CHILDREN'S CORE COLLECTION

TWENTIETH EDITION

CORE COLLECTION SERIES

Formerly Standard Catalog Series

JOHN GREENFIELDT, GENERAL EDITOR

CHILDREN'S CORE COLLECTION
MIDDLE AND JUNIOR HIGH CORE COLLECTION
SENIOR HIGH CORE COLLECTION
PUBLIC LIBRARY CORE COLLECTION: NONFICTION
FICTION CORE COLLECTION

CHILDREN'S
CORE COLLECTION

TWENTIETH EDITION

EDITED BY

ANNE PRICE

ASSISTED BY

MARGUERITA ROWLAND

NEW YORK • DUBLIN

THE H. W. WILSON COMPANY

2010

Printed in the United States of America

Abridged Dewey Decimal Classification and Relative Index, Edition 14 is © 2004-2010 OCLC Online Computer Library Center, Incorporated. Portions reprinted with Permission. DDC, Dewey, Dewey Decimal Classification, and WebDewey are registered trademarks of OCLC.

ISBN 978-0-8242-1106-6

Library of Congress Cataloging-in-Publication Data

Children's core collection. — 20th ed. / edited by Anne Price ; assisted by Marguerita Rowland.
      p. cm. — (Core collection series)
   Updated ed. of: Children's catalog. 19th ed. c2006.
   Kept up-to-date by annual supplements.
   Includes index.

   ISBN 978-0-8242-1106-6 (alk. paper)

   1. Children's literature—Bibliography.   2. Children's libraries—United States—Book lists. 3. School libraries—United States—Book lists. 4. Children—Books and reading—United States. I. Price, Anne, 1946- II. Rowland, Marguerita. III. Children's catalog.

Z1037.C5443 2010
011.62—dc22

                                                   2010026413

Visit H.W. Wilson's Web site at: www.hwwilson.com

CONTENTS

CONTENTS

PREFACE

Children's Core Collection is a comprehensive list of fiction and nonfiction books for children from preschool through grade six, together with professional aids for children's librarians and school media specialists. A new edition of this work is published every four years. Three annual supplements, to be published in 2011, 2012, and 2013, are intended for use with this volume.

In this Edition. This twentieth edition of *Children's Core Collection* (formerly titled *Children's Catalog*) includes entries for over 11,000 books. Of special note in this edition are a new abundance of graphic novels and books on environmental protection, natural sciences, and the arts. Another new feature is the addition of a star (*) on the bibliographic records to indicate the most highly recommended titles.

Preparation. In producing this edition the editor has worked closely with an advisory committee of distinguished librarians, who are listed below. Over the past four years they have participated in selecting the books that have entered the Collection. In preparation for this new edition they have re-evaluated all the material in the previous edition of the Core Collection and its supplements and proposed additional titles. Reviews in the professional literature have also been an important source of information in selecting the material for this Collection.

Scope and Purpose. This Core Collection is aimed at the needs of school and public libraries in providing materials for young children. Materials for the librarian or school media specialist are also included, such as works on the history and development of children's literature, literary criticism, bibliographies, selection aids, and guides to the operation of media centers.

Books listed are published in the United States, or published in Canada or the United Kingdom and distributed in the United States. All titles are in print at the time this Collection is published. Original paperback editions are included, and information is provided on paperback reprints of hardcover editions.

The convention of citing the first book in a fiction series in full with brief listings for other works in the series has been retained. In cases where more than one edition of a work illustrated by a notable artist is available, a listing of editions is provided with complete bibliographic information. Notes specify prizes or medals won and identify sequels or companion volumes.

The Core Collection excludes textbooks and materials in languages other than English, except for dictionaries and bilingual works. A non-English version of an English-language work is cited in the main entry for the work.

Organization. The Core Collection consists of two parts. Part 1, the Classified Collection, arranged according to the Dewey Decimal Classification, followed by Fiction (Fic), Story Collections (S C), and Easy Books (E); and Part 2, an Author, Title, and Subject Index. The section that follows this Preface, entitled How to Use Children's Core Collection, contains more detailed information about the uses, contents, and arrangement of the volume.

Acknowledgments

The H. W. Wilson Company is indebted to the publishers who supplied copies of their books and information about editions and prices. This Core Collection could not have been published without the efforts of the advisory committee, who gave so generously of their time and expertise.

Committee of Advisors

Betty Carter (Chair)
Professor emerita
School of Library and Information Studies
Texas Woman's University
Denton, Texas

John Edward Peters
Supervising Librarian
Children's Center at 42nd Street
The New York Public Library
New York, New York

Thom Barthelmess
Curator, Butler Children's Literature Center
Graduate School of Library and
    Information Science
Dominican University
River Forest, Illinois

Judith Rovenger
Youth Services Consultant
Westchester Library System
Ardsley, New York

Leslie M. Molnar
Youth Services Selection Supervisor
Cuyahoga County Public Library
Parma, Ohio

Linda Ward-Callaghan
Lead Professional, Youth Services
Joliet Public Library
Joliet, Ilinois

HOW TO USE CHILDREN'S CORE COLLECTION

USES OF THE CORE COLLECTION

Children's Core Collection is designed to serve these purposes:

As an aid in collection development. The annotations and grade level designation provided for each work in the Core Collection, along with information concerning publisher, ISBN, and price, are intended to assist in the selection and ordering of titles. The arrangement of the Classified Collection according to the Dewey Decimal Classification expedites the process of identifying areas of a library's collection that should be strengthened or updated.

As an aid in user service. Every item in this Core Collection is a highly recommended work of its kind and can be given with confidence to a user who expresses a need based on topic, genre, etc. Reference work and user service are further aided by information about grade level, sequels, and companion volumes; by the descriptive and critical annotations; and by the series and subject headings in the Index. In addition, the Index includes entries under names of illustrators and headings for Newbery and Caldecott medal winners.

As an aid in curriculum support. The classification, subject indexing, annotations, and grade level designations are helpful in identifying materials appropriate for classroom use.

As an aid in collection maintenance. Items elected to this edition of the Children's Core Collection comprise newly published works along with works listed in the previous edition or its supplements that have retained their usefulness. Information about the range of titles available in a field facilitates decisions to rebind, replace, or discard materials in the library's collection.

As an aid in professional development. The Collection is useful in courses that deal with children's literature and book selection, especially in the creation of bibliographies and reading lists.

DESCRIPTION OF THE CORE COLLECTION

Children's Core Collection is arranged in two parts: Part 1. Classified Collection, and Part 2. Author, Title, and Subject, Index.

Part 1. Classified Collection

The Classified Collection is arranged with the nonfiction books first, classified by the Dewey Decimal Classification. Individual biographies are classed in 92 and follow the 920s (collective biography). Three sections follow the nonfiction: Fiction

(Fic); Story Collections (S C); and Easy Books (E), consisting chiefly of picture books of interest to children from preschool to grade three.

An Outline of Classification is reproduced on page xiii. Within classes, works are arranged alphabetically under the main entry, usually the author. An exception is made for works of individual biography, classed in 92, which are arranged alphabetically under the name of the person written about.

The following is a sample entry and a description of its parts:

> **Silverstein, Alvin**
> Wildfires; the science behind raging infernos; [by] Alvin and Virginia Silverstein and Laura Silverstein Nunn. Enslow Publishers 2010 48p il map (The science behind natural disasters) lib bdg $23.93 *
> Grades: 4 5 6   **634.9**
> 1. Wildfires
> ISBN 978-0-7660-2973-6 (lib bdg); 0-7660-2973-5 (lib bdg)
> LC 2004-13282
> "Examines the science behind wildfires, including what causes them, the different types of wildfires, their devastating effects, and how to stay safe during a wildfire" Publisher's note
> "Scientific explanations are accompanied by plentiful color diagrams that will help students to grasp causes and effect. . . . Photos . . . are effective, and are sometimes turning into helpful, lively diagrams by the addition of such features as wind-direction arrows." SLJ
> Includes glossary and bibliographical references

The name of the author is inverted and printed in bold-face type. It is followed by the title, responsibility statement, and publisher. Next are the date of publication, pagination, illustration note, map note, series note, binding note, price, a star (indicating that this a most highly recommended title), and grade levels.

The number printed in bold face on the last line of type in the body of the entry is the classification number derived from the most recent information on the *Abridged Web Dewey,* the online version of the *Abridged Dewey Decimal Classification.* The numbered term that follows is a subject heading based on the twentieth edition of the *Sears List of Subject Headings.*

The ISBN (International Standard Book Number) or ISSN (International Standard Serial Number) is included to facilitate identification of the item. The Library of Congress control number is provided when available.

Notes supply additional information about the book. Most entries include both a note describing the book's contents and a critical note, which is useful in evaluating books for selection and in determining which of several books on the same subject is best suited for the individual reader. Other notes list special features, such as glossaries or bibliographical references, or describe sequels and companion volumes, editions available, awards, and publication history.

Part 2. Author, Title, and Subject Index

This is an alphabetical index to all the books in the Collection. Each book is entered under author, title (if distinctive), and subject, with added entries for joint author, illustrator, editor, and publisher's series as necessary. The classification number in bold-face type is the key to the location of the main entry of the book in the Classified Collection. "See" references are made from forms of names or subjects not used as headings. "See also" references are made to related or more specific headings.

Examples of entries in the Index:

Author	**Silverstein, Alvin** Wildfires	**634.9**
Title	**This** is rocket science. Skurzynski, G.	**629.4**
Subject	**Wildfires** Silverstein, A. Wildfires	**634.9**
Biography subject	**Edison, Thomas A. (Thomas Alva), 1847-1931** **About** Brown, D. A wizard from the start: the incredible boyhood & amazing inventions of Thomas Edison	**92**
Publisher's series	**The science behind natural disasters** [series] Silverstein, A. Wildfires	**634.9**
Joint authors	**Silverstein, Virginia B.** (jt. auth) Silverstein, A. Wildfires	**634.9**
Illustrator	**Diaz, David** (il) Krull, K. Wilma unlimited: how Wilma Rudolph became the world's fastest woman	**92**
Editor	**Hopkins, Lee Bennett, 1938-** (ed) Sharing the seasons. *See* Sharing the seasons	**811.008**

Outline of Classification

Reproduced below is the Second Summary of the Dewey Decimal Classification. It will serve as a table of contents for the nonfiction section of the Classified Collection. Note that the inclusion of this outline is not intended as a substitute for consulting the Dewey Decimal Classification itself. This outline is reproduced from Edition 14 of the Abridged Dewey Decimal Classification and Relative Index, published in 2004, by permission of OCLC Online Computer Library Center, Inc., owner of copyright.

000	**Computer science, knowledge & systems**		**500**	**Science**
010	Bibliographies		510	Mathematics
020	Library & information sciences		520	Astronomy
030	Encyclopedias & books of facts		530	Physics
040	[Unassigned]		540	Chemistry
050	Magazines, journals & serials		550	Earth sciences & geology
060	Associations, organizations & museums		560	Fossils & prehistoric life
070	News media, journalism & publishing		570	Life sciences; biology
080	Quotations		580	Plants (Botany)
090	Manuscripts & rare books		590	Animals (Zoology)
100	**Philosophy**		**600**	**Technology**
110	Metaphysics		610	Medicine & health
120	Epistemology		620	Engineering
130	Parapsychology & occultism		630	Agriculture
140	Philosophical schools of thought		640	Home & family management
150	Psychology		650	Management & public relations
160	Logic		660	Chemical engineering
170	Ethics		670	Manufacturing
180	Ancient, medieval & eastern philosophy		680	Manufacture for specific uses
190	Modern western philosophy		690	Building & construction
200	**Religion**		**700**	**Arts**
210	Philosophy & theory of religion		710	Landscaping & area planning
220	The Bible		720	Architecture
230	Christianity & Christian theology		730	Sculpture, ceramics & metalwork
240	Christian practice & observance		740	Drawing & decorative arts
250	Christian pastoral practice & religious orders		750	Painting
260	Christian organization, social work & worship		760	Graphic arts
270	History of Christianity		770	Photography & computer art
280	Christian denominations		780	Music
290	Other religions		790	Sports, games & entertainment
300	**Social sciences, sociology & anthropology**		**800**	**Literature, rhetoric & criticism**
310	Statistics		810	American literature in English
320	Political science		820	English & Old English literatures
330	Economics		830	German & related literatures
340	Law		840	French & related literatures
350	Public administration & military science		850	Italian, Romanian & related literatures
360	Social problems & social services		860	Spanish & Portuguese literatures
370	Education		870	Latin & Italic literatures
380	Commerce, communications & transportation		880	Classical & modern Greek literatures
390	Customs, etiquette & folklore		890	Other literatures
400	**Language**		**900**	**History**
410	Linguistics		910	Geography & travel
420	English & Old English languages		920	Biography & genealogy
430	German & related languages		930	History of ancient world (to ca. 499)
440	French & related languages		940	History of Europe
450	Italian, Romanian & related languages		950	History of Asia
460	Spanish & Portuguese languages		960	History of Africa
470	Latin & Italic languages		970	History of North America
480	Classical & modern Greek languages		980	History of South America
490	Other languages		990	History of other areas

CHILDREN'S CORE COLLECTION

TWENTIETH EDITION

CLASSIFIED COLLECTION

000 COMPUTER SCIENCE, KNOWLEDGE & SYSTEMS

001.4 Research; statistical methods

Cefrey, Holly
Researching people, places, and events. Rosen Central 2010 48p il (Digital and information literacy) lib bdg $26.50 *
Grades: 5 6 7 8   **001.4**
1. Internet research 2. Research 3. Report writing
ISBN 978-1-4358-5317-1 (lib bdg); 1-4358-5317-2 (lib bdg)   LC 2008-46785
Describes researching people, places, and events on the Internet, including using primary and secondary sources, evaluating source material, and avoiding plagiarism
"Colorful photos, diagrams, and sidebars and [a] lively [text creates an] appealing, user-friendly [presentation]. . . . . Students and teachers will find [this title] useful in keeping up-to-date on and utilizing online resources and today's technology in a rapidly changing digital world." SLJ
Includes glossary and bibliographical references

Gaines, Ann
Ace your Internet research; [by] Ann Graham Gaines. Enslow Publishers 2009 48p il (Ace it! information literacy) lib bdg $23.93
Grades: 3 4 5   **001.4**
1. Internet research 2. Internet searching
ISBN 978-0-7660-3392-4 (lib bdg); 0-7660-3392-9 (lib bdg)   LC 2008032351
"Readers will learn what the internet is, and how to do effective research while staying safe online" Publisher's note
Includes bibliographical references

Jakubiak, David J.
A smart kid's guide to doing Internet research. PowerKids Press 2009 c2010 24p il (Kids online) lib bdg $21.25; pa $8.25
Grades: 3 4 5 6   **001.4**
1. Internet research
ISBN 978-1-4042-8116-5 (lib bdg); 1-4042-8116-9 (lib bdg); 978-1-4358-3352-4 (pa); 1-4358-3352-X (pa)
                                LC 2009002879
In this title "readers are shown how to read URL tags, use browsers, and develop search-term strings. Readers are told that Wikipedia is not reliable because anybody

can add to it. . . . [This is a] worthwhile [purchase] for . . . updating collections in this area." SLJ
Includes glossary

001.9 Controversial knowledge

Allen, Judy
Unexplained. Kingfisher 2006 144p il $19.95 *
Grades: 5 6 7 8   **001.9**
1. Parapsychology 2. Curiosities and wonders
ISBN 978-0-7534-5950-8; 0-7534-5950-7
This addresses such topics as ghosts, psychic phenomena, superstitions, mysterious natural phenomena, alleged monsters, disappearances, secrets and mysteries of ancient history, and possible extraterrestrials.
"A seamless combination of absorbing fact-filled text and stunning visuals in an investigation of mysteries that continue to baffle, tantalize, and spark endless debate." SLJ
Includes glossary

Bardhan-Quallen, Sudipta
The real monsters; written by Sudipta Bardhan-Quallen; illustrated by Josh Cochran. Sterling 2008 88p il (Mysteries unwrapped) pa $5.95
Grades: 5 6 7 8   **001.9**
1. Monsters 2. Ghosts
ISBN 978-1-4027-3776-3 (pa); 1-4027-3776-9 (pa)
                                LC 2009275635
Investigates whether ghosts, werewolves, vampires, mummies, zombies and other such monsters exist
The book has "an ample number of clear black-and-white and full-color photographs and illustrations. . . . Perfect for libraries that need a boost or an update to their scary-story collections." SLJ
Includes bibliographical references

Gee, Joshua, fl. 1725-1750
Encyclopedia horrifica; the terrifying truth! about vampires, ghosts, monsters, and more. Scholastic Inc. 2007 129p il $14.99 *
Grades: 4 5 6 7   **001.9**
1. Vampires 2. Ghosts 3. Monsters
ISBN 978-0-439-92255-5; 0-439-92255-0
                                LC 2007061733
A visual reference contains true stories of such creatures as vampires, aliens, werewolves, and ghosts, accompanied by photographic evidence, eyewitness accounts, and original interviews.
"Each topic is replete with color illustrations and pho-

Gee, Joshua, fl. 1725-1750—*Continued*
tos and is accompanied by a light, readable text that tries
to separate fact from fiction." Voice Youth Advocates
Includes bibliographical references

Halls, Kelly Milner, 1957-
Tales of the cryptids; mysterious creatures that
may or may not exist; by Kelly Milner Halls, Rick
Spears, Roxyanne Young; [illustrated by Rick
Spears] Darby Creek 2006 72p il map $18.95 *
Grades: 4 5 6 7   **001.9**
  1. Monsters
  ISBN 1-58196-049-2
This considers the existance of creatures such as
Bigfoot, the Loch Ness Monster, Marozi of Kenya, the
Orang-pendek of Sumatra, and the Thylacine of Tasma-
nia.
"The conversational text makes for fun reading, and a
plethora of pictures . . . will prove enticing." SLJ

Kallen, Stuart A., 1955-
Crop circles. ReferencePoint Press 2010 104p il
(The mysterious & unknown) $25.95
Grades: 4 5 6 7   **001.9**
  1. Crop circles
  ISBN 978-1-60152-103-3; 1-60152-103-0
                     LC 2009034368
In an attempt to explain the phenomenon of crop circles, "Kallen reaches back to a 1678 account of a 'mowing devil' before considering numerous potential culprits:
plasma vortexes, psychokenesis, UFOs, the military, and
even wallabies stoned on opium. Equal time is spent between cereologists (those who study these formations)
and plain old hoaxsters—and both are equally interesting." Booklist
Includes bibliographical references

Nardo, Don, 1947-
Martians; by Don Nardo. KidHaven Press 2008
48p il (Monsters) lib bdg $26.20
Grades: 4 5 6 7   **001.9**
  1. Extraterrestrial beings 2. Popular culture
  ISBN 978-0-7377-3639-7 (lib bdg); 0-7377-3639-9 (lib
  bdg)   LC 2007-30616
"Nardo walks readers through everything from early
astronautical observations of the Red Planet to Martians
in the movies and on television. His writing is clear, informative and often humorous." SLJ
Includes glossary and bibliographical references

004   Data processing. Computer science

Jackson, Cari
Revolution in computers. Marshall Cavendish
Benchmark 2010 32p il (It works!) lib bdg $19.95
Grades: 3 4 5   **004**
  1. Computers—History
  ISBN 978-0-7614-4375-9 (lib bdg); 0-7614-4375-4 (lib
  bdg)   LC 2008-54517

"Discusses the history of computers, how the technology was developed, and the science behind it." Publisher's note
"This interesting, information packed [book] . . . motivates students to do their own exploring. . . . The appealing cartoon-like photographs add humor. . . . This
. . . just may be that spark needed to create eager budding scientists." Libr Media Connect
Includes glossary and bibliographical references

Oxlade, Chris
My first computer guide. Heinemann Library
2007 32p il (My first computer guides) lib bdg
$25.36; pa $7.99
Grades: K 1 2   **004**
  1. Computers
  ISBN   978-1-4329-0018-2   (lib   bdg);
  978-1-4329-0022-9 (pa)   LC 2006100905
This beginner's guide to computers answers such
questions as: How do you use a computer mouse? How
does a computer program work? What do you find on
the desktop?
This is "composed in easy-to-understand language.
. . . Packed with bright photographs and fact-filled word
balloons." SLJ
Includes glossary and bibliographical references

Rooney, Anne
Computers; faster, smaller, and smarter; [by]
Anne Rooney. Heinemann Library 2006 56p il
(The cutting edge) lib bdg $32.86; pa $8.99
Grades: 5 6 7 8   **004**
  1. Computers
  ISBN 1-4034-7426-5 (lib bdg); 1-4034-7432-X (pa)
                     LC 2005018014
This "describes early machines and then looks at em-
bedded computers, robotics, communication, imaging and
simulation, viruses, spyware, hackers, and the future of
computers. . . . Informative, fascinating, and useful for
reports." SLJ
Includes glossary and bibliographical references

Sherman, Josepha
The history of the personal computer. Watts
2003 63p il (Watts library) lib bdg $25.50
paperback o.p.
Grades: 4 5 6 7   **004**
  1. Computers—History
  ISBN 0-531-12166-6 (lib bdg); 0-531-16213-3 (pa)
                     LC 2002-8507
Discusses the inventors and scientists that contributed
to the development of computers and more recently, personal computers
This offers "fascinating and useful content." Libr Media Connect
Includes glossary and bibliographical references

004.6 Interfacing and communications

Jakubiak, David J.
A smart kid's guide to avoiding online predators. PowerKids Press 2009 c2010 24p il (Kids online) lib bdg $21.25; pa $8.95 *
Grades: 3 4 5 6   **004.6**
    1. Internet—Security measures 2. Internet and children 3. Safety education
    ISBN 978-1-4042-8117-2 (lib bdg); 1-4042-8117-7 (lib bdg); 978-1-4358-3354-8 (pa); 1-4358-3354-6 (pa)
                LC 2009004343
In this title "the focus is on treating the Internet as you would any other public place: avoiding strangers and telling someone if you see or read something you are uncomfortable with. . . . [This is a] worthwhile [purchase] for teaching online safety and updating collections in this area." SLJ
    Includes glossary

Oxlade, Chris
My first E-Mail guide; [by] Chris Oxlade. Heinemann Library 2007 32p il (My first computer guides) lib bdg $25.36; pa $7.99
Grades: K 1 2   **004.6**
    1. Electronic mail systems
    ISBN 978-1-4329-0017-5 (lib bdg); 978-1-4329-0021-2 (pa)   LC 2006100904
This beginner's introduction to e-mail is "composed in easy-to-understand language. . . . Packed with bright photographs and fact-filled word balloons." SLJ
    Includes glossary and bibliographical references

My first Internet guide; [by] Chris Oxlade. Heinemann Library 2007 32p il (My first computer guides) lib bdg $25.36; pa $7.99
Grades: K 1 2   **004.6**
    1. Internet
    ISBN 978-1-4329-0019-9 (lib bdg); 978-1-4329-0023-6 (pa)   LC 2006100906
This beginner's introduction to the internet is "composed in easy-to-understand language. . . . Packed with bright photographs and fact-filled word balloons." SLJ
    Includes glossary and bibliographical references

005 Computer programming, programs, data

Orr, Tamra
Creating multimedia presentations. Rosen Central 2010 48p il (Digital and information literacy) lib bdg $26.50 *
Grades: 5 6 7 8   **005**
    1. Multimedia 2. Presentation software
    ISBN 978-1-4358-5319-5 (lib bdg); 1-4358-5319-9 (lib bdg)   LC 2008-54736
Describes how to create a multimedia presentation, including adding graphs, images, sounds, and video, and

how to integrate these elements to form an informative presentation
    "Colorful photos, diagrams, and sidebars and [a lively text creates an] appealing, user-friendly [presentation]. . . . Students and teachers will find [this title] useful in keeping up-to-date on and utilizing online resources and today's technology in a rapidly changing digital world." SLJ
    Includes glossary and bibliographical references

005.8 Data security

Jakubiak, David J.
A smart kid's guide to Internet privacy. PowerKids Press 2009 c2010 24p il (Kids online) lib bdg $21.25; pa $8.25
Grades: 3 4 5 6   **005.8**
    1. Internet—Security measures 2. Internet and children 3. Computer crimes 4. Right of privacy
    ISBN 978-1-4042-8118-9 (lib bdg); 1-4042-8118-5 (lib bdg); 978-1-4358-3356-2 (pa); 1-4358-3356-2 (pa)
                LC 2009005369
This title "is straightforward about not sharing information without parental permission and also gives support and suggestions in case something does happen. . . . [A] worthwhile [purchase] for teaching online safety and updating collections in this area." SLJ
    Includes glossary and bibliographical references

006.7 Multimedia systems

Jakubiak, David J.
A smart kid's guide to social networking online. PowerKids Press 2009 c2010 24p il (Kids online) lib bdg $21.25; pa $8.95 *
Grades: 3 4 5 6   **006.7**
    1. Internet and children 2. Internet—Security measures 3. Safety education
    ISBN 978-1-4042-8119-6 (lib bdg); 1-4042-8119-3 (lib bdg); 978-1-4358-3358-6 (pa); 1-4358-3358-9 (pa)
                LC 2009006377
This book explains online social networking and explores kid-friendly networking options.
    "This . . . is easy to read, has vibrant photos on each page, and offers Tips. Additional links can be found at the publisher's portal, which is regularly updated." Libr Media Connect
    Includes glossary

Selfridge, Benjamin
A teen's guide to creating Web pages and blogs; [by] Benjamin Selfridge, Peter Selfridge, and Jennifer Osburn. Prufrock Press 2009 148p il pa $16.95
Grades: 5 6 7 8 9 10   **006.7**
    1. Web sites—Design 2. Weblogs 3. Internet and teenagers
    ISBN 978-1-59363-345-5 (pa); 1-59363-345-9 (pa)
                LC 2008-40044
First published 2004 by Zephyr Press with title: Kid's guide to creating Web pages for home and school

Selfridge, Benjamin—*Continued*
"This guide begins with basic step-by-step information about HTML, fonts, images, lists, and tables. . . . The book's last half introduces more advanced techniques, such as JavaScript, functions, loops, and applications like Flash and Instant Messenger. . . . Illustrated, with references and a glossary, this attractive paperback has lots of practical content." Voice Youth Advocates
Includes glossary and bibliographical references

Woog, Adam, 1953-
YouTube. Norwood House Press 2008 48p il (A great idea) lib bdg $25.27
Grades: 3 4 5 6   **006.7**
1. YouTube, Inc. 2. Internet
ISBN 978-1-59953-198-4 (lib bdg); 1-59953-198-4 (lib bdg)   LC 2008010724
"Describes the invention and development of YouTube." Publisher's note
This "offers a fresh topic and handles it extremely well. . . . Woog's account is interesting and informative and written in simple yet uncondescending prose that's spot-on for the intended audience. . . . The attractive design features full-color photographs, while fast facts appear throughout the narrative in eye-catching sidebars." Booklist
Includes glossary and bibliographical references

011.6 General bibliographies of works for specific kinds of users and libraries

Adventuring with books; a booklist for pre-K—grade 6; [by] Amy A. McClure and Janice V. Kristo, editors, and the Committee to Revise the Elementary School Booklist; with a foreword by Rudine Sims Bishop. 13th ed. National Council of Teachers of English 2002 536p il pa $39.95
Grades: Professional   **011.6**
1. Reference books 2. Children's literature—Bibliography 3. Best books
ISBN 0-8141-0073-2   LC 2003-265339
First published 1950
"In this edition of Adventuring with Books, teachers and librarians will find descriptions of more than 850 . . . texts suitable for student use in background research, unit study, or pleasure reading. . . . [divided] under the 24 general topics, including Science Nonfiction; Struggle and Survival; Fantasy Literature; Sports, Games, and Hobbies; and Mathematics in Our World." Publisher's note

Barr, Catherine
Best books for children: preschool through grade 6; [by] Catherine Barr, John T. Gillespie. 8th ed. Libraries Unlimited 2006 1783p $80 *
Grades: Professional   **011.6**
1. Reference books 2. Children's literature—Bibliography 3. Best books
ISBN 1-59158-085-4
First published 1978

This "guide to children's books includes more than 25,000 in-print titles recommended for children in grades K-6. . . . [It offers] thematic organization, concise annotations, and complete bibliographic data plus review citations." Publisher's note
"This is a standard reference for a reason, and this edition continues the tradition of providing an abundance of information in an easily navigated form." Bull Cent Child Books

Best new media, K-12; a guide to movies, subscription web sites, and educational software and games. Libraries Unlimited 2008 237p (Children's and young adult literature reference series) $50
Grades: Professional   **011.6**
1. Libraries—Special collections 2. Libraries—Collection development 3. Reference books
ISBN 978-1-59158-467-4; 1-59158-467-1   LC 2008020191
This "guides readers to the best movies, educational software and games, and subscription Web sites for children and teens. Entries feature full bibliographic information (including grade level), a descriptive annotation, and review citations. An introduction addresses selection, acquisition, cataloging, shelving, and security of new media." Publisher's note
"The book is a convenient compilation of resources that are otherwise hard to identify, making it a desirable purchase, particularly for libraries that are just starting to build game collections." SLJ

Barstow, Barbara
Beyond picture books; subject access to best books for beginning readers; [by] Barbara Barstow, Judith Riggle, Leslie Molnar. 3rd ed. Libraries Unlimited 2008 645p $75 *
Grades: Professional   **011.6**
1. Reference books 2. Children's literature—Bibliography 3. Best books
ISBN 978-1-59158-545-9; 1-59158-545-7   LC 2007042282
First published 1989
"The short preface defines first readers as kindergarten to third grade, and clearly defines the criteria used for inclusion of titles. The list of 200 'outstanding first readers' will be welcomed by anyone charged with developing an opening day collection or looking to beef up existing collections. The book's 3,600 titles are well-balanced between fiction and nonfiction. . . . The brief annotations provide rich descriptions of plot, illustrations, and overall tone." Libr Media Connect
Includes bibliographical references

Blakemore, Catherine
Faraway places; your source for picture books that fly children to 82 countries. Adams-Pomeroy Press 2002 468p pa $28.95
Grades: Professional   **011.6**
1. Reference books 2. Picture books for children—Bibliography 3. Travel—Bibliography
ISBN 0-9661009-2-1   LC 2001-132599

Blakemore, Catherine—_Continued_

"The bibliography is divided by region. . . . Each region is divided alphabetically by country; each country is divided (as applicable) into Specific Locations (such as cities), General (fables, fairy tales, folktales, legends, etc.), Historical Figures, Nonfiction, Stories, Poetry and Songs, and Books. Succinct summaries of more than 900 recommended titles are offered in a narrative format under each section. . . . An impressive guide that will not only aid collection development but serve as a useful reference tool as well." Bull Cent Child Books

Includes bibliographical references

Dale, Doris Cruger

Bilingual children's books in English and Spanish; an annotated bibliography, 1942 through 2001. McFarland & Co. 2003 174p pa $39.95 *

Grades: Professional   011.6
    1. Reference books 2. Children's literature—Bibliography
    ISBN 0-7864-1316-6   LC 2002-13462

A revised edition of Bilingual books in Spanish and English for children published 1985 by Libraries Unlimited

Title page in English and Spanish

In the introduction "the author discusses the four awards that have been established for books by Latino authors or with Latino themes, the publishers that produce bilingual books for children, and journals that review the books. . . . The annotated bibliography, the main body of the work, is comprised of 433 entries, mostly picture, alphabet, and counting books. A welcome addition to the literature in this growing field." Am Ref Books Annu, 2003

East, Kathy

Across cultures; a guide to multicultural literature for children. Libraries Unlimited 2007 342p il (Children's and young adult literature reference series) $55 *

Grades: Professional   011.6
    1. Reference books 2. Children's literature—Bibliography 3. Multiculturalism—Bibliography
    ISBN 978-1-59158-336-3; 1-59158-336-5
                                      LC 2007013573

This "introduces more than 400 . . . fiction and nonfiction multicultural resources for preschool through grade 6 . . . arranged in thematic groupings. . . . It presents both annotations and . . . advice on programming strategies. Connections are made to projects, graphic organizers, and activities." Publisher's note

This is "user-friendly and extremely helpful both in terms of the choices and the descriptions." SLJ

Includes bibliographical references

Freeman, Judy

Books kids will sit still for 3; a read-aloud guide; [by] Judy Freeman; Catherine Barr, series editor. Libraries Unlimited 2006 915p il (Children's and young adult literature reference series) $70; pa $55 *

Grades: Professional   011.6
    1. Reference books 2. Children's literature—Bibliography 3. Best books
    ISBN 1-59158-163-X; 1-59158-164-8 (pa)

First published 1984 by Alleyside with title: Books kids will sit still for

"The author features 2,000 . . . selected titles [for] children in grades K through 6. . . . All [are] published [from 1995 to 2005]. . . . Each annotated entry provides a brief plot summary, related titles, and subject designations. In addition, there are curriculum tie-ins and suggested activities including drama, crafts, research, and problem solving. The book . . . [offers] tips on effective reading aloud, storytelling, and classroom and library activities. There is also a bibliography of professional books." Publisher's note

"This excellent resource will be a favorite with teachers who need assistance finding quality children's literature, and it will also aid librarians and media specialists." SLJ

Gillespie, John Thomas, 1928-

The children's and young adult literature handbook; a research and reference guide. Libraries Unlimited 2005 393p (Children's and young adult literature reference series) $55

Grades: Professional   011.6
    1. Reference books 2. Children's literature—Bibliography 3. Children's literature—History and criticism 4. Young adult literature—Bibliography 5. Young adult literature—History and criticism
    ISBN 1-56308-949-1

This is "a selection guide and collection development aid for librarians, as well as a navigation tool for researchers. Describing and evaluating more than 1,000 publications, the book covers . . . general reference, bibliographies, and biographies to review sources, literary awards, professional organizations, and special library collections. Internet and other nonprint media are included, as are major English-language resources from Britain, Canada, Australia, and South Africa." Publisher's note

"This reference should meet the needs of librarians, teachers, and scholars." Choice

Harms, Jeanne McLain

Picture books to enhance the curriculum; [by] Jeanne McLain Harms, Lucille J. Lettow. Wilson, H.W. 1996 521p $60

Grades: Professional   011.6
    1. Reference books 2. Picture books for children—Indexes 3. Picture books for children—Bibliography
    ISBN 0-8242-0867-6   LC 94-42653

This is "a list of approximately 1,500 picture-book titles for use in literature-based programs in elementary schools implementing the whole language concept. The focus rests on language arts, graphic and performing arts, social studies, and science. Chapters cover a key to

Harms, Jeanne McLain—*Continued*
themes; a themes index listing related titles; a picture book index containing bibliographic information, a brief annotation of contents, and a list of themes; and a title index." Choice

Lima, Carolyn W.
A to zoo; subject access to children's picture books; [by] Carolyn W. Lima and John A. Lima. 7th ed. Libraries Unlimited 2006-2008 xxiii, 1692p (Children's and young adult literature reference series) $84; 2008 supplement $45
Grades: Professional   **011.6**
   1. Reference books 2. Picture books for children—Bibliography
   ISBN   978-1-59158-232-8;   1-59158-232-6; 978-1-59158-672-2 (supplement); 1-59158-672-0 (2008 supplement)   LC 2005030879
First published 1982
This "subject index to picture books for pre-school through grade 2 . . . covers nearly 28,000 in-print and out-of-print titles. . . . The volume is . . . divided into five sections: 'Subject Headings,' a list of the 1,350 subjects under which the books are classified; 'Subject Guide,' where the books are listed under the appropriate headings; 'Bibliographic Guide,' arranged by author and containing bibliographic information for each title; and title and illustrator indexes. . . . [An] essential [resource] for school and public libraries." Booklist
Includes bibliographical references

Polette, Nancy, 1930-
Find someone who; introducing 200 favorite picture books; [by] Nancy Polette. Libraries Unlimited 2006 205p pa $35
Grades: Professional   **011.6**
   1. Reference books 2. Picture books for children—Bibliography 3. Children—Books and reading
   ISBN 1-59158-465-5 (pa); 978-1-59158-465-0 (pa)
       LC 2006027318
"Polette shows a new way to present well-known picture books to preschoolers and primary-grade students. A one-paragraph booktalk introduces the story and is followed by 10 questions based upon the characters or situations. Children are instructed to find someone in their group who can relate to a portion of the story. . . . The book will be useful for quick, spur-of-the-moment planning as well as for quality lesson plans in working with ESL groups." SLJ

Reid, Rob
Reid's read-alouds; selections for children and teens. American Library Association 2009 xiii, 121p pa $45
Grades: Professional   **011.6**
   1. Books and reading 2. Children's literature—Bibliography 3. Young adult literature—Bibliography
   ISBN 978-0-8389-0980-5 (pa); 0-8389-0980-9 (pa)
       LC 2008045376
"Reid has collected 200 titles published between 2000 and 2008 that have both readability and general kid appeal. The titles are organized alphabetically by author,

and the book includes subject and age-level indexes. Each selection has a cursory summary, grade-level range, and a suggestion for a 10-minute read-aloud, which either provides an introduction to the main characters or a glimpse into the story. . . . This last part is what makes the book so useful." SLJ
Includes bibliographical references

Schon, Isabel
Recommended books in Spanish for children and young adults, 2004-2008. Scarecrow Press 2009 414p $55
Grades: Professional   **011.6**
   1.   Latin   American   literature—Bibliography 2. Spanish literature—Bibliography 3. Children's literature—Bibliography 4. Young adult literature—Bibliography 5. Reference books
   ISBN 978-0-8108-6386-6; 0-8108-6386-3
       LC 2008-33390
Also available volumes covering titles published 1991-1995, 1996-1999, and 2000-2004
"Schon evaluates 1231 reference books, fiction, and nonfiction. . . . Entries are arranged alphabetically by author and include a grade level for each book. . . . Schon examines and recommends materials based on the quality of the Spanish language, literary appeal, and the versatility of the translators, paying special attention to the effective use of Peninsular Spanish or the Spanish from the Americas. This annotated bibliography will help selectors in public libraries and media centers to develop existing Spanish-language collections." SLJ

Silvey, Anita
100 best books for children. Houghton Mifflin 2004 184p $20 *
Grades: Professional   **011.6**
   1. Reference books 2. Children's literature—Bibliography 3. Best books
   ISBN 0-618-27889-3   LC 2003-56899
"A former editor and reviewer for The Horn Book Magazine recommends one hundred of the best books for children, including a variety of works to suit diverse interests, reading levels, and special needs." Publisher's note
The author's "long experience as a book reviewer and editor makes her list pretty much spot-on. . . . Each title gets a short essay that not only discusses the book and what it has meant to its audience but that also supplies wonderful behind-the-scenes information. . . . A helpful list, 'Beyond the 100 Best,' points parents in the right direction for more good reads." Booklist
Includes bibliographical references

York, Sherry, 1947-
Ethnic book awards; a directory of multicultural literature for young readers. Linworth Pub. 2005 157p pa $36.95
Grades: Professional   **011.6**
   1. Reference books 2. Children's literature—Bibliography 3. Young adult literature—Bibliography 4. Multiculturalism—Bibliography
   ISBN 1-58683-187-9   LC 2005004332

York, Sherry, 1947-—*Continued*

"Part one provides basic background information and Web sites for the Sydney Taylor Book Award, the Coretta Scott King Award, the Carter G. Woodson Award, the Américas Award, the Tomás Rivera Mexican American Children's Literature Award, the Pura Belpré Award, and the Asian Pacific American Award for Literature. Part two, the bulk of the book, lists the books alphabetically by title, along with a one or two-sentence annotation and the honor citation(s). An extensive subject index is included, as is an index of authors, editors, illustrators, and translators." SLJ

016.3   Bibliographies of the social sciences

The **best** children's books of the year; selected by the Children's Book Committee at Bank Street College of Education. Teacher's College Press pa $8.95
Grades: Professional   **016.3**
1. Reference books 2. Children's literature—Bibliography
ISSN 1523-6471
First published 1998
"This is a comprehensive annotated book list for children, aged infant–14." Publisher's note

Crew, Hilary S., 1942-

Women engaged in war in literature for youth; a guide to resources for children and young adults. Scarecrow Press 2007 303p (Literature for youth) pa $55
Grades: Professional   **016.3**
1. Reference books 2. War—Bibliography 3. Women—Bibliography 4. Children's literature—Bibliography 5. Young adult literature—Bibliography
ISBN 978-0-8108-4929-7 (pa); 0-8108-4929-1 (pa)
LC 2006-101112
"Crew's guide to print and online sources documents women's roles in wars over the centuries and throughout the world, divided by time periods. . . . This is a great addition for libraries looking for a way to move Women's Studies beyond the month of March." SLJ
Includes bibliographical references

Notable social studies trade books for young people. Children's Bk. Council * pa $2
Grades: Professional   **016.3**
1. Reference books 2. Social sciences—Bibliography 3. Best books 4. Children's literature—Bibliography 5. Young adult literature—Bibliography
An annual annotated list, reprinted from an issue of the periodical Social Education, of the preceding year's best trade books in the field of social studies of interest to children in grades K-8. Prepared by the Book Review Panel of the National Council for the Social Studies—Children's Book Council Joint Committee. Titles are selected for emphasis on human relations, originality, readability and, when appropriate, illustrations. General reading levels (primary, intermediate, advanced) are indicated

Walter, Virginia A.

War & peace; a guide to literature and new media, grades 4-8; [by] Virginia A. Walter. Libraries Unlimited 2007 276p (Children's and young adult literature reference series) pa $40 *
Grades: Professional   **016.3**
1. Reference books 2. War—Bibliography 3. Peace—Bibliography 4. Children's literature—Bibliography 5. Young adult literature—Bibliography
ISBN 1-59158-271-7 (pa); 978-1-59158-271-7 (pa)
LC 2006030671
"Walter addresses the issue of war—and peace—by examining the information needs of children and how we as professionals can meet them. . . . The bulk of the book is the annotated listing of resources that is divided topically. . . . The well-annotated bibliography includes books, DVDs, Web sites, and CDs, as well as suggestions for using the materials. . . . This book should be a 'must purchase.'" SLJ
Includes bibliographical references

Wesson, Lindsey Patrick

Green reads; best environmental resources for youth, K-12. Libraries Unlimited 2009 219p (Children's and young adult literature reference series) $50
Grades: Professional   **016.3**
1. Environmental protection—Bibliography 2. Conservation of natural resources—Bibliography 3. Children's literature—Bibliography 4. Young adult literature—Bibliography 5. Reference books
ISBN 978-1-59158-834-4; 1-59158-834-0
LC 2009-17353
"This well-organized bibliography offers 450 annotated resources that can be integrated into the classroom to introduce students to environmental concepts. The five chapters focus on global warming, pollution, the Earth's resources, recycling, and conservation. Subchapters follow a uniform organization, including fiction; DVDs and CDs; nonfiction; seminal works, which are labeled 'Recycled Favorites'; and a storytime lesson plan with a variety of activities including songs and tactile learning activities. . . . This reference will delight educators and professionals interested in making students aware of environmental issues and to help youngsters rediscover the outside and natural worlds around them." SLJ
Includes bibliographical references

016.3058   Bibliographies of racial, ethnic, national groups

Al-Hazza, Tami Craft

Books about the Middle East; selecting and using them with children and adolescents; [by] Tami Craft Al-Hazza and Katherine T. Bucher. Linworth Pub. 2008 168p pa $39.95
Grades: Professional   **016.3058**
1. Reference books 2. Middle East—Bibliography 3. Children's literature—Bibliography 4. Young adult literature—Bibliography
ISBN 978-1-58683-285-8 (pa); 1-58683-285-9 (pa)
LC 2007-40149

Al-Hazza, Tami Craft—*Continued*
"This book examines the body of literature about the diverse groups of people who inhabit the Middle East, and it also explores a variety of ways in which this literature can be used. . . . It fills a huge gap and should not be overlooked. This powerhouse book will be tremendously helpful to media specialists, educators, and public librarians." Voice Youth Advocates
Includes bibliographical references

The **Black** experience in children's books; selected by the New York Public Library, Black Experience in Children's Books Committee. New York Public Lib. 2004 64p pa $8
Grades: Professional   **016.3058**
1. Reference books 2. African Americans—Bibliography 3. Blacks—Bibliography
ISBN 0-87104-768-3
First published 1946 with title: Books about Negro life for children
An annotated bibliography of titles portraying African American life in the United States and the Black experience in Africa and the Caribbean. Includes picture books, fiction, folklore, poetry, history, biography, and other nonfiction books for children from preschool through junior high school

Garcha, Rajinder
The world of Islam in literature for youth; a selective annotated bibliography for K-12; [by] Rajinder Garcha, Patricia Yates Russell. Scarecrow Press 2006 xx, 221p (Literature for youth) pa $35
Grades: Professional   **016.3058**
1. Reference books 2. Islam—Bibliography 3. Children's literature—Bibliography 4. Young adult literature—Bibliography
ISBN 978-0-8108-5488-8 (pa); 0-8108-5488-0 (pa)
LC 2005-26645
"This annotated bibliography has more than 700 selected print and electronic resources. Each numbered entry includes complete bibliographic information, a recommended grade level, and a one-paragraph summary and critique." SLJ
"This highly useful bibliography fills a conspicuous gap in a much-needed cultural area." Voice Youth Advocates
Includes bibliographical references

016.5 Bibliographies of science

Outstanding science trade books for students K-12. Children's Bk. Council * pa $2
Grades: Professional   **016.5**
1. Reference books 2. Science—Bibliography 3. Best books 4. Children's literature—Bibliography 5. Young adult literature—Bibliography
An annual annotated list, reprinted from an issue of the periodical Science and Children, of the preceding year's best trade books in the field of science of interest to children in grades K-8. Prepared by a Book Review Committee appointed by the National Science Teachers Association in cooperation with the Children's Book Council. Titles are selected for accuracy, readability and pleasing format. General reading levels (primary, intermediate, advanced) are indicated

016.7 Bibliographies of the arts

Pawuk, Michael G.
Graphic novels; a genre guide to comic books, manga, and more; foreword by Brian K. Vaughn. Libraries Unlimited 2007 xxxv, 633p il (Genreflecting advisory series) $65 *
Grades: Professional   **016.7**
1. Reference books 2. Graphic novels—Bibliography
ISBN 1-59158-132-X; 978-1-59158-132-1
LC 2006-34156
"This guide is intended to help you start, update, or maintain a graphic novel collection and advise readers about the genre. It covers more than 2,400 titles, including series titles, and organizes them according to genre, subgenre, and theme—from super-heroes and adventure to crime, humor, and nonfiction. Reading levels, awards/recognition, and core titles are identified; and tie-ins with gaming, film, anime, and television are noted." Publisher's note
Includes bibliographical references

016.8 Bibliographies of literature

Gillespie, John Thomas, 1928-
Historical fiction for young readers (grades 4-8); an introduction. Libraries Unlimited 2008 489p $60 *
Grades: Professional   **016.8**
1. Reference books 2. Children's literature—Bibliography 3. Young adult literature—Bibliography 4. Historical fiction—Bibliography
ISBN 978-1-59158-621-0; 1-59158-621-6
LC 2008031343
"Gillespie begins with chapters that suggest the criteria by which fiction, and historical fiction specifically, should be evaluated. He gives a detailed and enlightening look at the development of the genre that serves as a useful guide for building a collection of must-haves or classics. He also includes a generic chapter on how to bring books and children together. . . . The strength of the volume is the in-depth coverage of the 81 featured novels, organized geographically, and then chronologically. Historical background, information about the author, a lengthy synopsis, passages for booktalking, and discussions of themes are all provided." SLJ
Includes bibliographical references

Hall, Susan, 1940-
Using picture storybooks to teach literary devices; recommended books for children and young adults. Libraries Unlimited 2007 282p (Using picture books to teach) pa $42 *
Grades: Professional   **016.8**
1. Literature—Study and teaching
ISBN 978-1-59158-493-3 (pa); 1-59158-493-0 (pa)
Additional volumes published 1990, 1994, and 2002
"This fourth volume of the series, . . . gives teachers and librarians the . . . tool to teach literary devices in grades K-12. With this volume, the author has added:

Hall, Susan, 1940-—*Continued*

colloquialism; counterpoint; solecism; archetype; and others to the list of devices. The entries have been reorganized to include all the information under the book listing itself. Each entry includes an annotation, a listing of curricular tie-ins for the book and the art style used, and a listing and explanation of all the literary devices taught by that title." Publisher's note

Includes bibliographic references

Leeper, Angela

Poetry in literature for youth. Scarecrow Press 2006 303p (Literature for youth) pa $40

Grades: Professional   **016.8**
1. Reference books 2. Poetry—Bibliography
ISBN 0-8108-5465-1   LC 2005030719
This "provides annotated listings of titles arranged by subjects. . . . More than 900 entries describe collections, anthologies, performance poetry, poet biographies, and more, for kindergarten through high school." Booklist

"This title is packed with innovative ways to integrate poetry into the K-12 curriculum." SLJ

Includes bibliographical references

Lynn, Ruth Nadelman, 1948-

Fantasy literature for children and young adults; a comprehensive guide. 5th ed. Libraries Unlimited 2005 1128p (Children's and young adult literature reference series) $65

Grades: Professional   **016.8**
1. Reference books 2. Fantasy fiction—Bibliography
3. Fairy tales—Bibliography
ISBN 1-59158-050-1
First published 1979 with title: Fantasy for children
This describes and categorizes "fantasy novels and story collections published between 1900 and 2004. More than 7,500 titles . . . for readers grades 3-12 are organized in chapters based on fantasy subgenres and themes, including animal, alternate worlds, time travel, witchcraft, and sorcery. Lynn provides complete bibliographic information, grade level, a brief annotation, and a list of review citations, and notes recommended titles." Publisher's note

"This is an excellent resource." Booklist

Thomas, Rebecca L.

Popular series fiction for K-6 readers; a reading and selection guide; [by] Rebecca L. Thomas and Catherine Barr. 2nd ed. Libraries Unlimited 2008 1002p (Children's and young adult literature reference series) $65 *

Grades: Professional   **016.8**
1. Reference books 2. Children's literature—Bibliography
ISBN 978-1-59158-659-3; 1-59158-659-3
        LC 2008-38124
First published 2004
"Using standard review sources and bibliographies as well as author, publisher, bookseller, and library Web sites, the authors have identified nearly 2,200 in-print series appropriate for K-6 readers. . . . Entries are arranged by the series title and contain author, most recent

publisher, grade level, notation for availability of accelerated-reader resources, genre, a descriptive three to five-sentence annotation, and a list of individual titles in the series, arranged by publication date. Following the entries are author, title, and genre/subject indexes as well as appendixes that list books for boys, girls, and reluctant readers. . . . [This is] essential as reference and selection tools in all school, public, and academic libraries." Booklist

Includes bibliographical references

What do children and young adults read next? a reader's guide to fiction for children and young adults. Gale Res. $125

Grades: Professional   **016.8**
1. Reference books 2. Best books 3. Children's literature—Bibliography 4. Young adult literature—Bibliography
ISSN 1540-5060
Annual. First published 2002; previously published separately as: What do children read next? and What do young adults read next?

Each volume contains over 2,000 entries arranged alphabetically by author, for fiction for children and young adults. Each annotation includes basic bibliographic information, suggested age range, subject(s) and genre, names and descriptions of major characters, time period, locale(s), plot summary, citations of selected reviews, awards received and additional titles on a similar theme

016.9   Bibliographies of geography and history

Barancik, Sue, 1944-

Guide to collective biographies for children and young adults. Scarecrow Press 2005 447p pa $44.95

Grades: Professional   **016.9**
1. Reference books 2. Biography—Bibliography
3. Children's literature—Bibliography 4. Young adult literature—Bibliography
ISBN 0-8108-5033-8   LC 2004-19560
"This text indexes 721 titles for children and young adults in order to provide access to 5,760 notable individuals from early to modern times. All of the referenced titles were published between 1988 and 2002." Booklist

"A current guide such as this one is essential. . . . A must-have for libraries serving grades 4 through 12." SLJ

020   Library & information sciences

Gaines, Ann

Master the library and media center; [by] Ann Graham Gaines. Enslow Publishers, Inc. 2009 48p il (Ace it! information literacy) lib bdg $23.93

Grades: 3 4 5   **020**
1. Research 2. Information resources 3. Information literacy 4. Libraries 5. Instructional materials centers
ISBN 978-0-7660-3393-1 (lib bdg); 0-7660-3393-7 (lib bdg)   LC 2008024886

Gaines, Ann—*Continued*
"Readers will learn about both the regular and electronic research materials available at the library" Publisher's note
Includes bibliographical references

Kenney, Karen Latchana, 1974-
Librarians at work; by Karen L. Kenney; illustrated by Brian Caleb Dumm; content consultant, Judith Stepan-Norris. Magic Wagon 2010 32p il (Meet your community workers!) lib bdg $18.95
Grades: K 1 2 3   **020**
   1. Librarians 2. Vocational guidance
   ISBN 978-1-60270-649-1 (lib bdg); 1-60270-649-2 (lib bdg)   LC 2009-2386
This book about librarians has "an uncluttered layout and consistent organization. . . . Chapter headings such as 'Problems on the Job,' and 'Technology at Work,' and 'Special Skills and Training' make it easy to pinpoint specific information." SLJ
   Includes glossary

Misakian, Jo Ellen Priest
The essential school library glossary; [by] Jo Ellen Priest Misakian. Linworth Pub. 2004 96p pa $36.95
Grades: Professional   **020**
   1. Reference books 2. School libraries—Dictionaries
   ISBN 1-58683-150-X   LC 2004-6746
"This useful compendium of terms from 'Abstract' to 'Online Computer Library Center' to 'W3C' is succinct and easy to read. . . . Misakian includes terms specific to library-media programs as well as those related to the whole school program. This is a valuable resource for school librarians at all stages in their career." SLJ

021   Relationships of libraries, archives, information centers

York, Sherry, 1947-
Booktalking authentic multicultural literature; fiction and history for young readers. Linworth Pub. 2009 112p pa $39.95
Grades: Professional   **021**
   1. Book talks 2. Teenagers—Books and reading 3. Youth—Books and reading 4. Young adult literature—Bibliography 5. Multiculturalism—Bibliography 6. Multicultural education
   ISBN 978-1-58683-300-8; 1-58683-300-6
                     LC 200843798
Companion to: Booktalking Authentic Multicultural Literature: Fiction, History, and Memoirs for Teens (2008)
This title "highlights 101 contemporary books by a variety of U.S. authors. Arranged alphabetically by title, entries include the cultural background of author, illustrator, and translator; their Web sites when available; reading and interest levels; genre; related titles; and the single-paragraph booktalk itself. Over 20 ethnic groups are represented. . . . Librarians will find this book helpful in expanding their collections to reflect our global society." SLJ

021.2   Relationships with the community

Langemack, Chapple
The author event primer; how to plan, execute and enjoy author events. Libraries Unlimited 2007 188p pa $35 *
Grades: Professional   **021.2**
   1. Libraries and community 2. Authors
   ISBN 978-1-59158-302-8 (pa); 1-59158-302-0 (pa)
                     LC 2006032405
"Langemack gives practical guidance that will be useful to experienced and novice planners on how to host an author event. She covers everything, from reasons for having author visits to carrying off 'the really big do,' with humor and experience. The text is supplemented with charts; sample event proposals, fact sheets, letters, forms, and emails. . . . This book will be an invaluable source." Libr Media Connect
   Includes bibliographical references

Squires, Tasha, 1972-
Library partnerships; making connections between school and public libraries. Information Today, Inc. 2009 203p pa $39.50
Grades: Professional   **021.2**
   1. Libraries and schools 2. Libraries and students 3. Library cooperation 4. Public libraries 5. School libraries
   ISBN 978-1-57387-362-8 (pa); 1-57387-362-4 (pa)
                     LC 2008-51647
The author "delves into the many possible avenues for partnership [between school and public libraries], from summer reading programs to book talks to resource sharing and more." Publisher's note
"Squires's confident advice can get beleaguered librarians through . . . difficulties and into mutually productive partnerships." Voice Youth Advocates
   Includes bibliographical references

021.7   Promotion of libraries, archives, information centers

Brown, Mary E.
Exhibits in libraries; a practical guide; [by] Mary E. Brown and Rebecca Power. McFarland & Co. 2006 250p il pa $45
Grades: Professional   **021.7**
   1. Libraries—Exhibitions
   ISBN 0-7864-2352-8   LC 2005018508
This explains "what embodies an exhibit, types of exhibits, skills that a librarian needs to put an exhibit together, and the importance of exhibits. . . . This book is appropriate for all libraries thinking about exhibitions." Booklist
   Includes bibliographical references

Imhoff, Kathleen R.
Library contests; a how-to-do-it manual; [by] Kathleen R.T. Imhoff, Ruthie Maslin. Neal-Schuman Publishers 2007 182p il (How-to-do-it manuals for librarians) pa $55 *
Grades: Professional   **021.7**
     1. Contests 2. Libraries—Public relations 3. Advertising—Libraries 4. Libraries and community
     ISBN 1-55570-559-6 (pa); 978-1-55570-559-6 (pa)
                     LC 2006-33177
"This comprehensive book covers planning, implementing, and evaluating contests of all kinds, for all kinds of libraries. It addresses setting budgets and schedules, choosing prizes and judges, establishing rules, promoting the contest, and evaluating it once it is over. . . . The authors . . . cover potential negatives as well as positives in plain language. . . . The illustrations are informative." SLJ
Includes bibliographical references

Keane, Nancy J.
The tech-savvy booktalker; a guide for 21st-century educators; [by] Nancy J. Keane and Terence W. Cavanaugh. Libraries Unlimited 2009 162p il pa $35 *
Grades: Professional   **021.7**
     1. Book talks 2. Information technology
     ISBN 978-1-59158-637-1 (pa); 1-59158-637-2 (pa)
                     LC 2008-38988
"Keane offers a way to enhance booktalks with technology and to invite students to explore new ways to talk about books using Web 2.0 tools. The volume is divided into 11 chapters from booktalking concepts to more advanced uses of technology including scanners, digital cameras, computer software, and audio recording. Also included are chapters on software programs such as PowerPoint and iMovie as well as Internet sites such as YouTube and Amazon. The sequence of chapters is designed to allow easy access to information for both novice and experienced computer users. . . . This excellent resource shows ways to use existing technology to augment booktalks and to expand the experience beyond the classroom." SLJ
Includes bibliographical references

Phillips, Susan P., 1945-
Great displays for your library step by step. McFarland & Co. 2008 234p il pa $45
Grades: Professional   **021.7**
     1. Libraries—Exhibitions
     ISBN 978-0-7864-3164-9 (pa); 0-7864-3164-4 (pa)
                     LC 2007-47450
This volume is a "tool for designing . . . visual statements for library spaces. Each display includes a brief introduction to the subject; an explanation of the genesis of the idea; specifics regarding the information included and its source; step-by-step instructions for assembly; and ideas on how to customize the display to any available space." Publisher's note
"Phillips' enthusiasm, creativity, and breadth of personal interests are evident throughout this book. . . . This text will inspire readers to locate and showcase the treasures in their own collections." SLJ
Includes bibliographical references

Skaggs, Gayle, 1952-
Look, it's books! marketing your library with displays and promotions; [by] Gayle Skaggs. McFarland & Co. 2008 188p il pa $45
Grades: Professional   **021.7**
     1. School libraries 2. Libraries—Exhibitions 3. Books and reading
     ISBN 978-0-7864-3132-8 (pa); 0-7864-3132-6 (pa)
                     LC 2007049517
"For the elementary or middle school librarian (or the classroom teacher) looking to encourage literacy, this volume provides . . . ideas for promoting reading and encouraging students to learn about and use the library. The work begins with . . . ideas to market library services, including curriculum suggestions such as lessons to teach the Dewey Decimal System. A second section focuses on . . . ideas for decorating library spaces and various themes for reading programs as well as instructions for carrying these themes school-wide." Publisher's note
"A good basic resource for anyone needing ideas to promote reading to elementary students." Booklist

025.04   Information storage and retrieval systems

Blowers, Helene
Weaving a library Web; a guide to developing children's websites; [by] Helene Blowers and Robin Bryan. American Library Association 2004 197p il pa $32
Grades: Professional   **025.04**
     1. Web sites
     ISBN 0-8389-0877-2   LC 2004-1806
"A detailed description of topics and issues involved in designing, implementing, and maintaining Web sites for children. . . . This book can be used as a beginner's first stop and as a webmaster's companion. It is uncomplicated and easy to read." SLJ
Includes bibliographical references

Eisenberg, Michael
The Super3; information skills for young learners; [by] Michael B. Eisenberg and Laura Eisenberg Robinson. Linworth Pub. 2007 106p pa $39.95
Grades: Professional   **025.04**
     1. Information literacy—Study and teaching 2. Research
     ISBN 1-58683-286-7 (pa); 978-1-58683-286-5 (pa)
                     LC 2007010592
"The authors instruct readers on the implementation of the BIG6 ideas at the pre-K through second-grade levels. They hone the concepts down to three encompassing ones 'Plan, Do, and Review' called the Super3. . . . Most of the book supports a hands-on approach and provides users with a plethora of lessons and worksheets. . . . While geared toward younger students, ESL and struggling middle school students will benefit from many of the study-skills worksheets that use pictographs and graphic organizers." SLJ

11

Furgang, Adam
Searching online for image, audio, and video files. Rosen Central 2010 48p il (Digital and information literacy) lib bdg $26.50 *
Grades: 5 6 7 8   **025.04**
  1. Pictures 2. Sound recordings 3. Internet research 4. Internet searching
  ISBN 978-1-4358-5318-8 (lib bdg); 1-4358-5318-0 (lib bdg)   LC 2008-51726
Describes how to search for multimedia files on the Internet, including multimedia search engines, fair use of media files, and evaluating reliable sources
"Colorful photos, diagrams, and sidebars and [a] lively [text creates an] appealing, user-friendly [presentation]. . . . Students and teachers will find [this title] useful in keeping up-to-date on and utilizing online resources and today's technology in a rapidly changing digital world." SLJ
  Includes glossary and bibliographical references

Gordon, Rachel Singer
Teaching the Internet in libraries. American Library Association 2001 143p pa $38 *
Grades: Professional   **025.04**
  1. Internet searching—Study and teaching 2. Computer networks
  ISBN 0-8389-0799-7   LC 00-52564
"Chapters cover the reasons and methods to initiate programs, including convincing others of the necessity of such training, the importance of choosing proper trainers and how to do so; techniques for reaching diverse audiences such as parents, senior citizens, and Hispanics; training techniques and considerations such as lists of popular searches requested by patrons; and criteria for evaluating the program. Each section of the book concludes with resources for further information." Book Rep
  An "excellent and readable volume." Voice Youth Advocates
  Includes bibliographical references

McClure, Charles R.
Public libraries and internet service roles; measuring and maximizing Internet services; [by] Charles R. McClure and Paul T. Jaeger. American Library Association 2009 112p il map pa $65
Grades: Professional   **025.04**
  1. Public libraries 2. Internet
  ISBN 978-0-8389-3576-7 (pa); 0-8389-3576-1 (pa)
                                              LC 2008-26622
The authors "summarize the existing research on the meanings of social roles and expectations of public libraries and the results of studies detailing those roles and expectations in relation to the Internet. . . . Their book raises our awareness of some very critical issues and is required reading for anyone who cares about public libraries." Booklist
  Includes bibliographical references

Porterfield, Jason
Conducting basic and advanced searches. Rosen Central 2010 48p il (Digital and information literacy) lib bdg $26.50 *
Grades: 5 6 7 8   **025.04**
  1. Internet searching 2. Internet resources
  ISBN 978-1-4358-5316-4 (lib bdg); 1-4358-5316-4 (lib bdg)   LC 2008-46783
Describes how to conduct both basic and advanced searches on the Internet, from the basics of online search engines, boolean search terms, and evaluating the content of search results
"Colorful photos, diagrams, and sidebars and [a] lively [text creates an] appealing, user-friendly [presentation]. . . . Students and teachers will find [this title] useful in keeping up-to-date on and utilizing online resources and today's technology in a rapidly changing digital world." SLJ
  Includes glossary and bibliographical references

Wan Guofang
Virtually true; questioning online media; by Guofang Wan. Capstone Press 2007 32p il (Fact Finders: Media literacy) lib bdg $23.93; pa $7.95 *
Grades: 4 5 6 7   **025.04**
  1. Internet 2. Information literacy
  ISBN 978-0-7368-6767-2 (lib bdg); 0-7368-6767-8 (lib bdg); 978-0-7368-7863-0 (pa); 0-7368-7863-7 (pa)
                                              LC 2006021446
"Describes what media is, how the Internet is part of media, and encourages readers to question the medium's influential messages." Publisher's note
  This is "written in a breezy style and [has] plenty of popping colors and photos. . . . Useful and attractive." SLJ
  Includes bibliographical references

Wolinsky, Art
Internet power research using the Big6 approach. rev ed. Enslow Publishers 2005 64p il (Internet library) lib bdg $22.60; pa $11.93
Grades: Professional   **025.04**
  1. Information systems 2. Research
  ISBN 0-7660-1563-7 (lib bdg); 0-7660-1564-5 (pa)
                                              LC 2004-22185
  First published 2002
Provides instructions for using the "Big6" research method and scenarios for applying the technique to research conducted on the Internet.
  The information is presented in "a friendly, informal writing style. . . . This is a helpful resource for students who want to hone their research strategies." SLJ
  Includes glossary and bibliographical references

025.1 Administration

Anderson, Cynthia, 1945-

Write grants, get money; [by] Cynthia Anderson and Kathi Knop. 2nd ed. Linworth Pub. 2008 128p pa $44.95

Grades: Professional   025.1
   1. Grants-in-aid
   ISBN 978-1-58683-303-9 (pa); 1-58683-303-0 (pa)
                      LC 2008-22038

First published 2002

"This practical, grant writing manual will prove invaluable to both novice and experienced grant writers. Written clearly and concisely, this title outlines the grant writing process step by step, from generating ideas to the nuts and bolts of writing an effective proposal. . . . Multiple appendices provide a plethora of supplemental information such as resources on grant writing, Web sites, awards and contests, listservs for media specialists, and a sample grant proposal format. . . . This book makes grant writing as simple as its title." Libr Media Connect

Includes glossary and bibliographical references

Curzon, Susan Carol

Managing change; a how-to-do-it manual for librarians. rev ed. Neal-Schuman Publishers 2005 129p (How-to-do-it manuals for librarians) pa $55

Grades: Professional   025.1
   1. Libraries—Administration
   ISBN 1-55570-553-7   LC 2005-22846

First published 1989

The author "outlines the step-by-step processes and . . . instructions necessary for conceptualizing the issues; planning; preparing; decision-making; controlling resistance; and implementing changes. Practical guidance for dealing with technology's impact on libraries, applying the latest research in change management, and developing new strategies for coping with change are included." Publisher's note

"The real-world approach makes the book a valuable addition to the professional collection." Booklist

Includes bibliographical references

Hall-Ellis, Sylvia Dunn, 1949-

Grants for school libraries; [by] Sylvia D. Hall-Ellis and Ann Jerabek. Libraries Unlimited 2003 197p il pa $35 *

Grades: Professional   025.1
   1. Grants-in-aid 2. School libraries
   ISBN 1-59158-079-X   LC 2003-54630

"Hall-Ellis and Jerabek provide a systematic approach to every aspect of the grant process. Each section breaks down important concepts and is clearly supported by reproducible forms, examples, and lists. Two important segments address budget and personnel considerations. The project-evaluation section includes data-collection instruments and time lines, while a final chapter discusses practical suggestions such as publicity and writing letters of appreciation. . . . This surprisingly readable guide should be on every school library media specialist's professional shelf." SLJ

Includes bibliographical references

Hallam, Arlita

Managing budgets and finances; a how-to-do-it manual for librarians and information professionals. Neal-Schuman Publishers 2005 233p il (How-to-do-it manuals for librarians) pa $65 *

Grades: Professional   025.1
   1. Library finance
   ISBN 1-55570-519-7

"This budgeting manual . . . offers the new or seasoned library administrators, board members, department heads, or finance professionals a way to budget carefully and clearly by offering a variety of strategies, definitions, and suggestions. The manual is divided into three parts: basics for librarians, special topics in financial management for libraries, and alternative library funding." Booklist

Includes bibliographical references

Lushington, Nolan, 1929-

Libraries designed for kids. Neal-Schuman Publishers 2008 173p il pa $85 *

Grades: Professional   025.1
   1. Libraries—Administration 2. Children's libraries
   3. Young adults' libraries
   ISBN 978-1-55570-631-9   LC 2008-32537

"Lushington's guide will be invaluable to librarians and boards of trustees as they consider renovating, expanding, or creating new service areas for children and teens. . . . Lushington guides the planning team through creating the library program utilizing demographics and community input, which will help with determining the size of the facility. However, the largest sections of the book focus on design considerations to both enhance the user's experience and to most efficiently organize and supervise the collection and facility." SLJ

Includes bibliographical references

MacDonell, Colleen

Essential documents for school libraries; I've-got-it! answers to I-need-it-now! questions. Linworth Pub. 2004 132p il pa $44.95 *

Grades: Professional   025.1
   1. Libraries—Administration
   ISBN 978-1-58683-174-5 (pa); 1-58683-174-7 (pa)
                      LC 2004-19392

Contents: Planning documents; Official reports; Publicity; Teaching documents; Programming documents; Procedure sheets and guides; Library rules and regulations; Interactive forms

"Each chapter begins with why the documents are needed, followed by practical advice for writing the documents, and examples of how the documents make an effective change in the library media program." Libr Media Connect

"An excellent addition for school librarians who always want to be prepared." SLJ

Includes bibliographical references

Martin, Barbara Stein, 1947-
Fundamentals of school library media management; a how-to-do-it manual; [by] Barbara Stein Martin and Marco Zannier. Neal-Schuman Publishers 2009 172p il (How-to-do-it manuals for libraries) pa $59.95 *
Grades: Professional   **025.1**
1. School libraries 2. Instructional materials centers
ISBN 978-1-55570-656-2 (pa); 1-55570-656-8 (pa)
        LC 2009-7930
This book "contains useful information to help school librarians manage a myriad of tasks and roles. . . . [The authors] have created a book that is helpful, accessible, and full of down-to-earth, concrete examples." Booklist
Includes bibliographical references

Pugh, Lyndon
Managing 21st century libraries; [by] Lyndon Pugh. Scarecrow Press 2005 211p pa $40 *
Grades: Professional   **025.1**
1. Libraries—Administration
ISBN 0-8108-5185-7   LC 2005014531
This "details ways library managers and staff can develop systems for managing contemporary library services while taking advantage of circumstances that provide innovative organization development in the library services of today. Additionally, Lyndon Pugh specifically relates important issues in personnel management to the characteristics of libraries that deal significantly with both digital and printed material." Publisher's note
"A valuable guide to creating an organization for the e-future." Booklist
Includes bibliographical references

School library management; [edited by] Judi Repman and Gail Dickinson. 6th ed. Linworth Pub. 2007 200p il pa $44.95 *
Grades: Professional   **025.1**
1. School libraries 2. Libraries—Administration
ISBN 978-1-58683-296-4 (pa); 1-58683-296-4 (pa)
        LC 2006-103468
"This collection of more than 35 articles written for *Library Media Connection* from 2003 to 2006 is a virtual treasure trove for library media specialists. . . . The book covers the very practical everyday issues such as scheduling and overdues, and also provides invaluable information on data gathering, facilities planning, professional development, the role of the library in the world of standardized testing, the technological future of libraries, and much more." SLJ
Includes bibliographical references

Stueart, Robert D.
Library and information center management. 7th ed. Libraries Unlimited 2007 xxviii, 492p (Library and information science text series) $70; pa $50
Grades: Professional   **025.1**
1. Libraries—Administration
ISBN 978-1-59158-408-7; 978-1-59158-406-3 (pa)
        LC 2007-7922
This "covers all the essential functions involved in library management. New theories, concepts, and practices

currently being developed and used are included. . . . Both novices and veteran managers will find this to be a valuable tool." Booklist
Includes bibliographical references

Thelen, Laurie Noble
Essentials of elementary library management; by Laurie Noble Thelen. Linworth Pub. 2003 113p il pa $39.95   **025.1**
1. School libraries 2. Libraries—Administration
ISBN 1-58683-076-7   LC 2003-12889
Contents: Planning a new library media center; Starting over: the library media specialist in a new school district; Time management and the library media center; Budget secrets; Grant my wish; Programs to motivate a student to read; The library media specialist as collaborator and reading advocate; Encouraging staff to use new technology; Guidelines for positive student behavior; Finding and keeping volunteers and media clerks
This "guide covers the basics of school librarianship, with special emphasis on the one-person operation. Facilities planning, budgeting, technology advocacy, reading motivation, and student discipline are among the topics included. . . . A handy and functional volume that will be appreciated by both newbies and veteran media specialists 'in transition.'" SLJ
Includes bibliographical references

The **whole** digital library handbook; edited by Diane Kresh for the Council on Library and Information Resources. American Library Association 2007 416p il pa $55
Grades: Professional   **025.1**
1. Digital libraries
ISBN 978-0-8389-0926-3 (pa); 0-8389-0926-4 (pa)
        LC 2006-27498
"Part 1 defines the digital library, e-reference, and the digital library federation. Additional parts cover users, tools, operations, and more. Besides librarians, other experts and commentators on the various technologies present their views on topics ranging from Google's digital book project, to interpretations of NextGen demographic data, to digital preservation. . . . [This] should engender raucous discussions and debates." Booklist
Includes bibliographical references

025.2 Acquisitions and collection development

Baumbach, Donna
Less is more; a practical guide to weeding school library collections. American Library Association 2006 194p il pa $32 *
Grades: Professional   **025.2**
1. Libraries—Collection development
ISBN 978-0-8389-0919-5 (pa); 0-8389-0919-1 (pa)
        LC 2006-7490
Contents: The role of weeding in collection development (why less is more); General weeding guidelines; Getting started and keeping on keeping on; Weeding criteria by topic and Dewey number; What automation hath wrought; What's next?

Baumbach, Donna—*Continued*

"This outstanding, easy-to-use guide makes weeding realistic and achievable. . . . This is an indispensable resource for every school library." Booklist

Includes bibliographical references

Brenner, Robin E., 1977-

Understanding manga and anime. Libraries Unlimited 2007 335p il pa $40 *

Grades: Professional   025.2

1. Manga—Study and teaching 2. Anime 3. Libraries—Special collections—Graphic novels 4. Libraries—Collection development

ISBN 978-1-59158-332-5 (pa); 1-59158-332-2 (pa)

LC 2007-9773

Contents: Short history of manga and anime; Manga and anime vocabulary; Culture clash: East meets West; Adventures with ninjas and schoolgirls: humor and realism; Samurai and shogun: action, war, and historical fiction; Giant robots and nature spirits: science fiction, fantasy, and legends; Understanding fans and fan culture; Draw in a crowd: promotion and programs; Collection development

The author "provides thorough explanations of manga and anime vocabulary, potential censorship issues because of cultural disparities, and typical Manga conventions. . . . No professional collection could possibly be complete without this all-inclusive and exceptional work." Voice Youth Advocates

Doll, Carol Ann

Managing and analyzing your collection; a practical guide for small libraries and school media centers; [by] Carol A. Doll, Pamela Petrick Barron. American Library Association 2002 93p il pa $30 *

Grades: Professional   025.2

1. Libraries—Collection development

ISBN 0-8389-0821-7   LC 2001-53747

This guide to collection development is divided into chapters covering management objectives, gathering and analyzing collection data, and weeding

This is a "book that librarians will actually read from cover to cover. . . . [It] isn't overwhelming and technical. Instead, it is rather chatty with solid, useful information." Book Rep

Includes bibliographical references

Gallaway, Beth, 1975-

Game on! gaming at the library. Neal-Schuman Publishers 2009 306p il pa $55 *

Grades: Professional   025.2

1. Libraries—Special collections 2. Video games

ISBN 978-1-55570-595-4 (pa); 1-55570-595-2 (pa)

LC 2009-14110

"An essential guide for any librarian who plans on embracing the video-game phenomenon, or at the very least, understanding it. . . . The chapters . . . are well organized and contain an abundance of practical information. The sections on selection, collection, and circulation of video games include relevant advice on policy, cataloging, marketing, storage, and displays. . . . The anno-

tated list of video games for a core collection is wonderful for selection purposes." SLJ

Includes bibliographical references

Goldsmith, Francisca

The readers' advisory guide to graphic novels. American Library Association 2010 124p (ALA readers' advisory series) pa $45

Grades: Professional   025.2

1. Libraries—Special collections 2. Graphic novels—Bibliography

ISBN 978-0-8389-1008-5 (pa); 0-8389-1008-4 (pa)

LC 2009-25239

"The American Library Association (ALA) adds another excellent and, in this case, much-needed volume to its readers' advisory library with this succinct guide. . . . After dispelling the two main myths that ghettoize graphic novels—they are just for adolescents and they are far less complex than texts without pictures—Goldsmith emphasizes that GNs are a format and not a genre. She suggests active and passive ways to offer readers' advisory (RA) from face-to-face encounters with patrons to book displays and book groups and offers guidance on helping established GN readers to find new titles they might enjoy. . . . All in all it is a valuable and quite readable resource that belongs in every library's professional collection." Voice Youth Advocates

Includes glossary and bibliographical references

Graphic novels beyond the basics; insights and issues for libraries; Martha Cornog and Timothy Perper, editors. Libraries Unlimited 2009 xxx, 281p il pa $45

Grades: Professional   025.2

1. Libraries—Special collections—Graphic novels 2. Graphic novels—History and criticism 3. Comic books, strips, etc.—History and criticism

ISBN 978-1-59158-478-0   LC 2009-16189

Editors Cornog and Perper have collected essays by experts Robin Brenner, Francisca Goldsmith, Trina Robbins, Michael R. Lavin, Gilles Poitras, Lorena O'English, Michael Niederhausen, Erin Byrne, and Cornog herself, all about graphic novels in libraries. Topics covered range from the appeal of superheroes to manga, the appeal of comics to women and girls, anime, independent comics, dealing with challenges to the material, and more. Appendices provide resource information on African American-interest graphic novels, Latino-Interest graphic novels, LGBT-interest graphic novels, religious-themed graphic novels, a bibliography of books about graphic novels in libraries, and online resources.

"Whether you are serious about the genre, interested in the history, or looking for ammunition, this book should be on your shelf. The wealth of knowledge and research that went into these essays is impressive, and reading this book will put you on the road to becoming an expert." Libr Media Connect

Includes bibliographical references

Greiner, Tony

Analyzing library collection use with Excel. American Library Association 2007 167p il pa $40 *

Grades: Professional   **025.2**
1. Library circulation 2. Libraries—Collection development 3. Excel (Computer program)
ISBN 978-0-8389-0933-1 (pa); 0-8389-0933-7 (pa)
                                        LC 2006-101539
The authors "show how to use Excel® to translate circulation and collection data into meaningful reports for making collection management decisions." Publisher's note
Includes bibliographical references

Hughes-Hassell, Sandra

Collection management for youth; responding to the needs of learners; [by] Sandra Hughes-Hassell, Jacqueline C. Mancall. ALA Editions 2005 103p il pa $35 *
Grades: Professional   **025.2**
1. Libraries—Collection development 2. Instructional materials centers
ISBN 0-8389-0894-2   LC 2004-26911
"The authors present 11 . . . tools for creating a learner-centered collection with suggestions on the best methods for easy implementation of these procedures. . . . Every library media specialist wanting a more practical approach to collection management would find this book an important addition to his or her professional development library." Libr Media Connect
Includes bibliographical references

Lyga, Allyson A. W.

Graphic novels in your media center; a definitive guide; by Allyson A. W. Lyga with Barry Lyga. Libraries Unlimited 2004 180p il pa $35
Grades: Professional   **025.2**
1. Graphic novels—Administration 2. Book selection 3. Books and reading
ISBN 1-59158-142-7   LC 2004-46517
In the first section the authors "make cogent arguments for the inclusion of graphic novels. A second section introduces common terms and includes an extremely useful 'how to read' subsection, complete with sample pages. The remaining sections provide recommended titles for all ages, testimonials from teachers and comic book store proprietors, resource lists, and a set of 17 lesson plans." Booklist
"This indispensable, well-organized guide will provide school librarians with all of the necessary information for implementing and developing a graphic-novels collection." SLJ

Miller, Steve

Developing and promoting graphic novel collections. Neal-Schuman Publishers 2005 130p il (Teens @ the library series) pa $49.95
Grades: Professional   **025.2**
1. Graphic novels—Administration 2. Book selection 3. Books and reading
ISBN 1-55570-461-1   LC 2004-40159

This is an "overview of graphic novels and their use as reader development tools. Miller explores the evolution, categories, and genres of graphic novels; he then addresses the . . . details of collection development, acquisition, cataloging, and maintenance for this unique format. A special section shows how to promote graphic novels (include display ideas)." Publisher's note
"This volume is filled with practical information and savvy advice." SLJ
Includes bibliographical references

Scales, Pat R.

Protecting intellectual freedom in your school library; scenarios from the front lines; [by] Pat R. Scales for the Office for Intellectual Freedom. American Library Association 2009 148p (Intellectual freedom front lines) pa $55 *
Grades: Professional   **025.2**
1. School libraries 2. Intellectual freedom
ISBN 978-0-8389-3581-1 (pa); 0-8389-3581-8 (pa)
                                        LC 2008-39893
"Scales uses court opinions, federal and state laws, and ALA documents to offer solutions for responding to infringements. A broad range of potential scenarios—from challenges to materials in both the library and the classroom, the legality of film rating systems, using computerized reading programs as selection tools and labeling books by reading levels, policies for interlibrary loans and reserves to confidentiality of children's and teens' circulation records—are covered. . . . This resource should be in every school library's professional collection." Voice Youth Advocates
Includes bibliographical references

Serchay, David S., 1971-

The librarian's guide to graphic novels for children and tweens. Neal-Schuman Publishers 2008 272p pa $55 *
Grades: Professional   **025.2**
1. Graphic novels 2. Children—Books and reading 3. Libraries—Special collections—Graphic novels
ISBN 978-1-55570-626-5 (pa); 1-55570-626-5 (pa)
                                        LC 2008-6487
This book provides a brief history of graphic novels, describes genres, discusses manga, gives librarians reasons to include graphic novels in library collections and in school curricula. It also discusses some of the major comic book publishers in the U.S., suggests how to purchase graphic novels, and how to process, catalog, and shelve them, and also how to use them in programming. Several lengthy appendices provide annotated lists of titles that are suitable for children and tween readers, online resources for purchasing, reviews, and news, and additional, comics-related books
"An insightful introduction to this format as well as an effective selection tool, this guide is highly recommended." Booklist
Includes bibliographical references

Symons, Ann K.

Protecting the right to read; a how-to-do-it manual for school and public librarians; [by] Ann K. Symons, Charles Harmon; illustrations by Pat Race. Neal-Schuman 1995 211p il (How-to-do-it manuals for librarians) pa $55 *

Grades: Professional   **025.2**

1. Libraries—Censorship 2. Intellectual freedom

ISBN 1-55570-216-3   LC 95-42444

"The authors take readers from discussion of the policies and principles of intellectual freedom to considerations specific to school and public libraries to the protection of freedom on the Internet. . . . Appendixes consist of reprints of documents put out by the ALA and the Minnesota Coalition Against Censorship." Book Rep

"Intellectual freedom issues and guiding principles get a thorough and comprehensive treatment. . . . An essential book." Voice Youth Advocates

Includes bibliographical references

025.3 Bibliographic analysis and control

Cataloging correctly for kids; an introduction to the tools; edited by Sheila S. Intner, Joanna F. Fountain, Jane E. Gilchrist; Association for Library Collections and Technical Services. 4th ed. American Library Association 2006 136p bibl il tab pa $32 *

Grades: Professional   **025.3**

1. Reference books 2. Cataloging

ISBN 0-8389-3559-1   LC 2005018838

First published 1989 by the Cataloging for Children's Materials Committee

Among the topics discussed are: guidelines for standardized cataloging for children; how children search; using AACR2 and MARC 21; Sears List of Subject Headings; LC Children's headings; sources for Dewey numbers; cataloging nonbook materials; authority control; how the CIP program helps children; automating the children's catalog; vendors of cataloging for children's materials

Includes bibliographical references

Gorman, Michael, 1941-

The concise AACR2; prepared by Michael Gorman. 4th ed. American Library Association 2004 179p pa $40

Grades: Professional   **025.3**

1. Anglo-American cataloguing rules 2. Reference books 3. Cataloging

ISBN 0-8389-3548-6   LC 2004-16088

First published 1981

"This practical guidebook . . . [is] in concordance with AACR2, 2002 Revision 2004 Update. Michael Gorman . . . explains the more generally applicable AACR2 rules for cataloging library materials in simplified terms that make the rules more accessible and practical for practitioners and students who are in less complex library and bibliographic environments." Publisher's note

Kaplan, Allison G.

Catalog it! a guide to cataloging school library materials; [by] Allison G. Kaplan, Ann Marlow Riedling. 2nd ed. Linworth Publishing 2006 212p il $44.95 *

Grades: Professional   **025.3**

1. Reference books 2. Cataloging 3. School libraries 4. Instructional materials centers

ISBN 978-1-58683-197-4; 1-58683-197-6

"This practical, how-to manual provides a breakdown of the theories, rules, and issues that anyone cataloging school library materials needs to know. The first part . . . includes a condensed history of cataloging, basic tools for copy cataloging, and information on theory and the MARC record. The second part is devoted to application. . . . Using clear summaries and a nice variety of examples, this section also offers exercises. . . . This is a must for school libraries and academic libraries that have K-12 collections." Booklist

025.4 Subject analysis and control

Sears list of subject headings; Joseph Miller, editor; Susan McCarthy, associate editor. 20th ed. H.W. Wilson Co. 2010 847p $150 *

Grades: Professional   **025.4**

1. Subject headings

ISBN 978-0-8242-1105-9; 0-8242-1105-7

LC 2010005731

Also available Canadian companion. 6th edition published 2001

First published 1923 with title: List of subject headings for small libraries, by Minnie Earl Sears

"The Sears List of Subject Headings delivers a core list of key headings, together with patterns and examples to guide the cataloger in creating additional headings as required. It features: agreement with the Dewey Decimal Classification system to ensure that subject headings conform with library standards; [a] thesaurus-like format; accompanying list of canceled and replacement headings; and legends within the list that identify earlier forms of headings; scope notes accompanying all new and revised headings where clarification of the specialized use of a term may be required." Publisher's note

Includes bibliographical references

025.5 Services for users

Bell, Suzanne S.

Librarian's guide to online searching. 2nd ed. Libraries Unlimited 2009 287p il pa $45

Grades: Professional   **025.5**

1. Internet searching

ISBN 978-1-59158-763-7 (pa); 1-59158-763-8 (pa)

LC 2008-35924

First published 2006

This "online searching guide will be invaluable to anyone starting out or looking for a refresher course on this topic. In clear concise language, the author covers everything from Boolean searching to using specific topic-based databases. . . . This easy-to-use manual, written with just a touch of humor and not a drop of condescen-

Bell, Suzanne S.—*Continued*

sion, is sure to be embraced by librarians of all skill levels." Voice Youth Advocates

Includes bibliographical references

Duncan, Donna

I-search for success; a how-to-do-it manual for linking the I-search process with standards, assessment, tests, and evidence-based practice; [by] Donna Duncan and Laura Lockhart. Neal-Schuman Publishers 2005 xxi, 277p il (How-to-do-it manuals for librarians) pa $75 *

Grades: Professional   025.5

1. Research 2. Libraries

ISBN 1-55570-510-3   LC 2004-54665

"Extending the authors' previous book, *I-Search, You Search, We All Learn to Research* (Neal-Schuman, 2000), this title takes readers step-by-step through a unit for grades three and four, from planning to assessment. . . . Large boxed figures interspersed throughout the text include I-Search forms, worksheets, organizational tools, and lists of resources for further information. The accompanying CD-ROM contains the collaborative planning guide, the I-Search journal for students, and a PowerPoint presentation for professional development found in the book, with all of the figures incorporated for easy modification and printing. This is a valuable resource guide for teachers and librarians using, or planning to use, the I-Search method." Booklist

Includes bibliographical references

Gaines, Ann

Ace your research paper; [by] Ann Graham Gaines. Enslow Publishers 2009 48p il (Ace it! information literacy) lib bdg $23.93

Grades: 3 4 5   025.5

1. Report writing 2. English language—Composition and exercises 3. Research

ISBN 978-0-7660-3390-0 (lib bdg); 0-7660-3390-2 (lib bdg)   LC 2008024884

"Readers will learn how to research, take notes, write, and revise their research papers" Publisher's note

Includes glossary and bibliographical references

Grassian, Esther Stampfer

Information literacy instruction; theory and practice; [by] Esther S. Grassian and Joan R. Kaplowitz. 2nd ed. Neal-Schuman Publishers 2009 412p pa $75 *

Grades: Professional   025.5

1. Information literacy

ISBN 978-155570-666-1 (pa); 1-55570-666-5 (pa)
LC 2009-23647

First published 2001

This "is designed for anyone involved in the creation and management of information literacy programming. Sixteen well-written chapters, organized into five sections, provide both theory and practical applications, with the emphasis on the practical. . . . Several extras appear in the accompanying CD-ROM. . . . A timely, thorough, and endlessly useful must-have title for librarians, teaching librarians, and library schools." Booklist

Includes bibliographical references

Miller, Pat

Library skills. UpstartBooks 2003 56p il (Stretchy library lessons) pa $15.95

Grades: Professional   025.5

1. Bibliographic instruction 2. Children's libraries

ISBN 1-57950-083-8   LC 2003-245

Contents: Genre relay; Caldecott challenge; Fairy tale or folktale?; Where in the library?; Real or imagined?; Selecting a book; Book care; Meet Melvil; What's my line?; Life stories

This includes ten library skills lesson plans which can be presented in 20 minutes or expanded to an hour, focusing "on basic skills such as parts of a book, fiction and nonfiction, genres and the Dewey Decimal System." Publisher's note

This book is "great for lesson plans for school media specialists, and . . . [it also has] some interesting ideas for crafts and activities for public librarians. . . . [A must-have] for anyone working in a school library." SLJ

Includes bibliographical references

Reading activities. UpstartBooks 2003 80p il (Stretchy library lessons) pa $15.95

Grades: Professional   025.5

1. Books and reading 2. Children's libraries

ISBN 1-57950-082-X   LC 2003-279132

This includes ten reading activity lesson plans which can be presented in 20 minutes or expanded to an hour, focusing "on basic reading skills such as cause and effect, fact and opinion, main idea with supporting details, story mapping, graphic organizers and retelling in sequence." Publisher's note

This book is "great for lesson plans for school media specialists, and . . . [it also has] some interesting ideas for crafts and activities for public librarians. . . . [A must-have] for anyone working in a school library." SLJ

Research skills. UpstartBooks 2003 79p il (Stretchy library lessons) pa $15.95

Grades: Professional   025.5

1. Research 2. Children's libraries

ISBN 1-57950-084-6   LC 2003-271646

This includes ten research skills lesson plans which can be presented in 20 minutes or expanded to an hour focusing on "using electronic and print resources, forming questions and locating answers and gathering and organizing information." Publisher's note

This book is "great for lesson plans for school media specialists, and . . . {it also has} some interesting ideas for crafts and activities for public librarians. . . . [A must-have] for anyone working in a school library." SLJ

Includes bibliographical references

Standards for the 21st-century learner in action. American Association of School Librarians 2009 120p pa $39

Grades: Professional   025.5

1. Information literacy 2. Libraries—Standards

ISBN 978-0-8389-8507-6 (pa); 0-8389-8507-6 (pa)

"Standards in Action attempts to expand upon AASL's Standards for the 21st Century Learner by providing benchmarks and action examples. The original document was a nine-page brochure that outlined nine common beliefs, four learning standards, four strands, and indicators under each strand. It was an excellent starting point, but

Standards for the 21st-century learner in action—*Continued*

the addition of benchmarks at grades two, five, eight, ten, and twelve helps flesh out the original vision. . . . School libraries should own a copy of this professional, which has a role within any program." Voice Youth Advocates

Includes glossary and bibliographical references

027 General libraries, archives, information centers

Munro, Roxie, 1945-

The inside-outside book of libraries; paintings by Roxie Munro; text by Julie Cummins. Dutton Children's Bks. 1996 unp il hardcover o.p. pa $7.99 *

Grades: 2 3 4   **027**

1. Libraries

ISBN 0-525-45608-2; 0-375-84451-1 (pa)

LC 96-12111

Illustrations and brief text present various types of libraries, from bookmobiles and home libraries to the New York Public Library and the Library of Congress

"Cummins's text flows smoothly and is easy to comprehend, and the vast array of facilities discussed will add greatly to children's understanding of the concept of library services. Munro's excellent watercolor illustrations are extremely detailed and reveal an incredible sense of each architectural space." SLJ

Sawa, Maureen

The library book; the story of libraries from camels to computers; illustrated by Bill Slavin. Tundra Books 2006 72p il $18.95

Grades: 3 4 5 6   **027**

1. Libraries

ISBN 0-88776-698-6

"This information-packed picture book is an excellent tribute to libraries around the world, describing the development of libraries from ancient times to today. . . . The picture-book format, filled with earth-toned illustrations, adds appeal. . . . The book is also filled with interesting sidebars and highlighted sections of information." Voice Youth Advocates

Includes bibliographical references

Trumble, Kelly

The Library of Alexandria; illustrated by Robina MacIntyre Marshall. Clarion Bks. 2003 72p il maps $17

Grades: 5 6 7 8   **027**

1. Alexandrian Library (Egypt) 2. Egypt—Civilization 3. Ancient civilization

ISBN 0-395-75832-7   LC 2003-150

Contents: A city of learning; Collecting books; Pergamum; Astronomy; Geography; Mathematics; Medicine; Decline and destruction; The fate of the Library of Alexandria

An introduction to the largest and most famous library in the ancient world, discussing its construction in Alexandria, Egypt, its vast collections, rivalry with the Pergamum Library, famous scholars, and destruction by fire

This is a "well-organized and thorough resource." SLJ

Includes glossary and bibliographical references

027.6 Libraries for special groups and organizations

Alire, Camila

Serving Latino communities; a how-to-do-it manual for librarians; [by] Camila Alire, Jacqueline Ayala. 2nd ed. Neal-Schuman Publishers 2007 229p bibl il (How-to-do-it manuals for librarians) pa $59.95 *

Grades: Professional   **027.6**

1. Libraries and Hispanic Americans

ISBN 978-1-55570-606-7 (pa); 1-55570-606-1 (pa)

LC 2007-7783

First published 1998

"The information covered helps library staff understand the needs of their library's Latino community; develop successful programs and services; obtain funding for projects and programs; prepare staff to work more effectively with Latinos; establish partnerships with relevant external agencies and organizations; improve collection development; and perform effective outreach and public relations. . . . There are few resources widely available on this topic and none as complete." Libr Media Connect

Includes bibliographical references

Diamant-Cohen, Betsy

Early literacy programming en Español; Mother Goose on the Loose programs for bilingual learners. Neal-Schuman Publishers 2010 xxii, 177p il pa $65

Grades: Professional   **027.6**

1. Children's libraries 2. Nursery rhymes 3. Bilingual education

ISBN 978-1-55570-691-3; 1-55570-691-6

LC 2009049594

"Diamant-Cohen has developed this manual to encourage librarians to present Spanish-language MGOL programs. . . . The author proposes recruiting community partners fluent in Spanish who will be trained by the children's librarian and will copresent the sessions. Five parts cover the basics on how to run the program successfully. The manual is complemented with illustrations that can be replicated and used as flannel-board figures; bibliographies, worksheets, and a CD with instructions; nursery rhymes in English and Spanish; and graphics and templates of documents. This volume is infused with enthusiasm to serve the children of Spanish-speakers. It will not only help English-speaking librarians, but also the bilingual ones to present and enjoy MGOL." SLJ

Includes bibliographical references

The **family-centered** library handbook; Sandra Feinberg . . . [et al.] Neal-Schuman Publishers 2007 xv, 324p il pa $65

Grades: Professional   **027.6**
1. Children's libraries
ISBN 978-1-55570-541-1 (pa); 1-55570-541-3 (pa)
LC 2006102709

"This volume encourages libraries to increase services to children and those who care for these children, make programming developmentally appropriate, incorporate early intervention and primary prevention strategies, build relationships with family service professionals, and make children's library spaces inviting. . . . This highly organized handbook provides a wealth of information for libraries wanting to enhance their children's programming." Booklist

Includes bibliographical references

MacMillan, Kathy, 1975-
A box full of tales; easy ways to share library resources through story boxes. American Library Association 2008 222p pa $45

Grades: Professional   **027.6**
1. Children's libraries 2. Library cooperation 3. Storytelling
ISBN 978-0-8389-0960-7 (pa); 0-8389-0960-4 (pa)
LC 2007-48794

"The author, a veteran librarian and storyteller, here offers up the story box model of program resource sharing pioneered at Maryland's Carroll County Library System. Story boxes contain all the resources necessary to conduct a theme-based story time session; the boxes are created by children's librarians to be shared with other librarians at different locations within a system. . . . Even children's librarians who don't work in multibranch systems will find this guide extremely valuable for its theme-based program outlines, whether or not they choose to create story boxes. Strongly recommended for public libraries." Libr J

Includes bibliographical references

027.62 Libraries for specific age groups

Bauer, Caroline Feller, 1935-
Leading kids to books through crafts. American Lib. Assn. 2000 145p (Mighty easy motivators) pa $30

Grades: Professional   **027.62**
1. Reference books 2. Children's libraries 3. Books and reading 4. Handicraft 5. Children's literature—Bibliography
ISBN 0-8389-0769-5   LC 99-41387

"Bauer gives basic, practical information on presenting programs that introduce preschool and primary-grade youngsters to stories and poems and demonstrates related crafts that are easy to prepare and execute." SLJ

Leading kids to books through magic; illustrated by Richard Laurent. American Lib. Assn. 1996 128p il (Mighty easy motivators) pa $35

Grades: Professional   **027.62**
1. Reference books 2. Children's libraries 3. Books and reading 4. Magic tricks 5. Children's literature—Bibliography
ISBN 978-0-8389-0684-2 (pa); 0-8389-0684-2 (pa)
LC 95-53049

"Bauer shows how she uses magic tricks to entertain children as she leads them to good books. . . . Each section includes instructions for performing at least one trick as well as a short, annotated list of related books and, occasionally, a story or poem to present as part of the magician's patter." Booklist

The author's "concise yet thorough directions accompanied by Richard Laurent's delightful line drawings make this book a useful tool for teachers and librarians looking for ways to promote children's enthusiasm for reading." J Youth Serv Libr

Includes bibliographical references

Leading kids to books through puppets; illustrated by Richard Laurent. American Lib. Assn. 1997 156p il (Mighty easy motivators) pa $35

Grades: Professional   **027.62**
1. Reference books 2. Children's libraries 3. Books and reading 4. Puppets and puppet plays 5. Children's literature—Bibliography
ISBN 978-0-8389-0706-1 (pa); 0-8389-0706-7 (pa)
LC 97-1357

This "book suggests ways to promote books and reading to children through simple puppetry. . . . [It offers] a number of theme-based programs complete with stories to act out, poems, and lists of related books." Booklist

"Even the most reluctant performer will be encouraged by this practical, concise, easy-to-use book." SLJ

Includes bibliographical references

Benton, Gail, 1950-
Ready-to-go storytimes; fingerplays, scripts, patterns, music, and more; [by] Gail Benton, Trisha Waichulaitis. Neal-Schuman 2003 239p il pa $65

Grades: Professional   **027.62**
1. Storytelling 2. Children's libraries
ISBN 978-1-55570-449-0 (pa); 1-55570-449-2 (pa)
LC 2002-5806

"The six chapters represent six themed programs that include a welcome song, a read-aloud book, and various enrichment activities such as fingerplays, props, songs, coloring projects, and games. The accompanying CD includes 14 songs appropriate for the specific themes." SLJ

"This resource is excellent for beginning librarians and teachers and for any professionals who seek new ideas to freshen up their repertoires." Booklist

Includes bibliographical references

Bird, Elizabeth, 1978-

Children's literature gems; choosing and using them in your library career. American Library Association 2009 125p pa $45

Grades: Professional   **027.62**

   1. Children's libraries 2. Children—Books and reading 3. Children's literature—Bibliography 4. Book selection

   ISBN 978-0-8389-0995-9 (pa); 0-8389-0995-7 (pa)

                    LC 2009003079

"Bird writes in a chatty tone reminiscent of her popular blog, A Fuse #8 Production, and her love of children's literature shines through on every page. This slim volume is not meant to be an in-depth textbook, but rather a brief overview of the field and an introduction to the stars of children's literature. . . . Highlighted boxes throughout feature questions and answers from seasoned professionals on how they handle various parts of their collections and aspects of their work. Readers who are new to the field may find this a comforting basic guide to managing their collections. " SLJ

Includes bibliographical references

Bromann, Jennifer

More storytime action! 2,000+ more ideas for making 500+ picture books interactive. Neal-Schuman Publishers 2009 326p pa $55

Grades: Professional   **027.62**

   1. Children's libraries 2. Storytelling 3. Picture books for children—Bibliography

   ISBN 978-1-55570-675-3 (pa); 1-55570-675-4 (pa)

                    LC 2009031724

"Bromann presents more than 2,000 activities related to more than 500 picture books published since 2003. Beginning chapters cover 10 elements of interactive stories; storytelling, including how to select and prepare stories; and how to select books for interactive storytimes, identifying clues found in reviews. . . . The final chapter lists the more than 500 books alphabetically by author with bibliographic information, summary, and storytime activities. . . . For librarians looking to hold the attention of their youngest patrons or to spice up storytime, this title will be a welcome resource." Booklist

Includes bibliographical references

Storytime action! 2000+ ideas for making 500 picture books interactive. Neal-Schuman 2003 295p pa $45

Grades: Professional   **027.62**

   1. Reference books 2. Children's libraries 3. Storytelling 4. Picture books for children—Bibliography

   ISBN 1-55570-459-X   LC 2002-31994

The author "provides readers with ideas and tools to add interactivity to their programs. Tips include incorporating props, questions, movement, etc.; selecting the right books for your style; and adding simple crafts. Most of the book consists of an alphabetical listing (by author) of 500 recommended titles." SLJ

This "is packed with practical and fun activities for educators, parents, public librarians, and school media specialists." Booklist

Includes bibliographical references

Cerny, Rosanne

Outstanding library service to children; putting the core competencies to work; [by] Rosanne Cerny, Penny Markey, and Amanda Williams. American Library Association 2006 94p pa $25 *

Grades: Professional   **027.62**

   1. Children's libraries

   ISBN 978-0-8389-0922-5 (pa); 0-8389-0922-1 (pa)

   Contents: Knowledge of client group; Administrative and management skills; Communication skills; Materials and collection development; Programming skills; Advocacy, public relations, and networking skills; Professionalism and professional development

"The Association for Library Service to Children (ALSC) has outlined seven core competencies—skills and best practices that are the building blocks for professional development for children's librarians. . . . Each chapter, focusing on one of the competencies, [aims to get] new and experienced librarians up to speed . . . by offering explanations, examples, and a substantial bibliography for more in-depth learning." Publisher's note

"This slim volume should be required reading for all future children's services librarians." Booklist

Includes bibliiographical references

Cobb, Jane

What'll I do with the baby-o? nursery rhymes, songs, and stories for babies. Black Sheep 2007 255p pa $39.95

Grades: Professional   **027.62**

   1. Children's libraries

   ISBN 978-0-9698666-1-9

"Extensive preliminary chapters cover such things as identifying the audience, considering the developmental needs of the babies, and selecting and teaching the rhymes and books. The remainder of the book contains thoughtful suggestions of specific rhymes and songs, as well as comments to use with parents. . . . A musical CD provides samples of songs. . . . This book is a must-have for those embarking upon 'Baby and Me' or 'Mother Goose'-type programs." SLJ

Cullum, Carolyn N.

The storytime sourcebook II; [a compendium of 3500+ new ideas and resources for storytellers] Neal-Schuman Publishers 2007 489p pa $75 *

Grades: Professional   **027.62**

   1. Storytelling 2. Children's libraries

   ISBN 978-1-55570-589-3 (pa); 1-55570-589-8 (pa)

                    LC 2006-35096

First published 1990 with title: The storytime sourcebook

Subtitle from cover

"Each of the 146 themed programs, designed for children ages two to eight, appears on two facing pages that include appropriate calendar tie-ins, videos, books, music, movements, crafts, activities, and songs. . . . [The author] presents clear and simple directions for crafts and activities, quick and uncomplicated for librarians to prepare, and easy for children to follow. . . . This sourcebook is an essential purchase for libraries serving this audience." SLJ

Includes bibliographical references

Dixon, Tiara

The sound of storytime; [by] Tiara Dixon and Paula Blough. Neal-Schuman Publishers 2006 206p il pa $65

Grades: Professional **027.62**
1. Reference books 2. Children's libraries 3. Storytelling 4. Children's literature—Bibliography
ISBN 978-1-55570-552-7 (pa); 1-55570-552-9 (pa)
LC 2006001299

"This book takes the traditional storytime for early childhood and adds singing and simple instruments such as bells and rhythm sticks. Forty-two lesson plans centered around specific books are given in detail, with song suggestions and lists of additional appropriate books. Simple crafts complete each program. The inclusion of a CD-ROM with Ellison die cuts and original lyrics matched to commonly known songs such as 'Three Blind Mice' adds to the lessons." Booklist

Includes bibliographical references

Ernst, Linda L.

Baby rhyming time; [by] Linda L. Ernst. Neal-Schuman Publishers 2008 235p il pa $59.95

Grades: Professional **027.62**
1. Children's libraries
ISBN 978-1-55570-540-4 (pa); 1-55570-540-5 (pa)
LC 2007043246

Includes audio CD

"This useful resource provides background, logistics, and a wealth of practical ideas for programs. Ernst describes brain development and language acquisition clearly, with quotes and references for support. She does a good job of tying the science to infant/toddler growth and explaining the librarian's important role in sharing the information with caregivers. She discusses broader factors to consider when planning baby-time programs, including community, facilities, staffing, and potential partnerships." SLJ

Includes bibliographical references

Fasick, Adele M., 1930-

Managing children's services in the public library; [by] Adele M. Fasick and Leslie E. Holt. 3rd ed. Libraries Unlimited 2008 248p bibl il tab pa $45

Grades: Professional **027.62**
1. Children's libraries 2. Public libraries 3. Children—Books and reading
ISBN 978-1-59158-412-4 (pa); 1-59158-412-4 (pa)
LC 2007032759

First published 1991

"Section I deals with planning services in the context of a community. Section II covers maintaining a productive work environment, recruiting and retaining staff, communicating with colleagues, annual reports, budgeting and fundraising, planning facilities, and keeping the department safe and secure. Section III focuses on collection development, electronic resources, intellectual freedom, and reaching out to the community through programs and special events, working with other youth service organizations, and marketing children's services. Section IV suggests ways in which children's librarians can participate in the larger professional community of librarians." Publisher's note

"Excellent support for newbies and as a basis for professional development." Booklist

Includes bibliographical references

Fiore, Carole D.

Fiore's summer library reading program handbook. Neal-Schuman Publishers 2005 xxiii, 312p pa $65

Grades: Professional **027.62**
1. Children's libraries 2. Books and reading
ISBN 1-55570-513-8 LC 2004-31104

"This research-laden handbook . . . serves as a 'comprehensive program-planning and implementation tool' for public libraries seeking to revamp, revise, or develop a summer library reading program. . . . This is an invaluable resource, both for its concrete guidance and its abstract exploration of the meaning of summer library programs." Bull Cent Child Books

Includes bibliographical references

Follos, Alison M. G.

Reviving reading; school library programming, author visits, and books that rock! [by] Alison M. G. Follos; foreword by Jack Gantos. Libraries Unlimited 2006 xx, 143p bibl pa $32 *

Grades: Professional **027.62**
1. Books and reading 2. Children's libraries 3. Young adults' libraries
ISBN 1-59158-356-X LC 2006017616

This is an "idea-packed manual on innovative literacy programs for elementary, middle, and high-school students. . . . Three sections address why, how, and what needs to be done to instill lifelong reading habits in children and young adults. . . . This realistic and reasonable guide is recommended for school and public library professional collections." Booklist

Includes bibliographical references

Harker, Christa

Library research with emergent readers; meeting standards through collaboration; [by] Christa Harker and Dorette Putonti. Linworth Books 2008 112p il pa $39.95 *

Grades: Professional **027.62**
1. Research 2. Information literacy 3. School libraries
ISBN 978-1-58683-288-9 (pa); 1-58683-288-3 (pa)
LC 2007042179

This "is an all-encompassing look at the needs of emergent readers along with examples of standards-based library research projects. Definitely a great resource for those serving kindergarten or first-grade classrooms." Booklist

Includes bibliographical references

Lowe, Joy L.

Puppet magic; [by] Joy L. Lowe and Kathryn I. Matthew. Neal-Schuman Publishers 2008 173p il pa $45

Grades: Professional   **027.62**
1. Puppets and puppet plays 2. Storytelling 3. Children's libraries
ISBN 978-1-55570-599-2 (pa); 1-55570-599-5 (pa)
LC 2007024108

"Adults who are looking for a quick, unfussy way to present stories, songs, and rhymes to children will find enough material in *Puppet Magic* to launch them into a timeless art form. . . . Lowe and Matthew's title gives beginners just enough material and easy puppets—made primarily from socks, felt, and paper plates—to get them started without much of an investment of time or effort. . . . Photos, patterns, online resources, and a good resource list are included." SLJ

Includes bibliographical references

MacMillan, Kathy, 1975-

Storytime magic; 400 fingerplays, flannelboards, and other activities; [by] Kathy MacMillan and Christine Kirker. American Library Association 2009 139p il pa $45

Grades: Professional   **027.62**
1. Storytelling 2. Children's libraries
ISBN 978-0-8389-0977-5 (pa); 0-8389-0977-9 (pa)
LC 2008030266

"Both new and veteran storytellers will appreciate this book. Sixteen chapters are arranged by themes such as 'All About Me,' 'Animals,' and 'Holidays.' Whenever a flannelboard idea is listed, a thumbnail pen-and-ink sketch of the necessary pieces is included next to a Web icon. Readers can then proceed to an ALA Web page to view the actual-sized pattern. An appendix gives further instruction on how to use other props or costumes along with a story." SLJ

Includes bibliographical references

Marino, Jane

Babies in the library! Scarecrow Press 2003 149p hardcover o.p. pa $32 *

Grades: Professional   **027.62**
1. Children's libraries
ISBN 0-8108-4576-8; 0-8108-6044-9 (pa)
LC 2002-12022

Contents: Babies in the library; What works for prewalkers; What works for walkers; Rhymes to take home; Puppet rhymes

The author presents "arguments for holding library programs specifically geared toward babies. Organizing and presenting her ideas in a thoughtful and philosophical manner, she addresses many relevant topics: making babies feel comfortable in the library, creating programs for prewalkers and walkers, handling registration, and offering suggestions for planning and executing programs. She also includes various activities that introduce books, rhymes, puppets, and other tools that enhance language skills." SLJ

Includes bibliographical references

Mother Goose time; library programs for babies and their caregivers; by Jane Marino and Dorothy F. Houlihan; music arrangements by Jane Marino; photographs by Susan G. Drinker. Wilson, H.W. 1992 172p il music $55

Grades: Professional   **027.62**
1. Children's libraries 2. Nursery rhymes
ISBN 0-8242-0850-1   LC 91-46986

"The book was inspired by a program designed by the authors, librarians . . . who conducted 'Mother Goose Time' sessions for more than five years at the White Plains, New York, Public Library. These interactive sessions involved sharing songs and rhymes with babies and adults. . . . There are musical arrangements for the songs; bibliographies of picture books, display books, and resource books; an evaluation of form; and various indexes categorizing the rhymes and songs by title, first line, and developmental level." J Youth Serv Libr

Includes bibliographical references

Nichols, Judy, 1947-

Storytimes for two-year-olds; [by] Judy Nichols; illustrated by Lori D. Sears. 3rd ed. American Library Association 2007 252p bibl il pa $40

Grades: Professional   **027.62**
1. Storytelling 2. Children's libraries
ISBN 0-8389-0925-6 (pa); 978-0-8389-0925-6 (pa)
LC 2006023915

First published 1987

This outlines techniques for creating library programs for two-year-olds using books, rhymes, songs, fingerplays, puppets, and crafts on such themes as farms, animals, seasons, and bedtimes.

"The variety of programs, the diverse and excellent book selections, and the other program components . . . make this book useful for librarians, nursery-school teachers, and homeschoolers." Booklist

Includes bibliographical references

Pavon, Ana-Elba

25 Latino craft projects; [by] Ana-Elba Pavon, Diana Borrego. American Library Association 2003 80p il (Celebrating culture in your library) pa $35 *

Grades: Professional   **027.62**
1. Children's libraries 2. Hispanic Americans—Social life and customs 3. Handicraft
ISBN 978-0-8389-0833-4 (pa); 0-8389-0833-0 (pa)
LC 2002-5750

Following a "chapter on planning, the projects are organized around important Latino holidays and are inspired by *artesenias* (Latino folk art). . . . For each celebration, there is a suggested program for preschoolers, after-schooler, and families; each program incorporates the craft with songs, poems, and books. Activities include making piñatas, paper flowers, sweet tamales, and salsa." SLJ

Includes glossary and bibliographical references

Peck, Penny

Crash course in storytime fundamentals. Libraries Unlimited 2009 154p (Crash course) pa $30

Grades: Professional   **027.62**
   1. Storytelling 2. Children's libraries
   ISBN 978-1-59158-715-6 (pa); 1-59158-715-8 (pa)
                              LC 2008031234

"Practical and concise, this well-organized and readable guide is for inexperienced staff members who are not necessarily children's librarians. . . . The 75 themed storytimes include different types of books and Web sites and sources for songs, musical instruments, fingerplays, games, puppets, and crafts. The author discusses best times and settings for programs; special issues, such as children's and parents' behavior; selection and training of volunteers; the 'registration' question, and more." SLJ

   Includes bibliographical references

Reid, Rob

More family storytimes; twenty-four creative programs for all ages. American Library Association 2009 181p pa $45

Grades: Professional   **027.62**
   1. Children's libraries 2. Storytelling
   ISBN 978-0-8389-0973-7   LC 2008015377

"This volume contains 24 programs, each lasting 30 minutes, that promote learning readiness and reading skills. . . . Clearly presented and easy to follow, this is an excellent resource for librarians who want to come up with winning story hours that have broad appeal." Booklist

   Includes bibliographical references

Shake & shout; 16 noisy, lively story programs. Upstart Books 2008 110p il pa $17.95

Grades: Professional   **027.62**
   1. Children's libraries 2. Songs 3. Children—Books and reading 4. Storytelling 5. Dance
   ISBN 978-1-60213-006-7 (pa); 1-60213-006-X (pa)
                              LC 2009535346

"This book centers on the idea of using one song as the jumping-off point for a thematic storytime. Each program features two to three picture books that support the theme, along with one or two movement activities. There's also a 'backup picture book' listed as well as more related songs. . . . The featured songs are listed within the programs, where recordings can be found, and are also printed at the end of the chapter with suggested guitar chords. The themes run the gamut from seasonal, to various animals and their environments, to pretend activities and emotions. This volume will spark creativity and imagination." SLJ

   Includes bibliographical references

Something funny happened at the library; how to create humorous programs for children and young adults. American Library Association 2003 163p pa $42 *

Grades: Professional   **027.62**
   1. Children's libraries 2. Young adults' libraries 3. Storytelling
   ISBN 978-0-8389-0836-5 (pa); 0-8389-0836-5 (pa)
                              LC 2002-8970

Contents: Tricks of the trade; Humor programs for younger children: preschool and primary school age; Humor programs for intermediate school age children; Humor programs for middle and high school students; Reader's theater; Lively library tours & visits to schools; Raps and closings; The funniest books in the library; Two last treats

This is "an excellent resource for adding wit to your library repertoire." SLJ

   Includes bibliographical references

Serving young teens and 'tweens; edited by Sheila B. Anderson; foreword by James M. Rosinia. Libraries Unlimited 2007 xxv, 158p (Libraries Unlimited professional guides for young adult librarianship) pa $40

Grades: Professional   **027.62**
   1. Reference books 2. Young adults' libraries 3. Teenagers—Books and reading 4. Young adult literature—Bibliography
   ISBN 1-59158-259-8 (pa); 978-1-59158-259-5 (pa)
                              LC 2006030666

This "is aimed at librarians serving middle school, roughly ages 10-14. The book defines tweens developmentally and describes nonfiction and fiction resources, programming, and booktalking for this group. Well-qualified contributors provide practical ideas, balanced and specific examples, up-to-date book lists, and citations to research-oriented works." Booklist

   Includes bibliographical references

Sierra, Judy

The flannel board storytelling book. 2nd ed rev & expanded. Wilson, H.W. 1997 241p il music $65

Grades: Professional   **027.62**
   1. Children's libraries 2. Storytelling
   ISBN 978-0-8242-0932-2; 0-8242-0932-X
                              LC 97-15107

First published 1987

"Fifty stories, poems, and songs and over three hundred patterns are included for presenting stories to children in a flannel board medium, including classic children's stories, nursery rhymes, folk tales, and songs. . . . Sierra's experience telling stories with children is reflected throughout her book." J Youth Serv Libr

Sima, Judy

Raising voices; creating youth storytelling groups and troupes; [by] Judy Sima, Kevin Cordi. Libraries Unlimited 2003 xxviii, 241p pa $32.50

Grades: Professional   **027.62**
   1. Storytelling
   ISBN 1-56308-919-X   LC 2003-47631

This offers a "blueprint for beginning and sustaining a successful group or troupe of storytellers from grades 4 to 12. . . . The book includes reproducible forms that will save a lot of work and lists of valuable resources. . . . Raising Voices is the complete, and essential, handbook for this special group of storytellers." SLJ

   Includes bibliographical references

Simpson, Martha Seif, 1954-
Bringing classes into the public library; a handbook for librarians; [by] Martha Seif Simpson and Lucretia I. Duwel. McFarland & Co. 2007 175p il pa $45 *
Grades: Professional   **027.62**
  1. Children's libraries 2. Young adults' libraries 3. Libraries and schools 4. Public libraries
  ISBN 978-0-7864-2806-9 (pa); 0-7864-2806-6 (pa)
                    LC 2006037527
"This handbook articulates the reasons and defines a strategy for promoting a program of class visits to the public library, and provides . . . instructions and . . . templates to assist librarians in initiating an organized program of class visits." Publisher's note

Soltan, Rita
Reading raps; a book club guide for librarians, kids, and families; [by] Rita Soltan. Libraries Unlimited 2006 354p pa $35
Grades: Professional   **027.62**
  1. Reference books 2. Children's libraries 3. Books and reading 4. Children's literature—Bibliography
  ISBN 1-59158-234-2   LC 2005030842
"The author provides librarians with a guide to book discussion groups for children and adults, with plans for 100 books geared to grades 3-8. Ideas for forming groups and choosing titles, discussion questions, and ice-breakers are included. Titles range from older classics to books published in 2004 and cover all fiction genres. . . . The novice group leader will find this book helpful, and the experienced facilitator will find many new ideas." Booklist
Includes bibliographical references

Summer reading renaissance; an interactive exhibits approach; [by] Rita Soltan; illustrations by Jill Reichenbach Fill. Libraries Unlimited 2008 248p il pa $45
Grades: Professional   **027.62**
  1. Children's literature 2. Children—Books and reading
  ISBN 978-1-59158-572-5 (pa); 1-59158-572-4 (pa)
                    LC 2008025702
"A children's librarian explores a new mode of summer-reading programming through an innovative, family-oriented series utilizing hands-on approaches for a six- to eight-week period, as done in many museums. . . . Well organized, with detailed directions and ideas, the book is good for any librarian working with children from beginning readers to sixth grade." Booklist
Includes bibliographical references

Stover, Lynne Farrell
Magical library lessons; [by] Lynne Farrell Stover. UpstartBooks 2003 85p il pa $17.95
Grades: Professional   **027.62**
  1. Children's libraries 2. Bibliographic instruction
  ISBN 978-1-57950-094-8 (pa); 1-57950-094-3 (pa)
                    LC 2004-269620
Also available More magical library lessons (2004)
"Stover presents 15 stand-alone exercises designed to teach and reinforce library skills, research techniques, and literary concepts. . . . Each entry begins with a quote and a story synopsis of a book by a popular writer. . . . An introduction, time involved, objectives, materials, procedure, a subjective evaluation, and an enrichment extension are included, as are visuals and activity sheets. Up-to-date library and literacy lessons are always welcome, and these are winners." SLJ
Includes bibliographical references

Sullivan, Michael
Fundamentals of children's services. American Library Association 2005 255p bibl il (ALA fundamentals series) pa $45 *
Grades: Professional   **027.62**
  1. Children's libraries
  ISBN 0-8389-0907-8
This "covers the underlying principles and mission of library work for children and then discusses the collection, services, programming, and management. . . . Sections on homework, interlibrary loan, and reference services are especially well done, and lists of good story hour books for infants and toddlers as well as for older children are valuable." Booklist
Includes bibliographical references

Totten, Kathryn, 1955-
Family literacy storytimes; readymade storytimes suitable for the whole family. Neal-Schuman Publishers 2009 168p pa $59.95
Grades: Professional   **027.62**
  1. Children's libraries 2. Storytelling 3. Books and reading
  ISBN 978-1-55570-671-5 (pa); 1-55570-671-1 (pa)
                    LC 2009027770
"Part I explains the basics of family literacy storytimes and how to meet the needs of adults and children in this format. Special attention is given to working with low-income families who are struggling with, or are new to, the English language. The author suggests that, with an adjustment in focus, storytimes can provide a language-learning environment for parents as well as children. Part II gives detailed planning ideas and 25 ready-to-use themed programs. Other chapters include music (with original songs), nursery rhymes, stories, and action rhymes, all with reproducible illustrations." SLJ
Includes bibliographical references

Treviño, Rose Zertuche
Read me a rhyme in Spanish and English = Léame una rima en español e inglés. American Library Association 2009 155p pa $45
Grades: Professional   **027.62**
  1. Children's libraries 2. Libraries and Hispanic Americans 3. Latin American literature—Bibliography 4. Children's literature—Bibliography 5. Children—Books and reading 6. Bilingual books—English-Spanish
  ISBN 978-0-8389-0982-9 (pa); 0-8389-0982-5 (pa)
                    LC 2008045379
"This essential collection of Latino rhymes, songs, finger plays, and riddles offers a variety of flexible program ideas for babies, toddlers, preschoolers, and school-age

Treviño, Rose Zertuche—*Continued*

children. . . . Programs were developed by an experienced children's librarian who fully understands the needs of her colleagues serving Latino populations. . . . This volume can easily become a basic reference resource for English-speaking and bilingual librarians and teachers." SLJ

Includes bibliographical references

Van Orden, Phyllis J.

Library service to children; a guide to the history, planning, policy, and research literature; [by] Phyllis Van Orden, Patricia Pawelak-Kort. Rowman & Littlefield 2005 154p pa $37

Grades: Professional   **027.62**
1. Reference books 2. Children's libraries—Bibliography 3. Children—Books and reading—Bibliography
ISBN 978-0-8108-5169-6 (pa); 0-8108-5169-5 (pa)

"There are 428 works written or published between 1876 and 2003 in this annotated bibliography, which updates the 1992 edition of the same title. Every format is included, from journal articles to books, to brochures, to government documents, to electronic resources. . . . This is an amazingly complete resource for researchers." Booklist

Walter, Virginia A.

Children and libraries; getting it right. American Library Association 2000 155p pa $34

Grades: Professional   **027.62**
1. Children's libraries 2. Young adults' libraries
ISBN 978-0-8389-0795-5 (pa); 0-8389-0795-4 (pa)
LC 00-57600

Walter "examines changing routines, educational practices, and social patterns that have had a profound effect on our communities and from these trends drafts a slate of suggested goals for those of us who strive to serve children. She also examines the impact of digital technology and looks at the future of the book." SLJ

Includes bibliographical references

Twenty-first-century kids, twenty-first-century librarians. American Library Association 2010 104p pa $45

Grades: Professional   **027.62**
1. Children's libraries 2. Young adults' libraries 3. Librarians
ISBN 978-0-8389-1007-8 (pa); 0-8389-1007-6 (pa)
LC 2009016972

"This volume more than updates Walter's 2001 Children and Libraries; it revisits the nature of children, addressing social changes and encouraging a new generation of children's librarians. Chapter 1 provides a fine history about U.S. library services to children, primarily in public libraries. Subsequent chapters detail six enduring core values of children's library services and add two emerging themes: the need for information (and information literacy) and collaboration. Walter's main contribution lies in her description of five models of children relative to the library: as reader, as a child of the information age, as a community member, as global, and as an empowered person. Another chapter focuses on management principals. . . . Walter's core values are worth reading and implementing." Booklist

Includes bibliographical references

Weissman, Annie, 1948-

Do tell! storytelling for you and your students. Linworth Pub. 2002 86p il pa $36.95

Grades: Professional   **027.62**
1. Storytelling 2. Children's libraries
ISBN 1-58683-074-0   LC 2002-32969

"This concise beginner's guide encourages school librarians and teachers to incorporate storytelling into the elementary curriculum. It discusses how to select a story; how to learn it; and how to present it, including voice, pace, dialects, facial expressions, sound effects, and audience participation. . . . Proverbs, myths, fables, and folktales, all in the public domain and selected with beginning storytellers in mind, make this a handy one-volume source." SLJ

Includes bibliographical references

027.8   School libraries

Adams, Helen R., 1943-

Ensuring intellectual freedom and access to information in the school library media program. Libraries Unlimited 2008 xxi, 254p il map pa $40 *

Grades: Professional   **027.8**
1. School libraries 2. Censorship 3. Freedom of information
ISBN 978-1-59158-539-8 (pa); 1-59158-539-2 (pa)
LC 2008-16753

This is "an extremely helpful guide for dealing with intellectual-freedom and information-access issues. In chapters geared to school situations and covering topics including selection of resources, the First Amendment, privacy, challenges to resources, the Internet, and access for students with disabilities, Adams offers background on the topic and bulleted lists of strategies for dealing with the issue. . . . This is a book that every school librarian needs to keep handy and share with administrators, colleagues, and parents." Booklist

Includes bibliographical references

American Association of School Librarians

Information power; building partnerships for learning; prepared by the American Association of School Librarians [and] Association for Educational Communications and Technology. American Library Association 1998 205p il pa $42 *

Grades: Professional   **027.8**
1. School libraries 2. Instructional materials centers
ISBN 978-0-8389-3470-8 (pa); 0-8389-3470-6 (pa)
LC 98-23291

First published 1988

This resource "relates the library-media program to the entire educational infrastructure. The authors explicate their themes in terms of standards, indicators, levels of proficiency, goals, principles, and examples of student activities. The appendixes contain essential information on Library Power, AASL's ICON-nect project, the Library Bill of Rights, confidentiality, censorship, access equity, and ethics." SLJ

Includes bibliographical references

Bishop, Kay, 1942-
The collection program in schools; concepts, practices, and information sources. 4th ed. Libraries Unlimited 2007 xx, 269p il (Library and information science text) $65; pa $50
Grades: Professional   **027.8**
  1. School libraries 2. Libraries—Collection development
  ISBN 978-1-59158-583-1; 1-59158-583-X; 978-1-59158-360-8 (pa); 1-59158-360-8 (pa)
                    LC 2007-9005
First published 1988 under the authorship of Phyllis J. Van Orden
Contents: The collection; Collection development; Community analysis and needs assessment; The media center program; Policies and procedures; Selection; General selection criteria; Criteria by format; Acquisitions and processing; Maintenance and preservation; Circulation and promotion of the collection; Evaluation of the collection; Ethical issues and the collection; The curriculum; Special groups of students; Fiscal issues relating to the collection; Opening, moving, or closing the collection
"Media specialists who read this book will be renewed in their quest for excellence in their collections. . . . The book covers A-Z: Acquisitions, Evaluation, Ethical Issues, Inventory, Procedure Manual, Selection, Special Groups of Students, Weeding, etc. . . . This is a must purchase for every school library media center." Libr Media Connect
Includes bibliographical references

Buzzeo, Toni, 1951-
Collaborating to meet standards: teacher/librarian partnerships for K-6; [by] Toni Buzzeo. 2nd ed. Linworth Pub. 2007 246p pa $39.95
Grades: Professional   **027.8**
  1. School libraries
  ISBN 1-58683-302-2 (pa); 978-1-58683-302-2 (pa)
            LC 2007015406
First published 2002
This "addresses the assessment-driven educational environment of the No Child Left Behind Act. In the first section, Buzzeo focuses on the benefits of an involved school librarian to the educational process and how best to achieve this collaboration. She includes a template for collaborative planning and instruction. Sample lessons for specific grades from librarians around the United States complete the book. Practical suggestions and examples from school librarians across the country appear in separate text boxes. . . . Buzzeo gives worthwhile advice." SLJ
Includes bibliographical references

The collaboration handbook. Linworth Pub. 2008 132p il pa $42.95
Grades: Professional   **027.8**
  1. School libraries
  ISBN 978-1-58683-298-8 (pa); 1-58683-298-0 (pa)
          LC 2008-18119
"In this succinct guide, Buzzeo paints a picture of how media specialists can use instructional collaboration to transform a media program and increase student achievement. . . . Those new to the field will appreciate the step-by-step approach to increasing collaboration, while experienced media specialists will likely benefit most from the chapters on data-driven collaboration and assessment. The book concludes with a substantial amount of information on how to overcome common barriers to collaboration, the role of advocacy, and the importance of integrating new technologies into collaborative projects." SLJ
Includes bibliographical references

Downs, Elizabeth, 1953-
The school library media specialist's policy & procedure writer. Neal-Schuman 2009 195p pa $75 *
Grades: Professional   **027.8**
  1. School libraries
  ISBN 978-1-55570-621-0 (pa); 1-55570-621-5 (pa)
"School library media specialists who need policies or procedures will surely find what they are looking for in this thorough book. Downs lays the foundation by describing necessary forms and policies for a school library media center, then provides a variety of examples and templates. The book includes mission statements, goals and objectives, budgeting, facilities use, circulation, collection development, disaster management, weeding, copyright, ILL, ethics, and accessibility policies." SLJ

Erikson, Rolf
Designing a school library media center for the future; [by] Rolf Erikson and Carolyn Markuson. 2nd ed. American Library Association 2007 117p il pa $45
Grades: Professional   **027.8**
  1. Instructional materials centers—Design and construction 2. School libraries—Design and construction
  ISBN 978-0-8389-0945-4 (pa); 0-8389-0945-0 (pa)
          LC 2006-37644
First published 2000
"The first chapter offers an overview of the various steps involved in any project. Succeeding chapters cover technology planning, space allocations, furniture and placement, lighting and acoustics, ADA requirements, specifications, and bids." Booklist
Includes bibliographical references

Farmer, Lesley S. Johnson, 1949-
Collaborating with administrators and educational support staff; [by] Lesley S. J. Farmer. Neal-Schuman Publishers 2007 217p (Best practices for school library media professionals) pa $65 *
Grades: Professional   **027.8**
  1. School libraries 2. Instructional materials centers 3. Schools—Administration
  ISBN 978-1-55570-572-5 (pa); 1-55570-572-3 (pa)
          LC 2006-11171
"Farmer begins by exploring how schools work, the role of the library media specialist, and the background on collaboration. She then discusses, in some depth, how to work with different levels of administrators and key service personnel, such as technology directors, reading specialists, special-education educators, pupil services

Farmer, Lesley S. Johnson, 1949——*Continued*
personnel, and physical health and co-curricular personnel. Farmer concludes with ways of measuring the impact of collaboration and improving literacy, and provides suggestions for becoming a collaborative leader. This book is a must for school districts and a school library media specialists' personal collections." SLJ

Includes bibliographical references

Student success and library media programs; a systems approach to research and best practice; [by] Lesley S. J. Farmer. Libraries Unlimited 2003 180p pa $45
Grades: Professional   **027.8**
1. School libraries 2. Academic achievement
ISBN 1-59158-058-7   LC 2003-53881
"Designed for school library media specialists, this book focuses on library media programs and examines the factors that influence student achievement." Publisher's note

This is a "comprehensive and thoroughly researched book. . . . An invaluable guide for media specialists." SLJ

Includes bibliographical references

Grimes, Sharon
Reading is our business; how libraries can foster reading comprehension. American Library Association 2006 155p il pa $35 *
Grades: Professional   **027.8**
1. School libraries 2. Books and reading 3. Reading comprehension
ISBN 0-8389-0912-4   LC 2005028263
Grimes "led a school-wide research study with classroom teachers to transform the reading program at Lansdowne Elementary School in Baltimore. The study resulted in dramatic and measurable gains in student reading achievement. This book can be used as a toolkit to duplicate those results. Grimes's work is informed by solid educational research in the field of reading comprehension. The text is lively and clearly written, accessible to teachers and librarians." SLJ

Includes bibliographical references

Harada, Violet H.
Assessing learning; librarians and teachers as partners. Libraries Unlimited 2005 149p diag il tab pa $40
Grades: Professional   **027.8**
1. School libraries 2. Instructional materials centers
ISBN 1-59158-200-8
"After reviewing the topic of assessment, the authors look at library media centers to determine where and how students should be assessed and then examine assessment tools and explain a wide array of effective graphic organizers. . . . Close to 100 illustrations demonstrate the many forms of assessment described. Chapters are well constructed and the writing is clear." SLJ

Includes bibliographical references

Harlan, Mary Ann
Personal learning networks; professional development for the isolated school librarian. Libraries Unlimited 2009 96p il pa $30
Grades: Professional   **027.8**
1. Librarians—In-service training 2. Library education 3. Library science 4. Vocational guidance
ISBN 978-1-59158-790-3 (pa); 1-59158-790-5 (pa)
      LC 2008-45519
"Harlan offers commonsense information about professional development opportunities using both old and new technologies. From attendance at conferences to online courses and discussion lists, she moves to the newer Web 2.0 technologies such as podcasts, blogs and social networks. . . . Related information, hints and Web sites are set off within the text but do not break the flow of the narrative." Booklist

Includes bibliographical references

Hart, Thomas L.
The school library media facilities planner. Neal-Schuman Publishers 2006 253p diag il (Best practices for school library media professionals) pa $95 *
Grades: Professional   **027.8**
1. School libraries—Design and construction 2. Instructional materials centers—Design and construction
ISBN 1-55570-503-0   LC 2004047424
"This book presents timely information on designing, building, remodeling, and equipping library media centers. Chapters cover every phase of the process, from assessing needs, allocating space, selecting furniture, and working with the architect to moving into the new facility. . . . A CD 'view book' of several Florida libraries allows the user to see and hear librarians describe the pros and cons of their individual libraries." Booklist

Includes bibliographical references

Hughes-Hassell, Sandra
School reform and the school library media specialist; [by] Sandra Hughes-Hassell and Violet H. Harada. Libraries Unlimited 2007 xxiii, 204p il (Principles and practice series) pa $40 *
Grades: Professional   **027.8**
1. School libraries
ISBN 978-1-59158-427-8 (pa); 1-59158-427-2 (pa)
      LC 2007-16437
"This volume covers critical issues impacting school libraries today and offers practical solutions to meet these challenges. Written by leaders in the field such as Pam Berger, Carol Gordon, Barbara Stripling, and Ross Todd, the articles expound on implications of No Child Left Behind legislation, 21st-century literacy requirements, population diversity, and professional growth. . . . This volume will empower current and future school librarians as they embrace its guidelines." SLJ

The **Information-powered** school; [by] Public Education Network, American Association of School Librarians; edited by Sandra Hughes-Hassell, Anne Wheelock. American Library Association 2001 138p il pa $40
Grades: Professional   **027.8**
   1. Library Power (Program) 2. School libraries 3. Instructional materials centers
   ISBN 978-0-8389-3514-9 (pa); 0-8389-3514-1 (pa)
                        LC 2001-22561
"This volume presents a variety of articles highlighting various aspects and activities of Information Powered Schools and giving tips for putting the principles and practices to work. . . . Checklists, surveys, and planning forms are included to determine the status of current practices. The collaborative planning worksheets, request forms, unit evaluation and collaborative-unit evaluation forms will be of special interest to librarians already involved in this process." SLJ
   Includes bibliographical references

Johnson, Doug, 1952-
   School libraries head for the edge; rants, recommendations, and reflections. Linworth Pub. 2010 196p pa $35
Grades: Professional   **027.8**
   1. School libraries
   ISBN 978-1-58683-392-3; 1-58683-392-8
                        LC 2009-22053
"A Linworth Publishing book"
"Eighty long-running 'Head for the Edge' columns in Library Media Connection and its predecessor, Technology Connection, are collected here, in topical clusters dealing with professional issues relevant to both veterans and newbies. . . . The columns are reflective, conversational, and characteristically humorous. . . . Chapters end with quotes, questions, and self-evaluative reflection that readers will be inspired to mirror. For all practitioners." SLJ

Johnson, Mary
   Primary sources in the library; a collaboration guide for library media specialists; [by] Mary J. Johnson. Linworth Pub. 2003 145p il pa $39.95
Grades: Professional   **027.8**
   1. School libraries 2. History—Study and teaching
   ISBN 978-1-58683-075-5 (pa); 1-58683-075-9 (pa)
                        LC 2003-12887
This offers ideas for school librarians for developing collaborative units with teachers in grades 4 through 12 that incorporate primary source material
"A treasure trove of ideas, lessons, and strategies for teaching the concept of primary sources." SLJ
   Includes bibliographical references

Martin, Ann M., 1955-
   7 steps to an award-winning school library program; [by] Ann M. Martin; foreword by Ruth Toor. Libraries Unlimited 2005 129p diag il tab pa $38 *
Grades: Professional   **027.8**
   1. School libraries 2. Instructional materials centers
   ISBN 978-1-59158-173-4; 1-59158-173-7
"The author's purpose in this book is to describe how to use *Information Power* effectively and how to achieve the goal of winning a national award. . . . Her description of the process is organized in seven clearly explained steps. Appendixes contain helpful forms and policy statements. . . . [This is a] well-written, unique, and important book." Booklist

Ray, Virginia Lawrence
   School wide book events; how to make them happen; [by] Virginia Lawrence Ray. Libraries Unlimited 2003 133p pa $28
Grades: Professional   **027.8**
   1. School libraries 2. Books and reading
   ISBN 978-1-59158-038-6 (pa); 1-59158-038-2 (pa)
                        LC 2003-47724
"The author's intent is to present ideas on how to celebrate reading across grade levels and curriculum, involving teachers, administration, faculty, and students both in preparation and actual activities. She proposes that school libraries have a Book Event for the whole school. . . . All events require simple resources and are easy to follow even for school systems with extremely limited budgets." SLJ
   Includes bibliographical references

Schuckett, Sandy
   Political advocacy for school librarians; you have the power! Linworth Pub. 2004 128p pa $39.95
Grades: Professional   **027.8**
   1. School libraries 2. Libraries and community 3. Lobbying
   ISBN 1-58683-158-5   LC 2004-4869
"Schuckett motivates and explicitly details an exciting 'how-to' of political lobbying at all levels—from the school site and local board all the way to the national level. . . . School librarians need political clout, and Schuckett shows us how to get it." SLJ
   Includes bibliographical references

Schultz-Jones, Barbara
   An automation primer for school library media centers and small libraries. Linworth Pub. 2006 280p pa $39.95
Grades: Professional   **027.8**
   1. School libraries—Automation 2. Instructional materials centers—Automation 3. Libraries—Automation
   ISBN 1-58683-180-1   LC 2006005798
"This thorough guide to library automation provides an in-depth look at the many components and options available to school libraries. Topics discussed include defining automation systems, features of systems, Web access, technical considerations, and emerging technologies.

Schultz-Jones, Barbara—*Continued*
In addition, the book outlines a step-by-step process of project planning, selection, and site preparation."
Booklist
Includes bibliographical references

Stephens, Claire Gatrell
Library 101; a handbook for the school library media specialist; [by] Claire Gatrell Stephens and Patricia Franklin. Libraries Unlimited 2007 233p il pa $35
Grades: Professional   027.8
  1. School libraries 2. Instructional materials centers 3. Libraries—Handbooks, manuals, etc.
  ISBN 978-1-59158-324-0 (pa); 1-59158-324-1 (pa)
                  LC 2007-18420
"This handbook provides information for brand-new and inexperienced librarians preparing for a first job in a school library media center. Articles are divided into four subcategories covering day-to-day operations (library organization, circulation policies, media management, scheduling, staffing, and media center arrangement); collaboration with teachers; collection development and management; and equipment." Booklist
Includes bibliographical references

The **Whole** school library handbook; edited by Blanche Woolls and David V. Loertscher. American Library Association 2005 448p pa $45
Grades: Professional   027.8
  1. School libraries 2. Instructional materials centers
  ISBN 0-8389-0883-7   LC 2004-20198
This reference resource to the school media center includes "facts, . . . articles, checklists, organization contact information, trivia, [and] advice from the field's experts. . . . [It also features] information on fundraising, grant writing, flexible scheduling, promoting the school library, and advocating its value in the school community." Publisher's note
Includes bibliographical references

028.1   Reviews

Baxter, Kathleen A.
From cover to cover; evaluating and reviewing children's books. rev. ed. Collins 2010 229p $14.99 *
Grades: Professional   028.1
  1. Books—Reviews 2. Children's literature—History and criticism
  ISBN 978-0-06-077757-9; 0-06-077757-5
  First published 1997
The author addresses the distinctions between evaluation and review, and what makes a good children's book. She discusses categories of children's books including nonfiction; traditional literature (folktales, myths, legends, etc.); poetry, verse, rhymes, and songs; picture books; easy readers and transitional books; and fiction. She then describes the process of writing a review.
  This is a "very complete resource that will continue to be the venerable reference tool and required reading for education and library-science students, youth librarians, teachers, and anyone else interested in kids, reading, and children's literature." SLJ

Blass, Rosanne J., 1937-
Celebrate with books; booktalks for holidays and other occasions; [by] Rosanne J. Blass. Libraries Unlimited 2005 226p pa $35
Grades: Professional   028.1
  1. Reference books 2. Children's literature—Bibliography 3. Holidays—Bibliography 4. Book talks
  ISBN 1-59158-076-5
"This collection of booktalks for children in kindergarten through sixth grade emphasizes picture books, chapter books, and poetry published from 2000 to 2004. The volume begins with general holidays celebrated by cultures around the world . . . and then takes a month-by-month approach. Additional year-round celebrations . . . are appended. For each observation, at least two selections are suggested and include a complete citation, genre, age level, culture (where appropriate), summary, the booktalk itself, and a learning extension. . . . A great aid for collection development and for thematic planning." SLJ

028.5   Reading and use of other information media by young people

Allyn, Pam
What to read when; the books and stories to read with your child, and all the best times to read them. Avery 2009 318p pa $16.95
Grades: Adult Professional   028.5
  1. Children—Books and reading
  ISBN 978-1-58333-334-1   LC 2008-54501
The author "provides many ways to promote a love of reading to children and offers top-ten lists of reasons to read to kids that incorporate practical, easy-to-use tips to encourage literacy from a young age. . . . This is an indispensable guide to choosing age-appropriate books for children. Allyn provides a list of more than 300 titles on 50 themes including such issues as adoption, feelings about school, sharing, and coping with illness. This valuable resource for children's librarians, educators, and parents is highly recommended." Libr J

Bauer, Caroline Feller, 1935-
This way to books; drawings by Lynn Gates. Wilson, H.W. 1983 363p il $80
Grades: Professional   028.5
  1. Books and reading 2. Children's literature
  ISBN 978-0-8242-0678-9; 0-8242-0678-9
                  LC 82-19985
"Designed to involve children in books, this compendium is chock-full of ideas for programs, booktalks, games, crafts, and exhibits. Bauer's upbeat tone lends enthusiasm, and her numerous suggestions, which include easy-to-implement activities, short poems, directions for crafts, recipes, and unusual but effective bibliographies, will inspire readers with new ideas. . . . Teachers, librarians, and other adults working with children will find the collection worthwhile and helpful as a springboard to their own variations." Booklist

Baxter, Kathleen A.

Gotcha covered! more nonfiction booktalks to get kids excited about reading. Libraries Unlimited 2005 219p bibl il pa $35

Grades: Professional   **028.5**
1. Books and reading 2. Children's literature—Bibliography 3. Young adult literature—Bibliography

ISBN 1-59158-225-3

"This title presents more than 300 titles published since 2001. Titles range in interest and reading ability from third grade through middle school. Each thematically organized chapter concludes with a bibliography. . . . The authors suggest booktalk themes, key passages to read aloud, exciting and intriguing images to share from the books, and background information about the subjects. . . . Useful for professionals new to collection development, as well as support for nonfiction booktalks." SLJ

Gotcha for guys! nonfiction books to get boys excited about reading; [by] Kathleen A. Baxter and Marcia Agness Kochel. Libraries Unlimited 2007 269p il pa $35

Grades: Professional   **028.5**
1. Boys—Books and reading 2. Children's literature—Bibliography 3. Young adult literature—Bibliography

ISBN 1-59158-311-X (pa); 978-1-59158-311-0 (pa)
                                        LC 2006030667

This "focuses on nonfiction books to get boys excited about reading. There are citations for more than 1,100 books grouped by themes such as 'Prehistoric Creatures,' 'All Things Gross,' and 'Disasters and Unsolved Mysteries.' The last chapter, 'Hot Topics,' includes books on things such as riddles, games, and fascinating facts. With the exception of this last chapter, each chapter offers complete booktalks, short annotations and talks for additional books, and lists of titles that have been well reviewed. . . . This title is helpful for nonfiction collection development and can be used as a starting point for creating attractive, themed displays." Booklist

Includes bibliographical references

Gotcha good! nonfiction books to get kids excited about reading; [by] Kathleen A. Baxter and Marcia Agness Kochel. Libraries Unlimited 2008 259p pa $35

Grades: Professional   **028.5**
1. Books and reading 2. Children's literature—Bibliography 3. Young adult literature—Bibliography

ISBN 978-1-59158-654-8 (pa); 1-59158-654-2 (pa)
                                        LC 2008010350

"In addition to annotations for over 1000 nonfiction titles, [the authors] profile eight prolific authors and provide fun top-10 features for the various subjects covered. . . . The titles chosen are truly high quality, relevant, and up-to-date, with suggested ages provided, most ranging from grades three through eight. . . . A must-have for all librarians who want to get kids excited about nonfiction." SLJ

Includes bibliographical references

Bishop, Rudine Sims, 1937-

Free within ourselves; the development of African American children's literature. Heinemann/Greenwood 2007 295p bibl il $65; pa $22

Grades: Professional   **028.5**
1. American literature—African American authors—History and criticism 2. African Americans in literature 3. Children—Books and reading 4. Children's literature—History and criticism

ISBN 978-0-325-07135-0 (Heinemann); 978-0-313-34093-2 (pa Greenwood)
                                        LC 2007000612

"Bishop traces the evolution of fiction written for black children and by black authors and illustrators within the context of African-American social and literary history. . . . Her writing is precise and engaging, and it really comes alive when presenting primary-source material. . . . Librarians as well as teachers will be enriched by this work." SLJ

Includes bibliographical references

Casement, Rose

Black history in the pages of children's literature. Scarecrow Press 2008 317p pa $55

Grades: Professional   **028.5**
1. African Americans in literature 2. Children's literature—History and criticism 3. Children's literature—Bibliography

ISBN 978-0-8108-5843-5 (pa); 0-8108-5843-6 (pa)
                                        LC 2007018137

"Casement has organized her book along a time line from the initial presence of Africans in America before colonization to the present day. Each chapter begins with a brief description of important historical events that have often been left out of our history books. This is followed by an annotated bibliography that includes excerpts from each title and a description of the content. Books listed are primarily straight nonfiction but some fantasy, realistic fiction, biography, and poetry are included. The final two chapters address criteria for selecting children's literature for classroom use and introduce several talented African-American writers and illustrators. Putting this eminently accessible book into the hands of teachers should greatly increase the use of accurate books about African Americans and help to identify and pass on a more truthful historical picture than most of us were given in school." SLJ

Includes bibliographical references

Children's books in children's hands; an introduction to their literature; [by] Charles Temple, Miriam Martinez, Junko Yokota; with contributions by Evelyn B. Freeman. 4th ed. Pearson Allyn & Bacon 2010 pa $137.40

Grades: Professional   **028.5**
1. Children's literature—History and criticism 2. Books and reading

ISBN 978-0-1370-7403-7; 0-1370-7403-4
                                        LC 2010018237

First published 1998

The authors focus on creating an understanding of how literature works and how children respond to literature, they provide a wide range of good books to use

Children's books in children's hands—*Continued*

with children, and they suggest ways to guide children into books and help them enjoy the experience.

Includes bibliographical references

Codell, Esmé Raji, 1968-
How to get your child to love reading. Algonquin Bks. 2003 531p il pa $18.95 *
Grades: Adult Professional   **028.5**
    1. Reference books 2. Books and reading
    3. Children's literature—Bibliography
    ISBN 1-56512-308-5   LC 2003-40405
The author presents her "theory that interest (finding the right books for the child), integration (using reading as a springboard into other disciplines) and invention (when a child's unique ideas are inspired by the writing) can make the difference in how a youngster approaches reading. . . . The witty, comical 'Madame Esme' (as she calls herself) offers scores of thematic book lists parents can use to inspire young readers. . . . Codell creates a contagious enthusiasm for the enormous value of children's literature." Publ Wkly
Includes bibliographical references

The **Coretta** Scott King awards, 1970-2009; edited by Henrietta M. Smith. 4th ed. American Library Association 2009 131p pa $50 *
Grades: Professional   **028.5**
    1. Coretta Scott King Award 2. Children's literature—History and criticism 3. American literature—African American authors 4. African Americans in literature
    ISBN 978-0-8389-3584-2 (pa); 0-8389-3584-2 (pa)
                                    LC 2009000628
First published 1994
    This guide to the Coretta Scott King awards includes "comprehensive coverage of the award winning books; biographical profiles that introduce the creative artists and illustrators; color plates that give a . . . sense of the story and art; a subject index." Publisher's note
Includes bibliographical references

Cox Clark, Ruth E.
Tantalizing tidbits for middle schoolers; quick booktalks for the busy middle school and jr. high library media specialist; [by] Ruth E. Cox Clark. Linworth Pub. 2005 140p pa $36.95
Grades: Professional   **028.5**
    1. Book talks 2. Books and reading 3. Children's literature—Bibliography 4. Young adult literature—Bibliography
    ISBN 1-58683-195-X   LC 2005013159
    "In the first sections, the author provides information on annual recommended reading lists and children's book awards and describes different booktalking techniques. Section 5, the heart of the book, offers 75 booktalk examples. For each, the author provides bibliographic information, subjects and genres, references to pertinent reading lists and awards, and interest levels. This information is followed by a brief annotation, a booktalk, a page reference for an excerpt to read, a curriculum connection, and a list of similar books. A list of themes and an index of the books and authors mentioned conclude the volume, which is highly recommended for librarians, teachers, and students." Booklist

Crossing boundaries with children's books; edited by Doris Gebel. Scarecrow Press 2006 431p il pa $40
Grades: Professional   **028.5**
    1. Children—Books and reading 2. Children's literature—Bibliography
    ISBN 978-0-8108-5203-7 (pa); 0-8108-5203-9 (pa)
                                    LC 2005032774
    "Sponsored by the United States Board on Books for Young People"
    This "opens with several thoughtful essays that examine the complex issues related to international publishing and translations. . . . Part two is a carefully prepared, comprehensive, annotated bibliography organized by countries and regions of the world. . . . This is an important resource for all libraries to build and promote collections that reflect a global vision." SLJ
Includes bibliographical references

Diamant-Cohen, Betsy
Booktalking bonanza; ten ready-to-use multimedia sessions for the busy librarian. American Library Association 2009 240p bibl il pa $40
Grades: Professional   **028.5**
    1. Book talks 2. Books and reading 3. Children's literature
    ISBN 978-0-8389-0965-2 (pa); 0-8389-0965-5 (pa)
                                    LC 2008-15371
    "This volume is a collection of scripts for multimedia-enriched booktalks. After an introductory chapter that explains the reasoning for this approach, 10 scripts are outlined. Books, music, video, and Web sites are included for each one. The programs are geared toward elementary-aged children, although suggestions for adapting them for a middle or high school audience are included." SLJ
Includes bibliographical references

Embracing, evaluating, and examining African American children's and young adult literature; edited by Wanda M. Brooks, Jonda C. McNair; foreword by Rudine Sims Bishop. Scarecrow Press 2008 251p pa $45
Grades: Professional   **028.5**
    1. American literature—African American authors—History and criticism 2. Children's literature—History and criticism 3. Young adult literature—History and criticism 4. Children—Books and reading 5. African Americans in literature
    ISBN 978-0-8108-6027-8 (pa); 0-8108-6027-9 (pa)
                                    LC 2007025703
    "Brooks and McNair have compiled 12 scholarly studies about the use of books by and about African-American children and young adults in classrooms across the United States. Selections include a detailed textual analysis of the work of Arna Bontemps and Langston Hughes; a sociolinguistic perspective on readers' response to books containing African-American Vernacular English; and a detailed study of the books used as classroom read-alouds by teachers in rural schools, which found that only three percent were about African Americans. While each study is complete in and of itself, the text as a whole gives a broad picture of what is currently being done in this field, both in K-12 classrooms and

Embracing, evaluating, and examining African American children's and young adult literature—*Continued*

college classes that emphasize children's literature." SLJ

Includes bibliographical references

The **Essential** guide to children's books and their creators; Anita Silvey, editor. Houghton Mifflin 2002 542p $28; pa $17

Grades: Adult Professional   028.5

1. Reference books 2. Children's literature—Biobibliography 3. Children's literature—History and criticism

ISBN 0-618-19083-X; 0-618-19082-1 (pa)

LC 2002-32288

Updates Children's books and their creators, published 1995

This "volume contains 475 alphabetically ordered entries . . . covering authors, illustrators, genres, publishing trends and more. Writers and artists sound off in entries marked 'Voices of the Creators'; incidental illustrations appear throughout." Publ Wkly

"This guide offers brief but meaty articles. . . . While the original work featured over 800 authors and topics representing classic children's literature, the updated version retains only 375 of the older work's entries. This poses a difficulty for libraries, which will want to acquire this volume for the necessary updates but also retain the prior volume for the 400-plus entries not replicated here. Recommended for most reference collections." Libr J

Includes bibliographical references

Feinberg, Barbara

Welcome to Lizard Motel; children, stories, and the mystery of making things up: a memoir. Beacon Press 2004 256p $20

Grades: Adult Professional   028.5

1. Children—Books and reading 2. Imagination

ISBN 0-8070-7144-7   LC 2004-710

This "is a memoir about the place of stories in children's lives. It began when Barbara Feinberg noticed that her twelve-year-old son, Alex . . . hated reading many of the novels assigned to him in school. These stories of abandonment, kidnapping, abuse, and more—called 'problem novels'—were standard fare in his middle school classroom." Publisher's note

"Feinberg, who's spent years working with children in a creativity workshop she designed, has the independence and experience to raise important questions. Her critique . . . should stir some much-needed controversy." Publ Wkly

Includes bibliographical references

Fox, Mem, 1946-

Reading magic; why reading aloud to our children will change their lives forever. Harcourt 2001 156p il $23; pa $12 *

Grades: Adult Professional   028.5

1. Storytelling 2. Books and reading

ISBN 0-15-100624-5; 0-15-601076-3 (pa)

LC 2001-24631

"An introduction for parents about reading aloud to their children. Fox explains that babies are born learners, discusses the importance of books in the home, and stresses the value of a read-aloud ritual." SLJ

"In a cheerful, chatty style that's totally jargon-free . . . Fox makes a passionate case for reading aloud to children. . . . Her examples are personal, many from her own family and friends and from her own books, and occasional cartoons by Judy Horacek add to the fun." Booklist

Gelman, Judy, 1962-

The kids' book club book; reading ideas, recipes, activities, and smart tips for organizing terrific kids' book clubs; [by] Judy Gelman and Vicki Levy Krupp. Penguin Group 2007 460p pa $16.95

Grades: Professional   028.5

1. Children—Books and reading 2. Teenagers—Books and reading 3. Children's literature—Bibliography 4. Young adult literature—Bibliography

ISBN 978-1-58542-559-4   LC 2006-101469

"Stellar advice on running book clubs is presented in a friendly format. . . . The first section covers types of clubs, recruitment, organization, location, and duration. . . . In the second part, comprising the bulk of the text, the authors describe the top 50 recommended books arranged by grade level." SLJ

Includes bibliographical references

Gillespie, John Thomas, 1928-

The Newbery/Printz companion; booktalk and related materials for award winners and honor books; [by] John T. Gillespie and Corinne J. Naden. 3rd ed. Libraries Unlimited 2006 503p (Children's and young adult literature reference series) $75 *

Grades: Professional   028.5

1. Newbery Medal 2. Michael L. Printz award 3. Children's literature—History and criticism 4. Authors 5. Book talks

ISBN 1-59158-313-6   LC 2006-14955

First published 1996 with title: The Newbery companion

This guide to the "Newbery and Printz awards for children's and young adult literature provides information on each year's winners and honor books, as well as on the awards themselves and the librarians for whom they are named. For each award-winning book, there is a plot summary, list of characters and themes, background on the author, incidents for booktalking, related reads, and . . . ideas for introducing the book to young readers." Publisher's note

"This invaluable source should be in every school and public library." Booklist

Includes bibliographical references

Gilmore, Barry

Speaking volumes; how to get students discussing books, and much more. Heinemann 2006 128p pa $17.95 *

Grades: Professional   **028.5**

1. Books and reading

ISBN 978-0-325-00915-5 (pa); 0-325-00915-5 (pa)

LC 2005-28371

"Gilmore provides practical, hands-on methods to involve students in oral and written classroom conversations that encourage reflection and ultimately polished, coherent expression. . . . Both new and seasoned discussion leaders will want a copy for repeated reference." Voice Youth Advocates

Includes bibliographical references

Gilton, Donna L.

Multicultural and ethnic children's literature in the United States; [by] Donna L. Gilton. Scarecrow Press 2007 236p $45

Grades: Professional   **028.5**

1. Minorities in literature 2. Children's literature—History and criticism 3. Multiculturalism

ISBN 978-0-8108-5672-1 (pa); 0-8108-5672-7 (pa)

LC 2007006391

"Gilton writes with authority, clarity, and conviction, presenting a strong rationale for the necessity for teachers to use multicultural literature whether or not their schools and/or classrooms have diverse populations. . . . The author offers a wealth of information. . . . She gives a history of multicultural literature in the U.S. . . . Gilton addresses current issues. . . . There is ample information on how to find the best books that appropriately represent a variety of cultures. Finally, Gilton looks closely at groups that are growing in the U.S." SLJ

Includes bibliographical references

Golding, Jacqueline M.

Healing stories; picture books for the big & small changes in a child's life; [by] Jacqueline Golding. M. Evans 2006 343p pa $17.95

Grades: Professional   **028.5**

1. Reference books 2. Picture books for children—Bibliography 3. Children's literature—Bibliography 4. Books and reading

ISBN 1-59077-097-8 (pa); 978-1-59077-097-9 (pa)

"Golding has compiled an annotated list of more than 500 picture books on topics ranging from simple friendship to more complex themes of illness and divorce. In her introduction, she gives practical tips for adults who will be choosing books from this collection. . . . Both parents and librarians can use these suggested books either for bibliotherapy or for theme-building for storytimes." SLJ

Hearne, Betsy Gould, 1942-

Choosing books for children; a commonsense guide; [by] Betsy Hearne with Deborah Stevenson. 3rd ed. University of Ill. Press 1999 229p il hardcover o.p. pa $21

Grades: Adult Professional   **028.5**

1. Reference books 2. Books and reading 3. Children's literature—Bibliography

ISBN 0-252-02516-4; 0-252-06928-5 (pa)

LC 99-6144

First published 1981 by Delacorte Press

"The focus is on books since 1950; the 14 chapter-opening illustrations mainly represent books of the last decade. Chapters divide books by age and genre; one chapter considers the value of controversial books while another affectionately revisits classics." Publ Wkly

Helbig, Alethea

Dictionary of American children's fiction, 1995-1999; books of recognized merit; [by] Alethea K. Helbig and Agnes Regan Perkins. Greenwood Press 2002 614p $115

Grades: Adult Professional   **028.5**

1. Reference books 2. Children's literature—Dictionaries 3. Best books

ISBN 0-313-30389-4   LC 2001-23871

Also available volumes in series covering the years 1859-1959, 1960-1984, 1985-1989 and 1990-1994

"This dictionary is arranged alphabetically by title entries, author entries, character entries, and miscellaneous entries. . . . Entries include award winning and notable books from 1995-1999, as well as a few from previous years. Descriptions of each book are concise and include an overview of the characters, plot, setting, and awards received." Book Rep

"The extensive, detailed index is an excellent resource for locating fiction about a wide range of specific topics, characters, authors, and genres." Booklist

Includes bibliographical references

Herb, Steven

Connecting fathers, children, and reading; a how-to-do it manual for librarians; [by] Steven Herb, Sara Willoughby-Herb. Neal-Schuman 2001 196p (How-to-do-it manuals for librarians) pa $45

Grades: Professional   **028.5**

1. Books and reading 2. Fathers

ISBN 1-55570-390-9   LC 2001-18315

This "book looks at both the importance and effect of father involvement in children's reading. . . . Case studies, anecdotes, and interesting sidebars abound in this well-organized, well-written source. . . . An extensive bibliography includes more than 450 children's books about fathers and fathering." SLJ

Hey! listen to this; stories to read aloud; edited by Jim Trelease. Viking 1992 414p pa $15 hardcover o.p.

Grades: Adult Professional   **028.5**

1. Books and reading 2. Literature—Collections 3. Authors

ISBN 0-14-014653-9 (pa)   LC 91-37668

Hey! listen to this—*Continued*

"Divided into categories such as 'Animal Tales,' 'Children of Courage,' or 'Classic Tales,' the forty-eight selections cover a wide spectrum from folktales to fantasy, classics to contemporary stories. More than half are complete stories, while the remainder are one or two chapters from longer books. Trelease skillfully weaves his choices into a cohesive whole. Beyond merely categorizing them, he refers to other authors or stories in the discussions that precede and follow each story." J Youth Serv Libr

Includes bibliographical references

Kitain, Sandra

Shelf-esteem; [by] Sandra Kitain. Neal-Schuman Publishers 2008 183p pa $49.95
Grades: Professional   028.5
   1. Reference books 2. Book talks 3. Children's literature—Bibliography 4. Books and reading 5. Children's libraries
   ISBN 978-1-55570-568-8 (pa); 1-55570-568-5 (pa)
                                        LC 2007034737
"Kitain offers an array of books that 'help children relate to their personal lives and individual challenges.' Chapters are based on themes including but not limited to friendship, courage, emotions, moving, new siblings, physical challenges, and bullies. Tough subjects like alcoholism, illness and death, and homelessness are also included. . . . The quality and variety of texts are excellent. The remaining chapters of the book explore working with community partners. This text is highly recommended for all librarians, teachers, caregivers, and parents of younger readers." SLJ

Includes bibliographical references

Knowles, Elizabeth, 1946-

Boys and literacy; practical strategies for librarians, teachers, and parents; [by] Elizabeth Knowles and Martha Smith. Libraries Unlimited 2005 xxi, 164p il pa $35
Grades: Professional   028.5
   1. Boys—Books and reading 2. Children's literature—Bibliography 3. Young adult literature—Bibliography
   ISBN 1-59158-212-1
"Boys don't seem to like to read. . . . This book briefly explores the research about this situation, outlines strategies to reverse this trend, and lists books within genres that boys enjoy reading. . . . The best part of the book is the author section. . . . For each author covered, there is a complete list of books, contact information, . . . and Web sites. . . . This is a wonderful resource for teachers and parents to begin working on improving literacy with boys." Booklist

More reading connections; bringing parents, teachers, and librarians together; [by] Elizabeth Knowles and Martha Smith. Libraries Unlimited 1999 148p il pa $26.50
Grades: Professional   028.5
   1. Books and reading
   ISBN 1-56308-723-5
   Also available Reading connections pa $23 (ISBN 1-56308-436-8)

The authors present "information about starting and participating in elementary and middle school book clubs. The authors introduce 13 topics such as the arts, humor, families in transition, folklore and mythology, sports fiction, the Internet, and banned books. Each chapter contains guided reading questions, a related journal article . . . and an additional annotated list of articles." SLJ

Larson, Jeanette C.

Bringing mysteries alive for children and young adults; [by] Jeanette Larson. Linworth Pub. 2004 134p il pa $39.95
Grades: Professional   028.5
   1. Children—Books and reading 2. Teenagers—Books and reading 3. Mystery fiction
   ISBN 1-58683-012-0   LC 2003-22064
   Contents: Introducing mystery; Defining mystery; Appreciating mysteries; Looking at series mysteries; Suggestions for integrating mysteries into the curriculum; Programming with mysteries
"The book has excellent ideas for beginning as well as seasoned professionals." SLJ

Includes bibliographical references

Latrobe, Kathy Howard

The children's literature dictionary; definitions, resources, and teaching activities; [by] Kathy Latrobe, Carolyn S. Brodie, Maureen White. Neal-Schuman 2002 282p pa $59.95
Grades: Adult Professional   028.5
   1. Reference books 2. Children's literature—Dictionaries
   ISBN 1-55570-424-7   LC 2001-44434
"The first section is an alphabetical dictionary of 325 terms found in reviews, lesson plans, and other resources. Definitions of terms contain meanings and examples from popular children's literature and activities related to the term. The activities descriptions provide a starting point for teaching or demonstrating the term. This reference book supports resources and materials that librarians or teachers should have in their collection." Book Rep

Lerer, Seth, 1955-

Children's literature; a reader's history, from Aesop to Harry Potter. University of Chicago Press 2008 385p il $30 *
Grades: Professional   028.5
   1. Children's literature—History and criticism
   ISBN 978-0-226-47300-0; 0-226-47300-7
                                        LC 2007046708
"This work presents a true critical history of [children's literature], from Aesop to the present. Scholarly, erudite, and all but exhaustive, it is also entertaining and accessible. . . . [Lerer] asks important questions about writers' intentions and readers' reactions, about why some texts endure and others do not, about the influence of science and religion on children's literature, and even about the impact of libraries and literary prizes upon the genre." Libr J

Includes bibliographical references

Lukenbill, W. Bernard

Biography in the lives of youth; culture, society, and information. Libraries Unlimited 2006 251p il pa $45

Grades: Professional   **028.5**

1. Children—Books and reading 2. Teenagers—Books and reading 3. Biography 4. Children's libraries 5. Young adults' libraries

ISBN 1-59158-284-9   LC 2006007466

"Reflecting on the different and varied uses of biography depending on the age, interests, and developmental needs of students, Lukenbill breaks the genre down into the different types of biographies and how they have changed over time. He includes author and literature suggestions throughout the text and concludes with an extensive bibliography of selection aids, including books and periodicals, for locating recommended titles." SLJ

Includes bibliographical references

Marks, Diana F.

Children's book award handbook. Libraries Unlimited 2006 412p bibl il tab pa $40

Grades: Professional   **028.5**

1. Children's literature—Awards 2. Young adult literature—Awards

ISBN 1-59158-304-7

The author "has compiled a valuable resource that will be much appreciated by teachers and school librarians. Her handbook provides details on the history and origins of 24 major children's book awards from the Jane Addams Book Award to the Charlotte Zolotow Award and includes lesson plans and student activity sheets for 21 of them." Libr J

McDaniel, Deanna

Gentle reads; great books to warm hearts and lift spirits, grades 5-9; [by] Deanna J. McDaniel. Libraries Unlimited 2008 318p (Children's and young adult literature reference series) $45

Grades: Professional   **028.5**

1. Children's literature—Bibliography 2. Young adult literature—Bibliography

ISBN 978-1-59158-491-9   LC 2008018878

This includes "500 recommended titles. Here readers will find books with divorce, drug use, attempted suicides, and more but they all meet the criteria the author has set by being either inspiring, heartwarming, or in some way uplifting. . . . Arranged by genres, the entries include full bibliographic information, an annotation, and a description of why the book fits the 'gentle criteria.'" SLJ

Includes bibliographical references

Nespeca, Sue McCleaf

Picture books plus; 100 extension activities in art, drama, music, math, and science; [by] Sue McCleaf Nespeca, Joan B. Reeve. American Lib. Assn. 2003 133p il pa $38

Grades: Professional   **028.5**

1. Picture books for children 2. Books and reading

ISBN 0-8389-0840-3   LC 2002-11822

Contents: Why use picture books with children?; Extending picture books through art; Extending picture books through drama; Extending picture books through music; Extending picture books through math; Extending picture books through science

"This book is intended for use by teachers, librarians, and others working with children in preschool through grade three and features extension activities for use with a variety of materials. . . . Each chapter includes titles with annotations, 20 activities, and a list of resource books that will introduce readers to further activities. . . . Librarians and teachers will find many useful ideas here." Booklist

Includes bibliographical references

The **Newbery** and Caldecott awards; a guide to the medal and honor books; [by] Association for Library Service to Children. American Lib. Assn. il $18

Grades: Professional   **028.5**

1. Newbery Medal 2. Caldecott Medal

ISSN 1070-4493

Annual

"An annotated listing of winning titles since the inception of the awards (1922 and 1938 respectively). . . . Annotations serve as a reliable guide for colllection development, reader's advisory, curriculum development, and a host of other programs." Publisher's note

Pearl, Nancy

Book crush; for kids and teens; recommended reading for every mood, moment, and interest. Sasquatch Books 2007 288p $16.95 *

Grades: Professional   **028.5**

1. Books and reading 2. Best books

ISBN 1-57061-500-4; 978-1-57061-500-9

LC 2007-13865

Presents lists of recommended book titles for children and teenagers divided into three age groups and then further subdivided into more than 118 categories, including animals, folktales, girl power, autobiographies, comic books, and many others.

"Librarians, parents, and young people will enjoy browsing this resource." Voice Youth Advocates

The **Pura** Belpré Awards; celebrating Latino authors and illustrators; Rose Zertuche Treviño, editor. American Library Association 2006 86p il pa $35 *

Grades: Professional   **028.5**

1. Pura Belpré award 2. American literature—Hispanic American authors—Bio-bibliography 3. Children's literature—Bibliography

ISBN 978-0-8389-3562-0 (pa); 0-8389-3562-1 (pa)

Includes DVD

This reference explains the significance of Pura Belpré, her work, and the partnership that launched this honor for Latino children's literature. It covers the first ten years of the Pura Belpré Awards, from 1996 to 2006, and includes annotations of the winning titles, brief biographies of the winning authors and illustrators, program ideas, activities, and book talks.

"A well-crafted addition to any professional-reading shelf. . . . This superb guide will be valuable to librarians, teachers, and children's literature enthusiasts." SLJ

Reid, Rob

Cool story programs for the school-age crowd. American Library Association 2004 181p il pa $32 *

Grades: Professional   **028.5**
    1. Books and reading 2. Children's literature
    ISBN 0-8389-0887-X   LC 2004-9933
This offers plans for story programs which incorporate poetry, picture books, chapter book excerpts, and short stories

"Eighteen well-developed plans with wacky themes that kids will love will bring literature to life with a minimum of stress for public librarians, teachers, and school media specialists. . . . A useful book with sure-fire suggestions for winning programs." SLJ

Includes bibliographical references

Stephens, Claire Gatrell

Coretta Scott King Award books; using great literature with children and young adults. Libraries Unlimited 2000 238p pa $27.50 *

Grades: Professional   **028.5**
    1. Coretta Scott King Award 2. Children's literature—History and criticism 3. Young adult literature—History and criticism 4. American literature—African American authors 5. African Americans in literature
    ISBN 1-56308-685-9   LC 99-51955
"Both author and illustrator award lists are followed by annotated bibliographies. Twelve of the author entries also feature biographical information. The book is chock-full of curricular units for 15 selected titles. The units include discussion questions, crossword puzzles, vocabulary exercises, performance activities, and integrated curriculum ideas. Additionally, lists of related materials and Internet sites are provided." Book Rep

Includes bibliographical references

Sullivan, Michael, 1967-

Connecting boys with books 2; closing the reading gap. American Library Association 2009 119p il pa $40 *

Grades: Professional   **028.5**
    1. Boys—Books and reading 2. Children's libraries 3. Young adults' libraries 4. School libraries
    ISBN 978-0-8389-0979-9 (pa); 0-8389-0979-5 (pa)
                           LC 2008-34925
Sullivan "looks at developmental differences between boys and girls and how our culture views reading as a leisure activity. He also looks at materials that will attract male readers. His concern is not necessarily the boy who cannot read but the aliterate boy—the one who can read but chooses not to." Booklist

"A must-read for all librarians and media specialists." SLJ

Includes bibliographical references

Sutherland, Zena, 1915-2002

Children & books; [by] Zena Sutherland; cover, frontispiece, and part opening illustrations by Trina Schart Hyman. 9th ed. Longman 1997 720p $119

Grades: Professional   **028.5**
    1. Children's literature—History and criticism 2. Children—Books and reading
    ISBN 0-673-99733-2
First edition by May Hill Arbuthnot published 1947 by Scott, Foresman

"This children's literature textbook emphasizes the best books and authors. The introductory sections about children and books in general are followed by genre overviews which emphasize the major authors in each category. A third section discusses ways to bring children and books together, while a final section covers issues such as censorship. Lavish color illustrations, viewpoint boxes, extensive bibliographies and useful appendices make this an attractive and stimulating work." Safford. Guide to Ref Materials for Sch Libr Media Cent. 5th edition

Trelease, Jim

The read-aloud handbook. 6th ed. Penguin Books 2006 xxvi, 340p il pa $15 *

Grades: Professional   **028.5**
    1. Books and reading 2. Children's literature—Bibliography
    ISBN 0-14-303739-0   LC 2006-41773
First published 1982
This handbook explains the importance of reading aloud to children, offers guidance on how to set up a read-aloud atmosphere in the home or classroom and suggests 1,500 titles for reading aloud.

Includes bibliographical references

Vardell, Sylvia M.

Children's literature in action; a librarian's guide. Libraries Unlimited 2008 323p (Library and information science text) $65; pa $50

Grades: Professional   **028.5**
    1. Children's literature—History and criticism 2. Children—Books and reading
    ISBN   978-1-59158-657-9;   1-59158-657-7; 978-1-59158-557-2 (pa); 1-59158-557-2 (pa)
                           LC 2007038012
"This excellent introduction to children's literature and its various genres and forms offers many activities and practical applications. Each chapter includes 'Action' components that highlight literature, authors, specific book titles, or history. . . . It also includes evaluation criteria, writing reviews, collection development of various genres, awards, and other programs of merit as well as additional information in numerous bibliographies and lists of recommended reading and Web sites." SLJ

Includes bibliographical references

Yolen, Jane

Touch magic; fantasy, faerie & folklore in the
literature of childhood. Expanded ed. August
House 2000 128p pa $11.95

Grades: Professional   **028.5**

   1. Children's literature—History and criticism
2. Folklore

   ISBN 0-87483-591-7   LC 00-27565

   First published 1981 by Philomel Bks.

   The author provides perspectives on reading, appreciating, and preserving fantasy and folklore for children.
Among topics discussed are the morality of fairy tales,
the definition of story, and the theme of time travel

   Includes bibliographical references

York, Sherry, 1947-

Children's and young adult literature by Latino
writers; a guide for librarians, teachers, parents,
and students. Linworth Pub. 2002 184p pa $36.95

Grades: Professional   **028.5**

   1. American literature—Hispanic American authors—
Bibliography 2. Young adult literature—Bibliography
3. Children's literature—Bibliography 4. Books and
reading

   ISBN 1-58683-062-7   LC 2002-67112

   This guide includes "bibliographic information for a
variety of titles in various genres including novels, chapter books, short stories, folklore, drama, poetry, and nonfiction. A list of additional resource materials, as well as
publisher information and an index, is also included."
Publisher's note

   "This publication fills a necessary void for professionals looking for all forms of Latino literature for primary
grades through high school. . . . This book should provide the framework for building a solid collection." SLJ

   Includes bibliographical references

Zbaracki, Matthew D.

Best books for boys; a resource for educators;
foreword by Jon Scieszka. Libraries Unlimited
2008 189p il (Children's and young adult literature
reference series) $45

Grades: Professional   **028.5**

   1. Boys—Books and reading 2. Best books
3. Children's literature—Bibliography 4. Young adult
literature—Bibliography

   ISBN 978-1-59158-599-2; 1-59158-599-6

                     LC 2007-51065

   "This guide offers ideas for educators, librarians, and
parents on fiction and nonfiction books that will interest
boys in grades three to 10." Publisher's note

   "Good source notes guide readers to additional writings on the topic and speak to the author's significant research in his field. Nicely indexed by author, title, and
subject, this [is an] easy-to-navigate resource." Voice
Youth Advocates

   Includes bibliographical references

028.7 Use of books and other information media as sources of information

Callison, Daniel, 1948-

The blue book on information age inquiry,
instruction and literacy; [by] Daniel Callison and
Leslie Preddy. Libraries Unlimited 2006 643p il pa
$45 *

Grades: Professional   **028.7**

   1. Information literacy

   ISBN 978-1-59158-325-7 (pa); 1-59158-325-X (pa)

                     LC 2006-23645

   A revised edition of Key Words, Concepts and Methods for Information Age Instruction, published 2003 by
LMS Associates

   "Part 1 introduces the concepts of information inquiry,
providing foundational documents and exploring search
and use models, information literacy, standards, the instructional role of library media specialists, online inquiry learning, and resource management. Part 2 offers concrete examples of inquiry applied to the middle-school
student research process and supplies reproducible pages
for classroom use. Part 3 discusses and defines 51 key
terms. Entries here are several pages in length and include citations and references. Indispensable for all
school media specialists, this book will also appeal to
other readers, who will be impressed by its well-
organized design, thoroughness, and practicality."
Booklist

   Includes bibliographical references

Taylor, Joie

Information literacy and the school library
media center. Libraries Unlimited 2006 148p il
(Libraries Unlimited professional guides in school
librarianship) pa $35

Grades: Professional   **028.7**

   1. Information literacy 2. School libraries

   ISBN 0-313-32020-9

   "Beginning with a description of what it means to be
information literate, the author goes on to highlight how
the American Association of School Librarians (AASL)
and Association for Educational Communications and
Technology (AECT) standards can be integrated into the
curriculum in ways that complement state and district
standards, giving specific examples from several states.
She discusses how the library media specialist through
flexible scheduling and curriculum mapping can facilitate
an environment where students can hone their information literacy skills. . . . Two things make this book exceptional. First the chapter on collaboration is a
refreshingly frank discussion of the value of working
with classroom teachers that delineates the roles of the
teacher and the library media specialist, while being realistic in realizing that barriers do exist to real collaboration. Second the extensive bibliography is filled with
books, journal articles, and Web resources that will guide
readers to the bestpractices in information literacy at the
current time." Voice Youth Advocates

031 General encyclopedic works in American English

Britannica student encyclopedia. Encyclopedia
Britannica 2007 11v il set $499 *
Grades: 3 4 5 6 7   **031**
1. Encyclopedias and dictionaries 2. Reference books
ISBN 978-1-59339-300-7 (set); 1-59339-300-8 (set)
"With a clear grasp of the interests of the target audience, this attractive and engaging set is a delightful entry
into the student-encyclopedia market and a much-needed
addition for the age group. It provides just the right
amount of information without overwhelming young researchers." Booklist

Grolier student encyclopedia. Grolier 2004 17v il
map set $249
Grades: 3 4 5 6   **031**
1. Reference books 2. Encyclopedias and dictionaries
ISBN 0-7172-5865-3   LC 2003-42402
This is "a general encyclopedia with more than 700
entries arranged alphabetically. . . . The writing is clear
and should be accessible to students in grades three and
above. . . . Entries are enhanced with color photographs,
illustrations, diagrams, time lines, and maps. The picture
captions supplement the text nicely. . . . This set provides a solid introduction to general topics for students
in the primary grades." Booklist

Heinemann first encyclopedia. Heinemann Library
2006 14v il map set $520
Grades: K 1 2   **031**
1. Reference books 2. Encyclopedias and dictionaries
ISBN 1-4034-7122-3   LC 2005006176
First published 1999
A fourteen-volume encyclopedia covering animals,
plants, countries, transportation, science, ancient civilizations, US states, US presidents, and world history.
"This lovely encyclopedia is a wonderful entry to the
beginnings of book searching, and it is highly recommended for purchase in primary schools and in public libraries serving primary students." Booklist

The **New** book of knowledge; the children's
encyclopedia. Grolier 2006 21v il map set $699
Grades: 4 5 6 7   **031**
1. Reference books 2. Encyclopedias and dictionaries
ISBN 0-7172-0540-1
Also available on-line version
First published 1966 as successor to The Book of
knowledge. Frequently revised
Supplemented by The New book of knowledge annual
"Intended to interest a wide range of readers from
those in early childhood to students nearly ready to use
an adult encyclopedia; thus, articles are written at various
levels of understanding, with the main emphasis being
for children in grades three to six. Longer articles are
signed by contributors or consultants. Suggested activities
or projects are incorporated into some articles to further
the educational value." Guide to Ref Books. 11th edition
For a review of 2004 edition see: Booklist, Sept. 15,
2004

One million things; a visual encyclopedia; [by]
Kim Bryan . . . [et al.] DK Publishing 2008
304p il map $24.99 *
Grades: 5 6 7 8 9   **031**
1. Encyclopedias and dictionaries 2. Curiosities and
wonders 3. Science—Encyclopedias 4. Technology—
Encyclopedias 5. Art—Encyclopedias 6. Reference
books
ISBN 978-0-7566-3843-6; 0-7566-3843-7
                                           LC 2008-298840
"DK has put together a visual encyclopedia that runs
with the concept of cramming a million bits of information into one volume. . . . Arranged in sections from nature to nutrition, the human body to technology, people
and places to art and culture, the breadth of subject matter is impressive. Vital to the operation are the photographs. This may be the single largest collection of pictures kids have ever seen in one place, and each page
shows as much as it tells." SLJ

Scholastic children's encyclopedia. Scholastic
Reference 2004 710p il map $19.95
Grades: 4 5 6 7   **031**
1. Encyclopedias and dictionaries 2. Reference books
ISBN 0-439-43816-0   LC 2003-45591
"More than 600 entries are arranged alphabetically and
range in length from one-half page to just over four
pages. Entries are illustrated with more than 2,000 photographs, diagrams, charts, time lines, and maps. Longer
entries include subheadings that divide text into easy-to-
read sections. . . . Libraries serving younger students
will want multiple copies of this highly usable and user-
friendly tool." Booklist

Turner, Tracey
World of the weird. Firefly Books 2009 144p il
$14.95
Grades: 5 6 7 8   **031**
1. Curiosities and wonders
ISBN 978-1-55407-481-5; 1-55407-481-9
"A first-rate browsing item, from the bicycle-riding
frog on the front cover to the recipe for chocolate-
covered crickets at the end. . . . Turner presents barrages
of snippets on extreme sports ('chessboxing'), uncommon
maladies ('exploding head syndrome'), oddball festivals,
bizarre beliefs ('Eating stolen bacon is a cure for consti-
pation.' Do tell!), strange creatures real or otherwise, supernatural phenomena and . . . more. . . . Illustrated
with photos that are often startling but never gory or
gross, this compact page-turner will light up the imaginations of motivated young readers and jaded nonreaders
alike." Kirkus

Wilkes, Angela
My world of discovery. Kingfisher 2007 192p il
$14.95
Grades: 3 4 5 6   **031**
1. Encyclopedias and dictionaries 2. Reference books
ISBN 0-7534-5931-0
Contents: The universe; The world around us; Prehis-
toric life; Plant life; Animal world; Your body; People
and places; Transportation; How things work

Wilkes, Angela—*Continued*

This "is an excellent resource for a young person developing an interest in a diverse number of science topics. Many colorful, clear illustrations accompany the text. . . . The text is easy to read and follow." Sci Books Films

The **World** Book encyclopedia. World Book 2009 22v il map set $1,009 *

Grades: 4 5 6 7 8 9 10 11 12 Adult

031

1. Reference books 2. Encyclopedias and dictionaries
ISBN 978-0-7166-0109-8 (set); 0-7166-0109-5 (set)
LC 2008-28060

First published 1917-1918 by Field Enterprises. Frequently revised

Supplemented by: World Book's year in review; another available annual supplement is World Book's science year in review

"A 22-volume, highly illustrated, A-Z general encyclopedia for all ages, featuring sections on how to use World Book, other research aids, pronunciation key, a student guide to better writing, speaking, and research skills, and comprehensive index." Publisher's note

Includes bibliographical references

031.02 American books of miscellaneous facts

Aronson, Marc

For boys only; the biggest, baddest book ever; [by] Marc Aronson [and] H.P. Newquist. Feiwel and Friends 2007 157p il map $14.95

Grades: 4 5 6 7

031.02

1. Curiosities and wonders 2. Boys
ISBN 978-0-312-37706-9; 0-312-37706-1
LC 2007-32847

"In a tone both light and humorous, Newquist and Aronson aim to please by assembling a tantalizing miscellany—codes, puzzles, best lists, brief history and science facts, instructions for making fake blood and playing Ultimate Frisbee. . . . This offers lots of good fun." Booklist

Buchanan, Andrea J.

The daring book for girls; [by] Andrea J. Buchanan, Miriam Peskowitz; illustrations by Alexis Seabrook. Collins 2007 279p il map $24.95

Grades: 4 5 6 7

031.02

1. Girls 2. Amusements 3. Recreation 4. Curiosities and wonders
ISBN 978-0-06-147257-2 LC 2007031986

"In the introduction, the authors invite girls to explore their world . . . and they deliver a resource that will help them to do just that. The pages that follow are filled with interesting activities to try and important facts they may not know, but are sure to keep them busy for hours. The authors cover everything from making a lemon-powered clock to the history of writing and cursive, from how to paddle a canoe to the Periodic Table of the Elements in clear, thoughtful language that readers of all ages are sure to embrace." SLJ

Farndon, John

Do not open; written by John Farndon. DK Publishing 2007 256p il $24.99

Grades: 4 5 6 7

031.02

1. Curiosities and wonders
ISBN 978-0-7566-3205-2; 0-7566-3205-6
LC 2007300131

This encyclopedic tome catalogues "the mysterious and unusual. . . . Flaps, foldout pages and varied styles of illustration—from photomontage to digital cartoons and more conventional line art—keep the book visually fresh and ably complement the subject matter. . . . Taking in everything from weird weather like St. Elmo's fire and raining frogs to possible locations of Atlantis, the book incites curiosity—and expansively rewards it." Publ Wkly

Iggulden, Conn, 1971-

The dangerous book for boys; [by] Conn Iggulden, Hal Iggulden. Collins 2007 270p il map $24.95

Grades: 4 5 6 7

031.02

1. Curiosities and wonders 2. Amusements 3. Recreation 4. Boys
ISBN 0-06-124358-2; 978-0-06-124358-5
LC 2006-491918

"This eclectic collection addresses the undeniable boy-appeal of certain facts and activities. Dozens of short chapters, in fairly random order, cover a wide range of topics in conversational prose. Simple instructions for coin tricks and paper airplanes alternate with excerpts from history such as Famous Battles and facts about ancient wonders of the world and astronomy. . . . Tongue-in-cheek humor emerges throughout." SLJ

Kane, Joseph Nathan, 1899-2002

Famous first facts; a record of first happenings, discoveries, and inventions in American history; [by] Joseph Nathan Kane, Steven Anzovin, & Janet Podell. 6th ed. Wilson, H.W. 2006 1307p il $185 *

Grades: 5 6 7 8 9 10 11 12 Adult

031.02

1. Encyclopedias and dictionaries 2. United States—History—Dictionaries 3. Reference books
ISBN 978-0-8242-1065-6; 0-8242-1065-4
LC 2006-3096

Also available CD-ROM version and online

First published 1933

Over 7500 entries cover first occurences in American history, organized into 16 chapters each divided into sections. Sections are alphabetically organized, and individual entries are organized chronologically within each section. Includes five indexes: subject index, index by years, index by days, index to personal names, and geographical index

"Besides serving as an essential ready-reference source, the book is also fun to read out loud to colleagues—when was bubble gum first manufactured in the U.S.? When was the spray can introduced?" Booklist

Masoff, Joy, 1951-
Oh, yuck! the encyclopedia of everything nasty; illustrated by Terry Sirrell. Workman 2000 212p il pa $14.95
Grades: 4 5 6 7   **031.02**
1. Curiosities and wonders
ISBN 0-7611-0771-1   LC 99-43603
An alphabetical collection of articles about disgusting things, from acne, ants, and bacteria to worms, x-periments, and zits
"Amusing cartoons and well-chosen, black-and-white photographs with humorous captions support the text. . . . This delightful volume will be enjoyed by fans of grossness everywhere." SLJ
Includes bibliographical references

Thomas, Keltie
Planet Earth News presents: super humans. Maple Tree Press 2006 64p il $19.95; pa $9.95
Grades: 3 4 5 6   **031.02**
1. Curiosities and wonders
ISBN   978-1-897066-51-5;   1-897066-51-1; 978-1-897066-52-2 (pa); 1-897066-52-X (pa)
This "is a high-energy account of all things human that manages to include fun factoids about subject material ranging from biology and history to engineering and linguistics. . . . Each turn of the page gives us a landscape strewn with multiple brightly colored illustrations and up to eight blurbs covering subjects pulled from every direction." Sci Books Films

The **world** almanac and book of facts, 2010. World Almanac Books 2010 1008p il map $34.95; pa $12.99
Grades: 6 7 8 9 10 11 12 Adult
031.02
1. Almanacs 2. Reference books
ISSN 0084-1382
ISBN 978-1-60057-126-8; 978-1-60057-123-7 (pa)
Annual. First published 1868. Publisher varies
"This is the most comprehensive and well-known of almanacs. . . . Contains a chronology of the year's events, consumer information, historical anniversaries, annual climatological data, and forecasts. Color section has flags and maps. Includes detailed index." N Y Public Libr Book of How & Where to Look It Up

The **World** almanac for kids. World Almanac il maps * $18.95; pa $10.95
Grades: 4 5 6 7   **031.02**
1. Reference books 2. Almanacs
Annual. First published 1995 for 1996
This volume contains information on animals, art, religion, sports, books, law, language, science and computers. Includes a section of full-color maps and flags. Illustrated throughout with pictures, diagrams, and charts

032.02   English books of miscellaneous facts

Guinness world records. Guinness World Records il * $28.95
Grades: 5 6 7 8 9 10 11 12 Adult
032.02
1. Curiosities and wonders 2. Reference books
ISSN 1475-7419
Annual. First published 1955 in the United Kingdom; in the United States 1962. Variant titles: Guinness book of records; Guinness book of world records
"Ready reference for current record holders in all fields, some esoteric. Index provides access to information arranged in broad subject categories. Must be replaced annually." N Y Public Libr. Ref Books for Child Collect

050   Magazines, journals & serials

Botzakis, Stergios
Pretty in print; questioning magazines; by Stergios Botzakis. Fact Finders 2007 32p il (Media literacy) lib bdg $22.60; pa $7.95
Grades: 4 5 6 7   **050**
1. Periodicals 2. Publishers and publishing
ISBN 978-0-7368-6764-1 (lib bdg); 0-7368-6764-3 (lib bdg); 978-0-7368-7860-9 (pa); 0-7368-7860-2 (pa)
LC 2006021443
"Describes what media is, how magazines are part of media, and encourages readers to question the medium's influential messages." Publisher's note
This is "written in a breezy style and [has] plenty of popping colors and photos. . . . Useful and attractive." SLJ
Includes bibliographical references

051   General serial publications in American English

Hopkins, Lee Bennett, 1938-
Days to celebrate; a full year of poetry, people, holidays, history, fascinating facts, and more; written and edited by Lee Bennett Hopkins; illustrated by Stephen Alcorn. Greenwillow Books 2005 112p il $17.99; lib bdg $18.89 *
Grades: 3 4 5   **051**
1. Reference books 2. Almanacs 3. Poetry—Collections 4. Holidays
ISBN 0-06-000765-6; 0-06-000766-4 (lib bdg)
LC 2003-49288
"The writers represented include Robert Frost, Langston Hughes, Richard Wilbur, and Gwendolyn Brooks. Alcorn's large, vibrant, whimsical artwork perfectly enhances the prose and verse to make this book a delight to the eye and the ear." SLJ

069 Museology (Museum science)

Mark, Jan, 1943-2006

The museum book; a guide to strange and wonderful collections; written by Jan Mark; illustrated by Richard Holland. Candlewick Press 2007 54p il $15

Grades: 3 4 5 6   069

1. Museums

ISBN 978-0-7636-3370-7; 0-7636-3370-4

LC 2006-49055

Explains what a museum is, and what fascinating things you might find there.

This "tome will launch readers on a leisurely and edifying journey of discovery. . . . Holland . . . jolts readers . . . with his mixed-media collages, which sparingly employ color and liberally combine to look like Victorian engravings, pencil sketches, Gorey-like figures, and photos of various locales." Publ Wkly

070.4 Journalism

Sullivan, George

Journalists at risk; reporting America's wars; [by] George Sullivan. Twenty-First Century Books 2006 128p il (People's history) lib bdg $26.60

Grades: 5 6 7 8   070.4

1. Journalism 2. War

ISBN 0-7613-2745-2   LC 2003015855

Discusses the role of reporters during war time, including the risks they take and the censorship they face, and how their jobs have changed with each conflict since the Civil War.

"As a case study in the fluidity of First Amendment rights in wartime, it's thought-provoking reading." Booklist

Includes bibliographical references

070.5 Publishing

Donovan, Sandra, 1967-

Pingpong Perry experiences how a book is made; by Sandy Donovan; illustrated by Martin Haake. Picture Window 2010 24p il (In the library) lib bdg $25.32 *

Grades: 1 2 3   070.5

1. Publishers and publishing

ISBN 978-1-4048-5759-9 (lib bdg); 1-4048-5759-1 (lib bdg)

This volume "surprises and amuses with every page, while also neatly explaining the publishing process. . . . On the first page, Perry (digitally illustrated in an angular, retro-cool style) is clutching his own book: *Perry's Practical Guide to the Pizza Picks of Popular Pingpong Players*. Donovan then backtracks to relate Perry's meteoric transformation into publishing royalty. . . . The editing process, complete with a sample of a copyedited page, is admirably realistic, as is the portrayal of the savvy professional women Perry encounters at every turn." Booklist

Marcus, Leonard S., 1950-

Golden legacy; how Golden Books won children's hearts, changed publishing forever, and became an American icon along the way. Golden Books 2007 245p il $40

Grades: Adult Professional   070.5

1. Golden Books Publishing Co. Inc. 2. Publishers and publishing 3. Children's literature—History and criticism

ISBN 978-0-375-82996-3; 0-375-82996-2

LC 2006-939312

Presents a history of Golden Books, discussing how it was founded in the midst of World War II providing quality books at inexpensive prices and used innovative writers and marketing techniques to establish itself as a highly successful publishing firm

This is a "lavishly illustrated, handsomely designed volume. . . . The author unearths some startling facts. . . . The highly readable narrative is documented with thorough and detailed footnotes. . . . This winning combination of nostalgia and clear-eyed, meticulously researched history breaks new ground." SLJ

Minders of make-believe; idealists, entrepreneurs, and the shaping of American children's literature. Houghton Mifflin Co. 2008 402p $28 *

Grades: Adult Professional   070.5

1. Children's literature—History and criticism 2. Children—Books and reading 3. Publishers and publishing

ISBN 978-0-395-67407-9; 0-395-67407-7

LC 2008-00589

"This broad survey distills the history of American children's publishing and librarianship, from colonial times to British interloper Harry Potter, including children's periodicals, major publishers and changes in printing technology." Publ Wkly

"Marcus' approach and tone are always, and irresistibly, well informed, sensible, and intelligent. . . . It is hard to imagine any issue that he has overlooked, and the resulting book is, in word, *indispensable*." Booklist

Includes bibliographical references

Side by side; five favorite picture-book teams go to work. Walker & Co. 2001 64p il $22.95; lib bdg $23.85 *

Grades: 4 5 6 7   070.5

1. Picture books for children 2. Authors, American 3. Illustrators

ISBN 0-8027-8778-9; 0-8027-8779-7 (lib bdg)

LC 2001-26344

This "volume introduces five sets of collaborators in the field of picture books: Arthur Yorinks and Richard Egielski, Alice and Martin Provensen, Julius Lester and Jerry Pinkney, Joanna Cole and Bruce Degen, and Jon Scieszka, Lane Smith, and Molly Leach. Each chapter discusses how the writer and artist (and in Leach's case, designer) got together, and highlights their collaboration during various projects, as well as providing a wealth of interesting details about these creative individuals and their books. The clearly reproduced illustrations, many in color, include photographs, sketches for book illustrations, and finished art." Booklist

Includes glossary and bibliographical references

100 PHILOSOPHY

Law, Stephen
Really, really big questions; about the weird, the wonderful, and everything else; illustrated by Nishant Choksi. Kingfisher 2009 62p il $16.99
Grades: 5 6 7 8   **100**
1. Philosophy
ISBN 978-0-7534-6309-3; 0-7534-6309-1
An introduction to philosophy which uses clear analogies to explore some of life's biggest moral and scientific questions, including the origins of the universe and the meaning of life
"Through a combination of vibrant colors; hip, retro illustrations; and interesting quotes, Law has produced a stimulating work for young minds that is sure to spark conversation and, of course, more questions." SLJ

133.1 Apparitions

Stefoff, Rebecca, 1951-
Ghosts and spirits; [by] Rebecca Stefoff. Marshall Cavendish Benchmark 2007 c2008 94p il (Secrets of the supernatural) lib bdg $32.79
Grades: 5 6 7 8   **133.1**
1. Ghosts
ISBN 978-0-7614-2634-9 (lib bdg); 0-7614-2634-5 (lib bdg)   LC 2006031652
This is a history of beliefs in ghosts and spirits throughout the world, including haunted houses, spiritualism, hauxes, and investigations into paranormal phenomena.
"Nearly every other page has an illustration. . . . The text is accessible." Libr Media Connect
Includes glossary and bibliographical references

Wetzel, Charles
Haunted U.S.A.; written by Charles Wetzel; illustrated by Josh Cochran. Sterling 2008 86p il (Mysteries unwrapped) pa $5.95
Grades: 5 6 7 8   **133.1**
1. Ghosts
ISBN 978-1-4027-3735-0 (pa); 1-4027-3735-1 (pa)   LC 2007045905
"Wetzel tells stories of haunted America from the White House to Hollywood. Although some of the places and people mentioned, such as the Amityville house and Rudolph Valentino, might be unfamiliar to younger readers, the selections are still good ghost stories. . . . [The book has] an ample number of clear black-and-white and full-color photographs and illustrations. . . . Perfect for libraries that need a boost or an update to their scary-story collections." SLJ
Includes bibliographical references

133.3 Divinatory arts

Stefoff, Rebecca, 1951-
Prophets and prophecy; [by] Rebecca Stefoff. Marshall Cavendish Benchmark 2007 c2008 79p il (Secrets of the supernatural) lib bdg $32.79
Grades: 5 6 7 8   **133.3**
1. Prophets 2. Prophecies
ISBN 978-0-7614-2638-7 (lib bdg); 0-7614-2638-8 (lib bdg)   LC 2007008779
This is a history of prophecy and fortune-telling from ancient times to the present, discussing such topics as tarot cards, the Oracle of Delphi, astrology, fate, Nostradamus, Jean Dixon, omens, and the *I Ching*.
"Nearly every other page has an illustration. . . . The text is accessible." Libr Media Connect
Includes glossary and bibliographical references

133.4 Demonology and witchcraft

Hill, Douglas, 1935-2007
Witches & magic-makers; written by Douglas Hill; photographed by Alex Wilson. Dorling Kindersley 2000 61p il (DK eyewitness books) $15.99; lib bdg $19.99
Grades: 4 5 6 7   **133.4**
1. Witchcraft 2. Magic
ISBN 0-7894-5878-0; 0-7894-6619-8 (lib bdg)
First published 1997 by Knopf
This book on "witchcraft, shamanism, and mysticism . . . introduces magical charms, talismans, and amulets from around the world. . . . This title gives a colorful overview of the topic." [review of 1997 edition]

Jackson, Shirley, 1919-1965
The witchcraft of Salem Village. Random House 1987 c1956 146p pa $5.99 hardcover o.p.
Grades: 4 5 6 7   **133.4**
1. Witchcraft 2. Salem (Mass.)—History
ISBN 0-394-89176-7 (pa)   LC 87-4543
"Landmark books"
A reissue of the title first published 1956
"A simple, chilling account of the witchcraft trials of 1692 and '93 when, because of testimony given by a group of little girls, twenty persons were executed as witches and others died in jail. There is good introductory background and though the story's subject is by nature horrifying the book does not play on the emotions. . . . It presents a difficult theme lucidly and without condescension." Horn Book

Kent, Deborah, 1948-
Witchcraft trials; fear, betrayal, and death in Salem. Enslow Publishers, Inc. 2009 128p il (America's living history) lib bdg $31.93
Grades: 5 6 7 8   **133.4**
1. Salem (Mass.)—History 2. Witchcraft 3. Massachusetts—History—1600-1775, Colonial period
ISBN 978-0-7660-2906-4 (lib bdg); 0-7660-2906-9 (lib bdg)   LC 2008-18393

Kent, Deborah, 1948-—*Continued*

"Examines the witchcraft hysteria in Salem Village in 1692, including the history of witchcraft, the principal participants in the accusations, the trials and judgment, and its legacy in American history." Publisher's note

"Primary sources and sidebars add valuable perspective." Horn Book Guide

Includes glossary and bibliographical references

Kerns, Ann, 1959-

Wizards and witches. Lerner Publications 2010 48p il (Fantasy chronicles) lib bdg $27.93

Grades: 4 5 6 7   133.4

1. Witches
ISBN 978-0-8225-9983-8 (lib bdg); 0-8225-9983-X (lib bdg)   LC 2008050757

"The explanations and history behind . . . witches [and wizards] . . . will provide satisfaction for readers who want to know more about these familiar characters from myth, fantasy, and folk and fairy tales. Brief and concise." SLJ

Includes bibliographical references

Roach, Marilynne K.

In the days of the Salem witchcraft trials. Houghton Mifflin 1996 92p il map hardcover o.p. pa $5.95

Grades: 4 5 6 7   133.4

1. Witchcraft 2. Salem (Mass.)—History
ISBN 0-395-69704-2; 0-618-39196-7 (pa)
LC 94-32383

"After discussing the Salem Witchcraft trials in one short chapter, this attractive volume explores the social history of the times to show the context that made such events possible. Topics include the law and punishment, magic, social status, clothing, food, household goods, occupations, recreation, common activities, government, and the political troubles leading to widespread tension and unrest. Readers will come away with a much fuller picture of who lived in Salem and how they lived. Small ink drawings decorate the pages." Booklist

Includes bibliographical references

Stefoff, Rebecca, 1951-

Magic; [by] Rebecca Stefoff. Marshall Cavendish Benchmark 2007 c2008 92p il (Secrets of the supernatural) lib bdg $32.79

Grades: 5 6 7 8   133.4

1. Magic
ISBN 978-0-7614-2636-3 (lib bdg); 0-7614-2636-1 (lib bdg)   LC 2007006722

"A critical exploration of magic, its history, and practitioners." Publisher's note

"Nearly every other page has an illustration. . . . The text is accessible." Libr Media Connect

Includes glossary and bibliographical references

152 Sensory perception, movement, emotions, physiological drives

Woodward, John, 1954-

How to be a genius; written by John Woodward; consultants, David Hardman and Phil Chambers; illustrated by Serge Seidlitz and Andy Smith. DK 2009 192p il $19.95

Grades: 5 6 7 8   152

1. Brain 2. Psychology
ISBN 978-0-7566-5515-0; 0-7566-5515-3

Explores the working of the brain, the potential of the mind and how the brain makes a person unique. Includes puzzles, games, and optical illusions to sharpen the wit.

"The pages explode with information arranged in the publisher's signature format—little snippets illustrated by photographs and illustrations, creating a collage that is ideal for browsing. . . . The information is fun for all ages, making it a great choice for family sharing. Most suitable for middle school readers, the book is certainly an excellent purchase for both school and public libraries." Voice Youth Advocates

152.1 Sensory perception

Cobb, Vicki, 1938-

How to really fool yourself; illusions for all your senses; illustrated by Jessica Wolk-Stanley. Wiley 1999 120p il pa $12.95

Grades: 5 6 7 8   152.1

1. Senses and sensation 2. Perception 3. Optical illusions
ISBN 0-471-31592-3   LC 98-27723

A newly illustrated edition of the title first published 1981 by Lippincott

"The book begins with an explanation of perception and explores many different sensory aspects of it through experiments, definitions of important terms (italicized), background information and how illusions affect us in everyday life." SLJ

152.14 Visual perception

Dispezio, Michael A.

Eye-popping optical illusions. Sterling 2000 80p il $17.95

Grades: 4 5 6   152.14

1. Optical illusions
ISBN 0-8069-6641-6   LC 00-58319

"Page after page of visual images demonstrate how the eye and brain can be confused by tricky perspectives, varicolored patterns, and comparative lines and shapes." Horn Book Guide

The author "includes instructions for several projects—among them, a flip book and a zootrope. Whether used independently or in the classroom this lively book will entertain and educate." Booklist

Simon, Seymour, 1931-

Now you see it, now you don't; the amazing world of optical illusions; drawings by Constance Ftera. rev ed. Morrow Junior Bks. 1998 64p il $17.99 *

Grades: 4 5 6 7   **152.14**

1. Optical illusions

ISBN 0-688-16152-9   LC 97-49855

First published 1976 by FourWinds Press with title: The optical illusion book

The author explains optical illusions involving lines and spaces, changeable figures, depth and distance, brightness and contrast, and color

"One of the clearest and most interesting discussions of optical illusions ever written for children." Booklist

Wick, Walter, 1953-

Walter Wick's optical tricks; by Walter Wick. 10th anniversary edition. Cartwheel Books 2008 43p il $14.99 *

Grades: 4 5 6 7   **152.14**

1. Optical illusions

ISBN 978-0-439-85520-4; 0-439-85520-9

First published 1998

Presents a series of optical illustions and explains what is seen.

The author "has produced a stunning picture book of optical illusions. With crystal-clear photographs, he creates a series of scenes that fool the eye and the brain." Booklist [review of 1998 ed.]

152.4   Emotions

Aliki

Feelings. Greenwillow Bks. 1984 32p il $16; pa $5.95 *

Grades: K 1 2 3   **152.4**

1. Emotions

ISBN 0-688-03831-X; 0-688-06518-X (pa)

LC 84-4098

"Small pen-and-ink cartoons with vivid coloring depict boys and girls interacting and experiencing the full range of feelings which evolve in everyday settings. This creative, unique book would be ideal for parent/child interaction or use by elementary teachers in language arts classes. Children will enjoy the comic book 'frame' format." Child Book Rev Serv

153.7   Perceptual processes

Hillman, Ben

How big is it? a big book all about bigness. Scholastic 2007 47p il $14.99

Grades: 3 4 5   **153.7**

1. Size

ISBN 0-439-91808-1; 978-0-439-91808-4

LC 2006050609

"This oversize picture book . . . presents 22 giant creatures, objects, and plants, prehistoric and contempo-

rary. On each double-page spread there is a panel of chatty information next to a huge, unframed color picture, which uses digitally blended images to show comparative size. . . . These clear, astonishing pictures [are] both a magnet to browsers as well as a device to demonstrate gradations of bigness." Booklist

155.9   Environmental psychology

Brown, Laurene Krasny

When dinosaurs die; a guide to understanding death; [by] Laurie Krasny Brown and Marc Brown. Little, Brown 1996 32p il hardcover o.p. pa $5.95

Grades: K 1 2 3   **155.9**

1. Death 2. Bereavement

ISBN 0-316-10917-7; 0-316-11955-5 (pa)

LC 95-14511

"The text explains the inevitability of death, various reasons for death (including old age, sickness, accident, and suicide), and the difference between death and sleep; it then goes on to examine feelings about death and ways, both individual and cultural, of dealing with the loss of loved ones. . . . The simple watercolor illustrations help to make some scary situations more approachable. Quiet, respectful, and unthreatening, this will probably become a primary-grades standard on the subject." Bull Cent Child Books

Includes glossary

Krementz, Jill

How it feels when a parent dies. Knopf 1981 110p il pa $16 hardcover o.p.

Grades: 4 5 6 7   **155.9**

1. Death 2. Bereavement

ISBN 0-394-75854-4 (pa)   LC 80-8808

This book is "a hopeful tribute to the healing power sustained by young survivors, who are competently interviewed and photographed in their widely varied reactions and situations. The subjects range in age from 7 to 16 and cope with a variety of deaths by suicide, accident, and illness. Adults helping children through a hard time will better understand their charges' problems through the honest opinions expressed here, and young readers might feel less alone." Booklist

Murphy, Patricia J., 1963-

Death; [by] Patricia J. Murphy. Heinemann Library 2008 32p il (Tough topics) lib bdg $25.36; pa $7.99

Grades: PreK K 1 2 3   **155.9**

1. Death 2. Bereavement

ISBN   978-1-4034-9778-9   (lib   bdg); 978-1-4034-9783-3 (pa)   LC 2007007230

The author "discusses what death is, how it can happen, how it affects people, funerals and memories, and different ways of coping with such loss. . . . The two-page chapters include full-color photos and two paragraphs of text that are frank yet sensitive in their approach." SLJ

Includes glossary and bibliographical references

Raschka, Christopher

The purple balloon; [by] Chris Raschka. Schwartz & Wade Books 2007 unp il $16.99; lib bdg $19.99

Grades: PreK K 1 2   **155.9**
1. Death 2. Terminally ill
   ISBN   978-0-375-84146-0;   0-375-84146-6; 978-0-375-94259-4 (lib bdg); 0-375-94259-9 (lib bdg)
                   LC 2006-23725

"Dying is the subject of this sensitive and somber book intended for terminally ill children and their families and friends. . . . The focus is first on how support from those around us can help 'make dying not so hard' for an older person. The same case is then made for a child who faces death. . . . The illustrations are appropriately subdued, with balloons as the characters, all of them given loving and supportive faces and postures. . . . The book ends with suggestions on how to help a friend who is terminally ill." Booklist

Simons, Rae, 1957-

Survival skills; how to handle life's catastrophes. Mason Crest Publishers 2009 128p il (Survivors: ordinary people, extraordinary circumstances) lib bdg $24.95

Grades: 5 6 7 8   **155.9**
1. Life skills 2. Survival skills
   ISBN 978-1-4222-0456-6 (lib bdg); 1-4222-0456-1 (lib bdg)
                   LC 2008-50320

"Begins with a brief and accessible discussion of the psychology of stress and its role in adolescence, and offers twelve pieces of advice for overcoming difficult experiences and catastrophes. . . . [This book features] important, and sometimes complex, information in an easy-to-read format, offering high gloss photographs, marginal glossary notes, concept definitions, a bibliography, and further reading reccommendations." Voice Youth Advocates

Includes glossary and bibliographical references

158   Applied psychology

Andrews, Linda Wasmer

Meditation; [by] Linda Wasmer Andrews. F. Watts 2004 79p (Life balance) $19.50; pa $6.95 *

Grades: 5 6 7 8   **158**
1. Meditation
   ISBN 0-531-12219-0; 0-531-16609-0 (pa)
                   LC 2003-7153

Contents: Meditation myth-busters; The relaxation response; The mind/body/spirit link; Minding your mindfulness

"Andrews emphasizes that meditation is not a flaky practice, or a particularly religious one, but one that's designed to reduce stress and help individuals manage their lives. Four chapters explain the why and how of meditating. . . . [This offers] solid, easy-to-understand information" SLJ

Includes bibliographical references

Brown, Laurene Krasny

How to be a friend; a guide to making friends and keeping them; [by] Laurie Krasny Brown and Marc Brown. Little, Brown 1998 31p il $15.99; pa $6.99

Grades: K 1 2 3   **158**
1. Friendship
   ISBN 0-316-10913-4; 0-316-11153-8 (pa)
                   LC 97-10179

"Dino life guides for families"--Cover

Dinosaur characters illustrate the value of friends, how to make friends, and how to be and not to be a good friend

"Dialogue balloons personalize, enrich, and add humor to the main text. . . . *How to Be a Friend* will be very useful to parents, teachers, and other caregivers of young children." Horn Book

Burstein, John, 1949-

I said no! refusal skills. Crabtree Pub. Co. 2010 32p il (Slim Goodbody's life skills 101) lib bdg $26.60; pa $8.95

Grades: 1 2 3 4 5   **158**
1. Peer pressure 2. Decision making 3. Risk-taking (Psychology)
   ISBN 978-0-7787-4789-5 (lib bdg); 0-7787-4789-1 (lib bdg); 978-0-7787-4805-2 (pa); 0-7787-4805-7 (pa)
                   LC 2009022850

In this book children are taught to understand when and why they need to say "no," and how to refuse and still keep their friends

This book offers "clear and simple advice for children and [provides] adults with springboards for discussion and role-playing. [It has] appealing color photographs of a variety of types of kids, . . . opening scenarios, concrete coping suggestions, and solid reasoning." SLJ

Includes bibliographical references

Crist, James J.

What to do when you're sad & lonely; a guide for kids; [by] James J. Crist. Free Spirit Pub. 2006 124p il pa $9.95

Grades: 4 5 6 7   **158**
1. Depression (Psychology) 2. Solitude
   ISBN 978-1-57542-189-6 (pa); 1-57542-189-5 (pa)
                   LC 2005021794

"Advising his audience to read this book and work through negative feelings with an adult, Crist describes sad and lonely feelings, distinguishes them from more serious conditions such as depression, and then suggests 'Blues Busters' and ways to ask for help. . . . Crist's clear explanations and simple techniques . . . are relevant for both children and adults." Voice Youth Advocates

Includes bibliographical references

What to do when you're scared & worried; a guide for kids; [by] James Crist. Free Spirit Pub. 2004 128p il pa $9.95

Grades: 4 5 6 7   **158**
1. Fear 2. Worry
   ISBN 1-57542-153-4

"Part one deals with normal anxiety, offering detailed steps for developing 10 coping mechanisms. Expert help

Crist, James J.—*Continued*

is needed to deal with the more serious problems discussed in Part two (e.g., phobias, separation anxiety, obsessive-compulsive disorder). Throughout, the author provides information, case histories, and coping skills in a manner that is both reassuring and encouraging. . . . Illustrations lighten the tone of the subject matter." SLJ

Includes bibliographical references

Fox, Annie, 1950-

Real friends vs. the other kind. Free Spirit Pub. 2009 90p il pa $9.99

Grades: 5 6 7 8   158

1. Friendship 2. Interpersonal relations

ISBN 978-1-57542-319-7 (pa); 1-57542-319-7 (pa)

LC 2008031368

"Jack, Abby, Mateo, Jen, Chris, and Michelle are the middle school students of various ethnicities who take readers through this slim, interactive guide. Chapters cover such topics as friendship dilemmas, so-called friends, when friendships aren't working, crushes, and making new friends. Each chapter opens with a scene played out by the students in cartoon panels. Next, bits of text, along with a multitude of side boxes, address the topic at hand. . . . Lists of questions are offered, along with the answers. There's a lot packed into this colorful title that falls somewhere between self-help and peer advice." SLJ

McIntyre, Thomas, 1952-

The behavior survival guide for kids; how to make good choices and stay out of trouble; [by] Thomas McIntyre. Free Spirit Pub. 2003 167p pa $14.95

Grades: 5 6 7 8   158

1. Interpersonal relations 2. Conduct of life

ISBN 1-57542-132-1   LC 2003-4565

"The author provides skills and activities to learn and practice so that new behaviors can replace those that have resulted in getting students into trouble. . . . Those motivated to make better choices for how they behave in school or with friends and family will find much to help them." Voice Youth Advocates

Rogers, Fred

Making friends; photographs by Jim Judkis. Putnam 1987 unp il pa $6.99 hardcover o.p.

Grades: PreK K 1   158

1. Friendship

ISBN 0-698-11409-4 (pa)   LC 86-12353

"From its opening lines ('When people like each other and like to do things together, they're friends. Can you think of someone who's your friend?'), Rogers's inimitable voice reaches out to his small readers with understanding and reassurance. He describes the pleasures of friendship as well as potential problem areas. . . . Judkis's large color photos capture the range of emotions Rogers writes about." Publ Wkly

170   Ethics

MacGregor, Cynthia

Think for yourself; a kid's guide to solving life's dilemmas and other sticky problems; by Cynthia MacGregor; illustrator: Paula Becker. 2nd ed. Lobster Press 2008 142p il pa $14.95

Grades: 3 4 5 6   170

1. Ethics 2. Conduct of life

ISBN 978-1-897073-90-2 (pa); 1-897073-90-9 (pa)

First published 2003

This book "presents 53 real-life dilemmas that 21st century children might face. Topics range from cyberbullying, chat rooms, and online porn to situations with friends, family and adults. . . . Each dilemma is . . . followed by three questions. . . . The questions encourage readers to examine why the predicaments are dilemmas, to analyze possible solutions, and to arrive at acceptable decisions. . . . This indispensible book is recommended for school and public library collections." Libr Media Connect

Parker, Victoria

Making choices; [by] Vic Parker. Heinemann Library 2010 32p il (Exploring citizenship) $25.36; pa $7.99

Grades: 1 2 3 4   170

1. Choice (Psychology) 2. Decision making

ISBN   978-1-4329-3317-3;   1-4329-3317-5; 978-1-4329-3325-8 (pa); 1-4329-3325-6 (pa)

LC 2008-55310

This describes the different choices and decisions people have to make every day and why it is important to think for yourself, what to do if you are bullied, and how to make the right choices for your health.

"The text presents a multitude of realistic situations to which young children will relate. There are 'Think About It' fact boxes and checklists that aid in understanding and that will spark discussion. All are filled with captioned, color photographs that relate to the text. The information is relevant and current. . . . Strongly consider this." Libr Media Connect

Includes glossary and bibliographical references

174   Occupational ethics

Hartman, Eve

Science ethics and controversies; [by] Eve Hartman and Wendy Meshbesher. Raintree 2009 48p il (Sci-hi: life science) $31.43; pa $8.99

Grades: 5 6 7 8   174

1. Science—Ethical aspects

ISBN   978-1-4109-3330-0;   1-4109-3330-X; 978-1-4109-3338-6 (pa); 1-4109-3338-5 (pa)

LC 2009003475

In this introduction to science ethics and controversies "clear language, embedded definitions, and interesting examples illustrate abstract concepts through both text and well-chosen photographs. . . . [It] discusses topics such as global warming and animal research, and their implications for decision-making by scientists, policy

Hartman, Eve—*Continued*

makers, and voters. Because so many issues are raised in this book, it will be especially useful as a research starter in both science and social-studies classes. . . . [The] book also includes suggested activities to test ideas as well as a thorough glossary and a Webliography." SLJ

Includes glossary and bibliographical references

175 Ethics of recreation, leisure, public performances, communication

Barraclough, Sue

Fair play. Heinemann Library 2010 32p il (Exploring citizenship) $25.36; pa $7.99

Grades: 1 2 3 4   175

1. Sportsmanship 2. Respect

ISBN   978-1-4329-3313-5;   1-4329-3313-2; 978-1-4329-3321-0 (pa); 1-4329-3321-3 (pa)

LC 2008-55301

"Learn about how people should behave when they play sports and games. Find out why people need rules, why cheating is wrong, and how to cope when you lose." Publisher's note

"The text presents a multitude of realistic situations to which young children will relate. There are 'Think About It' fact boxes and checklists that aid in understanding and that will spark discussion. All are filled with captioned, color photographs that relate to the text. The information is relevant and current. . . . Strongly consider this." Libr Media Connect

Includes glossary and bibliographical references

177 Ethics of social relations

Barraclough, Sue

Sharing. Heinemann Library 2010 32p il (Exploring citizenship) $25.36; pa $7.99

Grades: 1 2 3 4   177

1. Etiquette 2. Kindness

ISBN   978-1-4329-3312-8;   1-4329-3312-4; 978-1-4329-3320-3 (pa); 1-4329-3320-5 (pa)

LC 2008-55300

"Learn about the different ways in which people share." Publisher's note

"The text presents a multitude of realistic situations to which young children will relate. There are 'Think About It' fact boxes and checklists that aid in understanding and that will spark discussion. All are filled with captioned, color photographs that relate to the text. The information is relevant and current. . . . Strongly consider this." Libr Media Connect

Includes glossary and bibliographical references

Parker, Victoria

Good relationships. Heinemann Library 2008 32p il (Exploring citizenship) $25.36; pa $7.99

Grades: 1 2 3 4   177

1. Interpersonal relations

ISBN   978-1-4329-3316-6;   1-4329-3316-7; 978-1-4329-3324-1 (pa); 1-4329-3324-8 (pa)

LC 2008-55306

This describes how important it is to get along with the people around us and what can happen when people do not try to listen to or understand each other.

"The text presents a multitude of realistic situations to which young children will relate. There are 'Think About It' fact boxes and checklists that aid in understanding and that will spark discussion. All are filled with captioned, color photographs that relate to the text. The information is relevant and current. . . . Strongly consider this." Libr Media Connect

Includes glossary and bibliographical references

Pryor, Kimberley Jane

Cooperation; by Kimberley Jane Pryor. Marshall Cavendish Benchmark 2008 32p il (Values) lib bdg $19.95

Grades: 1 2 3   177

1. Cooperation 2. Conduct of life

ISBN 978-0-7614-3124-4 (lib bdg); 0-7614-3124-1 (lib bdg)   LC 2008001617

In this book "cooperation is described as following instructions, sharing, and solving problems. [This] value is considered in a direct manner, which makes the [book] useful for the younger part of the age range, while the [title] will provide springboards for discussion among the older children. The brief [text is] accompanied by attractive, captioned color photographs." SLJ

Honesty; by Kimberley Jane Pryor. Marshall Cavendish Benchmark 2008 32p il (Values) lib bdg $19.95

Grades: 1 2 3   177

1. Honesty 2. Conduct of life

ISBN 978-0-7614-3125-1 (lib bdg); 0-7614-3125-X (lib bdg)   LC 2008001673

This "well-executed [book provides a] simple [definition] of [honesty], examples of how it can be demonstrated, and a breakdown of the behavior into individual actions. . . . The brief [text is] accompanied by attractive, captioned color photographs." SLJ

Kindness; by Kimberley Jane Pryor. Marshall Cavendish Benchmark 2008 32p il (Values) lib bdg $19.95

Grades: 1 2 3   177

1. Kindness 2. Conduct of life

ISBN 978-0-7614-3126-8 (lib bdg); 0-7614-3126-8 (lib bdg)   LC 2008001661

This "begins with a bulleted explanation of the word 'values.'. . . The rest of the text describes [kindness]. . . . The author then goes on to discuss examples of behaviors and emotions such as being kind to family and friends, feeling sympathy, and caring. The accompanying color photographs, showing children that appear to be unposed, are age-appropriate, culturally diverse, and complement the [narrative]." SLJ

Respect; by Kimberley Jane Pryor. Marshall Cavendish Benchmark 2008 32p il (Values) lib bdg $19.95

Grades: 1 2 3   177

1. Respect 2. Conduct of life

ISBN 978-0-7614-3128-2 (lib bdg); 0-7614-3128-4 (lib bdg)   LC 2008001669

Pryor, Kimberley Jane—*Continued*
This "begins with a bulleted explanation of the word 'values.' . . . The rest of the text describes [respect]. . . . The author then goes on to discuss examples of behaviors and emotions such as being kind to family and friends, feeling sympathy, and caring. The accompanying color photographs, showing children that appear to be unposed, are age-appropriate, culturally diverse, and complement the [narrative]." SLJ

Tolerance; by Kimberley Jane Pryor. Marshall Cavendish Benchmark 2008 32p il (Values) lib bdg $19.95
Grades: 1 2 3   **177**
    1. Toleration 2. Conduct of life
    ISBN 978-0-7614-3129-9 (lib bdg); 0-7614-3129-2 (lib bdg)   LC 2008001672
This "begins with a bulleted explanation of the word 'values.' . . . The rest of the text describes [tolerance]. . . . The author then goes on to discuss examples of behaviors and emotions such as being kind to family and friends, feeling sympathy, and caring. The accompanying color photographs, showing children that appear to be unposed, are age-appropriate, culturally diverse, and complement the [narrative]." SLJ

Verdick, Elizabeth
Words are not for hurting; illustrated by Marieka Heinlen. Free Spirit Pub. 2004 33p il pa $11.95; bd bk $7.95
Grades: K 1 2   **177**
    1. Conversation 2. Etiquette 3. Interpersonal relations
    ISBN 1-57542-156-9 (pa); 1-57542-155-0 (bd bk)
                                        LC 2003-21273
Also available Spanish language edition
Encourages toddlers and preschoolers to express themselves using helpful, not hurtful, words. Includes a note for parents and caregivers
"The brightly colored drawings, which bring the minimal text to life, are especially effective at showing the range of emotions children experience when they hear unkind language. An excellent resource for sharing at home and at preschools." Booklist

179 Other ethical norms

Barraclough, Sue
Honesty. Heinemann Library 2010 32p il (Exploring citizenship) $25.36; pa $7.99
Grades: 1 2 3 4   **179**
    1. Honesty 2. Citizenship
    ISBN   978-1-4329-3311-1;   1-4329-3311-6;
    978-1-4329-3319-7 (pa); 1-4329-3319-1 (pa)
                                        LC 2008-55297
"Learn what honest behavior is and why it is important." Publisher's note
"The text presents a multitude of realistic situations to which young children will relate. There are 'Think About It' fact boxes and checklists that aid in understanding and that will spark discussion. All are filled with captioned, color photographs that relate to the text. The information is relevant and current. . . . Strongly consider this." Libr Media Connect
Includes glossary and bibliographical references

Burstein, John, 1949-
Can we get along? dealing with differences. Crabtree Pub. Company 2010 32p il (Slim Goodbody's life skills 101) lib bdg $26.60; pa $8.95
Grades: 1 2 3 4 5   **179**
    1. Toleration
    ISBN 978-0-7787-4788-8 (lib bdg); 0-7787-4788-3 (lib bdg); 978-0-7787-4804-5 (pa); 0-7787-4804-9 (pa)
                                      LC 2009023634
This book helps students understand the need and importance for tolerance, and the steps they can take to increase peace in their lives and in the world.
These book offers "clear and simple advice for children and [provides] adults with springboards for discussion and roleplaying. All have appealing color photographs of a variety of types of kids, . . . opening scenarios, concrete coping suggestions, and solid reasoning." SLJ
Includes bibliographical references

Parker, Victoria
Acting responsibly; [by] Vic Parker. Heinemann Library 2010 32p il (Exploring citizenship) $25.36; pa $7.99
Grades: 1 2 3 4   **179**
    1. Responsibility
    ISBN   978-1-4329-3315-9;   1-4329-3315-9;
    978-1-4329-3323-4 (pa); 1-4329-3323-X (pa)
                                        LC 2008-55305
This describes how and why to behave in a responsible way
"The text presents a multitude of realistic situations to which young children will relate. There are 'Think About It' fact boxes and checklists that aid in understanding and that will spark discussion. All are filled with captioned, color photographs that relate to the text. The information is relevant and current. . . . Strongly consider this." Libr Media Connection
Includes glossary and bibliographical references

Pryor, Kimberley Jane
Courage; by Kimberley Jane Pryor. Marshall Cavendish Benchmark 2008 32p il (Values) lib bdg $19.95
Grades: 1 2 3   **179**
    1. Courage 2. Conduct of life
    ISBN 978-0-7614-3131-2 (lib bdg); 0-7614-3131-4 (lib bdg)   LC 2008001662
This "well-executed [book provides a] simple [definition] of [courage], examples of how it can be demonstrated, and a breakdown of the behavior into individual actions. . . . The brief [text is] accompanied by attractive, captioned color photographs." SLJ

200 RELIGION

Ajmera, Maya

Faith; [by] Maya Ajmera, Magda Nakassis, and Cynthia Pon. Charlesbridge 2009 unp il lib bdg $16.95; pa $7.95

Grades: 1 2 3   200

1. Religion 2. Religions

ISBN 978-1-58089-177-6 (lib bdg); 1-58089-177-2 (lib bdg); 978-1-58089-178-3 (pa); 1-58089-178-0 (pa)

LC 2008008282

This "explores through full-color photographs the many ways in which the world celebrates and practices religious belief, highlighting the common threads—praying and meditating, chants and songs, holy books, cleansing, holy places, holidays and festivals, important events, dress, food and drink, and helping others. Spare text accompanies the pictures of children and identifies the specific religion and practices. . . . The excellent photographs are clear and colorful and invite careful observation." SLJ

Buller, Laura

A faith like mine; a celebration of the world's religions . . . seen through the eyes of children. DK Pub. 2005 80p il maps $19.99

Grades: 4 5 6 7   200

1. Religions

ISBN 0-7566-1177-6

"Buller introduces Hinduism, Islam, Judaism, Christianity, Buddhism, and Sikhism through the eyes of children. . . . The amount of information is adequate and straightforward and focuses on aspects of the religion that would appeal to children. The clear, vibrant photographs are especially inviting." SLJ

Osborne, Mary Pope, 1949-

One world, many religions; the ways we worship. Knopf 1996 86p il map $19.95 *

Grades: 4 5 6 7   200

1. Religions

ISBN 0-679-83930-5   LC 96-836

This is an "overview of major world religions—Judaism, Christianity, Islam, Hinduism, Buddhism, and Taoism. . . . Each of six essay-styled chapters addresses themes of religious tenets, deities, morality, and ritual only as they are pertinent to a particular faith." Bull Cent Child Books

"The presentation is notable for its respect to each group, succinctness, and clarity. . . . The artful, full-page, color and black-and-white photographs tell much of the story." SLJ

Includes glossary and bibliographical references

201 Religious mythology, general classes of religion, interreligious relations and attitudes, social theology

Hamilton, Virginia, 1936-2002

In the beginning; creation stories from around the world; told by Virginia Hamilton; illustrated by Barry Moser. Harcourt Brace Jovanovich 1988 161p il hardcover o.p. pa $20 *

Grades: 5 6 7 8   201

1. Creation 2. Mythology

ISBN 0-15-238740-4; 0-15-238742-0 (pa)

LC 88-6211

A Newbery Medal honor book, 1989

"Hamilton has gathered 25 creation myths from various cultures and retold them in language true to the original. Images from the tales are captured in Moser's 42 full-page illustrations, tantalizing oil paintings that are rich with somber colors and striking compositions. Included in the collection are the familiar stories (biblical creation stories, Greek and Roman myths), and some that are not so familiar (tales from the Australian aborigines, various African and native American tribes, as well as from countries like Russia, China, and Iceland). At the end of each tale, Hamilton provides a brief commentary on the story's origin and originators." Booklist

Includes bibliographical references

Reinhart, Matthew

Gods & heroes; [by] Matthew Reinhart and Robert Sabuda. Candlewick Press 2010 unp il (Encyclopedia mythologica) $29.99

Grades: K 1 2 3   201

1. Mythology 2. Gods and goddesses 3. Pop-up books

ISBN 978-0-7636-3171-0; 0-7636-3171-X

LC 2009-15140

This is "a global tour of gods and other deities. Multiple stories unfold on each page within layered tableaus in miniature booklets, like treasures to be unveiled. . . . A fun and engaging assemblage that seamlessly marries its form and content." Publ Wkly

220 Bible

Brown, Alan

The Bible and Christianity; by Alan Brown. Smart Apple Media 2003 30p il (Sacred texts) $27.10

Grades: 5 6 7 8   220

1. Bible (as subject) 2. Christianity

ISBN 1-58340-243-8   LC 2003-41645

Explains how the Old and New Testaments came to be part of the Bible used by Christians and discusses some of the important messages found in the holy scriptures.

"Colorful strips of symbolic patterns adorn the pages and accent the informative text boxes. . . . The clear captioned . . . illustrations (photos and historical art) provide additional background." Horn Book Guide

Includes glossary

220.5 Bible—Modern versions and translations

Bible.

The Bible: Authorized King James Version; with an introduction and notes by Robert Carroll and Stephen Prickett. Oxford University Press 1998 lxxiv, 1039, 248, 445p il map (Oxford world's classics) pa $18.95

Grades: 5 6 7 8 9 10 11 12 Adult   **220.5**

ISBN 987-0-19-283525-3 (pa); 0-19-283525-4 (pa)

LC 96-28858

"Reissued as an Oxford world's classics paperback 1998" Verso of title page

The authorized or King James Version originally published 1611

Includes bibliographical references

The Holy Bible; containing the Old and New Testaments with the Apocryphal/Deuterocanonical books: New Revised Standard Version. Oxford University Press 1989 xxi, 996, 298, 284p map $29.99

Grades: 5 6 7 8 9 10 11 12 Adult   **220.5**

ISBN 0-19-528330-9; 978-0-19-528330-3

LC 90-222105

"Intended for public reading, congregational worship, private study, instruction, and meditation, it attempts to be as literal as possible while following standard American English usage, avoids colloquialism, and prefers simple, direct terms and phrases." Sheehy. Guide to Ref Books. 10th edition. suppl

220.9 Bible—Geography, history, chronology, persons of Bible lands in Bible times

Brown, Laaren

The Children's illustrated Jewish Bible; retold by Laaren Brown & Lenny Hort; illustrated by Eric Thomas. rev ed. DK Pub. 2007 192p il map $19.99

Grades: 1 2 3 4 5 6   **220.9**

1. Bible stories

ISBN 978-0-7566-2665-5

Includes CD

"This is indeed a Jewish Bible, written by Jewish authors, and successful in its inclusion of many popular stories retold in a lively, child-friendly style. Realistic and colorful pencil-drawn illustrations add to the telling, and as a treat for curious minds, the small photographs on the sidebars are really interesting." SLJ

Lottridge, Celia Barker

Stories from Adam and Eve to Ezekiel; retold from the Bible; by Celia Barker Lottridge; illustrated by Gary Clement. Douglas & McIntyre/Groundwood 2004 192p il $24.95

Grades: 4 5 6 7   **220.9**

1. Bible stories

ISBN 0-88899-490-7

"Lottridge uses her storyteller's ear to bring ancient stories from the Hebrew Bible to a young audience, tailoring them to make them more age appropriate. . . . The numerous, well-drawn ink-and-watercolor illustrations are reminiscent of Warwick Hutton's work. Some pictures . . . are quite spectacular." Booklist

Osborne, Mary Pope, 1949-

The Random House book of Bible stories; by Mary Pope Osborne and Natalie Pope Boyce; illustrated by Michael Welply. Random House 2009 165p il $24.99; lib bdg $27.99

Grades: 2 3 4 5   **220.9**

1. Bible stories

ISBN   978-0-375-82281-0;   0-375-82281-X; 978-0-375-92281-7 (lib bdg); 0-375-92281-4 (lib bdg)

LC 2007047308

"The retellers do a credible job of adapting more than 50 Old and New Testament selections in sequential order. Each story is related in language that evokes biblical storytelling, giving the collection the feel of a real Bible with the accessibility of a shared read-aloud. . . . Welply's realistic illustrations . . . will help readers contextualize the place and time." SLJ

Pirotta, Saviour

Children's stories from the Bible; stories retold; color art by Anne Yvonne Gilbert; monochrome art by Ian Andrew. Templar Books 2009 292p il map $19.99

Grades: 4 5 6   **220.9**

1. Bible stories

ISBN 978-0-7636-4551-9; 0-7636-4551-6

LC 2008944069

Recounts over seventy stories from the Bible, including "The Walls of Jericho," "The Prodigal Son," "Jesus and the Children," and "Rahab and the Spies"

Pirotta "adds, for example, kid-friendly details about the weather on the day Mary and Joseph travel to Bethlehem, and he resolves each story with a tidy ending. Softly textured illustrations enhance the mood of the tales." Horn Book Guide

Watts, Murray

The Bible for children from Good Books; retold by Murray Watts; illustrated by Helen Cann. Good Bks. (Pa.) 2002 352p il map $23.99

Grades: 3 4 5 6   **220.9**

1. Bible stories

ISBN 1-56148-362-1   LC 2002-20243

A collection of approximately two hundred and fifty illustrated stories from the Old and New Testaments, retold for children

Watts, Murray—*Continued*

"Watts' retellings from the Old and New Testaments are vivid and evocative. . . . The handsome pictures and decorated borders employ a rich palette of colors and patterns, giving the book a contemporary look." Booklist

221.9   Bible. Old Testament— Geography, history, stories

Hanft, Joshua E., 1956-

Miracles of the Bible; by Josh Hanft; illustrated by Seymour Chwast. Blue Apple Books 2007 unp il $16.95

Grades: K 1 2   **221.9**

    1. Miracles 2. Bible stories

    ISBN 978-1-59354-617-5; 1-59354-617-3

                     LC 2007007093

This retells "such familiar Bible stories as 'Daniel in the Lion's Den' and 'Jonah and the Fish' and 'Noah's Ark.' He also includes such dramatic episodes as the parting of the Red Sea and the conquests of Samson and David. . . . It's Chwast's full-page-and-more compositions, rendered in creamy, pastel-toned ink-and-watercolor that stand out—literally. A number of these illustrations, in Chwast's signature comics-influenced style, appear on foldout pages that boldly expand the scene, vertically or horizontally. Children will likely flock to this hands-on reading experience." Publ Wkly

Sasso, Sandy Eisenberg, 1947-

But God remembered; stories of women from creation to the promised land; illustrated by Bethanne Andersen. Jewish Lights Pub. 1995 31p il $16.95

Grades: 3 4 5   **221.9**

    1. Women in the Bible 2. Bible stories

    ISBN 1-879045-43-5   LC 95-3591

The author "weaves together the stories of: Lilith, the first woman in the garden of Eden, . . . Serach the musician, who, with her song, reveals to her grandfather Jacob that his son is still alive, . . . Bityah, who draws the baby Moses from the Nile, . . . and the bold-spirited Daughters of Z, who struggle against discrimination." Publisher's note

"Although part of the pleasure of the book lies in its strong feminist voice, Sasso also tells good stories; and these will have even more value for the discussions they can generate. Andersen's evocative paintings are beautiful additions to this carefully designed book." Booklist

Ward, Elaine M.

Old Testament women; [by] Elaine Ward. Enchanted Lion 2004 32p il (Art revelations) $18.95

Grades: 5 6 7 8   **221.9**

    1. Women in the Bible 2. Bible stories

    ISBN 1-59270-011-X

These Old Testament stories about women include "explanatory paragraphs, sidebars, and captions by the author. Art masterpieces . . . illustrate each story. . . . The captions provide background on the artist and the significance of each painting or mosaic. . . . The 18 women . . . include Rachel, Leah, Ruth, and Bathsheba. . . . Bosch, Botticelli, and Poussin are among the painters whose work appears here. . . . Visually stunning." SLJ

222   Historical books of Old Testament

Feiler, Bruce S.

Walking the Bible; an illustrated journey for kids through the greatest stories ever told; by Bruce Feiler; illustrated by Sasha Meret. HarperCollinsPublishers 2004 108p il map $16.99; lib bdg $17.89 *

Grades: 5 6 7 8   **222**

    1. Middle East 2. Bible (as subject)

    ISBN 0-06-051117-6; 0-06-051118-4 (lib bdg)

                     LC 2003-15861

Contents: Walking the Bible; Creating the world; Noah's ark; Abraham; Abraham in the promised land; Abraham and Isaac; Joseph in Egypt; Moses parts the Red Sea; The burning bush; Climbing Mt. Sinai

The author describes his journey through places mentioned in the Old Testament

"In this version of his adult book with the same title (Morrow, 2001), Feiler largely succeeds in slimming rather than dumbing down his account of his trip across the 10,000-mile setting of the earliest Bible stories. The author's unpretentious . . . tone and astute pacing help make the volume accessible, and his sincerity is palpable." SLJ

Fischer, Chuck

In the beginning: the art of Genesis; a pop-up book; by Chuck Fischer. Little, Brown 2008 unp il $35 *

Grades: 5 6 7 8   **222**

    1. Bible. O.T. Genesis 2. Bible stories 3. Pop-up books 4. Religious art

    ISBN 978-0-316-11842-2; 0-316-11842-7

                     LC 2007045411

Fischer "presents an impressive, three-dimensional view of the Book of Genesis. . . . Fischer and his collaborators offer a Garden of Eden scene executed in an artistic style that recalls ancient tile work; a huge Noah's Ark landed atop a mountain; and a Tower of Babel impressively high. . . . The text, more commentary than story, is hidden in inset mini-books and is accompanied by reproductions of biblical masterpieces. . . . This book becomes more amazing as the pages are turned." Booklist

Hodges, Margaret

Moses; illustrated by Barry Moser. Harcourt, Inc. 2006 c2007 unp il $16 *

Grades: 3 4 5   **222**

    1. Moses (Biblical figure) 2. Bible stories

    ISBN 978-0-15-200946-5; 0-15-200946-9

Retells the story of Moses, from his birth and trip in a boat of bulrushes to his bringing of the Ten Command-

Hodges, Margaret—*Continued*
ments down from Mount Sinai.

"The venerable story of Moses gets a brisk yet compelling treatment by Hodges. . . . The book is beautiful to page through, with cream-colored pages and the bordered watercolors in Moser's signature style." Booklist

Jules, Jacqueline, 1956-
Abraham's search for God; by Jacqueline Jules; illustrated by Natascia Ugliano. Kar-Ben Pub. 2007 unp il lib bdg $17.95
Grades: K 1 2 3   222
    1. Abraham (Biblical figure) 2. God
    ISBN 978-1-58013-243-5 (lib bdg); 1-58013-243-X
    (lib bdg)   LC 2006027429
"Jules retells a midrash (a legend based on biblical text) in which the youthful Abraham discovers the concept of monotheism. Rejecting worship of unresponsive idols, Abraham spends time outdoors where he senses an unseen hand directing the movements of the moon, sun, storm, and rainbow. He concludes that 'God is everywhere. God is in everything. God is something we know with our hearts.' . . . The energetic pastel illustrations are cheerful and warm. . . . This simply told tale is an excellent introduction to the concept of monotheism, and would be a great discussion starter for talking about God." SLJ
Includes bibliographical references

Benjamin and the silver goblet; illustrated by Natascia Ugliano. Kar-Ben Pub. 2009 unp il $17.95; pa $8.95
Grades: K 1 2 3   222
    1. Benjamin (Biblical figure) 2. Bible stories
    ISBN   978-0-8225-8757-6;   0-8225-8757-2;
    978-0-8225-8758-3 (pa); 0-8225-8758-0 (pa)
                      LC 2007048344
"When Jacob's sons arrive home from their travels in Egypt, they tell their father that one brother is being held as a hostage by the governor, who demands that they return with the youngest brother, Benjamin. The child, aching to see the world, is only too happy to oblige, though Jacob fears that he will lose this son the way he lost his eldest, Joseph, years before. . . . Well paced and well told, this familiar story makes itself fresh with a folkloric feel and a satisfying ending. Ugliano's heavily textured, colorful pastel illustrations ably support and extend the text." Kirkus

Sarah laughs; by Jacqueline Jules; illustrated by Natascia Ugliano. Kar-Ben Pub. 2008 32p il $17.95; pa $8.95
Grades: K 1 2 3   222
    1. Sarah (Biblical figure) 2. Abraham (Biblical figure)
    3. Bible stories
    ISBN   978-0-8225-7216-9;   0-8225-7216-8;
    978-0-8225-9934-0 (pa); 0-8225-9934-1 (pa)
                      LC 2006039738
"Through poetic language and sweeping illustrations, this picture book tells the story of the biblical patriarch and matriarch Abraham and Sarah from Sarah's point of view. . . . Sarah is portrayed as graceful, loving, and faithful. However, her sadness about remaining childless through the years has made her lose her bright laughter.

With the birth of Isaac, when she is gray-haired and wrinkled, she finally laughs again. . . . This lovely retelling deserves a place on the shelves of any library that collects religious materials." SLJ
Includes bibliographical references

Koralek, Jenny
The coat of many colors; illustrated by Pauline Baynes. Eerdmans Books for Young Readers 2004 unp il $16
Grades: K 1 2 3   222
    1. Joseph (Biblical figure) 2. Bible stories
    ISBN 0-8028-5277-7   LC 2004-6575
This "retelling of the story from the Book of Genesis highlights the key events in the life of Joseph . . . and explores timeless themes of sibling rivalry and the power of forgiveness. . . . Baynes enhances the straightforward text with atmospheric illustrations rendered in muted desert shades. . . . This appealing rendition of a well-known tale is perfect for reading aloud." SLJ

The story of Queen Esther; written by Jenny Koralek; illustrated by Grizelda Holderness. Eerdmans Books for Young Readers 2008 unp il $17.50
Grades: K 1 2 3   222
    1. Esther, Queen of Persia 2. Bible stories
    ISBN 978-0-8028-5348-6; 0-8028-5348-X
                      LC 2008017713
This is a "retelling of the biblical story of the Jewish queen of ancient Persia who saved her people from the plotting of the king's evil vizier, Haman. . . . The Jewish holiday of Purim, which commemorates the story of Queen Esther, is mentioned on the final spread. . . . The illustrations are the highlight of the book. Stylized, dreamy pastel spreads sing with deep color. . . . The dignified pictures support the solemn tone of the text." SLJ

Manushkin, Fran
Miriam's cup; a Passover story; illustrated by Bob Dacey. Scholastic 1998 unp il hardcover o.p. pa $6.99
Grades: K 1 2 3   222
    1. Miriam (Biblical figure) 2. Passover 3. Bible stories
    ISBN 0-590-67720-9; 0-439-81111-2 (pa)
                      LC 96-2480
A Jewish mother preparing for Passover tells her young children, the story of Miriam, the Biblical woman who prophesied the birth of Moses

"The text and the lush double-spread watercolors, which are painted to reflect a child's perspective, are framed on a papyrus background. Each illustration bursts with movement, immersing readers and pre-readers alike in the sequence and drama of the story." Booklist
Includes bibliographical references

Paterson, Katherine

The angel and the donkey; retold by Katherine Paterson; illustrated by Alexander Koshkin. Clarion Bks. 1996 34p il $15.95; pa $5.95

Grades: 3 4 5   222

1. Balaam (Biblical figure) 2. Bible stories

ISBN 0-395-68969-4; 0-618-37840-5 (pa)

LC 94-22430

"Paterson retells the story from the Book of Numbers in which the Moab King Balak summons soothsayer Balaam to curse the Israelites, but through the intervention of God, an angel, and a talking donkey, Balaam is inspired to bless this people instead." Bull Cent Child Books

"This faithful, graceful retelling is embellished with many equally graceful watercolor, tempera, and gouache paintings executed in a detailed and realistic manner." SLJ

Ray, Jane

Adam and Eve and the Garden of Eden; written and illustrated by Jane Ray. Eerdmans Books for Young Readers 2005 unp il $17

Grades: K 1 2 3   222

1. Adam (Biblical figure) 2. Eve (Biblical figure) 3. Bible stories

ISBN 0-8028-5278-5   LC 2004-6804

"Adam and Eve live harmoniously with the animals that have been named by the first man, until Eve is tempted by the serpent. In rich prose, the author describes the garden in lyrical detail. The descriptive passages are complemented by exquisite illustrations that lend a mystical aura to the narrative." SLJ

Sasso, Sandy Eisenberg, 1947-

Cain & Abel; finding the fruits of peace; illustrated by Joani Keller Rothenberg. Jewish Lights Pub. 2001 32p il $16.95

Grades: K 1 2 3   222

1. Cain (Biblical figure) 2. Abel (Biblical figure) 3. Bible stories

ISBN 1-58023-123-3   LC 2001-2206

Retells the story of two brothers who, after years of sharing everything, become angry enough to lose control and bring violence into the world

"In this simple yet effective book, Sasso leads children to think not only about how the brothers' personal relationship failed but also about the story's connection to today's violence. The eye-catching, folk-art-style illustrations, with thick swathes of color and inventive background designs, make as strong a statement as the text." Booklist

Spier, Peter, 1927-

Noah's ark; illustrated by Peter Spier. Doubleday 1977 unp il $16.95; pa $7.99 *

Grades: K 1 2   222

1. Noah's ark 2. Bible stories

ISBN 0-385-09473-6; 0-440-49693-8 (pa)

LC 76-43630

Awarded the Caldecott Medal, 1978

"A seventeenth-century Dutch poem, 'The Flood' by Jacobus Revius, opens the otherwise almost wordless book. Skillfully translated by the artist and set in a readable, appropriately archaic type, the artlessly reverent verses add an unexpected dimension to the full-color pictures. Peter Spier's characteristic panoramas are marvels of minute detail, activity, vitality, and humor." Horn Book

Stewig, John W.

The animals watched; by John Warren Stewig; illustrated by Rosanne Litzinger. Holiday House 2007 unp il $16.95

Grades: K 1 2   222

1. Noah's ark 2. Alphabet

ISBN 978-0-8234-1906-7; 0-8234-1906-1

LC 2006004784

"A simple account of the story of Noah's ark. The language is easy enough for young children to understand, but remains true to the basics of the Genesis text. . . . In alphabetical order from aardvarks to jaguars to zebras, animals tell a part of the tale. . . . The appealing illustrations are done in pencil, watercolor, gouache, and colored pencil." SLJ

223 Poetic books of Old Testament

Bible. O.T. Ecclesiastes.

To every thing there is a season; verses from Ecclesiastes; illustrations by Leo and Diane Dillon. Blue Sky Press (NY) 1998 unp il $16.95 *

Grades: 4 5 6 7 8   223

ISBN 0-590-47887-7   LC 97-35124

Presents that selection from Ecclesiastes which relates that everything in life has its own time and season

"The Dillons compellingly convey the relevance of the Ecclesiastes verse throughout history, via a stunning array of artwork that embraces motifs from cultures the world over." Publ Wkly

Delval, Marie-Hélène

Psalms for young children; by Marie-Helene Delval; illustrated by Arno. Eerdmans Books for Young Readers 2008 unp il $16

Grades: K 1 2 3   223

1. Bible. O.T. Psalms

ISBN 978-0-8028-5322-6; 0-8028-5322-6

LC 2006031831

"Each psalm expresses feelings familiar to children: fear and uncertainty, comfort and contentment, amazement and gratitude. The sacred songs, paraphrased in simple, child-friendly language, celebrate the beautiful world, which is protected by God's all-encompassing love, and provide a sense of reassurance. . . . Organized in numerical order, the selections are printed in a large, readable font. . . . The magical paintings feature exotic settings, bold outlines, and rich hues. They are filled with images of children and the natural world." SLJ

Lindbergh, Reeve

On morning wings; adapted from Psalm 139 by Reeve Lindbergh; illustrated by Holly Meade. Candlewick Press 2002 unp il $15.99

Grades: K 1 2 3   223

1. Bible. O.T. Psalms 2. God

ISBN 0-7636-1106-9   LC 2001-58169

"On morning wings" was previously published in the anthology In every tiny grain of sand: a child's book of prayers and praise, collected by Reeve Lindbergh, published by Candlewick Press, 2000

Retells, in simple words, a psalm of God's knowledge of and love for each of us

"Meade's visual story line shows four children spending an idyllic summer day together outdoors. The striking use of light, reflected in water or filtered by campfire, conveys the natural reverence of the text with seeming spontaneity." Publ Wkly

Moser, Barry

Psalm 23; illustrated by Barry Moser. Zonderkidz 2008 unp il $14.99

Grades: K 1 2   223

1. Bible. O.T. Psalms

ISBN 978-0-310-71085-1; 0-310-71085-5

LC 2006027616

"In a two-page introduction, Moser invites readers to see the venerable poem through a new prism: that of a boy tending goats and sheep on a Caribbean island such as Antigua, where the author-illustrator has spent much time. While watching the island animals, Moser says he has often recited the psalm, which he writes here in simple words. . . . Moser strives to accentuate mood and nature, and the paintings in this book . . . highlight the feeling that as God watches over us, we watch over those in our charge." Booklist

230   Christianity & Christian theology

Nardo, Don, 1947-

Christianity. Compass Point Books 2010 48p il map (World religions) lib bdg $27.99

Grades: 5 6 7 8   230

1. Christianity

ISBN 978-0-7565-4237-5 (lib bdg); 0-7565-4237-5 (lib bdg)   LC 2009-15811

This describes the "history and traditions of Christianity and how the religion fits into today's world." Publisher's note

"The colorful, attractive layout includes high-quality reproductions of photographs, maps, and paintings. Students who are new to religious studies, as well as those doing reports, will find that this . . . meets their needs." SLJ

Includes glossary and bibliographical references

Self, David

Christianity; [by] David Self. World Almanac Library 2005 48p il map (Religions of the world) lib bdg $30 *

Grades: 5 6 7 8   230

1. Christianity

ISBN 0-8368-5866-2   LC 2005041712

This is a summary of the Christian religion including history, beliefs, worship, festivals, practice, and current disagreements.

"Wonderfully colorful in images, language, and fact. . . . [This is] enumerated with full-color photographs on every page, charts, maps, and tables." SLJ

Includes bibliographical references

231   God

Fitch, Florence Mary, 1875-1959

A book about God; illustrated by Henri Sorensen. Lothrop, Lee & Shepard Bks. 1998 24p il hardcover o.p. lib bdg $15.93

Grades: K 1 2 3   231

1. God

ISBN 0-688-16128-6; 0-688-16129-4 (lib bdg)

LC 97-48682

A newly illustrated edition of the title first published 1953

The "text explains how people can understand God's nature by observing the world he created. Fitch describes the ways that characteristics of the sun, air, trees, mountains, and oceans reflect the character of God. Proponents of many faiths will embrace this book's message." Horn Book Guide

231.7   God—Relation to the world

Tutu, Desmond

God's dream; by Archbishop Desmond Tutu and Douglas Carton Adams; illustrated by LeUyen Pham. Candlewick Press 2008 unp il $16.99

Grades: PreK K   231.7

1. God 2. Peace 3. Multiculturalism

ISBN 978-0-7636-3388-2; 0-7636-3388-7

"In a series of energetic scenes, a multicultural cast of toddlers follow God's dreams about people caring, sharing . . . and playing together. Adding a touch of drama is the elemental scene in which two kids get in a fight. . . . The large, digitally enhanced pictures, alive with color and pattern, make clear the hurt, anger, and regret. Finally, the two fighters make up, and they join a big circle of laughing kids. . . . Praying together are Muslims, Jews, Buddhists, Christians, and more." Booklist

232.9   Family and life of Jesus

Bible. N.T.
Jesus; his life in verses from the King James
Holy Bible; art by Gennady Spirin. Marshall
Cavendish Children 2010 unp il $21
Grades: 5 6 7 8   **232.9**
   1. Jesus Christ
   ISBN 978-0-7614-5630-8; 0-7614-5630-9
                                        LC 2009005956
"In an unusual project, a tempera painting by Spirin
has been digitally dissected to create individual images
for this picture book that portrays 13 events from the life
of Jesus. . . . Details from the larger work illustrate key
moments—including the Annunciation, Jesus' baptism,
and the raising of Lazarus, among others—beside passages from the King James Bible (Jesus' words are printed in red). The result is an elegant, large-format volume
that offers a reverent and arresting visual interpretation
of biblical events." Publ Wkly

Crossley-Holland, Kevin
How many miles to Bethlehem? illustrated by
Peter Malone. Arthur A. Levine Books 2004 unp
il $16.95 *
Grades: K 1 2 3   **232.9**
   1. Jesus Christ—Nativity
   ISBN 0-439-67642-8   LC 2003-28079
This is a telling of the Nativity story, told from the
perspectives of Mary, the innkeeper, the ox, the donkey,
the shepherds, the Wise Men, King Herod, the child, the
lamb, and the angels.
   "The language is both colloquial and lyrical. . . . Malone's illustrations are reminiscent of early Renaissance
and medieval Eastern art in their wealth of detail and
color. . . . The paintings evoke both sumptuous glory
and a serene stillness." SLJ

Demi, 1942-
Jesus; written and illustrated by Demi. Margaret
K. McElderry Books 2005 unp il $19.95 *
Grades: 3 4 5 6   **232.9**
   1. Jesus Christ
   ISBN 0-689-86905-3   LC 2004-12854
"Brilliantly colored artwork and text based on the
King James version of the Bible tell the story of the life
of Jesus, beginning with the prophesies and the annunci-
ation and ending with his ascension into Heaven. Demi's
paintings are full of bright, intricate patterns, and bold
touches of gold produce a feeling of awe and splendor."
SLJ

Jones, Sally Lloyd
Little one, we knew you'd come; by Sally
Lloyd-Jones; illustrated by Jackie Morris. Little,
Brown 2006 unp il $16.99
Grades: PreK K 1 2   **232.9**
   1. Jesus Christ—Nativity
   ISBN 978-0-316-52391-2; 0-316-52391-7
                                        LC 2005024661

"Although the illustrations depicting Mary and Joseph's arrival in Bethlehem and the birth of Baby Jesus
make clear that this is a Christmas story, the simple text
sings a universal hymn of anticipation and love from a
parent to a child. . . . The sumptuous watercolor and
gold-leaf illustrations, bordered with cherries, peacock
feathers, flowers, and stars, portray an arid yet animal-
filled landscape enlivened by the gloriously bedecked angels and kings." SLJ

Lottridge, Celia Barker
Stories from the life of Jesus; retold from the
Bible by Celia Barker Lottridge; illustrated by
Linda Wolfsgruber. Doulgas & McIntyre 2004
140p il $24.95
Grades: 4 5 6 7   **232.9**
   1. Jesus Christ 2. Bible stories
   ISBN 0-88899-497-4
"A Groundwood book"
A retelling of selected events from the life of Christ
based on biblical accounts
   This is an "exceptional collection. . . . Each story is
retold in three or four pages of clear, concise prose that
is meant to be read aloud. . . . Each selection is enhanced by dramatic and atmospheric, mixed-media illustrations that are executed in warm earth tones." SLJ

Paterson, Katherine
The light of the world; the life of Jesus for
children; [by] Katherine Paterson; [illustrated by]
François Roca. Arthur A. Levine Books 2008 unp
il $17.99 *
Grades: K 1 2   **232.9**
   1. Jesus Christ
   ISBN 978-0-545-01172-3; 0-545-01172-8
                                        LC 2007-06811
"The incisive text . . . deftly moves through the story
of Jesus' life and death, and also highlights several of
the best-known parables. . . . Roca presents . . . close-
ups of the various people surrounding Jesus and . . .
handsome landscapes that give import to events."
Booklist

Skevington, Andrea
The story of Jesus; illustrated by Angelo Ruta.
Lion Children's 2009 127p il $16.95
Grades: 2 3 4 5   **232.9**
   1. Jesus Christ 2. Bible stories
   ISBN 978-0-7459-4982-6; 0-7459-4982-7
                                        LC 2008278094
"Skevington's collection of key New Testament stories
chronicles the life of Jesus beginning with his birth in a
humble stable in Bethlehem and concluding with the
feast of Pentecost when the Holy Spirit descends upon
the disciples. Retelling stories from all four gospels, the
author fictionalizes the scripture passages, adding dialogue and cultural details to enliven the characters and
the setting. . . . Explanatory margin notes supplement
the stories, and the neatly drawn illustrations portray Jesus and his followers in a palette of soft pastels." SLJ

Wildsmith, Brian, 1930-
Jesus. Eerdmans Bks. for Young Readers 2000
unp il $20
Grades: K 1 2 3   **232.9**
    1. Jesus Christ
    ISBN 0-8028-5212-2   LC 00-55126
This "picture book gives an overview of Jesus' life
beginning with the angel Gabriel's visit to Mary and
ending with Jesus' ascension into Heaven." Horn Book
Guide
    "Wildsmith's pictures are framed in windowlike arch-
es, set against backgrounds of pure colors. As with his
other works, gold embellishments add majesty." Booklist

232.91   Mary, mother of Jesus

Demi, 1942-
Mary; written and illustrated by Demi. Margaret
K. McElderry Books 2006 unp il $19.95
Grades: 3 4 5 6   **232.91**
    1. Mary, Blessed Virgin, Saint
    ISBN 0-689-87692-0; 978-0-689-87692-9
                                   LC 2005005844
"Demi begins her story before Mary is born, when her
parents, Anna and Joachim, learn that their prayers have
been heard, and that they will have a child whom they
will dedicate to the service of the Lord. . . . The words
simply serve as a backdrop for the glorious artwork. . . .
Along with her familiar beautiful borders and diminutive
characters, she incorporates many Jewish and Christian
symbols that tie the religions together." SLJ

242   Devotional literature

Billingsley, Mary
The life of Jesus; an illustrated rosary; written
and illustrated by Mary Billingsley; foreword by
Benedict J. Groeschel. Eerdmans Books for Young
Readers 2010 56p il $19.99
Grades: 3 4 5 6   **242**
    1. Jesus Christ 2. Prayer
    ISBN 978-0-8028-5362-2; 0-8028-5362-5
"Billingsley has divided this book according to the
four 'Mysteries' that are emblematic of Christ's life—
'Joyful,' 'Luminous,' 'Sorrowful,' and 'Glorious,' and
then into subsections about each of its five parts. The
book is remarkable in the accessibility it offers to readers
of all ages. The introductory page provides visual instruction—a painting of a rosary with labels and arrows
indicating which beads are meant for each prayer—followed by the prayers themselves. . . . Billingsley's unusual technique is what stands out; she has created
'shrines' of everyday objects, flowers, puppets, children's
toys arranged in a vignette, and then reproduced them in
gouache. The overall effect is child-friendly but also intensely emotionally evocative." SLJ

Brooks, Jeremy, 1925-1994
Let there be peace; prayers from around the
world; illustrated by Jude Daly. Frances Lincoln
2009 unp il $16.95
Grades: PreK K 1 2 3   **242**
    1. Prayers 2. Peace
    ISBN 978-1-8450-7530-9; 1-8450-7530-7
"This picture-book collection of prayers sends universal messages of peace and global unity. Brooks . . . has
pulled from diverse religious traditions. . . . Almost all
of the selections are simple, immediate, and rhythmic.
. . . Daly's delicately rendered, brightly hued paintings
greatly increase the impact of the words. . . . Children
of many backgrounds will be stirred by these prayers."
Booklist

Brooks, Jeremy, 1967-
My first prayers. Albert Whitman 2009 unp il
$16.95
Grades: K 1 2   **242**
    1. Prayers
    ISBN 978-1-84507-535-4; 1-84507-535-8
"Brooks has collected prayers from a variety of nations including Poland, South Africa, the United States,
and France, as well as several from his native England.
The book features prayers of thanks, requests for guidance, blessings, and bedtime prayers. . . . Young readers
will appreciate Brooks's gentle message of acceptance
and inclusiveness." SLJ

A world of prayers; illustrated by Elena Gomez.
Eerdmans Books for Young Readers 2006 unp il
$16
Grades: 1 2 3 4   **242**
    1. Prayers
    ISBN 0-8028-5285-8   LC 2004017482
"A collection of 26 prayers assembled under the headings, Prayers for the Morning, Mealtime Graces, Prayers
for Nighttime, and Blessings. A brief introduction and
comments at the beginning of each chapter reflect on the
place of prayer in our lives. Written in simple, easy-to-
read language, the entreaties are recited by children in a
variety of lands. . . . Dreamlike, decorative paintings
that reflect the various cultures greatly enhance the selections and emphasize the books message of inclusiveness." SLJ

A **child's** book of prayers; collected and illustrated
by Juli Kangas. Dial Books for Young Readers
2007 unp il $12.99
Grades: PreK K   **242**
    1. Prayers
    ISBN 978-0-8037-3054-0; 0-8037-3054-3
                                   LC 2006017595
"Simple meditations, both familiar and less well
known, are presented along with warmhearted illustrations for the purpose of exposing children to the spiritual
benefits of prayer. The well-chosen selections begin at
the start of the day and follow different youngsters and
their families through school, meals, and other typical
pursuits, offering prayers of blessing, thanksgiving, or
praise suited to each endeavor. The pencil, watercolor,
and oil-wash artwork skillfully depicts the charismatic
characters, who hale from a variety of ethnic backgrounds and live in both city and rural settings." SLJ

Field, Rachel, 1894-1942

Prayer for a child; pictures by Elizabeth Orton Jones. Diamond anniversary ed. Simon & Schuster Books for Young Readers 2004 c1944 unp il $10.95

Grades: K 1 2   **242**

1. Prayers

ISBN 0-689-87356-5   LC 2004-5259

Awarded the Caldecott Medal, 1945

A reissue of the title first published 1944 by Macmillan

"The complete prayer, written in rhymed couplets, appears on the first page; then a few lines per page accompany serene illustrations of a girl in tender moments—stargazing out a window or smiling up at her parents. . . . This lovely book lends itself to nightly repetition (a reference to Jesus tags it for a Christian audience)." Publ Wkly

Goble, Paul

Song of creation; written and illustrated by Paul Goble. Eerdmans Books for Young Readers 2004 unp il $16

Grades: K 1 2 3   **242**

1. Creation 2. Prayers

ISBN 0-8028-5271-8   LC 2004-6576

"An author's note introduces this story as an adaptation of the song from The Liturgy of the Hours and The Book of Common Prayer. . . . Goble includes the familiar verse, in which heavens, angels, sun, moon, and the entire Earth sing songs of praise, and includes animals and plants of America as additional elements that also send out prayers to God." SLJ

"In striking graphic compositions, Goble creates magical, yet concrete, scenes of birds, beasts, fish, and more, conveying a personal and a universal reverence for and connection to nature. A beautiful, praiseworthy volume that does, indeed, sing." Booklist

Jordan, Deloris

Baby blessings; a prayer for the day you are born; illustrated by James E. Ransome. Simon & Schuster Books for Young Readers 2010 unp il $16.99

Grades: PreK K   **242**

1. Prayers

ISBN 978-1-4169-5362-3; 1-4169-5362-0

LC 2008017131

"A Paula Wiseman book"

Jordan "offers a colloquial prayer to greet the newborn child, offers advice, and gives reassurance of family love and support as well as God's blessings. . . . Ransome's handsome . . . oil paintings follow an African American child growing from infancy to the start of kindergarten under the watchful eyes of his loving parents. . . . Tenderly portraying a child growing up within a warmhearted family, this appealing picture book clearly expresses the faith, love, and hopes that surround him." Booklist

264   Public worship

Alexander, Cecil Frances, 1818-1895

All things bright and beautiful; based on the hymn by Cecil F. Alexander. Atheneum Books for Young Readers 2010 unp il $16.99 *

Grades: PreK K 1 2 3   **264**

1. Hymns 2. Religious poetry

ISBN 978-1-4169-8939-4; 1-4169-8939-0

LC 2009032628

Bryan "interprets Cecil F. Alexander's 19th century hymn with cut-paper art defined by swirling geometrical shapes in neon hues, contributing to a pervasively jubilant atmosphere. Every spread is a riot of colors, movement, and natural splendors." Publ Wkly

Granfield, Linda

Out of slavery; the journey to Amazing Grace; illustrated by Janet Wilson. Tundra Books 2009 unp il map $15.95

Grades: 4 5 6 7   **264**

1. Newton, John, 1725-1807 2. Amazing grace (Hymn) 3. Clergy 4. Hymns 5. Slave trade

ISBN 978-0-88776-915-3; 0-88776-915-2

LC 2009502001

First published 1997 with title: Amazing Grace

This story of the hymn *Amazing Grace* "and its writer is beautifully written, evocative, and heart-wrenching. With an emphasis on John Newton and his years as a slave trader, Granfield shares how the events in his life led him to become an abolitionist, a pastor, and a writer of hymns. . . . Quotations from Newton's own writings are peppered throughout. Full-color, full-page illustrations add grandeur and appeal to the story. Rich in texture and color, the artwork is somber in tone and content." SLJ

271   Religious congregations and orders in church history

Kennedy, Robert Francis, 1954-

Saint Francis of Assisi; a life of joy; written by Robert F. Kennedy, Jr.; illustrated by Dennis Nolan. Hyperion Books for Children 2004 31p il $18.99

Grades: 2 3 4   **271**

1. Francis, of Assisi, Saint, 1182-1226 2. Christian saints

ISBN 0-7868-1875-1   LC 2003-60420

"The book paints Francis in glowing terms . . . weaving together the major threads of his life: his early kindness to beggars in his family's fabric shop; his call to and ultimate rejection of a military career; his estrangement from his wealthy father; and his ministry to lepers, the impoverished, and animals. . . . Nolan's oil paintings render realistic figures in carefully staged scenes." SLJ

Visconti, Guido

Clare and Francis; text by Guido Visconti, inspired by the biographies and written works of the two saints of Assisi collected in the Franciscan Sources. Eerdmans Books for Young Readers 2004 unp il $20

Grades: 4 5 6 7   **271**
1. Francis, of Assisi, Saint, 1182-1226 2. Clare, of Assisi, Saint, 1194-1253 3. Christian saints
ISBN 0-8028-5269-6   LC 2003-13441
Reviews the lives and works of two members of Assisi society, Francis and Clare, who renounced their wealth and founded religious orders dedicated to relying on God and living in peace, poverty, and humility.
"The familiar story of Francis (and to a lesser extent, Clare) is beautifully treated in this book, with luminous iconic artwork and a text that is both down-to-earth and stroking the stars." Booklist

282   Roman Catholic Church

Hawker, Frances

Christianity in Mexico; written by Frances Hawker and Noemi Paz; photography by Bruce Campbell. Crabtree Pub. Co. 2010 32p il (Families and their faiths) lib bdg $26.60; pa $8.95

Grades: 3 4 5   **282**
1. Catholics 2. Mexico
ISBN 978-0-7787-5007-9 (lib bdg); 0-7787-5007-8 (lib bdg); 978-0-7787-5024-6 (pa); 0-7787-5024-8 (pa)
LC 2009-14157
This "book introduces a child who practices [Christianity]. . . . Provides a solid introduction without overwhelming readers with complex regional variations in practices and beliefs. . . . Words and phrases that are unique to the faith appear in bold font and are defined at greater length in the glossary." SLJ
Includes glossary

289.3   Latter-Day Saints (Mormons)

Bial, Raymond

Nauvoo; Mormon city on the Mississippi River; [by] Raymond Bial. Houghton Mifflin Co. 2006 44p il map $17

Grades: 5 6 7 8   **289.3**
1. Mormons 2. Church of Jesus Christ of Latter-day Saints 3. Illinois—History
ISBN 978-0-618-39685-6; 0-618-39685-3
LC 2005027528
"Bial introduces readers to a city that was established by the Church of Jesus Christ of Latter Day Saints in 1839. . . . This effectively written account provides a sympathetic but balanced introduction to Mormon beliefs. . . . Excellent color photographs grace almost every page." SLJ

George, Charles, 1949-

What makes me a Mormon? by Charles George. KidHaven Press 2004 48p il map (What makes me a--?) $27

Grades: 3 4 5   **289.3**
1. Mormons 2. Church of Jesus Christ of Latter-day Saints
ISBN 978-0-7377-3083-8; 0-7377-3083-8
LC 2004-13636
Contents: How did Mormonism begin?; What do I believe?; How do I practice my faith?; What holidays do I celebrate?
This describes Morman origins, beliefs, practices, and holidays
"Presenting information about religion objectively for younger audiences poses a difficult challenge, but [this title does] an excellent job of it." Booklist
Includes bibliographical references

289.6   Society of Friends (Quakers)

Woog, Adam, 1953-

What makes me a Quaker? by Adam Woog. KidHaven Press 2004 48p il (What makes me a--?) $27

Grades: 3 4 5   **289.6**
1. Society of Friends
ISBN 978-0-7377-3082-1; 0-7377-3082-X
LC 2004-13096
Contents: How did Quakerism begin?; What do Quakers believe?; How do Quakers practice their faith?; What is the future of Quakerism?
This explains Quakerism's origins, beliefs, practices, and future
"Presenting information about religion objectively for younger readers poses a difficult challenge, but [this title does] an excellent job of it." Booklist
Includes glossary and bibliographical references

289.7   Mennonite churches

Bial, Raymond

Amish home. Houghton Mifflin 1993 40p il hardcover o.p. pa $5.95

Grades: 3 4 5   **289.7**
1. Amish
ISBN 0-395-59504-5; 0-395-72021-4 (pa)
LC 92-4406
Text and photographs depict the way of life of the Amish
The full-color photos depict "cozy kitchens, lovingly tended gardens, prized horses, and rolling landscapes. As well as being informative, these photographs create a mood through which readers enter another lifestyle." SLJ
Includes bibliographical references

292   Classical religion (Greek and Roman religion)

Aliki

The gods and goddesses of Olympus; written and illustrated by Aliki. HarperCollins Pubs. 1994 48p il $16; pa $6.95 *

Grades: 2 3 4 5   292

1. Classical mythology

ISBN 0-06-023530-6; 0-06-446189-0 (pa)

LC 93-17834

"After the Uranus-Gaea, Cronus-Rhea background is sketched, the occupants of the 12 golden thrones are each described, along with Hades (underground), Hestia (hearth-bound) and Eros (hovering). The author outlines the deities' characters and attributes, sometimes including a brief incident from their lives." SLJ

"This large-format book provides a quick, brightly illustrated introduction to the ancient Greek gods and goddesses." Booklist

Bryant, Megan E.

Oh my gods! a look-it-up guide to the gods of mythology. Franklin Watts 2009 128p il map (Mythlopedia) lib bdg $39; pa $13.95

Grades: 4 5 6 7   292

1. Classical mythology 2. Gods and goddesses

ISBN 978-1-60631-026-7 (lib bdg); 1-60631-026-7 (lib bdg); 978-1-60631-058-8 (pa); 1-60631-058-5 (pa)

LC 2009-17169

Presents a guide to Greek mythology, providing profiles of gods and goddesses along with information on monsters, heroes, and the underworld.

"The book is organized around entries on major gods and titans, each with vital stats and a Top 10 Things to Know about Me, followed by a few highlights from their lore and sidebars that delve into their cultural relevance. Illustrations abound, from embellished stock images to original cartoons, and the pastel-heavy color scheme may entice readers otherwise resistant to the grays and ivories that tend to dominate classicism." Booklist

Includes glossary and bibliographical references

She's all that! a look-it-up guide to the goddesses of mythology. Franklin Watts 2009 128p il map (Mythlopedia) lib bdg $39; pa $13.95

Grades: 4 5 6 7   292

1. Gods and goddesses 2. Classical mythology

ISBN 978-1-60631-027-4 (lib bdg); 1-60631-027-5 (lib bdg); 978-1-60631-059-5 (pa); 1-60631-059-3 (pa)

LC 2009-17168

Presents a guide to Greek mythology, providing profiles of goddesses and the myths surrounding them.

This "spices things up with sassy artwork, a pastel color scheme, and an OMG sensibility. . . . Aside from the heaps of information coming from all angles on just about every page. . . . [this] book also contains a decent family tree, a rudimentary star chart, and lists of further reading. . . . For kids unconvinced that anything so old and gray could have any bearing on their lives, . . . [this provides] a feisty . . . guide to the many cultural references lingering from antiquity." Booklist

Includes glossary and bibliographical references

Clayton, Sally Pomme

Persephone; a journey from winter to spring; by Sally Pomme Clayton; illustrated by Virginia Lee. Eerdmans Books for Young Readers 2009 unp il $18 *

Grades: 2 3 4   292

1. Persephone (Greek deity)

ISBN 978-0-8028-5349-3; 0-8028-5349-8

LC 2008018391

"Approaching the Greek myth of Persephone with the respect that a good storyteller holds for a great story, Clayton retells the tale with drama and grace. The mixed-media artwork creates a series of scenes defined by sweeping lines, broad views, and restrained use of color." Booklist

Craft, Marie

Cupid and Psyche; as told by M. Charlotte Craft; illustrated by K. Y. Craft. Morrow Junior Bks. 1996 unp il $16 *

Grades: 4 5 6 7   292

1. Eros (Greek deity) 2. Psyche (Greek deity) 3. Classical mythology

ISBN 0-688-13163-8   LC 95-14895

"In this Greek myth, Cupid falls in love with Psyche and treats her royally but does not reveal himself. When Psyche tries to discover his identity, Cupid leaves her, but she wins him back by accomplishing three difficult tasks. Recalling an earlier artistic era, the occasionally ornate romantic paintings—some of them quite dramatic—feature detailed landscapes and beautiful figures in flowing drapery." Horn Book Guide

Curlee, Lynn, 1947-

Mythological creatures; a classical bestiary: tales of strange beings, fabulous creatures, fearsome beasts, & hideous monsters from ancient Greek mythology. Atheneum Books for Young Readers 2008 35p il $17.99

Grades: 3 4 5   292

1. Classical mythology 2. Mythical animals

ISBN 978-1-4169-1453-2; 1-4169-1453-6

LC 2006-16980

"A preponderance of these sixteen fabulous beasts are half human (or, like Pan, minor deities). Most are monstrous in behavior as well as body; only the purely animal Pegasus and Phoenix possess some sort of nobility. Confining each within a broad, sober border, Curlee depicts all as classically statuesque. . . . Staightforward and clean, the accompanying text outlines without dramatization what these mythical beings were and their role in Greek lore. . . . The book is an eye-catching introduction to the world of ancient myth." Horn Book

Karas, G. Brian

Young Zeus. Scholastic Press 2010 unp il $17.99 *

Grades: 2 3 4 5   292

1. Zeus (Greek deity) 2. Classical mythology

ISBN 978-0-439-72806-5; 0-439-72806-1

LC 2009-10148

Karas, G. Brian—*Continued*

Karas "opens this spirited embellishment of Zeus's little-documented boyhood with an author's note explaining that he drew form early accounts of the Greek gods and 'true to the nature of myths, imagined the rest.' . . . But Kara's imagination serves him well in making Zeus a relatable character. . . . Droll dialogue and asides mitigate the tale's dark undertones [and] . . . energetic, airy gouache and pencil cartoons playfully skew scale and also keep the tone light." Publ Wkly

Kimmel, Eric A.

The McElderry book of Greek myths; [by] Eric A. Kimmel; illustrated by Pep Montserrat. M.K. McElderry Books 2008 96p il $21.99 *

Grades: K 1 2 3   292

1. Classical mythology
ISBN 1-4169-1534-6; 978-1-4169-1534-8
LC 2005031010

In this collection of retellings of Greek myths "Kimmel uses spare, direct language and lots of exciting action. . . . Montserrat's stylish computer-generated artwork picks up on ancient Greek design motifs and creates memorable characters from the mythical archetypes." Booklist

Lupton, Hugh

The adventures of Odysseus; [by] Hugh Lupton and Daniel Morden; [illustrated by] Christina Balit. Barefoot Books 2006 unp il $19.99

Grades: 3 4 5 6   292

1. Odysseus (Greek mythology) 2. Classical mythology
ISBN 1-84148-800-3   LC 2005032532

This "book retells Homer's epic of Odysseus' perilous journey home in a immediate, fast-paced narrative. . . . The text is beautifully framed with crisp, brightly colored, mosaic-style illustrations of the heroes and monsters, rendered in watercolor, gouache, and gold ink." Booklist

Mayer, Marianna, 1945-

Pegasus; as told by Marianna Mayer; illustrated by K. Y. Craft. Morrow Junior Bks. 1998 unp il $17.99 *

Grades: 4 5 6   292

1. Pegasus (Greek mythology) 2. Classical mythology
ISBN 0-688-13382-7; 0-688-13383-5 (lib bdg)
LC 96-32442

Retells how Bellerophon, son of the King of Corinth, secures the help of the winged horse Pegasus in order to fight the monstrous Chimera

"Dark, painterly illustrations set in gold frames heighten the mysticism in this lyrical interpretation of the Greek myth." Horn Book Guide

McCaughrean, Geraldine, 1951-

Hercules; retold by Geraldine McCaughrean. Cricket Books 2005 142p il (Heroes) $16.95 *

Grades: 5 6 7 8   292

1. Hercules (Legendary character) 2. Classical mythology
ISBN 978-0-8126-2737-4; 0-8126-2737-7
LC 2005004524

First published 2003 by Oxford University Press

This is a retelling of the twelve labors of Hercules including his battles with the Cretan Bull, the many-headed Hydra, the Nemean Lion, and the three-headed guardian of hell, Cerberus.

"This volume does a creditable job of making Hercules a dimensional character whose struggles against fate and the vindictiveness of the gods arouse readers' sympathy. . . . McCaughrean enlivens the familiar story with arresting imagery." SLJ

Odysseus; retold by Geraldine McCaughrean. Cricket Books 2004 148p il (Heroes) $16.95 *

Grades: 5 6 7 8   292

1. Odysseus (Greek mythology) 2. Classical mythology
ISBN 978-0-8126-2721-3; 0-8126-2721-0
LC 2004-10734

This is a retelling of the "adventures of Odysseus, including his encounters with the evil Cyclops, the monsters Scylla and Charybdis, the beautiful sorceress Circe, and . . . Poseidon." Publisher's note

"With mounting suspense, wild action, and simple, rhythmic prose, this dramatic retelling of Homer's classic makes a gripping read-aloud as well as an exciting introduction to the story." Booklist

Perseus; retold by Geraldine McCaughrean. Cricket Books 2005 118p il (Heroes) $16.95 *

Grades: 5 6 7 8   292

1. Perseus (Greek mythology) 2. Classical mythology
ISBN 978-0-8126-2735-0; 0-8126-2735-0

This follows the story of "Perseus as he lives the fate the oracles have declared, an impossible quest to kill the hideous, snake-haired Medusa to save his mother from marriage to an evil king." Publisher's note

This "makes a thrilling read-aloud. . . . McCaughrean blends the colloquial and contemporary into the heroic quest." Booklist

Osborne, Mary Pope, 1949-

Favorite Greek myths; retold by Mary Pope Osborne; illustrated by Troy Howell. Scholastic 1989 81p il lib bdg $18.95

Grades: 3 4 5 6   292

1. Classical mythology
ISBN 0-590-41338-4   LC 87-32332

Retells twelve tales from Greek mythology, including the stories of King Midas, Echo and Narcissus, the Golden Apples, and Cupid and Psyche

"Osborne's retellings are both lively and descriptive, while Howell's full-color, often iridescent illustrations set the scene and mood at the start of each tale." Publ Wkly

Includes glossary and bibliographical references

Otfinoski, Steven, 1949-
All in the family; a look-it-up guide to the in-laws, outlaws, and offspring of mythology. F. Watts 2009 128p il (Mythlopedia) lib bdg $39; pa $13.95
Grades: 4 5 6 7   292
1. Classical mythology
ISBN 978-1-60631-025-0 (lib bdg); 1-60631-025-9 (lib bdg); 978-1-60631-057-1 (pa); 1-60631-057-7 (pa)
LC 2009-20999
"Jam-packed with trivia, brief profiles, god and goddess relationships, stories, 'Top 10 Things to Know About Me' facts, and entertaining illustrations, this title explores 20 heroes and mortals of classic Greek mythology. The selections include the well-known Achilles, Heracles, Odysseus, and Pandora and the more obscure Meleager, Orion, Atalanta, and Bellerophon; each one is given lively treatment. . . . The lighthearted style and humorous collage and cartoon illustrations may draw even the most reluctant of readers. " SLJ
Includes glossary and bibliographical references

Rylant, Cynthia
The beautiful stories of life; six Greek myths, retold; illustrated by Carson Ellis. Harcourt 2009 71p il $16
Grades: 5 6 7 8   292
1. Classical mythology
ISBN 978-0-15-206184-5; 0-15-206184-3
LC 2007-34808
"Rylant retells the stories of Pandora, Persephone, Orpheus, Pygmalion, Narcissus, and Psyche in this trim, handsome book. Written in a modern style with an old-fashioned feel, the selections sit well with other titles in the genre. . . . Accompanied by full-page black-and-white illustrations and sprinkled with decorations, the whole package is nicely done." SLJ

Steer, Dugald
The mythology handbook; a course in ancient Greek myths; by Hestia Evans; edited by Dugald A. Steer and Clint Twist. Candlewick Press 2009 71p il map $12.99
Grades: 4 5 6 7   292
1. Classical mythology
ISBN 978-0-7636-4291-4
"Written by Dugald A. Steer and Clint Twist" - title page verso
"This follow-up to Mythology (Candlewick, 2007) again uses the voice of a fictional 19th-century scholar. Here, Lady Hestia Evans offers a guide to elements of Greek myth for her two children, providing information in 'lessons' . . . with exercises based on each topic. Some of the activities encourage students to do further research . . . while others suggest that they draw new monsters, write hymns with the Muses' help, or design a new pentathlon for the Olympics. Mazes and a word search (using Greek letters) are also included. . . . The activities are engaging, and the illustrations of creatures and maps of the ancient world will add to the knowledge of even more experienced myth fans." SLJ

Townsend, Michael, 1981-
Michael Townsend's amazing Greek myths of wonder and blunders. Dial Books for Young Readers 2010 160p il $14.99
Grades: 4 5 6 7   292
1. Greek mythology—Graphic novels
ISBN 978-0-8037-3308-4; 0-8037-3308-9
"Ten familiar myths—the stories of Pandora, Arachne, Midas, Perseus, and others—are embellished with humor, the gory parts glossed over, and served up in blazing color for fans of either comic books or Percy Jackson, or both. . . . Conversational, up-to-date language and broad jokes help to make the stories accessible and coordinate well with the simple, cartoon illustration style." SLJ

293   Germanic religion

Fisher, Leonard Everett, 1924-
Gods and goddesses of the ancient Norse. Holiday House 2001 unp il $16.95
Grades: 3 4 5 6   293
1. Norse mythology
ISBN 0-8234-1569-4   LC 00-32040
In this guide each "double-page spread is devoted to one or two of the major gods or goddesses, accompanied by a succinct description that includes significant characteristics and responsibilities. A pronunciation guide and family tree are appended." Horn Book Guide
Includes bibliographical references

Lunge-Larsen, Lise
The adventures of Thor the Thunder God; retold by Lise Lunge-Larsen; illustrated by Jim Madsen. Houghton Mifflin 2007 76p il $19.95
Grades: 3 4 5 6   293
1. Norse mythology
ISBN 0-618-47301-7; 978-0-618-47301-4
LC 2004015765
This "volume introduces the pantheon of Norse gods and giants and some of Thor's family members and then relates several well-known tales of the Thunder God." SLJ
"Madsen's . . . majestic digitally rendered illustrations bring the tales to life, echoing their humor. . . . These retellings offer an accessible and engaging doorway into the world of Norse mythology." Publ Wkly

294.3   Buddhism

Chödzin, Sherab
The wisdom of the crows and other Buddhist tales; retold by Sherab Chödzin & Alexandra Kohn; illustrated by Marie Cameron. Tricycle Press 1998 c1997 80p il pa $16.95
Grades: 4 5 6 7   294.3
1. Buddhism
ISBN 1-883672-68-6   LC 97-30441
First published 1997 in the United Kingdom with title: The Barefoot book of Buddhist tales

Chödzin, Sherab—*Continued*

A collection of thirteen retold Buddhist tales from all over Asia, illustrating various aspects of Buddhist thought

"Folktale lovers will find much to like here. Marie Cameron's clear, fresh watercolors, incorporating Asian artistic motifs and bordered with waves and origami, are handsomely rendered." Booklist

Includes bibliographical references

Demi, 1942-

Buddha. Holt & Co. 1996 unp il $21.95 *
Grades: 4 5 6　　　　　　　　　　　　**294.3**
　1. Gautama Buddha
　ISBN 0-8050-4203-2　　　　　　　LC 95-16906
The author "tells the story of Siddhartha's birth and the prophecies surrounding it, touches upon his childhood, and then follows his path to enlightenment." Booklist

Demi "uses clear, uncomplicated storytelling to present complex philosophical concepts. . . . The gilded illustrations (based, according to the jacket, on 'Indian, Chinese, Japanese, Burmese, and Indonesian paintings, sculptures, and sutra illustrations') are delicate, yet the colors and composition are bold, with central figures and action cascading beyond the careful borders." Bull Cent Child Books

Buddha stories. Holt & Co. 1997 unp il $21.95
Grades: 3 4 5 6　　　　　　　　　　　**294.3**
　1. Jataka stories
　ISBN 0-8050-4886-3　　　　　　　LC 96-31253
This "is a picture-book collection of eleven Jataka tales retold in a formal yet straightforward style. . . . An author's note gives the source of the tales as well as the historical basis for the design concept behind the elegantly sophisticated artwork. Both text and illustrations are done in gold ink on deep indigo paper, resulting in a striking visual impact." Bull Cent Child Books

Ganeri, Anita, 1961-

Buddhism; [by] Anita Ganeri. World Almanac Library 2006 48p il map (Religions of the world) lib bdg $30.60 *
Grades: 5 6 7 8　　　　　　　　　　　**294.3**
　1. Buddhism
　ISBN 0-8368-5865-4　　　　　　LC 2005041708
The author "presents a survey of Buddhist history, beliefs, sacred texts, festivals, and lifecycle events. . . . There is discussion of the art and folk literature associated with the religious tradition. Colorful photographs, illustrations, and art reproductions appear throughout." SLJ

Includes bibliographical references

George, Charles, 1949-

What makes me a Buddhist? by Charles George. KidHaven Press 2004 48p il (What makes me a--?) $23.70
Grades: 3 4 5　　　　　　　　　　　　**294.3**
　1. Buddhism
　ISBN 0-7377-2269-X　　　　　　LC 2003-24344

Contents: A religion or a philosophy?; How did my religion begin?; What do I believe?; How do I practice my faith?; What holidays do I celebrate?; My religion today and tomorrow

This describes the beliefs, origins, practices, holidays and future of Buddhism.

"An attractive, colorful design is the background for a map and numerous color photographs and diagrams. But best of all is the straightforward organization and the clarity of the text." Booklist

Includes bibliographical references

Hawker, Frances

Buddhism in Thailand; written by Frances Hawker and Sunantha Phusomsai; photography by Bruce Campbell. Crabtree Pub. Co. 2009 32p il map (Families and their faiths) lib bdg $26.60; pa $8.95
Grades: 3 4 5　　　　　　　　　　　　**294.3**
　1. Buddhism 2. Thailand
　ISBN 978-0-7787-5006-2 (lib bdg); 0-7787-5006-X (lib bdg); 978-0-7787-5023-9 (pa); 0-7787-5023-X (pa)　　　　　　　　　　　　LC 2009-14156
This "book introduces a child who practices [Buddhism]. . . . Provides a solid introduction without overwhelming readers with complex regional variations in practices and beliefs. . . . Words and phrases that are unique to the faith appear in bold font and are defined at greater length in the glossary." SLJ

Includes glossary

Nardo, Don, 1947-

Buddhism. Compass Point Books 2009 48p il map (World religions) lib bdg $27.99
Grades: 5 6 7 8　　　　　　　　　　　**294.3**
　1. Buddhism
　ISBN 978-0-7565-4236-8 (lib bdg); 0-7565-4236-7 (lib bdg)　　　　　　　　LC 2009-11453
This describes the "history and traditions of Buddhism and how the religion fits into today's world." Publisher's note

"The colorful, attractive layout includes high-quality reproductions of photographs, maps, and paintings. Students who are new to religious studies, as well as those doing reports, will find that this . . . meets their needs." SLJ

Includes glossary and bibliographical references

294.5　Hinduism

Ganeri, Anita, 1961-

The Ramayana and Hinduism. Smart Apple Media 2003 30p il (Sacred texts) $27.10
Grades: 5 6 7 8 9　　　　　　　　　　**294.5**
　1. Hinduism
　ISBN 1-58340-242-X　　　　　　LC 2003-42352
Contents: Origins; Texts and teaching; In daily life
Explains the history and practices of the religion of Hinduism, especially as revealed through its sacred book, the Ramayana

George, Charles, 1949-

What makes me a Hindu? by Charles George. KidHaven Press 2004 48p il map (What makes me a--?) $27

Grades: 3 4 5   **294.5**

1. Hinduism

ISBN 978-0-7377-2267-3; 0-7377-2267-3

LC 2003-24346

This describes Hindu origins, beliefs, practices, and holidays

"Presenting information about religion objectively for younger audiences poses a difficult challenge, but [this title does] an excellent job of it." Booklist

Includes bibliographical references

Hawker, Frances

Hinduism in Bali; written by Frances Hawker and Putu Resi; photography by Bruce Campbell. Crabtree Pub. Company 2009 32p il (Families and their faiths) lib bdg $26.60; pa $8.95

Grades: 3 4 5   **294.5**

1. Hinduism 2. Indonesia 3. Bali Island (Indonesia)

ISBN 978-0-7787-5008-6 (lib bdg); 0-7787-5008-6 (lib bdg); 978-0-7787-5008-6 (pa); 0-7787-5008-6 (pa)

LC 2009-14297

This "book introduces a child who practices [Hinduism]. . . . Provides a solid introduction without overwhelming readers with complex regional variations in practices and beliefs. . . . Words and phrases that are unique to the faith appear in bold font and are defined at greater length in the glossary," SLJ

Includes glossary

Heiligman, Deborah

Celebrate Diwali; [by] Deborah Heiligman; consultant, Dr. Vasudha Narayanan. National Geographic 2006 32p il map (Holidays around the world) $15.95; lib bdg $23.90 *

Grades: K 1 2 3   **294.5**

1. Divali

ISBN 0-7922-5922-X; 0-7922-5923-8 (lib bdg)

LC 2006003426

This "focuses on the Hindu celebration in India but mentions observance by the Sikh and Jain faiths and also show customs in four other countries. . . . Each spread features up to three high-quality color photographs." SLJ

Jani, Mahendra

What you will see inside a Hindu temple; [by] Mahendra Jani and Vandana Jani; with photographs by Neirah Bhargava and Vijay Dave. Skylight Paths 2005 32p il (What you will see inside–) $17.99

Grades: 3 4 5 6   **294.5**

1. Hinduism

ISBN 978-1-59473-116-7; 1-59473-116-0

"This introduces the beliefs and practices of the Hindu religion. The book opens with a traditional Sanskrit word of greeting . . . setting the respectful, inviting tone of the text, which leads readers into a temple. The book explains what can be seen there and discusses Hindu be-

liefs, worship practices, scriptures, celebrations, blessing ceremonies, and family shrines in homes. A typical double-page spread includes one large color photograph and a few small ones illustrating several paragraphs of clear, concise text." Booklist

Plum-Ucci, Carol, 1957-

Celebrate Diwali; [by] Carol Plum-Ucci. Enslow Publishers 2008 128p il map (Celebrate holidays) $31.93

Grades: 5 6 7 8   **294.5**

1. Divali

ISBN 978-0-7660-2778-7; 0-7660-2778-3

LC 2006028106

This describes the history, cultural significance, customs, symbols and celebrations around the world of the Hindu holiday of Diwali.

"Captioned photographs, maps, drawings, and sidebars combine with accessible text to present a thorough discussion of [Diwali]. . . . This . . . is a useful resource." Horn Book Guide

Includes glossary and bibliographical references

Rasamandala Das

Hinduism. World Almanac Library 2006 48p il map (Religions of the world) $30.60 *

Grades: 5 6 7 8   **294.5**

1. Hinduism

ISBN 0-8368-5867-0

Hinduism is "explored in an accessible introductory manner, including information on [its] history, teachings, religious practices, culture and lifestyle, and the [faith's role] in today's global society. Vibrant full-color photographs are appropriately placed within the [text]. Ideal for . . . school reports or for general interest." SLJ

Includes bibliographical references

294.6   Sikhism

Hawker, Frances

Sikhism in India; written by Frances Hawker and Mohini Kaur Bhatia; photography by Bruce Campbell. Crabtree Pub. Company 2009 32p il (Families and their faiths) lib bdg $26.60; pa $8.95

Grades: 3 4 5   **294.6**

1. Sikhism 2. India 3. Sikhs

ISBN 978-0-7787-5011-6 (lib bdg); 0-7787-5011-6 (lib bdg); 978-0-7787-5028-4 (pa); 0-7787-5028-0 (pa)

LC 2009-14160

This "book introduces a child who practices [Sikhism]. . . . Provides a solid introduction without overwhelming readers with complex regional variations in practices and beliefs. . . . Words and phrases that are unique to the faith appear in bold font and are defined at greater length in the glossary." SLJ

Includes glossary

296 Judaism

296.1 Judaism—Sources

Hawker, Frances

Judaism in Israel; written by Frances Hawker and Daniel Taub; photography by Bruce Campbell. Crabtree Pub. 2010 32p il (Families and their faiths) lib bdg $26.60; pa $8.95

Grades: 3 4 5   **296**

1. Judaism 2. Israel

ISBN 978-0-7787-5010-9 (lib bdg); 0-7787-5010-8 (lib bdg); 978-0-7787-5027-7 (pa); 0-7787-5027-2 (pa)

LC 2009-14159

This "book introduces a child who practices [Judaism]. . . . Provides a solid introduction without overwhelming readers with complex regional variations in practices and beliefs. . . . Words and phrases that are unique to the faith appear in bold font and are defined at greater length in the glossary." SLJ

Includes glossary

Keene, Michael

Judaism; [by] Michael Keene. World Almanac Library 2006 48p il map (Religions of the world) lib bdg $30.60 *

Grades: 5 6 7 8   **296**

1. Judaism

ISBN 0-8368-5869-7   LC 2005041734

This "volume presents fundamental beliefs and faith foundations, current status and practices of [Judaism] around the globe, and a time line of historically significant events. . . . The [book is] enumerated with full-color photographs on every page, charts, maps, and tables. . . . [This title] will enhance the education of diverse populations." SLJ

Includes bibliographical references

Rosinsky, Natalie M. (Natalie Myra)

Judaism. Compass Point Books 2009 48p il map (World religions) lib bdg $27.99

Grades: 5 6 7 8   **296**

1. Judaism

ISBN 978-0-7565-4240-5 (lib bdg); 0-7565-4240-5 (lib bdg)   LC 2009-15813

This describes the "history and traditions of Judaism and how the religion fits into today's world." Publisher's note

"The colorful, attractive layout includes high-quality reproductions of photographs, maps, and paintings. Students who are new to religious studies, as well as those doing reports, will find that this . . . meets their needs." SLJ

Includes glossary and bibliographical references

Chaikin, Miriam, 1928-

Angels sweep the desert floor; Bible legends about Moses in the wilderness; illustrated by Alexander Koshkin. Clarion Bks. 2002 102p il $19

Grades: 4 5 6 7   **296.1**

1. Moses (Biblical figure) 2. Angels—Fiction 3. Jewish legends 4. Bible stories

ISBN 0-395-97825-4   LC 2001-47501

A collection of eighteen stories based on the Bible which tell how angels respond to God's commands to ease the way for Moses and the Israelites as they cross the wilderness after being freed from slavery in Egypt

"The full-page watercolor, tempera, and gouache illustrations have a fanciful formality that complements the narrative. Capable of exciting the creative, as well as the spiritual imagination, these wonderful stories make great read-alouds." SLJ

Includes bibliographical references

Pinsker, Marlee

In the days of sand and stars; illustrated by François Thisdale. Tundra Books 2006 87p il $22.95

Grades: 5 6 7 8   **296.1**

1. Jewish legends 2. Women in the Bible 3. Bible stories

ISBN 978-0-88776-724-1; 0-88776-724-9

This is a collection of stories from the Midrash about women including Eve, Naamah, Sarai, Sarah, Rebecca, Leah, Rachel, Dina, and Yocheved.

"Pinsker works like a musician, playing with words instead of notes, but the result is just as lilting and lyrical. The stories are matched by unusual illustrations. Thisdale blends traditional artwork with digital technology. Pieces of photographs mix with ancient elements, giving the pictures a fresh, compelling look." Booklist

296.4 Judaism—Traditions, rites, public services

Chaikin, Miriam, 1928-

Menorahs, mezuzas, and other Jewish symbols; illustrated by Erika Weihs. Clarion Bks. 1990 102p il $17; pa $5.95 *

Grades: 5 6 7 8   **296.4**

1. Jewish art and symbolism 2. Judaism—Customs and practices

ISBN 0-89919-856-2; 0-618-37835-9 (pa)

LC 89-77719

Explains the history and significance of many Jewish symbols, such as the Shield of David, the menorah, and the mezuza, and discusses holiday symbols and rituals

"Embellished with bibliographical references as well as Weihs' simple yet elegant and wonderfully dramatic scratchboard illustrations, this smoothly woven patchwork of history and culture is a fine introduction that will attract browsers and be useful for children investigating the subject of symbolism in school." Booklist

Cooper, Ilene, 1948-
Jewish holidays all year round; a family
treasury; written by Ilene Cooper; illustrations by
Elivia Savadier; captions by Josh Feinberg; in
association with the Jewish Museum, New York.
Abrams 2002 80p il $19.95 *
Grades: 4 5 6 7   **296.4**
   1. Jewish holidays
   ISBN 0-8109-0550-7   LC 2001-56741
   As the author "explores the history and significance of
the holidays and festivals of the Jewish year, she . . .
links these to traditions and rituals. . . . Instructions for
holiday activities (crafts, recipes, etc.) are also included.
. . . Savadier's vignettes, mostly of busy, happy people,
underscore the liveliness of Jewish faith." Publ Wkly
   Includes bibliographical references

Fishman, Cathy, 1951-
On Hanukkah; by Cathy Goldberg Fishman;
illustrated by Melanie W. Hall. Atheneum Bks. for
Young Readers 1998 unp il $16
Grades: K 1 2 3   **296.4**
   1. Hanukkah
   ISBN 0-689-80643-4   LC 96-44696
   "Fishman and Hall focus on a family's celebration of
a Jewish holiday. The writing is simple and direct, yet
the coverage is ample. . . . The fanciful, mixed-media
paintings feature strong texturing and glowing, gilt-edged
colors." Booklist

On Rosh Hashanah and Yom Kippur; by Cathy
Goldberg Fishman; illustrated by Melanie W. Hall.
Atheneum Bks. for Young Readers 1997 unp il
hardcover o.p. pa $5.99
Grades: K 1 2 3   **296.4**
   1. Rosh ha-Shanah 2. Yom Kippur
   ISBN 0-689-80526-8; 0-689-83892-1 (pa)
                              LC 96-23258
   "Fishman explores and explains the traditions associated with the Jewish High Holidays. She focuses mainly
on Rosh Hashanah . . . and in a quiet, almost reverent
way uses the voice of a little girl to make readers party
to a family's celebrations. . . . Hall's beautiful, rosy, expressionistic pictures are a fine complement to Fishman's
text. They capture the warm glow of a family celebrating
together." Booklist

On Sukkot and Simchat Torah; [by] Cathy
Goldberg Fishman; illustrations by Melanie W.
Hall. Kar-Ben Pub. 2006 unp il lib bdg $17.95
Grades: K 1 2 3   **296.4**
   1. Sukkot 2. Simchath Torah
   ISBN 1-58013-165-4   LC 2001022789
   "Readers watch a family get ready for the Sukkot by
building a small shelter, a sukkah . . . In evocative
prose, Fishman not only explains the holiday but also
captures the joyous mood that infuses it. . . . She also
captures the celebratory feel of Simchat Torah, complete
with the marching and singing that take place as the Torah is carried around the synagogue. The lively text is
matched by Hall's stirring artwork, in shades of blue,
green, gold, and orange, which is ethereal yet full of
sweet, everyday detail." Booklist

Had gadya; a Passover song; paintings by
Seymour Chwast; afterword by Michael
Strassfeld. Roaring Brook Press 2005 unp il
$16.95; pa $7.95
Grades: K 1 2 3   **296.4**
   1. Passover 2. Songs
   ISBN 1-59643-033-8; 1-59643-298-5 (pa)
                             LC 2003-17831
   "A Deborah Brodie book"
   This is an illustrated version of "a folk song often
sung at the end of the Passover Seder. [It] tells a cumulative story that begins with a man's purchase of a goat.
In the tradition of chain folk stories, the cat eats the
goat, the dog chases the cat, the stick beats the dog, and
so on. . . . The Angel of Death appears, but then God
comes and destroys the Angel of Death." Bull Cent
Child Books
   "The bright, acrylic folk-art paintings express the
rhythm of the chant. . . . The book, complete with musical notation and Hebrew and English words, is bound to
add to the pleasure of the seder." Booklist

Hanft, Joshua E., 1956-
The miracles of Passover; [by] Josh Hanft;
illustrated by Seymour Chwast. Blue Apple Books
2007 unp il $15.95
Grades: PreK K 1 2   **296.4**
   1. Passover
   ISBN 978-1-59354-600-7; 1-59354-600-9
                             LC 2006031585
   "The story of Moses, Pharaoh, the 10 plagues, and the
crossing of the Red Sea is explained in child-friendly
language with additional information included about the
traditions of the Seder. What distinguishes this book
from others of its kind is the overall excellence of the
colorful artwork." SLJ

Heiligman, Deborah
Celebrate Hanukkah; [by] Deborah Heiligman;
consultant, Shira Stern. National Geographic 2006
32p il (Holidays around the world) $15.95; lib bdg
$23.90 *
Grades: K 1 2 3   **296.4**
   1. Hanukkah
   ISBN 0-7922-5924-6; 0-7922-5925-4 (lib bdg)
                             LC 2005032427
   This "introduces children to the Jewish Festival of
Lights. Heiligman recounts the holiday's history and ori-
gins and describes how it is celebrated today. . . . The
main text is succinct and appropriate for reading aloud.
. . . Decorating the pages are sumerous crisp, full-color
photos." Booklist
   Includes glossary and bibliographical references

Celebrate Passover; [by] Deborah Heiligman.
National Geographic 2007 32p il (Holidays around
the world) $15.95; lib bdg $23.90 *
Grades: K 1 2 3   **296.4**
   1. Passover
   ISBN 978-1-4263-0018-9; 978-1-4263-00196 (lib bdg)
                             LC 2006020676

Heiligman, Deborah—*Continued*

This "begins with a short recitation of the Passover story and then moves directly into how the holiday is celebrated. . . . A concluding essay by a rabbi offers thoughts on the meaning of the holiday. The clean format evokes the spring holiday, but the book's visual emphasis is also on Jewish communities in Africa, Asia, the Middle East, and elsewhere." Booklist

Includes bibliographical references

Celebrate Rosh Hashanah and Yom Kippur; [by] Deborah Heiligman; consultant, Shira Stern. National Geographic 2007 31p il (Holidays around the world) $15.95; lib bdg $23.90 *

Grades: K 1 2 3   **296.4**
1. Rosh ha-Shanah 2. Yom Kippur
ISBN 978-1-4263-0076-9; 978-1-4263-0077-6 (lib bdg)   LC 2006100317

"Lush color photographs show the diversity of the celebrants and bring an immediacy to these observances. Clear, simple [text provides] history and background information, descriptions of customs, and basic analyses of each celebration's deeper meaning. . . . Exemplary back matter includes quick facts and extra information to provide context. There is even a map showing where all of the fascinating photos were taken." SLJ

Includes glossary and bibliographical references

Heller, Esther Susan

Menorah under the sea; photographs by David Ginsburg. Kar-Ben Pub. 2009 29p il lib bdg $17.95

Grades: K 1 2 3   **296.4**
1. Hanukkah 2. Marine biology 3. Antarctica
ISBN 978-0-8225-7386-9 (lib bdg); 0-8225-7386-5 (lib bdg)   LC 2007043175

Describes how, while studying sea urchins in Antarctica, marine biologist David Ginsburg celebrated Hanukkah by creating his own menorah on the sea floor

"The vibrant color photography and surprising thematic juxtaposition—readers will learn as much about urchins as about the holiday—makes this a memorable selection, even for readers who don't celebrate Hanukkah." Publ Wkly

Hoffman, Lawrence A., 1942-

What you will see inside a synagogue; [by] Lawrence Hoffman and Ron Wolfson; with photographs by Bill Aron. SkyLight Paths 2004 31p il (What you will see inside--) $17.99

Grades: 3 4 5 6   **296.4**
1. Judaism
ISBN 1-59473-012-1   LC 2004-11178

Contents: Welcome; Gathering for Shabbat; Preparing for prayer; The holiest place in the synagogue; How Jews pray; Reading the Torah; Enjoying Shabbat; Prayer and learning go together; Fixing the world; Bar and bat mitzvah; Celebrating holidays; The High Holy Days; Showing our thanks; How we remember; L'hitra'ot. come again

"The authors focus on the synagogues and services of three branches of North American Judaism—Conservative, Reconstruction, and Reform. . . . They introduce

readers to Sabbath customs, prayer, the sanctuary and its contents, the Torah, important holidays and life cycle events, and key tenets of the faith." Booklist

"This book provides a warm and thorough welcome to the center of Jewish life. . . . Numerous clear color photos and pronunciation guides for Hebrew words are included. . . . An excellent overview." SLJ

Hoyt-Goldsmith, Diane

Celebrating Hanukkah; photographs by Lawrence Migdale. Holiday House 1996 31p il hardcover o.p. pa $6.95 *

Grades: 3 4 5   **296.4**
1. Hanukkah
ISBN 0-8234-1252-0; 0-8234-1411-6 (pa)
                                                       LC 96-5110

"Leora, the 11-year-old daughter of a San Francisco rabbi, explains the history of Hanukkah and describes how her family observes it." Publ Wkly

The photographs "are warm and inviting, with Migdale catching celebrations at home, at school, and in the synagogue. . . . The text is equally fine, well organized and rich in detail but also friendly." Booklist

Includes glossary

Celebrating Passover; photographs by Lawrence Migdale. Holiday House 2000 32p il lib bdg $16.95 *

Grades: 3 4 5   **296.4**
1. Passover
ISBN 0-8234-1420-5   LC 99-49006

Uses one family's celebration of Passover to describe the religious significance, traditions, customs, and symbols of this Jewish holiday

"An attractive and useful choice for the holiday shelf; recipes, songs, and a glossary are a bonus." Booklist

Kimmel, Eric A.

Wonders and miracles; a Passover companion; illustrated with art spanning three thousand years; written and compiled by Eric A. Kimmel. Scholastic Press 2004 136p il $18.95 *

Grades: 4 5 6 7   **296.4**
1. Passover
ISBN 0-439-07175-5   LC 2002-4732

Presents the steps performed in a traditional Passover Seder, plus stories, songs, poetry, and pictures that celebrate the historical significance of this holiday to Jews all over the world.

"The marvelous selection of art—paintings, photographs, artifacts, and illustrations from historical Haggadahs—illuminates each step in the service. . . . Both the presentation of information and the overall design attest to the careful and loving attention given to every detail. This inviting, handsome, and informative compendium should find a place of honor in every library." SLJ

Includes bibliographical references

Lehman-Wilzig, Tami

Hanukkah around the world; by Tami Lehman-Wilzig; illustrated by Vicki Wehrman. Kar-Ben Pub. 2009 48p il map $16.95

Grades: 2 3 4 5   296.4

1. Hanukkah

ISBN 978-0-8225-8761-3; 0-8225-8761-0

LC 2008031196

"This tour of Hanukkah includes information on its historical significance and the ways in which it is celebrated in places like New York City, Turin, Sydney and Warsaw. After an introductory section about the history, terminology and customs associated with the holiday, the book features a story of a child living in each city." Publ Wkly

"The engaging text and attractive illustrations will make this a good choice for families wishing to explore diverse ways of celebrating." Booklist

Leon, Carol Boyd

Dayenu! a Passover Haggadah for families and children; illustrated by Gwen Connelly. KTAV Pub. House 2008 32p il $16.95 *

Grades: 1 2 3   296.4

1. Passover

ISBN 978-1-60280-040-3; 1-60280-040-5

LC 2008025641

Text in English; portions of the Haggadah in Hebrew and romanized Hebrew with English translation

"This Haggadah offers colorful, child-friendly illustrations and interweaves the traditional prayers with songs that explain the Passover Seder rituals in simple terms. In nearly an hour of audio on the accompanying CD, Leon and a choir of children narrate the Haggadah, chant the prayers, and sing Passover songs that flesh out the story of Moses and Pharoah." SLJ

Metter, Bert

Bar mitzvah, bat mitzvah; the ceremony, the party, and how the day came to be; by Bert Metter; illustrated by Joan Reilly. Clarion Books 2007 unp il $16; pa $5.95

Grades: 4 5 6 7   296.4

1. Bar mitzvah 2. Bat mitzvah

ISBN 978-0-618-76772-4; 0-618-76772-X; 978-0-618-76773-1 (pa); 0-618-76773-8 (pa)

LC 2006032942

"Portions of this text were originally published as Bar mitzvah, bat mitzvah: how Jewish boys and girls come of age, copyright (c) 1984 by Bert Metter"--T.p. verso.

The author "describes a typical ceremony and explains how this custom began for boys during the Middle Ages and how it was adapted for girls beginning in 1922. He also discusses the recent custom of adult bar and bat mitzvahs and celebratory parties. The writing is clear and concise; ink illustrations . . . help break up the text." Booklist

Includes bibliographical references

Podwal, Mark H., 1945-

Built by angels; the story of the old-new synagogue; by Mark Podwal. Harcourt Children's Books 2009 unp il $16

Grades: 1 2 3 4   296.4

1. Synagogues 2. Jews—Czech Republic

ISBN 978-0-15-206678-9; 0-15-206678-0

LC 2007052091

"Legend, history and spiritual significance intertwine in Podwal's illustrated free-verse poem paying homage to Prague's Altneuschul, or Old-New Synagogue, which is the oldest in Europe, dating back to 1270, and is treasured for its early Gothic architecture. . . . Childlike yet abstract drawings in acrylic, gouache and colored pencil-dominated by a combination of reds . . . delineate the building's history as a haven for worship throughout the centuries. . . . A beautiful, Impressionistic introduction to a portion of Judaic lore and a European architectural marvel." Kirkus

A sweet year; a taste of the Jewish holidays; [by] Mark Podwal. Doubleday Bks. for Young Readers 2003 unp il hardcover o.p. lib bdg $14.99 *

Grades: K 1 2 3   296.4

1. Jewish holidays 2. Food

ISBN 0-385-74637-7; 0-385-90869-5 (lib bdg)

LC 2002-155442

Pictures and easy-to-read text introduce Jewish holidays, focusing on the foods associated with each

This offers "beautifully crafted poetic text and symbolic paintings in gouache and acrylics." SLJ

Includes bibliographical references

Schecter, Ellen

The family Haggadah; illustrated by Neil Waldman. Viking 1999 66p il music pa $13.99 *

Grades: 4 5 6 7   296.4

1. Passover

ISBN 0-670-88341-7   LC 98-28597

"This book interweaves original writing with traditional Haggadah, prayer book, and biblical texts, as well as with midrash (rabbinic stories and commentaries)." Verso of title page

"Although really intended for parents to use with their children at a family Passover seder, this attractive book may also be useful to children wanting to plan their own model celebration." Booklist

Woog, Adam, 1953-

What makes me a Jew? Kidhaven Press 2004 48p il (What makes me a-- ?) $23.70

Grades: 3 4 5   296.4

1. Judaism

ISBN 0-7377-2266-5   LC 2003-20951

Contents: How Judaism began; What I believe; The ceremonies I observe; The holidays I celebrate; The food I eat; Judaism in the modern world

This describes Jewish origins, beliefs, practices, foods, and holidays.

"Presenting information about religion objectively for younger audiences poses a difficult challenge, but [this title does] and excellent job of it." Booklist

Includes bibliographical references

Ziefert, Harriet

Hanukkah haiku; [by] Harriet Ziefert; paintings by Karla Gudeon. Blue Apple Books 2008 unp il $16.95 *

Grades: PreK K 1   **296.4**
   1. Hanukkah 2. Haiku
   ISBN 978-1-934706-33-6; 1-934706-33-7
       LC 2008005877
"Combining festive illustrations and a playful format, this title uses haiku to celebrate the eight nights of Hanukkah. . . . Each turn of the stepped pages brings fresh excitement as another lit candle and verse are revealed. Illustrations have a lovely folkloric quality in which Chagall-like figures, surrounded by richly colored flowers and stars, float across a fibrous tan background." SLJ

Passover; celebrating now, remembering then; paintings by Karla Gudeon. Blue Apple Books 2010 unp il $17.99

Grades: PreK K 1 2 3   **296.4**
   1. Passover
   ISBN 978-1-60905-020-7; 1-60905-020-7
"Ziefert provides a simplified adaptation of Exodus, a description of holiday preparations, and a concise *Haggadah*, or service for this ritual meal. Throughout, Ziefert contrasts current practice . . . with ancient origins. . . . On every page, Gudeon's Chagall-like paintings exhibit a folkloric style. . . . This title is one that families with young children will appreciate and want to own." Booklist

297   Islam, Babism, Bahai Faith

Demi, 1942-

Muhammad; written and illustrated by Demi. Margaret K. McElderry Bks. 2003 unp il $19.95 *

Grades: 4 5 6 7   **297**
   1. Muḥammad, d. 632 2. Islam
   ISBN 0-689-85264-9   LC 2002-2985
"With dramatic scenes extending past the borders of the intricately patterned frames, the art will be a continual source of interest for young people. . . . [An] excellent retelling of the Prophet's life that combines beauty and scholarship." Booklist
Includes bibliographical references

Hawker, Frances

Islam in Turkey; written by Frances Hawker and Leyla Alicavusoglu; photography by Bruce Campbell. Crabtree Pub. Company 2010 32p il (Families and their faiths) lib bdg $26.60; pa $8.95

Grades: 3 4 5   **297**
   1. Islam 2. Turkey
   ISBN 978-0-7787-5009-3 (lib bdg); 0-7787-5009-4 (lib bdg); 978-0-7787-5026-0 (pa); 0-7787-5026-4 (pa)
       LC 2009-14158
This "book introduces a child who practices [Islam]. . . . Provides a solid introduction without overwhelming readers with complex regional variations in practices and beliefs. . . . Words and phrases that are unique to the

faith appear in bold font and are defined at greater length in the glossary." SLJ
Includes glossary

Raatma, Lucia

Islam. Compass Point Books 2010 48p il map (World religions) lib bdg $27.99

Grades: 5 6 7 8   **297**
   1. Islam
   ISBN 978-0-7565-4239-9 (lib bdg); 0-7565-4239-1 (lib bdg)   LC 2009-15812
This describes the "history and traditions of Islam and how the religion fits into today's world.history and traditions of Islam and how the religion fits into today's world." Publisher's note
"The colorful, attractive layout includes high-quality reproductions of photographs, maps, and paintings. Students who are new to religious studies, as well as those doing reports, will find that this . . . meets their needs." SLJ
Includes glossary and bibliographical references

297.3   Islamic worship

Brown, Tricia

Salaam; a Muslim American boy's story. Henry Holt 2006 unp il $17.95

Grades: K 1 2 3   **297.3**
   1. Muslims 2. Islam
   ISBN 978-0-8050-6538-1; 0-8050-6538-5
       LC 2005013147
"A gentle and informative look at a Muslim-American boy and the way he practices his faith. The book does a good job of explaining each of the Five Pillars of Islam. . . . Good-quality black-and-white photos enhance the presentation and effectively show the warmth of Imran's family life." SLJ
Includes glossary

Douglass, Susan L., 1950-

Ramadan; illustrations by Jeni Reeves. Carolrhoda Books 2004 48p il (On my own holidays) lib bdg $23.93; pa $4.95 *

Grades: 1 2 3   **297.3**
   1. Ramadan 2. Id al-Adha 3. Islam
   ISBN 0-87614-932-8 (lib bdg); 1-57505-584-8 (pa)
       LC 2002-6781
An introduction to Islamic observances during the month of Ramadan and the subsequent festival of Eid-al-Fitr
"Reeves's abundant, framed illustrations in pastel colors provide detailed windows on the observance. . . . An easy-to-read, well-organized introduction." SLJ

Heiligman, Deborah

Celebrate Ramadan & Eid al-Fitr; [by] Deborah Heiligman; consultant, Neguin Yavari. National Geographic 2006 31p il map (Holidays around the world) $15.95; lib bdg $23.90 *

Grades: K 1 2 3   **297.3**

1. Ramadan 2. Id al-Adha 3. Islam
ISBN 0-7922-5926-2; 0-7922-5927-0 (lib bdg)
LC 2006008889

"Heiligman offers a simple, accessible introduction to the traditions of this solemn month and its concluding festival. Numerous clear, expressive photos feature captions that describe the experiences of children from varying countries and cultures and how they observe Ramadan." Publ Wkly

Includes glossary and bibliographical references

Hoyt-Goldsmith, Diane

Celebrating Ramadan; Ramadan al-mu'azzam; photographs by Lawrence Migdale. Holiday House 2001 32p il map $16.95 *

Grades: 3 4 5   **297.3**

1. Ramadan 2. Islam
ISBN 0-8234-1581-3   LC 2001-16643

"This picture book for older readers follows devout muslim Ibraheem, a fourth-grader living in New Jersey, through the holy month of Ramadan. . . . This is a sensitive introduction to Ramadan; the quality of the photographs and the eloquent text make the book the one of the best introductions in recent memory." Booklist

Jeffrey, Laura S.

Celebrate Ramadan; [by] Laura S. Jeffrey. Enslow Publishers 2007 112p il (Celebrate holidays) lib bdg $31.93

Grades: 5 6 7 8   **297.3**

1. Ramadan 2. Id al-Adha 3. Islam
ISBN 978-0-7660-2774-9 (lib bdg); 0-7660-2774-0 (lib bdg)
LC 2006028107

"This book opens by introducing a contemporary Muslim, Bushra, who celebrated Ramadan as a girl growing up in England [and] later immigrated to the United States. . . . An informative chapter surveys the history, beliefs, and practices of Islam. . . . The remainder of the book offers a detailed discussion of Ramadan, prayer, and spiritual awareness, and of l'Id al Fitr. . . . Punctuated by sidebars and illustrated with color photos, this clearly written book offers a good overview of how the holidays of Islam are celebrated." Booklist

Includes glossary and bibliographical references

Khan, Aisha Karen, 1967-

What you will see inside a mosque; photographs by Aaron Pepis. Skylight Paths Pub. 2003 31p il (What you will see inside--) $16.95; pa $8.99

Grades: 3 4 5 6   **297.3**

1. Islam 2. Mosques
ISBN 1-893361-60-8; 1-594732-57-4 (pa)
LC 2002-153436

Describes what happens inside a mosque and introduces the Muslim faith

This is an "excellent introduction. . . . Full-page photographs are supplemented by smaller photos with informative captions." SLJ

MacMillan, Dianne M., 1943-

Ramadan and Id al-Fitr; [by] Dianne M. MacMillan. rev and updated ed. Enslow Elementary 2008 48p il map (Best holiday books) $23.93

Grades: 2 3 4   **297.3**

1. Ramadan 2. Id al-Adha 3. Islam
ISBN 978-0-7660-3045-9; 0-7660-3045-8
LC 2007002425

First published 1994

This describes the history of the Muslim holidays of Ramadan and Id al-Fitr and how they are celebrated in the United States

"The well-written [text] aptly [describes] the traditions and customs and capture the flavor of the [holidays]. The open, spacious format makes the [book] accessible, and the full-color and black-and-white photos lend interest." SLJ

Includes glossary and bibliographical references

Marchant, Kerena

Id-ul-Fitr. Millbrook Press 1998 32p il (Festivals) lib bdg $21.90

Grades: 3 4 5   **297.3**

1. Id al-Adha 2. Islam
ISBN 0-7613-0963-2   LC 97-46035

Looks at some of the ways Muslims around the world celebrate the joyous festival of Id-ul-Fitr

Includes bibliographical references

Petrini, Catherine M.

What makes me a Muslim? [by] Catherine M. Petrini. KidHaven Press 2005 48p il map (What makes me a-- ?) $27 *

Grades: 3 4 5   **297.3**

1. Islam
ISBN 978-0-7377-2265-9; 0-7377-2265-7
LC 2004014526

"This overview explains what Islam is, where it came from, and how it has spread over time. Petrini provides a look at the background, beliefs, practices, holidays, and challenges of the religion today. . . . The full-color photographs and religious paintings throughout the book are as informative as they are appealing." SLJ

Includes bibliographical references

Whitman, Sylvia, 1961-

Under the Ramadan moon; [by] Sylvia Whitman; illustrated by Sue Williams. A. Whitman & Co. 2008 unp il $15.99

Grades: PreK K 1 2   **297.3**

1. Ramadan 2. Moon
ISBN 978-0-8075-8304-3; 0-8075-8304-9
LC 2008001307

"This delightful picture book describes the month-long Muslim observance of Ramadan by a modern family. . . . The images of the waxing, full, and waning moon progress along with the spare, lyrical text. Practices such as fasting, speaking kind words, giving to the poor, decorating with bright lights, and praying all take place, 'under the moon, under the Ramadan moon.' Williams uses soft, luminous pastels in richly textured, detailed spreads." SLJ

299 Religions not provided for elsewhere

Fisher, Leonard Everett, 1924-

The gods and goddesses of ancient China. Holiday House 2003 unp il $16.95 *

Grades: 3 4 5 6   **299**

1. Gods and goddesses 2. China—Religion

ISBN 0-8234-1694-1   LC 2002-68802

"Beginning with an introduction that mentions Qin Shi Huangdi, China's First Supreme Emperor, Fisher offers very brief historical and cultural background to China's deities. . . . Profiles of 17 gods and goddesses follow, each one presented on a double-page spread that includes a roughly brushed portrait opposite a few paragraphs summarizing the figure's corresponding legend. . . . Fisher combines concise, accessible language, colorful art, and exciting stories about figures that aren't often covered in books for youth." Booklist

Includes bibliographical references

Kramer, Ann, 1946-

Egyptian myth; a treasury of legends, art, and history. M. E. Sharpe 2008 96p il map (The world of mythology) $35.95

Grades: 5 6 7 8   **299**

1. Egyptian mythology 2. Egyptian art 3. Egypt—History

ISBN 978-0-7656-8105-8; 0-7656-8105-6

       LC 2007005876

This "handsomely designed [book is] illustrated with works of art from the culture. [It] is a well-organized presentation that includes information and tales about the gods and the pharoahs as well as magical stories and legends, providing an excellent introduction to this fascinating culture." SLJ

Includes glossary and bibliographical references

299.5 Religions of East and Southeast Asian origin

Demi, 1942-

The legend of Lao Tzu and the Tao te ching. Margaret K. McElderry Books 2007 unp il $21.99 *

Grades: 4 5 6 7   **299.5**

1. Lao-tzu, 6th cent. B.C. 2. Taoism

ISBN 1-4169-1206-1; 978-1-4169-1206-4

       LC 2005029695

"This is the legend of Lao Tzu . . . who may or may not have founded Taoism, one of the greatest religions of the world. Demi's elegant picture-book introduction to the legendary Chinese philosopher . . . combines nuggets of his purported life with 20 verses from the Tao Te Ching. . . . The narrative and graceful paintings are contained in a gold circular frame on each parchment shaded page." SLJ

Levin, Judith, 1956-

Japanese mythology; [by] Judith Levin. The Rosen Pub. Group 2008 64p il map (Mythology around the world) $29.95

Grades: 5 6 7 8   **299.5**

1. Japanese mythology 2. Shinto 3. Buddhism 4. Japan—Civilization

ISBN 978-1-4042-0736-3; 1-4042-0736-8

       LC 2005035279

This "presents not only an introduction to Shinto and Buddhist beliefs, but also Japanese history and mythology in general. . . . The most remarkable part of [this book] . . . is the respect [it shows] for the mythological customs, treating them throughout with the same care that writers of books on major religions might offer. The illustrations show both ancient and modern incarnations of the deities and heroes." SLJ

Includes glossary and bibliographical references

299.7 Religions of North American native origin

Swamp, Jake, 1941-

Giving thanks; a Native American good morning message; by Chief Jake Swamp; illustrated by Erwin Printup, Jr. Lee & Low Bks. 1995 unp il $16.95; pa $6.95

Grades: K 1 2 3   **299.7**

1. Mohawk Indians 2. Native Americans

ISBN 1-880000-15-6; 1-880000-54-7 (pa)

       LC 94-5955

"Drawing on Six Nation (Iroquois) ceremonial tradition, the text speaks concise thanks to Mother Earth, to water, grass, fruits, animals, to the wind and rain, sun, moon and stars, to the Spirit Protectors of our past and present . . . and to the Great Spirit, giver of all. . . . The entire text is reproduced in Mohawk on the last page." SLJ

"Its simple, timeless language bears witness to the Native American reverence for the natural world and sense of unity with all living things. . . . The gifts of the earth . . . are richly depicted in paintings of wildlife and bountiful harvests." Publ Wkly

300　SOCIAL SCIENCES, SOCIOLOGY & ANTHROPOLOGY

302.23　Media (Means of communication)

Ali, Dominic

Media madness; an insider's guide to media; written by Dominic Ali; illustrated by Michael Cho. Kids Can Press 2005 64p il hardcover o.p. pa $8.95

Grades: 4 5 6 7　　　　　　　　　　**302.23**

1. Mass media

ISBN 1-55337-174-7; 1-55337-175-5 (pa)

Host Max McLoon gives pointers on how to analyze media, and takes readers behind the scenes to reveal media workplaces in action. The book also includes activities for readers to further explore concepts or try their own media-making.

"The hip illustrations and wry sidebars prevent the book from coming off as goofy or childish, while the humorous treatment takes a bit of the edge off of otherwise 'heavy' issues like stereotypes, sexism, and violence. Light and loony, but enlightening, too." SLJ

302.3　Social interaction within groups

Burstein, John, 1949-

Why are you picking on me? dealing with bullies. Crabtree Pub. Company 2009 32p il (Slim Goodbody's life skills 101) lib bdg $26.60; pa $8.95

Grades: 1 2 3 4 5　　　　　　　　　　**302.3**

1. Bullies

ISBN 978-0-7787-4792-5 (lib bdg); 0-7787-4792-1 (lib bdg); 978-0-7787-4808-3 (pa); 0-7787-4808-1 (pa)

LC 2009022427

This book about dealing with bullies offers "clear and simple advice for children and [provides] adults with springboards for discussion and roleplaying. All have appealing color photographs of a variety of types of kids, . . . opening scenarios, concrete coping suggestions, and solid reasoning." SLJ

Includes bibliographical references

Fox, Debbie, 1958-

Good-bye bully machine; written by Debbie Fox and Allan L. Beane; illustrated by Debbie Fox. Free Spirit Pub. 2009 39p il $12.99; pa $8.95 *

Grades: K 1 2 3 4 5　　　　　　　　　**302.3**

1. Bullies

ISBN 978-1-57542-326-5; 1-57542-326-X; 978-1-57542-321-0 (pa); 1-57542-321-9 (pa)

LC 2008-41025

Kids learn what bullying is, why it hurts, and what they can do to end it with this fresh, compelling book including contemporary collage art, lively layout, and straightforward text.

"The authors provide tips for dealing with negative behaviors and encourage readers to take a stand against bullying and unplug the bully machine. Fox's enticing, edgy, collage artwork will draw readers in. . . . This offering will be a great discussion springboard for teachers and counselors." SLJ

Jakubiak, David J.

A smart kid's guide to online bullying. PowerKids Press 2009 c2010 24p il (Kids online) lib bdg $21.25; pa $8.95

Grades: 3 4 5 6　　　　　　　　　　**302.3**

1. Bullies 2. Internet—Security measures 3. Safety education

ISBN　978-1-4042-8114-1　(lib　bdg); 978-1-4358-3348-7 (pa)　　　　LC 2009000695

This describes how to identify bullies online, how to deal with them, and how to avoid becoming a bully.

"This . . . is easy to read, has vibrant photos on each page, and offers Tips. Additional links can be found at the publisher's portal, which is regularly updated." Libr Media Connect

Includes glossary

Kevorkian, Meline

101 facts about bullying; what everyone should know; [by] Meline Kevorkian and Robin D'Antona. Rowman & Littlefield Pub. 2008 148p $32.95 *

Grades: Professional　　　　　　　　**302.3**

1. Bullies

ISBN 978-1-57886-849-0; 1-57886-849-1

This "is designed to break down what the research says about bullying and its effects, offering ideas for what can and should be done to minimize or reduce it. Meline Kevorkian . . . discusses topics ranging from relational bullying to cyber bullying to media and video violence to the legal ramifications of bullying." Publisher's note

"A user-friendly, accessible, and well-organized resource. . . . The format will lend itself well to group discussions and give teachers and others who work with young people a solid basis upon which to explore the issues surrounding this prevalent problem." SLJ

303.3　Coordination and control

Barraclough, Sue

Leadership. Heinemann Library 2009 32p il (Exploring Citizenship) $25.36; pa $7.99

Grades: 1 2 3 4　　　　　　　　　　**303.3**

1. Leadership

ISBN　978-1-4329-3314-2;　1-4329-3314-0; 978-1-4329-3322-7 (pa); 1-4329-3322-1 (pa)

LC 2008-55302

"Learn about why people need leaders. Find out how leaders are chosen, what makes a good role model, and why everyone should try to be a leader sometimes." Publisher's note

Barraclough, Sue—*Continued*

"The text presents a multitude of realistic situations to which young children will relate. There are 'Think About It' fact boxes and checklists that aid in understanding and that will spark discussion. All are filled with captioned, color photographs that relate to the text. The information is relevant and current. . . . Strongly consider this." Libr Media Connect

Includes glossary and bibliographical references

Evans, G. Edward, 1937-

Leadership basics for librarians and information professionals; [by] G. Edward Evans, Patricia Layzell Ward. Scarecrow Press 2007 246p pa $40 *

Grades: Professional   **303.3**
    1. Leadership 2. Libraries—Administration
    ISBN 0-8108-5229-2 (pa); 978-0-8108-5229-7 (pa)
                                           LC 2006026885

"Evans and Ward provide an extensive collection of valuable research and recommendations for the current and future leaders. Arranged in three sections, their book offers background followed by an important section on the development of leadership skills and, finally, real-world experiences drawn from survey responses and conversations with colleagues. . . . Up-and-coming information professionals will gain insight and knowledge from this inspirational work." Booklist

Includes bibliographical references

303.4   Social change

Solway, Andrew

Communication; the impact of science and technology. Gareth Stevens Pub. 2010 64p il (Pros and cons) lib bdg $35

Grades: 5 6 7 8   **303.4**
    1. Information technology 2. Telecommunication
    3. Communication
    ISBN 978-1-4339-1986-2 (lib bdg); 1-4339-1986-9 (lib bdg)   LC 2009-12435

"Looks at how scientific and technological advances in recent decades have dramatically altered the way we live and examines both positive and negative impacts of these changes." Publisher's note

An "active layout that features color photographs, maps, graphs or charts on every spread, this . . . [book] has much to offer. . . . It conveniently outlines the range of views . . . helping students to learn how to view both sides of [the] issue[s]." SLJ

Includes glossary and bibliographical references

303.6   Conflict and conflict resolution

Ellis, Deborah, 1960-

Off to war; voices of soldiers' children. Groundwood Books/House of Anansi Press 2008 175p il $15.95; pa $9.95

Grades: 5 6 7 8   **303.6**
    1. Children and war 2. Iraq War, 2003-
    3. Afghanistan
    ISBN   978-0-88899-894-1;   0-88899-894-5;
    978-0-88899-895-8 (pa); 0-88899-895-3 (pa)

The wars in Iraq and Afghanistan have impacted the children of soldiers—men and women who have been called away from their families to fight in a faraway war. In their own words, some of these children describe how their experience has marked and shaped their lives

"Accessible and utterly readable. . . . The book is an excellent resource for opening discussions about the current events." SLJ

Includes glossary and bibliographical references

Engle, Dawn

PeaceJam; a billion simple acts of peace; written by Ivan Suvanjieff and Dawn Gifford Engle. Puffin Books 2008 194p il pa $16.99

Grades: 5 6 7 8 9   **303.6**
    1. PeaceJam Foundation 2. Peace 3. Youth
    ISBN 978-0-14-241234-3 (pa); 0-14-241234-1 (pa)
                                           LC 2008-24865
    Includes DVD

"This visually impressive and well-organized book would work well as a reference tool, how-to handbook, or promotional device for classroom altruistic activities or civil service clubs. Each stand-alone chapter uses a Noble Peace Laureate as the catalyst for a particular crisis, introduces the reader to a courageous young person who has been inspired to help with a specific problem, and ends with a list of ten very 'doable' suggestions of ways that every concerned citizen can help. The resources listed in the back of the book are extensive and current. An excellent addition to the text is a snappy thirty-minute DVD that could serve as a book talk, review tool or promotional device." Voice Youth Advocates

Gilley, Jeremy

Peace one day; illustrated by Karen Blessen. Putnam 2005 48p il $16.99 *   **303.6**
    1. Peace
    ISBN 0-399-24330-5   LC 2004-20475

The author "tells how he persuaded world leaders to establish World Peace Day. . . . His personal account of filming the consequences of war in several countries . . . draws attention to the issue, as do his accounts of meeting with world leaders. . . . Most powerful are the double-page collage illustrations . . . which blend some of Gilley's film images of kids caught up in war and portraits of world peace leaders with colored pencil drawings, posters, and even news headlines. [This offers] passionate prose and stirring images." Booklist

Polland, Barbara K., 1939-

We can work it out; conflict resolution for children; photographs by Craig DeRoy. Tricycle Press 2000 64p il hardcover o.p. pa $9.95 *

Grades: K 1 2 3   **303.6**

1. Interpersonal relations 2. Conflict management

ISBN 1-58246-031-0; 1-58246-029-9 (pa)

      LC 00-23852

Text and photographs designed to create opportunities for children to talk about their experiences of conflict and the varieties of ways to resolve them

"DeRoy's candid photos of kids caught in the act, both positive and negative, should be powerful incentives for thought and discussion." Booklist

Woolf, Alex

Why are people terrorists? Raintree 2005 48p il (Exploring tough issues) lib bdg $31.43 *

Grades: 4 5 6 7   **303.6**

1. Terrorism

ISBN 0-7398-6686-9   LC 2003-11571

Contents: What is terrorism?; Why do people become terrorists?; What methods do terrorists use?; The supporters of terrorism; What can be done about terrorism?; What is the war on terrorism?

Explores issues related to terrorism, such as who becomes a terrorist and why, and options such as the "War Against Terrorism" for fighting against these acts of violence agains innocent people.

"Up-to-date information for young people who are concerned about security and want to learn more about important political issues." SLJ

304.6   Population

Smith, David J.

If the world were a village; a book about the world's people; written by David J. Smith; illustrated by Shelagh Armstrong. Kids Can Press 2002 32p il $15.95 *

Grades: 3 4 5   **304.6**

1. Population 2. Human geography

ISBN 1-55074-779-7

The author compresses the earth's population of over six billion "down to a more understandable figure, 100 persons, and in 9 spreads offers data on such topics as nationalities, languages, ages, religions, and education as represented in a condensed global village." SLJ

"Though understated, the artwork contains accurate details. . . . Thought-provoking and highly effective, this world-in-miniature will open eyes to a wider view of our planet and its human inhabitants." Horn Book

Includes bibliographical references

304.8   Movement of people

Andryszewski, Tricia, 1956-

Walking the earth; a history of human migration; [by] Tricia Andryszewski. Twenty-First Century Books 2007 80p il map lib bdg $27.23

Grades: 5 6 7 8   **304.8**

1. Immigration and emigration 2. Prehistoric peoples 3. Population

ISBN 978-0-7613-3458-3 (lib bdg); 0-7613-3458-0 (lib bdg)   LC 2005033430

"The long history of humankind from 150,000 years ago to the present is examined in terms of how populations spread slowly around the globe. Along the way, the book describes innovations in food, clothing, and shelter that enabled people to progress." Voice Youth Advocates

"Copious sepia-toned visuals, including drawings, photographs, maps, and charts, create an attractive and accessible presentation of complex material." SLJ

Includes bibliographical references

305.23   Young people

Come and play; snapshots of our world's children having fun; poems by children; edited by Ayana Lowe; photographs from the Magnum Collection. Bloomsbury 2008 unp il $16.95 *

Grades: K 1 2 3   **305.23**

1. Play 2. Children—Pictorial works

ISBN 978-1-59990-245-6; 1-59990-245-1

      LC 2007039970

"Beautiful, clear photos by top professional photographers show children across the world at play. Each full-page picture is placed opposite a few simple lines of free verse, which are based on 'word-riffs' by students in the editor's New York City grade-school classes. . . . The images reflect the kids' individuality and connections, and their anger, hurt, joy, and loneliness—which will spark discussion and more 'word-riffs.'" Booklist

Freedman, Russell

Children of the Great Depression. Clarion Books 2005 118p il lib bdg $20 *

Grades: 4 5 6 7   **305.23**

1. Children—United States 2. Great Depression, 1929-1939 3. United States—Social conditions

ISBN 0-618-44630-3   LC 2005-06506

"Eight chapters cover the causes of the Great Depression, schooling, work life, migrant work, the lives of children who rode the rails, entertainment, and the economic resurgence of the early '40s." SLJ

"This stirring photo-essay combines . . . unforgettable personal details with a clear historical overview of the period and black-and-white photos by Dorothea Lange, Walker Evans, and many others." Booklist

Kerley, Barbara

One world, one day. National Geographic 2009 unp il map $17.95; lib bdg $26.90 *

Grades: PreK K 1 2   305.23

1. Children—Pictorial works

ISBN   978-1-4263-0460-6;   1-4263-0460-9;
978-1-4263-0461-3 (lib bdg); 1-4263-0461-7 (lib bdg)

LC 2008-29315

"In this visually engaging book, former Peace Corps volunteer Kerley brings together excellent photographs of children around the world. Beginning at dawn and continuing through the day until nightfall, the pictures depict young people doing similar things." Booklist

"An arresting, eye-opening compilation." Publ Wkly

Kindersley, Barnabas

Children just like me; by Barnabas & Anabel Kindersley. Dorling Kindersley 1995 79p il maps $19.95 *

Grades: 3 4 5 6   305.23

1. Children—Pictorial works

ISBN 0-7894-0201-7   LC 95-10199

"In association with United Nations Children's Fund"

This is a "compilation of facts, photographs, and interviews with thirty-seven children from thirty-two countries, including the U.S. Each child gets a full-page or double spread built around a large color photograph of the child and, often, his or her siblings; smaller photos show other family members, home and school, favorite foods and toys, homework or schoolbooks, and file photos of famous sights." Bull Cent Child Books

"A delightful, attractive look at children from around the world. . . . This book is factual, respectful, and insightful. It provides just the right balance of information and visual interest for the intended audience." SLJ

A **Life** like mine. DK Pub. 2002 127p il maps hardcover o.p. pa $12.99

Grades: 3 4 5 6   305.23

1. Children

ISBN 0-7894-8859-0; 0-7566-1803-7 (pa)

LC 2002-11197

"In association with UNICEF, United Nations Children's Fund"

Looks at what life is like for children of different countries and how each child can fulfill his or her hopes and ambitions no matter how little or much their human rights are infringed

"This book gives the reader a remarkable look at the lives of children around the world. . . . The text is varied within each page and is written in language easy for a child to understand. The photographs are dispersed throughout all pages and enhance the meaning of the text." Libr Media Connect

Making it home; real-life stories from children forced to flee; with an introduction by Beverley Naidoo. Dial Books 2005 c2004 117p $17.99; pa $6.99

Grades: 4 5 6 7   305.23

1. Refugees 2. Children and war

ISBN 0-8037-3083-7; 0-14-240455-1 (pa)

LC 2005045904

First published 2004 in the United Kingdom

This includes 20 "brief narratives by young people escaping their war-torn lands and lives. . . . Narrators from Kosovo, Bosnia, Afghanistan, Iraq, Congo, Liberia, Sudan, and Burundi reveal the injustices of their lives, forced by fate to have anything but normal childhoods. A short introduction precedes each narrative or set of narratives and gives the history of the country's conflict, providing much-needed background information. . . . A centerfold features full-color photos of several of the young people." SLJ

The **Milestones** Project; celebrating childhood around the world; photography by Richard Steckel and Michele Steckel. Tricycle 2004 64p il $17.95; pa $12.95

Grades: 3 4 5 6   305.23

1. Children

ISBN 1-58246-132-5; 1-58246-228-3 (pa)

"Milestones such as losing a first tooth, starting school, birthdays, haircuts, responsibilities, and so on are documented with stunning images of children from all corners of the globe, along with their observations. . . . The book has a clean design, with blocks of color and text and brilliantly animated photographs. This is a volume to share with younger children and to be enjoyed by many ages." SLJ

Rimm, Sylvia B., 1935-

See Jane win for girls; a smart girl's guide to success; [by] Sylvia Rimm. Free Spirit 2003 131p il pa $13.95

Grades: 5 6 7 8   305.23

1. Girls 2. Success 3. Conduct of life

ISBN 1-57542-122-4   LC 2002-155780

Adapted from the author's title for adults See Jane win, published 1999 by Crown

Presents tips, quizzes, activities, and words of wisdom from successful women for girls trying to make positive changes and choices in all areas of their lives and develop confidence, inner strength, and the desire to learn

"The message is strong and simple, the advice is practical, and readers looking for guidance and direction will respond positively to the book's format. . . . A useful self-help book and practical guide to life." SLJ

Includes bibliographical references

Wilson, Janet, 1962-

One peace; true stories of young activists; written and illustrated by Janet Wilson. Orca Book Publishers 2008 43p il $19.95

Grades: 4 5 6 7   305.23

1. Children and war 2. Peace

ISBN 978-1-55143-892-4; 1-55143-892-5

"The stories of young people who have been refugees from war, injured by land mines, or learned about the consequences of violence through other means are interspersed with children's poems, quotes, artwork, and photographs. The brief, powerful accounts document how these children ages 8 to 15 worked for or became symbols of peace." SLJ

305.4   Women

33 things every girl should know about women's history; from suffragettes to skirt lengths to the E.R.A.; edited by Tonya Bolden. Crown 2002 240p il hardcover o.p. pa $12.95 *
Grades: 5 6 7 8   **305.4**
1. Women—United States—History 2. Feminism 3. Women's rights
ISBN 0-375-91122-7; 0-375-81122-2 (pa)
     LC 2001-47131
Uses poems, essays, letters, photographs and more to present the actions and achievements of women in the United States, from its beginnings up through the twentieth century
"This is a very strong, highly readable offering that gives context to the feminist movement." Booklist

Heinemann, Sue, 1948-
The New York Public Library amazing women in American history; a book of answers for kids. Wiley 1998 192p (New York Public Library answer books for kids series) pa $12.95 *
Grades: 5 6 7 8   **305.4**
1. Women—United States—History
ISBN 0-471-19216-3   LC 97-18465
"A Stonesong Press book"
Consists of short answers to questions about the roles and achievements of women in America from prehistory to the end of the twentieth century
"The text is succinct, easy to read, and informative. . . . Pertinent black-and-white photos appear throughout." SLJ
Includes glossary and bibliographical references

Rossi, Ann
Created equal; women campaign for the right to vote 1840-1920. National Geographic 2005 40p il (Crossroads America) $12.95; lib bdg $21.90 *
Grades: 4 5 6   **305.4**
1. Women—Suffrage 2. Women—United States—History
ISBN 0-7922-8275-2; 0-7922-8285-X (lib bdg)
A history of the movement for women's suffrage in the United States
"Period photographs, drawings, and cartoons; primary-source material; and biographical content make [this] introductory [title] interesting and accessible." SLJ
Includes glossary

305.8   Ethnic and national groups

Birdseye, Debbie Holsclaw
Under our skin; kids talk about race; by Debbie Holsclaw Birdseye and Tom Birdseye; photographs by Robert Crum. Holiday House 1997 30p il $15.95
Grades: 4 5 6 7   **305.8**
1. United States—Race relations 2. Ethnic relations
ISBN 0-8234-1325-X   LC 97-9395

Six young people discuss their feelings about their own ethnic backgrounds and about their experiences with people of different races
"This book provides an excellent starting point for discussion. It gives readers a chance to see what life is like through someone else's eyes, and in someone else's skin." SLJ
Includes bibliographical references

The **Black** Americans; a history in their own words, 1619-1983; edited by Milton Meltzer. Harper & Row 1987 c1984 306p il pa $12.99
Grades: 5 6 7 8 9 10   **305.8**
1. African Americans—History—Sources
ISBN 0-06-446055-X
"A Harper trophy book"
This is a revised and updated edition of In their own words: a history of the American Negro, edited by Milton Meltzer and published in three volumes, 1964-1967
A history of Black people in the United States, as told through letters, speeches, articles, eyewitness accounts, and other documents

Bolden, Tonya
Tell all the children our story; memories and mementos of being young and Black in America. Abrams 2001 128p il $24.95
Grades: 5 6 7 8   **305.8**
1. African American children 2. United States—Race relations
ISBN 0-8109-4496-0   LC 2001-1353
"This compilation of the African American experience, from colonial times through the twentieth century, reads and looks like a family scrapbook. . . . Photographs, excerpts from diaries and memoirs, and reproductions of artwork by black artists such as Charles Altson beautifully bring the story of each generation to life. Bolden vibrantly delivers her historical message through a contemporary perspective." Booklist
Includes bibliographical references

Cha, Dia, 1962-
Dia's story cloth; written by Dia Cha; stitched by Chue and Nhia Thao Cha. Lee & Low Bks. 1996 unp il $15.95; pa $6.95 *
Grades: 3 4 5   **305.8**
1. Hmong (Asian people)
ISBN 1-880000-34-2; 1-880000-63-6 (pa)
     LC 95-41465
The story cloth made for her by her aunt and uncle chronicles the life of the author and her family in their native Laos and their eventual emigration to the United States
"An interesting and unusual title that resists neat categorization. . . . Part autobiography, part history, part description of a changing culture adapting life and art to new circumstances, the book serves as a brief introduction to the Hmong people." SLJ
Includes bibliographical references

Haskins, James, 1941-2005

The rise of Jim Crow; by James Haskins and Kathleen Benson; with Virginia Schomp. Marshall Cavendish Benchmark 2008 80p il (Drama of African-American history) lib bdg $23.95 *

Grades: 5 6 7 8 **305.8**

1. African Americans—Segregation 2. African Americans—History 3. United States—Race relations

ISBN 978-0-7614-2640-0

"Provides a history of the decades of poverty, oppression, and terror that African Americans suffered under the system of segregation in the United States, from the end of the Reconstruction era through the early decades of the twentieth century." Publisher's note

Includes glossary and bibliographical references

Hernández, Roger E.

1898 to World War II. Marshall Cavendish Benchmark 2009 78p il (Hispanic America) lib bdg $34.21

Grades: 4 5 6 7 **305.8**

1. Hispanic Americans—History 2. United States—History—1898-1919 3. United States—History—1919-1933 4. United States—History—1933-1945

ISBN 978-0-7614-4176-2 (lib bdg); 0-7614-4176-X (lib bdg)   LC 2008041140

"Provides comprehensive information on the history of the Spanish coming to the United States, focusing on the time from 1898 to the start of World War II." Publisher's note

Includes glossary and bibliographical references

Hoobler, Dorothy

The African American family album; [by] Dorothy and Thomas Hoobler; introduction by Phylicia Rashad. Oxford University Press 1995 127p il (American family albums) hardcover o.p. pa $24.95

Grades: 5 6 7 8 **305.8**

1. African Americans

ISBN 0-19-509460-3; 0-19-512419-7 (pa)
                                    LC 94-34697

"Beginning with life in pre-colonial Africa, the Hooblers make superb use of personal histories, autobiographies, slave narratives, and other original documents to paint a vivid picture of life in medieval Africa, in Africa during the slave trade, and of the lives of slaves and former slaves in the U.S. Readers are introduced to a complex set of historical events, presented in a simple, yet moving manner. . . . An excellent addition to any collection." SLJ

Includes bibliographical references

The Chinese American family album; [by] Dorothy and Thomas Hoobler; introduction by Bette Bao Lord. Oxford University Press 1994 128p il map (American family albums) hardcover o.p. pa $24.95

Grades: 5 6 7 8 **305.8**

1. Chinese Americans

ISBN 0-19-509123-X; 0-19-512421-9 (pa)
                                    LC 93-11873

"This sourcebook on the Chinese immigrant experience is divided into six topics: the homeland, the voyage to America, arrival in America, first-generation life, the integration of . . . generations, and Chinese Americans today. The authors introduce each chapter with a summary essay, then let the immigrants and their descendents speak for themselves in excerpts from oral reminiscences, written histories, and fiction spanning the years from the Gold Rush to the 1980s. Period photographs and drawings, maps, and sidebars enhance the text. The result resembles a well-organized, handsomely designed scrapbook. . . . A valuable resource." SLJ

Includes bibliographical references

The Irish American family album; [by] Dorothy and Thomas Hoobler; introduction by Joseph P. Kennedy II. Oxford University Press 1995 128p il (American family albums) hardcover o.p. pa $24.95

Grades: 5 6 7 8 **305.8**

1. Irish Americans

ISBN 0-19-509461-1; 0-19-512418-9 (pa)
                                    LC 94-19569

"Selections from diaries, letters, interviews, newspaper and magazine articles, and books provide an arresting picture of what it has meant to be of Irish heritage in America. . . . Topics such as prejudice, working conditions and labor unions; politics; and the importance of family, friends, and the Catholic Church are touched upon." SLJ

Includes bibliographical references

The Italian American family album; [by] Dorothy and Thomas Hoobler; introduction by Governor Mario M. Cuomo. Oxford University Press 1994 127p il map (American family albums) hardcover o.p. pa $24.95

Grades: 5 6 7 8 **305.8**

1. Italian Americans

ISBN 0-19-509124-8; 0-19-512420-0 (pa)
                                    LC 93-46918

This volume includes selections from "diaries, letters, and oral histories. . . . Each of the six chapters begins with background information and then goes on to discuss life in the old country, coming to America, first impressions, working, forming a new life, and becoming a part of America." SLJ

Includes bibliographical references

The Jewish American family album; [by] Dorothy and Thomas Hoobler; introduction by Mandy Patinkin. Oxford University Press 1995 127p il (American family albums) pa $17.95

Grades: 5 6 7 8 **305.8**

1. Jews—United States

ISBN 0-19-512417-0   LC 94-43460

This volume "begins with a five-page thumbnail sketch of Jewish history from Abraham to the rise of the State of Israel. Successive chapters detail Jewish life in 'the old country', immigration to America, and the contributions Jews have made to their new homeland." Book Rep

"What makes this title unique is the high quality of the carefully researched and varied historical information and the Hooblers' judicious selection of primary-source

Hoobler, Dorothy—*Continued*

excerpts, many of which are by well-known writers, politicians, and celebrities." SLJ

Includes bibliographical references

The Mexican American family album; [by] Dorothy and Thomas Hoobler; introduction by Henry G. Cisneros. Oxford University Press 1994 127p il (American family albums) hardcover o.p. pa $24.95

Grades: 5 6 7 8   **305.8**

1. Mexican Americans
ISBN 0-19-509459-X; 0-19-512426-X (pa)
LC 94-7785

"Using almost exclusively first-person accounts, the Hooblers present vignettes of history, culture, and experience from the first Mexican American settlers to the Chicano Movement. . . . Gathered together, these accounts present a powerful portrait of a strong people, rich in history and culture. A must for multicultural studies." Book Rep

Includes bibliographical references

The Scandinavian American family album; [by] Dorothy and Thomas Hoobler; introduction by Hubert H. Humphrey, III. Oxford University Press 1997 127p il (American family albums) hardcover o.p. pa $24.95

Grades: 5 6 7 8   **305.8**

1. Scandinavian Americans
ISBN 0-19-510579-6; 0-19-512424-3 (pa)
LC 95-45540

"The Hooblers begin with a chapter on life in Scandinavia and the conditions that caused people to emigrate. Scandinavian-Americans who have played an influential role in our society are featured throughout the book. . . . Photographs and captions add personal narratives that explain what life was like for Scandinavian Americans." Book Rep

Includes bibliographical references

Keedle, Jayne

Americans from the Caribbean and Central America. Marshall Cavendish Benchmark 2009 c2010 80p il map (New Americans) lib bdg $35.64

Grades: 5 6 7 8   **305.8**

1. Caribbean Americans 2. Central American Americans 3. Immigrants—United States
ISBN 978-0-7614-4302-5 (lib bdg); 0-7614-4302-9 (lib bdg)
LC 2009003171

This title looks at Caribbean and Central American "communities in America today, detailing earlier generations of immigrants and current arrivals who are making new lives, changing the American culture, and looking to the future. [The] title includes many full-color photos, maps, and charts. . . . The [book does] a good job of helping readers to understand the differences between undocumented and documented immigrants and describe the citizenship process. The topics of racism, stereotypes, and other issues related to integration into American society are sensitively covered." SLJ

Includes glossary and bibliographical references

Mexican Americans. Marshall Cavendish Benchmark 2009 c2010 80p il map (New Americans) lib bdg $35.64

Grades: 5 6 7 8   **305.8**

1. Mexican Americans 2. Immigrants—United States
ISBN 978-0-7614-4307-0 (lib bdg); 0-7614-4307-X (lib bdg)
LC 2008052101

This describes the history of Mexican Americans
"Consistent in content, and providing a mix of facts and personal accounts, this . . . will be [a] . . . very useful addition to the collection." Libr Media Collect

Includes glossary and bibliographical references

West African Americans. Marshall Cavendish Benchmark 2009 c2010 80p il map (New Americans) lib bdg $35.64

Grades: 5 6 7 8   **305.8**

1. Africans—United States 2. African Americans 3. Immigrants—United States
ISBN 978-0-7614-4313-1 (lib bdg); 0-7614-4313-4 (lib bdg)
LC 2008055753

This title looks at West African "communities in America today, detailing earlier generations of immigrants and current arrivals who are making new lives, changing the American culture, and looking to the future. [The] title includes many full-color photos, maps, and charts. . . . [The book does] a good job of helping readers to understand the differences between undocumented and documented immigrants and describe the citizenship process. The topics of racism, stereotypes, and other issues related to integration into American society are sensitively covered." SLJ

Includes glossary and bibliographical references

Kuklin, Susan

How my family lives in America. Bradbury Press 1992 unp il hardcover o.p. pa $5.99 *

Grades: K 1 2 3   **305.8**

1. African Americans 2. Chinese Americans 3. Puerto Ricans—United States 4. Family
ISBN 0-02-751239-8; 0-689-82221-9 (pa)
LC 91-22949

"Sanu's father was born in Senegal, Eric's father came from Puerto Rico, and both of April's parents were born in Taiwan. Each section provides special words, foods, games, clothes, music and other ways in which families transmit their heritages and integrate them with the lifestyles of the United States. The photographs provide insights as to how cultures are cherished and continued." Child Book Rev Serv

"Each child's first-person narration is simple and uncomplicated, with occasional humorous touches. . . . The full-color photographs are well composed and serviceable." SLJ

Lester, Julius

Let's talk about race; illustrated by Karen Barbour. HarperCollinsPublishers 2005 unp il $15.99; lib bdg $16.89 *

Grades: K 1 2 3   **305.8**

1. Racism 2. Prejudices
ISBN 0-06-028596-6; 0-06-028598-2 (lib bdg)
LC 2002-10979

Lester, Julius—*Continued*

This "picture book introduces race as just one of many chapters in a person's story. . . . Throughout the narrative, [the author] asks questions that young readers can answer, creating a dialogue about who they are and encouraging them to tell their own tales. He also discusses 'stories' that are not always true, pointing out that we create prejudice by perceiving ourselves as better than others. . . . The pairing of text and dazzling artwork is flawless." SLJ

Masoff, Joy, 1951-

The African American story; the events that shaped our nation—and the people that changed our lives. Five Ponds 2007 95p il map $26.50 *

Grades: 4 5 6 7   **305.8**

1. African Americans—History
ISBN 978-0-9727156-9-0

This "covers the history of the African people in America from the 1400s to the present. Historical photographs, archival documents, maps, and a fact-filled time line provide a visually stimulating introduction to the subject. . . . Masoff provides a tremendous amount of material in an exciting, appealing title that is useful for browsing, introductory lessons, quick reference, and beginning research." SLJ

Includes bibliographical references

McClaurin, Irma

Facing the future; by Irma McClaurin with Virginia Schomp. Marshall Cavendish Benchmark 2008 80p il (Drama of African-American history) lib bdg $23.95 *

Grades: 5 6 7 8   **305.8**

1. African Americans—History 2. United States—Race relations
ISBN 978-0-7614-2644-8 (lib bdg); 0-7614-2644-2 (lib bdg)

"Covers the struggle for racial equality from the end of the civil rights movement in the 1960s to the present day." Publisher's note

Includes glossary and bibliographical references

Myers, Walter Dean, 1937-

Now is your time! the African-American struggle for freedom. HarperCollins Pubs. 1991 292p il pa $14.99 hardcover o.p. *

Grades: 6 7 8 9   **305.8**

1. African Americans—History
ISBN 0-06-446120-3 (pa)   LC 91-314

Coretta Scott King Award for text

A history of the African-American struggle for freedom and equality, beginning with the capture of Africans in 1619, continuing through the American Revolution, the Civil War, and into contemporary times

"Myers's unique episodic approach makes this history a compelling exploration of the African-American experience. . . . This fascinating book will engender pride in heritage for young African Americans and provide insight into American history for all of us." Horn Book

Includes bibliographical references

Park, Ken

Americans from India and other South Asian countries. Marshall Cavendish Benchmark 2009 c2010 80p il map (New Americans) lib bdg $35.64

Grades: 5 6 7 8   **305.8**

1. East Indians—United States 2. Asian Americans 3. Immigrants—United States
ISBN 978-0-7614-4305-6 (lib bdg); 0-7614-4305-3 (lib bdg)   LC 2009002599

This title looks at Indian and other South Asian "communities in America today, detailing earlier generations of immigrants and current arrivals who are making new lives, changing the American culture, and looking to the future. [The] title includes many full-color photos, maps, and charts. . . The [book does] a good job of helping readers to understand the differences between undocumented and documented immigrants and describe the citizenship process. The topics of racism, stereotypes, and other issues related to integration into American society are sensitively covered." SLJ

Includes glossary and bibliographical references

Petrillo, Valerie

A kid's guide to Latino history; more than 70 activities. Chicago Review Press 2009 214p il pa $14.95 *

Grades: 4 5 6 7   **305.8**

1. Hispanic Americans—History
ISBN 978-1-55652-771-5 (pa); 1-55652-771-3 (pa)
LC 2008040433

"This big, lively overview examines the history of Latinos in the U.S. . . . The chatty, informative text, presented in readable, spacious layouts, will draw kids with lots of fun, illustrated instructions for related activities. . . . The accessible facts and the individual portraits of notable authors, athletes, entertainers, and politicians portray Latinos' rich contribution to U.S. heritage, and kids will want to talk about the well-presented issues." Booklist

Includes bibliographical references

Rappaport, Doreen, 1939-

Free at last! stories and songs of Emancipation; illustrated by Shane W. Evans. Candlewick Press 2004 63p il $19.99; pa $7.99 *

Grades: 3 4 5 6   **305.8**

1. African Americans—History 2. African Americans—Civil rights 3. Southern States—Race relations
ISBN 0-7636-1440-8; 0-7636-3147-7 (pa)
LC 2003-43853

"Stories, poems, and songs about events from the Emancipation Proclamation of 1863 through the Brown v. Board of Education decision of 1954 are perfectly matched with vibrant oil paintings. The result is a glorious tribute to the lives of African-American heroes and heroines." SLJ

Schomp, Virginia, 1953-
Marching toward freedom; by Virginia Schomp. Marshall Cavendish Benchmark 2008 80p il (Drama of African-American history) lib bdg $23.95
Grades: 5 6 7 8   **305.8**
    1. African Americans—History 2. United States—Race relations
    ISBN 978-0-7614-2643-1
"Explores the period between 1929 and 1954 in African-American history, when the 'New Negro' emerged, proud of his or her racial heritage and determined to topple the barriers to black advancement." Publisher's note
Includes glossary and bibliographical references

Thomas, William David, 1947-
Korean Americans. Marshall Cavendish Benchmark 2009 c2010 80p il (New Americans) lib bdg $35.64
Grades: 5 6 7 8   **305.8**
    1. Korean Americans 2. Immigrants—United States
    ISBN 978-0-7614-4306-3 (lib bdg); 0-7614-4306-1 (lib bdg)   LC 2008054846
    This describes the history of Korean Americans
"Consistent in content, and providing a mix of facts, and personal accounts, this . . . will be [a] . . . very useful addition to the collection." Libr Media Connect
Includes glossary and bibliographical references

Wachtel, Alan
Southeast Asian Americans. Marshall Cavendish Benchmark 2009 c2010 80p il map (New Americans) lib bdg $35.64
Grades: 5 6 7 8   **305.8**
    1. Immigrants—United States 2. Asian Americans
    ISBN 978-0-7614-4312-4 (lib bdg); 0-7614-4312-6 (lib bdg)   LC 2008055752
    This title looks at Southeast Asian "communities in America today, detailing earlier generations of immigrants and current arrivals who are making new lives, changing the American culture, and looking to the future. [The] title includes many full-color photos, maps, and charts. . . . The books [does] a good job of helping readers to understand the differences between undocumented and documented immigrants and describe the citizenship process. The topics of racism, stereotypes, and other issues related to integration into American society are sensitively covered." SLJ
Includes glossary and bibliographical references

Weiss, Gail Garfinkel
Americans from Russia and Eastern Europe. Marshall Cavendish Benchmark 2009 c2010 80p il (New Americans) lib bdg $35.64
Grades: 5 6 7 8   **305.8**
    1. Russian Americans 2. East European Americans 3. Immigrants—United States
    ISBN 978-0-7614-4310-0 (lib bdg); 0-7614-4310-X (lib bdg)   LC 2008046350
    This title looks at Russian and Eastern European "communities in America today, detailing earlier generations of immigrants and current arrivals who are making

new lives, changing the American culture, and looking to the future. [The] title includes many full-color photos, maps, and charts. . . . The [book does] a good job of helping readers to understand the differences between undocumented and documented immigrants and describe the citizenship process. The topics of racism, stereotypes, and other issues related to integration into American society are sensitively covered." SLJ
Includes glossary and bibliographical references

Wolf, Bernard, 1930-
Coming to America; a Muslim family's story. Lee & Low Bks. 2003 unp il hardcover o.p. pa $7.95 *
Grades: 3 4 5   **305.8**
    1. Arab Americans 2. Muslims—United States
    ISBN 1-58430-086-8; 1-58430-177-5 (pa)
                                    LC 2002-67115
Depicts the joys and hardships experienced by a Muslim family that immigrates to New York City from Alexandria, Egypt, in the hope of making a better life for themselves
"The tone is low-key but optimistic; the large, mostly full-page color photos seem like those of a welcomed visitor." Horn Book

306.8   Marriage and family

Charlip, Remy
Hooray for me! by Remy Charlip & Lilian Moore; paintings by Vera B. Williams. Tricycle Press 1996 unp il $14.95
Grades: PreK K 1 2   **306.8**
    1. Family 2. Children 3. Self-perception
    ISBN 1-88367-243-0   LC 96-2449
A reissue of the title first published 1975 by Parents' Magazine Press
Explores an individual's relationship to family, friends, and even pets.
"Two kids realize they are both 'me' and then continue the discussion with a whole crowd, discovering that 'me' can be an aunt, a nephew, a second cousin, a great-grandfather. Bright, dreamlike watercolors enhance this joyful look at self-discovery." Horn Book Guide

Cole, Joanna
The new baby at your house; photographs by Margaret Miller. rev ed. Morrow Junior Bks. 1998 unp il hardcover o.p. pa $6.99 *
Grades: K 1 2 3   **306.8**
    1. Infants 2. Siblings
    ISBN 0-688-13897-7; 0-688-13898-5 (lib bdg); 0-688-16698-9 (pa)   LC 97-29267
A revised and newly illustrated edition of the title first published 1985
Describes the activities and changes involved in having a new baby in the house and the feelings experienced by the older brothers and sisters
"Miller captures many intimate and touching moments with her pictures. . . . There is a good balance of families from varied ethnic backgrounds. . . . This book

Cole, Joanna—*Continued*

opens with a clear and precise note to parents that gives honest, practical advice." SLJ

Includes bibliographical references

Crist, James J.

Siblings; you're stuck with each other so stick together; by James J. Crist & Elizabeth Verdick; illustrated by Steve Mark. Free Spirit Pub. 2010 118p il (Laugh & learn) pa $8.95

Grades: 3 4 5 6   **306.8**

1. Siblings

ISBN 978-1-57542-336-4 (pa); 1-57542-336-7 (pa)

"Starting with the wry subtitle and the colorful cover cartoon of two fuming kids standing back to back, this lively title uses accessible humor to approach sibling-related topics, such as birth order, privacy, jealousy, bullying, and bonding. The authors discuss each subject in a child-centered, casual, and humorous tone. . . . The book's open design and interactive features, such as quick checklists and quizzes, help make this a great choice for kids and grownups to talk and laugh about together." Booklist

Includes bibliographical references

Garza, Carmen Lomas, 1948-

Family pictures; paintings and stories [by] Carmen Lomas Garza. 15th anniversary edition. Children's Book Press 2005 30p il $16.95; pa $7.95 *

Grades: K 1 2 3   **306.8**

1. Family 2. Mexican Americans 3. Bilingual books—English-Spanish

ISBN 0-89239-206-1; 0-89239-207-X (pa)

A re-designed edition with a new introduction of the title first published 1990

Text and title page in English and Spanish

The "Mexican-American artist shares memories of her childhood in Kingsville, Texas, through . . . paintings depicting the traditions of her family and community life. A fair in Mexico, the author's sixth birthday party, and a visit from a curandera (healer) represent a few of the scenes presented." Booklist

"An inspired celebration of American cultural diversity. . . . The English text is simple and reads smoothly, but it is Zubizarreta's Spanish rendition that has real verve and style. From the exquisite cut-paper images on the text pages, to the brilliant paintings, to the strong family bonds expressed in the text, Family Pictures/Cuadros de familia is a visual feast, and an aural delight." SLJ

In my family; pictures and stories by Carmen Lomas Garza; as told to Harriet Rohmer; edited by David Schecter; Spanish translation by Francisco X. Alarcón. Children's Bk. Press 1996 unp il $15.95; pa $7.95 *

Grades: K 1 2 3   **306.8**

1. Family 2. Bilingual books—English-Spanish

ISBN 0-89239-138-3; 0-89239-163-4 (pa)

LC 96-7471

Text in English and Spanish

"Lomas Garza uses her narrative paintings to relate her memories of growing up in Kingsville, Texas, near the Mexican border, and to reflect her pride in her Mexican American heritage. The artist portrays everyday events as well as special moments of family history in crisply colorful, vibrantly peopled paintings and provides brief, bilingual background stories for each of the 13 paintings." Booklist

Kuklin, Susan

Families. Hyperion Books for Children 2006 36p il $15.99 *

Grades: 3 4 5   **306.8**

1. Family

ISBN 0-7868-0822-5

"This book consists of interviews with the children from 15 different families, including mixed-race, immigrant, gay, lesbian, and divorced, as well as single parents and families for whom religion is a focal point. The children may be adopted, have special needs, be only children or have multiple siblings. . . . The voices are natural, and the children come across as individuals. . . . Kuklin has composed sharp and vibrant photos that capture the essence of each of them. This book will be both attractive to browsers and an excellent impetus for discussing relationships and diversity in America." SLJ

MacGregor, Cynthia

Jigsaw puzzle family; the stepkids' guide to fitting it together. Impact Pub. 2005 106p (RebuildingBooks, relationships, divorce and beyond) pa $12.95 *

Grades: 5 6 7 8   **306.8**

1. Stepfamilies

ISBN 1-886230-63-3

"MacGregor offers simple guidelines, practical advice, and lots of fictional examples about living with a new blended family. . . . This title offers healthy and helpful suggestions for resolving much of the conflict that arises when family situations change." SLJ

Includes bibliographical references

Rotner, Shelley

Lots of grandparents! by Shelley Rotner and Sheila Kelly; photographs by Shelley Rotner. Millbrook Press 2001 unp il hardcover o.p. pa $7.95

Grades: K 1   **306.8**

1. Grandparents

ISBN 0-7613-2313-9; 0-7613-1896-8 (pa)

LC 00-66827

In this photo-essay "color photographs show grandparents of different ages, ethnic groups, shapes, and sizes sharing happy times with grandchildren." SLJ

"The brief text offers sensible comments about grandparents and their bond with their grandchildren, but teachers will particularly appreciate the variety of photographs that can lead to classroom discussions." Booklist

Rubel, Nicole
Twice as nice; what it's like to be a twin.
Farrar, Straus and Giroux 2004 32p il $16.50 *
Grades: K 1 2 3   **306.8**
1. Twins
ISBN 0-374-31836-0   LC 2003-54168
Presents facts, anecdotes, studies, opinions, and advice
on the topic of twins
"The layout is colorful and inviting, blending light-hearted cartoon illustrations with black-and-white and full-color photos. Dialogue balloons present additional factual tidbits as well as humorous one-liners." SLJ

Sheldon, Annette
Big sister now; a story about me and our new baby; written by Annette Sheldon; illustrated by Karen Maizel. Magination Press 2006 32p il $14.95; pa $8.95 *
Grades: PreK   **306.8**
1. Infants 2. Siblings
ISBN 1-59147-243-1; 1-59147-244-X (pa)
                                      LC 2005005839
"An Educational Publishing Foundation book"
"Among the flood of titles about older siblings and new babies, this book, published under the auspices of the American Psychological Association, stands out for its appealing illustrations and direct story, which wraps a clear, comforting message. . . . An appended section offers parents solid ideas for helping a child adjust to a new baby." Booklist

Snow, Judith E.
How it feels to have a gay or lesbian parent; a book by kids for kids of all ages. Harrington Park Press 2004 110p $19.95; pa $12.95
Grades: 5 6 7 8 9 10   **306.8**
1. Gay parents 2. Parent-child relationship
ISBN 1-56023-419-9; 1-56023-420-2 (pa)
                                      LC 2003-18008
In their own words, children of different ages talk about how and when they learned of their gay or lesbian parent's sexual orientation and the effect it has had on them.
"This inspirational, eye-opening title gives readers who have gay and lesbian parents a much-deserved voice." SLJ

306.89   Separation and divorce

Brown, Laurene Krasny
Dinosaurs divorce; a guide for changing families; [by] Laurene Krasny Brown and Marc Brown. Atlantic Monthly Press 1986 31p il $15.95; pa $7.95 *
Grades: K 1 2 3   **306.89**
1. Divorce
ISBN 0-316-11248-8; 0-316-10996-7 (pa)
                                      LC 86-1079
Text and illustrations of dinosaur characters introduce aspects of divorce such as its causes and effects, living with a single parent, spending holidays in two separate households, and adjusting to a stepparent
"The picture-book, almost comic-book, format, the touches of humor, and the distancing effect of the dinosaurs as surrogate humans may make the book accessible to young or extremely anxious children. A thoughtful, useful book." Horn Book

Holyoke, Nancy
A smart girl's guide to her parents' divorce; how to land on your feet when your world turns upside down; illustrated by Scott Nash. American Girl Pub. 2009 120p il pa $9.95
Grades: 3 4 5   **306.89**
1. Divorce 2. Children of divorced parents
ISBN 978-1-59369-488-3 (pa); 1-59369-488-1 (pa)
"Short chapters illustrated with bright cartoon drawings cover many important concerns and offer explanations of the divorce process. Topics range from how to deal with negative emotions, family changes, and new living arrangements, to tougher issues such as violence and financial troubles. The text has a compassionate tone, and sprinkled throughout are answers to questions that readers might have as well as snippets of advice from girls who have found what works for them." SLJ

Krementz, Jill
How it feels when parents divorce. Knopf 1984 115p il pa $15 hardcover o.p.
Grades: 4 5 6 7   **306.89**
1. Divorce
ISBN 0-394-75855-2 (pa)   LC 83-48856
In a personal interview format "19 boys and girls, ranging in age from 7 to 16 years, tell of their parents' divorces and of the effects the divorce has had on them and their families." SLJ
"The full-page portraits that precede each piece are exceptionally expressive. While the accounts have many similarities, experiences and personalities are unique; Krementz' ear for language ensures that the children project their own individuality." Horn Book

Murphy, Patricia J., 1963-
Divorce and separation; [by] Patricia J Murphy. Heinemann Library 2008 32p il (Tough topics) $25.36; pa $7.99
Grades: 1 2 3   **306.89**
1. Divorce
ISBN   978-1-4034-9775-8;   1-4034-9775-3;
978-1-4034-9780-2 (pa); 1-4034-9780-X (pa)
                                      LC 2007005347
"Murphy addresses these emotionally charged topics in a basic and direct manner. The book defines the terms and explains the differences between separation and divorce. It also covers various emotions and feelings that are often associated with them. The writing is frank yet sensitive enough in its approach and the accompanying full-color photographs effectively illustrate the text. A solid introduction to a tough topic." SLJ
Includes bibliographical references

Rogers, Fred

Divorce; photographs by Jim Judkis. Putnam 1996 unp il (Lets talk about it) hardcover o.p. pa $6.99 *

Grades: K 1 2   **306.89**
  1. Divorce
  ISBN 0-399-22449-1; 0-698-11670-4 (pa)
                                                    LC 94-2312

Rogers "defines a family as anyone who gives a child food, care, love, and a place to feel safe. He explains that these main ingredients should remain constant even in the event of a divorce. Children are advised to ask about changes in living arrangements and other aspects of their lives. . . . The author prescribes activities like talking, drawing, and playing with friends to deal with normal feelings of sadness, anger, and crying. . . . Judkis's sensitive full-color photographs of three families work well with the text." SLJ

307   Communities

Ajmera, Maya

Be my neighbor; [by] Maya Ajmera & John D. Ivanko. Shakti for Children, Charlesbridge 2004 unp il $15.95; pa $6.95

Grades: K 1 2   **307**
  1. Community life
  ISBN 1-57091-504-0; 1-57091-685-3 (pa)
                                                    LC 2003-21230

A simple introduction to the characteristics of a neighborhood

"This beautifully crafted book explores the concept of community, using well-chosen words from the late Mr. Rogers as a starting point. . . . Illustrated with bright, beautiful full-color photos of children around the world, the gorgeous spreads are organized by themes." SLJ

307.7   Specific kinds of communities

Kent, Peter, 1949-

Peter Kent's city across time. Kingfisher 2010 48p $16.99

Grades: 4 5 6   **307.7**
  1. Cities and towns—Growth
  ISBN 978-0-7534-6400-7; 0-7534-6400-4

"Kent offers a quick tour of modern civilization as seen through the archaeological lens of an imagined European city in this detail-rich picture book. Beginning in the Stone Age, each spread uses the same vantage point to show a cutaway snapshot of what the landscape and city would look like in each era. . . . It's a winning format, and Kent knows how to provide the mini-dramas . . . that make it such a fun, flip back-and-forth experience." Booklist

Includes glossary

320   Political science

Giesecke, Ernestine, 1945-

National government. 2nd ed. Heinemann Library 2010 32p il map (Kids' guide to government) $29.29; pa $7.99

Grades: 3 4 5   **320**
  1. United States—Politics and government
  ISBN 978-1-4329-2708-0; 1-4329-2708-6;
  978-1-4329-2713-4 (pa); 1-4329-2713-2 (pa)
  First published 2000

Introduces the purpose and function of national government, the significance of the Constitution, the three branches of government, how the government raises money, and how a bill becomes a law

"This . . . would be a great asset. . . . Students will learn about a different, but related government every two pages. The font is large and easy to read. The photos, diagrams, charts, maps, and illustrations supplement the text well." Libr Media Connect

Includes glossary

320.3   Comparative government

Giesecke, Ernestine, 1945-

Governments around the world. 2nd ed. Heinemann Library 2010 32p il map (Kids' guide to government) $29.29; pa $7.99

Grades: 3 4 5   **320.3**
  1. Comparative government
  ISBN 978-1-4329-2705-9; 1-4329-2705-1;
  978-1-4329-2710-3 (pa); 1-4329-2710-8 (pa)
  First published 2000

Introduces the concept of government, exploring various types of systems, including democracy, communism, and socialism, and presenting international organizations such as the UN and NATO

"This . . . would be a great asset. . . . Students will learn about a different, but related government every two pages. The font is large and easy to read. The photos, diagrams, charts, maps, and illustrations supplement the text well." Libr Media Connect

Includes glossary and bibliographical references

320.4   Structure and functions of government

Wyatt, Valerie

How to build your own country; written by Valerie Wyatt; illustrated by Fred Rix. Kids Can Press 2009 40p il (CitizenKid) $17.95

Grades: 3 4 5   **320.4**
  1. Citizenship 2. Political science
  ISBN 978-1-55453-310-7; 1-55453-310-4

"This unique, odd, and informative book offers a guide for readers to create their own personal countries. Everything from finding unclaimed land and coming up with a name . . . to holding elections and serving one's citizens is covered. Despite the silliness, useful informa-

Wyatt, Valerie—*Continued*

tion is given, teaching readers about the value of diplomacy and how actual governments function." Horn Book Guide

Includes glossary

320.8   Local government

Giesecke, Ernestine, 1945-

Local government. 2nd ed. Heinemann Library 2009 32p il map (Kids' guide to government) $29.29; pa $7.99

Grades: 3 4 5   **320.8**

1. Local government 2. United States—Politics and government

ISBN   978-1-4329-2706-6;   1-4329-2706-X; 978-1-4329-2711-0 (pa); 1-4329-2711-6 (pa)

First published 2000

Introduces the purpose and function of local governments, explores the three branches of government at the city and county level, and presents the relationships between city and suburban governments and between various governments and schools

"This . . . would be a great asset. . . . Students will learn about a different, but related government every two pages. The font is large and easy to read. The photos, diagrams, charts, maps, and illustrations supplement the text well." Libr Media Connect

Includes glossary

322.4   Political action groups

Schwartz, Heather E.

Political activism; how you can make a difference; by Heather E. Schwartz. Capstone Press 2009 32p il (Take action) lib bdg $19.99

Grades: 3 4 5 6   **322.4**

1. Lobbying 2. Political activists 3. Social action

ISBN 978-1-4296-2799-3 (lib bdg); 1-4296-2799-9 (lib bdg)   LC 2008026939

"Whether the issue is animal rights, global warming, or student representation in government, this lively hands-on title . . . combines personal profiles of activist teens with the politics of what they are fighting for, and includes realistic advice about how to do research, set goals, ask questions, and take one step at a time to reach those in power. The open, attractive design will draw readers with color photos of young activists." Booklist

Includes bibliographical references

323   Civil and political rights

Every human has rights; a photographic declaration for kids; based on the United Nations Universal Declaration of Human Rights; with poetry from the ePals community; foreword by Mary Robinson. National Geographic 2009 30p il $26.90 *

Grades: 4 5 6 7 8   **323**

1. Human rights

ISBN 978-1-4263-0511-5; 1-4263-0511-7

"On the sixtieth anniversary of the Universal Declaration of Human Rights, this full-color photo-essay combines prize-winning poems by young people with beautiful photographs from all over the world. . . . The stirring pictures will stimulate classroom discussion about the declaration, which is quoted in full at the back." Booklist

Thomas, William David, 1947-

What are citizens' basic rights? [by] William David Thomas. Gareth Stevens Pub. 2008 32p il (My American government) lib bdg $23.93; pa $8.95

Grades: 3 4 5   **323**

1. Civil rights

ISBN 978-0-8368-8861-4 (lib bdg); 0-8368-8861-8 (lib bdg); 978-0-8368-8866-9 (pa); 0-8368-8866-9 (pa)

LC 2007032425

This describes the basic legal rights of United States citizens

This book has "an accessible format and clear writing. . . . Black-and-white and full-color vintage and more recent photographs appear throughout." SLJ

Includes glossary and bibliographical references

We are all born free. Frances Lincoln Children's Books 2008 unp il $19.95 *

Grades: K 1 2 3   **323**

1. Human rights

ISBN 978-1-84507-650-4; 1-84507-650-8

[Published] in association with Amnesty International

A commemorative edition of the Universal Declaration of Human Rights as adopted in 1948 by the United Nations General Assembly offers insight into the world's shared views about the rights of all people.

"Amnesty International has taken the 30 articles that comprise the Declaration and simplified them in such a way that they are clear to elementary school students. Each right is illustrated by an international array of well-known artists . . . [including] Bob Graham, . . . Alan Lee, . . . John Burningham, Niki Daly, Polly Dunbar, Jessica Souhami, and Satoshi Kitamura. This is an important book, best shared with children in a setting where discussion of both the rights and the illustrations is encouraged." SLJ

323.1 Civil and political rights of nondominant groups

Aretha, David

Sit-ins and freedom rides. Morgan Reynolds Pub. 2009 128p il lib bdg $28.95

Grades: 5 6 7 8   323.1

    1. African Americans—Civil rights 2. Southern States—Race relations

    ISBN 978-1-59935-098-1 (lib bdg); 1-59935-098-X (lib bdg)   LC 2008039600

"Aretha opens with an introduction to the four college students who orchestrated the famous sit-in at Woolworth's in Greensboro, NC, in 1960. He follows that with chapters that describe slavery, Reconstruction, and Jim Crow in terms of how they set the stage for the resistance efforts. . . . [The book] offers insight into to workings of the protests at the grassroots level. Individual anecdotes interspersed thoughout the detailed narrative provide personal and effective accounts that go beyond mere facts. Black-and-white and some color photographs appear on almost every page." SLJ

Includes bibliographical references

Bausum, Ann

Freedom Riders; John Lewis and Jim Zwerg on the front lines of the civil rights movement; by Ann Bausum; forewords by Freedom Riders Congressman John Lewis and Jim Zwerg. National Geographic 2006 79p il por $18.95; lib bdg $28.90

Grades: 5 6 7 8   323.1

    1. Lewis, John, 1940- 2. Zwerg, Jim, 1939- 3. African Americans—Civil rights 4. Southern States—Race relations

    ISBN 0-7922-4173-8; 0-7922-4174-6 (lib bdg)   LC 2005012947

"Eschewing a general overview of the 1961 Freedom Rides for specific, personal histories of real participants in the dangerous bus integration protests, Bausum focuses on two college students from strikingly different backgrounds: Jim Zwerg, a white Wisconsin native who became involved during an exchange visit to Nashville, and John Lewis, a black seminarian and student leader of the nonviolence movement." Booklist

"Bausum's narrative style, fresh, engrossing, and at times heart-stopping, brings the story of the turbulent and often violent dismantling of segregated travel alive in vivid detail. The language, presentation of material, and pacing will draw readers in and keep them captivated." SLJ

Includes bibliographical references

Brimner, Larry Dane, 1949-

Birmingham Sunday. Calkins Creek 2010 48p il $17.95 *

Grades: 5 6 7 8   323.1

    1. Sixteenth Street Baptist Church (Birmingham, Ala.) 2. Birmingham (Ala.)—Race relations 3. African Americans—Civil rights 4. Bombings 5. Hate crimes

    ISBN 978-1-59078-613-0; 1-59078-613-0   LC 2009-35716

"This moving photo-essay covers much more than just an account of the Birmingham, Alabama, Baptist Church bombing that killed four young girls in 1963. The detailed text, illustrated with black-and-white photos on every spacious double-page spread, sets the shocking assassination of the children within a general overview of both the racist segregation of the times and the struggle against it." Booklist

Freedman, Russell

Freedom walkers; the story of the Montgomery bus boycott. Holiday House 2006 114p il $18.95 *

Grades: 4 5 6 7   323.1

    1. Montgomery (Ala.)—Race relations 2. African Americans—Civil rights

    ISBN 978-0-8234-2031-5; 0-8234-2031-0   LC 2006-41148

This account of the Montgomery bus boycott of 1955 focuses on Jo Ann Robinson, Claudette Colvin, Rosa Parks, Martin Luther King, and other participants.

This offers "expertly paced text, balanced but impassioned. . . . The narrative arc is compelling; well-captioned black-and-white photographs enhance the impact." Horn Book

Includes bibliographical references

Holland, Leslie J.

Dr. Martin Luther King Jr.'s I have a dream speech in translation; what it really means. Capstone Press 2009 32p il (Fact finders. Kids' translations) lib bdg $23.99; pa $7.95

Grades: 3 4 5   323.1

    1. King, Martin Luther, Jr., 1929-1968 2. American speeches 3. African Americans—Civil rights

    ISBN 978-1-4296-2793-1 (lib bdg); 1-4296-2793-X (lib bdg); 978-1-4296-3449-6 (pa); 1-4296-3449-9 (pa)   LC 2008-32867

"Presents Dr. Martin Luther King Jr.'s speech and explains its meaning using everyday language. Describes the events that led to the speech and its significance through history." Publisher's note

Includes glossary and bibliographical references

King, Casey

Oh, freedom! kids talk about the Civil Rights Movement with the people who made it happen: illustrated with photographs; by Casey King and Linda Barrett Osborne; foreword by Rosa Parks; portraits by Joe Brooks. Knopf 1997 137p il hardcover o.p. pa $10.99

Grades: 5 6 7 8   323.1

    1. African Americans—Civil rights 2. United States—Race relations

    ISBN 0-679-85856-3; 0-679-89005-X (pa)   LC 96-13014

Interviews between young people and people who took part in the civil rights movement accompany essays that describe the history of efforts to make equality a reality for African Americans

"King and Osborne present a carefully unbiased overview of the civil rights movement. . . . But most

King, Casey—*Continued*

impressive is the way the authors use interesting interviews by students . . . [that] humanize history and add depth to the bare facts of the historical account." Book Rep

Includes bibliographical references

King, Martin Luther, Jr., 1929-1968

I have a dream; foreword by Coretta Scott King; paintings by fifteen Coretta Scott King Award and Honor Book artists, Ashley Bryan . . . [et al.] Scholastic 1997 40p il $16.95 *

Grades: K 1 2 3   323.1
1. African Americans—Civil rights 2. United States—Race relations
ISBN 0-590-20516-1   LC 95-45189

"Martin Luther King, Jr.'s classic speech is creatively illustrated by 15 Coretta Scott King Award-winning artists. Signed statements from the artists explain the emotions they were trying to capture and why and how they used certain colors and tones. . . . From cover to cover this is a beautiful book." SLJ

McClaurin, Irma

The civil rights movement; by Irma McClaurin. Marshall Cavendish Benchmark 2008 80p il (Drama of African-American history) lib bdg $23.95 *

Grades: 5 6 7 8   323.1
1. African Americans—Civil rights 2. United States—Race relations
ISBN 978-0-7614-2642-4

"Covers the struggle of African Americans to gain their civil rights, from Brown v. Board of Education in 1954 through the turbulent Sixties." Publisher's note

McWhorter, Diane

A dream of freedom; the Civil Rights Movement from 1954 to 1968; foreword by Reverend Fred Shuttlesworth. Scholastic Nonfiction 2004 160p il $19.95 *

Grades: 5 6 7 8   323.1
1. African Americans—Civil rights 2. United States—Race relations
ISBN 0-439-57678-4

The author discusses "the national civil rights movement from Brown v. the Board of Education to the assassination of Martin Luther King Jr. . . . This account is both factual and personal. She discusses her feelings as a white child in the South, and she focuses in on the many ways in which both white and black children were involved in the movement. . . . The breadth and depth of McWhorter's book is exemplary." Booklist

Pinkney, Andrea Davis

Sit-in; how four friends stood up by sitting down; [by] Andrea Davis Pinkney and Brian Pinkney. Little, Brown and Company 2010 unp il $16.99 *

Grades: K 1 2 3   323.1
1. African Americans—Civil rights 2. Southern States—Race relations
ISBN 978-0-316-07016-4; 0-316-07016-5
LC 2009-19470

"This compelling picture book is based on the historic sit-in 50 years ago by four college students who tried to integrate a Woolworth's lunch counter in Greensboro, North Carolina. Food-related wordplay adds layers to free verse. . . . At the core of the exciting narrative are scenes that show the difficulty of facing hatred. . . . Even young children will grasp the powerful, elemental, and historic story." Booklist

Rappaport, Doreen, 1939-

Nobody gonna turn me 'round; stories and songs of the civil rights movement; illustrated by Shane W. Evans. Candlewick Press 2006 63p il $19.99 *

Grades: 3 4 5 6   323.1
1. African Americans—Civil rights 2. United States—Race relations
ISBN 0-7636-1927-2; 978-0-7636-1927-5
LC 2005-53184

"Rappaport draws on songs, poems, memories, letters, court testimony, and first-person accounts to provide a moving portrayal of the experiences of African Americans from the 1955 Montgomery Bus Boycott to the Voting Rights Act in July 1965. . . . Evans's earth-toned oil paintings enhance the stories with images that are by turns poignant, sad, hurtful, resigned, determined, hopeful, and triumphant." SLJ

Includes bibliographical references

Shelton, Paula Young

Child of the civil rights movement; illustrated by Raul Colón. Schwartz & Wade Books 2010 unp il $17.99; lib bdg $20.99 *

Grades: K 1 2 3   323.1
1. Young, Andrew, 1932- 2. African Americans—Civil rights 3. Selma (Ala.)—Race relations
ISBN 978-0-375-84314-3; 0-375-84314-0; 978-0-375-95414-6 (lib bdg); 0-375-95414-7 (lib bdg)
LC 2008045855

The daughter of Andrew Young recalls her memories of her father and other African American Civil Rights activists, including Martin Luther King Jr., Dorothy Cotton and Ralph Abernathy, and the march from Selma to Montgomery Alabama.

"Colón's . . . soft-focus art features his customarily rich textural backdrop of speckles, scratches, and waves. Both contributors evoke the drama and emotion of the times . . . and a triumphal sense of community and family." Publ Wkly

Includes bibliographical references

Weatherford, Carole Boston, 1956-
The beatitudes; from slavery to civil rights; written by Carole Boston Weatherford; illustrated by Tim Ladwig. Eerdmans Books for Young Readers 2010 unp il $16.99

Grades: 1 2 3 4 **323.1**
1. African Americans—Civil rights 2. African Americans—History
ISBN 978-0-8028-5352-3; 0-8028-5352-8

"Using the Beatitudes of blessings found in the Sermon on the Mount as an underpinning, Weatherford . . . highlights the faith that bolstered the African American struggle for freedom and civil rights. . . . The words serve as a refrain to puncuate Ladwig's elegant watercolors and lend a dreamlike quality to the stirring depictions." Booklist

323.44 Freedom of action (Liberty)

Intellectual freedom manual; compiled by the Office for Intellectual Freedom of the American Library Association. 7th ed. American Library Association 2006 xx, 521p pa $57 *

Grades: Professional **323.44**
1. Intellectual freedom 2. Libraries—Censorship
ISBN 978- 0-8389-3561-3 (pa); 0-8389-3561-3 (pa)
LC 2005-22409

First published 1974

This guide to preserving intellectual freedom includes: ALA interpretations to the Library Bill of Rights; recommendations for special libraries and specific situations; information about legal decisions affecting school and public libraries; a section on the ALA's Intellectual Freedom Action Network.

"This manual details the professional standards to which librarians aspire and offers practical information about how to achieve those goals; it's a must for any librarian's professional library." Book Rep

Includes bibliographical references

Scales, Pat R.
Teaching banned books; 12 guides for young readers. American Library Association 2001 134p pa $28

Grades: Professional **323.44**
1. Books—Censorship 2. Children's literature—Study and teaching 3. School libraries
ISBN 0-8389-0807-1
LC 01-22340

The author "offers twelve strategies for teaching books that have been challenged or censored in the United States. Designed to accompany teaching about the First Amendment, 'each strategy includes a summary of the novel, a pre-reading activity, discussion questions to encourage critical thinking, and activities to broaden students' knowledge of topics in the novel.'" Bull Cent Child Books

"Scales knows her material inside out. She also knows how to inspire others to take up this cause and gives them an effective handbook to do just that." Booklist

Includes bibliographical references

323.6 Citizenship and related topics

Hamilton, John, 1959-
Becoming a citizen; [by] John Hamilton. ABDO Pub. Co. 2004 32p il (Government in action!) $22.78

Grades: 3 4 5 **323.6**
1. Citizenship 2. Naturalization
ISBN 1-59197-642-1
LC 2003-69698

This describes the process of naturalization, with samples of the documents required and questions from citizenship tests

This "has an interesting assortment of vintage and recent color photos, all well captioned, and is logically arranged." SLJ

Raum, Elizabeth
The Pledge of Allegiance in translation; what it really means; by Elizabeth Raum. Capstone Press 2009 32p il map (Fact finders. Kids' translations) lib bdg $23.93; pa $7.95

Grades: 3 4 5 **323.6**
1. Pledge of Allegiance
ISBN 978-1-4296-1931-8 (lib bdg); 1-4296-1931-7 (lib bdg); 978-1-4296-2846-4 (pa); 1-4296-2846-4 (pa)
LC 2007-51304

"Presents the full text of the Pledge of Allegiance in both its original version and in a translated version using everyday language. Describes the events that led to the creation of the pledge and its significance through history." Publisher's note

Provides "a nearly line-by-line translation that makes . . . the written word accessible and meaningful." SLJ

Includes glossary and bibliographical references

324 The political process

Christelow, Eileen, 1943-
Vote! Clarion 2003 47p il $16 *

Grades: K 1 2 3 **324**
1. Elections 2. Politics
ISBN 0-618-24754-8
LC 2002-152288

Using a campaign for mayor as an example, shows the steps involved in an election, from the candidate's speeches and rallies, to the voting booth where every vote counts, to the announcement of the winner

"It's hard to imagine a more accessible introduction to voting. The words are straightforward, the art whimsical and creative, and two darling dogs provide color commentary on the action." Booklist

Includes glossary

The **encyclopedia** of U.S. presidential elections; David C. Saffell, general editor. Franklin Watts 2004 128p il map (Watts reference) $39 *

Grades: 5 6 7 8 **324**
1. Presidents—United States—Election 2. Reference books
ISBN 0-531-12051-1
LC 2002-38009

The encyclopedia of U.S. presidential elections—*Continued*

Chronicles the candidates, issues, platforms, campaign slogans, and influences of presidential elections in the United States from 1789 through 2000

"Enjoyably readable, this compilation devotes a clearly written, two to three-page treatment to each election. . . . Casual readers will enjoy the way historical figures come to life, foibles and all." SLJ

Includes glossary and bibliographical references

Goodman, Susan, 1952-

See how they run; campaign dreams, election schemes, and the race to the White House; [by] Susan E. Goodman; illustrated by Elwood H. Smith. Bloomsbury Children's Books 2008 96p il lib bdg $16.95; pa $9.95 *

Grades: 4 5 6 7   324
1. Presidents—United States—Election
ISBN 978-1-59990-285-2 (lib bdg); 1-59990-285-0 (lib bdg); 978-1-59990-171-8 (pa); 1-59990-171-4 (pa)
LC 2007044452

"A lighthearted, fact-filled look at elections in the United States. The engaging conversational narrative and funny cartoons lend appealing irreverence to [the] topic. . . . The book covers a lot of ground and introduces concepts and personalities in ways that readers will understand and remember. Coverage includes the electoral college, campaigning, and many other aspects of elections. . . . Plentiful illustrations utilize humor to demonstrate content. . . . Informative, entertaining, and timely." SLJ

Includes bibliographical references

Hamilton, John, 1959-

Running for office; [by] John Hamilton. ABDO Pub. Co. 2005 32p il (Government in action!) $22.78

Grades: 3 4 5   324
1. Elections 2. Politics
ISBN 1-59197-822-X   LC 2004-46289

This describes a political campaign and discusses differences between Republicans and Democrats

This "book has an interesting assortment of vintage and recent color photos, all well captioned, and is logically arranged." SLJ

Includes bibliographical references

Steele, Philip

Vote. DK Pub. 2008 72p il (Eyewitness books) $15.99

Grades: 4 5 6 7 8   324
1. Elections
ISBN 978-0-7566-3382-0; 0-7566-3382-6

"Engaging visual material and a wealth of assorted facts trace the history of voting and its impact on human rights, politics, and other related areas. The first half moves chronologically from ancient Greece to modern times, with current information into the 21st century. Later sections look at political structures, election logistics, and even nongovernmental elections (including trade unions, the Oscars, and Britain's Pop Idol). Several high-quality photographs and reproductions appear on each spread. . . . The book does a nice job of pulling together an impressive array of topics, events, and ideas within the broad concept of global suffrage. The book comes with a poster-size wall chart and a clip-art CD with downloadable images of many of the illustrations." SLJ

Stier, Catherine

If I ran for president; illustrated by Lynne Avril. Albert Whitman & Co. 2007 unp il $16.99; pa $6.99 *

Grades: 1 2 3   324
1. Presidents—United States—Election
ISBN 978-0-8075-3543-1;   0-8075-3543-5; 978-0-8075-3544-5 (pa); 0-8075-3544-3 (pa)

"This candidate's eye view of a presidential campaign takes readers from initial questions . . . to the first day in the Oval Office." Booklist

"This title is a step above the usual election books, both in content and entertainment value. . . . The lively cartoons cheerfully clarify the action and reinforce the concepts." SLJ

Thomas, William David, 1947-

How do we elect our leaders? by William David Thomas. Gareth Stevens 2008 32p il map (My American government) lib bdg $23.93; pa $8.95

Grades: 3 4 5   324
1. Elections—United States 2. United States—Politics and government
ISBN 978-0-8368-8860-7   (lib   bdg); 978-0-8368-8865-2 (pa)   LC 2007028173

This describes the electoral process in the United States.

This book has "an accessible format and clear writing. . . . Black-and-white and full-color vintage and more recent photographs appear throughout." SLJ

Includes glossary and bibliographical references

Wagner, Heather Lehr

How the president is elected; [by] Heather Lehr Wagner. Chelsea House 2007 95p il map (The U.S. government: how it works) lib bdg $30

Grades: 5 6 7 8   324
1. Presidents—United States—Election
ISBN 978-0-7910-9418-1 (lib bdg); 0-7910-9418-9 (lib bdg)   LC 2006102365

"Wagner opens with the controversial election of 2000 between George W. Bush and Al Gore, and uses it as a springboard to discuss how the Electoral College works. Subsequent chapters discuss the two-party system, presidential campaigns, and what types of qualifications presidential candidates need. . . . The writing is clear and concise, facts are easy to find, and the prose is fluid." SLJ

Includes glossary and bibliographical references

325.73 Immigration to the United States

Bial, Raymond

Ellis Island; coming to the land of liberty. Houghton Mifflin Books for Children 2009 56p il $18

Grades: 4 5 6 7   325.73

1. Ellis Island Immigration Station 2. United States—Immigration and emigration

ISBN 978-0-618-99943-9; 0-618-99943-4

LC 2008-36794

"Bial examines the history of the famed immigration station. . . . He looks at the socio-historical roots of the mass exodus to America and provides a detailed look at the immigrant experience from ship to shore, with Ellis Island in between. Primary-source quotes and period photos pair eloquently with the modern narrative voice and color photographs of the museum exhibits. . . . The generously sized period photos and Bial's museum shots tell a vivid and poignant tale." SLJ

Includes bibliographical references

Freedman, Russell

Immigrant kids. Dutton 1980 72p il pa $8.99 hardcover o.p. *

Grades: 4 5 6 7   325.73

1. Children of immigrants 2. United States—Immigration and emigration 3. City and town life

ISBN 0-14-037594-5 (pa)   LC 79-20060

The author has "assembled an interesting collection of old photographs for a book that gives a broad view of the experiences of immigrant children in an urban environment. The text is divided into such areas as the journey to America, schools, play, work (much of it illegal), and home life. Photographs are carefully placed in relation to textual references, and the text itself is enlivened by quotations from the reminiscences of several people about their first days in the United States as child immigrants. Large, clear print and an index add to the book's usefulness." Horn Book

I was dreaming to come to America; memories from the Ellis Island Oral History Project; selected and illustrated by Veronica Lawlor; foreword by Rudolph W. Giuliani. Viking 1995 38p il hardcover o.p. pa $6.99 *

Grades: 4 5 6 7   325.73

1. Ellis Island Immigration Station 2. United States—Immigration and emigration

ISBN 0-670-86164-2; 0-14-055622-2 (pa)

LC 95-1281

In their own words, coupled with hand-painted collage illustrations, immigrants recall their arrival in the United States. Includes brief biographies and facts about the Ellis Island Oral History Project

"There is a flavor of Chagall in the peasant figures dancing above the ship or hopping ashore near the turreted towers of the huge building on Ellis Island. The elegant rendering offers a timeless view of this significant journey that is at once personal and universal." Horn Book

Kroll, Steven

Ellis Island; doorway to freedom; illustrated by Karen Ritz. Holiday House 1995 32p il maps $15.95

Grades: 3 4 5   325.73

1. Ellis Island Immigration Station 2. United States—Immigration and emigration

ISBN 0-8234-1192-3   LC 95-714

Describes how the immigration station on Ellis Island served as a gateway into the United States for more than sixteen million immigrants between 1892 and 1954

This is an "informative, approachable introduction. . . . Illustration done in pen and ink and in pencil and watercolor give an authentic, old-fashioned feeling to the artwork." Horn Book Guide

Includes glossary

Levine, Ellen, 1939-

. . . if your name was changed at Ellis Island; illustrated by Wayne Parmenter. Scholastic 1993 80p il pa $6.99 hardcover o.p. *

Grades: 3 4 5   325.73

1. Ellis Island Immigration Station 2. United States—Immigration and emigration

ISBN 0-590-43829-8 (pa)   LC 92-27940

Describes, in question and answer format, the great migration of immigrants to New York's Ellis Island, from the 1880s to 1914. Features quotes from children and adults who passed through the station

The author "writes in a clear, direct style that's packed with information and lively case histories. . . . There are many illustrations, sometimes full-page, sometimes small, in acrylic earth colors . . . they are an attractive part of a clear and accessible design." Booklist

Maestro, Betsy, 1944-

Coming to America: the story of immigration; illustrated by Susannah Ryan. Scholastic 1996 unp il $15.95 *

Grades: K 1 2 3   325.73

1. United States—Immigration and emigration

ISBN 0-590-44151-5   LC 94-31110

"In an introductory look at immigration, all inhabitants of the United States are considered immigrants or descendants of immigrants, whether they crossed the land bridge from Asia, came across the oceans voluntarily, or were brought as slaves. The clear, simple text and bright, animated illustrations convey excitement and adventure as well as hardship and loss." Horn Book Guide

Masoff, Joy, 1951-

We are all Americans; understanding diversity. Five Ponds 2006 63p il $26.50

Grades: 4 5 6 7   325.73

1. United States—Immigration and emigration 2. Multiculturalism

ISBN 0-9727156-2-2

"Gloriously supported by photographs, diagrams, and maps, this five-chapter overview offers information about America's immigrants. 'In the Beginning' describes diversity and how it is created. 'A New Start' focuses on the mechanisms in place for journeying from country to

Masoff, Joy, 1951-—*Continued*

country—passports and visas, Ellis Island and Angel Island. The most comprehensive section, 'Who Are We?,' chronicles those who have come from Africa, Asia, Europe, North America, South America, and Oceania to make a home in the United States. . . . 'Coming Together,' . . . features plants and animals, food, sports, games, holidays, and music from myriad backgrounds that Americans now enjoy. The last section, 'All Together Now,' discusses the strengths of diversity, featuring significant Americans." SLJ

Sandler, Martin W.

Island of hope; the story of Ellis Island and the journey to America. Scholastic Nonfiction 2004 144p il $18.95

Grades: 5 6 7 8   **325.73**

   1. Ellis Island Immigration Station 2. United States—Immigration and emigration

   ISBN 0-439-53082-2   LC 2003-54448

Relates the story of immigration to America through the voices and stories of those who passed through Ellis Island, from its opening in 1892 to the release of the last detainee in 1954.

"This engagingly written, inspirational account will give children, particularly immigrants or descendants of immigrants, some sharp insight into the trials and triumphs of their predecessors." Booklist

Includes bibliographical references

Solway, Andrew

Graphing immigration. Raintree 2010 32p il (Real world data) $28.21; pa $7.99

Grades: 4 5 6 7   **325.73**

   1. United States—Immigration and emigration 2. Statistics 3. Graphic methods

   ISBN   978-1-4329-2617-5;   1-4329-2617-9; 978-1-4329-2626-7 (pa); 1-4329-2626-8 (pa)

                     LC 2009001185

"A line graph in [this] title shows the estimated number of illegal immigrants in the U.S. from 1980 to 2005. Arguments about costs and benefits of all kinds of immigrants include a pie chart that shows where immigrants in the U.S. come from and pairs thoughts on why people migrate with a discussion of costs and benefits. . . . The clear design, with lots of full-color photos and sidebars, will encourage browsers as much as the up-to-date examples and the clear directions for remaining 'chart smart.'" Booklist

Includes glossary and bibliographical references

Staton, Hilarie

Ellis Island. Chelsea Clubhouse 2009 48p il (Symbols of American freedom) $30

Grades: 3 4 5   **325.73**

   1. Ellis Island Immigration Station 2. United States—Immigration and emigration 3. New York (N.Y.)

   ISBN 978-1-60413-519-0; 1-60413-519-0

                     LC 2009-12067

This book about Ellis Island Immigration Station "provides nearly as much information as a guided tour by a park ranger. [It begins] with the story of how the place

came to be, and where it fits into U.S. history. Information boxes offer additional background and some surprising facts, such as the stages an immigrant would pass through at Ellis Island. . . . The final chapter shows the landmark today and includes maps and photographs of the visitors' center and some of the things individuals might see or do while visiting the site. Much information is packed into [this] slim [book]. Excellent . . . for state reports or to complement U.S. history units." SLJ

Includes glossary

326   Slavery and emancipation

Bial, Raymond

The strength of these arms; life in the slave quarters. Houghton Mifflin 1997 40p il $16

Grades: 4 5 6 7   **326**

   1. Slavery—United States 2. Plantation life 3. African Americans—Social life and customs

   ISBN 0-395-77394-6   LC 96-39860

Describes how slaves were able to preserve some elements of their African heritage despite the often brutal treatment they experienced on Southern plantations

"This volume features clear, color photographs of plantation sites and artifacts, as well as a few early photos of people living under slavery. . . . This makes slavery in America more concrete than many other books on the subject." Booklist

Includes bibliographical references

The Underground Railroad. Houghton Mifflin 1995 48p il map hardcover o.p. pa $6.95

Grades: 4 5 6 7   **326**

   1. Underground railroad 2. Slavery—United States

   ISBN 0-395-69937-1; 0-395-97915-3 (pa)

                     LC 94-19614

Using first-person accounts, historical documents, and his own photographs, the author "focuses on the history of the Underground Railroad, building on the experiences of both riders and conductors as he outlines the political climate and the moral beliefs that allowed slavery to thrive and those that helped bring about its downfall." Publ Wkly

"Although the text covers ground often trodden by other works on this popular subject, Bial's shots of places and things which now appear tidy and innocent conjure spirits of desperate freedom-seekers as handily as do more detailed narratives." Bull Cent Child Books

Includes bibliographical references

Currie, Stephen, 1960-

Escapes from slavery; [by] Stephen Currie. Lucent Books 2003 112p il map (Great escapes) $28.70

Grades: 5 6 7 8   **326**

   1. Slavery—United States

   ISBN 1-59018-276-6   LC 2002-154078

Contents: Introduction: fugitive slaves; Ellen and William Craft; Josiah Henson; Harriet Tubman; William Wells Brown; Henry Brown

Narratives of five escapes from slavery, each of which was typical in many ways but featured unusual personal characteristics or circumstances that made these trips to

Currie, Stephen, 1960-—*Continued*

freedom extraordinary

"These exciting tales are written in lively language and are accompanied by black-and-white illustrations and informative sidebars." SLJ

Includes bibliographical references

Ford, Carin T.

Slavery and the underground railroad; bound for freedom. Enslow 2004 48p il map lib bdg $23.93

Grades: 3 4 5   326

1. Slavery—United States 2. Underground railroad 3. Abolitionists

ISBN 0-7660-2251-X   LC 2003-6824

Contents: The growth of slavery; The life of a slave; Running from slavery; Riding the underground railroad; Working on the railroad

This "explores the roots of the Civil War, and offers a profusion of true stories about 'passengers' and 'conductors' on the railroad. Well-chosen, primary-source quotations, culled from a variety of sources, bring the drama up close. . . . Compelling archival images illustrate . . . [this] thoughtfully executed [volume]." Booklist

Includes glossary and bibliographical references

Hamilton, Virginia, 1936-2002

Many thousand gone; African Americans from slavery to freedom; illustrated by Leo and Diane Dillon. Knopf 1993 151p il hardcover o.p. pa $12.95 *

Grades: 5 6 7 8   326

1. Underground railroad 2. Slavery—United States

ISBN 0-394-92873-3; 0-679-87936-6 (pa)

LC 89-19988

In this book the author tells "the story of slavery through a series of dramatic biographical vignettes. . . . Her book includes such famous historical figures as Frederick Douglass, Sojourner Truth and Harriet Tubman. She also presents some more obscure individuals. . . . All of these profiles drive home the sickening realities of slavery in a personal way. . . . These are powerful stories eloquently told." N Y Times Book Rev

Includes bibliographical references

Haskins, James, 1941-2005

Get on board: the story of the Underground Railroad. Scholastic 1993 152p il map hardcover o.p. pa $4.50

Grades: 5 6 7 8   326

1. Tubman, Harriet, 1820?-1913 2. Brown, John, b. ca. 1810 3. Underground railroad 4. Slavery—United States

ISBN 0-590-45419-6; 0-590-45418-8 (pa)

LC 92-13247

The author "relates the history of the Underground Railroad in the U.S., and introduces those who made it a success." SLJ

"Weaving together poignant personal stories and carefully researched historical data, Haskins has produced a stirring account of the founding and the workings of the Underground Railroad." Publ Wkly

Includes bibliographical references

Heinrichs, Ann

The Underground Railroad. Compass Point Bks. 2001 48p il map (We the people) lib bdg $21.26 *

Grades: 2 3 4   326

1. Underground railroad 2. Slavery—United States

ISBN 0-7565-0102-4   LC 00-11020

This book briefly describes the Underground Railroad, slavery, and important abolitionists in the U.S.

"Short chapters, succinct text, large print, and well-chosen illustrations make this book a good starting point for young readers embarking on a study of the topic." SLJ

Includes glossary and bibliographical references

Jordan, Anne Devereaux, 1943-

Slavery and resistance; by Anne Devereaux Jordan; with Virginia Schomp. Marshall Cavendish Benchmark 2007 70p il (Drama of African-American history) lib bdg $23.95

Grades: 5 6 7 8   326

1. Slavery—United States

ISBN 978-0-7614-2178-8 (lib bdg); 0-7614-2178-5 (lib bdg)   LC 2006012313

"Describes slavery in the United States from colonial times up to the Civil War." Publisher's note

This "is a standout, with elements both well done and well balanced. Foremost is the text, which is as engaging as it is solidly written. . . . The handsome art, which includes paintings and photos . . . is compelling." Booklist

Includes glossary and bibliographical references

Lester, Julius

From slave ship to freedom road; paintings by Rod Brown. Dial Bks. 1998 40p il hardcover o.p. pa $6.99 *

Grades: 5 6 7 8   326

1. Slavery—United States

ISBN 0-8037-1893-4; 0-14-056669-4 (pa)

LC 96-44422

"Lester uses empathy-provoking exercises, open-ended questions, and the paintings of Rod Brown to help readers understand the experience of African-American slaves." Bull Cent Child Books

"Lester's impassioned questions grow from his visceral response to Brown's narrative paintings. . . . The combination of history, art, and commentary demands interaction." Booklist

To be a slave; paintings by Tom Feelings. 30th anniversary ed. Dial Bks. 1998 160p il hardcover o.p. pa $6.99 *

Grades: 6 7 8 9   326

1. Slavery—United States

ISBN 0-8037-2347-4; 0-14-131001-4 (pa)

LC 98-5213

A reissue of the title first published 1968

"Through the words of the slave, interwoven with strongly sympathetic commentary, the reader learns what it is to be another man's property; how the slave feels about himself; and how he feels about others. Every aspect of slavery, regardless of how grim, has been pain-

Lester, Julius—*Continued*
fully and unrelentingly described." Read Ladders for Hum Relat. 6th edition

Includes bibliographical references

McKissack, Patricia C., 1944-
Rebels against slavery; by Patricia C. McKissack and Fredrick McKissack. Scholastic 1996 181p il $15.95
Grades: 5 6 7 8   326
    1. Slavery—United States
    ISBN 0-590-45735-7   LC 94-41089
    A Coretta Scott King honor book for text, 1997
The authors "explore slave revolts and the men and women who led them, weaving a tale of courage and defiance in the face of tremendous odds. Readers learn not only about Nat Turner and Denmark Vesey, but also about Cato, Gabriel Prosser, the maroons, and the relationship between escaped slaves and Seminole Indians. The activities of abolitionists are described as well. The authors' careful research, sensitivity, and evenhanded style reveal a sad, yet inspiring story of the will to be free." SLJ

Newman, Shirlee Petkin, 1924-
Child slavery in modern times; [by] Shirlee P. Newman. Watts 2000 63p il (Watts library) lib bdg $24
Grades: 5 6 7 8   326
    1. Child abuse 2. Child labor 3. Slavery
    ISBN 0-531-11696-4   LC 00-38199
Discusses cases where children are forced to work against their wills in difficult and dangerous conditions in various countries around the world
This "includes numerous black-and-white and color photographs of exploited young people, guaranteed to raise readers' level of consciousness." SLJ

Includes bibliographical references

Rappaport, Doreen, 1939-
No more! stories and songs of slave resistance; illustrated by Shane Evans. Candlewick Press 2002 60p il $17.99; pa $7.99 *
Grades: 3 4 5 6   326
    1. Slavery
    ISBN 0-7636-0984-6; 0-7636-2876-X (pa)
                     LC 00-29756
"Rappaport has collected slave narratives, biographies, and songs that tell the history of resistance from the Middle Passage to the plantation and then the Underground Railroad and the Civil War." Booklist
"Evans's large, bold, dramatic oil paintings capture the despair, fear, and hope of the slaves. Taken together, the text and illustrations make a powerful statement." SLJ

Sharp, S. Pearl
The slave trade and the middle passage; by S. Pearl Sharp with Virginia Schomp. Marshall Cavendish Benchmark 2007 70p il map (Drama of African-American history) lib bdg $34.21
Grades: 5 6 7 8   326
    1. Slave trade 2. Slavery
    ISBN 978-0-7614-2176-4 (lib bdg); 0-7614-2176-9 (lib bdg)   LC 2006005321
"Traces the history of the transatlantic slave trade and the development of slavery in the New World." Publisher's note

Includes glossary and bibliographical references

327   International relations

Deedy, Carmen Agra
14 cows for America; [by] Carmen Agra Deedy in collaboration with Wilson Kimeli Naiyomah; illustrated by Thomas Gonzalez. Peachtree 2009 unp il $17.95
Grades: K 1 2 3   327
    1. September 11 terrorist attacks, 2001 2. Masai (African people) 3. Kenya
    ISBN 978-1-56145-490-7; 1-56145-490-7
"A native of Kenya, Naiyomah was in New York City on September 11, 2001. In his and Deedy's . . . lyrical account, he returns to his homeland and tells the members of his Maasai tribe the story that had 'burned a hole in his heart.' . . . Featuring luminous images . . . Gonzalez's pastel, colored pencil and airbrush paintings appear almost three-dimensional in their realism. A moving tale of compassion and generosity." Publ Wkly

327.1   Foreign policy and specific topics in international relations

Kerley, Barbara
A little peace; by Barbara Kerley; with a note by Richard H. Solomon. National Geographic 2007 unp il $16.95; lib bdg $25.90
Grades: 1 2 3 4   327.1
    1. Peace
    ISBN   978-1-4263-0086-8;   1-4263-0086-7; 978-1-4263-0087-5 (lib bdg); 1-4263-0087-5 (lib bdg)
                     LC 2006026367
Juxtaposes photographs from around the world with a simple message about our responsibilities for making and keeping peace on the planet.
This is a "simple, beautiful photo-essay. . . . The colorful pictures are supported by limited, yet powerful text, illustrating how each person can work to achieve peace." SLJ

Includes bibliographical references

327.12   Espionage and subversion

Earnest, Peter

The real spy's guide to becoming a spy; by Peter Earnest and Suzanne Harper, in association with the Spy Museum. Abrams Books for Young Readers 2009 144p il $16.95

Grades: 4 5 6 7   327.12

1. Spies 2. Intelligence service 3. Espionage
ISBN 978-0-8109-8329-8; 0-8109-8329-X
LC 2009-00518

"This guide, written by the executive director of the International Spy Museum, gives readers a glimpse at how spies work. Along with descriptions of the different types of intelligence officers and agencies and the tasks they perform, the text includes brief stories of spies in action." Horn Book Guide

Fridell, Ron, 1943-

Spy technology. Lerner Publications Co. 2007 48p il (Cool science) lib bdg $27.93; pa $8.95

Grades: 4 5 6 7   327.12

1. Espionage
ISBN 978-0-8225-5934-4 (lib bdg); 0-8225-5934-X (lib bdg); 978-0-8225-6675-5 (pa); 0-8225-6675-3 (pa)
LC 2005-33043

Readers of this book "will be delighted to learn that such ingenius gadgets as pistols in lipstick cases are not just the stuff of James Bond, but have been used by organizations like the CIA and the KGB. . . . This attractive book is an excellent introduction to the motivations of governments to look into the military and political secrets of enemy groups as well as within their own countries." SLJ

Includes bibliographical references

Gilbert, Adrian

Secret agents. Firefly 2009 32p il (Spy files) pa $6.95

Grades: 3 4 5 6   327.12

1. Secret service 2. Spies
ISBN 978-1-55407-574-4; 1-55407-574-2

First published 2008 in the United Kingdom

Discusses American, British, and Russian spies and secret agents, and the history of espionage. Includes profiles of famous spies and double agents.

The text's "short paragraphs and great pictures are combined in a collage style that will draw readers quickly through the information. Useful for reports and browsing." SLJ

Includes glossary

Spy school. Firefly 2009 32p il (Spy files) pa $6.95

Grades: 3 4 5 6   327.12

1. Espionage 2. Spies
ISBN 978-1-55407-575-1 (pa); 1-55407-575-0 (pa)

"Gilbert reveals how spies are recruited and trained, discussing methods of disguise, surveillance, interrogation, evasion, and escape. . . . The [text's] short paragraphs and great pictures are combined in a collage style that will draw readers quickly through the information. Useful for reports and browsing." SLJ

Includes glossary

Spyology; the complete book of spycraft. Candlewick Press 2008 unp il $22.99 *

Grades: 3 4 5 6   327.12

1. Espionage 2. Spies
ISBN 978-0-7636-4048-4; 0-7636-4048-4

This "poses as a collection of items assembled in 1958 and stored in national archives, now declassified under the 'fifty-year rule.' Agent K, a British spy, is tracking down the evil international Operation Codex, using his mission to ground a training manual for spies. Readers can match wits with Agent K as they pick up clues." Publ Wkly

328.73   Legislative process in the United States

Hamilton, John, 1959-

How a bill becomes a law; [by] John Hamilton. ABDO Pub. Co. 2004 32p il (Government in action!) lib bdg $15.95

Grades: 3 4 5   328.73

1. Legislation 2. Law
ISBN 1-59197-646-4   LC 2003-69305

This describes the steps in passing a federal law in the United States

This "book has an interesting assortment of vintage and recent color photos, all well captioned, and is logically arranged." SLJ

Obama, Barack, 1961-

Change has come; an artist celebrates our American spirit; the drawings of Kadir Nelson; with the words of Barack Obama. Simon & Schuster 2009 unp il $12.99

Grades: 1 2 3   328.73

1. Presidents—United States—Election—2008 2. United States—Politics and government—2001-
ISBN 978-1-4169-8955-4; 1-4169-8955-2

"Weaving Obama's words with his own extraordinary graphite drawings, Nelson has created a moving celebration of the election of our 44th president." SLJ

331.1   Labor force and market

Lynette, Rachel

What to do when your parent is out of work. PowerKids Press 2010 24p il (Let's work it out) lib bdg $21.25; pa $8.25

Grades: 2 3 4   331.1

1. Unemployed
ISBN 978-1-4358-9338-2 (lib bdg); 1-4358-9338-7 (lib bdg); 978-1-4358-9764-9 (pa); 1-4358-9764-1 (pa)
LC 2009-23067

A guide to unemployment, what it is, what it may mean for your family, and how you can help.

"Full-page color photographs appear opposite the [narrative], depicting multicultural children, parents, grandparents, social workers, and others, whose demeanors match the hopeful tone of the [title]. This . . . will help promote empathy and understanding for the plight of others and is a key purchase." SLJ

Includes glossary

331.3   Workers by age group

Bartoletti, Susan Campbell, 1958-
Growing up in coal country. Houghton Mifflin 1996 127p il $17; pa $7.95 *
Grades: 5 6 7 8   **331.3**
1. Child labor 2. Coal mines and mining
ISBN 0-395-77847-6; 0-395-97914-5 (pa)
LC 96-3142

This is an "account of working and living conditions in Pennsylvania coal towns. The first half of the volume details various duties in the mines, from jobs performed by the youngest boys to the tasks of adult miners, while the second half describes the company village, common customs and recreational activities, and the accidents and diseases that frequently beset the workers." Horn Book

"With compelling black-and-white photographs of children at work in the coal mines of northeastern Pennsylvania about 100 years ago, this handsome, spacious photo-essay will draw browsers as well as students doing research on labor and immigrant history." Booklist

Includes bibliographical references

Brown, Don, 1949-
Kid Blink beats the world. Roaring Brook Press 2004 unp il $16.95 *
Grades: 2 3 4   **331.3**
1. Newspaper carriers 2. Strikes 3. Child labor 4. New York (N.Y.)—History
ISBN 1-59643-003-6   LC 2003-21896

This "details the events in the summer of 1899, during which hundreds of young news vendors stood up to two of the most powerful men in the U.S.—William Randolph Hearst and Joseph Pulitzer." Booklist

"The accessible text presents a cogent, kid-empowering tale of underprivileged youngsters whose actions really made a difference . . . The loosely drawn pencil-and-watercolor illustrations convey great energy." Horn Book

Freedman, Russell
Kids at work; Lewis Hine and the crusade against child labor; with photographs by Lewis Hine. Clarion Bks. 1994 104p il $20; pa $9.95 *
Grades: 5 6 7 8   **331.3**
1. Hine, Lewis Wickes, 1874-1940 2. Child labor
ISBN 0-395-58703-4; 0-395-79726-8 (pa)
LC 93-5989

"Using the photographer's work throughout, Freedman provides a documentary account of child labor in America during the early 1900s and the role Lewis Hine played in the crusade against it. He offers a look at the man behind the camera, his involvement with the National Child Labor Committee, and the dangers he faced trying to document unjust labor conditions." SLJ

Freedman "does an outstanding job of integrating historical photographs with meticulously researched and highly readable prose." Publ Wkly

Includes bibliographical references

331.4   Women workers

Colman, Penny
Rosie the riveter; women working on the home front in World War II. Crown 1995 120p il hardcover o.p. pa $10.99 *
Grades: 5 6 7 8   **331.4**
1. Women—Employment 2. World War, 1939-1945—United States
ISBN 0-517-59790-X; 0-517-88567-0 (pa)
LC 94-3614

This is an account of women's employment in wartime industry during the Second World War. "Colman looks at the jobs women took, the impact women had on the workplace, and what happened to working women at war's end. . . . [She also discusses] the public relations campaign that not only 'wooed' women into the workplace, but also sought to change firmly entrenched attitudes about women's role in society." Booklist

"A thoughtfully prepared look at women's history and wartime society, this dynamic book is characterized by extensive research." Horn Book

Includes bibliographical references

331.7   Labor by industry and occupation

Coulter, Laurie
Cowboys and coffin makers; one hundred 19th-century jobs you might have feared or fancied; by Laurie Coulter; art by Martha Newbigging. Annick Press 2007 96p il $25.95; pa $16.95 *
Grades: 3 4 5 6   **331.7**
1. Occupations 2. World history—19th century
ISBN   978-1-55451-068-9;   1-55451-068-6; 978-1-55451-067-2 (pa); 1-55451-067-8 (pa)

"Short job descriptions, usually one or two per page, are written in an entertaining style and grouped according to headings. . . . The author considers a variety of economic and social classes, from robber barons to forced laborers and slaves, and acknowledges how locations affect available occupations. . . . Bright watercolor, cartoon-style illustrations accompany each job description." SLJ

Hopkinson, Deborah
Up before daybreak; cotton and people in America. Scholastic Nonfiction 2005 120p il $18.99 *
Grades: 5 6 7 8   **331.7**
1. Cotton 2. Textile industry—History 3. Working class
ISBN 0-439-63901-8   LC 2005-8128

"From the industrial revolution to the 1950s demise of the Lowell cotton mills, Hopkinson discusses the history and sociology of king cotton, frequently emphasizing the children who labored under slave masters, endured dead-end mill jobs, or helped sharecropping parents claw out a living. . . . Stories of real people . . . sharply focus

Hopkinson, Deborah—*Continued*
the dramatic history, as do arresting archival photos of stern youngsters manipulating hoes, cotton sags, or bobbins." Booklist

331.8 Labor unions, labor-management bargaining and disputes

Bartoletti, Susan Campbell, 1958-
Kids on strike! Houghton Mifflin 1999 208p il $20; pa $8.95 *
Grades: 5 6 7 8   **331.8**
    1. Jones, Mother, 1830-1930 2. Strikes 3. Child labor
    ISBN 0-395-88892-1; 0-618-36923-6 (pa)
                                        LC 98-50575
Describes the conditions and treatment that drove workers, including many children, to various strikes, from the mill workers strikes in 1828 and 1836 and the coal strikes at the turn of the century to the work of Mother Jones on behalf of child workers
"This well-researched and well-illustrated account creates a vivid portrait of the working conditions of many American children in the 19th and early 20th centuries." SLJ
Includes bibliographical references

332.024 Personal finance

Bochner, Arthur Berg
The new totally awesome money book for kids (and their parents); [by] Arthur Bochner & Rose Bochner; foreword by Adriane G. Berg. 3rd ed., rev & updated. Newmarket Press 2007 189p il pa $9.95
Grades: 4 5 6 7   **332.024**
    1. Personal finance
    ISBN 978-1-55704-738-0   LC 2006038930
First published 1993 with title: The totally awesome money book for kids (and their parents)
An introduction to money for kids including the basics of saving, investing, working, and taxes.
"Using an easy and comfortable style that young people will find unthreatening, the book presents a wealth of information. . . . The cute illustrations are also fun." Voice Youth Advocates
Includes bibliographical references

Hall, Alvin
Show me the money; [by] Alvin Hall. DK 2008 96p il $15.99 *
Grades: 4 5 6   **332.024**
    1. Personal finance 2. Money
    ISBN 978-0-7566-3762-0; 0-7566-3762-7
"Four main sections cover the history of money, expenses/income, the basics of economics, and the world of work and business. Brief profiles of eight wealthy entrepreneurs and their paths to prosperity and eight significant economists and their theories are included. The lively writing features real-life examples that will be meaningful to students and is presented in a balanced, nonjudgmental style that encourages them to decide for themselves among the various ideas concerning economic policies. . . . Color photos and graphics excel at conveying the concepts presented and represent diversity well." SLJ
Includes glossary

Hall, Margaret, 1947-
Your allowance. [2nd ed] Heinemann Library 2008 32p il (Earning, saving, spending) $25.36; pa $7.99
Grades: 3 4 5   **332.024**
    1. Personal finance
    ISBN   978-1-4034-9817-5;   1-4034-9817-2;
    978-1-4034-9822-9 (pa); 1-4034-9822-9 (pa)
                                        LC 2007015113
Also available Spanish language edition
First published 2000
Offers young people information on how to manage the money they have, providing advice on spending, saving, and donating money to help others
Includes bibliographical references

Holyoke, Nancy
A smart girl's guide to money; how to make it, save it, and spend it; illustrated by Ali Douglass. Pleasant Co. 2006 95p il pa $9.95 *
Grades: 4 5 6 7   **332.024**
    1. Personal finance
    ISBN 1-59369-103-3
"American Girl"
This "offers advice on earning, saving, and spending money. Holyoke addresses topics such as feelings about money, launching a business, becoming a smart shopper, and investing. . . . The text is upbeat and informal. . . . This book is an engaging introduction to personal economics." Booklist

Lynette, Rachel
What to do when your family has to cut costs. PowerKids Press 2010 24p il (Let's work it out) lib bdg $21.25; pa $8.25
Grades: 2 3 4   **332.024**
    1. Personal finance
    ISBN 978-1-4358-9340-5 (lib bdg); 1-4358-9340-9 (lib bdg); 978-1-4358-9768-7 (pa); 1-4358-9768-4 (pa)
                                        LC 2009-23737
Learn about prioritizing needs over wants and ways to be cost-conscious and frugal.
"Full-page color photographs appear opposite the [narrative], depicting multicultural children, parents, grandparents, social workers, and others, whose demeanors match the hopeful tone of the [title]. This . . . will help promote empathy and understanding for the plight of others and is a key purchase." SLJ
Includes glossary

Lynette, Rachel—*Continued*

What to do when your family is in debt. PowerKids Press 2010 24p il (Let's work it out) lib bdg $21.25; pa $8.25

Grades: 2 3 4   **332.024**

1. Consumer credit 2. Debt

ISBN 978-1-4358-9341-2 (lib bdg); 1-4358-9341-7 (lib bdg); 978-1-4358-9770-0 (pa); 1-4358-9770-6 (pa)

A guide to debt, what it is, what it may mean for your family, and how you can help.

"Full-page color photographs appear opposite the [narrative], depicting multicultural children, parents, grandparents, social workers, and others, whose demeanors match the hopeful tone of the [title]. This . . . will help promote empathy and understanding for the plight of others and is a key purchase." SLJ

Includes glossary

Morrison, Jessica

Saving. Weigl Publishers 2009 32p il (Everyday economics) lib bdg $26; pa $9.95

Grades: 5 6 7   **332.024**

1. Saving and investment

ISBN 978-1-60596-647-2 (lib bdg); 1-60596-647-9 (lib bdg); 978-1-60596-648-9 (pa); 1-60596-648-7 (pa)

LC 2009018567

This "informative [book introduces savings in] U.S. economic theory and practices using everyday language and real-life examples. [It] includes history, a brief annotated chronology, sidebar and intext explanations of terminology, and helpful diagrams. . . . With brief paragraphs; large, captioned photographs; ample margins; and well-organized graphics, the [book's] design makes economics accessible without sacrificing content. . . . [This is] easy to navigate and full of solid information and interesting facts." SLJ

Includes glossary

Roderick, Stacey

Centsibility; the Planet Girl guide to money; [by] Stacey Roderick and Ellen Warwick; illustrated by Monika Melnychuk. Kids Can Press 2008 80p il (Planet girl) $12.95

Grades: 5 6 7 8   **332.024**

1. Personal finance

ISBN 978-1-55453-208-7

"This book presents handy methods for managing money. . . . Chapters are broken down into subsections . . . which are peppered with quizzes and craft projects to keep readers engaged. . . . The book's sound advice is both practical and approachable." Horn Book Guide

Thomas, Keltie

The kids guide to money cent$; written by Keltie Thomas; illustrated by Stephen MacEachern. Kids Can Press 2004 56p il $14.95; pa $7.95

Grades: 4 5 6   **332.024**

1. Personal finance

ISBN 1-55337-389-8; 1-55337-391-X (pa)

"As a social-studies assignment, Alicia, Dan, and Jeff form the Money Cent$ Gang and embark on a journey into the world of consumerism, banks, credit cards, phi-

lanthropy, employment, and the stock market. Complex subjects are presented in short, easy-to-understand chapters. . . . Explanations are clear, concise, and age appropriate. . . . The accessible layout and colorful cartoon artwork will grab readers' attention." SLJ

Wiseman, Blaine

Budgeting. Weigl Publishers 2009 32p il (Everyday economics) lib bdg $26; pa $9.95

Grades: 5 6 7   **332.024**

1. Budget

ISBN 978-1-60596-643-4 (lib bdg); 1-60596-643-6 (lib bdg); 978-1-60596-644-1 (pa); 1-60596-644-4 (pa)

LC 2009018439

This "informative [book introduces budgeting in] U.S. economic theory and practices using everyday language and real-life examples. [It] includes history, a brief annotated chronology, sidebar and intext explanations of terminology, and helpful diagrams. . . . With brief paragraphs; large, captioned photographs; ample margins; and well-organized graphics, the [book's] design makes economics accessible without sacrificing content. . . . [This is] easy to navigate and full of solid information and interesting facts." SLJ

Includes glossary

332.1 Banks

Hall, Margaret, 1947-

Banks; [by] Margaret Hall. 2nd ed. Heinemann Library 2008 32p il (Earning, saving, spending) lib bdg $28.21; pa $7.95

Grades: 1 2 3   **332.1**

1. Banks and banking

ISBN 978-1-4034-9814-4 (lib bdg); 978-1-4034-9819-9 (pa)   LC 2007015147

First published 2000

"This book looks at the history of banks and how they help people take care of their money." Publisher's note

"Illustrated with sharp, clear photographs, each spread presents a different concept in a logical procession. The author uses simple sentences, highlighting important words." SLJ

Includes glossary and bibliographical references

332.4 Money

Adler, David A., 1947-

Money madness; by David A. Adler; illustrated by Edward Miller. Holiday House 2009 unp il $16.95 *

Grades: PreK K 1 2   **332.4**

1. Money

ISBN 978-0-8234-1474-1; 0-8234-1474-4

LC 2008004223

"This brightly illustrated picture book introduces the concept of money, first by looking at its development as an alternative to bartering and then by explaining the many forms of money, from primitive rocks, feathers, and metal lumps to the familiar coins and paper bills to

Adler, David A., 1947-—_Continued_

alternatives such as checks, credit cards, and digital forms of payment. Adler does a particularly good job explaining the inconvenience of bartering through child-friendly examples. . . . Using flat colors and stylized designs, Miller's upbeat digital artwork helps to clarify points made in the text, while adding occasional bits of visual humor. Photos of coins and bills are incorporated where appropriate." Booklist

Cribb, Joe

Money; written by Joe Cribb. rev ed. DK Pub. 2005 72p il (DK eyewitness books) lib bdg $15.99 *

Grades: 4 5 6 7   332.4

  1. Money

  ISBN 0-7566-1389-2

First published 1990 by Knopf

Examines, in text and photographs, the symbolic and material meaning of money, from shekels, shells, and beads to gold, silver, checks, and credit cards. Also discusses how coins and banknotes are made, the value of money during wartime, and how to collect coins

Forest, Christopher

The dollar bill in translation; what it really means. Capstone Press 2009 32p il (Fact finders. Kids' translations) lib bdg $23.99; pa $7.95

Grades: 3 4 5   332.4

  1. Dollar 2. Paper money 3. Signs and symbols 4. Money

  ISBN 978-1-4296-2794-8 (lib bdg); 1-4296-2794-8 (lib bdg); 978-1-4296-3448-9 (pa); 1-4296-3448-0 (pa)

                             LC 2008-28981

"Presents the dollar bill and explains its meaning and symbolism using everyday language. Describes the events that led to the creation of currency and its significance through history." Publisher's note

Includes glossary and bibliographical references

Kummer, Patricia K.

Currency; [by] Patricia K. Kummer. Franklin Watts 2004 80p il (Inventions that shaped the world) lib bdg $30.50; pa $9.95

Grades: 4 5 6 7   332.4

  1. Money

  ISBN 0-531-12341-3 (lib bdg); 0-531-16734-8 (pa)

                             LC 2003-16309

Contents: What is currency?; Barter and early currency; Important developers of modern currency; Development of modern currency: coins and paper money; Role of currency in daily life and in the life of countries

"Kummer covers the history of currency around the world, how money is made, and its prospective use in the future. Information about early barter systems and the role that currency plays in modern society are also included. . . . [The book has] appropriate color and black-and-white photographs, reproductions, and/or diagrams on virtually every spread. [This offering is an] excellent [resource] for reports and should also appeal to readers." SLJ

Leedy, Loreen, 1959-

Follow the money! written and illustrated by Loreen Leedy. Holiday House 2002 unp il $16.95; pa $6.95 *

Grades: K 1 2 3   332.4

  1. Money 2. Coins

  ISBN 0-8234-1587-2; 0-8234-1794-8 (pa)

                             LC 2001-39418

A quarter describes all the ways it is used from the time it is minted until it is taken back to a bank

"Leedy includes a good deal of information, while keeping the book light, energetic, and entertaining." Booklist

Includes glossary

Maestro, Betsy, 1944-

The story of money; illustrated by Giulio Maestro. Clarion Bks. 1993 43p il maps $17; pa $7.99

Grades: 3 4 5   332.4

  1. Money

  ISBN 0-395-56242-2; 0-688-13304-5 (pa)

                             LC 91-24997

A history of money, beginning with the barter system in ancient times, to the first use of coins and paper money, to the development of modern monetary systems

"A successful, readable presentation of a complicated subject. . . . Giulio Maestro's meticulously drawn watercolor illustrations brighten each page." SLJ

Orr, Tamra

Coins and other currency; a kid's guide to coin collecting; by Tamra Orr. Mitchell Lane Publishers 2009 48p il map (Money matters: a kid's guide to money) lib bdg $29.95

Grades: 4 5 6   332.4

  1. Money 2. Coins

  ISBN 978-1-58415-640-6 (lib bdg); 1-58415-640-6 (lib bdg)   LC 2008-2262

"When Charlie brings a box of his grandpa's old coins to school, his classmates want to learn . . . about collecting coins and other currency. . . . [This book describes] how the idea of money started and the . . . things people used before they invented metal coins and paper bills; . . . how coins are made, what secrets can be found on a dollar bill, and how to start your own coin collection; . . . [and] facts about the history and culture of currency from countries all over the world." Publisher's note

"Photos feature multigenerational and diverse subjects and illustrate related locations and historical figures, while graphs and sidebars enhance the [text]. Well-documented and informative." SLJ

Includes glossary and bibliographical references

Robinson, Elizabeth Keeler, 1959-

Making cents; by Elizabeth Keeler Robinson; illustrated by Bob McMahon. Tricycle Press 2008 unp il $14.95

Grades: K 1 2   332.4

  1. Money 2. Arithmetic

  ISBN 978-1-58246-214-1   LC 2007018197

Robinson, Elizabeth Keeler, 1959-—*Continued*
"This book introduces American coins and paper money in a clear and entertaining way. A group of children from a variety of ethnic backgrounds is hard at work earning money, saving, and planning for a neighborhood clubhouse. Readers see the purchasing power of the different coins and bills in terms of nails, screws, marking pencils, sandpaper, and other building supplies. They also view different ways that coins can be combined to equal a nickel, dime, quarter, dollar, etc. . . . The text is well paced, and the layout is attractive. . . . The colorful . . . computer-generated cartoons have child appeal." SLJ

332.6   Investment

Minden, Cecilia, 1949-
Investing; making your money work for you. Cherry Lake Pub. 2008 32p il (Real world math: personal finance) lib bdg $25.26
Grades: 3 4 5 6   332.6
    1. Investments 2. Personal finance
    ISBN 978-1-60279-003-2 (lib bdg); 1-60279-003-5 (lib bdg)   LC 2007005917
This "examines the importance of short-term and long-term savings and explains the pros and cons of savings accounts, certificates of deposit, government bonds, and stocks. Engaging full-color photographs on every page feature diverse children and families, and plenty of white space." SLJ
    Includes bibliographical references

Morrison, Jessica
Investing. Weigl Publishers 2009 32p il (Everyday economics) lib bdg $26; pa $9.95
Grades: 5 6 7   332.6
    1. Investments
    ISBN 978-1-60596-649-6 (lib bdg); 1-60596-649-5 (lib bdg); 978-1-60596-650-2 (pa); 1-60596-650-9 (pa)   LC 2009018568
This explains the advantages of investing money, how to read a stock report, interest, and the types of investments provided by different companies.
This "informative [book introduces] U.S. economic theory and practices using everyday language and real-life examples. . . . [This is] easy to navigate and full of solid information and interesting facts." SLJ
    Includes glossary

332.7   Credit

Hall, Margaret, 1947-
Credit cards and checks; [by] Margaret Hall. 2nd ed. Heinemann Library 2008 32p il (Earning, saving, spending) lib bdg $28.21; pa $7.99
Grades: 1 2 3   332.7
    1. Credit cards 2. Debit cards 3. Personal finance
    ISBN   978-1-4034-9816-8   (lib   bdg); 978-1-4034-9821-2 (pa)   LC 2007015150
    First published 2000

This offers an overview of spending money without using cash, including details on credit, checkbooks, debt and interest.
"Illustrated with sharp, clear photographs, each spread presents a different concept in a logical procession. The author uses simple sentences, highlighting important words." SLJ
    Includes glossary and bibliographical references

Tomljanovic, Tatiana
Borrowing. Weigl Pub. 2009 32p il (Everyday economics) lib bdg $26; pa $9.95
Grades: 5 6 7   332.7
    1. Credit
    ISBN 978-1-60596-645-8 (lib bdg); 1-60596-645-2 (lib bdg); 978-1-60596-646-5 (pa); 1-60596-646-0 (pa)   LC 2009018444
This "informative [book introduces borrowing in] U.S. economic theory and practices using everyday language and real-life examples. [It] includes history, a brief annotated chronology, sidebar and intext explanations of terminology, and helpful diagrams. . . . With brief paragraphs; large, captioned photographs; ample margins; and well-organized graphics, the [book's] design makes economics accessible without sacrificing content. . . . [This is] easy to navigate and full of solid information and interesting facts." SLJ
    Includes glossary

333.7   Land, recreational and wilderness areas, energy

Gazlay, Suzy
Managing green spaces; careers in wilderness and wildlife management. Crabtree 2010 64p il (Green-collar careers) lib bdg $30.60; pa $10.95
Grades: 4 5 6 7   333.7
    1. Wilderness areas 2. Wildlife 3. Vocational guidance
    ISBN 978-0-7787-4855-7 (lib bdg); 0-7787-4855-3 (lib bdg); 978-0-7787-4866-3 (pa); 0-7787-4866-9 (pa)   LC 2009-28145
"Passions often lead to professions, as this upbeat title . . . shows. . . . There is inevitable overlap among the categories: government-run parks and forestry, outdoor adventure, science, and wildlife sanctuaries. The browsable format, combining many crisp color photos with blocks of narrative texts and sidebars featuring specific ecoprofessionals, will easily lead students through the survey of nature-focused careers." Booklist

333.72   Conservation and protection

Dell, Pamela
Protecting the planet; environmental activism. Compass Point Books 2010 64p il (Green generation) lib bdg $31.99; pa $6.95
Grades: 5 6 7 8 9   333.72
    1. Environmental movement 2. Environmental protection
    ISBN 978-0-7565-4248-1 (lib bdg); 0-7565-4248-0 (lib bdg); 978-0-7565-4295-5 (pa); 0-7565-4295-2 (pa)   LC 2009-8782

Dell, Pamela—_Continued_

"The cover design, layout, and graphics feel hip and of the moment. The clear writing is easy to understand and includes many concrete examples of environmentally friendly practices. . . . [A] good choice[s] for both leisure reading and reports." SLJ

Includes glossary and bibliographical references

Fuoco, Gina Dal

Earth. Compass Point Books 2009 40p il (Mission: science) lib bdg $26.60

Grades: 4 5 6   **333.72**
1. Earth
ISBN 978-0-7565-4070-8 (lib bdg); 0-7565-4070-4 (lib bdg)   LC 2008-37575
Discusses the basic parts systems (atmosphere, hydrosphere, and geosphere) of Earth and how important it is to protect Earth's resources
Includes glossary

Hewitt, Sally

Your local environment. Crabtree Pub. Co. 2009 32p il (Green team) lib bdg $26.60; pa $8.95

Grades: 3 4 5 6   **333.72**
1. Environmental protection
ISBN 978-0-7787-4100-8 (lib bdg); 0-7787-4100-1 (lib bdg); 978-0-7787-4107-7 (pa); 0-7787-4107-9 (pa)
                                    LC 2008023292
This offers suggestions for improving local environments, such as keeping schools and playgrounds clean and tidy, planning and creating gardens, attracting wildlife, controlling litter, planting trees, and maintaining parks

"The color graphics and layouts are highly appealing and will definitely be attractive to young readers. . . . This . . . is an excellent resource for school libraries, science teachers, and community sponsors." Libr Media Connect

Hirsch, Rebecca E., 1969-

Protecting our natural resources; by Rebecca Hirsch. Cherry Lake Pub. 2010 32p il (Save the planet) lib bdg $27.07

Grades: 3 4 5 6   **333.72**
1. Conservation of natural resources
ISBN 978-1-60279-661-4 (lib bdg); 1-60279-661-0 (lib bdg)   LC 2009-38097
"Language Arts Explorer"
Explains what natural resources are, how they are being exploited, and what should be done to protect them

"At the beginning of . . . [the] book, readers are given a mission and advised to be alert to the facts provided so that they can successfully answer the questions at the end. . . . Children are made to feel part of the process; suggestions for how they can become involved abound." SLJ

Includes glossary and bibliographical references

Kelsey, Elin

Not your typical book about the environment; illustrated by Clayton Hammer. Owlkids 2010 64p il pa $10.95; $22.95

Grades: 3 4 5 6   **333.72**
1. Environmental protection
ISBN 978-1-897349-84-7 (pa); 1-897349-84-X (pa); 978-1-897349-79-3; 1-897349-79-3
Written to allay children's fears about the environment, this book shows how smart technologies, innovative ideas, and a growing commitment to alternative lifestyles are exploding around the world, creating a future that will be brighter than we sometimes might think. Includes profiles of unexpected personalities.

"Imaginative, comic-booklike illustrations add to a lively layout that will keep readers moving from one paragraph to the next, and funny wordplay prevents the facts from becoming overwhelming or dry. . . . This hilarious, information-packed work is an excellent addition." SLJ

McKay, Kim

True green kids; 100 things you can do to save the planet; [by] Kim McKay and Jenny Bonnin. National Geographic 2008 143p il $15.95

Grades: 4 5 6 7   **333.72**
1. Environmental protection
ISBN 978-1-4263-0442-2; 1-4263-0442-0
Presents an overview of global warming and describes 100 simple ways to be more environmentally friendly in the bedroom, in the house, at school, and on vacation.

"Accompanied by attractive, up-to-date pictures in a lively design, the one hundred suggestions are direct . . . and generally practical." Horn Book Guide

Includes glossary

Parr, Todd

The Earth book. Little, Brown Books for Young Readers 2010 unp il $15.99

Grades: PreK K 1   **333.72**
1. Environmental protection
ISBN 978-0-316-04265-9; 0-316-04265-X
                                    LC 2008047562
"With illustrations that look as though they might have been done by enthusiastic children themselves, Parr's book offers first-person advice about ways to take care of the earth. . . . The strong appeal comes from the simple artwork done in Parr's signature style, which features pure colors, objects and people outlined in thick black ink, and kids whose round faces are comprised of two dots for eyes and upturned lines for mouths. Young children will get a kick out of the vivid art." Booklist

Raatma, Lucia

Green living; no action too small. Compass Point Books 2009 64p il (Green generation) lib bdg $31.99; pa $6.95

Grades: 5 6 7 8 9   **333.72**
1. Environmental movement 2. Environmental protection
ISBN 978-0-7565-4245-0 (lib bdg); 0-7565-4245-6 (lib bdg); 978-0-7565-4293-1 (pa); 0-7565-4293-6 (pa)
                                    LC 2009-8779

Raatma, Lucia—*Continued*

Shows children how can they make a difference. From fighting global warming to protecting wildlife, this book contains the information young environmentalists need to change the world

"The cover design, layout, and graphics feel hip and of the moment. The clear writing is easy to understand and includes many concrete examples of environmentally friendly practices. . . . [A] good [choice] for both leisure reading and reports." SLJ

Includes glossary and bibliographical references

Recycle this book; 100 top children's book authors tell you how to go green; edited by Dan Gutman. Yearling 2009 267p pa $5.99 *
Grades: 5 6 7 8   **333.72**
  1. Environmental protection 2. Recycling 3. Authors
ISBN 978-0-385-73721-0 (pa); 0-385-73721-1 (pa)
                  LC 2008-10800

"This lively collection of brief essays (and a poem) by 100 outstanding children's and young adult authors teaches through example. Each selection highlights a small step (or steps) taken by the writer toward a greener Earth. . . . The essays also provide insight into the lives and thoughts of many familiar and beloved authors such as Laurie Halse Anderson, Ralph Fletcher, Gary Schmidt, Lois Lowry, Susan Patron, and Rick Riordan. Several pages of Web sites offer a starting point for action and information. Highly useful for classroom and family discussions and science-project ideas." SLJ

Reilly, Kathleen M.

Planet Earth; 25 environmental projects you can build yourself. Nomad Press 2008 122p il (Projects you can build yourself) $21.95; pa $14.95
Grades: 4 5 6 7   **333.72**
  1. Environmental sciences 2. Science projects
  ISBN   978-1-934670-05-7;   1-934670-05-7;
978-1-934670-04-0 (pa); 1-934670-04-9 (pa)

"Both comprehensive and approachable, this title . . . combines explanations of science concepts and environmental issues with hands-on projects. . . . Elementary- and middle-school students will find the succinct overview of the facts very useful, and they'll welcome the clearly presented projects." Booklist

Ride, Sally K.

Mission: save the planet; things you can do to help fight global warming; [by] Sally Ride and Tam O'Shaughnessy; illustrated by Andrew Arnold. Roaring Brook Press 2009 61p il (Sally Ride science) pa $7.99
Grades: 5 6 7 8   **333.72**
  1. Environmental protection
  ISBN 978-159643-379-3 (pa); 1-59643-379-5 (pa)
                  LC 2009-29254

"The first chapter in this slim volume discusses our energy use, dependence on fossil fuels, and the environmental impact of these practices. The remaining chapters are packed with facts and suggestions on reducing our carbon footprint. . . . The authors' background in science education is evident, as the writing style is clear, precise, and kid-friendly. Black-and-white cartoon illustrations provide excellent visuals for many of the recommendations." SLJ

Rohmer, Harriet

Heroes of the environment; true stories of people who are helping to protect our planet; illustrated by Julie McLaughlin. Chronicle Books 2009 109p il map $16.99 *
Grades: 4 5 6   **333.72**
  1. Environmentalists
  ISBN 978-0-8118-6779-5; 0-8118-6779-X
                  LC 2009004366

"This title spotlights 12 contemporary conservationists who are working to fight pollution in cities, oceans, and wetlands, from Alaska to Mexico City. Many of the featured activists are young people." Booklist

"Engaging graphics and clear writing combine to provide a compelling reading experience." Sci Books Films

Sirett, Dawn, 1966-

Love your world; how to take care of the plants, the animals, and the planet; written by Dawn Sirett; illustrations by Rachael Parfitt; special photography by Howard Shooter and Dave King. Dorling Kindersley Pub. 2009 unp il pa $8.99
Grades: K 1 2 3   **333.72**
  1. Environmental protection
  ISBN 978-0-7566-4590-8 (pa); 0-7566-4590-5 (pa)

"Using bright photographs, this cheery book teaches ways to be green as kids demonstrate planting seeds, recycling, reusing and reducing." Pub Wkly

"This is a vivid, cheerful introduction to going green." SLJ

Smalley, Carol Parenzan, 1960-

Green changes you can make around your home. Mitchell Lane Publishers 2010 47p il (Tell your parents) lib bdg $21.50
Grades: 4 5 6 7   **333.72**
  1. Environmental protection 2. Environmental movement
  ISBN 978-1-58415-764-9 (lib bdg); 1-58415-764-X (lib bdg)   LC 2009-4527

This book that explains how to be environmentally friendly "offers numerous facts and statistics, all of which are cited. . . . Chapters cover present-day issues and . . . are interspersed with full-color photographs and short 'Did You Know' trivia boxes. . . . Back matter includes detailed resource lists and 'Try This!' experiments." SLJ

Includes glossary and bibliographical references

Try this at home; planet-friendly projects for kids; Jackie Farquhar, D.I.Y. editor. Owlkids 2009 c2008 93p il pa $10.95
Grades: 5 6 7 8   **333.72**
  1. Environmental protection
  ISBN 978-2-89579-192-8 (pa); 2-89579-192-9 (pa)

"Many of these projects are unique or innovative, featuring ideas like growing your own pizza ingredients and making a foosball game out of recycled corks, clothespins, and plastic fruit baskets. One of the best projects provides tips on making sure a bike is road ready, offering advice on checking the cables, gears, and oiling the chain. The book also includes sections designed to in-

Try this at home—*Continued*

crease environmental awareness, including information on carbon footprint and 'eco all-stars.' Interactive elements, like a game board, should appeal to children. Illustrations are hip collages of full-color photographs and cartoons." SLJ

Includes bibliographical references

Walsh, Melanie

10 things I can do to help my world. Candlewick Press 2008 unp il $15.99 *

Grades: PreK K 1   333.72

1. Waste minimization
ISBN 978-0-7636-4144-3; 0-7636-4144-8
LC 2007051888

"A thoroughly successful presentation on how even small changes in lifestyle can make a big difference. On each spread, a large and colorful acrylic painting is accompanied by a sturdy die-cut flap and eco-friendly tips. Each suggestion opens with 'I,' followed by a verb, such as 'remember,' 'try,' and 'always.' The sentence is completed under the flap, along with a reason why the tip is conservation friendly. The recommendations are those that children can easily relate to, such as turning off the water while brushing your teeth, . . . using both sides of the paper, recycling, etc. Visually appealing and effective in its presentation, this title will serve as an introduction to environmental studies." SLJ

333.79 Energy

Barnham, Kay

Save energy; [by] Kay Barnham. Crabtree Pub. 2007 32p il (Environment action!) lib bdg $22.60; pa $7.95 *

Grades: K 1 2 3   333.79

1. Energy conservation 2. Energy resources
ISBN 978-0-7787-3660-8 (lib bdg); 0-7787-3660-1 (lib bdg); 978-0-7787-3670-7 (pa); 0-7787-3670-9 (pa)
LC 2007030001

This "book explores different sources of energy, how we use it, and how this affects the environment. It is also full of ideas for saving energy at home and at school, and encourages children to take an active part in preserving the environment and their future." Publisher's note

This book "exposes young children to concepts that can truly make a difference. . . . [The book has] plenty of colorful, relevant, and interesting glossy color photographs." Sci Books Films

Includes glossary

Bowden, Rob

Energy; by Rob Bowden. KidHaven Press 2004 48p (Sustainable world) lib bdg $23.70

Grades: 5 6 7 8   333.79

1. Renewable energy resources 2. Energy development
ISBN 0-7377-1897-8   LC 2003-52953

This "briefly introduces various forms of sustainable energy—water, wind, sun, geothermal sources—and takes a look at where sustainable technology is headed. . . . Bowden writes with admirable simplicity about compli-

cated subjects, and he's careful to separate facts from opinions when he quotes others. [This book includes] excellent color photos . . . and gripping statistics." Booklist

Includes glossary and bibliographical references

Farrell, Courtney

Using alternative energies. Cherry Lake Pub. 2010 32p il (Save the planet) lib bdg $27.07

Grades: 3 4 5 6   333.79

1. Renewable energy resources
ISBN 978-1-60279-663-8 (lib bdg); 1-60279-663-7 (lib bdg)

"Language Arts Explorer"

Examines the climate change and the problems caused by the use of traditional fossil fuels, and looks at alternatives such wind, solar, and hydroelectric energy

"At the beginning of . . . [the] book, readers are given a mission and advised to be alert to the facts provided so that they can successfully answer the questions at the end. . . . Children are made to feel part of the process; suggestions for how they can become involved abound." SLJ

Includes glossary and bibliographical references

Guillain, Charlotte

Saving energy; [by] Charlotte Guillain. Heinemann Library 2008 24p il (Help the environment) $21.70; pa $5.99

Grades: PreK K 1 2   333.79

1. Energy conservation
ISBN   978-1-4329-0887-4;   1-4329-0887-1; 978-1-4329-0893-5 (pa); 1-4329-0893-6 (pa)
LC 2007-41172

This describes ways to save energy.

"A great jumping-off point for a broader discussion of environmentalism. . . . The bright, vibrant photographs will grab readers' attention as they reinforce the simple sentences." Libr Media Connect

Includes glossary

Hewitt, Sally

Using energy. Crabtree Pub. Co. 2009 32p il (Green team) $26.60; pa $8.95

Grades: 3 4 5 6   333.79

1. Energy conservation 2. Energy resources
ISBN   978-0-7787-4096-4;   0-7787-4096-X; 978-0-7787-4103-9 (pa); 0-7787-4103-6 (pa)
LC 2008023288

"Looks at various types of energy resources, explains their effect on the environment, offers suggestions for conserving energy, and shows how local actions can have a global impact." Publisher's note

"The color graphics and layouts are highly appealing and will definitely be attractive to young readers. . . . This . . . is an excellent resource for school libraries, science teachers, and community sponsors." Libr Media Connect

Hirschmann, Kris, 1967-

Solar energy. KidHaven Press 2006 48p il (Our environment) lib bdg $23.70

Grades: 5 6 7 8   **333.79**
  1. Solar energy
  ISBN 0-7377-3049-8

"This book examines all aspects of the solar energy question-how solar energy works, its problems and potential, where it is being used today and more." Publisher's note

Juettner, Bonnie, 1968-

Energy; by Bonnie Juettner. KidHaven Press 2004 48p il map (Our environment) lib bdg $23.70

Grades: 5 6 7 8   **333.79**
  1. Energy resources
  ISBN 0-7377-1821-8   LC 2003-876

Contents: What does the world use for energy?; How is energy managed?; Are we running out of energy?; What will happen in the future?

"The liberal use of vibrant colors, the inclusion of a photograph or diagram on most pages, and the generous print size will appeal to reluctant readers. [This title] will help students examine cause and effect (and possible solutions), and challenge them to live green." SLJ

Includes glossary and bibliographical references

Leedy, Loreen, 1959-

The shocking truth about energy; written and illustrated by Loreen Leedy. Holiday House 2010 32p il $17.95

Grades: 1 2 3   **333.79**
  1. Energy resources
  ISBN 978-0-8234-2220-3; 0-8234-2220-8

An imaginary bolt of pure energy named Erg introduces the nature of energy, offers tips on how to use energy sensibly, and shows different ways energy can be harnessed.

"Leedy's experience selecting facts that are most relevant and engaging for young readers is evident, and the information is eminently digestible. The design moves from energetic to near-frenetic. Her brightly colored mixed-media illustrations are filled with animated appliances, bursts of information, and decorated fonts." Booklist

Rau, Dana Meachen, 1971-

Alternative energy beyond fossil fuels. Compass Point Books 2010 64p il (Green generation) lib bdg $31.99; pa $6.95

Grades: 5 6 7 8 9   **333.79**
  1. Renewable energy resources 2. Energy resources
  ISBN 978-0-7565-4247-4 (lib bdg); 0-7565-4247-2 (lib bdg); 978-0-7565-4289-4 (pa); 0-7565-4289-8 (pa)
  LC 2009-08778

"This great little book introduces the topics of fossil fuel usage, the limited nature of fossil fuels, and alternative energy options. It is particularly praiseworthy for its refreshingly objective, but still enthusiastic, presentations on solar, wind, geothermal, hydro, and biomass energy. . . . Interesting, well-written, and appropriately illustrated, the book is entertaining enough for general reading, but factual enough for use as a science text." Sci Books Films

Includes glossary and bibliographical references

Slade, Suzanne, 1964-

What can we do about the energy crisis? PowerKids Press 2010 24p il (Protecting our planet) lib bdg $21.25; pa $8

Grades: 2 3 4   **333.79**
  1. Energy resources 2. Energy development
  ISBN 978-1-4042-8081-6 (lib bdg); 1-4042-8081-2 (lib bdg); 978-1-4358-2481-2 (pa); 1-4358-2481-4 (pa)
  LC 2008-51935

"Learn about both the fossil fuels we depend upon today and the alternative energy sources we are likely to become reliant upon in the future." Publisher's note

This book provides "straightforward information . . . complemented by full-page, color photographs. . . . Links for further information . . . are housed at the publisher's Web site (which allows feedback so that readers can suggest more sites)." SLJ

Includes glossary

Solway, Andrew

Renewable energy sources. Raintree 2010 48p il (Sci-hi: Earth and space science) lib bdg $31.43; pa $8.99

Grades: 4 5 6 7   **333.79**
  1. Renewable energy resources
  ISBN 978-1-4109-3351-5 (lib bdg); 1-4109-3351-2 (lib bdg); 978-1-4109-3361-4 (pa); 1-4109-3361-X (pa)
  LC 2009-3535

"Explores the energy sources that will power the future. . . . Learn about everything from wind energy to biofuels." Publisher's note

"Multiple colorful sidebars and large and small diagrams and photographs will help students to grasp the fundamentals being discussed, and the easy but interesting science experiments will act as further reinforcements." SLJ

Includes glossary and bibliographical references

Woodford, Chris, 1943-

Energy; written by Chris Woodford. DK 2007 64p il (See for yourself) $14.99

Grades: 4 5 6 7   **333.79**
  1. Energy resources 2. Force and energy
  ISBN 978-0-7566-2561-0

The author "defines energy, giving examples of both potential and kinetic forms; explains how energy is released and travels; and provides detailed discussions of many energy sources. Chapters are composed of heavily illustrated double-page spreads that offer a main text and several sidebar comments. Most illustrations are full-color photographs, but captioned diagrams . . . offer much detail for readers to ponder." Booklist

333.8 Subsurface resources

Hartman, Eve
Fossil fuels; [by] Eve Hartman and Wendy Meshbesher. Raintree 2010 48p il map (Sci-hi: Earth and space science) lib bdg $31.43; pa $8.99
Grades: 4 5 6 7   **333.8**
  1. Coal 2. Oils and fats
  ISBN 978-1-4109-3350-8 (lib bdg); 1-4109-3350-4 (lib bdg); 978-1-4109-3360-7 (pa); 1-4109-3360-1 (pa)
                                    LC 2009-3548
"Fossil Fuels' explores the fuels that we use every day. . . . Learn about everything from how coal forms to the many products made from oil." Publisher's note
"Multiple colorful sidebars and large and small diagrams and photographs will help students to grasp the fundamentals being discussed, and the easy but interesting science experiments will act as further reinforcements." SLJ
Includes glossary and bibliographical references

White, Nancy, 1942-
Using Earth's underground heat. Bearport Pub. 2009 32p il (Going green) lib bdg $25.27
Grades: 4 5 6 7   **333.8**
  1. Geothermal resources
  ISBN 978-1-59716-963-9 (lib bdg); 1-59716-963-3 (lib bdg)   LC 2009-15119
Explains "how people around the world are finding creative ways to use the heat deep inside Earth to warm and cool their homes, grow food, and even make electricity." Publisher's note
"Color photographs (most full page) and a few diagrams accompany the informative text[s]. . . . Overall, the [book] . . . is user-friendly and covers topics that are not easily found elsewhere." SLJ
Includes glossary and bibliographical references

333.91 Water and lands adjoining bodies of water

Barnham, Kay
Save water; [by] Kay Barnham. Crabtree Pub. 2008 32p il (Environment action!) lib bdg $22.60; pa $7.95 *
Grades: K 1 2 3   **333.91**
  1. Water conservation
  ISBN 978-0-7787-3661-5 (lib bdg); 0-7787-3661-X (lib bdg); 978-0-7787-3671-4 (pa); 0-7787-3671-7 (pa)
                                    LC 2007030002
This "book explores where the water we use comes from, how water can become polluted, and why we should save water. Tips on saving water at home and at school encourage kids to think about conservation and caring for our environment." Publisher's note
This book "exposes young children to concepts that can truly make a difference. . . . [The book has] plenty of colorful, relevant, and interesting glossy color photographs." Sci Books Films
Includes glossary

Guillain, Charlotte
Saving water; [by] Charlotte Guillain. Heinemann Library 2008 24p il (Help the environment) $21.70; pa $5.99
Grades: PreK K 1 2   **333.91**
  1. Water conservation
  ISBN 978-1-4329-0886-7; 1-4329-0886-3; 978-1-4329-0892-8 (pa); 1-4329-0892-8 (pa)
                                    LC 2007-41175
This describes ways in which water is used and how to save water.
"A great jumping-off point for a broader discussion of environmentalism. . . . The bright, vibrant photographs will grab readers' attention as they reinforce the simple sentences." Libr Media Connect
Includes glossary

Vogel, Carole Garbuny
Human impact; [by] Carole G. Vogel. F. Watts 2003 95p il (Restless sea) $29.59 paperback o.p.
Grades: 5 6 7 8   **333.91**
  1. Marine pollution 2. Human influence on nature
  ISBN 0-531-12323-5; 0-531-16680-5 (pa)
                                    LC 2003-5301
Contents: Troubled waters; Sea sick; Too many fishermen; The impact of global warming; The human footprint
This "provides a detailed description of the results of population growth, global warming, and the development of coastal areas. The devastation to marine life resulting from occurrences such as oil spills and the dead zones caused by oxygen-depleted water are described through both heart-wrenching photographs and informative text." SLJ
Includes bibliographical references

333.95 Biological resources

Barnham, Kay
Protect nature; [by] Kay Barnham. Crabtree Pub. 2008 32p il (Environment action!) lib bdg $22.60; pa $7.95 *
Grades: K 1 2 3   **333.95**
  1. Nature conservation 2. Environmental protection
  ISBN 978-0-7787-3658-5 (lib bdg); 0-7787-3658-X (lib bdg); 978-0-7787-3668-4 (pa); 0-7787-3668-7 (pa)
                                    LC 2007029998
This "book explores how the everyday actions of humans can harm nature. . . . Ideas for protecting nature at home, at school, and on vacation encourage children to take an active part in preserving and caring for our environment." Publisher's note
This book "exposes young children to concepts that can truly make a difference. . . . [The book has] plenty of colorful, relevant, and interesting glossy color photographs." Sci Books Films
Includes glossary

Bortolotti, Dan

Tiger rescue; changing the future for endangered wildlife. Firefly 2003 64p il map lib bdg $19.95; pa $9.95

Grades: 4 5 6 7   **333.95**

1. Tigers 2. Wildlife conservation

ISBN 1-55297-599-1 (lib bdg); 1-55297-558-4 (pa)

This describes the tiger's "natural habitat, habits, physiology, and behavior in captivity. [It also includes] a time line of conservation efforts, profiles of conservationists in the field, and forecasts of the animals' future. Throughout, the author makes clear the factors that can threaten animal populations, and discusses human attitudes toward the animals throughout history. . . . Written in accessible, lively language and nicely illustrated with exciting color photos, [this] will be useful for reports and browsing." Booklist

Gallant, Roy A.

The wonders of biodiversity. Benchmark Bks. 2003 80p il maps (Story of science) lib bdg $19.95

Grades: 5 6 7 8   **333.95**

1. Biological diversity

ISBN 0-7614-1427-4   LC 2002-916

Partial contents: Beetles, bacteria, and biodiversity; Critters galore, what they are; Critters galore, where they live; Major ecosystems; Tragedy of the rain forests; Gaia

Discusses the many different life forms that have existed on Earth, their importance, and how they have changed over time

"Readers will find accurate, readable explanations for the scientific principles here addressed. . . . Up-to-date controversies and predictions conclude the [book] . . . illustrated with well-captioned photos." Horn Book Guide

Includes glossary and bibliographical references

Guillain, Charlotte

Caring for nature; [by] Charlotte Guillain. Heinemann Library 2008 24p il (Help the environment) $21.70; pa $5.99

Grades: PreK K 1 2   **333.95**

1. Nature conservation

ISBN   978-1-4329-0889-8;   1-4329-0889-8; 978-1-4329-0895-9 (pa); 1-4329-0895-2 (pa)

LC 2007-41174

The book "focus[es] on things children can do to help the environment and keep the world around us clean." Publisher's note

This book is "a great jumping–off point for a broader discussion of environmentalism. . . . The bright, vibrant photographs will grab readers' attention as they reinforce the simple sentences." Libr Media Connect

Includes glossary

Patent, Dorothy Hinshaw

Biodiversity; photographs by William Muñoz. Clarion Bks. 1996 109p il hardcover o.p. pa $7.95 *

Grades: 5 6 7 8   **333.95**

1. Biological diversity 2. Nature conservation

ISBN 0-395-68704-7; 0-618-31514-4 (pa)

LC 95-49982

Provides a global perspective on environmental issues while demonstrating the concept which encompasses the many forms of life on earth and their interdependence on one another for survival

"Patent imbues her lucid scientific discussion with many examples of her personal experience both in childhood and as an adult, and she employs a wide array of examples from many parts of the world to demonstrate current problems and scientific and conservation activity. Illustrated with plentiful and helpful photos." Horn Book

Includes glossary

Salmansohn, Pete, 1947-

Saving birds; heroes around the world; [by] Pete Salmansohn and Stephen W. Kress. Tilbury House 2003 39p il $16.95; pa $7.95

Grades: 5 6 7 8   **333.95**

1. Birds—Protection 2. Wildlife conservation 3. Endangered species

ISBN 0-88448-237-5; 0-88448-276-6 (pa)

LC 2002-6710

Profiles adults and children working in six habitats around the world to save wild birds, some of which are on the brink of extinction.

"As a teaching aid, this volume is an exceptional supplement. The six articles relating the heroic rescue of the endangered birds are accurate and enhanced by appropriate color photographs." Sci Books Films

Sheehan, Sean, 1951-

Endangered species; by Sean Sheehan. Gareth Stevens Pub. 2009 48p il map (What if we do nothing?) lib bdg $31

Grades: 5 6 7 8   **333.95**

1. Endangered species

ISBN 978-1-4339-0086-0 (lib bdg); 1-4339-0086-6 (lib bdg)   LC 2008029167

"Some scientists predict that, if we do nothing, half of all species alive today will be extinct by 2100. This book looks at the many animals and plants that have become endangered through hunting, poaching, pollution, habitat loss, and climate change. It also discusses the steps conservationists are taking to protect threatened species." Publisher's note

"Using intelligent, focused text; an open design; vivid photos; and excellent maps, [this] book demands attention." Booklist

Includes bibliographical references

Swinburne, Stephen R.

Once a wolf; how wildlife biologists fought to bring back the gray wolf; with photographs by Jim Brandenburg. Houghton Mifflin 1999 48p il hardcover o.p. pa $6.95 *

Grades: 4 5 6 7   **333.95**

1. Wolves 2. Wildlife conservation

ISBN 0-395-89827-7; 0-618-11120-4 (pa)

LC 98-16865

Surveys the history of the troubled relationship between wolves and humans, examines the view that these predators are a valuable part of the ecosystem, and describes the conservation movement to restore them to the

Swinburne, Stephen R.—*Continued*
wild

The "crisp color photographs showing wolves in their natural environment are exceptional. Swinburne's text adds suspense and excitement to the story. . . . This is an involving study . . . which makes fascinating reading." Bull Cent Child Books

Includes bibliographical references

Turner, Pamela S.

Gorilla doctors; saving endangered great apes. Houghton Mifflin 2005 64p il map (Scientists in the field) $17 *

Grades: 5 6 7 8   **333.95**
   1. Gorillas 2. Wildlife conservation
   ISBN 0-618-44555-2   LC 2004-9213

This describes The Mountain Gorilla Veterinary Project which works to save the mountain gorilla population in Rwanda and Uganda.

This offers "readable text . . . accompanied by striking, full-color photographs." SLJ

Includes bibliographical references

342 Constitutional and administrative law

Finkelman, Paul, 1949-

The Constitution. National Geographic 2006 32p il (American documents) $15.95; lib bdg $23.90 *
Grades: 4 5 6 7   **342**
   1. United States. Constitution 2. Constitutional history
   ISBN 0-7922-7937-9; 0-7922-7975-1 (lib bdg)

An introduction to the American Constitution, including why and how it was written and how it is amended.

This title is "clear and concise. . . . The superior layout and illustrations enhance and reinforce the [text] through a combination of high-quality reproductions, photographs, artwork, and biographical sidebars." SLJ

Includes glossary

Fritz, Jean

Shhh! we're writing the Constitution; illustrated by Tomie dePaola. Putnam 1987 64p il $15.99; pa $5.99 *
Grades: 2 3 4   **342**
   1. Constitutional history—United States
   ISBN 0-399-21403-8; 0-698-11624-0 (pa)
                                   LC 86-22528

"This book discusses how the Constitution came to be written and ratified. It includes the full text of the document produced by the Constitutional Convention of 1787." Bull Cent Child Books

"Jean Fritz gives a vivid, vibrant picture of the 1787 Constitutional Convention. The wonderful, full-color illustrations are a perfect match for the captivating text." Child Book Rev Serv

Krull, Kathleen, 1952-

A kid's guide to America's Bill of Rights; curfews, censorship, and the 100-pound giant; illustrated by Anna DiVito. Avon Bks. 1999 226p il $15.99
Grades: 4 5 6 7   **342**
   1. United States. Constitution. 1st-10th amendments
   2. Civil rights
   ISBN 0-380-97497-5   LC 99-17324

"After describing how the first 10 amendments came to be added to the Constitution, the book considers each one from a historical point of view, examining Supreme Court cases and famous challenges, and explaining in what ways each amendment applies to children and teenagers. Anna Divito's cartoonlike drawings add a visually appealing touch." Booklist

Includes bibliographical references

Leavitt, Amie Jane

The Bill of Rights in translation; what it really means; by Amie Jane Leavitt. Capstone Press 2009 32p il (Fact finders. Kids' translations) lib bdg $23.93; pa $7.95
Grades: 3 4 5   **342**
   1. United States. Constitution. 1st-10th amendments
   2. Civil rights
   ISBN 978-1-4296-1928-8 (lib bdg); 1-4296-1928-7 (lib bdg); 978-1-4296-2843-3 (pa); 1-4296-2843-X (pa)
                                   LC 2007-51307

"Presents the Bill of Rights in both its original version and in a translated version using everyday language. Describes the events that led to the creation of the document and its significance through history." Publisher's note

Provides "a nearly line-by-line translation that makes . . . the written word accessible and meaningful." SLJ

Includes glossary and bibliographical references

Maestro, Betsy, 1944-

A more perfect union; the story of our Constitution; illustrated by Giulio Maestro. Lothrop, Lee & Shepard Bks. 1987 48p il pa $7.99 hardcover o.p.
Grades: 2 3 4   **342**
   1. Constitutional history—United States
   ISBN 0-688-10192-5 (pa)   LC 87-4083

The Maestros "cover the birth of the Constitution from the initial decision to hold the convention, through the summer meetings in Philadelphia, the ratification struggle, the first election, and the adoption of the Bill of Rights." SLJ

"A simple, straightforward account using an oversize format with full-color illustration throughout. There is an excellent, fact-filled addenda that also includes the Preamble, chronologies and summaries of the Articles of the Constitution, the Bill of Rights, the Amendments and the Connecticut Compromise. This fine book places important events in historical context." Publ Wkly

Mortensen, Lori, 1955-

Writing the U.S. Constitution; illustrated by Siri Weber Feeney. Picture Window Books 2010 32p il (Our American story) lib bdg $23.99 *

Grades: 2 3 4   **342**

1. United States—Politics and government—1783-1809 2. United States—Constitution—History 3. Constitutional history

ISBN 978-1-4048-5540-3 (lib bdg); 1-4048-5540-8 (lib bdg)   LC 2009-6895

Discusses the history of the writing of the United States Constitution

This title is "illustrated with well-executed, full-page, color illustrations, maps, and photos. . . . [It has] accurate, clearly written information that students can use for either leisure reading or reports." SLJ

Includes glossary and bibliographical references

Thomas, William David, 1947-

What is a constitution? [by] William David Thomas. Gareth Stevens Pub. 2008 32p il (My American government) lib bdg $23.93; pa $8.95

Grades: 3 4 5   **342**

1. United States. Constitution 2. Constitutions 3. Democracy

ISBN 978-0-8368-8863-8 (lib bdg); 0-8368-8863-4 (lib bdg); 978-0-8368-8868-3 (pa); 0-8368-8868-5 (pa)   LC 2007027281

This describes the United States constitution as well as the constitutions of state governments.

This book has "an accessible format and clear writing. . . . Black-and-white and full-color vintage and more recent photographs appear throughout." SLJ

Includes glossary and bibliographical references

344   Labor, social service, education, cultural law

Chmara, Theresa

Privacy and confidentiality issues; a guide for libraries and their lawyers. American Library Association 2009 98p pa $40 *

Grades: Professional   **344**

1. Libraries—Law and legislation 2. Right of privacy 3. Library services

ISBN 978-0-8389-0970-6 (pa); 0-8389-0970-1 (pa)   LC 2008-34902

"This slim title is a must read. Chmara, a First Amendment attorney and litigation expert, clarifies privacy and confidentiality issues such as requests or subpoenas for patron-use records (both book and Internet), hostile-work-environment issues, state and federal privacy and confidentiality statutes, and minors' First Amendment rights and rights to privacy." Booklist

Includes bibliographical references

Good, Diane L.

Brown v. Board of Education; a civil rights milestone. Children's Press 2004 48p il (Cornerstones of freedom, Second series) $25; pa $5.95 *

Grades: 4 5 6   **344**

1. Brown, Oliver, 1919-1961 2. Topeka (Kan.). Board of Education 3. Segregation in education

ISBN 0-516-24225-3; 0-531-18686-5 (pa)   LC 2003-9097

Explains the history of segregation in the United States and cases that tested the law allowing "separate but equal" treatment, including the five cases that came together as Brown v. Board of Education

"Text divided into short sections, numerous photographs, and generous use of white space combine to make [this title] inviting." SLJ

Includes bibliographical references

345   Criminal law

Crewe, Sabrina

The Scottsboro case; [by] Sabrina Crewe and Michael V. Uschan. Gareth Stevens Pub. 2005 32p il map (Events that shaped America) lib bdg $24.67; pa $11.95

Grades: 4 5 6 7   **345**

1. Scottsboro case 2. Trials 3. African Americans—Civil rights

ISBN 0-8368-3407-0 (lib bdg); 0-8368-5416-0 (pa)   LC 2004-44240

An account of the 1931 court case in which nine African American youths were charged with rape

"The authors do a good job of a taking a subject that is rife with conflict, duplicity, and ugly words and actions . . . and shaping it into a useful, informative book for middle-graders. . . . [It] is attractively designed with plenty of crisply reproduced, black-and-white photos, and historical art, such as posters, in color. The writing is clear and the text doesn't pull punches." Booklist

Includes bibliographical references

Olson, Steven P.

The trial of John T. Scopes; a primary source account; by Steven P. Olson. Rosen Pub. Group 2004 64p il (Great trials of the 20th century) lib bdg $29.25 *

Grades: 5 6 7 8   **345**

1. Scopes, John Thomas 2. Evolution—Study and teaching

ISBN 0-8239-3974-X   LC 2002-153354

Contents: The meeting at the drugstore; Evolution vs. creation; The nation takes sides; The trial begins; The prosecution; The defense; Darrow vs. Bryan; The meaning of the Scopes trial

An account of the trial of John T. Scopes, prosecuted in 1925 for teaching evolution.

This title utilizes "photographs, copies of original transcripts, political cartoons, and quotations from those involved. [This] is written with respectful attention to the issues of evolution and creationism, the separation of church and state, and the power of the government.

Olson, Steven P.—*Continued*

Readers interested in the law will be captivated by the complexities of the arguments." SLJ

Includes bibliographical references

346.04 Property

Butler, Rebecca P.

Copyright for teachers and librarians. Neal-Schuman Publishers 2004 248p il pa $59.95

Grades: Professional 346.04

1. Copyright 2. Fair use (Copyright)

ISBN 1-55570-500-6 LC 2004-46013

"The five chapters in Part I are . . . reviews of copyright law, the concept of fair use, determining what is in public domain, how to obtain permissions, and other general guidelines on such topics as licensing, loaning, penalties, plagiarism, and exemptions. The bulk of the book is in Part II, which deals with specific applications, such as Internet and public access, videos and DVDs, television, software, music, multimedia, distance learning and—oh, yes!—print! . . . An indispensable addition." SLJ

Includes bibliographical references

Smart copyright compliance for schools; a how-to-do-it manual. Neal-Schuman Publishers 2009 154p il (How-to-do it manuals for libraries) pa $75 *

Grades: Professional 346.04

1. Copyright 2. Fair use (Copyright) 3. School libraries

ISBN 978-1-55570-646-3 (pa); 1-55570-646-0 (pa)

LC 2009-3621

This provides "step-by-step directions for developing and implementing a copyright policy for school districts and schools. . . . The clean layout with wide margins makes for easy reading. An excellent addition to the professional shelf." Booklist

Includes bibliographical references

Crews, Kenneth D.

Copyright law for librarians and educators; creative strategies and practical solutions; with contributions from Dwayne K. Buttler . . . [et al.] 2nd ed. American Library Association 2006 141p il pa $45

Grades: Professional 346.04

1. Copyright

ISBN 0-8389-0906-X LC 2005-13804

First published 2000 with title: Copyright essentials for librarians and educators

The author "addresses 18 areas of copyright in 5 parts. He begins with the scope of protectable works as well as works without copyright protection. Next, he discusses the rights of ownership, including duration and exceptions. He then explains fair use and its related guidelines. Part 4 focuses on the TEACH Act, Section 108, and responsibilities and liabilities. Lastly, Crews examines special issues such as the Digital Millennium Copyright Act." Booklist

Includes bibliographical references

347 Civil procedure and courts

Horn, Geoffrey

The Supreme Court; by Geoffrey M. Horn. World Almanac Library 2003 48p il (World Almanac Library of American government) lib bdg $30 paperback o.p. *

Grades: 5 6 7 8 347

ISBN 0-8368-5459-4 (lib bdg); 0-8368-5464-0 (pa)

LC 2002-38091

Contents: First Monday in October; What the Constitution says; Getting Confirmed; Arguing a case; The Chief Justices; Great dissenters; Finding a balance

This describes "the organization of the Court, the extent and limits of its powers, and how it checks and balances the president and Congress. . . . the history of the Court, how a person becomes a Supreme Court justice, how cases come before the Court, the role of the chief justice, and the importance of dissenting opinions." Publisher's note

"An amazing array of historical photos, statistics, primary-source documents, tables, graphs, and case studies supports the [text]." SLJ

Includes bibliographical references

352.13 State and provincial administration

Giesecke, Ernestine, 1945-

State government. Rev. and updated. Heinemann Library 2010 32p il map (Kids' guide to government) $29.29; pa $7.99

Grades: 3 4 5 352.13

1. State governments 2. United States—Politics and government

ISBN 978-1-4329-2707-3; 1-4329-2707-8; 978-1-4329-2712-7 (pa); 1-4329-2712-4 (pa)

First published 2000

Introduces the purpose and function of state government, the function of the three branches, how states raise money, how state government operates. and how a bill becomes a state law.

"This . . . would be a great asset. . . . Students will learn about a different, but related government every two pages. The font is large and easy to read. The photos, diagrams, charts, maps, and illustrations supplement the text well." Libr Media Connect

Includes glossary

352.23 Chief executives

Horn, Geoffrey

The presidency; by Geoffrey M. Horn. World Almanac Library 2003 48p il (World Almanac Library of American government) hardcover o.p. pa $11.95 *

Grades: 5 6 7 8 352.23

1. Presidents—United States 2. United States—Politics and government

ISBN 0-8368-5458-6 (lib bdg); 0-8368-5463-2 (pa)

LC 2002-33129

Horn, Geoffrey—*Continued*

Contents: A presidential inauguration; What the Constitution says; Getting elected; Using presidential power; Life in the White House; The first family; Leaving office

This discusses the jobs of the president, the history of the presidency, presidential elections and the electoral college, the transfer of power from one president to the next, the vice presidency, life in the White House, impeachment, and the role of the first lady.

"An amazing array of historical photos, statistics, primary-source documents, tables, graphs, and case studies supports the [text]. Highly readable for casual information seekers, yet perfect for research." SLJ

Includes bibliographical references

Obama, Barack, 1961-

Our enduring spirit; President Barack Obama's first words to America; with illustrations by Greg Ruth. Harper 2009 unp il $17.99; lib bdg $18.89
Grades: 2 3 4 5 6   **352.23**
1. Presidents—United States—Inaugural addresses 2. United States—Politics and government
ISBN   978-0-06-183455-4;   0-06-183455-6; 978-0-06-183456-1 (lib bdg); 0-06-183456-4 (lib bdg)
LC 2009014361

"The selected excerpts from Obama's speech (also printed in its entirety at the end of the book) only obliquely note the nation's current crises, but make ample use of Obama's numerous historical references. . . . Dramatic washes of color are juxtaposed with Ruth's inky paintings of the president and of Americans past and present, as strong brushstrokes define their subjects while creating a tangible sense of movement. With the book's emphasis on common values and backgrounds, readers are likely to come away with a sense of pride, hope and belonging, while recognizing that freedom doesn't come without work." Publ Wkly

355   Military science

Chapman, Caroline, 1941-

Battles & weapons: exploring history through art; [by] Caroline Chapman. Two-Can 2007 64p il (Picture that!) $19.95
Grades: 5 6 7 8   **355**
1. Military art and science 2. Military history 3. War in art
ISBN 978-1-58728-588-2   LC 2006033229

"Period paintings from ancient times through World War II are used as a vehicle for introducing battles and weapons and discussing how they have changed over the centuries." Publisher's note

"High quality reproductions of paintings, murals, sculptures, and artifacts show military customs and equipment over the centuries. . . . The lively, informative text creates a 'you are there' sense that will engage even reluctant readers." SLJ

Includes bibliographical references

Clinton, Catherine, 1952-

The Black soldier; 1492 to the present. Houghton Mifflin 2000 117p il $17
Grades: 5 6 7 8   **355**
1. African American soldiers
ISBN 0-395-67722-X   LC 99-48935

Chronicles the military accomplishments of African Americans who fought for the independence and preservation of the United States while struggling to be treated as equals and recognized for their valor and achievement

"Numerous black-and-white archival photographs and reproductions appear throughout this well-organized, readable resource." SLJ

Includes bibliographical references

Murrell, Deborah Jane, 1963-

Greek warrior; by Deborah Murrell. QEB Pub. 2010 32p il map (QEB warriors) lib bdg $28.50
Grades: 4 5 6 7   **355**
1. Military art and science—History 2. Greece—Military history
ISBN 978-1-59566-759-5 (lib bdg); 1-59566-759-8 (lib bdg)   LC 2009-3542

"Learn all about the devious tactics, wicked weapons, and courageous battles fought by Greek warriors." Publisher's note

"Bold, comprehensible type and full-color and black-and-white illustrations; reproductions; and photographs will make this offering a hit with its target audience, including reluctant readers." SLJ

Includes glossary

Park, Louise, 1961-

The Japanese samurai; [by] Louise Park and Timothy Love. Marshall Cavendish Benchmark 2010 32p il map (Ancient and medieval people) lib bdg $28.50
Grades: 4 5 6   **355**
1. Samurai 2. Military art and science—History 3. Japan—History—0-1868
ISBN 978-0-7614-4448-0 (lib bdg); 0-7614-4448-3 (lib bdg)   LC 2009-3573

"An introduction to the history and lifestyle of Japanese samurai." Publisher's note

This title has "a simple and elegant design with the proper balance of quality writing and quantity of information. . . . Handy time lines, well-chosen photos of ruins and artifacts, quality illustrations, inset 'Quick Facts', and 'What You Should Know About' features will grab reluctant readers and captivate even those with short attention spans." SLJ

Includes glossary

The Pharaohs' armies; by Louise Park and Timothy Love. Marshall Cavendish Benchmark 2009 32p il map (Ancient and medieval people) lib bdg $28.50
Grades: 4 5 6   **355**
1. Egypt—Civilization 2. Military art and science—History
ISBN 978-0-7614-4451-0 (lib bdg); 0-7614-4451-3 (lib bdg)

"An introduction to the history and lifestyle of the Pharaohs' armies." Publisher's note

Park, Louise, 1961-—Continued

This title has "a simple and elegant design with the proper balance of quality writing and quantity of information. . . . Handy time lines, well-chosen photos of ruins and artifacts, quality illustrations, inset 'Quick Facts', and 'What You Should Know About' features will grab reluctant readers and captivate even those with short attention spans." SLJ

Includes glossary

Solway, Andrew

Graphing war and conflict. Raintree 2010 32p il (Real world data) $28.21; pa $7.99

Grades: 4 5 6 7   355

1. Military history 2. Graphic methods

ISBN   978-1-4329-2620-5;   1-4329-2620-9; 978-1-4329-2629-8 (pa); 1-4329-2629-2 (pa)

LC 2009001188

This "uses graphs and charts to talk about global conflicts between 1990 and 2005, from guerilla warfare and civil war to nuclear attacks, with a special section on terrorism, including 9/11 and suicide bombers. . . . The clear design, with lots of full-color photos and sidebars, will encourage browsers as much as the up-to-date examples and the clear directions for remaining 'chart smart.'" Booklist

Includes glossary and bibliographical references

355.7   Military installations

Adams, Simon

Castles & forts; foreword by Clifford J. Rogers. Kingfisher (NY) 2003 63p il (Kingfisher knowledge) hardcover o.p. pa $8.95

Grades: 5 6 7 8   355.7

1. Fortification 2. Castles

ISBN   978-0-7534-5620-0;   0-7534-5620-6; 978-0-7534-6119-8 (pa); 0-7534-6119-6 (pa)

LC 2003-44631

An illustrated exploration of a wide array of castles and fortifications throughout the world, from Norman mottes to Maori forts, including how and why they were built and their importance in history

This title includes "stunning, captioned photos and illustrations that emphasize the many intriguing factual details in the text." SLJ

Includes glossary

355.8   Military equipment and supplies (Matériel)

Byam, Michèle

Arms & armor; written by Michéle Byam. rev ed. DK Pub. 2004 72p il (DK eyewitness books) $15.99

Grades: 4 5 6 7   355.8

1. Weapons 2. Armor

ISBN 0-7566-0654-3   LC 2004-558979

First published 1988 by Knopf

A photo essay examining the design, construction, and uses of hand weapons and armor from a Stone Age axe to the revolvers and rifles of the Wild West

361.2   Social action

Lewis, Barbara A., 1943-

The kid's guide to social action; how to solve the social problems you choose—and turn creative thinking into positive action; edited by Pamela Espeland and Caryn Pernu. rev, expanded, updated ed. Free Spirit 1998 211p il pa $18.95

Grades: 4 5 6 7   361.2

1. Social action 2. Social problems

ISBN 1-57542-038-4   LC 98-11036

"A Do something! book"

First published 1991

Resource guide for children for learning political action skills that can help them make a difference in solving social problems at the community, state, and national levels

"Clearly but informally written, the book is packed with well-organized, practical information and includes plenty of inspiring quotes and anecdotes. . . . This is an exemplary reference and curricular resource that works as enlightening browsing material as well." Bull Cent Child Books

Includes bibliographical references

Olien, Rebecca

Kids care! 75 ways to make a difference for people, animals & the environment; [by] Rebecca Olien; illustrations by Michael Kline. Williamson Books 2007 128p il (Williamson kids can! book) $16.99; pa $12.99

Grades: 3 4 5 6   361.2

1. Social action

ISBN   978-0-8249-6793-2;   0-8249-6793-3; 978-0-8249-6792-5 (pa); 0-8249-6792-5 (pa)

LC 2006036186

"This book is filled with ideas that children can implement in order to make a positive impact on the world around them. It is divided into five sections: people, pets, wildlife, environment, and kids joining together. . . . Throughout, material is neatly organized and the book has plenty of factual insets; color cartoon illustrations appear on every spread. . . . This is an excellent resource." SLJ

Includes bibliographical references

361.7   Private action

Shoveller, Herb

Ryan and Jimmy; and the well in Africa that brought them together. Kids Can Press 2006 55p il $16.95; pa $9.95

Grades: 3 4 5 6   361.7

1. Hreljac, Ryan 2. Social action 3. International cooperation 4. Wells 5. Uganda

ISBN   978-1-55337-967-6;   1-55337-967-5; 978-1-55453-271-1 (pa); 1-55453-271-X (pa)

This is an account of the a Canadian boy named Ryan Hreljac, whose efforts helped provide clean drinking water to a village in Uganda, and who befriended and ulti-

Shoveller, Herb—*Continued*
mately rescued a boy named Akana Jimmy from Ugandan rebels

"Clearly written and illustrated with full-color family photographs set against colorful backgrounds, this story is both personal and representative of the many people living in developing countries, the individuals working against all odds to help them, and the power of young people to make a difference." SLJ

362.1   Physical illness

Barber, Nicola
Going to the hospital. PowerKids Press 2009 24p il (The big day!) lib bdg $21.25; pa $8.25
Grades: PreK K 1   362.1
1. Hospitals 2. Medical care
ISBN 978-1-4358-2840-7 (lib bdg); 1-4358-2840-2 (lib bdg); 978-1-4358-2896-4 (pa); 1-4358-2896-8 (pa)
LC 2008025812
"Children in kindergarten will enjoy [this book] as a read-aloud] . . . while those at the end of first grade will be able to read [it] independently. The writing is straightforward and reassuring, and the content provides a realistic view of what youngsters might experience in [a hospital]. . . . [The book] discusses sickness, admission and surroundings, fasting for surgery, and blood tests." SLJ
Includes bibliographical references

Fleischman, John
Phineas Gage: a gruesome but true story about brain science. Houghton Mifflin 2002 86p il $16; pa $8.95 *
Grades: 5 6 7 8 9   362.1
1. Gage, Phineas P., d. 1861 2. Brain—Wounds and injuries
ISBN 0-618-05252-6; 0-618-49478-2 (pa)
LC 2001-39253
"Phineas, a railroad construction foreman, was blasting rock near Cavendish, Vermont, in 1848 when a thirteen-pound iron rod was shot through his brain. Miraculously, he survived to live another eleven years and become a textbook case in brain science." Publisher's note
"The author deftly introduces readers to a diverse range of relevant scientific history as well as more specific beliefs that influenced the medical establishment's understanding of Gage, then goes on to examine subsequent neurological discoveries that have changed and enhanced our understanding of Gage's fate. The book's present-tense narrative is inviting and intimate, and the text is crisp and lucid." Bull Cent Child Books
Includes glossary and bibliographical references

Peacock, Carol Antoinette
Sugar was my best food; diabetes and me; [by] Carol Antoinette Peacock, Adair Gregory, and Kyle Carney Gregory; illustrated by Mary Jones. Whitman, A. 1998 55p il $13.95; pa $4.95
Grades: 3 4 5 6   362.1
1. Diabetes
ISBN 0-8075-7646-8; 0-8075-7648-4 (pa)
LC 97-27869

Adair Gregory, an eleven-year-old boy describes how he learned that he had diabetes, the effect of this disease on his life, and how he learned to cope with the changes in his life
"What is truly exceptional here is the boy's emotional candor. . . . This appealing book is packaged with a colorful cover and has charming black-and-white illustrations. . . . A useful title for children with this disease and those who want to know more about it." SLJ

Rogers, Fred
Going to the hospital; photographs by Jim Judkis. Putnam 1988 unp il pa $5.99 hardcover o.p.
Grades: PreK K 1 2   362.1
1. Hospitals 2. Medical care
ISBN 0-698-11574-0 (pa)   LC 87-19170
Describes what happens during a stay in the hospital, including some of the common forms of medical treatment
"The author's style is just right for this level of information book: reassuring yet candid, matter-of-fact about those aspects of hospitalization that may be frightening or painful, yet not in itself alarming." Bull Cent Child Books

362.29   Substance abuse

Gottfried, Ted, 1928-
Marijuana; by Ted Gottfried with Lisa Harkrader. Marshall Cavendish Benchmark 2010 32p il (Drug facts) $19.95
Grades: 4 5 6 7   362.29
1. Marijuana
ISBN 978-0-7614-4351-3; 0-7614-4351-7
LC 2008-52761
"Rockets"
"Discusses the history, effects, and dangers of Marijuana as well as addiction treatment options." Publisher's note
"Provides clear explanations about effects, followed by diagrams of the body to clarify the specific organs/body systems that suffer the most damage. . . . An excellent starting point." SLJ
Includes glossary

LeVert, Suzanne
Ecstasy; by Suzanne LeVert with Jeff Hendricks. Marshall Cavendish Benchmark 2010 32p il (Drug facts) $19.95
Grades: 4 5 6 7   362.29
1. Ecstasy (Drug) 2. Designer drugs 3. Drug abuse
ISBN 978-0-7614-4349-0; 0-7614-4349-5
LC 2008-52753
"Rockets"
"Discusses the history, effects, and dangers of Ecstasy as well as addiction treatment options." Publisher's note
"Provides clear explanations about effects, followed by diagrams of the body to clarify the specific organs/body systems that suffer the most damage. . . . An excellent starting point." SLJ
Includes glossary

LeVert, Suzanne—*Continued*

Steroids; by Suzanne LeVert with Jim Whiting. Marshall Cavendish Benchmark 2010 32p il (Drug facts) $19.95

Grades: 4 5 6 7   **362.29**
1. Steroids 2. Sports—Corrupt practices
ISBN 978-0-7614-4352-0; 0-7614-4352-5
LC 2008-52752
"Rockets"
"Discusses the history, effects, and dangers of steroids as well as addiction treatment options." Publisher's note
"Provides clear explanations about effects, followed by diagrams of the body to clarify the specific organs/body systems that suffer the most damage. . . . An excellent starting point." SLJ
Includes glossary

Menhard, Francha Roffe

The facts about inhalants; by Francha Roffe Menhard with Laura Purdie Salas. Marshall Cavendish Benchmark 2010 32p il (Drug facts) $19.95

Grades: 4 5 6 7   **362.29**
1. Inhalant abuse
ISBN 978-0-7614-4350-6; 0-7614-4350-9
LC 2008-52739
"Rockets"
"Discusses the history, effects, and dangers of inhalants as well as addiction treatment options." Publisher's note
"Provides clear explanations about effects, followed by diagrams of the body to clarify the specific organs/body systems that suffer the most damage. . . . An excellent starting point." SLJ
Includes glossary

362.292 Alcohol

Gottfried, Ted, 1928-

Alcohol; by Ted Gottfried with Katherine Follett. Marshall Cavendish Benchmark 2010 32p il (Drug facts) $19.95

Grades: 4 5 6 7   **362.292**
1. Alcoholism 2. Alcohol—Physiological effect 3. Drinking of alcoholic beverages
ISBN 978-0-7614-4348-3; 0-7614-4348-7
LC 2008-52751
"Discusses the history, effects, and dangers of alcohol as well as addiction treatment options." Publisher's note
"Provides clear explanations about effects, followed by diagrams of the body to clarify the specific organs/body systems that suffer the most damage. . . . An excellent starting point." SLJ
Includes glossary

362.4 Problems of and services to people with physical disabilities

Patent, Dorothy Hinshaw

The right dog for the job; Ira's path from service dog to guide dog; photographs by William Muñoz. Walker & Co. 2004 unp il $16.95 *

Grades: 2 3 4   **362.4**
1. Guide dogs 2. Animals—Training 3. Animals and the handicapped
ISBN 0-8027-8914-5
LC 2003-65785
This "photo-essay follows a puppy from his training to become a service dog to becoming a guide dog. . . . The author . . . manages to slip in an extraordinary amount of information about the raising and training of guide dogs. . . . Myriad full-color photographs that will capture kids' interest accompany the text." SLJ

362.5 Problems of and services to poor people

Lynette, Rachel

What to do when your family loses its home. PowerKids Press 2010 24p il (Let's work it out) lib bdg $21.25; pa $8.25

Grades: 2 3 4   **362.5**
1. Homeless persons
ISBN 978-1-4358-9339-9 (lib bdg); 1-4358-9339-5 (lib bdg); 978-1-4358-9766-3 (pa); 1-4358-9766-8 (pa)
"Moving is stressful anytime, but when a family is forced to move because they cannot afford to pay their mortgage it is a whole different experience. . . . [This] text helps young readers make sense of it all." Publisher's note
"Full-page color photographs appear opposite the [narrative], depicting multicultural children, parents, grandparents, social workers, and others, whose demeanors match the hopeful tone of the [title]. This . . . will help promote empathy and understanding for the plight of others and is a key purchase." SLJ
Includes glossary

Mason, Paul, 1967-

Poverty; [by] Paul Mason. Heinemann Library 2006 48p il map (Planet under pressure) lib bdg $31.43

Grades: 4 5 6 7   **362.5**
1. Poverty
ISBN 1-4034-7743-4
LC 2005017166
"Mason presents common factors for poverty worldwide, such as lack of money and education, as well as natural disasters. He also addresses the effects of outsourcing jobs from wealthier countries to poorer ones and how poverty affects environment. The book should make the global situation clearer. [This has] numerous quality color visuals, and sidebars. Up-to-date and informative." SLJ
Includes bibliographical references

362.7 Problems of and services to young people

Krementz, Jill

How it feels to be adopted. Knopf 1982 107p il pa $15 hardcover o.p.

Grades: 4 5 6 7   362.7

1. Adoption

ISBN 0-394-75853-6 (pa)   LC 82-48011

"Nineteen youngsters ranging in age from 8 to 16 voice their feelings about being adopted. . . . Several of the accounts are by youngsters who 'have' found their birth mothers and are in the process of getting to know them. Single-parent adoptees are included, too." Booklist

This "is an important contribution to literature on adoption and the question of searching for biological parents." SLJ

Includes bibliographical references

Lynette, Rachel

What to do when your family is on welfare. PowerKids Press 2010 24p il (Let's work it out) lib bdg $21.25; pa $8.25

Grades: 2 3 4   362.7

1. Public welfare

ISBN 978-1-4358-9337-5 (lib bdg); 1-4358-9337-9 (lib bdg); 978-1-4358-9762-5 (pa); 1-4358-9762-5 (pa)

LC 2009-19863

"Explores some of the stresses, feelings, and fallout involved in starting and using the welfare system; and offers strategies for coping." Publisher's note

"Full-page color photographs appear opposite the [narrative], depicting multicultural children, parents, grandparents, social workers, and others, whose demeanors match the hopeful tone of the [title]. This . . . will help promote empathy and understanding for the plight of others and is a key purchase." SLJ

Includes glossary

Parr, Todd

We belong together; a book about adoption and families. Little, Brown 2007 32p il $15.99

Grades: PreK K   362.7

1. Adoption 2. Family

ISBN 0-316-01668-3

"Parr illustrates the rewards of family ties in this heartfelt, supportive book geared toward adopted children and their parents. In each double-page spread, Parr completes the phrase 'We belong together because . . .' with poignant explanations that touch upon basic, tangible needs . . . as well as emotional ones. . . . Cheerful, friendly artwork, with thickly outlined forms and characters and a bold rainbow palette, inclusively depicts an array of children and families—including one with a single parent and one with two dads." Booklist

Warren, Andrea

We rode the orphan trains. Houghton Mifflin 2001 132p il $18; pa $8.95 *

Grades: 4 5 6 7   362.7

1. Orphans

ISBN 0-618-11712-1; 0-618-11712-1 (pa)

LC 00-47279

The author "interviews eight orphan train riders concerning their childhood experiences during 'the largest children's migration in history' between 1854 and 1929 as part of a 'placing out' program run by the Children's Aid Society of New York City." Publ Wkly

"This is powerful nonfiction for classroom and personal reading and for discussion." Booklist

Includes bibliographical references

363.2 Police services

Arroyo, Sheri L.

How crime fighters use math; math curriculum consultant: Rhea A. Stewart. Chelsea Clubhouse 2010 32p il (Math in the real world) lib bdg $28

Grades: 4 5 6   363.2

1. Criminal investigation 2. Mathematics 3. Vocational guidance

ISBN 978-1-60413-602-9 (lib bdg); 1-60413-602-2 (lib bdg)   LC 2009-23330

"The layout for [this] slim [title] is bright and colorful with a photograph and a 'You Do the Math' problem to solve and large, easy-to-read text on every spread. An answer key is included in the back matter, along with a page detailing the career choices and the educational requirements. [It] touches on crime-scene grids, the importance of shoe prints in tracking a criminal, cracking secret codes, and more. . . . [This title] would be useful to supplement lessons on mathematics. [It] will also appeal to students wanting to learn more about math as it relates to specific careers." SLJ

Includes glossary and bibliographical references

Denega, Danielle, 1978-

Gut-eating bugs; maggots reveal the time of death! by Danielle Denega. Franklin Watts 2007 64p il map (24/7, science behind the scenes) lib bdg $27; pa $7.95

Grades: 5 6 7 8   363.2

1. Forensic sciences 2. Death 3. Insects 4. Criminal investigation

ISBN 978-0-531-11824-5 (lib bdg); 0-531-11824-X (lib bdg); 978-0-531-17525-5 (pa); 0-531-17525-1 (pa)

LC 2006020871

"Denega shows how forensic entomologists use insect evidence to narrow down the times of criminal and other deaths. . . . [This] will both rivet and inform true-crime fans." SLJ

Includes glossary and bibliographical references

Denega, Danielle, 1978-—_Continued_

Have you seen this face? the work of forensic artists; [by] Danielle Denega. Franklin Watts 2007 64p il map (24/7, science behind the scenes) lib bdg $27; pa $7.95

Grades: 5 6 7 8 **363.2**
1. Drawing 2. Forensic sciences 3. Criminal investigation
ISBN 978-0-531-11823-8 (lib bdg); 0-531-11823-1 (lib bdg); 978-0-531-15458-8 (pa); 0-531-15458-0 (pa)
LC 2006020870

"A forensic artist uses her talent to construct a lifelike replica of a murder victim found in New York. This book focuses on the process of reconstruction. . . . Further sections highlight important advances in forensic art such as the introduction of computers to the field and offer examples of how forensic artists can use their skills." Voice Youth Advocates

"Concise and interesting." SLJ

Includes glossary and bibliographical references

Fridell, Ron, 1943-

Forensic science. Lerner Publications Co. 2007 48p il (Cool science) lib bdg $26.60

Grades: 4 5 6 7 **363.2**
1. Forensic sciences 2. Criminal investigation
ISBN 978-0-8225-5935-1 (lib bdg); 0-8225-5935-8 (lib bdg)
LC 2005-33039

This is a "history of forensic science, from its beginnings in 1910 through the present. Examples of investigations abound and are brought to life by photos. Most riveting are the descriptions of professionals involved in a murder case, including a medical examiner who dissects corpses and a forensic entomologist who examines dead flesh." SLJ

Includes bibliographical references

Jackson, Donna M., 1959-

The wildlife detectives; how forensic scientists fight crimes against nature; by Donna M. Jackson; photographs by Wendy Shattil and Bob Rozinski. Houghton Mifflin 2000 47p il $16 *

Grades: 4 5 6 7 **363.2**
1. U.S. Fish and Wildlife Service. Forensics Laboratory 2. Forensic sciences 3. Game protection
ISBN 0-395-86976-5 LC 99-34857

Describes how the wildlife detectives at the National Fish and Wildlife Forensics Laboratory in Ashland, Oregon, analyze clues to catch and convict people responsible for crimes against animals

This book features "a smoothly written text that unfolds almost like a mystery novel. . . . Engaging full-color photographs help clarify the text and will appeal to browsers. A list of follow-up suggestions and a glossary of terms are appended. A book that will be welcomed by mystery fans and anyone who cares about animals." Booklist

Kenney, Karen Latchana, 1974-

Police officers at work; by Karen L. Kenney; illustrated by Brian Caleb Dumm; content consultant: Judith Stepan-Norris. Magic Wagon 2009 32p il (Meet your community workers!) lib bdg $18.95

Grades: K 1 2 3 **363.2**
1. Police 2. Vocational guidance
ISBN 978-1-60270-652-1 (lib bdg); 1-60270-652-2 (lib bdg)
LC 2009-2391

This book about police officers has "an uncluttered layout and consistent organization. . . . Chapter headings such as 'Problems on the Job,' and 'Technology at Work,' and 'Special Skills and Training' make it easy to pinpoint specific information." SLJ

Includes glossary

Platt, Richard, 1953-

Forensics. Kingfisher 2005 63p il (Kingfisher knowledge) $12.95 *

Grades: 5 6 7 8 **363.2**
1. Forensic sciences 2. Criminal investigation
ISBN 0-7534-5862-4

"This book looks at the . . . topic of collecting and analyzing evidence. Each spread focuses on a subtopic under the categories Signs of the Crime, Who Is It? and Crime Lab. Abundant, closeup color photographs illustrate everything from ballistics to counterfeit money. . . . This visually appealing book gives a basic overview of everything that goes into investigating a crime and is good for browsing." SLJ

Includes glossary

Spilsbury, Richard, 1963-

Counterfeit! stopping fakes and forgeries. Enslow Publishers 2009 48p il (Solve that crime!) lib bdg $23.93

Grades: 5 6 7 8 **363.2**
1. Forgery 2. Fraud
ISBN 978-0-7660-3378-8 (lib bdg); 0-7660-3378-3 (lib bdg)
LC 2008-33310

"Learn how forensics solves the mystery of counterfeit and forged objects, from fake money to false Vermeers." Publisher's note

This "title boasts in-depth information, sidebars detailing events of true crime, and activities that will increase understanding. . . . Photographs are colorful, well-captioned, and related to the text." SLJ

Includes glossary and bibliographical references

363.3 Other aspects of public safety

Nolan, Janet, 1956-

The firehouse light; illustrations by Marie Lafrance. Tricycle Press 2010 unp il $15.99; lib bdg $18.95

Grades: K 1 2 3 **363.3**
1. Electric lamps 2. Fire departments
ISBN 978-1-58246-298-1; 1-58246-298-4; 978-1-58246-346-9 (lib bdg); 1-58246-346-8 (lib bdg)
LC 2009-7964

Nolan, Janet, 1956-—*Continued*

The true story of a lightbulb in a firehouse located in Livermore, California, that has stayed lit for more than one hundred years.

"The narrative successfully knits firefighting and history into a fast dash through the twentieth century. . . . Flat, folk-style acrylic illustrations feature fluid, sinewy human figures amid a variety of vintage fire trucks." Booklist

363.34   Disasters

Fradin, Judith Bloom

Droughts; [by] Judy & Dennis Fradin. National Geographic 2008 48p il map (Witness to disaster) $16.95; lib bdg $20.90 *

Grades: 4 5 6 7   363.34

1. Droughts
ISBN   978-1-4263-0339-5;   1-4263-0339-4; 978-1-4263-0340-1 (lib bdg); 1-4263-0340-8 (lib bdg)
LC 2008020424

"This book examines the lessons from the Dust Bowl droughts for farmers, including the importance of topsoil. The history of droughts around the world compares impacts on a wide variety of societies. The final chapter looks at the latest tools and technologies developed to help us survive future droughts." Publisher's note

Includes glossary and bibliographical references

Hurricane Katrina; [by] Judith Bloom Fradin, Dennis Brindell Fradin. Marshall Cavendish Benchmark 2009 c2010 47p il map (Turning points in U.S. history) lib bdg $21.95

Grades: 3 4 5   363.34

1. Hurricane Katrina, 2005
ISBN 978-0-7614-4261-5 (lib bdg); 0-7614-4261-8 (lib bdg)
LC 2008038268

"Covers Hurricane Katrina as a watershed event in U.S. history, influencing social, economic, and political policies that shaped the nation's future." Publisher's note

This book provides "accurate, nonsensationalized information in [a] well-organized, clearly written, and politically neutral [text]. The photos are crisp, and, due to the subject matter, heartrending." SLJ

Includes glossary and bibliographical references

Karwoski, Gail, 1949-

Tsunami; the true story of an April Fools' Day disaster; [by] Gail Langer Karwoski; illustrated by John MacDonald. Darby Creek Pub. 2006 64p il $17.95

Grades: 4 5 6 7   363.34

1. Tsunamis 2. Hawaii
ISBN 1-58196-944-1

The author "opens with a description of the tsunami waves that struck the northern coast of the Hawaiian Islands in 1946, destroying a school and sweeping many children and adults out to sea. The book goes on to provide broader information about tsunamis, from scientific understanding of how they occur to ongoing efforts at early warning systems. . . . Clearly written and informative." Booklist

Langley, Andrew

Hurricanes, tsunamis, and other natural disasters; [by] Andrew Langley. Kingfisher 2006 63p il map (Kingfisher knowledge) $12.95

Grades: 5 6 7 8   363.34

1. Natural disasters
ISBN 978-0-7534-5975-1; 0-7534-5975-2
LC 2005027200

This briefly describes such natural disasters as hurricanes, tsunamis, avalanches, brush fires, earthquakes, floods, tornadoes, drought and famine, pandemics, with many color illustrations and maps

"This book presents a high-interest topic in an attractively designed format that features colorful, eye-catching graphics and a solidly written text." Booklist

Includes glossary and bibliographical references

Markle, Sandra, 1946-

Rescues! Millbrook Press 2006 88p il map lib bdg $25.26 *

Grades: 4 5 6 7   363.34

1. Rescue work 2. Survival after airplane accidents, shipwrecks, etc.
ISBN 978-0-8225-3413-6 (lib bdg); 0-8225-3413-4 (lib bdg)
LC 2005-09707

"From the collapse of a Pennsylvania coal mine in 2002 to the tsunami that struck 11 countries in 2004 to Hurricane Katrina in 2005, the 11 disasters Markle describes are straight from news headlines. In this full-color photo-essay, she uses individual experiences of rescue and survival to bring each drama close." Booklist

Includes bibliographical references

Miller, Mara, 1968-

Hurricane Katrina strikes the Gulf Coast; disaster & survival; [by] Mara Miller. Enslow Publishers 2006 48p il map (Deadly disasters) $23.93

Grades: 4 5 6 7   363.34

1. Hurricane Katrina, 2005 2. Hurricanes 3. Rescue work
ISBN 0-7660-2803-8   LC 2005030989

Contents: Katrina gains strength; What is a hurricane?; Katrina strikes; New Orleans floods; After Katrina; The next hurricane

"Miller begins with an account of the development of Hurricane Katrina as it struck Florida and then threatened the Gulf Coast. She discusses the subsequent flooding of New Orleans, the damage it caused, rescue and recovery attempts, and planning for the aftermath of future hurricanes. The author includes a clear scientific description of hurricanes, defining key terms. Color photos and graphics help explain concepts such as the structure of a hurricane, Katrina's path, and the conditions endured by the victims." SLJ

Includes glossary and bibliographical references

363.6 Public utilities and related services

Brown, Cynthia Light
Discover National Monuments, National Parks; natural wonders; illustrated by Blair Shedd. Nomad Press 2009 106p il (Discover your world) pa $19.95
Grades: 5 6 7 8   **363.6**
  1. National parks and reserves
  ISBN 978-1-9346702-8-6 (pa); 1-9346702-8-6 (pa)
  "With an inviting, browsable design and a chatty style, this large-sized volume . . . covers 15 national monuments and parks in the U.S. that celebrate and protect natural phenomena . . . The science will excite readers, with detailed explanations of tectonic plates, radiometric dating, and dendrochronology." Booklist

Burgan, Michael
Not a drop to drink; water for a thirsty world; Peter H. Gleick, consultant. National Geographic 2008 64p il map (National Geographic investigates) $17.95
Grades: 4 5 6 7   **363.6**
  1. Water 2. Water supply
  ISBN 978-1-4263-0360-9; 1-4263-0360-2
Explores the important connections between human activity and the water cycle and shows how researchers are working to understand such issues as how climate change affects water supplies and how the oceans can help solve the water crisis.

Hollyer, Beatrice
Our world of water; children and water around the world; foreword by Zadie Smith. Henry Holt and Co. 2009 47p il map $16.99 *
Grades: 3 4 5   **363.6**
  1. Water supply 2. Water
  ISBN 978-0-8050-8941-7; 0-8050-8941-1
                                    LC 2008040596
  "Seven and eight-year-olds share what water means to them by revealing their everyday uses of it. An opening spread introduces the children and their countries—Peru, Ethiopia, Mauritania, Tajikistan, Bangladesh, and the United States—on an outline world map. Locations vary from mountaintop to seaside and from scarcity to abundance. . . . There is no order to the countries and the text is matter-of-fact, leaving readers to draw their own conclusions about the subjects' varying circumstances. Several full-color, captioned photos appear on each spread. . . . Questions will inevitably arise from this revealing look at the status of water in the world." SLJ
  Includes bibliographical references

Kerley, Barbara
A cool drink of water. National Geographic Soc. 2002 unp il map $16.95; pa $7.95
Grades: K 1 2 3   **363.6**
  1. Water supply 2. Water
  ISBN 0-7922-6723-0; 0-7922-5489-9 (pa)
                                    LC 2001-2479

Depicts people around the world collecting, chilling, and drinking water
  "Children will be entranced by the beautiful images of a basic substance that connects us all. Excellent for cross-cultural discussions." Booklist

363.7 Environmental problems

Albee, Sarah
Poop happened! a history of the world from the bottom up; illustrated by Robert Leighton. Walker 2010 170p il lib bdg $20.89; pa $15.99 *
Grades: 4 5 6 7   **363.7**
  1. Toilets 2. Feces 3. Sanitation 4. Refuse and refuse disposal
  ISBN 978-0-8027-9825-1 (lib bdg); 0-8027-9825-X (lib bdg); 978-0-8027-2077-1 (pa); 0-8027-2077-3 (pa)
  "Albee deposits a heaping history of human sanitation—or rather lack thereof— and its effects. . . . She pumps out a steady stream of comments on the miasmic effects of urbanization, waste disposal, and the roles of (not) bathing in ancient Greece, Rome, medieval Europe, . . . and the 'Reeking Renaissance.' She then digs into the gradual adoption of better practices in the nineteenth century. . . . The cartoon illustrations feature sludgy green highlights." Booklist

Bang, Molly, 1943-
Nobody particular; one woman's fight to save the bays. Holt & Co. 2000 46p il $18
Grades: 4 5 6 7   **363.7**
  1. Wilson, Diane 2. Pollution 3. Environmental protection
  ISBN 0-8050-5396-4   LC 99-33348
  "Bang tells the story of activist Diane Wilson, a commercial shrimper who almost single-handedly forced Formosa Plastics to agree to stop polluting the Texas bays." Horn Book Guide
  "The story, in hand-lettered text and speech balloons, is in bordered squares containing panels of black-and-white cartoon art, which are printed over double-page spreads of beautifully executed full-color depictions of the bays' ecosystem, chemical pollution, and shrimp farming. . . . A riveting, emotional story." Booklist

Barnham, Kay
Recycle; [by] Kay Barnham. Crabtree Pub. 2008 32p il (Environment action!) lib bdg $22.60; pa $7.95 *
Grades: K 1 2 3   **363.7**
  1. Recycling
  ISBN 978-0-7787-3659-2 (lib bdg); 0-7787-3659-8 (lib bdg); 978-0-7787-3669-1 (pa); 0-7787-3669-5 (pa)
                                    LC 2007030000
  This "book explores how our garbage is processed, the problems it creates for the environment, and how we can change that." Publisher's note
  This book "exposes young children to concepts that can truly make a difference. . . . [The book has] plenty of colorful, relevant, and interesting glossy color photographs." Sci Books Films
  Includes glossary

Barraclough, Sue

Reusing things; by Sue Barraclough. Sea to Sea Publications 2008 30p il (Making a difference) lib bdg $27.10

Grades: 1 2 3   **363.7**

1. Environmental protection 2. Recycling

ISBN 978-1-59771-109-8 (lib bdg); 1-59771-109-8 (lib bdg)   LC 2006051277

This suggests ways in which people can reduce waste by reusing paper or junk, repairing or repainting old items, borrowing or giving away things, and buying or using second-hand things.

This features "clear, concise information that is simple to read and understand, alternating between giving simple facts and dispersing helpful hints and suggestions. The full-color photographs are crisp and attractive." SLJ

Bowden, Rob

Waste; by Rob Bowden. KidHaven Press 2004 48p il (Sustainable world) lib bdg $23.70

Grades: 5 6 7 8   **363.7**

1. Refuse and refuse disposal

ISBN 0-7377-1902-8   LC 2003-52951

This "discusses innovations in reuse and recycling, ingenious ways to use what would be discarded, and changes in taxation policy. The many full-color photographs clarify the [text]. [This] will be highly useful for both reports and in classroom discussions." SLJ

Includes bibliographical references

Bridges, Andrew

Clean air. Roaring Brook Press 2009 40p il (Sally Ride science) pa $7.99

Grades: 5 6 7 8   **363.7**

1. Greenhouse effect 2. Air pollution

ISBN 978-1-59643-576-6 (pa); 1-59643-576-3 (pa)

"Rb Flash Point"

"This volume examines how burning fossil fuels, clearing forests, and other human activities affect the Earth's climate by contributing large amounts of greenhouse gases to the atmosphere." Publisher's note

This is a "well-written, engaging book. . . . The [book's] best feature is the conversational tone that simply and clearly conveys important, and sometimes complicated, scientific concepts. Illustrations and layout are well done, and include colorful photographs and charts. Excellent." SLJ

Bryan, Nichol, 1958-

Exxon Valdez oil spill. World Almanac Library 2004 48p il map (Environmental disasters) lib bdg $29.27 paperback o.p.

Grades: 5 6 7 8   **363.7**

1. Exxon Valdez (Ship) 2. Oil spills

ISBN 0-8368-5506-X (lib bdg); 0-8368-5513-2 (pa)   LC 2003-47991

Describes the oil tanker Exxon Valdez, the events that led up to its disastrous oil spill in 1989, and the effects of the spill on the Alaskan environment.

This is "well-illustrated. . . . [It does] a fine job of placing [the] disaster within a larger context by including detailed background about America's industrial and environmental history; quotes from eyewitnesses, politicians, and journalists; and clear explanations of the changes in policy that [the] disaster instigated." Booklist

Includes glossary and bibliographical references

Cherry, Lynne, 1952-

How we know what we know about our changing climate; scientists and kids explore global warming; by Lynne Cherry and Gary Braasch; with a foreword by David Sobel. Dawn Publications 2008 66p il $18.95; pa $11.95 *

Grades: 4 5 6 7   **363.7**

1. Greenhouse effect 2. Climate—Environmental aspects

ISBN 978-1-58469-103-7; 0-1-58469-103-4; 978-1-58469-130-3 (pa); 1-58469-130-1 (pa)   LC 2007-37255

"This volume describes where scientists look to find evidence of climate change—from changes in bird migration patterns and fruit blossom dates, to obtaining tree rings and mud cores—and especially how students and other citizen-scientists are assisting to monitor climate change, as well as what can be done to mitigate global warming." Publisher's note

"The can-do emphasis helps to make the topic less depressing, and the intriguing color photographs are thoughtful and upbeat." Booklist

Cole, Joanna

The magic school bus and the climate challenge; illustrated by Bruce Degen. Scholastic 2010 37p il $16.99

Grades: 2 3 4   **363.7**

1. Greenhouse effect 2. Climate—Environmental aspects 3. Environmental protection

ISBN 978-0-590-10826-3; 0-590-10826-3

"Ms. Frizzle and her class challenge readers to go green. After traveling in their bus-plane and showing in storyboard style example after example of the Earth's changing climate, Ms. Frizzle, reluctant traveler Arnold, new South Korean classmate Joon, and the gang ride sun rays to the Earth, and then get back on the bus as those rays (and riders) get caught by heat-trapping gases." SLJ

David, Laurie

The down-to-earth guide to global warming; [by] Laurie David and Cambria Gordon. Orchard Books 2007 112p il map pa $15.99 *

Grades: 4 5 6 7   **363.7**

1. Greenhouse effect 2. Climate—Environmental aspects

ISBN 978-0-439-02494-5 (pa); 0-439-02494-3 (pa)   LC 2006-35705

The authors "put forth the basics on global warming, climate change, and how readers can green up the environment. They temper the book's often troubling subject matter with kid-friendly humor, some celebrity shout-outs, and explanations of the scientific underpinnings. An amply illustrated layout, featuring attention-grabbing sidebars, dramatic photos, and diagrams, will sustain reader interest." Booklist

Includes bibliographical references

Delano, Marfe Ferguson

Earth in the hot seat; bulletins from a warming world. National Geographic 2009 63p il (Preserve our planet) $19.95; lib bdg $28.90 *

Grades: 5 6 7 8   **363.7**

1. Greenhouse effect 2. Climate—Environmental aspects

ISBN   978-1-4263-0434-7;   1-4263-0434-X; 978-1-4263-0435-4 (lib bdg); 1-4263-0435-8 (lib bdg)

LC 2008029317

"This book lays out . . . the evidence for global warming and the part that human activity plays in it. Five chapters lay out the signs and evidences of a warming world. . . . Subsequent chapters of the book are devoted to what humankind can expect in a warming world and steps that must be taken to avert catastrophe for humans and the planet. . . . The illustrative photos are fully up to National Geographic high standards. This [is a] fine book, reasonably priced and carefully researched." Voice Youth Advocates

Includes bibliographical references

Farrell, Courtney

Keeping water clean. Cherry Lake Pub. 2010 32p il (Save the planet) lib bdg $27.04

Grades: 3 4 5 6   **363.7**

1. Water pollution

ISBN 978-1-60279-659-1 (lib bdg); 1-60279-659-9 (lib bdg)

"Language Arts Explorer"

Teaches young readers the importance of unpolluted water, and describes how to keep water clean by using gray water processes, conserving drinking water, and reducing overall pollution

"At the beginning of . . . [the] book, readers are given a mission and advised to be alert to the facts provided so that they can successfully answer the questions at the end. . . . Children are made to feel part of the process; suggestions for how they can become involved abound." SLJ

Includes glossary and bibliographical references

Geiger, Beth, 1958-

Clean water. Roaring Brook Press 2009 40p il (Sally Ride science) pa $7.99

Grades: 5 6 7 8   **363.7**

1. Water pollution 2. Water supply

ISBN 978-1-59643-577-3 (pa); 1-59643-577-1 (pa)

"Rb Flash Point"

This describes "developing technologies for recycling and desalinating water that are helping to bring clean water to people all over the world." Publisher's note

This is a "well-written, engaging book. . . . The [book']s best feature is the conversational tone that simply and clearly conveys important, and sometimes complicated, scientific concepts. Illustrations and layout are well done, and include colorful photographs and charts. Excellent." SLJ

Gifford, Clive

Pollution; [by] Clive Gifford. Heinemann Library 2006 48p il map (Planet under pressure) lib bdg $31.43 *

Grades: 4 5 6 7   **363.7**

1. Pollution

ISBN 1-4034-7742-6   LC 2005017064

"Gifford discusses the many types of pollution, global warming and the greenhouse effect, the worldwide impact on human lives and well-being, and possible solutions. . . . [This has] numerous quality color visuals, and sidebars. Up-to-date and informative." SLJ

Includes bibliographical references

Gore, Al, Jr., 1948-

An inconvenient truth; the crisis of global warming; adapted for young readers by Jane O'Connor. rev ed. Viking 2007 191p il map $23; pa $16 *

Grades: 5 6 7 8   **363.7**

1. Greenhouse effect 2. Climate—Environmental aspects

ISBN 978-0-670-06271-3; 978-0-670-06272-0 (pa)

Adapted from the title for adults published 2006 by Rodale Press

This explains what global warming is, what causes it, and explains how to take action to stop this crisis.

This is illustrated with "easy-to-grasp graphics and revealing before-and-after photos. . . . O'Connor rephrases Gore's arguments in briefer, simpler language without compromising their flow." SLJ

Guiberson, Brenda Z., 1946-

Earth feeling the heat; illustrated by Chad Wallace. Henry Holt and Company 2010 unp il map $16.99 *

Grades: K 1 2 3   **363.7**

1. Greenhouse effect 2. Climate—Environmental aspects 3. Animals

ISBN 978-0-8050-7719-3; 0-8050-7719-7

LC 2009012219

"This handsome picture book shows the threat of global warming, one creature at a time. . . . On each double-page spread, the detailed oil paintings pair with rhythmic text. . . . An accompanying world map shows the habitat of each creature and emphasizes the sense of global connections among living beings, while a final page features detailed suggestions for kids to practice conservation in their daily lives." Booklist

Hall, Eleanor J.

Recycling. KidHaven Press 2004 c2005 48p il (Our environment) lib bdg $23.70 *

Grades: 5 6 7 8   **363.7**

1. Recycling

ISBN 0-7377-1517-0   LC 2003-21682

Contents: What is recycling?; The challenges of recycling; The benefits of recycling; What does the future hold?

"The liberal use of vibrant colors, the inclusion of a photograph or diagram on most pages, and the generous

Hall, Eleanor J.—Continued

print size will appeal to reluctant readers. [This title] will help students examine cause and effect (and possible solutions), and challenge them to live green." SLJ

Includes glossary and bibliographical references

Hanel, Rachael

Climate fever; stopping global warming. Compass Point Books 2010 64p il (Green generation) lib bdg $31.99; pa $6.95

Grades: 5 6 7 8 9   **363.7**

1. Greenhouse effect 2. Climate

ISBN 978-0-7565-4246-7 (lib bdg); 0-7565-4246-4 (lib bdg); 978-0-7565-4291-7 (pa); 0-7565-4291-X (pa)

LC 2009-11448

"The cover design, layout, and graphics feel hip and of the moment. The clear writing is easy to understand and includes many concrete examples of environmentally friendly practices. . . . [A] good choice[s] for both leisure reading and reports." SLJ

Includes glossary and bibliographical references

Lorbiecki, Marybeth

Planet patrol; a kids' action guide to earth care; by Marybeth Lorbiecki; illustrated by Nancy Meyers. Two-Can Pub. 2005 48p il $15.95; pa $8.95

Grades: 3 4 5   **363.7**

1. Environmental protection

ISBN 1-58728-514-2; 1-58728-518-5 (pa)

LC 2005012476

"An introduction to ecology that uses examples of real-life human endeavors, action tips and factoids to show how environmental problems can be slowed or reversed." Publisher's note

"The amazing facts . . . the immediate action tips . . . the chatty, interactive style . . . and the urgent message about global warming and pollution will draw young readers to this lively, browsable conservation manual." Booklist

Includes bibliographical references

Martin, Laura C.

Recycled crafts box; [by] Laura C. Martin. Storey Publishing 2004 88p il $19.95; pa $10.95

Grades: 3 4 5 6   **363.7**

1. Recycling 2. Handicraft

ISBN 1-58017-523-6; 1-58017-522-8 (pa)

LC 2003-16703

Contents: All about garbage; Getting started; Paper; Plastics; Meta; Fabric and clothing; Glass

Discusses recycling and provides information and instructions for making art projects from a variety of recycled materials

"Illustrated with cheerful cartoon drawings and color photos of the finished projects, and bolstered by many resource lists, this is a surprisingly attractive, substantive offering." Booklist

Metz, Lorijo

What can we do about global warming? Rosen Pub. Group 2010 24p il (Protecting our planet) lib bdg $21.25; pa $8

Grades: 2 3 4   **363.7**

1. Greenhouse effect 2. Climate—Environmental aspects 3. Environmental protection

ISBN 978-1-4042-8079-3 (lib bdg); 1-4042-8079-0 (lib bdg); 978-1-4358-2479-9 (pa); 1-4358-2479-2 (pa)

LC 2008-50766

"Learn how global warming occurs, what causes it, and what we can do to lessen its effects." Publisher's note

This book provides "straightforward information . . . complemented by full-page, color photographs. . . . Links for further information . . . are housed at the publisher's Web site (which allows feedback so that readers can suggest more sites)." SLJ

Includes glossary

What can we do about trash and recycling? PowerKids Press 2010 24p il (Protecting our planet) lib bdg $21.25; pa $8

Grades: 2 3 4   **363.7**

1. Recycling

ISBN 978-1-4042-8082-3 (lib bdg); 1-4042-8082-0 (lib bdg); 978-1-4358-2483-6 (pa); 1-4358-2483-0 (pa)

LC 2008-53812

"Examines how we can reduce the average American trash intake through reducing, recycling, and reusing." Publisher's note

This book provides "straightforward information . . . complemented by full-page, color photographs. . . . Links for further information . . . are housed at the publisher's Web site (which allows feedback so that readers can suggest more sites)." SLJ

Includes glossary

Minden, Cecilia, 1949-

Reduce, reuse, and recycle. Cherry Lake Pub. 2010 32p il (Save the planet) lib bdg $27.07

Grades: 3 4 5 6   **363.7**

1. Conservation of natural resources 2. Waste minimization 3. Recycling

ISBN 978-1-60279-662-1 (lib bdg); 1-60279-662-9 (lib bdg)

"Language Arts Explorer"

Presents tips for how to reduce the amount of garbage thrown away, from buying items that have less packaging at the store to precycling and making art from trash

"At the beginning of . . . [the] book, readers are given a mission and advised to be alert to the facts provided so that they can successfully answer the questions at the end. . . . Children are made to feel part of the process; suggestions for how they can become involved abound." SLJ

Includes glossary and bibliographical references

Morris, Neil, 1946-

Global warming. World Almanac Library 2007 48p il (What if we do nothing?) lib bdg $22.95; pa $11.95 *

Grades: 5 6 7 8   363.7

1. Greenhouse effect 2. Climate—Environmental aspects

ISBN 978-0-8368-7755-7 (lib bdg); 0-8368-7755-1 (lib bdg); 978-0-8368-155-4 (pa); 0-8368-8155-9 (pa)

LC 2006-30444

This "explains how we can measure [global warming] and what is likely to happen to our world as a result of warming. It discusses both human activity and natural cycles that contribute to global warming, and it urges the reader to think about what we can do to preserve: Land from being lost, Human health, Endangered species." Publisher's note

This "boasts an attractive format, with large pages that allow room for pictures, excellent charts and graphs, as well as a thoughtful, clear discussion of the topic." Booklist

Includes bibliographical references

Nardo, Don, 1947-

Climate crisis; the science of global warming; by Don Nardo. Compass Point Books 2009 47p il map (Headline science) lib bdg $27.93; pa $7.95

Grades: 5 6 7   363.7

1. Greenhouse effect 2. Climate—Environmental aspects

ISBN 978-0-7565-3571-1 (lib bdg); 0-7565-3571-9 (lib bdg); 978-0-7565-3948-1 (pa); 0-7565-3948-X (pa)

LC 2008-7259

"Presents an introduction to global warming, discussing the impact of rising temperatures, melting ice, water shortages, increased rate of animal extinctions, and the current human efforts underway to lessen the effects." Publisher's note

"Color photos and graphics provide visual information; a timeline is helpful to find fast facts, and the Facthound Web site provides students with additional information." Libr Media Connect

Includes glossary and bibliographical references

Parker, Steve

Population. QEB Pub. 2010 32p il (QEB changes in . . .) lib bdg $28.50

Grades: 3 4 5 6   363.7

1. Human influence on nature 2. Human ecology

ISBN 978-1-59566-774-8 (lib bdg); 1-59566-774-1 (lib bdg)   LC 2008-56070

"The information is presented in brief paragraphs and sidebars. Suggestions for kids to help improve the planet are sprinkled throughout. . . . Students will enjoy this appealing layout and the information can spark further research on the topic[s]. . . . Either digitally or on paper, students could make fantastic presentations using a similar design." Libr Media Connect

Includes glossary

Parks, Peggy J., 1951-

Global warming. KidHaven Press 2004 48p il (Our environment) lib bdg $23.70

Grades: 5 6 7 8   363.7

1. Greenhouse effect 2. Climate—Environmental aspects

ISBN 0-7377-1822-6   LC 2002-156050

Contents: What is global warming?; Caused by humans or caused by nature?; Signs and effects of global warming; What can be done?

"The liberal use of vibrant colors, the inclusion of a photograph or diagram on most pages, and the generous print size will appeal to reluctant readers. [This title] will help students examine cause and effect (and possible solutions), and challenge them to live green." SLJ

Includes glossary and bibliographical references

Pringle, Laurence P.

Global warming; the threat of Earth's changing climate; [by] Laurence Pringle. SeaStar Bks. 2001 48p il $16.95 paperback o.p.

Grades: 4 5 6 7   363.7

1. Greenhouse effect 2. Climate—Environmental aspects

ISBN 1-58717-009-4; 1-58717-28-3 (pa)

LC 00-63740

Replaces the edition published 1990 by Arcade Pub.

"Pringle covers the science of global warming . . . from detailed discussion of atmospheric phenomena to concerns about human production of emissions." Horn Book Guide

"Well-illustrated . . . this offers students a solid, factual overview of the subject." Booklist

Includes glossary and bibliographical references

Rapp, Valerie

Protecting Earth's air quality; by Valerie Rapp. Lerner Publications 2009 72p il map (Saving our living Earth) lib bdg $30.60

Grades: 5 6 7 8   363.7

1. Air pollution

ISBN 978-0-8225-7558-0 (lib bdg); 0-8225-7558-2 (lib bdg)   LC 2008-907

"Provides a thorough, interesting discussion of multiple aspects of [protecting Earth's air quality], including historical origins, the current situation, and potential solutions. . . . Photos from around the world accompany discussions. . . . [This is a] solid choice to replace outdated books." SLJ

Includes glossary and bibliographical references

Rockwell, Anne F., 1934-

Why are the ice caps melting? the dangers of global warming; by Anne Rockwell; illustrated by Paul Meisel. HarperCollins 2006 33p il (Let's-read-and-find-out science) $15.99; pa $4.99 *

Grades: K 1 2 3   363.7

1. Greenhouse effect 2. Climate—Environmental aspects

ISBN 0-06-054669-7; 0-06-054671-9 (pa)

LC 2005-17972

Rockwell, Anne F., 1934-—_Continued_
Tells about the greenhouse effect, recycling, and what you can do to help fight global warming
"The information is detailed, but not overwhelming. . . . Colorful illustrations provide details that support the [text]." SLJ

Royston, Angela
Global warming. Heinemann 2008 32p il (Protect our planet) lib bdg $25.36; pa $7.99
Grades: 1 2 3   363.7
1. Greenhouse effect 2. Climate—Environmental aspects
ISBN 978-1-4329-0924-6 (lib bdg); 1-4329-0924-X (lib bdg); 978-1-4329-0930-7 (pa); 1-4329-0930-4 (pa)
This is a "very basic introduction to some of the causes and effects of global warming. . . . [The author] discusses extreme weather, changing climates, melting ice caps, alternative sources of energy . . . and low-carbon living. Young readers will come away not frightened, but understanding why they should be concerned." Booklist
Includes glossary and bibliographical references

Simon, Seymour, 1931-
Global warming. Collins 2010 31p il $17.99; lib bdg $18.89 *
Grades: 3 4 5   363.7
1. Greenhouse effect 2. Climate—Environmental aspects
ISBN 978-0-06-114250-5; 0-06-114250-6; 978-0-06-114251-2 (lib bdg); 0-06-114251-4 (lib bdg)
LC 2009001265
This takes "on the timely matter of climate change. Informative and noncondescending, this boils down large, complex issues into understandable concepts, even as it covers the range of current understanding on how we are impacting the planet. . . . Thoughtfully chosen full-page photos complement and reflect the text." Booklist
Includes glossary

Sohn, Emily
The environment; series editor, Tara Koellhoffer; with a foreword by Emily Sohn. Chelsea Clubhouse 2006 122p il (Science news for kids) $22.50 *
Grades: 4 5 6 7   363.7
1. Environmental sciences
ISBN 0-7910-9123-6   LC 2005037548
Articles written chiefly by Emily Sohn
"Lively writing style, good organization, an attractive design, and thought-provoking study questions help introduce the interwoven topics relating to the environment and global warming. Succinct overviews prefacing each section and plenty of color photographs make for an accessible presentation." Booklist
Includes bibliographical references

Thornhill, Jan, 1955-
This is my planet; the kids' guide to global warming. Maple Tree Press 2007 64p il map $21.95; pa $10.95 *
Grades: 4 5 6   363.7
1. Greenhouse effect 2. Climate—Environmental aspects
ISBN 978-1-897349-06-9; 1-897349-06-8; 978-1-897349-07-6 (pa); 1-897349-07-6 (pa)
"This is a thorough, accurate, interesting guide to global warming. . . . Helpful diagrams and appealing photographs accompany the easy-to-understand narrative." Sci Books Films

Wells, Robert E.
Polar bear, why is your world melting? Albert Whitman & Co. 2008 unp il $16.99; pa $6.99
Grades: 1 2 3 4   363.7
1. Greenhouse effect 2. Arctic regions 3. Ice
ISBN 978-0-8075-6598-8; 0-8075-6598-9; 978-0-8075-6599-5 (pa); 0-8075-6599-7 (pa)
LC 2008-01308
"Two children sail in a red research vessel through the pages of this clear and simple explanation of global warming. Colorful, cartoon drawings show the youngsters rescuing a mother polar bear and her two cubs by hauling them onto their boat. Then, beginning with an explanation of the sun's effect on the Earth's atmosphere, they pursue the reasons that the Arctic ice is melting. Without oversimplifying, Wells makes the large concepts of the Greenhouse Effect and the sources of CO_2 understandable for young children. . . . An excellent introduction to the topic." SLJ

363.8   Food supply

Bowden, Rob
Food and farming; [by] Rob Bowden. KidHaven Press 2004 48p il map (Sustainable world) lib bdg $23.70
Grades: 5 6 7 8   363.8
1. Food 2. Agriculture
ISBN 0-7377-1899-4   LC 2003-52952
This "first presents conventional techniques of food production, but focuses primarily on sustainable agriculture methods. . . . Bowden writes with admirable simplicity about complicated subjects, and he's careful to separate facts from opinions when he quotes others. . . . [The book includes] excellent color photos, and gripping statistics." Booklist
Includes glossary and bibliographical references

363.9   Population problems

Mason, Paul, 1967-
Population; [by] Paul Mason. Heinemann Library 2006 48p il map (Planet under pressure) lib bdg $31.43
Grades: 4 5 6 7   363.9
1. Population 2. Human ecology
ISBN 1-4034-7741-8   LC 2005017063

Mason, Paul, 1967-—*Continued*

"Mason describes the many factors that cause population levels to increase or decline; the impact of overpopulation, such as the depletion of food and clean-water supplies; current population figures; future forecasts; and more. Facts and figures show that overpopulation is affecting both rich and poor countries. The ethical question of whether societies and governments have the right to control personal choices is also addressed. . . . [This title has] numerous quality color visuals, and sidebars. Up-to-date and informative." SLJ

Includes bibliographical references

364 Criminology

Somervill, Barbara A., 1948-

Graphing crime. Raintree 2010 32p il (Real world data) $28.21; pa $7.99

Grades: 4 5 6 7   364

1. Crime 2. Statistics 3. Graphic methods

ISBN   978-1-4329-2623-6;   1-4329-2623-3;
978-1-4329-2632-8 (pa); 1-4329-2632-2 (pa)

LC 2009001292

This "discusses juvenile offenders, drug money, terrorism, and more, and teaches readers how to evaluate statistics in the various charts, such as the difference between crimes committed and crimes reported, or between total numbers and rate per population. . . . The clear design, with lots of full-color photos and sidebars, will encourage browsers as much as the up-to-date examples and the clear directions for remaining 'chart smart.'" Booklist

Includes glossary and bibliographical references

364.1 Criminal offenses

St. George, Judith, 1931-

In the line of fire; presidents' lives at stake. Holiday House 1999 144p il lib bdg $22.95 *

Grades: 4 5 6 7   364.1

1. Presidents—United States—Assassination

ISBN 0-8234-1428-0   LC 98-39030

"The first of the two main sections concerns the four slain U.S. presidents as well as their respective assassins, and also discusses the effects of these fatal events on the country. Each chapter preface relays the day's events preceding the murder in a dramatic fashion. The second half concerns the assassination attempts on six presidents and their would-be assassins. St. George includes intriguing anecdotes. . . . Nicely placed illustrations and photos add power to the text." SLJ

Includes bibliographical references

368.3   Old-age insurance and insurance against death, illness, injury

Lynette, Rachel

What to do when your family can't afford healthcare. PowerKids Press 2010 24p il (Let's work it out) $21.25; pa $8.25

Grades: 2 3 4   368.3

1. Health insurance 2. Medicaid

ISBN   978-1-4358-9342-9;   1-4358-9342-5;
978-1-4358-9772-4 (pa); 1-4358-9772-2 (pa)

This book explains what healthcare and insurance are and why they are so crucial. It also explains the many different low-cost insurance options that are available so that every family can get the care they need.

"Full-page color photographs appear opposite the [narrative], depicting multicultural children, parents, grandparents, social workers, and others, whose demeanors match the hopeful tone of the [title]. This . . . will help promote empathy and understanding for the plight of others and is a key purchase." SLJ

Includes glossary

370.1   Philosophy and theory, education for specific objectives, educational psychology

Barker, Dan

Maybe right, maybe wrong; a guide for young thinkers; by Dan Barker; illustrated by Brian Strassburg. Prometheus Bks. 1992 76p il pa $17.98

Grades: 4 5 6   370.1

1. Conduct of life 2. Human rights 3. Moral education

ISBN 978-0-87975-731-1 (pa); 0-87975-731-0 (pa)

LC 92-416

Discusses learning right from wrong, stressing such aspects as the difference between rules and principles and the importance of an individual's rights

370.9   Education—Historical, geographic, persons treatment

Aillaud, Cindy Lou, 1955-

Recess at 20 below. Alaska Northwest Books 2005 unp il hardcover o.p. pa $8.95 *

Grades: K 1 2 3   370.9

1. Schools—Alaska 2. Alaska

ISBN 0-88240-604-3; 0-88240-609-4 (pa)

"Aillaud, who wrote the text and took the photos here, teaches elementary physical education in Delta Junction, Alaska, a town at the end of the Alaska Highway, above the Arctic Circle. By focusing on one school activity—outdoor recess . . . she demonstrates how cold things get and how kids deal with it and still have plenty of fun. . . . Twenty-five color photographs capture marvelous details." Booklist

Ruurs, Margriet, 1952-

My school in the rain forest; how children attend school around the world. Boyds Mills Press 2009 31p il map $17.95

Grades: 1 2 3 4 5   **370.9**

1. Schools 2. Students

ISBN 978-1-59078-601-7; 1-59078-601-7

LC 2009000366

"The book introduces 13 schools, including home schools in Australia and the U.S., a floating school on a Cambodian lake, a village school in Guatemala, a monastery school in Myanmar, and one operated by a global charity. Each double-page spread includes several paragraphs of text, four color photos, and fact box with information about the country, a drawing of its flag, and a map. . . . The book as a whole gives a good sense of the vastly different educational experiences of children around the world." Booklist

371.1   Teachers and teaching, and related activities

Harada, Violet H.

Inquiry learning through librarian-teacher partnerships; [by] Violet H. Harada and Joan M. Yoshina. Linworth Pub. 2004 172p il pa $39.95

Grades: Professional   **371.1**

1. Teaching teams 2. School libraries

ISBN 1-58683-134-8   LC 2004-662

"The authors describe what happens in an inquiry-based classroom and library media center and show teachers/librarians how to develop a curriculum that incorporates essential questions and important habits of mind, all aligned with content standards. . . . The volume contains everything a teacher-librarian team would need to create, teach, research, and assess major interdisciplinary units." SLJ

Includes bibliographical references

Kenney, Karen Latchana, 1974-

Teachers at work; by Karen L. Kenney; illustrated by Brian Caleb Dumm; content consultant, Judith Stepan-Norris. Magic Wagon 2009 32p il (Meet your community workers!) lib bdg $18.95

Grades: K 1 2 3   **371.1**

1. Teachers 2. Vocational guidance

ISBN 978-1-60270-653-8 (lib bdg); 1-60270-653-0 (lib bdg)

LC 2009-2395

This book about teachers has "an uncluttered layout and consistent organization. . . . Chapter headings such as 'Problems on the Job,' and 'Technology at Work,' and 'Special Skills and Training' make it easy to pinpoint specific information." SLJ

Includes glossary

371.3   Methods of instruction and study

Bell, Ann, 1945-

Handheld computers in schools and media centers; [by] Ann Bell. Linworth Pub. 2007 134p il pa $39.95

Grades: Professional   **371.3**

1. Computer-assisted instruction 2. Wireless communication systems 3. School libraries—Automation 4. Instructional materials centers

ISBN 1-58683-212-3   LC 2006025691

"This guide will be a tremendous resource for students and teachers who are using handheld devices. Thoroughly indexed and easy to read and follow, it will give teachers and media specialists a means to integrate handheld computers into their curricula and library-media programs. Bell discusses using the devices to meet national and state academic standards and curriculum integration; selecting appropriate hardware and software; finding, assimilating, circulating, and designing digital media, like e-books and e-audiobooks; and common copyright issues with this format." SLJ

Includes bibliographical references

Crane, Beverley E.

Using WEB 2.0 tools in the K-12 classroom. Neal-Schuman Publishers 2009 189p il pa $59.95

Grades: Professional   **371.3**

1. Internet in education 2. Education—Curricula 3. Web 2.0

ISBN 978-1-55570-653-1 (pa); 1-55570-653-3 (pa)

LC 2008-46167

"In this extensive resource, teachers will find a wealth of suggestions, ideas, unit plans, and answers to questions pertaining to how to integrate and use Web 2.0 tools throughout the curriculum." SLJ

"This excellent resource should be widely appealing to teachers, librarians, and school media specialists." Voice Youth Advocates

Includes glossary and bibliographical references

Fontichiaro, Kristin

Podcasting at school; foreword by Diane R. Chen. Libraries Unlimited 2008 170p il pa $30 *

Grades: Professional   **371.3**

1. Podcasting

ISBN 978-1-59158-587-9 (pa); 1-59158-587-2 (pa)

LC 2007-35040

This title presents "incentives for implementing podcasting within the school curriculum. Part I explains the basics of Web 2.0 and dispels popular myths. [It includes] a review of necessary equipment and software; how to develop effective vocal techniques; and the mechanics of recording, publishing, and distributing a podcast. . . . Ideas for utilizing this technology are given in the second section." SLJ

"The book provides simple, clear explanations of podcasting terms, procedures, and protocols. . . . This book is an essential purchase for professional development collections." Libr Media Connect

Includes bibliographical references

Fox, Janet S.

Get organized without losing it; by Janet S. Fox; edited by Pamela Espeland. Free Spirit Pub. 2006 105p il (Laugh & learn) pa $8.95

Grades: 5 6 7 8   **371.3**
    1. Study skills 2. Time management 3. Life skills
    ISBN 978-1-57542-193-3 (pa); 1-57542-193-3 (pa)
                       LC 2005032809

"In this handbook for students, Fox uses humor to provide practical, easy-to-follow ideas for organizing desks, backpacks, and lockers; managing time for homework and after school activities; planning long-term projects; and taking better notes. . . . Fox writes in a conversational style. . . . Humorous illustrations complement the text." Voice Youth Advocates

Includes bibliographical references

Kraus, Jeanne, 1950-

Annie's plan; taking charge of schoolwork and homework; written by Jeanne Kraus; illustrated by Charles Beyl. Magination Press 2007 47p il $14.95; pa $8.95

Grades: 2 3 4 5   **371.3**
    1. Homework 2. Study skills 3. Attention deficit disorder
    ISBN 978-1-59147-481-4; 1-59147-481-7; 978-1-59147-482-1 (pa); 1-59147-482-5 (pa)
                       LC 2006009948

"Annie is smart but she just can't stay focused on anything so she is always behind in class. With the help of her parents and teacher, she learns how to organize her work and is given other tips for completing her assignments. The book offers 10 easy-to-follow steps that begin with a clean, organized desk at school and a quiet, organized work space at home, and end with a signed reward contract. . . . Comical color illustrations and a conversational tone explain that a youngster with ADHD is neither dumb nor an incurable behavioral problem. . . . An extensive note for adults is included. This is an excellent resource for school libraries, professional collections, and parenting collections, and a great shared read for parent and child." SLJ

Technologies for education; a practical guide; [by] Ann E. Barron . . . [et al.] 5th ed. Libraries Unlimited 2006 189p il pa $48

Grades: Professional   **371.3**
    1. Teaching—Aids and devices
    ISBN 1-59158-250-4 (pa); 978-1-59158-250-2 (pa)
                       LC 2006012708

This offers an "overview of the technologies that are impacting education. . . . [It includes] information on a variety of educational technology topics (with a . . . chapter featuring PDAs) and demonstrates how technologies can best be applied in educational settings. . . . Chapters include: Teaching With Technology; Digital Audio; Digital Video; Computer Graphics; Telecommunications; Distance Learning and others." Publisher's note

Includes bibliographical references

371.5 School discipline and related activities

Beaudoin, Marie-Nathalie

Responding to the culture of bullying and disrespect; new perspectives on collaboration, compassion, and responsibility; [by] Marie-Nathalie Beaudoin, Maureen Taylor. rev 2nd ed. Corwin Press 2009 281p il $76.95; pa $36.95

Grades: Professional   **371.5**
    1. Bullies 2. School discipline
    ISBN 978-1-4129-6853-9; 1-4129-6853-4; 978-1-4129-6854-6 (pa); 1-4129-6854-2 (pa)
                       LC 2008-55933

First published 2004 with title: Breaking the culture of bullying and disrespect

"This profound resource explores the behaviors that cultivate a culture of bullying and disrespect. . . . Concrete solutions to issues are offered, and the authors make sure to load this title with practical suggestions for affecting change. They delve into ways to work directly with young people to better address their concerns. . . . This purchase is essential for any educator, counselor, or parent. It should be a staple of the school library reference collection because the information provided should be used daily. It will be a title that can be referenced for years to come and will help with adults struggling to overcome bullying." Voice Youth Advocates

Includes glossary and bibliographical references

Bott, C. J., 1947-

The bully in the book and in the classroom; [by] C. J. Bott. Scarecrow Press 2004 185p il pa $30

Grades: Professional   **371.5**
    1. Reference books 2. Bullies 3. Children's literature—Bibliography 4. Young adult literature—Bibliography
    ISBN 0-8108-5048-6   LC 2004-8536

This "was written to address the . . . problem of bullying in the halls, offices, and classrooms of our schools and to help educators know what to look for and how to react when they witness harassment. . . . Bott also reviews books recommended for each reading level. . . . Each review contains . . . [a] summary, activities, and quotes from the book." Publisher's note

"The volume may be useful as a beginning effort in dealing with this very real and pervasive problem." SLJ

Includes bibliographical references

More bullies in more books. Scarecrow Press 2009 197p il pa $35

Grades: Professional   **371.5**
    1. Bullies 2. Reference books 3. Children's literature—Bibliography 4. Young adult literature—Bibliography
    ISBN 978-0-8108-6654-6 (pa); 0-8108-6654-4 (pa)
                       LC 2009-923

This "offers more than 350 annotated titles published since 2000 to create awareness of the many types of harassment and bullying. . . . Although the text is written for educators and librarians for use in classroom settings, the information is equally helpful for parents, caregivers, and public librarians." SLJ

Includes bibliographical references

Winkler, Kathleen

Bullying; how to deal with taunting, teasing, and tormenting. Enslow Pubs. 2005 104p il (Issues in focus today) lib bdg $31.93

Grades: 5 6 7 8   **371.5**

1. Bullies

ISBN 0-7660-2355-9

"Winkler examines the impact of bullying on both the victim and the victimizer. In straightforward and clear language, she uses conversations with teens, quotes from magazine and newspaper articles, interviews with professional therapists and school officials, plus excerpts from titles such as Rachel Simmons's *Odd Girl Out: The Hidden Culture of Aggression in Girls* (Harcourt, 2002) to provide a readable discussion of what bullying is, why bullies do what they do, and why victims take it." SLJ

Includes glossary and bibliographical references

371.82   Specific kinds of students; schools for specific kinds of students

Mortenson, Greg, 1957-

Listen to the wind; the story of Dr. Greg and *Three Cups of Tea*; by Greg Mortenson and Susan L. Roth; collages by Susan L. Roth. Dial Books for Young Readers 2009 unp il $16.99 *

Grades: K 1 2 3   **371.82**

1. Schools—Pakistan 2. Humanitarian intervention

ISBN 978-0-8037-3058-8; 0-8037-3058-6

LC 2008-12268

"Greg Mortenson stumbled, lost and delirious, into a remote Himalayan village after a failed climb up K2. The villagers saved his life, and he vowed to return and build them a school. . . . Told in the voice of Korphe's children, this story illuminates the humanity and culture of a relevant and distant part of the world." Publisher's note

Roth "pairs the words with her signature mixed-media collage work . . . using scraps of cloth along with a variety of papers. Her work has a welcoming, tactile dimension." Publ Wkly

Includes bibliographical references

Three cups of tea; one man's mission to promote peace—one school at a time; [by] Greg Mortenson and David Oliver Relin; adapted for young readers by Sarah Thomson. Dial Books for Young Readers 2009 209p il $16.99; pa $8.99

Grades: 4 5 6 7   **371.82**

1. Schools—Pakistan 2. Schools—Afghanistan 3. Humanitarian intervention

ISBN 978-0-8037-3392-3; 0-8037-3392-5; 978-0-14-241412-5 (pa); 0-14-241412-3 (pa)

Based on Three cups of tea: one man's mission to fight terrorism and build nations one school at a time, published 2006 by Viking for adults

"In 1993, while climbing one of the world's most difficult peaks, Mortenson became lost and ill, and eventually found aid in the tiny Pakistani village of Korphe. He vowed to repay his generous hosts by building a school; his efforts have grown into the Central Asia Institute. . . . Retold for middle readers, the story remains inspirational and compelling. . . . Illustrated throughout with

b&w photos, it also contains two eight-page insets of color photos." Publ Wkly

A **school** like mine; a unique celebration of schools around the world. DK 2007 79p il map $19.99

Grades: 3 4 5 6   **371.82**

1. Schools 2. Children

ISBN 978-0-7566-2913-7; 0-7566-2913-6

LC 2007298451

Published in association with UNICEF, United Nations Children's Fund

Introduces children from around the world and discusses where they live, how they play, and what their schools are like

Winter, Jeanette, 1939-

Nasreen's secret school; a true story from Afghanistan. Beach Lane Books 2009 unp il $16.99 *

Grades: 2 3 4   **371.82**

1. Schools—Afghanistan 2. Girls—Education 3. Afghanistan—Social conditions

ISBN 978-1-4169-9437-4; 1-4169-9437-8

LC 2009-08285

"This story begins with an author's note that succinctly explains the drastic changes that occurred when the Taliban came to power in Afghanistan in 1996. The focus is primarily on the regime's impact on women, who were no longer allowed to attend school or leave home without a male chaperone, and had to cover their heads and bodies with a burqa. After Nasreen's parents disappeared, the child neither spoke nor smiled. Her grandmother, the story's narrator, took her to a secret school, where she slowly discovered a world of art, literature, and history obscured by the harsh prohibitions of the Taliban. . . . Winter manages to achieve that delicate balance that is respectful of the seriousness of the experience, yet presents it in a way that is appropriate for young children. Winter's acrylic paintings make effective use of color. . . . This is an important book that makes events in a faraway place immediate and real." SLJ

371.9   Special education

Lauren, Jill, 1961-

That's like me! stories about amazing people with learning differences; foreword by Jerry Pinkney. Star Bright Books 2009 unp il $17.95; pa $7.95

Grades: 3 4 5   **371.9**

1. Learning disabilities

ISBN 978-1-59572-207-2; 1-59572-207-6; 978-1-59572-208-9 (pa); 1-59572-208-4 (pa)

LC 2009028647

"This colorful book spotlights people of different ages, backgrounds, and interests who have coped with learning disabilities and succeeded in their chosen fields. . . . Each entry includes several photos showing the person at different ages. A good resource for encouraging children with learning disabilities." Booklist

Includes bibliographical references

Stanley, Jerry, 1941-

Children of the Dust Bowl; the true story of the school at Weedpatch Camp. Crown 1992 85p il map hardcover o.p. pa $9.95 *

Grades: 5 6 7 8   **371.9**

1. Migrant labor 2. Great Depression, 1929-1939 3. Education—Social aspects

ISBN 0-517-88094-6; 0-517-58782-3 (pa)

LC 92-393

Describes the plight of the migrant workers who traveled from the Dust Bowl to California during the Depression and were forced to live in a federal labor camp and discusses the school that was built for their children

"Stanley's text is a compelling document. . . . The story is inspiring and disturbing, and Stanley has recorded the details with passion and dignity." Booklist

Includes bibliographical references

372 Elementary education

Barber, Nicola

First day of school. PowerKids Press 2009 24p il (The big day!) lib bdg $21.25; pa $8.25

Grades: PreK K 1   **372**

1. Schools

ISBN 978-1-4358-2839-1 (lib bdg); 1-4358-2839-9 (lib bdg); 978-1-4358-2895-7 (pa); 1-4358-2895-X (pa)

LC 2008025816

"Children in kindergarten will enjoy [this book] as [a read-aloud] . . . while those at the end of first grade will be able to read [it] independently. The writing is straightforward and reassuring, and the content provides a realistic view of what youngsters might experience in [school]. . . .The author discusses the activities of a typical day as well as feelings of sadness or loneliness that may occur." SLJ

Includes bibliographical references

Carlow, Regina

Exploring the connection between children's literature and music. Libraries Unlimited 2008 124p il pa $30

Grades: Professional   **372**

1. Music—Study and teaching 2. Children's literature—Bibliography

ISBN 978-1-59158-439-1 (pa); 1-59158-439-6 (pa)

LC 2007-40134

"Carlow sees music as part of developmental human activity and issues a plea to introduce it as direct participation. . . . This collection of methods and lessons encourages adults to broaden the possibilities of interacting with music, thereby using it to introduce young children to language, literature, and culture. Text is divided into chapters on singing and other ways to be musical. . . . The succeeding chapters are devoted to specific grade levels. . . . Each chapter includes an explanation of methods appropriate for the age group, followed by numerous lesson ideas for classrooms. The organization of this book makes it a solid addition to enhance curriculum materials." SLJ

Includes bibliographical references

MacDonell, Colleen

Thematic inquiry through fiction and nonfiction, PreK to grade 6. Linworth Pub. 2009 121p il pa $44.95

Grades: Professional   **372**

1. Education—Curricula 2. Active learning

ISBN 978-1-58683-350-3 (pa); 1-58683-350-2 (pa)

LC 2008-33365

This describes "how outstanding fiction and nonfiction titles can be integrated into thematic inquiry in preschool and elementary classrooms. Each thematic inquiry unit has four sections: Read it! describes a sample dialogic reading of one of the fiction or nonfiction books; Integrate it! gives concrete examples of how specialized subjects and technology can be integrated with the fiction or nonfiction selections; Do it! describes hands-on activities that are integral to the use of fiction and nonfiction for inquiry; and Assess it! enumerates across-the-curriculum standards met in the thematic inquiry." Publisher's note

"This is an excellent guide for classroom teachers and school media specialists interested in adding inquiry-based collaborative lessons to their repertoire." Libr Media Connect

Includes bibliographical references

Mackey, Bonnie

A librarian's guide to cultivating an elementary school garden; [by] Bonnie Mackey and Jennifer Mackey Stewart. Linworth Pub. 2009 124p il pa $39.95

Grades: Professional   **372**

1. School libraries—Activity projects 2. Gardening

ISBN 978-1-58683-328-2 (pa); 1-58683-328-6 (pa)

LC 2008-34963

"In this comprehensive guide to designing and implementing a school garden, Mackay and Stewart offer practical advice on acquiring funding sources and developing community partnerships, as well as specific instructions for developing various types of gardens: vegetable, butterfly, natural habitat, etc. A wide variety of activities is included, each one linked to the National Science Standards. Annotated book lists and webliographies of appropriate material for both students and faculty are presented throughout." SLJ

"Its unusual topic makes this book a standout." Libr Media Connect

Includes bibliographical references

372.2 Specific levels of elementary education

Howe, James, 1946-

When you go to kindergarten; text by James Howe; photographs by Betsy Imershein. rev & updated ed. Morrow Junior Bks. 1994 unp il hardcover o.p. pa $6.99 *

Grades: PreK K   **372.2**

1. Kindergarten

ISBN 0-688-12912-9; 0-688-14387-3 (pa)

LC 93-48152

First published 1986 by Knopf

Howe, James, 1946-—*Continued*

"The author tells youngsters what school might look like and how they might get there, and describes some of the possible activities. . . . Multicultural children are welcomed and taught by both male and female teachers. Smiling, busy kids engaged in many activities portray school as an exciting, interesting, and happy place." SLJ

372.4   Reading

Bouchard, Dave

The gift of reading; [by] David Bouchard, with Wendy Sutton. Orca Bk. Pubs. 2001 158p il pa $16.95

Grades: Professional   **372.4**

1. Reading 2. Books and reading

ISBN 1-55143-214-5   LC 2001-92682

This "overview of what young people need to become independent readers . . . targets families, teachers, and school administrators, claiming that nothing extravagant is required to promote reading. . . . All groups will find the grade-level reading lists and abundant literacy strategies helpful." Voice Youth Advocates

Bradbury, Judy

Children's book corner: a read-aloud resource with tips, techniques, and plans for teachers, librarians and parents: grades 5 and 6; photographs by Gene Bradbury. Libraries Unlimited 2006 463p il pa $32

Grades: Professional   **372.4**

1. Reading 2. Books and reading

ISBN 1-59158-045-5   LC 2006017478

This book promotes the reading aloud of books for grades 5 and 6 by teachers, librarians, and parents and includes suggestions for introducing each book, for questions to pose while reading, and for follow-up discussion.

Includes bibliographical references

Children's book corner: a read-aloud resource with tips, techniques, and plans for teachers, librarians, and parents: level grades 1 and 2; photographs by Gene Bradbury. Libraries Unlimited 2004 245p il pa $34

Grades: Professional   **372.4**

1. Reading 2. Books and reading

ISBN 1-59158-047-1

This book promotes "the reading aloud of quality picture books and early chapter books by teachers, librarians, and parents. 'Read-Aloud Plans' for 53 different titles include suggestions for introducing each book, for questions to pose while reading, and for follow-up discussion. . . . This fresh and original book should be a winner for schools, libraries, and homes." Booklist

Includes bibliographical references

Children's book corner: a read-aloud resource with tips, techniques, and plans for teachers, librarians, and parents: level grades 3 and 4; photographs by Gene Bradbury. Libraries Unlimited 2005 xvii, 337p pa $35

Grades: Professional   **372.4**

1. Reading 2. Books and reading

ISBN 1-59158-046-3   LC 2005011401

This book promotes the reading aloud of books for grades 3 and 4 by teachers, librarians, and parents and includes suggestions for introducing each book, for questions to pose while reading, and for follow-up discussion.

Includes bibliographical references

Children's book corner: a read-aloud resource with tips, techniques, and plans for teachers, librarians, and parents: level pre-K–K; photographs by Gene Bradbury. Libraries Unlimited 2003 163p il pa $35

Grades: Professional   **372.4**

1. Reading 2. Books and reading

ISBN 1-59158-048-X   LC 2003-53879

This book promotes the reading aloud of books for preschool and kindergarten children by teachers, librarians, and parents and includes suggestions for introducing each book, for questions to pose while reading, and for follow-up discussion.

Includes bibliographical references

Buzzeo, Toni, 1951-

Collaborating to meet literacy standards; teacher/librarian partnerships for K-2; [by] Toni Buzzeo. Linworth Pub. 2007 271p il pa $39.95 *

Grades: Professional   **372.4**

1. Reading 2. School libraries

ISBN 1-58683-189-5 (pa); 978-1-58683-189-9 (pa)

LC 2006-24926

"The author proposes specific strategies for collaboration to overcome imposed roadblocks and presents a template for unit and lesson development that addresses national standards and satisfies NCLB requirements while still dealing constructively with the nine information literacy standards developed by AASL. The 15 units, complete with black-line masters and written by several different library media professionals, make up most of the book and can help struggling school librarians in their attempts to integrate their philosophy with the difficult currency of present reality." SLJ

Includes bibliographical references

Hutchins, Darcy J.

Family reading night; [by] Darcy J. Hutchins, Marsha D. Greenfeld, Joyce L. Epstein. Eye on Education 2008 126p il pa $29.95

Grades: Professional   **372.4**

1. Family literacy programs 2. Reading

ISBN 978-1-59667-063-1 (pa); 1-59667-063-0 (pa)

LC 2007034492

"This guide presents clear examples of how to plan and implement thematic, monthly programs to help engage families with elementary-age children in literacy activities that they can do together. . . . This title would

Hutchins, Darcy J.—*Continued*
be an excellent tool for any school librarian, educator, or administrator working to devise a successful and strategically planned school-wide family reading program." SLJ

Knowles, Elizabeth, 1946-
Talk about books! a guide for book clubs, literature circles, and discussion groups, grades 4-8. Libraries Unlimited 2003 147p il pa $30 *
Grades: Professional   **372.4**
    1. Books and reading
    ISBN 1-59158-023-4   LC 2003-51582
"Each of the fifteen chapters focuses on a different book that serves as a prototype for a particular subject or genre. . . . Each focal book is briefly summarized, followed by a bit of biographical information about its author. Then a list of discussion questions is offered. . . . The questions nicely probe both concrete and abstract understanding of the book. . . . In addition, each chapter includes activities for all areas of the curriculum, an annotated list of related books, an annotated list of the author's other works, dozens of Web site suggestions, and the publisher's information." Voice Youth Advocates
Includes bibliographical references

Moreillon, Judi
Collaborative strategies for teaching reading comprehension; maximizing your impact; [by] Judi Moreillon. American Library Association 2007 170p il $38
Grades: Professional   **372.4**
    1. Reading comprehension
    ISBN 978-0-8389-0929-4; 0-8389-0929-9
                        LC 2006036132
This "begins by emphasizing the importance of collaboration between classroom teachers and teacher-librarians. . . . The bulk of the book focuses on seven reading comprehension strategies and how to teach them. . . . Overall this book is a cut above other 'how-to' books with its plethora of suggestions and resources for teachers and librarians." Voice Youth Advocates
Includes glossary and bibliographical references

Raines, Shirley C., 1945-
Story stretchers for infants, toddlers, and twos; experiences, activities, and games for popular children's books; [by] Shirley Raines, Karen Miller, and Leah Curry-Rood; illustrations by Kathy Dobbs. Gryphon House 2002 240p il pa $19.95
Grades: Professional   **372.4**
    1. Preschool education
    ISBN 0-87659-274-4   LC 2002-4803
"A book that offers numerous activities as well as a wealth of information for anyone instituting early childhood programs. The first chapter discusses emergent literacy and the role books play in this critical time. Sections on 'making the right selections' and 'techniques for reading books' will be especially valuable to new librarians, early childhood teachers, and other adults interested in promoting age-appropriate material. . . . The activities . . . include object play, music, movement, and more." SLJ
Includes bibliographical references

372.6   Language arts (Communication skills)

Bauer, Caroline Feller, 1935-
Caroline Feller Bauer's new handbook for storytellers; with stories, poems, magic, and more; illustrations by Lynn Gates Bredeson. American Library Association 1993 550p il pa $45 hardcover o.p. *
Grades: Professional   **372.6**
    1. Storytelling
    ISBN 0-8389-0664-8 (pa)   LC 93-14959
First published 1977 with title: Handbook for storytellers
Bauer's introduction "incorporates a broad variety of media and props into the storytelling process. . . . Beginners and veterans alike can benefit from this practical approach to program planning and promotion, story selection and preparation, and activities extending various themes or occasions." Bull Cent Child Books
Includes bibliographical references

Briggs, Diane
Preschool favorites; 35 storytimes kids love; [by] Diane Briggs; illustrated by Thomas Briggs. American Library Association 2007 227p bibl il pa $40
Grades: Professional   **372.6**
    1. Storytelling
    ISBN 0-8389-0938-8 (pa); 978-0-8389-0938-6 (pa)
                        LC 2006103159
"This book presents suggestions and resources for a variety of themes, from 'Animal Oddballs' to 'A Woggle of Witches.' Each session includes a variety of books and activities per topic. . . . Several fingerplays and folk rhymes per theme come with clear instructions for accompanying motions. . . . A useful discography provides sources for musical selections. Each theme also incorporates a flannel board poem, story, or song, with simple reproducible patterns and instructions on how to present them. . . . The thematic groupings and quantity of ideas should be useful to beginners and some experienced presenters looking to freshen up their programs." SLJ
Includes bibliographical references

Toddler storytimes II; [by] Diane Briggs; illustrations by Thomas Briggs. Scarecrow Press 2008 165p il pa $45
Grades: Professional   **372.6**
    1. Storytelling
    ISBN 978-0-8108-6057-5 (pa); 0-8108-6057-0 (pa)
                        LC 2008006243
"With 25 theme-based chapters, this is a handy resource. Each theme includes book recommendations, often 10 or more, with a nice mixture of classic and newer titles, and a suggestion to choose two or three per session. Words and instructions for fingerplays, rhymes, and songs are provided, while a discography provides melody sources for all songs. Each theme includes a flannel-board activity, complete with reproducible patterns and brief directions on how to present the story or song on the board." SLJ
Includes discography and bibliographical references

Champlin, Connie

Storytelling with puppets. 2nd ed. American Library Association 1998 249p il pa $35 *

Grades: Professional   **372.6**

1. Storytelling 2. Puppets and puppet plays

ISBN 0-8389-0709-1   LC 97-24810

First published 1985 under the authorship of Connie Champlin and Nancy Renfro

This book covers "such topics as puppet types and styles, developing a puppet collection, participatory storytelling, and presentation formats. . . . A very useful choice for professional shelves in both school and public libraries." Booklist

Includes bibliographical references

Ellis, Sarah, 1952-

From reader to writer; teaching writing through classic children's books. Douglas & McIntyre 2000 176p hardcover o.p. pa $14.95

Grades: Professional   **372.6**

1. Rhetoric—Study and teaching 2. Children's literature—Study and teaching

ISBN 0-88899-372-2; 0-88899-440-0 (pa)

"A Groundwood book"

The author discusses the work of seventeen British, Canadian and American authors of children's literature. "With each classic book, there's a 'sneak preview' (i.e., booktalk), a suggested read-aloud, exercises to help students and adult writers find their own stories, and a short annotated bibliography of related children's books." Booklist

Greene, Ellin, 1927-

Storytelling: art & technique; [by] Ellin Greene and Janice Del Negro. 4th ed. Libraries Unlimited 2010 xxvii, 455p il $55

Grades: Professional   **372.6**

1. Storytelling

ISBN 978-1-59158-600-5; 1-59158-600-3

First published 1977 by Bowker under the authorship of Augusta Baker and Ellin Greene

This "provides both a history of storytelling in libraries and . . . instruction for bringing storytelling to contemporary listeners. It details the selection, preparation, and presentation of stories, as well as planning and administration of a storytelling program. Full texts of 13 stories for various ages and occasions are included, as is an extensive list of resources. Bonus essays offer . . . international perspective through a survey of storytelling in Ireland and the British Isles and a look at storytelling in contemporary China." Publisher's note

"The fourth edition of this storytelling standby includes a wealth of updated and new materials." Bull Cent Child Books

Includes bibliographical references

Heitman, Jane, 1957-

Once upon a time; fairy tales in the library and language arts; [by] Jane Heitman. Linworth Pub. 2007 132p pa $36.95 *

Grades: Professional   **372.6**

1. Language arts 2. Reading 3. Fairy tales

ISBN 1-58683-231-X (pa); 978-1-58683-231-X (pa)

LC 2007006890

"Heitman presents a well-organized and comprehensive look at how fairy tales can be infused into the curriculum. . . . The book includes ways in which various lessons can be adapted for special and English-language learners, as well as numerous templates for writing, speaking, and listening activities. . . . This excellent resource deserves a place in most professional collections." SLJ

Includes bibliographical references

MacDonald, Margaret Read

Look back and see; twenty lively tales for gentle tellers; illustrations by Roxane Murphy. Wilson, H.W. 1991 178p il $60

Grades: Professional   **372.6**

1. Storytelling 2. Folklore

ISBN 978-0-8242-0810-3; 0-8242-0810-3

LC 91-2539

Stories included are: The snow bunting's lullaby; Look back and see; Kanji-jo, the nestlings; Domingo siete; Turkey girl; Little Cricket's marriage; Please all . . . please none; Why Koala has no tale; Katchi Katchi Blue Jay; Biyera well; The strawberries of the little men; The elk and the wren; The bear-child; Two women hunt for ground squirrels; Quail song; Grandfather Bear is hungry; Tiny Mouse goes traveling; The singing turtle; The Teeny Weeny Bop; A penny and a half

The author presents twenty non-violent folktales from around the world, with background notes and suggestions for storytelling uses

"Delightfully varied in mood, the tales range from silly and rowdy to contemplative and touching. . . . MacDonald's useful, informative, and entertaining notes follow each story. . . . The notes alone are worth the price of the book." J Youth Serv Libr

Includes bibliographical references

Shake-it-up tales! stories to sing, dance, drum, and act out. August House 2000 174p il music $24.95; pa $14.95

Grades: Professional   **372.6**

1. Storytelling 2. Folklore

ISBN 0-87483-590-9; 0-87483-570-4 (pa)

LC 00-36228

"With help from Jen and Nat Whitman, Wajuppa Tossa, and the Mahasarakham Storytellers"

This is a collection of "participation tales from different cultures. Each of the 20 stories is easy to learn and MacDonald provides wonderful ideas on how to inspire elementary-aged children to join in and become part of the storytelling tradition." SLJ

Includes bibliographical references

The storyteller's start-up book; finding, learning, performing, and using folktales including twelve tellable tales. August House 1993 215p $26.95; pa $14.95 *

Grades: Professional   **372.6**

1. Storytelling 2. Folklore

ISBN 0-87483-304-3; 0-87483-305-1 (pa)

LC 93-1580

Stories included are: Turtle of Koka; The little old woman who lived in a vinegar bottle; Puchika Churika; Marsh Hawk; Gecko; Kudu break!; What are their names!; Aayoga with many excuses; Kanu above and Kanu below; Ko Kóngole; Ningun; Yonjwa seeks a bride

MacDonald, Margaret Read—*Continued*

The author's advice on storytelling "covers the practical ground, from selection, learning (in one hour!), performance, and setting to classroom applications. . . . A dozen texts of proven success follow, with performance tips and source notes. Equally valuable are the selected and annotated bibliographies appended to every chapter." Libr J

Includes bibliographical references

When the lights go out; twenty scary tales to tell; illustrations by Roxane Murphy. Wilson, H.W. 1988 176p il $70 *
Grades: Professional   372.6
1. Storytelling 2. Horror fiction 3. Folklore
ISBN 0-8242-0770-X   LC 88-14197
Stories included are: Little Buttercup; The Wee Little Tyke; Looking for home; Wicked John and the Devil; The Great Red Cat; The wizard clip; The tinker and the ghost; The conjure wives; Sop doll; The Hobyahs; Old Ben; Sam'l; The cat with the beckoning paw; Totanguak; The red silk handkerchief; The strange visitor; Who lives in the skull?

"Divided into six sections—Not Too Scary, Scary in the Dark, Gross Stuff, Jump Tales, Tales to Act Out, and Tales to Draw or Stir Up—the selections will be especially useful around Halloween, although, as the author points out, the book can be used year round. Following each inclusion are helpful notes on telling the stories and a section that gives sources on origins and variants. Murphy's decorative drawings introduce chapters and are scattered throughout the text. Several concluding chapters list bibliographies and provide other helpful information." Booklist

Includes bibliographical references

Miller, Donalyn, 1967-

The book whisperer; awakening the inner reader in every child; [by] Donalyn Miller; foreword by Jeff Anderson. Jossey-Bass 2009 227p $22.95 *
Grades: Professional   372.6
1. Books and reading
ISBN 978-0-4703-7227-2; 0-4703-7227-3
                                                LC 2008055666
Donalyn Miller's approach to reading promotion "is simple yet provocative: affirm the reader in every student, allow students to choose their own books, carve out extra reading time, model authentic reading behaviors, discard time-worn reading assignments such as book reports and comprehension worksheets, and develop a classroom library filled with high-interest books. . . . Miller provides many tips for teachers and parents and includes a useful list of ultimate reading suggestions picked by her students. This outstanding contribution to the literature is highly recommended." Libr J
Includes bibliographical references

Pellowski, Anne, 1933-

The storytelling handbook; a young people's collection of unusual tales and helpful hints on how to tell them; illustrated by Martha Stoberock. Simon & Schuster Bks. for Young Readers 1995 129p il hardcover o.p. pa $7.99 *
Grades: Professional   372.6
1. Storytelling
ISBN 0-689-80311-7; 978-1-4169-7598-4 (pa);
1-4169-7598-5 (pa)   LC 95-2991
This work "addresses the young person who wants to tell stories in a public setting. It is similar in format to many adult books on storytelling how-tos, with sections on getting started and selecting and preparing stories, as well as a selection of sample tales. Pellowski's notes are extensive and will be very useful to novices looking for ways to research stories." Booklist
Includes bibliographical references

The world of storytelling. expanded and rev ed. Wilson, H.W. 1990 xxi, 311p il $75
Grades: Professional   372.6
1. Storytelling
ISBN 978-0-8242-0788-5; 0-8242-0788-2
                                                LC 90-31151
First published 1977
A practical guide to the origins, development, and applications of storytelling

This guide "reviews the oral traditions from which literature for children grew, addresses the controversy between storytellers and folklorists, and offers a modern-day definition for storytelling. *The world of storytelling* also includes chapters on: types of storytelling—bardic, folk, religious, theatrical, library and institutional, campground and playground, hygienic and therapeutic storytelling; format and style of storytelling—opening and closing of a story session; language, voice, and audience response; musical accompaniment; pictures and objects used; training of storytellers—history and survey of training methods; visuality, orality, and literacy; storytelling festivals." Publisher's note

"This is an important work for collections serving adult students of storytelling and the oral tradition." J Youth Serv Libr
Includes bibliographical references

Roth, Rita

The story road to literacy; [by] Rita Roth. Teacher Ideas Press 2006 176p il pa $30
Grades: Professional   372.6
1. English language—Study and teaching
2. Language arts 3. Children of immigrants
ISBN 1-59158-323-3   LC 2005030835
"Roth advances the idea that using traditional literature with students who are learning English will help them acquire critical communication skills while tying unfamiliar new places to familiar elements of their own heritages. The author provides practical, ready-to-use lesson plans, story samples, and suggested activities." SLJ
Includes bibliographical references

Sawyer, Ruth, 1880-1970

The way of the storyteller. Viking 1962 360p il pa $16 hardcover o.p.

Grades: Professional   372.6

1. Storytelling 2. Literature—Collections
ISBN 0-14-004436-1 (pa)
First published 1942

Stories included are: Wee Meg Barnileg and the fairies; The magic box; Señora, will you snip? Señora will you sew?; The peddler of Ballaghadereen; Where one is fed a hundred can dine; A matter of brogues; The juggler of Notre Dame; The deserted mine; The legend of Saint Elizabeth; The princess and the vagabone; The bird who spoke three times

"This is not primarily a book on how to tell stories; it is rather the whole philosophy of story telling as a creative art. From her own rich experience the author writes inspiringly of the background, experience, creative imagination, technique and selection essential to this art. A part of the book is devoted to a few well-loved stories with suggestions and comments." Booklist

Includes bibliographical references

373.1 Organization and activities in secondary education

Farrell, Juliana

Middle school, the real deal; from cafeteria food to combination locks; [by] Juliana Farrell, Beth Mayall. rev ed. Collins 2007 167p il pa $7.99 *

Grades: 4 5 6 7   373.1

1. Middle schools
ISBN 978-0-06-122742-4 (pa); 0-06-122742-0 (pa)
LC 2006102931

First published 2001

"New middle school students are given advice about living through the first day of school, handling the changing classroom schedule after being in a single elementary classroom, the benefits of extracurricular activities, making and keeping friends, and how to get along with parents." Voice Youth Advocates [review of 2001 ed.]

Pipkin, Gloria

At the schoolhouse gate; lessons in intellectual freedom; [by] Gloria Pipkin and ReLeah Cossett Lent; foreword by Susan Ohanian. Heinemann (Portsmouth) 2002 xx, 235p pa $21

Grades: Professional   373.1

1. Academic freedom 2. Censorship 3. Public schools
ISBN 0-325-00395-5   LC 2001-39909

"Two English teachers share their . . . personal battle to support students intellectual rights in the Bay County School District in Florida in the 1980s when censorship cases were looming in schools throughout the nation. . . . This book is one of inspiration, and teachers, librarians, and school administrators may find it encouraging as they face similar battles." SLJ

Includes bibliographical references

379 Public policy issues in education

Haskins, James, 1941-2005

Separate, but not equal; the dream and the struggle. Scholastic 1998 184p il hardcover o.p. pa $4.99 *

Grades: 5 6 7 8   379

1. African Americans—Education 2. School integration 3. Segregation in education
ISBN 0-590-45911-2; 0-590-45910-4 (pa)
LC 96-51507

The author traces "the history of the African American struggle for equal rights to education, from the enforced illiteracy of slavery times to the present debate about affirmative action." Booklist

"With his knack for blending historical facts and thoughtful interpretation, Haskins offers an informative, closeup look at the course of black education in America." SLJ

Includes bibliographical references

Morrison, Toni, 1931-

Remember; the journey to school integration. Houghton Mifflin Co. 2004 78p il $18

Grades: 3 4 5   379

1. School integration 2. Discrimination in education 3. African Americans—Education 4. United States—Race relations
ISBN 978-0-618-39740-2; 0-618-39740-X
LC 2003-22884

Historical real photo/portraits combined with simple factual statement from the point of view of African American children tells the history of the school integration in this country

"The provocative, candid images and conversational text should spark questions and discussion, a respect for past sacrifices, and inspiration for facing future challenges." SLJ

Walker, Paul Robert

Remember Little Rock; the time, the people, the stories; by Paul Robert Walker. National Geographic 2008 61p il map $17.95; lib bdg $27.90 *

Grades: 5 6 7 8 9   379

1. Central High School (Little Rock, Ark.) 2. School integration 3. Segregation in education 4. African Americans—Education 5. Arkansas—Race relations
ISBN   978-1-4263-0402-6;   1-4263-0402-1;
978-1-4263-0403-3 (lib bdg); 1-4263-0403-X (lib bdg)
LC 2008-24959

"The story of the battle to integrate Central High School in 1957 Little Rock, Arkansas, is presented through photographs and firsthand accounts from those who were there. . . . The multitude of eyewitness accounts, the poignant photographs, and the contextual background make this text a must-have addition to any classroom or library." Voice Youth Advocates

Includes bibliographical references

381 Commerce (Trade)

Krull, Kathleen, 1952-
Supermarket; illustrated by Melanie Hope Greenberg. Holiday House 2001 unp il $16.95
Grades: K 1 2 3   **381**
   1. Supermarkets
   ISBN 0-8234-1546-5   LC 99-88042
Explains modern supermarkets and how they work, discussing how they organize, display, and keep track of the items they sell
"Written in a clear and lively style. . . . Best of all, however, are the vibrant double-page gouache cartoon-style pictures using flat, decorative forms." SLJ

Lewin, Ted, 1935-
How much? visiting markets around the world. HarperCollins Pubs. 2006 31p il $17.99; lib bdg $17.89
Grades: K 1 2 3   **381**
   1. Markets
   ISBN 0-688-17552-X; 0-688-17553-8 (lib bdg)
                      LC 2004-30198
"From pet markets in Cairo to a flea market in New Jersey, stalls and vendors in five countries are described with brief, evocative text that captures small details. . . . The elaborate watercolors have a photorealistic authenticity that softened by impressionistic dabs of color." Bull Cent Child Books

Market! Lothrop, Lee & Shepard Bks. 1996 unp il $16.95 paperback o.p. *
Grades: K 1 2 3   **381**
   1. Markets
   ISBN 0-688-12161-6; 0-688-17520-1 (pa)
                      LC 95-7439
"An Irish horse market, New York City's Fulton Fish Market, a countryside market in Uganda, and a city market square in Nepal are among the six venues visited in this thoughtful exploration of long-standing social practices. Lewin's richly detailed watercolors convey the color and bustle of the marketplace as a human arena common worldwide, yet having distinctive characteristics according to country." Horn Book Guide

383 Postal communication

Brown, Craig McFarland, 1947-
Mule train mail. Charlesbridge Pub. 2009 unp il lib bdg $16.95; pa $7.95 *
Grades: 1 2 3   **383**
   1. Postal service—West (U.S.) 2. Grand Canyon (Ariz.)
   ISBN 978-1-58089-187-5 (lib bdg); 1-58089-187-X (lib bdg); 978-1-58089-188-2 (pa); 1-58089-188-8 (pa)
                      LC 2008007252
"Brown relates the daily trip made by Anthony the Postman from the top of the Grand Canyon to the village of Supai far below on the canyon floor. . . . An author's note gives additional details that children will appreciate.

. . . He also describes the expedition he made with Anthony Paya, lead muleteer, to appreciate firsthand the journey and the rigors of the landscape. Brown's wonderful pastel and colored pencil illustrations are a testament to the time he spent on the trail. . . . A fascinating and informative addition." SLJ

Kay, Verla, 1946-
Whatever happened to the Pony Express? illustrated by Kimberley Bulcken Root & Barry Root. G. P. Putnam's Sons 2010 unp il $16.99
Grades: K 1 2 3   **383**
   1. Pony express 2. Postal service 3. West (U.S.)—History
   ISBN 978-0-399-24483-4; 0-399-24483-2
"Through a series of letters between a brother and sister, Kay examines changes in mail delivery during the time period 1851-1870. . . . The rhymed text flows well. . . . While the brief phrases provide the larger historical context, the illustrations, rendered in pencil, ink, gouache, and watercolor, are crucial in developing the personal drama of the siblings and their families. . . . Libraries will want to accept delivery of this attractive and informative package." SLJ

Kenney, Karen Latchana, 1974-
Mail carriers at work; by Karen L. Kenney; illustrated by Brian Caleb Dumm; content consultant: Judith Stepan-Norris. Magic Wagon 2009 32p il (Meet your community!) lib bdg $18.95
Grades: K 1 2 3   **383**
   1. Letter carriers 2. Vocational guidance
   ISBN 978-1-60270-650-7 (lib bdg); 1-60270-650-6 (lib bdg)   LC 2009-2398
This book about mail carriers has "an uncluttered layout and consistent organization. . . . Chapter headings such as 'Problems on the Job,' and 'Technology at Work,' and 'Special Skills and Training' make it easy to pinpoint specific information." SLJ
Includes glossary

Spradlin, Michael P.
Off like the wind! the first ride of the pony express; illustrated by Layne Johnson. Walker Books for Young Readers 2010 unp il map $17.99; lib bdg $18.89
Grades: 3 4 5   **383**
   1. Pony express 2. Postal service 3. West (U.S.)—History
   ISBN 978-0-8027-9652-3; 0-8027-9652-4; 978-0-8027-9653-0 (lib bdg); 0-8027-9653-2 (lib bdg)
                      LC 2009-10827
"Basing his book, as much as possible, on scanty historical records . . . Spradlin re-creates the Pony Express' first rides east from Sacramento and west from St. Joseph, Missouri—naming riders and horses when he can, and providing a composite of various Express riders' adventures. Johnson heightens the drama with evocative full-bleed oils." Booklist
Includes bibliographical references

Thompson, Gare

Riding with the mail; the story of the Pony Express; by Gare Thompson. National Geographic 2007 40p il map (National Geographic history chapters) lib bdg $17.90

Grades: 2 3 4   **383**

     1. Pony express 2. West (U.S.)—History

     ISBN 978-1-4263-0192-6 (lib bdg); 1-4263-0192-8 (lib bdg)   LC 2007007897

"After an introduction sets the historical scene, this engaging volume provides a comprehensive introduction to the rise and fall of America's first postal service, the Pony Express. . . . Archival photographs, . . . maps, and . . . sidebars extend the text." Horn Book Guide

384.55   Television

Wan Guofang

TV takeover; questioning television; by Guofang Wan. Fact Finders 2007 32p il (Media literacy) lib bdg $22.90; pa $7.95

Grades: 4 5 6 7   **384.55**

     1. Television broadcasting

     ISBN 978-0-7368-6763-4 (lib bdg); 0-7368-6763-5 (lib bdg); 978-0-7368-7859-3 (pa); 0-7368-7859-9 (pa)   LC 2006021442

"Describes what media is, how television is part of media, and encourages readers to question the medium's influencial messages." Publisher's note

This is "written in a breezy style and [has] plenty of popping colors and photos. . . . Useful and attractive." SLJ

Includes bibliographical references

385   Railroad transportation

Zimmermann, Karl R.

All aboard! passenger trains around the world; [by] Karl Zimmermann; photography by the author. Boyds Mills Press 2006 48p il $19.95 *

Grades: 5 6 7 8   **385**

     1. Railroads

     ISBN 1-59078-325-5   LC 2005-24990

Zimmermann "has traveled by train across six continents, and his beautiful, big color photos appear on every double-page spread of this enthusiastic account, which blends history, geography, business, and engineering with his personal focus." Booklist

385.09   Railroad transportation— Historical and geographic treatment

Curlee, Lynn, 1947-

Trains. Atheneum Books for Young Readers 2009 40p il $19.99 *

Grades: 4 5 6   **385.09**

     1. Railroads—History

     ISBN 978-1-4169-4848-3; 1-4169-4848-1

                   LC 2007-40425

"Curlee illuminates . . . trains . . . with stunning, clean-lined illustrations and informative narration. He opens with a romantic reminiscence about the mighty engines that rumbled through his North Carolina hometown. . . . Launching into a chronological account of the evolution of the 'iron horse,' subsequent pages highlight major developments in (mostly American) railroad history, from the first steam engines to run on rails to the high-speed trains of Europe and Asia. Flatly styled and employing limited color palettes, several of Curlee's acrylic paintings will impress and awe readers." Publ Wkly

Halpern, Monica

Railroad fever; building the Transcontinental Railroad, 1830-1870; [by] Monica Halpern. National Geographic 2004 40p il map (Crossroads America) $21.90; pa $12.95 *

Grades: 4 5 6   **385.09**

     1. Union Pacific Railroad Company 2. Central Pacific Railroad 3. Railroads—History 4. Frontier and pioneer life

     ISBN 0-7922-6767-2; 0-7922-6767-2 (pa)

                   LC 2003-17858

Presents a history of the building of the transcontinental railroad and its effects on American life

"This is a first-choice purchase for its visually appealing presentation and its succinct yet thorough treatment of the topic." SLJ

Includes glossary

Perritano, John, 1962-

The transcontinental railroad. Children's Press 2010 48p il map (True book) lib bdg $26; pa $6.95

Grades: 3 4 5   **385.09**

     1. Union Pacific Railroad Company 2. Central Pacific Railroad 3. Railroads—History 4. West (U.S.)—Exploration

     ISBN   978-0-531-20585-3   (lib   bdg); 978-0-531-21248-6 (pa)   LC 2009014185

This introduction to the history of the transcontinental railroads provides "elementary readers with clear explanations, maps, illustrations, time lines, and engaging reproductions of primary resources. [This] volume contains eye-catching quick facts; illustrations and photographs are representational of regional Native Americans, pioneers, and explorers. This is ideal material for reports on the Westward expansion." SLJ

Includes bibliographical references

Zimmermann, Karl R.

Steam locomotives; whistling, chugging, smoking iron horses of the past. Boyds Mills Press 2004 48p il $19.95 *

Grades: 4 5 6 7   **385.09**

     1. Locomotives 2. Steam engines

     ISBN 1-59078-165-1

"In this photo-essay, Zimmermann shares his excitement for steam locomotives with young readers, tracing the development of the early engines and their impact on the history of the U.S. He includes a clear explanation

Zimmermann, Karl R.—*Continued*

. . . of how a steam engine works. The photographs, some archival and some from the present day, are excellent. . . . The engaging text clearly imparts the author's enthusiasm and love for the subject." SLJ

Includes glossary

386 Inland waterway and ferry transportation

Harness, Cheryl

The amazing impossible Erie Canal. Macmillan Bks. for Young Readers 1995 unp il map hardcover o.p. pa $5.99 *

Grades: 3 4 5   **386**

   1. Erie Canal (N.Y.)

   ISBN 0-02-742641-6; 0-689-82584-6 (pa)

                     LC 94-11114

"Focusing on the celebration that marked the completion of the Erie Canal in 1825, Harness uses words, maps, and pictures to explain the history and commerce of the canal. The book discusses the need for the canal, the politics of its planning and building, the workings of the locks and canals, the pleasure and pride people took in the accomplishment of this engineering feat, and the reasons for its demise." Booklist

"Harness has done a wonderful job of making the history and construction of the Erie Canal come alive. . . . The narrative is matched with illustrations that cover each page." SLJ

Includes bibliographical references

Kendall, Martha E., 1947-

The Erie Canal; by Martha E. Kendall. National Geographic 2008 128p il $18.95; lib bdg $28.90

Grades: 4 5 6   **386**

   1. Erie Canal (N.Y.)

   ISBN 978-1-4263-0022-6; 978-1-4263-0023-3 (lib bdg)   LC 2007029386

"This handsomely packaged introduction to our country's first great public works project pairs plenty of period prints and photos to a fluidly written account of the canal's origins, construction, uses and the folklore surrounding it." Booklist

387.1 Ports

House, Katherine L.

Lighthouses for kids; history, science, and lore with 21 activities; [by] Katherine L. House. Chicago Review Press 2008 118p il pa $14.95

Grades: 4 5 6 7 8   **387.1**

   1. Lighthouses

   ISBN 978-1-55652-720-3 (pa); 1-55652-720-9 (pa)

                 LC 2007-27093

"This book is noteworthy for the way in which the activities are related to the information in the text. . . . Readers learn about the challenges of building . . . [lighthouses], inventions to make them more reliable, and how lighthouses function as historical relics today." SLJ

Includes glossary and bibliographical references

Plisson, Philip

Lighthouses; photographs by Philip Plisson; text by Francis Dreyer; drawings by Daniel Dufour. Harry N. Abrams 2005 78p il $18.95 *

Grades: 4 5 6 7   **387.1**

   1. Lighthouses

   ISBN 0-8109-5958-5   LC 2005011781

"Plisson's magnificent color photos will draw young people to this introduction to lighthouses and the work of tending them. Each spread in the oversize volume introduces a different aspect of the history and technology of the structures or the work of maintaining them, from the lighthouses of ancient Egypt to the automated towers of today. Dreyer's engaging text . . . will pull readers to the facts through anecdotes about lighthouse keepers' lives." Booklist

387.2 Ships

Barton, Byron

Boats. Crowell 1986 unp il lib bdg $16.89; bd bk $6.99 *

Grades: K 1   **387.2**

   1. Boats and boating 2. Ships

   ISBN 0-690-04536-0 (lib bdg); 0-694-01165-7 (bd bk)

                 LC 85-47900

Depicts a variety of boats and a cruise ship docking and unloading passengers

"Thick black outlines contain vivid colors . . . clean lines, bright hues, and undemanding text." Booklist

Floca, Brian

Lightship. Atheneum Books for Young Readers 2007 unp il $16.99 *

Grades: K 1 2   **387.2**

   1. Lightships

   ISBN 978-1-4169-2436-4; 1-4169-2436-1

                 LC 2005-28028

"A Richard Jackson book"

"Lightships—floating lighthouses—were retired in 1983, but they live on in Floca's handsome picture book, which uses simple words and repeated phrases to emphasize the vessels' purpose and uniqueness as well as their day-to-day operation. . . . Some pictures include elements of humor, while other scenes are notable for their quiet beauty." Booklist

Gibbons, Gail

Boat book. Holiday House 1983 unp il $17.95 paperback o.p.

Grades: K 1 2 3   **387.2**

   1. Boats and boating 2. Ships

   ISBN 0-8234-0478-1; 0-8234-0709-8 (pa)

                 LC 82-15851

An introduction to "all sorts of seafaring craft . . . [including] speedboats, sailboats, canoes, cruise ships, police and fire boats, and commercial and military vessels. Various means of propulsion (wind, oars and paddles, engine power) are explained, as are the uses of each type of boat." Publ Wkly

The text "is logically presented in a non-

Gibbons, Gail—*Continued*
condescending manner. Bright color illustrations through-out show an array of boats moving through the water."
SLJ

O'Brien, Patrick, 1960-
The great ships. Walker & Co. 2001 39p il pa $7.95 *
Grades: 4 5 6 7   387.2
1. Ships
ISBN 0-8027-8774-6; 0-8027-8775-4 (lib bdg); 0-8027-7716-3 (pa)   LC 2001-17873
"O'Brien tells the stories of 17 of the world's most il-lustrious vessels (or groups of vessels). . . . The author includes accounts of Sir Francis Drake's *Golden Hind*, Blackbeard's *Queen Anne's Revenge*, Columbus's trio of Spanish caravels, and the disaster-destined *Titanic*. A double-page spread is devoted to each story, with a dra-matic watercolor-and-gouache illustration on the left and history on the right. . . . A captivating and beautiful vol-ume." SLJ

Sandler, Martin W.
On the waters of the USA; ships and boats in American life. Oxford Univ. Press 2004 63p il (Transportation in America) $19.95
Grades: 5 6 7 8   387.2
1. Shipping—United States 2. Ships 3. Boats and boating
ISBN 0-19-513227-0
Explores the evolving role of boats and ships in American history, from the dugout and birchbark canoes of Native Americans to twenty-first century container ships and supertankers.
This is a "fascinating account. . . . Drawings, maps, and photographs are well placed and fully captioned. . . . The large type is reader friendly, and the writing is clear and engaging." SLJ
Includes bibliographical references

Zimmermann, Karl R.
Ocean liners; crossing and cruising the seven seas; photographs by the author. Boyds Mills Press 2008 48p il $17.95 *
Grades: 5 6 7 8   387.2
1. Ocean liners 2. Ocean travel
ISBN 978-1-59078-552-2; 1-59078-552-5
LC 2007049323
This is "a comprehensive overview of ships from sail to steam to diesel, from the important modes of transpor-tation to the modern resorts at sea. The information is or-ganized in chapters about the history and development of the ships, the star ships of the Atlantic crossings and the conversion to modern cruising. . . . All is accompanied by photographs taken over the years by the author and supplemented by historic drawings, photos and docu-ments. . . . A fascinating voyage." Kirkus
Includes glossary

387.7   Air transportation

Barton, Byron
Airplanes. Crowell 1986 unp il lib bdg $15.89 *
Grades: PreK K 1   387.7
1. Airplanes
ISBN 0-690-04532-8   LC 85-47899
Brief text and illustrations present a variety of air-planes and what they do, "as well as some of the usual scenes surrounding each (e.g., workers checking a pas-senger plane). Brightly colored illustrations outlined in heavy black convey a bold and simple first impression, yet they portray a good number of accurate details that preschoolers find so fascinating." SLJ

Airport. Crowell 1982 unp il lib bdg $18.89; pa $6.99 *
Grades: PreK K 1   387.7
1. Airports 2. Airplanes
ISBN 0-690-04169-1 (lib bdg); 0-06-443145-2 (pa)
LC 79-7816
"In a brightly illustrated book, the author/artist cap-tures the hustle and bustle of passenger traffic from ar-rival at the terminal to take off." Kobrin Letter

388   Transportation Ground transportation

Flatt, Lizann, 1966-
Let's go! the story of getting from there to here; [by] Lizann Flatt; illustrated by Scot Ritchie. Maple Tree 2007 unp il $16.95
Grades: K 1 2   388
1. Transportation
ISBN 978-1-897349-02-1; 1-897349-02-5
"A breezy picture book introduction to modes of North American transportation from foot power to space vehicle. The book is rich in descriptive language and fol-lows a logical time line. . . . Vivid, double-page spreads of artwork, rendered in rainbow colors, provide added details." SLJ

Herbst, Judith
The history of transportation; [by] Judith Herbst. Twenty-First Century Books 2006 56p il (Major inventions through history) lib bdg $26.60 *
Grades: 5 6 7 8   388
1. Transportation—History
ISBN 0-8225-2496-1   LC 2004-23020
Contents: The wheel; Boats; The steam engine; The internal combustion engine; Air travel; Timeline
This history of transportation "covers the wheel, sail, steam engine, internal combustion engine, and airplane. . . . The text . . . is breezy but informative; unfamiliar terms are defined. Illustrations are a mixture of period black-and-white and color photos." SLJ
Includes bibliographical references

388.3   Vehicular transportation

Ammon, Richard, 1942-
Conestoga wagons; illustrated by Bill Farnsworth. Holiday House 2000 unp il lib bdg $16.95
Grades: 2 3 4 5   **388.3**
1. Carriages and carts 2. Transportation
ISBN 0-8234-1475-2   LC 99-19726
Explains how Conestoga wagons were built and driven as well as their historical significance and importance to the early American economy
Includes bibliographical references

388.4   Local transportation

DuTemple, Lesley A., 1952-
The New York subways. Lerner Publs. 2003 80p il (Great building feats) lib bdg $27.93 *
Grades: 5 6 7 8   **388.4**
1. Subways 2. New York (N.Y.)—History
ISBN 0-8225-0378-6   LC 2001-6143
Traces the history of the underground transportation system in New York City, discussing the politics involved, how it was financed, the men who built it, and the construction techniques
"DuTemple does a fine job. . . . [Photos] sidebars, maps, and archival material work beautifully together to supplement the information." Booklist
Includes bibliographical references

Miller, Heather, 1971-
Subway ride; illustrated by Sue Rama. Charlesbridge 2009 unp il lib bdg $15.95 *
Grades: PreK K 1   **388.4**
1. Subways
ISBN 978-1-58089-111-0 (lib bdg); 1-58089-111-X (lib bdg)   LC 2008-7249
"Take a ride on subway trains all around the world. Beginning in Cairo, a multicultural group of children rides the trains in ten cities, zigzagging from stop to stop around the globe. . . . Vivid colors and blurred lines evoke a bustling cheer. Cleverly composed to suggest both depth and action, the pictures tell most of the story. . . . The offbeat idea is deftly handled and should trigger further study." Kirkus

389   Metrology and standardization

Murphy, Stuart J., 1942-
Mighty Maddie; comparing weights; illustrated by Bernice Lum. HarperCollins Publishers 2004 31p il (MathStart) hardcover o.p. pa $4.99
Grades: K 1 2   **389**
1. Weights and measures 2. Cleanliness
ISBN 0-06-053159-2; 0-06-053161-4 (pa)
LC 2003-17610

As Maddie cleans up her room, she learns how to compare the weights of various objects
"Childlike line drawings with bright colors give readers a sense of action. This appealing book has uses beyond the math concept, and offers messages about family life, self-image, and responsibility." SLJ

391   Costume and personal appearance

Finley, Carol
The art of African masks; exploring cultural traditions. Lerner Publs. 1999 64p il map (Art around the world) $23.93
Grades: 5 6 7 8   **391**
1. Masks (Facial) 2. African art
ISBN 0-8225-2078-8   LC 98-10570
Describes how different types of masks are made and used in Africa and how they reflect the culture of their ethnic groups
"Clear, sharp full-color photographs of museum artifacts are well placed on the pages. . . . Pictures of modern members of still-existing cultures add to the attractiveness of this volume." SLJ
Includes bibliographical references

McLaren, Chesley
When royals wore ruffles; a funny & fashionable alphabet! written by Chesley McLaren and Pamela Jaber; illustrated by Chesley McLaren. Schwartz & Wade Books 2009 unp il $16.99; lib bdg $19.99
Grades: K 1 2 3   **391**
1. Clothing and dress—History 2. Fashion—History 3. Alphabet
ISBN   978-0-375-85166-7;   0-375-85166-6; 978-0-375-95166-4 (lib bdg); 0-375-95166-0 (lib bdg)
LC 2008017374
McLaren and "Jaber cover the fashion waterfront, enlightening readers on both history . . . and the less tangible aspects of glamour. . . . The commentary is smart and accessible. . . . Witty as the writing may be, the illustrations are irresistible. Like the best fashion, the lines and colors feel effortlessly right." Publ Wkly

Morris, Ann
Hats, hats, hats; photographs by Ken Heyman. Lothrop, Lee & Shepard Bks. 1989 unp il $16; pa $4.95
Grades: PreK K 1   **391**
1. Hats
ISBN 0-688-06338-1; 0-688-12274-4 (pa)
LC 88-26676
This book introduces a variety of hats worn around the world
"The vivid color photographs, one or two per page, show people engaged in lively activities while . . . wearing their hats. Each picture offers a strong ethnic identity or a thought-provoking human interaction, with captions of only a few words in large print. An unusual index . . . gives background information about the pictures, citing the countries of origin and a few facts about each . . . kind of hat." SLJ

Morris, Ann—*Continued*

Shoes, shoes, shoes. Lothrop, Lee & Shepard Bks. 1995 32p il hardcover o.p. pa $4.95

Grades: PreK K 1   **391**
1. Shoes
ISBN 0-688-13666-4; 0-688-16166-9 (pa)
                           LC 94-46649

"Morris gives a world-tour of shoes . . . in [a] picture book illustrated by various photographers. In rhyming text, she talks about shoes for all kinds of activities. . . . [The] book includes a map and a photograph key of the places visited." Bull Cent Child Books

Platt, Richard, 1953-

They wore what?! the weird history of fashion and beauty; [by] Richard Platt. Two-Can 2007 48p il $16.95; pa $9.95

Grades: 4 5 6   **391**
1. Fashion—History 2. Personal appearance
ISBN   978-1-58728-582-0;   1-58728-582-7; 978-1-58728-584-4 (pa); 1-58728-584-3 (pa)
                        LC 2006039159

Published in the United Kingdom with title: Would you believe in 1500, platform shoes were outlawed?

"Busy, colorful pages recount the historical, social, and political sides of clothing, hair, hats, and shoes, from legal and moral issues such as wearing fur to dangerous practices like cinched waists and bound feet. . . . Ever-fluctuating ideas of beauty and body image are also explored." Horn Book Guide

Includes glossary and bibliographical references

Rowland-Warne, L.

Costume; written by L. Rowland-Warne; [special photography, Liz McAulay] Dorling Kindersley 2000 63p il (DK eyewitness books) $15.99; lib bdg $19.99

Grades: 4 5 6 7   **391**
1. Costume 2. Clothing and dress 3. Fashion—History
ISBN 0-7894-5586-2; 0-7894-6584-1 (lib bdg)
First published 1992 by Knopf

Photographs and text document the history and meaning of clothing, from loincloths to modern children's clothes

Shaskan, Kathy

How underwear got under there; a brief history; illustrated by Regan Dunnick. Dutton 2007 47p il $16.99 *

Grades: 4 5 6   **391**
1. Underwear 2. Fashion—History
ISBN 978-0-525-47178-3; 0-525-47178-2

A humorous look at the science, fashion, and social ramifications of underwear throughout history.

This is a "lighthearted but thoughtful discourse on dainties. . . . [Illustrated with] Dunnick's watercolor cartoons." Bull Cent Child Books

Sills, Leslie

From rags to riches; a history of girls' clothing in America; [by] Leslie Sills. Holiday House 2005 48p il $16.95; pa $6.95 *

Grades: 5 6 7 8   **391**
1. Children's clothing 2. Girls 3. Fashion—History
ISBN 0-8234-1708-5; 0-8234-2048-5 (pa)
                        LC 2003-67600

A history of the clothing of American girls from colonial times to the present

"The sparkling design of Sills' overview makes this a pleasure to page through. . . . A marvelous collection of paintings and photographs show off the apparel." Booklist

Includes glossary and bibliographical references

Swain, Ruth Freeman

Hairdo! what we do and did to our hair; illustrated by Cat Bowman Smith. Holiday House 2002 unp il $16.95

Grades: 1 2 3 4   **391**
1. Hair
ISBN 0-8234-1522-8   LC 99-13350

Depicts how people have viewed, worn, and changed their hairstyles throughout history and in various cultures

"Smith's cartoons are well suited to the lighthearted tone of the narrative." SLJ

Includes bibliographical references

Underwear; what we wear under there; by Ruth Freeman Swain; illustrated by John O'Brien. Holiday House 2008 32p il $16.95

Grades: 2 3 4 5   **391**
1. Underwear 2. Fashion—History
ISBN 978-0-8234-1920-3; 0-8234-1920-7
                        LC 2008-4041

"Swain packs a lot of detail into the text as she quickly and chronologically progresses through a discussion of different types of underwear throughout the ages and how it has accommodated people's lifestyles. Children will find a multitude of interesting historical tidbits. . . . The winsome, imaginative illustrations vary in size and are rendered in watercolor over ink." SLJ

392   Customs of life cycle and domestic life

Hoyt-Goldsmith, Diane

Celebrating a Quinceañera; a Latina's 15th birthday celebration; photographs by Lawrence Migdale. Holiday House 2002 30p il $16.95 *

Grades: 3 4 5   **392**
1. Quinceañera (Social custom) 2. Mexican Americans—Social life and customs
ISBN 0-8234-1693-3   LC 2001-59424

Describes the customs and traditions connected with the celebration of a Mexican-American girl's fifteenth birthday, marking her coming of age

This offers "eye-catching, full-color photos. . . . The clearly written, engaging text conveys both the social and religious significance of the event." SLJ

Lauber, Patricia, 1924-

What you never knew about beds, bedrooms, and pajamas; illustrated by John Manders. Simon & Schuster Books for Young Readers 2007 unp il (Around-the-house history) $16.95 *

Grades: 2 3 4   **392**
1. Sleeping customs
ISBN 0-689-85211-8   LC 2004-20654

"Focusing on sleeping customs through the ages, Lauber begins with the Stone Age and moves up to the 1700s, but includes some more contemporary facts as well. . . . Manders's engaging artwork varies between full-page and spot illustrations. The humorous asides from characters in the comic-style pictures will entertain youngsters." SLJ

Includes bibliographical references

Onyefulu, Ifeoma, 1959-

Welcome Dede! an African naming ceremony; [by] Ifeoma Onyefulu. Frances Lincoln 2003 unp il map pa $7.95

Grades: K 1 2 3   **392**
1. Birth customs 2. Ghana—Social life and customs 3. Personal names
ISBN 1-84507-311-8

"Onyefulu opens this photo-essay with an enlightening one-page introduction that succinctly addresses the significance of names in African culture. Amarlai, who lives in Ghana, has a new cousin. . . . Through Amarlai's engaging voice, the process of naming a child is described—how and why one is chosen, and by whom. Each step is documented in a series of insightful, well-positioned photographs that capture the richness of this tradition and the importance of the extended family and community." SLJ

393   Death customs

Deem, James M.

Bodies from the ice; melting glaciers and the recovery of the past. Houghton Mifflin 2008 58p il map $17 *

Grades: 5 6 7 8 9 10   **393**
1. Mummies 2. Glaciers
ISBN 978-0-618-80045-2; 0-618-80045-X
                                      LC 2008-01868

A Sibert Medal honor book, 2009

This describes the discovery of human remains preserved in glaciers in the Alps, the Andes, The Himalayas, and other places around the world and what can be learned from them

"Full-color photographs, reproductions, and maps are clearly captioned; grand images of glaciated mountain peaks span entire pages, and detailed pictures of recovered objects . . . are presented. . . . [This] is a fantastic resource. Deem superbly weaves diverse geographical settings, time periods, and climate issues into a readable work that reveals the increasing interdisciplinary dimensions of the sciences." SLJ

Includes bibliographical references

Halls, Kelly Milner, 1957-

Mysteries of the mummy kids. Darby Creek Pub. 2007 72p il map $18.95

Grades: 4 5 6 7   **393**
1. Mummies
ISBN 978-1-58196-059-4; 1-58196-059-X

"Halls presents an eerily fascinating exploration of mummified children and teens found in South and North America, Europe, and Asia. . . . The writing style is plain yet absorbing, presenting scientific and historical information in simple terms." Voice Youth Advocates

Includes bibliographical references

Markle, Sandra, 1946-

Outside and inside mummies. Walker & Co. 2005 40p il $17.95; lib bdg $18.85 *

Grades: 4 5 6 7   **393**
1. Mummies
ISBN 0-8027-8966-8; 0-8027-8967-6 (lib bdg)
                                      LC 2004-66128

"Markle explores a global smorgasbord of mummy varieties, both those created by human procedures and those caused by nature. Crisp (if gruesome) color photos accompany the readable, informative text, which discusses not only the mummification process, but also the cutting-edge technologies used by forensic anthropologists and others to study the mummies themselves." SLJ

Includes glossary

Sloan, Christopher

Bury the dead; tombs, corpses, mummies, skeletons, & rituals; foreword by Bruno Frohlich. National Geographic Soc. 2002 64p il $18.95 *

Grades: 5 6 7 8   **393**
1. Funeral rites and ceremonies 2. Burial
ISBN 0-7922-7192-0   LC 2001-7507

Examines the customs and practices related to burial that have existed from ancient times to the present

The author "does a terrific job of providing an intriguing, reader-friendly text that is not overshadowed by the fabulous color photographs." Booklist

Includes bibliographical references

Tanaka, Shelley

Mummies; the newest, coolest, and creepiest from around the world; archaeological consultation by Paul Bahn. Harry N. Abrams 2005 48p il map $16.95 *

Grades: 4 5 6 7   **393**
1. Mummies
ISBN 0-8109-5797-3   LC 2005-00984

"After a brief discussion of mummification and the sorts of places in which mummified bodies have been found, Tanaka organizes her text by continent. Simple outlined and colored maps display the countries featured, supplementing the author's descriptions of the local conditions. . . . The main text for each mummy or cache of mummies is generally a few paragraphs, often supported by a shorter text, both of which are illustrated by photographs or reproductions." SLJ

"Not for the squeamish, the descriptions are graphic, and, like the riveting photos, they will draw kids right into the science." Booklist

Includes bibliographical references

394.1 Eating, drinking; using drugs

Ichord, Loretta Frances
Double cheeseburgers, quiche, and vegetarian burritos; American cooking from the 1920s through today; by Loretta Frances Ichord; illustrated by Jan Davey Ellis. Millbrook Press 2007 63p il (Cooking through time) lib bdg $25.26 *

Grades: 3 4 5 6   **394.1**
1. Eating customs 2. Cooking
ISBN 978-0-8225-5969-6 (lib bdg); 0-8225-5969-2 (lib bdg)   LC 2005-24535
"Each chapter, illustrated with lighthearted drawings, presents a quick, cogent overview of an American eating trend—from the first processed foods through TV dinners, fast food, the mainstreaming of organic foods, and more—ending with the influential fad diets of the 1990s. The examples are clear and lively, and relevant recipes close each chapter." Booklist
Includes bibliographical references

Lauber, Patricia, 1924-
What you never knew about fingers, forks, & chopsticks; illustrated by John Manders. Simon & Schuster Bks. for Young Readers 1999 unp il (Around-the-house history) $16 *
Grades: 2 3 4   **394.1**
1. Tableware 2. Table etiquette 3. Eating customs
ISBN 0-689-80479-2   LC 97-17041
Describes changes in eating customs throughout the centuries and the origins of table manners
"A delicious blend of humor and fascinating facts. . . . The lively, linear drawings incorporate amusing asides in dialogue balloons that will entertain readers as the text enlightens them about the subject." SLJ
Includes bibliographical references

394.25 Carnival

Hoyt-Goldsmith, Diane
Mardi Gras: a Cajun country celebration; photographs by Lawrence Migdale. Holiday House 1995 32p il music $15.95 *
Grades: 3 4 5   **394.25**
1. Carnival 2. Cajuns—Social life and customs
ISBN 0-8234-1184-2   LC 94-42707
This is a "photo essay and introduction to a Cajun Mardi Gras celebration in Eunice, Louisiana. The text follows Joel, a young fiddle player, as he prepares for and participates in the festivities. This lively and informative look at an ethnic and regional holiday is presented with clear text and bright, attractive photographs." Horn Book Guide
Includes glossary

394.26 Holidays

Ada, Alma Flor, 1938-
Merry Navidad! Christmas carols in Spanish and English; [by] Alma Flor Ada [and] F. Isabel Campoy; illustrated by Vivi Escrivá; English version by Rosalma Zubizarreta; musical consultant, Suni Paz. Rayo 2007 63p il $16.99; lib bdg $17.89
Grades: 2 3 4 5   **394.26**
1. Christmas 2. Carols 3. Poetry 4. Bilingual books—English-Spanish 5. Latin America—Social life and customs
ISBN   0-06-058434-3;   978-0-06-058434-4; 0-06-058435-1 (lib bdg); 978-0-06-058435-1 (lib bdg)   LC 2006-28710
A collection of Christmas carols and *villancicos* (folk poems), along with descriptions of Christmas traditions of Spain and Latin America, presented in English and Spanish.

Altman, Linda Jacobs, 1943-
Celebrate Kwanzaa; [by] Linda Jacobs Altman. Enslow Pub. 2008 104p il map (Celebrate holidays) lib bdg $31.93
Grades: 5 6 7 8   **394.26**
1. Kwanzaa 2. African Americans—Social life and customs
ISBN 978-07660-2862-3 (lib bdg); 0-7660-2862-3 (lib bdg)   LC 2007002421
This offers an introduction to harvest festivals around the world, outlines the life of Ronald Everett, who changed his name to Maulana Karenga and started the African American celebration of Kwanzaa in 1966, and describes how Kwanzaa is celebrated today.
"This is a useful look at the origins and greater context of Kwanzaa." SLJ
Includes glossary and bibliographical references

Ancona, George, 1929-
The fiestas. Benchmark Bks. 2002 48p il (Viva Mexico!) $16.95 *
Grades: 2 3 4   **394.26**
1. Festivals 2. Mexico—Social life and customs
ISBN 0-7614-1327-8   LC 00-65080
This photo-essay describes the festivals of Mexico, including carnaval, folk plays, saints days, and national holidays such as Dia de la Bandera, Cinco de Mayo, and El Dia del Charro
Includes glossary and bibliographical references

Pablo remembers; the fiesta of the Day of the Dead. Lothrop, Lee & Shepard Bks. 1993 42p il hardcover o.p. lib bdg $16.89 *
Grades: K 1 2 3   **394.26**
1. All Souls' Day 2. Mexico—Social life and customs
ISBN 0-688-11249-8; 0-688-11250-1 (lib bdg)   LC 92-22819
During the three-day celebration of the Day of the Dead, a young Mexican boy and his family make elaborate preparations to honor the spirits of the dead

Ancona, George, 1929---*Continued*

"The photography has the intimacy of high-quality family snapshots, and the tone of the text is clear and natural." Bull Cent Child Books

Includes glossary

Barth, Edna

Hearts, cupids, and red roses; the story of the valentine symbols; illustrated by Ursula Arndt. Clarion Bks. 2001 64p il $16 paperback o.p.

Grades: 3 4 5 6   **394.26**

1. Valentine's Day 2. Signs and symbols

ISBN 0-618-06789-2; 0-618-06791-4 (pa)

LC 2001-265787

A reissue of the title first published 1974 by Seabury Press

The history of Valentine's Day and the little-known stories behind its symbols

This offers "interesting and concise text along with lists of stories, poems, and sources." SLJ

Includes bibliographical references

Holly, reindeer, and colored lights; the story of the Christmas symbols; illustrated by Ursula Arndt. Clarion Bks. 2000 96p il hardcover o.p. pa $7.95

Grades: 3 4 5 6   **394.26**

1. Christmas 2. Signs and symbols

ISBN 0-618-06786-8; 0-618-06788-4 (pa)

LC 00-702874

A reissue of the title first published 1971 by Seabury Press

Examines the origins of Christmas symbols—trees, ornaments, Yule logs, Santa Claus, cards, Christmas colors, and many other holiday observances

"The well-written text is concise and interesting and the two-colored marginal drawings are festive. A selected list of books containing Christmas stories and poems is appended." Booklist

Includes bibliographical references

Lilies, rabbits, and painted eggs; the story of the Easter symbols; illustrated by Ursula Arndt. Clarion Bks. 2001 c1998 63p il $16 paperback o.p.

Grades: 3 4 5 6   **394.26**

1. Easter 2. Signs and symbols

ISBN 0-618-09646-9; 0-618-09648-5 (pa)

A reissue of the title first published 1970 by Seabury Press

Traces the history of Easter symbols from their Christian and pagan origins to such present-day additions as rabbits and new clothes

"The small pen drawings which illustrate the symbols and the celebrations will please the children, and an index and a bibliography of other Easter books will please the librarian." Horn Book

Shamrocks, harps, and shillelaghs; the story of the St. Patrick's Day symbols; illustrated by Ursula Arndt. Clarion Bks. 2001 95p il hardcover o.p. pa $7.95

Grades: 3 4 5 6   **394.26**

1. Saint Patrick's Day 2. Signs and symbols

ISBN 0-618-09649-3; 0-618-09651-5 (pa)

A reissue of the title first published 1977 by Seabury Press

"Irish history, lore, and legend are part of a wealth of information provided about Patrick the real missionary, St. Patrick's Day, and its celebration. Includes lists of stories for St. Patrick's Day and sources." LC. Child Books, 1977

Turkeys, Pilgrims, and Indian corn; the story of the Thanksgiving symbols; illustrated by Ursula Arndt. Clarion Bks. 2000 96p il hardcover o.p. pa $7.95

Grades: 3 4 5 6   **394.26**

1. Thanksgiving Day 2. Pilgrims (New England colonists) 3. Signs and symbols

ISBN 0-618-06783-3; 0-618-06785-X (pa)

LC 00-702873

A reissue of the title first published 1975 by Seabury Press

This book provides "information about the Pilgrims' voyage to and life in America and their dealings with the Indians. (The point is made, but not belabored, that the settled land was taken from the Indians.) Interesting sidelights are included about prominent men and women, myths such as Plymouth Rock, and harvest feasts in cultures around the world." SLJ

Includes bibliographical references

Witches, pumpkins, and grinning ghosts; the story of the Halloween symbols; illustrated by Ursula Arndt. Clarion Bks. 2000 95p il hardcover o.p. pa $7.95

Grades: 3 4 5 6   **394.26**

1. Halloween 2. Signs and symbols

ISBN 0-618-06780-9; 0-618-06782-5 (pa)

LC 00-712796

A reissue of the title first published 1972 by Seabury Press

Explains the origins of and relates stories associated with familiar Halloween symbols

"A diverting as well as useful account appropriately illustrated with drawings in black and orange." Booklist

Includes bibliographical references

Chase's calendar of events; the ultimate go-to guide for special days, weeks and months. McGraw-Hill il pa $74.95

Grades: Professional   **394.26**

1. Calendars 2. Holidays 3. Almanacs 4. Reference books

ISSN 1083-0588

Annual. First published 1958 by Contemporary Bks. under the editorship of William D. and Helen M. Chase with title: Chase's calendar of annual events. Variant title: Chase's annual events

Includes CD-ROM

Chase's calendar of events—*Continued*

"Day-by-day listing of national and state holidays, religious observances, special events, festivals and fairs, and historical anniversaries and birthdays. Covers U.S. events primarily, but some international occasions and anniversaries are included." N Y Public Libr Book of How & Where to Look It Up

Chocolate, Debbi, 1954-

My first Kwanzaa book; illustrated by Cal Massey. Scholastic 1992 unp il hardcover o.p. pa $5.99

Grades: K 1 2   **394.26**

1. Kwanzaa 2. African Americans—Social life and customs

ISBN 0-590-45762-4; 0-439-12926-5 (pa)

                  LC 92-1200

"Cartwheel books"

Introduces Kwanzaa, the holiday in which Afro-Americans celebrate their cultural heritage

"The book effectively conveys the spirit of the holiday through the text and the acrylic paint and colored-pencil illustrations, all outlined in a thin line of earthy brown." SLJ

Includes glossary

Demi, 1942-

Happy, happy Chinese New Year! Crown Pubs. 2003 c1997 unp il $8.95

Grades: K 1 2 3   **394.26**

1. Chinese New Year 2. China—Social life and customs

ISBN 0-375-82642-4   LC 2003-43469

First published in different form 1997 with title: Happy New Year! Kung-Hsi Fa-ts'ai!

Examines the customs, traditions, food, and lore associated with the celebration of Chinese New Year

Ditchfield, Christin

Memorial Day; by Christin Ditchfield. Children's Press 2003 47p il lib bdg $25 paperback o.p.

Grades: 2 3 4   **394.26**

1. Memorial Day

ISBN 0-516-22783-1 (lib bdg); 0-516-27821-5 (pa)

               LC 2003-4532

"A true book"

Contents: A very special holiday; How it all got started; America at war; To protect and serve; A day of remembrance

This looks at the history of Memorial Day and how Americans celebrate it.

"The discussions . . . of how people came to wear red poppies to honor the war dead and of the Tomb of the Unknowns add interest to the presentation. . . . Appropriate black-and-white and color photographs reflect the diversity of the U.S. and enhance the [text]. [This] up-to-date [title] will add depth to holiday collections." SLJ

Includes bibliographical references

Erlbach, Arlene

Merry Christmas, everywhere! by Arlene Erlbach with Herb Erlbach; illustrated by Sharon Lane Holm. Millbrook Press 2002 48p il map lib bdg $23.90; pa $8.95

Grades: K 1 2 3   **394.26**

1. Christmas

ISBN 0-7613-1956-5 (lib bdg); 0-7613-1699-X (pa)

               LC 2001-44758

Presents Christmas greetings and traditions, with related activities, from around the world

"The artwork is bright and festive, and the instructions are easy enough for even the most craft-challenged adults to follow." SLJ

Includes bibliographical references

Fisher, Aileen Lucia, 1906-2002

The story of Easter; by Aileen Fisher; illustrated by Stefano Vitale. HarperCollins Pubs. 1997 unp il hardcover o.p. pa $5.95

Grades: 3 4 5   **394.26**

1. Jesus Christ—Resurrection 2. Easter

ISBN 0-06-027296-1; 0-06-443490-7 (pa)

               LC 96-17395

A newly illustrated edition of Easter published 1968 by Crowell

"This book begins with the story of Jesus' crucifixion and resurrection, but focuses on the origins of various Easter and vernal equinox traditions, with an emphasis on the history of egg decorating. . . . The folk-art illustrations are defined by strong black outlines, simple shapes, and natural colors." Horn Book Guide

Gibbons, Gail

Easter. Holiday House 1989 unp il lib bdg $16.95; pa $6.95

Grades: K 1 2 3   **394.26**

1. Easter

ISBN 0-8234-0737-3 (lib bdg); 0-8234-0866-3 (pa)

               LC 88-23292

Examines the background, significance, symbols, and traditions of Easter

Gibbons "simplifies complex beliefs and traditions in a straightforward way, though transitions are occasionally abrupt. Pleasing watercolors outlined in black ink illustrate the text." Booklist

Groundhog day! shadow or no shadow? by Gail Gibbons. Holiday House 2007 32p il $16.95

Grades: K 1 2 3   **394.26**

1. Groundhog Day 2. Marmots

ISBN 978-0-8234-2003-2; 0-8234-2003-5

               LC 2006003456

"A look at some fascinating facts about this red-letter day, presented in Gibbons's signature style. Readers will learn about the traditions that led to the big celebration now held each year on February 2nd in Punxsutawney, PA. The author includes tidbits about the groundhog's diet, habitat, burrows, newborns/kits and looks at past cultures that depended on hibernating animals to help them determine the arrival of spring." SLJ

Gibbons, Gail—_Continued_
Halloween is—. Holiday House 2002 unp il
$16.95; pa $6.95
Grades: K 1 2 3 **394.26**
1. Halloween
ISBN 0-8234-1758-1; 0-8234-1797-2 (pa)
LC 2001-59429
Replaces the author's Halloween, published 1984
Describes the origins and history of Halloween traditions and festivities from ancient times to the present day
"The new version of Gibbons' _Halloween_ (1984) features a larger format, new illustrations, and a revised and slightly longer text as well as the new title. . . . Libraries with multiple copies of the earlier book will still find this version useful when the holiday rush is on, and given a choice, children will reach for this bigger, brighter, new edition." Booklist

St. Patrick's Day. Holiday House 1994 unp il
lib bdg $16.95; pa $6.95
Grades: K 1 2 3 **394.26**
1. Saint Patrick's Day
ISBN 0-8234-1119-2 (lib bdg); 0-8234-1173-7 (pa)
LC 93-29570
"A basic introduction to the holiday—how it began, the life and works of St. Patrick, and the various ways in which the day is celebrated. The text is clear and concise, and the pages are full of information. Gibbons's simple, clean, full-page watercolor-and-ink illustrations flow logically from one to the next." SLJ

Grace, Catherine O'Neill, 1950-
1621; a new look at Thanksgiving; [by] Catherine O'Neill Grace and Margaret M. Bruchac with Plimoth Plantation; photographs by Sisse Brimberg and Cotton Coulson. National Geographic Soc. 2001 47p il map $17.95; pa $7.95 *
Grades: 3 4 5 **394.26**
1. Plimoth Plantation, Inc. (Plymouth, Mass.)
2. Thanksgiving Day 3. Pilgrims (New England colonists) 4. Wampanoag Indians
ISBN 0-7922-7027-4; 0-7922-6139-1 (pa)
LC 2001-124
This is a "pictorial presentation of the reenactment of the first Thanksgiving, held at Plimoth Plantation museum in October, 2000. Countering the prevailing, traditional story of the first Thanksgiving . . . this lushly illustrated photo-essay presents a more measured, balanced, and historically accurate version of the three-day harvest celebration in 1621." SLJ
Includes bibliographical references

Heiligman, Deborah
Celebrate Christmas; [by] Deborah Heiligman; consultant, Reverend Father Nathan J.A. Humphrey. National Geographic 2007 31p il (Holidays around the world) $15.95; lib bdg $23.90 *
Grades: K 1 2 3 **394.26**
1. Christmas
ISBN 978-1-4263-0122-3; 978-1-4263-0123-0 (lib bdg)
LC 2007012659

"Brief text accompanies captivating and colorful photographs that demonstrate customs around the world. The use of bonfires and candles, Nativity plays, Advent wreaths, Three Kings Day, and Yule logs are among the topics touched upon. . . . A solid addition." SLJ
Includes glossary and bibliographical references

Celebrate Halloween; [by] Deborah Heiligman; consultant, Jack Santino. National Geographic Society 2007 31p il (Holidays around the world) $15.95; lib bdg $23.90 *
Grades: K 1 2 3 **394.26**
1. Halloween
ISBN 978-1-4263-0120-9; 978-1-4263-0121-6 (lib bdg)
LC 2007003121
In this introduction to Halloween "children will recognize familiar customs, such as carving pumpkins, dressing up, and hanging decorations, explained in simple, yet satisfying, text. The holiday is made accessible and inviting. . . . Lovely, well-captioned color photographs feature children around the world joyfully taking part in festivities." SLJ
Includes glossary and bibliographical references

Celebrate Independence Day; [by] Deborah Heiligman; consultant, Matthew Dennis. National Geographic 2007 31p il map (Holidays around the world) $15.95; lib bdg $23.90 *
Grades: K 1 2 3 **394.26**
1. Fourth of July
ISBN 978-1-4263-0074-5; 978-1-4263-0075-2 (lib bdg)
LC 2006100316
"Heiligman captures the festiveness of Independence Day, also reminding readers of its origin and relevence. . . . Her writing is clear and easy to read. . . . Plentiful photographs depict varied community celebrations." Horn Book Guide
Includes glossary and bibliographical references

Celebrate Thanksgiving; [by] Deborah Heiligman; consultant, Elizabeth Pleck. National Geographic 2006 32p il map (Holidays around the world) $15.95; lib bdg $23.90 *
Grades: K 1 2 3 **394.26**
1. Thanksgiving Day
ISBN 0-7922-5928-9; 0-7922-5929-7 (lib bdg)
LC 2006008685
This briefly describes the history of Thanksgiving Day and how it is celebrated.
Includes glossary and bibliographical references

Hess, Debra
The Fourth of July; [by] Debra Hess. Benchmark Books 2004 40p il map (Symbols of America) lib bdg $25.64; pa $6.99
Grades: 4 5 6 **394.26**
1. Fourth of July
ISBN 0-7614-1711-7 (lib bdg); 0-7614-3390-2 (pa)
LC 2003-4934
Contents: Taxation without representation; A nation is born; The American dream
The author explains why we celebrate the Fourth of July, offers a brief history of American independence from Britain, and describes how the holiday is celebrated around the country.

Hoyt-Goldsmith, Diane

Celebrating Chinese New Year; photographs by Lawrence Migdale. Holiday House 1998 32p il $16.95; pa $6.95 *

Grades: 3 4 5   **394.26**

1. Chinese New Year 2. Chinese Americans—Social life and customs

ISBN 0-8234-1393-4; 0-8234-1520-1 (pa)

LC 98-17028

Depicts a San Francisco boy and his family preparing for and enjoying their celebration of the Chinese New Year, their most important holiday

This book offers "big, bright photographs and a clear, easy-to-follow text. . . . Hoyt-Goldsmith's excellent book makes the Chinese New Year celebration accessible and understandable." SLJ

Includes glossary

Cinco de Mayo; celebrating the traditions of Mexico; by Diane Hoyt-Goldsmith; photographs by Lawrence Migdale. Holiday House 2007 30p il $16.95 *

Grades: 3 4 5   **394.26**

1. Cinco de Mayo 2. Mexico—Social life and customs

ISBN 978-0-8234-2107-7; 0-8234-2107-4

LC 2006101433

"This colorful photo-essay introduces Rosie, whose family celebrates their Mexican American traditions in California. After discussing Benito Juárez, the history of Cinco de Mayo, and three major waves of immigration from Mexico, Hoyt-Goldsmith presents elements of Rosie's heritage such as food, language, and mariachi music. . . . The clearly written text and the many fine, color photos provide readers with information as well as glimpses of the life in Rosie's community." Booklist

Includes glossary

Las Posadas; an Hispanic Christmas celebration; photographs by Lawrence Migdale. Holiday House 1999 32p il music hardcover o.p. pa $6.95 *

Grades: 3 4 5   **394.26**

1. Christmas 2. Hispanic Americans—Social life and customs

ISBN 0-8234-1449-3; 0-8234-1635-6 (pa)

LC 99-17337

Follows a Hispanic American family in a small New Mexican community as they prepare for and celebrate the nine-day religious festival which occurs just before Christmas

"Numerous clear, colorful photos bring the text to life. . . . A recipe for Las Posadas cookies, biscochitos, is provided, along with *The Song of Las Posadas* in both Spanish and English." Booklist

Includes glossary

Three Kings Day; a celebration at Christmastime; photographs by Lawrence Migdale. Holiday House 2004 30p il map $16.95 *

Grades: 3 4 5   **394.26**

1. Epiphany 2. Puerto Ricans—United States

ISBN 0-8234-1839-1   LC 2003-67625

This "photo-essay introduces Three Kings Day, or Dia de los Tres Reyes, and shows the celebration as experienced by a 10-year-old girl in New York's Puerto Rican community. . . . The clearly written text conveys a good deal of information in a lively, accessible manner. The many photographs capture the joyful spirit of the holiday." Booklist

Includes glossary

Jango-Cohen, Judith

Chinese New Year; illustrations by Jason Chin. Carolrhoda Books 2005 48p il (On my own holidays) lib bdg $23.93; pa $5.95

Grades: 1 2 3   **394.26**

1. Chinese New Year

ISBN 1-57505-653-4 (lib bdg); 1-57505-763-8 (pa)

LC 2004-4472

This "book describes the celebration of Chinese New Year. . . . Among the topics discussed are the Chinese zodiac, traditional symbols of the new year, family feasts and traditions for the holiday, and community activities, such as parades. . . . Clearly written, informative, and child-centered without talking down to children, this provides a good introduction to the holiday." Booklist

Jeffrey, Laura S.

Celebrate Martin Luther King, Jr., Day; [by] Laura S. Jeffrey. Enslow 2006 104p il (Celebrate holidays) lib bdg $31.93

Grades: 5 6 7 8   **394.26**

1. King, Martin Luther, Jr., 1929-1968 2. Martin Luther King Day 3. African Americans—Civil rights

ISBN 0-7660-2492-X   LC 2005028110

This offers a brief introduction to the life of Martin Luther King and the Civil Rights movement in the United States and how Martin Luther King Day became a holiday and is celebrated.

Includes glossary and bibliographical references

Celebrate Tet; [by] Laura S. Jeffrey. Enslow Publishers 2008 104p il map (Celebrate holidays) lib bdg $31.93

Grades: 5 6 7 8   **394.26**

1. Vietnamese New Year

ISBN 978-0-7660-2775-6 (lib bdg); 0-7660-2775-9 (lib bdg)

LC 2006031922

"Captioned photographs, maps, drawings, and sidebars combine with an accessible text to present a thorough discussion of the Vietnamese New Year celebration. Jeffrey discusses the holiday's legendary origins and ancient traditions along with people's modern-day observances." Horn Book Guide

Includes glossary and bibliographical references

Jones, Lynda

Kids around the world celebrate! the best feasts and festivals from many lands. Wiley 1999 c2000 124p il pa $12.95

Grades: 4 5 6   **394.26**

1. Festivals 2. Holidays

ISBN 0-471-34527-X   LC 99-14639

Introduces a variety of festivals celebrated around the world. Includes recipes and hands-on activities to give a taste of what it is like to be part of a feast or ceremony in another country

Junior Worldmark encyclopedia of world holidays; [edited by Robert Griffin and Ann H. Shurgin] U.X.L 2000 4v il set $185
Grades: 6 7 8 9   **394.26**
 1. Holidays 2. Festivals 3. Reference books
 ISBN 0-7876-3927-3   LC 00-23425
Alphabetically arranged entries provide descriptions of celebrations around the world of some thirty holidays and festivals, including national and cultural holidays, such as Independence Day and New Year's Day, which are commemorated on different days for different reasons in a number of countries
Includes bibliographical references

Kindersley, Anabel
Celebrations; written by Anabel Kindersley; photographed by Barnabas Kindersley. DK Pub. 1997 63p il (Children just like me) $17.95 *
Grades: 3 4 5   **394.26**
 1. Festivals 2. Holidays
 ISBN 0-7894-2027-9   LC 97-20108
 Published in association with UNICEF
"The celebrations are arranged by season and include: Christmas in Germany, Halloween in Canada, Hanukkah in the U.S., Diwali in India, Hina Matsuri in Japan, and Egemenlik Bayrami in Turkey. Each holiday is shown on a two-page spread with a large photograph of a featured child or children and many smaller captioned photographs of the festivities and the culture. . . . A superb addition to country/cultural teaching units." SLJ

Kule, Elaine A.
Celebrate Chinese New Year; [by] Elaine A. Kule. Enslow Publishers 2006 112p il map (Celebrate holidays) lib bdg $31.93
Grades: 5 6 7 8   **394.26**
 1. Chinese New Year
 ISBN 0-7660-2577-2   LC 2005028106
This describes the history of Chinese New Year, its cultural significance and traditions, and its signs and symbols, and includes instructions for making a paper lantern.
Includes glossary and bibliographical references

Landau, Elaine
Easter; parades, chocolates, and celebration; [by] Elaine Landau. Enslow Publishers 2004 48p il (Finding out about holidays) lib bdg $23.93 *
Grades: 2 3 4   **394.26**
 1. Easter
 ISBN 0-7660-2172-6   LC 2003-27483
Contents: Was that the Easter Bunny?; It started this way; A holiday that is more than a day; Easter symbols; Celebrating Easter; Still more celebrations!
This introduction to Easter covers "historical origins and [includes] descriptions of the symbols from eggs and bunnies to lambs and lilies, as well as both religious and secular celebrations, such as sunrise services, parades, and egg hunts. . . . The informative text is enhanced with colorful photographs." SLJ
Includes glossary and bibliographical references

St. Patrick's Day; parades, shamrocks, and leprechauns. Enslow Pubs. 2002 48p il (Finding out about holidays) lib bdg $18.95 *
Grades: 2 3 4   **394.26**
 1. Saint Patrick's Day
 ISBN 0-7660-1777-X   LC 2001-5560
"The story of St. Patrick is told, with legend and fact delineated. The significance of the color green is explained, as is that of shamrocks, four-leaf clovers, and pots of gold. Parades, festivals, athletic events, and special foods are all discussed. The text is clear and engaging, and the attractive color photos, reproductions, and drawings add interest and detail." SLJ
Includes glossary and bibliographical references

Valentine's day; candy, love, and hearts. Enslow Pubs. 2002 48p il (Finding out about holidays) lib bdg $18.95 *
Grades: 2 3 4   **394.26**
 1. Valentine's Day
 ISBN 0-7660-1779-6   LC 2001-989
"Three origins of the holiday are presented, followed by ways in which the day is celebrated around the world. . . . The large print and the well-placed, attractive color photos and illustrations make this book accessible to its intended audience." SLJ
Includes glossary and bibliographical references

Lankford, Mary D., 1932-
Christmas around the world; illustrated by Karen Dugan. Morrow Junior Bks. 1995 47p il map hardcover o.p. pa $5.95 *
Grades: 3 4 5   **394.26**
 1. Christmas
 ISBN 0-688-12166-7; 0-688-12167-5 (lib bdg);
 0-688-16323-8 (pa)   LC 93-38566
This book "looks at the rich diversity of Christmas traditions found in 12 distinctly different cultures. A small amount of pertinent background information serves as an introduction to each entry, but the majority of the text discusses the special ways each culture celebrates the holiday. The book's attractive layout effectively uses repetition of color and theme, with each double-page spread of text and art surrounded by a decorative border. . . . The book features a small selection of craft activities. . . . A helpful pronunciation guide, and an interesting selection of Christmas superstitions." Booklist
Includes bibliographical references

Christmas USA; [by] Mary D. Lankford; illustrated by Karen Dugan. HarperCollins 2006 unp il $16.99; lib bdg $16.89 *
Grades: 3 4 5   **394.26**
 1. Christmas 2. United States—Social life and customs
 ISBN 0-688-15012-8; 0-06-000861-X (lib bdg)
This "book takes readers on a region-by-region tour of the U.S. as well as discusses Christmas in the White House and offers a series of craft instructions and holiday recipes. . . . Warm and cheery, the illustrations and decorative borders enhance the book's appeal. A pleasant, useful addition." Booklist
Includes bibliographical references

Levy, Janice

Celebrate! It's cinco de mayo! written by Janice Levy; illustrated by Loretta Lopez; translated by Miguel Arisa. Albert Whitman 2007 unp $16.95; pa $6.95

Grades: PreK K 1   **394.26**
    1. Cinco de Mayo 2. Bilingual books—English-Spanish 3. Mexico—Social life and customs
    ISBN 978-0-8075-1176-3; 978-0-8075-1177-0 (pa)
                                   LC 2006024234

"A family demonstrates how it celebrates Cinco de Mayo. . . . Levy provides brief information about the history and the cultural traditions that surround the holiday. The simple text appears in both English and Spanish. Lopez's brightly colored illustrations add to the festive air of the narrative, and the family's excitement is palpable." SLJ

MacMillan, Dianne M., 1943-

Diwali—Hindu festival of lights; [by] Dianne M. MacMillan. rev and updated ed. Enslow Elementary 2008 48p il (Best holiday books) lib bdg $23.93

Grades: 2 3 4   **394.26**
    1. Divali 2. Hindu holidays
    ISBN 978-0-7660-3060-2 (lib bdg); 0-7660-3060-1 (lib bdg)   LC 2007002420
First published 1997

This describes the history of the Hindu festival of Diwali and how it is celebrated in the United States
Includes glossary and bibliographical references

Mattern, Joanne, 1963-

Celebrate Christmas; [by] Joanne Mattern. Enslow Publishers 2007 112p il (Celebrate holidays) lib bdg $31.93

Grades: 5 6 7 8   **394.26**
    1. Christmas
    ISBN 978-0-7660-2776-3 (lib bdg); 0-7660-2776-7 (lib bdg)   LC 2006025258

The author "devotes several pages to the origins of Christmas, first as a pagan holiday, then as a celebration of Jesus' birth, and its evolution into the holiday as it is observed today. Symbols of Christmas, important people, and traditions from around the world are explored, and there is a fair amount of discussion about the commercialization of the holiday. . . . Full-color photos and reproductions appear throughout. There is plenty here for reports." SLJ
Includes glossary and bibliographical references

Celebrate Cinco de Mayo; [by] Joanne Mattern. Enslow Pub. 2006 104p il map (Celebrate holidays) lib bdg $31.93

Grades: 5 6 7 8   **394.26**
    1. Cinco de Mayo 2. Mexico—History 3. Mexico—Social life and customs
    ISBN 0-7660-2579-9   LC 2005028107

This describes the history of Cinco de Mayo and how it is celebrated.
Includes glossary and bibliographical references

Matthew, Kathryn I.

Neal-Schuman guide to celebrations & holidays around the world; [by] Kathryn I. Matthew, Joy L. Lowe. Neal-Schuman Publishers 2004 xx, 452p il pa $65

Grades: Professional   **394.26**
    1. Holidays—Bibliography 2. Festivals—Bibliography 3. Children's literature—Bibliography 4. Reference books
    ISBN 1-55570-479-4   LC 2003-59940

"The first section provides bibliographic information and suggested grade levels for titles on specific days. Sections that follow offer longer, more detailed explanations of the meaning and significance of a holiday and a . . . description of the content of each recommended book or media choice. 'Explorations,' or activities for sharing specific titles with students, are included." SLJ

"Selecting books that represent favorite authors who will appeal to children, the authors have designed a work that will be useful to elementary librarians and teachers looking for culturally sensitive resources and activities to teach K-8 students about more than 80 holidays." Booklist
Includes bibliographical references

Nelson, Vaunda Micheaux

Juneteenth; by Vaunda Micheaux Nelson and Drew Nelson; illustrations by Mark Schroder. Millbrook Press 2006 48p il (On my own holidays) lib bdg $23.93 *

Grades: 2 3 4   **394.26**
    1. Juneteenth 2. African Americans—Social life and customs
    ISBN 978-1-57505-876-4 (lib bdg); 1-57505-876-6 (lib bdg)   LC 2005-15334

This is an introduction to the holiday "which celebrates the belated arrival of emancipation news to Texas slaves on June 19, 1865. . . . [This] offers a solid introduction to the holiday for independent readers or for presenting to small groups." Booklist

Old, Wendie

The Halloween book of facts and fun; [by] Wendie Old; illustrated by Paige Billin-Frye. Albert Whitman & Co. 2007 40p il $15.95 *

Grades: K 1 2 3   **394.26**
    1. Halloween
    ISBN 978-0-8075-3133-4; 0-8075-3133-2
                                   LC 2007001342

"This book provides a well-researched and accessible history of Halloween customs and celebrations, from the ancient Romans and Celts to the modern day. Halloween-themed jokes and riddles are interspersed throughout, and a chapter on party tips and ideas adds to the fun. A list of safety rules is appended." Horn Book Guide
Includes bibliographical references

Otto, Carolyn

Celebrate Chinese New Year; [by] Carolyn Otto; consultant, Haiwang Yuan. National Geographic 2008 32p il (Holidays around the world) $15.95; lib bdg $23.90 *

Grades: K 1 2 3   **394.26**
    1. Chinese New Year 2. China—Social life and customs
    ISBN 978-1-4263-0381-4; 1-4263-0381-5; 978-1-4263-0382-1 (lib bdg); 1-4263-0382-3 (lib bdg)
                               LC 2008024678

"Vivid, colorful photographs of fireworks, lion dancers, and food fill the pages of this introduction to Chinese New Year. The concise but informative narrative notes when the event occurs, cites a few of the countries where it is observed, and explains the reasons behind the customs and symbols, especially those traditions involving children. The well-captioned pictures capture the intense excitement and raucous exuberance of the festivities." Booklist
Includes glossary and bibliographical references

Celebrate Cinco de Mayo; [by] Carolyn Otto; consultant, Jose M. Alamillo. National Geographic 2008 32p il map (Holidays around the world) $15.95; lib bdg $23.90 *

Grades: K 1 2 3   **394.26**
    1. Cinco de Mayo 2. Mexico—Social life and customs
    ISBN 978-1-4263-0215-2; 1-4263-0215-0; 978-1-4263-0216-9 (lib bdg); 1-4263-0216-9 (lib bdg)

This "combines a clear, read-aloud-friendly text with big, beautiful color photos. After introducing Cinco de Mayo's 1862 origins, Otto shows and tells how the celebration has become an annual, joyous festival of Mexican culture, both north and south of the border. . . . Excellent back matter includes bibliography, recipes, a glossary and an informative afterword." Booklist

Celebrate Kwanzaa; [by] Carolyn Otto; consultant, Keith A. Mayes. National Geographic 2007 32p il (Holidays around the world) $15.95; lib bdg $23.90 *

Grades: K 1 2 3   **394.26**
    1. Kwanzaa 2. African Americans—Social life and customs
    ISBN 978-1-4263-0319-7; 978-1-4263-0320-3 (lib bdg)   LC 2007041221

This describes the history of the African American holiday of Kwanzaa and how it is celebrated and includes a craft activity and a recipe
Includes glossary and bibliographical references

Celebrate Valentine's Day; [by] Carolyn Otto; consultant, Jack Santino. National Geographic 2008 32p il map (Holidays around the world) $15.95; lib bdg $23.90 *

Grades: K 1 2 3   **394.26**
    1. Valentine's Day
    ISBN 978-1-4263-0213-8; 1-4263-0213-4; 978-1-4263-0214-5 (lib bdg); 1-4263-0214-2 (lib bdg)
                               LC 2007033764

This describes how Valentine's Day is celebrated and includes a game and a recipe
Includes glossary and bibliographical references

Perl, Lila

Piñatas and paper flowers; holidays of the Americas in English and Spanish; illustrated by Victoria de Larrea. Clarion Bks. 1983 91p il pa $7.95 hardcover o.p.

Grades: 4 5 6 7   **394.26**
    1. Holidays 2. Folklore—Latin America 3. Bilingual books—English-Spanish
    ISBN 0-89919-155-X (pa)   LC 82-1211

Text and title page in English and Spanish; Spanish version by Alma Flor Ada
A brief overview of eight holidays and their customs as celebrated in the Americas. Holidays covered include: The New Year, Three Kings' Day; Carnival and Easter; St. John the Baptist Day; Columbus Day; Halloween; The Festival of the Sun; and Christmas

Pfeffer, Wendy, 1929-

The longest day; celebrating the summer solstice; illustrated by Linda Bleck. Dutton Children's Books 2010 unp il $17.99

Grades: K 1 2 3   **394.26**
    1. Summer solstice 2. Summer
    ISBN 978-0-525-42237-2; 0-525-42237-4

"Science, myth and custom merge into a celebratory introduction to the Summer Solstice. . . . Bleck's sprightly, colorful illustrations offer a visual celebration as they faithfully track the text. A comfortable, multidimensional investigation of the Summer Solstice that transcends time and place." Kirkus

A new beginning; celebrating the spring equinox; illustrated by Linda Bleck. Dutton Children's Books 2008 unp il $17.99

Grades: K 1 2 3   **394.26**
    1. Vernal equinox 2. Spring
    ISBN 978-0-525-47874-4; 0-525-47874-4
                                LC 2007-18123

This "covers the spring equinox and how people mark its passage in the northern hemisphere. . . . [It includes] five multicultural activities. The free-verse text is clear and simple, and the colorful illustrations blanket every page with celebrants clad in traditional, festive clothing." Booklist
Includes bibliographical references

The shortest day; celebrating the winter solstice; illustrated by Jesse Reisch. Dutton Children's Books 2003 unp il $16.99

Grades: K 1 2 3   **394.26**
    1. Winter solstice
    ISBN 0-525-46968-0   LC 2003-40811

Describes how and why daylight grows shorter as winter approaches, the effect of shorter days on animals and people, and how the winter solstice has been celebrated throughout history. Includes activities
This uses "clear, concise language. . . . Pfeffer uses an easy, comfortable tone for conveying the basic information. . . . Reisch's realistic craypas illustrations provide serviceable interpretations of the author's ideas." SLJ

Pfeffer, Wendy, 1929-—*Continued*

We gather together; celebrating the harvest season; illustrated by Linda Bleck. Dutton Children's Books 2006 unp il $17.99
Grades: K 1 2 3　　　　　　　　　**394.26**
　1. Autumn 2. Festivals
　ISBN 0-525-47669-5　　　　　LC 2006-04340
The author "describes the changes in the weather and the ways in which people and animals prepare for the coming winter. She provides specific information as to why seasons change and describes the way the harvest has been celebrated by different cultures throughout history. Back matter includes equinox facts, a recipe for Equinox corn muffins, and a craft activity. Although a substantial amount of information is presented, Pfeffer's lively writing style will keep readers engaged. Bleck's vibrantly hued illustrations . . . are carefully interwoven with the text and enhance the book." SLJ
　Includes bibliographical references

Shea, Pegi Deitz, 1960-

Ten mice for Tet! by Pegi Deitz Shea and Cynthia Weill; illustrations by Tô Ngoc Trang; embroidery by Pham Viêt Dinh. Chronicle Books 2003 unp il $15.95
Grades: K 1 2 3　　　　　　　　　**394.26**
　1. Vietnamese New Year 2. Counting 3. Mice—Fiction
　ISBN 0-8118-3496-4　　　　　LC 2002-7456
A village of mice prepares for Tet, or Vietnamese New Year, as different numbers of mice give gifts, cook food, and celebrate in other traditional ways. Includes an afterword with facts about the holiday
　"This accessible counting book is a lovely introduction to the Vietnamese New Year. . . . Remarkable, vividly colored, embroidered artwork enhances the text." SLJ

Simonds, Nina

Moonbeams, dumplings & dragon boats; a treasury of Chinese holiday tales, activities & recipes; [by] Nina Simonds, Leslie Swartz, & the Children's Museum of Boston; illustrated by Meilo So. Harcourt 2002 74p il $20 *
Grades: 4 5 6 7　　　　　　　　　**394.26**
　1. Festivals—China
　ISBN 0-15-201983-9　　　　　LC 2001-4280
　"Gulliver books"
Presents background information, related tales, and activities for celebrating five Chinese festivals—Chinese New Year, the Lantern Festival, Qing Ming, the Dragon Boat Festival, and the Moon Festival
　"The ample white space surrounding the text is filled with small, whimsical watercolor illustrations. . . . [This] is a useful, visually appealing addition to any holiday collection." SLJ
　Includes bibliographical references

Tokunbo, Dimitrea

The sound of Kwanzaa; illustrated by Lisa Cohen. Scholastic Press 2009 unp il $16.99
Grades: PreK K 1 2　　　　　　　**394.26**
　1. Kwanzaa 2. African Americans—Social life and customs
　ISBN 978-0-545-01865-4; 0-545-01865-X
　　　　　　　　　　　　　　　LC 2007025916
"This picture book provides readers with an introduction to Kwanzaa's seven principles. . . . Rhythmic text includes the definitions, pronunciations, and significances of the principles. Uncluttered, vibrantly colored illustrations extend the meanings of each of the seven candles of Kwanzaa." Horn Book Guide
　Includes bibliographical references

Waters, Kate

Lion dancer: Ernie Wan's Chinese New Year; by Kate Waters and Madeline Slovenz-Low; photographs by Martha Cooper. Scholastic 1990 unp il pa $4.99 hardcover o.p.
Grades: K 1 2 3　　　　　　　　　**394.26**
　1. Chinese New Year 2. Chinese Americans—Social life and customs
　ISBN 0-590-43047-5 (pa)　　　　LC 89-6423
Describes six-year-old Ernie Wan's preparations, at home and in school, for the Chinese New Year celebrations and his first public performance of the lion dance
　"While some of the pictures look posed, the marvelously colorful photographs successfully capture Ernie's pride and anticipation as he is dressed in his gorgeous costume and the excitement and swirling movement of the subsequent parade. Illustrations of a Chinese lunar calendar and a Chinese horoscope are extra dividends in a useful and appealing book." Horn Book

395　Etiquette (Manners)

Aliki

Manners. Greenwillow Bks. 1990 unp il $16; lib bdg $15.93; pa $5.95 *
Grades: K 1 2 3　　　　　　　　　**395**
　1. Etiquette
　ISBN 0-688-09198-9; 0-688-09199-7 (lib bdg);
　0-688-04579-0 (pa)　　　　　　LC 89-34622
The author discusses etiquette and good manners
　"Aliki makes manners accessible to children through colorful cartoon-style illustrations. . . . Her lively primer sparkles with examples of the proper and the poor." Booklist

Joslin, Sesyle

What do you do, dear? pictures by Maurice Sendak. Harper & Row 1985 c1961 unp il pa $6.95 hardcover o.p. *
Grades: PreK K 1 2　　　　　　　**395**
　1. Etiquette
　ISBN 0-06-443113-4 (pa)　　　　LC 84-43139
　First published 1961 by Addison-Wesley
A "handbook of etiquette for young ladies and gentlemen to be used as a guide for everyday social behavior."

Joslin, Sesyle—*Continued*

The Author

"The propriety of what the well-mannered child will do is related to extraordinary situations, as for example: The Sheriff of Nottingham interrupts you while you are reading, to take you to jail; you will, naturally, 'Find a bookmark to save your place.'" Horn Book

A "wonderful spoof on manners in a hilarious picture-book made for laughing aloud." Child Study Assoc of Am

What do you say, dear? pictures by Maurice Sendak. Harper & Row 1986 c1958 unp il lib bdg $15.89; pa $5.95 *

Grades: PreK K 1 2   395

  1. Etiquette

  ISBN 0-06-023074-6 (lib bdg); 0-06-443112-6 (pa)
                                 LC 84-43140

A Caldecott Medal honor book, 1959

First published 1958 by Addison-Wesley

A "handbook of etiquette for young ladies and gentlemen to be used as a guide for everyday social behavior." The Author

"A rollicking introduction to manners for the very young. A series of delightfully absurd situations—being introduced to a baby elephant, bumping into a crocodile, being rescued from a dragon—are posed and appropriately answered. The illustrations are among Sendak's best—and funniest." Bull Cent Child Books

Post, Peggy, 1945-

Emily Post's table manners for kids. Collins 2009 96p $15.99

Grades: 4 5 6 7   395

  1. Etiquette

  ISBN 978-0-06-111709-1; 0-06-111709-9
                               LC 2008010655

"This deceptively slim guide teems with advice about everything from meal courses to table settings, from the art of conversation to dining out. The tone is measured and mildly proscriptive, offset by Bjorkman's amusing cartoons. . . . A strength: the excellent troubleshooting for specific concerns, such as eating fondue and using chopsticks." Kirkus

Emily Post's The guide to good manners for kids; by Peggy Post & Cindy Post Senning. HarperCollins 2004 144p il $15.99; lib bdg $16.89

Grades: 4 5 6 7   395

  1. Etiquette

  ISBN 0-06-057196-9; 0-06-057197-7 (lib bdg)
                               LC 2003-26426

This offers advice on etiquette at home, at school, and other places, including letter writing and on-line communication, table manners, phone answering, and behavior at social gatherings, and public places.

"The writing is clear, friendly, and sometimes clever. . . . The advice is consistently practical and simple." SLJ

Emily's everyday manners; [by] Peggy Post and Cindy Post Senning; illustrated by Steve Bjorkman. HarperCollins 2006 unp il $16.99; lib bdg $17.89

Grades: PreK K 1 2   395

  1. Etiquette

  ISBN 0-06-076174-1; 0-06-076177-6 (lib bdg)

"Cheerful illustrations set the upbeat (and updated) tone for this introduction to manners. A succinct running text introduces young Emily and her neighbor Ethan and comments on how and why they use manners as well as how etiquette can differ according to the time and place." Booklist

Other titles in this series are:

Emily's magic words (2007)

Emily's Christmas gifts (2008)

Emily's sharing and caring book (2008)

Emily's out and about book (2009)

398 Folklore

Beeler, Selby B.

Throw your tooth on the roof; tooth traditions from around the world; illustrated by G. Brian Karas. Houghton Mifflin 1998 unp il $16; pa $6.95

Grades: K 1 2 3   398

  1. Teeth—Folklore

  ISBN 0-395-89108-6; 0-618-15238-5 (pa)
                               LC 97-46042

Consists of brief statements relating what children from around the world do with a tooth that has fallen out. Includes facts about teeth

"This book will be an eye-opener for young Americans who may have assumed that the Tooth Fairy holds a worldwide visa." Publ Wkly

Berk, Ariel

Secret history of mermaids and creatures of the deep; or the Liber Aquaticum; written and collected by Ari Berk, magister and scribe; illuminated by Wayne Anderson, Gary Chalk, Matt Dangler, Virginia Lee. Candlewick Press 2009 unp il $16.99

Grades: 4 5 6   398

  1. Mermaids and mermen

  ISBN 978-0-7636-4515-1; 0-7636-4515-X

"This volume details merfolk from tales and mythologies around the world. A wide variety of creatures, their customs, and habitats are touched on. The often ornately scripted text is accompanied by intricate illustrations and numerous foldouts." Horn Book Guide

The **Dictionary** of folklore; David Adams Leeming, general editor. Watts 2002 128p il $35

Grades: 4 5 6 7   398

  1. Folklore—Dictionaries 2. Reference books

  ISBN 0-531-11985-8   LC 2001-22034

This work answers such questions as "Why was Abraham Lincoln known as 'Honest Abe?' Did George Washington really cut down his father's cherry tree? How

The Dictionary of folklore—*Continued*

much truth is there to the tall tale of John Henry, the 'natural-born steel-driving man,' or Paul Bunyon and Babe the Blue Ox?" Publisher's note

"The layout of the book is pleasing. It is organized in alphabetical order and the content is understandable with many cross-references. The illustrations complement the text. . . . Leeming does an excellent job of enticing the reader to be curious." Book Rep

Includes bibliographical references

Gibbons, Gail

Behold . . . the dragons! Morrow Junior Bks. 1999 unp il $16; lib bdg $15.89

Grades: K 1 2 3   **398**

1. Dragons 2. Folklore
ISBN 0-688-15526-X; 0-688-15527-8 (lib bdg)
      LC 98-20205

Explains how myths about dragons developed, different types of dragons, what draconologists do, and how different cultures portray dragons

"Numerous bright illustrations accompany the well-researched text. This is a solid, informative presentation." Horn Book Guide

Grant, John, 1949-

Life-size dragons; illustrated by Fred Gambino. Sterling Pub. 2006 48p il $9.95   **398**

1. Dragons   Grades: 3 4 5 6
ISBN 1-4027-2536-1

Explores the origins, varieties, and history of dragons, presenting them as if they are real creatures.

Harpur, James, 1956-

Mythical creatures; illustrated by Stuart Martin. Barron's 2009 unp il $22.99

Grades: 3 4 5   **398**

1. Mythical animals
ISBN 978-0-7641-6204-6; 0-7641-6204-7

"Mythical creatures like the Minotaur, the kraken and the selkies are featured in this sturdy, encyclopedia-style book. There are plenty of unique components: a pull-tab box addresses how to tell if a unicorn is real or not. . . . and an impressive pop-up 'Arabian Phoenix' spreads its red wings and opens its beak above a roaring fire. . . . [This] will give fantasy fans food for thought." Publ Wkly

Kallen, Stuart A., 1955-

Werewolves. Reference Point Press 2010 104p il (The mysterious & unknown) $25.95

Grades: 4 5 6 7   **398**

1. Werewolves
ISBN 978-1-60152-097-5; 1-60152-097-2

Describes the history and lore surrounding the topic of werewolves, examining how the shape-shifting beast has been feared by various cultures around the world, and its continuing influence on popular culture.

This is "surprisingly exhaustive. . . . Breakout summaries and quotes enliven the layout. . . . There is . . . plenty of creepy stuff to scrutinize." Booklist

Includes bibliographical references

Kelly, Sophia

What a beast! a look-it-up guide to the monsters and mutants of mythology. Scholastic 2010 128p il map (Mythlopedia) lib bdg $39; pa $13.95

Grades: 4 5 6 7   **398**

1. Monsters 2. Classical mythology
ISBN 978-1-60631-028-1 (lib bdg); 1-60631-028-3 (lib bdg); 978-1-60631-060-1 (pa); 1-60631-060-7 (pa)
      LC 2009-20998

Describes some of the creatures and monsters in Greek mythology.

This "spices things up with sassy artwork, a pastel color scheme, and an OMG sensibility. . . . [This title is] loaded with information on the inspired methods with which various nasty creatures could put an end to bothersome heroes. Aside from the heaps of information coming from all angles on just about every page, . . . [the] book also contains a decent family tree, a rudimentary star chart, and lists of further reading. . . . For kids unconvinced that anything so old and gray could have any bearing on their lives, . . . [this book provides] a feisty . . . guide to the many cultural references lingering from antiquity." Booklist

Includes glossary and bibliographical references

Knudsen, Shannon, 1971-

Fairies and elves. Lerner 2010 48p il (Fantasy chronicles) lib bdg $27.93

Grades: 4 5 6 7   **398**

1. Fairies
ISBN 978-0-8225-9979-1 (lib bdg); 0-8225-9979-1 (lib bdg)
      LC 2008050207

"The explanations and history behind . . . fairies [and elves] . . . will provide satisfaction for readers who want to know more about these familiar characters from myth, fantasy, and folk and fairy tales. Brief and concise." SLJ

Includes bibliographical references

Fantastical creatures and magical beasts. Lerner Publications 2010 48p il (Fantasy chronicles) lib bdg $27.93

Grades: 4 5 6 7   **398**

1. Mythical animals
ISBN 978-0-8225-9987-6 (lib bdg); 0-8225-9987-2 (lib bdg)
      LC 2009004794

This describes mythical beasts such as dragons, unicorns, Hydra, Medusa, the labyrinth, and basilisks

"The explanations and history behind well-known fantastical creatures . . . will provide satisfaction for readers who want to know more about these familiar characters from myth, fantasy, and folk and fairy tales. Brief and concise." SLJ

Includes bibliographical references

MacDonald, Margaret Read

The storyteller's sourcebook; a subject, title, and motif index to folklore collections for children, 1983-1999; by Margaret Read MacDonald and Brian W. Sturm. Gale Group 2001 712p $125 *

Grades: Professional   **398**

1. Reference books 2. Folklore—Indexes
ISBN 0-8103-5485-3   LC 00-48395

Also available original volume covering the years 1961-1982 $125 (ISBN 0-8103-0471-6)

MacDonald, Margaret Read—*Continued*

This sourcebook "provides descriptions of folktales and references to more than 700 published sources of folktales. . . . [Includes] indexing by subject, motif, title, ethnic group and country of origin and a comprehensive bibliography." Publisher's note

Mitton, Jacqueline

Zodiac; celestial circle of the sun; [by] Jacqueline Mitton; illustrated by Christina Balit. Frances Lincoln 2005 32p il $16.95; pa $7.95
Grades: 2 3 4   **398**
    1. Zodiac 2. Constellations
    ISBN 1-84507-074-7; 1-84507-279-0 (pa)
"Mitton covers the 12 well-known constellations belonging to the Zodiac, beginning with a brief introduction that is followed by a spread devoted to each of the signs. . . . Striking jewel-toned, classically inspired illustrations highlighted by metallic stars complement the text. This attractive survey of the symbols of the Zodiac should serve as an appealing starting point for budding astronomers and astrologers." SLJ

Ogburn, Jacqueline K.

A dignity of dragons; collective nouns for magical beasts; by Jacqueline K. Ogburn, Nicoletta Ceccoli; illustrated by Nicoletta Ceccoli. Houghton Mifflin Books for Children 2010 il $16
Grades: 2 3 4   **398**
    1. Mythical animals
    ISBN 978-0-618-86254-2; 0-618-86254-4
"Gorgeous mixed-media illustrations complement dozens of inventive collective nouns. . . . These creative descriptions comprise the only text in the book. A four-page glossary defines each fantastic creature and identifies the culture(s) of its origin. Ceccoli has created a stylized and luminous fantasyland energetically inhabited by Ogburn's enchanting bestiary. Fans of mythology and fantasy as well as budding lexophiles will savor this sophisticated picture book." SLJ

Regan, Sally

The vampire book. DK Pub. 2009 93p il $19.99
Grades: 5 6 7 8   **398**
    1. Vampires
    ISBN 978-0-7566-5551-8; 0-7566-5551-X
"This guide covers the origins and evolution of vampires throughout history, giving a worldwide perspective on legends, mythology, and lore, from African tales of terror to blood-drinking witches of Southeast Asia. It also covers vampires in literature, film, and television. . . . The vivid colors in the often full-page art leap from the pages, and the bold font demands attention." SLJ

Reinhart, Matthew

Fairies and magical creatures; [by] Matthew Reinhart and Robert Sabuda. Candlewick Press 2008 unp il (Encyclopedia mythologica) $27.99 *
Grades: K 1 2 3   **398**
    1. Fairies 2. Mythical animals 3. Pop-up books
    ISBN 978-0-7636-3172-7; 0-7636-3172-8
This pop-up book depicts and describes such magical creatures as Shakespeare's fairy queen Titania, hobgoblins, trolls, a humanoid magical tree, brownies, Pegasus, satyrs, Serbian enchanted birds, and merfolk.
"A dramatic pop-up towers over each spread, surrounded by flaps and corner gatefolds that open up more surprises. . . . The paper engineering consistently enhances the text. . . . The emphasis on global legends as well as a palette heavy on blues, purples and reds widen the audience way past the girly-girl set." Publ Wkly

Sierra, Judy

The gruesome guide to world monsters; illustrated by Henrik Drescher. Candlewick Press 2005 63p il $18.99
Grades: 5 6 7 8   **398**
    1. Monsters 2. Folklore
    ISBN 0-7636-1727-X   LC 2004-57470
This presents "brief introductions to dozens of ugly customers from world folklore. . . . [The author] offers wonderfully provocative warnings against creatures as diverse as the giant skunk Aniwye, the bloodsucking bat Mansusopsop, and Bloody Mary, an evil specter who lives on the other side of mirrors." SLJ

Thong, Roseanne

Wish; wishing traditions around the world; illustrated by Elisa Kleven. Chronicle Books 2008 unp il $16.99
Grades: K 1 2 3   **398**
    1. Wishes
    ISBN 978-0-8118-5716-1   LC 2007038299
"'The many ways to make a wish wherever home may be' come in for lighthearted yet respectful exploration in this attractive square-format book. Thong . . . entices readers with consistently well-rhymed verses . . . following up each with a brief description of a national custom. . . . Rendered in Kleven's . . . kaleidoscopic style, many of the full-bleed spreads nearly shimmer. . . . Endnotes include more information along with an invitation to find 15 lucky symbols hidden in the pictures." Publ Wkly

398.2   Folk literature

Sagas, romances, legends, ballads, and fables in prose form, and fairy tales, folk tales, and tall tales are included here, instead of with the literature of the country of origin, to keep the traditional material together and to make it more readily accessible. Modern fairy tales are classified with Fiction, Story collections (SC), or Easy books (E)

Aardema, Verna

Anansi does the impossible! an Ashanti tale; retold by Verna Aardema; illustrated by Lisa Desimini. Atheneum Bks. for Young Readers 1997 unp il $16; pa $5.99 *

Grades: K 1 2 3   398.2
1. Anansi (Legendary character) 2. Folklore—West Africa
ISBN 0-689-81092-X; 0-689-83933-2 (pa)
                   LC 96-20033
"An Anne Schwartz book"
"Anansi the Spider is determined to buy back the stories taken from the people and kept by the Sky God. With the assistance of his clever wife, Aso, he takes the Sky God the live python, the real fairy, and the 47 stinging hornets required to regain the stories." SLJ
"Vivid, stylized collage illustrations convey the frightening force and power of the Sky God yet also reveal Anansi's own pluck and boldness. Perfect for reading or telling aloud." Booklist
Includes glossary and bibliographical references

Borreguita and the coyote; a tale from Ayutla, Mexico; retold by Verna Aardema; illustrated by Petra Mathers. Knopf 1991 unp il pa $6.99 hardcover o.p. *

Grades: K 1 2 3   398.2
1. Folklore—Mexico 2. Coyote (Legendary character) 3. Sheep—Folklore
ISBN 0-679-88936-1 (pa)   LC 90-33302
A little lamb uses her clever wiles to keep a coyote from eating her up
This folk tale "is energetically told and comfortably packed with many recognizable motifs. Mathers enlarges upon the humorous elements of the story in her boldly colored paintings. . . . Aardema and Mathers are felicitously paired in a tale of trickery rewarded that begs to be read aloud." Horn Book
Includes glossary

Bringing the rain to Kapiti Plain; a Nandi tale; retold by Verna Aardema; pictures by Beatriz Vidal. Dial Bks. for Young Readers 1981 unp il $16.99; pa $5.99 *

Grades: K 1 2 3   398.2
1. Folklore—Africa 2. Stories in rhyme 3. Droughts—Folklore
ISBN 0-8037-0809-2; 0-8037-0904-8 (pa)
                   LC 80-25886
"Retold from an African folk tale, this is a cumulative rhyming tale with the rhythm and repetition of 'The House that Jack Built.' It tells of how Ki-pat, the herdsman, works out a clever method to save the plain from a long drought." SLJ
"Effective both in the rhythm of its metered storytell-

ing and in the brilliance of its stylized paintings, the panoramic picture book quickly engages both eye and ear." Horn Book

Rabbit makes a monkey of lion; a Swahili tale; retold by Verna Aardema; pictures by Jerry Pinkney. Dial Bks. for Young Readers 1989 unp il pa $5.99 hardcover o.p.

Grades: K 1 2 3   398.2
1. Folklore—Zanzibar 2. Animals—Folklore
ISBN 0-14-054593-X (pa)   LC 86-11523
Text adapted from The hare and the lion, published 1901 in Zanzibar tales
With the help of his friends Bush-rat and Turtle, smart and nimble Rabbit makes a fool of the mighty but slow-witted king of the forest
"Aardema's version of the tale reinforces the amusing trickster qualities of rascally Rabbit, making it a sure-fire choice for sharing with groups of children, who will instantly root for his success. Pinkney's lovely watercolor and pencil paintings in hues of green, brown, and gold fill the pages with lush scenes which evoke the East African setting." Horn Book

Who's in Rabbit's house? a Masai tale; retold by Verna Aardema; pictures by Leo and Diane Dillon. Dial Bks. for Young Readers 1977 unp il pa $6.99 hardcover o.p.

Grades: K 1 2 3   398.2
1. Masai (African people)—Folklore 2. Animals—Folklore 3. Folklore—East Africa
ISBN 0-14-054724-X (pa)   LC 77-71514
This "tale relates the attempts of Rabbit to regain possession of her house after it is taken over by an intruder. Rabbit's friends offer suggestions on how to solve the problem, but the solution comes from 'an unexpected source.' The story, adapted from the Masai tale 'The Long One,' uses repetition of key phrases to produce a rhythmic read-aloud text. The Dillons skillfully present their artistry in a vivid, colorful and impressive manner which contributes to the story and sets the tone." Child Book Rev Serv

Why mosquitoes buzz in people's ears; a West African tale retold; pictures by Leo and Diane Dillon. Dial Bks. for Young Readers 1975 unp il $16.99; pa $6.99 *

Grades: K 1 2 3   398.2
1. Folklore—West Africa 2. Mosquitoes—Folklore 3. Animals—Folklore
ISBN 0-8037-6089-2; 0-14-054905-6 (pa)
Awarded the Caldecott Medal, 1976
This tale relates "how a mosquito's silly lie to an iguana sets in motion a cumulative series of events that finally causes Mother Owl not to call up the sun. The resulting hardship ends only after King Lion traces the problem back to its source." Booklist
"Stunning full-color illustrations—watercolor sprayed with air gun, overlayed with pastel, cut out and repasted—give an eye-catching abstract effect and tell the story with humor and power." SLJ

Alley, Zöe B.

There's a wolf at the door; pictures by R. W. Alley. Roaring Brook Press 2008 40p il $19.95 *

Grades: K 1 2 3   **398.2**

1. Wolves—Folklore—Graphic novels 2. Humorous graphic novels 3. Graphic novels

ISBN 978-1-59643-275-8; 1-59643-275-6

LC 2007-44025

"A Neal Porter book"

Contents: The three little pigs; The boy who cried wolf; Little Red Riding Hood; The wolf in sheep's clothing; The wolf and the seven little goslings

As his plans are spoiled over and over again, the wolf keeps trying to find his dinner, in this retelling of five well-known stories and fables.

This is a "hilarious romp. . . . Illustrated with softly colored pen-and-ink drawings, these five stories meld seamlessly together. The text is full of puns, alliteration, and occasional rhymes." SLJ

Andrews, Jan, 1942-

Stories at the door; [retold] by Jan Andrews; illustrations by Francis Blake. Tundra Books 2007 79p il $18.95

Grades: 2 3 4   **398.2**

1. Folklore

ISBN 978-0-88776-811-8; 0-88776-811-3

This is a "collection of six folktales from around the world. Selections include a Scandinavian story, . . . an amusing Palestinian tale, . . . and an Indian story. . . . Andrews contributes a short poem before each selection and retells the stories in simple language. . . . With humor running through them like a bright thread, the lively stories are well matched by Blake's jaunty, colorful, and often comical line-and-wash artwork." Booklist

Includes bibliographical references

The **Arabian** nights entertainments; selected and edited by Andrew Lang; with numerous illustrations by H. J. Ford. Dover Publs. 1969 424p il pa $9.95

Grades: 5 6 7 8   **398.2**

1. Arabs—Folklore 2. Fairy tales

ISBN 0-486-22289-6

First published 1898 in the United Kingdom

"A collection of popular tales assembled over many centuries, and well known in Europe from the 18th cent. It contains the stories of 'Aladdin, Alibaba, and Sindbad the sailor.' . . . The framing story in which the tales are set concerns Scheherazade, who is determined to delay her royal husband's plan of killing her—he has taken to murdering his wives because the first was unfaithful to him—by telling him a story every evening. She leaves each evening's tale incomplete until the next day, so that he has to spare her life in order to hear its conclusion. He is so entertained that he finally abandons his murderous plan." Oxford Companion to Child Lit

The **August** House book of scary stories; spooky tales for telling out loud; edited by Liz Parkhurst. August House 2009 144p $15.95

Grades: 4 5 6 7 8   **398.2**

1. Folklore 2. Horror fiction 3. Short stories 4. Storytelling

ISBN 978-0-87483-915-9; 0-87483-915-7

LC 2009008711

Contents: Mean John and the Jacko-lantern (an Irish folktale) by Michael J. Caduto; The vain girl and the handsome visitor (based on a Mexican urban legend) by Olga Loya; The gingerbread boy (a Kentucky folktale) by Mary Hamilton; The mournful Lady of Binnorie (based on a Scottish ballad) by Bobbie Pell; The angel of River Road (based on a family story) by Larry G. Brown; One lace glove (a Civil War ghost story) by Lorna Macdonald Czarnota; The boy who drew cats (a Japanese folktale) by Judy Sima; The Greyman of Pawleys Island (based on maritime legend) by Timothy E. Dillinger; Simon and the magic catfish (a folktale from the southern United States) by Nat Whitman; The red satin ribbon (an American variant of a European legend) by Martha Hamilton and Mitch Weiss; The dauntless girl (a British folktale) by Margaret Read MacDonald; Shut up, Billy! (an original tale with a traditional twist) by Jim May; Ain't nobody here (an African-American folktale) by Lyn Ford; Outside the door (based on U.S. campus lore) by Richard and Judy Dockrey Young; Tío Mono y La Lechusa (based on Mexican folk legend) by Gregorio C. Pedroza; Johnny and the dead man's liver (an African-American folktale) by James "Sparky" Rucker; Aaron Kelly's bones (based on Appalachian and African-American folklore) by Kevin Cordi; The snow ghost (based on Irish and Scottish folklore) by Wendy Welch; Pretty maid Ibronka (a Hungarian folktale) by Mary Grace Ketner; Mia's ghost (an original story) by Robert D. San Souci.

An anthology of spooky stories drawn from folklore, local history, and the storytellers' imaginations, and divided into the categories "Just Desserts and Lessons Learned," "Ghostly Guardians," "Dark Humor," "Urban Legends and Jump Tales," and "Fearless Females."

"Each of these 20 chilling tales is meant to be told out loud and includes author notes about how to maximize the spooky effect. Middle schoolers will relish reading and sharing these tales, hoping to creep each other out." SLJ

Aylesworth, Jim, 1943-

The Gingerbread man; retold by Jim Aylesworth; illustrated by Barbara McClintock. Scholastic 1998 unp il $15.95

Grades: K 1 2 3   **398.2**

1. Folklore

ISBN 0-590-97219-7   LC 96-52781

A freshly baked gingerbread man escapes when he is taken out of the oven and eludes a number of pursuers until he meets a clever fox

"This hearty retelling of the well-known tale is distinguished by cheery, lively illustrations. . . . The scenery resembles that of the eighteenth-century English artist Thomas Bewick. With even a recipe included, this is altogether an old-fashioned and enjoyable version of a favorite tale." Horn Book Guide

Goldilocks and the three bears; retold by Jim Aylesworth; illustrated by Barbara McClintock. Scholastic Press 2003 unp il $15.95

Grades: K 1 2 3   **398.2**

1. Folklore 2. Bears—Folklore

ISBN 0-439-39545-3   LC 2002-15964

A little girl walking in the woods finds the house of the three bears and helps herself to their belongings

Aylesworth, Jim, 1943--*Continued*

"Aylesworth's text is faithful to the traditional elements of the original, juicing up the plot with folksy, conversational asides. . . . The artist's watercolor, sepia ink, and gouache illustrations are pastel and dainty yet full of life and action." SLJ

The mitten; retold by Jim Aylesworth; illustrated by Barbara McClintock. Scholastic Press 2009 unp il $16.99 *

Grades: PreK K 1 2   **398.2**
   1. Folklore—Ukraine 2. Animals—Folklore
   3. Winter—Folklore
   ISBN 978-0-439-92544-0; 0-439-92544-4
                LC 2006-37115

A retelling of the traditional tale of how a boy's lost mitten becomes a refuge from the cold for an increasing number of animals.

"Aylesworth's polished story together with McClintock's energetic pictures prove that *The Mitten* can hold one more. Aylesworth's text shows its storytelling roots with its perfect pacing, precisely chosen details, and most of all its particapatory repetition." Horn Book

The tale of Tricky Fox; a New England trickster tale; retold by Jim Aylesworth; illustrated by Barbara McClintock. Scholastic Press 2001 unp il $15.95

Grades: K 1 2 3   **398.2**
   1. Foxes—Folklore 2. Folklore—New England
   ISBN 0-439-09543-3   LC 00-35773

Tricky Fox uses his sack to trick everyone he meets into giving him ever more valuable items

"The romping good humor of the story is carried by the old-fashioned illustrations in sepia tones." SLJ

Badoe, Adwoa

The pot of wisdom: Ananse stories; pictures by Baba Wagué Diakité. Douglas & McIntyre 2001 63p il hardcover o.p. pa $12.95

Grades: 3 4 5 6   **398.2**
   1. Anansi (Legendary character) 2. Folklore—West
   Africa
   ISBN 0-88899-429-X; 0-88899-869-4 (pa)

"A Groundwood book"

Includes the following stories: Why Ananse lives on the ceiling; Ananse and the feeding pot; Ananse becomes the owner of stories; Ananse the even-handed judge; Ananse the forgetful guest; The mat confidences; Ananse and the pot of wisdom; Ananse and the singing cloak; Why pig has a short snout; Ananse and the birds

"Badoe remembers hearing these trickster stories in her youth in Ghana, and she retells them with the freshness and verve of the spoken word. . . . Each tale is illustrated with a brilliantly colored polychrome tile by Diakite, the Mali-born illustrator. The tiles employ strong black linear motifs and sun-and-earth colors: gold, orange, brown, blue, lemon." Booklist

Barton, Byron

The little red hen. HarperCollins Pubs. 1993 unp il $15.95; lib bdg $15.89; pa $24.99; bd bk $7.99 *

Grades: K 1 2   **398.2**
   1. Folklore 2. Chickens—Folklore
   ISBN 0-06-021675-1; 0-06-021676-X (lib bdg);
   0-06-443379-X (pa); 0-694-00999-7 (bd bk)
                LC 91-4051

The little red hen finds none of her lazy friends willing to help her plant, harvest, or grind wheat into flour, but all are eager to eat the bread she makes from it

"Barton here skillfully pares down a well-known tale for the youngest readers and listeners. Vibrant hues abound in his full-page, collage-like illustrations." Publ Wkly

The three bears. HarperCollins Pubs. 1991 unp il $15.95; lib bdg $15.89; bd bk $7.99 *

Grades: K 1   **398.2**
   1. Folklore 2. Bears—Folklore
   ISBN 0-06-020423-0; 0-06-020424-9 (lib bdg);
   0-694-00998-9 (bd bk)   LC 90-43151

"Here's the familiar tale of the three bears and their blond gal pal drawn for the very youngest. Byron uses large simple shapes, bright colors, and a spare text to tell his story. . . . The size of the art makes this a good choice for mother-toddler story hours." Booklist

Bateman, Teresa

The Frog with the Big Mouth; retold by Teresa Bateman; illustrated by Will Terry. Albert Whitman & Co. 2008 unp il $16.99

Grades: K 1 2   **398.2**
   1. Frogs—Folklore 2. Rain forest animals—Folklore
   3. Folklore—South America
   ISBN 978-0-8075-2621-7; 0-8075-2621-5
                LC 2007052157

An Argentine wide-mouthed frog sets out through the rain forest to brag about his fly-eating abilities and encounters a toco toucan, a coati, a capybara, and a jaguar. Includes a note about the animals.

"Terry's shiny, verdant rain forest capably offsets myriad greens with shadows of lavender, an electric-blue beetle, and wine-red berries. The spreads swirl with movement and beckon forward via fluid lines. . . . This is an inventive version of a long-favored tale." SLJ

Baynes, Pauline, 1922-2008

Questionable creatures; a bestiary; [by] Pauline Baynes. Eerdmans Books for Young Readers 2006 47p il $18

Grades: 4 5 6 7   **398.2**
   1. Mythical animals 2. Bestiaries
   ISBN 978-0-8028-5284-7; 0-8028-5284-X
                LC 2005033658

"Baynes introduces readers to the creatures and myths found in medieval bestiaries and explains how the books were made and how they were viewed by the general public. The rest of the volume details the commonly held beliefs that both peasants and scholars embraced about specific animals. . . . Baynes's detailed gouache and colored-pencil illustrations . . . are done in the style of me-

Baynes, Pauline, 1922-2008—*Continued*
dieval illuminations. . . . The artist shows great respect for the early bestiary creators while also giving the stories relevance for modern readers." SLJ

Includes bibliographical references

Bell, Anthea, 1936-
The porridge pot; 1854 by the Brothers Carl and Theodor Colshorn; retold from the German by Anthea Bell; pictures by Claudia Carls. Minedition 2007 unp il $16.99
Grades: 2 3 4 5   398.2
1. Folklore—Germany 2. Fairy tales
ISBN 978-0-698-40073-3

"A starving miller chases his porridge pot-toting wife into the woods, followed by their young daughter. The daughter loses her parents and her shoe, but is befriended by an eccentric-looking old woman who . . . directs her to her destiny as wife of the kingdom's prince. . . . Carls uses an amalgamation of computer-enhanced images and paintings to create an oddly textured folktale world. Claymation figures parade with Meer cats and ostriches in outlandish costumes. . . . and hyperrealistic, imagination-stretching details." Booklist

Beneduce, Ann
Jack and the beanstalk; retold by Ann Keay Beneduce; illustrated by Gennady Spirin. Philomel Bks. 1999 32p il $16.99
Grades: 2 3 4   398.2
1. Fairy tales 2. Folklore—Great Britain
ISBN 0-399-23118-8   LC 98-5722

A boy climbs to the top of a giant beanstalk, where he uses his quick wits to outsmart an ogre and make his and his mother's fortune

"Beneduce bases her version of Jack and the Beanstalk on a Victorian version, complete with a fairy guardian. . . . Spirin contributes some glorious borders for the text as well as many impressively detailed paintings, notable for their dark muted colors and mysterious, foggy look." Booklist

Berger, Barbara, 1945-
All the way to Lhasa; a tale from Tibet; retelling & art by Barbara Helen Berger. Philomel Bks. 2002 unp il $17.99
Grades: K 1 2 3   398.2
1. Folklore—Tibet (China)
ISBN 0-399-23387-3   LC 2001-54560

Based on a story told to the author by Lama Tharchin Rinpoche

A boy and his yak persevere along the difficult way to the holy city of Lhasa and succeed where others fail

"Berger distills the pilgrim's quest into a simply told, evocative tale. . . . Berger's paint-and-pencil illustrations are gloriously colored and filled with subtle details borrowed from Tibetan Buddhism." Booklist

Berner, Rotraut Susanne, 1948-
Definitely not for little ones; some very Grimm fairy-tale comics; translated by Shelley Tanaka. Groundwood Books 2009 unp il $18.95
Grades: 4 5 6   398.2
1. Grimm, Jacob, 1785-1863—Adaptations 2. Fairy tales 3. Folklore
ISBN 978-0-88899-957-3; 0-88899-957-7

"In a comic book format, Berner retells the Brothers Grimm tales of the Frog Prince, Mother Holle, Tom Thumb, Rapunzel, Jorinda & Jorindel, Lucky Hans, Hans the Hedgehog, and Little Red Cap, using a humorous, breezy and somewhat ironic tone. . . . Older elementary-school readers who like sneaky humor, slightly violent demises of villains, and humorous takes on familiar tales will enjoy these comics. . . . Tanaka's translation lets the narration and dialogue flow seamlessly." Booklist

Blackstone, Stella
Storytime; first tales for sharing; told by Stella Blackstone; illustrated by Anne Wilson. Barefoot Books 2005 94p il $19.99; pa $12.99
Grades: K 1   398.2
1. Folklore 2. Animals—Folklore
ISBN 1-84148-345-1; 1-84686-165-9 (pa)
LC 2004029542

Contents: The cock, the mouse and the little red hen; The gingerbread man; The ugly duckling; Goldilocks and the three bears; The timid hare

"Seven familiar nursery tales are accompanied by bright, stylized, folk-art illustrations, done in paper collage and acrylic. Selections include The Cock, the Mouse and the Little Red Hen, The Gingerbread Man, The Ugly Duckling, Goldilocks, The Timid Hare (a Henny Penny story from India), The Three Little Pigs, and Stone Soup. The retellings are straightforward; most are faithful to the most commonly known versions and retain the familiar refrains. . . . The collection as a whole is delightful; the art is fresh, vibrant, and full of child appeal." SLJ

Includes bibliographical references

Blackwood, Gary L.
Legends or lies? Marshall Cavendish Benchmark 2006 72p il (Unsolved history) lib bdg $34.21
Grades: 4 5 6 7   398.2
1. Legends
ISBN 978-0-7614-1891-7 (lib bdg); 0-7614-1891-1 (lib bdg)

Describes several legends that have intrigued people for centuries: the lost civilization of Atlantis, the Amazons, King Arthur, St Brendon, Pope Joan, and El Dorado

This collection "of tidbits about lingering mysteries of the past . . . [offers] more substance than most. . . . [It offers] a full-page illustration opening each chapter; reproductions, many in color; and a generously spaced format." SLJ

Includes glossary and bibliographical references

Blia Xiong

Nine-in-one, Grr! Grr! a folktale from the Hmong people of Laos; told by Blia Xiong; adapted by Cathy Spagnoli; illustrated by Nancy Hom. Children's Bk. Press 1989 30p il hardcover o.p. pa $7.95

Grades: K 1 2   **398.2**
   1. Folklore—Laos 2. Tigers—Folklore 3. Hmong (Asian people)—Folklore
   ISBN 0-89239-048-4; 0-89239-110-3 (pa)
                          LC 89-9891

When the great god Shao promises Tiger nine cubs each year, Bird comes up with a clever trick to prevent the land from being overrun by tigers

"Simply and eloquently told, this *pourquoi* tale from a minority Laotian culture is boldly illustrated in a style adapted from the multi-imaged embroidered story cloths of the Hmong people. Its rhythmic text and appealing, brightly colored pictures make it a good choice for pre-school story hours." Booklist

The **Blue** fairy book; edited by Andrew Lang; with numerous illustrations by H. J. Ford and G. P. Jacomb Hood. Dover Publs. 1965 390p il pa $10.95

Grades: 4 5 6   **398.2**
   1. Folklore 2. Fairy tales
   ISBN 0-486-21437-0

Also available in paperback $10.95 each: The Green fairy book; The Grey fairy book; The Lilac fairy book; The Olive fairy book; The Orange fairy book; The Pink fairy book; The Red fairy book; The Yellow fairy book

A reprint of the title first published 1889 by Longmans

A collection of thirty-seven fairy tales from various countries, consisting largely of old favorites from such sources as Perrault, the Brothers Grimm, Madame D'Aulnoy, Asbjörnsen and Möe, the Arabian Nights and Swift's Gulliver's travels

Bodkin, Odds

The crane wife; retold by Odds Bodkin; illustrated by Gennady Spirin. Gulliver Bks. 1998 unp il hardcover o.p. pa $7

Grades: 3 4 5   **398.2**
   1. Folklore—Japan
   ISBN 0-15-201407-1; 0-15-216350-6 (pa)
                        LC 96-35488

A retelling of the traditional Japanese tale about a poor sail maker who gains a beautiful but mysterious wife skilled at weaving magical sails

"Capturing the tale's mystery and tragedy, Spirin's watercolor-and-gouache paintings take their inspiration from Japanese art. Delicate shades of tawny gray and burnished gold predominate in the illustrations." Booklist

Bolt, Ranjit

The hare and the tortoise and other fables of La Fontaine; translated by Ranjit Bolt; illustrated by Giselle Potter. Barefoot Books 2006 64p il $19.99

Grades: 3 4 5 6   **398.2**
   1. La Fontaine, Jean de, 1621-1695—Adaptations 2. Fables
   ISBN 1-905236-54-9; 978-1-905236-54-1
                        LC 2005-30378

"Bolt translates and recasts La Fontaine's work in rhyming, contemporary English. . . . The Fox and the Stork, The Lion and the Rat, and other familiar tales appear among these 19 selections, along with a few that are less well known. . . . Potter's double-page, naive paintings echo the humor, effectively portraying the animal and human characters. The rhymed phrasing offers an entertaining introduction to the literature of fable and pleasing read-aloud and storytelling material." SLJ

Boughn, Michael

Into the world of the dead; astonishing adventures in the underworld. Annick Press 2006 56p il lib bdg $24.95; pa $12.95

Grades: 5 6 7 8   **398.2**
   1. Death—Folklore 2. Future life—Folklore
   ISBN 1-55037-959-3 (lib bdg); 1-55037-958-5 (pa)

"Boughn retells stories from many cultures on every continent except South America, including quite a few from Mesoamerica, Asia, Africa, and Oceania. Readers will find heroes who have traveled to and returned from the underworld as well as the gods and monsters who dwell there. Full-color and black-and-white illustrations, including reproductions, photos, and plenty of graphics of skulls, appear on every page. . . . This is a book that many young people may find appealing." SLJ

Brett, Jan, 1949-

Beauty and the beast; retold and illustrated by Jan Brett. Clarion Bks. 1989 unp il lib bdg $16; pa $6.95

Grades: 1 2 3   **398.2**
   1. Folklore—France 2. Fairy tales
   ISBN 0-89919-497-4 (lib bdg); 0-395-55702-X (pa)
                        LC 88-16965

Through her great capacity to love, a kind and beautiful maid releases a handsome prince from the spell which has made him an ugly beast

"A Beauty of distinguished appearance, a delightful set of animal servants, and a suitably hideous Beast are presented in Jan Brett's distinctive, decorative style. Small details, such as tapestries mirroring the action of the tale, add to the effect of the simply written story." Horn Book Guide

Gingerbread baby. Putnam 1999 unp il $16.99

Grades: K 1 2 3   **398.2**
   1. Folklore
   ISBN 0-399-23444-6   LC 98-52310

A young boy and his mother bake a gingerbread baby that escapes from their oven and leads a crowd on a chase

"Although the story remains true to the original tale, Brett has added her own touches and a surprise ending. . . . The illustrations are pure Brett and feature warm colors against a snow-white landscape." SLJ

Brett, Jan, 1949——*Continued*

The mitten; a Ukrainian folktale; adapted and illustrated by Jan Brett. anniversary ed. Penguin Young Readers Group 2009 c1989 unp il $17.99
Grades: K 1 2   398.2
    1. Folklore—Ukraine 2. Animals—Folklore
    ISBN 978-0-399-25296-9; 0-399-25296-7
    First published 1989 by Putnam
After Nicki accidentally drops his mitten in the forest it becomes an object of curiosity for a mole, a rabbit, a badger, a tiny brown mouse, and a big brown bear, as they all crawl into it
"Readers will enjoy the charm and humor in the portrayal of the animals as they make room for each newcomer in the mitten and sprawl in the snow after the big sneeze." Horn Book

The three snow bears; [by] Jan Brett. G. P. Putnam's Sons 2007 unp il $16.99
Grades: K 1 2 3   398.2
    1. Polar bear—Folklore 2. Inuit—Folklore
    ISBN 978-0-399-24792-7   LC 2007007373
Retells the story of Goldilocks, set in an Inuit village and featuring a family of polar bears.
"Filled with the gorgeously detailed watercolor and gouache illustrations that distinguish her work, this Arctic version of the classic tale is pure Brett. . . . The plot remains true to the progression of the traditional tale and the narrative moves swiftly." SLJ

Town mouse, country mouse. Putnam 1994 unp il $16.99; pa $6.99
Grades: K 1 2 3   398.2
    1. Aesop—Adaptations 2. Fables 3. Mice—Folklore
    ISBN 0-399-22622-2; 0-698-11986-X (pa)
                          LC 93-41227
A retelling of the Aesop fable. After trading houses, the country mice and the town mice discover there's no place like home
"In Brett's version, the town mice are as charming and naive as their country cousins. . . . Brett's narrative alternates the parallel mishaps of the two sets of mice with lively, smooth writing and a deft touch of humor. . . . The illustrations are rich with meticulous detail." SLJ

Who's that knocking on Christmas Eve. Putnam 2002 unp il $16.99
Grades: K 1 2   398.2
    1. Christmas—Fiction 2. Folklore—Norway
    ISBN 0-399-23873-5   LC 2001-48253
A boy from Finnmark and his ice bear help scare away some hungry trolls so that Kyri and her father can enjoy their Christmas Eve meal
This is a "vivid, well-paced retelling of an old Norwegian folktale. . . . Gorgeous endpapers depicting nightsky constellations studded with trolls, bears, and other mythical symbols complement the exquisitely detailed winter-wonderland artistry within." Booklist

Brown, Marcia, 1918-
Once a mouse; a fable cut in wood. Atheneum Pubs. 1961 unp il $16; pa $5.99
Grades: K 1 2 3   398.2
    1. Folklore—India 2. Fables
    ISBN 0-684-12662-1; 0-689-71343-6 (pa)
    Awarded the Caldecott Medal, 1962
A "fable from the Indian 'Hitopadesa.' There is lively action in spreads showing how a hermit 'thinking about big and little' suddenly saves a mouse from a crow and then from larger enemies by turning the little creature into the forms of bigger and bigger animals—until as a royal tiger it has to be humbled." Horn Book
"The illustrations are remarkably beautiful. The emotional elements of the story . . . are conveyed with just as much intensity as the purely visual ones." New Yorker

Stone soup; an old tale; told and pictured by Marcia Brown. Scribner 1947 unp il $16.95; pa $6.99
Grades: K 1 2 3   398.2
    1. Folklore—France
    ISBN 0-684-92296-7; 0-689-71103-4 (pa)
    A Caldecott Medal honor book, 1948
"When the people in a French village heard that three soldiers were coming, they hid all their food for they knew what soldiers are. However, when the soldiers began to make soup with water and stones the pot gradually filled with all the vegetables which had been hidden away. The simple language and quiet humour of this folktale are amplified and enriched by gay and witty drawings of clever light-hearted soldiers, and the gullible 'light-witted' peasants." Cont Libr Rev

Bruchac, James
The girl who helped thunder and other Native American folktales; retold by James Bruchac and Joseph Bruchac; illustrated by Stefano Vitale. Sterling Pub. Co. 2008 96p il (Folktales of the world) $14.95 *
Grades: 3 4 5 6   398.2
    1. Native Americans—Folklore
    ISBN 978-1-4027-3263-8; 1-4027-3263-5
                          LC 2007-16876
"The Bruchacs retell Native North American folktales in a clear yet bold voice. The anthology is arranged geographically, a logical organization that reveals the diversity of Native peoples. . . . Descriptions of each region introduce the original inhabitants of those places, as the authors provide succinct yet enriching historical and cultural context for the stories that follow. . . . Vitale's stylized oil-on-wood illustrations vividly reveal the colorful spirit of the tales, as bright blues and reds complement the earth tones found throughout." SLJ

Bruchac, Joseph, 1942-

Between earth & sky; legends of Native American sacred places; written by Joseph Bruchac; illustrated by Thomas Locker. Harcourt Brace & Co. 1996 unp il map hardcover o.p. pa $7

Grades: 3 4 5   **398.2**

1. Native Americans—Folklore

ISBN 0-15-200042-9; 0-15-202062-4 (pa)

LC 95-10862

"In response to Little Turtle's questions about places sacred to the Delaware Indians, Old Bear explains that all people have sacred places and shares 10 legends from different tribes." Booklist

"Each tale is a model of economy, gracefully distilling its message, while Locker's landscapes capture the mysticism inherent in each setting." Horn Book Guide

The first strawberries; a Cherokee story; retold by Joseph Bruchac; pictures by Anna Vojtech. Dial Bks. for Young Readers 1993 unp il hardcover o.p. pa $6.99 *

Grades: K 1 2 3   **398.2**

1. Cherokee Indians—Folklore 2. Strawberries—Folklore

ISBN 0-8037-1331-2; 0-14-05409-8 (pa)

LC 91-31058

A quarrel between the first man and the first woman is reconciled when the Sun causes strawberries to grow out of the earth

"This retelling . . . is simply and clearly written, and as sweet as the berries the woman stops to taste. The attractive watercolors and colored-pencil illustrations show an idealized pastoral world." SLJ

The great ball game; a Muskogee story; retold by Joseph Bruchac; illustrated by Susan L. Roth. Dial Bks. for Young Readers 1994 unp il $15 *

Grades: K 1 2 3   **398.2**

1. Creek Indians—Folklore 2. Animals—Folklore

ISBN 0-8037-1539-0   LC 93-6269

Bat, who has both wings and teeth, plays an important part in a game between the Birds and the Animals to decide which group is better

"Roth's dynamic collages combine cut papers of varied textures and hues to create a series of effective illustrations. Short and well told, this appealing *pourquoi* tale lends itself to reading aloud." Booklist

How Chipmunk got his stripes; a tale of bragging and teasing; as told by Joseph Bruchac & James Bruchac; pictures by Jose Aruego & Ariane Dewey. Dial Bks. for Young Readers 2001 unp il hardcover o.p. pa $6.99

Grades: K 1 2 3   **398.2**

1. Native Americans—Folklore 2. Bears—Folklore 3. Squirrels—Folklore 4. Chipmunks—Folklore

ISBN 0-8037-2404-7; 0-14-250021-6 (pa)

LC 99-16793

"Bears brags that he can do anything, so Brown Squirrel dares him to keep the sun from rising. When Bear fails, Brown Squirrel teases him and gets scratched down his back." Horn Book Guide

"This *pourquoi* story is succinctly written in simple, concrete language, and repeated chants give listeners an opportunity to participate actively in the narrative's unfolding. . . . The pictures are large enough to be seen and enjoyed by a group." Bull Cent Child Books

Raccoon's last race; a traditional Abenaki story; as told by Joseph Bruchac & James Bruchac; pictures by Jose Aruego & Ariane Dewey. Dial Books for Young Readers 2004 unp il $15.99

Grades: K 1 2 3   **398.2**

1. Abnaki Indians—Folklore 2. Raccoons—Folklore

ISBN 0-8037-2977-4   LC 2003-9104

Tells the story of how Raccoon, the fastest animal on earth, loses his speed because he is boastful and breaks his promises

"A solid retelling of an Abenaki legend. . . . The text reads aloud smoothly and keeps the action moving quickly. Done in pen-and-ink, gouache, and pastel, the illustrations accentuate the humor of the tale." SLJ

Turtle's race with Beaver; a traditional Seneca story; as told by Joseph Bruchac & James Bruchac; pictures by Jose Aruego & Ariane Dewey. Dial Bks. for Young Readers 2003 unp il $15.99; pa $5.99

Grades: K 1 2 3   **398.2**

1. Seneca Indians—Folklore 2. Beavers—Folklore 3. Turtles—Folklore

ISBN 0-8037-2852-2; 0-14-240466-7 (pa)

LC 2002-4001

When Beaver challenges Turtle to a swimming race for ownership of the pond, Turtle outsmarts Beaver, and Beaver learns to share

"Done in pen and ink, gouache, and pastel, the cheerful artwork is a wonderful match for this well-told tale." SLJ

Bryan, Ashley, 1923-

Ashley Bryan's African tales, uh-huh. Atheneum Bks. for Young Readers 1998 198p $22 *

Grades: 4 5 6   **398.2**

1. Folklore—Africa

ISBN 0-689-82076-3   LC 97-77743

This volume combines three previously published titles: The ox of the wonderful horns and other African folktales (1971), Beat the story-drum, pum-pum (1980), Lion and the ostrich chicks and other African folktales (1986)

This collection of African folktales is "told with Bryan's distinctive rhythmic word patterns and filled with humor, life lessons, and the antics of trickster Ananse. . . . Quality reproductions of the original woodcuts enrich this handsome volume." Horn Book Guide

Beautiful blackbird. Atheneum Bks. for Young Readers 2003 unp il $16.95 *

Grades: K 1 2 3   **398.2**

1. Folklore—Zambia 2. Birds—Folklore

ISBN 0-689-84731-9   LC 2002-5290

In a story of the Ila people, the colorful birds of Africa ask Blackbird, whom they think is the most beautiful of birds, to decorate them with some of his "blackening brew"

"Bryan employs boldly colored, cut-paper artwork to

Bryan, Ashley, 1923-—_Continued_

dramatize the action. The overlapping collage images fill the pages with energy. . . . Ready-made for participative storytelling." Booklist

Buehner, Caralyn

Goldilocks and the three bears; [by] Caralyn Buehner; pictures by Mark Buehner. Dial Books for Young Readers 2007 unp il $16.99

Grades: PreK K 1 2   398.2
  1. Folklore 2. Bears—Folklore
  ISBN 0-8037-2939-1   LC 2005036401
In this variation on the classic folktale, a rhyming, rope-skipping, little girl rudely helps herself to the belongings of a genteel family of bears.

"This warm and pleasing retelling of the classic include a rope-jumping Goldilocks in red cowboy boots who bursts with personality. . . . The luminous oil-over-acrylic illustrations enhance the story with delightful details." SLJ

Bunting, Eve, 1928-

Finn McCool and the great fish; written by Eve Bunting; illustrated by Zachary Pullen. Sleeping Bear Press 2010 unp il $16.95

Grades: K 1 2 3   398.2
  1. Finn MacCumhaill, 3rd cent.—Legends
  2. Folklore—Ireland 3. Giants—Folklore 4. Fishes—Folklore
  ISBN 978-1-58536-366-7; 1-58536-366-9
                                 LC 2009036936
Irish giant Finn McCool is told that in order to become wise he much catch and eat the salmon that possesses knowledge, but Finn finds that he cannot bring himself to kill the miraculous fish

"Bunting makes this unfamiliar story accessible to readers. The art beautifully illustrates the green Irish countryside and makes Finn a real gentle giant." SLJ

Burleigh, Robert, 1936-

Pandora; illustrated by Raul Colón. Silver Whistle/Harcourt 2002 unp il $16

Grades: 3 4 5 6   398.2
  1. Pandora (Legendary character) 2. Classical mythology
  ISBN 0-15-202178-7   LC 2001-1282
"Burleigh relates Pandora's battle to obey the stricture of Zeus that the jar remain unopened. Inevitably, she opens the vessel and releases greed, pestilence, war, and all manner of ills on an unsuspecting mankind, with only Hope remaining in the jar." Bull Cent Child Books

"The text, arranged in lines like free verse, is rhythmic and clear, with short, simple sentences. . . . The romantic watercolor/colored-pencil illustrations have narrow borders and textured grounds. Blues and greens dominate the muted palette." SLJ

Burns, Batt

The king with horse's ears and other Irish folktales; [by] Batt Burns; illustrated by Igor Oleynikov. Sterling Pub. Co. 2009 96p il (Folktales of the world) $14.95 *

Grades: 4 5 6 7   398.2
  1. Fairy tales 2. Folklore—Ireland
  ISBN 978-1-4027-3772-5; 1-4027-3772-6
                                 LC 2007035258
Contents: The king with horse's ears; Fionn Mac Cumhail and the Fianna of Ireland; The greedy barber; The charm setter; A famous thief; Back from the fairies; Oisin in the Land of the Ever Young; Just one choice; Paying the rent; The naming of Cuchulainn; The boy and the Pooka; A strange night; A clever leprechaun; The Lost Island of Lonesome Seals

"These 13 Irish tales retold by storyteller Burns follow fairies and warriors, heroes and clever thieves. . . . The stories are cleanly retold in contemporary, accessible language, and each is introduced with a short paragraph providing cultural or other information. . . . Oleynikov's paintings have a rough texture that suits the energy of the retellings and adds to the lively tone. This is a hearty collection, handsomely produced with Celtic-knot borders and gouache full-page and spot illustrations." Booklist
Includes glossary

Bushyhead, Robert H., 1914-2001

Yonder mountain; a Cherokee legend; as told by Robert H. Bushyhead; written by Kay Thorpe Bannon; foreword by Joseph Bruchac; illustrated by Kristina Rodanas. Marshall Cavendish 2002 unp il $16.95

Grades: K 1 2 3   398.2
  1. Cherokee Indians—Folklore 2. Folklore—Southern States
  ISBN 0-7614-5113-7   LC 2001-32319
A Cherokee chief chooses his successor by asking three candidates to climb a mountain, thus testing their character and strength

"Beautifully illustrated with rich watercolors that fill most of the pages, this story folds its altruistic message into a vivid, entertaining tale." Booklist

Byrd, Robert, 1942-

The hero and the minotaur; the fantastic adventures of Theseus; retold and illustrated by Robert Byrd. Dutton Children's Books 2005 unp il $16.99 *

Grades: 3 4 5 6   398.2
  1. Theseus (Greek mythology) 2. Minotaur (Greek mythology) 3. Classical mythology
  ISBN 0-525-47391-2   LC 2004-21585
The author "interweaves the legends of Aegeus, Heracles, the Minotaur, Ariadne, and Icarus with the story of Theseus. Myths that are normally quite complicated become easy to decipher in this outstanding version, for Byrd tells the tales simply and clearly. . . . The pen-and-watercolor illustrations are painstakingly drawn and include numerous small period details that heighten the sense of history." SLJ

Caduto, Michael J.

Keepers of the night; Native American stories and nocturnal activities for children; [by] Michael J. Caduto and Joseph Bruchac; story illustrations by David Kanietakeron Fadden; chapter illustrations by Jo Levasseur and Carol Wood; foreword by Merlin D. Tuttle. Fulcrum 1994 146p il pa $15.95

Grades: Professional   **398.2**
   1. Native Americans—Folklore 2. Nature study 3. Night—Folklore

ISBN 1-55591-177-3   LC 94-2602

Also available Keepers of the Earth (1988); Keepers of the animals (1991) and Keepers of life (1994)

Includes the following stories: How the bat came to be; Moth, the fire dancer; Oot-Kwah-Tah, the seven star dancers; Chipmunk and the Owl Sisters; The great Lacrosse game; How Grizzly Bear climbed the mountain

"Caduto and Bruchac use stories from various American Indian tribes as the basis for activities and lessons about the nighttime world. Written as a guide for teachers, outdoor education leaders, and other adults working with children in a nature setting, the guide gives detailed instructions for preparing, conducting, and evaluating a variety of activities that focus on the nocturnal habits of animals, on astronomy and nighttime weather, and on campfire activities, such as storytelling, dances, and games." Booklist

"The well-written chapters include discussions with illuminating scientific information." Sci Books Films

Includes glossary and bibliographical references

Campoy, F. Isabel, 1946-

Tales our abuelitas told; a Hispanic folktale collection; [by] F. Isabel Campoy and Alma Flor Ada; illustrated by Felipe Dávalos . . . [et al.] Simon & Schuster 2006 118p il $19.95 *

Grades: 3 4 5 6   **398.2**
   1. Hispanic Americans—Folklore 2. Folklore—Latin America

ISBN 0-689-82583-5

Presents the authors' retellings of twelve traditional tales accompanied by information on origins and different versions

"All of the selections are peppered with energetic dialogue and witty detail. Children will relish their humor, especially if read aloud." SLJ

Cárdenas, Teresa, 1970-

Oloyou; pictures by Margarita Sada; translated by Elisa Amado. Groundwood Books 2008 unp il $18.95

Grades: 2 3 4 5   **398.2**
   1. Yoruba (African people)—Folklore 2. Folklore—Cuba 3. Bilingual books—English-Spanish 4. Cats—Folklore

ISBN 978-0-88899-795-1; 0-88899-795-7

"In this striking bilingual retelling of a Yoruba myth, Oloyou the Cat is the very first creature created by the Godchild while he is still too young to know what he is doing. More importantly, Oloyou becomes God's first friend. They are happy until Oloyou falls into Nothing, which is an oceanic kingdom presided over by Okun

Aró. . . . The clarity of the writing makes this book suitable for reading aloud, while the complexity of the story will hold the interest of older readers. The oil-on-canvas illustrations are rich and bold with a mythic scope that incorporates the story's African-Caribbean roots." SLJ

Carrasco, Xavier

Rumpelstiltskin; adaptation by Xavier Carrasco; illustrated by Francesc Infante. Chronicle Books 2007 unp il $14.95; pa $6.95

Grades: K 1 2 3   **398.2**
   1. Fairy tales 2. Folklore—Germany 3. Bilingual books—English-Spanish

ISBN 978-0-8118-5971-4; 0-8118-5971-1; 978-0-8118-5972-1 (pa); 0-8118-5972-X (pa)
         LC 2006034846

A strange little man helps the miller's daughter spin straw into gold for the king on the condition that she will give him her first-born child.

In this bilingual English-Spanish adaptation, the illustrations use "sharp angles to exaggerate the humor." Horn Book Guide

Casanova, Mary

The hunter; a Chinese folktale; retold by Mary Casanova; illustrations by Ed Young. Atheneum Bks. for Young Readers 2000 unp il $16.95

Grades: K 1 2 3   **398.2**
   1. Folklore—China

ISBN 0-689-82906-X   LC 99-32166

After learning to understand the language of animals, Hai Li Bu the hunter sacrifices himself to save his village

Casanova "tells the tale in a dignified yet moving way that is complemented by the stark artwork. Arid-looking, dun-colored paper is the background for Young's masterful brush strokes." Booklist

Casey, Dawn

The great race; the story of the Chinese zodiac; written by Dawn Casey; illustrated by Anne Wilson. Barefoot Books 2006 unp il $16.99

Grades: 1 2 3 4   **398.2**
   1. Zodiac 2. Animals—Folklore 3. Folklore—China

ISBN 1-905236-77-8   LC 2005032544

Relates how the Jade Emperor chose twelve animals to represent the years in his calendar. Also discusses the Chinese calendar, zodiac, the qualities associated with each animal, and what animal rules the year in which the reader was born

"In this retelling of the ancient legend, Casey maintains the pace well. . . . The book is a visual treat, with illustrations in simple collage designs on acrylic and painted backgrounds placed in such a way as to keep the eye engaged and moving." SLJ

Casey, Dawn, 1975-

The Barefoot book of Earth tales; retold by Dawn Casey; illustrated by Anne Wilson. Barefoot Books 2009 95p il $19.99

Grades: 2 3 4 5 6   **398.2**

    1. Folklore 2. Ecology—Folklore

    ISBN 978-1-84686-224-3; 1-84686-224-8

    Contents: The Sun Mother (Australia); Why the sky Is far away (Nigeria); She who is alone (American Southwest); Grumpy gecko (Bali); The magic garden (Kazakhstan); Amrita's tree (India); Stink water (Wales)

"This enchanting collection of folk tales and creation myths from different cultures encourages readers to live a more harmonious life with nature. . . . Well chosen and crafted with broad appeal, the tales are woven with subtle morals and wisdom. Each story is introduced by a brief overview about the featured locale and culture . . . and followed by a related, easy-to-replicate activity or craft. Full-page and spot illustrations and colorful decorative borders reflect the spirit and origins of each offering. Done with collaged papers with acrylic and printed backgrounds." SLJ

Cech, John

Jack and the beanstalk; retold by John Cech; illustrated by Robert Mackenzie. Sterling Pub. Co. 2008 unp il $14.95

Grades: 1 2 3   **398.2**

    1. Fairy tales 2. Giants—Folklore 3. Folklore—Great Britain

    ISBN 978-1-4027-3064-1; 1-4027-3064-0

                     LC 2007001783

A boy climbs to the top of a giant beanstalk where he uses his quick wits to outsmart an ogre and make his and his mother's fortune. Includes historical notes on versions of this tale, other heroic stories, and alternate "ascension" tales.

Cech "knits fresh strands into the . . . story. This smoothly paced version, which begins with some hilarious wordplay, runs close to traditional tellings until the end, when the giant's wife joins Jack in his hasty escape. . . . MacKenzie ably ramps up the drama in the pencil-and-paint scenes." Booklist

Puss in boots; retold by John Cech; illustrated by Bernhard Oberdieck. Sterling Pub. 2010 unp il (Classic fairy tale collection) $14.95

Grades: K 1 2 3   **398.2**

    1. Fairy tales 2. Folklore—France

    ISBN 978-1-4027-4436-5; 1-4027-4436-6

                     LC 2008052496

A clever cat helps his poor master win fame, fortune, and the hand of a beautiful princess. Includes historical notes on versions of this tale and other fairy tales

This "offers an enjoyable retelling of the timeless story. . . . The narrative is descriptive, lively, and droll, and the colorful watercolor-and-ink illustrations, filled with period details, are intricately rendered." Booklist

The twelve dancing princesses; by John Cech; illustrated by Lucy Corvino. Sterling 2009 unp il $14.95

Grades: K 1 2 3 4   **398.2**

    1. Folklore 2. Fairy tales

    ISBN 978-1-4027-4435-8; 1-4027-4435-8

A retelling of the traditional tale of how the king's twelve daughters wear out their shoes every night while supposedly sleeping in their locked bedroom

"In this retelling of the Grimm Brothers' tale called 'The Dancing Shoes,' several significant details have been changed. . . . Corvino has used acrylic and watercolor paints and inks, with pencil detail–particularly on faces–to create lovely illustrations in the classic fairy-tale style. This adaptation is a worthy purchase for most collections." SLJ

Chase, Richard, 1904-1988

The Jack tales; told by R.M. Ward and his kindred in the Beech Mountain section of western North Carolina and by other descendants of Council Harmon (1803-1896) elsewhere in the southern mountains; with three tales from Wise County, Virginia; set down from these sources and edited by Richard Chase; with an appendix compiled by Herbert Halpert; and illustrated by Berkeley Williams, Jr. Houghton Mifflin 2003 c1943 216p il pa $7.95

Grades: 5 6 7 8 Professional   **398.2**

    1. Folklore—Southern States

    ISBN 978-0-618-34692-9 (pa); 0-618-34692-9 (pa)

                     LC 2003276676

First published 1943

"Collected and retold by Richard Chase" - book cover

A collection of folk tales from the southern Appalachians that center on a single character, the irrepressible Jack

"Humor, freshness, colorful American background, and the use of one character as a central figure in the cycle mark these 18 folk tales, told here in the dialect of the mountain country of North Carolina. A scholarly appendix by Herbert Halpert, giving sources and parallels, increases the book's value as a contribution to American folklore. Black-and-white illustrations in the spirit of the text." Booklist

Includes bibliographical references

Chen, Jiang Hong, 1963-

The magic horse of Han Gan; [by] Chen Jiang Hong; translated by Claudia Zoe Bedrick. Enchanted Lion Books 2006 37p il $16.95

Grades: 2 3 4   **398.2**

    1. Han, Kan, ca. 715-ca. 781—Legends 2. Artists—Folklore 3. Horses—Folklore 4. Folklore—China

    ISBN 1-59270-063-2   LC 2006046393

Master artist Han Gan's painted horse comes alive to help save ancient China from attack

This is an "elegant picture book. . . . The tale is crisply and concisely told. The double-page illustrations are dominated by strong browns, blacks, and reds, and are painted directly on silk." SLJ

Chichester-Clark, Emma, 1955-
    Goldilocks and the three bears. Candlewick
Press 2010 unp il $14.99
Grades: PreK K 1   **398.2**
    1. Folklore 2. Bears—Folklore
    ISBN 978-0-7636-4680-6; 0-7636-4680-6
                                        LC 2009-14601
    A retelling of the adventures of a nosy, naughty, and
sassy little girl who finds the house of the three bears
and helps herself to their belongings.
    "This large-format edition of the traditional story of-
fers plenty of scope for Clark's colorful illustrations.
While the plot remains the same, the telling is a little
more elaborate here than in most versions, with a couple
of new refrains and added dialogue. . . . The controlled
profusion of patterns gives the pencil-and-acrylic illustrations a busy but cheerful look. . . . Recommended for
the freshness and energy of its artwork." Booklist

Clayton, Sally Pomme
    Amazons! women warriors of the world;
illustrated by Sophie Herxheimer. Frances Lincoln
2009 93p il $19.95
Grades: 3 4 5 6   **398.2**
    1. Folklore 2. Women—Folklore
    ISBN 978-1-84507-660-3; 1-84507-660-5
    Contents: Queen of the Amazons (Greece); Dragon
girl (China); Winning eagle feathers (Native American);
Durga demon-slayer (India); The Maiden Knight and the
Northern Lights (Siberia); Hand of glory (England); The
warrior princess (Egypt)
    "This handsome collection of folktales showcases sev-
en empowering females, each with her own unique
strengths and abilities. . . . Filled with lively language
and fast-paced action, the tales introduce a pleasing
range of characters and moods. . . . The illustrations employ swirling lines and vibrant color washes to reflect the
setting and tone of each tale. The stories are separated by
two-page interludes that provide brief facts or activities."
SLJ
    Includes glossary

    Tales told in tents; stories from central Asia;
written by Sally Pomme Clayton; illustrated by
Sophie Herxheimer. Frances Lincoln 2005 64p il
map $16.95; pa $8.95
Grades: 2 3 4   **398.2**
    1. Folklore—Asia
    ISBN   978-1-84507-066-3;   1-84507-066-6;
978-1-84507-278-0 (pa); 1-84507-278-2 (pa)
    "In 12 traditional stories from the nomadic cultures of
Central Asia, folklorist Clayton retells myth and folklore
she heard in Kazakhstan, Afghanistan, and elsewhere.
The lively tales include epic creation myths, rhyming riddles, trickster tales, songs, and stories of magic carpets
and music. The large picture book is illustrated with
richly colored line-and-watercolor paintings that evoke
Central Asian traditional culture. . . . A rich resource,
even for older readers, this anthology has stories that
travel across the world." Booklist
    Includes glossary

Climo, Shirley, 1928-
    The Egyptian Cinderella; illustrated by Ruth
Heller. Crowell 1989 unp il $15.95; pa $5.95
Grades: K 1 2 3   **398.2**
    1. Folklore—Egypt 2. Fairy tales
    ISBN 0-690-04822-X; 0-06-443279-3 (pa)
                                        LC 88-37547
    In this version of Cinderella set in Egypt in the sixth
century B.C., Rhodopes, a slave girl, eventually comes to
be chosen by the Pharaoh to be his queen
    "The beauty of the language is set off to perfection by
Heller's arresting full-color illustrations." SLJ

    The Korean Cinderella; illustrated by Ruth
Heller. HarperCollins Pubs. 1993 unp il $15.95; pa
$6.95
Grades: K 1 2 3   **398.2**
    1. Folklore—Korea 2. Fairy tales
    ISBN 0-06-020432-X; 0-06-443397-8 (pa)
                                        LC 91-23268
    In this version of Cinderella set in ancient Korea, Pear
Blossom, a stepchild, eventually comes to be chosen by
the magistrate to be his wife
    "Heller's paintings are exotically lush and colorful as
well as engaging. Climo includes an explanatory note
about Cinderella variants (the Korean version in particular), and Heller explains the decorations, costumes, and
settings she used in the illustrations. An agreeable retelling of the Cinderella story." Booklist

    Monkey business; stories from around the
world; illustrated by Erik Brooks. H. Holt 2005
118p il $18.95
Grades: 3 4 5 6   **398.2**
    1. Folklore 2. Monkeys—Folklore
    ISBN 0-8050-6392-7   LC 2003-63956
    A collection of monkey lore, fables, and stories from
around the world
    "This well-told and entertaining book . . . draws on
pourquoi and folktales, mythology, facts, and trivia. . . .
Numerous colored-pencil-and-watercolor illustrations capture the myriad cultures and creatures represented. This
collection is unique, well written, and fun." SLJ

    Tuko and the birds; a tale from the Philippines;
illustrated by Francisco X. Mora. Holt & Co. 2008
unp il $16.95
Grades: 1 2 3   **398.2**
    1. Folklore—Philippines 2. Birds—Folklore
    3. Geckos—Folklore
    ISBN 978-0-8050-6559-6; 0-8050-6559-8
                                        LC 2007002826
    When Tuko the gecko cries so loudly that the birds
stop singing and cannot sleep, they try to trick him into
moving from their home on the Philippine island of Lu-
zon.
    "Climo's retelling . . . is infused with humor. . . .
Watercolor illustrations depict a village with bamboo
houses and people going about their daily lives of fishing, food preparation, and play. . . . A lively choice for
storytime." SLJ

Coburn, Jewell Reinhart

Domitila; a Cinderella tale from the Mexican tradition; adapted by Jewell Reinhart Coburn; illustrated by Connie McLennan. Shen's Bks. 2000 unp il $16.95

Grades: 2 3 4   **398.2**

1. Folklore—Mexico
ISBN 1-88500-813-9   LC 99-56173

By following her mother's admonition to perform every task with care and love, a poor young Mexican girl wins the devotion of the governor's son

"The full-page oil-on-cavas illustrations are bright, sumptuous, and visually enticing. The text is bordered by proverbs rendered in both Spanish and English. Well-written and strongly illustrated." SLJ

Cohen, Caron Lee

The mud pony; a traditional Skidi Pawnee tale; retold by Caron Lee Cohen; illustrated by Shonto Begay. Scholastic 1988 unp il pa $4.99 hardcover o.p.

Grades: K 1 2 3   **398.2**

1. Pawnee Indians—Folklore 2. Horses—Folklore
ISBN 0-590-41526-3 (pa)   LC 87-23451

A poor boy becomes a powerful leader when Mother Earth turns his mud pony into a real one, but after the pony turns back to mud, he must find his own strength

"The text is powerful because it is spare and unadorned. It is extended well by the softly toned, full-color, impressionistic pictures." Helbig. This land is our land

Cousins, Lucy

Yummy; eight favorite fairy tales. Candlewick Press 2009 121p il $18.99 *

Grades: PreK K 1   **398.2**

1. Fairy tales 2. Folklore
ISBN 978-0-7636-4474-1; 0-7636-4474-9

Contents: Little Red Riding Hood; The three billy goats gruff; The enormous turnip; Henny Penny; Goldilocks and the three bears; The little red hen; The three little pigs; The musicians of Bremen

"Beloved classics are successfully served by these bold, striking renditions. . . . Large, arresting gouache spreads in Cousins's signature style utilize saturated colors and thick, dark outlines against solid backgrounds. Expressive characters enhance the stories' shifting moods. Large type accentuates the dynamic texts, building each spare entry to its powerful climax." SLJ

Craft, Charlotte

King Midas and the golden touch; as told by Charlotte Craft; illustrated by K.Y. Craft. Morrow 1999 32p il $16; pa $6.99 *

Grades: 2 3 4   **398.2**

1. Midas (Legendary character)
ISBN 0-688-13165-4; 0-06-054063-X (pa)
LC 98-24035

A king finds himself bitterly regretting the consequences of his wish that everything he touches would turn to gold

"This sophisticated retelling, set in the Middle Ages, places King Midas in a sumptuous palace. . . . The elaborate oil-over-watercolor illustrations show the wondrous, tragic effects of the golden touch." Horn Book Guide

Cruz, Alejandro

The woman who outshone the sun; the legend of Lucia Zenteno; from a poem by Alejandro Cruz Martinez; pictures by Fernando Olivera; story by Rosalma Zubizarreta, Harriet Rohmer, David Schecter. Children's Bk. Press 1991 30p hardcover o.p. pa $7.95

Grades: K 1 2 3   **398.2**

1. Zapotec Indians—Folklore 2. Bilingual books—English-Spanish
ISBN 0-89239-101-4; 0-89239-126-X (pa)
LC 91-16646

Title page and text in English and Spanish

Retells the Zapotec legend of Lucia Zenteno, a beautiful woman with magical powers who is exiled from a mountain village and takes its water away in punishment

This "Hispanic folktale is skillfully told, and is solid and colorfully steeped with imagery of the earth and sky. Both the Spanish and English read gracefully, and the poetic use of language suits the story well for telling. The illustrations have a sense of volume that is reminiscent of Orozco." SLJ

Cummings, Pat, 1950-

Ananse and the lizard; a West African tale; retold and illustrated by Pat Cummings. Holt & Co. 2002 unp il $16.95 *

Grades: K 1 2 3   **398.2**

1. Anansi (Legendary character) 2. Folklore—Ghana
ISBN 0-8050-6476-1   LC 2001-1679

Ananse the spider thinks he will marry the daughter of the village chief, but instead he is outsmarted by Lizard

"Cummings' lively prose and humor are a perfect match for the story. The boxed text is accompanied by gorgeous watercolor, gouache, and pencil illustrations, rich in color and lively pattern." Booklist

Curry, Jane Louise, 1932-

Hold up the sky: and other Native American tales from Texas and the Southern Plains; illustrated by James Watts. Margaret K. McElderry Bks. 2003 159p il $17.95

Grades: 4 5 6 7   **398.2**

1. Native Americans—Folklore 2. Folklore—Southern States
ISBN 0-689-85287-8   LC 2002-16519

Contents: The beginning of the world; Coyote makes the sun; Why Bear waddles when he walks; The quarrel between Wind and Thunder; Thunderbird Woman, Skiwis, and Little Big-Belly Boy; The monsters and the flood; Coyote and the seven brothers; Slaying the monsters; Hold up the sky; Coyote and Mouse; Coyote and the smallest snake; Coyote flies with the geese; Coyote frees the buffalo; The great meatball; The fight between the animals and insects; How Rabbit stole Mountain Lion's teeth; Fox and Possum; Sendeh sings to the prai-

Curry, Jane Louise, 1932-—*Continued*

ries dogs; The deserted children; Mountain lion and the four sisters; How Poor Boy won his wife; The ghost woman; The boy who killed the hill; White Fox; The tonkawa and the bear; Young Boy Chief and his sister

Retells twenty-six tales from Native Americans whose traditional lands were in Texas and the Southern Plains, and provides a brief introduction to the history of each tribe

"Curry has carefully researched and sensitively retold tales from fourteen Native American nations. Attractive pencil drawings enhance the stories." Horn Book Guide

Includes bibliographical references

Dabcovich, Lydia, 1935-

The polar bear son; an Inuit tale; retold and illustrated by Lydia Dabcovich. Clarion Bks. 1997 37p il hardcover o.p. pa $5.95

Grades: K 1 2 3   398.2

1. Inuit—Folklore 2. Polar bear—Folklore
ISBN 0-395-72766-9; 0-395-97567-0 (pa)
                                   LC 96-4780

An old woman adopts and raises a polar bear cub which grows up and provides for her even after she has had to send it away to save it from the jealous men of the village

"Illustrated in muted pastel colors, the pictures capture this stark, yet beautiful, winter world." SLJ

D'Aulaire, Ingri, 1904-1980

The terrible troll-bird; [by] Ingri and Edgar Parin d'Aulaire. New York Review Books 2007 41p il $15.95

Grades: K 1 2 3   398.2

1. Fairy tales 2. Trolls 3. Folklore—Norway
ISBN 978-1-59017-252-0; 1-59017-252-3
                                   LC 2007-13020

First published 1976 by Doubleday

When four children defeat the terrible troll-bird who has terrified their Norwegian valley for years, everyone celebrates in a merry feast.

"The d'Aulaires illustrate this rousing Scandinavian folktale in exuberant pictures using both sketchy black-and-white lines and mottled color." Horn Book Guide

Dayrell, Elphinstone, 1869-1917

Why the Sun and the Moon live in the sky; an African folktale; illustrated by Blair Lent. Houghton Mifflin 1968 26p il $16; pa $6.95 *

Grades: K 1 2 3   398.2

1. Folklore—Nigeria 2. Sun—Folklore 3. Moon—Folklore
ISBN 0-395-29609-9; 0-395-53963-3 (pa)
A Caldecott Medal honor book, 1969

First told by the author in his book: Folk stories from Southern Nigeria, West Africa, published 1910 in England

"When the Sun and the Moon extended an invitation to Water and his people to visit their earthly home, they underestimated the number of Water's followers and thus were forced to seek a habitation in the sky." SLJ

"The beautifully detailed and stylized art work is based on African sources; the artist uses cool colors for the water, a pale blue-grey for the moon, and shades of gold and white for the sun." Sutherland. The Best in Child Books

De Paola, Tomie, 1934-

Adelita; a Mexican Cinderella story; written and illustrated by Tomie de Paola. Putnam 2002 unp il hardcover o.p. pa $6.99 *

Grades: K 1 2 3   398.2

1. Fairy tales 2. Folklore—Mexico
ISBN 0-399-23866-2; 0-14-240187-0 (pa)
                                   LC 2001-57873

After the death of her mother and father, Adelita is badly mistreated by her stepmother and stepsisters until she finds her own true love at a grand fiesta

"The prose is straightforward and crisp. . . . Making perfect use of clear, warm hues, the full-color acrylic illustrations are a feast for the eye." SLJ

The clown of God; an old story; told and illustrated by Tomie de Paola. Harcourt Brace Jovanovich 1978 unp il $16; pa $7

Grades: K 1 2 3   398.2

1. Legends 2. Miracles—Folklore 3. Christmas—Folklore
ISBN 0-15-219175-5; 0-15-618192-4 (pa)
                                   LC 78-3845

An orphan whose juggling skill led him to a career as a traveling entertainer has grown old and clumsy and returns as a hungry beggar to his birthplace. On Christmas Eve in the monastery church a miracle occurs as he summons his last strength to make his only possible offering

"Mr. de Paola has written the tale with love, tenderness, and joy. He has executed authentic Renaissance illustrations that are magnificent in design and beauty." Child Book Rev Serv

Jamie O'Rourke and the big potato; an Irish folktale; retold and illustrated by Tomie dePaola. Putnam 1992 unp il hardcover o.p. pa $5.99; bd bk $5.99

Grades: K 1 2 3   398.2

1. Folklore—Ireland
ISBN 0-399-22257-X; 0-698-11603-8 (pa); 0-448-45090-9 (bd bk)   LC 91-10626

The laziest man in all of Ireland catches a leprechaun, who offers a potato seed instead of a pot of gold for his freedom

"Illustrated in dePaola's signature style, this has an inviting look. Buoyant watercolors are framed by thin orange borders, but the potato simply can't be contained and bulges beyond the boundaries, graphic proof of its enormous size, an engaging read-aloud choice for Saint Patrick's Day." Booklist

The legend of the Indian paintbrush; retold and illustrated by Tomie dePaola. Putnam 1988 unp il $16.99; pa $7.99 *

Grades: K 1 2 3   398.2

1. Native Americans—Folklore
ISBN 0-399-21534-4; 0-698-11360-8 (pa)
                                   LC 87-20160

De Paola, Tomie, 1934-—*Continued*

A "folktale of the Plains Indians that reveals how the Indian Paintbrush, the state flower of Wyoming, first bloomed. An Indian boy's dream to recreate the colors of the sunset comes true when he discovers paintbrushes filled with the colors he needs. A voice in the night had promised him this because he had shared his artistic talent with his people." Child Book Rev Serv

"The native American motifs are rendered simply and authentically; the night sky and glorious sunset spreads are truly beautiful with line, color, and form perfectly balanced to capture the text." Horn Book

The legend of the poinsettia; retold and illustrated by Tomie de Paola. Putnam 1994 unp il $16.99; pa $6.99

Grades: K 1 2 3   **398.2**
1. Folklore—Mexico 2. Flowers—Folklore 3. Christmas—Folklore
ISBN 0-399-21692-8; 0-698-11567-8 (pa)
LC 92-20459
When Lucida is unable to finish her gift for the Baby Jesus in time for the Christmas procession, a miracle enables her to offer the beautiful flower we now call the poinsettia

"dePaola establishes a sense of place in his use of glowing colors and architectural details as he retells another legend of miraculous transcendence." Horn Book

Tomie dePaola's front porch tales and North Country whoppers. G.P. Putnam's Sons 2007 51p il $17.99

Grades: 2 3 4 5   **398.2**
1. Folklore—New England
ISBN 978-0-399-24754-5; 0-399-24754-8
LC 2007-17646
Contents: Inquirin'; Mud season; Mothah Skunk meets Sherman Curtis; Lookin'; Big Gertie and love at first sight; Countin'; Settin'; Bessie tells time; Wonderin'; The fahmah who hated wintah; Askin'

This is an "illustrated compendium of original stories, tall tales, jokes, and quips related to northern New England. . . . Warm, good-humored artwork in dePaola's signature style provides an inviting setting for this flavorful collection of regional humor." Booklist

De Regniers, Beatrice Schenk, 1914-2000

Little sister and the month brothers; retold by Beatrice Schenk de Regniers; pictures by Margot Tomes. Marshall Cavendish Children 2009 c1976 unp il $17.99

Grades: K 1 2 3   **398.2**
1. Fairy tales 2. Slavs—Folklore
ISBN 978-0-7614-5546-2; 0-7614-5546-9
A reissue of the title first published 1976 by Seabury Press

A retelling of the Slavic fairy tale in which the Month Brothers' magic helps Little Sister fulfill seemingly impossible tasks which prove the undoing of her greedy stepmother and stepsister.

"Tomes's intimate, unpretentious illustrations extend the text brilliantly. A timeless treasure." Horn Book Guide

Deedy, Carmen Agra

Martina the beautiful cockroach; a Cuban folktale; retold by Carmen Agra Deedy; illustrated by Michael Austin. Peachtree 2007 unp il $16.95 *

Grades: 2 3 4 5   **398.2**
1. Cockroaches—Folklore 2. Folklore—Cuba
ISBN 978-1-56145-399-3   LC 2007003108
In this humorous retelling of a Cuban folktale, a cockroach interviews her suitors in order to decide whom to marry

"Deedy's masterful retelling . . . has a rollicking voice imbued with sly tongue-in-cheek humor. The acrylic illustrations, in a hyperrealistic style . . . are rendered in a vivid tropical palette." Booklist

Delacre, Lulu, 1957-

Golden tales; myths, legends, and folktales from Latin America; [retold by] Lulu Delacre. Scholastic 1996 73p pa $5.99 hardcover o.p.

Grades: 5 6 7 8   **398.2**
1. Folklore—Latin America 2. Native Americans—Folklore
ISBN 0-439-24398-X (pa)   LC 94-36724
Contents: How the sea was born; Guanina; The eleven thousand Virgins; The laughing skull; Sención, the Indian girl; When the sun and the moon were children; How the rainbow was born; The miracle of Our Lady of Guadalupe; El Dorado; Manco Capac and the rod of gold; Kákuy; The courier

This includes 12 "stories from four native cultures (Taino, Zapotec, Muisca, and Quechua), including *pourquoi* tales, legends of the conquistadores, and folktales from before and after the age of Columbus. . . . [The author's] . . . retellings are done in a clear and confident voice and are accompanied by her robust, colorful oil paintings. . . . This impressively presented and referenced collection will inspire readers and tellers alike." Booklist

Includes bibliographical references

Demi, 1942-

The empty pot. Holt & Co. 1990 unp il $16.95; pa $6.95 *

Grades: K 1 2 3   **398.2**
1. Folklore—China
ISBN 0-8050-1217-6; 0-8050-4900-2 (pa)
LC 89-39062
"Ping is a Chinese boy with an emerald green thumb; he can make anything grow 'as if by magic.' One day the Emperor announces that he needs a successor. . . . He gives each child one seed, and the one who grows the best flower will take over after him. . . . On the day of the competition, [Ping] is the only child with an empty pot; all the others bring lush plants. But the Emperor has tricked everyone by distributing cooked seeds, unable to grow; and Ping, with his empty pot, is the only honest gardener—and the winner." Publ Wkly

"This simple story with its clear moral is illustrated with beautiful paintings. . . . A beautifully crafted book that will be enjoyed as much for the richness of its illustrations as for the simplicity of its story." SLJ

Demi, 1942-—*Continued*

The hungry coat; a tale from Turkey. Margaret K. McElderry Books 2004 unp il $19.95 *

Grades: K 1 2 3   **398.2**

    1. Folklore—Turkey

    ISBN 0-689-84680-0   LC 2002-155129

After being forced to change to a fancy new coat to attend a party, Nasrettin Hoca tries to feed his dinner to the coat, reasoning that it was the coat that was the invited guest.

"Demi's retelling of this tale is compelling and includes many details that help bring both time and place into focus. Her paint-and-ink illustrations are resplendent with her trademark gold leaf and intricate borders." SLJ

King Midas; the golden touch. Margaret K. McElderry Bks. 2002 unp il $19.95

Grades: 2 3 4   **398.2**

    1. Midas (Legendary character)

    ISBN 0-689-83297-4   LC 99-89389

A king finds himself bitterly regretting the consequences of his wish that everything he touches would turn to gold

Demi's "unsourced but briskly amusing retelling begins with the contest when Midas's preference for Pan's shrill discord so angers the great musician Apollo that he gives the king donkey's ears. . . . The gilded special effects take center stage; still, Demi's glowing colors, decorative figures, and delicate drafting are also worthy of note. . . . This handsome book breathes new life into one of the oldest of cautionary tales." Horn Book

Doherty, Berlie

Fairy tales; told by Berlie Doherty; illustrated by Jane Ray. Candlewick Press 2000 223p il $19.99

Grades: 4 5 6   **398.2**

    1. Fairy tales 2. Folklore

    ISBN 0-7636-0997-8   LC 99-89380

Contents: Cinderella; The sleeping beauty in the forest; Rumpelstiltskin; Rapunzel; Snow White; Aladdin and the enchanted lamp; Little Red Riding Hood; The firebird; Hansel and Gretel; Frog prince; The wild swans

A collection of well-known fairy tales, such as Cinderella, Rapunzel, Aladdin and the enchanted lamp, and The fire-bird

These are "superb retellings on the earliest available sources in fresh versions sure to captivate readers anew. Ray's gold paint and folk art motifs prevail, but she also peppers the spreads with striking silhouette-collage compositions in a sumptuously designed volume." Publ Wkly

Downard, Barry

The race of the century; retold, written, and illustrated by Barry Downard. Simon & Schuster Books for Young Readers 2008 unp il $15.99

Grades: 2 3 4   **398.2**

    1. Fables 2. Turtles—Folklore 3. Rabbits—Folklore

    ISBN 978-1-4169-2509-5; 1-4169-2509-0

                            LC 2006028791

Fed up with his incessant taunting, Tom Tortoise challenges Flash Harry Hare to the race of the century, which turns into a worldwide media event complete with television and newspaper coverage, photographers, and many other distractions.

"Digitally created photocollages of an animal cast, [the illustrations are] packed with silly exaggeration and humorous visual personification. . . . The sheer ludicrousness of this scenario will elicit snickering even in kids allergic to fables." Bull Cent Child Books

Doyle, Malachy, 1954-

Tales from old Ireland; retold by Malachy Doyle; illustrated by Niamh Sharkey. Barefoot Bks. (NY) 2000 95p il $19.99; pa $16.99

Grades: 3 4 5 6   **398.2**

    1. Folklore—Ireland

    ISBN 978-1-902283-97-5; 1-902283-97-X; 978-1-905236-32-9 (pa); 1-905236-32-8 (pa)

Contents: The children of Lir; Fair, Brown, and Trembling; The twelve wild geese; Lusmore and the fairies; Son of an otter, son of a wolf; The soul cages; Oisin in Tir na nOg

A collection of seven Irish folk tales

Doyle's "retellings are simple and economical, yet contain all the lilting rhythm and musical quality for which Irish tales are famous. Sharkey's illustrations, prepared in oil and gesso on canvas, are a perfect match." SLJ

Includes bibliographical references

Egielski, Richard

The gingerbread boy. HarperCollins Pubs. 1997 unp il $15.95; pa $5.95 *

Grades: K 1 2 3   **398.2**

    1. Folklore 2. New York (N.Y.)—Fiction

    ISBN 0-06-026030-0; 0-06-443708-6 (pa)

                            LC 95-50026

"A Laura Geringer book"

The "Gingerbread Boy pops out of an oven in an apartment somewhere in lower Manhattan. As he runs down the New York City streets, the arrogant little cookie is chased by his family, a rat, construction workers, subway musicians, and a mounted policeman." Horn Book

"Egielski's retelling is straightforward and retains the traditional refrain: 'Run run run as fast as you can'—it sounds just right, making a satisfying modern variation. The illustrations . . . adroitly evoke the city setting while giving a solid three-dimensionality and unique individuality to the Gingerbread Boy and his pursuers." SLJ

Saint Francis and the wolf; [by] Richard Egielski. Laura Geringer Books 2005 unp il $15.99; lib bdg $16.89 *

Grades: 1 2 3   **398.2**

    1. Francis, of Assisi, Saint, 1182-1226—Legends 2. Wolves—Folklore 3. Italy—Fiction

    ISBN 0-06-623870-6; 0-06-623871-4 (lib bdg)

                            LC 2003-09615

"A wolf is terrorizing the Italian town of Gubbio. Knights, armies, and a threatening-looking war machine have all failed to put a stop to his terrible behavior. Only St. Francis, who can speak the wolf's language, is able to find a workable compromise for the creature and the town. The expressive cartoon art is done in Egielski's characteristic style and is full of child appeal." SLJ

Ehlert, Lois, 1934-

Cuckoo. Cucú; a Mexican folktale; translated into Spanish by Gloria de Aragón Andújar. Harcourt Brace & Co. 1997 unp il $16; pa $7 *
Grades: K 1 2 3   **398.2**
    1. Mayas—Folklore 2. Folklore—Mexico 3. Bilingual books—English-Spanish
    ISBN 0-15-200274-X; 0-15-202428-X (pa)
                    LC 95-39560
A traditional Mayan tale which reveals how the cuckoo lost her beautiful feathers

"This tale, charmingly told in both English and Spanish, is boldly illustrated with large, brightly colored, cut-paper pictures. Inspired by folk art and crafts, the images evoke the tin work and cutout fiesta banners of Mexico." SLJ

Moon rope. Un lazo a la luna; a Peruvian folktale; translated into Spanish by Amy Prince. Harcourt Brace Jovanovich 1992 unp il $17 *
Grades: K 1 2 3   **398.2**
    1. Folklore—Peru 2. Moon—Folklore 3. Bilingual books—English-Spanish
    ISBN 0-15-255343-6   LC 91-36438
An adaptation of the Peruvian folktale in which Fox and Mole try to climb to the moon on a rope woven of grass

"Designed as a bilingual book from title page to the concluding double-page spread, this handsome addition to material for multicultural education impels young audiences to try reading the story in both languages. . . . The text moves smoothly, just right for reading aloud; the pictures are dramatic abstractions that glow like jewels against richly toned, calendared pages." Horn Book

Ehrlich, Amy, 1942-

A treasury of princess stories; retold by Amy Ehrlich; illustrated by Gary Blythe; [paper engineering by Keith Finch] Candlewick Press 2009 unp il lib bdg $19.99
Grades: 1 2 3   **398.2**
    1. Pop-up books 2. Fairy tales 3. Folklore 4. Princesses—Fiction
    ISBN 978-0-7636-4478-9 (lib bdg); 0-7636-4478-1 (lib bdg)
Contents: The wild swans; The sleeping beauty in the wood; The princess and the pea; Snow White; The twelve dancing princesses; The frog prince

"Six fairy tales previously retold by Ehrlich are here compiled, repackaged, and reillustrated with pop-ups. Each begins with a sort of title page/frontispiece designed to resemble a miniature book; when the cover is opened, a beautifully rendered pop-up illustration is revealed. The stories themselves are recounted faithfully and rhythmically. Each features at least two lush illustrations as well as spot decorations." Horn Book Guide

Eilenberg, Max

Beauty and the beast; retold by Max Eilenberg; illustrated by Angela Barrett. Candlewick Press 2006 unp il $17.99 *
Grades: 2 3 4   **398.2**
    1. Fairy tales 2. Folklore—France
    ISBN 978-0-7636-3160-4; 0-7636-3160-4
                    LC 2006-43171
Through her great capacity to love, a kind and beautiful maid releases a handsome prince from the spell which has made him an ugly beast

"Writer and artist are both at their best in the luxury of the Beast's palace. Collectors of sumptuous fairy tale editions will not want to miss this one." Publ Wkly

Emberley, Ed

Chicken Little. Roaring Brook Press 2009 unp il $16.95 *
Grades: PreK K 1 2   **398.2**
    1. Folklore 2. Animals—Folklore
    ISBN 978-1-59643-464-6; 1-59643-464-3
                    LC 2008-49329
"A Neal Porter Book"
A retelling of the classic story of Chicken Little, who has an acorn fall on his head and runs in a panic to his friends Henny Penny, Lucky Ducky, and Loosey Goosey, to tell them the sky is falling.

"The punchy text is perfectly complemented by high-impact illustrations in collage-like planes of electric hues. The bold splashes of countless colors, contrasted against sharp fields of white, brilliantly jump out from the square pages. This is certain to become a favorite version of this story, and young readers will gleefully welcome an ending that offers no pedantic lesson." Bull Cent Child Books

Endredy, James

The journey of Tunuri and the Blue Deer; a Huichol Indian story; illustrated by Maria Hernández de la Cruz and Casimiro de la Cruz López. Bear Cub Books 2003 32p il $15.95
Grades: 1 2 3   **398.2**
    1. Native Americans—Folklore—Mexico
    ISBN 1-59143-016-X   LC 2003-52298
Retells a traditional Huichol folktale in which the young Tunuri learns his place in the natural world when he meets the magical Blue Deer, and follows him on an enlightening journey.

"The colorful artwork is made from yarn that is applied to a piece of wood, an elaborate process that is a long-practiced art of the Huichol. The illustrations enhance the feel and authenticity of the story. Elaborate notes explain the sacred symbols, who the Huichol are, and how the art was created. A strong addition to folktale collections." SLJ

English folktales; edited by Dan Keding and Amy Douglas. Libraries Unlimited 2005 231p il map (World folklore series) $35
Grades: Professional   **398.2**
    1. Folklore—Great Britain
    ISBN 1-59158-260-1   LC 2005016075

English folktales—*Continued*

"This collection of more than 50 English folktales contains a variety of stories arranged by common themes: The Fool in All His Glory, Wily Wagers and Tall Tales, Dragons and Devils, etc. The work of 22 storytellers is represented and their tellings are lively and inflected with the rhythms and speech of the regions from which their stories emanate. It is a delightful compendium for storytellers." SLJ

Ernst, Lisa Campbell, 1957-

Little Red Riding Hood: a newfangled prairie tale. Simon & Schuster Bks. for Young Readers 1995 unp il $16; pa $5.99

Grades: K 1 2 3   **398.2**

1. Folklore 2. Wolves—Folklore

ISBN 0-689-80145-9; 0-689-82191-3 (pa)

LC 94-45723

In this "contemporary rendering of the old tale, Little Red Riding Hood wears a hooded sweatshirt and rides her bicycle, while Grandma is a robust farmer who turns the tables on the wolf. Ernst's inventive plot, enjoyable characters, and characteristic cartoon-style drawings demonstrate her mastery of the picture-book form." Horn Book Guide

Fang, Linda

The Ch'i-lin purse; a collection of ancient Chinese stories; retold by Linda Fang; pictures by Jeanne M. Lee. Farrar, Straus & Giroux 1994 127p il hardcover o.p. pa $5.95

Grades: 5 6 7 8   **398.2**

1. Folklore—China

ISBN 0-374-31241-9; 0-374-41189-1 (pa)

LC 94-9909

Contents: The Ch'i-lin purse; Dog steals and Rooster crows; Two Miss Peonys; The Ho Shi jade; The prime minister and the General; The clever magistrate; Mr. Yeh's New Year; The miracle doctor; The royal bridegroom

A collection of "Chinese stories derived from the history of the Warring States Period (770-221 B.C.E.) and from operatic versions of popular tales. Retellings are vivid, lively, and read aloud well. Many have a moral, and all are entertaining. . . . The black-and-white illustrations—one per selection—are graceful, depicting widely different epochs with amazing accuracy." SLJ

Includes glossary and bibliographical references

Fleischman, Paul

Glass slipper, gold sandal; a worldwide Cinderella; illustrated by Julie Paschkis. Henry Holt 2007 unp il $16.95 *

Grades: K 1 2 3 4   **398.2**

1. Folklore 2. Fairy tales

ISBN 978-0-8050-7953-1; 0-8050-7953-X

LC 2006-30615

"This inspired retelling blends many versions of Cinderella into a single, extraordinary tale. . . . As . . . Fleischman's . . . strong storytelling voice incorporates sometimes small details from different traditions, text and illustrations nimbly morph from one Cinderella story to

the next, creating this brand-new version. Paschkis . . . makes use of folk art and textile patterns throughout the world in the clever background paintings behind each of her vibrant panel illustrations." Publ Wkly

Forest, Heather

The contest between the Sun and the Wind; an Aesop's fable; retold by Heather Forest; illustrated by Susan Gaber. August House Little Folk 2008 unp il $16.95

Grades: K 1 2 3   **398.2**

1. Aesop—Adaptations 2. Fables 3. Folklore

ISBN 978-0-87483-832-9; 0-87483-832-0

LC 2007018813

The sun and the wind test their strength by seeing which of them can cause a man to remove his coat, demonstrating the value of using gentle persuasion rather than force as a means of achieving a goal.

"Forest recasts this fable from Aesop in simple, crystalline language and occasional rhyme. . . . Gaber's wild and vivid images reflect, augment, and illuminate the story." Booklist

The little red hen; an old fable; retold by Heather Forest; illustrated by Susan Gaber. August House Little Folk 2006 unp il $16.95 *

Grades: K 1 2 3   **398.2**

1. Folklore 2. Animals—Folklore

ISBN 0-87483-795-2   LC 2006040727

A rhymed retelling of the traditional tale about the industrious little red hen and her lazy friends

"Gaber's bold acrylic artwork and varied use of space . . . and the infectious, familiar refrain . . . make this an appealing storytime and readers' theater selection." SLJ

Fowles, Shelley

The bachelor and the bean. Farrar, Straus & Giroux 2003 unp il $16

Grades: K 1 2 3   **398.2**

1. Jews—Folklore 2. Folklore—Morocco

ISBN 0-374-30478-5   LC 2002-23160

In this Jewish folktale from Morocco, a bachelor receives a magic pot from an imp, but it is stolen by an old woman

"Fowles' retelling . . . is lively, funny, and perfectly paced for read-alouds. But it's her watercolor-and-ink illustrations that are most distinctive. Young children will enjoy the shimmering colors and swirling patterns . . . that show the town bustle and the humor." Booklist

French, Vivian

Henny Penny; [by] Vivian French; illustrated by Sophie Windham. Bloomsbury Children's Books 2006 unp il $16.95

Grades: PreK K 1 2   **398.2**

1. Folklore 2. Animals—Folklore

ISBN 1-58234-706-9   LC 2005053688

Henny Penny and her barnyard friends are on their way to tell the king that the sky is falling when they meet a hungry fox, but Henny Penny's quick thinking saves the day

French, Vivian—Continued

"A charmingly fleshed-out version of the traditional story. . . . Brightly colored and skillfully drawn illustrations balance perfectly with the delightful text and draw readers into their depths." SLJ

Fritz, Jean

Brendan the Navigator; a history mystery about the discovery of America; illustrated by Enrico Arno. Coward, McCann & Geoghegan 1979 31p il hardcover o.p. pa $5.99

Grades: 3 4 5   **398.2**
  1. Brendan, Saint, the Voyager, ca. 483-577
  2. America—Exploration
  ISBN 0-698-20473-5; 0-698-11759-X (pa)
                                            LC 78-13247
Recounts St. Brendan's life and voyage to North America long before the Vikings arrived

"Jean Fritz's narrative is beautifully cadenced, lively and wry. Her historical postscript is all right, too, and the two-color illustrations are appropriately convoluted and Celtic." N Y Times Book Rev

Galdone, Joanna

The tailypo; a ghost story; told by Joanna Galdone; illustrated by Paul Galdone. Clarion Bks. 1984 unp il pa $7.95 hardcover o.p. *

Grades: K 1 2 3   **398.2**
  1. Folklore—United States
  ISBN 0-395-30084-3 (pa)   LC 77-23289
  First published by Seabury Press

"An old man lives in the Tennessee backwoods with his three hunting dogs. . . . The old man sees an odd animal squeezing through a crack in his cabin and grabs it. All he gets is its tail but he makes a snack of that and gets into bed with a satisfied appetite. But the dismembered [creature] wants its tail back." Publ Wkly

"The energetic postures of the old man and his dogs form a strong accompaniment to the clean, vigorous storytelling, and the subtly underplayed color in the paintings not only suggests the ghostliness of the story but is pleasing in itself." Horn Book

Galdone, Paul, 1914-1986

The elves and the shoemaker; retold and illustrated by Paul Galdone. Clarion Bks. 1984 unp il pa $6.95 hardcover o.p.

Grades: PreK K 1 2   **398.2**
  1. Folklore—Germany 2. Fairy tales
  ISBN 0-89919-422-2 (pa)   LC 83-14979
  "Based on Lucy Crane's translation from the German of the Brothers Grimm." Title page

A pair of elves help a poor shoemaker become successful, and the shoemaker and his wife reward them with elegant outfits

"The pictures in flashing hues emphasize the secret helpers' impishness; they seem to be performing the service more for a lark than in the name of sweet charity." Publ Wkly

The gingerbread boy. Clarion Bks. 1975 unp il $16; pa $6.95 *

Grades: PreK K 1 2   **398.2**
  1. Folklore 2. Fairy tales
  ISBN 0-395-28799-5; 0-89919-163-0 (pa)
  Also available Big Book edition
  First published by Seabury Press

"A lively version of the tale of the gingerbread boy who sprang into action as soon as he was baked and gleefully eluded all would-be captors until he was finally outwitted by a fox. The artist's gingerbread boy is a strong-legged, cocky individual, who sets out on a merry race through the countryside. The action of the tale is well-paced; large, humorous illustrations with stone fences, a covered bridge, and hearty rural folk suggest a New England background, while the triumphant fox is the epitome of all slyness." Horn Book

Henny Penny; retold and illustrated by Paul Galdone. Clarion Bks. 1968 unp il $16; pa $6.95 *

Grades: PreK K 1 2   **398.2**
  1. Folklore 2. Animals—Folklore
  ISBN 0-395-28800-2; 0-89919-225-4 (pa)
  First published by Seabury Press
A folktale also popularly known as Chicken Little. "The simple retelling has a different ending which makes the fox seem somewhat less villainous—when Henny Penny and her credulous friends follow Foxy Loxy into the cave they are never seen again and the king is never told that the sky is falling, but Foxy Loxy, his wife, and seven little foxes (appealingly portrayed in a picture as a family group) still remember the fine feast they had that day." Booklist

The little red hen. Clarion Bks. 1973 unp il $15; pa $5.95 *

Grades: PreK K 1 2   **398.2**
  1. Folklore 2. Chickens—Fiction
  ISBN 0-395-28803-7; 0-89919-349-8 (pa)
  First published by Seabury Press

"A domesticated little hen, . . . busies herself . . . while her three house mates—a cat, a dog, and a mouse—doze blissfully. The industry of the little hen produces a cake; and only when 'a delicious smell filled the cozy little house,' do her lazy companions come to life." Horn Book

"The large, clear, colorful pictures perfectly suit the book for pre-school story hours; the simple text, with one or two lines per page, will make it a success with beginning readers." SLJ

The monkey and the crocodile; a Jataka tale from India. Clarion Bks. 1969 unp il pa $6.95 hardcover o.p. *

Grades: PreK K 1 2   **398.2**
  1. Folklore—India 2. Fables 3. Monkeys—Folklore
  4. Crocodiles—Folklore 5. Jataka stories
  ISBN 0-89919-524-5 (pa)
  First published by Seabury Press
Illustrated by Galdone, this is a retelling of one of the Jataka fables about Buddha in his animal incarnations. "The crocodile wants a meal of monkey, but the intended prey is far wilier than his antagonist." SLJ

Galdone, Paul, 1914-1986—*Continued*

The story "has the humor, plot, and movement to make it a good book for any young child, even one unused to stories: the brilliant colors, clear pictures, and brief text should make it very successful for sharing with groups of children." Horn Book

Puss in boots. Clarion Bks. 1976 unp il pa $7.95 hardcover o.p. *

Grades: K 1 2   **398.2**
  1. Folklore—France 2. Fairy tales 3. Cats—Folklore
  ISBN 0-89919-192-4 (pa)

First published by Seabury Press

"Galdone follows Perrault's story line faithfully, as Puss works mischief to obtain a fortune for his master. The writing, fluid and readable, makes even this familiar tale sound fresh—no mean feat. Galdone's large, humorous caricatures—easily seen for story hour—have great gusto, and Puss is the embodiment of cleverness and knavery." SLJ

The teeny-tiny woman; a ghost story. Clarion Bks. 1984 unp il $16; pa $5.95 *

Grades: PreK K 1 2   **398.2**
  1. Folklore—Great Britain 2. Ghost stories
  ISBN 0-89919-270-X; 0-89919-463-X (pa)
                   LC 84-4311

Retold and illustrated by Galdone, this is an English folk tale about a "teeny-tiny woman who lives in a teeny-tiny house in a teeny-tiny village goes for a teeny-tiny walk, etc. Opening the gates to a churchyard, she finds a bone that will add flavor to the soup she plans for supper. Back home, she goes to bed but is alarmed by a voice . . . demanding, 'Give me back my bone!'" Publ Wkly

"Quarter-inch type will attract reticent readers, and the comfortable, cozy country and cottage scenes defuse whatever scariness young readers might conjure up. Fences, trees, balustrades and cupboards in murky, inky tones are designed to suggest watchful faces and add to the atmospheric tension of the narrative." SLJ

The three bears. Clarion Bks. 1972 unp il $15; pa $6.95 *

Grades: PreK K 1 2   **398.2**
  1. Folklore 2. Bears—Folklore
  ISBN 0-395-28811-8; 0-89919-401-X (pa)

First published by Seabury Press

In Galdone's illustrations for his retelling of the tale of Goldilocks, "his three bears are beautifully groomed, civilized creatures, living a life of rustic contentment in an astonishingly verdant forest, while his Goldilocks is a horrid, be-ringletted, overdressed child who rampages wantonly through the bears' tidy home." Times Lit Suppl

The three Billy Goats Gruff. Clarion Bks. 1973 unp il $16; pa $6.95 *

Grades: PreK K 1 2   **398.2**
  1. Folklore—Norway 2. Goats—Folklore
  ISBN 0-395-28812-6; 0-89919-035-9 (pa)

First published by Seabury Press

In this retelling of the old Norwegian folk tale, "the goats flummox the wicked troll and send him over the rickety bridge to a watery grave." Publ Wkly

"Galdone's illustrations are in his usual bold, clear style. The three Billy Goats Gruff are expressively drawn, and the troll looks appropriately ferocious and ugly. The large, lively, double-page spreads are sure to win a responsive audience at story hour." SLJ

Garland, Sherry, 1948-

Children of the dragon; selected tales from Vietnam; with illustrations by Trina Schart Hyman. Harcourt 2001 58p il $18

Grades: 3 4 5 6   **398.2**
  1. Folklore—Vietnam
  ISBN 0-15-224200-7   LC 00-8300

Contents: How the tiger got its stripes; Chu Cuoi—the man in the moon; The legend of the monsoon rains; The boatman's flute; The raven and the star fruit; The bowmen and the sisters

An illustrated collection of Vietnamese folktales with explanatory notes following each story

"This handsome volume gathers six well-told traditional tales not readily available elsewhere. . . . [The book is] greatly enhanced by Hyman's strong color work, romantic sensibility, and dramatic characterizations." SLJ

Gerson, Mary-Joan

Why the sky is far away; a Nigerian folktale; retold by Mary-Joan Gerson; pictures by Carla Golembe. Little, Brown 1992 unp il pa $5.95 hardcover o.p.

Grades: K 1 2 3   **398.2**
  1. Folklore—Nigeria
  ISBN 0-316-30874-9 (pa)   LC 91-24949

"Joy Street books"

A revised and newly illustrated edition of the title first published 1974 by Harcourt

The sky was once so close to the Earth that people cut parts of it to eat, but their waste and greed caused the sky to move far away

"Golembe's simple, theatrical illustrations combine monotype prints and collages in brilliant colors. . . . With its playfulness and drama, this is a fine book for story hour, especially in an ecology program." Booklist

Ginsburg, Mirra, 1909-2000

The Chinese mirror; adapted from a Korean folktale by Mirra Ginsburg; illustrated by Margot Zemach. Harcourt Brace Jovanovich 1988 unp il pa $6 hardcover o.p.

Grades: K 1 2 3   **398.2**
  1. Folklore—Korea
  ISBN 0-15-217508-3 (pa)   LC 86-22940

"Gulliver books"

"A man brings a mirror—an object unknown to his fellow villagers—home from a trip to China. He secretes it in a chest, but when his curious family each indulge in a peek and see a different image (his or her own face, of course), each has a different reaction." Booklist

"This elegantly simple little story is a seamless blend of folk-tale adaptation with illustrations that were inspired by Korean genre paintings of the eighteenth century." Horn Book

Ginsburg, Mirra, 1909-2000—*Continued*

Clay boy; adapted from a Russian folk tale by Mirra Ginsburg; pictures by Jos. A. Smith. Greenwillow Bks. 1997 unp il $16

Grades: K 1 2 3   **398.2**
    1. Folklore—Russia
    ISBN 0-688-14409-8; 0-688-14410-1 (lib bdg)
                                 LC 96-33820

Wanting a son, an old man and woman make a clay boy who comes to life and begins eating everything in sight until he meets a clever goat

"The tale is adapted from a Russian folktale, and the storytelling voice is very simple and immediate. . . . In their play with scale, the illustrations express a wonderful combination of the monstrous and the cozy." Booklist

Goble, Paul

Buffalo woman; story and illustrations by Paul Goble. Bradbury Press 1984 unp il hardcover o.p. pa $5.99

Grades: 2 3 4   **398.2**
    1. Native Americans—Folklore 2. Bison—Folklore
    ISBN 0-02-737720-2; 0-689-71109-3 (pa)
                                 LC 83-15704

A young hunter marries a female buffalo in the form of a beautiful maiden, but when his people reject her he must pass several tests before being allowed to join the buffalo nation

"Each page sparkles with the lupins and yuccas of the Southwest and teems with native birds, butterflies, and small animals, the richness of detail never detracting from the overall design of the handsome illustrations. The author-artist successfully combines a compelling version of an old legend with his own imaginative and striking visual interpretation." Horn Book

Includes bibliographical references

The girl who loved wild horses; story and illustrations by Paul Goble. Bradbury Press 1978 unp il $14.95; pa $5.99

Grades: K 1 2 3   **398.2**
    1. Native Americans—Folklore 2. Horses—Folklore
    ISBN 0-02-736570-0; 0-689-71696-6 (pa)
                                 LC 77-20500

Awarded the Caldecott Medal, 1979

"After becoming lost in a storm, a young Indian girl joins and lives with a herd of wild horses until finally, she becomes one herself." SLJ

"Elaborate double-page spreads burst with life, revealing details of flowers and insects, animals and birds. . . . The story is told in simple language, and the author has included verses of a Navaho and Sioux song about horses. Both storytelling and art express the harmony with and the love of nature which characterize Native American culture." Horn Book

The legend of the White Buffalo Woman. National Geographic Soc. 1998 unp il hardcover o.p. pa $7.95

Grades: 3 4 5   **398.2**
    1. Native Americans—Folklore
    ISBN 0-7922-7074-6; 0-7922-6552-1 (pa)
                                 LC 97-24086

A Lakota Indian legend in which the White Buffalo Woman presents her people with the Sacred Calf Pipe which gives them the means to pray to the Great Spirit

"In his fluid retelling of the legend of the first peace pipe, Goble . . . handles sweeping Lakota history succinctly and assuredly, largely due to his compelling artwork." Publ Wkly

Includes bibliographical references

González, Lucía M., 1957-

Señor Cat's romance and other favorite stories from Latin America; retold by Lucía M. González; illustrated by Lulu Delacre. Scholastic 1997 46p il hardcover o.p. pa $5.99

Grades: 2 3 4   **398.2**
    1. Folklore—Latin America
    ISBN 0-590-48537-7; 0-439-27863-5 (pa)
                                 LC 95-34144

Contents: The little half-chick; Juan Bobo and the three-legged pot; Martina, the little cockroach; The billy goat and the vegetable garden; How Uncle Rabbit tricked Uncle Tiger; Señor Cat's romance

"González and Delacre introduce six . . . folktales popular throughout Latin America." Booklist

González tells these tales "with style and humor. The retellings are peppered with Spanish words, all of which are easily understood through context. Each story is followed by a short glossary and an author's note with information on the tale's origins and its variants. The vivid, sprightly paintings contain many regional details." Horn Book Guide

Graham, Lorenz B., 1902-1989

How God fix Jonah; by Lorenz Graham; illustrated by Ashley Bryan; foreword by W.E.B. Du Bois; new foreword by Effie Lee Morris. Boyds Mills Press 2000 156p il $17.95

Grades: 4 5 6 7   **398.2**
    1. Folklore—West Africa 2. Bible stories
    ISBN 1-56397-698-6

A newly illustrated edition of the title first published 1946 by Reynal & Hitchcock

"These stories from the Bible are offered in the idiom of the West African native." Introduction

Contents: How God fix Jonah [story]; Good in she heart; He no be keeper for him brother; David he no fear; Don't nobody sing; God wash the world and start again; Samson he weak for woman palaver; Hongry catch the foolish boy; Pican in river grass; God make a road down in the sea; They be slaves too long; She got hard head you know; Death take him hand off pican heart; The Shushan king love peace; Yam-leaf greens and rice; Old Satan try Job plenty; Brothers got bad heart for Joseph; Wise sword find true mommy; The Babylonia princes vex; Joshua be God's man; Every man heart lay down; Small boy teach wise men; God make plenty chop

"Ashley Bryan's magnificent black-and-white woodblock illustrations lend an added power and dignity to the text of this most unusual and captivating book." Horn Book Guide

Grandfather tales; American-English folk tales; selected and edited by Richard Chase; illustrated by Berkeley Williams, Jr. Houghton Mifflin 1948 239p il pa $7.95

Grades: 4 5 6 7   **398.2**
    1. Folklore—Southern States
    ISBN 0-395-06692-1; 0-618-34690-2 (pa)

Folklore gathered in Alabama, "North Carolina, Virginia and Kentucky. Written down only after many tellings, these [twenty-four] humorous tales are told in the vernacular of the region with added touches of local color provided by the storytellers as they meet together to keep Old-Christmas Eve. . . . Of special interest to storytellers." Booklist

Green, Roger Lancelyn, 1918-1987
King Arthur and his Knights of the Round Table; retold out of the old romances; with illustrations by Aubrey Beardsley. Knopf 1993 355p il $14.95

Grades: 5 6 7 8   **398.2**
    1. Arthur, King—Legends 2. Arthurian romances
    ISBN 0-679-42311-7   LC 92-55073

"Everyman's library children's classics"

A newly illustrated edition of the title first published 1953 in the United Kingdom

Relates the exploits of King Arthur and his knights from the birth of Arthur to the destruction of Camelot

Greene, Ellin, 1927-
The little golden lamb; retold by Ellin Greene; illustrated by Roseanne Litzinger. Clarion Bks. 2000 32p il $15

Grades: K 1 2 3   **398.2**
    1. Folklore 2. Sheep—Folklore
    ISBN 0-395-71526-1   LC 99-36025

A retelling of the traditional tale in which a poor, but good-hearted lad finds his fortune with the aid of a little golden lamb to which everyone that touches it sticks

"Greene's storytelling style is at once classic and relaxed, and the illustrations, in a soft, springtime palette, are fittingly buoyant." Horn Book Guide

Gregorowski, Christopher, 1940-
Fly, eagle, fly! an African tale; retold by Christopher Gregorowski; pictures by Niki Daly. Margaret K. McElderry Bks. 2000 unp il hardcover o.p. pa $12.99

Grades: K 1 2 3   **398.2**
    1. Folklore—Africa 2. Eagles—Folklore
    ISBN 0-689-82398-3; 1-4169-7599-3 (pa)
                                    LC 98-45302

Original two-color illustrated edition published 1982 in South Africa

A farmer finds an eagle and raises it to behave like a chicken, until a friend helps the eagle learn to find its rightful place in the sky

This "is a powerful celebration of the human spirit and its need for independence. It is beautifully complemented by watercolors, rich in the vibrant tones of earth and sky." Booklist

Grifalconi, Ann
The village of round and square houses. Little, Brown 1986 unp il lib bdg $16.95

Grades: K 1 2 3   **398.2**
    1. Folklore—Africa
    ISBN 0-316-32862-6   LC 85-24150

A Caldecott Medal honor book, 1987

A grandmother explains to her listeners why in their village on the side of a volcano the men live in square houses and the women in round ones

The author "illustrates her own tale, told to her by a young girl who grew up in Tos. The resting purple volcano, suddenly erupting into orange; the eerie orange sun; the villagers covered with ash; the fiery colored skies; the dense, lush jungles—all are captured beautifully by Grifalconi's art." Publ Wkly

Grimm, Jacob, 1785-1863
Grimm's fairy tales; illustrated by Arthur Rackam. Seastar Books 2001 160p il $19.95

Grades: 4 5 6   **398.2**
    1. Folklore—Germany 2. Fairy tales
    ISBN 978-158717-092-8; 1-58717-092-2

"A Peter Glassman book"

A collection of twenty-two favorite fairy tales from the Brothers Grimm, including "Rapunzel," "The Bremen Town Musicians," "The Valiant Tailor", "The Frog Prince," "Ashenputtel," and "The Elves and the Shoemaker."

"This handsome facsimile of the 1909 edition is illustrated with twenty-one color plates and twenty-eight black-and-white drawings with an afterword by Peter Glassman." Horn Book Guide

Hansel and Gretel; a fairy tale; by Jacob and Wilhelm Grimm; illustrated by Dorothée Duntze; translated by Anthea Bell. North-South Bks. 2001 unp il $15.95; lib bdg $15.88

Grades: 3 4 5 6   **398.2**
    1. Fairy tales 2. Folklore—Germany
    ISBN 0-7358-1422-8; 0-7358-1423-6 (lib bdg)
                                    LC 2001-34537

Translated from the German

When they are left in the woods by their parents, two children find their way home despite an encounter with a wicked witch

"*Hansel and Gretel* is perhaps the most terrifying fairy tale of all, and this book doesn't cover up the universal nightmare. . . . Duntze's large, beautiful, stylized pictures show the children huddled in their home, hearing their wild monster parent shout, 'We must get rid of the children.' . . . This is not a book for the very young, but it will lead to some great discussions among older kids studying heroes and monsters." Booklist

Little Red Cap; [by] The Brothers Grimm; illustrated by Lisbeth Zwerger; translated from the German by Elizabeth D. Crawford. Minedition 2006 unp il $16.99

Grades: K 1 2 3   **398.2**
    1. Folklore—Germany 2. Wolves—Folklore
    ISBN 0-698-40053-4   LC 2006048142

A reissue of the title first published 1983 by Morrow

Grimm, Jacob, 1785-1863—*Continued*

In this translation of Little Red Riding Hood "Little Red Cap strays from the path while taking wine and cake to grandmother. The wolf then gobbles up grandmother and Red Cap. Justice ultimately prevails when the hunter cuts open the wolf, frees the child and grandmother and finishes off the wolf." SLJ

This translation "gives the text a smooth pace and natural-sounding dialogue. . . . Washes in muted earth tones provide suggestions of backgrounds against which expressively drawn figures play out their familiar roles." Horn Book

Little Red Riding Hood; [by] the Brothers Grimm; illustrated by Bernadette Watts. North-South 2009 unp il $16.95

Grades: K 1 2 3   **398.2**
    1. Fairy tales 2. Folklore—Germany 3. Wolves—Folklore
ISBN 978-0-7358-2256-6; 0-7358-2256-5

A reissue of the edition first published 1968

A sweet little girl meets a hungry wolf in the forest while on her way to visit her grandmother.

"The well-known story is told simply and without embellishment, including some violent elements (e.g., the wolf's belly is slit open and filled with stones). The expansive illustrations use Old World folk-art elements to envelope readers in the forest landscapes." Horn Book Guide

Snow White; [by] the Brothers Grimm; illustrated by Quentin Gréban. NorthSouth Books 2009 unp il $16.95

Grades: 1 2 3   **398.2**
    1. Fairy tales 2. Folklore—Germany
ISBN 978-0-7358-2257-3; 0-7358-2257-3

Original Belgian edition 2007

"Gréban illustrates this faithful Grimm version of the classic story with a minimum of hocus-pocus. With the notable exception of the seven dwarfs, who are dead ringers for garden gnomes, the characters are realistic-looking. Snow White is a frightened and confused young girl, the wicked queen (in disguise) becomes a stooped, old peasant woman, the jodhpurs-clad prince is appropriately regal." Horn Book Guide

Haley, Gail E.

A story, a story; an African tale retold and illustrated by Gail E. Haley. Atheneum Pubs. 1970 unp il $18; pa $7.99 *

Grades: K 1 2 3   **398.2**
    1. Folklore—Africa 2. Anansi (Legendary character)
ISBN 0-689-20511-2; 0-689-71201-4 (pa)

Awarded the Caldecott Medal, 1971

"The story explains the origin of that favorite African folk material, the spider tale. Here Ananse, the old spider man, wanting to buy the Sky God's stories, completes by his cleverness three seemingly impossible tasks set as the price for the golden box of stories which he takes back to earth." Sutherland. The Best in Child Books

Hamilton, Martha

The ghost catcher; a Bengali folktale; [by] Martha Hamilton & Mitch Weiss; illustrated by Kristen Balouch. August House Little Folk 2008 unp il $16.95

Grades: PreK K 1 2   **398.2**
    1. Folklore—India 2. Ghosts—Folklore
ISBN 978-0-87483-835-0; 0-87483-835-5
                    LC 2007-14308

A retelling of a traditional Bengali tale in which a kind and generous Indian barber, pressed by his father then his wife to earn more money, cleverly persuades a ghost to bring him riches.

"Hamilton and Weiss relate the tale with economy and wit. . . . The illustrations' lyrical lines, colorful forms, and linen-textured backdrop create a distinctive look." Booklist

Hamilton, Virginia, 1936-2002

Bruh Rabbit and the tar baby girl; paintings by James E. Ransome. Blue Sky Press (NY) 2003 unp il $16.95 *

Grades: K 1 2 3   **398.2**
    1. Rabbits—Folklore 2. Wolves—Folklore 3. African Americans—Folklore
ISBN 0-590-47376-X   LC 2002-15529

In this retelling of the African American story, the wily Brer Rabbit outwits Brer Wolf who has set out to trap him

"Retold in Gullah, Hamilton's narrative is meticulously paced, lyrical, hilarious, and a joy to read aloud. Ransome's lush watercolors suit the story perfectly." SLJ

The girl who spun gold; illustrated by Leo & Diane Dillon. Blue Sky Press (NY) 2000 unp il $16.95 *

Grades: K 1 2 3   **398.2**
    1. Fairy tales 2. Folklore—West Indies
ISBN 0-590-47378-6   LC 99-86365

In this West Indian retelling of "Rumpelstiltskin," Lit'mahn spins thread into gold cloth for the Quashiba, the King's new bride

"The source of this folktale is apparent in the distinctive and lilting West Indian dialect that pervades this humorous and, at times, scary telling. The lavish use of gold within the acrylic illustrations and their frames is sumptuous." SLJ

The people could fly: American Black folktales; told by Virginia Hamilton; illustrated by Leo and Diane Dillon 2009 c1985 178p il $24.99; pa $13 *

Grades: 5 6 7 8   **398.2**
    1. African Americans—Folklore
ISBN   978-0-394-86925-4;   0-394-86925-7;
978-0-679-84336-8 (pa); 0-679-84336-1 (pa)

Coretta Scott King honor book for illustration, 1986

A reissue of the title first published 1985

"Hamilton retells 24 representative black folktales. . . . The stories are organized into four sections: tales of animals; the supernatural; the real, extravagent, and fanciful; and freedom tales." Booklist

The author "has been successful in her efforts to write

Hamilton, Virginia, 1936-2002—*Continued*

these tales in the Black English of the slave storytellers. Her scholarship is unobtrusive and intelligible. She has provided a glossary and notes concerning the origins of the tales and the different versions in other cultures. Handsomely illustrated." NY Times Book Rev

Includes bibliographical references

The people could fly: the picture book; illustrated by Leo and Diane Dillon. Knopf 2004 unp il $16.95 *

Grades: 3 4 5 6   **398.2**
   1. Slavery—Folklore 2. African Americans—Folklore
   ISBN 0-375-82405-7   LC 2003-25579

This is a retelling of the story first published in the author's collection, The people could fly: American black folktales, published 1985

In this retelling of a folktale, a group of slaves, unable to bear their sadness and starvation any longer, calls upon the African magic that allows them to fly away

"Familiar as it is, we have never seen the story like this. Not with all these evocative images, vivid, bright and moving, leading us on a journey through territory we thought we knew." NY Times Book Rev

A ring of tricksters; animal tales from America, the West Indies, and Africa; illustrated by Barry Moser. Blue Sky Press (NY) 1997 111p il $19.95

Grades: 3 4 5 6   **398.2**
   1. Folklore 2. Animals—Folklore
   ISBN 0-590-47374-3   LC 96-37543

"Divided into sections on American, West Indian, and African tricksters, these eleven tales each feature an animal tricksters either getting his comeuppance or giving as good as he gets." Bull Cent Child Books

"Hamilton's prose infuses the dialogue with depth and dimension, while Moser's spectacular, lively watercolors nearly render the impish creatures human." Publ Wkly

Han, Suzanne Crowder, 1953-

The rabbit's tail; a story from Korea; illustrated by Richard Wehrman. Holt & Co. 1999 unp il $16.95

Grades: K 1 2 3   **398.2**
   1. Folklore—Korea 2. Rabbits—Folklore 3. Tigers—Folklore
   ISBN 0-8050-4580-5   LC 98-16627

Tiger is afraid of being eaten by a fearsome dried persimmon, but when Rabbit tries to convince him he is wrong, Rabbit loses his long tail

"The tale is vividly retold. . . . An amusing entertainment about misperceptions." SLJ

Harris, John, 1950 July 7-

Strong stuff; Herakles and his labors; fierce words by John Harris; powerful art by Gary Baseman. J. Paul Getty Museum 2005 unp il map $16.95

Grades: 4 5 6 7   **398.2**
   1. Hercules (Legendary character) 2. Classical mythology
   ISBN 0-89236-784-9   LC 2004-7904

This is a "simplified version of the 12 labors of Hercules (Herakles as the Greeks called him). . . . Each labor is allotted a spread with bright and bold illustrations featuring Herakles locked in mortal combat with the monster of the moment, accompanied by a chatty, humorous commentary." SLJ

Hausman, Gerald

Horses of myth; [by] Gerald and Loretta Hausman; pictures by Robert Florczak. Dutton Children's Books 2004 100p il $12

Grades: 4 5 6 7   **398.2**
   1. Horses—Folklore 2. Folklore
   ISBN 0-525-46964-8   LC 2002-40809

Contents: The Arabian: Abjer, the horse of the Saharan sands; The Mustang: Snail, the horse of the American plains; The Mongolian pony: Humpy, the horse of the Russian steppes; The Timor: Ghost Chaser, the horse of the Tahitian shadows; The Karabair: Kourkig Jelaly, the horse of the Armenian Highlands

"These five tales each feature a different type of horse, remarkable for both its individuality and the qualities representative of its breed. . . . Florczak's illustrations adapt characteristics appropriate to the locations and time periods of each selection's origins. . . . This is an attractive volume, useful to teachers and librarians for read-alouds and of interest to horse-loving youngsters." SLJ

Hayes, Joe, 1945-

Dance, Nana, dance; Cuban folktales in English and Spanish; retold by Joe Hayes; illustrated by Mauricio Trenard Sayago. Cinco Puntos Press 2008 128p il $20.95

Grades: 5 6 7 8 9   **398.2**
   1. Folklore—Cuba 2. Bilingual books—English-Spanish
   ISBN 978-1-933693-17-0; 1-933693-17-7
                       LC 2007-38295

Contents: Yams don't talk; The fig tree; The gift; Dance, Nana, dance; The lazy old crows; Pedro Malito; Born to be poor; Young Heron's new clothes; We sing like this; Buy me some salt; The hairy old devil man; Compay Monkey and Comay Turtle; You can't dance

A collection of stories from Cuban folklore, representing the cultures of Spain, Africa, and the Caribbean.

"Each tale is accompanied by a full-page illustration that is colorful and contributes to the text. This book is a great addition to folktale and Spanish language collections. Students will enjoy these stories that could easily be incorporated into the curriculum." Libr Media Connect

Little Gold Star; a Cinderella cuento/Estrellita de oro; retold in Spanish & English by Joe Hayes; illustrated by Gloria Osuna Perez & Lucia Angela Perez. Cinco Puntos Press 2000 30p il $15.95

Grades: K 1 2 3   **398.2**
   1. Fairy tales 2. Hispanic Americans—Folklore 3. Bilingual books—English-Spanish
   ISBN 0-938317-49-0   LC 99-57104

In this variation of the Cinderella story, coming from the Hispanic tradition in New Mexico, Arciá and her

Hayes, Joe, 1945—*Continued*

wicked stepsisters have different encounters with a magical hawk and are left physically changed in ways that will affect their meeting with the prince

"The English text, which is made full-bodied by its many details, appears with a Spanish translation. The impressive acrylic illustrations, done in a sturdy folk-art style, are thick with color and bright with humor." Booklist

Henderson, Kathy

Lugalbanda; the boy who got caught up in a war; illustrated by Jane Ray. Candlewick Press 2006 72p il $16.99 *

Grades: 3 4 5 6   **398.2**
  1. Folklore—Iraq
  ISBN 0-7636-2782-8   LC 2004-65950

An ancient Sumerian tale about the youngest and weakest of eight brothers who, caught up in an ill-advised war, uses his wits and courage and eventually becomes king.

"The adventure story and the luminous, beautifully detailed watercolors of young men and gods will easily capture today's children. The background facts about the Sumerians . . . also makes this title a valuable nonfiction resource." Booklist

Hennessy, B. G. (Barbara G.)

The boy who cried wolf; retold by B.G. Hennessy; illustrated by Boris Kulikov. Simon & Schuster Books for Young Readers 2006 unp il $15.95

Grades: K 1 2   **398.2**
  1. Folklore 2. Wolves—Folklore 3. Sheep—Folklore
  ISBN 0-689-87433-2   LC 2004-21672

A boy tending sheep on a lonely mountainside thinks it a fine joke to cry "wolf" and watch the people come running—and then one day a wolf is really there, but no one answers his call

"The story begs to be read aloud, and the large, colorful, and amusing watercolor-and-gouache paintings are perfect for group viewing. . . . A clever take on an old favorite." SLJ

Heo, Yumi, 1964-

The green frogs; a Korean folktale; retold by Yumi Heo. Houghton Mifflin 1996 unp il $16; pa $6.95

Grades: K 1 2 3   **398.2**
  1. Folklore—Korea 2. Frogs—Folklore
  ISBN 0-395-68378-5; 0-618-43228-8 (pa)
          LC 95-19129

"Two young frogs delight in being contrary whenever their mother asks them to do something. . . . When she is dying, she asks to be buried by the creek, thinking they will contrarily bury her on a sunny hill. But the saddened frogs decide to carry out her wish." Child Book Rev Serv

"Using delicate tones, flat perspectives, and somewhat abstract figures set against busy backgrounds, [Heo] creates a quaint, comic effect. . . . This is a quirkier pourquoi tale than most, but it's too mischievous to be morbid." Horn Book

Hickox, Rebecca

The golden sandal; a Middle Eastern Cinderella story; illustrated by Will Hillenbrand. Holiday House 1998 unp il $16.95; pa $6.95

Grades: K 1 2 3   **398.2**
  1. Fairy tales 2. Folklore—Iraq
  ISBN 0-8234-1331-4; 0-8234-1513-9 (pa)
          LC 97-5071

Based on a Cinderella story from Iraq called "The little red fish and the clog of gold" in Inea Bushnaq's Arab folktales

An Iraqi version of the Cinderella story in which a kind and beautiful girl who is mistreated by her stepmother and stepsister finds a husband with the help of a magic fish

"The story is charmingly told and illustrated with paintings on vellum, giving the pictures a soft, luxurious quality." N Y Times Book Rev

Hirsh, Marilyn, 1944-1988

The rabbi and the twenty-nine witches. Marshall Cavendish Children 2009 c1976 unp il $17.99

Grades: K 1 2 3   **398.2**
  1. Jews—Folklore 2. Witches—Folklore 3. Moon—Folklore 4. Rain—Fiction
  ISBN 978-0-7614-5586-8; 0-7614-5586-8
          LC 2008022985

"Marshall Cavendish Classics"

A reissue of the title first published 1976 by Holiday House

A wise old rabbi finally rids the village of the witches that terrorize it every night that the moon is full.

Hodges, Margaret

Dick Whittington and his cat; retold by Margaret Hodges; illustrated by Melisande Potter. Holiday House 2006 unp il $16.95 *

Grades: K 1 2 3   **398.2**
  1. Whittington, Richard, d. 1423—Legends 2. Folklore—Great Britain 3. Cats—Folklore
  ISBN 0-8234-1987-8   LC 2005-46222

Retells the legend of the poor boy in medieval England who trades his beloved cat for a fortune in gold and jewels and eventually becomes Lord Mayor of London.

"In this spare retelling of the British legend, the narrative keeps buoyant with droll dialogue. The humorous illustrations, created with colorful inks and gouache, enhance the story with expressive faces and movement that delight the eye." SLJ

The kitchen knight; a tale of King Arthur; retold by Margaret Hodges and illustrated by Trina Schart Hyman. Holiday House 1990 unp il $16.95

Grades: 3 4 5 6   **398.2**
  1. Gareth (Legendary character) 2. Arthurian romances
  ISBN 0-8234-0787-X   LC 89-11215

A retelling of the Arthurian legend of how Sir Gareth becomes a knight and rescues the lady imprisoned by the fearsome Red Knight of the Red Plain

"Hyman's richly romantic illustrations are lush watercolors, framed and broken with framed insets for closeups and framed text inside the panoramic picture.

Hodges, Margaret—*Continued*
The format is horizontal, capturing the sweep of the story. While not a tale of King Arthur, it's a wonderful taste of Arthurian legend, hopefully whetting young appetites for more." SLJ

Merlin and the making of the king; illustrated by Trina Schart Hyman. Holiday House 2004 unp il $16.95

Grades: 3 4 5 6   398.2
1. Arthur, King—Legends 2. Arthurian romances 3. Merlin (Legendary character)
ISBN 0-8234-1647-X   LC 2003-47861
"Retold from Sir Thomas Malory's Morte d'Arthur"
"With its fairly simple vocabulary and succinct style, the lyrical narrative can be enjoyed if read independently or in a group setting. The truly distinguishing feature of this book is Hyman's detailed, colorful acrylic artwork. . . . In keeping with the feel of a medieval illuminated manuscript, each page has an attractive, elaborate border partially painted with gold ink that glows with all the richness of gold leaf." SLJ

Saint George and the dragon; a golden legend; adapted by Margaret Hodges from Edmund Spenser's Faerie Queene; illustrated by Trina Schart Hyman. Little, Brown 1984 32p il $16.95; pa $6.95 *

Grades: 2 3 4 5   398.2
1. George, Saint, d. 303 2. Knights and knighthood—Folklore 3. Dragons—Folklore
ISBN 0-316-36789-3; 0-316-36795-8 (pa)
LC 83-19980
Awarded the Caldecott Medal, 1985
Retells the segment from Spenser's The Faerie Queene, in which George, the Red Cross Knight, slays the dreadful dragon that has been terrorizing the countryside for years and brings peace and joy to the land
"Hyman's illustrations are uniquely suited to this outrageously romantic and appealing legend. . . . The paintings are richly colored, lush, detailed and dramatic. . . . This is a beautifully crafted book, a fine combination of author and illustrator." SLJ

Hogrogian, Nonny, 1932-
The contest; adapted and illustrated by Nonny Hogrogian. Greenwillow Bks. 1976 unp il lib bdg $15.89

Grades: K 1 2 3   398.2
1. Folklore—Armenia
ISBN 0-688-84042-6
A Caldecott Medal honor book, 1977
A "gently humorous retelling of an Armenian folk tale about two robbers who not only share the same occupation but are engaged to the same girl." SLJ
"The symmetrical elements of the tale, which create arabesques of humor, are well-served by the full-color, full-page illustrations and by the pencil drawings scattered through the text. Some of the colored illustrations are bordered by oriental rug patterns, and all of the paintings and drawings are strong in their depiction of Armenian physiognomy." Horn Book

One fine day. Macmillan 1971 unp il $16; pa $5.99 *

Grades: K 1 2 3   398.2
1. Folklore—Armenia 2. Foxes—Folklore
ISBN 0-02-744000-1; 0-02-043620-3 (pa)
Awarded the Caldecott Medal, 1972
When a fox drinks the milk in an old woman's jug, she chops off his tail and refuses to sew it back on unless he gives her milk back. The author-illustrator's cumulative tale, based on an Armenian folktale, tells of the many transactions the fox must go through before his tail is restored
"A charming picture book that is just right for reading aloud to small children, the scale of the pictures also appropriate for group use." Sutherland. The Best in Child Books

Hong, Lily Toy, 1958-
Two of everything; a Chinese folktale; retold and illustrated by Lily Toy Hong. Whitman, A. 1993 unp il $15.95 *

Grades: K 1 2 3   398.2
1. Folklore—China
ISBN 0-8075-8157-7   LC 92-29880
A poor old Chinese farmer finds a magic brass pot that doubles or duplicates whatever is placed inside it, but his efforts to make himself wealthy lead to unexpected complications
The author "here paints with muted colors, defining rounded forms with broad outlines. Retold with verve and gentle humor, this Chinese folktale could become a read-aloud favorite." Booklist

Hooks, William H.
Moss gown; illustrations by Donald Carrick. Clarion Bks. 1987 48p il pa $6.95 hardcover o.p.

Grades: K 1 2 3   398.2
1. Fairy tales
ISBN 0-395-54793-8 (pa)   LC 86-17199
After failing to flatter her father as much as her two evil sisters, Candace is banished from his plantation and only after much time and meeting her Prince Charming, is her father able to appreciate her love
"Many children and most adults will recognize in 'Moss Gown' the Cinderella story, while the most astute may note its resemblance to 'King Lear.' But everyone will enjoy this beautifully told North Carolina tale from the oral tradition. Carrick, a master of the dark and mysterious, has created haunting illustrations that are a wonderful complement to the story." Child Book Rev Serv

Houston, James A., 1921-2005
James Houston's Treasury of Inuit legends. Harcourt 2006 268p $18; pa $8.95

Grades: 5 6 7 8   398.2
1. Inuit—Folklore
ISBN 978-0-15-205924-8; 978-0-15-205930-9 (pa)
LC 2006043577
"An Odyssey Harcourt young classic"
"This collection includes four previously published stories: 'Tiktaliktak' (1965), 'The White Archer' (1967), 'Akavak' (1968), and 'Wolf Run' (1971). Noted artist

Houston, James A., 1921-2005—*Continued*

Houston lived among the Inuit people for fourteen years and brought their culture to life through his books and artwork." Horn Book Guide

Huck, Charlotte S., 1922-2005

Princess Furball; retold by Charlotte Huck; illustrated by Anita Lobel. Greenwillow Bks. 1989 unp il pa $6.99 hardcover o.p.

Grades: 1 2 3   **398.2**
  1. Fairy tales
  ISBN 0-688-13107-7 (pa)   LC 88-18780

This book is about a "princess who rebels against her tyrannical father and makes the most of her gifts to survive in another kingdom and win the hand of the king. This narrative focuses on the ingenuity of a girl who plots her own destiny." N Y Times Book Rev

"The paintings glimmer with intense colors—Lobel's flair for both historical and humorous detail has never been more apparent, nor more luxuriously bold." SLJ

Hyman, Trina Schart, 1939-2004

Little Red Riding Hood; by the Brothers Grimm retold and illustrated by Trina Schart Hyman. Holiday House 1983 unp il lib bdg $16.95; pa $6.95 *

Grades: K 1 2   **398.2**
  1. Folklore—Germany 2. Wolves—Folklore
  ISBN 0-8234-0470-6 (lib bdg); 0-8234-0653-9 (pa)
                                        LC 82-7700

This retelling "basically follows the Grimm story, although the text has been fleshed out with some extraneous details (for instance, the little girl is called Elisabeth). . . . The illustrations seem to be a labor of love; richly colored paintings of the forest teem with exquisitely detailed plant and animal life, and the interior scenes, awash with atmospheric light, are beautifully composed and executed." Horn Book

Index to fairy tales; including folklore, legends, and myths in collections. Scarecrow Press 1985-1994 4v

Grades: Professional   **398.2**
  1. Folklore—Indexes 2. Fairy tales 3. Legends—Indexes 4. Reference books 5. Mythology—Indexes

Volumes covering 1949-1972 and 1973-1977 first published by Faxon 1973 and 1979 respectively

A continuation of Index to fairy tales, myths and legends and its two supplements, compiled by Mary Huse Eastman, published 1926-1952 by Faxon (o.p.)

Volume covering 1949-1972 compiled by Norma Olin Ireland $85 (ISBN 0-8108-2011-0); volume covering 1973-1977 compiled by Norma Olin Ireland (o.p) (ISBN 0-8108-1855-8); volume covering 1978-1986 compiled by Norma Olin Ireland and Joseph W. Sprug $95 (ISBN 0-8108-2194-X); volume covering 1987-1992 compiled by Joseph W. Sprug $95 (ISBN 0-8108-2750-6)

"Although this is an essential reference book for the children's department, it is also a valuable source for the location of much folklore and fairy-tale material and should be available in adult book collections as well." Ref Sources for Small & Medium-sized Libr. 6th edition

Isadora, Rachel

The fisherman and his wife; written by the Brothers Grimm; retold and illustrated by Rachel Isadora. G. P. Putnam's Sons 2008 unp il $16.99

Grades: K 1 2 3   **398.2**
  1. Fairy tales 2. Folklore
  ISBN 978-0-399-24771-2; 0-399-24771-8
                                        LC 2007-18385

The fisherman's greedy wife is never satisfied with the wishes granted her by an enchanted fish.

"Isadora uses collages of paint-striated paper in tropical colors, plus occasional scraps of fabric, to give this familiar tale a generic African setting. . . . Compared to other retellings, dialogue here is minimal, suiting the story to listeners and beginning readers. . . . It's a handsome book, and a tale that sits comfortably in its new setting." Horn Book

Hansel and Gretel; written by the Brothers Grimm; retold and illustrated by Rachel Isadora. G.P. Putnam's Sons 2009 unp il $16.99

Grades: PreK K 1 2   **398.2**
  1. Fairy tales 2. Folklore
  ISBN 978-0-399-25028-6; 0-399-25028-X
                                        LC 2008018580

When they are left in the woods by their parents, two children find their way home despite an encounter with a wicked witch.

"Isadora's abbreviated retelling of the popular Grimm Brothers tale closely follows the original in both plot and detail while making the story more accessible to a younger audience. . . . She again sets her tale in Africa, piecing colorfully patterned and hand-painted papers together to create bold, busy eye-catching scenes with a strong ethnic feel." SLJ

Rapunzel; written by the Brothers Grimm; retold and illustrated by Rachel Isadora. G. P. Putnam's Sons 2008 unp il $16.99

Grades: K 1 2 3   **398.2**
  1. Fairy tales 2. Folklore—Germany
  ISBN 978-0-399-24772-9; 0-399-24772-6
                                        LC 2007047104

Recasts in an African setting the familiar fairy tale in which a beautiful girl with extraordinarily long hair is imprisoned in a lonely tower by a witch.

"The story remains true to the original. . . . Colorful, vibrant oil paints and collages brighten up the story. The artwork has rich brushstrokes and is heavily patterned, and details abound." SLJ

The twelve dancing princesses; [originally] written by the Brothers Grimm; [adapted and] illustrated by Rachel Isadora. G.P. Putnam's Sons 2007 unp il $16.99

Grades: K 1 2 3   **398.2**
  1. Folklore 2. Fairy tales
  ISBN 978-0-399-24744-6; 0-399-24744-0
                                        LC 2007-08160

A retelling, set in Africa, of the story of twelve princesses who dance secretly all night long and how their secret is eventually discovered.

"Working in collages of painted, textured paper, Isadora evokes an archetypal African kingdom through sumptuous, kente cloth textiles and Serengeti-like land-

Isadora, Rachel—*Continued*

scapes that pop vibrantly agains primarily white backgrounds." Booklist

Jacobs, Joseph, 1854-1916

English fairy tales; with illustrations by John Batten. Knopf 1993 428p il $13.95

Grades: 4 5 6 **398.2**

1. Fairy tales 2. Folklore—Great Britain

ISBN 0-679-42809-7 LC 93-13878

Also available in paperback from Dover Pubs.

"Everyman's library children's classics"

A reissue in one volume of the author's English fairy tales (1891) and More English fairy tales (1894)

Contents: Tom Tit Tot; The three sillies; The rose-tree; The old woman and her pig; How Jack went to seek his fortune; Mr Vinegar; Nix nought nothing; Jack Hannaford; Binnorie; Mouse and mouser; Cap o' Rushes; Teeny-tiny; Jack and the beanstalk; The story of the three little pigs; The master and his pupil; Titty Mouse and Tatty Mouse; Jack and his golden snuff-box; The story of the three bears; Jack the Giant-Killer; Henny-penny; Childe Rowland; Molly Whuppie; The Red Ettin; The golden arm; The history of Tom Thumb; Mr Fox; Lazy Jack; Johnny-cake; Earl Mar's daughter; Mr Miacca; Whittington and his cat; The strange visitor; The Laidly Worm of Spindleston Heugh; The cat and the mouse; The fish and the ring; The magpie's nest; Kate Crackernuts; The Cauld Lad of Hilton; The ass, the table and the stick; Fairy ointment; The Well of the World's End; Master of all masters; The three heads of the well; The Pied Piper; Hereafterthis; The golden ball; My own self; Black Bull of Norroway; Yallery Brown; Three feathers; Sir Gammer Vans; Tom Hickathrift; The Hedley Kow; Gobborn Seer; Tattercoats; The wee bannock; Johnny Gloke; Coat o' clay; The three cows; The blinded giant; Scrapefoot; The pedlar of

Swaffham; The old witch; The three wishes; The buried moon; A son of Adam; The Hobyahs; A pottle o' brains; The King of England and the Abbot of Canterbury; Rushen Coatie; The King o' the Cats; Tamlane; The stars in the sky; News!; The little bull-calf; The wee, wee mannie; Habetrot and Scantlie Mab; Catskin; Stupid's cries; The Lambton worm; The wise men of Gotham; Princess of Canterbury

A collection of more than eighty traditional stories that recount the adventures of giants, witches, princes, princesses, and animals

Jaffe, Nina

The cow of no color: riddle stories and justice tales from around the world; [by] Nina Jaffe and Steve Zeitlin; pictures by Whitney Sherman. Holt & Co. 1998 159p il $17

Grades: 4 5 6 7 **398.2**

1. Folklore

ISBN 0-8050-3736-5 LC 98-14167

Contents: The cow of no color; The sound of work; Ximen Bao and the river spirit; The cloak; The thief and the pig; The testimony of the fly; Susannah and the elders; The jury; The magic seed; The bird lovers; An ounce of mud; The dance of Elegba; The three wives of Nenpetro; The flask; Kim Son Dal and the water-carriers; The land; Sharing the soup; A higher truth; The walnut and the pumpkin; The wise king; Josephus in the cave; The water pot and the necklace; The test

In each of these stories, collected from around the world, a character faces a problem situation which requires that he make a decision about what is fair or just

"Sherman's black-and-white line drawings have a stark gracefulness that complements the tales' form and structure; the tales themselves are simply told with little embellishment." Bull Cent Child Books

Includes bibliographical references

The way meat loves salt; a Cinderella tale from the Jewish tradition; illustrated by Louise August. Holt & Co. 1998 unp il music $15.95

Grades: K 1 2 3 **398.2**

1. Jews—Folklore

ISBN 0-8050-4384-5 LC 97-41286

The youngest daughter of a rabbi is sent away from home in disgrace, but thanks to the help of the prophet Elijah, marries the son of a renowned scholar and is reunited with her family. Includes words and music to a traditional Yiddish wedding song

"Vibrant oils of reds, yellows, and blues set off the inky black, which defines the trees and rocks, and the sashes on the women's provincial gowns. Both the writing and the art contribute to the abundant good spirit." Horn Book

James, Elizabeth

The woman who married a bear; retold by Elizabeth James; illustrated by Atanas. Simply Read Books 2008 unp il $16.95

Grades: 2 3 4 **398.2**

1. Native Americans—Folklore 2. Bears—Folklore

ISBN 978-1-894965-49-1; 1-894965-49-3

"In this retelling of a West Coast First Nations' myth, a young woman tells her friends that bears are ugly, filthy, dumb animals. The Chief of the Bear People wants to punish her, but his nephew asks for her as his wife. From Mouse Woman she learns that bears can transform into humans and then into bears again. . . . Atanas's exquisite watercolor illustrations capture the natural beauty of the Pacific Coast and the distinctive culture of the First Nations people. . . . This is a welcome addition to units on Native American cultures." SLJ

Jiang, Ji-li

The magical Monkey King; mischief in heaven; classic Chinese tales retold by Ji-Li Jiang; illustrated by Hui Hui Su-Kennedy. HarperCollins Pubs. 2002 122p il hardcover o.p. pa $4.95 *

Grades: 3 4 5 **398.2**

1. Folklore—China 2. Monkeys—Folklore

ISBN 0-06-029544-9 (lib bdg); 0-06-442149-X (pa)

LC 2001-39672

Contents: Stone Monkey is born; Monkey accepts a challenge; Monkey behind the waterfall; Monkey goes searching; Monkey meets a sage; Monkey becomes a student; Monkey transforms himself; Monkey meets a demon; Monkey goes to the sea; Monkey visits Heaven; Monkey as a Heavenly horse deity; Monkey in the heavenly Peach Garden; Monkey goes to a banquet; Monkey at the peach banquet; Monkey under attack; Monkey meets Magician Lang; Monkey is captured; What finally happened to Monkey King

Jiang, Ji-li—*Continued*

The mischievous Monkey King attempts to achieve immortality the easy way, gains god-like powers, and wreaks havoc in heaven

The author "provides a lively telling, and the stories move briskly. Accompanying black-and-white pictures have the look of woodcuts." Booklist

Johnson, Paul Brett

Fearless Jack; adapted and illustrated by Paul Brett Johnson. Margaret K. McElderry Bks. 2001 unp il hardcover o.p. pa $10.99 *

Grades: K 1 2 3   **398.2**
1. Folklore—Appalachian Mountains
ISBN 0-689-83296-6; 1-416-96833-4 (pa)
                  LC 99-89184

In this Appalachian folktale, Jack wins fame and fortune after killing ten yellow jackets with one whack

"In an Appalachian twang, complete with distinct vocabulary and speech patterns, Johnson's colorful, comical, sturdy pictures are just as energetic as the story which is told." Booklist

Jack outwits the giants; adapted and illustrated by Paul Brett Johnson. Margaret K. McElderry Bks. 2002 unp il hardcover o.p. pa $11.99 *

Grades: K 1 2 3   **398.2**
1. Folklore—Appalachian Mountains 2. Giants—Folklore
ISBN 0-689-83902-2; 1-4169-7861-5 (pa)
               LC 2001-30811

Companion volume to Fearless Jack

In this Appalachian folktale, Jack outwits two giants who want fresh meat for breakfast

"Johnson interweaves several familiar motifs from many traditions while bringing an authentic mountain twang to his telling. Johnson's lively acrylics leave no doubt that these events are as comical as they are suspenseful; the equally lively dialogue makes this an especially good read-aloud." Horn Book Guide

Johnson-Davies, Denys

Goha the wise fool; retold by Denys Johnson-Davies; sewing by Hany El Saed Ahmed from drawings by Hag Hamdy Mohamed Fattouh. Books 2005 40p il $16.99 *

Grades: 2 3 4   **398.2**
1. Folklore—Turkey
ISBN 0-399-24222-8   LC 2004-15739

A collection of fourteen tales about the folk hero Nasreddin Hoca, also known as Goha, a man with a reputation for being able to answer difficult questions in a clever way.

The book is "illustrated by a team of Cairo tent makers in the form of traditional khiyamiya tapestries, with bits of bright, solid-colored fabric stitched to roughly woven, oatmeal-toned backgrounds. Many of the tales expose familiar human foibles. . . . Others amusingly illustrate wise principles." Booklist

Johnston, Tony

The tale of Rabbit and Coyote; illustrated by Tomie de Paola. Putnam 1994 unp il hardcover o.p. pa $5.99

Grades: K 1 2 3   **398.2**
1. Zapotec Indians—Folklore 2. Rabbit (Legendary character) 3. Coyote (Legendary character)
ISBN 0-399-22258-8; 0-698-11630-5 (pa)
              LC 92-43652

Rabbit outwits Coyote in this Zapotec tale which explains why coyotes howl at the moon

"DePaola's vivid, spicy palette of gold, red, and turquoise tones and his use of folk-art borders evoke the desert setting and complement the broad humor of Johnston's text. A glossary of the Spanish phrases that pepper the illustrations is appended." Booklist

Kajikawa, Kimiko

Tsunami! illustrated by Ed Young. Philomel Books 2009 unp il $16.99 *

Grades: K 1 2 3   **398.2**
1. Folklore—Japan 2. Tsunamis—Folklore
ISBN 978-0-399-25006-4; 0-399-25006-9
             LC 2008-25747

A wealthy man in a Japanese village, who everyone calls Ojiisan, which means grandfather, sets fire to his rice fields to warn the innocent people of an approaching tsunami.

"Kajikawa imbues the story with a sense of nobility. . . . Young's rough, impressionistic collages of handpainted papers, fabric, and organic material are dark and stirring." Booklist

Karlin, Barbara

James Marshall's Cinderella; illustrated by James Marshall; retold by Barbara Karlin. Dial Bks. for Young Readers 2001 unp il hardcover o.p. pa $6.99

Grades: K 1 2   **398.2**
1. Fairy tales 2. Folklore
ISBN 0-8037-2730-5; 0-14-230048-9 (pa)
             LC 2001-23097

This is a reissue of Barbara Karlin's Cinderella, published 1989 by Little, Brown

"Those seeking a condensed version of the classic fairy tale will find just what they want in Karlin's brief retelling; . . . James Marshall's witty, warts-and-all illustrations add the sparkle that brings out the best in Karlin's straightforward retelling." Horn Book

Keats, Ezra Jack, 1916-1983

John Henry; an American legend; story and pictures by Ezra Jack Keats. Pantheon Bks. 1965 unp il pa $5.99 hardcover o.p.

Grades: K 1 2 3   **398.2**
1. John Henry (Legendary character) 2. African Americans—Folklore 3. Folklore—United States
ISBN 0-394-89052-3 (pa)   LC 86-27453

This is a picture book retelling of the legend of the Black American folk hero who drove spikes for the railroads

"The dynamic power with which John Henry wields

Keats, Ezra Jack, 1916-1983—*Continued*
his hammer is matched by the strong illustrations: brilliant oranges and reds contrast with grays and blacks that are often silhouettes; unusual backgrounds produce startling effects. A good picture-story to show to a group." Horn Book

Kellogg, Steven, 1941-
Chicken Little; retold & illustrated by Steven Kellogg. Morrow 1985 unp il pa $5.95 hardcover o.p.
Grades: K 1 2 3   398.2
1. Folklore 2. Animals—Folklore
ISBN 0-688-07045-0 (pa)   LC 84-25519
Also available Spanish language edition
Chicken Little and his feathered friends, alarmed that the sky seems to be falling, are easy prey to hungry Foxy Loxy when he poses as a police officer in hopes of tricking them into his truck
"Kellogg has enlivened the text [by] giving it some modern touches (Turkey Lurkey carries golf clubs, Foxy Loxy is caught when a 'hippoliceman' tumbles out of a patrol helicopter to land him). Children have always enjoyed the repetition and cumulation of the story, as well as the silliness of the fowls who believe the sky is falling; here there's added fun." Bull Cent Child Books

Jack and the beanstalk; retold and illustrated by Steven Kellogg. Morrow Junior Bks. 1991 unp il $16; lib bdg $16.89; pa $6.95
Grades: K 1 2 3   398.2
1. Fairy tales 2. Folklore—Great Britain 3. Giants—Folklore
ISBN 0-688-10250-6; 0-688-10251-4 (lib bdg); 0-688-15281-3 (pa)   LC 90-45990
A boy climbs to the top of a giant beanstalk, where he uses his quick wits to outsmart a giant and make his and his mother's fortune
"Seldom has the ogre at the top of the beanstalk been depicted with such gusto! The warty, fanged, pug-nosed lout dressed in animal skins and a necklace of teeth is a wonder to behold. Steven Kellogg's humorous detail provides witty embellishment for savoring. His story line is quite faithful to the Joseph Jacobs version of the story, the sturdy text offering a strong framework for the energetic illustrations." Horn Book

Mike Fink; a tall tale; retold and illustrated by Steven Kellogg. Morrow Junior Bks. 1992 unp il hardcover o.p. pa $6.95
Grades: K 1 2 3   398.2
1. Fink, Mike, 1770-1823?—Fiction 2. Tall tales
ISBN 0-688-07003-5; 0-688-13577-3 (pa)
                                          LC 91-46014
Relates the extraordinary deeds of the frontiersman who became King of the Keelboatmen on the Mississippi River
"Steven Kellogg's ebullient retelling of Mike's tall-tale feats—illustrated with large, glowing scenes suffused with blue and yellow and with smaller vignettes emphasizing comic detail—follows Mike's prodigious childhood exploits, his teenage wrestling practice with Rocky Mountain grizzlies, and his years as King of the Keelboatmen, and closes with a final showdown with enormous steamboats taking over the river trade." Horn Book

Paul Bunyan; a tall tale; retold and illustrated by Steven Kellogg. Morrow 1984 unp il lib bdg $16.89; pa $5.95 *
Grades: K 1 2 3   398.2
1. Bunyan, Paul (Legendary character) 2. Tall tales
ISBN 0-688-03850-6 (lib bdg); 0-688-05800-0 (pa)
                                          LC 83-26684
"Numerous events from the legendary north woodsman's life have been linked together as Bunyan and Babe, his big blue ox, traverse the U.S." Booklist
"Kellogg uses oversize pages for busy, detail-crowded illustrations that have vitality and humor, echoing the exaggeration and ebullience of the story." Bull Cent Child Books

Pecos Bill; a tall tale; retold and illustrated by Steven Kellogg. Morrow 1986 unp il $17; pa $5.95
Grades: K 1 2 3   398.2
1. Pecos Bill (Legendary character) 2. Tall tales
ISBN 0-688-05871-X; 0-688-09924-6 (pa)
                                          LC 86-784
Incidents from the life of Pecos Bill, from his childhood among the coyotes to his unusual wedding day
"Although there's a lot going on in these pictures, they're not cluttered; both the gradations of color and the page design smooth the lines of continuous action and tumult of humorous detail. Kellogg's portrayal of Pecos Bill as a perpetual boy will appeal to children. The retelling is a smooth adaptation for introducing young listeners to longer versions or to accompany storytelling sessions centered around tall-tale heroes." Bull Cent Child Books

Sally Ann Thunder Ann Whirlwind Crockett; a tall tale; retold and illustrated by Steven Kellogg. Morrow Junior Bks. 1995 unp il $17 paperback o.p. *
Grades: K 1 2 3   398.2
1. Crockett, Sally Ann Thunder Ann Whirlwind—Fiction 2. Tall tales
ISBN 0-688-14042-4; 0-688-14043-2 (lib bdg); 0-688-17113-3 (pa)   LC 94-43782
Sally Ann is "Davy's wife and a match for any bear, alligator, or macho man in the West. As retold (and scrupulously sourced) by Kellogg, Sally Ann's early life outracing and outswimming her nine big brothers and beating all comers at the state fair . . . is but a prelude to her flight to the frontier and subsequent rescue of and marriage to Davy Crockett. . . . Kellogg's characteristically energetic paintings meet their match in this story's kinetic hyperbole; the fact that his Sally Ann and Davy look like rambunctious big kids will only add to their story-hour appeal." Bull Cent Child Books

The three little pigs; retold and illustrated by Steven Kellogg. Morrow Junior Bks. 1997 unp il hardcover o.p. pa $6.99 *
Grades: K 1 2 3   398.2
1. Folklore 2. Pigs—Folklore 3. Wolves—Folklore
ISBN 0-688-08731-0; 0-688-08732-9 (lib bdg); 0-06-443779-5 (pa)   LC 96-34434
In this retelling of a well-known tale, Serafina Sow starts her own waffle-selling business in order to enable her three offspring to prepare for the future, which in-

Kellogg, Steven, 1941-—*Continued*

cludes an encounter with a surly wolf

"Much of the broad humor is carried in the lively, colorful illustrations, though there's wordplay aplenty in the text and pictures too." Booklist

Kim, So-Un

Korean children's favorite stories; retold by Kim So-un; illustrated by Jeong Kyoung-Sim. Tuttle 2004 95p il $16.95

Grades: 3 4 5 6   **398.2**

1. Folklore—Korea

ISBN 0-8048-3591-8

A newly illustrated edition of The story bag, published 1955

This collection of 13 Korean folktales "includes elements shared by many cultures, such as a flood story, and others with a unique sensibility. A variety of animals appear, including tigers, both good and bad, and snakes, depicted as dragons. The delicate watercolor illustrations make the stories accessible to children." SLJ

Kimmel, Eric A.

The adventures of Hershel of Ostropol; retold by Eric A. Kimmel; with drawings by Trina Schart Hyman. Holiday House 1995 64p il hardcover o.p. pa $7.95

Grades: 3 4 5   **398.2**

1. Ostropoler, Hershele, 18th cent.—Legends 2. Jewish legends

ISBN 0-8234-1210-5; 0-8234-1404-3 (pa)

LC 95-8907

Contents: What Hershel's father did; The goose's foot; The bandit; Money from a table; Potatoes!; The miracle; An incredible story; The cow; The candlesticks; Hershel goes to heaven

"Kimmel retells ten stories about Hershel of Ostropol, a Jewish folk hero who lived during the first part of the nineteenth century. A man quick with a humorous saying or jest, Hershel lived by his wits, traveling from town to town in Eastern Europe." Horn Book Guide

"Hyman's wild, beautifully detailed drawings . . . capture Hershel's farcical interchange with the village creatures and characters, including the miser, the bandit, and the rabbi. With their wry idiom, these are stories for telling across generations." Booklist

Anansi and the magic stick; illustrated by Janet Stevens. Holiday House 2001 unp il $16.95; pa $6.95

Grades: K 1 2 3   **398.2**

1. Folklore—Africa 2. Anansi (Legendary character)

ISBN 0-8234-1443-4; 0-8234-1763-8 (pa)

LC 00-39608

Anansi the Spider steals Hyena's magic stick so he won't have to do the chores, but when the stick's magic won't stop, he gets more than he bargained for

"Kimmel tells it with cheerful energy, and Stevens' chaotic mixed-media illustrations, with lots of bright pink and green, show Anansi's friends and neighbors . . . caught up in the mess." Booklist

Anansi and the moss-covered rock; retold by Eric A. Kimmel; illustrated by Janet Stevens. Holiday House 1988 unp il lib bdg $17.95

Grades: 1 2 3 4   **398.2**

1. Anansi (Legendary character) 2. Spiders—Folklore 3. Animals—Folklore 4. Folklore—West Africa

ISBN 0-8234-0689-X   LC 87-31766

Anansi the Spider uses a strange moss-covered rock in the forest to trick all the other animals, until Little Bush Deer decides he needs to learn a lesson

"The text is rhythmic, nicely building suspense to the inevitable conclusion. Stevens' complementary, colorful illustrations add detail, humor, and movement to the text." SLJ

Anansi and the talking melon; retold by Eric A. Kimmel; illustrated by Janet Stevens. Holiday House 1994 unp il $16.95; pa $6.95

Grades: K 1 2 3   **398.2**

1. Folklore—Africa 2. Anansi (Legendary character)

ISBN 0-8234-1104-4; 0-8234-1167-2 (pa)

LC 93-4239

Anansi the Spider tricks Elephant and some other animals into thinking the melon in which he is hiding can talk

"The snappy narration is well suited for individual reading or group sharing. The colorful line-and-wash illustrations are filled with movement and playful energy." SLJ

Anansi goes fishing; retold by Eric A. Kimmel; illustrated by Janet Stevens. Holiday House 1992 unp il $16.95; pa $6.95 *

Grades: K 1 2 3   **398.2**

1. Folklore—Africa 2. Anansi (Legendary character)

ISBN 0-8234-0918-X; 0-8234-1022-6 (pa)

LC 91-17813

Anansi the spider plans to trick Turtle into catching a fish for his dinner, but Turtle proves to be smarter and ends up with a free meal. Explains the origin of spider webs

"Children able to comprehend the wordplay will be delighted when the lazy but lovable trickster figure is outwitted by the clever turtle, and Stevens' colorful, comical illustrations are perfect for this contemporary rendition of the tale." Booklist

Anansi's party time; by Eric A. Kimmel; illustrated by Janet Stevens. Holiday House 2008 unp il $16.95; pa $6.95

Grades: K 1 2 3   **398.2**

1. Folklore—West Africa 2. Anansi (Legendary character) 3. Turtles—Folklore 4. Spiders—Folklore

ISBN 978-0-8234-1922-7; 0-8234-1922-3; 978-0-8234-2241-8 (pa); 0-8234-2241-0 (pa)

LC 2007002206

When Anansi the spider invites Turtle to a party just to play a trick on him, Turtle gets revenge at a party of his own

"Children will delight in hearing this tale of the spider's comeuppance. . . . Almost every page, illustrated in acrylic ink and colored pencils, has some comical element." SLJ

Kimmel, Eric A.—*Continued*

Even higher! Holiday House 2009 unp il $16.95
Grades: K 1 2 3   **398.2**
1. Jews—Folklore 2. Rosh ha-Shanah—Fiction
ISBN 978-0-8234-2020-9; 0-8234-2020-5
                                      LC 2008019710
A skeptical visitor to the village of Nemirov finds out
where its rabbi really goes just before the Jewish New
Year, when the villagers claim he goes to heaven to
speak to God.
"Kimmel's wise, reassuring voice embellishes the story with wonderful details. . . . while keeping the narrative taut. . . . Weber's colorful, openhearted drawings
immerse readers in a lost world where piety defined life
and the quest for truth was the biggest adventure of all."
Publ Wkly

The fisherman and the turtle; adapted by Eric A.
Kimmel; illustrated by Martha Aviles. Marshall
Cavendish Children 2008 unp il $16.99
Grades: K 1 2   **398.2**
1. Fairy tales 2. Folklore 3. Turtles—Folklore
4. Aztecs—Folklore
ISBN 978-0-7614-5387-1; 0-7614-5387-3
A retelling of the Grimm tale about the fisherman's
greedy wife, set in the land of the Aztecs
"The vivid colors of the acrylic-and-watercolor illus-
trations and pages bordered with motifs from Aztec art
give the tale an authentic flavor." Booklist

The frog princess; a Tlingit legend from Alaska;
retold by Eric A. Kimmel; illustrated by Rosanne
Litzinger. Holiday House 2006 unp il $16.95
Grades: 2 3 4   **398.2**
1. Tlingit Indians—Folklore 2. Frogs—Folklore
ISBN 0-8234-1618-6   LC 2004049347
After rejecting all of her human suitors, the beautiful
daughter of a Tlingit tribal leader declares that she would
rather marry a frog from the lake
The story "is gracefully told, and [readers] will enjoy
the shape-shifting magic and cultural details, which are
extended in the uncluttered paintings of villagers in Tlingit costume." Booklist

Gershon's monster; a story for the Jewish New
Year; retold by Eric A. Kimmel; illustrated by Jon
J. Muth. Scholastic Press 2000 unp il $16.95 *
Grades: K 1 2 3   **398.2**
1. Jews—Folklore 2. Rosh ha-Shanah—Fiction
ISBN 0-439-10839-X   LC 99-46986
"Retelling of a Hasidic legend featuring Rabbi Israel
ben Eliezer"—Author's note
When his sins threaten the lives of his beloved twin
children, a Jewish man finally repents of his wicked
ways
"This presentation of a Hasidic legend has everything
a reader could want: a suspenseful story, an insightful
lesson and brilliantly conceived, airy pictures that accel-
erate the delivery of both." Publ Wkly

The gingerbread man; retold by Eric A.
Kimmel; illustrated by Megan Lloyd. Holiday
House 1993 unp il $16.95; pa $6.95
Grades: K 1 2   **398.2**
1. Folklore
ISBN 0-8234-0824-8; 0-8234-1137-0 (pa)
                                      LC 90-33202
A freshly baked gingerbread man escapes when he is
taken out of the oven and eludes a number of animals
until he meets a clever fox
"This version softens the ending with a final page of
fresh, recently baked gingerbread men. This is a story
that calls for energetic art, and Lloyd provides just that
in warm-toned watercolors that feature the gingerbread
man zipping across the pages. A compact text and suitably large pictures make this just right for groups."
Booklist

Iron John; adapted from the Brothers Grimm by
Eric A. Kimmel; illustrated by Trina Schart
Hyman. Holiday House 1994 unp il $16.95; pa
$6.95
Grades: 2 3 4 5   **398.2**
1. Fairy tales 2. Folklore—Germany
ISBN 0-8234-1073-0; 0-8234-1248-2 (pa)
                                      LC 93-7534
With help of Iron John, the wild man of the forest
who is under a curse, a young prince makes his way in
the world and finds his true love
"Abridged and, as the afterword explains, somewhat
changed from the Grimms' tale, Kimmel's dramatic narrative flows from scene to scene with a clear sense of
adventure and romance and an underlying sense of mystery. Hyman's beautifully composed illustrations . . . are
notable for their rich colors and subtle interplay of light
and darkness." Booklist

The runaway tortilla; illustrated by Randy Cecil.
Winslow Press (Delray Beach) 2000 unp il $16.95
Grades: K 1 2 3   **398.2**
1. Fairy tales 2. Folklore 3. Hispanic Americans—
Folklore
ISBN 1-89081-718-X   LC 00-20487
In this Southwestern version of the Gingerbread Man,
a tortilla runs away from Tia Lupe and Tio Jose in Texas
"The primitive oil paintings feature a palette of sunset
colors, a rotund Tia and Tio, and a lipsticked, scowling
tortilla. . . . Kimmel's saucy story joins a swarm of sim-
ilar, albeit popular, retellings of traditional tales with a
Southwestern setting." SLJ

Three sacks of truth; a story from France;
adapted by Eric A. Kimmel; illustrated by Robert
Rayevsky. Holiday House 1993 unp il $15.95
Grades: 2 3 4   **398.2**
1. Fairy tales 2. Folklore—France
ISBN 0-8234-0921-X   LC 91-19265
With the aid of a perfect peach, a silver fife, and his
own resources, Petit Jean outwits a dishonest king and
wins the hand of a princess
"In this crisp and sprightly interpretation, storyteller
Kimmel takes full advantage of the plot's sly humor,
which he accentuates through many colorful, deft turns
of phrase. . . . Rayevsky adds rich, predominantly earth-
toned illustrations that emphasize character and expression with a slight ironic bite." Publ Wkly

Kimmelman, Leslie

The Little Red Hen and the Passover matzah; illustrated by Paul Meisel. Holiday House 2010 unp il $16.95 *

Grades: PreK K 1 2   **398.2**

    1. Folklore 2. Passover—Folklore 3. Jews—Folklore 4. Chickens—Folklore

    ISBN 978-0-8234-1952-4; 0-8234-1952-5

                                LC 2008-48488

No one will help the Little Red Hen make the Passover matzah, but they all want to help her eat it. Includes information about Passover, a recipe for matzah, and a glossary of Yiddish words used in the story.

    "Such a clever idea! . . . By the time Kimmelman, . . . a terrifically conversational storyteller, and Meisel, . . . a slyly astute cartoonist, . . . are done, readers of all faiths will know a lot more than some emotionally evocative Yiddish words." Publ Wkly

Knutson, Barbara

Love and roast chicken; a trickster tale from the Andes. Lerner Pub. Group 2004 unp il map lib bdg $16.95

Grades: K 1 2 3   **398.2**

    1. Guinea pigs—Folklore 2. Foxes—Folklore 3. Folklore—Peru 4. Native Americans—South America—Folklore

    ISBN 1-57505-657-7   LC 2003-18045

In this folktale from the Andes, a clever guinea pig repeatedly outsmarts the fox that wants to eat him for dinner

    "Knutson's boldly outlined, vibrant woodcut-and-watercolor artwork captures the mischievous nature of the guinea pig. . . . A thoroughly enjoyable tale that deserves a place in most libraries." SLJ

Krasno, Rena, 1923-

Cloud weavers; ancient Chinese legends; [by] Rena Krasno and Yeng-Fong Chiang; illustrations from the collection of Yeng-Fong Chiang. Pacific View Press 2003 96p il $22.95

Grades: 5 6 7 8   **398.2**

    1. Folklore—China

    ISBN 1-881896-26-9   LC 2002-35911

Presents legends and tales from China, including ancient folktales, stories that reflect Chinese traditions and virtues, historical tales, and selections from literature

This collection "provides a showcase for some remarkable pieces of Chinese calendar art and advertising posters from the 1920s and 1930s. . . . Prefaces provide cultural insight for some stories, and the brisk retellings weave important background unobtrusively into the narrative." Booklist

Krensky, Stephen, 1953-

Anansi and the box of stories; a West African folktale; adapted by Stephen Krensky; illustrations by Jeni Reeves. Millbrook Press 2007 48p il (On my own folklore) lib bdg $25.26

Grades: 1 2 3 4   **398.2**

    1. Anansi (Legendary character) 2. Folklore—West Africa

    ISBN 978-0-8225-6741-7   LC 2006037783

Long ago in Africa, the sky god Nyame keeps all of the stories to himself, but when Anansi the spider asks their price, Nyame agrees to trade his stories if Anansi can perform four seemingly impossible tasks

    "Krensky's retelling is simple and fast-moving, ably supported by Reeve's illustrations." SLJ

John Henry; adapted by Stephen Krensky; illustrations by Mark Oldroyd. Millbrook Press 2007 48p il (On my own folklore) lib bdg $25.26

Grades: 1 2 3 4   **398.2**

    1. John Henry (Legendary character) 2. African Americans—Folklore 3. Folklore—United States

    ISBN 978-1-57505-887-0 (lib bdg); 1-57505-887-1 (lib bdg)   LC 2005010187

Retells the life of the legendary African American hero who raced against a steam drill to cut through a mountain.

    This is "written in a comfortably folksy tone. . . . While the narrative has its moments of understated humor, it also involves readers. . . . Full of light and movement, Oldroyd's impressionistic pictures effectively illustrate the story." Booklist

Paul Bunyan; adapted by Stephen Krensky; illustrated by Craig Orback. Millbrook Press 2007 42p il (On my own folklore) lib bdg $25.26

Grades: 1 2 3 4   **398.2**

    1. Bunyan, Paul (Legendary character) 2. Tall tales 3. Folklore—United States

    ISBN 978-1-57505-888-7 (lib bdg); 1-57505-888-X (lib bdg)   LC 2005033157

Relates some of the exploits of Paul Bunyan, a lumberjack said to be taller than the trees whose pet was a blue ox named Babe.

    "With simple vocabulary and some dialogue, Krensky gives children a feeling for the characters as well as the flavor of the time and the story's setting." SLJ

    Includes bibliographical references

Pecos Bill; adapted by Stephen Krensky; illustrations by Paul Tong. Millbrook Press 2007 44p il (On my own folklore) lib bdg $25.26

Grades: 1 2 3 4   **398.2**

    1. Pecos Bill (Legendary character) 2. Tall tales 3. Folklore—United States

    ISBN 978-1-57505-889-4 (lib bdg); 1-57505-889-8 (lib bdg)   LC 2005033174

Relates some of the exploits of Pecos Bill, the extraordinary cowboy who was raised by coyotes, rode a mountain lion, and used a rattle snake as a rope.

    "With simple vocabulary and some dialogue, Krensky gives children a feeling for the characters as well as the flavor of the time and the story's setting." SLJ

Kurtz, Jane

Fire on the mountain; illustrated by E. B. Lewis. Simon & Schuster Bks. for Young Readers 1994 unp il pa $5.99 hardcover o.p.

Grades: 1 2 3 4   **398.2**

    1. Folklore—Ethiopia

    ISBN 0-689-81896-3 (pa)   LC 93-11477

A clever young shepherd boy uses his wits to gain a fortune for himself and his sister from a haughty rich

Kurtz, Jane—*Continued*

man

"Lewis uses color to achieve intriguing contrast and articulates characters' faces with expression and power. Kurtz, who heard the story as a child in Ethiopia, retells it in a strong narrative voice: her language is simple and spare yet evocative." Booklist

Laird, Elizabeth

A fistful of pearls; and other tales from Iraq; illustrated by Shelley Fowles. Frances Lincoln Children's 2008 90p il hardcover o.p. pa $7.95

Grades: 3 4 5   398.2

1. Folklore—Iraq

ISBN   978-1-84507-811-9;   1-84507-811-X;
978-1-84507-641-2 (pa); 1-84507-641-9 (pa)

Mythical creatures, enchanted encounters, strange serpents, and wise magicians are brought together in a compilation of Iraqi folk tales.

"This collection introduces young readers to a host of interesting characters. . . . In the introduction, Laird recalls memories of living in Iraq and provides some background for the tales. Her retellings of these folktales are flavored with humor and cultural details, as is Fowles's clever black-and-white spot art." SLJ

Lamadrid, Enrique R., 1948-

Juan the bear and the water of life; La acequia de Juan del oso; retold and translated by Enrique R. Lamadrid & Juan Estevan Arellano; illustrations by Amy Córdova. University of New Mexico Press 2008 unp il $17.95

Grades: 3 4 5   398.2

1. Folklore—New Mexico 2. Irrigation—Folklore
3. Bears—Folklore 4. Tall tales 5. Bilingual books—
English-Spanish

ISBN 978-0-8263-4543-1; 0-8263-4543-3

LC 2008008846

Although treated as outcasts, three superhuman friends, including Juan del Oso whose father was a bear, create an irrigation system for New Mexico's Mora Valley.

"The English and Spanish versions of this engaging tall tale sit side by side. Córdova's bold colors and brushstrokes evoke the rustic folk-art styles of the Southwest." SLJ

Includes glossary and bibliographical references

Langton, Jane

Saint Francis and the wolf; by Jane Langton; illustrated by Ilse Plume. Godine 2007 unp il $16.95

Grades: K 1 2   398.2

1. Francis, of Assisi, Saint, 1182-1226—Legends
2. Wolves—Folklore 3. Folklore—Italy

ISBN 1-56792-320-8

An old and hungry wolf terrorizes the townspeople of Gubbio until Saint Francis shows the villagers how to live peacefully with the wolf.

This is written "with a smooth storyteller's pacing and an eye for kid-friendly detail. . . . Plume . . . alternates spot illustrations of flowers and plants with slightly larg-

er scenes of Gubbio framed in Renaissance-inspired shapes. Her delicate lines and sunny watercolor palette depict the flourishing flora, fauna and stone dwellings of the Italian countryside." Publ Wkly

Lesser, Rika

Hansel and Gretel; illustrated by Paul O. Zelinsky; retold by Rika Lesser. Dutton Children's Bks. 1999 unp il $16.99; pa $6.99 *

Grades: K 1 2 3   398.2

1. Fairy tales 2. Folklore—Germany

ISBN 0-525-46152-3; 0-698-11407-8 (pa)

LC 99-10198

A Caldecott Medal honor book, 1985

A reissue of the edition first published 1984 by Dodd, Mead

A retelling of the well-known tale in which two children are left in the woods but find their way home despite an encounter with a wicked witch

"Direct and unembellished, Lesser's retelling resembles that of the earliest German edition of Grimm, published in 1812. . . . A visual feast, the illustrations frequently recall Flemish and French genre painting of the seventeenth century, while the idyllic woodland scenes reflect a later Romantic mood." Horn Book Guide

Lester, Julius

John Henry; pictures by Jerry Pinkney. Dial Bks. for Young Readers 1994 unp il $17.99; pa $6.99 *

Grades: K 1 2 3   398.2

1. John Henry (Legendary character) 2. African Americans—Folklore 3. Folklore—United States

ISBN 0-8037-1606-0; 0-14-056622-8 (pa)

LC 93-34583

A Caldecott Medal honor book, 1995

"The original legend of John Henry and how he beat the steam drill with his sledgehammer has been enhanced and enriched, in Lester's retelling, with wonderful and contemporary details and poetic similes that add humor, beauty, and strength. Pinkney's evocative illustrations—especially the landscapes, splotchy and impressionistic, yet very solid and vigorous—are little short of magnificent." Horn Book Guide

The tales of Uncle Remus; the adventures of Brer Rabbit; as told by Julius Lester; illustrated by Jerry Pinkney. Dial Bks. 1987 151p il $19.99; pa $8.99

Grades: 4 5 6 7   398.2

1. African Americans—Folklore 2. Animals—Folklore

ISBN 0-8037-0271-X; 0-14-130347-6 (pa)

LC 85-20449

This adaptation of 48 Brer Rabbit stories "is the work of a writer familiar with the methodology of folkloristic and historical research but also with the techniques of flavoring fiction. . . . Pinkney's illustrations—black-and-white drawings with occasional double-page spreads in full color—are well drafted, fresh, and funny." Bull Cent Child Books

Lester, Julius—*Continued*

Uncle Remus, the complete tales; with a new introduction; as told by Julius Lester; illustrated by Jerry Pinkney 1999 xxi, 686p il lib bdg $35 *
Grades: 4 5 6 7   **398.2**
1. African Americans—Folklore 2. Animals—Folklore
ISBN 0-8037-2451-9   LC 99-17121

Reprint in one volume of works originally published separately, 1987-1994

Contents: book 1. The tales of Uncle Remus; book 2. More tales of Uncle Remus; book 3. Further tales of Uncle Remus; book 4. The last tales of Uncle Remus

Lester retells stories of the trickster rabbit from African American folklore collected by Joel Chandler Harris

"This is a landmark collection. . . . Lester's retellings are sharp and flavorful and grounded in the here and now." [review of book 1] Booklist

L'Homme, Erik

Tales of a lost kingdom; a journey into Northwest Pakistan; written by Erik L'Homme; illustrated by François Place; translated by Claudia Zoe Bedrick. Enchanted Lion Books 2007 47p il $17.95
Grades: 3 4 5 6   **398.2**
1. Folklore—Pakistan
ISBN 978-1-59270-072-1; 1-59270-072-1

A collection of three authentic folktales from the ancient kingdom of Chitral at the border between Pakistan and Afghanistan. Includes a travelogue with photographs, illustrations, and a map.

"Sardonic, bittersweet, and often tragic, these three tales reflect the hardscrabble life of this country. . . . The retellings are flavored with detail and language suitable to the oral tradition. . . . Place's elegantly simple, naive watercolor and pen-and-ink illustrations add to the attractive, hand-crafted design." SLJ

Light, Steven

Puss in boots; retold and illustrated by Steven Light. Abrams 2002 unp il $14.95
Grades: K 1 2 3   **398.2**
1. Fairy tales 2. Folklore—France 3. Cats—Folklore
ISBN 0-8109-4368-9   LC 2001-3746

A clever cat helps his poor master win fame, fortune, and the hand of a beautiful princess

"Inspired by the work of the French Rococo artist Jean-Honor Fragonard and by French decorative wallpapers, Light created patterned papers onto which he collaged the main illustrations for this story. The results are bright, busy, cheery spreads that suit his lighthearted retelling." SLJ

Livo, Norma J., 1929-

Tales to tickle your funny bone; humorous tales from around the world; [by] Norma J. Livo; foreward by Pat Mendoza. Libraries Unlimited 2007 xxvii, 206p il pa $30
Grades: Professional   **398.2**
1. Folklore 2. Wit and humor
ISBN 978-1-59158-504-6   LC 2007003331

"Tall tales, noodlehead stories, urban legends, riddles, and songs fill this delightful collection of humorous tales. The selections are in shortened but lively formats for easy reading or telling. Introductory notes discuss folklore and the healing power of humor. The more than 70 stories are arranged by genre and labeled with the country of origin. . . . The bibliography includes books and Internet sources as well as VHS and DVD materials. An excellent resource for teachers, librarians, and students." SLJ

Includes bibliographical references

Long, Laurel

The lady & the lion; a Brothers Grimm tale; retold by Laurel Long & Jacqueline K. Ogburn; illustrated by Laurel Long. Dial Books 2003 unp il $16.99
Grades: 2 3 4   **398.2**
1. Folklore—Germany 2. Fairy tales
ISBN 0-8037-2651-1

With help from Sun, Moon, and North Wind, a lady travels the world seeking to save her beloved from the evil enchantress who turned him first into a lion, then into a dove

"The dramatic tale is smoothly told, but the illustrations, with even more drama and lush with romance, take center stage here. The oil paintings use flowing compositions, swirling lines, rich colors, and a profusion of subtle patterns to create a series of detailed scenes combining European and Middle Eastern elements." Booklist

Louie, Ai-Ling, 1949-

Yeh-Shen; a Cinderella story from China; retold by Ai-Ling Louie; illustrated by Ed Young. Philomel Bks. 1982 unp il $16.99; pa $6.99 *
Grades: 2 3 4   **398.2**
1. Folklore—China 2. Fairy tales
ISBN 0-399-20900-X; 0-698-11388-8 (pa)
                                   LC 80-11745

This version of the Cinderella story, in which a young girl overcomes the wickedness of her stepsister and stepmother to become the bride of a prince, is based on ancient Chinese manuscripts written 1000 years before the earliest European version

"The reteller has cast the tale in well-cadenced prose, fleshing out the spare account with elegance and grace. In a manner reminiscent of Chinese scrolls and of decorated folding screens, the text is chiefly set within vertical panels, while the luminescent illustrations—less narrative than emotional—often increase their impact by overspreading the narrow framework or appearing on pages of their own." Horn Book

Lowery, Linda, 1949-

The tale of La Llorona; a Mexican folktale; adapted by Linda Lowery and Richard Keep; illustrations by Janice Lee Porter. Millbrook Press 2008 48p il (On my own folklore) lib bdg $25.26
Grades: 1 2 3 4   **398.2**
1. Folklore—Mexico 2. Ghost stories
ISBN 978-0-8225-6378-5 (lib bdg); 0-8225-6378-9 (lib bdg)   LC 2006005478

Lowery, Linda, 1949-—*Continued*

Expands on a popular Mexican folktale about a ghost that haunts riverbanks at night, crying as she searches for her lost children

"The illustrations are done in soft earth tones in a style reminiscent of Mexican folk art. . . . Given the limitations of the easy-reader format and the necessity of not terrifying young audiences too much, this is a creditable retelling." SLJ

Includes bibliographical references

Lunge-Larsen, Lise

The hidden folk; stories of fairies, dwarves, selkies, and other secret beings; illustrated by Beth Krommes. Houghton Mifflin 2004 72p il $18 *

Grades: 3 4 5   398.2

1. Fairy tales 2. Folklore

ISBN 0-618-17495-8   LC 2002-5089

Contents: The ivory cups; Tulips and parsley; The nisse's revenge; The battle for Bornholm; The wedding feast; The silver king; The long horse; Playing the fourth part; The selkie wife

Brief stories featuring such creatures as flower fairies, elves, dwarves, and river spirits.

"The author draws on a rich tradition of legends and myths, retelling them in an accessible manner that will captivate readers. Handsome scratchboard illustrations decorate the pages with stylized figures and landscapes. The vivid hues and interesting textures make an eye-catching combination." SLJ

The troll with no heart in his body and other tales of trolls from Norway; retold by Lise Lunge-Larsen; woodcuts by Betsy Bowen. Houghton Mifflin 1999 92p il hardcover o.p. pa $7.95

Grades: 3 4 5 6   398.2

1. Folklore—Norway

ISBN 0-395-91371-3; 0-618-35403-4 (pa)

                                         LC 98-43244

Contents: The Three Billy Goats Gruff; The boy who became a lion, a falcon, and an ant; Butterball; The handshake; The boys and the North Wind; The white cat in the Dovre Mountain; The sailors and the troll; The eating competition; The troll with no heart in his body

"Lunge-Larsen presents nine Norwegian tales about the greed and foolishness of trolls in a casual style that makes these stories ripe for reading aloud and storytelling. Her liveliness of language and easy turn of phrase give these retellings a comforting tone despite the sometimes scary events. Bowen's colored-ink woodblock prints, inspired by traditional Norwegian woodcarving and design, suit the monumental nature of the subject." Bull Cent Child Books

Includes bibliographical references

Lupton, Hugh

Pirican Pic and Pirican Mor; retold by Hugh Lupton; illustrated by Yumi Heo. Barefoot Bks. (NY) 2003 unp il $16.99

Grades: K 1 2 3   398.2

1. Folklore—Scotland

ISBN 1-84148-070-3

The story of two friends who go off to pick walnuts. Their adventure begins after one friend has been busy picking the walnuts, while the other has eaten every one. Based on a Scottish folktale

This adaptation "has a robust rhythm and language that lends itself easily to reading or telling aloud. That energetic, oral immediacy is enhanced by Heo's light-hearted oil paintings. Human and animal characters sporting eccentric physiologies free-float among varying planes and perspectives in foreground-focused compositions infused with color and light." Bull Cent Child Books

Lyons, Mary E.

Roy makes a car; based on a story collected by Zora Neale Hurston; illustrated by Terry Widener. Atheneum 2005 unp il $16.95 *

Grades: K 1 2 3   398.2

1. Folklore—United States 2. African Americans—Folklore 3. Tall tales 4. Automobiles—Folklore

ISBN 0-689-84640-1   LC 2004-03221

Roy Tyle, the best mechanic in the state of Florida, can clean spark plugs just by looking at them, and he takes a two dollar bet that he can make an accident-proof car.

"Perfect for reading aloud, the funny rhythmic words are well matched to Widener's exaggerated acrylic illustrations." Booklist

MacDonald, Margaret Read

Bat's big game; retold by Margaret Read MacDonald; illustrated by Eugenia Nobati. Albert Whitman & Co. 2008 unp il $16.95

Grades: K 1 2 3   398.2

1. Bats—Folklore 2. Soccer—Folkore 3. Animals—Folklore 4. Fables

ISBN 978-0-8075-0587-8; 0-8075-0587-0

"In this retelling of a traditional fable, Bat cannot decide whether he wants to be on the Animals' or the Birds' soccer team. At first he chooses the Animals, but when they start to fall behind, he switches to the Birds. When they start to lose, he tries to switch back. . . . The text is compact and has an innate rhythm characteristic of a veteran storyteller. Nobati's full-page, digitally created color illustrations are highly stylized. . . . The pictures are full of action and recreate the mood of a heated soccer game." SLJ

Conejito; a folktale from Panama; illustrated by Geraldo Valério. August House 2006 unp il $16.95

Grades: K 1 2 3   398.2

1. Folklore—Panama 2. Rabbits—Folklore

ISBN 0-87483-779-0   LC 2005-52567

"LittleFolk"

In this folktale from Panama, a little rabbit and his Tia Monica outwit a fox, a tiger, and a lion, all of whom

MacDonald, Margaret Read—*Continued*

want to eat him for lunch.

"Rhyming refrains invite the participation of young listeners. . . . Valerio's splashy tropical colors and elongated, rubbery characters . . . capture the tale's bouncing energy." Booklist

Fat cat; a Danish folktale; retold by Margaret Read MacDonald; illustrated by Julie Paschkis. August House 2001 unp il $15.95; pa $7.95 *

Grades: K 1 2 3   **398.2**

    1. Folklore—Denmark 2. Cats—Folklore 3. Mice—Folklore

    ISBN 0-87483-616-6; 0-87483-765-0 (pa)

                                LC 00-68939

A greedy cat grows enormous as he eats everything in sight, including his friends and neighbors who call him fat

"The book's huge, bright illustrations are glorious. . . . The large, funny illustrations will carry well for a bigger crowd and, combined with refrain that invites chanting along, make this a surefire hit for reading aloud." Booklist

Five-minute tales; more stories to read and tell when time is short; [by] Margaret Read MacDonald. August House Publishers 2007 159p $24.94; pa $14.95

Grades: Professional   **398.2**

    1. Folklore 2. Storytelling

    ISBN   978-0-87483-781-0;   0-87483-781-2;
978-0-87483-782-7 (pa); 0-87483-782-0 (pa)

                               LC 2007014511

"Quick tales in storytellers' pockets are like money in the bank. They fill in when programs are delayed, and when class periods are cut short or interrupted so that lengthier stories are no longer suitable. . . . This collection fits the bill with participation, animal, origin, riddle, romance, strange, trickster, and moral tales from around the world and for all ages. . . . Her practical guidance enables newer as well as veteran tellers to proceed confidently with these engaging stories." SLJ

Includes bibliographical references

Go to sleep, Gecko! a Balinese folktale; retold by Margaret Read MacDonald; illustrated by Geraldo Valério. August House Little Folk 2006 unp il $16.95

Grades: K 1 2   **398.2**

    1. Folklore—Indonesia 2. Geckos—Folklore

    ISBN 978-0-87483-780-3; 0-87483-780-4

                               LC 2006-40748

Retells the folktale of the gecko who complains to the village chief that the fireflies keep him awake at night but then learns that in nature all things are connected

"MacDonald's lyrical language and use of repetition help bring this folktale to life. There is just the right touch of humor in both the text and the art. The pacing is perfectly matched to the richly colored acrylic illustrations." SLJ

The great smelly, slobbery, small-tooth dog; a folktale from Great Britain; retold by Margaret Read MacDonald; illustrated by Julie Paschkis. August House Little Folk 2007 unp il $16.95

Grades: PreK K 1 2   **398.2**

    1. Dogs—Folklore 2. Folklore—Great Britain

    ISBN 978-0-87483-808-4   LC 2007005504

In this British variant of a traditional tale, a great smelly, slobbery, small-tooth dog rescues a rich man from bandits and demands that the man bring his beautiful daughter to live in his castle.

"The text is perfectly paced for interactive read-alouds . . . but the active, richly colored gouache paintings, which include beautiful details, . . . will work best with small groups." Booklist

How many donkeys? an Arabic counting tale; retold by Margaret Read MacDonald and Nadia Jameel Taibah; illustrations by Carol Liddiment. Albert Whitman 2009 unp il $16.99

Grades: K 1 2   **398.2**

    1. Arabs—Folklore 2. Counting

    ISBN 978-0-8075-3424-3; 0-8075-3424-2

                               LC 2008056047

When Jouha counts the ten donkeys carrying his dates to market, he repeatedly forgets to count the one he is riding on, causing him great consternation. Includes numbers written out in Arabic and in English transliteration, as well as the numerals one through ten, and a note on the origins and other versions of the story

"Bright, painterly illustrations depict the sunny desert setting; jewel-toned robes, turban, and blankets enliven the sandy palette. . . . A winning, witty, and surprisingly effective combination." Booklist

Little Rooster's diamond button; retold by Margaret Read MacDonald; illustrated by Will Terry. Albert Whitman 2007 unp il $16.95

Grades: K 1 2 3   **398.2**

    1. Roosters—Fiction 2. Folklore—Hungary

    ISBN 978-0-8075-4644-4; 0-8075-4644-5

                               LC 2006-23979

In this Hungarian folktale, a rooster with a magic stomach retrieves the diamond button which was stolen from him by a greedy king

"This fine paean to cleverness and persistence is given extra zest by Terry's acrylic illustrations, which are as colorful as sparkling gems." Booklist

Mabela the clever; retold by Margaret Read MacDonald; illustrated by Tim Coffey. Whitman, A. 2001 unp il music hardcover o.p. pa $6.95 *

Grades: K 1 2 3   **398.2**

    1. Folklore—Africa 2. Mice—Folklore 3. Cats—Folklore

    ISBN 0-8075-4902-9; 0-8075-4903-7 (pa)

                                LC 00-8307

An African folktale about a mouse who pays close attention to her surroundings and avoids being tricked by the cat

"MacDonald's retelling of this Limba tale is engineered for storytime success. . . . Coffey's thatch-strewn paintings, rendered in acrylic on watercolor paper textured with gesso, feature lots of visibly clueless, wide-eyed mice, and his cat oozes predatory shrewdness to the very end." SLJ

MacDonald, Margaret Read—*Continued*

Surf war! a folktale from the Marshall Islands; illustrated by Geraldo Valerio. August House LittleFolk 2009 unp il $16.95

Grades: K 1 2   **398.2**

1. Folklore—Marshall Islands 2. Ecology—Folklore

ISBN 978-0-87483-889-3; 0-87483-889-4

LC 2008042589

A bragging contest between Whale and Sandpiper turns into a battle over the beach and sea, until both parties realize that the beach and the sea, as well as sea creatures and shorebirds, are interdependent

"The illustrations dominate the pages, with the birds and their backgrounds painted with bright shades of yellow, pink, and orange, while the sea and its creatures are deeper blues, grays, and purples. This charming story provides a moral about getting along with others and caring for the environment." SLJ

Three-minute tales; stories from around the world to tell or read when time is short. August House 2004 160p $24.95; pa $17.95

Grades: Professioinal   **398.2**

1. Folklore 2. Storytelling

ISBN 0-87483-728-6; 0-87483-729-4 (pa)

LC 2004-46257

"Easy to tell, easy to teach to children and adults, and easy to remember, the 80 very short tales in this global collection are for sharing in the classroom, library, and home and around the campfire. . . . The informal, highly practical suggestions for beginners make storytelling sound easy." Booklist

Includes bibliographical references

Too many fairies; a Celtic Tale; retold by Margaret Read MacDonald; illustrated by Susan Mitchell. Marshall Cavendish Children 2010 unp il $17.99

Grades: K 1 2 3   **398.2**

1. Folklore—Scotland 2. Fairies—Folklore

ISBN 978-0-7614-5604-9; 0-7614-5604-X

LC 2009007128

An old woman complains about all the housework she has to do, but when some fairies come to help her she finds that they are more trouble than they are worth

"This Scottish folktale is subtle but effective in its message of humility. The illustrations are folksy and warm with amusing detail. . . . A fun read-aloud." SLJ

Tunjur! Tunjur! Tunjur! a Palestinian folktale; retold by Margaret Read MacDonald; collected by Ibrahim Muhawi and Sharif Kanaana; illustrated by Alik Arzoumanian. Marshall Cavendish Children 2006 unp il $16.95

Grades: K 1 2   **398.2**

1. Palestinian Arabs—Folklore 2. Theft—Fiction

ISBN 978-0-7614-5225-6; 0-7614-5225-7

LC 2005009719

"In this lively Palestinian tale, a woman wishes for a child to love, 'even if it is nothing more than a cooking pot.' Voila! Her wish comes true, and red Little Pot appears. . . . Reluctantly, the mother lets her pot outdoors, and its adventures include meetings with a merchant and even the royal family. Little Pot manages to roll away

from each encounter with valuable stolen goods tucked inside her lid, but after her petty thefts are discovered, she receives a stinky comeuppance that is sure to please read-aloud crowds. Folklorist MacDonald's briskly paced text brims with repetitive phrases that evoke the sounds and rhythm of Little Pot's tumbling, rolling movement, and Arzoumanian's richly hued, stylized acrylics, bordered with Islamic motifs, add subtle cultural detail." Booklist

Maddern, Eric

The cow on the roof; illustrated by Paul Hess. Frances Lincoln 2006 unp il $15.95

Grades: PreK K 1 2   **398.2**

1. Folklore

ISBN 1-84507-374-6

Shon thinks his work as a farmer is much harder than his wife's housework, so he trades places with her and both soon discover that they appreciate each other for who they are and what they do.

"Maddern recasts this familiar folktale in Wales. . . . Hess's droll, folksy watercolors are bright and humorous." SLJ

Nail soup; illustrated by Paul Hess. Frances Lincoln Children's Books 2007 unp il $16.95

Grades: K 1 2 3   **398.2**

1. Folklore

ISBN 978-1-84507-479-1; 1-84507-479-3

"Maddern retells the familiar tale of a traveler who begs hospitality from a cottage dweller, promising to prepare her a delicious soup from only a nail and then hoodwinking her into providing a collection of savory ingredients. . . . The stylized views in the watercolor art favor scenes of backs and hands, but they also emphasize the playful possibilities of the text." Bull Cent Child Books

Mahy, Margaret

The seven Chinese brothers; illustrated by Jean and Mou-Sien Tseng. Scholastic 1990 unp pa $5.99 hardcover o.p. *

Grades: 1 2 3   **398.2**

1. Folklore—China 2. Fairy tales

ISBN 0-590-42057-7 (pa)   LC 88-33668

A story about "seven brothers, each of whom was blessed with an extraordinary power. Together, they use their amazing talents to avoid death at the hands of Emperor Ch'in Shih Huang, while trying to help the exhausted conscripted laborers working on the Great Wall." Child Book Rev Serv

"The handsome watercolor illustrations show a sensitivity to landscape and character portrayal . . . a hint of humor, and a flair for the dramatic. Written with Mahy's accustomed storytelling skill, this book will find an eager audience as a read-aloud for elementary school children." Booklist

Malam, John, 1957-

Dragons. QEB Pub. 2010 32p il map (QEB mythologies) lib bdg $28.50

Grades: 4 5 6 7   **398.2**
  1. Dragons
  ISBN 978-1-59566-982-7; 1-59566-982-5
                                             LC 2008-56082

"Describes dragons, discussing behavior and characteristics, relating dragon tales from various cultures, and exploring their presence in popular culture." Publisher's note

"A wealth of sidebars and captions . . . adds depth to the compelling [narrative]. Supported by vibrant color illustrations, . . . [this] fascinating and well-written [tale] will integrate well with social-science curriculums." SLJ

Includes glossary

Fairies. QEB Pub. 2010 32p il (QEB mythologies) lib bdg $28.50

Grades: 4 5 6 7   **398.2**
  1. Fairies
  ISBN 978-1-59566-979-7; 1-59566-979-5
                                             LC 2008-56083

"Presents the lore and mythology of fairies, discussing beliefs about their origins, behavior, where they live, and describes their interactions with humans." Publisher's note

"A wealth of sidebars and captions . . . adds depth to the compelling [narrative]. Supported by vibrant color illustrations, . . . [this] fascinating and well-written [tale] will integrate well with social-science curriculums." SLJ

Includes glossary

Giants. QEB Pub. 2010 32p il (QEB mythologies) lib bdg $28.50

Grades: 4 5 6 7   **398.2**
  1. Giants—Folklore
  ISBN 978-1-59566-980-3; 1-59566-980-9
                                             LC 2009000389

"Explores the myths of giants, includes information on their interactions with humans, and describes the different giant legends from around the world." Publisher's note

"A wealth of sidebars . . . adds depth to the compelling [narrative]. Supported by vibrant color illustrations, . . . [this] fascinating and well-written [tale] will integrate well with social-science curriculums." SLJ

Includes glossary

Monsters. QEB Pub. 2010 32p il map (QEB mythologies) $28.50

Grades: 4 5 6 7   **398.2**
  1. Monsters
  ISBN 978-1-59566-981-0; 1-59566-981-7
                                             LC 2008056090

This "is filled with some of the weirdest creatures ever conceived. . . . Take the Hambaba (Iraqi myth), the hideous giant with a face of coiled intestines. Or the Flying Head (Iroquois folktale). . . . The layout, designed as if printed upon an ancient map or scroll, is great, and Follenn's artwork is a rousing example of graphic novel-style menace." Booklist

Marshall, James, 1942-1992

Goldilocks and the three bears; retold and illustrated by James Marshall. Dial Bks. for Young Readers 1988 unp il $15.99; pa $5.99 *

Grades: PreK K 1 2   **398.2**
  1. Folklore 2. Bears—Folklore
  ISBN 0-8037-0542-5; 0-14-056366-0 (pa)
                                             LC 87-32983

A Caldecott Medal honor book, 1989

"Marshall's Goldilocks, the naughty little girl who disrupts a placid bear household, is no adorable blond moppet led more by curiosity than by mischievous intent. Instead, she is a sturdy, brazen, mini-hussy who stomps over the doorsill with a determined set to her mouth and a confident bounce in her step. . . . The big cartoonlike pictures depict a cozy modern setting for the respectable, suburban bears with snug rooms cluttered with books, bulbous upholstered furniture and a messy little bear's room. . . . The story contains a genuine enjoyment of Goldilock's adventures as they are reflected in Marshall's usual slapdash and rollicking illustrations." Horn Book

Hansel and Gretel; retold and illustrated by James Marshall. Dial Bks. for Young Readers 1990 unp il pa $5.99 hardcover o.p.

Grades: PreK K 1 2   **398.2**
  1. Folklore—Germany 2. Fairy tales
  ISBN 0-14-050836-8 (pa)   LC 89-26011

A poor woodcutter's children, lost in the forest, come upon a house made of cookies, cakes, and candy, occupied by a wicked witch who likes to have children for dinner

"Marshall's trademark wit and slyness mark every page of this effervescent interpretation. Never has there been a more horribly magnificent witch than his—an overstuffed, cackling harridan resplendent in scarlet costume, lipstick and rouge, her hair bedecked with incongruously delicate bows." Publ Wkly

Red Riding Hood; retold and illustrated by James Marshall. Dial Bks. for Young Readers 1987 unp il $15.99; pa $5.99 *

Grades: PreK K 1 2   **398.2**
  1. Folklore—Germany 2. Wolves—Folklore
  ISBN 0-8037-0344-9; 0-14-054693-6 (pa)
                                             LC 86-16722

A "retelling of the familiar tale . . . maintaining the integrity of the Grimm Brothers' version, with both Grandma and Red Riding Hood eaten and later rescued by a hunter." SLJ

This version "will have both children and their parents gripped with the drama and amused by the up-to-date dialogue. . . . The humorous, slightly sinister illustrations display Marshall's wacky style to its best advantage. Funny and wonderful for reading aloud." Horn Book

The three little pigs; retold and illustrated by James Marshall. Dial Bks. for Young Readers 1989 unp il hardcover o.p. pa $6.99 *

Grades: PreK K 1 2   **398.2**
  1. Folklore—Great Britain 2. Pigs—Folklore
  3. Wolves—Folklore
  ISBN 0-8037-0591-3; 0-14-055742-3 (pa)
                                             LC 88-33411

Marshall, James, 1942-1992—*Continued*

"In his spiffed-up version of the story, the three porkers follow the traditional course of straw, sticks, and bricks with the traditional results, but the players and accoutrements have a bit more zip than those in other versions. . . . The large, exuberant, cartoonlike illustrations provide much additional entertainment, jouncing readers along delightfully from one amusing scene to the next." Horn Book

Marshall, James Vance, 1924-

Stories from the Billabong; retold by James Vance Marshall; illustrated by Francis Firebrace. Frances Lincoln Children's Books 2009 61p il $19.95

Grades: 3 4 5 6   398.2
1. Aboriginal Australians—Folklore
ISBN 978-1-84507-704-4; 1-84507-704-0

"With the help of Aboriginal storytellers who have collected the tales and myths of their people, Marshall has assembled 10 fascinating stories of the Dreamtime. . . . Each selection is beautifully told and is illustrated by a traditional artist who uses the distinctive symbols and colors of the Aboriginal people. . . . This is an engaging, colorful book that belongs in most libraries." SLJ

Martin, Rafe, 1946-

The Shark God; story by Rafe Martin; pictures by David Shannon. Levine Bks. 2001 unp il hardcover o.p. pa $5.99

Grades: K 1 2 3   398.2
1. Folklore—Hawaii 2. Sharks—Folklore
ISBN 0-590-39500-9; 0-590-39570-X (pa)
LC 00-40570

Because they freed a shark caught in a net, the fearsome Shark God rescues a brother and sister from the cruel king's imprisonment and helps them find a new, peaceful kingdom across the sea

"Shannon's vigorous illustrations provide a dramatic backdrop for this well-told tale." SLJ

The world before this one; a novel told in legend; with paper sculpture by Calvin Nicholls. Levine Bks. 2002 195p il hardcover o.p. pa $5.99
*

Grades: 4 5 6 7   398.2
1. Seneca Indians—Folklore
ISBN 0-590-37976-3; 978-0-590-37980-9 (pa);
0-590-37980-1 (pa)   LC 2001-23403

Contents: Dangers; Moving; Gaqka, crow; The bow; The rock; Questions; New day; Two boys; Allies; Men's tales; Dream; Stories; The council; The people and the stone; Farewell

"Written in the style of a novel, this collection of 14 Seneca tales is presented through the retelling of one central story into which all of the others are artfully woven. . . . Martin offers sources for the tales along with an introductory note by Seneca Elder Peter Jemison. Each chapter includes a painstakingly detailed white paper sculpture of a character (often an animal) from one of the stories." SLJ

Martinez, Rueben, 1940-

Once upon a time; traditional Latin American tales = Habia una vez: cuentos tradicionales latinoamericanos; illustrated by Raúl Colón; translated by David Unger. Rayo 2010 95p il $19.99

Grades: 1 2 3 4   398.2
1. Folklore—Latin America 2. Folklore—Caribbean region 3. Folklore—Spain 4. Bilingual books—English-Spanish
ISBN 978-0-06-146895-7; 0-06-146895-9
LC 2009014445

Contents: The wedding rooster; The tlacuache and the coyote; The mother of the jungle; Martina the cockroach and Pérez the mouse; The flower of lirolay; The king and the riddle; Pedro Urdemales and the giant

A collection of seven traditional tales from Latin America, the Caribbean, and Spain retold in English and Spanish. Includes notes about each story

"Each story features a colorful, appealing full-page illustration. . . . [Martinez's] interpretations read aloud well (especially in Spanish) and make a strong contribution to a still relatively empty canon of bilingual, Latin American folktale offerings." SLJ

Matthews, Caitlin, 1952-

Fireside stories; tales for a winter's eve; retold by Caitlin Matthews; illustrated by Helen Cann. Barefoot Books 2007 94p il $19.99

Grades: 2 3 4 5   398.2
1. Winter—Folklore 2. Folklore
ISBN 978-1-846860-65-2; 1-846860-65-2
LC 2006100360

"This collection of seasonal folklore introduces readers to the Celtic and Gaelic festival of Samhain, or Summer's End; Christmas Eve in Austria; the Jewish New Year of the Trees (Tu B'Shevat); the Twelve Days of Christmas in the Czech Republic; the Twelfth Night in Russia; and Candlemas observed by the Slavey people of Canada. Each tale is accompanied by a brief introduction, setting the time and place for the story and providing necessary background information. Exquisite borders frame the text and lush watercolor illustrations enhance the narratives. Magical, mystical, humorous, and thoughtful." SLJ

Matthews, John, 1948-

Trick of the tale; a collection of trickster tales; [by] John & Caitlin Matthews; illustrated by Tomislav Tomic. Candlewick Press 2008 85p il $18.99

Grades: 3 4 5 6 7 8 9 10   398.2
1. Folklore
ISBN 978-0-7636-3646-3; 0-7636-3646-0
LC 2007038675

An illustrated collection of tales featuring notable trickster characters such as Raven and Hare, from the folk traditions of many countries.

"Each of the 20 folktales is introduced with a detailed, full-page ink drawing that resembles a fine print, and illustrations in varying sizes appear throughout. The pictures are both energetic and eloquent, and their formal tone is echoed in generally well-shaped narrative." SLJ

Mayer, Marianna, 1945-

Baba Yaga and Vasilisa the brave; as told by Marianna Mayer; illustrated by K. Y. Craft. Morrow Junior Bks. 1994 unp il $16.95

Grades: 3 4 5   **398.2**
    1. Fairy tales 2. Folklore—Russia
    ISBN 0-688-08500-8   LC 90-38514

A retelling of the old Russian fairy tale in which beautiful Vasilisa uses the help of her doll to escape from the clutches of the witch Baba Yaga, who in turn sets in motion the events which lead to the once ill-treated girl's marrying the tzar

"Mayer's graceful prose conveys both the wonder and power of the tale. Complementing the text are Craft's il-lustrations done in a mixture of watercolor, gouache, and oils. The palette of red and gold set against a dark back-ground resembles Russian folk-art paintings on black-lacquered wood." SLJ

McBratney, Sam

One voice, please; [retold by] Sam McBratney; illustrated by Russell Ayto. Candlewick Press 2008 167p il $15.99

Grades: 1 2 3 4   **398.2**
    1. Folklore
    ISBN 978-0-7636-3479-7; 0-7636-3479-4
                              LC 2007038294

"McBratney offers an attractive collection of 56 short, pithy traditional stories from around the world, including folktales, fables, and Biblical parables. Most are retold in two or three pages, and some are illustrated with small stylized ink drawings, which add a decorative touch and occasionally underscore a selection's humor. The tales are well chosen, and the tellings are concise, nimble, and often amusing." Booklist

McCaughrean, Geraldine, 1951-

The epic of Gilgamesh; retold by Geraldine McCaughrean; illustrated by David Parkins. Eerdmans Bks. for Young Readers 2003 c2002 95p il $18 *

Grades: 5 6 7 8   **398.2**
    1. Gilgamesh 2. Folklore—Iraq
    ISBN 0-8028-5262-9   LC 2003-1086
    Cover title: Gilgamesh the hero

A retelling, based on seventh-century B.C. Assyrian clay tablets, of the wanderings and adventures of the god king, Gilgamesh, who ruled in ancient Mesopotamia (now Iraq) in about 2700 B.C., and of his faithful com-panion, Enkidu

This is "clearly a telling for our time, but one that honors its source. Parkins captures the epic's primitive power and universal emotions in rough, broadly rendered portraits." Horn Book

Grandma Chickenlegs; illustrated by Moira Kemp. Carolrhoda Bks. 1999 unp il $15.95

Grades: K 1 2 3   **398.2**
    1. Folklore—Russia
    ISBN 1-57505-415-9   LC 99-19161

In this variation of the traditional Baba Yaga story, a young girl must rely on the advice of her dead mother and her special doll when her wicked stepmother sends her to get a needle from Grandma Chickenlegs

"McCaughrean's well-paced narrative is rich in imag-ery and humor. . . . Kemp's colored-pencil illustrations are rendered with accessibly childlike simplicity, but she also uses sophisticated composition and perspectives to enhance the drama." Horn Book

McClintock, Barbara, 1955-

Cinderella; retold and illustrated by Barbara McClintock; from the Charles Perrault version. Scholastic Press 2005 32p il $15.99

Grades: 2 3 4   **398.2**
    1. Fairy tales 2. Folklore—France
    ISBN 0-439-56145-0   LC 2003-24883

Although mistreated by her stepmother and stepsisters, Cinderella meets her prince with the help of her fairy godmother

"McClintock's faithful adaptation combines readable text and enchanting pen-and-ink and watercolor illustra-tions filled with minute details of architecture and dress from the era of Louis XIV." SLJ

McClure, Gillian, 1948-

The land of the dragon king and other Korean stories. Frances Lincoln 2008 59p il $19.95

Grades: 2 3 4 5   **398.2**
    1. Folklore—Korea
    ISBN 978-1-84507-805-8; 1-84507-805-5
    Contents: The herdsman and the weaver; Clever Rab-bit; Why the sea is salty; The goblin's magic stick; A bit of shade; Why pigs have snouts; The fierce old dried persimmon; Me first!; The land of the dragon king

"McClure retells and illustrates nine brief folktales in this collection, which also includes an introduction and source list. McClure's pen, ink, and watercolor drawings gracefully wrap themselves around the text, adding detail and flavor. . . . Retold in a lightly humorous vein, there's nonetheless a keen sense of justice underpinning these tales. . . . Related in straightforward yet lively prose, with just enough detail and repetition, this collec-tion is sure to become a read-aloud favorite." SLJ

McDermott, Gerald

Anansi the spider; a tale from the Ashanti; adapted and illustrated by Gerald McDermott. Holt & Co. 1972 unp il $16.95; pa $6.95 *

Grades: K 1 2 3   **398.2**
    1. Folklore—Ghana 2. Ashanti (African people)—Folklore 3. Anansi (Legendary character)
    ISBN 0-8050-0310-X; 0-8050-0311-8 (pa)
    A Caldecott Medal honor book, 1973

The adaptation of this traditional tale of Ghana is based on an animated film by McDermott. It tells of Anansi, a spider, who is saved from terrible fates by his six sons and is unable to decide which of them to re-ward. The solution to his predicament is also an explana-tion for how the moon was put into the sky

This offers "brief poetic text, complemented by geo-metric African folk-style illustrations in pure, bold col-ors." SLJ

McDermott, Gerald—*Continued*

Arrow to the sun; a Pueblo Indian tale; adapted and illustrated by Gerald McDermott. Viking 1974 unp il $16.99; pa $6.99 *

Grades: K 1 2 3   **398.2**
   1. Pueblo Indians—Folklore
   ISBN 0-670-13369-8; 0-14-050211-4 (pa)
   Awarded the Caldecott Medal, 1975

This myth tells how Boy searches for his immortal father, the Lord of the Sun, in order to substantiate his paternal heritage. Shot as an arrow to the sun, Boy passes through the four chambers of ceremony to prove himself. Accepted by his father, he returns to earth to bring the Lord of the Sun's spirit to the world of men

"The simple, brief text—which suggests similar stories in religion and folklore—is amply illustrated in full-page and doublespread pictures. . . . The strong colors and the bold angular forms powerfully accompany the text." Horn Book

Coyote: a trickster tale from the American Southwest; told and illustrated by Gerald McDermott. Harcourt Brace & Co. 1994 unp il $15; pa $6 *

Grades: K 1 2 3   **398.2**
   1. Native Americans—Folklore 2. Coyote (Legendary character)
   ISBN 0-15-220724-4; 0-15-201958-8 (pa)
                       LC 92-32979

"Coyote persuades the crows to help him fly, but he becomes so obnoxious and boastful that they abandon him in midair, so he falls back to earth. Told with playful illustrations against the glowing orange of a desert sky, the humorous Zuni tale explains how Coyote, who once had blue fur, got his dust-colored coat and black-tippped tail." Horn Book Guide

Jabuti the tortoise; a trickster tale from the Amazon; told and illustrated by Gerald McDermott. Harcourt 2001 unp il hardcover o.p. pa $7

Grades: K 1 2 3   **398.2**
   1. Native Americans—Folklore 2. Amazon River valley—Folklore 3. Turtles—Folklore
   ISBN 0-15-200496-3; 0-15-205374-3 (pa)
                       LC 00-11977

All the birds enjoy the song-like flute music of Jabuti, the tortoise, except Vulture who, jealous because he cannot sing, tricks Jabuti into riding his back toward a festival planned by the King of Heaven

"The story succeeds by embracing what McDermott refers to as a universal trickster theme. . . . Utilizing a radiant palette to evoke the brilliance and vitality of the region, McDermott's spreads feature his familiar geometrically drawn characters that seem to vibrate against the lush-green stylized foliage set upon hot-pink backgrounds." SLJ

Musicians of the sun. Simon & Schuster Bks. for Young Readers 1997 unp il $17; pa $6.99 *

Grades: K 1 2 3   **398.2**
   1. Folklore—Mexico
   ISBN 0-689-80706-6; 0-689-93907-3 (pa)
                       LC 96-19891

In this retelling of an Aztec myth, Lord of the Night sends Wind to free the four musicians that the Sun is holding prisoner so they can bring joy to the world

"This work bears the hallmarks of McDermott's style: vivid colors, illustrations informed by cultural iconography and mythology, an engaging story, and complete source notes." Bull Cent Child Books

Pig-Boy; a trickster tale from Hawai'i. Harcourt Children's Books 2009 unp il $16

Grades: PreK K 1 2 3   **398.2**
   1. Folklore—Hawaii 2. Pigs—Folklore
   ISBN 978-0-15-216590-1; 0-15-216590-8
                    LC 2006-35426

The mischievous, shape-shifting Pig-Boy gets in trouble with both the King and Pele, the goddess of fire, but always manages to slip away as his grandmother has told him to do.

"The boldly colored art is dynamic and reflects both the humor of the sprightly text and the author/illustrator's background as an animator in its visual pacing. The tale itself has just enough folkloric elements to convey action, character and setting without bogging down in detail. . . . Good rascally fun." Kirkus

Raven; a trickster tale from the Pacific Northwest; told and illustrated by Gerald McDermott. Harcourt Brace Jovanovich 1993 unp il $16; pa $7

Grades: K 1 2 3   **398.2**
   1. Native Americans—Folklore
   ISBN 0-15-265661-8; 0-15-202449-2 (pa)
                    LC 91-14563

A Caldecott Medal honor book, 1994

Raven, a Pacific Coast Indian trickster, sets out to find the sun

"Raven, whether he appears as a bird or child, is always marked with a distinctive design of clear-cut red, green, and blue on black, sharply contrasting with the softer hues and forms of the backgrounds and the other characters. In this way, Raven is always recognizable, even when he shifts his shape to human form. . . . Read this picture book aloud for the full effect of its simple, rhythmic text and striking artwork." Booklist

Zomo the Rabbit; a trickster tale from West Africa; told and illustrated by Gerald McDermott. Harcourt Brace Jovanovich 1992 unp il $14.95; pa $6 *

Grades: K 1 2 3   **398.2**
   1. Folklore—Africa 2. Rabbits—Folklore
   ISBN 0-15-299967-1; 0-15-201010-6 (pa)
                    LC 91-14558

"Zomo the Rabbit, an African trickster . . . goes to Sky God and requests wisdom. Sky God informs him that he must earn it and assigns him three impossible tasks." Child Book Rev Serv

"Like the spare text, the shapes here are boldly controlled—ideal for sharing with a group of very young children. Because of their rich patterns and sharp color contrasts, the images in the gouache paintings, although simple, never become simplistic." Bull Cent Child Books

McGill, Alice

Sure as sunrise; stories of Bruh Rabbit & his walkin' talkin' friends; illustrated by Don Tate. Houghton Mifflin 2004 48p il $17

Grades: 2 3 4 5   **398.2**

     1. African Americans—Folklore

     ISBN 0-618-21196-9   LC 2003-12289

     Contents: Please don't fling me in the briar patch; Bruh Possum & the snake; How the critters got groceries; Bruh Rabbit's mystery bag; Looking to get married.

     "Drawing on the tales she heard from her African American family and community growing up in rural North Carolina more than 50 years ago, McGill tells five trickster stories with warmth, wit, and simple immediacy that's just right for reading aloud. . . . Based on clay models, the animal characters in human clothes are reminiscent of puppets in the big, clear oil-and-acrylic illustrations; their body language and exaggerated expressions are wonderful." Booklist

Way up and over everything; illustrated by Jude Daly. Houghton Mifflin 2008 unp il $16

Grades: 2 3 4 5   **398.2**

     1. Folklore—United States 2. African Americans—Folklore 3. Slavery—Folklore

     ISBN 978-0-618-38796-0; 0-618-38796-X

                        LC 2003-19384

     In this retelling of a folktale, five Africans escape the horrors of slavery by flying away

     "Daly's delicate and elongated figures, small in scale against the vast watercolor landscapes of the Georgia countryside, present a bird's eye view of the story and suggest the enormity of such an escape." Booklist

McGovern, Ann

Too much noise; illustrated by Simms Taback. Houghton Mifflin 1967 44p il $16; pa $6.95

Grades: K 1 2 3   **398.2**

     1. Folklore

     ISBN 0-395-18110-0; 0-395-62985-3 (pa)

     "The too crowded house of a familiar old tale becomes a too noisy house in this entertaining picture-book story. Bothered by the noises in his house, an old man follows the advice of the village wise man by first acquiring and then getting rid of a cow, donkey, sheep, hen, dog, and cat. Only then can he appreciate how quiet his house is. The simplicity and straightforwardness of the folktale are evident in both the telling of the cumulative story and in the amusing colored illustrations." Booklist

Menchú, Rigoberta

The honey jar; [by] Rigoberta Menchu with Dante Liano; pictures by Domi; translated by David Unger. Groundwood Books/House of Anansi Press 2006 64p il $18.95

Grades: 4 5 6   **398.2**

     1. Mayas—Folklore

     ISBN 978-0-88899-670-1; 0-88899-670-5

     This is a collection of 12 Mayan folktales that the author "heard as a child. The stories range from creation stories and pourquoi tales about animals to selections that reflect a distinctive worldview, a broad awareness of na-

ture, and a sense of humor. Using vivid colors, the naturalistic, folk-art oil paintings . . . illustrate the stories in a manner that reflects the simple spirit and directness of the tellings. An expressive collection that lends insight into the Mayan culture in which Menchu grew up." Booklist

     Includes glossary

The secret legacy; [by] Rigoberta Menchu with Dante Liano; pictures by Domi; translated by David Unger. Groundwood Books/House of Anansi Press 2008 64p il $19.95

Grades: 4 5 6 7 8   **398.2**

     1. Mayas—Folklore 2. Folklore—Guatemala

     ISBN 978-0-88899-896-5; 0-88899-896-1

     "On her first day watching over her Mayan grandfather's cornfields, young Ixkem is invited by the *b'e'n*, spirits in the form of small humans, to visit them underground. They feed her generously and she tells them stories that explain Mayan customs and include bits of folklore. . . . The Mexican artist Domi has provided bright paintings in a naturalistic, folk-art style. The lyrical translation preserves the storyteller's voice." SLJ

Mhlophe, Gcina

African tales; a Barefoot collection; written by Gcina Mhlophe; illustrated by Rachel Griffin. Barefoot Books 2009 95p il map $19.99

Grades: 5 6 7 8   **398.2**

     1. Folklore—Africa

     ISBN 978-1-84686-118-5; 1-84686-118-7

                        LC 2008028042

     "Each of these eight tales is preceded by information and interesting facts about the country from which it originated. A basic map of Africa helps orient readers to the location of the various countries represented. Extensive source notes are appended. . . . There are many choices that could be read aloud or told using a call-and-response format. The book design . . . is a feast for the eyes. Griffin employs a collage technique using colored beads, sewn fabric, and textured papers, and incorporates them into shapes and faces of animals and humans. . . . This compilation contains a wealth of information and will enhance folklore collections." SLJ

     Includes bibliographical references

Miller, Bobbi

Davy Crockett gets hitched; retold by Bobbi Miller; illustrated by Megan Lloyd. Holiday House 2009 unp il $16.95

Grades: K 1 2 3   **398.2**

     1. Crockett, Davy—Legends. 2. Crockett, Sally Ann Thunder Ann Whirlwind—Legends. 3. Crockett, Davy—Legends. 4. Crockett, Sally Ann Thunder Ann Whirlwind—Legends. 5. Folklore—United States 6. Tall tales

     ISBN 978-0-8234-1837-4; 0-8234-1837-5

                        LC 2006050063

     An accidental encounter with a thorn bush on his way to the spring dance has Davy Crockett kicking up his heels and out-dancing even the audacious Miss Sally Ann Thunder Ann Whirlwind.

     "Lloyd's energetic artwork propels the narrative with

Miller, Bobbi—*Continued*

effective use of light and line. . . . The text sings with rich vocabulary, making this tall tale a great choice for reading aloud." Booklist

One fine trade; retold by Bobbi Miller; illustrated by Will Hillenbrand. Holiday House 2009 unp il $16.95

Grades: K 1 2 3   **398.2**

1. Folklore—United States 2. Peddlers and peddling—Folklore 3. Weddings—Folklore

ISBN 978-0-8234-1836-7; 0-8234-1836-7

        LC 2007-25493

Georgy Piney Woods, the best peddler who ever lived, makes several trades so his daughter can buy a wedding dress.

This is an "entertaining romp. . . . The ink and pencil scenes were scanned and digitally manipulated, with colored pencil and gouache additions to the final work. This creates a convincing depth. . . . The outlandish events and droll caricatures are supported by lively language that is full of rhythm and fun to read aloud." SLJ

Milligan, Bryce, 1953-

Brigid's cloak; an ancient Irish story; written by Bryce Milligan; illustrated by Helen Cann. Eerdmans Bks. for Young Readers 2002 unp il $16; pa $8

Grades: K 1 2 3   **398.2**

1. Brigid, Saint, d. ca. 525—Legends 2. Jesus Christ—Nativity 3. Folklore—Ireland

ISBN 0-8028-5224-6; 0-8028-5297-1 (pa)

        LC 2001-40174

Relates a legend about the Irish slave girl who became Saint Brigid, beginning with a celestial song, a mysterious gift, and a prophecy on the night of her birth

"Borders of Celtic designs frame Cann's mixed-media pictures and add both authenticity and wonder to the tale." Booklist

Mitchell, Stephen, 1943-

Genies, meanies, and magic rings; three tales from the Arabian Nights; retold by Stephen Mitchell; illustrations by Tom Pohrt. Walker & Co. 2007 181p il $16.95

Grades: 3 4 5 6   **398.2**

1. Fairy tales 2. Arabs—Folklore

ISBN 978-0-8027-9639-4; 0-8027-9639-7

        LC 2006-27620

A retelling of three tales from the "Arabian Nights:" "Ali Baba and the 40 thieves," "Abu Keer and Abu Seer," and "Aladdin and the magic lamp"

"The retellings are lengthy but tension builds successfully even for those familiar with the stories. Appealing pen-and-ink drawings are sprinkled throughout." SLJ

Iron Hans; a Grimm's fairy tale; retold by Stephen Mitchell; illustrated by Matt Tavares. Candlewick Press 2007 unp il $16.99

Grades: K 1 2 3   **398.2**

1. Fairy tales 2. Folklore—Germany

ISBN 978-0-7636-2160-5; 0-7636-2160-9

        LC 2006047520

With the help of Iron Hans, the wild man of the forest, a young prince makes his own way in the world and wins the hand of a princess

"Clamoring knights, galloping steeds and scenes of palace splendor crowd the pages, which rise in a vertical format as if to stress Iron Hans's nine-foot stature. . . . Complex and muscular, this is a good bet for readers who demand lots of action." Publ Wkly

Mitton, Tony, 1951-

The storyteller's secrets; illustrated by Peter Bailey. David Fickling Books 2010 118p il $15.99

Grades: 4 5 6   **398.2**

1. Folklore 2. Storytelling—Fiction

ISBN 978-0-385-75190-2; 0-385-75190-7

Contents: The woodcutter's daughter; St Brigid's cloak; The seal hunter; The pedlar of Swaffham; Tam Lin; The Map of Marvels; Five fragments

"In a handsome volume profusely illustrated with a mix of silhouettes and vigorous line drawings, Mitton presents verse renditions of European tales and legends. . . . Written in ballad-style quatrains with unforced, natural sounding rhymes and cadences, the stories offer enthralling, easy-to-follow plots with clear themes. . . . Mitton links all of his selections with prose encounters between two marveling children and a mysterious old Storyteller. . . . This gathering will cast the same sort of profound spell on readers and listeners." Booklist

Mollel, Tololwa M. (Tololwa Marti)

Ananse's feast; an Ashanti tale; retold by Tololwa M. Mollel; illustrated by Andrew Glass. Clarion Bks. 1997 31p il $14.95; pa $6.95

Grades: K 1 2 3   **398.2**

1. Anansi (Legendary character) 2. Ashanti (African people)—Folklore 3. Folklore—Ghana

ISBN 0-395-67402-6; 0-618-19598-X (pa)

        LC 95-17358

Unwilling to share his feast, Ananse the spider tricks Akye the turtle so that he can eat all the food himself, but Akye finds a way to get even

"Varied in composition and bright with layers of color, the oil-and-colored-pencil artwork captures the actions, reactions, and emotions of the two main characters with a great sense of playfulness and humor." Booklist

The orphan boy; a Maasai story; illustrated by Paul Morin. Clarion Bks. 1990 unp il hardcover o.p. pa $6.95

Grades: K 1 2 3   **398.2**

1. Masai (African people)—Folklore 2. Folklore—Africa

ISBN 0-89919-985-2; 0-395-72079-6 (pa)

        LC 90-2358

"A solitary old man on the wide plains welcomes into his compound an orphan boy, Kileken, who helps with the work and the cattle and brings prosperity even in times of drought. But when the old man insists on knowing the boy's secret, Kileken returns to his place in the sky. He is the steadily shining star . . . that is the planet Venus." Booklist

"Infused with an aura of mystery, Mollel's compelling story is told skillfully and dramatically. Morin's richly textured paintings, evoking in bold colors an Africa of

Mollel, Tololwa M. (Tololwa Marti)—*Continued*
both parched desert and lush vegetation, are worthy companions." Publ Wkly

Monte, Richard
The dragon of Krakow and other Polish stories.
Frances Lincoln 2008 83p il hardcover o.p. pa
$7.95
Grades: 3 4 5 6   398.2
1. Folklore—Poland
ISBN 978-1-84507-812-6; 1-84507-812-8;
978-1-84507-752-5 (pa); 1-84507-752-0 (pa)
A collection of Polish legends, myths, and lore with
black-and-white illustrations.
"Monte has gathered eight beloved stories in this easy-to-read book. In the title story, a fierce dragon ravages
the city until the king, with the help of a clever shoemaker, comes up with a solution. Life lessons are taught
in a few of the stories. . . . The black-and-white pen-and-ink drawings are amusing and unique. A suitable addition to most fairy-tale and folklore collections." SLJ
Includes bibliographical references

Montes, Marisa, 1951-
Juan Bobo goes to work; a Puerto Rican
folktale; retold by Marisa Montes; illustrated by
Joe Cepeda. HarperCollins Pubs. 2000 unp il
$15.95; lib bdg $15.89 *
Grades: K 1 2 3   398.2
1. Folklore—Puerto Rico
ISBN 0-688-16233-9; 0-688-16234-7 (lib bdg)
                                    LC 99-28799
Although he tries to do exactly as his mother tells
him, foolish Juan Bobo keeps getting things all wrong
"The funny, well-paced retelling smoothly incorporates
Spanish words and phrases. . . . Using bold, bright Caribbean colors, Cepeda's oil paintings amplify Juan's silliness and charm. Brush strokes add texture, and background details establish the Puerto Rican setting."
Booklist
Includes glossary

Morales, Yuyi
Just a minute; a trickster tale and counting book.
Chronicle Books 2003 unp il $15.95 *
Grades: K 1 2 3   398.2
1. Folklore—Mexico 2. Counting 3. Bilingual books—
English-Spanish
ISBN 0-8118-3758-0   LC 2002-151386
In this version of a traditional tale, Senor Calavera arrives at Grandma Beetle's door, ready to take her to the
next life, but after helping her count, in English and
Spanish, as she makes her birthday preparations, he
changes his mind
"Like the text, the rich, lively artwork draws strongly
upon Mexican culture. . . . The splendid paintings and
spirited storytelling—along with useful math and
multicultural elements—augur a long, full life for this
original folktale." Booklist

Morpurgo, Michael
Beowulf; illustrated by Michael Foreman.
Candlewick Press 2006 92p il $17.99 *
Grades: 5 6 7 8   398.2
1. Beowulf 2. Monsters—Folklore 3. Folklore—Europe
ISBN 978-0-7636-3206-9; 0-7636-3206-6
"Morpurgo retells the classic story of the courageous
young warrior . . . who used his brute strength to save
the neighboring Danes, then his own kinsmen, by slaying
two horrible monsters, a sea serpent, and a massive dragon. . . . Many attractive full-page watercolor and pastel
paintings illustrate important action-filled scenes. . . .
This is a fine retelling." SLJ

Hansel and Gretel; retold by Michael Morpurgo;
illustrated by Emma Chichester Clark. Candlewick
Press 2008 c2009 unp il $18.99
Grades: 2 3 4   398.2
1. Fairy tales 2. Folklore—Germany
ISBN 978-0-7636-4012-5; 0-7636-4012-3
                                    LC 2007052335
When they are left in the woods by their parents, Hansel and Gretel find their way home despite an encounter
with a wicked witch
"Leaving the basic framework of the Grimm Brothers'
tale intact, Morpurgo has altered details of the plot, creating a story in which strong familial bonds allow the innocent brother and sister to overcome evil. . . . Folk-art-style paintings, in watercolor with colored-pencil outlines
and facial features, range in size from small decorations
and vertical strips of various widths to full-page scenes."
SLJ

The McElderry book of Aesop's fables;
illustrations by Emma Chichester Clark. Margaret
K. McElderry Books 2005 94p il $19.95 *
Grades: K 1 2   398.2
1. Aesop—Adaptations 2. Fables
ISBN 1-4169-0290-2   LC 2004-58160
First published 2004 in the United Kingdom with title:
The Orchard book of Aesop's fables
Retellings of twenty-one classic Aesop fables, including "The Hare and the Tortoise" and "Belling the Cat,"
in updated language.
"This large, spacious hardcover is perfectly designed
for reading aloud. The text appears in big, clear type on
thick paper, and Clark's gorgeous watercolors show the
characters. . . . Morpurgo's adaptations of 21 short tales
stay true to the tradition of humanlike animal characters
and lessons that eschew heavy philosophizing in favor of
warnings about ordinary folk and their foolishness."
Booklist

Sir Gawain and the Green Knight; as told by
Michael Morpurgo; illustrated by Michael
Foreman. Candlewick Press 2004 114p il $18.99
*
Grades: 5 6 7 8   398.2
1. Arthurian romances 2. Gawain (Legendary character)
ISBN 0-7636-2519-1   LC 2003-65527
The quest of Sir Gawain for the Green Knight teaches
him a lesson in pride, humility, and honor
"Morpurgo's sprightly writing brings out all the humor

Morpurgo, Michael—*Continued*
as well as the horror of the original tale, and Foreman's profuse, evocative watercolor-and-pastel illustrations highlight the drama in each scene." SLJ

Mosel, Arlene
The funny little woman; retold by Arlene Mosel; pictures by Blair Lent. Dutton 1972 unp il pa $5.99 hardcover o.p.
Grades: K 1 2   **398.2**
1. Folklore—Japan
ISBN 0-14-054753-3 (pa)
Awarded the Caldecott Medal, 1973
Based on Lafcadio Hearn's The old woman and her dumpling
While chasing a dumpling, a little lady is captured by wicked creatures from whom she escapes with the means of becoming the richest woman in Japan
"The tale unfolds in a simple tellable style. . . . Using elements of traditional Japanese art, the illustrator has made marvelously imaginative pictures. . . . All the inherent drama and humor of the story are manifest in the illustrations." Horn Book

Tikki Tikki Tembo; retold by Arlene Mosel; illustrated by Blair Lent. Holt & Co. 1968 unp il $16.95; pa $6.95
Grades: K 1 2   **398.2**
1. Folklore—China 2. Personal names—Folklore
ISBN 0-8050-0662-1; 0-312-36748-1 (pa)
A "Chinese folk tale about a first son with a very long name. When Tikki Tikki Tembo-No Sa Rembo-Chari Bari Ruchi-Pip Peri Pembo fell into the well, it took his little brother so long to say his name and get help that Tikki almost drowned." Hodges. Books for Elem Sch Libr
"In this polished version of a story hour favorite, beautifully stylized wash drawings of serene Oriental landscapes are in comic contrast to amusingly visualized folk and the active disasters accruing to the possessor of a 21-syllable, irresistibly chantable name." Best Books of the Year, 1968

Mueller, Doris L.
The best nest; by Doris L. Mueller; illustrated by Sherry Neidigh. Sylvan Dell 2008 unp il $16.95; pa $8.95
Grades: 2 3 4   **398.2**
1. Birds—Nests 2. Folklore—Great Britain 3. Birds—Folklore
ISBN   978-1-934359-09-9;   1-934359-09-2;
978-1-934359-25-9 (pa); 1-934359-25-4 (pa)
LC 2007-935084
In this retelling of an old English folktale featuring birds native to the U.S., Magpie explains to the other birds how to build a nest. Some birds are impatient and fly off without listening to all the instructions, however. That is why, to this day, birds' nests come in different shapes and sizes
"The author provides support for additional activities, information about each bird, 'bird math' (problems based upon the number of broods and eggs for each species), bird care, and a 'match the nest' activity. Illustrations show each bird in mixed media with watercolor and pen and ink details." SLJ

Muth, Jon J.
Stone soup; retold and illustrated by Jon J. Muth. Scholastic Press 2003 unp il $16.95 *
Grades: K 1 2 3   **398.2**
1. Folklore 2. China—Fiction
ISBN 0-439-33909-X   LC 2002-3776
"Three Zen monks arrive in a Chinese mountain village where hard times have made villagers distrustful of strangers and selfish toward one another. Undeterred by a lack of welcome, the monks set about preparing dinner soup, which . . . draws the villagers from their sheltered homes with ingredients to enrich the pot, thereby reinvigorating the community." Booklist
"Muth's muted blue-and-gray watercolors are ideally suited to portraying the inhospitable village. . . . His respect for Chinese people and their culture makes this serving of fusion cuisine delicious and satisfying." Horn Book

Myers, Christopher
Lies and other tall tales; collected by Zora Neale Hurston; adapted and illustrated by Christopher Myers. HarperCollins Pub. 2005 unp il $15.99; lib bdg $16.89   **398.2**
1. Hurston, Zora Neale, 1891-1960—Adaptations 2. African Americans—Folklore 3. Tall tales
ISBN 0-06-000655-2; 0-06-000656-0 (lib bdg)
LC 2004-22252
"Myers has adapted and illustrated some of the wild, very short, wicked stories collected by . . . Zora Neale Hurston. . . . True to the spirit of the tall-tale oral tradition, Myers' quiltlike pictures in paper and fabric collage are minimalist and exaggerated, magical and mundane. . . . Perfect for sharing with many age groups." Booklist

Myers, Tim, 1953-
The furry-legged teapot; retold by Tim Myers; illustrated by Robert McGuire. Marshall Cavendish Children 2007 unp il $16.99
Grades: 1 2 3 4   **398.2**
1. Folklore—Japan
ISBN 978-0-7614-5295-9   LC 2005016935
In ancient Japan, a young tanuki, a raccoon dog that can change shapes, becomes stuck in the form of a teapot
"McGuire's acrylic spreads place the farmer's hut and monk's quarters in a lush Japanese countryside with mountains in the background. . . . Myers provides source notes for his entertaining version of the tanuki-turned-teapot story." SLJ

Nanji, Shenaaz, 1954-
Indian tales; written by Shenaaz Nanji; illustrated by Christopher Corr. Barefoot Books 2007 92p il $19.99
Grades: 3 4 5 6   **398.2**
1. Folklore—India
ISBN 978-1-846860-83-6   LC 2006100357
"This anthology presents eight fluid retellings of folktales from different Indian states. . . . An introduction offers a brief overview of the country's history. . . . Each folktale is preceded by a note with facts about the

Nanji, Shenaaz, 1954-—*Continued*

state from which it originated, including explanations of festivals or terms that appear in the text. Illustrations and page borders support the texts perfectly as the folk-style paintings reflect colors of rural life." SLJ

Nesbit, E. (Edith), 1858-1924

Jack and the beanstalk; [by] E. Nesbit; illustrated by Matt Tavares. Candlewick Press 2006 unp il $16.99

Grades: 2 3 4   **398.2**

1. Fairy tales 2. Giants—Folklore 3. Folklore—Great Britain

ISBN 0-7636-2124-2   LC 2005050190

After climbing to the top of a huge beanstalk, a boy uses his quick wits to outsmart a giant and gain a fortune for himself and his mother

"First published in Nesbit's *The Old Nursery Stories* (1908), this lively retelling adds character and wit to the timeless fairy tale, and Tavares' large pencil-and-watercolor illustrations, in shades of dusky brown and green, are a fitting accompaniment to the young boy's scary encounter with the giant." Booklist

Nishizuka, Koko

The beckoning cat; based on a Japanese folktale; illustrated by Rosanne Litzinger. Holiday House 2009 unp il $16.95

Grades: K 1 2 3   **398.2**

1. Folklore—Japan 2. Cats—Folklore

ISBN 978-0-8234-2051-3; 0-8234-2051-5

LC 2008007266

A retelling of the traditional Japanese tale describing the origins of the beckoning cat and how it came to be a symbol of good luck.

Litzinger's "full-bleed pictures—a highly tactile mix of watercolor, colored pencil, ink and gouache—combine comfortably rounded, stylized forms and a gently shaded palette to evoke a contemplative mood." Publ Wkly

Norman, Howard

Between heaven and earth; bird tales from around the world; illustrated by Leo & Diane Dillon. Harcourt 2004 78p il lib bdg $22

Grades: 4 5 6 7   **398.2**

1. Folklore 2. Birds—Folklore

ISBN 0-15-201982-0   LC 2003-7874

"Gulliver books"

A collection of folktales from around the world, all of which have a bird as a main character

This is "a collection of stories that are rich in cultural references from the lands of their origins. . . . The Dillons' luminous watercolor-and-pencil illustrations, detailed with patterns drawn from each tale's culture of origin, will draw readers and listeners back to the stories." Booklist

Oberman, Sheldon, 1949-2004

Solomon and the ant; and other Jewish folktales; retold by Sheldon Oberman; introduction and commentary by Peninnah Schram. Boyds Mills Press 2006 165p $19.95

Grades: 5 6 7 8   **398.2**

1. Jews—Folklore

ISBN 1-59078-307-7   LC 2005020115

"This collection of 43 traditional Jewish stories is authoritative as well as immensely entertaining. . . . The stories, from both Ashkenazi and Sephardic traditions, are arranged more or less chronologically—from biblical days through the talmudic period to more contemporary times. There are legends, medieval fables, trickster tales, and more. . . . The stories, wonderful for storytelling and sharing, are accessible even to listeners younger than the target audience, and the notes and commentary will provide older children with context and history." Booklist

Includes bibliographical references

Olson, Arielle North, 1932-

Ask the bones: scary stories from around the world; selected and retold by Arielle North Olson and Howard Schwartz; illustrated by David Linn. Viking 1999 145p il hardcover o.p. pa $5.99

Grades: 4 5 6 7   **398.2**

1. Folklore

ISBN 0-670-87581-3; 0-14-230140-X (pa)

LC 98-19108

Contents: The haunted forest; The murky secret; Next-of-kin; The bloody fangs; Ask the bones; The four-footed horror; Beginning with the ears; Fiddling with fire; The Laplander's drum; A night of terror; Nowhere to hide; The handkerchief; The mousetrap; The speaking head; The dripping cutlass; The black snake; The hand of death; The invisible guest; A trace of blood; The bridal gown; The greedy man and the goat; The evil eye

A collection of scary folktales from countries around the world including China, Russia, Spain, and the United States

"David Linn's bone-chilling black-and-white illustrations . . . will stay with the reader long after the book is closed. Excellent for reading aloud, this collection will satisfy even jaded genre fans." Booklist

Includes bibliographical references

More bones; scary stories from around the world; selected and retold by Arielle North Olson and Howard Schwartz; illustrated by E.M. Gist. Viking 2008 162p il $15.99

Grades: 4 5 6 7   **398.2**

1. Folklore

ISBN 978-0-670-06339-0; 0-670-06339-8

Contents: A story to tell; Courting Astriah; The shaggy gray arm; The prince's fate; The headless horseman; The knife; The werewolf in the forest; The secret; The severed head; The dangerous dead; The haunted bell; The gruesome test; The enchanted cave; The witch of the woods; Wishes gone awry; The ghost of the rainbow maiden; The wife's tale; Youth without age; The haunted violin; The evil sea ghost; The peasant's revenge; The wizard's apprentice

"This tour of the world's shadowy corners is full of dark wizards, unkind witches, and other untrustworthy

Olson, Arielle North, 1932-—*Continued*

creatures. . . . The 22 tales, as retold by Olson and Schwartz, give a vivid glimpse into unfamiliar, unnerving territory. . . . The atmospheric illustrations, while not intricately detailed, are somewhat startling in their imagery." Booklist

Orgel, Doris, 1929-

Doctor All-Knowing; a folk tale from the Brothers Grimm; retold by Doris Orgel; illustrated by Alexandra Boiger. Atheneum Books for Young Readers 2008 unp il $16.99
Grades: PreK K 1 2   398.2
  1. Folklore—Germany
  ISBN 978-1-4169-1246-0; 1-4169-1246-0
  "A Richard Jackson book"
Desperate to provide enough food for himself and his daughter, a poor man sets himself up as Doctor All-Knowing and is soon called upon by a rich man to find a thief.
  "Consistent in style, yet varied in size, composition, and perspective, the watercolor paintings use comic exaggeration to good effect. Vivid in both the telling and art." Booklist

Osborne, Mary Pope, 1949-

American tall tales; wood engravings by Michael McCurdy. Knopf 1991 115p il map $22 *
Grades: 3 4 5 6   398.2
  1. Tall tales 2. Folklore—United States
  ISBN 0-679-80089-1   LC 89-37235
  Contents: Davy Crockett; Sally Ann Thunder Ann Whirlwind; Johnny Appleseed; Stormalong; Mose; Febold Feboldson; Pecos Bill; John Henry; Paul Bunyan
  A collection of tall tales about such American folk heroes as Sally Ann Thunder Ann Whirlwind, Pecos Bill, John Henry, and Paul Bunyan
  "As tantalizing as Osborne's storytelling are McCurdy's . . . elaborate, full-color wood engravings, which in their robust stylization dramatically render the grandeur of these engrossing yarns." Publ Wkly
  Includes bibliographical references

The brave little seamstress; written by Mary Pope Osborne; illustrated by Giselle Potter. Atheneum Bks. for Young Readers 2002 unp il $16 paperback o.p. *
Grades: K 1 2 3   398.2
  1. Fairy tales 2. Folklore
  ISBN 0-689-84486-7; 1-4169-1620-2 (pa)
                   LC 2001-33018
  "An Anne Schwartz book"
  A seamstress who kills seven flies with one blow outwits the king and, with the help of a kind knight, becomes a wise and kind queen
  "The whimsically perky, generous text is perfectly matched to the illustrations, in Potter's signature ink-gouache-gesso-water-colors, which affix just the right amount of sauciness to the cheeky heroine." Booklist

Kate and the beanstalk; written by Mary Pope Osborne; illustrated by Giselle Potter. Atheneum Bks. for Young Readers 2000 unp il pa $7.99 *
Grades: K 1 2 3   398.2
  1. Fairy tales 2. Folklore—Great Britain 3. Giants—Folklore
  ISBN 0-689-82550-1; 1-4169-0818-8 (pa)
                   LC 99-27029
  "An Anne Schwartz book"
  In this version of the classic tale, a girl climbs to the top of a giant beanstalk, where she uses her quick wits to outsmart a giant and make her and her mother's fortune
  "The text is straightforward but punctuated by some delicious dialogue. . . . Using a variety of mediums—pencil, ink, gouache, and watercolor—the illustrations are executed in Potter's signature folk-art style. They are immediate, innovative, and just the right size for story hours." Booklist

Osborne, Will

Sleeping Bobby; [by] Will Osborne and Mary Pope Osborne; illustrated by Giselle Potter. Atheneum Books for Young Readers 2005 unp il $16.95 *
Grades: K 1 2 3   398.2
  1. Fairy tales 2. Folklore—Germany
  ISBN 0-689-87668-8   LC 2004-06346
  "An Anne Schwartz Book"
  A retelling of the Grimm tale featuring a handsome prince who is put into a deep sleep by a curse until he is awakened by the kiss of a brave princess.
  This "is written in a breezy, readable style, and most details of the original story have been included. . . . Potter's folk-style characters are dressed in Elizabethan garb with details such as puffed sleeves, high lace collars, and ruffs." SLJ

Ōtsuka, Yūzō, 1921-

Suho's white horse; a Mongolian legend; retold by Yuzo Otsuka; illustrated by Suekichi Akaba; translated by Richard McNamara and Peter Howlett; instrumental by Li Bo. R.I.C. 2007 47p il $17.95
Grades: 2 3 4   398.2
  1. Folklore—Mongolia 2. Horses—Folklore 3. Musical instruments—Folkore
  ISBN 1-74126-021-3
  Relates how the tragic parting of a boy and his horse led to the creation of the horsehead fiddle, or *morin khuur*, of the Mongolian shepherds.
  "First published 40 years ago in Japan . . . this big, beautiful picture book tells [a] stirring legend. . . . Children will love [Akaba's] clear watercolor paintings. . . . This includes an audio CD that features music played by a *morin khuur* master." Booklist

Palatini, Margie

Lousy rotten stinkin' grapes; illustrated by Barry Moser. Simon & Schuster Books for Young Readers 2009 unp il $15.99 *

Grades: PreK K 1 2   **398.2**

1. Aesop—Adaptations 2. Folklore 3. Fables 4. Foxes—Folklore

ISBN 978-0-689-80246-1; 0-689-80246-3

LC 2007015727

Retells the fable of a frustrated fox that, after many tries to reach a high bunch of grapes, decides they must be sour anyway.

"Moser's wonderful watercolor illustrations of the doubting animals executing Fox's convoluted plans are rich in humor. . . . Matched by a text that rolls off the tongue and is full of action and repetitive phrases, the book is a delight." SLJ

Park, Janie Jaehyun

The love of two stars; a Korean legend; retold and pictures by Janie Jaehyun Park. Groundwood Books 2005 unp il $16.95

Grades: K 1 2 3   **398.2**

1. Folklore—Korea 2. Stars—Folklore

ISBN 0-88899-672-1

"High in the starry sky, Kyonu works as a farmer and Jingnyo as a weaver. After they fall in love, they neglect their work, leaving the people hungry and ragged, so the king allows them to meet only on the seventh day of the seventh moon month. When that day comes, however, they can't reach one another, and their tears flood the earth. Finally, the birds . . . fly up and make a bridge across the Milky Way to enable the lovers to embrace. Park's unframed double-page illustrations, painted on gessoed paper to add attractive texture, show the romantic costume drama of the Korean lovers together and apart. At the same time, the rich, dark-blue mystery of the night sky, with stars and swirling curves, will touch kids everywhere." Booklist

Partridge, Elizabeth

Kogi's mysterious journey; adapted by Elizabeth Partridge; illustrated by Aki Sogabe. Dutton Children's Bks. 2003 unp il $17.99

Grades: K 1 2 3   **398.2**

1. Artists—Folklore 2. Fishes—Folklore 3. Folklore—Japan

ISBN 0-525-47078-6

Kogi paints the shore of Lake Biwa, but is unable to capture the vigor and beauty that inspire him. One day, Kogi wades into the water to release a fish, and unable to resist follows in its wake, eventually becoming a fish himself, and learning what it is to be a fish in the lake

"Partridge's spare, poetic recasting of a Japanese folktale ends with the artist and his creations coming to life again as fish. Dignified and handsome, Sogabe's carefully composed cut-paper art employs muted colors to bring Kogi's inner and outer worlds to life." SLJ

Paterson, Katherine

Parzival; the quest of the Grail Knight; retold by Katherine Paterson. Lodestar Bks. 1998 127p hardcover o.p. pa $5.99

Grades: 5 6 7 8   **398.2**

1. Arthurian romances

ISBN 0-525-67579-5; 0-14-130573-8 (pa)

LC 97-23891

"From the thirteenth-century epic poem by Wolfram von Eschenbach. This retelling is based on A.T. Hatto's English translation"—Publisher

A retelling of the Arthurian legend in which Parzival, unaware of his noble birth, comes of age through his quest for the Holy Grail

"Nearly 800 years old, the story has freshness, humor, grace, and depth. . . . Paterson clarifies much of the Christian doctrine that is the basis of the story, but she is never dull or pedantic." SLJ

The tale of the mandarin ducks; illustrated by Leo & Diane Dillon. Lodestar Bks. 1989 unp il hardcover o.p. pa $6.99

Grades: 1 2 3   **398.2**

1. Folklore—Japan 2. Ducks—Folklore

ISBN 0-525-67283-4; 0-14-055739-3 (pa)

LC 88-30484

"A Japanese fairy tale, in picture-book format, about a Mandarin duck caught and caged at the whim of a wealthy Japanese lord. Separated from his mate, the bird languishes in captivity until a compassionate servant girl sets him free. The lord sentences the girl and her beloved to death, but they in turn are freed and rewarded with happiness." Booklist

"Paterson's story is rich with magic, compassion and love. The Dillons' elegantly detailed watercolor and pastel drawings, in the style of 18th-century Japanese woodcuts, are exquisite." Publ Wkly

Paye, Won-Ldy

Head, body, legs; a story from Liberia; retold by Won-Ldy Paye & Margaret H. Lippert; illustrated by Julie Paschkis. Holt & Co. 2002 unp il $16.95; pa $7.95 *

Grades: K 1 2 3   **398.2**

1. Folklore—Liberia

ISBN 0-8050-6570-9; 0-8050-7890-8 (pa)

LC 00-44856

In this tale from the Dan people of Liberia, Head, Arms, Body, and Legs learn that they do better when they work together

"This simple fable about working together is told in a straightforward text; humor is inherent in the situation. Enticing illustrations in ripe fruit colors enhance the strange, silly tale." Horn Book Guide

Mrs. Chicken and the hungry crocodile; [by] Won-Ldy Paye & Margaret H. Lippert; illustrated by Julie Paschkis. Holt & Co. 2003 unp il $16.95 *

Grades: K 1 2 3   **398.2**

1. Folklore—Liberia 2. Chickens—Folklore 3. Crocodiles—Folklore

ISBN 0-8050-7047-8   LC 2002-1755

Paye, Won-Ldy—*Continued*

"A version of this story was previously published in Why Leopard Has Spots: Dan Stories from Liberia by Won-Ldy Paye and Margaret H. Lippert, illustrated by Ashley Bryan, by Fulcrum Publishing, Inc., Golden, Colorado, 1998"

When a crocodile captures Mrs. Chicken and takes her to an island to fatten her up, clever Mrs. Chicken claims that she can prove they are sisters and that, therefore, the crocodile shouldn't eat her

"Told in straightforward language this trickster tale is smart and funny. . . . The stylized gouache artwork is strong and streamlined. . . . The flat paintings recall folk art, and Crocodile's checkerboard skin reflects the patterns found in her home." SLJ

The talking vegetables; retold by Won-Ldy Paye and Margaret H. Lippert; illustrated by Julie Paschkis. Henry Holt 2006 unp il $16.95 *
Grades: K 1 2 3   **398.2**
  1. Anansi (Legendary character) 2. Folklore—West Africa 3. Vegetables—Folklore
  ISBN 978-0-8050-7742-1; 0-8050-7742-1
                     LC 2005019757
After Spider refuses to help the villagers plant the vegetables, he is in for a surprise when he goes to pick some for himself

"From the Dan people of northeastern Liberia comes this traditional tale. . . . Paschkis's brightly colored folk-art illustrations . . . show the villagers to be an elephant, a hen, a crocodile, a leopard, a monkey, a snake, and a butterfly. . . . Read aloud, this simple but solid moralistic tale will delight youngsters and make them want to participate in the telling." SLJ

Penner, Lucille Recht

Dragons; illustrated by Peter Scott. Random House 2004 42p il hardcover o.p. pa $3.99
Grades: 3 4 5   **398.2**
  1. Dragons 2. Folklore
  ISBN 0-307-26417-2; 0-307-46417-3 (pa)
                     LC 2003-12427
"A Stepping Stone book"
Contents: Dragon myth; Scaly and scary
Relates myths about dragons from different countries, including where they live, what they eat, and how they look, as well as how the myths may have developed

"Carefully differentiating between reality and myth, the author intersperses bits of dragon lore . . . through the text. . . . Color illustrations showing different types of dragons add interest." Booklist

Perrault, Charles, 1628-1703

Cinderella; or, The little glass slipper; a free translation from the French of Charles Perrault; with pictures by Marcia Brown. Scribner 1954 unp il $16; pa $5.99
Grades: K 1 2 3   **398.2**
  1. Folklore—France 2. Fairy tales
  ISBN 0-684-12676-1; 0-689-81474-7 (pa)
  Awarded the Caldecott Medal, 1955
This is the classic story of the poor, good-natured girl who works for her selfish step-sisters until a fairy god-

mother transforms her into a beautiful 'princess' for just one night

"With soft, delicate colors and lines that subtly suggest, Miss Brown creates a thoroughly fairyland atmosphere, at the same time recreating the sophistication of the French Court with its golden coach, canopied bed, dazzling chandeliers, liveried footmen, curled and pompadoured ladies, and peruked (bewigged) courtiers." Libr J

Puss in boots; illustrated by Fred Marcellino; translated by Malcolm Arthur. Farrar, Straus & Giroux 1990 unp il $16; pa $8.95
Grades: K 1 2 3   **398.2**
  1. Folklore—France 2. Fairy tales 3. Cats—Folklore
  ISBN 0-374-36160-6; 0-374-46034-5 (pa)
                     LC 90-82136
A Caldecott Medal honor book, 1991

"Opulently designed and handsomely illustrated, this picture book provides a fitting showcase for Perrault's artful tale of deceit and resourcefulness. Unsullied by type, the striking front of the book features a close-up portrait of the cat's face. Befitting a fairy tale, the artwork inside is suffused with a golden light that proclaims the story to be from a sunnier, more dreamlike world." Booklist

Philip, Neil

Horse hooves and chicken feet: Mexican folktales; selected by Neil Philip; illustrated by Jacqueline Mair. Clarion Bks. 2003 83p il $19
Grades: 4 5 6 7   **398.2**
  1. Folklore—Mexico
  ISBN 0-618-19463-0   LC 2002-154886
  Contents: The flea; The story of the sun and the moon; The tailor who sold his soul to the Devil; The hog; Pedro the trickster; The shadow; Horse hooves and chicken feet; The seven oxen; The mule drivers who lost their feet; The two Marias; The priest who had a glimpse of glory; The brave widow; The endless tale; Cinder Juan
This is a "selection of 14 folktales from Mexico and people of Mexican descent from the American Southwest. The stories are simply yet effectively retold. . . . Adding considerably to the overall appeal of the book are Mair's exuberant illustrations, accomplished in the style of Mexican folk art." Booklist
Includes bibliographical references

The pirate princess and other fairy tales; by Neil Philip; illustrated by Mark Weber. Arthur A. Levine Books 2005 88p il $19.99 *
Grades: 4 5 6 7   **398.2**
  1. Jewish legends 2. Fairy tales
  ISBN 0-590-10855-7   LC 2004-16949
  Contents: The pirate princess; The fixer; The gem prince; The treasure; The merchant and the poor man; The turkey prince; The lost princess
This "volume contains seven fairy tales adapted from the stories written by seventeenth-century Hasidic rabbi Nahman ben Simha. . . . An informative four-page introduction discusses Nahman and his storytelling. The lively collection of varied tales begins with the story of a princess who turns pirate to escape unwanted suitors and re-

Philip, Neil—*Continued*

join the man she loves. Several of the other stories share elements of adventure, true love, promises, quests, and fortune. . . . Weber's many gouache paintings have the stylistic feeling of Chagall. . . . They capture the wit, drama, and occasional comedy of the tales." Booklist

Includes bibliographical references

Pinkney, Jerry, 1939-

The little red hen. Dial Books for Young Readers 2006 unp il $16.99 *

Grades: K 1 2 3   398.2
  1. Folklore 2. Chickens—Folklore
  ISBN 0-8037-2935-9   LC 2005-13301

A newly illustrated edition of the classic fable of the hen who is forced to do all the work of baking bread and of the animals who learn a bitter lesson from it.

This is "a lush, light-filled rendition of a folktale staple. . . . The animal's names appear in color-coded font (red for the hen, brown for the dog, etc.), making it extra-easy even for pre-readers to chime in, and the glorious, generous paintings are a real gift." SLJ

Little Red Riding Hood; [written and illustrated by] Jerry Pinkney. Little, Brown 2007 unp il $16.99 *

Grades: PreK K   398.2
  1. Fairy tales 2. Folklore—Germany 3. Wolves—Folklore
  ISBN 978-0-316-01355-0; 0-316-01355-2
                                    LC 2006025291

A sweet little girl meets a hungry wolf in the forest while on her way to visit her grandmother.

This is a "delightful, old-fashioned version of a familiar tale. . . . With lively detail . . . and lots of pattern and colors, Pinkney's watercolors show the predator in nightcap and glasses under Grandmother's patchwork quilt." Booklist

Pirotta, Saviour

The McElderry book of Grimms' fairy tales; retold by Saviour Pirotta; illustrated by Emma Clark. Margaret K. McElderry Books 2006 c2002 126p il $19.95

Grades: 2 3 4   398.2
  1. Grimm, Jacob, 1785-1863—Adaptations 2. Fairy tales 3. Folklore—Germany
  ISBN 1-4169-1798-5

First published 2002 in the United Kingdom with title: The sleeping princess and other fairy tales from Grimm

Contents: Sleeping Beauty: the story of Briar Rose; Magic gingerbread house: the story of Hansel and Gretel; Magic bear and the handsome prince: the story of Snow White and Rose Red; Golden-haired girl in the tower: the story of Rapunzel; Little mouse and lazy cat: the story of the cat and mouse in partnership; Princess and the seven dwarves: the story of Snow White; The swans and the brave princess: the story of the six swans; The naughty princess and the frog: the story of the frog prince; Girl who spun straw into gold: the story of Rumpelstiltskin; Twelve dancing princesses: the story of the shoes that were danced to pieces

"An appealing collection of 10 fairy tales. . . . Pirotta writes like a storyteller, with great imagery and description, and the lively stories read aloud beautifully. . . . Clark's dark, twisty branches in the forest enhance the mood of this story. The large typeface, generous use of white space, and overall design make this book one children can read themselves, and the artist's expressive illustrations contribute to the appeal." SLJ

Polacco, Patricia

Luba and the wren. Philomel Bks. 1999 unp il hardcover o.p. pa $6.99 *

Grades: K 1 2 3   398.2
  1. Fairy tales 2. Folklore—Russia 3. Birds—Folklore
  ISBN 0-399-23168-4; 0-698-11922-3 (pa)
                                    LC 98-16353

In this variation on the story of "The Fisherman and His Wife," a young Ukrainian girl must repeatedly return to the wren she has rescued to relay her parents' increasingly greedy demands

"Polacco's signature illustrations are lush and vibrant. The regal colors of royal blue and crimson play against deep green, dappled brown, and ocher of the natural world." SLJ

Poole, Amy Lowry

How the rooster got his crown; retold and illustrated by Amy Lowry Poole. Holiday House 1999 unp il $15.95 *

Grades: K 1 2 3   398.2
  1. Folklore—China 2. Roosters—Folklore
  ISBN 0-8234-1389-6   LC 98-12311

In the early days of the world, when the sun refuses to come out for fear of a skillful archer's arrows, a small rooster saves the day by coaxing the sun out with his crowing

"The illustrations reflect the traditions of ancient scroll paintings; the pacing of the story is synchronized with the pictures so that the visual and verbal elements form a seamless unit." Horn Book Guide

Princess stories; a classic illustrated edition; compiled by Cooper Edens. Chronicle Books 2004 133p il $19.95

Grades: 2 3 4   398.2
  1. Fairy tales 2. Folklore
  ISBN 0-8118-4032-8   LC 2003-20890

Contents: The princess and the pea; Rapunzel; The frog prince; Cinderella; Sleeping Beauty; Snow White and the seven dwarfs; The little mermaid; Beauty and the beast

"This edition of classic princess stories showcases artists from the Golden Age of Illustration, roughly the 1880s to the 1920s. . . . Arthur Rackham, Walter Crane, Jesse Wilcox Smith, Charles Robinson, Kay Nielsen, and Edmund Dulac are among the American and European artists represented. The edition is rich in language, tone, and picture and despite the disparate nature of each artist's style, it somehow comes together as a classic whole." SLJ

Pringle, Laurence P.

Imagine a dragon; [by] Laurence Pringle; illustrated by Eujin Kim Neilan. Boyds Mills Press 2008 unp il $16.95

Grades: 3 4 5   398.2

1. Dragons

ISBN 978-1-56397-328-4; 1-56397-328-6

LC 2007017575

This is a history of dragons in various world cultures

"The book is interesting with lots of materials without being overwhelming. It provides a good introduction to dragon myths in world literature. The pictures, done in acrylic, are strong and powerful." Libr Media Connect

Pullman, Philip, 1946-

Aladdin and the enchanted lamp; retold by Philip Pullman; illustrated by Sophy Williams. Arthur A. Levine Books 2005 67p il $16.95 *

Grades: 3 4 5   398.2

1. Fairy tales 2. Arabs—Folklore

ISBN 0-439-69255-5   LC 2004-8586

Recounts the tale of a poor tailor's son who becomes a wealthy prince with the help of a magic lamp he finds in an enchanted cave

"Pullman's spin on Aladdin's serendipitous adventures is satisfyingly festooned with exotic vocabulary and details. He also enlivens the telling with knowing wit. . . . Williams' numerous paintings follow Pullman's lead, with a bazaar of burnished colors and dramatic, imagination-tickling scenes." Booklist

Puttapipat, Niroot

The musicians of Bremen; a brothers Grimm tale; retold and illustrated by Niroot Puttapipat. Candlewick Press 2005 unp il $15.99

Grades: K 1 2 3   398.2

1. Folklore—Germany 2. Animals—Folklore

ISBN 0-7636-2758-5   LC 2005-46907

While on their way to Bremen, four aging animals who are no longer of any use to their masters find a new home after outwitting a gang of robbers

"Puttipipat makes music the strong focus of this lively version of the old Grimm folktale. . . . The dramatic ink-and-watercolor illustrations show the characters as real barnyard animals." Booklist

Quattlebaum, Mary, 1958-

Sparks fly high; the legend of Dancing Point; retold by Mary Quattlebaum; pictures by Leonid Gore. Farrar, Straus & Giroux 2006 unp il $16

Grades: K 1 2 3   398.2

1. Dance—Folklore 2. Devil—Folklore 3. Contests—Folklore 4. Folklore—Virginia

ISBN 978-0-374-34452-8; 0-374-34452-3

"Melanie Kroupa Books"

When Colonel Lightfoot and the devil hold a lengthy dance contest to see who will control a plot of land along the James River in Virginia, the result is a surprise for both participants

"Gore's textured illustrations convey the story's energy and comedy in beautifully composed scenes. . . . What really shines here, though, are the folksy words, which have all the infectious rhythm of a country dance." Booklist

Rapunzel and other magic fairy tales; selected and illustrated by Henriette Sauvant; translated by Anthea Bell. Trafalgar Square 2008 157p il $15.95

Grades: 5 6 7 8   398.2

1. Fairy tales 2. Folklore

ISBN 1-4052-2702-8

Contents: Rapunzel; Jack and the beanstalk; The master cat, or Puss in boots; The sea rabbit; The iron stove; Cinderella, or The little glass slipper; The Bremen town band; The girl with no hands; The drummer; Mother Holle; The wishing-table, the gold-donkey and the cudgel in the sack; The frog king, or Iron Henry; The goosegirl; Hansel and Gretel

"Sauvant has selected 14 tales of German, English, and French origin, many of them written down by the Grimm brothers. While most of them are familiar . . . others will be unknown to most readers. . . . The illustrations, which range in size from tiny fillers to full-page and double-page pictures, appear to be painted in watercolor or acrylic on a textured surface. While some are painted in classic fairy-tale style, others are best described as surreal. . . . The sophistication of both stories and artwork makes this collection most suitable for older readers." SLJ

Rascol, Sabina I.

The impudent rooster; adapted by Sabina I. Rascol; illustrated by Holly Berry. Dutton Children's Books 2004 unp il $16.99 *

Grades: K 1 2 3   398.2

1. Roosters—Folklore 2. Folklore—Romania

ISBN 0-525-47179-0   LC 2003-53141

"From a Romanian story by Ion Creanga"

Using his amazing swallowing ability, a rooster foils the evil plans of a greedy nobleman and brings back riches to his poor master.

"The language flows smoothly and reads aloud well. The large folk-art paintings, done in watercolors and colored pencils, depict brightly clothed characters, detailed backdrops, and a hero who grows in stature along with his deeds." SLJ

Ray, Jane

Snow White. Candlewick Press 2009 unp il $19.99

Grades: 3 4 5   398.2

1. Pop-up books 2. Fairy tales 3. Folklore—Germany

ISBN 978-0-7636-4473-4; 0-7636-4473-0

LC 2009007774

Retells, in six dioramas with accompanying text, the tale of the beautiful princess whose lips were red as blood, skin was white as snow, and hair was black as ebony.

"Unusual paper engineering makes this a particularly memorable version of the familiar tale. . . . Birds, squirrels, and other wildlife join viewers in looking through a die-cut screen of trees (or in interior scenes an archway) at gracefully posed, richly clad figures. The jewel-like colors, as well as Ray's almond-eyed Snow White and dusky-skinned Prince, give the tale an otherworldly air." SLJ

Robbins, Ruth

Baboushka and the three kings; illustrated by Nicolas Sidjakov; adapted from a Russian folk tale. Houghton Mifflin 1960 unp il $16; pa $6.95

Grades: 1 2 3 4   **398.2**

    1. Folklore—Russia 2. Christmas—Folklore

    ISBN 0-395-27673-X; 0-395-42647-2 (pa)

    Awarded The Caldecott Medal, 1961

    First published by Parnassus Press

A retelling of the Christmas legend about the old woman who declined to accompany the three kings on their search for the Christ Child and has ever since then searched for the Child on her own. Each year as she renews her search she leaves gifts at the homes she visits, acting, in this respect, as a Russian equivalent to Santa Claus

"Mystery and dignity are in the retelling. . . . At the end of the book is the story in verse set to original music." Horn Book

Rogasky, Barbara, 1933-

The golem; a version; illustrated by Trina Schart Hyman. Holiday House 1996 96p il $18.95 *

Grades: 4 5 6 7   **398.2**

    1. Jews—Folklore 2. Monsters—Folklore

    ISBN 0-8234-0964-3   LC 94-13040

This is "the legend of the golem—a monster created of clay—who, under the guidance of the chief rabbi of Prague, rescued the Jews from persecution by anti-Semitic Christians in the late 16th century. Rogasky's strong storytelling skills are evident. . . . Hyman's colorful, fairy tale-like illustrations bring the story to life." SLJ

Rohmer, Harriet

Uncle Nacho's hat; adapted by Harriet Rohmer; illustrations by Veg Reisberg; Spanish version, Rosalma Zubizarreta. Children's Bk. Press 1989 31p il pa $7.95 hardcover o.p.

Grades: K 1 2 3   **398.2**

    1. Folklore—Nicaragua 2. Bilingual books—English-Spanish

    ISBN 0-89239-112-X (pa)   LC 88-37090

    Title page and text in English and Spanish

"Adaptation of a Nicaraguan folktale. . . . When his niece, Ambrosia, gives Uncle Nacho a new hat, he tries unsuccessfully several times to get rid of the old, holey one. Seeing him dejected because his hat keeps coming back, Ambrosia suggests he put his mind on the new one instead. Flattened primitive paintings in brilliant, clear tropical colors and motifs enhance the fun of this comedy of errors." Helbig. This land is our land

Ros, Roser

Beauty and the beast = La bella y la bestia; illustrated by Cristina Losantos. Chronicle Books 2007 unp il $14.95; pa $6.95

Grades: K 1 2 3   **398.2**

    1. Fairy tales 2. Folklore—France 3. Bilingual books—English-Spanish

    ISBN 978-0-8118-5969-1; 0-8118-59609-X; 978-0-8118-5970-7 (pa); 0-8118-5969-X (pa)

    LC 2006034843

Through her great capacity to love, a kind and beautiful maid releases a handsome prince from the spell which has made him an ugly beast.

In this bilingual English-Spanish adaptation, the illustrations "are Tin-Tin-style cartoons." Horn Book Guide

Rose, Naomi C.

Tibetan tales from the top of the world; written and illustrated by Naomi C. Rose; bilingual with Tibetan translation by Pasang Tenzin. Clear Light Pub. 2009 62p il $19.95

Grades: 2 3 4   **398.2**

    1. Folklore—Tibet (China) 2. Bilingual books—English-Tibetan

    ISBN 978-1-57416-089-5; 1-57416-089-3

                           LC 2006024077

    Contents: Prince Jampa's surprise; Sonam and the stolen cow; Tashi's gold

"In 'Prince Jampa's Surprise,' a young prince gathers 5000 horsemen to attack a neighboring kingdom believed to be savage and bloodthirsty. He is surprised to find the people gentle and welcoming, totally unlike the stories he has heard. 'Sonam and the Stolen Cow' tells of a young nun falsely accused of stealing a cow and then convicted in her own heart for something she stole years before. . . . In 'Tashi's Gold,' a lazy boy learns of a magical lake full of gold. Its guardian allows him to take a little but warns that true riches never come from gold. . . . The expressive faces of the Tibetan people are carefully rendered while backgrounds are more impressionistic. Rose's palette is rich with periwinkle, teals, reds, golds, pinks, and purples. . . . Containing both English and Tibetan texts, these tales shine a light on the hearts of the Tibetan people." SLJ

Rounds, Glen, 1906-2002

Ol' Paul, the mighty logger. Holiday House 1976 93p il pa $5.95 hardcover o.p.

Grades: 3 4 5 6   **398.2**

    1. Bunyan, Paul (Legendary character)

    ISBN 0-8234-0713-6 (pa)

    First published 1936

"Being a true account of the seemingly incredible exploits and inventions of the great Paul Bunyan, profusely illustrated by drawings made at the scene by the author, Glen Rounds, and now republished in this special fortieth anniversary edition." Subtitle

Rumford, James, 1948-

Beowulf; a hero's tale retold. Houghton Mifflin Company 2007 unp il $17 *

Grades: 4 5 6 7   **398.2**

    1. Beowulf 2. Monsters—Folklore 3. Folklore—Europe

    ISBN 0-618-75637-X; 978-0-618-75637-7

A simplified and illustrated retelling of the exploits of the Anglo-Saxon warrior, Beowulf, and how he came to defeat the monster Grendel, Grendel's mother, and a dragon that threatened the kingdom.

"Superb on all counts—from the elegant bookmaking to the vigorous, evocative prose . . . to the pen-and-ink and watercolor illustrations that strikingly recall the work of Edmund Dulac." Horn Book

Ryan, Pam Muñoz

Nacho and Lolita; illustrated by Claudia Rueda. Scholastic Press 2005 unp il $16.99

Grades: 2 3 4   **398.2**
1. Folklore—Mexico 2. Swallows—Folklore 3. California—Folklore
ISBN 0-439-26968-7   LC 2004-793
Also available Spanish language edition

A very rare pitacochi bird falls in love with a swallow and plucks his colorful feathers to transform dry, barren San Juan Capistrano into a haven of flowers and flowing water, which the swallows can easily find when returning from their annual migration

"Ryan's cozy storytelling will draw listeners close, and the Colombian-born illustrator cleverly exploits the contrast between the drought-scarred backdrops and Nacho's brilliance to achieve a vibrancy that is unusual in colored-pencil illustrations." Booklist

Rylant, Cynthia

Hansel and Gretel; pictures by Jen Corace. Hyperion Books for Children 2008 unp il $16.99
Grades: K 1 2   **398.2**
1. Folklore 2. Fairy tales
ISBN 978-1-4231-1186-3; 1-4231-1186-9

A retelling of the well-known tale in which two children lost in the woods find their way home despite an encounter with a wicked witch who wants to eat them.

"The language is forceful and direct throughout. . . . Complementing this retelling, Corace's pen-and-ink artwork features neutral hues and sober-faced children." SLJ

Sakade, Florence

Japanese children's favorite stories; compiled by Florence Sakade; illustrated by Yoshisuke Kurosaki. 3rd ed. Tuttle 2003 109p il $16.95
Grades: 2 3 4   **398.2**
1. Folklore—Japan
ISBN 0-8048-3449-0
First published 1953
50th anniversary edition
Contents: Peach boy; The magic teakettle; Monkey-dance and sparrow dance; The long-nosed goblins; The rabbit and the moon; The tongue-cut sparrow; Silly Saburo; The toothpick warriors; The Sticky-sticky pine; The spider weaver; Little one-inch; The badger and the magic fan; Mr. Lucky straw; Why the jellyfish has no bones; The old man who made trees blossom; The crab and the monkey; The ogre and the rooster; The rabbit who crossed the sea; The grateful statues; The bobtail monkey

A collection of Japanese folktales.

"This enduring collection presents 20 stories to enchant and enlighten young readers. . . . Minor text revisions have little effect on the stories. . . . The text remains simple, clear, and accessible to beginning readers and storytellers alike. The 'sparkling new color illustrations' are simply Kurosaki's original stylized scenes, repainted in bright dabs of watercolor." SLJ

Salley, Coleen

Epossumondas; written by Coleen Salley; illustrated by Janet Stevens. Harcourt 2002 unp il $16
Grades: K 1 2 3   **398.2**
1. Folklore—Southern States 2. Opossums—Folklore
ISBN 0-15-216748-X   LC 2001-4906

A retelling of a classic tale in which a well-intentioned young possum continually takes his mother's instructions much too literally

"All of the elements of a good story are here. . . . Salley's text rolls off the page (and off the tongue) easily, and is accompanied by delightful watercolor and colored-pencil art." SLJ
Other titles about Epossumondas are:
Epossumondas saves the day (2006)
Epossumondas plays possum (2009)
Why Epossumondas has no hair on his tail (2004)

San Souci, Robert, 1946-

As luck would have it; from the Brothers Grimm; [by] Robert D. San Souci; illustrated by Daniel San Souci. August House/Little Folk 2008 unp il $16.95
Grades: K 1 2 3 4   **398.2**
1. Folklore—Germany
ISBN 978-0-87483-833-6; 0-87483-833-9
     LC 2008000965
"Lively, comical illustrations enhance the abundant droll humor in this noodle-head tale that plays off the Grimm Brothers' 'Clever Elsie.' . . . The expressive, lucent watercolors highlighted with Prismacolor pencils portray the foolish escapades adeptly, and the anthropomorphized animal characters evocatively represent human characteristics and foibles." SLJ

Cendrillon; a Caribbean Cinderella; [by] Robert D. San Souci; illustrated by Brian Pinkney. Simon & Schuster Bks. for Young Readers 1998 unp il hardcover o.p. pa $8.99 *
Grades: K 1 2 3   **398.2**
1. Fairy tales 2. Folklore—Martinique
ISBN 0-689-80668-X; 0-689-84888-9 (pa)
     LC 96-53142
A Creole variant of the familiar Cinderella tale set in Martinique and narrated by the godmother who helps Cendrillon find true love

"The narrative is full of French Creole words and phrases. . . . A *fruit à pain* (breadfruit) is transformed into the coach; six agoutis (a kind of rodent) become the horses. . . . Pinkney's art perfectly conveys the lush beauty and atmosphere of the island setting." SLJ

Cut from the same cloth; American women of myth, legend, and tall tale; collected and told by Robert D. San Souci; illustrated by Brian Pinkney; introduction by Jane Yolen. Philomel Bks. 1993 140p il hardcover o.p. pa $6.99 *
Grades: 4 5 6 7   **398.2**
1. Folklore—United States 2. Tall tales 3. Women—Folklore
ISBN 0-399-21987-0; 0-698-11811-1 (pa)
     LC 92-5233

San Souci, Robert, 1946-—*Continued*

Contents: The Star Maiden; Bess Call; Drop Star; Molly Cottontail; Annie Christmas; Susanna and Simon; Sal Fink; Sweet Betsey from Pike; Old Sally Cato; Pale-Face Lightning; Pohaha; Sister Fox and Brother Coyote; Hekeke; Otoonah; Hiiaka

A collection of fifteen stories about legendary American women from Anglo-American, African American, and Native American folklore

"San Souci's language is vigorous and action verbs abound; Pinkney's black-and-white block prints match the strength of the telling. The inclusion of notes on the sources and a general bibliography make this an academic resource as well as a good collection of rolicking stories." Child Book Rev Serv

The faithful friend; [by] Robert D. San Souci; illustrated by Brian Pinkney. Simon & Schuster Bks. for Young Readers 1995 unp il $16; pa $5.99
Grades: 2 3 4   398.2
   1. Folklore—Martinique
   ISBN 0-02-786131-7; 0-689-82458-0 (pa)
                                    LC 93-40672

A Caldecott Medal honor book, 1996

"A West Indian folktale from Martinique. . . . When Clement seeks the lovely Pauline as his wife, it is Hippolyte who protects the couple from the zombies and her vengeful uncle." Child Book Rev Serv

"Pinkney's scratchboard and oil artwork switches from bright daytime hues for most of the book to purples and grays for scenes with the zombies and snakes, which are very effective. . . . This excellent title contains all the elements of a well-researched folktale, and convincingly conveys the richness of the West Indian culture." SLJ

Includes bibliographical references

Little Gold Star; a Spanish American Cinderella tale; retold by Robert D. San Souci; illustrated by Sergio Martinez. HarperCollins Pubs. 2000 unp il $15.95; lib bdg $15.89
Grades: 2 3 4   398.2
   1. Fairy tales 2. Folklore—Southern States 3. Hispanic Americans—Folklore
   ISBN 0-688-14780-1; 0-688-14781-X (lib bdg)
                                    LC 99-50290

A Spanish American retelling of the familiar story of a kind girl who is mistreated by her jealous stepmother and stepsisters. In this version, the Virgin Mary replaces the traditional fairy godmother

"Martinez' watercolors depict homes with Spanish architectural influences in an arid, southwest desert landscape; his characters have lively, expressive faces and evocative body language. . . . This is effective fairy-tale magic transported to new terrain." Bull Cent Child Books

The secret of the stones; a folktale; retold by Robert D. San Souci; pictures by James Ransome. Phyllis Fogelman Bks. 2000 unp il $16.99
Grades: K 1 2 3   398.2
   1. African Americans—Folklore 2. Folklore—United States
   ISBN 0-8037-1640-0   LC 93-43952

When they try to find out who is doing their chores while they are working in the field, a childless couple

discovers that the two stones they have brought home are actually two bewitched orphans

"Based on a tale found in both the Bantu and African-American cultures . . . the clearly told tale (which includes dialect in the dialogue) is accompanied by expressive, deep-toned illustrations." Horn Book Guide

Short & shivery; thirty chilling tales; retold by Robert D. San Souci; illustrated by Katherine Coville. Doubleday 1987 175p il pa $5.50 hardcover o.p.
Grades: 4 5 6 7   398.2
   1. Folklore 2. Ghost stories
   ISBN 0-440-41804-6 (pa)   LC 86-29067

Contents: The robber bridegroom; Jack Frost; The waterfall of ghosts; The ghost's cap; The witch cat; The green mist; The Cegua; The ghostly little girl; The midnight mass of the Dead; Tailypo; Lady Eleanore's mantle; The soldier and the vampire; The skeleton's dance; Scared to death; Swallowed alive; The deacon's ghost; Nuckelavee; The adventure of the German student; Billy Mosby's night ride; The hunter in the haunted forest; Brother and sister; The lovers of Dismal Swamp; Boneless; The death waltz; The ghost of Misery Hill; The loup-garou; The golem; Lavender; The goblin spider; The Halloween pony

"A collection of spooky stories, competently adapted and retold (sometimes quite freely) from world folklore, including Japan, Africa, and Latin America, as well as Europe and the U.S. . . . The stories drawn from collections of regional American folklore are not only the freshest, but often the scariest. Sources are fully documented. . . . There are some delicious shivers here, with plenty of fodder for an active imagination, as well as excitement." SLJ

Sister tricksters; rollicking tales of clever females; retold by Robert D. San Souci; illustrated by Daniel San Souci. August House Pubs. 2006 69p il $19.95 *
Grades: 3 4 5 6   398.2
   1. Folklore—Southern States 2. Animals—Folklore
   ISBN 978-0-87483-791-9; 0-87483-791-X
                                    LC 2006-40793

"Little Folk"

"These eight stories, featuring characters like Molly Cottontail, Miz Grasshopper, and Miz Goose, are energetically retold from Anne Virginia Culbertsons long out-of-print At the Big House (Bobbs-Merrill, 1904). . . . Delicious dialect and expressions convey a rural Southern flavor, yet the text is never hard to read or understand. . . . Stunning, richly colored, detailed, and playful paintings showing animals dressed in lavish finery introduce each lively tale." SLJ

Sootface; an Ojibwa Cinderella story; retold by Robert D. San Souci; illustrated by Daniel San Souci. Doubleday Bks. for Young Readers 1994 unp il pa $6.99 hardcover o.p.
Grades: 1 2 3 4   398.2
   1. Ojibwa Indians—Folklore
   ISBN 0-440-41363-X (pa)   LC 93-10553

Although she is mocked and mistreated by her two older sisters, Sootface, an Ojibwa Indian maiden, wins a mighty invisible warrior for her husband with her kind

San Souci, Robert, 1946-—*Continued*
and honest heart
"The San Souci version reads aloud well, and the watercolor artwork illustrates the story with quiet grace." Booklist

Sukey and the mermaid; [by] Robert D. San Souci; illustrated by Brian Pinkney. Four Winds Press 1992 unp il hardcover o.p. pa $5.95 *
Grades: 1 2 3 4   **398.2**
  1. Mermaids and mermen 2. African Americans—Folklore
  ISBN 0-02-778141-0; 0-689-80718-X (pa)
                                    LC 90-24559
Unhappy with her life at home, Sukey receives kindness and wealth from Mama Jo the mermaid
  San Souci "outdoes himself here with pungent, lyrical prose that reverberates with the cadences of the South Carolina islands. . . . The supple lines of Pinkney's fluid scratchboard technique capture the grace and spirit of this magical tale and serve as the perfect foil to its darker undertones." Publ Wkly

The talking eggs; a folktale from the American South; retold by Robert D. San Souci; pictures by Jerry Pinkney. Dial Bks. for Young Readers 1989 unp il $16 *
Grades: K 1 2 3   **398.2**
  1. Folklore—Southern States
  ISBN 0-8037-0619-7   LC 88-33469
  A Caldecott Medal honor book, 1990
  A Southern folktale in which kind Blanche, following the instructions of an old witch, gains riches, while her greedy sister makes fun of the old woman and is duly rewarded
  "Adapted from a Creole folk tale originally included in a collection of Louisiana stories by folklorist Alcee Fortier, this tale captures the flavor of the nineteenth-century South in its language and story line. . . . Jerry Pinkney's watercolors are chiefly responsible for the excellence of the book; his characters convey their moods with vivid facial expressions." Horn Book

Sanderson, Ruth, 1951-
  Goldilocks; retold and illustrated by Ruth Sanderson. Little, Brown Books for Young Readers 2009 unp il $16.99
Grades: K 1 2 3   **398.2**
  1. Folklore 2. Bears—Folklore
  ISBN 978-0-316-77885-5; 0-316-77885-0
                                 LC 2008045298
  After finding the bears' cottage in the woods and making a mess inside, Goldilocks helps the family clean up and enjoys a nice meal
  "The artist warms her version of this oft-told tale with lavish accoutrements, costumes, and furniture that suggest a Scandinavian setting, which will entice viewers to explore the far corners of the pages. . . . The large, richly colored images make this an ideal classroom read-aloud, and Mama Bear's recipe for blueberry muffins offers a nice finishing touch." SLJ

Sanfield, Steve
  The adventures of High John the Conqueror; [illustrated by John Ward] August House 1995 113p il hardcover o.p. pa $11.95
Grades: 4 5 6 7   **398.2**
  1. Folklore—United States 2. African Americans—Folklore
  ISBN 0-87483-433-3; 0-87483-774-X (pa)
                                 LC 95-35825
  A reissue of the title first published 1988 by Orchard Books
  Contents: Master's walking stick; Just possum; You better not do it; In a box; Off limits; John wins a bet; This one and that one; Who's the fool now; George's dream; Deer hunting; John's memory; Freedom; An epidemic of ducks; John in court; Tops and bottoms; The Christmas turkey
  A collection of folk tales about High John the Conqueror, the traditional trickster hero of blacks during and immediately after the time of slavery
  "Simply told in language comprehensible to very young readers, these tales are short, funny, and entertaining. . . . Fourteen full-page black-and-white pencil drawings illustrate some of the more dramatic moments in the stories." SLJ
  Includes bibliographical references

Schlitz, Laura Amy
  The Bearskinner; a tale of the Brothers Grimm; retold by Laura Amy Schlitz; illustrated by Max Grafe. Candlewick Press 2007 unp il $16.99 *
Grades: 3 4 5 6   **398.2**
  1. Fairy tales 2. Folklore—Germany
  ISBN 978-0-7636-2730-0; 0-7636-2730-5
                                 LC 2007-22787
  A retelling of the Grimm fairy tale in which a despondent soldier makes a pact to do the devil's bidding for seven years in return for as much money and property as he could ever want
  "Schlitz narrates with clarity, grace, and sensitivity. . . . Except for the devil's coat of darkest green, Grafe's atmospheric full-page illustrations are almost monochromatic. . . . A provocative edition that should set older children thinking about the meaning of endurance and heroism." Horn Book

Schram, Peninnah, 1934-
  The magic pomegranate; by Peninnah Schram; illustrated by Melanie Hall. Millbrook Press 2008 48p il (On my own folklore) lib bdg $25.26; pa $6.95
Grades: 1 2 3 4   **398.2**
  1. Fairy tales 2. Pomegranates—Folklore 3. Jews—Folklore
  ISBN 978-0-8225-6742-4 (lib bdg); 0-8225-6742-3 (lib bdg); 978-0-8225-6746-2 (pa); 0-8225-6746-6 (pa)
                                 LC 2006036722
  Three handsome and clever brothers compete to find the world's most unusual gift. Includes a note on doing good deeds, or mitzvah, and discusses the symbolism of the pomegranate in Judaism
  The "tale is paired with an illustration style that nicely reflects the culture." Horn Book Guide
  Includes bibliographical references

Schwartz, Alvin, 1927-1992

All of our noses are here, and other noodle tales; retold by Alvin Schwartz; pictures by Karen Ann Weinhaus. Harper & Row 1985 64p il (I can read book) lib bdg $15.89 *

Grades: K 1 2   **398.2**

1. Folklore 2. Wit and humor
ISBN 0-06-025288-X   LC 84-48330
Contents: Jane gets a donkey; Grandpa misses the boat; All of our noses are here; The best boy in the world; Sam's girl friend

This companion volume to There is a carrot in my ear, and other noodle tales, contains additional stories about members of the Brown family

"The illustrations show them looking very much like mice and always smiling and cheerful. Cousins, no doubt, to the Stupids, the family is bound to be as appealing to young readers. With a list of sources." Horn Book

Ghosts! ghostly tales from folklore; retold by Alvin Schwartz; illustrated by Victoria Chess. HarperCollins Pubs. 1991 63p il lib bdg $15.89; pa $3.95 *

Grades: K 1 2   **398.2**

1. Ghost stories 2. Folklore
ISBN 0-06-021797-9 (lib bdg); 0-06-444170-9 (pa)
LC 90-21746
Contents: The haunted house; Susie; A little green bottle; The umbrella; Three little ghosts; The teeny-tiny woman; Ghost, get lost

Presents seven, easy-to-read ghost stories based on traditional folk tales and legends from various countries

"All of the pen-and-watercolor illustrations are tidy and cheery and creepy. . . . Retold in a style that is simple but not choppy . . . and accompanied by a page of brief notes, all the tales will lend themselves to elaboration and innovation." Bull Cent Child Books

I saw you in the bathtub, and other folk rhymes; collected by Alvin Schwartz; pictures by Syd Hoff. Harper & Row 1989 64p il (I can read book) pa $3.99 hardcover o.p.

Grades: K 1 2   **398.2**

1. Folklore
ISBN 0-06-444151-2 (pa)   LC 88-16111
Presents an illustrated collection of traditional folk rhymes, some composed by children

"Kids may be surprised to see their recess yells on the printed page but will relish the confirmation of significance. Hoff's full-color cartoons interpret the rhymes literally, an approach that leads to some pretty surreal results." Bull Cent Child Books

In a dark, dark room, and other scary stories; retold by Alvin Schwartz; illustrated by Dirk Zimmer. Harper & Row 1984 63p il (I can read book) $15.95; pa $3.95 *

Grades: K 1 2   **398.2**

1. Folklore 2. Ghost stories 3. Horror fiction
ISBN 0-06-025271-5; 0-06-444090-7 (pa)
LC 83-47699
Contents: The teeth; In the graveyard; The green ribbon; In a dark, dark room; The night it rained; The pirate

This is a collection of "seven traditional tales from around the world retold in simple yet effective language. . . . The chill here springs from suspense, an eerie setting or a ghostly surprise, rather than from blood and gore. Though pared down somewhat from longer versions, the stories retain their genuine creepiness. . . . The colorfully dark illustrations are sinister without being gruesome and add a comic touch." SLJ

More scary stories to tell in the dark; collected & retold from folklore by Alvin Schwartz; drawings by Stephen Gammell. Lippincott 1984 100p il $15.99; lib bdg $16.89; pa $5.99 *

Grades: 4 5 6 7   **398.2**

1. Ghost stories 2. Horror fiction 3. Folklore—United States
ISBN 0-397-32081-7; 0-397-32082-5 (lib bdg); 0-06-440177-4 (pa)   LC 83-49494
This volume contains stories of ghosts, murders, graveyards and other horrors

"The stories are all short and lively, very tellable, and greatly enhanced by the gray, ghoulish, horrifying illustrations of dismembered bodies, hideous creatures, and mysterious lights. A fine compendium by a well-known collector, easily accessible to young readers." Horn Book

Includes bibliographical references

Scary stories 3; more tales to chill your bones; collected from folklore and retold by Alvin Schwartz; drawings by Stephen Gammell. HarperCollins Pubs. 1991 115p il music $15.99; lib bdg $16.89; pa $5.99 *

Grades: 4 5 6 7   **398.2**

1. Ghost stories 2. Horror fiction 3. Folklore—United States
ISBN 0-06-021794-4; 0-06-021795-2 (lib bdg); 0-06-440418-8 (pa)   LC 90-47474
Traditional and modern-day stories of ghosts, haunts, superstitions, monsters, and horrible scary things

"The book is well paced and continually captivates, surprises, and entices audiences into reading just one more page. Gammell's gauzy, cobwebby, black-and-white pen-and-ink drawings help to sustain the overall creepy mood." SLJ

Includes bibliographical references

Scary stories to tell in the dark; collected from American folklore by Alvin Schwartz; with drawings by Stephen Gammell. Lippincott 1981 111p il $15.99; lib bdg $16.89; pa $5.99 *

Grades: 4 5 6 7   **398.2**

1. Ghost stories 2. Horror fiction 3. Folklore—United States
ISBN 0-397-31926-6; 0-397-31927-4 (lib bdg); 0-06-440170-7 (pa)   LC 80-8728
"A collection of scary, semi-scary, and humorous stories about ghosts and witches collected from American folklore. Most of the stories (poems and songs also) are very short and range from the traditional to the modern. The author includes suggestions on how to tell scary stories effectively." Bull Cent Child Books

"The scholarship in the source notes and bibliography will be useful to serious literature students." SLJ

Schwartz, Alvin, 1927-1992—*Continued*

There is a carrot in my ear, and other noodle tales; retold by Alvin Schwartz; pictures by Karen Ann Weinhaus. Harper & Row 1982 64p il hardcover o.p. pa $3.95 *

Grades: K 1 2   **398.2**
1. Folklore 2. Wit and humor
ISBN 0-06-025234-0; 0-06-444103-2 (pa)
        LC 80-8442
"An I can read book"

Contents: The Browns take the day off; Sam and Jane go camping; Mr. Brown washes his underwear; Jane grows a carrot; Grandpa buys a pumpkin egg; It is time to go to sleep

This "is a collection of six stories from sources . . . as diverse as American 'Little Moron' stories, ancient Greek tales and vaudeville pieces. Explaining in his foreword that a 'noodle is a silly person,' reteller Alvin Schwartz goes on to introduce the noodly Brown family and reveal their various foibles. . . . Most of the stories don't appear in other beginning noodle collections and will provide laughs for readers who catch the puns and absurdities the stories hinge on. The drawings by Karen Ann Weinhaus . . . show funny, pointy-proboscised folk blissfully unaware of their own goofiness." SLJ

Schwartz, Howard, 1945-

Before you were born; retold by Howard Schwartz; illustrated by Kristina Swarner. Roaring Brook Press 2005 unp il $16.95

Grades: K 1 2 3   **398.2**
1. Jews—Folklore
ISBN 1-59643-028-1   LC 2003-17845
"A Deborah Brodie Book"

Retells a folktale in which Lailah, a guardian angel, places the indentation that everyone has on the upper lip just before a baby is born

"In spare, serene language, Schwartz reshapes a rabbinic legend. . . . Swarner's ethereal, mixed-media illustrations illuminate the spirituality of the telling." Booklist

A coat for the moon and other Jewish tales; selected and retold by Howard Schwartz and Barbara Rush; illustrated by Michael Iofin. Jewish Publ. Soc. 1999 81p il hardcover o.p. pa $13

Grades: 4 5 6 7   **398.2**
1. Jews—Folklore
ISBN 0-8276-0596-X; 0-8276-0736-9 (pa)
        LC 98-52704

Contents: The Queen of the Sea; The enchanted spring; The lamp on the mountain; The underground world; The demon in the wine cellar; The rusty plate; The witch Barusha; The Sabbath walking stick; Amsha the giant; The king's secret; The fisherman and the silver fish; The weaving that saved the prince; A family of demons; The royal artists and the clever king; A coat for the moon

A collection of Jewish folktales from around the world, including "The Lamp on the Mountain," "The Witch Barusha," "The Sabbath Walking Stick," and "The Fisherman and the Silver Fish"

"These tales incorporate everything from the magical to the bizarre, all while imparting specific Jewish values that have transcended time and cultural dispersion.

. . . Each retelling opens with a delightfully detailed pen-and-ink illustration encircled by a key sentence or phrase from the text that gives a hint of what's to come." SLJ

A journey to paradise and other Jewish tales; retold by Howard Schwartz; illustrated by Giora Carmi. Pitspopany Press 2000 48p il $16.95; pa $9.95

Grades: 3 4 5   **398.2**
1. Jews—Folklore
ISBN 0-943706-21-1; 0-943706-16-5 (pa)

Contents: An apple from The Tree of Life; King Solomon tests fate; The flight of the midwife; The heavenly court; A student in magic; The finger; A messenger from the World to Come; A journey to paradise

"This collection of traditional tales from the world's far-flung Jewish community is ably selected by a well-known scholar. . . . The volume is abundantly illustrated with both spot and full-spread drawings in subdued colors." Horn Book Guide

Includes bibliographical references

Scott, Nathan Kumar

The sacred banana leaf; an Indonesian trickster tale; by Nathan Kumar Scott; illustrated by Radhashyam Raut. Tara 2008 unp il $16.95

Grades: 2 3 4   **398.2**
1. Animals—Folklore 2. Folklore—Indonesia
ISBN 978-81-86211-28-1; 81-86211-28-4

"Kanchil, the beloved trickster mouse-deer of Indonesian folklore, falls into a pit. With only a banana leaf for company, he invents a prophecy to trick some unlikely animals into helping him out." Publisher's note

"Scott's retelling has verve and humor, and the illustrations, rendered in *patachitra* (a traditional style of temple painting originating in eastern India) are both accessible and graceful. Saturated colors gleam from sand-toned pages, and the patterned skins of the clearly delineated animals add texture." Booklist

Seeger, Pete

Abiyoyo; based on a South African lullaby and folk story; text by Pete Seeger; illustrations by Michael Hays. Simon & Schuster Bks. for Young Readers 2001 unp il $19.95; pa $6.99 *

Grades: K 1 2 3   **398.2**
1. Folklore—South Africa 2. Giants—Folklore
ISBN 0-689-84693-2; 0-689-71810-1 (pa)

Also available: Abiyoyo returns (2001)

A reissue of the title first published 1986 by Macmillan

Includes audio CD

Banished from the town for making mischief, a little boy and his father are welcomed back when they make the giant Abiyoyo disappear

"Told in the familiar Seeger style, with brief musical phrases of the one-word song incorporated in the text and printed complete at the end, and with illustrations full of light and color, this rendering of a South African tale is a pleasure. The giant is imposing but not too scary for the youngest listener leaning over the book while a parent tells the story." N Y Times Book Rev

Shannon, George, 1952-

More stories to solve; fifteen folktales from around the world; told by George Shannon; illustrated by Peter Sis. Greenwillow Bks. 1991 64p il hardcover o.p. pa $4.99 *

Grades: 3 4 5 6   **398.2**
  1. Folklore 2. Riddles
  ISBN 0-688-09161-X; 0-380-73261-0 (pa)

"Shannon combines the folktale and the riddle in a brief collection that brings together 15 international stories." Booklist

Includes bibliographical references

Rabbit's gift; a fable from China; told by George Shannon; illustrated by Laura Dronzek. Harcourt 2007 unp il $16

Grades: PreK K 1   **398.2**
  1. Fables 2. Folklore—China 3. Rabbits—Folklore 4. Animals—Folklore
  ISBN 978-0-15-206073-2; 0-15-206073-1
                                                   LC 2006-04789

Woodland animals, each thinking of his neighbor, share a turnip left on their doorstep.

"The uncluttered illustrations, many framed in purple to compliment the purple of the turnip, perfectly capture the action of the story. The expressive faces of the animals are charming." Booklist

Stories to solve; folktales from around the world; illustrated by Peter Sis. Greenwillow Bks. 1985 55p il hardcover o.p. pa $4.99 *

Grades: 3 4 5 6   **398.2**
  1. Folklore 2. Riddles
  ISBN 0-688-04303-8; 0-380-73260-2 (pa)
                                                   LC 84-18656

"Each of these 14 delightful folktales is a short puzzle to be solced through clevernes, common sense or careful observations of details in the text. . . . Sis' pointillistic pen-and-ink drawings illustrate each puzzle, and sometimes clarify the solutions." SLJ

Sharpe, Leah Marinsky

The goat-faced girl; a classic Italian folktale; retold by Leah Marinsky Sharpe; illustrated by Jane Marinsky. David R. Godine 2009 unp il $16.95 *

Grades: K 1 2 3   **398.2**
  1. Folklore—Italy 2. Fairy tales
  ISBN 978-1-56792-393-3; 1-56792-393-3
                                                   LC 2009-22383

When Isabella, a beautiful but lazy young woman, agrees to marry an equally lazy prince, the sorceress who raised her gives her the head of a goat in hopes that she will learn to do things for herself.

"Rich storytelling and intricately imagined artwork make this debut a standout. . . . Marinsky's paintings, in the chalky, sun-bleached colors of the Italian renaissance, contain many small pleasures." Publ Wkly

Shelby, Anne

The adventures of Molly Whuppie and other Appalachian folktales; [by] Anne Shelby; illustrations by Paula McArdle. The University of North Carolina Press 2007 88p il $14.95

Grades: 4 5 6 7   **398.2**
  1. Folklore—Appalachian Mountains
  ISBN 978-0-8078-3163-2   LC 2007013789

A collection of Appalachian folktales featuring Molly Whuppie and her adventures.

"Shelby has captured the language of Appalachia. . . . Her adaptations are true to the traditional folktales. . . . Young readers and listeners will make these stories their own and enjoy retelling them." SLJ

Includes bibliographical references

Shepard, Aaron

One-Eye! Two-Eyes! Three-Eyes! a very Grimm fairy tale; pictures by Gary Clement. Atheneum Books for Young Readers 2007 unp il $16.95 *

Grades: K 1 2 3   **398.2**
  1. Folklore 2. Fairy tales
  ISBN 978-0-689-86740-8; 0-689-86740-9
                                                   LC 2005-00459

A retelling of the Grimm's fairy tale about a little girl who has two eyes and is horribly teased by her sisters who have one and three eyes respectively.

"The alterations to the story are consistent with the lighthearted watercolor-and-pencil illustrations. . . . Children will enjoy the humor in this reincarnation, and it will make excellent fodder for reader's theater, with a script available on the author's Web site." SLJ

The princess mouse; a tale of Finland; told by Aaron Shepard; illustrated by Leonid Gore. Atheneum Bks. for Young Readers 2003 unp il hardcover o.p. pa $13.99 *

Grades: K 1 2 3   **398.2**
  1. Fairy tales 2. Folklore—Finland 3. Mice—Folklore
  ISBN 0-689-82912-4; 1-4169-8969-2 (pa)
                                                   LC 2001-55273

A retelling of a Finnish folk tale about a young man who plans to marry his mouse sweetheart

"Shepard's charmingly droll version of a Finnish folktale combines classic elements with unexpected, witty details. . . . The jewel-toned art has beautiful luminescence; the elongated, somewhat blocky look of the characters reinforces the fantasy; and the mice are downright irresistible." Booklist

The sea king's daughter; a Russian legend; retold by Aaron Shepard; illustrated by Gennady Spirin. Atheneum Bks. for Young Readers 1997 28p il pa $11.99

Grades: 3 4 5 6   **398.2**
  1. Folklore—Russia 2. Musicians—Folklore
  ISBN 0-689-80759-7; 0-689-84259-7 (pa)
                                                   LC 96-3391

A talented musician from Novgorod plays so well that the Sea King wants him to marry one of his daughters

"The telling is descriptive yet very accessible, with the art, in Spirin's majestic signature style, evoking both the mythical feel of the legend and the folk-music roots from which the story sprang." Booklist

Sherman, Pat

The sun's daughter; a story based on an Iroquois legend; illustrated by R. Gregory Christie. Clarion Bks. 2005 31p il $16

Grades: 2 3 4   **398.2**

1. Iroquois Indians—Folklore

ISBN 0-618-32430-5   LC 2004-17820

"Inspired by Iroquois tales of the Corn Maiden and her sisters, this original story tells how Maize, Red Bean, and Pumpkin walked the earth spreading a bounty of food in their wake. . . . The story is charmingly told with eloquent phrasing and vocabulary. The artwork, done in a folk-art style, is energetic and exuberant, and the brush strokes are used to dramatic effect across the spreads." SLJ

Shulevitz, Uri, 1935-

The treasure. Farrar, Straus & Giroux 1978 unp il hardcover o.p. pa $6.95 *

Grades: K 1 2 3   **398.2**

1. Folklore

ISBN 0-374-37740-5; 0-374-47955-0 (pa)

A Caldecott Medal honor book, 1980

This is the "tale of a poor man, here named Isaac, who three times dreams of a voice telling him to go to the capital and look for a treasure under the bridge by the palace. When he gets to the capital, the captain of the guard tells him of his dream: a treasure is buried under the stove of a man named Isaac back in Isaac's home city. So Isaac returns home, finds the treasure under his own stove, and lives happily ever after." SLJ

"Although the story is known in many cultures the retelling suggests the Hassidic tradition. . . . The eastern European influence is extended in the illustrations." Horn Book

Sierra, Judy

Can you guess my name? traditional tales around the world; selected and retold by Judy Sierra; illustrated by Stefano Vitale. Clarion Bks. 2002 110p il $20

Grades: 3 4 5 6   **398.2**

1. Folklore

ISBN 0-618-13328-3   LC 2002-3509

Contents: The three little piggies and Old Mister Fox; Big Pig, Little Pig, Speckled Pig, and Runt; The three geese; How Jack went to seek his fortune; Medio Pollito; Master Thumb; Titeliture; How Ijapa the tortoise tricked the hippopotamus; Oniroku; Princess tombi-ende and the frog; How a warty toad became an emperor; Little singing frog; Jean and Jeannette; The cake tree; The runaway children

A collection of fifteen folktales from all over the world, including stories that resemble "The Three Pigs," "The Bremen Town Musicians," "Rumpelstiltskin," "The Frog Prince," and "Hansel and Gretel"

"All of the selections have dramatic dialogue and repetitive phrases and refrains, and are easy to learn. . . . Vitale's engaging folk illustrations are painted on wood. . . . This collection provides a fascinating experience with comparative literature, one that can open doors to other cultures. A must purchase for most collections." SLJ

Includes bibliographical references

The gift of the Crocodile; a Cinderella story; illustrated by Reynold Ruffins. Simon & Schuster Bks. for Young Readers 2000 unp il $17

Grades: K 1 2 3   **398.2**

1. Fairy tales 2. Folklore—Indonesia

ISBN 0-689-82188-3   LC 98-40592

In this Indonesian version of the Cinderella story, a girl named Damura escapes her cruel stepmother and stepsister and marries a handsome prince with the help of Grandmother Crocodile

"Sierra's unadorned retelling is straightforward. . . . Ruffins's brightly colored, patterned paintings, with their angular figures and wavy landscapes, express and evoke the story's island setting." Horn Book

Nursery tales around the world; selected and retold by Judy Sierra; illustrated by Stefano Vitale. Clarion Bks. 1996 114p il $20 *

Grades: K 1 2 3 4 5   **398.2**

1. Folklore

ISBN 0-395-67894-3   LC 93-2068

Contents: The gingerbread man; The pancake; The bun; I know an old lady who swallowed a fly; The boy who tried to fool his father; The cat and the parrot; Sody sallyraytus; The ram in the chile patch; Odon the giant; This is the house that Jack built; Anansi and the pig; The rooster and the mouse; The hare and the tortoise; The coyote and the rabbit; The fox and the crab; The gunny wolf; Groundhog's dance; The three pigs

Presents eighteen simple stories from international folklore, grouped around six themes, such as "Runaway Cookies," "Slowpokes and Speedsters," and "Chain Tales." Includes background information and storytelling hints

"This richly illustrated compendium of folktales does double duty as a nursery story book for lap-sharing and as a sourcebook for parents and professionals. . . . Most entries feature strong rhythms and repetition that invite audience participation and develop memory. . . . Top this engaging text with Vitale's lavish oil-on-wood ethnic borders, motif vignettes, and full-page illustrations, and you have a handsome work to be valued by readers and treasured by listeners." Bull Cent Child Books

Includes bibliographical references

Tasty baby belly buttons; a Japanese folktale; illustrated by Meilo So. Knopf 1998 unp il $17 paperback o.p. *

Grades: K 1 2 3   **398.2**

1. Folklore—Japan

ISBN 0-679-89369-5; 0-440-41738-4 (pa)

LC 98-22524

Urikohime, a girl born from a melon, battles the monstrous onis, who steal babies to eat their tasty belly buttons

"Graced with occasional delicate brushwork that seems distinctly Japanese, So's fluid, sweeping watercolors add freshness to a traditional tale of swashbuckling heroics." Booklist

Silverman, Erica

Raisel's riddle; story by Erica Silverman; pictures by Susan Gaber. Farrar, Straus & Giroux 1999 unp il hardcover o.p. pa $5.95

Grades: K 1 2 3   398.2

1. Fairy tales 2. Jews—Folklore

ISBN 0-374-36168-1; 0-374-46199-6 (pa)

LC 97-29421

A Jewish version of the Cinderella story, in which a poor but educated young woman captivates her "Prince Charming" a rabbi's son, at a Purim ball

"Gaber's softly stippled spreads evoke a quiet seriousness appropriate to this thoughtful retelling." Bull Cent Child Books

Singer, Isaac Bashevis, 1904-1991

Zlateh the goat, and other stories; pictures by Maurice Sendak; translated from the Yiddish by the author and Elizabeth Shub. Harper & Row 1966 90p il $15.95; pa $6.95

Grades: 4 5 6 7   398.2

1. Jews—Folklore

ISBN 0-06-028477-3; 0-06-440147-2 (pa)

A Newbery Award honor book, 1967

Contents: Fool's paradise; Grandmother's tale; The snow in Chelm; The mixed-up feet and the silly bridegroom; The first shlemiel; The Devil's trick; Zlateh the goat

"Seven tales drawn from middle-European Jewish village life, with illustrations which extend the humor and subtlety of the situations." Hodges. Books for Elem Sch Libr

Smith, Chris, 1947-

One city, two brothers; written by Chris Smith, illustrated by Aurélia Fronty. Barefoot Books 2007 unp il $16.99 *

Grades: 2 3 4   398.2

1. Folklore—Middle East 2. Jerusalem—Folklore 3. Brothers—Folklore

ISBN 978-1-846860-42-3

To settle an inheritance dispute between two brothers, King Solomon tells a tale of how Jerusalem came to be founded.

"Based on a folktale told by both Jews and Arabs, this picture book beautifully captures the spirit of brotherhood. . . . The accomplished folk-style artwork, in shades of verdant green, heavenly blue, and harvest orange . . . adds an air of peace and hope." Booklist

Snyder, Dianne

The boy of the three-year nap; illustrated by Allen Say. Houghton Mifflin 1988 32p il $16.95; pa $6.95

Grades: 1 2 3   398.2

1. Folklore—Japan

ISBN 0-395-44090-4; 0-395-66957-X (pa)

LC 87-30674

A Caldecott Medal honor book, 1989

"Japan's contribution to the trickster folktale, in which a lazy son cons a rich man, only to be outsmarted by his own, even trickier mother. Lilting prose and shimmering illustrations combine in perfect harmony." SLJ

Souhami, Jessica

King Pom and the fox; [by] Jessica Souhami. Frances Lincoln 2007 unp il $16.95

Grades: K 1 2 3   398.2

1. Folklore

ISBN 978-1-84507-478-4; 1-84507-478-5

"In this Chinese version of 'Puss in Boots,' a young man is called King Pom because he owns a grand pomegranate tree. When a fox is caught stealing its fruit, he strikes a bargain. The fox arranges for King Pom to be rescued from the river and presented to the Emperor as a rich man, unfortunately attacked by robbers. . . . Souhami's bright, uncluttered collages are made of Ingres papers adorned with watercolor, ink, and pencil and lightly positioned on creamy backgrounds. . . . The spareness of the text matches the simplicity of the artwork." SLJ

The little, little house. Frances Lincoln 2006 32p il $15.95

Grades: K 1 2   398.2

1. Jews—Folklore

ISBN 1-84507-108-5

"Souhami's adaptation of this eastern European Jewish folktale features a poor man named Joseph, his wife, and three children, who live together in a cramped little house. Joseph seeks advice from wise Aunty Bella, who recommends that he bring his six chickens, his rooster, his cow, and his goat inside. The results are predictably disastrous. . . . Finally, Aunty Bella gives permission to turn the animals outside again, and, suddenly, the house seems just the right size for Joseph's family." Booklist

"A delightful retelling. . . . The vibrant colors and strong contrast of the cut-paper shapes against neutral backgrounds provide great visual energy. The simple yet dramatic text makes it especially well suited to reading aloud." SLJ

Mrs. McCool and the giant Cuhullin; an Irish tale. Holt & Co. 2002 unp il $16.95

Grades: K 1 2 3   398.2

1. Finn MacCumhaill, 3rd cent.—Fiction 2. Folklore—Ireland 3. Giants—Folklore

ISBN 0-8050-6852-X

LC 2001-2884

The very clever Oona saves her husband, the giant Finn McCool, by outwitting Cuhullin, who seeks to prove that he is the strongest giant in the world by beating Finn

"Painted and cut-paper illustrations in bold colors and simple shapes echo the basic drama. This is a clever, amusing version of an oft-told story." Booklist

Sausages. Frances Lincoln Children's Books 2006 unp il hardcover o.p. pa $8.95

Grades: PreK K 1 2   398.2

1. Folklore

ISBN 978-1-84507-397-8; 1-84507-397-5; 978-1-84507-601-6 (pa); 1-84507-601-X (pa)

"In this vibrant retelling of the Grimms' *The Three Wishes*, brilliantly designed paper collages capture every trace of humor in this cautionary tale. . . . A woodcutter rescues an elf from a rosebush and is granted three wishes. . . . The woodcutter asks for sausages. His wife responds with an angry reply that leaves the sausages stuck on his nose, and, of course, the last wish must be used to remove them. The story begs to be read aloud or told—the language is rich with sound effects." SLJ

Spirin, Gennadiĭ

Goldilocks and the three bears; retold and illustrated by Gennady Spirin. Marshall Cavendish Children 2009 unp il $17.99

Grades: PreK K 1 2   **398.2**

1. Folklore 2. Bears—Folklore

ISBN 978-0-7614-5596-7; 0-7614-5596-5

LC 2008026984

A simplified retelling of the adventures of a little girl walking in the woods who finds the house of the three bears and helps herself to their belongings. Includes a note on the history of the tale

"Spirin's version of this classic pairs a simple, straightforward retelling with lush Renaissance costumes and elegant page designs. The bears, rendered in watercolor and colored pencil, are solid, realistic creatures, revealing sharp teeth and claws. . . . The setting is created with richly realized essentials: solid porridge bowls, carved chairs, ornate beds, a massive stucco and wood-trimmed dwelling. . . . This . . . will be embraced for its visual clarity and sumptuous style." SLJ

The tale of the Firebird; translated by Tatiana Popova. Philomel Bks. 2002 32p il $16.99 *

Grades: 2 3 4   **398.2**

1. Fairy tales 2. Folklore—Russia 3. Birds—Folklore

ISBN 0-399-23584-1   LC 2001-36660

When Prince Ivan sets out to find the Firebird for his father the tsar, he must complete a series of tasks before obtaining the Firebird and winning the hand of a beautiful princess

"The storytelling is dramatic and controlled, the language rising and falling in a cadence that encourages reading aloud. . . . Detailed and dramatic, with a golden palette that echoes crown jewels, the illustrations have an adventurous fairy-tale sweep." Bull Cent Child Books

Stampler, Ann Redisch

Shlemazel and the remarkable spoon of Pohost; illustrated by Jacqueline M. Cohen. Clarion Books 2006 39p il $16

Grades: K 1 2 3   **398.2**

1. Jews—Folklore

ISBN 978-0-618-36959-1; 0-618-36959-7

LC 2005023602

A retelling of an Eastern European Jewish tale in which Shlemazel, the laziest man in town, is tricked into believing that the lucky spoon given to him by a neighbor will bring him fortune and fame, if it is used in the right way

"Employing a lively Yiddish cadence, the text is a storyteller's delight, full of humor, hyperbole, and delicious adjectives that make it a pleasure to read aloud. Jewel-toned panoramic watercolors are infused with a joyful folkloric quality well suited to the story." SLJ

Steptoe, John, 1950-1989

Mufaro's beautiful daughters; an African tale. Lothrop, Lee & Shepard Bks. 1987 unp il $15.95; lib bdg $15.89 *

Grades: K 1 2 3   **398.2**

1. Folklore—Africa

ISBN 0-688-04045-4; 0-688-04046-2 (lib bdg)

LC 84-7158

A Caldecott Medal honor book, 1988; Coretta Scott King Award for illustration, 1988; Boston Globe-Horn Book Award, picture book 1987

Mufaro's two beautiful daughters, one bad-tempered, one kind and sweet, go before the king, who is choosing a wife

"The pace of the text matches the rhythm of the illustrations—both move in dramatic unity to the climax. By changing perspective the artist not only captures the lush, rich background but also the personalities of the characters with revealing studies of their faces." Horn Book

The story of Jumping Mouse; a native American legend; retold and illustrated by John Steptoe. Lothrop, Lee & Shepard Bks. 1984 unp il $15.95; pa $5.95 *

Grades: 1 2 3   **398.2**

1. Native Americans—Folklore 2. Mice—Folklore

ISBN 0-688-01902-1; 0-688-08740-X (pa)

LC 82-14848

A Caldecott Medal honor book, 1985

"By keeping hope alive within himself, a mouse is successful in his quest for the far-off land. Steptoe's retelling of an unattributed tribal legend is exquisite in its use of language and in its expansive drawings which employ dazzling subtleties of light and shadow." SLJ

Stevens, Janet, 1953-

Coyote steals the blanket; an Ute tale; retold and illustrated by Janet Stevens. Holiday House 1993 unp il lib bdg $17.95; pa $6.95

Grades: K 1 2 3   **398.2**

1. Ute Indians—Folklore 2. Coyote (Legendary character)

ISBN 0-8234-0996-1 (lib bdg); 0-8234-1129-X (pa)

LC 92-54415

"When Coyote swipes a blanket, thus angering the spirit of the desert, he is pursued by a rock on a rampage. This traditional trickster tale features a scraggly, scruffy yet lovable character, a narrative that will roll right off storytellers' tongues, and hilarious pictures of boastful animals trying to halt the furious boulder." SLJ

Old bag of bones; a Coyote tale; retold and illustrated by Janet Stevens. Holiday House 1996 unp il hardcover o.p. pa $6.95

Grades: K 1 2 3   **398.2**

1. Shoshoni Indians—Folklore 2. Coyote (Legendary character)

ISBN 0-8234-1215-6; 0-8234-1337-3 (pa)

LC 95-31443

"Now an aging, decidedly mangy creature who yearns for youth, Coyote begs a stalwart young buffalo for 'a drop of strength.' Transformed into a strapping 'Buffote,' Coyote misjudges the extent of his new powers, as well as the virtues of age, and is stripped of his buffalo guise." Publ Wkly

"Expressive, darkly hued illustrations complement the lively retelling, loosely based on a Shoshoni tale, which blends dialogue and a clipped narration for an animated, appealing story." Horn Book Guide

Stevens, Janet, 1953-—*Continued*

Tops and bottoms; adapted and illustrated by Janet Stevens. Harcourt Brace & Co. 1995 unp il $16 *

Grades: K 1 2 3   398.2
　　1. African Americans—Folklore 2. Rabbits—Folklore
　　3. Bears—Folklore
　　ISBN 0-15-292851-0   LC 93-19154
　　A Caldecott Medal honor book, 1996

"Bear agrees to enter into a farming partnership with Hare, but first Hare makes Bear choose which half he will receive at harvest time: tops or bottoms. Because Bear picks tops, Hare sows all root vegetables. For the second crop, Bear chooses bottoms; this time Hare grows lettuce, broccoli, and celery. Finally, the frustrated Bear demands tops and bottoms from the final season's crop. But Hare is still the winner: he grows corn [and] keeps the ears 'in the middle' for his family. . . . Steven's bold, well-composed watercolor, pencil, and gesso illustrations cover every inch of each vertically oriented double-page spread. . . . The story contains enough sly humor and reassuring predictability to captivate listeners." Horn Book

Stewig, John W.

King Midas; a golden tale; told by John Warren Stewig; pictured through the mind of Omar Rayyan. Holiday House 1999 unp il $15.95

Grades: 2 3 4   398.2
　　1. Midas (Legendary character)
　　ISBN 0-8234-1423-X   LC 98-21222

A king finds himself bitterly regretting the consequences of his wish that everything he touches would turn to gold

"Rayyan's watercolors are a phantasmagoria of irreverent details, from the statue of a fresh minotaur sticking his tongue out to a rubber duck floating in a fountain." Bull Cent Child Books

Stockings of buttermilk: American folktales; edited by Neil Philip; illustrated by Jacqueline Mair. Clarion Bks. 1999 124p il $20

Grades: 4 5 6 7   398.2
　　1. Folklore—United States
　　ISBN 0-395-84980-2   LC 98-54366

These "stories and anecdotes, rooted in Europe but harvested in America, and often from African American tellers, are nearly all surprising variants on familiar folktales. . . . Philip generally lays editorial hands on the tales lightly, if at all, learnedly discusses tale types and other matters in appended notes. . . . Jacqueline Mair's small paintings add atmosphere by mimicking folk art patchwork and embroidery patterns." Booklist

Includes bibliographical references

Storace, Patricia

Sugar Cane; a Caribbean Rapunzel; pictures by Raúl Colón. Jump at the Sun/Hyperion Books for Children 2007 48p il $16.99 *

Grades: 1 2 3 4   398.2
　　1. Folklore—Caribbean region
　　ISBN 0-7868-0791-1; 978-0-7868-0791-8
　　　　　　　　　　　　　LC 2006-36449

"The fisherman's pregnant wife wants sugar cane, and in an attempt to satisfy her cravings he cuts some from the garden of Madame Fate, an infamous 'conjure-woman.' In return, the sorceress demands the couple's unborn child, who will be named Sugar Cane. On the girl's first birthday, the woman takes her to live in a tower without stairs. . . . One evening the lonely girl's voice attracts King, a young man renowned for his songs. Colón's colored-pencil-and-watercolor illustrations mirror the lyrical text." SLJ

Sturges, Philemon

The Little Red Hen (makes a pizza); retold by Philemon Sturges; illustrated by Amy Walrod. Dutton Children's Bks. 1999 unp il $15.99 *

Grades: K 1 2 3   398.2
　　1. Folklore 2. Chickens—Folklore
　　ISBN 0-525-45953-7   LC 99-20066

In this version of the traditional tale, the duck, the dog, and the cat refuse to help the Little Red Hen make a pizza but do get to participate when the time comes to eat it and then they wash the dishes

"There's a keen sense of the absurd here, and the hilarious cut-paper illustrations are right in tune with the zany plot." SLJ

Taback, Simms, 1932-

Kibitzers and fools; tales my zayda (grandfather) told me. Viking 2005 unp il $16.99 *

Grades: K 1 2 3   398.2
　　1. Jews—Folklore
　　ISBN 0-670-05955-2   LC 2005-03859

Contents: The sign; A made-to-order suit; Chicken soup; A philosophical dispute; The umbrella; An important question; A shlemiel and a shlimazel; Two brothers; A case of mistaken identity; The caretaker; The restaurant; If I were a Rockefeller; The rabbi is so smart, or How Chelm got bigger

Thirteen brief, illustrated, traditional Jewish tales, each accompanied by an appropriate saying.

"This uproarious book celebrates the shtetl scene with energetic, mixed-media pictures in bright, folk-art style. . . . Families will want to share this." Booklist

Talbott, Hudson

King Arthur and the Round Table; written and illustrated by Hudson Talbott. Books of Wonder 1995 unp il $18.99

Grades: 3 4 5   398.2
　　1. Arthur, King—Legends 2. Arthurian romances
　　ISBN 0-688-11340-0   LC 94-43766

"Talbott recounts the battles immediately following Arthur's accession to the throne, the young king's fateful meeting with beautiful Guinevere, and the acquisition of the Round Table." Horn Book Guide

"The rich watercolor tableaux . . . paint war as bloody and painful, not all glorious. The love scenes glow golden. The Round Table, huge and decorated with the signs of the zodiac, exhibits its power more than the words do. Overall, this is a rousing addition to the current pickings of Arthurian stories." SLJ

Tatanka and the Lakota people; a creation story; illustrated by Donald F. Montileaux. South Dakota State Historical Society Press 2006 unp il $16.95

Grades: 1 2 3 4   **398.2**

1. Teton Indians—Folklore 2. Creation—Folklore
ISBN 0-9749195-8-6   LC 2006016009

The transformaton of the Buffalo Nation into the Ordinary People and their salvation by Tatanka comes from this traditional creation story of the Lakota, or Sioux, Indians.

"Montileaux, an Oglala Lakota artist, illustrates the text with paintings rendered in a two-dimensional format that reflects traditional buffalo-hide paintings. The colorful, stylized images match the formal tone of the story. The English telling is clear and concise, with the corresponding Lakota text appearing alongside." SLJ

Taylor, C. J. (Carrie J.), 1952-
Spirits, fairies, and merpeople; Native stories of other worlds. Tundra Books 2009 39p il $19.95

Grades: 3 4 5 6   **398.2**

1. Native Americans—Folklore
ISBN 978-0-88776-872-9; 0-88776-872-5

Contents: The mermaid; The little people; The lodge eater; Water Lily finds her love; The fairy village; Spirits of heaven and earth; Souls in the mist

"The seven brief legends in this collection hail from a range of Native cultures. Mohawk artist/storyteller Taylor includes one from her own heritage, along with one each from the Mi'kmaq, Dakota, Coos, Ojibwa, Ute, and Cree. . . . Taylor's retellings are crisp and lend themselves well to reading aloud. Each story is accompanied by a lushly hued, surrealistic painting. The powerful images featuring fearsome creatures and tiny human figures balance the taut economy of the text." SLJ

Taylor, Harriet Peck
Coyote places the stars; retold and illustrated by Harriet Peck Taylor. Bradbury Press 1993 unp il pa $5.99 hardcover o.p.

Grades: K 1 2 3   **398.2**

1. Chinook Indians—Folklore 2. Coyote (Legendary character) 3. Stars—Folklore
ISBN 0-689-81535-2 (pa)   LC 92-46431

"Based on a Wasco Native American legend, this . . . pourquoi tale explains the designs of the constellations. It is the curious coyote who decides to discover the secrets of the heavens by creating a ladder of arrows he shoots into the sky. Once in the heavens, he moves the stars around forming the shapes of his animal friends." SLJ

"Taylor's batik-and-dye paintings are a good match for the casual, playful rhythm of her retelling." Booklist

Taylor, Sean
The great snake; stories from the Amazon; [by] Sean Taylor; illustrated by Fernando Vilela. Frances Lincoln Children's 2008 60p il $19.95

Grades: 3 4 5 6   **398.2**

1. Folklore—Brazil 2. Amazon River valley—Folklore
ISBN 978-1-84507-529-3; 1-84507-529-3

Contents: The Legend of Jurutaí; The Tortoise and the Vulture; The Mother of the Water; The Great Snake; A Long Way to Go; The Dolphin and the Fisherman; The Curupira; Mani's Mystery; I Really Must be Gone; About the stories; Glossary; The burning rainforest

A collection of nine South American folktales from sly jaguars and the slowest of sloths to spine-tingling giant serpents and white-suited strangers.

"Youngsters will be caught up in this journey, following the river from place to place, meeting kind and welcoming people who share their stories. Woodcuts stamped in black, gold, green, turquoise, and red ink on white or orange backgrounds brilliantly capture the mystery of this unfamiliar world." SLJ

Tchana, Katrin Hyman, 1963-
Changing Woman and her sisters; stories of goddesses from around the world; retold by Katrin Hyman Tchana; illustrated by Trina Schart Hyman. Holiday House 2006 80p il $18.95

Grades: 5 6 7 8   **398.2**

1. Gods and goddesses 2. Folklore
ISBN 978-0-8234-1999-9; 0-8234-1999-1
                                      LC 2005-52504

An illustrated collection of traditional tales which feature goddesses from different cultures, including Navajo, Mayan, and Fon. Notes explain each goddess's place in her culture, the reason for the book, and how the illustrations were developed

"This large, handsome volume assembles well-chosen, well-told stories. . . . Hyman . . . contributed distinctive portrayals of the goddesses using a technique that melded photographs and found materials into full-page ink and acrylic paintings." Booklist

Includes bibliographical references

Sense Pass King; a story from Cameroon; retold by Katrin Tchana; illustrated by Trina Schart Hyman. Holiday House 2002 unp il $16.95 *

Grades: K 1 2 3   **398.2**

1. Folklore—Cameroon
ISBN 0-8234-1577-5   LC 00-35094

Despite a jealous king's repeated attempts to get rid of her, Ma'antah continually manages to outwit him and proves herself worthy of the name Sense Pass King

The author "gives enough details to set the scene, and her smooth pacing will keep readers on the edge of their seats. . . . Hyman's artwork suggests the African heat—layers of gold silhouettes of trees and straw-colored huts on stilts with palm-frond rooftops are artfully set off by geometrically patterned fabrics in citrus tones." Publ Wkly

Tchana, Katrin Hyman, 1963-—Continued

The serpent slayer: and other stories of strong women; retold by Katrin Tchana; illustrated by Trina Schart Hyman. Little, Brown 2000 113p il $22.99 *

Grades: 4 5 6 7   **398.2**
  1. Women—Folklore
  ISBN 0-316-38701-0   LC 95-35077

Contents: The serpent slayer; The barber's wife; Nesoowa and the Chenoo; Clever Marcela; Sister Lace; The rebel princess; Beebyeebyee and the Water God; Kate Crackernuts; The old woman and the Devil; The magic lake; Grandmother's skull; Three whiskers from a lion's chin; Duffy the Lady; Sun-Girl and Dragon-Prince; Staver and Vassilissa; Tokoyo; The lord's daughter and the blacksmith's son; The marriage of two masters

"These 18 folktales emphasize feminine strength, courage, and wit. . . . The selections come from places as diverse as China, Scotland, and the Gambia." SLJ

"Tchana offers solid retellings of the oft-anthologized ('Kate Crackernuts') and the not oft-anthologized ('Sister Lace'). . . . The thematic variety of the stories provides something for everyone. . . . Humor, suspense, romance, and horror are reflected through the medium of Hyman's powerful art." Bull Cent Child Books

Includes bibliographical references

Thomas, Joyce Carol

The six fools; collected by Zora Neale Hurston; adapted by Joyce Carol Thomas; illustrated by Ann Tanksley. HarperCollins 2006 unp il $15.99; lib bdg $16.89 *

Grades: K 1 2 3   **398.2**
  1. Hurston, Zora Neale, 1891-1960—Adaptations
  2. African Americans—Folklore 3. Folklore—United States
  ISBN 0-06-000646-3; 0-06-000647-1 (lib bdg)
        LC 2004-30055

Adapted from a story collected by Zora Neale Hurston and previously published in *Every tongue got to confess*

A young man searches for three people more foolish than his fiancée and her parents

"This adaptation of the fool story from Hurston's *Every Tongue Got to Confess* . . . is light and adept. . . . The result is wonderful in voice: rich, hilarious, and satisfying. Tanksley's oil monoprints done in a folk-art style set the story in Hurston's 1920s-'30s with humor and vibrant color in a wide-ranging palette." SLJ

The skull talks back and other haunting tales; collected by Zora Neale Hurston; adapted by Joyce Carol Thomas; illustrated by Leonard Jenkins. HarperCollins 2004 56p $15.99; lib bdg $16.89 *

Grades: 4 5 6 7   **398.2**
  1. Hurston, Zora Neale, 1891-1960—Adaptations
  2. Horror fiction 3. African Americans—Folklore
  ISBN 0-06-000631-5; 0-06-000634-X (lib bdg)
        LC 2003-22215

Contents: Big, bad Sixteen; Bill, the talking mule; High Walker; The witch who could slip off her skin; The skull talks back; The haunted house

"Thomas retells six supernatural folktales selected from Hurston's Every Tongue Got to Confess." SLJ

"Using a direct style that loses none of the colloquial immediacy of the original voices, Thomas has done a great job of retelling six of Hurston's supernatural tales, and Jenkins' monochromatic collages and silhouettes capture the delicious, shivery glow of skeletons and graveyards." Booklist

The three witches; collected by Zora Neale Hurston; adapted by Joyce Carol Thomas; illustrated by Faith Ringgold. HarperCollins 2006 unp il $15.99; lib bdg $16.89 *

Grades: K 1 2 3   **398.2**
  1. Hurston, Zora Neale, 1891-1960—Adaptations
  2. Witches—Folklore 3. African Americans—Folklore
  4. Folklore—Southern States
  ISBN 978-0-06-000649-5; 0-06-000649-8; 978-0-06-000650-1 (lib bdg); 0-06-000650-1 (lib bdg)
        LC 2005-14553

Three hungry witches set out to eat two orphaned children while their grandmother is away at the market.

"Adapting a story from Hurston's 1930s folklore collection, *Every Tongue Got to Confess*, Thomas makes a fast, fun, but also scary tale more accessible to young readers, while Ringgold's paintings, with thick black lines and vibrant colors, reflect both the comic exaggeration and the shivery action." Booklist

What's the hurry, Fox? and other animal stories; collected by Zora Neale Hurston; illustrated by Bryan Collier; adapted by Joyce Carol Thomas. HarperCollins Publishers 2004 unp il $15.99; lib bdg $16.89

Grades: K 1 2 3   **398.2**
  1. Hurston, Zora Neale, 1891-1960—Adaptations
  2. Animals—Folklore 3. Folklore—Southern States
  ISBN 0-06-000643-9; 0-06-000644-7 (lib bdg)
        LC 2003-7014

Presents a volume of pourquoi tales collected by Zora Neale Hurston from her field research in the Gulf states in the 1930s.

In her adaptations Thomas uses "simplicity, humor, wit, and a colloquial style true to the spirit of the originals. . . . Collier's double-page-spread pictures combine painting and collage to show the animal characters' sly human machinations. The stories are very short, leaving lots of space for storyteller and audience." SLJ

Tomie dePaola's Favorite nursery tales. Putnam 1986 127p il $24.99

Grades: K 1 2 3   **398.2**
  1. Folklore 2. Fables
  ISBN 0-399-21319-8   LC 85-28302

The book begins "with a verse about reading picture books from Stevenson's *Child's Garden of Verses*, followed by Longfellow's 'Children's Hour.' The story selections—'Johnny Cake,' 'The Little Red Hen,' 'Rumpelstiltskin,' 'The Princess and the Pea,' 'The Tortoise and the Hare,' 'The House on the Hill,' and 22 more." Booklist

"DePaola's droll, witty, and very funny illustrations capture the essence of each story from a child's point of view. . . . The beautiful layout of these pages, in which the print and pictures are perfectly at ease with one another, invites confident new readers as well as adults for reading aloud." SLJ

Trickster: Native American tales; a graphic collection; edited by Matt Dembicki. Fulcrum 2010 il pa $22.95 *

Grades: 5 6 7 8   **398.2**

1. Native Americans—Folklore 2. Folklore—Graphic novels 3. Graphic novels

ISBN 978-1-55591-724-1; 1-55591-724-0

"More than 40 storytellers and cartoonists have contributed to this original and provocative compendium of traditional folklore presented in authentic, colorful, and engaging sequential art. The stories are drawn from a variety of Native peoples across North America, and so the trickster character appears variously as Rabbit, a raccoon, Coyote, and in other guises; landscapes, clothing and rhythms of speech and action also vary in keeping with distinct traditions. Realistic, impressionistic, painterly, and cartoon styles of art are employed to echo and announce the tone of each tale and telling style, making this a rich visual treasure as well as cultural trove." SLJ

Tseng, Grace

White tiger, blue serpent; illustrated by Jean and Mou-Sien Tseng. Lothrop, Lee & Shepard Bks. 1999 unp il $16; lib bdg $16.84

Grades: 2 3 4   **398.2**

1. Fairy tales 2. Folklore—China

ISBN 0-688-12515-8; 0-688-12516-6 (lib bdg)

LC 94-9757

Based on tale from Drung tribe of Yunnan Province

When his mother's beautiful brocade is snatched away by a greedy goddess, a young Chinese boy faces many perils as he attempts to get it back

"Lush paintings in the manner of fifteenth-century Chinese art animate a full-bodied folktale retelling about the search for beauty." Booklist

Valeri, M. Eulalia

The hare and the tortoise = La liebre y la tortuga; adaptation by Maria Eulàlia Valeri; illustrated by Max. Chronicle 2006 unp il $14.95; pa $6.95

Grades: K 1 2   **398.2**

1. Rabbits—Folklore 2. Turtles—Folklore 3. Fables 4. Folklore 5. Bilingual books—English-Spanish

ISBN 0-8118-5057-9; 0-8118-5058-7 (pa)

Recounts the traditional tale of the race between the persevering tortoise and the boastful hare in English and Spanish

"Told in a simple but richly descriptive style, the story is both entertaining and lends itself very well to reading out loud. . . . The story is aptly rendered in the English and the Spanish versions, and overall, this is handsomely executed." Booklist

Vallverdú, Josep, 1923-

Aladdin and the magic lamp = Aladino y la lámpara marvillosa; from The thousand and one nights; adaptation by Josep Vallverdu; illustrated by Pep Montserrat. Chronicle Books 2006 unp il $14.95; pa $6.95

Grades: K 1 2   **398.2**

1. Arabs—Folklore 2. Fairy tales 3. Bilingual books—English-Spanish

ISBN 0-8118-5061-7; 0-8118-5062-5 (pa)

Aladdin outwits an evil magician who first tries to trick him into handing over an old lamp with a genie inside and later steals Aladdin's wife and possessions.

"Told in a simple but richly descriptive style, the story is both entertaining and lends itself very well to reading out loud. . . . This is a handsomely executed English-Spanish version that will make a great addition to a child's library of favorite bedtime readings." Booklist

Van Kampen, Vlasta, 1943-

It couldn't be worse! Annick Press 2003 unp il lib bdg $18.95; pa $6.95

Grades: K 1 2 3   **398.2**

1. Folklore

ISBN 1-55037-783-3 (lib bdg); 1-55037-782-5 (pa)

The farmer's family was so crowded in their one-room house that they knew that it couldn't get worse but couldn't see how to make it better. So the farmer's wife asked for advice

"Bright, cheery watercolors match the puckish charm of this folktale." Booklist

Van Laan, Nancy

The magic bean tree; a legend from Argentina; retold by Nancy Van Laan; paintings by Beatriz Vidal. Houghton Mifflin 1998 unp il $15

Grades: K 1 2 3   **398.2**

1. Native Americans—Folklore 2. Folklore—Argentina

ISBN 0-395-82746-9   LC 96-38632

A young Quechuan boy sets out on his own to bring the rains back to his parched homeland and is rewarded by a gift of carob beans that come to be prized across Argentina

"Vidal's shimmering, folk art-style paintings are well matched to the elegant simplicity and drama of Van Laan's retelling." Booklist

Includes glossary and bibliographical references

Shingebiss; an Ojibwe legend; retold by Nancy Van Laan; woodcuts by Betsy Bowen. Houghton Mifflin 1997 unp il $16

Grades: 2 3 4   **398.2**

1. Ojibwa Indians—Folklore 2. Ducks—Folklore

ISBN 0-316-89627-6   LC 95-40274

Shingebiss the duck bravely challenges the Winter Maker and manages to find enough food to survive a long, harsh winter

Van Laan's "lyric text flows like a soft drum beat and, although lengthy, wastes no words. . . . The artist's rustic, spirited woodcuts appear within circular frames of thick, loose lines that give one the sense of peering through ice holes." Publ Wkly

Includes glossary and bibliographical references

Wada, Stephanie

Momotaro and the island of ogres; a Japanese folktale; as told by Stephanie Wada; paintings by Kano Naganobu. George Braziller 2005 47p il $19.95

Grades: 3 4 5 6   **398.2**
    1. Folklore—Japan
    ISBN 0-8076-1552-8

Found floating on the river inside a peach by an old couple, Momotaro grows up and fights the terrible demons who have terrorized the village for years.

"Nineteenth-century silk handscrolls, painted by master Naganobu and housed in the New York Public Library's Spencer Collection, illustrate this handsome retelling of a much-loved Japanese folktale." Booklist

Wagué Diakité, Baba

The hatseller and the monkeys; a West African folktale; retold and illustrated by Baba Wagué Diakité. Scholastic Press 1999 unp il $15.95 *

Grades: K 1 2 3   **398.2**
    1. Folklore—West Africa 2. Monkeys—Folklore
    ISBN 0-590-96069-5   LC 98-16250

An African version of the familiar story of a man who sets off to sell his hats, only to have them stolen by a treeful of mischievous monkeys

"Ceramic-tile paintings on each spread depict the action in fluid, bold brushwork. . . . In this retelling, Diakité's use of language is as colorful and unusual as his artwork." Publ Wkly

The hunterman and the crocodile; a West African folktale; retold and illustrated by Baba Wagué Diakité. Scholastic 1997 unp il $15.95

Grades: 2 3 4   **398.2**
    1. Folklore—West Africa 2. Crocodiles—Folklore
    ISBN 0-590-89828-0   LC 95-25975

"After Donso rescues a crocodile family, they turn on him and threaten to eat him. Several creatures . . . refuse his appeals for help, saying that Man has always misused them in the past. Only clever Rabbit is willing to assist him. Bold figures painted on ceramic tiles illustrate this teaching tale about 'living in harmony with nature.'" Horn Book Guide

Includes bibliographical references

The magic gourd. Scholastic Press 2003 32p il $16.95

Grades: 2 3 4   **398.2**
    1. Folklore—Mali 2. Rabbits—Folklore 3. Chameleons—Folklore
    ISBN 0-439-43960-4   LC 2002-4731

"In a time of famine, Chameleon rewards Brother Rabbit for a kind deed with a magic gourd that fills with whatever its owner desires. King Mansa Juga steals the gourd, but clever Rabbit recovers it and teaches the greedy king a lesson. Photos of exquisitely crafted ceramic plates, bowls, and tiles bordered with traditional Mali patterns illustrate this West African tale, which is retold with both economy and flair." Horn Book Guide

Includes glossary

Mee-An and the magic serpent; a folktale from Mali. Groundwood Books 2007 unp il $16.95

Grades: K 1 2 3 4   **398.2**
    1. Folklore—Mali 2. Snakes—Folklore
    ISBN 978-0-88899-719-7; 0-88899-719-1

"Beautiful Mee-An has decided she will accept only a perfect husband, someone without a single scratch, scar, or blemish. Her magical little sister, Assa, turns herself into a fly and believes she has found such a paragon. However, he is really a serpent who plans to fatten both girls and devour them. . . . Diakité's trademark ceramic-tile illustrations are on the recto while the cleanly framed text is on the verso. A well-designed and elegantly told addition to folktale shelves." SLJ

Waldman, Debby

Clever Rachel; story by Debby Waldman; illustrations by Cindy Revell. Orca Book Publishers 2009 unp il $19.95

Grades: K 1 2 3   **398.2**
    1. Jews—Folklore 2. Riddles—Fiction
    ISBN 978-1-55469-081-7; 1-55469-081-1

Retells a traditional Jewish folktale about a clever girl named Rachel who clashes with a boy named Jacob when he challenges her with his riddles, until a woman with an urgent problem shows them that they are at their best when they work together.

"The lighthearted text includes occasional Yiddish words. Energetic illustrations convey Rachel and Jacob's competitive spirits." Horn Book Guide

A sack full of feathers; story by Debby Waldman; illustrations by Cindy Revell. Orca Book Publishers 2006 unp il $19.95

Grades: K 1 2 3   **398.2**
    1. Jews—Folklore 2. Gossip—Folklore
    ISBN 1-55143-332-X

"Yankel loves to tell stories and repeat the gossip that he hears in his father's store in the shtetl. . . . Unfortunately, Yankel only hears the bits and pieces that make trouble, not how things turn out. So the rabbi decides to teach the boy a lesson by making him see that stories spread and that they can be hurtful. The fun in this retelling of a Jewish folktale is not in the lesson, but in the setting, the people, and the stories they tell. The bright acrylic folk art shows the characters gossiping, quarreling . . . and, finally, getting together." Booklist

Wang Ping, 1957-

The dragon emperor; a Chinese folktale; retold by Wang Ping; illustrations by Tang Ge. Millbrook Press 2008 48p il (On my own folklore) lib bdg $25.26

Grades: 1 2 3 4   **398.2**
    1. Folklore—China 2. Dragons—Folklore
    ISBN 978-0-8225-6740-0 (lib bdg); 0-8225-6740-7 (lib bdg)   LC 2006036718

A jealous warrior challenges the leadership of the dragon emperor. End note discusses the dragon in Chinese folklore and culture.

The "tale is paired with an illustration style that nicely reflects the culture." Horn Book Guide

Ward, Helen, 1962-
The hare and the tortoise; a fable from Aesop; retold & illustrated by Helen Ward. Millbrook Press 1999 unp il $16.95; lib bdg $24.90
Grades: K 1 2 3 **398.2**
1. Aesop—Adaptations 2. Fables 3. Folklore 4. Rabbits—Folklore 5. Turtles—Folklore
ISBN 0-7613-0988-8; 0-7613-1318-4 (lib bdg)
LC 98-26100
Retells the events of the famous race between the boastful hare and the persevering tortoise. Includes a key to the various animals pictured in the illustrations
"A straightforward, elegant, witty retelling of an old favorite. . . . With black ink outlines meticulously delineating the creatures' fur and markings, Ward's watercolor-and-gouache paintings show each animal as both warmly cuddly and realistic." Booklist

Unwitting wisdom; an anthology of Aesop's fables; retold & illustrated by Helen Ward. Chronicle Books 2004 unp il $18.95 *
Grades: 3 4 5 6 **398.2**
1. Aesop—Adaptations 2. Fables
ISBN 0-8118-4450-1 LC 2003-22990
Contents: Sour grapes; The trappings of power; All dressed up; Pot luck; A time to dance; A dinner invitation; Steady and slow; Upon reflection; Size isn't everything; Not flying, but falling; Fool's gold; Hard cheese
"Familiar entries from Aesop are extravagantly extended in this stunning, oversized compendium. . . . Beautifully rendered in pen and watercolor, the illustrations incorporate cunning details. . . . [Ward's] language blends formal, even florid, phrases with jocular observations and some colloquial quips." SLJ

Wargin, Kathy-Jo, 1965-
The frog prince; by the Brothers Grimm; as retold by Kathy-jo Wargin; illustrated by Anne Yvonne Gilbert. Mitten Press 2007 unp il $18.95
Grades: K 1 2 3 **398.2**
1. Fairy tales 2. Folklore—Germany
ISBN 978-1-58726-279-1; 1-58726-279-7
LC 2006020283
As payment for retrieving the princess's ball, the frog exacts a promise which the princess is reluctant to fulfill
"Intricate, gloriously lush illustrations highlight this retelling of the familiar tale. Wargin has preserved much of the tone of the original text while editing the length to make it more palatable for younger audiences." Booklist

Washington, Donna L., 1967-
A pride of African tales; illustrated by James Ransome. HarperCollinsPublishers 2004 70p il $16.99; lib bdg $17.89
Grades: 3 4 5 **398.2**
1. Folklore—Africa
ISBN 0-06-024929-3; 0-06-024932-3 (lib bdg)
LC 94-18697
Contents: Anansi's fishing expedition; The boy who wanted the moon; Shansa Mutongo Shima; The roof of leaves; The wedding basket; The talking skull

A collection of African folktales originating in the storytelling tradition
"Ransome contributes lush, naturalistic watercolors. . . . Storytellers looking for material will welcome this versatile offering, as will educators seeking to deepen children's understanding of Africa's diversity and the richness of its narrative tradition." Booklist
Includes bibliographical references

Willey, Margaret
Clever Beatrice; an Upper Peninsula conte; illustrated by Heather McWhorter. Atheneum Bks. for Young Readers 2001 unp il $16
Grades: K 1 2 3 **398.2**
1. Folklore—United States 2. Giants—Folklore
ISBN 0-689-83254-0 LC 00-42019
A small, but clever young girl outwits a rich giant and wins all his gold
"Set in Michigan's Upper Peninsula, this is a winning tale of brain vs. brawn. . . . Willey's telling is simple but spirited, and her dialogue, with its slight French-Canadian cadence, is pitch perfect. Heather Solomon's illustrations are remarkable: watercolors augmented with collage, they have unusual texture and depth." Horn Book
Other titles about Clever Beatrice by this author are:
Clever Beatrice and the best little pony (2004)
A Clever Beatrice Christmas (2006)

The 3 bears and Goldilocks; illustrated by Heather M. Solomon. Atheneum Books for Young Readers 2008 unp il $16.99 *
Grades: PreK K 1 2 3 **398.2**
1. Folklore 2. Bears—Folklore
ISBN 978-1-4169-2494-4; 1-4169-2494-9
LC 2007-13857
Goldilocks, ignoring her father's warning not to rush in where she does not belong, enters a cabin in the woods, cleans it to meet her standards, plucks from the porridge items unappealing to her before eating a bowlful, and falls asleep on the bed that suits her best.
"There is a rustic feel to the illustrations, rendered in watercolor, collage, colored pencil, acrylic, and oil paint. . . . This satisfying read-aloud offers a new twist on an old favorite." SLJ

Wisnewski, Andrea
Little Red Riding Hood; retold and illustrated by Andrea Wisnewski. David R. Godine 2006 unp il $18.95
Grades: K 1 2 3 **398.2**
1. Fairy tales 2. Folklore—Germany
ISBN 1-56792-303-8; 978-1-56792-303-2
LC 2006022122
A version of the classic story about a little girl, her grandmother, and a not-so-clever wolf, set in nineteenth-century rural New England
"A handsomely illustrated version of a folktale favorite. Wisnewski's retelling is straightforward and the language has a comfortable, folksy cadence." SLJ

Wisniewski, David

Golem; story and pictures by David Wisniewski. Clarion Bks. 1996 unp il $15.95; pa $6.95 *
Grades: 3 4 5   **398.2**
 1. Jews—Folklore 2. Monsters—Folklore
 ISBN 0-395-72618-2; 0-618-89424-1 (pa)
                                        LC 95-21777
Awarded the Caldecott Medal, 1997
This "is the tale of a clay giant formed in the image of man to protect the Jewish people of medieval Prague from destruction by their enemies." SLJ
 "The fiery, crisply layered paper illustrations, portraying with equal drama and precision the ornamental architecture of Prague and the unearthly career of the Golem, match the specificity and splendor of the storytelling." Publ Wkly

Wolkstein, Diane

The magic orange tree, and other Haitian folktales; collected [and told] and with a new preface by Diane Wolkstein; drawings by Elsa Henriquez; [new] foreword by Edwidge Danticat. Schocken Books 1997 xii, 212p il pa $15
Grades: 5 6 7 8   **398.2**
 1. Folklore—Haiti
 ISBN 0-8052-1077-6   LC 97-118784
First published 1978 by Knopf
 "A rare collection of folktales and songs is presented in this volume. Miss Wolkstein travelled throughout Haiti listening to the many storytellers in all areas. Each of the twenty-eight tales is preceded by an introduction which details the circumstances surrounding the collection of each story. The blend of cultures found in Haiti is well-depicted in her selections. The introduction in itself is as spellbinding as are the stories. . . . An added delight is the inclusion of music and words in both English and Creole." Bibliophile

Wooldridge, Connie Nordhielm, 1950-

Wicked Jack; adapted by Connie Nordhielm Wooldridge; illustrated by Will Hillenbrand. Holiday House 1995 unp il $16.95; pa $6.95
Grades: K 1 2 3   **398.2**
 1. Folklore—Southern States
 ISBN 0-8234-1101-X; 0-8234-1292-X (pa)
                                        LC 93-13248
 "The mean blacksmith defeats the devil and his young sons with a chair that won't stop rocking, a sledgehammer that won't stop pounding, and a fire bush that keeps on sticking. In the delectable ending, Jack, now deceased, is turned away from the underworld by terrified demons. . . . Hillenbrand's imaginative mixed-media paintings (with smudges of coal) have thin, robust lines, angular figures, subtle colors, and a distinctive style." Booklist

Wormell, Christopher

Mice, morals, & monkey business; lively lessons from Aesop's Fables. Running Press 2005 unp il $18.95
Grades: K 1 2 3   **398.2**
 1. Aesop—Adaptations 2. Fables
 ISBN 0-7624-2404-4
 "Wormell uses linocut prints to illuminate 21 of Aesop's famous life lessons. . . . The bold, black lines of the expertly rendered images and colorful accents primarily in earth tones create instantly recognizable figures. The subtle use of light and shadow adds clarity, expression, and often drama without extraneous detail." SLJ

Yolen, Jane

Meow; cat stories from around the world; illustrated by Hala Wittwer. HarperCollins 2005 40p il $16.99; lib bdg $17.89 *
Grades: K 1 2 3   **398.2**
 1. Cats—Folklore 2. Folklore
 ISBN 0-06-029161-3; 0-06-029162-1 (lib bdg)
                                        LC 2002-06380
 "A collection of 10 cat stories, plus nursery rhymes and lore drawn from sources around the world. Yolen captures the heart of each story, and the resulting text begs to be told or read aloud. . . . Wittwer's richly colored paintings fill the pages with the essence of feline charm, power, and wit. " SLJ

Mightier than the sword; world folktales for strong boys; collected and told by Jane Yolen; with illustrations by Raul Colón. Silver Whistle/Harcourt 2003 112p il $19
Grades: 4 5 6 7   **398.2**
 1. Folklore
 ISBN 0-15-216391-3   LC 2002-9886
 Contents: The magic brocade; The young man protected by the river; The devil with the three golden hairs; Eating with trolls; Knee-high man; Language of the birds; Thick-head; The fisherman and the chamberlain; Jack and his companions; The truthful shepherd; And who cured the princess?; The false knight on the road; Hired hands; Mighty mikko
 A collection of folktales from around the world which demonstrate the triumph of brains over brawn
 Yolen's "versions of these stories are lively, expressively written, ready for reading aloud or telling, and illustrative of her point." SLJ
 Includes bibliographical references

Not one damsel in distress; world folktales for strong girls; collected and told by Jane Yolen; with illustrations by Susan Guevara. Silver Whistle Bks. 2000 116p il $17
Grades: 4 5 6 7   **398.2**
 1. Fairy tales 2. Women—Folklore
 ISBN 0-15-202047-0   LC 99-18509
 Contents: Atalanta the huntress; Nana Miriam; Fitcher's bird; The girl and the puma; Li Chi slays the serpent; Brave woman counts coup; Pretty Penny; Burd Janet; Mizilca; The pirate princess; The samurai maiden; Bradamante; Molly Whuppie

Yolen, Jane—*Continued*

A collection of thirteen traditional tales from various parts of the world, each of whose main character is a fearless, strong, heroic, and resourceful woman

"This is a spirited collection with a lively pace. . . . The stories sing and soar in Yolen's supple language, and each is contained enough for a read-aloud." Booklist

Includes bibliographical references

Young, Ed

Cat and Rat; the legend of the Chinese zodiac. Holt & Co. 1995 unp il $15.95; pa $6.95

Grades: K 1 2 3   398.2

1. Folklore—China 2. Zodiac 3. Cats—Folklore 4. Rats—Folklore

ISBN 0-8050-2977-X; 0-8050-6049-9 (pa)

LC 94-49147

"Cat and Rat were best friends, according to this Chinese legend, until the Jade Emperor of Heaven held a race to determine which animals would be included in the zodiac. . . . In the author's note, Young comments on the Chinese New Year, the 12 traditional signs, and the birth years and personality traits for each one." Booklist

"Young tells the story in lively, spare prose. . . . His charcoal and pastel drawings on dark blue and buff rice paper are elegant and full of action." SLJ

Lon Po Po; a Red-Riding Hood story from China; translated and illustrated by Ed Young. Philomel Bks. 1989 unp il $16.99; pa $6.99 *

Grades: 1 2 3   398.2

1. Folklore—China 2. Wolves—Folklore

ISBN 0-399-21619-7; 0-698-11382-9 (pa)

LC 88-15222

Awarded the Caldecott Medal, 1990

Three sisters staying home alone are endangered by a hungry wolf who is disguised as their grandmother

"The text possesses that matter-of-fact veracity that characterizes the best fairy tales. The watercolor and pastel pictures are remarkable: mystically beautiful in their depiction of the Chinese countryside, menacing in the exchanges with the wolf, and positively chilling in the scenes inside the house." SLJ

Seven blind mice. Philomel Bks. 1992 unp il $17.99; pa $7.99

Grades: K 1 2 3   398.2

1. Fables 2. Elephants—Folklore 3. Folklore—India 4. Mice—Folklore

ISBN 0-399-22261-8; 0-698-11895-2 (pa)

LC 90-35396

A Caldecott Medal honor book, 1993

"In Young's version of the familiar Indian folktale of the blind men and the elephant, seven blind mice approach an elephant, ask what it is, explore various parts of the beast, and arrive at different conclusions. . . . Many preschool and primary grade teachers will find that the book reinforces their students' learning of colors, days of the week, and ordinal numbers, while heeding the story's admonition not to lose sight of the whole in their enthusiasm for identifying the parts. Graphically, this picture book is stunning, with the cut-paper figures of the eight characters dramatically silhouetted against black backgrounds. . . . At once profound and simple, intelligent and playful." Booklist

The sons of the Dragon King; a Chinese legend. Atheneum Bks. for Young Readers 2004 unp il $16.95 *

Grades: 3 4 5   398.2

1. Folklore—China

ISBN 0-689-85184-7   LC 2002-154321

The nine immortal sons of the Dragon King set out to make something of themselves, and each, with help from a watchful father, finds a role that suits his individual strengths.

"The text is engrossing and includes an informative author's note. The illustrations, rendered in brush, ink, and cut paper, use softly smudged lines for the part of the story focused on the legend, and sharper, cleaner lines augmented by a minimal but dramatically effective use of color for the present-day segments. This elegant addition to folklore shelves should be a first purchase for most libraries." SLJ

What about me? Philomel Bks. 2002 unp il $16.99

Grades: K 1 2 3   398.2

1. Folklore—Middle East

ISBN 0-399-23624-4   LC 2001-45927

A young boy determinedly follows the instructions of the Grand Master in the hope of gaining knowledge, only to be surprised as how he acquires it. Based on a Sufi tale.

"Dazzling collage illustrations set the personae of the tale against muted, spatter-paint backgrounds. The figures are agile, rhythmic, graceful, and emotionally charged, interpreting the story in perfect synchronization with mood and tempo." Horn Book

Zelinsky, Paul O.

Rapunzel; retold and illustrated by Paul O. Zelinsky. Dutton Children's Bks. 1997 unp il $16.99 *

Grades: 3 4 5   398.2

1. Fairy tales 2. Folklore

ISBN 0-525-45607-4   LC 96-50260

Awarded the Caldecott Medal, 1998

A retelling of the folktale in which a beautiful girl with long golden hair is kept imprisoned in a lonely tower by a sorceress

"An elegant and sophisticated retelling that draws on early French and Italian versions of the tale. Masterful oil paintings capture the Renaissance setting and flesh out the tragic figures." SLJ

Rumpelstiltskin; from the German of the Brothers Grimm; retold & illustrated by Paul O. Zelinsky. Dutton 1986 unp il lib bdg $16.99; pa $6.99

Grades: K 1 2 3   398.2

1. Folklore—Germany 2. Fairy tales

ISBN 0-525-44265-0 (lib bdg); 0-14-055864-0 (pa)

LC 86-4482

A Caldecott Medal honor book, 1987

A strange little man helps the miller's daughter spin straw into gold for the king on the condition that she will give him her first-born child

"Zelinsky's painterly style and rich colors provide an evocative backdrop to this story. The medieval setting

Zelinsky, Paul O.—*Continued*

and costumes and the spools of gold thread which shine on the page like real gold are suggestive of an illuminated manuscript. . . . Zelinsky's smooth retelling and glowing pictures cast the story in a new and beautiful light." SLJ

Zemach, Margot

The little red hen; an old story. Farrar, Straus & Giroux 1983 unp il hardcover o.p. pa $4.95 *

Grades: K 1 2   **398.2**

1. Folklore 2. Chickens—Folklore

ISBN 0-374-34621-6; 0-374-44511-7 (pa)

LC 83-14159

A retelling of the traditional tale about the little red hen whose lazy friends are unwilling to help her plant, harvest, or grind the wheat into flour, but all are willing to help her eat the bread that she makes from it

"The pleasingly retold, rhythmical text is appropriately extended by scrappy, cartoonish, softly glowing color illustrations. The animals are anthropomorphized just enough, and their characters perfectly caught." Child Book Rev Serv

The three little pigs; an old story. Farrar, Straus & Giroux 1989 unp il hardcover o.p. pa $5.95

Grades: K 1 2   **398.2**

1. Folklore—Great Britain 2. Pigs—Folklore 3. Wolves—Folklore

ISBN 0-374-37527-5; 0-374-47717-5 (pa)

LC 87-73488

"Michael di Capua books"

Zemach "has brought a familiar, often-told tale to life with marvelous ink-and-watercolor illustrations. Her wolf, wearing a dapper green hat and radiating slyness with every inch of his furry self, cuts a spendidly sinister figure as he attempts to wile his way to three pork chop dinners. With simple, lively sentences Zemach has related the complete story, including the apple-picking and country fair episodes." Horn Book

Ziefert, Harriet

Little Red Riding Hood; retold by Harriet Ziefert; illustrated by Emily Bolam. Viking 2000 unp il hardcover o.p. pa $3.99

Grades: K 1 2   **398.2**

1. Fairy tales 2. Folklore—Germany 3. Wolves—Folklore

ISBN 0-670-88389-1; 0-14-056529-9 (pa)

LC 99-23210

"A Viking easy-to-read"

A little girl meets a hungry wolf in the forest while on her way to visit her gandmother

This adaptation of the Grimm's fairy tale "tells the story in a brisk, straightforward style . . . [with] simple, colorful illustrations. . . . The vocabulary is appropriate for beginning readers. The lively illustrations and familiarity of the story should provide a successful reading experience." SLJ

398.8 Rhymes and rhyming games

Anna Banana: 101 jump-rope rhymes; compiled by Joanna Cole; illustrated by Alan Tiegreen. Morrow Junior Bks. 1989 64p il pa $7.95 hardcover o.p.

Grades: 3 4 5   **398.8**

1. Jump rope rhymes 2. Games

ISBN 0-688-08809-0 (pa)   LC 88-29108

An illustrated collection of jump rope rhymes arranged according to the type of jumping they are meant to accompany

"Heavily inked drawings provide cartoon-style humor; sources for jump-rope rhymes and an index of first lines are appended." Booklist

The **Arnold** Lobel book of Mother Goose. Knopf 1997 176p il $21 *

Grades: PreK K 1 2   **398.8**

1. Nursery rhymes

ISBN 0-679-88736-9; 0-679-98736-3 (lib bdg)

LC 97-1762

First published 1986 with title: The Random House book of Mother Goose

This nursery rhyme collection is "a true classic, with more than three hundred verses and Lobel's vigorous, lively, narrative-filled illustrations." Horn Book Guide

Arrorró mi niño; Latino lullabies and gentle games; selected and illustrated by Lulu Delacre; musical arrangements by Cecilia Esqivel and Diana Sáez. Lee & Low Books 2004 unp il $16.95 *

Grades: K 1 2 3   **398.8**

1. Nursery rhymes 2. Finger play 3. Lullabies 4. Bilingual books—English-Spanish

ISBN 1-58430-159-7   LC 2003-9234

An illustrated collection of nursery rhymes, finger play games, and lullabies from the major Latino groups living in the United States today

"The bright, beautiful oil-wash illustrations . . . reflect the diversity of the Latino experience. . . . The bilingual text appears first in Spanish, with the English translation beneath or by its side. . . . Musical notation and comments about the melodies are at the back." Booklist

Baker, Keith, 1953-

Big fat hen; illustrated by Keith Baker. Harcourt Brace & Co. 1994 unp il $15; pa $6; bd bk $6.95 *

Grades: PreK K 1 2   **398.8**

1. Nursery rhymes 2. Counting 3. Chickens—Folklore

ISBN 0-15-200294-4; 0-15-201951-0 (pa); 0-15-201331-8 (bd bk)   LC 93-19160

"The text is the old rhyme, 'One, two, buckle my shoe,' and the double-page spreads show the hen and her chicks (first appearing as eggs) enacting the words. . . . Children who want to skip the counting altogether can just enjoy the singsong text and the pictures executed in acrylic paints. The big fat hen is very large and quite beautiful, with iridescent green feathers accented with purple and red; her friends are just as lovely, all colors, some with delicate patterns in their feathers." Booklist

Bodden, Valerie

Nursery rhymes. Creative Education 2010 32p il (Poetry basics) $28.50

Grades: 5 6 7 8   **398.8**

1. Nursery rhymes
ISBN 978-1-58341-778-2; 1-58341-778-8
LC 2008009157

This book describes nursery rhymes' "history, characteristics, and variations. Many examples are provided as well as ideas for how children can write their own pieces. The information is accessible, and the writing is sufficiently lively to engage readers. The well-designed pages feature a variety of art reproductions from different literary eras and some photographs." Horn Book Guide

Includes glossary and bibliographical references

Cabrera, Jane, 1968-

Old Mother Hubbard. Holiday House 2001 unp il hardcover o.p. bd bk $6.95

Grades: K 1 2   **398.8**

1. Nursery rhymes
ISBN 0-8234-1659-3; 0-8234-2132-5 (bd bk)
LC 00-59715

Based on The comic adventures of Old Mother Hubbard and her dog, by Sarah Catherine Martin, originally published in London, 1805, by John Harris

Light-hearted illustrations accompany this version of the familiar nursery rhyme about an old woman and her playful dog

"The big, close-up pictures, with thick black lines and blazing color combine slapstick and coziness. . . . The chanting rhymes and exuberant illustrations make a great read-aloud for young preschoolers." Booklist

Chapman, Jane

Sing a song of sixpence; a pocketful of nursery rhymes and tales; [by] Jane Chapman. Candlewick Press 2004 61p il $15.99

Grades: K 1   **398.8**

1. Nursery rhymes
ISBN 0-7636-2545-0   LC 2003-69565

An illustrated collection of twenty-five traditional nursery rhymes and stories, including "Jack and Jill," "Wee Willie Winkie," "Little Miss Muffet," "Three Blind Mice," "Goldilocks and the Three Bears," and "The Little Red Hen"

"With clear, bright acrylic pictures, Chapman brings an action-packed collection to preschoolers. . . . The type is large and clear, and lots of boisterous pictures decorate the big, spacious pages." Booklist

Chwast, Seymour, 1931-

She sells sea shells; world class tongue twisters. Applesauce Press 2008 64p il $19.95

Grades: 3 4 5 6   **398.8**

1. Tongue twisters
ISBN 978-1-60433-009-0; 1-60433-009-0

Chwast's "visual exposé of tongue twisters teems with humor and cheek. . . . The lines and use of color are posterlike. . . . The humor can . . . be goofy or dark. . . . The punchy illustrations capture [the tongue twisters'] buoyant essence. Few will be able to resist saying them aloud." Publ Wkly

Collins, Heather

Out came the sun; a day in nursery rhymes. Kids Can Press 2007 91p il $19.95

Grades: PreK K   **398.8**

1. Nursery rhymes
ISBN 978-1-55337-881-5; 1-55337-881-4

"Collins arranges 45 mostly familiar nursery rhymes in a sun-up to sun-down romp starring a multi-species stuffed animal family. . . . Collins's watercolors display just enough verve and domestic humor to keep her subjects from turning twee. . . . The manageable size and good-natured fun make this volume stand out." Publ Wkly

Dillon, Leo, 1933-

Mother Goose numbers on the loose; [by] Leo & Diane Dillon. Harcourt 2007 unp il $17

Grades: PreK K 1 2   **398.8**

1. Nursery rhymes 2. Counting
ISBN 0-15-205676-9; 978-0-15-205676-6
LC 2005-37763

Presents an illustrated collection of twenty-four counting rhymes, from "Baa, baa black sheep" to "Wash the dishes, wipe the dishes"

This "is so imaginative and playful that each reading yields something new and unexpected. A cast of humans and animals parades across the stark white pages like carnival-goers, some of them sporting elaborate Renaissance masks and clothing. . . . Inventive, artistically dazzling, and full of wit." Publ Wkly

Emberley, Barbara, 1932-

Drummer Hoff; adapted by Barbara Emberley; illustrated by Ed Emberley. Simon & Schuster 1987 c1967 unp il $16; pa $5.95

Grades: PreK K 1 2   **398.8**

1. Nursery rhymes
ISBN 0-671-66248-1; 0-671-66249-X (pa)
LC 87-35755

Awarded the Caldecott Medal, 1968

First published 1967 by Prentice-Hall

"A cumulative folk rhyme is adapted in spirited style and illustrated with arresting black woodcuts accented with brilliant color. The characters who participate in the building and firing of a cannon—'Sergeant Crowder brought the powder, Corporal Farrell brought the barrel,' etc.—are hilariously rugged characters, while 'Drummer Hoff who fired it off stands by, deadpan, waiting to touch off the marvelously satisfying explosion.'" Hodges. Books for Elem Sch Libr

Favorite nursery rhymes from Mother Goose; illustrated by Scott Gustafson. Greenwich Workshop Press 2007 96p il $19.95

Grades: PreK K 1   **398.8**

1. Nursery rhymes
ISBN 978-0-86713-097-3; 0-86713-097-0

"These 45 rhymes include the very well known (Itsy Bitsy Spider) and the somewhat familiar (Hickety, Pickety, My Black Hen). . . . [The illustrations include] an anthropomorphic baking bear, a pelican sea captain, and Peter Piper as a pug on two legs." Publisher's note

This "showcases lavish illustrations that are perfect for

Favorite nursery rhymes from Mother Goose—
Continued
sharing with a group. Suffused in color and charm, the visual interpretations include many delightful details." SLJ

Fitzgerald, Joanne, 1956-
Yum! yum!! delicious nursery rhymes; [compiled and illustrated by] Joanne Fitzgerald. Fitzhenry & Whiteside 2007 unp il $18.95
Grades: PreK 398.8
    1. Nursery rhymes 2. Food—Poetry
    ISBN 978-1-55041-888-0; 1-55041-888-2
"A farmer's market is the setting for this charming story, set around 13 well-known nursery rhymes that deal with food. The characters are animals dressed in human clothes. Listeners will have fun hunting for the piggy who appears in every scene. . . . The small pictures, all in light pastels, are beautifully detailed. . . . Subtle humor abounds." SLJ

Galdone, Paul, 1914-1986
The cat goes fiddle-i-fee; adapted and illustrated by Paul Galdone. Clarion Bks. 1985 unp il pa $6.95 hardcover o.p.
Grades: K 1 398.8
    1. Nursery rhymes 2. Animals—Poetry
    ISBN 0-89919-705-1 (pa) LC 85-2686
An old English rhyme names all the animals a farm boy feeds on his daily rounds
"Galdone's line-and-watercolor illustrations have all the verve and accessible good humor associated with his work, and the varied and irresistible rhythm of the verses carries the nonsense along at a good pace, enhancing its appeal to the very young. Whether told or sung, this is a diverting selection for preschool story times." Booklist

Three little kittens. Clarion Bks. 1986 unp il $15; pa $5.95
Grades: PreK K 1 2 398.8
    1. Nursery rhymes 2. Cats—Poetry
    ISBN 0-89919-426-5; 0-89919-796-5 (pa)
    LC 86-2655
Three little kittens lose, find, soil, and wash their mittens
"Galdone's characteristically exuberant pen-and-wash drawings fill these pages with feline faces, first rueful then joyful, then repentant, and finally excited about the prospects of catching 'a rat close by.' This is one of those sustained nursery rhymes that initiates youngest listeners into the concentration required for stories, and there's enough dramatic movement and color contrast in the art to hold toddlers' attention." Bull Cent Child Books

The **Helen** Oxenbury nursery collection. Alfred A. Knopf 2004 91p il $19.95; lib bdg $21.99 *
    Grades: K 1 2 3 398.8
    1. Nursery rhymes 2. Poetry—Collections
    ISBN 0-375-82992-X; 0-375-92992-4 (lib bdg)
    LC 2004-58446
This "anthology draws from three previous books: five poems from Tiny Tim—Verses for Children (1981), a dozen rhymes from Cakes and Custard—The Helen Oxenbury Nursery Rhyme Book (1975), and seven tales from The Helen Oxenbury Nursery Story Book (1985)." Booklist
"The stories all feature Oxenbury's trademark winsome pencil-and-watercolor pictures. They include such favorites as 'Little Red Riding Hood,' 'Henny-Penny,' and 'The Three Little Pigs,' and are retold with drama and humor." SLJ

Here comes Mother Goose; edited by Iona Opie; illustrated by Rosemary Wells. Candlewick Press 1999 107p il $21.99 *
    Grades: PreK K 1 2 398.8
    1. Nursery rhymes
    ISBN 0-7636-0683-9 LC 99-14256
Presents more than sixty traditional nursery rhymes, including "Old Mother Hubbard," "I'm a Little Teapot," and "One, Two, Buckle My Shoe"
"Wells's watercolor-and-ink pictures of somersaulting guinea pigs, mischievous rabbits, and fluffy ducklings capture the sheer joy and exuberance of the rhymes. . . . Make room on the shelves for this must-have title." SLJ

Hoberman, Mary Ann, 1930-
Miss Mary Mack; a hand-clapping rhyme; adapted by Mary Ann Hoberman; illustrated by Nadine Bernard Westcott. Little, Brown 1998 unp il music hardcover o.p. pa $6.99; bd bk $6.99
    Grades: PreK K 1 398.8
    1. Nursery rhymes
    ISBN 0-316-93118-7; 0-316-07614-7 (pa); 0-316-36642-0 (bd bk) LC 96-34829
"In this expanded version of the popular hand-clapping rhyme, the elephant (who's 'jumped so high' . . ./ He reached the sky/) . . . lands in the middle of a picnic where Mary Mack promises him her silver buttons if he doesn't go back to the zoo. Westcott's loose and humorous illustrations add to the necessarily limited text. A melody line and instructions for hand-clapping are included on the front endpapers." Horn Book Guide

I saw Esau; the schoolchild's pocket book; edited by Iona and Peter Opie; illustrated by Maurice Sendak. Candlewick Press 1992 160p il $19.99; pa $9.99
    Grades: Professional 398.8
    1. Folklore—Great Britain 2. English poetry—Collections
    ISBN 1-56402-046-0; 0-7636-1199-9 (pa)
    LC 91-71845
A revised and newly illustrated edition of the title first published 1947 in the United Kingdom
A collection of rhymes and riddles traditionally passed on orally from child to child
"From lamentation, pun, and insult to rebuttal, tongue-twister, and comic complaint, these schoolyard folk rhymes are vulgar, absurd, fierce, and utterly compelling. . . . [The book features] Sendak's wicked, joyful illustrations. Blending the factual and the surreal, the pictures (most in color, some in sepia or in black and white) extend the rhymes with characters and scenarios that are gross and tender. Sendak knows kids' ferocity and their fear." Booklist

If you love a nursery rhyme; illustrated by Susanna Lockheart. Barrons Educational Series 2009 unp il $18.99

Grades: PreK K   **398.8**
1. Nursery rhymes
ISBN 978-0-7641-6186-5; 0-7641-6186-5

"This large-format volume features just a dozen nursery rhymes but illustrates them with grace, style, and imaginative details. Some of the rhymes are featured on single pages, but five appear on double-page spreads accompanied with gatefold pages that, when opened out, move the vertical panels in the picture's central, cur-out oval to reveal a new scene. . . . Well designed and illustrated for active toddlers as well as older preschoolers." Booklist

Muu, moo! rimas de animales = animal nursery rhymes; selected by Alma Flor Ada and F. Isabel Campoy; English versions by Rosalma Zubizarreta; illustrated by Vivi Escriva. Rayo 2010 unp il $16.99; lib bdg $17.89

Grades: PreK K 1 2   **398.8**
1. Nursery rhymes 2. Latin American poetry—Collections 3. Animals—Poetry 4. Bilingual books—English-Spanish
ISBN   978-0-06-134613-2;   0-06-134613-6;
978-0-06-134614-9 (lib bdg); 0-06-134614-4 (lib bdg)
LC 2009014444

A collection of animal-themed nursery rhymes in Spanish, from Spain and Latin America, with English translations

"Rather than a verbatim translation of the Spanish, the English versions retain the rhythm and musicality of the originals. Escriva's watercolor illustrations include fun details. . . . In addition to being a perfect resource for bilingual programs, this book will be enjoyed as a bedtime read-aloud." SLJ

My very first Mother Goose; edited by Iona Opie; illustrated by Rosemary Wells. Candlewick Press 1996 107p il $21.99 *

Grades: PreK K 1 2   **398.8**
1. Nursery rhymes
ISBN 1-56402-620-5   LC 96-4904

"The 60 plus rhymes in this collection are mostly the old-time favorites, but include some more recent ones such as 'Shoo Fly' and 'Down by the Station.' Wells illustrates the selections with her usual winsome, quirky, anthropomorphic mice, rabbits, cats, pigs, bears, etc., and even includes some people. The lavish ink-and-watercolors are filled with action and delightful details." SLJ

The neighborhood Mother Goose; [illustrated by] Nina Crews. Greenwillow Books 2004 63p il $15.99; lib bdg $16.89 *

Grades: PreK K 1 2 3   **398.8**
1. Nursery rhymes
ISBN 0-06-051573-2; 0-06-051574-0 (lib bdg)
LC 2003-41763

"Amistad"

A collection of nursery rhymes, both familiar and lesser known, illustrated with photographs in a city setting.

"Nina Crews' clear, beautiful color photographs and computer manipulations bring children closeup to people like them. . . . She uses computer tools to combine photos of joyful kids in her Brooklyn neighborhood with all kinds of scenarios, realistic and wild." Booklist

Opie, Iona Archibald
Mother Goose's little treasures; [edited by] Iona Opie; illustrated by Rosemary Wells. Candlewick Press 2007 52p il $17.99

Grades: PreK K   **398.8**
1. Nursery rhymes
ISBN 978-0-7636-3655-5; 0-7636-3655-X
LC 2007-24959

A collection of nursery rhymes featuring such little-known characters as the wee melodie man and Handy Spandy, Mrs. Whirly and little bonny Button-cap

"This gem . . . shines with the charm of old-time rhymes and with Wells' beloved animal and child characters, set down in her signature style." Booklist

The Oxford dictionary of nursery rhymes; edited by Iona and Peter Opie. 2nd ed. Oxford Univ. Press 1997 xxix, 559p il $55

Grades: Adult Professional   **398.8**
1. Reference books 2. Nursery rhymes—Dictionaries
ISBN 0-19-860088-7   LC 98-140995

First published 1951

An anthology of "over 500 rhymes, songs, nonsense jingles, and lullabies. . . . Complementing the rhymes are nearly a hundred illustrations, including reproductions of early art found in ballad sheets and music books, which highlight the development of children's illustrations over the last two centuries. . . . [The editors note] the earliest known publications of the rhyme, describing how it originated, illustrating changes in wording over time, and indicating variations and parallels in other languages." Publisher's note

"The novice as well as the professional will find it an enjoyable read, as well as a learning experience." Am Ref Books Annu, 1999

¡Pio peep! traditional Spanish nursery rhymes; selected by Alma Flor Ada & F. Isabel Campoy; English adaptations by Alice Schertle; illustrated by Vivi Escrivá. HarperCollins Pubs. 2003 64p il $14.99; lib bdg $16.89 *

Grades: K 1 2 3   **398.8**
1. Nursery rhymes 2. Bilingual books—English-Spanish
ISBN 0-688-16019-0; 0-688-16020-4 (lib bdg)
LC 2001-51641

A collection of more than two dozen nursery rhymes in Spanish, from Spain and Latin America, with English translations

"Deeply rhythmic verses, compelling rhyme schemes, and words that 'play trippingly on the tongue' characterize every verse. Schertle's excellent English adaptations are not literal translations but poetic re-creations. They retain the rhythm, meter, and general meaning of the originals. . . . Escrivá's watercolor and colored-pencil illustrations use brilliant hues and detail to reconstruct a young child's world." SLJ

Polacco, Patricia

Babushka's Mother Goose. Philomel Bks. 1995 64p il hardcover o.p. pa $7.99

Grades: PreK **398.8**

1. Nursery rhymes

ISBN 0-399-22747-4; 0-698-11860-X (pa)

LC 94-32332

"The collection includes original rhymes written by Polacco as well as Ukrainian folktales and retellings from Mother Goose and Aesop that Polacco heard as a child from her own Babushka. The distinctive and humorous folk-art illustrations and delightful verses and stories make this book a joy to share with children." Horn Book Guide

The **real** Mother Goose; illustrated by Blanch Fisher Wright. Scholastic 1994 128p il $9.95

Grades: PreK K 1 2 **398.8**

1. Nursery rhymes

ISBN 0-590-22517-0

First published 1916 by Rand McNally

A comprehensive collection of over three-hundred traditional nursery rhymes

Reinhart, Matthew

A pop-up book of nursery rhymes. Little Simon 2009 unp il (Classic collectible pop-up) $26.99

Grades: PreK K **398.8**

1. Nursery rhymes 2. Pop-up books

ISBN 978-1-4169-1825-7; 1-4169-1825-6

Matthew Reinhart adapts Mother Goose's nursery rhymes, as the characters spring to life as intricate pop-up surprises.

"Ingenious details abound—the thoughtfulness put into every movement is evident." Pub Wkly

Ross, Tony, 1938-

Three little kittens and other favorite nursery rhymes; selected and illustrated by Tony Ross. Henry Holt and Co. 2009 90p il $16.95

Grades: PreK **398.8**

1. Nursery rhymes

ISBN 978-0-8050-8885-4; 0-8050-8885-7

LC 2008-925587

This is a "collection of nearly fifty classic nursery verses. . . . Illustrator Ross has sensibly taken a broad and pragmatic interpretation of the genre, so classic anonymous verse rubs shoulders with Lewis Carroll and lullabies. The presentation is invitingly simple. . . . Ross' visual style remains his usual rumply, comfortable, personable line and watercolor, his figures imbued with a gentle sense of comedy and individuality, and the illustrative vignettes are spirited and deft, sometimes approaching the masterful." Bull Cent Child Books

Rufus and friends: rhyme time; traditional poems extended and illustrated by Iza Trapani. Charlesbridge 2008 33p il $16.95; pa $7.95

Grades: PreK K **398.8**

1. Nursery rhymes

ISBN 978-1-58089-206-3; 978-1-58089-207-0 (pa)

LC 2007026200

In this collection of tongue-twisting nursery rhymes, the reader is asked to find hidden objects in the illustrations.

"The lively artwork was created using watercolor, ink, and colored pencils. Each actor/pooch is a different breed; they all have priceless facial expressions and vary with the situations. Children will ask for repeated readings as they search for the pictures again and again." SLJ

Another title about Rufus is:

Rufus and friends: school days (2010)

Sierra, Judy

Schoolyard rhymes; kids' own rhymes for rope skipping, hand clapping, ball bouncing, and just plain fun; illustrated by Melissa Sweet. Knopf 2005 31p il $15.95; lib bdg $17.89

Grades: K 1 2 3 **398.8**

1. Singing games 2. Jump rope rhymes

ISBN 0-375-82516-9; 0-375-92516-3 (lib bdg)

LC 2004-4273

"Sierra has selected 50 traditional playground chants and rhymes for inclusion in this illustrated collection. . . . Sweet's comical, mixed-media art adds to the wackiness of the rhymes, with jump ropes commanding a prominent position." Booklist

Sylvia Long's Mother Goose. Chronicle Bks. 1999 109p il $22.95

Grades: PreK **398.8**

1. Nursery rhymes

ISBN 0-8118-2088-2

LC 98-52311

"Human beings are replaced by animals, reptiles, and insects, all elegantly dressed, in this exuberant nursery-rhyme collection, which includes 82 familiar and less familiar verses." SLJ

Taback, Simms, 1932-

This is the house that Jack built. Putnam 2002 unp il $15.99; pa $6.99 *

Grades: K 1 2 3 **398.8**

1. Nursery rhymes

ISBN 0-399-23488-8; 0-14-240200-1 (pa)

LC 00-28057

The cumulative nursery rhyme about the chain of events that started when Jack built a house

"Taback's version of the age-old cumulative rhyme is an explosion of color, energy, zaniness, and pore-over-able detail." Horn Book

This little piggy; lap songs, finger plays, clapping rhymes, and pantomime rhymes; edited by Jane Yolen; illustrated by Will Hillenbrand; musical arrangements by Adam Stemple. Candlewick Press 2006 c2005 80p il $19.99 *

Grades: PreK K 1 2 **398.8**

1. Nursery rhymes 2. Finger play 3. Songs

ISBN 0-7636-1348-7

An "anthology of approximately 60 lap rhymes, songs, clapping rhymes, and finger and foot rhymes, all presented with explanations and simple instructions for parents to play with their babies and toddlers. . . . Hillenbrand has framed the rhymes with lovely mixed-

This little piggy—*Continued*

media pictures in an array of sherbet pastel colors with happy piggy families acting out the rhymes. . . . A delightful accompanying CD includes 13 songs from the text, beautifully done with vivacious accompaniment. The result is a perfect book for one-on-one sharing." SLJ

Tomie dePaola's Mother Goose. Putnam 1985
127p il $24.99
Grades: PreK K   **398.8**
1. Nursery rhymes
ISBN 0-399-21258-2   LC 84-26314

This "is a large, ample, unfussy edition of every child's first staple of literature. . . . The neat, flat illustrations are darkly outlined and colored generally in the illustrator's favorite palette of clear pinks, blues, and violets and surrounded with a lot of white space. Each verse is pictured in a simple and unmistakable interpretation. . . . A perfectly basic and lovely Mother Goose, lavish yet simple, and a splendid beginning for the youngest listener." Horn Book

Tortillitas para mamá and other nursery rhymes; Spanish and English; selected and translated by Margot C. Griego . . . [et al.]; illustrated by Barbara Cooney. Holt & Co. 1981 unp il pa $5.95 hardcover o.p.
Grades: PreK K 1 2   **398.8**
1. Nursery rhymes 2. Folklore—Latin America 3. Bilingual books—English-Spanish
ISBN 0-8050-0317-7   LC 81-4823

A bilingual collection of 13 popular Latin American nursery rhymes

The purpose of this book "is to preserve a unique aspect of Hispanic culture which deserves to be passed down to all children. . . . The illustrations are strikingly beautiful, capturing the rich color and texture of some parts of South America. . . . [But their] homogenized view of Latin Americans can easily lead to the perpetuation of some familiar stereotypes." Interracial Books Child Bull

Will Moses Mother Goose. Philomel Bks. 2003
61p il $17.99
Grades: PreK K   **398.8**
1. Nursery rhymes
ISBN 0-399-23744-5   LC 2003-731

Folk art paintings accompany this compilation of over sixty of the best-loved Mother Goose rhymes

"In a marvelous match of style and content Moses's . . . sprightly folk-art oil paintings make this a 'must have' Mother Goose volume. The book's tempo is set from the first page, which intersperses thumbnail vignettes with individual rhymes. . . . A turn of the page then blends the vignettes into a full-bleed panorama of busy village life." Publ Wkly

Winter, Jeanette, 1939-
The house that Jack built. Dial Bks. for Young Readers 2000 unp il hardcover o.p. pa $6.99
Grades: PreK K 1   **398.8**
1. Nursery rhymes
ISBN 0-8037-2524-8; 0-14-230126-4 (pa)
     LC 99-36344

Simple rebus illustrations are used to present the familiar cumulative nursery rhyme about the antics that go on in the house built by an unsuspecting Jack

"Readers can predict who will enter the story next by watching for visual clues. The small trim size of the book and the clear, vibrant colors and simple shapes of the artwork are appealing." Horn Book Guide

398.9   Proverbs

The **Night** has ears; African proverbs; selected and illustrated by Ashley Bryan. Atheneum Bks. for Young Readers 1999 unp il $16
Grades: K 1 2 3   **398.9**
1. Proverbs 2. Folklore—Africa
ISBN 0-689-82427-0   LC 98-48772

"A Jean Karl book"

A collection of twenty-six proverbs, some serious and some humorous, from a variety of African tribes

"Illustrated in Bryan's distinctive multishape, multicolor style, the tempera-and-gouache art resembles stained glass. . . . A worthy supplement to cultural studies, this will also inspire students to write and illustrate their own proverbs." Booklist

400   LANGUAGE

411   Writing systems of standard forms of languages

Donoughue, Carol, 1935-
The story of writing; [by] Carol Donoughue. Firefly Books 2007 48p il map $19.95
Grades: 4 5 6 7   **411**
1. Alphabet—History 2. Writing—History
ISBN 978-1-55407-306-1; 1-55407-306-5

This is an "introduction to the history of the Roman alphabet. . . . Beginning sections about early civilizations' alphabets, starting with Sumerian cuniforms, include a you-are-there narrative. . . . Later spreads cover European illuminated manuscripts and the development of printing technology. A final section [covers] Chinese characters. . . . Numerous carefully chosen color photos of artifacts . . . greatly enhance the book's appeal." Booklist

Includes bibliographical references

Jeffrey, Laura S.
All about Braille; reading by touch. Enslow Publishers 2004 48p il (Transportation & communication series) lib bdg $23.93
Grades: 2 3 4   **411**
1. Blind—Books and reading
ISBN 0-7660-2184-X   LC 2003-17617

Contents: A girl named Helen; Finger reading; Changing a secret code; Communicating and getting around; From teachers to musicians; Today and tomorrow

This offers a brief history of braille, describes the braille alphabet and how it is used for communication for the blind.

Includes glossary and bibliographical references

Robb, Don

Ox, house, stick; the history of our alphabet; illustrated by Anne Smith. Charlesbridge 2007 48p il $16.95; pa $7.95 *

Grades: 4 5 6 7   **411**

1. Alphabet—History 2. Writing—History
ISBN 978-1-57091-609-0; 978-1-57091-610-6 (pa)
                                        LC 2005-06015

"Robb traces the history of each letter from its origin to its modern appearance in the Roman alphabet. He explains the birth of writing in pictogram form and the eventual transition to written symbols that stand for sounds. . . . Smith's whimsical paintings are a fitting companion to Robb's lighthearted text." SLJ

Werner, Sharon

Alphabeasties and other amazing types; by Sharon Werner and Sarah Forss. Blue Apple Books 2009 unp il $19.99

Grades: K 1 2 3   **411**

1. Alphabet 2. Animals
ISBN 978-1-934706-78-7; 1-934706-78-7
                                        LC 2009-12599

"An alphabet of animals is presented, each one cleverly composed of its initial letter in a typeface that often suits the characteristics of that creature—a spiky alligator, shaggy sheep, etc. Foldout pages allow for the impressive height of the giraffe or the length of the alligator to be revealed. . . . Young readers will enjoy the animals while older children will have a greater appreciation for the book's artistry." SLJ

413   Dictionaries of standard forms of languages

Evans, Lezlie

Can you greet the whole wide world? 12 common phrases in 12 different languages; by Lezlie Evans; illustrated by Denis Roche. Houghton Mifflin 2006 unp il $16

Grades: K 1 2 3   **413**

1. Polyglot materials 2. Vocabulary
ISBN 0-618-56327-X   LC 2005020612

Introduces young readers to common phrases such as "good morning," "thank you," and "please" in German, Hebrew, Spanish, Arabic, Russian, Hindi, Chinese, Zulu, Japanese, Italian, French, and Portuguese.

"This book is a great way to introduce the many similarities and interests of children around the world. . . . Flat, cartoon-style illustrations done in bright colors reinforce action and concepts." SLJ

Includes bibliographical references

Park, Linda Sue, 1960-

Mung-mung! a foldout book of animal sounds; illustrated by Diane Bigda. Charlesbridge 2004 unp il $9.95

Grades: K 1 2   **413**

1. Polyglot materials 2. Vocabulary
ISBN 1-57091-486-9   LC 2003-3765

"A multilingual guessing game for the youngest children. Each spread begins with the question, 'What kind of animal says.' and features a variety of sounds in playful handwritten typefaces. Opening a flap reveals the answer. Several languages from Europe, Asia, and the Middle East are included, as well as the sound in English to tip off youngsters. Bigda's cotton-candy-colored gouache artwork displays a lightness of line and a jazzy, freeform feel that blends well with the simple fare." SLJ

Yum! Yuck! a foldout book of people sounds from around the world; [by] Linda Sue Park, Julia Durango; illustrated by Sue Rama. Charlesbridge 2005 unp il $9.95

Grades: K 1 2   **413**

1. Polyglot materials 2. Vocabulary
ISBN 1-57091-659-4   LC 2004-18955

Presenting sounds that people make to utter or cry out abruptly in various languages to express such emotion as distaste, excitement, and surprise

"This original offering is a delightful addition to the canon of multicultural picture books and a fun read-aloud guessing game." SLJ

Stojic, Manya

Hello world! greetings in 42 languages around the globe! Scholastic 2002 38p il $14.95

Grades: K 1 2   **413**

1. Polyglot materials 2. Vocabulary
ISBN 0-439-36202-4   LC 2001-43615

"Cartwheel books"

Children from around the world say "hello" in forty-two languages, from Amharic to Zulu

"Greetings appear with a bold nearly full-page acrylic painting of a child. . . . This deceivingly simple book encourages interest in and awareness of other languages." SLJ

Weinstein, Ellen, 1959-

Everywhere the cow says "Moo!"; [by] Ellen Weinstein; illustrated by Kenneth Andersson. Boyds Mills Press 2008 unp il $14.95

Grades: PreK K   **413**

1. Polyglot materials 2. Vocabulary
ISBN 978-1-59078-458-7; 1-59078-458-8
                                        LC 2007-17566

"Via simple text and illustrations, children are told what a dog, frog, duck, rooster, and cow say in English, Spanish, French, and Japanese. . . . Each phrase has its own page featuring the animal and an iconic item (the Eiffel Tower, a bullfighter, etc.). . . . The spare and colorful cartoonlike pictures mix the look of folk art and digital precision. Bold primary colors and heavy black lines abound. A glossary includes proper and phonetic spellings." SLJ

Includes glossary

419   Sign languages

Ault, Kelly

Let's sign! every baby's guide to communicating with grownups; written by Kelly Ault; illustrated by Leo Landry. Houghton Mifflin Co. 2005 77p il $17 *

Grades: PreK K 1   **419**
  1. Sign language
  ISBN 0-618-50774-4

"After a brief and informative introduction that details the benefits of using sign language with babies, Ault presents three simple stories: Mealtime, Playtime, and Bedtime. . . . Landry's pencil-and-watercolor illustrations are child-friendly, and his depictions of the signs are both appealing and informative. . . . The signs are well chosen to reflect a child's world." SLJ

Baker, Pamela J., 1947-

My first book of sign; illustrations by Patricia Bellan Gillen. Gallaudet Univ. Press 1986 76p il $11.96

Grades: K 1 2 3   **419**
  1. Sign language
  ISBN 0-930323-20-3   LC 86-14937

"A Kendall Green publication"

Pictures of children demonstrate the forming in sign language of 150 basic alphabetically arranged words, accompanied by illustrations of the words themselves. Includes a discussion of fingerspelling and general rules for signing

"Looking like an ABC book, this is both appealing and useful. . . . Illustrations are brightly colored and have an even mixture of boys and girls of various racial backgrounds, some with hearing aids, some without." SLJ

Heller, Lora

Sign language for kids; a fun & easy guide to American sign language; [by] Lora Heller. Sterling 2004 95p il $14.95 *

Grades: 3 4 5 6   **419**
  1. Sign language
  ISBN 1-4027-0672-3   LC 2003-19011

Color photos illustrate sign language for numbers, letters, colors, feelings, animals, and clothes

"Clear color photos and simple text combine to form an excellent introduction to American Sign Language (ASL)." SLJ

Lowenstein, Felicia

All about sign language; talking with your hands. Enslow Publishers 2004 48p il (Transportation & communication series) lib bdg $23.93

Grades: 2 3 4   **419**
  1. Sign language
  ISBN 0-7660-2028-2   LC 2003-26608

Contents: The unspoken language; Signs of the times; The history of sign language; People who sign; Jobs with sign language; The future of sign language

This discusses "how sign language came about, the jobs where it is useful to know sign language, and people who are important to sign language. Also [includes] the manual alphabet." Publisher's note

Includes glossary and bibliographical references

Rankin, Laura

The handmade alphabet. Dial Bks. 1991 unp il $16.99; pa $5.99 *

Grades: K 1 2 3   **419**
  1. Sign language 2. Alphabet
  ISBN 0-8037-0974-9; 0-14-055876-4 (pa)
                          LC 90-24593

Presents the handshape for each letter of the American manual alphabet accompanied by an object whose name begins with that letter

"This [is] an excellent introduction to American sign, as well as an engaging ABC book. The art work is multiethnic, visually appealing, anatomically correct, and full of life. Clever use of props, light, and reflections add to the enjoyment." SLJ

Warner, Penny

Signing fun; American sign language vocabulary, phrases, games & activities; illustrated by Paula Gray. Gallaudet Univ. Press 2006 225p il pa $19.95

Grades: 4 5 6 7 8   **419**
  1. Sign language
  ISBN 1-56368-292-3

This "offers 441 . . . signs on a variety of favorite topics. . . . Each chapter includes practice sentences using everyday phrases. . . . *Signing Fun* provides dozens of . . . games and activities, too." Publisher's note

"This book is a great resource for readers who want to learn more signs, or for teachers and librarians looking for fun ways to share them with kids." SLJ

420   English and Old English (Anglo-Saxon)

Dubosarsky, Ursula, 1961-

The word snoop; illustrated by Tohby Riddle. Dial Books 2009 246p il $16.99

Grades: 5 6 7 8   **420**
  1. English language—History
  ISBN 978-0-8037-3406-7; 0-8037-3406-9
                          LC 2009-8306

First published 2008 in Australia with title: The word spy

A tour of the English language from the beginning of the alphabet in 4000 BC to modern text messaging and emoticons

"Short chapters, clear explanations, and humorous examples bring the subject to life, while word puzzles and coded messages at the end of each section invite reader participation. The attractive design adds to the appeal." Booklist

422 Etymology of standard English

Baker, Rosalie F.
In a word; 750 words and their fascinating stories and origins; by Rosalie Baker; illustrated by Tom Lopes. Cobblestone Pub. 2003 221p il $17.95
Grades: 5 6 7 8   **422**
    1. English language—Etymology
    ISBN 0-8126-2710-5   LC 2003-25582
    Contents: Cultural creations; Worldly words & power people; Math magic & science synergy; Religious rituals, fabulous folklore, & marvelous myths; Exceptional expressions; Clothing collection; Glorious gizmos & great grub; Spectacular sports; Joyful journeys; Natural necessities; Awesome archaeology; Political powerhouse; Military madness; Tantalizing tidbits; Fickle finances; Fantastic foreigners
    "The entries in this book discuss the meanings and derivations of 750 words and phrases. . . . While exploring word origins, Baker also touches on interesting facets of European history and Greek mythology. The jaunty illustrations are reproduced in black and shades of gray. . . . This informative book fosters an appreciation for the richness of the English language." Booklist

423 Dictionaries of standard English

The **American** Heritage children's dictionary; by the editors of the American Heritage dictionaries. Houghton Mifflin Harcourt 2009 896p il $19.95 *
Grades: 3 4 5 6   **423**
1. English language—Dictionaries 2. Reference books
ISBN 978-0-547-21255-5; 0-547-21255-0
                   LC 2009012324
First published 1986
This dictionary includes over 25,000 entries, with more than 16,000 example sentences, hundreds of special feature notes, a separate phonics and spelling guide, and 1,500 full-color photographs, illustrations, and diagrams.
    "This dictionary will have a general appeal to students and teachers and is perfect for ready-reference sections. An excellent choice." Booklist

The **American** Heritage first dictionary. rev ed. Houghton Mifflin 2009 405p il $17.95 *
Grades: PreK K 1 2   **423**
1. English language—Dictionaries 2. Reference books
ISBN 978-0-547-21597-6; 0-547-21597-5
First published 2007
This dictionary includes more than 2,000 entry words, and 850 full-color photographs and drawings

The **American** Heritage picture dictionary. rev ed. Houghton Mifflin 2009 138p il $15.95 *
Grades: PreK K 1   **423**
1. English language—Dictionaries 2. Reference books
ISBN 978-0-547-21596-9; 0-547-21596-7
First published 2003

This book introduces preschoolers and beginning readers to the idea of alphabetical order, helps prepare them for higher-level dictionaries, and includes 900 entry words

Bollard, John K.
Scholastic children's thesaurus; illustrated by Mike Reed. [new and updated ed] Scholastic Reference 2006 240p il $16.99
Grades: 4 5 6 7   **423**
    1. English language—Synonyms and antonyms
    2. Reference books
    ISBN 0-43979-831-0   LC 2005050010
    First published 1998
    An illustrated thesaurus for young readers defines more than five hundred headwords and 2,500 synonyms, providing example sentences for each synonym and including an extensive cross-referencing index.

The **Cat** in the Hat beginner book dictionary; by the Cat himself and P. D. Eastman. Beginner Bks. 1964 133p il $21
Grades: K 1 2 3   **423**
1. Reference books 2. Picture dictionaries 3. English language—Dictionaries
ISBN 0-394-81009-0; 978-0-394-91009-3
Also available Spanish-English edition
    "This alphabetically arranged dictionary, illustrated with rollicking funny drawings, explains word meanings with sentences and pictures. It intends to help preschoolers 'recognize, remember, and really enjoy a basic vocabulary of 1,350 words.' Despite its age, this book will still appeal to young children." Peterson. Ref Books for Child. 4th edition

Delahunty, Andrew
Barron's first thesaurus; compiled by Andrew Delahunty; illustrated by Steve Cox. Barron's Educational Series 2005 127p il pa $12.95
Grades: 1 2 3 4   **423**
    1. English language—Synonyms and antonyms
    2. Reference books
    ISBN 0-7641-3159-1
This "volume presents more than 100 headwords—one headword to a page—then provides a short definition that includes synonyms an example sentence, a separate list of synonyms, and where appropriate, an antonym. Young readers will find a total of more than 1,000 synonyms." Publisher's note
    An "excellent, easy-to-use resource. . . . The relevant, color cartoon illustrations are eye-catching." SLJ

DK Merriam-Webster children's dictionary. rev ed. Dorling Kindersley 2005 911p il map $19.99
Grades: 3 4 5 6   **423**
    1. Reference books 2. English language—Dictionaries
    ISBN 0-7566-1143-1
    First published 2000
    Presents definitions for over 32,000 entries and includes some 3,000 illustrations interspersed throughout the text

Foster, John, 1941-
Barron's junior rhyming Dictionary; illustrated by Melanie Williamson and Rupert Van Wyk. Barron's 2006 160p il pa $12.99
Grades: 3 4 5   **423**
    1. English language—Rhyme 2. Poetics 3. Reference books
    ISBN 0-7641-3424-8
First published 2005 in the United Kingdom with title: Oxford junior rhyming dictionary
    "Young poets will have fun perusing this book in search of the perfect rhyme. . . . Short rhymes scattered throughout are likely to encourage and inspire readers to try their hand at creating their own poems. [Illustrated with] fanciful cartoons. . . . Tips for writing limericks, nonsense nursery rhymes, and various other rhymes are included in this useful resource." SLJ

Hellweg, Paul
The American Heritage children's thesaurus. updated ed. Houghton Mifflin 2009 280p il $18.95 *
Grades: 3 4 5 6   **423**
    1. English language—Synonyms and antonyms 2. Reference books
    ISBN 978-0-547-21599-0; 0-547-21599-1
First published 1997
    This presents more than 4,000 entries and 36,000 synonyms divided into two groups: "best choices" and "other choices." Every sense of each entry word is illustrated by an example sentence showing typical usage. Includes more than 150 full-color photographs

The American Heritage student thesaurus. updated ed. Houghton Mifflin 2009 378p il $18.95 *
Grades: 5 6 7 8 9 10   **423**
    1. English language—Synonyms and antonyms 2. Reference books
    ISBN 978-0-547-21601-0; 0-547-21601-7
First published 1994
    This thesaurus presents 6,000 main entries and more than 70,000 synonyms with illustrative sentences

Macmillan dictionary for children; general editor, Christopher G. Morris. [rev and updated ed.] Simon & Schuster Books for Young Readers 2007 832p il map $19.99 *
Grades: 2 3 4 5   **423**
    1. Reference books 2. English language—Dictionaries
    ISBN 978-1-4169-3959-7; 1-4169-3959-8
              LC 2007297593
First published 1975
    "With 35,000 entries and more than 3,000 full-color illustrations, this attractive dictionary is a browser's delight. An introductory section explains how to find a word and includes a helpful spelling guide. . . . Eye-catching feature panels provide detailed information about words of particular interest to children. . . . An accessible and enticing addition." SLJ

Macmillan first dictionary; general editor, Christopher G. Morris. Newly updated. Simon & Schuster Book for Young Readers 2008 400p il map $17.99
Grades: K 1 2 3   **423**
    1. English language—Dictionaries 2. Reference books
    ISBN 978-1-4169-5043-1; 1-4169-5043-5
Replaces the edition published 1990 by Macmillan
    This dictionary "starts with a brief section on how to use a dictionary. The reference section offers maps of the U.S., the world, and the solar system and tables listing U.S. states and presidents. The dictionary proper is very cleanly laid out in two columns per page. Definitions are numbered and include sample sentences as well as multiple forms, such as plurals and tenses. The more than 1,400 colorful illustrations make this volume especially appealing." Booklist

The **McGraw-Hill** children's dictionary; by the Wordsmyth Collaboratory. McGraw-Hill Children's Pub. 2003 various paging il (Wordsmyth reference series) $24.95
Grades: 4 5 6 7   **423**
    1. Reference books 2. English language—Dictionaries
    ISBN 1-57768-298-X   LC 2002-18796
    A dictionary with word histories, synonyms, illustrations, and spelling, grammar, and usage features
    "The more than 30,000 entries are easy to read, with definitions arranged in three columns. 'Word History,' 'Homophone Note,' and 'Synonyms' boxes give extra information about some words. . . . This attractive dictionary is a fine work." Booklist

The **McGraw-Hill** children's thesaurus; by the Wordsmyth Collaboratory. McGraw-Hill Children's Pub. 2003 294p (Wordsmyth reference series) $19.95
Grades: 4 5 6 7   **423**
    1. English language—Synonyms and antonyms 2. Reference books
    ISBN 1-57768-296-3   LC 2002-18797
    Presents an alphabetical list of more than 3000 entries, with explanations of the different meanings of each headword and its synonyms
    This is "a valuable addition to the upper elementary classroom, library, or any place where children write or do homework." Am Ref Books Annu, 2003

McIllwain, John
DK Children's illustrated dictionary. Dorling Kindersley 2009 256p il $19.99
Grades: K 1 2 3   **423**
    1. English language—Dictionaries 2. Reference books
    ISBN 978-0-7566-5196-1; 0-7566-5196-4
First published 1994 with title: The Dorling Kindersley children's illustrated dictionary
    This dictionary offers concise definitions with numerous illustrations, and information about abbreviations, spelling, word building, facts and figures, and countries of the world

Merriam-Webster's elementary dictionary. New and expanded ed. Merriam-Webster 2009 24a, 824p il map $17.95
Grades: 3 4 5 6   **423**
1. English language—Dictionaries
ISBN 978-0-87779-675-6; 0-87779-675-0
LC 2008041753
First published 1986 with title: Webster's elementary dictionary
More than 36,000 entries with expanded definitions, usage examples, and nearly 1,300 quotes from classic and contemporary children's literature.
Includes bibliographical references

Merriam-Webster's intermediate dictionary. Merriam-Webster 2004 18a, 1005p il $17.95
Grades: 5 6 7 8   **423**
1. English language—Dictionaries 2. Reference books
ISBN 0-87779-579-7   LC 2004-45792
First published 1994 as a replacement for Webster's intermediate dictionary (1986)
This dictionary includes over 70,000 words and more than 1,000 illustrations, providing definitions, pronunciation, etymology, part of speech designation, and other appropriate information.

Merriam-Webster's primary dictionary; with illustrations by Ruth Heller. Merriam-Webster 2005 436p il $16.95
Grades: K 1 2 3   **423**
1. Reference books 2. English language—Dictionaries
ISBN 0-87779-174-0
"A beginner's dictionary. . . . Nearly 1,000 entries include definitions, example sentences, and word histories. Introduces basic dictionary skills such as alphabetization, spelling, pronunciations, use of synonyms and antonyms, and using words in context. [Includes] jokes, poems, and fun facts." Publisher's note
This work "displays an extraordinary level of care in its presentation. . . . A gift to budding wordsmiths." SLJ

Scholastic children's dictionary. Scholastic Inc 2010 c2011 800p il $19.99 *
Grades: 3 4 5 6   **423**
1. English language—Dictionaries 2. Reference books
ISBN 978-0-545-21858-0; 0-545-21858-6
LC 2010001521
First published 1996
Offers a dictionary that includes pronunciations, definitions, parts of speech, sample sentences, etymologies, synonyms, and cross-references

Scholastic first dictionary. updated ed. Scholastic Reference 2006 256p il $16.99
Grades: 1 2 3   **423**
1. English language—Dictionaries 2. Reference books
ISBN 0-439-79834-5   LC 2005049911
First published 1998
This offers definitions for approximately 1,500 words, illustrated with approximately 600 full-color photographs, and includes alternate forms for nouns, verbs, and adjectives, illustrative example sentences, and a phonetic pronunciation guide for each word

Scholastic first picture dictionary. rev ed. Scholastic Reference 2009 92p il $15.99
Grades: PreK K 1   **423**
1. Picture dictionaries 2. English language—Dictionaries 3. Reference books
ISBN 978-0-545-13769-0; 0-545-13769-1
First published 2005
This visual dictionary "features more than 700 clearly labeled images of inanimate objects, food items and living things. A section called 'The Living Room' contains common items including a remote control, telephone and DVD player. . . . The artwork (and assorted reader-directed questions) will engage the curious." Publ Wkly

Simon & Schuster thesaurus for children; [edited by] Jonathan P. Latimer and Karen Stray Nolting. Simon & Schuster Bks. for Young Readers 2001 288p $16.95
Grades: 4 5 6   **423**
1. English language—Synonyms and antonyms 2. Reference books
ISBN 0-689-84322-4   LC 2001-31083
"This volume offers cross-references leading to a number of related terms. The main entries generally focus on one thread of meaning; for example, for 'correct,' the entry lists 'adjust' and 'revise' as synonyms with a see-also for 'change' and 'fix.' Each main entry word and synonym are separately defined and include a sample sentence. . . . Different colors highlight sidebars and distinguish main-entry words from synonyms. There is a useful 23-page index. Clear print and an easy-to-use format make this serviceable resource a good choice for novices." SLJ

Terban, Marvin
Mad as a wet hen! and other funny idioms; illustrated by Giulio Maestro. Clarion Bks. 1987 64p il pa $7.95 hardcover o.p.
Grades: 3 4 5   **423**
1. English language—Idioms 2. English language—Terms and phrases
ISBN 0-89919-479-6 (pa)   LC 86-17575
Illustrates and explains over 100 common English idioms, in categories including animals, body parts, and colors
"Maestro's two-color cartoonlike illustrations are amusing and informative themselves, providing visual clues that support the textual explanations. . . . Although some of the expressions included are dated, the alphabetical index enables teachers and librarians to pick and choose. This book might be particularly beneficial in schools having a large ESL program, especially for older, more advanced students." SLJ

Scholastic dictionary of idioms. new & updated. Scholastic 2006 298p il pa $19.85 *
Grades: 4 5 6 7   **423**
1. English language—Idioms 2. Reference books
ISBN 978-0-439-77083-5 (pa); 0-439-77083-1 (pa)
First published 1996
This "introduction to American slang and phrase origins identifies and defines more than six hundred commonly used idioms, complementing the entries with . . . sample sentences and . . . illustrations." Publisher's note

Webster's New World children's dictionary; editor in chief, Michael Agnes. 2nd ed., rev. Wiley Pub. 2006 928p il map $17.95

Grades: 3 4 5 6   **423**

1. English language—Dictionaries 2. Reference books
ISBN 978-0-471-78688-7; 0-471-78688-8

LC 2005053750

First published 1991

This dictionary includes more than 33,000 entries, more than 800 notes and tips on synonyms, homonyms, prefixes, spelling, and word histories, over 750 photographs and illustrations, a thesaurus, an album of U.S. presidents, tables of weights and measures, an atlas of the world, and an album of U.S. states

"This dictionary is almost three reference books in one. . . . [It] is enjoyable to read and makes learning easy." Libr Media Connect

425   Grammar of standard English Syntax of standard English

Cleary, Brian P., 1959-

But and for, yet and nor; what is a conjunction? illustrated by Brian Gable. Millbrook Press 2010 31p il (Words are categorical) lib bdg $15.95

Grades: 2 3 4   **425**

1. English language—Grammar
ISBN 978-0-8225-9153-5 (lib bdg); 0-8225-9153-7 (lib bdg)   LC 2009015861

"This colorful book offers information about conjunctions and examples of how they work, all in easy-to-read rhymes. . . . The cartoon-style artwork depicts brightly colored, catlike creatures in human dress dramatizing a variety of situations. The high-energy illustrations rev up the comic intensity of the lightly humorous verse and promise to engage children in the subject." Booklist

Lawlor, Laurie

Muddy as a duck puddle and other American similes; illustrated by Ethan Long. Holiday House 2010 unp il $16.95

Grades: 1 2 3   **425**

1. Simile
ISBN 978-0-8234-2229-6; 0-8234-2229-1

LC 2009-29944

"Sly and irreverent, the folk sayings collected here, one for each letter of the alphabet, stretch back over history and reflect Americans' restlessness. . . . For each letter, big, clear, brightly colored cartoons show the literal meaning in the imagery expressed in such phrases as 'crooked as a barrel of snakes,' as well as the words' sly double meanings. . . . Kids will relish the boisterous insults and ornery frontier references in both the words and the pictures." Booklist

427   Historical and geographic variations, modern nongeographic variations

O'Reilly, Gillian

Slangalicious; where we got that crazy lingo; text by Gillian O'Reilly; illustrations by Krista Johnson. Annick Press 2004 84p il $24.95; pa $12.95

Grades: 4 5 6 7   **427**

1. English language—Slang 2. English language—Etymology
ISBN 1-55037-765-5; 1-55037-764-7 (pa)

"This volume explores the origins and meanings of slang words by tracing the efforts of a fictional student doing an assignment. . . . After a general introduction to slang, succeeding chapters explore the colorful terminology used in the food industry, in different types of work, and in the world of sports. Also discussed are words used for money, musical terms, criminal jargon, and slang used during wartime and in different countries. . . . This is a clever way for younger students to learn about the topic. . . . Colorful, amusing illustrations appear throughout." SLJ

Includes bibliographical references

428   Standard English usage (Prescriptive linguistics) Applied linguistics

Bacon, Pamela S., 1964-

100+ literacy lifesavers; a survival guide for librarians and teachers K-12; [by] Pamela S. Bacon and Tammy K. Bacon. Libraries Unlimited 2009 363p il pa $40

Grades: Professional   **428**

1. Reading 2. Teaching teams
ISBN 978-1-59158-669-2 (pa); 1-59158-669-0 (pa)

LC 2008-45514

"This wonderful professional resource's focus is mainly school librarians and teachers, but it could be used by public librarians to generate ideas for educational programs. . . . This book is an insightful tool that provides the skills and plans for successful collaboration and evaluation of literacy efforts between teachers and librarians." Voice Youth Advocates

Includes glossary and bibliographical references

Bruno, Elsa Knight

A punctuation celebration! illustrated by Jenny Whitehead. Henry Holt and Co. 2009 unp il $17.95

Grades: 1 2 3 4   **428**

1. Punctuation
ISBN 978-0-8050-7973-9; 0-8050-7973-4

LC 2008018337

"Young readers will receive a better-than-average introduction to punctuation marks and their uses in this cheerfully illustrated collection of poems. Each selection

Bruno, Elsa Knight—*Continued*

presents an individual punctuation mark through rhyming verse. . . . Bruno's writing is clear and lively throughout. . . . Bright collages of children of various ethnicities engaged in diverse activities complement the text." SLJ

Cleary, Brian P., 1959-

Hairy, scary, ordinary; what is an adjective? illustrated by Jenya Prosmitsky. Carolrhoda Bks. 2000 32p il (Words are categorical) $12.95 paperback o.p. *

Grades: 2 3 4   **428**

1. English language—Grammar

ISBN 1-57505-401-9; 1-57505-419-1 (pa)

LC 98-32132

"Descriptive words of many kinds are presented in bouncy, rhyming text. . . . The adjectives are colorfully highlighted and readers will see their function demonstrated in a wide variety of contexts. Little round cats and quirky humans, both with fat noses and wide eyes, humorously illustrate the meanings." SLJ

How much can a bare bear bear? what are homonyms and homophones? by Brian P. Cleary; illustrated by Brian Gable. Millbrook Press 2005 unp il (Words are categorical) lib bdg $15.95 *

Grades: 2 3 4   **428**

1. English language—Homonyms

ISBN 1-57505-824-3   LC 2004031106

"Through rhyming wordplay, Cleary explains two parts of speech that are often difficult to understand. . . . Gable took ample advantage of the pairings to create zany cartoons that provide visual clues for readers. The grouping of each set of homophones and homonyms by color is also a helpful tool." SLJ

I and you and don't forget who; what is a pronoun? illustrated by Brian Gable. Carolrhoda Books 2004 unp il (Words are categorical) lib bdg $14.95 *

Grades: 2 3 4   **428**

1. English language—Grammar

ISBN 1-57505-596-1   LC 2003-1712

Rhyming text and illustrations of comical cats present numerous examples of pronouns and their functions, from "he" and "she" to "anyone," "neither," and "which."

The "text presents the major uses of pronouns with precision, brevity, and wit. The cartoon-style ink drawings brim with irrepressible humor, while the bold use of color in the artwork adds to the high-spirited look of the pages." Booklist

Lazily, crazily, just a bit nasally; more about adverbs; by Brian P. Cleary; illustrations by Brian Gable. Millbrook Press 2008 31p il (Words are categorical) lib bdg $15.95

Grades: 2 3 4   **428**

1. English language—Grammar

ISBN 978-0-8225-7848-2 (lib bdg); 0-8225-7848-4 (lib bdg)   LC 2006033800

"A professorial feline opens this offbeat lecture with a definition of adverbs and a color-coded guide to the types found throughout the book. Readers are then drawn into another of Cleary's signature rhyming narratives, which tumbles across each page verbally and visually. . . . Knob-nosed felines done in a rainbow of colors mime numerous examples of actions that can be performed with adverbial panache." SLJ

The punctuation station; illustrations by Joanne Lew-Vriethoff. Millbrook Press 2010 37p il lib bdg $16.95

Grades: K 1 2 3   **428**

1. Punctuation

ISBN 978-0-8225-7852-9 (lib bdg); 0-8225-7852-2 (lib bdg)   LC 2009015860

"Perky rhymes, animal characters, and a chaotic train-station setting provide an entertaining introduction to seven oft-used punctuation marks: periods, commas, apostrophes, quotation marks, question marks, hyphens, and exclamation points. . . . . The young audience will enjoy learning the concepts as they pore over the details in the cheerful, wittily detailed cartoon art." Booklist

Quirky, jerky, extra-perky; more about adjectives; by Brian P. Cleary; illustrations by Brian Gable. Millbrook Press 2007 30p il (Words are categorical) lib bdg $15.95

Grades: 2 3 4   **428**

1. English language—Grammar

ISBN 978-0-8225-6709-7 (lib bdg); 0-8225-6709-1 (lib bdg)   LC 2006010756

"Cleary offers more examples of the descriptive words in this upbeat, energetically illustrated book. Beginning with a straightforward definition of the word adjective, Cleary takes off with a series of imaginative examples presented in rhythmic, rhyming verses. . . . Colorful, comical, cartoon-style illustrations help create the madcap quality that distinguishes the series." Booklist

Stop and go, yes and no; what is an antonym? by Brian P. Cleary; illustrations by Brian Gable. Millbrook Press 2006 unp il (Words are categorical) lib bdg $15.95

Grades: 2 3 4   **428**

1. English language—Synonyms and antonyms
2. Opposites

ISBN 978-1-57505-860-3 (lib bdg); 1-57505-860-X (lib bdg)   LC 2005013991

"Cleary describes and illustrates antonyms from the obvious stop and go, yes and no, front and back, fast and slow, to the more obscure: excite and soothe, hefty and diminutive. He elaborates on reasons for celebrating opposites and also describes how to create them through the use of powerful prefixes such as un, dis, im, and non. . . . The bouncy lettering style enhances the whimsical rhymes and makes for yet another strong addition to collections of books about the English language." SLJ

Stroll and walk, babble and talk; more about synonyms; by Brian P. Cleary; illustrated by Brian Gable. Millbrook Press 2008 31p il (Words are categorical) lib bdg $15.95

Grades: 2 3 4   **428**

1. English language—Synonyms and antonyms

ISBN 978-0-8225-7850-5 (lib bdg); 0-8225-7850-6 (lib bdg)   LC 2007040360

Cleary, Brian P., 1959-—*Continued*

This book "shows the fun of words with light non-sense rhymes and color cartoons of animal characters that brag and boast, lie and deceive. . . . With all the slapstick fun, the pages show and tell about shades of meaning and the importance of choosing just the right word." Booklist

Heller, Ruth

Behind the mask; a book about prepositions; written and illustrated by Ruth Heller. Grosset & Dunlap 1995 unp il hardcover o.p. pa $7.99
Grades: K 1 2   **428**
   1. English language—Grammar
   ISBN 0-448-41123-7; 0-698-11698-4 (pa)
                                        LC 95-9535
Explores through rhyming text the subject of preposi-tions and how they're used
"Large, colorful drawings illustrate the words imagina-tively." Booklist

A cache of jewels and other collective nouns; written and illustrated by Ruth Heller. Grosset & Dunlap 1987 unp il hardcover o.p. pa $7.99
Grades: K 1 2   **428**
   1. English language—Grammar
   ISBN 0-448-19211-X; 0-698-11354-3 (pa)
                                        LC 87-80254
"In light verse and brightly colored pictures, Heller provides an introduction to a specialized part of speech, the collective noun. She lists and depicts more than 25, including such familiar terms as 'batch of bread' and 'bunch of bananas,' as well as more unusual phrases. . . . The concept will stimulate the curiosity and imagi-nations of children with an ear for language. The illustra-tions, containing large, bold objects in simple yet striking compositions, ensure a visually inspiring exploration as well." Publ Wkly

Fantastic! wow! and unreal! a book about interjections and conjunctions; written and illustrated by Ruth Heller. Grosset & Dunlap 1998 unp il hardcover o.p. pa $7.99
Grades: K 1 2   **428**
   1. English language—Grammar
   ISBN 0-448-41862-2; 0-698-11875-8 (pa)
                                        LC 98-36361
Rhyming text and illustrations introduce and explain various interjections and conjunctions, including "awe-some," "alas," and "yet."

Kites sail high: a book about verbs; written and illustrated by Ruth Heller. Grosset & Dunlap 1988 unp il hardcover o.p. pa $7.99
Grades: K 1 2   **428**
   1. English language—Grammar
   ISBN 0-448-10480-6; 0-698-11389-6 (pa)
                                        LC 87-82718
This "book explicates and celebrates verbs of all kinds, in ebullient verses which themselves sail and soar. . . . The verses are accompanied by bold, gaily colored graphics that are especially striking for their skillful use of pattern and design." Publ Wkly

Many luscious lollipops: a book about adjectives; written and illustrated by Ruth Heller. Grosset & Dunlap 1989 unp il hardcover o.p. pa $7.99
Grades: K 1 2   **428**
   1. English language—Grammar
   ISBN 0-448-03151-5; 0-698-11641-0 (pa)
                                        LC 88-83045
"The text begins: 'An adjective's terrific/when you want to be specific/It easily identifies/by number, color or by size/TWELVE LARGE, BLUE, GORGEOUS but-terflies.' And there they are, blue and yellow, filling a double-page spread. . . . There is great diversity and technical brilliance in the art work, and the text has rhyme, rhythm, humor, and a very clear presentation of the concepts of different kinds of adjectives and what they do." Bull Cent Child Books

Merry-go-round; a book about nouns; written and illustrated by Ruth Heller. Grosset & Dunlap 1990 unp il hardcover o.p. pa $7.99
Grades: K 1 2   **428**
   1. English language—Grammar
   ISBN 0-448-40085-5; 0-698-11642-9 (pa)
                                        LC 90-80645
Rhyming text and illustrations present explanations of various types of nouns and rules for their usage
"While the text will be helpful to children struggling with noun usage, the large, bountiful illustrations will ap-peal to everyone." Horn Book Guide

Mine, all mine; a book about pronouns; written and illustrated by Ruth Heller. Grosset & Dunlap 1997 unp il hardcover o.p. pa $7.99
Grades: K 1 2   **428**
   1. English language—Grammar
   ISBN 0-448-41606-9; 0-698-11797-2 (pa)
                                        LC 97-10051
Introduces various types of pronouns, explains how and when to use them, and provides whimsical glimpses of what our language would be without them
"Heller has taken a part of speech and made its func-tion perfectly and entertainingly clear. . . . The stylishly drawn, brilliantly colored, double-paged illustrations grab readers and don't let go. The exceptionally fluent, rhyth-mic text is printed in an unobtrusive font with pronouns highlighted in bright blue." SLJ

Up, up and away; a book about adverbs; written and illustrated by Ruth Heller. Grosset & Dunlap 1991 unp il hardcover o.p. pa $7.99
Grades: K 1 2   **428**
   1. English language—Grammar
   ISBN 0-448-40249-1; 0-698-11663-1 (pa)
                                        LC 91-70668
"Here the author explains concisely how adverbs an-swer precisely the questions of How? How often? When? and Where? The adverbs, in capital letters, stand out boldly and cannot be missed. . . . In the large, appealing illustrations, her penguins stand proudly, her pandas eat daintily, and her cat stares piercingly. . . . The cheerful volume . . . offers a clever introduction to kinds of words." Booklist

L is for lollygag; quirky words for a clever tongue. Chronicle Books 2008 125p $12.99

Grades: 4 5 6 7   **428**
1. Vocabulary
ISBN 978-0-8118-6021-5; 0-8118-6021-3
                                        LC 2007021061
"Budding and accomplished wordsmiths will delight in this specialized dictionary showcasing oft-overlooked gems of the English language. . . . Each definition is related with humor, sometimes including word origination and listing equally interesting synonyms. . . . Black-and-white engravings juxtaposed with cartoons in Picassoesque profile give an old-fashioned yet offbeat air to this unusual compendium." SLJ

Includes bibliographical references

Leedy, Loreen, 1959-

There's a frog in my throat; 440 animal sayings a little bird told me; written by Loreen Leedy & Pat Street; illustrated by Loreen Leedy. Holiday House 2003 48p il $16.95 *

Grades: 2 3 4 5   **428**
1. English language—Terms and phrases 2. Animals—Folklore
ISBN 0-8234-1774-3   LC 2002-68920
"The sayings are loosely grouped by types of animals—domestic, barnyard, winged, etc.—and each adage is accompanied by a short definition. For example, 'It's raining cats and dogs. *It's raining hard.*' . . . Children will pore over the pages. The collaboration of text and art makes the volume lively and humorous." SLJ

Moses, Will, 1956-

Raining cats and dogs; [by] Will Moses. Philomel Books 2008 unp il $17.99

Grades: 1 2 3 4 5   **428**
1. English language—Idioms
ISBN 978-0-399-24233-5; 0-399-24233-3
                                        LC 2008-10339
"In this highly appropriate pairing of folk art and sayings, Moses explains many common idioms. A colorful definition . . . a sample sentence, and one of Moses's old-fashioned Americana-style oil paintings accompany each phrase. The lesson is kept lighthearted through examples that play upon the literal meanings of each phrase, often to comedic effect." SLJ

O'Conner, Patricia T.

Woe is I Jr; the junior grammarphobes' guide to better English in plain English; [by] Patricia O'Conner; drawings by Tom Stiglich. G.P. Putnam's Sons 2007 152p il $16.99

Grades: 4 5 6 7 8   **428**
1. English language—Grammar 2. English language—Usage
ISBN 978-0-399-24331-8   LC 2006020575
An adaptation of Woe is I, published 2003 for adults by Riverhead Books
The author "covers pronouns, plurals, possessives, verb usage, subject-verb agreement, capitalization, and punctuation with jargon-free explanations and entertaining examples. . . . She knows her subject, can convey her message with wit and ease, and does it all in a compact, easy-to-read format." SLJ

Reid, Alastair, 1926-

Ounce, dice, trice; drawings by Ben Shahn. New York Review Books 2009 57p il $15.95

Grades: K 1 2 3   **428**
1. Vocabulary 2. Wit and humor
ISBN 978-1-59017-320-6; 1-59017-320-1
                                        LC 2008050325
A reissue of the title first published 1958 by Atlantic-Little
"'Words have a sound and shape, in addition to their meanings. Sometimes the sound *is* the meaning.' This 'odd collection of words and names' includes 'light words' (*lisssom, sibilant*), 'heavy words' (*befuddled*), and other fascinating categories. The author's poetic lists have been turned into picture-and-word amusement through collaboration with an illustrator whose Lear-like sketches have originality, joy, and absurdity." Horn Book Guide

Roy, Jennifer Rozines

You can write using good grammar; [by] Jennifer Rozines Roy. Enslow 2004 64p il (You can write) lib bdg $22.60

Grades: 4 5 6   **428**
1. English language—Grammar
ISBN 0-7660-2084-3   LC 2002-156035
Contents: Why learn grammar?; Parts of speech; Sentences and paragraphs; Using parts of speech; Punctuation, proofreading, and other word forms; Common grammar goofs
This "discusses parts of speech, punctuation, and proofreading. A list of 'Common Grammar Goofs' is appended. . . . Students will find [this book] useful." Horn Book Guide

Includes glossary and bibliographical references

Terban, Marvin

Scholastic dictionary of spelling. rev ed. Scholastic Reference 2006 272p il pa $9.99 *

Grades: 4 5 6   **428**
1. Spellers 2. Reference books
ISBN 978-0-439-76421-6; 0-439-76421-1
First published 1998
This spelling dictionary gives instructions for looking up a word the reader does not know how to spell, offers more than 150 memory tricks to correct commonly misspelled words, explains general spelling rules and their exceptions, and includes sections such as "The Four Longest Words in the English Language" and "The Spelling Words That Made Kids Champions." To aid pronunciation, each word is divided into syllables with the accented syllable in boldface.

Truss, Lynne

Eats, shoots & leaves; why, commas really do make a difference! illustrated by Bonnie Timmons. G.P. Putnam's Sons 2006 unp il $15.99 *

Grades: 2 3 4   **428**
1. Punctuation
ISBN 0-399-24491-3   LC 2005-28559
"Truss's picture-book version of her adult bestseller tackles the topic of commas and what can go wrong

Truss, Lynne—*Continued*

when they are misused. . . . Versions of two identically worded sentences are presented side by side, demonstrating the difference in meaning achieved when a comma is added or subtracted. Timmons's humorous watercolor cartoons bring the point home." SLJ

The girl's like spaghetti; why, you can't manage without apostrophes! illustrated by Bonnie Timmons. G. P. Putnam's Sons 2007 unp il $16.99 *

Grades: 2 3 4   **428**
    1. Punctuation
    ISBN 978-0-399-24706-4; 0-399-24706-8
                         LC 2006-34456
"This book presents readers with two identical sentences whose meaning changes with the simple placement of the apostrophe. The plural versus the possessive is depicted through lively cartoons illustrating the sentences. Truss . . . manages to keep her lessons funny and full of kid appeal." SLJ

Twenty-odd ducks; why, every punctuation mark counts! [by] Lynne Truss; illustrated by Bonnie Timmons. G.P. Putman's Sons 2008 unp il $16.99
Grades: 2 3 4   **428**
    1. Punctuation
    ISBN 978-0-399-25058-3; 0-399-25058-1
                         LC 2007045386
This "emphasizes the importance of punctuation in general. Truss . . . makes the case that careless application can dramatically change one's meaning. To prove her point, she provides contrasting examples of the same sentence, punctuated in different ways. Timmons's charming watercolors make the change in meaning clearer." SLJ

439   Other Germanic languages

Sussman, Joni Kibort

My first Yiddish word book; edited by Joni Kibort Sussman; pictures by Pepi Marzel. Kar-Ben Pub. 2008 32p il $17.95
Grades: K 1 2   **439**
    1. Yiddish language 2. Picture dictionaries
    3. Reference books
    ISBN 978-0-8225-8755-2   LC 2007028347
"With this [Yiddish] picture dictionary, select vocabulary is accessible to young readers. Basic words for parts of the body, members of the family, clothing, the house, school, playground, city, grocery store, bedtime, the zoo, colors, etc., are included. All are written in block letters with English transliteration and translation. Each spread includes a large, detailed illustration with the individual items clearly identified along the bottom. The pictures are cheerful and contemporary." SLJ

443   Dictionaries of standard French

Corbeil, Jean-Claude

My first French English visual dictionary; [by] Jean-Claude Corbeil; Ariane Archambault. Firefly Books 2006 80p il $14.95 *
Grades: 3 4 5 6   **443**
    1. Reference books 2. French language—Dictionaries
    3. Picture dictionaries
    ISBN 978-1-55407-193-7; 1-55407-193-3
"There are 36 themes-among them 'Clothing,' 'Colors and Shapes,' 'Dinosaurs,' 'Space,' and 'Sports' selected to appeal to primary-age children. Each theme has a double-page spread of small to medium-sized individual illustrations of items allied to the theme. The other 1,300 illustrations are large and in full color and are accompanied by the English word in boldface letters with the word in the other language underneath. The typeface is large and uncluttered and easy to see. . . . Separate English and French indexes complete the book." Booklist

Kudela, Katy R.

My first book of French words; translator, Translations.com. Capstone Press 2009 32p il (A+ books: bilingual picture dictionaries) lib bdg $23.99
Grades: K 1 2 3   **443**
    1. French language—Dictionaries 2. Picture dictionaries
    ISBN 978-1-4296-3295-9 (lib bdg); 1-4296-3295-X (lib bdg)   LC 2009005510
"This simple bilingual picture dictionary is illustrated with attractive, colorful photos. Each themed spread introduces 10 words, first in English and then in French, followed by the approximate French pronunciation. . . . The 130 words cover family, body parts, clothes, toys, bedroom, bathroom, kitchen, food, farm, garden, colors, classroom, city, numbers, and useful phrases. . . . Overall, this book is appealing, useful, and easy to comprehend." SLJ
Includes bibliographical references

463   Dictionaries of standard Spanish

Corbeil, Jean-Claude

My first Spanish English visual dictionary; [by] Jean-Claude Corbeil; Ariane Archambault. Firefly Books 2006 80p il $14.95 *
Grades: 3 4 5 6   **463**
    1. Reference books 2. Spanish language—Dictionaries
    3. Picture dictionaries
    ISBN 978-1-55407-194-4; 1-55407-194-1
A Spanish/English visual dictionary for children: 1,600 terms annotate 1,300 realistic illustrations organized in 36 themes that children experience in their lives. Two indexes, by language, and Spanish terms include gender.

Kudela, Katy R.

My first book of Spanish words. Capstone Press 2009 32p il (A+ books: bilingual picture dictionaries) lib bdg $23.99

Grades: K 1 2 3   **463**

1. Spanish language—Dictionaries 2. Picture dictionaries

ISBN 978-1-4296-3298-0 (lib bdg); 1-4296-3298-4 (lib bdg)   LC 2009005518

This picture dictionary introduces common Spanish words with color photos.

Includes bibliographical references

468   Standard Spanish usage (Prescriptive linguistics) Applied linguistics

Elya, Susan Middleton, 1955-

Say hola to Spanish, otra vez; illustrated by Loretta Lopez. Lee & Low Bks. 1997 unp il $15.95; pa $6.95

Grades: 1 2 3 4   **468**

1. Spanish language—Vocabulary

ISBN 1-880000-59-8; 1-880000-83-0 (pa)
                                                   LC 97-6851

Also available: Say hola to Spanish $15.95 (ISBN 1-880000-29-6); pa $6.95 (ISBN 1-880000-64-4) and Say hola to Spanish at the circus $15.95 (ISBN 1-880000-92-X)

"A rhyming text and bright cartoon illustrations introduce 72 Spanish words." SLJ

"The playful design scatters the text throughout Lopez's gouache and colored-pencil two-page spreads; the most effective scenes group the words thematically. . . . Lopez provides images bound to aid early elementary students' retention and recall of these Spanish words." Publ Wkly

Includes glossary

Emberley, Rebecca

My big book of Spanish words; by Rebecca Emberley. LB Kids/Little, Brown and Co. 2008 unp il $8.99

Grades: PreK K 1 2   **468**

1. Spanish language—Vocabulary 2. Vocabulary 3. Board books for children

ISBN 978-0-316-11803-3; 0-316-11803-6
                                                   LC 2008297866

"This oversize book contains the Spanish and English terms for colors, foods, toys, clothing, animals, things that go, shapes, numbers 1-10, and items familiar to bath and bedtime routines. Each noun is accompanied by a brilliant collage illustration. The bright page borders and white backgrounds will draw readers' eyes to the marvelous art." SLJ

492.4   Hebrew

Groner, Judyth Saypol

My first Hebrew word book; [by Judye Groner and Madeline Wikler]; pictures by Pepi Marzel. Kar-Ben Pub. 2005 32p il lib bdg $17.95

Grades: K 1 2   **492.4**

1. Hebrew language 2. Picture dictionaries 3. Reference books

ISBN 1-58013-126-3   LC 2004-13504

Contents: Me; My family; House; Kitchen; Bedroom; Bathroom; Living room; School; Playground; Community; People in neighborhood; Food; Meals; Transportation; Zoo; Farm; Beach; Park; Birthday party; Clothing; Weather; Seasons; Synagogue; Holidays; Verbs

"Basic Hebrew words . . . are included. All are written in block letters with English transliteration and translation. Each spread includes a large, detailed illustration with the individual items clearly identified along the bottom. The color cartoon art is cheerful and contemporary. At the back of the book, a word list is organized alphabetically in English and includes the Hebrew words and corresponding page numbers. All in all, this is a wonderful resource." SLJ

493   Non-Semitic Afro-Asiatic languages

Giblin, James, 1933-

The riddle of the Rosetta Stone; key to ancient Egypt; [by] James Cross Giblin. Crowell 1990 85p il pa $7.99 hardcover o.p. *

Grades: 5 6 7 8   **493**

1. Rosetta stone 2. Egyptian language 3. Hieroglyphics

ISBN 0-06-446137-8 (pa)   LC 89-29289

Describes how the discovery and deciphering of the Rosetta Stone unlocked the secret of Egyptian hieroglyphics

"Suspense keeps the reader glued to this fine piece of nonfiction as the mystery of hieroglyphs is slowly unraveled. . . . The author has done a masterful job of distilling information, citing the highlights, and fitting it all together in an interesting and enlightening look at a puzzling subject." Horn Book

Includes bibliographical references

495.1   Chinese

Lee, Huy Voun, 1969-

1, 2, 3 go! Holt & Co. 2000 unp il $17.95

Grades: K 1 2 3   **495.1**

1. Chinese language 2. Counting

ISBN 0-8050-6205-X   LC 99-48326

Parallel title on cover in Chinese characters

An introduction to Chinese writing describing the construction, meaning, and pronunciation of simple characters used for a variety of words and the numbers one through ten

"Lee effectively displays boldly contrasted cut-paper

Lee, Huy Voun, 1969-—*Continued*
shapes on stark white backgrounds. . . . With masterful simplicity, Lee leads readers to a preliminary appreciation of Chinese culture." Booklist

At the beach; written and illustrated by Huy Voun Lee. Holt & Co. 1994 unp il hardcover o.p. pa $7.95
Grades: K 1 2 3   **495.1**
1. Chinese language
ISBN 0-8050-2768-8; 0-8050-5822-2 (pa)
LC 93-25462
A mother amuses her young son at the beach by drawing in the sand Chinese characters, many of which resemble the objects they stand for
"The intricate, visually captivating cut-paper collages have borders with sea motifs. Useful for beginning language study and interesting due to its artistic innovation, the book includes a pronunciation guide." Horn Book Guide
Other titles in this series are:
In the leaves (2005)
In the park (1998)
In the snow (1995)

500   SCIENCE

Bryson, Bill
A really short history of nearly everything. Delacorte Press 2009 c2008 169p il $19.99
Grades: 4 5 6 7   **500**
1. Science
ISBN 978-0-385-73810-1; 0-385-73810-2
A newly illustrated, abridged and adapted edition of A short history of nearly everything, published 2003 by Broadway Books for adults; this edition first published in the United Kingdom 2008
Bryson "whirls through mind-numbing notions such as the creation of the universe and the life span of an atom with good cheer and accessible, even exciting, writing. The two-page spreads meander their way through the various recesses of science with a combination of explanatory prose, historical anecdotes, wry asides, and illustrations that range from helpful to comical." Booklist

Dotlich, Rebecca Kai
What is science? illustrated by Sachiko Yoshikawa. H. Holt 2006 unp il $16.95
Grades: K 1 2   **500**
1. Science
ISBN 978-0-8050-7394-2; 0-8050-7394-9
LC 2005-20050
"Dotlich begins and ends with the line, What is science?/So many things. In between, she enumerates some of the areas of study—astronomy, geology, paleontology, oceanography, botany, meteorology, and zoology. Each page has just a few words, in large print, superimposed on a background of boldly colored acrylic, pastel, and collage art. The rhyming text flows nicely. . . . With its large illustrations, simple text, and important concepts, this title will be enjoyed by newly independent readers, or will ignite excitement in a group. A unique look at the topic." SLJ

Goldsmith, Mike
Everything you need to know about science. Kingfisher 2009 160p il $18.99
Grades: 1 2 3 4 5   **500**
1. Science
ISBN 978-0-7534-6302-4; 0-7534-6302-4
"This broad, accessible encyclopedia will appeal to browsers because of the 500-plus highly realistic computer-generated illustrations, large fonts, and short paragraphs. . . . Science enthusiasts will enjoy browsing this smorgasbord of information." SLJ

Hillman, Ben
How weird is it; a freaky book all about strangeness. Scholastic 2009 47p il $15.99
Grades: 5 6 7 8   **500**
1. Science
ISBN 978-0-439-91868-8; 0-439-91868-5
LC 2008-09787
Strange but facinating facts about everyday things that turn out to be extraordinary.
"Humor adds interest to the random but readable text. Large, vivid computer-manipulated photographs illustrate the information." Horn Book Guide

Hoaxed!; fakes & mistakes in the world of science; written by editors of YES mag. Kids Can Press 2009 il lib bdg $16.95; pa $8.95
Grades: 5 6 7 8   **500**
1. Fraud 2. Science
ISBN 978-1-55453-206-3 (lib bdg); 1-55453-206-X (lib bdg); 978-1-55453-207-0 (pa); 1-55453-207-8 (pa)
"Piltdown man, Richard Meinertzhagen the light-fingered bird collector, 'Stone Age' Tasaday in the Philippines, crop circles in England, cold fusion energy and UFOs in Roswell, N.M., are the fakes and mistakes described in this lively introduction to fraud in science. The breezy text opens with a clear description of the scientific process of hypothesis, experiment, publication in professional magazines and replication of results before proceeding to the many colorful fakes exposed." Kirkus

Murphy, Glenn
Why is snot green; and other extremely important questions (and answers). Roaring Brook Press 2009 236p il pa $9.95
Grades: 4 5 6 7   **500**
1. Science 2. Technology
ISBN 978-1-59643-500-1 (pa); 1-59643-500-3 (pa)
"Conservation, evolution, technology, animal life, space travel, physics, and much more are discussed in this lively science book. . . . [This offers] chatty questions and answers . . . with text that is compelling, never intimidating, and sometimes deliberately outrageous. . . . Children will have fun browsing the spacious pages and sharing what they read with adults." Booklist

O'Meara, Stephen James, 1956-

Are you afraid yet? the science behind scary stuff; written by Stephen James O'Meara; illustrated by Jeremy Kaposy. Kids Can Press 2009 78p il $17.95; pa $9.95

Grades: 5 6 7 8   **500**

1. Science 2. Supernatural

ISBN 978-1-55453-294-0; 1-55453-294-9; 978-1-55453-295-7 (pa); 1-55453-295-7 (pa)

"This book cleverly weaves together the supernatural and the scientific in an entertaining read that answers questions about ghosts, UFOs, vampires, werewolves, and how long a decapitated head can remain conscious. Examples depicting such things in classical fiction and popular movies are seamlessly interjected between the factual explanations. Each page is filled with detailed black-and-white illustrations, emphasizing the sometimes-humorous, yet often-macabre descriptions." SLJ

Richardson, Gillian

Kaboom! explosions of all kinds. Annick Press 2009 83p il $22.95; pa $12.95

Grades: 4 5 6 7   **500**

1. Science 2. Explosions

ISBN 978-1-55451-204-1; 1-55451-204-2; 978-1-55451-203-4 (pa); 1-55451-203-4 (pa)

"With comic-style sound-effect headings and fact boxes galore, Kaboom! highlights the supercharged of the natural and manmade worlds, from astronomy, geology, biology, herbology, and entomology to chemistry, mechanics, pyrotechnics, and art. Text is broken into asymmetrical panels for bite-size explanations. Some explosions are captured in sequence and detail with historical and high-speed photography and illustrations in comic-style panel frames. . . . Kaboom! is an engrossing attention-getter, effectively tapping the sensationalism of all types of blasts." SLJ

Schwartz, David M., 1951-

Q is for quark; a science alphabet book; written by David M. Schwartz; illustrated by Kim Doner. Tricycle Press 2001 64p il $15.95

Grades: 4 5 6 7   **500**

1. Science 2. Alphabet

ISBN 1-58246-021-3   LC 00-10659

Explains the meaning of scientific terms which begin with the different letters of the alphabet such as atom, black hole, and clone

"The text is filled with readable and clear explanations for some very complex concepts. . . . [Readers] will enjoy browsing through this funny and informative book." SLJ

Swanson, Diane, 1944-

Nibbling on Einstein's brain; the good, the bad & the bogus in science; illustrated by Warren Clark. Annick Press 2001 104p il $24.95; pa $14.95

Grades: 5 6 7 8   **500**

1. Science—Methodology

ISBN 1-55037-687-X; 1-55037-686-1 (pa)

The author "discusses topics such as the difference between correlation and cause-and-effect relationships, the importance of asking the right questions about advertisers' claims, and the links between superstition, coincidence, and probability. With a highly readable text and jaunty line illustrations, the book encourages critical thinking and skepticism when evaluating science reporting and media hype." Booklist

Thimmesh, Catherine

The sky's the limit; stories of discovery by women and girls; illustrated by Melissa Sweet. Houghton Mifflin 2002 73p il hardcover o.p. pa $7.95

Grades: 5 6 7 8   **500**

1. Science 2. Women scientists

ISBN 0-618-07698-0; 0-618-49489-8 (pa)

     LC 2001-39111

"This collection highlights a variety of women discoverers from the well known, including Jane Goodall and Mary Leakey, to budding pioneers, such as eleven-year-old science-lover Katie Murray." Voice Youth Advocates

"The lively design and the mixed-media collage artwork is a creative delight, and the intricate ink-and-watercolor borders, inventive paintings, and childlike pictures will draw readers in. The best thing about the book, however, is Thimmesh's sparkling writing style. . . . Report writers will appreciate this, but the book will also charm browsers." Booklist

Includes bibliographical references

Watts, Claire

The most explosive science book in the universe; by the Brainwaves; illustrated by Lisa Swerling and Ralph Lazar; written by Claire Watts. DK Pub. 2009 60p il $19.99

Grades: 3 4 5 6   **500**

1. Science

ISBN 978-0-7566-5152-7; 0-7566-5152-2

The Brainwaves are pint-sized pals that explore the world of science including the building blocks of matter, chemistry, light, electricity and the future of science

"A sprawling, unique overview of the various scientific fields. Although students will have to hunt through the dense layout to find facts, they will likely encounter what they are searching for. . . . Appealing enough to inspire pleasure reading, the book will also serve those looking for scientific facts." SLJ

500.5   Space sciences

Space science. Grolier 2004 8v il map set $309

Grades: 5 6 7 8   **500.5**

1. Space sciences—Encyclopedias 2. Reference books

ISBN 0-7172-5825-4   LC 2003-61836

Contents: v1 How the universe works; v2 Sun and solar system; v3 Earth and Moon; v4 Rocky planets; v5 Gas giants; v6 Journey into space; v7 Shuttle to space station; v8 What satellites see

This set "provides general coverage of astronomy and cosmology, . . . [discusses] the technology and engineering aspects of understanding and exploring space, and [covers] the solar system and its central star. . . . The books all make excellent use of fantastic photographs and drawings. . . . The text is well-written and complete. . . . [This is] a must-have set." Sci Books Films

502 Miscellany

Murphy, Glenn
How loud can you burp? more extremely important questions (and answers!). Roaring Book Press 2009 284p il pa $10.99
Grades: 4 5 6 7   502
1. Science 2. Questions and answers
ISBN 978-1-59643-506-3 (pa); 1-59643-506-2 (pa)
"'Why does pollen give you hay fever?' 'Why don't big metal ships just sink?' These are but a couple of the questions that Murphy received on the Web site he set up to solicit inquiries from kids. Written in an informal, question-and-answer format, he delivers serious scientific information in an easygoing, humorous manner, with several pages dedicated to each topic. . . . A few line drawings break up the text and sidebars highlight interesting facts or are, at times, simply funny. . . . This is an entertaining, accessible approach to science that's sure to appeal to science buffs and general browsers alike." SLJ

502.8 Auxiliary techniques and procedures; apparatus, equipment, materials

Glass, Susan
Watch out! science tools and safety; [by] Susan Glass. Heinemann Library 2007 48p il (How to be a scientist) lib bdg $21; pa $8.99
Grades: 3 4 5 6   502.8
1. Scientific apparatus and instruments 2. Measurement 3. Science—Experiments
ISBN 978-1-4034-8360-7 (lib bdg); 978-1-4034-8364-5 (pa)   LC 2006010840
Contents: Observation; Measurement; Using models; Putting it all together; Make your own science tools; Science safety; Using science tools; The metric system
Includes bibliographical references

Kramer, Stephen
Hidden worlds: looking through a scientist's microscope; photographs by Dennis Kunkel. Houghton Mifflin 2001 57p il (Scientists in the field) $16; pa $5.95
Grades: 4 5 6 7   502.8
1. Kunkel, Dennis 2. Microscopes
ISBN 0-618-05546-0; 0-618-35405-0 (pa)
                                                    LC 00-58083
This book takes a "look at the work of a microscopist. Kunkel works with microscopes to explore science. . . . This book contains many of his photos, most taken with electron microscopes. . . . Several opening pages, along with the front and back endpapers, are visually dazzling. The heart of the book, though, is what readers learn about how Kunkel produces these images, and to what uses scientists put them. . . . This title offers a wealth of scientific information along with an insightful look at the world of an individual scientist." SLJ
Includes bibliographical references

Levine, Shar
The ultimate guide to your microscope; [by] Shar Levine & Leslie Johnstone. Sterling Pub. 2008 143p il pa $9.95 *
Grades: 5 6 7 8 9   502.8
1. Microscopes
ISBN 978-1-4027-4329-0 (pa); 1-4027-4329-7 (pa)
                                                 LC 2006-100967
"Through this fun and inviting book, readers can begin to explore the world using a microscope. Students are encouraged to learn the basics in the two first chapters and then undertake the 41 hands-on activities in the next eight chapters. Activities are presented in manageable one or two-page uniformly formatted modules." SLJ

503 Dictionaries, encyclopedias, concordances

Britannica illustrated science library. Encyclopaedia Britannica 2008 16v il map set $425 *
Grades: 5 6 7 8 9   503
1. Science—Encyclopedias 2. Reference books
ISBN 978-1-59339-382-3 (set); 1-59339-382-2 (set)
These "volumes cover a wide range of topics correlating nicely with science curriculums in the fields of the earth sciences, the life sciences, and the physical sciences. Each topic is addressed in no more than two pages with well-organized information and simple language. The editors have carefully linked their scientific explanations to topics of interest and the student's experience. . . . These volumes contain more than 10,000 engaging pictures and illustrations that fill an entire page and help the reader grasp complex scientific topics." Libr J

DK first science encyclopedia; [senior editors, Currie Love, Caroline Stamps and Ben Morgan] DK Publishing 2008 127p il map $16.99 *
Grades: K 1 2 3 4   503
1. Science—Encyclopedias
ISBN 978-0-7566-4296-9; 0-7566-4296-5
                                                  LC 2009277384

DK first science encyclopedia
Provides a basic reference guide to life, materials, physical, earth, and space science
"On flipping to any page, readers' first impressions will be the vibrancy and beauty of the photography, but further examination reveals a wealth of interesting facts and information about the topics presented, along with real-world context for their importance." Sci Books Films

Everything you need to know; an encyclopedia for inquiring young minds. Kingfisher 2007 320p il map $24.95
Grades: PreK K 1 2 3 4   503
1. Science—Encyclopedias 2. Technology—Encyclopedias 3. Reference books
ISBN 978-0-7534-6089-4; 0-7534-6089-0
"The encyclopedia is arranged thematically into 10 sections ('Our Earth,' 'Plants,' 'Animals,' 'Dinosaurs,' 'People and Places,' 'People Through Time,' 'My Body,' 'Science,' 'Space,' and 'Machines') with between 11 and

Everything you need to know—*Continued*
17 topics grouped under each. Most topics are treated in two-page spreads. . . . There is plenty of worthwhile information to answer questions and spark curiosity. . . . The volume is visually appealing, with full-color illustrations." Booklist

Jakab, Cheryl
The encyclopedia of junior science; [by] Cheryl Jakab, David Keystone. Chelsea Clubhouse 2009 10v il map set $230
Grades: 4 5 6 7   **503**
  1. Science—Encyclopedias 2. Reference books
  ISBN 978-1-60413-554-1 (set); 1-60413-554-9 (set)
                LC 2008-38113
"This set introduces students to basic science concepts. Approximately 270 entries are arranged alphabetically. . . . The writing is basic, and much of the information is presented in the form of charts and bulleted lists. . . . This set would be useful for school and public libraries seeking a science encyclopedia." Booklist

The **Kingfisher** science encyclopedia; contributors, Clive Gifford . . . [et al.] updated ed. Kingfisher 2006 488p il map $24.95
Grades: 5 6 7 8   **503**
  1. Science—Encyclopedias 2. Reference books
  ISBN 0-7534-5886-1
First published 2000
An illustrated science encyclopedia arranged in such categories as "Planet Earth," "Living Things," "Chemistry and the Elements," "Materials and Technology," "Space and Time," and "Conservation and the Environment"
"This attractive, browsable, reasonably priced encyclopedia definitely has a place beside titles offering more depth." Booklist

507   Education, research, related topics

Cleary, Brian P., 1959-
"Mrs. Riley Bought Five Itchy Aardvarks" and other painless tricks for memorizing science facts; illustrated by J. P. Sandy. Millbrook Press 2008 48p il (Adventures in memory) lib bdg $23.93
Grades: 3 4 5 6   **507**
  1. Science 2. Memory 3. Scientific recreations
  ISBN 978-0-8225-7819-2 (lib bdg); 0-8225-7819-0 (lib bdg)   LC 2007-52125
"A brief introductory chapter defines mnemonics, illustrates a few of the techniques with widely known examples, and encourages readers to begin developing their own. With no further jargon, the remaining chapters apply these strategies to random scientific facts in the areas of 'Earth and Space Science,' 'Physical Science,' 'Life Science,' and 'The Scientific Method.' Acronyms, acrostic sentences, visualizations, rhymes, songs, and even a pseudo theatrical script are all demonstrated. . . . Colorful cartoons match the lightheartedness of the presentation." SLJ
"This short (48 pages), well-written, often cleverly

phrased, entertaining, humorous, engaging, colorfully illustrated book should be in every school and public library. . . . [It includes] a short, informative chapter on the scientific method." Sci Books Films

Glass, Susan
Analyze this! understanding the scientific method; [by] Susan Glass. Heinemann Library 2007 48p il (How to be a scientist) lib bdg $21; pa $8.99
Grades: 3 4 5 6   **507**
  1. Science—Methodology
  ISBN 978-1-4034-8358-4 (lib bdg); 978-1-4034-8362-1 (pa)   LC 2006010638
  Contents: Yellow fever; The scientific method; A brief history of science; Other scientists, other methods; Modern science; Testing things out; Moving forward; Scientific method flowchart; Timeline of discoveries
  Includes bibliographical references

Prove it! the scientific method in action; [by] Susan Glass. Heinemann Library 2007 48p il (How to be a scientist) lib bdg $21 paperback o.p.
Grades: 3 4 5 6   **507**
  1. Science—Methodology 2. Science—Experiments
  ISBN 978-1-4034-8359-1 (lib bdg); 978-1-4034-8363-8 (pa)   LC 2006010639
  Contents: The scientific method; Classroom experiments; Taking it further; Tying it together; Careers using the scientific method; Scientific method flowchart
  Includes bibliographical references

Kramer, Stephen
How to think like a scientist; answering questions by the scientific method; [by] Stephen P. Kramer; illustrated by Felicia Bond. Crowell 1987 44p il $16.89
Grades: 3 4 5   **507**
  1. Science—Methodology
  ISBN 978-0-690-04565-9; 0-690-04565-4
               LC 85-43604
An "exploration of the ways questions are asked and how scientists try to make sure that the questions are answered correctly. Relying on concrete story examples, Kramer shows how observed information can result in different or incorrect conclusions. Examples are also used to explain the principles of the scientific method." Booklist
"This is a pleasant book with an open format; an amusing halftone cartoon on almost every page illustrates the child oriented experiments and supports the light tone of the book." SLJ

Science detectives; how scientists solved six real-life mysteries; by the editors of Yes Mag; illustrated by Rose Cowles. Kids Can Press 2006 48p il $15.95; pa $8.95
Grades: 4 5 6   **507**
  1. Science—Methodology
  ISBN 978-1-55337-994-2; 1-55337-994-2; 978-1-55337-995-9; 1-55337-995-0 (pa)
This describes how scientists solved mysteries such as the spread of typhoid in 1906, the death of vultures in India in 1999, and the crash of a Swissair flight in 1998. Includes related projects.

507.8 Use of apparatus and equipment in study and teaching

Bardhan-Quallen, Sudipta

Last-minute science fair projects; when your Bunsen's not burning but the clock's really ticking. Sterling Pub. 2006 112p il $19.95

Grades: 5 6 7 8   507.8

1. Science projects 2. Science—Experiments
ISBN 978-1-4027-1690-4; 1-4027-1690-7

LC 2005-34455

"The introduction goes through a stripped-down summary of things to consider in choosing a project . . . a description of what to include in the project report, and some tips on presentation. . . . The description of each project is succinct and specific, with question, hypothesis, materials, and procedures clearly outlined." Sci Books Films

Becker, Helaine

Science on the loose; amazing activities and science facts you'll never believe; illustrated by Claudia Dávila. Maple Tree Press 2008 64p il $22.95; pa $10.95 *

Grades: 3 4 5 6   507.8

1. Science—Experiments
ISBN   978-1-897349-18-2;   1-897349-18-1;
978-1-897349-19-9 (pa); 1-897349-19-X (pa)

LC 2007939081

This is a collection of science facts and experiments. "Each experiment features a 'What's Going On?' component that explains the science behind the results." Publisher's note

This "is thought provoking, imaginative, and engaging, with a wonderful blend of intelligent writing, intriguing ideas and easy-to-perform experiments. There is also plenty of humor." Sci Books Films

Challen, Paul C., 1967-

What just happened? reading results and making inferences; [by] Paul Challen. Crabtree 2010 32p il (Step into science) lib bdg $26.60; pa $8.95

Grades: 4 5 6   507.8

1. Science—Methodology
ISBN 978-0-7787-5156-4 (lib bdg); 0-7787-5156-2 (lib bdg); 978-0-7787-5171-7 (pa); 0-7787-5171-6 (pa)

This "shows the reader how to make sense of the data that have been collected and recorded during the experiment. . . . The examples of charts and graphs, along with colorful photographs and illustrations, enhance the text. A time line showing scientific discoveries and inventions, a glossary, a list of books, and websites for further information, and an index are presented at the back of the book. This . . . would be a wonderful addition to a school classroom." Sci Books Films

Includes glossary and bibliographical references

What's going to happen? making your hypothesis; [by] Paul Challen. Crabtree 2010 32p il (Step into science) lib bdg $26.60; pa $8.95

Grades: 4 5 6   507.8

1. Science—Methodology
ISBN 978-0-7787-5157-1 (lib bdg); 0-7787-5157-0 (lib bdg); 978-0-7787-5172-4 (pa); 0-7787-5172-4 (pa)

Learn how scientists make educated guesses called hypotheses to test their theories. . . . Readers will learn how to construct a measurable and focused hypothesis to test in an experiment.

"A time line showing important hypotheses, a glossary, a list of books and websites for further information, and an index are provided at the back of the book. This . . . would be a wonderful addition to a school classroom." Sci Books Films

Includes glossary and bibliographical references

Cobb, Vicki, 1938-

Science experiments you can eat; illustrated by David Cain. rev & updated. HarperCollins Pubs. 1994 214p il hardcover o.p. pa $5.95

Grades: 5 6 7 8   507.8

1. Science—Experiments 2. Cooking
ISBN 0-06-023551-9; 0-06-446002-9 (pa)

LC 93-13679

First published 1972

Experiments with food demonstrate various scientific principles and produce an eatable result. Includes rock candy, grape jelly, cupcakes, and popcorn

Includes glossary

Squirts and spurts; science fun with water; illustrated by Steve Haefele. Millbrook Press 2000 48p il hardcover o.p. pa $7.95

Grades: 3 4 5 6   507.8

1. Science—Experiments 2. Water
ISBN 0-7613-1572-1 (lib bdg); 0-8225-7024-6 (pa)

LC 00-22113

Explains the physics of water pressure, showing how it makes everyday products such as faucets, spray bottles, and water pistols work. Includes experiments

"The text succeeds in conveying sophisticated concepts through accessible language, and Steve Haefele's drawings of an exuberant, grinning narrator and her robot sidekick clearly illustrate both the broad, abstract concepts and the concrete activity steps." Booklist

We dare you! hundreds of science bets, challenges, and experiments you can do at home; [by] Vicki Cobb and Kathy Darling. Skyhorse Pub. 2007 321p il hardcover o.p. pa $14.94

Grades: 4 5 6 7   507.8

1. Science—Experiments
ISBN   978-1-60239-225-0;   1-60239-225-0;
978-1-60239-775-0 (pa); 1-60239-775-9 (pa)

LC 2007-51236

"Divided into chapters with titles such as 'The Human Wonder,' 'Fluid Feats,' 'Energy Entrapments,' and 'Mathematical Duplicity,' this volume has more than 200 experiments with clear how-to instructions. All of the projects are doable and the science behind them is explained in a kid-accessible manner. . . . Black-and-white line drawings add humor and clarify instructions. This is

Cobb, Vicki, 1938-—*Continued*
a great resource for teachers, parents, and budding scientists—and for any youngster who can't resist a challenge." SLJ

Includes bibliographical references

Gabrielson, Curt
Stomp rockets, catapults, and kaleidoscopes; 30+ amazing science projects you can build for less than $1. Chicago Review Press 2008 159p il $16.95
Grades: 3 4 5 6   **507.8**
1. Science—Experiments 2. Science projects
ISBN 978-1-55652-737-1; 1-55652-737-3
                                    LC 2007-37917
"Projects include building a working model of the human hand's muscles, bones, and tendons using drinking straws, tape, and string; using a pair of two-liter bottles and a length of rubber tubing to learn how a toilet flushes; and discovering how musical instruments make sounds by fashioning a harmonica, saxophone, drum, flute, or oboe. All devices are designed to use recycled or nearly free materials and common tools." Publisher's note

Goodstein, Madeline
Ace your sports science project; great science fair ideas; [by] Madeline Goodstein, Robert Gardner, and Barbara Gardner Conklin. Enslow Publishers 2009 128p il (Ace your physics science project) lib bdg $31.93
Grades: 5 6 7 8   **507.8**
1. Physics 2. Sports 3. Science projects 4. Science—Experiments
ISBN 978-0-7660-3229-3 (lib bdg); 0-7660-3229-9 (lib bdg)   LC 2008-4689
"Presents several science experiments and project ideas dealing with the physics of sports." Publisher's note
Includes bibliographical references

Goal! science projects with soccer. Enslow Publishers 2009 104p il (Score! Sports science projects) lib bdg $31.93
Grades: 5 6 7 8   **507.8**
1. Soccer 2. Force and energy 3. Motion 4. Science—Experiments 5. Science projects
ISBN 978-0-7660-3106-7 (lib bdg); 0-7660-3106-3 (lib bdg)   LC 2008-2999
"Presents several science experiments using physics and soccer." Publisher's note
"Introductions include information about the history of the sport, safety steps to follow, and the scientific method. . . . Detailed diagrams help clarify many of the directions." SLJ

Includes glossary and bibliographical references

Haduch, Bill
Science fair success secrets; how to win prizes, have fun, and think like a scientist; illustrated by Philip Scheuer. Dutton 2002 134p il pa $10.99 *
Grades: 5 6 7 8   **507.8**
1. Science projects 2. Science—Experiments
ISBN 0-525-46534-0   LC 2002-23536
Explains the scientific method and describes a variety of actual science fair projects in such fields as engineering, botany, behavioral science, and chemistry
"The often jaunty tone of the text and the cartoon-style drawings make this an unusually appealing book on the topic, while the respect for science and the solid presentation make it a highly useful book as well." Booklist
Includes bibliographical references

Hammond, Richard, 1969-
Super science lab. DK Pub. 2009 96p il pa $8.99
Grades: 3 4 5   **507.8**
1. Science—Experiments
ISBN 978-0-7566-5341-5 (pa); 0-7566-5341-X (pa)
"With more than 30 scientific experiments, ranging from more traditional science-fair projects . . . this fun book has plenty of ideas to sample. Also offered are magnified images. . . . In between experiments, Hammond explores the science behind the subjects. . . . The active approach to science and scrapbook-style design, with plenty of photos, notes and asides, should win over curious kids." Publ Wkly

Harris, Elizabeth Snoke, 1973-
Save the Earth science experiments; science fair projects for eco-kids; [illustrator, Orrin Lundgren] Lark Books 2008 112p il $19.95
Grades: 4 5 6   **507.8**
1. Science projects 2. Science—Experiments 3. Environmental protection
ISBN 978-1-60059-322-2; 1-60059-322-4
                                    LC 2008017826
Contents: Save the Earth with your science fair project!; How to make a great science fair project; Rethinking energy; Alternative oils; Power plants; A bright idea; Running on air; The sun solution; Methane madness; Blowing in the wind; Putting the sun to work; Out the window; Rethinking garbage; Garbage diet; Recycled paper; Is bulk better?; Disappearing waste; Rethinking pollution; Heating up; No-zone; Lights out!; Clean up your act; Rethinking water; Down the drain; Water power; Not so fast grass; Solar still; Deadly fertilizers
This describes science fair projects such as how to harness energy with windmills, make a biogas generator, create alternative fuels, and recycle paper

Yikes! wow! yuck! fun experiments for your first science fair; illustrated by Nora Thompson. Lark Books 2008 64p il $12.95
Grades: 3 4 5 6   **507.8**
1. Science—Experiments 2. Science projects
ISBN 978-1-57990-930-7; 1-57990-930-2
                                    LC 2007-19770

Harris, Elizabeth Snoke, 1973-—*Continued*

"The experiments in this collection are based on everyday things in students' lives, such as Jell-O, potatoes, cereal, foggy mirrors, and exploding soda. Each one has clear, step-by-step directions and culminating questions. Ways to expand and change the projects are also included. Jokes are interspersed to add a bit of fun. . . . The illustrations offer a glimpse of what the experiment will include." SLJ

Includes glossary

Hauser, Jill Frankel

Super science concoctions; 50 mysterious mixtures for fabulous fun; illustrations by Michael Kline. Williamson 1997 160p il pa $12.95 *

Grades: 3 4 5   **507.8**

1. Science—Experiments 2. Scientific recreations
ISBN 1-885593-02-3   LC 95-47894

"A Williamson kids can! book"

Over 75 science experiments with mixtures that illustrate changes in form and chemical composition

"The sequential logic of the text make[s] this title valuable for teaching basic chemistry principles. Pen-and-ink cartoon illustrations are well placed, informative, and humorous. Safety precautions are emphasized." SLJ

Hopwood, James, 1964-

Cool distance assistants; fun science projects to propel things; [by] James Hopwood. ABDO Pub. 2008 32p il (Cool science) lib bdg $25.65

Grades: 4 5 6   **507.8**

1. Science—Experiments 2. Science projects
ISBN 978-1-59928-906-9 (lib bdg); 1-59928-906-7 (lib bdg)   LC 2007015625

This offers science projects about propulsion, including "Awesome Air & Water Rockets"

The experiments "will attract boys and girls. [The] book begins with [an] upbeat introduction and three chapters about the scientific method, keeping a journal, and safety. . . . Background on the science concepts involved is presented along with a complete list of supplies. . . . The numbered instructions are easy to follow and are accompanied by small, closeup photos." SLJ

Cool dry ice devices; fun science projects with dry ice; [by] James Hopwood. ABDO Pub. 2008 32p il (Cool science) lib bdg $25.65

Grades: 4 5 6   **507.8**

1. Science—Experiments 2. Science projects
ISBN 978-1-59928-907-6 (lib bdg); 1-59928-907-5 (lib bdg)   LC 2007010257

This offers science projects using dry ice, including "Fast Frozen Confections"

The experiments "will attract boys and girls. [The] book begins with [an] upbeat introduction and three chapters about the scientific method, keeping a journal, and safety. . . . Background on the science concepts involved is presented along with a complete list of supplies. . . . The numbered instructions are easy to follow and are accompanied by small, closeup photos." SLJ

Hyde, Natalie, 1963-

What's the plan? designing your experiment. Crabtree 2010 32p il (Step into science) lib bdg $26.60; pa $8.95

Grades: 4 5 6   **507.8**

1. Science—Methodology
ISBN 978-0-7787-5154-0 (lib bdg); 0-7787-5154-6 (lib bdg); 978-0-7787-5169-4 (pa); 0-7787-5169-4 (pa)

This "shows readers how to gather materials and create a step-by-step procedure to test their hypotheses. . . . Colorful photographs and illustrations enhance the text. A time line showing scientific discoveries and inventions, a glossary, a list of books and websites for further information, and an index are presented at the back of the book. This . . . would be a wonderful addition to a school classroom." Sci Books Films

Includes glossary and bibliographical references

Kenda, Margaret

Science wizardry for kids; [by] Margaret Kenda [and] Phyllis S. Williams; illustrated by Deborah Gross. 2nd ed. Barron's Educational Series 2009 242p il spiral $14.99

Grades: 3 4 5 6   **507.8**

1. Science—Experiments 2. Scientific recreations
ISBN 978-0-7641-4177-5 (spiral); 0-7641-4177-5 (spiral)   LC 2008049689

First published 1992

This includes over two hundred science projects including "creating an indicator out of red cabbage to test acids and bases, making an electric lemon, building a simple camera, and designing a terrarium. The directions are presented in easy-to-follow, numbered steps, and simple color drawings appear on every page." SLJ

Levine, Shar

Bathtub science; [by] Shar Levine & Leslie Johnstone; illustrations by Dave Garbot; photography by Jeff Connery. Sterling 2000 80p il hardcover o.p. pa $9.95

Grades: 3 4 5   **507.8**

1. Science—Experiments 2. Water
ISBN 0-8069-7185-1; 1-4027-4094-8 (pa)   LC 2001-273784

"From a simple, familiar sink-and-float experiment to the more complicated construction of a miniature diving bell, this book covers a wide array of science experiments that can be performed in water. Clear descriptions of how to perform and understand the experiments, as well as photos of the different steps involved, make the book particularly easy to use." Horn Book Guide

Includes glossary

Sports science; [by] Shar Levine & Leslie Johnstone; illustrated by Dave Garbot; photography by Stephen Ogilvy. Sterling Pub. Co. 2006 80p il $19.95

Grades: 3 4 5   **507.8**

1. Science—Experiments 2. Sports
ISBN 1-4027-1520-X   LC 2005-24367

"These 26 activities will allow children to see some real-life applications of science principles. A paragraph-length explanation of the concept being explored opens

Levine, Shar—*Continued*

each chapter, along with mention of a specific sport or type of sport (swimming/buoyancy, various balls/aerodynamics) it relates to. . . . This book will be an appealing choice for children and for adults teaching basic science concepts to tactile and kinesthetic learners." SLJ

Murphy, Pat, 1955-

Exploratopia; by Pat Murphy, Ellen Macaulay, and the staff of the Exploratorium; illustrated by Jason Gorski. Little, Brown and Co. 2006 373p il $29.99

Grades: 3 4 5 6   **507.8**

1. Science—Experiments

ISBN 978-0-316-61281-4; 0-316-61281-2

LC 2006-40942

"Practiced young experimenters ready to strike out on their own will find enticing science demonstrations on nearly every page of this inviting collection. Each of the 21 sections contains a half dozen or more entries that feature easily gathered ingredients, clear directions, and color photos or diagrams that are not only informative but often arresting as well." SLJ

Includes bibliographical references

Newcomb, Rain

Smash it! crash it! launch it! 50 mind-blowing, eye-popping science experiments; [by] Rain Newcomb & Bobby Mercer. Lark Books 2006 80p il $14.95

Grades: 4 5 6 7   **507.8**

1. Science—Experiments

ISBN 978-1-57990-795-2; 1-57990-795-4

LC 2006-05518

"Science teachers will find entertaining ways to impress their students with Newton's laws if they're willing to break a few eggs as described in this engaging book. The study of physics becomes appealing when combined with marshmallow catapults, potato popguns, and water-balloon launchers. The authors provide a brief explanation of the physical principles involved and emphasize that cleanup is required on some of the messier projects. . . . Humorous cartoon illustrations and sketchy templates supplement the descriptions of how to set up the projects. Typical household ingredients like straws, pop bottles, fruits, and lots of eggs are the materials required." SLJ

Pilger, Mary Anne

Science experiments index for young people. 4th ed. Libraries Unlimited 2005 184p $65

Grades: Professional   **507.8**

1. Science—Experiments—Indexes 2. Reference books

ISBN 1-59158-237-7

This is a guide to science books that contain elementary and intermediate-level projects and experiments. Organized alphabetically by subject and including a list of headings, the book has 7000 entries that consist of a brief description, book and page numbers, and cross-references.

Rhatigan, Joe

Prize-winning science fair projects for curious kids; [by] Joe Rhatigan & Rain Newcomb. Lark Books 2004 112p il hardcover o.p. pa $7.95

Grades: 5 6 7 8   **507.8**

1. Science projects 2. Science—Experiments

ISBN 1-57990-478-5; 1-57990-750-4 (pa)

LC 2003-24957

"Fifty experiments in biology, the physical sciences, and chemistry are presented in an attractive and easy-to-follow format and illustrated with sharp photographs of children and of the materials needed. One of the book's strengths is the first chapter about choosing and doing a project. Ideas include checking out the validity of horoscopes, mummifying fish, testing the effectiveness of sunscreens, and testing spray-on water repellents." SLJ

Science activities for all students; edited by Aviva Ebner. Facts on File 2009 2v il loose-leaf $370

Grades: Professional   **507.8**

1. Science—Experiments 2. Science projects

ISBN 978-0-8160-7396-2 (loose-leaf); 0-8160-7396-1 (loose-leaf)   LC 2008043827

Replaces *Science Projects for All Students* and *More Science Projects for All Students*, published 1998 and 2002 respectively

These "binders enable students in grades 4 through 9 with developmental or physical challenges to join their classmates in . . . hands-on [science] activities. There are 60 experiments in each binder—designed to be as inclusive as possible—in the areas of basic skills, Earth science, weather, space science, life science, and physical science. Each binder is also enhanced by approximately 250 black-and-white line illustrations." Publisher's note

Includes glossary and bibliographical references

Tocci, Salvatore

More simple science fair projects, grades 3-5; illustrated by Bob Wiacek. Chelsea House Pub. 2006 48p il (Scientific American winning science fair projects) $27

Grades: 3 4 5   **507.8**

1. Science projects 2. Science—Experiments

ISBN 0-7910-9055-8   LC 2005-57097

This "begins by describing how to exhibit information on a trifold display with the following information: background, the experimental question, materials, procedures, results, and explanations. The author then describes 18 experiments following that format. The language is clear and easy to follow. Simple drawings add a great deal to the explanations." Sci Books Films

VanCleave, Janice Pratt

Janice VanCleave's 201 awesome, magical, bizarre & incredible experiments. Wiley 1994 118p pa $12.95 *

Grades: 4 5 6 7   **507.8**

1. Science—Experiments

ISBN 0-471-31011-5   LC 93-29807

The experiments in this book "are organized by field: astronomy, biology, chemistry, earth science, and physics; the purpose, materials needed, procedure, results, and an explanation are included for each demonstration. The

VanCleave, Janice Pratt—*Continued*
author writes in a clear, easy-to-understand style. . . .
The book will be especially useful to teachers looking
for ideas that can be adapted as hands-on activities." SLJ
Includes glossary

Janice VanCleave's 202 oozing, bubbling,
dripping & bouncing experiments. Wiley 1996
120p pa $12.95 *
Grades: 4 5 6 7   **507.8**
   1. Science—Experiments
   ISBN 0-471-14025-2   LC 95-46398
Provides instructions for over 200 short experiments in
astronomy, biology, chemistry, earth science, and physics
"Some activities consist merely of observation, such
as 'To study parts of a feather.' Some are more complex,
but all are clearly and concisely explained. Many are repeats from prior VanCleave books, but 40 are supposedly
new." SLJ
Includes glossary

Janice VanCleave's 203 icy, freezing, frosty,
cool & wild experiments. Wiley 1999 122p pa
$12.95 *
Grades: 4 5 6 7   **507.8**
   1. Science—Experiments
   ISBN 0-471-25223-9   LC 98-49721
This includes "experiments in astronomy, biology,
chemistry, earth science, and physics. . . . Each activity
includes a purpose, a list of materials, a step-by-step procedure, results, and an explanation. Experiments address
such topics as the Moon's 'changing' size, how environment affects body temperature, and why ice pops are
softer than ice. An excellent resource." SLJ

Janice VanCleave's big book of play and find
out science projects. Wiley 2007 213p il pa $19.95
Grades: K 1 2 3   **507.8**
   1. Science projects 2. Science—Experiments
   ISBN 978-0-7879-8928-6 (pa); 0-7879-8928-2 (pa)
                         LC 2006-52572
This "is a compilation of 56 hands-on activities based
on authentic questions asked by children. The four-part
book contains activities in each of the following content
areas: 'Physical Science,' 'Nature,' 'Bugs,' and 'Human
Body.' . . . Adults and children will likely find it a useful tool." Sci Books Films
Includes glossary and bibliographical references

Janice VanCleave's engineering for every kid;
easy activities that make learning science fun.
Jossey-Bass 2007 205p il (Science for every kid
series) pa $14.95
Grades: 4 5 6 7   **507.8**
   1. Engineering 2. Science projects 3. Science—Experiments
   ISBN 978-0-471-47182-0 (pa); 0-471-47182-8 (pa)
                         LC 2006-10540
Explains some of the basic physical principles of engineering, accompanied by activities that illustrate those
principles

Janice VanCleave's guide to more of the best
science fair projects. Wiley 2000 156p il pa
$14.95 *
Grades: 5 6 7 8   **507.8**
   1. Science projects 2. Science—Experiments
   ISBN 0-471-32627-5   LC 99-25575
Companion volume to Janice VanCleave's guide to
the best science fair projects
This volume includes "fifty experiments . . . in the
areas of astronomy, biology, earth science, engineering,
physical science, and mathematics. . . . A valuable addition to science collections." SLJ
Includes bibliographical references

Janice VanCleave's guide to the best science
fair projects; [by] Janice VanCleave. Wiley 1997
156p il pa $14.95 *
Grades: 4 5 6 7   **507.8**
   1. Science projects 2. Science—Experiments
   ISBN 0-471-14802-4   LC 96-27512
"In the first section, VanCleave discusses scientific
methodology: how to organize a project from selecting a
topic through the investigatory process, the importance of
keeping records, writing a final report, and the value of
a nicely crafted presentation. . . . The next section—the
largest by far—presents a number of double-page projects in a variety of fields. . . . A clear and informative
addition." SLJ
Includes glossary and bibliographical references

Janice VanCleave's science around the year.
Wiley 2000 122p il pa $12.95
Grades: 4 5 6 7   **507.8**
   1. Science—Experiments
   ISBN 0-471-33096-5   LC 99-53778
Presents experiments and activities in such fields as
astronomy, biology, chemistry, earth science, and physics
that are in some way related to one of the four seasons

Walker, Pamela, 1958-
Science experiments on file; [by] Pamela
Walker and Elaine Wood. Facts on File 2004-2005
2v unp il loose-leaf ea $185
Grades: Professional   **507.8**
   ISBN 0-8160-5734-6   LC 2004-47230
   Also available CD-ROM version
   First published 1988
This offers 120 science experiments with over 250 il-
lustrations, tables, and diagrams, listing time required,
safety precautions, materials, procedure, principles illus-
trated, data tables, connections, and additional activities,
which may be reproduced for classroom use
Includes glossaries and bibliographical references

Williams, Jennifer, 1971-
Oobleck, slime, & dancing spaghetti; twenty
terrific at-home science experiments inspired by
favorite children's books. Bright Sky Press 2009
192p il pa $14.95
Grades: Professional   **507.8**
   1. Science—Experiments 2. Children's literature
   ISBN 978-1-933979-34-2 (pa); 1-933979-34-8 (pa)
                       LC 2009000876

Williams, Jennifer, 1971-—*Continued*

"Using children's literature as a springboard, this title provides a series of science experiments designed to explore concepts and ideas that spring from various stories. At the beginning of each chapter, a children's book is nicely summarized. The author then explains a related science concept, suggests discussion questions that connect the experiment to the story, and offers ideas for taking the project further. This is serious science. . . . The experiments do a really wonderful job of emphasizing the importance of observation and data collection. The writing is relatively clear. . . . This book is great choice for home use and science units." SLJ

Includes bibliographical references

508   Natural history

Baker, Stuart

Climate change in the Antarctic. Marshall Cavendish Benchmark 2009 32p il map (Climate change) lib bdg $19.95

Grades: 3 4 5 6   508

1. Antarctica 2. Greenhouse effect 3. Climate—Environmental aspects

ISBN 978-0-7614-4438-1 (lib bdg); 0-7614-4438-6 (lib bdg)

"Antarctica holds 90 percent of the planet's ice, which could, if melted, potentially raise sea levels and submerge coastal cities worldwide. This slim title . . . explores how global warming is affecting this fascinating frozen world in fact-packed, concise pages fille with color photos . . . and digitally rendered charts and maps." Booklist

In the Antarctic. Marshall Cavendish Benchmark 2010 32p il map (Climate change) lib bdg $19.95

Grades: 5 6 7 8   508

1. Antarctica 2. Greenhouse effect

ISBN 978-0-7614-4438-1 (lib bdg); 0-7614-4438-6 (lib bdg)   LC 2009-5766

The book about climate change in the Antarctic "is perfectly organized for students. . . . Unique layout features serve as signposts and will help focus readers' attention. . . . [The book] features an outstanding chart of possible effects of global warming on the area in question, listing 'Possible Event', 'Predicted Result', and 'Impact' in short, bulleted statements." SLJ

Includes glossary

In the tropics. Marshall Cavendish Benchmark 2010 32p il map (Climate change) lib bdg $19.95

Grades: 5 6 7 8   508

1. Tropics 2. Greenhouse effect

ISBN 978-0-7614-4440-4 (lib bdg); 0-7614-4440-8 (lib bdg)   LC 2009-5768

The book about climate change in the Tropics "is perfectly organized for students. . . . Unique layout features serve as signposts and will help focus readers' attention. . . . [The book] features an outstanding chart of possible effects of global warming on the area in question, listing 'Possible Event', 'Predicted Result', and 'Impact' in short, bulleted statements." SLJ

Includes glossary

Lynch, Wayne

The Everglades; text and photographs by Wayne Lynch. NorthWord Books for Young Readers 2007 64p il (Our wild world: ecosystems) $16.95; pa $8.95

Grades: 4 5 6 7   508

1. Everglades (Fla.) 2. Natural history—Florida

ISBN 978-1-55971-970-4; 1-55971-970-2; 978-1-55971-971-1 (pa); 1-55971-971-0 (pa)

LC 2006-101497

This "provides an up-close look at the fascinating flora and fauna of the world-famous Everglades. . . . Lynch . . . smoothly pairs engaging prose with numerous color photographs that capture the beauty of the region in both sweeping panorama and close-up detail." Booklist

McMillan, Bruce

Summer ice; life along the Antarctic peninsula; written and photo-illustrated by Bruce McMillan. Houghton Mifflin 1995 48p il map $16

Grades: 3 4 5 6   508

1. Natural history—Antarctica 2. Antarctica

ISBN 0-395-66561-2   LC 93-38831

"This photo-essay introduces readers to the animals and plants of the Antarctic Peninsula. . . . After showing the landforms and glacial iceforms there, McMillan turns to the unexpected wealth of summer wildlife: algae and moss, plankton and krill, humpback whales and orcas, skuas and shags, seals and (of course) penguins." Booklist

"The full-color photography is brilliant in its beauty and attention to detail. However, the text is lively and knowledgeable, and could stand alone and still catch readers' interest." SLJ

Includes glossary and bibliographical references

Morrison, Gordon

Nature in the neighborhood; [by] Gordon Morrison. Houghton Mifflin Company 2004 32p il $16 *

Grades: 3 4 5 6   508

1. Natural history 2. Seasons

ISBN 0-618-35215-5   LC 2004-2354

"Walter Lorraine books"

The author "focuses on plants and animals in a single neighborhood in an unnamed North American city, beginning in spring as the snow melts and following them through the seasons." SLJ

"Morrison offers another quiet, layered view of a natural world that is familiar to many children. . . . His precise, pencil-and-watercolor artwork encourages viewers to look closely at common neighborhood scenes." Booklist

Potter, Jean, 1947-

Nature in a nutshell for kids; over 100 activities you can do in ten minutes or less. Wiley 1995 136p il pa $12.95

Grades: 2 3 4   508

1. Nature study

ISBN 0-471-04444-X   LC 94-28953

Potter, Jean, 1947-—*Continued*

"Each of the 102 experiments is easy, uses safe and mostly readily available household supplies, and is fun at the same time. Divided into seasonal sections, the activities have catchy titles, state hypotheses, list materials, lay out procedures, and finish with clear explanations. Among the noteworthy investigations are: how duck feathers react to water, how mountains are formed, what keeps a seal from freezing in icy weather, whether ants prefer sugar or aspertame, and more." SLJ

Includes glossary and bibliographical references

Rau, Dana Meachen, 1971-

Day and night. Marshall Cavendish Benchmark 2010 31p il (Bookworms. Nature's cycles) lib bdg $22.79

Grades: PreK K 1   **508**
1. Day 2. Night
ISBN 978-0-7614-4094-9 (lib bdg); 0-7614-4094-1 (lib bdg)   LC 2008-42512

"Introduces the idea that many things in the world around us are cyclical in nature and discusses how day changes to night each day." Publisher's note

"Well composed, simple sentences tie directly to colorful, carefully chosen photos [and] . . . accurate information flows naturally. . . . A great resource for sharing one-on-one with the youngest readers." Libr Media Connect

Includes glossary

Wood, A. J. (Amanda Jane)

Charles Darwin and the Beagle adventure; countries visited during the voyage round the world of HMS Beagle under the command of Captain Fitzroy, Royal Navy, including extracts from the works of Charles Darwin; written by A.J. Wood & Clint Twist. Candlewick Press 2009 unp il map $19.99

Grades: 4 5 6 7 8   **508**
1. Darwin, Charles, 1809-1882 2. Beagle Expedition (1831-1836) 3. Evolution
ISBN 978-0-7636-4538-0; 0-7636-4538-9
          LC 2009-921214

"This beautifully illustrated large-format book immediately appeals to both the eye and the mind. Imitating a 19th-century scrapbook to a certain extent, including various pullouts . . . the book draws the young reader in. . . . Included are copious quotes from Darwin's journals and other writings, as well as reproductions . . . of numerous 19th-century engravings, drawings, and watercolors, some from the Beagle voyage itself. . . . Integrated into the 19th-century material are modern illustrations and well-written narratives relating background information, the story of the Beagle's voyage . . . and notes on Darwin's life and work. . . . This volume provides an excellent introduction to Darwin and his accomplishments." Sci Books Films

508.2   Seasons

Anderson, Maxine

Explore spring! 25 great ways to learn about spring; [by Maxine Anderson; illustrated by Alexis Frederick-Frost] Nomad Press 2007 92p il pa $12.95

Grades: 2 3 4 5   **508.2**
1. Spring 2. Science—Experiments
ISBN 978-0-9785037-4-1

Explains what spring is and why it occurs. Includes projects, activities, and experiments.

"Bold, black-and-white cartoons and occasional jokes add levity to the science. . . . The information is sound, with engaging activities to test and illuminate spring events." SLJ

Includes glossary and bibliographical references

Explore winter! 25 great ways to learn about winter; [by Maxine Anderson; illustrated by Alexis Frederick-Frost] Nomad Press 2007 92p il pa $12.95

Grades: 2 3 4 5   **508.2**
1. Winter 2. Science—Experiments
ISBN 978-0-9785037-5-8

Explains what winter is and why it occurs. Includes projects, activities, and experiments.

"Pages of basic information are interspersed with 'Wow' facts, black-and-white cartoon illustrations, and jokes. . . . Curious readers will gain a new level of understanding about winter after reading, laughing at, and experimenting with this book." SLJ

Includes glossary and bibliographical references

Anderson, Sheila

Are you ready for fall? by Sheila M. Anderson. Lerner Publications 2010 32p il (Lightning bolt books. Seasons) lib bdg $25.26; pa $7.95

Grades: PreK K 1 2   **508.2**
1. Autumn
ISBN 978-0-7613-4586-2 (lib bdg); 0-7613-4586-8 (lib bdg); 978-0-7613-5672-1 (pa); 0-7613-5672-X (pa)
          LC 2009-16408

"The book explores, in simplest terms, things that we see and experience in the fall. . . . Vivid photographs accompany the text, with explanatory balloons to highlight certain points. . . . This wouid be an excellent book to read, chapter by chapter, to younger preschoolers and to be read by older readers and used for research up to third grade. It lends itself well to science and social studies lessons, as well as other activities." Sci Books Films

Includes glossary

Are you ready for spring? by Sheila M. Anderson. Lerner Publications 2010 32p il (Lightning bolt books. Seasons) lib bdg $25.26; pa $7.95

Grades: PreK K 1 2   **508.2**
1. Spring
ISBN 978-0-7613-4584-8 (lib bdg); 0-7613-4584-1 (lib bdg); 978-0-7613-5670-7 (pa); 0-7613-5670-3 (pa)
          LC 2009-16409

Anderson, Sheila—*Continued*

This "explores those attributes we most often associate with spring. The book has a lot of 'kid appeal' with its pictures and descriptions of mud puddles, rain, and flying kites. Changes in nature are subtly woven in with everyday experiences to provide a full overview of the season. The descriptions and explanations are scientifically accurate, and a diversity of ethncity and climates is shown in the colorful pictures." Sci Books Films

Includes glossary

Branley, Franklyn Mansfield, 1915-2002

Sunshine makes the seasons; illustrated by Michael Rex. newly illustrated ed. HarperCollins Pubs. 2005 31p il (Let's-read-and-find-out science) hardcover o.p. pa $4.99 *

Grades: K 1 2 3   508.2

1. Seasons

ISBN 0-06-059203-6; 0-06-059205-2 (pa)

LC 2003-25457

First published 1974; this is a newly illustrated edition of the text revised for the 1985 edition

Describes how sunshine and the tilt of the earth's axis are responsible for the changing seasons

Includes bibliographical references

Esbaum, Jill

Everything spring. National Geographic 2010 15p il (Picture the seasons) pa $5.95

Grades: PreK K 1   508.2

1. Spring

ISBN 978-1-4263-0607-5; 1-4263-0607-5

"These pages burst with vibrant photographs of baby animals and closeups of buds and growth. Esbaum uses poetic prose to connect children with the joy of the season." SLJ

Hawk, Fran

Count down to Fall; illustrated by Sherry Neidigh. Sylvan Dell 2009 unp il $16.95

Grades: PreK K 1 2 3   508.2

1. Autumn 2. Trees 3. Forest animals 4. Counting

ISBN 978-1-934359-94-5; 1-934359-94-7

"Bold, full-spread illustrations with inset details feature a variety of trees and woodland animals in this informational picture book. As the facts about trees count down, the images represent the numbers 10 to 1, while corner insets show the tree, spring and fall leaves, a seed, and occasionally the flower of the specific tree pictured, such as birch, dogwood, oak, and maple. Children will be drawn to examine the expressive images of animals and find additional ones along the detailed border featuring closeups of the tree's bark." SLJ

Lin, Grace, 1974-

Our seasons; [by] Grace Lin and Ranida McNeally; illustrated by Grace Lin. Charlesbridge 2006 unp il $15.95

Grades: K 1 2 3   508.2

1. Seasons

ISBN 978-1-57091-360-0; 1-57091-360-9

LC 2005-06016

"Following a brief explanation of the science behind the seasons, Lin takes readers from autumn to summer, pairing haiku verses on one page with explanations of seasonal changes on the other. . . . The gouache illustrations have plenty of child appeal and effectively tie together the poetry and the facts." SLJ

Rau, Dana Meachen, 1971-

Seasons. Marshall Cavendish Benchmark 2009 31p il (Bookworms. Nature's cycles) lib bdg $22.79

Grades: PreK K 1   508.2

1. Seasons

ISBN 978-0-7614-4098-7 (lib bdg); 0-7614-4098-4 (lib bdg)

LC 2008-42507

"Introduces the idea that many things in the world around us are cyclical in nature and discusses how the seasons change." Publisher's note

"Well composed, simple sentences tie directly to colorful, carefully chosen photos [and] . . . accurate information flows naturally. . . . A great resource for sharing one-on-one with the youngest readers." Libr Media Connect

Includes glossary

Rotner, Shelley

Every season; by Shelley Rotner & Anne Love Woodhull; photographs by Shelley Rotner. Roaring Brook Press 2007 unp il $16.95

Grades: PreK K 1   508.2

1. Seasons

ISBN 978-1-59643-136-2; 1-59643-136-9

LC 2006-12009

"A Neal Porter book"

With simple text and bright photographs presents a portrait of nature through the seasons of the year.

"Beautiful color photographs illustrate this picture-book. . . . What distinguishes this is the quality and selection of the photos and the lovely spare words, which repeat sounds and lines with an easy, circular rhythm that echoes the cycle of seasons and encourages child participation." Booklist

Schuette, Sarah L., 1976-

Let's look at fall; by Sarah L. Schuette. Capstone Press 2007 24p il (Investigate the seasons) $19.93

Grades: K 1 2   508.2

1. Animal behavior 2. Autumn

ISBN 978-0-7368-6705-4; 0-7368-6705-8

LC 2006020449

"Pebble plus"

"Simple text and photographs present what happens to the weather, animals, and plants in fall." Publisher's note

"The format consists of about three descriptive sentences per page in a large font, a vivid color photograph opposite, and colorful chapter titles in a larger typeface. . . . [This book is] excellent . . . for unit study and wonderful for sharing or browsing." SLJ

Includes bibliographical references

Schuette, Sarah L., 1976-—*Continued*

Let's look at spring; by Sarah L. Schuette. Capstone Press 2007 24p il (Investigate the seasons) $19.93

Grades: K 1 2   **508.2**
1. Animal behavior 2. Spring
ISBN 978-0-7368-6707-8; 0-7368-6707-4
LC 2006020451

"Pebble plus"

"Simple text and photographs present what happens to the weather, animals, and plants in spring." Publisher's note

"The format consists of about three descriptive sentences per page in a large font, a vivid color photograph opposite, and colorful chapter titles in a larger typeface. . . . [This book is] excellent . . . for unit study and wonderful for sharing or browsing." SLJ

Includes bibliographical references

Let's look at summer; by Sarah L. Schuette. Capstone Press 2007 24p il (Investigate the seasons) $19.93

Grades: K 1 2   **508.2**
1. Animal behavior 2. Summer
ISBN 978-0-7368-6708-5; 0-7368-6708-2
LC 2006020452

"Pebble plus"

"Simple text and photographs present what happens to the weather, animals, and plants in summer." Publisher's note

"The format consists of about three descriptive sentences per page in a large font, a vivid color photograph opposite, and colorful chapter titles in a larger typeface. . . . [This book is] excellent . . . for unit study and wonderful for sharing or browsing." SLJ

Includes bibliographical references

Let's look at winter; by Sarah L. Schuette. Capstone Press 2007 24p il (Investigate the seasons) $19.93

Grades: K 1 2   **508.2**
1. Animal behavior 2. Winter
ISBN 978-0-7368-6706-1; 0-7368-6706-6
LC 2006020508

"Pebble plus"

"Simple text and photographs present what happens to the weather, animals, and plants in winter." Publisher's note

"The format consists of about three descriptive sentences per page in a large font, a vivid color photograph opposite, and colorful chapter titles in a larger typeface. . . . [This book is] excellent . . . for unit study and wonderful for sharing or browsing." SLJ

Includes bibliographical references

Smith, Siân

Fall. Heinemann Library 2009 24p il (Seasons) lib bdg $20.71; pa $5.99

Grades: K 1   **508.2**
1. Autumn
ISBN 978-1-4329-2727-1 (lib bdg); 1-4329-2727-2 (lib bdg); 978-1-4329-2732-5 (pa); 1-4329-2732-9 (pa)
LC 2008049155

This describes the clothing, weather, and human and animal activities of the Autumn.

"What distinguishes [this book] from others on the same [subject is] the vibrant, eye-catching photographs. The sentences are simple and repetitive. . . . Reading teachers will want to use this . . . for instructional purposes while early readers will feel successful mastering the text. Students will delight in the color photographs of animals and children enjoying the activities." SLJ

Spring. Heinemann Library 2009 24p il (Seasons) lib bdg $20.71; pa $5.99

Grades: K 1   **508.2**
1. Spring
ISBN 978-1-4329-2728-8 (lib bdg); 1-4329-2728-0 (lib bdg); 978-1-4329-2733-2 (pa); 1-4329-2733-7 (pa)
LC 2008049156

This describes the clothing, weather, and human and animal activities of spring

"What distinguishes [this book] from others on the same [subject is] the vibrant, eye-catching photographs. The sentences are simple and repetitive. . . . Reading teachers will want to use this . . . for instructional purposes while early readers will feel successful mastering the text. Students will delight in the color photographs of animals and children enjoying the activities." SLJ

Summer. Heinemann Library 2009 24p il (Seasons) lib bdg $20.71; pa $5.99

Grades: K 1   **508.2**
1. Summer
ISBN 978-1-4329-2729-5 (lib bdg); 1-4329-2729-9 (lib bdg); 978-1-4329-2734-9 (pa); 1-4329-2734-5 (pa)
LC 2008049157

This describes the clothing, weather, and human and animal activities of summer

"What distinguishes [this book] from others on the same [subject is] the vibrant, eye-catching photographs. The sentences are simple and repetitive. . . . Reading teachers will want to use this . . . for instructional purposes while early readers will feel successful mastering the text. Students will delight in the color photographs of animals and children enjoying the activities." SLJ

Winter. Heinemann Library 2009 24p il (Seasons) lib bdg $20.71; pa $5.99

Grades: K 1   **508.2**
1. Winter
ISBN 978-1-4329-2730-1 (lib bdg); 1-4329-2730-2 (lib bdg); 978-1-4329-2735-6 (pa); 1-4329-2735-3 (pa)
LC 2008049162

This describes the clothing, weather, and human and animal activities of winter

"What distinguishes [this book] from others on the same [subject is] the vibrant, eye-catching photographs. The sentences are simple and repetitive. . . . Reading teachers will want to use this . . . for instructional purposes while early readers will feel successful mastering the text. Students will delight in the color photographs of animals and children enjoying the activities." SLJ

509 Historical, geographic, persons treatment

Beshore, George W.

Science in ancient China; [by] George Beshore. Watts 1998 63p il map (Science of the past) hardcover o.p. pa $8.95 *

Grades: 4 5 6 7   509

   1. Science—China—History 2. Science and civilization

   ISBN 0-531-11334-5 (lib bdg); 0-531-15914-0 (pa)

                LC 97-3519

First published 1988 in the First book series

Surveys the achievements of the ancient Chinese in science, medicine, astronomy, and cosmology, and describes such innovations as rockets, wells, the compass, water wheels, and movable type

Includes glossary and bibliographical references

Cole, Joanna

The magic school bus and the science fair expedition; illustrated by Bruce Degen. Scholastic Press 2006 45p il $15.99 *

Grades: 2 3 4   509

   1. Science—History 2. Scientists

   ISBN 0-590-10824-7

Ms. Frizzle takes her class on a tour through the history of science so they can get ideas for their science fair

"This has all the hallmarks of the winning series: humorous cartoon speech bubbles; instructive, funny, appealing illustrations; and clear language that explains basic concepts without condescension." Booklist

Fradin, Dennis B.

With a little luck; surprising stories of amazing discoveries; [by] Dennis Brindell Fradin. Dutton Children's Books 2006 183p il $17.99 *

Grades: 5 6 7 8   509

   1. Science—History

   ISBN 0-525-47196-0   LC 2005-04798

This describes 11 scientific discoveries, including gravity, fossils, rubber, anesthesia, hygienic medicine, prehistoric cave paintings, penicillin, the planet Pluto, nuclear fission, the Dead Sea Scrolls, and pulsars

The author "smoothly combines personal stories . . . with fascinating science, technology, and history. His style is open and chatty, and the book design is very attractive." Booklist

Includes bibliographical references

Harris, Jacqueline L., 1929-

Science in ancient Rome. Watts 1998 64p il map (Science of the past) hardcover o.p. pa $8.95 *

Grades: 4 5 6 7   509

   1. Science—Rome—History 2. Science and civilization

   ISBN 0-531-20354-9; 0-531-15916-7 (pa)

                LC 97-1901

First published 1988 in the First book series

Describes how the Romans put to use and expanded the scientific achievements of earlier civilizations

This "includes clear, easy-to-read text; simple yet effective topic headings; excellent-quality, full-color photographs and reproductions; and Internet sites." SLJ

Includes glossary and bibliographical references

Jackson, Donna M., 1959-

Extreme scientists; exploring nature's mysteries from perilous places. Houghton Mifflin Harcourt 2009 63p il (Scientists in the field) $18 *

Grades: 5 6 7 8   509

   1. Barton, Hazel 2. Sillett, Steve 3. Flaherty, Paul 4. Scientists 5. Explorers

   ISBN 978-0-618-77706-8; 0-618-77706-7

                LC 2008-36796

This volume "profiles three scientists working far out in the field. Hurricane hunter Paul Flaherty, . . . Hazel Barton, a microbiologist specializing in single-cell organisms living in extreme conditions, . . . [and] ecologist and college professor Steve Sillett, who . . . climbs into the canopies to study redwoods. While the clearly written text includes vivid passages about the dangers these scientists face, it goes on to discuss what drives them to pursue their subjects and what they have discovered along the way. . . . The many excellent color photos portray these adventures as scientists intently focused on their work." Booklist

Includes glossary and bibliographical references

January, Brendan, 1972-

Science in colonial America. Watts 1999 64p il (Science of the past) hardcover o.p. pa $8.95

Grades: 4 5 6 7   509

   1. Science—United States—History 2. Science and civilization

   ISBN 0-531-11525-9; 0-531-15940-X (pa)

                LC 98-10450

Describes the scientific contributions made by people in colonial America, including natural history, medicine, astronomy, and electricity

"Attractive and accessible. . . . Plentiful, accurate material." SLJ

Includes glossary and bibliographical references

McCutcheon, Marc

The kid who named Pluto; and the stories of other extraordinary young people in science; illustrated by Jon Cannell. Chronicle Books 2004 85p il $15.95 *

Grades: 4 5 6   509

   1. Scientists

   ISBN 0-8118-3770-X   LC 2003-3662

Contents: The boy who dreamed of Mars; The girl who named Pluto; The bookworm who became a science fiction writer; The teenager who invented television; The curious girl who discovered sea-monster skeletons; The high schooler who created an incredible secret code; The math whiz who calculated the movement of the moon; The fourth-grader who outsmarted medical experts; The blind boy who developed a new way to see

McCutcheon, Marc—*Continued*

"This book profiles nine people who made significant contributions to science while still quite young. Louis Braille and Robert Goddard are among the more famous, while others, such as television pioneer Philo Farnsworth and Venetia Burney, the girl who named Pluto, are less well known. . . . The lively and lighthearted text conveys a sense of the excitement of discovery, with an appropriate amount of background information, along with the biographical facts. . . . Lively cartoon pen-and-ink illustrations, all in greens and grays, help to unify the individual chapters. " Booklist

Woods, Geraldine, 1948-

Science in ancient Egypt. Watts 1998 64p il (Science of the past) hardcover o.p. pa $8.95 *

Grades: 4 5 6 7   **509**

1. Science—Egypt—History 2. Science and civilization

ISBN 0-531-20341-7; 0-531-15915-9 (pa)

                       LC 97-649

First published 1988 in the First book series

Discusses the achievements of the ancient Egyptians in science, mathematics, astronomy, medicine, agriculture, and technology

"Well-researched and easy-to-understand. . . . Woods offers a fascinating look at the ancient Egyptians' accomplishments." SLJ

Includes glossary and bibliographical references

510   Mathematics

Bodach, Vijaya

Bar graphs; by Vijaya Khisty Bodach. Capstone Press 2008 32p il (Making graphs) lib bdg $23.93; pa $7.95

Grades: K 1 2   **510**

1. Graphic methods

ISBN 978-1-4296-0040-8 (lib bdg); 1-4296-0040-3 (lib bdg); 978-1-4296-2870-9 (pa); 1-4296-2870-7 (pa)

                     LC 2007004670

"A+ books"

This "book illustrates how to sort items and represent quantity using horizontal and vertical bars on a graph. Toy animals, fruit, pet type, and hair color are used as examples. . . . [The] title encourages readers to create their own graphs. Large, colorful photographs depict the concepts and feature ethnically diverse children. The photos and graphs complement the controlled-vocabulary [text]." SLJ

Includes glossary and bibliographical references

Pictographs; by Vijaya Khisty Bodach. Capstone Press 2008 32p il (Making graphs) lib bdg $23.93; pa $7.95

Grades: K 1 2   **510**

1. Graphic methods

ISBN 978-1-4296-0041-5 (lib bdg); 1-4296-0041-1 (lib bdg); 978-1-4296-2871-6 (pa); 1-4296-2871-5 (pa)

                     LC 2007006948

"A+ books"

This "introduces the idea of organizing data to 'show how many' with picture representations. Comparisons are made on a variety of topics: spotted and solid-color bunnies, how students get to school (walking, bus, and bikes), beverage preferences, and the kinds of flowers in an arrangement. . . . [The] title encourages readers to create their own graphs. Large, colorful photographs depict the concepts and feature ethnically diverse children. The photos and graphs complement the controlled-vocabulary [text]." SLJ

Includes glossary and bibliographical references

Pie graphs; by Vijaya Khisty Bodach. Capstone Press 2007 c2008 32p il (Making graphs) lib bdg $23.93; pa $7.95

Grades: K 1 2   **510**

1. Graphic methods

ISBN 978-1-4296-0042-2 (lib bdg); 1-4296-0042-X (lib bdg); 978-1-4296-2872-3 (pa); 1-4296-2872-3 (pa)

                     LC 2007011075

"A+ books"

"It's hard to find books that effectively explain math concerts for young children; this crystal clear entry in the Making Graphs series does just that. The book sensibly opens with an episode involving slices of strawberry pie, then points out that 'pie graphs are not just for pies.' The examples, eight in all, stay close to children's immediate concerns. . . . A big strength of this title are the pictures, primarily professional photographs of children in scenes set up to closely match the text." Booklist

Includes bibliographical references

Tally charts; by Vijaya Khisty Bodach. Capstone Press 2008 32p il (Making graphs) lib bdg $23.93; pa $7.95

Grades: K 1 2   **510**

1. Counting 2. Graphic methods

ISBN 978-1-4296-0043-9 (lib bdg); 1-4296-0043-8 (lib bdg); 978-1-4296-2873-0 (pa); 1-4296-2873-1 (pa)

                     LC 2007010814

"A+ books"

This "is devoted to keeping count with tally marks recorded in groups of five. This concept is illustrated with pickup sticks and then translated to pen and paper. Sports preferences, the probability of heads or tails on coin flips, and score keeping are shown. [The] title encourages readers to create their own graphs. Large, colorful photographs depict the concepts and feature ethnically diverse children. The photos and graphs complement the controlled-vocabulary [text.]" SLJ

Includes glossary and bibliographical references

Lee, Cora

The great number rumble; [a story of math in surprising places]; [by] Cora Lee & Gillian O'Reilly; illustrations by Virginia Gray. Annick Press 104p il $24.95; pa $14.95

Grades: 4 5 6   **510**

1. Mathematics

ISBN   978-1-55451-032-0;   1-55451-032-5; 978-1-55451-031-3 (pa); 1-55451-031-7 (pa)

When his school district cuts math from the curriculum, saying it causes too much stress for students, one student, a self-proclaimed "mathnik," sets out to prove

Lee, Cora—*Continued*

that math is everywhere, necessary, and not as hard as everyone thinks, in a story that includes real mathematical facts, problems, and solutions

"Interspersed with the story line are one-page biographies of Pythagoras, Archimedes, Hypatia of Alexandria, Sophie Germain, Charles Ludwig Dodgson, Srinivasa Ramanujan, and Andrew Wiles. Sidebars with Jeremy's thoughts on chaos theory, cash prizes for new prime numbers, laws of probability, and palindrome numbers add to the information. Full-color cartoons, diagrams, and photos appear throughout." SLJ

McKellar, Danica

Math doesn't suck; how to survive middle school math without losing your mind or breaking a nail; [by] Danica McKellar. Hudson Street Press 2007 297p il $23.95

Grades: 5 6 7 8   **510**
    1. Mathematics
    ISBN 978-1-59463-039-2; 1-59463-039-9
                               LC 2007017091

This "covers some of the most basic ideas of middle-grade math, including concepts relating to fractions, decimals, and ratios, making each comprehensible, interesting, and fun. Using real-world constructions, such as tangled necklaces, boyfriends, and pizza, concepts are thoroughly explained." Voice Youth Advocates

Merriam, Eve, 1916-1992

12 ways to get to 11; written by Eve Merriam; illustrated by Bernie Karlin. Simon & Schuster Bks. for Young Readers 1993 unp il pa $6.99 hardcover o.p.

Grades: K 1 2 3   **510**
    1. Mathematics 2. Counting
    ISBN 0-689-80892-5 (pa)   LC 91-25810

Uses ordinary experiences to present twelve combinations of numbers that add up to eleven. Example: At the circus, six peanut shells and five pieces of popcorn

"Some of the double-page spreads are simpler to solve than others, which allows children to progress as they learn more about counting. The huge, vibrant cut-paper and colored-pencil pictures make the book fun, lively, and painlessly educational." Horn Book Guide

Schwartz, David M., 1951-

G is for googol; a math alphabet book; written by David M. Schwartz; illustrated by Marissa Moss. Tricycle Press 1998 57p il $15.95 *

Grades: 4 5 6 7   **510**
    1. Mathematics 2. Alphabet
    ISBN 1-883672-58-9   LC 98-15162

Explains the meaning of mathematical terms which begin with the different letters of the alphabet from abacus, binary, and cubit to zillion

"The text is lively and clear and will appeal to even those who think math is as dull as the kitchen floor. . . . The cartoon illustrations are colorful, amusing, and informative." SLJ

Includes glossary

Tang, Greg

Math-terpieces; the art of problem-solving; illustrated by Greg Paprocki. Scholastic Press 2003 31p il $16.95

Grades: 2 3 4   **510**
    1. Set theory 2. Counting 3. Art appreciation
    ISBN 0-439-44388-1   LC 2002-5361

A series of rhymes about artists and their works introduces counting and grouping numbers, as well as such artistic styles as cubism, pointillism, and surrealism

"Clearly written solutions to these exercises are given at the end of the book along with art definitions and brief explanations. This math-concept book is far more appealing than most." SLJ

Wyatt, Valerie

The math book for girls and other beings who count; written by Valerie Wyatt; illustrated by Pat Cupples. Kids Can Press 2000 64p il hardcover o.p. pa $9.95

Grades: 3 4 5 6   **510**
    1. Mathematics
    ISBN 1-55074-830-0; 1-55074-584-0 (pa)

This offers activities to entice "girls to stretch their math skills in measurement and probability, geometric construction and graphing, using a calculator and changing scale. . . . Activity directions are clear and simple, and cheerful line-and-watercolor cartoons keep the presentation breezy." Bull Cent Child Books

Includes glossary

511   General principles of mathematics

Murphy, Stuart J., 1942-

The sundae scoop; illustrated by Cynthia Jabar. HarperCollins Pubs. 2003 33p il (Mathstart) hardcover o.p. pa $4.99

Grades: 1 2 3   **511**
    1. Mathematics
    ISBN 0-06-028924-4; 0-06-028925-2 (lib bdg);
    0-06-446250-1 (pa)   LC 2001-24322

This "presents the concept of combinations in a story about a group of children who host an ice-cream booth at their school picnic. With two flavors of ice cream, two sauces, and two choices of toppings, the children are surprised that eight different sundaes are available. . . . Murphy easily folds the math concepts into a lively story that will capture young readers, and Jabar reinforces the lesson with colorful, whimsical drawings of delectable ice-cream scoops." Booklist

Nagda, Ann Whitehead, 1945-

Tiger math; learning to graph from a baby tiger; by Ann Whitehead Nagda and Cindy Bickel. Holt & Co. 2000 unp il $17.95; pa $7.95 *

Grades: 2 3 4   **511**
    1. Graphic methods 2. Tigers
    ISBN 0-8050-6248-3; 0-8050-7161-X (pa)
                               LC 99-46686

Nagda, Ann Whitehead, 1945-—*Continued*
Describes the growth of an orphan Siberian tiger cub, by means of words and graphs

"Easy-to-understand picture, pie or circle, bar, or line graphs, all with explanations, appear on the left; facing pages of text and clear full-color photographs are on the right." SLJ

511.3   Mathematical logic (Symbolic logic)

Murphy, Stuart J., 1942-
Dave's down-to-earth rock shop; illustrated by Cat Bowman Smith. HarperCollins Pubs. 2000 33p il (MathStart) hardcover o.p. pa $4.95

Grades: K 1 2 3   **511.3**
  1. Set theory 2. Rocks—Collectors and collecting
  ISBN 0-06-028018-2; 0-06-028019-0 (lib bdg);
  0-06-446729-5 (pa)   LC 98-32128
As they consider sorting their rock collection by color, size, type, and hardness, Josh and Amy learn that the same objects can be organized in many different ways

"Murphy's forte is explaining complex topics in a down-to-earth manner, and that's just what he's done here. Along the way, he also includes a good deal of information about rocks, minerals, and the scientific method. Smith's full-color illustrations capture the excitement of rock hunting and include many geological and equipment details." Booklist

Seaweed soup; by Stuart Murphy; illustrated by Frank Remkiewicz. HarperCollins Pubs. 2001 31p il (MathStart) hardcover o.p. pa $4.95

Grades: K 1 2 3   **511.3**
  1. Set theory
  ISBN 0-06-028032-8; 0-06-028033-6 (lib bdg);
  0-06-028036-8 (pa)   LC 99-87634
As he asks more and more friends to join him for lunch, Turtle must make up sets of dishes to accommodate them

"A graph will help children review what they've learned, and two pages of ideas for extending the book are appended. Remkiewicz's appealing illustrations encourage children to match sets and count items in each set." Booklst

512   Algebra

Anno, Masaichiro
Anno's mysterious multiplying jar; [by] Masaichiro and Mitsumasa Anno; illustrated by Mitsumasa Anno. Philomel Bks. 1983 unp il $19.99; pa $7.99

Grades: 2 3 4 5   **512**
  1. Factorials 2. Mathematics
  ISBN 0-399-20951-4; 0-698-11753-0 (pa)
                                       LC 82-22413
Simple text and pictures introduce the mathematical concept of factorials

This book "begins with a painting of a handsome blue and white lidded jar, moves into fantasy with pictures of

the water in the jar becoming a sea on which an old sailing ship is moving, transfers to an island on the sea, and goes on to describe the rooms in the houses in the kingdoms on the mountains in the countries on the island. Each time the number grows: one island, two countries, three mountains, etc. How many jars, then, were in the boxes that were in the cupboards in the rooms? . . . The explanation is in itself clear, and is expanded by other examples of factorials." Bull Cent Child Books

Murphy, Stuart J., 1942-
Safari Park; illustrated by Steve Björkman. HarperCollins Pubs. 2002 31p il (Mathstart) hardcover o.p. pa $4.99

Grades: 2 3 4   **512**
  1. Equations
  ISBN 0-06-028914-7; 0-06-028915-5 (lib bdg);
  0-06-446245-5 (pa)   LC 00-63201
"At the new amusement park, Grandpa gives his grandkids twenty tickets each. With a little help, the kids add up the cost in tickets for rides and figure out the 'unknowns,' the number of tickets left over for snacks and games. Cartoony watercolors keep up the carnival atmosphere, while a plot about Paul's lost tickets and the Terrible Tarantula ride adds a hint of suspense. Related activities are appended." Horn Book Guide

513   Arithmetic

Adler, David A., 1947-
Fraction fun; illustrated by Nancy Tobin. Holiday House 1996 unp il $16.95; pa $6.95

Grades: 2 3 4   **513**
  1. Fractions
  ISBN 0-8234-1259-8; 0-8234-1341-1 (pa)
                                       LC 96-10773
"Adler presents the concept of fractions with the tried-and-true example of dividing a pie (pizza pie, in this case), then directs readers to draw lines across paper plates and color the eight resultant wedges in various color combinations. . . . Adler doesn't shy away from correct terminology—numerators and denominators—in this primary-grade introduction. Next he launches into some hands-on experimentation. . . . Tobin supplies a jazzy, eye-popping color scheme and diagrams of exceptional clarity to illuminate the straightforward text." Bull Cent Child Books

Fractions, decimals, and percents; illustrated by Edward Miller. Holiday House 2010 unp il $16.95

Grades: 2 3 4   **513**
  1. Fractions 2. Decimal fractions 3. Percentage
  ISBN 978-0-8234-2199-2; 0-8234-2199-6
                                      LC 2008048464
"This brightly illustrated book . . . quickly presents several math concepts related to fractions, decimals, and percents. Using a county fair as a backdrop, Adler discusses how to change a number in one form to its equivalent in another; and how the value of a digit depends upon its placement in relation to a decimal point. Miller's digital artwork illustrates the ideas clearly." Booklist

Adler, David A., 1947-—*Continued*

Fun with Roman numerals; by David A. Adler; illustrated by Edward Miller. Holiday House 2008 unp il lib bdg $16.95

Grades: 2 3 4 **513**
1. Roman numerals
ISBN 978-0-8234-2060-5 (lib bdg); 0-8234-2060-4 (lib bdg) LC 2007-43531

"This book provides basic information on the symbols, arrangements, and mathematical processes involving Roman numerals. Details are shared in a clear and logical manner with appropriate graphics to illustrate the concepts." Sci Books Films

Anno, Mitsumasa, 1926-

Anno's magic seeds; written and illustrated by Mitsumasa Anno. Philomel Bks. 1995 unp il hardcover o.p. pa $6.99

Grades: K 1 2 3 **513**
1. Mathematics
ISBN 0-399-22538-2; 0-698-11618-6 (pa)
LC 92-39309

The reader is asked to perform a series of mathematical operations integrated into the story of a lazy man who plants magic seeds and reaps an increasingly abundant harvest

"Anno has succeeded in combining both the moral issue of conservation of resources and arithmetical games in a charming story for young readers. A tour de force from a most original author-illustrator." Horn Book

Campbell, Sarah C.

Growing patterns; Fibonacci numbers in nature; photographs by Sarah C. Campbell and Richard P. Campbell. Boyds Mills Press 2010 32p il $17.95

Grades: 3 4 5 **513**
1. Numbers 2. Nature study
ISBN 978-1-59078-752-6; 1-59078-752-8
LC 2009-24075

The authors "turn their attention to the Fibonacci sequence of numbers, employing photographs from nature, basic addition, and reader-directed text to explain it. . . . Besides being eye-catching, the photographs ought to prove invaluable for visual learners. . . . Kids should be left with a clear understanding of the pattern and curious about its remarkable prevalence in nature." Publ Wkly

Includes glossary

Cleary, Brian P., 1959-

The action of subtraction; by Brian P. Cleary; illustrated by Brian Gable. Millbrook Press 2006 30p il lib bdg $15.95

Grades: 2 3 4 **513**
1. Subtraction
ISBN 978-0-7613-9461-7 (lib bdg); 0-7613-9461-3 (lib bdg) LC 2005025881

"Subtraction is explained in rhyming text and simple, silly cartoons with excellent examples that range from angry bulldogs, hornets, and bowling pins to pieces of birthday cake, sports time-outs, and stuffed animals. . . . The illustrations are colorful and attractive." SLJ

Clements, Andrew, 1949-

A million dots; illustrated by Mike Reed. Simon & Schuster Books for Young Readers 2006 unp il $16.95

Grades: K 1 2 3 **513**
1. Million (The number)
ISBN 0-689-85824-8 LC 2004-05349

"With one million dots printed on its pages, this large-format picture book shows how big a million really is. Along the way, the text and illustrations offer plenty to look at and think about besides the rows and rows of tiny dots. On each page, Clements selects one number and connects it to a numerical fact." Booklist

Dodds, Dayle Ann, 1952-

Full house; an invitation to fractions; [by] Dayle Ann Dodds; illustrated by Abby Carter. Candlewick Press 2007 unp il $16.99

Grades: 1 2 3 **513**
1. Fractions 2. Stories in rhyme
ISBN 978-0-7636-2468-2; 0-7636-2468-3
LC 2006051847

Miss Bloom uses fractions as the six-room Strawberry Inn fills with guests and she divides her pie into sixths

"Fresh, whimsical watercolor illustrations fairly float off the pages in this title. Rhyming text invites readers to enjoy every moment at the Strawberry Inn." SLJ

Fisher, Valorie

How high can a dinosaur count? and other math mysteries; [by] Valorie Fisher. Schwartz & Wade Books 2006 unp il $16.95

Grades: 1 2 3 **513**
1. Arithmetic 2. Counting
ISBN 0-375-83608-X LC 2005010851

"The text for each of the 15 problems is presented on the left, using a large, clean font on a spectrum of soft pastel backgrounds. The problems are clearly explained, but lots of alliteration and some unexpected vocabulary make for interesting reading. The illustration on the right features Fisher's unique photographic technique. Richly textured patterns and hand-drawn objects are cut out and arranged, then photographed in such a way as to create whimsical tableaux with a three-dimensional feel. The characters are charming." SLJ

Franco, Betsy

Zero is the leaves on the tree; illustrations by Shino Arihara. Tricycle Press 2009 unp il $15.99
*

Grades: PreK K 1 2 **513**
1. Zero (The number)
ISBN 978-1-58246-249-3; 1-58246-249-6
LC 2008042185

Using "evocative examples from children's everyday experiences throughout the seasons, Franco explores the concept of zero. The gouache illustrations are done in soft, muted tones and have a naive charm that will have substantial child appeal." SLJ

Geisert, Arthur

Roman numerals I to MM; Numerabilia romana uno ad duo mila: liber de difficillimo computando numerum. Houghton Mifflin 1996 xxxiip $16

Grades: K 1 2 3   **513**

1. Roman numerals 2. Counting

ISBN 0-395-74519-5   LC 95-36247

"Seven Roman numerals are introduced, accompanied by very detailed illustrations of . . . pigs engaged in a variety of activities. What little text there is . . . explains the concept of Roman numerals and how they build on one another." Child Book Rev Serv

"Geisert's detailed etchings reward extended perusal, and children will revel in the sheer abundance of pigs. A great lesson in Roman numerals." Publ Wkly

Leedy, Loreen, 1959-

2 x 2 = boo! a set of spooky multiplication stories; written and illustrated by Loreen Leedy. Holiday House 1995 32p il $17.95; pa $6.95

Grades: K 1 2 3   **513**

1. Multiplication

ISBN 0-8234-1190-7; 0-8234-1272-5 (pa)

LC 94-46711

This is an "introduction to basic multiplication, with witches, cats, and monsters demonstrating the consequences of multiplying numbers from 0 to 5. The illustrations are done in muted, autumnal tones of black, blue, orange, and mustard, and arranged in a comic-strip format. . . . The concepts are clear and understandable. . . . Leedy's book presents an entertaining alternative to rote memorization." SLJ

Fraction action; written and illustrated by Loreen Leedy. Holiday House 1994 31p il $17.95; pa $6.95 *

Grades: K 1 2 3   **513**

1. Fractions

ISBN 0-8234-1109-5; 0-8234-1244-X (pa)

LC 93-22800

Miss Prime and her animal students explore fractions by finding many examples in the world around them

"Thickly pigmented paintings loaded with sporty animal figures add to the humorous presentation, which should make fractions not only more understandable, but also more fun for young children." Bull Cent Child Books

Mission: addition; written and illustrated by Loreen Leedy. Holiday House 1997 unp il $17.95; pa $6.95 *

Grades: K 1 2 3   **513**

1. Addition

ISBN 0-8234-1307-1; 0-8234-1412-4 (pa)

LC 96-37149

Miss Prime and her animal students explore addition by finding many examples in the world around them

"Flat chalk-box colors predominate in the illustrations, which will please kids with their liveliness, their informality, and their cartoonlike speech balloons. . . . An attractive picture book to support the math curriculum." Booklist

Subtraction action. Holiday House 2000 32p il $17.95; pa $6.95 *

Grades: K 1 2 3   **513**

1. Subtraction

ISBN 0-8234-1454-X; 0-8234-1244-X (pa)

LC 99-49803

Introduces subtraction through the activities of animal students at a school fair. Includes problems for the reader to solve

This is "an action-packed volume that is perfectly suited to its audience. The softly hued cartoon animals and dialogue balloons are skillfully combined on pages divided into framed sequences." SLJ

Lewis, J. Patrick

Arithme-tickle; an even number of odd riddle-rhymes; illustrated by Frank Remkiewicz. Harcourt 2002 32p il $16

Grades: 2 3 4   **513**

1. Arithmetic 2. Mathematical recreations

ISBN 0-15-216418-9   LC 2001-3228

"Silver Whistle"

"Wordplay, riddles, and math problems test readers' skill at addition, subtraction, multiplication, division, telling time, logic, and even general knowledge in this colorfully illustrated collection. Clearly meant to make math more approachable and enjoyable, this compilation includes enough genuinely complex puzzles to keep hardcore young math buffs entertained." Booklist

Long, Lynette

Fabulous fractions; games and activities that make math easy and fun. Wiley 2001 122p il (Magical math) pa $12.95

Grades: 3 4 5 6   **513**

1. Fractions

ISBN 0-471-36981-0   LC 00-43386

This introduction to fractions includes activities using such materials as sandwiches, paper plates, cards, and dominoes

This book includes "lists of the required materials, clear and complete procedures, and a black-and-white illustration." SLJ

Marvelous multiplication; games and activities that make math easy and fun. Wiley 2000 122p il (Magical math) pa $12.95

Grades: 3 4 5 6   **513**

1. Multiplication

ISBN 0-471-36982-9   LC 00-20473

Presents a series of activities, arranged in order of difficulty, that teach the operation of multiplication

"The cheerful ink drawings help make the [book] more inviting." Booklist

Markel, Michelle

Tyrannosaurus math; illustrations by Doug Cushman. Tricycle Press 2009 unp il $15.99

Grades: 1 2 3   **513**

1. Arithmetic 2. Mathematics 3. Dinosaurs

ISBN 978-1-58246-282-0; 1-58246-282-8

LC 2008042389

Markel, Michelle—*Continued*

"From the moment he bursts out of his shell, T-Math thinks mathematically, making number sentences to express how many digits he has and the number of kids in his family. He counts footprints by twos and uses fives and tens to group and count a herd of triceratops. He checks his subtraction with addition, draws pictures to solve word problems, creates pictographs and thinks in pie graphs. And it is his estimation skills that save his sister, who gets stranded on the wrong side of a canyon after an earthquake. . . . Cushman's brightly colored acrylic illustrations nicely show readers the math involved without diminishing in any way the personalities of the dinosaurs. The ultimate melding of a topic kids love with knowledge they need." Kirkus

Murphy, Stuart J., 1942-

Divide and ride; illustrated by George Ulrich. HarperCollins Pubs. 1997 32p il (MathStart) hardcover o.p. pa $4.95 *

Grades: 1 2 3   513
  1. Division
  ISBN 0-06-026776-3; 0-06-026777-1 (lib bdg);
  0-06-446710-4 (pa)   LC 95-26134

"Eleven friends climb aboard the Dare-Devil roller coaster and three other rides, but before each ride can begin, all of the seats must be filled. Readers follow the children as they solve each problem by dividing and then filling the empty seats with new friends. Watercolor, pen, and ink illustrations and follow-up activities accompany the story." Horn Book Guide

Double the ducks; illustrated by Valeria Petrone. HarperCollins Pubs. 2003 31p il (MathStart) hardcover o.p. lib bdg $16.89; pa $4.99 *

Grades: K 1   513
  1. Multiplication
  ISBN 0-06-028922-8; 0-06-028923-6 (lib bdg);
  0-06-446249-8 (pa)   LC 2001-24321

"A young cowboy cares for his five little ducks, and he scurries around to bring them three sacks of food and four bundles of hay with his two hands. When each duck brings a friend, the boy has double the ducks, so he needs to double the hay and double the food. . . . In a double-page spread at the back of the book, Murphy suggests lots of activities and games for parents to use in the kitchen and at play to make preschoolers' first steps into addition and multiplication more fun." Booklist

Earth Day-hooray! illustrated by Renee Andriani. HarperCollins Pubs. 2004 32p il (MathStart) $15.99; pa $4.99

Grades: 1 2 3   513
  1. Place value (Mathematics) 2. Recycling
  ISBN 0-06-000127-5; 0-06-000129-1 (pa)
                                          LC 2002-155234

A drive to recycle cans on Earth Day teaches the children of the Maple Street School Save-the-Planet Club about place value

"Andriani's cheerful illustrations fairly teem with information about recycling and add humor and human interest to the story." SLJ

Includes bibliographical references

Elevator magic; illustrated by G. Brian Karas. HarperCollins Pubs. 1997 32p il (MathStart) hardcover o.p. pa $4.95 *

Grades: K 1 2   513
  1. Subtraction
  ISBN 0-06-026775-5; 0-06-446709-0 (pa)
                                          LC 96-5672

"A boy meets his mother on the 10th floor of a high rise. On the way down, Mom needs to do some errands. The first stop, two floors down, is to cash a check at the Farm Bank and Trust, which is (lo and behold!) filled with horses, barns, and hay fields. Farther down is the Hard Rock Candy Store, which is not only full of candy but also the sounds and lights of a heavy metal band. Karas's zany illustrations support the main concept being taught, while picking up on the humor in the word play." SLJ

The Grizzly Gazette; illustrated by Steve Björkman. HarperCollins Pubs. 2003 31p il (MathStart) $15.99; lib bdg $16.89; pa $4.99

Grades: 1 2 3   513
  1. Percentage
  ISBN 0-06-000027-9; 0-06-000025-2 (lib bdg);
  0-06-000026-0 (pa)   LC 2001-24633

At Camp Grizzly the camp newspaper takes a poll each day to see who has the greatest percentage of the vote so far in the election to chose a mascot. Includes activities for learning about percentages

Henry the fourth; illustrated by Scott Nash. HarperCollins Pubs. 1999 33p il (MathStart) $15.95; lib bdg $15.89; pa $4.95

Grades: K 1   513
  1. Numbers
  ISBN 0-06-027610-X; 0-06-027611-8 (lib bdg);
  0-06-446719-8 (pa)   LC 98-4960

A simple story about four dogs at a dog show introduces the ordinal numbers: first, second, third, and fourth

"The numerical concepts are sequential and simple enough for young children to follow. The watercolor cartoons fill the pages with action." SLJ

Jack the builder; illustrated by Michael Rex. HarperCollins Pubs. 2006 33p il (MathStart) hardcover o.p. pa $4.99 *

Grades: K 1   513
  1. Counting
  ISBN 0-06-055774-5; 0-06-055775-3 (pa)

"Jack stacks 2 blocks taken from a big pile. Turn the page, and a wild, colorful double-page spread shows what his simple stack becomes with the addition of a little imagination—a robot. A third block makes a hot-dog stand . . . and 2 more build 'a ferryboat out on the sea.' Eight blocks become a lookout tower, and, using 17, Jack creates a rocket ship. . . . Murphy begins and ends with simple hands-on activities for adults to help bring the math into kids' everyday life. Rex's bright illustrations will encourage even young preschoolers to point at shapes and colors as they count and add on." Booklist

Murphy, Stuart J., 1942-—*Continued*

Jump, kangaroo, jump! illustrated by Kevin O'Malley. HarperCollins Pubs. 1999 unp il (MathStart) hardcover o.p. pa $4.95

Grades: 1 2 3   **513**

1. Division 2. Fractions

ISBN 0-06-027614-2; 0-06-446721-X (pa)

LC 97-45814

Kangaroo and his Australian animal friends divide themselves up into different groups for the various field day events at camp

"The simple story line presents a real-world application of fractions and division, neatly reinforced by O'Malley's expressive illustrations. Related activities are suggested." Horn Book Guide

Just enough carrots; illustrated by Frank Remkiewicz. HarperCollins Pubs. 1997 31p il (MathStart) $14.95; lib bdg $15.89; pa $4.95

Grades: K 1   **513**

1. Counting

ISBN 0-06-026778-X; 0-06-026779-8 (lib bdg); 0-06-446711-2 (pa)   LC 96-19495

While a bunny and his mother shop in a grocery store for lunch guests, the reader may count and compare the amounts of carrots, peanuts, and worms in the grocery carts of other shoppers

"Bright, colorful illustrations, a surprise ending, and two pages of activities for adults and children extend and enhance the book's appeal." SLJ

Less than zero; illustrated by Frank Remkiewicz. HarperCollins Pubs. 2003 33p il (MathStart) $15.99; pa $4.99

Grades: K 1 2 3   **513**

1. Arithmetic 2. Zero (The number)

ISBN 0-06-000124-0; 0-06-000126-7 (pa)

LC 2002-20732

While trying to save enough money to buy a new ice scooter, Perry the Penguin learns about managing his money and about negative numbers

Includes bibliographical references

Mall mania; illustrated by Renée Andriani. HarperCollins 2006 33p il (MathStart) $15.99; pa $4.99

Grades: K 1 2   **513**

1. Addition 2. Counting

ISBN 0-06-055776-1; 0-06-055776-X (pa)

"The 100th person to enter Parkside Mall will get lots of promotional gifts, and four kids from Wilson Elementary School's chess club are on hand to count up the shoppers and add the numbers together. . . . The counters use a variety of addition strategies and activities, as always, Murphy adds greatly to the math lesson by making it seem a part of daily life. Suggestions for follow-up activities, both complex and easy . . . are appended." Booklist

Includes bibliographical references

More or less; illustrated by David T. Wenzel. HarperCollinsPublishers 2005 33p il (MathStart) $15.99; pa $4.99

Grades: K 1 2 3   **513**

1. Arithmetic

ISBN 0-06-053165-7; 0-06-053167-3 (pa)

LC 2003-27847

"In this story, Eddie works the 'guess the age' booth at the fair. . . . The way Eddie progresses . . . leads children into the world of logical, educated guesses. . . . Youngsters who need to understand the math concept in more depth will find several activities at the conclusion of the book. . . . Sprightly watercolor artwork makes math look like fun. " Booklist

Sluggers' car wash; illustrated by Barney Saltzberg. HarperCollins Pubs. 2002 33p il (MathStart) hardcover o.p. lib bdg $17.89; pa $4.99

Grades: 1 2 3   **513**

1. Addition

ISBN 0-06-028920-1; 0-06-028921-X (lib bdg); 0-06-446248-X (pa)   LC 00-54062

When the 21st Street Sluggers, a baseball team, have a car wash to raise money, they learn to keep careful track of their dollars and cents

"Colorful illustrations both enhance the story line and elucidate the math lesson with clear tabulations for the money counting and change." SLJ

Nagda, Ann Whitehead, 1945-

Cheetah math; learning about division from baby cheetahs; by Ann Whitehead Nagda in collaboration with the San Diego Zoo. Henry Holt 2007 29p il $16.95

Grades: 2 3 4   **513**

1. Division 2. Cheetahs

ISBN 978-0-8050-7645-5; 0-8050-7645-X

LC 2006030069

"Each spread includes division problems that revolve around the big cats on the left and facts about the birth and development of two baby cheetahs, Majani and Kubali, on the right. The color photography is outstanding. . . . This is a wonderful cross-curricular book and an appealing way to introduce math." SLJ

Panda math; learning about subtraction from Hua Mei and Mei Sheng. Holt & Co. 2005 29p il lib bdg $17.95

Grades: 2 3 4   **513**

1. Subtraction 2. Giant panda

ISBN 0-8050-7644-1

"This wonderful title featuring panda cubs born in the San Diego Zoo does double duty as a math book. The right side of each spread offers a captioned color photograph and text describing the growth and development of Hua Mei and Mei Sheng. The green left-hand pages provide additional details about pandas in general and these two specifically: their eating and sleeping habits, weight, and life expectancy and incorporates this information into a subtraction word problem." SLJ

Nagda, Ann Whitehead, 1945-—*Continued*

Polar bear math; learning about fractions from Klondike and Snow; by Ann Whitehead Nagda and Cindy Bickel. H. Holt and Co. 2004 29p il $16.95

Grades: 2 3 4   513
    1. Fractions 2. Polar bear
    ISBN 0-8050-7301-9   LC 2003-20996

"Following the lives of two cubs that were born at the Denver Zoo and abandoned by their mother, this book provides information about polar bears and fractions. Right-hand pages tell the story of Snow and Klondike, with excellent, full-color photos showing how zoo personnel raised them from newborns until their first birthday. . . . The explanations, which combine text with pictographs, are clear and well formulated." SLJ

Schmandt-Besserat, Denise

The history of counting; illustrated by Michael Hays. Morrow Junior Bks. 1999 45p il $17; lib bdg $16.93

Grades: 4 5 6 7   513
    1. Counting 2. Mathematics
    ISBN 0-688-14118-8; 0-688-14119-6 (lib bdg)
                LC 96-35316

"Beginning with a look at primitive expressions of numbers, the text goes on to explain abstract counting and the methods used by the Sumerians, the Phoenicians, the Greeks, the Romans, and finally the Arabs, who brought Hindu numerals from India to Europe about 1,000 years ago. . . . Imaginatively conceived and well composed, Hays' acrylic paintings feature warm, harmonious colors and delicate plays of light and shadow against textured-linen backings. Cogently written and beautifully made." Booklist
Includes glossary

Schwartz, David M., 1951-

On beyond a million; an amazing math journey; illustrated by Paul Meisel. Doubleday Bks. for Young Readers 1999 unp il hardcover o.p. pa $6.99

Grades: 2 3 4   513
    1. Counting
    ISBN 0-385-32217-8; 0-440-41177-7 (pa)
                LC 98-52990

"Schwartz helps youngsters conceptualize enormous numbers by introducing them to counting by powers of ten. Professor X, along with his dog Y, comes to the rescue of some children with an out-of-control popcorn popper as they futilely attempt to count the kernels." SLJ

"The design is busy, with sidebars and balloon comments. Each double-page spread is clearly meant to be talked about, and the discussions aren't overwhelming. . . . Awesome and yet accessible." Booklist

Slade, Suzanne, 1964-

What's new at the zoo? an animal adding adventure; illustrated by Joan Waites. Sylvan Dell 2009 unp il $16.95

Grades: PreK K 1 2   513
    1. Addition 2. Animals 3. Zoos
    ISBN 978-1-934359-93-8; 1-934359-93-9

"On a visit to the zoo, a young boy counts the animal babies and parents in each enclosure, the accompanying rhyme encouraging readers to do the math along with him. . . . Slade slyly sneaks in some great vocabulary, working the animal baby names into each verse. . . . Backmatter teaches two methods for adding all the numbers, a section about fact families and a matching game wherein readers can test their memories of baby names against some paragraphs of information about each animal's development. The solid math and informative backmatter make this a worthwhile addition to libraries and math programs." Kirkus

Tang, Greg

The best of times; math strategies that multiply; illustrated by Harry Briggs. Scholastic Press 2002 unp il $16.95 *

Grades: 2 3 4   513
    1. Multiplication
    ISBN 0-439-21044-5   LC 2002-23043
Simple rhymes offer hints on how to multiply any number by zero through ten without memorizing the multiplication tables

"Encouraging rhymes and colorful, jaunty illustrations bolster the multiplication lesson." Booklist

Math fables; lessons that count; illustrated by Heather Cahoon. Scholastic Press 2004 unp il $16.95 *

Grades: K 1 2   513
    1. Counting 2. Science
    ISBN 0-439-45399-2   LC 2002-5360
A series of rhymes about animals introduces counting and grouping numbers, as well as examples of such behaviors as cooperation, friendship, and appreciation.

"The text and perky, computer-generated cartoons show youngsters that there are many different ways of putting numbers together. . . . The enriching vocabulary is an added bonus. A fine addition to math shelves." SLJ

Math fables too; making science count; by Greg Tang; illustrated by Taia Morley. Scholastic Press 2007 unp il $16.99 *

Grades: K 1 2   513
    1. Counting 2. Science
    ISBN 978-0-439-78351-4   LC 2006028970
"Tang offers 10 rhymes about animals that teach science concepts as well as basic arithmetic. In addition . . . each selection contains a moral. . . . The bright, bold computer-generated illustrations bring personality to the animals and create colorful displays for counting and adding." SLJ

VanCleave, Janice Pratt

Janice VanCleave's play and find out about math; easy activities for young children. Wiley 1998 122p il $29.95; pa $12.95

Grades: K 1 2   **513**

    1. Mathematics

    ISBN 0-471-12937-2; 0-471-12938-0 (pa)

                    LC 96-53002

"Fifty simple activities that involve basic arithmetic such as using one's fingers to do simple addition and subtraction. . . . Most procedures are between four and eight steps and are clearly written and accompanied by pencil drawings." SLJ

515   Analysis

Murphy, Stuart J., 1942-

Beep beep, vroom vroom! illustrated by Chris Demarest. HarperCollins Pubs. 2000 33p il (MathStart) hardcover o.p. pa $4.95

Grades: K 1   **515**

    1. Patterns (Mathematics)

    ISBN 0-06-028016-6; 0-06-028017-4 (lib bdg);

    0-06-446728-7 (pa)   LC 98-51907

"Molly loves playing with cars, but her brother, Kevin, tells her she's too young. He lines up his 12 cars—four red, four green, four yellow—in special order on the shelf and tells her not to touch them while he's gone. . . . At the back are practical suggestions for adults and kids to find patterns on the pages and make their own patterns with pebbles, buttons, coins, and kitchen utensils. Demarest's clear, simple pastel pictures express the fun of playing with cars as the vrooming action reveals the patterns in everyday things." Booklist

Includes bibliographical references

516   Geometry

Adler, David A., 1947-

Shape up! illustrated by Nancy Tobin. Holiday House 1998 unp il $16.95; pa $6.95 *

Grades: 2 3 4   **516**

    1. Geometry 2. Shape

    ISBN 0-8234-1346-2; 0-8234-1638-0 (pa)

                    LC 97-22236

Uses cheese slices, pretzel sticks, a slice of bread, graph paper, a pencil, and more to introduce various polygons, flat shapes with varying numbers of straight sides

"Tobin's colorful diagrams and lanky, baseball-capped tour guide make each definition and direction crystal clear, making this a useful and appealing title for extending classroom lessons or encouraging beginners to charge beyond circle-square-triangle." Bull Cent Child Books

Murphy, Stuart J., 1942-

Bigger, Better, BEST! illustrated by Marsha Winborn. HarperCollins Pubs. 2002 33p il (MathStart) hardcover o.p. pa $4.99 *

Grades: K 1 2 3   **516**

    1. Size 2. Measurement

    ISBN 0-06-028918-X; 0-06-028919-8 (lib bdg);

    0-06-446247-1 (pa)   LC 00-54034

"Jeff and Jenny are always fighting about who has something bigger or better, while Jill just ignores them. When the family moves to a bigger house with a separate room for each child, the two start arguing about whose room and windows are bigger. Mom then has them measure the windows with sheets of paper and the floor with newspaper. . . . [The story] carefully incorporates math without being overwhelming. The colorful and humorous illustrations add to the story." SLJ

Captain Invincible and the space shapes; illustrated by Rémy Simard. HarperCollins Pubs. 2001 33p il (MathStart) hardcover o.p. pa $4.95 *

Grades: K 1 2 3   **516**

    1. Geometry 2. Shape

    ISBN 0-06-028022-0; 0-06-028023-9 (lib bdg);

    0-06-446731-7 (pa)   LC 00-39609

While piloting his spaceship through the skies, Captain Invincible encounters three-dimensional shapes, including cubes, cylinders, and pyramids

"An excellent tool for introducing a unit on three-dimensional shapes. . . . The bold cartoon art in deep, bright colors draws readers into this fun and exciting story. . . . The concluding reinforcement strategies and activities are very good." SLJ

Hamster champs; by Stuart J. Murphy; illustrated by Pedro Martin. HarperCollins 2005 31p il (MathStart) $15.99; pa $4.99 *

Grades: 1 2 3   **516**

    1. Angles 2. Hamsters—Fiction 3. Cats—Fiction

    ISBN 0-06-055772-9; 0-06-055773-7 (pa)

                    LC 2004-22471

This "book offers a lesson on angles. Three rodents that are racing-car enthusiasts create a series of ramps in an attempt to get the feisty house cat with attitude to stop bothering them." SLJ

"The humorous cartoonlike characters are fun, and plenty of good-natured banter between the hamsters and the cat helps make the concept clear." Booklist

Let's fly a kite; illustrated by Brian Floca. HarperCollins Pubs. 2000 33p il (MathStart) hardcover o.p. pa $4.95 *

Grades: K 1 2 3   **516**

    1. Symmetry 2. Kites

    ISBN 0-06-028034-4; 0-06-028035-2 (lib bdg);

    0-06-446737-6 (pa)   LC 99-26550

Two squabbling siblings learn about symmetry when their babysitter helps them build and fly a kite

"Floca's watercolor-and-inkline cartoons enhance the story and ably depict the method used to divide everyday objects into two equal parts." SLJ

Murphy, Stuart J., 1942-—*Continued*
Polly's pen pal; illustrated by Remy Simard. HarperCollins 2005 30p il (MathStart) $15.99; pa $4.99 *

Grades: K 1 2 3   516
  1. Metric system 2. Measurement
  ISBN 0-06-053168-1; 0-06-053170-3 (pa)
               LC 2003-27526

"Polly has an e-mail pen pal in Montreal. As Ally uses metrics to discuss height, weight, and distances, Polly learns what they mean. No comparisons to English measurements are made but the metric measurements are likened to common objects that kids will recognize. This title features colorful . . . computer-generated cartoons." SLJ

Olson, Nathan
Cones; by Nathan Olson. Capstone Press 2008 32p il (3-D shapes) lib bdg $23.93

Grades: K 1 2   516
  1. Cones 2. Shape 3. Geometry
  ISBN 978-1-4296-0048-4 (lib bdg); 1-4296-0048-9 (lib bdg)   LC 2006037424
  "A+ books"

This gives examples of cones such as megaphones, tops, and castle towers, and describes a simple activity.

Includes glossary and bibliographical references

Cubes; by Nathan Olson. Capstone Press 2008 32p il (3-D shapes) lib bdg $23.93

Grades: K 1 2   516
  1. Cubes 2. Shape 3. Geometry
  ISBN 978-1-4296-0049-1 (lib bdg); 1-4296-0049-7 (lib bdg)   LC 2006037423
  "A+ shapes"

This gives examples of cubes, such as blocks, dice, sugar cubes, and ice cubes, and describes a simple activity.

Includes glossary and bibliographical references

Cylinders; by Nathan Olson. Capstone Press 2008 32p il (3-D shapes) lib bdg $23.93

Grades: K 1 2   516
  1. Cylinders 2. Shape 3. Geometry
  ISBN 978-1-4296-0050-7 (lib bdg); 1-4296-0050-0 (lib bdg)   LC 2006037421
  "A+ books"

"Large color photographs show real-world examples of . . . cylinders (canned goods, birthday candles). Short descriptions flank each photo. . . . A hands-on activity will appeal to kids." Horn Book Guide

Includes glossary and bibliographical references

Pyramids; by Nathan Olson. Capstone Press 2008 32p il (3-D shapes) lib bdg $23.93

Grades: K 1 2   516
  1. Pyramids 2. Shape 3. Geometry
  ISBN 978-1-4296-0051-4 (lib bdg); 1-4296-0051-9 (lib bdg)   LC 2006037420
  "A+ books"

"Large color photographs show real-world examples of pyramids (Hindu temple, toy tepee). . . . Short descriptions flank each photo. . . . A hands-on activity will appeal to kids." Horn Book Guide

Includes glossary and bibliographical references

Spheres; by Nathan Olson. Capstone Press 2008 32p il (3-D shapes) lib bdg $23.93

Grades: K 1 2   516
  1. Shape 2. Geometry
  ISBN 978-1-4296-0052-1 (lib bdg); 1-4296-0052-7 (lib bdg)   LC 2006037247
  "A+ books"

This offers examples of spheres such as bubbles, snowballs, oranges, and soccer balls, and describes a simple activity.

Includes glossary and bibliographical references

Rissman, Rebecca
Shapes in art. Heinemann Library 2009 24p il (Spot the shape) $14.50; pa $5.99

Grades: PreK K 1   516
  1. Shape 2. Art
  ISBN   978-1-4329-2169-9;   1-4329-2169-X; 978-1-4329-2175-0 (pa); 1-4329-2175-4 (pa)
               LC 2008043206

This describes the shapes that can be found in works of art.

This offers "vibrant photography and clarion text." Booklist

Shapes in buildings. Heinemann Library 2009 24p il (Spot the shape) $14.50; pa $5.99

Grades: PreK K 1   516
  1. Shape 2. Buildings
  ISBN   978-1-4329-2172-9;   1-4329-2172-X; 978-1-4329-2178-1 (pa); 1-4329-2178-9 (pa)
               LC 2008043210

This describes the shapes that can be found in buildings.

This offers "vibrant photography and clarion text." Booklist

Shapes in music. Heinemann Library 2009 24p il (Spot the shape) $14.50; pa $5.99

Grades: PreK K 1   516
  1. Shape 2. Musical instruments
  ISBN   978-1-4329-2171-2;   1-4329-2171-1; 978-1-4329-2177-4 (pa); 1-4329-2177-0 (pa)
               LC 2008043209

This describes the shapes that can be found in musical instruments.

This offers "vibrant photography and clarion text." Booklist

Shapes in sports. Heinemann Library 2009 24p il (Spot the shape) $14.50; pa $5.99 *

Grades: PreK K 1   516
  1. Shape 2. Sports
  ISBN   978-1-4329-2170-5;   1-4329-2176-2; 978-1-4329-2176-7 (pa); 1-4329-2176-2 (pa)
               LC 2008043208

This describes the shapes that can be found in sports.

This "is a near-perfect union of concept and execution. Using . . . vibrant photography and clarion text . . . Rissman lays out a simple premise ('Shapes are all around us.') before introducing seven shapes to come: rectangle, square, semicircle, diamond, and so forth. . . . What is most impressive . . . are the stunning aerial photographs that turn baseball diamonds and tennis

Rissman, Rebecca—*Continued*
courts into dazzling intersections of geometric patterns. This is the kind of book that will wake readers up to the complexity of everyday items." Booklist

Shapes in the garden. Heinemann Library 2009 24p il (Spot the shape) $14.50; pa $5.99
Grades: PreK K 1   **516**
1. Shape 2. Gardens
ISBN   978-1-4329-2168-2;   1-4329-2168-1;
978-1-4329-2174-3 (pa); 1-4329-2174-6 (pa)
LC 2008043205
This describes the shapes that can be found in gardens.
This offers "vibrant photography and clarion text." Booklist

Sullivan, Navin
Area, distance, and volume; [by] Navin Sullivan. Marshall Cavendish Benchmark 2007 44p il (Measure up!) lib bdg $20.95
Grades: 4 5 6 7   **516**
1. Measurement 2. Geometry
ISBN 978-0-7614-2323-2 (lib bdg); 0-7614-2323-0 (lib bdg)
LC 2006026394
"This book opens with a chapter on the history of customary measurement and the metric system. After introducing a few physical and conceptual tools used in measuring, Sullivan explains how to determine distances, . . . areas of common two-dimensional geometric shapes, and volumes of three-dimensional objects." Booklist
An "engaging and informative [title]. . . . An excellent blend of photographs, charts, and diagrams complements the [text]." SLJ
Includes glossary and bibliographical references

VanCleave, Janice Pratt
Janice VanCleave's geometry for every kid; easy activities that make learning geometry fun. Wiley 1994 221p il hardcover o.p. pa $12.95
Grades: 4 5 6 7   **516**
1. Geometry
ISBN 0-471-31142-1; 0-471-31141-3 (pa)
LC 93-43049
This "introductory text covers many topics in geometry, from lines, optical illusions, and art-related activities to applications with protractors and the construction of basic solids. Terms are presented in a simplified fashion and are easily understood. Graphics are clear. The hands-on activities encourage learning, creativity, and excitement." Sci Books Films
Includes glossary

519.2   Probabilities

Leedy, Loreen, 1959-
It's probably Penny; written and illustrated by Loreen Leedy. Henry Holt 2007 unp il $16.95
Grades: 1 2 3   **519.2**
1. Probabilities
ISBN 978-0-8050-7389-8; 0-8050-7389-2
LC 2006-02872

"Lisa's teacher assigns the class to study probability by writing down predictions, determining results, and recording them. He demonstrates by using (and eating) jellybeans. Choosing Penny as her focal point, Lisa begins to calculate her results. . . . Leedy clearly and cleverly depicts the possibilities and choices in panels and segmented pages that feature Penny in funny poses." Booklist

Murphy, Stuart J., 1942-
Probably pistachio; illustrated by Marsha Winborn. HarperCollins Pubs. 2001 30p il (MathStart) hardcover o.p. pa $4.95 *
Grades: K 1 2 3   **519.2**
1. Probabilities
ISBN 0-06-028028-X; 0-06-028029-8 (lib bdg); 0-06-446734-1 (pa)   LC 99-27695
Readers are introduced to the concept of probability in a story about a boy who has a day in which nothing goes right
"Winborn's watercolors playfully depict Jack's misery as things go from bad to worse. . . . A closing section has follow-up activities to extend and enrich the lesson, as well as a short list of books with related themes." Booklist

519.5   Statistical mathematics

Goldstone, Bruce
Great estimations. H. Holt 2006 32p il $16.95 *
Grades: 1 2 3 4   **519.5**
1. Approximate computation
ISBN 978-0-8050-7446-8; 0-8050-7446-5
LC 2005-19776
"Laying out a mixed assemblage of toys, pipe cleaners, marbles, peanuts, and other small items, Goldstone helps viewers train themselves to estimate the size of groups of about 10 things on sight, then goes on to present similar, often fetchingly arranged, materials by hundreds and (!) thousands. He also describes 'clump counting' and 'box and count' methods. . . . This book lends itself equally well to skill building and to casual reading." Booklist

Greater estimations. Henry Holt and Company 2008 31p il $16.95 *
Grades: 1 2 3 4   **519.5**
1. Approximate computation
ISBN 978-0-8050-8315-6; 0-8050-8315-4
LC 2007-40894
"Goldstone builds on the topics introduced in Great Estimations (Holt, 2006) and also discusses how to estimate length, weight, area, and volume. He does an exceptional job of breaking down the process of so that even early elementary students can comprehend it. The author also effectively introduces different methods of estimation. . . . The vivid, eye-catching photographs are the highlight of the book. . . . This lively book would be an excellent addition." SLJ

Murphy, Stuart J., 1942-

Betcha! illustrated by S.D. Schindler. HarperCollins Pubs. 1997 33p il (MathStart) hardcover o.p. pa $4.95

Grades: 1 2 3   **519.5**
   1. Approximate computation 2. Arithmetic
   ISBN 0-06-026768-2; 0-06-026769-0 (lib bdg);
   0-06-446707-4 (pa)   LC 96-15486
"On their way to a store sponsoring a contest that involves guessing the number of jellybeans in a jar, two friends encounter situations that involve numerical determinations. . . . One boy counts one by one to obtain the answers, whereas the other one uses simple techniques to come up with near estimations. The easy-to-read picture-book format with only one or two sentences per page will appeal to reluctant readers. . . . The uncomplicated drawings show how the boy's brain is processing data and the skills he employs to arrive at an educated guess." SLJ

Coyotes all around; illustrated by Steve Björkman. HarperCollins Pubs. 2003 31p il (MathStart) $15.99; pa $4.99 *

Grades: 1 2 3   **519.5**
   1. Approximate computation 2. Coyotes
   3. Roadrunners 4. Counting
   ISBN 0-06-051529-5; 0-06-051531-7 (pa)
     LC 2002-151776
A pack of coyotes tries to determine how many road-runners and other creatures are in their vicinity, and while some count different groups and add their totals together, Clever Coyote rounds off and estimates
"Humorous watercolor cartoons depict the action and clarify the concept. . . . Factoids about coyotes and other desert creatures appear throughout, so readers learn not only math, but also get their fair share of science sprinkled into the mix." SLJ

520 Astronomy

Aguilar, David A.

Planets, stars, and galaxies; a visual encyclopedia of our universe; written and illustrated by David A. Aguilar; contributing writers Christine Pulliam & Patricia Daniels. National Geographic 2007 191p il $24.95; lib bdg $38.90 *

Grades: 5 6 7 8 9 10 11 12   **520**
   1. Solar system 2. Galaxies 3. Astronomy
   ISBN   978-1-4263-0170-4;   1-4263-0170-7;
   978-1-4263-0171-1 (lib bdg); 1-4263-0171-5 (lib bdg)
     LC 2007061234
"This text introduces readers to the most current information available about the universe. Informatiion is presented is a clear and easy-to-understand manner. . . . The book features bright, eye-catching illustrations that Aguilar created on his computer. In addition, there are many vibrant photographs in the book that were taken by cameras here on Earth as well as by satellites and telescopes." Booklist
Includes glossary and bibliographical references

Gardner, Robert, 1929-

Ace your space science project; great science fair ideas; [by] Robert Gardner and Madeline Goodstein. Enslow Publishers 2009 128p il (Ace your space science project) lib bdg $31.93

Grades: 5 6 7 8   **520**
   1. Space sciences 2. Science projects 3. Science—Experiments
   ISBN 978-0-7660-3230-9 (lib bdg); 0-7660-3230-2 (lib bdg)   LC 2008-4688
"Presents several science experiments and project ideas about space." Publisher's note
"Informative, practical, and not without dry wit, this is a good bet for replacing older books of science projects related to astronomny." Booklist
Includes bibliographical references

Garlick, Mark A., 1968-

Atlas of the universe. Simon & Schuster Books for Young Readers 2008 c2007 128p il map (Insiders) $19.99

Grades: 5 6 7 8   **520**
   1. Astronomy 2. Cosmology
   ISBN 978-1-4169-5558-0; 1-4169-5558-5
"Presents the latest findings about the Universe, covering such topics as the solar system and its stars, other galaxies, supernovas, star clusters, nebulas, and black holes, and examines man's effort to explore outer space and find signs of life on other planets." Publisher's note
"Seamlessly commingling luscious, color space photographs and dramatic, sharply detailed digital imagery, this tour of the universe earns high marks for visual impact. It's not too shabby in breadth of coverage either." SLJ

Green, Dan

Astronomy; out of this world! illustrated by Simon Basher. Kingfisher 2009 128p il pa $8.95

Grades: 5 6 7 8   **520**
   1. Astronomy
   ISBN 978-0-7534-6290-4 (pa); 0-7534-6290-7 (pa)
"Basher has created a portrait gallery of personified planets, comets, space probes, galaxies, several kinds of stars, and an array of other celestial bodies in a hyper-cute, pastel cartoon style. . . . Along with short bulleted lists of additional information, each figure offers a fact-based self-description. . . . Green's astro-narrative is both accurate and spiced with seldom-mentioned details." SLJ
Includes glossary

Jankowski, Connie

Space exploration. Compass Point Books 2009 40p il (Mission: science) lib bdg $26.60

Grades: 4 5 6   **520**
   1. Astronomy 2. Outer space—Exploration
   ISBN 978-0-7565-3958-0 (lib bdg); 0-7565-3958-7 (lib bdg)   LC 2008-7722
Discusses outer space exploration and examines future possibilities such as a permanent space station, colonies in space, and journeys outside the solar system
Includes glossary

Rhatigan, Joe

Out-of-this-world astronomy; 50 amazing activities & projects; [by] Joe Rhatigan & Rain Newcomb; with Gregg Doppmann, special consultant. Lark Books 2003 128p il hardcover o.p. pa $12.95

Grades: 5 6 7 8   **520**

1. Astronomy
ISBN 1-57990-410-6; 1-57990-675-3 (pa)

           LC 2003-5196

Contents: The view from here; The Moon; The Sun; The solar system; The stars and beyond

Introduces the study of "stuff in space," providing statistics, quizzes, activities, and experiments about the stars and planets

"An excellent introduction to astronomy. . . . Most [of the projects] are interesting, informative, and well within the abilities of the intended audience. . . . Spectacular color photos and other graphics, useful charts, and graphs augment the text." SLJ

Includes glossary

Sparrow, Giles

Cosmic! the ultimate 3-D guide to the universe; [author, Giles Sparrow; paper engineer, Richard Ferguson] DK Publishing 2008 unp il $24.99

Grades: 5 6 7 8   **520**

1. Astronomy 2. Cosmology 3. Outer space—Exploration 4. Pop-up books
ISBN 978-0-7566-4021-7; 0-7566-4021-0

           LC 2008-300768

This book "traces the history of the universe beginning with the Big Bang, discussing the structure of the solar system, planets, stars, galaxies, how the Hubble telescope functions, and the spaceships used in space exploration." Publisher's note

522   Techniques, procedures, apparatus, equipment, materials

Cole, Michael D.

Hubble Space Telescope; exploring the universe. Enslow Pubs. 1999 48p il (Countdown to space) lib bdg $23.93

Grades: 4 5 6 7   **522**

1. Astronomy 2. Hubble Space Telescope 3. Astronautics
ISBN 0-7660-1120-8   LC 98-3298

Details the initiation of the Hubble Space Telescope in April 1990 and the repair and servicing missions which followed; explains the telescope's role in answering questions about the universe

"Illustrated with color photographs, the book provides solid basic information." Horn Book

Includes glossary and bibliographical references

Jefferis, David

Star spotters; telescopes and observatories. Crabtree Pub. 2009 32p il (Exploring our solar system) lib bdg $26.60; pa $8.95

Grades: 3 4 5   **522**

1. Outer space—Exploration 2. Astronomy 3. Telescopes
ISBN 978-0-7787-3725-4 (lib bdg); 0-7787-3725-X (lib bdg); 978-0-7787-3742-1 (pa); 0-7787-3742-X (pa)   LC 2008-49242

"Focuses on important observatories—earthbound and orbiting—along with types of telescopes—and concludes with brief observations about binoculars and cameras. . . . [This book is] designed with easily digestible blocks of question-and-answer text sharing page space with large, sharply reproduced space photos and graphic art." SLJ

Includes glossary

Nardo, Don, 1947-

Telescopes. Kidhaven Press 2005 48p il (Kidhaven science library) $23.70

Grades: 4 5 6 7   **522**

1. Telescopes
ISBN 0-7377-3060-9

This "volume explains how telescopes work and traces their history, along with the major discoveries they made possible, from Galileo's time to the present. The final chapter deals with present and planned space telescopes." Publisher's note

Includes glossary and bibliographical references

523   Specific celestial bodies and phenomena

Cole, Joanna

The magic school bus, lost in the solar system; illustrated by Bruce Degen. Scholastic 1990 unp il pa $6.99 hardcover o.p. *

Grades: 2 3 4   **523**

1. Astronomy 2. Outer space—Exploration 3. Planets
ISBN 0-590-4429-1 (pa)   LC 89-10185

"The planetarium is closed for repairs, so the Magic School Bus blasts off on a real tour of the solar system. After their previous field trips, the children in Ms. Frizzle's class are all blasé about such things; as they land on the Moon, Venus, and Mars, and fly by the other planets and the Sun, they comment on what they see, generate a blizzard of one- or two-sentence reports on special topics and—even while Ms. Frizzle is temporarily left behind in the asteroid belt—crack terrible jokes." SLJ

Gardner, Robert, 1929-

Far-out science projects about Earth's sun and moon; illustrations by Tom Labaff. Enslow Publishers 2007 48p il (Rockin' earth science experiments) lib bdg $23.93

Grades: 3 4 5 **523**

1. Sun 2. Moon 3. Science—Experiments 4. Science projects

ISBN 978-0-7660-2736-7 (lib bdg); 0-7660-2736-8 (lib bdg) LC 2006-13789

A collection of science experiments such as getting direction and time from the sun, finding locations of sunrise and sunset, measuring heat from the sun, and observing the phases of the moon

This is "just right for students with limited experience looking for projects that are fairly interesting and manageable." SLJ

Includes glossary and bibliographical references

523.1 The universe, galaxies, quasars

Asimov, Isaac, 1920-1992

The Milky Way and other galaxies; by Isaac Asimov; with revisions and updating by Richard Hantula. Gareth Stevens Pub. 2005 32p (Isaac Asimov's 21st century library of the universe) lib bdg $24.67

Grades: 4 5 6 **523.1**

1. Galaxies 2. Milky Way

ISBN 0-8368-3968-4 LC 2004-58313

First published 1995 with title: Our vast home

This "examines various galactic types, structures, and superstructures, as observed by a wide array of specialized telescopes. . . . The pictures . . . are striking. . . . [An] excellent collection [enhancer]." SLJ

Includes bibliographical references

Fox, Karen

Older than the stars; [by] Karen C. Fox; illustrated by Nancy Davis. Charlesbridge 2010 unp il lib bdg $15.95

Grades: 2 3 4 5 **523.1**

1. Cosmology 2. Big bang theory 3. Atoms

ISBN 978-1-57091-787-5 (lib bdg); 1-57091-787-6 (lib bdg) LC 2009-04304

"Fox and Davis tackle the challenge of creating an engaging read-aloud about the Big Bang theory with energy and style. Employing the structure of a familiar nursery rhyme, the text takes readers through the steps of the universe's expansion. . . . A text box on each spread offers a clear, concise explanation of what happened in that particular stage of the universe. . . . Perfect for the classroom, this is an intriguing introduction to a difficult-to-understand concept." SLJ

Gibbons, Gail

Galaxies, galaxies! Holiday House 2006 32p il $16.95

Grades: K 1 2 3 **523.1**

1. Galaxies

ISBN 978-0-8234-2002-5; 0-8234-2002-7 LC 2006-02504

"Between an opening description of the Milky Way and a closing claim that galaxy formation is still going on, the author depicts ancient astronomers at work, describes several kinds of telescopes, and profiles five distinctive galactic forms, from irregular to lenticular. Pairing brief, matter-of-fact generalizations leavened with digestible doses of specific information to painted scenes that link diverse groups of human observers to galaxies seen in blobby, broadly brushed portraits, this introduction to some of the universe's largest structures will put stars in the eyes of the most Earthbound young readers." SLJ

Jefferis, David

Galaxies; immense star islands. Crabtree Pub. 2009 32p il (Exploring our solar system) lib bdg $26.60; pa $8.95

Grades: 3 4 5 **523.1**

1. Galaxies 2. Milky Way

ISBN 978-0-7787-3723-0 (lib bdg); 0-7787-3723-3 (lib bdg); 978-0-7787-3740-7 (pa); 0-7787-3740-3 (pa) LC 2008-46248

This "begins with a summary look at galactic types and origins, then goes on to describe cores, halos, and other structures with special reference to the Milky Way. It closes with a smattering of advice for young sky watchers and a spread of general facts about galaxies. . . . Designed with easily digestible blocks of question-and-answer text sharing page space with large, sharply reproduced space photos and graphic art." SLJ

Includes glossary

Rau, Dana Meachen, 1971-

The Milky Way and other galaxies; by Dana Meachen Rau. Compass Point Books 2005 32p il (Our solar system) $22.60

Grades: 3 4 5 **523.1**

1. Galaxies 2. Milky Way

ISBN 0-7565-0853-3 LC 2004-15571

Contents: A milky path of stars; A spinning pinwheel; Where in the galaxy are we?; Parts of the Milky Way; Types of galaxies; Groups of galaxies; Always on the move

The author "describes the nature of our own galaxy, then presents a gallery of other types, along with brief mentions of quasars, clusters, and superclusters. [The book is] illustrated with a mix of photos and digital art. . . . [This earns] high marks for visual appeal, and for clear, specific presentation of material." SLJ

Includes glossary and bibliographical references

Simon, Seymour, 1931-
Galaxies. Morrow Junior Bks. 1988 unp il hardcover o.p. pa $6.95 *
Grades: 3 4 5 6	**523.1**
1. Galaxies
ISBN 0-688-08002-2; 0-688-10992-6 (pa)
LC 87-23967
"This is a step-by-step introduction to and description of the many galaxies in the universe. . . . He includes discussions of the ways in which astronomers classify galaxies, black holes, smaller satellite galaxies such as the Magellanic Clouds and supernovas. The terms are explained within the text." Publ Wkly
"This fine introduction to an awe-inspiring subject will surely stimulate interest in stargazing, further reading, and investigation." Horn Book

The universe. rev ed. HarperCollins 2006 unp il pa $6.99
Grades: 4 5 6 7	**523.1**
1. Cosmology
ISBN 978-0-06-087725-5 (pa); 0-06-087725-1 (pa)
LC 2007272350
First published 1998
"This quick tour of the universe stops at galaxies, the solar system (Pluto is still labeled a planet), nebulas, and quasars. . . . Simon has a unique ability to make the big and vast tangible and real. Full-page light and radio telescope images are fittingly set against white text on a black, space-like background." Horn Book Guide
Includes bibliographical references

Solway, Andrew
What's inside a black hole? deep space objects and mysteries. Heinemann Library 2006 48p il (Stargazers' guides) lib bdg $22; pa $8.99
Grades: 4 5 6	**523.1**
1. Cosmology 2. Astronomy 3. Stars 4. Black holes (Astronomy)
ISBN 1-4034-7710-8 (lib bdg); 1-4034-7717-5 (pa)
LC 2005029113
Contents: The universe in the sky; Shapes in the sky; Looking into the past; Types of stars; A star is born; Black holes and wormholes; Gas and dust; Galaxies; Quasars and red shift; Rewinding the tape; What's next?; Timeline of the universe; Ten brightest stars
Includes bibliographical references

523.2   Planetary systems

Baines, Rebecca
Every planet has a place; a book about our solar system; by Becky Baines. National Geographic 2008 27p il (Zig zag) $14.95; lib bdg $19.90
Grades: PreK K 1	**523.2**
1. Solar system
ISBN   978-1-4263-0313-5;   1-4263-0313-0; 978-1-4263-0314-2 (lib bdg); 1-4263-0314-9 (lib bdg)
LC 2008-24447
Presents "factual, clearly-written information on [the solar system]. . . . Readers curiosity will be piqued by the vibrant color photographs, accommodating illustra-

tions, large font size, and helpful captions. Special features include drawings superimposed over photographs, and a zigzag path at the end of . . . [the] book prompting readers to further explore the topic in new and fun ways." SLJ

Bredeson, Carmen
What is the solar system? Enslow Elementary 2008 32p il (I like space!) lib bdg $22.60
Grades: K 1 2 3	**523.2**
1. Solar system 2. Planets
ISBN 978-0-7660-2944-6 (lib bdg); 0-7660-2944-1 (lib bdg)
LC 2007-02745
This answers such questions as "Is Pluto a planet? Do all planets have moons? What are asteroids and comets?" Publisher's note
This book "is beautifully illustrated, with photographs from NASA and other sources, and is well organized." Sci Books Films
Includes glossary and bibliographical references

Carson, Mary Kay, 1964-
Exploring the solar system; a history with 22 activities; [by] Mary Kay Carson. Chicago Review Press 2006 168p il pa $17.95
Grades: 5 6 7 8	**523.2**
1. Solar system 2. Astronomy 3. Outer space—Exploration
ISBN 1-55652-593-1	LC 2005028284
This "traces the history of human exploration of the solar system, and, even better, conveys a sense of the enthusiasm that often drives astronomers, engineers, and others involved in the process. . . . Carson highlights the achievements of historical figures as well as contemporary space scientists, and each chapter includes a few simple activities. . . . Excellent color photos and clear drawings and diagrams appear throughout the book." Booklist
Includes bibliographical references

Greathouse, Lisa E.
Solar system. Compass Point Books 2009 40p il (Mission: science) lib bdg $26.60
Grades: 4 5 6	**523.2**
1. Solar system
ISBN 978-0-7565-4071-5 (lib bdg); 0-7565-4071-2 (lib bdg)
LC 2008-35728
Introduces the solar system and the specific characteristics of its planets
Includes glossary

Kudlinski, Kathleen V., 1950-
Boy were we wrong about the solar system! illustrated by John Rocco. Dutton Children's Books 2008 unp il $15.99
Grades: K 1 2 3	**523.2**
1. Solar system
ISBN 978-0-525-46979-7; 0-525-46979-6
LC 2007-50557
This is a "debunking of such erstwhile astronomical theories as solar revolution around the Earth, concentric

Kudlinski, Kathleen V., 1950-—*Continued*

glass spheres dividing planetary orbits, Martian canals, and, of course, the overly elevated status of Pluto. . . . [This is illustrated with] jewel-hued, cartoonishly exaggerated paintings. . . . The concept of adults getting it dead wrong is realiably engaging." Bull Cent Child Books

Simon, Seymour, 1931-

Our solar system; [by] Seymour Simon. updated ed. Collins 2007 62p il $19.99; lib bdg $20.89 *
Grades: 3 4 5 6   **523.2**
    1. Solar system
    ISBN   978-0-06-114008-2;   0-06-114008-2;
    978-0-06-114009-9 (lib bdg); 0-06-114009-0 (lib bdg)
                      LC 2007279969
    First published 1992
    Describes the origins, characteristics, and future of the sun, planets, moons, asteroids, meteoroids, and comets
    This "is a fine, comprehensive work on the solar system. . . . [The book includes] excellent photographs. Beautifully designed and a pleasure to use." Horn Book Guide

Trammel, Howard K., 1957-

The solar system. Children's Press 2009 c2010 48p il (True book) lib bdg $26; pa $6.95 *
Grades: 3 4 5   **523.2**
    1. Solar system
    ISBN 978-0-531-16898-1 (lib bdg); 0-531-16898-0 (lib bdg); 978-0-531-22805-0 (pa); 0-531-22805-3 (pa)
                      LC 2008049376
    "The Solar System begins with a lineup of the usual suspects (yes, Pluto is off the hook). The way the chapters move from inner to outer planets is no surprise, but the called-out details are cunningly illustrated and plenty fascinating. . . . Short but solid back matter closes out [this] impressive [offering]." Booklist

VanCleave, Janice Pratt

Janice VanCleave's solar system; mind-boggling experiments you can turn into science fair projects. Wiley 2000 90p il map pa $10.95
Grades: 4 5 6 7   **523.2**
    1. Solar system 2. Science projects 3. Science—Experiments
    ISBN 0-471-32204-0   LC 99-15479
    Provides instructions for a variety of experiments and science fair projects exploring the solar system, including the sun, moon, planets, comets, and meteorites
    "Welcome and valuable." SLJ
    Includes glossary

Wittenstein, Vicki Oransky, 1954-

Planet hunter; Goeff Marcy and the search for other earths. Boyds Mills Press 2010 48p il $17.95
Grades: 5 6 7 8   **523.2**
    1. Marcy, Geoffrey W. 2. Extrasolar planets 3. Life on other planets
    ISBN 978-1-59078-592-8; 1-59078-592-4
    "The profound thrill of searching for (and finding!) planets orbiting stars other than our own is deftly cap-

tured in this profile of Geoff Marcy, one of the great hunt's most successful practitioners. Matched to big, sharp color photos of scientists (mostly) at work and compelling speculative views of exotic suns and landscapes, Wittenstein's matter-of-fact narrative first introduces readers to Marcy and his team on the night shift . . . at the W. M. Keck Observatory atop Hawaii's Mauna Kea. . . . This handsomely packaged introduction is just the ticket for turning earthbound (for now) children into budding skywatchers." SLJ
    Includes glossary and bibliographical references

523.3   Moon

Branley, Franklyn Mansfield, 1915-2002

The moon seems to change; by Franklyn M. Branley; illustrations by Barbara and Ed Emberley. rev ed. Crowell 1987 29p il (Let's-read-and-find-out science book) pa $4.95 hardcover o.p.
Grades: K 1 2 3   **523.3**
    1. Moon
    ISBN 0-06-445065-1 (pa)   LC 86-47747
    A revised and newly illustrated edition of the title first published 1960
    The author "explains the waxing and waning of the moon and compares the length of a day on earth and on the moon. Each page has colorful explanatory illustrations. . . . Branley's brief-easy-to-read text and the Emberleys' diagrams make this book a welcome addition to science collections for young children or the picture book section." SLJ

What the moon is like; by Franklyn M. Branley; illustrated by True Kelley. newly illustrated ed. HarperCollins Pubs. 2000 30p il (Let's-read-and-find-out science) hardcover o.p. lib bdg $15.89; pa $4.95
Grades: K 1 2 3   **523.3**
    1. Moon
    ISBN 0-06-027992-3; 0-06-027993-1 (lib bdg); 0-06-445185-2 (pa)   LC 98-54072
    A revised and newly illustrated edition of the title first published 1963 by Crowell
    This book "invites readers simply to observe the moon from Earth before it delves into facts. . . . The following pages, all illustrated with clear, colorful pictures of astronauts and the lunar landscape, explore the moon's actual surface, climate, and temperature; briefly discuss lunar landings (with a map); and draw comparisons between the moon and Earth." Booklist

Gibbons, Gail

The moon book. Holiday House 1997 unp il $16.95; pa $6.95
Grades: K 1 2 3   **523.3**
    1. Moon
    ISBN 0-8234-1297-0; 0-8234-1364-0 (pa)
                      LC 96-36826
    Identifies the moon as our only natural satellite, describes its movement and phases, and discusses how we have observed and explored it over the years

Gibbons, Gail—*Continued*

"Gibbons presents a great deal of information in a deceptively simple format by combining inviting illustrations with clear writing." Horn Book Guide

Landau, Elaine

The moon; [by] Elaine Landau. Children's Press 2007 c2008 48p il lib bdg $26

Grades: 2 3 4   **523.3**
1. Moon
ISBN 0-531-12562-9 (lib bdg); 978-0-531-12562-5 (lib bdg)   LC 2007004183
"A True book"

This describes the phases of the moon, its composition and geography, and moon exploration.

This "matches a clearly reasoned, matter-of-fact text to plenty of small but sharply reproduced photos." SLJ

Includes glossary and bibliographical references

Simon, Seymour, 1931-

The moon. rev ed. Simon & Schuster Bks. for Young Readers 2003 unp il $17.95 *

Grades: 4 5 6 7   **523.3**
1. Moon
ISBN 0-689-83563-9   LC 2001-31303
First published 1984 by Four Winds Press

A basic introduction to Earth's closest neighbor, its composition, and man's missions to it

"The digitally remastered color photographs in this update are incredible. . . . The text has undergone minimal change. . . . The facts remain true and relevant, and the writing reflects the graphics: beautiful. This is a must-have for astronomy sections." SLJ

Stewart, Melissa, 1968-

Why does the moon change shape? Marshall Cavendish Benchmark 2009 32p il (Tell me why, tell me how) lib bdg $20.95

Grades: 3 4 5   **523.3**
1. Moon
ISBN 978-0-7614-2921-0 (lib bdg); 0-7614-2921-2 (lib bdg)   LC 2007025247
"Provides comprehensive information on the moon and the phases it goes through in a month" Publisher's note

"One or two large, well-captioned color photographs are provided per spread. [The] book concludes with an activity. [This is a] solid [introduction]." SLJ

Includes glossary and bibliographical references

Tomecek, Steve

Moon; illustrated by Liisa Chauncy Guida. National Geographic 2005 31p il (Jump into science) $16.95; lib bdg $25.90 *

Grades: K 1 2   **523.3**
1. Moon
ISBN 0-7922-5123-7; 0-7922-8304-X (lib bdg)
LC 2004-8761

"A cartoon cat and bug explain scientific history and concepts regarding the Earth's moon: its ever-changing appearance, composition, comparisons to Earth and the sun, Galileo's observations and discoveries in 1609, astronauts, orbits, and other topics." SLJ

"Guida's artwork, in bright, saturated colors, will easily draw children into the science. . . . Tomecek's words encourage a sense of awe and wonder." Booklist

523.4   Planets

Aguilar, David A.

11 planets; a new view of the solar system. National Geographic 2008 47p il $16.95; lib bdg $25.90 *

Grades: 5 6 7 8   **523.4**
1. Planets 2. Solar system
ISBN   978-1-4263-0236-7;   1-4263-0236-3; 978-1-4263-0237-4 (lib bdg); 1-4263-0237-1 (lib bdg)

"Aguilar uses the classification by the International Astronomical Union (which demoted Pluto to dwarf status in 2006). In addition to the eight full-fledged planets, the group of 11 includes the three dwarf planets, Ceres . . . and Eris. . . . The book offers a visually impressive tour of major objects in the solar system. . . . An attractive and timely addition to astronomy collections." Booklist

Includes glossary and bibliographical references

Bjorklund, Ruth

Venus. Marshall Cavendish Benchmark 2009 c2010 64p il (Space!) lib bdg $22.95

Grades: 4 5 6 7   **523.4**
1. Venus (Planet)
ISBN 978-0-7614-4251-6 (lib bdg); 0-7614-4251-0 (lib bdg)   LC 2009014665

"Describes Venus, including its history, its composition, and its role in the solar system." Publisher's note

This stands out for its "clear, accurate [presentation] of basic facts punctuated by lively turns of phrase and, sometimes, details not commonly found in the plethora of similar tours of the solar system and beyond. Bjorklund enhances her introduction to Venus . . . with explanations of why its occasional transits across the Sun's face are important to astronomers, and goes on to an ominous comparison of the greenhouse-gas effect there with the same phenomenon on our planet." SLJ

Includes glossary and bibliographical references

Bortolotti, Dan

Exploring Saturn. Firefly Bks. 2003 64p il $19.95; pa $9.95

Grades: 5 6 7 8   **523.4**
1. Saturn (Planet)
ISBN 1-55297-766-8; 1-55297-765-X (pa)

This "introduction to the sixth planet [describes] . . . what we know, don't know, and hope to find out soon. The author . . . lays out Saturn's probable origins and inner structure, provides . . . glimpses of [its] rings, and describes each moon in turn—including one, as yet unnamed, discovered in 2003. He then covers the Cassini-Huygens mission in detail." SLJ

"This appealing presentation features a well-organized and engaging text as well as many exceptionally clear, colorful illustrations: photographs, space-telescope images, paintings, and drawings." Booklist

Capaccio, George

Jupiter. Marshall Cavendish Benchmark 2009 c2010 64p il (Space!) lib bdg $22.95

Grades: 4 5 6 7   **523.4**

1. Jupiter (Planet)
ISBN 978-0-7614-4244-8 (lib bdg); 0-7614-4244-8 (lib bdg)   LC 2008037276

"Describes Jupiter, including its history, its composition, and its role in the solar system." Publisher's note

This stands out for its "clear, accurate [presentation] of basic facts punctuated by lively turns of phrase and, sometimes, details not commonly found in the plethora of similar tours of the solar system and beyond. . . . The author provides an unusual perspective on planetary dynamics by opening his coherent account of what and how we have learned about the planet and its moons through ground, orbital, and space-probe observations with an explanation of how a gravitational 'snow line' governed whether newly formed planets turned out rocky or largely gas and ice." SLJ

Includes glossary and bibliographical references

Mars. Marshall Cavendish Benchmark 2010 64p il (Space!) lib bdg $22.95

Grades: 4 5 6 7   **523.4**

1. Mars (Planet)
ISBN 978-0-7614-4247-9 (lib bdg); 0-7614-4247-2 (lib bdg)   LC 2008037280

Describes Mars, including its history, its composition, and its role in the solar system

Includes glossary and bibliographical references

Colligan, L. H.

Mercury. Marshall Cavendish Benchmark 2009 c2010 64p il (Space!) lib bdg $22.95

Grades: 4 5 6 7   **523.4**

1. Mercury (Planet)
ISBN 978-0-7614-4239-4 (lib bdg); 0-7614-4239-1 (lib bdg)   LC 2008037278

"Describes Mercury, including its history, its composition, and its role in the solar system." Publisher's note
Includes glossary and bibliographical references

Croswell, Ken

Ten worlds; everything that orbits the sun. Boyds Mills Press 2006 56p il $19.95 *

Grades: 5 6 7 8   **523.4**

1. Planets 2. Solar system
ISBN 1-59078-423-5   LC 2005-35316

This describes the planets of our solar system and their moons, plus comets, meteors, and asteroids

"On the basis of its striking design and photographs, this handsome, large-format volume is well worthy of praise. And astronomer Crosswell's . . . concise yet conversational, information-packed text wins it sky-high accolades in the narrative sphere as well." Publ Wkly

Hicks, Terry Allan

Saturn. Marshall Cavendish Benchmark 2010 64p il (Space!) lib bdg $22.95

Grades: 4 5 6 7   **523.4**

1. Saturn (Planet)
ISBN 978-0-7614-4249-3 (lib bdg); 0-7614-4249-9 (lib bdg)   LC 2008037453

"Describes Saturn, including its history, its composition, and its role in the solar system." Publisher's note
Includes glossary and bibliographical references

Landau, Elaine

Beyond Pluto; [by] Elaine Landau. Children's Press 2007 c2008 48p il lib bdg $26

Grades: 2 3 4   **523.4**

1. Planets
ISBN 0-531-12565-3 (lib bdg); 978-0-531-12565-6 (lib bdg)   LC 2007012280

"A True book"

This "looks past Pluto into the Kuiper Belt, the Oort Cloud, and the search for extrasolar planets. . . . [This] matches a clearly reasoned, matter-of-fact text to plenty of small but sharply reproduced color photos." SLJ

Includes glossary and bibliographical references

Jupiter; [by] Elaine Landau. Children's Press 2007 c2008 48p il (True book) lib bdg $26; pa $6.95

Grades: 2 3 4   **523.4**

1. Jupiter (Planet)
ISBN 978-0-531-12559-5 (lib bdg); 0-531-12559-9 (lib bdg); 978-0-531-14789-4 (pa); 0-531-14789-4 (pa)   LC 2007003869

First published 1991

This describes the atmosphere and geographic features of Jupiter and the missions which have explored the planet

This "matches a clearly reasoned, matter-of-fact text to plenty of small but sharply reproduced color photos." SLJ

Includes glossary and bibliographical references

Mars; [by] Elaine Landau. Children's Press 2007 c2008 48p il (True book) lib bdg $26; pa $6.95

Grades: 2 3 4   **523.4**

1. Mars (Planet)
ISBN 978-0-531-12560-1 (lib bdg); 0-531-12560-2 (lib bdg); 978-0-531-14790-0 (pa); 0-531-14790-8 (pa)   LC 2007-12260

This describes the place of Mars in the solar system, the composition of the planet, its moons and missions to Mars

This "matches a clearly reasoned, matter-of-fact text to plenty of small but sharply reproduced color photos." SLJ

Includes glossary and bibliographical references

Mercury; [by] Elaine Landau. Children's Press 2007 c2008 48p il (True book) lib bdg $26; pa $6.95

Grades: 2 3 4   **523.4**

1. Mercury (Planet)
ISBN 978-0-531-12561-8 (lib bdg); 0-531-12561-0 (lib bdg); 978-0-531-14791-7 (pa); 0-531-14791-6 (pa)   LC 2007012277

This describes Mercury's place in the solar system, its atmosphere and composition, and missions to Mercury

This "matches a clearly reasoned, matter-of-fact text to plenty of small but sharply reproduced color photos." SLJ

Includes glossary and bibliographical references

Landau, Elaine—*Continued*

Neptune; [by] Elaine Landau. Children's Press 2007 c2008 48p il (True book) lib bdg $26; pa $6.95

Grades: 2 3 4   **523.4**
  1. Neptune (Planet)
  ISBN 978-0-531-12563-2 (lib bdg); 0-531-12563-7 (lib bdg); 978-0-531-14793-1 (pa); 0-531-14793-2 (pa)
                         LC 2007008257

This describes Neptune's place in the solar system, its atmosphere and composition

This "matches a clearly reasoned, matter-of-fact text to plenty of small but sharply reproduced color photos." SLJ

Includes glossary and bibliographical references

Pluto; from planet to dwarf; [by] Elaine Landau. Children's Press 2007 c2008 48p il (True book) lib bdg $26; pa $6.95

Grades: 2 3 4   **523.4**
  1. Pluto (Planet)
  ISBN 978-0-531-12566-3 (lib bdg); 0-531-12566-1 (lib bdg); 978-0-531-14794-8 (pa); 0-531-14794-0 (pa)
                         LC 2007012279

This describes Pluto's place in the solar system, its change in status from planet to dwarf, its moons, and missions to Pluto

This "matches a clearly reasoned, matter-of-fact text to plenty of small but sharply reproduced color photos." SLJ

Includes glossary and bibliographical references

Saturn; [by] Elaine Landau. Children's Press 2007 c2008 48p il (True book) lib bdg $26; pa $6.95

Grades: 2 3 4   **523.4**
  1. Saturn (Planet)
  ISBN 978-0-531-12567-0 (lib bdg); 0-531-12567-X (lib bdg); 978-0-531-14795-5 (pa); 0-531-14795-9 (pa)
                         LC 2007004181

This describes Saturn's place in the solar system, its composition, its moons and rings and missions to Saturn

This "matches a clearly reasoned, matter-of-fact text to plenty of small but sharply reproduced color photos." SLJ

Includes glossary and bibliographical references

Uranus; [by] Elaine Landau. Children's Press 2007 c2008 48p il (True book) lib bdg $26; pa $6.95

Grades: 2 3 4   **523.4**
  1. Uranus (Planet)
  ISBN 978-0-531-12569-4 (lib bdg); 0-531-12569-6 (lib bdg); 978-0-531-14797-9 (pa); 0-531-14797-5 (pa)
                         LC 2007012258

This describes Uranus's place in the solar system, its atmosphere, moons, and rings, and exploration

This "matches a clearly reasoned, matter-of-fact text to plenty of small but sharply reproduced color photos." SLJ

Includes glossary and bibliographical references

Venus; [by] Elaine Landau. Children's Press 2007 c2008 48p il (True book) lib bdg $26; pa $6.95

Grades: 2 3 4   **523.4**
  1. Venus (Planet)
  ISBN 978-0-531-12564-9 (lib bdg); 0-531-12564-5 (lib bdg); 978-0-531-14798-6 (pa); 0-531-14798-3 (pa)
                         LC 2007004449

This describes Venus's place in the solar system, its atmosphere and composition, and missions to Venus

This "matches a clearly reasoned, matter-of-fact text to plenty of small but sharply reproduced color photos." SLJ

Includes glossary and bibliographical references

Leedy, Loreen, 1959-

Messages from Mars; by Loreen Leedy and Andrew Schuerger; illustrated by Loreen Leedy. Holiday House 2006 40p il $16.95

Grades: K 1 2 3   **523.4**
  1. Mars (Planet) 2. Space flight to Mars
  ISBN 978-0-8234-1954-8; 0-8234-1954-1
                         LC 2005-50267

"In 2106 six children, their team leader, and a 'hoverbot' (floating robot) take a voyage to Mars. . . . Along the way, they send messages back home, informally relaying information about space travel and conditions on the red planet. Cartoonlike images of the fictional characters and their spacecraft are digitally combined with photos of Mars. . . . Clever, and a good starting point for those intrigued by Mars." Booklist

Includes glossary

Lew, Kristi, 1968-

The dwarf planet Pluto. Marshall Cavendish Benchmark 2009 c2010 64p il (Space!) lib bdg $22.95

Grades: 4 5 6 7   **523.4**
  1. Pluto (Planet)
  ISBN 978-0-7614-4243-1 (lib bdg); 0-7614-4243-X (lib bdg)   LC 2008037272

"Describes the dwarf planet Pluto, including its history, its composition, and its role in the solar system." Publisher's note

Includes glossary and bibliographical references

Miller, Ron, 1947-

Saturn. Twenty-First Century Books 2003 80p il (Worlds beyond) lib bdg $27.90

Grades: 5 6 7 8   **523.4**
  1. Saturn (Planet)
  ISBN 0-7613-2360-0   LC 2002-14098

Contents: Lord of the rings; Exploring Saturn; The crown jewel of the solar system; Moons, moons, and more moons; The future of Saturn

Chronicles the discovery and exploration of the planet Saturn and discusses its rings and moons, its place in the solar system, and more.

"Concepts are explained clearly, and helpful diagrams and carefully chosen illustrations assist understanding." SLJ

Includes bibliographical references

Scott, Elaine, 1940-
When is a planet not a planet? the story of Pluto. Clarion Books 2007 43p il $17 *
Grades: 3 4 5 6   **523.4**
1. Planets
ISBN 978-0-618-89832-9; 0-618-89832-8
"Scott takes the 2006 downgrading of Pluto from planet to dwarf planet as a teachable moment for discussing questions such as how the number of planets has changed through the centuries, what can be called a planet, and how scientists come to conclusions—and occasionally change their minds. . . . Beautifully designed, the book includes many well-captioned, color illustrations, from period portraits to NASA images to artist's conceptions." Booklist

Sherman, Josepha
Asteroids, meteors, and comets. Marshall Cavendish Benchmark 2009 c2010 64p il (Space!) lib bdg $22.95
Grades: 4 5 6 7   **523.4**
1. Asteroids 2. Meteors 3. Comets
ISBN 978-0-7614-4252-3 (lib bdg); 0-7614-4252-9 (lib bdg)   LC 2008037281
"Describes asteroids, meteors, and comets, including their histories, their compositions, and their roles in the solar system." Publisher's note
This stands out for its "clear, accurate [presentation] of basic facts punctuated by lively turns of phrase and, sometimes, details not commonly found in the plethora of similar tours of the solar system and beyond." SLJ
Includes glossary and bibliographical references

Neptune. Marshall Cavendish Benchmark 2009 c2010 63p il (Space!) lib bdg $22.95
Grades: 4 5 6 7   **523.4**
1. Neptune (Planet)
ISBN 978-0-7614-4246-2 (lib bdg); 0-7614-4246-4 (lib bdg)   LC 2008037279
"Describes Neptune, including its history, its composition, and its role in the solar system." Publisher's note
This stands out for its "clear, accurate [presentation] of basic facts punctuated by lively turns of phrase and, sometimes, details not commonly found in the plethora of similar tours of the solar system and beyond." SLJ
Includes glossary and bibliographical references

Uranus. Marshall Cavendish Benchmark 2010 63p il (Space!) lib bdg $22.95
Grades: 4 5 6 7   **523.4**
1. Herschel, Sir William, 1738-1822 2. Uranus (Planet)
ISBN 978-0-7614-4248-6 (lib bdg); 0-7614-4248-0 (lib bdg)   LC 2008037274
"Describes Uranus, including its history, its composition, and its role in the solar system." Publisher's note
This stands out for its "clear, accurate [presentation] of basic facts punctuated by lively turns of phrase and, sometimes, details not commonly found in the plethora of similar tours of the solar system and beyond." SLJ
Includes glossary and bibliographical references

Ward, David J. (David John)
Exploring Mars; [by] D. J. Ward. Lerner Publications Co. 2007 48p il (Cool science) lib bdg $27.93; pa $8.95
Grades: 4 5 6   **523.4**
1. Mars (Planet)
ISBN 978-0-8225-5936-8 (lib bdg); 0-8225-5936-6 (lib bdg); 978-0-8225-6673-1 (pa); 0-8225-6673-7 (pa)
LC 2005032346
This describes what is known about the planet Mars and its moons, the possiblity of life on Mars, and past and possible future missions to the planet
Includes glossary and bibliographical references

Winrich, Ralph
Pluto; a dwarf planet; by Ralph Winrich; revised and updated by Thomas K. Adamson. rev and updated. Capstone Press 2007 24p il (First facts: the solar system) lib bdg $21.26
Grades: K 1 2 3   **523.4**
1. Pluto (Planet)
ISBN 978-1-4296-0727-8 (lib bdg); 1-4296-0727-0 (lib bdg)   LC 2006037427
First published 2005
This describes the dwarf planet Pluto, as well as other dwarf planets Ceres and Eris
"Information present in the simply phrased [narrative] is supplemented by boxes of facts . . . and sharply reproduced photos or other art." SLJ
Includes glossary and bibliographical references

523.6   Comets

Cole, Michael D.
Comets and asteroids; ice and rocks in space. Enslow Pubs. 2003 48p il (Countdown to space) lib bdg $18.95
Grades: 4 5 6 7   **523.6**
1. Comets
ISBN 0-7660-1954-3   LC 2002-8520
Explores what comets and asteroids are, how scientists have studied them throughout history, and the effects of space debris on the Earth when it enters our atmosphere
Includes glossary and bibliographical references

Simon, Seymour, 1931-
Comets, meteors, and asteroids. Morrow Junior Bks. 1994 unp il pa $6.95 hardcover o.p. *
Grades: 3 4 5 6   **523.6**
1. Comets 2. Meteors 3. Asteroids
ISBN 0-688-15843-9 (pa)   LC 93-51251
"Simon presents basic information about comets, meteors, and asteroids in an attractive oversize book. . . . Blocks of text appear in fairly large type, usually facing a full-page illustration. . . . Simon writes in plain language, without talking down to his audience. The intriguing photographs include shots of comets and meteor showers in the sky, a meteorite in Antarctica, and an enormous impact crater in Arizona." Booklist

523.7 Sun

Branley, Franklyn Mansfield, 1915-2002

The sun, our nearest star; by Franklyn M. Branley; illustrated by Edward Miller. HarperCollins Pubs. 2002 25p il (Let's-read-and-find-out science) hardcover o.p. pa $4.95 *

Grades: K 1 2   523.7

1. Sun

ISBN 0-06-028534-6; 0-06-028535-4 (lib bdg); 0-06-445202-6 (pa)   LC 2001-24951

A revised and newly illustrated edition of the title first published 1961

Describes the sun and how it provides the light and energy which allow plant and animal life to exist on the earth

"This edition marks the third incarnation of an old standby. . . . The gently edited text reads better than the old one. The new design features a larger format, bolder typography, and eye-catching artwork." Booklist

Capaccio, George

The sun. Marshall Cavendish Benchmark 2009 c2010 64p il (Space!) lib bdg $22.95

Grades: 4 5 6 7   523.7

1. Sun

ISBN 978-0-7614-4242-4 (lib bdg); 0-7614-4242-1 (lib bdg)   LC 2008037275

"Describes the Sun, including its history, its composition, and its role in the solar system." Publisher's note

This stands out for its "clear, accurate [presentation] of basic facts punctuated by lively turns of phrase and, sometimes, details not commonly found in the plethora of similar tours of the solar system and beyond." SLJ

Includes glossary and bibliographical references

Gibbons, Gail

Sun up, sun down; written and illustrated by Gail Gibbons. Harcourt Brace Jovanovich 1983 unp il hardcover o.p. pa $7

Grades: K 1 2 3   523.7

1. Sun

ISBN 0-15-282781-1; 0-15-282782-X (pa)
LC 82-23420

The author explains "the sun and its effect on the earth. Narrated by a little girl who notices the sun shining when she wakes up one morning, this . . . [book covers] what the sun does, what makes shadows, how the sun helps form rain clouds, and how it keeps the planet warm." Booklist

"The illustrations clarify the text with bold, clear drawings in full color." SLJ

Landau, Elaine

The sun; [by] Elaine Landau. Children's Press 2007 c2008 48p il (True book) lib bdg $26; pa $6.95

Grades: 2 3 4   523.7

1. Sun

ISBN 978-0-531-12568-7 (lib bdg); 0-531-12568-8 (lib bdg); 978-0-531-14796-2 (pa); 0-531-14796-7 (pa)
LC 2007012259

This describes the sun as a star, the sun's place in the solar system, its relationship to Earth, and how astronomers study the sun

This "matches a clearly reasoned, matter-of-fact text to plenty of small but sharply reproduced color photos." SLJ

Includes glossary and bibliographical references

523.8 Stars

Aguilar, David A.

Super stars; the biggest, hottest, brightest, and most explosive stars in the Milky Way. National Geographic 2010 48p il $16.95; lib bdg $27.90

Grades: 4 5 6 7   523.8

1. Stars

ISBN 978-1-4263-0601-3; 1-4263-0601-6; 978-1-4263-0602-0 (lib bdg); 1-4263-0602-4 (lib bdg)
LC 2009037124

"Pairing dramatic space art with souped-up prose, Aguilar introduces more than a dozen types of stars and stellar phenomena. . . . . Aside from the occasional alien or interstellar spacecraft set against glowing star fields, the information in both pictures and texts sticks to the facts, accurately reflecting current knowledge without ever coming close to turning into a dry recitation of data. . . . [This is an] unusually exuberant ticket to ride for young sky watchers and armchair space travelers." SLJ

Includes glossary and bibliographical references

Asimov, Isaac, 1920-1992

The life and death of stars; by Isaac Asimov. rev and updated ed, with revisions and updating by Richard Hantula. Gareth Stevens Pub. 2005 32p il lib bdg $24.67

Grades: 4 5 6   523.8

1. Stars

ISBN 0-8368-3967-6   LC 2004-57842

First published 1995 with title: Star cycles

This "begins with the birth of stars in dust cloud nurseries; goes on to profile the different types of stars; describes supernovas, neutron stars, and other late-stage developments; then closes with an account of our Sun's probable fate. . . . [This is an] excellent collection [enhancer]." SLJ

Includes bibliographical references

Branley, Franklyn Mansfield, 1915-2002

The Big Dipper; by Franklyn M. Branley; illustrated by Molly Coxe. rev ed. HarperCollins Pubs. 1991 32p il (Let's-read-and-find-out science book) pa $4.95 hardcover o.p.

Grades: K 1   **523.8**

1. Ursa Major

ISBN 0-06-445100-3 (pa)   LC 90-31199

A revised and newly illustrated edition of the title first published 1962

Explains basic facts about the Big Dipper, including which stars make up the constellation, how its position changes in the sky, and how it points to the North Star

Croswell, Ken

The lives of stars. Boyds Mills Press 2009 72p il $19.95 *

Grades: 5 6 7 8   **523.8**

1. Stars 2. Astronomy

ISBN 978-1-59078-582-9; 1-59078-582-7

LC 2008033913

"Extensive, detailed information about stars is coupled with amazing colorful photographs, many from the Hubble Space Telescope, in this stunning book. Packed with facts about the stars and their life cycle, the text often relates them to situations or objects familiar to readers." SLJ

Includes glossary

Jackson, Ellen B., 1943-

The mysterious universe; supernovae, dark energy, and black holes; text by Ellen Jackson; photographs and illustrations by Nic Bishop. Houghton Mifflin 2008 60p il (Scientists in the field) $18 *

Grades: 5 6 7 8   **523.8**

1. Filippenko, Alexei V. 2. Supernovas 3. Black holes (Astronomy)

ISBN 978-0-618-56325-8; 0-618-56325-3

LC 2007-41165

This "follows prominent astronomer Alex Filippenko and associates from the Keck Observatory in Hawaii to the Lick Observatory in California on a hunt for supernovae and related large-scale astronomical phenomena. . . . Along with depicting the scientists, the images also include massive telescopes and photos or digital simulations of galaxies, exploding stars, and other astronomical phenomena." SLJ

Includes glossary and bibliographical references

Jefferis, David

The stars; glowing spheres in the sky. Crabtree Pub. 2009 32p il (Exploring our solar system) lib bdg $26.60; pa $8.95

Grades: 3 4 5   **523.8**

1. Stars

ISBN 978-0-7787-3726-1 (lib bdg); 0-7787-3726-8 (lib bdg); 978-0-7787-3743-8 (pa); 0-7787-3743-8 (pa)

LC 2008-46250

"Learn about the stars: what is a star, how stars are formed and more." Publisher's note

"Provides an interesting, well-illustrated introduction." Sci Books Films

Inlcudes glossary

Kim, F. S.

Constellations. Children's Press 2009 c2010 48p il (True book) lib bdg $26; pa $6.95 *

Grades: 3 4 5   **523.8**

1. Constellations

ISBN 978-0-531-16895-0 (lib bdg); 0-531-16895-6 (lib bdg); 978-0-531-22802-9 (pa); 0-531-22802-9 (pa)

LC 2008050629

Though this title "dabbles in the science of planetary orbits and early stargazing gear, . . . it mostly focuses on the rich myths surrounding the constellations, in one illustration transforming the night sky into a draped tapestry of monsters and gods. . . . Short but solid back matter closes out [this] impressive [offering]." Booklist

Mack, Gail

The stars. Marshall Cavendish Benchmark 2009 c2010 64p il (Space!) lib bdg $32.79

Grades: 4 5 6 7   **523.8**

1. Stars 2. Galaxies

ISBN 978-0-7614-4250-9 (lib bdg); 0-7614-4250-2 (lib bdg)   LC 2009014655

"Describes the stars, including their history, their composition, and their roles in the solar system." Publisher's note

This stands out for its "clear, accurate [presentation] of basic facts punctuated by lively turns of phrase and, sometimes, details not commonly found in the plethora of similar tours of the solar system and beyond." SLJ

Includes glossary and bibliographical references

Mitton, Jacqueline

Once upon a starry night; a book of constellations; [illustrated by] Christina Balit. National Geographic 2004 c2003 unp il $16.95 *

Grades: K 1 2 3   **523.8**

1. Constellations 2. Classical mythology

ISBN 0-7922-6332-4   LC 2003-10993

Companion volume to Zoo in the sky (1998)

First published 2003 in the United Kingdom

Presents facts about stars, nebulas, galaxies, and constellations and recounts the Greek myths that provided widely-known names for ten constellations, from Andromeda to Pegasus.

"Although the stories are quite short, Mitton's vivid word choices make the text as dynamic as Balit's striking pictures. Partly abstract and partly representational, the artwork features bold figures of mythological characters with silver-foil stars highlighting the points of light that make up the constellations." Booklist

Rau, Dana Meachen, 1971-

Black holes; by Dana Meachen Rau. Compass Point Books 2005 32p il (Our solar system) $22.60

Grades: 3 4 5   **523.8**

1. Black holes (Astronomy)

ISBN 0-7565-0849-5   LC 2004-15567

Rau, Dana Meachen, 1971-—_Continued_

Contents: Invisible spots in outer space; Imagining a visit; The life of stars; Types of black holes; Thinking about black holes; Studying black holes

"Rightly noting . . . that black holes by their very nature can neither be seen nor directly measured, [the author] discusses what we can infer and theorize from indirect observations, then closes with a revealing 2004 discovery. . . . [This earns] high marks for visual appeal, and for clear, specific presentation of material." SLJ

Includes glossary and bibliographical references

Rey, H. A. (Hans Augusto), 1898-1977

Find the constellations. 2nd ed. Houghton Mifflin Harcourt 2008 72p il $20; pa $9.99 *

Grades: 3 4 5 6   **523.8**

1. Constellations 2. Stars
ISBN   978-0-547-13140-5;   0-547-13140-2;
978-0-547-13178-8 (pa); 0-547-13178-X (pa)
First published 1954

This book contains "star charts, a guide to the constellations, and details about seasons and the movement of the objects we see in the sky." Publisher's note

"This much-needed update of Rey's classic work . . . features a cleaner typeface but retains the layout and most of the graphics of the previous edition. . . . The primary update . . . involves the change in Pluto's status; a great touch is the inclusion of definitions for 'planet' and 'dwarf planet.' . . . Statistical data . . . are updated; the planet finder now covers the years 2007 through 2016; and there is a new list of books for further reading. With its enduring appeal, current information, and exceptional sky charts . . . this revision should be an essential purchase for all libraries." SLJ

Rockwell, Anne F., 1934-

Our stars; written and illustrated by Anne Rockwell. Silver Whistle Bks. 1999 unp il hardcover o.p. pa $6.99

Grades: K 1 2   **523.8**

1. Stars 2. Planets 3. Outer space
ISBN 0-15-201868-9; 0-15-216360-0 (pa)
LC 97-49518

A simple introduction to the stars, planets, and outer space

"This book clearly explains many science facts without 'talking down' to youngsters. The storybook-style illustrations, . . . invite children to look at the night sky and think about the information presented in the text." Sci Books Films

Than, Ker, 1980-

Stars. Children's Press 2009 c2010 48p il (True book) lib bdg $26; pa $6.95 *

Grades: 3 4 5   **523.8**

1. Stars
ISBN 978-0-531-16899-8 (lib bdg); 0-531-16899-9 (lib bdg); 978-0-531-22806-7 (pa); 0-531-22806-1 (pa)
LC 2008051630

This introduction to stars "is simply gorgeous. The ghostly veils of the Cat's Eye Nebula, the ominous gas pillars of the Eagle Nebula, the coral-reef depths of the Crab Nebula—the only complaint will be that the photos aren't bigger. The diagrams (including the cradle-to-grave 'A Star's Life') are remarkably educational. Short but solid back matter closes out [this] impressive [offering]." Booklist

525   Earth (Astronomical geography)

Bailey, Jacqui

Sun up, sun down; the story of day and night; written by Jacqui Bailey; illustrated by Matthew Lilly. Picture Window Books 2004 31p il (Science works) lib bdg $23.93

Grades: 2 3 4   **525**

1. Day 2. Night 3. Sun 4. Earth 5. Moon
ISBN 1-4048-0567-2   LC 2003-20119

Follows the sun from dawn to dusk to explain how light rays travel, how shadows are formed, how the moon lights up the night sky, and more

This "excellent science [book explains its subject] lucidly and sometimes amusingly. . . . Children will be illuminated and engaged." SLJ

Includes bibliographical references

Gibbons, Gail

The reasons for seasons. Holiday House 1995 unp il $16.95; pa $6.95

Grades: K 1 2 3   **525**

1. Seasons 2. Earth
ISBN 0-8234-1174-5; 0-590-90735-2 (pa)
LC 94-32904

"Gibbons uses simple words and clear, colorful pictures to explain the seasons, the solstices, and the equinoxes. Besides discussing the earth's tilt and orbit, she also comments on what people and animals do in each season of the year." Booklist

Hicks, Terry Allan

Earth and the moon. Marshall Cavendish Benchmark 2009 c2010 64p il (Space!) lib bdg $22.95

Grades: 4 5 6 7   **525**

1. Earth 2. Moon
ISBN 978-0-7614-4254-7 (lib bdg); 0-7614-4254-5 (lib bdg)
LC 2009014663

"Describes Earth and its Moon, including their history, their composition, and their roles in the solar system." Publisher's note

Includes glossary and bibliographical references

Karas, G. Brian

On Earth; written and illustrated by G. Brian Karas. Putnam 2005 unp il $16.99 *

Grades: K 1 2   **525**

1. Earth
ISBN 0-399-24025-X   LC 2004-18204

"Karas covers the earth's rotation and revolution, space and time, hemispheres, and gravity. The spare text

Karas, G. Brian—*Continued*

alternates between technical descriptions and personal experiences. Artistic renderings of the earth and its cycles introduce diagrams and offer concrete images showing what happens as day turns to night, seasons change, and the earth rotates on its axis." Horn Book Guide

Landau, Elaine

Earth; [by] Elaine Landau. Children's Press 2007 48p il (True book) lib bdg $26; pa $6.95

Grades: 2 3 4   **525**
    1. Earth
    ISBN 978-0-531-12558-8 (lib bdg); 0-531-12558-0 (lib bdg); 978-0-531-14788-7 (pa); 0-531-14788-6 (pa)
                                                    LC 2007012278

Describes the planet Earth, exploring its composition, the conditions which support life, theories about how it formed, and its relationship with the moon

This "matches a clearly reasoned, matter-of-fact text to plenty of small but sharply reproduced color photos." SLJ

Includes glossary and bibliographical references

Martin, Bill, 1916-2004

I love our Earth; [by] Bill Martin, Jr., and Michael Sampson; photographs by Dan Lipow. Charlesbridge 2006 unp il $14.95

Grades: PreK K 1 2   **525**
    1. Earth
    ISBN 978-1-58089-106-6; 1-58089-106-3
                                                    LC 2005-06008

"Martin's simple poem celebrates the colors of varied landscapes and the glories of the seasons. Each line of text appears on half a page, under a photo of a child. The rest of each spread is devoted to a panoramic vista. The boys and girls, of varying ages, come from many racial and ethnic groups from around the globe." SLJ

Miller, Ron, 1947-

Earth and the moon. 21st Cent. Bks. (Brookfield) 2003 96p il (Worlds beyond) lib bdg $25.90

Grades: 5 6 7 8   **525**
    1. Earth 2. Moon
    ISBN 0-7613-2358-9   LC 2001-8479

Contents: Discovering a planet; The beginning; The story of the moon; Earth, air, fire, and water; The birth of life; The first animals; Earth takes shape; The rise and fall of the dinosaurs; Earth today; Earth around us; A planet on the move; A visit to the moon; The end of the world

Chronicles the origin, evolution, and exploration of the Earth and the Moon, and discusses their composition, their place in our solar system, and more

This is illustrated "with a mix of NASA photos and wide-angle, computer-generated art. . . . Students with a serious interest in the physical history of the Earth and its moon will be engrossed by his account of our planet's first few billion years, the Moon's probable origin, and the rise of life." SLJ

Includes glossary and bibliographical references

Ride, Sally K.

Mission: planet Earth; our world and its climate—and how humans are changing them; [by] Sally Ride & Tam O'Shaughnessy. Roaring Brook Press 2009 80p il map (Sally Ride science) $19.95

Grades: 5 6 7 8   **525**
    1. Earth 2. Climate—Environmental aspects
    ISBN 978-1-59643-310-6; 1-59643-310-8
                                                    LC 2009-29253

"This environmental-science primer introduces a range of important concepts necessary to understand climate change and global warming. Topics include the carbon cycle, water cycle, long-range carbon emissions data, biological evidence of climate change, and much more. The authors have an extensive background in science education, and their text exhibits an excellent balance of concept thoroughness with ease of comprehension. Attractive photographs and colorful graphics, including many charts and diagrams, are incorporated throughout." SLJ

Ross, Michael Elsohn, 1952-

Earth cycles; illustrated by Gustav Moore. Millbrook Press 2001 unp il (Cycles) hardcover o.p. pa $7.95

Grades: K 1 2 3   **525**
    1. Earth
    ISBN 0-7613-1815-1; 0-7613-1977-8 (pa)
                                                    LC 00-41860

"Ross discusses Earth's daily cycle of light and dark, the thirteen lunar cycles, and Earth's yearly trip around the sun. The simple text provides very basic information about periodicity and uses familiar examples to introduce new concepts. . . . Pleasing watercolors expand the text." Horn Book Guide

Simon, Seymour, 1931-

Earth: our planet in space. rev ed. Simon & Schuster Bks. for Young Readers 2003 unp il $17.95 *

Grades: 4 5 6 7   **525**
    1. Earth
    ISBN 0-689-83562-0   LC 2001-31304
    First published 1984 by Four Winds Press

This describes the relationship between the Earth, the sun, and the moon and explains the seasons, day and night, the atmosphere, and changes in the planet's surface. Illustrated with photographs taken from space

Wells, Robert E.

What's so special about planet Earth? Albert Whitman & Co. 2009 unp il $16.99

Grades: K 1 2 3   **525**
    1. Earth
    ISBN 978-0-8075-8815-4; 0-8075-8815-6
                                                    LC 2008056045

"Wells elaborates on the idea that our planet is 'a pretty good place for people to live' by, first, giving each of the other seven planets a quick flyby, then explaining how Earth's water and atmosphere create conditions suitable for life. His lively cartoon illustrations feature a pair of overall-clad young explorers (and a span-

Wells, Robert E.—*Continued*

iel) boarding a jalopy-like spaceship for their spin around the solar system, then landing back on their home planet to demonstrate recycling, energy conservation, and other environmentally friendly activities." Booklist

526   Mathematical geography

Borden, Louise, 1949-

Sea clocks; the story of longitude; illustrated by Erik Blegvad. Margaret K. McElderry Bks. 2003 unp il $18.95

Grades: 3 4 5 6   **526**
    1. Harrison, John, 1693-1776 2. Clocks and watches
    3. Longitude 4. Navigation
    ISBN 0-689-84216-3   LC 00-45599
This "picture book introduces John Harrison, the 18th-century English carpenter turned clockmaker who spent more than 40 years perfecting a device that solved the centuries-old problem of determining longitude. . . . The writing has a measured pace that helps readers to keep the details straight and the scientific concepts are clearly explained and smoothly incorporated into the text. Blegvad's precise illustrations create a strong sense of time and place." SLJ

Lasky, Kathryn

The man who made time travel; pictures by Kevin Hawkes. Farrar, Straus & Giroux 2003 unp il $17 *

Grades: 3 4 5   **526**
    1. Harrison, John, 1693-1776 2. Clocks and watches
    3. Longitude 4. Navigation
    ISBN 0-374-34788-3   LC 2001-33266
    "Melanie Kroupa books"
Describes the need for sailors to be able to determine their position at sea and the efforts of John Harrison, an eighteenth century man who spent his life refining instruments to enable them to do this
    "With Hawkes's luminous full-color paintings on every page, its clear science, and its compelling social commentary, this title is not to be missed." SLJ
    Includes bibliographical references

529   Chronology

Gardner, Robert, 1929-

It's about time! Science projects; How long does it take? Enslow Pubs. 2003 48p il (Sensational science experiments) $18.95

Grades: 3 4 5 6   **529**
    1. Time 2. Clocks and watches 3. Science—Experiments 4. Science projects
    ISBN 0-7660-2012-6   LC 2002-4621
    Contents: Time before clocks; Measuring time with the sun; A water clock; A problem with water clocks; A sand clock; A candle clock; Heart time; From heart clock to pendulum clock; A pendulum clock; Running time; Time to breathe; Quick as a wink or a squeeze; Time to fall; How fast can you react?; Decay time; Estimating time; Using time to stop motion; A year of change

This offers 18 experiments in time measurement
    This is an "approachable, hands-on-book. . . . This volume is not casual reading; it deserves and requires some attention as well as adult guidance and will be rewarding to those who make the effort." Sci Books Films
    Includes bibliographical references

Gleick, Beth

Time is when; [by] Beth Gleick; illustrated by Marthe Jocelyn. Tundra Books 2008 unp il $15.95

Grades: PreK K 1   **529**
    1. Time
    ISBN 978-0-88776-870-5; 0-88776-870-9
    A newly illustrated edition of the title first published 1960 by Rand McNally
    "Gleick successfully answers the age-old question, 'What is time?.'. . . Breaking down time into all of its components, the author explains each one, using events that children face daily. . . . The story then builds upon each part of time as it is woven back together to make up the four seasons, explaining that a year is the time between one birthday and the next—a concept readers are sure to grasp. Jocelyn's illustrations give this account a fresh look with multicultural characters and digital clocks while still keeping an old-fashioned, nostalgic feel in the paper and fabric collages, which have bright colors and fun, busy patterns. The simple, lyrical text has a timeless quality that works well as a read-aloud and is still easy enough for beginning readers to work out on their own." SLJ

Hutchins, H. J. (Hazel J.), 1952-

A second is a hiccup; a child's book of time; by Hazel Hutchins; illustrated by Kady MacDonald Denton. Arthur A. Levine Books 2007 unp il $16.99

Grades: PreK K 1 2   **529**
    1. Time
    ISBN 0-439-83106-7   LC 2006007561
    "The abstract concept of time is explained in child-friendly terms. . . . Denton's charming watercolor-and-ink vignettes, showing three friends interacting with one another and with their families, celebrate their joys and accomplishments with warmth and affection. The lyrical, rhyming text answers deceptively simple childhood questions with great flair." SLJ

Jenkins, Martin

The time book; a brief history from lunar calendars to atomic clocks; illustrated by Richard Holland. Candlewick Press 2009 57p il map lib bdg $18.99

Grades: 4 5 6 7   **529**
    1. Time 2. Calendars 3. Clocks and watches
    ISBN 978-0-7636-4112-2 (lib bdg); 0-7636-4112-X
    (lib bdg)   LC 2008-19706
    "Defines time through an examination of what it means and how it is measured as well as an overview of the history of clocks and calendars, the process of time-keeping, the studies that have been done on time, and more." Publisher's note
    "Conversational text, whimsical mixed-media artwork, and elegant book design combine to present an informative and entertaining romp through time." SLJ

Koscielniak, Bruce

About time; a first look at time and clocks; by Bruce Koscielniak. Houghton Mifflin 2004 unp il map $16 *

Grades: 3 4 5   **529**

1. Time 2. Calendars 3. Clocks and watches
ISBN 0-618-39668-3   LC 2003-17469

Describes the concept of time and how it has been measured throughout history, using water clocks, sundials, calendars, and atomic vibrations.

"Koscielniak gives an instructive yet entertaining march through the ages. . . . Attractive watercolor illustrations in green and tan tones enhance the text." SLJ

Maestro, Betsy, 1944-

The story of clocks and calendars; marking a millennium; illustrated by Giulio Maestro. Lothrop, Lee & Shepard Bks. 1999 48p il hardcover o.p. pa $9.99

Grades: 3 4 5 6   **529**

1. Calendars 2. Clocks and watches 3. Time
ISBN 0-688-14548-5; 0-688-14549-3 (lib bdg);
0-06-058945-0 (pa)   LC 98-21305

"This overview of timekeeping begins with prehistoric 'calendar sticks' and stone structures, and continues through today's ultra-precise atomic clocks. The text takes a broad multicultural approach, showing how science, history, and societal differences have influenced the calendar; the color illustrations are executed in styles that match the eras and cultures discussed in the volume." Horn Book Guide

Murphy, Stuart J., 1942-

It's about time! illustrated by John Speirs. HarperCollins Publishers 2005 33p il (MathStart) $15.99; pa $4.99 *

Grades: K 1 2   **529**

1. Time 2. Day 3. Night
ISBN 0-06-055768-0; 0-06-055769-9 (pa)
                                  LC 2003-27524

"Each page shows an analog clock and a digital clock displaying the time, from seven o'clock one morning through the day and night to seven the next morning. The illustrations show the child's activities and, in the night, his dreams. . . . Soft pencil drawings deliniate the rounded forms of children engaged in their daily activities. The rich colors of the washes glow against the white backgrounds." Booklist

Rodeo time; by Stuart J. Murphy; illustrated by David T. Wenzel. HarperCollins 2006 33p il (MathStart) $15.99; pa $4.99

Grades: 2 3 4   **529**

1. Time 2. Rodeos
ISBN 0-06-055779-6; 0-06-055778-8 (pa)
                                  LC 2005002665

"Katie and Cameron visit a rodeo with their uncle, Cactus Joe. . . . Joe gives Katie and Cameron some chores and activities, and Katie makes out a schedule to keep track of them all. Then, Katie and Cameron have to keep watch so that they don't miss any of the rodeo events. . . . The short length, light tone, and bright illustrations will help put across the concept." Booklist

Includes bibliographical references

Nagda, Ann Whitehead, 1945-

Chimp math; learning about time from a baby chimpanzee; by Ann Whitehead Nagda and Cindy Bickel. Holt & Co. 2002 29p il $16.95

Grades: 2 3 4   **529**

1. Time 2. Chimpanzees
ISBN 0-8050-6674-8   LC 00-57529

The authors "integrate the elementary-level mathematical skills of telling and representing time with the story of [a] . . . chimp, Jiggs. . . . Jiggs's growth and feeding are shown through representations of time: timelines, graphs of variables over time, calendars, and daily charts." Horn Book

"The details of the chimp's young life will fascinate readers. . . . The time lines, in particular, illuminate the narrative and can lead to classroom projects." SLJ

Older, Jules, 1940-

Telling time; how to tell time on digital and analog clocks! written by Jules Older; illustrated by Megan Halsey. Charlesbridge Pub. 2000 unp il $16.95; pa $6.95

Grades: K 1 2 3   **529**

1. Time 2. Clocks and watches
ISBN 0-88106-396-7; 0-88106-397-5 (pa)
                                  LC 99-18764

Humorous text explains the concept of time, from seconds to hours on both analog and digital clocks, from years to millennia on the calendar

"The cartoon illustrations, showing children and many, many types of clocks are colorful, plentiful, and inviting. . . . This jovial look at time and time telling is as handy as they come." SLJ

Raum, Elizabeth

The story behind time. Heinemann Library 2009 32p il (True stories) lib bdg $28.21

Grades: 3 4 5   **529**

1. Time 2. Clocks and watches 3. Calendars
ISBN 978-1-4329-2343-3 (lib bdg); 1-4329-2343-9 (lib bdg)   LC 2008037393

This offers information about time, including a history of time measurement

Includes bibliographical references

Skurzynski, Gloria, 1930-

On time; from seasons to split seconds. National Geographic Soc. 2000 41p il $17.95

Grades: 4 5 6 7   **529**

1. Time
ISBN 0-7922-7503-9   LC 99-33927

Examines the ways humans have measured time throughout history and discusses the various units that are used to keep track of it

"This attractive offering is brimming with information. . . . The conversational tone helps readers get through the more difficult concepts. . . . The book is heavily illustrated with full-color drawings, photographs, and diagrams." SLJ

530   Physics

Baxter, Roberta, 1952-
The particle model of matter. Raintree 2009 48p
il (Sci-hi: physical science) lib bdg $31.43; pa
$8.99
Grades: 4 5 6 7   **530**
　1. Matter 2. Atoms
　ISBN   978-1-4109-3244-0   (lib   bdg);
　978-1-4109-3259-4 (pa)   LC 2008030582
　This takes a look at atoms, the building blocks of matter. It describes the different kinds of atoms, the particles
that make up an atom, and the different states that matter
can take
　Includes bibliographical references

Bonnet, Robert L.
Home run! science projects with baseball and
softball; [by] Robert L. Bonnet and Dan Keen.
Enslow Publishers 2009 104p il (Score! Sports
science projects) lib bdg $31.93
Grades: 5 6 7 8   **530**
　1. Baseball 2. Motion 3. Force and energy
4. Science—Experiments 5. Science projects
　ISBN 978-0-7660-3365-8 (lib bdg); 0-7660-3365-1 (lib
bdg)   LC 2008-3005
　"Provides several science experiments using physics
and baseball or softball." Publisher's note
　"In addition to colorful, digital drawings illustrating
the projects, a few photos and period prints also brighten
the pages. . . . [This] will appeal to those looking for
fresh science-project ideas." Booklist
　Includes glossary and bibliographical references

Gaff, Jackie
Looking at solids, liquids, and gases; how does
matter change? [by] Jackie Gaff. Enslow
Publishers 2008 32p il (Looking at science: how
things change) lib bdg $22.60
Grades: 1 2 3   **530**
　1. Matter
　ISBN 978-0-7660-3092-3 (lib bdg); 0-7660-3092-X
(lib bdg)   LC 2007-24514
　"Provides an introduction for readers on the differ-
ences between the states of matter." Publisher's note
　"Fills a huge void in elementary science collections.
. . . Text is arranged in succinct 'chunks,' giving impor-
tant facts without overwhelming readers. . . . [This] is
an essential addition." Libr Media Connect
　Includes glossary and bibliographical references

Gardner, Robert, 1929-
Ace your physical science project; great science
fair ideas; [by] Robert Gardner, Madeline
Goodstein, and Thomas R. Rybolt. Enslow
Publishers 2009 128p il (Ace your physics science
project) lib bdg $31.93
Grades: 5 6 7 8   **530**
　1. Physics 2. Science projects 3. Science—Experiments
　ISBN 978-0-7660-3225-5 (lib bdg); 0-7660-3225-6 (lib
bdg)   LC 2008-29637

　"Presents several science projects and science fair
ideas that use physics." Publisher's note
　"Dozens of . . . science activities are presented with
background information, step-by-step instructions, and
suggestions for extending to the science fair level. . . .
Color illustrations and important safety information are
included." Horn Book Guide
　Includes bibliographical references

Science projects about physics in the home.
Enslow Publishers 1999 112p il (Science projects)
lib bdg $26.60 *
Grades: 5 6 7 8   **530**
　1. Physics 2. Science—Experiments 3. Science proj-
ects
　ISBN 0-89490-948-7   LC 98-6822
　Presents instructions for physics projects and experi-
ments that can be done at home and exhibited at science
fairs
　"This volume is well organized with lots of hands-on
activities that use relatively simple pieces of equipment.
. . . A good starting point in the understanding of the
physics of objects and events in our daily life." Sci
Books Films
　Includes bibliographical references

Slam dunk! science projects with basketball;
[by] Robert Gardner and Dennis Shortelle. Enslow
Publishers 2009 104p il (Score! sports science
projects) lib bdg $31.93
Grades: 5 6 7 8   **530**
　1. Physics 2. Science—Experiments 3. Basketball
4. Science projects
　ISBN 978-0-7660-3366-5 (lib bdg); 0-7660-3366-X
(lib bdg)   LC 2008-24879
　"Presents several science experiments and science
project ideas using physics and basketball." Publisher's
note
　"Introductions include information about the history of
the sport, safety steps to follow, and the scientific method. . . . Detailed diagrams help clarify many of the directions." SLJ
　Includes glossary and bibliographical references

Goodstein, Madeline
Wheels! science projects with bicycles,
skateboards, and skates. Enslow Publishers 2009
104p il (Score! sports science projects) lib bdg
$31.93
Grades: 5 6 7 8 9 10   **530**
　1. Physics 2. Science—Experiments 3. Wheels
4. Science projects
　ISBN 978-0-7660-3107-4 (lib bdg); 0-7660-3107-1 (lib
bdg)   LC 2008-24880
　"Presents several science experiments and science
project ideas using physics and bicycles, skateboards, and
roller skates." Publisher's note
　"Introductions include information about the history of
the sport, safety steps to follow, and the scientific method. . . . Detailed diagrams help clarify many of the directions." SLJ
　Includes glossary and bibliographical references

Green, Dan

Physics; why matter matters! [by] Dan Green; Simon Basher, illustrator. Kingfisher 2008 128p il pa $8.95

Grades: 5 6 7 8   530

1. Physics

ISBN 978-0-7534-6214-0 (pa); 0-7534-6214-1 (pa)

LC 2007-31805

This "introduces the elements of physics as anthropomorphic, cartoon-style characters. . . . Each of the groupings begins with an introduction and each concept is given its own spread that shows the cartoon figure and describes its 'personality.' The information is presented in a chatty and conversational tone. . . . Along with the narrative, which is written in the first person from the concept's point of view, other key facts are presented. This book would be handy as a supplement to a physics curriculum." SLJ

Includes glossary

Hartman, Eve

Light and sound; [by] Eve Hartman and Wendy Meshbesher. Raintree 2008 48p il (Sci-hi: physical science) lib bdg $22; pa $8.99

Grades: 5 6 7 8   530

1. Sound 2. Light

ISBN 978-1-4109-3378-2 (lib bdg); 1-4109-3378-4 (lib bdg); 978-1-4109-3383-6 (pa); 1-4109-3383-0 (pa)

LC 2009-3506

This describes "what causes sound, heat, and light energy." Publisher's note

A "compelling read for both browsers and science buffs. . . . Information is clearly presented and flows smoothly. . . . A treasure trove of information." SLJ

Includes glossary and bibliographical references

Lee, Cora

The great motion mission; a surprising story of physics in everyday life; illustrated by Steve Rolston. Annick Press 2009 114p il $24.95; pa $14.95

Grades: 4 5 6   530

1. Physics

ISBN 978-1-55451-185-3; 1-55451-185-2; 978-1-55451-184-6 (pa); 1-55451-184-4 (pa)

"This book is a combination of narrative and concepts about physics. . . . Jeremy and his friends are distraught when the local summer fair is canceled in order to host a physics conference. While Jeremy helps his uncle campaign to save the fair, his new neighbor, Aubrey, sets out to prove that physics isn't only necessary, but also fun. The text is chatty and accessible to students. Topics include 'Physics and Sight,' 'Physics and Sound,' and 'Physics in Motion.' Each chapter profiles a featured physicist, from Albert Einstein to Richard Feynman. . . . Cartoon illustrations help to explain concepts such as the water cycle and wave patterns. Photographs are scattered throughout, and boxed areas highlight specific topics. This title would be especially useful for students wanting a good introduction to physics." SLJ

Includes glossary and bibliographical references

Mason, Adrienne

Change it! solids, liquids, gases and you; written by Adrienne Mason; illustrated by Claudia Davila. Kids Can Press 2006 32p il (Primary physical science) $12.95; pa $5.95

Grades: K 1 2   530

1. Matter 2. Science—Experiments

ISBN 978-1-55337-837-2; 1-55337-837-7; 978-1-55337-838-9 (pa); 1-55337-838-5 (pa)

This describes the three states of matter and includes experiments

This uses "colorful eye-catching graphics." Sci Books Films

Includes glossary

Ross, Michael Elsohn, 1952-

Toy lab; illustrations by Tim Seeley. Carolrhoda Bks. 2003 48p il (You are the scientist) lib bdg $23.29

Grades: 3 4 5 6   530

1. Toys 2. Physics 3. Science—Experiments

ISBN 0-87614-456-3   LC 2001-5456

"Using the scientific method, youngsters are encouraged to experiment with toys like Slinkies, Silly Putty, Frisbees, and blocks to learn about flight, gravity, matter, pressure and waves, and objects in motion. . . . Toy Lab should pique youngsters' interest, even those who are not usually drawn to scientific experiments, and will give students some ideas for science fair projects as well." SLJ

Includes glossary

Silverstein, Alvin

Matter; by Alvin Silverstein, Virginia Silverstein, Laura Silverstein Nunn. Twenty-First Century Books 2009 112p il (Science concepts) lib bdg $31.93

Grades: 5 6 7 8   530

1. Matter

ISBN 978-0-8225-7515-3 (lib bdg); 0-8225-7515-9 (lib bdg)   LC 2007049493

This is a "simple and straightforward [discussion] of the [subject]. The layout . . . is attractive and inviting, with full-color photographs and/or diagrams on almost every spread. In addition, the authors make good use of fact boxes. . . . [This] discusses the states of matter, the elements, chemical reactions, and more. [This title] will interest browsers and provide ample information for reports." SLJ

Includes glossary and bibliographical references

Weir, Jane, 1976-

Matter. Compass Point Books 2009 40p il (Mission: science) lib bdg $26.60

Grades: 4 5 6   530

1. Matter

ISBN 978-0-7565-4069-2 (lib bdg); 0-7565-4069-0 (lib bdg)   LC 2008-37624

An introduction to the scientific concept of matter, including elements, atoms, and molecules

Includes glossary

530.4   States of matter

Boothroyd, Jennifer, 1972-

What is a gas? by Jennifer Boothroyd. Lerner Publications Co. 2007 23p il (First step nonfiction: states of matter) lib bdg $21.27

Grades: K 1 2   530.4

   1. Gases

   ISBN 978-0-8225-6837-7 (lib bdg); 0-8225-6837-3 (lib bdg)   LC 2006006303

"This small book introduces a single state of matter: a gas. Each page in the main section offers one or more colorful photographs and a brief line or two of large-print text. After a brief introduction to matter, the discussion moves on to the characteristics of gases and a few examples." Booklist

What is a liquid? by Jennifer Boothroyd. Lerner Publications Co. 2007 23p il (First step nonfiction: states of matter) lib bdg $21.27; pa $5.95

Grades: K 1 2   530.4

   1. Liquids

   ISBN 978-0-8225-6838-4 (lib bdg); 0-8225-6838-1 (lib bdg); 978-0-8225-6817-9 (pa); 0-8225-6817-9 (pa)   LC 2006006304

This explains liquids "along with basic vocabulary. The layout is bright with many color photographs featuring children of different ethnicities. The text is spare; each spread includes, on average, three sentences." SLJ

What is a solid? by Jennifer Boothroyd. Lerner Publications Co. 2007 23p il (First step nonfiction: states of matter) lib bdg $21.27; pa $5.95

Grades: K 1 2   530.4

   1. Solids

   ISBN 978-0-8225-6836-0 (lib bdg); 0-8225-6836-5 (lib bdg); 978-0-8225-6816-2 (pa); 0-8225-6816-0 (pa)   LC 2006006307

This explains solids "along with basic vocabulary. The layout is bright with many color photographs featuring children of different ethnicities. The text is spare; each spread includes, on average, three sentences." SLJ

Bradley, Kimberly Brubaker

Pop! a book about bubbles; photographs by Margaret Miller. HarperCollins Pubs. 2001 33p il (Let's-read-and-find-out science) hardcover o.p. pa $4.95

Grades: K 1   530.4

   1. Bubbles

   ISBN 0-06-028700-4; 0-06-028701-2 (lib bdg); 0-06-445208-5 (pa)   LC 99-57794

Simple text explains how soap bubbles are made, why they are always round, and why they pop

"A simple, accurate text that is also fun to read. . . . Delightful color photographs of charming children making bubbles and of bubbles floating freely reinforce and extend the text. . . . This is science learning at its best." SLJ

Claybourne, Anna

The nature of matter; [by] Anna Claybourne. Gareth Stevens Pub. 2007 48p il (Gareth Stevens vital science: physical science) lib bdg $26.60; pa $11.95

Grades: 4 5 6 7   530.4

   1. Matter

   ISBN 978-0-8368-8088-5 (lib bdg); 978-0-8368-8097-7 (pa)   LC 2006033732

This describes uses for matter and what happens when it changes from one form to another, the basic physical laws and properties of matter, and the various ways in which we control how matter behaves.

This is "straightforward and clear. . . . The layout is bright and colorful, with photographs and illustrations on almost every page." SLJ

Includes glossary and bibliographical references

Gardner, Robert, 1929-

Melting, freezing, and boiling science projects with matter; [by] Robert Gardner. Enslow Elementary 2006 48p il (Fantastic physical science experiments) lib bdg $23.93

Grades: 4 5 6   530.4

   1. Matter 2. Temperature 3. Science—Experiments

   ISBN 0-7660-2589-6   LC 2005033753

This offers experiments on the nature of solids, liquids, and gases and temperature.

"The ink-and-wash pictures illustrate the scientific principles as well as the equipment used in various activities. . . . Gardner's explanations are clear and his discussions lead readers to think about causes as well as what is happening to matter . . . as it changes form." Booklist

Includes glossary and bibliographical references

Hurd, Will

Changing states; solids, liquids, and gases. Heinemann Library 2009 48p il (Do it yourself) lib bdg $31.43; pa $8.99

Grades: 3 4 5 6   530.4

   1. Matter 2. Solids 3. Liquids 4. Gas

   ISBN 978-1-4329-2312-9 (lib bdg); 1-4329-2312-9 (lib bdg); 978-1-4329-2319-8 (pa); 1-4329-2319-6 (pa)   LC 2008034939

The describes the fluctuating states of matter and includes experiments

This "would make an ideal supplement to science classes. A modular layout and dynamic photos keep things moving, while the experiments . . . feature lists of readily available materials, steps required to pull off the magic, and warnings as the when adult supervision is required." Booklist

Includes bibliographical references

Mason, Adrienne

Touch it! materials, matter and you; written by Adrienne Mason; illustrated by Claudia Dávila. Kids Can Press 2005 32p il (Primary physical science) $12.95; pa $5.95

Grades: K 1 2   **530.4**

1. Materials 2. Matter

ISBN 1-55337-760-5; 1-55337-761-3 (pa)

"Large-scale digital illustrations show children, animals, and adults commenting on and exploring the properties of matter. Some sections discuss ideas such as mass, buoyancy, or magnetism, while others suggest informal activities, for example describing different foods. Five double-page spreads present very simple science projects, beginning with a question-and-answer section followed by a short list of materials, a few steps to follow, and a brief concluding paragraph. . . . This colorful beginning science series is suitable for primary-grade students in groups and even younger children one-on-one." Booklist

Includes glossary

Oxlade, Chris

Changing materials; [by] Chris Oxlade. Crabtree Publishing Company 2008 32p il (Working with materials) lib bdg $26.60; pa $7.95 *

Grades: 2 3 4   **530.4**

1. Chemical reactions 2. Matter 3. Strength of materials

ISBN 978-0-7787-3638-7 (lib bdg); 0-7787-3638-5 (lib bdg); 978-0-7787-3648-6 (pa); 0-7787-3648-2 (pa)
LC 2007027419

This describes how materials change by such processes as bending, breaking, melting, boiling, evaporating, dissolving, and burning

This "title has numerous captioned color photographs. . . . The [book offers] three simple, easy, and safe reproducible experiments. . . . Students will appreciate the pleasing design, easy-to-read font, and direct, clear writing style." Libr Media Connect

Includes glossary and bibliographical references

Cooling. Heinemann Library 2009 32p il (Changing materials) lib bdg $25.36; pa $7.99

Grades: K 1 2   **530.4**

1. Cold

ISBN 978-1-4329-3273-2 (lib bdg); 1-4329-3273-X (lib bdg); 978-1-4329-3278-7 (pa); 1-4329-3278-0 (pa)

Introduces the concept of freezing points.

"A few simple activities provide opportunities to experiment. The color photographs are engaging." SLJ

Includes glossary and bibliographical references

Heating. Heinemann Library 2009 32p il (Changing materials) lib bdg $25.36; pa $7.99

Grades: K 1 2   **530.4**

1. Heat

ISBN 978-1-4329-3272-5 (lib bdg); 1-4329-3272-1 (lib bdg); 978-1-4329-3277-0 (pa); 1-4329-3277-2 (pa)

Introduces the concept of boiling points.

"A few simple activities provide opportunities to experiment. The color photographs are engaging." SLJ

Includes glossary and bibliographical references

Spilsbury, Richard, 1963-

What are solids, liquids, and gases? exploring science with hands-on activities; [by] Richard and Louise Spilsbury. Enslow Elementary 2008 32p il (In touch with basic science) lib bdg $22.60

Grades: 3 4 5   **530.4**

1. Matter 2. Science—Experiments

ISBN 978-0-7660-3094-7 (lib bdg); 0-7660-3094-6 (lib bdg)
LC 2007024516

This book "covers the three phases of matter described in its title. . . . Properties of each are explored. . . . The activities are all doable with simple household items, and they definitely reinforce the concepts being explored. This volume would a plus for budding scientists." Sci Books Films

Includes glossary and bibliographical references

Zoehfeld, Kathleen Weidner

What is the world made of? all about solids, liquids, and gases; illustrated by Paul Meisel. HarperCollins Pubs. 1998 32p il (Let's-read-and-find-out science) hardcover o.p. pa $4.95

Grades: K 1 2 3   **530.4**

1. Matter

ISBN 0-06-027143-4; 0-06-027144-2 (lib bdg); 0-06-445163-1 (pa)
LC 97-30658

In simple text, presents the three states of matter, solid, liquid, and gas, and describes their attributes

"The explanations are clear with a simple, informal text for the new reader, and the lively line-and-watercolor pictures bring in humor and common-sense." Booklist

530.8 Measurement

Adler, David A., 1947-

How tall, how short, how faraway; illustrated by Nancy Tobin. Holiday House 1999 unp il $16.95; pa $6.95 *

Grades: K 1 2 3   **530.8**

1. Measurement

ISBN 0-8234-1375-6; 0-8234-1632-1 (pa)
LC 98-18802

Introduces several measuring systems such as the Egyptian system, the inch-pound system, and the metric system

"In this wonderful hands-on concept book, easy technological measuring tools are superbly introduced and explained. . . . The informative text and colorful illustrations clearly explain the difference between customary and metric systems." Sci Child

Ball, Johnny, 1938-

Why pi; how math applies to everyday life. DK Pub. 2009 93p il map $16.99

Grades: 4 5 6 7   **530.8**

1. Measurement 2. Mathematics 3. Pi

ISBN 978-0-7566-5164-0; 0-7566-5164-6

"Author Johnny Ball focuses on how people have used numbers to measure things through the ages, from the

Ball, Johnny, 1938-—*Continued*
ways the ancient Egyptians measured the pyramids to how modern scientists measure time and space." Publisher's note

Cleary, Brian P., 1959-
How long or how wide? a measuring guide; illustrated by Brian Gable. Millbrook Press 2007 30p il (Math is categorical) lib bdg $15.95
Grades: K 1 2   **530.8**
1. Measurement
ISBN 978-0-8225-6694-6 (lib bdg); 0-8225-6694-X (lib bdg)   LC 2006-10754
A rhyming text filled with humorous examples explains how to use and compare metric and U.S. customary units of length and introduces such tools of measurement as rulers and yardsticks.
"The book is very kid friendly, whimsical, vivid, and lively." Sci Books Films

On the scale; a weighty tale; by Brian P. Cleary; illustrated by Brian Gable. Millbrook Press 2008 31p il (Math is categorical) lib bdg $15.95
Grades: 2 3 4 5   **530.8**
1. Weights and measures
ISBN 978-0-8225-7851-2 (lib bdg); 0-8225-7851-4 (lib bdg)   LC 2007033670
"In bubbly verse, Cleary presents a basic introduction to weights and measures. . . . Cheery, child-friendly examples are used for both English and metric measurements, progressing from smaller to larger weights in this approachable explanation of the topic. . . . Gable's watercolor cartoons depict rainbow-hued cats engaged in all manner of activities. This humorous title should prove useful in both classroom and family discussions." SLJ

Gardner, Robert, 1929-
Ace your math and measuring science project; great science fair ideas. Enslow Publishers 2009 128p il (Ace your physics science project) lib bdg $31.93
Grades: 5 6 7 8   **530.8**
1. Measurement 2. Weights and measures 3. Science projects 4. Science—Experiments
ISBN 978-0-7660-3224-8 (lib bdg); 0-7660-3224-8 (lib bdg)   LC 2008-23926
"Presents several science projects and science fair ideas using math and measuring." Publisher's note
"Dozens of . . . science activities are presented with background information, step-by-step instructions, and suggestions for extending to the science fair level. . . . Color illustrations and important safety information are included." Horn Book Guide
Includes bibliographical references

Far-out science projects with height and depth; How high is up? How low is down? Enslow Pubs. 2003 48p il (Sensational science experiments) lib bdg $18.95
Grades: 3 4 5 6   **530.8**
1. Measurement 2. Science—Experiments 3. Science projects
ISBN 0-7660-2016-9   LC 2002-4619

Contents: Introduction; How to measure; Safety first; How tall are you?; How high is your ceiling?; How high are your stairs?; How high is your roof?; How high is a flagpole?; How high is a tall tree?; How high is a skyscraper?; How high is a mountain?; How high are low clouds?; How high are high clouds?; How do we know cloud heights?; How deep is this book?; How deep is one page?; How deep is your bathtub?; How deep is your basement?; How deep is a pond or lake?; What is the farthest "down"?
"Following a brief introduction to measurement, a review of units (metric and English standard), and a list of safety tips, Gardner presents a series of 17 measurement activities for readers. . . . The colorful illustrations provide additional clarity for the narrative directions. . . . The activities provide hands-on, mind-on measurement experiences with real-world applications." Sci Books Films
Includes glossary and bibliographical references

Heavy-duty science projects with weight; how much does it weigh? Enslow Pubs. 2003 48p il (Sensational science experiments) lib bdg $18.95
Grades: 3 4 5 6   **530.8**
1. Gravitation 2. Measurement 3. Science—Experiments 4. Science projects
ISBN 0-7660-2013-4   LC 2002-8460
Contents: Safety first; Weighing in; More weighing in; Weight and position; Gravity and different weights; Measuring weight: a "spring" scale; Weight and friction; Becoming weightless; Seesaws, weights, distances, and levers; Levers to lift weights; An inclined plane; Measuring weight with a balance; Can you weigh air?; Weighing air; Some effects of air's weight; Defying gravity; Defying gravity again; Using a siphon to defy gravity; Forces other than gravity
This "includes a variety of hands-on activities that use everyday cheap materials to introduce students to many significant physics concepts related to gravity. . . . While challenging, the activities are accessible and interesting to all students. . . . The language used in the volume is simple, accurate, and scientific." Sci Books Films
Includes glossary and bibliographical references

Super-sized science projects with volume; how much space does it take up? Enslow Pubs. 2003 48p il (Sensational science experiments) lib bdg $18.95
Grades: 3 4 5 6   **530.8**
1. Volume (Cubic content) 2. Measurement 3. Science—Experiments 4. Science projects
ISBN 0-7660-2014-2   LC 2002-153850
Contents: Measuring—how big is it?; Safety first; Measuring with cubes; Cubic friends; Inch, foot, and yard; Cup, pint, quart, and gallon; Liter vs. quart and milliliter; Volume of a drop; Air takes up space; Underwater mystery; Displacing water; Seeds and water; How much air is in sand?; What fraction of air is oxygen?; Temperature and the volume of a gas; Temperature and the volume of a liquid; Freezing and the volume of water; The volume of a breath; Volume of a deep breath; Testing paper towels; Words to know
This "explores topics ranging from determining the volume of a quart and a liter to the amount of air in a container of sand. Gardner's clear, informal explanations are echoed in LaBaff's colorful illustrations." Booklist
Includes glossary and bibliographical references

Leedy, Loreen, 1959-

Measuring Penny; written and illustrated by Loreen Leedy. Holt & Co. 1997 unp il $16.95; pa $6.95 *

Grades: 1 2 3   **530.8**
  1. Measurement 2. Dogs
  ISBN 0-8050-5360-3; 0-8050-6572-5 (pa)
                        LC 97-19108

"For a measuring project, Lisa decides to measure her dog, Penny, and a cast of other dogs at the park. Noses, tails, ears, paws—nothing escapes her measuring zeal. Also, time, temperature, cost, and even value are creatively calculated throughout a day spent caring for Penny. Leedy cleverly incorporates Lisa's notebook recordings into the illustrations, which depict a wide range of shapes and sizes for easy visual comparison." Horn Book Guide

Long, Lynette

Measurement mania; games and activities that make math easy and fun. Wiley 2001 122p il (Magical math) pa $12.95

Grades: 3 4 5 6   **530.8**
  1. Measurement
  ISBN 0-471-36980-2   LC 00-43383

In this introduction to measurement "the activities range from using hands and feet to measure distance to making a sundial. . . . [This book provides] valuable activities and games to help children learn about the concepts." SLJ

Murphy, Stuart J., 1942-

Room for Ripley; illustrated by Sylvie Wickstrom. HarperCollins Pubs. 1999 33p il (MathStart) hardcover o.p. pa $4.95 *

Grades: 1 2 3   **530.8**
  1. Measurement 2. Aquariums
  ISBN 0-06-027621-5 (lib bdg); 0-06-446724-4 (pa)
                        LC 98-26109

Uses a story about a young boy who is getting a fish bowl ready for his new pet to introduce various units of liquid measure

"The writing is breezy and reads like a story about a boy who wants a pet, but the text constantly reinforces the mathematical concepts (how many cups in a pint, a quart, etc.). The illustrations are painted in muted primary colors against a lot of white space. . . . A fun, painless math lesson." SLJ

Robbins, Ken, 1945-

For good measure; the ways we say how much, how far, how heavy, how big, how old. Roaring Brook Press 2010 44p il $17.99 *   **530.8**
  1. Measurement   Grades: 3 4 5 6
  ISBN 978-1-59643-344-1; 1-59643-344-2

"A Neal Porter book"

"By tossing in tidbits of history, word origins and meanings, Robbins takes the everyday subject of measurement and makes it accessible, interesting and memorable. Beginning with the units for lengths and distances, readers will not only learn about feet and inches, but also hands . . . and cubits. . . . From distances, the author

moves on to area—measured in acres, hectares and sections—and then on to weigh—pound, ounce, ton, stone, dram and carat. . . . Liquid measures, dry capacity and time round out the volume. The photographs are a good complement, clearly illustrating the concepts without distracting from the text." Kirkus

Schwartz, David M., 1951-

Millions to measure; pictures by Steven Kellogg. HarperCollins Pubs. 2003 unp il $16.99; lib bdg $17.89 *

Grades: 2 3 4   **530.8**
  1. Measurement 2. Weights and measures
  ISBN 0-688-12916-1; 0-06-623784-X (lib bdg)
                        LC 2001-39683

Marvelosissimo the Magician explains the development of standard units of measure, and shows the simplicity of calculating length, height, weight, and volume using the metric system

"Schwartz not only manages to impart a good deal of basic information . . . but also entertains the reader. He receives ample support from illustrator Kellogg, who contributes enough merry madness to make learning fun. Bright with shining colors, the large, detailed pictures brim with action and humor as well as history and math." Booklist

531 Classical mechanics. Solid mechanics

Bradley, Kimberly Brubaker

Energy makes things happen; illustrated by Paul Meisel. HarperCollins Pubs. 2003 33p il (Let's-read-and-find-out science) hardcover o.p. lib bdg $16.89; pa $4.99

Grades: K 1 2 3   **531**
  1. Force and energy
  ISBN 0-06-028908-2; 0-06-028909-0 (lib bdg); 0-06-445213-1 (pa)   LC 2001-39520

This book shows how energy comes originally from the sun and can be transferred from one thing to another

"This worthy title uses familiar examples and a clear focus to introduce basic scientific concepts. . . . Meisel's color illustrations of cheerful multiethnic children match the level and tone of the text perfectly, make it more comprehensible, and add to the book's appeal." SLJ

Forces make things move; illustrated by Paul Meisel. HarperCollins 2005 33p il (Let's-read-and-find-out science) $15.99; lib bdg $16.89; pa $4.99

Grades: K 1 2 3   **531**
  1. Force and energy 2. Gravity
  ISBN 0-06-028906-6; 0-06-028907-4 (lib bdg); 0-06-445214-X (pa)   LC 2002-14763

Simple language and humorous illustrations show how forces make things move, prevent them from starting to move, and stop them from moving

"Colorful line-and-watercolor-wash illustrations brighten the pages. . . . A practical starting place for understanding forces." Booklist

Claybourne, Anna

Forms of energy. Raintree 2008 48p il (Sci-hi: physical science) lib bdg $22; pa $8.99

Grades: 5 6 7 8   531

1. Force and energy

ISBN 978-1-4109-3377-5 (lib bdg); 1-4109-3377-6 (lib bdg); 978-1-4109-3382-9 (pa); 1-4109-3382-2 (pa)
    LC 2009-3504

This describes "what causes sound, heat, and light energy." Publisher's note

A "compelling read for both browsers and science buffs. . . . Information is clearly presented and flows smoothly. . . . A treasure trove of information." SLJ

Includes glossary and bibliographical references

Cobb, Vicki, 1938-

I fall down; illustrated by Julia Gorton. HarperCollins Publishers 2004 unp il (Science play) $17.99; lib bdg $18.89

Grades: K 1 2   531

1. Gravity 2. Science—Experiments

ISBN 0-688-17842-1; 0-688-17843-X (lib bdg)
    LC 2003-1822

Simple experiments introduce the basic concept of gravity and its relationship to weight

"The digital illustrations offer clearly defined images with a distinctive, retro look. Their eye-catching pizzazz will help hold the attention of the audience. . . . Attuned to the learning style of young children, Cobb's questions and suggestions offer kids the experience of the scientific process." Booklist

Gardner, Robert, 1929-

Ace your forces and motion science project; great science fair ideas; [by] Robert Gardner and Madeline Goodstein. Enslow Publishers 2009 128p il (Ace your physics science project) lib bdg $31.93

Grades: 5 6 7 8   531

1. Force and energy 2. Science—Experiments 3. Science projects

ISBN 978-0-7660-3222-4 (lib bdg); 0-7660-3222-1 (lib bdg)
    LC 2008-49778

"Presents several science experiments and project ideas about forces and motion." Publisher's note

Includes bibliographical references

Split-second science projects with speed; how fast does it go? Enslow Pubs. 2003 48p il (Sensational science experiments) lib bdg $18.95

Grades: 3 4 5 6   531

1. Speed 2. Science—Experiments 3. Science projects

ISBN 0-7660-2017-7   LC 2002-4618

Contents: Introduction; Speedometer readings; An odometer and a clock; Walking speeds; Running speeds; Animals: fast and slow; Wind speeds by observation; Wind speeds by meter; Wind direction and velocity; The speed of falling leaves; Speed and parachutes; Growth speed; How fast do your fingernails grow?; How fast do you read?; Speed of melting; Speed of dissolving; Speed while falling; Speed of a chemical reaction

This serves as an "introduction to speed and velocity by providing introductory explanations and step-by-step

instructions on how to set up and conduct different simple experiments. . . . Perhaps the book's strongest point is its readability. . . . The book is nicely illustrated and appealing." Sci Books Films

Includes glossary and bibliographical references

Hillman, Ben

How fast is it? a zippy book all about speed. Scholastic 2008 47p il $14.99

Grades: 3 4 5   531

1. Speed

ISBN 978-0-439-91867-1; 0-439-91867-7
    LC 2007039983

"Twenty-two full-color, full-page spreads convey the quickness (or lack) of the most ordinary things in a unique and amazing way. Examples: * How fast is a bullet-bike? * Which one is faster? A coyote or a roadrunner? * Can a sneeze be faster than a tennis serve? * How fast is the population growing? * What is the fastest-growing plant?" Publisher's note

Hopwood, James, 1964-

Cool gravity activities; fun science projects about balance; [by] James Hopwood. ABDO Pub. 2008 32p il (Cool science) lib bdg $16.95

Grades: 4 5 6   531

1. Gravity 2. Science projects 3. Science—Experiments

ISBN 978-1-59928-908-3 (lib bdg); 1-59928-908-3 (lib bdg)
    LC 2007010204

This offers science projects about gravity, including "The Old Cane Trick"

The projects "will attract boys and girls. [The] book begins with [an] upbeat introduction and three chapters about the scientific method, keeping a journal, and safety. . . . Background on the science concepts involved is presented along with a complete list of supplies. . . . The numbered instructions are easy to follow and are accompanied by small, closeup photos." SLJ

Macdonald, Wendy

Galileo's leaning tower experiment; a science adventure; illustrated by Paolo Rui. Charlesbridge 2009 32p il $16.95; pa $7.95

Grades: 3 4 5   531

1. Galilei, Galileo, 1564-1642 2. Gravity 3. Physics

ISBN 978-1-57091-869-8; 1-57091-869-4; 978-1-57091-870-4 (pa); 1-57091-870-8 (pa)
    LC 2008010652

"In this fictionalized account of Galileo's legendary experiments on the speed of falling objects, the young professor meets a poor farm boy, Massimo, who drops bread and cheese to his uncle passing under a bridge in a boat. Stunned that the bread and cheese hit the boat at the same time, contradicting Aristotle's teachings, Galileo begins experimenting with other pairs of falling objects. . . . The story excels at teaching the concept involved and is admirably enhanced by Rui's attractive, colorful, and informative acrylics." SLJ

Mason, Adrienne

Move it! motion, forces and you; written by Adrienne Mason; illustrated by Claudia Dávila. Kids Can Press 2005 32p il (Primary physical science) $12.95; pa $5.95

Grades: K 1 2   531

1. Motion 2. Force and energy

ISBN 1-55337-758-3; 1-55337-759-1 (pa)

This explores the physics of why and how things move with simple activities such as pushing, pulling or lifting objects.

Includes glossary

Parker, Barry R.

The mystery of gravity. Benchmark Bks. 2003 78p il (Story of science) lib bdg $28.50

Grades: 5 6 7 8   531

1. Gravitation

ISBN 0-7614-1428-2   LC 2002-970

Defines gravity and discusses how our knowledge of the natural force has broadened and evolved

"Readers will find accurate, readable explanations for the phenomenon of gravity. The text moves from classical attempts to understand why and how objects fall to the work of Kepler, Galileo, Newton, and Einstein's general theory of relativity. The book is ably illustrated by well-captioned photos and clear diagrams, such as the wormhole of a black hole." Horn Book Guide

Includes glossary and bibliographical references

Phelan, Glen

Invisible force; the quest to define the laws of motion; [by] Glen Phelan. National Geographic 2006 59p il (Science quest) $17.95; lib bdg $25.90

Grades: 5 6 7 8   531

1. Motion 2. Gravity

ISBN 0-7922-5539-9; 0-7922-5540-2 (lib bdg)
                                        LC 2005027350

This "traces the historical and scientific path to man's understanding of motion and gravity." Publisher's note

Includes glossary and bibliographical references

Royston, Angela

Looking at forces and motion; how do things move? [by] Angela Royston. Enslow Publishers 2008 32p il (Looking at science: how things change) lib bdg $22.60

Grades: 1 2 3   531

1. Force and energy 2. Motion

ISBN 978-0-7660-3089-3 (lib bdg); 0-7660-3089-X (lib bdg)   LC 2007-24508

"A look at the basics of force and motion, including what makes swings move, why we use tools, natural forces, gravity, magnetic force, and friction." Publisher's note

"Fills a huge void in elementary science collections. . . . Text is arranged in succinct 'chunks,' giving important facts without overwhelming readers. . . . [This] is an essential addition." Libr Media Connect

Includes glossary and bibliographical references

Silverstein, Alvin

Forces and motion; [by Alvin & Virginia Silverstein & Laura Silverstein Nunn] Twenty-First Century Books 2008 c2009 112p il (Science concepts) lib bdg $31.93

Grades: 5 6 7 8   531

1. Force and energy 2. Motion

ISBN 978-0-8225-7514-6 (lib bdg); 0-8225-7514-0 (lib bdg)   LC 2007-48826

"The breadth of material the authors cover in this volume is impressive. They discuss energy (kenetic and potential), forces (friction, gravity, electricity, and magnetism), simple machines (lever, wheel, pulley, ramp, and wedge), motion in fluids, and Newton's laws of motion. . . . [This offers] simple writing, many colorful pictures, and lots of examples." Sci Books Films

Includes glossary and bibliographical references

Spilsbury, Richard, 1963-

What are forces and motion? exploring science with hands-on activities; [by] Richard and Louise Spilsbury. Enslow Publishers 2008 32p il (In touch with basic science) lib bdg $22.60

Grades: 3 4 5   531

1. Force and energy 2. Motion 3. Science—Experiments

ISBN 978-0-7660-3095-4 (lib bdg); 0-7660-3095-4 (lib bdg)   LC 2007024517

This book "introduces children to forces through a simple introduction to Newton's three laws, simple machines, the relationship of energy and motion through potential and kinetic energy, buoyant forces, and structural forces. . . . This volume is an excellent resource for any child who is interested in science." Sci Books Films

Includes glossary and bibliographical references

Sullivan, Navin

Speed. Marshall Cavendish Benchmark 2007 48p il (Measure up!) lib bdg $20.90

Grades: 4 5 6 7   531

1. Speed 2. Measurement

ISBN 978-0-7614-2325-6 (lib bdg); 0-7614-2325-7 (lib bdg)

"Have you ever wondered how we measure different speeds? How do we know how fast an airplane travels or how much speed a shuttle needs to travel to outer space? What does speed have to do with satellites? How does the speed of light compare with the speed of sound? *Speed* answers these questions and explores the history of humankind's discoveries about speed." Publisher's note

Includes glossary and bibliographical references

Weight. Marshall Cavendish Benchmark 2007 48p il (Measure up!) lib bdg $20.90

Grades: 4 5 6 7   531

1. Gravity 2. Weights and measures

ISBN 978-0-7614-2324-9 (lib bdg); 0-7614-2324-9 (lib bdg)

This "explains concepts such as how gravity affects weight on Earth and in space, the relationship between volume and density, and why some objects float better than others." Publisher's note

Sullivan, Navin—*Continued*

"Examples using familiar objects and excellent full-color graphics help to bring concepts to life." SLJ

Includes glossary and bibliographical references

VanCleave, Janice Pratt

Janice VanCleave's energy for every kid; [by] Janice VanCleave. J. Wiley & Sons 2006 221p il (Science for every kid series) pa $12.95

Grades: 4 5 6 7   **531**

1. Force and energy 2. Energy resources 3. Science projects 4. Science—Experiments

ISBN 978-0-471-33099-8 (pa); 0-471-33099-X (pa)
LC 2004-27114

Presents problems and experiments that introduce the different types of energy

532   Fluid mechanics Liquid mechanics

Cobb, Vicki, 1938-

I get wet; illustrated by Julia Gorton. HarperCollins Pubs. 2002 unp il $15.99; lib bdg $17.89

Grades: K 1 2   **532**

1. Water 2. Science—Experiments

ISBN 0-688-17838-3; 0-688-17839-1 (lib bdg)
LC 00-49882

In this book "a boy learns some of the properties of water through pouring it into different containers, observing it drip and flow, and trying to absorb it with waxed paper and paper toweling." Booklist

"The simple yet well-conceived activities engage children in more than just observations—the questions and explanations are constructed to help young kids draw conclusions from their observations. Remarkably, all this is accomplished in a child-friendly, straightforward text. The illustrations are bright and energetic." Horn Book

Farndon, John

Water. Benchmark Bks. 2001 32p il (Science experiments) lib bdg $16.95

Grades: 3 4 5 6   **532**

1. Water 2. Science—Experiments

ISBN 0-7614-1087-2   LC 00-60187

A collection of experiments exploring the properties of water, including ice, water, and steam, floating and sinking, heavy water, and surface tension

Includes glossary

Meiani, Antonella

Water. Lerner Publs. 2003 40p il (Experimenting with science) lib bdg $23.93

Grades: 4 5 6 7   **532**

1. Water 2. Science—Experiments

ISBN 0-8225-0083-3   LC 2001-50773

Contents: The force of water; To float or not to float?; The transformation of water; Water solutions; The force of water; Fact finder; Metric conversion chart

Describes experiments with water which answer such questions as "Why are water droplets round?" and "Why do some things, like salt, dissolve in water and other things, like fish, don't?"

This offers "straightforward, well-designed experiments. . . . Numerous clear diagrams, some photos, and occasional historical sidebars extend this material, which is notable for its substance." Horn Book Guide

Includes glossary and bibliographical references

Parker, Steve

The science of water; projects with experiments with water and power; [by] Steve Parker. Heinemann Library 2005 32p il (Tabletop scientist) lib bdg $29.29; pa $7.85

Grades: 4 5 6 7   **532**

1. Water 2. Science—Experiments

ISBN 1-4034-7282-3 (lib bdg); 1-4034-7289-0 (pa)
LC 2005007027

This "has experiments on the water cycle, water density, water as a solvent, surface tension, capillary action, buoyancy, water power, and water propulsion. . . . The colorful illustrations, organization, and ease of use of [this title makes it an] excellent [addition]." SLJ

Includes glossary

Simon, Seymour, 1931-

Let's try it out in the water; by Seymour Simon and Nicole Fauteux; illustrated by Doug Cushman. Simon & Schuster Bks. for Young Readers 2000 unp il $15

Grades: K 1 2   **532**

1. Water 2. Science—Experiments

ISBN 0-689-82919-1   LC 99-20371

Presents simple activities and experiments that demonstrate buoyancy by observing why some things sink and others float in water

This does "a great job of using hands-on activities in daily life to explain basic science to young children. . . . The writers include helpful information for adults about how to teach the science as an active part of the child's ordinary experience. The exuberant, colorful pictures add to the fun." Booklist

533   Pneumatics (Gas mechanics)

Meiani, Antonella

Air. Lerner Publs. 2003 40p il (Experimenting with science) lib bdg $23.93

Grades: 4 5 6 7   **533**

1. Air 2. Science—Experiments

ISBN 0-8225-0082-5   LC 2001-37730

Explains the properties of air through experiments which feature such topics as what air is, how much force wind has, what shape is best for flying, and how sound travels

This offers "straightforward, well-designed experiments. . . . Numerous clear diagrams, some photos, and occasional historical sidebars extend this material, which is notable for its substance." Horn Book Guide

Includes glossary and bibliographical references

Parker, Steve

The science of air; projects and experiments on air and flight; [by] Steve Parker. Heinemann Library 2005 32p il (Tabletop scientist) lib bdg $29.29; pa $7.85

Grades: 4 5 6 7   **533**

1. Air 2. Science—Experiments

ISBN 1-4034-7280-7 (lib bdg); 1-4034-7287-4 (pa)

LC 2005006940

"The 12 experiments in [this] book have a materials list and step-by-step photo instructions. Boxed text explains the scientific ideas in each project and the processes that make it work, and offer ideas for further experimentation. The activities are followed by a history of the topic. . . . [This] title introduces air movement, air pressure, wind resistance, lift, flight, and energy from the wind. . . . The colorful illustrations, organization, and ease of use [this title makes it an] excellent [addition]." SLJ

Includes glossary

534   Sound and related vibrations

Farndon, John

Sound and hearing. Benchmark Bks. 2001 32p il (Science experiments) lib bdg $16.95

Grades: 3 4 5 6   **534**

1. Sound 2. Hearing 3. Science—Experiments

ISBN 0-7614-1091-0   LC 99-89262

A collection of experiments that explore the nature of sound and how we hear it. Activities include making a string telephone, a megaphone, and a bottle organ

Includes glossary

Gardner, Robert, 1929-

Jazzy science projects with sound and music; [by] Robert Gardner. Enslow Publishers 2006 48p il (Fantastic physical science experiments) lib bdg $23.93

Grades: 4 5 6   **534**

1. Sound 2. Science—Experiments

ISBN 0-7660-2588-8   LC 2005018729

This offers science experiments illustrating such concepts as pitch, vibration, how sound travels and how it is perceived

Includes glossary and bibliographical references

Guillain, Charlotte

Different sounds. Heinemann Library 2009 24p il (Sounds all around us) lib bdg $20.71; pa $5.99

Grades: PreK K 1   **534**

1. Sound 2. Sound waves

ISBN 978-1-4329-3202-2 (lib bdg); 1-4329-3202-0 (lib bdg); 978-1-4329-3208-4 (pa); 1-4329-3208-X (pa)

LC 2008-51740

This book "introduces the basics of sound through vibrant photographs, large text, and simple sentences. . . . [A] great introduction[s] and worthy addition[s]." SLJ

Includes glossary and bibliographical references

Making sounds. Heinemann Library 2008 24p il (Sounds all around us) lib bdg $20.71; pa $5.99

Grades: PreK K 1   **534**

1. Sound

ISBN 978-1-4329-3200-8 (lib bdg); 1-4329-3200-4 (lib bdg); 978-1-4329-3206-0 (pa); 1-4329-3206-3 (pa)

LC 2008-51682

This book "introduces the basics of sound through vibrant photographs, large text, and simple sentences. . . . [A] great introduction[s] and worthy addition[s]." SLJ

Includes glossary and bibliographical references

What is sound? Heinemann Library 2009 24p il (Sounds all around us) lib bdg $20.71; pa $5.99

Grades: PreK K 1   **534**

1. Sounds 2. Sound waves

ISBN 978-1-4329-3199-5 (lib bdg); 1-4329-3199-7 (lib bdg); 978-1-4329-3205-3 (pa); 1-4329-3205-5 (pa)

LC 2008-51681

This describes vibrations, sound waves, and echoes. This book "introduces the basics of sound through vibrant photographs, large text, and simple sentences. . . . [A] great introduction[s] and worthy addition[s]." SLJ

Inlcudes glossary

Oxlade, Chris

Experiments with sound; explaining sound. Heinemann Library 2009 48p il (Do it yourself) $22; pa $8.99

Grades: 3 4 5 6   **534**

1. Sound 2. Science—Experiments

ISBN 978-1-4329-2311-2; 978-1-4329-2318-1 (pa)

LC 2008034938

This explains the science of sound and includes such experiments as making a pan flute from straws and a homemade record player

This "would make an ideal supplement to science classes. A modular layout and dynamic photos keep things moving, while the experiments . . . feature lists of readily available materials, the steps required to pull off the magic, and warnings when adult supervision is required." Booklist

Includes bibliographical references

Parker, Steve

The science of sound; projects with experiments with music and sound waves; [by] Steve Parker. Heinemann Library 2005 32p il (Tabletop scientist) lib bdg $29.29; pa $7.85

Grades: 4 5 6 7   **534**

1. Sound 2. Music 3. Science—Experiments

ISBN 1-4034-7281-5 (lib bdg); 1-4034-7288-2 (pa)

LC 2005006960

This book of experiments "covers sound waves as they travel through air and underwater, high and low sounds, how we hear, the Doppler effect, soundproofing, and recorded sound. . . . The colorful illustrations, organization, and ease of use of [this title makes it an] excellent [addition]." SLJ

Includes glossary

Spilsbury, Richard, 1963-

What is sound? exploring science with hands-on activities; [by] Richard and Louise Spilsbury. Enslow Publishers 2008 32p il (In touch with basic science) lib bdg $22.60

Grades: 3 4 5   **534**
   1. Sound 2. Sound waves 3. Science—Experiments
   ISBN 978-0-7660-3098-5 (lib bdg); 0-7660-3098-9 (lib bdg)   LC 2007024520

This book "covers topics about sound, such as reflecting waves, the speed of sound, resonance, standing waves, beats, noise, and the sounds of strings. Each of seven hands-on activities for children is fully illustrated with photos of children doing the experiment. . . . This book would appeal to elementary children." Sci Books Films

Includes glossary and bibliographical references

535 Light and infrared and ultraviolet phenomena

Branley, Franklyn Mansfield, 1915-2002

Day light, night light; where light comes from; by Franklyn M. Branley; illustrated by Stacey Schuett. newly il ed. HarperCollins Pubs. 1998 32p col il (Let's-read-and-find-out science) hardcover o.p. pa $4.95 *

Grades: K 1 2 3   **535**
   1. Light
   ISBN 0-06-027294-5; 0-06-027295-3 (lib bdg); 0-06-445171-2 (pa)   LC 96-33316

First published 1975 with title: Light and darkness

Discusses the properties of light, particularly its source in heat

"This is a beautifully illustrated children's book about a basic concept in science. The pictures add to the clearly written text." Sci Books Films

Bulla, Clyde Robert, 1914-2007

What makes a shadow? illustrated by June Otani. rev ed. HarperCollins Pubs. 1994 32p il (Let's-read-and-find-out science) lib bdg $15.89

Grades: K 1   **535**
   1. Shades and shadows
   ISBN 0-06-022916-0   LC 92-36350

A revised and newly illustrated edition of the title first published 1962 by Crowell

"Using short sentences and developmentally appropriate language, the author explains how shadows are formed, gives numerous examples of shadows, and describes how to make shadow pictures on the wall. Each page is illustrated with bright, colorful drawings, and the gender and cultural representation is excellent." Sci Books Films

Burnie, David

Light; written by David Burnie. DK Pub. 1999 64p il (DK eyewitness books) $15.99

Grades: 5 6 7 8   **535**
   1. Light
   ISBN 978-0-7894-4885-9; 0-7894-4885-8

A guide to the origins, principles, and historical study of light.

Cobb, Vicki, 1938-

I see myself; illustrated by Julia Gorton. HarperCollins Pubs. 2002 unp il (Science play) $15.99; lib bdg $17.89

Grades: K 1 2   **535**
   1. Optics 2. Light
   ISBN 0-688-17836-7; 0-688-17837-5 (lib bdg)   LC 00-57220

This book "features a girl who finds out a little about vision, light, and reflection by playing with a mirror, a flashlight, and a bouncing ball." Booklist

"The simple yet well-conceived activities engage children in more than just observations—the questions and explanations are constructed to help young kids draw conclusions from their observations. Remarkably, all this is accomplished in a child-friendly, straightforward text. The illustrations are bright and energetic." Horn Book

Farndon, John

Light and optics. Benchmark Bks. 2000 32p il (Science experiments) lib bdg $16.95

Grades: 3 4 5 6   **535**
   1. Light 2. Optics 3. Science—Experiments
   ISBN 0-7614-1090-2   LC 99-89898

A collection of experiments that explore the nature of light and how it is measured and perceived. Activities include making a shadow theater, a periscope, a microscope, a telescope, and a pinhole camera

Includes glossary

Gardner, Robert, 1929-

Dazzling science projects with light and color. Enslow Elementary 2006 48p il (Fantasic physical science experiments) lib bdg $23.93

Grades: 4 5 6   **535**
   1. Light 2. Color 3. Science—Experiments
   ISBN 0-7660-2587-X   LC 2005-09498

This "title is devoted to light and seeing, mixing colors, and more. Each of 10 chapters includes an experiment, followed by an explanation of why it works, and offers ideas for devising projects to present at a science fair. . . . Large colorful, cartoonlike drawings complement the [text]. . . . [This offers] solid information." SLJ

Includes glossary and bibliographical references

Lauw, Darlene

Light; [by Darlene Lauw & Lim Cheng Puay; series illustrator, Roy Chan Yoon Loy] Crabtree 2002 31p il (Science alive!) $25.27; pa $7.95

Grades: 3 4 5 6   **535**
   1. Light 2. Optics 3. Science—Experiments
   ISBN 0-7787-0560-9; 0-7787-0606-0 (pa)   LC 2001-42423

Lauw, Darlene—*Continued*

Presents activities that demonstrate how light works in our everyday lives. History boxes feature the scientists who made significant discoveries in the field of light

This book explains its subject matter "in a colorful and easy to understand format. . . . All experiments use easily obtainable parts and in some cases actual household items." Sci Books Films

Includes glossary

Meiani, Antonella

Light. Lerner Publs. 2003 40p il (Experimenting with science) lib bdg $23.93

Grades: 4 5 6 7   **535**

1. Light 2. Science—Experiments

ISBN 0-8225-0084-1   LC 2001-38947

Experiments with light explain shadows and colors, and demonstrate such concepts as reflection and refraction

This offers "straightforward, well-designed experiments. . . . Numerous clear diagrams, some photos, and occasional historical sidebars extend this material, which is notable for its substance." Horn Book Guide

Includes glossary and bibliographical references

Spilsbury, Richard, 1963-

What is light? exploring science with hands-on activities; [by] Richard and Louise Spilsbury. Enslow Publishers 2008 32p il (In touch with basic science) lib bdg $22.60

Grades: 3 4 5   **535**

1. Light 2. Optics 3. Science—Experiments

ISBN 978-0-7660-3097-8 (lib bdg); 0-7660-3097-0 (lib bdg)   LC 2007024550

This book "introduces the reader to concepts such as reflection, refraction, taking pictures, using lenses, and light waves—specifically as manifested in rainbows and spectrometers. . . . What makes this volume so useful is that children are learning while they are doing the experiments. The graphics are excellent." Sci Books Films

Includes glossary and bibliographical references

535.6 Color

Barton, Chris

The Day-Glo brothers; the true story of Bob and Joe Switzer's bright ideas and brand-new colors; illustrated by Tony Persiani. Charlesbridge 2009 unp il $18.95 *

Grades: K 1 2 3   **535.6**

1. Switzer, Bob, 1914-1997 2. Switzer, Joe, d. 1973 3. Fluorescence 4. Color 5. Paint

ISBN 978-1-57091-673-1; 1-57091-673-X

    LC 2008-26959

ALA ALSC Siebert Medal Honor Book (2010)

"Still in their teens in 1933, brothers Bob and Joe Switzer began experimenting with fluorescent colors and trying to create paints that would glow in the dark. . . . After years of experimentation, they succeeded in creating paints that glowed in daylight as well as ultraviolet light. . . . In stylized, digital artwork with a retro feel,

Persiani illustrates early scenes of the Switzers' life in black, white, and shades of gray, then gradually introduces colors. . . . Organizing his material well and writing with a sure sense of what will interest children, Barton creates a picture book that celebrates ingenuity and invention." Booklist

Color; illustrations and photos by Ella Doran, David Goodman & Zoe Miller. Abrams 2006 unp il $19.95

Grades: K 1 2 3   **535.6**

1. Color

ISBN 978-1-85437-697-8; 1-85437-697-7

"This riotous and bold concept book presents the basic ideas about color with simple text and clear, inviting images. . . . Arty photo collages [introduce] each of the three primary colors. . . . [The book introduces] the idea of color mixing, followed by spreads for each of the secondary colors. . . . Black and white provide an introduction to the concepts of shading and tinting. The language of color, including word associations (e.g., blue: cool, calm, sad), and different shades printed in their appropriate hues are included as are some craft activities and a few trompe l'oeils." SLJ

Farndon, John

Color. Benchmark Bks. 2000 32p il (Science experiments) lib bdg $16.95

Grades: 3 4 5 6   **535.6**

1. Color 2. Science—Experiments

ISBN 0-7614-1092-9   LC 99-86994

A collection of experiments that explore the nature of color and how it is created and perceived

"Activities include creating a spectrum using a bottle of water and a piece of black cardboard, and making a color wheel. . . . The clearly illustrated, step-by-step directions for the science activities will make this a useful addition to many libraries." Booklist

Includes glossary

Houblon, Marie

A world of colors; seeing colors in a new way. National Geographic 2009 43p il $16.95; lib bdg $25.90

Grades: K 1 2 3   **535.6**

1. Color

ISBN 978-1-4263-0556-6; 1-4263-0556-7; 978-1-4263-0559-7 (lib bdg); 1-4263-0559-1 (lib bdg)

Original French edition, 2004

"This sophisticated book shows the uses of color and encourages children to find examples in their own environments. Most hues are allotted two spreads. The first one features a solid, saturated page with the color's name in a contrasting shade, facing a closeup photograph framed in black. The second includes two or three additional photos with engaging commentary or questions. . . . The images are unexpected and captivating." SLJ

536   Heat

Gardner, Robert, 1929-
Easy genius science projects with temperature and heat; great experiments and ideas; by Robert Gardner and Eric Kemer. Enslow Publishers 2009 128p il (Easy genius science projects) lib bdg $31.93
Grades: 5 6 7 8   **536**
   1. Temperature 2. Heat 3. Science projects 4. Science—Experiments
   ISBN 978-0-7660-2939-2 (lib bdg); 0-7660-2939-5 (lib bdg)   LC 2008-4675
"Presents several science experiments and science project ideas dealing with temperature and heat." Publisher's note
Includes glossary and bibliographical references

Really hot science projects with temperature; how hot is it? how cold is it? Enslow Pubs. 2003 48p il (Sensational science experiments) lib bdg $18.95
Grades: 3 4 5 6   **536**
   1. Temperature 2. Heat 3. Cold 4. Science—Experiments 5. Science projects
   ISBN 0-7660-2015-0   LC 2002-153849
Contents: Introduction; Thermometer liquid rises and falls; Go on a temperature hunt; Moving liquids by temperature difference; What is your temperature?; Temperature and evaporation; Temperatures all day long!; Temperatures above and below ground; Sun, color, and temperature; Sun and seasonal temperatures; Earth, sun, and temperature; Diffusion and temperature; Temperature and chemistry; Temperature and speed of a chemical reaction; How cold can you make water ice?; Temperature of melting ice or snow; Make your own thermometer; Measuring dew point; Temperature and the greenhouse effect
"Includes such experiments as observing diffusion in hot and cold water and measuring the dew point. . . . Gardner's clear, informal explanations are echoed in LaBaff's colorful illustrations." Booklist
Includes glossary and bibliographical references

Sizzling science projects with heat and energy; [by] Robert Gardner. Enslow Elementary 2006 48p il (Fantastic physical science experiments) $23.93
Grades: 4 5 6   **536**
   1. Heat 2. Force and energy 3. Science—Experiments
   ISBN 0-7660-2586-1   LC 2005033755
This offers science experiments concerning heat and temperature, kinetic energy, elastic potential energy, light and electric energy, insulation, and ice.
Includes glossary and bibliographical references

Sullivan, Navin
Temperature; [by] Navin Sullivan. Marshall Cavendish Benchmark 2007 48p il (Measure up!) lib bdg $20.90
Grades: 4 5 6 7   **536**
   1. Heat 2. Thermometers 3. Temperature
   ISBN 978-0-7614-2322-5 (lib bdg); 0-7614-2322-2 (lib bdg)   LC 2006011981

This "explains how molecules react to heat, how different types of thermometers measure heat energy, and shows the immense impact temperature has on every part of our lives." Publisher's note
This is "engaging and informative. . . . The excellent blend of photographs, charts, and diagrams complements the [text]." SLJ
Includes glossary and bibliographical references

537   Electricity and electronics

Berger, Melvin, 1927-
Switch on, switch off; illustrated by Carolyn Croll. Crowell 1989 32p il (Let's-read-and-find-out science book) hardcover o.p. pa $4.95
Grades: K 1 2 3   **537**
   1. Electricity
   ISBN 0-690-04786-X (lib bdg); 0-06-445097-X (pa)   LC 88-17638
"This book presents rudimentary exploration of electricity and how electrical current flows to the light switch in a child's room. Follow the current from the generator to a power plant to the switch on the wall. Includes instructions for a simple generator. A good, first look at a topic that mystifies young scientists." Sci Child

Farndon, John
Electricity. Benchmark Bks. 2001 32p il (Science experiments) lib bdg $16.95
Grades: 3 4 5 6   **537**
   1. Electricity 2. Science—Experiments
   ISBN 0-7614-1086-4   LC 00-39752
A collection of activities that explore electricity "discussing charges, circuits, conductors, and insulators. Activities include creating a Xerox effect and making an electroscope." SLJ
Includes glossary

Gardner, Robert, 1929-
Easy genius science projects with electricity and magnetism; great experiments and ideas. Enslow Publishers 2009 128p il (Easy genius science projects) lib bdg $31.93
Grades: 5 6 7 8   **537**
   1. Electricity 2. Magnetism 3. Science projects 4. Science—Experiments
   ISBN 978-0-7660-2923-1 (lib bdg); 0-7660-2923-9 (lib bdg)   LC 2007-38470
"Science projects and experiments about electricity and magnetism." Publisher's note
Includes glossary and bibliographical references

Energizing science projects with electricity and magnetism; [by] Robert Gardner. Enslow Elementary 2006 48p il (Fantastic physical science experiments) lib bdg $23.93
Grades: 4 5 6   **537**
   1. Electricity 2. Magnetism 3. Science—Experiments
   ISBN 0-7660-2584-5   LC 2005018730
This offers science experiments concerning electric charges, magnetism and compasses, batteries, electric bulbs, and wires, and electromagnets
Includes glossary and bibliographical references

Meiani, Antonella

Electricity. Lerner Publs. 2003 40p il (Experimenting with science) lib bdg $23.93

Grades: 4 5 6 7   537

1. Electricity 2. Science—Experiments

ISBN 0-8225-0086-8   LC 2001-50517

Experiments and text illustrate characteristics of static electricity, circuits and switches, and electrical currents

This offers "straightforward, well-designed experiments. . . . Numerous clear diagrams, some photos, and occasional historical sidebars extend this material, which is notable for its substance." Horn Book Guide

Includes glossary and bibliographical references

Parker, Steve

Electricity; written by Steve Parker. rev ed. DK Pub. 2005 64p il (DK eyewitness books) $15.99

Grades: 4 5 6 7   537

1. Electricity

ISBN 0-7566-1388-4

First published 1992

Discusses the properties of electricity and describes how it is made and used

Spilsbury, Richard, 1963-

What is electricity and magnetism? exploring science with hands-on activities; [by] Richard and Louise Spilsbury. Enslow Elementary 2008 32p il (In touch with basic science) lib bdg $22.60

Grades: 3 4 5   537

1. Electricity 2. Magnetism 3. Science—Experiments

ISBN 978-0-7660-3096-1 (lib bdg); 0-7660-3096-2 (lib bdg)   LC 2007024518

This book "covers topics such as making and storing electricity, magnetic fields, electromagnets, and motors. Each chapter focuses on activities related to these topics. . . . There are more than enough hands-on activities to provide a child with a solid basic understanding of the relationship between magnetism and electricity." Sci Books Films

Includes glossary and bibliographical references

VanCleave, Janice Pratt

Janice VanCleave's electricity; mind-boggling experiments you can turn into science fair projects; [by] Janice VanCleave. Wiley 1994 89p il $10.95

Grades: 4 5 6 7   537

1. Electricity 2. Science projects 3. Science—Experiments

ISBN 0-471-31010-7   LC 93-40913

"The experiments move from the simple, which do not require the use of batteries, to those that require small batteries, sizes AA, AAA, C, or D. An appendix shows how to make strips of aluminum foil that can be used to form the electrical circuits that are part of some of the experiments. By encouraging students to move beyond the basic problems (with adult supervision), the author encourages them to be creative in designing science fair projects." Booklist

Includes glossary

Woodford, Chris, 1943-

Electricity; [by] Chris Woodford. Blackbirch Press 2004 40p il (Routes of science) hardcover o.p. pa $18.70

Grades: 5 6 7 8   537

1. Electricity

ISBN 1-4103-0165-6; 1-4103-0304-7 (pa)
                                LC 2004-301790

Contents: The mysteries of electric fluid; From frogs' legs to batteries; Electricity meets magnetism; The power of electricity; Electricity makes waves; The electronic age; Into the future

"This book traces the history of electrical discovery from ancient Greek experiments with static electricity to Benjamin Franklin's famous kite experiment to today's work with superconductivity." Publisher's note

This "volume contains color photographs, illustrations, and diagrams to help explain the important concepts and discoveries. [This volume] would be [an] excellent [supplement] to the science curriculum." SLJ

Includes glossary and bibliographical references

538   Magnetism

Branley, Franklyn Mansfield, 1915-2002

What makes a magnet? by Franklyn M. Branley; illustrated by True Kelley. HarperCollins Pubs. 1996 31p il (Let's-read-and-find-out science) hardcover o.p. pa $4.95

Grades: K 1 2 3   538

1. Magnets

ISBN 0-06-026441-1; 0-06-445148-8 (pa)
                                LC 95-32181

Describes how magnets work and includes instructions for making a magnet and a compass

"Kelley's happy line drawings incorporate a humorous mouse to add safety warnings and goofy side comments. The clear diagrams and lucid explanations are both informative and engaging." Horn Book

Farndon, John

Magnetism. Benchmark Bks. 2001 32p il (Science experiments) lib bdg $16.95

Grades: 3 4 5 6   538

1. Magnetism 2. Science—Experiments

ISBN 0-7614-1343-X   LC 2001-25168

A collection of activities that explore magnetism, discussing magnetic materials, magnetic poles, electricity and magnetism, Earth's magnetism, and magnetism in space

Includes glossary

Meiani, Antonella

Magnetism. Lerner Publs. 2003 40p il (Experimenting with science) lib bdg $23.93

Grades: 4 5 6 7   538

1. Magnetism 2. Science—Experiments

ISBN 0-8225-0085-X   LC 2001-50464

Describes a variety of experiments that explore the world of magnets and magnetism, arranged in the categories "Magnets," "Magnetic Poles," "Magnetic Force," and

Meiani, Antonella—Continued
"Magnetism and Electricity"

This offers "straightforward, well-designed experiments. . . . Numerous clear diagrams, some photos, and occasional historical sidebars extend this material, which is notable for its substance." Horn Book Guide

Includes glossary and bibliographical references

539.7   Atomic and nuclear physics

Cregan, Elizabeth R.
The atom. Compass Point Books 2009 40p il (Mission: science) lib bdg $26.60

Grades: 4 5 6   **539.7**
   1. Atoms 2. Atomic theory 3. Nuclear energy
   ISBN 978-0-7565-3953-5 (lib bdg); 0-7565-3953-6 (lib bdg)   LC 2008007724

"Cregan discusses the structure of the atom, key scientists, cathode rays and electrons, radioactivity, and atom smashers. . . . The [book has an] open [layout] and large, easy-to-read type. . . . Large eye-catching and colorful photographs and illustrations appear on every page. The [book] includes a simple activity." SLJ

Includes glossary and bibliographical references

Jerome, Kate Boehm
Atomic universe; the quest to discover radioactivity; by Kate Boehm Jerome. National Geographic 2006 59p il (Science quest) $17.95; lib bdg $25.90

Grades: 5 6 7 8   **539.7**
   1. Nuclear physics 2. Radioactivity
   ISBN 0-7922-5543-7; 0-7922-5544-5 (lib bdg)
       LC 2006001316

This "traces the path to the discovery of radioactivity and places this major scientific breakthrough in the context of history." Publisher's note

The text offers "key concepts in a pleasing and readable format that would appeal to reluctant readers." SLJ

Includes glossary and bibliographical references

540   Chemistry

Baxter, Roberta, 1952-
Chemical reaction. Kidhaven Press 2005 48p il (Kidhaven science library) $27

Grades: 4 5 6 7   **540**
   1. Chemistry
   ISBN 0-7377-2072-7

"Baxter defines her subject and describes many different types of reactions, including acid-base reactions, oxidation, and photosynthesis. The explanations are clear and succinct. The final chapter presents some potential uses for chemical reactions, citing the development of molecular computers." SLJ

Includes glossary and bibliographical references

Juettner, Bonnie, 1968-
Molecules. Kidhaven Press 2005 48p il (Kidhaven science library) $27

Grades: 4 5 6 7   **540**
   1. Molecules 2. Chemistry
   ISBN 0-7377-2076-X

"Juettner gives an overview of the building blocks of elements and compounds, including atoms, molecules, and the various states of matter, and describes their characteristics. The last chapter offers information on some extreme materials, such as plasma and the recently discovered Bose-Einstein condensates (BEC)." SLJ

Newmark, Ann
Chemistry; written by Ann Newmark. rev ed. DK Pub. 2005 72p il (DK eyewitness books) $15.99

Grades: 4 5 6 7   **540**
   1. Chemistry
   ISBN 0-7566-1385-X
   First published 1993

Explores the world of chemical reactions and shows the role that chemistry plays in our world.

Townsend, John, 1955-
Crazy chemistry. Raintree 2007 56p il (Weird history of science) lib bdg $23; pa $9.49

Grades: 4 5 6 7   **540**
   1. Chemistry
   ISBN   978-1-4109-2378-3   (lib   bdg);
   978-1-4109-2383-7 (pa)   LC 2006-07031

"This book shows how chemists through the ages risked their lives with poison gases, lethal liquids and dangerous reactions. Read how they tried to turn ordinary metals into gold, how urine was made into a glow-in-the-dark explosive, and how chemistry can catch murderers." Publisher's note

"This is an unusual book that gets its message across very effectively." Sci Books Films

Includes bibliographical references

Van Gorp, Lynn
Elements. Compass Point Books 2009 40p il (Mission: science) lib bdg $26.60

Grades: 4 5 6   **540**
   1. Chemical elements
   ISBN 978-0-7565-3951-1 (lib bdg); 0-7565-3951-X (lib bdg)   LC 2008007284

"Van Gorp provides an overview of matter and the elements and how the latter combine to form compounds; ionic and covalent bonds; the periodic table of the elements; reactions; and mixtures and solutions. The [book has an] open [layout] and large, easy-to-read type. . . . Large eye-catching and colorful photographs and illustrations appear on every page. . . . The [book] includes a simple activity." SLJ

Includes glossary and bibliographical references

Woodford, Chris, 1943-
Atoms and molecules; [by] Chris Woodford [and] Martin Clowes. Blackbirch Press 2004 40p il (Routes of science) hardcover o.p. pa $18.70 *
Grades: 5 6 7 8 **540**
1. Atoms 2. Molecules
ISBN 1-4103-0295-4; 1-4103-0324-1 (pa)
Contents: Philosophers and alchemists; Discovering the elements; The periodic table; Molecules, matter, and motion; Inside the atom; Into the future
"This book traces the history of atomic discovery from ancient Greek theories about four basic elements to today's research into nanotechnology." Publisher's note
This "volume contains color photographs, illustrations, and diagrams to help explain the important concepts and discoveries. [This] up-to-date [volume] would be [an] excellent [supplement] to the science curriculum." SLJ

540.7 Chemistry—Education and related topics

Gardner, Robert, 1929-
Ace your chemistry science project; great science fair ideas; [by] Robert Gardner, Salvatore Tocci, and Kenneth G. Rainis. Enslow Publishers 2009 112p il (Ace your science project) lib bdg $31.93
Grades: 5 6 7 8 **540.7**
1. Chemistry 2. Science projects 3. Science—Experiments
ISBN 978-0-7660-3227-9 (lib bdg); 0-7660-3227-2 (lib bdg) LC 2008-30800
"Presents several science projects and science project ideas about chemistry." Publisher's note
Includes bibliographical references

Ace your science project using chemistry magic and toys; great science fair ideas. Enslow Publishers 2009 128p il (Ace your science project) lib bdg $31.93
Grades: 5 6 7 8 **540.7**
1. Chemistry 2. Toys 3. Science projects 4. Science—Experiments
ISBN 978-0-7660-3226-2 (lib bdg); 0-7660-3226-4 (lib bdg) LC 2008-4685
"Presents several fun science experiments and project ideas using toys and chemistry magic." Publisher's note
"Dozens of . . . science activities are presented with background information, step-by-step instructions, and suggestions for extending to the science fair level. . . . Color illustrations and important safety information are included." Horn Book Guide
Includes bibliographical references

Easy genius science projects with chemistry; great experiments and ideas. Enslow Publishers 2009 112p il (Easy genius science projects) lib bdg $31.93
Grades: 5 6 7 8 **540.7**
1. Chemistry 2. Science—Experiments 3. Science projects
ISBN 978-0-7660-2925-5 (lib bdg); 0-7660-2925-5 (lib bdg) LC 2007-38469

This book offers science projects and experiments about chemistry divided into the following chapters: atoms, molecules, elements, and compounds; chemical reactions; oxygen and oxidation; separating and testing substances
"Illustrations are bright and useful in explaining the techniques presented. . . . An excellent resource." Sci Books Films
Includes glossary and bibliographical references

Meiani, Antonella
Chemistry. Lerner Publs. 2003 40p il (Experimenting with science) lib bdg $23.93
Grades: 4 5 6 7 **540.7**
1. Chemistry 2. Science—Experiments
ISBN 0-8225-0087-6 LC 2001-50503
Uses experiments to explore such topics as how heat changes a substance, the purpose of chemical analysis, and how the human stomach digests food
"This book makes chemistry both accessible and exciting." Sci Books Films
Includes glossary and bibliographical references

Rhatigan, Joe
Cool chemistry concoctions; 50 formulas that fizz, foam, splatter & ooze; [by] Joe Rhatigan & Veronika Gunter; illustrated by Tom LaBaff. Lark Books 2005 80p il hardcover o.p. pa $7.95
Grades: 3 4 5 6 **540.7**
1. Chemistry 2. Science—Experiments
ISBN 1-57990-620-6; 1-57990-882-9 (pa)
LC 2004-13287
This describes such experiments as how to make slime, volcanoes, stalactites, water bombs, and shrunken heads (using apples and Epsom salts)
"This lively book offers an engaging introduction to science experiments. The projects . . . are simple and require household materials. . . . The zany cartoon illustrations are the perfect accompaniment to the text, which is fun and informative." SLJ

541 Physical chemistry

Ballard, Carol
Mixtures and solutions. Raintree 2010 48p il (Sci-hi: physical science) lib bdg $22; pa $8.99
Grades: 5 6 7 8 **541**
1. Molecules 2. Chemistry
ISBN 978-1-4109-3376-8 (lib bdg); 1-4109-3376-8 (lib bdg); 978-1-4109-3381-2 (pa); 1-4109-3381-4 (pa)
LC 2009-13452
This describes "different types of mixtures, how solutions can be made, and how different solvents can be used." Publisher's note
A "compelling read for both browsers and science buffs. . . . Information is clearly presented and flows smoothly. . . . A treasure trove of information." SLJ
Includes glossary and bibliographical references

Oxlade, Chris

Mixing and separating. Heinemann Library 2009 32p il (Changing materials) lib bdg $25.36; pa $7.99

Grades: K 1 2   **541**

1. Materials

ISBN 978-1-4329-3274-9 (lib bdg); 1-4329-3274-8 (lib bdg); 978-1-4329-3279-4 (pa); 1-4329-3279-9 (pa)

LC 2008-55124

"Discusses the ideas of mixtures, materials that combine to form a new marterial, and materials that cannot be combined. A few simple activities provide opportunities to experiment. The color photographs are engaging." SLJ

Includes glossary and bibliographical references

546   Inorganic chemistry

Dingle, Adrian

The periodic table; elements with style! [created by Simon Basher; written by Adrian Dingle] Kingfisher 2007 128p il pa $8.95

Grades: 4 5 6 7   **546**

1. Chemical elements

ISBN 978-0-7534-6085-6 (pa); 0-7534-6085-8 (pa)

LC 2006022515

"After a brief introduction to Mendeleev's famous table and a spread on the chart-topping loner, hydrogen, Dingle presents the elements by group. . . . Data on featured elements includes symbol, atomic number and weight, color, standard state, classification, density, boiling and melting points, . . . a diagram of the position in the periodic table, a full-page original anime-styled icon, . . . and descriptive paragraphs that rise from informative all the way to entertaining." Bull Cent Child Books

The **Elements**. Benchmark Bks. 1999-2007 40v il ea $25.64

Grades: 5 6 7 8   **546**

1. Chemical elements

Contents: Aluminum, by J. Farndon; Arsenic, by C. Cooper; Boron, by R. Beatty; Bromine, by Krista West; Cadmium, by Allan Cobb; Calcium, by J. Farndon; Carbon, by G. Sparrow; Chlorine, by S. Watt; Chromium, by N. Lepora; Cobalt, by S. Watt; Copper, by R. Beatty; Fluorine, by T. Jackson; Gold, by S. Angliss; Hydrogen, by J. Farndon; Iodine, by L. Gray; Iron, by G. Sparrow; The Lanthanides, by Richard Beatty; Lead, by S. Watt; Lithium, by T. Jackson; Magnesium, by C. Uttley; Manganese, by R. Beatty; Mercury, by Susan Watt; Molybdenum, by N. Lepora; Nickel, by G. Sparrow; Nitrogen, by J. Farndon; Noble gases, by J. Thomas; Oxygen, by J. Farndon; Phosphorus, by R. Beatty; Platinum, by I. Wood; Potassium, by C. Woodford; Radioactive elements, by T. Jackson; Silicon, by J. Thomas; Silver, by S. Watt; Sodium, by A. O'Daly; Sulfur, by R. Beatty; Tin, by L. Gray; Titanium, by C. Woodford; Tungsten, by K. Turrell; Zinc, by L. Gray; Zirconium, by S. Watt

These "titles cover where these substances are found, how they were discovered, their characteristics and reactions, and their importance in the human body and the environment. Each volume includes a double-page spread on the element's position in the periodic table. The captioned, full-color drawings, photographs, and diagrams

clarify the text while boxed 'Did you Know?' items offer interesting extensions to it. . . . Informative, accessible science books that will be of interest for both general reading and report writing." SLJ

Includes glossaries

Just add water; science projects you can sink, squirt, splash & sail. Children's Press 2008 32p il (Experiment with science) lib bdg $25; pa $7.95

Grades: 5 6 7 8   **546**

1. Water 2. Science—Experiments

ISBN 978-0-531-18545-2 (lib bdg); 0-531-18545-1 (lib bdg); 978-0-531-18762-3 (pa); 0-531-18762-4 (pa)

LC 2007-21682

"The book consists of nine hands-on activities that target physical science concepts inherent in water (e.g. density, buoyancy, and hardness.) . . . Students . . . will likely find the age-appropriate activities engaging and purposeful. . . . The colorful photos augment the narrative and the science is sound." Sci Books Films

Includes glossary and bibliographical references

Oxlade, Chris

Mixing and separating; [by] Chris Oxlade. Crabtree Pub. 2008 32p il (Working with materials) lib bdg $26.60; pa $7.95 *

Grades: 2 3 4   **546**

1. Matter 2. Materials

ISBN 978-0-7787-3640-0 (lib bdg); 0-7787-3640-7 (lib bdg); 978-0-7787-3650-9 (pa); 0-7787-3650-4 (pa)

LC 2007027421

This defines and gives examples of mixtures and describes how materials are mixed or separated by such processes as sieving, dissolving, straining, using magnets, settling and skimming, filtering, and evaporating.

This "title has numerous captioned color photographs. . . . The [book offers] three simple, easy, safe reproducible experiments. . . . Students will appreciate the pleasing design, easy-to-read font, and direct, clear writing." Libr Media Connect

Includes glossary and bibliographical references

548   Crystallography

Stangl, Jean, 1928-

Crystals and crystal gardens you can grow. Watts 1990 64p il (First book) lib bdg $23

Grades: 4 5 6 7   **548**

1. Crystals 2. Science—Experiments

ISBN 0-531-10889-9   LC 89-38999

The author discusses the nature and structure of crystals and presents experiments in crystal formation

With "clear explanatory background on crystal formations, and easy directions for experiments, this will meet a real need in every classroom and public library collection." Bull Cent Child Books

Includes bibliographical references

Symes, R. F.

Crystal & gem; written by R.F. Symes and R.R. Harding. rev ed. DK Pub. 2007 72p il (DK eyewitness books) $15.99

Grades: 4 5 6 7 **548**

1. Crystals 2. Precious stones
ISBN 978-0-7566-3001-0; 0-7566-3001-0
LC 2007-277721

First published 1991

Includes CD-Rom

Describes the seven basic shapes of crystals and other aspects of crystallography, including how they form in nature and how crystals are studied and identified

549 Mineralogy

Farndon, John

Rocks and minerals. Benchmark Bks. 2003 32p il (Science experiments) lib bdg $25.64

Grades: 5 6 7 8 **549**

1. Rocks 2. Minerals 3. Science—Experiments
ISBN 0-7614-1468-1 LC 2002-908

Discusses the physical properties of various rocks and minerals and gives instructions for experiments that identify their unique characteristics

Includes glossary

Pellant, Chris

Minerals; [by] Chris and Helen Pellant. Gareth Stevens Pub. 2009 24p il (Rock stars) lib bdg $23

Grades: 2 3 4 **549**

1. Minerals
ISBN 978-0-8368-9224-6 (lib bdg); 0-8368-9224-0 (lib bdg) LC 2008016121

This describes "the different types of minerals, each with its own special characteristics. This book includes a guide to help beginning collectors find and identify minerals." Publisher's note

"Accessible and action-oriented, short but info-packed. . . . Photographs are fine, and graphics are kept extremely simple." SLJ

Includes glossary

550 Earth sciences & geology

Gaff, Jackie

Looking at earth; how does it change? [by] Jackie Gaff. Enslow Publishers 2008 32p il (Looking at science: how things change) lib bdg $22.60

Grades: 1 2 3 **550**

1. Earth
ISBN 978-0-7660-3088-6 (lib bdg); 0-7660-3088-1 (lib bdg) LC 2007-24507

"Provides a look at Earth, its relationship to the sun, earthquakes, volcanoes, and how people can help the planet." Publisher's note

"Fills a huge void in elementary science collections. . . . Text is arranged in succinct 'chunks,' giving important facts without overwhelming readers. . . . [This] is an essential addition." Libr Media Connect

Includes glossary and bibliographical references

Gardner, Robert, 1929-

Earth-shaking science projects about planet Earth; illustrations by Tom Labaff. Enslow 2007 c2008 48p il (Rockin' earth science experiments) lib bdg $23.90

Grades: 3 4 5 **550**

1. Earth 2. Geophysics 3. Science—Experiments 4. Science projects
ISBN 978-0-7660-2733-6 (lib bdg); 0-7660-2733-3 (lib bdg) LC 2006-18656

This offers experiments on such topics as the roundness of Earth, the Earth's layers, the continents, plate movements, earthquakes, and volcanoes.

Includes glossary and bibliographical references

Gibbons, Gail

Planet earth/inside out. Morrow Junior Bks. 1995 unp il maps hardcover o.p. pa $4.95

Grades: K 1 2 3 **550**

1. Earth 2. Geology
ISBN 0-688-09681-6 (lib bdg); 0-688-15849-8 (pa) LC 94-41926

"From Pangaea to recycling, Gibbons skims the surface of geology, touching on plate tectonics, volcanoes, earthquakes, and climates." SLJ

Gibbons' "explanations of the earth's interior are enlivened by comparisons . . . and her plentiful pictures, with their sharp outlines and broad blocks of color, will help clarify the concepts for the youngest learners." Booklist

Lauber, Patricia, 1924-

You're aboard Spaceship Earth; illustrated by Holly Keller. HarperCollins Pubs. 1996 32p il (Let's-read-and-find-out science) pa $4.95 hardcover o.p.

Grades: K 1 2 3 **550**

1. Earth sciences
ISBN 0-06-445159-3 (pa) LC 94-18704

In this book "life on our planet is compared with a manned shuttle mission that must take special care to insure the health and safety of its crew. . . . Once that concept is established, youngsters learn interesting facts about the supplies needed to survive—food, air with oxygen, and water. Lauber is adept at writing for this audience, using simple vocabulary and straightforward sentences. . . . Keller's bright and colorful drawings further explain complicated concepts such as the water cycle." SLJ

Solway, Andrew

Understanding cycles and systems. Raintree 2008 48p il map (Sci-hi: Earth and space science) lib bdg $31.43; pa $8.99

Grades: 4 5 6 7 **550**

1. Earth sciences 2. Earth
ISBN 978-1-4109-3348-5 (lib bdg); 1-4109-3348-2 (lib bdg); 978-1-4109-3358-4 (pa); 1-4109-3358-X (pa) LC 2009-3531

"Explores the constant processes that surround us. . . . Learn about everything from the movement of rocks to the changing forms of water. . . . Discover how invis-

Solway, Andrew—*Continued*

ible elements and the Sun's energy are the keys to all living things." Publisher's note

"Multiple colorful sidebars and large and small diagrams and photographs will help students to grasp the fundamentals being discussed, and the easy but interesting science experiments will act as further reinforcements." SLJ

Includes glossary and bibliographical references

VanCleave, Janice Pratt

Janice VanCleave's earth science for every kid; 101 easy experiments that really work. Wiley 1991 231p il pa $12.95 hardcover o.p.

Grades: 4 5 6 7   **550**

1. Earth sciences 2. Science—Experiments
ISBN 0-471-53010-7 (pa)   LC 90-42724

Instructions for experiments, each introducing a different earth science concept

"An entertaining, educational, and nonthreatening aid to understanding earth science. The easy experiments are carefully organized." SLJ

Woodward, John, 1954-

Planet Earth; written by John Woodward; consultant Kim Bryan. DK Pub. 2009 123p il (One million things) $18.99

Grades: 5 6 7 8   **550**

1. Earth
ISBN 978-0-7566-5235-7; 0-7566-5235-9

This book features "photographic spreads that . . . showcase the rocks, minerals, streams, oceans, layers, clouds, ancient sediments, and brand-new islands that make up our planet." Publisher's note

"The artwork is a balanced mix of stunning photography, effective illustrations, and somewhat depth-challenged Photoshop jobs. An eye-catching catchall on the natural world, this . . . is great browsing material, packed full of well-articulated information." Booklist

551   Geology, hydrology, meteorology

Blobaum, Cindy, 1966-

Geology rocks! 50 hands-on activities to explore the earth; illustrations by Michael Kline. Williamson 1999 96p il pa $10.95

Grades: 4 5 6   **551**

1. Geology 2. Science—Experiments
ISBN 1-885593-29-5   LC 98-53299

Presents fifty hands-on activities to introduce the science of geology and explain the formation and history of the earth

"The text is witty but conveys much factual material. The experiments can be done easily with household items and include safety precautions. . . . The book is illustrated with red-and-purple tinted cartoons and photographs." SLJ

Includes bibliographical references

Kelly, Erica

Evolving planet; [by] Erica Kelly & Richard Kissel. Harry N. Abrams 2008 136p il map $19.95 *

Grades: 5 6 7 8   **551**

1. Field Museum of Natural History 2. Earth 3. Evolution
ISBN 978-0-8109-9486-7; 0-8109-9486-0
            LC 2007-36342

"Published in association with The Field Museum, Chicago."

"Based on a exhibit at Chicago's Field Museum, this big spacious volume packs in a wealth of information about evolution over four billion years. . . . There are detailed, beautiful photographs and glorious paintings on every double-page spread and the chatty text is accessible for grade-schoolers." Booklist

Includes glossary and bibliographical references

551.1   Gross structure and properties of the earth

Cole, Joanna

The magic school bus inside the Earth; illustrated by Bruce Degen. Scholastic 1987 40p il hardcover o.p. pa $4.95 *

Grades: 2 3 4   **551.1**

1. Earth—Internal structure 2. Geology
ISBN 0-590-40759-7; 0-590-40760-0 (pa)
            LC 87-4563

In this book Ms. Frizzle teaches "geology via a field trip through the center of the earth. As her class learns about fossils, rocks, and volcanoes, so will readers, absorbing information painlessly as they vicariously travel through the caves, tunnels, and up through the cone of a volcanic island shortly before it erupts. . . . Degen's bright, colorful artwork includes many witty details to delight observant children. Carried in cartoonlike balloons, the schoolmates' thoughts, banter, and asides add spice to the geology lesson. Bright, sassy, and savvy, the magic school bus books rate high in child appeal." Booklist

Snedden, Robert

Earth's shifting surface. Raintree 2010 48p il (Sci-hi: Earth and space science) lib bdg $31.43; pa $8.99

Grades: 4 5 6 7   **551.1**

1. Plate tectonics 2. Earth—Surface
ISBN 978-1-4109-3349-2 (lib bdg); 1-4109-3349-0 (lib bdg); 978-1-4109-3359-1 (pa); 1-4109-3359-8 (pa)
            LC 2009-3532

Explains "how the surface of Earth is constantly moving . . . [and] what causes the movements in Earth's crust." Publisher's note

"Multiple colorful sidebars and large and small diagrams and photographs will help students to grasp the fundamentals being discussed, and the easy but interesting science experiments will act as further reinforcements." SLJ

Includes glossary and bibliographical references

Storad, Conrad J.

Earth's crust. Lerner Publications Co. 2006 c2007 48p il map (Early bird Earth science) lib bdg $25.26

Grades: 3 4 5 6   **551.1**
  1. Earth—Crust
  ISBN 978-0-8225-5944-3 (lib bdg); 0-8225-5944-7 (lib bdg)   LC 2005-16423
This "introduces the earth's crust. Four chapters discuss the planet's overall structure, plate tectonics, changes in the crust, and features such as mountains, faults, and volcanoes. . . . With short sentences, generously spaced lines, and large type, the text has an inviting look for young readers. The colorful illustrations include several clear diagrams and maps as well as many captioned photos. . . . A clearly written, accessible introduction." Booklist
  Includes glossary

551.2 Volcanoes, earthquakes, thermal waters and gases

Branley, Franklyn Mansfield, 1915-2002

Earthquakes; by Franklyn M. Branley; illustrated by Megan Lloyd. newly il ed. HarperCollinsPublishers 2005 33p il (Let's-read-and-find-out science) hardcover o.p. pa $4.99

Grades: K 1 2 3   **551.2**
  1. Earthquakes
  ISBN 0-06-028008-5; 0-06-028009-3 (lib bdg); 0-06-445188-7 (pa)   LC 2003-25458
A newly illustrated edition of the title first published 1990
This "introduction to earthquakes explores what causes them, how they are measured, and what to do when you are in one." Publisher's note
"The most effective pictures are those that show the unseen and unseeable, such as cross-sections of mountains, volcanoes, and faults in the earth's moving crust." Booklist

Volcanoes; by Franklyn M. Branley; illustrated by Megan Lloyd. newly illustrated ed. Collins 2008 30p il map (Let's-read-and-find-out science) $16.99; pa $5.99

Grades: 2 3 4   **551.2**
  1. Volcanoes
  ISBN 978-0-06-028011-6; 0-06-028011-5; 978-0-06-445189-5 (pa); 0-06-445189-5 (pa)   LC 2006000465
A newly illustrated edition of the title first published 1985
Discusses volcanoes, what causes an eruption, and the warning signs
"The new illustrations excel at depicting ideas presented in the text and include scenes of destruction. . . . This work remains a sound, basic introduction to the topic." SLJ

Burleigh, Robert, 1936-

Volcanoes; journey to the crater's edge; photographs by Philippe Bourseiller; adapted by Robert Burleigh; text by Helene Montardre; drawings by David Giraudon. H.N. Abrams 2003 75p il map $14.95

Grades: 4 5 6 7   **551.2**
  1. Volcanoes
  ISBN 0-8109-4590-8   LC 2003-971
Over thirty photographs and accompanying text reveal the facts about the world's volcanoes
"Photographer Bourseiller takes young readers to the crater's edge with truly spectacular full-color photographs. . . . The book does an excellent job of documenting the effect of volcanoes on the lives of those who live close to them, and small watercolor paintings further enliven the sense of human history." Booklist

Fradin, Judith Bloom

Earthquakes; witness to disaster; by Judy and Dennis Fradin. National Geographic 2008 48p map (Witness to disaster) $16.95; lib bdg $26.90 *

Grades: 4 5 6 7   **551.2**
  1. Earthquakes
  ISBN 978-1-4263-0211-4; 1-4263-0211-8; 978-1-4263-0212-1 (lib bdg); 1-4263-0212-6 (lib bdg)   LC 2007044164
"The first chapter documents the 1964 Alaskan quake that shook Prince William Sound with a 9.2 magnitude force, and set off a tsunami that ultimately caused most of the deaths attributed to this frightening act of nature. The following chapters explore the deadly history of earthquakes and the seismic and geological science of this phenomenon." Publisher's note
"The combination of good writing and excellent graphics paired with archival and personal perspectives makes this book a valuable addition." SLJ
  Includes glossary and bibliographical references

Volcanoes; by Judy and Dennis Fradin. National Geographic 2007 48p il map (Witness to disaster) $16.95; lib bdg $26.90 *

Grades: 4 5 6 7   **551.2**
  1. Volcanoes
  ISBN 978-0-7922-5376-1; 0-7922-5376-0; 978-0-7922-5377-8 (lib bdg); 0-7922-5377-9 (lib bdg)   LC 2006-102817
This "introduces readers to these violent eruptions, using eyewitness accounts to explain the history and science involved. They begin with a report of the 1943 birth of a volcano in Paricutín, Mexico. . . . Subsequent chapters describe other celebrated volcanoes, explain their causes and types, note the benefits of these eruptions, and clarify how they are currently predicted. . . . Numerous clear, well-chosen photographs and diagrams help to convey the great power of volcanic activity and the consequences to humans. . . . This will be useful for report writers, and a fascinating pick for browsers." Booklist
  Includes bibliographical references

Grace, Catherine O'Neill, 1950-
Forces of nature; the awesome power of volcanoes, earthquakes, and tornadoes; by Catherine O'Neill Grace. National Geographic Society 2004 62p il $17.95 *
Grades: 4 5 6 7 **551.2**
    1. Stein, Ross S. 2. Wurman, Joshua 3. Edmonds, Marie 4. Herd, Richard 5. Volcanoes 6. Earthquakes 7. Tornadoes
    ISBN 0-7922-6328-6 LC 2003-18929
    Contents: On the rim of a volcano; In an earthquake zone; In the path of a storm
    "A companion volume to the National Geographic film of the same title, this book presents the basics of these phenomena with a focus on the work of four scientists who study them: Richard Herd, Marie Edmonds, Ross Stein, and Joshua Wurman. . . . Outstanding color and black-and-white photos and diagrams augment the very readable text." SLJ

Harrison, David Lee, 1937-
Volcanoes: nature's incredible fireworks; by David L. Harrison; illustrated by Cheryl Nathan. Boyds Mills Press 2002 unp il (Earthworks) $15.95 *
Grades: 1 2 3 **551.2**
    1. Volcanoes
    ISBN 1-56397-996-9 LC 2001-94536
    "The author and illustrator offer a look at volcanoes and the forces at work deep beneath the earth. The book addresses basic questions such as how rocks get so hot that they melt and what causes a volcano." SLJ
    "The surprisingly graceful text is illuminated with dynamic artwork. . . . The expressive compositions, rich in color and subtle texture, serve as literal scenes of what's happening on the earth, and there are plenty of cross sections and diagrams of what's happening beneath the earth's crust." Booklist
    Includes bibliographical references

Jennings, Terry, 1938-
Earthquakes and tsunamis. Smart Apple Media 2010 32p il map (Amazing planet earth) lib bdg $28.50
Grades: 4 5 6 **551.2**
    1. Earthquakes 2. Tsunamis
    ISBN 978-1-59920-372-0 (lib bdg); 1-59920-372-3 (lib bdg) LC 2008-55496
    This book shows readers how the shifting plates far below the earth's surface can result in violent earthquakes and tsunamis
    "Chapters are labeled as 'Case Study' or 'Science Report,' making the presentation lively. The concise explanations include just the right number of examples and clear diagrams, and have perfect color photo accompaniments." SLJ
    Includes glossary

Violent volcanoes. Smart Apple Media 2010 32p il map (Amazing planet earth) lib bdg $28.50
Grades: 4 5 6 **551.2**
    1. Volcanoes
    ISBN 978-1-59920-374-4 (lib bdg); 1-59920-374-X (lib bdg) LC 2008-55499

This explains how powerful forces beneath the Earth's crust cause volcanoes to erupt
    "Chapters are labeled as 'Case Study' or 'Science Report,' making the presentation lively. The concise explanations include just the right number of examples and clear diagrams, and have perfect color photo accompaniments." SLJ
    Includes glossary

Levy, Matthys
Earthquakes, volcanoes, and tsunamis; projects and principles for beginning geologists; [by] Matthys Levy and Mario Salvadori. Chicago Review Press 2009 136p il pa $14.95
Grades: 5 6 7 8 **551.2**
    1. Earthquakes 2. Volcanoes 3. Tsunamis
    ISBN 978-1-55652-801-9 (pa); 1-55652-801-9 (pa) LC 2008040143
    This "is an excellent introduction for young minds to the subject of earthquakes, volcanoes, and related phenomena. . . . The book is filled with projects to help young people understand the occurrence and consequences of earthquakes, volcanoes, and tsunamis." Sci Books Films

Silverstein, Alvin
Earthquakes; the science behind seismic shocks and tsunamis; [by] Alvin Silverstein, Virginia Silverstein, and Laura Silverstein Nunn. Enslow Publishers 2010 48p il map (The science behind natural disasters) lib bdg $23.93
Grades: 4 5 6 **551.2**
    1. Earthquakes 2. Tsunamis
    ISBN 978-0-7660-2975-0 (lib bdg); 0-7660-2975-1 (lib bdg) LC 2008-38589
    "Examines the science behind earthquakes and tsunamis, including what makes them happen, where they occur, how they are measured, and tips to stay safe during an earthquake." Publisher's note
    "Scientific explanations are accompanied by plentiful color diagrams that will help students to grasp causes and effects. . . . Photos . . . are effective, and are sometimes turned into helpful, lively diagrams by the addition of such features as wind-direction arrows." SLJ
    Includes glossary and bibliographical references

Volcanoes; the science behind fiery eruptions; [by] Alvin Silverstein, Virginia Silverstein, and Laura Silverstein Nunn. Enslow Publishers 2010 48p il map (The science behind natural disasters) lib bdg $23.93
Grades: 4 5 6 **551.2**
    1. Volcanoes
    ISBN 978-0-7660-2972-9 (lib bdg); 0-7660-2972-7 (lib bdg) LC 2008-42866
    "Examines the science behind volcanoes, including what causes them to erupt, the inner-workings of a volcano, underwater volcanoes, and how to stay safe during an eruption." Publisher's note
    "Scientific explanations are accompanied by plentiful color diagrams that will help students to grasp causes and effects. . . . Photos . . . are effective, and are sometimes turned into helpful, lively diagrams by the addition of such features as wind-direction arrows." SLJ
    Includes glossary and bibliographical references

Simon, Seymour, 1931-

Earthquakes. rev ed. Collins 2006 30p il map pa $6.99 *

Grades: 3 4 5 6   **551.2**
1. Earthquakes
ISBN 978-0-06-087715-6 (pa); 0-06-087715-4 (pa)
LC 2006279219
First published 1991 by Morrow Junior Books
Examines the phenomenon of earthquakes, describing how and where they occur, how they can be predicted, and how much damage they can inflict

Stille, Darlene R., 1942-

Great shakes; the science of earthquakes. Compass Point Books 2009 43p il map (Headline science) lib bdg $27.93; pa $7.95

Grades: 5 6 7 8   **551.2**
1. Earthquakes
ISBN 978-0-7565-3947-4 (lib bdg); 0-7565-3947-1 (lib bdg); 978-0-7565-3368-7 (pa); 0-7565-3368-6 (pa)
LC 2008-05739
This "is an accessible, technically accurate introduction to [earthquakes]. . . . In addition to the ludic writing, this slim volume offers . . . readers comprehensive coverage of the fundamentals of earthquakes, including the effects, plate tectonics, fault systems, seismic waves, forecasting, and safer building designs. . . . The many charts and graphs enrich the volume and clarify technical issues." Sci Books Films
Includes glossary and bibliographical references

Tagliaferro, Linda

How does a volcano become an island? Raintree 2010 32p il (How does it happen?) lib bdg $27.50; pa $7.99

Grades: 3 4 5   **551.2**
1. Volcanoes 2. Islands
ISBN 978-1-4109-3447-5 (lib bdg); 1-4109-3447-0 (lib bdg); 978-1-4109-3455-0 (pa); 1-4109-3455-1 (pa)
LC 2008-52652
This addresses questions such as "How do mountains grow underwater? Why does the 'Ring of Fire' feature so many volcanoes? Why might the island of Surtsey soon disappear?" Publisher's note
"Information is clearly presented using a large font, diagrams, and photographs formatted to resemble Polaroid pictures. . . . A first-rate job answering some important scientific questions." SLJ
Includes glossary and bibliographical references

Waldron, Melanie, 1972-

Volcanoes; [by] Melanie Waldron. Heinemann 2007 c2008 32p il map (Mapping earthforms) lib bdg $28.21 paperback o.p.

Grades: 3 4 5   **551.2**
1. Volcanoes
ISBN 978-1-4034-9606-5 (lib bdg); 1-4034-9606-4 (lib bdg); 978-1-4034-9616-4 (pa); 1-4034-9616-1 (pa)
LC 2006037722
After defining volcanoes, this describes "the actions that produce them, their effects on animals and plants, related science, . . . future possibilities, . . . and [lists]

significant examples around the world. Maps, diagrams, tables, and high-quality color photographs complement the text." SLJ
Includes glossary and bibliographical references

Woods, Michael, 1946-

Volcanoes; by Michael Woods and Mary B. Woods. Lerner Publications Co. 2007 64p il map (Disasters up close) lib bdg $27.93

Grades: 4 5 6   **551.2**
1. Volcanoes
ISBN 978-0-8225-4715-0 (lib bdg); 0-8225-4715-5 (lib bdg)
LC 2005-17132
This describes how volcanoes "are formed, where they are located, and the devastation wreaked by them." SLJ
"Each page of the colorful, eye-catching book has several paragraphs of text, sidebars, and small photos, with a large photo or graphic on the facing page." Sci Books Films
Includes bibliographical references

551.3 Surface and exogenous processes and their agents

Harrison, David Lee, 1937-

Glaciers; nature's icy caps; [by] David L. Harrison; illustrated by Cheryl Nathan. Boyds Mills Press 2006 unp il (Earthworks) $15.95

Grades: K 1 2 3   **551.3**
1. Glaciers
ISBN 1-59078-372-7   LC 2005-24988
The author "provides a straightforward introduction to glaciers. Opening with the sinking of the *Titanic*, he explains how they form, move, and drop icebergs into the sea, going on to discuss where glaciers can be found and how their range shifts as Earth cycles in and out of ice ages. . . . The text reads like clear, informational prose. Nathan's digital illustrations vary in quality, but the best double-page spreads . . . are exceptionally fine." Booklist

Sepehri, Sandy

Glaciers; [by] Sandy Sepehri. Rourke Pub. 2008 32p il (Landforms) lib bdg $28.50; pa $7.95

Grades: 1 2 3 4   **551.3**
1. Glaciers
ISBN 978-1-60044-544-6 (lib bdg); 1-60044-544-6 (lib bdg); 978-1-60044-705-1 (pa); 1-60044-705-8 (pa)
LC 2007012143
Contents: What Is a glacier?; A close look; Types of glaciers; How glaciers move; How glaciers benefit people; Life among glaciers; Glaciers and global warming
"The illustrations and photographs are plentiful and colorful. . . . The [volume is] well written and successfully [conveys] the basics of the topic." Sci Books Films
Includes glossary and bibliographical references

Simon, Seymour, 1931-
Icebergs and glaciers. Morrow 1987 unp il pa
$6.99 hardcover o.p. *
Grades: 3 4 5 6   **551.3**
1. Glaciers 2. Icebergs
ISBN 0-688-16705-5 (pa)   LC 86-18142
"After an explanation of the consistency of snowflakes, packed snow, and ice fields, the text describes the
movement of glaciers by sliding or creeping, various processes of measurement, landscape alteration, geological
effects of glacial movement, and the formation of icebergs." Bull Cent Child Books
The author "chronicles the development of glaciers
and icebergs with a wonderfully clear, almost Spartan
text that receives all of the support necessary from the
magnificent color photographs which accompany it. . . .
This book would be an excellent addition to any elementary school library or any personal juvenile collection."
Appraisal

551.4   Geomorphology and hydrosphere

Brimner, Larry Dane, 1949-
Caves. Children's Press 2000 47p il (True book)
hardcover o.p. pa $6.95
Grades: 2 3 4   **551.4**
1. Caves
ISBN 0-516-21567-1; 0-516-27189-X (pa)
     LC 99-58037
Describes the different kinds of caves, how they are
formed, and the wildlife that lives within them
Includes bibliographical references

Jennings, Terry, 1938-
Massive mountains. Smart Apple Media 2010
32p il map (Amazing planet earth) lib bdg $28.50
Grades: 4 5 6   **551.4**
1. Mountains
ISBN 978-1-59920-370-6 (lib bdg); 1-59920-370-7 (lib
bdg)   LC 2008-55497
This book explains how mountains form and change
over time
"Chapters are labeled as 'Case Study' or 'Science Report,' making the presentation lively. The concise explanations include just the right number of examples and
clear diagrams, and have perfect color photo accompaniments." SLJ
Includes glossary

Lindop, Laurie
Cave sleuths. Twenty-First Century Books 2006
80p il (Science on the edge) lib bdg $26.90
Grades: 5 6 7 8   **551.4**
1. Caves
ISBN 0-7613-2702-9   LC 2003-16946
Discusses the science of speleology and what scientists have learned about caves, how they are formed, and
what lives in them.
"The science is intriguing here. . . . The photos . . .
are all intriguing and lend interest." Voice Youth Advocates
Includes glossary and bibliographical references

Sheehan, Thomas F., 1928-
Islands; [by] Thomas F. Sheehan. Rourke Pub.
2008 32p il map (Landforms) lib bdg $28.50; pa
$7.95
Grades: 1 2 3 4   **551.4**
1. Islands
ISBN 978-1-60044-545-3 (lib bdg); 1-60044-545-4 (lib
bdg); 978-1-60044-706-8 (pa); 1-60044-706-6 (pa)
     LC 2007012183
Contents: What do you know about islands?; Continental islands; Oceanic islands; Atolls; Island cays; Ar-
chipelagos; Island reefs; Island plants and animals; Islands in danger
"The illustrations and photographs are plentiful and
colorful. . . . The [volume is] well written and successfully [conveys] the basics of the topic." Sci Books Films
Includes glossary and bibliographical references

Mountains; [by] Thomas Sheehan. Rourke Pub.
2008 32p il map (Landforms) lib bdg $28.50; pa
$7.95
Grades: 1 2 3 4   **551.4**
1. Mountains
ISBN 978-1-60044-547-7 (lib bdg); 1-60044-547-0 (lib
bdg); 978-1-60044-708-2 (pa); 1-60044-708-2 (pa)
     LC 2007012290
Contents: What do you know about mountain ranges?;
United States mountain ranges; The making of mountains; Mountain ecosystems; Mountain and people; What
can we do to protect our mountains?
"The illustrations and photographs are plentiful and
colorful. . . . The [volume is] well written and successfully [conveys] the basics of the topic." Sci Books Films
Includes glossary and bibliographical references

Simon, Seymour, 1931-
Mountains. Morrow Junior Bks. 1994 unp il pa
$6.99 hardcover o.p. *
Grades: 4 5 6 7   **551.4**
1. Mountains
ISBN 0-688-15477-8 (pa)   LC 93-11398
Introduces various mountain ranges, how they are
formed and shaped, and how they affect vegetation and
animals, including humans
"The striking color photographs work well with the
clear text to illustrate key points and highlight the diver-
sity among the Earth's mountain ranges." Horn Book
Guide

Zoehfeld, Kathleen Weidner
How mountains are made; illustrated by James
Graham Hale. HarperCollins Pubs. 1995 29p il
maps (Let's-read-and-find-out science) hardcover
o.p. pa $4.95
Grades: K 1 2 3   **551.4**
1. Mountains 2. Geology
ISBN 0-06-024510-7; 0-06-445128-3 (pa)
     LC 93-45436
"Four children and a dog climbing a forest trail provide the framework for this discussion of mountains.
Along the way, the knowledgeable characters explain the
earth's structure and tectonic plates as well as the different types of mountains and how they are formed."

Zoehfeld, Kathleen Weidner—*Continued*
Booklist

"The text and illustrations work together well in this sequential, well-organized book. Much credit goes to Hale's engaging watercolor illustrations done in cheery colors; they are simply drawn but add effective examples and diagrams." SLJ

551.46 Hydrosphere and submarine geology. Oceanography

Adamson, Thomas K.
Tsunamis; with Walter C. Dudley, consultant. Capstone Press 2005 c2006 24p il $22.26
Grades: 2 3 4   551.46
1. Tsunamis
ISBN 0-7368-5248-4   LC 2005-01640
"Bridgestone books"

"Adamson explains how tsunamis are caused and how they move through the ocean and grow in height as they approach the shore. He describes the damage they cause, the kinds of warning systems used to detect them, and the impact of the 2004 Indian Ocean disaster. The writing is concise but clear, and the layout features a full-page illustration facing each page of easy-to-read text. Excellent photos of the 2004 tsunami are featured, and the diagrams of the earth's plates and earthquakes are simple but informative." SLJ

Includes bibliographical references

Burns, Loree Griffin
Tracking trash; flotsam, jetsam, and the science of ocean motion. Houghton Mifflin 2007 56p il map (Scientists in the field) $18 *
Grades: 5 6 7 8   551.46
1. Ocean currents 2. Pollution
ISBN 978-0-618-58131-3; 0-618-58131-6
                                    LC 2006-11534
"The book profiles two oceanographers who devised experiments using computer-modeling programs of ocean surface current movement to predict the landfall of . . . drifting objects. . . . Spacious layout, exceptionally fine color photos, and handsome maps give this book an inviting look. . . . A unique and often fascinating book." Booklist

Includes glossary and bibliographical references

Earle, Sylvia A., 1935-
Dive! my adventures in the deep frontier. National Geographic Soc. 1999 64p il map $18.95
Grades: 4 5 6   551.46
1. Underwater exploration 2. Submarine diving
ISBN 0-7922-7144-0   LC 98-11480
The author relates some of her adventures studying and exploring the world's oceans, including tracking whales, living in an underwater laboratory, and helping to design a deep water submarine

"In this extraordinary photo-essay, an eminent marine biologist and ocean explorer combines personal adventure and scientific fact with glorious color action pictures." Booklist

Includes glossary

Fradin, Judith Bloom
Tsunamis; witness to disaster; [by] Judy & Dennis Fradin. National Geographic 2008 48p il map (Witness to disaster) $16.95; lib bdg $20.90 *
Grades: 4 5 6 7   551.46
1. Tsunamis
ISBN 978-0-7922-5380-8; 0-7922-5380-9; 978-0-7922-5381-5 (lib bdg); 0-7922-5381-7 (lib bdg)
                                    LC 2008010536
This "explores the science, history, and personal experience of tsunamis and shows kids what scientists are doing to develop early warning systems so we can survive such disasters in the future." Publisher's note

Includes glossary and bibliographical references

Gibbons, Gail
Exploring the deep, dark sea. Little, Brown 1999 unp il $14.95; pa $5.95
Grades: K 1 2 3   551.46
1. Underwater exploration 2. Ocean bottom 3. Marine biology
ISBN 0-316-30945-1; 0-316-75549-4 (pa)
                                    LC 98-14443
"From the sunlight zone to the abyss, Gibbons follows the crew of a deep-diving submersible craft into the ocean depths, noting the changes in terrain and animal life at the various levels. Labels identify parts of the craft and the many animals, and explanations of the differing ecologies of the many levels are brief. Thoughtful attention to page design and narrative produce an account that is both spare and surprisingly rich." Horn Book Guide

Green, Jen
The world's oceans. Smart Apple Media 2010 32p il map (Amazing planet earth) lib bdg $28.50
Grades: 4 5 6   551.46
1. Ocean
ISBN 978-1-59920-373-7 (lib bdg); 1-59920-373-1 (lib bdg)   LC 2008-55500
This covers how ocean waves shape the seashore, the makeup of the ocean bed, underwater hazards, storm surges, and the effects of global warming. Interspersed with these are six "Case Study" chapters, which take an in-depth look at various oceanic events throughout history such as the creation of Iceland or the deadly tsunami that hit Indonesia in December, 2004

"Chapters are labeled as 'Case Study' or 'Science Report,' making the presentation lively. The concise explanations include just the right number of examples and clear diagrams, and have perfect color photo accompaniments." SLJ

Includes glossary

Hamilton, John, 1959-
Tsunamis; [by] John Hamilton. ABDO Pub. Co. 2006 32p il map lib bdg $27.07
Grades: 2 3 4   551.46
1. Tsunamis
ISBN 1-59679-333-3   LC 2005040427

Hamilton, John, 1959-—*Continued*
"Hamilton describes the 2004 Indian Ocean disaster and explains the causes and nature of tsunamis. . . . The brief but readable text adequately presents the phenomenon and the specific events. Excellent, informative color photos include several that are not common to many of the other recent books on the topic." SLJ

Includes bibliographical references

Lindop, Laurie
Venturing the deep sea. Twenty-First Century Books 2006 80p il map (Science on the edge) lib bdg $27.93 *
Grades: 5 6 7 8　　　　　　　　　**551.46**
　1. Ocean bottom 2. Underwater exploration
　ISBN 0-7613-2701-0　　　　　LC 2004-29729
"Comparing exploration of the ocean with that of outer space, Lindop covers the equipment used and knowledge sought by underwater biologists and geologists. She presents the different zones of the sea, traces the development of diving equipment, and describes a typical dive. Topics include the mid-ocean ridge, plate tectonics, and continental drift; hydrothermal vents; bioluminescence; underwater cameras; and deep-sea remotely operated robot explorers." SLJ
"The science is intriguing here. . . . The photos of undersea projects, creatures, weird cave and underwater tube formations are all intriguing." Voice Youth Advocates

Includes bibliographical references

Mallory, Kenneth
Diving to a deep-sea volcano. Houghton Mifflin Company 2006 60p il map (Scientists in the field) $17 *
Grades: 5 6 7 8　　　　　　　　　**551.46**
　1. Lutz, Richard A. 2. Ocean bottom 3. Underwater exploration 4. Marine biology
　ISBN 978-0-618-33205-2; 0-618-33205-7
　　　　　　　　　　　　　　LC 2005-25449
This describes the exploration by marine biologist Rich Lutz and his crew of deep sea hydrothermal vents and the creatures that survive there.
"The profile of an enthusiastic scientist injects excitement into even unassuming facts." Booklist

Includes glossary and bibliographical references

Matsen, Bradford
The incredible record-setting deep-sea dive of the bathysphere; [by] Brad Matsen. Enslow Pubs. 2003 48p il map (Incredible deep-sea adventures) lib bdg $18.95
Grades: 4 5 6 7　　　　　　　　　**551.46**
　1. Beebe, William, 1877-1962 2. Barton, Otis 3. Underwater exploration 4. Ocean bottom
　ISBN 0-7660-2188-2　　　　　LC 2002-13822
Contents: Heroes of the deep; The voyage into the depths; A record is broken, a record is set; Explorers of the abyss; The ultimate dive to the bottom of the sea
Describes the 1934 dive of a bathysphere, or "sphere of the deep," in which two explorers, William Beebe and Otia Barton, set the world depth record and saw mysteri-

ous creatures of the deep ocean
"Attractive color photos contribute to the content." SLJ

Includes glossary and bibliographical references

Schuh, Mari C., 1975-
Tsunamis. Capstone Press 2010 24p il (Earth in action) lib bdg $21.32
Grades: K 1 2　　　　　　　　　**551.46**
　1. Tsunamis
　ISBN 978-1-4296-3438-0 (lib bdg); 1-4296-3438-3 (lib bdg)　　　　　　　　　　LC 2009-2175
"Describes tsunamis, how they occur, and the damage they cause." Publisher's note
This book "boasts a full-page color photograph. . . . [It shows] the aftermath of a disaster . . . but there are also some diagrams showing physical mechanisms and maps highlighting commonly affected places. The left side of each spread provides a few sentences of large-print text, with short, clear explanations." SLJ

Includes glossary and bibliographical references

Simon, Seymour, 1931-
Oceans. Morrow Junior Bks. 1990 unp il $16 *
Grades: 3 4 5 6　　　　　　　　　**551.46**
　1. Ocean
　ISBN 0-688-09453-8　　　　　LC 89-28452
This book "covers the geography of the ocean floor, major currents, and El Nino (a shift in the prevailing currents that causes severe climactic changes). Tides, tsunami, waves, coastal erosion, and marine life are also touched upon." Booklist
"Simon presents clear, simplified explanations of natural phenomena with well-chosen full-color photographs that go beyond decoration. He includes good black-and-white diagrams of how tides work and how waves form and transfer energy. The endpapers are maps of the world showing how and where the major currents flow." SLJ

Stille, Darlene R., 1942-
Oceans. Children's Press 1999 47p il maps (True book) $22; pa $6.95
Grades: 2 3 4　　　　　　　　　**551.46**
　1. Ocean
　ISBN 0-516-21510-8; 0-516-26768-X (pa)
　　　　　　　　　　　　　　LC 98-53857
An introduction to the ocean describing its physical characteristics, the plants and animals that live in or near it, and its importance to life on Earth
Includes bibliographical references

Tagliaferro, Linda
How does an earthquake become a tsunami? Raintree 2008 32p il map (How does it happen?) lib bdg $27.50; pa $7.99
Grades: 3 4 5　　　　　　　　　**551.46**
　1. Tsunamis 2. Waves 3. Earthquakes 4. Plate tectonics
　ISBN 978-1-4109-3446-8 (lib bdg); 1-4109-3446-2 (lib bdg); 978-1-4109-3454-3 (pa); 1-4109-3454-3 (pa)
　　　　　　　　　　　　　　LC 2008-52643

Tagliaferro, Linda—*Continued*

This addresses questions such as "What causes earthquakes? Why does the tide go out right before a tsunami hits? How can the damage of tsunamis be minimized?" Publisher's note

"Information is clearly presented using a large font, diagrams, and photographs formatted to resemble Polaroid pictures. . . . A first-rate job answering some important scientific questions." SLJ

Includes glossary and bibliographical references

VanCleave, Janice Pratt

Janice VanCleave's oceans for every kid; easy activities that make learning science fun. Wiley 1996 245p il map (Science for every kid series) pa $12.95 hardcover o.p.

Grades: 4 5 6 7   **551.46**
1. Oceanography
ISBN 0-471-12453-2 (pa)   LC 95-9201

Includes information on techniques and technologies of oceanography, the topology of the ocean floor, movement of the sea, properties of sea water, and life in the sea

"An engaging overview of marine sciences. Each chapter explores a topic in two to four pages, then poses questions accompanied by lucid explanations." SLJ

Includes glossary

Woodward, John, 1954-

Voyage: Ocean: a full-speed-ahead tour of the oceans. DK Pub. 2009 128p il $24.99

Grades: 3 4 5   **551.46**
1. Ocean
ISBN 978-0-7566-4548-9; 0-7566-4548-4

"This eclectic and informative book is shaped like the porthole of a submarine. After readers open the hatch, the ocean comes alive with full-color photographs. . . . Images from the book are featured on collector's cards housed in a pocket at the end, along with stickers and a poster of ocean life. The breadth of information and special features will appeal to intrepid readers." Publ Wkly

551.48 Hydrology

Chambers, Catherine, 1954-

Rivers; [by] Catherine Chambers and Nicholas Lapthorn. rev and updated. Heinemann 2007 32p il map (Mapping earthforms) lib bdg $28.21 paperback o.p.

Grades: 3 4 5   **551.48**
1. Rivers
ISBN 978-1-4034-9604-1 (lib bdg); 1-4034-9604-8 (lib bdg); 978-1-4034-9614-0 (pa); 1-4034-9614-5 (pa)
LC 2006037720

First published 2002

After defining rivers, this work describes "the actions that produce them, their effects on animals and plants, related science, . . . [lists] future possibilities . . . Maps, diagrams, tables, and high-quality color photographs complement the text." SLJ

Includes glossary and bibliographical references

Cole, Joanna

The magic school bus at the waterworks; illustrated by Bruce Degen. Scholastic 1986 39p il hardcover o.p. pa $4.95 *

Grades: 2 3 4   **551.48**
1. Water 2. Water supply
ISBN 0-590-43739-9; 0-590-40360-5 (pa)
LC 86-6672

The author presents "specific facts about water and a memorable image of the water cycle process. The story involves a 'strange' teacher who takes her class on a magical trip: up to the clouds—down to earth in raindrops—down a stream into a reservoir where the water is purified—finally into the underground pipes leading back to school. The illustrations both enhance the humor and provide visual presentation of the water cycle." Appraisal

Dorros, Arthur, 1950-

Follow the water from brook to ocean; written and illustrated by Arthur Dorros. HarperCollins Pubs. 1991 32p il (Let's-read-and-find-out science book) $13.95; lib bdg $13.89

Grades: K 1 2 3   **551.48**
1. Water
ISBN 0-06-021598-4; 0-06-021599-2 (lib bdg)
LC 90-1438

Explains how water flows from brooks, to streams, to rivers, over waterfalls, through canyons and dams, to eventually reach the ocean

"An excellent presentation of introductory material about water. . . . The illustrations are simple, almost childlike, in soft colors." SLJ

Gallant, Roy A.

Water. Benchmark Bks. 2001 48p il (Kaleidoscope) lib bdg $15.95

Grades: 3 4 5   **551.48**
1. Water
ISBN 0-7614-1040-6   LC 99-49627

Explains why water, although common, has characteristics which make it an unusual substance

"The large-print [text is] easy to read, and the explanations are clear and concise. Outstanding full-page, full-color photographs appear throughout." SLJ

Includes glossary and bibliographical references

Green, Jen

Mighty rivers. Smart Apple Media 2010 32p il map (Amazing planet earth) lib bdg $28.50

Grades: 4 5 6   **551.48**
1. Rivers
ISBN 978-1-59920-371-3 (lib bdg); 1-59920-371-5 (lib bdg)
LC 2008-55498

Starting with a quick introduction to the water cycle, this book shows readers how rivers are formed, and how they, in turn, form waterfalls, carve out canyons, create fertile deltas, cause flooding, and have a great impact on the daily lives of people all over the world

"Chapters are labeled as 'Case Study' or 'Science Report,' making the presentation lively. The concise explanations include just the right number of examples and

Green, Jen—*Continued*
clear diagrams, and have perfect color photo accompaniments." SLJ
  Includes glossary

Rauzon, Mark J.
  Water, water everywhere; [by] Mark J. Rauzon and Cynthia Overbeck Bix. Sierra Club Bks. for Children 1994 32p il $14.95; pa $6.95
Grades: K 1 2 3   **551.48**
  1. Water
  ISBN 0-87156-598-6; 0-87156-383-5 (pa)
                           LC 92-34521
  Describes the forms water takes, how it has shaped Earth, and its importance to life
  "Water's vital role in the life of our planet is vividly portrayed in a crisp, economical text that cultivates respect for the environment. . . . Striking, often full-page, color photographs will engage the imagination of young readers." Horn Book Guide

Sepehri, Sandy
  Rivers; [by] Sandy Sepehri. Rourke Pub. 2008 32p il (Landforms) lib bdg $28.50 paperback o.p.
Grades: 1 2 3 4   **551.48**
  1. Rivers
  ISBN 978-1-60044-546-0 (lib bdg); 1-60044-546-2 (lib bdg); 978-1-60044-707-5 (pa); 1-60044-707-4 (pa)
                        LC 2007012292
  Contents: What Is a river?; The parts of a river; A river's journey; How rivers sculpt the land; The importance of rivers in America; Rivers in danger; Major American rivers
  "The illustrations and photographs are plentiful and colorful. . . . The [volume is] well written and successfully [conveys] the basics of the topic." Sci Books Films
  Includes glossary and bibliographical references

Waldman, Neil, 1947-
  The snowflake; a water cycle story; [by] Neil Waldman. Millbrook Press 2003 unp il $14.95
Grades: K 1 2 3   **551.48**
  1. Water 2. Snow
  ISBN 0-7613-2347-3   LC 2003-4806
  Follows the journey of a water droplet through the various stages of the water cycle, from precipitation to evaporation and condensation
  "The clear text is undeniably lyrical. . . . The real stunners here, though, are the dazzling, cool-toned paintings that convey the wonders of nature with delicate precision." SLJ

Wells, Robert E.
  Did a dinosaur drink this water? A. Whitman 2006 unp il $15.95; pa $6.95
Grades: K 1 2 3   **551.48**
  1. Water
  ISBN 978-0-8075-8839-0; 978-0-8075-8840-6 (pa)
                        LC 2006-01039
  This describes "the water cycle, explaining that the earth's water has been constantly recycled not just since dinosaur days but for billions of years. The simple text asks good questions and offers clearly worded answers, enhanced by lively, colorful ink-and-watercolor illustrations." Booklist

551.5   Meteorology

Banqueri, Eduardo, 1966-
  Weather. Enchanted Lion Books 2006 33p il (Field guides) $16.95
Grades: 4 5 6 7   **551.5**
  1. Weather
  ISBN 1-59270-059-4   LC 2006-42864
  This "book is filled with information about all aspects of weather, from why there are seasons to predicting the weather. Complementing the scientifically accurate text is an excellent mix of drawings and photographs." Sci Books and Films

Branley, Franklyn Mansfield, 1915-2002
  Air is all around you; by Franklyn M. Branley; illustrated by John O'Brien. newly illustrated ed. HarperCollinsPublishers 2006 36p il (Let's-read-and-find-out science) hardcover o.p. pa $4.99
Grades: K 1 2   **551.5**
  1. Air
  ISBN 0-06-059413-6; 0-06-059414-4 (lib bdg); 0-06-059415-2 (pa)   LC 2004005043
  A revised and newly illustrated edition of the title first published 1962
  This "title introduces the concept of air, its presence in our world, and its importance to the environment. The text describes several interesting facts, clearly explaining ideas and incorporating experiments that are easy to reproduce at home or in the classroom. The appealing artwork supports the narrative. . . . Produced in pen and warm, earthy watercolors, the pictures are filled with amusing details." SLJ

Carson, Mary Kay, 1964-
  Weather projects for young scientists; experiments and science fair ideas. Chicago Review Press 2007 134p il $14.95
Grades: 4 5 6 7   **551.5**
  1. Weather 2. Science—Experiments
  ISBN 978-1-55652-629-9; 1-55652-629-6
                        LC 2006-16430
  This covers "fundamentals about the water cycle and seasons as well as more sophisticated topics, such as pressure systems, greenhouse gases, and forecasting. The information alternates with more than 40 activities." Booklist
  This "presents difficult concepts in a very concrete, basic manner." Sci Books Films

Cosgrove, Brian, 1926-

Weather; written by Brian Cosgrove. rev ed. DK Publishing 2007 72p il map (DK eyewitness books) $15.99; lib bdg $19.99

Grades: 4 5 6 7   **551.5**
   1. Weather 2. Climate 3. Atmosphere
   ISBN   978-0-7566-3006-5;   0-7566-3006-1;
   978-0-7566-0737-1 (lib bdg); 0-7566-0737-X (lib bdg)
                                              LC 2007-281112

First published 1991 by Knopf

"Discover the world's weather—from heat waves and droughts to blizzards and floods"—Cover. Includes discussion of why the climate may change in the future.

"Accompanying the book are a poster, additional images on CD-ROM, and a useful glossary. Altogether, this book and its supplements are well crafted to motivate young learners about the importance of weather, to deepen their conceptual understanding of it, and to pique their interest in participating in its study." Sci Books Films

Includes glossary

Gardner, Robert, 1929-

Ace your weather science project; great science fair ideas; [by] Robert Gardner and Salvatore Tocci. Enslow Publishers 2009 104p il (Ace your physics science project) lib bdg $31.93

Grades: 5 6 7 8   **551.5**
   1. Weather 2. Science projects 3. Science—Experiments
   ISBN 978-0-7660-3223-1 (lib bdg); 0-7660-3223-X
   (lib bdg)   LC 2008-49779

"Presents several science experiments and project ideas about weather." Publisher's note

Includes bibliographical references

Easy genius science projects with weather; great experiments and ideas. Enslow Publishers 2009 128p il (Easy genius science projects) lib bdg $31.93

Grades: 5 6 7 8   **551.5**
   1. Weather 2. Science projects 3. Science—Experiments
   ISBN 978-0-7660-2924-8 (lib bdg); 0-7660-2924-7 (lib
   bdg)   LC 2008-23972

"Science experiments and science project ideas about weather." Publisher's note

Includes glossary and bibliographical references

Stellar science projects about Earth's sky; [by] Robert Gardner; illustrations by Tom Labaff. Enslow Elementary 2007 c2008 48p il (Rockin' earth science experiments) lib bdg $23.93

Grades: 3 4 5   **551.5**
   1. Sky 2. Science—Experiments 3. Science projects
   ISBN 978-0-7660-2732-9 (lib bdg); 0-7660-2732-5 (lib
   bdg)   LC 2006-13790

This offers experiments on topics such as the weight of air, air pressure, why the sky is blue, why sunsets are red, clouds, stars, and balloons in sky and water

This is "just right for students with limited experience looking for projects that are fairly interesting and manageable." SLJ

Includes glossary and bibliographical references

Wild science projects about Earth's weather; illustrations by Tom LaBaff. Enslow 2007 48p il (Rockin' earth science experiments) lib bdg $23.93

Grades: 3 4 5   **551.5**
   1. Weather 2. Science projects 3. Science—Experiments
   ISBN 978-0-7660-2734-3 (lib bdg); 0-7660-2734-1 (lib
   bdg)   LC 2006-05897

This presents experiments on such topics as air temperature and pressure, wind direction, rainfall, and clouds.

"Each experiment is enhanced by a topical fact box and includes a supply list and step-by-step explanation." SLJ

Includes glossary and bibliographical references

Lauw, Darlene

Weather; [by Darlene Lauw and Lim Cheng Puay] Crabtree 2003 29p il (Science alive!) lib bdg $21.28; pa $7.95

Grades: 3 4 5 6   **551.5**
   1. Weather 2. Science—Experiments
   ISBN 0-7787-0565-X (lib bdg); 0-7787-0611-7 (pa)
                                          LC 2002-11641

Includes index

Contents: The power of the sun!; The weight of air affects weather; Windy days are fun!; Water, water everywhere!; Light rain, heavy rain; What a muggy day!; Flash, crash, boom!

Introduces concepts related to weather through various activities and projects

"The directions are kid friendly, and the graphics that support them are very helpful. . . . The science content is within the range of understanding of an upper elementary school student." Sci Books Films

Includes glossary

VanCleave, Janice Pratt

Janice VanCleave's weather; mind-boggling experiments you can turn into science fair projects; [by] Janice VanCleave. Wiley 1995 89p il (Spectacular science projects series) pa $10.95

Grades: 4 5 6 7   **551.5**
   1. Weather 2. Science projects 3. Science—Experiments
   ISBN 0-471-03231-X   LC 94-25646

"Using everyday household items, the reading audience can demonstrate to itself such phenomena as differences in climate at different points on the Earth, lightning, wind direction and intensity, clouds, rain, fronts, etc. Through excellent directions and adequate illustrations, the reader can do 20 simple experiments at little or no cost that demonstrate many aspects of the weather." Sci Books Films

Includes glossary

551.51   Composition, regions, dynamics of atmosphere

Bauer, Marion Dane, 1938-
Wind; illustrated by John Wallace. Aladdin 2004 32p il (Ready-to-read) hardcover o.p. pa $3.99
Grades: K 1 2   **551.51**
   1. Winds
   ISBN 0-689-85442-0; 0-689-85443-9 (pa)
                      LC 2002-9656
Illustrations and simple text explain what wind is, how it is used by plants, birds, and people, and how wind can become a storm

Cobb, Vicki, 1938-
I face the wind; illustrated by Julia Gorton. HarperCollins Pubs. 2003 unp il (Science play) $16.99
Grades: K 1 2   **551.51**
   1. Winds 2. Science—Experiments
   ISBN 0-688-17840-5; 0-688-17841-3 (lib bdg)
                      LC 2001-26480
Introduces the characteristics and actions of the wind through simple hands-on activities
"All demonstrations . . . are conducted with readily available materials. . . . Streamlined and jargon-fee though the text may be, it gets the basics across in kid-friendly terms. . . . Gorton's strong, angular graphics feature a redheaded little gal with wide-set eyes and a powerful curiosity who alternately serves as wind-tousled subject of forces real but unseen and as demonstrator for each experiment." Bull Cent Child Books

Friend, Sandra
Earth's wild winds. 21st Cent. Bks. (Brookfield) 2002 32p il maps (Exploring planet earth) lib bdg $24.90
Grades: 5 6 7 8   **551.51**
   1. Winds
   ISBN 0-7613-2673-1   LC 2001-6515
Examines different aspects of the wind, including its measurement, effects on weather, potential destructiveness, and uses
"This attractive and fact-filled book will be useful for earth-science reports. . . . The full-color charts, maps, and photos contribute immeasurably to the success of the presentation." SLJ
Includes bibliographical references

Gallant, Roy A.
Atmosphere; sea of air. Benchmark Bks. 2002 79p il (Earthworks) lib bdg $19.95
Grades: 5 6 7 8   **551.51**
   1. Atmosphere 2. Meteorology
   ISBN 0-7614-1366-9   LC 2001-43301
Describes the atmosphere which makes life on earth possible, explores its effects on weather and climate, and examines what causes air pollution and what can be done it

"Gallant's prose is nearly conversational in its easy delivery, but his facts are always thorough and his ideas clearly explained. . . . Crisp graphs, maps, and excellent color photos illustrate [this] fine [volume]." Booklist
Includes glossary and bibliographical references

Kaner, Etta, 1947-
Who likes the wind? written by Etta Kaner; illustrated by Marie Lafrance. Kids Can Press 2006 unp il (Exploring the elements) $14.95
Grades: PreK K 1 2   **551.51**
   1. Winds
   ISBN 1-55337-839-3
"On each double-page spread, a child expresses why he or she likes the wind ('because it pushes my boat'). The child then wonders how the event happens ('I wonder why the wind blows') and lifts a flap for a scientific explanation. The narrative sections are illustrated in child-friendly acrylics, with the explantions set off in white. Clear diagrams supplement the scientific details." Horn Book Guide

Malone, Peter, 1953-
Close to the wind; the Beaufort scale. G.P. Putnam's Sons 2007 unp il $16.99
Grades: 3 4 5 6   **551.51**
   1. Beaufort, Sir Francis, 1774-1857 2. Winds
   ISBN 0-399-24399-2; 978-0-399-24399-8
                      LC 2005-32672
"Captain Francis Beaufort of the Royal Navy spent the years 1805-1810 developing a graduated scale for measuring the wind. In a treatment that manages at once to be entirely informative and utterly charming, the author presents the captain's work through a rousing story. Young William Bentley . . . is a fictional midshipman on the *Zephyr*, a man-of-war making a voyage from Portsmouth to Naples and then to Jamaica and back. The Beaufort scale of the prevailing conditions is given on the versos, while the rectos sport exquisite watercolor-and-gouache paintings. . . . A truly lovely job of book-making that covers a topic rarely treated in children's literature." SLJ

Sayre, April Pulley
Stars beneath your bed; the surprising story of dust; pictures by Ann Jonas. Greenwillow Books 2005 unp il $15.99; lib bdg $16.89 *
Grades: K 1 2 3   **551.51**
   1. Dust
   ISBN 0-06-057188-8; 0-06-057189-6 (lib bdg)
                      LC 2004-2108
"Dust gets a poetic treatment in a picture book that tells all about dust's what and where, and sometimes its why. Using free verse, Sayre explains how dust is made everywhere. . . . The watercolors in the well-composed two-page spreads sometimes soar . . . but there are also smaller images . . . that are equally effective." Booklist

551.55 Atmospheric disturbances and formations

Branley, Franklyn Mansfield, 1915-2002
Flash, crash, rumble, and roll; by Franklyn M. Branley; illustrated by True Kelley. newly il ed. HarperCollins Pubs. 1999 32p il (Let's-read-and-find-out science) hardcover o.p. pa $4.95
Grades: K 1 2 3   551.55
1. Thunderstorms 2. Lightning
ISBN 0-06-027858-7; 0-06-027859-5 (lib bdg); 0-06-445179-8 (pa)   LC 97-43599
A revised and newly illustrated edition of the title first published 1964 by Crowell
Explains how and why a thunderstorm occurs and gives safety steps to follow when lightning is flashing
This offers "clear and informative explanations . . . [and] colorful cartoonlike pictures." Horn Book Guide

Ceban, Bonnie J.
Hurricanes, typhoons, and cyclones; disaster & survival; [by] Bonnie J. Ceban. Enslow Pubs. 2005 48p il map (Deadly disasters) lib bdg $23.93
Grades: 4 5 6 7   551.55
1. Hurricanes 2. Typhoons 3. Cyclones
ISBN 0-7660-2388-5
This briefly explains the science of hurricanes, typhoons, and cyclones; describes Cyclone Tracy in Australia in 1974, Hurricanes Andrew and Floyd in Florida in 1991 and 1999 respectively, and Typhoon Tokage in Japan in 2004; and suggests safety precautions
Includes glossary and bibliographical references

Tornadoes; disaster & survival; [by] Bonnie J. Ceban. Enslow Publishers 2005 48p il map (Deadly disasters) lib bdg $23.93
Grades: 4 5 6 7   551.55
1. Tornadoes
ISBN 0-7660-2383-4   LC 2004-11700
This explores the causes of tornadoes, how people survive these storms, and how they are predicted
Includes glossary and bibliographical references

Challoner, Jack
Hurricane & tornado; written by Jack Challoner. rev ed. DK Pub. 2004 72p il map (DK eyewitness books) $15.99; lib bdg $19.99
Grades: 4 5 6 7   551.55
1. Storms 2. Natural disasters 3. Weather
ISBN 0-7566-0690-X; 0-7566-0689-6 (lib bdg)
LC 2004302408
First published 2000
Describes dangerous and destructive weather conditions around the world, such as thunderstorms, tornadoes, hurricanes, lightning, hail, and drought with photographs, historical background, and legends.

Cole, Joanna
The magic school bus inside a hurricane; illustrated by Bruce Degen. Scholastic 1995 unp il hardcover o.p. pa $4.99 *
Grades: 2 3 4   551.55
1. Hurricanes 2. Weather 3. Meteorology
ISBN 0-590-44686-X; 0-590-44687-8 (pa)
LC 94-34703
"The magic school bus changes into a weather balloon and then into an airplane as the class experiences the hurricane and a spin-off tornado firsthand. As usual, Ms. Frizzle's wardrobe is as changeable as the weather. The familiar format features lots of weather information delivered via students' written reports and spoken comments." SLJ
"Cole presents the science in easy-to-understand terms, with Degen clarifying the concepts and adding comic relief through double-page-spread pictures that brim with details." Booklist

Demarest, Chris L., 1951-
Hurricane hunters! riders on the storm; [by] Chris L. Demarest. Margaret K. McElderry Books 2006 unp il $17.95
Grades: K 1 2 3   551.55
1. Hurricanes 2. Weather forecasting
ISBN 978-0-689-86168-0; 0-689-86168-0
LC 2005011292
This "picture book explains the work of the large converted cargo planes that fly into hurricanes to collect weather data. . . . The pastels are particularly effective at capturing the look and feel of the powerful winds and swirling water caused by a hurricane at its height." SLJ
Includes bibliographical references

Fradin, Judith Bloom
Hurricanes; by Judy and Dennis Fradin. National Geographic 2007 48p il (Witness to disaster) $16.95; lib bdg $26.90 *
Grades: 4 5 6 7   551.55
1. Hurricanes
ISBN 978-1-4262-0111-0; 1-4262-0111-7; 978-1-4262-0112-7 (lib bdg); 1-4262-0112-5 (lib bdg)
LC 2006-103003
This describes Hurricane Katrina, the science of hurricanes, some hurricanes of the past, and the prediction of hurricanes.
This offers "dramatic first-person quotes and an array of impressive photographs." Horn Book Guide
Includes glossary and bibliographical references

Gibbons, Gail
Hurricanes! Holiday House 2009 32p il $17.95
Grades: K 1 2   551.55
1. Hurricanes
ISBN 978-0-8234-2233-3; 0-8234-2233-X
LC 2009-8761
"Gibbons uses a picture-book format to detail [hurricanes'] destructive power without the information ever becoming too frightening. . . . Gentle watercolors are Gibbons' main weapons here, and the painted panoramas . . . are engagingly tumultuous. . . . Famous hurricanes,

Gibbons, Gail—*Continued*

from Andrew to Katrina, are among the multitude of . . . topics broached in this intriguing introduction." Booklist

Tornadoes! Holiday House 2009 32p il $16.95
Grades: K 1 2 3   551.55
  1. Tornadoes
  ISBN 978-0-8234-2216-6; 0-8234-2216-X
                                        LC 2008035828

"Gail Gibbons explains how tornadoes form, the scale used for classifying them, and what to do in case one should be near you." Publisher's note

"Gibbons uses her trademark watercolor cartoon images and simple text to introduce readers to scientific information. . . . Gibbons's style is appealing and accessible." SLJ

Godkin, Celia, 1948-

Hurricane! Fitzhenry & Whiteside 2008 unp il $19.95
Grades: 2 3 4   551.55
  1. Hurricanes
  ISBN 978-1-55455-080-7; 1-55455-080-7

"An attractive, simple introduction to the effects of a hurricane on humans and on wildlife. . . . Godkin's gentle illustrations—paintings in water-soluble oil on canvas and drawings in ink and watercolor on paper—add luminous grace to this simple look at the effects of violent tropical storms. Handsome and useful." SLJ

Goin, Miriam Busch

Storms. National Geographic 2009 32p il (National Geographic kids) lib bdg $11.90; pa $3.99
Grades: K 1 2   551.55
  1. Storms
  ISBN   978-1-4263-0395-1   (lib   bdg);
  978-1-4263-0394-4 (pa)   LC 2008-51883

"Blizzards, monsoons, hurricanes: the excitement of wild, stormy weather will draw beginning readers to this dramatic title with color photos and an interactive text." Booklist

Harris, Caroline, 1964-

Wild weather. Kingfisher 2005 53p il map (Kingfisher voyages) $14.95
Grades: 4 5 6 7   551.55
  1. Storms 2. Weather
  ISBN 0-7534-5931-0; 978-0-7534-5911-9

This describes weather phenomena such as monsoons, tsunamis, blizzards, tornadoes, cyclones, mirages, and El Niño.

This "book has bright and exciting pictures. . . . The organization . . . is great, and the text is easy to read." Sci Books Films

  Includes glossary

Jennings, Terry, 1938-

Extreme weather. Smart Apple Media 2009 32p il map (Amazing planet earth) lib bdg $28.50
Grades: 4 5 6   551.55
  1. Weather 2. Storms
  ISBN 978-1-59920-369-0 (lib bdg); 1-59920-369-3 (lib bdg)   LC 2009-3401

This book explains how extreme weather conditions can have devastating effects on our lives

"Chapters are labeled as 'Case Study' or 'Science Report,' making the presentation lively. The concise explanations include just the right number of examples and clear diagrams, and have perfect color photo accompaniments." SLJ

  Includes glossary

Schuh, Mari C., 1975-

Tornadoes. Pebble Plus 2010 24p il map (Earth in action) lib bdg $21.32
Grades: K 1 2   551.55
  1. Tornadoes
  ISBN 978-1-4296-3434-2 (lib bdg); 1-4296-3434-0 (lib bdg)   LC 2009-2174

"Describes tornadoes, how they form, and the tools scientists use to predict them." Publisher's note

This book "boasts a full-page color photograph. . . . [It shows] the aftermath of a disaster . . . but there are also some diagrams showing physical mechanisms and maps highlighting commonly affected places. The left side of each spread provides a few sentences of large-print text, with short, clear explanations." SLJ

  Includes glossary and bibliographical references

Silverstein, Alvin

Hurricanes; the science behind killer storms; [by] Alvin Silverstein, Virginia Silverstein, and Laura Silverstein Nunn. Enslow Publishers 2009 48p il map (The science behind natural disasters) lib bdg $23.93
Grades: 4 5 6   551.55
  1. Hurricanes
  ISBN 978-0-7660-2971-2 (lib bdg); 0-7660-2971-9 (lib bdg)   LC 2008-26264

"Examines the science behind hurricanes, including how and where tropical storms form, the various types of tropical storms, how scientists track hurricanes, and provides hurricane safety tips." Publisher's note

"Scientific explanations are accompanied by plentiful color diagrams that will help students to grasp causes and effects. . . . Photos . . . are effective, and are sometimes turned into helpful, lively diagrams by the addition of such features as wind-direction arrows." SLJ

  Includes glossary and bibliographical references

Tornadoes; the science behind terrible twisters; [by] Alvin Silverstein, Virginia Silverstein, and Laura Silverstein Nunn. Enslow Publishers 2009 48p il map (The science behind natural disasters) lib bdg $23.93
Grades: 4 5 6   551.55
  1. Tornadoes
  ISBN 978-0-7660-2976-7 (lib bdg); 0-7660-2976-X (lib bdg)   LC 2008-29635

Silverstein, Alvin—*Continued*

"Discusses the science behind tornadoes, including how and where they form, the scientific methods to track and predict them, and tornado safety tips." Publisher's note

"Scientific explanations are accompanied by plentiful color diagrams that will help students to grasp causes and effects. . . . Photos . . . are effective, and are sometimes turned into helpful, lively diagrams by the addition of such features as wind-direction arrows." SLJ

Includes glossary and bibliographical references

Simon, Seymour, 1931-

Hurricanes. updated ed. Collins 2007 31p il map $16.99; pa $6.99 *

Grades: 3 4 5 6   **551.55**
   1. Hurricanes
   ISBN   978-0-06-117072-0;   0-06-117072-0;
   978-0-06-117071-3 (pa); 0-06-117071-2 (pa)
                                               LC 2007-280766
   First published 2003

Discusses where and how hurricanes are formed, the destruction caused by legendary storms, and the precautions to take when a hurricane strikes

This is written "in a simple and precise manner. . . . The photos include computer-enhanced radar images and shots of storm damage from recent (Katrina in 2005) and historical (Glaveston in 1900) times." Sci Books Films

Includes bibliographical references

Storms. Morrow Junior Bks. 1989 unp il pa $5.95 hardcover o.p.

Grades: 4 5 6 7   **551.55**
   1. Storms
   ISBN 0-688-11708-2 (pa)   LC 88-22045

This book describes the atmospheric conditions which create thunderstorms, hailstorms, lightning, tornadoes, and hurricanes and how violent weather affects the environment and people

"The half- to full-page glossy color photographs are sure to attract young readers as will the subject. *Storms* is an excellent way to introduce the science of meteorology to children." Sci Books Films

Tornadoes. Morrow Junior Bks. 1999 unp il map hardcover o.p. pa $6.99 *

Grades: 4 5 6 7   **551.55**
   1. Tornadoes
   ISBN 0-688-14646-5; 0-06-443791-4 (pa)
                                               LC 98-27953

Describes the location, nature, development, measurement, and destructive effects of tornadoes, as well as how to stay out of danger from them

"Incredible full-color photographs and diagrams, clearly portraying the different formations and devastating power of the windstorms, complement the text perfectly." Booklist

Stewart, Mark, 1960-

Blizzards and winter storms. Gareth Stevens Pub. 2009 48p il map (The ultimate 10. Natural disasters) lib bdg $31

Grades: 5 6 7 8   **551.55**
   1. Blizzards 2. Storms
   ISBN 978-0-8368-9150-8 (lib bdg); 0-8368-9150-3 (lib bdg)   LC 2008-28230

A "look at how winter storms form and how they wreak havoc in different parts of the world." Publisher's note

Blizzards and winter storms "are described, while color photos illustrate the resulting damage, conveying a significant part of the information through their captions. . . . An especially useful book." SLJ

Includes glossary and bibliographical references

Treaster, Joseph B.

Hurricane force; in the path of America's deadliest storms. Kingfisher 2007 128p il map $16.95

Grades: 4 5 6 7 8   **551.55**
   1. Hurricanes 2. Storms
   ISBN 978-0-7534-6086-3   LC 2006-22517

Describes how violent storms and hurricanes are formed and notes some of history's greatest storms to hit the U.S. such as Hurricane Katrina.

This is a "gripping photo-essay. . . . There are lots of full-color photographs that bring close the high winds and surging seas of hurricanes, the shattered homes, and pictures of people rescued or lost. The extensive back matter is an integral part of the book." Booklist

Includes bibliographical references

551.56   Atmospheric electricity and optics

Kramer, Stephen

Lightning; photographs by Warren Faidley. Carolrhoda Bks. 1992 48p il (Nature in action) hardcover o.p. pa $7.95

Grades: 4 5 6   **551.56**
   1. Lightning
   ISBN 0-87614-659-0; 0-87614-617-5 (pa)
                                               LC 91-21793

This introduction to lightning "explains how a thunderhead develops, how lightning results from negatively and positively charged electrons, kinds of lightning, and [includes] safety information." Bull Cent Child Books

"Diagrams supplement the well-written narrative in describing scientific concepts. Exceptionally fine, full-color photographs—each a work of art—perfectly illustrate the text, powerfully and spectacularly showing the majesty and might of this phenomenon." SLJ

Includes glossary

Simon, Seymour, 1931-

Lightning. Morrow Junior Bks. 1997 unp il hardcover o.p. pa $6.99

Grades: 4 5 6 7   **551.56**
   1. Lightning
   ISBN 0-688-14638-4; 0-06-088435-5 (pa)
                                               LC 96-16962

Simon, Seymour, 1931—*Continued*

Photographs and text explore the natural phenomenon of lightning

"The subject is exciting, the information is amazing, and the full-color photographs are riveting. . . . Simon's explanations are concise but thorough." Booklist

551.57   Hydrometeorology

Branley, Franklyn Mansfield, 1915-2002

Down comes the rain; by Franklyn M. Branley; illustrated by James Graham Hale. HarperCollins Pubs. 1997 31p il (Let's-read-and-find-out science) hardcover o.p. pa $4.95

Grades: K 1 2 3   **551.57**

1. Rain 2. Clouds

ISBN 0-06-025338-X; 0-06-445166-6 (pa)

LC 96-3519

A revised and newly illustrated edition of Rain & hail published 1983 by Crowell

The author explains "how water is recycled, how clouds are formed, and why rain and hail occur. A few easy science activities are included. . . . The pen-and-ink with watercolor wash paintings clearly interpret the concepts presented on each page." SLJ

Snow is falling; by Franklyn M. Branley; illustrated by Holly Keller. HarperCollins Pubs. 2000 33p il (Let's-read-and-find-out science) hardcover o.p. pa $4.95

Grades: K 1   **551.57**

1. Snow

ISBN 0-06-027990-7; 0-06-027991-5 (lib bdg); 0-06-445186-0 (pa)   LC 98-23106

A revised and newly illustrated edition of the title first published 1963 by Crowell

Describes snow's physical qualities and how quantities of it can be fun as well as dangerous

"Keller's new illustrations are a good match for the spare, informative text. A few easy activities explore snow's different properties, and a list of websites is appended." Horn Book Guide

Cassino, Mark

The story of snow; the science of winter's wonder; by Mark Cassino, with Jon Nelson; illustrations by Nora Aoyagi. Chronicle Books 2009 33p il $16.99 *

Grades: 2 3 4 5   **551.57**

1. Snow

ISBN 978-0-8118-6866-2; 0-8118-6866-4

LC 2009-04368

"Simple sentences in large type offer basic information about the formation and structure of snow crystals while additional explanations and detail are presented in two sets of progressively smaller fonts. Aoyagi's watercolor and ink drawings show how a snow crystal develops from a tiny speck of soil, pollen, or other substances to become a complex six-sided structure." SLJ

"Aoyagi's clean ink-and-watercolor diagrams and backgrounds allow the spectacular photographs to take center stage and provide supplemental information. Sure to get young scientists outside in the cold, particularly as it helpfully includes crystal-catching instructions." Kirkus

De Paola, Tomie, 1934-

The cloud book; words and pictures by Tomie de Paola. Holiday House 1975 30p il lib bdg $16.95; pa $6.95

Grades: K 1 2 3   **551.57**

1. Clouds

ISBN 0-8234-0259-2 (lib bdg); 0-8234-0531-1 (pa)

The author instructs "young readers about the ten most common types of clouds, how they were named, and what they mean in terms of changing weather. Actually a very good text to use for early science instruction. Includes a scattering of traditional myths that have clouds as a basis." Adventuring with Books

Kaner, Etta, 1947-

Who likes the rain? written by Etta kaner; llustrated by Marie Lafrance. Kids Can Press 2007 unp il (Exploring the elements) $14.95

Grades: PreK K 1 2   **551.57**

1. Rain

ISBN 978-1-55337-841-9; 1-55337-841-5

On each double-page spread, a child expresses why he or she likes the rain ("because I can jump in puddles"). The child then wonders how the event happens ("I wonder where puddles come from") and lifts a flap for a scientific explanation

"An attractive, straight-forward presentation of concepts related to rain." Booklist

Who likes the snow? written by Etta Kaner; illustrated by Marie Lafrance. Kids Can Press 2006 unp il (Exploring the elements) $14.95

Grades: PreK K 1 2   **551.57**

1. Snow

ISBN 978-1-55337-842-6; 1-55337-842-3

"This slim book is packed with fascinating information about snow. Each spread is divided into three parts: a statement, a query, and, with the turn of a flap, a simply stated scientific explanation. . . . Lafrance's naive acrylic paintings have a flat appearance, as if they were carved of wood, and clearly depict the topics being discussed." SLJ

Libbrecht, Kenneth G., 1958-

The secret life of a snowflake; an up-close look at the art & science of snowflakes; [by] Kenneth Libbrecht. Voyageur Press 2010 48p il $17

Grades: 3 4 5 6   **551.57**

1. Snow

ISBN 978-0-7603-3676-2; 0-7603-3676-8

LC 2009-07892

"Extraordinary photographs of individual snowflakes are the true highlight of this informational book. With crisp detail and lit up with colored light, the crystals are mesmerizing in their clarity and brilliance. Libbrecht uses a first-person narration to describe the microphotography process that he uses to create the images and then goes on to outline the life cycle of a snowflake. . . . A solid addition to any science collection, this book will draw in young enthusiasts, and the beautiful photographs will engage casual browsers." SLJ

Marsico, Katie, 1980-

Snowy weather days; [by] Katie Marsico. Children's Press 2007 24p il (Scholastic news nonfiction readers) lib bdg $19

Grades: K 1 2 3   **551.57**

1. Snow

ISBN 978-0-531-16773-1 (lib bdg); 0-531-16773-9 (lib bdg)   LC 2006013306

Simple facts about snow.

"Young readers will take pleasure in learning simple facts while discovering new words along the way. . . . These full-color pictures show the featured conditions, as well as a variety of outdoor scenes of children and adults enjoying nature." SLJ

Includes glossary and bibliographical references

Rockwell, Anne F., 1934-

Clouds; by Anne Rockwell; illustrated by Frané Lessac. Collins 2008 33p il (Let's-read-and-find-out-science) $16.99; pa $5.99

Grades: 1 2 3   **551.57**

1. Clouds

ISBN 978-0-06-029101-3; 0-06-029101-X; 978-0-06-445220-5 (pa); 0-06-445220-4 (pa)

"Rockwell introduces 11 different types of clouds according to their positions in the atmosphere. . . . The author describes each type of cloud formation, explains where it is found in the sky, and tells what kind of weather is associated with it. Attractive folk-art-style paintings show the clouds and children playing or working outside. The information is solid." SLJ

Schuh, Mari C., 1975-

Avalanches. Pebble Plus 2010 24p il (Earth in action) lib bdg $21.32

Grades: K 1 2   **551.57**

1. Avalanches

ISBN 978-1-4296-3437-3 (lib bdg); 1-4296-3437-5 (lib bdg)   LC 2009-2163

Describes avalanches, how they occur, and the damage they cause

This book "boasts a full-page color photograph. . . . [It shows] the aftermath of a disaster . . . but there are also some diagrams showing physical mechanisms and maps highlighting commonly affected places. The left side of each spread provides a few sentences of large-print text, with short, clear explanations." SLJ

Includes glossary and bibliographical references

551.6 Climatology and weather

Arnold, Caroline, 1944-

El Niño; stormy weather for people and wildlife. Clarion Bks. 1998 48p il $16; pa $5.95

Grades: 4 5 6 7   **551.6**

1. El Niño Current 2. Climate

ISBN 0-395-77602-3; 0-618-55110-7 (pa)

LC 98-4826

Explores the nature of the El Niño current and its effects on people and wildlife

This book has a "readable, informative text. . . . Full-color photos, a computer-image series, diagrams, and Internet sources bolster the narrative." SLJ

Includes glossary and bibliographical references

Baker, Stuart

In temperate zones. Marshall Cavendish Benchmark 2009 32p il map (Climate change) lib bdg $19.95

Grades: 5 6 7 8   **551.6**

1. Greenhouse effect 2. Forest ecology

ISBN 978-0-7614-4441-1 (lib bdg); 0-7614-4441-6 (lib bdg)   LC 2009-5769

The book about climate change in the temperate zones "is perfectly organized for students. . . . Unique layout features serve as signposts and will help focus readers' attention. . . . [The book] features an outstanding chart of possible effects of global warming on the area in question, listing 'Possible Event', 'Predicted Result', and 'Impact' in short, bulleted statements." SLJ

Includes glossary

Gibbons, Gail

Weather words and what they mean. Holiday House 1990 unp il $16.95; pa $6.95

Grades: K 1 2 3   **551.6**

1. Weather

ISBN 0-8234-0805-1; 0-8234-0952-X (pa)

LC 89-39515

The author discusses the meaning of meteorological terms such as temperature, air pressure, thunderstorm and moisture

"Gibbons' easily identifiable artistic style works well with her explanations of sometimes misunderstood weather-related terms. Drawings are appealing, attractively arranged, and closely matched to the textual information. . . . An attractive introduction for weather units in the primary grades." SLJ

Hartman, Eve

Climate change; [by] Eve Hartman and Wendy Meshbesher. Raintree 2010 48p il map (Sci-hi: Earth and space science) lib bdg $31.43; pa $8.99

Grades: 4 5 6 7   **551.6**

1. Greenhouse effect 2. Climate—Environmental aspects

ISBN 978-1-4109-3352-2 (lib bdg); 1-4109-3352-0 (lib bdg); 978-1-4109-3362-1 (pa); 1-4109-3362-8 (pa)

LC 2009-3538

Examine the causes of climate change, and how scientists gather data about global warming. Learn about the different ways people and nations are combating climate change, and how people and animals adapt to a new climate.

"Multiple colorful sidebars and large and small diagrams and photographs will help students to grasp the fundamentals being discussed, and the easy but interesting science experiments will act as further reinforcements." SLJ

Includes glossary and bibliographical references

Parker, Steve

Climate. QEB Pub. 2010 32p il (QEB changes in . . .) lib bdg $28.50

Grades: 3 4 5 6   **551.6**
1. Climate
ISBN 978-1-59566-776-2 (lib bdg); 1-59566-776-8 (lib bdg)   LC 2008-56068
"The information is presented in brief paragraphs and sidebars. Suggestions for kids to help improve the planet are sprinkled throughout. . . . Students will enjoy this appealing layout and the information can spark further research on the topic[s]. . . . Either digitally or on paper, students could make fantastic presentations using a similar design." Libr Media Connect

Includes glossary

Royston, Angela

Looking at weather and seasons; how do they change? [by] Angela Royston. Enslow Publishers 2008 32p il (Looking at science: how things change) lib bdg $22.60

Grades: 1 2 3   **551.6**
1. Seasons 2. Weather
ISBN 978-0-7660-3093-0 (lib bdg); 0-7660-3093-8 (lib bdg)   LC 2007-24515
"An introductory look at what causes Earth's weather and seasons." Publisher's note
"Fills a huge void in elementary science collections. . . . Text is arranged in succinct 'chunks,' giving important facts without overwhelming readers. . . . [This] is an essential addition." Libr Media Connect

Includes glossary and bibliographical references

Rupp, Rebecca

Weather; with journal illustrations by Melissa Sweet and experiment illustrations by Dug Nap. Storey Kids 2003 136p il map hardcover o.p. pa $14.95

Grades: 4 5 6 7   **551.6**
1. Weather
ISBN 1-58017-469-8; 1-58017-420-5 (pa)   LC 2002-152310
Contents: The atmosphere: what's up?; Wind: huffs, puffs, & hurricanes; Sunshine: beams, burns, & blue skies; Clouds: white sheep & little cat feet; Rain: drops, drizzles, & downpours; Thunder & lightning: Thor's hammer & Zeus's spear; Snow & ice: frost, flurries, and blizzards; Predicting the weather: reading the skys
This includes facts about weather with instructions for 22 science projects
"A lively, upbeat presentation. Chock-full of solid information, this compendium includes lots of slightly offbeat, appealing observations. . . . Numerous, attention-grabbing visuals illustrate experiments." SLJ

Includes glossary

Simpson, Kathleen

Extreme weather; science tackles global warming and climate change; by Kathleen Simpson; Jonathan D.W. Kahl, consultant. National Geographic 2008 64p il map (National Geographic investigates) $17.95; lib bdg $27.90 *

Grades: 4 5 6 7   **551.6**
1. Greenhouse effect 2. Climate—Environmental aspects
ISBN   978-1-4263-0359-3;   1-4263-0359-9; 978-1-4263-0281-7 (lib bdg); 1-4263-0281-9 (lib bdg)
"An exploration of extreme weather explains how weather is created, shows how hurricanes and tornadoes form and are rated, covers types of clouds and precipitation, and looks at the link between climate and weather." Publisher's note
This "is a well-written and engaging book. . . . Excellent descriptions of how and why these various weather patterns occur are presented. The book includes dramatic photographs and clear diagrams." Sci Books Films

Includes glossary and bibliographical references

551.63   Weather forecasting and forecasts, reporting and reports

Breen, Mark, 1960-

The kids' book of weather forecasting; build a weather station, "read" the sky & make predictions; with meteorologist Mark Breen and Kathleen Friestad; illustrations by Michael Kline. Williamson 2000 140p il maps music pa $12.95 *

Grades: 4 5 6 7   **551.63**
1. Weather forecasting 2. Science—Experiments
ISBN 1-88559-339-2   LC 99-89954
"A Williamson kids can! book"
A hands-on introduction to the science of meteorology, explaining how to make equipment to measure rainfall, wind direction, and humidity, record measurements and observations in a weather log, make weather predictions, and perform other related activities
"A useful, accessible book illustrated with black-and-white diagrams and cartoons." SLJ

Includes bibliographical references

Gibbons, Gail

Weather forecasting. Four Winds Press 1987 unp il pa $5.99 hardcover o.p.

Grades: K 1 2 3   **551.63**
1. Weather forecasting
ISBN 0-689-71683-4 (pa)   LC 86-7602
"The book is divided into four sections, one per season, which treat different kinds of weather as they're observed, recorded, and reported at a weather station." Bull Cent Child Books
"Any child can learn the basic concepts from the text at the bottom of each page, while the precocious can garner an impressive weather vocabulary by absorbing the terms labeled and defined within the artwork. Brightly illustrated with the artist's usual bold, flat colors, this book will serve as an appealing introduction to weather forecasting for young children." Booklist

552 Petrology

Davis, Barbara J., 1952-
Minerals, rocks, and soil. Raintree 2010 48p il map (Sci-hi: Earth and space science) lib bdg $31.43; pa $8.99
Grades: 4 5 6 7   **552**
    1. Rocks 2. Minerals 3. Petrology
    ISBN 978-1-4109-3347-8 (lib bdg); 1-4109-3347-4 (lib bdg); 978-1-4109-3357-7 (pa); 1-4109-3357-1 (pa)
        LC 2009-13459
This title "shows . . . how minerals, soil, and rocks form." Publisher's note
"Multiple colorful sidebars and large and small diagrams and photographs will help students to grasp the fundamentals being discussed, and the easy but interesting science experiments will act as further reinforcements." SLJ
Includes glossary and bibliographical references

Extreme rocks & minerals! Q & A. Collins 2007 47p il $17.99; pa $6.99
Grades: 4 5 6   **552**
    1. Rocks 2. Minerals
    ISBN 978-0-06-089982-0; 0-06-089982-4; 978-0-06-089981-3 (pa); 0-06-089981-6 (pa)
        LC 2007001760
This describes types of rocks and minerals, how they are formed, and how people use them.
"It's hard to beat this title for a clear, accurate, and appealing survey. Illustrations are key to this subject, and the range of crisp photos is excellent." SLJ
Includes bibliographical references

Faulkner, Rebecca
Igneous rock; [by] Rebecca Faulkner. Raintree 2007 48p il (Geology rocks!) lib bdg $31.43; pa $8.99
Grades: 4 5 6   **552**
    1. Rocks
    ISBN 978-1-4109-2747-7 (lib bdg); 1-4109-2747-4 (lib bdg); 978-1-4109-2755-2 (pa); 1-4109-2755-5 (pa)
        LC 2006037174
"Raintree freestyle express"
This "describes all three categories of rocks and what distinguishes them from each other, minerals, identification of igneous rocks, and their formation through volcanic activity. . . . [The book] includes quality color photographs and diagrams that do an exemplary job of expanding on the topics covered." SLJ
Includes glossary and bibliographical references

Metamorphic rock. Raintree 2007 48p il (Geology rocks!) lib bdg $31.43; pa $8.99
Grades: 4 5 6   **552**
    1. Rocks
    ISBN 978-1-4109-2749-1 (lib bdg); 1-4109-2749-0 (lib bdg); 978-1-4109-2757-6 (pa); 1-4109-2757-1 (pa)
        LC 2006037063
"Raintree freestyle express"
"This title covers the following: Squeeze and heat; Crust, mantle, and core; The world's rocks; Marvelous Metamorphism; Metamorphic rock types; Hard beauty; Metamorphic landforms." Publisher's note
Includes glossary and bibliographical references

Sedimentary rock; [by] Rebecca Faulkner. Raintree 2007 48p il (Geology rocks!) lib bdg $31.43; pa $8.99
Grades: 4 5 6   **552**
    1. Rocks
    ISBN 978-1-4109-2748-4 (lib bdg); 1-4109-2748-2 (lib bdg); 978-1-4109-2756-9 (pa); 1-4109-2756-3 (pa)
        LC 2006037173
"Raintree freestyle express"
This "covers the Earth's structure, how these rocks are formed, fossils, and the various types. [The] book includes quality color photographs and diagrams that do an exemplary job of expanding on the topics covered." SLJ
Includes glossary and bibliographical references

Gans, Roma, 1894-1996
Let's go rock collecting; illustrated by Holly Keller. newly il ed. HarperCollins Pubs. 1997 31p il (Let's-read-and-find-out science) hardcover o.p. pa $5.99
Grades: K 1 2   **552**
    1. Rocks—Collectors and collecting
    ISBN 0-06-027282-1; 0-06-027283-X (lib bdg); 0-06-027283-X (pa)   LC 95-44999
A revised and newly illustrated edition of Rock collecting, published 1984 by Crowell
Describes the formation and characteristics of igneous, metamorphic, and sedimentary rocks and how to recognize and collect them
"The excellent diagrams, full-color photographs of specimens, and minor textual changes clarify the concepts (for example, Mohs' scale of hardness) and extend the presentation. . . . The pair of youngsters featured in Keller's brightly colored illustrations . . . convey the joys of being a rock hound." SLJ

Gardner, Robert, 1929-
Smashing science projects about Earth's rocks and minerals; [by] Robert Gardner; illustrations by Tom Labaff. Enslow Elementary 2007 c2008 48p il (Rockin' earth science experiments) lib bdg $23.93
Grades: 3 4 5   **552**
    1. Minerals 2. Rocks 3. Science—Experiments 4. Science projects
    ISBN 978-0-7660-2731-2 (lib bdg); 0-7660-2731-7 (lib bdg)   LC 2006013788
This offers experiments about minerals and crystals, testing materials for hardness, soil, igneos, sedimentary, and metamorphic rock, and core samples.
Includes glossary and bibliographical references

Green, Dan

Rocks and minerals; a gem of a read! by Dan Green and Simon Basher; illustrated by Simon Basher. Kingfisher 2009 128p il pa $8.99

Grades: 5 6 7 8   **552**

   1. Rocks 2. Minerals

   ISBN 978-0-7534-6314-7 (pa); 0-7534-6314-8 (pa)

This "presents a portrait gallery of 56 rocks and minerals (plus four kinds of fossils) composed of smiling, round-headed, usually peanut-shaped cartoon figures wearing or bearing distinctive identifiers. . . . The entries make lighthearted but unexpectedly meaty reading." Booklist

Hynes, Margaret, 1970-

Rocks & fossils; foreword by Jack Horner. Kingfisher 2006 63p il (Kingfisher knowledge) $12.95

Grades: 5 6 7 8   **552**

   1. Rocks 2. Fossils

   ISBN 978-0-7534-5974-4; 0-7534-5974-4

                              LC 2005-23897

This covers "the history of rock, . . . the minerals that make them, and . . . their different uses, from building materials to pigments for paints and dyes. The formation of fossils is also explained." Publisher's note

This is a "lavishly illustrated book. . . . The well-written text is pithy and comprehensible." Voice Youth Advocates

Includes glossary and bibliographical references

Trueit, Trudi Strain

Rocks, gems, and minerals. Watts 2003 63p il (Watts library) $24; pa $8.95

Grades: 4 5 6 7   **552**

   1. Rocks 2. Minerals 3. Precious stones

   ISBN 0-531-12195-X; 0-531-16241-9 (pa)

                              LC 2001-7222

Contents: World of wonders; Mineral magic; The circle of stone; A rocky road; Where do you stand?

"The formation of basic rocks— sedimentary, igneous, and metamorphic—are covered, as are rock crystals and crystallization. Chemical symbols for elements, charts such as the Mohs scale and the geographic location of major gem finds, and fun facts are included." SLJ

This includes "attention-grabbing photography, excellent charts and diagrams, short articles with or without photographs, and vocabulary terms that appear in bold and are explained in context." Sci Books Films

Includes glossary and bibliographical references

VanCleave, Janice Pratt

Janice VanCleave's rocks and minerals; mind-boggling experiments you can turn into science fair projects. Wiley 1996 90p il (Spectacular science projects series) pa $10.95

Grades: 4 5 6 7   **552**

   1. Rocks 2. Minerals 3. Science projects 4. Science—Experiments

   ISBN 0-471-10269-5   LC 95-10324

"The experiments lead the investigator through a range of topics such as crystal shapes; mineral characteristics

. . . magnetism in minerals; sedimentary, metamorphic, and igneous rock formation; rock weathering; fossil types and formation; and how to put together a mineral, rock, or fossil collection." Sci Books Films

"VanCleave presents stunningly clear, direct, and informative projects. They are generally simple enough for self-directed students to do on their own, but a teacher's guidance would be helpful." SLJ

Includes glossary

553.2   Carbonaceous materials

Green, Robert, 1969-

Coal. Cherry Lake Pub. 2010 32p il (21st century skills library. Power up!) lib bdg $27.07

Grades: 4 5 6   **553.2**

   1. Coal

   ISBN 978-1-60279-508-2 (lib bdg); 1-60279-508-8 (lib bdg)   LC 2008-44184

This "provides a basic introduction to [coal]. . . . The writing is clear and succinct, and the information is accurate, timely and unbiased. The plentiful photographs are outstanding and reinforce the text. . . . Certain to appeal to young readers and their teachers." Libr Media Connect

Includes glossary and bibliographical references

Tagliaferro, Linda

How does a plant become oil? Raintree 2010 32p il (How does it happen?) lib bdg $27.50; pa $7.99

Grades: 3 4 5   **553.2**

   1. Petroleum 2. Gasoline

   ISBN 978-1-4109-3443-7 (lib bdg); 1-4109-3443-8 (lib bdg); 978-1-4109-3451-2 (pa); 1-4109-3451-9 (pa)

                              LC 2008-52290

This addresses questions such as "What tiny sea plants decompose to form oil? How did ancient Egyptians use oil to preserve mummies? What are the dangers of using fossil fuels?" Publisher's note

"Information is clearly presented using a large font, diagrams, and photographs formatted to resemble Polaroid pictures. . . . A first-rate job answering some important scientific questions." SLJ

Includes glossary and bibliographical references

553.4   Metals and semimetals

Raum, Elizabeth

The story behind gold. Heinemann Library 2009 32p il map (True stories) lib bdg $28.21

Grades: 3 4 5   **553.4**

   1. Gold 2. Gold mines and mining

   ISBN 978-1-4329-2340-2 (lib bdg); 1-4329-2340-4 (lib bdg)   LC 2008037525

This offers history, ephemera, and basic facts about gold, gold mining, and the uses of gold

Includes bibliographical references

553.6 Other economic materials

Kurlansky, Mark

The story of salt; [illustrated by] S. D. Schindler. G.P. Putnam's Sons 2006 48p il map $16.99 *

Grades: 3 4 5 6   553.6

    1. Salt

    ISBN 0-399-23998-7   LC 2005-032629

An adaptation of the author's title for adults: Salt: a world history (2002)

"The informal narrative and the exquisitely detailed, sometimes playful ink-and-watercolor illustrations dramatize the sweeping world history of salt's essential role in human life—from prehistoric times and the early voyages of discovery through the breakthrough of refrigeration and the latest drilling technology." Booklist

Includes bibliographical references

Moore, Heidi, 1976-

The story behind salt. Heinemann Library 2009 32p il map (True stories) lib bdg $28.21

Grades: 3 4 5   553.6

    1. Salt

    ISBN 978-1-4329-2348-8 (lib bdg); 1-4329-2348-X (lib bdg)   LC 2008037390

This describes the properties of salt and how it is used, including its history and miscellaneous facts, answering such questions as: Why is the sea salty? Why is it so easy to float in the Dead Sea? Why do people put salt on icy roads?

Includes bibliographical references

553.7 Water

Gallant, Roy A.

Water; our precious resource. Benchmark Bks. 2002 c2003 79p il map (Earthworks) lib bdg $29.93

Grades: 5 6 7 8   553.7

    1. Water

    ISBN 0-7614-1365-0   LC 2001-43290

Contents: What is water?; Some properties of water; Where is all the water?; Our needs for water; Water pollution and purification; Whose water is it?

An in-depth look at Earth's waters and mankind's uses of water throughout history which includes ideas about planning better use of this critical resource in the future

"Gallant's prose is nearly conversational in its easy delivery, but his facts are always thorough and his ideas clearly explained. Best of all, he raises informed points that will help readers rethink their habits and realize the complexity of the issues. . . . Crisp graphs, maps, and excellent color photos illustrate [this] fine [volume]." Booklist

Includes glossary and bibliographical references

Lauw, Darlene

Water; [by Darlene Lauw and Lim Cheng Puay] Crabtree 2003 31p il (Science alive!) lib bdg $21.28; pa $7.95

Grades: 3 4 5 6   553.7

    1. Water 2. Science—Experiments

    ISBN 0-7787-0567-6 (lib bdg); 0-7787-0613-3 (pa)   LC 2002-11640

Contents: What is water made of?; Solid, liquid, gas; Keeping cool; Water pressure; Water seeks its own level; Water flows up!; Water pollution and water treatment

Uses simple experiments to demonstrate the properties of water

"The directions are kid friendly, and the graphics that support them are very helpful. . . . The science content is within the range of understanding of an upper elementary school student." Sci Books Films

Includes glossary

Strauss, Rochelle, 1967-

One well; the story of water on Earth; written by Rochelle Strauss; illustrated by Rosemary Woods. Kids Can Press 2007 32p il $17.95 *

Grades: 4 5 6   553.7

    1. Water

    ISBN 978-1-55337-954-6; 1-55337-954-3

"Looking at all the water on Earth . . . as 'One Well' into which all life dips to survive, Strauss presents a timely discussion of the use and abuse of a not-so-limitless resource. Liberally sprinkled with interesting facts, . . . [the book has a] readable text. . . . Woods's delicate paintings keep perfect step and provide a gentle framework for the plentiful statistical snippets." SLJ

Wick, Walter, 1953-

A drop of water; a book of science and wonder; written and photographed by Walter Wick. Scholastic 1997 40p il $16.95 *

Grades: 4 5 6   553.7

    1. Water

    ISBN 0-590-22197-3   LC 95-30068

The author "uses simple techniques to show water properties such as surface tension, adhesion, capillary attraction, molecular motion, freezing, evaporation, and condensation." Booklist

"This title is an elegant synthesis of science and art. . . . The close-up photographs are breathtakingly distinct; and the clarity provided by the combination of concept, text, and photography of this quality is noteworthy." Bull Cent Child Books

553.8 Gems

Moore, Heidi, 1976-

The story behind diamonds. Heinemann Library 2009 32p il (True stories) lib bdg $28.21

Grades: 3 4 5   553.8

    1. Diamonds

    ISBN 978-1-4329-2345-7 (lib bdg); 1-4329-2345-5 (lib bdg)   LC 2008043374

This describes the history, ephemera, basic facts, and uses of diamonds

Includes bibliographical references

560   Fossils & prehistoric life

Aliki

Fossils tell of long ago. rev ed. Crowell 1990 32p il (Let's-read-and-find-out science book) pa $4.95 hardcover o.p.

Grades: K 1 2 3   560

1. Fossils

ISBN 0-06-445093-7 (pa)   LC 89-17247

Also available Spanish language edition

First published 1972

"Information about how fossils are formed and discovered is presented in simple text and an appealing variety of colorful illustrations. Includes directions for creating a fossil." Sci Child

Barner, Bob

Dinosaurs roar, butterflies soar! Chronicle Books 2009 unp il $16.99

Grades: K 1 2 3   560

1. Butterflies 2. Fossils 3. Dinosaurs

ISBN 978-0-8118-5663-8; 0-8118-5663-1

LC 2008016783

"This gently informative book describes the role butterflies played in helping dinosaurs and their environment flourish. The main text offers a simpler narrative than the supplementary and more detailed one in small type that appears below or next to it. . . . A few of the predominant theories about the dinosaurs' extinction and explanations of the continuing survival of butterflies are put forth. . . . Barner's illustrations are, as always, fantastically bright, eye-catching cut-paper collages. A useful, engaging, and illuminating book." SLJ

Bonner, Hannah

When bugs were big, plants were strange, and tetrapods stalked the earth; a cartoon prehistory of life before dinosaurs; written and illustrated by Hannah Bonner. National Geographic 2004 c2003 44p il $16.95 *

Grades: 3 4 5 6   560

1. Prehistoric animals 2. Fossils

ISBN 0-7922-6326-X   LC 2003-7818

"The Carboniferous and Permian periods spanned 100 million years or so just before the better-known Mesozoic Era. The author describes many of the unusual plant and animal species from those times." SLJ

The information is "presented with verve and humor that don't shortchange the young natural historian's quest for good explanations of the earth's distant past. . . . An exemplary curriculum support resource, but kids who dig dinosaurs will read the book purely for pleasure." Booklist

When fish got feet, sharks got teeth, and bugs began to swarm; a cartoon prehistory of life long before dinosaurs; written and illustrated by Hannah Bonner. National Geographic 2007 45p il $16.95; lib bdg $25.90 *

Grades: 2 3 4 5   560

1. Prehistoric animals

ISBN   978-1-4263-0078-3;   1-4263-0078-6; 978-1-4263-0079-0 (lib bdg); 1-4263-0079-4 (lib bdg)

LC 2006-20768

"Bonner explores life on Earth during the Silurian and Devonian periods. . . . Bonner's clear, engaging writing conveys plenty of information without overwhelming readers, and her illustrations offer fascinating visual representations of unusual creatures and landscapes." SLJ

Bradley, Timothy J.

Paleo bugs; survival of the creepiest; written and illustrated by Timothy J. Bradley. Chronicle Books 2008 44p il $15.99 *

Grades: 4 5 6 7   560

1. Insects 2. Fossils 3. Prehistoric animals

ISBN 978-0-8118-6022-2; 0-8118-6022-1

LC 2007-18174

This offers an "eye-widening gallery of extinct arthropods, from the mayfly-like heptagenia to a seven-foot-long arthropleura. . . . Bradley decks out each of his painted figures in bright hues, poses them in natural settings . . . and sets them aside a human hand or body in silhouette to suggest scale. . . . Readers will . . . pore over the pictures and come away knowing more about both these extinct animals and their modern descendants." Booklist

Includes glossary and bibliographical references

Brown, Charlotte Lewis

Beyond the dinosaurs; monsters of the air and sea; by Charlotte Lewis Brown; pictures by Phil Wilson. HarperCollinsPublishers 2007 30p il (I can read!) $15.99; lib bdg $16.89

Grades: K 1 2 3   560

1. Prehistoric animals 2. Fossils

ISBN   978-0-06-053056-3;   0-06-053056-1; 978-0-06-053057-0 (lib bdg); 0-06-053057-X (lib bdg)

LC 2007014462

"This introduction to creatures 'just as strange and wonderful as any dinosaur' pairs a straightforward text with action-packed, life-like illustrations. . . . [It has] a spread devoted to each of 11 prehistoric animals, including the Elasmosaurus, Hainosaurus, and Archaeopteryx. Helpful pronunciation guides are included. Readers of this book will get a closeup feel for life millions of years ago." SLJ

Burton, Virginia Lee, 1909-1968

Life story. updated ed. Houghton Mifflin 2009 67p il $22; pa $7.99

Grades: 3 4 5   560

1. Fossils 2. Evolution 3. Natural history

ISBN   978-0-547-19508-7;   0-547-19508-7; 978-0-547-20359-1 (pa); 0-547-20359-4 (pa)

First published 1962

Burton, Virginia Lee, 1909-1968—*Continued*

"Burton's 1962 exploration of the history of life on Earth, framed as a five-act play, returns in a newly updated edition that takes current scientific information into account (Pluto, for instance, is not among the planets shown orbiting the sun). Beginning with the birth of the Sun and continuing through the Earth's creation, the emergence and evolution of animal life, up to the changing seasons of the present, it's a lyrical and informative journey." Publ Wkly

Camper, Cathy

Bugs before time; prehistoric insects and their relatives; illustrated by Steve Kirk. Simon & Schuster Bks. for Young Readers 2002 unp il $16.95 *

Grades: 4 5 6 7   560
1. Insects 2. Fossils
ISBN 0-689-82092-5   LC 98-22872
Describes the physical characteristics, habits, and natural environment of various prehistoric insects some of which, including cockroaches, centipedes, and dragonflies, have survived into the present day

"A handsome introduction to prehistoric insects and other arthropods. . . . [Includes] up-to-date, conversational text and informative captions and date boxes. . . . Kirk's eye-catching, realistic watercolors portray a fascinating array of creatures." SLJ

Includes glossary and bibliographical references

Faulkner, Rebecca

Fossils; [by] Rebecca Faulkner. Raintree 2007 48p il map (Geology rocks!) lib bdg $31.43; pa $8.99

Grades: 4 5 6   560
1. Fossils
ISBN 978-1-4109-2752-1 (lib bdg); 1-4109-2752-0 (lib bdg); 978-1-4109-2760-6 (pa); 1-4109-2760-1 (pa)
LC 2006037065
"Raintree freestyle express"

This "discusses plate tectonics, common fossils and where they are found, dinosaurs, fossil fuels, and the contributions of the study of these relics to paleontology. . . . [The] book includes quality color photographs and diagrams that do an exemplary job of expanding on the topics covered." SLJ

Includes glossary and bibliographical references

Gallant, Roy A.

Fossils. Benchmark Bks. 2000 48p il map (Kaleidoscope) lib bdg $15.95

Grades: 3 4 5   560
1. Fossils
ISBN 0-7614-1041-4   LC 99-47494
Describes what fossils are, how they are formed, and what they tell scientists about the earth's past

"The easy-to-read text offers clear explanations. . . . Well-selected, beautifully reproduced photographs and computer graphics." SLJ

Includes glossary and bibliographical references

Goldish, Meish

The fossil feud; Marsh and Cope's bone wars; by Meish Goldish. Bearport Pub. 2007 32p il map (Fossil hunters) lib bdg $23.96

Grades: 3 4 5 6   560
1. Cope, E. D. (Edward Drinker), 1840-1897 2. Marsh, Othniel Charles, 1831-1899 3. Fossils
ISBN 978-1-59716-256-2 (lib bdg); 1-59716-256-6 (lib bdg)   LC 2006011319
This "tells of the Bone Wars, a clash between two American paleontologists. In 1868, at the Haddonfield, New Jersey, marl pit, Othniel Marsh and Edward Cope established a cooperative relationship, but it deteriorated rapidly. Over the next two decades, each man established dinosaur digs in Wyoming and Colorado, spied on the other's work, and engaged in bribery, theft, and sabotage, even dynamiting fossil sites. Finally, their newspaper attacks on each other's expertise, honor, and sanity alienated the scientific community and led to the end of the Bone Wars. Goldish writes in a clear, straightforward manner, letting the story's inherent drama speak for itself. . . . The presentation is enhanced by attractive page design, which includes a paragraph or two on each page and a photo of an artifact, individuals, sites, or fossils." Booklist

Includes bibliographical references

Harrison, David Lee, 1937-

Cave detectives; unraveling the mystery of an Ice Age cave; written by David L. Harrison; illustrated by Ashley Mims; cave photographs by Edward Biamonte. Chronicle Books 2007 47p il $15.95 *

Grades: 4 5 6 7   560
1. Caves 2. Prehistoric animals 3. Fossils 4. Ice Age
ISBN 978-0-8118-5006-3; 0-8118-5006-4
LC 2005-30067
This "documents the discovery of a cave found in Greene County, Missouri, in 2001. . . . The book focuses on the investigations of a team of scientists . . . to map and explore the cave's many mysteries and wonders. . . . [The book] does a nice job explaining the ice age and how caves are formed and fossils created. It includes illustrations of animals and fossils found in or around Riverbluff Cave." Sci Books Films

Holmes, Thom

Dinosaur scientist; careers digging up the past. Enslow Publishers 2009 128p il (Wild science careers) lib bdg $31.93 *

Grades: 5 6 7 8   560
1. Fossils 2. Vocational guidance
ISBN 978-0-7660-3053-4 (lib bdg); 0-7660-3053-9 (lib bdg)   LC 2008-19634
"Explores the science of and careers in paleontology using several examples of real-life scientists." Publisher's note

"A great read for middle school students, the book provides vocational guidance while introducing the reader to a challenging, but very exciting, career as a paleontologist." Sci Books Films

Includes glossary and bibliographical references

Jenkins, Steve

Prehistoric actual size. Houghton Mifflin Co. 2005 unp il $16 *

Grades: K 1 2 3   **560**

1. Prehistoric animals

ISBN 0-618-53578-0   LC 2004-25124

Illustrated with cut-paper artwork, "the animals pictured here include the minuscule protozoa; . . . the eight-foot-tall 'terror bird'; and the Giganotosaurus. . . . The most arresting spreads are those in which the animal is too large to picture in its entirety. . . . Information about and an illustration of the entire creature (not to scale) completes this colorful volume." Booklist

Larson, Peter L.

Bones rock! everything you need to know to be a paleontologist; [by] Peter Larson and Kristin Donnan. Invisible Cities Press 2004 204p il pa $19.95

Grades: 5 6 7 8   **560**

1. Fossils

ISBN 1-93122-935-X   LC 2004-413

"Revealing true stories about kids who have made paleo-discoveries and providing young readers with the tools necessary to make the next big discovery, this book shows kids how to collect, clean, and study fossil samples in order to develop and further their own research interests." Publisher's note

"Illustrations include high-quality color photographs and helpful diagrams and drawings. There's fascinating information here, and Larson's enthusiasm and sound advice give plenty of encouragement to young scientists." SLJ

Includes bibliographical references

Pellant, Chris

Fossils; [by] Chris and Helen Pellant. Gareth Stevens Pub. 2009 24p il (Rock stars) lib bdg $23

Grades: 2 3 4   **560**

1. Fossils

ISBN 978-0-8368-9223-9 (lib bdg); 0-8368-9223-2 (lib bdg)   LC 2008016116

This describes "how fossils form, and . . . what these traces of ancient life tell us. This book includes a collector's guide and amazing fossil facts." Publisher's note

"Accessible and action-oriented, short but info-packed. . . . Photographs are fine, and graphics are kept extremely simple." SLJ

Includes glossary

Sabuda, Robert

Sharks and other sea monsters; [by] Robert Sabuda & Matthew Reinhart. Candlewick Press 2006 unp il (Encyclopedia prehistorica) $27.99

Grades: 3 4 5 6 7   **560**

1. Prehistoric animals 2. Pop-up books

ISBN 0-7636-2229-X   LC 2005-44866

This pop-up book introduces such prehistoric creatures as giant sharks, sea scorpions, and squids

"Gatefolds and inset minibooks expand the capacity of the book's seven spreads. . . . The sheer wonder generated by the collaborators' dimensional sleight-of-hand will more than justify purchase." Booklist

Stewart, Melissa, 1968-

How does a bone become a fossil? Raintree 2010 32p il (How does it happen?) lib bdg $27.50; pa $7.99

Grades: 3 4 5   **560**

1. Fossils

ISBN 978-1-4109-3445-1 (lib bdg); 1-4109-3445-4 (lib bdg); 978-1-4109-3453-6 (pa); 1-4109-3453-5 (pa)
                     LC 2008-52596

This answers such questions as "How do minerals collect in ancient bones? Why are fish fossils sometimes found on land? How can some feathers be preserved for millions of years?" Publisher's note

"Information is clearly presented using a large font, diagrams, and photographs formatted to resemble Polaroid pictures. . . . A first-rate job answering some important scientific questions." SLJ

Includes glossary and bibliographical references

Taylor, Paul D., 1953-

Fossil; written by Paul D. Taylor. rev ed. DK Pub. 2004 72p il map (DK eyewitness books) $15.99; lib bdg $19.99

Grades: 4 5 6 7   **560**

1. Fossils

ISBN 0-7566-0682-9; 0-7566-0681-0 (lib bdg)

First published 1990 by Knopf

This book describes different types of fossils, from algae to birds and mammals

567 Fossil cold-blooded vertebrates Fossil Pisces (fishes)

Arnold, Caroline, 1944-

Giant shark: megalodon, prehistoric super predator; illustrated by Laurie Caple. Clarion Bks. 2000 32p il $15

Grades: 3 4 5 6   **567**

1. Sharks 2. Prehistoric animals 3. Fossils

ISBN 0-395-91419-1   LC 99-86991

Describes Megalodon, an extinct shark that was more than fifty feet long and could swallow an object the size of a small car

"This book's glowing artwork, clearly accessible text, and engrossing subject will attract readers." SLJ

Bradley, Timothy J.

Paleo sharks; survival of the strangest; written and illustrated by Timothy J. Bradley. Chronicle Books 2007 46p il $15.95

Grades: 4 5 6 7   **567**

1. Sharks 2. Prehistoric animals 3. Fossils

ISBN 978-0-8118-4878-7; 0-8118-4878-7
                     LC 2006-11652

This is "an intelligent, handsomely designed look at the ancient fish that are the forerunners of today's efficient predator, the shark. . . . Bradley uses bright colors and hard edges to delineate the best informed guesses as to what these sharks might have looked like." Booklist

Includes glossary and bibliographical references

O'Brien, Patrick, 1960-
Megatooth! Holt & Co. 2001 unp il $16.95
Grades: K 1 2 3   **567**
  1. Sharks 2. Prehistoric animals 3. Fossils
  ISBN 0-8050-6214-9   LC 00-28135
  "Megatooth, or Megalodon, was an ancient shark three
times as large as today's great white shark. O'Brien supplies . . . several interesting facts that scientists have
surmised about this fascinating creature from the huge
teeth that have been found. . . . The brief text is accompanied by oversized watercolor-and-gouache illustrations." SLJ

567.9   Reptilia

Arnold, Caroline, 1944-
Giant sea reptiles of the dinosaur age; illustrated
by Laurie Caple. Clarion Books 2007 40p il $17
Grades: 3 4 5 6   **567.9**
  1. Marine animals 2. Prehistoric animals 3. Reptiles
  4. Fossils
  ISBN 978-0-618-50449-7; 0-618-50449-4
                       LC 2005-14733
  Provides information about enormous reptiles who
swam the seas during the dinosaur age
  "Caple painstakingly re-creates the creatures Arnold
introduces, but it is the undersea paintings . . . that are
most effective." Booklist

Global warming and the dinosaurs; fossil
discoveries at the Poles; illustrated by Laurie
Caple. Clarion Books 2009 40p il map $17
Grades: 4 5 6   **567.9**
  1. Dinosaurs 2. Arctic regions 3. Antarctica 4. Fossils
  ISBN 978-0-618-80338-5; 0-618-80338-6
                       LC 2008026651
  "Arnold tallies recent fossil discoveries inside or close
to the Arctic and Antarctic Circles proving that dinosaurs
weren't just tropical animals but could adapt to cold climates and long nights too." Kirkus
  "The best of Caple's watercolors . . . convincingly
portray individual animals while creating beautiful effects
with fine-textured surfaces and suffused light. . . . [This
is a] clearly written, informative, and handsome book."
Booklist

Pterosaurs; rulers of the skies in the dinosaur
age; illustrated by Laurie Caple. Clarion Books
2004 40p il map $16
Grades: 3 4 5 6   **567.9**
  1. Pterosaurs 2. Fossils
  ISBN 0-618-31354-0   LC 2003-27698
  Contents: Wing lizards; The age of reptiles; The first
pterosaurs; The "wing fingers;" Bodies built for flight;
Mealtime for pterosaurs; Baby pterosaurs; Discovering
pterosaur fossils; Pterodactyl; A Jurassic lagoon; In the
air over western Kansas; The Brazilian pterosaurs; A
"hairy" pterosaur; The last of the pterosaurs; Where you
can see pterosaur fossils
  This "covers pterosaurs' ancestry, their peculiar physiology, theories about their behavior, and major fossil discoveries, frequently making abstract facts concrete
through vivid comparisons. . . . Caple's neatly labeled

watercolors emphasize clarity over drama, but her subjects' exotic physical oddities . . . will draw kids into
the diorama-like tableaus." Booklist

Ashby, Ruth
Pteranodon; the life story of a pterosaur; by
Ruth Ashby; art by Phil Wilson. Harry N. Abrams
2005 unp il map $14.95
Grades: 1 2 3   **567.9**
  1. Pterosaurs
  ISBN 0-8109-5778-7   LC 2004-15612
  "Ashby imagines the life of a Pteranodon from its
hatching to its successful mating years later. . . . Wilson's colorful interpretations of the fossil record provide
eye-catching images to enhance the narrative. Appended
notes provide the reasoning behind the author's extrapo-
lations on the pterosaur's life cycle and behaviors and
the artist's bright palette. . . . this is an attractive and a
rewarding look at the possibilities in a long-lost life history." SLJ
  Includes bibliographical references

Bailey, Jacqui
Monster bones; the story of a dinosaur fossil;
written by Jacqui Bailey; illustrated by Matthew
Lilly. Picture Window Books 2004 31p il (Science
works) lib bdg $23.93
Grades: 2 3 4   **567.9**
  1. Dinosaurs 2. Fossils
  ISBN 1-4048-0565-6   LC 2003-20117
  Describes how the bones of a dinosaur became fossilized, were discovered by a paleontologist, and were ultimately displayed in a museum.
  This "excellent science [book explains its subject] lucidly and sometimes amusingly. . . . Children will be illuminated and engaged." SLJ

Benton, Mike
The Kingfisher dinosaur encyclopedia.
Kingfisher 2010 159p il $19.99
Grades: 3 4 5 6   **567.9**
  1. Dinosaurs 2. Fossils
  ISBN 978-0-7534-6440-3; 0-7534-6440-3
  "This thorough, fact-filled dinosaur encyclopedia contains full-color digital images of dinosaurs, in order of
their appearance through geological time. . . . Profiles
offer descriptions of various species' anatomy and speculations on issues like mobility, diet, and predation. Easy-
to-read time lines and charts discuss the origins of and
extinctions of species, while abundant photographs of
skeletans, dig sites, and paleontogists at work integrate
relevance and texture." Publ Wkly

Bergen, David
Life-size dinosaurs. Sterling Pub. 2004 48p il
$9.95
Grades: 3 4 5 6   **567.9**
  1. Dinosaurs
  ISBN 1-4027-1755-X
  This includes life-size illustrations of such dinosaurs
as Atreipus, Oviraptor, and Therizinosaurus in three 8-

Bergen, David—*Continued*

page-long gatefolds and four 6-page ones.

"This slim, oversize title will be eye candy indeed to dinophiles. . . . These vivid color illustrations are surrounded by chatty explanatory paragraphs and information boxes." SLJ

Berkowitz, Jacob

Jurassic poop; what dinosaurs (and others) left behind; written by Jacob Berkowitz; illustrated by Steve Mack. Kids Can Press 2006 40p il $14.95; pa $7.95 *

Grades: 4 5 6 7   **567.9**

1. Fossils 2. Feces 3. Dinosaurs

ISBN   978-1-55337-860-0;   1-55337-860-1; 978-1-55337-867-9 (pa); 1-55337-867-9 (pa)

This describes fossilized feces, or coprolites, and what we can learn from them

"Berkowitz' style is goofy and lighthearted, but there's plenty of real information. . . . The browsable format combines cartoony digital art, photographs . . . and design elements such a spiky borders and background shading." Bull Cent Child Books

Includes glossary

Bishop, Nic, 1955-

Digging for bird-dinosaurs; an expedition to Madagascar. Houghton Mifflin 2000 48p il $16; pa $4.95 *

Grades: 4 5 6 7   **567.9**

1. Forster, Cathy 2. Dinosaurs 3. Birds 4. Fossils 5. Madagascar

ISBN 0-395-96056-8; 0-618-1982-X (pa)

LC 99-36145

The story of Cathy Forster's experiences as a member of a team of paleontologists who went on an expedition to the island of Madagascar in 1998 to search for fossil birds

"Throughout the engaging, personal story, Bishop presents a great deal of information in highly readable, age-appropriate language, well matched by exceptional full-color images of scientists at work and the Malagasy landscape and people." Booklist

Includes bibliographical references

Brewster, Hugh

Dinosaurs in your backyard; illustrated by Alan Barnard. Abrams Books for Young Readers 2009 32p il $15.95

Grades: 3 4 5   **567.9**

1. Dinosaurs

ISBN 978-0-8109-7099-1; 0-8109-7099-6

LC 2008030406

First published 2008 in Canada with title: Breakout dinosaurs

"This informative book . . . transports readers back to a time when North America was defined by substantially different coastlines and divided by a broad inland seaway. Introducing some of the dinosaurs living there . . . the book uses double-page spreads that typically describe one animal in a paragraph of descriptive or dramatic text as well as a section of fast facts relating its size, weight,

era, diet, and range. Large, painterly illustrations set the tone, supported by smaller maps and photos of fossils. The occasional dramatic tooth-and-claw scene is more than balanced by the weight of accessible, interesting information." Booklist

Includes bibliographical references

Brown, Charlotte Lewis

The day the dinosaurs died; written by Charlotte Lewis Brown; illustrated by Phil Wilson. HarperCollins Publishers 2006 48p il (I can read book) $15.99; lib bdg $16.89

Grades: K 1 2 3   **567.9**

1. Dinosaurs

ISBN   978-0-06-000528-3;   0-06-000528-9; 978-0-06-000529-0 (lib bdg); 0-06-000529-7 (lib bdg)

LC 2005-15135

"Beginning with a pronunciation guide for the names of various dinosaurs, this book describes what probably happened to those reptiles 65 million years ago, when a comet or an asteroid most likely slammed into the Earth in the area of the Yucatán Peninsula. . . . Second graders will be able to read this book independently, and with its expressive, fairly naturalistic illustrations, younger children will find that it answers the question of how the dinosaurs became extinct." SLJ

Cole, Joanna

The magic school bus: in the time of the dinosaurs; illustrated by Bruce Degen. Scholastic 1994 unp il hardcover o.p. pa $4.99 *

Grades: 2 3 4   **567.9**

1. Dinosaurs

ISBN 0-590-44688-6; 0-590-44639-4 (pa)

LC 93-5753

"The fashionable Ms. Frizzle warps her students back to the late Triassic period, where they begin a journey forward through time in search of Maiasaura eggs for Jeff, the Friz's paleontologist friend from high school." Bull Cent Child Books

"An eye-catching, humorous book with bright, busy illustrations . . . packed with information." Sci Books Films

Collard, Sneed B., III

Reign of the sea dragons; illustrated by Andrew Plant. Charlesbridge 2008 61p il $17.95; pa $8.95 *

Grades: 5 6 7 8 9   **567.9**

1. Marine animals 2. Prehistoric animals

ISBN 978-1-58089-124-0; 978-1-58089-125-7 (pa)

LC 2007-26201

"An arresting dust jacket depicting a humongous pliosaur snapping huge toothy jaws at a small, long-necked plesiosaur is an attention-grabber, but it is the informative text that brings these real sea monsters to life. Collard follows his usual pattern of careful organization, with a readable text and up-to-date information. . . . Plant has provided five full-color paintings, but it is his numerous black-and-white drawings that lend sturdy anatomical and physical information. . . . Collard's discussion on extinction theories is cogent." SLJ

Includes glossary, bibliographical references, and websites

Dixon, Dougal, 1947-

Amazing dinosaurs; [by] Dougal Dixon. 2nd ed. Boyds Mills Press 2007 128p il $19.95

Grades: 3 4 5 6   **567.9**

1. Dinosaurs

ISBN 978-1-59078-537-9; 1-59078-537-1

LC 2006038922

First published 2000 with title: Dougal Dixon's amazing dinosaurs

This guide to dinosaurs is divided into four sections representing meat eaters, long-necked plant eaters, armored dinosaurs, and two-footed plant eaters. Each illustrated entry includes pronunciation, meaning of name, classification, size, weight, time, place, and food of a dinosaur species.

Includes glossary and bibliographical references

Dougal Dixon's dinosaurs; [by] Dougal Dixon. 3rd ed. Boyds Mills Press 2007 160p il $19.95

Grades: 4 5 6 7   **567.9**

1. Dinosaurs

ISBN 978-1-59078-470-9   LC 2006037876

First published 1993

The life and times of dinosaurs, from their evolution to the present-day discovery of their fossils.

Includes glossary

World of dinosaurs and other prehistoric life. Barron's 2008 112p il pa $9.99

Grades: 3 4 5   **567.9**

1. Dinosaurs 2. Fossils

ISBN 978-0-7641-4082-2 (pa); 0-7641-4082-5 (pa)

This book "starts off with a color coded contents page for easy reference. Each two-page spread highlights a different creature from prehistoric life, including many lesser-known animals. . . . Wonderful illustrations capture each creature as it might have lived. Many photographs are included highlighting fossils, skeletons, and other prehistoric finds. Large font makes it more accessible to a younger reader where interest is at its highest. . . . This is a treasure trove of interesting facts without being overwhelming." Libr Media Connect

Includes glossary

DK first dinosaur encyclopedia. DK Pub. 2007 127p il $15.99

Grades: 2 3 4 5   **567.9**

1. Reference books 2. Dinosaurs—Encyclopedias

ISBN 978-0-7566-2539-9   LC 2006016039

"Solid introductory information and strong visual appeal make this a fine choice for dinosaur fans. Crystal-clear photographs of models and artifacts fill every spread. . . . The text is clear, with enough intriguing facts to fascinate without overwhelming." SLJ

Farlow, James Orville, 1951-

Bringing dinosaur bones to life; how do we know what dinosaurs were really like? [by] James O. Farlow; with illustrations by James E. Whitcraft. Watts 2001 63p il lib bdg $25 *

Grades: 5 6 7 8   **567.9**

1. Dinosaurs 2. Fossils

ISBN 0-531-11403-1   LC 00-38150

This "describes how paleontologists draw conclusions from the dinosaur fossils they study. Separate chapters examine physical appearance, diet, fighting, and reproduction." SLJ

"Clearly written and well organized, this book will interest children intrigued by the process of scientific thinking as well as its results." Booklist

Includes glossary and bibliographical references

French, Vivian

T. Rex; illustrated by Alison Bartlett. Candlewick Press 2004 29p il $15.99; pa $6.99; pa with audio CD $8.99

Grades: K 1 2 3   **567.9**

1. Dinosaurs

ISBN   978-0-7636-2184-1;   0-7636-2184-6; 978-0-7636-3177-2 (pa);   0-7636-3177-9 (pa); 978-0-7636-3999-0 (pa with audio CD); 0-7636-3999-0 (pa with audio CD)

LC 2003-69563

In a "dialogue with his grandfather, a boy discovers the thrill of the intellectual hunt while touring a T. Rex exhibition. . . . Bartlett . . . working in saturated acrylics and bold shapes, travels back to the era when T. Rex was indeed king. . . . The author eloquently makes the case that a willingness to seek answers, rather than merely receive them, has its own rewards." Publ Wkly

Funston, Sylvia

Dino–why? the dinosaur question and answer book. updated and rev. Maple Tree Press 2008 64p il $22.95; pa $10.95

Grades: 4 5 6 7   **567.9**

1. Dinosaurs

ISBN   978-1-897349-24-3;   1-897349-24-6; 978-1-897349-25-0 (pa); 1-897349-25-4 (pa)

LC 2007-939082

First published 1992 by Joy Street Books with title: The dinosaur question and answer book

"This book is an excellent and highly readable introduction to dinosaurs. . . . The questions are well conceived, and the answers . . . are scientifically sound and up to date. . . . The illustrations, a few of them cartoon-like, are nicely drawn and useful." Sci Books Films

Gibbons, Gail

Dinosaurs! by Gail Gibbons. Holiday House 2008 32p il $16.95

Grades: K 1 2 3   **567.9**

1. Dinosaurs

ISBN 978-0-8234-2143-5; 0-8234-2143-0

LC 2007034425

Simple text and illustrations introduce young readers to dinosaurs

"The combination of clear writing and lively artwork makes this an accessible choice for young dinosaur enthusiasts." Booklist

Henry, Michel, 1962-
Raptor; the life of a young deinonychus; illustrations by Rich Penney. Abrams Books for Young Readers 2007 unp il map $15.95
Grades: 2 3 4   **567.9**
   1. Dinosaurs
   ISBN 978-0-8109-5775-6; 0-8109-5775-2
                     LC 2004-12588
"A Byron Preiss book"
This "is a beautifully illustrated book that brings a dinosaur and his environment to life. Based on informed speculation . . . this book follows the life experiences of several raptors that are part of a pack that lived in the western part of North America 100 million years ago." Sci Books Films
   Includes glossary and bibliographical references

Hort, Lenny
Did dinosaurs eat pizza? mysteries science hasn't solved; illustrated by John O'Brien. Henry Holt and Co. 2006 unp il $15.95
Grades: K 1 2 3   **567.9**
   1. Dinosaurs
   ISBN 978-0-8050-6757-6; 0-8050-6757-4
                     LC 2005-12171
"The discussion opens with the idea that even though much is known about dinosaurs, there are still mysteries to solve. The pages that follow introduce a series of unanswered questions. . . . Clearly written and filled with fascinating facts for dinosaur enthusiasts. . . . O'Brien's detailed, often-witty ink drawings, brightened with colorful washes, interpret the facts imaginatively." Booklist

Judge, Lita, 1968-
Born to be giants; how baby dinosaurs grew to rule the world. Flash Point 2010 unp il $17.99
Grades: 2 3 4   **567.9**
   1. Dinosaurs
   ISBN 978-1-59643-443-1; 1-59643-443-0
"Expanding on the idea that the hugest dinosaurs hatched from (relatively speaking) small eggs, Judge depicts cute hatchlings with outsized heads and feet wobbling about as their gargantuan parents look on indulgently. Along with a full measure of visual appeal, she also delivers a terse but clear explanation of how scientists gain insight into dino parenting from both fossil evidence." Booklist
   Includes glossary and bibliographical references

Kudlinski, Kathleen V., 1950-
Boy, were we wrong about dinosaurs! illustrated by S. D. Schindler. Dutton Children's Books 2005 unp il $15.99 *
Grades: K 1 2 3   **567.9**
   1. Dinosaurs
   ISBN 0-525-46978-8   LC 2003-53140
Examines what is known about dinosaur bones, behavior, and other characteristics and how different the facts often are from what scientists, from ancient China to the recent past, believed to be true.
"Intelligently designed and imaginatively conceived, the artwork makes the text more understandable and the

whole book more beautiful. . . . Best of all, the closing paragraph acknowledges that the search is not over yet." Booklist
   Includes bibliographical references

Lessem, Don
The fastest dinosaurs; by Don Lessem; illustrations by John Bindon. Lerner Publications 2005 32p il (Meet the dinosaurs) lib bdg $23.93; pa $6.95
Grades: 2 3 4   **567.9**
   1. Dinosaurs
   ISBN 0-8225-1422-2 (lib bdg); 0-8225-2620-4 (pa)
                     LC 2004-7055
This "looks at how paleontologists determine living speed when only the fossil record remains, and cites some prime examples of dinosprinters, such a Gallimimus and Troodon. The realistic, soft illustrations . . . are lively enough to please budding paleontologists. Simple, eye-catching, and informative." SLJ

Feathered dinosaurs; by Don Lessem; illustrations by John Bindon. Lerner Publications 2005 32p il (Meet the dinosaurs) lib bdg $23.93; pa $6.95
Grades: 2 3 4   **567.9**
   1. Dinosaurs 2. Birds
   ISBN 0-8225-1423-0 (lib bdg); 0-8225-2621-2 (pa)
                     LC 2004-19651
This covers the "links between dinosaurs and birds. . . . Lessem writes in simple language and short sentences appropriate for children transitioning out of early readers. But the brief text . . . will also read well to younger dino fans. . . . Bindon's detailed illustrations imagine the creatures in dramatic settings that will bring the drama of the ancient age alive." Booklist

Flying giants of dinosaur time. Lerner Publications Co. 2005 32p il map (Meet the dinosaurs) lib bdg $23.93; pa $6.95
Grades: 2 3 4   **567.9**
   1. Pterodactyls 2. Pterosaurs
   ISBN 0-8225-1424-9 (lib bdg); 0-8225-2622-0 (pa)
                     LC 2004-17918
   Contents: Meet the flying reptiles; The world of flying reptiles; Wings, necks, and tails; The lives of pterosaurs; Mysteries of the flying giants
This "covers the pterosaurs and pterodactyls, extrapolating some behaviors using modern birds as models, and speculates on beak shapes and sizes in the food-gathering process. . . . The realistic, soft illustrations . . . are lively enough to please budding paleontologists. Simple, eye-catching, and informative." SLJ

Sea giants of dinosaur time. Lerner Publications Co. 2005 32p il map (Meet the dinosaurs) lib bdg $23.93; pa $6.95
Grades: 2 3 4   **567.9**
   1. Dinosaurs
   ISBN 0-8225-1425-7 (lib bdg); 0-8225-2623-9 (pa)
                     LC 2004-17916
   Contents: Meet the sea giants; Water wonders; Life in the sea; What happened to the sea giants?

Lessem, Don—*Continued*

"A quick glimpse at eight of the larger prehistoric marine reptiles, ranging in eras from 220 million to 65 million years ago. The simple text presents a time line for these creatures, a global map of fossil finds, and some details of their physiology and distribution. The colorful double-page illustrations on blue backgrounds are accompanied by a paragraph or two of particulars." SLJ

The smartest dinosaurs; by Don Lessem; illustrations by John Bindon. Lerner Publications 2005 32p il (Meet the dinosaurs) lib bdg $23.93; pa $6.95

Grades: 2 3 4   **567.9**
　　1. Dinosaurs
　　ISBN 0-8225-1373-0 (lib bdg); 0-8225-2618-2 (pa)
　　　　　　　　　　　　　　　LC 2004-11152

Contents: Meet the smartest dinosaurs; How smart were dinosaurs?; Big brains; Which dinosaurs were the smartest?

"After a discussion of brain/body-size ratios, Lessem goes on to describe the importance of fossil finds in determining intelligence possibilities, leading to brief descriptions of seven dinosaurs that scientists feel may have been brighter than their contemporaries. . . . This is a clear look at a facet of dinosaur makeup not often touched on in other works." SLJ

Long, John A., 1957-

Dinosaurs; [by] John Long. Simon & Schuster Books for Young Readers 2007 64p il (Insiders) lib bdg $16.99 *

Grades: 4 5 6 7   **567.9**
　　1. Dinosaurs
　　ISBN 978-1-4169-3857-6 (lib bdg); 1-4169-3857-5 (lib bdg)　　　　　　　　　LC 2007-61735

"The first section includes paleontological periods, extinction theories, and a . . . pictorial time line tracing the first bird archaeopteryx to the earliest feathered dinosaurs. The second section contains profiles of a diverse selection of species." Booklist

"Richly hued, crisp computer-generated art and 3D model imagery serve as a stunning and sophisticated graphic counterpoint to the educational text." Publ Wkly

Includes glossary

MacLeod, Elizabeth

Monster fliers; from the time of the dinosaurs; written by Elizabeth MacLeod; illustrated by John Bindon. Kids Can Press 2010 31p il $16.95

Grades: K 1 2 3   **567.9**
　　1. Dinosaurs 2. Birds 3. Pterosaurs
　　ISBN 978-1-55453-199-8; 1-55453-199-3

"This attractive picture book [is] sure to appeal to dinophiles eager to learn more about dinosaurs' flying cousins. Nineteen pterosaurs, a few early birds, and a dromaeosaur (a dinosaur that both walked and flew) are briefly described and illustrated in their presumed native habitats. . . . The realistic illustrations [are] painted with remarkable detail." Booklist

Manning, Phillip Lars, 1967-

Dinomummy; the life, death, and discovery of Dakota, a dinosaur from Hell Creek; foreword by Tyler Lyson. Kingfisher 2007 64p il map $18.95 *

Grades: 4 5 6 7   **567.9**
　　1. Dinosaurs 2. North Dakota
　　ISBN 978-0-7534-6047-4; 0-7534-6047-5
　　　　　　　　　　　　　　　LC 2007-02878

Tells about the discovery of the fossil remains of a hadrosaur in the hills of the Hell Creek Formation in North Dakota.

"The color photographs and simple text offer a detailed account of carefully unearthing the fossil and transporting it safely to the laboratory, where many tests were performed. Dinosaurs buffs and young scientists will love this book. It is a thrilling story that is part narrative, part mystery, and part science lesson." Voice Youth Advocates

Markle, Sandra, 1946-

Outside and inside dinosaurs. Atheneum Bks. for Young Readers 2000 40p il hardcover o.p. pa $7.99 *

Grades: 2 3 4   **567.9**
　　1. Dinosaurs 2. Fossils
　　ISBN 0-689-82300-2; 0-689-85778-0 (pa)
　　　　　　　　　　　　　　　LC 99-45808

Describes the inner and outer workings of dinosaurs, discussing what has been learned about their anatomy, diet, and behavior from fossils

"Excellent, large color photos march hand in hand with Markle's readable, informative text." SLJ

Includes glossary

Munro, Roxie, 1945-

Inside-outside dinosaurs. Marshall Cavendish Children 2009 unp il $17.99

Grades: PreK K   **567.9**
　　1. Dinosaurs
　　ISBN 978-0-7614-5624-7; 0-7614-5624-4
　　　　　　　　　　　　　　　LC 2008055322

"This large-format book offers paired double-page spreads showing each featured dinosaur twice. In the first spread, a black-and-gray skeleton in a dramatic pose stands out clearly against a white background. . . . The second spread portrays the living dinosaur within its habitat. Typically these pictures, india-ink drawings washed with colors, depict action in the background or foreground. . . . An appended section offers a bit of information about each species and identifies all the dinosaurs in the action scenes. . . . Eye-catching illustrations and minimal text make this a good choice for young dino fans." Booklist

Includes bibliographical references

Myers, Tim, 1953-

If you give a T-rex a bone; illustrated by Anisa Claire Hovemann. Dawn Publications 2007 unp il (A sharing nature with children book) $16.95; pa $8.95

Grades: PreK K 1 2   **567.9**
  1. Dinosaurs
  ISBN   978-1-58469-097-9;   1-58469-097-6;
  978-1-58469-098-6 (pa); 1-58469-098-4 (pa)
                              LC 2007-08332

"Dinosaurs and other ancient reptiles appear in their ancient habitats as if witnessed by a modern day child. Includes information about the animals and resources for additional learning." Publisher's note

"The book is illustrated throughout with bright, and quite beautiful, watercolors. . . . This is a fine first introduction to prehistoric reptiles for the very young." Sci Books Films

Includes bibliographical references

Podesto, Martine

Dinosaurs; by Martine Podesto. Gareth Stevens 2009 102p il (My science notebook) lib bdg $31

Grades: 4 5 6   **567.9**
  1. Dinosaurs
  ISBN 978-0-8368-9213-0 (lib bdg); 0-8368-9213-5 (lib
  bdg)   LC 2008-12427

Provides "exciting information—like what the Earth might have looked like when dinosaurs lived, which dinosaur had the biggest teeth of all, and which dinosaur has gotten a bad reputation that it didn't deserve." Publisher's note

"Designed to resemble a notebook with illustrated paper clips, pasting, and tape appearing on most pages, this [book] . . . offers comprehensive information. . . . supplemented by colorful drawings, diagrams, and photographs." SLJ

Includes glossary and bibliographical references

Prap, Lila, 1955-

Dinosaurs?! North South Books 2010 unp il $16.95

Grades: K 1 2 3   **567.9**
  1. Dinosaurs 2. Birds 3. Evolution
  ISBN 978-0-7358-2284-9; 0-7358-2284-0

"In this humorous look at evolution, Prap makes the case that all modern-day birds, including chickens, are descended from dinosaurs. The book's illustrations are fun and well-laid-out, and the witty text is chock-full of information. A group of chickens makes snarky comments about their disparate relatives . . . and side notes provide interesting details about the 'terrible lizards.' Dino lovers will clamor for this title." SLJ

Ray, Deborah Kogan, 1940-

Dinosaur mountain; digging into the Jurassic Age. Frances Foster Books 2010 unp il map $16.99 *

Grades: 3 4 5 6   **567.9**
  1. Douglass, Earl, 1862-1931 2. Dinosaur National
  Monument (Colo. and Utah) 3. Dinosaurs 4. Fossils
  ISBN 978-0-374-31789-8; 0-374-31789-5
                           LC 2008027877

This describes how, beginning in 1908, Earl Douglass set out to discover "a mountain in Utah that would reveal some of the grandest dinosaur skeletons anyone had ever seen. . . . Ray's expressive art . . . excels in capturing the grandeur and wonder of key moments. . . . Excited journal entries from Douglass enliven the informative text, and small sketch book-style drawings of fossils and tools add a scholarly touch." Booklist

Includes glossary and bibliographical references

Relf, Patricia

A dinosaur named Sue: the story of the colossal fossil: the world's most complete T. rex; by Pat Relf; with the SUE Science Team of the Field Museum. Scholastic 2000 64p il $15.95 *

Grades: 5 6 7 8   **567.9**
  1. Fossils 2. Dinosaurs
  ISBN 0-439-09985-4   LC 00-38038

"Sue, named after discoverer Susan Hendrickson, is the most complete *Tyrannosaurus Rex* in existence. The reader follows the scientific journey from the fossil excavation in 1990 to its display at Chicago's Field Museum." Sci Child

"Readers will get a real sense of the team effort that science can be. . . . Many color photographs, as well as diagrams and paintings, appear throughout the book." Booklist

Rushby, Pamela

Discovering Supercroc; by Pamela Rushby. National Geographic 2007 40p il (National Geographic science chapters) lib bdg $17.90

Grades: 3 4 5 6   **567.9**
  1. Fossils 2. Prehistoric animals 3. Crocodiles
  ISBN 978-1-4263-0186-5 (lib bdg); 1-4263-01863- (lib
  bdg)   LC 2007007906

"This book describes the discovery of first the jaw and then other bones belonging to SuperCroc: a forty-foot-long prehistoric crocodile. The accessible text explains how paleontologists removed the fossils and reassembled them into a skeleton, and how SuperCroc compares to today's reptiles. The many eye-catching photographs include close-ups of crocodile teeth on the striking endpapers." Horn Book Guide

Sabuda, Robert

Dinosaurs; by Robert Sabuda and Matthew Reinhart. Candlewick Press 2005 unp il (Encyclopedia prehistorica) $26.99

Grades: 3 4 5 6 7   **567.9**
  1. Dinosaurs 2. Pop-up books
  ISBN 0-7636-2228-1   LC 2004-51899

"With Sabuda lending deft paper engineering to artwork rendered by Reinhart, who also wrote this book's text, the Mesozoic's major players leap into three dimensions. Pop-ups featured on the six spreads include a gargantuan brachiosaurus; an anklyosaurus studded with paper spikes; and, perhaps most impressive from a technical standpoint, a minutely detailed T. rex skeleton." Booklist

Sloan, Christopher

Bizarre dinosaurs; some very strange creatures and why we think they got that way; [by] Christopher Sloan; with a foreword by James Clark and Cathy Forster. National Geographic 2008 31p il $16.95; lib bdg $25.90

Grades: 4 5 6 7   567.9
    1. Dinosaurs
    ISBN 978-1-4263-0330-2; 1-4263-0330-0; 978-1-4263-0331-9 (lib bdg); 1-4263-0331-9 (lib bdg)

This "book should engage children of all ages who are fascinated by dinosaurs. . . . The illustrations are of uniformly high quality. . . . Each species gets two pages of text, including a full-page illustration; an inset with basic facts such as range, diet, and geological period in which it lived; a silhouette comparing their size with that of humans; and a paragraph of text." Sci Books Films

How dinosaurs took flight; the fossils, the science, what we think we know, and the mysteries yet unsolved; foreword by Dr. Xu Xing. National Geographic 2005 64p il $17.95 *

Grades: 5 6 7 8   567.9
    1. Dinosaurs 2. Birds 3. Fossils
    ISBN 0-7922-7298-6

This explains the evolutionary relationships between dinosaurs and birds, based on fossils and the latest research.

Includes glossary and bibliographical references

Supercroc and the origin of crocodiles; introduction by Paul Sereno. National Geographic Soc. 2002 55p il map $18.95

Grades: 5 6 7 8   567.9
    1. Fossil reptiles 2. Crocodiles
    ISBN 0-7922-6691-9   LC 2001-3976

Discusses prehistoric crocodiles, including the discovery of SuperCroc in the Sahara Desert, and the lifestyles, habitats, and conservation of modern crocodiles

"Fans of paleontology or of crocodiles will find a great deal of information clearly explained. The illustrations are up to the high National Geographic standard." Booklist

Includes glossary

Tanaka, Shelley

New dinos; The latest finds! The coolest dinosaur discoveries! written by Shelley Tanaka; illustrated by Alan Barnard. Atheneum Bks. for Young Readers 2003 48p il maps hardcover o.p. pa $9.95

Grades: 3 4 5 6   567.9
    1. Dinosaurs 2. Fossils
    ISBN 0-689-85183-9; 1-897330-55-3 (pa)
                            LC 2002-9809

"Madison Press book"

Describes some of the newly discovered dinosaurs and what paleontologists have learned about these prehistoric creatures in recent years

"Vivid, dramatic illustrations are a sure draw to an already hot topic. . . . Tanaka's lively, brief text provides enough data to satisfy many readers, including true aficionados." SLJ

Includes glossary and bibliographical references

Thomson, Sarah L.

Extreme dinosaurs! Q & A; Smithsonian; [written by Sarah L. Thomson] Collins 2007 unp il $16.99; pa $6.99

Grades: 3 4 5   567.9
    1. Dinosaurs 2. Fossils
    ISBN 978-0-06-089971-4; 0-06-089971-9; 978-0-06-089967-7 (pa); 0-06-089967-0 (pa)
                            LC 2006935100

"This title poses 21 questions about these perennially popular creatures and answers them with a simple text accompanied by crisp photos and/or attractive artwork. . . . [This] will surely appeal to most young dinophiles." SLJ

Includes glossary and bibliographical references

Williams, Judith

The discovery and mystery of a dinosaur named Jane. Enslow Publishers 2007 c2008 48p il map lib bdg $23.93; pa $13.26

Grades: 3 4 5 6   567.9
    1. Dinosaurs 2. Fossils
    ISBN 0-7660-2730-9 (lib bdg); 978-0-7660-2730-5 (lib bdg); 0-7660-2709-0 (pa); 978-0-7660-2709-1 (pa)
                            LC 2006-10475

This describes "the 2001 discovery of a fossilized dinosaur skeleton in Montana's Hell Creek Formation. . . . Williams carefully reports the entire event, from discovery through excavation and preparation to exhibition at the Burpee Museum of Natural History in Rockford, IL. Small color photos and artwork, simple diagrams, and a map help readers to visualize the complex process." SLJ

Includes bibliographical references

Woodward, John, 1954-

Dinosaurs eye to eye; zoom in on the world's most incredible dinosaurs; digital sculptor Peter Minister. Dorling Kindersley 2010 96p il map $19.99

Grades: 3 4 5 6   567.9
    1. Dinosaurs 2. Fossils
    ISBN 978-0-7566-5760-4; 0-7566-5760-1

"This oversize reference book features striking digital images of dinosaurs, along with abundant information about them and the Triassic, Jurassic, and Cretaceous periods in which they thrived. . . . Action scenes . . . offer visual excitement, while diagrams, sidebars with dino-stats, and photographs of fossils emphasize the educational." Publ Wkly

Zoehfeld, Kathleen Weidner

Dinosaur parents, dinosaur young; uncovering the mystery of dinosaur families; with full-color paintings by Paul Carrick and line drawings by Bruce Shillinglaw. Clarion Bks. 2001 58p il map $17

Grades: 4 5 6 7   567.9
    1. Dinosaurs 2. Fossils
    ISBN 0-395-91338-1   LC 00-43101

The author "guides readers through the complex historical trail of evidence collection and theory develop-

Zoehfeld, Kathleen Weidner—*Continued*
ment that make up what we currently believe we know
about dinosaur family life." Horn Book Guide
   "High-quality, color photographs of fossils of eggs
and embryos and of paleontologists at work as well as
line drawings and full-color paintings add to this inviting, thought-provoking book." SLJ
   Includes glossary and bibliographical references

   Dinosaur tracks; by Kathleen Weidner Zoehfeld;
illustrated   by   Lucia   Washburn.
HarperCollinsPublishers   2007   33p   il
(Let's-read-and-find-out science) $15.99; lib bdg
$16.89; pa $5.99
Grades: K 1 2 3   **567.9**
   1. Dinosaurs 2. Fossils
   ISBN   0-06-029024-2;   978-0-06-02904-5;
   0-06-029025-0 (lib bdg); 978-0-06-029025-2 (lib bdg);
   0-06-445217-4 (pa); 978-0-06-445217-5 (pa)
                              LC 2004-06242
   Describes how footprints made by the dinosaurs have
been preserved and what these impressions tell scientists
about the animals which made them.
   "The clear text is illustrated with informal, colorful
spreads of kids at play on the beach where millions of
years earlier dinosaurs may have 'splooshed through
gloppy mud . . . [leaving] footprints behind them.'"
Booklist

568   Fossil Aves (birds)

Zoehfeld, Kathleen Weidner
   Did dinosaurs have feathers? illustrated by Lucia
Washburn. HarperCollins Publishers 2004 33p il
(Let's-read-and-find-out science) $15.99; lib bdg
$16.89; pa $4.99
Grades: K 1 2 3   **568**
   1. Dinosaurs 2. Birds 3. Fossils 4. Archaeopteryx
   ISBN 0-06-029026-9; 0-06-029027-7 (lib bdg);
   0-06-029027-7 (pa)   LC 2002-10585
   Discusses the discovery and analysis of Archaeopteryx, a feathered dinosaur which may have been an ancestor of modern birds
   "Using short sentences and simple words, Zoehfeld
clearly explains what we know about dinosaurs with
feathers. . . . Iridescent shades of blue and orange give
the theropods and their settings an appealing glow."
Horn Book Guide

569   Fossil mammalia

Aliki
   Wild and woolly mammoths; written and
illustrated by Aliki. rev ed. HarperCollins Pubs.
1996 32p il pa $6.95 hardcover o.p.
Grades: K 1 2 3   **569**
   1. Mammoths
   ISBN 0-06-446179-3 (pa)   LC 94-48217
   A revised and newly illustrated edition of the title first
published 1977

An easy-to-read account of the woolly mammoth, a
giant land mammal which has been extinct for over
11,000 years
   "With concise text and informative art, Aliki illuminates the timeless appeal of these long-gone animals—
and drops a gentle warning about the possible fate of
tusked decendants." Publ Wkly

Arnold, Caroline, 1944-
   When mammoths walked the earth; illustrated
by Laurie Caple. Clarion Bks. 2002 40p il $16 *
Grades: 3 4 5 6   **569**
   1. Mammoths
   ISBN 0-618-09633-7   LC 2001-47192
   Describes the physical characteristics, known habits,
and fossil sites of mammoths, prehistoric animals closely
related to the elephant
   "The information is brief but thorough, with realistic
watercolor illustrations depicting the giant animals and
their surroundings." Booklist

Bardoe, Cheryl
   Mammoths and mastodons; titans of the Ice
Age. Abrams Books for Young Readers 2010 43p
il map $18.95
Grades: 4 5 6 7   **569**
   1. Mammoths 2. Mastodons 3. Fossils
   ISBN 978-0-8109-8413-4; 0-8109-8413-X
   "Published in conjunction with the Field Museum of
Chicago"
   "This well-designed book opens with two boys finding
a strange animal dead on the arctic tundra. Their father
hikes four days to a village where the news can be
spread; then scientists take away the frozen baby mammoth, the first example found intact, and study it inten-
sively. The book intersperses accounts of the scientists'
research and deductions with general information about
mammoths and mastodons as well as imagined scenes
taking place when they walked the earth. . . . A handsome introduction." Booklist
   Includes glossary and bibliographical references

Brown, Charlotte Lewis
   After the dinosaurs; mammoths and fossil
mammals; written by Charlotte Lewis Brown,
pictures by Phil Wilson. HarperCollinsPublishers
2006 unp il (I can read!) $15.99; lib bdg $16.89
Grades: K 1 2 3   **569**
   1. Fossil mammals
   ISBN   978-0-06-053053-2;   0-06-053053-7;
   978-0-06-053054-9 (lib bdg); 0-06-053054-5 (lib bdg)
                              LC 2005028662
   "This title examines a variety of ancient mammals. It
opens with a brief introduction, followed by a spread devoted to each animal. . . . The pronunciation guide is a
welcome feature. The finely detailed watercolor illustrations emphasize the unusual features of each species."
SLJ

Manning, Mick

Woolly mammoth; [by] Mick Manning [and] Brita Granström. Frances Lincoln 2009 unp il $16.95

Grades: K 1 2 3   569

1. Mammoths

ISBN 978-1-84507-860-7; 1-84507-860-8

"Manning and Granström pair rhyming couplets, in this case describing the life of a mammoth, alongside columns of information. Simple pencil drawings fill sidebars with specific details about these huge beasts, including their habitat and natural enemies, their physical characteristics and behavior. . . . Bright watercolor-over-pencil paintings dominate the pages, which feature simple stanzas that deliver the mammoth's side of the story." SLJ

Markle, Sandra, 1946-

Outside and inside woolly mammoths. Walker & Co. 2007 40p il $17.95; lib bdg $18.85 *

Grades: 4 5 6   569

1. Mammoths

ISBN 978-0-8027-9589-2; 0-8027-9589-7; 978-0-8027-9590-8 (lib bdg); 0-8027-9590-0 (lib bdg)
LC 2006027621

"Markle explains what scientists have discovered from the preserved remains of mammoths: their food, and the structure of their hair, their soft tissues, and even their DNA. Asking readers leading questions and systematically noting similarities to and differences from modern elephants, she speculates about why mammoths became extinct. . . . Except for the cover picture, the illustrations are all big, sharp color photos and digital tomography images rather than artistic re-creations. A closing multimedia resource list that is accurately pitched to the level of her intended audience makes this as valuable for student use as for pleasure reading." Booklist

O'Brien, Patrick, 1960-

Sabertooth. Henry Holt and Co. 2008 unp il $16.95

Grades: 2 3 4   569

1. Saber-toothed tigers 2. Dinosaurs

ISBN 978-0-8050-7105-4; 0-8050-7105-9
LC 2007-02792

O'Brien "offers this large-format, fully illustrated volume on prehistoric cats with canine teeth so long, sharp, and curving that they are called sabertooths. After introducing several kinds of sabertooths, O'Brien focuses mainly on the Smilodon genus. . . . O'Brien writes clearly. . . . The book's main strength, though, is its excellent artwork, which portrays dramatic scenes and quiet studies of the animals with equal skill and attention to detail. A visually strong introduction." Booklist

Sabuda, Robert

Mega beasts; [by] Robert Sabuda & Matthew Reinhart. Candlewick Press 2007 unp il (Encyclopedia prehistorica) $27.99

Grades: 3 4 5 6 7   569

1. Prehistoric animals 2. Pop-up books

ISBN 978-0-7636-2230-5; 0-7636-2230-3
LC 2006052791

Pop-up illustrations and text about such prehistoric creatures as quetzalcoatlus, therapsids, megatherium, saber-toothed tiger, and woolly mammoth

"Thick with layers of carefully painted, cut, folded, and glued papers, this book is designed to amaze, and so it does." Booklist

Turner, Alan, 1947-

National Geographic prehistoric mammals; illustrated by Mauricio Antón. National Geographic 2004 192p il map $29.95; lib bdg $49.90 *

Grades: 5 6 7 8   569

1. Fossil mammals

ISBN 0-7922-7134-3; 0-7922-6997-7 (lib bdg)
LC 2004-1189

This describes the Age of Mammals and profiles over 100 prehistoric mammals, including time lines, fact boxes, distribution maps, photos of fossils, and illustrations

"Dramatic full-color pictures . . . and captions enhance the brief, informative text." SLJ

Wheeler, Lisa, 1963-

Mammoths on the move. Harcourt, Inc. 2006 unp il $16

Grades: K 1 2   569

1. Mammoths

ISBN 0-15-204700-X   LC 2004-19112

"The text describes a group of female mammoths and their young traveling south for the winter, reaching their destination only to turn around and begin their long trek back. Wheeler uses wordplay skillfully, her verse shows originality. . . . The beautifully composed scratchboard illustrations offer strong line work, subtle use of color, and a fine sense of what migrating mammoths may have looked like." Booklist

570 Life sciences; biology

Biology matters! Grolier 2004 10v il set $389 *

Grades: 5 6 7 8 9 10   570

1. Biology 2. Reference books

ISBN 0-7172-5979-X   LC 2003-56942

Contents: v1 Introduction to biology; v2 Cell biology; v3 Genetics; v4 Microorganisms; v5 Plants; v6 Animals; v7 The human body; v8 Reproduction; v9 Evolution; v10 Ecology

"This set presents the fundamentals of the life sciences in a clear format. . . . Volumes contain between six and eight articles in 80 pages . . . introducing its subject, presenting a brief history, and covering many aspects of its current study and applications. . . . The text is large and easy to read, and the writing is straightforward. . . . This title . . . would be a useful addition for public and school libraries." Booklist

Exploring life science. Marshall Cavendish 2000 11v set $329.95

Grades: 4 5 6   570

1. Reference books 2. Life sciences—Encyclopedias

ISBN 0-7614-7135-9   LC 98-52925

Based on the high school level Encyclopedia of life sciences (1966)

Exploring life science—*Continued*

"Arranged into a single alphabet, these more than 300 specific, easily digestible articles cover living things, the environment, and the life sciences themselves. Entries are enhanced by numerous crisply detailed photos, full-color drawings, and boxed closer looks at special issues or topics." SLJ

VanCleave, Janice Pratt

Janice VanCleave's play and find out about nature; easy experiments for young children. Wiley 1997 122p il $29.95; pa $12.95

Grades: K 1 2   **570**
  1. Biology 2. Nature 3. Science—Experiments
  ISBN 0-471-12939-9; 0-471-12940-2 (pa)
                                  LC 96-2865
Provides instructions for fifty nature experiments and activities involving both plants and animals
"VanCleave's explanations are straightforward and concise. The book has a clear and uncluttered look." SLJ
Includes glossary

571.4 Biophysics

Winner, Cherie

Cryobiology. Lerner Publications Co. 2006 48p il (Cool science) lib bdg $26.60

Grades: 4 5 6   **571.4**
  1. Cryobiology
  ISBN 978-0-8225-2907-1 (lib bdg); 0-8225-2907-6 (lib bdg)
                                  LC 2005006158
This book "discusses how different life forms survive low temperatures, e.g., hibernating animals. . . . [The book provides] clear explanations of the science and [covers] possible benefits to humans. A variety of photos and information boxes provide an eye-catching . . . layout." Horn Book Guide
Includes glossary and bibliographical references

571.6 Cell biology

Johnson, Rebecca L., 1956-

Mighty animal cells; [by] Rebecca L. Johnson; illustrations by Jack Desrocher; diagrams by Jennifer E. Fairman. Millbrook Press 2007 48p il (Microquests) lib bdg $29.27

Grades: 4 5 6   **571.6**
  1. Cells
  ISBN 978-0-8225-7137-7 (lib bdg); 0-8225-7137-4 (lib bdg)
                                  LC 2006-36394
In this introduction to animal cells, "Johnson builds one scientific concept at a time using authentic terminology and connecting new information to familiar things. . . . Full-color microscope images, drawings, and cartoons appear in a clean, uncluttered format, combining solid science with humor." Horn Book Guide
Includes glossary and bibliographical references

Lee, Kimberly Fekany

Cells. Compass Point Books 2009 40p il (Mission: science) lib bdg $26.60

Grades: 4 5 6   **571.6**
  1. Cells
  ISBN 978-0-7565-3954-2 (lib bdg); 0-7565-3954-4 (lib bdg)
                                  LC 2008007719
"Lee describes the difference between plant and animal cells, and their contents; diffusion; and cell storage, movement, and reproduction. . . . Large eye-catching and colorful photographs and illustrations appear on every page. . . . The [book] includes a simple activity." SLJ
Includes glossary and bibliographical references

571.8 Reproduction, development, growth

Mitchell, Susan K., 1972-

Animal body-part regenerators; growing new heads, tails, and legs; by Susan K. Mitchell. Enslow Publishers 2009 48p il (Amazing animal defenses) lib bdg $23.93

Grades: 4 5 6   **571.8**
  1. Regeneration (Biology)
  ISBN 978-0-7660-3295-8 (lib bdg); 0-7660-3295-7 (lib bdg)
                                  LC 2008-11453
"Readers will learn about animals that can re-grow parts of their bodies, such as tails and legs." Publisher's note
"The closeup photos are frequent and well chosen, and accompanied by clear, simply phrased [text], which [is] more detailed than average and [takes] up most or all of the space on each page." SLJ
Includes glossary and bibliographical references

Royston, Angela

Looking at life cycles; how do plants and animals change? [by] Angela Royston. Enslow Publishers 2008 32p il (Looking at science: how things change) lib bdg $22.60

Grades: 1 2 3   **571.8**
  1. Life cycles (Biology)
  ISBN 978-0-7660-3091-6 (lib bdg); 0-7660-3091-1 (lib bdg)
                                  LC 2007-24513
"An explanation of life cycles of different types of plants and animals, as well as people." Publisher's note
"Fills a huge void in elementary science collections. . . . Text is arranged in succinct 'chunks,' giving important facts without overwhelming readers. . . . [This] is an essential addition." Libr Media Connect
Includes glossary and bibliographical references

Silverstein, Alvin

Growth and development; by Alvin Silverstein, Virginia Silverstein, and Laura Silverstein Nunn. Twenty-First Century Books 2008 112p il (Science concepts) lib bdg $31.93 *

Grades: 4 5 6 7   **571.8**
  1. Growth 2. Biology
  ISBN 978-0-8225-6057-9 (lib bdg); 0-8225-6057-7 (lib bdg)
                                  LC 2006030299

Silverstein, Alvin—*Continued*

This "considers the growth process, animals with and without skeletons, human and plant growth, and future trends as a result of medical technology. Clear organization, engaging anecdotes, and generally good photos and diagrams are strengths of the [volume]." Horn Book Guide

Includes glossary and bibliographical references

Wade, Mary Dodson, 1930-

Plants grow! Enslow Elementary 2009 24p il (I like plants!) lib bdg $21.26; pa $6.95

Grades: K 1 2   **571.8**
1. Growth 2. Plants
ISBN 978-0-7660-3152-4 (lib bdg); 0-7660-3152-7 (lib bdg); 978-0-7660-3612-3 (pa); 0-7660-3612-X (pa)
LC 2007039453

"The life cycle and parts of a plant are discussed in a clear, concise manner. Beautifully detailed professional photographs of plants, animals, and people complement the subject matter. [The] book includes a simple activity." SLJ

Includes glossary and bibliographical references

572   Biochemistry

Bang, Molly, 1943-

Living sunlight; how plants bring the Earth to life; by Molly Bang & Penny Chisholm; illustrated by Molly Bang. Blue Sky Press 2009 unp il $16.99 *

Grades: PreK K 1 2 3   **572**
1. Photosynthesis 2. Sun
ISBN 978-0-545-04422-6; 0-545-04422-7
LC 2008-14238

This book "talks to young children about photosynthesis . . . in a way that tells what is actually happening on a molecular level. It also tells children why this process matters and leads them into a broad understanding of their personal connection with plant life and energy from the sun. . . . The amiable, well-informed narrator is the sun. Alight with unusual intensity, the artwork fills the pages with vibrant images. . . . Each double-page spread illustrates its lines of text with intelligence and originality." Booklist

Includes bibliographical references

Collard, Sneed B., III

In the deep sea; by Sneed B. Collard III. Marshall Cavendish Benchmark 2005 43p il (Science adventures) lib bdg $29.93

Grades: 4 5 6   **572**
1. Widder, Edith 2. Bioluminescence 3. Ocean bottom
ISBN 0-7614-1952-7   LC 2004026489

"Describes the work of Dr. Edith Widder and other biologists in the field of bioluminescence research." Publisher's note

Includes glossary and bibliographical references

Sitarski, Anita

Cold light; creatures, discoveries, and inventions that glow. Boyds Mills Press 2007 48p il $16.95 *

Grades: 5 6 7 8   **572**
1. Bioluminescence 2. Light
ISBN 1-59078-468-5; 978-1-59078-468-6

"A clearly written, chatty text not only discusses the expected bioluminescent critters (think fireflies), but delves into the realms of chemiluminescence, photoluminescence, and LEDs (light-emitting diodes) as well. . . . The text lays out the historical hows and whys of cold light, its success in the natural world, and its application in medicine and domestic/industrial illumination. Clear color photos and information boxes abound." SLJ

572.8   Biochemical genetics

Johnson, Rebecca L., 1956-

Amazing DNA; [by] Rebecca L. Johnson; illustrations by Jack Desrocher; diagrams by Jennifer E. Fairman. Millbrook Press 2008 48p il (Microquests) lib bdg $29.27

Grades: 4 5 6   **572.8**
1. DNA 2. Genetics
ISBN 978-0-8225-7139-1 (lib bdg); 0-8225-7139-0 (lib bdg)   LC 2006-102324

This describes DNA structure, cell replication and genetic transmission.

"Johnson builds one scientific concept at a time using authentic terminology and connecting new information to familiar things. . . . Full-color microscope images, drawings, and cartoons appear in a clean, uncluttered format, combining solid science with humor." Horn Book Guide

Includes glossary and bibliographical references

Phelan, Glen

Double helix; the quest to uncover the structure of DNA. National Geographic 2006 59p il (Science quest) $17.95 *

Grades: 5 6 7 8   **572.8**
1. DNA 2. Genetics
ISBN 0-7922-5541-0

This "offers a brief but informative overview of the quest to understand heredity. The book focuses on the accomplishments of Francis Crick and James Watson, who eventually uncovered the structure of DNA, but begins with Gregor Mendel's experiments, which were used as the foundation of modern genetic research. . . . Attractively designed and abundantly illustrated." Booklist

Includes glossary and bibliographical references

573.4 Endocrine and excretory systems

Goodman, Susan, 1952-
The truth about poop; by Susan E. Goodman; illustrated by Elwood H. Smith. Viking 2004 40p il $15.99 *

Grades: 2 3 4 5   **573.4**
1. Feces 2. Animal behavior
ISBN 0-670-03674-9   LC 2003-22547

"Chock-full of . . . facts about animal and human excrement, Goodman's free-range text discusses everything from Tyrannosaurus rex dung to the evolution of toilet paper. The three main sections outline animal elimination practices, the processes of human excretion and plumbing, and helpful uses for poop (e.g., for fertilizer or scientific research)." SLJ

This book is "very readable, appropriately visual, and exceedingly encompassing. . . . The well-executed cartoon artwork successfully goes for the clever" Booklist

573.8 Nervous and sensory systems

Jenkins, Steve
What do you do with a tail like this? [by] Steve Jenkins & Robin Page. Houghton Mifflin 2003 unp il $15 *

Grades: K 1 2 3   **573.8**
1. Senses and sensation
ISBN 0-618-25628-8   LC 2002-11673

A Caldecott Medal honor book, 2004

"Tandem spreads treat each body part, with the first posing the question ('What do you do with a nose like this?') and offering five examples . . . positioned on the page so as to obscure the rest of their owners. A turn of the page not only reveals the animals in question . . . but also offers brief answers to the question for each, outlining the special functions of each variant of the featured body part." Bull Cent Child Books

"Jenkins' handsome paper-cut collages are both lovely and anatomically informative. . . . This is a striking, thoughtfully created book with intriguing facts made more memorable through dynamic art." Booklist

573.9 Miscellaneous systems and organs, regional histology and physiology

Souza, D. M. (Dorothy M.)
Look what feet can do; by D. M. Souza. Lerner Publications Co. 2007 48p il (Look what animals can do) lib bdg $25.26

Grades: 2 3 4   **573.9**
1. Foot 2. Animals
ISBN 978-0-7613-9460-0 (lib bdg); 0-7613-9460-5 (lib bdg)

Simple text and color photographs describe the many ways that animals use their feet

"The clean, uncluttered format, excellent color photos, and very readable type make this an attractive choice for independent reading or sharing with classroom groups." Booklist

Includes glossary and bibliographical references

Look what mouths can do; by D. M. Souza. Lerner Publications Co. 2007 48p il (Look what animals can do) lib bdg $25.26

Grades: 2 3 4   **573.9**
1. Mouth 2. Animals
ISBN 978-0-7613-9462-4 (lib bdg); 0-7613-9462-1 (lib bdg)   LC 2005032481

This describes the many ways that animals use their mouths

This has "fun facts and sharp, clear photos. . . . Those interested in animals will be fascinated by the information provided here." SLJ

Includes bibliographical references

Look what tails can do; by D. M. Souza. Lerner Publications Co. 2007 48p il (Look what animals can do) lib bdg $25.26

Grades: 2 3 4   **573.9**
1. Tails 2. Animals
ISBN 978-0-7613-9458-7 (lib bdg); 0-7613-9458-3 (lib bdg)   LC 2005032480

This describes the many ways in which animals use their tails

This has "fun facts and sharp, clear photos. . . . Those interested in animals will be fascinated by the information provided here." SLJ

Includes bibliographical references

575 Specific parts of and physiological systems in plants

Farndon, John
Leaves. Blackbirch Press 2006 24p il (World of plants) lib bdg $24.90

Grades: 2 3 4 5   **575**
1. Leaves
ISBN 978-1-4103-0422-3 (lib bdg); 1-4103-0422-1 (lib bdg)   LC 2005047048

This book examines leaf shapes, the process of photosynthesis, the turning of leaves in the fall season, and unusual leaves that can trap insects

This uses "clear language and short sentences. . . . Helpful diagrams and sharp, colorful photographs supplement the [text]. . . . [This book offers] solid information in an attractive format." SLJ

Includes bibliographical references

576.5 Genetics

Gallant, Roy A.
The treasure of inheritance. Benchmark Bks. 2003 78p il (Story of science) lib bdg $19.95

Grades: 5 6 7 8   **576.5**
1. Genetics 2. Heredity
ISBN 0-7614-1426-6   LC 2002-10

Gallant, Roy A.—*Continued*

Discusses how living things inherit traits, chronicles the history of the study of heredity, and examines current research on genetic engineering and mapping the human gene

"Readers will find accurate, readable explanations for the scientific principles here addressed. . . . Up-to-date controversies and predictions conclude the [book] . . . illustrated with well-captioned photos." Horn Book Guide

Includes glossary and bibliographical references

Simpson, Kathleen

Genetics; from DNA to designer dogs; Sarah Tishkoff, consultant. National Geographic 2008 64p il map (National Geographic investigates) $27.90 *

Grades: 4 5 6 7   **576.5**
    1. Genetics
    ISBN   978-1-4263-0361-6;   1-4263-0361-0;
978-1-4263-0327-2 (lib bdg); 1-4263-0327-0 (lib bdg)

This discusses topics in genetics such as the identification of an Egyptian mummy by DNA testing, the genetics of pea plants studied by Gregor Mendel, cloning, the Human Genome Project, and stem cell research.

"The content is fairly exciting and should grab the attention of its target audience. . . . The photographs throughout are of high quality. . . . An engaging look at a complex topic." Booklist

Walker, Richard, 1951-

Genes & DNA; foreword by Steve Jones. Kingfisher 2003 63p il (Kingfisher knowledge) $11.95 *

Grades: 5 6 7 8   **576.5**
    1. Genetics
    ISBN 0-7534-5621-4   LC 2004-269108

This briefly discusses such topics as the role of genes in inheritance, the structure of the DNA molecule, mutations, The Human Genome Project, and genetic technology such as DNA fingerprinting, gene therapy, genetic engineering, and cloning

Includes glossary and bibliographical references

576.8   Evolution

Berkowitz, Jacob

Out of this world; the amazing search for an alien earth. Kids Can Press 2009 48p il $16.95; pa $8.95

Grades: 4 5 6 7   **576.8**
    1. Life on other planets 2. Outer space—Exploration
    ISBN   978-1-55453-197-4;   1-55453-197-7;
978-1-55453-198-1 (pa); 1-55453-198-5 (pa)

The author "has written a miniencyclopedic, profusely illustrated, picture book that describes, in much detail, what we all know about the universe in which we live and about the conditions that must be present on any planet in our solar system, or on an exoplanet . . . for life as we know it to exist." Sci Books Films

Bortz, Alfred B., 1944-

Astrobiology. Lerner Publications 2008 48p il map (Cool science) lib bdg $26.60

Grades: 4 5 6   **576.8**
    1. Space biology 2. Life on other planets
    ISBN 978-0-8225-6771-4 (lib bdg); 0-8225-6771-7 (lib bdg)   LC 2006033268

This describes "the search for life in the universe. Astrobiologists compare life on Earth to signs of life on other planets. They test meteorites for evidence of alien bacteria. They collect soil and atmospheric samples from other planets. They study photographs taken on space missions. And they listen for signals from alien civilizations on enormous radio dishes." Publisher's note

Includes bibliographical references

Branley, Franklyn Mansfield, 1915-2002

Is there life in outer space? illustrated by Edward Miller. HarperCollins Pubs. 1999 31p il (Let's-read-and-find-out science) hardcover o.p. pa $4.95

Grades: K 1 2 3   **576.8**
    1. Life on other planets 2. Outer space—Exploration
    ISBN 0-06-028146-4; 0-06-028145-6 (lib bdg); 0-06-445192-5 (pa)   LC 99-10904

A newly illustrated edition of the title first published 1984 by Crowell

Discusses some of the ideas and misconceptions about life in outer space and speculates on the existence of such life in light of recent space explorations

"Children curious about the possibility of life on distant planets will find much to think about in this speculative yet scientifically accurate text. The new illustrations, which incorporate photographs of planets, are bright and colorful." Horn Book Guide

Gamlin, Linda

Evolution; written by Linda Gamlin. rev ed. DK Pub. 2009 72p il (DK eyewitness books) $16.99

Grades: 4 5 6 7   **576.8**
    1. Evolution
    ISBN 978-0-7566-5028-5; 0-7566-5028-3
    First published 1993

Text about and photography of experiments, animals, plants, bones, and fossils reveal the ideas and discoveries that have changed our understanding of the natural world and how life began. Includes a CD and wall chart.

Hartman, Eve

Changing life on Earth; [by] Eve Hartman and Wendy Meshbesher. Raintree 2009 48p il (Sci-hi: life science) lib bdg $31.43; pa $8.99

Grades: 5 6 7 8   **576.8**
    1. Evolution
    ISBN 978-1-4109-3324-9 (lib bdg); 1-4109-3324-5 (lib bdg); 978-1-4109-3332-4 (pa); 1-4109-3332-6 (pa)
                                      LC 2009003459

In this introduction to evolution "clear language, embedded definitions, and interesting examples illustrate abstract concepts through both text and well-chosen photographs. . . . [The book] provides a clear and useful explanation of the theory of evolution, with multiple

Hartman, Eve—*Continued*

sources of evidence and a discussion of how it helps scientists to predict the implications of changes to the environment. . . . [The] book also includes suggested activities to test ideas as well as a thorough glossary and a Webliography." SLJ

Includes glossary and bibliographical references

Jackson, Ellen B., 1943-

Looking for life in the universe; the search for extraterrestrial intelligence; by Ellen Jackson; with photographs by Nic Bishop. Houghton Mifflin 2002 57p il (Scientists in the field) $16 *

Grades: 4 5 6 7   576.8

1. Tarter, Jill Cornell, 1944- 2. Life on other planets
ISBN 0-618-12894-8   LC 2001-51312

Investigates how scientists, particularly Jill Tarter, Director of the SETI Institute in Mountain View, California, use twenty-first century technology to investigate whether life exists on other planets

"An exciting, visually awesome look at frontier science." SLJ

Includes glossary and bibliographical references

Jenkins, Steve

Life on earth: the story of evolution. Houghton Mifflin 2002 unp il $16 *

Grades: 3 4 5 6   576.8

1. Evolution
ISBN 0-618-16476-6   LC 2002-472

Provides an overview of the origin and evolution of life on earth and of what has been learned from the study of evolution

"Jenkins presents a superb introduction to evolution. . . . His signature cut-paper illustrations placed on white backgrounds work well. . . . Jenkins's explanations of science concepts are comprehensive and comprehensible. . . . Particularly admirable is his avoidance of any over-simplifications." Horn Book

Includes bibliographical references

Mehling, Randi

Great extinctions of the past; by Randi Mehling. Chelsea House 2007 72p il (Scientific American) lib bdg $30

Grades: 5 6 7 8   576.8

1. Mass extinction of species
ISBN 978-0-7910-9049-7 (lib bdg); 0-7910-9049-3 (lib bdg)   LC 2006014851

Examines extinctions of prehistoric species including the dinosaurs, looks at the five largest extinctions ever, and explores the idea of a future mass extinction.

"The ideas in this book are . . . clearly explained. . . . [The book has] captioned color photos throughout." SLJ

Includes glossary and bibliographical references

Scott, Elaine, 1940-

Mars and the search for life. Clarion Books 2008 60p il $17 *

Grades: 4 5 6 7   576.8

1. Mars (Planet) 2. Life on other planets
ISBN 978-0-618-76695-6; 0-618-76695-2
                                      LC 2008-07243

The author discusses "the Mars Exploration Rover (MER) and tantalizing findings that suggest that conditions on the red planet may once have been hospitable to life. . . . Illustrations are arresting and clearly captioned." Bull Cent Child Books

Includes glossary and bibliographical references

Skurzynski, Gloria, 1930-

Are we alone? scientists search for life in space. National Geographic Society 2004 92p il $18.95 *

Grades: 5 6 7 8   576.8

1. Life on other planets
ISBN 0-7922-6567-X   LC 2003-17732

The author begins with a "history of how the idea of flying saucers and extraterrestrials became part of the American consciousness. Later chapters trace specific quests . . . for signs of life beyond earth. . . . The text remains readable even while explaining intricate scientific concepts and complex . . . ideas. The vibrant full-color photos enhance the work impressively." Booklist

Includes glossary and bibliographical references

Turner, Pamela S.

Life on earth—and beyond; an astrobiologist's quest. Charlesbridge 2008 109p il map lib bdg $19.95; pa $11.95 *

Grades: 5 6 7 8   576.8

1. McKay, Christopher P. 2. Life on other planets 3. Space biology
ISBN 978-1-58089-133-2 (lib bdg); 1-58089-133-0 (lib bdg); 978-1-58089-134-9 (pa); 1-58089-134-9 (pa)
                                      LC 2007-01475

"Astrobiologists look outward from the Earth seeking evidence of life elsewhere in the universe. But, as this fascinating book shows, they also travel to places on Earth where extreme conditions may be similar to those on distant worlds. Turner follows astrobiologist Chris McKay as he looks for life in apparently hostile environments. . . . Illustrated with many excellent color photos and other images." Booklist

Includes bibliographical references

Weaver, Anne H., 1947-

The voyage of the beetle; a journey around the world with Charles Darwin and the search for the solution to the mystery of mysteries, as narrated by Rosie, an articulate beetle; [by] Anne H. Weaver; illustrated by George Lawrence. University of New Mexico Press 2007 80p il map $16.95

Grades: 4 5 6   576.8

1. Darwin, Charles, 1809-1882 2. Beagle Expedition (1831-1836) 3. Naturalists 4. Evolution
ISBN 978-0-8263-4304-8; 0-8263-4304-X
                                      LC 2007008924

Weaver, Anne H., 1947-—*Continued*

This book "is playful, creative, and beautifully conceived and executed, in terms of both the writing and the wonderful illustrations. . . . Through the eyes and narration of Darwin's fictional beetle friend Rosie, the reader is taken on the outer journey of Darwin's voyage (1831-1836) on the H.M.S. Beagle and the inner intellectual journey of Darwin's formulation of the theory of natural selection and the origin of the species." Sci Books Films

Includes bibliographical references

Winston, Robert M. L.

Evolution revolution; [by] Robert Wilson. DK Pub. 2009 96p il $16.99 *

Grades: 5 6 7 8   **576.8**

1. Evolution

ISBN 978-0-7566-45243-; 0-7566-4524-7

"The first two thirds of the book are devoted to the history of thought and research on evolution, from stories of Creation, through Darwin, to genetics. The last third looks at 'Evolution in Action.' Information on the fetuses of related species rubs shoulders with variations within species and a time line of the Earth. Visually, the book snaps with colored backgrounds, cool graphics, topflight photos, and clever word balloons coming from vintage black-and-white reproductions." SLJ

577 Ecology

Gardner, Robert, 1929-

Ace your ecology and environmental science project; great science fair ideas; [by] Robert Gardner, Phyllis J. Perry, and Salvatore Tocci. Enslow Publishers 2009 128p il (Ace your science project) lib bdg $31.93

Grades: 5 6 7 8   **577**

1. Environmental sciences 2. Ecology 3. Science projects 4. Science—Experiments

ISBN 978-0-7660-3216-3 (lib bdg); 0-7660-3216-7 (lib bdg)   LC 2008-4683

"Presents several science projects and science fair ideas dealing with ecology and environmental studies." Publisher's note

"Dozens of . . . science activities are presented with background information, step-by-step instructions, and suggestions for extending to the science fair level. . . . Color illustrations and important safety information are included." Horn Book Guide

Includes bibliographical references

Godkin, Celia, 1948-

Wolf island. Fitzhenry & Whiteside 2007 unp il $17.95; pa $9.95

Grades: K 1 2 3   **577**

1. Ecology 2. Food chains (Ecology)

ISBN 1-55455-007-6; 1-55455-008-4 (pa)

A newly formatted edition of the title first published 1989 in Canada; first U.S. edition 1993 by Scientific American Books for Young Readers

When a family of wolves is removed from the food chain on a small island, the impact on the island's ecology is felt by the other animals living there.

"The food chain, especially its harsher aspects, can be difficult to explain to young children, but this gentle narrative conveys the realism without mawkish sentimentality. . . . With a large format, arresting cover, and beautiful soft-edged illustrations, this presentation offers an effective balance between a documentary and a nature story." Booklist

Habitats of the world. Marshall Cavendish 2005 c2006 11v il map set $359.95

Grades: 5 6 7 8   **577**

1. Habitat (Ecology) 2. Reference books

ISBN 0-7614-7523-0   LC 2004-52782

Contents: v1 Abbey-Badlands; v2 Baikal-coral reef; v3 Cousteau-estuary and delta; v4 Etosha-Great Barrier Reef; v5 Habitat-island; v6 Kilimanjaro-Muir; v7 Nile River-pollution; v8 Pond-severe weather; v9 Shrubland-tree; v10 Tropical ocean-Yellowstone National Park; v11 Index

"This encyclopedia informs students about ecology and the connections between people and the natural environment. Emphasizing how humans make a difference, articles on particular habitats draw attention to the threat of species extinction, the promise of sustainability, and personal responsibilities for stewardship of the earth. Biographies of ecologists and articles discussing broad environmental concerns contribute to students' knowledge of concepts central to the science curriculum." Publisher's note

Housel, Debra J., 1961-

Ecosystems. Compass Point Books 2009 40p il map (Mission: science) lib bdg $26.60

Grades: 4 5 6   **577**

1. Ecology

ISBN 978-0-7565-4068-5 (lib bdg); 0-7565-4068-2 (lib bdg)   LC 2008-35730

An introduction to the ways in which plants and animals interact with each other

Includes glossary

Latham, Donna

Ecology. Raintree 2009 48p il (Sci-hi: life science) lib bdg $31.43; pa $8.99

Grades: 5 6 7 8   **577**

1. Ecology

ISBN 978-1-4109-3328-7 (lib bdg); 1-4109-3328-8 (lib bdg); 978-1-4109-3336-2 (pa); 1-4109-3336-9 (pa)   LC 2009003465

In this introduction to ecology "clear language, embedded definitions, and interesting examples illustrate abstract concepts through both text and well-chosen photographs. . . . [It] includes suggested activities to test ideas as well as a thorough glossary and a Webliography." SLJ

Includes glossary and bibliographical references

Lauber, Patricia, 1924-

Who eats what? food chains and food webs; illustrated by Holly Keller. HarperCollins Pubs. 1995 32p il (Let's-read-and-find-out science) hardcover o.p. pa $4.95

Grades: K 1 2 3   577
   1. Food chains (Ecology)
   ISBN 0-06-022981-0; 0-06-022982-9 (lib bdg); 0-06-445130-5 (pa)   LC 93-10609

The author "demonstrates the interconnectedness of nature by showing how creatures form chains through the foods they eat. . . . Lauber gives several examples, from short chains (apple to child) to the web of connections between sea creatures. She uses sea otters to show how the disappearance of one link in the chain can disrupt the flow of food both up and down." Bull Cent Child Books

"Clear, simple ink-and-watercolor drawings illustrate the clear, simple text. Informative and intriguing, this basic science book leads children to think about the complex and interdependent web of life on Earth." Booklist

Munro, Roxie, 1945-

Ecomazes; 12 Earth adventures. Sterling 2010 unp il $14.95 *

Grades: 2 3 4   577
   1. Ecology 2. Maze puzzles
   ISBN 978-1-4027-6393-9; 1-4027-6393-X

"These simple, themed mazes are set in full-spread renditions of biomes ranging from a tropical rain forest to a rocky, penguin-packed Antarctic beach. Munro invites viewers to trace each wandering, easy-to-follow pathway with a finger, noting distinctive landforms and keeping their eyes peeled for the tiny but precisely rendered wildlife visible on either side of the path. . . . This is truly a complete package: it's engrossing and interactive, featuring finely and accurately detailed art and covering the basics of an organizational concept that is central to our understanding of the natural world." SLJ

Pollock, Steve

Ecology; written by Steve Pollock. rev ed. DK Pub. 2005 72p il (DK eyewitness books) $15.99; lib bdg $19.99

Grades: 4 5 6 7   577
   1. Ecology
   ISBN 0-7556-1387-6; 0-7556-1396-5 (lib bdg)
   First published 1993

Illustrations and text provide information about ecology in general, specific ecosystems, and our changing understanding of life around us.

Rau, Dana Meachen, 1971-

Food chains. Marshall Cavendish Benchmark 2009 31p il (Bookworms. Nature's cycles) lib bdg $22.79

Grades: PreK K 1   577
   1. Food chains (Ecology)
   ISBN 978-0-7614-4095-6 (lib bdg); 0-7614-4095-X (lib bdg)   LC 2008-42508

"Introduces the idea that many things in the world around us are cyclical in nature and explores the food chain." Publisher's note

"Well composed, simple sentences tie directly to colorful, carefully chosen photos [and] . . . accurate information flows naturally. . . . A great resource for sharing one-on-one with the youngest readers." Libr Media Connect

Includes glossary

Rompella, Natalie

Ecosystems; [by] Natalie Rompella. Heinemann Library 2008 48p il (Science fair projects) $30

Grades: 5 6 7 8   577
   1. Ecology 2. Science—Experiments 3. Science projects
   ISBN 978-1-4034-7915-0   LC 2006039543

This "describes 10 inquiry-based science projects related to life science and ecosystems. . . . Students from mid-elementary through middle school would find little difficulty following the clearly written instructions and suggestions. . . . The illustrations consist of colorful photographs and well-labeled diagrams." Sci Books Films

Includes bibliographical references

Sayre, April Pulley

Trout are made of trees; [by] April Pulley Sayre; illustrated by Kate Endle. Charlesbridge 2008 unp il lib bdg $15.95; pa $6.95

Grades: K 1 2 3   577
   1. Food chains (Ecology)
   ISBN 978-1-58089-137-0 (lib bdg); 1-58089-137-3 (lib bdg); 978-1-58089-138-7 (pa); 1-58089-138-1 (pa)
                                 LC 2007-02268

"A boy and girl, one white, one black, are exploring the stream and its inhabitants with their parents. In clear sentences, young readers follow autumn leaves as they fall from a tree into the water, are softened by algae and eaten by other creatures, which are then consumed by the trout. A more detailed explanation is included at the end of the book. Attractive collage illustrations in natural colors fill the spreads and help to explain the text. This unique introduction to how changes in nature create the food web illustrates how the whole world is interconnected." SLJ

Includes bibliographical references

Somervill, Barbara A., 1948-

Our living world; earth's biomes. Tradition 2006 7v il map set $350 *

Grades: 5 6 7 8   577
   1. Ecology 2. Reference books
   ISBN 1-59187-052-6

"Seven volumes . . . examine the biomes: Oceans, Seas, and Reefs; Tundra; Rivers, Streams, Lakes, and Ponds; Wetlands; Deserts; Grasslands; and Forests. Each is truly a visual and informational feast for the intermediate-grades researcher. Following a solid definition of the pertinent ecosystem, eight chapters of readable text describe the indigenous animals and plants. Chapters include discussions on the key species, predators, prey, flora, herbivores, and life cycle. . . . All entries contain vibrant color photographs and maps, colored sidebars, and a variety of boxed supplemental reference features." Booklist

Stille, Darlene R., 1942-

Nature interrupted; the science of environmental chain reactions. Compass Point Books 2009 48p il map (Headline science) lib bdg $27.93

Grades: 5 6 7 8   577
    1. Ecology 2. Food chains (Ecology) 3. Environmental degradation
    ISBN 978-0-7565-3949-8 (lib bdg); 0-7565-3949-8 (lib bdg)   LC 2008007282

This "reviews the importance of subtle links in the environmental chain and the far-reaching consequences of its disruption. The possible harm to the food chain caused by the use of antibacterial soap is one case study. The flow of energy from one organism to the next in the food web and the unexpected results when this relationship is disrupted are shown in examinations of monarch butterflies, zebra mussels, and algal blooms. The color illustrations and charts . . . are clear and helpful, and the text, although information rich, is not overly difficult." SLJ

Includes glossary and bibliographical references

Toft, Kim Michelle

The world that we want; [by] Kim Michelle Toft. Charlesbridge 2005 unp il $16.95

Grades: K 1 2 3   577
    1. Habitat (Ecology)
    ISBN 1-58089-114-4   LC 2004-20717

"This book offers two-page vistas that incorporate animals found in a variety of habitats, including a mangrove, a tide pool, and a reef. As viewers move from flying pelican to gliding barracuda, Toft creates ever-widening perspectives to reveal how various ecosystems relate to one another. . . . This process culminates in an impressive four-page, foldout panorama that includes all 45 animals. The minimal text cumulates as well. . . . The arresting, brilliantly hued illustrations were drawn and painted on silk." SLJ

VanCleave, Janice Pratt

Janice Vancleave's ecology for every kid; easy activities that make learning science fun. Wiley 1996 219p il maps (Science for every kid series) hardcover o.p. pa $10.95

Grades: 4 5 6 7   577
    1. Ecology 2. Habitat (Ecology) 3. Science—Experiments
    ISBN 0-471-10100-1; 0-471-10086-2 (pa)
                           LC 95-6112

This book of science activities covers "25 topics, ranging from plant and animal food chains to the effect of plastics on the environment. Subjects are introduced in a 'What You Need to Know' section that gives explanation of the scientific principles, plus plenty of everyday examples. A brief preparatory exercise follows, usually in the form of an imaginative game. . . . Simple black-line drawings are crisp, uncluttered, and well placed. . . . Solid information and a generous portion of fun are combined to elevate this selection above the standard collection of experiments." SLJ

Includes glossary

577.2   Specific factors affecting ecology

Godkin, Celia, 1948-

Fire! Fitzhenry & Whiteside 2006 unp il $17.95

Grades: 2 3 4   577.2
    1. Forest fires 2. Forest ecology
    ISBN 1-55041-889-0

"Focusing on events in one location, this handsome volume presents the cycle of forest fires in words and pictures. . . . Clear, concise writing and vivid artwork make this a fine presentation on the subject." Booklist

Peluso, Beth A., 1974-

The charcoal forest; how fire helps animals and plants; written and illustrated by Beth A. Peluso. Mountain Press Pub. Co. 2007 56p il pa $12

Grades: 3 4 5 6   577.2
    1. Forest fires 2. Forest ecology 3. Forest animals 4. Forest plants 5. Rocky Mountains
    ISBN 978-0-87842-532-7 (pa); 0-87842-532-2 (pa)
                          LC 2007003358

This "explores the new habitat created by [a forest] fire. Focusing on the Northern Rocky Mountains of the United States and Canada, the book describes twenty species of animals and plants that contribute to the reclamation and renewal of the charcoal forest." Publisher's note

"Each featured plant, animal, or fungus gets a clear, two-page spread with several informative paragraphs accompanied by vibrant illustrations. The writing is accessible and engaging." Sci Books Films

Simon, Seymour, 1931-

Wildfires. Morrow Junior Bks. 1996 unp il pa $6.99 hardcover o.p.

Grades: 4 5 6 7   577.2
    1. Forest fires 2. Forest ecology
    ISBN 0-688-17530-9 (pa)   LC 95-12653

"Exploring the place of fire in nature, Simon explains that . . . forest fires have important functions in the ecosystem. With a brilliantly clear and colorful photograph facing each page of text, the book describes the causes and the progression of the wildfires that burned areas of Yellowstone National Park in 1988, explains how the fires were beneficial in many ways. . . . Lucid writing and excellent book design." Booklist

577.3   Forest ecology

Brenner, Barbara, 1925-

One small place in a tree; illustrated by Tom Leonard. HarperCollins Publishers 2004 unp il $15.99; lib bdg $16.89

Grades: 2 3 4   577.3
    1. Forest ecology
    ISBN 0-688-17180-X; 0-688-17181-8 (lib bdg)
                          LC 2002-1181

Brenner, Barbara, 1925-—*Continued*

A child visitor observes as one tiny scratch in a tree develops into a home for a variety of woodland animals over many years, even after the tree has fallen.

"Brenner makes the science enjoyable and understandable, and Leonard's highly detailed, realistic illustrations provide great visual aid." Booklist

Burnie, David

Shrublands. Raintree Steck-Vaughn Pubs. 2003 64p il map (Biomes atlases) lib bdg $31.42

Grades: 5 6 7 8   **577.3**

   1. Forest ecology

   ISBN 0-7398-5514-X   LC 2002-68093

A comprehensive look at the shrubland biome, describing the climate, plants, animals, people, and future of these areas, and providing detailed views of some major shrubland regions

"Especially effective are the maps. Brief notes for 10 to 12 highlights appear on each one, commenting on the diversity of flora, fauna, and landforms that occurs. . . . [The book includes] excellent-quality, full-color photographs and related sidebars." SLJ

Includes glossary and bibliographical references

Collard, Sneed B., III

Forest in the clouds; by Sneed Collard III; illustrated by Michael Rothman. Charlesbridge Pub. 2000 unp il map $16.95; pa $7.95

Grades: 2 3 4   **577.3**

   1. Forest ecology 2. Cloud forests 3. Natural history—Costa Rica

   ISBN 0-88106-985-X; 0-88106-986-8 (pa)

                           LC 98-6150

Describes some of the exotic plants and animals that live in the cloud forest of Costa Rica, and discusses some environmental threats faced by this region

"Rothman's detailed acrylic paintings, dominated by rich greens and browns, cover the better part of each spread. . . . Although valuable for reports, Collard's book will interest browsers as well." SLJ

Fleisher, Paul

Forest food webs. Lerner Publications Co. 2008 48p il (Early bird food webs) lib bdg $26.60

Grades: 2 3 4 5   **577.3**

   1. Forest ecology 2. Food chains (Ecology)

   ISBN 978-0-8225-6729-5   LC 2007-01373

"This colorful volume introduces the forest, with an emphasis on food webs. Clearly written chapters focus on topics such as plants, herbivores, carnivores, decomposers, and people's enjoyment, use, and destruction of forests in the U.S." Booklist

Includes glossary and bibliographical references

Fusco Castaldo, Nancy, 1962-

Rainforests; an activity guide for ages 6-9; [by] Nancy F. Castaldo. Chicago Review Press 2003 133p il $14.95

Grades: 2 3 4 5   **577.3**

   1. Rain forest ecology

   ISBN 1-55652-476-5   LC 2002-152661

Provides facts and activities that explore tropical and temperate ancient forests, discusses how individuals can help preserve them, and describes well-known and unfamiliar creatures of the rain forest

"The activities are varied and interesting, ranging from science projects to crafts to recipes. . . . The book would serve as a valuable resource." SLJ

Includes bibliographical references

Gibbons, Gail

Nature's green umbrella; tropical rain forests. Morrow Junior Bks. 1994 unp il maps hardcover o.p. pa $5.95

Grades: K 1 2 3   **577.3**

   1. Rain forest ecology

   ISBN 0-688-12353-8; 0-688-12354-6 (lib bdg); 0-688-15411-5 (pa)

                           LC 93-17569

Describes the climatic conditions of the rain forest as well as the different layers of plants and animals that comprise the ecosystem

The language is "simple, yet poetic and evocative. . . . Colorful maps pinpoint the locations of these global resources. Green vines entwine around the borders of each page and enclose the text and bright illustrations." Sci Books Films

Greenaway, Theresa, 1947-

Jungle; written by Theresa Greenaway; photographed by Geoff Dann. rev ed. DK Pub. 2004 71p il map (DK eyewitness books) $15.99

Grades: 4 5 6 7   **577.3**

   1. Rain forest ecology

   ISBN 0-7566-0694-2   LC 2004558978

First published 1994

Color photographs, drawings, and brief text describe the animals, plants, and ecology of tropical forests of the world

Guiberson, Brenda Z., 1946-

Rain, rain, rain forest; illustrated by Steve Jenkins. Henry Holt 2004 unp il $16.95

Grades: K 1 2 3   **577.3**

   1. Rain forest ecology

   ISBN 0-8050-6582-2   LC 2003-12250

"Vibrant words and sensory impressions bring the creatures' noisy cacophony and slithering, swooping motions up close, while gracefully incorporated facts convey a surprising amount of information. . . . The artist's colorful, textured images create a rich sense of atmosphere, and the precise details and lively compositions will easily draw children back to the text." Booklist

Jackson, Kay, 1959-

Rain forests; by Kay Jackson. KidHaven Press 2007 48p il (Our environment) lib bdg $23.70

Grades: 5 6 7 8   **577.3**

   1. Rain forests 2. Rain forest ecology

   ISBN 978-0-7377-3624-3   LC 2007006892

"Jackson defines rain forests. . . . She explains why rain forests are important, . . . the causes of rain forest destruction, and current efforts to save diverse eco-

Jackson, Kay, 1959-—*Continued*
systems. The writing is clear and succinct. . . . Full-color, captioned photographs and drawings appear on nearly every page." Booklist
Includes bibliographical references

Jackson, Tom, 1972-
Tropical forests. Raintree Steck-Vaughn Pubs. 2003 64p il map (Biomes atlases) lib bdg $31.42
Grades: 5 6 7 8   **577.3**
   1. Rain forest ecology
   ISBN 0-7398-5250-7   LC 2002-68094
A comprehensive look at the tropical forest biome, examining its climate, plants, animals, people, and future, plus detailed views of some particular tropical forest locations
"Especially effective are the maps. Brief notes for 10 to 12 highlights appear on each one, commenting on the diversity of flora, fauna, and landforms that occurs. . . . [The book includes] excellent-quality, full-color photographs and related sidebars." SLJ
Includes glossary and bibliographical references

Johansson, Philip
The forested Taiga; a web of life. Enslow Pubs. 2004 48p il map (World of biomes) lib bdg $18.95
Grades: 3 4 5   **577.3**
   1. Forest ecology
   ISBN 0-7660-2197-1   LC 2003-4436
Contents: A wolf's dining room; The Taiga biome; Biome communities; Taiga plants; Taiga animals
This describes the ecology of dark evergreen forests of northern Europe, Asia and North America
This book is "extremely well written, and [it contains] ample information presented in a way that is easy to understand." Sci Books Films
Includes glossary and bibliographical references

The temperate forest; a web of life. Enslow Pubs. 2004 48p il map (World of biomes) lib bdg $18.95
Grades: 3 4 5   **577.3**
   1. Forest ecology
   ISBN 0-7660-2198-X   LC 2003-3614
Contents: A forest for bears; The temperate forest biome; Forest communities; Temperate forest plants; Temperate forest animals
This describes the ecology of temperate forests
This book is "extremely well written, and [it contains] ample information presented in a way that is easy to understand." Sci Books Films
Includes glossary and bibliographical references

The tropical rain forest; a web of life. Enslow Pubs. 2004 48p il map (World of biomes) lib bdg $18.95
Grades: 3 4 5   **577.3**
   1. Rain forest ecology
   ISBN 0-7660-2199-8   LC 2003-6481
Contents: The eating machines; The rain forest biome; Tropical rain forest communities; Tropical rain forest plants; Tropical rain forest animals

This describes the ecology of the tropical rain forests
This book is "extremely well written, and [it contains] ample information presented in a way that is easy to understand." Sci Books Films
Includes glossary and bibliographical references

Johnson, Rebecca L., 1956-
A walk in the boreal forest; with illustrations by Phyllis V. Saroff. Carolrhoda Bks. 2001 48p il map (Biomes of North America) lib bdg $23.93
Grades: 3 4 5 6   **577.3**
   1. Forest ecology
   ISBN 1-57505-156-7   LC 00-8240
Describes the climate, seasons, plants, animals, and soil of the boreal forest, a biome or land zone, which stretches across the northern parts of North America, Europe, and Asia
"A fine overview of the plant and animal life of the boreal forest. . . . Excellent full-color photographs." SLJ
Includes glossary and bibliographical references

A walk in the deciduous forest; with illustrations by Phyllis V. Saroff. Carolrhoda Bks. 2001 48p il map (Biomes of North America) lib bdg $23.93
Grades: 3 4 5 6   **577.3**
   1. Forest ecology
   ISBN 1-57505-155-9   LC 00-8243
Takes readers on a walk through a forest of trees that lose their leaves in the fall, showing examples of how the animals and plants depend on each other and their environment to survive
"The simple design and clearly written, informative text will appeal to readers who enjoy nature." Horn Book Guide
Includes glossary and bibliographical references

Lasky, Kathryn
The most beautiful roof in the world; exploring the rainforest canopy; photographs by Christopher G. Knight. Harcourt Brace & Co. 1997 unp il hardcover o.p. pa $9
Grades: 4 5 6 7   **577.3**
   1. Lowman, Margaret 2. Rain forest ecology
   ISBN 0-15-200893-4; 0-15-200897-7 (pa)
                                LC 95-48193
"Gulliver Green"
Describes the work of Meg Lowman in the rainforest canopy, an area unexplored until the last ten years and home to previously unknown species of plants and animals
"Fresh in out-look and intriguing in details, this memorable book features colorful photographs that reflect the you-are-there quality of the text." Booklist
Includes glossary

Levinson, Nancy Smiler, 1938-

Rain forests; illustrated by Diane Dawson Hearn. Holiday House 2008 40p il (Holiday House reader) lib bdg $15.95 *

Grades: K 1 2   577.3

1. Rain forest ecology

ISBN 978-0-8234-1899-2 (lib bdg); 0-8234-1899-5 (lib bdg)

"Levinson offers a straightforward, simple introduction to rain forests and some of the flora and fauna found there. Most of the book deals with tropical forests and the characteristics of each of their four layers. Hearn clearly identifies the locales of her illustrations and labels the plants and animals depicted." SLJ

Levy, Janey

Discovering rain forests; [by] Janey Levy. PowerKids Press 2007 32p il map (World habitats) lib bdg $23.95

Grades: 3 4 5   577.3

1. Rain forest ecology 2. Rain forests

ISBN 978-1-4042-3782-7 (lib bdg); 1-4042-3782-8 (lib bdg)   LC 2006036867

This book about rain forest ecology "includes 10 chapters with information on climate, location, plants, animals, people, conservation, and page of relevant facts and figures. Clear, colorful photographs show the landscape and the varied plants and wildlife." SLJ

Includes glossary

Lundgren, Julie K.

Forest fare; studying food webs in the forest; [by] Julie K. Lundgren. Rourke Pub. 2009 32p il map (Studying food webs) lib bdg $28.50

Grades: 3 4 5   577.3

1. Forest ecology 2. Food chains (Ecology)

ISBN 978-1-60472-316-8 (lib bdg); 1-60472-316-5 (lib bdg)   LC 2008-24858

This book has "stunning photos, fascinating facts, and intriguing examples. . . . Herbivores, omnivores, and carnivores specific to . . . [the forest] ecosystem are presented. . . . 'Chew on this' insets add further interest and information. . . . [This] will appeal to readers." SLJ

Includes glossary and bibliographical references

Pfeffer, Wendy, 1929-

A log's life; illustrations by Robin Brickman. Simon & Schuster Bks. for Young Readers 1997 unp il $16

Grades: K 1 2 3   577.3

1. Oak 2. Forest ecology

ISBN 0-689-80636-1   LC 95-30020

This is an "introduction to the life, death, and decay of an oak tree. The simple, informative text presents the complex cast of characters residing in or on the living tree as well as the decomposing log. . . . The verbal descriptions of this rich ecosystem are enhanced by striking illustrations of three-dimensional paper sculptures, often so realistic as to seem to be preserved natural specimens." SLJ

Stille, Darlene R., 1942-

Tropical rain forest. Children's Press 1999 47p il (True book) lib bdg $22

Grades: 2 3 4   577.3

1. Rain forest ecology

ISBN 0-516-21511-6   LC 98-50753

Differentiates a tropical rain forest from all others, and describes its typical plant and animal life

"The plain style, accessible design, and beautiful photographs of landscapes and wildlife make this a good [title] for children's first research presentations." Booklist

Includes glossary and bibliographical references

Tagliaferro, Linda

Explore the tropical rain forest; by Linda Tagliaferro. Capstone Press 2007 32p il map (Explore the biomes) $16.95; pa $6.95

Grades: PreK K 1 2   577.3

1. Rain forest ecology

ISBN   978-0-7368-6407-7;   0-7368-6407-5; 978-0-7368-9630-6 (pa); 0-7368-9630-9 (pa)
                                           LC 2006004107

"Fact finders"

This is an introduction to the tropical rain forest habitat and some of its plants and animals.

This book "uses vivid, sense-appealing language. . . . An attractive . . . format displays the captions to colorful photographs." Sci Books Films

Includes bibliographical references

Tocci, Salvatore

The chaparral; life on the scrubby coast. Franklin Watts 2003 63p il map (Biomes and habitats) lib bdg $25.50; pa $8.95

Grades: 4 5 6 7   577.3

1. Chaparral ecology

ISBN 0-531-12303-0 (lib bdg); 0-531-16671-6 (pa)
                                           LC 2003-16574

"Watts library"

A look at the plants, animals, locations, and various habitats that make up the chaparral ecosystems of the world

Life in the temperate forests. Franklin Watts 2005 63p il map (Biomes and habitats) lib bdg $25.50

Grades: 4 5 6 7   577.3

1. Forest ecology

ISBN 0-531-12363-4   LC 2004027303

"Watts library"

Describes the plants and animals that live in temperate forests and the threats facing them

Includes glossary and bibliographical references

Life in the tropical forests. Franklin Watts 2005 63p il map (Biomes and habitats) lib bdg $25.50

Grades: 4 5 6 7   577.3

1. Rain forest ecology

ISBN 0-531-12364-2   LC 2004027054

"Watts library"

Describes the animals, plants, and people that live in rainforests and the threats to their existence

Includes glossary and bibliographical references

Vogt, Richard Carl

Rain forests. Simon & Schuster Books for Young Readers 2009 64p il (Insiders) $16.99 *
Grades: 4 5 6 7   **577.3**
1. Rain forests
ISBN 978-1-4169-3866-8; 1-4169-3866-4
LC 2008061111

"The layers of a rain forest are drawn with exacting detail in every imaginable shade of green, while circular inserts zoom in on flora with accompanying stats. Running down the length of the spread are markers delineating the cutoff points for each layer—emergent, canopy, and so on. The rest of the book is similarly fine, bringing animals, reptiles, and insects into the mix. . . . Some photographs join the mostly hand-illustrated affair. . . . What will grab browsers are the 3D cover and vivid drawings on thick, oversize pages, but what will keep them reading is a cumulative sense of the rain forest as a verdant universe nearly festering with life." Booklist

Welsbacher, Anne, 1955-

Protecting Earth's rain forests; by Anne Welsbacher. Lerner Publications 2009 72p il map (Saving our living Earth) lib bdg $30.60
Grades: 5 6 7 8   **577.3**
1. Rain forests 2. Environmental protection
ISBN 978-0-8225-7562-7 (lib bdg); 0-8225-7562-0 (lib bdg)
LC 2007-38859

"Provides a thorough, interesting discussion of multiple aspects of [rain forest protection], including historical origins, the current situation, and potential solutions. . . . Photos from around the world accompany discussions. . . . Solid choice to replace outdated books." SLJ

Includes glossary and bibliographical references

577.4 Grassland ecology

Collard, Sneed B., III

The prairie builders; reconstructing America's lost grasslands; written and photographed by Sneed B. Collard III. Houghton Mifflin Co. 2005 66p il (Scientists in the field) $17; pa $8.95
Grades: 4 5 6 7   **577.4**
1. Prairies 2. Nature conservation
ISBN 978-0-618-39687-0; 0-618-39687-X; 978-0-547-01441-8 (pa); 0-547-01441-4 (pa)
LC 2004-13201

This describes an effort to restore part of the native tallgrass prairie in the the 8,000-acre Neal Smith National Wildlife Refuge in Iowa

"The engaging text is accompanied by large, inviting color photographs. . . . An essential purchase for libraries in prairie regions and a worthwhile choice for others." SLJ

Includes bibliographical references

Dunphy, Madeleine

Here is the African savanna; illustrated by Tom Leonard. Hyperion Books for Children 1999 unp il $14.99; lib bdg $15.99
Grades: K 1 2 3   **577.4**
1. Grassland ecology 2. Natural history—Africa
ISBN 0-7868-0162-X; 0-7868-2134-5 (lib bdg)
LC 98-30007

Cumulative text describes the interdependence among the plants and animals of an African savanna

"The acrylic illustrations are rich with detail and gold-toned radiance. An endnote provides some additional information about conservation. This is an attractive, effective way to introduce ecology to young readers." Horn Book Guide

Hoare, Ben

Temperate grasslands. Raintree Steck-Vaughn Pubs. 2003 64p il map (Biomes atlases) lib bdg $31.42
Grades: 5 6 7 8   **577.4**
1. Grassland ecology
ISBN 0-7398-5249-3   LC 2002-12818

Contents: Biomes of the world; Temperate grasslands of the world; Grassland climate; Grassland plants; Grassland animals; People and grasslands; The future

This offers a look at temperate grasslands of the world describing their climate, plants, animals, people, and future

"Especially effective are the maps. Brief notes for 10 to 12 highlights appear on each one, commenting on the diversity of flora, fauna, and landforms that occurs. . . . [The book includes] excellent-quality, full-color photographs and related sidebars." SLJ

Includes glossary and bibliographical references

Jackson, Kay, 1959-

Explore the grasslands; by Kay Jackson. Capstone Press 2007 32p il map (Explore the biomes) $16.95; pa $6.95
Grades: PreK K 1 2   **577.4**
1. Grassland ecology
ISBN 978-0-7368-6405-3; 0-7368-6405-9; 978-0-7368-9628-3 (pa); 0-7368-9628-7 (pa)
LC 2006005641

"Fact finders"

This is a introduction to grassland ecology and some of its plants and animals

This book "uses vivid, sense-appealing language. . . . An attractive . . . format displays the captions to colorful photographs." Sci Books Films

Includes bibliographical references

Johnson, Rebecca L., 1956-

A walk in the prairie; with illustrations by Phyllis V. Saroff. Carolrhoda Bks. 2001 48p il map (Biomes of North America) lib bdg $23.93
Grades: 3 4 5 6   **577.4**
1. Prairie ecology
ISBN 1-57505-153-2   LC 00-8252

Describes the climate, soil, seasons, plants, and animals of the North American prairie and the ways in

Johnson, Rebecca L., 1956-—*Continued*
which the plants and animals depend on each other and
their environment to survive
Includes glossary and bibliographical references

Levy, Janey
Discovering the tropical savanna; [by] Janey
Levy. PowerKids Press 2008 32p il map (World
habitats) lib bdg $23.95
Grades: 3 4 5   577.4
   1. Grassland ecology
   ISBN 978-1-4042-3783-4 (lib bdg); 1-4042-3783-6 (lib
bdg)   LC 2006103368
This book about the ecology of the tropical savanna
"includes 10 chapters with information on climate, location, plants, animals, people, conservation, and page of
relevant facts and figures. The [text is] concise and accessible. Clear, colorful photographs show the landscape
and the varied plants and wildlife." SLJ
   Includes glossary

Lion, David C., 1948-
A home on the prairie; by David C. Lion.
Children's Press 2007 24p il (Scholastic news
nonfiction readers) $20
Grades: 1 2 3   577.4
   1. Prairie ecology
   ISBN 0-516-25346-8; 978-0-516-25346-6
                         LC 2006002308
An introduction to prairie ecology
"Simple, easy-to-read. . . . Everything students need
for reports is beautifully depicted with scenic full-color
photographs of the land, the plants, and the animals that
live there." SLJ
   Includes bibliographical references

Lundgren, Julie K.
Grassland buffet; studying food webs in the
grasslands and savannahs; [by] Julie K. Lundgren.
Rourke Pub. 2009 32p il map (Studying food
webs) lib bdg $28.50
Grades: 3 4 5   577.4
   1. Grassland ecology 2. Food chains (Ecology)
   ISBN 978-1-60472-318-2 (lib bdg); 1-60472-318-1 (lib
bdg)   LC 2008-24859
This book has "stunning photos, fascinating facts, and
intriguing examples. . . . Herbivores, omnivores, and
carnivores specific to . . . [the grassland] ecosystem are
presented. . . . 'Chew on this' insets add further interest
and information. . . . [This] will appeal to readers." SLJ
   Includes glossary and bibliographical references

Stille, Darlene R., 1942-
Grasslands. Children's Press 1999 47p il (True
book) lib bdg $22; pa $6.95
Grades: 2 3 4   577.4
   1. Grassland ecology
   ISBN 0-516-21509-4 (lib bdg); 0-516-26762-0 (pa)
                         LC 98-49728
Examines the different types of grasslands and the
plant and animal life they support
   Includes glossary and bibliographical references

Toupin, Laurie, 1963-
Life in the temperate grasslands. Franklin Watts
2005 63p il map (Biomes and habitats) lib bdg
$25.50
Grades: 4 5 6 7   577.4
   1. Grassland ecology
   ISBN 0-531-12385-5   LC 2004-13282
   "Watts library"
   Contents: No trees, no problem; Tough as grass; Graz-
ers big and small; Predators feathery, furry, and slippery;
Giving mother nature a hand; In your hands
This describes the ecology of grasslands such as the
North American prairie, the South American pampas, the
African veldt and the European steppes
This is "written in an accessible and interesting, con-
versational style. The [author conveys] a good deal of in-
formation about topics such as adaptation, environmental
threats, seasonal changes, and other essentials important
to report writers and general readers." SLJ
   Includes bibliographical references

Savannas; life in the tropical grasslands; [by]
Laurie Peach Toupin. Franklin Watts 2005 63p il
map (Biomes and habitats) lib bdg $25.50
Grades: 4 5 6 7   577.4
   1. Grassland ecology
   ISBN 0-531-12386-3   LC 2004-13281
   "Watts library"
   Contents: Too dry, too wet . . . ah, home!; Grasses
rule; Landscapers and gardeners; Hoofed vegetarians;
Tooth and claw; People and the grasslands
This introduces "readers to the climate characteristics
as well as plants and animals of [tropical grasslands. It
is] written in an accessible and interesting, conversational
style. The authors convey a good deal of information
about topics such as adaptation, environmental threats,
seasonal changes, and other essentials important to report
writers and general readers." SLJ
   Includes bibliographical references

577.5   Ecology of miscellaneous environments

Bial, Raymond
A handful of dirt. Walker & Co. 2000 32p il
$16.95 *
Grades: 3 4 5 6   577.5
   1. Soils 2. Soil ecology
   ISBN 0-8027-8698-7   LC 99-53632
The author "discusses how plant, animal, and mineral
matter are broken down to create soil, as well as the vast
amount of life forms soil supports, such as protozoa,
earthworms, insects, moles, snakes, and prairie dogs.
Tips on how to compost are included. The book is illustrated with crisp color photos, including several using an
electron microscope." Horn Book Guide
   Includes bibliographical references

Fridell, Ron, 1943-

Life in the desert. Franklin Watts 2005 63p il map (Biomes and habitats) lib bdg $25.50

Grades: 4 5 6 7 **577.5**

1. Desert ecology 2. Deserts
ISBN 0-531-12384-7   LC 2004027254

"Watts library"

Presents an introduction to desert environments, in simple text with illustrations, providing information on its average temperature, climate, plant and animal life, and people

Includes glossary and bibliographical references

Hooks, Gwendolyn, 1951-

Arctic appetizers; studying food webs in the arctic; [by] Gwendolyn Hooks. Rourke Pub. 2009 32p il map (Studying food webs) lib bdg $28.50

Grades: 3 4 5 **577.5**

1. Arctic regions 2. Food chains (Ecology)
ISBN 978-1-60472-314-4 (lib bdg); 1-60472-314-9 (lib bdg)   LC 2008-24855

This book has "stunning photos, fascinating facts, and intriguing examples. . . . Herbivores, omnivores, and carnivores specific to . . . [the arctic] ecosystem are presented. . . . 'Chew on this' insets add further interest and information. . . . [This] will appeal to readers." SLJ

Includes glossary and bibliographical references

Jackson, Kay, 1959-

Explore the desert; by Kay Jackson. Capstone Press 2007 32p il map (Explore the biomes) $16.95; pa $6.95

Grades: PreK K 1 2 **577.5**

1. Desert ecology
ISBN   978-0-7368-6404-6;   0-7368-6404-0; 978-0-7368-9627-6 (pa); 0-7368-9627-9 (pa)
          LC 2006004109

"Fact finders"

This is an introduction to desert ecology and some of its plants and animals.

This book "uses vivid, sense-appealing language. . . . An attractive . . . format displays the captions to colorful photographs." Sci Books Films

Includes bibliographical references

Johansson, Philip

The dry desert; a web of life. Enslow Publishers 2004 48p il (World of biomes) lib bdg $18.95

Grades: 3 4 5 **577.5**

1. Desert ecology
ISBN 0-7660-2200-5   LC 2003-20443

Contents: Life in the slow lane; The desert biome; Desert communities; Desert plants; Desert animals

This describes the plants, animals, and ecology of deserts of the world

Includes glossary and bibliographical references

The frozen tundra; a web of life. Enslow Pubs. 2004 48p il map (World of biomes) lib bdg $18.95

Grades: 3 4 5 **577.5**

1. Tundra ecology
ISBN 0-7660-2176-9   LC 2003-2271

Contents: Learning the bear facts; The Tundra biome; Biome communities; Tundra plants; Tundra animals

This describes the ecology of the arctic tundra

This book is "extremely well written, and [it contains] ample information presented in a way that is easy to understand." Sci Books Films

Includes glossary and bibliographical references

Johnson, Rebecca L., 1956-

A walk in the desert; with illustrations by Phyllis V. Saroff. Carolrhoda Bks. 2001 48p il map (Biomes of North America) lib bdg $23.93; pa $8.95

Grades: 3 4 5 6 **577.5**

1. Desert ecology
ISBN 1-57505-152-4 (lib bdg); 1-57505-529-5 (pa)
          LC 00-8251

Describes the climate, soil, plants, and animals of North American deserts and the ways in which the plants and animals depend on each other and their environment to survive

"The many full-color, close-up photographs and black-and-white drawings are sure to engage readers' interest." SLJ

Includes glossary and bibliographical references

A walk in the tundra; with illustrations by Phyllis V. Saroff. Carolrhoda Bks. 2001 48p il map (Biomes of North America) lib bdg $23.93; pa $8.95

Grades: 3 4 5 6 **577.5**

1. Tundra ecology
ISBN 1-57505-157-5 (lib bdg); 1-57505-526-0 (pa)
          LC 00-8245

Takes readers on a walk in the tundra, showing examples of how the animals and plants of the tundra are connected and dependent on each other and the tundra's soil and climate

"A visually pleasing title with plenty of clear, colorful photographs of the biome's flora and fauna throughout the year." SLJ

Includes glossary and bibliographical references

Levinson, Nancy Smiler, 1938-

Death Valley; a day in the desert; illustrated by Diane Dawson Hearn. Holiday House 2001 29p il $14.95

Grades: 1 2 3 **577.5**

1. Desert ecology
ISBN 0-8234-1566-X   LC 00-23305

"A Holiday House reader"

Describes the desert habitat of Death Valley and the plants and animals that live there

"Newly independent readers will appreciate the simple text of this nonfiction easy reader. . . . The illustrations are clear and attractive." Horn Book Guide

Levy, Janey

Discovering mountains; [by] Janey Levy. PowerKids Press 2008 32p il map (World habitats) lib bdg $23.95

Grades: 3 4 5 **577.5**

1. Mountain ecology 2. Mountains
ISBN 978-1-4042-3785-8 (lib bdg); 1-4042-3785-2 (lib bdg)   LC 2006103369

Levy, Janey—*Continued*

This book about mountain ecology "includes 10 chapters with information about climate, location, plants, animals, people, conservation, and a page of relevant facts and figures. The [text is] concise and accessible. Clear, colorful photographs show the landscape and the varied plants and wildlife." Booklist

Includes glossary

Discovering the Arctic tundra; [by] Janey Levy. PowerKids Press 2008 32p il map (World habitats) lib bdg $23.95

Grades: 3 4 5   **577.5**

1. Tundra ecology 2. Arctic regions
ISBN 978-1-4042-3787-2 (lib bdg); 1-4042-3787-9 (lib bdg)   LC 2006103405

This book about the ecology of the Arctic tundra "includes 10 chapters with information on climate, location, plants, animals, people, conservation, and a page of relevant facts and figures. The [text is] concise and accessible. Clear, colorful photographs show the landscape and the varied plants and wildlife." Booklist

Includes glossary

Lundgren, Julie K.

Desert dinners; studying food webs in the desert; [by] Julie K. Lundgren. Rourke Pub. 2009 32p il map (Studying food webs) lib bdg $28.50

Grades: 3 4 5   **577.5**

1. Desert ecology 2. Food chains (Ecology)
ISBN 978-1-60472-315-1 (lib bdg); 1-60472-315-7 (lib bdg)   LC 2008-24856

This book has "stunning photos, fascinating facts, and intriguing examples. . . . Herbivores, omnivores, and carnivores specific to . . . [the desert] ecosystem are presented. . . . 'Chew on this' insets add further interest and information. . . . [This] will appeal to readers." SLJ

Includes glossary and bibliographical references

Lynch, Wayne

Sonoran Desert; text and photographs by Wayne Lynch; assisted by Aubrey Lang. NorthWord Books 2009 64p il (Our wild world ecosystems) $16.95

Grades: 5 6 7 8   **577.5**

1. Natural history—Sonoran Desert 2. Desert ecology 3. Sonoran Desert
ISBN 978-1-58979-389-7; 1-58979-389-7
        LC 2008036635

"An in-depth look at a vibrant ecosystem. Spilling over the Mexican border into Arizona and New Mexico, the Sonoran Desert is especially rich in varied plants, animals, insects, and other critters that call it home. Lynch shares his expertise and experiences in a clearly written, conversational text, lavishly illustrated with his own crisp color photos." SLJ

Marsico, Katie, 1980-

A home on the tundra; by Katie Marsico. Children's Press 2007 24p il (Scholastic news nonfiction readers) $20

Grades: 1 2 3   **577.5**

1. Tundra ecology
ISBN 0-516-25345-X; 978-0-516-25345-9
        LC 2006002306

An introduction to tundra ecology

"Simple, easy-to-read. . . . Everything students need for reports is beautifully depicted with scenic full-color photographs of the land, the plants, and the animals that live there." SLJ

Includes bibliographical references

Pascoe, Elaine

Soil; text by Elaine Pascoe; photographs by Dwight Kuhn. Blackbirch Press 2005 24p il (Nature close-up juniors) $21.20

Grades: K 1 2 3   **577.5**

1. Soil ecology
ISBN 1-4103-0311-X   LC 2004-13975

"This book introduces young readers to the wildlife lurking in the soil right under their feet and to the role of soil in plant growth. Activities include starting plants from seed and watching earthworms tunnel." Publisher's note

Includes bibliographical references

Stille, Darlene R., 1942-

Deserts. Children's Press 1999 47p il (True book) hardcover o.p. pa $6.95

Grades: 2 3 4   **577.5**

1. Desert ecology
ISBN 0-516-21508-6 (lib bdg); 0-516-26760-4 (pa)
        LC 98-53856

Presents a general description of deserts and describes specific desert plants, animals, people, and activities

Includes glossary and bibliographical references

Tagliaferro, Linda

Explore the tundra; by Linda Tagliaferro. Capstone Press 2007 32p il map (Explore the biomes) $16.95; pa $6.95

Grades: PreK K 1 2   **577.5**

1. Tundra ecology
ISBN   978-0-7368-6408-4;   0-7368-6408-3; 978-0-7368-9631-3 (pa); 0-7368-9631-7 (pa)
        LC 2006004108

"Fact finders"

This is an introduction to the tundra and some of its plants and animals.

This book "uses vivid, sense-appealing language. . . . An attractive . . . format displays the captions to colorful photographs." Sci Books Films

Includes bibliographical references

Tocci, Salvatore

Alpine tundra; life on the tallest mountain; [by] Salvatore Tocci. Franklin Watts 2005 63p il (Biomes and habitats) lib bdg $25.50

Grades: 4 5 6 7   **577.5**

1. Tundra ecology

ISBN 978-0-531-12365-2 (lib bdg); 0-531-12365-0 (lib bdg)   LC 2004-13583

"Watts library"

Contents: A land high up; The season to grow; The season to prepare; The season to hide; The season to re-appear; People of the tundra

This introduces "readers to the climate characteristics as well as plants and animals of [the Alpine tundra. It is] written in an accessible and interesting, conversational style. The authors convey a good deal of information about topics such as adaptation, environmental threats, seasonal changes, and other essentials important to report writers and general readers." SLJ

Includes bibliographical references

Arctic tundra; life at the North Pole; [by] Salvatore Tocci. Franklin Watts 2005 63p il map (Biomes and habitats) lib bdg $25.50

Grades: 4 5 6 7   **577.5**

1. Tundra ecology

ISBN 978-0-531-12366-9 (lib bdg); 0-531-12366-9 (lib bdg)   LC 2004-13283

"Watts library"

This introduces "readers to the climate characteristics as well as plants and animals of [the Arctic tundra. It is] written in an accessible and interesting, conversational style. The authors convey a good deal of information about topics such as adaptation, environmental threats, seasonal changes, and other essentials important to report writers and general readers." SLJ

Includes bibliographical references

Wojahn, Rebecca Hogue

An Australian outback food chain; a who-eats-what adventure; [by] Rebecca Hogue Wojahn, Donald Wojahn. Lerner Publications 2009 64p il map (Follow that food chain) lib bdg $30.60

Grades: 3 4 5 6   **577.5**

1. Food chains (Ecology) 2. Animals—Australia 3. Natural history—Australia

ISBN 978-0-8225-7499-6 (lib bdg); 0-8225-7499-3 (lib bdg)   LC 2008021117

"Numerous photos of plants and animals in their habitats appear on these pages, accompanied by an explanation of the basic elements of a food chain and definitions of terms such as predators, consumers, producers, and decomposers. What sets [this book] apart . . . is [its] 'choose your own adventure' style. . . . The authors instruct [readers] to choose one of the region's carnivores and explore its food chain. . . . [including the] dingo, saltwater crocodile, wedge-tailed eagle, [and] Gould's monitor. . . . Choices result in returning to some pages more than once and sometimes discovering a 'dead end,' a critically endangered or extinct animal. . . . The interconnections created by the choices effectively illustrate the complexity of food webs while providing information about the plants and animals that form the components. Lively, engaging writing helps sustain interest." SLJ

Includes glossary and bibliographical references

A tundra food chain; a who-eats-what adventure in the Arctic; [by] Rebecca Hogue Wojahn, Donald Wojahn. Lerner Publications 2009 64p il map (Follow that food chain) lib bdg $30.60

Grades: 3 4 5 6   **577.5**

1. Tundra ecology 2. Food chains (Ecology) 3. Animals—Arctic regions

ISBN 978-0-8225-7500-9 (lib bdg); 0-8225-7500-0 (lib bdg)   LC 2008027092

"Numerous photos of plants and animals in their habitats appear on these pages, accompanied by an explanation of the basic elements of a food chain and definitions of terms such as predators, consumers, producers, and decomposers. What sets [this book] apart . . . is [its] 'choose your own adventure' style. . . . The authors instruct [readers] to choose one of the region's carnivores and explore its food chain. Six animals (grizzly bear, snowy owl, Arctic wolf, polar bear, wolverine, and peregrine falcon) are presented. . . . Choices result in returning to some pages more than once and sometimes discovering a 'dead end,' a critically endangered or extinct animal. . . . The interconnections created by the choices effectively illustrate the complexity of food webs while providing information about the plants and animals that form the components. Lively, engaging writing helps sustain interest." SLJ

Includes glossary and bibliographical references

577.6   Aquatic ecology. Freshwater ecology

Arnosky, Jim

The brook book; exploring the smallest streams. Dutton Children's Books 2008 unp il $15.99

Grades: K 1 2 3   **577.6**

1. Stream animals 2. Stream plants 3. Freshwater ecology

ISBN 978-0-525-47716-7; 0-525-47716-0

This "looks at brooks . . . and invites children to explore them. Guiding readers, Arnosky introduces the rocks at the brook's bottom, the creatures in the water, and the flowers and birds living nearby, and the animals that leave their tracks in the soft banks. [Illustrated with] luminous paintings in spring colors. . . . Attractive and useful." Booklist

Brenner, Barbara, 1925-

One small place by the sea; illustrated by Tom Leonard. HarperCollins Publishers 2004 unp il hardcover o.p. lib bdg $16.89

Grades: 2 3 4   **577.6**

1. Tide pool ecology

ISBN 0-688-17182-6; 0-688-17183-4 (lib bdg)
                                                    LC 2002-1180

For one afternoon, a child visitor observes the cycle of change within a tidepool, a small place at the edge of the sea that is home to many plants and animals

"The contents of the book are well organized, current, and accurate. The content is well illustrated, with colored pictures of the organisms, as well as many of their life habits, discussed." Sci Books Films

Fusco Castaldo, Nancy, 1962-

River wild; an activity guide to North American rivers; [by] Nancy F. Castaldo. Chicago Review Press 2006 147p il pa $14.95

Grades: 4 5 6   577.6

1. River ecology 2. Rivers

ISBN 1-55652-585-0   LC 2005-22976

Thirty games, activites, and experiments provide an introduction to learning about how rivers are formed, the water cycle, and the animals and habitats that exist along rivers

"This book serves as a good source of information and projects." Booklist

Includes bibliographical references

Gibbons, Gail

Marshes & swamps. Holiday House 1998 unp il $16.95; pa $6.95

Grades: K 1 2 3   577.6

1. Wetlands 2. Ecology

ISBN 0-8234-1347-0; 0-8234-1515-5 (pa)

LC 97-17995

Defines marshes and swamps, discusses how conditions in them may change, and examines the life found in and around them

"Gibbons balances a succinct, informative text with well-labeled watercolors." Horn Book Guide

Halpern, Monica

All about tide pools; by Monica Halpern. National Geographic 2007 40p il (National Geographic science chapters) $17.90

Grades: 3 4 5 6   577.6

1. Tide pool ecology

ISBN 978-1-4263-0184-1; 1-4263-0184-7

LC 2007007907

This is an introduction to animals and plants in tide pools and how they survive which offers suggestions for exploring this ecosystem

This "book provides a clear, engaging introduction to the topic. . . . The [book's] clear design features many well-captioned photographs . . . charts, and diagrams." Horn Book Guide

Includes glossary and bibliographical references

Hooks, Gwendolyn, 1951-

Freshwater feeders; studying food webs in freshwater. Rourke Pub. 2009 32p il map (Studying food webs) lib bdg $28.50

Grades: 3 4 5   577.6

1. Freshwater ecology 2. Food chains (Ecology)

ISBN 978-1-60472-317-5 (lib bdg); 1-60472-317-3 (lib bdg)   LC 2008-24857

This book has "stunning photos, fascinating facts, and intriguing examples. . . . Herbivores, omnivores, and carnivores specific to . . . [the freshwater] ecosystem are presented. . . . 'Chew on this' insets add further interest and information. . . . [This] will appeal to readers." SLJ

Includes glossary

Johansson, Philip

Lakes and rivers; a freshwater web of life; [by] Philip Johansson. Enslow Elementary 2007 48p il (Wonderful water biomes) lib bdg $23.93

Grades: 3 4 5   577.6

1. Freshwater ecology 2. Lakes 3. Rivers

ISBN 978-0-7660-2812-8 (lib bdg); 0-7660-2812-7 (lib bdg)   LC 2006100470

This describes the plants, animals, and ecology of lakes and rivers.

Includes glossary and bibliographical references

Marshes and swamps; a wetland web of life; [by] Philip Johansson. Enslow Elementary 2007 48p il (Wonderful water biomes) lib bdg $23.93

Grades: 3 4 5   577.6

1. Marsh ecology 2. Wetlands

ISBN 978-0-7660-2814-2 (lib bdg); 0-7660-2814-3 (lib bdg)   LC 2006039769

This describes the plants, animals, and ecology of marshes and swamps.

This has "good-quality color photos. . . . Well written and engaging." SLJ

Includes glossary and bibliographical references

The seashore; a saltwater web of life. Enslow Elementary 2008 48p il (Wonderful water biomes) lib bdg $23.93

Grades: 3 4 5   577.6

1. Seashore ecology

ISBN 978-0-7660-2811-1 (lib bdg); 0-7660-2811-9 (lib bdg)   LC 2006-100600

This describes the plants, animals, and ecology of the seashore.

This has "good-quality color photos. . . . Well written and engaging." SLJ

Includes glossary and bibliographical references

Kudlinski, Kathleen V., 1950-

The seaside switch; illustrated by Lindy Burnett. NorthWord Books for Young Readers 2007 unp il $16.95

Grades: PreK K 1 2   577.6

1. Tide pool ecology 2. Marine biology

ISBN 978-1-55971-964-3; 1-55971-964-8

LC 2006-11608

"Kudlinski's picture book uses poetic words to describe the seashore during a cycle of tides. . . . The gouache illustrations show tidal changes on a beach through the eyes of a boy, who often sketches what he sees." Booklist

Marx, Trish, 1948-

Everglades forever; restoring America's great wetland; photographs by Cindy Karp. Lee & Low Books 2004 40p il map $17.95; pa $8.95 *

Grades: 3 4 5 6   577.6

1. Everglades (Fla.) 2. Wetlands

ISBN   978-1-58430-164-6;   1-58430-164-3; 978-1-60060-339-6 (pa); 1-60060-339-4 (pa)

LC 2004-2934

Marx, Trish, 1948—*Continued*

The author offers an "introduction to the natural history and environment of the Everglades by documenting the studies of a fifth-grade class. . . . Complementing the excellent, informative text are high-quality color photographs and maps." Booklist

Morrison, Gordon

Pond. Houghton Mifflin 2002 30p il $16

Grades: 2 3 4   **577.6**

1. Pond ecology

ISBN 0-618-10271-X   LC 2002-3494

Observes how a glacial pond and the abundance of plants and animals that draw life from it change over the course of a year

"Lovely, realistic watercolor paintings illustrate the text; small, detailed pencil drawings and diagrams accompany each note. . . . This lovingly crafted sketchbook has the potential to awaken in readers an awareness of the workings of nature." SLJ

Sill, Cathryn P., 1953-

Wetlands; written by Cathryn Sill; illustrated by John Sill. Peachtree 2008 unp il (About habitats) $16.95

Grades: PreK K 1 2 3   **577.6**

1. Wetlands

ISBN 978-1-56145-432-7; 1-56145-432-X

LC 2007031280

This introduction to wetland ecology "features full-page watercolor paintings that strikingly illustrate the factual information conveyed by a sentence or two on the facing pages. . . . The artwork is stunning, filled with realistic details and a beautiful balance of colors. The format would work well as a read-aloud choice. . . . Independent readers or browsers could enjoy perusing the book themselves." SLJ

Toupin, Laurie, 1963-

Freshwater habitats; life in freshwater ecosystems. F. Watts 2005 63p il map (Biomes and habitats) lib bdg $25.50; pa $8.95

Grades: 4 5 6 7   **577.6**

1. Freshwater ecology

ISBN 0-531-12305-7 (lib bdg); 0-531-16675-9 (pa)

LC 2003-16572

"Watts library"

A look at the plants, animals, locations, and various habitats that make up the freshwater ecosystems of the world

Wechsler, Doug

Frog heaven; ecology of a vernal pool; [by] Doug Wechsler; photographs by the author. Boyds Mills Press 2006 48p il $17.95

Grades: 3 4 5 6   **577.6**

1. Vernal pool ecology 2. Frogs 3. Natural history—Delaware

ISBN 978-1-59078-253-8; 1-59078-253-4

LC 2005037562

"Wechsler offers a close-up view of a vernal pool in Delaware as it cycles through the year. . . . Wechsler's clear, color photos provide an excellent visual counterpoint to the text. This well-focused book will open readers' eyes." Booklist

Includes glossary and bibliographical references

577.7   Marine ecology

Collard, Sneed B., III

On the coral reefs; by Sneed B. Collard III. Marshall Cavendish Benchmark 2005 43p il (Science adventures) lib bdg $25.64

Grades: 4 5 6   **577.7**

1. Grutter, Alexandra 2. Coral reefs and islands 3. Marine ecology

ISBN 0-7614-1953-5   LC 2004030316

This describes the ecology of coral reefs and the research of marine biologist Dr. Alexandra Grutter.

Includes glossary and bibliographical references

Crenson, Victoria

Horseshoe crabs and shorebirds; the story of a food web; illustrated by Annie Cannon. Marshall Cavendish 2003 unp il lib bdg $16.95 *

Grades: 2 3 4   **577.7**

1. Food chains (Ecology) 2. Crabs 3. Delaware Bay (Del. and N.J.)

ISBN 0-7614-5115-3   LC 2002-156473

Presents a portrait of the Delaware Bay in the spring when a wide variety of animals, including minnows, mice, turtles, raccoons, and especially migrating shorebirds, come to feed on the billions of eggs laid by horseshoe crabs

"Crenson's text is highly descriptive and reads like an adventure story, conveying the action and excitement of nature. Cannon's watercolors fill the pages with atmosphere and motion." SLJ

Gibbons, Gail

Coral reefs. Holiday House 2007 32p il $16.95

Grades: K 1 2 3   **577.7**

1. Coral reefs and islands

ISBN 978-0-8234-2080-3; 0-8234-2080-9

LC 2006-37959

"Gibbons introduces a complex ecosystem with accessible words and inviting watercolor-washed pictures. . . . [The author explains] coral types and anatomy, how reefs form, and the symbiotic . . . relationship among reef creatures." Booklist

Hooks, Gwendolyn, 1951-

Makers and takers; studying food webs in the ocean; [by] Gwendolyn Hooks. Rourke Pub. 2009 32p il map (Studying food webs) lib bdg $28.50

Grades: 3 4 5   **577.7**

1. Marine ecology 2. Food chains (Ecology)

ISBN 978-1-60472-319-9 (lib bdg); 1-60472-319-X (lib bdg)

LC 2008-24860

Hooks, Gwendolyn, 1951-—*Continued*

This book has "stunning photos, fascinating facts, and intriguing examples. . . . Herbivores, omnivores, and carnivores specific to . . . [The ocean] ecosystem are presented. . . . 'Chew on this' insets add further interest and information. . . . [This] will appeal to readers." SLJ

Includes glossary and bibliographical references

Jackson, Kay, 1959-

Explore the ocean; by Kay Jackson. Capstone Press 2007 32p il (Explore the biomes) $16.95; pa $6.95

Grades: PreK K 1 2   **577.7**
1. Marine ecology
ISBN   978-0-7368-6406-0;   0-7368-6406-7; 978-0-7368-9629-0 (pa); 0-7368-9629-5 (pa)
                      LC 2006004110
"Fact finders"

This an introduction to the ocean habitat and some of its plants and animals.

This book "uses vivid, sense-appealing language. . . . An attractive . . . format displays the captions to colorful photographs." Sci Books Films

Includes bibliographical references

Johansson, Philip

The coral reef; a colorful web of life. Enslow Publishers 2007 48p il (Wonderful water biomes) lib bdg $17.95

Grades: 3 4 5   **577.7**
1. Coral reefs and islands
ISBN 978-0-7660-2813-5 (lib bdg); 0-7660-2813-5 (lib bdg)
                      LC 2006-17903
"Following a lively account of a team of divers' underwater observations, the chapters discuss types of coral reefs, their formation, and the plants and animals that inhabit them. . . . Johansson writes knowledgably and vividly, and his text, along with the well-chosen color photos, will inspire interest." Booklist

Includes glossary and bibliographical references

Parker, Steve

Seashore; written by Steve Parker. rev ed. DK Pub. 2004 72p il (DK eyewitness books) $15.99

Grades: 4 5 6 7   **577.7**
1. Seashore 2. Marine animals 3. Marine plants
ISBN 0-7566-0721-3; 0-7566-0720-5 (lib bdg)
First published 1989 by Knopf

Brief text and photos introduce the animal inhabitants of the seashore, including fish, crustaceans, snails, and shorebirds

Pfeffer, Wendy, 1929-

Life in a coral reef; illustrated by Steve Jenkins. Collins 2009 32p il (Let's-read-and-find-out science) $16; pa $5.99 *

Grades: K 1 2 3   **577.7**
1. Coral reefs and islands
ISBN   978-0-06-029553-0;   0-06-029553-8; 978-0-06-445222-9 (pa); 0-06-445222-0 (pa)
                      LC 2008000498

"Jenkins' striking paper-collage illustrations nicely complement Pfeffer's clear and engaging text in this successful explanation of what lies beneath the surface of the ocean in and around a coral reef." Booklist

Pringle, Laurence P.

Come to the ocean's edge; a nature cycle book; illustrated by Michael Chesworth. Boyds Mills Press 2003 32p il $15.95

Grades: K 1 2 3   **577.7**
1. Seashore ecology
ISBN 1-56397-779-6
"Spanning sunrise to sunset, Pringle gives [an] . . . account of a coastline environment." Horn Book Guide

This offers "a poetic text and beautifully composed watercolor paintings. . . . While providing a realistic view of this environment, the artwork also echoes the expressive tone of the narrative." SLJ

Taylor-Butler, Christine, 1959-

A home in the coral reef; by Christine Taylor-Butler. Childrens Press 2007 24p il (Scholastic news nonfiction readers) $20

Grades: 1 2 3   **577.7**
1. Coral reefs and islands
ISBN 0-516-25344-1; 978-0-516-25344-2
                      LC 2006002305
An introduction to coral reef ecology

"Simple, easy-to-read. . . . Everything students need for reports is beautifully depicted with scenic full-color photographs of the land, the plants, and the animals that live there." SLJ

Includes bibliographical references

Tocci, Salvatore

Coral reefs; life below the sea. Franklin Watts 2003 63p il map (Biomes and habitats) lib bdg $25.50; pa $8.95

Grades: 4 5 6 7   **577.7**
1. Coral reefs and islands 2. Ecology
ISBN 0-531-12304-9 (lib bdg); 0-531-16669-4 (pa)
                      LC 2003-16566
"Watts library"

Explores coral reefs, ridges of rocky materials just below the ocean's surface, which are inhabited by thousands of diverse organisms

Includes glossary and bibliographical references

577.8   Synecology and population biology

Aruego, Jose

Weird friends; unlikely allies in the animal kingdom; [by] Jose Aruego and Ariane Dewey. Harcourt 2002 unp il $16

Grades: K 1 2 3   **577.8**
1. Symbiosis
ISBN 0-15-202128-0   LC 2001-1154
"Gulliver books"

Aruego, Jose—*Continued*

"This book offers an overview of fourteen symbiotic animal relationships, such as that between rhinos and cattle egrets. . . . The brief text provides a short description of the animals, what their functions are, and how they cooperate with their allies. The brightly colored illustrations feature anthropomorphized creatures, which may attract younger naturalists." Horn Book Guide

578   Natural history of organisms and related subjects

Collard, Sneed B., III

In the rain forest canopy. Marshall Cavendish Benchmark 2006 43p il (Science adventures) lib bdg $25.70

Grades: 4 5 6   **578**
1. Nadkarni, Nalini, 1954- 2. Rain forests 3. Natural history—Costa Rica
ISBN 0-7614-1954-3   LC 2004-27940
This describes the rain forest canopy and the research of Dr. Nalini Nadkarni in Monteverde, Costa Rica
Includes glossary and bibliographical references

Kelsey, Elin

Strange new species; astonishing discoveries of life on earth. Maple Tree Press 2005 96p il $24.95; pa $16.95

Grades: 5 6 7 8   **578**
1. Natural history 2. Biology 3. Scientists
ISBN 1-897066-31-7; 1-897066-32-5 (pa)
"This large-format book showcases new species . . . and the scientists who have discovered them. . . . The discussion ends with information on cloning, genetically modified food, and the future of life. . . . With many excellent photos, this introductory book on new species will be an intriguing addition to classroom units on classification or biology." Booklist

Strauss, Rochelle, 1967-

Tree of life; the incredible biodiversity of life on Earth. Kids Can Press 2004 40p il $16.95

Grades: 5 6 7 8   **578**
1. Biology—Classification 2. Biological diversity
ISBN 1-55337-669-2
The "text first introduces the concept of a family tree for all living things, then goes on to name the five kingdoms of scientific classification. . . . The author describes the life-forms included in each species, with specific examples shown in the softly colorful illustrations accompanied by informative captions. . . . Striking, lucid, and deceptively simple." SLJ

Wildlife and plants. 3rd ed. Marshall Cavendish 2007 20v il set $359.95

Grades: 4 5 6 7   **578**
1. Animals—Encyclopedias 2. Plants—Encyclopedias 3. Reference books
ISBN 978-0-7614-7693-1

First published 1994 with title: Wildlife and plants of the world

This set includes "more than 500 entries covering animals, plants, microorganisms, fungi, habitats, biomes, and overviews. . . . Entries provide a concise introduction followed by more detailed information including behavior, reproduction, characteristics, and survival tactics. . . . With its captivating information and photographs, students are sure to come to this easy-to-use set again and again." Booklist

578.4   Adaptation

Silverstein, Alvin

Adaptation; by Alvin Silverstein, Virginia Silverstein, and Laura Silverstein Nunn. Twenty-First Century Books 2008 112p il (Science concepts) lib bdg $31.93 *

Grades: 4 5 6 7   **578.4**
1. Adaptation (Biology)
ISBN 978-0-8225-3434-1 (lib bdg); 0-8225-3434-7 (lib bdg)   LC 2007-02862
This "provides an accessible introduction to how living beings adapt to survive in diverse habitats. . . . The narrative gains clarity from abundant examples, colorful photos and diagrams, and fascinating sidebars." Booklist
Includes bibliographical references

578.6   Miscellaneous nontaxonomic kinds of organisms

Batten, Mary

Aliens from Earth; when animals and plants invade other ecosystems; written by Mary Batten; illustrated by Beverly Doyle. Peachtree Pubs. 2003 unp il $15.95

Grades: 3 4 5 6   **578.6**
1. Nonindigenous pests 2. Biological invasions
ISBN 1-56145-236-X   LC 2002-13170
Explores how and why plants and animals enter ecosystems to which they are not native, as well as the consequences of these invasions for other animals, plants, and humans

"From the book title and first line of text . . . to the information-packed, full-page color illustrations, this overview of ecological missteps is nonstop intriguing." Booklist

Collard, Sneed B., III

Science warriors; the battle against invasive species; written by Sneed B. Collard III. Houghton Mifflin 2008 48p il (Scientists in the field) $17 *

Grades: 5 6 7 8   **578.6**
1. Nonindigenous pests 2. Biological invasions
ISBN 978-0-618-75636-0; 0-618-75636-1
                                      LC 2008-01867
"Collard focuses on four major invader species in the U.S.: the brown tree snake, . . . the red imported fire ant, . . . the melaleuca tree, . . . and the zebra mussel. . . . These are useful and thought-provoking case studies of a very large problem." Bull Cent Child Books
Includes glossary and bibliographical references

Drake, Jane

Alien invaders; species that threaten our world; [by] Jane Drake & Ann Love; illustrated by Mark Thurman. Tundra Books 2008 56p il map $19.95
Grades: 3 4 5 6   **578.6**

1. Nonindigenous pests 2. Biological invasions
ISBN 978-0-88776-798-2; 0-88776-798-2

"This book discusses non-native flora and fauna that endanger native species. The authors present historical cases (Irish potato blight, toad invasion in Australia), the most notorious invasive species, and threatened communities. Each double-page spread features a detailed gouache illustration, a conversational overview of problems, and some species-specific facts." Horn Book Guide

Jackson, Cari

Alien invasion; invasive species become major menaces. Gareth Stevens Pub. 2010 48p il (Current science) lib bdg $31
Grades: 4 5 6   **578.6**

1. Nonindigenous pests 2. Biological invasions
ISBN 978-1-4339-2057-8 (lib bdg); 1-4339-2057-3 (lib bdg)   LC 2009002279

This "lively, well-organized [text profiles] dozens of organisms that threaten our health and well-being. Jackson succinctly describes the characteristics of more than three dozen invasive species of plants and animals. . . . One or more illustrations accompany the text on every page—a mix of sharp, color photographs and some color drawings, maps, life cycle diagrams, etc." SLJ

Includes glossary and bibliographical references

Metz, Lorijo

What can we do about invasive species? PowerKids Press 2010 24p il (Protecting our planet) lib bdg $21.25; pa $8
Grades: 2 3 4   **578.6**

1. Biological invasions 2. Nonindigenous pests
ISBN 978-1-4042-8084-7 (lib bdg); 1-4042-8084-7 (lib bdg); 978-1-4358-2487-4 (pa); 1-4358-2487-3 (pa)
LC 2008-55828

"Some introduced species just naturally drive out native plants and animals from their environments. . . . Learn how experts are dealing with each ecological threat." Publisher's note

This book provides "straightforward information . . . complemented by full-page, color photographs. . . . Links for further information . . . are housed at the publisher's Web site (which allows feedback so that readers can suggest more sites)." SLJ

Includes glossary

578.68 Rare and endangered species

Pobst, Sandy, 1959-

Animals on the edge; science races to save species threatened with extinction; by Sandra Pobst; Todd K. Fuller, consultant. National Geographic 2008 64p il (National Geographic investigates) $17.95; lib bdg $27.90 *
Grades: 4 5 6 7   **578.68**

1. Endangered species 2. Wildlife conservation
ISBN 978-1-4263-0358-6; 1-4263-0358-0; 978-1-4263-0265-7 (lib bdg); 1-4263-0265-7 (lib bdg)

This "examines numerous threats to animals in the wild, raising awareness of each species, and detailing the extent and urgency of the problem. The book also encourages young animal lovers to take an active role in the preservation of creatures great and small." Publisher's note

This "eye-catching [title features] full-color photographs. . . . The approach is to understand the challenges to protecting endangered animals, including global warming, destruction of habitat, tagging and tracking, poaching, captive breeding, and cloning." Voice Youth Advocates

Includes glossary and bibliographical references

578.7 Organisms characteristic of specific kinds of environments

Arnosky, Jim

Beachcombing; exploring the seashore. Dutton Children's Bks. 2004 unp il $15.99 *
Grades: K 1 2 3   **578.7**

1. Seashore
ISBN 0-525-47104-9

Illustrations and text describe some of the many things that can be found on a walk along a beach, including coconuts, shark teeth, jellyfish, crabs and different kinds of shells.

"Young beachcombers will discover old and new ideas about collecting or just identifying their finds, and the book will appeal to those children who are looking for relaxing fun." SLJ

Parrotfish and sunken ships; exploring a tropical reef; by Jim Arnosky. Collins 2007 unp il map $16.99; lib bdg $17.89
Grades: 2 3 4 5   **578.7**

1. Natural history—Florida 2. Coral reefs and islands
ISBN 978-0-688-17123-0; 978-0-688-17124-7 (lib bdg)   LC 2007010994

"With stunning watercolors and a brief, easy-to-follow text, Arnosky chronicles a boat trip he took with his wife through the coral reefs off the Florida Keys." Booklist

Cerullo, Mary M., 1949-

Life under ice; photography by Bill Curtsinger. Tilbury House 2003 37p il map $16.95

Grades: 3 4 5   **578.7**

1. Marine animals 2. Marine plants 3. Natural history—Antarctica

ISBN 0-88448-246-4   LC 2002-154451

Follows marine photographer Bill Curtsinger as he dives under the ice at Antarctica to learn about the plants and animals that thrive in this extreme habitat

"Illustrated with stunning color undersea photographs, this offers a fascinating look at the many creatures living near and beneath the waters of Antarctica. . . . The text is clear and well written, but it is the wonderful photography that distinguishes the book." Booklist

Includes glossary and bibliographical references

Conlan, Kathy

Under the ice. Kids Can Press 2002 55p il $16.95; pa $8.95

Grades: 4 5 6 7   **578.7**

1. Marine biology 2. Marine pollution 3. Polar regions

ISBN 1-55337-001-5; 1-55337-060-0 (pa)

"A Canadian Museum of Nature book."

"In this photo-essay, Conlan details her three-month stay in Antarctica, highlighting some of her experiences and her involvement in ongoing experiments relating to the effects of human waste on marine life." SLJ

"The first-person text creates a feeling of immediacy. . . . Well-captioned, color photos appear throughout the book. . . . Conlan . . . offers readers an engaging account of her adventurous career in scientific field research." Booklist

Guiberson, Brenda Z., 1946-

Life in the boreal forest; paintings by Gennady Spirin. Henry Holt and Co. 2009 unp il $16.99 *

Grades: 2 3 4 5   **578.7**

1. Forest ecology

ISBN 978-0-8050-7718-6; 0-8050-7718-9

LC 2008-18329

"Gorgeously intricate illustrations perfectly complement equally evocative text in this introduction to the great northern, or boreal, forest, which sprawls across the entire northern hemisphere. . . . Any child interested in animals or the outdoors will be fascinated by the array portrayed here in a series of vignettes, each of which intersperses factual information information with lively action scenes." Booklist

Kummer, Patricia K.

The Great Barrier Reef; by Patricia K. Kummer. Marshall Cavendish Benchmark 2008 c2009 96p il map (Nature's wonders) lib bdg $24.95

Grades: 5 6 7 8   **578.7**

1. Coral reefs and islands 2. Great Barrier Reef (Australia)

ISBN 978-0-7614-2852-7 (lib bdg); 0-7614-2852-6 (lib bdg)   LC 2007026661

"Provides comprehensive information on the geography, history, wildlife, peoples, and environmental issues of the Great Barrier Reef." Publisher's note

Includes glossary and bibliographical references

O'Neill, Michael Patrick

Ocean magic. Batfish 2008 45p il $19.95

Grades: 1 2 3 4   **578.7**

1. Marine animals 2. Ocean

ISBN 978-0-9728653-5-7; 0-9728653-5-7

LC 2007-904079

"O'Neill introduces readers to coral reefs, kelp forests, and the ocean bottom. Especially stunning are the photos of the Hairy Frogfish, an incredibly camouflaged member of the Anglerfish family that prowls off the coast of Florida. Nevertheless, the colorful creatures of the coral reef are the stars of this book. The author's strong support of conservation comes through loud and clear in his narrative, and photographs amplify this message by showing the amazing life-forms that could be lost." SLJ

Person, Stephen

The coral reef; a giant city under the sea; consultant, Rod Salm. Bearport Pub. 2009 32p il map (Spectacular animal towns) lib bdg $25.27

Grades: 2 3 4   **578.7**

1. Coral reefs and islands

ISBN 978-1-59716-869-4 (lib bdg); 1-59716-869-6 (lib bdg)   LC 2009-12952

"Through excellent photographs, high-interest texts, sidebars, maps, and other material, children learn about both the animals and their habitats. The . . . book also provides brief profiles of animals with similar habitats. . . . [This book is] much better than average 'report' titles." SLJ

Includes glossary and bibliographical references

Serafini, Frank

Looking closely across the desert. Kids Can Press 2008 unp il (Looking closely) $16.95

Grades: K 1 2 3   **578.7**

1. Deserts

ISBN 978-1-55453-211-7; 1-55453-211-6

"An extreme closeup color photo of a section of a plant, animal, or other natural object set in a circle on a black background challenges readers to guess its identity. Turning the page reveals a large photo of the item in its natural setting, accompanied by two paragraphs of descriptive and informative text." SLJ

Looking closely along the shore; [by] Frank Serafini. Kids Can Press 2008 unp il (Looking closely) $16.95

Grades: K 1 2 3   **578.7**

1. Seashore

ISBN 978-1-55453-141-7; 1-55453-141-1

This title about plants and animals of the seashore "will pique the interest of children and encourage them to seek out more information. . . . [It is] set up like a guessing game, allowing for interaction. . . . Each entry opens with a white page with large black type that asks viewers to 'Look very closely. What do you see?' The facing page is black with what seems like a hole to peep through to the next spread. . . . Readers are given a couple of possibilities to start them guessing on what image might be depicted, and, when the page is turned, an enlarged closeup is in full view, along with a few interesting facts about the plant or animal." SLJ

Serafini, Frank—*Continued*

Looking closely inside the garden. Kids Can Press 2008 unp il (Looking closely) $16.95

Grades: K 1 2 3   **578.7**

1. Gardens

ISBN 978-1-55453-210-0; 1-55453-210-8

"An extreme closeup color photo of a section of a plant, animal, or other natural object set in a circle on a black background challenges readers to guess its identity. Turning the page reveals a large photo of the item in its natural setting, accompanied by two paragraphs of descriptive and informative text." SLJ

Looking closely through the forest. Kids Can Press 2008 unp il (Looking closely) $16.95

Grades: K 1 2 3   **578.7**

1. Forest animals 2. Forest plants

ISBN 978-1-55453-212-4; 1-55453-212-4

This book about forest plants and animals "will pique the interest of children and encourage them to seek out more information. . . . [It is] set up like a guessing game, allowing for interaction. . . . Each entry opens with a white page with large black type that asks viewers to 'Look very closely. What do you see?' The facing page is black with what seems like a hole to peep through to the next spread. . . . Readers are given a couple of possibilities to start them guessing on what image might be depicted, and, when the page is turned, an enlarged closeup is in full view, along with a few interesting facts about the plant or animal." SLJ

Somervill, Barbara A., 1948-

Marine biologist. Cherry Lake Pub. 2009 32p il (Cool science careers) lib bdg $27.07

Grades: 3 4 5 6   **578.7**

1. Marine biology 2. Vocational guidance

ISBN 978-1-60279-504-4 (lib bdg); 1-60279-504-5 (lib bdg)   LC 2008045234

This describes the career of marine biologist, including ways to become involved in the profession, the interests and skills required, and activities for learning more

This is "highly readable. . . . Colorful photographs illustrate [the] book." SLJ

Includes glossary and bibliographical references

Wallace, Marianne D.

America's forests; guide to plants and animals. Fulcrum Pub. 2009 47p il (America's ecosystems) pa $11.95

Grades: 5 6 7 8   **578.7**

1. Forests and forestry 2. Forest plants 3. Forest animals 4. Forest ecology

ISBN 978-1-55591-595-7 (pa); 1-55591-595-7 (pa)   LC 2008041005

This "is a guide to plants and animals within the context of forest communities. Marianne Wallace . . . expertly crafts this introduction to forests. . . . The book contains abundant illustrations." Sci Books Films

Includes glossary

Wechsler, Doug

Marvels in the muck; life in the salt marshes. Boyds Mills Press 2008 48p il $17.95

Grades: 4 5 6 7   **578.7**

1. Salt marshes 2. Marsh ecology

ISBN 978-1-59078-588-1   LC 2007052583

"A season-by-season look at the ecology of an oft-overlooked habitat. Wechsler's lucid text introduces the insects, birds, reptiles, crustaceans, and other critters that claim this salty expanse as home. . . . Clear color photos present species mentioned in the text." SLJ

Includes glossary and bibliographical references

Winner, Cherie

Life on the edge. Lerner Publications Co. 2006 48p il (Cool science) lib bdg $26.60

Grades: 4 5 6   **578.7**

1. Adaptation (Biology)

ISBN 978-0-8225-2499-1 (lib bdg); 0-8225-2499-6 (lib bdg)   LC 2005011071

This book "introduces creatures in extreme conditions such as thermal pools, Antarctica, and the deep sea. [The book provides] clear explanations of the science and [covers] possible benefits to humans. A variety of photos and information boxes provide an eye-catching . . . layout." Horn Book Guide

Includes glossary and bibliographical references

579   Microorganisms, fungi, algae

Arato, Rona

Protists; algae, amoebas, plankton, and other protists. Crabtree Pub. Co. 2010 48p il (A class of their own) lib bdg $29.27; pa $9.95

Grades: 5 6 7 8   **579**

1. Protists 2. Protozoa 3. Algae

ISBN 978-0-7787-5377-3 (lib bdg); 0-7787-5377-8 (lib bdg); 978-0-7787-5391-9 (pa); 0-7787-5391-3 (pa)   LC 2009-51386

Looks at the protist kingdom, providing information and examples of species from the major phyla, as well as information about the role of protists in the food chain and in various diseases.

"Lively section headings . . . and notes on uncommon achievements, . . . lighten the substantial load of biological terminology. Illustrated with a plethora of closeup color photos and microphotos, and closing with annotated lists of recommended Web sites, . . . [this captures] the remarkable diversity of life." SLJ

Includes glossary and bibliographical references

Brown, Jordan

Micro mania; a really close-up look at bacteria, bedbugs & the zillions of other gross little creatures that live in, on & all around you! [by] Jordan D. Brown. Imagine! 2010 80p il $19.95

Grades: 4 5 6   **579**

1. Microorganisms

ISBN 978-0-9823064-2-0; 0-9823064-2-3

"This engrossing book goes into squirm-inducing detail about the bacteria, microbes, and other assorted mini-

Brown, Jordan—*Continued*

organisms that dwell in our bodies and our homes. Each spread is well laid out with plenty of white space, large text, and colorful photos of these little critters . . . and the havoc they wreak. The writing is vivid without being breathless." SLJ

Latta, Sara L.

The good, the bad, the slimy; the secret life of microbes; [by] Sara Latta; photographs by Dennis Kunkel. Enslow Publishers 2006 128p il lib bdg $31.93 *

Grades: 5 6 7 8 9   **579**
    1. Microorganisms
    ISBN 0-7660-1294-8   LC 2005-35405

This describes how bacteria, viruses, fungi and other microbes "live in and on our bodies, help make food, live in extreme environments, and even change history." Publisher's note

"Explanations are simple and clear, and the layout is appeling, open, and colorful." SLJ

Includes glossary and bibliographical references

Walker, Richard, 1951-

Microscopic life; [by] Richard Walker; foreword by Peter C. Doherty. Kingfisher 2004 63p il (Kingfisher knowledge) $12.95

Grades: 4 5 6 7   **579**
    1. Microorganisms
    ISBN 0-7534-5778-4   LC 2004-1321

"Double-page spreads introduce viruses, bacteria, 'mini animals' (e.g., Hydra and dust mites), and other microorganisms and explain how these unseen entities affect humanity in both harmful and helpful ways. The accompanying photographic enlargements . . . are fascinating." Horn Book Guide

Wearing, Judy

Fungi; mushrooms, toadstools, molds, yeasts, and other fungi. Crabtree 2010 48p il (A class of their own) lib bdg $29.27; pa $9.95

Grades: 5 6 7 8   **579**
    1. Fungi
    ISBN 978-0-7787-5375-9 (lib bdg); 0-7787-5375-1 (lib bdg); 978-0-7787-5389-6 (pa); 0-7787-5389-1 (pa)

Features an examination of the four major groups of fungi: yeasts, toadstools, chytrids, and bread molds.

"Lively section headings . . . and notes on uncommon achievements, . . . lighten the substantial load of biological terminology. Illustrated with a plethora of closeup color photos and microphotos, and closing with annotated lists of recommended Web sites, . . . [thi scaptures] the remarkable diversity of life." SLJ

Includes glossary and bibliographical references

Zabludoff, Marc

The protoctist kingdom. Benchmark Books 2006 95p il (Family trees) lib bdg $29.92

Grades: 5 6 7 8   **579**
    1. Protoctista
    ISBN 0-7614-1818-0   LC 2004-21821

This examines the physical traits, adaptations, diets, habitats, and life cycles of such life forms as bacteria, amoebas, slime nets, molds, algae, coccoliths, forams, and diatoms.

"Fact-filled, yet surprisingly readable. . . . [This] title contains a wide variety of excellent-quality, full-color photographs; interesting sidebars; and diagrams." SLJ

Zamosky, Lisa

Simple organisms. Compass Point Books 2009 40p il (Mission: science) lib bdg $26.60

Grades: 4 5 6   **579**
    1. Microorganisms
    ISBN 978-0-7565-3955-9 (lib bdg); 0-7565-3955-2 (lib bdg)   LC 2008-7723

An introduction to microscopic organisms, including germs

Includes glossary and bibliographical references

579.3   Prokaryotes

Barker, David M.

Archaea; salt-lovers, methane-makers, thermophiles, and other archaeans; by David Barker. Crabtree Pub. 2010 48p il (A class of their own) lib bdg $23.41; pa $9.95

Grades: 5 6 7 8   **579.3**
    1. Bacteria
    ISBN 978-0-7787-5373-5 (lib bdg); 0-7787-5373-5 (lib bdg); 978-0-7787-5387-2 (pa); 0-7787-5387-5 (pa)
                                    LC 2009-51393

Looks at the archaea domain, providing information and examples of species from the three major phyla, as well as information about why so little is known about this diverse domain.

"Lively section headings . . . and notes on uncommon achievements, . . . lighten the substantial load of biological terminology. Illustrated with a plethora of closeup color photos and microphotos, and closing with annotated lists of recommended Web sites, . . . [this captures] the remarkable diversity of life." SLJ

Includes glossary and bibliographical references

Wearing, Judy

Bacteria; staph, strep, clostridium, and other bacteria. Crabtree 2010 48p il (A class of their own) lib bdg $29.27; pa $9.95

Grades: 5 6 7 8   **579.3**
    1. Bacteria
    ISBN 978-0-7787-5374-2 (lib bdg); 0-7787-5374-3 (lib bdg); 978-0-7787-5388-9 (pa); 0-7787-5388-3 (pa)

Examines bacteria that are found in virtually every environment-including those that are characterized by extreme heat, cold, and depth-and, of course, bacteria that are found inside our bodies.

"Lively section headings . . . and notes on uncommon achievements, . . . lighten the substantial load of biological terminology. Illustrated with a plethora of closeup color photos and microphotos, and closing with annotated lists of recommended Web sites, . . . [this captures] the remarkable diversity of life." SLJ

Includes glossary and bibliographical references

579.6 Mushrooms

Royston, Angela

Life cycle of a mushroom. rev and updated ed. Heinemann Library 2009 32p il (Life cycle of a) $25.36; pa $7.99

Grades: 2 3 4   **579.6**

1. Mushrooms

ISBN   978-1-4329-2530-7;   1-4329-2530-X; 978-1-4329-2547-5 (pa); 1-4329-2547-4 (pa)

LC 2009517694

Introduces the life cycle of a mushroom, from formation of spores through underground growth of the mycelia to formation of mature mushrooms

This offers "easily accessible information in [an] attractive [package]." SLJ

Includes glossary and bibliographical references

579.8 Algae

Cerullo, Mary M., 1949-

Sea soup: phytoplankton; photography by Bill Curtsinger. Tilbury House 1999 39p il $16.95 *

Grades: 5 6 7 8   **579.8**

1. Phytoplankton

ISBN 0-88448-208-1   LC 99-39210

Discusses the microscopic organisms known as phytoplankton and the important functions they serve in replenishing earth's atmosphere, in the marine food chain, and more

"Outstanding full-color photomicroscopy dominates this slim volume on the microscopic plants at the bottom of the ocean food chain. The clearly presented information is not available in another single volume for this audience." SLJ

Includes glossary and bibliographical references

580 Plants (Botany)

Goodman, Emily

Plant secrets; illustrated by Phyllis Limbacher Tildes. Charlesbridge 2009 unp il $16.95; pa $7.95

Grades: PreK K 1 2   **580**

1. Plants

ISBN   978-1-58089-204-9;   1-58089-204-3; 978-1-58089-205-6 (pa); 1-58089-205-1 (pa)

LC 2008-07256

"Children will look at plants with new eyes after reading this fresh introduction. The plant cycle is introduced, beginning and ending with seeds. . . . The text will draw readers into the wonder of the topic. Bold color-coded headings introduce each of the four stages. Realistic spot illustrations, beginning with the endpapers, present the variety described in the text." SLJ

Levine, Shar, 1953-

Plants; flowering plants, ferns, mosses, and other plants; by Shar Levine and Leslie Johnstone. Crabtree Pub. 2010 48p il (A class of their own) lib bdg $29.27; pa $9.95

Grades: 5 6 7 8   **580**

1. Plants

ISBN 978-0-7787-5376-6 (lib bdg); 0-7787-5376-X (lib bdg); 978-0-7787-5390-2 (pa); 0-7787-5390-5 (pa)

LC 2009-51342

Describes the main groups of plants, including mosses, ferns, conifers, and flowering plants.

"Lively section headings . . . and notes on uncommon achievements, . . . lighten the substantial load of biological terminology. Illustrated with a plethora of closeup color photos and microphotos, and closing with annotated lists of recommended Web sites, . . . [this captures] the remarkable diversity of life." SLJ

Includes glossary and bibliographical references

Rau, Dana Meachen, 1971-

Plants. Marshall Cavendish Benchmark 2009 31p il (Bookworms. Nature's cycles) lib bdg $22.79

Grades: PreK K 1   **580**

1. Life cycles (Biology) 2. Plants

ISBN 978-0-7614-4097-0 (lib bdg); 0-7614-4097-6 (lib bdg)   LC 2008-42515

"Introduces the idea that many things in the world around us are cyclical in nature and discusses the plant cycle from seed to plant to flower to seed again." Publisher's note

"Well composed, simple sentences tie directly to colorful, carefully chosen photos [and] . . . accurate information flows naturally. . . . A great resource for sharing one-on-one with the youngest readers." Libr Media Connect

Includes glossary

Wade, Mary Dodson, 1930-

Trees, weeds, and vegetables—so many kinds of plants! Enslow Elementary 2009 24p il (I like plants!) lib bdg $21.26; pa $6.95

Grades: K 1 2   **580**

1. Plants

ISBN 978-0-7660-3156-2 (lib bdg); 0-7660-3156-X (lib bdg); 978-0-7660-3616-1 (pa); 0-7660-3616-2 (pa)

LC 2007039460

"Presents information about different types of plants" Publisher's note

This does "an excellent job of introducing basic concepts about seeds and plants. Large text on colored pages explains terms and covers a lot of ground in the simplest manner imaginable. The full-color illustrations amplify the narrative." SLJ

Includes glossary and bibliographical references

580.7 Education, research, related topics

Benbow, Ann

Lively plant science projects; [by] Ann Benbow and Colin Mably; illustrations by Tom Labaff. Enslow Publishers 2009 48p il (Real life science experiments) lib bdg $23.93

Grades: 3 4 5   **580.7**

1. Botany 2. Plants 3. Science projects

ISBN 978-0-7660-3146-3 (lib bdg); 0-7660-3146-2 (lib bdg)   LC 2008-01745

"Presents several easy-to-do science experiments using plants." Publisher's note

"Color drawings, photographs, a glossary, and suggestions for further research enliven . . . [this] title . . . [and provide] solid curricular support." Booklist

Includes glossary and bibliographical references

Sprouting seed science projects; [by] Ann Benbow and Colin Mably; illustrations by Tom Labaff. Enslow Publishers 2009 48p il (Real life science experiments) lib bdg $23.93

Grades: 3 4 5   **580.7**

1. Seeds 2. Germination 3. Science projects

ISBN 978-0-7660-3147-0 (lib bdg); 0-7660-3147-0 (lib bdg)   LC 2008-1731

"Presents several easy-to-do science experiments using seeds." Publisher's note

"Color drawings, photographs, a glossary, and suggestions for further research enliven . . . [this] title . . . [and provide] solid curricular support." Booklist

Includes glossary and bibliographical references

Gardner, Robert, 1929-

Ace your plant science project; great science fair ideas; [by] Robert Gardner and Phyllis J. Perry. Enslow Publishers 2009 104p il (Ace your biology science project) lib bdg $31.93

Grades: 5 6 7 8   **580.7**

1. Plants 2. Science projects 3. Science—Experiments

ISBN 978-0-7660-3221-7 (lib bdg); 0-7660-3221-3 (lib bdg)   LC 2008-4687

"Presents several science experiments and project ideas using plants." Publisher's note

Includes bibliographical references

VanCleave, Janice Pratt

Janice VanCleave's plants; mind-boggling experiments you can turn into science fair projects. Wiley 1997 90p il (Spectacular science projects series) pa $10.95

Grades: 5 6 7 8   **580.7**

1. Botany 2. Plants 3. Science projects 4. Science—Experiments

ISBN 0-471-14687-0   LC 96-2744

Presents facts about plants and includes experiments, projects, and activities related to each topic

This book "is inspiring without being flashy. . . . The black-and-white line drawings are sketchy but helpful.

. . . This is a fine example of helpful information that is neither academically dry nor ingratiatingly slangy." SLJ

Includes glossary

Whitehouse, Patricia, 1958-

Plants; [by] Patricia Whitehouse. Heinemann Library 2008 48p il (Science fair projects) $30

Grades: 5 6 7 8   **580.7**

1. Plants 2. Science—Experiments 3. Science projects

ISBN 978-1-4034-7918-1   LC 2006039547

This guide to science fair projects about plants "is one of the better 'how-to-do-a-science-fair project' books on the market. . . . [It] guides students with initial concrete suggestions and ideas for projects, but continues to challenge students to extend their investigations. . . . The content is presented in a colorful and engaging format." Sci Books Films

Includes glossary and bibliographical references

581 Specific topics in natural history of plants

Wade, Mary Dodson, 1930-

Plants live everywhere! Enslow Elementary 2009 24p il (I like plants!) lib bdg $21.26; pa $6.95

Grades: K 1 2   **581**

1. Plants

ISBN 978-0-7660-3155-5 (lib bdg); 0-7660-3155-1 (lib bdg); 978-0-7660-3615-4 (pa); 0-7660-3615-4 (pa)
                                                   LC 2007039457

"Information about plants living in different habitats for young readers" Publisher's note

This book does "an excellent job of introducing basic concepts about seeds and plants. Large text on colored pages explains terms and covers a lot of ground in the simplest manner imaginable. The full-color illustrations amplify the narrative." SLJ

Includes glossary and bibliographical references

581.4 Adaptation

Aston, Dianna Hutts, 1964-

A seed is sleepy; by Dianna Hutts Aston; illustrated by Sylvia Long. Chronicle Books 2007 unp il $16.95 *

Grades: K 1 2 3   **581.4**

1. Seeds

ISBN 978-0-8118-5520-4; 0-8118-5520-1
                                                   LC 2006-13302

"The topic is seeds, and . . . Long's masterful watercolors dominate each spread, which includes text on two levels. Short poetic phrases in large print, aimed at younger children, give seeds accessible, anthropomorphic qualities. . . . Paragraphs in smaller print, which tackle science concepts and expand on the phrases, are geared to older readers." Booklist

Farndon, John
  Fruits. Blackbirch Press 2006 24p il (World of plants) lib bdg $27.44
  Grades: 2 3 4 5   **581.4**
    1. Fruit
    ISBN 978-1-4103-0424-7 (lib bdg); 1-4103-0424-8 (lib bdg)   LC 2005052412
  This book examines the various types of fruits, including nuts; regions in which various fruits are grown; animals that rely on fruit for food; and fruits in the human diet
  Includes bibliographical references

  Roots. Blackbirch Press 2006 24p il (World of plants) lib bdg $27.44
  Grades: 2 3 4 5   **581.4**
    1. Roots (Botany)
    ISBN 978-1-4103-0421-6 (lib bdg); 1-4103-0421-3 (lib bdg)   LC 2005047045
  This book examines root functions, root growth, kinds of roots including climbing roots, and roots as food for both humans and animals
  This uses "clear language and short sentences. . . . Helpful diagrams and sharp, colorful photographs supplement the [text]. . . . [This book offers] solid information in an attractive format." SLJ
  Includes bibliographical references

  Seeds. Blackbirch Press 2006 24p il (World of plants) lib bdg $27.44
  Grades: 2 3 4 5   **581.4**
    1. Seeds
    ISBN 978-1-4103-0419-3 (lib bdg); 1-4103-0419-1 (lib bdg)   LC 2005047047
  This book examines germination, the ways seeds are spread, types and sizes of seeds, and the role of seeds in the diets of both humans and animals
  This uses "clear language and short sentences. . . . Helpful diagrams and sharp, colorful photographs supplement the [text]. . . . [This book offers] solid information in an attractive format." SLJ
  Includes bibliographical references

  Stems. Blackbirch Press 2006 24p il (World of plants) lib bdg $27.44
  Grades: 2 3 4 5   **581.4**
    1. Stems (Plants)
    ISBN 978-1-4103-0420-9 (lib bdg); 1-4103-0420-5 (lib bdg)   LC 2005047049
  This book examines how stems grow, the sizes of various types of stems, underground stems, and the ways people and animals use stems for food and shelter
  This uses "clear language and short sentences. . . . Helpful diagrams and sharp, colorful photographs supplement the [text]. . . . [This book offers] solid information in an attractive format." SLJ
  Includes bibliographical references

Goodman, Susan, 1952-
  Seeds, stems, and stamens; the ways plants fit into their world; by Susan E. Goodman; photographs by Michael Doolittle. Millbrook Press 2001 48p il $22.90
  Grades: 2 3 4   **581.4**
    1. Adaptation (Biology) 2. Plants 3. Ecology
    ISBN 0-7613-1874-7   LC 00-68367
  The author describes "a variety of ways plants adapt to their environment in order to survive. . . . The text is clearly and concisely written, and Doolittle's color photography is outstanding." Booklist

Macken, JoAnn Early, 1953-
  Flip, float, fly; seeds on the move; by JoAnn Early Macken; illustrated by Pam Paparone. Holiday House 2008 unp il $16.95
  Grades: K 1 2 3   **581.4**
    1. Seeds
    ISBN 978-0-8234-2043-8; 0-8234-2043-4
                                                LC 2006-37278
  This book introduces "methods of seed distribution. Each is introduced on a double-page spread, in which a few lines of poetic text provide information succinctly. . . . Pleasing in their colors, compositions, and decorative elements, the pictures clearly show points made in the text. . . . Satisfying and well designed for both classroom sharing and individual reading." Booklist
  Includes glossary and bibliographical references

Richards, Jean, 1940-
  A fruit is a suitcase for seeds; illustrated by Anca Hariton. Millbrook Press 2002 unp il lib bdg $21.90
  Grades: K 1 2   **581.4**
    1. Seeds 2. Fruit
    ISBN 0-7613-1622-1   LC 2001-32959
  Provides an illustrated description of seed dispersal by which plants, most specifically fruits, travel from one place to another
  "Richard's carefully worded information provides an excellent introduction to seeds, their purpose, and growth that should be easy for young children to grasp. . . . Hariton's use of bright watercolors adds sensual appeal to her illustrations." SLJ

Robbins, Ken, 1945-
  Seeds; text and pictures by Ken Robbins. Atheneum Books for Young Readers 2005 unp il $15.95 *
  Grades: K 1 2 3   **581.4**
    1. Seeds
    ISBN 0-689-85041-7
  This "book focuses on seed basics: differences in shapes and sizes, and links between structure and function. . . . Seeds are show alongside the whole plants and fruits they come from. . . . The superb photographs lend themselves to scientific scrutiny: the details are sharp and clear." Horn Book

Wade, Mary Dodson, 1930-

Seeds sprout! Enslow Elementary 2009 24p il (I like plants!) lib bdg $21.26; pa $6.95

Grades: K 1 2   **581.4**

    1. Seeds 2. Plants

    ISBN 978-0-7660-3154-8 (lib bdg); 0-7660-3154-3 (lib bdg); 978-0-7660-3614-7 (pa); 0-7660-3614-6 (pa)

                    LC 2007039461

"Presents information about seeds, including where they come from, how they grow, and how they travel" Publisher's note

This book does "an excellent job of introducing basic concepts about seeds and plants. Large text on colored pages explains terms and covers a lot of ground in the simplest manner imaginable. The full-color illustrations amplify the narrative." SLJ

Includes glossary and bibliographical references

581.6   Miscellaneous nontaxonomic kinds of plants

Souza, D. M. (Dorothy M.)

Plant invaders; [by] D. M. Souza. F. Watts 2003 63p il lib bdg $25.50; pa $8.95

Grades: 3 4 5   **581.6**

    1. Plant ecology 2. Biological invasions 3. Nonindigenous pests

    ISBN 0-531-12211-5 (lib bdg); 0-531-16247-8 (pa)

                    LC 2002-8887

Discusses non-native plants, such as the kudzu vine and the tree-of-heaven, which were imported from other countries and now pose a significant threat to the ecosystems of North America

"Large, brightly colored close-up photos ranging from beautiful to bizarre are nicely placed to support the well-written [narrative.]" SLJ

Wade, Mary Dodson, 1930-

People need plants! Enslow Elementary 2009 24p il (I like plants!) lib bdg $21.26; pa $6.95

Grades: K 1 2   **581.6**

    1. Plants

    ISBN 978-0-7660-3153-1 (lib bdg); 0-7660-3153-5 (lib bdg); 978-0-7660-3613-0 (pa); 0-7660-3613-8 (pa)

                    LC 2007039458

"Presents information about how humans and animals use plants for housing, food, clothing, and other necessities" Publisher's note

"Beautifully detailed professional photographs of plants, animals, and people complement the subject matter. [The] book includes a simple activity." SLJ

Includes glossary and bibliographical references

582   Plants notable for specific vegetative characteristics and flowers

Schaefer, Lola M., 1950-

Pick, pull, snap! where once a flower bloomed; illustrated by Lindsay Barrett George. Greenwillow Bks. 2003 unp il $15.99 *

Grades: K 1 2 3   **582**

    1. Plants 2. Flowers 3. Fruit 4. Seeds

    ISBN 0-688-17834-0   LC 2002-66818

Describes how raspberries, peanuts, corn, and other foods are produced as various plants flower, create seeds, and finally bear fruit

"On each spread, rhythmic, poetic text describes a plant's flower or husk and shows a cross section that reveals the seeds inside. A few lines of text explain a plant's growth, and then the page folds out to reveal the mature plant. . . . George's inviting, realistic color art brings youngsters up close to plants that produce familiar foods." Booklist

Includes glossary

582.13   Plants noted for their flowers

Pascoe, Elaine

Flowers; text by Elaine Pascoe; photographs by Dwight Kuhn. Blackbirch Press 2003 48p il lib bdg $23.70

Grades: 3 4 5   **582.13**

    1. Flowers

    ISBN 1-56711-432-6   LC 2002-151824

Describes the parts of different flowers, their role in the plants' reproduction, how to grow flowers, and how to press them. Includes activites and experiments related to flowers

This is "well organized. . . . Different-sized, sharply focused pictures complement the text on almost every page; many are remarkably detailed, extreme close-ups." SLJ

Includes bibliographical references

Souza, D. M. (Dorothy M.)

Freaky flowers. Watts 2002 63p il (Watts library) lib bdg $24.50; pa $8.95

Grades: 5 6 7 8   **582.13**

    1. Flowers

    ISBN 0-531-11981-5 (lib bdg); 0-531-16221-4 (pa)

                    LC 2001-17573

"The book begins with a short course in botany that stresses vocabulary and processes. Subsequent chapters discuss different ways plants attract pollinators through colors, odors, and habitats. The last chapter acts as a warning that many plants are endangered because their pollinators are threatened, emphasizing the balance of nature. The outstanding full-color photos feature some of the most spectacular flowers found anywhere. Small sidebars offer interesting bits of trivia about similar plants. The text is packed with biological information and pertinent vocabulary." SLJ

Includes bibliographical references

Wade, Mary Dodson, 1930-
Flowers bloom! Enslow Elementary 2009 24p il
(I like plants!) lib bdg $21.26; pa $6.95
Grades: K 1 2   **582.13**
1. Flowers
ISBN 978-0-7660-3157-9 (lib bdg); 0-7660-3157-8 (lib
bdg); 978-0-7660-3617-8 (pa); 0-7660-3617-0 (pa)
LC 2007039462
"Presents basic information about flowers, including
colors, shapes, sizes, and parts" Publisher's note
"Beautifully detailed professional photographs of
plants, animals, and people complement the subject mat-
ter. [The] book includes a simple activity." SLJ
Includes glossary and bibliographical references

582.16 Trees

Bulla, Clyde Robert, 1914-2007
A tree is a plant; illustrated by Stacey Schuett.
HarperCollins   Pubs.   2001   31p   il
(Let's-read-and-find-out science) hardcover o.p. pa
$4.95
Grades: K 1 2   **582.16**
1. Trees 2. Apples
ISBN 0-06-028171-5; 0-06-028172-3 (lib bdg);
0-06-445196-8 (pa)   LC 00-40797
A newly illustrated edition of the title first published
1960 by Crowell
The text "follows an apple plant from seed to sprout
to tree, including the development of blossoms, leaves,
and fruit. The functions of roots, trunk, branches, and
leaves are also discussed, as well as the seasonal changes
in the tree. Schuett's colorful paintings clearly illustrate
topics explained in the text, while their pleasing colors,
rounded forms, and small, playful animals will help keep
children involved in the topic." Booklist

Ehlert, Lois, 1934-
Red leaf, yellow leaf. Harcourt Brace
Jovanovich 1991 unp il $16 *
Grades: K 1 2 3   **582.16**
1. Trees
ISBN 0-15-266197-2   LC 90-21195
"In a quiet, first-person narrative, a young child details
the life cycle of a sugar maple tree. . . . The story is
quite brief, and the choice of a very large typeface
makes the main portion of the book accessible to beginning readers. The concluding section offers more detailed
and concrete botanical information and provides hints on
selecting and planting one's own tree. . . . Ehlert has
combined many media to create the book's dazzling illustrations." Horn Book

Gardner, Robert, 1929-
Science project ideas about trees. Enslow Pubs.
1997 96p il (Science project ideas) lib bdg $25.26
Grades: 5 6 7 8   **582.16**
1. Trees 2. Science projects 3. Science—Experiments
ISBN 978-0-89490-846-0 (lib bdg); 0-89490-846-4 (lib
bdg)   LC 97-6515

Contains many experiments introducing the processes
that take place in plants and trees
The directions "are easy to understand, and the vocabulary is fairly accessible. The accompanying diagrams
are particularly sharp and clear." SLJ
Includes bibliographical references

Gerber, Carole
Winter trees; illustrated by Leslie Evans.
Charlesbridge 2008 unp il $15.95
Grades: PreK K 1 2   **582.16**
1. Trees 2. Winter
ISBN 978-1-58089-168-4; 1-58089-168-3
LC 2007-26197
"Alone in the snowy woods with his dog, a boy discovers the wonder of winter trees. . . . On every double-
page spread, four lines of simple verse and bright linoleum block prints decorated with watercolor and collage
capture the stark outlines and the details of what he sees,
hears, and touches. . . . The blend of play, science, poetry, and art is beautiful; and notes at the back provide
more facts about each tree." Booklist

Gibbons, Gail
Tell me, tree; all about trees for kids. Little,
Brown 2002 unp il $15.95
Grades: K 1 2 3   **582.16**
1. Trees
ISBN 0-316-30903-6   LC 00-64967
"Gibbons discusses the parts of the tree and their
functions, types of fruits and seeds, kinds of bark, and
uses for trees. She includes a discussion of photosynthesis and gives directions for students to make their own
tree identification books." SLJ
"The bright, watercolor illustrations show cheerful
children and adults observing, planting, using, and enjoying many kinds of trees. In this simple, informative
book, Gibbons provides a basic guide that is sure to
please parents and teachers as well as children." Booklist

Lauber, Patricia, 1924-
Be a friend to trees; illustrated by Holly Keller.
HarperCollins   Pubs.   1994   32p   il
(Let's-read-and-find-out science) hardcover o.p. pa
$4.95
Grades: K 1 2 3   **582.16**
1. Trees
ISBN 0-06-021529-1 (lib bdg); 0-06-445120-8 (pa)
LC 92-24082
In this book "photosynthesis is explained, as well as
the beauty and usefulness of trees. Easy conservation
suggestions are also offered." Horn Book Guide
"This conveys a lot of information in a simple text
with clear line-and-watercolor illustrations." Booklist

Maestro, Betsy, 1944-

Why do leaves change color? illustrated by Loretta Krupinski. HarperCollins Pubs. 1994 32p il (Let's-read-and-find-out science) hardcover o.p. pa $4.95

Grades: K 1 2 3   **582.16**
1. Leaves 2. Autumn
ISBN 0-06-022874-1 (lib bdg); 0-06-445126-7 (pa)
LC 93-9611

Explains how leaves change their colors in autumn and then separate from the tree as the tree prepares for winter

"This is an informative concept book. . . . Krupinski's bright gouache-and-colored pencil illustrations show a boy and a girl playing in a country landscape that changes with weather and light. There are also detailed pictures of leaves in different sizes, shapes, and colors. Maestro includes simple instructions for making a leaf rubbing and for pressing leaves, as well as suggestions for places to visit where the fall foliage is special." Booklist

Pallotta, Jerry

Who will plant a tree? written by Jerry Pallotta; illustrated by Tom Leonard. Sleeping Bear Press 2010 unp il $15.95

Grades: PreK K 1 2   **582.16**
1. Trees 2. Seeds
ISBN 978-1-58536-502-9; 1-58536-502-5
LC 2009037411

"Each spread features an animal in a different habitat that, by simply going about its everyday activities, unknowingly plants a tree. . . . The range of habitats and animals shown is impressive, from monkeys throwing figs in the jungle to Amazon River fish excreting seeds from their fruit dinners. . . . With simple, rhythmic language and engaging illustrations, this book encourages readers to see how the actions of each creature impact the Earth. An excellent accompaniment to science lessons." SLJ

Rene, Ellen

Investigating why leaves change their color. Rosen/PowerKids 2008 24p il (Science detectives) lib bdg $15.95

Grades: 3 4 5   **582.16**
1. Trees 2. Leaves
ISBN 978-1-4042-4485-6 (lib bdg); 1-4042-4485-9 (lib bdg)

"With a chatty text, oversize font, and beautiful, full-page color photos, the open design of this . . . book . . . will invite young readers to look at the astonishing science happening around them. The page headings are appealing . . . leading into text that details the process of photosynthesis and chlorophyll's role in trapping sunlight; the botany is quite technical and will encourage kids to talk about it in the classroom and at home. . . . [This is a] fine account of one of nature's most vibrant transformations, leading kids to an elementary understanding of how the sun and sky affect each and every leaf." Booklist

583 Magnoliopsida (Dicotyledons)

Bash, Barbara

Desert giant; the world of the saguaro cactus. Sierra Club Bks. 1989 unp il pa $6.95 hardcover o.p.

Grades: 3 4 5   **583**
1. Cactus 2. Desert ecology
ISBN 1-57805-085-5 (pa)   LC 88-4706

"Animals find food and shelter in the towering plant of the Sonoran desert, and the local Tohono O'odom Indians have multiple uses for it. The cactus's 200-year life cycle is depicted as part of the ecosystem with colorful illustrations and clear text." Sci Child

Ganeri, Anita, 1961-

From bean to bean plant; [by] Anita Ganeri. Heinemann Library 2006 32p il (How living things grow) lib bdg $25.36; pa $7.99

Grades: K 1 2 3   **583**
1. Beans
ISBN 1-4034-7861-9 (lib bdg); 1-4034-7870-8 (pa)
LC 2005026925

"Heinemann first library"
This describes the life cycle of the fava bean plant
This is "well-illustrated and informative." Sci Books Films
Includes glossary and bibliographical references

From seed to apple; [by] Anita Ganeri. Heinemann Library 2006 32p il (How living things grow) lib bdg $25.36; pa $7.99

Grades: K 1 2 3   **583**
1. Apples
ISBN 1-4034-7862-7 (lib bdg); 1-4034-7871-6 (pa)
LC 2005026926

"Heinemann first library"
This describes the life cycle of the apple from seed to blossom to fruit

"The eye-catching color photos on each spread are bright and substantial. . . . Young readers will find [this title] interesting and [its] size manageable." SLJ
Includes glossary and bibliographical references

From seed to sunflower; [by] Anita Ganeri. Heinemann Library 2006 32p il (How living things grow) lib bdg $25.36; pa $7.99

Grades: K 1 2 3   **583**
1. Sunflowers
ISBN 1-4034-7857-0 (lib bdg); 1-4034-7866-X (pa)
LC 2005026921

"Heinemann first library"
This describes the life cycle of the sunflower.
This is "well-illustrated and informative." Sci Books Films
Includes glossary and bibliographical references

Guiberson, Brenda Z., 1946-
Cactus hotel; illustrated by Megan Lloyd. Holt & Co. 1991 unp il $16.95; pa $6.95
Grades: K 1 2 3   **583**
1. Cactus 2. Desert ecology
ISBN 0-8050-1333-4; 0-8050-2960-5 (pa)
LC 90-41748
Describes the life cycle of the giant saguaro cactus, with an emphasis on its role as a home for other desert dwellers
"Guiberson's simple, understandable text gives an enjoyable lesson in desert ecology. Crisply attractive illustrations in color pencil and watercolor show the beauty of the desert landscape and its variety of wildlife." Booklist

Johnson, Jinny
Dandelion; illustrations by Graham Rosewarne. Smart Apple Media 2010 32p il (How does it grow?) lib bdg $28.50
Grades: 1 2 3   **583**
1. Dandelions 2. Life cycles (Biology)
ISBN 978-1-59920-351-5 (lib bdg); 1-59920-351-0 (lib bdg)   LC 2009-5693
Explains the life cycle of a dandelion
"Each stage is described on a spread that features clearly written, oversized text and a caption opposite a full-page, realistic watercolor, or, occasionally, a photograph. . . . A worthwhile purchase." SLJ
Includes glossary

Oak tree; illustrations by Graham Rosewarne. Smart Apple Media 2010 32p il (How does it grow?) lib bdg $28.50
Grades: 1 2 3   **583**
1. Oak 2. Life cycles (Biology)
ISBN 978-1-59920-356-0 (lib bdg); 1-59920-356-1 (lib bdg)   LC 2009-3399
Presents a basic overview of how an acorn grows into an oak tree and explains each stage in its development
"Each stage is described on a spread that features clearly written, oversized text and a caption opposite a full-page, realistic watercolor, or, occasionally, a photograph. . . . A worthwhile purchase." SLJ
Includes glossary and bibliographical references

Pfeffer, Wendy, 1929-
From seed to pumpkin; illustrated by James Graham Hale. HarperCollins 2004 33p il (Let's-read-and-find-out science) hardcover o.p. lib bdg $16.89; pa $4.99
Grades: K 1   **583**
1. Pumpkin
ISBN 0-06-028038-7; 0-06-028039-5 (lib bdg); 0-06-445190-9 (pa)   LC 00-54039
This explains the stages in the development of a seed into a pumpkin
Written "in simple, clear language. . . . A couple of easy recipes and experiments are appended. Appealing watercolor-and-pencil illustrations show children involved in planting and tending the pumpkins, and help make the process and the passage of time understandable to this audience." SLJ

Posada, Mia
Dandelions; stars in the grass. Carolrhoda Bks. 2000 unp il lib bdg $15.95
Grades: 2 3 4   **583**
1. Dandelions
ISBN 1-57505-383-7   LC 98-53000
Rhyming text presents the dandelion, not as a weed, but as a flower of great beauty. Includes information about the flower, a recipe, and science activities
"This cheerful book is a nice combination of rhyme and information. . . . Bright and pleasing acrylic illustrations extend the text. . . . Posada includes just enough botanical detail for beginning dandelion pickers." SLJ
Includes bibliographical references

Royston, Angela
Life cycle of an oak tree. rev and updated ed. Heinemann Library 2009 32p il (Life cycle of a) $25.36; pa $7.99
Grades: 2 3 4   **583**
1. Oak
ISBN 978-1-4329-2531-4; 1-4329-2531-8; 978-1-4329-2548-2 (pa); 1-4329-2548-2 (pa)
LC 2009517688
First published 2000
Introduces the life cycle of an oak tree, from the sprouting of an acorn through its more than 100 years of growth
This offers "easily accessible information in [an] attractive [package]." SLJ
Includes glossary and bibliographical references

585   Pinophyta (Gymnosperms) Coniferales (Conifers)

Chin, Jason, 1978-
Redwoods. Roaring Brook Press 2009 unp il $16.95 *
Grades: PreK K 1 2   **585**
1. Redwood
ISBN 978-1-59643-430-1; 1-59643-430-9
'A Neal Porter book.'
"The framing story opens with a boy finding a copy of *Redwoods* on a subway station bench (he's even on the cover). He delves in, and facts about the ancient trees spring to life around him. . . . Emerging from the station to find himself in the middle of a redwood forest, his adventures mirror what he's learning. . . . The straightforward narrative is given enormous energy by the inventive format and realistic watercolor illustrations. . . . Chin adeptly captures the singular and spectacular nature of redwoods in this smartly layered book." Publ Wkly

586   Cryptogamia (Seedless plants)

Pascoe, Elaine
Plants without seeds; photography by Dwight Kuhn. PowerKids Press 2003 32p il (Kid's guide to the classification of living things) $20.65
Grades: 2 3 4 5   **586**
1. Mosses 2. Ferns
ISBN 0-8239-6315-2   LC 2001-7794

Pascoe, Elaine—*Continued*

An introduction to the life cycles and characteristics of bryophytes, or plants without seeds, such as mosses and ferns

This "slim, well-organized . . . [introduction is] a must for schools in which plant studies are a part of the curriculum. . . . Useful for reports, with browsing appeal as well." SLJ

Includes glossary and bibliographical references

590 Animals (Zoology)

Ablow, Gail, 1962-

A horse in the house, and other strange but true animal stories; illustrated by Kathy Osborn. Candlewick Press 2007 unp il $17.99

Grades: 2 3 4 5   590

1. Animals

ISBN 978-0-7636-2838-3; 0-7636-2838-7

LC 2006051855

"Some of these 16 short tales would be very hard to believe, had Ablow, a journalist, not provided specific source notes for each at the end. It wouldn't be too hard to buy the moose that does laps in a Spokane swimming pool . . . —but a man successfully giving mouth-to-mouth to a distressed ornamental fish? . . . Osborn's stylized paintings capture the humor in each report. . . . Even skeptical young readers will come back for more." Booklist

Includes bibliographical references

Arnosky, Jim

Wild tracks! a guide to nature's footprints; [by] Jim Arnosky. Sterling Pub. Co. 2008 32p il $14.95 *

Grades: 1 2 3   590

1. Animal tracks

ISBN 978-1-4027-3985-9; 1-4027-3985-0

LC 2007033972

"Features giant fold-out pages of life-size prints"-- Jacket

"Tracks are separated into categories (bear, deer, cat, and so on), each presented in a two-page spread. On the left, a full-color painting displays an animal, and its tracks, in its natural habitat. On the right, information about the tracks, and how to read them, appears as pencil-sketch reproductions from Arnosky's own notebook. . . . Arnosky supplements the track identification information with fascinating related material in notebook-style entries. . . . The uniformly lovely illustrations and the compelling concept make this a book that young naturalists will enjoy year-round." Booklist

Bayrock, Fiona

Bubble homes and fish farts; illustrated by Carolyn Conahan. Charlesbridge 2009 45p il $16.95; pa $7.95

Grades: 2 3 4   590

1. Animals 2. Bubbles

ISBN 978-1-57091-669-4; 1-57091-669-1; 978-1-57091-670-0 (pa); 1-57091-670-5 (pa)

LC 2008-06151

"Fast Repetitive Tick (FaRT) is the term scientists use to describe the flatulencelike noise that herring make as they communicate their locations to one another. That might be the most amusing description of the uses of bubbles in the natural world, but this entire book is enjoyable and engaging. . . . The illustrations are pale and less-detailed versions of scientifically accurate drawings overlaid with entertaining comments. . . . Creative, accessible, and fact-filled." SLJ

BishopRoby, Joshua

Animal kingdom. Compass Point Books 2009 40p il (Mission: science) lib bdg $26.60

Grades: 4 5 6   590

1. Animals—Classification

ISBN 978-0-7565-4057-9 (lib bdg); 0-7565-4057-7 (lib bdg)

LC 2008-37574

An introduction to the animal kingdom, which is made up of a variety of animals that are organized into categories based on physical attributes or ancestors

Includes glossary

Davies, Nicola, 1958-

Extreme animals; the toughest creatures on Earth; illustrated by Neal Layton. Candlewick Press 2006 61p il $12.99; pa $7.99 *

Grades: 3 4 5 6   590

1. Animals 2. Adaptation (Biology)

ISBN 978-0-7636-3067-6; 0-7636-3067-5; 978-0-7636-4127-6 (pa); 0-7636-4127-8 (pa)

LC 2005-43544

"There is life everywhere on Earth . . . and much of that life thrives in conditions that humans could not endure for five minutes or less. This funny and appealing little book describes who these amazing life-forms are and how they manage to survive. Simple and inviting cartoon drawings enliven the text and convey the types of extremes in an easy-to-understand manner." SLJ

Includes glossary

Gannij, Joan

Hidden hippo; written by Joan Gannij; illustrated by Clare Beaton. Barefoot Books 2008 unp il $15.99

Grades: PreK K 1 2   590

1. Hippopotamus 2. Animals

ISBN 978-1-84686-170-3; 1-84686-170-5

LC 2007042677

Companion to: Elusive moose (2006)

"On safari, an unseen narrator hopes 'to see/A hippo or two,/Perhaps even three?' Clever rhyming verse details the spectacular sights along the way, such as lions, chimpanzees, and sleepy leopards. . . . This expansive tour of the African Plains is brought to life through Beaton's signature fabric appliqué collages. . . . The vibrant colors capture the hot, arid habitat. . . . Young adventurers and conservationists alike will pore over this visually stunning story." SLJ

Jenkins, Steve

Biggest, strongest, fastest. Ticknor & Fields Bks. for Young Readers 1995 unp il $16; pa $5.95 *

Grades: K 1 2   **590**

1. Animals

ISBN 0-395-69701-8; 0-395-86136-5 (pa)

LC 94-21804

Companion volume to Hottest, coldest, highest, deepest

"Here are 14 creatures of distinction, including elephants, ants, jellyfish, cheetahs and fleas. The collage illustrations show them at work, and silhouette graphics with captions provide scientific information about comparative achievement." N Y Times Book Rev

"A helpful chart at the end contains further information about each creature, such as diet and habitat. An all-round superlative effort." SLJ

Johnson, Jinny

Animal tracks & signs. National Geographic Society 2008 192p il $24.95; lib bdg $32.90 *

Grades: 5 6 7 8   **590**

1. Animal tracks 2. Animals 3. Tracking and trailing

ISBN 978-1-4263-0253-4; 1-4263-0253-3; 978-1-4263-0254-1 (lib bdg); 1-4263-0254-1 (lib bdg)

"This attractive book describes the tracks (paw prints, bird claw prints, slimy trails) and signs (molted skin, food remains, scat, tree markings) that animals leave in their wake. . . . A typical two-page layout includes a photo and short paragraph about the animal category, three or four colored boxes containing a photo or drawing of a specific animal (serval, bobcat), and a description of its size, geographic range, habitat, food, tracks and signs, and comments. . . . The beautiful photos vary from action . . . to informational. . . . The language is simple and readable." Voice Youth Advocates

Includes glossary and bibliographical references

Komiya, Teruyuki

Life-size zoo; from tiny rodents to gigantic elephants, an actual-size animal encyclopedia; editorial supervisor of Japanese edition, Teruyuki Komiya; photographer, Toyofumi Fukuda; Japanese translation by Makiko Oku; English language adaptation by Kristin Earhart. Seven Footer Kids 2009 43p il $17.95

Grades: PreK K 1 2   **590**

1. Animals 2. Size 3. Zoos

ISBN 978-1-934734-20-9; 1-934734-20-9

"The claim to fame for this oversize collection of animal portraits is that each animal is shown at 'actual size.' The striking photographs, taken at Japanese zoos, provide a rare opportunity to see animal faces up close. . . . Animal facts are provided in side panels that feature stick figures who engage readers. . . . The stellar photographs, playful format and informative content create a highly appealing package." Publ Wkly

Levine, Shar

Animals; mammals, birds, reptiles, amphibians, fish, and other animals; by Shar Levine and Leslie Johnstone. Crabtree Pub. 2010 48p il (A class of their own) lib bdg $29.27; pa $9.95

Grades: 5 6 7 8   **590**

1. Animals—Classification

ISBN 978-0-7787-5372-8 (lib bdg); 0-7787-5372-7 (lib bdg); 978-0-7787-5386-5 (pa); 0-7787-5386-7 (pa)

Looks at the animal kingdom, providing information and examples of species from the major phyla and classes, as well as case histories of newly discovered endangered species.

"Lively section headings . . . and notes on uncommon achievements, . . . lighten the substantial load of biological terminology. Illustrated with a plethora of closeup color photos and microphotos, and closing with annotated lists of recommended Web sites, . . . [this captures] the remarkable diversity of life." SLJ

Includes glossary and bibliographical references

Lewin, Ted, 1935-

Tooth and claw; animal adventures in the wild. HarperCollins Pubs. 2003 97p il maps $15.99; lib bdg $16.89

Grades: 4 5 6 7   **590**

1. Wildlife 2. Dangerous animals

ISBN 0-688-14105-6; 0-688-14106-4 (lib bdg)

LC 2002-4588

Contents: Beach master; Grizzly; Macaco meojor; Waiting for puff adder; Bears, bears, bears; Roar; The meat eaters of Kibale; Barnstorming; Sleeping with bison; Rattler; Deputy Dawg; Downwind of a dung beetle; The joker; Garbage elephants

Author/illustrator Ted Lewin relates fourteen of his experiences with wild animals while travelling the world, following each anecdote with facts about the featured animal and its habitat

"This is outstanding nature storytelling, related in a distinctive voice imbued with humor and personality; it's even better when read aloud." Horn Book

Includes glossary

McKay, Sindy

Animals under our feet; illustrated by Judith Hunt. Treasure Bay 2007 40p il (We both read) $7.99; pa $3.99

Grades: K 1 2   **590**

1. Burrowing animals

ISBN 978-1-60115-003-5; 1-60115-003-2; 978-1-60115-004-2 (pa); 1-60115-004-0 (pa)

LC 2006-932224

"This book takes a . . . look at many animals that live or spend much of their life underground. It [provides] . . . information about why the animals go underground and how they live there. Animals covered in the book include the desert tortoise, moles, ants, meerkats, armadillos, burrowing owls, and many more." Publisher's note

This "is a marvelous series for beginning readers. . . . The parent reads the left-hand page, which has complex text and new or complex words in boldface print. The child's side has supporting, but less complex, text. . . .

McKay, Sindy—*Continued*

The illustrations are well done, and the boldface type used to introduce new words to the young reader is invaluable." Sci Books Films

Myers, Jack

The puzzle of the platypus; and other explorations of science in action; [by] Jack Myers; illustrated by John Rice. Boyds Mills Press 2008 64p il map (Scientists probe 11 animal mysteries) $17.95

Grades: 3 4 5 6   **590**

1. Animals

ISBN 978-1-59078-556-0; 1-59078-556-8

LC 2007023741

"This collection of 11 articles originally appeared in *Highlights* magazine during the 1990s and early 2000s. Each article tells how a scientist was able to unravel a mystery about some kind of animal. Myers's stories about dolphins, polar bears, elephants, and other animals contain many interesting scientific facts and are written in accessible and engaging prose. . . . Most of the pages have attractive watercolor illustrations." SLJ

Post, Hans, 1959-

Creepy crawlies; [by] Hans Post & [illustrated by] Irene Goede; translated by Nancy Forest-Flier. Front Street 2006 unp il $16.95

Grades: 2 3 4   **590**

1. Animals

ISBN 1-932425-65-9   LC 2005020813

Original Dutch edition 2005

A cat named "Lika spends the early morning in the living room, where a housefly zooms around. Six other insects living in this room are described in informative paragraphs on the facing page. These descriptions are enhanced by realistic colorful drawings. Each two page spread portrays the cat's setting and the organisms found in this area. This is a beautifully illustrated book, full of valuable facts and details about the natural world." Sci Child

Rau, Dana Meachen, 1971-

Animals. Marshall Cavendish Benchmark 2009 31p il (Bookworms. Nature's cycles) lib bdg $22.79

Grades: PreK K 1   **590**

1. Life cycles (Biology) 2. Animals

ISBN 978-0-7614-4093-2 (lib bdg); 0-7614-4093-3 (lib bdg)   LC 2008-42513

"Introduces the idea that many things in the world around us are cyclical in nature and discusses the life cycle of animals—how they grow, mate, and procreate." Publisher's note

"Well composed, simple sentences tie directly to colorful, carefully chosen photos [and] . . . accurate information flows naturally. . . . A great resource for sharing one-on-one with the youngest readers." Libr Media Connect

Includes glossary

Selsam, Millicent Ellis, 1912-1996

Big tracks, little tracks; following animal prints; illustrated by Marlene Hill Donnelly. rev ed. HarperCollins Pubs. 1999 31p il (Let's-read-and-find-out science) hardcover o.p. pa $4.95

Grades: K 1 2 3   **590**

1. Animal tracks 2. Tracking and trailing

ISBN 0-06-028209-6; 0-06-445194-1 (pa)

LC 98-18315

"An I can read book"

First published with this title 1995; originally published with title How to be a nature detective

This book "teaches young readers how to track animals by finding footprints and other clues. . . . Included is a new Find Out More page with lots of hands-on activites." Publisher's note

Seuling, Barbara

Cows sweat through their noses; and other freaky facts about animal habits, characteristics, and homes; by Barbara Seuling; illustrated by Matthew Skeens. Picture Window Books 2008 40p il (Freaky facts) lib bdg $16.95

Grades: 2 3 4 5   **590**

1. Animals

ISBN 978-1-4048-3749-2 (lib bdg); 1-4048-3749-3 (lib bdg)   LC 2007004028

"This delightful little book contains a potpourri of facts about many members of the animal kingdom, large and small, from insects to elephants. . . . The information presented . . . is . . . fascinating." Sci Books Films

Includes glossary and bibliographical references

Siwanowicz, Igor

Animals up close; zoom in on the world's most incredible creatures. DK Pub. 2009 96p il $19.99

Grades: 4 5 6   **590**

1. Animals

ISBN 978-0-7566-4513-7; 0-7566-4513-1

"An eye-catching cover will attract readers to this amazing look at some of the world's insects, fish, mammals, reptiles, amphibians, and birds. The focus is on animals small enough to fit in a child's hand. Siwanowicz showcases each creature with a spread containing a full-color, high-quality, close-up photo surrounded by multiple factual asides. . . . The book is packed with interesting material that captures the author's fascination for small creatures." SLJ

Includes glossary

Swanson, Diane, 1944-

Animal aha! thrilling discoveries in wildlife science. Annick Press 2009 48p il $19.95; pa $9.95

Grades: 4 5 6   **590**

1. Animals

ISBN 978-1-55451-165-5; 1-55451-165-8; 978-1-55451-164-8 (pa); 1-55451-164-X (pa)

"An olio of 'AHA!' moments in natural science. Who knew that a Burmese python's heart enlarges to aid in

Swanson, Diane, 1944-—*Continued*
digestion? Or that a parrot might comprehend human language and be able to use it creatively? Such are the tidbits in this browsable book. 'Fun Facts' and 'Fast Facts' boxes abound, and a color photo pops up on almost every page. With a lively text, this interesting pastiche will be enjoyed by kids pawing through the classroom library seeking an engaging nonfiction read." SLJ

Walker, Richard, 1961-
Animal life; written by Richard Walker; consultant Kim Bryan. DK Pub. 2009 123p il (One million things) $18.99
Grades: 5 6 7 8   **590**
    1. Animals
    ISBN 978-0-7566-52340; 0-7566-5234-0
    This "chronicles the lives of animals around the globe." Publisher's note
    "The artwork is a balanced mix of stunning photography, effective illustrations, and somewhat depth-challenged Photoshop jobs. An eye-catching catchall on the natural world, this . . . is great browsing material, packed full of well-articulated information." Booklist

590.3   Encyclopedias and dictionaries

Animals; a children's encyclopedia. DK Pub. 2008
   304p il map $29.99 *
   Grades: 4 5 6 7   **590.3**
    1. Animals—Encyclopedias 2. Reference books
    ISBN 978-0-7566-4027-9; 0-7566-4027-X
                      LC 2008-04654
    "A visual encyclopedia of the major animal groups. . . . Succinct but important details are provided for each animal including size, location, life span, habitat, and conservation status, using special colored icons. . . . This is a true children's encyclopedia and a must-have reference for every library." Libr Media Connect

Animals: a visual encyclopedia. DK Pub. 2008
   304p il map $29.95 *
   Grades: K 1 2 3 4   **590.3**
    1. Animals—Encyclopedias 2. Reference books
    ISBN 978-0-7566-4027-9; 0-7566-4027-X
                      LC 2008004654
    "Arranged by the major groups of animals, this volume offers a thorough introduction to the animal kingdom for young readers. Vibrant and abundant color photographs add to its appeal for both browsers and researchers." Booklist

McGhee, Karen
   Encyclopedia of animals; [by] Karen McGhee, George McKay. National Geographic 2007 192p il map $24.95; lib bdg $38.90 *
   Grades: 4 5 6 7 8   **590.3**
    1. Animals—Encyclopedias 2. Reference books
    ISBN 0-7922-5936-X; 0-7922-5937-8 (lib bdg)
                      LC 2006299476

"This lavish, ambitious volume contains full-color illustrations of more than 1500 species. Each brief entry includes common and scientific names and mention of an interesting physical or behavioral trait. Range maps show where each animal is found, and conservation data notes which species are extinct, endangered, or vulnerable. In addition to the realistic drawings, there are dramatic photos of animals in their habitats." SLJ

590.7   Animals—Education, research, related topics

Benbow, Ann
   Awesome animal science projects; [by] Ann Benbow and Colin Mably; illustrations by Tom Labaff. Enslow Publishers 2010 48p il (Real life science experiments) lib bdg $23.93
   Grades: 3 4 5   **590.7**
    1. Animal behavior 2. Science projects
    ISBN 978-0-7660-3148-7 (lib bdg); 0-7660-3148-9 (lib bdg)   LC 2008-23932
    "Presents several easy-to-do science experiments about animals and animal behavior." Publisher's note
    "Color drawings, photographs, a glossary, and suggestions for further research enliven . . . [this] title . . . [and provide] solid curricular support." Booklist
    Includes glossary and bibliographical references

Gardner, Robert, 1929-
   Ace your animal science project; great science fair ideas; [by] Robert Gardner . . . [et al.] Enslow Publishers 2009 128p il (Ace your biology science project) lib bdg $31.93
   Grades: 5 6 7 8   **590.7**
    1. Animal behavior 2. Science—Experiments 3. Science projects
    ISBN 978-0-7660-3220-0 (lib bdg); 0-7660-3220-5 (lib bdg)   LC 2008-4234
    "Presents several science projects and science project ideas about animals." Publisher's note
    "Dozens of . . . science activities are presented with background information, step-by-step instructions, and suggestions for extending to the science fair level. . . . Color illustrations and important safety information are included." Horn Book Guide
    Includes bibliographical references

590.73   Collections and exhibits of living animals

Aliki
   My visit to the zoo. HarperCollins Pubs. 1997 33p il hardcover o.p. pa $6.95
   Grades: K 1 2 3   **590.73**
    1. Zoos 2. Animals
    ISBN 0-06-024939-0; 0-06-446217-X (pa)
                      LC 96-9897
    A day at the zoo introduces the different animals that exist in the world, where they come from, what their nat-

Aliki—*Continued*

ural habitats are like, and whether or not they are endangered

"Aliki's accessible text and lush illustrations bring the animal world to life." SLJ

591.3 Genetics, evolution, young animals

Baillie, Marilyn

Small wonders; baby animals in the wild; illustrated by Romi Caron. Maple Tree Press 2006 unp il (Canadian geographic kids) $17.95

Grades: K 1 2 3   **591.3**

1. Animals—North America 2. Animal babies

ISBN 978-1-897066-72-0; 1-897066-72-4

"Realistic watercolors of North American animal parents and their young sprawl across facing pages, leaving ample space for two paragraphs of simple text. . . . This oversize, attractive, and easy-to-read book is a pleasing introduction." SLJ

Eamer, Claire

Super crocs & monster wings; modern animals' ancient past; [by] Claire Eamer. Annick Press 2008 93p il $19.95; pa $9.95

Grades: 4 5 6 7   **591.3**

1. Animals 2. Evolution 3. Prehistoric animals

ISBN   978-1-55451-130-3;   1-55451-130-5; 978-1-55451-129-7 (pa); 1-55451-129-1 (pa)

"The author's conversational and often-humorous voice slides readers effortlessly through a great deal of fascinating scientific information in this title on animal evolution. After a brief but clear introduction to geologic time and Linnaean taxonomy, six chapters compare ancient and modern dragonflies, crocodilians, camelids, sloths, glyptodonts (armadillos), and beavers. . . . Jazzy fonts; crisp photos and paintings; and tilted illustrations, titles, and captions create an up-to-the-minute feel." SLJ

Kajikawa, Kimiko

Close to you; how animals bond; [by] Kimiko Kajikawa. Henry Holt 2008 unp il $16.95

Grades: PreK K 1   **591.3**

1. Animal babies

ISBN 978-0-8050-8123-7; 0-8050-8123-2

LC 2007002959

"This tender title about the bonding between baby and adult animals gets some punch from additional facts appended at the end. The body of the book has a brief rhyming text, notable for its precise and engaging verbs. . . . Large, heartwarming stock photos of animal families clearly illustrate each verse. . . . The information seems carefully selected to be understandable and interesting to young children." SLJ

Patkau, Karen

Creatures yesterday and today; [by] Karen Patkau. Tundra Books 2008 unp il $18.95

Grades: K 1 2 3   **591.3**

1. Animals 2. Evolution 3. Prehistoric animals 4. Fossils

ISBN 978-0-88776-833-0; 0-88776-833-4

"On the first page of this oversize book a huge diplodocus speaks. . . . Turn the page, and his descendant, a little skylark high in a tree, speaks. . . . Then there are the mollusks. . . . With large computer-created graphics in dramatic colors and a few lines of text, each double-page spread makes a similar connection for reptiles, fish, arachnids, birds, amphibians, mammals, crustaceans, and insects. . . . The amazing science will engage dinosaur fans with the wonder of evolution and the evidence of fossils." Booklist

Includes glossary

Rose, Deborah Lee, 1955-

Ocean babies; illustrations by Hiroe Nakata. National Geographic 2005 unp il $16.95; lib bdg $25.90

Grades: K 1 2   **591.3**

1. Marine animals 2. Animal babies

ISBN 0-7922-6669-2; 0-7922-8312-0 (lib bdg)

LC 2003-14075

Describes baby animals that live in the ocean, pointing out their many differences as well as the most important similarity.

"Nakata's cheerful watercolor paintings clearly illustrate the book's ideas while creating a beautiful undersea setting, bright with colors, teeming with varied creatures, and studded with intriguing details. Many books present information in this format, but few manage to stay as focused on the topic and sensitive to the intended audience as this one." Booklist

591.4 Physical adaptation

Aston, Dianna Hutts, 1964-

An egg is quiet; illustrated by Sylvia Long. Chronicle Books 2006 unp il $16.95 *

Grades: K 1 2 3   **591.4**

1. Eggs 2. Animals

ISBN 978-0-8118-4428-4; 0-8118-4428-5

LC 2005-12090

"An exceptionally handsome book on eggs, from the delicate ova of the green lacewing to the rosy roe of the Atlantic salmon to the mammoth bulk of an ostrich egg. Aston's simple, readable text celebrates their marvelous diversity, commenting on size, shape, coloration, and where they might be found." SLJ

Baines, Rebecca

What's in that egg? a book about life cycles; by Becky Baines. National Geographic 2009 27p il $16.95; lib bdg $25.90

Grades: PreK K 1   **591.4**

1. Eggs 2. Animals

ISBN   978-1-4263-0408-8;   1-4263-0408-0; 978-1-4263-0409-5 (lib bdg); 1-4263-0409-9 (lib bdg)

LC 2008-47895

Baines, Rebecca—_Continued_

"A Zigzag book"

This describes the eggs of various animals, including turtles, frogs, fish, butterflies, and swans

This title engages "children through humor, clear language, interesting facts, and abundant photos. . . . [An] excellent [introduction] for young science students." SLJ

Burnie, David

How animals work. Dorling Kindersley 2010 132p il $24.99

Grades: 5 6 7 8   **591.4**

1. Animals 2. Animal behavior

ISBN 978-0-7566-5897-7; 0-7566-5897-7

Describes the anatomy of many animal species and explains how their bodies work to help them survive. Covers such animals as birds, butterflies, elephants, crocodiles, and wolves, and includes color photos, illustrations, and diagrams.

"This beautifully photographed encyclopedia of animals is divided into categories that include movement, diet, senses, and animal families. . . . Diagrams showing internal organs and intimate closeups of eyes, skin, fur, and wings, should engage budding biologists." Publ Wkly

Cusick, Dawn

Animal tongues. EarlyLight Books 2009 36p il $14.95

Grades: 3 4 5   **591.4**

1. Animals 2. Tongue

ISBN 978-0-9797455-1-5; 0-9797455-1-9

Looks at the varied types of animal tongues and their different uses in adaption to their environment, from the sticky tongue of a chameleon, to the tongue of the lizardfish lined with teeth, to the tongue of the parrot used to make sounds.

"The facts presented are fascinating, the activities connect the reader to the text, and the photos are attention grabbing. . . . A great addition to a public or school library." Sci Books Films

Davies, Nicola, 1958-

Just the right size; why big animals are big and little animals are little; illustrated by Neal Layton. Candlewick Press 2009 61p il $14.99

Grades: 3 4 5 6   **591.4**

1. Animals 2. Size

ISBN 978-0-7636-3924-2; 0-7636-3924-9

This "book uses the 'Big Thing, Little Thing' rule (which explains how the length, surface area and cross section of an object or creature are relative to its volume and weight) . . . to explore how size affects living things. Davies's often humorous text and Layton's energetic illustrations demonstrate why humans don't have superpowers . . . and later spreads discuss the advantages and limitations of being very small or very big. . . . The spot-on comic delivery and readily comprehensible explanations make this a prime pick for readers curious about physical science in the natural world." Publ Wkly

Goodman, Susan, 1952-

Claws, coats, and camouflage; the ways animals fit into their world; photographs by Michael Doolittle. Millbrook Press 2001 48p il lib bdg $22.90

Grades: 2 3 4   **591.4**

1. Adaptation (Biology) 2. Animals

ISBN 0-7613-1865-8   LC 00-48167

"After a short introduction about adaptation, the photographs and text demonstrate how animals fit into their environment, stay safe, obtain food, and reproduce. . . . Both narrative and photographs are understandable, engaging, and informative." Booklist

Jenkins, Steve

Actual size. Houghton Mifflin 2004 unp il $16
*

Grades: K 1 2 3   **591.4**

1. Animals 2. Size

ISBN 0-618-37594-5   LC 2003-17462

In "torn-and-cut paper collages, Jenkins depicts 18 animals and insects—or a part of their body—in actual size. . . . The end matter offers full pictures of the creatures and more details about their habitats and habits. Mixing deceptive simplicity with absolute clarity, this beautiful book is an enticing way to introduce children to the glorious diversity of our natural world, or to illustrate to budding scientists the importance of comparison, measurement, observation, and record keeping. A thoroughly engaging read-aloud and a must-have for any collection." SLJ

Big & little. Houghton Mifflin 1996 unp il $16

Grades: K 1 2   **591.4**

1. Animals 2. Size

ISBN 0-395-72664-6   LC 95-41162

Jenkins "points out the differences in size between animals who are similar in other ways. The artwork combines cuttings of colored, textured papers to form animals that stand out strikingly against white backgrounds. . . . One line of text comments on the two animals' sizes, habits, or habitats. The final pages include a presentation of the comparative sizes of all the animals, [and] a paragraph of additional information about each species." Booklist

Includes bibliographical references

Miller, Debbie S.

Arctic lights, arctic nights; illustrations by Jon Van Zyle. Walker & Co. 2003 unp il map $16.95; pa $7.95

Grades: 2 3 4   **591.4**

1. Animals—Arctic regions 2. Natural history—Alaska

ISBN 0-8027-8856-4; 0-8027-9636-2 (pa)

                       LC 2002-191047

Describes the unique light phenomena of the Alaskan Arctic and the way animals adapt to the temperature and daylight changes each month of the year

The "brief text includes not only lyrical messages about light and its partner, darkness, but also references to the reaction of wildlife to the waxing and waning. . . . Wrapped about this unfamiliar (to many of us) swirl of seasons of light are Van Zyle's superb and quietly

Miller, Debbie S.—*Continued*

beautiful acrylic paintings, which capture both light and dark in perfect harmony with the text." SLJ

Includes glossary

Miller, Sara Swan

All kinds of ears. Marshall Cavendish Benchmark 2007 48p il (All kinds of . . .) lib bdg $29.93 *

Grades: 3 4 5 6   591.4

1. Ear 2. Animals

ISBN 978-0-7614-2518-2 (lib bdg); 0-7614-2518-7 (lib bdg)

This describes the various forms and functions of animal ears

Includes glossary and bibliographical references

All kinds of eyes. Marshall Cavendish Benchmark 2007 48p il (All kinds of . . .) lib bdg $29.93 *

Grades: 3 4 5 6   591.4

1. Eye 2. Animals

ISBN 978-0-7614-2519-9 (lib bdg); 0-7614-2519-5 (lib bdg)

This describes the various forms and functions of eyes in animals

"The excellent content and rare photographs will appeal to children, whether for research or leisure reading." SLJ

Includes glossary and bibliographical references

All kinds of feet. Marshall Cavendish Benchmark 2007 48p il (All kinds of . . .) lib bdg $29.93 *

Grades: 3 4 5 6   591.4

1. Foot 2. Animals

ISBN 978-0-7614-2520-5 (lib bdg); 0-7614-2520-9 (lib bdg)

This describes the various forms and functions of animal feet

"The excellent content and rare photographs will appeal to children, whether for research of leisure reading." SLJ

Includes glossary and bibliographical references

All kinds of mouths. Marshall Cavendish Benchmark 2007 48p il (All kinds of . . .) lib bdg $29.93 *

Grades: 3 4 5 6   591.4

1. Mouth 2. Animals

ISBN 978-0-7614-2521-2 (lib bdg); 0-7614-2521-7 (lib bdg)

This describes the various forms and functions of animal mouths

"The excellent content and rare photographs will appeal to children, whether for research or leisure reading." SLJ

Includes glossary and bibliographical references

All kinds of noses. Marshall Cavendish Benchmark 2007 48p il (All kinds of . . .) lib bdg $29.93 *

Grades: 3 4 5 6   591.4

1. Nose 2. Animals

ISBN 978-0-7614-2522-9 (lib bdg); 0-7614-2522-5 (lib bdg)

This describes the various forms and functions of animal noses

"The excellent content and rare photographs will appeal to children, whether for research or leisure reading." SLJ

Includes glossary and bibliographical references

All kinds of skin. Marshall Cavendish Benchmark 2007 48p il (All kinds of . . .) lib bdg $29.93 *

Grades: 3 4 5 6   591.4

1. Skin 2. Animals

ISBN 978-0-7614-2713-1 (lib bdg); 0-7614-2713-9 (lib bdg)

This describes the shapes and functions of animal exteriors found in nature, including skin, feathers, fur, and scales

Includes glossary and bibliographical references

Patkau, Karen

Creatures great and small. Tundra Books 2006 unp il $17.95

Grades: K 1 2 3   591.4

1. Animals 2. Size

ISBN 978-0-88776-754-8; 0-88776-754-0

"Each spread in this informational picture book shows a large animal filling a page-and-a-half scene and a small one from a similar classification on the right edge. . . . Sharp lines, bold colors, and careful composition of the computer-generated art successfully convey the rich variety of creatures and environments, accentuating similarities and differences. . . . Labeled illustrations at the back of the book introduce concepts of scale in a clear and inviting way." SLJ

Includes glossary

Posada, Mia

Guess what is growing inside this egg. Millbrook Press 2007 unp il lib bdg $15.95

Grades: K 1 2 3   591.4

1. Eggs 2. Animals

ISBN 978-0-8225-6192-7 (lib bdg); 0-8225-6192-1 (lib bdg)   LC 2006-16250

"This attractive picture book presents six animals that hatch from eggs: penguins, alligators, ducklings, sea turtles, spiders, and octopuses. . . . The first spread is a guessing game, telling a little about the animal in two rhymed couplets, showing a closeup of an egg in its natural setting, and asking 'Can you guess what is growing inside this egg?' The next spread reveals the answer to the riddle and offers information about the featured animal's physical attributes and behaviors. Distinctive collage-and-watercolor artwork offers eye-catching views of the animals within their habitats." Booklist

Rodriguez, Ana Maria, 1958-
Secret of the puking penguins . . . and more!
Enslow Publishers 2008 c2009 48p il (Animal
secrets revealed!) lib bdg $23.93
Grades: 5 6 7 8   **591.4**
    1. Reptiles 2. Birds
    ISBN 978-0-7660-2955-2 (lib bdg); 0-7660-2955-7 (lib
    bdg)   LC 2007-39490
In this title "readers learn not only why King penguin
fathers regurgitate food to feed their newborn chicks, but
also how chameleons grip prey with their powerful
tongue, along with some unusual information about alligators, cuckoos, and peacock feathers. Each topic is covered in six to nine pages with a short Meet the Scientists
section. The methodology used by each scientist or team
of scientists to make the discoveries is carefully explained is a lively and accessible manner. . . . The photo
illustrations . . . are of excellent quality, well placed,
and helpful." Booklist
    Includes glossary and bibliographical references

Schwartz, David M., 1951-
Where else in the wild? more camouflaged
creatures concealed and revealed; by David M.
Schwartz and Yael Schy; eye-tricking photographs
by Dwight Kuhn. Tricycle Press 2009 unp il
$16.99
Grades: 2 3 4   **591.4**
    1. Camouflage (Biology) 2. Animals 3. Poetry—By
    individual authors
    ISBN 978-1-58246-283-7; 1-58246-283-6
Presents poems and brief facts about eleven animals
that rely on the ability to camouflage within nature to
survive in the wilderness
    "Poetry and photography work well together in this
beautifully illustrated book. . . . Notable for its finesse
and variety, the poetry includes rhymed verse, as well as
haiku and concrete poems. A playful, informative introduction to camouflage in nature." Booklist

Where in the wild? camouflaged creatures
concealed—and revealed; ear-tickling poems by
David M. Schwartz and Yael Schy; eye-tricking
photos by Dwight Kuhn. Tricycle Press 2007 unp
il $15.95
Grades: 2 3 4   **591.4**
    1. Camouflage (Biology) 2. Animals 3. Poetry—By
    individual authors
    ISBN 978-1-58246-207-3; 1-58246-207-0
      LC 2006-101406
    "Ten creatures await, camouflaged in . . . full-page
photographs, while . . . poems offer clues about each
animal's identity and whereabouts." Publisher's note
    "The well-crafted, short poems . . . offer clues to the
hidden animals' identities. Beautifully photographed and
designed with great attention to detail, this book will intrigue and challenge children." Booklist

Singer, Marilyn, 1948-
Eggs; illustrated by Emma Stevenson. Holiday
House 2008 unp il $16.95
Grades: 1 2 3 4   **591.4**
    1. Eggs 2. Animals
    ISBN 978-0-8234-1727-8; 0-8234-1727-1
    Explains the varieties, functions, and characteristics of
the eggs of a multitude of creatures, including insects,
birds, and reptiles
    "Smoothly written, the text creates an even, almost
conversational flow from page to page. . . . Stevenson
contributes large and small gouache paintings in a precise yet fluid style that suits the subject well." Booklist
    Includes glossary

Zoehfeld, Kathleen Weidner
What lives in a shell? illustrated by Helen K.
Davie. HarperCollins Pubs. 1994 32p il
(Let's-read-and-find-out science) pa $5.99
hardcover o.p.
Grades: K 1   **591.4**
    1. Shells 2. Animal defenses
    ISBN 0-06-445124-0 (pa)   LC 93-12428
    Describes such animals as snails, turtles, and crabs,
which live in shells and use these coverings as protection
    This book uses "interesting and accurate illustrations
and just the right words. . . . The science here is good,
and the explanations should cause young readers to want
to learn more." Sci Books Films

591.47   Protective and locomotor adaptations, color

Bishop, Nic, 1955-
The secrets of animal flight. Houghton Mifflin
1997 31p il $16
Grades: 3 4 5 6   **591.47**
    1. Flight 2. Animal behavior
    ISBN 0-395-77848-4   LC 96-23131
    "The mechanics of birds' flight are explored first; the
author then turns his attention to bats, and, finally, to insects. In conclusion, he discusses unanswered questions
that are still being researched." SLJ
    "The many colorful photographs (bolstered by a few
diagrams) expand the text with precision and beauty.
. . . A good choice for curious browsers as well as information seekers." Booklist
    Includes bibliographical references

Collard, Sneed B., III
Teeth; illustrated by Phyllis Saroff.
Charlesbridge 2008 32p il lib bdg $16.95; pa
$7.95
Grades: 1 2 3   **591.47**
    1. Teeth 2. Animals
    ISBN 978-1-58089-120-2 (lib bdg); 1-58089-120-9 (lib
    bdg); 978-1-58089-121-9 (pa); 1-58089-121-7 (pa)
      LC 2007-02266
    This describes types of animal teeth, how they are
used, how they grow, and the differences between teeth

Collard, Sneed B., III—*Continued*
and horns or antlers
"Packed with exciting information, this large-size picture book combines chatty prose . . . and clear, full-color illustrations to tell amazing facts." Booklist

Wings; illustrated by Robin Brickman. Charlesbridge 2008 31p il lib bdg $16.95; pa $7.95
Grades: 1 2 3   591.47
1. Wings 2. Flight 3. Animals
ISBN 978-1-57091-611-3 (lib bdg); 1-57091-611-X (lib bdg); 978-1-57091-612-0 (pa); 1-57091-612-8 (pa)
LC 2007-02265
This "looks at wing design and the shapes of birds, insects, and mammals, as well as at prehistoric flyers and birds that no longer fly. Human fascination with flying rounds out the discussion. Brickman's paper collages of winged animals are . . . impressive in texture and color." SLJ
Includes glossary and bibliographical references

Cooper, Jason, 1942-
Camouflage and disguise; [by] Jason Cooper. Rourke Pub. 2007 24p il (Let's look at animals) $22.79
Grades: K 1 2   591.47
1. Camouflage (Biology) 2. Animal defenses
ISBN 1-60044-170-X   LC 2006012744
This describes how animals are defended by camouflage and disguise.
Illustrated "with colorful lifelike photographs. Stimulating and relevant information is presented in a concise manner." Sci Books Films
Includes glossary and bibliographical references

Hooves and claws; [by] Jason Cooper. Rourke Pub. 2007 24p il (Let's look at animals) $22.79
Grades: K 1 2   591.47
1. Claws 2. Hoofs
ISBN 1-60044-173-4   LC 2006012633
This book describes how hooves and claws grow, their functions, and which animals have them.
Illustrated "with colorful lifelike photographs. Stimulating and relevant information is presented in a concise manner." Sci Books Films
Includes glossary and bibliographical references

Fielding, Beth
Animal colors; a rainbow of colors from animals around the world. EarlyLight Books 2009 32p il $14.95
Grades: K 1 2 3 4 5   591.47
1. Animals 2. Color
ISBN 978-0-9797455-4-6; 0-9797455-4-3
"A gorgeous, in-depth look at animal colors as they occur in nature. Highly graphic and visually appealing, the book is organized first by singular colors, followed by common combinations. . . . For the youngest readers, this book can be enjoyed as simply an excellent introduction to color and to identifying the animals. For older readers, this book holds appeal as it also provides factual information, such as habitat, behavior, and diet, in bite-size doses beneath each picture. The photography is sharp and clear. . . . Simply stunning." SLJ

Halpern, Monica
Underground towns, treetops, and other animal hiding places; by Monica Halpern. National Geographic 2007 40p (National Geographic science chapters) lib bdg $17.90
Grades: 3 4 5 6   591.47
1. Animals—Habitations 2. Animal defenses
ISBN 978-1-4263-0183-4 (lib bdg); 1-4263-0183-9 (lib bdg)
LC 2007007894
This is an introduction to hidden animal habitats, such as underground burrows, underwater, or treetops
This "book provides a clear, engaging introduction to the topic. . . . The [book's] clear design features many well-captioned photographs . . . charts, and diagrams." Horn Book Guide

Helman, Andrea, 1946-
Hide and seek; nature's best vanishing acts; photographs by Gavriel Jecan. Walker Pub. Co. 2008 unp il $16.95; lib bdg $17.85
Grades: 2 3 4   591.47
1. Camouflage (Biology) 2. Animal defenses
ISBN   978-0-8027-9690-5;   0-8027-9690-7; 978-0-8027-9691-2 (lib bdg); 0-8027-9691-5 (lib bdg)
LC 2007024242
"Animals' camouflage is equally effective at hiding prey from predators and predators from prey. This large-format book offers plenty of excellent photographs of animals in each category, arranged by type of habitat. . . . Throughout the book, the words seem to elaborate on the pictures." Booklist

Hickman, Pamela M., 1958-
Animals in motion; how animals swim, jump, slither and glide; written by Pamela Hickman; illustrations by Pat Stephens. Kids Can Press 2000 40p il hardcover o.p. pa $5.95
Grades: 3 4 5   591.47
1. Animal locomotion
ISBN 1-55074-573-5; 1-55074-575-1 (pa)
"The chapters are organized according to method of locomotion ('Swimmers and floaters,' 'Hoppers and jumpers,' 'Runners and walkers,' etc.). There's a lot of information to be found here, but what gives this book a different twist is that it encourages kids to think about the ways animals move and compare them to their own means of locomotion." SLJ

Higginson, Mel, 1942-
Feathers and fur; [by] Mel Higginson. Rourke Pub. 2007 24p il (Let's look at animals) $21.35
Grades: K 1 2   591.47
1. Feathers 2. Fur 3. Animals
ISBN 1-60044-171-8   LC 2006012748
This describes feathers and fur of birds and mammals
Illustrated "with colorful lifelike photographs. Stimulating and relevant information is presented in a concise manner." Sci Books Films
Includes glossary and bibliographical references

James, Raymond H., 1917-2001

Teeth and fangs; [by] Ray James. Rourke Pub. 2007 24p il (Let's look at animals) $21.35

Grades: K 1 2   **591.47**

1. Teeth 2. Animals

ISBN 1-60044-174-2   LC 2006012629

This "explains how teeth are used to eat different foods, and how some animals, such as alligators, grow more when the originals wear out." SLJ

Illustrated "with colorful lifelike photographs. Stimulating and relevant information presented in a concise manner." Sci Books Films

Includes glossary and bibliographical references

Jenkins, Steve

Living color. Houghton Mifflin 2007 unp il $17 *

Grades: 3 4 5 6   **591.47**

1. Animals—Color

ISBN 978-0-618-70897-0; 0-618-70897-9

                          LC 2007-12751

This "offers a pageant of the most stunning, vividly hued creatures on the planet. . . . This book opens by explaining that bright coloration goes beyond mere decoration. . . . Arranged by color, subsequent spreads feature a rainbow of animals rendered in Jenkins' celebrated cut-paper style. Each picture is accompanied by a paragraph of nicely distilled information." Booklist

What do you do when something wants to eat you? Houghton Mifflin 1997 unp il $16 *

Grades: K 1 2 3   **591.47**

1. Animal defenses

ISBN 0-395-82514-8   LC 96-44993

Describes how various animals, including an octopus, a bombadier beetle, a puff adder, and a gliding frog, escape danger

"Jenkins achieves remarkable anatomical detail in his boldly textured cut-paper collages; simple backgrounds keep attention tightly focused on the animals and their survival strategies." Bull Cent Child Books

Mitchell, Susan K., 1972-

Animal chemical combat; poisons, smells, and slime; [by] Susan K. Mitchell. Enslow Publishers 2009 48p il (Amazing animal defenses) lib bdg $23.93

Grades: 4 5 6   **591.47**

1. Animal defenses

ISBN 978-0-7660-3294-1 (lib bdg); 0-7660-3294-9 (lib bdg)   LC 2008-11075

"Readers will learn how animals defend themselves using a variety of weapons including poisons and scents." Publisher's note

"The closeup photos are frequent and well chosen, and accompanied by clear, simply phrased [text], which [is] more detailed than average and [takes] up most or all of the space on each page." SLJ

Includes glossary and bibliographical references

Animal mimics; look-alikes and copycats; [by] Susan K. Mitchell. Enslow Publishers 2009 48p il (Amazing animal defenses) lib bdg $23.93

Grades: 4 5 6   **591.47**

1. Animal defenses

ISBN 978-0-7660-3293-4 (lib bdg); 0-7660-3293-0 (lib bdg)   LC 2008-11449

"Find out how animals mimic other, and more dangerous animals to keep themselves safe from predators." Publisher's note

"The closeup photos are frequent and well chosen, and accompanied by clear, simply phrased [text], which [is] more detailed than average and [takes] up most or all of the space on each page." SLJ

Includes glossary and bibliographical references

Animals with awesome armor; shells, scales, and exoskeletons; [by] Susan K. Mitchell. Enslow Publishers 2009 48p il (Amazing animal defenses) lib bdg $23.93

Grades: 4 5 6   **591.47**

1. Animal defenses

ISBN 978-0-7660-3296-5 (lib bdg); 0-7660-3296-5 (lib bdg)   LC 2008-11456

"Readers will learn how animals such as armadillos and crabs protect themselves from predators." Publisher's note

"The closeup photos are frequent and well chosen, and accompanied by clear, simply phrased [text], which [is] more detailed than average and [takes] up most or all of the space on each page." SLJ

Includes glossary and bibliographical references

Animals with crafty camouflage; hiding in plain sight; [by] Susan K. Mitchell. Enslow Publishers 2009 48p il (Amazing animal defenses) lib bdg $23.93

Grades: 4 5 6   **591.47**

1. Camouflage (Biology) 2. Animal defenses

ISBN 978-0-7660-3291-0 (lib bdg); 0-7660-3291-4 (lib bdg)   LC 2008-11073

"Readers will find out about animals who blend in with their surroundings to avoid predators." Publisher's note

"The closeup photos are frequent and well chosen, and accompanied by clear, simply phrased [text], which [is] more detailed than average and [takes] up most or all of the space on each page." SLJ

Includes glossary and bibliographical references

Animals with wicked weapons; stingers, barbs, and quills; [by] Susan K. Mitchell. Enslow Publishers 2009 48p il (Amazing animal defenses) lib bdg $23.93

Grades: 4 5 6   **591.47**

1. Animal defenses

ISBN 978-0-7660-3292-7 (lib bdg); 0-7660-3292-2 (lib bdg)   LC 2008-11075

"Readers will learn about the weapons that different animals have to protect themselves from predators." Publisher's note

"The closeup photos are frequent and well chosen, and accompanied by clear, simply phrased [text], which [is] more detailed than average and [takes] up most or all of the space on each page." SLJ

Includes glossary and bibliographical references

Pryor, Kimberley Jane

Amazing armor. Marshall Cavendish Benchmark 2009 32p il (Animal attack and defense) $19.95
Grades: 2 3 4   **591.47**
  1. Animal defenses
  ISBN 978-0-7614-4424-4; 0-7614-4424-6
                          LC 2009-4996
"Discusses how animals use armor to protect themselves from predators or to catch prey." Publisher's note
"Students will enjoy the large vivid photographs that allow for a closeup look at the animal, along with the excellent descriptions of the different survival methods. . . . Pryor does a good job of bringing the information down to a level that an elementary student would understand without losing any of the important details. . . . [This] would be a great addition to any nonfiction collection." Libr Media Connect
  Includes glossary

Clever camouflage. Marshall Cavendish Benchmark 2009 32p il (Animal attack and defense) $19.95
Grades: 2 3 4   **591.47**
  1. Camouflage (Biology) 2. Animal defenses
  ISBN 978-0-7614-4420-6; 0-7614-4420-3
                          LC 2009-4997
"Discusses how animals use camouflage to protect themselves from predators or to catch prey." Publisher's note
"Students will enjoy the large vivid photographs that allow for a closeup look at the animal, along with the excellent descriptions of the different survival methods. . . . Pryor does a good job of bringing the information down to a level that an elementary student would understand without losing any of the important details. . . . [This] would be a great addition to any nonfiction collection." Libr Media Connect
  Includes glossary

Mimicry and relationships. Marshall Cavendish Benchmark 2009 32p il (Animal attack and defense) $19.95
Grades: 2 3 4   **591.47**
  1. Animal defenses
  ISBN 978-0-7614-4421-3; 0-7614-4421-1
                          LC 2009-4995
"Discusses how animals use mimicry and relationships to protect themselves from predators or to catch prey." Publisher's note
"Students will enjoy the large vivid photographs that allow for a closeup look at the animal, along with the excellent descriptions of the different survival methods. . . . Pryor does a good job of bringing the information down to a level that an elementary student would understand without losing any of the important details. . . . [This] would be a great addition to any nonfiction collection." Libr Media Connect
  Includes glossary

Tricky behavior. Marshall Cavendish Benchmark 2009 32p il (Animal attack and defense) $19.95
Grades: 2 3 4   **591.47**
  1. Animal defenses
  ISBN 978-0-7614-4425-1; 0-7614-4425-4
                          LC 2009-4993

"Discusses how animals use tricky behavior to protect themselves from predators or to catch prey." Publisher's note
"Students will enjoy the large vivid photographs that allow for a closeup look at the animal, along with the excellent descriptions of the different survival methods. . . . Pryor does a good job of bringing the information down to a level that an elementary student would understand without losing any of the important details. . . . [This] would be a great addition to any nonfiction collection." Libr Media Connect
  Inlcudes glossary

Warning colors. Marshall Cavendish Benchmark 2009 32p il (Animal attack and defense) $19.95
Grades: 2 3 4   **591.47**
  1. Animal defenses
  ISBN 978-0-7614-4419-0; 0-7614-4419-X
                          LC 2009-4992
"Discusses how animals use warning colors to protect themselves from predators or to catch prey." Publisher's note
"Students will enjoy the large vivid photographs that allow for a closeup look at the animal, along with the excellent descriptions of the different survival methods. . . . Pryor does a good job of bringing the information down to a level that an elementary student would understand without losing any of the important details. . . . [This] would be a great addition to any nonfiction collection." Libr Media Connect
  Includes glossary

Racanelli, Marie

Animals with armor. PowerKids Press 2010 24p il (Crazy nature) lib bdg $21.25; pa $8.25
Grades: 2 3 4 5   **591.47**
  1. Animal defenses
  ISBN 978-1-4358-9386-3 (lib bdg); 1-4358-9386-7 (lib bdg); 978-1-4358-9864-6 (pa); 1-4358-9864-8 (pa)
                        LC 2009036527
This describes the different animals that have adapted defensive coverings, from turtles and snakes to armadillos, snails, and bugs
This book "combines attention-grabbing information with a well-organized format. . . . [The book has] spectacular color photography and eye-popping facts." SLJ

Camouflaged creatures. PowerKids 2010 24p il (Crazy nature) lib bdg $21.25; pa $8.25
Grades: 2 3 4 5   **591.47**
  1. Camouflage (Biology) 2. Animals
  ISBN 978-1-4358-9383-2 (lib bdg); 1-4358-9383-2 (lib bdg); 978-1-4358-9858-5 (pa); 1-4358-9858-3 (pa)
This explains how color, texture, and body shape allow animals to blend in seamlessly with their surroundings, with examples of camouflage in lizards, moths, beetles and other creatures
This book "combines attention-grabbing information with a well-organized format. . . . [The book has] spectacular color photography and eye-popping facts. . . . Excellent for reports." SLJ

591.5   Behavior

Batten, Mary
Please don't wake the animals; a book about
sleep; written by Mary Batten; illustrated by
Higgins Bond. Peachtree 2008 unp il $16.95
Grades: PreK K 1 2 3   **591.5**
  1. Animal behavior 2. Sleep
  ISBN 978-1-56145-393-1; 1-56145-393-5
                        LC 2007-31904
"This big bright picture book is an exciting way to
talk about the biology that connects humans with many
kinds of animals. 'All animals sleep,' and in all kinds of
places. Predators can sleep quite safely. . . . Their prey,
however, must stay alert, hardly daring to sleep at all.
. . . There's also information about animals that hibernate." Booklist

Fielding, Beth
Animal baths; wild & wonderful ways animals
get clean! illustrations by Susan Greenelsh.
EarlyLight Books 2009 47p il $14.95
Grades: 3 4 5   **591.5**
  1. Animal behavior 2. Baths 3. Cleanliness
  ISBN 978-0-9797455-2-2; 0-9797455-2-7
"Written in a conversational tone, this book is divided
into three parts based on how animals clean themselves.
. . . Each section begins with a brief description of how
and why they engage in specific activities, followed by
a spread about which ones utilize this method. A full-
page, softly colored drawing of the animals 'bathing'
faces each page of text. This fascinating book provides
some unusual details about the unique behavior of the
featured creatures." SLJ

Fraser, Mary Ann
Where are the night animals? HarperCollins
Pubs. 1999 29p il (Let's-read-and-find-out science)
$15.95; lib bdg $15.89; pa $4.95
Grades: K 1   **591.5**
  1. Animal behavior 2. Night
  ISBN 0-06-027717-3; 0-06-027718-1 (lib bdg);
  0-06-445176-3 (pa)   LC 97-34683
Describes various nocturnal animals and their nighttime activities, including the opossum, brown bat, and
tree frog
"The narrative approach and affable, realistic paintings
make this basic science lesson accessible and engaging to
the preschool audience." Horn Book Guide

Hirschi, Ron
Lions, tigers, and bears; why are big predators
so rare? [by] Ron Hirschi; photographs by Thomas
D. Mangelsen. Boyds Mills Press 2007 40p il
$16.95 *
Grades: 3 4 5 6   **591.5**
  1. Predatory animals 2. Wildlife conservation
  ISBN 978-1-59078-435-8; 1-59078-435-9
                        LC 2006037956

"Cougars, polar bears, lions, cheetahs, tigers, grizzly
bears, and killer whales are nature's threatened giants.
Each one gets its due in this important book. Hirschi's
approach is gentle and engaging, but the urgency of his
message is not lost—these animals need human help.
. . . The text is clear and easy to follow, and the problems are balanced with hope. . . . Mangelsen's crisp col-
or photographs are beautifully composed and heart-
grabbing." SLJ
Includes bibliographical references

Jenkins, Steve
How many ways can you catch a fly? [by]
Steve Jenkins & Robin Page. Houghton Mifflin
Company 2008 unp il $16 *
Grades: PreK K 1 2 3   **591.5**
  1. Food chains (Ecology) 2. Animal behavior
  ISBN 978-0-618-96634-9; 0-618-96634-X
                        LC 2008-01864
"This picture book is about the food chain. . . . The
facts about how particular animals escape danger and
evade predators to stay alive are just as exciting as the
facts about hunting. With clear, gorgeous, freestanding
images in cut- and torn-paper collage, each double-page
spread shows detailed species close up, as well as the
connections between animals." Booklist
Includes bibliographical references

Kaner, Etta, 1947-
Animals migrating; how, when, where and why
animals migrate; written by Etta Kaner; illustrated
by Pat Stephens. Kids Can Press 2005 40p il
$12.95; pa $5.95
Grades: 2 3 4   **591.5**
  1. Animals—Migration
  ISBN 1-55337-547-5; 1-55337-548-3 (pa)
This briefly describes the migration of mammals,
birds, insects, sea life, and reptiles and amphibians.
"Packed with fascinating facts about a wide range of
migrating animals and relayed in chatty style, this attractive picture book is illustrated with handsome line-and-
watercolor pictures." Booklist

Krautwurst, Terry, 1946-
Night science for kids; exploring the world after
dark; by Terry Krautwurst. Lark Books 2003 144p
il $19.95
Grades: 4 5 6   **591.5**
  1. Animals 2. Night
  ISBN 1-57990-411-4   LC 2003-4388
  Contents: Into the night; Becoming a night explorer;
Night animals; The fly-by-nights; Insects in the night;
Eyes to the sky; The edges of night
  Provides ideas and activities for discovering what
changes in the world after dark, including the arrival of
moths and owls, fog, and the stars
"The writing is clear and readable, with a light and
sometimes humorous tone. Outstanding full-color photos
illustrate the projects well." SLJ

Pipe, Jim, 1966-

Swarms; written by Jim Pipe; created and designed by David Salariya. Franklin Watts 2009 32p il (Scary creatures) lib bdg $26; pa $8.95

Grades: 3 4 5   **591.5**

1. Animal behavior

ISBN 978-0-531-21674-3 (lib bdg); 0-531-21674-8 (lib bdg); 978-0-531-21045-1 (pa); 0-531-21045-6 (pa)

LC 2009010800

This describes the behavior of large groups of similar animals such as insects, birds, or fish, all moving in the same direction

This title has "two-page chapters of accessible, large-type text and bright color photos and illustrations. . . . The series distinguishes itself with 'X-Ray Vision.' When readers hold the page with this prompt up to the light, an image emerges. The X-rays mostly show the skeletal structures of the animals. Text boxes throughout add to the visual appeal. . . . [This is an] excellent [resource] for school assignments and browsing." SLJ

Includes glossary

Racanelli, Marie

Animal mimics. PowerKids Press 2010 24p il (Crazy nature) lib bdg $21.25; pa $8.25

Grades: 2 3 4 5   **591.5**

1. Animal behavior

ISBN 978-1-4358-9382-5 (lib bdg); 1-4358-9382-4 (lib bdg); 978-1-4358-9856-1 (pa); 1-4358-9856-7 (pa)

Mimicry is an animal adaptation used both by prey and predators to disguise them in their habitats. The different kinds of mimicry are explored, along with specific examples of each type

This book "combines attention-grabbing information with a well-organized format. . . . [The book has] spectacular color photography and eye-popping facts. . . . Excellent for reports." SLJ

Underground animals. PowerKids 2010 24p il (Crazy nature) lib bdg $21.25; pa $8.25

Grades: 2 3 4 5   **591.5**

1. Animals

ISBN 978-1-4358-9384-9 (lib bdg); 1-4358-9384-0 (lib bdg); 978-1-4358-9860-8 (pa); 1-4358-9860-5 (pa)

This describes animals that live underground from burrowers to cave-dwellers, such as earthworms, moles, ants, badgers, desert tortoises

This book "combines attention-grabbing information with a well-organized format. . . . [The book has] spectacular color photography and eye-popping facts. . . . Excellent for reports." SLJ

Settel, Joanne

Exploding ants; amazing facts about how animals adapt. Atheneum Bks. for Young Readers 1999 40p il $16.95

Grades: 4 5 6 7   **591.5**

1. Animal behavior

ISBN 0-689-81739-8   LC 97-35395

Describes examples of animal behavior that may strike humans as disgusting, including the "gross" ways animals find food, shelter, and safety in the natural world

"This attractive volume presents its material as wondrous science instead of sensational effect." Booklist

Includes glossary and bibliographical references

591.56   Behavior relating to life cycle

Bancroft, Henrietta

Animals in winter; by Henrietta Bancroft and Richard G. Van Gelder; illustrated by Helen K. Davie. rev ed. HarperCollins Pubs. 1997 32p il (Let's-read-and-find-out science) hardcover o.p. pa $4.95

Grades: K 1   **591.56**

1. Animal behavior 2. Winter

ISBN 0-06-027158-2; 0-06-445165-8 (pa)

LC 95-36246

First published 1963

Describes the many different ways animals cope with winter, including migration, hibernation, and food storage

"The words are immediate . . . and the clear, active illustrations will draw new readers to a popular subject." Booklist

Collard, Sneed B., III

Animal dads; [by] Sneed B. Collard III; illustrated by Steve Jenkins. Houghton Mifflin 1997 unp il $15.95; pa $5.95

Grades: K 1 2 3   **591.56**

1. Animal behavior

ISBN 0-395-83621-2; 0-618-03299-1 (pa)

LC 96-22171

"The text highlights the roles and responsibilities of male parents in the wild, primarily the protection and care of their young." Horn Book Guide

"Each father and his offspring are presented on a single or double-page spread, illustrated with striking, cut-paper collage figures. The large, lifelike creatures are set against backgrounds that are true to each animal's natural habitat." SLJ

Animals asleep; illustrated by Anik McGrory. Houghton Mifflin 2004 unp il $15

Grades: K 1 2 3   **591.56**

1. Animal behavior 2. Sleep

ISBN 0-618-27697-1

Provides a look at the many different ways in which animals sleep, from a snoozing orangutan to a sleeping whale, as well as facts about each animal pictured.

"A parent or child could read just a few words appearing in large type or dip into the smaller-print paragraph of related information below. . . . McGrory's paintings offer graceful, well-composed depictions of beasts, birds, and butterflies in a series of beautifully lit settings." Booklist

Fraser, Mary Ann

How animal babies stay safe. HarperCollins Pubs. 2002 33p il (Let's-read-and-find-out science) hardcover o.p. pa $4.95

Grades: K 1   **591.56**

1. Animal babies

ISBN 0-06-028803-5; 0-06-445211-5 (pa)

LC 00-57267

Fraser, Mary Ann—*Continued*

The author "describes how animal babies are cared for by their parents, including alligator babies who are carried about in their mother's mouth and young elephants who are placed in the middle of the herd for protection. Watercolor illustrations in muted colors help expand the simple text." Horn Book Guide

Hickman, Pamela M., 1958-

Animals and their mates; how animals attract, fight for and protect each other; written by Pamela Hickman; illustrated by Pat Stephens. Kids Can Press 2004 40p il $10.95; pa $5.95

Grades: 3 4 5   **591.56**
   1. Animal behavior
   ISBN 1-55337-545-9; 1-55337-546-7 (pa)

"From insects and worms to birds and mammals, this colorfully illustrated introduction considers the who, what, when, where and how of mating. Though not detailed about the mechanics of reproduction, the book discusses matters such as amusing, bizarre, or aggressive courtship behaviors and the reasons certain animals mate at specific times of the year. . . . Tinted with colorful washes, the attractive artwork shows many different animals in a variety of habitats." Booklist

Animals and their young; how animals produce and care for their babies; written by Pamela Hickman; illustrated by Pat Stephens. Kids Can Press 2003 40p il $10.95; pa $5.95

Grades: 3 4 5   **591.56**
   1. Animal babies
   ISBN 1-55337-061-9; 1-55337-062-7 (pa)

The author compares "human babies and animals such as an Atlantic puffin chick, branching out to show how creatures that lay eggs are similar and different, and then . . . [discusses] mammals and marsupials." SLJ

"Young naturalists will appreciate this picture-book-size take on animals' habits. . . . [It is a] clear, colorfully illustrated exposition of animals' reproductive habits." Booklist

It's moving day! written by Pamela Hickman; illustrated by Geraldo Valério. Kids Can Press 2008 unp il $16.95

Grades: PreK K 1 2   **591.56**
   1. Animals—Habitations 2. Forest animals
   ISBN 978-1-55453-074-8

"This book depicts woodland animals that share a common experience: inhabiting the same burrow for a time and moving from it. . . . The bright acrylic artwork depicts realistic animals with some subtle cartoon-like expressions. This book with delight young animal lovers, offering them some scientific information." Libr Media Connect

Jenkins, Steve

Sisters & brothers; sibling relationships in the animal world; [by] Steve Jenkins & Robin Page. Houghton Mifflin 2008 unp il $16 *

Grades: 2 3 4   **591.56**
   1. Animal behavior 2. Siblings
   ISBN 978-0-618-37596-7; 0-618-37596-1
                              LC 2007-34305

"Steve Jenkins and Robin Page investigate sibling relationships throughout the animal kingdom." Publisher's note

"This riveting picture book . . . is packed with amazing facts. . . . [The subjects are] depicted in crisp, gorgeous, cut-and-torn paper collages set against lots of white space. . . . The sibling focus is a way to include a wealth of fascinating facts." Booklist

Roemer, Heidi B.

Whose nest is this? by Heidi Bee Roemer; illustrated by Connie McLennan. NorthWord Books for Young Readers 2009 unp il $16.95

Grades: PreK K 1 2   **591.56**
   1. Birds—Nests 2. Animals—Habitations
   ISBN 978-1-58979-386-6; 1-58979-386-2
                            LC 2007021870

"This picture book describes the nests of various birds, insects, mammals, fish, and reptiles. Whether it's an elf owl's cavity in a giant Saguaro, a Caribbean flamingo's mound of mud in shallow water, or a sea turtle's sandy pit, these shelters are described in brief rhymed texts. . . . The creatures are brought to life in the engaging rhymes and vivid art." SLJ

Rylant, Cynthia

The journey; stories of migration; illustrated by Lambert Davis. Blue Sky Press 2006 unp il $16.99 *

Grades: 2 3 4   **591.56**
   1. Animals—Migration
   ISBN 0-590-30717-7   LC 2004-20762

"This large-format book begins with a brief introduction to animal migration before relating six tales of migration. These are . . . narratives relating the migratory habits of six species: the desert locust, the blue whale, the American silver eel, the monarch butterfly, the caribou, and the Arctic tern. . . . Well matched with Rylant's measured prose, Davis' paintings offer clearly delineated, well-composed views of the animals in different stages of growth and habitats." Booklist

Schubert, Ingrid, 1953-

Like people; [by] Ingrid and Dieter Schubert. Lemniscaat 2008 unp il $16.95

Grades: PreK K 1   **591.56**
   1. Animal behavior
   ISBN 978-1-59078-576-8   LC 2007018429
   Original Dutch edition 2006

This focuses "on the bonds between parent and child that cut across all species. Taking advantage of the large trim size, full-bleed watercolors and even small panels brim with details that construct an irresistible if imaginary animal kingdom. . . . The prose is warm and soothing, but the art, packed with quasirealistic, playful animals, will have readers fully alert and poring over the pages." Publ Wkly

Stockdale, Susan, 1954-

Carry me! animal babies on the move; written and illustrated by Susan Stockdale. Peachtree Publishers 2005 unp il $15.95

Grades: K 1 2   **591.56**

1. Animal behavior

ISBN 1-56145-328-5   LC 2004-16585

"The facts of zoology are both exciting and cuddly in this science picture book with clear, bright acrylic illustrations that show how various animals carry their babies. The settings give the big picture—from the African savannah and Antarctica to South America. Then children can look closely and find animal babies tucked into pouches, clinging to bellies, propped on shoulders, perched on feet, gripped between teeth." Booklist

Includes bibliographical references

Swinburne, Stephen R.

Safe, warm, and snug; illustrated by Jose Aruego and Ariane Dewey. Harcourt Brace & Co. 1999 unp il hardcover o.p. pa $7

Grades: K 1 2 3   **591.56**

1. Animal behavior 2. Animal babies

ISBN 0-15-201734-8; 0-15-216378-6 (pa)

LC 98-9978

"Gulliver books"

Describes how a variety of animals, including kangaroos cockroaches, and pythons, protect their unhatched eggs and young offspring from predators

"Swinburne's informative verses combine with Aruego and Dewey's delightful artwork. . . . Appended with notes offering additional details for each species, this will be useful for primary science units and story hours." Booklist

591.59   Communication

Baines, Rebecca

What did one elephant say to the other; a book about communication; by Becky Baines. National Geographic Society 2008 26p il (Zig zag) $14.95; lib bdg $19.90

Grades: PreK K 1   **591.59**

1. Animal communication

ISBN 978-1-4263-0307-4; 1-4263-0307-6; 978-1-4263-0308-1 (lib bdg); 1-4263-0308-4 (lib bdg)

LC 2008-07218

"Readers will learn a lot about elephants, habitats, [and] animal communication." Publisher's note

"Curiosity will be piqued by the vibrant color photographs, accommodating illustrations, large font size, and helpful captions. Special features include drawings superimposed over photographs, and a zigzag path at the end of . . . [the] book prompting readers to further explore the topic in new and fun ways." SLJ

Sayre, April Pulley

Secrets of sound; studying the calls and songs of whales, elephants, and birds. Houghton Mifflin 2002 63p il (Scientists in the field) $16 *

Grades: 4 5 6 7   **591.59**

1. Animal communication

ISBN 0-618-01514-0   LC 2001-51877

Examines the work of several bioacousticians, scientists who study the sounds made by living creatures, discussing the results and importance of their research

"This fascinating title shows the thrill of scientific discovery up close. . . . Lots of well-edited quotes from the scientists convey their contagious enthusiasm for what they do, and sharp color photos, sound charts, and activity boxes break up the text, making it even more readable." Booklist

Includes glossary and bibliographical references

591.6   Miscellaneous nontaxonomic kinds of animals

Davies, Nicola, 1958-

What's eating you? parasites—the inside story; [by] Nicola Davies; illustrated by Neal Layton. Candlewick Press 2007 60p il $12.99

Grades: 3 4 5 6   **591.6**

1. Parasites

ISBN 978-0-7636-3460-5; 0-7636-3460-3

LC 2007-25634

"Davies uses a conversational approach to introduce readers to those weird critters that consider their host to be 'just a pantry.' . . . The subject is inherently fascinating for kids and those who settle into read will find a good deal of information about some of the more familiar parasites. . . . The artwork adds a welcome comic veneer." Booklist

Gilpin, Daniel

Life-size killer creatures. Sterling 2006 28p il $9.95

Grades: 3 4 5 6   **591.6**

1. Dangerous animals

ISBN 1-4027-2701-1

"Life-size illustrations and foldout pages highlight this examination of predators. Each spread offers basic background and interesting facts about several creatures. . . . Life-size views are mixed in with smaller, detailed drawings, always clearly labeled." SLJ

Graham, Ian, 1953-

Microscopic scary creatures; written by Ian Graham; created and designed by David Salariya. Franklin Watts 2009 32p il (Scary creatures) lib bdg $26; pa $8.95

Grades: 3 4 5   **591.6**

1. Protozoa 2. Microorganisms 3. Parasites

ISBN 978-0-531-21673-6 (lib bdg); 0-531-21673-X (lib bdg); 978-0-531-21044-4 (pa); 0-531-21044-8 (pa)

LC 2009-11224

This defines microscopic creatures and describes their habitats and life cycles, and their relationships to humans.

This title has "two-page chapters of accessible, large-type text and bright color photos and illustrations. . . . The series distinguishes itself with 'X-Ray Vision.' When readers hold the page with this prompt up to the light, an image emerges. The X-rays mostly show the skeletal structures of the animals. Text boxes throughout

Graham, Ian, 1953-—*Continued*
add to the visual appeal. . . . [This title is an] excellent
[resource] for school assignments and browsing." SLJ
   Includes glossary

Jenkins, Steve
   Never smile at a monkey; and 17 other
important things to remember. Houghton Mifflin
Books for Children 2009 unp il $16 *
Grades: 1 2 3 4   **591.6**
   1. Dangerous animals
   ISBN 978-0-618-96620-2; 0-618-96620-X
                              LC 2009-32964
   "Eighteen alliterative rules showcase the dangerous
defense mechanisms of animals found in the wild."
Kirkus
   "A visually stunning book illustrated with cut paper
and torn collages. . . . This superlative illustrator has
given children yet another work that educates and
amazes." SLJ

Pryor, Kimberley Jane
   Venom, poison, and electricity. Marshall
Cavendish Benchmark 2009 32p il (Animal attack
and defense) $19.95
Grades: 2 3 4   **591.6**
   1. Poisonous animals 2. Animal defenses
   ISBN 978-0-7614-4422-0; 0-7614-4422-X
                               LC 2009-4994
   "Discusses how animals use venom, poison, and electricity to protect themselves from predators or to catch
prey." Publisher's note
   "Students will enjoy the large vivid photographs that
allow for a close-up look at the animal, along with the
excellent descriptions of the different survival methods.
. . . Pryor does a good job of bringing the information
down to a level that an elementary student would understand without losing any of the important details. . . .
[This] would be a great addition to any nonfiction collection." Libr Media Connect
   Inlcudes glossary

Racanelli, Marie
   Albino animals. PowerKids Press 2010 24p il
(Crazy nature) lib bdg $21.25; pa $8.25
Grades: 2 3 4 5   **591.6**
   1. Albinos and albinism 2. Animals—Color
   ISBN 978-1-4358-9381-8 (lib bdg); 1-4358-9381-6 (lib
bdg); 978-1-4358-9854-7 (pa); 1-4358-9854-0 (pa)
   This explains why different types of animals are born
without skin pigmentation and about the challenges they
must face in their natural environments
   This book "combines attention-grabbing information
with a well-organized format. . . . [The book has] spectacular color photography and eye-popping facts. . . .
Excellent for reports." SLJ

Singer, Marilyn, 1948-
   Venom. Darby Creek 2007 96p il $19.95 *
Grades: 5 6 7 8   **591.6**
   1. Poisonous animals
   ISBN 978-1-58196-043-3; 1-58196-043-3
   "Singer introduces a teeming menagerie of creatures
. . . that use venom for attack, defense, or, commonly,
both. . . . The close-up, color photos . . . include not
only views of many creepy crawlies but also such arresting scenes as wood ants spraying formic acid. . . .
Browsers and dedicated young naturalists alike will enthusiastically dig their teeth into this substantial survey."
Booklist

Wilkes, Angela
   Dangerous creatures; foreword by Steve
Leonard. Kingfisher 2003 63p il (Kingfisher
knowledge) $11.95 *
Grades: 5 6 7 8   **591.6**
   1. Dangerous animals
   ISBN 0-7534-5622-2   LC 2003-40063
   Describes various kinds of dangerous animals, such as
lions, piranhas, killer bees, and vampire bats

591.68   Rare and endangered
animals

Barry, Frances
   Let's save the animals; a flip-the-flap book.
Candlewick Press 2010 unp il $12.99
Grades: PreK K   **591.68**
   1. Endangered species 2. Wildlife conservation
   ISBN 978-0-7636-4501-4; 0-7636-4501-X
                              LC 2009022117
   "Barry's engaging entry brings young children into the
conversation [about wildlife conservation] without sacrificing an ounce of kid appeal. Sporting a rounded cover,
sturdy pages, and inventive die-cut flaps, this primer
presents 10 endangered species in their natural habitats.
. . . Barry's superb, colorful paper-collage illustrations
feature close-ups of friendly looking animals." Booklist

Collard, Sneed B., III
   In the wild. Marshall Cavendish Benchmark
2006 43p il (Science adventures) lib bdg $25.64
Grades: K 1 2 3   **591.68**
   1. Endangered species 2. Zoos 3. Primates 4. Wildlife
conservation
   ISBN 0-7614-1955-1
   This "explains the vital role zoos are playing in the
world by sending their scientists out into the field to
save animals such as Africa's great apes and Brazil's
golden lion tamarins." Publisher's note
   This is a "little gem of a book." Sci Books Films
   Includes glossary and bibliographical references

Hirsch, Rebecca E., 1969-
Helping endangered animals; by Rebecca Hirsch. Cherry Lake Pub. 2010 32p il (Save the planet) lib bdg $27.07
Grades: 3 4 5 6   **591.68**
  1. Endangered species
  ISBN 978-1-60279-658-4 (lib bdg); 1-60279-658-0 (lib bdg)   LC 2009-38094
"Language Arts Explorer"
Examines endangered species, how human activities have contributed to shrinking numbers, and what is being done to protect animals for the future
"At the beginning of . . . [the] book, readers are given a mission and advised to be alert to the facts provided so that they can successfully answer the questions at the end. . . . Children are made to feel part of the process; suggestions for how they can become involved abound." SLJ

Includes glossary and bibliographical references

Jenkins, Steve
Almost gone; the world's rarest animals. HarperCollins Pubs. 2006 33p il (Let's-read-and-find-out science) $16.99; pa $5.99
*
Grades: K 1 2 3   **591.68**
  1. Rare animals 2. Endangered species
  ISBN 0-06-053598-9; 0-06-053600-4 (pa)
    LC 2004-30199
The author "shows 21 endangered species, accompanying each image with a few sentences about the animal's habitat, a particular characteristic, and, sometimes, the reason for its endangered status." Booklist
"This engaging title is informative as well as visually stunning." SLJ

Taylor, Barbara, 1954-
Planet animal; saving Earth's disappearing animals. Barron's 2009 unp il $22.99
Grades: 3 4 5 6   **591.68**
  1. Endangered species 2. Rare animals
  ISBN 978-0-7641-6205-3; 0-7641-6205-5
"This interactive, oversize book pairs information about endangered species and their habitats with attention-grabbing details. Accompanying full-color photographs are panels, tabs and removable cards that enliven animal descriptions . . . along with reasons that each is endangered." Publ Wkly

591.7 Animal ecology, animals characteristic of specific environments

Arnosky, Jim
Watching desert wildlife. National Geographic Soc. 1998 unp il hardcover o.p. pa $7.95
Grades: 3 4 5 6   **591.7**
  1. Desert animals
  ISBN 0-7922-7304-4; 0-7922-6737-0 (pa)
    LC 98-13189

Illustrations and text describe some of the animals the author encountered in the deserts of the American Southwest
"An informative and well-illustrated addition to science units on desert wildlife." Booklist

Barnhill, Kelly Regan
Monsters of the deep; deep sea adaptation; by Kelly Regan Barnhill. Capstone Press 2008 32p il (Fact finders. Extreme life) lib bdg $22.60
Grades: 2 3 4   **591.7**
  1. Ocean bottom 2. Marine animals
  ISBN 978-1-4296-1264-7 (lib bdg); 1-4296-1264-9 (lib bdg)   LC 2007-20897
This reveals "the world of deep-sea creatures. A conversational text explains how the animals have adapted to the incredible depth and darkness of the ocean's 'midnight zone.' Readers will be fascinated—or terrified—by the unusual-looking fish." Horn Book Guide
Includes glossary and bibliographical references

Bateman, Donna M.
Deep in the swamp; [by] Donna M. Bateman; illustrated by Brian Lies. Charlesbridge 2007 unp il lib bdg $15.95; pa $6.95
Grades: K 1 2 3   **591.7**
  1. Swamp animals 2. Counting
  ISBN 978-1-57091-596-3 (lib bdg); 978-1-57091-597-0 (pa)   LC 2006009026
"This stunning book spotlights the flora and fauna of Florida's Okefenokee Swamp. . . . The text is a version of the familiar poem 'Over in the Meadow,' with impeccable meter. . . . Lie's meticulous and glowing acrylic illustrations feature myriad shades of green, yellow, and blue." SLJ

Berger, Melvin, 1927-
Penguins swim but don't get wet; and other amazing facts about polar animals; [by] Melvin and Gilda Berger. Scholastic 2004 48p il (Speedy facts) pa $7.99
Grades: 2 3 4   **591.7**
  1. Animals—Arctic regions 2. Animals—Antarctica
  ISBN 0-439-62535-1
Introduction to polar animals.
"The facts are amazing and entertaining in this title . . . and a wealth of information is presented with clarity and excitement in pages that are packed with color photos and lots of boxed facts." Booklist

Bredeson, Carmen
Baby animals of the desert. Enslow Publishers 2008 c2009 24p il map (Nature's baby animals) lib bdg $21.26
Grades: 1 2 3   **591.7**
  1. Desert animals 2. Animal babies
  ISBN 978-0-7660-3007-7 (lib bdg); 0-7660-3007-5 (lib bdg)   LC 2007029287
"Up-close photos and information about baby animals of the desert biome." Publisher's note
"Well-chosen, exceedingly endearing photos highlight this [book]. . . . Accessible to new readers." SLJ
Includes glossary and bibliographical references

Bredeson, Carmen—*Continued*

Baby animals of the frozen tundra. Enslow Publishers 2009 24p il map (Nature's baby animals) lib bdg $21.26

Grades: 1 2 3   **591.7**
1. Animals—Arctic regions 2. Animal babies
ISBN 978-0-7660-3002-2 (lib bdg); 0-7660-3002-4 (lib bdg)   LC 2007039472
"Up-close photos and information about baby animals of the tundra biome" Publisher's note
Includes glossary and bibliographical references

Baby animals of the grasslands. Enslow Publishers 2008 23p il map (Nature's baby animals) lib bdg $21.26

Grades: 1 2 3   **591.7**
1. Grasslands 2. Animal babies
ISBN 978-0-7660-3006-0 (lib bdg); 0-7660-3006-7 (lib bdg)   LC 2007-29284
"Up-close photos and information about baby animals of the grasslands biome." Publisher's note
"Well chosen, exceedingly endearing photos highlight this [book]. . . . Accessible to new readers." SLJ
Includes glossary and bibliographical references

Baby animals of the ocean. Enslow Publishers 2009 24p il (Nature's baby animals) lib bdg $21.26

Grades: 1 2 3   **591.7**
1. Marine animals 2. Animal babies
ISBN 978-0-7660-3003-9 (lib bdg); 0-7660-3003-2 (lib bdg)   LC 2007039469
"Up-close photos and information about baby animals of the ocean biome" Publisher's note
Includes glossary and bibliographical references

Baby animals of the tropical rain forest. Enslow Publishers 2008 c2009 24p il map (Nature's baby animals) lib bdg $21.26

Grades: 1 2 3   **591.7**
1. Rain forest animals 2. Animal babies
ISBN 978-0-7660-3004-6 (lib bdg); 0-7660-3004-0 (lib bdg)   LC 2007-29285
"Up-close photos and information about baby animals of the tropical rain forest biome." Publisher's note
"Well chosen, exceedingly endearing photos highlight this [book]. . . . Accessible to new readers." SLJ
Includes glossary and bibliographical references

Baby animals of the woodland forest. Enslow Publishers 2008 c2009 24p il map (Nature's baby animals) lib bdg $21.26

Grades: 1 2 3   **591.7**
1. Forest animals 2. Animal babies
ISBN 978-0-7660-3005-3 (lib bdg); 0-7660-3005-9 (lib bdg)   LC 2007039470
"Up-close photos and information about baby animals of the temperate forest biome." Publisher's note
"Well-chosen, exceedingly endearing photos highlight this [book]. . . . Accessible to new readers." SLJ
Includes glossary and bibliographical references

Carlson-Voiles, Polly, 1943-
Someone walks by; the wonders of winter wildlife; story and illustrations by Polly Carlson-Voiles. Raven Productions 2008 unp il $18.95; pa $12.95

Grades: K 1 2 3   **591.7**
1. Forest animals 2. Winter
ISBN 978-0-9801045-5-4; 0-9801045-5-6; 978-0-9801045-6-1 (pa); 0-9801045-6-4 (pa)   LC 2008036871
"Set in the northern woodland in winter, this picture book shows how a variety of animals adapt to the frigid, snowy environment. . . . Poetic metaphors, internal rhymes, and repeated sounds give a lyrical tone to the prose. A typical double-page spread introduces several animals . . . in a few lines of text and two collage illustrations that combine cut papers into effective compositions enhanced with ink drawings and watercolors for details and patterns." Booklist

Cerullo, Mary M., 1949-
The truth about dangerous sea creatures; written by Mary M. Cerullo; photographs by Jeffrey L. Rotman; illustrated by Michael Wertz. Chronicle Books 2003 46p il $15.95

Grades: 3 4 5   **591.7**
1. Marine animals
ISBN 0-8118-4050-6   LC 2003-828
Contents: Giant squid; Giant octopus; Blue-ringed octopus; Giant clam; Spiny sea urchin; Crown-of-thorns sea star; Jellies; Sea wasp; Surgeonfish; Cone shel; Stonefish; Lionfish; Coral reefs; Damselfish; Sea anemone; Sea snake;- Barracuda; Giant grouper; Puffer fish; Manta ray; Stingray; Torpedo ray; Basking shark and whale shark; Tiger shark; Bull shark; Great white shark
"This book looks at a variety of 'dangerous' sea animals, such as sharks, jellies, and a giant squid, and provides readers with solid information. . . . The amount of text is brief enough to keep the material accessible. Full-color photos and childlike drawings add a lot of visual appeal." SLJ
Includes bibliographical references

Cole, Joanna
The magic school bus on the ocean floor; illustrated by Bruce Degen. Scholastic 1992 unp il hardcover o.p. pa $6.99 *

Grades: 2 3 4   **591.7**
1. Ocean 2. Marine animals
ISBN 0-590-41430-5; 0-590-41431-3 (pa)   LC 91-17695
On another special field trip on the magic school bus, Ms. Frizzle's class learns about the ocean and the different creatures that live there
"Cole's straightforward text explains the main action while energetic (but never hectic), colorful doublespread pictures supply a wealth of detail. . . . A perfect match of text and art, this is another first-class entry in a stellar series that makes science fascinating and fun." Booklist

Dawes, John

Exploring the world of aquatic life; [consultant editor, John P. Friel; authors, John Dawes and Andrew Campbell] Chelsea House Publishers 2009 6v il set $210 *

Grades: 5 6 7 8   **591.7**

1. Marine animals—Encyclopedias 2. Reference books
ISBN 978-1-60413-255-7 (set); 1-60413-255-8 (set)
LC 2008-30416

This set "offers an introduction to the diversity of animals that inhabit oceans, rivers, and lakes. . . . Entries are arranged alphabetically. . . . [The set includes] more than 100 articles. . . . Large photographs and illustrations appear on every two-page spread. . . . With its large typeface, clear explanations, and open layout, this set will appeal to younger students and would be a useful addition to school and public libraries." Booklist

Includes bibliographical references

Ganeri, Anita, 1961-

The oceans' most amazing animals; [by] Anita Ganeri. Raintree 2008 32p il map (Animal top tens) lib bdg $27.50; pa $7.99

Grades: 3 4 5 6   **591.7**

1. Marine animals
ISBN 978-1-4109-3088-0 (lib bdg); 1-4109-3088-2 (lib bdg); 978-1-4109-3097-2 (pa); 1-4109-3097-1 (pa)
LC 2007-47399

"Interesting and unique animals . . . including mammals, reptiles, and insects are covered in [this book]. . . . Stylized pages include simply written descriptions, captioned color photographs of the animals, and sidebar blurbs of additional information. . . . [This book] serves as an excellent starting point for beginner animal researchers." Libr Media Connect

Includes bibliographical references

Grupper, Jonathan

Destination: deep sea. National Geographic Soc. 2000 31p il $16.95 *

Grades: 3 4 5 6   **591.7**

1. Marine animals
ISBN 0-7922-7693-0   LC 00-27643

Describes the physical characteristics, behavior, and habitat of various sea creatures, from familiar crabs to giant whales to tube worms

"Every stunning photograph is a celebration of ocean life." SLJ

Himmelman, John, 1959-

Who's at the seashore? written and illustrated by John Himmelman. NorthWord Books 2009 unp il $15.95

Grades: K 1   **591.7**

1. Seashore ecology 2. Animal behavior
ISBN 978-1-58979-387-3; 1-58979-387-0
LC 2008038264

"This quiet little book introduces some seaside creatures via a simple rhyming text and realistic illustrations. A ruddy turnstone uncovers a sand hopper, a watchful gull hits on the hopper, while a moon snail creates a sand collar to hold her eggs, and so on in a soft litany of beach denizens and their activities. Himmelman's larger-than-life watercolors spread across the facing pages, revealing not only the action described in the text, but also the participants in the next sequence." SLJ

Hodge, Deborah, 1954-

Desert animals; written by Deborah Hodge; illustrated by Pat Stephens. Kids Can Press 2008 24p il (Who lives here?) $14.95; pa $5.95

Grades: K 1 2 3   **591.7**

1. Desert animals
ISBN 978-1-55453-047-2; 1-55453-047-4; 978-1-55453-048-9 (pa); 1-55453-048-2 (pa)

This introduces animals that are built for living in the extremes of deserts, including Elf owls, sand cats, and scorpions.

Forest animals; written by Deborah Hodge; illustrated by Pat Stephens. Kids Can Press 2009 24p il (Who lives here?) $14.95; pa $5.95

Grades: K 1 2 3   **591.7**

1. Forest animals
ISBN 978-1-55453-070-0; 1-55453-070-9; 978-1-55453-071-7 (pa); 1-55453-071-7 (pa)

"This mini-guide to creatures of the northern forest features one animal per spread. A brief introduction . . . includes facts about the animal's home, diet, young, unique features and abilities, and/or survival techniques. The text provides enough detail to engage readers without overwhelming them. Uncluttered design and finely crafted realistic illustrations are strengths." Horn Book Guide

Polar animals; written by Deborah Hodge; illustrated by Pat Stephens. Kids Can Press 2008 24p il (Who lives here?) $14.95; pa $5.95

Grades: K 1 2 3   **591.7**

1. Animals—Arctic regions
ISBN 978-1-55453-043-4; 1-55453-043-1; 978-1-55453-044-1 (pa); 1-55453-044-X (pa)

This book describes "the animal inhabitants of [the arctic region]. . . . Each double-page spread highlights a specific animal [and] . . . muted illustrations . . . effectively supplement and help explain the text." Horn Book Guide

Rain forest animals; written by Deborah Hodge; illustrated by Pat Stephens. Kids Can Press 2008 24p il (Who lives here?) $14.95; pa $5.95

Grades: K 1 2 3   **591.7**

1. Rain forest animals
ISBN 978-1-55453-041-0; 1-55453-041-5; 978-1-55453-042-7 (pa); 1-55453-042-3 (pa)

This book describes "the animal inhabitants of [the rain forest]. . . . Each double-page spread highlights a specific animal [and] . . . muted illustrations . . . effectively supplement and help explain the text." Horn Book Guide

Hodge, Deborah, 1954-—*Continued*

Savanna animals; written by Deborah Hodge; illustrated by Pat Stephens. Kids Can Press 2009 24p il (Who lives here?) $14.95; pa $5.95
Grades: K 1 2 3   **591.7**
  1. Grassland ecology 2. Animals—Africa
  ISBN   978-1-55453-072-4;   1-55453-072-5; 978-1-55453-073-1 (pa); 1-55453-073-3 (pa)
"This well-illustrated book introduces . . . readers to . . . animals that live in the African savanna. . . . Basic information about the elephant, wildebeest (aka, the gnu), giraffe, meerkat, zebra, black mamba (a snake), lion, and ostrich is presented to two-page spreads. . . . The highlight of the book is the excellent illustrations that complement the brief text." Sci Books Films

Wetland animals; written by Deborah Hodge; illustrated by Pat Stephens. Kids Can Press 2008 24p il (Who lives here?) $14.95; pa $5.95
Grades: K 1 2 3   **591.7**
  1. Wetlands 2. Freshwater animals
  ISBN   978-1-55453-045-8;   1-55453-045-8; 978-1-55453-046-5 (pa); 1-55453-046-6 (pa)
Introduces the animals that are built for living in or on the water of swamps, ponds, bogs, and marshes, including hippos, moose, capybaras, and bullfrogs.

Jenkins, Steve

Down, down, down; a journey to the bottom of the sea. Houghton Mifflin Harcourt 2009 unp il $17 *
Grades: 2 3 4 5   **591.7**
  1. Marine animals 2. Ocean bottom
  ISBN 978-0-618-96636-3; 0-618-96636-6
                 LC 2008-36082
"Starting at the surface of the Pacific Ocean, Jenkins introduces some of the animals that inhabit descending layers of water all the way down to the Marianas Trench. At nearly 36,000 feet, this zone has been visited only once, by human passengers of a research vessel. Depicted in Jenkins's signature handsome collages, the denizens of each level swim against ever-darkening backgrounds ranging from sunny blue to deepest black. . . . The repeated message that humans have much to explore and learn in the deeper ocean is intriguing and inviting. " SLJ

How to clean a hippopotamus; a look at unusual animal partnerships; by Steve Jenkins and Robin Page; illustrations by Steve Jenkins. Houghton Mifflin 2010 32p il $16 *
Grades: K 1 2 3   **591.7**
  1. Symbiosis
  ISBN 978-0-547-24515-7; 0-547-24515-7
This picture book "explores unexpected animal partnerships. . . . The spreads have an exciting, comics-inspired feel. Each page combines panels of multiple images, rendered in Jenkins' superbly crafted paper-collage style, with brief lines of concise, clear text and attention-grabbing headlines. . . . These fascinating stories from the natural world will easily interest young people." Booklist

I see a kookaburra! discovering animal habitats around the world; [by] Steve Jenkins & Robin Page. Houghton Mifflin Co. 2005 unp il map $16 *
Grades: K 1 2 3   **591.7**
  1. Habitat (Ecology) 2. Animals
  ISBN 0-618-50764-7   LC 2004-13188
A pictorial introduction to desert, tide pool, jungle, savana, forest, and pond habitats, with examples of the animals that live in each
"Filled with vibrant colors and palpable textures, the illustrations are breathtaking and give a real sense of the vitality, diversity, and beauty of nature. A first-rate foray into ecology that will encourage readers to explore the world around them." SLJ
Includes bibliographical references

Johnson, Jinny

Simon & Schuster children's guide to sea creatures. Simon & Schuster Bks. for Young Readers 1998 80p il $21.95
Grades: 4 5 6 7   **591.7**
  1. Marine animals
  ISBN 0-689-81534-4   LC 97-8227
Describes the major groups of marine animals, including fish, birds, mammals, and crustaceans
"A beautifully illustrated guide, with a full-color drawing of each animal. . . . The book has enough information to be a useful research tool in the library. The organization, by habitat, is outstanding." Book Rep
Includes glossary

Kratter, Paul, 1956-

The living rain forest; an animal alphabet. Charlesbridge 2004 unp il $17.95
Grades: K 1 2 3   **591.7**
  1. Rain forest animals 2. Alphabet
  ISBN 1-57091-603-9   LC 2003-3761
Introduces twenty-six rain forest animals from A to Z, providing the name, favorite foods, and unique characteristics of each.
"The uncluttered layouts position the text blocks and the exquisite, photorealistic paintings of the animals against lots of white space. . . . With eye-catching visuals, an engaging theme, and basic information, the book will appeal to a wide age range." Booklist

Landstrom, Lee Ann, 1954-

Nature's yucky! 2: the desert southwest; by Lee Landstrom and Karen I. Shragg; illustrated by Rachel Rogge. Mountain Press Pub. Co. 2007 48p il pa $12
Grades: K 1 2 3   **591.7**
  1. Desert animals 2. Natural history—Southwestern States
  ISBN 978-0-87842-529-7 (pa); 0-87842-529-2 (pa)
                 LC 2006032479
This explains "the significance of adaptations of animals of the southwestern desert. . . . The illustrations are detailed and well done. . . . Each of the animals is well described." Sci Books Films

Mannis, Celeste Davidson

Snapshots; the wonders of Monterey Bay; words and pictures by Celeste Davidson Mannis. Viking 2006 unp il $16.99

Grades: K 1 2 3   591.7
  1. Marine animals 2. Natural history—California
3. Monterey (Calif.)
  ISBN 0-670-06062-3   LC 2005026407
Introduces young readers to the marine animals of Monterey Bay and the unique places that they inhabit there, offering facts and images to provide a closer look at the region's ecosystem.
  "The simple text can be shared with younger children while the boxed sections provide enough detail to interest older students. With stunning photographs and text that will meet the needs of a wide range of ages, this title will be a welcome addition to most collections." SLJ

McLimans, David

Gone fishing; ocean life by the numbers; [by] David McLimans. Walker 2008 unp il $16.99; lib bdg $17.89

Grades: 3 4 5   591.7
  1. Marine animals 2. Endangered species
  ISBN   978-0-8027-9770-4;   0-8027-9770-9;
978-0-8027-9564-9 (lib bdg); 0-8027-9564-1 (lib bdg)
                                            LC 2008014475
"Using animal-shaped numbers from 1 to 10 and back again, McLimans introduces various marine creatures and their survival status. An African penguin, sea lamprey, tiger tail sea horse, and blue-ringed octopus are among the featured species. . . . The black silhouetted numbers are sinuous and compelling in this unique and imaginative description of the dangers facing ocean life today." SLJ
  Includes bibliographical references

Miller, Debbie S.

Survival at 40 below; illustrations by Jon Van Zyle. Walker & Co. 2010 unp il $17.99; lib bdg $18.89

Grades: 2 3 4   591.7
  1. Natural history—Alaska 2. Animals—Arctic regions
  ISBN   978-0-8027-9815-2;   0-8027-9815-2;
978-0-8027-9816-9 (lib bdg); 0-8027-9816-0 (lib bdg)
                                            LC 2009013328
"Miller describes the terrain of Alaska's Gates of the Arctic National Park and explains how the seasonal changes affect a diverse array of animals . . . that live in the area year-round. . . . The text moves smoothly and quickly, offering interesting glimpses of varied hibernation patterns and the physical characteristics enabling some animals to survive winter's deep chill aboveground. . . . Van Zyle's acrylic paintings span the spreads, offering good impressionistic views of varied landscapes and fauna." SLJ

Mitton, Tony, 1951-

Rainforest romp; [by] Tony Mitton and [illustrated by] Ant Parker. Kingfisher 2009 unp il (Amazing animals) $9.99   591.7
  1. Rain forest animals
  ISBN 978-0-7534-6298-0; 0-7534-6298-2
  "In bouncy rhymes, Mitton describes animals that live in the rainforest. . . . Parker's vibrant cartoon illustrations show three animal friends, dressed in safari gear, exploring in the rainforest, along with the smiling creatures they encounter." Horn Book Guide

Parker, Steve

Animal habitats. QEB Pub. 2010 32p il (QEB changes in . . .) lib bdg $28.50

Grades: 3 4 5 6   591.7
  1. Habitat (Ecology)
  ISBN 978-1-59566-773-1 (lib bdg); 1-59566-773-3 (lib bdg)   LC 2008-56067
  "Outstanding photography and informative summaries uniquely combine to make this text a must have for any elementary school library. . . . Short, succinct paragraphs and marginalia combine to appeal to readers of all ages and literary abilities. The author guides the juvenile reader through a series of environmental concerns such as the preservation of rare and endangered species, sustainability, overpopulation, biodiversity hot spots, conservation techniques, and introduced and invasive species." Sci Books Films
  Includes glossary

Rose, Deborah Lee, 1955-

Into the A, B, sea; an ocean alphabet; pictures by Steve Jenkins. Scholastic Press 2000 unp il $15.95

Grades: K 1 2 3   591.7
  1. Marine animals 2. Alphabet
  ISBN 0-439-09696-0   LC 99-50034
  An alphabet book featuring twenty-six animals found in the ocean and including endnotes giving additional details about each of these sea creatures
  "The text reads aloud smoothly, with natural-sounding rhymes and an even pace. The collage artwork is breathtaking. Using a variety of textures and a palette of deep blues and purples, Jenkins captures the grace and vitality of his subjects." SLJ

Savage safari. Kingfisher 2010 il $14.99
  Grades: 2 3 4 5   591.7
  1. Animals—Africa
  ISBN 978-0-7534-6456-4; 0-7534-6456-X
                                            LC 2010015767
  "This look at the many dangerous beasts that are found in Africa describes their habitat, species name, measurements, and weight. A graph measures their level of intelligence, strength, speed, agility, and endurance. Each animal's enemies and prey are also pictured. An excellent photograph of a representative of each species is highlighted with bullet points around it describing specific traits. . . . The book is well organized and informative and would be useful for short reports. The artwork and the photography are excellent and fully complement the text." SLJ

Stewart, Melissa, 1968-
Under the snow; written by Melissa Stewart; illustrated by Constance R. Bergum. Peachtree 2009 unp il $16.95
Grades: K 1 2 3　　　　　**591.7**
　　1. Animal behavior 2. Snow 3. Winter
　　ISBN 978-1-56145-493-8; 1-56145-493-1
This describes how animals live under the snow in fields, forests, ponds, and wetlands
　　This is a "lyrical portrait. . . . Bergum's watercolor illustrations painted in panels suggest the passage of time and include close-up insets of wildlife in various habitats. . . . Many of the facts will wow children . . . and pique interest to read more." Booklist

When rain falls; written by Melissa Stewart; illustrated by Constance R. Bergum. Peachtree 2008 unp il $16.95
Grades: PreK K 1 2　　　　　**591.7**
　　1. Animal behavior 2. Rain
　　ISBN 978-1-56145-438-9; 1-56145-438-9
　　　　　　　　　　　LC 2007-31395
"After two children hurry inside to escape the rain, they gaze outdoors and wait for the end of the storm. Stewart elaborates on how various animals react to rain in different habitats: a forest, a field, a wetland, and a desert. The examples are clearly presented and interesting. . . . Bergum's well-rendered watercolors will facilitate group sharing." SLJ

Swinburne, Stephen R.
Ocean soup; tide pool poems; illustrated by Mary Peterson. Charlesbridge 2010 unp il lib bdg $16.95
Grades: 1 2 3　　　　　**591.7**
　　1. Animals—Poetry 2. Marine animals 3. Tide pool ecology
　　ISBN 978-1-58089-200-1 (lib bdg); 1-58089-200-0 (lib bdg)　　　　LC 2008026960
"This brightly illustrated, large-format book offers a collection of poems in the voices of tide-pool animals. . . . Each species is presented through first-person verse and a paragraph of information. . . . Clean, curving pencil lines with digitally added colors portray the animals in child-friendly, cartoon-style pictures." Booklist
　　Includes glossary and bibliographical references

The woods scientist; with photographs by Susan C. Morse. Houghton Mifflin 2002 41p il map (Scientists in the field) $16 *
Grades: 4 5 6 7　　　　　**591.7**
　　1. Morse, Susan 2. Forest animals
　　ISBN 0-618-04602-X　　　　LC 2002-302
A devoted nature lover and animal tracker, Sue Morse shares her knowledge and love of some of the creatures that inhabit America's woodlands
　　"The language is immediate, clear, and filled with moment-by-moment observations and well-presented facts. . . . Readers will come away with a much more informed view of wildlife at risk, enriched by Morse's superb color photographs." Booklist
　　Includes glossary and bibliographical references

Turner, Pamela S.
Prowling the seas; exploring the hidden world of ocean predators. Walker & Co. 2009 39p il map $17.99; lib bdg $18.89
Grades: 4 5 6　　　　　**591.7**
　　1. Marine animals 2. Predatory animals 3. Ocean
　　ISBN　　978-0-8027-9748-3;　　0-8027-9748-2; 978-0-8027-9749-0 (lib bdg); 0-8027-9749-0 (lib bdg)
"In 2000, a multinational group of scientists created the Tagging of Pacific Predators project (TOPP) to study the dwindling numbers of ocean predators and find ways to save them. This book reports on the work of scientists who fitted four species with satellite tags—loggerhead turtles, great white sharks, bluefin tuna, and sooty shearwater seabirds." SLJ
　　"In each chapter, a clearly delineated map makes it easy to follow the animals' routes, and many clear color photos show the animals and the scientists who study them. . . . A clearly written presentation of an unusual topic." Booklist

Woodward, John, 1954-
Creatures of the deep; written by John Woodward. Barron's Educational Series 2009 30p il (Discoverology) $18.99
Grades: 5 6 7 8　　　　　**591.7**
　　1. Marine animals 2. Ocean 3. Pop-up books
　　ISBN 978-0-7641-6232-9; 0-7641-6232-2
"Noting how little is known about the ocean depths, this volume . . . offers bits of information about that mysterious world and its inhabitants. Double-page spreads present topics such as the history of undersea exploration, modern research, food chains, hydro-thermal vents, and the ocean's sunlit zone, twilight zone, and dark zone." Booklist
　　"Flaps, foldouts, wheels, and pop-ups spill across the pages of this colorful title. . . . Each facing page unit . . . contains an introductory paragraph and a collection of color photos, realistic illustrations, and a sampling of the aforementioned doohickeys accompanied by brief, informative captions." SLJ

591.9　Treatment of animals by specific continents, countries, localities

Ganeri, Anita, 1961-
Africa's most amazing animals; [by] Anita Ganeri. Raintree 2008 32p il map (Animal top tens) lib bdg $27.50; pa $7.99
Grades: 3 4 5 6　　　　　**591.9**
　　1. Animals—Africa
　　ISBN 978-1-4109-3083-5 (lib bdg); 1-4109-3083-1 (lib bdg); 978-1-4109-3092-7 (pa); 1-4109-3092-0 (pa)
　　　　　　　　　　　LC 2007-47419
"Interesting and unique animals [of Africa] . . . including mammals, reptiles, and insects are covered in [this book]. . . . Stylized pages include simply written descriptions, captioned color photographs of the animals, and sidebar blurbs of additional information. . . . [This book] serves as an excellent starting point for beginner animal researchers." Libr Media Connect
　　Includes bibliographical references

Ganeri, Anita, 1961-—*Continued*

Asia's most amazing animals; [by] Anita Ganeri. Raintree 2008 32p il map (Animal top tens) lib bdg $27.50; pa $7.99

Grades: 3 4 5 6   **591.9**
    1. Animals—Asia
    ISBN 978-1-4109-3084-2 (lib bdg); 1-4109-3084-X (lib bdg); 978-1-4109-3093-4 (pa); 1-4109-3093-9 (pa)
                           LC 2007-47550
"Interesting and unique animals [of Asia] . . . including mammals, reptiles, and insects are covered in [this book]. . . . Stylized pages include simply written descriptions, captioned color photographs of the animals, and sidebar blurbs of additional information. . . . [This book] serves as an excellent starting point for beginner animal researchers." Libr Media Connect

Includes bibliographical references

Europe's most amazing animals; [by] Anita Ganeri. Raintree 2008 32p il map (Animal top tens) lib bdg $27.50; pa $7.99

Grades: 3 4 5 6   **591.9**
    1. Animals—Europe
    ISBN 978-1-4109-3086-6 (lib bdg); 1-4109-3086-6 (lib bdg); 978-1-4109-3095-8 (pa); 1-4109-3095-5 (pa)
                           LC 2007-47552
"Interesting and unique animals [of Europe] . . . including mammals, reptiles, and insects are covered in [this book]. . . . Stylized pages include simply written descriptions, captioned color photographs of the animals, and sidebar blurbs of additional information. . . . [This book] serves as an excellent starting point for beginner animal researchers." Libr Media Connect

Includes bibliographical references

South America's most amazing animals; [by] Anita Ganeri. Raintree 2008 32p il map (Animal top tens) lib bdg $27.50; pa $7.99

Grades: 3 4 5 6   **591.9**
    ISBN 978-1-4109-3090-3 (lib bdg); 1-4109-3090-4 (lib bdg); 978-1-4109-3099-6 (pa); 1-4109-3099-8 (pa)
                           LC 2007-47400
"Interesting and unique animals [of South America] . . . including mammals, reptiles, and insects are covered in [this book]. . . . Stylized pages include simply written descriptions, captioned color photographs of the animals, and sidebar blurbs of additional information. . . . [This book] serves as an excellent starting point for beginner animal researchers." Libr Media Connect

Includes bibliographical references

Haas, Robert B.
African critters. National Geographic 2008 91p il $17.95; lib bdg $26.90

Grades: 3 4 5   **591.9**
    1. Animals—Africa
    ISBN   978-1-4263-0317-3;   1-4263-0317-3; 978-1-4263-0318-0 (lib bdg); 1-4263-0318-1 (lib bdg)
This is a "beautiful photo-essay about African wildlife, which features pictures [Haas] took over several years in southern African game preserves. . . . Each of the chapters . . . provides fascinating details about animal behavior, and numerous boxed notes fill in more

facts about numbers and anatomy. . . . This book is a must-purchase. . . . An exceptionally strong combination of action, information, and conservation." Booklist

Hooper, Meredith
Antarctic journal; the hidden worlds of Antarctica's animals; illustrated by Lucia deLeiris. National Geographic Soc. 2000 35p il maps $16.95

Grades: 3 4 5 6   **591.9**
    1. Animals—Antarctica 2. Antarctica
    ISBN 0-7922-7188-2   LC 00-35496
"Hooper describes the three-and-a-half months she and deLeiris spent at Palmer Station, Antarctica, observing marine life. . . . The realistic watercolors and black-and-white sketches work well with the detailed text." Horn Book Guide

Lewin, Ted, 1935-
Elephant quest; [by] Ted & Betsy Lewin. HarperCollins Pubs. 2000 47p il $15.95; lib bdg $15.89

Grades: 3 4 5 6   **591.9**
    1. Animals—Africa
    ISBN 0-688-14111-0; 0-688-14112-9 (lib bdg)
                           LC 99-55369
Recounts an expedition through the Moremi Wildlife Reserve in Botswana, describing the vegetation and wildlife, and culminating in the sighting of an African elephant herd

"Each encounter is accompanied by glorious watercolors—Betsy Lewin's humorous, emotive sketches and Ted Lewin's full-page paintings. . . . Throughout, a cheerful, humorous tone combines with reverence for the beauty and variety of nature." Horn Book

592 Invertebrates

Cerullo, Mary M., 1949-
Sea soup: zooplankton; [by] Mary M. Cerullo; photography by Bill Curtsinger. Tilbury House 2001 39p il $16.95

Grades: 5 6 7 8   **592**
    1. Zooplankton
    ISBN 0-88448-219-7   LC 00-46721
This book "opens a pellucid window into the drifting world of mostly minute animals that, along with phytoplankton, form an aqueous 'soup' that nourishes a wide variety of sea creatures. . . . Curtsinger's often extraordinary color photos allow readers to envision the often microscopically small creatures delineated in the text. . . . This is a fascinating look at a watery zoo of creatures whose ecological importance is far beyond the measure of their size." SLJ

Includes glossary and bibliographical references

Dixon, Norma

Lowdown on earthworms. Fitzhenry & Whiteside 2005 32p il $16.95

Grades: 3 4 5   **592**

    1. Worms

    ISBN 1-55041-114-8

"This project-oriented study combines basic facts about worm anatomy and behavior with general instructions for building, maintaining, and performing simple experiments with both a 'plastic-bottle wormery'; and a more ambitious compost bin. A mix of color photos and simple paintings offer cutaways views of worms and their burrows, representations of several types of earthworms, and pictures of finished projects." Booklist

Includes bibliographical references

Pfeffer, Wendy, 1929-

Wiggling worms at work; illustrated by Steve Jenkins. HarperCollins Publishers 2004 33p il (Let's-read-and-find-out science) $15.99; lib bdg $16.89; pa $4.99

Grades: K 1 2 3   **592**

    1. Worms

    ISBN 0-06-028448-X; 0-06-028449-8 (lib bdg); 0-06-445199-2 (pa)

"This book is filled with clear explanations. . . . The concluding activities . . . are important because Jenkins's cut-paper illustrations, while lovely, include only a few anatomical details." Horn Book Guide

Trueit, Trudi Strain

Worms. Marshall Cavendish Benchmark 2009 23p il (Benchmark rebus. Creepy critters) lib bdg $22.79

Grades: PreK K 1   **592**

    1. Worms

    ISBN 978-0-7614-3966-0 (lib bdg); 0-7614-3966-8 (lib bdg)   LC 2008-15997

"Easy to read text with rebuses explores the different places worms can be found." Publisher's note

"Brilliant closeup photos will help beginning readers make meaning and appeal to students who like these creatures. . . . Glossary, print and media resources for further learning, and an about the author section conclude . . . [the] book. Reading specialists will want to be advised about [this book] . . . as will teachers. . . . This . . . is an excellent resource for beginning research projects." Publisher's note

Includes glossary and bibliographical references

593.4   Porifera (Sponges)

Coldiron, Deborah

Sea sponges; by Deborah Coldiron. ABDO Pub. 2008 32p il (Underwater world) lib bdg $24.21

Grades: 2 3 4   **593.4**

    1. Sponges

    ISBN 978-1-59928-812-3 (lib bdg); 1-59928-812-5 (lib bdg)   LC 2007-17851

"Present[s] basic information about [sea sponges]. . . . Vibrant captioned photos enhance the accessible text." Horn Book Guide

Includes glossary

593.5   Cnidaria (Coelenterata)

King, David C., 1933-

Jellyfish; by David C. King. Marshall Cavendish Benchmark 2006 48p il map (Animals, animals) lib bdg $23.64

Grades: 3 4 5 6   **593.5**

    1. Jellyfishes

    ISBN 0-7614-1867-9   LC 2004-21441

Describes the physical characteristics, behavior, and habitat of jellyfish

Includes glossary and bibliographical references

Wearing, Judy

Jellyfish. Weigl Publishers 2010 24p il (World of wonder: underwater life) lib bdg $24.45; pa $8.95

Grades: K 1 2   **593.5**

    1. Jellyfishes

    ISBN 978-1-60596-100-2 (lib bdg); 1-60596-100-0 (lib bdg); 978-1-60596-101-9 (pa); 1-60596-101-9 (pa)   LC 2009-25986

This book about jellyfish begins "with introductory information and progress[es] to more unique details of the featured creatures. Bold photographs juxtaposed on colorful background graphic will hold the attention of even the most novice readers. . . . [This book is] sure to make a splash with budding marine biologists everywhere." SLJ

Includes glossary

593.6   Anthozoa

Collard, Sneed B., III

One night in the Coral Sea; [by] Sneed B. Collard III; illustrated by Robin Brickmann. Charlesbridge 2005 32p il $15.95; pa $6.95 *

Grades: 3 4 5   **593.6**

    1. Corals 2. Coral reefs and islands

    ISBN 1-57091-389-7; 1-57091-390-0 (pa)   LC 2004-3307

"On a single spring night . . . the coral in the Great Barrier Reef releases millions of eggs into the ocean. . . . Collard explains the unique spawning event and provides some background about coral and the sea creatures that share the reef. . . . Whether or not children understand the specifics of fertilization, they will be captivated by Brickman's realistic, astonishingly detailed colored-paper collages of the brilliant underwater world." Booklist

Includes glossary and bibliographical references

593.9 Echinodermata and hemichordata

Blaxland, Beth
Sea stars, sea urchins, and their relatives; echinoderms; [by] Beth Blaxland for the Australian Museum. Chelsea House 2003 c2002 32p il (Invertebrates) $18.95
Grades: 3 4 5 6 **593.9**
1. Echinoderms
ISBN 0-7910-6996-6 LC 2002-3177
First published 2002 in Australia
Defines echinoderms, such as sand dollars and crown-of-thorns sea stars, and describes their physical characteristics, life cycles, habitats, sense, food, and means of self-defense
"One or two clear, color photographs complement the text on almost every page; many are close-ups of body parts, with labels. . . . [The text is] well organized." SLJ
Includes glossary

Coldiron, Deborah
Starfish; [by] Deborah Coldiron. ABDO Pub. Co. 2008 32p il (Underwater world) lib bdg $24.21
Grades: 2 3 4 **593.9**
1. Starfishes
ISBN 978-1-59928-813-0 (lib bdg); 1-59928-813-3 (lib bdg) LC 2007-16263
This presents "basic information about [starfish]. . . . Vibrant captioned photos enhance the accessible text." Horn Book Guide
Includes glossary

Lunis, Natalie
Prickly sea stars. Bearport 2008 24p il (No backbones! the world of invertebrates) lib bdg $21.28
Grades: K 1 2 3 **593.9**
1. Starfishes
ISBN 978-1-59716-508-2 (lib bdg); 1-59716-508-5 (lib bdg) LC 2007-6928
Text and photographs present amazing facts about sea stars
"Presents underwater creatures in a way that makes you feel like you're snorkeling. . . . This is a wonderful choice to use with even PreK students during an ocean unit." Libr Media Connect
Includes glossary and bibliographical references

594 Mollusca and Molluscoidea

Blaxland, Beth
Octopuses, squids, and their relatives; cephalopods; [by] Beth Blaxland for the Australian Museum. Chelsea House 2003 c2002 32p il (Invertebrates) $18.95
Grades: 3 4 5 6 **594**
1. Cephalopods
ISBN 0-7910-6992-3 LC 2002-3181

First published 2002 in Australia
Defines cephalopods, such as blue-ringed octopuses and giant squids, and describes their physical characteristics, life cycles, habitats, senses, food, and means of self-defense
This offers "basic report-worthy information, mesmerizing photographs, and a layout that will please young readers." Booklist
Includes glossary

Snails, clams, and their relatives; mollusks; [by] Beth Blaxland for the Australian Museum. Chelsea House 2003 c2002 32p il (Invertebrates) $18.95
Grades: 3 4 5 6 **594**
1. Mollusks
ISBN 0-7910-6997-4 LC 2002-3176
First published 2002 in Australia
Defines mollusks, such as land snails and pearl oysters, and describes their physical features, life cycles, habitats, sense, food, and means of self-defense
Includes glossary

Campbell, Sarah C.
Wolfsnail; a backyard predator; photographs by Sarah C. Campbell and Richard P. Campbell. Boyds Mills Press 2008 32p il $16.95 *
Grades: PreK K 1 2 **594**
1. Snails
ISBN 978-1-59078-554-6; 1-59078-554-1 LC 2007-30838
A Geisel Award honor book, 2009
"The tiny wolfsnail eats garden snails and slugs. This dramatic photo-essay . . . shows the predator stalking its prey, . . . eating it, and leaving the empty shell behind. The back matter includes a small photo of the tiny wolfsnail at its true size and lots of fascinating facts about where snails live, how they mate, and more." Booklist

Coldiron, Deborah
Octopuses. ABDO Pub. 2008 32p il (Underwater world) lib bdg $24.21
Grades: 2 3 4 **594**
1. Octopuses
ISBN 978-1-59928-815-4 (lib bdg); 1-59928-815-X (lib bdg) LC 2007-14852
This presents "basic information about [the octopus]. . . . Vibrant captioned photos enhance the accessible text." Horn Book Guide
Includes glossary

Gray, Susan Heinrichs
Giant African snail. Cherry Lake Pub. 2009 32p il map (Animal invaders) lib bdg $27.07
Grades: 3 4 5 **594**
1. Snails 2. Biological invasions
ISBN 978-1-60279-241-8 (lib bdg); 1-60279-241-0 (lib bdg) LC 2008000803
Looks at the qualities of giant African snails and examines how they became an invasive species in many of the world's tropical and subtropical regions, how they cause problems in their new environments, and the ways

Gray, Susan Heinrichs—*Continued*
that people have attempted to deal with them
"Clear color photographs, most of which are closeups, accompany the [text] on about every other page. . . . [This title provides] report writers with in-depth and up-to-date information on these invaders and the serious problems they cause." SLJ
Includes glossary and bibliographical references

Jango-Cohen, Judith
Octopuses. Marshall Cavendish 2004 47p il map (Animals, animals) lib bdg $17.95
Grades: 3 4 5 6   **594**
1. Octopuses
ISBN 0-7614-1614-5   LC 2003-739
Contents: Introducing octopuses; Dodging danger; A cunning hunter; Batches of hatchlings; Octopuses and us
Describes the physical characteristics, behavior, and habitat of octopuses
This has "excellent, full-color photographs and lively [text] that [brings] these animals to life." SLJ
Includes glossary and bibliographical references

Markle, Sandra, 1946-
Octopuses. Lerner Pubs. 2007 39p il (Animal prey) lib bdg $25.26 *
Grades: 3 4 5   **594**
1. Octopuses
ISBN 978-0-8225-6063-0 (lib bdg); 0-8225-6063-1 (lib bdg)   LC 2005-36350
"This title about octopuses, both predator and prey, features eye-popping color photographs of the animals on nearly every spread. Markel's lively prose brings readers right into the underwater world with sensory descriptions and details kids can relate to." Booklist
Includes bibliographical references

Outside and inside giant squid. Walker & Co. 2003 35p il hardcover o.p. pa $8.95 *
Grades: 2 3 4   **594**
1. Squids
ISBN 0-8027-8872-6; 0-8027-8873-4 (lib bdg); 0-8027-7724-4 (pa)   LC 2002-191044
Describes the inner and outer workings of giant squids, enormous deep-sea creatures that have never been seen alive, discussing their diet, anatomy, and reproduction
The book "benefits from its color photos. The volume is a treasure trove of facts sure to intrigue budding biologists and the merely curious to an equal degree." Booklist
Includes glossary

Redmond, Shirley-Raye
Tentacles! tales of the giant squid; illustrated by Bryn Barnard. Random House 2003 44p il $11.99; pa $3.99
Grades: 1 2 3   **594**
1. Squids
ISBN 0-375-91307-6; 0-375-81307-1 (pa)   LC 2002-10238
"Step into reading"

Describes some of the exaggerated stories that have been told about giant squids and also what scientists have learned about their real physical characteristics and behavior
"An excellent choice to introduce early elementary students to nonfiction titles." Booklist

Waxman, Laura Hamilton
Let's look at snails. Lerner Publications Company 2010 32p il (Lightning bolt books: Animal close-ups) lib bdg $25.26
Grades: PreK K 1 2   **594**
1. Snails
ISBN 978-0-8225-7899-4 (lib bdg); 0-8225-7899-9 (lib bdg)   LC 2007-29226
Introduces snails, describing their physical characteristics, life cycle, habitat, and predators
"Fresh photography, a creative use of graphics, and a collagelike layout make[s] . . . [this book] eye-catching. . . . [The] book ends with a labeled diagram of the animal, a range map, and a further-reading list that includes print and online resources in a single list, a nice way of validating both types of materials." SLJ
Includes glossary

595   Arthropoda

Bonotaux, Gilles, 1956-
Dirty rotten bugs? arthropods unite to tell their side of the story; written and illustrated by Gilles Bonotaux. Two-Can 2007 45p il $14.95
Grades: 2 3 4   **595**
1. Arthropoda
ISBN 978-1-58728-593-6   LC 2006-38121
"Insects, arachnids, centipedes, and millipedes speak out against their reputation as dirty rotten bugs and explain why they deserve respect from humans." Publisher's note

595.3   Crustacea

Blaxland, Beth
Crabs, crayfishes, and their relatives; crustaceans; [by] Beth Blaxland for the Australian Museum. Chelsea House 2003 c2002 32p il (Invertebrates) $18.95
Grades: 3 4 5 6   **595.3**
1. Crustaceans
ISBN 0-7910-6994-X   LC 2002-3178
First published 2002 in Australia
Defines crustaceans, such as slaters and freshwater crayfishes, and describes their physical characteristics, life cycles, habitats, senses, food and means of self-defense
"One or two clear, color photographs complement the text on almost every page. . . . [The text is] well organized." SLJ
Includes glossary

Greenaway, Theresa, 1947-

Crabs; [illustrated by Colin Newman] Raintree Steck-Vaughn Pubs. 2001 48p il (Secret world of) lib bdg $18.98

Grades: 4 5 6 7   **595.3**

1. Crabs

ISBN 0-7398-3506-8   LC 00-62833

This describes the anatomy, habits, and life cycle of crabs and their place in the ecosystem

"The well-designed pages consist of text broken up with blocks of related facts and colorful, close-up photographs and labeled drawings. . . . [This offers] a balance of research material and interest-piquing detail." SLJ

Includes glossary and bibliographical references

Sill, Cathryn P., 1953-

About crustaceans; a guide for children; written by Cathryn Sill; illustrated by John Sill. Peachtree Publishers 2004 unp il $15.95

Grades: K 1 2   **595.3**

1. Crustaceans

ISBN 1-56145-301-3   LC 2003-16838

Describes the anatomy, behavior, and habitat of various crustaceans, including the lobster, crab, and shrimp

"Done in bright watercolors, the illustrations give a sense of these creatures' different habitats. . . . This is an excellent example of easy nonfiction, perfect for beginning readers or for sharing aloud with budding naturalists." SLJ

Tokuda, Yukihisa, 1940-

I'm a pill bug; written by Yukihisa Tokuda; illustrated by Kiyoshi Takahashi. Kane/Miller 2006 unp il pa $7.95

Grades: K 1 2   **595.3**

1. Woodlice

ISBN 1-929132-95-6

"In this picture book, a pill bug narrates a fascinating account of life among his humble yet admirable fellow crustaceans. In an easy-to-follow, conversational style, he explains what pill bugs eat and excrete, why they live near people, how they protect themselves against predators, why they shed and then eat their shells . . . how they reproduce, and more. . . . The lucid, matter-of-fact text answers the main questions children may have about the critters as well as some they might not have thought to ask. Meanwhile, handsome cut-paper collages recreate the pill bugs' world in realistic yet simplified terms." Booklist

595.4 Chelicerata Arachnida

Berger, Melvin, 1927-

Spinning spiders; illustrated by S.D. Schindler. HarperCollins Pubs. 2003 33p il (Let's-read-and-find-out science) hardcover o.p. pa $4.99

Grades: K 1 2 3   **595.4**

1. Spiders

ISBN 0-06-028696-2; 0-06-445207-7 (pa)
LC 2001-39507

Describes the characteristics of spiders and the methods they use to trap their prey in webs

Written "in a clear, easy-to-read style. . . . Detailed, full-color illustrations, often on spreads, highlight the well-organized text." SLJ

Bishop, Nic, 1955-

Spiders. Scholastic Nonfiction 2007 48p il $16.99 *

Grades: 1 2 3 4   **595.4**

1. Spiders

ISBN 0-439-87756-3; 978-0-439-87756-5
LC 2006-47179

"This photo-rich picture book is packed with astonishing facts about these highly successful predators. . . . General facts are here: the difference between spiders and insects; body parts; . . . how they eat; and more. Each double-page spread includes a dramatic, brilliantly colored close-up of a spider." Booklist

Bredeson, Carmen

Tarantulas up close; [by] Carmen Bredeson. Enslow Elementary 2008 24p il (Zoom in on animals!) lib bdg $21.26

Grades: 1 2 3   **595.4**

1. Tarantulas

ISBN 978-0-7660-3076-3 (lib bdg); 0-7660-3076-8 (lib bdg)   LC 2007025609

In this introduction to tarantulas, "short, large-print paragraphs describe key body parts . . . and how they function; . . . [the book outlines] hunting techniques, defense mechanisms, diet, and life cycle. Complementing the text is a large, usually full-page, sharp, color close-up of a representative species. . . . The text is well-organized and clearly written. . . . Bredeson's excellent illustrations and lucid text provide valuable insights into the nature of these hairy, and unjustly feared, spiders." SLJ

Camisa, Kathryn

Hairy tarantulas; by Kathryn Camisa. Bearport Pub. 2009 24p il (No backbone!: The world of invertebrates) lib bdg $21.28

Grades: 1 2 3   **595.4**

1. Tarantulas

ISBN 978-1-59716-704-8 (lib bdg); 1-59716-704-5 (lib bdg)   LC 2008-12106

"Describes different types of tarantulas and their behavior." Publisher's note

"Spreads include four or five simple sentences, each neatly spaced by a carriage return, facing a vivid, close-up view of the spider in action. Word balloon captions highlight details when needed and smaller photographs on the text pages provide further visual reference." SLJ

Includes glossary and bibliographical references

Gonzales, Doreen

Scorpions in the dark. PowerKids Press 2010 24p il (Creatures of the night) lib bdg $21.25; pa $8.05

Grades: 2 3 4   **595.4**

1. Scorpions

ISBN 978-1-4042-8100-4 (lib bdg); 1-4042-8100-2 (lib bdg); 978-1-4358-3257-2 (pa); 1-4358-3257-4 (pa)

                         LC 2009-2076

A look at scorpions and their world in the dark.

"Basic details are complemented by eclectic trivia, . . . [and] each volume concludes with a defense of the animal . . . and why it is vital to humans. The layout is attractive, with easy-to-read text and eye-catching photography. Good for reports." SLJ

Includes glossary

Lunis, Natalie

Deadly black widows; by Natalie Lunis. Bearport Pub. 2009 24p il (No backbone!: The world of invertebrates) lib bdg $21.28

Grades: 1 2 3   **595.4**

1. Spiders

ISBN 978-1-59716-667-6 (lib bdg); 1-59716-667-7 (lib bdg)   LC 2008-1997

A discussion of the black widow spider, the most dangerous kind of spider in the United States

"Spreads include four or five simple sentences, each neatly spaced by a carriage return, facing a vivid, close-up view of the spider in action. Word balloon captions highlight details when needed and smaller photographs on the text pages provide further visual reference." SLJ

Includes glossary and bibliographical references

Markle, Sandra, 1946-

Sneaky, spinning, baby spiders; [by] Sandra Markle. Walker & Company 2008 32p il $16.99; lib bdg $17.89

Grades: 3 4 5   **595.4**

1. Spiders 2. Animal babies

ISBN   978-0-8027-9697-4;   0-8027-9697-4; 978-0-8027-9698-1 (lib bdg); 0-8027-9698-2 (lib bdg)

                         LC 2007-49139

"Markle's intimate style beckons readers into her text and immediately immerses them in the world of spiderlings. . . . The full-color photographs are the work of many photographers and are filled with energy. . . . [Markle] introduces about 14 species (of the 30,000 spiders worldwide), but she does it in such vivid detail and with such respect and appreciation that youngsters will feel connected to these spider moms and their babies." SLJ

Spiders; biggest! littlest! photographs by Simon Pollard. Boyds Mills Press 2004 unp il $15.95

Grades: K 1 2 3   **595.4**

1. Spiders 2. Size

ISBN 1-59078-190-2   LC 2003-26794

This "focuses on seven spiders and explains why their size gives them an edge over other species. . . . The book also incorporates information about the arachnid's role as predator, its use of venom, molting, feeding methods, reproduction, etc. . . . Amazingly detailed, closeup, color photographs appear on every spread. . . . Well organized and clearly written, this engaging work offers important insights into spider physiology not present in many other overviews." SLJ

Montgomery, Sy

The tarantula scientist. Houghton Mifflin Co. 2004 80p il map (Scientists in the field) $18; pa $7.95 *

Grades: 4 5 6 7   **595.4**

1. Marshall, Samuel D. 2. Tarantulas

ISBN 0-618-14799-3; 0-618-91577-X (pa)

                        LC 2003-20125

Describes the research that Samuel Marshall and his students are doing on tarantulas, including the largest spider on earth, the Goliath birdeating tarantula

"Enthusiasm for the subject and respect for both Marshall and his eight-legged subjects come through on every page of the clear, informative, and even occasionally humorous text. Bishop's full-color photos . . . are amazing." Booklist

Includes glossary and bibliographical references

Morley, Christine

Freaky facts about spiders; [written by Christine Morley; illustrated by Phillip Morrison] Two-Can 2007 32p il (Freaky facts) $13.95; pa $8.95

Grades: 2 3 4 5   **595.4**

1. Spiders

ISBN 978-1-58728-596-7; 978-1-58728-597-4 (pa)

                        LC 2006-22589

"Competent cartoons, full-color photos, boxes, sidebars, and facts are pulled together on busy but appealing pages that deliver a shower of brief, tantalizing fact bites. In this book readers will find plenty of closeups of spiders as well as information about what they eat, how they behave, where they live, and more. The tone is casual, and the cartoons provide a light coat of comedy." Booklist

Murawski, Darlyne

Spiders and their webs; [by] Darlyne A. Murawski. National Geographic 2004 31p il $16.95

Grades: 2 3 4 5   **595.4**

1. Spiders

ISBN 0-7922-6979-9   LC 2004-397

This describes nine species of spiders and how they make and use webs

"Even fainthearted arachnophobes will appreciate this gallery of spider profiles featuring full-color, telephoto views. . . . Murawski writes about her subjects with an awe and a reverence that will encourage reluctant children to move beyond spiders' creepy reputation to their fascinating features." Booklist

Includes bibliographical references

Ross, Michael Elsohn, 1952-

Spiderology; photographs by Brian Grogan; illustrations by Darren Erickson. Carolrhoda Bks. 2000 48p il (Backyard buddies) lib bdg $19.93; pa $6.95

Grades: 3 4 5 6   **595.4**
    1. Spiders
    ISBN 1-57505-387-X (lib bdg); 1-57505-438-8 (pa)
                           LC 98-51406

Describes the physical characteristics and habits of spiders and provides instructions for finding, collecting, and keeping spiders

"Clear color photographs and black-and-white diagrams enhance the text. . . . The experiments . . . are creative and easily replicable for a classroom demonstration or science fair project." Booklist

Includes glossary

Simon, Seymour, 1931-

Spiders; [by] Seymour Simon. updated ed. Smithsonian 2008 31p il $16.99; pa $6.99 *

Grades: 3 4 5 6   **595.4**
    1. Spiders
    ISBN   978-0-06-089104-6;   0-06-089104-1; 978-0-06-089103-9 (pa); 0-06-089103-3 (pa)
    First published 2003 by HarperCollins

An introduction to the physical characteristics, behavior, and life cycle of different kinds of spiders.

"The fantastic color photos of the original edition are all here, as is Simon's crisp, informative text. . . . An attention grabber." SLJ

Stewart, Melissa, 1968-

How do spiders make webs? Marshall Cavendish Benchmark 2009 32p il (Tell me why, tell me how) lib bdg $20.95

Grades: 3 4 5   **595.4**
    1. Spiders
    ISBN 978-0-7614-2920-3 (lib bdg); 0-7614-2920-4 (lib bdg)
                           LC 2007025092

This "explains the differences between [spiders] and other arachnids, and how and why they spin webs. One or two large, well-captioned color photographs are provided per spread. [The] book concludes with an activity. [This is a] solid [introduction]." SLJ

Includes glossary and bibliographical references

Trueit, Trudi Strain

Spiders. Marshall Cavendish Benchmark 2009 23p il (Benchmark rebus. Creepy critters) lib bdg $22.79

Grades: PreK K 1   **595.4**
    1. Spiders
    ISBN 978-0-7614-3965-3 (lib bdg); 0-7614-3965-X (lib bdg)
                           LC 2008-14426

"Easy to read text with rebuses explores the different varieties of spiders." Publisher's note

"Brilliant closeup photos will help beginning readers make meaning and appeal to students who like these creatures. . . . Glossary, print and media resources for further learning, and an about the author section conclude . . . [the] book. Reading specialists will want to be advised about [this book] . . . as will teachers. . . . This . . . is an excellent resource for beginning research projects." Libr Media Connect

Includes glossary and bibliographical references

Wadsworth, Ginger

Up, up, and away; illustrated by Patricia J. Wynne. Charlesbridge 2009 unp il lib bdg $16.95

Grades: PreK K 1 2   **595.4**
    1. Spiders
    ISBN 978-1-58089-221-6 (lib bdg); 1-58089-221-3 (lib bdg)
                           LC 2008040752

This traces the life cycle of a garden spider

"Simply told with well-chosen words and phrases, the story reads aloud well. . . . Wynne uses watercolor, gouache, and colored pencil to add hue and shading to the precise ink drawings that define the spiders and their surroundings." Booklist

595.6   Myriapoda

Blaxland, Beth

Centipedes, millipedes, and their relatives; myriapods; [by] Beth Blaxland for the Australian Museum. Chelsea House 2003 c2002 32p il (Invertebrates) $28

Grades: 3 4 5 6   **595.6**
    1. Millipedes 2. Centipedes
    ISBN 0-7910-6995-8   LC 2002-3179
    First published 2002 in Australia

Defines myriapods, such as centipedes and three groups of millipedes, and describes their physical characteristics, life cycles, habitats, senses, food, and means of self-defense

"One or two clear, color photographs complement the text on almost every page. . . . [The text is] well organized." SLJ

Includes glossary

Povey, Karen D.

Centipede; [by] Karen Povey. KidHaven Press 2004 32p il (Bugs) $22.45

Grades: 3 4 5   **595.6**
    1. Centipedes
    ISBN 0-7377-1766-1   LC 2003-15274

Describes the physical characteristics, behavior, and habitat of centipedes.

Ross, Michael Elsohn, 1952-

Millipedeology; photographs by Brian Grogan; illustrations by Darren Erickson. Carolrhoda Bks. 2000 48p il (Backyard buddies) hardcover o.p. pa $6.95

Grades: 3 4 5 6   **595.6**
    1. Millipedes
    ISBN 1-57505-398-5 (lib bdg); 1-575505-436-1 (pa)
                           LC 99-35398

Describes the physical characteristics and behavior of the millipede and presents millipede-related activities

"Illustrated with diagrams, cartoons, and color photos." Horn Book Guide

Includes glossary

595.7   Insecta (Insects)

Aronin, Miriam

The ant's nest; a huge underground city. Bearport Pub. 2009 32p il (Spectacular animal towns) lib bdg $18.95

Grades: 2 3 4   595.7

1. Ants

ISBN 978-1-59716-868-7 (lib bdg); 1-59716-868-8 (lib bdg)   LC 2009-3065

"Introduces ants, describing their physical characteristics and how they build structures, take care of their queen, and raise their young." Publisher's note

"Through excellent photographs, high-interest texts, sidebars, maps, and other material, children learn about both the animals and their habitats. The . . . book also provides brief profiles of animals with similar habitats. . . . [This book is] much better than average 'report' titles." SLJ

Includes glossary and bibliographical references

Bailer, Darice

How do caterpillars become butterflies? Marshall Cavendish Benchmark 2009 32p il (Tell me why, tell me how) lib bdg $20.95

Grades: 3 4 5   595.7

1. Butterflies 2. Caterpillars

ISBN 978-0-7614-3987-5 (lib bdg); 0-7614-3987-0 (lib bdg)   LC 2008-19732

This provides "information on the process of caterpillars changing into butterflies," Publisher's note

"Students will enjoy the large, beautiful color photographs of various species and the uncrowded layout of [this] title. Its strengths include close-ups of a curling proboscis and a compound eye. A catch-and-release caterpillar/butterfly observation activity is included." SLJ

Includes glossary and bibliographical references

Baker, Nick, 1973-

Bug zoo. DK 2010 64p il $12.99

Grades: 2 3 4   595.7

1. Insects 2. Collectors and collecting

ISBN 978-0-7566-6166-3; 0-7566-6166-8

             LC 2010-279437

Naturalist Nick Baker shows the reader how to make miniature habitats for insects, snails and worms, some interesting aspects of their lives and how to feed the contained creatures

"This is a colorful, informative, and engaging book about keeping insects-if not as pets, then as creatures worthy of intense study. . . . Baker's enthusiasm for the subject is evident throughout. Because it provides interesting facts about insects as well as how-to tips, this title will find an audience with curious readers and would-be zookeepers alike. It may even intrigue avowed entomophobes." SLJ

Berger, Melvin, 1927-

Chirping crickets; illustrated by Megan Lloyd. HarperCollins Pubs. 1998 32p il (Let's-read-and-find-out science) lib bdg $15.89; pa $4.95

Grades: K 1 2 3   595.7

1. Crickets

ISBN 0-06-024962-5 (lib bdg); 0-06-445180-1 (pa)

             LC 96-51661

Describes the physical characteristics, behavior, and life cycle of crickets while giving particular emphasis to how they chirp

"Clear and detailed, the ink-and-watercolor artwork is often visually striking as well as educationally sound. . . . A well-rounded introduction." Booklist

How do flies walk upside down? questions and answers about insects; by Melvin and Gilda Berger; illustrated by Jim Effler. Scholastic Ref. 1999 48p il (Scholastic question and answer series) $12.95; pa $5.95

Grades: 3 4 5   595.7

1. Insects

ISBN 0-590-13089-7; 0-439-08572-1 (pa)

             LC 98-18457

A series of questions and answers provides information about the physical characteristics, senses, eating habits, life cycles, and behavior of different insects

"The colorful illustrations are detailed, vivid, and well conceived. . . . Attractive enough for browsers, yet solid enough to help support the curriculum." Booklist

Bishop, Nic, 1955-

Nic Bishop butterflies and moths. Scholastic Nonfiction 2009 48p il $17.99 *

Grades: 2 3 4   595.7

1. Butterflies

ISBN 978-0-439-87757-2; 0-439-87757-1

             LC 2008-15290

"The text covers the all-important topic of metamorphosis, of course, but also discusses feeding and predation, migration, and reproduction. . . . The real draw here, though, is the art; even for Bishop, the photographs are breathtaking. . . . Kids will be drawn to this like Bishop's subject to flame." Bull Cent Child Books

Blobaum, Cindy, 1966-

Insectigation! 40 hands-on activities to explore the insect world; [by] Cindy Blobaum. Chicago Review Press 2005 133p il pa $12.95

Grades: 3 4 5 6   595.7

1. Insects

ISBN 1-55652-568-0

"Raising mealworms, testing the visual acuity of bees, setting up a watering hole for butterflies—these are just a few of the 40 activities included in this earnest introduction to entomology. Each of eight chapters focuses on a different topic, such as physical and behavioral characteristics; metamorphosis; communication; methods to attract, collect and keep insects, etc. . . . Clear line drawings, diagrams of body parts and project materials, plus the occasional black-and-white photograph are found on almost every page. . . . The text is clearly written and

Blobaum, Cindy, 1966-—*Continued*
well organized." SLJ
Includes bibliographical references

Bredeson, Carmen
Monarch butterflies up close; [by] Carmen Bredeson. Enslow Elementary 2006 24p il $21.26
Grades: 1 2 3   595.7
  1. Butterflies
  ISBN 0-7660-2494-6   LC 2005020034
This describes the anatomy, behavior, and life cycle of the monarch butterfly
Includes glossary and bibliographical references

Cole, Joanna
The magic school bus inside a beehive; illustrated by Bruce Degen. Scholastic 1996 47p il hardcover o.p. pa $4.99 *
Grades: 2 3 4   595.7
  1. Bees
  ISBN 0-590-44684-3; 0-590-025721-8 (pa)
                                        LC 95-38288
Ms. Frizzle "introduces her class to the insect kingdom via an excursion through a honeybee hive. Garbed in bee costumes complete with antennae, and sprayed with the proper pheromones, the students are accepted by the workers and allowed to perform such chores as foraging for nectar and pollen, building honeycombs, making honey, and feeding larvae. . . . A plethora of pseudo school reports provide additional information on the topic. Degen's colorful and amusing cartoons heighten the adventures. Clearly written and well organized." SLJ

Cusick, Dawn
Bug butts; illustrations by Haude Levesque. Earlylight Books 2009 48p il $14.95
Grades: 3 4 5   595.7
  1. Insects
  ISBN 978-0-9797455-0-8; 0-9797455-0-0
This describes the diverse ways insects use their butt ends to survive and thrive.
  "Provides interesting information on the posterior anatomy of insects, discussing a variety of modifications of the abdomen and anus. . . . The book is well written, informative, and very nicely illustrated." Sci Books Films

Davies, Andrew, 1955-
Super-size bugs; written by Andrew Davies; photographed by Igor Siwanowicz. Sterling Publishing 2007 48p il $9.95
Grades: 3 4 5 6   595.7
  1. Insects
  ISBN 978-1-4027-5340-4; 1-4027-5340-3
"From the scarlet whiplike tails of a Puss Moth caterpillar to the glittering armor of the Blue Ground Beetle, from the clustered eyes of a Greenbottle Blue Tarantula to the eerily alien face of the Devil's Flower Mantis, Davies introduces a host of insects made 'supersize' by the camera lens. Paragraphs of text and detailed captions provide interesting snippets of information, but it is the superb photos that rivet the eye to these oversize pages." SLJ

Derzipilski, Kathleen
Beetles; by Kathleen Derzipilski. Benchmark Books 2004 46p il map (Animals, animals) lib bdg $25.64 *
Grades: 3 4 5 6   595.7
  1. Beetles
  ISBN 0-7614-1751-6   LC 2003-24841
Contents: What is a beetle; The beetle's body; How beetles grow; How beetles live; Beetles and people
This describes the life cycles and characteristics of beetles, illustrated with color photographs
Includes glossary and bibliographical references

Dixon, Norma
Focus on flies. Fitzhenry & Whiteside 2008 32p il $18.95
Grades: 4 5 6 7   595.7
  1. Flies
  ISBN 978-1-55005-128-5; 1-55005-128-8
This "chatty, informative title, illustrated with many clear color photos and diagrams, will hook readers with its fascinating view of a fly's 'creepy cool world.' . . . The gross details will appeal to middle-grade readers, who will then go on to learn about anatomy, metamorphosis, adaptation, diversity, classification, and flies' roles in plant pollination." Booklist
Includes bibliographical references

Dorros, Arthur, 1950-
Ant cities; written and illustrated by Arthur Dorros. Crowell 1987 28p il (Let's-read-and-find-out science book) hardcover o.p. lib bdg $11.89; pa $5.99
Grades: K 1 2 3   595.7
  1. Ants
  ISBN 0-690-04568-9; 0-690-04570-0 (lib bdg); 0-06-445079-1 (pa)   LC 85-48244
Also available Spanish language edition
"Using harvester ants as a basic example, Dorros shows how the insects build tunnels with rooms for different functions and how workers, queens, and males have distinct roles in the ant hill. Along the way, she works in details of food and reproduction, ending with descriptions of other kinds of ants and suggestions for ways to observe them (including instructions for making an ant farm). The text is simple without becoming choppy, the full-color illustrations are inviting as well as informative." Bull Cent Child Books

Gibbons, Gail
Monarch butterfly. Holiday House 1989 unp il $16.95; pa $6.95
Grades: K 1 2 3   595.7
  1. Butterflies
  ISBN 0-8234-0773-X; 0-8234-0909-0 (pa)
                                        LC 89-1880
"Large-scale paintings, clearly detailed, and a simply written, sequential text describe the life cycle of the monarch butterfly and its migratory patterns. This is Gibbons at her best, providing information in a text that is cohesive and comprehensible." Bull Cent Child Books

Glaser, Linda

Brilliant bees; illustrated by Gay W. Holland. Millbrook Press 2003 unp il lib bdg $22.90; pa $8.95

Grades: K 1 2 3   **595.7**
1. Bees
ISBN 0-7613-2670-7 (lib bdg); 0-7613-1943-3 (pa)
LC 2001-8630
Simple text and illustrations describe the physical characteristics, habits, and life cycle of the honey bee.

This "features excellent, large-scale pictures in colored pencil. Printed in uneven lines that look like verse, the first-person, large-type text frequently includes poetic rhythm and rhyme." Booklist

Dazzling dragonflies; a life cycle story; illustrated by Mia Posada. Millbrook Press 2008 unp il (Linda Glaser's classic creatures) lib bdg $22.60

Grades: K 1 2 3   **595.7**
1. Dragonflies
ISBN 978-0-8225-6753-0 (lib bdg); 0-8225-6753-9 (lib bdg)
LC 2007-21886
"Clearly written text and bright-hued watercolor collage illustrations introduce the life cycle of that zip-a-dipping aerialist, the dragonfly, from newly laid eggs, through months of aquatic life as a nymph, to the final metamorphosis into a glitter-winged creature. . . . [This] is basic, attractive, and easy to read." SLJ

Goldish, Meish

Deadly praying mantises. Bearport Pub. 2008 24p il (No backbone! The world of invertebrates) lib bdg $21.28

Grades: K 1 2 3   **595.7**
1. Praying mantis
ISBN 978-1-59716-582-2 (lib bdg); 1-59716-582-4 (lib bdg)
Introduces the praying mantis, describing its physical characteristics, life cycle, habitat, diet, and behavior

"The closeup photos are vivid and engaging . . . [and] the text is . . . thorough enough to sustain interest." Horn Book Guide

Includes glossary and bibliographical references

Smelly stink bugs. Bearport Pub. 2008 24p il (No backbone! The world of invertebrates) lib bdg $21.28

Grades: K 1 2 3   **595.7**
1. Stink bugs
ISBN 978-1-59716-580-8 (lib bdg); 1-59716-580-8 (lib bdg)
LC 2007-31228
Introduces the stink bug, describing its physical characteristics, life cycle, habitat, diet, and behavior

"The closeup photos are vivid and engaging . . . [and] the text is . . . thorough enough to sustain interest." Horn Book Guide

Includes glossary and bibliographical references

Gonzales, Doreen

Crickets in the dark. PowerKids Press 2010 24p il (Creatures of the night) lib bdg $21.25; pa $8.05

Grades: 2 3 4   **595.7**
1. Crickets
ISBN 978-1-4042-8098-4 (lib bdg); 1-4042-8098-7 (lib bdg); 978-1-4358-3253-4 (pa); 1-4358-3253-1 (pa)
LC 2009-483
A look at crickets and their world in the dark.

"Basic details are complemented by eclectic trivia, . . . [and] each volume concludes with a defense of the animal . . . and why it is vital to humans. The layout is attractive, with easy-to-read text and eye-catching photography. Good for reports." SLJ

Includes glossary

Gray, Susan Heinrichs

Emerald ash borer; by Susan H. Gray. Cherry Lake Pub. 2008 32p il map (Animal invaders) lib bdg $27.07

Grades: 3 4 5 6   **595.7**
1. Emerald ash borer 2. Biological invasions
ISBN 978-1-60279-112-1 (lib bdg); 1-60279-112-0 (lib bdg)
LC 2007-34973
This describes the Emerald ash borers' "outstanding physical and behavioral characteristics at each stage in their life cycle, diet, and natural habitat, and then [explains] how they were introduced into areas outside their natural range . . . and the nature and extent of the ecological damage they have caused, and various attempts to eradicate or at least control the animals. . . . Larvae of the emerald ash borer have infested and destroyed thousands of valuable ash trees in the Midwest. . . . Clear color photographs . . . accompany the texts on about every other page. . . . [This title is] clearly written and well organized, and [has] up-to-date information." SLJ

Includes glossary

Hansen, Amy

Bugs and bugsicles; insects in the winter; [by] Amy S. Hansen; illustrations by Robert C. Kray. Boyds Mills Press 2010 32p il $17.95

Grades: 3 4 5   **595.7**
1. Insects 2. Winter
ISBN 978-1-59078-269-9; 1-59078-269-0
"This colorful book describes what happens in winter to seven different insects: a praying mantis, a field cricket, a ladybug, a honeybee, a pavement ant, a monarch butterfly, and an Arctic woolly bear caterpillar. . . . The title concludes with an author's note and two science activities related to freezing water. A typical double-page spread includes a few paragraphs of text accompanied by large-scale illustrations." Booklist

Includes glossary and bibliographical references

Heiligman, Deborah

From caterpillar to butterfly; illustrated by Bari Weissman. HarperCollins Pubs. 1996 31p il (Let's-read-and-find-out science) $15.95; pa $4.95

Grades: K 1   **595.7**
1. Butterflies 2. Caterpillars
ISBN 0-06-024264-7; 0-06-024268-X (lib bdg); 0-06-445129-1 (pa)
LC 93-39055

Heiligman, Deborah—*Continued*

Young children observe the metamorphosis of a caterpillar into a butterfly in a jar in their classroom

"Pen-and-ink and watercolor illustrations create a cheerful setting. . . . A small collection of butterflies commonly found in most parts of the U.S. and a list of addresses of butterfly centers are appended. An inviting book that young children can relate to and one that teachers will find valuable to support nature-study projects." SLJ

Jackson, Donna M., 1959-

The bug scientists; by Donna M. Jackson. Houghton Mifflin 2002 48p il (Scientists in the field) $16; pa $5.95 *

Grades: 4 5 6 7   **595.7**

1. Insects
ISBN 0-618-10868-8; 0-618-43232-9 (pa)
     LC 2001-39256

Bug scientists, called entomologists, present information on insects and explain how they use that information in their work

"The much-maligned world of insects becomes fascinating in this . . . entry in the excellent Scientists in the Field series. . . . The highly readable text weaves in plenty of science. . . . With its crisp photos and lively story angles and language, this is sure to attract young readers." Booklist

Includes glossary and bibliographical references

Jango-Cohen, Judith

Bees; by Judith Jango-Cohen. Marshall Cavendish Benchmark 2006 48p il (Animals, animals) lib bdg $19.95

Grades: 3 4 5 6   **595.7**

1. Bees
ISBN 978-0-7614-2235-8 (lib bdg); 0-7614-2235-8 (lib bdg)   LC 2005025610

"Describes the physical characteristics, behavior, and habitat of bees." Publisher's note

"Sharp color photographs accompany the text. . . . [This is] clearly written, [and] well organized." SLJ

Includes glossary and bibliographical references

Johnson, Jinny

Butterfly; illustrations by Michael Woods. Smart Apple Media 2010 32p il (How does it grow?) lib bdg $28.50

Grades: 1 2 3   **595.7**

1. Butterflies 2. Life cycles (Biology)
ISBN 978-1-59920-352-2 (lib bdg); 1-59920-352-9 (lib bdg)   LC 2009-3397

Introduces children to the lifecycle of a butterfly

"Each stage is described on a spread that features clearly written, oversized text and a caption opposite a full-page, realistic watercolor, or, occasionally, a photograph. . . . A worthwhile purchase." SLJ

Includes glossary

Simon & Schuster children's guide to insects and spiders. Simon & Schuster Bks. for Young Readers 1996 80p il $19.95

Grades: 4 5 6 7   **595.7**

1. Insects 2. Spiders
ISBN 0-689-81163-2   LC 96-27600

Provides an introduction to more than 100 insects and arachnids, giving general information about family characteristics and habits, and more specific facts about some species

"Crisp and well-designed, this is an inviting visual introduction to insects and arachnids." Booklist

Includes glossary

Knudsen, Shannon, 1971-

From egg to butterfly. Lerner Publs. 2003 24p il (Start to finish) lib bdg $18.60

Grades: K 1 2   **595.7**

1. Butterflies
ISBN 0-8225-0713-7   LC 2001-4652

Follows the development of a butterfly from the egg its mother lays on a plant to the fully developed insect that flies away

"Readers will be transfixed by the incredibly crisp and clear photographs accompanying the text. This up-close and intimate look at the life stages of a monarch butterfly will be an asset to any young entomologist's library." Sci Teach

Koontz, Robin Michal

What's the difference between a butterfly and a moth? by Robin Koontz; illustrated by Bandelin-Dacey. Picture Window Books 2010 24p il (What's the difference) lib bdg $25.32

Grades: K 1 2   **595.7**

1. Butterflies 2. Moths
ISBN 978-1-4048-5543-4 (lib bdg); 1-4048-5543-2 (lib bdg)   LC 2009-6884

"Compares and contrasts the habitats, physical characteristics, location, and lifestyles of [butterflies and moths]. The picture-book format is used to great effect as it allows the two animals to be compared side by side on each spread. The bold, expressive watercolors provide the same visual impact as photographs. . . . Short sentences and highlighted fun facts make this a . . . [book] with broad appeal for both researchers and browsers." SLJ

Includes glossary

Latimer, Jonathan P.

Butterflies; [by] Jonathan P. Latimer, Karen Stray Nolting; illustrations by Amy Bartlett Wright; foreword by Virginia Marie Peterson. Houghton Mifflin 2000 48p il (Peterson field guides for young naturalists) hardcover o.p. pa $6.99

Grades: 4 5 6 7   **595.7**

1. Butterflies
ISBN 0-395-97943-9; 0-395-97944-7 (pa)
     LC 99-38605

A guide to help identify various butterflies, using the Peterson System of identification

Latimer, Jonathan P.—*Continued*

Caterpillars; [by] Jonathan P. Latimer, Karen Stray Nolting; illustrations by Amy Bartlett Wright; foreword by Virginia Marie Peterson. Houghton Mifflin 2000 48p il (Peterson field guides for young naturalists) $15; pa $5.95

Grades: 4 5 6 7   595.7
  1. Caterpillars
  ISBN 0-395-97942-0; 0-395-97945-5 (pa)
                                            LC 99-38944

Describes the physical characteristics, behavior, and habitat of a variety of caterpillars, arranged by the categories "Smooth," "Bumpy," "Sluglike," "Horned," "Hairy," "Bristly," and "Spiny"

Lerner, Carol, 1927-

Butterflies in the garden. HarperCollins Pubs. 2002 29p il $16.95; lib bdg $16.89

Grades: K 1 2 3   595.7
  1. Butterflies
  ISBN 0-688-17478-7; 0-688-17479-5 (lib bdg)
                                            LC 00-61408

The "text describes how butterflies eat, introduces distinguishing characteristics of a few species, gives a basic overview of the life cycle from caterpillar to butterfly, and describes plants that attact butterflies to the garden." Booklist

This "is very attractive. Watercolors done in spring shades rest neatly in precise outlines of lovely butterflies and flowers. . . . The text . . . is lively and clear." SLJ

Lockwood, Sophie

Ants; by Sophie Lockwood. Child's World 2008 40p il map (World of insects) lib bdg $29.93

Grades: 4 5 6   595.7
  1. Ants
  ISBN 978-1-59296-817-6 (lib bdg); 1-59296-817-1 (lib bdg)   LC 2006103452

This describes ants' "basic anatomy, outstanding physical and behavioral characteristics, [diet, life cycle], roles in myths and legends, and effects on humans. . . . With [its] well-organized, succinct [text] and excellent photography, [this] solid [introduction] will be [a] valuable [resource]." SLJ

Includes glossary and bibliographical references

Dragonflies; by Sophie Lockwood. Child's World 2008 40p il map (World of insects) lib bdg $29.93

Grades: 4 5 6   595.7
  1. Dragonflies
  ISBN 978-1-59296-821-3 (lib bdg); 1-59296-821-X (lib bdg)   LC 2006103454

This describes dragonflies' "basic anatomy, outstanding physical and behavioral characteristics, [diet, life cycle], roles in myths and legends, and effects on humans. . . . With [its] well-organized, succinct [text] and excellent photography, [this] solid [introduction] will be [a] valuable [resource]." SLJ

Includes glossary and bibliographical references

Flies; by Sophie Lockwood. Child's World 2008 40p il (World of insects) lib bdg $29.93

Grades: 4 5 6   595.7
  1. Flies
  ISBN 978-1-59296-822-0 (lib bdg); 1-59296-822-8 (lib bdg)   LC 2007000182

This describes flies' "basic anatomy, outstanding physical and behavioral characteristics, [diet, life cycle], roles in myths and legends, and effects on humans. . . . With [its] well-organized, succinct [text] and excellent photography, [this] solid [introduction] will [a] be valuable [resource]." SLJ

Includes glossary and bibliographical references

Markle, Sandra, 1946-

Hornets; incredible insect architects; by Sandra Markle. Lerner Publications Company 2008 48p il (Insect world) lib bdg $27.93

Grades: 2 3 4 5   595.7
  1. Hornets and yellowjackets
  ISBN 978-0-8225-7297-8 (lib bdg); 0-8225-7297-4 (lib bdg)   LC 2007022290

This describes the anatomy, life cycle, and behavior of hornets

This "will please report writers, budding entomologists, and anyone who expects children's nonfiction to be as carefully documented as adult nonfiction. . . . The [book is] notable for the sharp photos placed precisely to enhance understanding. . . . The main [text is] clear and [flows] well." SLJ

Includes glossary and bibliographical references

Insects; biggest! littlest! photographs by Simon Pollard. Boyds Mills Press 2009 32p il $16.95

Grades: 2 3 4 5   595.7
  1. Insects 2. Size
  ISBN 978-1-59078-512-6; 1-59078-512-6
                                            LC 2008-33524

"This simply written introduction examines insects from the perspective of size. Employing over a dozen kinds as examples, Markle explains why those that are unusually large, small, or equipped with extraordinary body parts have an edge over predators or competing species. . . . An amazingly detailed, closeup color photograph of one or more of the insects discussed complements the text on almost every page. . . . Well organized and clearly written in an engaging style." SLJ

Includes glossary and bibliographical references

Luna moths; masters of change; by Sandra Markle. Lerner Publications Co. 2008 48p il (Insect world) lib bdg $27.93

Grades: 2 3 4 5   595.7
  1. Moths
  ISBN 978-0-8225-7302-9 (lib bdg); 0-8225-7302-4 (lib bdg)   LC 2007025260

This describes the anatomy, life cycle, and behavior of luna moths

This "will please report writers, budding entomologists, and anyone who expects children's nonfiction to be as carefully documented as adult nonfiction. . . . The [book is] notable for the sharp photos placed precisely to enhance understanding. . . . The main [text is] clear and [flows] well." SLJ

Includes glossary and bibliographical references

Markle, Sandra, 1946-—*Continued*

Outside and inside killer bees; [by] Sandra Markle. Walker & Company 2004 37p il $17.95; lib bdg $18.85 *

Grades: 2 3 4   **595.7**
   1. Bees
   ISBN 0-8027-8906-4; 0-8027-8907-2 (lib bdg)
                      LC 2003-70500

The author presents "factual information about bee anatomy, social behavior, honey production, and the like. . . . She imbeds these facts in a deeper examination of the greater ecological topic of invasive species." Horn Book

"The subject of this photo-essay . . . is highly dramatic, and the [book has an] attractive design, with big, clear, full-color pictures and spacious type. . . . This is . . . an excellent introduction to the excitement of entomology." Booklist

Praying mantises; hungry insect heroes. Lerner Publications Company 2008 48p il (Insect world) lib bdg $27.93 *

Grades: 2 3 4 5   **595.7**
   1. Praying mantis
   ISBN 978-0-8225-7300-5 (lib bdg); 0-8225-7300-8 (lib bdg)   LC 2007-25961

This describes the anatomy, life cycle, and behavior of praying mantises.

This "will please report writers, budding entomologists, and anyone who expects children's nonfiction to be as carefully documented as adult nonfiction. . . . The [book is] notable for the sharp photos placed precisely to enhance understanding. . . . The main [text is] clear and [flows] well." SLJ

Includes glossary and bibliographical references

Termites; hard-working insect families; by Sandra Markle. Lerner Publications Co. 2008 48p il (Insect world) lib bdg $27.93

Grades: 2 3 4 5   **595.7**
   1. Termites
   ISBN 978-0-8225-7301-2 (lib bdg); 0-8225-7301-6 (lib bdg)   LC 2007025963

This describes the anatomy, life cycle, and behavior of termites

This "will please report writers, budding entomologists, and anyone who expects children's nonfiction to be as carefully documented as adult nonfiction. . . . The [book is] notable for the sharp photos placed precisely to enhance understanding. . . . The main [text is] clear and [flows] well." SLJ

Includes glossary and bibliographical references

Markovics, Joyce L.

The honey bee's hive; a thriving city; by Joyce Markovics; consultant, Brian V. Brown. Bearport Pub. 2009 32p il map (Spectacular animal towns) lib bdg $25.27

Grades: 2 3 4   **595.7**
   1. Bees
   ISBN 978-1-59716-867-0 (lib bdg); 1-59716-867-X (lib bdg)   LC 2009-11295

Describes the activities within a honey bee hive

"Through excellent photographs, high-interest texts, sidebars, maps, and other material, children learn about both the animals and their habitats. The . . . book also provides brief profiles of animals with similar habitats. . . . [This book is] much better than average 'report' titles." SLJ

Includes glossary and bibliographical references

Martin, Ruth

Bugs; [illustrated by Peter Scott; written by Ruth Martin; paper engineering by Andy Mansfield] Silver Dolphin Books 2009 unp il (Kaleidopops) $15.95

Grades: K 1 2 3   **595.7**
   1. Insects 2. Pop-up books
   ISBN 978-1-59223-889-7; 1-59223-889-0

In this book about insects "iridescent insect pop-ups (which change color thanks to lenticular panels) are accompanied by brief, descriptive classifications of each species. . . . The vibrant and shiny images . . . emphasize the alien beauty of the various creepy crawlies, with less of a focus on insect anatomy." Publ Wkly

Merrick, Patrick

Cockroaches. Child's World 2003 32p il (Naturebooks) lib bdg $25.64

Grades: 1 2 3 4   **595.7**
   1. Cockroaches
   ISBN 1-56766-206-4   LC 2002-151471

Describes the physical characteristics, behavior, habitat, and life cycle of cockroaches

This gives "children a firm grasp of the basics. . . . Most pages of text alternate with large, sharp, color close-up photographs . . . [The text is] succinctly written and well organized." SLJ

Micucci, Charles, 1959-

The life and times of the ant. Houghton Mifflin 2003 32p hardcover o.p. pa $6.95 *

Grades: 2 3 4   **595.7**
   1. Ants
   ISBN 0-618-00559-5; 0-618-68949-4 (pa)
                      LC 2002-478

Describes the evolution, physical characteristics, behavior, and social nature of ants

This "offers succinct text and an impressive amount of information presented in an attractive, picture-book format." Booklist

Includes bibliographical references

The life and times of the honeybee. Ticknor & Fields Bks. for Young Readers 1995 32p il pa $6.95 hardcover o.p. *

Grades: 2 3 4   **595.7**
   1. Bees 2. Honey
   ISBN 0-395-86139-X (pa)   LC 93-8135

The author "covers everything from distribution, reproduction, behavior, and honey manufacture to the honeybee's niche in history." Booklist

"The multitude of original watercolors bring the subject to life, provide a sense of scale and amplify the text. . . . A must acquisition for a library." Appraisal

Miller, Heather, 1971-

This is your life cycle; by Heather Lynn Miller; illustrated by Michael Chesworth. Clarion Books 2008 32p il $16

Grades: K 1 2 3   **595.7**

   1. Dragonflies 2. Life cycles (Biology)

   ISBN 978-0-618-72485-7; 0-618-72485-0

                         LC 2007-7245

Told in the form of a TV show, this describes the different stages of the life of Dahlia the dragonfly, including the various predators she faced, what she ate, and other facts.

"Lively, vibrant watercolor illustrations supplement the ambitious text. . . . Children will find this playful science book memorable." Libr Media Connect

Miller, Sara Swan

Ants, bees, and wasps of North America. Watts 2003 47p il (Animals in order) lib bdg $25; pa $6.95

Grades: 4 5 6   **595.7**

   1. Ants 2. Bees 3. Wasps

   ISBN 0-531-12244-1 (lib bdg); 0-531-16658-9 (pa)

                        LC 2002-1731

Introduces the different animals in the hymenoptra order, their similarities and differences, environments in which they live, and how to observe them

This book makes "fascinating reading. . . . Photographs are glorious." Libr Media Connect

Includes glossary and bibliographical references

Mortensen, Lori, 1955-

In the trees, honeybees! illustrated by Cris Arbo. Dawn Publications 2009 unp il $16.95; pa $8.95

Grades: PreK K 1 2 3   **595.7**

   1. Bees

   ISBN 978-1-58469-114-3; 1-58469-114-X; 978-1-58469-115-0 (pa); 1-58469-115-8 (pa)

                      LC 2008038513

"Short, simple rhyming words and phrases, printed in large type on realistic illustrations, describe the amazing life cycle of the honeybee. The vibrantly colored scenes center on a beehive hidden in a tree trunk and the grass and gardens surrounding it. Brief paragraphs in a smaller font provide more information about the insect's depicted activities. . . . A wonderful choice for sharing aloud, Mortensen's finely crafted book makes a solid addition." SLJ

Mound, L. A. (Laurence Alfred), 1934-

Insect; written by Laurence Mound. rev ed. DK Pub. 2007 72p il (Eyewitness books) $15.99; lib bdg $19.99

Grades: 4 5 6 7   **595.7**

   1. Insects

   ISBN 978-0-7566-3004-1; 0-7566-3004-5; 978-0-7566-0691-6 (lib bdg); 0-7566-0691-8 (lib bdg)

                      LC 2007-281241

   First published 1990 by Knopf

   Includes CD-ROM with wall chart and clip art

   Contents: The parts of an insect; What is an insect?; The first insects; Wings and flight; Through an insect's

eyes; Touch, smell, and hearing; Legwork; Mouthparts and feeding; Battling beetles; Complete metamorphosis; Incomplete metamorphosis; Beetles; Flies; Butterflies and moths; Wasps, bees, and ants; Other insects; Living with plants; Hide and seek; How to avoid being eaten; A watery life; Building a nest; Insect architects; Social ants; Honeybees and hives; Helpful and harmful; Looking at insects; Did you know?; Insect classification

   Includes glossary and bibliographical references

Murawski, Darlyne

Face to face with caterpillars; by Darlyne A. Murawski. National Geographic 2007 32p il (Face to face) $16.95; lib bdg $25.90 *

Grades: 3 4 5 6   **595.7**

   1. Caterpillars

   ISBN 978-1-4263-0052-3; 1-4263-0052-2; 978-1-4263-0053-0 (lib bdg); 1-4263-0053-0 (lib bdg)

                      LC 2006-20499

"Murawski tells how to find caterpillars and discusses their developmental stages, body parts, diet problems, and self-defense mechanisms. . . . Attractive, well written, and fascinating." SLJ

Includes bibliographical references

Nirgiotis, Nicholas

Killer ants; illustrated by Emma Stevenson. Holiday House 2009 29p il $17.95

Grades: 2 3 4 5   **595.7**

   1. Ants

   ISBN 978-0-8234-2034-6; 0-8234-2034-5

                      LC 2007-46922

This "volume presents four species of flesh-eating killer ants: army, driver, fire, and bulldog. After a dramatic opening scene and a general introduction to ants, the book spotlights each featured species in turn, devoting the most space to the army ants of the Amazon rain forest. Readers drawn by the book's title will enjoy the stories of ants attacking animals, but just as fascinating are the details of the ants' abilities, adaptations, and survival skills. . . . Stevenson . . . contributes a series of precisely drawn, useful, and sometimes dramatic gouache paintings. An informative, visually dynamic presentation." Booklist

Perritano, John, 1962-

Bugs on your body; nature's creepiest creatures live on you! Gareth Stevens Pub. 2010 48p il (Current science) lib bdg $31

Grades: 4 5 6   **595.7**

   1. Parasites 2. Insects

   ISBN 978-1-4339-2058-5 (lib bdg); 1-4339-2058-1 (lib bdg)

                      LC 2009006687

This has a "lively, well-organized [text]. . . . Perritano briefly discusses the distinctive physical and behavioral characteristics of about a dozen common parasites that live on or inside human bodies and how they affect their hosts. Featured invertebrates include bedbugs, fleas, head lice, tapeworms, and mosquitoes. . . . One or more illustrations accompany the text on every page—a mix of sharp, color photographs and some color drawings, maps, life cycle diagrams, etc." SLJ

   Includes glossary and bibliographical references

Posada, Mia

Ladybugs; red, fiery, and bright; written and illustrated by Mia Posada. Carolrhoda Bks. 2002 unp il hardcover o.p. pa $6.95

Grades: K 1 2   **595.7**

  1. Ladybugs

  ISBN 0-87614-334-6; 0-8225-6989-2 (pa)

"The description of the life cycle of ladybugs begins with fully developed insects . . . and progresses through a . . . study of behavior, birth, and development." SLJ

"A colorful description of the ladybug's life cycle, depicted in beautiful illustrations and expressed in poetic verse." Soc Educ

Prischmann, Deirdre A.

Poop-eaters; dung beetles in the food chain; by Deirdre A. Prischmann. Capstone Press 2008 32p il (Fact finders. Extreme life) lib bdg $23.93

Grades: 2 3 4   **595.7**

  1. Beetles

  ISBN 978-1-4296-1265-4 (lib bdg); 1-4296-1265-7 (lib bdg)   LC 2007-20440

"The beetles' features, traits, and development are explained in breezy text, accompanied by vivid photographs and additional 'Gross!' fact boxes. . . . The volume provides an informative introduction to an underappreciated insect." Horn Book Guide

Includes glossary and bibliographical references

Rockwell, Anne F., 1934-

Becoming butterflies; by Anne Rockwell; pictures by Megan Halsey. Walker & Co. 2002 unp il map hardcover o.p. pa $6.95

Grades: K 1 2   **595.7**

  1. Butterflies

  ISBN 0-8027-8797-5; 0-8027-8798-3 (lib bdg); 0-8027-7686-8 (pa)   LC 2001-26935

A class observes the various stages caterpillars go through to become butterflies

"Without an unneccessary word of explanation, the text makes clear the science of metamorphosis, and leavens the story with the humor of the children's comments. The illustrations are watercolors with pieces of cut paper layered to give depth." SLJ

Bugs are insects; by Anne Rockwell; illustrated by Steve Jenkins. HarperCollins Pubs. 2001 29p il (Let's-read-and-find-out science) hardcover o.p. lib bdg $15.89; pa $4.95

Grades: K 1 2 3   **595.7**

  1. Insects

  ISBN 0-06-028568-0; 0-06-028569-9 (lib bdg); 0-06-445203-4 (pa)   LC 99-39846

Introduces common backyard insects and explains the basic characteristics of these creatures

This is a "well-written and informative book. . . . The collage illustrations are beautifully rendered with layered colored papers of a variety of textures that add both depth and details to the creatures." SLJ

Honey in a hive; by Anne Rockwell; illustrated by S. D. Schindler. HarperCollinsPublishers 2005 33p il (Let's-read-and-find-out science) $15.99; lib bdg $16.89; pa $4.99

Grades: K 1 2 3   **595.7**

  1. Bees 2. Honey

  ISBN 0-06-028566-4; 0-06-028567-2 (lib bdg); 0-06-445204-2 (pa)   LC 2003-10357

An introduction to the behavior and life cycle of honeybees, with particular emphasis on the production of honey

"Schindler's realistic artwork is both colorful and nicely matched to the text. . . . This attractive introduction to honey production will serve students well." Booklist

Rodriguez, Ana Maria, 1958-

Secret of the plant-killing ants . . . and more! Enslow Publishers 2008 c2009 48p il (Animal secrets revealed!) lib bdg $23.93

Grades: 5 6 7 8   **595.7**

  1. Insects 2. Ants

  ISBN 978-0-7660-2953-8 (lib bdg); 0-7660-2953-0 (lib bdg)   LC 2007039494

"Explains why ants in the Amazon rainforest kill all but one species of plant and details other strange abilities of different types of animals." Publisher's note

Includes glossary and bibliographical references

Rompella, Natalie

Don't squash that bug! the curious kid's guide to insects; written by Natalie Rompella; [Margo Burian, illustrator] Lobster 2007 unp il (Lobster learners) $14.95

Grades: 2 3 4   **595.7**

  1. Insects

  ISBN 978-1-897073-50-6

"This appealing introduction to insects uses colorful photographs and a consistent layout to engage and inform readers. . . . An excellent glossary is included. The conversational text will hold readers' interest without overwhelming them." SLJ

Rotner, Shelley

The buzz on bees; why are they disappearing? by Shelley Rotner and Anne Woodhull; photographs by Shelley Rotner. Holiday House 2010 unp il $16.95

Grades: 2 3 4   **595.7**

  1. Beekeeping 2. Bees 3. Fertilization of plants

  ISBN 978-0-8234-2247-0; 0-8234-2247-X

"Excellent color photos provide an eye-catching backdrop for a simple, readable text that explains the importance of bees as pollinators and the current mystery of CCD (Colony Collapse Disorder) as hundreds of thousands of bees vanish without a trace. . . . Rotner and Woodhull offer a look at a variety of bees and other pollinators and a sample of the many products dependent on their efforts. . . . This title is eye-catching and informative." SLJ

Includes bibliographical references

Schwabacher, Martin

Butterflies. Benchmark Bks. 2004 45p il map (Animals, animals) lib bdg $17.95 *

Grades: 3 4 5 6   **595.7**

1. Butterflies

ISBN 0-7614-1618-8   LC 2003-3627

Contents: Beautiful butterflies; The butterfly family; The big change; Butterfly enemies; Butterflies and people

This describes the life cycles and characteristics of butterflies, illustrated with color photographs

Includes glossary and bibliographical references

Siy, Alexandra

Mosquito bite; [by] Alexandra Siy & Dennis Kunkel. Charlesbridge 2005 32p il $16.95; pa $6.95 *

Grades: 3 4 5   **595.7**

1. Mosquitoes

ISBN 1-57091-591-1; 1-57091-592-X (pa)

LC 2004-18959

"Black-and-white photographs of an evening game of hide-and-seek are interspersed with stunning color-enhanced microphotographs that record the life cycle of another seeker: a female Culex pipiens mosquito looking for a meal. . . . This title is fascinating for its photography and the informative text and captions." SLJ

Stewart, Melissa, 1968-

How do bees make honey? Marshall Cavendish Benchmark 2009 32p il (Tell me why, tell me how) lib bdg $20.95

Grades: 3 4 5   **595.7**

1. Bees 2. Honey

ISBN 978-0-7614-2923-4 (lib bdg); 0-7614-2923-9 (lib bdg)   LC 2007022935

"Provides comprehensive information on bees and the process of how they make honey." Publisher's note

"One or two large, well-captioned color photographs are provided per spread. [The] book concludes with an activity. [This is a] solid [introduction]." SLJ

Includes glossary and bibliographical references

Stradling, Jan

Bugs and spiders. Silver Dolphin Books 2009 90p il (The wonders inside) $19.95 *

Grades: 1 2 3 4   **595.7**

1. Insects 2. Spiders

ISBN 978-1-57145-907-7; 1-57145-907-3

This is a introduction to the life cycles and anatomy of a variety of insects and spiders

"The most outstanding innovation in the book consists of a series of five clear plastic overlays interspersed among the pages: these colorful overlays fit exactly over the figures on the page and bring out internal anatomic features. . . . The plethora of gorgeous drawings [is] accompanied by [an] easy-to-read, generally reliable, and highly informative text." Sci Books Films

Includes glossary

Swanson, Diane, 1944-

Bugs up close; written by Diane Swanson; photographed by Paul Davidson. Kids Can Press 2008 40p il pa $16.95

Grades: 3 4 5 6   **595.7**

1. Insects

ISBN 978-1-55453-138-7 (pa); 1-55453-138-1 (pa)

This describes "basic insect anatomy, major body parts and how they function, special adaptations of close to three dozen kinds of insects, egg-laying, metamorphosis, defense mechanisms, etc. . . . Most of the photos are so highly magnified that individual hairs, spines, and antennae segments are clearly visible. . . . This attractive, informative overview will appeal to both browsers and budding entomologists." SLJ

Tait, Noel

Insects & spiders. Simon & Schuster Books for Young Readers 2008 64p il map (Insiders) $16.99

Grades: 5 6 7 8   **595.7**

1. Insects 2. Spiders

ISBN 978-1-4169-3868-2; 1-4169-3868-0

LC 2008-61110

Provides an overview of insects and spiders in a book that includes detailed three-dimensional illustrations.

"Sharp, hyper-realistic, larger-than-life drawings . . . are . . . set against a plain colored background or within a natural setting. . . . [This] title succinctly describes basic anatomy; physical and behavioral characteristics common to all [insects and spiders]." SLJ

Includes glossary

Thomson, Ruth, 1949-

The life cycle of a ladybug. PowerKids Press 2009 24p il (Learning about life cycles) lib bdg $21.25; pa $8.25

Grades: K 1 2   **595.7**

1. Ladybugs

ISBN 978-1-4358-2835-3 (lib bdg); 1-4358-2835-6 (lib bdg); 978-1-4358-2885-8 (pa); 1-4358-2885-2 (pa)

LC 2008025780

This describes the life cycle of the ladybug

The text is "clear and graceful. . . . Crisp, closeup color photos appear on every page." SLJ

Trueit, Trudi Strain

Ants; reading consultant, Nanci R. Vargus. Marshall Cavendish Benchmark 2009 23p il (Benchmark rebus. Creepy critters) lib bdg $22.79

Grades: PreK K 1   **595.7**

1. Ants

ISBN 978-0-7614-3961-5; 0-7614-3961-7

LC 2008-12152

"Easy to read text with rebuses explores the strength of the ant.". Publisher's note

"Brilliant close-up photos will help beginning readers make meaning and appeal to students who like these creatures. . . . Glossary, print and media resources for further learning, and an about the author section conclude . . . [the] book. Reading specialists will want to be advised about [this book] . . . as will teachers. . . . This . . . is an excellent resource for beginning research projects." Libr Media Connect

Includes glossary and bibliographical references

Trueit, Trudi Strain—*Continued*

Beetles. Marshall Cavendish Benchmark 2010 23p il (Benchmark rebus. Creepy critters) lib bdg $22.79

Grades: PreK K 1   **595.7**
1. Beetles
ISBN 978-0-7614-3962-2; 0-7614-3962-5
                                    LC 2008-23153
"Easy to read text with rebuses explores beetle varieties." Publisher's note

"Brilliant closeup photos will help beginning readers make meaning and appeal to students who like these creatures. . . . Glossary, print and media resources for further learning, and an about the author section conclude . . . [the] book. Reading specialists will want to be advised about [this book] . . . as will teachers. . . . This . . . is an excellent resource for beginning research projects." Libr Media Connect

Includes glossary and bibliographical references

Caterpillars. Marshall Cavendish Benchmark 2009 23p il (Benchmark rebus. Creepy critters) lib bdg $22.79

Grades: PreK K 1   **595.7**
1. Caterpillars
ISBN 978-0-7614-3963-9 (lib bdg); 0-7614-3963-3 (lib bdg)   LC 2008-17108
"Easy to read text with rebuses explores the busy day of a caterpillar." Publisher's note

"Brilliant closeup photos will help beginning readers make meaning and appeal to students who like these creatures. . . . Glossary, print and media resources for further learning, and an about the author section conclude . . . [the] book. Reading specialists will want to be advised about [this book] . . . as will teachers. . . . This . . . is an excellent resource for beginning research projects." Libr Media Connect

Includes glossary and bibliographical references

Grasshoppers. Marshall Cavendish Benchmark 2009 23p il (Benchmark rebus. Creepy critters) lib bdg $22.79

Grades: PreK K 1   **595.7**
1. Grasshoppers
ISBN 978-0-7614-3964-6 (lib bdg); 0-7614-3964-1 (lib bdg)   LC 2008-24210
"Easy to read text with rebuses explores the different things grasshoppers like to eat." Publisher's note

"Brilliant closeup photos will help beginning readers make meaning and appeal to students who like these creatures. . . . Glossary, print and media resources for further learning, and an about the author section conclude . . . [the] book. Reading specialists will want to be advised about [this book] . . . as will teachers. . . . This . . . is an excellent resource for beginning research projects." Publisher's note

Includes glossary and bibliographical references

VanCleave, Janice Pratt

Janice VanCleave's insects and spiders; mind-boggling experiments you can turn into science fair projects. Wiley 1998 92p il (Spectacular science projects series) pa $10.95

Grades: 4 5 6 7   **595.7**
1. Insects 2. Spiders 3. Science projects 4. Science—Experiments
ISBN 0-471-16396-1   LC 97-12595

Presents facts about insects and spiders and includes experiments, projects, and activities related to each topic

"This title is chock-full of meaningful, but not difficult, projects. . . . Clear line drawings illustrate the text on almost every page. . . . The lucid text is well organized and liberally sprinkled with safety warnings." SLJ

Includes glossary and bibliographical references

Voake, Steve

Insect detective; illustrated by Charlotte Voake. Candlewick Press 2010 28p il $16.99 *

Grades: K 1 2 3   **595.7**
1. Insects
ISBN 978-0-7636-4447-5; 1-4063-1051-4
                                    LC 2009011152
"This charming collaboration . . . gently encourages young readers to explore their natural surroundings and observe some of the more commonly found insects in it. In spare prose, brief facts about a variety of creatures, such as leaf-miner caterpillars, ground beetles, ants, earwigs, and dragonflies, are shared, as are hints on where and how to find them. . . . Simple but elegant pen and watercolor illustrations show the creatures in their habitats." SLJ

Walker, Sally M.

Fireflies. Lerner Publs. 2001 47p il (Early bird nature books) lib bdg $22.60

Grades: K 1 2 3   **595.7**
1. Fireflies
ISBN 0-8225-3047-3
Describes the physical characteristics, behavior and life cycle of fireflies

"The text is well organized and clearly written. . . . One or two good-quality color photographs or diagrams with informative captions appear on almost every page." SLJ

Whalley, Paul Ernest Sutton

Butterfly & moth; written by Paul Whalley; [special photography, Colin Keates, Kim Taylor, and Dave King] Dorling Kindersley 2000 63p il (DK eyewitness books) $15.99; lib bdg $19.99

Grades: 4 5 6 7   **595.7**
1. Butterflies 2. Moths
ISBN 0-7894-5832-2; 0-7894-6556-6 (lib bdg)
First published 1988 by Knopf

Photographs and text explore the behavior and life cycles of butterflies and moths, examining mating rituals, camouflage, habitat, growth from pupa to larva to adult, and other aspects

Wilkes, Sarah, 1964-

Insects; [by] Sarah Wilkes. World Almanac Library 2006 48p il (World Almanac Library of the animal kingdom) lib bdg $30.60

Grades: 5 6 7 8   **595.7**

1. Insects

ISBN 0-8368-6211-2 (lib bdg); 978-0-8368-6211-9 (lib bdg)   LC 2005052629

This "discusses a range of insects that help keep the natural world in balance. . . . [It describes] the common physical and behavioral traits of this . . . animal category . . . [and] what makes each species unique and how it fits into the natural world." Publisher's note

"One or two fine-quality, color close-up photos of representative species accompany the text on almost every page. . . . [This title is] precisely written, with unusual scientific terms defined as they appear." SLJ

Includes bibliographical references

597   Cold-blooded vertebrates Pisces (Fishes)

Arnosky, Jim

All about sharks. Scholastic Press 2003 unp il $15.95; pa $5.95

Grades: K 1 2 3   **597**

1. Sharks

ISBN 0-590-48166-5; 0-545-02600-8 (pa)

            LC 2002-67004

Describes the physical characteristics, behavior, and survival techniques of different kinds of sharks

"Different species and families are illustrated in simple drawings, and the various parts of a shark's body are labeled and explained in a basic, easy-to-read text." SLJ

Butterworth, Christine

Sea horse; the shyest fish in the sea; [by] Chris Butterworth; illustrated by John Lawrence. Candlewick Press 2006 27p il $16.99; pa $6.99 *

Grades: K 1 2   **597**

1. Sea horses

ISBN   978-0-7636-2989-2;   0-7636-2989-8; 978-0-7636-4140-5 (pa); 0-7636-4140-5 (pa)

            LC 2005-50755

First published 2005 in the United Kingdom with title: Sea-steady sea horse

"Pairing a central narrative about a male Barbour's sea horse with facts in smaller type, Butterworth first pinpoints the creatures' most immediately appealing attributes . . . then goes on to discuss the males' gestational role in reproduction and survival tactics of newly independent offspring. . . . Butterworth has a flair for dynamic writing. . . . Lawrence has created vinyl engravings that masterfully capture the delicate textures of sea horses' graceful, spiny bodies and of their undersea habitats." Booklist

Cerullo, Mary M., 1949-

The truth about great white sharks; written by Mary M. Cerullo; photographs by Jeffrey L. Rotman; illustrations by Michael Wertz. Chronicle Bks. 2000 48p il $14.95 paperback o.p.

Grades: 4 5 6 7   **597**

1. Sharks

ISBN 0-8118-2467-5; 0-8118-5759-X (pa)

            LC 00-31506

This provides information "about shark anatomy, senses, eating habits, and their relationships with humans. . . . The book also contains unusual information such as how these fish are measured and photographed and why they are not able to survive in an aquarium. The attractive layout blends line drawings, full-color photographs, varied typefaces, and eye-catching graphics. Rotman's pictures are clear and informative. . . . This title will be accessible to reluctant readers and is a must for most collections." SLJ

Includes bibliographical references

Coldiron, Deborah

Eels; by Deborah Coldiron. ABDO Pub. 2008 32p il (Underwater world) lib bdg $24.21

Grades: 2 3 4   **597**

1. Eels

ISBN 978-1-59928-818-5 (lib bdg); 1-59928-818-4 (lib bdg)   LC 2007-14850

"The captioned photographs are engaging. . . . 'Fast Facts' appear on some pages. . . . Provide[s] solid information for elementary school reports." Horn Book Guide

Includes glossary

Stingrays; by Deborah Coldiron. ABDO Pub. 2008 32p il (Underwater world) lib bdg $24.21

Grades: 2 3 4   **597**

1. Rays (Fishes)

ISBN 978-1-59928-817-8 (lib bdg); 1-59928-817-6 (lib bdg)   LC 2007-14856

"The captioned photographs are engaging. . . . 'Fast Facts' appear on some pages. . . . Provide[s] solid information for elementary school reports." Horn Book Guide

Includes glossary

De la Bédoyère, Camilla

Sharks. Silver Dolphin 2009 24p il (Action files) $15.95

Grades: K 1 2 3   **597**

1. Sharks

ISBN 978-1-59223-933-7; 1-59223-933-1

"This lively interactive guide . . . delivers plenty of highly accessible shark-related information in tabbed chapters that cover anatomy, . . . shark life and conservation issues." Publ Wkly

Doubilet, David

Face to face with sharks; by David Doubilet and Jennifer Hayes. National Geographic 2009 31p il (Face to face) $16.95; lib bdg $25.90 *

Grades: 3 4 5 6   **597**

1. Sharks

ISBN   978-1-4263-0404-0;   1-4263-0404-8; 978-1-4263-0405-7 (lib bdg); 1-4263-0405-6 (lib bdg)

            LC 2008038244

Doubilet, David—*Continued*

The authors describe the life cycle and behavior of sharks and their own experiences with sharks in the wild

Includes glossary and bibliographical references

George, Twig C., 1950-

Seahorses. Millbrook Press 2003 31p il lib bdg $24.90

Grades: K 1 2 3   597

1. Sea horses

ISBN 0-7613-2869-6   LC 2003-10124

Describes the physical characteristics, behavior, and habitats of different species of seahorses, sea dragons, and pipefish, through simple text and photographs

"Some of the photographs are simply quite beautiful. Others stand out for their subjects. . . . The text is well cadenced and informative." Booklist

Gibbons, Gail

Sharks. Holiday House 1992 unp il $16.95; pa $6.95

Grades: K 1 2 3   597

1. Sharks

ISBN 0-8234-0960-0; 0-8234-1068-4 (pa)

LC 91-31524

Describes shark behavior and different kinds of sharks

The author's "bold, appealing illustrations (many of them labeled and explained) are the strength of the presentation. An excellent choice for even the youngest shark fan, this will be useful for simple reports as well." Booklist

Gray, Susan Heinrichs

Walking catfish; by Susan H. Gray. Cherry Lake Pub. 2009 32p il map (Animal invaders) lib bdg $27.07

Grades: 3 4 5   597

1. Catfish 2. Biological invasions

ISBN 978-1-60279-242-5 (lib bdg); 1-60279-242-9 (lib bdg)   LC 2008000804

"Walking catfish can move from water to land and back again, but it is humans that have carried them thousands of miles from their native Southeast Asia. In their new locations, they have upset the balance of ecosystems and hurt the local economies. [This book describes] walking catfish, the problems they create, and what is being done to control their spread." Publisher's note

"Clear color photographs, most of which are closeups, accompany the [text] on about every other page. . . . [This title provides] report writers with in-depth and up-to-date information on these invaders and the serious problems they cause." SLJ

Includes glossary and bibliographical references

Macquitty, Miranda

Shark; written by Miranda MacQuitty. rev ed. DK Pub. 2004 72p il (DK eyewitness books) hardcover o.p. lib bdg $19.99 *

Grades: 4 5 6 7   597

1. Sharks

ISBN 0-7566-0725-6; 0-7566-0724-8 (lib bdg)

First published 1992 by Knopf

Describes, in text and photographs, the physical characteristics, behavior, and life cycle of various types of sharks

Mallory, Kenneth

Swimming with hammerhead sharks. Houghton Mifflin 2001 48p il (Scientists in the field) $16

Grades: 4 5 6 7   597

1. Klimley, A. Peter 2. Sharks

ISBN 0-618-05543-6   LC 00-61401

"A New England Aquarium book"

Published "in association with the New England Aquarium."

This book follows "marine biologist Pete Klimley and an IMAX film team to seamounts off Cocos Island in the Pacific Ocean to observe and film schooling hammerhead sharks. . . . A fascinating record of research and investigation, this inviting book is larded with numerous dramatic color photos." SLJ

Includes bibliographical references

Markle, Sandra, 1946-

Great white sharks; by Sandra Markle. Carolrhoda Books 2004 40p il (Animal predators) lib bdg $25.26; pa $7.95

Grades: 3 4 5 6   597

1. Sharks

ISBN 1-57505-731-X (lib bdg); 1-57505-747-6 (pa)

LC 2003-23180

"Markle observes great whites' hunting techniques and includes information about their physical characteristics, physiology, habitats, and care of young." Horn Book Guide

"The role of camouflage is aptly explained in flowing text and illustrated in clear photography. . . . The full-color photography bedazzles on almost every page." SLJ

Includes bibliographical references

Sharks; biggest! littlest! photographs by Doug Perrine. Boyds Mills Press 2008 32p il map $16.95

Grades: 2 3 4   597

1. Sharks 2. Size

ISBN 978-1-59078-513-3; 1-59078-513-4

LC 2007052629

"Bright, clear color photos and informative text introduce young readers to the biggest and littlest sharks as well as sharks with some of the strangest features. . . . With just the right amount of detail for the intended audience, the large-print text is interspersed between fascinating pictures of sharks in their environments." Booklist

Includes glossary and bibliographical references

Otfinoski, Steven, 1949-

Sea horses; by Steven Otfinoski. Marshall Cavendish Benchmark 2007 48p il map (Animals, animals) lib bdg $28.50 *

Grades: 3 4 5 6   597

1. Sea horses

ISBN 978-0-7614-2529-8

"Describes the physical characteristics, habitat, behavior, diet, life cycle, and conservation status of the sea

Otfinoski, Steven, 1949-—*Continued*
horse." Publisher's note

This "solid, smoothly written [introduction is] compelling for [its] well-organized and attractively formatted presentation." SLJ

Includes glossary and bibliographical references

Pfeffer, Wendy, 1929-
What's it like to be a fish? illustrated by Holly Keller. HarperCollins Pubs. 1996 32p il (Let's-read-and-find-out science) hardcover o.p. pa $4.95
Grades: K 1   597
  1. Fishes
  ISBN 0-06-024429-1 (lib bdg); 0-06-445151-8 (pa)
                                  LC 94-6543

"By comparing goldfish to wild fish and human beings, this book describes the basic physiology of fish. The colorful illustrations are done in watercolors and pastels. . . . In a very accessible narrative that flows from point to point, the basic external anatomy of fish and such behaviors as movement, breathing, eating, and maintenance of temperature are defined in terms of caring for a goldfish in a bowl." Sci Books Films

Pringle, Laurence P.
Sharks!: strange and wonderful; by Laurence Pringle; illustrated by Meryl Henderson. Boyds Mills Press 2001 32p il $15.95
Grades: 3 4 5   597
  1. Sharks
  ISBN 1-56397-863-6

"Basic information about sharks—including physical characteristics, feeding habits, and their role in the chain of ocean life—is presented in clear, accessible prose. The acrylic paintings serve as a veritable catalog showcasing the variety of known sharks." Horn Book Guide

Rockwell, Anne F., 1934-
Little shark; [by] Anne Rockwell; pictures by Megan Halsey. Walker & Co. 2005 unp il $15.95; lib bdg $16.85
Grades: K 1 2   597
  1. Sharks
  ISBN 0-8027-8955-2; 0-8027-8956-0 (lib bdg)
                                LC 2004-52611

"Rockwell invites her readers to follow a newborn shark pup as it grows, explores its ocean home on its own, and develops at last into an adult blue shark. Strung throughout the narrative . . . are interesting facts about shark physiology, behaviors, and deep-sea dangers. . . . The whole is decorated with soft watercolor-and-pencil collage illustrations that are both attractive and . . . informative." SLJ

Rodriguez, Ana Maria, 1958-
Secret of the suffocating slime trap . . . and more! Enslow Publishers 2008 c2009 48p il (Animal secrets revealed!) lib bdg $23.93
Grades: 5 6 7 8   597
  1. Fishes
  ISBN 978-0-7660-2954-5 (lib bdg); 0-7660-2954-9 (lib bdg)
                          LC 2007039493

"Explains how hagfish excrete slime to evade predators and details other strange abilities of different types of animals." Publisher's note

This book offers "fascinating accounts of how scientists systematically analyzed, tested, and proved their theories or how their findings led to other, serendipitous discoveries. . . . Science experiments are thoughtfully placed to inspire exploration, and captioned, full-color photos appear throughout." SLJ

Includes glossary and bibliographical references

Simon, Seymour, 1931-
Sharks. HarperCollins Pubs. 1995 unp il $16.95; pa $6.95 *
Grades: 2 3 4   597
  1. Sharks
  ISBN 0-06-023029-0; 0-06-446187-4 (pa)
                                LC 95-1593

The author "explores the fascinating undersea life of sharks, examining the truths and myths about these amazing creatures. Astounding close-up photographs enhance the informative and exciting text." Sci Child

Stockdale, Susan, 1954-
Fabulous fishes; written and illustrated by Susan Stockdale. Peachtree 2008 unp il $15.95 *
Grades: PreK K 1 2 3   597
  1. Fishes
  ISBN 978-1-56145-429-7; 1-56145-429-X
                                LC 2007-29749

"With simple, rhyming text and full-page illustrations in acrylic and collage, this picture book introduces dramatic facts about more than 20 different fishes. . . . Young children will enjoy pointing out the various fish in the illustrations, while older children will switch back and forth from the pictures to the fascinating biological facts about fish behavior, habitat, and camouflage gathered in notes at the back." Booklist

Walker, Sally M.
Fossil fish found alive; discovering the coelacanth. Carolrhoda Bks. 2002 72p il map lib bdg $17.95
Grades: 5 6 7 8   597
  1. Coelacanth
  ISBN 1-57505-536-8   LC 2001-3815

Describes the 1938 discovery of the coelacanth, a fish previously believed to be extinct, and subsequent research about it

"Walker writes well, making this relatively unknown area of science history an exciting story of exploration and discovery. Excellent, full-color photos illustrate the text." Booklist

Includes bibliographical references

Rays. Carolrhoda Bks. 2003 48p il (Carolrhoda nature watch book) lib bdg $23.93
Grades: 3 4 5 6   597
  1. Rays (Fishes)
  ISBN 1-57505-172-9   LC 2001-6586

Describes the physical characteristics, behavior, life cycle, and endangered status of rays

Walker, Sally M.—*Continued*

"The crisp, well-captioned color photos highlight the many varieties of this unusual fish. Information is presented clearly." Horn Book Guide

Includes glossary

Wallace, Karen

Think of an eel; illustrated by Mike Bostock. Candlewick Press 1993 unp il hardcover o.p. pa $6.99; pa with audio CD $8.99

Grades: K 1 2 3   **597**
  1. Eels
  ISBN 1-56402-180-7; 978-0-7636-1522-2 (pa); 0-7636-1522-6 (pa); 978-0-7636-3994-5 (pa with audio CD); 0-7636-3994-X (pa with audio CD)
                            LC 92-53131

Text and illustrations discuss the characteristics and life cycle of the eel

"Bostock's watercolor paintings illustrate the places and creatures in the text without diminishing the mystery of the eel's journey. . . . The short phrases of the prose create a rhythm almost like unrhymed verse that will please readers." Booklist

Wearing, Judy

Manta rays. Weigl Publishers 2010 24p il (World of wonder: underwater life) lib bdg $24.45; pa $8.95

Grades: K 1 2   **597**
  1. Rays (Fishes)
  ISBN 978-1-60596-104-0 (lib bdg); 1-60596-104-3 (lib bdg); 978-1-60596-105-7 (pa); 1-60596-105-1 (pa)
                            LC 2009-25988

This book about mantra rays begins "with introductory information and progress[es] to more unique details of the featured creatures. Bold photographs juxtaposed on colorful background graphic will hold the attention of even the most novice readers. . . . [This book is] sure to make a splash with budding marine biologists everywhere." SLJ

Includes glossary

Seahorses. Weigl 2010 24p il (World of wonder: underwater life) lib bdg $24.45; pa $8.95

Grades: K 1 2   **597**
  1. Sea horses
  ISBN 978-1-60596-102-6 (lib bdg); 1-60596-102-7 (lib bdg); 978-1-60596-103-3 (pa); 1-60596-103-5 (pa)
                            LC 2009-4986

This book about seahorses begins "with introductory information and progress[es] to more unique details of the featured creatures. Bold photographs juxtaposed on colorful background graphic will hold the attention of even the most novice readers. . . . [This book is] sure to make a splash with budding marine biologists everywhere." SLJ

Includes glossary

Wilkes, Sarah, 1964-

Fish; [by] Sarah Wilkes. World Almanac Library 2006 48p il (World Almanac Library of the animal kingdom) lib bdg $30.60

Grades: 5 6 7 8   **597**
  1. Fishes
  ISBN 0-8368-6210-4 (lib bdg); 978-0-8368-6210-2 (lib bdg)
                        LC 2005051693

This "introduces a wide range of aquatic creatures that contribute to the diversity of Earth's oceans and lakes. [It describes] the common physical and behavioral traits of this . . . animal category . . . [and] what makes each species unique and how it fits into the natural world." Publisher's note

"One or two fine-quality, color close-up photos of representative species accompany the text on almost every page. . . . [This title is] precisely written, with unusual scientific terms defined as they appear." SLJ

Includes bibliographical references

597.8   Amphibia (Amphibians)

Arnosky, Jim

All about frogs. Scholastic Press 2002 unp il $15.95

Grades: K 1 2 3   **597.8**
  1. Frogs
  ISBN 0-590-48164-9   LC 2001-20680

"Beginning with a discussion of amphibians, the book goes on to talk specifically about frogs: their distinctive characteristics, habits, habitats, range, life cycle, diet, and the threats to their existence. The attractive acrylic paintings, well designed to illustrate particular points, zoom in for details. . . . Always informative, yet casual in tone, the text will engage young readers without talking down to them." Booklist

Bishop, Nic, 1955-

Nic Bishop frogs. Scholastic Nonfiction 2008 48p il $17.99 *

Grades: 2 3 4   **597.8**
  1. Frogs
  ISBN 978-0-439-87755-8; 0-439-87755-5
                        LC 2007-08699

Boston Globe-Horn Book Award honor book: Nonfiction (2008)

Bishop "presents a number of large, striking photos illustrating a clearly written discussion of the physical characteristics and habits of frogs. Dominating the book are Bishop's remarkably fine color photographs of frogs from around the world." Booklist

Includes glossary

Bluemel Oldfield, Dawn

Leaping ground frogs. Bearport 2010 24p il map (Amphibiana) lib bdg $22.61

Grades: 3 4 5 6   **597.8**
  1. Frogs
  ISBN 978-1-936087-35-8 (lib bdg); 1-936087-35-9 (lib bdg)

This book about ground frogs "is informative, eye-catching, well organized, and useful for reports. . . .

Bluemel Oldfield, Dawn—*Continued*

Large, clear color photos depict the animals in their natural habitats." SLJ

Includes glossary and bibliographical references

Bredeson, Carmen

Poison dart frogs up close; [by] Carmen Bredeson. Enslow Elementary 2008 24p il (Zoom in on animals!) lib bdg $21.26

Grades: 1 2 3   **597.8**

  1. Frogs

  ISBN 978-0-7660-3077-0 (lib bdg); 0-7660-3077-6 (lib bdg)   LC 2007039467

"Short paragraphs of simply written text describe [poison dart frogs'] key body parts and how they function. . . . Behavior, diet, and care and development of the young are briefly addressed. Facing the text on each spread is a full-page, sharp, color close-up of one or more of the . . . animals in their natural habitat. . . . Bredeson's simply written and colorful [title] will provide younger readers with [a] satisfying first [introduction] to these fascinating creatures." SLJ

Includes glossary and bibliographical references

Carney, Elizabeth, 1981-

Frogs! National Geographic 2009 32p il (National Geographic kids) $11.90; pa $3.99

Grades: K 1 2   **597.8**

  1. Frogs

  ISBN   978-1-4263-0393-7;   1-4263-0393-9; 978-1-4263-0392-0 (pa); 1-4263-0392-0 (pa)   LC 2008014028

This "volume employs simple sentence structures to convey basic facts about frogs . . . including life cycles, habitats, and feeding information. The excellent photographs showcase a variety of species in vivid detail. Vocabulary-word text boxes and goofy jokes . . . increase accessibility." Horn Book Guide

Firestone, Mary, 1951-

What's the difference between a frog and a toad? illustrated by Bandelin-Dacey. Picture Window Books 2010 24p il (What's the difference) lib bdg $25.32

Grades: K 1 2   **597.8**

  1. Frogs 2. Toads

  ISBN 978-1-4048-5544-1 (lib bdg); 1-4048-5544-0 (lib bdg)   LC 2009-6885

"Compares and contrasts the habitats, physical characteristics, location, and lifestyles of [frogs and toads]. The picture-book format is used to great effect as it allows the two animals to be compared side by side on each spread.The bold, expressive watercolors provide the same visual impact as photographs. . . . Short sentences and highlighted fun facts make this . . . [a book] with broad appeal for both researchers and browsers." SLJ

Includes glossary

Gibbons, Gail

Frogs. Holiday House 1993 unp il $16.95; pa $6.95

Grades: K 1 2 3   **597.8**

  1. Frogs

  ISBN 0-8234-1052-8; 0-8234-1134-6 (pa)   LC 93-269

An introduction to frogs, discussing their tadpole beginnings, noises they make, their hibernation, body parts, and how they differ from toads

"Gibbons' distinctive, labeled drawings identify the features described in the text, and her subjects float, swim, jump, and dive in colorful, lifelike illustrations. . . . This attractive book will appeal to prereaders, beginning readers, and the adults who read to those groups." Booklist

Goldish, Meish

Amazing water frogs. Bearport 2010 24p il map (Amphibiana) lib bdg $22.61

Grades: 3 4 5 6   **597.8**

  1. Frogs

  ISBN 978-1-936087-34-1 (lib bdg); 1-936087-34-0 (lib bdg)

This book about water frogs "is informative, eye-catching, well organized, and useful for reports. . . . Large, clear color photos depict the animals in their natural habitats." SLJ

Includes glossary and bibliographical references

Little newts. Bearport 2010 24p il map (Amphibiana) lib bdg $22.61

Grades: 3 4 5 6   **597.8**

  1. Newts

  ISBN 978-1-936087-38-9 (lib bdg); 1-936087-38-3 (lib bdg)

This book about newts "is informative, eye-catching, well organized, and useful for reports. . . . Large, clear color photos depict the animals in their natural habitats." SLJ

Includes glossary and bibliographical references

Slimy salamanders. Bearport 2010 24p il map (Amphibiana) lib bdg $22.61

Grades: 3 4 5 6   **597.8**

  1. Salamanders

  ISBN 978-1-936087-37-2 (lib bdg); 1-936087-37-5 (lib bdg)

This book about salamanders "is informative, eye-catching, well organized, and useful for reports. . . . Large, clear color photos depict the animals in their natural habitats." SLJ

Includes glossary and bibliographical references

Warty toads. Bearport 2010 24p il (Amphibiana) lib bdg $22.61

Grades: 3 4 5 6   **597.8**

  1. Toads

  ISBN 978-1-936087-36-5 (lib bdg); 1-936087-36-7 (lib bdg)

This book about toads "is informative, eye-catching, well organized, and useful for reports. . . . Large, clear color photos depict the animals in their natural habitats." SLJ

Includes glossary and bibliographical references

Hamilton, Garry, 1962-
Frog rescue; changing the future for endangered wildlife. Firefly Books 2004 64p il (Firefly animal rescue series) $19.95; pa $9.95
Grades: 5 6 7 8 **597.8**
    1. Frogs 2. Endangered species 3. Wildlife conservation
    ISBN 1-55297-597-5; 1-55297-506-7 (pa)
This describes endangered species of frogs, how and why they are in danger, and explains what efforts are being made to protect them.
This is "well-written. . . . Stunning, full-color photographs bring each species to life and depict a number of individuals in the field and laboratory working to save these animals." SLJ

Johnson, Jinny
Frog; illustrations by Graham Rosewarne. Smart Apple Media 2010 32p il (How does it grow?) lib bdg $28.50
Grades: 1 2 3 **597.8**
    1. Frogs 2. Life cycles (Biology)
    ISBN 978-1-59920-355-3 (lib bdg); 1-59920-355-3 (lib bdg)   LC 2008-53341
Presents an introduction to the life cycle of a frog, from its beginning as an egg, to its life as a tadpole, to its maturity as an adult frog
"Each stage is described on a spread that features clearly written, oversized text and a caption opposite a full-page, realistic watercolor, or, occasionally, a photograph. . . . A worthwhile purchase." SLJ
Includes glossary

Lunis, Natalie
Tricky tree frogs. Bearport 2010 24p il map (Amphibiana) lib bdg $22.61
Grades: 3 4 5 6 **597.8**
    1. Frogs
    ISBN 978-1-936087-33-4 (lib bdg); 1-936087-33-2 (lib bdg)
This book about tree frogs "is informative, eye-catching, well organized, and useful for reports. . . . Large, clear color photos depict the animals in their natural habitats." SLJ
Includes glossary and bibliographical references

Magloff, Lisa
Frog; written and edited by Lisa Magloff. Dorling Kindersley 2003 24p il (Watch me grow) $7.99
Grades: K 1 2 **597.8**
    1. Frogs
    ISBN 0-7894-9629-1   LC 2003-1578
Shows the frog as it grows up in its natural environment
"The full-color photographs . . . are not only exceptionally well chosen but downright dynamic. . . . Outstanding for browsing, with solid content for animal reports." Booklist
Includes glossary

Markle, Sandra, 1946-
Hip-pocket papa; illustrated by Alan Marks. Charlesbridge 2010 unp il lib bdg $15.95
Grades: K 1 2 3 **597.8**
    1. Frogs 2. Natural history—Australia
    ISBN 978-1-57091-708-0 (lib bdg); 1-57091-708-6 (lib bdg)   LC 2008025334
"Markle and Marks present this tiny Australian frog in the context of its natural environment. Both male and female hip-pocket frogs guard their developing eggs, but after they've hatched, the male keeps his tadpoles safe in hip pockets until they have used up their yolks and developed lungs. The poetic text follows one male journeying to a new and wetter home, describing the creatures he eats and those that want to eat him along the way." Kirkus
"Markle writes with clarity and precision, while Marks' evocative watercolor, ink, and pencil artwork brings the frogs' world to life." Booklist

Slippery, slimy baby frogs. Walker & Co. 2006 31p il map $16.95
Grades: 3 4 5 **597.8**
    1. Frogs
    ISBN 978-0-8027-8062-1; 0-8027-8062-8; 978-0-8027-8063-8 (lib bdg); 0-8027-8063-6 (lib bdg)   LC 2005-27542
"This book describes various types of frogs, from mating to adulthood. . . . The large, full-color photos provide crystal-clear closeup views of tadpoles and frogs in their natural environments, and a world map shows where the photographs were taken. While there are many other books about the life cycle of frogs, none contain the detailed information found here." SLJ

Moffett, Mark W.
Face to face with frogs. National Geographic 2008 31p il map (Face to face) $16.95; lib bdg $25.90
Grades: 3 4 5 6 **597.8**
    1. Frogs
    ISBN 978-1-4263-0205-3; 1-4263-0205-3; 978-1-4263-0206-0 (lib bdg); 1-4263-0206-1 (lib bdg)   LC 2007-12445
This is an overview of frogs, "from metamorphosis to diet [and] from habitat to distinctive features." Publisher's note
This book has "personal accounts of [Moffett's] own explorations providing entertaining specifics to go with the arresting visuals, as casual sidebars offer information on random hoppy topics." Bull Cent Child Books
Includes glossary and bibliographical references

Pfeffer, Wendy, 1929-
From tadpole to frog; illustrated by Holly Keller. HarperCollins Pubs. 1994 32p il (Let's-read-and-find-out science) $15.95; pa $4.95
Grades: K 1 **597.8**
    1. Frogs
    ISBN 0-06-023044-4; 0-06-445123-2 (pa)
    LC 93-3135
This "introduction sketches the most basic aspects of frog life—the laying and hatching of eggs, the stages of

Pfeffer, Wendy, 1929- —*Continued*
growth, eating and the danger of being eaten, and hibernation." Horn Book Guide
  "The illustrations are simple, interesting, and just right
for young children. The science is accurate and presented
in a way to excite young readers to get outside and look
for some frogs and tadpoles." Sci Books Films

Salas, Laura Purdie, 1966-
  Amphibians; water-to-land animals; illustrated
by Kristin Kest. Picture Window Books 2010 24p
il (Amazing science. Animal classification) lib bdg
$25.32
Grades: K 1 2   **597.8**
  1. Amphibians
  ISBN 978-1-4048-5521-2 (lib bdg); 1-4048-5521-1 (lib
  bdg)   LC 2009-3290
  "This is the way to introduce kids to science as well
as lead them to a deeper level of understanding how the
animal kingdom is divided into phylum, class, order,
family, genus, and species. Excellent picture book-quality
illustrations fill each page with a few well chosen words
to extend visual understanding. . . . The writing is clear,
age-appropriate science writing. Every school should purchase this book." Libr Media Connect
  Includes glossary

Schwabacher, Martin
  Frogs. Benchmark Bks. 2004 47p il map
(Animals, animals) lib bdg $17.95
Grades: 3 4 5 6   **597.8**
  1. Frogs
  ISBN 0-7614-1619-6   LC 2003-13124
  Contents: Introducing frogs; Many kinds of frogs;
Frog bodies; A frog's life; Frogs and people
  Describes the physical characteristics, behavior, habi-
tat, and endangered status of the frog
  This has "excellent, full-color photographs and lively
[text] that [brings] these animals to life." SLJ
  Includes glossary and bibliographical references

Somervill, Barbara A., 1948-
  Cane toad; by Barbara A. Somervill. Cherry
Lake Pub. 2008 32p il map (Animal invaders) lib
bdg $26.26
Grades: 3 4 5 6   **597.8**
  1. Toads 2. Biological invasions
  ISBN 978-1-60279-115-2 (lib bdg); 1-60279-115-5 (lib
  bdg)   LC 2007-33510
  This describes the cane toads' "outstanding physical
and behavioral characteristics at each stage in their life
cycle, diet, and natural habitat, and then [explains] how
they were introduced into areas outside their natural
range . . . and the nature and extent of the ecological
damage they have caused, and various attempts to eradicate or at least control the animals. . . . The prolific
cane toads, which are fast supplanting native amphibians
in Australia, excrete a toxin powerful enough to kill the
animals, and some humans unfortunate enough to ingest
them. . . . Clear color photographs . . . accompany the
[text] on about every other page. . . . [This title is]
clearly written and well organized, and [has] up-to-date
information." SLJ
  Includes glossary

Stewart, Melissa, 1968-
  A place for frogs; written by Melissa Stewart;
illustrated by Higgins Bond. Peachtree Publishers
2010 unp il $16.95
Grades: K 1 2 3   **597.8**
  1. Frogs 2. Wildlife conservation
  ISBN 978-1-5614-5521-8; 1-5614-5521-0
  "This wide-format book shows how people's actions
have endangered frogs and what has been done to reverse those environmental threats. A typical double-page
spread includes a large, detailed acrylic painting showing
various frogs in their habitats. . . . Written and illustrated with young children in mind, this book is a good
starting place for environmental studies." Booklist

Turner, Pamela S.
  The frog scientist; photographs by Andy
Comins. Houghton Mifflin Books for Children
2009 58p il (Scientists in the field) lib bdg $18 *
Grades: 5 6 7 8   **597.8**
  1. Hayes, Tyrone 2. Frogs
  ISBN 978-0-618-71716-3 (lib bdg); 0-618-71716-1 (lib
  bdg)   LC 2008-39770
  This volume "opens with biologist Tyrone Hayes and
his team collecting frogs at a pond in Wyoming. After
a short chapter on Hayes' background, the discussion returns to his work: he addresses the general question of
why amphibian populations world-wide are declining by
studying the effects of atrizine, an agricultural pesticide,
on the reproductive organs of leopard frogs from a particular pond. Well organized and clearly written. . . .
Excellent color photos offer clear pictures of frogs and
of this scientific team at work in the field and in the lab.
. . . A vivid, realistic view of one scientist at work."
Booklist
  Includes glossary and bibliographical references

Whiting, Jim, 1943-
  Frogs in danger; by Jim Whiting. Mitchell Lane
Publishers 2007 32p il (On the verge of extinction:
crisis in the environment) lib bdg $25.27
Grades: 3 4 5   **597.8**
  1. Frogs
  ISBN 978-1-58415-585-0   LC 2007000802
  "A Robbie reader"
  This describes threats to the survival of frog species,
including global warming and other environmental dangers.
  "Short chapters, large font, and pronunciation guides
to key words engage children doing research, but the
depth of information is not compromised. . . . Colorful,
up-close photographs are accompanied by satisfying captions." SLJ
  Includes glossary and bibliographical references

Winer, Yvonne, 1934-
  Frogs sing songs; written by Yvonne Winer;
illustrated by Tony Oliver. Charlesbridge Pub.
2003 unp il $16.95; pa $6.95
Grades: K 1 2 3   **597.8**
  1. Frogs 2. Animal communication
  ISBN 1-57091-548-2; 1-57091-549-0 (pa)
                                          LC 2002-6234

Winer, Yvonne, 1934-—*Continued*
First published 2002 in the United Kingdom
Describes how, when, where, and why frogs sing songs. Includes frog identification guide
"One of Winer's short, simple poems appears under a spot illustration of a frog. Opposite is a full-page, vivid, realistic watercolor illustration of that particular species in its natural habitat." Booklist

597.9   Reptilia (Reptiles)

Arnosky, Jim
Slither and crawl; eye to eye with reptiles. Sterling Pub. 2009 31p il $14.95 *
Grades: 2 3 4 5   597.9
  1. Reptiles
  ISBN 978-1-4027-3986-6; 1-4027-3986-9
                                        LC 2008022493
"Arnosky's painterly eye and personal observations match handsomely in this face-to-face experience. The slim volume presents-head-on-life-size depictions of a plethora of scaly or otherwise armored critters, along with a nice selection of data included in the conversational text. Neat foldouts of a passel of snakes, an American crocodile, . . . a skitter of lizards, and the heads of a variety of sea turtles add an interactive touch to the artist's outstanding acrylics." SLJ
Includes bibliographical references

McCarthy, Colin, 1951-
Reptile; written by Colin McCarthy; [special photography, Karl Shone . . . [et al.]] Dorling Kindersley 2000 63p il (DK eyewitness books) $15.99
Grades: 4 5 6 7   597.9
  1. Reptiles
  ISBN 0-7894-5786-5
  First published 1991 by Knopf
Photographs and text depict the many different kinds of reptiles, their similarities and differences, habitats, and behavior

Wilson, Hannah
Life-size reptiles; written by Hannah Wilson. Sterling 2007 48p il $9.95
Grades: 3 4 5 6   597.9
  1. Reptiles
  ISBN 1-4027-4542-7
This "covers lizards, crocodilians, and others of their cold-blooded kin. Colorful, realistic illustrations fill the pages, depicting reptiles in all their scaly/shelled splendor, many—as promised in the title—life-sized." SLJ

Zabludoff, Marc
The reptile class. Benchmark Books 2005 95p il (Family trees) lib bdg $29.92
Grades: 6 7 8 9   597.9
  1. Reptiles
  ISBN 0-7614-1820-2   LC 2004-21820

This examines physical traits, adaptations, diets, habitats, and life cycles of reptiles.
"Fact-filled, yet surprisingly readable. . . . [This] title contains a wide variety of excellent-quality, full-color photos; interesting sidebars; and diagrams." SLJ

597.92   Chelonia

Berger, Melvin, 1927-
Look out for turtles! illustrated by Megan Lloyd. HarperCollins Pubs. 1992 32p il (Let's-read-and-find-out science book) hardcover o.p. pa $4.95
Grades: K 1 2 3   597.92
  1. Turtles
  ISBN 0-06-022540-8 (lib bdg); 0-06-445156-9 (pa)
                                        LC 90-36894
"This simple introductory resource provides an overview of the different types of turtles and their characteristics and habits. It is a good resource for young children to use independently." Sci Child

Christopherson, Sara Cohen
Top 50 reasons to care about marine turtles; animals in peril. Enslow Publishers 2009 103p il (Top 50 reasons to care about endangered animals) lib bdg $31.93
Grades: 4 5 6 7   597.92
  1. Sea turtles 2. Endangered species
  ISBN 978-0-7660-3455-6 (lib bdg); 0-7660-3455-0 (lib bdg)   LC 2009-10555
This describes marine turtles-their life cycles, diets, young, habitats, and reasons why they are endangered animals
"The illustrations, mostly color photographs, represent a wonderful selection of the animals and their habitats. Reluctant readers may be enticed by this . . . simply because of the great images. This . . . would make a substantial supplement to the science curriculum when studying endangered animals." Libr Media Connect
Includes glossary and bibliographical references

Davies, Nicola, 1958-
One tiny turtle; illustrated by Jane Chapman. Candlewick Press 2001 29p il hardcover o.p. pa with audio CD $9.99
Grades: K 1 2 3   597.92
  1. Turtles
  ISBN 0-7636-1549-8; 978-0-7636-4193-1 (pa with audio CD)   LC 00-52326
"This story follows one female loggerhead turtle from infancy to adulthood, when she lays her own eggs." Horn Book Guide
This offers "simple, lyrical words and bright, acrylic double-page pictures. . . . Without condescension, this tells a powerful nature story for a young audience." Booklist

Gibbons, Gail

Sea turtles. Holiday House 1995 unp il $16.95;
pa $6.95

Grades: K 1 2 3   **597.92**

1. Sea turtles

ISBN 0-8234-1191-5; 0-8234-1373-X (pa)
                                 LC 94-48579

This book examines "the size, habitat, and diet of the
eight kinds of sea turtles and efforts environmentalists
are making to protect them." Sci Child

This is "a very appealing book. . . . The illustrations
are lovely paintings, highlighted with black outlines and
clear labels. Children should find the diagram that shows
differences between sea turtles and other turtles fascinating because they are often familiar only with the latter."
Sci Books Films

Guiberson, Brenda Z., 1946-

Into the sea; illustrated by Alix Berenzy. Holt &
Co. 1996 unp il $16.95; pa $6.95

Grades: K 1 2 3   **597.92**

1. Sea turtles

ISBN 0-8050-2263-5; 0-8050-6481-8 (pa)
                                 LC 95-46757

The author "recounts the life of a sea turtle from its
days as a hatchling on a sandy beach through its return
to the same island as an egg-laying adult many years later." Booklist

"Guiberson uses italicized sound words such as *tap,
tap,* and *scritch* to draw readers into the story. Berenzy
captures the essence of the text with her colored-pencil
and gouache illustrations that alternate from dark to light,
reflecting the various habitats." SLJ

Hall, Kirsten, 1974-

Leatherback turtle; the world's heaviest reptile.
Bearport Pub. 2007 24p il map (Super sized!) lib
bdg $21.28

Grades: K 1 2   **597.92**

1. Sea turtles

ISBN 978-1-59716-393-4 (lib bdg); 1-59716-393-7 (lib
bdg)   LC 2006033247

This describes the size, habitat, diet, and life cycle of
the leatherback turtle

This is "attractive. . . . Most spreads include two to
five large-type sentences, a boxed fact, and a large colorful photograph." SLJ

Includes glossary and bibliographical references

Hickman, Pamela M., 1958-

Turtle rescue; changing the future for
endangered wildlife. Firefly 2005 64p il map
(Firefly animal rescue) $19.95; pa $9.95

Grades: 5 6 7 8   **597.92**

1. Turtles 2. Endangered species 3. Wildlife conservation

ISBN 1-55297-916-4; 1-55297-915-6 (pa)

This "overview of the plight of the world's turtles and
tortoises describes the general problems that all turtles
face and then explains what is being done to rescue certain species from near extinction. . . . The book is illustrated with excellent-quality photographs that are closely

tied to the text. Maps and charts are useful. . . . Other
books on the topic cannot match this, one for its thorough
approach as well as the current information." SLJ

Lockwood, Sophie

Sea turtles; by Sophie Lockwood. Child's World
2006 40p il map (World of reptiles) lib bdg
$29.93

Grades: 4 5 6   **597.92**

1. Sea turtles

ISBN 1-59296-550-4   LC 2005024792

"Conservation is the dominant theme of this attractive
photo-essay. . . . which has beautiful full-page color
photos that bring readers close to the subject. Fast-fact
boxes focus on particular species, providing spot statistics on weight, length, color, habitat, threatened or endangered status, and more." Booklist

Includes glossary and bibliographical references

Rebman, Renee C., 1961-

Turtles and tortoises. Marshall Cavendish
Benchmark 2007 48p il map (Animals, animals)
lib bdg $19.95 *

Grades: 3 4 5 6   **597.92**

1. Turtles

ISBN 978-0-7614-2239-6 (lib bdg); 0-7614-2239-0 (lib
bdg)

"Describes the physical characteristics, behavior, habitat, and endangered status of turtles and tortoises." Publisher's note

"Sharp color photographs accompany the text. . . .
[This is] clearly written [and] well organized." SLJ

Includes glossary and bibliographical references

Rodriguez, Cindy

Sea turtles. Rourke Pub. 2010 24p il map (Eye
to eye with endangered species) lib bdg $27.07

Grades: 2 3 4   **597.92**

1. Sea turtles

ISBN 978-1-60694-405-9 (lib bdg); 1-60694-405-3 (lib
bdg)   LC 2009-5996

Text examines the issues endangered sea turtles face
and how they can be saved

"Sets out to introduce readers to [sea turtles] . . . explain the dangers they face, and detail the efforts of biologists and conservationists to save them. . . . Serviceable and informative." SLJ

Includes glossary

Stone, Lynn M.

Box turtles; written and photographed by Lynn
M. Stone. Lerner Publications 2007 48p il map
(Nature watch) lib bdg $25.26

Grades: 4 5 6   **597.92**

1. Turtles

ISBN 978-1-57505-869-6 (lib bdg); 1-57505-869-3 (lib
bdg)   LC 2006012867

This describes the habitats, feeding habits, and reproductive behavior of the four species of box turtles found
in North America.

Includes glossary and bibliographical references

Swinburne, Stephen R.

Turtle tide; the ways of sea turtles; illustrated by Bruce Hiscock. Boyds Mills Press 2005 unp il $15.95

Grades: 2 3 4   **597.92**
  1. Sea turtles
  ISBN 1-59078-081-7   LC 2004-16856

"A mother loggerhead crawls onto an Atlantic beach, lays a hundred eggs in a deep nest, and heaves her way back to the sea. . . . Predators quickly reduce the clutch to a solitary hatchling. . . . [The book] closes with a view of the lone survivor, intrepidly paddling off into the wide, sunrise-lit sea." Booklist

"Simple, lyrical prose accompanies brilliant watercolors in this account." SLJ

Wearing, Judy

Sea turtle. Weigl 2010 24p il (World of wonder: underwater life) lib bdg $24.45; pa $8.95

Grades: K 1 2   **597.92**
  1. Sea turtles
  ISBN 978-1-60596-106-4 (lib bdg); 1-60596-106-X (lib bdg); 978-1-60596-107-1 (pa); 1-60596-107-8 (pa)   LC 2009-4987

This book about sea turtles begins "with introductory information and progress[es] to more unique details of the featured creatures. Bold photographs juxtaposed on colorful background graphic will hold the attention of even the most novice readers. . . . [This book is] sure to make a splash with budding marine biologists everywhere." SLJ

Includes glossary

597.95   Sauria (Lizards)

Cowley, Joy

Chameleon chameleon; story by Joy Cowley; illustrated with photographs by Nic Bishop. Scholastic Press 2005 unp il $16.95 *

Grades: K 1 2   **597.95**
  1. Chameleons
  ISBN 0-439-66653-8   LC 2004-7291

A chameleon creeps through the rain forest avoiding danger and searching for food

This is a "stunning photo-essay. . . . Crisp, clear, full-color photos portray this reptile and its habitat. . . . An informative, thoughtfully produced science book that will be popular with a wide range of animal lovers. Excellent for browsing as well as learning." Booklist

Jango-Cohen, Judith

Let's look at iguanas. Lerner Publications Co. 2010 32p il map (Lightning bolt books: Animal close-ups) lib bdg $25.26; pa $7.95

Grades: PreK K 1 2   **597.95**
  1. Iguanas
  ISBN 978-0-7613-3888-8 (lib bdg); 0-7613-3888-8 (lib bdg); 978-0-7613-5005-7 (pa); 0-7613-5005-5 (pa)   LC 2008-51857

Introduces desert iguanas, describing their physical characteristics, habitat, and predators.

"Fresh photography, a creative use of graphics, and a collagelike layout make[s] . . . [this book] eye-catching. . . . [The] book ends with a labeled diagram of the animal, a range map, and a further-reading list that includes print and online resources in a single list, a nice way of validating both types of materials." SLJ

Includes glossary

Stewart, Melissa, 1968-

How do chameleons change color? Marshall Cavendish Benchmark 2009 32p il (Tell me why, tell me how) lib bdg $20.95

Grades: 3 4 5   **597.95**
  1. Chameleons
  ISBN 978-0-7614-2922-7 (lib bdg); 0-7614-2922-0 (lib bdg)   LC 2007024099

"Provides comprehensive information on chameleons and explains how and why they change color" Publisher's note

"One or two large, well-captioned color photographs are provided per spread. [The] book concludes with an activity. [This is a] solid [introduction]." SLJ

Includes glossary and bibliographical references

597.96   Serpentes (Snakes)

Gibbons, Gail

Snakes. Holiday House 2007 32p il map $16.95

Grades: K 1 2 3   **597.96**
  1. Snakes
  ISBN 978-0-8234-2122-0; 0-8234-2122-8   LC 2007-24585

"Gibbons injects a healthy dose of snake basics, delivered in her customary matter-of-fact style and illustrated with watercolor portraits of dozens of different species, pictured mostly in natural settings." Booklist

Holub, Joan, 1956-

Why do snakes hiss? and other questions about snakes, lizards, and turtles; illustrations by Anna DiVito. Dial Books for Young Readers 2004 46p il (Dial easy-to-read) hardcover o.p. pa $3.99

Grades: K 1 2   **597.96**
  1. Reptiles 2. Snakes
  ISBN 0-8037-3000-4; 0-14-240105-6 (pa)   LC 2003-64948

Questions and answers present information about the behavior and characteristics of snakes, lizards, and turtles

"The photos and attractive ink drawings with color washes that come two to three to a page result in a colorful presentation with illustrations in different styles from many sources." Booklist

Markle, Sandra, 1946-

Rattlesnakes. Lerner Publications 2009 39p il (Animal predators) lib bdg $26.60

Grades: 4 5 6   **597.96**
  1. Rattlesnakes
  ISBN 978-1-58013-539-9 (lib bdg); 1-58013-539-0 (lib bdg)   LC 2008-38038

Markle, Sandra, 1946——*Continued*

Introduces the physical characteristics, habitat, and predatory behavior of rattlesnakes.

"Vivid close-up photographs accompany a narrative." Horn Book Guide

Includes glossary and bibliographical references

Menon, Sujatha

Discover snakes. Enslow Publishers 2008 47p il (Discover animals) lib bdg $23.93

Grades: 4 5 6 7   **597.96**
1. Snakes
ISBN 978-0-7660-3471-6 (lib bdg); 0-7660-3471-2 (lib bdg)   LC 2008013867

First published 2005 in the United Kingdom

This "introduces readers to a variety of snakes, from pythons to boa constrictors and cobras. . . . Images and text explain about a snake's fangs, life cycle, senses, and how they fight and move. The book also discusses the different snake families and the hunting styles of each." Publisher's note

Includes glossary and bibliographical references

Montgomery, Sy

The snake scientist; photographs by Nic Bishop. Houghton Mifflin 1999 48p il map $16; pa $5.95
*

Grades: 4 5 6 7   **597.96**
1. Mason, Bob 2. Snakes
ISBN 0-395-87169-7; 0-618-11119-0 (pa)
LC 98-6124

Discusses the work of Bob Mason and his efforts to study and protect snakes, particularly red-sided garter snakes

"The lively text communicates both the meticulous measurements required in this kind of work and the thrill of new discoveries. Large, full-color photos of the zoologist and young students at work, and lots of wriggly snakes, pull readers into the presentation." SLJ

Includes bibliographical references

Pringle, Laurence P.

Snakes! strange and wonderful; by Laurence Pringle; illustrated by Meryl Henderson. Boyds Mills Press 2004 31p il $15.95; pa $10.95

Grades: 3 4 5 6   **597.96**
1. Snakes
ISBN 1-59078-003-5; 1-59078-744-7 (pa)
LC 2003-26418

"Short paragraphs describe [snakes'] major physical and behavioral characteristics and highlight some distinctive traits of several different species. . . . More than three dozen species from around the world are depicted in the realistic watercolors. . . . The narrative is well organized and clearly written." SLJ

Simon, Seymour, 1931-

Giant snakes; [by] Seymour Simon. Chronicle Books 2006 unp il (See more readers) lib bdg $14.95; pa $3.95

Grades: K 1 2 3   **597.96**
1. Snakes
ISBN 978-0-8118-5410-8 (lib bdg); 0-8118-5410-8 (lib bdg); 978-0-8118-5411-5 (pa); 0-8118-5411-6 (pa)
LC 2005-25360

An easy-to-read illustrated introduction to large snakes.

"The text is lively, well organized, and clear, with the many facts it presents cleverly woven into the story. The illustrations, which are beautiful, show distinctly the intricate patterns of the snakes' skin." Sci Books Films

Stewart, Melissa, 1968-

Snakes! National Geographic 2009 31p il (National Geographic kids) lib bdg $11.90; pa $3.99

Grades: K 1 2   **597.96**
1. Snakes
ISBN   978-1-4263-0429-3   (lib   bdg);
978-1-4263-0428-6 (pa)   LC 2008-47001

An introduction to the types, physical features, behavior, and pet potential of snakes.

"The excellent photographs showcase a variety of species in vivid detail. Vocabulary-word text boxes and goofy jokes . . . increase accessibility." Horn Book Guide

597.98   Crocodilia (Crocodilians)

Feigenbaum, Aaron

American alligators; freshwater survivors. Bearport Pub. Company, Inc. 2008 32p il map (America's animal comebacks) lib bdg $25.27

Grades: 2 3 4   **597.98**
1. Alligators
ISBN 978-1-59716-503-7 (lib bdg); 1-59716-503-4 (lib bdg)   LC 2007-13160

Explains why American alligators became an endangered species, and describes the efforts of scientists to bring them back from the brink of extinction

"Closeup photos, maps, and an accessible text provide solid information for readers and report writers. Statistics and information about other endangered alligators are appended." Horn Book Guide

Includes glossary and bibliographical references

Gibbons, Gail

Alligators and crocodiles. Holiday House 2010 32p il map $17.95

Grades: K 1 2 3   **597.98**
1. Alligators 2. Crocodiles
ISBN 978-0-8234-2234-0; 0-8234-2234-8

Gibbons "draws young readers into the world of alligators and crocodiles by first asking readers to distinguish between them. She describes the physical similarities and differences between the two most common species of the world's largest reptiles, as well as their habi-

Gibbons, Gail—*Continued*

tats, habits, prey, locomotion, senses, communication, mating and nesting behavior, and status as endangered species. The author has chosen facts that will engage her readers, organized the information logically, and presented it in straightforward exposition. Pen-and-ink and watercolor illustrations show both species in their likely environment." Booklist

Markle, Sandra, 1946-

Crocodiles; by Sandra Markle. Carolrhoda Books 2004 39p il (Animal predators) lib bdg $25.26; pa $7.95 *
Grades: 3 4 5 6   **597.98**
1. Crocodiles
ISBN 1-57505-726-3 (lib bdg); 1-57505-742-5 (pa)
LC 2003-15402
"Markle observes Nile crocodiles' hunting techniques and includes information about their physiology, habitats, and care of young." Horn Book Guide
"The straightforward, descriptive text and superb photos give [this title] surefire appeal to middle readers." Booklist
Includes glossary and bibliographical references

Otfinoski, Steven, 1949-

Alligators; by Steven Otfinoski. Marshall Cavendish Benchmark 2009 47p il (Animals animals) lib bdg $20.95 *
Grades: 3 4 5 6   **597.98**
1. Alligators
ISBN 978-0-7614-2930-2 (lib bdg); 0-7614-2930-1 (lib bdg)   LC 2007-25448
"Provides comprehensive information on the anatomy, special skills, habitats, and diet of alligators." Publisher's note
Includes glossary

Pringle, Laurence P.

Alligators and crocodiles! strange and wonderful; [by] Laurence Pringle; illustrated by Meryl Henderson. Boyds Mills Press 2009 32p il $16.95
Grades: 3 4 5   **597.98**
1. Alligators 2. Crocodiles
ISBN 978-1-59078-256-9; 1-59078-256-9
LC 2008-30018
This describes alligators' and crocodiles' "habitats and nesting behavior, and explains their common anatomical features and distinguishing characteristics. . . . Henderson presents a gallery of full-body portraits of 21 crocodilian species, as well as a series of close-ups. These illustrations are drawn and colored in . . . clear, precise detail." Booklist

Rockwell, Anne F., 1934-

Who lives in an alligator hole? by Anne Rockwell; illustrated by Lizzy Rockwell. HarperCollins 2006 33p il (Let's-read-and-find-out science) $15.99; pa $4.99
Grades: K 1 2 3   **597.98**
1. Alligators 2. Ecology
ISBN 0-06-028530-3; 0-06-445200-X (pa)
Describes the habitats of these reptiles which scientists call a "keystone species" because they change the environment for their own use in a way that helps many other plants and animals.
"Information and illustration work well together in this picture book presentation. . . . Simplified yet not anthropomorphized, the clearly delineated paintings feature alligators and other animals as the focal points of well-composed scenes." Booklist

Simon, Seymour, 1931-

Crocodiles & alligators. HarperCollins Pubs. 1999 unp il hardcover o.p. pa $6.99
Grades: 4 5 6 7   **597.98**
1. Crocodiles 2. Alligators
ISBN 0-06-027473-5; 0-06-443829-5 (pa)
LC 98-34705
Describes the physical characteristics and behavior of various members of the family of animals known as crocodilians
"The book is filled with interesting information, and the vivid, well-composed, full-color photographs and entertaining text will draw in browsers." SLJ

Snyder, Trish

Alligator & crocodile rescue; changing the future for endangered wildlife. Firefly Books 2006 64p il (Firefly animal rescue) lib bdg $19.95; pa $9.95
Grades: 5 6 7 8   **597.98**
1. Alligators 2. Crocodiles 3. Wildlife conservation
ISBN 1-55297-920-2 (lib bdg); 1-55297-919-9 (pa)
This "outlines the various threats to survival of [alligators and crocodiles] and introduces readers to organizations and individuals trying to save them. . . . Numerous photographs document the work of scientists, conservationists, educators, and other people around the world who are committed to wildlife preservation." SLJ

598 Aves (Birds)

Arnold, Caroline, 1944-

Birds; nature's magnificent flying machines; illustrated by Patricia J. Wynne. Charlesbridge Pub. 2003 32p il $16.95; pa $6.95
Grades: 3 4 5 6   **598**
1. Birds—Flight
ISBN 1-57091-516-4; 1-57091-572-5 (pa)
LC 2002-10441
An introduction to the science that explains how birds fly
"A clear, interesting book. . . . Each spread contains one or two paragraphs with a large, full-color illustration

Arnold, Caroline, 1944-—*Continued*
as well as smaller, captioned pictures that cover such topics as bone structure and preening. The colorful artwork consistently clarifies the concepts being discussed." SLJ

Includes glossary and bibliographical references

A penguin's world; written and illustrated by Caroline Arnold. Picture Window Books 2005 24p il $23.93
Grades: K 1 2 3   598
1. Penguins
ISBN 1-4048-1323-3   LC 2005023159
"This title follows an Adelie penguin family from scenes in which the parents build a nest and warm their eggs to final pages showcasing the four-month-old, newly independent chicks. The simple, well-paced text weaves basic concepts into the captivating narrative, and the artwork's strong colors and bold, uncluttered compositions capture the expression and movement of the birds." Booklist

Includes glossary and bibliographical references

Arnosky, Jim
Watching water birds. National Geographic Soc. 1997 unp il hardcover o.p. pa $7.95 *
Grades: 2 3 4   598
1. Water birds
ISBN 0-7922-7073-8; 0-7922-6739-7 (pa)
                                        LC 97-7594
Provides a personal look at various species of fresh- and saltwater birds, including loons and grebes, mergansers, mallards, wood ducks, Canada geese, gulls, and herons
Arnosky "weaves facts and many personal observations in the breezy conversational blocks of text and informative captions that surround the naturalistic, almost photoreal, watercolor paintings. . . . He offers marvelous anatomical detail and captures close-up views of that casual observers rarely get to see." SLJ

Bardhan-Quallen, Sudipta
Flying eagle; illustrated by Deborah Kogan Ray. Charlesbridge 2009 unp il $15.95
Grades: 1 2 3   598
1. Eagles
ISBN 978-1-57091-671-7; 1-57091-671-3
                                        LC 2007-17186
"The setting is a big part of the drama in this large picture book about an eagle's search for prey in the Serengeti wildlife refuge in Tanzania. Each double-page spread includes a very short, simple rhyme with a soaring, unframed watercolor and colored-pencil picture of the bird in flight. . . . Long notes at the back about the eagle and about the Seregenti will fascinate young readers." Booklist

Barner, Bob
Penguins, penguins, everywhere! Chronicle Books 2007 unp il $14.95
Grades: PreK K 1   598
1. Penguins
ISBN 978-0-8118-5664-5; 0-8118-5664-X
                                        LC 2006-20960

"Colorful collages depict plump penguins performing a plethora of penguiny pastimes. . . . Barner's simply rhyming text presents a variety of the birds. . . . A final spread proffers a parade of all 17 species, including data on global location, size, and weight." SLJ

Bash, Barbara
Urban roosts: where birds nest in the city. Sierra Club Bks. 1990 unp il pa $6.95 hardcover o.p. *
Grades: 1 2 3 4   598
1. Birds—Nests
ISBN 0-316-08312-7 (pa)   LC 89-70187
"Excellent treatment of an unusual subject reveals that human-made places of steel, stone, and concrete are home to a variety of birds. Includes information on sparrows, finches, barn and snowy owls, swallows, swifts, nighthawks, killdeers, pigeons, wrens, crows, starlings, and falcons that have successfully adapted to city life." Sci Child

Birds of the world; editorial adviser, Jason A. Mobley. Marshall Cavendish Reference 2008 11v il map set $359.95 *
Grades: 5 6 7 8 9   598
1. Birds—Encyclopedias 2. Reference books
ISBN 978-0-7614-7775-4 (set); 0-7614-7775-6 (set)
                                        LC 2008-62300
"This encyclopedia, designed to introduce birds in all their varieties, contributes to and encourages student research. Nearly 140 . . . articles are arranged alphbetically. . . . Articles range in length from two to eight pages and include numerous full-color photographs, diagrams, and maps. . . . Clear and concise information is provided in an appealing layout most appropriate for upper-elementary through middle-school users." Booklist

Burnie, David
Bird; written by David Burnie. rev ed. DK Pub. 2008 72p il (DK eyewitness books) $15.99
Grades: 4 5 6 7   598
1. Birds
ISBN 978-0-7566-3768-2; 0-7566-3768-6
First published 1988 by Knopf
Includes CD-ROM
A photo essay on the world of birds examining such topics as body construction, feathers and flight, the adaptation of beaks and feet, feeding habits, courtship, nests and eggs, and bird watching.
Includes glossary

Cherry, Lynne, 1952-
Flute's journey; the life of a wood thrush; written and illustrated by Lynne Cherry. Harcourt Brace & Co. 1997 unp il $17; pa $9.87
Grades: 2 3 4   598
1. Wood thrush
ISBN 0-15-292853-7; 0-15-314369-X (pa)
                                        LC 96-17024
"A Gulliver green book"
A young wood thrush makes his first migration from his nesting ground in a forest preserve in Maryland to his winter home in Costa Rica and back again

Cherry, Lynne, 1952-—*Continued*

This features "detailed watercolors. . . . The story and illustrations contain much useful information." Horn Book Guide

Collard, Sneed B., III

Beaks! illustrated by Robin Brickman. Charlesbridge Pub. 2002 unp il hardcover o.p. pa $6.95

Grades: K 1 2 3   **598**
1. Birds
ISBN 1-57091-387-0; 1-57091-388-9 (pa)
                                 LC 2001-4362

Simple text describes various bird beaks and how birds use them to eat, hunt, and gather food. Includes a quiz

"The intricate characteristics of a variety of birds' beaks are presented skillfully through words and vividly painted, cut-and-sculpted-paper illustrations. . . . The clear text is easy to follow." SLJ

Includes bibliographical references

Daigle, Evelyne

The world of penguins; [by] Evelyne Daigle; illustrated by Daniel Grenier; translated by Geneviève Wright. Tundra Books 2007 47p il map $18.95

Grades: 4 5 6   **598**
1. Penguins
ISBN 978-0-88776-799-9; 0-88776-799-0

This describes the life cycles and habitats of various species of penguins.

"Nicely illustrated with realistic acrylic paintings and some photos, slender and oversized, this book is eye-catching and attractive." SLJ

Includes bibliographical references

Evert, Laura, 1967-

Birds of prey; explore the fascinating worlds of eagles, falcons, owls, vultures; by Laura Evert and Wayne Lynch; illustrations by Sherry Neidigh and John F. McGee. NorthWord 2005 191p il (Our wild world) $16.95

Grades: 3 4 5 6   **598**
1. Birds of prey
ISBN 1-55971-925-7   LC 2005000189

This "volume is divided into four sections, each addressing one of the major groups of raptors: eagles, falcons, owls, and vultures. The chapters, which have color-coded pages for quick reference, are similarly organized, making for easier reading, and deal with all aspects of the birds' life cycles and habits. Plentiful, high-quality photographs . . . and clear illustrations elucidate the narrative." SLJ

Gibbons, Gail

Gulls—gulls—gulls. Holiday House 1997 unp il $16.95; pa $6.95

Grades: K 1 2 3   **598**
1. Gulls
ISBN 0-8234-1323-3; 0-8234-1664-X (pa)
                                 LC 97-1266

Describes the life cycle, behavior patterns, and habitat of various species of gulls, focusing on those found in North America

"Both illustration and text provide basic, easy-to-understand facts. . . . The format is attractive with framed, simply drawn watercolor illustrations showing the birds in the foreground against bright colorful seashore or seascape backgrounds of dominant blues and greens." SLJ

Owls; [by] Gail Gibbons. Holiday House 2005 32p il $16.95; pa $6.95

Grades: K 1 2 3   **598**
1. Owls
ISBN 0-8234-1880-4; 0-8234-2014-0 (pa)
                                 LC 2004-48225

A "factual look at raptors of the night, full of information tied specifically to the owls of North America. General facts on physiology, hunting tactics, digestion, habitats, and communication are offered, as is a section on mating, egg laying and incubation, and owlet development. . . . Gibbons's trademark watercolors provide lively renditions of a variety of these silent hunters. . . . This is a bright addition to owl lore for younger readers." SLJ

Penguins! Holiday House 1998 unp il maps $16.95; pa $6.95

Grades: K 1 2 3   **598**
1. Penguins
ISBN 0-8234-1388-8; 0-8234-1516-3 (pa)
                                 LC 98-5194

Describes the habitat, physical characteristics, and behavior of different kinds of penguins

This book has "simply written, clear text. . . . The oversized format, brightly colored illustrations, and large type font result in an eye-catching appearance that will attract young researchers and the curious minded alike." SLJ

Soaring with the wind; the bald eagle. Morrow Junior Bks. 1998 unp il $16.99; lib bdg $17.89

Grades: K 1 2 3   **598**
1. Bald eagle
ISBN 0-688-13730-X; 0-688-13731-8 (lib bdg)
                                 LC 97-20497

Describes the characteristics, behavior, and life cycle of the bald eagle

"Appealing watercolor illustrations, labeled diagrams, definitions, and well-researched facts come together to form a perfect connection for teachers seeking to expand science units." SLJ

Goldin, Augusta R.

Ducks don't get wet; by Augusta Goldin; illustrated by Helen K. Davie. newly il ed. HarperCollins Pubs. 1999 32p il (Let's-read-and-find-out science) hardcover o.p. pa $4.95

Grades: K 1 2 3   **598**
1. Ducks
ISBN 0-06-027881-1; 0-06-027882-X (lib bdg); 0-06-445187-9 (pa)   LC 97-43597

A newly illustrated edition of the title first published 1965 by Crowell

Goldin, Augusta R.—*Continued*

Describes the behavior of different kinds of ducks and, in particular, discusses how all ducks use preening to keep their feathers dry

"The text is well focused throughout. . . . Notable for its clarity, subtlety, and beauty, the artwork illustrates the text with precision and imagination." Booklist

Goldish, Meish

California condors; saved by captive breeding. Bearport Pub. 2009 32p il map (America's animal comebacks) lib bdg $25.27

Grades: 2 3 4   **598**

1. Condors 2. Wildlife conservation
ISBN 978-1-59716-741-3 (lib bdg); 1-59716-741-X (lib bdg)   LC 2008-32803

Through this true tale of wildlife survival, young readers discover the bold and creative ideas that Americans and their government have used to protect and care for the country's endangered California condors

"Crisp photos and maps on every page work well with the text and give faces to the scientists and animals. The back matter includes a facts page, information on related species, and an up-to-date reading list." SLJ

Includes glossary and bibliographical references

Gonzales, Doreen

Owls in the dark. PowerKids Press 2010 24p il (Creatures of the night) lib bdg $21.25; pa $8.05

Grades: 2 3 4   **598**

1. Owls
ISBN 978-1-4042-8097-7 (lib bdg); 1-4042-8097-9 (lib bdg); 978-1-4358-3251-0 (pa); 1-4358-3251-5 (pa)

A look at owls and their world in the dark.

"Basic details are complemented by eclectic trivia, . . . [and the] volume concludes with a defense of the animal . . . and why it is vital to humans. The layout is attractive, with easy-to-read text and eye-catching photography. Good for reports." SLJ

Includes glossary

Guiberson, Brenda Z., 1946-

The emperor lays an egg; illustrated by Joan Paley. Holt & Co. 2001 unp il $16.95; pa $7.99 *

Grades: K 1 2 3   **598**

1. Penguins
ISBN 0-8050-6204-1; 0-8050-7636-3 (pa)   LC 00-40980

"Beginning with the laying of an egg, Guiberson describes the care given to a baby emperor penguin by both parents from the time it hatches until it is on its own." SLJ

"Guiberson's vivid prose fleshes out the bare bones of the penguin's life cycle. . . . Paley's collages of painted and cut papers provide exceptionally beautiful scenes of the birds." Booklist

Mud city; a flamingo story; [by] Brenda Z. Guiberson. Henry Holt and Co. 2005 unp il $16.95

Grades: 2 3 4   **598**

1. Flamingos
ISBN 0-8050-7177-6   LC 2004-9199

On a muddy mound in a salty lake, a mother and father flamingo take turns shading their egg from the blistering sun. Soon a fluffy white chick hatches in the nest by the mangrove shrub. Thus begins a life cycle of a baby flamingo

"Guiberson's brightly colored watercolor/gouache illustrations are a perfect complement for her informative, conversational text." SLJ

Hanel, Rachael

Penguins. Smart Apple Media 2009 46p il (Living wild) lib bdg $32.80

Grades: 4 5 6 7   **598**

1. Penguins
ISBN 978-1-58341-658-7 (lib bdg); 1-58341-658-7 (lib bdg)   LC 2007008503

"The 17 species of penguins . . . fill [this] slim, informative [volume]. [The] overview is divided into several chapters . . . describing the shared and distinct physical characteristics of the various species, the location of their particular habitats, life cycle, social behavior, and the history of human awareness of and impact on these animals. Fine color photographs face pages of text with smaller views placed in colored sidebars or insets. The [book concludes] with current environmental threats and conservation efforts. . . . Handsome and appealing." SLJ

Harkins, Susan Sales

Threat to the whooping crane; [by] Susan Sales Harkins and William H. Harkins. Mitchell Lane Pub. 2008 32p il map (On the verge of extinction: crisis in the environment) lib bdg $17.95

Grades: 3 4 5   **598**

1. Cranes (Birds) 2. Endangered species
ISBN 978-1-58415-685-7 (lib bdg); 1-58415-685-6 (lib bdg)   LC 2008-08037

"A Robbie Reader"

Describes the physical characteristics and behavior of the whooping crane, including their yearly migration patterns, and details the history of threats to the species and what steps are being made to return the crane from endangerment.

This book "provide[s] a wealth of information . . . [and is] accurate and easy for young readers to comprehend." Sci Books Films

Includes glossary and bibliographical references

Helget, Nicole Lea, 1976-

Swans; by Nicole Helget. Smart Apple Media 2009 46p il (Living wild) lib bdg $32.80

Grades: 4 5 6 7   **598**

1. Swans
ISBN 978-1-58341-659-4 (lib bdg); 1-58341-659-5 (lib bdg)   LC 2007015242

The "7 [species] of swans fill [this] slim, informative [volume]. [The] overview is divided into several chapters . . . describing the shared and distinct physical characteristics of the various species, the location of their particular habitats, life cycle, social behavior, and the history of human awareness of and impact on these animals. Fine color photographs face pages of text with smaller views placed in colored sidebars or insets. The [book concludes] with current environmental threats and conservation efforts. . . . Handsome and appealing." SLJ

Includes bibliographical references

Higginson, Mel, 1942-
Beaks and bills; [by] Mel Higginson. Rourke Pub. 2007 24p il (Let's look at animals) hardcover o.p. pa $6.95
Grades: K 1 2   **598**
  1. Bills (Birds)
  ISBN 1-60044-169-6; 1-59515-527-9 (pa)
                 LC 2006012745
This describes how birds' beaks and bills grow and function.
Illustrated "with colorful lifelike photographs. Stimulating and relevant information is presented in a concise manner." Sci Books and Films
Includes glossary and bibliographical references

Hiscock, Bruce, 1940-
Ookpik; the travels of a snowy owl. Boyds Mills Press 2008 unp il map $16.99
Grades: 2 3 4   **598**
  1. Owls 2. Birds—Migration
  ISBN 978-1-59078-461-7; 1-59078-461-8
                 LC 2007-17327
A snowy owl hatches on Baffin Island and migrates over the taiga, past Ottawa, spends the winter in northern New York, and returns to his arctic home.
"An informative author's note comments on the range, size, food, courtship, nesting, growth, and survival of snowy owls. Varied in composition, well focused, and often panoramic in effect, the watercolor paintings depict the snowy owl's world as well as the bird himself. . . . The owl's journey becomes an involving story for children." Booklist

Holub, Joan, 1956-
Why do birds sing? illustrations by Anna DiVito. Dial Books for Young Readers 2004 47p il (Dial easy-to-read) hardcover o.p. pa $3.99 *
Grades: K 1 2   **598**
  1. Birds
  ISBN 0-8037-2999-5; 0-14-240106-4 (pa)
                 LC 2003-64945
Questions and answers present information about the behavior and characteristics of birds
"The photos and attractive ink drawings with color washes that come two to three to a page result in a colorful presentation with illustrations in different styles from many sources." Booklist

Jacquet, Luc
March of the penguins; [by] Luc Jacquet; including narration written by Jordan Roberts; photographs by Jérôme Maison; translated and adapted by Donnali Fifield. National Geographic 2006 160p il $30
Grades: K 1 2 3   **598**
  1. Penguins 2. Antarctica
  ISBN 0-7922-6190-9
"From summer's end in Antarctica, the book takes the reader on a journey through a year's cycle in the life of emperor penguins. . . . The quality of the photographs makes this simple story accessible to a wide audience." Sci Books Films

Johnson, Jinny
Duck; illustrations by Michael Woods. Smart Apple Media 2010 32p il (How does it grow?) lib bdg $28.50
Grades: 1 2 3   **598**
  1. Ducks 2. Life cycles (Biology)
  ISBN 978-1-59920-353-9 (lib bdg); 1-59920-353-7 (lib bdg)
                 LC 2008-53338
Introduces the life cycle of a duck and explains each stage in its development
"Each stage is described on a spread that features clearly written, oversized text and a caption opposite a full-page, realistic watercolor, or, occasionally, a photograph. . . . A worthwhile purchase." SLJ
Includes glossary

Johnson, Sylvia A.
Crows; by Sylvia A. Johnson. Carolrhoda Books 2005 48p il (Carolrhoda nature watch book) lib bdg $25.26
Grades: 3 4 5 6   **598**
  1. Crows
  ISBN 1-57505-628-3   LC 2004-564
  Contents: Crows all around us; The crow family tree; Country birds, city birds; Studying crows; Crows and people
This "book introduces the American crow, its broader family of corvids, and its range, habitats, cooperative breeding system, life cycle, winter migration, roosting behavior, language, and relations with people. . . . Though the clear, color photographs take up most of the space on the pages, the text offers a well-organized, informative discussion of the species." Booklist

Kalman, Bobbie, 1947-
The life cycle of an emperor penguin; [by] Bobbie Kalman & Robin Johnson. Crabtree Pub. 2007 32p il lib bdg $25.27; pa $6.95
Grades: 2 3 4   **598**
  1. Penguins
  ISBN 978-0-7787-0630-4 (lib bdg); 0-7787-0630-3 (lib bdg); 978-0-7787-0704-2 (pa); 0-7787-0704-0 (pa)
                 LC 2006018781
"The information is presented in a flowing narrative accompanied by color photographs and drawings that perfectly illustrate the [text]. . . . Facts are . . . outlined in a lively manner. [This work has] a wealth of factual information and would be excellent for reports." SLJ

Kelly, Irene, 1957-
Even an ostrich needs a nest; where birds begin. Holiday House 2009 unp il map $16.95 *
Grades: K 1 2 3   **598**
  1. Birds—Nests
  ISBN 978-0-8234-2102-2; 0-8234-2102-3
                 LC 2007-51059
"This nonfiction picture book describes materials used by 40 species of birds from all parts of the world to build their unique nests and how they go about building them. . . . The diversity of materials and designs . . . make this a topic that will appeal to many. The pleasant format features text, creatively placed with the softly colored illustrations, and makes the engaging subject matter even more accessible." Booklist

Kelly, Irene, 1957-—*Continued*

It's a hummingbird's life. Holiday House 2003 unp il $16.95
Grades: 2 3 4   **598**
   1. Hummingbirds
   ISBN 0-8234-1658-5   LC 00-53544
"Kelly follows the activities of the ruby-throated hummingbird throughout the seasons, relating facts and bits of trivia. . . . The tiny pen-and-ink and watercolor illustrations effectively show the features described and comparisons drawn in the narrative." SLJ

Kenyon, Linda, 1956-
Rainforest bird rescue; changing the future for endangered wildlife. Firefly Books 2006 64p il (Firefly animal rescue) $19.95 paperback o.p.
Grades: 5 6 7 8   **598**
   1. Birds 2. Rain forest animals 3. Wildlife conservation
   ISBN 1-55407-153-4; 1-55407-152-6 (pa)
Provides details and facts about rainforest birds from around the world, their endangerment and a range of conservation programs to save them, including profiles of individual conservationists and rainforest bird species

Lynch, Wayne
Penguins! text and photographs by Wayne Lynch. Firefly Bks. (Willowdale) 1999 64p il map $19.95; pa $9.95
Grades: 4 5 6 7   **598**
   1. Penguins
   ISBN 1-55209-421-9; 1-55209-424-3 (pa)
In a "first-person narrative, peppered with journal excerpts, personal observations, and anecdotes, Lynch discusses penguins' evolution, varied habitats, physical and behavioral adaptations, diet, predators, mating and nesting habits, and chick development." Horn Book Guide
This "is a delightful book. . . . The beautiful color photographs and the text tell a fascinating, exciting, and revealing story." Sci Books Films

Mara, Wil
Ducks; by Wil Mara. Marshall Cavendish Benchmark 2009 47p il (Animals animals) $20.95 *
Grades: 3 4 5 6   **598**
   1. Ducks
   ISBN 978-0-7614-2927-2; 0-7614-2927-1
       LC 2007-26004
"Provides comprehensive information on the anatomy, special skills, habitats, and diet of ducks." Publisher's note
"The material is well researched and would be an excellent source for reports, and the [book has] a narrative flow that makes [it] easy and enjoyable to read. [The] title includes expert full-color photography." SLJ
Includes glossary and bibliographical references

Markle, Sandra, 1946-
Eagles. Lerner Publications Company 2009 39p il (Animal predators) lib bdg $26.60
Grades: 4 5 6   **598**
   1. Eagles
   ISBN 978-1-58013-519-1; 1-58013-519-6
       LC 2008038119
Introduces the physical characteristics, habitat, and predatory behavior of different types of eagles.
"Crisp photographs illustrate the hunting activities of eagles. . . . Facts are presented in a dramatic and informational manner." Horn Book Guide
Includes glossary and bibliographical references

A mother's journey; illustrated by Alan Marks. Charlesbridge 2005 32p il $15.95; pa $6.95 *
Grades: K 1 2 3   **598**
   1. Penguins
   ISBN 1-57091-621-7; 1-57091-622-5 (pa)
       LC 2004-18954
"A simple, lyrical text follows the fortunes of an Emperor penguin from laying her first egg through her epic journey to open sea seeking food and culminating in her timely return with a belly full to regurgitate for her newly hatched chick. The whole is perfectly accompanied by Marks's luminous blue-toned watercolors." SLJ

McMillan, Bruce
Days of the ducklings; written and photo-illustrated by Bruce McMillan. Houghton Mifflin 2001 32p il hardcover o.p. pa $6.95
Grades: 2 3 4   **598**
   1. Ducks
   ISBN 0-618-04878-2; 0-618-86270-6 (pa)
       LC 00-13258
"Walter Lorraine books"
The author focuses on a remote island off the coast of Iceland "and its eider duck population. . . . A girl named Drifa, daughter of one of the island's new owners, takes on the task of fostering the ducklings and ensuring their safety until their return to the wild." Bull Cent Child Books
"McMillan's photographs are of extremely high quality, a wonderful blend of artistry and emotion, and his text flows well." Booklist
Includes bibliographical references

Nights of the pufflings; written and photo-illustrated by Bruce McMillan. Houghton Mifflin 1995 32p il $16; pa $5.95
Grades: 2 3 4   **598**
   1. Puffins
   ISBN 0-395-70810-9; 0-395-85693-0 (pa)
       LC 94-14808
"For two weeks every year, the children of Heimaey Island, Iceland, stay out late rescuing hundreds of stranded pufflings. Many of the birds are confused by the village lights and need help flying toward the sea." Sci Child
"This fascinating story, combined with gorgeous color photographs, a simple, clear text, and handsome book design, makes an appealing package. McMillan includes the pronunciation of unfamiliar Icelandic names and words within the text and follows his story with an afterwood about the North Atlantic puffins." Horn Book
Includes bibliographical references

McMillan, Bruce—*Continued*

Penguins at home; gentoos of Antarctica; written and photo-illustrated by Bruce McMillan. Houghton Mifflin 1993 32p il $17

Grades: 2 3 4   598
1. Penguins
ISBN 0-395-66560-4   LC 92-34769

Describes the physical characteristics, behavior, and life cycle of the timid gentoo penguin

"First-rate photographs illustrate a text that supplies interesting information. . . . Large captions summarize important facts and detailed descriptions are provided to enrich the volume." Sci Child

Includes bibliographical references

Wild flamingos; written and photo-illustrated by Bruce McMillan. Houghton Mifflin 1997 32p il $17

Grades: 2 3 4   598
1. Flamingos
ISBN 0-395-84545-9   LC 97-1521

A photo essay describing the physical characteristics, natural habitat, and behavior of the flamingos of Bonaire, Netherlands Antilles

"Children can learn a great deal from the readable text. . . . The striking full-color photographs capture the birds in a variety of interesting poses." SLJ

Includes bibliographical references

Miller, Sara Swan

Woodpeckers, toucans, and their kin. Watts 2003 47p il (Animals in order) lib bdg $25; pa $6.95

Grades: 4 5 6   598
1. Woodpeckers 2. Toucans 3. Honeyguides (Birds)
ISBN 0-531-12243-3 (lib bdg); 0-531-16661-9 (pa)
LC 2002-1732

Introduces the different animals in the piciform order, their similarities and differences, environments in which they live, and how to observe them

This book makes "fascinating reading. . . . Photographs are glorious." Libr Media Connect

Includes glossary and bibliographical references

Momatiuk, Yva, 1940-

Face to face with penguins; by Yva Momatiuk and John Eastcott. National Geographic 2009 31p il (Face to face) $16.99; lib bdg $25.90 *

Grades: 3 4 5 6   598
1. Penguins
ISBN   978-1-4263-0561-0;   1-4263-0561-3;
978-1-4263-0562-7 (lib bdg); 1-4263-0562-1 (lib bdg)
LC 2009011439

The authors describe the life cycle and behavior of penguins and their own experiences with penguins in the wild.

"The exquisite photos and firsthand information provide an in-depth and personal look into the lives of these animals." SLJ

Includes glossary and bibliographical references

Mudd-Ruth, Maria

Owls; by Maria Mudd Ruth. Benchmark Books 2004 46p il map (Animals, animals) lib bdg $25.64

Grades: 3 4 5 6   598
1. Owls
ISBN 0-7614-1752-4   LC 2004-364

Contents: Introducing owls; Who's an owl; The silent hunters; Life cycle; A promising future?

This describes the life cycles and characteristics of owls, illustrated with color photographs

Includes glossary and bibliographical references

Nobleman, Marc Tyler

Eagles; by Marc Tyler Nobleman. Marshall Cavendish Benchmark 2007 48p il (Animals, animals) lib bdg $19.95 *

Grades: 3 4 5 6   598
1. Eagles
ISBN 978-0-7614-2236-5 (lib bdg); 0-7614-2236-6 (lib bdg)   LC 2005025609

"Describes the physical characteristics, behavior, habitat, and endangered status of eagles." Publisher's note

Includes glossary and bibliographical references

Osborn, Elinor, 1939-

Project UltraSwan; written and photographed by Elinor Osborn. Houghton Mifflin 2002 64p il map (Scientists in the field) $16; pa $6.99

Grades: 4 5 6 7   598
1. Swans
ISBN 0-618-14528-1; 0-618-58545-1 (pa)
LC 2002-223

Describes the life of large trumpeter swans, how they nearly became extinct, and efforts to reintroduce them to the Northeastern United States and to help them relearn migration routes

"Beautifully illustrated with crisp, colorful photographs and maps, *Project UltraSwan* describes in clear, succinct language all that the scientists must take into account in their work, as well as what they have learned about their subject so far." Booklist

Otfinoski, Steven, 1949-

Hummingbirds; by Steven Otfinoski. Marshall Cavendish Benchmark 2009 47p il (Animals animals) $20.95 *

Grades: 3 4 5 6   598
1. Hummingbirds
ISBN 978-0-7614-2932-6; 0-7614-2932-8
LC 2007-24325

"Provides comprehensive information on the anatomy, special skills, habitats, and diet of hummingbirds." Publisher's note

Includes glossary and bibliographical references

Patent, Dorothy Hinshaw

The bald eagle returns; [by] Dorothy Hinshaw Patent; [photographs by] William Muñoz. Clarion Bks. 2000 68p il map $15

Grades: 4 5 6 7   598

1. Bald eagle 2. Birds—Protection

ISBN 0-395-91416-7   LC 00-21751

"A revised version of the author's and photographer's earlier book *Where the Bald Eagles Gather.*" Title page

Describes how bald eagles have recovered from the threat of extinction, how they raise their families, and why they are the national bird of the United States

This offers "exciting new information about the status of our national bird; and crisp, beautiful, full-color photos." SLJ

Pigeons; photographs by William Muñoz. Clarion Bks. 1997 78p il $16

Grades: 4 5 6 7   598

1. Pigeons

ISBN 0-395-69848-0   LC 96-42072

Describes the physical characteristics, behavior, and usefulness of these birds, which have lived with people since prehistoric times

"This informative book offers a well-researched and readable text illustrated with clear, full-color photographs." Booklist

Includes glossary

Peterson, Roger Tory, 1908-1996

Peterson field guide to birds of North America; with contributions from Michael DiGiorgio . . . [et al.] Houghton Mifflin Co. 2008 527p il map (Peterson field guide series) $26 *

Grades: 5 6 7 8 9 10 11 12 Adult   598

1. Birds—North America

ISBN 978-0-618-96614-1; 0-618-96614-5

LC 2007-39803

First published 1934 with title: A field guide to the birds. Previously published in two separate parts as A field guide to western birds (1990) and A field guide to the birds of eastern and central North America (2002)

This guide to birds found in North America contains colored illustrations painted by the author, with a description of each species on the facing page. Views of young birds and seasonal variations in plumage are included. The book also includes a URL to video podcasts.

"This field guide is of high quality and should be in millions of birders' and other nature lovers' backpacks." Sci Books Films

Peterson field guide to birds of Western North America; with contributions from Michael DiGiorgio . . . [et al.] 4th ed. Houghton Mifflin Harcourt 2010 493p il map (Peterson field guide series) pa $19.95

Grades: 5 6 7 8 9 10 11 12 Adult   598

1. Birds—North America

ISBN 978-0-547-15270-7   LC 2009-39158

First published 1941 with title: A field guide to western birds

This guide illustrates over 600 species of birds on 176 color plates. In addition, over 588 range maps are included.

Piehl, Janet

Let's look at pigeons. Lerner Publications Co. 2010 32p il (Lightning bolt books: Animal close-ups) lib bdg $25.26; pa $7.95

Grades: PreK K 1 2   598

1. Pigeons

ISBN 978-0-8225-7897-0 (lib bdg); 0-8225-7897-2 (lib bdg); 978-1-58013-863-5 (pa); 1-58013-863-2 (pa)

LC 2007-29224

Introduces pigeons, describing their physical characteristics, habitat, and predators

"Fresh photography, a creative use of graphics, and a collagelike layout make[s] . . . [this book] eye-catching. . . . [The] book ends with a labeled diagram of the animal, a range map, and a further-reading list that includes print and online resources in a single list, a nice way of validating both types of materials." SLJ

Includes glossary

Post, Hans, 1959-

Sparrows; [by Hans Post & Kees Heij; illustrated by Irene Goede] Lemniscaat 2008 unp il $16.95

Grades: PreK K 1 2   598

1. Sparrows

ISBN 978-1-59078-570-6; 1-59078-570-3

LC 2008-02563

Original Dutch edition 2006

"A year in the life of the European House Sparrow is conveyed to young readers through a friendly text and beguiling illustrations. . . . The tone of the text is both playful and informative. . . . The realistic illustrations intersperse views from the birds' prespective . . . with field guide-like pages that help illustrate bird anatomy and behavior and introduce other animals in the sparrow habitat." Horn Book

Pringle, Laurence P.

Penguins! strange and wonderful; illustrated by Meryl Henderson. Boyds Mills Press 2007 unp il $16.95

Grades: 3 4 5   598

1. Penguins

ISBN 978-1-59078-090-9; 1-59078-090-6

LC 2006000521

This "highlights the diversity among the habitats, physical traits, and behaviors of the 17 amazingly adaptable species. Pringle's succinct text provides an engaging overview of penguin life. . . . Henderson's realistic paintings vary between double-page spreads of penguins in their diverse Southern Hemisphere environments and finely detailed insets that echo the text." Booklist

Includes bibliographical references

Sattler, Helen Roney

The book of North American owls; illustrated by Jean Day Zallinger. Clarion Bks. 1995 64p il maps hardcover o.p. pa $7.95

Grades: 4 5 6 7   598

1. Owls

ISBN 0-395-60524-5; 0-395-90017-4 (pa)

LC 91-43626

Sattler, Helen Roney—*Continued*

This volume "includes owl classification and history, hunting and habitat, courtship and nesting, and the complex relationship between owls and humans. The comprehensive glossary includes all of the 21 North American species." Sci Child

This "is a superb ornithological primer. . . . The book is lavishly illustrated." Appraisal

Includes bibliographical references

Savage, Stephen, 1965-

Duck. PowerKids Press 2009 32p il map (Animal neighbors) lib bdg $23.95

Grades: 3 4 5 6   **598**
    1. Ducks
    ISBN 978-1-4358-4988-4 (lib bdg); 1-4358-4988-4 (lib bdg)   LC 2008-5401

This describes the life cycle, habitat, and behavior of ducks

This title features "beautiful, detailed, close-up photos of animals displayed on child-friendly page layouts. The information is well organized for reports." SLJ

Includes glossary and bibliographical references

Sayre, April Pulley

Honk, honk, goose! Canada geese start a family; illustrated by Huy Voun Lee. Henry Holt and Company 2009 unp il $16.95 *

Grades: K 1 2 3   **598**
    1. Geese
    ISBN 978-0-8050-7103-0; 0-8050-7103-2
                                    LC 2008013423

"A pair of Canada geese is starting a family. The female builds a nest, lays her eggs, and keeps the chicks warm until they're ready to hatch. Her mate protects their nesting site. Soon they will have six wobbly-legged chicks." Publisher's note

"A fun read-aloud grounded by informational back matter. . . . Lee's cut-paper collage illustrations wonderfully complement the text—they're simple yet expressive." Booklist

Vulture view; illustrated by Steve Jenkins. Henry Holt 2007 unp il $16.95 *

Grades: K 1 2   **598**
    1. Vultures
    ISBN 978-0-8050-7557-1; 0-8050-7557-7
                                    LC 2006-30766

"Sayre's poetic text begins with the sun rising. . . . The words, almost startling in their brevity, describe a group of turkey vultures as they soar in the sky, seeking food that reeks. . . . Jenkins . . . places the birds against strong, vivid colors—brilliant sky blues, hot desert reds—and gives them wide wingspans that make them seem to soar across the pages. . . . A final two-page spread . . . does a solid job of explaining how turkey vultures live." Booklist

Schulman, Janet, 1933-

Pale Male; citizen hawk of New York City; by Janet Schulman; illustrated by Meilo So. Knopf 2008 unp il $16.99; lib bdg $19.99 *

Grades: 3 4 5 6   **598**
    1. Hawks 2. New York (N.Y.)
    ISBN 978-0-375-84558-1; 0-375-84558-5; 978-0-375-94558-8 (lib bdg); 0-375-94558-X (lib bdg)
                                    LC 2007-14661

This is "about the first red-tailed hawk to take up residence in New York City's Central Park since its construction in 1857. . . . The artist's evocative watercolor and colored pencil pictures perfectly capture the power and grace of the majestic raptors. . . . Readers experience New Yorkers' excitement about Pale Male and his various mates and their offspring and understand why his story has captured the interest of so many people." SLJ

Simon, Seymour, 1931-

Penguins. HarperCollins Publishers 2007 31p il (Smithsonian) $16.99; lib bdg $17.89

Grades: 2 3 4   **598**
    1. Penguins
    ISBN 978-0-06-028395-7; 0-06-028395-5; 978-0-06-028396-4 (lib bdg); 0-06-028396-3 (lib bdg)
                                    LC 2006-24116

This describes penguin behavior, reproduction, and feeding

This is written "in a voice perfectly attuned to the conceptual level of elementary-age readers. . . . The full-page color photographs competently capture . . . penguin appeal and are skillfully discussed in the narrative." Horn Book

Solway, Andrew

Eagles and other birds. Heinemann Library 2007 48p il (Adapted for success) lib bdg $31.43; pa $8.99

Grades: 3 4 5   **598**
    1. Birds
    ISBN 978-1-4034-8222-8 (lib bdg); 1-4034-8222-5 (lib bdg); 978-1-4034-8229-7 (pa); 1-4034-8229-2 (pa)
                                    LC 2006-14291

This explores how birds are adapted to their environment and covers habitat, defenses, camouflage, and the way birds find food.

Includes glossary and bibliographical references

Stearns, Precious McKenzie

Whooping cranes; [by] Precious McKenzie. Rourke Pub. 2010 24p il map (Eye to eye with endangered species) lib bdg $27.07

Grades: 2 3 4   **598**
    1. Cranes (Birds)
    ISBN 978-1-60694-401-1 (lib bdg); 1-60694-401-0 (lib bdg)   LC 2009-5992

Examines the issues endangered whooping cranes face and how they can be saved

"Sets out to introduce readers to [whooping cranes] . . . explain the dangers they face, and detail the efforts of biologists and conservationists to save them. . . . Serviceable and informative." SLJ

Includes glossary

Stewart, Melissa, 1968-

A place for birds; written by Melissa Stewart; illustrated by Higgins Bond. Peachtree 2009 unp il $16.95

Grades: K 1 2 3   **598**
  1. Birds
  ISBN 978-1-56145-474-7; 1-56145-474-5
                                    LC 2008036744
"This title focuses on the effects, good and bad, that human behavior has on birds, highlighting the progress that we've made toward living in harmony with our winged friends and acknowledging problems still not solved. The rhythmic main text highlights birds' needs and what people can do to see that they are met. Insets on each page then provide specific examples to drive the point home. . . . This format . . . is effective and engaging, and Bond's acrylic illustrations depict realistic scenes with a crisp vibrancy." Kirkus

Swans; by Melissa Stewart. Marshall Cavendish Benchmark 2007 48p il map (Animals, animals) lib bdg $28.50

Grades: 3 4 5 6   **598**
  1. Swans
  ISBN 978-0-7614-2530-4   LC 2006019716
"Describes the physical characteristics, habitat, behavior, diet, life cycle, and conservation status of the swan." Publisher's note
  Includes glossary and bibliographical references

Tatham, Betty

Penguin chick; illustrated by Helen K. Davie. HarperCollins Pubs. 2002 33p il (Let's-read-and-find-out science) $15.95; pa $4.95

Grades: K 1 2 3   **598**
  1. Penguins
  ISBN 0-06-028594-X; 0-06-445206-9 (pa)
                                    LC 00-59696
This book "follows the growth of one penguin chick from egg to adulthood. The story has been told before, but the clear, simple text provides intriguing details and inherent drama that will keep young children involved straight through till the end." Booklist

Thompson, Bill, III, 1962-

The young birder's guide to birds of eastern North America; [by] Bill Thompson III; illustrations by Julie Zickefoose. Houghton Mifflin Co. 2008 256p il map (Peterson field guide series) $14.95

Grades: 3 4 5 6   **598**
  1. Birds 2. Bird watching
  ISBN 978-0-547-11934-2; 0-547-11934-8
                                    LC 2007-43904
This describes 200 species of birds of eastern North America, with color photos, black & white drawings, and range maps.
  Includes glossary and bibliographical references

Thomson, Ruth, 1949-

The life cycle of an owl. PowerKids Press 2009 24p il lib bdg $21.23; pa $8.25

Grades: K 1 2   **598**
  1. Owls
  ISBN 978-1-4358-2833-9 (lib bdg); 1-4358-2833-X (lib bdg); 978-1-4358-2883-4 (pa); 1-4358-2883-6 (pa)
                                    LC 2008026176
This introduction to the life cycle of the owl is "arranged in a series of spreads, each of which covers a subtopic. Pages feature one to three simple sentences of large-print text and a clear, color photograph of one or more animals in various stages of growth. . . . With [its] easily accessible format, and clear [text] and photographs, [this book] will appeal to both browsers and report writers." SLJ

Underwood, Deborah, 1962-

Colorful peacocks; by Deborah Underwood. Lerner Publications Co. 2007 32p il (Pull ahead books) lib bdg $22.60; pa $5.95

Grades: K 1 2 3   **598**
  1. Peacocks
  ISBN 978-0-8225-5930-6 (lib bdg); 0-8225-5930-7 (lib bdg); 978-0-8225-6507-9 (pa); 0-8225-6507-2 (pa)
                                    LC 2005017977
"This charming introduction to the peafowl family presents facts and color photographs in an easy-to-read format. Underwood covers what they eat, where they sleep, and how they care for their young. An outline drawing of a peafowl with the parts labeled and a map showing countries native to the species are included. An informative and enjoyable book." SLJ
  Includes bibliographical references

Vogel, Carole Garbuny

The man who flies with birds; [by] Carole G. Vogel and Yossi Leshem. Kar-Ben Pub. 2009 64p il map lib bdg $18.95

Grades: 5 6 7 8   **598**
  1. Birds—Migration 2. Aircraft accidents
  ISBN 978-0-8225-7643-3 (lib bdg); 0-8225-7643-0 (lib bdg)   LC 2008-31198
Discusses the work of the bird expert whose lifelong study of the patterns of bird migration in Israel has led to a significant reduction in the number of collisions between aircraft and bird flocks.
  "The book is heavily illustrated with good-quality color photos, maps, and diagrams, many of them captioned with incredible facts about wildlife and migration. This inspiring title on a most timely topic will appeal to those who are fascinated with wildlife, Earth science, and technology." SLJ
  Includes bibliographical references

Webb, Sophie, 1958-

Looking for seabirds; journal from an Alaskan voyage. Houghton Mifflin Co. 2004 48p il $16

Grades: 4 5 6 7   **598**
  1. Birds 2. Alaska
  ISBN 0-618-21235-3   LC 2003-12420

Webb, Sophie, 1958-—*Continued*

A journal of the author's observations and adventures while working on a research vessel counting seabirds through Alaska's Aleutian Island chain

The "immediacy of the narrative . . . and the clear and colorful watercolor-and-gouache landscapes and drawings of the birds form an appealing travelogue that is as exciting as it is informative." SLJ

My season with penguins; an Antarctic journal. Houghton Mifflin 2000 48p il map $15; pa $5.95 *

Grades: 4 5 6 7 **598**
1. Penguins 2. Antarctica
ISBN 0-395-92291-7; 0-618-43234-5 (pa)
LC 99-54781

Describes the author's two-month stay in Antarctica to study and draw penguins

"Webb presents a great deal of scientific information through an effective blend of journal entries and illustrations. . . . Done in gouache and watercolor, the paintings range from scenes of mountains and moving ice to depictions of penguins engaged in typical behaviors. . . . Webb offers a fine look at the scientific method in action." SLJ

Includes glossary

Wilcox, Charlotte

Bald eagles; photographs by Jerry Boucher. Carolrhoda Bks. 2003 48p il (Carolrhoda nature watch book) lib bdg $25.26

Grades: 3 4 5 6 **598**
1. Bald eagle
ISBN 1-57505-170-2
LC 2001-6803

Describes the physical characteristics, life cycle, and behavior of bald eagles, as well as efforts to protect them

Willis, Nancy Carol, 1952-

Red knot; a shorebird's incredible journey. Birdsong Books 2006 unp il map $15.95; pa $6.95

Grades: 2 3 4 **598**
1. Sandpipers 2. Birds—Migration
ISBN 0-9662761-4-0; 0-9662761-5-9 (pa)

"This title introduces an endangered sandpiper and chronologically documents her journey from Tierra del Fuego along a 20,000-mile route to the Arctic where she has her young and then makes her way back down south for the winter. . . . The smooth, simple text is complemented with well-composed, colored-pencil drawings." SLJ

Winter, Jeanette, 1939-

The tale of Pale Male; a true story. Harcourt, Inc. 2007 unp il $16

Grades: K 1 2 3 **598**
1. Hawks 2. New York (N.Y.)
ISBN 978-0-15-205972-9; 0-15-205972-5
LC 2006-08741

"When Pale Male and his mate built a nest high on the side of a Fifth Avenue apartment building, they attracted the attention of local bird-watchers. . . . However, some residents complained about bird droppings and animal remains falling from the hawks' living space. In December 2004, the nest was removed, generating local protests and national media attention. Eventually, the nesting spot was restored." SLJ

"Working with acrylics on watercolor paper, Winter uses Easter-egg colors to frame her appealing cityscapes. . . . Winter blends the realistic with the fanciful throughout the story." Booklist

599   Mammalia (Mammals)

Exploring mammals. Marshall Cavendish 2007 20v il map set $399.95 *

Grades: 5 6 7 8 9 10 **599**
1. Mammals—Encyclopedias 2. Reference books
ISBN 978-0-76147-719-8
LC 2007060864

"About 90 animals . . . are described in these volumes. Each article includes . . . a 'Profile,' with introductory information; a discussion of anatomy, with diagrams; a discussion of habitat; descriptions of various behaviors; and a consideration of factors determining survival. Each article also has numerous boxed sections . . . as well as many color photographs and other illustrations. . . . This set has just about everything a student requires." Booklist

Includes bibliographical references

Exploring the world of mammals; [edited by Nancy Simmons, Richard Beatty, Amy Jane Beer] Chelsea House 2008 6v il map set $210 *

Grades: 5 6 7 8 **599**
1. Mammals—Encyclopedias 2. Reference books
ISBN 978-0-7910-9651-2 (set); 0-7910-9651-3 (set)
LC 2007028223

"This colorful and appealing set offers an introduction to the world of mammals. Most of entries are 2 to 4 pages in length. Sidebars offer extra details, and bright photographs and illustrations appear on every 2-page spread." Booklist

Phillips, Dee, 1967-

Mammals. Two-Can Pub. 2006 96p il map (Blue zoo guides) lib bdg $18.95

Grades: K 1 2 3 **599**
1. Mammals
ISBN 1-58728-519-3
LC 2005-17711

"Introduces mammals from around the world, including information about where they live, what they eat, and how they grow and survive." Publisher's note

"The photographs enhance the text and bring the animal to life. . . . The print is large and the layout of each page is child friendly. The information included will provide a solid introduction for each of the mammals presented." Libr Media Connect

Includes glossary

Rodriguez, Ana Maria, 1958-
Secret of the singing mice . . . and more! [by] Ana Maria Rodriguez. Enslow Publishers 2008 c2009 48p il (Animal secrets revealed!) lib bdg $23.93
Grades: 5 6 7 8   **599**
  1. Mammals
  ISBN 978-0-7660-2956-9 (lib bdg); 0-7660-2956-5 (lib bdg)   LC 2007-39495
  "Explains how mice use ultrasonic vocalizations to attract mates and details other strange abilities of different types of animals." Publisher's note
  This book offers "fascinating accounts of how scientists systematically analyzed, tested and proved their theories or how their findings led to other, serendipitous discoveries. . . . Science experiments are thoughtfully placed to inspire exploration, and captioned, full-color photos appear throughout." SLJ
  Includes glossary and bibliographical references

599.2 Marsupialia and monotremata

Arnold, Caroline, 1944-
A platypus' world; written and illustrated by Caroline Arnold. Picture Window Books 2008 24p il map (Caroline Arnold's animals) lib bdg $26.60
Grades: PreK K 1 2   **599.2**
  1. Platypus
  ISBN 978-1-4048-3985-4 (lib bdg); 1-4048-3985-2 (lib bdg)   LC 2007032890
  "Arnold opens with a brief entry stating where the [platypus] lives and its habitat, food, length, weight, animal class, and scientific name. Her narrative of a female's life from birthing preparations through raising the young cleverly contrasts with distinctly hued boxes of fast facts. . . . The cut-paper illustrations in scenic spreads feature a night-time palette of indigo, olive, mocha, and burnt sienna. . . . Visually engaging and brimming with data." SLJ
  Includes glossary

A wombat's world; written and illustrated by Caroline Arnold. Picture Window Books 2008 24p il (Caroline Arnold's animals) lib bdg $26.60
Grades: PreK K 1 2   **599.2**
  1. Wombats
  ISBN 978-1-4048-3986-1   LC 2007032891
  "This introduction to wombats combines a narrative story with boxed facts about the animals. The uncluttered cut-paper collages and simple, straightforward text show and tell events in a wombat's life over a year's time. . . . Arnold gives a mostly clear, compelling sense of the lives and characteristics of these unique animals." Booklist

Bishop, Nic, 1955-
Nic Bishop marsupials. Scholastic 2009 48p il $17.99 *
Grades: 3 4 5 6   **599.2**
  1. Marsupials
  ISBN 978-0-439-87758-9; 0-439-87758-X
                                     LC 2008-53379

"This broad-ranging discussion includes the Virginia opossum and related animals in the Americas before turning to the main topic, the varied marsupials of Australia. Large in scale and often exceptionally clear, the many color photos will attract animal lovers to the book. . . . This inviting title pairs some remarkable photos with a wealth of intriguing facts." Booklist

Bredeson, Carmen
Kangaroos up close; [by] Carmen Bredeson. Enslow Elementary 2008 c2009 24p il (Zoom in on animals!) lib bdg $21.26
Grades: 1 2 3   **599.2**
  1. Kangaroos
  ISBN 978-0-7660-3079-4 (lib bdg); 0-7660-3079-2 (lib bdg)
  "Short paragraphs of simply written text describe [kangaroos'] key body parts and how they function. . . . Behavior, diet, and care and development of the young are briefly addressed. Facing the text on each spread is a full-page, sharp, color closeup. . . . Bredeson's simply written and colorful [title] will provide younger readers with [a] satisfying first [introduction] to these fascinating creatures." SLJ
  Includes glossary and bibliographical references

Collard, Sneed B., III
Platypus, probably; [by] Sneed B. Collard III; illustrated by Andrew Plant. Charlesbridge 2005 unp il $16.95; pa $6.95 *
Grades: K 1 2 3   **599.2**
  1. Platypus
  ISBN 1-57091-583-0; 1-57091-584-9 (pa)
                                     LC 2004-18957
  This "introduces the platypus, which lives only in Australia, and describes the physical characteristics and behaviors of this unusual animal. . . . Richly detailed and atmospheric, the acrylic-and-gouache paintings illustrate the text with many large-scale, horizontal spreads." Booklist

Pocket babies and other amazing marsupials. Darby Creek 2007 72p il map $18.95 *
Grades: 4 5 6 7   **599.2**
  1. Marsupials
  ISBN 978-1-58196-046-4; 1-58196-046-8
  "This large-format book provides an attractive introduction to marsupials around the world. . . . Attractive, informative side-bars, excellent maps, and many clear, color photos appear throughout the book. . . . This handsomely designed volume introduces marsupials with panache." Booklist
  Includes glossary and bibliographical references

Doudna, Kelly, 1963-
It's a baby kangaroo! ABDO Pub. Co. 2009 24p il (Baby Australian animals) $13.95
Grades: K 1 2 3   **599.2**
  1. Kangaroos
  ISBN 978-1-60453-576-1; 1-60453-576-8
                                     LC 2008055075

Doudna, Kelly, 1963-—*Continued*
The "book opens with a page of vital statistics: the 'baby name,' number in litter, 'weight at birth,' 'age of independence,' 'adult weight,' and 'life expectancy.' The [book] then [goes] on to describe where the animals live and their predators and conclude with a 'Fun Fact.' The photography is excellent. Sidebars on some pages include more facts or reinforce the text." SLJ

French, Jackie, 1950-
How to scratch a wombat; where to find it . . . what to feed it . . . why it sleeps all day; illustrated by Bruce Whatley. Clarion Books 2009 85p il $16 *
Grades: 2 3 4 5   **599.2**
   1. Wombats
   ISBN 978-0-618-86864-3; 0-618-86864-X
                             LC 2008-02581
"Between detailed notes about wombat anatomy, behavior and habitat, French weaves in personal anecdotes from her 30-plus years of observing local wombats and caring for orphaned baby wombats. . . . French uses a friendly tone, discussing how wombats have influenced her writing career. Whatley's spot maps, diagrams and realistic b&w pencil sketches further amplify key points. A nifty blend of field notebook and memoir." Publ Wkly

Jango-Cohen, Judith
Kangaroos; by Judith Jango-Cohen. Benchmark Books 2006 48p il (Animals, animals) lib bdg $25.64 *
Grades: 3 4 5 6   **599.2**
   1. Kangaroos
   ISBN 0-7614-1869-5   LC 2004-21621
Describes the physical characteristics, behavior, and habitat of kangaroos
Includes glossary and bibliographical references

Markle, Sandra, 1946-
Finding home; [by] Sandra Markle; illustrated by Alan Marks. Charlesbridge 2008 unp il lib bdg $15.95 *
Grades: K 1 2 3   **599.2**
   1. Koalas
   ISBN 978-1-58089-122-6   LC 2007-01473
"Based on the true story of a koala that survived multiple bushfires and wandered into a residential area, this picture book, narrated in dramatic free verse, tells a gripping story of animal survival. . . . Markle's smooth, elegant poetry and Marks' expressive, realistic mixed-media images give a strong sense of the animals' terror and the mother's intense bond with her child." Booklist
Includes bibliographical references

Markovics, Joyce L.
Tasmanian devil; nighttime scavenger; by Joyce L. Markovics. Bearport Pub. 2009 32p il map (Uncommon animals) lib bdg $25.27
Grades: 1 2 3   **599.2**
   1. Tasmanian devils
   ISBN 978-1-59716-733-8 (lib bdg); 1-59716-733-9 (lib bdg)   LC 2008-9307

"Describes the physical characteristics, habits, and habitat of the Tasmanian devil." Publisher's note
"The explanatory text works spendidly, with large photographs that bring readers as close as they'll ever get to such beasts." Booklist
Includes glossary and bibliographical references

Montgomery, Sy
Quest for the tree kangaroo; an expedition to the cloud forest of New Guinea; text by Sy Montgomery; photographs by Nic Bishop. Houghton Mifflin 2006 79p il map (Scientists in the field) $18 *
Grades: 5 6 7 8   **599.2**
   1. Dabek, Lisa 2. Tree kangaroos 3. New Guinea
   ISBN 0-618-49641-6   LC 2005-34849
"The writer and photographer of this exemplary description of science field work accompanied researcher Lisa Dabek on an expedition high in New Guinea's mountains to study tree kangaroos and promote the conservation of this elusive and endangered species. . . . Montgomery . . . paces her narrative well . . . keeping the reader engaged and concerned. . . . Bishop's photographs . . . are beautifully reproduced." Publ Wkly

Otfinoski, Steven, 1949-
Koalas; by Steven Otfinoski. Marshall Cavendish Benchmark 2007 48p il map (Animals, animals) lib bdg $28.50 *
Grades: 3 4 5 6   **599.2**
   1. Koalas
   ISBN 978-0-7614-2526-7   LC 2006019709
"Describes the physical characteristics, habitat, behavior, diet, life cycle, and conservation status of the koala." Publisher's note
"The clearly written text; simple, spacious design; and appealing illustrations make this a good choice for children intrigued by koalas." Booklist
Includes glossary and bibliographical references

Racanelli, Marie
Animals with pockets. PowerKids Press 2010 24p il (Crazy nature) lib bdg $21.25; pa $8.25
Grades: 2 3 4 5   **599.2**
   1. Marsupials
   ISBN 978-1-4358-9385-6 (lib bdg); 1-4358-9385-9 (lib bdg); 978-1-4358-9862-2 (pa); 1-4358-9862-1 (pa)
                             LC 2009036517
This book takes a look at different kinds of marsupials, and what makes them unique from other mammals.
This book "combines attention-grabbing information with a well-organized format. . . . [The book has] spectacular color photography and eye-popping facts. . . . Excellent for reports." SLJ
Includes glossary

Sill, Cathryn P., 1953-
About marsupials; a guide for children; [by] Cathryn Sill; illustrated by John Sill. Peachtree 2006 unp il $15.95
Grades: K 1 2 3   **599.2**
   1. Marsupials
   ISBN 1-56145-358-7   LC 2005-20582

Sill, Cathryn P., 1953-—_Continued_

This introduces the characteristics and behavior of 17 marsupials, such as the marsupial mole, the red kangaroo, the numbat, the spotted cuscus, the koala and tasmanian devil.

"Written with simplicity and dignity. . . . Well-suited to classroom sharing, the paintings are attractively composed and clearly delineated." Booklist

Includes glossary and bibliographical references

Webster, Christine

Opossums; [by] Christine Webster. Weigl Publishers Inc. 2008 24p il map (Backyard animals) lib bdg $24.45; pa $6.95

Grades: 2 3 4   **599.2**

1. Opossums

ISBN   978-1-59036-677-6   (lib   bdg); 978-1-59036-678-3 (pa)   LC 2006-102107

This describes the physical characteristics, behavior, and life cycle of the opossum.

"Large, full-color photos appear throughout, and the [text is] clearly written and well organized." SLJ

Includes glossary and bibliographical references

599.3   Miscellaneous orders of Eutheria (placental mammals)

Aronin, Miriam

The prairie dog's town; a perfect hideaway. Bearport Pub. 2009 32p il map (Spectacular animal towns) lib bdg $25.27

Grades: 2 3 4   **599.3**

1. Prairie dogs

ISBN 978-1-59716-870-0 (lib bdg); 1-59716-870-X (lib bdg)   LC 2009-4064

"Introduces prairie dogs and how they live, covering the building of burrows and towns for families, different types of communication skills, and conservation efforts to protect them." Publisher's note

"Through excellent photographs, high-interest texts, sidebars, maps, and other material, children learn about both the animals and their habitats. The . . . book also provides brief profiles of animals with similar habitats. . . . [This book is] much better than average 'report' titles." SLJ

Includes glossary and bibliographical references

Diemer, Lauren

Squirrels; [by] Lauren Diemer. Weigl Publishers 2008 24p il map (Backyard animals) lib bdg $24.45; pa $6.95

Grades: 2 3 4   **599.3**

1. Squirrels

ISBN 978-1-59036-671-4 (lib bdg); 1-59036-671-9 (lib bdg); 978-1-59036-672-1 (pa); 1-59036-672-7 (pa)
LC 2006102029

This describes the physical characteristics, behavior, and life cycle of the squirrel

"Large, full-color photos appear throughout, and the [text is] clearly written and well organized." SLJ

Includes glossary and bibliographical references

Gibbons, Gail

Rabbits, rabbits, & more rabbits! Holiday House 2000 unp il $16.95; pa $6.95

Grades: K 1 2 3   **599.3**

1. Rabbits

ISBN 0-8234-1486-8; 0-8234-1660-7 (pa)
LC 99-16765

Describes different kinds of rabbits, their physical characteristics, behavior, where they live, and how to care for them

"Colored washes and crayon shading enliven the clearly delineated ink drawings." Booklist

Glaser, Linda

Hello, squirrels! scampering through the seasons; by Linda Glaser; illustrated by Gay W. Holland. Millbrook Press 2006 32p il lib bdg $22.60

Grades: K 1 2   **599.3**

1. Squirrels

ISBN 978-0-7613-2887-2 (lib bdg); 0-7613-2887-4 (lib bdg)   LC 2005003692

"The book documents a year in a squirrel's life in a first-person narration that imitates a child's voice and cadences. . . . The text is filled with the kind of natural details that a child would observe. Holland's realistic colored-pencil drawings . . . are complemented by generous white space and easy-to-read print. More scientific information is provided in the answers to four questions at the end of the book." Booklist

Jango-Cohen, Judith

Armadillos. Benchmark Bks. 2004 47p il map (Animals, animals) lib bdg $25.64 *

Grades: 3 4 5 6   **599.3**

1. Armadillos

ISBN 0-7614-1617-X   LC 2003-3824

Contents: Introducing armadillos; Digging up dinner; Little pink pups; Armadillo defenses; Armadillos and people

Describes the physical characteristics, behavior, and habitat of armadillos

Includes glossary and bibliographical references

Kalman, Bobbie, 1947-

The life cycle of a beaver; [by] Bobbie Kalman. Crabtree 2007 32p il lib bdg $25.27; pa $6.95

Grades: 2 3 4   **599.3**

1. Beavers

ISBN 978-0-7787-0628-1 (lib bdg); 0-7787-0628-1 (lib bdg); 978-0-7787-0702-8 (pa); 0-7787-0702-4 (pa)
LC 2006023330

The beaver "is described as a mammal (a term that is explained) belonging to the rodent family. Its habitat is outlined, along with information on how it builds lodges, dams, and burrows. Diet, growth, and facts about the young are included. The information is presented in a flowing narrative accompanied by color photographs and drawings that perfectly illustrate the [text]." SLJ

Mara, Wil

Beavers; by Wil Mara. Marshall Cavendish Benchmark 2007 48p il map (Animals, animals) lib bdg $28.50 *

Grades: 3 4 5 6   **599.3**

1. Beavers

ISBN 978-0-7614-2524-3   LC 2006019710

"Describes the physical characteristics, habitat, behavior, diet, life cycle, and conservation status of the beaver." Publisher's note

This "solid, smoothly written [introduction is] compelling for [its] well-organized and attractively formatted presentation." SLJ

Includes glossary and bibliographical references

Markle, Sandra, 1946-

Prairie dogs. Lerner Publications Company 2007 39p il map (Animal prey) lib bdg $25.26; pa $7.95

Grades: 4 5 6   **599.3**

1. Prairie dogs

ISBN 978-0-8225-6438-6 (lib bdg); 0-8225-6438-6 (lib bdg); 978-0-8225-6441-6 (pa); 0-8225-6441-6 (pa)

LC 2006-598

Describes the behavior of prairie dogs in their native habitat, where they are the prey of larger animals and birds and where they must work together as a colony to create burrows and warning systems to protect themselves and their young

Includes glossary and bibliographical references

Rebman, Renee C., 1961-

Anteaters. Marshall Cavendish Benchmark 2007 48p il map (Animals, animals) lib bdg $19.95 *

Grades: 3 4 5 6   **599.3**

1. Anteaters

ISBN 978-0-7614-2234-1 (lib bdg); 0-7614-2234-X (lib bdg)

"Describes the physical characteristics, behavior, habitat, and endangered staus of anteaters." Publisher's note

"Sharp color photographs accompany the text. . . . [This is] clearly written [and] well organized." SLJ

Includes glossary and bibliographical references

Reingold, Adam

The beaver's lodge; building with leftovers. Bearport Pub. 2009 32p il map (Spectacular animal towns) lib bdg $25.27

Grades: 2 3 4   **599.3**

1. Beavers

ISBN 978-1-59716-872-4 (lib bdg); 1-59716-872-6 (lib bdg)

LC 2009-11723

Explores the remarkable homes built by beavers.

"Through excellent photographs, high-interest texts, sidebars, maps, and other material, children learn about both the animals and their habitats. The . . . book also provides brief profiles of animals with similar habitats. . . . [This book is] much better than average 'report' titles." SLJ

Includes glossary and bibliographical references

Stewart, Melissa, 1968-

Rabbits; by Melissa Stewart. Marshall Cavendish Benchmark 2007 48p il map (Animals, animals) lib bdg $28.50 *

Grades: 3 4 5 6   **599.3**

1. Rabbits

ISBN 978-0-7614-2528-1   LC 2006019717

"Describes the physical characteristics, habitat, behavior, diet, life cycle, and conservation status of the rabbit." Publisher's note

This "solid, smoothly written [introduction is] compelling for [its] well-organized and attractively formatted presentation." SLJ

Includes glossary and bibliographical references

Sloths. Carolrhoda Books 2005 48p il map (Carolrhoda nature watch book) lib bdg $25.26

Grades: 3 4 5 6   **599.3**

1. Sloths

ISBN 1-57505-577-5   LC 2003-23223

Contents: Sloths through time; At home in the tropical forest; Food facts; Avoiding enemies; Raising a family; Can sloths survive?

In this "book, two and three-toed sloths' physical features, habitat, and environmental issues are featured. The well-composed text traces their evolution from prehistoric progenitors' to the current day. . . . With its well-captioned, full-color photos on every page and informative text, Sloths offers enough information for solid reports and general interest." SLJ

Swinburne, Stephen R.

Armadillo trail; the northward journey of the armadillo; illustrated by Bruce Hiscock. Boyds Mills Press 2009 unp il $16.95

Grades: K 1 2 3   **599.3**

1. Armadillos

ISBN 978-1-59078-463-1   LC 2008028774

"In a burrow beneath a Texas field, an armadillo gives birth to four pups. As the little ones grow, they venture outside with her to hunt for food. . . . This handsome picture book offers enough detail to engage them in understanding armadillos, and a refreshing lack of sensationalism and sentimentality about events in the animals' lives." Booklist

Tagholm, Sally

The rabbit; written by Sally Tagholm; illustrated Bert Kitchen. Kingfisher (NY) 2000 32p il (Animal lives) $9.95; pa $4.95

Grades: 2 3 4   **599.3**

1. Rabbits

ISBN 0-7534-5214-6; 0-7534-5607-9 (pa)

LC 99-45787

Describes how the European rabbit, now found on every continent, burrows, breeds, feeds, plays, and lives

"Charming illustrations and an attractive layout support the lyrical and engaging text." Sci Child

Includes glossary

Zuchora-Walske, Christine
Let's look at prairie dogs. Lerner Publications Co. 2010 32p il map (Lightning bolt books: Animal close-ups) lib bdg $25.26
Grades: PreK K 1 2   **599.3**
1. Prairie dogs
ISBN 978-0-7613-3891-8 (lib bdg); 0-7613-3891-8 (lib bdg)   LC 2008-51856
Introduces prairie dogs, describing their physical characteristics, habitat, and predators
"Fresh photography, a creative use of graphics, and a collagelike layout make[s] . . . [this book] eye-catching. . . . [The] book ends with a labeled diagram of the animal, a range map, and a further-reading list that includes print and online resources in a single list, a nice way of validating both types of materials." SLJ
Includes glossary

599.35   Rodents

Bill, Tannis
Pika; life in the rocks; photographs by Jim Jacobson. Boyds Mills Press 2010 32p il $18.95
Grades: K 1 2 3   **599.35**
1. Pikas
ISBN 978-1-59078-803-5; 1-59078-803-6
"The pika is a cousin to the rabbit. . . . Using short, declarative sentences, Tannis follows the laborious life of a pika living in the Rocky Mountains. It is a daily grind of gathering leaves and branches for his hay pile, a massive thatch that can grow as large as a bathtub and that serves as a food reserve, particularly during winter months. . . . The photos capture the pika at his cutest. . . . Loaded with rich back matter on the pika and its predators, this is a cycle-of-life book that satisfies to the end." Booklist
Includes glossary and bibliographical references

Jango-Cohen, Judith
Porcupines; by Judith Jango-Cohen. Benchmark Books 2005 48p il (Animals, animals) lib bdg $25.64
Grades: 3 4 5 6   **599.35**
1. Porcupines
ISBN 0-7614-1868-7   LC 2004-21443
Describes the physical characteristics, behavior, and habitat of porcupines
This is "eye-catching . . . smoothly written and informative . . . [This includes] numerous clear, closeup color photographs." SLJ
Includes glossary and bibliographical references

Markle, Sandra, 1946-
Outside and inside rats and mice. Atheneum Bks. for Young Readers 2001 39p il hardcover o.p. pa $10.99
Grades: 2 3 4   **599.35**
1. Rats 2. Mice
ISBN 0-689-82301-0; 1-4169-7571-3 (pa)
       LC 00-29290

Describes the external and internal physical characteristics of mice and rats and their behavior
"Markle skillfully draws readers into careful observation of outstanding close-up photographs of mice and rats. . . . The friendly text maintains its scientific rigor." Horn Book
Includes glossary

Porcupines; [by] Sandra Markle. Lerner Publications Company 2007 39p il (Animal prey) lib bdg $25.26 *
Grades: 3 4 5   **599.35**
1. Porcupines
ISBN 978-0-8225-6439-3 (lib bdg); 0-8225-6439-4 (lib bdg)   LC 2006000601
This describes the physical characteristics, habits, and life cycle of porcupines
"An outstanding combination of fascinating [text] and informative, appealing photos." SLJ
Includes glossary and bibliographical references

Marrin, Albert, 1936-
Oh, rats! the story of rats and people; illustrated by C.B. Mordan. Dutton Children's Books 2006 48p il $16.99 *
Grades: 3 4 5 6   **599.35**
1. Rats
ISBN 0-525-47762-4   LC 2004-24512
"Along with portraying rats in many roles, from pests to pets, Marrin . . . introduces rodent relatives and provides glimpses of rats' habits and innate intelligence, as well as their history as disease carriers, lab animals, predators, and . . . even entrees." Booklist
This is "lively and informative. . . . The nine short chapters are set in a handsome slim book with striking black-and-white scratchboard illustrations and muted red framing on many pages." SLJ
Includes bibliographical references

Pascoe, Elaine
Mice; text by Elaine Pascoe; photographs by Dwight Kuhn. Blackbirch Press 2005 48p il (Nature close-up) $23.70
Grades: 4 5 6 7   **599.35**
1. Mice
ISBN 1-4103-0537-6   LC 2005007650
This introduces mouse breeds, physical characteristics, and life cycles, and offers tips on keeping mice as pets, and activities for studying them, and information on scientific research.
"Clear photographs that show every mouse whisker and toe will attract browsers as well as report writers. . . . The language presents concepts in easily understood, straightforward language, and the surprising facts . . . are sure to illicit newfound appreciation." Booklist
Includes glossary and bibliographical references

Savage, Stephen, 1965-
Mouse. PowerKids Press 2009 32p il (Animal neighbors) lib bdg $23.95
Grades: 3 4 5 6   **599.35**
1. Mice
ISBN 978-1-4358-4990-7 (lib bdg); 1-4358-4990-6 (lib bdg)   LC 2008-5414

Savage, Stephen, 1965- — *Continued*

This describes the life cycle, habitat, and behavior of mice

Rat. PowerKids Press 2009 32p il (Animal neighbors) lib bdg $23.95

Grades: 3 4 5   **599.35**

1. Rats

ISBN 978-1-4358-4991-4 (lib bdg); 1-4358-4991-4 (lib bdg)   LC 2008-5451

This describes the life cycle, habitat, and behavior of rats

This title features "beautiful, detailed, close-up photos of animals displayed on child-friendly page layouts. The information is well organized for reports." SLJ

Sill, Cathryn P., 1953-

About rodents; [by] Cathryn Sill; illustrated by John Sill. Peachtree 2008 unp il $15.95

Grades: K 1 2 3   **599.35**

1. Rodents

ISBN 978-1-56145-454-9; 1-56145-454-0

Explains what rodents are, how they live, and what they do.

"Beautifully illustrated with clear, well-composed paintings of animals, this book shows respect for its audience as well as its subject." Booklist

Includes glossary and bibliographical references

599.4   Chiroptera (Bats)

Berman, Ruth, 1958-

Let's look at bats. Lerner Publications Co. 2010 32p il (Lightning bolt books: Animal close-ups) lib bdg $25.26

Grades: PreK K 1 2   **599.4**

1. Bats

ISBN 978-0-7613-3885-7 (lib bdg); 0-7613-3885-3 (lib bdg)   LC 2008-51858

Introduces bats, describing their physical characteristics, habitat, nocturnal behavior, and feeding habits

"Fresh photography, a creative use of graphics, and a collagelike layout make[s] . . . [this book] eye-catching. . . . [The] book ends with a labeled diagram of the animal, a range map, and a further-reading list that includes print and online resources in a single list, a nice way of validating both types of materials." SLJ

Includes glossary

Dornfeld, Margaret

Bats; [by] Margaret Dornfeld. Benchmark Books 2004 46p il map (Animals, animals) lib bdg $25.64 *

Grades: 3 4 5 6   **599.4**

1. Bats

ISBN 0-7614-1754-0   LC 2004-9342

Contents: Introducing bats; Bat basics; Calling all bats; Living upside down; Bats at risk

This describes the life cycles and characteristics of bats, illustrated with color photographs.

Includes glossary and bibliographical references

Earle, Ann

Zipping, zapping, zooming bats; illustrated by Henry Cole. HarperCollins Pubs. 1995 32p il (Let's-read-and-find-out science) hardcover o.p. pa $4.95

Grades: K 1 2 3   **599.4**

1. Bats

ISBN 0-06-023480-6; 0-06-445133-X (pa)   LC 93-11052

"Brown bats are introduced as fliers, hunters, and contributors to good ecology in this simple discussion of the flying mammals' physical characteristics and behavior. The illustrations include realistic close-ups, informative diagrams, and scenes incorporating children. Instructions for building a bat house are included." Horn Book Guide

Gibbons, Gail

Bats. Holiday House 1999 unp il $16.95; pa $6.95

Grades: K 1 2 3   **599.4**

1. Bats

ISBN 0-8234-1457-4; 0-8234-1637-2 (pa)   LC 99-12051

Describes different kinds of bats, their physical characteristics, habits and behavior, and efforts to protect them

"The occasional splashes of color light up brilliantly against the dark backgrounds. Well suited for classroom use, this book makes a good case for bats as an admirable part of the natural world." Booklist

Gonzales, Doreen

Bats in the dark. PowerKids Press 2010 24p il (Creatures of the night) lib bdg $21.25; pa $8.05

Grades: 2 3 4   **599.4**

1. Bats

ISBN 978-1-4042-8096-0 (lib bdg); 1-4042-8096-0 (lib bdg); 978-1-4358-3249-7 (pa); 1-4358-3249-3 (pa)   LC 2008-53802

A look at bats and their world in the dark

"Basic details are complemented by eclectic trivia, . . . [and] each volume concludes with a defense of the animal . . . and why it is vital to humans. The layout is attractive, with easy-to-read text and eye-catching photography. Good for reports." SLJ

Includes glossary

Lockwood, Sophie

Bats; by Sophie Lockwood. Child's World 2008 40p il map (World of mammals) lib bdg $29.93

Grades: 4 5 6   **599.4**

1. Bats

ISBN 978-1-59296-926-5 (lib bdg); 1-59296-926-7 (lib bdg)   LC 2007013565

This book about bats provides "all the basics for reports: an introduction to the creatures' challenges, the role humans play, physical traits and behaviors, habitats, and struggles for survival. Every part of their life [cycle], including sexual maturity, birth, and family relationships, is explained. . . . Clear bright photographs pump up the content. . . . The detail that Lockwood imparts is startlingly high. The [text is] written in a dynamic and engaging style." SLJ

Includes glossary and bibliographical references

Lunde, Darrin P.

Hello, bumblebee bat; [by] Darrin Lunde; illustrated by Patricia J. Wynne. Charlesbridge 2007 unp il lib bdg $15.95

Grades: PreK K 1 2   **599.4**
    1. Bats
    ISBN 978-1-57091-374-7 (lib bdg); 1-57091-374-9 (lib bdg)   LC 2006-20952

A Geisel Award honor book, 2008

"Meet the inch-long bumblebee bat, the smallest bat species in the world. Each left-hand page poses a question to a little bat. . . . Beginning each question with the bat's memorable name heightens the pleasing sense of pattern in the text, which offers information that children can understand, but avoids overwhelming them with too many facts. Wynne . . . contributes an appealing set of pictures that complement the text." Booklist

Markovics, Joyce L.

The bat's cave; a dark city; by Joyce Markovics. Bearport Pub. 2009 32p il map (Spectacular animal towns) lib bdg $25.27

Grades: 2 3 4   **599.4**
    1. Bats
    ISBN 978-1-59716-871-7 (lib bdg); 1-59716-871-8 (lib bdg)   LC 2009-8146

A look inside a bat's dark world, how bats hunt, sleep, and raise their young, and more

"Through excellent photographs, high-interest texts, sidebars, maps, and other material, children learn about both the animals and their habitats. The . . . book also provides brief profiles of animals with similar habitats. . . . [This book is] much better than average 'report' titles." SLJ

Includes glossary and bibliographical references

Rodriguez, Cindy

Bats. Rourke Pub. 2010 24p il map (Eye to eye with endangered species) lib bdg $27.07

Grades: 2 3 4   **599.4**
    1. Bats
    ISBN 978-1-60694-406-6 (lib bdg); 1-60694-406-1 (lib bdg)   LC 2009-5997

Text examines the issues endangered bats face and how they can be saved

"Sets out to introduce readers to [bats] . . . explain the dangers they face, and detail the efforts of biologists and conservationists to save them. . . . Serviceable and informative." SLJ

Includes glossary

Stewart, Melissa, 1968-

How do bats fly in the dark? Marshall Cavendish Benchmark 2009 32p il (Tell me why, tell me how) lib bdg $20.95

Grades: 3 4 5   **599.4**
    1. Bats
    ISBN 978-0-7614-2924-1 (lib bdg); 0-7614-2924-7 (lib bdg)   LC 2007023821

"Provides comprehensive information on bats and the process of how they use their sensory system to find their way in the dark" Publisher's note

Includes glossary and bibliographical references

Vogel, Julia, 1958-

Bats; by Julia Vogel; illustrations by Andrew Recher. NorthWord 2007 47p il (Our wild world) $10.95; pa $7.95

Grades: 3 4 5 6   **599.4**
    1. Bats
    ISBN 978-1-55971-968-1; 978-1-55971-969-8 (pa)   LC 2006021917

The "text describes the major physical characteristics shared by all [bats], . . . behavior, distinctive characteristics of several large groups and more than two dozen species, habitats, defense mechanisms, diets, and life cycles. . . . A sharp color photograph . . . illustrates the text on most pages." Booklist

599.5   Cetacea and Sirenia

Arnold, Caroline, 1944-

Super swimmers; whales, dolphins, and other mammals of the sea; illustrated by Patricia J. Wynne. Charlesbridge 2007 32p il $16.95

Grades: 3 4 5 6   **599.5**
    1. Marine mammals
    ISBN 978-1-57091-588-8; 1-57091-588-1   LC 2005-06018

This "introduction to marine mammals begins with whales, dolphins, and porpoises and then goes on to discuss seals, sea lions, walruses, manatees, dugongs, sea otters, and polar bears. . . . The well-organized, succinct text is accompanied by clearly delineated ink drawings, washed with delicate colors. Precise yet lively." Booklist

Includes glossary

Arnosky, Jim

Jim Arnosky's All about manatees. Scholastic Nonfiction 2008 unp pa $5.99

Grades: K 1 2 3   **599.5**
    1. Manatees
    ISBN 0-439-90361-0 (pa); 978-0-439-90361-5 (pa)   LC 2007061717

This is an "introductory guide to manatees. . . . Artwork, captions, and paragraphs of information work together seamlessly to present the physical characteristics, behaviors, and habitats of manatees living in Florida waters, as well as the threats to their survival. Fluid paintings illustrate points in the text and depict the animals' lumbering grace." Booklist

Christopherson, Sara Cohen

Top 50 reasons to care about whales and dolphins; animals in peril. Enslow Publishers 2010 103p il (Top 50 reasons to care about endangered animals) lib bdg $31.93

Grades: 4 5 6 7   **599.5**
    1. Whales 2. Dolphins 3. Endangered species
    ISBN 978-0-7660-3453-2 (lib bdg); 0-7660-3453-4 (lib bdg)   LC 2008-48695

This describes whales and dolphins—their life cycles, diets, young, habitats, and reasons why they are endangered animals

"The illustrations, mostly color photographs, represent

Christopherson, Sara Cohen—*Continued*

a wonderful selection of the animals and their habitats. Reluctant readers may be enticed by this . . . simply because of the great images. This . . . would make a substantial supplement to the science curriculum when studying endangered animals." Libr Media Connect

Includes glossary and bibliographical references

Davies, Nicola, 1958-

Big blue whale; illustrated by Nick Maland. Candlewick Press 1997 27p il hardcover o.p. pa $6.99

Grades: K 1 2 3   **599.5**
1. Whales
ISBN 1-56402-895-X; 0-7636-1080-1 (pa)
     LC 96-42327

Examines the physical characteristics, habits, and habitats of the blue whale

"Davies's brief overview offers young readers exactly what they want to know about this magnificent animal, and her judicious use of comparison makes the abstract more understandable. . . . Maland's cross-hatched pen-and-ink drawings rest on blue watercolor wash backgrounds." Horn Book Guide

Dudzinski, Kathleen

Meeting dolphins; my adventures in the sea. National Geographic Soc. 2000 64p il $17.95

Grades: 4 5 6 7   **599.5**
1. Dolphins 2. Animal communication
ISBN 0-7922-7129-7   LC 99-39069

The author describes her work studying dolphin communication and her invention of a listening device that allows researchers to tell which of a group of dolphins is vocalizing underwater

"The lively, first-person narrative incorporates abundant facts and entertaining anecdotes, infused with Dudzinski's infectious enthusiasm for her subjects and her work. Beautiful, full-color photos are breathtaking and well chosen for explication." Booklist

Esbensen, Barbara Juster

Baby whales drink milk; illustrated by Lambert Davis. HarperCollins Pubs. 1994 32p il (Let's-read-and-find-out science) pa $4.95 hardcover o.p.

Grades: K 1   **599.5**
1. Whales 2. Mammals
ISBN 0-06-445119-4 (pa)   LC 92-30375

Describes the behavior of the humpback whale, with an emphasis on the fact that it is a mammal and shares the characteristics of other mammals

"Full-color paintings, mainly in watery greens and blues, show the animals in their habitat, along with a scene of a whale model in a museum and a map of migration. The book's strong point, though, is Esbensen's simple, informative text, which keeps its young audience clearly in view." Booklist

Goldish, Meish

Florida manatees; warm water miracles; by Meish Goldish. Bearport Pub. 2007 c2008 32p il map (America's animal comebacks) lib bdg $18.95

Grades: 2 3 4   **599.5**
1. Manatees 2. Wildlife conservation
ISBN 978-1-59716-507-5 (lib bdg); 1-59716-507-7 (lib bdg)   LC 2007010311

"This accessible title discusses the environmental threats facing the Florida manatee and the efforts that saved this appealing sea creature from extinction. . . . Double-page spread feature attention-grabbing fact boxes and large, full-color photos." Booklist

Includes glossary and bibliographical references

Greenaway, Theresa, 1947-

Whales; [illustrated by Colin Newman] Raintree Steck-Vaughn Pubs. 2001 48p il (Secret world of) lib bdg $18.98

Grades: 4 5 6 7   **599.5**
1. Whales
ISBN 0-7398-3508-4   LC 00-62828

This describes the anatomy, habits, and life cycle of whales and their place in the ecosystem

"The accessible presentation and clear writing style combined with a high level of detail make . . . [this] valuable for simple reports." Booklist

Includes glossary and bibliographical references

Greenberg, Daniel A.

Whales; [by] Dan Greenberg, with Nina Hess. Marshall Cavendish Benchmark 2010 24p il map (Benchmark rockets. Animals) lib bdg $16.95

Grades: 3 4 5   **599.5**
1. Whales
ISBN 978-0-7614-4346-9; 0-7614-4346-0
     LC 2008-52110

"Describes the physical characteristics, habitat, behavior, diet, life cycle, and conservation status of whales." Publisher's note

"The straightforward presentation of the information and the uncluttered and attractive layout make [this] . . . good . . . for reports. Color photographs . . . are well utilized and complete a solid package." SLJ

Includes glossary

Hodgkins, Fran, 1964-

The whale scientists; solving the mystery of whale strandings. Houghton Mifflin Co. 2007 63p il map (Scientists in the field) $18 *

Grades: 5 6 7 8   **599.5**
1. Whales
ISBN 978-0-618-55673-1; 0-618-55673-7
     LC 2006-34634

This describes the evolution of whales and their relationship to humans and offers various scientific theories about their strandings.

"Hodgkins packs her text with an impressive amount of information. . . . Well-chosen color photographs amply illustrate the well-organized discussion." SLJ

Includes glossary and bibliographical references

Hoyt, Erich, 1950-
Whale rescue; changing the future for endangered wildlife. Firefly 2005 64p il $19.95; pa $9.95
Grades: 5 6 7 8   **599.5**
1. Whales 2. Wildlife conservation
ISBN 1-55297-601-7; 1-55297-600-9 (pa)
"Hoyt examines the impact of commercial whaling on global whale populations and the efforts being made by scientists, environmentalists, and some governments to protect these endangered mammals. Crisp, color photos portray these leviathans in their natural habitat and also show scientists hard at work on cetacean projects, whaling ships and their harvest on the high seas, and seagoing environmentalists in action." SLJ

Kant, Tanya
The migration of a whale; written by Tanya Kant; illustrated by Mark Bergin. Children's Press 2008 32p il map (Amaze) lib bdg $26; pa $8.95
Grades: K 1 2 3   **599.5**
1. Animals—Migration 2. Whales
ISBN 978-0-531-24049-6 (lib bdg); 0-531-24049-5 (lib bdg); 978-0-531-23803-5 (pa); 0-531-23803-5 (pa)
This describes the journey of a whale as it migrates across the oceans.
"Well-organized chapters promote inquiry, using questions as titles, which are followed by clearly written answers and other facts, distinguished by different-size fonts. . . . Children will love holding pages up to the light to see 'inside' the gray whale. . . Excellent, simple illustrations using colorful mixed media enhance the [text]." SLJ
Inlcudes glossary

Lockwood, Sophie
Whales; by Sophie Lockwood. Child's World 2008 40p il map (World of mammals) lib bdg $29.93
Grades: 4 5 6   **599.5**
1. Whales
ISBN 978-1-59296-930-2 (lib bdg); 1-59296-930-5 (lib bdg)   LC 2007020890
This book about whales presents "all the basics for reports: an introduction to the creatures' challenges, the role humans play, physical traits and behaviors, habitats, and struggles for survival. Every part of their life [cycle], including sexual maturity, birth, and family relationships, is explained. . . . Clear bright photographs pump up the content. . . . The detail that Lockwood imparts is startlingly high. The [text is] written in a dynamic and engaging style." SLJ
Includes glossary and bibliographical references

Lourie, Peter
Whaling season; a year in the life of an arctic whale scientist. Houghton Mifflin Books for Children 2009 80p il map (Scientists in the field) $18 *
Grades: 4 5 6 7   **599.5**
1. George, John Craighead 2. Whales 3. Alaska 4. Inuit
ISBN 978-0-618-77709-9; 0-618-77709-1
                                        LC 2009-18596

Profiles the work of John Craighead George, an Arctic whale scientist, as he studies the bowhead whale and works with the indigenous people of Alaska to better understand the history of the animal.
"Combining exemplary color photos and simple, vivid language, the chapters detail not only George's day-today methodology but also his motivation." Booklist
Includes glossary and bibliographical references

Markle, Sandra, 1946-
Killer whales; [by] Sandra Markle. Carolrhoda Books 2004 39p il (Animal predators) lib bdg $25.26; pa $7.95
Grades: 3 4 5 6   **599.5**
1. Whales
ISBN 1-57505-728-X (lib bdg); 1-57505-743-3 (pa)
                                        LC 2003-25944
The author observes killer whales' "hunting techniques and includes information about their physical characteristics, physiology, habitats, and care of young." Horn Book Guide
"Dramatic, large color photos keep step with informative, readable [text]." SLJ
Includes glossary and bibliographical references

Nicklin, Flip
Face to face with dolphins; by Flip and Linda Nicklin. National Geographic 2007 32p il (Face to face) $16.95; lib bdg $25.90 *
Grades: 3 4 5 6   **599.5**
1. Dolphins
ISBN 978-1-4263-0141-4; 1-4263-0141-3; 978-1-4263-0142-1 (lib bdg); 1-4263-0142-1 (lib bdg)
                                        LC 2006-36273
"The Nicklins outline the special abilities and physical features of dolphins, such as echolocation, as well as diet, reproduction, swimming habits, and threats to their existence. . . . [This] attractive, smoothly written [book], topped off with advice about self-directed research, will catch the attention of enthusiasts and motivate them toward personal investigation." SLJ
Includes glossary and bibliographical references

Face to face with whales; by Flip & Linda Nicklin. National Geographic 2008 31p il map (Face to face) $16.95; lib bdg $25.95 *
Grades: 3 4 5 6   **599.5**
1. Whales
ISBN 978-1-4263-0244-2; 1-4263-0244-4; 978-1-4263-0245-9 (lib bdg); 1-4263-0245-2 (lib bdg)
                                        LC 2007-34249
The authors describe the life cycle and behavior of whales and their own experiences with whales in the wild.
Includes glossary and bibliographical references

Pfeffer, Wendy, 1929-

Dolphin talk; whistles, clicks, and clapping jaws; illustrated by Helen K. Davie. HarperCollins Pubs. 2003 33p il (Let's-read-and-find-out science) hardcover o.p. pa $4.99

Grades: K 1 2   **599.5**
    1. Dolphins 2. Animal communication
    ISBN 0-06-028801-9; 0-06-028802-7 (lib bdg);
    0-06-445210-7 (pa)   LC 2001-39518

Describes how dolphins communicate with each other in squeaks, whistles, and pops

"Pfeffer does a great job of keeping the concept understandable and comparing human and animal communication. . . . Davie's watercolor illustrations are pleasant and upbeat." SLJ

Rake, Jody Sullivan, 1961-

Blue whales up close. Capstone Press 2010 24p il (First facts. Whales and dolphins up close) lib bdg $21.32

Grades: K 1 2 3   **599.5**
    1. Whales
    ISBN 978-1-4296-3336-9 (lib bdg); 1-4296-3336-0 (lib
    bdg)   LC 2009-6005

"Presents an up-close look at blue whales, including their body features, habitat, and life cycle." Publisher's note

This "title has colorful pages and chapter heading to capture the interest of young readers as well as short, straightforward sentence structure to keep them reading. Captivating photographs of whales in the wild are present on each spread and feature up close images of body parts such as blow holes and baleen. . . . This . . . will be a fabulous addition to any elementary school library collection." Libr Media Connect

Includes glossary and bibliographical references

Humpback whales up close. Capstone Press 2010 24p il (First facts. Whales and dolphins up close) lib bdg $21.32

Grades: K 1 2   **599.5**
    1. Whales
    ISBN 978-1-4296-3337-6 (lib bdg); 1-4296-3337-9 (lib
    bdg)   LC 2009-6004

"Presents an up-close look at humpback whales, including their body features, habitat, and life cycle'." Publisher's note

This "title has colorful pages and chapter heading to capture the interest of young readers as well as short, straightforward sentence structure to keep them reading. Captivating photographs of whales in the wild are present on each spread and feature up close images of body parts such as blow holes and baleen. . . . This . . . will be a fabulous addition to any elementary school library collection." Libr Media Connect

Includes glossary and bibliographical references

Simon, Seymour, 1931-

Dolphins. Smithsonian/Collins 2009 32p il $17.99; lib bdg $18.89

Grades: 1 2 3 4   **599.5**
    1. Dolphins
    ISBN 978-0-06-028393-3; 0-06-028393-9;
    978-0-06-028394-0 (lib bdg); 0-06-028394-7 (lib bdg)
                                          LC 2008010654

"Simon presents fascinating facts about these playful mammals and describes the difference between dolphins, porpoises, and whales in terms that children can understand. Without being didactic, he discusses the physiology and habits of dolphins, as well as the greatest threat to the species—humans. Accompanied by full-page color photographs of dolphins, the text is presented with considerable white space in the margins." Booklist

Stearns, Precious McKenzie

Manatees; [by] Precious McKenzie. Rourke 2010 24p il map (Eye to eye with endangered species) lib bdg $27.07

Grades: 2 3 4   **599.5**
    1. Manatees
    ISBN 978-1-60694-403-5 (lib bdg); 1-60694-403-7 (lib
    bdg)   LC 2009-6011

This describes manatees and why they are threatened with extinction

"Sets out to introduce readers to [manatees] . . . explain the dangers they face, and detail the efforts of biologists and conservationists to save them. . . . Serviceable and informative." SLJ

Includes glossary and bibliographical references

Thomson, Sarah L.

Amazing whales! written by Sarah L. Thomson; photographs provided by the Wildlife Conservation Society. HarperCollins 2004 27p il (I can read book) $15.99; lib bdg $16.89 *

Grades: 1 2 3   **599.5**
    1. Whales
    ISBN 0-06-054465-1; 0-06-054466-X (lib bdg)
                                          LC 2004-2473

"Thomson takes a look at blue whales, killer whales, sperm whales, dolphins, and porpoises, describing common physical characteristics of the group as well as hunting and feeding habits, methods of communication, and endangered status." Booklist

"Thomson's superior text sustains readers' attention with interesting facts and apt comparisons. . . . Spectacular color photographs add detail and drama." SLJ

599.63　Artiodactyla (Even-toed ungulates)

Anderson, Jill, 1968-

Giraffes; by Jill Anderson. NorthWord 2005 unp il (Wild ones) $12.95; pa $8.95

Grades: K 1 2   **599.63**
    1. Giraffes
    ISBN 978-1-55971-928-5; 1-55971-928-1;
    978-1-55971-929-2 (pa); 1-55971-929-X (pa)
                                          LC 2004031117

This describes the physiology, habitat, and life cycle of giraffes

"With simple, direct words and clear, closeup color photo images, this . . . does an excellent job of introducing preschoolers to basic facts about giraffe physiology and habitat, and, especially, how the animals get their food and digest it, and how they care for their young." Booklist

Bredeson, Carmen

Giraffes up close. Enslow Elementary 2008 c2009 24p il (Zoom in on animals!) lib bdg $21.26

Grades: 1 2 3   **599.63**

  1. Giraffes

  ISBN 978-0-7660-3081-7 (lib bdg); 0-7660-3081-4 (lib bdg)

This describes the anatomy, behavior, and life cycle of the giraffe.

Includes glossary and bibliographical references

Clarke, Penny

Hippos; written by Penny Clarke. F. Watts 2009 32p il (Scary creatures) lib bdg $26; pa $8.95 *

Grades: 3 4 5   **599.63**

  1. Hippopotamus

  ISBN 978-0-531-21671-2 (lib bdg); 0-531-21671-3 (lib bdg); 978-0-531-21042-0 (pa); 0-531-21042-1 (pa)

                     LC 2009010798

This describes the hippo's life cycle, habitat, behavior, and relationship to humans

This title has "two-page chapters of accessible, large-type text and bright color photos and illustrations. . . . The series distinguishes itself with 'X-Ray Vision.' When readers hold the page with this prompt up to the light, an image emerges. The X-rays mostly show the skeletal structures of the animals. Text boxes throughout add to the visual appeal. . . . [This title is an] excellent [resource for school assignments and browsing." SLJ

  Includes glossary

Hatkoff, Isabella

Owen & Mzee; the true story of a remarkable friendship; told by Isabella Hatkoff, Craig Hatkoff, and Paula Kahumbu; with photographs by Peter Greste. Scholastic Press 2006 unp il map $16.99 *

Grades: K 1 2 3   **599.63**

  1. Hippopotamus 2. Turtles 3. Indian Ocean earthquake and tsunami, 2004 4. Kenya

  ISBN 0-439-82973-9   LC 2005-21341

The "true story of two great friends, a baby hippo named Owen and a 130-yr-old giant tortoise named Mzee (Mm-ZAY). When Owen was stranded after the Dec 2004 tsunami, villagers in Kenya worked tirelessly to rescue him. Then, to everyone's amazement, the orphan hippo and the elderly tortoise adopted each other." Publisher's note

"The text and the back matter are brimming with information about the animals, their caregivers, and the locale. This touching story of the power of a surprising friendship to mitigate the experience of loss is full of heart and hope." SLJ

Owen & Mzee: the language of friendship; told by Isabella Hatkoff, Craig Hatkoff, and Paula Kuhumbu; with photographs by Peter Greste. Scholastic Press 2007 unp il $16.99 *

Grades: K 1 2 3   **599.63**

  1. Hippopotamus 2. Turtles 3. Kenya

  ISBN 978-0-439-89959-8; 0-439-89959-1

                     LC 2006015612

"Owen & Mzee: The True Story of a Remarkable Friendship (Scholastic, 2006) chronicled the fascinating story of a baby hippo who was orphaned by the December 2004 tsunami and the bond he formed with Mzee, a 130-year-old Alhambra tortoise at a wildlife sanctuary in Kenya. This sequel updates readers on the status of that friendship a year and a half later, particularly with regard to the way this unusual duo has learned to communicate with one another. . . . The text is clearly written and accompanied by numerous high-quality, full-color photos of this unique pair." SLJ

Includes bibliographical references

Jango-Cohen, Judith

Camels; [by] Judith Jango-Cohen. Benchmark Books 2004 c2005 47p il map (Animals, animals) lib bdg $25.64 *

Grades: 3 4 5 6   **599.63**

  1. Camels

  ISBN 0-7614-1750-8   LC 2003-24842

  Contents: Introducing camels; A camel's diet; Blasting sand and blazing sun; Birth and growth; From caravan to race track

This describes the life cycle and behavior of camels, and their relationships to humans

This "beautifully crafted [book presents] information in a lively, readable manner. [It includes] excellent-quality, candid full-color photographs." SLJ

Includes glossary and bibliographical references

Hippopotamuses; by Judith Jango-Cohen. Marshall Cavendish Benchmark 2006 47p il (Animals, animals) lib bdg $19.95

Grades: 3 4 5 6   **599.63**

  1. Hippopotamus

  ISBN 978-0-7614-2238-9 (lib bdg); 0-7614-2238-2 (lib bdg)   LC 2005026015

"Describes the physical characteristics, behavior, habitat, and endangered status of hippopotamuses." Publisher's note

Includes glossary and bibliographical references

Rumford, James, 1948-

Chee-lin; a giraffe's journey; by James Rumford. Houghton Mifflin 2008 unp il map $17 *

Grades: 1 2 3   **599.63**

  1. Giraffes 2. China

  ISBN 978-0-618-71720-0; 0-618-71720-X

                     LC 2008001863

"Linking the Chinese mythological creature, the 'chee-lin', to a 1414 Chinese portrait of a giraffe, Rumford imagines how a giraffe may have journeyed to China. . . . Tweega (Swahili for 'giraffe') survives frightening voyages, cruel and tender caretakers, and cramped quarters, ending up in the emperor's spacious grounds. . . . The narrative—moving, even tender in many places—is accompanied by handsome full-page paintings, beautifully bordered with evocative motifs." Booklist

St. George, Judith, 1931-
Zarafa; the giraffe who walked to the king; illustrated by Britt Spencer. Philomel Books 2009 unp il $16.99
Grades: 2 3 4   **599.63**
1. Giraffes 2. France—Kings and rulers 3. Exotic animals
ISBN 978-0-399-25049-1; 0-399-25049-2
                                        LC 2008-32609
This "highlights a unique historical episode, following a 19th-century giraffe, a gift from the viceroy of Egypt to Charles X, as she journeys from Africa to France. Fanciful flourishes fill Spencer's watercolor, gouache and ink art. . . . St. George's breezy, conversational text . . . moves this voyage along briskly." Publ Wkly

Tourville, Amanda Doering, 1980-
A giraffe grows up; by Amanda Doering Tourville; illustrated by Michael Denman and William J. Huiett. Picture Window Books 2007 24p il map lib bdg $25.26 paperback o.p.
Grades: PreK K 1 2   **599.63**
1. Giraffes
ISBN 978-1-4048-3158-2 (lib bdg); 1-4048-3158-4 (lib bdg); 978-1-4048-3565-8 (pa); 1-4048-3565-2 (pa)
                                        LC 2006027307
"Each spread has an acrylic painting with a paragraph or two of text. . . . Easy-to-read . . . with enough information for basic reports." SLJ
Includes glossary and bibliographical references

Walden, Katherine
Warthogs. PowerKiDS Press 2009 24p il (Safari animals) lib bdg $21.25
Grades: PreK K 1 2   **599.63**
1. Warthogs
ISBN 978-1-4358-2688-5 (lib bdg); 1-4358-2688-4 (lib bdg)   LC 2008019531
Includes glossary and bibliographical references
This book provides "succinctly written introductory information about [warthogs'] range, habitat, social groups, and diet. Spreads consist of one to three short, simply constructed sentences opposite crisp, color photographs, most of which represent the subject perfectly." SLJ

599.64   Bovidae

Caper, William
American bison; a scary prediction; by William Caper. Bearport 2007 32p il map (America's animal comebacks) lib bdg $25.27
Grades: 2 3 4   **599.64**
1. Hornaday, William Temple, 1854-1937 2. Bronx Zoo 3. Bison 4. Wildlife conservation
ISBN 978-1-59716-504-4 (lib bdg); 1-59716-504-2 (lib bdg)   LC 2007010863
This describes how the American bison was saved from extinction by William Temple Hornaday, the American Bison Society, and the The Bronx Zoo.
This book is "well organized and [has] an easy style and an accessible vocabulary and text size . . . [and] color photographs." SLJ
Includes glossary and bibliographical references

George, Jean Craighead, 1919-
The buffalo are back; paintings by Wendell Minor. Dutton Children's Books 2010 unp il $16.99
Grades: 3 4 5   **599.64**
1. Bison 2. West (U.S.)—History
ISBN 978-0-525-42215-0; 0-525-42215-3
"This handsome book discusses the history of the buffalo on the American plains. Succinctly and gracefully written, it envisions the centuries when Indians carefully managed the land, using the buffalo for food, shelter, and clothing. . . . Illustrated with beautiful landscape paintings and striking close-ups of people and animals, this book offers a very effective presentation of the buffalo's story." Booklist

Marrin, Albert, 1936-
Saving the buffalo. Scholastic Nonfiction 2006 128p il $18.99 *
Grades: 4 5 6 7   **599.64**
1. Bison
ISBN 0-439-71854-6   LC 2005-51827
"In characteristically robust prose, Marrin retraces the American bison's roller-coaster ride from Lord of the Great Plains to near extinction at the end of the 19th century, and slow recovery. Along with showing how the buffalo fit into the habitat's complex, interdependent ecology, he describes in vivid detail how the animals were hunted and utilized by indigenous peoples. . . . A generous array of accompanying illustrations includes crisply reproduced photos, both new and old; prints; paintings; and pictures of artifacts." SLJ
Includes glossary and bibliographical references

Perry, Phyllis J., 1933-
Buffalo. Benchmark Books 2005 48p il (Animals, animals) lib bdg $29.93 *
Grades: 3 4 5 6   **599.64**
1. Bison
ISBN 978-0-7614-1866-5 (lib bdg); 0-7614-1866-0 (lib bdg)   LC 2004-21438
Contents: The buffalo; What are buffalo?; A native species; The herd; Saving the buffalo
Describes the physical characteristics, behavior, and habitat of buffalo
This is "eye-catching . . . smoothly written and informative. . . . [It includes] numerous clear, closeup color photographs." SLJ
Includes glossary and bibliographical references

Walden, Katherine
Wildebeests. Rosen Pub. Group's PowerKids Press 2009 24p il (Safari animals) lib bdg $21.25; pa $8.25
Grades: PreK K 1 2   **599.64**
1. Gnus
ISBN 978-1-4358-2692-2 (lib bdg); 1-4358-2692-2 (lib bdg); 978-1-4358-3066-0 (pa); 1-4358-3066-0 (pa)
                                        LC 2008021587
This book provides "succinctly written introductory information about [wildebeests'] range, habitat, social groups, and diet. Spreads consist of one to three short,

Walden, Katherine—_Continued_
simply constructed sentences opposite crisp, color photographs, most of which represent the subject perfectly." SLJ

Includes glossary

599.65 Cervidae (Deer)

Estigarribia, Diana
Moose. Benchmark Books 2006 48p il (Animals, animals) lib bdg $29.93 *
Grades: 3 4 5 6   **599.65**
1. Moose
ISBN 0-7614-1870-9   LC 2004-21444
Describes the physical characteristics, behavior, and habitat of moose
This is "eye-catching . . . smoothly written and informative. . . . [It includes] numerous clear, close-up color photographs." SLJ
Includes glossary and bibliographical references

Heuer, Karsten
Being caribou; five months on foot with a caribou herd. Walker & Co. 2007 48p il map $17.95; lib bdg $18.95 *
Grades: 4 5 6 7   **599.65**
1. Caribou 2. Arctic regions
ISBN   978-0-8027-9565-6;   0-8027-9565-X; 978-0-8027-9566-3 (lib bdg); 0-8027-9566-8 (lib bdg)
LC 2006-27651
This is an adaptation of an adult title by the same name, published 2005 by Mountaineers Books
"Heuer recounts in short chapters of text and handsome color photographs a venture with his wife to follow on foot a herd of female caribou on their summer trek to their Arctic birthing grounds." SLJ
"The caribou calving grounds in the Arctic National Wildlife Refuge are being threatened by oil exploration. [This title] will help make kids aware of what is at stake and give them a glimpse of an extraordinary part of the world and the lengths the caribou go to traverse it. It is an important book." Quill Quire
Includes bibliographical references

Mara, Wil
Deer; by Wil Mara. Marshall Cavendish Benchmark 2009 47p il (Animals animals) $20.95 *
Grades: 3 4 5 6   **599.65**
1. Deer
ISBN 978-0-7614-2926-5; 0-7614-2926-3
LC 2007-27328
"Provides comprehensive information on the anatomy, special skills, habitats, and diet of deer." Publisher's note
"The material is well researched and would be an excellent source for reports, and the [book has] a narrative flow that makes [it] easy and enjoyable to read. [The] title includes expert full-color photography." SLJ
Includes glossary and bibliographical references

Patent, Dorothy Hinshaw
White-tailed deer; photographs by William Muñoz. Lerner Publications Co. 2005 47p il map (Early bird nature books) lib bdg $25.26
Grades: 2 3 4   **599.65**
1. Deer
ISBN 0-8225-3052-X   LC 2004-2381
Contents: Deer around the world; The whitetail; Raising a family; Life in fall and winter; Whitetails and people
"Short chapters introduce children first to the larger deer family, then provide information on whitetails' life cycles, adaptations for survival, and interactions with humans. . . . A solid offering." Booklist

599.66 Perissodactyla (Odd-toed ungulates)

Carson, Mary Kay, 1964-
Emi and the rhino scientist; [by] Mary Kay Carson; with photographs by Tom Uhlman. Houghton Mifflin Company 2007 57p il (Scientists in the field) $18 *
Grades: 5 6 7 8   **599.66**
1. Roth, Terri 2. Rhinoceros
ISBN 978-0-618-64639-5; 0-618-64639-6
LC 2006-34517
This describes "how Terri Roth, an expert in endangered-species reproduction at the Cincinnati Zoo, helped Emi to give birth to the first Sumatran rhino born in captivity in more than 100 years. . . . The text is full of important details, and the photographs are unfailingly crisp, bright, and full of variety." SLJ

Firestone, Mary, 1951-
Top 50 reasons to care about rhinos; animals in peril. Enslow Publishers 2010 103p il (Top 50 reasons to care about endangered animals) lib bdg $31.93
Grades: 4 5 6 7   **599.66**
1. Rhinoceros 2. Endangered species
ISBN 978-0-7660-3457-0 (lib bdg); 0-7660-3457-7 (lib bdg)
LC 2008048692
This describes the different types of rhino, their life cycle, diet, young, habitat, and reasons why they are endangered animals
"The illustrations, mostly color photographs, represent a wonderful selection of the animals and their habitats. Reluctant readers may be enticed by this . . . simply because of the great images. This . . . would make a substantial supplement to the science curriculum when studying endangered animals." Libr Media Connect
Includes glossary and bibliographical references

Holmes, Mary Tavener
My travels with Clara; illustrated by Jon Cannell. J. Paul Getty Museum 2007 unp il $17.95
Grades: 2 3 4   **599.66**
1. Rhinoceros
ISBN 978-0-89236-880-8   LC 2006-35719

Holmes, Mary Tavener—*Continued*

"In the mid-eighteenth century, a Dutch sea captain bought an orphaned baby rhinoceros in India, named her Clara, and toured with her around western Europe. . . . His first-person, fictionalized narrative affectionately tells of his kindness, his bond with his extraordinary companion, and the public excitement she caused. . . . Illustrations include costumed period figures and reproductions of the art Clara inspired. . . . The facts about Clara . . . are as fascintating as the art and pet story." Booklist

Jango-Cohen, Judith

Rhinoceroses. Benchmark Books 2004 c2005 47p il map (Animals, animals) lib bdg $25.64 *

Grades: 3 4 5 6   **599.66**

1. Rhinoceros

ISBN 0-7614-1753-2   LC 2004-839

Contents: Introducing rhinoceroses; Horns, hides, and hooves; Mud baths and back scratches; Rhino reproduction; Rhino survival

This describes the life cycle and behavior of rhinoceroses

This "beautifully crafted [book presents] information in a lively, readable manner. [It includes] excellent-quality, candid full-color photographs." SLJ

Includes glossary and bibliographical references

Lockwood, Sophie

Zebras; by Sophie Lockwood. Child's World 2008 40p il map (World of mammals) lib bdg $29.93

Grades: 4 5 6   **599.66**

1. Zebras

ISBN 978-1-59296-931-9 (lib bdg); 1-59296-931-3 (lib bdg)   LC 2007-21689

This book about Zebras looks "at all aspects of the mammal's life including where they live, how they live, and their unique habits. . . . Detailed and labeled color photographs enhance the information provided. Enjoyable and full of information." Libr Media Connect

Includes glossary and bibliographical references

Momatiuk, Yva, 1940-

Face to face with wild horses; by Yva Momatiuk and John Eastcott. National Geographic 2009 31p il (Face to face) $16.95; lib bdg $25.90 *

Grades: 3 4 5 6   **599.66**

1. Horses

ISBN   978-1-4263-0466-8;   1-4263-0466-8; 978-1-4263-0467-5 (lib bdg); 1-4263-0467-6 (lib bdg)   LC 2008-38247

The authors describe the behavior of wild horses and their personal encounters with them.

Includes bibliographical references

Noble-Goodman, Katherine

Zebras; by Katherine Noble-Goodman. Benchmark Books 2006 48p il (Animals, animals) lib bdg $25.64 *

Grades: 3 4 5 6   **599.66**

1. Zebras

ISBN 0-7614-1871-7

Describes the physical characteristics, behavior, and habitat of zebras

Includes glossary and bibliographical references

Walden, Katherine

Rhinoceroses. PowerKids Press 2009 24p il (Safari animals) lib bdg $21.25

Grades: PreK K 1 2   **599.66**

1. Rhinoceros

ISBN 978-1-4358-2687-8 (lib bdg); 1-4358-2687-6 (lib bdg)   LC 2008019534

This book provides "succinctly written introductory information about [rhinoceroses'] range, habitat, social groups, and diet. Spreads consist of one to three short, simply constructed sentences opposite crisp, color photographs, most of which represent the subject perfectly." SLJ

Includes glossary and bibliographical references

599.67   Proboscidea (Elephants)

Arnold, Katya

Elephants can paint, too! pictures and text by Katya Arnold. Atheneum Books for Young Readers 2005 unp il $16.95 *

Grades: K 1 2 3   **599.67**

1. Elephants 2. Painting

ISBN 0-689-86985-1   LC 2004-17387

"An Anne Schwartz book"

The author "tells how she trains elephants to paint and compares the work of her human and elephant pupils. The spare narrative is easy to understand and reads like a picture book. . . . Arnold's amusing and colorful photographs—of elephants and children at work—will have readers laughing as they view them side-by-side." SLJ

Buckley, Carol

Tarra & Bella; the elephant and dog who became best friends; text and photography by Carol Buckley. G.P. Putnam's Sons 2009 unp il $16.99

Grades: K 1 2 3 4   **599.67**

1. Elephants 2. Dogs 3. Animal behavior

ISBN 978-0-399-25443-7; 0-399-25443-9   LC 2009-18888

Spotlights the true-life friendship between Tarra, a retired circus elephant, and one of the Tennessee Elephant Sanctuary's stray dogs, Bella

"Shots of Tarra petting Bella with her trunk are among the book's most endearing pictures, which range from snapshotlike to skillfully framed images; also notable are photographs that underscore the dramatic difference in the animals' sizes. . . . The animals' friendship will inspire young readers." Publ Wkly

Firestone, Mary, 1951-

Top 50 reasons to care about elephants; animals in peril. Enslow Publishers 2010 103p il (Top 50 reasons to care about endangered animals) lib bdg $31.93

Grades: 4 5 6 7   599.67

1. Elephants 2. Endangered species
ISBN 978-0-7660-3454-9 (lib bdg); 0-7660-3454-2 (lib bdg)   LC 2008-48690

This describes an elephant's ears, trunk and teeth, what they eat, their ancestors, the different kinds of elephants, and why they are on the endangered animals list

"The illustrations, mostly color photographs, represent a wonderful selection of the animals and their habitats. Reluctant readers may be enticed by this . . . simply because of the great images. This . . . would make a substantial supplement to the science curriculum when studying endangered animals." Libr Media Connect

Includes glossary and bibliographical references

Gibbons, Gail

Elephants of Africa. Holiday House 2008 32p il $16.95

Grades: K 1 2 3   599.67

1. Elephants
ISBN 978-0-8234-2168-8; 0-8234-2168-6
LC 2007-51619

"Gibbons introduces young readers to [African elephants]. Each page is filled with illustrations and a succinct but informative text that details the habitats, physical characteristics, diet, offspring development, and behavior of these dwellers of Africa's savannas and forests. . . . The text is well organized and simple to understand, enhanced by the pen-and-ink and watercolor artwork." SLJ

Joubert, Beverly

Face to face with elephants; by Beverly and Dereck Joubert. National Geographic 2008 31p il map (Face to face) $16.95; lib bdg $25.90 *

Grades: 3 4 5 6   599.67

1. Elephants
ISBN   978-1-4263-0325-8;   1-4263-0325-4;
978-1-4263-0326-5 (lib bdg); 1-4263-0326-2 (lib bdg)
LC 2007-41229

The authors describe the life cycle and behavior of elephants and their own experiences with elephants in the wild

"The photographs are stunning, sometimes intimate, sometimes epic. . . . [This book] conveys [elephants'] magnificence and fascination." Bull Cent Child Books

Includes glossary and bibliographical references

Morgan, Jody

Elephant rescue; changing the future for endangered wildlife. Firefly Books 2004 64p il $19.95; pa $9.95

Grades: 5 6 7 8   599.67

1. Elephants 2. Wildlife conservation
ISBN 1-55297-595-9; 1-55297-594-0 (pa)

This "photo-essay . . . combines an urgent message about conservation with a close-up view of elephant

physiology, behavior, and habitat in Africa and Asia." Booklist

This is "well-written. . . . Stunning, full-color photographs bring [these animals] to life." SLJ

Schwabacher, Martin

Elephants; by Martin Schwabacher, with Lori Mortensen. Marshall Cavendish Benchmark 2010 24p il map (Animals) lib bdg $16.95

Grades: 3 4 5   599.67

1. Elephants
ISBN 978-0-7614-4343-8 (lib bdg); 0-7614-4343-6 (lib bdg)   LC 2008-52103

"Rockets"

"Describes the physical characteristics, habitat, behavior, diet, life cycle, and conservation status of elephants." Publisher's note

"The straightforward presentation of the information and the uncluttered and attractive layout make [this] . . . good . . . for reports. Color photographs . . . are well utilized and complete a solid package." SLJ

Includes glossary and bibliographical references

599.7   Carnivora Fissipedia (Land carnivores)

Gonzales, Doreen

Raccoons in the dark. PowerKids Press 2010 24p il (Creatures of the night) lib bdg $21.25; pa $8.05

Grades: 2 3 4   599.7

1. Raccoons
ISBN 978-1-4042-8101-1 (lib bdg); 1-4042-8101-0 (lib bdg); 978-1-4358-3259-6 (pa); 1-4358-3259-0 (pa)
LC 2009-2758

A look at raccoons and their world in the dark.

"Basic details are complemented by eclectic trivia, . . . [and] each volume concludes with a defense of the animal . . . and why it is vital to humans. The layout is attractive, with easy-to-read text and eye-catching photography. Good for reports." SLJ

Includes glossary

Skunks in the dark. PowerKids Press 2010 24p il (Creatures of the night) lib bdg $21.25; pa $8.05

Grades: 2 3 4   599.7

1. Skunks
ISBN 978-1-4042-8099-1 (lib bdg); 1-4042-8099-5 (lib bdg); 978-1-4358-3255-8 (pa); 1-4358-3255-8 (pa)
LC 2009-718

A look at skunks and their world in the dark.

"Basic details are complemented by eclectic trivia, . . . [and] each volume concludes with a defense of the animal . . . and why it is vital to humans. The layout is attractive, with easy-to-read text and eye-catching photography. Good for reports." SLJ

Includes glossary

Leardi, Jeanette
Southern sea otters; fur-tastrophe avoided; by Jeanette Leardi. Bearport Pub. 2008 32p il map (America's animal comebacks) lib bdg $25.27
Grades: 2 3 4   **599.7**
   1. Otters 2. Wildlife conservation
   ISBN 978-1-59716-534-1 (lib bdg); 1-59716-534-4 (lib bdg)   LC 2007012593
This describes efforts by scientists and environmentalists to protect southern sea otters from hunting, pollution, and other dangers
This book is "well organized and [has] an easy style and an accessible vocabulary and text size . . . [and] color photographs." SLJ
Includes glossary and bibliographical references

Mara, Wil
Otters; by Wil Mara. Marshall Cavendish Benchmark 2007 48p il map (Animals, animals) lib bdg $28.50 *
Grades: 3 4 5 6   **599.7**
   1. Otters
   ISBN 978-0-7614-2527-4   LC 2006020823
"Describes the physical characteristics, habitat, behavior, diet, life cycle, and conservation status of the otter." Publisher's note
Includes glossary and bibliographical references

Mason, Adrienne
Skunks; written by Adrienne Mason; illustrated by Nancy Gray Ogle. Kids Can Press 2006 32p (Kids Can Press wildlife series) $10.95
Grades: 2 3 4   **599.7**
   1. Skunks
   ISBN 1-55337-733-8
"Focusing primarily on the four types of skunks found in North America, Mason has provided readers with an accurate, fun-to-read look at this sometimes misunderstood animal. She offers a straightforward description of the mammals habitat, appearance, predators, diet, reproduction, and human interaction. Realistically rendered watercolor illustrations appear on every spread." SLJ
Includes glossary

Otfinoski, Steven, 1949-
Skunks; by Steven Otfinoski. Marshall Cavendish Benchmark 2009 47p il (Animals animals) lib bdg $20.95 *
Grades: 3 4 5 6   **599.7**
   1. Skunks
   ISBN 978-0-7614-2929-6 (lib bdg); 0-7614-2929-8 (lib bdg)   LC 2007-24117
"Provides comprehensive information on the anatomy, special skills, habitats, and diet of skunks." Publisher's note
"The material is well researched and would be an excellent source for reports, and the [book has] a narrative flow that makes [it] easy and enjoyable to read. [The] title includes expert full-color photography." SLJ
Includes glossary

Tatham, Betty
Baby sea otter; illustrated by Joan Paley. Holt & Co. 2005 unp il $16.95
Grades: K 1 2   **599.7**
   1. Otters
   ISBN 0-8050-7504-6   LC 2004-23393
"A baby sea otter is born and cared for by her mother, who grooms her, hunts for food, feeds her, and saves her from a hungry eagle. . . . The clear, simple paragraphs of text, interspersed with the drama that the otters face daily, will keep young readers interested. Paley's lush blue and aqua-toned collages add texture and richness." SLJ

599.74 Feloidea

Goldish, Meish
Fossa; a fearsome predator; by Meish Goldish. Bearport Pub. 2009 32p il map (Uncommon animals) lib bdg $25.27
Grades: 1 2 3   **599.74**
   1. Fossa (Mammals)
   ISBN 978-1-59716-732-1 (lib bdg); 1-59716-732-0 (lib bdg)   LC 2008-4817
"Describes the physical characteristics, habits, and habitat of the fossa." Publisher's note
"The explanatory text works spendidly, with large photographs that bring readers as close as they'll ever get to such beasts." Booklist
Includes glossary and bibliographical references

Walden, Katherine
Meerkats. PowerKids Press 2009 24p il (Safari animals) lib bdg $21.25
Grades: PreK K 1 2   **599.74**
   1. Meerkats
   ISBN 978-1-4358-2691-5 (lib bdg); 1-4358-2691-4 (lib bdg)   LC 2008020793
This book provides "succinctly written introductory information about [meerkats'] range, habitat, social groups, and diet. Spreads consist of one to three short, simply constructed sentences opposite crisp, color photographs, most of which represent the subject perfectly." SLJ

599.75 Felidae (Cat family)

Becker, John E., 1942-
Wild cats: past & present; illustrations by Mark Hallett. Darby Creek 2008 80p il $18.95 *
Grades: 5 6 7 8   **599.75**
   1. Wild cats
   ISBN 978-1-58196-052-5; 1-58196-052-2
"Becker provides an informative introduction to wild cats, including an account of their ancient ancestors, an overview of the family Felidae and its subdivisions, accounts of wild cats alive in the world today, and woven throughout, discussions of the endangered status of many species. . . . Clearly written and well organized, the text is enhanced by many side-bars, maps, photos, and paintings." Booklist

Bredeson, Carmen

Lions up close; [by] Carmen Bredeson. Enslow Elemenatry 2008 24p il (Zoom in on animals!) $21.26

Grades: 1 2 3   **599.75**
1. Lions
ISBN 978-0-7660-3080-0; 0-7660-3080-6
            LC 2007025610

This describes the anatomy, behavior, and life cycle of lions.

Includes glossary and bibliographical references

Clutton-Brock, Juliet

Cat; written by Juliet Clutton-Brock. rev ed. Dorling Kindersley 2004 72p il (DK eyewitness books) $15.99

Grades: 4 5 6 7   **599.75**
1. Wild cats 2. Cats
ISBN 0-7566-0662-4
First published 1991

Text and photographs present the anatomy, behavior, habitats, and other aspects of wild and domestic cats

Estigarribia, Diana

Cheetahs; by Diana Estigarribia. Benchmark Books 2004 c2005 46p il map (Animals, animals) lib bdg $25.64

Grades: 3 4 5 6   **599.75**
1. Cheetahs
ISBN 0-7614-1749-4   LC 2003-22600

Contents: Introducing cheetahs; Built for speed; A cheetah's life; The hunter; Cheetahs and us

Describes the physical characteristics, behavior, hunting methods, and habitat of cheetahs

This "beautifully crafted [book presents] information in a lively, readable manner. [It includes] excellent-quality, candid full-color photographs." SLJ

Includes glossary and bibliographical references

Firestone, Mary, 1951-

Top 50 reasons to care about tigers; animals in peril. Enslow Publishers 2010 103p il (Top 50 reasons to care about endangered animals) lib bdg $31.93

Grades: 4 5 6 7   **599.75**
1. Tigers 2. Endangered species
ISBN 978-0-7660-3452-5 (lib bdg); 0-7660-3452-6 (lib bdg)   LC 2008-48689

This describes a tiger's life, how they hunt, the purpose of its stripes, caring for young, competing with people for space, and that these animals are very close to extinction

"The illustrations, mostly color photographs, represent a wonderful selection of the animals and their habitats. Reluctant readers may be enticed by this . . . simply because of the great images. This . . . would make a substantial supplement to the science curriculum when studying endangered animals." Libr Media Connect

Includes glossary and bibliographical references

Hanel, Rachael

Tigers. Creative Education 2008 46p il map (Living wild) lib bdg $22.95

Grades: 3 4 5   **599.75**
1. Tigers
ISBN 978-1-58341-660-0 (lib bdg); 1-58341-660-9 (lib bdg)   LC 2007-08504

This describes the behavior, life cycle, and physical characteristics of tigers and their relationships to humans.

"Children will turn first to the excellent, informatively captioned photos. . . . But this . . . also has solid, informative content to accompany the captivating visuals." Booklist

Johns, Chris

Face to face with cheetahs; by Chris Johns with Elizabeth Carney. National Geographic 2008 32p il map (Face to face) $16.95; lib bdg $25.90 *

Grades: 3 4 5 6   **599.75**
1. Cheetahs
ISBN   978-1-4263-0323-4;   1-4263-0323-8; 978-1-4263-0324-1 (lib bdg); 1-4263-0324-6 (lib bdg)   LC 2007041220

Chris Johns describes the life cycle and behavior of cheetahs and his own experiences with cheetahs in the wild.

Includes glossary and bibliographical references

Joubert, Beverly

Face to face with leopards; by Beverly and Dereck Joubert. National Geographic 2009 31p il (Face to face) $16.95; lib bdg $25.90 *

Grades: 3 4 5 6   **599.75**
1. Leopards
ISBN   978-1-4263-0636-5;   1-4263-0636-9; 978-1-4263-0637-2 (lib bdg); 1-4263-0637-7 (lib bdg)   LC 2009011441

The authors describe the life cycle and behavior of leopard and their own experiences with leopards in the wild.

"The exquisite photos and firsthand information provide an in-depth and personal look into the lives of these animals." SLJ

Includes glossary and bibliographical references

Face to face with lions; by Beverly and Dereck Joubert. National Geographic 2008 31p il (Face to face) $16.95; lib bdg $25.90 *

Grades: 3 4 5 6   **599.75**
1. Lions
ISBN   978-1-4263-0207-7;   1-4263-0207-X; 978-1-4263-0208-4 (lib bdg); 1-4263-0208-8 (lib bdg)   LC 2007-11118

The authors describe the life cycle and behavior of lions and their own experiences with lions in the wild.

This is "well written and complete. . . . [It contains] many beautiful color photographs." Sci Books Films

Includes glossary and bibliographical references

Landau, Elaine

Big cats; hunters of the night. Enslow Publishers 2007 32p il (Animals after dark) $16.95

Grades: 1 2 3 4   **599.75**

1. Wild cats

ISBN 978-0-7660-2770-1; 0-7660-2770-8

LC 2006-16805

This "book presents basic information on the night-hunting big cats—lions, tigers, leopards, and jaguars—in an entertaining and informative format. . . . The photographs and clear text on mostly black pages add to a rewarding reading experience." Sci Books Films

Includes bibliographical references

Markle, Sandra, 1946-

Lions; by Sandra Markle. Carolrhoda 2004 39p il (Animal predators) lib bdg $25.26; pa $7.95 *

Grades: 3 4 5 6   **599.75**

1. Lions

ISBN 1-57505-727-1 (lib bdg); 1-57505-744-1 (pa)

LC 2003-11198

The author observes lions' "hunting techniques and includes information about their physical characteristics, physiology, habitats, and care of young." Horn Book Guide

"The straightforward, descriptive text and superb photos give [this title] surefire appeal to middle readers." Booklist

Includes glossary and bibliographical references

Outside and inside big cats. Atheneum Bks. for Young Readers 2003 39p il $16.95 *

Grades: 2 3 4   **599.75**

1. Wild cats

ISBN 0-689-82299-5   LC 2001-46368

The author "gives readers a close-up view of a variety of cat species, including lions and tigers and cheetahs and panthers. She guides animal enthusiasts through the basics of organism structure and function, anatomy, and animal behavior. . . . Excellent color photographs capture all aspects of big cats, from cuddly views of baby animals to detailed pictures of interior organs to grisly scenes of feeding frenzies." Horn Book

Includes glossary

Montgomery, Sy

The man-eating tigers of Sundarbans; with photographs by Eleanor Briggs. Houghton Mifflin 2001 57p il map hardcover o.p. pa $6.95 *

Grades: 4 5 6 7   **599.75**

1. Tigers

ISBN 0-618-07704-9; 0-618-49490-1 (pa)

LC 00-32031

"The author introduces readers to the geography of India and the ecology of Sundarbans, gives a brief overview of tiger behavior . . . discusses the man-eating habits of the tigers of Sundarbans, and puts forth some possible explanations for their unusual behavior." Bull Cent Child Books

"To draw readers into this scientific puzzle, Montgomery integrates science, storytelling, anthropology, and adventure in a unique treatment, illustrated with excellent color photos and diagrams." Horn Book Guide

Includes bibliographical references

Saving the ghost of the mountain; an expedition among snow leopards in Mongolia; text by Sy Montgomery; photographs by Nic Bishop. Houghton Mifflin Books for Children 2009 48p il map (Scientists in the field) $18

Grades: 5 6 7 8   **599.75**

1. McCarthy, Tom 2. Snow leopard 3. Mongolia

ISBN 978-0-618-91645-0; 0-618-91645-8

LC 2008-36762

Author Sy Montgomery and photographer Nic Bishop accompany conservationist Tom McCarthy and his team as they travel to Mongolia's Altai Mountains to gather data about snow leopard populations in an attempt to save this endangered species

"Montgomery's enthusiasm translates well to the page and will have readers cheering for the entourage as they attempt to spot a snow leopard. This slender book abounds with information. Bishop's trademark stunning photography fills out the book with breathtaking views of the extreme environs of Central Asia and warm portraits of the charming people who live there." SLJ

Nuzzolo, Deborah

Cheetahs; by Deborah Nuzzolo. Capstone Press 2008 24p il map (African animals) lib bdg $19.93

Grades: PreK K 1 2   **599.75**

1. Cheetahs

ISBN 978-1-4296-1244-9 (lib bdg); 1-4296-1244-4 (lib bdg)   LC 2007-28674

Discusses cheetahs, their African habitat, food, and behavior

This book about Cheetahs has "gorgeous, large photographs with grade-appropriate, fascinating text. . . . [It] will be very popular with the youngest readers and will match many educational science standards." Libr Media Connect

Includes glossary and bibliographical references

O'Neal, Claire

Threat to the Bengal tiger. Mitchell Lane Publishers 2009 32p il map (On the verge of extinction: crisis in the environment) lib bdg $17.95

Grades: 3 4 5   **599.75**

1. Tigers 2. Endangered species

ISBN 978-1-58415-688-8 (lib bdg); 1-58415-688-8 (lib bdg)   LC 2008-20891

"A Robbie Reader"

Information about the physiology, lifestyle, and human threat to the Bengal tiger.

"A charming fable that begins the book eases young readers into empathy for the topic. Full-color photos and graphics relate to the whole picture. . . . Technical or specialized words are given a phonetic pronunciation and a glossary further details meanings." Sci Books Films

Includes glossary and bibliographical references

Patent, Dorothy Hinshaw

Big cats; illustrations by Kendahl Jan Jubb. Walker & Co. 2005 unp il map $17.95

Grades: 2 3 4   **599.75**

1. Wild cats

ISBN 0-8027-8968-4

"After mentioning the physical features and behaviors common to all or most big cats, the book looks more closely at the lion, leopard, cheetah, tiger, snow leopard, cougar, and jaguar. Patent writes with clarity, economy, and a knack for finding apt descriptions. . . . The watercolor paintings clearly represent the animals in their habitats." Booklist

Rodriguez, Cindy

Cougars. Rourke Pub. 2009 24p il map (Eye to eye with endangered species) lib bdg $27.07

Grades: 2 3 4   **599.75**

1. Pumas

ISBN 978-1-60694-404-2 (lib bdg); 1-60694-404-5 (lib bdg)   LC 2009-5995

Text examines the issues endangered cougars face and how they can be saved

"Sets out to introduce readers to [cougars] . . . explain the dangers they face, and detail the efforts of biologists and conservationists to save them. . . . Serviceable and informative." SLJ

Includes glossary

Schafer, Susan

Lions; by Susan Schafer, with Susan Markowitz Meredith. Marshall Cavendish Benchmark 2010 24p il map (Animals) lib bdg $16.95

Grades: 3 4 5   **599.75**

1. Lions

ISBN 978-0-7614-4344-5 (lib bdg); 0-7614-4344-4 (lib bdg)   LC 2008-52104

"Rockets"

"Describes the physical characteristics, habitat, behavior, diet, life cycle, and conservation status of lions." Publisher's note

"The straightforward presentation of the information and the uncluttered and attractive layout make [this] . . . good . . . for reports. Color photographs . . . are well utilized and complete a solid package." SLJ

Includes glossary and bibliographical references

Tigers; by Susan Schafer, with Fay Robinson. Marshall Cavendish Benchmark 2010 24p il map (Animals) lib bdg $16.95

Grades: 3 4 5   **599.75**

1. Tigers

ISBN 978-0-7614-4345-2 (lib bdg); 0-7614-4345-2 (lib bdg)   LC 2008-52109

"Rockets"

"Describes the physical characteristics, habitat, behavior, diet, life cycle, and conservation status of tigers." Publisher's note

"The straightforward presentation of the information and the uncluttered and attractive layout make [this] . . . good . . . for reports. Color photographs . . . are well utilized and complete a solid package." SLJ

Includes glossary and bibliographical references

Simon, Seymour, 1931-

Big cats. HarperCollins Pubs. 1991 unp il hardcover o.p. pa $6.95 *

Grades: 3 4 5 6   **599.75**

1. Wild cats

ISBN 0-06-021647-6; 0-06-446119-X (pa)   LC 90-36374

Simon "begins with a general overview of the big cats, and then presents details on the tiger, lion, leopard, jaguar, puma, cheetah and snow leopard. . . . The author also discusses concerns about wildlife conservation." Appraisal

The author "offers a clear, succinct text illuminated with stunning, large color photographs." Booklist

Squire, Ann

Cheetahs; by Ann O. Squire. Children's Press 2005 47p il (True book) lib bdg $25; pa $6.95

Grades: 2 3 4   **599.75**

1. Cheetahs

ISBN 0-516-22792-0 (lib bdg); 0-516-27932-7 (pa)   LC 2003-5174

Contents: Meet a cheetah; Built for speed; What's for dinner?; Cheetah cubs

"Beginning with cheetahs' best-known quality, their speed, this very readable volume goes on to discuss their prowess and limitations as hunters as well as their prey, social habits, life cycle, and use of camouflage. . . . Remarkably clear, often-dramatic color photos of cheetahs in the wild offer unusually good views of the animals." Booklist

Includes bibliographical references

Stone, Lynn M.

Tigers; written and photographed by Lynn M. Stone. Carolrhoda Books 2005 48p il map (Carolrhoda nature watch book) lib bdg $25.26

Grades: 3 4 5 6   **599.75**

1. Tigers

ISBN 1-57505-578-3   LC 2003-23230

Contents: Tigers are cats; Tiger country; Becoming a tiger; Born to kill; Tracking tigers; Saving the perfect predator

An introduction to the physical characteristics, habits, natural habitat, relationship to humans, and future of the tiger, one of the largest meat-eating animals in the world.

Includes glossary

Tourville, Amanda Doering, 1980-

A jaguar grows up; by Amanda Doering Tourville; illustrated by Michael Denman and William J. Huiett. Picture Window Books 2007 24p il map (Wild animals) lib bdg $25.26

Grades: PreK K 1 2   **599.75**

1. Jaguars

ISBN 978-1-4048-3159-9 (lib bdg); 1-4048-3159-2 (lib bdg)   LC 2006027305

Examines a jaguar from birth to adulthood

Includes bibliographical references

599.77 Canidae (Dog family)

Brandenburg, Jim

Face to face with wolves; by Jim and Judy Brandenburg. National Geographic 2008 31p il map (Face to face) $16.95; lib bdg $25.90 *
Grades: 3 4 5 6   **599.77**
　1. Wolves
　ISBN   978-1-4263-0242-8;   1-4263-0242-8;
　978-1-4263-0243-5 (lib bdg); 1-4263-0243-6 (lib bdg)
　　　　　　　　　　　　　　　　LC 2007-41217
The authors describe the life cycle and behavior of wolves and their own experiences with wolves in the wild.

This is "well written and complete. . . . [It contains] many beautiful color photographs." Sci Books Films

Includes glossary and bibliographical references

Cohn, Scotti

One wolf howls; by Scotti Cohn; illustrated by Susan Detwiler. Sylvan Dell Pub. 2009 unp il $16.95; pa $8.95
Grades: PreK K 1   **599.77**
　1. Wolves 2. Counting 3. Months 4. Stories in rhyme
　ISBN   978-1-934359-92-1;   1-934359-92-0;
　978-1-607180-37-1 (pa); 1-607180-37-5 (pa)
The months of the year and the numbers 1 through 12 are used in rhyming text to introduce children to the behavior of wolves in natural settings

"Readers should be captivated by the animals' resilient joie de vivre as well as by their habitats' seasonal glories. The educational guide offers wolf facts, activities and details about their life cycle." Publ Wkly

George, Jean Craighead, 1919-

The wolves are back; paintings by Wendell Minor. Dutton Children's Books 2008 unp il lib bdg $16.99 *
Grades: 2 3 4 5   **599.77**
　1. Wolves 2. Yellowstone National Park
　ISBN 978-0-525-47947-5   LC 2007017064
"In 1995, wolves were reintroduced to Yellowstone Park. . . . The emphasis here is not as much on the wolves and their habits, but on how their presence has changed the ecosystem and returned its natural balance. . . . George writes . . . in simple, rhythmic, informative prose. Adding to the book's appeal are Minor's finely detailed illustrations, featuring spectacularly rendered animals in the foreground of the bold, western landscapes." Booklist

Gibbons, Gail

Wolves. Holiday House 1994 unp il $16.95; pa $6.95
Grades: K 1 2 3   **599.77**
　1. Wolves
　ISBN 0-8234-1127-3; 0-8234-1202-4 (pa)
　　　　　　　　　　　　　　　　LC 94-2108
"A simply written introduction that focuses on the gray, or timber, wolf. . . . Material covered includes

physical characteristics, behavior within a pack, and communication by howling and body language. . . . The format is open and spacious, the print is large, and the realistic, watercolor illustrations are set against backgrounds of white and deep blues." SLJ

Goldish, Meish

Red wolves; and then there were (almost) none. Bearport Pub. 2009 32p il map (America's animal comebacks) lib bdg $25.27
Grades: 2 3 4   **599.77**
　1. Wolves 2. Wildlife conservation
　ISBN 978-1-59716-742-0 (lib bdg); 1-59716-742-8 (lib bdg)   LC 2008-30831
Through this true tale of wildlife survival, young readers discover the bold and creative ideas that Americans and their government have used to protect and care for the countrys endangered red wolves

"Crisp photos and maps on every page work well with the text and give faces to the scientists and animals. The back matter includes a facts page, information on related species, and an up-to-date reading list." SLJ

Includes glossary and bibliographical references

Johnson, Jinny

Fox; illustrations by Graham Rosewarne. Smart Apple Media 2010 32p il (How does it work?) lib bdg $28.50
Grades: 1 2 3   **599.77**
　1. Foxes 2. Life cycles (Biology)
　ISBN 978-1-59920-354-6; 1-59920-354-5
　　　　　　　　　　　　　　　　LC 2008-53340
Explains the life cycle of a fox.

"Each stage is described on a spread that features clearly written, oversized text and a caption opposite a full-page, realistic watercolor, or, occasionally, a photograph. . . . A worthwhile purchase." SLJ

Includes glossary

Mara, Wil

Coyotes. Marshall Cavendish Benchmark 2009 48p il (Animals animals) $20.95 *
Grades: 3 4 5 6   **599.77**
　1. Coyotes
　ISBN 978-0-7614-2928-9; 0-7614-2928-X
　　　　　　　　　　　　　　　　LC 2007023411
"Provides comprehensive information on the anatomy, special skills, habitats, diet, and hunting strategies of coyotes." Publisher's note

"The material is well researched and would be an excellent source for reports, and the [book has] a narrative flow that makes [it] easy and enjoyable to read. [The] title includes expert full-color photography." SLJ

Includes glossary and bibliographical references

Markle, Sandra, 1946-

Wolves; by Sandra Markle. Lerner Publications 2004 40p il (Animal predators) hardcover o.p. pa $7.95 *
Grades: 3 4 5 6   **599.77**
　1. Wolves
　ISBN 1-57505-732-8; 1-57505-748-4 (pa)
　　　　　　　　　　　　　　　　LC 2003-11197

Markle, Sandra, 1946-—*Continued*

The author "describes the birth, physical growth, and education of three gray wolf cubs during the several seasons that it takes them to mature to adulthood." SLJ

"The text works well with the often striking full-color photos that illustrate the book." Booklist

Includes glossary and bibliographical references

Nobleman, Marc Tyler

Foxes; by Marc Tyler Nobleman. Marshall Cavendish Benchmark 2007 47p il (Animals, animals) lib bdg $19.95 *

Grades: 3 4 5 6   599.77
1. Foxes
ISBN 978-0-7614-2237-2 (lib bdg); 0-7614-2237-4 (lib bdg)   LC 2005025608
"Describes the physical characteristics, behavior, habitat, and endangered status of foxes." Publisher's note

Includes glossary and bibliographical references

Patent, Dorothy Hinshaw

When the wolves returned; restoring nature's balance in Yellowstone; photographs by Dan Hartman and Cassie Hartman. Walker 2008 39p il $17.95; lib bdg $18.85

Grades: 3 4 5   599.77
1. Wolves 2. Yellowstone National Park
ISBN 978-0-8027-9686-8; 0-8027-9686-9; 978-0-8027-9687-5 (lib bdg); 0-8027-9687-7 (lib bdg)   LC 2007-37141
NCTE Orbis Pictus Award honor book (2009)
When wolves were eliminated from Yellowstone National Park the natural system was out of balance. Shows the return of the wolves to the park and the natural balance being restored.

"Outstanding historical and present-day photographs of Yellowstone, its inhabitants, and its visitors capture the rugged natural beauty of the park." Horn Book

Includes bibliographical references

Person, Stephen

Arctic fox; very cool! by Stephen Person. Bearport Pub. 2009 32p il map (Uncommon animals) lib bdg $25.27

Grades: 1 2 3   599.77
1. Foxes
ISBN 978-1-59716-730-7 (lib bdg); 1-59716-730-4 (lib bdg)   LC 2008-10637
"Easily readable sections detail the bitter natural habitat of the arctic fox and highlight the ways in which the animal is uniquely outfitted to survive such harsh conditions. The text works splendidly with the large, clear photographs on each page that will delight readers." Booklist

Includes glossary and bibliographical references

Swinburne, Stephen R.

Coyote; North America's dog. Boyds Mills Press 1999 32p il $16.95; pa $8.95

Grades: 4 5 6   599.77
1. Coyotes
ISBN 1-56397-765-6; 1-59078-485-5 (pa)
The author describes the lifestyles of this "canine, its place in Native American folklore, the conflict between ranchers/farmers and this elusive predator, and the problems the animal faces as it struggles to thrive in pristine wilderness areas and in congested suburbs." SLJ

This book "packs a lot of information about North American coyotes into a small space. The author, a veteran park ranger, knows his subject well and succeeds in making it interesting to his audience. . . . The full-color photographs are clean and clear and enliven the text." Booklist

599.78   Ursidae (Bears)

Baines, Rebecca

A den is a bed for a bear; a book about bears; by Becky Baines. National Geographic 2008 29p il (Zig zag) $14.95; lib bdg $19.90

Grades: PreK K 1   599.78
1. Bears 2. Hibernation
ISBN 978-1-4263-0309-8; 1-4263-0309-2; 978-1-4263-0310-4 (lib bdg); 1-4263-0310-6 (lib bdg)   LC 2008-07221
"Explore [bear dens] . . . and find out how, when, and why they are used." Publisher's note

"Readers curiosity will be piqued by the vibrant color photographs, accommodating illustrations, large font size, and helpful captions. Special features include drawings superimposed over photographs, and a zigzag path at the end of . . . [the] book prompting readers to further explore the topic in new and fun ways." SLJ

Berman, Ruth, 1958-

Let's look at brown bears. Lerner Publications Co. 2010 32p il map (Lightning Bolt Books: Animal close-ups) lib bdg $25.26

Grades: PreK K 1 2   599.78
1. Bears
ISBN 978-0-7613-3890-1 (lib bdg); 0-7613-3890-X (lib bdg)   LC 2008-51855
Introduces the Alaskan brown bear, describing its physical characteristics, hibernation behavior, and feeding habits

"Fresh photography, a creative use of graphics, and a collagelike layout make[s] . . . [this book] eye-catching. . . . [The] book ends with a labeled diagram of the animal, a range map, and a further-reading list that includes print and online resources in a single list, a nice way of validating both types of materials." SLJ

Includes glossary

Bortolotti, Dan

Panda rescue; changing the future for endangered wildlife. Firefly 2003 64p il map lib bdg $19.95; pa $9.95

Grades: 4 5 6 7   **599.78**

1. Giant panda 2. Wildlife conservation

ISBN 1-55297-598-3 (lib bdg); 1-55297-557-6 (pa)

This describes the panda's "natural habitat, habits, physiology, and behavior in captivity. [It also includes] a time line of conservation efforts, profiles of conservationists in the field, and forecasts of the animals' future. Throughout, the author makes clear the factors that can threaten animal populations, and discusses human attitudes toward the animals throughout history. . . . Written in accessible, lively language and nicely illustrated with exciting color photos, [this] will be useful for reports and browsing." Booklist

Davies, Nicola, 1958-

Ice bear; in the steps of the polar bear; illustrated by Gary Blythe. Candlewick Press 2005 unp il $16.99 *

Grades: K 1 2 3   **599.78**

1. Polar bear

ISBN 0-7636-2759-3

Describes how the polar bear, also called Nanuk, thrives in the Arctic and explains the lessons that the Inuit people have learned from watching the creature.

"This inviting picture book delivers facts about polar bears and conveys respect for their adaptive success. . . . Children will be fascinated by the impressionistic oil paintings of stunning polar settings and bears at play, tenderly nursing young, and, yes, hunting seals, an activity represented by a stark image of a bear's crimson-stained muzzle that may startle the youngest readers." Booklist

Firestone, Mary, 1951-

Top 50 reasons to care about giant pandas; animals in peril. Enslow Publishers 2010 103p il (Top 50 reasons to care about endangered animals) lib bdg $31.93

Grades: 4 5 6 7   **599.78**

1. Giant panda 2. Endangered species

ISBN 978-0-7660-3451-8 (lib bdg); 0-7660-3451-8 (lib bdg)   LC 2008-48953

This describes the giant panda's life cycle, habitat, young, diet, living in the wild and in captivity, and why it is endangered

"The illustrations, mostly color photographs, represent a wonderful selection of the animals and their habitats. Reluctant readers may be enticed by this . . . simply because of the great images. This . . . would make a substantial supplement to the science curriculum when studying endangered animals." Libr Media Connect

Includes glossary and bibliographical references

Gibbons, Gail

Giant pandas. Holiday House 2002 unp $16.95; pa $6.95

Grades: K 1 2 3   **599.78**

1. Giant panda

ISBN 0-8234-1761-1; 0-8234-1828-2 (pa)

LC 2002-19057

An introduction to the physical characteristics, behavior, life cycle, and habitat of giant pandas

"Fascinating panda facts abound. . . . Gibbons encourages early readers by sticking to the facts and keeping her sentence structure simple. Stylized, instructive watercolor paintings convey a genuine affection for this appealing animal." Booklist

Polar bears. Holiday House 2001 unp il map $16.95; pa $6.95

Grades: K 1 2 3   **599.78**

1. Polar bear

ISBN 0-8234-1593-7; 0-8234-1768-9 (pa)

LC 00-54075

An introduction to polar bear behavior discussing "where it lives, what it eats, how it gets its food, when it mates, how it rears its young, and the dangers it faces." SLJ

"Written in brief, engaging sentences with facts that inform but don't overwhelm, this is a good selection for beginning report writers; it will also work well as nonfiction read-aloud for young ones." Booklist

Greene, Jacqueline Dembar

Grizzly bears; saving the silvertip; by Jacqueline Dembar Greene. Bearport Pub. 2008 32p il map (America's animal comebacks) lib bdg $25.27

Grades: 2 3 4   **599.78**

1. Grizzly bear 2. Wildlife conservation

ISBN 978-1-59716-533-4 (lib bdg); 1-59716-533-6 (lib bdg)   LC 2007012606

This describes efforts by environmentals to save the silvertip grizzly bear from extinction in the American West

This book is "well organized and [has] an easy style and an accessible vocabulary and text size . . . [and] color photographs." SLJ

Includes glossary and bibliographical references

Guiberson, Brenda Z., 1946-

Ice bears; [by] Brenda Z. Guiberson; illustrated by Ilya Spirin. Henry Holt & Co. 2008 unp il $16.95

Grades: 1 2 3 4   **599.78**

1. Polar bear 2. Arctic regions

ISBN 978-0-8050-7607-3; 0-8050-7607-7

LC 2007040895

"This story of the struggle of a polar bear mother and her two cubs to survive introduces both the harsh conditions of the Arctic and the challenges of global warming for polar bears in general. Guiberson uses precise verbs and onomatopoeia to paint a picture of the daily activities of the bears while gracefully weaving in facts about their weight, diet, and climate. Spirin's detailed watercolors are surprisingly varied in depicting an essentially frozen world, using interesting perspectives." SLJ

Moon bear; illustrated by Ed Young. Henry Holt & Co. 2010 unp il $16.99 *

Grades: PreK K 1 2 3   **599.78**

1. Bears

ISBN 978-0-8050-8977-6; 0-8050-8977-2

LC 2009017931

Guiberson, Brenda Z., 1946-—*Continued*
"This picture book both celebrates the endangered black moon bear in Southeast Asia and warns about the urgent threats against the species. Filled with physical details, the spare, question-and-answer text . . . is illustrated with Young's stark, large silhouette images of a beautiful, dark bear throughout the seasons." Booklist

Hatkoff, Juliana
Knut; how one little polar bear captivated the world; told by Juliana, Isabella, and Craig Hatkoff, and Gerald R. Uhlich. Scholastic Press 2007 unp il $16.99
Grades: 2 3 4　　　　　　　　　**599.78**
　　1. Polar bear
　　ISBN 978-0-545-04716-6; 0-545-04716-1
　　　　　　　　　　　　　　　LC 2007-21379
"Knut is a German polar bear born in captivity. His story is told in simple language and accompanied by adorable, engaging close-ups of him and his primary handler, a zookeeper named Thomas Dörflein. . . . Consider this well-written, well-documented title an essential addition to every collection." SLJ

Hirsch, Rebecca E., 1969-
Top 50 reasons to care about polar bears; animals in peril. Enslow Publishers 2010 103p il (Top 50 reasons to care about endangered animals) lib bdg $31.93
Grades: 4 5 6 7　　　　　　　　　**599.78**
　　1. Polar bear 2. Endangered species
　　ISBN 978-0-7660-3458-7 (lib bdg); 0-7660-3458-5 (lib bdg)　　　　　　　　　LC 2008-48693
This describes polar bears--their life cycle, diet, young, habitat, and reasons why they are endangered animals
"The illustrations, mostly color photographs, represent a wonderful selection of the animals and their habitats. Reluctant readers may be enticed by this . . . simply because of the great images. This . . . would make a substantial supplement to the science curriculum when studying endangered animals." Libr Media Connect
Includes glossary and bibliographical references

Hirschi, Ron
Our three bears; [by] Ron Hirschi; photographs by Thomas D. Mangelsen. Boyds Mills Press 2008 32p il $16.95
Grades: 2 3 4 5　　　　　　　　　**599.78**
　　1. Bears
　　ISBN 978-1-59078-015-2　　　　LC 2007049380
"North America's bears—black, grizzly, and polar—are introduced in this attractive presentation made compelling by Mangelsen's full-color photographic delights. . . . Hirschi reveals the differences in each bear's hibernation patterns, habitats, diets, size, and population estimates. These short paragraphs are chock-full of information. Beginning researchers as well as young wildlife enthusiasts will find Our Three Bears well suited to their interests." SLJ
Includes bibliographical references

Searching for grizzlies; photographs by Thomas D. Mangelsen; drawings by Deborah Cooper. Boyds Mills Press 2005 unp il $15.95 *
Grades: 3 4 5　　　　　　　　　**599.78**
　　1. Bears
　　ISBN 1-59078-014-0
Describes the physical characteristics, behavior, and habitat primarily of grizzly bears, with some comparisons to black bears and polar bears.
"Mangelsen's fine photos and Cooper's attractive sketches accompany Hirschi's readable text bursting with the bear facts." SLJ

Leathers, Dan
Polar bears on the Hudson Bay; by Dan Leathers. Mitchell Lane Publishers 2008 32p il map (On the verge of extinction: crisis in the environment) lib bdg $17.95
Grades: 3 4 5　　　　　　　　　**599.78**
　　1. Polar bear
　　ISBN 978-1-58415-586-7　　　　LC 2007000797
"A Robbie reader"
This describes the life cycle of polar bears on the Hudson Bay and how they are threatened by climate change and other environmental dangers.
"Short chapters, large font, and pronunciation guides to key words engage children doing research, but the depth of information is not compromised. . . . Colorful, up-close photographs are accompanied by satisfying explanatory captions." SLJ
Includes glossary and bibliographical references

Lockwood, Sophie
Polar Bears. Child's World 2005 40p il (World of mammals) lib bdg $29.93
Grades: 4 5 6　　　　　　　　　**599.78**
　　1. Polar bear
　　ISBN 1-59296-501-6
"The first chapter of *Polar Bears* discusses the bond between the animal and the Inuit people, who have depended on hunting the bears for survival. Then the discussion turns to the bears themselves: their physical features, behaviors, and relatives as well as the threats to their survival." Booklist
Includes glossary and bibliographical references

Markle, Sandra, 1946-
Grizzly bears. Lerner Publications Company 2010 39p il (Animal predators) $26.60
Grades: 4 5 6　　　　　　　　　**599.78**
　　1. Grizzly bear
　　ISBN 978-1-58013-537-5; 1-58013-537-4
　　　　　　　　　　　　　　　LC 2008-38120
Introduces the physical characteristics, habitat, and predatory behavior of grizzly bears.
"Vivid photographs alongside Markle's narrative, which provides factual information about grizzly bears' physical characteristics and hunting behaviors, introduce readers to these majestic and dangerous creatures." Horn Book Guide
Includes glossary and bibliographical references

Markle, Sandra, 1946-—*Continued*

How many baby pandas? Walker 2009 23p il map $15.99; lib bdg $16.89 *

Grades: K 1 2 3   **599.78**

1. Giant panda 2. Animal babies

ISBN   978-0-8027-9783-4;   0-8027-9783-0; 978-0-8027-9784-1 (lib bdg); 0-8027-9784-9 (lib bdg)

"Clear accessible text . . . and sharp photos provide an engaging, informative introduction to baby pandas, highlighting those born at China's Wolong Giant Panda Breeding Center in 2005. . . . Scientific concepts are well explained, and pages are filled with panda facts." Booklist

Includes glossary and bibliographical references

Polar bears; [by] Sandra Markle. Carolrhoda Books 2004 40p il (Animal predators) lib bdg $25.26; pa $7.95

Grades: 3 4 5 6   **599.78**

1. Polar bear

ISBN 1-57505-730-1 (lib bdg); 1-57505-746-8 (pa)

LC 2003-19515

The author observes polar bears' "hunting techniques and includes information about their physical characteristics, physiology, habitats and care of young." Horn Book Guide

Includes glossary and bibliographical references

Montgomery, Sy

Search for the golden moon bear; science and adventure in the Asian tropics. Houghton Mifflin 2004 80p il $17 *

Grades: 5 6 7 8   **599.78**

1. Bears

ISBN 0-618-35650-9   LC 2004-5236

The author reports on an expedition into Laos and Thailand in search of a rare species of bear

"The exciting narrative is complemented by an array of full-color photos. . . . This attractive and informative offering is an intelligent reportage of science as it happens." SLJ

Includes bibliographical references

Rosing, Norbert

Face to face with polar bears; by Norbert Rosing with Elizabeth Carney. National Geographic 2007 32p il (Face to face) $16.95; lib bdg $25.90

Grades: 3 4 5 6   **599.78**

1. Polar bear

ISBN 978-1-4263-0139-1; 978-1-4263-0140-7 (lib bdg)   LC 2006032847

"Rosing tells how he and his wife tried to fend off a polar bear 'with a toothache' and a yen for their spaghetti dinner while they waited for a helicopter rescue. The book describes the animal's diet, physical features, and habitat, and the dangers of global warming. . . . [This] attractive, smoothly written [book], topped off with advice about self-directed research, will catch the attention of enthusiasts and motivate them toward personal investigation." SLJ

Includes glossary and bibliographical references

Ryder, Joanne, 1946-

Little panda; the world welcomes Hua Mei at the San Diego Zoo. Simon & Schuster 2001 unp il $16.95; pa $7.99

Grades: K 1 2 3   **599.78**

1. Giant panda

ISBN 0-689-84310-0; 0-689-86616-X (pa)

"Ryder's photo-essay chronicles the life of Hua Mei, born at the World Famous San Diego Zoo in 1999. . . . Ryder's brief, almost haiku-like text is bolstered by informative paragraphs set in smaller type. The crisp, engaging photos were provided by the zoo." Booklist

A pair of polar bears; twin cubs find a home at the San Diego Zoo; photos by the world-famous San Diego Zoo. Simon & Schuster Books for Young Readers 2006 unp il $16.95

Grades: K 1 2   **599.78**

1. Polar bear

ISBN 0-689-85871-X   LC 2005014013

"This photo-essay introduces children to an engaging, true story from the San Diego Zoo. . . . The stars are rescued polar bear twins Tatqiq and Kalluk, who progress through the photo-rich pages from needy, quarantined cubs to fully acclimated adults with mastery over their outdoor habitat. The images, all provided by the zoo and most sharply focused and closeup, will elicit coos from readers." Booklist

Sartore, Joel

Face to face with grizzlies. National Geographic 2007 32p il (Face to face) $16.95; lib bdg $25.90 *

Grades: 3 4 5 6   **599.78**

1. Grizzly bear

ISBN   978-1-4263-0050-9;   1-4263-0050-6; 978-1-4263-0051-6 (lib bdg); 1-4263-0051-4 (lib bdg)

LC 2006-20500

"In accessible, exciting language, Sartore . . . describes his close encounters with bears while on assignment. . . . He matches stunning photographs of bears playing, fighting, eating, and chasing prey . . . with basic information about bears' bodies, habitats, and behavior." Booklist

Includes bibliographical references

Schwabacher, Martin

Bears; by Martin Schwabacher with Terry Miller Shannon. Marshall Cavendish Benchmark 2010 24p il map (Animals) lib bdg $16.95

Grades: 3 4 5   **599.78**

1. Bears

ISBN 978-0-7614-3820-5 (lib bdg); 0-7614-3820-3 (lib bdg)

"Rockets"

"Describes the physical characteristics, habitat, behavior, diet, life cycle, and conservation status of bears." Publisher's note

"The straightforward presentation of the information and the uncluttered and attractive layout make [this] . . . good . . . for reports. Color photographs . . . are well utilized and complete a solid package." SLJ

Includes glossary and bibliographical references

Swinburne, Stephen R.

Black bear; North America's bear. Boyds Mills 2003 32p il map $15.95 *

Grades: 3 4 5   **599.78**

1. Bears

ISBN 1-59078-023-X

An examination of black bears, their behavior and habitat.

"Stunning, full-color photos and a lively text make for an intriguing introduction to these fascinating animals." SLJ

Thomas, Keltie

Bear rescue; changing the future for endangered wildlife. Firefly Books 2006 64p il (Firefly animal rescue series) $19.95

Grades: 5 6 7 8   **599.78**

1. Bears 2. Endangered species 3. Wildlife conservation

ISBN 1-55297-922-9

Provides details and facts about bears from around the world, their endangerment and a range of conservation programs to save them, including profiles of individual conservationsists and bear species

Thomson, Sarah L.

Where do polar bears live? illustrated by Jason Chin. Collins 2010 37p il (Let's-read-and-find-out science) $16.99; pa $5.99

Grades: K 1 2 3   **599.78**

1. Polar bear 2. Arctic regions

ISBN   978-0-06-157518-1;   0-06-157518-6; 978-0-06-157517-4 (pa); 0-06-157517-8 (pa)

LC 2008056030

"This title explores a year in the life of a polar bear, focusing on facts about the animal's diet, hunting techniques, and habitat. Thomson also covers the impact of global warming on polar bears' food sources. . . . This is an affecting introduction to polar bears and their threatened existence for young children." Booklist

599.79   Pinnipedia (Marine carnivores)

Hengel, Katherine, 1982-

It's a baby Australian fur seal! ABDO 2010 24p il (Baby Australian animals) lib bdg $19.93

Grades: K 1 2 3   **599.79**

1. Seals (Animals) 2. Animal babies

ISBN 978-1-60453-574-7 (lib bdg); 1-60453-574-1 (lib bdg)

LC 2008-55073

This book about fur seals "is a great choice. Though the focus of . . . [the] book is the animal baby, the reader will learn a great many facts. Information includes how they are born, how they are fed, age of independence, food, habitat, predators, and features that help them find food and protect themselves. . . . This . . . is a sound addition for any school library." Libr Media Connect

Includes glossary

Malam, John, 1957-

Pinnipeds; written by John Malam; created and designed by David Salariya. Franklin Watts 2009 32p il (Scary creatures) lib bdg $26; pa $8.95

Grades: 3 4 5   **599.79**

1. Marine mammals 2. Seals (Animals) 3. Walruses

ISBN 978-0-531-21672-9 (lib bdg); 0-531-21672-1 (lib bdg); 978-0-531-21043-7 (pa); 0-531-21043-X (pa)

LC 2009010799

This defines pinnipeds and describes their life cycles, habitats, behavior, and relationship to humans

This title has "two-page chapters of accessible, large-type text and bright color photos and illustrations. . . . The series distinguishes itself with 'X-Ray Vision.' When readers hold the page with this prompt up to the light, an image emerges. The X-rays mostly show the skeletal structures of the animals. Text boxes throughout add to the visual appeal. . . . [This title is an] excellent [resource] for school assignments and browsing." SLJ

Includes glossary

Markovics, Joyce L.

Weddell seal; fat and happy; by Joyce L. Markovics. Bearport Pub. 2009 32p il map (Uncommon animals) lib bdg $25.27

Grades: 1 2 3   **599.79**

1. Seals (Animals)

ISBN 978-1-59716-734-5 (lib bdg); 1-59716-734-7 (lib bdg)

LC 2008-14391

"Describes the physical characteristics, habits, and habitat of the Weddell seal." Publisher's note

"The explanatory text works spendidly, with large photographs that bring readers as close as they'll ever get to such beasts." Booklist

Includes glossary and bibliographical references

Stearns, Precious McKenzie

Steller sea lions; [by] Precious Stearns. Rourke Pub. 2009 24p il map (Eye to eye with endangered species) lib bdg $27.07

Grades: 2 3 4   **599.79**

1. Seals (Animals)

ISBN 978-1-60694-402-8 (lib bdg); 1-60694-402-9 (lib bdg)

LC 2009-5993

Examines the issues endangered Steller Sea lions face and how they can be saved

"Sets out to introduce readers to [sea lions] . . . explain the dangers they face, and detail the efforts of biologists and conservationists to save them. . . . Serviceable and informative." SLJ

Includes glossary

599.8   Primates

Aronin, Miriam

Aye-aye; an evil omen; by Miriam Aronin. Bearport Pub. 2009 32p il map (Uncommon animals) lib bdg $25.27

Grades: 1 2 3   **599.8**

1. Aye-aye (Animal) 2. Lemurs

ISBN 978-1-59716-731-4 (lib bdg); 1-59716-731-2 (lib bdg)

LC 2008-15387

Aronin, Miriam—*Continued*

This describes the aye-aye, a lemur from Madagascar, believed, according to legend, to be an evil omen

"The explanatory text works splendidly, with large photographs that bring readers as close as they'll ever get to such beasts." Booklist

Includes glossary and bibliographical references

Barker, David, 1959-

Top 50 reasons to care about great apes; animals in peril. Enslow Publishers 2010 103p il (Top 50 reasons to care about endangered animals) lib bdg $31.93

Grades: 4 5 6 7   599.8

1. Apes 2. Endangered species

ISBN 978-0-7660-3456-3 (lib bdg); 0-7660-3456-9 (lib bdg)   LC 2008048691

This describes the great apes—their life cycle, habitats, young, and why these animals are endangered

"The illustrations, mostly color photographs, represent a wonderful selection of the animals and their habitats. Reluctant readers may be enticed by this . . . simply because of the great images." Libr Media Connect

Includes glossary and bibliographical references

Bow, Patricia

Chimpanzee rescue; changing the future for endangered wildlife. Firefly Books 2004 64p il (Firefly animal rescue series) $19.95; pa $9.95

Grades: 5 6 7 8   599.8

1. Chimpanzees 2. Wildlife conservation

ISBN 1-55297-909-1; 1-55297-908-3 (pa)

This introduces chimpanzees, how and why they are in danger, and explains what efforts are being made to protect them.

This is "well-written. . . . Stunning, full-color photographs bring [this] species to life and depict a number of individuals in the field and laboratory working to save these animals." SLJ

Bredeson, Carmen

Orangutans up close; [by] Carmen Bredeson. Enslow Elementary 2008 c2009 24p il (Zoom in on animals!) lib bdg $21.26

Grades: 1 2 3   599.8

1. Orangutan

ISBN 978-0-7660-3078-7 (lib bdg); 0-7660-3078-4 (lib bdg)   LC 2007039466

"Short paragraphs of simply written text describe [orangutans'] key body parts and how they function. . . . Behavior, diet, and care and development of the young are briefly addressed. Facing the text on each spread is a full-page, sharp, color closeup. . . . Bredeson's simply written and colorful [title] will provide younger readers with [a] satisfying first [introduction] to these fascinating creatures." SLJ

Includes glossary and bibliographical references

Costa-Prades, Bernadette

Little gorillas; [by] Bernadette Costa-Prades. Gareth Stevens Pub. 2005 23p il (Born to be wild) lib bdg $22

Grades: 3 4 5   599.8

1. Gorillas

ISBN 0-8368-4437-8   LC 2004-59721

Originally published in French

"The text introduces a variety of facts, beginning with the lives of gorilla babies. Children will be fascinated by the clearly drawn parallels between the behaviors of gorillas and humans. . . . The concise, simply worded paragraphs are written at a suitable level for elementary-school report writers." Booklist

Coxon, Michèle, 1950-

Termites on a stick; a chimp learns to use a tool; by Michèle Coxon. Star Bright Books 2008 unp il $17.95; pa $7.95

Grades: PreK K 1 2   599.8

1. Chimpanzees 2. Termites

ISBN 978-1-59572-121-1; 1-59572-121-5; 978-1-59572-183-9 (pa); 1-59572-183-5 (pa)

"A young chimpanzee is rewarded with a tasty treat once he figures out how to fish termites out of their nest. Simple text and realistic paintings follow Little Chimp and his mother through a day in which the youngster emulates his mother's use of a handy tool. . . . Carefully crafted, this picture-book introduction to tool-using chimps could work as a read-aloud story or as independent reading." SLJ

Goodall, Jane, 1934-

The chimpanzees I love; saving their world and ours. Scholastic Press 2001 80p il map $17.95

Grades: 4 5 6 7   599.8

1. Chimpanzees

ISBN 0-439-21310-X   LC 00-47080

"A Byron Preiss book"

"Goodall presents her long involvement with the chimpanzees of Gombe, describing the amazing discoveries she has made over 40 years." SLJ

"Striking an admirable balance between scientific reporting and deep affection, Goodall's . . . impassioned introduction to the creatures to whom she's dedicated her life's work may well ignite in readers a similar appreciation." Publ Wkly

Includes bibliographical references

Greenberg, Daniel A.

Chimpanzees; by Dan Greenberg, with Christina Wilsdon. Marshall Cavendish Benchmark 2010 24p il map (Benchmark rockets. Animals) lib bdg $16.95

Grades: 3 4 5   599.8

1. Chimpanzees

ISBN 978-0-7614-4341-4; 0-7614-4341-X
                                             LC 2008-52102

"Describes the physical characteristics, habitat, behavior, diet, life cycle, and conservation status of chimpanzees." Publisher's note

"The straightforward presentation of the information

Greenberg, Daniel A.—*Continued*

and the uncluttered and attractive layout make [this title] . . . good . . . for reports. Color photographs . . . are well utilized and complete a solid package." SLJ

Includes glossary and bibliographical references

Jenkins, Martin

Ape; illustrated by Vicky White. Candlewick Press 2007 45p il $16.99 *

Grades: K 1 2 3　　　　　　　　　**599.8**

1. Apes

ISBN 978-0-7636-3471-1; 0-7636-3471-9

　　　　　　　　　　　　　　LC 2007023456

Close-up illustrations and facts about five great apes: chimps, orangutans, bonobos, gorillas, and humans.

"Working in oil and pencil, White portrays [the apes] . . . as having psychologically complex, fully realized personalities. The pictures are consistently stunning. . . . Jenkins's . . . economical, conservation-oriented text ably sets each scene . . . while occasional captions add information about the apes' habitat or behavior." Publ Wkly

Laman, Tim

Face to face with orangutans; by Tim Laman & Cheryl Knott. National Geographic 2009 31p il (Face to face) $16.95; lib bdg $25.90 *

Grades: 3 4 5 6　　　　　　　　　**599.8**

1. Orangutan

ISBN 978-1-4263-0464-4; 1-4263-0464-1; 978-1-4263-0465-1 (lib bdg); 1-4263-0465-X (lib bdg)

　　　　　　　　　　　　　　LC 2009-00170

The authors describe orangutan behavior and their personal encounters with orangutans in Borneo.

Includes glossary and bibliographical references

Lockwood, Sophie

Chimpanzees; by Sophie Lockwood. Child's World 2008 40p il map (World of mammals) lib bdg $29.93

Grades: 4 5 6　　　　　　　　　**599.8**

1. Chimpanzees

ISBN 978-1-59296-927-2 (lib bdg); 1-59296-927-5 (lib bdg)

　　　　　　　　　　　　　　LC 2007-20870

This book about chimpanzees looks "at all aspects of the mammal's life including where they live, how they live, and their unique habits. . . . Detailed and labeled color photographs enhance the information provided. Enjoyable and full of information." Libr Media Connect

Includes glossary and bibliographical references

Looking for Miza; the true story of mountain gorilla family who rescued one of their own; told by Juliana Hatkoff, Isabella Hatkoff, Craig Hatkoff and Dr. Paula Kahumbu; with photographs by Peter Greste. Scholastic Press 2008 unp il $16.99

Grades: 2 3 4 5　　　　　　　　　**599.8**

1. Gorillas

ISBN 978-0-545-08540-3; 0-545-08540-3

　　　　　　　　　　　　　　LC 2008-09544

"In the Democratic Republic of the Congo's Virunga National Park, two rangers receive disturbing news that Miza, a baby mountain gorilla, and her mother have disappeared. When they reach Miza's family, her father, Kabirizi, has already left to look for the missing. He returns with Miza. . . . Readers will quickly respond to the vulnerable little gorilla's story, told in large color photographs as well as text." Booklist

Includes bibliographical references

McDaniel, Melissa

Monkeys. Benchmark Bks. 2004 47p il map (Animals, animals) lib bdg $25.64 *

Grades: 3 4 5 6　　　　　　　　　**599.8**

1. Monkeys

ISBN 0-7614-1615-3　　　　　　　LC 2003-1837

Contents: Introducing monkeys; A monkey's world; Family life; Monkey food; Monkeys and man

Describes the life of monkeys, including social structure, reproduction and child rearing, diet, interaction with humans, and loss of habitat

Includes glossary and bibliographical references

Nichols, Michael, 1952-

Face to face with gorillas; by Michael "Nick" Nichols with Elizabeth Carney. National Geographic 2009 31p il map (Face to face) $16.95; lib bdg $25.90 *

Grades: 3 4 5 6　　　　　　　　　**599.8**

1. Gorillas

ISBN 978-1-4263-0406-4; 1-4263-0406-4; 978-1-4263-0407-1 (lib bdg); 1-4263-0407-2 (lib bdg)

　　　　　　　　　　　　　　LC 2008023002

"Nichols has spent much of his life raising awareness about the plight of gorillas, and through brief text and accompanying photographs he shares some of his experiences as well as information about their family structure, habits, habitats, and connections to humans. . . . The attractive format will appeal to the intended audience." Booklist

Includes glossary and bibliographical references

Redmond, Ian

Gorilla, monkey & ape; written by Ian Redmond; photographed by Peter Anderson & Geoff Brightling. Dorling Kindersley 2000 63p il (DK eyewitness books) $15.99; lib bdg $19.99

Grades: 4 5 6 7　　　　　　　　　**599.8**

1. Primates

ISBN 0-7894-6036-X; 0-7894-6613-9 (lib bdg)

First published 1995 by Knopf with title: Gorilla

An illustrated look at primates, including lemurs, monkeys, and apes.

Sayre, April Pulley

Meet the howlers; illustrated by Woody Miller. Charlesbridge 2010 unp il lib bdg $16.95

Grades: K 1 2　　　　　　　　　**599.8**

1. Monkeys

ISBN 978-1-57091-733-2 (lib bdg); 1-57091-733-7 (lib bdg)

　　　　　　　　　　　　　　LC 2009-3953

Sayre, April Pulley—_Continued_

"Sayre's . . . latest is a rhyming introduction to the howler monkeys of Central and South America. Verses appear in a jaunty typeface atop . . . Miller's full-bleed spreads; prose paragraphs in smaller type provide additional information. . . . A solid read-aloud for young animal enthusiasts." Publ Wkly

Simon, Seymour, 1931-

Gorillas. updated ed. Collins Smithsonian 2009 31p il $17.99; pa $6.99 *

Grades: 3 4 5 6   **599.8**
    1. Gorillas
    ISBN   978-0-06-089102-2;   0-06-089102-5;
    978-0-06-089101-5 (pa); 0-06-089101-7 (pa)
    First published 2000 by HarperCollins
    Describes the physical characteristics and behavior of various kinds of gorillas.
    "This book presents an accurate portrayal of these gentle animals. While the stunning, highly expressive photos dominate in space and impact, Simon's child-friendly writing also offers a fairly full picture of gorilla behavior, physiology, habitat, and daily life. The slightly redesigned and updated book ends on a strong conservationist note." Horn Book Guide

599.93 Genetics, sex and age characteristics, evolution

Goldenberg, Linda, 1941-

Little people and a lost world; an anthropological mystery. Twenty-First Century Books 2007 112p il (Discovery!) lib bdg $31.93 *

Grades: 5 6 7 8   **599.93**
    1. Fossil hominids 2. Excavations (Archeology)—Indonesia 3. Pygmies
    ISBN 978-0-8225-5983-2 (lib bdg); 0-8225-5983-8 (lib bdg)   LC 2005-33431
    This is an account of the 2003 discovery of small fossil hominids on Flores Island, Indonesia
    "This will add important insights to the study of early humans as well as, more broadly, how science and politics interact." Booklist
    Includes bibliographical references

Tattersall, Ian

Bones, brains and DNA; the human genome and human evolution; by Ian Tattersall & Rob DeSalle; illustrated by Patricia J. Wynne. Bunker Hill Pub., Inc. 2007 47p il $16.95 *

Grades: 5 6 7 8   **599.93**
    1. Human origins 2. Evolution 3. Genetics
    ISBN 978-1-59373-056-7; 1-59373-056-X
                                               LC 2006931578
    The "text follows the trail of human evolution, basing its factual content on current data exhibited in the New Hall of Human Origins in New York City's American Museum of Natural History. Using the skills of anthropologists, archaeologists, and paleontologists, the authors track clues laid down in the fossil record, and, more im-portantly, in our DNA. . . . The very unsimple concepts are presented clearly, in an attractive format, with splashings of small photos, colorful artwork, diagrams, and maps to attract the eye and elucidate the text." SLJ

Thimmesh, Catherine

Lucy long ago; uncovering the mystery of where we came from. Houghton Mifflin Harcourt 2009 63p il $18 *

Grades: 4 5 6 7   **599.93**
    1. Human origins 2. Fossil hominids
    ISBN 978-0-547-05199-4; 0-547-05199-9
                                               LC 2008-36761
    "The 1974 discovery of the fossilized partial skeleton of a small-brained primate who apparently walked upright 3.2 million years ago in what is now Ethiopia significantly changed accepted theories about human origins. Step by step, Thimmesh presents the questions the newly discovered bones raised and how they were answered. . . . Extensive research, clear organization and writing, appropriate pacing for new ideas and intriguing graphics all contribute to this exceptionally accessible introduction to the mystery of human origins." Kirkus

600 TECHNOLOGY

Macaulay, David, 1946-

The new way things work; [by] David Macaulay with Neil Ardley. Houghton Mifflin 1998 400p il $35

Grades: 4 5 6 7 8 9 10 11 12 Adult   **600**
    1. Technology 2. Machinery 3. Inventions
    ISBN 0-395-93847-3   LC 98-14224
    First published 1988 with title: The way things work
    Arranged in five sections this volume provides information on "the workings of hundreds of machines and devices—holograms, helicopters, airplanes, mobile phones, compact disks, hard disks, bits and bytes, cash machines. . . . Explanations [are also given] of the scientific principles behind each machine—how gears make work easier, why jumbo jets are able to fly, how computers actually compute." Publisher's note

Piddock, Charles

Future tech; from personal robots to motorized monocycles; by Charles Piddock; Dr. James Lee, consultant. National Geographic 2009 64p il (National Geographic investigates) $17.95

Grades: 5 6 7 8   **600**
    1. Technology 2. Forecasting
    ISBN 978-1-4263-0468-2; 1-4263-0468-4
    "This effort takes an appreciative, uncritical look at robots, transportation, bionics, nanotechnology and future life in general. It concludes with ten specific predictions for 2025. . . . Interesting color photographs appear on almost every page and entertaining text boxes with additional related information add appeal." Kirkus
    Includes glossary and bibliographical references

Solway, Andrew

Inventions and investigations. Raintree 2008 48p il (Sci-hi: physical science) lib bdg $22; pa $8.99

Grades: 5 6 7 8   **600**

1. Inventions 2. Inventors

ISBN 978-1-4109-3379-9 (lib bdg); 1-4109-3379-2 (lib bdg); 978-1-4109-3384-3 (pa); 1-4109-3384-9 (pa)

LC 2009-3508

This explores the scientific processes used by inventors throughout history.

A "compelling read for both browsers and science buffs. . . . Information is clearly presented and flows smoothly. . . . A treasure trove of information." SLJ

Includes glossary and bibliographical references

Woodford, Chris, 1943-

Cool Stuff 2.0 and how it works; written by Chris Woodford and Jon Woodcock. DK Pub. 2007 256p il $24.99 *

Grades: 5 6 7 8   **600**

1. Inventions 2. Technology

ISBN 978-0-7566-3207-6; 0-7566-3207-2

LC 2007-299442

"More than 100 entries present a wide variety of topics with high child appeal, from robot cars to high-tech toilets. . . . Full but uncluttered layouts mix photos, text boxes, diagrams, and captions to highlight key elements. . . . Readers should have an easy time understanding the basics of what each item does, how it is used, and how it works. Along with up-to-date scientific information on high-interest topics, this title has very strong browsing appeal and great booktalk potential." SLJ

Zuckerman, Amy

2030; a day in the life of tomorrow's kids; [by] Amy Zuckerman and James Daly; illustrated by John Manders. Dutton Children's Books 2009 unp il $16.99

Grades: K 1 2 3   **600**

1. Forecasting 2. Technology

ISBN 978-0-525-47860-7; 0-525-47860-4

LC 2008-14606

"A talking dog, a housecleaning robot, and a three-dimensional data orb are among the many cool features that kids might enjoy in the future, according to this lighthearted look at 2030. The breezy narrative follows one boy through a typical day, highlighting many interesting aspects of his world. Fanciful cartoon drawings show a lively and appealing world full of new and intriguing activities that correspond neatly to modern equivalents." SLJ

609 Historical, geographic, persons treatment

Barretta, Gene

Neo Leo; the ageless ideas of Leonardo da Vinci. Henry Holt & Co. 2009 unp il $16.99

Grades: 2 3 4 5   **609**

1. Leonardo, da Vinci, 1452-1519 2. Inventors 3. Inventions—History

ISBN 978-0-8050-8703-1; 0-8050-8703-6

LC 2008038220

"This book focuses on sketches found in Leonardo's writings that reveal an understanding of inventions that would not come into being until hundreds of years after the death of this quintessential Renaissance man. Vivid watercolor illustrations depict more than a dozen, including the hang glider, contact lenses, the tank, and robots. . . . Barretta provides clear information without veering into scientific explanations." SLJ

Includes bibliographical references

Now & Ben; the modern inventions of Benjamin Franklin; by Gene Barretta. Henry Holt & Co. 2006 unp il $16.95

Grades: 2 3 4 5   **609**

1. Franklin, Benjamin, 1706-1790 2. Inventions

ISBN 978-0-8050-7917-3; 0-8050-7917-3

LC 2005012491

"This humorous book covers twenty-two inventions, first by showing their use in today's world . . . and a second by explaining Franklin's role in their development. . . . Read this one aloud; the busy cartoon illustrations offer plenty for listeners to contemplate." Horn Book Guide

Includes bibliographical references

Becker, Helaine

What's the big idea? inventions that changed life on Earth forever; illustrated by Steve Attoe. Maple Tree Press 2010 96p il $27.95; pa $17.95

Grades: 3 4 5 6   **609**

1. Inventions—History

ISBN 978-1-897349-60-1; 1-897349-60-2; 978-1-897349-61-8 (pa); 1-897349-61-0 (pa)

This book shares the big ideas behind more than thirty of the world's greatest innovations

"Identifying significant inventions in a historic timeline, this book has wonderful kid appeal. It begins with prehistory to the Middle Ages, advancing to the 1900s, finishing with not so long ago. . . . Information is displayed in short paragraphs making it easier to read than many invention books. . . . Author Helaine Becker does an excellent job of crediting diverse cultural and female contributions known or presumed." Libr Media Connect

Bender, Lionel

Invention; written by Lionel Bender. rev ed. DK Pub. 2005 72p il (DK eyewitness books) $15.99; lib bdg $19.99

Grades: 4 5 6 7   **609**

1. Inventions

ISBN 0-7566-1076-1; 0-7566-1075-3 (lib bdg)

First published 1991 by Knopf

Photographs and text explore such inventions as the wheel, gears, levers, clocks, telephones, and rocket engines.

Crowther, Robert

Robert Crowther's pop-up house of inventions; hundreds of fabulous facts about your home. Candlewick Press 2009 unp il $17.99

Grades: 4 5 6 7 **609**

1. Inventions 2. Pop-up books

ISBN 978-0-7636-4253-2; 0-7636-4253-3

First published 2000 with title: Robert Crowther's amazing pop-up house of inventions

"As a beautifully engineered pop-up book, it is complex, highly visual, and inviting. . . . It is also durably manufactured. . . . The book is essentially an encyclopedic assortment of facts and anecdotes about the earliest forms of household appliances, furnishings, novelties, . . . games, clothing, and consumables such as soap, soda and candles. The author integrates history and science in a chatty, colorful, and humorous way that quickly draws readers into his subject." Sci Books Films

Harper, Charise Mericle

Imaginative inventions; the who, what, where, when, and why of roller skates, potato chips, marbles, and pie and more! Little, Brown 2001 32p il $14.95

Grades: K 1 2 3 **609**

1. Inventions

ISBN 0-316-34725-6   LC 00-62443

"Megan Tingley books"

This "volume explains how such everyday items as gum, roller skates and potato chips came to be, describing each item in doggerel verse. With its crazy-quilt visual patterns, bouncy stanzas and fun facts, this collection of miscellany zigzags between informational and whimsical." Publ Wkly

Jedicke, Peter

Great inventions of the 20th century; by Peter Jedicke. Chelsea House 2007 72p il (Scientific American) $30

Grades: 5 6 7 8 **609**

1. Inventions—History 2. Technology—History

ISBN 978-0-7910-9048-0; 0-7910-9048-5

LC 2006014773

This "presents a celebration of the inventors and inventions that transformed the world during the age of technology. Topics presented include cellophane, the microwave oven, liquid-filled rockets, ultrasound, and robotic machines, among many others." Publisher's note

"The text is simple, clear, and concise. . . . [The book has] captioned color photos throughout." SLJ

Includes glossary and bibliographical references

Landau, Elaine

The history of everyday life. 21st Century Bks. 2005 56p il (Major inventions through history) $26.60

Grades: 5 6 7 8 **609**

1. Inventions—History

ISBN 0-8225-3808-3

This "explores fireplaces and central heating, indoor plumbing, the washing machine, food and clothing production, and microwave ovens. . . . [It] presents information about daily living from ancient times to the present. . . . The text . . . is breezy but informative. . . . Illustrations are a mixture of period black-and-white and color photos." SLJ

Includes bibligraphical references

Podesto, Martine

Inventions; by Martine Podesto. Gareth Stevens 2009 104p il (My science notebook) lib bdg $31

Grades: 4 5 6 **609**

1. Inventions

ISBN 978-0-8368-9214-7 (lib bdg); 0-8368-9214-3 (lib bdg)   LC 2008-12429

This book answers questions from students sent to "Professor Brainy" about inventions

"Designed to resemble a notebook with illustrated paper clips, pasting, and tape appearing on most pages, this [book] . . . offers comprehensive information. . . . supplemented by colorful drawings, diagrams, and photographs." SLJ

Includes glossary and bibliographical references

Robinson, James

Inventions; foreword by James Dyson. Kingfisher 2006 63p il (Kingfisher knowledge) $12.95

Grades: 5 6 7 8 **609**

1. Inventions—History 2. Technology—History

ISBN 978-0-7534-5973-7; 0-7534-5973-6

This "examines the ideas, machines, and technology that have shaped the modern age. Divided into four chapters—Communication, Inventions in the Home, Transportation, and Microtechnology—it charts the developments that led to the cell phone revolution and reveals the incredible growth of the information superhighway." Publisher's note

"A slim, colorful overview of inventions." Kirkus

Includes glossary

Rossi, Ann

Bright ideas; the age of invention in America, 1870-1910; [by] Ann Rossi. National Geographic 2005 40p il (Crossroads America) $12.95 *

Grades: 4 5 6 **609**

1. Inventions—History

ISBN 0-7922-8276-0   LC 2003-19834

This describes the history of late 19th and early 20th century inventions such as the light bulb, the telegraph, the telephone, and the automobile.

This "solid [title] for report writers may even pull in a few curious browsers because of [its] plentiful, full-color photos and reproductions. The [layout is] inviting, and the [text is] clear, informative, and readable." SLJ

Includes glossary

St. George, Judith, 1931-

So you want to be an inventor? illustrated by David Small. Philomel Bks. 2002 53p il $16.99; pa $7.99 *

Grades: 3 4 5 6 **609**

1. Inventors 2. Inventions

ISBN 0-399-23593-0; 0-14-240460-8 (pa)

LC 2001-55447

St. George, Judith, 1931-—*Continued*

Presents some of the characteristics of inventors by describing the inventions of people such as Alexander Graham Bell, Thomas Edison, and Eli Whitney

"St. George and Small take a skewed, funny, and informative look at the history of inventions and their inventors and what it takes to become one. . . . Small's lively, fluid caricatures make for a winning collaboration." SLJ

Includes bibliographical references

Tomecek, Steve

What a great idea! inventions that changed the world; [by] Stephen M. Tomecek; illustrated by Dan Stuckenschneider. Scholastic Ref. 2003 112p il $22.99 *

Grades: 4 5 6 7   **609**

1. Inventions—History
ISBN 0-590-68144-3   LC 2001-20937

"Tomecek puts significant inventions and discoveries in a historical context. Dividing the text into five broad time periods, he offers a series of essays on important advances that occurred in each 'age'. . . . What emerges is a sense of interconnectedness that other books often lack. . . . Full-color diagrams and illustrations are well integrated into each spread." SLJ

Includes bibliographical references

610   Medicine & health

Auden, Scott

Medical mysteries; science researches conditions from bizarre to deadly; by Scott Auden; Elizabeth Brownell, consultant. National Geographic 2008 64p il (National Geographic investigates) $17.95; lib bdg $27.90

Grades: 4 5 6 7   **610**

1. Medicine—Research 2. Diseases
ISBN   978-1-4263-0356-2;   1-4263-0356-4;
978-1-4263-0261-9 (lib bdg); 1-4263-0261-4 (lib bdg)

This title features "full-color photographs that readers have come to expect from this publisher. . . . [It] focuses on diseases that are regarded as bizarre and are often deadly, including Creutzfeldt-Jakob, Progeria, and Morgellons. The approach is to examine the way in which these mysterious diseases were discovered and how they are being studied to find a cure. . . . [This book offers] explanations simple enough for middle school students but with enough content to make them a useful resource for high school students as well." Voice Youth Advocates

Includes glossary and bibliographical references

Goldsmith, Connie, 1945-

Cutting-edge medicine. Lerner Publications Co. 2008 48p il (Cool science) lib bdg $26.60

Grades: 4 5 6   **610**

1. Medicine
ISBN 978-0-8225-6770-7 (lib bdg); 0-8225-6770-9 (lib bdg)   LC 2007001946

"This book explains the many amazing ways new medical techniques are helping people live longer, healthier lives." Publisher's note

Includes glossary and bibliographical references

Murphy, Liz, 1964-

ABC doctor. Blue Apple 2007 unp il $15.95

Grades: PreK K 1   **610**

1. Medicine 2. Medical care
ISBN 978-1-593545-93-2; 1-593545-93-2

"The basics of seeing a doctor and/or nurse are . . . explained with clever, colorful collage illustrations setting the scene and clarifying the explanation. . . . Some medical tools are included. Physical conditions such as fever and vomit appear, and procedures such as a urine sample and X-ray take readers through the alphabet. Murphy has compiled an interesting array of terms to help children realize that medical professionals are there to help them." SLJ

Rooney, Anne

Health and medicine; the impact of science and technology. Gareth Stevens Pub. 2009 64p il (Pros and cons) lib bdg $35

Grades: 5 6 7 8   **610**

1. Medical technology 2. Medicine 3. Health
ISBN 978-1-4339-1988-6 (lib bdg); 1-4339-1988-5 (lib bdg)   LC 2008-54133

"Looks at how scientific and technological advances in recent decades have dramatically altered the way we live-and examines both positive and negative impacts of these changes." Publisher's note

An "active layout that features color photographs, maps, graphs or charts on every spread, this . . . [book] has much to offer. . . . It conveniently outlines the range of views . . . helping students to learn how to view both sides of [the] issue[s]." SLJ

Includes glossary and bibliographical references

Singer, Marilyn, 1948-

I'm getting a checkup; illustrated by David Milgrim. Clarion Books 2009 32p il $16

Grades: PreK K   **610**

1. Medicine 2. Medical care 3. Stories in rhyme
ISBN 978-0-618-99000-9; 0-618-99000-3
LC 2007034977

"Informative and fun, this rhyming picture book will help prepare preschoolers for a visit to the doctor's office. The digitally rendered oil-and-pastel pictures show three kids, each with a parent or caregiver, getting a checkup from three different doctors. . . . Each quick rhyme is followed by a long explanatory note. . . . The bright, cartoon-style pictures keep the visit playful." Booklist

610.3   Medical sciences—Encyclopedias and dictionaries

Encyclopedia of health. 4th ed. Marshall Cavendish 2009 c2010 18v il set $514.21

Grades: 5 6 7 8 9 10   **610.3**

1. Medicine—Encyclopedias 2. Reference books
ISBN 978-0-7614-7845-4   LC 2008033014

Encyclopedia of health—*Continued*

First published 1995 with title: The Marshall Cavendish encyclopedia of health

This reference features alphabetically arranged entries on body function; diet and nutrition; human behavior; illness, injury and disorders; and prevention and care

"Easy-to-understand language, an attractive design, and content that supports student research and interest lend value to the set." Booklist

Includes bibliographical references

610.73 Nursing and services of allied health personnel

Glasscock, Sarah, 1952-

How nurses use math; math curriculum consultant: Rhea A. Stewart. Chelsea Clubhouse 2010 32p il (Math in the real world) lib bdg $28

Grades: 4 5 6   **610.73**

1. Nurses 2. Mathematics 3. Vocational guidance
ISBN 978-1-60413-607-4 (lib bdg); 1-60413-607-3 (lib bdg)   LC 2009-20199

This describes how nurses use math in such tasks as giving eye tests, keeping records, taking the pulse, and measuring medicine and includes relevant math problems and information about how to become a nurse

Includes glossary and bibliographical references

Kenney, Karen Latchana, 1974-

Nurses at work; by Karen L. Kenney; illustrated by Brian Caleb Dumm; content consultant, Judith Stepan-Norris. Magic Wagon 2010 32p il (Meet your community workers!) lib bdg $18.95

Grades: K 1 2 3   **610.73**

1. Nurses 2. Vocational guidance
ISBN 978-1-60270-651-4 (lib bdg); 1-60270-651-4 (lib bdg)   LC 2009-2393

This book about nurses has "an uncluttered layout and consistent organization. . . . Chapter headings such as 'Problems on the Job' and 'Technology at Work,' and 'Special Skills and Training' make it easy to pinpoint specific information." SLJ

Includes glossary

610.9 Medical sciences—Historical and geographic treatment

Davis, Lucile

Medicine in the American West. Children's Press 2001 30p il (Cornerstones of freedom) lib bdg $21 *

Grades: 4 5 6   **610.9**

1. Medicine—History 2. West (U.S.)—History
ISBN 0-516-22004-7   LC 00-31608

The author provides an "overview of medical practices at the time Lewis and Clark set out, and builds from there to include the importance of Native American herbals, wagon-train surgeries, traveling elixir salesmen, continuing to the introduction of ether to anesthetize patients

in surgery. . . . High-quality, full-color illustrations add variety to the page layout." SLJ

Includes glossary

Sandvold, Lynnette Brent

Revolution in medicine. Marshall Cavendish Benchmark 2010 32p il (It works!) lib bdg $19.95

Grades: 3 4 5   **610.9**

1. Medicine—History 2. Medical technology
ISBN 978-0-7614-4376-6 (lib bdg); 0-7614-4376-2 (lib bdg)   LC 2008-54364

"Discusses the history of medicine, how the technology developed, and the science behind it." Publisher's note

"This interesting, information packed [book] . . . motivates students to do their own exploring. . . . The appealing cartoon-like photographs add humor. . . . This . . . just may be that spark needed to create eager budding scientists." Libr Media Connect

Includes glossary and bibliographical references

Woolf, Alex

Death and disease; [by] Alex Woolf. Lucent Books 2004 48p il map (Medieval realms) $29.95

Grades: 5 6 7 8   **610.9**

1. Medicine—History 2. Medieval civilization
ISBN 1-59018-533-1   LC 2003-61797

This "discusses topics such as medieval theories about the body and disease, the influence of the Church on health practices, the causes and effects of bubonic plague, and the emergence of modern medicine as the medieval era drew to an end." Booklist

"Clear, well-organized [text] along with full-color reproductions of art and artifacts and photos of period structures immerse readers in . . . medieval life and offer sufficient information for reports." SLJ

Includes glossary and bibliographical references

611 Human anatomy, cytology, histology

Allen, Kathy

The human head. Capstone Press 2010 32p il (Fact finders. Anatomy class) lib bdg $23.99; pa $7.95

Grades: 3 4 5   **611**

1. Head
ISBN 978-1-4296-3338-3 (lib bdg); 1-4296-3338-7 (lib bdg); 978-1-4296-3882-1 (pa); 1-4296-3882-6 (pa)
                                    LC 2009-2793

"Describes the anatomy of the human head, including organs, muscles, and the skull." Publisher's note

"The vivid scientific photographs . . . and micrographs . . . are a plus. . . . On-page definitions, current further-reading lists, and a webliography maintained at the publisher's FactHound Web site all add value." SLJ

Includes glossary and bibliographical references

Jackson, Donna M., 1959-

In your face; the facts about your features. Viking 2004 42p il $17.99 *

Grades: 3 4 5 6   **611**

1. Face

ISBN 0-670-03657-9   LC 2003-26331

"Jackson explains the physiology of facial features, their evolution, and their roles in survival and communication. . . . With its well-captioned and colorful photos, logical organization, interesting topics, and profusion of ideas and information, this thin volume offers an unusual array of scientific and cultural concepts." SLJ

Includes glossary and bibliographical references

Lew, Kristi, 1968-

Human organs. Capstone Press 2010 32p il (Fact finders. Anatomy class) lib bdg $23.99; pa $7.99

Grades: 3 4 5   **611**

1. Human body

ISBN 978-1-4296-3339-0 (lib bdg); 1-4296-3339-5 (lib bdg); 978-1-4296-3886-9 (pa); 1-4296-3886-9 (pa)
LC 2009-2775

"Describes the organs of the human body, including vital and non-vital organs." Publisher's note

"The vivid scientific photographs . . . and micrographs . . . are a plus. . . . On-page definitions, current further-reading lists, and a webliography maintained at the publisher's FactHound Web site all add value." SLJ

Includes glossary and bibliographical references

Rake, Jody Sullivan, 1961-

The human skeleton. Capstone Press 2010 32p il (Fact finders. Anatomy class) lib bdg $23.99; pa $7.95

Grades: 3 4 5   **611**

1. Skeleton 2. Bones

ISBN 978-1-4296-3340-6 (lib bdg); 1-4296-3340-9 (lib bdg); 978-1-4296-3888-3 (pa); 1-4296-3888-5 (pa)
LC 2009-2771

"Describes the human skeleton, including connective tissues, bone growth and repair." Publisher's note

"The vivid scientific photographs . . . and micrographs . . . are a plus. . . . On-page definitions, current further-reading lists, and a webliography maintained at the publisher's FactHound Web site all add value." SLJ

Includes glossary and bibliographical references

Walker, Richard, 1951-

Body; written by Richard Walker. DK Pub. 2005 96p il $19.99 *

Grades: 4 5 6 7   **611**

1. Human anatomy

ISBN 0-7566-1371-X

Subtitle on cover: an amazing tour of human anatomy

"This book features eye-catching views of the human body. The computer-generated, three-dimensional images were created by scanning successive horizontal slices of a specially treated human cadaver. . . . The accompanying CD allows users to examine interactive, 360-degree animations of the images. Suitable as a ready-reference source as well as for casual browsers, this informative title does a magnificent job of showing just how complicated and elaborate the human body is." SLJ

Wheeler-Toppen, Jodi

Human muscles. Capstone Press 2010 32p il (Fact finders. Anatomy class) lib bdg $23.99; pa $7.95

Grades: 3 4 5   **611**

1. Muscles

ISBN 978-1-4296-3341-3 (lib bdg); 1-4296-3341-7 (lib bdg); 978-1-4296-3884-5 (pa); 1-4296-3884-2 (pa)
LC 2009-2766

"Describes human muscles, including skeletal muscles and involuntary muscles, and how they work." Publisher's note

"The vivid scientific photographs . . . and micrographs . . . are a plus. . . . On-page definitions, current further-reading lists, and a webliography maintained at the publisher's FactHound Web site all add value." SLJ

Includes glossary and bibliographical references

612   Human physiology

Aliki

My feet. Crowell 1990 31p il (Let's-read-and-find-out science book) hardcover o.p. pa $5.99

Grades: PreK K 1   **612**

1. Foot

ISBN 0-690-04815-7 (lib bdg); 0-06-445106-2 (pa)
LC 89-49357

"An extensive discussion of feet, through simple text and playful illustration, demonstrates their parts, relative sizes, what they do, and what they wear in different seasons. Includes a handicapped child whose crutches supplement feet." Sci Child

My hands. rev ed. Crowell 1990 32p il (Let's-read-and-find-out science book) hardcover o.p. pa $5.99

Grades: PreK K 1   **612**

1. Hand

ISBN 0-690-04880-7 (lib bdg); 0-06-445096-1 (pa)
LC 89-49158

First published 1962

The author "calls attention to hand structure—fingers, nails, an opposable thumb—and the special ways we use our hands to carry on everyday activities. . . . The jaunty illustrations and simple but efficient text combine for a fresh take on some very basic information." Booklist

Bailey, Gerry

Body and health; discover science through facts and fun; by Gerry Bailey & Steve Way. Gareth Stevens Pub. 2009 32p il (Simply science) lib bdg $26

Grades: 3 4 5   **612**

1. Human body

ISBN 978-1-4339-0030-3 (lib bdg); 1-4339-0030-0 (lib bdg)   LC 2008-27573

Along with facts that explore concepts across a wide range of topics, comic-strip illustrations present historical background information and foster modern-day science connections.

"The brightly colored cover with its montage of peo-

Bailey, Gerry—*Continued*

ple and cartoon characters is a real eye-catcher. This is a wonderful little book that is packed with lots of information." Sci Books Films

Includes glossary and bibliographical references

Berger, Melvin, 1927-

Why don't haircuts hurt? questions and answers about the human body; [by] Melvin and Gilda Berger; illustrated by Karen Barnes. Scholastic Ref. 1999 48p il (Scholastic question and answer series) hardcover o.p. pa $5.95

Grades: 2 3 4   612

1. Human body

ISBN 0-590-13079-X; 0-439-08569-1 (pa)

LC 97-45874

Provides answers to a variety of questions about the human body including "Why do you blush?," "Why do you need two ears?," "How strong is hair?," and "What are goosebumps?"

"The student-friendly question-and-answer format is appealing, with simple and concise one or two paragraph answers and attractive, colorful illustrations." SLJ

Calabresi, Linda

Human body. Simon & Schuster Books for Young Readers 2008 unp il (Insiders) $16.99

Grades: 4 5 6 7   612

1. Human body

ISBN 978-1-4169-3861-3; 1-4169-3861-3

LC 2007-61744

This volume "offers excellent pictures of systems, organs, and even individual cells in the human body. . . . A visually dynamic introduction to the human package." Booklist

Cole, Joanna

The magic school bus inside the human body; illustrated by Bruce Degen. Scholastic 1989 unp il hardcover o.p. pa $5.99

Grades: 2 3 4   612

1. Human body

ISBN 0-590-41426-7; 0-590-41427-5 (pa)

LC 88-3070

"Ms. Frizzle's class leaves on a trip to the science museum, but stops for a snack along the way. Arnold is left behind when his classmates reboard the bus. Meanwhile, Ms. Frizzle has miniaturized the bus and its riders. Unwittingly, Arnold swallows it. Traveling through Arnold's insides, the class visits his digestive system, arteries, lungs, heart, brain, and muscles, finally departing through his nostrils when he sneezes." Booklist

"This is an enjoyable look at factual material painlessly packaged with the ribbons and balloons of jokes and asides meant to appeal to kids. Degen's zany, busy, full-color drawings fill the pages with action and information far beyond the text." SLJ

Ganeri, Anita, 1961-

Alive; the living, breathing human body book; [written by Anita Ganeri; paper engineering: Iain Smyth] DK Publishing 2007 unp il $24.99

Grades: 5 6 7   612

1. Human body 2. Pop-up books

ISBN 978-0-7566-3211-3; 0-7566-3211-0

This "riveting pop-up tour of human anatomy . . . kicks off with two glitzy special effects—a cutaway brain with a pushbutton cascade of sparkles on the cover, then the sound of a beating heart triggered by fully opening the first spread—and goes on for a seven-spread survey of the body's systems and cell biology. . . . A sure thing for display, for casual browsing, and to crank science units up a notch." SLJ

Gardner, Robert, 1929-

Ace your human biology science project; great science fair ideas; [by] Robert Gardner and Barbara Gardner Conklin. Enslow Publishers 2009 128p il (Ace your biology science project) lib bdg $31.93

Grades: 5 6 7 8   612

1. Biology 2. Science projects 3. Science—Experiments

ISBN 978-0-7660-3219-4 (lib bdg); 0-7660-3219-1 (lib bdg)

LC 2008-30799

"Presents several science projects and science project ideas about human biology." Publisher's note

"Dozens of . . . science activities are presented with background information, step-by-step instructions, and suggestions for extending to the science fair level. . . . Color illustrations and important safety information are included." Horn Book Guide

Includes bibliographical references

Gray, Susan Heinrichs

The human body [series] Child's World 2004 6v il set $162.42

Grades: 3 4 5 6   612

1. Human body

Also available as separate volumes $27.07 each

Contents: The circulatory system (1-59296-036-7); The digestive system (1-59296-037-5); The muscular system (1-59296-038-3); The nervous system (1-59296-039-1); The respiratory system (1-59296-040-5); The skeletal system (1-59296-041-3)

This series introduces the systems of the human body

These titles "provide an unusually sound overview of a topic represented in most upper-elementary science curricula. Each book opens with a child performing a familiar activity . . . that introduces the featured system in a concrete way. This tactic reflects Gray's consistently child-centered approach, which is reinforced by clear, vivid explanations." Booklist

Includes glossaries and bibliographical references

Johnson, Rebecca L., 1956-
Ultra-organized cell systems; by Rebecca L. Johnson; illustrations by Jack Desrocher; diagrams by Jennifer Fairman. Millbrook Press 2008 48p il (Microquests) lib bdg $29.27 *
Grades: 5 6 7 8   612
1. Human body 2. Tissues
ISBN 978-0-8225-7138-4   LC 2006036395
This "is an introductory anatomy and physiology book. . . . The book contains a wealth of accurate information presented clearly in a logical arrangement. Clever cartoon diagrams . . . are fun and add to the understanding of the concepts illustrated. . . . The organization of cells into tissues, tissues into organs, and organs into organ systems is explained clearly and concisely." Sci Books Films
Includes glossary and bibliographical references

Manning, Mick
Under your skin; your amazing body; [by] Mick Manning and Brita Granström. Albert Whitman 2007 23p il $16.95
Grades: 1 2 3   612
1. Human body
ISBN 978-0-8075-8313-5; 0-8075-8313-8
                              LC 2007-02350
"This well-designed introduction to human body parts and their functions features eight half-page flaps that lift up to reveal simple views of internal organs. The terminology allows for different levels of comprehension . . . and the cartoon illustrations in bright colors help make the science aproachable." Horn Book Guide

Parker, Nancy Winslow
Organs! how they work, fall apart, and can be replaced (gasp!). Greenwillow Books 2009 48p il $17.99; lib bdg $18.89 *
Grades: 1 2 3 4   612
1. Human body
ISBN 978-0-688-15105-8;   0-688-15105-1; 978-0-688-15106-5 (lib bdg); 0-688-15106-X (lib bdg)
                              LC 2008-20718
"This is an engaging children's textbook on human anatomy and functioning. . . . Spot illustrations, charmingly rendered in colored pencil, show people with their organs in action. . . . Author Nancy Winslow Parker admirably tackles the challenge of visualizing objects that are typically masked from everyday view. . . . This fun and lighthearted book is . . . recommend[ed] for every child's library and one that will easily become a go-to reference for many years." Sci Books Films

Podesto, Martine
The body; by Martine Podesto. Gareth Stevens Pub. 2009 104p il (My science notebook) lib bdg $31
Grades: 4 5 6   612
1. Human body
ISBN 978-0-8368-9212-3 (lib bdg); 0-8368-9212-7 (lib bdg)   LC 2008-12428

This book answers questions about the human body
"Designed to resemble a notebook with illustrated paper clips, pasting, and tape appearing on most pages, this [book] . . . offers comprehensive information. . . . supplemented by colorful drawings, diagrams, and photographs." SLJ
Includes glossary and bibliographical references

Rau, Dana Meachen, 1971-
What's inside me? [series] Benchmark Books 2005 6v il set $128.14 *
Grades: K 1 2 3   612
1. Human body
ISBN 0-7614-1776-1
Also available as separate volumes $21.36 each
Contents: My bones and muscles; My brain; My heart and blood; My lungs; My skin; My stomach
"These titles provide descriptions, photographs, and illustrations of the body and some of its systems. . . . The photographs in each book depict a diverse group of children, and diagrams, illustrations, and X-rays provide age-appropriate and specific details. The books are written for proficient readers and make excellent additions to most collections." SLJ

Reilly, Kathleen M.
The human body; 25 fantastic projects illuminate how the body works; illustrated by Shawn Braley. Nomad Press 2008 120p il $21.95; pa $15.95
Grades: 5 6 7 8   612
1. Human body
ISBN   978-1-934670-25-5;   1-934670-25-1; 978-1-934670-24-8 (pa); 1-934670-24-3 (pa)
"The workings of the human body are expertly summarized in 11 tidy chapters, which include experiments that explain how the body works by creating models that either imitate or test its functions. . . . Many of the activities require adult supervision due to the materials required. . . . Simple drawings and cartoons enliven and illuminate the text. . . . The scientific explanations are superb." SLJ

Rockwell, Lizzy
The busy body book; a kid's guide to fitness. Crown 2004 unp il $15.95
Grades: K 1   612
1. Physiology 2. Exercise
ISBN 0-375-82203-8; 0-375-92203-2 (lib bdg)
An introduction to the human body, how it functions, and its need for exercise.
"The text is purposely motivating, yet easy to understand and informative. The age-appropriate artwork is colorful and lively, and provides just the right amount of detail." SLJ

Seuling, Barbara

Your skin weighs more than your brain; and other freaky facts about your skin, skeleton, and other body parts; by Barbara Seuling; illustrated by Matthew Skeens. Picture Window Books 2008 40p il (Freaky facts) lib bdg $23.93; pa $4.95

Grades: 2 3 4 5   612

1. Human body

ISBN 978-1-4048-3751-5 (lib bdg); 1-4048-3751-5 (lib bdg); 978-1-4048-3756-0 (pa); 1-4048-3756-6 (pa)

LC 2007004030

A collection of amazing facts and statistics about the human body

"This quick read is a light, fun, and at times fascinating collection of various facts about the human body. . . . The book is eye-catching—a convenient and kid-friendly small size, with illustrations on every couple of pages." Sci Books Films

Includes glossary and bibliographical references

Simon, Seymour, 1931-

The human body. HarperCollins Children's Books 2008 64p il $19.99; lib bdg $20.89 *

Grades: 3 4 5   612

1. Human body

ISBN 978-0-06-055541-2; 0-06-055541-6; 978-0-06-055542-9 (lib bdg); 0-06-055542-4 (lib bdg)

LC 2007-33300

"In this survey of the twelve body systems and the senses, Simon's explanations are complemented by captivating full-page false-color images, photomicrographs, and diagrams of the interior of the human body. . . . Simon works his usual magic to keep the narrative flowing smoothly yet rigorously." Horn Book

Somervill, Barbara A., 1948-

The human body. Gareth Stevens Pub. 2008 48p il (Gareth Stevens vital science: life science) lib bdg $26.60; pa $11.95 *

Grades: 5 6 7 8   612

1. Human body

ISBN 978-0-8368-8441-8 (lib bdg); 978-0-8368-8450-0 (pa) LC 2007-16175

First published 2006 in the United Kingdom

This describes "human anatomy and physiology. . . . Factoids are scattered throughout the text in a fashion that captures the reader's attention and interest. . . . [The book offers] excellent graphics, namely photos and diagrams. The artwork complements and enhances the written content." Sci Books Films

Includes glossary and bibliographical references

Stewart, David Evelyn, 1954-

How your body works; a good look inside your insides; written by David Stewart; illustrated by Carolyn Franklin. Children's Press 2008 32p il (Amaze) $26; pa $8.95

Grades: K 1 2   612

1. Human body

ISBN 978-0-531-20444-3; 0-531-20444-8; 978-0-531-20455-9 (pa); 0-531-20455-3 (pa)

This "is a bright, colorful, vivid, and easy-to-digest children's book about the basics of physiology. The book includes simple, well-illustrated chapters on the eyes, ears, intestines, cardiovascular system, liver and kidneys. . . . Organs are represented with big, colorful blocks, with very little distracting detail." Sci Books Films

Stradling, Jan

The human body. Silver Dolphin 2009 90p il (The wonders inside) $19.95 *

Grades: 1 2 3 4   612

1. Human body

ISBN 978-1-57145-718-9; 1-57145-718-6

This is an introduction to human anatomy and physiology

This "is a winner. The artwork is terrific. . . . [It includes] excellent large illustrations, many with overlaying transparencies to show depth or layers of complexity." Sci Books Films

Includes glossary

Swanson, Diane, 1944-

You are weird; your body's peculiar parts and funny functions; written by Diane Swanson; illustrated by Kathy Boake. Kids Can Press 2009 40p il $16.95; pa $7.95

Grades: 2 3 4 5   612

1. Human body

ISBN 978-1-55453-282-7; 1-55453-282-5; 978-1-55453-283-4 (pa); 1-55453-283-3 (pa)

"This chatty, interactive humorous science book make[s] human physiology accessible and interesting, with lots of wild facts about hair, bacteria, sweat, skin, joints, muscles, and more. . . . The irreverence is right on . . . and the sound of words extend the fun without jargon." Booklist

VanCleave, Janice Pratt

Janice VanCleave's the human body for every kid; easy activities that make learning science fun. Wiley 1995 223p hardcover o.p. pa $12.95

Grades: 4 5 6 7   612

1. Human body 2. Science—Experiments

ISBN 0-471-02413-9; 0-471-02408-2 (pa)

LC 94-20862

"The book's 23 chapters cover cells, skin, the brain, the senses, lungs, blood and the heart, the digestive system, bones, muscles, and genetics. Each chapter includes . . . background information, problem-solving strategies, and simple activities." Sci Child

"The activities described are easy to follow, are inexpensive, use readily obtainable supplies, and, most importantly, make the learning of human anatomy and

VanCleave, Janice Pratt—*Continued*
physiology fun and exciting. Moreover, the material is presented in an organized, clear, and accurate manner." Sci Books Films

Walker, Richard, 1951-
Dr. Frankenstein's human body book; the monstrous truth about how your body works; [author, Richard Walker; artist, Nick Abadzis] DK Pub. 2008 93p il $24.99
Grades: 4 5 6 7	612
   1. Human body
   ISBN 978-0-7566-4091-0; 0-7566-4091-1
"This anatomy book is as engrossing as any science fiction. Dr. Frankenstein, shown in a sepia photograph standing in a laboratory, gazing at a skull he holds in one hand, invites readers to join him as he creates a human being. . . . The story line is sustained with brief, pun-happy journal entries. . . . Gothic fonts and engraved illustrations and vignettes (in red and black and also hand-colored) blend with state-of-the-art images from MEG scans, gamma scans and other advanced technology. Clear explanations broken into easily assimilable captions and text blocks encourage the reader." Publ Wkly
Includes glossary

How the incredible human body works—by the Brainwaves; written by Richard Walker; illustrated by Lisa Swerling and Ralph Lazar. DK Pub. 2007 61p il $19.99
Grades: 4 5 6	612
   1. Human body
   ISBN 978-0-7566-3145-1; 0-7566-3145-9
   LC 2007-299595
"Colorful diagrams take center stage in this introduction to various systems and organs of the . . . human body. Cartoon characters, Brainwaves, . . . run rampant through the images, adding additional humor to the lighthearted text." Booklist

Human body; written by Richard Walker. DK Pub. 2009 72p il (DK eyewitness books) $16.99; lib bdg $19.95
Grades: 4 5 6 7	612
   1. Human body
   ISBN	978-0-7566-4545-8;	0-7566-4545-X;
   978-0-7566-4545-8 (lib bdg); 0-7566-4533-6 (lib bdg)
   LC 2009419529
Includes CD-ROM
In this book, text and illustrations present information on the parts of the body and how they work
Includes glossary and bibliographical references

Ouch! how your body makes it through a very bad day; written by Richard Walker. DK Pub. 2007 71p il $16.99
Grades: 4 5 6 7	612
   1. Human body
   ISBN 978-0-7566-2536-8; 0-7566-2536-X
"Tag along on a rotten day as a body copes with sneezing, getting cut, being stung by a bee, and vomiting, as well as performing more mundane actions such as

urinating, tapping into its melanin supply, acting reflexively, and sweating. . . . Dramatic color graphics, both large and small, are accompanied by a multitude of informative captions. Researchers who find the information on the busy pages hard to grasp can pop in the accompanying CD-ROM and catch a ride up the esophagus on a wave of vomit. . . . Eye-catching, highly pictorial, informative, and with a megadose of ick! factor." SLJ
Includes glossary

612.1   Blood and circulation

Corcoran, Mary K.
The circulatory story; illustrated by Jef Czekaj. Charlesbridge 2010 41p il lib bdg $17.95
Grades: 2 3 4	612.1
   1. Blood—Circulation 2. Cardiovascular system
   ISBN 978-1-58089-208-7 (lib bdg); 1-58089-208-6 (lib bdg)
   LC 2008025332
"The author and illustrator of *The Quest to Digest* (2006) take young readers on an equally engaging ride through the heart, lungs, arteries, veins, capillaries, and back again. In the big, labeled cartoon illustrations a small, green Smoo-like creature rides a red blood cell down a river of plasma. . . . Corcoran's breezy commentary lays out the whole 60,000-mile system in easy-to-understand terms. . . . An irresistable invitation to go with the flow." Booklist

Showers, Paul, 1910-1999
A drop of blood; illustrated by Edward Miller. HarperCollins	Pub.	2004	32p	il (Let's-read-and-find-out science) hardcover o.p. pa $4.99
Grades: K 1 2 3	612.1
   1. Blood
   ISBN 0-06-009108-8; 0-06-009109-6 (lib bdg); 0-06-009110-X (pa)
A newly illustrated edition of the title first published 1967 and revised in 1989
A simple introduction to the composition and functions of blood
"Showers's classic introduction to this vital fluid is cleverly updated by Miller's amusing illustrations featuring a Dracula-like vampire and his Igorish friend. . . . High-quality, closeup photographs of blood cells, platelets, and fibrin under the microscope are well placed within the illustrations, and science concepts are presented with just the right amount of detail for the intended audience." SLJ

Hear your heart; illustrated by Holly Keller. HarperCollins	Pubs.	2001	33p	il (Let's-read-and-find-out science) hardcover o.p. pa $4.95
Grades: K 1 2 3	612.1
   1. Heart
   ISBN 0-06-025410-6; 0-06-025411-4 (lib bdg); 0-06-445139-9 (pa)
   LC 99-41336
A revised and newly illustrated edition of the title first published 1968

Showers, Paul, 1910-1999—*Continued*

A simple explanation of the structure of the heart and how it works

"This is an excellent introduction to the heart and how it works. . . . The open, informal design brings the physiology right into daily life. Factual, accurate, and fun." Booklist

Simon, Seymour, 1931-

The heart; our circulatory system; [by] Seymour Simon. rev ed. Collins 2006 30p il hardcover o.p. pa $6.99 *

Grades: 4 5 6 7   612.1

1. Cardiovascular system 2. Cardiovascular system 3. Heart

ISBN   978-0-06-087720-0;   0-06-087720-0; 978-0-06-087721-7 (pa); 0-06-087721-9 (pa)

LC 2006-279215

First published 1996

Describes the heart, blood, and other parts of the body's circulatory system and explains how each component functions

"The text is succinct and direct, making the details understandable without losing the sense that the whole process of circulation is 'strange and wonderful.' . . . The often striking pictures include many computer-enhanced photographs as well as diagrams and highly enlarged images made possible by electron microscopes. Handsome and well-conceived in every way." Booklist [review of 1996 edition]

612.2   Respiration

Jakab, Cheryl

Respiratory system. Smart Apple Media 2006 32p il (Our body) lib bdg $28.50

Grades: 3 4 5   612.2

1. Respiratory system

ISBN 978-1-58340-736-3 (lib bdg); 1-58340-736-7 (lib bdg)

LC 2005-56798

This "clear, approachable book contains six chapters that describe the [respiratory] system, how it works, diseases, treatment, and more. A final chapter promotes a healthy lifestyle and educates readers on first aid and avoiding possible problems associated with the system. Health tips appear throughout, and an activity is included. [This book is] interactive in tone and [provides] plenty of sidebar material, along with color photographs, drawings, charts, and diagrams, and a fascinating 'under the microscope' look at parts of the body." SLJ

Includes glossary

Simon, Seymour, 1931-

Lungs; your respiratory system; [by] Seymour Simon. Smithsonian/Collins 2007 30p il $16.77 paperback o.p.; lib bdg $17.89

Grades: 3 4 5 6   612.2

1. Respiratory system

ISBN 978-0-06-054654-0; 978-0-06-054655-7 (lib bdg); 0-06-054655-7 (lib bdg); 0-06-054656-5 (pa)

LC 2006003768

"This straightforward overview of the respiratory system follows the journey of a breath through the body. Color diagrams, X-rays, and photos provide visual support. . . . The writing is concise and full of clear examples meaningful to kids." SLJ

Includes glossary and bibliographical references

Siy, Alexandra

Sneeze! [by] Alexandra Siy and Dennis Kunkel. Charlesbridge 2007 45p il lib bdg $16.95; pa $6.95 *

Grades: 4 5 6 7   612.2

1. Sneezing

ISBN   978-1-57091-653-3   (lib   bdg); 978-1-57091-654-0 (pa)   LC 2005-27567

This describes some causes of sneezing, including "air-pollen, dust mites, mold spores, dust, goose down, cat hair, pepper, flu viruses, and bright light." Publisher's note

"Kunkel's big, clear, beautiful color electron micrographs on every double-page spread show everything from dust mites, mildew, and pollen to the influenza A virus." Booklist

Includes glossary and bibliographical references

612.3   Digestion

Corcoran, Mary K.

The quest to digest; illustrated by Jef Czekaj. Charlesbridge 2006 32p il lib bdg $16.95; pa $6.95

Grades: 2 3 4   612.3

1. Digestion

ISBN   978-1-57091-664-9   (lib   bdg); 978-1-57091-665-6 (pa)   LC 2005-19622

"This graphically appealing, colorful, and fact-rich story describes the importance of food to the body by following an apple as it goes through the human digestion system. . . . Abundant, humorous cartoons and clever text handle explanations of belching, passing gas, and diarrhea." SLJ

Includes glossary

Donovan, Sandra, 1967-

Hawk & Drool; gross stuff in your mouth; by Sandy Donovan; illustrated by Michael Slack. Millbrook Press 2010 48p il (Gross body science) lib bdg $29.27

Grades: 4 5 6   612.3

1. Saliva 2. Mouth—Diseases

ISBN 978-0-8225-8966-2 (lib bdg); 0-8225-8966-4 (lib bdg)

LC 2008-50699

Presents disgusting facts about the human mouth, how it works to aid in digestion, the organisms that live there, and ways to keep it clean and healthy

"Solid information layered between sarcastic comments and kid-friendly terminology like fart, poop, barf, and puke will keep readers engaged. . . . Labeled, captioned (and graphic) photographs, cartoon-style illustrations, and micrographs add information." SLJ

Includes glossary and bibliographical references

Donovan, Sandra, 1967-—*Continued*
Rumble & spew; gross stuff in your stomach and intestines; by Sandy Donovan; illustrated by Michael Slack. Lerner Publications Company 2010 48p il (Gross body science) lib bdg $29.27
Grades: 4 5 6   **612.3**
1. Intestines
ISBN 978-0-8225-8899-3 (lib bdg); 0-8225-8899-4 (lib bdg)   LC 2008-37713
Presents disgusting facts about the human digestive system and its functions
"Solid information layered between sarcastic comments and kid-friendly terminology like fart, poop, barf, and puke will keep readers engaged. . . . Labeled, captioned (and graphic) photographs, cartoon-style illustrations, and micrographs add information." SLJ
Includes glossary and bibliographical references

Jakab, Cheryl
The digestive system; by Cheryl Jakab. Smart Apple Media 2006 32p il (Our body) lib bdg $28.50
Grades: 3 4 5   **612.3**
1. Digestion
ISBN 978-1-58340-737-0 (lib bdg); 1-58340-737-5 (lib bdg)   LC 2005057881
This "clear, approachable book contains six chapters that [describes] the [digestive] system, how it works, diseases, treatment, and more. A final chapter promotes a healthy lifestyle and educates readers on first aid and avoiding possible problems associated with the system. Health tips appear throughout, and an activity is included. [This book is] interactive in tone and [provides] plenty of sidebar material, along with color photographs, drawings, charts, and diagrams, and a fascinating 'under the microscope' look at parts of the body." SLJ
Includes glossary

Showers, Paul, 1910-1999
What happens to a hamburger? illustrated by Edward Miller. HarperCollins Pubs. 2001 33p il (Let's-read-and-find-out science) hardcover o.p. pa $5.99
Grades: K 1 2 3   **612.3**
ISBN 0-06-027947-8; 0-06-027948-6 (lib bdg); 0-06-445183-6 (pa)   LC 97-39007
A newly illustrated edition of the title first published 1970
Explains the processes by which a hamburger and other foods are used to make energy, strong bones, and solid muscles as they pass through the digestive system
This edition offers "attractive new illustrations, enhanced in a few places with photos that show body parts such as the epiglottis and the stomach lining. . . . Miller's digital artwork has a jaunty, retro look." Booklist

Simon, Seymour, 1931-
Guts; our digestive system; [by] Seymour Simon. HarperCollins 2005 unp il $16.99; lib bdg $17.89 *
Grades: 4 5 6 7   **612.3**
1. Digestion
ISBN 0-06-054651-4; 0-06-054652-2 (lib bdg)
LC 2004-14508

This "explains how the digestive system works. . . . [The author] describes the complex facts and processes of the physiology, from the time food enters the mouth until all the various organs transform it into energy, nutrients, and waste." Booklist
"Simon's specialty of drawing in readers through large, detailed, breathtaking photos and then entertaining them with facts is again in evidence. . . . The text is enhanced with detailed colored X rays, computer-generated pictures, and microscopic photos." SLJ

612.4   Hematopoietic, lymphatic, glandular, urinary systems

Goodman, Susan, 1952-
Gee whiz! it's all about pee! by Susan E. Goodman; illustrated by Elwood H. Smith. Viking 2006 39p il $15.99
Grades: 2 3 4 5   **612.4**
1. Urine
ISBN 0-670-06064-X   LC 2006001957
The author "explains the biological necessity of pee, cultural and historical variations in toilet practices, . . . urinary habits among other species, and the various uses to which humans have put urine. . . . Smith's compact, angular cartoons offer jocular interpretations of the historical and biological trivia, with occasional extremely silly but helpful diagrams." Bull Cent Child Books
Includes bibliographical references

612.6   Reproduction, development, maturation

Butler, Dori Hillestad
My mom's having a baby! illustrated by Carol Thompson. Albert Whitman & Co. 2005 unp il $15.95 *
Grades: 2 3 4   **612.6**
1. Pregnancy 2. Childbirth 3. Sex education
ISBN 0-8075-5344-1   LC 2004-18585
"Elizabeth describes the month-by-month development of the baby as well as the changes in Mom's body. . . . Through very direct language and clear illustrations, children will learn about a man's testicles where sperm are made and the fallopian tube where an egg is fertilized. . . . Mom answers Elizabeth's big question, 'how do Dad's sperm and your egg get together?' . . . Details are not spared when the birth is described. The playful and colorful illustrations add exuberance to the text, combining full-page paintings, cartoon panels, word balloons, and free-floating images. The joy and love felt by all of the family members is palpable. This volume is an excellent choice for those readers who are ready to ask and be told some of life's basic facts." SLJ

Cocovini, Abby

What's inside your tummy, Mommy? [by] Abby Cocovini. Henry Holt & Co. 2008 unp il pa $8.95 *

Grades: PreK K 612.6

1. Pregnancy

ISBN 978-0-8050-8760-4 (pa); 0-8050-8760-5 (pa)

"Cocovini has designed this oversize guide so that 'if the mommy holds the book up to her belly, you will see what the baby looks like (actual size) inside her every month!' . . . This book is warm and nonthreatening to the max, its crayoned and watercolor spot illustrations and hand-drawn timeline lending it a homey, scrapbook/journal feel. The five or so factoids on each page are shaped around easy-to-grasp, domestic concepts." Publ Wkly

Cole, Joanna

How you were born; photographs by Margaret Miller. rev & expanded ed. Morrow Junior Bks. 1993 48p il $15.95; pa $6.99 *

Grades: K 1 2 612.6

1. Pregnancy 2. Childbirth 3. Infants

ISBN 0-688-12059-8; 0-688-12061-X (pa)

LC 92-23970

A revised and newly illustrated edition of the title first published 1984

"Illustrated with photographs of culturally diverse families, Cole's text explains conception, the development of the fetus, and the birth process. A note to parents and a suggested reading list are included." J Youth Serv Libr

When you were inside Mommy; illustrated by Maxie Chambliss. HarperCollins Pubs. 2001 unp il $7.99

Grades: PreK K 1 612.6

1. Pregnancy 2. Childbirth 3. Infants

ISBN 0-688-17043-9 LC 00-40890

This "begins with a simple explanation of a baby's development in the mother's uterus. It goes on to show the baby's birth, followed by his growth to a child of perhaps three or four years old. An appended 'Note to Parents' offers a sound approach to talking with children. . . . The simplicity and sensitivity of the writing is well matched by Chambliss' line and watercolor wash illustrations." Booklist

Gaff, Jackie

Looking at growing up; how do people change? [by] Jackie Gaff. Enslow Publishers 2008 32p il (Looking at science: how things change) lib bdg $22.60

Grades: 1 2 3 612.6

1. Growth

ISBN 978-0-7660-3090-9 (lib bdg); 0-7660-3090-3 (lib bdg) LC 2007-24509

"A beginner's look at how people grow and change." Publisher's note

"Fills a huge void in elementary science collections. . . . Text is arranged in succinct 'chunks,' giving important facts without overwhelming readers. . . . [This] is an essential addition." Libr Media Connect

Includes glossary and bibliographical references

Gravelle, Karen

The period book; everything you don't want to ask (but need to know); by Karen Gravelle & Jennifer Gravelle; illustrations by Debbie Palen. updated ed. Walker & Co. 2006 126p il $16.95

Grades: 4 5 6 7 612.6

1. Menstruation

ISBN 978-0-8027-8072-0; 0-8027-8072-5

LC 2008270981

First published 1996

Explains what happens at the onset of menstruation, discussing what to wear, going to the gynecologist, and how to handle various problems

"The cartoonlike illustrations and conversational tone make this updated edition a friendly, reassuring resource as well as a thorough one." Horn Book Guide

Harris, Robie H.

It's not the stork! a book about girls, boys, babies, bodies, families, and friends; illustrated by Michael Emberley. Candlewick Press 2006 59p il $16.99 *

Grades: K 1 2 3 612.6

1. Sex education 2. Childbirth 3. Pregnancy

ISBN 0-7636-0047-4 LC 2005-54280

"Harris opens by introducing two cartoon characters— a green-feathered bird clad in a purple shirt and blue hightop sneakers and his spike-haired friend, a bee. They wonder, 'So where DO babies come from?' Their conversational commentary, given in word balloons, is a lighthearted supplement to a more focused narrative. Told in the second person, the text is straightforward, informative, and personable. Facts are presented step-by-step, starting from the similarities and differences between boys' and girls' bodies, moving to a baby's conception, growth in the womb, and birth, ending with an exploration of different configurations of families as well as a section on 'okay' versus 'not okay' touches." SLJ

It's so amazing! a book about eggs, sperm, birth, babies, and families; illustrated by Michael Emberley. Candlewick Press 1999 81p il $21.99; pa $10.99 *

Grades: 2 3 4 612.6

1. Pregnancy 2. Childbirth 3. Sex education

ISBN 0-7636-0051-2; 0-7636-1321-5 (pa)

LC 98-33119

Uses bird and bee cartoon characters to present straightforward explanations of topics related to sexual development, love, reproduction, adoption, sexually transmitted diseases, and more

"While the illustrations are engaging and often hilarious, factual information is effectively presented in a clear, nonjudgmental tone that will inform and assure readers." SLJ

Jukes, Mavis

Growing up: it's a girl thing; straight talk about first bras, first periods, and your changing body; illustrations by Debbie Tilley. Knopf 1998 72p il pa $10 hardcover o.p. *

Grades: 4 5 6 7 612.6

1. Adolescence 2. Girls 3. Menstruation

ISBN 0-679-89027-0 (pa) LC 98-18113

Jukes, Mavis—*Continued*

This is a slightly revised version of chapters from the author's It's a girl thing

This "covers body hair and shaving, perspiration and deodorant, and how to buy your first bra. The second half of the book is devoted to what to expect and how to plan for your first period. . . . The narration has an easy, comfortable voice and imparts accurate and important information." SLJ

Katz, Anne

Girl in the know; your inside-and-out guide to growing up; written by Anne Katz; illustrated by Monika Melnychuk. Kids Can Press 2010 111p il $18.95

Grades: 4 5 6 7   **612.6**
1. Puberty 2. Girls—Health and hygiene
ISBN 978-1-5545-3303-9; 1-5545-3303-1

"This reassuring title is aimed at girls who want clear facts about puberty but who may not be ready to read in-depth specifics of sex and birth-control. The author . . . offers a holistic guide that covers the body changes puberty brings as well as tips about maintaining physical and emotional health. . . . The warm, straightforward, useful advice on a broad range of topics . . . will captivate both middle graders and middle-schoolers, and the frequent color drawings of stylish, diverse girls . . . reinforce the book's appeal to a wide age group." Booklist

Madaras, Lynda, 1947-

On your mark, get set, grow! a "what's happening to my body?" book for younger boys; [by] Lynda Madaras; illustrations by Paul Gilligan. Newmarket Press 2008 123p il $22; pa $12 *
Grades: 3 4 5 6   **612.6**
1. Puberty 2. Boys—Health and hygiene
ISBN 978-1-55704-780-9; 1-55704-780-4; 978-1-55704-781-6 (pa); 1-55704-781-2 (pa)
LC 2007043095

"Madaras draws on her experience teaching sex education (called puberty classes here) to inform boys about the physical changes they will experience as they start to mature. . . . The age-appropriate presentation includes cartoon art on almost every page and a sprinkling of humor. Along with covering sex-organ growth, height, weight, and muscle gain, Madaras also discusses health and nutrition, hygiene, and 'becoming your own self.' A reassuring tone pervades the text. . . . This is an excellent resource for both children and parents." SLJ

Ready, set, grow! a "what's happening to my body?" book for younger girls; illustrations by Linda Davick. Newmarket Press 2003 127p il $22; pa $12 *
Grades: 3 4 5 6   **612.6**
1. Puberty 2. Girls—Health and hygiene
ISBN 1-55704-587-9; 1-55704-565-8 (pa)
LC 2003-9489

Contents: A note from the author: Hi, I'm Lynda Madaras; What's happening to me? puberty is about change; Buds, boobs, and bras: your growing breasts; Hair, there and everywhere: all about body hair; You grow, girl! the height spurt; Bigger Is beautiful: the weight spurt; BO and zits: a survival guide; What's up down there? a look at your private parts; The inside story: changes you can't see; That time of the month: all about getting your period; Yours alone: respecting and protecting your body

This "introduces the basics of puberty and the physical changes that come with it." Publ Wkly

This "is a timely and important book. In a consistently sensitive and encouraging tone, Madaras reassures preadolescents that the changes they know are approaching or they are beginning to experience are normal, natural, and cause for celebration. Humorous sketches illustrate the emotions and stages of puberty, and keep the tone light." SLJ

The "what's happening to my body?" book for boys; [by] Lynda Madaras with Area Madaras; drawings by Simon Sullivan. 3rd rev ed. Newmarket Press 2007 xx, 233p il $24.95; pa $12.95 *
Grades: 4 5 6 7   **612.6**
1. Adolescence 2. Puberty 3. Sex education 4. Boys—Health and hygiene
ISBN 978-1-55704-769-4; 1-55704-769-3; 978-1-55704-765-6 (pa); 1-55704-765-0 (pa)
LC 2007009874

First published 1984

Discusses the changes that take place in a boy's body during puberty, including information on the body's changing size and shape, the growth spurt, reproductive organs, pubic hair, beards, pimples, voice changes, wet dreams, and puberty in girls

Includes bibliographical references

The "what's happening to my body?" book for girls; [by] Lynda Madaras with Area Madaras; drawings by Simon Sullivan. 3rd rev ed. Newmarket Press 2007 xxvi, 259p il $24.95; pa $12.95 *
Grades: 4 5 6 7   **612.6**
1. Adolescence 2. Puberty 3. Sex education 4. Girls—Health and hygiene
ISBN 978-1-55704-768-7; 1-55704-768-5; 978-1-55704-764-9 (pa); 1-55704-764-2 (pa)
LC 2007009862

Discusses the changes that take place in a girl's body during puberty, including information on the body's changing size and shape, pubic hair, breasts, reproductive organs, the menstrual cycle, and puberty in boys

Includes bibliographical references

Movsessian, Shushann

Puberty girl. Allen & Unwin 2005 128p $15.95
Grades: 4 5 6 7   **612.6**
1. Puberty 2. Girls
ISBN 1-74114-104-4

"In addition to chapters about the basic body changes during female puberty, including one about menstruation and the necessary equipment, the author offers helpful suggestions for conflict resolution, listening to one's feelings, and understanding personal boundaries (and when they are breached). She also includes a brief list of boys' puberty changes, and a closing chapter mentions homosexuality. The glossy, girl-magazine design, with lots of

Movsessian, Shushann—*Continued*
color photos of attractive preteens, is matched by the bubbly, girl-power tone." Booklist

Parker, Steve
Reproduction. Raintree 2004 48p il (Our bodies) lib bdg $31.43
Grades: 5 6 7 8   **612.6**
  1. Reproduction 2. Sex education 3. Growth
  ISBN 0-7398-6623-0   LC 2003-10547
  Contents: Female reproductive organs; The menstrual cycle; Egg production; Male reproductive organs; Sperm production; The reproductive process; The first week; Reproductive problems; The early embryo; Growth in the uterus; Life support in the uterus; Toward birth; The day of birth; A new baby; Birth problems; Growing up; The young child; The older child; Child to adult; The next generation
  This "discusses the male and female reproductive organs and how they work, the process of fertilization, growth of the embryo and fetus, birth, and stages of life from infancy to adulthood. . . . The anatomy is accurate, and the format, with plenty of pictures, diagrams, and magnified photos, is very accessible. There are also lots of lively boxed facts." Booklist
  Includes bibliographical references

Price, Geoff
Puberty boy. Allen & Unwin 2006 122p il pa $15.95
Grades: 4 5 6 7   **612.6**
  1. Puberty 2. Boys
  ISBN 1-74114-563-5   LC 2006-482082
  This "is a frank, reassuring discussion of male adolescence. Chapters on physiology present information clearly, in a colloquial voice that is never stuffy or condescending, and the questions that are asked and answered seem straight from kids. . . . The mechanics of sex aren't addressed, but there is some discussion of STDs and the emotional maturity intimacy requires. The book's unusual holistic approach includes coverage of the emotional changes, independence, and responsibility that come with puberty. There are also excellent suggestions to help boys connect respectfully with girls, find a mentor, develop emotional intelligence, and distinguish between 'boy thinking' and 'young man thinking.'" Booklist
  Includes glossary and bibliographical references

Pringle, Laurence P.
Everybody has a bellybutton; your life before you were born; by Laurence Pringle; illustrated by Clare Wood. Boyds Mills Press 1997 unp il $14.95
Grades: PreK K 1 2 3   **612.6**
  1. Fetus 2. Pregnancy 3. Childbirth
  ISBN 1-56397-009-0   LC 95-83168
  Pringle "offers a gently phrased, solidly scientific look at the growth of a baby. . . . The narrative gives specific, sensorial details that will keep even young children engaged, and the description of childbirth is matter-of-fact and undisturbing. . . . Illustrations are softly realis-

tic pencil drawings on pink and blue backgrounds." Booklist
  Includes bibliographical references

Rand, Casey
Human reproduction. Raintree 2009 48p il (Sci-hi: life science) lib bdg $31.43; pa $8.99
Grades: 5 6 7 8   **612.6**
  1. Reproduction 2. Sex education
  ISBN 978-1-4109-3327-0 (lib bdg); 1-4109-3327-X (lib bdg); 978-1-4109-3335-5 (pa); 1-4109-3335-0 (pa)
                               LC 2009003464
  In this introduction to human reproduction "clear language, embedded definitions, and interesting examples illustrate abstract concepts through both text and well-chosen photographs. . . . [It] includes suggested activities to test ideas as well as a thorough glossary and a Webliography." SLJ
  Includes glossary and bibliographical references

Saltz, Gail
Amazing you; getting smart about your private parts; illustrated by Lynne Avril Cravath. Dutton Children's Books 2005 unp il $15.99 *
Grades: PreK K 1   **612.6**
  1. Sex education 2. Reproduction 3. Growth
  ISBN 0-525-47389-0   LC 2004-22014
  "This upbeat picture book, illustrated with sunny cartoon drawings, introduces kids to basic reproductive physiology. Saltz offers simple, accessible definitions of terms, accompanied by pictures of unclothed kids and labeled diagrams of internal organs. Subsequent drawings show three stages of body development from baby to young adult, followed by an abbreviated explanation, illustrated with a heart-shaped drawing of a smiling egg and sperm, of reproduction. . . . Saltz presents the information clearly in a cheerful, positive tone." Booklist

Changing you! a guide to body changes and sexuality; [by] Gail Saltz; illustrated by Lynne Avril Cravath. Dutton Children's Books 2007 unp il $16.99
Grades: 3 4 5   **612.6**
  1. Puberty 2. Sex education
  ISBN 978-0-525-47817-1; 0-525-47817-5
                               LC 2006035593
  "This is an introduction to puberty and sexual intercourse in the context of a loving relationship between a man and woman. The book covers topics that kids often inquire about, such as bodily changes and how babies are born. Bright, cartoon illustrations of the human body at different stages and ages and labeled diagrams fill the pages. The clear, straightforward text uses language that young children can easily grasp while the running commentary that accompanies the art takes a lighter, more conversational approach." SLJ

Schwartz, John
Short; walking tall when you're not tall at all. Roaring Brook Press 2010 132p il $16.99
Grades: 4 5 6 7 8   **612.6**
  1. Growth 2. Size 3. Body image 4. Prejudices
  ISBN 978-1-59643-323-6; 1-59643-323-X
  "Flash Point"

Schwartz, John—*Continued*

"In a humorous, personal voice, . . . Schwartz combines his own memories of growing up short with related discussions about physiology, statistics, popular culture, and societal prejudice, always returning to his own self-image. . . . Short kids will want every word. . . . and many readers will move on to the resource list of articles, Web sites, and scientific papers in the detailed, informal back matter." Booklist

Includes bibliographical references

Sears, William

Baby on the way; [by] William Sears, Martha Sears, and Christie Watts Kelly; illustrated by Renée Andriani. Little, Brown 2001 unp il (Sears children's library) $12.95

Grades: PreK K 1 2   **612.6**
1. Pregnancy 2. Childbirth 3. Infants
ISBN 0-316-78767-1   LC 00-38451

This book describes how a family prepares for the arrival of a new baby and explains pregnancy and childbirth to an older sibling

"Andriani's brightly colored, cartoon-style illustrations help create the books' upbeat, yet realistic tone." Booklist

Includes bibliographical references

612.7   Musculoskeletal system, integument

Baines, Rebecca

The bones you own; a book about the human body; by Becky Baines. National Geographic 2009 27p il (Zigzag) $16.95; lib bdg $25.90

Grades: PreK K 1   **612.7**
1. Bones 2. Skeleton
ISBN   978-1-4263-0410-1;   1-4263-0410-2;
978-1-4263-0411-8 (lib bdg); 1-4263-0411-0 (lib bdg)
LC 2008-47900

This describes functions that bones perform in a human body.

This title engages "children through humor, clear language, interesting facts, and abundant photos. . . . [An] excellent [introduction] for young science students." SLJ

Your skin holds you in; a book about your skin; by Becky Baines. National Geographic 2008 29p il (Zigzag) $14.95; lib bdg $19.90

Grades: PreK K 1   **612.7**
1. Skin
ISBN   978-1-4263-0311-1;   1-4263-0311-4;
978-1-4263-0312-8 (lib bdg); 1-4263-0312-2 (lib bdg)
LC 2007-44156

"Thirteen short sentences describe skin . . . in all its glory. Additional facts appear in smaller print . . . on the same pages with the main idea sentences. Photographs of people, outlined in white and reproduced on brightly colored pages, serve as diagrams for important elements. . . . Exuberant double-page spreads encourage looking and talking." Horn Book

Ballard, Carol

The skeleton and muscular system. Raintree Steck-Vaughn Pubs. 1998 48p il (Human body) lib bdg $27.12

Grades: 5 6 7 8   **612.7**
1. Musculoskeletal system 2. Skeleton
ISBN 0-8172-4805-6   LC 96-29688

Explains the various parts of the human skeleton and different types of muscles and their functions

The text is "well organized and well written. The full-color photos, diagrams, and illustrations are clear and complement the text." SLJ

Includes glossary and bibliographical references

Barner, Bob

Dem bones; [illustrations and informational bone text by] Bob Barner. Chronicle Bks. 1996 unp il $16.99

Grades: K 1 2 3   **612.7**
1. Skeleton 2. Bones
ISBN 0-8118-0827-0   LC 95-29

An "introduction to the human skeleton, this picture book is based on the African American spiritual 'Dem bones.'. . . Each double-page spread illustrates one phrase from the song, which dances through the spread, while in smaller letters Barner discusses one of the 10 bones named in the song in a few lines of simple, informative text." Booklist

"A rollicking read-aloud, sing-along treat for children as they learn anatomy, rhyme, and language. . . . Scientific facts and names combined with lyrics make this a fascinating book." Exploring Sci in the Libr

Berger, Melvin, 1927-

Why I sneeze, shiver, hiccup, and yawn; illustrated by Paul Meisel. HarperCollins Pubs. 2000 unp il (Let's-read-and-find-out science) hardcover o.p. pa $4.99

Grades: K 1 2 3   **612.7**
1. Reflexes 2. Nervous system
ISBN 0-06-028144-8; 0-06-445193-3 (pa)
LC 98-55542

A revised and newly illustrated edition of Why I cough, sneeze, shiver, hiccup & yawn, published 1983 by Crowell

An introduction to reflex acts that explains why we sneeze, shiver, hiccup, and yawn

"The writing is simple but effective, and the charming, colorful pen-and-ink and watercolors are [detailed]. . . . Attractive introductory nonfiction." SLJ

Jakab, Cheryl

Muscular system. Smart Apple Media 2007 32p il (Our body) $18.95

Grades: 3 4 5   **612.7**
1. Musculoskeletal system
ISBN 978-1-58340-734-9   LC 2005-56804

"Diagrams shown throughout the book are useful in understanding muscle contraction. Muscle and tendon problems are discussed with several methods of treating them, even surgery. Sound suggestions are given for keeping muscles healthy. . . . This is a valuable book that provides good tips for everyone." Sci Books Films

Jakab, Cheryl—*Continued*

Skeletal system. Smart Apple Media 2007 32p il (Our body) $18.95

Grades: 3 4 5   **612.7**
1. Skeleton
ISBN 978-1-58340-738-7   LC 2005-57882

"The book contains 'Fascinating Facts' about the skeletal system, as well as 'Health Tips.' . . . Both sections are quite useful. Diagrams showing different parts of the skeletal system are helpful in identifying the bones related to the 'Heath Tips.' . . . This very useful book will serve the reader well." Sci Books Films

Includes glossary

Macnair, Patricia Ann, 1958-

Movers & shapers; bones, muscles, and joints; consultant, Richard Walker. Kingfisher 2004 40p il (Bodyscope) $9.95

Grades: 3 4 5   **612.7**
1. Musculoskeletal system
ISBN 0-7534-5791-1   LC 2003-27315

Contents: Bony framework; Where the bones meet: joints; Cartilage; Muscles that get us moving; The skull; From a smile to a frown: the face; The secrets of skeletons; The ribs and spine; Legs and feet; Artificial limbs; Arms and hands; The story of a broken bone; Health and exercise

This describes the musculoskeletal system including how limbs move, the importance of exercise, and how bones heal.

The author has "a flair for kid-friendly trivia. . . . Macnair is . . . adept at describing complex processes for young readers without too much distracting detail." Booklist

Includes glossary

Parker, Steve

The skeleton and muscles; [by] Steve Parker. Raintree 2004 48p il (Our bodies) lib bdg $29.93

Grades: 5 6 7 8   **612.7**
1. Musculoskeletal system
ISBN 0-7398-6622-2   LC 2003-6594

This "takes a look at bones, muscles, and joints; how they are connected and function; and how to keep them healthy. The anatomy is accurate, and the format, with plenty of pictures, diagrams, and magnified photos, is very accessible. There are also lots of lively boxed facts." Booklist

Includes bibliographical references

Simon, Seymour, 1931-

Bones; our skeletal system. Morrow Junior Bks. 1998 unp il hardcover o.p. pa $6.99

Grades: 4 5 6 7   **612.7**
1. Bones 2. Skeleton
ISBN 0-688-14645-7 (lib bdg); 0-688-17721-2 (pa)
                                LC 97-44751

Describes the skeletal system and outlines the many important roles that bones play in the healthy functioning of the human body

"Simon once again proves his remarkable facility for making complicated science clear and understandable." Booklist

Muscles; our muscular system. Morrow Junior Bks. 1998 unp il hardcover o.p. pa $6.99

Grades: 4 5 6 7   **612.7**
1. Muscles
ISBN 0-688-14642-2; 0-688-14643-0 (lib bdg); 0-688-17720-4 (pa)   LC 97-44758

Describes the nature and work of muscles, the different kinds, and the effects of exercise and other activities on them

"The full-paged illustrations are great and include full-color photographs, MRI scans, X rays, and excellent drawings." SLJ

612.8   Nervous system. Sensory functions

Aliki

My five senses. rev ed. Crowell 1989 31p il (Let's-read-and-find-out science book) $16.95; pa $4.99

Grades: PreK K 1   **612.8**
1. Senses and sensation
ISBN 0-690-04792-4; 0-06-445083-X (pa)
                                LC 88-35350

First published 1962

The faculties of touch, hearing, sight, smelling and taste are introduced in relation to everyday experiences

"Each sense is used independently to observe common phenomena. Next, the author demonstrates more than one sense being used. . . . The book effectively introduced the five senses to young people." Appraisal

Boothroyd, Jennifer, 1972-

What is hearing? Lerner Publications Co. 2010 32p il (Lightning Bolt Books TM-Your amazing senses) lib bdg $25.26

Grades: K 1 2   **612.8**
1. Hearing 2. Sound
ISBN 978-0-7613-4250-2 (lib bdg); 0-7613-4250-8 (lib bdg)   LC 2008-51848

Describes the properties of sound and hearing, including everyday examples and information on how an ear functions

"Given [its] . . . simple sentences, colorful layout, full-page photos, and well-chosen diagrams, [this title] . . . will be useful for reports." SLJ

Includes glossary and bibliographical references

What is sight? Lerner Publications Co. 2010 32p il (Lightning Bolt Books TM-Your amazing senses) lib bdg $25.26

Grades: K 1 2   **612.8**
1. Vision
ISBN 978-0-7613-4248-9 (lib bdg); 0-7613-4248-6 (lib bdg)   LC 2008-51849

Describes the importance of the sense of sight and how the human eye works, including information on color, depth perception, and protecting sight

"Given [its] . . . simple sentences, colorful layout, full-page photos, and well-chosen diagrams, [this title] . . . will be useful for reports." SLJ

Includes glossary and bibliographical references

Boothroyd, Jennifer, 1972-—*Continued*

What is smell? Lerner Publications Co. 2010 32p il (Lightning Bolt Books TM-Your amazing senses) lib bdg $25.26
Grades: K 1 2   **612.8**
1. Smell
ISBN 978-0-7613-4253-3 (lib bdg); 0-7613-4253-2 (lib bdg)   LC 2008-51850
Provides information on the sense of smell, including why there are good and bad smells and how noses function
"Given [its] . . . simple sentences, colorful layout, full-page photos, and well-chosen diagrams, [this title] . . . will be useful for reports." SLJ
Includes glossary and bibliographical references

What is taste? Lerner Publications Co. 2010 32p il (Lightning Bolt Books TM-Your amazing senses) lib bdg $25.26
Grades: K 1 2   **612.8**
1. Taste
ISBN 978-0-7613-4251-9 (lib bdg); 0-7613-4251-6 (lib bdg)   LC 2008-51847
Explains how human beings use their sense of taste and illustrates good and bad tastes
"Given [its] . . . simple sentences, colorful layout, full-page photos, and well-chosen diagrams, [this title] . . . will be useful for reports." SLJ
Includes glossary and bibliographical references

What is touch? Lerner Publications Co. 2010 32p il (Lightning Bolt Books TM-Your amazing senses) lib bdg $25.26
Grades: K 1 2   **612.8**
1. Touch
ISBN 978-0-7613-4252-6 (lib bdg); 0-7613-4252-4 (lib bdg)   LC 2008-51587
The book about touch has "simple sentences, colorful layout, full-page photos, and well-chosen diagrams . . . [and] will be useful for reports." SLJ

Cobb, Vicki, 1938-

Feeling your way; discover your sense of touch; illustrations by Cynthia C. Lewis. Millbrook Press 2001 unp il (Five senses) lib bdg $22.90; pa $7.95
Grades: 2 3 4   **612.8**
1. Touch
ISBN 0-7613-1657-4 (lib bdg); 0-7613-1980-8 (pa)   LC 00-32916
"A look at over a dozen ways to explore this sense. . . . The experiments are simple to carry out and include little or no equipment. The illustrations include photographed heads superimposed on drawings and simple cartoons with dialogue balloons." SLJ

Follow your nose; discover your sense of smell; illustrated by Cynthia C. Lewis. Millbrook Press 2000 unp il (Five senses) lib bdg $22.60; pa $7.95
Grades: 2 3 4   **612.8**
1. Smell
ISBN 0-7613-1521-7 (lib bdg); 0-7613-1978-6 (pa)   LC 99-47872

Examines the sense of smell, how the nose detects different odors, and how we react to different smells. Includes simple experiments to test the sense of smell
An "entertaining and colorful book. . . . The science is accurate, and the pictorial and written anecdotes are cleverly directed toward advanced elementary school . . . students." Sci Books Films

Open your eyes; discover your sense of sight; illustrations by Cynthia C. Lewis. Millbrook Press 2001 unp il (Five senses) lib bdg $22.90
Grades: 2 3 4   **612.8**
1. Vision 2. Eye
ISBN 0-7613-1705-8   LC 2001-30394
"A discussion of the science of the eye, its parts, and how it works, and easy, child-friendly experiments on sensory perception and optical illusions result in an interesting and amusing look at one of our five senses. The collage illustrations are done with photographs, newspapers, and drawings. Many have humorous captions." SLJ

Perk up your ears; discover your sense of hearing; illustrated by Cynthia C. Lewis. Millbrook Press 2001 unp il (Five senses) lib bdg $22.90
Grades: 2 3 4   **612.8**
1. Hearing
ISBN 0-7613-1704-X   LC 00-68099
"Lots of hands-on activities and easy experiments invite readers to explore sound, normal human hearing, auditory illusions, and exceptional ears such as those with perfect pitch. Cobb uses questions and second-person address to engage readers with the facts. Kids will laugh at the illustrations: combinations of cartoons, collage, dialogue balloons, and goofy comments and captions." Horn Book Guide

Your tongue can tell; discover your sense of taste; illustrations by Cynthia C. Lewis. Millbrook Press 2000 unp il (Fivr senses) lib bdg $22.60; pa $7.95
Grades: 2 3 4   **612.8**
1. Taste
ISBN 0-7613-1473-3 (lib bdg); 0-7613-1979-4 (pa)   LC 99-47873

Text and suggested activities explore the sense of taste, how it works, and how it can help us detect which foods are sweet, sour, salty, or spicy

Cole, Joanna

The magic school bus explores the senses; illustrated by Bruce Degen. Scholastic Press 1999 47p il hardcover o.p. pa $5.99
Grades: 2 3 4   **612.8**
1. Senses and sensation
ISBN 0-590-44697-5; 0-590-44698-3 (pa)   LC 98-18662
Ms. Frizzle and her class explore the senses by traveling on the magic school bus in and out of an eye, ear, mouth, nose, and other parts of both human and animal bodies
"Along the margins are snippets of information in the form of Frizzle Facts and excerpts from kids' school reports. Degen's clever illustrations are both humorous and informative, acting as excellent visual aids for little learners." Booklist

Funston, Sylvia

It's all in your head; a guide to your brilliant brain; [by] Sylvia Funston, Jay Ingram; illustrated by Gary Clement. 2nd ed. Maple Tree Press 2005 64p il $16.95; pa $9.95

Grades: 3 4 5 6   **612.8**
  1. Brain 2. Psychology
  ISBN 1-897066-43-0; 1-897066-44-9 (pa)
First published 1994 with title: A kid's guide to the brain

This "explains how the brain controls our senses, emotions, memory, and thinking. Each chapter includes experiments, with easy-to-find items such as buttons and jelly beans, brain teasers, . . . historical information, and current theories on brain function. . . . Color photographs and whimsical illustrations make the presentation appealing." SLJ

Gardner, Robert, 1929-

Ace your science project about the senses; great science fair ideas; [by] Robert Gardner . . . [et al.] Enslow Publishers 2009 112p il (Ace your biology science project) lib bdg $31.93

Grades: 5 6 7 8   **612.8**
  1. Senses and sensation 2. Science projects 3. Science—Experiments
  ISBN 978-0-7660-3217-0 (lib bdg); 0-7660-3217-5 (lib bdg)   LC 2008-30797
"Presents several science projects and science project ideas about the senses." Publisher's note

Includes glossary and bibliographical references

Guillain, Charlotte

How do we hear? Heinemann Library 2008 24p il (Sounds all around us) lib bdg $20.71; pa $5.99

Grades: PreK K 1   **612.8**
  1. Hearing 2. Sound waves 3. Sound
  ISBN 978-1-4329-3201-5 (lib bdg); 1-4329-3201-2 (lib bdg); 978-1-4329-3207-7 (pa); 1-4329-3207-1 (pa)
                                                  LC 2008-51738
Learn about sound waves, how the human ear works, and how animals can have a special sense of hearing.

This book "introduces the basics of sound through vibrant photographs, large text, and simple sentences. . . . [A] great introduction[s] and worthy addition[s]." SLJ

Includes glossary and bibliographical references

Hewitt, Sally

Hear this! [by] Sally Hewitt. Crabtree Pub. 2008 24p il (Let's start! science) pa $6.95

Grades: PreK K 1 2   **612.8**
  1. Sounds 2. Hearing
  ISBN 978-0-7787-4058-2 (pa); 0-7787-4058-7 (pa)
                                                  LC 2008-5007
First published 2005 by QEB publications

"Five fun activities help children discover the answers in this . . . introduction to the sense of sound." Publisher's note

This book about hearing "will provide a good starting point for younger students to learn more about their senses. . . . Most chapters are accompanied by a related activity, none are too complex for the intended audience." Libr Media Connect

Includes glossary and bibliographical references

Look here! [by] Sally Hewitt. Crabtree 2008 24p il (Let's start! science) pa $6.95

Grades: PreK K 1 2   **612.8**
  1. Vision
  ISBN 978-0-7787-4059-9 (pa); 0-7787-4059-5 (pa)
                                                  LC 2008-5008
First published 2005 by QEB publications with title: Look out!

"Five fun activities help children discover the answers in this . . . introduction to the sense of sight." Publisher's note

This book about vision "will provide a good starting point for younger students to learn more about their senses. . . . Most chapters are accompanied by a related activity, none are too complex for the intended audience." Libr Media Connect

Includes glossary and bibliographical references

Smell it! Crabtree Pub. Company 2008 24p il (Let's start! science) pa $6.95

Grades: PreK K 1 2   **612.8**
  1. Smell
  ISBN 978-0-7787-4060-5 (pa); 0-7787-4060-9 (pa)
                                                  LC 2008-5009
First published 2005 by QEB publications with title: Smell that!

"Five fun activities help children discover the answers in this . . . introduction to the sense of smell." Publisher's note

This book "will provide a good starting point for younger students to learn more about their senses. . . . Most chapters are accompanied by a related activity, none are too complex for the intended audience." Libr Media Connect

Includes glossary and bibliographical references

Tastes good! [by] Sally Hewitt. Crabtree Pub. Company 2008 24p il (Let's start! science) pa $6.95

Grades: PreK K 1 2   **612.8**
  1. Taste
  ISBN 978-0-7787-4061-2 (pa); 0-7787-4061-7 (pa)
                                                  LC 2008-5010
First published 2005 by QEB publications

"Five fun activities help children discover the answers in this . . . introduction to the sense of taste." Publisher's note

This book "will provide a good starting point for younger students to learn more about their senses. . . . Most chapters are accompanied by a related activity, none are too complex for the intended audience." Libr Media Connect

Includes glossary and bibliographical references

Touch that! [by] Sally Hewitt. Crabtree Pub. Co. 2008 24p il (Let's start! science) pa $6.95

Grades: PreK K 1 2   **612.8**
  1. Touch
  ISBN 978-0-7787-4062-9 (pa); 0-7787-4062-5 (pa)
                                                  LC 2008-5011
First published 2005 by QEB publications

"Five fun activities help children discover the answers in this . . . introduction to the sense of touch." Publisher's note

This book "will provide a good starting point for

Hewitt, Sally—*Continued*

younger students to learn more about their senses. . . . Most chapters are accompanied by a related activity, none are too complex for the intended audience." Libr Media Connect

Includes glossary and bibliographical references

Larsen, C. S., 1966-

Crust and spray; gross stuff in your eyes, ears, nose, and throat; illustrated by Michael Slack. Millbrook Press 2010 48p il (Gross body science) lib bdg $29.27

Grades: 4 5 6   **612.8**

1. Eye 2. Nose 3. Ear 4. Throat

ISBN 978-0-8225-8964-8 (lib bdg); 0-8225-8964-8 (lib bdg)   LC 2008-33777

"Learn all about the nasty stuff in your eyes, ears, nose, and throat and find out how it can actually help you by flushing germs out of your body and keeping you in good health." Publisher's note

"Solid information layered between sarcastic comments and kid-friendly terminology like fart, poop, barf, and puke will keep readers engaged. . . . Labeled, captioned (and graphic) photographs, cartoon-style illustrations, and micrographs add information." SLJ

Includes glossary and bibliographical references

Read, Leon

My senses. Sea-to-Sea Publications 2010 23p il (Tiger talk. All about me) lib bdg $24.25

Grades: PreK K   **612.8**

1. Senses and sensation

ISBN 978-1-59771-188-3 (lib bdg); 1-59771-188-8 (lib bdg)   LC 2008-45010

This book about the senses "makes learning fun. . . . [The] book employs a simplified game of 'Where's Waldo?' by hiding a cartoon tiger on almost every page. This approach, combined with questions . . . will encourage discussion and involvement." SLJ

Royston, Angela

Why do I sleep? QEB Pub. 2010 24p il (QEB my body) lib bdg $28.65

Grades: PreK K 1 2   **612.8**

1. Sleep

ISBN 978-1-59566-974-2 (lib bdg); 1-59566-974-4 (lib bdg)   LC 2009-15226

Introduces the function and importance of sleep, and outlines good sleeping habits

"This . . . is meant to be read to young children because it is written at a higher reading level than its intended audience. The information is straightforward, well presented, and easy to understand. . . . [This] title is well designed, filled with color photographs, and scattered with fact boxes. . . . This . . . will be useful in preschool and primary classrooms where health and hygiene are stressed." Libr Media Connect

Includes glossary and bibliographical references

Scott, Elaine, 1940-

All about sleep from A to ZZZZ; by Elaine Scott; illustrated by John O'Brien. Viking 2008 58p il $17.99

Grades: 5 6 7 8 9 10   **612.8**

1. Sleep

ISBN 978-0-670-06188-4; 0-670-06188-3   LC 2008-6074

"The book covers a range of topics, including circadian rhythms, dreams, and the functions and stages of sleep." Booklist

"This excellent overview is packed with interesting tidbits. . . . Scott is careful to point out which information is factual and which is theory, an important distinction. . . . The fanciful cartoon illustrations add to the book's appeal. . . . It is interesting, highly engaging, and fun to read." SLJ

Showers, Paul, 1910-1999

Sleep is for everyone; illustrated by Wendy Watson. HarperCollins Pubs. 1997 32p il (Let's-read-and-find-out science) hardcover o.p. pa $4.99

Grades: K 1 2   **612.8**

1. Sleep

ISBN 0-06-025392-4; 0-06-025393-s (lib bdg); 0-06-445141-0 (pa)   LC 96-49375

A newly illustrated edition of the title first published 1974 by Crowell

This volume examines "how different animals sleep, why we sleep, and what happens while we sleep and when we don't sleep enough. Colorful paper cut-out illustrations are simple and light-hearted with mottled paper as background creating a restful, gentle feeling." Horn Book Guide

Silverstein, Alvin

Sleep; [by] Alvin Silverstein, Virginia Silverstein, and Laura Silverstein Nunn. Watts 2000 48p il (My health) lib bdg $24.50; pa $6.95

Grades: 3 4 5   **612.8**

1. Sleep

ISBN 0-531-11636-0 (lib bdg); 0-531-16452-7 (pa)   LC 98-53647

Discusses the activities of the body during sleep, the importance of sleep, common sleep disorders, and the phenomenon of dreams

Includes bibliographical references

Simon, Seymour, 1931-

The brain; our nervous system; [by] Seymour Simon. rev ed. Collins 2006 30p il $17.99; pa $6.99 *

Grades: 4 5 6 7   **612.8**

1. Brain 2. Nervous system

ISBN 978-0-06-087718-7;   0-06-087718-9; 978-0-06-087718-4 (pa); 0-06-087719-7 (pa)   LC 2007-272349

First published 1997

Describes the various parts of the brain and the nervous system and how they function to enable us to think, feel, move, and remember.

Simon, Seymour, 1931-—*Continued*

Simon's "clear, concise writing style is complemented by stunning color images taken with radiological scanners, such as CAT scans, MRIs, and SEMs (scanning electron microscopes.)" SLJ [review of 1997 edition]

Includes bibliographical references

Eyes and ears. HarperCollins Pubs. 2003 unp il hardcover o.p. pa $6.99 *

Grades: 4 5 6 7   **612.8**

1. Eye 2. Ear 3. Vision 4. Hearing

ISBN 0-688-15303-8; 978-0-06-073302-5 (pa); 0-06-073302-0 (pa)   LC 2002-19060

Describes the anatomy of the eye and ear, how those organs function and some ways in which they may malfunction, and how the brain is also involved in our seeing and hearing

"Simon is at his very best here. . . . The large, exquisitely reproduced photographs from a number of sources look like fiery planets, galaxies, and monster creatures. . . . The anatomy and physiology are detailed and accurate, with clear diagrams." Booklist

Simpson, Kathleen

The human brain; inside your body's control room. National Geographic 2009 64p il (National Geographic investigates) lib bdg $27.90

Grades: 5 6 7 8   **612.8**

1. Brain

ISBN 978-1-4263-0421-7 (lib bdg); 1-4263-0421-8 (lib bdg)

"Readers will learn about . . . new brain research in this title, which includes a basic discussion of the parts of the brain, their functions, and how neurons send messages throughout the body. Information is also included about the role of the brain during sleep, dreaming, and various emotional states, as well as explanations of the various technologies available to measure brain activity. This is a well-organized, compelling introduction, sure to pique the curiosity of many children. Full-color photographs and illustrations enliven the text." SLJ

Includes bibliographical references

Stewart, Melissa, 1968-

Why do we see rainbows? Marshall Cavendish Benchmark 2009 32p il (Tell me why, tell me how) lib bdg $20.95

Grades: 3 4 5   **612.8**

1. Eye 2. Color 3. Rainbow

ISBN 978-0-7614-2919-7 (lib bdg); 0-7614-2919-0 (lib bdg)   LC 2007024628

"Provides comprehensive information on how the human eye sees color." Publisher's note

Veitch, Catherine

Sound and hearing. Heinemann Library 2009 24p il (Sounds all around us) lib bdg $20.71; pa $5.99

Grades: PreK K 1   **612.8**

1. Hearing 2. Sound waves 3. Sound

ISBN 978-1-4329-3224-4 (lib bdg); 1-4329-3224-1 (lib bdg); 978-1-4329-3225-1 (pa); 1-4329-3225-X (pa)   LC 2008-51741

This book "introduces the basics of sound through vibrant photographs, large text, and simple sentences. . . . [A] great introduction[s] and worthy addition[s]." SLJ

Includes glossary

613 Personal health and safety

American Medical Assocation boy's guide to becoming a teen. Jossey-Bass 2006 128p il pa $12.95

Grades: 4 5 6 7   **613**

1. Boys—Health and hygiene 2. Puberty 3. Adolescence

ISBN 0-7879-8343-8

Contents: Welcome to puberty; Eating, exercise, and a healthy weight; Your height; Your skin, teeth, and hair; Your reproductive system-inside and out; Erections, wet dreams, and masturbation; Your feelings; Relationships; What about sex?

"This guide addresses puberty's changes clearly. . . . The text's approach is straightforward, accessible, and nonjudgmental, whether the topic is same-sex attraction or divorcing parents. The volume closes with an extensive resource section, including hotlines." Booklist

Includes bibliographical references

American Medical Association girl's guide to becoming a teen. Jossey-Bass 2006 128p pa $12.95

Grades: 4 5 6 7   **613**

1. Girls—Health and hygiene 2. Puberty 3. Adolescence

ISBN 0-7879-8344-6

Contents: What is puberty?; Eating, exercise, and a healthy weight; Your height; Your skin and teeth; Your hair; Your changing body; Menstruation; Your emotions; Relationships; For more information

This "covers the physical and emotional changes that puberty brings, along with solid tips about grooming, diet, exercise, and other health issues, such as eating disorders. . . . The clear text communicates concepts clearly . . . and girls will find plenty of useful information." Booklist

Includes bibliographical references

Cheung, Lilian W. Y., 1951-

Be healthy! it's a girl thing; food, fitness, and feeling great; [by] Lilian Cheung and Mavis Jukes. Crown Publishers 2003 117p il lib bdg $18.99; pa $12.95

Grades: 5 6 7 8   **613**

1. Girls—Health and hygiene 2. Nutrition 3. Physical fitness

ISBN 0-679-99029-1 (lib bdg); 0-679-89029-7 (pa)   LC 2003-10114

This "offers girls going through puberty advice on nutrition, fitness, self-image, and appearance." SLJ

"Given the alarmingly high rates of eating disorders, girls definitely need to hear some of the straight talk more often. . . . A chapter devoted to advertising is also helpful in countering the unrealistic images portrayed in the media." Booklist

Gardner, Robert, 1929-
Ace your exercise and nutrition science project: great science fair ideas; [by] Robert Gardner, Barbara Gardner Conklin, and Salvatore Tocci. Enslow Publishers 2009 128p il (Ace your biology science project) lib bdg $31.93
Grades: 5 6 7 8   **613**
     1. Exercise 2. Nutrition 3. Science projects 4. Science—Experiments
     ISBN 978-0-7660-3218-7 (lib bdg); 0-7660-3218-3 (lib bdg)   LC 2008-30798
     "Presents several science projects and science project ideas about exercise and nutrition." Publisher's note
     Includes bibliographical references

Miller, Edward, 1964-
The monster health book; a guide to eating healthy, being active, & feeling great for monsters & kids! [by] Edward Miller. Holiday House 2006 40p il $16.95 *
Grades: 2 3 4   **613**
     1. Nutrition 2. Health
     ISBN 978-0-8234-1956-2; 0-8234-1956-8
     LC 2005046383
     "Featuring a friendly, rotund, green monster determined to make healthy choices, this book presents basic information about food, exercise, and health. . . . Subjects include food nutrients, counting calories and understanding food labels, tips for making healthy lunches and snacks, the benefits of getting enough sleep and exercise, and ways to improve self-esteem. Miller's retro-style illustrations fill the pages with color, shapes, and humorous details, and silly jokes are tucked everywhere. . . . This lively, visually appealing book . . . belongs in children's hands." SLJ

Read, Leon
Keeping well. Sea-to-Sea Publications 2010 23p il (Tiger talk. All about me) lib bdg $24.25
Grades: PreK K   **613**
     1. Health 2. Hygiene
     ISBN 978-1-59771-186-9 (lib bdg); 1-59771-186-1 (lib bdg)   LC 2008-45008
     This book about keeping well "makes learning fun. . . . [The] book employs a simplified game of 'Where's Waldo?' by hiding a cartoon tiger on almost every page. This approach, combined with questions . . . will encourage discussion and involvement." SLJ

Royston, Angela
Why do I wash my hands? QEB Pub. 2010 24p il (QEB my body) lib bdg $28.65
Grades: PreK K 1 2   **613**
     1. Hygiene
     ISBN 978-1-59566-972-8 (lib bdg); 1-59566-972-8 (lib bdg)   LC 2009-15228
     Introduces the effects of germs on the skin and outlines the principles of personal hygiene.
     "The information is straightforward, well presented, and easy to understand. . . . [This] title is well designed, filled with color photographs, and scattered with fact boxes." Libr Media Connect
     Includes glossary and bibliographical references

Schaefer, Adam, 1976-
Staying healthy; [by] A. R. Schaefer. Heinemann Library 2010 32p il (Health and fitness) lib bdg $25.36; pa $7.99
Grades: PreK K 1   **613**
     1. Health 2. Hygiene 3. Exercise
     ISBN 978-1-4329-2769-1 (lib bdg); 1-4329-2769-8 (lib bdg); 978-1-4329-2774-5 (pa); 1-4329-2774-4 (pa)
     LC 2008-52298
     Find out about the importance of a good diet, exercise, staying clean, and what to do if you are injured or sick.
     "Spare, declarative sentences coupled with bright, full-color photos . . . [makes this book] appropriate for reading aloud in the classroom or even during a themed story hour. . . . While each spread introduces a new topic . . . [a] solid [introduction] and [conclusion] make for [a] cohesive [package]." SLJ
     Includes glossary and bibliographical references

613.2   Dietetics

Doeden, Matt, 1974-
Eat right! how you can make good food choices; [by] Matt Doeden; illustrations by Jack Desrocher. Lerner Publications 2008 64p il (Health zone) lib bdg $30.60
Grades: 4 5 6 7   **613.2**
     1. Nutrition
     ISBN 978-0-8225-7552-8 (lib bdg); 0-8225-7552-3 (lib bdg)   LC 2007043322
     "This offers a highly readable, never preachy exploration into the benefits of providing quality fuel for your body. It opens with an anecdote of a kid who snacks on soda and chips while playing volleyball. A friend challenges him to to eat better for a week, and he comes back with more sustained energy and a fresh outlook. . . . The following chapters do a great job of detailing everything from the food pyramid and benefits of different nutrients to warnings against following the faddish, ineffective diets." Booklist
     Includes bibliographical references

King, Hazel, 1962-
Carbohydrates for a healthy body. 2nd ed. Heinemann Library 2009 48p il (Body needs) $17.99; pa $8.99
Grades: 4 5 6   **613.2**
     1. Carbohydrates 2. Nutrition
     ISBN 978-1-4329-2186-6; 1-4395-3782-8; 978-1-4329-2192-7 (pa); 1-4329-2192-4 (pa)
     LC 2009290513
     First published 2003
     Describes what carbohydrates are, what types of foods contain them, how they are digested and used to produce energy, and their role in a healthy diet.
     This is "written in a clear, organized style and the full-color illustrations and photos complement the [text]." SLJ [review of 2003 edition]
     Includes bibliographical references

Leedy, Loreen, 1959-

The edible pyramid; good eating every day; written and illustrated by Loreen Leedy. rev ed. Holiday House 2007 unp il $17.95; pa $6.95

Grades: K 1 2 3   **613.2**
    1. Nutrition 2. Diet
    ISBN   978-0-8234-2074-2;   0-8234-2074-4;
    978-0-8234-2075-9 (pa); 0-8234-2075-2 (pa)
                            LC 2006036590

First published 1994

This is a "picture-book guide to healthy, delicious eating. . . . Featuring the smart cat waiter at the Edible Pyramid restaurant who recommends the menu to stylishly dressed animal customers, the bright, clear pictures show breads and grains, pasta in amazing shapes, vegetables and fruits in delicious colors, an abundance of beans, and more." Booklist

Powell, Jillian

Fats for a healthy body. 2nd ed. Heinemann Library 2009 48p il (Body needs) lib bdg $31.43

Grades: 4 5 6   **613.2**
    1. Oils and fats 2. Nutrition
    ISBN 978-1-4329-2187-3 (lib bdg); 1-4329-2187-8 (lib
    bdg)   LC 2009290512
First published 2003

Discusses what fats are, how they are absorbed and stored in the body, how the body uses fats, and health problems caused by fats.

Includes bibliographical references

Royston, Angela

Proteins for a healthy body. 2nd ed. Heinemann Library 2009 48p il (Body needs) lib bdg $31.43; pa $8.99

Grades: 4 5 6   **613.2**
    1. Proteins 2. Nutrition
    ISBN 978-1-4329-2188-0; 1-4329-2188-6 (lib bdg);
    978-1-4329-2194-1 (pa); 1-4329-2194-0 (pa)
                            LC 2009290511
First published 2003

"Royston looks at different kinds of proteins—antibodies, hormones, enzymes—and how vegetarians and vegans can get enough of them. . . . [This is] written in a clear, organized style and the full-color illustrations and photos complement the [text]." SLJ [review of 2003 edition]

Vitamins and minerals for a healthy body. 2nd ed. Heinemann Library 2009 48p il (Body needs) lib bdg $31.43; pa $8.99

Grades: 4 5 6   **613.2**
    1. Vitamins 2. Minerals 3. Nutrition
    ISBN 978-1-4329-2189-7; 1-4329-2189-4 (lib bdg);
    978-1-4329-2195-8 (pa); 1-4329-2195-9 (pa)
                            LC 2009293230
First published 2003

Discusses what vitamins and minerals are, how they are digested, absorbed, and used by the body, and the role of these substances in a healthy diet

Includes bibliographical references

Water and fiber for a healthy body. 2nd ed. Heinemann Library 2009 48p il (Body needs) lib bdg $31.43; pa $8.99

Grades: 4 5 6   **613.2**
    1. Water 2. Food—Fiber content 3. Nutrition
    ISBN 978-1-4329-2190-3 (lib bdg); 1-4329-2190-8;
    978-1-4329-2196-5 (pa); 1-4329-2196-7 (pa)
                            LC 2009293229
First published 2003

Discusses what water and fiber are, what foods they can be found in, and how the body absorbs, digests, and uses these ingredients

Includes bibliographical references

Schaefer, Adam, 1976-

Healthy food; [by] A. R. Schaefer. Heinemann Library 2010 32p il (Health and fitness) lib bdg $25.36; pa $7.99

Grades: PreK K 1   **613.2**
    1. Nutrition 2. Diet
    ISBN 978-1-4329-2768-4 (lib bdg); 1-4329-2768-X
    (lib bdg); 978-1-4329-2773-8 (pa); 1-4329-2773-6 (pa)
                            LC 2008-52367

Find out what the main food groups are, and the best ways to eat these foods

"Spare, declarative sentences coupled with bright, full-color photos . . . [makes this book] appropriate for reading aloud in the classroom or even during a themed story hour. . . . While each spread introduces a new topic . . . [a] solid [introduction] and [conclusion] make for [a] cohesive [package]." SLJ

Includes glossary and bibliographical references

Zahensky, Barbara A.

Diet fads. Rosen 2007 64p il (Danger zone: dieting and eating disorders) lib bdg $27.95

Grades: 4 5 6 7 8   **613.2**
    1. Weight loss 2. Obesity
    ISBN 978-1-4042-1999-1

"This clearly written overview emphasizes the impact of super-thin celebrity images on general self-esteem. . . . Zahensky considers the reasons people overeat and walks readers through practical steps to recognizing true hunger, making a weight-loss plan, and establishing good diet and exercise habits. She examines different types of fad and crash diets, pointing out their inherent dangers." SLJ

613.6 Personal safety and special topics of health

Miller, Edward, 1964-

Fireboy to the rescue! a fire safety book. Holiday House 2010 unp il $16.95

Grades: K 1 2   **613.6**
    1. Safety education 2. Fire prevention 3. Fire fighting
    ISBN 978-0-8234-2222-7; 0-8234-2222-4

"Fireboy is a superhero intent on keeping the world's children safe from fire. After heralding all the great things fire can do . . . the cut paper-style artwork bursts

Miller, Edward, 1964-—*Continued*
into reds and yellows and oranges as all manners of
things—including homes—catch aflame. . . . The snazzy
presentation is entertaining in its own right. . . . Some
of the especially vital details (fire alarms, extinguishers)
are incorporated as photos." Booklist

Raatma, Lucia
Safety in your neighborhood. Child's World
2005 32p il (Living well) lib bdg $25.64
Grades: 4 5 6 7   **613.6**
1. Crime prevention 2. Safety education
ISBN 1-59296-240-8   LC 2003-27214
Contents: Who is that man?; Your home and neighborhood; Knowing your neighbors; Strangers on your
street; Someone's at your door; Keeping your neighborhood safe; Glossary; Questions and answers about neighborhood safety; Helping a friend learn about neighborhood safety; Did you know?; How to learn more about
neighborhood safety
This book teaches young readers how to keep their
neighborhood a safe place and what to do if that safety
is compromised.
This "clearly written [title has] an appealing layout
with plenty of full-color photos and a triple-spaced text.
. . . [It] provides solid tips." SLJ
Includes glossary and bibliographical references

Schaefer, Adam, 1976-
Staying safe. Heinemann Library 2009 32p il
(Health and fitness) lib bdg $25.36; pa $7.99
Grades: PreK K 1   **613.6**
1. Safety education
ISBN 978-1-4329-2770-7 (lib bdg); 1-4329-2770-1 (lib
bdg); 978-1-4329-2775-2 (pa); 1-4329-2775-2 (pa)
                                       LC 2008-52300
Find out what to do in a fire, how to stay safe in the
street, and who to call in an emergency.
"Spare, declarative sentences coupled with bright, full-
color photos . . . [makes this book] appropriate for reading aloud in the classroom or even during a themed story
hour. . . . While each spread introduces a new topic
. . . [a] solid [introduction] and [conclusion] make for
[a] cohesive [package]." SLJ
Includes glossary and bibliographical references

613.7 Physical fitness

Birkemoe, Karen, 1974-
Strike a pose; the Planet Girl guide to yoga;
written by Karen Birkemoe; illustrated by Heather
Collett. Kids Can Press 2007 96p il (Planet girl)
spiral $12.95 *
Grades: 5 6 7 8   **613.7**
1. Yoga 2. Girls—Health and hygiene
ISBN 978-1-55337-004-8
"This compact book offers a well-rounded overview of
Hatha yoga. Using an easy conversational tone,
Birkemoe relates the general practice and specific poses
to reader's lives. The simple line drawings and color il-
lustrations partner effectively with text to explain each
move." SLJ
Includes glossary

Chryssicas, Mary Kaye
I love yoga; written by Mary Kaye Chryssicas;
photography by Angela Coppola. DK Pub. 2005
47p il $12.99
Grades: 3 4 5   **613.7**
1. Yoga
ISBN 0-7566-1400-7
The author "offers a vicarious tour of a typical [yoga]
class. Opening spreads discuss equipment, clothing, and
camaraderie among the young learners. Later spreads
showcase poses. . . . The mostly sharp, clear photos of
accomplished kids having fun . . . may inspire some
children to dip into their first 'Downward Dog,' while
others will marvel at yoga's mental benefits." Booklist

Dalgleish, Sharon
Exercise and rest; [by] Sharon Dalgleish. Smart
Apple Media 2007 32p il (Healthy choices) $27.10
Grades: 2 3 4   **613.7**
1. Exercise 2. Rest
ISBN 978-1-58340-755-4   LC 2005057878
"The square pages include bright color photographs of
kids playing basketball, doing judo, and making snow
angels, as well as occasional, simple diagrams of body
parts, such as a healthy heart muscle, biceps, and triceps.
The importance of sleep, too, gets attention. . . . The
mix of simple physiology with fun activities makes exercise a natural part of daily life." Booklist

Royston, Angela
Why do I run? QEB Pub. 2010 24p il (QEB my
body) lib bdg $28.65
Grades: PreK K 1 2   **613.7**
1. Running 2. Physical fitness 3. Exercise
ISBN 978-1-59566-971-1 (lib bdg); 1-59566-971-X
(lib bdg)   LC 2009-15223
Introduces the effects of running and other exercise on
the body, and outlines the principles of physical fitness
and healthy, safe exercise
"The information is straightforward, well presented,
and easy to understand. . . . [This] title is well designed,
filled with color photographs, and scattered with fact
boxes." Libr Media Connect
Includes glossary and bibliographical references

Schaefer, Adam, 1976-
Exercise; [by] A. R. Schaefer. Heinemann
Library 2010 32p il (Health and fitness) lib bdg
$25.36; pa $7.99
Grades: PreK K 1   **613.7**
1. Exercise
ISBN 978-1-4329-2767-7 (lib bdg); 1-4329-2767-1 (lib
bdg); 978-1-4329-2772-1 (pa); 1-4329-2772-8 (pa)
                                       LC 2008-52297
This book about exercise has "spare, declarative sentences coupled with bright, full-color photos. . . . While
each spread introduces a new topic . . . [a] solid [intro-
duction] and [conclusion] make for [a] cohesive [pack-
age]." SLJ
Includes glossary and bibliographical references

Whitford, Rebecca

Little yoga; a toddler's first book of yoga; [by] Rebecca Whitford & Martina Selway. Holt & Co. 2005 unp il $9.95

Grades: PreK K 1   **613.7**

1. Yoga

ISBN 0-8050-7879-7

"This small, square book offers a simple sequence of yoga poses designed especially for toddlers. On each cheerfully designed spread, a simple, black-outlined illustration shows a smiling toddler in a pose; on the opposite page, an animal mimics the same motion. . . . Appended material includes tips for adults to help guide children through the motions and photos of toddlers performing the poses." Booklist

613.9 Birth control, reproductive technology, sex hygiene

Brown, Laurene Krasny

What's the big secret? talking about sex with girls and boys; [by] Laurie Krasny Brown and Marc Brown. Little, Brown 1997 31p il hardcover o.p. pa $5.95

Grades: K 1 2 3   **613.9**

1. Sex education

ISBN 0-316-10915-0; 0-316-10183-4 (pa)

LC 96-15521

This "picture book's subject is sex and sexuality: not simply physical differences but also gender roles, the issue of privacy, and reproduction. . . . The Browns do an outstanding and very responsible job of introducing a wide variety of terms (everything from the expected, *umbilical cord*, to the unexpected, *masturbation*, which is handled with honesty but restraint), synthesizing a great deal of information kids want to know at this age, and presenting facts in a nonthreatening but forthright context. They even manage a good deal of humor along the way. . . . The words and illustrations work extremely well together, with the busy, bright cartoon art and balloon dialogue conveying as much of the information as the text." Booklist

Cole, Joanna

Asking about sex & growing up; a question-and-answer book for kids; illustrated by Bill Thomas. rev ed. Collins 2009 89p il $15.99; pa $6.99

Grades: 4 5 6   **613.9**

1. Sex education

ISBN   978-0-06-142987-3;   0-06-142987-2;
978-0-06-142986-6 (pa); 0-06-142986-4 (pa)

LC 2008022710

First published 1988 by Morrow Junior Books

This book "offers straightforward information about topics such as physical changes in puberty, masturbation, birth control, pregnancy, homosexuality, and STDs. . . . Libraries . . . should consider adding it as a source of basic information for curious preteens." SLJ

Harris, Robie H.

It's perfectly normal; a book about changing bodies, growing up, sex & sexual health; illustrated by Michael Emberley. 3rd ed. Candlewick Press 2009 93p il $22.99; pa $12.99 *

Grades: 4 5 6 7   **613.9**

1. Sex education 2. Puberty

ISBN   978-0-7636-4483-3;   0-7636-4483-8;
978-0-7636-4484-0 (pa); 0-7636-4484-6 (pa)

LC 2009008457

First published 1994

This provides information about sex, puberty, family relationships and reproduction, sexual decision-making and birth control, abortion laws, sexual abuse, sexual health, sexually transmitted diseases, and (new in this edition) internet safety.

"This caring, conscientious, and well-crafted book will be a fine library resource as well as a marvelous adjunct to the middle-school sex-education curriculum. . . . The bold color cartoon drawings are very candid. . . . Harris' text [is] as forthright as Emberley's art." Booklist [review of 1994 ed.]

614 Forensic medicine; incidence of injuries, wounds, disease; public preventive medicine

Spilsbury, Richard, 1963-

Bones speak! solving crimes from the past. Enslow Publishers 2009 48p il (Solve that crime!) lib bdg $23.93

Grades: 5 6 7 8   **614**

1. Forensic anthropology 2. Forensic sciences

ISBN 978-0-7660-3377-1 (lib bdg); 0-7660-3377-5 (lib bdg)   LC 2008-33309

"Learn how forensics helps solve old crimes and mysteries." Publisher's note

This "title boasts in-depth information, sidebars detailing events of true crime, and activities that will increase understanding. . . . Photographs are colorful, well-captioned, and related to the text." SLJ

Includes glossary and bibliographical references

614.4 Incidence of and public measures to prevent disease

Barnard, Bryn

Outbreak; plagues that changed history; written and illustrated by Bryn Barnard. Crown Publishers 2005 47p il maps $17.95 *

Grades: 5 6 7 8   **614.4**

1. Epidemics 2. Diseases

ISBN 0-375-82986-5   LC 2005-15086

This "volume explores specific plagues that have impacted society. Barnard begins with an introduction to microbes and the positive and negative effects that they can have on humans. A history of the study of microorganisms follows. The bulk of the book then focuses on specific plagues with a chapter devoted to each, includ-

Barnard, Bryn—*Continued*
ing the Black Death, smallpox, yellow fever, cholera, tuberculosis, and influenza. The final chapter discusses the modern struggle against disease. . . . The evocative paintings help to clarify the text. Browsers and report writers alike will find this to be a fascinating and informative resource." SLJ

Piddock, Charles
Outbreak; science seeks safeguards for global health; [Caryn Oryniak, consultant] National Geographic 2008 64p il (National Geographic investigates) $17.95; lib bdg $27.90
Grades: 4 5 6 7   **614.4**
     1. Epidemics 2. Diseases 3. Medicine—Research
     ISBN   978-1-4263-0357-9;   1-4263-0357-2;
     978-1-4263-0263-3 (lib bdg); 1-4263-0263-0 (lib bdg)
                         LC 2009-275290
This is an "introduction to the fight against infectious diseases, including scientists who discovered various viruses and bacteria. The text outlines how we have learned to fight nature's harmful strains and to use others to our advantage; it also provides the latest findings on bird flu and SARS, Ebola and AIDS, and highly resistant strains of tuberculosis." Publisher's note

Walker, Richard, 1951-
Epidemics & plagues; foreword by Denise Grady. Kingfisher 2006 63p il (Kingfisher knowledge) $12.95 paperback o.p.
Grades: 4 5 6 7   **614.4**
     1. Epidemics 2. Diseases
     ISBN   978-0-7534-6035-1;   0-7534-6035-1;
     978-0-7534-6161-7 (pa); 0-7534-6161-7 (pa)
Discusses the spread of infectious diseases and their impact on human populations, from the Black Death in medieval Europe to such modern diseases as AIDS and West Nile virus, as well as efforts to stop the spread of these diseases.
Includes glossary

614.5   Incidence of and public measures to prevent specific diseases and kinds of diseases

Ballard, Carol
AIDS and other epidemics. Gareth Stevens Pub. 2008 48p il map (What if we do nothing?) lib bdg $31
Grades: 5 6 7 8   **614.5**
     1. AIDS (Disease) 2. Epidemics 3. Communicable diseases
     ISBN 978-1-4339-0085-3 (lib bdg); 1-4339-0085-8 (lib bdg)   LC 2008029189
"This book looks at the causes of major infectious diseases, how they spread, and how they can be treated. It also discusses different steps that governments and health organizations can take to handle and prevent epidemics and pandemics." Publisher's note
"Using intelligent, focused text; an open design; vivid photos; and excellent maps, [this] book demands attention." Booklist
Includes bibliographical references

Marrin, Albert, 1936-
Dr. Jenner and the speckled monster; the search for the smallpox vaccine. Dutton Children's Bks. 2002 120p il $19.99 *
Grades: 5 6 7 8   **614.5**
     1. Jenner, Edward, 1749-1823 2. Smallpox
     ISBN 0-525-46922-2   LC 2002-2698
This is a "social history of smallpox, with an emphasis on Dr. Edward Jenner's contributions to eradicate the disease. . . . Marrin's writing is direct and succinct, and his scientific explanations are lucid and well detailed. Numerous black-and-white period illustrations (some appropriately gruesome) appear in most chapters, adding interest to the text." Booklist
Includes bibliographical references

Murphy, Jim, 1947-
An American plague; the true and terrifying story of the yellow fever epidemic of 1793. Clarion Bks. 2003 165p il map $18 *
Grades: 5 6 7 8   **614.5**
     1. Yellow fever
     ISBN 0-395-77608-2   LC 2002-151355
     A Newbery Medal honor book, 2004
     Contents: No one noticed; "All was not right;" Church bells tolling; Confusion, distress, and utter desolation; "It was our duty;" The prince of bleeders; "By twelve only;" "This unmerciful enemy;" "A delicate situation;" Improvements and the public gratitude; "A modern-day time bomb"
"Murphy culls from a number of historical records the story of the yellow fever epidemic that swept Philadelphia in 1793, skillfully drawing out from these sources the fear and drama of the time and making them immediate to modern readers. . . . Thoroughly documented, with an annotated source list, the work is both rigorous and inviting." Horn Book

615   Pharmacology and therapeutics

Phelan, Glen
Killing germs, saving lives; the quest for the first vaccines. National Geographic 2006 59p il (Science quest) $17.95; lib bdg $25.90
Grades: 5 6 7 8   **615**
     1. Vaccination
     ISBN   0-7922-5537-2;   978-0-7922-5537-6;
     0-7922-5538-0 (lib bdg); 978-0-7922-5538-3 (lib bdg)
                         LC 2005-22143
This "traces the path to the creation of the vaccines that revolutionized modern medicine. [It includes] profiles [of such] figures [as] Louis Pasteur, Joseph Lister, and Florence Nightingale." Publisher's note
Includes glossary and bibliographical references

615.9 Toxicology

Bjorklund, Ruth
Food-borne illnesses. Marshall Cavendish Benchmark 2006 64p il (Health alert) $19.95
Grades: 4 5 6 7   615.9
1. Food contamination 2. Diseases
ISBN 0-7614-1917-9
"Discusses food-borne illnesses and their effects on people and society." Publisher's note
"Children seeking up-to-date and reliable information about the many kinds of food-borne illnesses, treatments, preventions, and coping strategies, as well as a historical overview of food-safety efforts in the United States, will appreciate this easy-to-use and information-rich resource. . . . Useful features include color photos, diagrams, and sidebars." SLJ
Includes glossary and bibliographical references

Day, Jeff, 1980-
Don't touch that! the book of gross, poisonous, and downright icky plants and critters. Chicago Review Press 2008 108p il pa $9.95
Grades: 3 4 5 6   615.9
1. Poisons and poisoning 2. Poisonous plants 3. Poisonous animals
ISBN 978-1-55652-711-1 (pa); 1-556527-11-X (pa)
                                LC 2007027466
"Packed with potentially lifesaving information, this guide is humorous without sacrificing usefulness. The author, a medical doctor, begins with some basic plants (poison ivy, poison oak, and poison sumac) that might be encountered. Drawings of the leaves are carefully labeled and accompanied by the warning not to touch any part of the plant, and not to burn it as even the smoke can irritate. Poisonous insects, spiders, amphibians, reptiles, and mammals are also included, and every entry explains why the creature's venom causes the bad reaction it does and how to treat it. . . . Genuinely funny, colorful drawings on every page amplify the text and make it memorable." SLJ

Silverstein, Alvin
The food poisoning update; [by] Alvin and Virginia Silverstein and Laura Silverstein Nunn. Enslow Publishers 2007 128p il (Disease update) lib bdg $31.93
Grades: 5 6 7 8   615.9
1. Food poisoning
ISBN 978-0-7660-2748-0 (lib bdg); 0-7660-2748-1 (lib bdg)
                                LC 2006032822
This describes the history of food poisoning, its causes, detection, treatment and prevention.
"This timely, well-written title . . . combines practical food-safety tips with clear science facts and concise, historical survey of foodborne illnesses." Booklist
Includes glossary and bibliographical references

616 Diseases

Calamandrei, Camilla
Fever; by Camilla Calamandrei. Marshall Cavendish Benchmark 2009 64p il (Health alert) $22.95
Grades: 4 5 6 7   616
1. Fever
ISBN 978-0-7614-2915-9; 0-7614-2915-8
                                LC 2007-26002
"Provides comprehensive information on the causes, treatment, and history of fever." Publisher's note
Includes glossary

Dendy, Leslie A., 1946-
Guinea pig scientists; bold self-experimenters in science and medicine; [by] Leslie Dendy and Mel Boring; with illustrations by C. B. Mordan. Henry Holt & Co. 2005 213p il $19.95 *
Grades: 5 6 7 8   616
1. Medicine—Research 2. Scientists
ISBN 0-8050-7316-7   LC 2004-52364
"The authors offer 10 . . . case studies of scientists from the past several centuries who became their own test subjects. . . . The accounts are lively, compelling, and not always for the squeamish. . . . The authors cogently discuss each experiment's significance in advancing our understanding of science and medicine. Illustrated with a mix of period black-and-white photos and Mordan's nineteenth-century-style portraits . . . the episodes make riveting reading." Booklist
Includes bibliographical references

Murphy, Patricia J., 1963-
Illness; [by] Patricia J Murphy. Heinemann Library 2008 32p il (Tough topics) lib bdg $25.36; pa $7.99
Grades: PreK K 1 2 3   616
1. Diseases
ISBN   978-1-4034-9777-2   (lib   bdg); 978-1-4034-9782-6 (pa)   LC 2007005345
This "book talks about different kinds of illnesses, coping mechanisms, and varieties of medical treatments available. . . . Murphy gives an overview of the topic in a way that young readers can understand. . . . The two-page chapters include full-color photos and two paragraphs of text that are frank yet sensitive in their approach." SLJ
Includes glossary and bibliographical references

Nardo, Don, 1947-
Cure quest; the science of stem cell research; by Don Nardo. Compass Point Books 2009 48p il (Headline science) lib bdg $27.93; pa $7.95
Grades: 5 6 7   616
1. Stem cell research
ISBN 978-0-7565-3371-7 (lib bdg); 0-7565-3371-6 (lib bdg); 978-0-7565-3374-8 (pa); 0-7565-3374-0 (pa)
                                LC 2008-5738

Nardo, Don, 1947——*Continued*

Explains the science behind stem cell research.

"Color photos and graphics provide visual information; a timeline is helpful to find fast facts, and the Facthound Web site provides student with additional information." Libr Media Connect

Includes glossary and bibliographical references

Ollhoff, Jim, 1959-

What are germs? ABDO Pub. Co. 2010 32p il (A history of germs) $27.07

Grades: 3 4 5 6   **616**

1. Germ theory of disease 2. Bacteria

ISBN 978-1-60453-502-0; 1-60453-502-4

"What Are Germs? includes kinds of germs and germ-fighting organizations. The short, informative chapters provide plenty of details for reports. The illustrations, many of which are color photos, enhance the information." SLJ

Includes glossary

616.1   Diseases of cardiovascular system

Silverstein, Alvin

The sickle cell anemia update; [by] Alvin and Virginia Silverstein, and Laura Silverstein Nunn. Enslow Publishers 2006 112p il (Disease update) lib bdg $31.93 *

Grades: 5 6 7 8   **616.1**

1. Sickle cell anemia

ISBN 0-7660-2479-2   LC 2005018727

This describes the history, diagnosis, treatment, prevention, and future of sickle cell anemia.

Includes glossary and bibliographical references

616.2   Diseases of respiratory system

Cobb, Vicki, 1938-

Your body battles a cold; written by Vicki Cobb; photomicrographs by Dennis Kunkel; illustrated by Andrew N. Harris. Millbrook Press 2009 32p il (Body battles) lib bdg $25.26

Grades: 3 4 5   **616.2**

1. Cold (Disease) 2. Immune system

ISBN 978-0-8225-6813-1 (lib bdg); 0-8225-6813-6 (lib bdg)   LC 2008002839

Color illustrations and photomicrographs show what happens when a human body is attacked by a cold virus

"The body's immune system has never looked like this before with plasma cells using sling shots to fire antibodies into viruses, platelets riding inner tubes down a stream of blood, and viruses multiplying in a 'Germco' factory. [The] title introduces five or six defense cells, disguised as superheroes protecting the body from adversarial viruses. . . . The oversize text uses metaphors that readers will understand. . . . The micrographs will fascinate and compel young readers to read everything." SLJ

Includes glossary and bibliographical references

Hoffmann, Gretchen

The flu; [by] Gretchen Hoffmann. Marshall Cavendish Benchmark 2007 64p il (Health alert) lib bdg $31.36

Grades: 4 5 6 7   **616.2**

1. Influenza

ISBN 978-0-7614-2208-2 (lib bdg); 0-7614-2208-0 (lib bdg)   LC 2006011980

"Explores the history, causes, symptoms, treatments, and future of different types of influenza." Publisher's note

Includes glossary and bibliographical references

Landau, Elaine

Asthma; by Elaine Landau. Marshall Cavendish Benchmark 2009 32p il (Head-to-toe health) lib bdg $19.95

Grades: 2 3 4   **616.2**

1. Asthma

ISBN 978-0-7614-2845-9 (lib bdg); 0-7614-2845-3 (lib bdg)   LC 2007-34998

"Provides basic information about asthma and its prevention." Publisher's note

"Photo illustrations are apt and age appropriate. . . . Pervading the [book] . . . is an overall sense of reassurance that even if something hurts, 'all better' is never too far away. Appealing and readable nonfiction." SLJ

Includes glossary and bibliographical references

The common cold; by Elaine Landau. Marshall Cavendish Benchmark 2009 32p il (Head-to-toe health) lib bdg $19.95

Grades: 2 3 4   **616.2**

1. Cold (Disease)

ISBN 978-0-7614-2844-2 (lib bdg); 0-7614-2844-5 (lib bdg)   LC 2007-35005

"Provides basic information about the common cold and its prevention." Publisher's note

"Photo illustrations are apt and age appropriate. . . . Pervading the [book] . . . is an overall sense of reassurance that even if something hurts, 'all better' is never too far away. Appealing and readable nonfiction." SLJ

Includes glossary and bibliographical references

Moore-Mallinos, Jennifer

I have asthma; illustrated by Rosa M. Cirto. Barron's 2007 35p il (What do I know about?) pa $6.99

Grades: K 1 2 3   **616.2**

1. Asthma

ISBN 0-7641-3785-9

After a young boy has trouble breathing during soccer practice, he is taken to his doctor who says that he has asthma, but he learns that with proper treatment and medical supervision, his asthma can be kept under control.

"The easy text, combined with soft, rounded figures in the colorful illustrations, results in a sensitively told story that offers encouragement to children suffering from this condition, complete with helpful advice." SLJ

Ollhoff, Jim, 1959-
The flu. ABDO Pub. Co. 2010 32p il (A history
of germs) $27.07
Grades: 3 4 5 6 **616.2**
1. Influenza 2. Viruses
ISBN 978-1-60453-498-6; 1-60453-498-2
LC 2008055063
"*Flu* provides a concise look at the illness, pandemics,
treatments, and recent strains, including H1N1. . . . The
short, informative chapters provide plenty of details for
reports. The illustrations, many of which are color photos, enhance the information." SLJ
Includes glossary

Robbins, Lynette
How to deal with asthma. PowerKids Press
2010 24p il (Kids' health) lib bdg $21.25
Grades: 2 3 4 **616.2**
1. Asthma
ISBN 978-1-4042-8141-7 (lib bdg); 1-4042-8141-X
(lib bdg) LC 2009-7653
"Hypothetical situations with fictional characters put
readers in the moment and provide a solid foundation for
comprehending [asthma]. . . . Robbins maintains a comforting tone, reassuring readers that it is possible to lead
active lives with proper attention to diet and guidance
from parents and doctors." SLJ
Includes glossary

Royston, Angela
Asthma. Black Rabbit Books 2009 30p il
(How's your health) lib bdg $27.10
Grades: 1 2 3 **616.2**
1. Asthma
ISBN 978-1-59920-219-8 (lib bdg); 1-59920-219-0 (lib
bdg) LC 2007-35689
First published 2004 by Heinemann Library
"Describes the symptoms and treatment of asthma."
Publisher's note
"Encourages further learning with sidebars that help
readers think concretely about the subject. . . . Altogeth-
er a pitch perfect presentation." SLJ
Includes glossary and bibliographical references

Colds, the flu, and other infections. Black
Rabbit Books 2009 30p il (How's your health) lib
bdg $27.10
Grades: 1 2 3 **616.2**
1. Cold (Disease) 2. Influenza
ISBN 978-1-59920-217-4 (lib bdg); 1-59920-217-4 (lib
bdg)
"Describes the causes, symptoms, treatment of colds
and flu, and how to prevent them." Publisher's note
"Encourages further learning with sidebars that help
readers think concretely about the subject. . . . Altogether a pitch perfect presentation." SLJ
Includes glossary and bibliographical references

Explaining asthma. Smart Apple Media 2010
45p il (Explaining) lib bdg $34.25
Grades: 5 6 7 8 **616.2**
1. Asthma
ISBN 978-1-59920-315-7 (lib bdg); 1-59920-315-4 (lib
bdg) LC 2008-49284

Describes what living with asthma is like, discussing
symptoms, triggers, treatments, and lifestyle changes that
may be necessary to prevent asthma attacks
The book provides a "basic [overview] of the health
concerns related to the disease; information on diagnosis
and treatment; and a discussion of the challenges or complications experienced by the affected person and their
family/friends, and how to manage those problems. . . .
The incorporation of quotes and personal accounts in
'Case Notes' sidebars adds to the sensitive tone found
throughout [the title]." SLJ
Includes glossary

Silverstein, Alvin
The asthma update; [by] Alvin and Virginia
Silverstein, and Laura Silverstein Nunn. Enslow
Publishers 2006 128p il (Disease update) lib bdg
$31.93
Grades: 5 6 7 8 **616.2**
1. Asthma
ISBN 0-7660-2482-2 LC 2005-18728
This describes the history, causes, diagnosis, treat-
ment, prevention, and future of asthma
This "provides a clearly written, well-organized, and
well-documented account of a disease that is increasingly
prevalent among young people." Booklist
Includes glossary and bibliographical references

The flu and pneumonia update; [by] Alvin and
Virginia Silverstein, and Laura Silverstein Nunn.
Enslow Publishers 2006 104p il (Disease update)
lib bdg $31.93
Grades: 5 6 7 8 **616.2**
1. Influenza 2. Pneumonia
ISBN 0-7660-2480-6 LC 2005005988
This "provides a clear idea of the etiology, common
symptoms, and treatment of both influenza and its secondary bacterial infection, pneumonia. The tone is serious but reassuring as the authors discuss the great flu epidemic of 1918, then go on to consider the nature of both
illnesses and what readers can do to prevent or minimize
effects." Booklist
Includes glossary and bibliographical references

The tuberculosis update; [by] Alvin and Virginia
Silverstein, and Laura Silverstein Nunn. Enslow
Elementary 2006 112p il (Disease update) lib bdg
$31.93
Grades: 5 6 7 8 **616.2**
1. Tuberculosis
ISBN 0-7660-2481-4 LC 2005-05989
This covers the "history, transmission, symptoms, di-
agnosis, treatment, current advances, and potential out-
breaks [of tuberculosis]. . . . [It includes] numerous
high-quality color illustrations and diagrams, information-
al sidebars highlighting important facts and statistics."
SLJ
Includes bibliographical references

616.3   Diseases of digestive system

Bjorklund, Ruth
Cystic fibrosis; by Ruth Bjorklund. Marshall Cavendish Benchmark 2009 64p il (Health alert) $22.95
Grades: 4 5 6 7   616.3
1. Cystic fibrosis
ISBN 978-0-7614-2912-8; 0-7614-2912-3
                                    LC 2007-46674
"Provides comprehensive information on the causes, treatment, and history of cystic fibrosis." Publisher's note

Cobb, Vicki, 1938-
Your body battles a stomachache; written by Vicki Cobb; with photomicrographs by Dennis Kunkel; illustrations by Andrew N. Harris. Millbrook Press 2009 32p il (Body battles) lib bdg $25.26
Grades: 3 4 5   616.3
1. Stomach 2. Intestines 3. Immune system
ISBN 978-0-8225-7166-7 (lib bdg); 0-8225-7166-8 (lib bdg)   LC 2008002852
Color illustrations and photomicrographs show what happens when a human digestive system is attacked by a rotavirus
"The body's immune system has never looked like this before with plasma cells using sling shots to fire antibodies into viruses, platelets riding inner tubes down a stream of blood, and viruses multiplying in a 'Germco' factory. [The] title introduces five or six defense cells, disguised as superheroes protecting the body from adversarial viruses. . . . The oversize text uses metaphors that readers will understand. . . . The micrographs will fascinate and compel young readers to read everything." SLJ
Includes glossary and bibliographical references

Hicks, Terry Allan
Obesity; by Terry Allan Hicks. Marshall Cavendish Benchmark 2009 63p il (Health alert) $22.95
Grades: 4 5 6 7   616.3
1. Obesity
ISBN 978-0-7614-2911-1; 0-7614-2911-5
                                    LC 2007-31246
"Provides comprehensive information on the causes, treatment, and history of obesity." Publisher's note
Includes glossary

Powell, Jillian
Explaining cystic fibrosis. Smart Apple Media 2010 45p il (Explaining) lib bdg $34.25
Grades: 5 6 7 8   616.3
1. Cystic fibrosis
ISBN 978-1-59920-312-6 (lib bdg); 1-59920-312-X (lib bdg)   LC 2008-49288
Describes the illness, including its causes, how it is diagnosed, current treatments for the illness, and how those with cystic fibrosis lead everyday lives

The book provides a "basic [overview] of the health concerns related to the disease; information on diagnosis and treatment; and a discussion of the challenges or complications experienced by the affected person and their family/friends, and how to manage those problems. . . . The incorporation of quotes and personal accounts in 'Case Notes' sidebars adds to the sensitive tone found throughout [the title]." SLJ
Includes glossary and bibliographical references

Robbins, Lynette
How to deal with obesity. PowerKids Press 2010 24p il (Kids' health) lib bdg $21.25
Grades: 2 3 4   616.3
1. Obesity
ISBN 978-1-4042-8143-1 (lib bdg); 1-4042-8143-6 (lib bdg)   LC 2009-8902
"Hypothetical situations with fictional characters put readers in the moment and provide a solid foundation for comprehending [obesity]. . . . Robbins maintains a comforting tone, reassuring readers that it is possible to lead active lives with proper attention to diet and guidance from parents and doctors." SLJ
Includes glossary

616.4   Diseases of hematopoietic, lymphatic, glandular systems Diseases of endocrine system

Loughrey, Anita
Explaining diabetes. Smart Apple Media 2010 45p il (Explaining) lib bdg $34.25
Grades: 5 6 7 8   616.4
1. Diabetes
ISBN 978-1-59920-314-0 (lib bdg); 1-59920-314-6 (lib bdg)   LC 2008-49290
Provides an overview of Type 1 and Type 2 diabetes, discussing causes and symptoms, recommended and required lifestyle changes, how the disease is managed, and possible complications that may occur
The book provides a "basic [overview] of the health concerns related to the disease; information on diagnosis and treatment; and a discussion of the challenges or complications experienced by the affected person and their family/friends, and how to manage those problems. . . . The incorporation of quotes and personal accounts in 'Case Notes' sidebars adds to the sensitive tone found throughout [the title]." SLJ
Includes glossary and bibliographical references

Pirner, Connie White
Even little kids get diabetes; pictures by Nadine Bernard Westcott. Whitman, A. 1991 unp il hardcover o.p. pa $6.95
Grades: K 1   616.4
1. Diabetes
ISBN 0-8075-2158-2; 0-8075-2159-0 (pa)
                                    LC 90-12738
A young girl who has had diabetes since she was two years old describes her adjustments to the disease
"Language is simple, age appropriate, and effectively

Pirner, Connie White—*Continued*
gets the point across. The ink-and-watercolor drawings are lively and often upbeat. . . . Perhaps the most valuable part of the book is the 'note for parents,' which relates Pirner's personal experience over the last three years in caring for a diabetic child." SLJ

Robbins, Lynette
How to deal with diabetes. PowerKids Press 2010 24p il (Kids' health) lib bdg $21.25
Grades: 2 3 4   **616.4**
  1. Diabetes
  ISBN 978-1-4042-8144-8 (lib bdg); 1-4042-8144-4 (lib bdg)   LC 2009-10467
"Hypothetical situations with fictional characters put readers in the moment and provide a solid foundation for comprehending [diabetes]. . . . Robbins maintains a comforting tone, reassuring readers that it is possible to lead active lives with proper attention to diet and guidance from parents and doctors." SLJ
  Includes glossary

Silverstein, Alvin
The diabetes update; [by] Alvin and Virginia Silverstein, and Laura Silverstein Nunn. Enslow Publishers 2006 128p il (Disease update) lib bdg $31.93
Grades: 5 6 7 8   **616.4**
  1. Diabetes
  ISBN 0-7660-2483-0   LC 2005-05991
This describes the symptoms and causes of diabetes, the history of the disease, diagnosis and treatments, and future possibilities
  Includes glossary and bibliographical references

616.5   Diseases of integument

Caffey, Donna, 1954-
Yikes-lice! illustrations by Patrick Girouard. Whitman, A. 1998 unp il $14.95; pa $5.95
Grades: K 1 2 3   **616.5**
  1. Lice
  ISBN 0-8075-9374-5; 0-8075-9375-3 (pa)
                       LC 97-30679
Rhyming text describes what happens when a family discovers lice in the home and fights against them. Includes factual information about how lice live, spread, and can be eradicated

DerKazarian, Susan, 1969-
You have head lice! by Susan DerKazarian. Children's Press 2005 31p il (Rookie read-about health) $20.50; pa $5.95
Grades: PreK K 1 2   **616.5**
  1. Lice
  ISBN 0-516-25879-6; 0-516-27920-3 (pa)
                       LC 2004-15308
This "approaches the sometimes-touchy subject of head lice in a straightforward, reassuring manner. . . . Adults wanting to explain head lice to children will find this a helpful source of basic information." Booklist

Hirschmann, Kris, 1967-
Lice; by Kris Hirschmann. KidHaven Press 2004 32p il (Parasites) $22.45
Grades: 4 5 6   **616.5**
  1. Lice
  ISBN 978-0-7377-1784-6; 0-7377-1784-X
                       LC 2003-12157
Contents: Human-loving parasites; Infestation; Lice in action; The fight against lice
"Several short chapters briefly describe the distinctive physical and behavioral characteristics of [lice] and special characteristics of particular species. [The book] also [highlights] the symptoms, victims' experiences, the organisms' potential threats as disease vectors, current treatments, and prevention methods. . . . Clear, color photographs illustrate the [text]. . . . Well organized and clearly written." SLJ
  Includes bibliographical references

Lew, Kristi, 1968-
Itch & ooze; gross stuff on your skin; illustrations by Michael Slack. Millbrook Press 2010 48p il (Gross body science) lib bdg $29.27
Grades: 4 5 6   **616.5**
  1. Skin—Diseases 2. Skin
  ISBN 978-0-8225-8963-1 (lib bdg); 0-8225-8963-X (lib bdg)   LC 2008-45591
Presents disgusting facts about human skin, the diseases and parasites that can cause problems with it, and how it functions to protect the body and itself.
"Solid information layered between sarcastic comments and kid-friendly terminology like fart, poop, barf, and puke will keep readers engaged. . . . Labeled, captioned (and graphic) photographs, cartoon-style illustrations, and micrographs add information." SLJ
  Includes glossary and bibliographical references

Royston, Angela
Head lice. Black Rabbit Books 2009 30p il (How's your health) lib bdg $27.10
Grades: 1 2 3   **616.5**
  1. Lice
  ISBN 978-1-59920-218-1 (lib bdg); 1-59920-218-2 (lib bdg)
First published 2001 by Heinemann Library
"Describes the causes, symptoms, and treatment of head lice and how to prevent yourself from getting them." Publisher's note
"Encourages further learning with sidebars that help readers think concretely about the subject. . . . Altogether a pitch perfect presentation." SLJ
  Includes glossary

616.7   Diseases of musculoskeletal system

Gray, Susan Heinrichs
Living with juvenile rheumatoid arthritis. Child's World 2003 32p il (Living well) lib bdg $25.64
Grades: 5 6 7 8   **616.7**
  1. Arthritis
  ISBN 1-56766-104-1   LC 2002-2870

Gray, Susan Heinrichs—Continued

This title "leads off with an introduction to a young person who has [juvenile rheumatoid arthritis]. Subsequent chapters explain the physiology of the illness, what causes it, and what it's like to live with it. [The concluding section looks] at possible treatments and potential cures. [The text is] clear and simple, double spaced, and punctuated by colorful exemplary photos of kids dealing with the disease." SLJ

Includes glossary and bibliographical references

Hoffmann, Gretchen

Osteoporosis; [by] Gretchen Hoffmann. Marshall Cavendish Benchmark 2007 c2008 64p il (Health alert) lib bdg $21.95

Grades: 4 5 6 7   **616.7**
   1. Osteoporosis
   ISBN 978-0-7614-2702-5   LC 2007008787

This describes what it is like to have osteoporosis, what it is, its history and its diagnosis and treatment

Includes glossary and bibliographical references

616.8 Diseases of nervous system and mental disorders

Ali-Walsh, Rasheda

I'll hold your hand so you won't fall; a child's guide to Parkinson's disease; [by] Rasheda Ali; foreword for Muhammad Ali. Merit 2005 40p il $19.95 *

Grades: 2 3 4   **616.8**
   1. Parkinson's disease
   ISBN 1-873413-13-0

"Ali's father, Muhammad Ali, suffers from Parkinson's disease, and she answers questions children may have about the illness. . . . The text is well written and basic, without being oversimplified. . . . A short CD-ROM of the author introducing the book and its contents is included. An excellent overview written in an approachable style that will be reassuring to young readers." SLJ

Bender, Lionel

Explaining epilepsy. Smart Apple Media 2010 45p il (Explaining) lib bdg $34.25

Grades: 5 6 7 8   **616.8**
   1. Epilepsy
   ISBN 978-1-59920-309-6 (lib bdg); 1-59920-309-X (lib bdg)   LC 2008-49292

Describes the nature, symptoms, and possible causes of epilepsy, gives a history of its study, and discusses its treatment

The book provides a "basic [overview] of the health concerns related to the disease; information on diagnosis and treatment; and a discussion of the challenges or complications experienced by the affected person and their family/friends, and how to manage those problems. . . . The incorporation of quotes and personal accounts in 'Case Notes' sidebars adds to the sensitive tone found throughout [the title]." SLJ

Includes glossary and bibliographical references

Bjorklund, Ruth

Cerebral palsy. Marshall Cavendish Benchmark 2007 64p il (Health alert) lib bdg $31.36 *

Grades: 4 5 6 7   **616.8**
   1. Cerebral palsy
   ISBN 978-0-7614-2209-9 (lib bdg); 0-7614-2209-9 (lib bdg)   LC 2006-15818

"Explores the history, causes, symptoms, treatments, and future of cerebral palsy." Publisher's note

Includes glossary and bibliographical references

Epilepsy. Marshall Cavendish Benchmark 2007 63p il (Health alert) lib bdg $21.95 *

Grades: 4 5 6 7   **616.8**
   1. Epilepsy
   ISBN 978-0-7614-2206-8 (lib bdg); 0-7614-2206-4 (lib bdg)   LC 2006-15816

"Explores the history, causes, symptoms, treatments, and future of epilepsy and seizure disorders." Publisher's note

Includes glossary and bibliographical references

Brill, Marlene Targ, 1945-

Multiple sclerosis; [by] Marlene Targ Brill. Marshall Cavendish Benchmark 2007 c2008 64p il (Health alert) lib bdg $21.95

Grades: 4 5 6 7   **616.8**
   1. Multiple sclerosis
   ISBN 978-0-7614-2699-8   LC 2007008789

This describes what it is like to have mulitiple sclerosis, what it is, its history, and living with the disease.

Includes glossary and bibliographical references

Colligan, L. H.

Sleep disorders; by L. H. Colligan. Marshall Cavendish Benchmark 2009 64p il (Health alert) $22.95

Grades: 4 5 6 7   **616.8**
   1. Sleep disorders
   ISBN 978-0-7614-2913-5; 0-7614-2913-1

"Provides comprehensive information on the causes, treatment, and history of sleep disorders." Publisher's note

Includes glossary

Klosterman, Lorrie

Meningitis; [by] Lorrie Klosterman. Marshall Cavendish Benchmark 2007 64p il (Health alert) lib bdg $31.36 *

Grades: 4 5 6 7   **616.8**
   1. Meningitis
   ISBN 978-0-7614-2211-2 (lib bdg); 0-7614-2211-0 (lib bdg)   LC 2006015819

"Explores the history, causes, symptoms, treatments, and future of different types of meningitis." Publisher's note

Includes glossary and bibliographical references

Levete, Sarah

Explaining cerebral palsy. Smart Apple Media 2010 45p il (Explaining) lib bdg $34.25

Grades: 5 6 7 8 **616.8**

1. Cerebral palsy

ISBN 978-1-59920-311-9 (lib bdg); 1-59920-311-1 (lib bdg) LC 2008-49287

Describes the illness, including its causes, how it is diagnosed, current treatment methods, and how those with cerebral palsy live everyday lives

The book provides a "basic [overview] of the health concerns related to the disease; information on diagnosis and treatment; and a discussion of the challenges or complications experienced by the affected person and their family/friends, and how to manage those problems. . . . The incorporation of quotes and personal accounts in 'Case Notes' sidebars adds to the sensitive tone found throughout [the title]." SLJ

Includes glossary and bibliographical references

Petreycik, Rick

Headaches; [by] Rick Petreycik. Marshall Cavendish Benchmark 2007 64p il (Health alert) lib bdg $31.36 *

Grades: 4 5 6 7 **616.8**

1. Headache

ISBN 978-0-7614-2210-5 (lib bdg); 0-7614-2210-2 (lib bdg) LC 2006015815

"Explores the history, causes, symptoms, treatments, and future of different types of headaches." Publisher's note

Includes glossary and bibliographical references

616.85 Miscellaneous diseases of nervous system and mental disorders

Bjorklund, Ruth

Eating disorders. Marshall Cavendish Benchmark 2005 c2006 64p il (Health alert) lib bdg $32.79

Grades: 4 5 6 7 **616.85**

1. Eating disorders

ISBN 978-0-7614-1914-3 (lib bdg); 0-7614-1914-4 (lib bdg)

"Discusses eating disorders and their effects on people and society." Publisher's note

"Clear archival photos and photomicrographs support the text." Horn Book Guide

Includes glossary and bibliographical references

Brill, Marlene Targ, 1945-

Autism; [by] Marlene Targ Brill. Marshall Cavendish Benchmark 2007 c2008 64p il (Health alert) lib bdg $21.95

Grades: 4 5 6 7 **616.85**

1. Autism

ISBN 978-0-7614-2700-1 LC 2007008786

This describes what it is like to have autism, what it is, its history, and living with the disease.

Includes glossary and bibliographical references

Down syndrome. Marshall Cavendish Benchmark 2007 64p il (Health alert) lib bdg $31.36 *

Grades: 4 5 6 7 **616.85**

1. Down syndrome

ISBN 978-0-7614-2207-5 (lib bdg); 0-7614-2207-2 (lib bdg) LC 2006-15817

"Explores the history, causes, symptoms, treatments, and future of Down syndrome." Publisher's note

Includes glossary and bibliographical references

Capaccio, George

ADD and ADHD; [by] George Capaccio. Marshall Cavendish Benchmark 2007 c2008 64p il (Health alert) lib bdg $21.95

Grades: 4 5 6 7 **616.85**

1. Attention deficit disorder

ISBN 978-0-7614-2705-6 LC 2007008790

This describes what it is like to have Attention Deficit Disorder or Attention Deficit Hyperactivity Disorder, what they are, their history, and living with the disorders.

Includes glossary and bibliographical references

Landau, Elaine

Dyslexia; by Elaine Landau. Franklin Watts 2004 79p (Life balance) lib bdg $19.50; pa $6.95 *

Grades: 5 6 7 8 **616.85**

1. Dyslexia

ISBN 0-531-12217-4 (lib bdg); 0-531-16612-0 (pa) LC 2003-7142

Contents: Being dyslexic; Dyslexia; Getting help; Questions and answers about dyslexia

"Narration by dyslexics combines with an overview of the disorder to give readers an informative and thought-provoking look at this often misunderstood condition. Beginning with the struggles of a young student to cover for his difficulties, the book goes on to describe the various manifestations of dyslexia, therapies, and outcomes." SLJ

Includes glossary and bibliographical references

Lynette, Rachel

Anorexia. Kidhaven Press 2006 48p il (Understanding diseases and disorders) $23.70

Grades: 4 5 6 **616.85**

1. Anorexia nervosa

ISBN 0-7377-3176-1

This book explains who is at risk for developing anorexia, possible causes, the physical and psychological effects of the disorder and how it is treated.

Includes glossary and bibliographical references

Quinn, Patricia O.

Attention, girls! a guide to learn all about your AD/HD; illustrated by Carl Pearce. Magination Press 2009 119p il $16.95; pa $12.95

Grades: 4 5 6 7 **616.85**

1. Attention deficit disorder

ISBN 978-1-4338-0447-2; 1-4338-0447-6; 978-1-4338-0448-9 (pa); 1-4338-0448-4 (pa) LC 2008054524

Quinn, Patricia O.—*Continued*

"Quinn has attention deficit hyperactivity disorder and is a medical doctor; she addresses the types of AD/HD; who can help; differences between girls and boys with AD/HD; making friends; talking with adults about the condition; relaxation techniques; and medication. Her aim is to give girls a variety of ways to manage their disorders. . . . The book is attractive and inviting with colorful cartoon illustrations, sidebars, and highlighted reminders." SLJ

Robbins, Lynette

How to deal with ADHD. PowerKids Press 2010 24p il (Kids' health) lib bdg $21.25

Grades: 2 3 4   **616.85**

1. Attention deficit disorder

ISBN 978-1-4042-8140-0 (lib bdg); 1-4042-8140-1 (lib bdg)   LC 2009-6412

"Hypothetical situations with fictional characters put readers in the moment and provide a solid foundation for comprehending [ADHD]. . . . Robbins maintains a comforting tone, reassuring readers that it is possible to lead active lives with proper attention to diet and guidance from parents and doctors." SLJ

Includes glossary

How to deal with autism. PowerKids Press 2010 24p il (Kids' health) lib bdg $21.25

Grades: 2 3 4   **616.85**

1. Autism

ISBN 978-1-4042-8142-4 (lib bdg); 1-4042-8142-8 (lib bdg)   LC 2009-7862

"Hypothetical situations with fictional characters put readers in the moment and provide a solid foundation for comprehending [autism]. . . . Robbins maintains a comforting tone, reassuring readers that it is possible to lead active lives with proper attention to diet and guidance from parents and doctors." SLJ

Includes glossary

Routh, Kristina, 1961-

Down syndrome; [by] Kristina Routh. Heinemann Library 2004 56p il (Just the facts) $23

Grades: 5 6 7 8   **616.85**

1. Down syndrome

ISBN 1-4034-5145-1   LC 2003-22568

Provides an overview of Down's syndrome, describing what it is, the history of this disorder, what it is like to live with Down's syndrome, and some of the available treatments

This is "well written and substantive without being overly technical." SLJ

Roy, Jennifer Rozines

Depression. Benchmark Books 2005 64p il (Health alert) lib bdg $28.50 *

Grades: 4 5 6 7   **616.85**

1. Depression (Psychology)

ISBN 0-7614-1800-8   LC 2004-5970

Contents: What depression is like; Defining the disease; The history of depression; Living with depression; Coping with depression; Conclusion

The author explains "the causes, physiology, treatments, and complications associated with [depression]. The [book is] well organized. . . . The photos are colorful and . . . some are startling, including the brain scans of a patient . . . who suffers from depression." SLJ

Includes bibliographical references

Royston, Angela

Explaining down syndrome. Smart Apple Media 2010 45p il (Explaining) lib bdg $34.25

Grades: 5 6 7 8   **616.85**

1. Down syndrome

ISBN 978-1-59920-308-9 (lib bdg); 1-59920-308-1 (lib bdg)   LC 2008-49291

This book about down syndrome provides a "basic [overview] of the health concerns related to the disease; information on diagnosis and treatment; and a discussion of the challenges or complications experienced by the affected person and their family/friends, and how to manage those problems. . . . The incorporation of quotes and personal accounts in 'Case Notes' sidebars adds to the sensitive tone found throughout [the title]." SLJ

Includes glossary

Shapiro, Ouisie

Autism and me; sibling stories; photographs by Steven Vote. Albert Whitman 2009 unp il $16.99

Grades: 3 4 5 6   **616.85**

1. Autism 2. Siblings

ISBN 978-0-8075-0487-1; 0-8075-0487-4

LC 2008-31700

Children tell their stories of what it is like to live with a sibling who has autism.

"The children's emotions ring true, telling what they love about their sibling; the preaching comes from their hearts. This book would be useful in families and in classrooms to help explain both the struggles and the triumphs of living with someone who has this disorder." SLJ

Silverstein, Alvin

The ADHD update; understanding attention-deficit/hyperactivity disorder; [by] Alvin and Virginia Silverstein and Laura Silverstein Nunn. Enslow Publishers 2008 112p il (Disease update) lib bdg $31.93

Grades: 5 6 7 8   **616.85**

1. Attention deficit disorder

ISBN 978-0-7660-2800-5 (lib bdg); 0-7660-2800-3 (lib bdg)   LC 2007-13853

This describes Attention-deficit hyperactivity disorder (ADHD) and its history, diagnosis and treatment, living with it, and its future

"This book is an excellent primer on AD/HD." Sci Books Films

Includes glossary and bibliographical references

Silverstein, Alvin—*Continued*

The eating disorders update; understanding anorexia, bulimia, and binge eating; [by] Alvin and Virginia Silverstein and Laura Silverstein Nunn. Enslow Publishers 2008 128p il (Disease update) lib bdg $31.93

Grades: 5 6 7 8 **616.85**

    1. Eating disorders 2. Anorexia nervosa 3. Bulimia

    ISBN 978-0-7660-2802-9 (lib bdg); 0-7660-2802-X (lib bdg)   LC 2007013985

"An introduction to the history and most up-to-date research and treatment of eating disorders." Publisher's note

Includes glossary and bibliographical references

Skotko, Brian

Fasten your seatbelt; a crash course on Down syndrome for brothers and sisters; [by] Brian G. Skotko and Susan P. Levine. Woodbine House 2009 191p il pa $18.95

Grades: 4 5 6 7 **616.85**

    1. Down syndrome 2. Siblings

    ISBN 978-1-890627-86-7 (pa); 1-890627-86-0 (pa)   LC 2008049753

"Skotko and Levine address preteens and teenagers who have a sibling with Down syndrome, answering questions that have been generated through their work with this population. . . . With a wealth of information, numerous resources, and the reassurance that all siblings of people with disabilities sometimes go through periods of contradictory feelings, this is an excellent guide for young people who are trying to figure out how to negotiate an often-confusing relationship." SLJ

Includes bibliographical references

Snedden, Robert

Explaining autism. Smart Apple Media 2010 45p il (Explaining) lib bdg $34.25

Grades: 5 6 7 8 **616.85**

    1. Autism 2. Asperger's syndrome

    ISBN 978-1-59920-307-2 (lib bdg); 1-59920-307-3 (lib bdg)   LC 2008-49285

Describes the illness, including its symptoms, how it affects physical and mental health, current treatments, and how people with autism live everyday lives

"The incorporation of quotes and personal accounts in 'Case Notes' sidebars adds to the sensitive tone found throughout [the title]." SLJ

Includes glossary and bibliographical references

Taylor, John F., 1944-

The survival guide for kids with ADD or ADHD; [by] John F. Taylor. Free Spirit Pub. 2006 119p il pa $13.95

Grades: 3 4 5 **616.85**

    1. Attention deficit disorder

    ISBN 978-1-57542-195-7 (pa); 1-57542-195-X (pa)   LC 2005033737

This "opens with suggestions on how to use the book and . . . definitions of the disorders, including quotations from attention deficit disorder (ADD) and attention defi-

cit hyperactivity disorder (ADHD) youth themselves. The book's following chapters deal with controlling behavior, making decisions, taking medicine, eating properly, getting along with family members, working well in school, and making and keeping friends. The last chapter gives . . . advice about managing 'strong feelings,' such as using relaxation techniques and talking with others." Voice of Youth Advocates

"Packed with good advice, this guide will catch readers' eyes with its bright cover, varied fonts, and cartoon-style illustrations. The writing is clear and kid-friendly." SLJ

Van Niekerk, Clarabelle, 1952-

Understanding Sam and Asperger Syndrome; [by] Clarabelle van Niekerk and Liezl Venter; illustrated by Clarabelle van Niekerk. Skeezel Press 2008 unp il $17.95

Grades: PreK K 1 2 **616.85**

    1. Asperger's syndrome

    ISBN 978-0-9747217-1-2; 0-9747217-1-9

"A third-person past-tense narrative tells the story of Sam, a boy with Asperger Syndrome. . . . Because of the interesting story line, the positive approach, and the notion that others can learn to help Sam instead of expecting him to change, this is an excellent introduction to the topic. The pictures are bright and lively, showing mostly happy faces. The book concludes with 10 helpful tips to remember when a friend or a classmate has Asperger's." SLJ

616.89   Mental disorders

Rashkin, Rachel

Feeling better; a kid's book about therapy; by Rachel Rashkin; illustrated by Bonnie Adamson. Magination Press 2005 48p il $14.95; pa $8.95

Grades: 4 5 6 7 **616.89**

    1. Psychotherapy

    ISBN 1-59147-237-7; 1-59147-238-5 (pa)   LC 2004022727

"Using a journal format, 12-year-old Maya chronicles her emotional ups and downs and describes the process of psychotherapy." Publisher's note

"Clearly written and well-organized. . . . Animated black-and-white sketches portray the girl's various emotions. This title gently encourages kids who are struggling with issues to seek help." SLJ

616.9   Other diseases

Berger, Melvin, 1927-

Germs make me sick! illustrated by Marylin Hafner. rev ed. HarperCollins Pubs. 1995 32p il (Let's-read-and-find-out science) hardcover o.p. pa $4.99

Grades: K 1 2 3 **616.9**

    1. Bacteria 2. Viruses

    ISBN 0-06-024250-7 (lib bdg); 0-06-445154-2 (pa)   LC 93-27059

First published 1985

Berger, Melvin, 1927-—*Continued*

Explains how bacteria and viruses affect the human body and how the body fights them

This features "Hafner's lively color cartoon illustrations. . . . [It offers a] lively combination of fact and narrative that has made this a great title for easy reading and for sharing aloud." Booklist

Colligan, L. H.

Tick-borne illnesses; by L. H. Colligan. Marshall Cavendish Benchmark 2009 64p il (Health alert) $22.95

Grades: 4 5 6 7   **616.9**

1. Tick-borne diseases

ISBN 978-0-7614-2914-2; 0-7614-2914-X

                   LC 2007-38517

"Provides comprehensive information on the causes, treatment, and history of tick-borne illnesses." Publisher's note

Includes glossary

Hoffmann, Gretchen

Chicken pox; by Gretchen Hoffmann. Marshall Cavendish Benchmark 2009 62p il (Health alert) $22.95

Grades: 4 5 6 7   **616.9**

1. Chickenpox

ISBN 978-0-7614-2916-6; 0-7614-2916-6

"Provides comprehensive information on the causes, treatment, and history of chickenpox." Publisher's note

Includes glossary

Mononucleosis; [by] Gretchen Hoffmann. Marshall Cavendish Benchmark 2006 64p il (Health alert) lib bdg $28.50 *

Grades: 4 5 6 7   **616.9**

1. Mononucleosis

ISBN 0-7614-1915-2   LC 2005005001

This describes the symptoms and causes of mononucleosis, its history, diagnosis and treatment.

This is "well-designed and easy-to-use . . . with accurate and reliable information. Colorful photos, micrographs, and sidebars appear throughout." SLJ

Includes glossary and bibliographical references

Jarrow, Gail, 1952-

Chiggers; [by] Gail Jarrow. KidHaven Press 2004 32p il (Parasites) $22.45

Grades: 4 5 6   **616.9**

1. Mites

ISBN 0-7377-1778-5   LC 2003-9614

Contents: The chigger: a young mite; Attack on humans; The chigger disease; Avoiding chigger bites

"Several short chapters briefly describe the distinctive physical and behavioral characteristics of [chiggers] and special characteristics of particular species. [The book] also [highlights] the symptoms, victims' experiences, the organisms' potential threats as disease vectors, current treatments, and prevention methods. . . . Clear, color photographs illustrate the [text]. . . . Well organized and clearly written." SLJ

Klosterman, Lorrie

Rabies; [by] Lorrie Klosterman. Marshall Cavendish Benchmark 2007 c2008 64p il (Health alert) lib bdg $21.95

Grades: 4 5 6 7   **616.9**

1. Rabies

ISBN 978-0-7614-2704-9   LC 2007008788

This describes what it is like to have rabies, what it is, its history, and its prevention, diagnosis, and treatment.

Includes glossary and bibliographical references

Kornberg, Arthur, 1918-2007

Germ stories; illustrations by Adam Alaniz; photography by Roberto Kolter. University Science Books 2007 70p il $22

Grades: 2 3 4   **616.9**

1. Microbiology 2. Bacteria

ISBN 978-1-891389-51-1; 1-891389-51-3

                  LC 2007-09960

"This book of poems is a visual and lyrical journey into the wonderful world of . . . germs. . . . Nobel Prize winner Arthur Kornberg gives readers a look at the structures, methods, and cycles of germs. . . . The poetry is easy and flowing. Cartoon germs—fanged slime bacteria and wispy penicillin—are bright additions. After each poem is an electron micrograph, plus a visual comparison to help children understand just how small germs are." Libr Media Connect

Includes glossary

Landau, Elaine

Chickenpox. Marshall Cavendish Benchmark 2010 32p il (Head-to-toe health) $28.50

Grades: 2 3 4   **616.9**

1. Chickenpox

ISBN 978-0-7614-3498-6; 0-7614-3498-4

                  LC 2008-10782

"Provides basic information about chickenpox and its prevention." Publisher's note

"The book will satisfy researchers as well as those with a personal interest in the virus. . . . [This is] well-organized, informative." SLJ

Includes glossary and bibliographical references

Lynette, Rachel

Leprosy; [by] Rachel Lynette. KidHaven Press 2006 48p il (Understanding diseases and disorders) $23.70

Grades: 4 5 6   **616.9**

1. Leprosy

ISBN 0-7377-3172-9   LC 2005012168

This describes the history, causes, diagnosis, and treatment of leprosy.

"A solid, up-to-date examination of the disease. . . . Lucid text . . . presents the factual material in an understandable style that is unburdened by medical jargon." SLJ

Includes bibliographical references

Ollhoff, Jim, 1959-
The Black Death. ABDO Pub. Co. 2010 32p il map (A history of germs) lib bdg $27.07
Grades: 3 4 5 6 **616.9**
1. Plague
ISBN 978-1-60453-497-9 (lib bdg); 1-60453-497-4 (lib bdg) LC 2008-55061
This book "examines the plague's origins, causes, effects, cures, and historical legacy. . . . The short, informative chapters provide plenty of details for reports. The illustrations, many of which are color photos, enhance the information." SLJ
Includes glossary

The germ detectives. ABDO Pub. Co. 2010 32p il (A history of germs) lib bdg $27.07
Grades: 3 4 5 6 **616.9**
1. Leeuwenhoek, Antoni van, 1632-1723
2. Semmelweis, Ignác Fülöp, 1818-1865 3. Lister, Joseph, Baron, 1827-1912 4. Pasteur, Louis, 1822-1895
5. Koch, Robert, 1843-1910 6. Bacteria
7. Microbiology 8. Scientists
ISBN 978-1-60453-499-3 (lib bdg); 1-60453-499-0 (lib bdg) LC 2008-55062
This book "highlights the work of Antoni van Leeuwenhoek, Ignaz Semmelweis, Joseph Lister, Louis Pasteur, and Robert Koch, all of whom contributed to current knowledge about germs. . . . The short, informative chapters provide plenty of details for reports. The illustrations, many of which are color photos, enhance the information." SLJ
Includes glossary

Malaria. ABDO Pub. Co. 2010 32p il (A history of germs) lib bdg $27.07
Grades: 3 4 5 6 **616.9**
1. Malaria
ISBN 978-1-60453-500-6 (lib bdg); 1-60453-500-8 (lib bdg)
"*Malaria* explains why the disease is so deadly, notes types of treatments, looks at efforts to control it, and suggests the future development of a vaccine. . . . The short, informative chapters provide plenty of details for reports. The illustrations, many of which are color photos, enhance the information." SLJ

Smallpox. ABDO Pub. Co. 2010 32p il (A history of germs) lib bdg $27.07
Grades: 3 4 5 6 **616.9**
1. Jenner, Edward, 1749-1823 2. Smallpox
ISBN 978-1-60453-501-3 (lib bdg); 1-60453-501-6 (lib bdg)
"*Smallpox* discusses the disease's symptoms, highlights Edward Jenner's work in developing a vaccine, and touches upon the potential use of the virus as a biological weapon. . . . The short, informative chapters provide plenty of details for reports. The illustrations, many of which are color photos, enhance the information." SLJ
Includes glossary

616.97   Diseases of immune system

Ballard, Carol
Explaining food allergies. Smart Apple Media 2010 45p il (Explaining) $23.95
Grades: 5 6 7 8 **616.97**
1. Food allergy
ISBN 978-1-59920-316-4; 1-59920-316-2
LC 2008049936
This "does an excellent job of discussing complex clinical science while showing what daily life is like for kids living with food allergies, from the signs and symptoms to the tests and treatments. . . . This blend of the technical and the personal will have wide appeal." Booklist

Hicks, Terry Allan
Allergies. Marshall Cavendish Benchmark 2006 64p il (Health alert) lib bdg $28.50 *
Grades: 4 5 6 7 **616.97**
1. Allergy
ISBN 0-7614-1918-7 LC 2005-05000
This describes the causes of allergies, their history, and how to live with them.
This is "well-designed and easy-to-use . . . with accurate and reliable information. Colorful photos, micrographs, and sidebars appear throughout." SLJ
Includes glossary and bibliographical references

Landau, Elaine
Food allergies. Marshall Cavendish Benchmark 2010 32p il (Head-to-toe health) lib bdg $28.50
Grades: 2 3 4 **616.97**
1. Food allergy
ISBN 978-0-7614-3500-6 (lib bdg); 0-7614-3500-X (lib bdg) LC 2008-10785
"Provides basic information about food allergies and their prevention." Publisher's note
"Color photographs appear throughout. . . . [This is] well-organized, informative." SLJ
Includes glossary and bibliographical references

Robbins, Lynette
How to deal with allergies. PowerKids Press 2010 24p il (Kids' health) lib bdg $21.25
Grades: 2 3 4 **616.97**
1. Allergy
ISBN 978-1-4042-8139-4 (lib bdg); 1-4042-8139-8 (lib bdg) LC 2009-2616
"Hypothetical situations with fictional characters put readers in the moment and provide a solid foundation for comprehending [allergies]. . . . Robbins maintains a comforting tone, reassuring readers that it is possible to lead active lives with proper attention to diet and guidance from parents and doctors." SLJ
Includes glossary

Royston, Angela
Allergies. Black Rabbit Books 2009 30p il (How's your health?) lib bdg $27.10
Grades: 1 2 3   **616.97**
1. Allergy
ISBN 978-1-59920-220-4 (lib bdg); 1-59920-220-4 (lib bdg)   LC 2007-35174
First published 2004 by Heinemann Library
"Describes the symptoms and treatment of food allergies, skin allergies, and breathing allergies." Publisher's note
"Encourages further learning with sidebars that help readers think concretely about the subject. . . . Altogether a pitch perfect presentation." SLJ
Includes glossary and bibliographical references

Silverstein, Alvin
The AIDS update; [by] Alvin and Virginia Silverstein and Laura Silverstein Nunn. Enslow Publishers 2007 c2008 128p il (Disease update) lib bdg $31.93
Grades: 5 6 7 8   **616.97**
1. AIDS (Disease)
ISBN 978-0-7660-2746-6 (lib bdg); 0-7660-2746-5 (lib bdg)   LC 2006100475
"Discusses the causes, diagnoses, treatment methods, and future of AIDS." Publisher's note
Includes glossary and bibliographical references

Taylor-Butler, Christine, 1959-
Food allergies. Children's Press 2008 48p il (True book) $26
Grades: 3 4 5   **616.97**
1. Food allergy
ISBN 0-531-16858-1; 978-0-531-16858-5
LC 2007-036016
"With a lively format featuring a colorful, image-rich layout and conversational text, this entry in the True Book: Health and the Human Body series provides an accessible introduction to food allergies. . . . Book and Web resources, along with a somewhat scattershot glossary and index, conclude this useful title." Booklist
Includes glossary and bibliographical references

Thomas, Pat, 1959-
I think I am going to sneeze; a first look at allergies; [by] Pat Thomas; illustrated by Lesley Harker. Barron's Educational Series 2008 29p il pa $6.99
Grades: PreK K 1 2   **616.97**
1. Allergy
ISBN 978-0-7641-3900-0 (pa); 0-7641-39002 (pa)
This "title covers the causes and effects of allergies and treatments and reassures youngsters that they don't have to be left out of school activities. Sidebars . . . ask questions about children's personal experiences and thoughts, which can be used as discussion starters. [The] title ends with an extensive note to parents, with practical advice for . . . helping children cope with allergies. [This is a] solid [addition] for most collections." SLJ

616.99 Tumors and miscellaneous communicable diseases

Buckmaster, Marjorie L.
Skin cancer; [by] Marjorie L. Buckmaster. Marshall Cavendish Benchmark 2007 c2008 60p il (Health alert) lib bdg $21.95
Grades: 4 5 6 7   **616.99**
1. Cancer 2. Skin—Diseases
ISBN 978-0-7614-2703-2   LC 2007024623
This describes what it is like to have skin cancer, what it is, its history, and diagnosing and treating skin cancer.
Includes glossary and bibliographical references

Silverstein, Alvin
The breast cancer update; [by] Alvin and Virginia Silverstein and Laura Silverstein Nunn. Enslow Publishers 2008 128p il (Disease update) lib bdg $31.93
Grades: 5 6 7 8   **616.99**
1. Breast cancer
ISBN 978-0-7660-2747-3 (lib bdg); 0-7660-2747-3 (lib bdg)   LC 2006-32821
This offers a history of breast cancer, a definition of it, and describes its diagnosis and treatment, prevention, and future
Includes glossary and bibliographical references

Watters, Debbie, 1961-
Where's Mom's hair? a family's journey through cancer; by Debbie Watters; with Haydn and Emmett Watters; photographs by Sophie Hogan. Second Story Press 2005 31p il pa $10.95
Grades: 2 3 4   **616.99**
1. Cancer 2. Hair
ISBN 1-896764-94-0
"When the author underwent chemotherapy following cancer surgery, she faced the loss of her hair with courage and humor. Family and friends gathered for a 'haircutting party,' where her husband and two young sons . . . joined her in getting buzz cuts. . . . The gentle kindness conveyed in the often-humorous writing will reassure young children facing similar circumstances." SLJ

617 Miscellaneous branches of medicine. Surgery

Woog, Adam, 1953-
The bionic hand. Norwood House Press 2009 48p il (A great idea) lib bdg $25.27
Grades: 3 4 5 6   **617**
1. Artificial limbs 2. Bionics
ISBN 978-1-59953-341-4 (lib bdg); 1-59953-341-3 (lib bdg)   LC 2009-15640
"Explores the development and creation of the i-LIMB which is the first commercially available bionic hand." Publisher's note

Woog, Adam, 1953-—*Continued*

"With a mix of scientific terminology and accessible sentence structure, the [book] effectively [describes] how the [idea] took shape and [was] put into practice by the scientists involved. . . . [This] is a fascinating look at how biology and technology are being used to create more useful prostheses for those who have lost a limb." SLJ

Includes glossary and bibliographical references

617.1   Injuries and wounds

Cobb, Vicki, 1938-

Your body battles a broken bone; written by Vicki Cobb; photomicrographs by Dennis Kunkel; illustrations by Andrew N. Harris. Millbrook Press 2009 32p il (Body battles) lib bdg $25.26

Grades: 3 4 5   617.1

  1. Fractures 2. Bones

  ISBN 978-0-8225-7468-2 (lib bdg); 0-8225-7468-3 (lib bdg)   LC 2008002837

This book provides comic illustrations and photomicrographs that describe how the body heals a broken bone

"Many of the vibrant illustrations anthropomorphize various cells and other 'battle' participants, making the science explained approachable and easy to understand. Photomicrographs further illuminate the text. These amazing pictures, taken with a scanning electron microscope, are greatly magnified and colored to highlight certain features." SLJ

Includes glossary and bibliographical references

Your body battles a skinned knee; written by Vicki Cobb; photomicrographs by Dennis Kunkel; illustrations by Andrew N. Harris. Millbrook Press 2009 32p il (Body battles) lib bdg $25.26

Grades: 3 4 5   617.1

  1. Wounds and injuries 2. Skin 3. Immune system

  ISBN 978-0-8225-6814-8 (lib bdg); 0-8225-6814-4 (lib bdg)   LC 2008002826

"By combining simple yet engaging text; comic-like illustrations; and greatly magnified photomicrographs, this book describes the healing process of a bloodied knee in a fashion that is both entertaining and easy to understand." Booklist

Includes glossary and bibliographical references

Landau, Elaine

Bites and stings; by Elaine Landau. Marshall Cavendish Benchmark 2009 32p il (Head-to-toe health) lib bdg $28.50

Grades: 2 3 4   617.1

  1. Bites and stings

  ISBN 978-0-7614-2850-3 (lib bdg); 0-7614-2850-X (lib bdg)   LC 2007-43022

"Provides basic information about bites and stings and their prevention." Publisher's note

"Photo illustrations are apt and age appropriate. . . . Pervading the [book] . . . is an overall sense of reassurance that even if something hurts, 'all better' is never too far away. Appealing and readable nonfiction." SLJ

Includes glossary and bibliographical references

Broken bones; [by] Elaine Landau. Marshall Cavendish Benchmark 2009 32p il (Head-to-toe health) lib bdg $28.50

Grades: 2 3 4   617.1

  1. Fractures 2. Bones

  ISBN 978-0-7614-2847-3 (lib bdg); 0-7614-2847-X (lib bdg)   LC 2007-26665

"Provides basic information about the skeletal system, broken bones, and prevention." Publisher's note

"Photo illustrations are apt and age appropriate. . . . Pervading the [book] . . . is an overall sense of reassurance that even if something hurts, 'all better' is never too far away. Appealing and readable nonfiction." SLJ

Includes glossary and bibliographical references

Bumps, bruises, and scrapes; by Elaine Landau. Marshall Cavendish Benchmark 2009 32p il (Head-to-toe health) lib bdg $28.50

Grades: 2 3 4   617.1

  1. Wounds and injuries

  ISBN 978-0-7614-2849-7 (lib bdg); 0-7614-2849-6 (lib bdg)   LC 2007-26959

"Provides basic information about minor bumps, bruises, and scrapes, and their prevention." Publisher's note

"Photo illustrations are apt and age appropriate. . . . Pervading the [book] . . . is an overall sense of reassurance that even if something hurts, 'all better' is never too far away. Appealing and readable nonfiction." SLJ

Includes glossary and bibliographical references

Lew, Kristi, 1968-

Clot & scab; gross stuff about your scrapes, bumps, and bruises; illustrations by Michael Slack. Millbrook Press 2010 48p il (Gross body science) lib bdg $29.27

Grades: 4 5 6   617.1

  1. Wounds and injuries

  ISBN 978-0-8225-8965-5 (lib bdg); 0-8225-8965-6 (lib bdg)   LC 2008-45626

"Learn how your body repairs itself and what happens when something goes wrong." Publisher's note

"Solid information layered between sarcastic comments and kid-friendly terminology like fart, poop, barf, and puke will keep readers engaged. . . . Labeled, captioned (and graphic) photographs, cartoon-style illustrations, and micrographs add information." SLJ

Includes glossary and bibliographical references

Royston, Angela

Cuts, bruises, and breaks. Black Rabbit Books 2009 30p il (How's your health) lib bdg $27.10

Grades: 1 2 3   617.1

  1. Wounds and injuries

  ISBN 978-1-59920-222-8 (lib bdg); 1-59920-222-0 (lib bdg)

"Describes the causes and treatment of cuts, bruises, and broken bones, and how to prevent injuries." Publisher's note

"Encourages further learning with sidebars that help readers think concretely about the subject. . . . Altogether a pitch perfect presentation." SLJ

Includes glossary

617.6 Dentistry

Cobb, Vicki, 1938-
Your body battles a cavity; written by Vicki Cobb; photomicrographs by Dennis Kunkel; illustrations by Andrew N. Harris. Millbrook Press 2009 32p il (Body battles) lib bdg $25.26
Grades: 3 4 5   **617.6**
1. Teeth 2. Immune system
ISBN 978-0-8225-7469-9 (lib bdg); 0-8225-7469-1 (lib bdg)   LC 2008002827
With comic illustrations and photomicrographs, this shows what happens when a person gets a cavity, depicting the body's defenses as superheroes
Includes glossary and bibliographical references

Landau, Elaine
Cavities and toothaches; by Elaine Landau. Marshall Cavendish Benchmark 2008 32p il (Head-to-toe health) lib bdg $28.50
Grades: 2 3 4   **617.6**
1. Teeth 2. Dentistry
ISBN 978-0-7614-2848-0 (lib bdg); 0-7614-2848-8 (lib bdg)   LC 2007-19192
"Provides basic information about teeth, tooth decay, and the benefits of good oral hygiene." Publisher's note
"Photo illustrations are apt and age appropriate. . . . Pervading the [book] . . . is an overall sense of reassurance that even if something hurts, 'all better' is never too far away. Appealing and readable nonfiction." SLJ
Includes glossary and bibliographical references

Miller, Edward, 1964-
The tooth book; a guide to healthy teeth and gums; [by] Edward Miller. Holiday House 2008 unp il $16.95 *
Grades: K 1 2 3   **617.6**
1. Teeth 2. Dentistry
ISBN 978-0-8234-2092-6; 0-8234-2092-2
                                    LC 2007018302
"In this brightly illustrated picture book, Miller goes well beyond the basics of brushing, flossing, and visiting the dentist. Readers view the inside of a tooth and learn about primary and permanent teeth, decay, losing teeth, and dental first aid. Especially welcome is the emphasis on eating healthy foods and avoiding sugar. . . . The cleanly designed, computer-generated artwork is appealing, lively, and instructive." SLJ

Royston, Angela
Tooth decay. Black Rabbit Books 2009 30p il (How's your health) lib bdg $27.10
Grades: 1 2 3   **617.6**
1. Teeth
ISBN 978-1-59920-221-1 (lib bdg); 1-59920-221-2 (lib bdg)
First published 2004 by Heinemann Library
"Describes the causes, symptoms, and treatment of tooth decay and cavities and how to prevent them." Publisher's note

"Encourages further learning with sidebars that help readers think concretely about the subject. . . . Altogether a pitch perfect presentation." SLJ
Includes glossary

Why do I brush my teeth? QEB Pub. 2010 24p il (QEB my body) lib bdg $28.65
Grades: PreK K 1 2   **617.6**
1. Dentistry 2. Teeth
ISBN 978-1-59566-973-5 (lib bdg); 1-59566-973-6 (lib bdg)   LC 2009-15219
Introduces the structure and growth of the teeth, and outlines the principles of dental health and hygiene
"The information is straightforward, well presented, and easy to understand. . . . [This] title is well designed, filled with color photographs, and scattered with fact boxes." Libr Media Connect
Includes glossary and bibliographical references

Schuh, Mari C., 1975-
All about teeth; by Mari Schuh. Capstone Press 2008 24p il (Pebble plus. Healthy teeth) lib bdg $21.26; pa $5.95
Grades: K 1 2 3   **617.6**
1. Teeth
ISBN 978-1-4296-1238-8 (lib bdg); 1-4296-1238-X (lib bdg); 1-4296-1784-5 (pa); 978-1-4296-1784-0 (pa)
                                    LC 2007-27115
"Simple text, photographs, and diagrams present information about teeth, including how to take care of them properly." Publisher's note
"Feature[s] bright close-up photographs . . . and simple vocabulary and sentences to engage pre-readers as well as new readers." Horn Book Guide
Includes glossary and bibliographical references

Loose tooth; by Mari Schuh. Capstone Press 2008 24p il (Pebble plus. Healthy teeth) lib bdg $21.26; pa $6.95
Grades: K 1 2 3   **617.6**
1. Teeth
ISBN 978-1-4296-1243-2 (lib bdg); 1-4296-1243-6 (lib bdg); 978-1-4296-1789-5 (pa); 1-4296-1789-6 (pa)
                                    LC 2007-27208
"Simple text, photographs, and diagrams present information about having a loose tooth, including how they feel and how to take care of all teeth properly." Publisher's note
"Feature[s] bright close-up photographs . . . and simple vocabulary and sentences to engage pre-readers as well as new readers." Horn Book Guide
Includes glossary and bibliographical references

Thomas, Pat, 1959-
Do I have to go to the dentist? a first look at healthy teeth; [by] Pat Thomas; illustrated by Lesley Harker. Barron's Educational Series 2008 29p il pa $6.99
Grades: PreK K 1 2   **617.6**
1. Dentistry 2. Teeth
ISBN 978-0-7641-3901-7 (pa); 0-7641-3901-0 (pa)
This "book addresses the purpose of dental visits, what to expect, the dental exam and tooth cleaning, and

Thomas, Pat, 1959——*Continued*

cavities. . . . Sidebars . . . ask questions about children's personal experiences and thoughts, which can be used as discussion starters. [The] title ends with an extensive note to parents, with practical advice for lessening anxiety about going to the dentist. . . . [This is a] solid [addition] for most collections." SLJ

Ziefert, Harriet

ABC dentist; illustrated by Liz Murphy. Blue Apple Books 2008 unp il $15.95
Grades: K 1 2 3   **617.6**
  1. Dentistry 2. Alphabet
  ISBN 978-1-934706-31-2; 1-934706-31-0
                                        LC 2008005875
"From A ('appointment') to Z ('zillion times cleaner'), the bright, collage-filled pages feature facts about teeth and gums, assurances that a visit to the dentist won't hurt too much, and images of children getting care from friendly dentists and hygienists. The facts range from the basics . . . to the more specialized . . . while the . . . illustrations . . . offer a variety of views of mouths and teeth, including one nice use of an actual X-ray. . . . The book seeks to offer plenty of knowledge as well as comfort." Booklist

617.7   Ophthalmology

Bender, Lionel

Explaining blindness. Smart Apple Media 2010 45p il (Explaining) lib bdg $34.25
Grades: 5 6 7 8   **617.7**
  1. Blind
  ISBN 978-1-59920-310-2 (lib bdg); 1-59920-310-3 (lib bdg)
                                        LC 2008-49286
Describes blindness, including its possible causes, the different types of visual impairment, current treatments and cures, and how blind and visually impaired people live everyday lives
"The incorporation of quotes and personal accounts in 'Case Notes' sidebars adds to the sensitive tone found throughout [the title]." SLJ
Includes glossary

Silverstein, Alvin

Can you see the chalkboard? [by] Alvin Silverstein, Virginia Silverstein, and Laura Silverstein Nunn. Watts 2001 48p il (My health) lib bdg $22.50
Grades: 3 4 5   **617.7**
  1. Eye 2. Vision
  ISBN 0-531-11783-9   LC 00-28983
Describes the human eye and how it functions, various visual problems and how they are corrected, and how to take care of one's eyes
The text is "easy to read and [contains] a lot of information. The illustrations, sharp and in bright colors, are a combination of well-placed photographs, cartoons, and diagrams." SLJ
Includes glossary and bibliographical references

617.8   Otology and audiology

Cobb, Vicki, 1938-

Your body battles an earache; written by Vicki Cobb; photomicrographs by Dennis Kunkel; illustrated by Andrew N. Harris. Millbrook Press 2009 32p il (Body battles) lib bdg $25.26
Grades: 3 4 5   **617.8**
  1. Ear infections 2. Immune system
  ISBN 978-0-8225-6812-4 (lib bdg); 0-8225-6812-8 (lib bdg)
                                        LC 2008002846
Microphotographs and comic illustrations show what happens when a person has an earache
"Many of the vibrant illustrations anthropomorphize various cells and other 'battle' participants, making the science explained approachable and easy to understand. Photomicrographs further illuminate the text." SLJ
Includes glossary and bibliographical references

Levete, Sarah

Explaining deafness. Smart Apple Media 2010 45p il (Explaining) lib bdg $34.25
Grades: 5 6 7 8   **617.8**
  1. Deafness
  ISBN 978-1-59920-313-3 (lib bdg); 1-59920-313-8 (lib bdg)
                                        LC 2008-49289
Discusses the history, diagnosis, and treatment of deafness, including ways to cope with living with the condition
"The incorporation of quotes and personal accounts in 'Case Notes' sidebars adds to the sensitive tone found throughout [the title]." SLJ
Includes glossary, bibliographical references and filmography

617.9   Operative surgery and special fields of surgery

Jango-Cohen, Judith

Bionics; [by] Judith Jango-Cohen. Lerner Publications Co. 2007 48p il (Cool science) lib bdg $26.60
Grades: 4 5 6 7   **617.9**
  1. Bionics 2. Artificial organs
  ISBN 978-0-8225-5937-5 (lib bdg); 0-8225-5937-4 (lib bdg)
                                        LC 2005032221
This "introduction to the field of bionics is divided into four chapters: 'Replacing Parts,' 'Fixing Malfunctions,' 'Assisting the Senses,' and 'Facing the Future.' Jango-Cohen uses a number of personal stories and references to pop culture to engage readers. . . . The explanations are clearly written and easily understood. Colorful photographs and illustrations are featured throughout the text." SLJ
Includes bibliographical references

620.1 Engineering mechanics and materials

Hillman, Ben

How strong is it? a mighty book all about strength; [by] Ben Hillman. Scholastic Reference 2008 48p il (What's the big idea?) $14.99

Grades: 3 4 5   **620.1**

1. Power (Mechanics)

ISBN 978-0-439-91866-4; 0-439-91866-9

This describes the strength of such things as spiderwebs, bulldozers, wood, elephants, glue, lasers, hair, rope, and volcanoes.

"The conversational, fact-filled text and computer-manipulated illustrations add humor to this random sampling of awesome powers." Horn Book Guide

Langley, Andrew

Glass; [by] Andrew Langley. Crabtree Pub. Co. 2009 24p il (Everyday materials) lib bdg $21.27; pa $6.95

Grades: K 1 2 3   **620.1**

1. Glass

ISBN 978-0-7787-4126-8 (lib bdg); 0-7787-4126-5 (lib bdg); 978-0-7787-4134-3 (pa); 0-7787-4134-6 (pa)

LC 2008-24157

This title "introduces [glass] in an engaging style. The text and photos work together, progressing from a definition of the material to how it is manufactured and what it is used for. . . . [It] concludes with a recycling section, a simple comprehension quiz, and a topic web that offers extension ideas. The large type, bright photos, and uncluttered layout will allow large and small group use." SLJ

Includes glossary

Metal; [by] Andrew Langley. Crabtree Pub. Co. 2009 24p il (Everyday materials) lib bdg $21.27; pa $6.95

Grades: K 1 2 3   **620.1**

1. Metals

ISBN 978-0-7787-4127-5 (lib bdg); 0-7787-4127-3 (lib bdg); 978-0-7787-4134-3 (pa); 0-7787-4134-6 (pa)

LC 2008-24036

This title "introduces [metals] in an engaging style. The text and photos work together, progressing from a definition of the material to how it is manufactured and what it is used for. . . . [It] concludes with a recycling section, a simple comprehension quiz, and a topic web that offers extension ideas. The large type, bright photos, and uncluttered layout will allow large and small group use." SLJ

Includes glossary

Wood; [by] Andrew Langley. Crabtree Pub. Co. 2009 24p il (Everyday materials) lib bdg $21.27; pa $6.95

Grades: K 1 2 3   **620.1**

1. Wood

ISBN 978-0-7787-4130-5 (lib bdg); 0-7787-4130-3 (lib bdg); 978-0-7787-4137-4 (pa); 0-7787-4137-0 (pa)

LC 2008-24037

This title "introduces [wood] in an engaging style. The text and photos work together, progressing from a definition of the material to how it is manufactured and what it is used for. . . . [It] concludes with a recycling section, a simple comprehension quiz, and a topic web that offers extension ideas. The large type, bright photos, and uncluttered layout will allow large and small group use." SLJ

Includes glossary

Oxlade, Chris

Changing shape. Heinemann Library 2008 32p il (Changing materials) lib bdg $25.36; pa $7.99

Grades: K 1 2   **620.1**

1. Materials

ISBN 978-1-4329-3271-8 (lib bdg); 1-4329-3271-3 (lib bdg); 978-1-4329-3276-3 (pa); 1-4329-3276-4 (pa)

LC 2008-54586

Discusses "the properties of materials and whether or not they can bend or twist or are brittle, or are in liquid or gas form. . . . A few simple activities provide opportunities to experiment. The color photographs are engaging." SLJ

Includes glossary and bibliographical references

Joining materials; [by] Chris Oxlade. Crabtree Pub. Company 2008 32p il (Working with materials) lib bdg $26.60; pa $7.95

Grades: 2 3 4   **620.1**

1. Materials

ISBN 978-0-7787-3639-4 (lib bdg); 0-7787-3639-3 (lib bdg); 978-0-7787-3649-3 (pa); 0-7787-3649-0 (pa)

LC 2007027420

This describes how materials are joined with nuts, bolts, and screws, glue, wood joints, welding, soldering, sewing, tape, and velcro

This "title has numerous captioned color photographs. . . . The [book offers] three simple, easy, and safe reproducible experiments. . . . Students will appreciate the pleasing design, easy-to-read font, and direct, clear writing style." Libr Media Connect

Includes glossary and bibliographical references

Shaping materials; [by] Chris Oxlade. Crabtree Pub. Company 2008 32p il (Working with materials) lib bdg $26.60; pa $7.95

Grades: 2 3 4   **620.1**

1. Materials

ISBN 978-0-7787-3641-7 (lib bdg); 0-7787-3641-5 (lib bdg); 978-0-7787-3651-6 (pa); 0-7787-3651-2 (pa)

LC 2007027422

This describes how materials are shaped with scissors, molds, hammers, saws, chisels, and machine shapers, and by folding and bending, glassblowing, and clay modeling

This "title has numerous captioned color photographs. . . . The [book offers] three simple, easy, safe reproducible experiments. . . . Students will appreciate the pleasing design, easy-to-read font, and direct, clear writing." Libr Media Connect

Includes glossary and bibliographical references

Ward, David J. (David John)

Materials science; by D. J. Ward. Lerner Publications 2009 47p il (Cool science) lib bdg $26.60

Grades: 4 5 6   **620.1**
1. Materials
ISBN 978-0-8225-7588-7 (lib bdg); 0-8225-7588-4 (lib bdg)   LC 2007042176

This describes how scientists study the microscopic parts of materials such as plastic, glass, or stainless steel, how they learn how each part makes something hard or soft, strong or weak, or good or bad at carrying heat, and how they use that knowledge to create supermaterials to help make better sports equipment, tinier computer chips, and more.

Includes glossary and bibliographical references

621   Applied physics

Herweck, Don

Energy; science contributor, Sally Ride Science. Compass Point Books 2009 40p il (Mission: science) lib bdg $26.60

Grades: 4 5 6   **621**
1. Energy resources
ISBN 978-0-7565-3967-2 (lib bdg); 0-7565-3967-6 (lib bdg)   LC 2008-36546

Describes different forms of energy and how it is used.

Includes glossary and bibliographical references

Spilsbury, Richard, 1963-

What is energy? exploring science with hands-on activities; [by] Richard and Louise Spilsbury. Enslow Elementary 2008 32p il (In touch with basic science) lib bdg $22.60

Grades: 3 4 5   **621**
1. Power (Mechanics) 2. Energy resources 3. Force and energy 4. Science—Experiments
ISBN 978-0-7660-3099-2 (lib bdg); 0-7660-3099-7 (lib bdg)   LC 2007024521

This book includes "a discussion about what energy is and then moves on to examine heat energy, chemical energy, energy for life, electrical energy, and finally, renewable energy. Energy is such a broad topic, yet this small volume masterfully provides a good basis for understanding the concept." Sci Books Films

Includes glossary and bibliographical references

621.1   Steam engineering

O'Neal, Claire

How to use waste energy to heat and light your home. Mitchell Lane Publishers 2009 47p il (Tell your parents) lib bdg $21.50

Grades: 4 5 6 7   **621.1**
1. Recycling 2. Waste products as fuel
ISBN 978-1-58415-765-6 (lib bdg); 1-58415-765-8 (lib bdg)   LC 2009-4483

Explores how to reduce the amount of trash produced and stored by reusing items and recycling materials, and describes how these efforts can help protect the environment

This title "offers numerous facts and statistics, all of which are cited. . . . Chapters cover present-day issues and . . . are interspersed with full-color photographs and short 'Did You Know' trivia boxes. . . . Back matter includes detailed resource lists and 'Try This!' experiments." SLJ

Includes glossary and bibliographical references

621.3   Electrical, magnetic, optical, communications, computer engineering; electronics, lighting

Price, Sean, 1963-

The story behind electricity; [by] Sean Stewart Price. Heinemann Library 2009 32p il (True stories) $28.21

Grades: 3 4 5   **621.3**
1. Electrical engineering 2. Electricity
ISBN 978-1-4329-2339-6; 1-4329-2339-0   LC 2008043408

This answers such questions as: How does a lightning rod work? What animals use electricity? Why did Thomas Edison have to build a power station?

Includes bibliographical references

621.31   Generation, modification, storage, transmission of electric power

Bartholomew, Alan

Electric mischief; battery-powered gadgets kids can build; written by Alan Bartholomew; illustrated by Lynn Bartholomew. Kids Can Press 2002 48p il (Kids can do it) $12.95; pa $5.95

Grades: 4 5 6   **621.31**
1. Electric apparatus and appliances 2. Electricity
ISBN 1-55074-923-4; 1-55074-925-0 (pa)

This provides instructions for building 10 electric gadgets such as a bumper car, electric dice, and a robot hand

"Projects are clearly explained and easy to follow; colorful illustrations aid understanding. Materials required . . . are readily available at hardware stores." SLJ

Benduhn, Tea

Water power; by Tea Benduhn. Weekly Reader Pub. 2009 24p il (Energy for today) lib bdg $21; pa $5.95

Grades: 2 3 4   **621.31**
1. Water power 2. Energy resources
ISBN 978-0-8368-9264-2 (lib bdg); 0-8368-9264-X (lib bdg); 978-0-8368-9363-2 (pa); 0-8368-9363-8 (pa)   LC 2008012021

This explains how flowing water is used as an energy resource, and how it may be used in the future.

Benduhn, Tea—*Continued*

"New readers will be able to wrap their hands around the small, square size, and their minds around the clear, enlightening text. [This book has] crisp photos and strong back matter." Booklist

Includes glossary and bibliographical references

Wind power; by Tea Benduhn. Weekly Reader Pub. 2009 24p il (Energy for today) lib bdg $21; pa $5.95

Grades: 2 3 4   **621.31**

1. Wind power 2. Energy resources
ISBN 978-0-8368-9265-9 (lib bdg); 0-8368-9265-8 (lib bdg); 978-0-8368-9364-9 (pa); 0-8368-9364-6 (pa)
LC 2008012019

This explains how wind forms and the ways we may use it as an energy source in the future.

"New readers will be able to wrap their hands around the small, square size, and their minds around the clear enlightening text. [This book has] crisp photos and strong back matter." Booklist

Includes glossary and bibliographical references

Graf, Mike

How does a waterfall become electricity? Raintree 2008 32p il (How does it happen?) lib bdg $27.50; pa $7.99

Grades: 3 4 5   **621.31**

1. Water power 2. Electricity 3. Hydrodynamics
ISBN 978-1-4109-3448-2 (lib bdg); 1-4109-3448-9 (lib bdg); 978-1-4109-3456-7 (pa); 1-4109-3456-X (pa)
LC 2008-52653

The explains the cause and effect of waterfalls, and the many ways they can be used to make electricity.

"Information is clearly presented using a large font, diagrams, and photographs formatted to resemble Polaroid pictures. . . . A first-rate job answering some important scientific questions." SLJ

Includes glossary and bibliographical references

Lew, Kristi, 1968-

Goodbye, gasoline; the science of fuel cells. Compass Point Books 2009 48p il (Headline science) lib bdg $27.93

Grades: 5 6 7 8   **621.31**

1. Fuel cells
ISBN 978-0-7565-3521-6 (lib bdg); 0-7565-3521-2 (lib bdg)
LC 2008011729

This "clearly examines the history and technology of hydrogen fuel cells, including the various types such as proton exchange membrane and alkaline cells. An excellent description of how the technology works gives readers an understanding of both the successes and problems relating to these promising energy sources. . . . The color illustrations and charts . . . are clear and helpful, and the text, although information rich, is not overly difficult." SLJ

O'Neal, Claire

How to use wind power to light and heat your home. Mitchell Lane Publishers 2009 47p il map (Tell your parents) lib bdg $21.50

Grades: 4 5 6 7   **621.31**

1. Wind power 2. Renewable energy resources
ISBN 978-1-58415-762-5 (lib bdg); 1-58415-762-3 (lib bdg)
LC 2009-4530

Introduces wind power, including the history of harnessing the wind for work, how modern wind power generates electricity, and how to install a turbine to a home

This book "offers numerous facts and statistics, all of which are cited. . . . Chapters cover present-day issues and . . . are interspersed with full-color photographs and short 'Did You Know' trivia boxes. . . . Back matter includes detailed resource lists and 'Try This!' experiments." SLJ

Includes glossary and bibliographical references

621.319   Transmission

Cole, Joanna

The magic school bus and the electric field trip; illustrated by Bruce Degen. Scholastic 1997 48p il hardcover o.p. pa $6.99

Grades: 2 3 4   **621.319**

1. Electricity 2. Electric power
ISBN 0-590-44682-7; 0-590-44683-5 (pa)
LC 97-2080

Ms. Frizzle takes her class on a field trip through the town's electrical wires so they can learn how electricity is generated and how it is used

"Spiced with plenty of puns and jokes, the writing and the colorful artwork continue the series' unbeatable combination of clearly presented information and plenty of fun." Booklist

Suen, Anastasia

Wired; illustrated by Paul Carrick. Charlesbridge 2007 32p il lib bdg $16.95; pa $6.95

Grades: 2 3 4 5   **621.319**

1. Electric power 2. Electricity
ISBN   978-1-57091-599-4   (lib   bdg); 978-1-57091-494-2 (pa)   LC 2005-19623

"This introduction to electricity traces the path of electrons from the power station to electronic devices used in the home. . . . Acrylic mixed-media illustrations are informative, with clear labels to identify specific components. The uncrowded layout and three-dimensional look are especially effective . . . The fundamental information comes through in an appealing way that kids can fully understand." SLJ

Includes glossary and bibliographical references

621.382 Communications engineering

Perritano, John, 1962-
Revolution in communications. Marshall Cavendish Benchmark 2010 32p il (It works!) lib bdg $19.95
Grades: 3 4 5   **621.382**
  1. Telecommunication
  ISBN 978-0-7614-4373-5 (lib bdg); 0-7614-4373-8 (lib bdg)   LC 2008-54347
"Discusses the history of communication technology, how the technology was developed, and the science behind it." Publisher's note
"This interesting, information packed [book] . . . motivates students to do their own exploring. . . . The appealing cartoon-like photographs add humor. . . . This . . . just may be that spark needed to create eager budding scientists." Libr Media Connect
Includes glossary and bibliographical references

621.384 Radio and radar

Firestone, Mary, 1951-
Wireless technology. Lerner Publications 2009 48p il (Cool science) lib bdg $27.93
Grades: 4 5 6   **621.384**
  1. Wireless communication systems
  ISBN 978-0-8225-7590-0 (lib bdg); 0-8225-7590-6 (lib bdg)   LC 2007041102
This describes "how cutting-edge science helps people communicate better, live healthier, and have more fun!" Publisher's note
Includes glossary and bibliographical references

621.389 Security, sound recording, related systems

Gilbert, Adrian
Top technology. Firefly 2009 32p il (Spy files) pa $6.95
Grades: 3 4 5 6   **621.389**
  1. Espionage 2. Electronic surveillance
  ISBN 978-1-55407-576-8; 1-55407-576-9
First published 2008 in the United Kingdom
Discusses equipment and technology used by spies, including satellites, cameras, lie detectors, listening devices, and more.
The text's "short paragraphs and great pictures are combined in a collage style that will draw readers quickly through the information. Useful for reports and browsing." SLJ
Includes glossary

621.4 Prime movers and heat engineering

Cartlidge, Cherese
Home windmills; by Cherese Cartlidge. Norwood House Press 2008 48p il (A great idea) lib bdg $25.27
Grades: 3 4 5 6   **621.4**
  1. Windmills
  ISBN 978-1-59953-192-2 (lib bdg); 1-59953-192-5 (lib bdg)   LC 2008-24190
"Describes the invention and development of the home windmills." Publisher's note
Includes glossary and bibliographical references

Walker, Niki, 1972-
Generating wind power; [by] Niki Walker. Crabtree Pub. 2007 32p il (Energy revolution) lib bdg $25.20; pa $8.95
Grades: 5 6 7 8   **621.4**
  1. Wind power
  ISBN 978-0-7787-2913-6 (lib bdg); 0-7787-2913-3 (lib bdg); 978-0-7787-2927-3 (pa); 0-7787-2927-3 (pa)   LC 2006014370
This describes various ways of gathering and using wind power, and offers a brief history of wind power and energy conservation tips.
"Vivid color photographs with informative captions extend the [text], showing diverse people and applications." SLJ
Includes glossary

621.47 Solar-energy engineering

Bang, Molly, 1943-
My light. Blue Sky Press 2004 unp il $16.95 *
Grades: 1 2 3   **621.47**
  1. Solar energy 2. Electricity
  ISBN 0-439-48961-X
"Writing in the voice of the sun, the first-person narrative investigates various forms of energy on Earth, all derived in one way or another from the light and heat of this solar system's major star." SLJ
"Bang's strong design sense comes through in compositions that gracefully incorporate diagrams and strike a balance between graphic forms and delicate, decorative patterns. A lovely and illuminating book that presents sound science while expressing the wonder of flipping a switch and flooding a room with light." Booklist

Bearce, Stephanie
How to harness solar power for your home. Mitchell Lane Publishers 2009 47p il map (Tell your parents) lib bdg $21.50
Grades: 4 5 6 7   **621.47**
  1. Solar energy
  ISBN 978-1-58415-761-8 (lib bdg); 1-58415-761-5 (lib bdg)   LC 2009-4529

Bearce, Stephanie—*Continued*

This title about solar power "offers numerous facts and statistics, all of which are cited. . . . Chapters cover present-day issues and . . . are interspersed with full-color photographs and short 'Did You Know' trivia boxes. . . . Back matter includes detailed resource lists and 'Try This!' experiments." SLJ

Includes glossary and bibliographical references

Benduhn, Tea

Solar power; by Tea Benduhn. Weekly Reader Pub. 2008 c2009 24p il (Energy for today) lib bdg $21; pa $5.95

Grades: 2 3 4   **621.47**

1. Solar energy

ISBN 978-0-8368-9263-5 (lib bdg); 0-8368-9263-1 (lib bdg); 978-0-8368-9362-5 (pa); 0-8368-9362-X (pa)

LC 2008015515

"This title presents a surprising amount of information about solar power in brief sentences that are calibrated to newly confident readers' abilities. . . . The selection of well-chosen photos, which are crisply reproduced on each page, is particularly strong in the final chapters about solar technology. . . . The language is direct, clear, and enlightening." Booklist

Includes glossary and bibliographical references

621.48   Nuclear engineering

Benduhn, Tea

Nuclear power; by Tea Benduhn. Weekly Reader Pub. 2009 24p il (Energy for today) lib bdg $21; pa $5.95

Grades: 2 3 4   **621.48**

1. Nuclear energy

ISBN 978-0-8368-9262-8 (lib bdg); 0-8368-9262-3 (lib bdg); 978-0-8368-9361-8 (pa); 0-8368-9361-1 (pa)

LC 2008012020

This describes how nuclear power works and how it may be used in the future.

"New readers will be able to wrap their hands around the small, square size, and their minds around the clear, enlightening text. [This book has] crisp photos and strong back matter." Booklist

Includes glossary and bibliographical references

Feigenbaum, Aaron

Emergency at Three Mile Island; by Aaron Feigenbaum. Bearport Pub. 2007 32p il map (Code red) lib bdg $23.96

Grades: 3 4 5   **621.48**

1. Three Mile Island Nuclear Power Plant (Pa.) 2. Nuclear power plants

ISBN 978-1-59716-364-4 (lib bdg); 1-59716-364-3 (lib bdg)

LC 2006031635

This "discusses the 1979 malfunction of a nuclear reactor that could have cost thousands of lives and devastated the area but, fortunately, did not. . . . The writing is clear and concise. . . . The facts are allowed to speak for themselves. The [book is] liberally laced with pertinent period photographs and numerous quotes."

Includes glossary and bibliographical references

621.8   Machine engineering

Coppendale, Jean

The great big book of mighty machines; [by] Jean Coppendale and Ian Graham. Firefly Books 2009 160p il $19.95

Grades: PreK K 1 2 3   **621.8**

1. Vehicles 2. Machinery

ISBN 978-1-55407-521-8; 1-55407-521-1

"A vehicle-lover's dream come true, this meaty volume focuses on cars, bikes, trains, tractors, rescue vehicles, construction trucks and monster trucks. Each section . . . ends with an activity page. . . . The text is easy to read and understand. Brightly colored page edges draw eyes inward to the exciting full-color photos that fill the pages." Kirkus

Includes glossary

De Medeiros, James, 1975-

Pulleys. Weigl Publishers 2009 24p il (Science matters: simple machines) lib bdg $24.45; pa $8.95

Grades: 2 3 4   **621.8**

1. Pulleys

ISBN 978-1-60596-041-8 (lib bdg); 1-60596-041-1 (lib bdg); 978-1-60596-042-5 (pa); 1-60596-042-X (pa)

LC 2009-1947

Discusses what a pulley is, where it can be found, and how it is used.

"The bold, large-scale, colorful photographs . . . are sure to draw in even the most reluctant readers." SLJ

Includes glossary

De Medeiros, Michael

Screws. Weigl Publishers 2009 24p il (Science matters: simple machines) lib bdg $24.45; pa $8.95

Grades: 2 3 4   **621.8**

1. Screws

ISBN 978-1-60596-039-5 (lib bdg); 1-60596-039-X (lib bdg); 978-1-60596-040-1 (pa); 1-60596-040-3 (pa)

LC 2009-1941

Discusses what a screw is, where it can be found, and how it is used.

"De Medeiros' description of the object's function is unusually elegant: Screws convert movement in a circle to movement straight ahead. . . . The back matter (including online suggestions, a craft, a quiz, a well-chosen glossary, and more) is strong and features what is likely the only 10-word index in existence to feature the terms nuts, bolts, and King Nebuchadnezzar." Booklist

Includes glossary

Wheels and axles. Weigl Publishers 2010 24p il (Science matters: simple machines) lib bdg $24.45; pa $8.95

Grades: 2 3 4   **621.8**

1. Wheels 2. Axles

ISBN 978-1-60596-033-3 (lib bdg); 1-60596-033-0 (lib bdg); 978-1-60596-034-0 (pa); 1-60596-034-9 (pa)

LC 2009-7808

De Medeiros, Michael—*Continued*

Discusses wheels and axles and how they are used in everyday life.

"The bold, large-scale photographs . . . are sure to draw in even the most reluctant readers." SLJ

Includes glossary

Gardner, Robert, 1929-

Sensational science projects with simple machines; [by] Robert Gardner. Enslow Elementary 2006 48p il (Fantastic physical science experiments) $23.93

Grades: 4 5 6   **621.8**

  1. Simple machines 2. Science—Experiments

  ISBN 0-7660-2585-3   LC 2005008974

"The first chapter of [this book] explains force, friction, distance, and work. The book then introduces levers, inclined planes, pulleys, etc. . . . Large colorful, cartoonlike drawings complement the [text]. . . . [This offers] solid information." SLJ

Includes glossary and bibliographical references

Hoban, Tana

Construction zone. Greenwillow Bks. 1997 unp il $16.99

Grades: K 1 2   **621.8**

  1. Machinery

  ISBN 0-688-12284-1   LC 96-5696

Hoban uses "full-color photographs to introduce construction equipment. Each of the 13 machines presented is given a two-page spread, one picture taken at middle distance, the other close up. The final two pages match thumbnail photos with explanatory text." SLJ

The "photos have extraordinary depth and detail." Booklist

Howse, Jennifer

Inclined planes. Weigl Publishers 2009 24p il (Science matters: simple machines) lib bdg $24.45; pa $8.95

Grades: 2 3 4   **621.8**

  1. Inclined planes

  ISBN 978-1-60596-035-7 (lib bdg); 1-60596-035-7 (lib bdg); 978-1-60596-036-4 (pa); 1-60596-036-5 (pa)

      LC 2009-25972

Discusses what an inclined plane is, where it can be found, and how it is used.

"The bold, large-scale colorful photographs . . . are sure to draw in even the most reluctant readers." SLJ

Includes glossary

Levers. Weigl Publishers 2009 24p il (Science matters: simple machines) lib bdg $24.45; pa $8.95

Grades: 2 3 4   **621.8**

  1. Levers

  ISBN 978-1-60596-031-9 (lib bdg); 1-60596-031-4 (lib bdg); 978-1-60596-032-6 (pa); 1-60596-032-2 (pa)

      LC 2009-1921

Discusses what a lever is, where it can be found, and how it is used.

"The bold, large-scale, colorful photographs . . . are sure to draw in even the most reluctant readers." SLJ

Includes glossary

Low, William

Machines go to work. Holt & Co. 2009 unp il $14.95

Grades: PreK K 1   **621.8**

  1. Machinery

  ISBN 978-0-8050-8759-8; 0-8050-8759-1

"A fun and feisty tour of big, powerful and fascinating machines; each of them is ready, willing and eager to 'go to work.'" Kirkus

"The realistic digital paintings will delight youngsters; spreads alternate with three-page foldouts that show the machines at work. . . . This well-constructed picture book is a surefire hit." SLJ

Solway, Andrew

Castle under siege! simple machines; [by] Andrew Solway. Raintree 2005 32p il lib bdg $28.21; pa $7.85

Grades: 3 4 5   **621.8**

  1. Simple machines 2. Castles

  ISBN 1-4109-1918-8 (lib bdg); 1-4109-1949-8 (pa)

      LC 2005014549

"Raintree fusion"

"The author leads readers through the construction of a castle, the workings of the drawbridge, the execution of a siege and how the inhabitants would protect the castle from attack, methods the invaders might use, and what would happen afterward to repair the damage. While readers are drawn into the action, they are also introduced to the simple machines used during this period of time. . . . Detailed, easily interpreted diagrams are included for added understanding of concepts. Vivid and realistic photos add to the appeal. An excellent choice for research or for general interest." SLJ

Thales, Sharon

Inclined planes to the rescue. Capstone Press 2007 24p il (Simple machines to the rescue) lib bdg $21.26

Grades: K 1 2 3   **621.8**

  1. Inclined planes 2. Simple machines

  ISBN 978-0-7368-6752-8

"First facts"

"Describes inclined planes, including what they are, how they work, and common uses of these simple machines today." Publisher's note

This is "brightly colored, attractive . . . [and written] in language students can read and understand independently." SLJ

Includes glossary and bibliographical references

Levers to the rescue. Capstone Press 2007 24p il (Simple machines to the rescue) lib bdg $21.26

Grades: K 1 2 3   **621.8**

  1. Levers 2. Simple machines

  ISBN 978-0-7368-6747-4 (lib bdg); 0-7368-6747-3 (lib bdg)

"First facts"

"Describes levers, including what they are, how they work, past uses, and common uses of these simple machines today." Publisher's note

This is "brightly colored, attractive . . . [and written] in language students can read and understand independently." SLJ

Includes glossary and bibliographical references

Thales, Sharon—*Continued*

Pulleys to the rescue; by Sharon Thales. Capstone Press 2007 24p il (Simple machines to the rescue) lib bdg $21.26

Grades: K 1 2 3　　　　　　**621.8**

1. Pulleys 2. Simple machines
ISBN 978-0-7368-6748-1 (lib bdg); 0-7368-6748-1 (lib bdg)　　　　　　LC 2006021503

"First facts"

"Describes pulleys, including what they are, how they work, past uses, and common uses of these simple machines today." Publisher's note

"The presentation of the material . . . is impressive." Sci Books Films

Includes glossary and bibliographical references

Screws to the rescue; by Sharon Thales. Capstone Press 2007 24p il (Simple machines to the rescue) lib bdg $21.26

Grades: K 1 2 3　　　　　　**621.8**

1. Screws 2. Simple machines
ISBN 978-0-7368-6749-8 (lib bdg); 0-7368-6749-X (lib bdg)　　　　　　LC 2006021502

"First facts"

"Describes screws, including what they are, how they work, past uses, and common uses of these simple machines today" Publisher's note

"The presentation of the material . . . is impressive." Sci Books Films

Includes glossary and bibliographical references

Wedges to the rescue; by Sharon Thales. Capstone Press 2007 24p il (Simple machines to the rescue) lib bdg $21.26

Grades: K 1 2 3　　　　　　**621.8**

1. Wedges 2. Simple machines
ISBN 978-0-7368-6750-4 (lib bdg); 0-7368-6750-3 (lib bdg)　　　　　　LC 2006021495

"First facts"

"Describes wedges, including what they are, how they work, past uses, and common uses of these simple machines today." Publisher's note

"The presentation of the material . . . is impressive." Sci Books Films

Includes glossary and bibliographical references

Wheels and axles to the rescue. Capstone Press 2007 24p il (Simple machines to the rescue) lib bdg $21.26

Grades: K 1 2 3　　　　　　**621.8**

1. Wheels 2. Axles 3. Simple machines
ISBN 978-0-7368-6751-1

"First facts"

This describes "what wheels and axles are, how they work, and how these simple machines can save the day." Publisher's note

This is "brightly colored, attractive. . . [and written] in language students can read and understand independently." SLJ

Includes glossary and bibliographical references

Tomljanovic, Tatiana

Wedges. Weigl Publishers 2010 24p il (Science matters: simple machines) lib bdg $24.45; pa $8.95

Grades: 2 3 4　　　　　　**621.8**

1. Wedges
ISBN 978-1-60596-037-1 (lib bdg); 1-60596-037-3 (lib bdg); 978-1-60596-038-8 (pa); 1-60596-038-1 (pa)
　　　　　　LC 2009-1936

Discusses what a wedge is, where it can be found, and how it is used.

"The bold, large-scale, colorful, photographs . . . are sure to draw in even the most reluctant readers." SLJ

Includes glossary

621.9　Tools

Blaxland, Wendy

Helmets. Marshall Cavendish Benchmark 2011 32p il map (How are they made?) lib bdg $12.99

Grades: 4 5 6　　　　　　**621.9**

1. Helmets 2. Plastics
ISBN 978-0-7614-4755-9; 0-7614-4755-5
　　　　　　LC 2009039881

"The opening spread of *Helmets*, which shows both a football player and an astronaut, illustrates the wide range of protective headgear, which stretches back to the leather war apparel of 3,000 BCE. Shots of gleaming orbs shuttling down assembly lines accompany text on thermoplastics, testing methods, and laws." Booklist

Includes glossary

Clements, Andrew, 1949-

Workshop; illustrated by David Wisniewski. Clarion Bks. 1998 unp il $16

Grades: K 1 2　　　　　　**621.9**

1. Tools 2. Workshops
ISBN 0-395-85579-9　　　　　　LC 97-48534

"From ruler to wrench, 13 basic tools are described in short text and bright, bold cut-paper illustrations. In each large-scale, double-page spread, a young apprentice watches a different craftsman at work with saw, chisel, grinder, or knife." SLJ

"Wisniewski's cut-paper illustrations and collage ably illustrate Clements' spare, poetic text. . . . A unique introduction to the world of wood and art for budding artisans." Bull Cent Child Books

623.4　Ordnance

Fridell, Ron, 1943-

Military technology. Lerner Publications Co. 2008 48p il (Cool science) lib bdg $27.93

Grades: 4 5 6　　　　　　**623.4**

1. Weapons 2. Military art and science
ISBN 978-0-8225-6769-1 (lib bdg); 0-8225-6769-5 (lib bdg)　　　　　　LC 2006019404

A history of military technology from ancient to modern times

Includes glossary and bibliographical references

Gurstelle, William

The art of the catapult; build Greek ballistae, Roman onagers, English trebuchets, and more ancient artillery. Chicago Review Press 2004 172p il map $16.95

Grades: 5 6 7 8 **623.4**

1. Catapult

ISBN 1-55652-526-5

"This collection of 10 working catapult projects offers a fascinating look at world history, military strategy, and physics, related with an engaging yet lighthearted touch. . . . Instructions are clear, with full materials lists, helpful diagrams, and no skipped steps. . . . There's excellent booktalk potential here, and lively reading even for those who never get around to constructing a catapult." SLJ

Includes bibliographical references

623.74   Vehicles

Abramson, Andra Serlin

Fighter planes up close. Sterling 2008 48p (Up close) lib bdg $9.95

Grades: 2 3 4 **623.74**

1. Fighter planes

ISBN 978-1-4027-4796-0 (lib bdg); 1-4027-4796-9 (lib bdg)   LC 2007008215

An introduction to fighter planes

623.82   Nautical craft

Abramson, Andra Serlin

Submarines up close. Sterling 2008 c2007 48p il (Up close) lib bdg $9.95

Grades: 2 3 4 **623.82**

1. Submarines

ISBN 978-1-4027-4797-7 (lib bdg); 1-4027-4797-7 (lib bdg)   LC 2006102593

An introduction to submarines

Clark, Willow

Boats on the move. PowerKids Press 2010 24p il (Transportation station) lib bdg $21.25; pa $8.25

Grades: 2 3 **623.82**

ISBN 978-1-4358-9336-8 (lib bdg); 1-4358-9336-0 (lib bdg); 978-1-4358-9760-1 (pa); 1-4358-9760-9 (pa)   LC 2009-27410

Learn all about speedboats, military boats, boats used by the Coast Guard, and much more.

Includes glossary

Kirk, Shoshanna

T is for tugboat; navigating the seas from A to Z; [text by Shoshanna Kirk; designed by Sara Gillingham] Chronicle Books 2008 unp il $15.99

Grades: 2 3 4 **623.82**

1. Navigation 2. Ships

ISBN 978-0-8118-6094-9; 0-8118-6094-9   LC 2007018333

This is an introduction to sea-related terms such as buoy, figurehead, hornpipe, and sextant

"This attractive title is an eye-pleaser filled with a mix of photographs, illustrations, and graphic images set on textured, woodgrain backgrounds. Images are both vintage and contemporary, and range from black-and-white to full-color reproductions. . . . A spread depicting an array of sailors' knots, a page illustrating Morse code, a spread labeling the parts of a ship, and the endpapers with the international code of maritime flags will be of interest to older children." SLJ

Lindeen, Mary, 1962-

Ships; by Mary Lindeen. Bellwether Media 2007 24p il (Mighty machines) lib bdg $18.95

Grades: PreK K 1 2 3 **623.82**

1. Ships

ISBN 978-1-60014-060-0 (lib bdg); 1-60014-060-2 (lib bdg)   LC 2006035262

"Blastoff! readers"

This explains what a ship is, describes its major parts, and what it does

The glossary features "easy-to-read-and-understand definitions. . . . With [its] exciting, full-color photos on every spread [this] colorful [title] will certainly appeal to the mighty curiosity of young readers." SLJ

Includes glossary and bibliographical references

Sutherland, Jonathan, 1958-

Aircraft carriers; [by] Jonathan Sutherland and Diane Canwell. Gareth Stevens Pub. 2008 32p il (Amazing ships) lib bdg $23.93

Grades: 4 5 6 **623.82**

1. Aircraft carriers

ISBN 978-0-8368-8376-3   LC 2007017049

This is an illustrated introduction to aircraft carriers from various parts of the world

"Bright colors and eye-catching photos are an enticing invitation of younger readers. . . . Vocabulary is appropriate in both text and captions. . . . Attractive, accurate, and informative." SLJ

Includes glossary and bibliographical references

Container ships and oil tankers; [by] Jonathan Sutherland and Diane Canwell. Gareth Stevens Pub. 2008 32p il (Amazing ships) lib bdg $23.93

Grades: 4 5 6 **623.82**

1. Container ships 2. Tankers

ISBN 978-0-8368-8377-0   LC 2007020479

An illustrated introduction to container ships and oil tankers from various parts of the world

"Bright colors and eye-catching photos are an enticing invitation to younger readers. . . . Vocabulary is appropriate in both text and captions. . . . Attractive, accurate, and informative." SLJ

Includes glossary and bibliographical references

Cruise ships; [by] Jonathan Sutherland and Diane Canwell. Gareth Stevens Pub. 2008 32p il (Amazing ships) lib bdg $23.93

Grades: 4 5 6 **623.82**

1. Cruise ships 2. Ocean liners

ISBN 978-0-8368-8378-7   LC 2007017050

Sutherland, Jonathan, 1958——*Continued*

This is an illustrated introduction to cruise ships from various parts of the world

"Bright colors and eye-catching photos are an enticing invitation to younger readers. . . . Vocabulary is appropriate in both text and captions. . . . Attractive, accurate, and informative." SLJ

Includes glossary and bibliographical references

Submarines; [by] Jonathan Sutherland and Diane Canwell. Gareth Stevens Pub. 2008 32p il (Amazing ships) lib bdg $23.93
Grades: 4 5 6   **623.82**
1. Submarines
ISBN 978-0-8368-8379-4   LC 2007017051

This is an illustrated introduction to submarines from various parts of the world

"Bright colors and eye-catching photos are an enticing invitation to younger readers. . . . Vocabulary is appropriate in both text and captions. . . . Attractive, accurate, and informative." SLJ

Includes glossary and bibliographical references

623.89   Navigation

Morrison, Taylor, 1971-

The coast mappers. Houghton Mifflin Co. 2004 45p il map $16
Grades: 5 6 7 8   **623.89**
1. Davidson, George 2. Maps 3. Surveying 4. Pacific Coast (North America)
ISBN 0-618-25408-0   LC 2003-13534

Chronicles the difficulties encountered by George Davidson and others as they attempted to create nautical charts to complete the U.S. Coast Survey of the West Coast in the mid-nineteenth century

"Cartographic methods are clearly explained through both the carefully researched text and the precise illustrations. . . . The artwork clarifies the text, depicts the breathtaking beauty of the coastline, and adds a sense of adventure." SLJ

Includes glossary and bibliographical references

Young, Karen Romano, 1959-

Across the wide ocean; the why, how, and where of navigation for humans and animals at sea. Greenwillow Books 2007 78p il $18.99; lib bdg $19.89
Grades: 4 5 6 7   **623.89**
1. Navigation 2. Ocean 3. Marine animals
ISBN   978-0-06-009086-9;   0-06-009086-3; 978-0-06-009087-6 (lib bdg); 0-06-009087-1 (lib bdg)
                     LC 2005-46146

"Readers follow such disparate entities as a loggerhead sea turtle, a nuclear submarine, and a sailboat crew seeking scientific sightings of North Atlantic right whales as Young explores the concept of navigation. . . . Larded with photos, diagrams, and maps. . . . Deceptively simple in appearance, the informative text can push some intense mental activity." SLJ

624   Civil engineering

Caney, Steven

Steven Caney's ultimate building book. Running Press 2006 596p il $29.95 *
Grades: 4 5 6 7 8   **624**
1. Civil engineering 2. Building
ISBN 0-7624-0409-4

"Caney examines 'building' in its broadest sense, encompassing everything from skyscrapers and bridges to bird feeders and peanut-shell 'bricks.' Opening sections investigate the history and techniques of construction, with clearly written explanations supported by black-and-white photographs and diagrams. . . . The author reinforces important concepts of design in a way that is fascinating and effective." SLJ

Fantastic feats and failures; by the editors of YES magazine. Kids Can Press 2004 52p il hardcover o.p. pa $7.95
Grades: 4 5 6 7   **624**
1. Civil engineering
ISBN 1-55337-633-1; 1-55337-634-X (pa)

This "book spotlights 20 notable highs and lows in engineering. The 'feats' celebrated include the Sydney Opera House, the Brooklyn Bridge, and Canadarm (a huge, Canadian-built robotic arm used for repairs in space). Among the 'failures' are the space shuttle Challenger, the Tacoma Narrows Bridge, and the Chernobyl nuclear power plant. . . . Well organized and engagingly written. . . . Excellent photos . . . illustrate the places and events discussed, while colorful drawings visually represent concepts." Booklist

Macaulay, David, 1946-

Underground. Houghton Mifflin 1976 109p il hardcover o.p. pa $9.95 *
Grades: 5 6 7 8 9   **624**
1. Civil engineering
ISBN 0-395-24739-X; 0-395-34065-9 (pa)

In this "examination of the intricate support systems that lie beneath the street levels of our cities, Macaulay explains the ways in which foundations for buildings are laid or reinforced, and how the various utilities or transportation services are constructed." Bull Cent Child Books

"Introduced by a visual index—a bird's eye view of a busy, hypothetical intersection with colored indicators marking the specific locations analyzed in subsequent pages—detailed illustrations are combined with a clear, precise narrative to make the subject comprehensible and fascinating." Horn Book

Includes glossary

Sandvold, Lynnette Brent

Revolution in construction. Marshall Cavendish Benchmark 2010 32p il (It works!) lib bdg $19.95
Grades: 3 4 5   **624**
1. Building 2. Engineering
ISBN 978-0-7614-4378-0 (lib bdg); 0-7614-4378-9 (lib bdg)   LC 2008-54363

Sandvold, Lynnette Brent—*Continued*

"Discusses the history of construction, how the technology was developed, and the science behind it." Publisher's note

"This interesting, information packed [book] . . . motivates students to do their own exploring. . . . The appealing cartoon-like photographs add humor. . . . This . . . just may be that spark needed to create eager budding scientists." Libr Media Connect

Includes glossary and bibliographical references

Sullivan, George

Built to last; building America's amazing bridges, dams, tunnels, and skyscrapers. Scholastic Nonfiction 2005 128p il map $18.99

Grades: 5 6 7 8   **624**
1. Civil engineering
ISBN 0-439-51737-0   LC 2004-60996

This is a "survey of American building—from the Erie Canal to Boston's current 'Big Dig.' Chronological chapters describe the historical forces that helped drive each project as well as the specific technological feats linked to each pioneering structure. . . . The wide selection of captivating illustrations includes archival photos and engravings, architectural drawings, and color photos. . . . Sullivan's skillful integration of social and economic history distinguishes this clear, well-designed title." Booklist

624.1 Structural engineering and underground construction

Mason, Adrienne

Build it! structures, systems and you; written by Adrienne Mason; illustrated by Claudia Dávila. Kids Can Press 2006 32p il (Primary physical science) $14.95; pa $5.95

Grades: K 1 2   **624.1**
1. Structural engineering 2. Building
ISBN   978-1-55337-835-8;   1-55337-835-0;
978-1-55337-836-5 (pa); 1-55337-836-9 (pa)

This provides "a first glimpse of how structures and structural systems exist both in nature and in human-made designs. The author makes reading this book an easy and enjoyable reading experience. The book uses carefully worded descriptions, creative and vivid colors with striking graphics representations, and clear fonts." Sci Books Films

624.2 Bridges

Curlee, Lynn, 1947-

Brooklyn Bridge. Atheneum Bks. for Young Readers 2001 35p il map $18 *

Grades: 3 4 5 6   **624.2**
1. Roebling, John Augustus 2. Roebling, Washington Augustus, 1837-1926 3. Brooklyn Bridge (New York, N.Y.) 4. Bridges
ISBN 0-689-83183-8   LC 99-43771

This book "tells the history behind the bridge and its construction . . . explains the financing and final deci-

sion to build the bridge, and describes the roles of John A. Roebling and, later, his son, Washington, as Chief Engineer." SLJ

"Biography, social history, and introductory engineering are . . . precisely balanced, with human-interest angles. . . . This is a grand yet practical tribute to a grand yet practical edifice." Bull Cent Child Books

Includes bibliographical references

Johmann, Carol, 1949-

Bridges! amazing structures to design, build & test; [by] Carol Johmann & Elizabeth Rieth; illustrations by Michael Kline. Williamson 1999 96p il pa $12.95

Grades: 4 5 6 7   **624.2**
1. Bridges
ISBN 1-88559-330-9   LC 98-53272

"A Williamson Kaleidoscope Kids book"

Describes different kinds of bridges, their history, design, construction, and effects on populations, environmental dilemmas, safety, and more

"Eye-catching photographs and cartoon illustrations in blue and orange tones abound; clear organization of text and unifying page borders create an attractive graphic package. The volume includes a list of notable bridges by state and country." SLJ

625.1 Railroads

Barton, Byron

Trains. Crowell 1986 unp il lib bdg $16.89 *

Grades: PreK K 1   **625.1**
1. Railroads
ISBN 0-690-04534-4   LC 85-47898

Brief text and illustrations present a variety of trains and what they do

"The concepts are simple and Barton's illustrations are just enough, and no more." Publ Wkly

Big book of trains; [by] National Railway Museum, York, England. DK Pub. 1998 32p il $14.99

Grades: 4 5 6   **625.1**
1. Railroads
ISBN 0-7894-3436-9   LC 98-18830

Describes the locomotives, cars, tunnels, stations, and functions of such trains as freight trains, channel tunnel trains, bullet trains, mountain trains, and snow trains

Includes glossary

Clark, Willow

Trains on the move; [by] Willow Clark. PowerKids Press 2010 24p il (Transportation station) lib bdg $21.25; pa $8.025

Grades: 2 3   **625.1**
1. Railroads
ISBN 978-1-4358-9331-3 (lib bdg); 1-4358-9331-X (lib bdg); 978-1-4358-9750-2 (pa); 1-4358-9750-1 (pa)
                              LC 2009-21776

Learn all about the different types of trains, how they work, and how important they are

Clark, Willow—*Continued*

"Clark has done a fine job of including meaningful content in a limited space. . . . [This book] consists of 10 two-page chapters printed in a font of an inviting size. Full-page photos–all color except one vintage photograph–with informative captions face two-paragraph text blocks. . . . Will make readers feel they have learned something" SLJ

Includes glossary

Crowther, Robert

Trains: a pop-up railroad book. Candlewick Press 2006 unp il $17.99

Grades: 2 3 4 5   **625.1**
1. Railroads 2. Pop-up books
ISBN 978-0-7636-3082-9; 0-7636-3082-9

"With pop-up effects that, appropriately enough, tend to be long, narrow, and placed in parallel tracks, this history of railroading opens with outside and inside views of a small steam locomotive and closes with a full-spread, double-tiered train station. In between, the book covers methods of propulsion, the development of passenger cars, speed and other records, tunnels, bridges, and other engineering feats. . . . Crowther simplifies technological details in his neat, brightly colored collage illustrations." SLJ

Lindeen, Mary, 1962-

Trains; by Mary Lindeen. Bellwether Media 2007 24p il (Mighty machines) lib bdg $18.50

Grades: PreK K 1 2 3   **625.1**
ISBN 978-1-60014-062-4 (lib bdg); 1-60014-062-9 (lib bdg)   LC 2006035264

"Blastoff! readers"

This explains what a train is and discusses its major parts and what they do

The glossary features "easy-to-read-and-understand definitions. . . . With [its] exciting, full-color photos on every spread, [this] colorful [title] will certainly appeal to the mighty curiosity of young readers." SLJ

Includes glossary and bibliographical references

Simon, Seymour, 1931-

Seymour Simon's book of trains. HarperCollins Pubs. 2002 unp il $16.99; lib bdg $17.89; pa $6.99
*

Grades: K 1 2 3   **625.1**
1. Railroads
ISBN 0-06-028475-7; 0-06-028476-5 (lib bdg); 0-06-446223-4 (pa)   LC 2001-24020

"Each double-page spread in this picture book sets a dramatic close-up photo of a moving train opposite a few sentences about the train's source of power (steam, diesel, electric) and how it works. The full-color, close-up pictures by a number of photographers will grab even young preschoolers. . . . The astonishing facts will interest older train buffs." Booklist

625.4   Rapid transit systems

McKendry, Joe, 1972-

Beneath the streets of Boston; building America's first subway; written & illustrated by Joe McKendry. David R. Godine 2005 unp il maps $19.95

Grades: 4 5 6   **625.4**
1. Subways 2. Boston (Mass.)—History
ISBN 1-56792-284-8   LC 2004-16418

This book covers over twenty years of the early history of the Boston subway system

"The text is clear and well written. . . . The paintings convey the sense of story, while the drawings provide specific details. Both are equally well executed and contribute to the overall understanding of the text." SLJ

Weitzman, David L., 1936-

A subway for New York; [by] David Weitzman. Farrar, Straus and Giroux 2005 unp il map $17

Grades: 4 5 6 7   **625.4**
1. Subways 2. New York (N.Y.)—History
ISBN 0-374-37284-5   LC 2004-56286

"Weitzman recounts the construction of [New York's] first subterranean train system, beginning above ground with descriptions of [the city's] crowded streets in 1904. . . . The text and captivating images convey the awe-inspiring scope of the project and the engineering feats that produced what remains the fastest method of navigating the city." Booklist

Includes bibliographical references

627   Hydraulic engineering

Mann, Elizabeth, 1948-

Hoover Dam; with illustrations by Alan Witschonke. Mikaya Press 2001 44p il (Wonders of the world) $19.95; pa $9.95

Grades: 4 5 6 7   **627**
1. Hoover Dam (Ariz. and Nev.)
ISBN 978-1-931414-02-9;   1-931414-02-5; 978-1-931414-13-5 (pa); 1-931414-13-0 (pa)
                                     LC 2001-34520

Describes the engineering, construction, and social and historical contexts of the Hoover Dam

"A wonderfully readable, well-organized book filled with fascinating detail." SLJ

Zuehlke, Jeffrey, 1968-

The Hoover Dam. Lerner Publications Co. 2010 32p il map (Lightning Bolt Books. Famous places) lib bdg $25.26

Grades: 2 3 4   **627**
1. Hoover Dam (Ariz. and Nev.)
ISBN 978-0-8225-9408-6 (lib bdg); 0-8225-9408-0 (lib bdg)   LC 2008-31245

Describes the Hoover Dam and includes information on its design, construction, and environmental issues

This book uses "high-quality photos, illustrations,

Zuehlke, Jeffrey, 1968-—*Continued*
maps, and diagrams. . . . Readers will enjoy learning about [the Hoover Dam] . . . and the challenges of building and maintaining large structures." SLJ
Includes glossary and bibliographical references

628.1 Water supply

Cartlidge, Cherese
Water from air; water-harvesting machines; by Cherese Cartlidge. Norwood House Press 2008 48p il (A great idea) lib bdg $25.27
Grades: 3 4 5 6   **628.1**
1. Water resources development 2. Humidity 3. Water supply
ISBN 978-1-59953-196-0 (lib bdg); 1-59953-196-8 (lib bdg)   LC 2008-10780
"Describes the invention and development of water harvesting machines." Publisher's note
Includes glossary and bibliographical references

628.9 Other branches of sanitary and municipal engineering

Abramson, Andra Serlin
Fire engines up close. Sterling 2008 c2007 48p (Up close) lib bdg $9.95
Grades: 2 3 4   **628.9**
1. Fire engines
ISBN 978-1-4027-4798-4 (lib bdg); 1-4027-4798-5 (lib bdg)   LC 2007008214
An introduction to fire fighters and their equipment

Allman, Toney, 1947-
The Jaws of Life. Norwood House Press 2008 48p il (A great idea) lib bdg $25.27
Grades: 3 4 5 6   **628.9**
1. Rescue work
ISBN 978-159953-191-5 (lib bdg); 1-59953-191-7 (lib bdg)   LC 2008007041
This book takes a "look at how the Jaws of Life tool was invented, improved and used to help rescue people in life-threatening situations." Publisher's note
"Full-color photographs and copious fun facts help make this . . . enjoyable reading, but it's really the choice of [topic] that is so enthralling." Booklist
Includes glossary and bibliographical references

Bingham, Caroline, 1962-
Fire truck. DK Pub. 2003 29p il (Machines at work) $8.99
Grades: K 1 2 3   **628.9**
1. Fire engines 2. Fire fighting
ISBN 0-7894-9221-0
Introduces fire engines and the work that they help firefighters do in all kinds of settings
"Bingham immediately grabs the reader's attention with brilliantly colored pictures. . . . An excellent stimulant for a child's imagination." Sci Books Films
Includes glossary

Butler, Dori Hillestad
F is for firefighting; by Dori Hillestad Butler; illustrated by Joan C. Waites. Pelican 2007 unp il $15.95
Grades: PreK K 1   **628.9**
1. Fire fighting 2. Alphabet
ISBN 978-1-58980-420-3; 1-58980-420-1
                                                        LC 2006031113
"From 'A is for Alarm' to 'Z is for Zones,' each page introduces a different aspect of firefighting. Crisp, colorful illustrations depict the topics, and thick borders frame the artwork as well as the text boxes at the bottom of the pages." SLJ

Demarest, Chris L., 1951-
Firefighters A to Z. Margaret K. McElderry Bks. 2000 unp il lib bdg $16.95
Grades: K 1   **628.9**
1. Fire fighters 2. Alphabet
ISBN 0-689-83798-4   LC 99-56382
An alphabetic look at a firefighter's day
"There's nothing babyish or cute about the robust, action-oriented pastel artwork in *Firefighters A to Z*. . . . Permeated with intense primary colors, the images build on one another to convey the physical nature of this dramatic but serious job. The firefighters themselves, in their bulky yellow suits and oxygen masks, appear straight out of science fiction, but the smoothly rhyming text grounds their activities in reality." Horn Book

Kenney, Karen Latchana, 1974-
Firefighters at work; by Karen L. Kenney; illustrated by Brian Caleb Dumm. Magic Wagon 2010 32p il (Meet your community workers!) lib bdg $18.95
Grades: K 1 2 3   **628.9**
1. Vocational guidance 2. Fire fighters
ISBN 978-1-60270-648-4 (lib bdg); 1-60270-648-4 (lib bdg)   LC 2009-2384
This book about firefighters has "an uncluttered layout and consistent organization. . . . Chapter headings such as 'Problems on the Job,' and 'Technology at Work,' and 'Special Skills and Training' make it easy to pinpoint specific information." SLJ
Includes glossary

Landau, Elaine
Smokejumpers; photographs by Ben Klaffke. Millbrook Press 2002 48p il lib bdg $23.90
Grades: 3 4 5 6   **628.9**
1. Fire fighters 2. Forest fires
ISBN 0-7613-2324-4   LC 2001-30974
"The first half explains the physical training smokejumpers undergo and the fire-fighting theory they must learn. The second half shows what happens when a fire call comes in. . . . The pictures and text work together beautifully. . . . This is a must-purchase for libraries in places where forest fires occur, and the true-life-adventure aspect will make it popular in other libraries as well." Booklist
Includes glossary and bibliographical references

629.04   Transportation engineering

Perritano, John, 1962-
Revolution in transportation. Marshall Cavendish Benchmark 2010 32p il (It works!) lib bdg $19.95
Grades: 3 4 5   **629.04**
  1. Transportation
  ISBN 978-0-7614-4379-7 (lib bdg); 0-7614-4379-7 (lib bdg)   LC 2008-54366
"Discusses the history of transportation, how the technology was developed, and the science behind it." Publisher's note
"This interesting, information packed [book] . . . motivates students to do their own exploring. . . . The appealing cartoon-like photographs add humor. . . . This . . . just may be that spark needed to create eager budding scientists." Libr Media Connect
Includes glossary and bibliographical references

629.13   Aeronautics

Bailey, Gerry
Flight. Gareth Stevens Pub. 2009 32p il (Simply science) lib bdg $26
Grades: 3 4 5   **629.13**
  1. Flight 2. Aeronautics
  ISBN 978-1-4339-0032-7 (lib bdg); 1-4339-0032-7 (lib bdg)   LC 2008-27569
"In this little book, various vehicles associated with human flight are introduced . . . [and] fundamental principles underlying how these various vehicles are able to travel through the air are explained in a straightfoward and understandable manner. . . . This text will provide . . . an entertaining and informative introduction to aircraft and aerodynamic vehicles." Sci Books Films
Includes glossary and bibliographical references

Borden, Louise, 1949-
Touching the sky; the flying adventures of Wilbur and Orville Wright; [by] Louise Borden & Trish Marx; illustrated by Peter Fiore. Margaret K. McElderry Bks. 2003 unp il map $18.95
Grades: 3 4 5   **629.13**
  1. Wright, Wilbur, 1867-1912 2. Aeronautics—History
  ISBN 0-689-84876-5   LC 2002-12041
A look at how the Wright Brothers became the first celebrities of the twentieth century through their 1909 public flying exhibitions in New York City and Germany
"Fiore's detailed watercolors dramatically and accurately record the two venues. The narrative, too, is laced with engaging facts that are successfully married to the pictures." SLJ

Brown, Don, 1949-
Ruth Law thrills a nation; story and pictures by Don Brown. Ticknor & Fields 1993 unp il $16; pa $5.95
Grades: K 1 2 3   **629.13**
  1. Law, Ruth, b. 1887 2. Women air pilots
  ISBN 0-395-66404-7; 0-395-73517-3 (pa)
                                        LC 92-45701

Describes the record-breaking flight of a daring woman pilot, Ruth Law, from Chicago to New York in 1916
"Using a simple text and effective watercolors, Brown successfully re-creates the remarkable flying feat. He sets Law in her historical context with humor and precision." Booklist

Carson, Mary Kay, 1964-
The Wright Brothers for kids; how they invented the airplane: 21 activities exploring the science and history of flight; illustrations by Laura D'Argo. Chicago Review Press 2003 146p il pa $14.95 *
Grades: 4 5 6 7   **629.13**
  1. Wright, Orville, 1871-1948 2. Wright, Wilbur, 1867-1912 3. Aeronautics—History 4. Science—Experiments
  ISBN 1-55652-477-3   LC 2002-155449
This account of the Wright brothers' invention of the airplane, explains the forces of flight-lift, thrust, gravity, and drag and includes such activities as making a Chinese flying top, building a kite, bird watching, making a paper glider and a rubber-band-powered flyer
"A treasure trove of activities awaits readers of this wonderfully executed survey of the Wright brothers and their invention. The narrative flows easily and is complemented by numerous photographs that give a sense of history and this event. . . . This is a valuable resource for student reports and projects, and for classroom units." SLJ
Includes glossary and bibliographical references

Crowther, Robert
Flight: a pop-up book of aircraft. Candlewick Press 2007 unp il $17.99
Grades: 2 3 4 5   **629.13**
  1. Aeronautics 2. Pop-up books
  ISBN 978-0-7636-3459-9; 0-7636-3459-X
This is "a history of flight, from the ancient Chinese invention of the kite to the X-43A scramjet that NASA still has under development. Along with dozens of small, simplified but clean-lined portraits of renowned aircraft, many of which 'fly' along die-cut slots, [Crowther] includes a pop-up modern air terminal, a large two-sided globe on which famous firsts are traced, and a particularly well-designed 747 cockpit with moving control levers." SLJ

Goldish, Meish
Freaky-big airplanes. Bearport Pub. 2010 24p il (World's biggest) lib bdg $22.61
Grades: 2 3 4   **629.13**
  1. Airplanes
  ISBN 978-1-59716-959-2 (lib bdg); 1-59716-959-5 (lib bdg)   LC 2009-14620
Describes different types of aircraft used around the world, including information on their history, dimensions, weight, and performance
"The simply phrased narrative and captions describe what each vehicle carries, along with top speed, full weight, and other basic facts. . . . A visual glossary and a look at four other outsize flying machines . . . cap this

Goldish, Meish—*Continued*
awe-inspiring entry in the World's Biggest series."
Booklist
Includes glossary and bibliographical references

Hense, Mary
How fighter pilots use math; math curriculum
consultant: Rhea A. Stewart. Chelsea Clubhouse
2010 32p il (Math in the real world) lib bdg $28
Grades: 4 5 6   **629.13**
1. Aeronautics 2. Air pilots 3. Mathematics
4. Vocational guidance
ISBN 978-1-60413-605-0 (lib bdg); 1-60413-605-7 (lib
bdg)   LC 2009-20242
This describes how fighter pilots use math to judge
speed, attain altitude, and maintain safety, and includes
relevant math problems and information about how to
become a fighter pilot
Includes glossary and bibliographical references

Hodgkins, Fran, 1964-
How people learned to fly; by Fran Hodgkins;
illustrated by True Kelley. HarperCollinsPublishers
2007 33p il (Let's-read-and-find-out science)
$15.99; pa $5.99
Grades: K 1 2 3   **629.13**
1. Aeronautics 2. Flight
ISBN   978-0-06-029558-5;   0-06-029558-9;
978-0-06-445221-2 (pa); 0-06-445221-2 (pa)
                              LC 2006000482
"This book explains the development of aircraft and
the scientific principles behind them. Complex ideas,
such as gravity and lift, are made accessible through concise explanations and excellent illustrations and diagrams,
which are always bright, clear, and appealing." SLJ

629.133 Aircraft types

Clark, Willow
Planes on the move. PowerKids Press 2010 24p
il (Transportation station) lib bdg $21.25; pa $8.25
Grades: 2 3   **629.133**
1. Airplanes 2. Aeronautics
ISBN 978-1-4358-9332-0 (lib bdg); 1-4358-9332-8 (lib
bdg); 978-1-4358-9752-6 (pa); 1-4358-9752-8 (pa)
Learn about all kinds of planes, including passenger
planes, seaplanes, and planes used by the military.
"Clark has done a fine job of including meaningful
content in a limited space. . . . [This] title consists of 10
two-page chapters printed in a font of an inviting size.
Full-page photos–all color except one vintage photograph–with informative captions face two-paragraph text
blocks. . . . Will make readers feel they have learned
something." SLJ
Includes glossary

Graham, Ian, 1953-
Aircraft; [by] Ian Graham. Black Rabbit Books
2009 32p il (How machines work) $18.95
Grades: 3 4 5   **629.133**
1. Airplanes
ISBN 978-1-59920-292-1; 1-59920-292-1
                              LC 2008002399
"Describes in detail how the engines, wings, and controls of airplanes and helicopters work." Publisher's note
This "uses informational drawings, cutaway diagrams,
and photos—including some dazzling shots of cockpit
control panels. The layout is sufficiently busy to capture
interest." Booklist

Hosking, Wayne
Asian kites. Tuttle 2005 63p il (Asian arts &
crafts for creative kids) $12.95
Grades: 3 4 5 6   **629.133**
1. Kites 2. Handicraft
ISBN 0-8048-3545-4
"This survey offers brief anecdotes and legends along
with carefully annotated construction diagrams for 15
simple kites commonly flown in Asia. . . . Closing with
notes on running a kite-making workshop for children,
lists of associations and sources of supplies, and a relatively extensive bibliography, this title merits, and will
find, a wide audience in libraries large or small." SLJ

Nahum, Andrew
Flying machine; written by Andrew Nahum. rev
ed. DK Pub. 2004 72p il (DK eyewitness books)
$15.99; lib bdg $19.99
Grades: 4 5 6 7   **629.133**
1. Aeronautics—History
ISBN 0-7566-0680-2; 0-7566-0679-9 (lib bdg)
First published 1990 by Knopf
A photo essay tracing the history and development of
aircraft from hot-air balloons to jetliners. Includes information on the principles of flight and the inner workings
of various flying machines.

Oxlade, Chris
Airplanes; uncovering technology. Firefly Books
2006 52p il $16.95
Grades: 4 5 6 7   **629.133**
1. Airplanes
ISBN 1-55407-134-8
This "book covers civilian and military airplanes and
helicopters as well as the pilots and engineers that put
them in the air. . . . [The] book contains four acetate
overlays, used in some cases to show changes over time,
in others to show a cutaway interior." Publisher's note
This offers "appealing visuals and plenty of well-
chosen facts." SLJ

629.2 Motor land vehicles, cycles

Cooper, Wade
On the road. Cartwheel Books 2008 30p il
(Scholastic reader) pa $3.99
Grades: PreK K 1   629.2
    1. Vehicles
    ISBN 978-0-545-00720-7 (pa); 0-545-00720-8 (pa)
"Vehicles—from lumbering tractors and cement mix-
ers to sleek sports cars—roll across the pages of this
Level One entry in the Scholastic Reader series. Each
spread combines a large, crisp color photo of a vehicle,
with a banner of smaller photos. The rhyming sentences
are well tuned for brand-new readers." Booklist
    Includes glossary

Smith, Miranda
Speed machines; and other record-breaking
vehicles. Kingfisher 2009 63p il (Kingfisher
knowledge) $12.95
Grades: 5 6 7 8   629.2
    1. Vehicles 2. Speed
    ISBN 978-0-7534-6287-4; 0-7534-6287-7
"This well-organized, full-color book is packed with
facts, photos, and history. It covers all aspects in history
dealing with humankind's quest for speed, including
land, water and air. . . . There are short blocks of main
text and sidebars or blurbs to add additional information.
Besides the usual suspects in books that cover this topic—cars, motorcycles, and planes—this book includes
boats, gliders, hot air balloons, trains, and windsurfing
among other speed machines. . . . It is an essential purchase, especially where books about racing, cars, planes,
trucks, motorcycles, etc. are popular." Voice Youth Advocates

629.222 Passenger automobiles

Bearce, Stephanie
All about electric and hybrid cars; and who's
driving them. Mitchell Lane Publishers 2009 47p
il (Tell your parents) lib bdg $21.50
Grades: 4 5 6 7   629.222
    1. Electric automobiles
    ISBN 978-1-58415-763-2 (lib bdg); 1-58415-763-1 (lib
    bdg)   LC 2009004528
This describes how hybrid and electric cars work and
new inventions in the automotive industry, including vehicles powered by hydrogen and solar powered cars
    Includes bibliographical references

Clark, Willow
Cars on the move. PowerKids Press 2010 24p il
(Transportation station) lib bdg $21.25; pa $8.25
Grades: 2 3   629.222
    1. Automobiles
    ISBN 978-1-4358-9333-7 (lib bdg); 1-4358-9333-6 (lib
    bdg); 978-1-4358-9754-0 (pa); 1-4358-9754-4 (pa)
Explains how cars work and shows the many different
types of cars.

"Clark has done a fine job of including meaningful
content in a limited space. . . . [This] title consists of 10
two-page chapters printed in a font of an inviting size.
Full-page photos–all color except one vintage photograph–with informative captions face two-paragraph text
blocks. . . . Will make readers feel they have learned
something." SLJ
    Includes glossary

Crowther, Robert
Cars; a pop-up book of automobiles.
Candlewick Press 2009 unp il $17.99
Grades: K 1 2 3   629.222
    1. Automobiles 2. Pop-up books
    ISBN 978-0-7636-4448-2; 0-7636-4448-X
"This introduction to all things automotive begins with
the earliest examples that can be considered cars, finishes
with a nifty foldout track scene that doubles as both
stock car and Formula One, and features an intelligent
array of information on luxury, everyday, and record-
breaking cars in between. Most of the moving pieces are
sturdily designed . . . and go a long way toward adding
some pizzazz to the straightforward text." Booklist

Juettner, Bonnie, 1968-
Hybrid cars; by Bonnie Juettner. Norwood
House Press 2009 48p il (A great idea) lib bdg
$25.27
Grades: 3 4 5 6   629.222
    1. Electric automobiles
    ISBN 978-1-59953-193-9 (lib bdg); 1-59953-193-3 (lib
    bdg)   LC 2008-22970
"Describes the invention and development of hybrid
cars." Publisher's note
"Full-color photographs and copious fun facts help
make this . . . enjoyable reading, but it's really the
choice of [topic] that is so enthralling." Booklist
    Includes glossary and bibliographical references

Mitchell, Joyce Slayton, 1933-
Crashed, smashed, and mashed; a trip to
junkyard heaven; photographs by Steven Borns.
Tricycle Press 2001 unp il hardcover o.p. pa $7.95
Grades: 3 4 5 6   629.222
    1. Automobiles 2. Salvage
    ISBN 1-58246-034-5; 1-58246-156-2 (pa)
          LC 00-10713
This describes an automobile junkyard where old cars
are salvaged for parts and scrap metal
This book offers "excellent, clear, close-up photo-
graphs and a wealth of facts." Booklist
    Includes glossary

Steggall, Susan
The life of a car. Henry Holt & Co. 2008 unp
il $16.95
Grades: PreK K 1 2   629.222
    1. Automobiles
    ISBN 0-8050-8747-8
"With torn-paper collages in saturated color and just
three words for every spread except the last, Steggall

Steggall, Susan—*Continued*
presents the life cycle of a car from its manufacture to its destruction and recycling, when the process begins anew." SLJ

Wheeler, Jill C., 1964-
Alternative cars; [by] Jill C. Wheeler. ABDO 2008 32p il (Eye on energy) $16.95
Grades: 3 4 5   **629.222**
1. Alternative fuel vehicles
ISBN 978-1-59928-803-1; 1-59928-803-6
LC 2007007107
This "begins with an explantion of the internal-combustion engine and its shortcomings. Wheeler then introduces readers to more efficient methods of powering automobiles, including electricity, a combination of gas and electricty, diesel fuel, hydrogen, natural gas, and ethanol. For each alternative she describes advantages, disadvantages, and the current availability of this technology. Captioned, full-color photographs . . . appear on nearly every page, complementing the clearly written text." Booklist
Includes glossary

Woods, Bob
Hottest muscle cars; by Bob Woods. Enslow Publishers 2008 48p il (Wild wheels!) lib bdg $23.93; pa $7.95
Grades: 4 5 6 7   **629.222**
1. Automobiles
ISBN 978-0-7660-2872-2 (lib bdg); 0-7660-2872-0 (lib bdg); 978-0-7660-3611-6 (pa); 0-7660-3611-1 (pa)
LC 2007007423
This focuses on "the beginning of America's love for muscle cars, and see why they are still loved today." Publisher's note
Includes glossary and bibliographical references

Hottest sports cars; by Bob Woods. Enslow Publishers 2008 48p il (Wild wheels!) lib bdg $23.93; pa $7.95
Grades: 4 5 6 7   **629.222**
1. Automobiles
ISBN 978-0-7660-2873-9 (lib bdg); 0-7660-2873-9 (lib bdg); 978-0-7660-3609-3 (pa); 0-7660-3909-X (pa)
LC 2007007428
This focuses on "some of the world's most famous sports cars; how they began, and where they are going in the future." Publisher's note
Includes glossary and bibliographical references

629.224 Trucks

Barton, Byron
Trucks. Crowell 1986 unp il lib bdg $15.89 *
Grades: PreK K 1   **629.224**
1. Trucks
ISBN 0-690-04530-1   LC 85-47901
Brief text and illustrations present a variety of trucks from cement trucks to ice-cream trucks, and what they do

"A tightly focused (book) . . . featuring Barton's trademark bright, blocky graphics and spare text." Publ Wkly

Lindeen, Mary, 1962-
Trucks; by Mary Lindeen. Bellwether Media 2007 24p il (Mighty machines) lib bdg $18.50
Grades: PreK K 1 2 3   **629.224**
1. Trucks
ISBN 978-1-60014-063-1 (lib bdg); 1-60014-063-7 (lib bdg)   LC 2006035265
"Blastoff! readers"
This explains what a truck is and describes its major parts and that they do.
The glossary features "easy-to-read-and-understand definitions. . . . With [its] exciting, full-color photos on every spread, [this] will certainly appeal to the mighty curiosity of young readers." SLJ
Includes glossary and bibliographical references

Maass, Robert
Little trucks with big jobs; [by] Robert Maass. Henry Holt & Co. 2007 unp il $16.95
Grades: PreK K   **629.224**
1. Trucks
ISBN 978-0-8050-7748-3; 0-8050-7748-0
LC 2006030617
"Children are introduced to 15 little rigs and the important work they do. Simple, clear explanations accompany each full-page photograph. . . . Bright, primary colored backgrounds frame the pictures, and the text appears inside road-sign shapes. This high-interest book is sure to be popular with vehicle fans." SLJ

Murrell, Deborah Jane, 1963-
Mega trucks. Tangerine Press 2008 c2005 32p il $6.99
Grades: PreK K 1 2   **629.224**
1. Trucks
ISBN 0-439-85056-8
First published in 2005 by Scholastic
"Discusses the parts and functions of different kinds of trucks, including tractor-trailers, loaders, and monster trucks." Publisher's note

Simon, Seymour, 1931-
Seymour Simon's book of trucks. HarperCollins Pubs. 2000 unp il hardcover o.p. pa $6.99 *
Grades: K 1 2 3   **629.224**
1. Trucks
ISBN 0-06-028473-0; 0-06-028481-1 (lib bdg); 0-06-446224-2 (pa)   LC 99-14602
Describes various kinds of trucks and their functions, including a log truck, cement mixer truck, and sanitation truck
"The exciting photographs, many of them close-ups, will captivate youngsters. . . . The visual appeal of this book is very high and the information is clear and equally engaging." SLJ

Stille, Darlene R., 1942-

Trucks. Children's Press 1997 47p il (True book) lib bdg $22; pa $6.95

Grades: 2 3 4   629.224

1. Trucks

ISBN 0-516-20343-6 (lib bdg); 0-516-26179-7 (pa)
LC 96-25727

Describes different kinds of trucks, including tractor trailers and tank trucks, pick-ups, tow trucks, fire trucks, garbage trucks, vans, and recreational vehicles

Includes bibliographical references

629.225   Work vehicles

Abramson, Andra Serlin

Heavy equipment up close; [by] Andra Serlin Abramson. Sterling Pub. Co. 2008 47p il (Up close) $9.95 *

Grades: 2 3 4   629.225

1. Construction equipment

ISBN 978-1-4027-4799-1; 1-4027-4799-3
LC 2007019277

This is "packed with full-color photographs on pages measuring about 10 1/2 x 14 inches, many of which open out into eye-popping gatefolds. This . . . title is tailor-made for children known to gaze longingly at construction sites. Even preschoolers will enjoy the photos . . . but children who can read on their own, or sit still through each page's several pages of text, will get the most out the book's terrific mix of fun and technical vocabulary." Booklist

Lindeen, Mary, 1962-

Tractors; by Mary Lindeen. Bellwether Media 2007 24p il (Mighty machines) lib bdg $18.50

Grades: PreK K 1 2 3   629.225

1. Tractors

ISBN 978-1-60014-061-7 (lib bdg); 1-60014-061-0 (lib bdg)   LC 2006035263

"Blast off! readers"

This explains what a tractor is and discusses its major parts and what they do.

The glossary features "easy-to-read-and-understand definitions. . . . With [its] exciting, full-color photos on every spread, [this] colorful [title] will certainly appeal to the mighty curiosity of young readers." SLJ

Includes glossary and bibliographical references

629.227   Cycles

Clark, Willow

Bikes on the move. PowerKids Press 2010 24p il (Transportation station) lib bdg $21.25; pa $8.25

Grades: 2 3   629.227

1. Bicycles 2. Cycling

ISBN 978-1-4358-9334-4 (lib bdg); 1-4358-9334-4 (lib bdg); 978-1-4358-9756-4 (pa); 1-4358-9756-0 (pa)

Learn about mountain bikes, racing bikes and lowrider bikes.

"Clark has done a fine job of including meaningful content in a limited space. . . . [This] title consists of 10 two-page chapters printed in a font of an inviting size. Full-page photos–all color except one vintage photograph–with informative captions face two-paragraph text blocks. . . . Will make readers feel they have learned something." SLJ

Includes glossary

Motorcycles on the move. PowerKids Press 2010 24p il (Transportation station) lib bdg $21.25; pa $8.25

Grades: 2 3   629.227

1. Motorcycles

ISBN 978-1-4358-9335-1 (lib bdg); 1-4358-9335-2 (lib bdg); 978-1-4358-9758-8 (pa); 1-4358-9758-7 (pa)

Introduces the various kinds of motorcycles and their uses.

"Clark has done a fine job of including meaningful content in a limited space. . . . [This] title consists of 10 two-page chapters printed in a font of an inviting size. Full-page photos–all color except one vintage photograph–with informative captions face two-paragraph text blocks. . . . Will make readers feel they have learned something." SLJ

Includes glossary

Gibbons, Gail

Bicycle book. Holiday House 1995 unp il $16.95; pa $6.95

Grades: K 1 2 3   629.227

1. Bicycles 2. Cycling

ISBN 0-8234-1199-0; 0-8234-1408-6 (pa)
LC 95-5911

"The history of bicycles, the science behind their design, descriptions of different types, their care, and safety rules are all clearly and simply presented in Gibbons's typical, inimitable style. Lots of color, accurate explanations, and interesting facts make this a winning choice." SLJ

Haduch, Bill

Go fly a bike! the ultimate book about bicycle fun, freedom & science; illustrated by Chris Murphy. Dutton Children's Books 2004 83p il $16.99 *

Grades: 4 5 6 7   629.227

1. Bicycles 2. Cycling

ISBN 0-525-47024-7

Gives the history, science, types of cycles, safety and the basics and maintenance of bicycles

"Halftone cartoonlike illustrations are scattered throughout, and a funny fact or joke appears in an inset on most pages. . . . This is a versatile, fact-packed book that can work for both research and recreational reading." Booklist

Smedman, Lisa

From boneshakers to choppers; the rip-roaring history of motorcycles. Annick Press 2007 120p il $24.95; pa $14.95

Grades: 5 6 7 8   **629.227**

1. Motorcycles

ISBN 978-1-55451-016-0; 1-55451-016-3; 978-1-55451-015-3 (pa); 1-55451-015-5 (pa)

"Smedman defines 'motorcycles' broadly enough to include everything from Harleys to Vespas, and even bicycles, in this lively, wide-ranging history. . . . Illustrated with a generous array of action photos, historical shots, and period advertisements." Booklist

Includes bibliographical references

Woods, Bob

Hottest motorcycles; by Bob Woods. Enslow Publishers 2008 48p il (Wild wheels!) lib bdg $23.93; pa $7.95

Grades: 4 5 6 7   **629.227**

1. Motorcycles

ISBN 978-0-7660-2874-6 (lib bdg); 0-7660-2874-7 (lib bdg); 978-0-7660-3608-6 (pa); 0-7660-3608-1 (pa)

LC 2007007425

This focuses on "the motorcycle's beginning, the chopper phenomenon, and motorcycle racing." Publisher's note

Includes bibliographical references

629.228   Racing cars

Rex, Michael

My race car. Holt & Co. 2000 unp il lib bdg $15.95

Grades: PreK K 1   **629.228**

1. Automobile racing 2. Automobiles

ISBN 0-8050-6101-0   LC 99-31773

"'I have a race car. I drive it all the time,' says a boy sitting on the floor with his toy cars. As the pages turn, the toy world becomes reality: the boy finds himself on the track with his crew, checking his car engine, and then driving his laps. . . . Short, simple sentences create excitement . . . and Rex's bright, thick-lined cartoon drawings are appealingly energetic and clear. A great choice for young race car enthusiasts who are beginning to read on their own." Booklist

629.4   Astronautics

Aldrin, Buzz

Look to the stars. G. P. Putnam's Sons 2009 40p il $17.99

Grades: 2 3 4   **629.4**

1. Astronautics 2. Space flight 3. Outer space

ISBN 978-0-399-24721-7; 0-399-24721-1

LC 2008018575

This is "a quick overview of the past and near future of human space flight. Paired with Minor's clean-lined, realistically detailed scenes of significant aircraft, spacecraft, and high spots, [the] narrative opens with Galileo, [and] closes with the rousing suggestion that the opportunity to venture into space lies just a tantalizing few years down the road for many young readers." SLJ

Barchers, Suzanne I.

Revolution in space. Marshall Cavendish Benchmark 2010 32p il (It works!) lib bdg $19.95

Grades: 3 4 5   **629.4**

1. Outer space—Exploration 2. Astronautics

ISBN 978-0-7614-4377-3 (lib bdg); 0-7614-4377-0 (lib bdg)   LC 2008-54365

"Discusses the history of space exploration, how the technology was developed, and the science behind it." Publisher's note

"This interesting, information packed [book] . . . motivates students to do their own exploring. . . . [The] book starts with an invention from long ago and gradually builds on it. The scientist famous for each invention is highlighted; the brief synopsis shares his interests growing up. The ideas that ultimately inspired the invention are shown in visual 'idea clouds' sharing the process with students. Timelines show that the inventions not only took creative thought, they also took perseverance. The appealing cartoon-like photographs add humor. . . . This . . . just may be that spark needed to create eager budding scientists." Libr Media Connection

Includes glossary and bibliographical references

Bredeson, Carmen

John Glenn returns to orbit; life on the space shuttle. Enslow Pubs. 2000 48p il (Countdown to space) $18.95

Grades: 4 5 6 7   **629.4**

1. Glenn, John, 1921- 2. Space flight 3. Space shuttles 4. Astronauts

ISBN 0-7660-1304-9   LC 99-12490

Describes the activities aboard the space shuttle Discovery during its historic flight in 1998 when John Glenn, at age seventy-seven, returned to space

"The accessible [text is] accompanied by plenty of well-captioned photos and diagrams." Horn Book Guide

Includes glossary and bibliographical references

Harris, Joseph, 1982-

Space exploration; impact of science and technology. Gareth Stevens Pub. 2010 64p il map (Pros and cons) lib bdg $35

Grades: 5 6 7 8   **629.4**

1. Astronautics 2. Outer space—Exploration

ISBN 978-1-4339-1989-3 (lib bdg); 1-4339-1989-3 (lib bdg)   LC 2009-12436

"This book examines the politics of space—the space race, weapons in space, and international cooperation, the realities of living in space, the uses of satellites and space probes, space age technologies that changed life on Earth, the future of space exploration, from space tourism to space elevators." Publisher's note

An "active layout that features color photographs, maps, graphs or charts on every spread, this . . . [book] has much to offer. . . . It conveniently outlines the range of views . . . helping students to learn how to view both sides of [the] issue[s]." SLJ

Includes glossary and bibliographical references

Jedicke, Peter

Great moments in space exploration. Chelsea House 2007 72p il (Scientific American) $30

Grades: 5 6 7 8   **629.4**

1. Astronautics 2. Outer space—Exploration

ISBN 978-0-7910-9046-6; 0-7910-9046-9

LC 2006-14774

This "introduction to the history of space exploration is well illustrated with numerous photos, many from NASA. The history is well told, with the achievements of the Soviet Union, in particular, covered quite nicely." Sci Books Films

Includes glossary and bibliographical references

Skurzynski, Gloria, 1930-

This is rocket science; true stories of the risk-taking scientists who figure out ways to explore beyond Earth. National Geographic 2010 80p il $18.95; lib bdg $28.90 *

Grades: 5 6 7 8   **629.4**

1. Rocketry 2. Aerospace engineers 3. Aeronautics

ISBN   978-1-4263-0597-9;   1-4263-0597-4; 978-1-4263-0598-6 (lib bdg); 1-4263-0598-2 (lib bdg)

LC 2009-20386

"This concise book provides a historical, as well as contemporary, introduction to the field of aeronautical engineering with a decidedly human interest perspective. . . . This text will be a great introduction to many of the significant contributors to the field of rocket science." Sci Books Films

Includes glossary and bibliographical references

Stott, Carole

Space exploration; written by Carole Stott; photographed by Steve Gorton. Dorling Kindersley 2009 71p il (DK eyewitness books) $16.99

Grades: 4 5 6 7   **629.4**

1. Astronautics 2. Outer space—Exploration

ISBN 978-0-7566-5828-1; 0-7566-5828-4

First published 1997 by Knopf

Includes clip-art CD

Describes rockets, exploratory vehicles, and other technological aspects of space exploration, satellites, space stations, and the life and work of astronauts.

629.43   Unmanned space flight

Jefferis, David

Space probes; exploring beyond Earth. Crabtree Pub. 2009 32p il (Exploring our solar system) lib bdg $26.60; pa $8.95

Grades: 3 4 5   **629.43**

1. Space probes

ISBN 978-0-7787-3724-7 (lib bdg); 0-7787-3724-1 (lib bdg); 978-0-7787-3741-4 (pa); 0-7787-3741-1 (pa)

LC 2008-46249

"The author explains what space probes are for, names many that have visited each of the major planets, and then suggests where models and mock-ups (since they can't be observed directly) might be found. . . . [The book is] designed with easily digestible blocks of ques-

tion-and-answer text sharing page space with large, sharply reproduced space photos and graphic art." SLJ

Includes glossary

Miller, Ron, 1947-

Robot explorers. Twenty-First Century Books 2007 112p il (Space innovations) lib bdg $31.93

Grades: 4 5 6   **629.43**

1. Space probes 2. Robots

ISBN 978-0-8225-7152-0 (lib bdg); 0-8225-7152-8 (lib bdg)

LC 2007002864

This describes how robots are used for space exploration

Includes bibliographical references

Siy, Alexandra

Cars on Mars; roving the red planet. Charlesbridge 2009 57p il $18.95 *

Grades: 5 6 7 8   **629.43**

1. Mars (Planet)—Exploration 2. Space vehicles

ISBN 978-1-57091-462-1; 1-57091-462-1

LC 2008-40751

Presents an introduction to the Mars Exploration Rovers (MERS), 'Spirit' and 'Opportunity,' with photographs of the Mars landscape taken over a five-year period as the rovers searched for water on the red planet

"This title will sweep readers up in an exploratory mission that has come closer than any other so far to finding sure signs of extraterrestrial life." SLJ

Includes glossary and bibliographical references

629.44   Auxiliary spacecraft

Branley, Franklyn Mansfield, 1915-2002

The International Space Station; by Franklyn M. Branley; illustrated by True Kelley. HarperCollins Pubs. 2000 32p il (Let's-read-and-find-out science) hardcover o.p. pa $5.95

Grades: K 1 2 3   **629.44**

1. Space stations 2. Astronauts

ISBN 0-06-028702-0; 0-06-445209-3 (pa)

LC 99-31897

Explains the construction and purpose of the International Space Station and the life of the astronauts on board

"The facts, including a history and background of the station and descriptions of life in space, are presented in a clear, easy-to-read manner. . . . Kelley's clearly labeled drawings and configurations reinforce the concepts presented, and the watercolor illustrations add dimension to the presentation." SLJ

Cole, Michael D.

The Columbia space shuttle disaster; from first liftoff to tragic final flight. Enslow Pubs. 2003 48p il (Countdown to space) lib bdg $18.95

Grades: 4 5 6   **629.44**

1. Columbia (Space shuttle) 2. Space vehicle accidents

ISBN 0-7660-2295-1   LC 2003-4823

First published 1995 with title: Columbia

Cole, Michael D.—*Continued*

Contents: A new kind of spaceship; Columbia in orbit; Flight and reentry; Welcome home, Columbia!; Columbia's last mission

Details the first flight of the space shuttle Columbia, as well as its tragic final flight

"The account offers a lot of information, helping to make sense of a highly complicated subject. . . . The color and b&w photographs complement the story." Libr Media Connect

Includes glossary and bibliographical references

NASA space vehicles; capsules, shuttles, and space stations. Enslow Pubs. 2000 48p il (Countdown to space) lib bdg $18.95

Grades: 4 5 6 7   629.44

1. Space vehicles 2. Outer space—Exploration

ISBN 0-7660-1308-1   LC 99-35533

Describes American space vehicles and their uses, including various space probes, the Mercury, Gemini, and Apollo capsules, Skylab, the space shuttles, and the International Space Station

Includes glossary and bibliographical references

Kerrod, Robin, 1938-

Space shuttles; [by] Robin Kerrod. World Almanac Library 2005 48p il (History of space exploration) lib bdg $30 paperback o.p.

Grades: 5 6 7 8   629.44

1. Space shuttles

ISBN 0-8368-5709-7 (lib bdg); 0-8368-5716-X (pa)

LC 2004-49217

Explores the successes of the shuttle program, including the daring recovery and repair of satellites by space-walking astronauts, and examines the human and technological costs of its tragic failures, such as the losses the Challenger and Columbia

This "is profusely illustrated with sharply reproduced space photos and artists' conceptions. . . . [This] makes an important addition for any collection supporting avid young scientists or strong science curricula." SLJ

Includes bibliographical references

Space stations; [by] Robin Kerrod. World Almanac Library 2005 48p il (History of space exploration) lib bdg $30 paperback o.p.

Grades: 5 6 7 8   629.44

1. Space stations

ISBN 0-8368-5710-0 (lib bdg); 0-8368-5717-8 (pa)

LC 2004-49071

Explores the history of space homes such as the Soviet's Salyut 1, Mir, the United States's Skylab, and the International Space Station, a truly international venture between several space countries and scheduled for completion in 2008

This "is profusely illustrated with sharply reproduced space photos and artists' conceptions. . . . [This] makes an important addition for any collection supporting avid young scientists or strong science curricula." SLJ

Includes bibliographical references

629.45 Manned space flight

Bodden, Valerie

Man walks on the Moon. Creative Education 2009 48p il map (Days of change) $32.80

Grades: 5 6 7 8   629.45

1. Project Apollo 2. Space flight to the moon

ISBN 978-1-58341-735-5; 1-58341-735-4

LC 2008009166

"With elegant design and mature prose, the Days of Change series is an ideal starting point for all manner of school projects. . . . The very first page of *Man Walks on the Moon* questions whether or not the feat was worth the resources, before reveling in the tech-heavy details of spaceflight and offering up some telling photos." Booklist

Includes bibliographical references

Branley, Franklyn Mansfield, 1915-2002

Floating in space; by Franklyn M. Branley; illustrated by True Kelley. HarperCollins Pubs. 1998 32p il (Let's-read-and-find-out science) hardcover o.p. pa $4.95

Grades: K 1 2 3   629.45

1. Astronauts 2. Space shuttles

ISBN 0-06-025433-5 (lib bdg); 0-06-445142-9 (pa)

LC 97-13052

Examines life aboard a space shuttle, describing how astronauts deal with weightlessness, how they eat and exercise, some of the work they do, and more

"This is a beautifully illustrated children's book. . . . The textual information is clearly written, easy to read, and well organized." Sci Books Films

Mission to Mars; by Franklyn M. Branley; illustrated by True Kelley; foreword by Neil Armstrong. HarperCollins Pubs. 2002 33p il (Let's-read-and-find-out science) hardcover o.p. lib bdg $17.89; pa $4.99

Grades: K 1 2 3   629.45

1. Space flight to Mars 2. Mars (Planet)—Exploration

ISBN 0-06-029807-3; 0-06-029808-1 (lib bdg); 0-06-445233-6 (pa)   LC 00-54036

The author invites readers to envision "themselves as members of the first Mars Mission's crew. . . . Along with a sprinkling of black-and-white and full-color photos, the illustrations mix clearly drawn schematics with scenes of crew members working busily inside the Mars Station or outside in heavy protective suits. An informative, inspirational introduction." SLJ

Bredeson, Carmen

What do astronauts do. Enslow Elementary 2008 32p il (I like space!) lib bdg $22.60

Grades: K 1 2 3   629.45

1. Astronautics

ISBN 978-0-7660-2942-2 (lib bdg); 0-7660-2942-5 (lib bdg)   LC 2007-02742

This answers such questions as "What is it like to blast into space? What are spacewalks? What do astronauts eat and how do they go to the bathroom?" Pub-

Bredeson, Carmen—*Continued*

lisher's note

This book "is beautifully illustrated, with photographs from NASA and other sources, and is well organized." Sci Books Films

Includes bibliographical references

Burleigh, Robert, 1936-

One giant leap; paintings by Mike Wimmer. Philomel Books 2009 unp il $16.99 *

Grades: 1 2 3   **629.45**

1. Project Apollo (U.S.)—History—Juvenile literature. 2. Space flight to the moon 3. Apollo project 4. Astronautics

ISBN 978-0-399-23883-3; 0-399-23883-2

LC 2008-15695

"Distinguished language and compelling imagery make this commemoration of the first Moon landing's 40th anniversary particularly intense. . . . The sense of immediacy is irresistible." SLJ

Chaikin, Andrew, 1956-

Mission control, this is Apollo; the story of the first voyages to the moon; [by] Andrew Chaikin, with Victoria Kohl; [with paintings by] Alan Bean. Penguin Group 2009 114p il $23.99 *

Grades: 5 6 7 8 9   **629.45**

1. Project Apollo 2. Space flight to the moon 3. Astronautics

ISBN 978-0-670-01156-8; 0-670-01156-8

LC 2009000833

"Based on interviews with 28 astronauts, this history of the Apollo program masterfully describes the missions and personalizes them with astronauts' own words. Chaikin starts with a brief overview of its origins and of the Mercury and Gemini missions. He then highlights the significance of each manned Apollo mission in chronological chapters, with full-page sidebars on such topics as food, TV coverage, space sickness and going to the bathroom in space. The handsome design has many photographs, diagrams of the rockets and modules and more than 30 well-reproduced paintings by Apollo 12 astronaut Bean." Kirkus

Includes bibliographical references

Cole, Michael D.

Space emergency; astronauts in danger. Enslow Pubs. 2000 48p il (Countdown to space) lib bdg $18.95

Grades: 4 5 6 7   **629.45**

1. Astronautics 2. Space vehicle accidents

ISBN 0-7660-1307-3   LC 99-26855

Describes emergencies that occurred during several space missions, including Apollo 13, Friendship 7, Gemini 8, and Mir

Includes glossary and bibliographical references

Dyer, Alan, 1953-

Mission to the moon. Simon & Schuster Books for Young Readers 2009 80p il $19.99

Grades: 5 6 7 8   **629.45**

1. Project Apollo 2. Space flight to the moon 3. Moon—Exploration

ISBN 978-1-4169-7935-7; 1-4169-7935-2

LC 2008-61118

"A Weldon Owen production"

"Sporting a highly visual encyclopedic format, this informative book features 200 photographs documenting early research into mankind's history with the moon, early space exploration and the space race, and the Apollo missions. Detailed cross-sections of modules, space suits and other equipment offer a sound technological overview, while information on the phases, structure and surface of the moon provides added insight. . . . A DVD and poster are included." Publ Wkly

Dyson, Marianne J.

Home on the moon; living on a space frontier. National Geographic Soc. 2003 64p il $18.95

Grades: 4 5 6 7   **629.45**

1. Moon

ISBN 0-7922-7193-9   LC 2002-5280

Considers the moon as a frontier that has been only partially explored, looking at its history, geography, and weather, as well as what people would require to live and work there. Includes activities

"Clear writing, vivid images, interesting details, and quotes from astronauts and scientists make this a lively, fact-filled introduction." Booklist

Includes glossary and bibliographical references

Floca, Brian

Moonshot; the flight of Apollo 11; written and illustrated by Brian Floca. Atheneum Books for Young Readers 2008 unp il $17.99 *

Grades: K 1 2 3   **629.45**

1. Apollo 11 (Spacecraft) 2. Space flight to the moon 3. Astronautics

ISBN 978-1-4169-5046-2; 1-4169-5046-X

LC 2007-52358

ALA ALSC Siebert Medal Honor Book (2010)

"A Richard Jackson book"

"Forty years after NASA's Apollo II mission first landed astronauts on the moon, this striking nonfiction picture book takes young readers along for the ride. . . . Written with quiet dignity and a minimum of fuss, the main text is beautifully illustrated with line-and-wash artwork that provides human interest, technological details, and some visually stunning scenes." Booklist

Hense, Mary

How astronauts use math; math curriculum consultant: Rhea A. Stewart. Chelsea Clubhouse 2010 32p il (Math in the real world) lib bdg $28

Grades: 4 5 6   **629.45**

1. Astronautics 2. Astronauts 3. Mathematics 4. Vocational guidance

ISBN 978-1-60413-610-4 (lib bdg); 1-60413-610-3 (lib bdg)   LC 2009-23926

Hense, Mary—*Continued*

This describes how astronauts use math for such tasks as calculating distance, speed, and velocity, and includes relevant math problems and information about how to become an astronaut

Includes glossary and bibliographical references

McCarthy, Meghan

Astronaut handbook. Alfred A. Knopf 2008 unp il $16.99; lib bdg $19.99

Grades: K 1 2 3   **629.45**
1. Astronautics
ISBN   978-0-375-84459-1;   0-375-84459-7;
978-0-375-94459-8 (lib bdg); 0-375-94459-1 (lib bdg)
LC 2007-31951

"Readers follow four aspiring astronauts from classroom to cockpit as they focus, study, practice, and ultimately take off. McCarthy applies a light, comic tone to the subject, reflected in her simple, expressive, cartoony acrylic paintings. . . . McCarthy introduces the paraphernalia of rocket travel with direct humor that understands and respects its audience." Booklist

McNulty, Faith

If you decide to go to the moon; illustrated by Steven Kellogg. Scholastic Press 2005 unp il $16.99 *

Grades: K 1 2 3   **629.45**
1. Space flight to the moon 2. Moon
ISBN 0-590-48359-5   LC 2004-27755

In this "picture book, readers accompany a boy on a fascinating excursion to the moon. The lyrical text provides tips on what to pack and describes the distance to be covered. After blastoff, facts about space travel are mingled with descriptions of what the journey might be like. . . . Rich artwork complements the strong text." SLJ

Platt, Richard, 1953-

Moon landing; a pop-up celebration of Apollo 11; by Richard Platt; paper engineering by David Hawcock. Candlewick Press 2008 unp il $29.99 *

Grades: 4 5 6 7   **629.45**
1. Apollo 11 (Spacecraft) 2. Space flight to the moon 3. Pop-up books
ISBN 978-0-7636-4046-0; 0-7636-4046-8

"This is a handsome, carefully engineered compendium. The text begins with the so-called space race between the United States and the Soviet Union in the 1950s and '60s and then offers brief descriptions of the 17 flights that made up the Apollo program. Here the emphasis is on the famous landing of the *Eagle* on the Moon in July 1969. The pop-ups and foldout pages on sturdy, shiny paper demonstrate the mechanical aspects of the spacecraft and offer a bold sense of both the rocketry and the trip. Small photographs and drawings surround the larger views." SLJ

Ross, Stewart

Moon: science, history, and mystery. Scholastic 2009 128p il lib bdg $18.99

Grades: 4 5 6   **629.45**
1. Project Apollo 2. Space flight to the moon 3. Moon—Exploration 4. Astronautics
ISBN 978-0-545-12732-5 (lib bdg); 0-545-12732-7 (lib bdg)

"Jam-packed with information, this colorful oversize volume chronicles the race to land a person on the Moon. Alternating chapters describe Moon mythologies and superstitions, the history of astronomical study, and the efforts involved in launching a lunar expedition. . . . The photographs pop with color and action. . . . The invaluable contribution of Muslim scientists is included. . . . [The book's] multicultural history will expand any collection." SLJ

Includes glossary

Thimmesh, Catherine

Team moon; how 400,000 people landed Apollo 11 on the moon. Houghton Mifflin Company 2006 80p il $19.95 *

Grades: 5 6 7 8   **629.45**
1. Apollo 11 (Spacecraft) 2. Space flight to the moon
ISBN 0-618-50757-4   LC 2005-10755

"Thimmesh retraces the course of the space mission that landed an actual man, on the actual Moon. It's an oft-told tale, but the author tells it from the point of view not of astronauts or general observers, but of some of the 17,000 behind-the-scenes workers at Kennedy Space Center, the 7500 Grumman employees who built the lunar module, the 500 designers and seamstresses who actually constructed the space suits, and other low-profile contributors who made the historic flight possible. . . . This dramatic account will mesmerize even readers already familiar with the event. . . . This stirring, authoritative tribute to the collective effort . . . belongs in every collection." SLJ

Includes glossary and bibliographical references

Vogt, Gregory

Apollo moonwalks; the amazing lunar missions. Enslow Pubs. 2000 48p il (Countdown to space) lib bdg $18.95

Grades: 4 5 6 7   **629.45**
1. Project Apollo 2. Space flight to the moon 3. Moon—Exploration
ISBN 0-7660-1306-5   LC 99-16921

Discusses the six Apollo missions that landed on the moon, describing the work performed there, what it is like to walk on the moon, and the collection of moon rocks

Includes glossary and bibliographical references

Spacewalks; the ultimate adventure in orbit; [by] Gregory L. Vogt. Enslow Pubs. 2000 48p il (Countdown to space) lib bdg $18.95

Grades: 4 5 6 7   **629.45**
1. Extravehicular activity (Space flight) 2. Space flight
ISBN 0-7660-1305-7   LC 99-37094

Describes the training and preparation for spacewalking, the hazards faced by astronauts, as well as the construction of spacesuits

Includes glossary and bibliographical references

629.46   Engineering of unmanned spacecraft

Johnson, Rebecca L., 1956-
Satellites. Lerner Publications Co. 2006 48p il (Cool science) lib bdg $25.26
Grades: 4 5 6   629.46
   1. Artificial satellites
   ISBN 978-0-8225-2908-8 (lib bdg); 0-8225-2908-4 (lib bdg)   LC 2004-30298
This book has "an attractive, colorful layout that will appeal to readers. Each spread includes captioned, color photographs and/or illustrations; text boxes; and, often, a 'fun fact.' . . . [This] title explains what a satellite is and discusses many aspects of satellites, including how they pertain to television broadcasts, weather forecasting, and locating black holes. Numerous amazing facts are included to pique readers' interest." SLJ
   Includes bibliographical references

629.8   Automatic control engineering

Allman, Toney, 1947-
The Nexi robot. Norwood House Press 2009 48p il (A great idea) lib bdg $25.27
Grades: 3 4 5 6   629.8
   1. Breazeal, Cynthia 2. Robots
   ISBN 978-1-59953-342-1 (lib bdg); 1-59953-342-1 (lib bdg)   LC 2009-14714
"Nexi is one of a team of four small humanoid robots that have mobility, dexterity and 'social' communication skills." Publisher's note
"The real star of this title . . . is Cynthia Breazeal, the head of the Personal Robotics Group at MIT. . . . The challenge of creating a robot with personality is understandably complex, but Allman does a fine job of making it accessible by offering up examples, and numerous photographs. . . . It's all fascinating stuff, for sure, and presented in a simple yet informative manner." Booklist
   Includes glossary and bibliographical references

Robots: from everyday to out of this world; written by the editors of Yes mag. Kids Can Press 2008 48p il $16.95; pa $8.95
Grades: 3 4 5 6   629.8
   1. Robots
   ISBN   978-1-55453-203-2;   1-55453-203-5; 978-1-55453-204-9 (pa); 1-55453-204-3 (pa)
This "introduces robots that work (defusing bombs, assembling cars, assisting surgeons, exploring Mars) and play (riding camels, kicking soccer balls). . . . Each section is packed with fascinating information, entertaining cartoon graphics, and numerous full-color photographs. The text is hip and accessible. . . . Well-organized and engaging." Booklist
   Includes glossary

VanVoorst, Jennifer, 1972-
Rise of the thinking machines; the science of robots. Compass Point Books 2009 48p il (Headline science) lib bdg $27.93; pa $7.95
Grades: 5 6 7   629.8
   1. Robots
   ISBN 978-0-7565-3377-9 (lib bdg); 0-7565-3377-5 (lib bdg); 978-0-7565-3518-6 (pa); 0-7565-3518-2 (pa)
                         LC 2008-05732
"Describes various types of robots and their functions, discusses technological advancements in the field of robotics, and considers the ethical issues surrounding autonomous robots." Publisher's note
   Includes glossary and bibliographical references

630   Agriculture

Apte, Sunita
Eating green. Bearport Pub. 2009 32p il map (Going green) lib bdg $25.27
Grades: 4 5 6 7   630
   1. Sustainable agriculture 2. Natural foods
   ISBN 978-1-59716-965-3 (lib bdg); 1-59716-965-X (lib bdg)   LC 2009-19183
Explains "steps people are taking to 'eat green' as a way of conserving Earth's resources and helping protect the planet." Publisher's note
"Color photographs (most full page) and a few diagrams accompany the informative text. . . . Overall, the [book] . . . is user-friendly and covers topics that are not easily found elsewhere." SLJ
   Includes glossary and bibliographical references

Parker, Steve
Food and farming. QEB Pub. 2010 32p il (QEB changes in . . .) lib bdg $28.50
Grades: 3 4 5 6   630
   1. Agriculture 2. Farms 3. Food supply
   ISBN 978-1-59566-775-5 (lib bdg); 1-59566-775-X (lib bdg)   LC 2008-56069
"The information is presented in brief paragraphs and sidebars. Suggestions for kids to help improve the planet are sprinkled throughout. . . . Students will enjoy this appealing layout and the information can spark further research on the topic. . . . Either digitally or on paper, students could make fantastic presentations using a similar design." Libr Media Connect
   Includes glossary

Vogel, Julia, 1958-
Local farms and sustainable foods. Cherry Lake 2010 32p il (Save the planet) lib bdg $27.07
Grades: 3 4 5 6   630
   1. Sustainable agriculture 2. Farms
   ISBN 978-1-60279-660-7 (lib bdg); 1-60279-660-2 (lib bdg)   LC 2009-38096
Teaches young readers about locally grown fruits and vegetables
"At the beginning of . . . [the] book, readers are given a mission and advised to be alert to the facts provided so that they can successfully answer the questions at the

Vogel, Julia, 1958-—Continued

end. . . . Children are made to feel part of the process; suggestions for how they can become involved abound." SLJ

Includes glossary and bibliographical references

630.9   Agriculture—Historical and geographic treatment

Michelson, Richard

Tuttle's Red Barn; the story of America's oldest family farm; illustrated by Mary Azarian. G.P. Putnam's Sons 2007 unp il $17

Grades: K 1 2 3   630.9
   1. Tuttle family 2. Family farms
   ISBN 978-0-399-24354-7; 0-399-24354-2
                      LC 2007-07514

Michelson and Azarian "salute 12 generations of Tuttles from Dover, N.H., operators of the longest continuously running family farm in the country. . . . Each chapter focuses on the male Tuttle who inherits the farm, and that Tuttle, glimpsed in his youth, observes some history. . . . In Azarian's tableau-like woodcuts, styles change while character endures. Her hand-crafted aesthetic enhances the story's warmth and humanity." Publ Wkly

Rosen, Michael J., 1954-

Our farm; four seasons with five kids on one family's farm; written and photographed by Michael J. Rosen. Darby Creek Pub. 2008 144p il $18.95 *

Grades: 4 5 6 7 8   630.9
   1. Farm life—United States 2. Ohio 3. Family life
   ISBN 978-1-58196-067-9; 1-58196-067-0

A journal of one year on the Bennett farm in central Ohio. Shows how one family, with the help of relatives and friends, creates a life and livelihood on a 150-acre farm.

"This engaging book is an unsentimental, appreciative look into the world of one farm family." SLJ

631.3   Tools, machinery, apparatus, equipment

Peterson, Cris, 1952-

Fantastic farm machines; photographs by David R. Lundquist. Boyd Mills Press 2006 unp il $17.95 *

Grades: K 1 2 3   631.3
   1. Agricultural machinery
   ISBN 1-59078-271-2   LC 2005-33561

"Peterson gives readers an accurate firsthand view of modern, often computerized equipment used on today's farms. Her easy-to-understand text describes both the machines and their functions. . . . The short, informative paragraphs are surrounded by excellent color photographs that extend the text." SLJ

631.4   Soil science

Bourgeois, Paulette

The dirt on dirt; by Paulette Bourgeois with Kathy Vanderlinden; illustrated by Martha Newbigging. Kids Can Press 2008 48p il $15.95; pa $7.95

Grades: 3 4 5 6   631.4
   1. Soils 2. Soil ecology
   ISBN   978-1-55453-101-1;   1-55453-101-2;
   978-1-55453-1028 (pa); 1-55453-102-0 (pa)

"From dirty toes, fossils, earthworms, and animal burrows to buried treasure, cities, and dog bones, this engaging introduction to soil touches on a wide variety of topics clearly and concisely. 'Fun with Dirt' experiments and activities demonstrate concepts and stimulate imagination. Illustrated with well-captioned photographs and cartoon-style sketches." Booklist

Gardner, Robert, 1929-

Super science projects about Earth's soil and water; [by] Robert Gardner; illustrations by Tom Labaff. Enslow Elementary 2007 c2008 48p il (Rockin' earth science experiments) $17.95

Grades: 3 4 5   631.4
   1. Soils 2. Water 3. Science—Experiments 4. Science projects
   ISBN 978-0-7660-2735-0; 0-7660-2735-X
                 LC 2006006680

This is a "selection of earth-science projects, all focused on soil and water concepts, such as evaporation, the water cycle, and the components of soil. Each experiment is clearly explained in step-by-step instructions, illustrated with Labaff's clean-lined diagrams and formatted on uncluttered pages." Booklist

Includes glossary and bibliographical references

631.5   Cultivation and harvesting

Juettner, Bonnie, 1968-

The seed vault. Norwood House Press 2009 48p il (A great idea) lib bdg $25.27

Grades: 3 4 5 6   631.5
   1. Seeds 2. Plants—Collection and preservation 3. Endangered species 4. Biological diversity
   ISBN 978-1-59953-343-8 (lib bdg); 1-59953-343-X
   (lib bdg)   LC 2009-16567

"The seed vault in Norway houses plant seeds from around the world to be stored in the event that the plant needs to be re-introduced into the food supply." Publisher's note

"With a mix of scientific terminology and accessible sentence structure, the [book] effectively [describes] how the [idea] took shape and were put into practice by the scientists involved. . . . Color photographs are included on every page and provide a visual complement to the [text]." SLJ

Includes glossary and bibliographical references

631.8   Fertilizers, soil conditioners, growth regulators

Barker, David, 1959-
Compost it. Cherry Lake Pub. 2010 32p il (Save the planet) lib bdg $27.95
Grades: 3 4 5 6   631.8
1. Compost
ISBN 978-1-60279-656-0 (lib bdg); 1-60279-656-4 (lib bdg)   LC 2009038092
"Language Arts Explorer"
"Written as dispatches from an imaginary journalist, the pages follow several individuals who explain different types of composting: a soil ecologist, . . . a home owner, . . . an apartment dweller, . . . and, finally, the manager of large-scale, urban operation. The creative, uncrowded format features text printed in an old-fashioned typewriter font on a notebook-paper background, numerous color photos, and facts boxes. . . . This upbeat, lucid overview of compost and its benefits is a strong choice." Booklist

Glaser, Linda
Garbage helps our garden grow; a compost story; story by Linda Glaser; photography by Shelley Rotner. Millbrook 2010 32p il lib bdg $25.26
Grades: K 1 2 3   631.8
1. Compost
ISBN 978-0-7613-4911-2 (lib bdg); 0-7613-4911-1 (lib bdg)
"Clear, vivid photos give this simple introduction to composting a realistic look that makes the process look downright doable. . . . Most of Rotner's excellent photos feature one or two children as they scrape their dinner plates into a bucket indoors, add kitchen and yard waste to the compost bin outside, observe the leaves and food rotting over time, add the compost to their vegetable garden, put new plants into the ground, and watch them grow." Booklist

632   Plant injuries, diseases, pests

Mooney, Carla, 1970-
Sunscreen for plants. Norwood House Press 2009 48p il (A great idea) lib bdg $25.27
Grades: 3 4 5 6   632
1. Plants 2. Sun
ISBN 978-1-59953-344-5 (lib bdg); 1-59953-344-8 (lib bdg)   LC 2009-15641
This describes Purshade, "a new SPF 45 spray that can be applied to crops in order to prevent burning and dehydration." Publisher's note
"With a mix of scientific terminology and accessible sentence structure, the [book] effectively [describes] how the [idea] took shape and were put into practice by the scientists involved. . . . Color photographs are included on every page and provide a visual complement to the [text]." SLJ
Includes glossary and bibliographical references

633.1   Cereals

Aliki
Corn is maize; the gift of the Indians; written and illustrated by Aliki. Crowell 1976 33p il (Let's-read-and-find-out science book) hardcover o.p. pa $5.99
Grades: K 1 2 3   633.1
1. Corn
ISBN 0-690-00975-5 (lib bdg); 0-06-445026-0 (pa)
In this book, the author provides a history of corn, or maize, and "also the life cycle of the plant itself, its growth and reproductive patterns, and its many uses. Excellent illustrations by the author help convey both cultural aspects and technological uses of corn." Sci Child

Gibbons, Gail
Corn; by Gail Gibbons. Holiday House 2008 32p il $16.95
Grades: K 1 2 3   633.1
1. Corn
ISBN 978-0-8234-2169-5; 0-8234-2169-4
LC 2007051632
"Popcorn, corn on the cob, corn dogs, cornflakes—corn is used in many children's favorite foods. This book offers a cornucopia of information about the history of corn as well as details concerning planting, cultivation, harvesting, and its many uses." Publisher's note
"The colorful watercolors are sure to attract even the most reluctant readers. . . . A simple, yet informative and engaging look at an important food source." SLJ

Landau, Elaine
Corn. Children's Press 1999 47p il (True book) lib bdg $22; pa $6.95
Grades: 2 3 4   633.1
1. Corn
ISBN 0-516-21026-2 (lib bdg); 0-516-26759-0 (pa)
LC 98-47332
Examines the history, cultivation, and uses of corn
"Landau does her usual fine job of explaining a topic so that it is understandable to kids." Booklist
Includes glossary and bibliographical references

Wheat. Children's Press 1999 47p il (True book) lib bdg $22; pa $6.95
Grades: 2 3 4   633.1
1. Wheat
ISBN 0-516-21029-7 (lib bdg); 0-516-26792-2 (pa)
LC 98-47333
Examines the history, cultivation, and uses of wheat
Includes glossary and bibliographical references

Micucci, Charles, 1959-
The life and times of corn; written and illustrated by Charles Micucci. Houghton Mifflin Books for Children 2009 32p il $16
Grades: 2 3 4   633.1
1. Corn
ISBN 978-0-618-50751-1; 0-618-50751-5
LC 2008040466

Micucci, Charles, 1959-—*Continued*

This focuses on the science, uses and history of corn

This is an "entertaining and informative mix of bite-size scientific information and historical facts and mouth-watering watercolors." Booklist

Includes bibliographical references

Reynolds, Jan, 1956-

Cycle of rice, cycle of life; a story of sustainable farming. Lee & Low Books 2009 unp il map $19.95

Grades: 3 4 5   **633.1**

1. Rice 2. Sustainable agriculture 3. Bali Island (Indonesia)

ISBN 978-1-60060-254-2; 1-60060-254-1

LC 2008030518

This is a "photo-essay exploring the cultural and environmental aspects of traditional Balinese rice farming, a model of sustainable food production." Publisher's note

This is "filled with beautiful color images. . . . [It is written] in precise, accessible language. . . . Reynolds offers young readers a broad, deep understanding of the concept, even as she provides a fascinating introduction to a specific culture." Booklist

Includes glossary

633.3 Legumes, forage crops other than grasses and legumes

Bial, Raymond

The super soybean. Albert Whitman & Co. 2007 40p il $16.95

Grades: 4 5 6   **633.3**

1. Soybean

ISBN 978-0-8075-7549-9; 0-8075-7549-6

LC 2007-14165

"Pairing a densely informational text with color photos, mostly of soybeans being grown and harvested, [the author] traces their cultivation's historical background, catalogs many of the uses to which they are put, and . . . trumpets enthusiastic appreciation for their twin roles as a major U.S. export and a renewable natural resource." Booklist

633.5 Fiber crops

Moore, Heidi, 1976-

The story behind cotton. Heinemann Library 2009 32p il (True stories) $28.21

Grades: 3 4 5   **633.5**

1. Cotton

ISBN 978-1-4329-2341-9; 1-4329-2341-2

LC 2008043334

This offers history, ephemera, and basic facts about cotton and its production and uses.

Includes bibliographical references

634 Orchards, fruits, forestry

Esbaum, Jill

Apples for everyone. National Geographic 2009 16p il (Picture the seasons) pa $5.95

Grades: K 1 2   **634**

1. Apples

ISBN 978-1-4263-0523-8 (pa); 1-4263-0523-0 (pa)

LC 2009-12719

"National Geographic Kids"

Discusses how apples develop from blossoms to fruit, how they are harvested, how people use them, the history of apples in the United States, and different varieties of them

This does "a fabulous job of conjuring up the sights, smells, and sensations of a brisk autumn. Using minimal text with National Geographic's typically fine photographs, Esbaum brings out familiar, comforting details of the outdoors. . . . The writing flows with sensory details." Booklist

Farmer, Jacqueline

Apples; illustrated by Phyllis Limbacher Tildes. Charlesbridge 2007 unp il map lib bdg $16.95; pa $6.95

Grades: 1 2 3 4   **634**

1. Apples

ISBN 978-1-57091-694-6 (lib bdg); 1-57091-694-2 (lib bdg); 978-1-57091-695-3 (pa); 1-57091-695-0 (pa)

LC 2006-20942

"Farmer provides a wealth of information here. The process of grafting is clearly explained, as are the differences between apple juice and cider, the nutritional value of the popular fruit, and the apple in history and legend. A handy chart detailing the various kinds of apples and their appropriate uses is included, as is a page of facts and records and a recipe for apple pie. Watercolor illustrations feature a multicultural cast of smiling children. The pictures accurately reflect the text and are attractive." SLJ

Gibbons, Gail

Apples. Holiday House 2000 unp il $17.95; pa $6.95

Grades: K 1 2 3   **634**

1. Apples

ISBN 0-8234-1497-3; 0-8234-1669-0 (pa)

LC 99-54246

Explains how apples were brought to America, how they grow, their traditional uses and cultural significance, and some of the varieties grown

"With its cheerful, bright illustrations and clear, simple presentation, this title will be the perfect pick for the perennial fall apple-book requests." SLJ

The berry book. Holiday House 2002 unp il $16.95

Grades: K 1 2 3   **634**

1. Berries

ISBN 0-8234-1697-6   LC 2001-40602

Describes different types of berries and how they grow. Includes recipes with berry ingredients

Gibbons, Gail—*Continued*

This is a "brief, informative account. . . . Cheerful illustrations with clear labels enliven the accessible text." Horn Book Guide

Hall, Zoe, 1957-

The apple pie tree; illustrated by Shari Halpern. Blue Sky Press (NY) 1996 unp il $15.95

Grades: K 1   **634**

1. Apples

ISBN 0-590-62382-6   LC 95-31134

"From bud to fruit, two children follow the cycle of an apple tree as it is nurtured through the seasons. . . . The story ends with a nice, warm apple pie being taken from the oven. The large pictures and text are suitable for young children. The colorful, clear-cut illustrations use a paint and paper collage technique. An end note shows how bees pollinate the tree's flowers and offers a recipe for apple pie." SLJ

Landau, Elaine

Apples. Children's Press 1999 47p il (True book) lib bdg $25 paperback o.p.

Grades: 2 3 4   **634**

1. Apples

ISBN 0-516-21024-6 (lib bdg); 0-516-26571-7 (pa)
LC 98-47327

Surveys the history, cultivation, and uses of apples and describes the different kinds

This "will fill a need for young report writers." Booklist

Includes glossary and bibliographical references

Bananas. Children's Press 1999 47p il (True book) lib bdg $22; pa $6.95

Grades: 2 3 4   **634**

1. Banana

ISBN 0-516-21025-4 (lib bdg); 0-516-26574-1 (pa)
LC 98-47328

Examines the history, cultivation, and uses of bananas

Includes glossary and bibliographical references

Maestro, Betsy, 1944-

How do apples grow? illustrated by Giulio Maestro. HarperCollins Pubs. 1992 32p il (Let's-read-and-find-out science book) hardcover o.p. pa $5.99

Grades: K 1 2 3   **634**

1. Apples

ISBN 0-06-020056-1 (lib bdg); 0-06-445117-8 (pa)
LC 91-9468

Describes the life cycle of an apple from its initial appearance as a spring bud to that point in time when it becomes a fully ripe fruit

"Clear, complete. . . . Inquisitive children will find simple yet scientifically accurate answers to their questions about apple trees and their fruit. Large illustrations and limited text facilitate group-reading. The endearing, soft-toned drawings are clearly labelled, providing an excellent teaching tool or reference point for the science teacher." Sci Child

Smucker, Anna Egan

Golden delicious; a Cinderella apple story; by Anna Egan Smucker; illustrated by Kathleen Kemly. Albert Whitman & Company 2008 unp il $16.99

Grades: 1 2 3   **634**

1. Apples

ISBN 978-0-8075-2987-4; 0-8075-2987-7
LC 2007052792

This is "the story of the discovery and successful marketing of the Golden Delicious apple. The narrative is simple and direct, with an occasional flair. . . . Kemly's soft pastel illustrations provide interesting historical details, including dress and transportation, and help to move the story along. An author's note gives more background, along with details about the grafting process." SLJ

Ziefert, Harriet

One red apple; paintings by Karla Gudeon. Blue Apple Books 2009 unp il $16.99   **634**

1. Apples

ISBN 978-1-934706-67-1; 1-934706-67-1
LC 2009012663

This follows the life cycle of an apple: from fruit growing on the tree to market, to picnic, to seed, to sapling and tree, and finally to a new apple.

"With lyrical text and folk-style artwork, this handsome picture book celebrates the pleasures of a favorite food while accentuating nature's cycles and Earth's bounty." SLJ

634.9   Forestry

Morrison, Taylor, 1971-

Wildfire. Houghton Mifflin Co. 2006 48p il $17

Grades: 4 5 6   **634.9**

1. Wildfires 2. Forest fires

ISBN 978-0-618-50900-3; 0-618-50900-3
LC 2005-30483

"Walter Lorraine books"

This is an "overview of the people involved in fighting wildfires and the techniques and equipment they use. Detailed paintings aid in explaining how firefighters work and in describing the natural conditions that lead to initial fires and more dangerous developments. . . . The pages are packed with visual and textual information." SLJ

Includes glossary and bibliographical references

Silverstein, Alvin

Wildfires; the science behind raging infernos; [by] Alvin and Virginia Silverstein and Laura Silverstein Nunn. Enslow Publishers 2010 48p il map (The science behind natural disasters) lib bdg $23.93 *

Grades: 4 5 6   **634.9**

1. Wildfires

ISBN 978-0-7660-2973-6 (lib bdg); 0-7660-2973-5 (lib bdg)   LC 2008-48025

Silverstein, Alvin—*Continued*

"Examines the science behind wildfires, including what causes them, the different types of wildfires, their devastating effects, and how to stay safe during a wildfire." Publisher's note

"Scientific explanations are accompanied by plentiful color diagrams that will help students to grasp causes and effects. . . . Photos . . . are effective, and are sometimes turned into helpful, lively diagrams by the addition of such features as wind-direction arrows." SLJ

Includes glossary and bibliographical references

635   Garden crops (Horticulture) Vegetables

Creasy, Rosalind

Blue potatoes, orange tomatoes; illustrations by Ruth Heller. Sierra Club Bks. for Children 1994 40p il hardcover o.p. pa $6.95

Grades: 3 4 5   635

1. Vegetable gardening 2. Vegetables

ISBN 0-87156-576-5; 0-87156-919-1 (pa)

LC 92-38800

Describes how to plant and grow a variety of colorful vegetables, including red corn, yellow watermelons, and multicolored radishes, and includes recipes

"With interesting and authentic information about gardening accompanied by brilliant, life-like illustrations, this book will not only promote the delight in growing plants but enhance the wonder in the natural world right in your own backyard." Appraisal

Esbaum, Jill

Seed, sprout, pumpkin, pie. National Geographic 2009 16p il (Picture the seasons) pa $5.95

Grades: K 1 2   635

1. Pumpkin

ISBN 978-1-4263-0582-5 (pa); 1-4263-0582-6 (pa)

LC 2009-12735

"National Geographic Kids"

Discusses how pumpkins grow, the different varieties of pumpkins, and the many ways people use them

"Using minimal text with National Geographic's typically fine photographs, Esbaum brings out familiar, comforting details of the outdoors. . . . Perfect for Halloween, [this] is a veritable festival of orange featuring . . . panoramas of pumpkin fields and market stands, . . . the rarely appreciated pumpkin flower, pumpkins so big people make boats out of them, and . . . jack-'o-lanterns. . . . Fun, cozy, evocative stuff." Booklist

Fridell, Ron, 1943-

Life cycle of a pumpkin; [by] Ron Fridell and Patricia Walsh. rev ed. Heinemann Library 2009 32p il (Life cycle of a) $25.36; pa $7.99

Grades: 2 3 4   635

1. Pumpkin

ISBN   978-1-4329-2527-7;   1-4329-2527-X; 978-1-4329-2544-4 (pa); 1-4329-2544-X (pa)

LC 00011234

First published 2002

"From seed to seedling, vine, and finally full-grown fruit, the life cycle of the pumpkin is clearly and colorfully described. Bright and engaging full-color photographs amplify the text on each page." SLJ

Includes bibliographical references

Gibbons, Gail

The pumpkin book. Holiday House 1999 unp il $16.95; pa $6.95

Grades: K 1 2 3   635

1. Pumpkin

ISBN 0-8234-1465-5; 0-8234-1636-4 (pa)

LC 98-45267

Describes how pumpkins come in different shapes and sizes, how they grow, and their traditional uses and cultural significance. Includes instructions for carving a pumpkin and drying the seeds

"Bold, clear watercolor illustrations and a concise text work together. . . . Gibbons succeeds once again at covering a topic in a useful way at just the right level for beginning readers." SLJ

The vegetables we eat; by Gail Gibbons. Holiday House 2007 32p il $16.95

Grades: K 1 2 3   635

1. Vegetables

ISBN 0-8234-2001-9; 978-0-8234-2001-8

LC 2005052654

"A clear, informative introduction to eight groups of vegetables, categorized by the part of the plant that is eaten. For each group, Gibbons includes an illustration of one representative veggie as it grows in a garden. The rest of the page includes illustrations of related plants. . . . The author offers basic suggestions for starting a garden and shows how produce goes from large farms to processing plants and grocery stores. . . . Familiar paneled illustrations and accessible text combine to present a simple, effective approach to the topic." SLJ

Grow it, cook it. DK Pub. 2008 80p il $15.99

Grades: 3 4 5 6   635

1. Vegetable gardening 2. Cooking

ISBN 978-0-7566-3367-7; 0-7566-3367-2

This "title combines instructions for growing edible plants with recipes based on the harvest. . . . The lush photos of ripening vegetables . . . will spark children's curiosity and inspire them to learn more. . . . Most children will need help . . . as they prepare the delicious, often sophisticated culinary treats. . . . An attractive introduction to both gardening and healthy meals." Booklist

Hirsch, Rebecca E., 1969-

Growing your own garden; by Rebecca Hirsch. Cherry Lake Pub. 2010 32p il (Save the planet) lib bdg $27.07

Grades: 3 4 5 6   635

1. Vegetable gardening

ISBN 978-1-60279-657-7 (lib bdg); 1-60279-657-2 (lib bdg)   LC 2009-38093

"Language Arts Explorer"

"Teaches young readers how to grow a garden, including choosing the right seeds, weeding, watering, and har-

Hirsch, Rebecca E., 1969-—*Continued*
vesting." Publisher's note

"At the beginning of . . . [the] book, readers are given a mission and advised to be alert to the facts provided so that they can successfully answer the questions at the end. . . . Children are made to feel part of the process; suggestions for how they can become involved abound." SLJ

Includes glossary and bibliographical references

Morris, Karyn
The Kids Can Press jumbo book of gardening; written by Karyn Morris; illustrated by Jane Kurisu. Kids Can Press 2000 240p il pa $14.95 *
Grades: 4 5 6 7   **635**
  1. Gardening
  ISBN 1-55074-690-1
"Sections cover general information; fruit, vegetable, and flower gardens; noninvasive native plants; gardens that attract wildlife; and group projects. Projects range from a few annuals in a container and thickets designed with native wildlife in mind to community gardens. Directions are clear, with plenty of diagrams and illustrations." Booklist

Ready set grow! quick and easy gardening projects. DK Pub. 2010 79p il $12.99
Grades: 3 4 5   **635**
  1. Gardening
  ISBN 978-0-7566-5887-8; 0-7566-5887-X
"Sunny and energetic spreads feature more than 30 garden project ideas, aimed at getting kids outdoors and in the dirt. Photographs and illustrations teach the basics about plant cultivation. . . . Recycling is a recurring theme, . . . many of the garden-related projects tend toward the whimsical, . . . and there's a strong emphasis on growing edible plants. . . . The fun, easy, and green concepts should have readers eagerly awaiting spring." Publ Wkly

Robbins, Ken, 1945-
Pumpkins. Roaring Brook Press 2006 unp il $14.95
Grades: K 1 2   **635**
  1. Pumpkin
  ISBN 978-1-59643-184-3; 1-59643-184-9
               LC 2005-33023
"A Neal Porter book"
"Robbins traces the life cycle of the pumpkin, offering in each spread just enough read-aloud text and a framed photograph on one page, and a full-bleed photo on the facing page." Bull Cent Child Books
"With color photos that equal any painting for artistry of composition and sensitivity, Robbins has created a book that is certain to become an autumn favorite." SLJ

Rockwell, Anne F., 1934-
One bean; pictures by Megan Halsey. Walker & Co. 1998 unp il hardcover o.p. pa $6.95
Grades: K 1 2   **635**
  1. Beans
  ISBN 0-8027-8648-0; 0-8027-7572-1 (pa)
               LC 97-36249

"An easy-to-read text combines with lively illustrations to create the story of what happens to one small bean when it interacts with some soil, just a little water, a lot of sunlight, and a young child's tender care." Sci Child

635.9 Flowers and ornamental plants

Bearce, Stephanie
A kid's guide to container gardening. Mitchell Lane Publishers 2009 48p il (Gardening for kids) lib bdg $29.95
Grades: 3 4 5 6   **635.9**
  1. Container gardening
  ISBN 978-1-58415-814-1 (lib bdg); 1-58415-814-X (lib bdg)   LC 2009001314
This is a guide to growing plants in tubs, buckets, and other containers
This book is "filled with information, which is divided into neat chapters written in a chatty, enthusiastic voice. . . . [The book features] large type, embedded with bolded vocabulary words, . . . as well as sharp color photos on every page." Booklist
Includes bibliographical references

A kid's guide to making a terrarium. Mitchell Lane Publishers 2009 48p il (Gardening for kids) lib bdg $29.95
Grades: 3 4 5 6   **635.9**
  1. Terrariums
  ISBN 978-1-58415-813-4 (lib bdg); 1-58415-813-1 (lib bdg)   LC 2009001319
This book is "filled with information, which is divided into neat chapters written in a chatty, enthusiastic voice. . . . [The book features] large type, embedded with bolded vocabulary words, . . . as well as sharp color photos on every page." Booklist
Includes bibliographical references

636 Animal husbandry

Gunter, Veronika Alice
Pet science; 50 purr-fectly woof-worthy activities for you & your pets; by Veronika Alice Gunter and Rain Newcomb; illustrated by Tom LaBaff. Lark Books 2006 80p il $14.95
Grades: 3 4 5 6   **636**
  1. Pets 2. Science—Experiments
  ISBN 1-57990-786-5   LC 2005-4860
This "book of 50 activities encourages budding ethnologists to investigate, explore, and record their pet's behavior. . . . Delightful four-color illustrations fill the pages. . . . This engaging book is a delightful way to bring science to young children." Sci Books Films
Includes glossary

Jones, Charlotte Foltz, 1945-

The king who barked; real animals who ruled; illustrated by Yayo. Holiday House 2009 40p il $16.95

Grades: 3 4 5   **636**

1. Animals

ISBN 978-0-8234-1925-8; 0-8234-1925-8

LC 2008-25669

"The brief accounts in this whimsical collection of animal anecdotes introduce symbolic leaders such as goat mayors, dog-kings, and a rhinoceros who won a seat on the São Paulo city council in a write-in campaign. The stories, which are arranged by continent of origin, hail from legends and oral histories, though some are more recent and better documented. Yayo's acrylic-on-canvas paintings capture the topsy-turvy spirit of the tales and add playful details." SLJ

Includes bibliographical references

Keenan, Sheila, 1953-

Animals in the house; a history of pets and people. Scholastic Nonfiction 2007 112p il $17.99 *

Grades: 4 5 6   **636**

1. Pets

ISBN 978-0-439-69286-1; 0-439-69286-5

"Keenan provides an overview of pets and their people. Beginning with statistics about pet ownership, the text goes on to describe how animals and humans came together . . . and discusses how this relationship has changed and deepened. . . . Eye-catchingly designed, the format uses Photoshop to best advantage, providing interesting graphics, popping borders, and plenty of pictures featuring adorable animals." Booklist

Includes bibliographical references

Love, Ann, 1947-

Talking tails; the incredible connection between people and their pets; [by] Ann Love & Jane Drake; illustrated by Bill Slavin. Tundra Books 2010 80p il $22.95

Grades: 3 4 5 6   **636**

1. Pets

ISBN 978-0-88776-884-2; 0-88776-884-9

"Focusing mainly on dogs and cats but with some attention to fish, reptiles, rodents, and birds, Love and Drake celebrate the affection that connects people with their pets. Along with providing a historical overview of animal domestication, . . . the authors profile some famous real pets. . . . They run through major cat and dog breeds; discuss characteristic instincts, personalities, behavior, and body language; and explain how to plan for, choose, . . . and care for an animal. . . . Slavin skillfully captures the bountiful warmth here. . . . This will draw animal lovers like a magnet." Booklist

636.08   Specific topics in animal husbandry

Doner, Kim, 1955-

On a road in Africa; [by] Kim Doner; afterword by Chryssee Perry Martin. Tricycle Press 2008 unp il $15.95

Grades: PreK K 1 2   **636.08**

1. Wildlife conservation 2. Animals—Africa 3. Stories in rhyme

ISBN 978-1-58246-230-1; 1-58246-230-5

LC 2007-18199

"Doner celebrates the work of Chryssee Perry Martin, dubbed 'Mama Orphanage' for her work as an honorary warden of the Kenya Wildlife Service." SLJ

"This is a lovely picture book to share as a rhyming story, animal book, or cultural introduction." Libr Media Connect

Larson, Kirby, 1954-

Two Bobbies; a true story of Hurricane Katrina, friendship, and survival; [by] Kirby Larson and Mary Nethery; illustrations by Jean Cassels. Walker & Co. 2008 unp il $16.99

Grades: K 1 2 3   **636.08**

1. Dogs 2. Cats 3. Hurricane Katrina, 2005

ISBN 978-0-8027-9754-4; 0-8027-9754-7

"Abandoned during the [Hurricane] Katrina evacuations, pets Bobbi [the dog] and Bob Cat wander dangerous, debris-strewn streets seeking food and water. Eventually taken to a rescue shelter, the Bobbies show distress when separated but remain calm when together. Workers then discover that Bob Cat is blind and that Bobbi seems to serve as his seeing-eye dog. . . . The descriptive, sometimes folksy prose and realistically rendered gouache illustrations accessibly convey the Bobbies' experiences and mutual devotion. . . . This moving story about the importance of friendship and home highlights the plight of the hurricane's lost and left-behind animals, as well as the value of animal shelters." Booklist

636.088   Animals for specific purposes

Halls, Kelly Milner, 1957-

Saving the Baghdad Zoo; a true story of hope and heroes; by Kelly Milner Halls and Major William Sumner. Greenwillow Books 2010 64p il map $17.99

Grades: 4 5 6 7   **636.088**

1. Baghdad Zoo (Iraq) 2. Zoos 3. Wildlife conservation 4. Baghdad (Iraq)

ISBN 978-0-06-177202-3; 0-06-177202-X

"This eye-opening tale of compassion and cooperation chronicles the mission of an international team of military personnel, zoo staffers, veterinarians, and relief workers to rescue neglected animals in Baghdad. . . . Sobering and uplifting photographs—many taken by Sumner—underscore both the direness of the situation and the spirit of hope that drove the project." Publ Wkly

Includes bibliographical references

Kent, Deborah, 1948-
Animal helpers for the disabled. Watts 2003 63p il (Watts library) $25.50 paperback o.p. *
Grades: 4 5 6 7　　　　　　　　　　　**636.088**
  1. Animals and the handicapped 2. Animals—Training 3. Guide dogs
  ISBN 0-531-12017-1; 0-531-16663-5 (pa)
                  LC 2002-8885
Explores the history of guide dogs, service animals, and assistance dogs, and discusses the process of training them to help people who have physical disabilities
  This is an "informative, often inspirational and thought-provoking [book]." Booklist
  Includes bibliographical references

Laidlaw, Rob
Wild animals in captivity; [by] Rob Laidlaw. Fitzhenry & Whiteside 2008 48p il $19.95
Grades: 5 6 7 8　　　　　　　　　　　**636.088**
  1. Animal welfare 2. Zoos
  ISBN 978-1-55455-025-8; 1-55455-025-4
"A passionate, well-written, and well-researched argument against the practices of most zoos around the world. . . . Describes the damage done when animals are unnaturally confined and moved to inhospitable climates, and compares the wild and captive lives of polar bears, orcas, elephants, and great apes—the four species most harmed by captivity. . . . The issues raised in this important and powerful book will resonate with young and old." SLJ

Markle, Sandra, 1946-
Animal heroes; true rescue stories; by Sandra Markle. Millbrook Press 2009 64p il lib bdg $29.27
Grades: 4 5 6 7　　　　　　　　　　　**636.088**
  1. Pets 2. Animals 3. Rescue work
  ISBN 978-0-8225-7884-0 (lib bdg); 0-8225-7884-0 (lib bdg)　　　　　　　　　　　　　LC 2007-50435
"Nine stories, based on interviews with the grateful survivors, describe how brave animals rescued people in catastrophic circumstances. Each edgy retelling reveals details that only the participants could know, including sounds, smells, sights, and the knowledge that at any moment they could die, deepening the tension. Mixed in are Markle's broad and perfectly attuned insights about animal behavior." SLJ
  Includes glossary and bibliographical references

636.089　Veterinary sciences. Veterinary medicine

Jackson, Donna M., 1959-
ER vets; life in an animal emergency room. Houghton Mifflin 2005 88p il $17
Grades: 5 6 7 8　　　　　　　　　　　**636.089**
  1. Veterinary medicine
  ISBN 0-618-43663-4
"With plentiful, excellent-quality photographs, this highly visual book offers a behind-the-scenes look at an emergency animal hospital in Colorado. . . . A section

on grief counseling for families with critically ill pets and a spread on how to put together a pet first-aid kit are included. Well-researched and well-written, ER Vets is an engaging book on a hot topic." SLJ

636.1　Equines. Horses

Barnes, Julia, 1955-
Horses at work; [by] Julia Barnes. North American ed. Gareth Stevens 2006 32p il (Animals at work) lib bdg $23.93
Grades: 3 4 5　　　　　　　　　　　　**636.1**
  1. Horses 2. Working animals
  ISBN 0-8368-6225-2　　　　　LC 2005054066
This describes horses' uses throughout history, their relationship with humans, habitat, diet, and appearance.
  This is "well-written, well-organized, . . . visually appealing and fun to read." SLJ
  Includes bibliographical references

Bowers, Nathan, 1988-
4-H guide to training horses. Voyageur Press 2009 176p il $18.99
Grades: 5 6 7 8　　　　　　　　　　　**636.1**
  1. Horses—Training
  ISBN 978-0-7603-3627-4; 0-7603-3627-X
                  LC 2009015299
This provides "sound and comprehensive information. [The book] covers basic training techniques and riding skills such as mounting, saddling, reining, stopping and starting, and posture among other topics. The training techniques offer insight into equine behavior based on their history as prey animals. The authors also emphasize that horse owners' success will be determined by how much effort they are willing to expend on their relationship with their animals. The many color photographs clearly depict the methods and activities that are taking place, and the accompanying images further clarify what is happening and its significance." SLJ
  Includes glossary

Bozzo, Linda
My first horse; [by] Linda Bozzo. Enslow Elementary 2007 32p il (My first pet library from the American Humane Association) lib bdg $22.60
Grades: 1 2 3　　　　　　　　　　　　**636.1**
  1. Horses
  ISBN 978-0-7660-2753-4 (lib bdg); 0-7660-2753-8 (lib bdg)　　　　　　　　　　　LC 2006014969
  Also available English-Spanish bilingual edition
This offers brief basic advice on selecting a horse and caring for it.
  Includes glossary and bibliographical references

Draper, Judith

My first horse and pony book; [by] Judith Draper. Kingfisher 2005 47p il $9.95

Grades: K 1 2 3   **636.1**

1. Horses 2. Horsemanship

ISBN 0-7534-5878-0

This "guide covers the basics about horses and ponies, including physical characteristics, care and feeding, grooming, and stabling. After discussing proper clothing and tacking up, the author takes a look at English and Western riding. . . . The photos are excellent—bright and clear—and precisely illustrate what the text is describing." SLJ

My first horse and pony care book; [by] Judith Draper. Kingfisher 2006 48p il $9.95 *

Grades: K 1 2 3   **636.1**

1. Horses 2. Horsemanship

ISBN 978-0-7534-5989-8; 0-7534-5989-2

                    LC 2006005962

"Draper focuses on pony breeds commonly used in the United Kingdom and on English-style riding and tack. The information about feeding, grooming, and riding is detailed, accurate, and accessible. . . . The photographs are beautiful and in sharp focus. . . . This book is a must-have for young horse lovers." SLJ

Includes glossary

Gibbons, Gail

Horses! Holiday House 2003 unp il $17.95; pa $6.95

Grades: K 1 2 3   **636.1**

1. Horses 2. Horsemanship

ISBN 0-8234-1703-4; 0-8234-1875-8 (pa)

                    LC 2003-41683

Presents information on horses, including their physical characteristics, behavior, and how to ride a horse

"Attractive, full-color labeled illustrations fill every page, with many expanding on a particular point in the main text. . . . The book's accessible format will attract browsers as well as legions of young would-be equestrians." Booklist

Hamilton, Libby

Horse: the essential guide for young equestrians; writer, Libby Hamilton; illustrators: Sophie Allsopp . . . [et al.] Candlewick Press 2008 24p il $15.99

Grades: 2 3 4 5   **636.1**

1. Horses

ISBN 978-0-7636-3547-3; 0-7636-3547-2

"This clever and pleasing guide contains a wealth of information on horses, including history, breeds, care and grooming, equipment, riding, and shows. Facts and tips are presented in an imaginative and lively format. The excellent, realistic illustrations are colorful and accurate and even occasionally humorous." SLJ

Holub, Joan, 1956-

Why do horses neigh? illustrations by Anna DiVito. Dial Bks. for Young Readers 2003 46p il (Dial easy-to-read) hardcover o.p. pa $3.99 *

Grades: K 1 2   **636.1**

1. Horses

ISBN 0-8037-2770-4 (lib bdg); 0-14-230119-1 (pa)

                    LC 2001-47476

Questions and answers present information about the behavior and characteristics of horses and their interactions with humans

The book has "a bright, appealing format that combines jaunty original art and well-chosen photos." Booklist

Jeffrey, Laura S.

Horses; how to choose and care for a horse. Enslow Publishers 2004 48p il (American Humane pet care library) lib bdg $23.93 *

Grades: 3 4 5   **636.1**

1. Horses

ISBN 0-7660-2519-5   LC 2003-22970

Provides information on owning a horse, including how to choose among different breeds and how to groom, house, feed, and keep a horse healthy

This offers "children solid information . . . at a level they can understand. Many endearing photos . . . make [this book] fun to look at." Booklist

Includes glossary and bibliographical references

Lomberg, Michelle

Horse. Weigl Publishers 2009 32p il (My pet) lib bdg $26; pa $9.95

Grades: 3 4 5   **636.1**

1. Horses 2. Pets

ISBN 978-1-60596-092-0 (lib bdg); 1-60596-092-6 (lib bdg); 978-1-60596-093-7 (pa); 1-60596-093-4 (pa)

                    LC 2009-25974

Information about how to house, feed, and care for horses.

"With clear, formal writing, and extensive coverage . . . [this title is] useful for reports. . . . Numerous color photographs, charts . . . and question-and-answer boxes supplement the [text]." SLJ

Includes glossary

Lunis, Natalie

Miniature horses. Bearport 2010 24p il (Peculiar pets) lib bdg $22.61

Grades: 3 4 5   **636.1**

1. Horses

ISBN 978-1-59716-861-8 (lib bdg); 1-59716-861-0 (lib bdg)

                    LC 2009-10379

Introduces the miniature horse, describing its physical characteristics, history, and behavior, and discussing the care and diet that it needs

"The language . . . is lively . . . [and] the illustrations are vivid, with photos offering some amusing shots. . . . This [book] . . . will hold readers' attention, but also challenge them to consider the responsibilities required of owners of unusual creatures." SLJ

Includes glossary and bibliographical references

Mack, Gail

Horses. Marshall Cavendish Benchmark 2010
48p il (Great pets) lib bdg $29.93

Grades: 2 3 4   **636.1**
    1. Horses
    ISBN 978-0-7614-4147-2 (lib bdg); 0-7614-4147-6 (lib
bdg)   LC 2008037262

"Describes the characteristics and behavior of pet
horses, also discussing their physical appearance and
place in history." Publisher's note

Includes glossary and bibliographical references

MacLeod, Elizabeth

Why do horses have manes? Kids Can Press
2009 64p $14.95

Grades: 3 4 5 6   **636.1**
    1. Horses
    ISBN 978-1-55453-312-1; 1-55453-312-0

In a question and answer format "this slim volume
covers standard information . . . and branches out to the
more esoteric. . . . Freestanding text sections with a
light and engaging tone combined with glossy photo vignettes of horses vamping for the camera make the book
highly browsable." Horn Book Guide

Peterson, Cris, 1952-

Horsepower; the wonder of draft horses;
photographs by Alvis Upitis. Boyds Mills Press
1997 unp il $16.95; pa $9.95

Grades: K 1 2 3   **636.1**
    1. Horses
    ISBN 1-56397-626-9; 1-56397-943-8 (pa)
                   LC 96-84679

"This book focuses on three popular breeds of draft
horses, commonly known as work horses: Belgians, Per-
cherons, and Clydesdales. Peterson introduces the families who raise and care for the horses and discusses some
horse-training procedures." Horn Book Guide

"Crisp, full-color photographs accompany the short,
smoothly written text." SLJ

Ransford, Sandy

Horse & pony breeds; written by Sandy
Ransford; photographed by Bob Langrish.
Kingfisher (NY) 2003 64p il (Kingfisher riding
club) $14.95; pa $8.99

Grades: 4 5 6 7   **636.1**
    1. Horses
    ISBN 0-7534-5575-7; 0-7534-6075-0 (pa)
                   LC 2003-272944

An "overview of an international array of horse and
pony breeds including many that may be unfamiliar to
American children. The book covers the majority of
breeds in half-page treatments that feature at least a paragraph of commentary and a captioned side body, and a
full-color photograph that points out conformation differences particular to each breed. . . . An attractive, informative book that is sure to please both readers and
browsers." SLJ

Includes glossary

Horse & pony care; written by Sandy Ransford;
photographed by Bob Langrish. Kingfisher (NY)
2002 64p il (Kingfisher riding club) hardcover o.p.
pa $8.95

Grades: 4 5 6 7   **636.1**
    1. Horses
    ISBN 0-7534-5439-4; 0-7534-5744-X (pa)

This offers instructions on such topics as washing and
clipping a pony, exercise routines and caring for
pastureland, and includes information about types of feed
and how much feed a pony needs

"Children who have a horse or want one will find a
good deal of information in this attractive, photo-rich
book. There are clear instructions. . . . The full-color
photos are well composed, fully captioned, and quite
thorough." Booklist

The Kingfisher illustrated horse & pony
encyclopedia; written by Sandy Ransford;
photographed by Bob Langrish. Kingfisher 2004
224p il $24.95 *

Grades: 4 5 6 7   **636.1**
    1. Horses 2. Horsemanship
    ISBN 0-7534-5781-4   LC 2003-27293

"The first part of the book covers the life cycle, domestication, and types of horses and ponies. . . . The
second part deals with how to care for these animals and
discusses horsemanship from taking riding lessons to
training and driving a horse. . . . Filled with appealing
photos of young people interacting with their four-legged
friends, this title is an extremely useful addition to any
collection." SLJ

Simon, Seymour, 1931-

Horses. HarperCollins Pubs. 2006 unp il $15.99;
lib bdg $16.89 *

Grades: 2 3 4   **636.1**
    1. Horses
    ISBN 0-06-028944-9; 0-06-028945-7 (lib bdg)
                   LC 2004-30392

"Simon provides the basic facts, which include the importance of horses to humans throughout history, their
evolution, physical traits, interactions among themselves,
and the various breeds. The information is clear and accurate. The striking color photos will capture readers attention." SLJ

636.2   Ruminants and Camelidae
Bovidae Cattle

Barnes, Julia, 1955-

Camels and llamas at work; [by] Julia Barnes.
Gareth Stevens 2006 32p il map (Animals at
work) lib bdg $23.93

Grades: 3 4 5   **636.2**
    1. Camels 2. Llamas 3. Working animals
    ISBN 0-8368-6222-8   LC 2005054065

"Camels and llamas serve as traditional pack animals
in harsh environments on opposite sides of the world.
They also provide entertainment, produce nutrients, and
protect other livestock. Learn about the deep traditions

Barnes, Julia, 1955-—_Continued_
that bond these unusual animals to their respective cultures." Publisher's note

This is "well-written, well-organized, . . . visually appealing and fun to read." SLJ

Includes bibliographical references

Freedman, Russell
In the days of the vaqueros; America's first true cowboys. Clarion Bks. 2001 70p il $18; pa $9.99 *

Grades: 4 5 6 7   **636.2**
1. Cowhands 2. Mexican Americans 3. Ranch life 4. Southwestern States
ISBN   0-395-96788-0;   978-0-395-96788-1; 978-0-547-13365-2 (pa); 0-547-13365-0 (pa)
                                          LC 2001-17357

"Freedman explores the often-overlooked role of the Central American cowherders who preceded by centuries the cowboys of popular lore and legend." SLJ

The author "tells the story with depth, clarity, and a vigor that conveys the thrilling excitement of the work and the macho swagger of the culture. . . . The book's design is beautiful, with spacious type on thick paper, and the dazzling illustrations—prints, paintings, and photos on almost every page." Booklist

Includes glossary and bibliographical references

Peterson, Cris, 1952-
Clarabelle; making milk and so much more; [by] Cris Peterson; photographs by David R. Lundquist. Boyds Mills Press 2007 unp il $16.95
Grades: 1 2 3   **636.2**
1. Cattle 2. Dairying
ISBN 1-59078-310-7; 978-1-59078-310-8

This focuses on "a dairy farm in northern Wisconsin, introduced through the daily life of a single cow, Clarabelle. In describing the basics of cow physiology and care and the dairy's operations, Peterson illuminates facts with comparisons that will grab kids' attention. . . . Lundquist's sharp, close-up photographs . . . will easily draw curious kids back into the science." Booklist

Includes glossary

636.3   Smaller ruminants Sheep

Minden, Cecilia, 1949-
Sheep. Cherry Lake Pub. 2010 24p il (21st century junior library: farm animals) lib bdg $22.80
Grades: 1 2 3   **636.3**
1. Sheep
ISBN 978-1-60279-544-0 (lib bdg); 1-60279-544-4 (lib bdg)   LC 2009-3318

This is an introduction to sheep as farm animals

This manages "to parlay [its] low page count into surprisingly deep and wide-ranging discussions on the various aspects of [the sheep's] existence. . . . It's the text that is so impressive, with its use of simple, explanatory language to introduce unusually advanced vocabulary. . . . [The] animal is not only shown in its natural (and

often adorable) state but also as meat on a plate. Info boxes called 'Think!' expand the discussion even further." Booklist

Includes glossary and bibliographical references

Urbigkit, Cat
The shepherd's trail; [by] Cat Urbigkit. Boyds Mills Press 2008 32p il $16.95
Grades: 2 3 4   **636.3**
1. Sheep 2. Shepherds
ISBN 978-1-59078-509-6   LC 2007017475

This "discusses the migration of domestic sheep in the western U.S. . . . Clear color photos offer close-ups of individual animals and long-range views of the flocks and the often striking landscapes. Topics discussed in the text include the roles of sheepherders, camptenders, herding dogs, guardian dogs, and sheepshearers, as well as details of the sheep's lives through the cycle of a year." Booklist

A young shepherd. Boyd Mills Press 2006 unp il $15.95
Grades: K 1 2 3   **636.3**
1. Sheep 2. Shepherds
ISBN 1-59078-364-6

"This photo-essay features a 12-year-old 4-H member (Urbigkit's son) who tends his own flock of sheep. Urbigkit . . . communicates Cass' commitment to his task in compelling photos that showcase the gamboling baby animals. . . . The close-up look at a fascinating, animal-focused activity will appeal even to readers who rarely rub shoulders with livestock." Booklist

636.4   Swine

Gibbons, Gail
Pigs. Holiday House 1999 unp il $16.95; pa $6.95
Grades: K 1 2 3   **636.4**
1. Pigs
ISBN 0-8234-1441-8; 0-8234-1554-6 (pa)
                                          LC 98-28807

Examines the basic characteristics, common breeds, intelligence, behavior, life cycle, and uses of pigs

"Bright with spring greens and yellows, this attractive book introduces pigs through simple sentences and many colorful pictures." Booklist

King-Smith, Dick, 1922-
All pigs are beautiful; illustrated by Anita Jeram. Candlewick Press 1993 unp il (Read and wonder) pa $6.99 hardcover o.p.; pa with audio CD $9.99 *
Grades: K 1 2 3   **636.4**
1. Pigs
ISBN 978-0-7636-1433-1 (pa); 0-7636-1433-5 (pa); 978-0-7636-4195-5   (pa   with   audio   CD); 0-7636-4195-2 (pa with audio CD)   LC 92-53136

The author "interlards fond reminiscences of porkers he has known with interesting facts about them that are sure to keep children absorbed. His tone is affectionate,

King-Smith, Dick, 1922-—*Continued*

amusing, and informative. Jeram's pen-and-ink and watercolor illustrations, done in soft, earthy colors, are a warm match for the text." SLJ

Minden, Cecilia, 1949-

Pigs. Cherry Lake Pub. 2010 24p il (21st century junior library: farm animals) lib bdg $22.80

Grades: 1 2 3　　　　　　　　　　　**636.4**

1. Pigs

ISBN 978-1-60279-542-6 (lib bdg); 1-60279-542-8 (lib bdg)　　　　　　　　　　　　LC 2009-3676

This is an introduction to pigs as farm animals

This manages "to parlay [its] low page count into surprisingly deep and wide-ranging discussions on the various aspects of [the pig's] existence. . . . It's the text that is so impressive, with its use of simple, explanatory language to introduce unusually advanced vocabulary. . . . [The] animal is not only shown in its natural (and often adorable) state but also as meat on a plate. Info boxes called 'Think!' expand the discussion even further ([The book] encourages readers to ask why some of their friends may not eat pork)." Booklist

Includes glossary and bibliographical references

636.5　Poultry Chickens

Gibbons, Gail

Chicks & chickens. Holiday House 2003 unp il $17.95; pa $6.95

Grades: K 1 2 3　　　　　　　　　　　**636.5**

1. Chickens

ISBN 0-8234-1700-X; 0-8234-1939-8 (pa)

LC 2002-27472

An introduction to the physical characteristics, behavior, and life cycle of chickens, as well as a discussion of how chickens are raised on farms

The author "offers lots of solid information as well as bits of trivia that will be of interest to this audience. Cartoon illustrations are large, colorful, and plentiful." SLJ

Kindschi, Tara, 1970-

4-H guide to raising chickens. Voyageur Press 2010 176p il pa $18.99

Grades: 5 6 7 8　　　　　　　　　　　**636.5**

1. Chickens

ISBN 978-0-7603-3628-1 (pa); 0-7603-3628-8 (pa)

LC 2009015300

"This title has everything one ever wanted to know about chickens but didn't know enough to ask. Eight chapters divide the text into broad topics such as getting started, choosing a breed, housing equipment, and exhibiting chickens. . . . Line drawings and charts give additional information, and the excellent color photography is profuse." SLJ

Includes glossary and bibliographical references

Minden, Cecilia, 1949-

Ducks. Cherry Lake Pub. 2010 24p il (21st century junior library: farm animals) lib bdg $22.80

Grades: 1 2 3　　　　　　　　　　　**636.5**

1. Ducks

ISBN 978-1-60279-546-4 (lib bdg); 1-60279-546-0 (lib bdg)　　　　　　　　　　　　LC 2009-5033

This is an introduction to ducks as farm animals

This manages "to parlay [its] low page count into surprisingly deep and wide-ranging discussions on the various aspects of [the duck's] existence. . . . It's the text that is so impressive, with its use of simple, explanatory language to introduce unusually advanced vocabulary. In [this book] readers learn such terminology as clutch, dabbling, and gland. . . . [The] animal is not only shown in its natural (and often adorable) state but also as meat on a plate. Info boxes called 'Think!' expand the discussion even further." Booklist

Includes glossary and bibliographical references

Sklansky, Amy E., 1971-

Where do chicks come from? illustrated by Pam Paparone. HarperCollins Publishers 2005 unp il (Let's-read-and-find-out science) hardcover o.p. pa $4.99

Grades: K 1 2　　　　　　　　　　　**636.5**

1. Chickens 2. Eggs

ISBN 0-06-028892-2; 0-06-028893-0 (lib bdg); 0-06-445212-3 (pa)　　　　　　　LC 2003-7711

Describes what happens day-by-day for the three weeks from the time a hen lays an egg until the baby chick hatches

This offers "clear and accurate text. . . . The illustrations are soft and friendly, but retain enough realism for children to understand the subject matter. . . . This is an enjoyable and informative introduction to scientific information." SLJ

636.6　Birds other than poultry

Altman, Linda Jacobs, 1943-

Parrots. Benchmark Bks. 1999 32p il (Perfect pets) lib bdg $28.50

Grades: 3 4 5 6　　　　　　　　　　　**636.6**

1. Parrots

ISBN 0-7614-1102-X　　　　　　　LC 99-49672

Provides information about the history, physical characteristics, choosing, and care of all kinds of parrots

"The writing is clear and informative. . . . Colorful, nicely detailed, framed photographs and reproductions of the animals are interspersed throughout." SLJ

Includes glossary and bibliographical references

Bozzo, Linda

My first bird; [by] Linda Bozzo. Enslow Elementary 2007 32p il (My first pet library from the American Humane Association) lib bdg $22.60

Grades: 1 2 3　　　　　　　　　　　**636.6**

1. Cage birds

ISBN 978-0-7660-2749-7 (lib bdg); 0-7660-2749-X (lib bdg)　　　　　　　　　　LC 2006008405

Bozzo, Linda—*Continued*

Also available English-Spanish bilingual edition

"This book explores how to choose the right bird and how to care for your new pet." Publisher's note

"The material is brief, providing a general overview. . . . [Illustrated with] attractive, heartwarming color photographs." SLJ

Includes glossary and bibliographical references

Haney, Johannah

Parrots. Marshall Cavendish Benchmark 2008 48p il (Great pets) lib bdg $29.93

Grades: 2 3 4   **636.6**

    1. Parrots

    ISBN 978-0-7614-2998-2 (lib bdg); 0-7614-2998-0 (lib bdg)   LC 2008-24335

"Describes the characteristics and behavior of pet parrots, also discussing their physical appearance and place in history." Publisher's note

Includes glossary and bibliographical references

Small birds. Marshall Cavendish Benchmark 2010 46p il (Great pets) lib bdg $29.93

Grades: 2 3 4   **636.6**

    1. Cage birds

    ISBN 978-0-7614-4150-2 (lib bdg); 0-7614-4150-6 (lib bdg)   LC 2008037258

"Describes the characteristics and behavior of small pet birds, also discussing their physical appearance and place in history." Publisher's note

Includes glossary and bibliographical references

Jeffrey, Laura S.

Birds; how to choose and care for a bird. Enslow Publishers 2004 48p il (American humane pet care library) lib bdg $23.93

Grades: 3 4 5   **636.6**

    1. Birds

    ISBN 0-7660-2515-2   LC 2003-22966

Provides information on keeping birds as pets, including how to choose and care for a bird

Mead, Wendy

Top 10 birds for kids; [by] Wendy Mead. Enslow Publishers 2008 48p il (Top pets for kids with American Humane) lib bdg $23.93

Grades: 2 3 4 5   **636.6**

    1. Cage birds 2. Pets

    ISBN 978-0-7660-3072-5 (lib bdg); 0-7660-3072-5 (lib bdg)   LC 2007-38479

"Provides facts on the top ten bird breeds for kids and how to care for them." Publisher's note

"Includes beautiful full-color photos showing the animals at their best. Judicious use of text boxes, crisp fonts, and white space will make it easy for readers to follow the flow of information." SLJ

Includes glossary and bibliographical references

636.7 Dogs

Altman, Linda Jacobs, 1943-

Big dogs. Benchmark Bks. 2001 32p il (Perfect pets) lib bdg $15.95

Grades: 3 4 5 6   **636.7**

    1. Dogs

    ISBN 0-7614-1101-1   LC 99-49674

Provides information about the history, physical characteristics, choice, training and care of various breeds of large dogs

Includes glossary and bibliographical references

Barnes, Julia, 1955-

Pet dogs; [by] Julia Barnes. Gareth Stevens Pub. 2007 unp il (Pet pals) lib bdg $23.93

Grades: 2 3 4 5   **636.7**

    1. Dogs

    ISBN 0-8368-6777-7   LC 2006042378

This places dogs "within the context of [their] wild roots and [their] relationship to humans. . . . Barnes explains what makes the animal an ideal pet, recommends how to be a good caregiver, and reveals how the creature communicates (as well as how to answer). The [book mixes] practical advice with trivia in a way that children will find informative and easy to navigate. Crisp, full-color photos enhance the [text]." SLJ

Includes glossary and bibliographical references

Bidner, Jenni

Is my dog a wolf? how your pet compares to its wild cousin. Lark Books 2006 64p il $9.95

Grades: 3 4 5 6   **636.7**

    1. Dogs 2. Wolves

    ISBN 978-1-57990-732-7; 1-57990-732-6

                                       LC 2005-34865

"This book identifies instinctual behaviors in wolves, such as pack living, licking and biting at one another, and howling, and describes how they are manifested in the common house dog, even though the species changed thousands of years ago. . . . Clear color photographs beautifully illustrate the text. This informative, entertaining title is suitable for reports and for general reading." SLJ

Bozzo, Linda

My first dog; [by] Linda Bozzo. Enslow Elementary 2007 32p il (My first pet library from the American Humane Association) lib bdg $22.60

Grades: 1 2 3   **636.7**

    1. Dogs

    ISBN 978-0-7660-2754-1 (lib bdg); 0-7660-2754-6 (lib bdg)   LC 2006008404

"This book will help you choose the right dog and show how to care for your new pet. Learn what your new dog needs to stay healthy." Publisher's note

"The material is brief, providing a general overview. . . . [Illustrated with] attractive, heartwarming color photographs." SLJ

Includes glossary and bibliographical references

Calmenson, Stephanie

May I pet your dog? the how-to guide for kids meeting dogs (and dogs meeting kids); by Stephanie Calmenson; illustrated by Jan Ormerod. Clarion Books 2007 32p il $9.95

Grades: PreK K 1 2   **636.7**
1. Dogs
ISBN 978-0-618-51034-4; 0-618-51034-6
                                        LC 2005-34955

Harry the dog explains how to safely meet him and his friends.

"Straightforward guidelines and a positive, encouraging tone make this book appealing and practical. Young dog lovers will delight in the variety of breeds shown in the bright, clear illustrations." SLJ

Rosie; a visiting dog's story; photographs by Justin Sutcliffe. Clarion Bks. 1994 47p il hardcover o.p. pa $6.95

Grades: K 1 2 3   **636.7**
1. Dogs
ISBN 0-395-65477-7; 0-395-92722-6 (pa)
                                        LC 93-21243

"Rosie is the true story of an endearing Tibetan terrier who works as a therapy dog with Delta Society's Pet Partners Program of New York City. Rosie's tenderness and enthusiasm come through in Sutcliffe's fantastic photos that chronicle Rosie's training and first visit to a children's hospital and a nursing home." Child Book Rev Serv

The **Complete** dog book for kids; official publication of the American Kennel Club. Howell Book House 1996 274p il maps hardcover o.p. pa $22.95 *

Grades: 4 5 6 7   **636.7**
1. Dogs
ISBN 0-87605-458-0; 0-87605-460-2 (pa)
                                        LC 96-29228

This "begins with a general section that advises readers on buying a dog, responsibilities, rewards, and how to match a dog with one's situation. . . . More than 100 dogs are profiled, with information on history, appearance, health, and 'fun facts.' Crisp color photographs accompany each article. . . . A final section gives good advice about nutrition and health issues." Booklist

Coren, Stanley

Why do dogs have wet noses? Kids Can Press 2006 63p il $14.95; pa $9.95

Grades: 3 4 5 6   **636.7**
1. Dogs
ISBN 1-55337-657-9; 1-55337-658-7 (pa)

"This interesting, entertaining book has chapters on 'How Humans and Dogs Became Friends,' 'How Dogs See the World,' 'How Dogs Talk,' and 'How Dogs Think.' The question-and-answer format is interspersed with facts and stories in sidebars. . . . Beautiful full-color photos show many breeds." SLJ

Crosby, Jeff

Little lions, bull baiters & hunting hounds; a history of dog breeds; written and illustrated by Jeff Crosby and Shelley Ann Jackson. Tundra Books 2008 72p il $19.95

Grades: 2 3 4 5   **636.7**
1. Dogs
ISBN 978-0-88776-815-6; 0-88776-815-6
                                        LC 2007927387

"Featuring more than breeds that are categorized as hunting, herding, working, or companion dogs, this attractive volume includes interesting and sometimes unusual facts about canines. . . . The painterly illustrations are often action-packed. . . . There is also a brief history of the origin of dogs and a succinct look at mixed breeds. . . . This is a great browsing book." SLJ

Includes bibliographical references

Dennis, Brian, 1971-

Nubs; the true story of a mutt, a Marine & a miracle; by Brian Dennis, Kirby Larson, and Mary Nethery. Little, Brown Books for Young Readers 2009 unp il $17.99 *

Grades: K 1 2 3   **636.7**
1. Dogs 2. Iraq War, 2003-—Personal narratives
ISBN 978-0-316-05318-1; 0-316-05318-X
                                        LC 2009003808

"Nubs, an Iraqi dog of war, never had a home or a person of his own. He was the leader of a pack of wild dogs living off the land and barely surviving. But Nubs's life changed when he met Marine Major Brian Dennis." Publisher's note

This is a "hugely inspirational true account. . . . The gritty, low-res shots of the two companions against the bleak Iraqi horizon are married with text so gracefully that many of the compositions could be book jackets." Booklist

Gaines, Ann

Top 10 dogs for kids; [by] Ann Graham Gaines. Enslow Publishers 2008 48p il (Top pets for kids with American Humane) lib bdg $23.93

Grades: 2 3 4 5   **636.7**
1. Dogs
ISBN 978-0-7660-3070-1 (lib bdg); 0-7660-3070-9 (lib bdg)   LC 2007-24510

"Provides facts on the top ten dog breeds for kids and how to care for them." Publisher's note

"Includes beautiful full-color photos showing the animals at their best. Judicious use of text boxes, crisp fonts, and white space will make it easy for readers to follow the flow of information." SLJ

Includes glossary and bibliographical references

George, Jean Craighead, 1919-

How to talk to your dog; illustrated by Sue Truesdell. HarperCollins Pubs. 2000 26p il $9.95 *

Grades: 2 3 4   **636.7**
1. Dogs
ISBN 0-06-027092-6   LC 98-41515

George, Jean Craighead, 1919——*Continued*

Describes how dogs communicate with people through their behavior and sounds and explains how to talk back to them using sounds, behavior, and body language

"The mixed photography (of George, representing the humans) and illustration (an endearingly scruffy yellow mutt is the main canine representative) is . . . effective. . . . This will be an accessible and perhaps paradigm-shifting introduction for young readers." Bull Cent Child Books

Gibbons, Gail

Dogs. Holiday House 1996 32p il $16.95; pa $6.95

Grades: K 1 2 3   636.7

1. Dogs

ISBN 0-8234-1226-1; 0-8234-1335-7 (pa)

LC 95-24966

An introduction to dogs including their history, types of breeds, senses, and ways of communication

"There is something for all dog enthusiasts here. A good choice for both reports and pleasure reading." SLJ

Gorrell, Gena K. (Gena Kinton), 1946-

Working like a dog; the story of working dogs through history. Tundra 2003 156p il pa $16.95

Grades: 4 5 6 7   636.7

1. Working dogs

ISBN 0-88776-589-0

"Gorrell begins by tracing the evolution of 'household canids' from the wild into the civilized world. Other chapters delve into the many ways in which these animals have been viewed throughout history, what makes particular breeds right for certain jobs, dogs at war, famous pooches, etc. . . . The well-captioned, black-and-white photographs and reproductions add greatly to a narrative that's packed with intriguing details." SLJ

Includes bibliographical references

Grogan, John, 1957-

Marley; a dog like no other. Collins 2007 196p il $16.99; lib bdg $17.89

Grades: 4 5 6   636.7

1. Dogs

ISBN 978-0-06-124033-1; 978-0-06-124034-8 (lib bdg)   LC 2007-08600

"Grogan's anecdotal adaptation of his bestselling memoir, *Marley & Me: Life and Love with the World's Worst Dog* speaks to a middle-grade audience. . . . The narrative maintains all the energy, humor and poignancy of the adult book. . . . Grogan leaves young readers with fond memories of this exasperating yet thoroughly endearing creature." Publ Wkly

Hart, Joyce, 1954-

Big dogs; by Joyce Hart. Marshall Cavendish Benchmark 2008 48p il (Great pets) lib bdg $29.93

Grades: 2 3 4   636.7

1. Dogs

ISBN 978-0-7614-2707-0 (lib bdg); 0-7614-2707-4 (lib bdg)   LC 2007013042

"Describes the characteristics and behavior of big dogs as pets, also discussing the physical appearance and place in the history of big dogs." Publisher's note

This is an "enthusiastic, warm [introduction]. . . . [It is] clearly written and [is] the most thorough, honest [introduction] to owning [big dogs] for this audience." SLJ

Includes glossary and bibliographical references

Small dogs. Marshall Cavendish Benchmark 2008 48p il (Great pets) lib bdg $29.93

Grades: 2 3 4   636.7

1. Dogs

ISBN 978-0-7614-2995-1 (lib bdg); 0-7614-2995-6 (lib bdg)   LC 2007-36784

"Describes the characteristics and behavior of small dogs, also discussing their physical appearance and place in history." Publisher's note

Includes glossary and bibliographical references

Holub, Joan, 1956-

Why do dogs bark? Dial Bks. for Young Readers 2001 48p il (Dial easy-to-read) $13.99 *

Grades: K 1 2   636.7

1. Dogs

ISBN 0-8037-2504-3   LC 00-23984

Questions and answers present information about the origins, behavior, and characteristics of dogs and their interaction with humans

This book combines "appealing color photos and sprightly cartoons with an informative, easy-to-read text." Booklist

Houston, Dick

Bulu, African wonder dog. Random House 2010 323p il $15.99; lib bdg $18.99

Grades: 5 6 7 8   636.7

1. Dogs 2. Wildlife conservation 3. Zambia

ISBN 978-0-375-84723-3; 0-375-84723-5; 978-0-375-94720-9 (lib bdg); 0-375-94720-5 (lib bdg)

LC 2009015804

"In the Nyanja language, bulu means 'wild dog,' and that's what Steve and Anna Tolan named the beloved little Jack Russell mix they adopted. Disregarding warnings about the dangers of raising a dog in the bush, the Tolans moved from England to rural Zambia to fulfill their lifelong dream of setting up an animal rescue and conservation center. . . . Bulu's energy, high spirits, and loyalty to his masters make the book read like a praise song to dogs. Houston's account is an animal-lover's delight, complete with the action-adventure of surviving the bush, fighting poachers, and spreading a message of conservation." Booklist

Jackson, Emma, 1992-

A home for Dixie; the true story of a rescued puppy; by Emma Jackson, with full-color photographs by Bob Carey. Collins 2008 unp il $16.99; lib bdg $17.89

Grades: 1 2 3 4   636.7

1. Dogs

ISBN 978-0-06-144962-8; 0-06-144962-8; 978-0-06-144963-5 (lib bdg); 0-06-144963-6 (lib bdg)

LC 2008-006049

Jackson, Emma, 1992--—*Continued*

"In this photo-essay, the author, a high school student, chronicles her quest for a puppy, her family's decision to adopt one, and their trip to Aunt Mary's Doghouse—a nonprofit rescue agency—to find the right animal. . . . The book's strengths are the large, full-color, often full-page photos of the appealing pup and her new owner. The Web sites recommended for potential pet owners are regularly updated." SLJ

Jeffrey, Laura S.

Dogs; how to choose and care for a dog. Enslow Publishers 2004 48p il (American humane pet care library) lib bdg $23.93

Grades: 3 4 5   **636.7**

1. Dogs

ISBN 0-7660-2520-9   LC 2003-22971

Explains who to consult, where to go to pick the right dog, and how to keep them happy and healthy

Includes glossary and bibliographical references

Jenkins, Steve

Dogs and cats; written and illustrated by Steve Jenkins. Houghton Mifflin Co. 2007 unp il $16 *

Grades: 1 2 3 4   **636.7**

1. Dogs 2. Cats

ISBN 978-0-618-50767-2; 0-618-50767-1

          LC 2006-24654

"The lively narrative provides a copious amount of information, examining each species in human history, describing evolution and domestication, highlighting physical characteristics and behaviors, and finishing up with amazing facts about each animal. The layout is excellent, with images dominating the text. Jenkins's cut and torn-paper collages are stunning." SLJ

Johnson, Jinny

Dogs and puppies; [by] Jinny Johnson. Smart Apple Media 2008 32p il (Get to know your pet) $27.10

Grades: 3 4 5 6   **636.7**

1. Dogs

ISBN 978-1-59920-089-7; 1-59920-089-9

          LC 2007-52598

"Describes the behavior of dogs and puppies and how to choose and care for pet dogs." Publisher's note

"Spreads include in-depth care instruction, and 'Q & A' sidebars that answer common behavioral questions. . . . The layout is clear, with full color photos and illustrations breaking up the text." SLJ

Includes glossary

Kehret, Peg, 1936-

Shelter dogs; amazing stories of adopted strays. Whitman, A. 1999 unp il $14.95

Grades: 3 4 5   **636.7**

1. Dogs

ISBN 0-8075-7334-5   LC 98-34760

Tells the stories of eight stray dogs that were adopted from animal shelters and went on to become service dogs, actors, and heroes

"The writing is clear and straightforward, letting the drama and pathos of the dogs' triumphs, and the owners' dedication, carry the stories." SLJ

Kimmel, Elizabeth Cody

Balto and the great race; illustrated by Nora Koerber. Random House 1999 99p il map hardcover o.p. pa $3.99

Grades: 3 4 5   **636.7**

1. Sled dog racing 2. Nome (Alaska) 3. Diphtheria

ISBN 0-679-99198-0 (lib bdg); 0-679-89198-6 (pa)

          LC 98-35753

"A Stepping Stone book"

Recounts how the sled dog Balto saved Nome, Alaska, in 1925 from a diphtheria epidemic by delivering medicine through a raging snowstorm

"Kimmel's writing deftly combines geography, sled racing, and historical background with the gripping adventure of Balto's race to save lives. In many ways, the book reads like fast-paced fiction. Koerber's serviceable black-and-white illustrations appear throughout and reflect the action. Sure to appeal to beginning chapter-book readers." SLJ

Mehus-Roe, Kristin

Dogs for kids! everything you need to know about dogs; by Kristin Mehus-Roe. BowTie Press 2007 384p il pa $14.95

Grades: 4 5 6 7   **636.7**

1. Dogs

ISBN 978-1-931993-83-8 (pa); 1-931993-83-1 (pa)

          LC 2006035434

"If you are looking for a book about canines that is entertaining as well as immensely informative, this is it. In a lively, conversational tone, Mehus-Roe offers a vast amount of material, from the history of dogs to vacationing with a pet, and provides practical and upbeat explanations, ideas, offbeat tidbits, and pertinent details." SLJ

Includes bibliographical references

Rogers, Tammie

4-H guide to dog training and dog tricks. Voyageur Press 2009 176p il pa $18.99

Grades: 5 6 7 8 9 10   **636.7**

1. Dogs—Training

ISBN 978-0-7603-3629-8; 0-7603-3629-6

          LC 2009-17040

"This is not simply a how-to-train book; it is also a guide to cultivating a respectful relationship with your dog. The excellent information is comprehensive, and it is presented in a clear and detailed style. The author covers different training methods, discussing the tools needed from food to collar selection. Using this manual, dog owners can move through the basics (sit, down, etc.) to obedience competition and fun tricks and activities." SLJ

Includes bibliographical references

636.8 Cats

Simon, Seymour, 1931-

Dogs. HarperCollinsPublishers 2004 unp il
$17.99; lib bdg $18.89; pa $6.99 *

Grades: 1 2 3 4   **636.7**

1. Dogs

ISBN 0-06-028942-2; 0-06-028943-0 (lib bdg);
978-0-06-446255-6 (pa); 0-06-446255-2 (pa)

LC 2003-12484

Provides a basic introduction to the physical characteristics and behavior of dogs

"The striking color photos, including many close-ups,
create a feeling of intimacy. . . . Simon succeeds in addressing his topic in clear, easily understood vocabulary
without writing down to children." SLJ

Singer, Marilyn, 1948-

A dog's gotta do what a dog's gotta do; dogs at
work. Holt & Co. 2000 86p il $16

Grades: 3 4 5 6   **636.7**

1. Working dogs

ISBN 0-8050-6074-X

Describes how dogs use their physical abilities, intelligence, and training by humans to perform a variety of
jobs, including working in the movies, catching burglars,
delivering messages, and cheering up children in hospitals

"Dog lovers will appreciate this readable, informative
look at canines and the work they do." Booklist

Urbigkit, Cat

Brave dogs, gentle dogs; how they guard sheep.
Boyds Mills Press 2005 32p il $15.95; pa $8.95

Grades: K 1 2 3   **636.7**

1. Sheep dogs

ISBN 1-59078-317-4; 978-1-59078-674-1 (pa)

LC 2004-16855

A "photo-essay on guardian dogs. Accompanied by
clear, full-color photos, the simple, informative text describes the raising of these sheepdogs and their natural
proclivity for guarding 'their' flocks." SLJ

Whitehead, Sarah

How to speak dog. Scholastic Reference 2008
96p il pa $6.99

Grades: 4 5 6 7 8   **636.7**

1. Dogs

ISBN 978-0-545-02078-7 (pa); 0-545-02078-6 (pa)

Explains how to read a dog's body language and vocalizations and presents step-by-step instructions for
training, housebreaking, teaching tricks, and playing several types of games.

This is "well-organized and interesting. . . . Whitehead discusses, and clearly shows in good-quality, full-color photographs, various canine emotions." SLJ

Barnes, Julia, 1955-

Pet cats; [by] Julia Barnes. Gareth Stevens Pub.
2007 32p il (Pet pals) lib bdg $23.93

Grades: 2 3 4 5   **636.8**

1. Cats

ISBN 0-8368-6776-9   LC 2006042377

"In spreads filled with color photographs, Barnes presents a short explanation of the feline family tree, as well
as the history of cat-human relationships, before delving
into cat breeds, characteristics, and behavior. Final sections offer ideas for new cat owners." Booklist

Includes glossary and bibliographical references

Bidner, Jenni

Is my cat a tiger? how your cat compares to its
wild cousins. Lark Books 2006 64p il $9.95

Grades: 3 4 5 6   **636.8**

1. Cats 2. Wild cats

ISBN 1-57990-815-2   LC 2006023356

"This book shows how domestic cats compare with
their wild cousins. Specifically, it addresses what domestic behavior reveals about wild roots. . . . The color
photographs are fantastic. . . . This is a fascinating volume." SLJ

Bozzo, Linda

My first cat; [by] Linda Bozzo. Enslow
Elementary 2007 32p il (My first pet library from
the American Humane Association) lib bdg $22.60

Grades: 1 2 3   **636.8**

1. Cats

ISBN 978-0-7660-2750-3 (lib bdg); 0-7660-2750-3 (lib
bdg)   LC 2006008403

Also available English-Spanish bilingual edition

This offers brief basic advice on selecting a cat and
caring for it.

Includes glossary and bibliographical references

George, Jean Craighead, 1919-

How to talk to your cat; illustrated by Paul
Meisel. HarperCollins Pubs. 2000 28p il $9.95

Grades: 2 3 4   **636.8**

1. Cats

ISBN 0-06-027968-0   LC 98-41517

Describes how cats communicate with people through
their behavior and sounds and explains how to talk back
to them using sounds, behavior, and body language

"The writing style is breezy, conversational, and
amusing, and is helped along by the many color illustrations. The photographs of the author are cleverly combined with humorous cartoon drawings of cats that display a great deal of intelligence and comedic personality.
. . . A useful and readable addition to any pet collection." SLJ

Gibbons, Gail

Cats. Holiday House 1996 unp il $16.95 paperback o.p.

Grades: K 1 2 3   **636.8**

1. Cats

ISBN 0-8234-1253-9; 0-8234-1410-8 (pa)

LC 96-3953

Presents information about the physical characteristics, senses, and behavior of cats, as well as how to care for these animals and some general facts about them

"This easy-to-read picture book will appeal to lovers of the popular pet. Brightly colored illustrations identify different breeds, while the informative . . . text describes physical and behavioral traits of kittens and cats." Horn Book Guide

Hart, Joyce, 1954-

Cats; by Joyce Hart. Marshall Cavendish Benchmark 2008 48p il (Great pets) lib bdg $29.93

Grades: 2 3 4   **636.8**

1. Cats

ISBN 978-0-7614-2710-0 (lib bdg); 0-7614-2710-4 (lib bdg)   LC 2007016462

"Describes the characteristics and behavior of pet cats, also discussing the physical appearance and place in the history of pet cats." Publisher's note

This is an "enthusiastic, warm [introduction]. . . . [It is] clearly written and [is] the most thorough, honest [introduction] to owning [pet cats] for this audience." SLJ

Holub, Joan, 1956-

Why do cats meow? illustrations by Anna DiVito. Dial Books for Young Readers 2001 46p il (Dial easy-to-read) hardcover o.p. pa $3.99

Grades: K 1 2   **636.8**

1. Cats

ISBN 0-8037-2503-5; 0-14-056788-7 (pa)

LC 00-23985

Questions and answers present information about the history, behavior, and characteristics of cats and their interaction with humans

"Packed with interesting information and illustrated with an abundance of cartoon artwork and color photographs." Horn Book Guide

Jeffrey, Laura S.

Cats; how to choose and care for a cat. Enslow Publishers 2004 48p il (American humane pet care library) lib bdg $23.93

Grades: 3 4 5   **636.8**

1. Cats

ISBN 0-7660-2516-0   LC 2003-22967

Provides information on cats as pets, including how to choose among different breeds, find a cat to buy or adopt, and how to feed and keep a cat healthy

This offers "children solid information about pet selection and care at a level they can understand." SLJ

Includes glossary and bibliographical references

Johnson, Jinny

Cats and kittens; [by] Jinny Johnson. Black Rabbit Books 2009 32p il (Get to know your pet) $27.10

Grades: 3 4 5 6   **636.8**

1. Cats

ISBN 978-1-59920-088-0; 1-59920-088-0

LC 2007-43435

"Describes the behavior of cats and kittens and how to choose and care for pet cats." Publisher's note

"Spreads include in-depth care instruction, and 'Q & A' sidebars that answer common behavioral questions. . . . The layout is clear, with full color photos and illustrations breaking up the text." SLJ

Includes glossary

MacLeod, Elizabeth

Why do cats have whiskers? Kids Can Press 2008 64p il $14.95

Grades: 3 4 5 6   **636.8**

1. Cats

ISBN 978-1-55453-196-7; 1-55453-196-9

"With its lively text and copious photographs, this title offers readers an accessible introduction to the world of felines. . . . MacLeod's interesting facts and anecdotes are sure to keep young cat owners engaged." Horn Book Guide

Myron, Vicki

Dewey the library cat; a true story; [by] Vicki Myron with Bret Witter. Little, Brown 2010 214p $16.99

Grades: 4 5 6 7 8   **636.8**

1. Cats 2. Libraries

ISBN 978-0-316-06871-0; 0-316-06871-3

Adapted from: Dewey: the small town library cat who touched the world, published 2008 by Grand Central Publisher for adults

"From the opening chapter, when librarian Vicki Myron finds a fragile, freezing kitten in the book return, children will be hooked on her heartwarming story about Dewey Readmore Books. . . . Anecdotes such as Dewey's fascination with rubber bands, his bizarre behavior during a bat invasion, and his finicky eating habits are ideal booktalk material. So are descriptions of Dewey's tender, intuitive interactions with people of all ages and backgrounds." Booklist

Rau, Dana Meachen, 1971-

Top 10 cats for kids; [by] Dana Meachen Rau. Enslow Publishers 2008 48p il (Top pets for kids with American Humane) lib bdg $23.93

Grades: 2 3 4 5   **636.8**

1. Cats

ISBN 978-0-7660-3071-8 (lib bdg); 0-7660-3071-7 (lib bdg)   LC 2007-24440

"Provides facts on the top ten cat breeds for kids and how to care for them." Publisher's note

"Includes beautiful full-color photos showing the animals at their best. Judicious use of text boxes, crisp fonts, and white space will make it easy for readers to follow the flow of information." SLJ

Includes glossary and bibliographical references

Rebman, Renee C., 1961-

Cats. Marshall Cavendish Benchmark 2009 47p il (Animals, animals) lib bdg $20.95

Grades: 3 4 5   **636.8**

  1. Cats

  ISBN 978-0-7614-3975-2   LC 2008020918

Provides comprehensive information on the anatomy, special skills, habitats, and diet of cats.

Includes glossary and bibliographical references

Simon, Seymour, 1931-

Cats. HarperCollins Pub. 2004 unp il lib bdg $16.89; pa $6.99 *

Grades: 1 2 3 4   **636.8**

  1. Cats

  ISBN 0-06-028940-6; 0-06-028941-4 (lib bdg); 0-06-446254-4 (pa)   LC 2003-8337

Discusses the history, physical characteristics, behavior, and various breeds of cats, and provides basic information on caring for one as a pet.

"The striking color photos, including many closeups, create a feeling of intimacy. . . . Simon succeeds in addressing his topic in clear, easily understood vocabulary without writing down to children." SLJ

Tildes, Phyllis Limbacher

Calico's cousins; cats from around the world. Charlesbridge Pub. 1999 unp il lib bdg $15.95; pa $6.95

Grades: K 1 2 3   **636.8**

  1. Cats

  ISBN 0-88106-648-6 (lib bdg); 0-88106-649-4 (pa)   LC 98-4011

"Calico, a domestic longhair cat, introduces various breeds by describing both their origin and common traits. Each double-page spread features realistic illustrations of several cats in an environment appropriate to their origin, and a map at the end provides geographical reference." Horn Book Guide

Whitehead, Sarah

How to speak cat. Scholastic 2009 96p il pa $6.99

Grades: 4 5 6 7 8   **636.8**

  1. Cats

  ISBN 978-0-545-02079-4 (pa); 0-545-02079-4 (pa)

"This pet-care book focuses on developing a relationship with a pet. The author states that the communication process is a two-way street, and she describes how readers can translate a cat's body language and vocalizations. . . . the bright color photographs of children with their cats on every page will appeal greatly to readers. This is a fun book that offers a good understanding of its audience and subject." SLJ

636.9   Other mammals

Barnes, Julia, 1955-

Elephants at work; [by] Julia Barnes. Gareth Stevens 2006 32p il map (Animals at work) lib bdg $23.93

Grades: 3 4 5   **636.9**

  1. Elephants 2. Working animals

  ISBN 0-8368-6224-4   LC 2005054067

This describes uses of elephants throughout history, their relationship with humans, habitat, diet, and appearance

This is "well-written, well-organized, . . . visually appealing and fun to read." SLJ

Includes bibliographical references

Pet guinea pigs; [by] Julia Barnes. Gareth Stevens Pub. 2007 32p il (Pet pals) lib bdg $23.93

Grades: 2 3 4 5   **636.9**

  1. Guinea pigs

  ISBN 0-8368-6779-3   LC 2006042373

This places guinea pigs "within the context of [their] wild roots and [their] relationship to humans. From there, Barnes explains what makes the animal an ideal pet, recommends how to be a good caregiver, and reveals how the creature communicates (as well as how to answer). The [book mixes] practical advice with trivia in a way that children will find informative and easy to navigate. Crisp, full-color photos enhance the [text]." SLJ

Includes glossary and bibliographical references

Pet rabbits; [by] Julia Barnes. Gareth Stevens Pub. 2007 32p il (Pet pals) lib bdg $32.92

Grades: 2 3 4 5   **636.9**

  1. Rabbits

  ISBN 0-8368-6781-5   LC 2006042374

This places rabbits "within the context of [their] wild roots and [their] relationship to humans. From there, Barnes explains what makes the animal an ideal pet, recommends how to be a good caregiver, and reveals how the creature communicates (as well as how to answer). The [book mixes] practical advice with trivia in a way that children will find informative and easy to navigate. Crisp, full-color photos enhance the [text]." SLJ

Includes glossary and bibliographical references

Bjorklund, Ruth

Rabbits; by Ruth Bjorklund. Marshall Cavendish Benchmark 2008 48p il (Great pets) lib bdg $28.50

Grades: 2 3 4   **636.9**

  1. Rabbits

  ISBN 978-0-7614-2708-7 (lib bdg); 0-7614-2708-2 (lib bdg)   LC 2007013044

The offers an introduction to rabbits as pets and how to choose and care for them

This is an "enthusiastic, warm [introduction]. . . . [This is] clearly written and [is] the most thorough, honest [introduction] to owning a pet [rabbit] for this audience." SLJ

Includes glossary and bibliographical references

Bozzo, Linda

My first guinea pig and other small pets; [by] Linda Bozzo. Enslow Elementary 2007 32p il (My first pet library from the American Humane Association) lib bdg $22.60

Grades: 1 2 3   **636.9**
1. Pets
ISBN 978-0-7660-2752-7 (lib bdg); 0-7660-2752-X (lib bdg)   LC 2006014970

Also available English-Spanish bilingual edition

This offers advice on selecting and caring for small pets including guinea pigs, hamsters, gerbils, rabbits, ferrets, rats, and mice.

Includes glossary and bibliographical references

Ellis, Carol, 1945-

Hamsters and gerbils. Marshall Cavendish Benchmark 2009 46p il (Great pets) $20.95

Grades: 2 3 4   **636.9**
1. Hamsters 2. Gerbils
ISBN 978-0-7614-2999-9; 0-7614-2999-9
           LC 2008-24336

"Describes the characteristics and behavior of pet hamsters and gerbils, also discussing their physical appearance and place in history." Publisher's note

Includes glossary and bibliographical references

Foran, Jill

Guinea pig. Weigl 2010 32p il (My pet) lib bdg $26; pa $9.95

Grades: 3 4 5   **636.9**
1. Guinea pigs 2. Pets
ISBN 978-1-60596-090-6 (lib bdg); 1-60596-090-X (lib bdg); 978-1-60596-091-3 (pa); 1-60596-091-8 (pa)
           LC 2009-5128

Information about how to house, feed, and care for guinea pigs.

"With clear, formal writing, and extensive coverage . . . [this title is] useful for reports. . . . Numerous color photographs, charts . . . and question-and-answer boxes supplement the [text]." SLJ

Includes glossary

Gaines, Ann

Top 10 small mammals for kids; [by] Ann Graham Gaines. Enslow Publishers 2008 48p il (Top pets for kids with American Humane) lib bdg $23.93

Grades: 2 3 4 5   **636.9**
1. Pets 2. Mammals
ISBN 978-0-7660-3075-6 (lib bdg); 0-7660-3075-X (lib bdg)   LC 2007-38480

"Provides facts on the top ten small mammals for kids and how to care for them." Publisher's note

"Includes beautiful full-color photos showing the animals at their best. Judicious use of text boxes, crisp fonts, and white space will make it easy for readers to follow the flow of information." SLJ

Includes glossary and bibliographical references

Ganeri, Anita, 1961-

Rabbits. Heinemann 2009 32p il (A pet's life) $17.75 *

Grades: 3 4 5   **636.9**
1. Rabbits
ISBN 978-1-4329-3394-4; 1-4329-3394-9

"Pretty much everything a child needs to know about taking care of rabbits in this title. . . . The book is organized in a logical way that will keep kids focused. . . . [The book uses] a good-size typeface and clear, adorable photos. . . . Fact-filled, fun to look at, and a pleasure to read." Booklist

Holub, Joan, 1956-

Why do rabbits hop? and other questions about rabbits, guinea pigs, hamsters, and gerbils; illustrations by Anna DiVito. Dial Bks. for Young Readers 2002 46p il (Dial easy-to-read) hardcover o.p. pa $3.99 *

Grades: K 1 2   **636.9**
1. Rabbits 2. Guinea pigs 3. Hamsters 4. Gerbils
ISBN 0-8037-2771-2 (lib bdg); 0-14-230120-5 (pa)
           LC 2001-47477

Questions and answers present information about the behavior and characteristics of rabbits, guinea pigs, hamsters, and gerbils and their interaction with humans

"The text is both interesting and informative. . . . [The book has] a bright, appealing format that combines jaunty original art and well-chosen photos." Booklist

Jeffrey, Laura S.

Hamsters, gerbils, guinea pigs, rabbits, ferrets, mice, and rats; how to choose and care for a small mammal. Enslow Publishers 2004 48p il (American humane pet care library) lib bdg $23.93

Grades: 3 4 5   **636.9**
1. Hamsters 2. Guinea pigs 3. Rabbits 4. Ferrets 5. Mice 6. Rats
ISBN 0-7660-2518-7   LC 2003-22969

Explains the different personalities of several small mammals, where to go to pick the right one, and how to keep them happy and healthy

Includes glossary and bibliographical references

Johnson, Jinny

Guinea pigs; [by] Jinny Johnson. Black Rabbit Books 2009 32p il (Get to know your pet) $27.10

Grades: 3 4 5 6   **636.9**
1. Guinea pigs
ISBN 978-1-59920-211-2; 1-59920-211-5
           LC 2007-43437

"Describes the behavior of guinea pigs and how to choose and care for guinea pigs as pets." Publisher's note

"Spreads include in-depth care instruction, and 'Q & A' sidebars that answer common behavioral questions. . . . The layout is clear, with full color photos and illustrations breaking up the text." SLJ

Includes glossary

Johnson, Jinny—*Continued*
Hamsters and gerbils; [by] Jinny Johnson. Black Rabbit Books 2009 32p il (Get to know your pet) $27.10
Grades: 3 4 5 6 **636.9**
1. Hamsters 2. Gerbils
ISBN 978-1-59920-092-7; 1-59920-092-9
LC 2007-52813
"Describes the behavior of hamsters and gerbils and how to choose and care for hamsters and gerbils as pets." Publisher's note
"Spreads include in-depth care instruction, and 'Q & A' sidebars that answer common behavioral questions. . . . The layout is clear, with full color photos and illustrations breaking up the text." SLJ
Includes glossary

Rabbits; [by] Jinny Johnson. Black Rabbit Books 2009 32p il (Get to know your pet) $27.10
Grades: 3 4 5 6 **636.9**
1. Rabbits
ISBN 978-1-59920-090-3; 1-59920-090-2
LC 2007-43436
"Describes the behavior of rabbits and how to choose and care for pet rabbits." Publisher's note
"Spreads include in-depth care instruction, and 'Q & A' sidebars that answer common behavioral questions. . . . The layout is clear, with full color photos and illustrations breaking up the text." SLJ
Includes glossary

Rats and mice; [by] Jinny Johnson. Black Rabbit Books 2009 32p il (Get to know your pet) $27.10
Grades: 3 4 5 6 **636.9**
1. Rats 2. Mice
ISBN 978-1-59920-091-0; 1-59920-091-0
LC 2007-52815
"Describes the behavior of rats and mice and how to choose and care for rats and mice as pets." Publisher's note
"Spreads include in-depth care instruction, and 'Q & A' sidebars that answer common behavioral questions. . . . The layout is clear, with full color photos and illustrations breaking up the text." SLJ
Includes glossary

Lewin, Ted, 1935-
Balarama; a royal elephant; [by] Ted and Betsy Lewin. Lee & Low Books 2009 unp il $19.95 *
Grades: 3 4 5 6 **636.9**
1. Elephants 2. India
ISBN 978-1-60060-265-8; 1-60060-265-7
LC 2009-1499
"World travelers Ted and Betsy Lewin recount how the trained elephants of southern India, in particular the one chosen to be the lead elephant in the Mysore Dasara, are raised, cared for, and prepared for performing in ceremonial processions. Includes background information and glossary." Publisher's note
"Ted Lewin's brilliant, realistic watercolors capture the sun-drenched pageantry of Mysore as well as the dusty, filtered light of the forest, while Betsy Lewin's lively cartoons aptly depict the action and personalities involved. The story has pathos and tension." SLJ

McNicholas, June, 1956-
Rats. Heinemann Lib. 2003 48p il (Keeping unusual pets) $24.22
Grades: 4 5 6 7 **636.9**
1. Rats
ISBN 1-4034-0283-3 LC 2002-3164
Contents: What is a rat?; Ratty facts; Is a rat for you?; What do I need?; Routine care; Handling and play; Health issues; Major problems; A record of your rat
Describes how to select a pet rat, what to feed it, and when to take it to the vet, as well as how to keep a pet scrapbook
"A valuable, accessible resource." Booklist
Includes bibliographical references

Newcomb, Rain
Is my hamster wild? the secret lives of hamsters, gerbils & guinea pigs; by Rain Newcomb & Rose McLarney. Lark Books 2008 64p il $9.95
Grades: 2 3 4 **636.9**
1. Hamsters 2. Gerbils 3. Guinea pigs
ISBN 978-1-60059-242-3; 1-60059-242-2
LC 2007-44312
"Examines the behavior of pet hamsters, gerbils, and guinea pigs." Publisher's note
"Crisp photo album-style pictures with humorous captions reinforce the deft main text." Horn Book Guide

Petrylak, Ashley
Guinea pigs. Marshall Cavendish Benchmark 2009 44p il (Great pets) lib bdg $29.93
Grades: 2 3 4 **636.9**
1. Guinea pigs
ISBN 978-0-7614-4148-9 (lib bdg); 0-7614-4148-4 (lib bdg)
LC 2008037238
"Describes the characteristics and behavior of pet guinea pigs, also discussing their physical appearance and place in history." Publisher's note
Includes glossary and bibliographical references

Richardson, Adele, 1966-
Caring for your hamster; by Adele Richardson. Capstone Press 2007 24p il (Positively pets) $21.26
Grades: K 1 2 3 **636.9**
1. Hamsters
ISBN 978-0-7368-6387-2; 0-7368-6387-7
LC 2005035852
"First facts"
"Describes caring for a hamster, including supplies needed, feeding, cleaning, health, safety, and aging." Publisher's note
This is a "concise, competent [introduction] to the responsibility and fun of being a pet owner. . . . Attractive and well suited for young readers in both tone and content. The clear color photographs display the animals in all their glory." SLJ
Includes bibliographical references

Sobol, Richard
An elephant in the backyard; text and photographs by Richard Sobol. Dutton Children's Books 2004 unp il $17.99
Grades: K 1 2 3   **636.9**
1. Elephants 2. Thailand
ISBN 0-525-47288-6   LC 2003-52492
Describes how special elephants are in the village of Tha Kleng in Thailand and looks at the life of one particular young elephant named Wan Pen.
This is an "engaging photo-essay. Large, colorful photographs enhance the text. . . . The text is packed with interesting tidbits about these large mammals." SLJ

636.97   Fur farming

Hamilton, Lynn, 1964-
Ferret. Weigl 2010 32p il (My pet) lib bdg $26; pa $9.95
Grades: 3 4 5   **636.97**
1. Ferrets 2. Pets
ISBN 978-1-60596-096-8 (lib bdg); 1-60596-096-9 (lib bdg); 978-1-60596-097-5 (pa); 1-60596-097-7 (pa)
LC 2009-4985
Information about how to house, feed, and care for ferrets.
"With clear, formal writing, and extensive coverage . . . [this title is] useful for reports. . . . Numerous color photographs, charts . . . and question-and-answer boxes supplement the [text]." SLJ
Includes glossary

Haney, Johannah
Ferrets. Marshall Cavendish Benchmark 2010 46p il (Great pets) lib bdg $29.93
Grades: 2 3 4   **636.97**
1. Ferrets 2. Pets
ISBN 978-0-7614-4153-3 (lib bdg); 0-7614-4153-0 (lib bdg)
LC 2009020561
"Describes the characteristics and behavior of pet ferrets, also discussing their physical appearance and place in history." Publisher's note
Includes glossary and bibliographical references

Lunis, Natalie
Furry ferrets. Bearport 2010 24p il (Peculiar pets) lib bdg $22.61
Grades: 3 4 5   **636.97**
1. Ferrets 2. Pets
ISBN 978-1-59716-860-1 (lib bdg); 1-59716-860-2 (lib bdg)
LC 2009-10378
Introduces the furry ferret, describing its physical characteristics, habitat, and behavior, and discussing the care and diet that it needs if it is kept as a pet
"The language . . . is lively . . . [and] the illustrations are vivid, with photos offering some amusing shots. . . . This [book] . . . will hold readers' attention, but also challenge them to consider the responsibilities required of owners of unusual creatures." SLJ
Includes glossary and bibliographical references

637   Processing dairy and related products

Aliki
Milk from cow to carton. rev ed. HarperCollins Pubs. 1992 31p il (Let's-read-and-find-out science book) pa $5.95 hardcover o.p.
Grades: K 1 2 3   **637**
1. Dairying 2. Milk 3. Cattle
ISBN 0-06-445111-9 (pa)   LC 91-23807
First published 1974 by Crowell with title: Green grass and white milk
Briefly describes how a cow produces milk, how the milk is processed in a dairy, and how various other dairy products are made from milk
This features "full-color artwork. . . . An excellent primary-level introduction to dairy science." Booklist

Gibbons, Gail
The milk makers. Macmillan 1985 unp il hardcover o.p. pa $5.99
Grades: K 1 2 3   **637**
1. Dairying 2. Milk 3. Cattle
ISBN 0-02-736640-5; 0-689-71116-6 (pa)
LC 84-20081
Explains how cows produce milk and how it is processed before being delivered to stores
"Starting with dairy cows grazing at pasture, nothing is overlooked in the procedure, from the role of the calf to winter feed and shelter, the function of four stomachs, milking, milk handling, and the operation of a dairy. Diagrams of the cow stomachs as well as the machines used at farm and dairy leave no question unanswered, although city children will be unfamiliar with what it means to breed a cow. Finally, there is a pictorial list of the many other dairy products found in most homes." Sci Books Films

Peterson, Cris, 1952-
Extra cheese, please! mozzarella's journey from cow to pizza; photographs by Alvis Upitis. Boyds Mills Press 1994 unp il $16.95; pa $9.95
Grades: K 1 2 3   **637**
1. Dairying 2. Cheese
ISBN 1-56397-177-1; 1-59078-246-1 (pa)
LC 93-70876
In photographs and text, this book introduces "dairying and cheese making. Using her own farm as an example, Peterson describes the care and feeding of dairy cattle, the milking process, and the steps involved in producing mozzarella cheese." Booklist
"Nicely balanced pages contain brief blocks of clearly written text and many full-color photographs." SLJ
Includes glossary and bibliographical references

638 Insect culture

639 Hunting, fishing, conservation, related technologies

Burns, Loree Griffin

The hive detectives; chronicle of a honey bee catastrophe; with photographs by Ellen Harasimowicz. Houghton Mifflin Books for Children 2010 66p il (Scientists in the field) $18 *

Grades: 5 6 7 8 9 10   **638**
   1. Beekeeping
   ISBN 978-0-547-15231-8; 0-547-15231-0
                                   LC 2009-45249

"Not long after beekeepers encountered a devastating new problem in their hives in 2006, a team of bee scientists began working to discover the causes of colony collapse disorder (CCD), now attributed to a combination of factors possibly including pesticides, nutrition, mites and viruses. . . . Mock notebook pages break up the narrative with biographies of the individual scientists, information about who and what can be found inside the hive and the features of bee bodies. An appendix adds varied fascinating facts about bees—again using the format of an illustrated research journal. Harasimowicz's clear, beautifully reproduced photographs support and extend the text." Kirkus

Includes glossary and bibliographical references

Fujiwara, Yumiko

Honey; a gift from nature; written by Yumiko Fujiwara; illustrated by Hideko Ise. Kane/Miller 2006 unp il (Nature: a child's eye view) pa $7.95

Grades: PreK K 1   **638**
   1. Honey 2. Bees
   ISBN 1-929132-94-8 (pa); 978-1-929132-94-2 (pa)
                                   LC 2005-930528

Original Japanese edition 1997

A young Japanese girl spends the day with her beekeeping father in the mountains where he keeps his hives. Explains how bees gather nectar, how it is turned into honey, and how the honey is collected.

Harkins, Susan Sales

Design your own butterfly garden; by Susan Sales Harkins and William H. Harkins. Mitchell Lane Publishers 2008 48p il (Gardening for kids) lib bdg $29.95

Grades: 3 4 5 6   **638**
   1. Butterfly gardens
   ISBN 978-1-58415-638-3 (lib bdg); 1-58415-638-4 (lib bdg)   LC 2008-2245

Introduces the principles of butterfly gardening, discussing how to plan the garden, what flowers to plant there, and how to maintain it in all seasons

"All the tasks delineated are well within the scope of children's abilities, and the items needed to complete them are not hard to find. . . . [The book has] excellent full-color photography and include[s] charts and diagrams to assist in the completion of the projects." SLJ

Includes bibliographical references

Lomberg, Michelle

Spider. Weigl Publishers 2009 32p il (My pets) lib bdg $26; pa $9.95

Grades: 3 4 5   **639**
   1. Spiders 2. Pets
   ISBN 978-1-60596-094-4 (lib bdg); 1-60596-094-2 (lib bdg); 978-1-60596-095-1 (pa); 1-60596-095-0 (pa)
                                   LC 2009-25979

Information about how to house, feed, and care for spiders.

"With clear, formal writing, and extensive coverage . . . [this title is] useful for reports. . . . Numerous color photographs, charts . . . and question-and-answer boxes supplement the [text]." SLJ

Includes glossary

Richardson, Adele, 1966-

Caring for your hermit crab; by Adele Richardson. Capstone Press 2007 24p il (Positively pets) $21.26

Grades: K 1 2 3   **639**
   1. Crabs 2. Pets
   ISBN 978-0-7368-6388-9; 0-7368-6388-5
                                   LC 2006006390

"First facts"

"Describes caring for a hermit crab, including supplies needed, feeding, cleaning, health, and safety." Publisher's note

This is a "concise, competent [introduction] to the responsibility and fun of being a pet owner. . . . Attractive and well suited for young readers in both tone and content. The clear color photographs display the animals in all their glory." SLJ

Includes bibliographical references

639.2 Commercial fishing, whaling, sealing

Foster, Mark

Whale port; a history of Tuckanucket; written by Mark Foster; illustrated by Gerald Foster. Houghton Mifflin Company 2007 64p il $18 *

Grades: 4 5 6 7   **639.2**
   1. Whaling
   ISBN 978-0-618-54722-7; 0-618-54722-3
                                   LC 2006018772

"Walter Lorraine books"

This describes the history of whaling in New England through the fictional village of Tuckanucket and Zachariah Taber, his family and neighbors.

The village is "depicted in precisely detailed ink and crayon pictures. . . . The Fosters . . . have elegantly synthesized a tremendous amount of information into a beguiling format." Horn Book

Kurlansky, Mark

The cod's tale; illustrated by S.D. Schindler. Putnam 2002 43p il map $16.99 *

Grades: 3 4 5 6   **639.2**

1. Codfish 2. Commercial fishing

ISBN 0-399-23476-4   LC 00-68412

"Kurlansky traces the role that the once plentiful Atlantic cod has played in the history of North America and Europe." Publ Wkly

"Schindler's line-and-watercolor scenes are rendered with the delicate hatching of fine engraving and suffused with gentle humor. . . . This is a classic example of an unlikely subject made not only likely but fascinating and informative through authorial and illustrative craftsmanship." Bull Cent Child Books

Includes bibliographical references

McKissack, Patricia C., 1944-

Black hands, white sails; the story of African-American whalers; [by] Patricia C. McKissack & Fredrick L. McKissack. Scholastic Press 1999 xxiv, 152p il $17.95 *

Grades: 5 6 7 8   **639.2**

1. Whaling 2. African Americans

ISBN 0-590-48313-7   LC 99-11439

A Coretta Scott King honor book for text, 2000

A history of African-American whalers from 1730 and 1880, describing their contributions to the whaling industry and their role in the abolitionist movement

"A well-researched and detailed book." SLJ

Includes bibliographical references

McMillan, Bruce

Salmon summer; written and photo-illustrated by Bruce McMillan. Houghton Mifflin 1998 32p il $17

Grades: 2 3 4   **639.2**

1. Salmon 2. Fishing 3. Alaska

ISBN 0-395-84544-0   LC 97-29679

"Walter Lorraine books"

A photo essay describing a young native Alaskan boy fishing for salmon on Kodiak Island as his ancestors have done for generations

"McMillan documents the goings on with his trademark crystal-clear color photographs and an engaging text." Booklist

Includes glossary and bibliographical references

Sandler, Martin W.

Trapped in ice! an amazing true whaling adventure. Scholastic Nonfiction 2006 168p il $16.99 *

Grades: 5 6 7 8   **639.2**

1. Whaling

ISBN 0-439-74363-X   LC 2005-42644

"In 1871, people aboard 32 whaling ships discovered just how dangerous Arctic waters could be after they ignored warnings of an early winter. As conditions worsened, the ships were trapped by ice, forcing the 1,219 people to abandon the vessels or die. Sandler's account of this true story is both informative and absorbing. . . .

Well-chosen illustrations and side notes on such topics as life aboard ship and women at sea extend readers' understanding." Booklist

Includes glossary and bibliographical references

639.3   Culture of cold-blooded vertebrates. Of fishes

Bjorklund, Ruth

Lizards. Marshall Cavendish Benchmark 2009 48p il (Great pets) $20.95

Grades: 2 3 4   **639.3**

1. Lizards

ISBN 978-0-7614-2997-5; 0-7614-2997-2

LC 2008-17560

"Describes the characteristics and behavior of pet lizards, also discussing their physical appearance and place in history." Publisher's note

Includes glossary and bibliographical references

Cone, Molly, 1918-

Come back, salmon; how a group of dedicated kids adopted Pigeon Creek and brought it back to life; photographs by Sidnee Wheelwright. Sierra Club Bks. for Children 1992 48p il $16.95; pa $7.95 *

Grades: 3 4 5 6   **639.3**

1. Salmon 2. Wildlife conservation

ISBN 0-87156-572-2; 0-87156-489-0 (pa)

LC 91-29023

Describes the efforts of the Jackson Elementary School in Everett, Washington, to clean up a nearby stream, stock it with salmon, and preserve it as an unpolluted place where the salmon could return to spawn

"The photographs are superb. . . . Personal and inspiring, the text alternates between descriptions of the project, background information about pollution and renewal, and dialogue of the students recorded; additional scientific information is displayed in panels set off from the main text." Horn Book

Includes glossary

Craats, Rennay, 1973-

Gecko. Weigl Publishers 2009 32p il (My pet) lib bdg $26; pa $9.95

Grades: 3 4 5   **639.3**

1. Geckos 2. Pets

ISBN 978-1-60596-098-2 (lib bdg); 1-60596-098-5 (lib bdg); 978-1-60596-099-9 (pa); 1-60596-099-3 (pa)

LC 2009-25985

Information about how to house, feed, and care for geckos.

"With clear, formal writing, and extensive coverage . . . [this title is] useful for reports. . . . Numerous colorful photographs, charts . . . and question-and-answer boxes supplement the [text]." SLJ

Includes glossary

Gaines, Ann

Top 10 reptiles and amphibians for kids; [by] Ann Graham Gaines. Enslow Publishers 2008 48p il (Top pets for kids with American Humane) lib bdg $23.93

Grades: 2 3 4 5   **639.3**

    1. Reptiles 2. Amphibians 3. Pets

    ISBN 978-0-7660-3074-9 (lib bdg); 0-7660-3074-1 (lib bdg)   LC 2007047884

"Provides facts on the top ten reptiles and amphibians for kids and how to care for them." Publisher's note

"Includes beautiful full-color photos showing the animals at their best. Judicious use of text boxes, crisp fonts, and white space will make it easy for readers to follow the flow of information." SLJ

Includes glossary and bibliographical references

Hamilton, Lynn, 1964-

Turtle. Weigl Publishers 2009 32p il (My pet) lib bdg $26; pa $9.95

Grades: 3 4 5   **639.3**

    1. Turtles 2. Pets

    ISBN 978-1-60596-088-3 (lib bdg); 1-60596-088-8 (lib bdg); 978-1-60596-089-0 (pa); 1-60596-089-6 (pa)   LC 2009-25973

Information about how to house, feed, and care for turtles.

"With clear, formal writing, and extensive coverage . . . [this title is] useful for reports. . . . Numerous color photographs, charts . . . and question-and-answer boxes supplement the [text]." SLJ

Includes glossary

Haney, Johannah

Frogs. Marshall Cavendish Benchmark 2009 48p il (Great pets) lib bdg $29.93

Grades: 2 3 4   **639.3**

    1. Frogs 2. Pets

    ISBN 978-0-7614-4151-9 (lib bdg); 0-7614-4151-4 (lib bdg)   LC 2008037242

"Describes the characteristics and behavior of pet frogs, also discussing their physical appearance and place in history." Publisher's note

Includes glossary and bibliographical references

Turtles; [by] Johannah Haney. Marshall Cavendish Benchmark 2008 48p il (Great pets) lib bdg $28.50

Grades: 2 3 4   **639.3**

    1. Turtles 2. Pets

    ISBN 978-0-7614-2709-4 (lib bdg); 0-7614-2709-0 (lib bdg)   LC 2006038157

The offers an introduction to turtles as pets and how to choose and care for them

This is an "enthusiastic, warm [introduction]. . . . [It is] clearly written and [is] the most thorough, honest [introduction] to owning a pet [turtle] for this audience." SLJ

Includes glossary and bibliographical references

Hart, Joyce, 1954-

Snakes. Marshall Cavendish Benchmark 2008 48p il (Great pets) $20.95

Grades: 2 3 4   **639.3**

    1. Snakes 2. Pets

    ISBN 978-0-7614-2996-8; 0-7614-2996-4   LC 2008-24333

"Describes the characteristics and behavior of pet snakes, also discussing their physical appearance and place in history." Publisher's note

Includes glossary and bibliographical references

Hernandez-Divers, Sonia, 1969-

Geckos. Heinemann Lib. 2003 48p il (Keeping unusual pets) lib bdg $24.22

Grades: 3 4 5 6   **639.3**

    1. Geckos 2. Pets

    ISBN 1-4034-0282-5   LC 2002-3163

This offers information about geckos and advice about keeping them as pets

"Lively and informative, with photos scattered across and around the pages . . . [this offers] a wealth of valuable advice." SLJ

Includes glossary and bibliographical references

Lunis, Natalie

Green iguanas. Bearport Pub. 2010 24p il map (Peculiar pets) lib bdg $25.26

Grades: 3 4 5   **639.3**

    1. Iguanas 2. Pets

    ISBN 978-1-59716-863-2 (lib bdg); 1-59716-863-7 (lib bdg)   LC 2009-17545

Introduces the green iguana, describing its physical characteristics, habitat, and behavior, and discussing the care and diet that it needs if it is kept as a pet

"The language . . . is lively . . . [and] the illustrations are vivid, with photos offering some amusing shots. . . . This [book] . . . will hold readers' attention, but also challenge them to consider the responsibilities required of owners of unusual creatures." SLJ

Includes glossary and bibliographical references

Schafer, Susan

Lizards. Benchmark Bks. 2001 32p il (Perfect pets) lib bdg $15.95

Grades: 3 4 5 6   **639.3**

    1. Lizards 2. Pets

    ISBN 0-7614-1103-8   LC 99-58088

Describes various kinds of lizards while focusing on those which could best serve as pets by indicating the food they need and the care they require

Includes glossary and bibliographical references

639.34 Fish culture in aquariums

Aliki

My visit to the aquarium. HarperCollins Pubs. 1993 unp il $15.95; pa $6.95 *

Grades: K 1 2 3   639.34

1. Marine aquariums 2. Marine animals 3. Freshwater animals

ISBN 0-06-021458-9; 0-06-446186-6 (pa)

LC 92-18678

During his visit to an aquarium, a boy finds out about the characteristics and environments of many different marine and freshwater creatures

"Fish facts, selected for their child-appeal and delivered in a brisk, conversational tone, are neatly organized by marine environment. . . . The dominant blues and greens of Aliki's watercolors are not only cool and inviting; they also provide visual continuity amid the riot of brightly colored fish." Booklist

Bozzo, Linda

My first fish; [by] Linda Bozzo. Enslow Publishers 2007 32p il (My first pet library from the American Humane Association) lib bdg $22.60

Grades: 1 2 3   639.34

1. Fishes 2. Aquariums

ISBN 978-0-7660-2751-0 (lib bdg); 0-7660-2751-1 (lib bdg)   LC 2006010500

Also available English-Spanish bilingual edition

"This book explores how to choose the right fish and how to care for your new pet." Publisher's note

Includes glossary and bibliographical references

Buckmaster, Marjorie L.

Freshwater fishes; [by] Marjorie L. Buckmaster. Marshall Cavendish Benchmark 2007 c2008 48p il (Great pets) $19.95

Grades: 2 3 4   639.34

1. Aquariums 2. Fishes

ISBN 978-0-7614-2712-4   LC 2007017809

The offers an introduction to freshwater fish as pets and how to choose and care for them.

This is an "enthusiastic, warm [introduction]. . . . [It is] clearly written and [is] the most thorough, honest [introduction] to owning [pet fish] for this audience." SLJ

Jeffrey, Laura S.

Fish; how to choose and care for a fish. Enslow Publishers 2004 48p il (American humane pet care library) lib bdg $23.93

Grades: 3 4 5   639.34

1. Fishes 2. Aquariums

ISBN 0-7660-2517-9   LC 2003-22968

Explains how to set up a personalized aquarium, pick the right fish, and how to keep them happy and healthy

Includes glossary and bibliographical references

Rau, Dana Meachen, 1971-

Top 10 fish for kids; [by] Dana Meachen Rau. Enslow Publishers 2008 48p il (Top pets for kids with American Humane) lib bdg $23.93

Grades: 2 3 4 5   639.34

1. Aquariums 2. Fishes

ISBN 978-0-7660-3073-2 (lib bdg); 0-7660-3073-3 (lib bdg)   LC 2007-32319

"Provides facts on the top ten fish breeds for kids and how to care for them." Publisher's note

"Includes beautiful full-color photos showing the animals at their best. Judicious use of text boxes, crisp fonts, and white space will make it easy for readers to follow the flow of information." SLJ

Includes glossary and bibliographical references

Richardson, Adele, 1966-

Caring for your fish; by Adele Richardson. Capstone Press 2007 24p il (Positively pets) $21.26

Grades: K 1 2 3   639.34

1. Fishes 2. Aquariums

ISBN 978-0-7368-6386-5; 0-7368-6386-9

LC 2005035854

"First facts"

"Describes caring for a fish, including supplies needed, feeding, cleaning, health, safety, and aging." Publisher's note

This is a "concise, competent [introduction] to the responsibility and fun of being a pet owner. . . . Attractive and well suited for young readers in both tone and content. The clear color photographs display the animals in all their glory." SLJ

Includes bibliographical references

639.9 Conservation of biological resources

Buckley, Carol

Just for elephants. Tilbury House 2006 unp il $16.95

Grades: 3 4 5 6   639.9

1. Elephants 2. Wildlife conservation

ISBN 978-0-88448-283-3; 0-88448-283-9

LC 2006-22283

"Buckley records the arrival of Shirley, an elderly circus animal, at the Elephant Sanctuary, cofounded by the author, in Tennessee." Booklist

"This is a beautifully written, compelling story of a conscientious drive to care for these animals in a humane way." SLJ

Fleming, Denise, 1950-

Where once there was a wood. Holt & Co. 1996 unp il $16.95; pa $6.95 *

Grades: K 1 2   639.9

1. Habitat (Ecology) 2. Wildlife conservation

ISBN 0-8050-3761-6; 0-8050-6482-6 (pa)

LC 95-18906

Fleming, Denise, 1950-—*Continued*

"Fleming's brief text describes the many creatures who once lived in a wild area but whose homes have been destroyed by a new housing development. Fleming includes an afterword that describes the things families can do to create new backyard habitats for birds and animals." Horn Book Guide

"Lush, textured collage artwork features a stunning combination and arrangement of colors with brilliant hues juxtaposed against muted earth tones. . . . The gentle, poetic narration is never overpowered by the pictures." SLJ

Includes bibliographical references

Hatkoff, Juliana

Winter's tail; how one little dolphin learned to swim again; told by Juliana Hatkoff, Isabella Hatkoff, and Craig Hatkoff. Scholastic Press 2009 unp il $16.99

Grades: 3 4 5 6   **639.9**
    1. Dolphins 2. Artificial limbs
    ISBN 978-0-545-12335-8; 0-545-12335-6

"A compassionate look at the true odyssey of an orphaned Atlantic bottlenose dolphin. Rescued from a crab trap, with severe injuries, 'Winter' was brought to the Clearwater (FL) Marine Aquarium and, despite the heroic efforts of the staff, lost her tail. . . . Winter caught the attention of a prosthetic engineer, and the Hatkoffs' clear text follows the efforts of a mixed team from the aquarium and Hanger Prosthetics & Orthotics to design a workable 'tail' to keep her healthy. Full-color photos reveal the cooperative efforts of the human team and Winter in this journey toward a more normal life." SLJ

Lasky, Kathryn

Interrupted journey; illustrated by Christopher Knight. Candlewick Press 2001 unp il hardcover o.p. pa $6.99 *

Grades: 3 4 5 6   **639.9**
    1. Sea turtles 2. Rare animals 3. Wildlife conservation
    ISBN 0-7636-0635-9; 0-7636-2883-2 (pa)
                                          LC 99-57126
Describes efforts to protect sea turtles, particularly Kemp's ridley turtles, and help them reproduce and replenish their once-dwindling numbers

"There's a sense of wonder in the simple words and the huge, thrilling color pictures in this photo-essay." Booklist

Montgomery, Sy

Kakapo rescue; saving the world's strangest parrot; text by Sy Montgomery; photography by Nic Bishop. Houghton Mifflin 2010 74p il map (Scientists in the field) $18 *

Grades: 4 5 6 7   **639.9**
    1. Parrots 2. Wildlife conservation 3. Endangered species 4. New Zealand
    ISBN 978-0-618-49417-0; 0-618-49417-0
Montgomery and Bishop head "to a remote island off the southern tip of New Zealand, where they join a local government-sponsored research team that is working to save the Kakapo parrot from extinction. . . . Montgom-

ery's delight in her subject is contagious, and throughout her enthusiastic text, she nimbly blends scientific and historical facts with immediate, sensory descriptions of fieldwork. Young readers will be fascinated. . . . Bishop's photos of the creatures and their habitat are stunning." Booklist

Stetson, Emily, 1957-

Kids' easy-to-create wildlife habitats; [by] Emily Stetson. Williamson Books 2004 128p il map (Quick starts for kids!) pa $12.95

Grades: 2 3 4   **639.9**
    1. Wildlife conservation 2. Habitat (Ecology)
    ISBN 0-8249-8665-2   LC 2004-40871
This "book shows children how to observe and support wildlife around their homes, schools, and communities. Packed with useful information. . . . With sound advice and many helpful illustrations, precisely drawn in blue and gray ink, this offers children small ways to support wildlife close to home." Booklist

641.3   Food

Burleigh, Robert, 1936-

Chocolate; riches from the rainforest. Abrams 2002 unp il $16.95

Grades: 3 4 5 6   **641.3**
    1. Chocolate
    ISBN 0-8109-5734-5   LC 2001-3744
Traces the history of chocolate from a drink of the Olmec and Maya and later in Europe to its popularity around the world today

"Chocolate's fascinating story pairs with mouth watering photos in this handsome, picture-book-size overview." Booklist

Includes glossary and bibliographical references

D'Amico, Joan, 1957-

The science chef; 100 fun food experiments and recipes for kids; [by] Joan D'Amico, Karen Eich Drummond; illustrations by Tina Cash-Walsh. Wiley 1995 180p il $12.95

Grades: 4 5 6   **641.3**
    1. Food 2. Cooking 3. Science—Experiments
    ISBN 0-471-31045-X   LC 94-9045
This includes facts about food, recipes, and experiments with food

"Attractively illustrated with black-and-white line drawings, easy and interesting to read, and filled with tidbits of information." SLJ

Includes glossary

De Paola, Tomie, 1934-

The popcorn book. Holiday House 1978 unp il lib bdg $16.95; pa $6.95

Grades: K 1 2 3   **641.3**
    1. Popcorn
    ISBN 0-8234-0314-9 (lib bdg); 0-8234-0533-8 (pa)
                                          LC 77-21456

De Paola, Tomie, 1934-—*Continued*

"While one twin prepares the treat, the other stays close-by and reads aloud what popcorn is, how it's cooked, stored, and made, how the Indians of the Americas discovered it, and who eats the most. . . . The best thing about popcorn, the twins decide, is eating it. Two recipes are included." Babbling Bookworm

The author-artist's "amusing soft-color pictures—each bordered with a lavender frame—show action in the past or the present while a few lines of text or balloon speeches describe what is happening." Horn Book

Hewitt, Sally

Your food. Crabtree Pub. Co. 2009 32p il (Green team) $26.60; pa $8.95

Grades: 3 4 5 6   **641.3**
1. Food
ISBN   978-0-7787-4099-5;   0-7787-4099-4;
978-0-7787-4106-0 (pa); 0-7787-4106-0 (pa)
LC 2008023291

"Looks at ways to eat, cook, and grow foods that are healthy and eco-friendly and offers examples of positive actions being taken by children around the world to eat in a green way and to look after the environment." Publisher's note

"The color graphics and layouts are highly appealing and will definitely be attractive to young readers. . . . This . . . is an excellent resource for school libraries, science teachers, and community sponsors." Libr Media Connect

Includes glossary

Jango-Cohen, Judith

The history of food; [by] Judith Jango-Cohen. Twenty-First Century Books 2006 56p il (Major inventions through history) lib bdg $26.60

Grades: 5 6 7 8   **641.3**
1. Food—History
ISBN 0-8225-2484-8   LC 2004-23022

This history of food "discusses canning, pasteurization, refrigeration, supermarkets, and genetically modified foods. . . . The text . . . is breezy but informative; unfamiliar terms are defined. Illustrations are a mixture of period black-and-white and color photos." SLJ

Includes bibliographical references

Landau, Elaine

Popcorn; illustrated by Brian Lies. Charlesbridge Pub. 2003 32p il hardcover o.p. pa $7.95

Grades: 2 3 4   **641.3**
1. Popcorn
ISBN 1-57091-442-7 (lib bdg); 1-57091-443-5 (pa)
LC 2002-2271

Provides a history of one of America's favorite snack foods, presenting its origins, nutritional information and recipes

"Lies' brightly colored acrylic illustrations enhance the humor of the text. . . . This will be useful for classroom projects and report writers as well as entertaining reading." Booklist

Includes bibliographical references

Menzel, Peter

What the world eats; photographed by Peter Menzel; written by Faith D'Aluisio. Tricycle Press 2008 160p il map $22.99 *

Grades: 4 5 6 7 8   **641.3**
1. Food—Pictorial works 2. Diet 3. Eating customs
ISBN 978-1-58246-246-2; 1-58246-246-1
LC 2007-41439

An adaptation of *Hungry Planet*, published 2005 by Ten Speed Press for adults

"A photographic collection exploring what the world eats featuring portraits of twenty-five families from twenty-one countries surrounded by a week's worth of food." Publisher's note

"Stunning color photographs of mealtimes and daily activities illustrate the warm, informative, anecdotal narratives. . . . This is a fascinating, sobering, and instructive look at daily life around the world." Booklist

Includes bibliographical references

Micucci, Charles, 1959-

The life and times of the peanut. Houghton Mifflin 1997 31p il music hardcover o.p. pa $6.95 *

Grades: 2 3 4   **641.3**
1. Peanuts
ISBN 0-395-72289-6; 0-618-03314-9 (pa)
LC 96-1290

"The author presents information on how peanuts grow, how they are farmed, where they are produced . . . and how they are used worldwide. What sets this book apart is Micucci's amusing and creative techniques for bringing statistics to life. . . . The artwork is attractive . . . with great attention to line, movement, and color, all carefully placed on the pages." Booklist

Miller, Jeanne

Food science. Lerner Publications 2009 48p il (Cool science) lib bdg $27.93

Grades: 4 5 6   **641.3**
1. Food
ISBN 978-0-8225-7589-4 (lib bdg); 0-8225-7589-2 (lib bdg)

This describes how food scientists "explore how cooking changes food, create dishes that surprise the senses, and help farmers grow food in healthier ways." Publisher's note

Includes glossary and bibliographical references

Price, Sean, 1963-

The story behind chocolate; [by] Sean Stewart Price. Heinemann Library 2009 32p il map lib bdg $28.21

Grades: 3 4 5   **641.3**
1. Chocolate
ISBN 978-1-4329-2347-1 (lib bdg); 1-4329-2347-1 (lib bdg)   LC 2008037524

"Price explains how chocolate was discovered and became popular, its ingredients, the chocolate-making process, and how companies like Hershey and Cadbury became successful. . . . The well-organized [text is] informative and clearly written, and the numerous color pho-

Price, Sean, 1963-—*Continued*
tographs and drawings are eye-catching and complement the [narrative] well." SLJ
Includes bibliographical references

Solheim, James
It's disgusting—and we ate it! true food facts from around the world—and throughout history! illustrated by Eric Brace. Simon & Schuster Bks. for Young Readers 1998 37p il hardcover o.p. pa $6.99
Grades: 4 5 6 7   **641.3**
  1. Food 2. Eating customs
  ISBN 0-689-80675-2; 0-689-84393-3 (pa)
               LC 96-7406
This "look at culinary culture is divided into three sections, the first discussing the global breadth of tastes, the second describing some startling dishes of history, and the third revealing some of the colorful truths behind contemporary American favorites." Bull Cent Child Books
Includes bibliographical references

Sylver, Adrienne
Hot diggity dog; the history of the hot dog; illustrated by Elwood H. Smith. Dutton Children's Books 2010 unp il $16.99
Grades: K 1 2 3   **641.3**
  1. Frankfurters
  ISBN 978-0-525-47897-3; 0-525-47897-3
"How did hot dogs become so popular? asks Sylver in this popular history of the wiener. . . . Accompanied by Smith's handsomely goofy, retro artwork, the narrative offers sidebars with factual tidbits galore." Kirkus

641.5   Cooking

Arroyo, Sheri L.
How chefs use math; math curriculum consultant, Rhea A. Stewart. Chelsea Clubhouse 2010 32p il (Math in the real world) lib bdg $28
Grades: 4 5 6   **641.5**
  1. Cooking 2. Cooks 3. Mathematics 4. Vocational guidance
  ISBN 978-1-60413-608-1 (lib bdg); 1-60413-608-1 (lib bdg)   LC 2009-14180
This describes how chefs use math for such tasks as measuring ingredients, watching temperatures, buying food, setting menu prices, and managing restaurant and catering businesses, and includes relevant math problems and information about how to become a chef
Includes glossary and bibliographical references

Batmanglij, Najmieh, 1947-
Happy Nowruz; cooking with children to celebrate the Persian New Year; [by] Najmieh Batmanglij. Mage Publishers 2008 119p il $40
Grades: 4 5 6 7 8   **641.5**
  1. Middle Eastern cooking 2. New Year 3. Eating customs 4. Iran—Social life and customs
  ISBN 1-933823-16-X; 978-1-933823-16-4
              LC 2007-036047

"Combining a cookbook format with straightforward, informational text, this amply illustrated title offers a detailed introduction to the history and customs surrounding Nowruz, the Persian New Year. . . . The covered spiral binding allows pages to remain open while cooking, and the uncluttered, attractive format, featuring color photos of kids in the kitchen and whimsical illustrations, will attract interested browsers." Booklist

Bloomfield, Jill
Jewish holidays cookbook; by Jill Colella Bloomfield; Janet Ozur Bass, consultant; photography by Angela Coppola. DK Pub. 2008 128p il spiral bdg $19.99
Grades: 4 5 6 7   **641.5**
  1. Jewish cooking 2. Jewish holidays
  ISBN 978-0-7566-4089-7 (spiral bdg); 0-7566-4089-X (spiral bdg)
"More than 40 recipes are included for celebrations from Shabbat to Lag B'Omer. Several introductions explain cooking tools, kitchen safety, and the general principles of keeping kosher, and brief background information is given for each holiday. Simple step-by-step instructions make the recipes easy. . . . Beautiful color photographs, both full page and spot, whet the appetite." SLJ

Bowers, Sharon
Ghoulish goodies. Storey Pub. 2009 153p il pa $14.95
Grades: 3 4 5 6   **641.5**
  1. Halloween 2. Holiday cooking 3. Desserts
  ISBN 978-1-60342-146-1 (pa); 1-60342-146-7 (pa)
              LC 2009007802
This offers recipes for Halloween-themed desserts such as Monster Eyeballs, Chocolate Spider Clusters, Buried Alive Cupcakes, and Screaming Red Punch
"Perfect for Halloween and beyond, this conveniently organized, well-illustrated cookbook is sure to be a crowd-pleaser. . . . Most recipes are complemented by a full-color photograph of the finished product. . . . Hauntingly appetizing." SLJ

Braman, Arlette N., 1952-
Kids around the world cook! the best foods and recipes from many lands. Wiley 2000 116p il pa $12.95
Grades: 4 5 6   **641.5**
  1. Cooking
  ISBN 0-471-35251-9   LC 99-46110
Presents information on and recipes for a variety of foods from many countries, including Sweet Lassi from India, Challah from Israel, Strawberry Soup from Poland, Kushiyaki from Japan, and Prairie Berry Cake from Canada

Canfield, Jack, 1944-

Chicken soup for the soul: kids in the kitchen; tasty recipes and fun activities for budding chefs; [by] Jack Canfield, Mark Victor Hansen, and Antonio Frontera. Health Communications 2007 248p il pa $19.95

Grades: 5 6 7 8   **641.5**

1. Cooking 2. Anecdotes

ISBN 978-0-7573-0579-5 (pa); 0-7573-0579-2 (pa)
           LC 2007-020559

"This title has child-friendly recipes and good tips to help kids understand and appreciate cooking." SLJ

D'Amico, Joan, 1957-

The coming to America cookbook; delicious recipes and fascinating stories from America's many cultures; [by] Joan D'Amico, Karen Eich Drummond. Wiley 2005 180p il pa $14.95 *

Grades: 5 6 7 8   **641.5**

1. Cooking 2. United States—Immigration and emigration

ISBN 0-471-48335-4   LC 2004-14947

The authors "provide information about American immigrants from 18 nations as well as recipes representing each group. . . . Accompanied by line drawings of ethnic families choosing, preparing, and eating food, . . . chapters discuss each country's climate, history, major waves of emigration, and traditional foods. Typically, three recipes follow. . . . Teachers and students looking for recipes from American immigrant cultures will make good use of this handy resource." Booklist

The healthy body cookbook; over 50 fun activities and delicious recipes for kids; [by] Joan D'Amico, Karen Eich Drummond; illustrations by Tina Cash-Walsh. Wiley 1999 184p il pa $12.95

Grades: 5 6 7 8   **641.5**

1. Cooking 2. Nutrition

ISBN 0-471-18888-3   LC 98-2776

Discusses the various parts of the human body and what to eat to keep them healthy. Includes recipes that contain nutrients important for the heart, muscles, teeth, skin, nerves, and other parts of the body

"The line drawings are helpful and the writing is informal but straightforward. The recipes are clear, thoroughly explained, and tasty." SLJ

The math chef; over 60 math activities and recipes for kids; [by] Joan D'Amico, Karen Eich Drummond; illustrations by Tina Cash-Walsh. Wiley 1997 180p il pa $12.95

Grades: 4 5 6   **641.5**

1. Cooking 2. Mathematics

ISBN 0-471-13813-4   LC 96-22143

Relates math and cookery by presenting math concepts and reinforcing them with recipes. Provides practice in converting from English to metric system, multiplying quantities, measuring area, estimating, and more

"The instructional value of this book is excellent. . . . The illustrations and content are accurate and very well depicted." Sci Books Films

Includes glossary

Deen, Paula H., 1947-

Paula Deen's my first cookbook; by Paula Deen with Martha Nesbit; illustrated by Susan Mitchell. Simon & Schuster 2008 176p il spiral bdg $21.99

Grades: 3 4 5 6   **641.5**

1. Cooking

ISBN 978-1-4169-5033-2 (spiral bdg); 1-4169-5033-8 (spiral bdg)   LC 2008-4433

Easy-to-follow recipes, safety tips, and lessons on good manners are compiled in this cookbook along with detailed steps, informative illustrations, family photos, and anecdotes for aspiring young chefs.

"Watercolor illustrations of ingredients, finished dishes, and children at work are numerous and each page is framed with a colorful pattern. While the spiral format may shorten this book's shelf life, it will facilitate use for the youngest chefs." SLJ

Dodge, Abigail Johnson

Around the world cookbook; by Abigail Johnson Dodge. DK Publishing 2008 124p il map spiral bdg $19.99

Grades: 3 4 5 6   **641.5**

1. Cooking

ISBN 978-0-7566-3744-6 (spiral bdg); 0-7566-3744-9 (spiral bdg)

"This book presents more than 50 step-by-step recipes for ethnic cuisine. Dodge opens with instructions for basic cooking skills, an illustrated list of kitchen tools, a glossary of terms used in the recipes, and tips for working with different types of ingredients. . . . Possibly tricky steps are clarified with photographs and captions." SLJ

Easy menu ethnic cookbooks. rev ed. Lerner Publs. 2002-2005 37v ea $25.26

Grades: 5 6 7 8   **641.5**

1. Cooking

Some titles also available in paperback

Series first published 1982-1995

Available volumes in the revised series are: Cooking the Australian way, by E. Germaine & A. L. Burchhardt; Cooking the Austrian way, by H. Hughes; Cooking the Brazilian way, by A. Behnke & K. L. Duro; Cooking the Caribbean way, by C. D. Kaufman; Cooking the Central American way, by A. Behnke; Cooking the Chinese way, by L. Yu; Cooking the Cuban way, by A. Behnke & V. M. Valens; Cooking the East African way, by C. Nabwire & B. V. Montgomery; Cooking the English way, by B. W. Hill; Cooking the French way, by L. M. Waldee; Cooking the German way, by H. Parnell; Cooking the Greek way, by L. W. Villios; Cooking the Hungarian way, by M. Hargittai; Cooking the Indian way, by V. Madavan; Cooking the Indonesian way, by M. Anwar & K. Cornell; Cooking the Israeli way, by J. Bacon; Cooking the Italian way, by A. Bisignano; Cooking the Japanese way, by R. Weston; Cooking the Korean way, by O. Chung & J. Monroe; Cooking the Lebanese way, by S. Amari; Cooking the Mediterranean way, by A. Behnke; Cooking the Mexican way, by R. Coronado; Cooking the Middle Eastern way, by A. Behnke; Cooking the North African way, by M. Winget & H. Cahlbi; Cooking the Norwegian way, by S. Munsen; Cooking the Polish way, by D. Zamojska-Hutchins; Cooking the Rus-

Easy menu ethnic cookbooks—*Continued*

sian way, by G. & R. Plotkin; Cooking the South American way, by H. Parnell; Cooking the Southern African way, by K. Cornell & P. Thomas; Cooking the Spanish way, by R. Christian; Cooking the Thai way, by S. Harrison & J. Monroe; Cooking the Turkish way, by K. Cornell & N. Turkoglu; Cooking the Vietnamese way, by C. Nguyen & J. Monroe; Cooking the West African way, by C. Nabwire & B. V. Montgomery; Desserts aroung the world by L. Engfer; Holiday cooking around the world, by R. Wolfe & D. Wolfe; Vegetarian cooking around the world, by A. Behnke

"In each volume, the front matter comprises close to half the book. Geography, history, holidays, and festivals, typical ingredients, and sample menus are all covered. . . . Each book presents about 20 recipes, mostly focusing on lunch, dinner, and holiday foods. . . . The narrative pieces are smoothly written and offer some interesting tidbits. . . . The pages are a warm buff color, and the design allows plenty of space on the pages for the text and the nicely reproduced color photos." SLJ

Gerasole, Isabella, 1995-

The Spatulatta cookbook; by Isabella and Olivia Gerasole; photographs by John Zich. Scholastic 2007 128p il spiral bdg $16.99

Grades: 3 4 5 6   641.5

    1. Cooking

    ISBN 978-0-439-02250-7 (spiral bdg); 0-439-02250-9 (spiral bdg)

"This lively, colorful companion book to the Gerasole sisters' Web site . . . contains an enticing array of dishes both sweet and savory, easy and complicated. . . . Beautifully reproduced color photos show the completed dishes and smaller photos show some of the steps. . . . This book strikes a great balance between fun and practical." SLJ

    Includes glossary

Gillies, Judi

The jumbo vegetarian cookbook; written by Judi Gillies and Jennifer Glossop; illustrated by Louise Phillips. Kids Can Press 2002 256p il pa $14.95 *

Grades: 4 5 6 7   641.5

    1. Vegetarian cooking

    ISBN 1-55074-977-3

"Much more than just a cookbook, this sprawling title introduces basic nutrition and how to achieve it with a vegetarian diet. Beginning sections cover safety tips and culinary basics . . . as well as types of vegetarianism, the environmental and health reasons that have led many to a meatless diet, and a list of common vegetarian ingredients. The recipe sections are extensive, with well-chosen dishes from breakfast foods through entrées and desserts." Booklist

The Kids Can Press jumbo cookbook; written by Judi Gillies and Jennifer Glossop; illustrated by Louise Phillips. Kids Can Press 2000 256p il pa $14.95 *

Grades: 4 5 6 7   641.5

    1. Cooking

    ISBN 1-55074-621-9

A "collection of over 100 recipes, arranged by categories such as 'Soups and Chilis'; 'Salads and Vegetables'; 'Pasta, Noodles, Rice and Grains'; etc. All have simple, step-by-step instructions, call for commonly available ingredients, and range in difficulty from boiled rice to sushi and shepherd's pie." SLJ

"The book's format is kid-friendly, with large print and cartoon art, but many of the numerous recipes are quite grown-up." Booklist

Gold, Rozanne, 1954-

Kids cook 1-2-3; recipes for young chefs using only 3 ingredients; illustrated by Sara Pinto. Bloomsbury Children's Books 2006 144p il $17.95

Grades: 3 4 5 6   641.5

    1. Cooking

    ISBN 978-1-58234-735-6; 1-58234-735-2

                           LC 2006-00623

"This very basic cookbook offers 125 recipes for breakfast, lunch, dinner, healthy snacks, side dishes, and desserts. The recipes are clearly presented, and are broken into easy-to-follow steps." SLJ

Hopkinson, Deborah

Fannie in the kitchen; the whole story from soup to nuts of how Fannie Farmer invented recipes with precise measurements; pictures by Nancy Carpenter. Atheneum Bks. for Young Readers 2001 unp il hardcover o.p. pa $7.99 *

Grades: K 1 2 3   641.5

    1. Farmer, Fannie Merritt, 1857-1915 2. Cooking

    ISBN 0-689-81965-X; 0-689-86987-5 (pa)

                           LC 97-46712

"An Anne Schwartz book"

Fannie Farmer is a mother's helper in the Shaw house, where the daughter gives her the idea of writing down precise instructions for measuring and cooking, which eventually became one of the first modern cookbooks

"A clever introduction to the renowned nineteenth century cook. . . . The collage artwork is exceptional—elegant as well as whimsical. Carpenter brings together original pen-and-ink artwork and engravings, all washed in watercolor, to create a houseful of expressive characters and abundant, often witty details." Booklist

Ichord, Loretta Frances

Skillet bread, sourdough, and vinegar pie; cooking in pioneer days; illustrated by Jan Davey Ellis. Millbrook Press 2003 64p il map hardcover o.p. pa $8.95

Grades: 3 4 5   641.5

    1. Cooking 2. Frontier and pioneer life—West (U.S.)

    ISBN 0-7613-1864-X (lib bdg); 0-7613-9521-0 (pa)

                           LC 2002-8157

Ichord, Loretta Frances—*Continued*

Presents a look at what was eaten in the American West by pioneers on the trail, cowboys on cattle drives, and gold miners in California camps, with available ingredients, cooking methods, and equipment. Includes recipes and appendix of classroom cooking directions

"This unique title effectively combines recipes with history, a must for any collection needing information on the old West." Libr Media Connect

Includes bibliographical references

Katzen, Mollie, 1950-

Honest pretzels; and 64 other amazing recipes for cooks ages 8 & up. Tricycle Press 1999 177p il hardcover o.p. pa $17.99 *

Grades: 4 5 6   641.5
1. Vegetarian cooking
ISBN 1-88367-288-0; 978-1-58246-305-6 (pa);
1-58246-305-0 (pa)   LC 99-20184

Provides step-by-step instructions for a variety of vegetarian recipes, arranged in such categories as "Breakfast Specials," "Soups, Sandwiches & Salads for Lunch or Supper," and "Desserts and a Few Baked Things"

"Small, colorful drawings illustrate most of the cooking instructions and brighten many of the other pages as well." Booklist

Salad people and more real recipes; a new cookbook for preschoolers and up. Tricycle Press 2005 93p il $17.95 *

Grades: K 1 2 3   641.5
1. Cooking
ISBN 1-58246-141-4

"Katzen offers a range of vegetarian, kid-friendly recipes in an artistic, innovative format. Each recipe receives two spreads. The first contains detailed, step-by-step instructions for adults; the second, directed to children, illustrates stages of preparation in a series of clear, boxed drawings. Katzen's whimsical color pictures of dancing produce and animals decorate the pages. . . . These detailed, practical, and inspired ideas may extend far beyond the kitchen, helping adults approach parenting in new ways and helping kids develop a lifelong interest and confidence in healthy food." Booklist

Kids' first cookbook; delicious-nutritious treats to make yourself. American Cancer Soc. 2000 88p il $13.95

Grades: K 1 2 3   641.5
1. Cooking
ISBN 0-944235-19-0

A collection of easy-to-make recipes for breakfast foods, snacks, main dishes, drinks, and desserts

"A cookbook with a contemporary look filled with nutrition information. . . . A solid effort that will encourage healthy eating habits." SLJ

Lagasse, Emeril

Emeril's there's a chef in my family! recipes to get everybody cooking; illustrated by Charles Yuen; photographs by Quentin Bacon. HarperCollins Publishers 2004 209p il $22.99 *

Grades: 5 6 7 8   641.5
1. Cooking
ISBN 0-06-000439-8   LC 2003-5612

Provides tips for having fun and keeping safe in the kitchen, along with dozens of world-famous chef Emeril Lagasse's favorite recipes that families can make and eat together

"The step-by-step directions are clearly laid out, and most of the dishes look delicious. The fresh and attractive design includes a mix of simple paintings (for the food) and photos (for the people). Emeril himself is shown throughout, conveying his enthusiasm and sense of play." SLJ

Emeril's there's a chef in my world! recipes that take you places; illustrated by Charles Yuen; photographs of Emeril Lagasse and children by Quentin Bacon. HarperCollins Publishers 2006 210p il $22.99 *

Grades: 5 6 7 8   641.5
1. Cooking
ISBN 978-0-06-073926-3; 0-06-073926-6
                                        LC 2005-15133

"The famous chef introduces dishes from around the world, dividing the recipes into familiar food categories—sweets, snacks, sandwiches, entrees, etc. . . . The recipes, from latkes to egg-drop soup, are good choices for open-minded eaters. . . . Many children will enjoy the mix of maps, flags, cartoon drawings, and color photos . . . and the cultural facts woven into each recipe." Booklist

Lee, Frances, 1971-

Fun with Chinese cooking. PowerKids Press 2009 32p il (Let's get cooking!) lib bdg $18.95; pa $11.75

Grades: 4 5 6 7   641.5
1. Chinese cooking
ISBN 978-1-4358-3453-8 (lib bdg); 1-4358-3453-4 (lib bdg); 978-1-4358-3475-0 (pa); 1-4358-3475-5 (pa)
                                        LC 2009010337

This includes recipes for such Chinese dishes as spring rolls and braised mushrooms, and highlights the history and dishes that surround the Chinese New Year.

"The photography is exceptional, with children engaged in the cooking process. . . . Children, and the adults who assist them, will spend hours together mastering the techniques." SLJ

Locricchio, Matthew

The international cookbook for kids; by Matthew Locricchio; photographs by Jack McConnell. Marshall Cavendish 2004 175p il $18.95 *

Grades: 5 6 7 8   641.5
1. Cooking
ISBN 0-7614-5185-4   LC 2004-5894

Locricchio, Matthew—*Continued*

This includes "60 classic recipes from Italy, France, China, and Mexico, . . . chef's tips discussing ingredients, nutrition, and technique, safety section discussing basic kitchen precautions, cooking terms and definitions." Publisher's note

"This is a strong collection of popular dishes attractively presented." SLJ

The 2nd international cookbook for kids; photographs by Jack McConnell. Marshall Cavendish 2008 176p il $18.99 *

Grades: 5 6 7 8   **641.5**
1. Cooking
ISBN 978-0-7614-5513-4   LC 2008003178

"Chef Matthew Locricchio brings us . . . recipes from India, Greece, Thailand, and Brazil specially designed for kids and their families." Publisher's note

The recipes are "presented in a challenging yet teen-friendly step-by-step sequence. The book is best for patient chefs with kitchen experience and adventurous appetites. Informative sidebars provide facts about the recipes and cultures." Horn Book Guide

A **taste** of culture [series] Kidhaven Press 2005-2008 17v il map

Grades: 4 5 6   **641.5**
1. Cooking
Contents: Foods of Brazil by Barbara Sheen; Foods of China by Barbara Sheen; Foods of Ethiopia by Barbara Sheen; Foods of France by Peggy J. Parks; Foods of Germany by Barbara Sheen; Foods of Greece by Barbara Sheen; Foods of India by Barbara Sheen; Foods of Iran by Barbara Sheen; Foods of Italy by Barbara Sheen; Foods of Japan by Barbara Sheen; Foods of Mexico by Barbara Sheen; Foods of Russia by Barbara Sheen; Foods of Spain by Barbara Sheen; Foods of Thailand by Barbara Sheen; Foods of the Caribbean by Barbara Sheen; Foods of the Philippines by Barbara Sheen; Foods of Vietnam by Barbara Sheen

"These titles offer easy, delicious recipes . . . and insights into the cultures that produced them. . . . Each volume is well researched, and culture and food go hand-in-hand. . . . Each title ends with a metric conversion chart and extensive chapter notes. Clear, large full-color photographs spice up the texts. The language is inviting and not overly challenging." SLJ

Walker, Barbara Muhs, 1928-

The Little House cookbook; frontier foods from Laura Ingalls Wilder's classic stories; by Barbara M. Walker; illustrated by Garth Williams. Harper & Row 1979 240p il $16.95; pa $9.95

Grades: 5 6 7 8   **641.5**
1. Wilder, Laura Ingalls, 1867-1957 2. Cooking 3. Frontier and pioneer life
ISBN 0-06-026418-7; 0-06-446090-8 (pa)
                                                  LC 76-58733

Recipes based on the pioneer food written about in the "Little House" books of Laura Ingalls Wilder, along with quotes from the books and descriptions of the food and cooking of pioneer times

"Illustrated by Williams's familiar warm drawings, the adaptations of menus from pioneer days include paragaphs describing the Wilder and Ingalls families working together, preparing holiday meals, individual foods, special treats and staple fare." Publ Wkly

Includes bibliographical references

Webb, Lois Sinaiko, 1922-

Holidays of the world cookbook for students. Oryx Press 1995 xxxiv, 297p il maps pa $36.95

Grades: 5 6 7 8 9 10   **641.5**
1. Cooking 2. Holidays
ISBN 0-89774-884-0   LC 95-26019

In this cookbook "more than 136 countries are represented, with 388 recipes. The U.S. is divided into six sections with 10 recipes for regional celebrations. History behind the holiday is included where possible, as is pertinent background information on the culture represented. . . . A discussion of different calendars used around the world is an interesting inclusion. The recipes' directions are clear and include equipment lists." SLJ

Includes glossary and bibliographical references

Yolen, Jane

Fairy tale feasts; a literary cookbook for young readers and eaters; [by] Jane Yolen and Heidi E. Y. Stemple; illustrated by Philippe Beha. Crocodile Books 2006 197p il $24.95

Grades: 2 3 4 5   **641.5**
1. Cooking 2. Folklore
ISBN 1-56656-543-6

This "folds fairy tales into a cookbook of kid-friendly recipes. The stories, with the exception of one original story by Yolen, represent mostly European folktales, and Yolen retells them with her usual verve and ease. . . . Each story is paired with at least one recipe that connects with the story's themes or references. . . . Stemple's recipes require adult supervision, but the resulting dishes, as well as Beha's spare, whimsical spot illustrations, will capture children's fancy." Booklist

641.6 Cooking specific materials

MacLeod, Elizabeth

Chock full of chocolate; written by Elizabeth MacLeod; illustrated by June Bradford. Kids Can Press 2005 40p il (Kids can do it) hardcover o.p. pa $6.95

Grades: 4 5 6   **641.6**
1. Chocolate 2. Cooking
ISBN 1-55337-762-1; 1-55337-763-X (pa)

This includes recipes for chocolate cookies, cakes, and other desserts.

641.8 Cooking specific kinds of dishes, preparing beverages

Dunnington, Rose

Sweet eats; mmmore than just desserts; [by] Rose Dunnington. Lark Books 2008 112p $9.95

Grades: 3 4 5 6   **641.8**

1. Desserts 2. Baking

ISBN 978-1-60059-236-2; 1-60059-236-8

LC 2007037094

This "offers mouthwatering recipes, explains how to cook safely and efficiently, and introduces basic skills. In a breezy first-person style, the author covers such useful aspects as how to organize a work space, safety tips, the tools needed, and how and why to do things. The 35 recipes include a pie crust and various frostings/toppings and are accompanied by plenty of full-color visual aids along the way." SLJ

Includes glossary

Fleisher, Paul

Ice cream treats; the inside scoop; photographs by David O. Saunders. Carolrhoda Bks. 2001 48p il lib bdg $23.93

Grades: 4 5 6 7   **641.8**

1. Ice cream, ices, etc.

ISBN 1-57505-268-7   LC 00-9229

"Focusing on the production of ice cream novelties at a Good Humor-Breyers factory, this . . . describes the process from pasteurization of raw milk to the formation of ice cream bars to the trip through the wrapping machine. . . . The book includes several recipes for homemade ice cream." Horn Book Guide

"An appealing and instructive book." SLJ

Gibbons, Gail

Ice cream; the full scoop; by Gail Gibbons. Holiday House 2006 unp il $16.95

Grades: K 1 2 3   **641.8**

1. Ice cream, ices, etc.

ISBN 978-0-8234-2000-1; 0-8234-2000-0

LC 2005052575

"Gibbons explains how this favorite food developed from flavored ice to the creamy dessert we know today, describes the invention and workings of the ice-cream maker, follows the journey from cow to factory to grocery-store shelves, and mentions the innovative creation of the cone. . . . The narrative is simple and direct and the cartoon illustrations are colorful and cheerful." SLJ

Goodman, Susan, 1952-

All in just one cookie; by Susan E. Goodman; illustrated by Timothy Bush. Greenwillow Books 2006 unp il $16.99; lib bdg $17.89

Grades: 2 3 4   **641.8**

1. Cookies 2. Baking

ISBN   978-0-06-009092-0;   0-06-009092-8; 978-0-06-009093-7 (lib bdg); 0-06-009093-6 (lib bdg)

LC 2005040308

"As Grandma gathers the ingredients for her chocolate-chip cookies, her cat collects facts about the process of making butter, vanilla, baking soda, and other cookie components. . . . Cartoonlike illustrations show where each ingredient comes from, along with side comments from the cat and dog." Horn Book Guide

Love, Ann, 1947-

Sweet! the delicious story of candy; [by] Ann Love & Jane Drake; illustrated by Claudia Dávila. Tundra Books 2007 64p il map $19.95

Grades: 4 5 6 7   **641.8**

1. Candy

ISBN 978-0-88776-752-4

"This history of things sweet and sugary is a yummy feast. The prose is chatty and inviting. Color cartoon illustrations show multiethnic people in the process of making or enjoying everything from honey to ice cream to cotton candy (called candy floss here) to jelly beans and chocolate." SLJ

MacLeod, Elizabeth

Bake and make amazing cakes; written by Elizabeth MacLeod; illustrated by June Bradford. Kids Can Press 2001 40p il (Kids can do it) hardcover o.p. pa $5.95

Grades: 4 5 6   **641.8**

1. Cake

ISBN 1-55074-849-1; 1-55074-848-3 (pa)

In this book "there are four cake recipes; three icing recipes; and 19 different creations, including cakes in the shape of a mouse, a house, a butterfly, and a bus. . . . The directions are clear and the format is clean." SLJ

Bake and make amazing cookies; written by Elizabeth MacLeod; illustrated by June Bradford. Kids Can Press 2004 40p il (Kids can do it) hardcover o.p. pa $6.95

Grades: 4 5 6   **641.8**

1. Cookies

ISBN 1-55337-631-5; 1-55337-632-3 (pa)

This offers "32 recipes under four headings 'Holidays,' 'For Special People,' 'Seasons,' and 'Just for Fun.' This book is sure to please bakers. The step-by-step instructions . . . are easy to follow, and the ingredients/tools listed are readily available or easily obtainable. . . . Each recipe is accompanied by precise, softly colored illustrations." SLJ

Morris, Ann

Bread, bread, bread; photographs by Ken Heyman. Lothrop, Lee & Shepard Bks. 1989 unp il hardcover o.p. pa $5.95

Grades: PreK K 1   **641.8**

1. Bread

ISBN 0-688-06335-7; 0-688-12275-2 (pa)

LC 88-26677

This photo essay shows different kinds of bread around the world from baguettes to challah

"Each picture offers a strong ethnic identity or a thought-provoking human interaction, with captions of only a few words in large print. An unusual index . . .

Morris, Ann—*Continued*

gives background information about the pictures, citing the countries of origin and a few facts about each type of bread." SLJ

Paulsen, Gary

The tortilla factory; paintings by Ruth Wright Paulsen. Harcourt Brace & Co. 1995 unp il hardcover o.p. pa $7

Grades: K 1 2 3 **641.8**

1. Tortillas

ISBN 0-15-292876-6; 0-15-201698-8 (pa)

LC 93-48590

Also available Spanish language edition

"Paulsen traces the journey of the corn, from harvest and grinding, to the tortilla factory, where people turn the corn flour into tortillas that, filled with beans, 'give strength to the brown hands that work the black earth to plant yellow seeds.' . . . Replete with the lush greens of healthy plants, the rich browns of adobe buildings and fertile soil, and the vibrant gold of ears of corn, the highly satisfying illustrations reinforce the reverential mood established by the spare poetic narrative." Horn Book

Raum, Elizabeth

The story behind bread. Heinemann Library 2009 32p il (True stories) lib bdg $28.21

Grades: 3 4 5 **641.8**

1. Bread

ISBN 978-1-4329-2346-4 (lib bdg); 1-4329-2346-3 (lib bdg)

LC 2008037394

The story behind "bread covers the history of the staple and its importance, the harvesting of grains, and the equipment used to bring it 'From Fields to Tables.' Readers will learn, for example, that bagels were originally created in the shape of a stirrup to honor the King of Poland. . . . The well-organized [text is] informative and clearly written, and the numerous color photographs and drawings are eye-catching and complement the [narrative] well." SLJ

Includes bibliographical references

Smart, Denise

The children's baking book; recipes & styling by Denise Smart; photography by Howard Shooter. DK 2009 128p il $17.99

Grades: 3 4 5 **641.8**

1. Baking

ISBN 978-0-7566-5788-8; 0-7566-5788-1

Instructions for making bread, pastry, muffins, cakes and cookies. Includes more than 50 easy-to-follow recipes.

"This accessible baking book features more than 50 sweet and savory recipes . . . with full-color photographs that show both preparations and tasty end results. Divided into sections on cookies and baked goods, dough, cakes, and pastry, the recipes are further labeled with levels of difficulty. . . . The sweet-toothed should find the mouthwatering pictures and straightforward instructions hard to resist." Publ Wkly

646.2 Sewing and related operations

Sadler, Judy Ann, 1959-

Simply sewing; written by Judy Ann Sadler; illustrated by Jane Kurisu. Kids Can Press 2004 48p il (Kids can do it) hardcover o.p. pa $6.95

Grades: 4 5 6 **646.2**

1. Sewing

ISBN 1-55337-659-5; 1-55337-660-9 (pa)

This "book opens with a section on sewing supplies. . . . Subsequent chapters discuss fabric and the basics of hand and machine stitching. . . . Each of the 12 projects is accompanied by a color photo, step-by-step color illustrations, and a list of supplies needed. . . . This attractive book has a wide assortment of ideas to spark interest." SLJ

646.4 Clothing and accessories construction

D'Cruz, Anna-Marie

Make your own masks. PowerKids Press 2009 24p il (Do it yourself projects!) lib bdg $23.95; pa $9.40

Grades: 2 3 4 **646.4**

1. Masks (Facial) 2. Handicraft

ISBN 978-1-4358-2853-7 (lib bdg); 1-4358-2853-4 (lib bdg); 978-1-4358-2923-7 (pa); 1-4358-2923-9 (pa)

LC 2008033677

This offers "step-by-step instructions and full-color photos to illustrate the crafts. Projects have a broad cultural representation and are not gender specific. Materials are easily obtained. [The projects include] an Aztec skull, a Bwa sun mask, a Greek Medusa, and a Viking mask." SLJ

Includes glossary and bibliographical references

Make your own purses and bags. PowerKids Press 2009 24p il (Do it yourself projects!) lib bdg $23.95; pa $9.40

Grades: 2 3 4 **646.4**

1. Bags 2. Handicraft

ISBN 978-1-4358-2856-8 (lib bdg); 1-4358-2856-9 (lib bdg); 978-1-4358-2929-9 (pa); 1-4358-2929-8 (pa)

LC 2008033671

This offers "step-by-step instructions and full-color photos to illustrate the crafts. Projects have a broad cultural representation and are not gender specific. Materials are easily obtained. . . . A Didgeridoo pencil case and an MP3-player case are among the projects [included]." SLJ

Includes glossary and bibliographical references

Schwarz, Renée

Making masks; written and illustrated by Renée Schwarz. Kids Can Press 2002 40p il (Kids can do it) $12.95; pa $5.95

Grades: 4 5 6   **646.4**

   1. Masks (Facial) 2. Handicraft

   ISBN 1-55074-929-3; 1-55074-931-5 (pa)

This offers instructions for creating a variety of masks using such materials as cardboard, felt, paper, and pipe cleaners

This includes "appealing projects and easy-to-follow directions. . . . Schwarz does a good job constructing and illustrating a variety of masks." SLJ

646.7   Management of personal and family life

Boonyadhistarn, Thiranut

Fingernail art; dazzling fingers and terrific toes; by Thiranut Boonyadhistarn. Capstone Press 2007 32p il (Snap books) $25.26

Grades: 4 5 6 7   **646.7**

   1. Manicuring 2. Handicraft

   ISBN 978-0-7368-6474-9; 0-7368-6474-1

                   LC 2006004084

This is "lively and attractive. The projects use easily obtainable materials, and the directions are simple and well numbered. . . . [This] title demonstates how to decorate nails with paper dots, acrylic paints, emoticons, stickers, and so on." SLJ

Includes bibliographical references

648   Housekeeping

Barber, Nicola

Moving to a new house. PowerKids Press 2009 24p il (The big day!) lib bdg $21.25; pa $8.25

Grades: PreK K 1   **648**

   1. Moving

   ISBN   978-1-4358-2841-4   (lib   bdg); 978-1-4358-2897-1 (pa)   LC 2008026222

"Children in kindergarten will enjoy [this book] as [a read-aloud] . . . while those at the end of first grade will be able to read [it] independently. The writing is straightforward and reassuring, and the content provides a realistic view of what youngsters might experience in [a new home]. . . . [The book] mentions the possibility of feeling strange in the new environment, but also discusses how quickly the child will adjust and make new friends." SLJ

Includes bibliographical references

649   Child rearing; home care of persons with disabilities and illnesses

Buckley, Annie, 1968-

Be a better babysitter; by Annie Buckley. Child's World 2007 32p il (Girls rock!) lib bdg $24.21

Grades: 5 6 7 8   **649**

   1. Babysitting

   ISBN 1-59296-740-X   LC 2006001639

This "describes what babysitting entails, examines pros and cons, discusses safety issues, offers tips for doing a good job, and suggests saving as much as half of any money earned. . . . [This] realistic [title is] well written and [provides] excellent information." SLJ

Includes bibliographical references

Danzig, Dianne

Babies don't eat pizza; the big kids' book about baby brothers and baby sisters; by Dianne Danzig; illustrated by Debbie Tilley. Dutton Children's Books 2009 unp il $16.99

Grades: PreK K   **649**

   1. Infants 2. Siblings

   ISBN 978-0-525-47441-8; 0-525-47441-2

"Focusing on day-to-day living with an infant, the text adopts an unfussy tone that subtly flatters readers as being sensible and mature (relatively speaking). . . . Tilley's ink and watercolor cartoons are sunny and empathic . . . and include plenty of visual jokes to encourage anxious kids—and their parents—to bond. Headings on most spreads make this volume eminently browsable—and therefore a handy family resource." Publ Wkly

Raatma, Lucia

Safety for babysitters. Child's World 2005 32p il (Living well) lib bdg $25.64

Grades: 4 5 6 7   **649**

   1. Babysitting 2. Safety education

   ISBN 1-59296-239-4   LC 2003-27213

The offers advice on how to prepare for a babysitting job, what kinds of questions to ask the parents, what to do in emergencies

This has "an appealing layout with plenty of full-color photos and a triple-spaced text. . . . An excellent, easy-to-understand overview." SLJ

Includes glossary and bibliographical references

Sears, William

What baby needs; [by] William Sears, Martha Sears and Christie Watts Kelly; illustrated by Renée Andriani. Little, Brown 2001 unp il (Sears children's library) $12.95 *

Grades: K 1 2   **649**

   1. Infants 2. Siblings

   ISBN 0-316-78828-7   LC 00-37529

This "is a warm look at how life in the family changes to accommodate the needs of a newborn, and the care an infant requires. . . . The lighthearted, full-

Sears, William—*Continued*
color cartoons bring some welcome new images to baby books: breastfeeding, babywearing (including both a dad and a mom with an infant in a baby sling), and the newborn snoozing near the parents' bed." SLJ
Includes bibliographical references

650.1 Personal success in business

Orr, Tamra
A kid's guide to earning money; by Tamra Orr. Mitchell Lane Publishers 2008 47p il (Money matters: a kid's guide to money) lib bdg $29.95
Grades: 4 5 6   **650.1**
1. Money-making projects for children 2. Personal finance
ISBN 978-1-58415-643-7 (lib bdg); 1-58415-643-0 (lib bdg)   LC 2008-2253
"This chatty, interactive guide offers practical suggestions for finding jobs, from babysitting and dogwalking to delivering newspapers. . . . Also included is useful advice on setting price points, how to cut costs, and what the labor laws allow for kids under 18, as well as a frank view of the negatives associated with the working world. . . . Stress is laid on the importance of getting parental permission before setting out on the trail to riches." Booklist
Includes glossary and bibliographical references

652 Processes of written communication

Blackwood, Gary L.
Mysterious messages; a history of codes and ciphers; [by] Gary Blackwood; designed and illustrated by Jason Henry. Dutton Children's Books 2009 170p il $16.99
Grades: 5 6 7 8   **652**
1. Cryptography 2. Ciphers
ISBN 978-0-525-47960-4; 0-525-47960-0   LC 2008-48970
"This well-written history of cryptography begins with a pottery-glaze formula encrypted in cuneiform on a clay tablet (1500 BCE) and traces the uses of secret messages in statecraft, espionage, warfare, crime, literature, and business up to the present. Along the way, Blackwood . . . discusses the historical development of coding and encryption and tells many good stories of messages ciphered and deciphered. . . . The many sidebars and illustrations, including photos, reproductions of artworks and artifacts, and the pictures demonstrating the codes themselves, contribute to the book's approachable look." Booklist

Gilbert, Adrian
Codes and ciphers. Firefly 2009 32p il (Spy files) pa $6.95
Grades: 3 4 5 6   **652**
1. Ciphers 2. Cryptography 3. Espionage
ISBN 978-1-55407-573-7 (pa); 1-55407-573-4 (pa)
First published 2008 in the United Kingdom

Discusses the difference between codes and ciphers, common codes and ciphers that have been used during wars, and how to create simple ciphers
This "gives an excellent overview of the historical and practical use of codes and ciphers in spy work. . . . The [text's] short paragraphs and great pictures are combined in a collage style that will draw readers quickly through the information." SLJ
Includes glossary

Janeczko, Paul B., 1945-
Top secret; a handbook of codes, ciphers and secret writing; illustrated by Jenna LaReau. Candlewick Press 2004 136p il hardcover o.p. pa $7.99 *
Grades: 4 5 6 7   **652**
1. Cryptography 2. Ciphers
ISBN 978-0-7636-0971-9; 0-7636-0971-4; 978-0-7636-2972-4 (pa); 0-7636-2972-3 (pa)
This is a "guide to secret writing. Janeczko relates how different codes came to be and why they were needed, and gives some historical examples. The book also contains information and exercises (with answers) on deciphering codes and provides children with the tools to make their own field kit. . . . Humorous black-and-white sketches . . . are found throughout the book. The author's upbeat, positive tone is refreshing and his enthusiasm about his topic is contagious." SLJ

658 General management

Bochner, Arthur Berg
The new totally awesome business book for kids (and their parents); with twenty super businesses you can start right now! [by] Arthur Bochner & Rose Bochner; foreword by Andriane G. Berg. rev and updated 3rd ed. Newmarket Press 2007 188p il pa $9.95
Grades: 4 5 6 7   **658**
1. Small business 2. Money-making projects for children
ISBN 978-1-55704-757-1 (pa); 1-55704-757-X (pa)   LC 2007002637
First published 1995 with title: The totally awesome business book for kids
A comprehensive look at the basic financial and management aspects of moneymaking businesses for children
"This book can certainly be thought provoking for young people with an entrepreneurial spirit. . . . The illustrations are lively and engaging, and the text non-threatening." Voice Youth Advocates
Includes bibliographical references

659.1 Advertising

Hoban, Tana
I read signs. Greenwillow Bks. 1983 unp il hardcover o.p. pa $6.99
Grades: PreK K 1 2   **659.1**
1. Signs and signboards
ISBN 0-688-02317-7; 0-688-02318-5 (lib bdg); 0-688-07331-X (pa)   LC 83-1482

Hoban, Tana—*Continued*

In this book "30 verbal and 27 symbolic street signs have been caught on location in close-ups with a minimum of background to give just a soupçon of milieu (city, sky or apple tree) or hint of meaning ('Beware of dog' on chain link fence). Design is bold; primary colors are emphasized. The familiar predominates; more unusual signs . . . add interest." SLJ

660.6   Biotechnology

Fridell, Ron, 1943-

Genetic engineering. Lerner Pub. Group 2006 48p il (Cool science) lib bdg $25.26

Grades: 4 5 6   **660.6**

    1. Genetic engineering

    ISBN 978-0-8225-2633-9 (lib bdg); 0-8225-2633-6 (lib bdg)   LC 2004-22764

This book has "an attractive, colorful layout that will appeal to readers. Each spread includes captioned, color photographs and/or illustrations; text boxes; and, often, a 'fun fact.' . . . Fridell offers a brief explanation of the science and then discusses how genetics is being used to invent plants, improve animals, and engineer people. . . . Many intriguing examples are given. Glowing plants, supersized mice, and shrinking watermelons are among the topics included." SLJ

662   Technology of explosives, fuels, related products

Benduhn, Tea

Ethanol and other new fuels; by Tea Benduhn. Weekly Reader Pub. 2009 24p il (Energy for today) lib bdg $21; pa $5.95

Grades: 2 3 4   **662**

    1. Alcohol as fuel 2. Energy resources

    ISBN 978-0-8368-9260-4 (lib bdg); 0-8368-9260-7 (lib bdg); 978-0-8368-9359-5 (pa); 0-8368-9359-X (pa)   LC 2008014483

This describes how ethanol and other new fuels work and how they can be used in the future.

"New readers will be able to wrap their hands around the small, square size, and their minds around the clear, enlightening text. [This book has] crisp photos and strong back matter." Booklist

Includes glossary and bibliographical references

Cobb, Vicki, 1938-

Fireworks; photographs by Michael Gold. Millbrook Press 2005 48p il (Where's the science here?) lib bdg $23.93

Grades: 3 4 5   **662**

    1. Fireworks

    ISBN 0-7613-2771-1   LC 2004-29823

"From pictures of different types of display formations to those of chemicals being loaded into mortar tubes, readers will find interesting illustrations that support the text in *Fireworks*. They will learn about the science of pyrotechnics and be exposed to words like chemical re-

action, combustion, and lift charges. Sections offer a historical overview of the evolution of the study of fire, the mechanics of building fireworks . . . how explosions are timed, and how pyrotechnicians avoid nasty surprises." SLJ

664   Food technology

Bledsoe, Karen E., 1962-

Genetically engineered foods; written by Karen E. Bledsoe. Blackbirch Press 2006 48p il (Science on the edge) $23.70

Grades: 5 6 7 8   **664**

    1. Food—Biotechnology 2. Genetic engineering

    ISBN 1-4103-0602-X

This offers a brief summary of Mendel's discoveries and the discovery of DNA, then discusses how foods are modified by genetics and the issues associated with genetic engineering of foods.

Includes glossary and bibliographical references

Cobb, Vicki, 1938-

Junk food; photographs by Michael Gold. Millbrook 2005 48p il (Where's the science here?) lib bdg $23.93

Grades: 3 4 5   **664**

    1. Food industry 2. Food—Composition

    ISBN 0-7613-2773-8

The author "focuses on food chemistry, not nutrition, in examinations of six seductive snack foods (popcorn, corn chips, chocolate, candy, potato chips, and soda). Well-digested explanations and low-tech projects reinforce Cobb's reputation for snappy hands-on science writing for children. . . . Gold's photos stand well above those in most nonfiction science series and directly support Cobb's intentions." Booklist

Gardner, Robert, 1929-

Ace your food science project; great science fair ideas; [by] Robert Gardner, Salvatore Tocci, and Thomas R. Rybolt. Enslow Publishers 2009 128p il (Ace your science project) lib bdg $31.93

Grades: 5 6 7 8   **664**

    1. Food 2. Science projects 3. Science—Experiments

    ISBN 978-0-7660-3228-6 (lib bdg); 0-7660-3228-0 (lib bdg)   LC 2008-49780

"Presents several science experiments and project ideas using food." Publisher's note

Includes bibliographical references

McCarthy, Meghan

Pop! the accidental invention of bubble gum. Simon & Schuster Books for Young Readers 2010 40p il $15.99 *

Grades: 1 2 3   **664**

    1. Bubble gum

    ISBN 978-1-4169-7970-8; 1-4169-7970-0

            LC 2008049272

"A Paula Wiseman book"

McCarthy, Meghan—*Continued*

Traces the 1928 invention of bubble gum by a hardworking accountant at a candy company, describing how in his spare time he experimented with different recipes and ingredients to eventually create the product known today as Double Bubble.

"Kids who enjoy blowing gum bubbles may never have considered how the treat came to be, but here, in easy language and with amusing illustrations, McCarthy changes that. . . . The acrylic paintings portray humor throughout, in part by peopling the book with googly-eyed characters who are often chewing a wad of gum." Booklist

Ridley, Sarah, 1963-

A chocolate bar; [by] Sarah Ridley. Gareth Stevens Pub. 2006 32p il (How it's made) lib bdg $23.93

Grades: 3 4 5   **664**

1. Chocolate
ISBN 0-8368-6293-7   LC 2005054075
First published 2005 in the United Kingdom
This presents "the origins of a chocolate bar, from a Ghana cocoa farm to a factory. The facts are clear and well organized; each spread shows a logical progression in the process, and sharp color photos and maps will help cement the concepts in readers' minds." Booklist

Rotner, Shelley

Where does food come from? by Shelley Rotner and Gary Goss; photographs by Shelley Rotner. Millbrook Press 2006 32p il lib bdg $22.60

Grades: K 1 2   **664**

1. Food industry 2. Food
ISBN 0-7613-2935-8   LC 2005000874
Explains where various foods originate from, how food is grown, and brought to supermarkets and other stores, in simple text with illustrations.

"Large print, a well-spaced text, varied typeface, simple explanations, and appealing color photos of children on every page make this book a pleasant reading experience. . . . This is a book that teachers, librarians, and parents will find useful, informative, and fun to share." SLJ

665 Technology of industrial oils, fats, waxes, gases

Walker, Niki, 1972-

Hydrogen; running on water; [by] Niki Walker. Crabtree Pub. 2007 32p il (Energy revolution) lib bdg $25.20; pa $8.95

Grades: 5 6 7 8   **665**

1. Hydrogen as fuel
ISBN 978-0-7787-2915-0 (lib bdg); 0-7787-2915-X (lib bdg); 978-0-7787-2929-7 (pa); 0-7787-2929-X (pa)   LC 2006014369
This describes various sources of hydrogen power, including natural gas, gasified coal, fuel from water, and biomass gas, and how it is stored and distributed, and offers energy conservation tips.

Includes glossary

665.5 Petroleum

Benduhn, Tea

Oil, gas, and coal; by Tea Benduhn. Weekly Reader Pub. 2009 24p il (Energy for today) lib bdg $21; pa $5.95

Grades: 2 3 4   **665.5**

1. Gasoline 2. Natural gas 3. Coal 4. Energy resources
ISBN 978-0-8368-9261-1 (lib bdg); 0-8368-9261-5 (lib bdg); 978-0-8368-9360-1 (pa); 0-8368-9360-3 (pa)
LC 2008015517
This describes what fossil fuels are, how they work as energy sources, and their future.

"New readers will be able to wrap their hands around the small, square size, and their minds around the clear, enlightening text. [This book has] crisp photos and strong back matter." Booklist

Includes glossary and bibliographical references

Rockwell, Anne F., 1934-

What's so bad about gasoline? fossil fuels and what they do; by Anne Rockwell; illustrated by Paul Meisel. Collins 2009 33p il (Let's-read-and-find-out science) $16.99; pa $5.99

Grades: 1 2 3   **665.5**

1. Gasoline 2. Air pollution 3. Greenhouse effect 4. Energy conservation 5. Energy resources
ISBN 978-0-06-157528-0; 0-06-157528-3; 978-0-06-157527-3 (pa); 0-06-157527-5 (pa)
LC 2007-52947
"Rockwell presents the basic facts about how gasoline is produced, how it was first discovered, and its uses. She then discusses how gasoline and other fossil fuels . . . have contributed to polluting the environment. Suggestions are offered on how to cut back our gas consumption, and alternatives such as solar power, wind power, nuclear energy, and alternative fuels are addressed. . . . Detailed pen-and-ink and watercolor drawings in shades of blue and brown appear throughout, and text balloons help provide humor to various scenarios." SLJ

666 Ceramic and allied technologies

Koscielniak, Bruce

Looking at glass through the ages; by Bruce Koscielniak. Houghton Mifflin Co. 2006 unp $16

Grades: 3 4 5 6   **666**

1. Glass—History
ISBN 0-618-50750-7   LC 2005003916
"A handsome book on the history of glassmaking. Starting with faience, developed in Egypt around 2500 B.C., the author's precisely worded, carefully detailed text and watercolor artwork explain the steps for producing various types of glass and glassware. . . . Much information is compacted into the smoothly written narrative. Captioned illustrations are well matched with the text and extend the information value of the book." SLJ

Stewart, Melissa, 1968-

How does sand become glass? Raintree 2010 32p il (How does it happen?) lib bdg $27.50; pa $7.99

Grades: 3 4 5   **666**

   1. Sand 2. Erosion 3. Glass

   ISBN 978-1-4109-3449-9 (lib bdg); 1-4109-3449-7 (lib bdg); 978-1-4109-3457-4 (pa); 1-4109-3457-8 (pa)

                     LC 2008-52654

This addresses questions such as "What kind of fish can grind coral into sand? How did ancient people form glass from quartz pebbles? How does a mirror reflect an image?" Publisher's note

"Information is clearly presented using a large font, diagrams, and photographs formatted to resemble Polaroid pictures. . . . A first-rate job answering some important scientific questions." SLJ

Includes glossary and bibliographical references

668 Technology of other organic products

Rhatigan, Joe

Soapmaking; 50 fun & fabulous soaps to melt & pour. Lark Books 2003 112p il (Kids' crafts) $19.95

Grades: 3 4 5 6   **668**

   1. Soap 2. Handicraft

   ISBN 1-57990-416-5   LC 2003-883

This describes soapmaking projects beginning with choosing a soap base and selecting molds, adding fragrance, color, or other extras. Projects include eyeball soaps, making soap popsicles, smiley faces, a soapasaurus, alphabet soap, a soap bracelet and a clear bar with an embedded photo.

"This book has a wonderful, 'squeaky-clean' appearance and a perfect combination of text, color photography, design, and child models." SLJ

Wagner, Lisa, 1961-

Cool melt & pour soap; [by] Lisa Wagner. ABDO Pub. 2005 32p il (Cool crafts) lib bdg $22.78

Grades: 4 5 6   **668**

   1. Soap 2. Handicraft

   ISBN 1-59197-741-X   LC 2004-46291

This guide to soap crafting "discusses premade bases, coloring and fragrance, layered soaps, treasure-packed soaps, relief soaps, and packaging ideas." SLJ

668.4 Plastics

Langley, Andrew

Plastic; [by] Andrew Langley. Crabtree Pub. Co. 2009 24p il (Everyday materials) lib bdg $21.27; pa $6.95

Grades: K 1 2 3   **668.4**

   1. Plastics

   ISBN 978-0-7787-4129-9 (lib bdg); 0-7787-4129-X (lib bdg); 978-0-7787-4136-7 (pa); 0-7787-4136-2 (pa)

                     LC 2008-25324

This title "introduces [plastics] in an engaging style. The text and photos work together, progressing from a definition of the material to how it is manufactured and what it is used for. . . . [It] concludes with a recycling section, a simple comprehension quiz, and a topic web that offers extension ideas. The large type, bright photos, and uncluttered layout will allow large and small group use." SLJ

Includes glossary

670 Manufacturing

Slavin, Bill, 1959-

Transformed; how everyday things are made; written by Bill Slavin with Jim Slavin; illustrated by Bill Slavin. Kids Can Press 2005 160p il $24.95

Grades: 4 5 6 7   **670**

   1. Manufactures

   ISBN 1-55337-179-8

This describes the manufacture of such items "as baseballs, plastic dinosaurs, toothpaste, cereal, paper, and bricks. Each two-page spread covers the making of one of the 69 items in numbered paragraphs. The pictures are the best part—clear watercolor and ink images, made all the more engaging by folks in overalls directing the action." Booklist

Includes glossary and bibliographical references

676 Pulp and paper technology

Langley, Andrew

Paper products; [by] Andrew Langley. Crabtree Pub. Co. 2009 24p il (Everyday materials) lib bdg $21.27; pa $6.95

Grades: K 1 2 3   **676**

   1. Paper 2. Papermaking

   ISBN 978-0-7787-4128-2 (lib bdg); 0-7787-4128-1 (lib bdg); 978-0-7787-4135-0 (pa); 0-7787-4135-4 (pa)

                     LC 2008-24011

This title "introduces [paper products] in an engaging style. The text and photos work together, progressing from a definition of the material to how it is manufactured and what it is used for. . . . [It] concludes with a recycling section, a simple comprehension quiz, and a topic web that offers extension ideas. The large type, bright photos, and uncluttered layout will allow large and small group use." SLJ

Includes glossary

677 Textiles

Langley, Andrew

Wool; [by] Andrew Langley. Crabtree Pub. Co. 2009 24p il (Everyday materials) lib bdg $21.27; pa $6.95

Grades: K 1 2 3   **677**

   1. Wool

   ISBN 978-0-7787-4131-2 (lib bdg); 0-7787-4131-1 (lib bdg); 978-0-7787-4138-1 (pa); 0-7787-4138-9 (pa)

                     LC 2008-25323

Langley, Andrew—*Continued*

This title "introduces [wool] in an engaging style. The text and photos work together, progressing from a definition of the material to how it is manufactured and what it is used for. . . . [It] concludes with a recycling section, a simple comprehension quiz, and a topic web that offers extension ideas. The large type, bright photos, and uncluttered layout will allow large and small group use." SLJ

Includes glossary

678 Elastomers and elastomer products

Allman, Toney, 1947-

Recycled tires; by Toney Allman. Norwood House Press 2008 48p il (A great idea) lib bdg $25.27

Grades: 3 4 5 6   678

1. Tires 2. Recycling

ISBN 978-1-59953-197-7 (lib bdg); 1-59953-197-6 (lib bdg)   LC 2008-15736

"'Describes the invention and development of recycled rubber tires." Publisher's note

Includes glossary and bibliographical references

680 Manufacture for specific uses

Tunis, Edwin, 1897-1973

Colonial craftsmen and the beginnings of American industry; written and illustrated by Edwin Tunis. Johns Hopkins Univ. Press 1999 159p pa $18.95 *

Grades: 4 5 6 7   680

1. Decorative arts 2. United States—Social life and customs—1600-1775, Colonial period 3. Handicraft

ISBN 0-8018-6228-0   LC 99-20398

A reprint of the edition published 1965 by World Pub. Co.

The author describes the working methods and products, houses and shops, town and country trades, individual and group enterprises by which the early Americans forged the economy of the New World. He discusses such trades as papermaking, glassmaking, shipbuilding, printing, and metalworking

"An oversize book that is impressively handsome and that should be tremendously useful; well-organized and superbly illustrated, the text is comprehensive, lucid, and detailed. . . . An extensive index is appended." Chicago. Children's Book Center

685 Leather and fur goods, and related products

Blaxland, Wendy

Sneakers. Marshall Cavendish Benchmark 2009 32p il (How are they made?) $19.95

Grades: 4 5 6   685

1. Sneakers

ISBN 978-0-7614-3810-6; 0-7614-3810-6

LC 2008026211

This is an "introduction to athletic shoes and the global trade involved in their manufacture and marketing. . . . A typical page offers a paragraph or more of informative text as well as a color photo and, perhaps, a small sidebar." Booklist

Cobb, Vicki, 1938-

Sneakers; photographs by Michael Gold. Millbrook Press 2006 48p il (Where's the science here?) lib bdg $23.93

Grades: 3 4 5   685

1. Sneakers

ISBN 0-7613-2772-X   LC 2004-29816

"From photographs of the inside of a sneaker factory to X-rays of the foot to a picture of how rubber is extracted from a rubber tree, readers will find a new angle to spark their interest in *Sneakers*. They will learn about how sneakers are designed and made, and even how to test their fit. [An] attractive [choice] that [relates] science to [a topic] that fascinate kids." SLJ

D'Cruz, Anna-Marie

Make your own slippers and shoes. PowerKids Press 2009 24p il (Do it yourself projects!) lib bdg $23.95; pa $9.40

Grades: 2 3 4   685

1. Shoes 2. Handicraft

ISBN 978-1-4358-2852-0 (lib bdg); 1-4358-2852-6 (lib bdg); 978-1-4358-2921-3 (pa); 1-4358-2921-2 (pa)

LC 2008033669

Contents: All about shoes; Leaf shoes; Roman sandals; Funky flip-flops; Dutch clogs; Fun fur boots; Lotus shoes; Jutti slippers; Native American moccasins

Learn how to make different types of shoes from around the world using easy-to-find materials.

Includes glossary and bibliographical references

686 Printing and related activities

D'Cruz, Anna-Marie

Make your own books. PowerKids Press 2009 24p il (Do it yourself projects!) lib bdg $23.95; pa $9.40

Grades: 2 3 4   686

1. Books 2. Bookbinding 3. Handicraft

ISBN 978-1-4358-2855-1 (lib bdg); 1-4358-2855-0 (lib bdg); 978-1-4358-2927-5 (pa); 1-4358-2927-1 (pa)

LC 2008033659

Contents: All about books; Button holder; Folding book; Palm-leaf book; Lift the flaps; Pop-up book; Address book; Photo album; Eco-notebook

Projects for creating many different kinds of books from easy-to-find materials

Includes glossary and bibliographical references

686.2   Printing

Koscielniak, Bruce
Johann Gutenberg and the amazing printing
press. Houghton Mifflin Co. 2003 unp il $16
Grades: 2 3 4   **686.2**
1. Gutenberg, Johann, 1397?-1468 2. Printing—History
ISBN 0-618-26351-9   LC 2002-151176
A history of the modern printing industry, including
how paper and ink are made, looking particularly at the
printing press invented by Gutenberg around 1450 but
also at its precursors
"The pleasing line drawings and the subtle hues of
Boscielniak's watercolors give the illustrations an informal look that makes their informative content all the
more accessible." Booklist

688.7   Recreational equipment

Blaxland, Wendy
Basketballs. Marshall Cavendish Benchmark
2011 32p il map (How are they made?) lib bdg
$28.50
Grades: 3 4 5 6   **688.7**
1. Basketball 2. Sporting goods
ISBN 978-0-7614-4751-1; 0-7614-4751-2
                                LC 2009039874
This book "starts out with the raw materials used to
make [basketballs]. . . . Next, [a] time [line] handily
[sums] up basketball from 1891 to 1992, when composite
rubber balls were developed. . . . Design and stages of
production are then explained. . . . Nicely designed and
well executed." SLJ
Includes glossary

Fridell, Ron, 1943-
Sports technology. Lerner Publications 2009 48p
il (Cool science) lib bdg $27.93
Grades: 4 5 6   **688.7**
1. Sports 2. Technology
ISBN 978-0-8225-7587-0 (lib bdg); 0-8225-7587-6 (lib
bdg)   LC 2007050905
This describes "how science helps athletes stay safer,
perform better, and have more fun." Publisher's notes
Includes glossary and bibliographical references

Hirschmann, Kris, 1967-
LEGO toys. Norwood House Press 2008 48p il
(A great idea) lib bdg $25.27
Grades: 3 4 5 6   **688.7**
1. LEGO (Firm) 2. Toys
ISBN 978-1-59953-194-6 (lib bdg); 1-59953-194-1 (lib
bdg)   LC 2008010712
Describes the invention and development of LEGO
toys
"Full-color photographs and copious fun facts help
make this . . . enjoyable reading, but it's really the
choice of [topic] that is so enthralling." Booklist
Includes glossary and bibliographical references

Wulffson, Don L., 1943-
Toys! amazing stories behind some great
inventions; [by] Don Wulffson; with illustrations
by Laurie Keller. Holt & Co. 2000 137p il $16.95
Grades: 4 5 6 7   **688.7**
1. Toys 2. Inventions
ISBN 0-8050-6196-7   LC 99-58440
Describes the creation of a variety of toys and games,
from seesaws to Silly Putty and toy soldiers to Trivial
Pursuit
"Each of the 25 chapters is illustrated with small, humorous drawings and discusses a particular toy or
game's origin and development. The book ends with a
bibliography and a list of Web sites. Good, readable fare
for browsing or light research." Booklist
Includes bibliographical references

690   Building & construction

Barton, Byron
Building a house. Greenwillow Books 1981 unp
il lib bdg $17.89; pa $6.99
Grades: PreK K 1   **690**
1. House construction
ISBN 978-0-688-84291-8 (lib bdg); 0-688-84291-7 (lib
bdg); 978-0-688-09356-3 (pa); 0-688-09356-6 (pa)
"In the simplest possible book on building a house, a
step-by-step, one-line description is given of the major
factors in construction. Such workers as bricklayers, car-
penters, plumbers, electricians, and painters do their own
jobs until the small, bright red-and-green house is completed and a family moves in. Flat drawings in brilliant
primary colors enable the very young to visualize the
methods of housebuilding." Horn Book

Machines at work. Crowell 1987 unp il $17.99;
bd bk $7.99 *
Grades: PreK K 1   **690**
1. Building
ISBN 0-694-00190-2; 0-694-01107-X (bd bk)
                                LC 86-24221
"Double-page illustrations depict a busy day at a construction site as workers (with the positive inclusion of
women) knock down a building and start a new one."
SLJ
"The short, punchy narrative reinforces the dynamics
of the illustrations. . . . This should be a popular read-
aloud for preschoolers and satisfying read-alone for beginners." Publ Wkly

Gibbons, Gail
How a house is built. Holiday House 1990 unp
il $16.95; pa $6.95
Grades: K 1 2 3   **690**
1. Building 2. Houses
ISBN 0-8234-0841-8; 0-8234-1232-6 (pa)
                                LC 90-55107
This book describes how the surveyor, heavy machinery operators, carpenter crew, plumbers, and other
workers build a house
"With her customary bright illustrations, Gibbons
gives a fine introduction to the construction of a wood-

Gibbons, Gail—*Continued*

frame house. . . . Construction machines and materials as well as parts of the house are identified, and each stage of construction logically follows the others. Workers are drawn in both sexes and several skin tones." Booklist

Hudson, Cheryl Willis

Construction zone; photographs by Richard Sobol; text by Cheryl Willis Hudson. Candlewick Press 2006 unp il $15.99 *

Grades: 2 3 4   **690**

1. Building

ISBN 0-7636-2684-8

"Large photographs of the construction of the MIT Stata Center in Cambridge, MA, are the core of this book. The simple text explains the process from the design by Frank O. Gehry to the completed building. Construction-zone activity, equipment, and jargon are pictured and explained. . . . Words in bold . . . are defined and explained at the bottom of the page on which they appear. . . . Children will be fascinated by both the picture story and the informative text." SLJ

Macaulay, David, 1946-

Mill. Houghton Mifflin 1983 128p il $19; pa $9.95 *

Grades: 4 5 6 7 8 9 10   **690**

1. Mills 2. Textile industry—History

ISBN 0-395-34830-7; 0-395-52019-3 (pa)

LC 83-10652

This is an "account of the development of four fictional 19th-century Rhode Island cotton mills. In explaining the construction and operation of a simple waterwheel powered wooden mill, as well as the more complex stone, turbine and steam mills to follow, the author also describes the rise and decline of New England's textile industry." SLJ

"Well-researched, ambitious, and absorbing, this is another first-rate history lesson from a practiced, perfectionist hand." Booklist

Unbuilding. Houghton Mifflin 1980 78p il $18; pa $9.95 *

Grades: 4 5 6 7 8 9   **690**

1. Empire State Building (New York, N.Y.) 2. Building 3. Skyscrapers

ISBN 0-395-29457-6; 0-395-45425-5 (pa)

LC 80-15491

This fictional account of the dismantling and removal of the Empire State Building describes the structure of a skyscraper and explains how such an edifice would be demolished

"Save for the fact that one particularly stunning double-page spread is marred by tight binding, the book is a joy: accurate, informative, handsome, and eminently readable." Bull Cent Child Books

Newhouse, Maxwell, 1947-

The house that Max built. Tundra Books 2008 unp il $18.95

Grades: K 1 2 3   **690**

1. House construction

ISBN 978-0-88776-774-6; 0-88776-774-5

"When Max decides to build a house beside the lake, 'he needs a lot of help.' This simple introduction takes readers through the major steps of the construction, from the architect's drawings to the completed house. In one or two sentences per page, the present-tense narrative neatly applies the personal viewpoint of the homeowner to each construction phase. . . . Warmly rendered folk-art-style oil paintings show the house coming together over time. . . . [This has] strong visual appeal and just enough detail." SLJ

Schwarz, Renée

Birdfeeders. Kids Can Press 2005 40p il (Kids can do it) $12.95; pa $6.95

Grades: 4 5 6   **690**

1. Bird feeders

ISBN 1-55337-699-4; 1-55337-700-1 (pa)

This offers instructions for constructing nine types of bird feeders composed of recycled or common household materials such as flowerpots, juice cans, Frisbees and ketchup bottles.

Birdhouses. Kids Can Press 2005 40p il (Kids can do it) $12.95; pa $6.95

Grades: 4 5 6   **690**

1. Birdhouses 2. Woodwork

ISBN 1-55337-549-1; 1-55337-550-5 (pa)

This "shows and tells how to build nine birdhouses using inexpensive materials such as wood, plastic drainage pipes, flower pots, and even an old boot. . . . Small, clear pictures illustrate the step-by-step directions." Booklist

694 Wood construction Carpentry

Robertson, J. Craig

The kids' building workshop; 15 woodworking projects for kids and parents to build together; [by] J. Craig and Barbara Robertson, with their daughters Camille and Allegra. Storey Kids 2004 136p il $22.96; pa $12.95

Grades: 3 4 5 6   **694**

1. Woodwork

ISBN 1-58017-572-4; 1-58017-488-4 (pa)

LC 2004-1521

"The first section, 'Setting Up Shop: Getting to Know Your Tools,' includes a basic introduction to hammering, sawing, drilling, block planing, and measuring. Next, 'Down to Business: Building Your Own Projects' puts these tools and techniques to work in simple, yet cleverly designed, kid-friendly projects that increase in complexity. . . . Clear instructions, black-and-white photos, and cutting diagrams are included for each one. . . . Practical and enjoyable introduction to the subject." SLJ

Walker, Lester

Carpentry for children; preface by David Macaulay. Overlook Press 1982 208p il pa $14.95 hardcover o.p.

Grades: 4 5 6 7   **694**

  1. Carpentry 2. Handicraft

  ISBN 0-87951-990-8 (pa)   LC 82-3469

A step-by-step guide to carrying out such carpentry projects as a birdhouse, candle chandelier, doll cradle, puppet theater, and coaster car

696   Utilities

Raum, Elizabeth

The story behind toilets. Heinemann Library 2009 32p il (True stories) $19.75 *

Grades: 2 3 4   **696**

  1. Toilets

  ISBN 978-1-4329-2350-1; 1-4329-2350-1

           LC 2008037392

"Virtually everything related to toilets is covered, from the bodily functions that require such facilities all the way to the technology of the toilets of tomorrow. . . . 'A Short History of Toilets' is the most surprising chapter, with its running time line of toilet innovations. . . . Raum has the arcana down. . . . But there's real educational value here, too, notably in the discussion of sewage plants, the debate over pay toilets, the international scope of health problems related to poor sanitation, and the twisty time line that ends the book." Booklist

Includes bibliographical references

700   ARTS

Ajmera, Maya

To be an artist; [by] Maya Ajmera & John D. Ivanko; foreword by Jacques d'Amboise. Charlesbridge 2004 unp il $15.95 *

Grades: K 1 2 3   **700**

  1. Arts

  ISBN 1-57091-503-2   LC 2003-8154

"Shakti for Children"

This includes "photographs of youngsters from many different countries engaged in a variety of art forms, including dancing, singing, writing, and painting. The bold text introduces each discipline and is supported with more extensive descriptions of the individual endeavors and the nature of artistic expression in general. . . . This vibrant book pulsates with the energy and sense of accomplishment that accompanies participation in the arts." SLJ

Johnson, Dolores, 1949-

The Harlem Renaissance; by Dolores Johnson with Virginia Schomp. Marshall Cavendish Benchmark 2008 80p il (Drama of African-American history) lib bdg $23.95 *

Grades: 5 6 7 8   **700**

  1. Harlem Renaissance 2. African American arts

  ISBN 978-0-7614-2641-7   LC 2007034691

This is an account of the flowering of African American art, literature, music, and political commentary of the 1920s and 1930s centered in the Harlem section of New York City.

Includes glossary and bibliographical references

Worth, Richard, 1945-

The Harlem Renaissance; an explosion of African-American culture; [by] Richard Worth. Enslow Publishers 2008 128p il map (America's living history) lib bdg $31.93

Grades: 5 6 7 8   **700**

  1. Harlem Renaissance 2. African American arts

  ISBN 978-0-7660-2907-1 (lib bdg); 0-7660-2907-7 (lib bdg)   LC 2007025593

"Explores the Harlem Renaissance, a reawakening of African-American culture, including literature, the arts, theater, and music, motivated by a goal to achieve equal rights." Publisher's note

This "is well sourced, includes extensive back matter, and has a full complement of supporting color photographs or other illustrations that makes it accessible and useful to report writers and general readers." SLJ

Includes glossary and bibliographical references

701   Philosophy and theory of fine and decorative arts

Benduhn, Tea

What is color? Crabtree Pub. Co. 2009 24p il (Get art smart) lib bdg $15.95; pa $6.95

Grades: K 1 2 3   **701**

  1. Color in art

  ISBN 978-0-7787-5123-6 (lib bdg); 0-7787-5123-6 (lib bdg); 978-0-7787-5137-3 (pa); 0-7787-5137-6 (pa)   LC 2009-22914

Isolates the artistic element of color, discusses what thoughts and feelings can be conveyed by different colors, and examines how they contribute to a work of art through various examples

This book has a "first-person plural tone that uses accessible, well-thought-out phrases. Concrete visual examples are in the form of frequent and excellent reproductions of fine art in a variety of mediums. . . . [A] respectable and respectful resource[s]." SLJ

Includes glossary and bibliographical references

What is shape? Crabtree Pub. 2009 24p il (Get art smart) lib bdg $15.95; pa $6.95

Grades: K 1 2 3   **701**

  1. Shape

  ISBN 978-0-7787-5139-7 (lib bdg); 0-7787-5139-2 (lib bdg); 978-0-7787-5125-0 (pa); 0-7787-5125-2 (pa)

This describes how shapes of all kinds, including geometric shapes and the organic shapes found in nature, can be used in art.

This book has a "first-person plural tone that uses accessible, well-thought-out phrases. Concrete visual examples are in the form of frequent and excellent reproductions of fine art in a variety of mediums. . . . [A] respectable and respectful resource[s]." SLJ

Includes glossary and bibliographical references

Fitzgerald, Stephanie

What is texture? Crabtree Pub. Co. 2009 24p il (Get art smart) lib bdg $15.95; pa $6.95

701

1. Art—Technique 2. Handicraft
ISBN 978-0-7787-5127-4 (lib bdg); 0-7787-5127-9 (lib bdg); 978-0-7787-5141-0 (pa); 0-7787-5141-4 (pa)

LC 2009-22917

Introduces different kinds of texture and how they are used in art, and includes information on making a rubbing

This book has a "first-person plural tone that uses accessible, well-thought-out phrases. Concrete visual examples are in the form of frequent and excellent reproductions of fine art in a variety of mediums. . . . [A] respectable and respectful resource[s]." SLJ

Includes glossary and bibliographical references

Gonyea, Mark

A book about color. Henry Holt & Co. 2010 unp il $19.99 *
Grades: 1 2 3 4 5

701

1. Color in art
ISBN 978-0-8050-9055-0; 0-8050-9055-X

"Topics presented include primary and secondary colors, warm and cool colors, saturation, and the addition of black and white. In the digital illustrations, simple forms in solid colors stand out sharply against white or other solid backgrounds. . . . This attractive volume offers plenty to observe, ponder, and discuss." Booklist

Meredith, Susan

What is form? by Susan Markowitz Meredith. Crabtree Pub. Co. 2009 24p il (Get art smart) lib bdg $15.95; pa $6.95
Grades: K 1 2 3

701

1. Composition (Art)
ISBN 978-0-7787-5124-3 (lib bdg); 0-7787-5124-4 (lib bdg); 978-0-7787-5138-0 (pa); 0-7787-5138-4 (pa)

Introduces the concept of form, demonstrates how it is used in art, and includes information on reliefs, sculpture, and identifying forms in everyday life

This book has a "first-person plural tone that uses accessible, well-thought-out phrases. Concrete visual examples are in the form of frequent and excellent reproductions of fine art in a variety of mediums. . . . [A] respectable and respectful resource[s]." SLJ

Includes glossary and bibliographical references

What is line? by Susan Markowitz Meredith. Crabtree Pub. Co. 2009 24p il (Get art smart) lib bdg $15.95; pa $6.95
Grades: K 1 2 3

701

1. Line (Art)
ISBN 978-0-7787-5122-9 (lib bdg); 0-7787-5122-8 (lib bdg); 978-0-7787-5136-6 (pa); 0-7787-5136-8 (pa)

LC 2009-22912

Identifies lines in art and demonstrates how differently shaped lines are used to create texture, movement, patterns, and emotion.

This book has a "first-person plural tone that uses accessible, well-thought-out phrases. Concrete visual examples are in the form of frequent and excellent reproduc-

tions of fine art in a variety of mediums. . . . [A] respectable and respectful resource[s]." SLJ

Includes glossary and bibliographical references

What is space? by Susan Markowitz Meredith. Crabtree Pub. Co. 2009 24p il (Get art smart) lib bdg $15.95; pa $6.95
Grades: K 1 2 3

701

1. Space and time in art
ISBN 978-0-7787-5126-7 (lib bdg); 0-7787-5126-0 (lib bdg); 978-0-7787-5140-3 (pa); 0-7787-5140-6 (pa)

Introduces the concept of space; how differences in space are used in art; and includes information on distance, form, and overlap.

This book has a "first-person plural tone that uses accessible, well-thought-out phrases. Concrete visual examples are in the form of frequent and excellent reproductions of fine art in a variety of mediums. . . . [A] respectable and respectful resource[s]." SLJ

Includes glossary and bibliographical references

Renshaw, Amanda

The art book for children; [texts by Amanda Renshaw and Gilda Williams Ruggi] Phaidon Press 2005 79p il $19.95 *
Grades: 2 3 4 5

701

1. Art appreciation
ISBN 978-0-7148-4530-2

Invites the reader to take a closer look at art work while pointing out tiny details hidden in famous works of art, providing information about a work or an artist, or explaining the techniques used to create the pieces

This is "an excellent, accessible introduction to art that speaks directly to children without condescension." Booklist

The art book for children: book two; text by Amanda Renshaw. Phaidon Press 2007 79p il $19.95 *
Grades: 2 3 4 5

701

1. Art appreciation
ISBN 978-0-7148-4706-1

"Each double-page spread features a top-quality reproduction of an artwork, accompanied by simple text that will engage both young children and mature, independent readers. . . . The brief words . . . encourage viewers to imagine themselves in the scenes, to find objects in the compositions, or to reflect on the moods and activities depicted and in their own lives. This interactive approach creates a wonderful introduction to the history of Western art." Booklist

702.8 Techniques, procedures, apparatus, equipment, materials

Hanson, Anders, 1980-

Cool collage; the art of creativity for kids! [by] Anders Hanson. ABDO Pub. Co. 2009 32p il (Cool art) lib bdg $24.21
Grades: 2 3 4

702.8

1. Collage
ISBN 978-1-60453-146-6 (lib bdg); 1-60453-146-0 (lib bdg)

LC 2008-8641

Hanson, Anders, 1980-—_Continued_

This book about collage making is "well organized, with clearly written sections . . . and several clever projects and exercises. . . . [It] should have substantial child appeal." SLJ

Includes glossary

Luxbacher, Irene, 1970-

1 2 3 I can collage! [by] Irene Luxbacher. Kids Can Press 2009 23p il (Starting art) $14.95; pa $6.95

Grades: 2 3 4   **702.8**

1. Collage

ISBN   978-1-55453-313-8;   1-55453-313-9; 978-1-55453-314-5 (pa); 1-55453-314-7 (pa)

Collage activities with step-by-step instructions will help kids create a whale, a crab, a sea turtle and more.

The jumbo book of art; written and illustrated by Irene Luxbacher. Kids Can Press 2003 208p il pa $14.95 *

Grades: 4 5 6 7   **702.8**

1. Art—Study and teaching

ISBN 1-55074-762-2

"Each of the four chapters is devoted to instructing readers in the basics of one technique—drawing, creating with color, sculpture, and mixed-media projects, respectively—and then inspires those readers to let loose and have fun making something beautiful. . . . The book features clear layouts, well-written definitions of terms, full-color illustrations, and more than 90 projects. . . . This practical, lively, and smart package is a must-have for every art and elementary school classroom, and a welcome addition to most library collections." SLJ

Includes glossary

704   Special topics in fine and decorative arts

Barber, Nicola

Islamic empires; [by] Nicola Barber. Raintree 2005 48p il map (History in art) $31.43 *

Grades: 4 5 6 7   **704**

1. Islamic art 2. Islam

ISBN 1-4109-0522-5   LC 2004-7527

Contents: Art as evidence; The spread of Islam; The great empires; Life in the Islamic empires; Religion

This is an introduction to the art, culture, and history of Islamic empires.

This book has "a depth of content that is unusual in art-history books for this age group. . . . [It] is amply illustrated with full-color photographs and reproductions. . . . Well-written, informative." SLJ

Includes bibliographical references

Coyne, Jennifer Tarr

Come look with me: discovering women artists for children; [by] Jennifer Tarr Coyne. Lickle 2005 32p il $15.95

Grades: 3 4 5   **704**

1. Women artists 2. Art appreciation

ISBN 1-890674-08-7

Introduces twelve women artists, including Faith Ringgold, Mary Cassatt, Frida Kahlo, and Grandma Moses, each with a short biography, a full-page color plate, a description of the image, and a set of discussion questions.

"This offering encourages children to learn biographical facts about artists and to look closely at the images and think about artistic decisions. . . . Each spread features a beautifully reproduced image." Booklist

Rolling, James Haywood, Jr.

Come look with me: discovering African American art for children; [by] James Haywood Rolling, Jr. Lickle 2005 32p il $15.95

Grades: 3 4 5   **704**

1. African American art 2. Art appreciation

ISBN 1-890674-07-9

This volume presents 12 works of African American art "reproduced in full color and accompanied by descriptive information; the facing page contains several questions designed to engage young viewers and an adult in conversation as well as a few paragraphs of background. . . . Artists . . . include . . . Palmer Hayden and Clementine Hunter . . . Henry Ossawa Tanner, Romare Bearden, and Jacob Lawrence." SLJ

704.9   Iconography

Bingham, Jane

Emotion & relationships; [by] Jane Bingham. Raintree 2006 56p il map (Through artists' eyes) lib bdg $32.86

Grades: 4 5 6 7   **704.9**

1. Emotions in art 2. Interpersonal relations in art 3. Art appreciation

ISBN 1-4109-2238-3

"Using simple yet descriptive language and good-quality, full-color reproductions, Bingham describes works of art and links them to [emotions and relationships]. [The book] has chapters such as 'Family Feelings,' 'Happiness and Contentment,' and 'Sickness and Pain,' and includes works by Thomas Gainsborough, Frans Hals, and Frida Kahlo. . . . A variety of artwork is highlighted, including sculpture, paintings, jewelry and costume, literature, [and] opera." SLJ

Includes bibliographical references

Landscape & the environment; [by] Jane Bingham. Raintree 2006 56p il (Through artists' eyes) lib bdg $32.86

Grades: 4 5 6 7   **704.9**

1. Landscape in art 2. Art appreciation

ISBN 1-4109-2240-5   LC 2005024925

"Using simple yet descriptive language and good-quality, full-color reproductions, Bingham describes

Bingham, Jane—*Continued*

works of art and links them to [landscapes and environment]. . . . [The book] is broken down by location and/or time period into such topics as 'Ancient Gardens,' 'Romantic Landscapes,' and 'Landscapes of the Renaissance.' . . . A variety of artwork is highlighted, including sculpture, paintings, jewelry and costume, literature, opera, and . . . altered landscapes such as gardens and the large-scale work of Christo." SLJ

Includes bibliographical references

Science & technology; [by] Jane Bingham. Raintree 2006 56p il (Through artists' eyes) lib bdg $32.86

Grades: 4 5 6 7   **704.9**
    1. Science in art 2. Technology in art 3. Art appreciation
    ISBN 1-4109-2241-3   LC 2005025029

"Painters such as Rembrandt and, much later, Thomas Eakins were fascinated by the advancements in medicine. Steam engines intrigued Turner and Monet. These are just a few examples of the intersecting of technology and science with art. Throughout *Science & Technology*, printing, measuring time, engineering, and communications are touched upon along with the artwork inspired by various discoveries. . . . The full-color reproductions are well chosen and of good quality. The information is brief, but it provides a well-thought-out overview of these artistic interpretations." SLJ

Includes bibliographical references

Society & class; [by] Jane Bingham. Raintree 2006 56p il map (Through artists' eyes) lib bdg $32.86

Grades: 4 5 6 7   **704.9**
    1. Society in art 2. Social classes in art 3. Art appreciation
    ISBN 1-4109-2237-5   LC 2005025028

This "succinctly looks at how artists have depicted the lives of farmers, hunters, rulers, slaves, soldiers, and merchants throughout history. Social change such as the French and American Revolutions inspired artists, while the rise of Communism and Fascism had a chilling effect on art. . . . The full-color reproductions are well chosen and of good quality. The information is brief, but it provides a well-thought-out overview of these artistic interpretations." SLJ

Includes bibliographical references

Luxbacher, Irene, 1970-

The jumbo book of outdoor art; written and illustrated by Irene Luxbacher. Kids Can Press 2006 144p il pa $16.95 *

Grades: 3 4 5 6   **704.9**
    1. Nature craft 2. Art
    ISBN 978-1-55337-680-4 (pa); 1-55337-680-3 (pa)

"Four major sections (Digging Deep, Going Green, It's All Elemental, and Fertile Ground) each contain more than a dozen activities and/or experiments. Good-quality illustrations and photos bring these ideas to life. . . . Children will polish their creative skills with a wide variety of artistic experiences, such as a secret garden, silly sprouts, terrific topiaries, beautiful batik, super spider's web, weathervanes, great flowing fountain, sparkling ice chandeliers, and more." SLJ

Raczka, Bob

Action figures; paintings of fun, daring, and adventure. Millbrook Press 2010 31p il lib bdg $25.26

Grades: 1 2 3 4   **704.9**
    1. Art appreciation
    ISBN 978-0-7613-4140-6 (lib bdg); 0-7613-4140-4 (lib bdg)   LC 2008053976

"Eighteen paintings, and not a bowl of fruit in sight. Whether it is the knockout punch of George Bellows's Dempsey and Firpo or the fiery blasts of Diego Rivera's The Conquest of Mexico, this art is not about sitting still. Raczka threads selections together using few words. . . . The book includes works in various styles, dating from 1450 to 1962. Rounded out with some fun facts about the selections, this enjoyable collection presents an array of action-packed art fit for independent perusal or group discussion." SLJ

The art of freedom; how artists see America; by Bob Raczka. Millbrook Press 2008 32p il lib bdg $25.26

Grades: 1 2 3   **704.9**
    1. United States in art 2. American art 3. Art appreciation
    ISBN 978-0-8225-7508-5   LC 2007023831

"The 18 beautifully reproduced works of art in this collection cut a swath across the country—including farms and cities, baseball and jazz, hard work and sacrifice, native peoples and immigrants. . . . Concise notes about each picture at the back of the book will help children and those reading to them find out more about the artists and their work." Booklist

709 Art—Historical, geographic, persons treatment of fine and decorative arts

Ayres, Charlie

Lives of the great artists. Thames & Hudson 2008 96p il $19.95

Grades: 5 6 7 8   **709**
    1. Artists 2. Art—History
    ISBN 978-0-500-23853-0; 0-500-23853-7
                                            LC 2008-91000

Presents illustrated and age-appropriate imaginary tours of the studios of famous artists from Leonardo da Vinci and Michelangelo to Monet and van Gogh, in an anecdotal reference that is complemented by reproductions of famous works and introductory portraits

This is "brightly written and augmented with activities, Web resources, and fun facts. . . . The works of art chosen to represent each artist are heavy on the drama and detail, resulting in high kid appeal and interesting captions. . . . The layout is clean and clear." SLJ

Children's book of art; an introduction to the world's most amazing paintings and sculptures. DK Pub. 2009 139p il $24.99

Grades: 4 5 6 7					**709**

1. Art—History 2. Art appreciation

ISBN 978-0-7566-5511-2; 0-7566-5511-0

"From prehistoric to modern times, this expertly designed survey delivers a wealth of information. Much more than a mere time line, the focus shifts from artist to movement to medium with fluidity. Gallery pages examine how particular subjects are depicted in art from a variety of cultures and time periods. Hundreds of color reproductions are sure to hold readers' interest. . . . The vast amount of information presented is neither overwhelming nor superficial." SLJ

Guéry, Anne

Alphab'art; by Anne Guery, Olivier Dussutour. Frances Lincoln 2009 unp il $19.95

Grades: 3 4 5 6					**709**

1. Art appreciation 2. Alphabet

ISBN 978-1-84780-013-8; 1-84780-013-0

One letter of the alphabet is concealed in each of these 26 paintings by some of the masters of Western art, including Picasso, Dalí, Van Gogh, Matisse, Giotto, Chagall, Mondrian, Hopper, Kandinsky, Klee, Magritte, and Bosch.

"Readers are challenged by representational and abstract paintings spanning seven centuries, as the text encourages close inspection of the art. . . . This [is a] rich, well-thought-out book." SLJ

Johnson, Stephen, 1964-

A is for art; an abstract alphabet; [by] Stephen T. Johnson. Simon & Schuster Books for Young Readers 2008 unp il $16.99

Grades: K 1 2 3					**709**

1. Abstract art 2. Alphabet

ISBN 978-0-689-86301-1; 0-689-86301-2

LC 2007-30224

"A Paula Wiseman book"

"This exciting alphabetic compendium began with a dictionary. Following years of study and work as a realistic painter, Johnson found himself wanting to explore abstract art. He started by collecting words for each letter of the alphabet. Then, he created a piece based on their meanings. . . . The works vary from paintings and collages to sculptures to installations, and an index reveals the locations of the hidden letters as well as dimensions and materials for the pieces. Children will enjoy seeing everyday objects like candy used in his creations, and will no doubt be inspired to come up with some abstract art of their own." SLJ

Raczka, Bob

Name that style; all about isms in art; by Bob Raczka. Millbrook Press 2008 32p il (Art adventures) lib bdg $25.26; pa $9.95 *

Grades: 5 6 7 8					**709**

1. Art—History

ISBN 978-0-8225-7586-3 (lib bdg); 0-8225-7586-8 (lib bdg); 978-1-58013-824-6 (pa); 1-58013-824-1 (pa)

LC 2008000312

"Beginning with naturalism and ending with photorealism, with many stops along the way, this compact overview documents the shifts, both in terms of technique as well as subject matter, that differentiate each style from its predecessors. Each 'ism' gets a two-page spread, with a beautifully reproduced example. . . . This is . . . indispensible for any middle-grade classrooms introducing art history." Booklist

Where in the world? around the globe in 13 works of art; [by] Bob Raczka. Millbrook Press 2007 31p il map lib bdg $25.26; pa $9.95

Grades: 4 5 6 7 8					**709**

1. Art appreciation

ISBN 978-0-8225-6371-6 (lib bdg); 0-8225-6371-1 (lib bdg); 978-0-8225-6372-3 (pa); 0-8225-6372-X (pa)

LC 2006014895

"On this armchair tour around the world, Raczka introduces different artists and works of art. All evoke a strong sense of place. . . . Each reproduction is accompanied by a lively text describing the locale and time period, biographical information about the artist, and other interesting tidbits." SLJ

Schümann, Bettina

13 women artists children should know; [by] Bettina Schumann; [translated from German by Jane Michael] Prestel 2009 46p il $14.95

Grades: 5 6 7 8					**709**

1. Women artists 2. Art appreciation

ISBN 978-3-7913-4333-4; 3-7913-4333-5

This is profiles women artists such as Sofonisba Anguissola, Maria Sybilla Merian, Mary Cassatt, Georgia O'Keeffe, Frida Kahlo, Louise Bourgeois, and Cindy Sherma

This "large-format, brightly colored [survey proves a] solid, even inspiring [introduction] to the art world. . . . Leading questions encourage budding artists to use the featured subjects and artworks as inspiration." Horn Book Guide

Includes glossary

Wenzel, Angela

13 artists children should know; [translation by Jane Michael] Prestel 2010 46p il $14.95

Grades: 5 6 7 8					**709**

1. Artists 2. Art—History 3. Art appreciation

ISBN 978-3-7913-4173-6; 3-7913-4173-1

This profiles 13 artists such as Leonardo da Vinci, Vincent Van Gogh, Vermeer, and Henri Matisse

This "large-format, brightly colored [survey provides a] solid, even inspiring [introduction] to the art world. . . . Leading questions encourage budding artists to use the featured subjects and artworks as inspiration." Horn Book Guide

Includes glossary

709.04   Art—20th century, 1900-1999

Raimondo, Joyce

Express yourself! activities and adventures in expressionism. Watson-Guptill Publications 2005 48p il (Art explorers) $12.95 *

Grades: 2 3 4 5   **709.04**

1. Expressionism (Art) 2. Art appreciation

ISBN 0-8230-2506-3

An introduction to Expressionism which includes guidance for related activities as well as brief biographies of six artists: Edvard Munch, Vincent van Gogh, Ernst Ludwig Kirchner, Visily Kandinsky, Willem de Kooning, and Jackson Pollock

"The layout is particularly attractive, with crisp, full-color photos and drawings set against brightly colored borders; the text and captions are easy to read. . . . This book will be welcomed by teachers, parents, and would-be artists." Booklist

Imagine that! activities and adventures in surrealism. Watson-Guptill Publications 2004 48p il (Art explorers) $13.95 *

Grades: 2 3 4 5   **709.04**

1. Surrealism 2. Art appreciation

ISBN 0-8230-2502-0   LC 2003-19487

An introduction to Surrealism which includes guidance for related activities as well as brief biographies of six artists: Salvador Dali, Rene Magritte, Max Ernst, Joan Mir, Merit Oppenheim, and Frida Kahlo

"One of the strengths of this book is the inclusion of artwork produced by children. . . . It offers a wealth of intriguing and easy-to-do activities." SLJ

Make it pop! activities and adventures in Pop art; [by] Joyce Raimondo. Watson-Guptill Publications 2006 48p il (Art explorers) $12.95

Grades: 2 3 4 5   **709.04**

1. Pop art 2. Art appreciation

ISBN 0-8230-2507-1; 978-0-8230-2507-7

LC 2006012957

"Raimondo introduces six prominent Pop artists—Roy Lichtenstein, Andy Warhol, Robert Rauschenberg, Jasper Johns, Claes Oldenburg, and George Segal. First she describes each man's creative technique, and then she invites readers to observe one of their well-known works by asking questions. . . . Most of the required materials can be found around the house or are readily available at a craft store, and written instructions for each project are easy to follow." SLJ

What's the big idea? activities and adventures in abstract art. Watson-Guptill 2008 48p il (Art explorers) $13.95

Grades: 2 3 4 5   **709.04**

1. Abstract art 2. Art appreciation

ISBN 978-0-8230-9998-6; 0-8230-9998-9

"Using the works of famous abstract artists, Raimondo invites readers to discover this genre. Her tone is lively and inquisitive. . . . The activities encourage the investigation of shapes, colors, and patterns, as well as personal creativity. Instructions are clear and thorough. . . . The

color photos are reproductions are well chosen and the vivid layout will draw readers to the featured works and projects." SLJ

Spilsbury, Richard, 1963-

Pop art. Heinemann Library 2009 48p il (Art on the wall) lib bdg $23

Grades: 5 6 7 8 9 10   **709.04**

1. Pop art

ISBN 978-1-4329-1368-7 (lib bdg); 1-4329-1368-9 (lib bdg)   LC 2008020358

This describes how Pop art began, some of the movement's artists, and the influence of Pop art

This title succeeds "in presenting a bird's-eye view of [Pop art] without oversimplification. Information on individual artists is included in the broader context of the movement. Visually exciting, with plenty of color, [the layout is] hip and should appeal to the target audience." SLJ

Includes glossary and bibliographical references

709.38   Ancient Greek art

Langley, Andrew

Ancient Greece. Raintree 2005 48p il (History in art) lib bdg $31.43; pa $8.99 *

Grades: 4 5 6 7   **709.38**

1. Greek art 2. Greece—Civilization

ISBN 978-1-4109-0517-8 (lib bdg); 1-4109-0517-9 (lib bdg); 978-1-4109-2035-5 (pa); 1-4109-2035-6 (pa)

LC 2004-7523

Contents: Art as evidence; The story of ancient Greece; Inside the city-state; Everyday life; Religion and mythology; Time line

The author shows "how art provides primary-source information about everyday and family life, beliefs and religion, and philosophy and mythology in . . . ancient [Greece]. . . . The [book follows] a well-organized format that makes the history accessible for reports, but the [author takes the book] beyond a reports-only status. Captions for the two or three illustrations per spread are clear." SLJ

Includes glossary and bibliographical references

709.39   Art of other parts of ancient world

Campbell-Hinshaw, Kelly

Ancient Mexico; [by] Kelly Campbell-Hinshaw. Chronicle Books 2007 32p il (Art across the ages) hardcover o.p. pa $4.95

Grades: 2 3 4   **709.39**

1. Mexican art 2. Mexico—Antiquities

ISBN 0-8118-5670-4; 0-8118-5671-2 (pa)

"A brief text and striking photos introduce the art of ancient Mexico in this distinctive early reader, which features artifacts such as stone and clay sculptures, a jade mask, a wall painting, and a shield decorated with feathers and inlaid gold. . . . This offers a visually impressive introduction to the arts of Mexico's earliest cultures." Booklist

709.5   Asian art

Lane, Kimberly
Come look with me: Asian art. Charlesbridge
2008 32p il $15.95
Grades: 3 4 5   **709.5**
   1. Asian art 2. Art appreciation
   ISBN 978-1-890674-19-9; 1-890674-19-2
                LC 2007037926
   "The book is intended to introduce children to fine art
in various Asian countries in an accessible manner, and
it succeeds. . . . Lane presents a dozen full-color reproductions, done in various mediums and representing different time periods, along with background information
and discussion starters." SLJ

709.51   Chinese art

Anderson, Dale, 1953-
Ancient China; [by] Dale Anderson. Raintree
2005 48p il map (History in art) $22; pa $8.99 *
Grades: 4 5 6 7   **709.51**
   1. Chinese art 2. China—Civilization
   ISBN   978-1-4109-0519-2;   1-4109-0519-5;
978-1-4109-2037-9 (pa); 1-4109-2037-2 (pa)
                LC 2004-7587
   Contents: Art as evidence; The story of ancient China;
Imperial government; Daily life in ancient China; Beliefs
and philosophies; Timeline
   The author shows "how art provides primary-source
information about everyday and family life, beliefs and
religion, and philosophy and mythology in . . . ancient
[China]. . . . The [book follows] a well-organized format
that makes the history accessible for reports, but the [au-
thor takes the book] beyond a reports-only status. Captions for the two or three illustrations per spread are
clear." SLJ
   Includes glossary and bibliographical references

709.7   North American art

January, Brendan, 1972-
Native American art & culture; [by] Brendan
January. Raintree 2005 56p il map (World art &
culture) lib bdg $23; pa $9.99 *
Grades: 5 6 7 8   **709.7**
   1. Native American art 2. Native Americans
   ISBN 978-1-4109-1108-7 (lib bdg); 1-4109-1108-X
(lib bdg); 978-1-4109-2118-5 (pa); 1-4109-2118-2 (pa)
                LC 2004-8072
   Contents: Introduction; Beliefs and traditions; Rock
art; Land art; Architecture; Body art; Carving; Masks;
Images; Pottery; Weaving; Baskets; Kachina dolls; Painting; Clothing, decoration, and hair styles; Ceremonies,
songs, and dance; Metals and precious stones; The powwow; Cross currents
   "January investigates the many art forms of the Native
American tribes. . . . Chapters are dedicated to pottery,
textiles, carving, and painting as well as body art, architecture, ceremonies, songs, and dances. . . . Numerous

color photographs of both ancient and modern artwork
are included on each spread, and they are exceptional.
. . . This fresh look at Native American culture through
its artwork will be a welcome alternative for reports and
classroom discussion, and the popularity of the subject
matter and appealing design will attract readers outside
the classroom environment." SLJ
   Includes bibliographical references

   Native Americans; [by] Brendan January.
Raintree 2005 48p il map (History in art) lib bdg
$22; pa $8.99
Grades: 4 5 6 7   **709.7**
   1. Native American art 2. Native Americans
   ISBN 978-1-4109-0523-9 (lib bdg); 1-4109-0523-3 (lib
bdg); 978-1-4109-2041-6 (pa); 1-4109-2041-0 (pa)
                LC 2004-7526
   Contents: The Native Americans; A chronological history; Traditional ways; Everyday life; Beliefs and mythology
   This book has "a depth of content that is unusual in
art-history books for this age group. . . . [It] is amply illustrated with full-color photographs and reproductions.
. . . Well-written, informative." SLJ
   Includes bibliographical references

709.8   Latin American art

Lane, Kimberly
Come look with me: Latin American art; [by]
Kimberly Lane. Charlesbridge 2007 32p il $15.95
Grades: 3 4 5   **709.8**
   1. Latin American art 2. Art appreciation
   ISBN 978-1-890674-20-5   LC 2006034237
   This book provides an introduction to Latin American
art, pairing reproductions of works of art with questions
about the artists lives and work.
   "The paintings are reproduced in full color on high-
quality paper. The writing is lively and interesting, yet
the discussions of artistic ideas and theories are concise
and easy to understand." SLJ

711   Area planning (Civic art)

Macaulay, David, 1946-
   City: a story of Roman planning and
construction. Houghton Mifflin 1974 112p il $18;
pa $10.99 *
Grades: 4 5 6 7 8 9   **711**
   1. City planning—Rome 2. Civil engineering
3. Roman architecture
   ISBN 0-395-19492-X; 0-395-34922-2 (pa)
                LC 74-4280
   "By following the inception, construction, and development of an imaginary Roman city, the account traces
the evolution of Verbonia from the selection of its site
under religious auspices in 26 B.C. to its completion in
100 A.D." Horn Book
   Includes glossary

720   Architecture

Curlee, Lynn, 1947-
Skyscraper. Atheneum Books for Young Readers 2007 40p il $17.99 *
Grades: 3 4 5 6   720
1. Skyscrapers
ISBN 0-689-84489-1
"Dramatic paintings and lucid prose highlight this excellent history of skyscrapers." SLJ

Hosack, Karen, 1971-
Buildings; [by] Karen Hosack. Raintree 2009 32p il map (What is art?) lib bdg $27.50
Grades: 5 6 7 8   720
1. Buildings 2. Architecture
ISBN 978-1-4109-3165-8 (lib bdg); 1-4109-3165-X (lib bdg)   LC 2008-9700
This "features public spaces and private residences created from a variety of materials. Every page includes a paragraph about the structure with glossary terms in bold type. . . . [Title is] consistent in quality of design and content." SLJ
Includes glossary and bibliographical references

Laroche, Giles
What's inside; fascinating structures around the world. Houghton Mifflin Books for Children 2009 unp il $17
Grades: 4 5 6 7   720
1. Architecture
ISBN 978-0-618-86247-4; 0-618-86247-1
                                                    LC 2008-33832
"This beautiful book presents interior and exterior views of 14 extraordinary structures, from King Tut's tomb and the Temple of Kukulcan to the Sydney Opera House and the Georgia Aquarium. . . . The text is good, the organization is clever, but it's the art here that is truly masterful. The illustrations are made from layers and layers of cut and painted paper." SLJ

Macaulay, David, 1946-
Building big. Houghton Mifflin 2000 192p il $30; pa $12.95 *
Grades: 5 6 7 8 9 10   720
1. Architecture 2. Engineering
ISBN 0-395-96331-1; 0-618-46527-8 (pa)
                                                    LC 00-28116
"Walter Lorraine books"
This companion to the PBS series examines the architecture and engineering of "bridges, tunnels, dams, domes, and skyscrapers. Each section offers an implicitly chronological analysis as it focuses on several significant examples of that particular kind of structure." Bull Cent Child Books
"Macaulay combines his detailed yet vaguely whimsical illustrations with simple, straightforward prose that breaks down complex architectural and engineering accomplishments into easily digestible tidbits that don't insult the intelligence of the reader of any age." N Y Times Book Rev
Includes glossary

Oxlade, Chris
Skyscrapers; uncovering technology. Firefly Books 2006 52p il $16.95
Grades: 4 5 6 7   720
1. Skyscrapers
ISBN 1-55407-136-4
"This tour of big buildings flits around the world and through history with a kaleidoscopic mix of small, finely detailed artrists' renditions and five-sentence-or-less text munchies. . . . It also features four mylar overlays that offer an inside look at a few towering structures. . . . Blending eye-catching visuals with specific facts and comparisons, this quick survey will please both browsers and assignment-driven readers." Booklist

Price, Sean, 1963-
The story behind skyscrapers; [by] Sean Stewart Price. Heinemann Library 2009 32p il (True stories) $28.21
Grades: 3 4 5   720
1. Skyscrapers
ISBN 978-1-4329-2349-5; 1-4329-2349-8
                                                    LC 2008043411
This offers a history of skyscrapers along with miscellaneous facts about them.
Includes bibliographical references

Roeder, Annette
13 buildings children should know; [translator, Jane Michael] Prestel 2009 46p il $14.95
Grades: 5 6 7 8   720
1. Architecture
ISBN 978-3-7913-4171-2; 3-7913-4171-5
"The famous buildings featured in this pictorial collection include Notre Dame cathedral in Paris, Neuschwanstein Castle in Germany, New York City's Guggenheim Museum and the Beijing National Stadium (built for the 2008 Olympics), each pictured in color photographs, cross-sections and/or ground plans, with time lines tracing the buildings' developments and changes over time. . . . A sound introduction to some impressive structures." Publ Wkly

Spilsbury, Louise, 1963-
Can buildings speak? [by] Louise and Richard Spilsbury. Cherrytree Books 2009 24p il (Start-up art and design) lib bdg $24.25
Grades: 2 3 4   720
1. Architecture 2. Buildings
ISBN 978-1-84234-523-8 (lib bdg); 1-84234-523-0 (lib bdg)   LC 2007-46389
"Explores what the shape, patterns, and exterior of buildings can tell us about purpose of those buildings and compares historical building methods with modern ones. Includes project ideas." Publisher's note
This title has "readers examining all sorts of structures, from their local school to Antonio Gaudí's Casa Batlló in Barcelona, Spain. . . . Includes a wide range of possible activities to extend the information provided, often suggesting further research on the Internet. . . . [This book is] well designed, with a large, bold font; clear and ample photography; and interesting layout." SLJ

Stern, Steven L.
Building greenscrapers; consultant, Frank Robbins. Bearport Pub. 2009 32p il (Going green) lib bdg $25.27
Grades: 4 5 6 7   **720**
1. Skyscrapers 2. Sustainable architecture
ISBN 978-1-59716-962-2 (lib bdg); 1-59716-962-5 (lib bdg)   LC 2009-12494
Explains how "'greenscrapers' use the latest technology to meet the needs of the people who work and live in them while at the same time conserving and protecting Earth's precious resources." Publisher's note
"Color photographs (most full page) and a few diagrams accompany the informative text. . . . Overall, the [book] . . . is user-friendly and covers topics that are not easily found elsewhere." SLJ
Includes glossary and bibliographical references

720.9 Architecture—Historical, geographic, persons treatment

Zaunders, Bo
Gargoyles, girders, & glass houses; magnificent master builders; illustrated by Roxie Munro. Dutton Children's Books 2004 48p il $17.99 *
Grades: 3 4 5 6   **720.9**
1. Architecture—History 2. Architects
ISBN 0-525-47284-3   LC 2003-28192
The author and illustrator "tell the stories of Brunelleschi's dome of Santa Maria del Fiore, the mosques of Mimar Koca Sinan, the sculpture and architecture of Brazil's Lisboa, the Roeblings' Brooklyn Bridge, Eiffel's tower in Paris, the buildings of Barcelona's Gaudi, and Van Alen's Chrysler Building in New York City. Zaunders' narrative approach to nonfiction adds an appealing dimension to these artistic and engineering feats. Munro's often-beautiful ink drawings with color washes capture the special qualities of each construction." Booklist
Includes bibliographical references

725 Public structures

Low, William
Old Penn Station; [by] William Low. Henry Holt and Co. 2007 unp il $16.95
Grades: 3 4 5 6   **725**
1. Pennsylvania Station (New York, N.Y.) 2. Historic buildings 3. Railroad stations
ISBN 978-0-8050-7925-8; 0-8050-7925-4
                                     LC 2006015359
"Low contributes both words and pictures in this ode to New York City's Pennsylvania Station. Introductory pages describe why and how the glorious train station was erected. Later spreads focus on how the building was utilized before it fell into disuse and was finally demolished to make way for the smaller, subterranean station used today. . . . The artwork . . . is magnificent. Full-spread, oil-and-digital, mixed-media paintings depicting people moving through the beautiful structure will draw children into Low's underlying message:

'Buildings are not just concrete and steel. They are the heart and soul of all great cities.'" Booklist
Includes bibliographical references

Nardo, Don, 1947-
Roman amphitheaters. Watts 2002 63p il (Watts library) lib bdg $25.50; pa $8.95
Grades: 5 6 7 8   **725**
1. Colosseum (Rome, Italy) 2. Roman architecture
ISBN 0-531-12036-8 (lib bdg); 0-531-16224-9 (pa)
                                     LC 2001-17769
The author discusses the Colosseum in Rome as an example of how amphitheaters were constructed and "provides a brief cultural context; a history of the development of the building type; and a history of the . . . [Colosseum] including how it was built, what it was used for, and what happened after the society that created it lost prominence. . . . The writing is informative and engaging and not oversimplified. The illustrations are mainly clear, high-quality, full-color photographs." SLJ
Includes glossary and bibliographical references

726 Buildings for religious and related purposes

Curlee, Lynn, 1947-
Parthenon. Atheneum Books for Young Readers 2004 unp il $17.95 *
Grades: 3 4 5 6   **726**
1. Parthenon (Athens, Greece)
ISBN 0-689-84490-5   LC 2003-2615
A detailed history of the Parthenon exploring its construction and restoration.
This is a "splendid introduction to Greece's most renowned monument. . . . [The author's] examination of the architectural details is particularly accurate and absorbing. . . . The limpid, forthright prose matches artwork of similar clarity and elegant simplicity. The acrylic paintings balance areas of flat color with finely controlled line." SLJ

Hyman, Teresa L., 1971-
Pyramids; [by] Teresa Hyman. KidHaven Press 2004 48p il (Wonders of the world) lib bdg $23.70
Grades: 3 4 5 6   **726**
1. Pyramids
ISBN 0-7377-2055-7   LC 2004-12063
Contents: Pyramids of treasure; Pyramids of power; Pyramids of enlightenment; Pyramids of sacrifice
This "introduces structures in ancient Egypt, Africa, Cambodia, and Mexico and is full of large, colorful photos and illustrations. . . . Attractive, readable." SLJ
Includes bibliographical references

Macaulay, David, 1946-
Building the book Cathedral. Houghton Mifflin 1999 112p il $29.95 *
Grades: 4 5 6 7 8 9   **726**
1. Cathedrals 2. Gothic architecture
ISBN 0-395-92147-3   LC 99-17975

Macaulay, David, 1946-—*Continued*

"Walter Lorraine books"

"On its twenty-fifth anniversary, the author recounts the origins of his first book and suggests revisions he'd make in light of what he's learned. . . . Most of the original *Cathedral: the story of it's construction* is reproduced in this oversized celebratory volume, along with lots of preliminary sketches, new commentary, and revised, or newly deployed, art. . . . Touches of informal humor further enliven a book that's already mesmerizing for both its original content and its insights into this author-illustrator's incisive, ebulliently creative mind." Horn Book

Cathedral: the story of its construction. Houghton Mifflin 1973 77p il $18; pa $8.95 *

Grades: 4 5 6 7 8 9   726

1. Cathedrals 2. Gothic architecture

ISBN 0-395-17513-5; 0-395-31668-5 (pa)

LC 73-6634

This is a description, illustrated with black-and-white line drawings, of the construction of an imagined representative Gothic cathedral "in southern France from its conception in 1252 to its completion in 1338. The spirit that motivated the people, the tools and materials they used, the steps and methods of constructions, all receive . . . attention." Booklist

Includes glossary

Mosque. Houghton Mifflin 2003 96p il $18 *

Grades: 4 5 6 7 8 9   726

1. Mosques—Design and construction

ISBN 0-618-24034-9   LC 2003-177

"Walter Lorraine books"

Using "a fictional framework to hold his nonfictional material, the author introduces readers to Admiral Suha Mehmet Pasa, a wealthy aristocrat living in Istanbul, who decides in his declining years to fund the building of a mosque and its associated buildings—religious school, soup kitchen, public baths, public fountain, and tomb. Detailing the activities of the architect and workers, Macaulay creates a from-the-ground-up look not only at the actual construction, but also at the uses of the various buildings." SLJ

"Once again Macaulay uses clear words and exemplary drawings to explore a majestic structure's design and construction. . . . In his respectful, straightforward explanation of the mosque's design, Macaulay offers an unusual, inspiring perspective into Islamic society." Booklist

Includes glossary

Pyramid. Houghton Mifflin 1975 80p il $20; pa $9.95 *

Grades: 4 5 6 7 8 9   726

1. Pyramids 2. Egypt—Civilization

ISBN 0-395-21407-6; 0-395-32121-2 (pa)

LC 75-9964

The construction of a pyramid in 25th century B.C. Egypt is described. "Information about selection of the site, drawing of the plans, calculating compass directions, clearing and leveling the ground, and quarrying and hauling the tremendous blocks of granite and limestone is conveyed as much by pictures as by text." Horn Book

Includes glossary

Mann, Elizabeth, 1948-

The Parthenon; illustrations by Yuan Lee. Mikaya Press 2006 47p il (Wonders of the world) $22.95

Grades: 4 5 6 7   726

1. Parthenon (Athens, Greece) 2. Athens (Greece)—History 3. Greece—Civilization

ISBN 1-931414-15-7

This "volume introduces the history of ancient Athens culminating in the building of the Parthenon. . . . [The text is] well-researched and clearly written. . . . The color illustrations include an excellent map of Greece, photos of artifacts and sculptures, and many clearly deliniated, large-scale paintings." Booklist

727 Buildings for educational and research purposes

Vogel, Jennifer

A library story; by Jennifer Vogel. Millbrook Press 2006 64p il lib bdg $26.60

Grades: 4 5 6   727

1. Library architecture 2. Public libraries

ISBN 978-0-8225-5916-0 (lib bdg); 0-8225-5916-1 (lib bdg)   LC 2005023742

"A fact-filled look at the design and construction of the new Central Library of the Minneapolis Public Library, which opened its doors in May 2006. Vogel includes a brief overview of the library's history and plenty of details and trivia relating to this specific library system and public libraries in general. . . . A mix of color photographs and archival graphics enliven the text." SLJ

Includes bibliographical references

728.8 Large and elaborate private dwellings

Macaulay, David, 1946-

Castle. Houghton Mifflin 1977 74p il $20; pa $9.95 *

Grades: 4 5 6 7 8 9   728.8

1. Castles 2. Fortification

ISBN 0-395-25784-0; 0-395-32920-5 (pa)

LC 77-7159

Macaulay depicts "the history of an imaginary thirteenth-century castle—built to subdue the Welsh hordes—from the age of construction to the age of neglect, when the town of Aberwyfern no longer needs a fortified stronghold." Economist

Includes glossary

Scarre, Christopher
The Palace of Minos at Knossos; [by] Chris Scarre and Rebecca Stefoff. Oxford University Press 2003 47p il map (Digging for the past) $21.95
Grades: 4 5 6 7   **728.8**
  1. Evans, Sir Arthur John, 1851-1941 2. Palace of Knossos 3. Excavations (Archeology)—Greece 4. Crete (Greece)
  ISBN 0-19-514272-1   LC 2003-3712
  Contents: An unexplored world; Discovering a lost palace; In search of the Minoans; Knossos today; Interview with Chris Scarre
  Discusses the ancient Minoan civilization of Knossos, Crete, as manifested by the excavations of that city by the archaeologist Sir Arthur Evans.
  "Many excellent photos and diagrams, mainly in color; time lines . . . and explanations of archaeological stratigraphy and of the mysterious Linear B writing are included. The book is concise, clear, entertaining, and factual." SLJ
  Includes bibliographical references

729   Design and decoration of structures and accessories

Hill, Isabel
Urban animals. Star Bright Books 2009 unp il $17.95; pa $7.95
Grades: K 1 2 3   **729**
  1. Architectural decoration and ornament 2. Animals in art
  ISBN   978-1-59572-209-6;   1-59572-209-2; 978-1-59572-210-2 (pa); 1-59572-210-6 (pa)
                                        LC 2009028378
  "Vivid photographs invite children to look closely at a variety of city buildings to find a column adorned with a dog's face, a bronze frieze featuring flying geese, etc. On each double-page spread, lefthand pages show wide views while right-hand pages zoom in on the highlighted animal. The child-friendly topic and approach and the small trim size make this a winning introduction to architecture." Horn Book Guide

730   Sculpture, ceramics & metalwork

Raczka, Bob
3-D ABC; a sculptural alphabet; by Bob Raczka. Millbrook Press 2007 32p il lib bdg $23.93 *
Grades: K 1 2 3   **730**
  1. Sculpture 2. Alphabet
  ISBN 978-0-7613-9456-3 (lib bdg); 0-7613-9456-7 (lib bdg)   LC 2005013472
  "This alphabetically arranged primer on 20th-century sculpture includes Marcel Duchamp's Bicycle Wheel, Constantin Brancusi's The Kiss (paired with Robert Indiana's Love), and Claes Oldenburg's Spoonbridge and Cherry. The selections are international in scope, and the media range from scrap metal and found objects to wood and fluorescent lights." SLJ

730.9   Historical, geographic, persons treatment of sculpture

Fritz, Jean
Leonardo's horse; illustrated by Hudson Talbott. Putnam 2001 unp il $16.99
Grades: 4 5 6 7   **730.9**
  1. Leonardo, da Vinci, 1452-1519 2. Dent, Charlie, 1919-1994 3. Bronzes
  ISBN 0-399-23576-0   LC 00-41550
  "In 1482, Leonardo da Vinci began work on a mammoth bronze horse. But though he completed a twenty-four-foot clay model, it was never cast. . . . Half a millennium later, retired pilot Charles Dent dedicated himself to re-creating Leonardo's dream, a venture eventually realized with the help of sculptor Nina Akamu." Horn Book
  "Combining biography, history, and art, Fritz's absorbing text is both a lively introduction to Leonardo and a tribute to Dent." Booklist

Niepold, Mil
Oooh! Picasso; [by] Mil Niepold & Jeanyves Verdu. Tricycle Press 2009 unp il (The Oooh! artist) $14.95
Grades: 2 3 4   **730.9**
  1. Picasso, Pablo, 1881-1973 2. Sculpture 3. Art appreciation
  ISBN 978-1-58246-265-3; 1-58246-265-8
                                        LC 2008010646
  "Niepold and Verdu introduce five of Picasso's sculptures. For each one, a close-up detail of the artwork is shown first, along with the question, 'What is this?' Two more spreads present zoomed-in images with possible answers, followed by a third spread showing the entire sculpture along with a statement like, 'oooh! i am a guitar.' . . . Bold text floating on bright solid-color pages complements the pictures. A photo of the artist is appended along with reproductions of the artworks and identifying information. . . . This book will ignite readers' imaginations and is both an effective gateway to art appreciation for young children and a fun exercise for elementary students." SLJ

731   Processes, forms, subjects of sculpture

Kenney, Karen Latchana, 1974-
Super simple masks; fun and easy-to-make crafts for kids. ABDO Pub. Company 2010 32p il (Super simple crafts) lib bdg $17.95
Grades: K 1 2 3 4   **731**
  1. Masks (Sculpture) 2. Handicraft
  ISBN 978-1-60453-627-0 (lib bdg); 1-60453-627-6 (lib bdg)   LC 2009-357
  "Colorful photos; clean layout in a bright, primary palette; and large, abundant step-by-step instructional photos give [this book] great appeal. The . . . crafts . . . are functional and attractive. . . . Readily obtainable household materials and easy-to-follow instructions mean that children can do these crafts independently." SLJ
  Includes glossary

731.4 Sculpture—Techniques and procedures

Hanson, Anders, 1980-
Cool sculpture; the art of creativity for kids; [by] Anders Hanson. ABDO Pub. Co. 2009 32p il (Cool art) lib bdg $24.21
Grades: 2 3 4   **731.4**
    1. Sculpture—Technique
    ISBN 978-1-60453-144-2 (lib bdg); 1-60453-144-4 (lib bdg)   LC 2008-22324
This book about sculpture is "well organized, with clearly written sections . . . and several clever projects and exercises. . . . [It] should have substantial child appeal." SLJ
Includes glossary

Luxbacher, Irene, 1970-
1 2 3 I can build! Kids Can Press 2009 23p il (Starting art) $14.95; pa $6.95
Grades: 2 3 4   **731.4**
    1. Sculpture—Technique
    ISBN 978-1-55453-315-2; 978-1-55453-316-9 (pa)
"Illustrated step-by-step projects show kids how to build small structures out of household materials, encouraging both hands-on creativity and imaginative play. Clear photos of brightly colored materials appear on spacious layouts against white backgrounds. Each project looks sharp and appealing, with sketched cartoon characters adding liveliness and humor." SLJ

1 2 3 I can sculpt! Kids Can Press 2007 23p il (Starting art) $12.95
Grades: 2 3 4   **731.4**
    1. Sculpture—Technique
    ISBN 978-1-55453-038-0; 1-55453-038-5
This "introduces the various types of simple materials and techniques that can be used to create animal sculptures. This book is . . . project-oriented, although such concepts as three-dimensionality, texture, and balance are mentioned. Children can make an egg-carton crocodile, an aluminum-foil-and-clay snake, a clay-and-pipe-cleaner giraffe, a paper-bag dinosaur, and more. . . . [The book has] lively pages with color photos and easy-to-follow directions." SLJ

Spilsbury, Louise, 1963-
What is sculpture? [by] Louise and Richard Spilsbury. Cherrytree Books 2009 24p il (Start-up art and design) lib bdg $24.25
Grades: 2 3 4   **731.4**
    1. Sculpture
    ISBN 978-1-84234-525-2 (lib bdg); 1-84234-525-7 (lib bdg)   LC 2007-46393
"Describes forms of sculpture, the textures of materials used, and provides project ideas, including wire sculpture and junk art." Publisher's note
"Includes a wide range of possible activities to extend the information provided, often suggesting further research on the Internet. . . . [This book is] well designed, with a large, bold font; clear and ample photography; and interesting layout." SLJ

736 Carving and carvings

Alexander, Chris
Difficult origami; by Chris Alexander. Capstone Press 2009 32p il (Snap books) lib bdg $25.26
Grades: 3 4 5 6   **736**
    1. Origami
    ISBN 978-1-4296-2022-2 (lib bdg); 1-4296-2022-6 (lib bdg)   LC 2007-52196
"Provides step-by-step instructions for difficult origami models, including a cat, a lily, a crested bird, a lop-eared rabbit, a frog, a picture frame, and a speedboat." Publisher's note
This book includes "clearly illustrated diagrams and attractive photos of the completed projects using different colors and textures of paper." SLJ
Includes glossary and bibliographical references

Sort-of-difficult origami; by Chris Alexander. Capstone Press 2009 32p il (Snap books) lib bdg $25.26
Grades: 3 4 5 6   **736**
    1. Origami
    ISBN 978-1-4296-2023-9 (lib bdg); 1-4296-2023-4 (lib bdg)   LC 2007-52208
"Provides step-by-step instructions for moderately difficult origami models, including a fox mask, a tulip and stem, a masu box and insert, a penguin, a seal, a goldfish, a waterbomb, and an ornament." Publisher's note
This book includes "clearly illustrated diagrams and attractive photos of the completed projects using different colors and textures of paper." SLJ
Includes glossary and bibliographical references

Boursin, Didier
Folding for fun; origami for ages 4 and up. Firefly Books 2007 63p il $19.95
Grades: K 1 2 3 4 5   **736**
    1. Origami
    ISBN 978-1-55407-253-8; 1-55407-253-0
This offers instructions for 16 origami projects including balls, boats, twirlers, boxes, hats, and airplanes.
"The pages combine a dynamic array of images, including ink illustrations of the folding steps and color photos of young people playing with their finished work. . . . This how-to will appeal to a wide range of children . . . as well as the adults and teens who work with them." Booklist

Henry, Sally
Paper folding; [by] Sally Henry. PowerKids Press 2009 32p il (Make your own crafts) lib bdg $25.25
Grades: 3 4 5 6   **736**
    1. Paper crafts 2. Origami
    ISBN 978-1-4358-2507-9 (lib bdg); 1-4358-2507-1 (lib bdg)   LC 2008-4524
"After describing different kinds of paper, Henry explains the difference between a fold, a crease, and a burnished fold, and then lists all the other supplies besides paper (glue, rubber cement) that should be on hand. The rest of the book devotes two-page spreads to each proj-

Henry, Sally—*Continued*

ect. . . . The ideas are fantastic. . . . This will keep plenty of hands and minds busy." Booklist

Includes glossary

Jackson, Paul, 1956-

Origami toys; that tumble fly and spin. Gibbs Smith 2010 127p il $19.99 **736**

1. Origami 2. Toys

ISBN 978-1-4236-0524-9; 1-4236-0524-1

"In this handsomely packaged volume, Jackson offers 29 elegantly simple toys that he has either invented or modified. The models . . . include percussive 'instruments,' a wriggling fish, dogs, . . . a spinning star, two gliders, and even a catapult. . . . The particularly clear step diagrams use standard origami notation, and the directions that accompany them are just as easy to follow. . . . [This is an] above-average offering." SLJ

Krier, Ann Kristen, 1962-

Totally cool origami animals. Sterling Pub. 2007 96p il $19.95

Grades: 4 5 6 **736**

1. Origami

ISBN 978-1-4027-2448-0; 1-4027-2448-9

LC 2006029593

"Each of these twenty-eight origami animal projects is accompanied by clear step-by-step instructions and photos. Projects are conveniently labeled 'beginner,' 'intermediate,' or 'advanced.' . . . The projects . . . are typically well explained. Paper-folders of all abilities should be able to tackle these projects with success." Horn Book Guide

Meinking, Mary

Easy origami; by Mary Meinking. Capstone Press 2009 32p il (Snap books) lib bdg $25.26

Grades: 3 4 5 6 **736**

1. Origami

ISBN 978-1-4296-2020-8 (lib bdg); 1-4296-2020-X (lib bdg)

LC 2008-1677

"Provides step-by-step instructions for easy origami models, including a drinking cup, a spinning top, and a fortune-teller." Publisher's note

This book includes "clearly illustrated diagrams and attractive photos of the completed projects using different colors and textures of paper." SLJ

Includes glossary and bibliographical references

Not-quite-so-easy origami; by Mary Meinking. Capstone Press 2009 32p il (Snap books) lib bdg $25.26

Grades: 3 4 5 6 **736**

1. Origami

ISBN 978-1-4296-2021-5 (lib bdg); 1-4296-2021-8 (lib bdg)

LC 2008-1679

"Provides step-by-step instructions for moderately easy origami models, including a hopping frog, gliding airplane, and flapping crane." Publisher's note

This book includes "clearly illustrated diagrams and attractive photos of the completed projects using different colors and textures of paper." SLJ

Includes glossary and bibliographical references

Nguyen, Duy

Creepy crawly animal origami; [by] Duy Nguyen. Sterling Pub. 2003 96p il hardcover o.p. pa $9.95

Grades: 5 6 7 8 **736**

1. Origami 2. Animals in art

ISBN 0-8069-9012-0; 1-4027-2229-X (pa)

LC 2002-15507

This offers instructions for creating origami representations of animals such as alligators, turtles, tarantulas, geckos, lobsters, and grasshoppers

"Origami purists should be aware that all of the 13 creatures diagrammed here require scissors cuts, and several are assembled with glue. . . . Nguyen includes drawings and color photos of finished models, and uses standard origami notation in his easy-to-follow diagrams." SLJ

Monster origami. Sterling Pub. 2007 96p il pa $9.95

Grades: 5 6 7 8 **736**

1. Origami 2. Monsters

ISBN 978-1-4027-4014-5 (pa); 1-4027-4014-X (pa)

LC 2007003244

This "volume offers step-by-step instructions for using paper to create 'creatures of horror from books and movies.' . . . Nguyen begins with an overview of basic folds, each demonstrated in clear illustrations. . . . Nguyen shows, in easy-to-follow diagrams, how to use the folds in intricate combinations to create an array of familiar, frightening characters, ranging from Count Dracula to Godzilla's foe, King Ghidora. A final spread shows color photographs of the finished projects." Booklist

Origami birds. Sterling Pub. 2006 96p il $19.95

Grades: 5 6 7 8 **736**

1. Origami 2. Birds in art

ISBN 978-1-4027-1932-5; 1-4027-1932-9

LC 2005037669

This offers instructions for creating origami representions of 19 species of birds including cardinals, cockatoos, falcons, flying ducks, parakeets, and penguins

"The instructions are direct and thorough. . . . Spare line drawings show each step of construction, and color photos spotlight the finished project against a background photo of the bird's natural habitat." Booklist

Under the sea origami; [by] Duy Nguyen. Sterling Pub. 2004 96p il hardcover o.p. pa $9.95

Grades: 5 6 7 8 **736**

1. Origami 2. Marine animals in art

ISBN 1-4027-1541-2; 1-4027-2790-9 (pa)

LC 2004-3341

This "set of origami challenges includes step diagrams, with standard notation, for an elegant seahorse, two menacing-looking sharks, and 16 other marine models—all constructed from one or two sheets of origami paper, and many requiring scissors and/or glue." SLJ

738 Ceramic arts

Spilsbury, Louise, 1963-
Mother nature, designer; [by] Louise and Richard Spilsbury. Cherrytree Books 2008 24p il (Start-up art and design) lib bdg $24.25
Grades: 2 3 4   **738**
1. Nature craft
ISBN 978-1-84234-526-9 (lib bdg); 1-84234-526-5 (lib bdg)   LC 2007-46390
First published 2007 in the United Kingdom
"Examines the patterns and colors that exist naturally in habitats and animal life, tells how they have inspired great artists such as Henri Rousseau. . . . Includes a wide range of possible activities to extend the information provided, often suggesting further research on the Internet. . . . [This book is] well designed, with a large, bold font; clear and ample photography; and interesting layout." SLJ

738.1 Ceramic arts—Techniques, procedures, apparatus, equipment, materials

Kenney, Karen Latchana, 1974-
Super simple clay projects; fun and easy-to-make crafts for kids. ABDO Pub. Company 2010 32p il (Super simple crafts) lib bdg $17.95
Grades: K 1 2 3 4   **738.1**
1. Pottery 2. Clay 3. Handicraft
ISBN 978-1-60453-623-2 (lib bdg); 1-60453-623-3 (lib bdg)   LC 2009-351
"Colorful photos; clean layout in a bright, primary palette; and large, abundant step-by-step instructional photos give [this book] great appeal. The . . . crafts . . . are functional and attractive. . . . [The book] shows kids how to make a pencil holder out of an empty can, for example. . . . Readily obtainable household materials and easy-to-follow instructions mean that children can do these crafts independently." SLJ
Includes glossary

Llimós, Anna
Easy clay crafts in 5 steps. Enslow Elementary 2008 31p il (Easy crafts in 5 steps) lib bdg $22.60
Grades: 2 3 4   **738.1**
1. Clay 2. Ceramics
ISBN 978-0-7660-3085-5 (lib bdg); 0-7660-3085-7 (lib bdg)
Original Spanish edition 2005
The offers instructions for 14 clay craft projects, among them a pear-shaped box, a flower vase, and a paperweight
The text is "easy to read, and the results are quirky and pleasing; steps are illustrated with bright photographs." Horn Book Guide
Includes bibliographical references

738.5 Mosaics

Harris, Nathaniel
Mosaics. PowerKids Press 2009 30p il (Stories in art) lib bdg $25.25
Grades: 4 5 6 7   **738.5**
1. Mosaics
ISBN 978-1-4042-4438-2; 1-4042-4438-7   LC 2007052714
"After introducing the ancient roots of mosaic art in many cultures, this colorfully illustrated book discusses the methods used in making mosaics. Each of the next six double-page spreads presents a single, narrative mosaic. . . . Four mosaic craft ideas follow, with detailed instructions and photos of key construction steps as well as finished products. . . . [Illustrated with] fine color photos. . . . This book nicely combines art appreciation with hands-on learning." Booklist

739.27 Jewelry

Kenney, Karen Latchana, 1974-
Super simple jewelry; fun and easy-to-make crafts for kids. ABDO Pub. Co. 2010 32p il (Super simple crafts) lib bdg $17.95
Grades: K 1 2 3 4   **739.27**
1. Jewelry 2. Handicraft
ISBN 978-1-6045-3625-6 (lib bdg); 1-6045-3625-X (lib bdg)   LC 2009000354
"From bright jewelry pendants made from metal washers to necklaces made from scrap-paper beads, the likable projects featured in this slim title create bright baubles from easy-to-find, inexpensive materials. Each spread combines sharp photos both during construction and then in their finished state, and the book's design makes following along easy." Booklist

741.2 Drawing and drawings—Techniques, procedures, apparatus, equipment, materials

Emberley, Ed
Ed Emberley's big green drawing book. Little, Brown 1979 91p il pa $10.99 hardcover o.p.
Grades: 2 3 4 5   **741.2**
1. Drawing
ISBN 0-316-23596-2 (pa)   LC 79-16247
The author "combines basic shapes (circles, triangles, lines, squiggles) to create a variety of cartoon people and animals. The crisp green-and-black illustrations on a white background are large and well spaced. . . . As in his other drawing books, Emberley's wordless step-by-step method is easy to follow; even very young children can successfully reproduce the simple but appealing figures." SLJ

Ed Emberley's big red drawing book. Little, Brown 1987 unp il pa $10.99 hardcover o.p.
Grades: 2 3 4 5   **741.2**
1. Drawing
ISBN 0-316-23435-4 (pa)   LC 87-3091

Emberley, Ed—*Continued*

The author explains "how to create objects and figures by building up a series of simple lines and squiggles into a more complicated and complete whole. The color red suggests most of the subjects, among them a U.S. flag, a fire engine, and assorted red-and-green Christmas items." Booklist

Ed Emberley's drawing book: make a world. Little, Brown 1972 unp il pa $6.99 hardcover o.p.
Grades: 2 3 4 5   **741.2**
1. Drawing
ISBN 0-316-78972-0 (pa)

"Emberley gives directions for drawing, among a myriad of other things, 10 different kinds of cars, 16 varieties of trucks, and animals of all species including anteaters and dinosaurs." Book World

"The final three pages, which supply suggestions for making comic strips, posters, mobiles and games, help make the volume particularly appealing. For all developing artists and even plain scribblers." Horn Book

Ed Emberley's fingerprint drawing book. Little, Brown 2000 unp il hardcover o.p. pa $7.99 *
Grades: 2 3 4 5   **741.2**
1. Drawing
ISBN 0-316-23215-7; 0-316-78969-0 (pa)
                     LC 00-31026

"A step-by-step approach to drawing for beginners and those who are artistically challenged. Each figure introduced can be made with a basic fingerprint or more, and then lines and dots are placed beneath the form to take budding artists to a complete picture. It is so easy to do that even very young children can enjoy a simple art adventure." SLJ

Ed Emberley's great thumbprint drawing book. Little, Brown 1977 37p il lib bdg $15.95; pa $6.95
Grades: 2 3 4 5   **741.2**
1. Drawing
ISBN 0-316-23613-6 (lib bdg); 0-316-23668-3 (pa)
                     LC 76-57346

"The artist shows how to combine thumbprints and simple lines to create a multitude of animals, people, birds, and flowers." Booklist

"There is little text; most of the book consists of illustrations, step-by-step, of making pictures out of thumbprints. A few Emberley embellishments and a page that suggests other ways of making prints (carrot or potato) are included." Bull Cent Child Books

Hanson, Anders, 1980-

Cool drawing; the art of creativity for kids! [by] Anders Hanson. ABDO Pub. Co. 2009 32p il (Cool art) lib bdg $24.21
Grades: 2 3 4   **741.2**
1. Drawing
ISBN 978-1-60453-142-8 (lib bdg); 1-60453-142-8 (lib bdg)   LC 2008-8642

This book about drawing is "well organized, with clearly written sections . . . and several clever projects and exercises. . . . [It] should have substantial child appeal." SLJ

Includes glossary and bibliographical references

Luxbacher, Irene, 1970-

1 2 3 I can draw! Kids Can Press 2008 23p il (Starting art) $14.95; pa $5.95
Grades: 2 3 4   **741.2**
1. Drawing
ISBN 978-1-55453-039-7; 1-55453-039-3; 978-1-55453-152-3 (pa); 1-55453-152-7 (pa)

"A creative, eye-catching illustrated cover will attract kids to this book, and the large print; softly colored, childlike drawings; and simple sentences are sure to keep them interested in pursuing art on their own. A 'self-portrait' shows how position, figure, clothing, facial expressions, and hair are combined to create a lively piece of artwork. Materials needed are clearly labeled and accompanied by sharp color photos or neat sketches. In three easy steps, children can see how to use lines and shapes to draw faces, features, expressions, a figure drawing, or an astronaut. . . . This title is sure to please beginning artists." SLJ

Temple, Kathryn

Drawing; the only drawing book you'll ever need to be the artist you've always wanted to be; [by] Kathryn Temple. Lark Books 2005 112p il (Art for kids) $17.95 *
Grades: 5 6 7 8   **741.2**
1. Drawing
ISBN 1-57990-587-0   LC 2004-17909

Contents: Drawing basics; Line drawing; Light & shadow; Scale & proportion; Perspective; Faces & bodies; Still life and drawing nature; Drawing on the imagination; Composition

This "introduction to essential drawing techniques builds from the starting points of lines and simple shapes. . . . Eight concise chapters explore seeing with artist's eyes, line drawing, light and shadow, proportion and scale, perspective, drawing faces, drawing bodies, and using imagination. The succinct text reads smoothly and is written in a clear, understandable style. Sample sketches and crisp, color photographs extend the text." SLJ

741.5   Cartoons, caricatures, comics

Abadzis, Nick

Laika. First Second Books 2007 205p il $17.95 *
Grades: 5 6 7 8 9 10 11 12 Adult   **741.5**
1. Graphic novels 2. Space flight—Graphic novels
ISBN 978-1-59643-101-0; 1-59643-101-6
                     LC 2006-51907

Laika was the abandoned puppy destined to become Earth's first space traveler. This is her journey. Along with Laika, there is Korolev, once a political prisoner and now a driven engineer at the top of the Soviet space program, and Yelena, the lab technician responsible for Laika's health and life. The book includes a bibliography of books and websites

"Although the tightly packed and vividly inked panels of Abadzis's art tell an impressively complex tale . . . Laika's palpable spirit is what readers will remember." Publ Wkly

Artell, Mike, 1948-

Funny cartooning for kids. Sterling Pub. 2007 128p il $17.95

Grades: 3 4 5 6   **741.5**
1. Cartooning—Technique 2. Drawing
ISBN 978-1-4027-2260-8

"This volume approaches the basics of traditional cartooning with what is funny—what creates humor. Pointing out the difference between 'regular' illustrations and cartoons, the author divides the book into chapters that give readers instruction in six areas—exaggeration; simplification; animals and objects doing 'people' things; people in different poses; unusual body types and gestures; and monsters, weird creatures, and aliens. . . . Black-and-white pen-and-ink drawings throughout are designed to encourage readers to add and create their own individual changes to cartoon figures." SLJ

Baltazar, Art

Tiny Titans: welcome to the treehouse. DC Comics 2009 144p il $12.99

Grades: K 1 2 3   **741.5**
1. Graphic novels 2. Superhero graphic novels
3. Humorous graphic novels
ISBN 978-1-4012-2078-5

Here are the Teen Titans as never seen before: as little kids. They all attend Sidekick City Elementary School, where their principal and teachers are supervillains, and they get into playground showdowns with the Fearsome Five. Baltazar and Franco, who have created such characters as Patrick the Wolf Boy, present a series of short stories, most one or two pages long, featuring little kid versions of Robin, Starfire, Wonder Girl, Cassie, Speedy, Kid Flash, Cyborg, Beast Boy, Raven, and more. While these stories are written for the young readers, the humor may also appeal to teens and adults.

Other titles in this series are:
Tiny Titans: adventures in awesomeness (2009)
Tiny Titans: Sidekickin' it (2010)
Tiny Titans go camping (2010)
Tiny Titans and the science fair (2010)

Bannister (Person)

The shadow door; art by Bannister; story by Nykko; [colors by Jaffre; translation by Carol Klio Burrell] Graphic Universe 2009 46p il (The Elsewhere chronicles) lib bdg $27.93; pa $6.95

Grades: 4 5 6 7   **741.5**
1. Graphic novels 2. Horror graphic novels
ISBN 978-0-7613-4459-9 (lib bdg); 0-7613-4459-4 (lib bdg); 978-0-7613-3963-2 (pa); 0-7613-3963-9 (pa)
         LC 2008-39442

Four friends discover a movie projector that opens a passageway into a world threatened by creatures of shadow, where their only weapon is light

"This is an undeniably attractive offering, as the artwork, with deep darks and effervescent lights splayed across large, glossy pages, is strikingly rendered. . . . [This] should have no problem gaining an appreciative readership." Booklist

Other titles in this series are:
Shadow spies (2009)
Master of shadows (2009)

Barba, Corey

Yam: bite-size chunks. Top Shelf Productions 2008 88p il pa $10

Grades: PreK K 1 2 3   **741.5**
1. Graphic novels 2. Humorous graphic novels
3. Friendship—Graphic novels 4. Stories without words
ISBN 978-1-60309-014-8 (pa); 1-60309-014-2 (pa)

Yam is a little boy who wears a hooded suit and has a magical backpack. On the island of La Leche de la Luna, Yam meets a sentient cupcake, cheers up a crying raincloud with a lollipop, plays with his friends Gato and Mary, and has a four-legged pet TV that sleeps in bed with him. Along with short stories that originally appeared as mini comics and in Nickelodeon Magazine, the book includes an original story in which Yam develops a crush on a beautiful toy seller in town. He spends so much time daydreaming about her that he neglects all his friends.

"The wordless panels are quite effective with the tenderly drawn art powerfully conveying nuanced moments." SLJ

Big fat Little Lit; [edited by] Art Spiegelman and Francoise Mouly. Puffin 2006 144p il pa $14.99

Grades: 2 3 4 5 6 7 8   **741.5**
1. Graphic novels 2. Folklore—Graphic novels
ISBN 0-14-240706-2

This volume collects all three previously published Little Lit books: *Little Lit: Once Upon a Time*, *Little Lit: Strange Stories for Strange Kids*, and *Little Lit: It Was a Dark and Silly Night*. Many comics creators and children's book writers and illustrators contributed stories, including Ian Falconer, Daniel Clowes, Maurice Sendak, David Sedaris, Chris Ware, Jules Feiffer, Barbara McClintock, Crockett Johnson, J. Otto Siebold, Neil Gaiman, Art Spiegelman, and Lemony Snicket.

Bliss, Harry

Luke on the loose; a Toon Book. TOON Books 2009 32p il map $12.95 *

Grades: PreK K 1 2   **741.5**
1. Graphic novels 2. New York (State)—Graphic novels 3. Humorous graphic novels
ISBN 978-1-935179-00-9; 1-935179-00-4
         LC 2008-35699

A young boy's fascination with pigeons soon erupts into a full-blown chase around Central Park, across the Brooklyn Bridge, through a fancy restaurant, and into the sky

"The cartoon panels are so successful at engaging readers that young children do not have to be able to read the text to enjoy the story. Each drawing is filled with humorous details." SLJ

Bullock, Mike

Lions, tigers, and bears, vol. 1: Fear and pride; [by] Mike Bullock and Jack Lawrence. Image Comics 2006 128p il pa $12.99

Grades: 2 3 4 5 6   **741.5**
1. Graphic novels 2. Adventure graphic novels
ISBN 1-58240-657-X

When Joey Price has to move away from his grandmother, she gives him a new set of stuffed animals that

Bullock, Mike—*Continued*

she says will guard him from nightmares. And one night, he discovers that the stuffed animals are real, and unfortunately, so are the Beasties, the nightmares in his closet

Caldwell, Ben

Fantasy! cartooning; [by] Ben Caldwell. Sterling Pub. Co. 2005 95p il pa $9.95

Grades: 5 6 7 8   **741.5**

1. Cartooning—Technique 2. Fantasy in art
ISBN 1-4027-1612-5   LC 2005041676

Caldwell's "drawing style is . . . a blend of modern Disney (Hercules, Mulan), Don Bluth (Dragon's Lair), and the Cartoon Network (Powderpuff Girls, Samurai Jack, Star Wars: Clone Wars). . . . Caldwell shows original thinking, and his technique is exciting, modern, and unique." SLJ

Cammuso, Frank

Knights of the lunch table: the dodgeball chronicles. Graphix 2008 141p il pa $9.99

Grades: 3 4 5 6   **741.5**

1. Graphic novels 2. Humorous graphic novels 3. School stories—Graphic novels
ISBN 978-0-439-90322-6 (pa); 0-439-90322-X (pa)

Artie King's family has moved and now he has to start at a new school, Camelot Middle School. Dodgeball is the big game at Camelot, and the Horde is a champion team; the Horde members are also the worst bullies in the school. . . . Artie immediately gets into trouble with Joe, the leader of the Horde. . . . However, he manages to open the broken old locker . . . [which] provides mysterious, useful stuff, such as a lunch. Joe challenges Artie to a dodgeball game; Artie has new friends Percy and Wayne who'll help him, and then he meets Gwen. And science teacher Mr. Merlyn is also on his side.

"Arthurian legend gets an update for young readers in this outstanding graphic novel. . . . The funny, fast-paced tale of young Arthur's quest to defeat the bullies stands well on its own. The appealing illustrations are full of color, action, and life." SLJ

Another title in this series is:
Knights of the lunch table: the dragon players (2009)

Otto's orange day; a Toon Book; by Frank Cammuso & Jay Lynch. TOON Books 2008 40p il $12.95 *

Grades: K 1 2   **741.5**

1. Graphic novels 2. Cats—Graphic novels 3. Magic—Graphic novels 4. Color—Graphic novels
ISBN 978-0-9799238-2-1; 0-9799238-2-4
LC 2007040759

"When Otto the cat meets a magical genie, he knows just what to wish for: he makes the whole world orange! At first, this new, bright world seems like a lot of fun, but when his mom serves orange spinach for lunch, Otto realizes that his favorite color isn't the best color for everything." Publisher's note

"This is a text-book example of how to use page composition, expanding panel size, color, and stylized figures to make sequential art fresh, energetic, and lively." Booklist

Cavallaro, Michael, 1969-

L. Frank Baum's The Wizard of Oz; the graphic novel. Puffin Books 2005 176p pa $9.99

Grades: 3 4 5 6 7 8   **741.5**

1. Baum, L. Frank, 1856-1919—Adaptations 2. Graphic novels 3. Fantasy graphic novels
ISBN 0-14-240471-3   LC 2006-273599

"A Byron Preiss book"

This graphic novel adaptation remains true to the story by Baum: Dorothy and her dog Toto are whisked to Oz, where they meet the Tin Woodsman, the Cowardly Lion, and the Scarecrow and they all journey to find the Wizard to grant their desires.

"The black-and-white illustrations are action packed, and the characters, with their Bazooka Joe eyes, combine classic comic touches with the popular manga style. Reluctant readers will gravitate toward the cartoon cover." SLJ

Colfer, Eoin, 1965-

Artemis Fowl: the graphic novel; adapted by Eoin Colfer and Andrew Donkin; art by Giovanni Rigano; color by Paolo Lammana. Hyperion Books for Children 2007 unp il $18.99; pa $9.99 *

Grades: 4 5 6 7 8 9   **741.5**

1. Graphic novels 2. Fantasy graphic novels 3. Adventure graphic novels
ISBN 978-0-7868-4881-2; 0-7868-4881-2; 978-0-7868-4882-9 (pa); 0-7868-4882-0 (pa)

Twelve-year-old genius and criminal mastermind Artemis Fowl runs his missing father's crime empire and gets his hands on a book that will give him access to the underground fairy world. This graphic novel adaptation gives the book a European look and color palette

"Excellent use of color and shading gives the panels a tremendous sense of light with enchanting effect. Characters are expressively brought to life with fun, exaggerated style." SLJ

Collicutt, Paul

City in peril! Templar Books/Candlewick Press 2009 unp il (Robot City) pa $8.99

Grades: 3 4 5   **741.5**

1. Graphic novels 2. Science fiction graphic novels 3. Robots—Graphic novels 4. Mystery graphic novels
ISBN 978-0-7636-4120-7 (pa); 0-7636-4120-0 (pa)
LC 2009-931660

"Curtis is a walking, talking lighthouseheaded robot who protects the coast of Robot City with his trusty human crew, Ali and Steve. When an oil rig out at sea catches fire, Curtis rushes to the rescue and then investigates the fishy mystery of the causes of this near disaster. . . . The illustrations . . . are full of retro-comicbook-style action and classic movieserial banter." Kirkus

In Robot City, a metropolis of 15 million humans and 1 million robots, Curtis, the Colossal CoastGuard Robot works as part of a team of robots and humans to keep the Robot City Bay safe. In the middle of the night, the Red Star oil rig sends out a desperate distress call when something attacks it in the middle of a storm. Curtis, who looks like a light house on huge, long legs, helps to save the crew on the oil rig, but there's something out

Collicutt, Paul—*Continued*

there in the ocean, and it means to attack Robot City. He has suffered damage in one of his legs, but Curtis knows he has to stop the menace. This science fiction adventure is full of action and derring-do with colorful retro-style comic book illustrations. Young readers, as well as adults, will appreciate the twist in the story.

Craddock, Erik

Stone rabbit: Pirate Palooza. Random House Children's Books 2009 96p $11.99; pa $5.99

Grades: 2 3 4 5   **741.5**

1. Graphic novels 2. Adventure graphic novels 3. Humorous graphic novels 4. Pirates—Graphic novels

ISBN 978-0-375-95660-7; 978-0-375-85660-0 (pa)

Our unnamed bunny hero plays at pro wrestling with his friend Andy when they break a leg on the coffee table. On their way to buy a replacement leg, Andy gets sidetracked to the local comics store for new comics day; and the rabbit finds a wooden leg. It's the peg leg of Barnacle Bob, a legendary pirate. When the rabbit uses it to fix his coffee table, he releases the ghosts of Barnacle Bob, his crew, and his ship, the Biscotti. Andy becomes the cabin boy while our rabbit hero becomes the first mate, and there's all kinds of trouble.

"This book will give those children who love the ridiculous just what they want: a zany, mile-a-minute graphic novel. . . . The bold illustrations are bursting at the seams with energy." SLJ

Other titles in this series are:

BC Mambo (2009)

Deep-Space Disco (2009)

Superhero stampede (2009)

Crane, Jordan

The clouds above. Fantagraphics 2005 216p il $18.95

Grades: 3 4 5 6 7 8   **741.5**

1. Graphic novels 2. Fantasy graphic novels

ISBN 1-560976-27-6

Simon and his cat Jack embark on an adventure among the clouds one day when Simon skips school and finds a rickety stairway leading skyward. They find a friendly cloud, flee thunderstorms and trick a flock of belligerent birds, only to find themselves back at school.

"Everything's exciting . . . and the dialogue is witty and bubbly. . . . The book is a joy to look at—Crane's loose, gliding lines burst with character, and his compositional gifts make every panel worth contemplating on its own." Publ Wkly

Davis, Eleanor

The secret science alliance and the copycat crook. Bloomsbury 2009 153p il $18.99; pa $10.99 *

Grades: 3 4 5 6 7 8   **741.5**

1. Graphic novels 2. Inventors—Fiction 3. School stories 4. Humorous graphic novels 5. Adventure graphic novels

ISBN 978-1-59990-142-8; 1-59990-142-0; 978-1-59990-396-5 (pa); 1-59990-396-2 (pa)

LC 2008-45399

Eleven-year-old Julian Calendar thought changing schools would mean leaving his "nerdy" persona behind, but instead he forms an alliance with fellow inventors Greta and Ben and works with them to prevent an adult from using one of their gadgets for nefarious purposes

"With its frenetically eye-catching, full-color panels chock-full of humorous and informative detail, Davis's first (of many, one hopes) graphic adventure of the SSA pumps new life into the kids' secret society formula." Kirkus

Stinky; a Toon Book. RAW Junior 2008 40p il $12.95 *

Grades: K 1 2 3   **741.5**

1. Graphic novels 2. Humorous graphic novels 3. Friendship—Graphic novels 4. Monsters—Graphic novels

ISBN 978-0-9799238-4-5; 0-9799238-4-0

LC 2007-94387

A Geisel Award honor book, 2009

Stinky the monster is sort of a young Shrek—a little grumpy, he loves pickles and likes his swamp nicely yucky and mucky, with no kids. Kids are gross, they like to take baths. When a new boy dares to build a treehouse in the middle of his swamp, Stinky takes action with all kinds of crazy plans to scare the boy away. However, every plan backfires, so what's a monster to do?

"The charming cartoon artwork, full of humorous details, complements the text, and the muted color scheme makes Stinky endearing rather than scary. The simple vocabulary and repetition of words make the text accessible for emergent readers." SLJ

Davis, Jim, 1945-

Garfield: 30 years of laughs & lasagna; the life & times of a fat, furry legend! Ballantine Books 2008 287p il $35

Grades: 4 5 6 7 8   **741.5**

1. Comic books, strips, etc. 2. Cats—Graphic novels

ISBN 978-0-345-50379-4; 0-345-50379-1

"Davis calls Garfield 'a human in a catsuit,' and the sarcastic feline's wry, egotistical observations and love of lasagna, donuts, and naps are a winning and enduring formula. . . . Readers will find plenty of slapstick humor and visual gags in this collection to entertain them. Throughout the book, Davis offers occasional insights about his career and the development of Garfield. They are written in simple language." SLJ

De Campi, Alex

Kat & Mouse: Teacher torture; [by] Alex de Campi; art by Frederica Manfredi. Tokyopop 2006 96p il pa $5.99

Grades: 4 5 6 7 8 9   **741.5**

1. Graphic novels 2. Mystery fiction 3. Mystery graphic novels

ISBN 1-59816-548-8

Middle schooler Kat starts at a posh school where her father has been hired as the new science teacher, but all is not well. Accidents happen in the science lab, and an anonymous student threatens worse unless Kat's dad passes all the rich, popular students. Kat decides to investigate, aided by her one new friend, Mouse, the rebellious computer nerd and would-be CSI investigator.

Espinosa, Rod

The courageous princess. Dark Horse Comics 2007 c2003 240p il pa $9.95

Grades: 3 4 5 6 7 8 9   **741.5**

1. Graphic novels 2. Fantasy graphic novels 3. Princesses—Graphic novels

ISBN 978-1-59307-719-8

This new edition from Dark Horse is in black and white; the previous Antarctic Press editions were in color.

Plain Princess Mabelrose doesn't get along with the other, prettier princesses, but her intelligence helps her when a dragon kidnaps her. Instead of waiting for rescue, Mabelrose escapes, taking a friendly hedgehog and a few useful-looking items (a pouch, a length of rope) that she doesn't know are magic.

Farshtey, Greg, 1965-

Bionicle #1: rise of the Toa Nuva. Papercutz 2008 unp il $12.95; pa $7.95

Grades: 3 4 5 6   **741.5**

1. Graphic novels 2. Science fiction graphic novels 3. Adventure graphic novels

ISBN 978-1-59707-110-9; 978-1-59707-109-3 (pa)

Six mighty heroes the Toa arrive on a tropical island to find a land under siege. The Great Spirit Mata Nui has been cast into an unending sleep by the evil Makuta. Now Makuta is attacking the island's Matoran villagers with vicious Rahi beasts. The Toa must combine their skills and elemental and mask powers to defeat Makuta and restore peace to the island.

"The art is vivid and attention grabbing, and the story line, which weaves in Polynesian mythology, is exciting and action-packed." SLJ

Flight explorer; edited by Kazu Kibuiski. Villard

2008 112p il pa $10

Grades: 4 5 6 7   **741.5**

1. Graphic novels 2. Science fiction graphic novels 3. Fantasy graphic novels 4. Adventure graphic novels 5. Humorous graphic novels

ISBN 978-0-345-50313-8 (pa); 0-345-50313-9 (pa)

This anthology includes stories that Kibuishi kept from Flight Volume 4 because they had all-ages appeal, as well as stories submitted especially for this volume. Kibuishi's own Copper and his talking dog cross a deep canyon by leaping onto mushrooms, only to discover the vegetation is intelligent. Kean Soo's Jellaby and his human friends frolic in the snow. Missile Mouse by Jake Parker defends a village on another planet, only to discover his coming was prophesied (this story includes two uses of the word "crap"). The other stories will appeal to younger readers, while some of the humor will also appeal to older readers. Other than the one bad word in "Missile Mouse" (noted above), there shouldn't be any other content that would keep this book out of most elementary and middle schools.

"Every story has a layout that promotes an acute sense of pacing and showcases the crisp, defined, full-color art." SLJ

Frampton, Otis

Oddly Normal; volume 1; written & illustrated by Otis Frampton. Viper Comics 2006 unp il pa $11.95 *

Grades: 4 5 6 7 8 9   **741.5**

1. Graphic novels 2. Fantasy graphic novels 3. Humorous graphic novels

ISBN 0-9777883-0-X

"Oddly Normal, a half witch with green hair, pointed ears, and an aversion to rain, is miserable. She is an outcast at school, and her parents are clueless about how abnormal the Normal family is. When an accidental wish on her tenth birthday goes awry, causing her parents to disappear, Oddly goes to live with her great-aunt in Fignation. . . . Frampton's art is refreshingly quirky, with strong lines and bold use of color. The world he creates is full of fun and whimsy." Booklist

Friesen, Ray

Cupcakes of doom! Don't Eat Any Bugs Productions 2008 98p il pa $12.95

Grades: 3 4 5 6 7 8   **741.5**

1. Graphic novels 2. Adventure graphic novels 3. Humorous graphic novels 4. Pirates—Graphic novels

ISBN 978-0-9802314-1-0 (pa); 0-9802314-1-8 (pa)

The Pirate band led by Captain Scurvybeard must do battle with the Vikings to decide the fate of the kingdom called Pellmellia. With a decidedly shifty fellow named Flambe testing them to see if they deserve to be pirates, Yoho Joseph, Peglegless Pete (he's just a kid), Lester the parrot, Pete's sister Jamie, and the rest of the crew must find the long lost recipe for the Cupcakes of Doom, or the Deliciously-Evil Viking Pie will take over as the people's favorite baked good. The book is full of silly humor, wacky characters (including identical twin sea serpents and a Viking penguin), and a lot of action without violence or bad language. The book is suitable for younger readers, but adults will enjoy the silliness and catch more of the jokes

Fuji, Machiko

The big adventures of Majoko, volume 1; illustrated by Tomomi Mizuna. UDON Entertainment 2009 200p il (Manga for kids) pa $7.99

Grades: 3 4 5 6 7 8   **741.5**

1. Witches—Graphic novels 2. Graphic novels 3. Manga 4. Fantasy graphic novels

ISBN 978-1-89737-681-2 (pa); 1-89737-681-2 (pa)

"Young witch Majoko sends her diary to the human world to find an adventuring partner and through it finds shy, quiet Nana. Together the two girls have a rollicking series of escapades. . . . Characters are simply drawn, but the backgrounds are nicely detailed and the plot elements are clearly thought out and easy to follow. . . . The content is very appropriate for the intended audience." Booklist

Giarrano, Vince, 1960-

Comics crash course; [by] Vincent Giarrano. Impact Books 2004 127p il pa $19.99 *

Grades: 5 6 7 8   741.5
    1. Cartoons and caricatures 2. Drawing
    ISBN 1-58180-533-0   LC 2004-43969

This is a guide to creating comic book stories and characters.

This offers "plenty of great art advice, striking imagery, and just enough edginess to satisfy most aspiring comic-book artists. . . . An excellent introduction to comic drawing, composition, and graphic storytelling." SLJ

Goscinny, 1926-1977

Asterix the Gaul; [by] René Goscinny and Albert Uderzo. Orion Media 2004 48p il map $12.95; pa $9.95

Grades: 4 5 6 7 8 9 10 11 12   741.5
    1. Graphic novels 2. Humorous graphic novels
    3. France—History—Graphic novels
    ISBN 0-7528-6604-4; 0-7528-6605-2 (pa)
    Translated from the French

Meet Asterix, a diminutive but extremely strong Gaul living in ancient France during the time of the Roman Republic. Together with his friend Obelix, Asterix continually outwits the Roman Legionnaires sent to conquer Gaul for Julius Caesar. Full of puns and outrageous humor, the books also manage to teach a lot of history. This is the first in a long-running series of graphic novels translated from the original French.

Other titles in this series are:
Asterix and Caesar's Gift
Asterix and Cleopatra
Asterix and the actress
Asterix and the banquet
Asterix and the big fight
Asterix and the cauldron
Asterix and the Goths
Asterix and the Great Crossing
Asterix and the laurel wreath
Asterix the legionary
Asterix and the Normans
Asterix and the Roman Agent
Asterix and the soothsayer
Asterix at the Olympic Games
Asterix in Belgium
Asterix in Britain
Asterix in Corsica
Asterix in Spain
Asterix in Switzerland
Asterix Obelix and Co.
Asterix the gladiator
Asterix The Mansions of the Gods

Gownley, Jimmy

Amelia rules!: the whole world's crazy! ibooks 2003 176p $24.95; pa $14.95

Grades: 3 4 5 6   741.5
    1. Graphic novels 2. Humorous graphic novels
    3. Friendship—Graphic novels 4. Family life—Graphic novels
    ISBN 0-9712169-3-2; 0-9712169-2-4 (pa)

"Amelia . . . is getting used to life with her newly divorced mom and her hip, young aunt Tanner; settling in at a strange new school; and finding a group of friends. Amelia is no sweet innocent, nor are her three G.A.S.P (Gathering of Awesome Superpals) buddies: Reggie, superhero in the making; Rhonda, Amelia's tough bete noire with a fourth-grade 'thing' for Reggie; and quiet, mysterious Pajamaman. Jealousy, meanness, sadness, and confusion, as well as surprising generosity, and love crisscross the pages in energetic, freewheeling, full-color cartoon art that unwraps a kid's-eye view of life honestly, poignantly, and with a hefty dollop of melodrama." Booklist

Other titles in this series are:
Amelia rules!: What makes you happy? (2004)
Amelia rules! Superheroes (2005)
Amelia rules! a very ninja Christmas (2009)
Amelia rules! When the past is a present (2010)
Amelia rules! The tweenage guide to not being unpopular (2010)

Grant, Alan, 1949-

Robert Louis Stevenson's Strange case of Dr. Jekyll and Mr. Hyde; adapted by Alan Grant; illustrated by Cam Kennedy; colored and lettered by Jamie Grant. Tundra Books 2008 40p il pa $11.95

Grades: 6 7 8 9 10   741.5
    1. Stevenson, Robert Louis, 1850-1894—Adaptations
    2. Graphic novels 3. Horror graphic novels
    ISBN 978-0-88776-882-8 (pa); 0-88776-882-2 (pa)

"Stevenson's classic tale takes on a new format in a vivid graphic novel. This mysterious story of the struggle between good and evil is one that has been popular since its publication and continues to hold its appeal. Much about this adaptation honors the original version of the story—the language of the period remains true, and the drawings of 1880s London and the furnishings and fashion within it are realistic as well." Voice Youth Advocates

Guibert, Emmanuel, 1964-

Sardine in outer space; [by] Emmanuel Guibert; illustrated by Joann Sfar; translated by Sasha Watson; colorist, Walter Pezzali. First Second 2006 128p il pa $12.95

Grades: 3 4 5 6   741.5
    1. Graphic novels 2. Science fiction graphic novels
    3. Humorous graphic novels
    ISBN 978-1-59643-126-3 (pa); 1-59643-126-1 (pa)
                   LC 2005-21790

In this volume of twelve interconnected stories, little space pirate Sardine cruises in the spaceship Huckleberry with Uncle Yellow Shoulder and Little Louie. They do battle with Supermuscleman, who runs a tough space orphanage where children are taught "good behavior"

"Sfar's off-kilter, slightly uglified art, reminiscent of a toned-down Beavis and Butthead, gives the simple fun an unusual punch." Booklist

Other titles in this series are:
Sardine in outer space 2 (2006)
Sardine in outer space 3 (2007)
Sardine in outer space 4 (2007)
Sardine in outer space 5 (2008)
Sardine in outer space 6 (2009)

Hale, Shannon

Rapunzel's revenge; [by] Shannon and Dean Hale; illustrated by Nathan Hale. Bloomsbury 2008 144p il map $18.99; pa $14.99 *

Grades: 5 6 7 8   **741.5**
1. Graphic novels 2. Humorous graphic novels 3. Fantasy graphic novels 4. Fairy tales—Graphic novels
ISBN   978-1-59990-070-4;   1-59990-070-X; 978-1-59990-288-3 (pa); 1-59990-288-5 (pa)
LC 2007-37670
In this graphic novel Rapunzel is raised in a grand villa surrounded by towering walls. Rapunzel dreams of a different mother than Gothel, the woman she calls Mother. She climbs over the wall and finds out the truth. Her real mother, Kate, is a slave in Gothel's gold mine. In this Old West retelling, Rapunzel uses her hair as a lasso and to take on outlaws—including Gothel.
"The dialogue is witty, the story is an enticing departure from the original, and the illustrations are magically fun and expressive." SLJ
Another title about these characters is:
Calamity Jack (2009)

Hart, Christopher

The cartoonist's big book of drawing animals; [by] Christopher Hart. Watson-Guptill Publications 2008 224p il pa $21.95

Grades: 3 4 5 6   **741.5**
1. Animals in art 2. Cartoons and caricatures 3. Drawing
ISBN 978-0-8230-1421-7 (pa); 0-8230-1421-5 (pa)
LC 2007-29102
"Presents step-by-step instructions, illustrations, and guidelines on how to portray emotions, actions, and more for dozens of cartoon animals, including dogs, cats, elephants, bears, pigs, horses, and birds." Publisher's note
"The simple text that accompanies each drawing explains the artist's choices and focuses readers' attention on important details in each drawing. Children will love this thorough and easy-to-use how-to guide." SLJ

Drawing the new adventure cartoons; cool spies, evil guys and action heroes. Sixth & Spring Books 2008 126p il pa $19.95

Grades: 4 5 6 7   **741.5**
1. Cartoons and caricatures 2. Drawing
ISBN 978-1-933027-60-9 (pa); 1-933027-60-6 (pa)
"This fun guide works best for those with some previous figure-drawing experience. . . . Sections on 'Drawing the Head,' 'Drawing the Teen Action Body,' and 'Using Body Language to Convey Emotion' offer detailed and, for the most part, step-by-step instructions. Subsequent sections . . . provide examples of unique and zany aspects of adventure-style characters. . . . Throughout the book, Hart also includes useful tip boxes, often demonstrating how not to draw a character. These suggestions are invaluable, providing insight into creating kinetic and expressive cartoons." SLJ

Kids draw Manga Shoujo; [by] Christopher Hart. Watson Guptill Publications 2005 54p il (Kids draw) pa $10.95

Grades: 1 2 3 4   **741.5**
1. Cartoons and caricatures 2. Drawing
ISBN 0-8230-2622-1   LC 2004-19367

"Each page takes a character, then shows a step-by-step rendering starting with simple shapes and adding more detailed lines until the final figure is realized. *Manga Shoujo* is full of clean, bold colors and lines. . . . Hart's books are designed for young, casual fans who will appreciate the simplicity of the drawing style and will use these titles as an easy introduction to this art." SLJ

You can draw cartoon animals; a simple step-by-step drawing guide. Walter Foster 2009 120p il (Just for kids!) pa $12.99

Grades: 2 3 4 5 6   **741.5**
1. Drawing 2. Cartoons and caricatures
ISBN 978-1-60058-611-8 (pa); 1-60058-611-2 (pa)
"Hart begins by giving some general guidelines for drawing head and body shapes, and line thickness. Then he demonstrates, step by step, how to draw a variety of animals, both wild and domesticated. He includes an informative paragraph at the beginning of each set of instructions and side notes for some of the steps. . . . The projects are simple but yield a pleasing result reminiscent of animated characters the target age group might see on TV. Colored boarders at the top and bottom of each page unify the book and add visual appeal. Sure to be a favorite." SLJ

Hastings, Jon

Terrabella Smoot and the unsung monsters. SLG Publishing 2005 48p il $10.95

Grades: K 1 2 3   **741.5**
1. Graphic novels 2. Monsters—Graphic novels 3. Fantasy graphic novels
ISBN 1-59362-017-9
When she becomes separated from her family on the way to the Monster of the Year celebration, young monster Terrabella meets up with a loose-lipped dip and other creatures as she makes her way to Lord Thonk's castle. There, she discovers that Lord Thonk, the Monster of the Year, has imprisoned all the monster servants who actually performed the monstrous deeds, and she finds a way to bring justice to the celebration

Hayes, Geoffrey

Benny and Penny in just pretend; a Toon Book; [by] Geoffrey Hayes. RAW Junior 2008 32p il $12.95 *

Grades: PreK K 1   **741.5**
1. Mice—Graphic novels 2. Graphic novels 3. Siblings—Graphic novels
ISBN 978-0-9799238-0-7; 0-9799238-0-8
"How can Benny pretend to be a brave pirate when his pesky little sister, Penny, wants to tag along and is always asking for a hug? He tries to lose her, but when he does, he starts to feel a little lost himself. Then, Penny proves her bravery and saves Benny from a bug." Publisher's note
"The sweet, delicately colored illustrations have an old-fashioned feel that gives the familiar sibling story a timeless quality. . . . The text uses a limited vocabulary with sufficient repetition to help with word recognition. . . . A charmer that will invite repeated readings." Booklist
Other titles about Benny and Penny are:

Hayes, Geoffrey—*Continued*
Benny and Penny in the big no-no! (2009)
Benny and Penny in the toy breaker (2010)

Hergé, 1907-1983
The adventures of Tintin, vol. 1; Tintin in America, Cigars of the Pharaoh, The Blue Lotus. Little, Brown 1994 192p il $18.99
Grades: 4 5 6 7 8 9   **741.5**
  1. Graphic novels 2. Adventure graphic novels
  ISBN 0-316-35940-8
Tintin, the heroic boy reporter from France, travels to America where he outwits gangsters in Chicago of the 1930s and adventures in the Wild West; sails the Mediterranean Sea with faithful dog Snowy and finds himself in a mystery involving a movie tycoon, drugs, and cigars in an ancient Egyptian tomb; then he travels to India to finally solve the mystery. This Little, Brown edition reprints some of the early Tintin adventures published in the 1930s in a 3-in-1 volume. This is the first in a series that reprints most of the Tintin stories by Herge. Librarians and teachers should note that the books retain some stereotypical depictions of people of other cultures and remember that these were acceptable and expected at the time of original publication.

Hoena, B. A., 1966-
Jack and the beanstalk: the graphic novel; retold by Blake A. Hoena; illustrated by Ricardo Tercio. Stone Arch Books 2009 33p il $21.26
Grades: 2 3 4 5   **741.5**
  1. Graphic novels 2. Fairy tales—Graphic novels
  ISBN 978-1-4342-0766-1   LC 2008-6722
Part of the Graphic Spin series
When Jack sells the family cow for a handful of beans, his mother is not pleased. However, they are magic beans, and when Jack plants them, a giant beanstalk grows. Curious about where the beanstalk has gone, Jack climbs it, and finds a giant's home up there. As he brings back such things as a chicken that lays golden eggs, his mother exclaims that he is finding his father's old treasures. But sooner or later, the giant will catch Jack. This graphic novel adaptation includes information about the history of the tale, along with a short glossary and reading questions.

Holm, Jennifer L.
Babymouse: queen of the world. Random House Books for Young Readers 2005 91p il lib bdg $12.99; pa $5.95 *
Grades: 3 4 5 6   **741.5**
  1. Graphic novels 2. Mice—Graphic novels 3. Humorous graphic novels 4. Friendship—Graphic novels 5. Babymouse (Fictional character)
  ISBN 0-375-93229-1 (lib bdg); 0-375-83229-7 (pa)
          LC 2004-51166
"In this energetic comic . . . Babymouse, a wisecracking rodent stand-in for your average, adventure-seeking nine-year-old, strives to capture popular Felicia's goodwill, finally achieving her end at the expense of Wilson Weasel, truest of friends. But, wouldn't you know it, Felicia's world has little to offer a smart, fun-loving mouse, after all." Booklist

Other titles in this series are:
Babymouse: beach babe (2006)
Babymouse burns rubber (2010)
Babymouse: dragonslayer (2009)
Babymouse: heartbreaker (2006)
Babymouse: monster mash (2008)
Babymouse: our hero (2005)
Babymouse: puppy love (2007)
Babymouse: rock star (2006)
Babymouse: the musical (2009)
Babymouse: skater girl (2007)
Camp Babymouse (2007)

Horowitz, Anthony, 1955-
Stormbreaker: the graphic novel; [by] Anthony Horowitz; adapted Antony Johnston; illustrated by Kanako Damerum & Yusuru Takasaki. Philomel Books 2006 unp il (Alex Rider) pa $14.99
Grades: 5 6 7 8   **741.5**
  1. Spies—Graphic novels 2. Graphic novels
  ISBN 0-399-24633-9
In this graphic novel version on Horowitz's novel, fourteen-year-old Alex Rider is coerced into continuing his uncle's dangerous work for Britain's intelligence agency, MI6.
"If it's possible, this is even more rapidly paced than the novel. Alex remains an appealing hero here, and the idea of a heroic teen up against insidious adults continues to be an extremely powerful draw for readers." Booklist

Jolley, Dan
Guan Yu; blood brothers to the end: a Chinese legend; story by Dan Jolley; pencils and inks by Ron Randall. Graphic Universe TM 2008 48p il (Graphic myths and legends) lib bdg $26.60
Grades: 4 5 6   **741.5**
  1. Kuan, Yu, 160-220—Graphic novels 2. China—Graphic novels 3. Graphic novels
  ISBN 978-0-8225-7527-6 (lib bdg); 0-8225-7527-2 (lib bdg)   LC 2007019742
This graphic novel offers "a look at Guan Yu, a Chinese superwarrior circa 2,000 years ago. Here chronicled is his first meeting with his 'blood brothers' and his various battles both with and against them, battles that helped to shape ancient China. . . . Most effective . . . is the unfolding of Guan Yu's life, charted not by his incredible triumphs but his failures, which provide readers . . . with a worthwhile change of perspective." Booklist

Kibuishi, Kazu
Amulet, book one: The Stonekeeper. Graphix 2008 185p $21.99; pa $9.99
Grades: 3 4 5 6 7 8   **741.5**
  1. Graphic novels 2. Fantasy graphic novels 3. Mystery graphic novels 4. Adventure graphic novels
  ISBN 978-0-439-84680-6; 0-439-84680-3; 978-0-439-84681-3 (pa); 0-439-84681-1 (pa)
After a family tragedy, Emily, Navin, and their mother move to an ancestral home to start a new life. When their mother is kidnapped by a tentacled creature, Em and Navin have to figure out how to set things straight

Kibuishi, Kazu—*Continued*
and save their mother's life.

"Filled with excitement, monsters, robots, and mysteries, this fantasy adventure will appeal to many readers." SLJ

Another title in this series is:
Amulet: The Stonekeeper's curse (2009)

Copper. Graphix/Scholastic 2010 94p il $21.99; pa $12.99
Grades: 5 6 7 8   **741.5**
1. Graphic novels 2. Dogs—Graphic novels 3. Adventure graphic novels 4. Science fiction graphic novels
ISBN   978-0-545-09892-2;   0-545-09892-0; 978-0-545-09893-9 (pa); 0-545-09893-9 (pa)

A collection of graphic novel adventures about a boy named Copper and his dog, Fred, including "navigating a dangerous forest of giant mushrooms, [and] surviving a crash landing in a homemade airplane—that run from lyrical to the downright apocalyptic. Illustrated in a deceptively simple style, its solemn tenor and deep strangeness . . . will likely inspire heavy investment from those who prefer a somewhat off-kilter read." Booklist

Kim, Susan
City of spies; [by] Susan Kim [and] Laurence Klavan; illustrated by Pascal Dizin. First Second 2010 172p il pa $17 *
Grades: 4 5 6 7   **741.5**
1. Adventure graphic novels 2. World War, 1939-1945—Graphic novels 3. Spies—Graphic novels 4. Graphic novels
ISBN 978-1-59643-262-8 (pa); 1-59643-262-4 (pa)

"With her mother gone and a father who has better things to do than be bothered raising a daughter, Evelyn is sent to live with her unconventional Aunt Lia in the bohemian art world of 1942 New York City. . . . Evelyn spends much of her time in the company of imaginary superheroes, fouling up the plans of Nazi spies. Before long she finds an unlikely friend in the building superintendent's son, Tony. Together, they . . . stumble upon an actual Nazi plot. With stupefying precision, Dizin's art channels Hergé's Tintin in tone, palette, and with the remarkable expressiveness of the clean, flexible figures. . . . With villains and danger that just border on the genuinely scary, the tale is filled not only with a thrilling sense of excitement but also with a child's longing for a grown-up to believe in." Booklist

Kochalka, James
Dragon Puncher. Top Shelf 2010 il $9.95
Grades: PreK K 1 2   **741.5**
1. Graphic novels 2. Dragons—Graphic novels 3. Cats—Graphic novels
ISBN 978-1-60309-057-5; 1-60309-057-6

This is the story of The Dragon Puncher, a cute but ruthless kitty in an armored battle suit who is dedicated to defeating dangerous dragons, and his would-be sidekick Spoony-E (a fuzzy little fellow armed with a wooden spoon).

This is illustrated using Kochalka's "signature childlike figures collaged onto photographed backgrounds with the faces of himself, his son, and his cat. . . .

Through Kochalka's guerilla, one-man-and-a-pen style of creation, it magically captures the exact sense of zaniness often discovered in . . . playtime. . . . Remarkably, it does this without losing coherence; and with huge panels and spare dialogue that will amuse kids and adults, it's also the rare graphic novel that makes an excellent read-aloud." Booklist

Johnny Boo: the best little ghost in the world! Top Shelf Productions 2008 40p pa $9.95
Grades: K 1 2 3   **741.5**
1. Ghosts—Graphic novels 2. Graphic novels 3. Humorous graphic novels 4. Friendship—Graphic novels
ISBN 978-1-60309-013-1

"Johnny Boo may be the best little ghost in the world, with the best little ghost pet, Squiggle, but that doesn't mean he's ready to face down scary Ice Cream Monster. When the monster turns out not to be scary after all, Johnny and Squiggle take it on as a new, if unpredictable, friend. Kochalka's simple line drawings and bright crayon colors stand out in this sweet, silly graphic novel. . . . The dialogue is fairly simple but never simplistic, and the text is printed clearly enough to make the book accessible to children just beginning to pick up chapter books." Booklist

Other titles in this series are:
Johnny Boo: Twinkle power (2009)
Johnny Boo and the happy apples (2009)
Johnny Boo and The mean little boy (2010)

Kovac, Tommy
Wonderland; written by Tommy Kovac; illustrated by Sonny Liew. Disney Press 2008 159p il $19.99
Grades: 4 5 6 7 8   **741.5**
1. Graphic novels 2. Fantasy graphic novels
ISBN 978-1-4231-0451-3; 1-4231-0451-X

First published as single-issue comics by SLG Publishing

Based on the tale Alice in Wonderland by Lewis Carroll

"Ever wonder what happened in Wonderland after Alice left? Follow the quirky tale of Mary Ann, the meticulous and dutiful housekeeper for the White Rabbit, as she continues the tale. Her boss is now wanted for treason by the Queen of Hearts for allowing the Alice Monster to enter the kingdom–off with his head! On the run and fearing for their lives, Mary Ann and White Rabbit encounter the meddlesome Cheshire Cat, the ever-contentious troublemaker, sending the White Rabbit straight into the clutches of the queen and poor Mary Ann tumbling into the Treacle Well. . . . This is a terrific look at a great classic. The energetic, action-packed illustrations complement the story in Disney-cartoon style, making for a great read for all ages" SLJ

Krosoczka, Jarrett J.

Lunch Lady and the League of Librarians. Alfred A. Knopf 2009 unp il lib bdg $11.99; pa $5.99

Grades: 3 4 5 6 7 8   **741.5**

1. Graphic novels 2. School stories—Graphic novels 3. Humorous graphic novels 4. Librarians—Graphic novels 5. Games—Graphic novels 6. School children—Food—Graphic novels

ISBN 978-0-375-94684-4 (lib bdg); 0-375-94684-5 (lib bdg); 978-0-375-84684-7 (pa); 0-375-84684-0 (pa)

LC 2008043117

The school lunch lady, a secret crime fighter, sets out to stop a group of librarians bent on destroying a shipment of video games, while a group of students known as the Breakfast Bunch provides back-up

"The black-and-white pen-and-ink illustrations have splashes of yellow in nearly every panel. The clean layout, featuring lots of open space, is well suited for the intended audience. . . . With its appealing mix of action and humor, this clever, entertaining addition to the series should have wide appeal." SLJ

Other titles about the Lunch Lady are:
Lunch lady and the cyborg substitute (2009)
Lunch Lady and the author visit vendetta (2009)
Lunch Lady and the summer camp shakedown (2010)

Larson, Hope

Chiggers; [by] Hope Larson; lettered by Jason Azzopardi. Atheneum Books for Young Readers 2008 170p il $17.99; pa $9.99

Grades: 5 6 7 8 9   **741.5**

1. Camps—Fiction 2. Graphic novels 3. Friendship—Graphic novels

ISBN 978-1-4169-3584-1; 978-1-4169-3587-2 (pa)

LC 2008-09557

When Abby returns to the same summer camp she always goes to, she is dismayed to find that her old friends have changed, and the only person who wants to be her friend is the strange new girl, Shasta.

"Chiggers provides a ticket to summer fun. Larson delicately handles both the usual middle-school angst and the additional pressures that come with being somewhat different. . . . The content is perfect for upper elementary and middle school students." SLJ

Lemke, Donald

Zinc Alloy: Super Zero; illustrated by Douglas Holgate. Stone Arch Books 2009 33p il $21.26

Grades: 2 3 4 5 6 7   **741.5**

1. Graphic novels 2. Superhero graphic novels 3. Humorous graphic novels 4. Robots—Graphic novels 5. Bullies—Graphic novels

ISBN 978-1-4342-0762-3   LC 2008-6712

Part of the Graphic Sparks Zinc Alloy series

Zack Allen loves to read comics, especially Robo Hero; unfortunately, he's the kind of kid that bullies like to pick on, and they have done so. Then Zack builds his own robot suit; he was just going to get the bullies to stop, but when he hears about a runaway train, he uses the suit to become a new superhero Zinc Alloy! He's going to have to work on controlling things a lot better, though how will he explain broken doors to his mom? The book includes a short history of comic books and

the glossary includes definitions for "noogies" and "wet willies."

Lepp, Royden

David: Shepard's song, vol. 1. Cross Culture Entertainment/Alias Enterprises 2005 72p il pa $8.99

Grades: 3 4 5 6 7 8 9   **741.5**

1. David, King of Israel—Graphic novels 2. Samuel (Biblical figure)—Graphic novels 3. Graphic novels 4. Bible stories—Graphic novels

ISBN 1-933428-82-1

Anointed by the prophet Samuel as a young boy and mocked by his family, young David is hunted even by King Saul himself. While hiding in a cave, David looks back on the day that Samuel found him tending the sheep and anointed him to become the next King of Israel. This retelling can be exciting for any young reader.

Luciani, Brigitte

The meeting; illustrated by Eve Tharlet. Graphic Universe 2010 32p il (Mr. Badger and Mrs. Fox) lib bdg $25.26; pa $6.95

Grades: 1 2 3   **741.5**

1. Siblings—Graphic novels 2. Badgers—Graphic novels 3. Foxes—Graphic novels 4. Graphic novels

ISBN 978-0-7613-5625-7 (lib bdg); 0-7613-5625-8 (lib bdg); 978-0-7613-5631-8 (pa); 0-7613-5631-2 (pa)

LC 2009032617

Having lost their home, a fox and her daughter move in with a badger and his three children, but when the youngsters throw a big party hoping to prove that they are incompatible, their plan backfires.

"Rendered as a beginning graphic novel, the story and characters are presented with plenty of heart and soul: expressive anthropomorphic faces and postures and rich dialogue require and reward engagement. Watercolor panels vary in size on folio pages, and balloons contain an easy-to-read font." Booklist

Lynch, Jay

Mo and Jo: fighting together forever; a toon book; by [illustrator] Dean Haspiel & [writer] Jay Lynch. RAW Junior 2008 40p il $12.95

Grades: K 1 2 3   **741.5**

1. Graphic novels 2. Superhero graphic novels 3. Siblings—Graphic novels 4. Humorous graphic novels

ISBN 978-0-9799238-5-2

Mona and Joey are battling twins, and everything they do turns into a fight. They both love the same superhero, the Mighty Mojo. One day he comes to their house and says he needs to retire and gives them his costume, which has all his powers

"The text is peppered with puns and some clever idiom work, reinforced by repetition as well as what's happening in the clean panels and art." Booklist

Macdonald, Fiona

Journey to the Center of the Earth; by Jules Verne; Fiona Macdonald, adapter; illustrated by Penko Gelev. Barron's Educational Series, Inc. 2007 48p il (Graphic classics) $15.99; pa $8.99

Grades: 3 4 5 6 7 8   **741.5**

1. Verne, Jules, 1828-1905—Adaptations 2. Graphic novels 3. Adventure graphic novels

ISBN 978-0-7641-5982-4; 978-0-7641-3495-1 (pa)

In Hamburg, Germany in 1863, eccentric Professor Otto Lidenbrock acquires a book by the sixteenth-century alchemist, Arne Saknussemm; the book includes a parchment page written in coded runes, and Lidenbrock's nephew Axel helps him decode it. To Axel's horror, the message tells of a way to get to the Center of the Earth, and Lidenbrock drags him along on the adventure.

The "story progresses in short two-page episodes, helped along by a few sentences of narration under each frame. Detailed illustrations in muted colors work with . . . the dim underground setting. . . . Dramatic, action-filled scenes and highly expressive faces catch readers eyes and pull them into the [story]." SLJ

Kidnapped; by Robert Louis Stevenson; Fiona Macdonald, adapter; illustrated by Penko Gelev. Barron's Educational Series, Inc. 2007 48p il (Graphic classics) $15.99; pa $8.99

Grades: 3 4 5 6 7 8   **741.5**

1. Stevenson, Robert Louis, 1850-1894—Adaptations 2. Graphic novels 3. Adventure graphic novels

ISBN 978-0-7641-5980-0; 978-0-7641-3494-4 (pa)

Orphaned David Balfour goes to his uncle, who first tries to kill him and then tricks him into going onboard a ship that leaves Scotland with David aboard. David befriends a passenger, Alan Breck, then learns he's a Jacobite in exile. They survive a shipwreck, witness a murder, and become fugitives on the run back in Scotland.

The "story progresses in short two-page episodes, helped along by a few sentences of narration under each frame. Detailed illustrations in muted colors work with the stormy, furtive story. . . . Dramatic, action-filled scenes and highly expressive faces catch readers eyes and pull them into the [story]." SLJ

Martin, Ann M., 1955-

The Baby-sitter's Club: Kristy's great idea; a graphic novel; [text by Ann M. Martin; art] by Raina Telgemeier. Scholastic Graphix 2006 192p il $16.99; pa $8.99

Grades: 3 4 5 6   **741.5**

1. Graphic novels 2. Friendship—Graphic novels 3. Babysitting—Graphic novels

ISBN 0-439-80241-5; 0-439-73933-0 (pa)

LC 2005-37749

Follows the adventures of Kristy and the other members of the Baby-sitters Club as they deal with crank calls, uncontrollable two-year-olds, wild pets, and parents who do not always tell the truth. A graphic novel based on the 1988 book by the same name.

"Comics artist Telgemeier's clean-lined, black-and-white art with stark black details nicely differentiates the four personable seventh-graders who parlay their babysitting experience into a business." Booklist

Other titles about the Baby-sitters Club are:

The truth about Stacey (2006)

Mary Anne saves the day (2007)

Claudia and Mean Janine (2008)

Medley, Linda

Castle waiting. Fantagraphics 2006 456p il $29.95 *

Grades: 5 6 7 8 9 10 11 12   **741.5**

1. Graphic novels 2. Fairy tales—Graphic novels 3. Fantasy graphic novels

ISBN 1-56097-747-7

All of Medley's previously self-published comics are collected here in one volume for the first time. The titular castle was the home of Sleeping Beauty, whose story is retold from the viewpoint of the flibbertigibbet ladies in waiting. After the flighty princess awakens with the kiss of a handsome but not too bright prince, the castle becomes a sanctuary for various misfits. Readers will find references to many fairy tales, folk tales, and nursery rhymes in Medley's book, and her clean, clear black-and-white art reflects the works of classic illustrators such as Arthur Rackham.

Meister, Cari

Clues in the attic; illustrated by Rémy Simard. Stone Arch Books 2010 25p il (My 1st graphic novel) $21.32; pa $3.95

Grades: K 1 2   **741.5**

1. Graphic novels 2. Mystery graphic novels 3. Siblings—Graphic novels

ISBN   978-1-4342-1889-6;   1-4342-1889-9; 978-1-4342-2283-1 (pa); 1-4342-2283-7 (pa)

"Siblings Ben and Sofia investigate strange noises that they hear coming from above them. . . . [This title provides an] effective early-reader [equivalent] to comics and graphic novels. [Its] traditional beginning-reader trim size as well as bold and brightly colored illustrations are appealing to novice readers, while the inclusion of a 'How to Read a Graphic Novel' section, a glossary, discussion questions, and writing prompts will appeal to parents and teachers. The texts include simple sentences that closely match the art, while panels are limited to a maximum of four per page. Good fun for early graphic-novel readers." SLJ

Morse, Scott

Magic Pickle; with color by Jose Garibaldi. Scholastic/Graphix 2008 unp il pa $9.99 *

Grades: 2 3 4 5   **741.5**

1. Graphic novels 2. Humorous graphic novels 3. Superhero graphic novels

ISBN 978-0-439-87995-8 (pa); 0-439-87995-7 (pa)

"When Weapon Kosher, the Magic Pickle, erupts from the bedroom floor of little Jo Jo Wigman, she has to answer a lot of questions! What's the Magic Pickle's connection to the Brotherhood of Evil Produce? What is 'Dill Justice'? How did Danny Johnson get to be so cute?" Publisher's note

"Starting with an irresistibly goofy premise, Morse layers on sly humor, astute references, and blazing action, turning in a charming, slam-bang story." Booklist

Other titles in this series are:

Morse, Scott—*Continued*
Magic Pickle and the Planet of the Grapes (2008)
Magic Pickle vs. the Egg Poacher (2008)
Magic Pickle and the Garden of Evil (2009)
Magic Pickle and the Creature from the Black Legume
(2009)

Mortensen, Lori, 1955-
The missing monster card; illustrated by Rémy
Simard. Stone Arch Books 2010 25p il (My 1st
graphic novel) $21.32; pa $3.95
Grades: K 1 2   **741.5**
  1. Graphic novels 2. Mystery graphic novels
  ISBN   978-1-4342-1888-9;   1-4342-1888-0;
  978-1-4342-2284-8 (pa); 1-4342-2284-5 (pa)
  "Ethan has just found a rare Monster Card in the pack
he bought, and he wants to show it to his friend Zack,
but when he goes to Zack's house the next day, the card
isn't in his jacket pocket. The two friends search for the
card to solve the mystery. . . . The book provides a
short tutorial on how to navigate the panels and uses
sound effects, dialogue balloons, and brief narrative text
to tell the story. . . . A brief glossary, discussion questions, and writing prompts provide teachers with easy
lesson plans for classroom use. The bright colors and
cartoony illustrations add to the appeal for beginning
readers." Booklist

Mucci, Tim
The odyssey; by Homer and Tim Mucci;
illustrated by Ben Caldwell and others. Sterling
2010 unp il (All-action classics) pa $7.95 *
Grades: 5 6 7 8   **741.5**
  1. Homer—Adaptations 2. Graphic novels 3. Greek
mythology—Graphic novels
  ISBN 978-1-4027-3155-6 (pa); 1-4027-3155-8 (pa)
  This graphic novel adaptation of Homer's classic epic
is "a crackling adventure that also penetrates the recess-
ess of the human heart. . . . Caldwell's art has the force
and vibrant life of a Samurai Jack cartoon." Booklist

O'Brien, Anne Sibley, 1952-
The legend of Hong Kil Dong, the Robin Hood
of Korea. Charlesbridge 2006 unp il $14.95 *
Grades: 3 4 5 6 7   **741.5**
  1. Graphic novels 2. Korea—Graphic novels 3. Hong
Kil Dong (Legendary character)
  ISBN 978-1-58089-302-2; 1-58089-302-3
                                           LC 2005-56941
  Hong Kil Dong is the son of a powerful government
minister and one of his servants; this means the father
will not recognize his son as his own. The boy grows up
with great intelligence and wit, and leaves home to find
his fortune. He learns martial arts and magic, and when
he encounters thieves who rob only because corrupt government officials have ruined them, he turns the thieves
into an army to right the wrongs. This story is based on
a seventeenth century Korean legend.
  Includes bibliographical references

O'Connor, George
Zeus; king of the gods. Roaring Brook Press
2010 76p il (Olympians) $16.99; pa $9.99 *
Grades: 5 6 7 8   **741.5**
  1. Zeus (Greek deity) 2. Classical mythology
3. Graphic novels
  ISBN   978-1-59643-431-8;   1-59643-625-5;
  978-1-59643-432-5 (pa); 1-59643-431-7 (pa)
  Retells in graphic novel format stories from Greek
mythology about the exploits of the young Zeus and how
he rallied an army and overthrew his father, Kronos, to
become king of the gods
  "It's [the] balance between respect for myth and ad-
herence to comic-book form that works so wonderfully
well here." Bull Cent Child Books
  Followed by: Athena: grey-eyed goddess (2010)

O'Donnell, Liam, 1970-
Wild ride: a graphic guide adventure; written by
Liam O'Donnell; illustrated by Mike Deas. Orca
Book Publishers 2007 unp il pa $8.95
Grades: 3 4 5 6 7 8   **741.5**
  1. Graphic novels 2. Adventure graphic novels
3. Wilderness survival—Graphic novels
  ISBN 978-1-55143-756-9
  Devin, his sister Nadia, smart-mouthed Marcus (all
children of environmentalists), and government accountant Gerald Wiley all fly into the wilderness toward Big
Horn Valley in British Columbia, but they fly into a
storm and crash in the middle of nowhere. The pilot is
killed, and the three young people and Wiley must survive until rescue. However, the kids soon discover Wiley
is not on their side; he's taking bribes from a large corporation to stop the environmental study.
  "The easy-to-follow survival adventure will engage reluctant readers. . . . Deas' full-color art is packed with
action." Booklist
  Another title about Devin and Nadia is:
Soccer sabotage (2008)

Ottaviani, Jim
T-Minus: the race to the moon; [illustrated by]
Zander Cannon, Kevin Cannon. Aladdin 2009
124p il $21.99; pa $12.99
Grades: 4 5 6 7 8 9 10 11 12 Adult
                                                 741.5
  1. Graphic novels 2. Space flight to the moon—
Graphic novels 3. Gemini project—Graphic novels
4. Apollo project—Graphic novels
  ISBN   978-1-4169-8682-9;   1-4169-8682-0;
  978-1-4169-4960-2 (pa); 1-4169-4960-7 (pa)
                                           LC 2009-920999
  Ottaviani, Zander Cannon, and Kevin Cannon show
what happened when the U.S. and the U.S.S.R. started
the space race in the 1950s, and how it progressed to the
NASA Apollo 11 mission which landed two men on the
moon in July of 1969.
  "Organized as a countdown, making the outcome
seem inevitable, the frequent, prominent sidebars list a
type of rocket, the duration of its flight, and whether the
mission was a success or a failure. There are more than
30 attempts chronicled, and the shift between Soviet and
U.S. successes creates an interesting balance in the narrative. . . . Ottaviani is particular with facts and eager to
inspire readers with regard to the scientific process." SLJ

Parker, Jake

Missile Mouse: the star crusher. Graphix 2010 172p (Missile Mouse) $21.99; pa $10.99

Grades: 3 4 5 6 **741.5**

1. Graphic novels 2. Science fiction graphic novels 3. Mice—Graphic novels 4. Adventure graphic novels

ISBN 978-0-545-11714-2; 0-545-11714-3; 978-0-545-11715-9 (pa); 0-545-11715-1 (pa)

"When his mission to recover an ancient star compass goes wrong, intrepid Galactic Security Agent Missile Mouse finds himself saddled with a partner. . . . The two are to retrieve a missing scientist who holds the key to a horrible weapon, the Star Crusher, in his hereditary memory. . . . [This is] a gem in story and art. Bright, action-filled, at times wordless panels keep the pages turning. Intelligent space opera and a realistically rounded hero will have young fans of the future demanding the next volume." Kirkus

Petersen, David, 1977-

Mouse Guard: Fall 1152. Archaia Studios Press 2007 unp il $24.95 *

Grades: 5 6 7 8 **741.5**

1. Graphic novels 2. Fantasy graphic novels 3. Mice—Graphic novels

ISBN 978-1-932386-57-8; 1-932386-57-2

Originally published as Mouse Guard issues #1-6.

In a medieval world populated by animals, mice have their own civilization but live in constant peril from predators. They live in hidden towns protected by the Guard, who also escort travelers between towns. Three young members of the Guard, Lieam, Saxon, and Kenzie, go in search of a missing grain merchant. They find him dead in the belly of a snake who tried to eat them; but they also find evidence that the dead merchant is a traitor. Now they need to find out to whom he was betraying the Guard and why. While this story features animals and is suitable for most readers who can handle some fighting action, there's nothing cute or Disney-esque in the art. Characters die, this is a serious story, but readers who have read Bone or the Harry Potter series can handle the action in this book. This is the first in a series.

Another title is this series is:

Mouse Guard: Winter 1152 (2009)

Phelan, Matt

The storm in the barn. Candlewick Press 2009 201p il $24.99 *

Grades: 4 5 6 7 8 9 **741.5**

1. Graphic novels 2. Adventure graphic novels 3. Dust storms—Graphic novels 4. Monsters—Graphic novels 5. United States—History—1933-1945—Graphic novels 6. Kansas—Graphic novels

ISBN 978-0-7636-3618-0; 0-7636-3618-5

In Kansas of 1937, the land has been in the grip of the Dust Bowl for four years, and eleven-year-old Jack Carter has seen his family worn down by it. But the day Jack outruns a dust storm all the way home from town, he glimpses something odd in the abandoned Talbot barn, and he tries to find the courage to go into the barn and confront what is there.

"Children can read this as a work of historical fiction, a piece of folklore, a scary story, a graphic novel, or all four. Written with simple, direct language, it's an almost wordless book: the illustrations' shadowy grays and blurry lines eloquently depict the haze of the dust. A complex but accessible and fascinating book." SLJ

Pien, Lark

Long Tail Kitty. Blue Apple Books 2009 51p il $14.95

Grades: 1 2 3 4 **741.5**

1. Cats—Graphic novels 2. Graphic novels 3. Humorous graphic novels 4. Friendship—Graphic novels

ISBN 978-1-934706-44-2

Long Tail Kitty comes to children's books from Pien's webcomic. Pien colored Gene Yang's American Born Chinese. Here, she uses watercolor washes over precise ink to depict the everyday adventures of Long Tail Kitty. First, he introduces readers to where he lives; then in the meadow near his house, he encounters a bee who stings him on the nose for trying to pick a flower, but they end up making friends with each other and with the friendly wildflowers in the meadow. In the wintertime, Long Tail Kitty meets Good Tall Mouse at the frozen lake and they have fun on the ice. After buying groceries at the market, Long Tail Kitty, Good Tall Mouse, and Bernice the dog get together to cook a feast for dinner. Then Long Tail Kitty's alien friends come for a visit, and they do all the things on Kitty's long list of fun. Here, Pien provides a foldout page filled with small panels depicting all the different activities, ranging from doing handstands to folding origami to reading comics to playing ninja and lots more.

Renier, Aaron

Spiral-bound. Top Shelf Productions 2005 144p il pa $14.95

Grades: 4 5 6 7 8 9 **741.5**

1. Graphic novels 2. Mystery graphic novels

ISBN 1-891830-50-3

"Turnip the elephant is using the summer to find his artistic voice through sculpture, his friend Stucky the dog is building a submarine, and Ana the rabbit is working on the town's underground newspaper. Their stories all wind around the town's deep, dark secret about the monster that lives in the pond. . . . The characters seem like real children, wholesome without being too sweet, and Renier's art is light and fun, a sort of Babar meets underground comix." Booklist

The Unsinkable Walker Bean. First Second 2010 il pa $13.99 *

Grades: 5 6 7 8 **741.5**

1. Graphic novels 2. Adventure graphic novels

ISBN 978-1-59643-453-0; 1-59643-453-8

The story "centers around a cursed skull stolen from the lair of two deep-sea crustacean witches. Like all who look upon the skull, Walker's beloved grandpa falls deathly ill when he finds it, and the boy sets out to return the skull from whence it came. . . . The generous page size lets [the] reader dive into Renier's quavery and painstakingly detailed cartooning, and he really shows off his stuff with a bounty of full-splash dazzlers. . . . Exciting, deep, funny, and scary, with tremendous villains and valor galore." Booklist

Reynolds, Aaron, 1970-

Joey Fly, private eye in Creepy crawly crime; illustrations by Neil Numberman. Henry Holt & Co. 2009 96p il (Joey Fly, private eye) $16.95; pa $9.95

Grades: 3 4 5 6   **741.5**
  1. Graphic novels 2. Mystery graphic novels
  ISBN   978-0-8050-8242-5;   0-8050-8242-5;
  978-0-8050-8786-4 (pa); 0-8050-8786-9 (pa)
                                        LC 2007-40041

"In a city inhabited by insects, Joey fly is a private eye combating crime for a fee. . . . Young readers will be amused by this noir-type story filled with classic detective dialogue and swarms of insect humor." Booklist

Roberts, Scott

Patty-cake and friends: color collection. SLG Publishing 2006 104p il pa $12.95

Grades: 4 5 6 7 8 9 10 11 12   **741.5**
  1. Graphic novels 2. Humorous graphic novels
  3. Family life—Graphic novels 4. Friendship—Graphic novels
  ISBN 1-59362-030-6

Patty-Cake (real name Patricia Bakerman), her family and her neighborhood friends star in a series of true-to-life everyday adventures and misadventures, including getting even with her older sister at the pool, helping her best friend Irving get even with his pesky older brother, going on her first train ride with her dad, and more. Roberts' exaggerated cartoon style is reminiscent of old Tex Avery cartoons, as characters fully express their emotions particularly anger and surprise. Some use of frank language may keep this book in public library collections.

Roche, Art

Cartooning; the only cartooning book you'll ever need to be the artist you've always wanted to be. Lark Books 2005 111p il (Art for kids) $17.95 *

Grades: 3 4 5 6   **741.5**
  1. Cartooning—Technique 2. Drawing
  ISBN 1-57990-623-0

Contents: Cartoons everywhere!; Cartooning materials; Making faces; Drawing bodies; Drawing stuff; Drawing animals; Writing jokes; Putting it all together; Publishing your cartoons; Draw, draw, draw!

"This how-to guide is a step above the average cartooning instruction book. The glossy, full-color pages are visually attractive. . . . Roche's engaging writing style is informative and fun. . . . His loose, spacious cartooning style is perfect for beginners or kids who might be intimidated by more detail-oriented techniques." SLJ

Rosenstiehl, Agnès

Silly Lilly and the four seasons; [by] Agnes Rosenstiehl. Toon Books 2008 36p il $12.95 *
Grades: PreK K 1 2   **741.5**
  1. Graphic novels 2. Seasons—Graphic novels
  3. Humorous graphic novels
  ISBN 978-0-9799238-1-4

"Rosenstiehl follows Lilly . . . as she undertakes simple, familiar activities through the seasons. . . . Lilly is

bold and engaging. . . . The text is very brief, . . . the colors are warm and bright, and the panels are large enough to draw in children new to books and reading." Booklist

Rosinsky, Natalie M. (Natalie Myra)

Graphic content! the culture of comic books. Compass Point Books 2010 64p il (Pop culture revolutions) lib bdg $31.99
Grades: 5 6 7 8 9 10   **741.5**
  1. Comic books, strips, etc.—History and criticism
  ISBN 978-0-7565-4241-2 (lib bdg); 0-7565-4241-3 (lib bdg)

Traces the origins of comic books and discusses the emergence of superheroes, censorship issues, their depiction of increased social diversity, and their impact on society

"This slim and splashily designed book . . . does an admirable job of keeping things succinct yet thorough. . . . [The author] maintains a nice international scope throughout. . . . This is a super resource to have on hand to give a broader context of the medium and its fascinating history." Booklist

Write your own graphic novel. Compass Point Books 2009 64p il (Write your own) lib bdg $33.26
Grades: 5 6 7 8 9 10 11 12   **741.5**
  1. Graphic novels—Authorship
  ISBN 978-0-7565-3856-9 (lib bdg); 0-7565-3856-4 (lib bdg)   LC 2008-6506
  Part of the Write Your Own series

This book offers tips, advice, end encouragement to readers who might want to try their hand at writing their own comics and graphic novels. Rosinsky uses many examples from Stone Arch and Capstone Press books along with many others, and the "case study" side bars provide glimpses into the work of such graphic novelists as Marjane Satrapi, Art Spiegelman, and Craig Thompson. The back matter includes a list of suggested graphic novels that are suitable for teen readers

"Students wishing to explore the graphic-novel format will benefit from clear explanations of how to portray heroes and villains, use dramatic dialogue, and create a story map. Excerpts from several popular graphic novels are included." SLJ

Runton, Andy

Owly: The way home and The bittersweet summer; [by] Andy Runton. Top Shelf 2004 160p il pa $10
Grades: K 1 2 3 4 5 6 7 8 9 10 11 12
                                                   741.5
  1. Graphic novels 2. Owls—Graphic novels
  3. Friendship—Graphic novels
  ISBN 1-891830-62-7   LC 2005298860

Rotund little Owly befriends Wormy despite their differences, and together they help a couple of hummingbirds and learn that friendship doesn't end with separation.

"The whimsical black-and-white art is done with great facility for expressing emotion, and Runton's reliance on icons and pictures in lieu of the usual dialogue makes the story perfect for give-and-take between children and their parents." Booklist

Runton, Andy—*Continued*
Other titles in this series are:
Owly vol. 2: Just a little blue (2005)
Owly vol. 3: Flying lessons (2005)

Russell, P. Craig, 1951-
Coraline; based on the novel by Neil Gaiman; adapted and illustrated by P. Craig Russell; colorist, Lovern Kindzierski; letterer, Todd Klein. HarperCollins 2008 186p il $18.99; lib bdg $19.89 *

Grades: 4 5 6 7   **741.5**
1. Gaiman, Neil, 1960-—Adaptations 2. Graphic novels 3. Horror graphic novels
ISBN 978-0-06-082543-0; 978-0-06-082544-7 (lib bdg)   LC 2007-930658
"An adaptation of Gaiman's 2002 novel *Coraline*, . . . a tale of childhood nightmares. As in the original story, Coraline wanders around her new house and discovers a door leading into a mirror place, where she finds her button-eyed 'other mother,' who is determined to secure Coraline's love one way or another. This version is a virtuoso adaptation. . . . A master of fantastical landscapes, Russell sharpens the realism of his imagery, perserving the humanity of the characters and heightening the horror." Booklist

Sava, Scott Christian
Hyperactive; by Scott Christian Sava; artist, Joseph Bergin. IDW Publishing/Worthwhile Children's Books 2009 108p il pa $12.99 *
Grades: 3 4 5 6 7 8   **741.5**
1. Adventure graphic novels 2. Graphic novels 3. Humorous graphic novels 4. Superhero graphic novels
ISBN 978-1-60010-313-1; 1-60010-313-8
"Joey Johnson learns he can move at super speed and puts his power to good use doing household chores. But when word gets out, a shady executive sees the opportunity to make big bucks off of Joey's super DNA. . . . With its surprise ending, which suggests more to come, a readership of young boys will ensure that this one flies off the shelf at the speed of light." Booklist

Sfar, Joann
Little Vampire; stories and drawings by Joann Sfar; colors by Walter; translated by Alexis Siegel and Edward Gauvin. First Second 2008 92p il pa $13.95
Grades: 3 4 5 6   **741.5**
1. Vampires—Graphic novels 2. School stories—Graphic novels 3. Graphic novels
ISBN 978-1-59643-233-8 (pa); 1-59643-233-0 (pa)   LC 2007-38498
First published in France
An unusual friendship forms between a vampire and a human, when Little Vampire leaves notes on homework Michael has left at school.
"Joann Sfar's art is surreal, with vivid colors, busy panels and fabulous monsters." KLIATT

Shiga, Jason
Meanwhile. Abrams/Amulet 2010 unp il $15.95
*
Grades: 4 5 6 7 8 9   **741.5**
1. Science fiction graphic novels 2. Graphic novels
ISBN 978-0-8109-8423-3; 0-8109-8423-7
"In this graphic novel mind boggler . . . readers play the role of little Jimmy and on the first page make the seemingly innocuous decision of ordering a vanilla or chocolate ice-cream cone. Tubes connect panels in all directions and veer off into tabs to other pages, creating a head-spinningly tangled web of story. . . . The crux is that Jimmy stumbles into the lab of an affable mad scientist and is allowed to tinker with three inventions: a mind reader, a time machine, and the Killitron, which obliterates all life on earth aside from the user's. . . . It's maddening and challenging, all right, but that's precisely what makes it so crazy fun." Booklist

Shioya, Hitoshi, 1969-
Dinosaur hour!, vol. 1; story and art by Hitoshi Shioya; [translation, Katherine Schilling] Viz Media/Vizkids 2009 192p il $7.99
Grades: 3 4 5 6   **741.5**
1. Graphic novels 2. Manga 3. Humorous graphic novels 4. Dinosaurs—Graphic novels
ISBN 978-1-4215-2648-5
Shioya takes dinosaurs from the various prehistoric periods and puts them into slapstick situations. In short comics stories, herbivores such as Protoceratops and carnivores such as Tyrannosaurus Rex interact, often with the herbivores getting eaten. In one story, a couple of Protoceratops decide to check out the story that Tyrannosaurus Rex can't see well, but it doesn't stop the carnivore from chomping on both of them. In other stories, smaller carnivores try to tackle a stegosaurus, who uses its tail to sweep them away. Dinosaurs make bets with each other, play pranks, deal with ghosts and bullies. The almost inevitable getting eaten part isn't portrayed graphically (beyond a T. Rex holding a couple of Protoceratops in its mouth), so younger readers who like dinosaurs and enjoy silly humor can enjoy this manga.

Smith, Jeff, 1960 Feb. 27-
Little Mouse gets ready. TOON Books 2009 32p il $12.95 *
Grades: PreK K 1   **741.5**
1. Graphic novels 2. Mice—Graphic novels 3. Humorous graphic novels 4. Clothing and dress—Graphic novels
ISBN 978-1-935179-01-6; 1-935179-01-2   LC 2008-55403
ALA ALSC Geisel Award Honor Book (2010)
"Little Mouse is eager to go to the barn with his mother. He slowly and methodically gets dressed, which is quite an accomplishment for the little guy, only to be reminded, in classic noodlehead fashion, that mice don't wear clothes. . . . The cartoon illustrations are large and uncomplicated without being babyish, and the punch line is preceded with places for knowing giggles." SLJ

Sonishi, Kenji, 1969-

Leave it to PET!: the misadventures of a recycled super robot, vol. 1; story & art by Kenji Sonishi; translation, Katherine Schilling; touch-up art & lettering, John Hunt; editor, Traci N. Todd. Viz Media/VizKids 2009 192p il $7.99

Grades: 3 4 5 6 **741.5**

    1. Graphic novels 2. Manga 3. Humorous graphic novels 4. Recycling—Graphic novels

    ISBN 978-1-4215-2649-2

PET (polyethylene terephthalate, a type of recyclable plastic) was a simple plastic bottle until nine-year-old Noboru recycled him. Now PET is a super robot programmed to "repay" Noboru for recycling him by helping him. Unfortunately for Noboru, PET's help usually ends up causing even more trouble; being a super robot doesn't mean PET has a clue about what he is doing. The book includes lots of short stories that follow the formula of Noboru getting into a bit of a fix, calling for PET, then getting into more trouble as PET does the wrong thing. Some of the stories do include some information about recycling plastics and aluminum, which is done somewhat differently in Japan than in the U.S.

Spires, Ashley, 1978-

Binky the space cat. Kids Can Press 2009 64p il $16.95; pa $7.95 *

Grades: 2 3 4 5 **741.5**

    1. Graphic novels 2. Humorous graphic novels 3. Cats—Graphic novels 4. Space flight—Graphic novels

    ISBN 978-1-55453-309-1; 1-55453-309-0; 978-1-55453-419-7 (pa); 1-55453-419-4 (pa)

Binky the cat lives with two humans (an unnamed mother and son) in what he thinks of as a space station. He's determined to become a space cat and venture into outer space with his stuffed mousie Ted, and to that end he gets his space cat kit through the mail, complete with instructions to build a space ship.

"Spires's mix of sly, dry and slapstick humor in her first graphic novel is perfect. . . . Details in the muted watercolor illustrations, like mousie Ted covering his nose as Binky releases 'space gas,' will keep readers of all ages giggling, whether they're cat lovers or not." Kirkus

Stanley, John, 1914-1993

Little Lulu, vol. 1: My dinner with Lulu; [by] John Stanley and Irving Tripp. Dark Horse Comics 2005 200p il pa $9.95

Grades: 4 5 6 7 8 9 10 11 12 Adult

                                    741.5

    1. Graphic novels 2. Humorous graphic novels 3. Friendship—Graphic novels

    ISBN 1-59307-318-6

Lulu Moppet plays with best friend Tubby, except when he hangs out with the other neighborhood boys and tries to keep girls out of their clubhouse; she deals with terrible toddler Alvin by weaving extravagant tales featuring herself; and other everyday adventures. This is the first volume of a series that will eventually reprint every Little Lulu comic for new young readers.

Other titles in this series are:

Little Lulu vol. 2: Sunday afternoon
Little Lulu vol. 3: Lulu in the doghouse
Little Lulu vol. 4: Lulu goes shopping
Little Lulu vol. 5: Lulu takes a trip
Little Lulu vol. 6: Letters to Santa
Little Lulu vol. 7: Lulu's umbrella
Little Lulu vol. 8: Late for school
Little Lulu vol. 9: Lucky Lulu
Little Lulu vol. 10: All dressed up
Little Lulu vol. 11: April fools
Little Lulu vol. 12: Leave it to Lulu
Little Lulu vol. 13: Too much fun

Steinberg, David, 1962-

Sound off! by D. J. Steinberg; illustrated by Brian Smith. Grosset & Dunlap 2008 unp il (Adventures of Daniel Boom AKA Loud Boy) pa $5.99 *

Grades: 3 4 5 **741.5**

    1. Graphic novels 2. Superhero graphic novels

    ISBN 978-0-448-44698-1 LC 2007019009

"Being the new kid in town with no volume control on his voice, Daniel Boom discovers an even bigger problem—the evil Kid-Rid Corporation has silenced the entire world with their terrible Soundsucker LX machine! Daniel taps into his inner superhero to become Loud Boy." Publisher's note

"Bursting with action, color, and intriguing characters . . . this works in every way. Smith's visual wit, which puts a retro gloss on cartoon art of the 1950s, is on display without sidetracking the story, and pacing and plotting are superb." Booklist

Stephens, Jay, 1971-

Heroes! draw your own superheroes, gadget geeks & other do-gooders; [by] Jay Stephens. Lark Books 2007 64p il $12.95; pa $5.95

Grades: 4 5 6 7 **741.5**

    1. Superheroes 2. Drawing 3. Cartoons and caricatures

    ISBN 978-1-57990-934-5; 1-57990-934-5; 978-1-60059-179-2 (pa); 1-60059-179-5 (pa)

                                 LC 2006101661

"Stephens shows just how to draw [superheroes]. . . . Stephens does a good job organizing his material, beginning with a bit of history, then moving quickly to hero heads, . . . and on to masks, disguises, physical features, power effects, and action moves. The brightly colored illustrations offer plenty of how-to info and lots of great heroes, male and female, to use as models." Booklist

Monsters! draw your own mutants, freaks & creeps; [by] Jay Stephens. Lark Books 2007 64p il $12.95; pa $5.95

Grades: 4 5 6 7 **741.5**

    1. Monsters in art 2. Drawing 3. Cartoons and caricatures

    ISBN 978-1-57990-935-2; 1-57990-935-3; 978-1-60059-178-5 (pa); 1-60059-178-7 (pa)

                                 LC 2006036104

This offers instruction in drawing such cartoon monsters as Dockula, the aquatic nibbler; Skeeterman, the campground creep; and Spook Ook, the attic thumper

Stephens, Jay, 1971-—*Continued*

Robots! draw your own androids, cyborgs & fighting bots; [by] Jay Stephens. Lark Books 2007 64p il $12.95

Grades: 4 5 6 7   **741.5**
    1. Robots in art 2. Drawing 3. Cartoons and caricatures
    ISBN 978-1-57990-937-6; 1-57990-937-X
                                            LC 2007027637

"With simple detailed instructions, an inviting text, and entertaining cartoon scenarios, . . . Stephens explains, step by step, how to draw a variety of robots." Booklist

Storrie, Paul D.

Beowulf; monster slayer: a British legend; story by Paul D. Storrie; pencils and inks by Ron Randall. Lerner Publishing Group/Graphic Universe 2008 48p il (Graphic myths and legends) lib bdg $26.60 *

Grades: 4 5 6 7   **741.5**
    1. Beowulf—Graphic novels 2. Graphic novels 3. Monsters—Graphic novels
    ISBN 978-0-8225-6757-8 (lib bdg); 0-8225-6757-1 (lib bdg)   LC 2006-39094

An adaptation of the epic poem in which the hero Beowulf slays the monster Grendel

This "reads like ancient poetry. . . . The action and character design are strong and clear, with solid, comfortable storytelling that is strongly helped by capable color artwork." SLJ

Sturm, James, 1965-

Adventures in cartooning; how to turn your doodles into comics; [by] James Sturm, Andrew Arnold, Alexis Frederick-Frost. First Second 2009 109p il pa $12.95 *

Grades: 2 3 4 5   **741.5**
    1. Graphic novels—Authorship 2. Comic books, strips, etc.—Authorship 3. Drawing 4. Graphic novels
    ISBN 978-1-59643-369-4 (pa); 1-59643-369-8 (pa)

"In fairy-tale fashion, the Magic Cartooning Elf helps a young princess with writer's block produce her first comic. A story-within-a-story emerges. . . . Simple cartooning basics offered after the story are quite appealing; even the most reluctant artist may be inspired to pick up a pencil and give it a shot. Entertaining and surprisingly edifying." Kirkus

Taylor, Sarah Stewart

Amelia Earhart; this broad ocean; [illustrations by] Ben Towle; with an introduction by Eileen Collins. Disney/Hyperion Books 2010 78p il lib bdg $17.99

Grades: 5 6 7 8 9   **741.5**
    1. Earhart, Amelia, 1898-1937—Graphic novels 2. Women air pilots 3. Biographical graphic novels
    ISBN 978-1-4231-1337-9 (lib bdg); 1-4231-1337-3 (lib bdg)   LC 2009-29321

"This account follows Amelia Earhart through the eyes of young Grace, a resident of the small coastal Newfoundland village from where Earhart and her pilot hope to begin a transatlantic flight in 1927. . . . The aviator gives the girl an intimate interview. . . . This approach brings the legendary aviation pioneer and her fame into a manageable context. . . . Reluctant readers, adventure fans, and thos who themselves yearn for the skies will be sucked right into the immediacy here." Bull Cent Child Books

Includes bibliographical references

Telgemeier, Raina

Smile. Scholastic/Graphix 2010 213p il $21.99; pa $10.99

Grades: 5 6 7 8   **741.5**
    1. Dentistry—Graphic novels 2. Personal appearance—Graphic novels 3. Autobiographical graphic novels 4. Graphic novels 5. Friendship—Graphic novels
    ISBN   978-0-545-13205-3;   0-545-13205-3; 978-0-545-13206-0 (pa); 0-545-13206-1 (pa)
                                            LC 2008-51782

"The dental case that Telgemeier documents in this graphic memoir was extreme: a random accident led to front tooth loss when she was 12, and over the next several years, she suffered through surgery, implants, headgear, false teeth, and a rearrangement of her remaining incisors. . . . Both adults and kids . . . are vividly and rapidly portrayed. . . . Telgemeier's storytelling and full-color cartoony images form a story that will cheer and inspire any middle-schooler dealing with orthodontia." Booklist

Sixth grader Raina just wants to be normal, but when she falls down going home from a Girl Scout meeting, she severely injures her two front teeth, and this starts her down a long road with braces, surgery, retainers, embarrassing headgear all sure to make her stand out from her middle school classmates for all the wrong reasons. There's also a major earthquake, then boy confusion, friends who turn out not to be good friends, sibling jealousy, all the stuff that makes life interesting, if not fun. Telgemeier wrote and drew the autobiographical Smile as a webcomic; this volume collects the story in color.

Thompson, Jill, 1966-

Magic Trixie; written and illustrated by Jill Thompson; lettered by Jason Arthur. Harper Trophy 2008 93p il pa $7.99

Grades: 3 4 5   **741.5**
    1. Graphic novels 2. Humorous graphic novels 3. Fantasy graphic novels 4. Magic—Graphic novels
    ISBN 978-0-06-117045-4 (pa)   LC 2007-24298

Magic Trixie is feeling a bit put out; everything in her house seems to revolve around her baby sister, and she doesn't get to do anything fun. If that wasn't bad enough, Show & Tell time is coming up at Monstersorri School, and all her classmates have seen all her tricks too many times. She'll have to come up with a new one that's really special.

"Bright colors and a whimsical style make everything friendly rather than scary. Underneath the supernatural trappings lies a classical story of sibling envy to which every big sister and big brother can relate." Booklist

Other titles in this series are:
Magic Trixie sleeps over (2008)
Magic Trixie and the dragon (2009)

The **TOON** treasury of classic children's comics; selected and edited by Art Spiegelman and Françoise Mouly; introduction by Jon Scieszka. Abrams ComicArts 2009 350p il $40 *

Grades: 3 4 5 6   **741.5**

1. Comic books, strips, etc.

ISBN 978-0-8109-5730-5; 0-8109-5730-2

LC 2009009830

"This treasury created for young readers focuses on comic books, not strips, and contains humorous stories that range from a single-page to eight or even twenty-two pages. . . . The comics have been culled from the Golden Age of comic books, roughly the 1940s through the early 1960s, and feature . . . examples of works by such . . . artists and writers as Carl Barks, John Stanley, Sheldon Mayer, Walt Kelly, Basil Wolverton, and George Carlson, among many, many others." Publisher's note

"These stories are terrifically funny, joltingly exuberant, bafflingly bizarre, and best of all, compiled into one hearty, hefty, handsome volume." Booklist

Townsend, Michael, 1981-

Kit Feeny: on the move. Alfred A. Knopf 2009 unp il lib bdg $12.99; pa $5.99

Grades: 3 4 5   **741.5**

1. Graphic novels 2. Moving—Fiction 3. Friendship—Fiction 4. Bullies—Fiction

ISBN 978-0-375-95614-0 (lib bdg); 0-375-95614-X (lib bdg); 978-0-375-85614-3 (pa); 0-375-85614-5 (pa)

LC 2008-37443

When plucky Kit Feeny moves to a new town, he immediately makes an enemy of the sadistic school bully and must struggle to find friends who share his interests.

"Kit, a mischievous, silly, ambiguous anthropomorphic animal, . . . is an easy hero to cheer for in this graphic novel, which reluctant readers will find hard to put down." Booklist

Another title about Kit Feeny is:

Kit Feeny: the ugly necklace (2009)

Trondheim, Lewis

Tiny Tyrant; by Lewis Trondheim; translated from the French by Alexis Siegel; illustrated by Fabrice Parme. First Second Books 2007 124p il $12.95

Grades: 4 5 6 7 8 9 10 11 12 Adult

    741.5

1. Graphic novels 2. Humorous graphic novels

ISBN 978-1-59643-094-5   LC 2006021479

"Tiny child-king Ethelbert is spoiled and difficult, expecting to have his every whim fulfilled-or else. . . . In the end, though, he becomes a hero. The dynamic cartoons are filled with details and riddled with humor; most pages have between six and eight small pictures. . . . This title will have wide appeal. It's young and accessible enough for elementary-grade kids, but teens will also be charmed by the rascally king." SLJ

Varon, Sara, 1971-

Robot dreams. First Second 2007 205p il pa $16.95 *

Grades: 3 4 5 6 7 8 9 10 11 12 Adult

    741.5

1. Graphic novels 2. Dogs—Graphic novels 3. Robots—Graphic novels

ISBN 978-1-59643-108-9 (pa); 1-59643-108-3 (pa)

LC 2006-52640

"A Junior Library Guild book"

In this wordless book, a dog builds a robot from a kit and they become friends; everything is fine until one fateful day at the beach, when the robot goes into the water and later rusts into immobility.

"Varon's drawing style is uncomplicated, and her colors are clean and refeshing. Although her story seems equally simple, it is invested with true emotion." Booklist

Venable, Colleen AF

Hamster and cheese; illustrated by Stephanie Yue. Graphic Universe 45p il (Guinea PIG, Pet shop private eye) lib bdg $27.93; pa $6.95

Grades: 2 3 4   **741.5**

1. Hamsters—Graphic novels 2. Guinea pigs—Graphic novels 3. Animals—Graphic novels 4. Mystery graphic novels

ISBN 978-0-7613-4598-5 (lib bdg); 0-7613-4598-1 (lib bdg); 978-0-7613-5479-6 (pa); 0-7613-5479-4 (pa)

"Who is stealing Mr. Venezi's sandwiches? The befuddled pet-shop owner misidentifies the store's animals, leading the hamsters to think they're koalas. . . . Hamisher the koala-hamster thinks Sasspants the guinea pig is a private investigator because the second G on her cage's sign has fallen off, so he asks her to investigate. . . . Young readers will appreciate the zaniness of the pet shop and the fun mystery, and Yue's colorful art uses a straightforward panel design that's easy to follow." Booklist

Watson, Andi, 1969-

Glister and the haunted teapot. Image Comics 2007 unp il pa $5.99 *

Grades: 4 5 6   **741.5**

1. Ghosts—Graphic novels 2. Graphic novels

ISBN 978-1-58240-853-8 (pa); 1-58240-853-X (pa)

Cover reads "Glister" and title page reads "Glister and the haunted teapot."

"Strange things happen around Glister Butterworth, and that is why she does not bat an eye when a haunted teapot arrives at her door. It is haunted by the ghost of Phillip Bulwark-Stratton, whose long-winded literary works have fallen out of favor. . . . British author/artist Watson, creator of the fan-favorite *Skeleton Key* aims at a younger but still sophisticated audience with his new bi-monthly series. . . . Each issue will be digest-sized and include a self-contained story. Fans of the series will want to read every issue." Voice Youth Advocates

Weigel, Jeff, 1958-

Thunder from the sea; adventure on board the HMS Defender. G. P. Putnam's Sons 2010 46p il $17.99

Grades: 3 4 5 6   **741.5**
1. Great Britain. Royal Navy—Graphic novels 2. Graphic novels 3. Adventure graphic novels 4. Europe—History—1789-1815—Graphic novels 5. Naval art and science—Graphic novels
ISBN 978-0-399-25089-7   LC 2009-32801

In 1805, during the Napoleonic Wars, twelve-year-old Jack Hoyton becomes a member of the crew of HMS Defender, a midsize ship in the British Royal Navy. The Defender patrols along a portion of the French coast to block French ships, but a major gun emplacement in Dumont hampers the ship's efforts. When some of the crew land to fill their barrels with fresh water, French gunmen fire upon them, killing an officer and wounding a crewman. The Captain assigns Jack to be part of the crew that will land and take the guns; when the men arrive, they find that there is no small village, but a major shipbuilding facility, and they're captured.

"Weigel's old-fashioned comics art shows lots of authentic details of eighteenth-century shipboard life, and there is some battle violence. . . . This picture-book-size graphic novel should find a ready audience of young adventure-loving readers." Booklist

Includes bibliographical references

Wight, Eric, 1974-

Frankie Pickle and the closet of doom; written and illustrated by Eric Wight. Simon & Schuster Books for Young Readers 2009 79p il $9.99 *
Grades: 2 3 4 5   **741.5**
1. Cleanliness—Fiction 2. Imagination—Fiction 3. Family life—Fiction 4. Graphic novels 5. Humorous graphic novels 6. Family life—Graphic novels 7. Orderliness—Graphic novels
ISBN 978-1-4169-6484-1; 1-4169-6484-3
LC 2008-30865

Fourth-grader Frankie Piccolini has a vivid imagination when it comes to cleaning his disastrously messy room, but eventually even he decides that it is just too dirty.

"Wight's hilarious twists of language are matched with a wicked sense of fun in the illustrations and frequent sequential-paneled episodes of pretend play." Kirkus

Another title about Frankie Pickle is:
Frankie Pickle and the Pine Run 3000 (2010)

Zornow, Jeff

The legend of Sleepy Hollow; adapted and illustrated by Jeff Zornow; based upon the works of Washington Irving. Magic Wagon 2007 unp il (Graphic horror) $18.95
Grades: 5 6 7 8 9 10 11 12   **741.5**
1. New York (State)—Graphic novels
ISBN 978-1-60270-060-4; 1-60270-060-5
LC 2007-9615

This "is an entertaining and faithful, if much adapted version of Irving's classic story. Zornow's illustrations are the highlight of the work, successfully bringing the characters of the story to life." Booklist

741.6   Graphic design, illustration, commercial art

The **art** of reading; forty illustrators celebrate RIF's 40th anniversary; with a foreword by Leonard S. Marcus. Dutton Bks. 2005 96p il lib bdg $19.99
Grades: Adult Professional   **741.6**
1. Illustration of books 2. Illustrators
ISBN 0-525-47484-6

"Forty well-known, well-loved children's book illustrators share memories of a book . . . seminal to their development as readers and artists, and offer accompanying pieces of art—reimagined from those books. . . . This is a lovingly conceived, cohesive, and distinctively designed treasure. . . . Leonard S. Marcus's insightful and affecting foreword sets just the right anticipatory tone for readers who will be treated to spectacular pictures and often-moving personal statements." SLJ

Artist to artist; 23 major illustrators talk to children about their art. Philomel Books 2007 105p il $30 *
Grades: 4 5 6 7   **741.6**
1. Illustrators 2. Illustration of books 3. Picture books for children
ISBN 978-0-399-24600-5

"This anthology celebrates and elucidates contemporary picture-book art. . . . Ashley Bryan, Quentin Blake, Leo Lionni, Alice Provensen, and Gennady Spirin are among the contributors, whose comments are formatted as signed letters illustrated with childhood photographs. . . . Each artist includes glorious self-portraits and a gatefold page that reveals a marvelous array of sketches, color mixes, and studio scenes. All readers will find something that piques curiosity or provides insight." Booklist

Carle, Eric

The art of Eric Carle. Philomel Bks. 1996 125p il $35; pa $19.99
Grades: Adult Professional   **741.6**
1. Picture books for children 2. Illustration of books
ISBN 0-399-22937-X; 0-399-24002-0 (pa)
LC 95-24940

This is "both a textual and visual anthology: in addition to Carle's autobiographical chapter and the text of his 1990 speech at the Library of Congress, chapters include accolades from Ann Beneduce (Carle's U.S. editor) and from Dr. Viktor Christen (Carle's German editor). A photoessay on the artist's collage technique rubs shoulders with a forty-page gallery of his illustrations over the last quarter of a century, which precedes a look at some of his quick sketches and an illustrated bibliography of his oeuvre. The book's inviting layout may appeal to artistic youngsters as well as grown Carle fans, and the information about his working process, particularly the technical details, is absorbing." Bull Cent Child Books

Ellabbad, Mohieddine, 1940-

The illustrator's notebook; [translated from the Arabic by Sarah Quinn] Groundwood Books/House of Anansi Press 2006 30p il $16.95
Grades: 5 6 7 8   **741.6**
   1. Illustrators 2. Illustration of books
   ISBN 0-88899-700-0

"Part children's book, part autobiography, part design treatise, this hard-to-categorize Egyptian import is full of wonders from start to finish. Ellabbad uses excerpts from his notebooks to discuss ways of seeing art from an artist's perspective and as someone from an Arabic culture. Printed like the Egyptian edition—read right to left—the pages are magnificently and surprisingly illustrated, juxtaposing Arabic script (English translations appear in the margins), watercolor paintings, pasted-in photos and pictures from comic books, and all manner of characters from Eastern and Western cultures." SLJ

Evans, Dilys

Show & tell; exploring the fine art of children's book illustration; [by] Dilys Evans. Chronicle Books 2008 143p il $24.99 *
Grades: Professional   **741.6**
   1. Illustration of books 2. Illustrators
   ISBN 978-0-8118-4971-5; 0-8118-4971-6
                      LC 2006027981

This "book focuses on twelve illustrators, ranging from classic stars such as Hilary Knight and Trina Schart Hyman to new talents such as Bryan Collier and David Shannon; each . . . chapter talks about the artist's process and life and explores in depth the artistic achievements in particular books, with page reproductions included for close viewing and exploration. The style is chatty yet informed, and the careful scrutiny of the illustrations will be conceptually enlightening to many readers seeking to develop their skill in assessing art." Bull Cent Child Books

Kushner, Tony

The art of Maurice Sendak; 1980 to present; text by Tony Kushner. Abrams 2003 223p il $60
Grades: Adult Professional   **741.6**
   1. Sendak, Maurice
   ISBN 0-8109-4448-0   LC 2003-9293
   Companion volume to The art of Maurice Sendak by Selma Lanes, published 1981 by Harry Abrams

This "collection presents 350 illustrations, many of which are drawings for set and costume design work, . . . others of which are posters for plays and for events such as the New York is Book Country fair. . . . Sendak's precise, intensely shaded yet welcoming shapes and figures have lost none of their luster. They would ordinarily be enough in themselves in a survey like this, but Kushner's lovely, funny, partisan text . . . lifts the book to another level." Publ Wkly
   Includes bibliographical references

Maguire, Gregory

Making mischief; a Maurice Sendak appreciation. William Morrow 2009 200p il $27.50
Grades: Professional   **741.6**
   1. Sendak, Maurice 2. Illustrators
   ISBN 978-0-06-168916-1; 0-06-168916-5
                    LC 2009017357

"Maguire constructs a thoughtful and accessible overview of Sendak's works and artistic process, making for a tender homage to the famed artist that only a true fan could produce. . . . He presents a series of five essays, expounding upon the various influences seen in Sendak's work. . . as well as an analysis of motifs and techniques. Maguire often allows the art to speak for itself, displaying a generous selection of Sendak's illustrations, both famed and lesser known." Bull Cent Child Books

Marcus, Leonard S., 1950-

A Caldecott celebration; seven artists and their paths to the Caldecott medal. rev ed. Walker & Co. 2008 55p il $19.95; lib bdg $20.85 *
Grades: Professional   **741.6**
   1. Caldecott Medal 2. Illustrators 3. Illustration of books
   ISBN 978-0-8027-9703-2; 0-8027-9703-2; 978-0-8027-9704-9 (lib bdg); 0-8027-9704-0 (lib bdg)
                    LC 2007-23132
   First published 1998

Profiles seven Caldecott award winning books and their authors, including Robert McCloskey's "Make Way for Ducklings," Marcia Brown's "Cinderella," Maurice Sendak's "Where the Wild Things Are," William Steig's "Sylvester and the Magic Pebble," Chris Van Allsburg's "Jumanji," David Wiesner's "Tuesday," and Mordicai Gerstein's "The Man Who Walked Between the Towers"
   "The value of this volume is that Marcus makes these exceptional author/illustrators, and the processes by which they created their award-winning picture books, accessible to children and to adults who value children's literature." SLJ

Stevens, Janet, 1953-

From pictures to words; a book about making a book; written and illustrated by Janet Stevens. Holiday House 1995 unp il $16.95
Grades: K 1 2 3   **741.6**
   1. Picture books for children 2. Authorship
   ISBN 0-8234-1154-0   LC 94-18976

"Stevens, appearing as herself sketched in black-and-white, is the main character in her story. She's surrounded by . . . animal characters who encourage her to write a book starring them. With help from Cat, Koala Bear, and Rhino, she does, explaining as she goes along the basic elements of writing and illustrating—setting, plot, tension, and characterization." Booklist

"The straightforward text carefully presents information while maintaining the narrative flow. Dialogue balloons and funny asides from the characters keep the presentation lively." SLJ

Under the spell of the moon; art for children from the world's great illustrators; [edited by Patricia Aldana; texts translated by Stan Dragland] Groundwood Books 2004 80p il $25

Grades: Professional   **741.6**

1. Illustration of books 2. Illustrators

ISBN 0-88899-559-8

This "collection features the artwork of children's book illustrators who, together, represent more than 25 countries. Each double-page spread includes a different artist's image accompanied by a poem, nursery rhyme, song, or bit of nonsense that appears in both English and the illustrator's native language. . . . Katherine Paterson offers a stirring introduction that discusses IBBY (The International Board on Books for Young People)." Booklist

741.9   Collections of drawings

—I never saw another butterfly—; children's drawings and poems from Terezin concentration camp, 1942-1944; edited by Hana Volavková; foreword by Chaim Potok; afterword by Vaclav Havel. expanded 2nd ed, by U.S. Holocaust Memorial Mus. Schocken Bks. 1993 xxii, 106p il pa $17.50 hardcover o.p. *

Grades: 4 5 6 7   **741.9**

1. Child artists 2. Children's writings 3. Terezin (Czechoslovakia: Concentration camp) 4. Holocaust, 1933-1945

ISBN 0-8052-1015-6 (pa)   LC 92-50477

Original Czech edition, 1959; first American edition published 1964 by McGraw-Hill

"Of the 15,000 children who passed through Terezin before going to Auschwitz, only 100 lived. This book is a collection of poems and drawings by some of them. . . . This touching book adds another facet to library collections on the Holocaust." SLJ

Pericoli, Matteo

See the city; the journey of Manhattan unfurled; [by] Matteo Pericoli. Alfred A. Knopf 2004 unp il $15.95

Grades: 4 5 6 7   **741.9**

1. Drawing 2. Manhattan (New York, N.Y.)

ISBN 0-375-82469-3   LC 2003-25881

"This depiction of Manhattan began as two continuous scrolls, one of the East Side, one of the West Side, each 37 feet long, which were published in 2001 (Random). The drawings in pen and ink depict the city skyline from the perspective of a boat tour taken around the island by Pericoli. . . . A personal narrative accompanies the drawings, affording insight into the creative processes of writing and illustrating. This is a fascinating work." SLJ

743   Drawing and drawings by subject

Ames, Lee J., 1921-

[Draw 50 series] Doubleday 1974-2003 21v pa each $8.95

Grades: 4 5 6 7   **743**

1. Drawing

Available titles are: Draw 50 Airplanes, aircraft, and spacecraft; Draw 50 aliens; Draw 50 animal toons; Draw 50 animals; Draw 50 athletes; Draw 50 baby animals; Draw 50 beasties; Draw 50 birds; Draw 50 boats, ships, trucks, & trains; Draw 50 buildings and other structures; Draw 50 cats; Draw 50 dinosaurs and other prehistoric animals; Draw 50 dogs; Draw 50 endangered animals; Draw 50 famous faces; Draw 50 flowers, trees, and other plants; Draw 50 holiday decorations; Draw 50 horses; Draw 50 monsters; Draw 50 people; Draw 50 people from the Bible

Each volume presents step-by-step instructions for drawing a variety of animals, people, or objects

Court, Rob, 1956-

How to draw cars and trucks; [by] Rob Court. Child's World 2005 32p il (Scribbles Institute) lib bdg $21.36

Grades: 4 5 6   **743**

1. Drawing 2. Automobiles 3. Trucks

ISBN 1-59296-148-7   LC 2004-3729

Contents: Drawing cars and trucks; Drawing with shapes; Drawing with lines; Freehand drawing; Three-dimensional form; Light and shadows; Drawing ideas; Patterns; Space and composition; Drawing with color; The artist's studio

This volume does "more than deconstruct objects into basic shapes then reconstruct them to show budding artists how to draw. [It] also [provides] information about select information of what's being drawn . . . which makes artists look harder at details and helps them better understand what they are creating. . . . [The author] introduces a few drawing fundamentals—perspective, shading, and composition—and supplies tips on choosing drawing pencils and using color to enliven a picture. . . . There's a lot more than just drawing practice here." Booklist

Emberley, Ed

Ed Emberley's drawing book of faces. Little, Brown 1975 32p il pa $6.95 hardcover o.p.

Grades: 2 3 4 5   **743**

1. Drawing 2. Face in art

ISBN 0-316-23655-1 (pa)

Provides step-by-step instructions for drawing a wide variety of faces reflecting various emotions and professions

Lipsey, Jennifer, 1971-
I love to draw horses! [by] Jennifer Lipsey. Lark Books 2008 48p il (My very favorite art book) $9.95

Grades: 3 4 5 6   **743**
1. Horses in art 2. Drawing
ISBN 978-1-60059-152-5; 1-60059-152-3
         LC 2007-49048

"This drawing guide presents basics (starting with circles) for beginning artists. Readers will discover a wealth of information as they sketch a variety of equine subjects in action. . . . The accessible instructions are presented with finished, illustrated demonstrations in colored pen to create an easy-to-use and attractive how-to for young artists." SLJ

Peffer, Jessica, 1983-
DragonArt; how to draw fantastic dragons and fantasy creatures. Impact Books 2005 127p il pa $19.99

Grades: 5 6 7 8   **743**
1. Drawing 2. Dragons 3. Mythical animals
ISBN 1-58180-657-4   LC 2005013013

This is a guide to drawing dragons and other mythical beasts such as griffins, guardian gargoyles, and deadly basilisks.

"This book has great writing and superb illustrations and manages to do everything right from the front cover to the index." SLJ

745.2   Industrial art and design

Welsbacher, Anne, 1955-
Earth-friendly design; by Anne Welsbacher. Lerner Publications Company 2009 72p il (Saving our living Earth) lib bdg $30.60

Grades: 5 6 7 8   **745.2**
1. Industrial design 2. Environmental protection
ISBN 978-0-8225-7564-1 (lib bdg); 0-8225-7564-7 (lib bdg)   LC 2007-35925

"Provides a thorough, interesting discussion of multiple aspects of [Earth-friendly design], including historical origins, the current situation, and potential solutions. . . . Photos from around the world accompany discussions. . . . [This is a] solid choice to replace outdated books." SLJ

Includes glossary and bibliographical references

745.4   Pure and applied design and decoration

Gonyea, Mark
Another book about design; complicated doesn't make it bad. Henry Holt & Co. 2007 unp il $19.95 *

Grades: 3 4 5   **745.4**
1. Design
ISBN 978-0-8050-7576-2; 0-8050-7576-3
         LC 2006-43705

The author demonstrates "how ideas such as foreground and background, repetition and size of shapes, and positive and negative space can affect a final composition. The definitions of terms are as minimal and clear as the visuals. . . . [This] will leave kids eager to play with the concepts in their own pictures." Booklist

A book about design; complicated doesn't make it good. Henry Holt & Co. 2005 unp il $18.95 *

Grades: 3 4 5   **745.4**
1. Design
ISBN 0-8050-7575-5   LC 2004-08982

"This stylish, square volume delivers a cheerful manifesto on graphic design. . . . Chatty, brief chapters present principles of composition, line, color, and contrast, as well as techniques for drawing attention to 'what's important' on a page. . . . The text, set against pure white backdrops, is easy to read, and the artwork's elemental shapes and bright colors illustrate the theories in ways that children will readily grasp." Booklist

745.5   Handicrafts

Alter, Anna, 1974-
What can you do with an old red shoe? a green activity book about re-use; [by] Anna Alter. Henry Holt & Co. 2009 32p il $16.95

Grades: 1 2 3   **745.5**
1. Handicraft 2. Recycling 3. Salvage
ISBN 978-0-8050-8290-6; 0-8050-8290-5
         LC 2008018341

"Recycling becomes lots of fun in this sprightly activity book. Alter offers 13 projects, and . . . the finished products are usually items kids will want to use. . . . The instructions are clear and simple . . . and what really makes this a standout is Alter's adorable artwork featuring a coterie of animals at work and play. Short poems introduce each project." Booklist

Bell-Rehwoldt, Sheri, 1962-
The kids' guide to building cool stuff; by Sheri Bell-Rehwoldt. Capstone Press 2009 32p il (Kids' guides) lib bdg $23.99

Grades: 4 5 6 7   **745.5**
1. Handicraft 2. Amusements 3. Science—Experiments
ISBN 978-1-4296-2276-9 (lib bdg); 1-4296-2276-8 (lib bdg)   LC 2008-29687

"Edge books"

This provides instructions for building such items as a kite, a balloon rocket, a paper boat, a milk carton bird feeder, and a plastic plate hovercraft

Includes glossary and bibliographical references

Bull, Jane, 1957-
Make it! by Jane Bull. DK Pub. 2008 62p il $14.99 *

Grades: 1 2 3 4   **745.5**
1. Handicraft 2. Recycling
ISBN 978-0-7566-3837-5; 0-7566-3837-2
         LC 2008006636

Bull, Jane, 1957-—*Continued*
"From its unique cardboard cutout 'picture-frame' cover to its 3 'Rs' to recycling, this craft book lives up to its motto: 'Don't trash it-treasure it!' As good for its ideas in suggesting alternate materials as for its instructions, it will be sheer joy for young crafters. . . . The projects are easy and clever, and all of the pages are profusely illustrated with large, colorful photos of a boy and girl working on the crafts." SLJ

Check, Laura, 1958-
Create your own candles; 30 easy-to-make designs; illustrations by Norma Jean Martin-Jourdenais. Williamson Books 2004 62p il (Quick starts for kids!) pa $8.95
Grades: 5 6 7 8   745.5
1. Candles
ISBN 1-88559-352-X   LC 2004-40870
"Check begins this useful resource with 'Ten Hot Safety Tips.' . . . Next, she lists and describes basic equipment. . . . The projects range from simple beeswax candles to molded candles, hand-dipped candles, and gel candles." SLJ

Crafty activities; over 50 fun and easy things to make; by Judy Balchin . . . [et al.] Search 2007 unp il pa $19.95
Grades: 4 5 6 7   745.5
1. Handicraft
ISBN 978-1-84448-250-4 (pa); 1-84448-250-2 (pa)
"The book is divided into six chapters—mosaics, printing, lettering, papier-mâché, handmade cards, and origami—with projects ranging from simple leaf prints to an elaborate necklace made from dried pasta. . . . The photos of smiling kids showing off their creations, the attractive, spacious page design, and, above all the ingenious projects will attract kids—as well as teachers." Booklist

Dall, Mary Doerfler, 1949-
Little Hands create! art & activities for kids ages 3 to 6; [by] Mary Dall; illustrations by Sarah Rakitin. Williamson Books 2004 118p il pa $9.95
Grades: K 1 2   745.5
1. Handicraft
ISBN 1-88559-365-1   LC 2004-40872
"A Williamson Little Hands book"
"Although Dall's text is addressed to the little ones who will be making these projects . . . it's really for adult helpers, who can read the instructions aloud as they shepherd their charges through a wealth of crafts activities—from twisted-paper jewelry to pictures and sculptures. Most of the projects depend on readily available materials. . . . The directions are clear. . . . Dall extends the fun with some bright, silly poems and occasional suggestions of simple games to play or picture books that dovetail nicely with the craft. . . . Great for teachers, daycare providers, or anyone looking for rainy-day activities for the very young." Booklist

Fox, Tom
Snowball launchers, giant-pumpkin growers, and other cool contraptions; [by] Tom Fox. Sterling Pub. 2006 127p il pa $9.95 *
Grades: 4 5 6 7   745.5
1. Handicraft
ISBN 978-0-8069-5515-5 (pa); 0-8069-5515-5 (pa)
                              LC 2005032781
"The 20 projects in this collection range from a simple 'Heartbeat Monitor' to a fairly complex 'Moth-Bot,' a wheeled vehicle that moves toward light with the flick of a switch. Most have strong kid appeal. . . . Instructions are written in an engaging, conversational tone, with background information about concepts such as gravity and electricity woven into the text." SLJ

Garner, Lynne
African crafts; fun things to make and do from West Africa. Chicago Review Press 2008 48p il $12.95 *
Grades: 4 5 6   745.5
1. Handicraft 2. Ghana—Social life and customs 3. African art
ISBN 978-1-55652-748-7; 1-55652-748-9
First published 2004 in the United Kingdom
Presents an overview of West African culture and provides step-by-step instructions for using simple household materials to make such traditional items as a mask, a coiled pot, block-printed and woven cloths, and a drum.
"Despite the generic title, the focus is on one country, Ghana, and that is the strength of this hands-on crafts book, illustrated with clear step-by-step instructions and lots of color photos. . . . Written in chatty style, the spaciously laid out chapters cover *adinkra* block printing, pot coiling, mask making, music makers, and kente strip weaving. . . . An excellent source for school and home." Booklist

Haab, Sherri, 1964-
Dangles and bangles; 25 funky accessories to make and wear; by Sherri Haab and Michelle Haab; with illustrations by Barbara Pollak. Watson-Guptill Publications 2005 96p il pa $9.95 *
Grades: 5 6 7 8   745.5
1. Jewelry 2. Handicraft
ISBN 0-8230-0064-8
This describes "jewelry hardware, . . . tools, glues and adhesives, and . . . craft supplies, as well as ideas about where to purchase these materials. A spread on basic techniques explains how to work with cord and elastic, glue, rings/pins, etc. The projects . . . range from necklaces to key chains to hair accessories. . . . The mix of colorful photographs, full-page paintings of stylishly dressed youngsters, and varied typefaces makes for an attractive layout. Packed full of wonderful ideas, this irresistible title will be popular with young crafters as well as with adults who plan craft programs." SLJ

Hankin, Rosie

Crafty kids; fun projects for you and your toddler. Barron's 2006 64p il pa $8.99

Grades: PreK K   **745.5**

    1. Handicraft

    ISBN 0-7641-3542-2

"Designed for parents to use with young children, the 28 projects in this collection are both fun and simple to put together. . . . Most of the projects are constructed from paper plates and colored or painted papers that have been cut into simple, often geometric shapes and then adorned with cotton balls, stickers, or marker designs." Booklist

Hendry, Linda

Cat crafts; written and illustrated by Linda Hendry. Kids Can Press 2002 40p il (Kids can do it) $12.95; pa $5.95

Grades: 4 5 6   **745.5**

    1. Handicraft 2. Cats

    ISBN 1-55074-964-1; 1-55074-921-8 (pa)

This includes instructions for 17 craft projects including a spider cat toy, a scratch pad, a catnip fish, and decorated placemats, earrings, and bookends

"Nicely designed, double-page spreads show the project step-by-step, each one clearly and succinctly described and illustrated with a color drawing." Booklist

Dog crafts; written and illustrated by Linda Hendry. Kids Can Press 2002 40p il (Kids can do it) $12.95; pa $5.95

Grades: 4 5 6   **745.5**

    1. Handicraft 2. Dogs

    ISBN 1-55074-960-9; 1-55074-962-5 (pa)

This includes instructions for 17 craft projects including decorated jars, picture frames, placemats, jewelry, and bookends

"Nicely designed, double-page spreads show the project step-by-step, each one clearly and succinctly described and illustrated with a color drawing." Booklist

Horse crafts; written and illustrated by Linda Hendry. Kids Can Press 2006 40p il (Kids can do it) $12.95; pa $6.95

Grades: 4 5 6   **745.5**

    1. Handicraft 2. Horses

    ISBN 1-55337-646-3; 1-55337-647-1 (pa)

This includes instructions for craft projects including drawing a horse, making a silhouette, a pencil top, a lampshade, a pin, a browband cover, a mirror, a plaque, a clipboard, a pillow, a keepsake box, a blue jean bag, bookends, a CD box, and a sock horse.

Henry, Sandi, 1951-

Making amazing art; 40 activities using the 7 elements of art design; by Sandi Henry; illustrated by Sarah Rakitin Cole. Williamsonbooks 2007 128p il (Kids can) $16.99; pa $12.99

Grades: 2 3 4 5   **745.5**

    1. Handicraft 2. Art 3. Design

    ISBN   978-0-8249-6794-9;   0-8249-6794-1; 978-0-8249-6795-6 (pa); 0-8249-6795-X (pa)

                    LC 2006101173

"A Williamson Kids Can book"

"Each chapter in this well-organized, heavily illustrated book features one element—line, texture, color, etc.— with five or six projects that cleverly support it. . . . Icons display three challenge levels; step-by-step instructions help to ensure success." SLJ

Kenney, Karen Latchana, 1974-

Super simple art to wear; fun and easy-to-make crafts for kids. ABDO Pub. Company 2010 31p il (Super simple crafts) lib bdg $17.95

Grades: K 1 2 3 4   **745.5**

    1. Handicraft

    ISBN 978-1-60453-622-5 (lib bdg); 1-60453-622-5 (lib bdg)   LC 2009-349

"Colorful photos; clean layout in a bright, primary palette; and large, abundant step-by-step instructional photos give [this book] great appeal. The . . . crafts . . . are functional and attractive. [The book] demonstrates [for instatnce] how to paint shoelaces. . . . Readily obtainable household materials and easy-to-follow instructions mean that children can do these crafts independently." SLJ

Includes glossary

Llimós, Anna

Easy cardboard crafts in 5 steps. Enslow Elementary 2008 31p il (Easy crafts in 5 steps) lib bdg $22.60

Grades: 2 3 4   **745.5**

    1. Handicraft

    ISBN 978-0-7660-3083-1 (lib bdg); 0-7660-3083-0 (lib bdg)

    Original Spanish edition 2005

This "has instructions for 14 projects, among them a folder, drum, and hang-glider. . . . A materials list is provided for each item, with general supplies and recyclables sufficient for most crafts. The simple directions are adequately spaced on the page and accompanied by step-by-step color photos." SLJ

Includes bibliographical references

Easy cloth crafts in 5 steps. Enslow Elementary 2008 31p il (Easy crafts in 5 steps) lib bdg $22.60

Grades: 2 3 4   **745.5**

    1. Handicraft

    ISBN 978-0-7660-3084-8 (lib bdg); 0-7660-3084-9 (lib bdg)

    Original Spanish edition 2005

This "has instructions for 14 projects, among them . . . a tray, turtle, and clown. . . . A materials list is provided for each item, with general supplies and recyclables sufficient for most crafts. The simple directions are adequately spaced on the page and accompanied by step-by-step color photos." SLJ

Includes bibliographical references

Easy earth-friendly crafts in 5 steps. Enslow Elementary 2008 31p il (Easy crafts in 5 steps) lib bdg $22.60

Grades: 2 3 4   **745.5**

    1. Handicraft 2. Recycling

    ISBN 978-0-7660-3086-2 (lib bdg); 0-7660-3086-5 (lib bdg)

    Original Spanish edition 2005

Llimós, Anna—*Continued*

This offers instructions for 14 crafts using recycled materials such as bottle caps, egg cartons, and bottles, among them a coin purse, a spinning top, and a doll

The text is "easy to read, and the results are quirky and pleasing; steps are illustrated with bright photographs." Horn Book Guide

Includes bibliographical references

Monaghan, Kimberly

Organic crafts; 75 earth-friendly art activities; [by] Kimberly Monaghan. Chicago Review Press 2007 140p pa $14.95

Grades: 2 3 4 5   745.5
1. Handicraft 2. Nature craft
ISBN 978-1-55652-640-4 (pa); 1-55652-640-7 (pa)
LC 2006031659
"These activities, crafts, and games are arranged by type of material used, such as rocks, pebbles, and shells; soil, clay, and sand, etc. There's a wide range of interesting projects, including clay beads, a glittering sand castle, potpourri, a sea sparkler, a wind sock, a gourd birdhouse, broken-china mosaics, homemade paper, rock sculpture, and garden chimes. Children will also learn how to make natural glue, cornstarch paint, and salt clay." SLJ

Includes bibliographical references

Oldham, Todd

Kid made modern. AMMO 2009 184p il $22.95 *

Grades: 3 4 5 6   745.5
1. Handicraft 2. Design
ISBN 978-1-934429-36-5; 1-934429-36-8
LC 2009-934393
"This activity book from renowned designer Oldham uses the work of Mid-Century modern visual artists—including Isamu Noguchi, Alexander Calder, and Charles and Ray Eames—as springboards for 52 hands-on creative projects. Brief tutorials introduce skills and techniques, paired with full-color photos of kids and the various processes. . . . There's much here to capture the eye of ambitious, crafty readers." Publ Wkly

Owen, Cheryl

Gifts for kids to make. Hamlyn 2006 128p il pa $14.95

Grades: K 1 2 3 4 5   745.5
1. Handicraft 2. Gifts
ISBN 0-600-61502-2
"This useful volume is divided into six categories—bric-a-brac, stationery, scented gifts, floral garden gifts, accessories, and edible treats—with 7 to 10 projects in each. Examples are magnets, bookmarks, gift wrap, birdfeeder, glasses case, and cookies. . . . The items are appealing to children and age appropriate. Both the written and visual instructions are clear and easy to follow." SLJ

Press, Judy, 1944-

Around-the-world art & activities; visiting the 7 continents through craft fun; illustrations by Betsy Day. Williamson 2001 128p il (Williamson Little Hands book) pa $12.95 *

Grades: K 1 2   745.5
1. Handicraft
ISBN 1-88559-345-7   LC 00-60030
"North American totem poles, Hawaiian leis, Aboriginal bark painting, Japanese dolls in kimonos, Korean drums, egg-carton camels, Masai beaded necklaces, nesting Russian dolls, and South American gaucho belts are among the projects. While the ideas will not be new to veteran crafters, they are basic and solid for the intended audience." SLJ

ArtStarts for little hands! fun & discoveries for 3- to 7-year olds; illustrations by Karol Kaminski. Williamson 2000 118p il (Williamson Little Hands book) pa $12.95 *

Grades: K 1 2   745.5
1. Handicraft
ISBN 1-88559-337-6   LC 99-89956
Presents a variety of art projects and related activities grouped around such themes as the family, animals, nature, transportation, color, and more
"These simple activities use easy-to-find materials such as egg cartons, paper plates, craft sticks, and paper-towel tubes. The directions are easy to follow and are supplemented with clear, black-line drawings of almost every step." SLJ

The little hands big fun craft book; illustrated by Loretta Trezzo Braren. 2nd ed. Williamson 2008 142p il pa $12.99

Grades: PreK K 1   745.5
1. Handicraft
ISBN 978-0-8249-6827-4 (pa); 0-8249-6827-1 (pa)
First published 1996
This craft book for young children includes 70 projects

Robinson, Fay

Hispanic-American crafts kids can do! [by] Fay Robinson. Enslow Elementary 2006 32p il (Multicultural crafts kids can do!) $22.60 *

Grades: 3 4 5   745.5
1. Handicraft 2. Latin America—Social life and customs
ISBN 0-7660-2459-8   LC 2005033800
This offers instructions for creating 10 crafts from Mexico, Panama, and Central and South America including piñatas, maracas, molas, Mayan weavings, and Mexican pottery.

"The title gets it right. These are crafts kids can do, and, more important, will want to do. . . . Kids get to see each project in colorful, step-by-step photographs." Booklist

Includes bibliographical references

Ross, Kathy, 1948-

Bedroom makeover crafts; illustrated by Nicole in den Bosch. Millbrook Press 2008 47p il (Girl crafts) lib bdg $26.60; pa $7.95

Grades: 3 4 5   **745.5**

1. Handicraft

ISBN 978-0-8225-7593-1 (lib bdg); 0-8225-7593-0 (lib bdg); 978-1-58013-823-9 (pa); 1-58013-823-3 (pa)

LC 2007001894

"This title contains step-by-step directions for an array of room accessories that includes everything from earring dolls and doorknob covers to small tables and trash baskets. Materials are readily obtained and directions are clear and easy to follow." SLJ

Crafts for kids who are learning about dinosaurs; illustrated by Jan Barger. Millbrook Press 2008 48p il lib bdg $26.60

Grades: 2 3 4   **745.5**

1. Handicraft 2. Dinosaurs

ISBN 978-0-8225-6809-4 (lib bdg); 0-8225-6809-8 (lib bdg)

LC 2006100645

"These 22 projects include a necklace, a bathtub toy, puppets, a pencil topper, a tape dispenser, and more. Brief facts about dinosaurs are matched with each craft. Each project has a list of materials needed and illustrations for the 3 to 15 steps. . . . A welcome addition for young dinosaur fans." SLJ

Earth-friendly crafts; clever ways to reuse everyday items; [by] Kathy Ross; illustrated by Celine Malepart. Millbrook Press 2009 48p il lib bdg $26.60

Grades: 3 4 5 6   **745.5**

1. Handicraft 2. Recycling

ISBN 978-0-8225-9099-6 (lib bdg); 0-8225-9099-9 (lib bdg)

LC 2008025481

"This clear, colorful title offers a selection of environmentally focused projects that encourage kids to reduce, reuse, and recycle. Both practical and eye-catching, the projects, from pencil cups to decorative pins, rely on everyday discarded items that many kids will find around their homes. . . . [The crafts] are presented in line drawings that demonstrate the construction step by step along with color photos of the finished product." Booklist

Sadler, Judy Ann, 1959-

The new jumbo book of easy crafts; written by Judy Ann Sadler; illustrated by Caroline Price. Kids Can Press 2009 176p il pa $18.95

Grades: PreK K 1 2   **745.5**

1. Handicraft

ISBN 978-1-55453-239-1 (pa); 1-55453-239-6 (pa)

First published 2001 with title: The Kids Can Press jumbo book of easy crafts

This includes instructions for over 150 crafts divided into four themed sections: Imagine and Create, Wear and Use, Make and Play and Decorate and Celebrate

Schwarz, Renée

Funky junk; cool stuff to make with hardware. Kids Can Press 2003 40p il (Kids can do it) $12.95; pa $5.95

Grades: 4 5 6   **745.5**

1. Handicraft

ISBN 1-55337-387-1; 1-55337-388-X (pa)

This offers ideas for craft projects using materials found "at the hardware store. Directions are given for turning nuts, bolts, corner braces, and so on into jewelry, a chess set, and more." SLJ

Silver, Patricia

Face painting; written by Patricia Silver (Patty the clown); illustrated by Louise Phillips. Kids Can Press 2000 40p il (Kids can do it) $12.95; pa $5.95

Grades: 4 5 6   **745.5**

1. Face painting

ISBN 1-55074-845-9; 1-55074-689-8 (pa)

The author "includes step-by-step instructions for 16 of the most commonly requested faces, rules for safety, and the all-important cleanup tips. Clear, full-color photographs and drawings of children in the makeup accompany the instructions. These simple illustrations are charming and helpful." SLJ

Sirrine, Carol

Cool crafts with old jeans; green projects for resourceful kids. Capstone Press 2010 32p il (Snap books. Green crafts) lib bdg $26.65

Grades: 3 4 5 6   **745.5**

1. Jeans (Clothing) 2. Handicraft 3. Recycling

ISBN 978-1-4296-4006-0 (lib bdg); 1-4296-4006-5 (lib bdg)

"Step-by-step instructions for crafts made from old jeans and information about reusing and recycling." Publisher's note

"Steps are easy to follow and well documented, and the projects encourage experimentation and creativity. Materials are generally easy to find. . . . This . . . is original, well-presented, and bound to inspire classroom and individual projects." SLJ

Includes glossary and bibliographical references

Cool crafts with old t-shirts; green projects for resourceful kids. Capstone Press 2010 32p il (Snap Books. Green crafts) lib bg $26.65

Grades: 3 4 5 6   **745.5**

1. Handicraft 2. Salvage

ISBN 978-1-4296-4009-1 (lib bdg); 1-4296-4009-X (lib bdg)

"Step-by-step instructions for crafts made from old T-shirts and information about reusing and recycling." Publisher's note

"Steps are easy to follow and well documented, and the projects encourage experimentation and creativity. Materials are generally easy to find. . . . This . . . is original, well-presented, and bound to inspire classroom and individual projects." SLJ

Includes glossary and bibliographical references

Sirrine, Carol—_Continued_

Cool crafts with old wrappers, cans and bottles; green projects for resourceful kids. Capstone Press 2010 32p il (Snap books. Green crafts) lib bdg $26.65

Grades: 3 4 5 6   **745.5**

1. Handicraft 2. Salvage
ISBN 978-1-4296-4008-4 (lib bdg); 1-4296-4008-1 (lib bdg)

"Step-by-step instructions for crafts made from everyday items and information about reusing and recycling." Publisher's note

"Steps are easy to follow and well documented, and the projects encourage experimentation and creativity. Materials are generally easy to find. . . . This . . . is original, well-presented, and bound to inspire classroom and individual projects." SLJ

Includes glossary and bibliographical references

Warwick, Ellen

Everywear; written by Ellen Warwick; illustrated by Bernice Lum. Kids Can Press 2008 80p il (Planet girl) $14.95

Grades: 5 6 7 8   **745.5**

1. Handicraft 2. Dress accessories
ISBN 978-1-55337-799-3; 1-55337-799-0

"After several opening pages that introduce supplies, . . . very basic stitching skills, and terminology, girls turn to the . . . issue of hair: woven-ribbon bands, jazzed-up chopsticks; fabric-flower-bedecked combs; reversible ponytail wraps. Next come body adornments . . . followed by stuff to stow it in, of clutched, dangled, and toted varieties. Each project features a list of supplies, . . . clearly numbered steps with cartoon-styled illustrations . . . and full-color photograph of the finished item. . . . [This has] genuine sleepover appeal." Bull Cent Child Books

745.54   Paper handicrafts

Garza, Carmen Lomas, 1948-

Making magic windows; creating papel picado/cut-paper art with Carmen Lomas Garza. Children's Bk. Press 1999 61p il pa $9.95 *

Grades: 3 4 5 6   **745.54**

1. Paper crafts
ISBN 0-89239-159-6   LC 98-38518

Provides instructions for making paper banners and more intricate cut-outs. Includes diagrams for creating specific images

"Based on workshops conducted by the artist, the step-by-step instructions and illustrations have been fine-tuned and are clear and easy to follow. . . . Multiculturally authentic and a guaranteed kid-crowd pleaser, this workbook is enthusiastically recommended for all craft collections." Booklist

Llimós, Anna

Easy paper crafts in 5 steps. Enslow Elementary 2008 31p il (Easy crafts in 5 steps) lib bdg $22.60

Grades: 2 3 4   **745.54**

1. Paper crafts
ISBN 978-0-7660-3087-9 (lib bdg); 0-7660-3087-3 (lib bdg)

Original Spanish edition 2005

This offers instructions for 14 paper craft projects, among them a basket, a butterfly, and pop-up card

The text is "easy to read, and the results are quirky and pleasing; steps are illustrated with bright photographs." Horn Book Guide

Includes bibliographical references

Walsh, Danny

The cardboard box book; 25 things to make and do with empty boxes; by Danny, Jake, and Niall Walsh; [photographs by Martin Norris; illustrations by Josh Halloran] Watson-Guptill 2006 112p il pa $12.95

Grades: 3 4 5   **745.54**

1. Boxes 2. Handicraft
ISBN 0-8230-0610-7   LC 2005935223

"An eye-catching cover showcases a few of these projects designed for indoor or outdoor play, and the book's lively design and layout, featuring bold colors and various fonts, will draw in young crafters. Opening chapters discuss where to find boxes of different sizes, what a basic tool kit consists of, how to use paint and glitter, when adult help is needed, and the time involved in constructing the creations." SLJ

745.58   Handicrafts from beads, found and other objects

Boonyadhistarn, Thiranut

Beading; bracelets, barrettes, and beyond; by Thiranut Boonyadhistarn. Capstone Press 2007 32p il (Snap books) $25.26

Grades: 4 5 6 7   **745.58**

1. Beadwork
ISBN 978-0-7368-6472-5; 0-7368-6472-5
     LC 2006004102

This describes how to create such bead crafts as safety-pin bracelets and bag charms.

"Girls will appreciate these ideas for recreating fashion trends and for achieving the artistic effects that they want. . . . Page layouts are lively and attractive. The projects use easily obtainable materials, and the directions are simple and well numbered." SLJ

Includes bibliographical references

Llimós, Anna

Easy bead crafts in 5 steps. Enslow Elementary 2008 31p il (Easy crafts in 5 steps) lib bdg $22.60

Grades: 2 3 4   **745.58**

1. Beadwork
ISBN 978-0-7660-3083-1 (lib bdg); 0-7660-3083-0 (lib bdg)

Original Spanish edition 2005

Llimós, Anna—_Continued_

This offers instructions for 14 bead craft projects, among them a bracelet and ring, a bookmark, and a belt

The text is "easy to read, and the results are quirky and pleasing; steps are illustrated with bright photographs." Horn Book Guide

Includes bibliographical references

Ross, Kathy, 1948-

Beautiful beads; illustrated by Nicole in den Bosch. Millbrook Press 2009 48p il lib bdg $26.60

Grades: 2 3 4 5   **745.58**

1. Beadwork

ISBN 978-0-8225-9214-3 (lib bdg); 0-8225-9214-2 (lib bdg)   LC 2008044441

"A diverse collection of 21 fun and unique projects. Young readers will learn how to make different types of beads (fabric, textured, thread, ribbon, sparkle stem), two games, a felt-bead bracelet, a cluster pin, a seed-bead flower magnet, whimsical items (beaded dog, spaghetti doll, and others), a bookmark, a tissue box, and more. The colors are vivid, and the illustrations perfectly complement the text." SLJ

Scheunemann, Pam, 1955-

Cool beaded jewelry; [by] Pam Scheunemann. ABDO Pub. 2005 32p il (Cool crafts) $22.78 *

Grades: 4 5 6   **745.58**

1. Beadwork 2. Jewelry

ISBN 1-59197-739-8   LC 2004-46292

This "has an extensive section on bead history, sizes, shapes, types, and metal findings (clasps, etc.). Projects include a memory wire bracelet, a beaded necklace and bracelet, daisy chain necklace, and beaded rings." SLJ

Sirrine, Carol

Cool crafts with old CDs; green projects for resourceful kids. Capstone Press 2010 32p il (Snap books. Green crafts) lib bdg $26.65

Grades: 3 4 5 6   **745.58**

1. Salvage 2. Compact discs 3. Plastics craft

ISBN 978-1-4296-4007-7 (lib bdg); 1-4296-4006-5 (lib bdg)

"Step-by-step instructions for crafts made from old CDs and information about reusing and recycling." Publisher's note

"Steps are easy to follow and well documented, and the projects encourage experimentation and creativity. Materials are generally easy to find. . . . This . . . is original, well-presented, and bound to inspire classroom and individual projects." SLJ

Includes glossary and bibliographical references

745.59   Making specific objects

Hufford, Deborah

Greeting card making; send your personal message; by Deborah Hufford. Capstone Press 2006 32p il (Snap books crafts) lib bdg $25.26 *

Grades: 3 4 5   **745.59**

1. Greeting cards 2. Handicraft

ISBN 0-7368-4385-X   LC 2005006899

"A pop-up birthday cake, a dried flower-petal design, and a lacey valentine are among the homemade card ideas featured in this simple, easy-to-follow title. . . . Introductory pages cover basic paper folds and materials; later spreads present mostly clear, step-by-step instructions." Booklist

Includes glossary and bibliographical references

Kenney, Karen Latchana, 1974-

Super simple magnets; fun and easy-to-make crafts for kids. ABDO Pub. Co. 2010 32p il (Super simple crafts) lib bdg $17.95

Grades: K 1 2 3 4   **745.59**

1. Handicraft 2. Magnets

ISBN 978-1-60453-626-3 (lib bdg); 1-60453-626-8 (lib bdg)   LC 2009-355

"Colorful photos; clean layout in a bright, primary palette; and large, abundant step-by-step instructional photos give [this book] great appeal. The . . . crafts . . . are functional and attractive. . . . Readily obtainable household materials and easy-to-follow instructions mean that children can do these crafts independently." SLJ

Includes glossary

745.592   Toys, models, miniatures, related objects

Harbo, Christopher L.

The kids' guide to paper airplanes. Capstone Press 2009 32p il (Kids' guides) $23.93

Grades: 4 5 6 7   **745.592**

1. Airplanes—Models 2. Paper crafts

ISBN 978-1-4296-2274-5; 1-4296-2274-1   LC 2008029688

"Edge books"

"Provides instructions and diagrams for making a variety of traditional paper airplanes." Publisher's note

"Using colorful, vivid, and clear step-by-step illustrations, Harbo demonstrates how to construct everything from the classic Dart to the circular Space Ring to the 18-step Silent Huntress." Booklist

Includes glossary and bibliographical references

Rigsby, Mike

Amazing rubber band cars; easy-to-build wind-up racers, models, and toys; [by] Mike Rigsby. Chicago Review Press 2007 121p il lib bdg $12.95 *

Grades: 4 5 6 7   **745.592**

1. Automobiles—Models 2. Toys 3. Handicraft

ISBN 978-1-55652-736-4 (lib bdg); 1-55652-736-5 (lib bdg)   LC 2007013969

This offers instructions for making toy and model cars "using mostly cardboard, glue, pencils, rubber bands, and a few other easily obtainable materials. . . . Readers will learn about corrugated and flat cardboard, and how to use glue and work with templates. Excellent instructions are accompanied by black-and-white photos every step of the way. . . . These projects are fun to construct, and inquisitive minds will be fascinated by the moving cars." SLJ

Schwarz, Renée
Wind chimes and whirligigs. Kids Can Press 2007 40p il (Kids can do it) $12.95; pa $6.95
Grades: 4 5 6   **745.592**
    1. Wind chimes 2. Whirligigs 3. Handicraft
    ISBN   978-1-55337-868-6;   1-55337-868-7; 978-1-55337-870-9 (pa); 1-55337-870-9 (pa)
    "A colorfully designed and artfully arranged photographic cover is the perfect introduction to the 12 unique and creative projects within. An overall neat appearance and precise, vibrant illustrations or sharp photos add to the attractive layout. . . . The techniques, using plastic, nylon fishing line, tape, glue, and screwdrivers, are carefully explained." SLJ

Simon, Seymour, 1931-
The paper airplane book; illustrated by Byron Barton. Viking 1971 48p il pa $6.99 *
Grades: 3 4 5   **745.592**
    1. Airplanes—Models 2. Paper crafts
    ISBN 0-14-030925-X
    Step-by-step instructions for making paper airplanes with suggestions for experimenting with them

745.593   Useful objects

Maurer, Tracy, 1965-
Scrapbook starters; [by] Tracy Nelson Maurer. Rourke Pub. LLC 2009 32p il (Creative crafts for kids) lib bdg $29.95
Grades: 3 4 5 6   **745.593**
    1. Scrapbooks
    ISBN 978-1-6069-4343-4 (lib bdg); 1-6069-4343-X (lib bdg)   LC 2009003900
    "This attractive title . . . guides young readers through the basics of starting, designing, and maintaining a scrapbook. . . . Boxed tips, supply lists, and full-color photos of scrapbooking kids in action, along with completed projects, add visual interest. . . . A solid resource on a popular subject." Booklist

Price, Pamela S.
Cool scrapbooks; [by] Pam Price. ABDO Pub. 2005 32p il (Cool crafts) lib bdg $25.65 *
Grades: 4 5 6   **745.593**
    1. Scrapbooks
    ISBN 1-59197-744-4   LC 2004-46290
    This guide to scrapbooks "addresses the use of photos, embellishments, adding words, computer possibilities, and more. . . . [This book lists] required materials, [has] small color photos, and [includes] clearly explained, numbered steps." SLJ

745.594   Decorative objects

Ancona, George, 1929-
The piñata maker: El piñatero. Harcourt Brace & Co. 1994 unp il hardcover o.p. pa $9 *
Grades: K 1 2 3   **745.594**
    1. Paper crafts 2. Bilingual books—English-Spanish 3. Mexico—Social life and customs
    ISBN 0-15-261875-9; 0-15-200060-7 (pa)
               LC 93-2389
    Describes how Don Ricardo, a craftsman from Ejutla de Crespo in southern Mexico, makes piñatas for all the village birthday parties and other fiestas
    "Ancona tells his story in both English and Spanish, with both languages on every page. His clear, bright, full-color photographs complement the detailed text, giving the reader much additional information." Horn Book

Bledsoe, Karen E., 1962-
Chinese New Year crafts; [by] Karen E. Bledsoe. Enslow Publishers 2005 32p il (Fun holiday crafts kids can do) lib bdg $22.60
Grades: 2 3 4   **745.594**
    1. Handicraft 2. Chinese New Year
    ISBN 0-7660-2347-8   LC 2004-9622
    This includes directions for ten craft projects related to Chinese New Year including a dragon-streamer puppet, a ribbon lantern, and Chinese zodiac pictures
    This is "aesthetically pleasing with . . . bright colorful pages, clear concise instructions on the left side and photographs of various stages of the final product on the right. . . . Use of everyday items such as paper cups, cupcake liners, and construction paper makes these activities practical for both students and teachers." SLJ
    Includes bibliographical references

Di Salle, Rachel, 1976-
Junk drawer jewelry; written by Rachel Di Salle and Ellen Warwick; illustrated by Jane Kurisu. Kids Can Press 2006 40p il (Kids can do it) hardcover o.p. pa $6.95
Grades: 4 5 6   **745.594**
    1. Jewelry 2. Handicraft
    ISBN 978-1-55337-965-2; 978-1-55337-966-9 (pa)
    This introduces the "world of jewelry crafting. . . . Projects of varying difficulty include bracelets, necklaces, rings, wristbands, chokers, and earrings. Each project is accompanied by a color photo, a You Will Need list, and step-by-step instructions. This book will be a popular addition to libraries." SLJ

Gnojewski, Carol
Cinco de Mayo crafts; [by] Carol Gnojewski. Enslow Publishers 2004 32p il (Fun holiday crafts kids can do) lib bdg $22.66
Grades: 2 3 4   **745.594**
    1. Handicraft 2. Cinco de Mayo
    ISBN 0-7660-2344-3   LC 2004-9624
    This includes instructions for ten craft projects related the Cinco de Mayo including a peace votive, sombrero,

Gnojewski, Carol—*Continued*
and paper poncho

This is "aesthetically pleasing with . . . bright colorful pages, clear concise instructions on the left side and photographs of various stages of the final product on the right. . . . Use of everyday items such as paper cups, cupcake liners, and construction paper makes these activities practical for both students and teachers." SLJ

Includes bibliographical references

Jazzy jewelry. Kingfisher 2007 48p il (Ecocrafts) pa $7.95

Grades: 3 4 5 6   **745.594**
1. Jewelry 2. Handicraft 3. Recycling
ISBN 978-0-7534-5969-0 (pa); 0-7534-5969-8 (pa)

This offers instructions for making jewelry out of recycled materials such as buttons, bottle caps, beads, safety pins, fabric scraps, chop sticks, key rings, and plastic bags.

Levine, Shar

Extreme balloon tying; more than 40 over-the-top projects; [by] Shar Levine & Michael Ouchi. Sterling Pub. Co. 2006 91p il pa $9.95

Grades: 3 4 5 6   **745.594**
1. Balloons 2. Handicraft
ISBN 978-1-4027-2465-7 (pa); 1-4027-2465-9 (pa)
                                    LC 2006007319

This explains "how to make balloon figures. . . . The book offers complete, step-by-step directions for a variety of appealing projects, illustrated with exceptionally precise drawings and color photos." Booklist

McGee, Randel

Paper crafts for Chinese New Year; [by] Randel McGee. Enslow Elementary 2008 48p il (Paper craft fun for holidays) lib bdg $23.93

Grades: 2 3 4   **745.594**
1. Paper crafts 2. Chinese New Year
ISBN 978-0-7660-2950-7 (lib bdg); 0-7660-2950-6 (lib bdg)   LC 2007014026

This explains the significance of Chinese New Year and offers instructions for making paper crafts including a dancing dragon puppet, a lion dancer mask, a *lai see* or red gift envelope, shadow puppets, a tangram, a chinese lantern, firecracker decorations, and Chinese symbols and banners.

"The crafts contain materials lists and color photos of the steps and of the finished product. The directions are easy to follow, and enlargeable patterns are provided." SLJ

Includes bibliographical references

Paper crafts for Christmas; [by] Randel McGee. Enslow Elementary 2009 48p il (Paper craft fun for holidays) lib bdg $23.93

Grades: 2 3 4   **745.594**
1. Paper crafts 2. Christmas
ISBN 978-0-7660-2952-1 (lib bdg); 0-7660-2952-2 (lib bdg)

Provides a brief introduction to the history of Christmas, and Christmas-themed paper craft ideas

"Filled with cultural facts . . . [this book offers] much

more than just basic craft ideas. . . . Kids will . . . enjoy piecing together these appealing projects. . . . A pop-up card that sends Santa down the chimney is particularly inventive." Booklist

Paper crafts for Day of the Dead; [by] Randel McGee. Enslow Elementary 2008 48p il (Paper craft fun for holidays) lib bdg $23.93

Grades: 2 3 4   **745.594**
1. Paper crafts 2. All Souls' Day
ISBN 978-0-7660-2951-4 (lib bdg); 0-7660-2951-4 (lib bdg)   LC 2007013987

This explains the significance of the Mexican Day of the Dead, and offers instructions for paper crafts including paper marigolds, a skeleton candy basket, happy skeleton figures, skeleton pets, paper clothes for skeletons, a skull mask, *papel cortado* window banners, and Aztec animal decorations.

"The crafts contain materials lists and color photos of the steps and of the finished product. The directions are easy to follow, and enlargeable patterns are provided." SLJ

Includes bibliographical references

Paper crafts for Halloween; [by] Randel McGee. Enslow Elementary 2009 48p il (Paper craft fun for holidays) lib bdg $23.93

Grades: 2 3 4   **745.594**
1. Paper crafts 2. Halloween
ISBN 978-0-7660-2947-7 (lib bdg); 0-7660-2947-6 (lib bdg)   LC 2007014048

"Provides a brief introduction to the history of Halloween, and Halloween-themed paper craft ideas." Publisher's note

"Filled with cultural facts, [this book offers] . . . much more than just basic craft ideas. . . . Kids will . . . enjoy piecing together these appealing projects." Booklist

Includes bibliographical references

Paper crafts for Kwanzaa; [by] Randel McGee. Enslow Elementary 2008 48p il (Paper craft fun for holidays) lib bdg $23.93

Grades: 2 3 4   **745.594**
1. Paper crafts 2. Kwanzaa
ISBN 978-0-7660-2949-1 (lib bdg); 0-7660-2949-2 (lib bdg)   LC 2007014039

This explains the significance of Kwanzaa and offers instructions for paper crafts including a *kinara* pop-up card, a *mkeka* mat, a *muhindi* or ear of corn, standing Kwanzaa figures, a standing fruit tree, cut-outs of the *Nguzo Saba* or Seven Guiding Principles, a lion, and an African-style hat.

"The crafts are attractive and easy to make with adult help, and they use common supplies." SLJ

Includes bibliographical references

Paper crafts for Valentine's Day. Enslow Publishers 2008 48p il (Paper craft fun for holidays) lib bdg $23.93

Grades: 2 3 4   **745.594**
1. Paper crafts 2. Valentine's Day
ISBN 978-0-7660-2948-4 (lib bdg); 0-7660-2948-4 (lib bdg)   LC 2007014041

McGee, Randel—*Continued*

Explains the significance of Valentine's Day and offers instructions for making paper crafts including a Cupid figure, a heart sculpture, a lacy heart card, a pop-up heart card, a valentine heart crown, heart flowers, a stick puppet, and a Danish woven heart basket.

"These eight crafts are simple to complete, with easy-to-follow instructions. A color photo of the finished piece is included." SLJ

Includes bibliographical references

Sadler, Judy Ann, 1959-

Christmas crafts from around the world; written by Judy Sadler; illustrated by June Bradford. Kids Can Press 2003 40p il (Kids can do it) $12.95; pa $6.95

Grades: 4 5 6   745.594

1. Handicraft 2. Christmas decorations
ISBN 1-55337-427-4; 1-55337-428-2 (pa)

"From cranberry and popcorn garlands (U.S.) to woven hearts (Denmark) to a piñata (Mexico) to a crinkle-paper chain (South Africa), these 17 projects for craft-confident readers also include snippets of information on how and why the holiday is celebrated in a variety of countries. A photograph of each finished product is provided, along with a list of materials needed and succinct but clear instructions. Small but clear illustrations guide reader through each step." SLJ

745.6   Calligraphy, heraldic design, illumination

Hanson, Anders, 1980-

Cool calligraphy; the art of creativity for kids; [by] Anders Hanson. ABDO Pub. Co. 2009 32p il (Cool art) lib bdg $24.21

Grades: 2 3 4   745.6

1. Calligraphy
ISBN 978-1-60453-145-9 (lib bdg); 1-60453-145-2 (lib bdg)   LC 2008-19885

This book about calligraphy is "well organized, with clearly written sections . . . and several clever projects and exercises. . . . [It] should have substantial child appeal." SLJ

Includes glossary

Winters, Eleanor

1 2 3 calligraphy! letters and projects for beginners and beyond. Sterling Pub. Co. 2006 128p il $14.95 *

Grades: 4 5 6 7   745.6

1. Calligraphy
ISBN 1-4027-1839-X; 978-1-4027-1839-7
      LC 2005022071

"Twenty well-written, easy-to-follow explanatory chapters are filled with plenty of practical exercises. Chapters are grouped into three parts with the first reviewing calligraphy basics, vocabulary, and types of writing instruments. The second part teaches italic, swing gothic, and modern gothic alphabets. Finally, creative projects such as stationery, envelopes, signs, and 'calligrams' are described." SLJ

745.7   Decorative coloring

Wagner, Lisa, 1961-

Cool painted stuff; [by] Lisa Wagner. ABDO Pub. 2005 32p il (Cool crafts) $22.78 *

Grades: 4 5 6   745.7

1. Painting 2. Handicraft
ISBN 1-59197-742-8   LC 2004-53117

This guide to painted crafts "includes four projects (in six or seven steps): a flowered mini-tote, checkered frame, treasure box, and fancy flowerpot. [This book lists] required materials, [has] small color photos, and [includes] clearly explained, numbered steps." SLJ

746   Textile arts

Warwick, Ellen

Injeanuity; written by Ellen Warwick; illustrated by Bernice Lum. Kids Can Press 2006 80p il (Planet girl) spiral bdg $12.95

Grades: 5 6 7 8   746

1. Sewing 2. Handicraft
ISBN 978-1-55337-681-1 (spiral bdg); 1-55337-681-1 (spiral bdg)

"Warwick combines a love of denim with some simple crafts that will have readers thinking and feeling like fashion designers. . . . [The book] includes 17 projects from re-wearable jeans to purses and wallets to bolsters and footstools to halters and skirts and more. All include clear, easy-to-follow instructions and informative illustrations." SLJ

746.4   Needlework and handwork

The **jumbo** book of needlecrafts; written by Judy Ann Sadler . . . [et al.]; illustrated by Esperaça Melo . . . [et al.] Kids Can Press 2005 208p il $16.95 *

Grades: 4 5 6   746.4

1. Needlework
ISBN 1-55337-793-1

A compilation with a new introduction of 5 books previously published: Knitting by Judy Ann Sadler (2002); Crocheting by Gwen Blakely Kinsler (2003); Simply sewing by Judy Ann Sadler (2004); Embroidery by Judy Ann Sadler (2004); Quilting by Biz Storms (2001)

This is a "how-to guide to the basics of knitting, crocheting, embroidery, quilting, and sewing. . . . The volume begins with helpful suggestions on gathering supplies, measuring, selecting fabric, and stitching. The rest of the book presents detailed, step-by-step directions on basic techniques for projects that range from very simple to intricate. . . . Color drawings and photographs are appealing as well as instructive. . . . An excellent addition to needlework collections." SLJ

746.41 Weaving, braiding, matting unaltered vegetable fibers

Swett, Sarah

Kids weaving; [by] Sarah Swett; photographs by Chris Hartlove; illustrations by Lena Corwin. Stewart, Tabori & Chang 2005 128p il $19.95

Grades: 4 5 6 7 **746.41**

1. Weaving

ISBN 1-58479-467-4 LC 2005000650

"Swett introduces this craft with a simple weaving of a checkerboard note card—a task requiring two pieces of paper and a pair of scissors. After mastering the technique with several different small projects, she explains how to weave a hideout out of sticks and vines in the yard. She demonstrates techniques on a cardboard loom and progresses to skills for weaving on a pipe loom. These projects show the whimsical and the practical, the useful and the decorative aspects of the art. Hartlove's excellent-quality, full-color photos depict children enjoying the craft in many different settings. . . . In addition, the helpful step-by-step drawings clearly depict the processes and techniques." SLJ

Includes bibliographical references

746.42 Nonloom weaving and related techniques

Sadler, Judy Ann, 1959-

Hemp jewelry; written by Judy Ann Sadler; illustrated by June Bradford. Kids Can Press 2005 40p il (Kids can do it) hardcover o.p. pa $6.96

Grades: 4 5 6 **746.42**

1. Macramé 2. Beadwork 3. Jewelry

ISBN 1-55337-774-5; 1-55337-775-3 (pa)

This "provides instructions for making jewelry from strands of hemp that are woven in various patterns while incorporating beads, clasps, and other findings. . . . Attractive and easy to follow. . . . Detailed, step-by-step instructions, . . . are clearly illustrated with large-scale, colorful ink-and-wash drawings." Booklist

Knotting; make your own basketball nets, guitar straps, sports bags and more! written by Judy Ann Sadler; illustrated by Céleste Gagnon. Kids Can Press 2006 40p il (Kids can do it) $12.95; pa $6.99 *

Grades: 4 5 6 **746.42**

1. Knots and splices 2. Handicraft

ISBN 1-55337-541-6; 1-55337-834-2 (pa)

This describes how use rope to make various types of knots, lanyards, guitar straps, ladders, hanging holders, swings, dog leashes, and basketball nets.

746.43 Knitting, crocheting, tatting

Blakley Kinsler, Gwen, 1947-

Crocheting; written by Gwen Blakley Kinsler and Jackie Young; illustrated by Esperança Melo. Kids Can Press 2002 40p il (Kids can do it) $12.95; pa $5.95

Grades: 4 5 6 **746.43**

1. Crocheting

ISBN 1-55337-176-3; 1-55337-177-1 (pa)

This describes basic crochet techniques and projects including a fashion scarf, bookmarks, headbands, and purses

"Clearly written instructions and ideas, illustrated with color diagrams and photographs." SLJ

Blanchette, Peg, 1949-

12 easy knitting projects. Williamson Books 2006 63p il (Quick starts for kids!) pa $8.95

Grades: 3 4 5 6 **746.43**

1. Knitting

ISBN 0-8249-6785-2 LC 2005029247

"With its wide margins, color illustrations on every page, and well-spaced text, this book will appeal to beginners and accomplished knitters. It discusses the four basic yarn weights, lists materials, and offers step-by-step instructions for basic stitches, making fringe, and more. An icon indicates the complexity of each project." SLJ

Bradberry, Sarah

Kids knit! simple steps to nifty projects; [by] Sarah Bradberry. Sterling Pub. Co. 2004 96p il hardcover o.p. pa $9.95 *

Grades: 5 6 7 8 **746.43**

1. Knitting

ISBN 0-8069-7733-7; 978-1-4027-4057-2 (pa); 1-4027-4057-3 (pa) LC 2004-19375

Presents basic knitting techniques and instructions for making a backpack, pillow, doll, and other simple projects

This "book works equally well for beginners and experienced knitters. . . . Besides the requisite information on knitting and purling, there are invaluable tips about finishing garments, fixing mistakes, and adding embellishments. The projects have been chosen with an eye toward simplicity, yet they have real appeal." Booklist

Davis, Jane

Crochet; fantastic jewelry, hats, purses, pillows & more. Lark Books 2005 112p il (Kids' crafts) $19.95; pa $9.95 *

Grades: 5 6 7 8 **746.43**

1. Crocheting

ISBN 978-1-57990-477-7; 1-57990-477-7; 978-1-60059-138-9 (pa); 1-60059-138-8 (pa) LC 2004-13288

This describes basic crochet techniques and includes instructions for 50 projects

"The book is a pleasure to look at. . . . Photographs are large and crisp. . . . Davis clearly knows what kids

Davis, Jane—*Continued*

like. . . . Both visual and text explanations are very clear. . . . This is a must for your craft shelves." Booklist

Guy, Lucinda

Kids learn to crochet; [by] Lucinda Guy & François Hall. Trafalgar Square Books 2008 96p il pa $15.95

Grades: 2 3 4   **746.43**

1. Crocheting

ISBN 978-1-57076-395-3 (pa); 1-57076-395-X (pa)
                     LC 2008900190

"Softly hued, whimsical color illustrations are superimposed on sharp, vivid color photos in this eye-catching introduction. In step-by-step fashion, children will learn how (with adult guidance) to crochet a pen or pencil topper, cute critters, flowers, a bag, and more. Adorable mice guide children throughout with their 'Pip Says' and 'Peg Says' tips." SLJ

Kids learn to knit; [by] Lucinda Guy & Francois Hall. Trafalgar Square Pub. 2007 96p il pa $14.95

Grades: 2 3 4   **746.43**

1. Knitting

ISBN 1-56076-335-6

"After introducing the basics of knitting, the tools, and the materials, the handbook starts at the beginning (the slip knot, broken down into four steps); casting on (three steps); the knit stitch (five steps); and binding off (four steps). Each simply explained step is illustrated with at least one clear, larger-than-life illustration. Knitters . . . can proceed to sections on the purl stitch and the stockinette stitch, followed by six projects. . . . With breezy ink-and-watercolor cartoons of frolicking animals as well as bright photos, this book infuses instructions and advice with a welcome dose of fun." Booklist

Ronci, Kelli

Kids crochet; projects for kids of all ages; photographs by John Gruen; illustrations by Lena Corwin. Stewart, Tabori & Chang 2005 128p il $19.95 *

Grades: 4 5 6 7   **746.43**

1. Crocheting

ISBN 1-58479-413-5   LC 2004-17477

This offers instructions for "15 projects. All aspects of crocheting are covered. . . . Handcrafted items include a neck cozy, tool pouch, friendship cuffs, patchwork poncho, triangle-square quilt and pillow, and critter cushions." SLJ

This "has projects that kids will really enjoy making. . . . What will especially entice children are the sharply reproduced color photographs. . . . Also excellent are the attractive drawings." Booklist

Sadler, Judy Ann, 1959-

Knitting; written by Judy Ann Sadler; illustrated by Esperança Melo. Kids Can Press 2002 40p il (Kids can do it) hardcover o.p. pa $6.95

Grades: 4 5 6   **746.43**

1. Knitting

ISBN 1-55337-050-3; 1-55337-051-1 (pa)

This "book discusses yarn, needles and other supplies. Beyond instruction in the basic techniques of casting on, knit and purl stitches, increasing and decreasing, and binding off, it shows how to make fringe, pom-poms, and tassels, and how to combine stitches to create patterns. . . . There are complete instructions for a headband, a rolled-brim hat, slipper socks, a book bag, and more. The step-by-step instructions are easy to follow, and the large, softly colored, superior-quality diagrams show exactly how to perform each step in the process." SLJ

Quick knits; written by Judy Ann Sadler; illustrated by Esperança Melo. Kids Can Press 2006 40p il (Kids can do it) hardcover o.p. pa $6.95

Grades: 4 5 6   **746.43**

1. Knitting

ISBN   978-1-55337-963-8;   1-55337-963-2; 978-1-55337-964-5 (pa); 1-55337-964-0 (pa)

This provides instructions for basic knitting stitches and simple projects including scarves, hats, cuffs, a wallet, a pillow, foot mats, slippers, and a sweater

"This attractively designed title features clear, colorful illustrations and an easy-to-follow text." SLJ

746.44   Embroidery

Sadler, Judy Ann, 1959-

Embroidery; written by Judy Ann Sadler; illustrated by June Bradford. Kids Can Press 2004 40p il (Kids can do it) $12.95; pa $6.95

Grades: 4 5 6   **746.44**

1. Embroidery

ISBN 1-55337-616-1; 1-55337-617-X (pa)

This describes materials and techniques for simple embroidery stitches and includes instructions for creating such objects as a pincushion, a stitched greeting card, a beaded star ornament, and embroidered clothing.

"With an attractively designed cover featuring photos of sample projects, this book is sure to encourage interest in needlework." SLJ

746.46   Patchwork and quilting

Rau, Dana Meachen, 1971-

Quilting for fun! Compass Point Books 2009 48p il (For fun) lib bdg $25.26

Grades: 3 4 5   **746.46**

1. Quilting

ISBN 978-0-7565-3860-6 (lib bdg); 0-7565-3860-2 (lib bdg)   LC 2008008274

This covers the basics of quilting, a brief history, and instructions for five quilting projects

Rau, Dana Meachen, 1971-—*Continued*

"Varied typefaces and colors, large print, good spacing, and lively and creative arrangement make [this book] attractive, and color photos and other illustrations throughout are easy to follow. . . . Materials are easily obtainable from craft stores, and some are readily available at home." SLJ

Includes glossary and bibliographical references

Storms, Biz, 1955-

Quilting; written by Biz Storms; illustrated by June Bradford. Kids Can Press 2001 40p il (Kids can do it) $12.95; pa $5.95

Grades: 4 5 6   **746.46**

1. Quilting

ISBN 1-55074-967-6; 1-55074-805-X (pa)

"*Quilting* uses step-by-step instructions keyed to excellent color illustrations to present basics. Ten kid-pleasing projects of increasing difficulty follow—from an appliquéd tee shirt to a full-size quilt—each as appealingly and clearly presented as the last." Booklist

746.9 Textile products and fashion design

Bertoletti, John C.

How fashion designers use math; math curriculum consultant: Rhea A. Stewart. Chelsea Clubhouse 2010 32p il (Math in the real world) lib bdg $28

Grades: 4 5 6   **746.9**

1. Fashion design 2. Mathematics 3. Vocational guidance

ISBN 978-1-60413-606-7 (lib bdg); 1-60413-606-5 (lib bdg)   LC 2009-22683

This describes how designers use math to measure, create, and produce their fashions, and includes problems to solve and information about how to become a fashion designer

"Color photos of designers in action combine with diagrams that further clarify the easily digestible text." Booklist

Includes glossary and bibliographical references

Blaxland, Wendy

Sweaters. Marshall Cavendish Benchmark 2011 32p il map (How are they made?) lib bdg $12.99

Grades: 4 5 6   **746.9**

1. Knitting 2. Sweaters 3. Wool

ISBN 978-0-7614-4756-6; 0-7614-4756-3

LC 2009039882

This describes how sweaters are made, including their history, parts, design, wool and synthetic fibers, raw materials, manufacture, packaging and distribution, marketing and advertising, and their affects on the environment.

Includes glossary

747 Interior decoration

Weaver, Janice

It's your room; a decorating guide for real kids; [by] Janice Weaver and Frieda Wishinsky; illustrated by Claudia Dávila. Tundra Books 2006 63p il pa $14.95 *

Grades: 5 6 7 8   **747**

1. Interior design

ISBN 0-88776-711-7

"Budding interior designers and readers who want to personalize their rooms will appreciate this title. It is filled with step-by-step guidelines for creating a budget, selecting paint colors and fabrics, organizing closets and desks, laying everything out, and adding finishing touches. The illustrations will be a hit with first-time decorators just starting to develop their own color sense." SLJ

748.5 Stained, painted, leaded, mosaic glass

Kenney, Karen Latchana, 1974-

Super simple glass jar art; fun and easy-to-make crafts for kids. ABDO Pub. Co. 2010 32p il (Super simple crafts) lib bdg $17.95

Grades: K 1 2 3 4   **748.5**

1. Handicraft 2. Glass

ISBN 978-1-60453-624-9 (lib bdg); 1-60453-624-1 (lib bdg)   LC 2009-352

"Colorful photos; clean layout in a bright, primary palette; and large, abundant step-by-step instructional photos give [this book] great appeal. The . . . crafts . . . are functional and attractive. . . . Readily obtainable household materials and easy-to-follow instructions mean that children can do these crafts independently." SLJ

Includes glossary

750 Painting

Cressy, Judith

Can you find it? Abrams 2002 40p il $15.95 *

Grades: 2 3 4 5   **750**

1. Metropolitan Museum of Art (New York, N.Y.)
2. Painting 3. Art appreciation

ISBN 0-8109-3279-2   LC 2002-18358

"Nineteen paintings from New York City's Metropolitan Museum of Art were chosen for careful scrutiny in this book. Next to each striking, full-color reproduction is a list of items to search for: e.g., '2 cats, 6 lotus blossoms, 3 eye amulets,' etc., for a painting from ancient Egypt. The works of art are from around the globe and range from illuminated manuscripts to 20th-century canvases. Designed to encourage discovery, the tiny, sometimes indistinct details will keep children engrossed for hours." SLJ

Other titles in this series are:

Can you find it, too? by Judith Cressey (2004)

Can you find it inside? by by Jessica Schulte (2005)

Can you find it outside? by Jessice Schulte (2005)

Can you find it? America by Linda Falken (2010)

D'Harcourt, Claire, 1960-

Masterpieces up close; by Claire d'Harcourt. Chronicle Books 2006 63p il $22.95 *

Grades: 4 5 6 7   **750**

1. Painting 2. Art appreciation

ISBN 0-8118-5403-5   LC 2004-16341

"Western painting from the 14th to 20th centuries. Over 100 details to find."— jacket

"From Giotto to Warhol, d'Harcourt selects some of the most famous icons of Western art for a closer look. . . . The format of this oversize volume [consists of] boldly colored spreads featuring a central, large image surrounded by smaller details from it. Interesting tidbits and questions accompany each small picture, inviting viewers to wonder, think, and question what they see. . . . The last pages include lift-the-flap copies of the paintings and biographical sketches of the artists. A visually striking volume for browsers and art education." SLJ

Micklethwait, Lucy

Children; a first art book. Frances Lincoln Children's 2006 unp il $14.95

Grades: K 1 2 3   **750**

1. Painting 2. Art appreciation 3. Children in art

ISBN 1-84507-116-6

"This title uses works by 18 different artists to illustrate its theme. Children are shown in nine activities, from Reading and writing to Sleeping. . . . The artwork represents several cultures and ethnic groups, as well as styles and time periods. Text is minimal—just enough to encourage conversation about the reproductions. An excellent first exposure to fine art, and great preparation for museum visits." SLJ

Raczka, Bob

Artful reading; [by] Bob Raczka. Millbrook Press 2007 c2008 32p il lib bdg $25.26 *

Grades: 1 2 3 4   **750**

1. Painting 2. Art appreciation 3. Reading in art

ISBN 978-0-8225-6754-7   LC 2006035083

"Through 23 works of art, Raczka shows the timeless appeal of reading. . . . Simple sentences serve as captions to these masterpieces. . . . Each work is clearly labelled, and endnotes provide information about the artists and their paintings, among them Edgar Degas and Dante Gabriel Rossetti." SLJ

More than meets the eye; seeing art with all five senses; by Bob Raczka. Millbrook Press 2003 32p il hardcover o.p. pa $9.95 *

Grades: K 1 2 3   **750**

1. Painting 2. Art appreciation

ISBN 0-7613-2797-5 (lib bdg); 0-7613-1994-8 (pa)

     LC 2003-343

Provides images of paintings and new, sensory ways to experience them, such as tasting the milk in Vermeer's "The Milkmaid," hearing the music in Tanner's "The Banjo Lesson," or feeling the fur in da Vinci's "Lady with an Ermine."

"Raczka's short, rhyming text gives structure to the book, but the color reproductions of well-chosen, vivid paintings steal the show. This art book rests on a simple concept, beautifully executed." Booklist

Unlikely pairs; fun with famous works of art; [by] Bob Raczka. Millbrook Press 2006 31p il lib bdg $23.93; pa $9.95 *

Grades: 4 5 6 7   **750**

1. Painting 2. Art appreciation

ISBN 0-7613-2936-6 (lib bdg); 0-7613-2378-3 (pa)

     LC 2003-14078

Invites the reader to discover fourteen funny stories produced by pairing twenty-eight paintings from different eras and styles

"Raczka deserves an A+ for cleverness. . . . Rodin's *The Thinker* is juxtaposed with Klee's modernistic painting of a chessboard so that the statue looks as if it is contemplating the next move. Siméon-Chardin's picture of a boy blowing soap bubbles seems to be creating Kandinsky's *Several Circles*. Each selection takes up a page and is reproduced in crisp color. . . . This book is an amusing way to introduce children to famous works of art." SLJ

Wenzel, Angela

13 paintings children should know. Prestel 2009 il $14.95

Grades: 5 6 7 8   **750**

1. Painting 2. Art appreciation

ISBN 978-3-7913-4323-5; 3-7913-4323-8

This book examines "Mona Lisa's beguiling smile, Van Gogh's hypnotic night sky, and Frida Kahlo's depiction of herself with a monkey. These [paintings] and ten others are featured in the book in large reproductions with accompanying details. The . . . text offers biographical information about each artist and important facts about the painting's technical and historical aspects." Publisher's note

This "large-format, brightly colored [survey provides a] solid, even inspiring [introduction] to the art world. . . . Leading questions encourage budding artists to use the featured subjects and artworks as inspiration." Horn Book Guide

Includes glossary

750.1 Painting—Philosophy and theory

Richardson, Joy

Looking at pictures; an introduction to art for young people; with illustrations by Charlotte Voake. rev ed. Abrams Books for Young Readers 2009 80p il $21.95

Grades: 4 5 6 7   **750.1**

1. National Gallery (Great Britain) 2. Painting 3. Art appreciation

ISBN 978-0-8109-8288-8; 0-8109-8288-9

     LC 2008055684

First published 1997

This "exploration of thirteenth- to twentieth-century European paintings examines the subject matter and techniques used and also delves into how the pieces were restored. Other topics covered are pigments, the use of light and perspective, the depiction of special events and daily life, and painting people and nature. Occasional well-placed illustrations supplement the numerous color reproductions." Horn Book Guide

Includes bibliographical references

Wolfe, Gillian

Look! Drawing the line in art. Frances Lincoln 2008 44p il $17.95

Grades: 3 4 5   **750.1**

1. Art appreciation

ISBN 978-1-84507-824-9; 1-84507-824-1

"Each spread introduces a different technique, such as 'strong lines' and 'leafy lines' and shows a work of fine art demonstrating it, reproduced with clarity and in full color. Occasionally, the text defines artistic techniques, such as perspective and shading. Each spread has kid-friendly ideas for making one's own creations. . . . There is a wide range of dates for the art featured, beginning in the 1600s and ending in 2003. The text describes how each piece was created and includes some anecdotal stories about the artist and the work. . . . This is an accessible introduction to art history." SLJ

Look! Seeing the light in art. Frances Lincoln 2007 45p il $16.95

Grades: 3 4 5   **750.1**

1. Art appreciation

ISBN 978-1-84507-467-8; 1-84507-467-X

"Wolfe invites readers to examine how artists have tried to convey qualities of light in works that represent night, day, rainstorms, sunlight, heat, cold, and use light to create the texture and shape of objects. Each spread includes a suggestion for an art activity . . . as well as a page of accessible text, in large print, that presents questions and observations designed to draw viewers back into the well-reproduced artworks. With a few exceptions, the artists represented are well-known, male, European masters, such as Caravaggio and Renoir." Booklist

751.4 Painting—Techniques and procedures

Hanson, Anders, 1980-

Cool painting; the art of creativity for kids; [by] Anders Hanson. ABDO Pub. Co. 2009 32p il (Cool art) lib bdg $24.21

Grades: 2 3 4   **751.4**

1. Painting—Technique

ISBN 978-1-60453-143-5 (lib bdg); 1-60453-143-6 (lib bdg)   LC 2008-22243

This book about painting is "well organized, with clearly written sections . . . and several clever projects and exercises. . . . [It] should have substantial child appeal." SLJ

Includes glossary

Lipsey, Jennifer, 1971-

I love to finger paint! [by] Jennifer Lipsey. Lark Books 2006 48p il (My very favorite art book) $9.95 *

Grades: K 1 2 3   **751.4**

1. Finger painting

ISBN 1-57990-771-7   LC 2005034821

"Lipsey describes a variety of painting techniques that can be used to create intriguing designs—finger and hand-printing, patterning, scraping and scratching, textur-ing, even painting with feet and palms. Pictures in a rainbow of brilliant colors accompany the instructions, supplying children with examples to copy and inspiration to extend what they have learned to make more pictures. Excellent for teachers, and, with oversight from adults, for kids themselves." Booklist

I love to paint! Lark Books 2005 48p il (My very favorite art book) $9.95 *

Grades: K 1 2 3   **751.4**

1. Painting—Technique

ISBN 1-57990-630-3

This offers instruction in such techniques as finger painting, watercolors, scratch art, sponge painting, using straws to blow paint around the pages, and stenciling

"Here's a book that is as attractive as it is useful. . . . This is exceptionally well organized." Booklist

Luxbacher, Irene, 1970-

1 2 3 I can paint! Kids Can Press 2007 23p il (Starting art) $14.95; pa $5.95

Grades: 2 3 4   **751.4**

1. Painting—Technique

ISBN 978-1-55453-037-3; 1-55453-037-7; 978-1-55453-150-9 (pa); 1-55453-150-0 (pa)

This "introduces aspiring artists to some materials and techniques that can be successfully used to create pictures with paint. Luxbacher discusses primary and secondary colors; backgrounds; color tones; cool warm, and complementary colors; perspective and line; and several brush strokes. The brief text offers clear definitions of terms and easy-to-follow instructions for projects. . . . The artwork . . . will be easy for children to replicate." Booklist

751.7 Paintings—Specific forms

Bingham, Jane

Graffiti. Raintree 2009 32p il (Culture in action) $28.21; pa $7.99

Grades: 5 6 7 8   **751.7**

1. Graffiti 2. Mural painting and decoration

ISBN 978-1-4109-3401-7; 1-4109-3401-2; 978-1-4109-3418-5 (pa); 1-4109-3418-7 (pa)

LC 2008054323

"According to the time line in the . . . book, graffiti can be traced back to 60,000 BCE and paintings on cave walls. A note on the contents page states that it is illegal to draw on other people's property without permission. The different types of graffiti described are interesting, and some of the artwork is beautiful. A section on problems talks about ugly tags (short nicknames), the expense of cleanup, and how some cities have legal graffiti walls. . . . Well organized and with bright, colorful photography, [this] introductory [title gives] readers good basic knowledge." SLJ

Includes glossary and bibliographical references

Harris, Nathaniel
Wall paintings. PowerKids Press 2009 30p il
(Stories in art) lib bdg $25.25
Grades: 4 5 6 7   **751.7**
1. Mural painting and decoration
ISBN 978-1-4042-4440-5 (lib bdg); 1-4042-4440-9 (lib
bdg)   LC 2007-52739
"This title explains the concept of wall paintings and
how they were executed by using well-known examples.
. . . Pages are well-designed with a paragraph about the
painting and a section which gives some background in-
formation. . . . This is a useful addition to the art
shelves." Libr Media Connect
Includes glossary and bibliographical references

757   Human figures

Raczka, Bob
Here's looking at me; how artists see
themselves; [by] Bob Raczka. Millbrook Press
2006 32p il lib bdg $23.93 *
Grades: 3 4 5 6   **757**
1. Self-portraits 2. Artists
ISBN 978-0-7613-3404-0 (lib bdg); 0-7613-3404-1 (lib
bdg)   LC 2005006144
The author "leads children through a series of artists'
self-portraits, evidently chosen to represent a broad range
of styles within Western art. Each portrait appears on a
full page, facing a page of commentary. Artists, introduced in chronological order beginning with Albrecht
Durer (1472-1528) and concluding with Cindy Sherman
(1954), include Artemisia Gentileschi, Jan Vermeer, and
Chuck Close." Booklist
This is a "top-notch introduction to self-portraiture."
SLJ

Thomson, Ruth, 1949-
Portraits. Chelsea Clubhouse 2004 c2003 32p il
(First look at art) $14.95
Grades: 2 3 4 5   **757**
1. Portraits 2. Art appreciation
ISBN 0-7910-7948-1   LC 2003-14428
First published 2003 in the United Kingdom
Contents: What is a portrait?; People in profile; Looking sideways; Self-portraits; Picturing yourself; A magnificent queen; Portraying royalty; Multiple faces; Repeating portraits; Portraits of a hero; A heroic you!; A
made-up face; Collage portraits; Artists and answers
This describes various types of portraits including profiles and silhouettes, self-portraits, depictions of royalty,
multiple faces, heroic portraits, and collage portraits, and
includes related art activities.
"Teachers will find easy-to-understand art lessons and
projects and students will find inspiration in [this] well-
organized, attractive [title]." SLJ
Includes glossary

759.05   Painting—1800-1899

Raimondo, Joyce
Picture this! activities and adventures in
impressionism. Watson-Guptill 2004 48p il (Art
explorers) $12.95 *
Grades: 3 4 5   **759.05**
1. Impressionism (Art) 2. Art appreciation
ISBN 0-8230-2503-9   LC 2004-7356
"With step-by-step activities, full-color reproductions,
and examples of children's imitative art, this slim volume provides a creative and simple introduction to the
Impressionists. . . . Brief biographies of the painters are
appended. A highly useful and entertaining book." SLJ

Sabbeth, Carol, 1957-
Monet and the impressionists for kids; their
lives and ideas, 21 activities. Chicago Review
Press 2002 140p il pa $17.95 *
Grades: 5 6 7 8   **759.05**
1. Impressionism (Art) 2. Art appreciation
ISBN 1-55652-397-1   LC 2001-47191
Discusses the nineteenth-century French art movement
known as Impressionism, focusing on the works of Monet, Renoir, Degas, Cassatt, Cezanne, Gauguin, and Seurat
"A beautifully designed introduction to Impressionism.
. . . Sabbeth also includes 21 appealing extension activities such as recipes, crafts, games, and writing suggestions. Quality color reproductions on glossy pages, and
varied, attractive layouts add to the book." SLJ
Includes glossary and bibliographical references

Sellier, Marie
Renoir's colors. Getty 2010 il bd bk $16.95
Grades: PreK K 1 2   **759.05**
1. Renoir, Auguste, 1841-1919 2. Color in art
3. French painting 4. Board books for children
ISBN 978-1-60606-003-2 (bd bk); 1-60606-003-1 (bd
bk)
"Lift-the-flap windows spotlight pure colors in details
of the artist's work. Turn the page to see the entire work,
with a few simple lines of text guiding the eye to other
shades of the highlighted color or adding an anecdote
about the piece or model. Well-chosen paintings of familiar subjects . . . keep this small collection of fine art
accessible to even the youngest child. This fine-art concept book is simply designed and superbly printed." SLJ

759.06   Painting—1900-1999

Raczka, Bob
No one saw; ordinary things through the eyes of
an artist. Millbrook Press 2002 32p il lib bdg
$23.90; pa $9.95
Grades: K 1 2 3   **759.06**
1. Modern painting 2. Art appreciation
ISBN 0-7613-2370-8 (lib bdg); 0-7613-1648-3 (pa)
     LC 2001-30006

Raczka, Bob—*Continued*

"Reproductions of sixteen famous paintings, set against complementary backgrounds, reflect their creators' unique viewpoints, while a gentle rhyming text comments on the masterpieces ('No one saw mothers like Mary Cassatt. / No one saw Sunday like Georges Seurat'). The selections serve the impressionist through modern works well and conclude that 'nobody sees the world like you.'" Horn Book Guide

759.13   American painting

Honoring our ancestors; stories and pictures by fourteen artists; edited by Harriet Rohmer. Children's Bk. Press 1999 31p il $15.95

Grades: 3 4 5 6   **759.13**
1. Artists—United States
ISBN 0-89239-158-8   LC 98-38686

Fourteen artists and picture book illustrators present paintings with descriptions of ancestors or other sources of inspiration that have inspired them

This is "rewarding in its breadth and vivacity. The portraits are thematically rich yet accessible; generally, the texts are cheerful and resist sentimentality." Horn Book Guide

Lawrence, Jacob, 1917-2000

The great migration; an American story; paintings by Jacob Lawrence; with a poem in appreciation by Walter Dean Myers. HarperCollins Pubs. 1993 unp il hardcover o.p. pa $8.99

Grades: 4 5 6 7   **759.13**
1. African Americans in art
ISBN 0-06-023037-1; 0-06-443428-1 (pa)
                                  LC 93-16788

Published by The Museum of Modern Art, The Phillips Collection, and HarperCollins Pubs.

"A noted African-American artist chronicles the 1916-1919 migration of blacks from the South through a sequence of 60 paintings and accompanying narrative captions." SLJ

"Lawrence is a storyteller with words as well as pictures: his captions and his own 1992 introduction to this book are the best commentary on his work." Booklist

759.4   French painting

Monet, Claude, 1840-1926

Monet's impressions; words and pictures. Chronicle Books 2009 unp il $15.99

Grades: K 1 2 3   **759.4**
1. Impressionism (Art) 2. Art appreciation
ISBN 978-0-8118-7056-6; 0-8118-7056-1
                                  LC 2009004287

"This simple, stunning title pairs details from the artist's paintings with short quotations from his letters and from articles in which he was quoted. At the back of the book, each painting is reproduced in full, with captions (medium, size, location) and a source for each quote. High-quality printing ensures that each brushstroke is in clear focus, and that colors are true." SLJ

Niepold, Mil

Oooh! Matisse; [by] Mil Niepold and Jeanyves Verdu. Tricycle Press 2007 unp il $14.95

Grades: 2 3 4   **759.4**
1. Matisse, Henri
ISBN 978-1-58246-227-1; 1-58246-227-5
                                  LC 2006102319

"'What is this?' reads the text on the opening page of this vivid visual conundrum, which opens with four elongated, purplish-blue tear shapes set on a goldenrod background. The answer . . . is: 'Yellow, I am the sun and blue, I am the fingers that shield my eyes.' Four other color-and-shape constructs are presented in a similar manner. . . . The format seems simple, but this is really a sophisticated eye-opener." Booklist

759.9492   Dutch painting

Gogh, Vincent van, 1853-1890

Vincent's colors; words and pictures by Vincent van Gogh. Chronicle Books 2005 unp il $14.95 *

Grades: K 1 2 3   **759.9492**
1. Color in art 2. Artists, Dutch
ISBN 0-8118-5099-4

"This text is pulled directly from the letters Van Gogh wrote about his paintings to his brother, Theo. Each line of the rhyming stanzas is accompanied by a rich, full-color reproduction of one of the artist's key works. . . . Van Gogh's poetic descriptions will hold the attention of young readers; even preschoolers will enjoy the simple text and vibrant pictures. The brilliant colors and brush strokes are reproduced faithfully." SLJ

Raczka, Bob

The Vermeer interviews; conversations with seven works of art; as imagined by Bob Raczka. Millbrook Press 2009 32p il (Art adventures) lib bdg $25.27

Grades: 3 4 5 6   **759.9492**
1. Vermeer, Johannes, 1632-1675 2. Artists, Dutch 3. Art appreciation
ISBN 978-0-8225-9402-4 (lib bdg); 0-8225-9402-1 (lib bdg)   LC 2008024969

"Raczka makes Johannes Vermeer's masterpieces accessible by employing an interview format. Clearly stating that these 'conversations' are 'as imagined' by the author, 'Bob' asks the subjects of seven paintings a series of questions about themselves and their surroundings, allowing them to give details about the art techniques, historical context, and cultural elements." SLJ

Includes bibliographical references

760.2 Miscellany of printmaking and prints

Hanson, Anders, 1980-
Cool printmaking; the art of creativity for kids; [by] Anders Hanson. ABDO Pub. Co. 2009 32p il (Cool art) lib bdg $24.21
Grades: 2 3 4   **760.2**
    1. Prints 2. Printing
    ISBN 978-1-60453-147-3 (lib bdg); 1-60453-147-9 (lib bdg)   LC 2008-22323
This book about printmaking is "well organized, with clearly written sections . . . and several clever projects and exercises. . . . [It] should have substantial child appeal." SLJ
Includes glossary

Luxbacher, Irene, 1970-
1 2 3 I can make prints! Kids Can Press 2008 24p il (Starting art) $14.95; pa $5.95
Grades: 2 3 4   **760.2**
    1. Prints 2. Printing
    ISBN   978-1-55453-040-3;   1-55453-040-7; 978-1-55453-153-0 (pa); 1-55453-153-5 (pa)
"This book presents brightly colored, framed examples and ink cartoons to invite young readers to make prints. Simple stamp prints fill the pages, as well as relief, intaglio, and block prints, with examples of patterns and symmetry. . . . A child-friendly format introduces the prints: each art project entails only three easy-to-follow steps, and embellishments add creativity and instruction. . . . Luxbacher presents bold, eye-catching examples in an easy-to-understand, entertaining manner." SLJ

761 Relief processes (Block printing)

Boonyadhistarn, Thiranut
Stamping art; imprint your designs; by Thiranut Boonyadhistarn. Capstone Press 2007 31p il $25.26
Grades: 4 5 6 7   **761**
    1. Rubber stamp printing 2. Handicraft
    ISBN 978-0-7368-6477-0; 0-7368-6477-6   LC 2006004077
This "describes how to make stamps from common household objects, create 'embossed' cards, make a 'stained glass' lampshade, and more." SLJ
Includes bibliographical references

Price, Pamela S.
Cool rubber stamp art; [by] Pam Price. ABDO Pub. Co. 2005 32p il (Cool crafts) lib bdg $22.78 *
Grades: 4 5 6   **761**
    1. Rubber stamp printing 2. Handicraft
    ISBN 1-59197-743-6   LC 2004-53123

This describes five rubber stamp art projects: "a terracotta flowerpot, spring greeting card, wrapping paper, canvas beach bag, and homemade stamps (sponge, string, leaf). . . . [This book lists] required materials, [has] small color photos, and [includes] clearly explained, numbered steps. . . . [It will] will appeal to children." SLJ

Ross, Kathy, 1948-
One-of-a-kind stamps and crafts; illustrated by Nicole in den Bosch. Millbrook Press 2010 48p il (Girl crafts) lib bdg $25.26; pa $7.95
Grades: 3 4 5 6   **761**
    1. Rubber stamp printing 2. Handicraft
    ISBN 978-0-8225-9216-7 (lib bdg); 0-8225-9216-9 (lib bdg); 978-1-58013-885-7 (pa); 1-58013-885-3 (pa)   LC 2009020626
"This book describes how to create 20 stamps as well as an ink-pad storage shelf and a stamp storage box. . . . Decorative top borders add to the overall neat, well-spaced pages. The projects include readily available supplies, step-by-step instructions, and clear color illustrations. . . . An enhancement to craft collections." SLJ

770 Photography & computer art

Friedman, Debra, 1955-
Picture this; fun photography and crafts. Kids Can Press 2003 40p il (Kids can do it) hardcover o.p. pa $5.95 *
Grades: 4 5 6   **770**
    1. Photography 2. Handicraft
    ISBN 1-55337-046-5; 1-55337-047-3 (pa)
This focuses "on composition and presentation techniques adaptable for 35mm, disposable, and, to a more limited extent, digital cameras. Novices and enthusiasts will find hints on capturing shadows and motion, creating montaged panoramas and simple optical illusions, and adding interest to portraits with before/after, bug's-eye, and bird's-eye views. Suggestions for cropping, grouping, and sequencing raise the bar from simple scrapbook-style mounting." Bull Cent Child Books
"Clearly written instructions and ideas, illustrated with color diagrams and photographs . . . explores such concepts as light and shadow, action, and point of view. The crafts include framing and matting as well as suggestions for arranging pictures in a scrapbook." SLJ
Includes glossary

775 Digital photography

Bidner, Jenni
The kids' guide to digital photography; how to shoot, save, play with & print your digital photos. Lark Books 2004 96p il $14.95; pa $9.95 *
Grades: 5 6 7 8   **775**
    1. Digital photography
    ISBN 1-57990-604-4; 1-57990-643-5 (pa)   LC 2004-14465

Bidner, Jenni—*Continued*

"Beginning chapters address basics, including understanding camera features, using focus and flash functions, capturing motion, and so on. Bidner then delves into picture-editing software and even how to set up a Web site. . . . Final sections offer ideas for projects. . . . Bidner introduces sophisticated technical material in enthusiastic language that is kid-friendly without being condescending." Booklist

Includes glossary

Johnson, Daniel, 1984-

4-H guide to digital photography. Voyageur Press 2009 176p $18.99

Grades: 5 6 7 8   **775**
    1. Digital photography
    ISBN 978-0-7603-3652-6; 0-7603-3652-0
                                                LC 2009014679
This guide to digital photography offers "sound and comprehensive information. . . . [It] features numerous excellent photos that support the text. It explores types of digital cameras, how to take good photos, the complexities of lighting, managing images . . . and the importance of just enjoying this activity. Types of photography such as landscape and macro are explained. The author does an excellent job of discussing the importance of both technological details and artistic creativity." SLJ

Includes glossary

778.59   Video production

Shulman, Mark, 1962-

Attack of the killer video book; tips and tricks for young directors; by Mark Shulman and Hazlitt Krog; art by Martha Newbigging. Annick Press 2004 64p il $24.95; pa $12.95 *

Grades: 5 6 7 8   **778.59**
    1. Video recording
    ISBN 1-55037-841-4; 1-55037-840-6 (pa)
This "guide explores every stage of video production, from brainstorming, to organizing a shoot, to finally piecing it all together." Publisher's note

"This lighthearted primer uses lots of humor and colorful, cartoon-style illustrations. . . . A good choice for collections in need of an updated video-production guide that won't become dated too quickly." SLJ

779   Photographs

Delannoy, Isabelle

Our living Earth; a story of people, ecology, and preservation; by Isabelle Delannoy; photographs by Yann Arthus-Bertrand. Harry N. Abrams 2008 157p il $24.95 *

Grades: 5 6 7 8   **779**
    1. Aerial photography 2. Human geography
    ISBN 978-0-8109-7132-5; 0-8109-7132-1
                                                LC 2008010324
Published in association with the Field Museum

"Wrapped around Arthus-Bertrand's magnificent aerial photographs from around the world, Delannoy's text is organized thematically, covering fresh water, biodiversity, oceans, land, cities, people, food, and climate. . . . Readers will find surprising information and images to ponder. Almost every page supports the overarching theme that social justice and environmental protection are inextricably related. . . . This volume raises awareness, and the striking images, astonishing statistics, and brief explanations will stimulate readers to investigate further and possibly to take action." SLJ

780   Music

Aliki

Ah, music! written and illustrated by Aliki. HarperCollins Pubs. 2003 47p il $17.99; pa $6.99 *

Grades: K 1 2 3   **780**
    1. Music
    ISBN 0-06-028719-5; 0-06-446236-6 (pa)
                                                LC 2001-26476
This introduction to music defines such terms as rhythm, melody, pitch, and volume, gives a brief description of written music, instruments of the orchestra, vocal parts, harmony, dynamics, and tempo, cultural diversity in dance and music, and gives a brief outline of musical history

"Terms are explained in an easy, child-friendly manner. . . . Aliki's love of her subject shines through. This enjoyable title is best shared one-on-one and its format makes it ideal for browsing." SLJ

Lach, William, 1968-

Can you hear it? Abrams Books for Young Readers 2007 39p il $18.95 *

Grades: 2 3 4 5   **780**
    1. Art and music
    ISBN 978-0-8109-5721-3
Published in association with The Metropolitan Museum of Art

"This visual and aural feast invites parents, educators, and young listeners to 'listen and look' at 13 examples of pictorial music and visual masterpieces. The introduction prepares readers with an explanation of the connections between composers' notes and art images. A woodblock print by Utagawa Hiroshige, the pointillism of Seurat, and landscapes by Jacob van Ruisdael and Thomas Cole are among those included in the presentation. The paired examples invite listeners to identify solo instruments or orchestral themes that characterize an image found in the visual art." SLJ

Nathan, Amy

Meet the musicians; from prodigy (or not) to pro. Henry Holt and Co. 2006 168p il $17.95

Grades: 5 6 7 8   **780**
    1. Musicians 2. Music
    ISBN 978-0-8050-7743-8; 0-8050-7743-X
                                                LC 2005026508

Nathan, Amy—*Continued*

The author "interviewed 13 of the New York Philharmonic's members, representing 11 different instruments, and spun their articulate comments into brief, readable profiles, supplemented by various sidebars—among them, an invaluable feature outlining pros and cons of individual instruments. . . . The practical advice mixed with inspirational words strikes just the right note for children at many different stages in their musical education." Booklist

Includes bibliographical references

780.89 Music with respect to specific ethnic and national groups

Igus, Toyomi, 1953-

I see the rhythm; paintings by Michele Wood; text by Toyomi Igus. Children's Bk. Press 1998 32p il $18.95; pa $7.95 *

Grades: 4 5 6 7   **780.89**

1. African American music
ISBN 0-89239-151-0; 0-89239-212-9 (pa)
                   LC 97-29310

Coretta Scott King Award for illustration

Chronicles and captures poetically the history, mood, and movement of African American music

"The text, made up of free verse and music lyrics, incorporates different font sizes, shapes, and colors to underline the mood of each genre. . . . The colors of each full-page scenario underline the mood. . . . This book celebrates music with art and words and successfully blends all three." SLJ

780.9 Music—Historical, geographic, persons, treatment

Solway, Andrew

Africa; [by] Andrew Solway. Heinemann Library 2008 48p il (World of music) lib bdg $22

Grades: 5 6 7 8   **780.9**

1. African music
ISBN 978-1-4034-9891-5 (lib bdg); 1-4034-9891-1 (lib bdg)
                  LC 2006100578

This introduction to African music discusses "instruments, dance, and vocal styles. The photographs presented are wonderfully colorful in quality and narrative. Topics covered include history, famous players, current styles, pop-culture, politics, world-wide connections." Libr Media Connect

Includes glossary and bibliographical references

Latin America and the Caribbean; [by] Andrew Solway. Heinemann Library 2008 48p il (World of music) lib bdg $22

Grades: 5 6 7 8   **780.9**

1. Music—Latin America 2. Music—Caribbean region
ISBN 978-1-4034-9889-2 (lib bdg); 1-4034-9889-X (lib bdg)
                  LC 2006100579

This introduction to music of Latin America and the Caribbean discusses "instruments, dance, and vocal

styles. The photographs presented are wonderfully colorful in quality and narrative. Topics covered include history, famous players, current styles, pop-culture, politics, and world-wide connections." Libr Media Connect

Includes glossary and bibliographical references

Underwood, Deborah, 1962-

Australia, Hawaii, and the Pacific; [by] Deborah Underwood. Heinemann Library 2008 48p il (World of music) lib bdg $22

Grades: 5 6 7 8   **780.9**

1. Music—Australia 2. Music—Hawaii 3. Music—Oceania
ISBN 978-1-4034-9894-6 (lib bdg); 1-4034-9894-6 (lib bdg)
                  LC 2006100576

This introduction to the music of Australia, Hawaii, and the Pacific discusses "instruments, dance, and vocal styles. The photographs presented are wonderfully colorful in quality and narrative. Topics covered include history, famous players, current styles, pop-culture, politics, and world-wide connections." Libr Media Connect

Includes glossary and bibliographical references

780.94 Music of Europe

Allen, Patrick

Europe; [by] Patrick Allen. Heinemann Library 2008 48p il (World of music) lib bdg $22

Grades: 5 6 7 8   **780.94**

1. Music—Europe
ISBN 978-1-4034-9890-8 (lib bdg); 1-4034-9890-3 (lib bdg)
                  LC 2006100580

This introduction to European music discusses "instruments, dance, and vocal styles. The photographs presented are wonderfully colorful in quality and narrative. Topics covered include history, famous players, current styles, pop-culture, politics, and world-wide connections." Libr Media Connect

Includes glossary and bibliographical references

781 Music—General principles and musical forms

Sabbeth, Alex, 1950-

Rubber-band banjos and a java jive bass; projects and activities on the science of music and sound; project illustrations by Laurel Aiello. Wiley 1997 102p il pa $12.95 *

Grades: 4 5 6 7   **781**

1. Music 2. Sound 3. Musical instruments
ISBN 0-471-15675-2   LC 96-22144

This "presentation explores the world of sound and provides instructions for making musical instruments. Along the way, readers will learn about famous scientists who had musical inclinations. . . . Numerous, clear, pen-and-ink drawings illustrate the construction of instruments from a glass harmonica, to a violin, drums, and a foot-powered organ. . . . The scientific principles behind the creation of all the wonderful noises are explained, as is basic music notation." SLJ

Includes glossary

781.49   Recording of music

Miles, Liz
Making a recording. Raintree 2009 32p il
(Culture in action) $28.21; pa $7.99
Grades: 5 6 7 8   **781.49**
  1. Music industry—Vocational guidance 2. Sound recordings
  ISBN   978-1-4109-3392-8;   1-4109-3392-X;
978-1-4109-3409-3 (pa); 1-4109-3409-8 (pa)
                                              LC 2009000416
  This "is a must-read for any aspiring musician. A
brief history is followed by a discussion of modern techniques, and technical terms are explained in simple language. Fun activities include designing a label. . . . Well
organized and with bright, colorful photography, [this]
introductory [title gives] readers good basic knowledge."
SLJ
  Includes glossary and bibliographical references

781.62   Folk music

Handyside, Chris, 1972-
Folk. Heinemann Library 2006 48p il (A history
of American music) lib bdg $31.43 *
Grades: 5 6 7 8   **781.62**
  1. Folk music
  ISBN 1-4034-8150-4
  This history of folk music is an "excellent, clear [in-
troduction]. . . . [It] starts with the post-Civil War era,
when folklorists gathered slave songs. It describes the
music's commercial success beginning with early recordings of the Carter family and Jimmie Rodgers in the
1920s and continuing with Leadbelly, Woody Guthrie,
Pete Seeger, and the many musicians who became popular during the folk revival of the late 50s and early 60s.
. . . It concludes with sections on folk rock, punk rock,
and the future of folk music." SLJ
  Includes bibliographical references

781.642   Country music

Bertholf, Bret
Long gone lonesome history of country music;
by Bret Bertholf. Little, Brown 2007 unp il $18.99
*
Grades: 4 5 6   **781.642**
  1. Country music
  ISBN 978-0-316-52393-6; 0-316-52393-3
                                              LC 2005016036
  "This tongue-in-cheek overview features a folksy narrative of how and why country music developed in the
barns and back roads of rural America. The text . . .
covers instruments, early recordings, yodeling, . . . the
Great Depression, gospel, movie cowboys, a 'paper-doll'
spoof of singers' costumes, hillbilly jazz, World War II,
. . . and much more. While poking fun at itself . . . the
book offers a vast amount of historical fact amid a multitude of caricatures of country stars. . . . The ever-
changing backgrounds and fonts with colored-pencil and
crayon illustrations carry an amazing variation of detail."
SLJ

Handyside, Chris, 1972-
Country. Heinemann Library 2006 48p il (A
history of American music) lib bdg $31.43 *
Grades: 5 6 7 8   **781.642**
  1. Country music
  ISBN 1-4034-8151-2
  This history of Country music is an "excellent clear
[introduction]. . . . [It] follows the music's history
through honky-tonk, singing cowboys, Western Swing,
bluegrass, rockabilly, country rock, outlaw, and alternative country. Featured musicians include Uncle Dave Ma-
con, the Carter family, Jimmie Rodgers, Hank Williams,
Johnny Cash, Loretta Lynn, and John Denver." SLJ
  Includes bibliographical references

781.643   Blues

Handyside, Chris, 1972-
Blues; [by] Christopher Handyside. Heinemann
Library 2006 48p il (A history of American music)
lib bdg $31.43 *
Grades: 5 6 7 8   **781.643**
  1. Blues music
  ISBN 1-4034-8148-2   LC 2005019280
  "This book charts the development of this uniquely
American Music form from the 1600s through to the
present. It also shows how social, economic, and regional
factors have all helped to shape the blues over time and,
in turn, how this music has gone on to influence other
genres." Publisher's note
  Includes glossary and bibliographical references

781.644   Soul music

Handyside, Chris, 1972-
Soul and R&B; [by] Christopher Handyside.
Heinemann Library 2006 48p il (A history of
American music) lib bdg $31.43 *
Grades: 5 6 7 8   **781.644**
  1. Soul music 2. Rhythm and blues music
  ISBN 1-4034-8153-9   LC 2005019324
  "This book charts the development of this uniquely
American music form from the 1800s through to the
present. It also shows how social, economic, and regional
factors have all helped to shape soul and R&B over time
and, in turn, how this music has gone on to influence
other genres." Publisher's note
  Includes glossary and bibliographical references

781.65   Jazz

Dillon, Leo, 1933-
Jazz on a Saturday night; [by] Leo & Diane
Dillon. Blue Sky Press 2007 unp il $16.99 *
Grades: PreK K 1 2   **781.65**
  1. Jazz music 2. Jazz musicians
  ISBN 0-590-47893-1; 978-0-590-47893-1
                                              LC 2006-34009

Dillon, Leo, 1933-—_Continued_

This takes readers on "an imaginary Saturday night concert featuring seven . . . [jazz] greats, from Thelonius Monk to John Coltrane. Rhythmic text acts as an introduction to the legendary musicians. . . . The sophisticated illustrations . . . recall Harlem Renaissance paintings. . . . Brief biographies of the seven featured artists serve as endnotes, while a bonus CD briefly explores jazz instruments and features an original song that shares the book's title." Publ Wkly

Handyside, Chris, 1972-

Jazz; [by] Christopher Handyside. Heinemann Library 2006 48p il (A history of American music) lib bdg $31.43 *

Grades: 5 6 7 8   **781.65**

1. Jazz music

ISBN 1-4034-8149-0   LC 2005019305

"This book charts the development of this uniquely American Music form from the 1600s through to the present. It also shows how social, economic, and regional factors have all helped to shape Jazz over time and, in turn, how this music has gone on to influence other genres." Publisher's note

Includes glossary and bibliographical references

Marsalis, Wynton

Jazz A-B-Z; [by] Wynton Marsalis and Paul Rogers; with biographical sketches by Phil Schaap. Candlewick Press 2005 unp il $24.99 *

Grades: 5 6 7 8 9 10   **781.65**

1. Jazz music 2. Jazz musicians

ISBN 0-7636-2135-8   LC 2005-48448

This is an illustrated alphabetically arranged introduction to jazz musicians.

This is a "witty, stunningly designed alphabet catalog. . . . The biographical sketches and notes on poetic forms by Phil Schaap are concise and genuinely informative. . . . Rogers's pastiche full-page portraits, his use of expressive typography and the smaller vignettes he sprinkles throughout are bound to heighten any reader's appreciation of both the musicians and the music. . . . [Marsalis offers] clever . . . poems, wordplays, odes and limericks." N Y Times Book Rev

781.66   Rock (Rock 'n' roll)

Handyside, Chris, 1972-

Rock. Heinemann Library 2006 48p il (A history of American music) lib bdg $31.43 *

Grades: 5 6 7 8   **781.66**

1. Rock music

ISBN 1-4034-8150-4

This history of rock music is an "excellent, clear [introduction]. . . . [It] opens with the mid-1950s advent of rock n roll and continues with surf music, girl groups, the British invasion, psychedelic rock, heavy metal, punk, and grunge. Featured musicians range from Elvis Presley to Kurt Cobain." SLJ

Includes bibliographical references

Stamaty, Mark Alan

Shake, rattle & turn that noise down! how Elvis shook up music, me, and mom. Alfred A. Knopf 2010 unp il $17.99; lib bdg $20.99

Grades: 2 3 4   **781.66**

1. Presley, Elvis, 1935-1977 2. Rock music

ISBN   978-0-375-84685-4;   0-375-84685-9; 978-0-375-94685-1 (lib bdg); 0-375-94685-3 (lib bdg)

                    LC 2008-02231

"Mark first heard the howling thunder of Elvis Presley singing 'Hound Dog' on the radio one lazy day and his life was forever changed. . . . But his mother lived in constant fear that her son's new love of rock 'n' roll would turn him into a juvenile delinquent." Publisher's note

"Dividing each page into multiple panels with sizable chunks of text allows Stamaty to cram a lot of information into the picture-book format. . . . [The book] makes a convincing case that that old, dead singer really was cool." Booklist

782.25   Sacred songs

All night, all day; a child's first book of African-American spirituals; selected and illustrated by Ashley Bryan; musical arrangements by David Manning Thomas. Atheneum Pubs. 1991 48p il music hardcover o.p. pa $6.99

Grades: K 1 2 3 4   **782.25**

1. Spirituals (Songs)

ISBN 0-689-31662-3; 0-689-86786-7 (pa)

                    LC 90-753145

This is a "selection of 20 well-known spirituals." SLJ

"An exuberance of warm color and great variety in pattern and design distinguish the illustrations. . . . Excellent piano accompaniments and guitar chords further enrich the beautiful, wholly gratifying book." Horn Book

Let it shine; three favorite spirituals; [illustrated by] Ashley Bryan. Atheneum Books for Young Readers 2007 unp il $16.99 *

Grades: K 1 2 3   **782.25**

1. Spirituals (Songs)

ISBN 0-689-84732-7

"The inspiring words of three well-known spirituals, 'This Little Light of Mine,' 'Oh, When the Saints Go Marching In,' and 'He's Got the Whole World in His Hands,' are matched with powerful construction-paper collage illustrations. Each double-page spread of this oversize picture book is an explosion of shapes and bright colors." Booklist

Nelson, Kadir

He's got the whole world in his hands. Dial Books for Young Readers 2005 unp il $16.99 *

Grades: K 1 2   **782.25**

1. Spirituals (Songs)

ISBN 0-8037-2850-6   LC 2004-23075

An illustrated version of the well-known spiritual song

"Nelson uses pencils, oils, and watercolors to create a series of striking, beautifully composed pictures. . . .

Nelson, Kadir—*Continued*

Nelson envisions the song in a highly personal and involving manner while embodying its strength and spirit." Booklist

This little light of mine; illustrated by E. B. Lewis. Simon & Schuster Books for Young Readers 2005 32p il $16.95 *

Grades: K 1 2 3   **782.25**

1. Spirituals (Songs)

ISBN 0-689-83179-X

"A visual interpretation of an African-American spiritual. It is morning when the book opens, and readers are greeted by a smiling boy. Throughout the day, he spreads his own special brand of joy wherever he goes. . . . Lewis's watercolor illustrations across double pages effectively convey emotions of happiness and the giving and sharing of oneself." SLJ

782.28   Carols

Spirin, Gennadiĭ

We three kings; illustrated by Gennady Spirin. Atheneum Books for Young Readers 2007 unp il $16.99

Grades: K 1 2 3   **782.28**

1. Carols

ISBN 978-0-689-82114-1; 0-689-82114-X

"This handsome picture book illustrates the verses and repeated choruses of the Christmas carol 'We Three Kings.' . . . Created with watercolors and colored pencils, the formally composed and richly detailed illustrations create a distinctive world, with landscapes reminiscent of Renaissance paintings." Booklist

782.42   Songs

The **12** days of Christmas; a pop-up celebration by Robert Sabuda. anniversary edition. Little Simon 2006 unp il $26.95 *

Grades: K 1 2 3   **782.42**

1. Christmas—Songs 2. Folk songs 3. Pop-up books

ISBN 978-1-4169-2792-1; 1-4169-2792-1

A reissue of the edition first published 1996

This pop-up version of the popular Christmas folk song about gift-giving features "a partridge popping, snow scattering, and lords a-leaping off the page. . . . For this . . . anniversary edition . . . paper engineer Robert Sabuda encloses . . . extra pages with a pop-up Christmas tree with real lights aglow, and a . . . pop-up ornament of two turtledoves." Publisher's note

Arroz con leche; popular songs and rhymes from Latin America; selected and illustrated by Lulu Delacre; English lyrics by Elena Paz; musical arrangements by Ana-María Rosado. Scholastic 1989 32p il music pa $5.99 hardcover o.p. *

Grades: K 1 2 3   **782.42**

1. Folk songs 2. Folklore—Latin America 3. Bilingual books—English-Spanish

ISBN 0-590-041886-6 (pa)

A Lucas/Evans Bk.

This is a bilingual collection of twelve folk songs and rhymes from Puerto Rico, Mexico and Argentina. Instructions for fingerplays and games accompany some of the songs. Musical arrangements for nine of the entries are included at the end of the book

"Delacre has selected lilting verses that are pleasing to the ear—ones likely to encourage non-Spanish-speakers to join in the fun. . . . Fresh, springlike colors brighten the pictures. . . . An author's note explains that many of the scenes depict real places." Booklist

Bates, Ivan

Five little ducks; illustrated by Ivan Bates. Scholastic 2006 unp il $12.99 *

Grades: K 1 2   **782.42**

1. Ducks—Songs 2. Songs 3. Counting

ISBN 0-439-74693-0   LC 2005000112

"Orchard books"

One by one, five little ducks wander away from their mother until her lonely quack brings them all waddling back

"Bates's muted watercolors bring a lively energy . . . to this beloved song. The artist's sweet and nostalgic adaptation is unique for its gentle and warm tone." SLJ

Baum, Maxie

I have a little dreidel; illustrated by Julie Paschkis. Scholastic Press 2006 unp il $9.99

Grades: K 1 2   **782.42**

1. Hanukkah—Songs 2. Songs

ISBN 0-439-64997-8; 978-0-439-64997-1

          LC 2005-31318

"Cartwheel books"

An illustrated retelling of the classic Hannukah song, with directions for playing the dreidel game and a recipe for making latkes.

"A favorite Hanukkah song is given new life in this charmingly illustrated variation. . . . Distinctive, folk-art-style illustrations feature a mix of patterns and vibrant solids, thick lines and simple shapes, while the bottom third of each spread frames the text in a bold blue-and-white woodcutlike design." SLJ

Boynton, Sandra

Blue Moo; 17 jukebox hits from way back never; deluxe illustrated songbook; lyrics and drawings by Sandra Boynton; music by Sandra Boynton & Michael Ford. Workman Pub. Co. 2007 64p il $16.95

Grades: K 1 2 3   **782.42**

1. Songs

ISBN 978-0-7611-4775-6; 0-7611-4775-6

A book and audio CD of songs in the style of 1950s pop music.

"Grandparents, parents, and children alike can enjoy this collection. . . . Boynton has combined a roster of celebrity singers, good humor, and lots of creativity for a gift of music and fun for every member of the family." SLJ

Boynton, Sandra—*Continued*

Dog train; deluxe illustrated lyrics book of the unpredictable rock-and-roll journey; music by Sandra Boynton & Michael Ford; lyrics and drawings by Sandra Boynton. Workman Pub. 2005 64p il $17.95

Grades: K 1 2 3   **782.42**
   1. Songs 2. Rock music
   ISBN 0-7611-3966-4   LC 2005051801

"This collection of songs erupts with energy, humor, and a strong dose of rock n roll. . . . The book has a spread for each song—a colorful, cheerful illustration and excerpts of lyrics—followed by complete lyrics and musical scores at the end. An About the Artists section includes a photo and biographical sketch of each artist who performs on the accompanying CD." SLJ

Philadelphia chickens; a too-illogical zoological musical revue: deluxe illustrated lyrics book of the original cast recording of the unforgettable (though completely imaginary) stage spectacular; music by Sandra Boynton & Michael Ford; lyrics and drawings by Sandra Boynton. Workman Pub. 2002 64p il $16.95

Grades: K 1 2 3   **782.42**
   1. Musicals 2. Songs
   ISBN 0-7611-2636-8   LC 2002-27049

This is "a book-and-CD package billed as an 'imaginary musical revue.' The first 32 pages contain lyrics and illustrations, the second half of the book includes musical notation and additional lyrics for each song. An all-star cast, including Meryl Streep, Laura Linney, Eric Stoltz and the Bacon Brothers, headlines the musical recording, which features a variety of original show tunes." Publ Wkly

Sandra Boynton's One shoe blues; starring B.B. King. Workman 2009 59p il $10.95

Grades: PreK K 1 2 3   **782.42**
   1. King, B. B.—Fiction 2. Lost and found possessions—Fiction 3. Puppets and puppet plays—Fiction 4. Songs
   ISBN 978-0-7611-5138-8; 0-7611-5138-9
                                   LC 2009035847

"Boynton transforms a song from her 2007 book-and-CD title *Blue Moo: 17 Jukebox Hits from Way Back Never* into a stand-alone book-plus-DVD, starring blues legend B.B. King. Boynton weaves the lyrics of her original song into an extended tale about some colorful sock puppets who watch King perform the song in a cozy country house. . . . Still photographs from Boynton's music video and other complementary shots illustrate the story. . . . In addition to King's humorous and engaging performance (complete with sock puppet accompaniment), the DVD contains other kid-pleasing tidbits." Publ Wkly

Cabrera, Jane, 1968-

Old MacDonald had a farm; [by] Jane Cabrera. Holiday House 2008 unp il $16.95

Grades: PreK K   **782.42**
   1. Folk songs—United States 2. Farm life—Songs
   ISBN 978-0-8234-2141-1   LC 2007034036
   First published 2007 in the United Kingdom

"A gray-haired, rosy-cheeked Old MacDonald starts off by introducing his young-looking wife, with 'a kiss kiss here, and a kiss kiss there. . . .' Then it's off to the fields, barn, and pond to meet his dog, sheep, horse, hens, goat, ducks, cow, and pig. . . . Cabrera's bright, splotchy illustrations follow the text, with full spreads devoted to each verse. Young children can read along easily enough and can probably add their own verses to the mix." SLJ

Carle, Eric

Today is Monday; pictures by Eric Carle. Philomel Bks. 1993 unp il music hardcover o.p. pa $6.99 *

Grades: K 1 2 3   **782.42**
   1. Songs 2. Food—Songs 3. Animals—Songs
   ISBN 0-399-21966-8; 0-698-11563-5 (pa)
                                   LC 91-45866

Each day of the week brings a new food, until on Sunday all the world's children can come and eat it up

This song "gets new life in a picture book bursting with food, animals, and lots of energy. Beginning with the grinning cat on the cover . . . a zooful of animals act out the lyrics: snakes get tangled in spaghetti, elephants use their trunks to slurp 'Zoooop,' and pelicans catch fish on Friday. With text at a minimum, Carle's always innovative artwork steps center stage in an oversize format that allows gloriously colored collages to spread over two pages." Booklist

Coots, John Frederick, 1897-1985

Santa Claus is comin' to town; written by J. Fred Coots & Haven Gillespie; illustrated by Steven Kellogg. HarperCollins 2004 unp il hardcover o.p. pa $6.99

Grades: K 1 2 3   **782.42**
   1. Songs 2. Santa Claus—Songs 3. Christmas—Songs
   ISBN 0-688-14938-3; 0-06-443865-1 (pa)
                                   LC 2003-1821

"A little bear has just returned from visiting Santa at the North Pole. Armed with insider information, he uses the familiar words of this upbeat Christmas standard to warn the children that they had best behave themselves." SLJ

This "manages to get the rhythm of the music right onto the page. . . . The pictures are packed, and the design is witty." Horn Book

De colores = Bright with colors; illustrated by David Diaz. Marshall Cavendish 2008 unp il $16.99

Grades: K 1 2 3   **782.42**
   1. Songs 2. Bilingual books—English-Spanish
   ISBN 978-0-7614-5431-1; 0-7614-5431-4
                                   LC 2007022133

"This popular folk song, which is also the anthem of the United Farm Workers of America, celebrates the arrival of spring and the connectedness of humankind. Diaz's joyful pictures bring the words to life. Rendered in acrylic, colored pencil, and pencil, the vibrant, fanciful artwork features flying and floating people as well as giant-sized roosters, chickens, and birds. . . . Presented in Spanish and English, each line is illustrated on an expansive spread. Piano music and historical information about the song are included." SLJ

De colores and other Latin-American folk songs for children; selected, arranged, and translated by José-Luis Orozco; illustrated by Eliza Kleven. Dutton Children's Bks. 1994 56p il hardcover o.p. pa $7.99 *
Grades: K 1 2 3   **782.42**
1. Folk songs 2. Bilingual books—English-Spanish 3. Folklore—Latin America
ISBN 0-525-45260-5; 0-14-056548-5 (pa)
"Each of the 27 songs is presented with background notes; lyrics in both Spanish and English; simple arrangements for the voice, piano, and guitar; and suggestions for group sing-alongs and musical games. . . . The book is a delight for the eyes as well as the ear. . . . Kleven provides bountiful illustrations—the endpapers are sunshine bright with a crisp quilt of yellow flowers, and playful borders that ripple with colorful patterns and miniature pictures line the edge of every page." Booklist

Deck the halls; [illustrations by] Norman Rockwell. Atheneum Books for Young Readers 2008 unp il $16.99
Grades: PreK K 1 2   **782.42**
1. Christmas—Songs 2. Songs
ISBN 978-1-4169-1771-7; 1-4169-1771-3
LC 2007037461
"The traditional Christmas carol is illustrated with Rockwell's heartwarming visions of holiday cheer. The art come[s] from a variety of sources—magazine covers, advertisements, holiday cards—and matches the lyrics surprisingly well. . . . Handsomely nostalgic." SLJ

Diez deditos. Ten little fingers & other play rhymes and action songs from Latin America; selected, arranged, and translated by José-Luis Orozco; illustrated by Elisa Kleven. Dutton Children's Bks. 1997 56p il music $19.99; pa $7.99 *
Grades: K 1 2 3   **782.42**
1. Songs 2. Folklore—Latin America 3. Finger play 4. Bilingual books—English-Spanish
ISBN 0-525-45736-4; 0-14-230087-9 (pa)
"This collection of fingerplays and action songs in Spanish and English comes with clear instructions for physical movements and simple musical notation. A brief sentence or paragraph introduces each entry. . . . Orozco's selections, some traditional, some written by himself, include versifications on such child-appealing subjects as dancing, singing, animals, weather, and food. . . . Kleven's collage illustrations practically pop off the pages with flashy colors and rich details that make each bustling composition a viewer's delight." Bull Cent Child Books

DiPucchio, Kelly S.
Sipping spiders through a straw; campfire songs for monsters; lyrics by Kelly DiPucchio; pictures by Gris Grimly. Scholastic Press 2008 unp il $15.99
Grades: 2 3 4   **782.42**
1. Monsters 2. Songs
ISBN 978-0-439-58401-2; 0-439-58401-9
"This book of eighteen clever song parodies captures exactly the type of thing kids might come up with on

their own. Grisly watercolor and mixed-media illustrations awash in appropriately putrid shades of brown and gray will definitely appeal to its target readers: those with a ghoulish sense of humor who are not easily grossed out by disgusting monsters or bodily fluids." Horn Book Guide

The **Farmer** in the dell; illustrated by Alexandra Wallner. Holiday House 1998 unp il music $15.95
Grades: K 1   **782.42**
1. Folk songs—United States
ISBN 0-8234-1382-9   LC 97-44206
An illustrated version of the traditional game song accompanied by music
"Wallner's primitive folk art sparkles with life, action, and energy. The colored pen-and-ink illustrations are packed with details." SLJ

Fatus, Sophie
Here we go round the mulberry bush; [by] Sophie Fatus and Fred Penner. Barefoot Books 2007 unp il $16.99
Grades: PreK K 1 2   **782.42**
1. Songs
ISBN 978-1-84686-035-5; 1-84686-035-0
LC 2006025656
Includes audio CD with song performed by Fred Penner
Presents ten verses of the popular song, with illustrations of children from different cultures as they get ready for school.
"The double-page spreads, rendered in bold acrylics, are separated into fours to show the kids side by side. This artfully underscores cultural diversity while uniting the children through their similar routines. Music and a CD of the song are included." Horn Book Guide

Favorite folk songs; The Peter Yarrow songbook; [compiled by Peter Yarrow]; illustrated by Terry Widener. Sterling Pub. 2008 48p il (Peter Yarrow songbook series) $16.95
Grades: PreK K 1 2   **782.42**
1. Folk songs
ISBN 978-1-4027-5961-1; 1-4027-5961-4
LC 2008022435
Contents: The Golden Vanity; Skip to my Lou; Cockles and mussels; The fox; Springfield Mountain; The Erie Canal; Beautiful city; Rock-a my soul; The cruel war; O, Mary don't you weep; I've been workin' on the railroad; Sloop John B.
An illustrated compilation of folk songs with an audio CD of the songs performed by Peter Yarrow and his daughter Bethany.
"Widener's acrylic paintings are expansive and gorgeous, but the [CD is] the real treasure here." SLJ

Fiestas: a year of Latin American songs of celebration; selected, arranged, and translated by José-Luis Orozco; illustrated by Elisa Kleven. Dutton Children's Bks. 2002 48p il music $17.99 *

Grades: K 1 2 3   **782.42**
   1. Songs 2. Festivals 3. Latin America—Social life and customs 4. Bilingual books—English-Spanish
ISBN 0-525-45937-5

"Orozco presents 22 songs that center around holidays. . . . Arranged by month, each song is presented with a paragraph of background, the music for the melody (with guitar chords), and the lyrics in both Spanish and English. . . . Kleven's bright borders and busy illustrations . . . make this not only an exemplary songbook, but also a stunning visual experience." SLJ

The **Fox** went out on a chilly night; an old song; illustrated by Peter Spier. Doubleday 1961 unp il music hardcover o.p. pa $6.95

Grades: K 1 2 3   **782.42**
   1. Folk songs—United States 2. Foxes—Songs
ISBN 0-385-07990-7; 0-440-40829-6 (pa)

Set in New England, this old song tells about the trip the fox father made to town to get some of the farmer's plump geese for his family's dinner, and how he manages to evade the farmer who tries to shoot him

"A true picture book in the Caldecott-Brooke tradition. Fine drawings, lovely colors, and pictures so full of amusing details that young viewers will make fresh discoveries every time they . . . scrutinize these beautiful, action-filled pages." Horn Book

Harburg, E. Y. (Edgar Yipsel), 1896-1981
Over the rainbow; performed by Judy Collins; music by Harold Arlen; lyrics by E.Y. Harburg; paintings by Eric Puybaret. Imagine Pub. 2010 unp il $17.95

Grades: K 1 2 3   **782.42**
   1. Songs
ISBN 978-1-936140-00-8; 1-936140-00-4

Illustrates the well-known song with paintings of a young girl's search for happiness.

"A musical classic inspires the creation of new images of sweeping horizons and fanciful creatures. The book includes a CD by singer Judy Collins. Her crystal-clear voice floats seamlessly through the lyrics. . . . Two additional songs interpreted by Collins make this brief CD a treasure—'I See the Moon' . . . and 'White Coral Bells.' Readers are treated to deep jewel tones as Puybaret carefully pulls them from one image to another with a succession of dreamlike scenes. . . . The art is unique, delicate, and detailed." SLJ

Hillenbrand, Will, 1960-
Down by the station. Harcourt Brace & Co. 1999 unp il music $17; pa $6.99 *

Grades: K 1 2   **782.42**
   1. Songs 2. Animals—Songs 3. Railroads—Songs
ISBN 0-15-201804-2; 0-15-216790-0 (pa)
                                LC 98-41770

"Gulliver books"

In this version of a familiar song, baby animals ride to the children's zoo on the zoo train

"This twist on an old favorite combines sunny illustrations, playful humor, and appealing animals." SLJ

Hinojosa, Tish
Cada niño/Every child; a bilingual songbook for kids; illustrated by Lucia Angela Perez. Cinco Puntos Press 2002 56p il music hardcover o.p. pa $9.95

Grades: K 1 2 3   **782.42**
   1. Songs 2. Bilingual books—English-Spanish
ISBN 0-9383-1760-1; 0-9383-1779-2 (pa)

"Hinojosa has gathered 11 traditional, original, and adapted songs to celebrate both Hispanic culture and universal experiences and feelings. A brief author's note in English and Spanish prefaces the music, with chords and melody, and verses in both languages. . . . Lovely, bright, folk-art illustrations, brimming with pattern play and whimsical details, create magical worlds of familiar objects and experiences as they incorporate cultural elements. . . . A CD is available for separate purchase." Booklist

Hoberman, Mary Ann, 1930-
The eensy-weensy spider; adapted by Mary Ann Hoberman; illustrated by Nadine Bernard Westcott. Little, Brown 2000 unp il hardcover o.p. pa $6.99

Grades: K 1 2 3   **782.42**
   1. Songs 2. Finger play 3. Spiders—Songs
ISBN 0-316-36330-8; 0-316-73412-8 (pa)
                                LC 99-25701

An expanded version of the familiar children's finger-play rhyme describing what the little spider does after being washed out of the water-spout

"Whimsical, watercolor cartoons capture the light-hearted tone of the verse. . . . This sprightly adaptation lends itself to singing aloud and is sure to be a hit." SLJ

Mary had a little lamb; adapted by Mary Ann Hoberman; illustrated by Nadine Bernard Westcott. Little, Brown 2003 unp il (Sing-along stories) $15.95

Grades: K 1 2   **782.42**
   1. Songs 2. Sheep—Songs
ISBN 0-316-60687-1   LC 2002-72478

"Megan Tingley books"

This expanded version of the traditional rhyme shows what happens after the lamb gets to school. Includes music on the last page

"This playful extension of the original nursery rhyme adds to the nonsense with simple words and clear, slapstick watercolor-and-ink illustrations." Booklist

Hort, Lenny
The seals on the bus; illustrated by G. Brian Karas. Holt & Co. 2000 unp il $17.95 *

Grades: K 1 2   **782.42**
   1. Songs 2. Animals—Songs
ISBN 0-8050-5952-0   LC 99-33612

Hort, Lenny—*Continued*

Different animals—including seals, tigers, geese, rabbits, monkeys, and more—make their own sounds as they ride all around the town on a bus

"Karas' artwork combines cut paper, gouache, acrylic, and pencil to create a series of pleasingly varied scenes of cheerful chaos. A good story hour choice." Booklist

Hush, little baby; a folk song; with pictures by Marla Frazee. Harcourt Brace & Co. 1999 unp il hardcover o.p. pa $7

Grades: K 1 2   **782.42**
1. Folk songs—United States 2. Lullabies
ISBN 0-15-201429-2; 0-15-204761-1 (pa)
      LC 98-9608

In an old lullaby a baby is promised an assortment of presents from its adoring parent

"True to the song's Appalachian roots, Frazee sets the traditional lullaby in the hills of West Virginia, with big, detailed pictures that add character and exaggerated sibling rivalry to the nonsense story. . . . The music is on the last page, and Frazee's clear narrative pictures in acrylics and pencil capture the rhythm of the words, the historic particulars of the place, the nighttime farce, and the universal family scenarios of jealousy and love." Booklist

I hear America singing! folk songs for American families; collected and arranged by Kathleen Krull; illustrated by Allen Garns; introductory note by Arlo Guthrie. Knopf 2003 145p il $24.95 *

Grades: 3 4 5 6   **782.42**
1. Folk songs—United States
ISBN 0-375-82527-4
Includes audio CD

First published 1992 without CD with title: Gonna sing my head off!

"Work songs, love songs, ballads and blues, lullabies, spirituals, protest songs, and sheer nonsense make up this entertaining collection of 62 traditional and contemporary favorites. For each song, Krull provides the simplest piano and guitar arrangements in a clear double-page spread design that includes the words to all the verses. . . . The exuberant illustrations, mostly in bright pastels, manage to be both familiar and dramatic. . . . Informal notes at the head of each song give something about history, origin, performance, and possibilities for variation." Booklist

In the hollow of your hand; slave lullabies; collected by Alice McGill; pictures by Michael Cummings. Houghton Mifflin 2000 unp il music $18

Grades: 5 6 7 8   **782.42**
1. Lullabies 2. African Americans—Poetry 3. Slavery—Poetry
ISBN 0-395-85755-4   LC 97-20269

A collection of lullabies orally transmitted by African-American slaves revealing their hardships and sorrows as well as soothing notes of well-being and belief in a better time to come

"This moving collection of 13 folk lullabies is a powerful way to communicate what family life was like under slavery. . . . Opposite each song is a handsome full-

page quilt collage contributed by Michael Cummings. . . . There's full musical notation at the back, and a CD of the songs, sung by McGill, is included. The people's words are achingly beautiful, and the combination with history and personal experience makes this an enduring collection." Booklist

Jackson, Jill, 1913-1995

Let there be peace on earth; and let it begin with me; by Jill Jackson & Sy Miller; [illustrated by David Diaz] Tricycle Press 2009 unp il $18.99

Grades: PreK K 1 2   **782.42**
1. Songs 2. Peace—Songs
ISBN 978-1-58246-285-1; 1-58246-285-2
      LC 2008043122

Illustrates the award-winning song about each person's responsibility to help bring about world peace. Includes a history of the song and biographical notes on the husband and wife songwriting team.

"Diaz's luminous artwork brings [the song] to life for picture-book audiences. . . . The CD contains 12 peace-themed, secular songs. The arrangements are airy and fun for children." SLJ

Johnson, James Weldon, 1871-1938

Lift every voice and sing; by James Weldon Johnson; illustrated by Bryan Collier. Amistad 2007 unp il $16.99; lib bdg $17.89 *

Grades: K 1 2 3   **782.42**
1. African American music 2. Songs
ISBN 978-0-06-054147-7; 978-0-06-145897-2 (lib bdg)   LC 2007008602

An illustrated version of the song that has come to be considered the African American national anthem

"Collier's stirring textured collage-and-watercolor illustrations . . . express his Christian faith and his profound sense of connection with his people's historic struggle." Booklist

Katz, Alan

On top of the potty and other get-up-and-go songs; [by] Alan Katz; [illustrations] David Catrow. Margaret K. McElderry Books 2008 unp il $16.99

Grades: PreK   **782.42**
1. Songs 2. Toilet training—Songs
ISBN 978-0-689-86215-1; 0-689-86215-6
      LC 2007-9004

Well-known songs with new lyrics encourage toddlers to trade in their diapers for the potty chair, including 'If You Gotta Go Do Poopy,' sung to the tune of 'If You're Happy and You Know It.'

"Great for toilet training, this picture book provides adults with a different way to sing and talk about that crucial time when toddlers move from diapers to underwear, potty chair, and toilet. . . . Lots of youngsters and their caregivers will have fun with this." Booklist

Katz, Alan—*Continued*

Smelly locker; silly dilly school songs; illustrated by David Catrow. Margaret K. McElderry Books 2008 unp il $16.99

Grades: K 1 2 3   **782.42**
    1. Songs 2. Schools—Songs
    ISBN 978-1-4169-0695-7; 1-4169-0695-9
                          LC 2006-36814

Well-known songs, including "Oh Susannah" and "Take Me Out to the Ballgame," are presented with new words and titles, such as "Heavy Backpack!" and "I Don't Want to Do Homework!"

This is "an irreverent, entertaining commentary in song about school life. . . . With exaggerated features and hilarious body language, Catrow's expressive cartoon characters capture the bizarre and ridiculous elements of the text." SLJ

Take me out of the bathtub and other silly dilly songs; illustrated by David Catrow. Margaret K. McElderry Bks. 2001 unp il $15

Grades: K 1 2 3   **782.42**
    1. Songs
    ISBN 0-689-82903-5   LC 99-89390

Well-known songs, including "Oh Susannah" and "Row Row Row Your Boat," are presented with new words and titles, such as "I'm So Carsick" and "Go Go Go to Bed"

"Catrow's animated double-spread pictures are at least as silly as the song lyrics, offering action-filled scenes bursting with odd-looking creatures." Booklist

Knick knack paddy whack; illustrated by Christiane Engel; sung by SteveSongs. Barefoot Books 2008 unp il $16.99

Grades: PreK K   **782.42**
    1. Folk songs 2. Counting
    ISBN 978-1-84686-144-4; 1-84686-144-6
                          LC 2007-25046

Includes CD

An illustrated version of the traditional counting song that tells of the ten things 'this old man' played before he came rolling home.

"This bright, lively, new interpretation of the classic children's song incorporates numbers, musical-instrument families, and a multiethnic group of adorable children who march along with the 'old man' of the song. . . . With its inventive use of numbers, music, and collage illustrations, it's a worthy addition." SLJ

Langstaff, John M., 1920-2005

Frog went a-courtin'; retold by John Langstaff; with pictures by Feodor Rojankovsky. Harcourt Brace Jovanovich 1955 unp il music $16; pa $7

Grades: K 1 2 3   **782.42**
    1. Folk songs 2. Frogs—Songs 3. Mice—Songs
    ISBN 0-15-230214-X; 0-15-633900-5 (pa)

Awarded the Caldecott Medal, 1956

"Retelling of a merry old Scottish ballad with many-colored illustrations about the marriage between Mr. Frog and Miss Mouse. A composite American version set to Appalachian mountain music." Chicago Public Libr

Oh, a-hunting we will go; [by] John Langstaff; pictures by Nancy Winslow Parker. Atheneum Pubs. 1974 unp il music pa $6.99 hardcover o.p.

Grades: K 1 2   **782.42**
    1. Folk songs 2. Animals—Songs
    ISBN 0-689-71503-X (pa)

"A Margaret K. McElderry book"

The nonsense verses of this folk song trace the hunt for such animals as an armadillo, a fox, and a snake, and describe the imagined treatment of each animal once it is caught

"The 12 stanzas are complemented by Parker's droll crayon illustrations (the fox caught in the box is watching TV), and a score for guitar and piano is appended. An amusing addition to 'song' picture books." SLJ

Over in the meadow; with pictures by Feodor Rojankovsky. Harcourt Brace & Co. 1957 unp il music hardcover o.p. pa $7 *

Grades: K 1 2   **782.42**
    1. Folk songs 2. Counting 3. Animals—Songs
    ISBN 0-15-258854-X; 0-15-670500-1 (pa)

"This old counting rhyme tells of ten meadow families whose mothers advise them to dig, run, sing, play, hum, build, swim, wink, spin and hop. The illustrations, half in full color, show the combination of realism and imagination which little children like best. The tune, arranged simply, is on the last page, and children will have fun acting the whole thing out." Horn Book

Leodhas, Sorche Nic, 1898-1968

Always room for one more; illustrated by Nonny Hogrogian. Holt & Co. 1965 unp il music $14.95; pa $5.95

Grades: K 1 2 3   **782.42**
    1. Folk songs
    ISBN 0-8050-0331-2; 0-8050-0330-4 (pa)

Awarded the Caldecott Medal, 1966

"A picture book based on an old Scottish folk song about hospitable Lachie MacLachlan, who invited in so many guests that his little house finally burst. Rhymed text . . . a glossary of Scottish words, and music for the tune are combined into an effective whole." Hodges. Books for Elem Sch Libr

Let's sing together; The Peter Yarrow songbook; [selected by Peter Yarrow]; illustrated by Terry Widener. Sterling Pub. 2009 48p il (Peter Yarrow songbook series) $16.95

Grades: PreK K 1 2   **782.42**
    1. Folk songs
    ISBN 978-1-4027-5963-5; 1-4027-5963-0

Contents: This little light of mine; She'll be coming 'round the mountain; Hey, Lolly, Lolly; Home on the range; Blue-tail fly; Hey, ho, nobody home; My Bonnie lies over the ocean; John Jacob Jingleheimer Schmidt; I'm on my way; We shall not be moved; Down by the riverside; Oh, you can't get to heaven

"The lyrics of 12 folk songs, rooted in several cultural traditions, are illustrated in Widener's simple yet resonant folk art style, which creatively mingles conventional, earth-toned scenarios . . . with images featuring vividly hued, fanciful flourishes. . . . The author provides guitar chords, historical notes and personal anecdotes for

Let's sing together—*Continued*

each song. On the included CD, Yarrow sings each song, accompanied by his talented daughter Bethany Yarrow and a quartet of children. An energetic and uplifting package." Publ Wkly

Mallett, David

Inch by inch; the garden song; pictures by Ora Eitan. HarperCollins Pubs. 1995 unp il music pa $5.95 hardcover o.p. *

Grades: K 1 2   **782.42**

1. Songs 2. Gardens—Songs

ISBN 0-06-443481-8 (pa)   LC 93-38352

"In this picture-book version of the song first published in 1975 . . . a young child plants seeds . . . weeds and tends them, and finally, gleans a bountiful harvest. . . . Employing a variety of media including cut paper, Eitan uses color and space to create a striking effect." SLJ

Mora, Pat

A pinata in a pine tree; a Latino twelve days of Christmas; illustrated by Magaly Morales. Clarion Books 2009 28p il $16

Grades: PreK K 1   **782.42**

1. Songs 2. Christmas—Songs 3. Latin Americans—Songs 4. Spanish language—Vocabulary

ISBN 978-0-618-84198-1; 0-618-84198-9

LC 2008-32463

In this adaptation of the folk song 'The Twelve Days of Christmas,' friends exchange such gifts as a pinata and 'cuatro luminarias.' Includes pronunciation and glossary of Spanish words and a description of Christmas foods and other holiday traditions from different Latin American countries.

"Morales's acrylic illustrations glow with warm, festive colors, evoking lantern light. Phonetic pronunciations for the gifts and numbers are incorporated into the spreads, which lead up to a special final gift—a new sibling. A luminous holiday pick." Publ Wkly

National anthems of the world; edited by Michael Jamieson Bristow. 11th ed. Weidenfeld & Nicolson 2006 629p $90 *

Grades: 5 6 7 8 9 10 11 12 Adult

782.42

1. National songs

ISBN 0-304-36826-1

First published 1943 in the United Kingdom with title: National anthems of the United Nations and France

This volume contains national anthems of about 198 nations, including melody and accompaniment. Words are presented in the native language with transliteration provided where necessary. English translations follow. Brief historical notes on the adoption of each anthem are included

"An essential reference resource for all libraries." Libr J

Paxton, Tom, 1937-

The marvelous toy; words and music by Tom Paxton; illustrated by Steve Cox. Imagine Publishing 2009 unp il $17.95

Grades: PreK K 1 2   **782.42**

1. Toys—Songs 2. Songs

ISBN 978-0-9822939-2-8; 0-9822939-2-5

In this picture book adaptation of Paxton's song, a "boy receives [a] toy from his father, they enjoy it together, and the boy passes it on to his own son with similar enthusiasm. . . . Although the spindly, alien-looking toy is never completely visible, the rainbow-colored protrusions that are shown emit airbrushed beams, while sparks zoom and zip behind it, illuminating the night and leaving a trail of magic in its wake. . . . Four Paxton songs are enclosed on a CD." Publ Wkly

Pinkney, Brian, 1961-

Hush, little baby; adapted and illustrated by Brian Pinkney. Greenwillow Books 2006 unp il $15.99; lib bdg $17.89 *

Grades: K 1 2   **782.42**

1. Folk songs—United States 2. Lullabies

ISBN 978-0-06-055993-9; 0-06-055993-4; 978-0-06-055994-6 (lib bdg); 0-06-055994-2 (lib bdg)

LC 2005-08216

"Pinkney sets his version of the traditional Appalachian folksong in an African American household of the early 1900s. . . . Ink-on-clayboard scenes show a distraught toddler girl comforted by a playful father and older brother, who sing, dance, and, of course, offer a series of whimsical gifts. . . . An appended musical arrangement gives the tune a jazzy beat to match the wheeling, undulating figures in the story." Booklist

Raffi, 1948-

Baby Beluga; illustrated by Ashley Wolff. Crown 1990 unp il music (Raffi songs to read) pa $5.99 hardcover o.p.; bd bk $6.99

Grades: K 1 2   **782.42**

1. Songs 2. Whales—Songs

ISBN 0-517-58362-3 (pa); 0-517-70977-5 (bd bk)

LC 89-49367

Presents the illustrated text to the song about the little white whale who swims wild and free

"Wolff's striking double-page spreads show the young whale among its fellow Arctic Sea inhabitants. Diversifying her views, the illustrator eyes Baby Beluga and mother swimming together underwater; takes an aerial angle, looking down on the whales from a puffin's perspective; and observes the icy yet welcoming formations where seals, polar bears, and an Eskimo find shelter. . . . An inviting approach to reading encouragement." Booklist

Down by the bay; illustrated by Nadine Bernard Westcott. Crown 1987 unp il music (Raffi songs to read) pa $5.99 hardcover o.p.; bd bk $6.99

Grades: K 1 2   **782.42**

1. Songs

ISBN 0-517-56645-1 (pa); 0-517-80058-6 (bd bk)

LC 87-750291

Raffi, 1948-—*Continued*

This illustrated version of one of Raffi's songs depicts a variety of unusual sights to be seen "down by the bay"

The "cheerful nonsense verses are illustrated with equal cheer. Westcott's scraggly lines and bright, clear colors humorously portray the busy children, jolly animals, and frantic mothers that populate the song." SLJ

Five little ducks; illustrated by Jose Aruego and Ariane Dewey. Crown 1989 unp il (Raffi songs to read) hardcover o.p. pa $5.99; bd bk $6.99

Grades: K 1 2   782.42

  1. Songs 2. Ducks—Songs
  ISBN   0-517-58360-7;   0-517-56945-0   (pa);
0-517-80057-8 (bd bk)   LC 88-3752

  When her five little ducks disappear one by one, Mother Duck sets out to find them

Raven, Margot

Happy birthday to you! the mystery behind the most famous song in the world; by Margot Theis Raven; paintings by Chris K. Soentpiet. Sleeping Bear Press 2008 unp il $17.95

Grades: 1 2 3 4   782.42

  1. Hill, Mildred, 1859-1916 2. Hill, Patty Smith, 1868-1946 3. Songs
  ISBN 978-1-58536-169-4; 1-58536-169-0
                                        LC 2007037438

"In 1889 Patty and Mildred Hill, two Kentucky sisters, wrote the words and composed the melody of 'Good Morning to All' for their kindergarten students. They later changed the words and song is today known as the happy birthday song." Publisher's note

"A lovely succession of watercolor paintings depicts the latter half of the 19th century in Louisville and illuminates the thoughtful expressions and joyful faces of the Hill family. . . . [This is] an eye-opener for history and trivia lovers in all libraries." SLJ

Reid, Rob

Children's jukebox; the select subject guide to children's musical recordings. 2nd ed. American Library Association 2007 284p pa $55

Grades: Adult Professional   782.42

  1. Songs—Indexes 2. Children's libraries
3. Reference books
  ISBN 978-0-8389-0940-9 (pa); 0-8389-0940-X (pa)
                                        LC 2006103175

  First published 1995
  This is an index to 548 recordings for children with 147 subject headings, plus subcategories
  Includes discography

Roth, Susan L.

Hanukkah, oh Hanukkah; [by] Susan L. Roth. Dial Books for Young Readers 2004 unp il $10.99; pa $5.99 *

Grades: K 1 2   782.42

  1. Hanukkah—Songs 2. Songs
  ISBN 0-8037-2843-3; 0-14-240701-1 (pa)
                                        LC 2003-13165

A family of mice celebrates the eight days of Hannukah with friends in this illustrated version of the holiday song

"Cloth and paper collages done in many different patterns and textures add interest to the cozy tableaux. . . . The lovely colors and the appealing tune make this a good holiday choice." SLJ

Rueda, Claudia

Let's play in the forest while the wolf is not around; by Claudia Rueda. Scholastic Press 2006 unp il $16.99

Grades: PreK K 1   782.42

  1. Folk songs 2. Animals—Songs 3. Wolves—Songs
4. Singing games
  ISBN 0-439-82323-4   LC 2005030531

In this adaptation of the traditional French and Latin American song, animals play in the forest while a scary wolf slowly dresses and becomes hungrier and hungrier

"On flat backgrounds, the angular, minimally detailed but colorful digital images, enhanced with a few light pencil strokes, show the animals at play in the forest, always chanting the same line. . . . This is a great song for toddlers to act out as they are getting dressed." Booklist

Seeger, Ruth Crawford, 1901-1953

American folk songs for children in home, school, and nursery school; a book for children, parents, and teachers; by Ruth Crawford Seeger; illustrated by Barbara Cooney. Oak Publications 2002 190p il pa $24.95 *

Grades: PreK K 1 2 3 4 Professional

                                            782.42

  1. Folk music—United States 2. Songs
  ISBN 978-0-8256-0346-4 (pa); 0-8256-0346-3 (pa)
  First published 1948 by Doubleday

"Mrs. Seeger has collected the words and melodies of nearly a hundred traditional American songs, the greater number of them familiar only to folklorists, has given them easy accompaniments, and has added footnotes on how to improvise new words, clap out or make a play of each song. In a foreword, she gives her theories of how the book should be used, and there are several indexes." New Yorker

"This is a unique collection. It will probably be the authoritative source for American folk songs for children for many, many years." Saturday Review of Books

Seskin, Steve

Sing my song; a kid's guide to songwriting; starring Steve Seskin and a chorus of creative kids; illustrated by Eve Aldridge . . . [et al.] Tricycle Press 2008 32p il $18.99

Grades: 1 2 3 4 5   782.42

  1. Songwriters and songwriting
  ISBN 978-1-58246-266-0; 1-58246-266-6
                                        LC 2007046966

"Seskin has tapped a mother lode of musical enthusiasm in this book by showing young readers the 'how to' necessary to create songs and set them to music. Following 12 excellent examples and step-by-step instructions,

Seskin, Steve—*Continued*

readers discover how to put together the parts of a song. Musical terms are defined, song forms are suggested, and a CD of tunes provides sample accompaniment as Seskin backs up his relaxed vocals on guitar and with choruses from various schools." SLJ

Sleepytime songs; The Peter Yarrow songbook; [compiled by] Peter Yarrow; illustrated by Terry Widener. Sterling Pub. 2008 48p il (Peter Yarrow songbook series) $16.95

Grades: PreK K 1 2   **782.42**
1. Lullabies 2. Folk songs—United States
ISBN 978-1-4027-5962-8; 1-4027-5962-2

           LC 2008022530

Contents: All Through the Night; Puff, the Magic Dragon; Ol' Blue; All the Pretty Little Horses; Hush, Little Baby; Kum Ba Ya; The Water Is Wide; Down in the Valley; All My Trials; On Top of Old Smokey; Who's Gonna Shoe Your Pretty Little Foot?; Brahms Lullaby

"Yarrow, best known as the Peter of Peter, Paul, and Mary, here offers a wonderful compilation of bedtime songs, complete with CD. Beginning with a warm introduction from Yarrow about singing to children, the book continues with two-page spreads containing the lyrics of the songs, set against Widener's imaginative art." Booklist

Spirin, Gennadiĭ

The twelve days of Christmas; illustrated by Gennady Spirin. Marshall Cavendish 2009 unp il $16.99 *

Grades: K 1 2 3   **782.42**
1. Christmas—Songs 2. English folk songs
ISBN 978-0-7614-5551-6; 0-7614-5551-5

           LC 2008-06476

On each of the twelve days of Christmas, unusual and fanciful gifts arrive to celebrate the season.

"This holiday favorite is brought to life through Spirin's gorgeous illustrations. . . . The elaborately detailed and exquisitely executed artwork, rendered in watercolor and colored pencil, has a Renaissance feel. Roman numerals are placed on the tree or the base of the tree planter to indicate which day is being celebrated. As the oval inset fills with calling birds, golden rings, swans-a-swimming, etc., readers will enjoy trying to count all the gifts. A must-have." SLJ

Staines, Bill

All God's critters; song by Bill Staines; pictures by Kadir Nelson. Simon & Schuster Books for Young Readers 2009 unp il $16.99 *

Grades: PreK K 1   **782.42**
1. Songs 2. Animals—Songs
ISBN 978-0-689-86959-4; 0-689-86959-2

           LC 2008-23624

Celebrates how all the animals in the world make their own music in their own way, some singing low, some singing higher.

The song "is brought to rollicking life by Nelson's artwork. . . . Each delightful spread [is] full-to-bursting with . . . critters' energy. . . . The oversize type of the lyrics nearly shouts off the page." Booklist

Stotts, Stuart, 1957-

We shall overcome; a song that changed the world; by Stuart Stotts; foreword by Pete Seeger; with illustrations by Terrance Cummings. Clarion Books 2009 72p il $18

Grades: 5 6 7 8   **782.42**
1. African Americans—Civil rights—Songs
ISBN 978-0-547-18210-0; 0-547-18210-4

           LC 2009022578

"Stuart Stotts explores the roots of the tune and the lyrics in traditional African music and Christian hymns. He demonstrates the key role 'We Shall Overcome' played in the civil rights, labor, and antiwar movements in America. And he traces the song's transformation into an international anthem." Publisher's note

"This smart, effective telling has few missteps. From the informative black-and-white photographs to the solid back matter to the CD sung by Pete Seeger, it is a complete package." Booklist

Taback, Simms, 1932-

There was an old lady who swallowed a fly. Viking 1997 unp il $16.99 *

Grades: K 1 2 3   **782.42**
1. Folk songs 2. Animals—Songs
ISBN 0-670-86939-2

A Caldecott Medal honor book, 1998

Simms Taback's illustrated version of the folk song in which an old lady swallows a variety of progressively larger animals

"Each page is full of details and humorous asides. . . . A die-cut hole allows readers to see inside [the old lady's] belly, first the critters already devoured and, with the turn of the page, the new animal that will join the crowd in her ever-expanding stomach. . . . The text is handwritten on vivid strips of paper that are loosely placed on the patterned page, thus creating a lively interplay between the meaning of the words and their visual power." SLJ

They Might Be Giants (Musical group)

Kids go! [by] They Might Be Giants; illustrations by Pascal Campion. Simon & Schuster 2009 unp il $19.99

Grades: K 1 2 3   **782.42**
1. Songs
ISBN 978-0-7432-7275-9; 0-7432-7275-7

           LC 2009019668

An illustrated version of the song 'Go, Kid, Go,' exhorting the reader to get up and move around

"With just a hint of retro style about them, Campion's thick and loose black ink lines provide a sense of fluidity in riotous scenes that use a limited but appealing palette of green, gray, and peach, splashed over lots of white space. Befitting the action words in the text, the font size bounces from small to large, adding to the energetic tone. . . . An accompanying DVD features an animated video of the song." Publ Wkly

The **twelve** days of Christmas; illustrated by Ilse Plume. David R. Godine 2005 unp il $17.95 *

Grades: K 1 2 3   **782.42**
1. Christmas—Songs 2. Folk songs
ISBN 978-1-56792-300-1; 1-56792-300-3

           LC 2005013368

The twelve days of Christmas—*Continued*

A reissue of the edition first published 1990 by Harper & Row

"Plume has drawn on her studies of old manuscripts, books of hours, miniatures, and bestiaries, plus her knowledge of Italy to produce a rich tribute to the Italian Renaissance. Paintings, as if executed on old vellum or parchment, depict a young woman in fancy dress and her true love resplendent in garden and household settings enjoying each day's gifts. The text, variously framed, is surrounded by flower embellishments, birds, vines, and other natural bits. . . . Words and music with piano accompaniment and guitar chords in the key of F are included." SLJ

Vetter, Jennifer Riggs, 1968-

Down by the station; illustrations by Frank Remkiewicz. Tricycle Press 2009 unp il $15.99

Grades: PreK K   **782.42**

1. Songs 2. Vehicles

ISBN 978-1-58246-243-1; 1-58246-243-7

LC 2008011308

This illustrated version of the traditional song expands and describes more vehicles, different locations, and their unique sounds, from puffer-billies to racecars and rockets

"Remkiewicz uses candy-bright colors and a hint of goofy elasticity in his slightly busy watercolor art. With enough repetition to tempt early readers to try the text on their own, the book will also attract the lap-sit crowd." SLJ

Voake, Charlotte

Tweedle dee dee; [by] Charlotte Voake. Candlewick Press 2008 unp il $16.99 *

Grades: PreK K 1 2   **782.42**

1. Folk songs—United States

ISBN 978-0-7636-3797-2; 0-7636-3797-1

LC 2007040414

Illustrations of a forest in spring and simple text provide a variation on the traditional folk song, "The green leaves grew around"

The pages are "washed with pale green and covered with squiggly line drawings and watercolors. . . . The minimal text invites a read-aloud—and even before arriving at the musical score on the final spread, readers are likely to find themselves singing." Publ Wkly

Weave little stars into my sleep; Native American lullabies; edited by Neil Philip; photographs by Edward S. Curtis. Clarion Bks. 2001 unp il $16

Grades: 2 3 4   **782.42**

1. Lullabies 2. Native American literature

ISBN 0-618-08856-3   LC 00-60324

Published in the United Kingdom with title: Where did you fall from?

This is a "book of 15 lullabies, selected, adapted, and, in some cases, reworked from original Native American material. Striking, carefully chosen photographs, originally published in the early 1900s, portray the spirit of the words." Booklist

Includes bibliographical references

Yarrow, Peter, 1938-

Puff, the magic dragon; [by] Peter Yarrow [and] Leonard Lipton; with paintings by Eric Puybaret. Sterling Pub. 2007 unp il $16.95 *

Grades: PreK K 1 2 3   **782.42**

1. Dragons—Songs 2. Songs

ISBN 978-1-4027-4782-3; 1-4027-4782-9

LC 2007-02404

"Puff and his friend Jackie Paper frolic in the land of Honalee—traveling in a fantastic boat with billowed sails, climbing red castle stairs onto a balcony to meet with noble kings and princes, and watching pirate ships lower their flags for the roaring dragon." Publisher's note

"This handsome volume offers a charming interpretation of the 1960s folk song. . . . Featuring a soothing palette highlighted by greens and blues, Puybaret's graceful acrylic on linen paintings are intermittently misty and sunny. . . . Adding to the appeal of the book is a CD presenting a new recording of the song (and two others), sung by Yarrow and his daughter Bethany, accompanied by cellist Rufus Cappadocia." Publ Wkly

Yolen, Jane

Apple for the teacher; thirty songs for singing while you work; collected and introduced by Jane Yolen; music arranged by Adam Stemple; art edited by Eileen Michaelis Smiles. Harry N. Abrams 2005 117p il $24.95 *

Grades: 4 5 6 7   **782.42**

1. Songs 2. Work—Songs

ISBN 0-8109-4825-7   LC 2004-24404

"Yolen has brought together a collection of 30 work songs . . . which represent a wide variety of occupations. . . . She introduces each job, explaining unusual vocabulary and references in the songs. . . . The artwork . . . is elegant. Ranging from sculpture to paintings to needlework, each selection of Americana has been carefully matched to the occupation, beautifully reproduced on high-quality paper, and meticulously identified." Booklist

Zelinsky, Paul O.

Knick-knack paddywhack! a moving parts book; adapted from the counting song and illustrated by Paul O. Zelinsky; paper engineering by Andrew Baron. Dutton 2002 unp il $18.99 *

Grades: K 1 2 3   **782.42**

1. Counting 2. Songs

ISBN 0-525-46908-7

A young boy sets out on a walk—pull the tabs and tiny old men from One to Ten act out the familiar refrain of the traditional counting song on and all around him.

"This glorious title is a paper-engineering and bookmaking marvel as well as a freewheeling romp." SLJ

784.19   Musical instruments

D'Cruz, Anna-Marie
Make your own musical instruments. PowerKids Press 2009 24p il (Do it yourself projects!) lib bdg $23.95; pa $9.40
Grades: 2 3 4   **784.19**
   1. Musical instruments 2. Handicraft
   ISBN 978-1-4358-2854-4 (lib bdg); 1-4358-2854-2 (lib bdg); 978-1-4358-2925-1 (pa); 1-4358-2925-5 (pa)
                                        LC 2008033667
This offers "step-by-step instructions and full-color photos to illustrate the crafts. Projects have a broad cultural representation and are not gender specific. Materials are easily obtained. . . . [Projects include] castanets, bongo drums, and a jazz washboard." SLJ
Includes glossary and bibliographical references

Helsby, Genevieve
Those amazing musical instruments; [by] Genevieve Helsby; with Marin Alsop as your guide. Sourcebooks Jabberwocky 2007 176p il $19.95 *
Grades: 4 5 6 7 8 9   **784.19**
   1. Musical instruments
   ISBN 978-1-4022-0825-6; 1-4022-0825-1
                                        LC 2007013821
This is "a guide to instruments commonly found in an orchestra. . . . Utilizing large print; ample, colorful illustrations; and an open format, the book is logically organized into chapters about each of the musical instrument families, including keyboards, the voice, and modern electronic instruments. Throughout, readers are prompted to listen to the accompanying CD-ROM, which features more than 100 musical samples. Information is clearly presented, and the author's enthusiasm for her subject is contagious." SLJ

Wiseman, Ann Sayre, 1926-
Making music; [by] Ann Sayre Wiseman and John Langstaff; illustrations by Ann Sayre Wiseman. Storey Bks. 2003 96p il hardcover o.p. pa $9.95
Grades: 3 4 5 6   **784.19**
   1. Musical instruments 2. Handicraft
   ISBN 1-58017-513-9; 1-58017-512-0 (pa)
                                        LC 2003-54218
First published 1979 by Scribner with title: Making musical things
Includes instructions for making a variety of simple musical instruments from ordinary household items
Includes glossary and bibliographical references

784.2   Full orchestra (Symphony orchestra)

Ganeri, Anita, 1961-
The young person's guide to the orchestra; Benjamin Britten's composition on CD narrated by Ben Kingsley; book written by Anita Ganeri. Harcourt Brace & Co. 1996 56p il $25 *
Grades: 4 5 6 7   **784.2**
   1. Orchestra 2. Musical instruments 3. Music appreciation
   ISBN 0-15-201304-0   LC 95-41478
"Accompanying this book on orchestral music is a CD featuring Britten's *A Young Person's Guide to the Orchestra* . . . as well as Dukas' *The Sorcerer's Apprentice*. The book begins with an overview of the orchestra and then centers around groups of instruments, explaining a bit of their history and their sound's distinctive quality. . . . The book also introduces eight famous composers, world music, Benjamin Britten, and the background of *The Young Person's Guide to the Orchestra*. . . . Handsome and useful." Booklist
Includes glossary

Koscielniak, Bruce
The story of the incredible orchestra; an introduction to musical instruments and the symphony orchestra. Houghton Mifflin 2000 unp il $16; pa $6.95 *
Grades: 2 3 4   **784.2**
   1. Orchestra 2. Musical instruments
   ISBN 0-395-96052-5; 0-618-31112-2 (pa)
                                        LC 98-43933
Describes the orchestra, the families of instruments of which it is made, and the individual instruments in each family
"The illustrations are dense with gentle color and filled with scenes of musicians at play and pictures of instruments, with banner labels adding more information. . . . A lot of information about who invented what and how it's played is packed into these engaging pages." Booklist

787.87   Guitars

Blaxland, Wendy
Guitars. Marshall Cavendish Benchmark 2011 32p il map (How are they made?) lib bdg $12.99
Grades: 4 5 6   **787.87**
   1. Guitars
   ISBN 978-0-7614-4754-2; 0-7614-4754-7
                                        LC 2009039880
This describes how guitars are made including their history, parts, materials, design, manufacture, packaging and distribution, marketing and advertising, and affect on the environment.
"There is a bounty of color photos, including fascinating contructiion shots as well as pics of axe-wielding notables Les Paul, Bruce Springsteen, and Prince." Booklist
Includes glossary

790.1   General kinds of recreational activities

Ball, Jacqueline A.

Traveling green. Bearport Pub. 2009 32p il (Going green) lib bdg $25.27

Grades: 4 5 6 7   **790.1**

1. Travel—Environmental aspects

ISBN 978-1-59716-964-6 (lib bdg); 1-59716-964-1 (lib bdg)   LC 2009-19836

Explains the "steps people are taking to travel in ways that conserve Earth's precious resources and help protect the planet." Publisher's note

"Color photographs (most full page) and a few diagrams accompany the informative text[s]. . . . Overall, the [book] . . . is user-friendly and covers topics that are not easily found elsewhere." SLJ

Includes glossary and bibliographical references

Bell-Rehwoldt, Sheri, 1962-

The kids' guide to classic games. Capstone Press 2009 32p il (Kids' guides) lib bdg $23.99

Grades: 4 5 6 7   **790.1**

1. Games

ISBN 978-1-4296-2273-8 (lib bdg); 1-4296-2273-3 (lib bdg)   LC 2008-29686

"Edge books"

This provides instructions and rules for indoor and outdoor games such as ping-pong soccer, ringer, paper football, spiderweb, tug-of-war, and pipeline

Includes glossary and bibliographical references

Conner, Bobbi

Unplugged play; no batteries, no plugs, pure fun; illustrations by Amy Patacchiola. Workman Pub. 2007 xxv, 401p il $27.95; pa $16.95

Grades: Adult Professional   **790.1**

1. Games 2. Play

ISBN 978-0-7611-4114-3; 978-0-7611-4390-1 (pa)   LC 2007-23999

"Conner has compiled more than 710 games and activities sorted by age level. Good old-fashioned play and fun are the motto here with simple props from around the house or just an imagination. The book is separated into three major parts: 'Toddler Play,' 'Preschool Play,' and 'Grade School Play.' Each has a section on solo play, ideas for parent and child, playing with others, and birthday-party activities. Each chapter and section is loaded with ideas and suggestions for simple crafts. There is such a wealth of information in this book." SLJ

Davies, Huw, 1961-

The games book; written by Huw Davies; illustrated by Lisa Jackson. Scholastic 2009 c2008 118p il pa $9.99

Grades: 1 2 3 4 5 6   **790.1**

1. Games

ISBN 978-0-545-13403-3 (pa); 0-545-13403-X (pa)   LC 2009004292

"This small book takes a look at the games in simpler times. There are no electronics, batteries, cell phones, or videos involved. They mostly require physical and/or mental action along with the use of an imagination and some sweat, and maybe a little dirt. There are old favorites such as Red Rover and Simon Says as well as Rummy, Hangman, and I Spy. The clear instructions are easy for early readers to follow." SLJ

Drake, Jane

The kids winter handbook; [by] Jane Drake & Ann Love; illustrated by Heather Collins. Kids Can Press 2001 127p il $18.95; pa $12.95

Grades: 4 5 6 7   **790.1**

1. Recreation 2. Handicraft 3. Nature craft

ISBN 1-55337-033-3; 1-55074-969-2 (pa)

Companion volume to The kids' summer handbook

This offers ideas for winter activities such as sewing, observing the night sky, identifying animal tracks, storytelling, cooking, crafts, and games

"Most of the projects are inexpensive to make, and supplies are easy to obtain, making these interesting alternatives to holiday boredom or too much TV. Many of the activities, especially those that are science related, are also suitable for the classroom." SLJ

Hines-Stephens, Sarah

Show off; how to do absolutely everything one step at a time; [by] Sarah Hines Stephens and Bethany Mann. Candlewick Press 2009 224p il $18.99

Grades: 5 6 7 8   **790.1**

1. Recreation 2. Amusements 3. Handicraft

ISBN 978-0-7636-4599-1; 0-7636-4599-0   LC 2009015847

"This lively illustrated activity book delivers concise instructions for a variety of indoor and outdoor activities. Projects include crafts, pranks and magic tricks; ideas for nature exploration; and other purely entertaining feats. . . . The instructions are heavy on graphics and light on detail, making for an eye-catching but potentially frustrating experience. But readers should enjoy the irreverence and variety." Publ Wkly

791.3   Circuses

Helfer, Ralph

The world's greatest elephant; illustrated by Ted Lewin. Philomel Books 2006 unp il $16.99

Grades: 1 2 3   **791.3**

1. Circus 2. Elephants

ISBN 0-399-24190-6   LC 2005-06490

The true story of the lives and travels of the circus elephant Modoc who travelled widely and experienced dangerous adventures with his owner and trainer Bram Gunterstein.

"The large picture-book format is the typical choice for Lewin's fine watercolors, boldly portraying the dramatic episodes of the elephants life and the story of friendship, separation, and reunion. This bold and heartwarming adventure tale should have wide appeal." SLJ

791.43   Motion pictures

791.44   Radio

O'Brien, Lisa, 1963-
Lights, camera, action! making movies and TV from the inside out; [by] Lisa O'Brien; illustrated by Stephen MacEachern. 2nd ed. Maple Tree Press 2007 64p il $21.95; pa $12.95
Grades: 4 5 6 7   **791.43**
1. Motion pictures—Production and direction 2. Acting
ISBN   978-1-897066-88-1;   1-897066-88-0; 978-1-897066-89-8 (pa); 1-897066-89-9 (pa)
First published 1998 by Firefly Books
This book "follows Johnny, a young aspiring actor, as he auditions for and gets a part in a new movie called The Mists of Time. Author Lisa O'Brien examines the development and production of movies from early concept through final production. Along the way, readers get a guided tour of the world of acting, from finding an agent, through to 'acting' an audition, to handling the media." Publisher's note

McCarthy, Meghan
Aliens are coming! the true account of the 1938 War of the worlds radio broadcast. Knopf 2006 unp il $16.95; lib bdg $18.99 *
Grades: 1 2 3   **791.44**
1. War of the worlds (Radio program)
ISBN 0-375-83518-0; 0-375-93518-5 (lib bdg)
LC 2005-08941
"In an average American living room of 1938, folks gather around the radio for a night's entertainment, when there's a new bulletin: 'Aliens are coming!' Orson Welles' infamous Halloween trick, his October 30 broadcast of H. G. Wells' War of the Worlds, is greatly excerpted and put together with quirky, imaginative artwork that reinforces the fantasy. . . . Using a 1930's art style, and a palette comprising mostly muted grays and reds, McCarthy evokes an era gone by. . . . This is packed with age-appropriate thrills and scares." Booklist

791.5   Puppetry and toy theaters

Reinhart, Matthew
Star Wars: a pop-up guide to the galaxy. Orchard Books 2007 unp il $32.99 *
Grades: 4 5 6 7   **791.43**
1. Star Wars films 2. Pop-up books
ISBN 978-0-439-88282-8; 0-439-88282-6
LC 2007-19587
"Lucasfilm"
"The book has . . . six two-page spreads, each presenting a gigantic iconic character, creature, spaceship or location from the original 'Star Wars' movie trilogy. . . . The four corners of each spread contain sub-pages. These small doors open to reveal even more pop-up sculptures. . . . In all, there are 36 increasingly stunning pop-up displays." NY Times Book Rev

D'Cruz, Anna-Marie
Make your own puppets. PowerKids Press 2009 24p il (Do it yourself projects!) lib bdg $23.95; pa $9.40
Grades: 2 3 4   **791.5**
1. Puppets and puppet plays 2. Handicraft
ISBN 978-1-4358-2851-3 (lib bdg); 1-4358-2851-8 (lib bdg); 978-1-4358-2919-0 (pa); 1-4358-2919-0 (pa)
LC 2008033661
This offers "step-by-step instructions and full-color photos to illustrate the crafts. Projects have a broad cultural representation and are not gender specific. Materials are easily obtained. . . . [Projects include] a Venus flytrap and a Chinese dragon." SLJ
Includes glossary and bibliographical references

Reynolds, David West
Star wars: incredible cross sections; illustrated by Hans Jenssen & Richard Chasemore. DK Pub. 1998 32p il $19.95
Grades: 4 5 6 7   **791.43**
1. Star Wars films
ISBN 0-7894-3480-6   LC 98-22878
This book "includes diagrams for the *Millennium Falcon*, T-65 X-wing, Blockade Runner, Tie Fighters, Sandcrawler, and BLT-A4 Y-wing, among others. An elaborate four-page fold-out analyzes the Death Star in minute detail. . . . AT-AT Walkers, AT-STs, snowspeeders, and speeder bikes are also included. Diagrams are surrounded by inserts of fascinating trivia, history, and technical notes." Voice Youth Advocates

Exner, Carol R.
Practical puppetry A-Z; a guide for librarians and teachers; [by] Carol R. Exner. McFarland 2005 267p il pa $39.95
Grades: Professional   **791.5**
1. Puppets and puppet plays
ISBN 0-7864-1516-9   LC 2005010590
"Exner presents the art of puppetry as a creative and engaging way to snag the interests of both adults and children. Presented in alphabetical order, approximately 135 entries cover everything from starting a puppetry business to puppetry history to creating numerous kinds of puppets: glove, sponge, life-size, even marionettes. . . . This is an excellent resource for school or public libraries." Booklist
Includes bibliographical references

Kennedy, John E., 1967-
Puppet mania; the world's most incredible puppet making book ever. North Light Books 2003 79p il pa $14.99
Grades: 4 5 6 7   **791.5**
    1. Puppets and puppet plays
    ISBN 1-58180-372-9   LC 2003-59965
    This includes instructions for making 13 puppets and for animating them with techniques such as lip synching, body movements, eye contact and movement

Puppet planet. North Light Books 2006 79p il $16.99 *
Grades: 4 5 6 7   **791.5**
    1. Puppets and puppet plays
    ISBN 978-1-58180-794-3; 1-58180-794-5
         LC 2005033711
    This book offers twelve "puppet projects, each using a variety of techniques, [and] features 'action panels' so readers can see how each puppet comes to life. [It also] Includes staging ideas to play up each project's uniqueness." Publisher's note

Minkel, Walter
How to do "The three bears" with two hands; performing with puppets. American Lib. Assn. 2000 154p il pa $28 *
Grades: Professional   **791.5**
    1. Puppets and puppet plays 2. Children's libraries
    ISBN 0-8389-0756-3   LC 99-28228
    This guide to performing puppet plays in libraries offers advice on such topics as voice control and manipulation technique, script writing and adaptation, puppets, stages, scenery and props, and includes five puppet show scripts and stage-building plans
    Includes bibliographical references

791.8   Animal performances

Munro, Roxie, 1945-
Rodeo; by Roxie Munro. Bright Sky Press 2007 unp il $15.95
Grades: PreK K 1 2   **791.8**
    1. Rodeos
    ISBN 978-1-933979-03-8   LC 2007015245
    "This lift-the-flap, foldout book contains nearly 50 flaps to lift, plus a . . . rodeo event on every . . . spread: Grand Entry Parade, Saddle Bronc Riding, Steer Wrestling, Cutting Competition, Mutton Busting, Calf Scramble, Barrel Racing, Calf Roping, Bull Riding, and a Square Dance with a cowboy band." Publisher's note
    "Clear, concise text and clever lift-the-flap illustrations capture the action and excitement of a rodeo." SLJ

Schubert, Leda
Ballet of the elephants; illustrated by Robert Andrew Parker. Roaring Brook Press 2006 unp il $17.95 *
Grades: K 1 2 3   **791.8**
    1. Circus 2. Ballet 3. Elephants
    ISBN 1-59643-075-3   LC 2005-02670

"A Deborah Brodie Book"
    The story of how "Circus polka" a dance of 50 elephants and 50 ballerinas, conceived by John Ringling North, choreographed by George Balanchine to music written by Igor Stravinsky, was created
    "Schubert's book tells an astonishing true story. . . . The words are simple and lyrical . . . and the beautiful, freely sketched double-page ink-and-watercolor art celebrates the excitement of the animals' dance." Booklist

792   Stage presentations

Friedman, Lise
Break a leg! the kids' guide to acting and stagecraft; photographs by Mary Dowdle. Workman 2002 222p il hardcover o.p. pa $14.95 *
Grades: 4 5 6 7   **792**
    1. Acting 2. Theater
    ISBN 0-7611-2590-6; 0-7611-2208-7 (pa)
         LC 2001-26986
    A comprehensive manual for acting and theater, discussing improvisation, voice projection, breathing exercises, script analysis, and technical aspects of theater production
    "The information is solid and presented well, and the sidebars, in which young actors offer comments and tips, add life to the text." Booklist

Jacobs, Paul DuBois
Putting on a play; drama activities for kids; [by] Paul DuBois Jacobs and Jennifer Swender; illustrated by Debra Spina Dixon. Gibbs Smith 2005 64p il pa $9.95 *
Grades: 2 3 4   **792**
    1. Theater—Production and direction
    ISBN 1-58685-767-3   LC 2005011249
    Contents: Getting started; Casting call; Acting your part; Setting the stage; Scripts (or no scripts); Getting warmed up with theater games; Music Theatrical supplies; Makeup; Safety; Fun!; Pirate play; Princess play; Explorer play; Circus play; Cowboy and cowgirl play; Holiday plays; Cast party
    "This little book is a powerhouse of information. . . . An excellent beginning resource for any child or group of children interested in theater." SLJ

Kenney, Karen Latchana, 1974-
Cool costumes; how to stage your very own show. ABDO Pub. Company 2010 32p il (Cool performances) lib bdg $17.95
Grades: 4 5 6   **792**
    1. Costume 2. Theater
    ISBN 978-1-60453-714-7 (lib bdg); 1-60453-714-0 (lib bdg)   LC 2009-1751
    Includes step-by-step instructions on how to create royalty robes, animal ears, baseball T-Shirts and more
    "Simple language, colorful page design, and detailed step-by-step photos invite children to gather some easily available household items, apply paint and some imagination, and put on a play—or just play." SLJ
    Includes glossary and webliography

Kenney, Karen Latchana, 1974-—*Continued*

Cool makeup; how to stage your very own show. ABDO Pub. Company 2010 32p il (Cool performances) lib bdg $17.95

Grades: 4 5 6   **792**

1. Theatrical makeup

ISBN 978-1-60453-715-4 (lib bdg); 1-60453-715-9 (lib bdg)   LC 2009-1752

Offers instructions and step-by-step pictures to reveal how theatrical makeup can create the illusion of facial hair, bruises and wounds, animals, skeletons, or old age.

"Simple language, colorful page design, and detailed step-by-step photos invite children to gather some easily available household items, apply paint and some imagination, and put on a play—or just play." SLJ

Includes glossary and webliography

Cool productions; how to stage your very own show. ABDO Pub. Co. 2010 32p il (Cool performances) lib bdg $17.95

Grades: 4 5 6   **792**

1. Theater—Production and direction

ISBN 978-1-60453-716-1 (lib bdg); 1-60453-716-7 (lib bdg)   LC 2009-405

Includes step-by-step instructions on how to make flyers, tickets, programs and more

"Simple language, colorful page design, and detailed step-by-step photos invite children to gather some easily available household items, apply paint and some imagination, and put on a play—or just play." SLJ

Includes glossary

Cool scripts & acting; how to stage your very own show. ABDO Pub. Company 2010 32p il (Cool performances) lib bdg $17.95

Grades: 4 5 6   **792**

1. Drama—Technique 2. Acting 3. Theater—Production and direction

ISBN 978-1-60453-717-8 (lib bdg); 1-60453-717-5 (lib bdg)   LC 2009-406

Includes step-by-step instructions on how to write a script, use stage directions, play acting games and more

"Simple language, colorful page design, and detailed step-by-step photos invite children to gather some easily available household items, apply paint and some imagination, and put on a play—or just play." SLJ

Includes glossary

Cool sets & props; how to stage your very own show. ABDO Pub. Company 2010 32p il (Cool performances) lib bdg $17.95

Grades: 4 5 6   **792**

1. Theaters—Stage setting and scenery

ISBN 978-1-60453-718-5 (lib bdg); 1-60453-718-3 (lib bdg)   LC 2009-408

"This volume focuses on the primarily cardboard and paper objects that motivated youngsters can turn into backdrops, set pieces, and props. Photo examples set the bar high (though many are achievable), and the text breaks down the creation process into bite-size chunks. It's fairly challenging stuff, but the information is metered out so efficiently that patience, not artistic ability, will be the key to success." Booklist

Includes glossary and webliography

Cool special effects; how to stage your very own show. ABDO Pub. Company 2010 32p il (Cool performances) lib bdg $17.95

Grades: 4 5 6   **792**

1. Stage lighting 2. Theaters—Stage setting and scenery

ISBN 978-1-60453-719-2 (lib bdg); 1-60453-719-1 (lib bdg)   LC 2009-1753

Offers instructions on creating special effects for a theatrical production, including information on different light effects, keeping a prompt book, and recording your own sound effects

"Simple language, colorful page design, and detailed step-by-step photos invite children to gather some easily available household items, apply paint and some imagination, and put on a play—or just play." SLJ

Includes glossary and webliography

Schumacher, Thomas L.

How does the show go on? an introduction to the theater; by Thomas Schumacher with Jeff Kurtti. 2nd ed. Disney 2008 128p il $22.95

Grades: 4 5 6 7   **792**

1. Theater

ISBN 978-1-4231-2031-5; 1-4231-2031-0

"Filled with lavish color photos of Disney theater productions, this eye-catching volume has clever chapter titles, beginning with 'Overture,' which tells about 'styles of theaters' and 'kinds of shows.' In 'Act One' and 'Act Two,' aspects of the front and back of the house are discussed, including the marquee, the box office, props, special effects, and so on. Interspersed throughout the facts and photos are 'Stage Notes,' where bits of trivia are doled out." SLJ

Underwood, Deborah, 1962-

Staging a play. Raintree 2009 32p il (Culture in action) $28.21; pa $7.99

Grades: 5 6 7 8   **792**

1. Theater—Production and direction

ISBN 978-1-4109-3396-6; 1-4109-3396-2; 978-1-4109-3413-0 (pa); 1-4109-3413-6 (pa)
                                    LC 2009000417

This "discusses the various professionals involved in a production, such as actors, costume designers, prop masters, and stage handlers. Well organized and with bright, colorful photography, [this] introductory [title gives] readers good basic knowledge." SLJ

Includes glossary and bibliographical references

792.5   Opera

Siberell, Anne

Bravo! brava! a night at the opera; behind the scenes with composers, cast, and crew; introduction by Frederica von Stade. Oxford Univ. Press 2001 64p il $19.95 *

Grades: 4 5 6 7   **792.5**

1. Opera

ISBN 0-19-513966-6   LC 2001-21206

Siberell, Anne—*Continued*

This "book introduces all features of the opera, including stars, stagehands, set designers, conductors, and supernumeraries. . . . Cartoon artwork illustrates the text, and a world map highlighting the settings of well-known operas is also included, as are curtain diagrams, plot summaries of favorite operas, and sample costumes." Horn Book Guide

"An excellent resource for reports, this unusual book has an exceptional range of topics for younger students and is an essential purchase for upper elementary and middle school music programs." SLJ

Includes glossary and bibliographical references

792.6   Musical plays

Amendola, Dana

A day at the New Amsterdam Theatre; photos by Gino Domenico; written by Dana Amendola. Disney Editions 2004 125p il $24.95

Grades: 4 5 6 7   **792.6**
     1. New Amsterdam Theatre (New York, N.Y.)
     2. Theater
     ISBN 0-7868-5438-3

"This title covers a day in the life of Disney's *The Lion King*, the long-running Broadway musical. . . . A clock in a corner of each spread guides readers through the day as box-office personnel, makeup designers, dancers, actors, cleaning staff, and others do their jobs. Each spread includes several full-color photos that are often gritty, sometimes glamorous. . . . This unique volume provides an honest, realistic, eye-opening look at the behind-the-scenes work that goes into the running of a Broadway show." SLJ

792.8   Ballet and modern dance

Augustyn, Frank

Footnotes; dancing the world's best-loved ballets; [by] Frank Augustyn and Shelley Tanaka. Millbrook Press 2001 94p il $17.95 *

Grades: 5 6 7 8   **792.8**
     1. Ballet
     ISBN 0-7613-1646-9   LC 00-50075

"*Footnotes* uses seven classical ballets as a jumping-off point to talk about the evolution of this unique art form, partnering, dancer as actor, training, costumes, choreography, and some of the world's most well-known performers." SLJ

"Fine photographs, most in color, add enormously to the book's appeal. A well-crafted, readable volume." Booklist

Collins, Pat Lowery, 1932-

I am a dancer; by Pat Lowery Collins; illustrated by Mark Graham. Millbrook Press 2008 unp il lib bdg $22.60

Grades: PreK K 1 2 3   **792.8**
     1. Dance
     ISBN 978-0-8225-6369-3 (lib bdg); 0-8225-6369-X (lib bdg)   LC 2007021885

"This book shows girls and boys in various movements that can be defined as dance steps. . . . Graham's beautiful oil paintings are filled with solidly built children on the move, while some of the backgrounds are almost ethereal. Even the brushstrokes convey action. This book is a lovely merging of art and poetry and gives a delightful sense of joyful motion." SLJ

Gladstone, Valerie

A young dancer; the life of an Ailey student; photographs by Jose Ivey. Henry Holt and Co. 2009 unp il $18.95

Grades: 1 2 3 4   **792.8**
     1. Alvin Ailey American Dance Theater 2. Ballet
     3. African American dancers
     ISBN 978-0-8050-8233-3; 0-8050-8233-6
                     LC 2008-18343

"This book about a 13-year-old African American dancer . . . combines strong color photos and lively first-person text. Iman Bright is a student at New York City's Ailey School, founded by the late Alvin Ailey. . . . A wide range of readers will find inspiration in Iman's dedication and in her joyful approach to her discipline." Booklist

Goodman, Joan E., 1950-

Ballet bunnies; written and illustrated by Joan Elizabeth Goodman. Marshall Cavendish 2008 unp il $14.99

Grades: K 1 2   **792.8**
     1. Ballet
     ISBN 978-0-7614-5392-5; 0-7614-5392-X
                     LC 2007-11907

This ballet primer demonstrates basic technique in ballet, from warm-ups to the barre to the hop, skip, twirl, and wiggle fun of centerwork.

"The simply drawn acrylic illustrations show the boys and girls demonstrating positions, and the easy-to-understand text gives further guidance. . . . This is a gentle introduction." SLJ

Includes glossary

Mellow, Mary Kate

Ballet for beginners; featuring the School of American Ballet; by Mary Kate Mellow and Stephanie Troeller. Imagine! 2010 80p il $14.95

Grades: 3 4 5 6   **792.8**
     1. Ballet
     ISBN 978-1-936140-01-5; 1-936140-01-2

"A cartoon ballerina named Prima Princessa . . . hosts this introduction to the art form. Full-color photographs feature the essential steps of becoming a professional, beginning with an outdoor 'Creative Movement' class for girls under six, followed by lessons for children ages six to 13 and an advanced class, both photographed at the School of American Ballet in New York City." Publ Wkly

"The education of a dancer's body and mind is a long and complicated process, and this book tells that story with a lighthearted grace and brio." SLJ

Nelson, Marilyn, 1946-
Beautiful ballerina; photographs by Susan Kuklin. Scholastic Press 2009 unp il $17.99
Grades: PreK K 1 2   **792.8**
   1. Ballet 2. African American dancers
   ISBN 978-0-545-08920-3; 0-545-08920-4
                  LC 2009009135
"The description 'poetry in motion' may be taken quite literally in this paean to the young dancers who train at the Dance Theatre of Harlem. The heartfelt poem's playful words could make a lively read-aloud dance-along, and young balletomanes will be intrigued by the girls in the photographs. The phrase 'Beautiful ballerina, you are the dance' is repeated throughout and invites audience participation." SLJ

Solway, Andrew
Modern dance; [by] Andrew Solway. Heinemann Library 2009 48p il (Dance) lib bdg $31.43
Grades: 4 5 6 7 8   **792.8**
   1. Modern dance
   ISBN 978-1-4329-1376-2 (lib bdg); 1-4329-1376-X (lib bdg)
                  LC 2008-14295
This book "is enhanced by eye-catching photography that shows costumes, famous dancers, technique and people dancing. . . . [Those] thinking about dance as a career will find this . . . helpful. . . . [This] is a definite must have." Libr Media Connect
Includes glossary and bibliographical references

Thompson, Lauren, 1962-
Ballerina dreams; a true story; by Lauren Thompson; photographs by James Estrin. Feiwel & Friends 2007 unp il $16.95 *
Grades: PreK K 1 2   **792.8**
   1. Ballet 2. Cerebral palsy
   ISBN 978-0-312-37029-6; 0-312-37029-6
                  LC 2006036338
"Five adorable little girls are given the opportunity to learn to dance like ballerinas and eventually perform on stage. This is no small accomplishment since the girls have cerebral palsy and other muscle disorders and several wear leg braces. . . . This is an inspiring portrayal of determination and love that will foster empathy among young readers. The colorful photographs of this dancing community working toward a common goal accurately and sensitively capture the struggles and joyful enthusiasm of all of the participants." SLJ

Troupe, Thomas Kingsley
If I were a ballerina; illustrated by Heather Heyworth. Picture Window Books 2010 24p il (Dream big) lib bdg $25.32; pa $7.95
Grades: K 1 2 3   **792.8**
   1. Ballet
   ISBN 978-1-4048-5532-8 (lib bdg); 1-4048-5532-7 (lib bdg); 978-1-4048-5706-3 (pa); 1-4048-5706-0 (pa)
                  LC 2009-3295
This "begins with a small girl who imagines herself as a star onstage, dancing to beautiful music played by a glorious orchestra. Then the story tracks back to imag-

ined ballet classes, where she envisions the pointed shoes she would wear and the barre exercises she would do with the other dancers before practicing at home. The simple, first-person narrative and clear, digitally enhanced color drawings partner well together, and even young preschoolers will enjoy the fun blend of the fantasy . . . and facts, including ballet's five basic positions." Booklist
Includes glossary

Veitch, Catherine
Dancing. Heinemann Library 2009 24p il (Sports and my body) lib bdg $21.36; pa $6.49
Grades: 1 2   **792.8**
   1. Dance
   ISBN 978-1-4329-3501-6 (lib bdg); 1-4329-3501-1 (lib bdg); 978-1-4329-3502-3 (pa); 1-4329-3502-X (pa)
                  LC 2009-8962
Readers learn what dancing is, how it can help them stay healthy, and how they can dance safely.
This book relates "activity to health . . . [and] explains that in order to stay healthy, children should get plenty of rest, eat healthy food, and drink plenty of water." SLJ
Includes glossary

793   Indoor games and amusements

Gunter, Veronika Alice
The ultimate indoor games book; the 200 best boredom busters ever! [by] Veronika Alice Gunter. Lark Books 2005 128p il hardcover o.p. pa $7.95 *
Grades: 3 4 5 6   **793**
   1. Indoor games
   ISBN 1-57990-625-7; 1-60059-198-1 (pa)
                  LC 2005006054
"This compilation of brain games, ball games, pen-and-paper games, etc., provides a good supply of ideas that will appeal to most any player in a variety of circumstances. The activities are suitable for individuals or two or more players. Most of the suggestions require little or no equipment." SLJ

793.2   Parties and entertainments

McGillian, Jamie Kyle
Sleepover party! games and giggles for a fun night; [by] Jamie Kyle McGillian. Sterling Pub. 2007 95p il $14.95
Grades: 3 4 5 6   **793.2**
   1. Parties
   ISBN 978-1-4027-2978-2; 1-4027-2978-2
                  LC 2006029509
"An attractive, girl-friendly compendium of party-planning ideas. All of the basics are covered, such as house rules, what to make/buy, 'Top 10 Things to Get Straight before the Party,' invitations, menus, music, and more. . . . Dozens of indoor and outdoor games . . . and craft ideas are briefly described. The chapter on food includes snacks, dinners, desserts, breakfasts, and goodie-bag ideas." SLJ

Ross, Kathy, 1948-
The best birthday parties ever! a kid's do-it-yourself guide; art by Sharon Lane Holm. Millbrook Press 1999 78p il lib bdg $24.90; pa $9.95

Grades: 2 3 4   **793.2**
1. Parties 2. Birthdays
ISBN 0-7613-1410-5 (lib bdg); 0-7613-0989-6 (pa)
LC 98-27503

Provides instructions for the invitations, games, crafts, table decorations, and cakes for a dozen birthday parties based on such themes as outer space, puppets, and dinosaurs

"The book is appealing. The illustrations are colorful and plentiful." SLJ

793.3   Social, folk, national dancing

Ancona, George, 1929-
Capoeira; game! dance! martial art! [by] George Ancona. Lee & Low Books 2007 unp il $18.95 *

Grades: 3 4 5 6   **793.3**
1. Capoeira (Dance)
ISBN 978-1-58430-268-1   LC 2006028866

"Photo-essay about Capoeira, a game, dance, and martial art, as it is played in the United States and Brazil today, plus its history and origins in the African slave culture of Brazil during the seventeenth century." Publisher's note

This offers "uncomplicated words and engaging, step-by-step photographs of young capoeristas in action. . . . Ancona's . . . enthusiasm and awe for his subject is contagious." Booklist

Includes glossary and bibliographical references

Keeler, Patricia A.
Drumbeat in our feet. Lee & Low 2006 unp il $16.95 *

Grades: 3 4 5   **793.3**
1. Dance—Africa
ISBN 1-58430-264-X

This "book opens with a concise overview of the origins of African dance traditions that highlights the diversity of African peoples, cultures, and landscapes. Other two-page chapters cover how dances are passed on to children, different types of dances, image dances (those that mimic animal movements), costumes and body painting, honoring spirits and ancestors, musical instruments, drums, call-and-response songs, masked dancers, and performance. Keeler's watercolor-and-pencil illustrations impart a sense of vibrancy, movement, and joy. . . . A fresh, uplifting, and captivating offering." SLJ

793.73   Puzzles and puzzle games

Agee, Jon
Jon Agee's palindromania! Farrar, Straus & Giroux 2002 unp il hardcover o.p. pa $6.96

Grades: 3 4 5 6   **793.73**
1. Palindromes
ISBN 0-374-35730-7; 0-374-40025-3 (pa)
LC 2002-101771

In this collection "the pages are filled with whimsical black-and-white drawings of absurd or nonsensical situations. Some of the approximately 170 palindromes are monologues, some are comic-strip stories, and others are simply descriptive situations. From 'How Palindromes Are Formed in the Atmosphere' to 'AIBOHPHOBIA: Unusual Fear of Palindromes.'" SLJ

This "book on word play is a creative, comedic gem." Booklist

Smart feller fart smeller & other Spoonerisms. Hyperion Books 2006 unp il $14.95

Grades: 3 4 5 6   **793.73**
1. Spoonerisms
ISBN 0-7868-3692-X   LC 2005-929187

"Using full-page black-and-white cartoons that play with the mixed-up words, Agee captures the fun of spoonerisms. The farce of the verbal puns is extended by pictures that caricature everyone. . . . A brief introduction explains what a spoonerism is, and the last page summarizes 'what they said' with 'what they meant to say.'" Booklist

Chedru, Delphine
Spot it! find the hidden creatures. Abrams Books for Young Readers 2009 unp il $14.95

Grades: PreK K 1   **793.73**
1. Picture puzzles
ISBN 978-0-8109-0632-7; 0-8109-0632-5
LC 2008032549

"This rounded-corner volume employs op-art designs to hide 15 creatures, and a farm girl, for viewers to find. The searches vary in difficulty. . . . The bright patterns vary from packed geometrics to a gathering of flowers, mushrooms, or trees. . . . Great for one-on-one lap sharing." SLJ

Cole, Joanna
Why did the chicken cross the road? and other riddles, old and new; compiled by Joanna Cole and Stephanie Calmenson; illustrated by Alan Tiegreen. Morrow Junior Bks. 1994 64p il pa $7.95 hardcover o.p.

Grades: 3 4 5   **793.73**
1. Riddles
ISBN 0-688-12204-3   LC 94-2582

The authors "begin with a brief explanation about the origin of riddles and proceed with a collection of over two hundred, classic and new. Though many of the riddles appear in other collections, the book, illustrated with black-and-white line drawings, will be useful for its short bibliography and subject index." Horn Book Guide

Hall, Katy, 1947-
Creepy riddles; [by] Katy Hall and Lisa Eisenberg; pictures by S.D. Schindler. Dial Bks. for Young Readers 1998 48p il (Dial easy-to-read) hardcover o.p. pa $3.99 *

Grades: K 1 2   **793.73**
1. Riddles
ISBN 0-8037-1684-2; 0-14-130988-1 (pa)
LC 94-37524

Hall, Katy, 1947-—*Continued*

"A collection of riddles about vampires, ghosts, ghouls, and assorted monsters. . . . The illustrations are a scream. Schindler uses a find-nibbed pen to include lots of subtle details before adding vivid watercolor washes. . . . A superior choice for most joke or beginning-to-read collections." SLJ

Dino riddles; by Katy Hall and Lisa Eisenberg; pictures by Nicole Rubel. Dial Bks. for Young Readers 2002 40p il (Dial easy-to-read) hardcover o.p. pa $3.99 *

Grades: K 1 2   **793.73**
1. Riddles
ISBN 0-8037-2239-7; 0-14-250179-4 (pa)
LC 97-49947

A collection of riddles relating to dinosaurs, such as "What do you get if you cross a dinosaur with a rabbit? Tricerahops!" and "What did dinosaur campers cook over the fire? Dino-s'mores!"

"Rubel's informal ink-and-marker illustrations are suitably silly. . . . This will be just right for joke-book junkies, beginning readers, and teachers looking to breathe new life into staid dinosaur units." Bull Cent Child Books

Ribbit riddles; by Katy Hall and Lisa Eisenberg; pictures by Robert Bender. Dial Bks. for Young Readers 2001 40p il (Dial easy-to-read) hardcover o.p. pa $3.99

Grades: K 1 2   **793.73**
1. Riddles 2. Jokes
ISBN 0-8037-2525-6; 0-14-240056-4 (pa)
LC 99-89174

A collection of riddles and jokes about frogs. Example: What do little frogs like to eat on a hot summer day? Hopsicles!

"The distinctive art, cell-vinyl on layers of acetate, has a shimmery, almost fuzzy look that catches the eye—and the jokes." Booklist

Simms Taback's great big book of spacey, snakey, buggy riddles; riddles by Katy Hall and Lisa Eisenberg; [illustrated by Simms Taback] Viking 2008 unp il $17.99 *

Grades: K 1 2 3   **793.73**
1. Riddles
ISBN 978-0-670-01121-6; 0-670-01121-5

"Taback brings his vibrant trademark exuberance to this picture-book riddle collection, which fairly hums with fun. Rainbow-bright colors pop off black backgrounds, making the riddles bigger than life. As the title suggests, space, snakes, and bugs dominate the subject matter." Booklist

Snakey riddles; by Katy Hall and Lisa Eisenberg; pictures by Simms Taback. Dial Bks. for Young Readers 1990 48p il (Dial easy-to-read) pa $3.99 hardcover o.p.

Grades: K 1 2   **793.73**
1. Riddles
ISBN 0-14-037141-9 (pa)
LC 88-23687

An illustrated collection of riddles about snakes

"Riddle lovers will groan with delight at some of these riddles. . . . The best thing about the book is the cleverly drawn, lively cartoon illustrations. Long, colorful snakes form borders framing the text and picture for each riddle." SLJ

Turkey riddles; by Katy Hall and Lisa Eisenberg; pictures by Kristin Sorra. Dial Bks. for Young Readers 2002 40p il (Dial easy-to-read) hardcover o.p. pa $3.99

Grades: K 1 2   **793.73**
1. Riddles
ISBN 0-8037-2530-2; 0-14-240369-5 (pa)
LC 2001-47475

A collection of nearly three dozen riddles featuring turkeys, such as "What happened when Tom Turkey stepped up to the plate? He hit a fowl ball"

"The art, with cross-hatched details, is bright and appealing. . . . Great for a good time alone, with friends, or even in a classroom." Booklist

Lankford, Mary D., 1932-

Mazes around the world; by Mary D. Lankford; illustrated by Karen Dugan. Collins 2008 26p il $16.99; lib bdg $17.89

Grades: 3 4 5   **793.73**
1. Maze puzzles
ISBN 978-0-688-16519-2; 0-688-16519-2; 978-0-688-16520-8 (lib bdg); 0-688-16520-6 (lib bdg)
LC 2007008580

"Lankford traces the history of mazes from the ancient Egyptian Labyrinth . . . to today's mazes in North America's corn fields. . . . Each left-hand page offers an engaging account of a particular maze or type of maze, depicted on the facing page in a charming painting by Dugan. . . . Drawing from many cultures and historical periods, this well-researched, accessible book explores a topic with inherent child appeal." Booklist

Includes bibliographical references

Maestro, Giulio, 1942-

Riddle roundup; a wild bunch to beef up your word power. Clarion Bks. 1989 64p il pa $7.95 hardcover o.p.

Grades: 2 3 4   **793.73**
1. Riddles 2. Word games
ISBN 0-89919-537-7 (pa)   LC 86-33403

A collection of sixty-one riddles based on different kinds of word play such as puns, homonyms, and homographs

Maestro, Marco

What do you hear when cows sing? and other silly riddles; by Marco and Giulio Maestro; pictures by Giulio Maestro. HarperCollins Pubs. 1996 48p il (I can read book) pa $3.95 hardcover o.p.

Grades: K 1 2   **793.73**
1. Riddles
ISBN 0-06-444227-6 (pa)   LC 94-18686

"The subjects of the riddles will be familiar to most readers—trains, bugs, mice, fish, boats. . . . Most of the

Maestro, Marco—*Continued*

selections involve plays on words, but some are relatively straightforward. . . . Children will love the silly pictures, laugh at the riddles, enjoy sharing them with others, and expand their vocabularies all at the same time." SLJ

Munro, Roxie, 1945-

Amazement park; by Roxie Munro. Chronicle Books 2005 37p il $16.95
Grades: K 1 2 3   **793.73**
  1. Maze puzzles
  ISBN 0-8118-4581-8   LC 2004-8482

This book includes "12 . . . mazes to navigate. . . . All mazes lead from one page to the next and then back again to the first one. . . . The mazes do get tricky and sometimes completely confusing, but an answer key is included for those who get stuck. The cartoon art is eye-catching and colorful." SLJ
Another book of maze puzzles by this author is:
Mazescapes (2001)

Mazeways: A to Z; by Roxie Munro. Sterling Pub. Co., Inc. 2007 unp il $12.95
Grades: K 1 2 3   **793.73**
  1. Maze puzzles 2. Alphabet
  ISBN 978-1-4027-3774-9; 1-4027-3774--2
                                          LC 2007001586

"Each letter is featured on a spread or a page with directions for traveling through the maze and finding different objects along the way. . . . Back pages provide solutions. This engaging title works as an interactive alphabet book, an introduction to mapping skills, or to sharpen visual discrimination skills." SLJ

Nickle, John

Alphabet explosion! search and count from alien to zebra; [by] John Nickle. Schwartz & Wade Books 2006 unp il $16.95
Grades: K 1 2 3   **793.73**
  1. Alphabet 2. Puzzles
  ISBN 0-375-83598-9   LC 2005024372

"Each wordless page features animals and objects whose names begin with a featured letter. A number indicates how many items are buried within the picture. . . . Nickle's finely rendered scenes are imaginative, humorous, and sophisticated, and he incorporates a free-flowing range of artistic styles that adds energy to the pages." Booklist

Spot 7 School; by KIDSLABEL. Chronicle Books 2006 unp il (Seek & find) $12.95
Grades: K 1 2 3 4   **793.73**
  1. Puzzles
  ISBN 978-0-8118-5324-8; 0-8118-5324-1
                                          LC 2005026114

Original Japanese edition 2003
"This book has colorful, busy photos of objects and lists of items associated with school for readers to locate. . . . It also offers viewers some additional tasks: the two pages of each spread are identical except for seven differences, and each left-hand page contains a riddle, the answer to which is found on the page. . . . The clear

images depict imaginative groupings. . . . It offers entertainment and an opportunity to hone observational skills rolled into one." SLJ
Other titles in this series are:
Spot 7 Christmas (2006)
Spot 7 Animals (2007)
Spot 7 Spooky (2007)
Spot 7 Toys (2008)

Steig, William, 1907-2003

C D B. Simon & Schuster Bks. for Young Readers 2000 c1968 47p il $16; pa $4.99 *
Grades: 2 3 4 5   **793.73**
  1. Word games
  ISBN 0-689-83160-9; 0-671-66689-4 (pa)
                                          LC 99-32720

First published 1968 by Windmill Bks.
Letters and numbers are used to create the sounds of words and simple sentences 4 u 2 figure out with the aid of illustrations
Readers "will delight in puzzling out the letter-and-number messages, aided by the simple, thickly outlined drawings and an answer key." Booklist

C D C? Farrar, Straus & Giroux 2003 c1984 57p il $16
Grades: 2 3 4 5   **793.73**
  1. Word games
  ISBN 0-374-31233-8   LC 2002-111704

Also available in paperback with black & white illustrations
A color illustrated edition of the title first published 1984
Letters, numbers, and symbols are used to create the sounds of words and simple sentences which U R expected to figure out with the aid of illustrations. Includes an answer key
"Flawlessly executed, purely pleasurable, the book is definitely 'D-Q-R' for doldrums at any season." Horn Book

Steiner, Joan, 1943-

Look-alikes around the world; concept, constructions & text by Joan Steiner; design by Stephen Blauweiss; photography by Ogden Gigli. Little, Brown and Company 2007 unp il $15.99
Grades: K 1 2 3 4   **793.73**
  1. Puzzles
  ISBN 978-0-316-81172-9; 0-316-81172-6
                                          LC 2007012332

"Megan Tingley books"
"Using everyday objects . . . artist Joan Steiner has created three-dimensional scenes of more than 40 famous landmarks and familiar vacation locales. . . . Complete with photographs of the actual sites, . . . facts, and more than 500 look-alikes to search for, this [is in the format of a] postcard album." Publisher's note
Other titles in this series are:
Look-alikes (1998)
Look-alikes Jr (1999)
Look-alikes Christmas (2003)

Wick, Walter, 1953-

Can you see what I see? picture puzzles to search and solve. Scholastic 2002 35p il $13.95 *

Grades: PreK K 1 2   **793.73**

1. Puzzles

ISBN 0-439-16391-9   LC 2001-49032

"Cartwheel books"

Presents twelve brain-teasing hidden picture puzzles to solve

"With its range of activities and perspective-shifting challenges, this is sure to appeal to a wide age group of children, who won't be satisfied until they've solved the last puzzle." Booklist

Other titles in this series are:

Can you see what I see?: Cool collections (2004)

Can you see what I see?: Dream machine (2003)

Can you see what I see?: On a scary scary night (2008)

Can you see what I see?: Once upon a time (2006)

Can you see what I see?: Seymour and the juice box boat (2004)

Can you see what I see: Seymour makes new friends (2006)

Can you see what I see?: The night before Christmas (2005)

Can you see what I see?: Treasure ship (2010)

I spy; a book of picture riddles; photographs by Walter Wick; riddles by Jean Marzollo; design by Carol Devine Carson. Scholastic 1992 33p il $13.95 *

Grades: K 1 2 3 4   **793.73**

1. Puzzles

ISBN 0-590-45087-5   LC 91-28268

Also available I spy board books for younger readers and I spy easy readers

"Cartwheel books"

This visual game book consists of "a series of rhymed riddles listing objects that children must locate in the accompanying photographs. Each double-page spread features crisp, full-color shots featuring an abundance of familiar items. The objects range from large and easy-to-spot to tiny and partially hidden. . . . An appealing book for children and adults to share and enjoy together." SLJ

Other titles in this series are:

I spy Christmas (1992)

I spy extreme challenger! (2000)

I spy fantasy (1994)

I spy fun house (1993)

I spy gold challenger! (1998)

I spy mystery (1993)

I spy school days (1995)

I spy spooky night (1996)

I spy super challenger! (1997)

I spy treasure hunt (1999)

I spy ultimate challenger! (2003)

I spy year-round challenger! (2003)

793.74 Mathematical games and recreations

Ball, Johnny, 1938-

Go figure! DK Pub. 2005 96p il map $15.99

Grades: 4 5 6 7   **793.74**

1. Mathematical recreations 2. Mathematics

ISBN 0-7566-1374-4

A collection of math activities that include brainteasers, magic tricks, and mind-reading games

"A dynamic book. . . . Blocks of color, diagrams, and photo collages contribute to the exciting layout. . . . A fun romp for number and puzzle lovers." SLJ

Math for the very young; a handbook of activities for parents and teachers; [by] Lydia Plonsky . . . [et al.]; illustrated by Marcia Miller. Wiley 1995 210p il hardcover o.p. pa $14.95

Grades: Adult Professional   **793.74**

1. Mathematical recreations

ISBN 0-471-01671-3; 0-471-01647-0 (pa)

LC 94-20861

"This guide suggests ways to introduce math to children through everyday activities. Sections include making a record book about the child and the family as well as activities for each month of the year, geometric crafts, math games, counting rhymes and stories, and ways to use math in the home and on the road." Booklist

Includes bibliographical references

Tang, Greg

The grapes of math; mind-stretching math riddles; illustrated by Harry Briggs. Scholastic Press 2001 unp il $16.95

Grades: 2 3 4   **793.74**

1. Mathematical recreations

ISBN 0-439-21033-X   LC 00-30062

Illustrated riddles introduce strategies for solving a variety of math problems in using visual clues

"This clever collection of puzzles could spark the interest of even the mathematically challenged. . . . The simple, staccato rhymes and crisp lines of the artwork keep attention focused, while those who find themselves stumped can consult the 'Answers' section at the back of the book." Publ Wkly

Math appeal; mind-stretching math riddles; illustrated by Harry Briggs. Scholastic Press 2003 unp il $16.95

Grades: 2 3 4   **793.74**

1. Mathematical recreations

ISBN 0-439-21046-1   LC 2002-5354

Rhyming anecdotes present opportunities for simple math activities and hints for solving

"Bright, whimsical illustrations and clever rhymes introduce challenging exercises. . . . In a note, Tang states that his goal is 'to encourage clever, creative thinking,' and the questions posed do that." SLJ

Tang, Greg—*Continued*

Math potatoes; mind-stretching brain food; illustrated by Harry Briggs. Scholastic Press 2005 unp il $16.95 *

Grades: 2 3 4   **793.74**

1. Mathematical recreations

ISBN 0-439-44390-3   LC 2004-16638

"This picture book uses all kinds of visual tricks to demonstrate how to make arithmetic faster and easier. On each double-page spread, a rhyming verse has fun with a variety of subjects. Most rhymes are about foods . . . and the bright, computer-generated pictures are as playful as the words. . . . The games are complex, the visuals are tricky, and although the rhyme seems straightforward . . . readers must think carefully about adding, subtracting, and multiplying." Booklist

793.8   Magic and related activities

Barnhart, Norm

Amazing magic tricks: a beginner level; by Norm Barnhart. Capstone Press 2009 32p il (Magic Tricks) lib bdg $23.93

Grades: 4 5 6   **793.8**

1. Magic tricks

ISBN 978-1-4296-1942-4 (lib bdg); 1-4296-1942-2 (lib bdg)   LC 2008-2572

"Edge books"

"Instructions and . . . photos describe how to perform magic tricks at the beginner level." Publisher's note

"Numbered steps, clearly illustrated by crisp photographs, guide students through the preparation and performance of such classic magician's fare as 'The Magical Sailor's Knot.'. . . The books' design, with the text neatly packaged in boxes, will attract reluctant readers." SLJ

Includes glossary and bibliographical references

Amazing magic tricks: apprentice level; by Norm Barnhart. Capstone Press 2009 32p il (Magic Tricks) lib bdg $23.93

Grades: 4 5 6   **793.8**

1. Magic tricks

ISBN 978-1-4296-1943-1 (lib bdg); 1-4296-1943-0 (lib bdg)   LC 2008-2573

"Edge books"

"Instructions and . . . photos describe how to perform magic tricks at the apprentice level." Publisher's note

"Numbered steps, clearly illustrated by crisp photographs, guide students through the preparation and performance of such classic magician's fare as 'The Magical Sailor's Knot.'. . . The books' design, with the text neatly packaged in boxes, will attract reluctant readers." SLJ

Includes glossary and bibliographical references

Amazing magic tricks: expert level; by Norm Barnhart. Capstone Press 2009 32p il (Magic Tricks) lib bdg $23.93

Grades: 4 5 6   **793.8**

1. Magic tricks

ISBN 978-1-4296-1945-5 (lib bdg); 1-4296-1945-7 (lib bdg)   LC 2008-2574

"Edge books"

"Instructions and . . . photos describe how to perform magic tricks at the expert level." Publisher's note

"Numbered steps, clearly illustrated by crisp photographs, guide students through the preparation and performance of such classic magician's fare as 'The Magical Sailor's Knot.'. . . The books' design, with the text neatly packaged in boxes, will attract reluctant readers." SLJ

Includes glossary and bibliographical references

Amazing magic tricks: master level; by Norm Barnhart. Capstone Press 2009 32p il (Magic Tricks) lib bdg $23.93

Grades: 4 5 6   **793.8**

1. Magic tricks

ISBN 978-1-4296-1944-8 (lib bdg); 1-4296-1944-9 (lib bdg)   LC 2008-2575

"Edge books"

"Instructions and clear photos describe how to perform magic tricks at the master level." Publisher's note

"Numbered steps, clearly illustrated by crisp photographs, guide students through the preparation and performance of such classic magician's fare as 'The Magical Sailor's Knot.'. . . The books' design, with the text neatly packaged in boxes, will attract reluctant readers." SLJ

Includes glossary and bibliographical references

Becker, Helaine

Magic up your sleeve; amazing illusions, tricks, and science facts you'll never believe; illustrated by Claudia Dávila. Maple Tree Press 2010 64p il $22.95; pa $10.95

Grades: 3 4 5 6   **793.8**

1. Magic tricks 2. Science

ISBN   978-1-897349-75-5;   1-897349-75-0; 978-1-897349-76-2 (pa); 1-8973497-6-9 (pa)

"Thirty tricks are presented covering optical illusions, mind reading, 'math magic,' chemistry, and physics. All directions are clear and easy to follow. . . . The digital cartoon illustrations are nicely executed and add flashes of humor to the scenarios. . . . A welcome addition that should vanish off library shelves." SLJ

Wyler, Rose

Magic secrets; by Rose Wyler and Gerald Ames; pictures by Arthur Dorros. rev ed. Harper & Row 1990 63p il (I can read book) pa $3.99 hardcover o.p.

Grades: K 1 2   **793.8**

1. Magic tricks

ISBN 0-06-444153-9 (pa)   LC 89-35841

A revised and newly illustrated edition of the title first published 1967

Easy magic tricks for the aspiring young magician

"Most of the magic tricks presented here are easily understood and appear to be simple to learn and to execute with ample practice." SLJ

794.1 Chess

Basman, Michael
Chess for kids; written by Michael Basman. Dorling Kindersley 2001 45p il $12.99; pa $6.99
Grades: 4 5 6 7   **794.1**
   1. Chess
   ISBN 0-7894-6540-X; 0-7566-1807-X (pa)
                                    LC 00-59018
This guide to chess explains the rudiments of the game, techniques and winning strategies
"A solid introduction for novices and good for skilled players wanting to develop their strategies and find out about chess clubs and tournaments." Booklist

King, Daniel, 1963-
Chess; from first moves to checkmate. Kingfisher (NY) 2000 64p il $16.95; pa $8.95 *
Grades: 5 6 7 8 9 10 11 12   **794.1**
   1. Chess
   ISBN 0-7534-5387-8; 0-7534-5820-9 (pa)
                                    LC 00-26353
Introduces the rules and strategies of chess, as well as its history and some of the great players and matches
The author "offers training exercises, strategy quizzes, and trivia, all of which add depth and texture to his explanations. The computer-generated graphics are staggering. The colorful, multi-image illustrations are not only aesthetically appealing but also crystal clear and very effectively placed to enhance the text." Booklist

794.8 Electronic games. Computer games

Egan, Jill
How video game designers use math; math curriculum consultant: Rhea A. Stewart. Chelsea Clubhouse 2010 32p il (Math in the real world) lib bdg $28
Grades: 4 5 6   **794.8**
   1. Computer games 2. Computer animation 3. Video games 4. Mathematics 5. Vocational guidance
   ISBN 978-1-60413-603-6 (lib bdg); 1-60413-603-0 (lib bdg)   LC 2009-24173
This describes how video game designers use math to create and produce their games and includes relevant math problems and information about how to become a video game designer
Includes glossary and bibliographical references

Jakubiak, David J.
A smart kid's guide to playing online games. PowerKids Press 2009 c2010 24p il (Kids online) lib bdg $21.25; pa $8.95
Grades: 3 4 5 6   **794.8**
   1. Computer games 2. Video games 3. Computers and children
   ISBN 978-1-4042-8115-8 (lib bdg); 1-4042-8115-0 (lib bdg); 978-1-4358-3350-0 (pa); 1-4358-3350-3 (pa)
                                    LC 2009002615

This book instructs children on how to enjoy and safely partake in the online gaming community.
"This . . . is easy to read, has vibrant photos on each page, and offers Tips. Additional links can be found at the publisher's portal, which is regularly updated." Libr Media Connect
Includes glossary

796 Athletic and outdoor sports and games

Berman, Len
The greatest moments in sports. Sourcebooks 2009 136p il $16.99
Grades: 5 6 7 8   **796**
   1. Sports
   ISBN 978-1-4022-2099-9; 1-4022-2099-5
                                    LC 2009023686
"Forty years as a sportscaster gives Berman plenty of experience to choose the 25 greatest sports moments. His writing is lively, humorous, and informative—just right to sustain kids' (or adults') interest. Quality photos throughout are another plus. . . . An audio CD that includes many of the moments as they were broadcast live is part of the package." SLJ
Includes bibliographical references

Blumenthal, Karen
Let me play; the story of Title IX, the law that changed the future of girls in America; [by] Karen Blumenthal. Atheneum Books for Young Readers 2005 152p il $19.95
Grades: 6 7 8 9 10   **796**
   1. Women athletes 2. Sex discrimination
   ISBN 0-689-85957-0   LC 2004-1450
"The author looks at American women's evolving rights by focusing on the history and future of Title IX, which bans sex discrimination in U.S. education. . . . The images are . . . gripping, and relevant political cartoons and fact boxes add further interest. Few books cover the last few decades of American women's history with such clarity and detail." Booklist
Includes bibliographical references

Sierra, Judy
Children's traditional games; games from 137 countries and cultures; by Judy Sierra, Robert Kaminski. Oryx Press 1995 232p il pa $49.95
Grades: Professional   **796**
   1. Games
   ISBN 0-89774-967-7   LC 95-35623
The authors "describe popular games from 137 countries and cultures, including over 20 games from Native American groups. Each game . . . can be played by small groups in the classroom or on the playground." Publisher's note
Includes bibliographical references

Strother, Scott

The adventurous book of outdoor games; classic fun for daring boys and girls; [by] Scott Strother. Sourcebooks 2008 293p il pa $14.99 *

Grades: 4 5 6 7 Professional   796
1. Games
ISBN 978-1-4022-1443-1 (pa); 1-4022-1443-X (pa)

This book "outlines more than 100 games, each at different activity levels set by the amount of physical exertion required. . . . Each game discusses the number of players, ages, time allotted, and type of playing field, followed by a brief description of equipment, startup, object of the game, and how to play. . . . The easy-to-read, easy-to-follow format will provide hours of imaginative play for all of those who are willing to try. An excellent resource for parents, teachers, and activity directors and even for children themselves." SLJ

796.1   Miscellaneous games

The **Eentsy,** weentsy spider: fingerplays and action rhymes; compiled by Joanna Cole and Stephanie Calmenson; illustrated by Alan Tiegreen. Morrow Junior Bks. 1991 64p il music pa $8.99 hardcover o.p. *

Grades: K 1 2 3   796.1
1. Finger play 2. Songs
ISBN 0-688-10805-9 (pa)   LC 90-44594

"This collection of 38 fingerplays and action rhymes ranges from the familiar 'I'm a Little Teapot,' to the older 'Two Fat Gentlemen.' Simple musical arrangements are included where appropriate." SLJ

"Tiegreen uses a few simple lines to create a cast of multicultural characters whose enthusiasm is infectious. . . . An attractive, upbeat addition to the finger-play collection." Booklist

Includes bibliographical references

Miss Mary Mack and other children's street rhymes; compiled by Joanna Cole and Stephanie Calmenson; illustrated by Alan Tiegreen. Morrow Junior Bks. 1990 64p pa $7.95 hardcover o.p. *

Grades: K 1 2 3   796.1
1. Games 2. Nursery rhymes
ISBN 0-688-09749-9 (pa)   LC 89-37266

This is a collection of over 100 traditional childhood hand-clapping and street rhymes

"Tiegreen's lighthearted pen-and-ink illustrations are sure to tickle the fancy of young readers. . . . A book that's sure to produce smiles in any story hour or program." SLJ

796.22   Skateboarding

Fitzpatrick, Jim, 1948-

Skateboarding. Cherry Lake Pub. 2009 32p il (Innovation in sports) lib bdg $27.07

Grades: 4 5 6 7   796.22
1. Skateboarding
ISBN 978-1-60279-259-3 (lib bdg); 1-60279-259-3 (lib bdg)   LC 2008007548

This describes skateboarding history, equipment, safety, and health benefits

This "stands out by emphasizing monumental shifts and advances in the events themselves. . . . Concise and occasionally revelatory." Booklist

Includes glossary and bibliographical references

Spencer, Russ

Skateboarding; by Russ Spencer. Child's World 2005 32p il (Kids' guides) lib bdg $24.21

Grades: 4 5 6   796.22
1. Skateboarding
ISBN 1-59296-210-6   LC 2003-27370

Contents: Go rip!; Into the great wide open; Gear up!; In action; Stars and competition

This "opens with an explanation of the sport and gives reasons why people enjoy it. The four chapters that follow cover background and development, equipment, technique, and stars and competitions. The excellent color photos are clear and exciting." SLJ

Includes bibliographical references

796.3   Athletic ball games

Rosen, Michael J., 1954-

Balls!: round 2; illustrations by John Margeson. Darby Creek Pub. 2008 80p il $18.95

Grades: 3 4 5 6   796.3
1. Sporting goods 2. Sports
ISBN 978-1-58196-066-2; 1-58196-066-2

Companion volume to: Balls! (2006)

"Rosen offers a lighthearted look at a variety of balls, covering their production and history, and how they're used in sports. . . . The author highlights balls used in baseball, softball, bowling, bocce, croquet, shot put, billiards, and lacrosse. Each sport receives a brief introduction . . . complemented by color photographs, cartoons, and graphics. There's an emphasis on fun science, with simple puzzles and experiments. . . . Rosen serves up a feast of whimsical trivia and wordplay, and he rounds out this collection with sections on marbles and extreme goofballs." SLJ

Includes bibliographical references

796.323   Basketball

Doeden, Matt, 1974-

The greatest basketball records; by Matt Doeden. Capstone Press 2009 32p il (Sports records) lib bdg $17.95

Grades: 4 5 6 7 8   796.323
1. National Basketball Association 2. Basketball
ISBN 978-1-4296-2006-2 (lib bdg); 1-4296-2006-4 (lib bdg)   LC 2008-2033

"Short stories and tables of statistics describe the history and greatest records of the National Basketball Association." Publisher's note

This "has enough historical insight and trivia to remain appealing over time. . . . Brief, lively sentences sum up individual feats and set them in context. . . . [This] should appeal to a wide audience." SLJ

Includes glossary and bibliographical references

Gifford, Clive

Basketball. Marshall Cavendish Benchmark 2009 30p il (Tell me about sports) $19.95
Grades: 3 4 5   **796.323**
1. Basketball
ISBN 978-0-7614-4455-8; 0-7614-4455-6
LC 2008-55992
"An introduction to basketball, including techniques, rules, and the training regimen of professional athletes in the sport." Publisher's note
Includes glossary and bibliographical references

Basketball; [by] Clive Gifford. PowerKids Press 2009 32p il (Personal best) lib bdg $25.25
Grades: 4 5 6 7 8   **796.323**
1. Basketball
ISBN 978-1-4042-4444-3 (lib bdg); 1-4042-4444-1 (lib bdg)
LC 2007-42989
Contents: What is basketball?; Playing the game; Stance and pivoting; Passing; Dribbling; Court movement; Screening; Defending; Fouls and free throws; Jump and hook shots; Layups; Jumping and rebounding; Team plays
This guide to basketball "offers well-organized and easy-to-follow instructions, focusing on rules, clothing, specific skills, and competitions. . . . Informative, readable." SLJ
Includes bibliographical references

Ingram, Scott, 1948-

A basketball all-star. Heinemann Library 2005 48p il (Making of a champion) lib bdg $31.43; pa $8.90 *
Grades: 5 6 7 8   **796.323**
1. Basketball
ISBN 1-4034-5363-2 (lib bdg); 1-4034-5547-3 (pa)
LC 2004-3864
Contents: A worldwide sport; Basketball beginnings; The growth of the NBA; Changes in the rules; Basketball basics; Coaching; Nutrition for athletes; Running; Flexibility; Basketball fitness: strength; Injuries and recovery; Skills: dribbling; Skills: passing; Skills: shooting; On offense; Transition; Getting position; Game day; Olympic dreams; Being a champion; Records
This overview of basketball includes "basic skills and playing strategies, rules of the game, training, and typical injuries. . . . Fact boxes, short vignettes on past and present professional athletes, and lists of championships . . . are offered. . . . The clearly presented information is accompanied by a quality color or black-and-white photograph on every page." SLJ
Includes bibliographical references

Labrecque, Ellen

Basketball; by Ellen Labrecque. Cherry Lake Pub. 2009 32p il (Innovation in sports) lib bdg $27.07
Grades: 4 5 6 7   **796.323**
1. Basketball
ISBN 978-1-60279-256-2 (lib bdg); 1-60279-256-9 (lib bdg)
LC 2008002044
This describes basketball history, rules, equipment, training, and great players

This "stands out by emphasizing monumental shifts and advances in the events themselves. . . . Concise and occasionally revelatory." Booklist
Includes glossary and bibliographical references

Stewart, Mark, 1960-

Swish; the quest for basketball's perfect shot; by Mark Stewart and Mike Kennedy. Millbrook Press 2009 64p il lib bdg $25.26
Grades: 5 6 7 8   **796.323**
1. Basketball
ISBN 978-0-8225-8752-1 (lib bdg); 0-8225-8752-1 (lib bdg)
LC 2008-24958
"Stewart and Kennedy offer an engaging history of the sport, followed by profiles of some of the most impressive shots of all time and the players who made them." SLJ
"The wide pages offer plenty of room for well-spaced text, sidebars, and illustrations. Each page has at least one picture, with mostly color photos, and the many action shots make the book more exciting. With information on women's and men's basketball at both collegiate and professional levels, this is a nice addition to sports collections." Booklist
Includes bibliographical references

Thomas, Keltie

How basketball works. Maple Tree Press 2005 64p il $16.95 paperback o.p. *
Grades: 5 6 7 8   **796.323**
1. Basketball
ISBN 1-89706-618-X; 1-89706-619-8 (pa)
This guide to basketball offers information about the game's origins, history, and equipment as well as positions, training, skills, stats, & rules of the game. It also offers tips and fascinating factoids.
"The writing style is razzle-dazzle energetic. . . . The layout features numerous sidebars and brightly colored photos and digital drawings. Even longtime fans will learn something from this engaging, enthusiastic book." Booklist

796.325   Volleyball

Crossingham, John, 1974-

Spike it volleyball; [by] John Crossingham. Crabtree Pub. Co. 2008 32p il (Sports starters) lib bdg $18.95; pa $6.95
Grades: 2 3 4   **796.325**
1. Volleyball
ISBN 978-0-7787-3143-6 (lib bdg); 0-7787-3143-X (lib bdg); 978-0-7787-3175-7 (pa); 0-7787-3175-8 (pa)
LC 2008004853
This "offers a sturdy overview of volleyball, from rules and scoring to basic moves. The accessible text lays out clear explanations of terms and concepts. . . . The eye-catching design combines large color photos of athletes in action with smaller inset pictures." Booklist

796.332   American football

Buckley, James, Jr.
Ultimate guide to football; by James Buckley, Jr. Franklin Watts 2010 160p il $30; pa $7.99
Grades: 4 5 6 7   **796.332**
1. Football
ISBN 978-0-531-20752-9; 0-531-20752-8; 978-0-531-21023-9 (pa); 0-531-21023-5
LC 2009011003
This guide to football covers "historical highlights and delectable ephemera . . . with spreads covering each NFL team interspersed among chatty tales. . . . The highlighter-green color scheme matches the loud, vibrant layout and heightens the contrasting black-and-white player photos, while sporatic cartoons add some pep to the presenation." Booklist
Includes bibliographical references

The **Child's** World encyclopedia of the NFL; by James Buckley, Jr. . . . [et al.] Child's World 2007 4v il set $189
Grades: 3 4 5 6 7   **796.332**
1. National Football League 2. Football—Encyclopedias 3. Reference books
ISBN 978-1-59296-922-7 (v1); 978-1-59296-923-4 (v2); 978-1-59296-924-1 (v3); 978-1-59296-925-8 (v4)
LC 2007005662
This encyclopedia of the National Football League is "full of color photos; significant names, terms, and events; and plenty of popular football figures. The authors are all experienced sportswriters and editors." Booklist

Dougherty, Terri, 1964-
The greatest football records; by Terri Dougherty. Capstone Press 2009 32p il (Sports records) lib bdg $17.95
Grades: 4 5 6 7 8   **796.332**
1. National Football League 2. Football
ISBN 978-1-4296-2007-9 (lib bdg); 1-4296-2007-2 (lib bdg)
LC 2008-2035
"Short stories and tables of statistics describe the history and greatest records of the National Football League." Publisher's note
This "has enough historical insight and trivia to remain appealing over time. . . . Brief, lively sentences sum up individual feats and set them in context. . . . [This] should appeal to a wide audience." SLJ
Includes glossary and bibliographical references

Gibbons, Gail
My football book. HarperCollins Pubs. 2000 unp il $5.95
Grades: K 1 2   **796.332**
1. Football
ISBN 0-688-17139-7   LC 99-87202
Introduces the basics of the game of football, describing the players, field, and how the game is played
"What shines through [in this book] is Gibbons's dedication to presenting the game as fun. . . . The illustrations, especially those of the players, clearly reflect the action." SLJ
Includes glossary

Gifford, Clive
Football. Marshall Cavendish Benchmark 2009 30p il (Tell me about sports) $19.95
Grades: 3 4 5   **796.332**
1. Football
ISBN 978-0-7614-4456-5; 0-7614-4456-4
LC 2009-4828
"An introduction to football, including techniques, rules, and the training regimen of professional athletes in the sport." Publisher's note
Includes glossary and bibliographical references

Gigliotti, Jim
Defensive backs. Gareth Stevens Pub. 2010 48p il (Game day. Football) lib bdg $31
Grades: 3 4 5   **796.332**
1. Football
ISBN 978-1-4339-1964-0 (lib bdg); 1-4339-1964-8 (lib bdg)
LC 2009-6801
"Examines the position of defensive back, discussing its history, key skills and tactics, and top players." Publisher's note
"The attractive page design showcases a mix of colorful photographs along with some vintage black-and-white shots, all within an attractive green border that shows yardage marks on a field. . . . This [book] . . . will generate discussion and sharing of opinions about favorite players and record book statistics." SLJ
Includes glossary and bibliographical references

Football. Cherry Lake Pub. 2009 32p il (Innovation in sports) lib bdg $27.07
Grades: 4 5 6 7   **796.332**
1. Football
ISBN 978-1-60279-257-9 (lib bdg); 1-60279-257-7 (lib bdg)
LC 2008002305
This describes football history, rules, equipment, training and strategy, and innovators
This "stands out by emphasizing monumental shifts and advances in the events themselves. . . . Concise and occasionally revelatory." Booklist
Includes glossary and bibliographical references

Linebackers. Gareth Stevens Pub. 2010 48p il (Game day. Football) lib bdg $31
Grades: 3 4 5   **796.332**
1. Football
ISBN 978-1-4339-1959-6 (lib bdg); 1-4339-1959-1 (lib bdg)
LC 2009-6802
"Examines the position of linebacker, discussing its history, key skills and tactics, and top players." Publisher's note
"The attractive page design showcases a mix of colorful photographs along with some vintage black-and-white shots, all within an attractive green border that shows yardage marks on a field. . . . This [book] . . . will generate discussion and sharing of opinions about favorite players and record book statistics." SLJ
Includes glossary and bibliographical references

Linemen. Gareth Stevens Pub. 2010 48p il (Game day. Football) lib bdg $31
Grades: 3 4 5   **796.332**
1. Football
ISBN 978-1-4339-1960-2 (lib bdg); 1-4339-1960-5 (lib bdg)
LC 2009-2272

Gigliotti, Jim—_Continued_

"Examines the positions of offensive and defensive lineman, discussing history, key skills and tactics, and top players." Publisher's note

"The attractive page design showcases a mix of colorful photographs along with some vintage black-and-white shots, all within an attractive green border that shows yardage marks on a field. . . . This [book] . . . will generate discussion and sharing of opinions about favorite players and record book statistics." SLJ

Includes glossary and bibliographical references

Receivers. Gareth Stevens Pub. 2010 48p il (Game day. Football) lib bdg $31

Grades: 3 4 5   **796.332**

1. Football

ISBN 978-1-4339-1962-6 (lib bdg); 1-4339-1962-1 (lib bdg)   LC 2008-55595

"Examines the position of receiver, discussing its history, key skills and tactics, and top players." Publisher's note

"The attractive page design showcases a mix of colorful photographs along with some vintage black-and-white shots, all within an attractive green border that shows yardage marks on a field. . . . This [book] . . . will generate discussion and sharing of opinions about favorite players and record book statistics." SLJ

Includes glossary and bibliographical references

Ingram, Scott, 1948-

A football all-pro; [by] Scott Ingram. Heinemann Library 2005 48p il (The making of a champion) lib bdg $31.43 paperback o.p.

Grades: 5 6 7 8 9   **796.332**

1. Football

ISBN 1-4034-5364-0 (lib bdg); 1-4034-5548-1 (pa)   LC 2004-3870

Contents: Introduction: the Super Bowl; The beginnings of football; The rise of the National Football League; Equipment; Starting young; The football basics; Weight training; The dangers of steroids; Diet and training; What a coach expects; Master the pass; Heavy-duty runners; Gifted hands; Offensive linemen; Defensive line; Linebackers; Defensive backs; The kicking game; Injuries; Game day; What it takes to make a champion; Fascinating football facts

This provides an overview of football "from [its] beginnings to contemporary times. Basic skills and playing strategies, rules of the game, training, and typical injuries are discussed, and fact boxes, short vignettes on past and present professional athletes, and lists of championships . . . are offered." SLJ

Includes bibliographical references

Kelley, K. C., 1960-

Quarterbacks. Gareth Stevens Pub. 2010 48p il (Game day. Football) lib bdg $31

Grades: 3 4 5   **796.332**

1. Football

ISBN 978-1-4339-1961-9 (lib bdg); 1-4339-1961-3 (lib bdg)   LC 2008-55596

"Examines the position of quarterback, discussing its history, key skills and tactics, and top players." Publisher's note

"The attractive page design showcases a mix of colorful photographs along with some vintage black-and-white shots, all within an attractive green border that shows yardage marks on a field. . . . This [book] . . . will generate discussion and sharing of opinions about favorite players and record book statistics." SLJ

Includes glossary and bibliographical references

Running backs. Gareth Stevens Pub. 2010 48p il (Game day. Football) lib bdg $31

Grades: 3 4 5   **796.332**

1. Football

ISBN 978-1-4339-1963-3 (lib bdg); 1-4339-1963-X (lib bdg)   LC 2009-2277

"Examines the position of running back, discussing its history, key skills and tactics, and top players." Publisher's note

"The attractive page design showcases a mix of colorful photographs along with some vintage black-and-white shots, all within an attractive green border that shows yardage marks on a field. . . . This [book] . . . will generate discussion and sharing of opinions about favorite players and record book statistics." SLJ

Includes glossary and bibliographical references

LeBoutillier, Nate

The story of the Chicago Bears. Creative Education 2009 48p il (NFL today) lib bdg $32.80

Grades: 4 5 6 7   **796.332**

1. Chicago Bears (Football team) 2. Football

ISBN 978-1-58341-750-8 (lib bdg); 1-58341-750-8 (lib bdg)   LC 2008020707

"This narrative captures a sense of the team's continuity, from the beginning of George Halas' epic career through the 2008 season. . . . With an economy of words, the anecdotal and spirited text accurately informs without becoming a chore to read. . . . What will really get this book off the shelves is the eye-catching, classy design and abundance of oversize, gorgeously reproduced photos of electrifying gridiron action." Booklist

Includes bibliographical references

Marsico, Katie, 1980-

Football; by Katie Marsico and Cecilia Minden. Cherry Lake Pub. 2009 32p il (Real world math: Sports) lib bdg $27.07

Grades: 4 5 6   **796.332**

1. Football 2. Arithmetic

ISBN 978-1-60279-247-0 (lib bdg); 1-60279-247-X (lib bdg)   LC 2008-1165

This book "starts with a short story on the history of [football], fundamental rules, and a math challenge in every chapter. . . . [This book] will pique your imagination." Sci Books Films

Includes glossary and bibliographical references

Stewart, Mark, 1960-
Touchdown; the power and precision of football's perfect play; by Mark Stewart and Mike Kennedy. Millbrook Press 2009 64p il lib bdg $27.93
Grades: 5 6 7 8   **796.332**
  1. Football
  ISBN 978-0-8225-8751-4 (lib bdg); 0-8225-8751-3 (lib bdg)   LC 2008044295
"This attractive book opens with an intriguing history of American football. . . . Next, 10 double-page spreads feature 'Ten Unforgettable Touchdowns' in both professional and collegiate games from 1913 to 2006. After a chapter on 'touchdown makers,' spotlighting outstanding players . . . comes a short section on notable touchdown bloopers and another on trick plays and the element of surprise. . . . Photos, period prints, and reproductions of trading cards illustrate the text while adding color to the pages. . . . This nicely designed book provides plenty of on-the-field drama as well as pertinent information in a smoothly written overview of the touchdown." Booklist

796.334   Soccer

Gifford, Clive
The Kingfisher soccer encyclopedia. Kingfisher 2006 144p il $19.95 *
Grades: 5 6 7 8   **796.334**
  1. Soccer—Encyclopedias 2. Reference books
  ISBN 978-0-7534-5928-7; 0-7534-5928-0
     LC 2005023899
"Beginning with the history of the sport, Gifford covers the basic rules as well as skills such as defending the ball, goalkeeping, and attacking. He includes brief bios of the legends of the sport, both men and women, organized by their positions. Fascinating tales of great teams and memorable competitions in events . . . will entertain fans of the sport. . . . This book could be used as a reference guide for reports or to answer specific questions. A solid purchase where an all-encompassing encyclopedia is needed." SLJ
  Includes glossary

Soccer; [by] Clive Gifford. PowerKids Press 2009 32p il (Personal best) lib bdg $25.25
Grades: 4 5 6 7 8   **796.334**
  1. Soccer
  ISBN 978-1-4042-4441-2 (lib bdg); 1-4042-4441-7 (lib bdg)   LC 2007-42997
  Contents: What is soccer?; The pitch and play; Training and clothing; Passing the ball; Receiving the ball; Movement in play; Attacking play; Shooting; Heading; Goalkeeping; Defending; Tackling; Set pieces
This guide to soccer "offers well-organized and easy-to-follow instructions, focusing on rules, clothing, specific skills, and competitions. . . . Informative, readable." SLJ

Soccer; [by] Clive Gifford. Sea-to-Sea Publications 2009 30p il (Know your sport) lib bdg $27.10
Grades: 5 6 7 8   **796.334**
  1. Soccer
  ISBN 978-1-59771-152-4 (lib bdg); 1-59771-152-7 (lib bdg)   LC 2008-7320

Contents: The game; Training to play; Ball control; Passing; On the ball; Attacking; Goalscoring; Defending; Tackling; Goalkeeping; Statistics and records
"Describes the equipment, training, moves, and competitions of soccer. Includes step-by-step descriptions of moves." Publisher's note
  Includes glossary

Guillain, Charlotte
Soccer. Heinemann Library 2009 24p il (Sports and my body) lib bdg $21.36; pa $6.49
Grades: 1 2   **796.334**
  1. Soccer
  ISBN 978-1-4329-3456-9 (lib bdg); 1-4329-3456-2 (lib bdg); 978-1-4329-3461-3 (pa); 1-4329-3461-9 (pa)
     LC 2009-7082
Learn what soccer is, how it can help them stay healthy, and how they can play soccer safely.
This book relates "activity to health . . . [and] explains that in order to stay healthy, children should get plenty of rest, eat healthy food, and drink plenty of water." SLJ
  Includes glossary

Hornby, Hugh
Soccer; written by Hugh Hornby; photographed by Andy Crawford. DK Pub. 2008 70p il (DK eyewitness books) $15.99
Grades: 4 5 6 7   **796.334**
  1. Soccer
  ISBN 978-0-7566-3779-8; 0-7566-3779-1
     LC 2008276290
  First published 2000
  Includes CD ROM
Examines all aspects of the game of soccer: its history, rules, techniques, tactics, equipment, playing fields, competitive play, and more.

Hyde, Natalie, 1963-
Soccer science. Crabtree Pub. Co. 2009 32p il (Sports science) lib bdg $26.60; pa $8.95
Grades: 3 4 5 6   **796.334**
  1. Soccer
  ISBN 978-0-7787-4537-2 (lib bdg); 0-7787-4537-6 (lib bdg); 978-0-7787-4554-9 (pa); 0-7787-4554-6 (pa)
     LC 2008-46276
This book approachs soccer "from a scientific angle, describing some of the physics behind [the] pursuit and how athletes can use this knowledge to improve performance. . . . Fascinating facts . . . [such as] information about the soccer robots in the RoboCup, are presented in a captivating, lively manner. . . . The layout features colorful text boxes interspersed among photographs." SLJ
  Includes glossary

Kelley, K. C., 1960-
Soccer. Cherry Lake Pub. 2008 32p il (Innovation in sports) lib bdg $27.07
Grades: 4 5 6 7   **796.334**
  1. Soccer
  ISBN 978-1-60279-261-6 (lib bdg); 1-60279-261-5 (lib bdg)   LC 2008006749

Kelley, K. C., 1960-—*Continued*

This describes soccer history, rules, styles of play, equipment, and innovators

This "stands out by emphasizing monumental shifts and advances in the events themselves. . . . Concise and occasionally revelatory." Booklist

Includes glossary and bibliographical references

Stewart, Mark, 1960-

Goal!: the fire and fury of soccer's greatest moment; [by] Mark Stewart and Mike Kennedy. Millbrook Press 2010 64p il lib bdg $27.93 *

Grades: 5 6 7 8   **796.334**

1. Soccer

ISBN 978-0-8225-8754-5 (lib bdg); 0-8225-8754-8 (lib bdg)   LC 2009014098

"This well-written book explores the nuances of scoring in the world's most popular sport. A quick history of the game lays the groundwork with details that may be new to even hard-core fans. The second chapter jumps right into the good stuff with descriptions of 10 of the most famous goals. . . . Also included is a rundown of the best male and female scorers from the early twentieth century to the present and weird anomalies and amusing anecdotes from soccer lore." Booklist

796.342 Tennis

Bow, Patricia, 1946-

Tennis science. Crabtree Pub. Co. 2009 32p il (Sports science) lib bdg $26.60; pa $8.95

Grades: 3 4 5 6   **796.342**

1. Tennis

ISBN 978-0-7787-4539-6 (lib bdg); 0-7787-4539-2 (lib bdg); 978-0-7787-4556-3 (pa); 0-7787-4556-2 (pa)
                                                    LC 2008-48874

This book approachs tennis "from a scientific angle, describing some of the physics behind [the] pursuit and how athletes can use this knowledge to improve performance. . . . Fascinating facts . . . are presented in a captivating, lively manner. . . . The layout features colorful text boxes interspersed among photographs." SLJ

Includes glossary and bibliographical references

Ditchfield, Christin

Tennis. Children's Press 2003 47p il (True book) lib bdg $25; pa $6.95

Grades: 2 3 4   **796.342**

1. Tennis

ISBN 0-516-22589-8 (lib bdg); 0-516-26960-7 (pa)
                                                    LC 2001-8504

This examines the history, basic rules, terminology, and major events of the sport of tennis

This book is "just the thing for eager young sports fans. Brief, yet quite thorough. . . . Good-quality photos, most in color, appear on almost every page, and deftly illustrate the text." SLJ

Includes glossary and bibliographical references

Gifford, Clive

Tennis; [by] Clive Gifford. Sea-to-Sea Publications 2009 30p il (Know your sport) lib bdg $27.10

Grades: 5 6 7 8   **796.342**

1. Tennis

ISBN 978-1-59771-153-1 (lib bdg); 1-59771-153-5 (lib bdg)   LC 2008-7322

"Describes the equipment, courts, training, moves, and competitions of tennis. Includes step-by-step descriptions of moves." Publisher's note

Includes glossary

Marsico, Katie, 1980-

Tennis; [by] Katie Marsico and Cecilia Minden. Cherry Lake Pub. 2009 32p il (Real world math: Sports) lib bdg $27.07

Grades: 4 5 6   **796.342**

1. Tennis 2. Arithmetic

ISBN 978-1-60279-248-7 (lib bdg); 1-60279-248-8 (lib bdg)   LC 2008-1179

This book "starts with a short story on the history of [tennis], fundamental rules, and a math challenge in every chapter. . . . [This book] will pique your imagination." Sci Books Films

Includes glossary and bibliographical references

796.352 Golf

Ditchfield, Christin

Golf. Children's Press 2003 47p il (True book) lib bdg $25

Grades: 2 3 4   **796.352**

1. Golf

ISBN 978-0-516-22590-6 (lib bdg); 0-516-22590-1 (lib bdg)   LC 2002-5896

Contents: Tigermania; Years ago; The equipment; The rules; On the course; The professional tour

This examines the history, basic rules, terminology, and major events of the sport of golf

This book is "just the thing for eager young sports fans. Brief, yet quite thorough. . . . Good-quality photos, most in color, appear on almost every page, and deftly illustrate the text." SLJ

Includes glossary and bibliographical references

Kelley, K. C., 1960-

Golf. Cherry Lake Pub. 2009 32p il (Innovation in sports) lib bdg $27.07

Grades: 4 5 6 7   **796.352**

1. Golf

ISBN 978-1-60279-262-3 (lib bdg); 1-60279-262-3 (lib bdg)   LC 2008002045

This describes golf history, rules, balls, and club technology, and innovators

This "stands out by emphasizing monumental shifts and advances in the events themselves. . . . Concise and occasionally revelatory." Booklist

Includes bibliographical references

796.357   Baseball

Bertoletti, John C.

How baseball managers use math; math curriculum consultant: Rhea A. Stewart. Chelsea Clubhouse 2010 32p il (Math in the real world) lib bdg $28

Grades: 4 5 6   **796.357**

1. Baseball 2. Mathematics 3. Vocational guidance

ISBN 978-1-60413-604-3 (lib bdg); 1-60413-604-9 (lib bdg)   LC 2009-16265

"The layout for [this] slim [title] is bright and colorful with a photograph and a 'You Do the Math' problem to solve and large, easy-to-read text on every spread. An answer key is included in the back matter, along with a page detailing the career choices and the educational requirements. . . . [It] includes such topics as how managers rely on player statistics to make decisions and why the pitch count is important to monitor. [This title] would be useful to supplement lessons on mathematics. [It] will also appeal to students wanting to learn more about math as it relates to specific careers." SLJ

Includes glossary and bibliographical references

Bow, James

Baseball science. Crabtree Pub. 2009 32p il (Sports science) lib bdg $26.60; pa $8.95

Grades: 3 4 5 6   **796.357**

1. Baseball

ISBN 978-0-7787-4534-1 (lib bdg); 0-7787-4534-1 (lib bdg); 978-0-7787-4551-8 (pa); 0-7787-4551-1 (pa)   LC 2008-46274

This describes baseball skills and techniques from a scientific point of view.

Includes glossary and bibliographical references

Buckley, James, Jr.

Ultimate guide to baseball. Shoreline Pub. 2010 160p il $30; pa $7.99

Grades: 4 5 6 7   **796.357**

1. Baseball

ISBN   978-0-531-20750-5;   0-531-20750-1; 978-0-531-21021-5 (pa); 0-531-21021-9 (pa)   LC 2009043684

"This is a wide-ranging, brisk overview of the game. Sections briefly skim baseball history, hitting, pitching, defense and baserunning, and the World Series. Each major league team is introduced in a thumbnail sketch. . . . Other topics include baseball slang and nicknames, the 11 ways to get on base, and the author's choices for the best defensive players of all time. . . . Buckley writes with a lightly humorous touch that should appeal to fans and browsers." SLJ

Includes bibliographical references

Coleman, Janet Wyman

Baseball for everyone; stories from the great game; by Janet Wyman Coleman with Elizabeth V. Warren. Abrams 2003 48p il $16.95

Grades: 4 5 6   **796.357**

1. Baseball

ISBN 0-8109-4580-0   LC 2002-155971

An illustrated history of baseball, covering the origins of the game, some of its best-known players, and significant changes in rules and practices throughout the nineteenth and twentieth centuries

"Drawing on The Perfect Game, Warren's adult book and exhibit of the same name at New York's American Folk Art Museum, . . . this elegant volume may well be irresistible to fans of America's favorite pastime. . . . [This offers] lively, informative text . . . enticingly packaged with a plethora of photographs, memorabilia and often astonishing folk art." Publ Wkly

Cook, Sally

Hey batta batta swing! the wild old days of baseball; [by] Sally Cook & James Charlton; illustrated by Ross MacDonald. Margaret K. McElderry Books 2007 48p il $17.99

Grades: 3 4 5 6   **796.357**

1. Baseball

ISBN 978-1-4169-1207-1; 1-4169-1207-X   LC 2006-08132

"The authors present a lively, puckish history of baseball's earliest years, relating what young readers actually want to know. . . . Boldface words in the text identify jargon, most of which is still used today, and definitions stud the page borders. The jaunty tone is flawlessly matched by MacDonald's illustrations, with their wriggling lines and Katzenjammer Kids colors." Booklist

Curlee, Lynn, 1947-

Ballpark; the story of America's baseball fields. Atheneum Books for Young Readers 2005 41p il $17.95 *

Grades: 3 4 5 6   **796.357**

1. Baseball 2. Stadiums

ISBN 0-689-86742-5   LC 2003-23144

This is a "history of baseball parks in words and pictures. The text briefly recaps the history of the game, mentioning star players through the years . . . but emphasizing the game's growth through the evolution of its playing fields." Booklist

This is a "succinct and thoughtful overview. . . . Stylized, full-page acrylic paintings add to the nostalgic tone of the book." SLJ

Doeden, Matt, 1974-

The greatest baseball records; by Matt Doeden. Capstone Press 2009 32p il (Sports records) lib bdg $17.95

Grades: 4 5 6 7 8   **796.357**

1. Baseball

ISBN 978-1-4296-2005-5 (lib bdg); 1-4296-2005-6 (lib bdg)   LC 2008-2030

"Short stories and tables of statistics describe the history and greatest records of Major League Baseball." Publisher's note

This "has enough historical insight and trivia to remain appealing over time. . . . Brief, lively sentences sum up individual feats and set them in context. . . . [This] should appeal to a wide audience." SLJ

Includes glossary and bibliographical references

Kisseloff, Jeff

Who is baseball's greatest pitcher? Cricket Bks. 2003 181p il $15.95

Grades: 5 6 7 8   **796.357**
1. Baseball
ISBN 0-8126-2685-0   LC 2003-1245

Also available: Who is baseball's greatest hitter? (2000)

"A Marcato book"

Contents: So who's the best?; Grover Cleveland Alexander; Mordecai Brown; Steve Carlton; John Clarkson; Roger Clemens; Dizzy Dean; Bob Feller; Whitey Ford; James Galvin; Bob Gibson; Lefty Grove; Carl Hubbell; Randy Johnson; Walter Johnson; Addie Joss; Tim Keefe; Sandy Koufax; Greg Maddux; Juan Marichal; Pedro Martinez; Christy Mathewson; Joe McGinnity; Kid Nichols; Satchel Paige; Jim Palmer; Eddie Plank; Charles Radbourn; Amos Rusie; Nolan Ryan; Tom Seaver; Warren Spahn; Ed Walsh; Cy Young; Who's it gonna be?

Asks the reader to compare the statistics for thirty-three of baseball's greatest starting pitchers and decide who is the best

"Accomplishments and anecdotes are related in an informative and entertaining manner. . . . Anyone who enjoys baseball will be delighted with this information-packed, informal book." SLJ

Includes bibliographical references

Krasner, Steven

Play ball like the hall of famers; the inside scoop from 19 baseball greats; written by Steven Krasner; illustrations by Keith Neely. Peachtree 2005 221p il $14.95

Grades: 5 6 7 8   **796.357**
1. Baseball
ISBN 1-56145-339-0

"Krasner assembles an impressive group of subjects, from Johnny Bench and Gary Carter on catching, to Don Sutton, Phil Niekro, and Tom Seaver on aspects of pitching. . . . Each entry includes anecdotes, a glossary of key terms, and mention of how the advice can be put into action. Black-and-white photos and line drawings appear throughout the succinct and readable interviews, and the perspectives are both detailed and insightful." SLJ

Play ball like the pros; tips for kids from 20 big league stars; written by Steven Krasner. Peachtree Pubs. 2002 181p il pa $12.95 *

Grades: 5 6 7 8   **796.357**
1. Baseball
ISBN 1-56145-261-0   LC 2001-7342

Nearly two dozen professional baseball players, such as Pedro Martinez and Derek Jeter, provide insights into how they prepare for and play the game.

"This title is just the sort of finely tuned analysis of baseball that many young players are looking for. . . . The tips given are detailed and insightful. . . . This is a good reference for young people working to improve their skills." Booklist

Lipsyte, Robert

Heroes of baseball; the men who made it America's favorite game; [by] Robert Lipsyte. Atheneum Books for Young Readers 2006 92p il $19.95 *

Grades: 4 5 6 7   **796.357**
1. Baseball—Biography
ISBN 0-689-86741-7; 978-0-689-86741-5
LC 2005010841

"Using as a focus some of baseball's greats—Big Al Spalding, Babe Ruth, Mickey Mantle, Jackie Robinson, Curt Flood . . . —Lipsyte offers a strong history of the game and its place in American culture. . . . Although much of this material, including the pictures, might be familiar to young readers already absorbed in the game, it is nicely laid out and colorfully formatted. Lipsyte has a clear, vivid style." Booklist

Includes glossary and bibliographical references

McKissack, Patricia C., 1944-

Black diamond; the story of the Negro baseball leagues; [by] Patricia C. McKissack and Fredrick McKissack, Jr. Scholastic 1994 184p il pa $5.99 hardcover o.p. *

Grades: 6 7 8 9   **796.357**
1. Baseball 2. African American athletes
ISBN 0-590-68213-X (pa)   LC 93-22691

Traces the history of baseball in the Negro Leagues and its great heroes, including Monte Irwin, Buck Leonard, and Cool Papa Bell

This is "an engaging account. . . . It includes a chronology, player profiles and wonderful photographs from the Negro Leagues." N Y Times Book Rev

Includes bibliographical references

Nelson, Kadir

We are the ship; the story of Negro League baseball; words and paintings by Kadir Nelson; forward by Hank Aaron. Jump at the Sun 2008 88p il $18.99 *

Grades: 2 3 4   **796.357**
1. Baseball 2. Negro leagues 3. African American athletes
ISBN 978-0-7868-0832-8; 0-7868-0832-2

Awarded the Sibert Medal, 2009

The author "delivers a history of the Negro Leagues in a sumptuous volume that no baseball fan should be without. Using a folksy vernacular, a fictional player gives an insider account of segregated baseball. . . . As illuminating as the text is, Nelson's muscular paintings serve as the true draw. His larger-than-life players have oversized hands, elongated bodies and near-impossible athleticism." Publ Wkly

Smith, Charles R.

Diamond life; baseball sights, sounds, and swings. Orchard Bks. 2004 28p il $15.95

Grades: 2 3 4   **796.357**
1. Baseball
ISBN 0-439-43180-8

"A celebration of America's pastime that . . . utilizes a jazzed layout, multiple fonts, and enhanced photogra-

Smith, Charles R.—*Continued*

phy." Booklist

"Smith captures the colorful language and vivid images of the game. . . . The energetic, playful language begs to be read aloud. Combined with bright colors, bold print in a variety of fonts, and exceptional photography, this book is a winner." SLJ

Stewart, Mark, 1960-

Long ball; the legend and lore of the home run; [by] Mark Stewart and Mike Kennedy. Millbrook Press 2006 64p il lib bdg $22.60

Grades: 4 5 6 7   **796.357**

1. Baseball

ISBN 978-0-7613-2779-0 (lib bdg); 0-7613-2779-7 (lib bdg)   LC 2005015041

"Stewart and Kennedy offer an overview of the history and significance of the long ball." SLJ

"The highly readable text is extended by excellent graphics, photographs, and reproductions of baseball cards and magazine covers." Booklist

Includes bibliographical references

Teitelbaum, Michael, 1953-

Baseball; by Michael Teitelbaum. Cherry Lake Pub. 2009 32p il (Innovation in sports) lib bdg $18.95

Grades: 5 6 7 8   **796.357**

1. Baseball

ISBN 978-1-60279-255-5 (lib bdg); 1-60279-255-0 (lib bdg)   LC 2008-2310

This title "traces the many leaps forward in the history of baseball. [It] chronicles innovations that changed the game. . . . Nice-sized color photographs and sidebars . . . accompany the concise and easy-to-follow text." Booklist

Includes glossary and bibliographical references

Weatherford, Carole Boston, 1956-

A Negro league scrapbook; foreword by Buck O'Neil. Boyds Mills Press 2005 48p il $19.95 *

Grades: 4 5 6 7   **796.357**

1. Baseball 2. Negro leagues 3. African American athletes

ISBN 1-59078-091-4   LC 2004-19324

"Weatherford's text covers . . . a summation of the history of the Negro Leagues and sections on the pitchers, hitters, utility men, various teams, and so forth. Each topic is briefly covered on a spread of text with black-and-white photos and full-color realia designed to look like a scrapbook. Topics are introduced with a few lines of verse. . . . The book is especially successful in conveying the significance of the Negro Leagues to the black community, and in detailing the realities of segregation. . . . This title succeeds as a thoughtful introduction." SLJ

Wong, Stephen

Baseball treasures; by Stephen Wong; photographs by Susan Einstein. Collins 2007 58p il $16.99; lib bdg $17.89

Grades: 5 6 7 8   **796.357**

1. Baseball—Collectibles 2. Baseball—History

ISBN 978-0-06-114464-6; 0-06-114464-9; 978-0-06-114473-8 (lib bdg); 0-06-114473-8 (lib bdg)   LC 2006036069

This describes collectibles connected with the history of baseball, including balls, gloves and bats, jerseys, baseball cards, World Series memorabilia, and trophies.

This is "a well-designed, well-illustrated book for kids. . . . The text manages to impart the essential information without becoming bogged down in too much detail." Booklist

796.41   Weight lifting

Knotts, Bob

Weightlifting. Children's Press 2000 47p il (True book) hardcover o.p. pa $6.95

Grades: 2 3 4   **796.41**

1. Weight lifting

ISBN 0-516-21067-X; 0-516-27032-X (pa)   LC 99-15089

Describes the history of the sport of weight lifting, as well as the training, equipment, rules, and techniques involved

Includes bibliographical references

796.42   Track and field

Gifford, Clive

Track and field; [by] Clive Gifford. PowerKids Press 2009 32p il (Personal best) lib bdg $25.25

Grades: 4 5 6 7 8   **796.42**

1. Track athletics

ISBN 978-1-4042-4442-9 (lib bdg); 1-4042-4442-5 (lib bdg)   LC 2007-42984

Contents: What is track and field?; Training and preparation; Sprint start; Sprinting; Relay running; Hurdling; Distance running; Long jump; High jump; Throwing the javelin; Shot putting; Discus throwing; Other events

This guide to track and field "offers well-organized and easy-to-follow instructions, focusing on rules, clothing, specific skills, and competitions. . . . Informative, readable." SLJ

Includes bibliographical references

Track athletics; [by] Clive Gifford. Sea-to-Sea Publications 2009 30p il (Know your sport) lib bdg $27.10

Grades: 5 6 7 8   **796.42**

1. Track athletics

ISBN 978-1-59771-154-8 (lib bdg); 1-59771-154-3 (lib bdg)   LC 2008-7323

Contents: Training for success; In competition; The sprints: 1; The sprints: 2; Relay racing; Hurdles; Middle-distance running; Long-distance running; Marathon and race walking; The big competitions; Selected world records

Gifford, Clive—*Continued*

"Describes the equipment, training, moves, and running events of track competitions. Includes step-by-step descriptions of moves." Publisher's note

Includes glossary

Knotts, Bob

Track and field. Children's Press 2000 47p il (True book) lib bdg $25 paperback o.p.

Grades: 2 3 4   **796.42**

1. Track athletics
ISBN 0-516-21066-1 (lib bdg); 0-516-27031-1 (pa)
LC 99-15088

Describes the history of track competitions, the various events involved, as well as several of the stars in this sport

Includes bibliographical references

Marsico, Katie, 1980-

Running; [by] Katie Marsico and Cecilia Minden. Cherry Lake Pub. 2009 32p il (Real world math: Sports) lib bdg $27.07

Grades: 4 5 6   **796.42**

1. Running 2. Track athletics 3. Arithmetic
ISBN 978-1-60279-249-4 (lib bdg); 1-60279-249-6 (lib bdg)
LC 2008-1167

This book "starts with a short story on the history of [running], fundamental rules, and a math challenge in every chapter. . . . [This book] will pique your imagination." Sci Books Films

Includes glossary and bibliographical references

796.44 Sports gymnastics

Veitch, Catherine

Gymnastics. Heinemann Library 2009 24p il (Sports and my body) lib bdg $21.36; pa $6.49

Grades: 1 2   **796.44**

1. Gymnastics
ISBN 978-1-4329-3454-5 (lib bdg); 1-4329-3454-6 (lib bdg); 978-1-4329-3459-0 (pa); 1-4329-3459-7 (pa)
LC 2009-7084

Readers learn what gymnastics is, how it can help them stay healthy, and how they can do gymnastics safely.

This book relates "activity to health . . . [and] explains that in order to stay healthy, children should get plenty of rest, eat healthy food, and drink plenty of water." SLJ

Includes glossary

796.48 Olympic games

Macy, Sue, 1954-

Swifter, higher, stronger; a photographic history of the Summer Olympics; by Sue Macy; foreword by Bob Costas. updated for the 2008 Summer Olympics. National Geographic 2008 96p il $18.95; lib bdg $27.90 *

Grades: 4 5 6 7   **796.48**

1. Olympic games
ISBN 978-1-4263-0290-9; 1-4263-0290-8; 978-1-4263-0302-9 (lib bdg); 1-4263-0302-5 (lib bdg)
First published 2004

A detailed look at the history of the Olympic Games, from their origins in Ancient Greece, through their rebirth in nineteenth century France, to the present, highlighting the contributions of individuals to the Games' success and popularity.

"While other books on the topic go into more depth on specific sports, athletes, or historical events, none are as enthusiastically broad or as enjoyable to read as this one. And, it's superbly illustrated with colorful, well-chosen, and enticing photographs." SLJ [review of 2004 ed.]

Includes bibliographical references

796.5 Outdoor life

George, Jean Craighead, 1919-

Pocket guide to the outdoors; [by] Jean Craighead George; with Twig C. George . . . [et al.] Dutton Children's Books 2009 138p il pa $9.99 *

Grades: 5 6 7 8   **796.5**

1. Outdoor life 2. Wilderness survival 3. Camping
ISBN 978-0-525-42163-4 (pa); 0-525-42163-7 (pa)

"This survival guide is the book to read before a wilderness adventure. In short, clearly written chapters, it provides practical tips about ways to enjoy nature and includes information about building shelters, starting fires, making a fishing line and cleaning a fish, outdoor cooking, identifying animal tracks and edible and poisonous plants, and the basics of orienteering. Safety is always considered. Drawings and clearly labeled sketches help with identification." SLJ

Includes bibliographical references

Schofield, Jo

Make it wild; 101 things to make and do outdoors; [by] Jo Schofield and Fiona Danks. Frances Lincoln 159p il pa $24.95

Grades: 4 5 6 7 8   **796.5**

1. Outdoor life 2. Nature craft
ISBN 978-0-7112-2885-6; 0-7112-2885-X

"Using the raw materials nature has to offer, the authors offer clear, concise instructions on how to create ephemeral art, outdoor toys, jewelry, sculptures, and dozens of other things using materials like clay, ice, leaves, sand, and wood. The instructions offer good guidance but also encourage children to use their own creativity and

Schofield, Jo—*Continued*

imagination to craft the final product. The projects range in level of difficulty and, depending on the age of the child, can be done individually or in collaboration with siblings, peers, or parents. The authors include safety instructions and recommendations for further resources on outdoor creative exercises. The activities will teach problem solving and commonsense, useful skills; instill a deeper appreciation of nature; and encourage creativity and ingenuity. An excellent choice for any library collection." Booklist

796.52   Walking and exploring by kind of terrain

Jenkins, Steve

The top of the world; climbing Mount Everest. Houghton Mifflin 1999 unp il $16; pa $6.95 *
Grades: 2 3 4   **796.52**
1. Mountaineering 2. Mount Everest (China and Nepal)
ISBN 0-395-94218-7; 0-618-19676-5 (pa)
                     LC 98-42748

"Jenkins' papercut illustrations are extraordinary— feathery light to catch the effect of fog radiating off the mountains, mottled and striated to replicate rocky plateaus, pebbled to look like ice flowers. . . . A very attractive book, with plenty of substance for curious children." Booklist

Includes bibliographical references

Skreslet, Laurie

To the top of Everest; [by] Laurie Skreslet with Elizabeth MacLeod. Kids Can Press 2001 56p il hardcover o.p. pa $9.95
Grades: 4 5 6 7   **796.52**
1. Mountaineering 2. Mount Everest (China and Nepal)
ISBN 1-55074-721-5; 1-55074-814-9 (pa)

This is an account of Skreslet's "1982 trek up Everest when he became one of the first Canadians to make it to the top. Skreslet takes readers through every exciting, excruciating element of the climb. Beautiful color photographs abound." Booklist

Includes glossary

796.54   Camping

Brunelle, Lynn

Camp out! the ultimate kids' guide, from the backyard to the backwoods; [by] Lynn Brunelle; illustrations by Brian Biggs; technical illustrations by Elara Tanguy. Workman Pub. 2007 376p il pa $11.95
Grades: 5 6 7 8   **796.54**
1. Camping
ISBN 978-0-7611-4122-8 (pa); 0-7611-4122-7 (pa)
                 LC 2007297580

"This book is stuffed with information about gear, packing lists, where to go, what to do while you're camping, and what to do when you get back. There are 174 games, skills, projects, recipes, songs, experiments, crafts, and more to make, learn, play, and do outdoors. . . . Line drawings give a clear picture of the instructions they represent. The book is well organized. . . . Written on a kid's level from a kid's-eye view, this volume is perfect for would-be campers." SLJ

796.6   Cycling and related activities

Bow, James

Cycling science. Crabtree Pub. Co. 2009 32p il (Sports science) lib bdg $26.60; pa $8.95
Grades: 4 5 6   **796.6**
1. Cycling
ISBN 978-0-7787-4535-8 (lib bdg); 0-77874535-X (lib bdg); 978-0-7787-4552-5 (pa); 0-7787-4552-X (pa)
                 LC 2008-46275

This book approachs cycling "from a scientific angle, describing some of the physics behind [the] pursuit and how athletes can use this knowledge to improve performance. . . . Fascinating facts . . . are presented in a captivating, lively manner. . . . The layout features colorful text boxes interspersed among photographs." SLJ

Includes glossary and bibliographical references

Buckley, Annie, 1968-

Be a better biker; by Annie Buckley. Child's World 2007 32p il (Girls rock!) lib bdg $24.21
Grades: 5 6 7 8   **796.6**
1. Cycling 2. Bicycles
ISBN 1-59296-741-8   LC 2006001640

This "gives the history of bicycles and describes the different types available and what they are used for. A section on safety covers helmets, bike maintenance, and basic rules of the road. . . . [The book has] clear color photos. . . . [This] realistic [title is] well written and [provides] excellent information." SLJ

Includes bibliographical references

Guillain, Charlotte

Cycling. Heinemann Library 2009 24p il (Sports and my body) lib bdg $21.36; pa $6.49
Grades: 1 2   **796.6**
1. Cycling
ISBN 978-1-4329-3457-6 (lib bdg); 1-4329-3457-0 (lib bdg); 978-1-4329-3462-0 (pa); 1-4329-3462-7 (pa)
                 LC 2009-7085

Readers learn what cycling is, how it can help them stay healthy, and how they can cycle safely.

This book relates "activity to health . . . [and] explains that in order to stay healthy, children should get plenty of rest, eat healthy food, and drink plenty of water." SLJ

Includes glossary

Robinson, Laura

Cyclist bikelist; a book for every rider; illustrated by Ramón K. Pérez. Tundra Books 2010 55p il pa $17.95 *

Grades: 4 5 6 7   **796.6**

1. Cycling 2. Bicycles

ISBN 978-0-88776-784-5; 0-88776-784-2

The author "covers a broad range of topics, from choosing and caring for a bike to differences in tires, how gear ratios work, and even proper dress and nutrition. She also provides a quick overview of the bicycle's history and inspiring sketches of several renowned racers. . . . Supplemented by photos of different types of bikes, Pérez's bright, cartoon-style pictures add both humor and . . . sharply drawn details. A first-rate guide." Booklist

Schoenherr, Alicia

Mountain biking; by Alicia and Rusty Schoenherr. Child's World 2005 32p il (Kids' guides) lib bdg $24.21

Grades: 4 5 6   **796.6**

1. Mountain biking

ISBN 1-59296-209-2   LC 2003-27371

Contents: From street to trail; The klunkers; Gearing up to ride; Mountain biking in action; Superstars of the mountains

This "opens with an explanation of the sport and gives reasons why people enjoy it. The four chapters that follow cover background and development, equipment, technique, and stars and competitions. The excellent color photos are clear and exciting." SLJ

Includes bibliographical references

796.72   Automobile racing

Arroyo, Sheri L.

How race car drivers use math; math curriculum consultant: Rhea A. Stewart. Chelsea Clubhouse 2010 32p il (Math in the real world) lib bdg $28

Grades: 4 5 6   **796.72**

1. Automobile racing 2. Mathematics 3. Vocational guidance

ISBN 978-1-60413-609-8 (lib bdg); 1-60413-609-X (lib bdg)   LC 2009-21476

"The layout for [this slim [title] is bright and colorful with a photograph and a 'You Do the Math' problem to solve and large, easy-to-read text on every spread. An answer key is included in the back matter, along with a page detailing the career choices and the educational requirements. . . . In [this title], readers learn about qualifying times, track designs, and tracking fuel. . . . [This title] would be useful to supplement lessons on mathematics. [It] will also appeal to students wanting to learn more about math as it relates to specific careers." SLJ

Includes glossary and bibliographical references

Caldwell, Dave

Speed show; how NASCAR won the heart of America. Kingfisher 2006 126p il $16.95 *

Grades: 5 6 7 8   **796.72**

1. National Association for Stock Car Auto Racing 2. Automobile racing

ISBN 978-0-7534-6011-5; 0-7534-6011-4

"A New York Times book"

"Caldwell, a *New York Times* sports correspondent, gives a furiously fast but impressively thorough rundown on the National Association for Stock Auto Racing, better known as NASCAR. With his firsthand account, the history feels both personal and like fact-fueled reportage." Booklist

Includes bibliographical references

Eagen, Rachel, 1979-

NASCAR; written by Rachel Eagen. Crabtree Pub. Co. 2007 32p il (Automania!) lib bdg $25.20; pa $8.95

Grades: 4 5 6   **796.72**

1. National Association for Stock Car Auto Racing 2. Automobile racing

ISBN 978-0-7787-3007-1 (lib bdg); 0-7787-3007-7 (lib bdg); 978-0-7787-3029-3 (pa); 0-7787-3029-8 (pa)

LC 2006012406

"Eagen has done an excellent job explaining the National Association of Stock Car Automobile Racing—the history, the modification of the cars, the drivers, and the competitions—while conveying a sense of the magnitude of the sport's current fan base. Her lucid, interesting text gets a lift from plenty of high-energy photos." Booklist

Egan, Erin

Hottest race cars; by Erin Egan. Enslow Publishers 2007 c2008 48p il (Wild wheels!) $17.95 *

Grades: 4 5 6   **796.72**

1. Automobile racing

ISBN 978-0-7660-2871-5; 0-7660-2871-2

LC 2007007427

"Along with presenting a bit of racing's history, Egan unravels confusion about the three kinds of open-wheel competitions (Formula One, Indy, and Champ). Then she takes a quick but revealing look at major car components. . . . Information on driver's gear, race strategy, and more, along with a sprinkling of anecdotes . . . fill the rest of the pages, which are loaded with color photos." Booklist

Includes glossary and bibliographical references

Gigliotti, Jim

Hottest dragsters and funny cars; by Jim Gigliotti. Enslow Publishers 2008 47p il (Wild wheels!) lib bdg $23.93

Grades: 4 5 6 7   **796.72**

1. Automobile racing

ISBN 978-0-7660-2870-8 (lib bdg); 0-7660-2870-4 (lib bdg)   LC 2007007424

"Learn about drag racing, funny cars, and experience what it feels like to spend the day at a drag race." Publisher's note

Includes glossary and bibliographical references

Kelley, K. C., 1960-
Hottest NASCAR machines; by K. C. Kelley. Enslow Publishers 2008 48p il (Wild wheels!) lib bdg $23.93

Grades: 4 5 6 7   **796.72**
1. National Association for Stock Car Auto Racing 2. Automobile racing
ISBN 978-0-7660-2869-2 (lib bdg); 0-7660-2869-0 (lib bdg)   LC 2007007426
"Experience the thrill of a NASCAR race, and learn about the cars, personalities, and races associated with this sport." Publisher's note

Includes glossary and bibliographical references

796.8   Combat sports

Ditchfield, Christin
Wrestling. Children's Press 2000 47p il (True book) lib bdg $25 paperback o.p.

Grades: 2 3 4   **796.8**
1. Wrestling
ISBN 0-516-21611-2 (lib bdg); 0-516-27033-8 (pa)
LC 99-28191
Describes the history, rules, and styles of wrestling
Includes bibliographical references

Gifford, Clive
Martial arts. Marshall Cavendish Benchmark 2009 30p il (Tell me about sports) $19.95

Grades: 3 4 5   **796.8**
1. Martial arts
ISBN 978-0-7614-4457-2; 0-7614-4457-2
LC 2008-55993
"An introduction to martial arts, including techniques, rules, and the training regimen of professional athletes in the sport." Publisher's note
Includes glossary and bibliographical references

Lewin, Ted, 1935-
At Gleason's gym. Roaring Brook Press 2007 unp il $17.95 *

Grades: 2 3 4 5   **796.8**
1. Gleason's Gyms 2. Boxing
ISBN 978-1-59643-231-4; 1-59643-231-4
LC 2006-32176
"A Neal Porter book."
"Gleason's gym in Brooklyn is where 'the world works out.' . . . Nine-year-old Sugar Boy Younan, National Silver Gloves Champion, 110-pound division, goes there to shadow box and spar with partners. This glorious tribute to Gleason's . . . packs a punch of its own, with a text that is both moving and informative and with vibrant artwork so realistic that readers can practically smell the sweat." Booklist

Mason, Paul, 1967-
Judo; [by] Paul Mason. Sea-to-Sea Publications 2009 30p il (Know your sport) lib bdg $27.10

Grades: 5 6 7 8   **796.8**
1. Judo
ISBN 978-1-59771-151-7 (lib bdg); 1-59771-151-9 (lib bdg)   LC 2008-7318

"Describes the equipment, training, moves, and competitions of judo. Includes step-by-step descriptions of moves." Publisher's note
"Concise, readable. . . . Informative and enjoyable." SLJ
Includes glossary

Rielly, Robin L.
Karate for kids; [by] Robin Rielly. Tuttle Pub. 2004 48p il $11.95 *

Grades: 4 5 6 7   **796.8**
1. Karate
ISBN 0-8048-3534-9   LC 2003-27610
Contents: What is karate?; The uniform; The dojo; The class; Warming up; Practicing karate; Advancing in karate; Is karate good for me?
"Rielly begins with a history of karate before going on to information about the uniform, including the meaning of the belt colors, the rules and etiquette of the dojo, and the interaction between student and teacher. The actual stances are clearly portrayed in watercolor-and-ink artwork that features both boys and girls in a number of stances and practicing thrusts and kicks. The book ends with advice for advancing in karate." Booklist

796.9   Ice and snow sports

Woods, Bob
Snowboarding; by Bob Woods. Child's World 2005 32p il (Kids' guides) lib bdg $24.21

Grades: 4 5 6   **796.9**
1. Snowboarding
ISBN 1-59296-211-4   LC 2003-27365
Contents: Get on board; Snowboarding's cold, hard history; Gear up and go; Hit the slippery slopes; Snowboarding stars
This "opens with an explanation of the sport and gives reasons why people enjoy it. The four chapters that follow cover background and development, equipment, technique, and stars and competitions. The excellent color photos are clear and exciting." SLJ
Includes bibliographical references

796.91   Ice skating

Marsico, Katie, 1980-
Speed skating; [by] Katie Marsico and Cecilia Minden. Cherry Lake Pub. 2009 32p il (Real world math: Sports) lib bdg $27.07

Grades: 4 5 6   **796.91**
1. Ice skating 2. Arithmetic
ISBN 978-1-60279-250-0 (lib bdg); 1-60279-250-X (lib bdg)   LC 2008-806
This book "starts with a short story on the history of [speed skating], fundamental rules, and a math challenge in every chapter. . . . [This book] will pique your imagination." Sci Books Films

Thomas, Keltie

How figure skating works; illustrated by Stephen MacEachern. OwlKids 2009 64p il $22.95; pa $10.95

Grades: 3 4 5 6   **796.91**

1. Ice skating

ISBN 978-1-897349-58-8; 1-897349-58-0; 978-1-897349-59-5 (pa); 1-897349-59-9 (pa)

"This lively overview features clear, well-written explanations of the technical elements of figure skating and anecdotes from skating history. The readable text is supplemented with eye-catching photos, cartoon illustrations, and simple diagrams and charts." SLJ

Includes glossary

796.962 Ice hockey

Johnstone, Robb

Hockey. rev ed. Weigl Publishers 2009 24p il (In the zone) $24.45; pa $8.95

Grades: 4 5 6 7   **796.962**

1. Hockey

ISBN 978-1-6059-6130-9; 1-6059-6130-2; 978-1-6059-6131-6 (pa); 1-6059-6131-0 (pa)

LC 2009005607

First published 2001

"Colorful, informative. . . . For those just showing an interest in the bone-crushing sport, [this is] an excellent place to get their bearings. Using short, mostly two-page chapters, Johnstone explains the genesis of the sport, the gear needed, the rules, the positions, and the leagues, before concluding with biographies of eight legendary NHL players." Booklist

McKinley, Michael, 1961-

Ice time; the story of hockey. Tundra Books 2006 80p il $18.95

Grades: 5 6 7 8   **796.962**

1. Hockey

ISBN 978-0-88776-762-3; 0-88776-762-1

"This straightforward history of hockey emphasizes the professional game and Canadian players. . . . Hockey enthusiasts will find this a welcome arrival." Booklist

796.98 Winter Olympic games

Macy, Sue, 1954-

Freeze frame; a photographic history of the Winter Olympics. National Geographic 2006 96p il map $18.95 *

Grades: 5 6 7 8 9 10   **796.98**

1. Olympic games 2. Winter sports

ISBN 0-7922-7887-9; 978-0-7922-7887-0

Highlights in the history of the Winter Olympics from their inception in 1924 to today, including profiles of Olympic athletes and information on the lesser-known winter sports. Also includes an Olympic almanac with information about each Olympiad.

This book "has spectacular photographs and clear, captivating prose." SLJ

Includes bibliographical references

797.1 Boating

Bass, Scott

Kayaking; by Scott Bass. Child's World 2005 32p il (Kids' guides) lib bdg $24.21

Grades: 4 5 6   **797.1**

1. Kayaks and kayaking

ISBN 1-59296-208-4   LC 2003-27372

Contents: The freedom of kayaking; Climb in a kayak; Gear and events; Kayaks in action; Kayaking stars

This "opens with an explanation of the sport and gives reasons why people enjoy it. The four chapters that follow cover background and development, equipment, technique, and stars and competitions. The excellent color photos are clear and exciting." SLJ

Includes bibliographical references

Wurdinger, Scott D.

Kayaking; by Scott Wurdinger and Leslie Rapparlie. Creative Education 2006 48p il (Adventure sports) $21.95

Grades: 5 6 7 8   **797.1**

1. Kayaks and kayaking

ISBN 978-1-58341-397-5   LC 2005051057

"Strong, full-page color photographs illustrate this overview of kayaking. . . . Tracing the use of kayaks back thousands of years, the authors touch on the history of the boats before moving on to contemporary usage for sports and recreation. . . . The exciting views . . . will instantly draw browsers and serious readers alike." Booklist

Includes bibliographical references

797.2 Swimming and diving

Arroyo, Sheri L.

How deep sea divers use math; math curriculum consultant: Rhea A. Stewart. Chelsea Clubhouse 2010 32p il (Math in the real world) lib bdg $28

Grades: 4 5 6   **797.2**

1. Scuba diving 2. Mathematics 3. Vocational guidance

ISBN 978-1-60413-611-1 (lib bdg); 1-60413-611-1 (lib bdg)   LC 2009-18413

"The layout for [this] slim [title] is bright and colorful with a photograph and a 'You Do the Math' problem to solve and large, easy-to-read text on every spread. An answer key is included in the back matter, along with a page detailing the career choices and the educational requirements. . . . [It] discusses how divers use math to determine how much air they will need in their tanks and use grids to map underwater shipwrecks. The mathematical topics covered include measurement, estimation, data analysis, and problem solving. . . . [This title] would be useful to supplement lessons on mathematics. [It] will also appeal to students wanting to learn more about math as it relates to specific careers." SLJ

Includes glossary and bibliographical references

Boudreau, Helene
Swimming science. Crabtree Pub. Co. 2009 32p
il (Sports science) lib bdg $26.60; pa $8.95
Grades: 3 4 5 6   **797.2**
1. Swimming
ISBN 978-0-7787-4538-9 (lib bdg); 0-7787-4538-4 (lib
bdg); 978-0-7787-4555-6 (pa); 0-7787-4555-4 (pa)
LC 2008-48870
This book approachs swimming "from a scientific angle, describing some of the physics behind [the] pursuit
and how athletes can use this knowledge to improve performance. . . . Fascinating facts . . . [such as] a discussion of the swimmer who covered 3,270 miles down the
Amazon River . . . are presented in a captivating, lively
manner. . . . The layout features colorful text boxes interspersed among photographs." SLJ
Includes glossary and bibliographical references

Gifford, Clive
Swimming; [by] Clive Gifford. PowerKids Press
2009 32p il (Personal best) lib bdg $25.25
Grades: 4 5 6 7 8   **797.2**
1. Swimming
ISBN 978-1-4042-4443-6 (lib bdg); 1-4042-4443-3 (lib
bdg)   LC 2007-43003
Contents: What is swimming?; Training and equipment; Fast starts; Front crawl; More front crawl; Breaststroke; More breaststroke; Backstroke; More backstroke;
Butterfly; More butterfly; Racing turns; Relays and med-
leys
This guide to swimming "offers well-organized and
easy-to-follow instructions, focusing on rules, clothing,
specific skills, and competitions. . . . Informative, readable." SLJ

Guillain, Charlotte
Swimming. Heinemann Library 2009 24p il
(Sports and my body) lib bdg $21.36; pa $6.49
Grades: 1 2   **797.2**
1. Swimming
ISBN 978-1-4329-3455-2 (lib bdg); 1-4329-3455-4 (lib
bdg); 978-1-4329-3460-6 (pa); 1-4329-3460-0 (pa)
LC 2009-7083
Learn what swimming is, how it can help them stay
healthy, and how they can swim safely.
This book relates "activity to health . . . [and] ex-
plains that in order to stay healthy, children should get
plenty of rest, eat healthy food, and drink plenty of wa-
ter." SLJ
Includes glossary and bibliographical references

Lourie, Peter
First dive to shark dive. Boyds Mills Press 2006
48p il $17.95   **797.2**
1. Scuba diving 2. Bahamas
ISBN 1-59078-068-X   LC 2005-24987
"In this photo-essay, a father and his 12-year-old
daughter, Suzanna, fly to Andros, in the Bahamas, so
Suzanna can learn to scuba dive. During an intense seven
days, she becomes certified and makes four dives. The
narrative . . . also covers information about the island
. . . the ocean and its inhabitants . . . and the old Andros traditions. . . . Stunning color photographs . . . reveal why Suzanna wanted to be certified to dive."
Booklist

Minden, Cecilia, 1949-
Swimming; [by] Cecilia Minden and Katie
Marsico. Cherry Lake Pub. 2009 32p il (Real
world math: Sports) lib bdg $27.07
Grades: 4 5 6   **797.2**
1. Swimming 2. Arithmetic
ISBN 978-1-60279-246-3 (lib bdg); 1-60279-246-1 (lib
bdg)   LC 2008-1198
This book "starts with a short story on the history of
[swimming], fundamental rules, and a math challenge in
every chapter. . . . [This book] will pique your imagination." Sci Books Films
Includes glossary and bibliographical references

Timblin, Stephen
Swimming. Cherry Lake Pub. 2009 32p il
(Innovation in sports) lib bdg $27.07
Grades: 4 5 6 7   **797.2**
1. Swimming
ISBN 978-1-60279-258-6 (lib bdg); 1-60279-258-5 (lib
bdg)   LC 2008002046
This describes swimming history, rules, equipment,
training, and swimming stars
This "stands out by emphasizing monumental shifts
and advances in the events themselves. . . . Concise and
occasionally revelatory." Booklist
Includes glossary and bibliographical references

798.2 Horsemanship

Hayden, Kate
Horse show; written by Kate Hayden. DK Pub.
2001 32p il $12.95; pa $3.95
Grades: 1 2 3   **798.2**
1. Horsemanship
ISBN 0-7894-7372-0; 0-7894-7371-2 (pa)
LC 00-56975
"Dorling Kindersley readers"
"As three children prepare for a show, readers are introduced to the horses at White Lane Farm, the preparations, and the basic events. . . . Ample white space and
compelling color photographs of young equestrians competing in English-style riding are appealing and encouraging." SLJ

Kimball, Cheryl
Horse show handbook for kids; everything a
young rider needs to know to prepare, train, and
compete in English or Western events: plus
getting-ready checklists and show diary pages; [by]
Cheryl Kimball. Storey Pub. 2004 151p il $26.95;
pa $16.95 *
Grades: 4 5 6 7   **798.2**
1. Horsemanship
ISBN 1-58017-573-2; 1-58017-501-5 (pa)
LC 2003-21732

Kimball, Cheryl—*Continued*

Paperback edition has title: Horse showing for kids

Contents: Types of shows; Types of classes; Show personnel; Choosing the right horse; Conditioning and training; Trailering; Grooming; Attire and equipment (you & your horse); Planning for a show; On the big day; After the show; Moving up the competitive ladder

"For kids who have ever wondered if there is a certain color that complements their horse more than another, what last-minute checks they need to do before entering a show ring, how to dress for success, and much more, this handbook is invaluable. Presenting a wealth of information in a well-organized and enthusiastic manner, the author also addresses the more serious issues such as safety and good sportsmanship. The format is appealing, with lots of colorful photos." SLJ

798.4 Horse racing

McCarthy, Meghan

Seabiscuit; the wonder horse. Simon & Schuster Books for Young Readers 2008 unp il $15.99 *

Grades: K 1 2 3   **798.4**

1. Seabiscuit (Race horse) 2. Horse racing

ISBN 978-1-4169-3360-1; 1-4169-3360-3

LC 2008-06729

"A Paula Wiseman book"

"The book covers Seabiscuit's transformation from scruffy loser to—well, scruffy winner, his loyal team of owner, trainer, and jockey, and his appeal to the economically pinched crowds; the saga here culminates in Seabiscuit's famous match with War Admiral. . . . The account is simplified for the youngest audiences, and they'll get the high points of the story . . . without getting lost in detail. . . . The cartooning is genuinely comic at times; the acrylic paintings are subtly toned, though, with gray touches muting the colors slightly." Bull Cent Child Books

Tate, Nikki, 1962-

Behind the scenes: the racehorse. Fitzhenry & Whiteside 2008 72p il $22.95; pa $18.95

Grades: 5 6 7 8   **798.4**

1. Horse racing

ISBN 978-1-55455-018-0; 1-55455-018-1; 978-1-55455-032-6 (pa); 1-55455-032-7 (pa)

"A short history of horse racing opens this attractive and informative book. Tate discusses the breeding, training, and care of the horses but devotes plenty of space to the people who are involved in the sport. . . . The many color photos . . . are quite clear and well matched to the text." Booklist

798.8 Dog racing

Miller, Debbie S.

The great serum race; blazing the Iditarod Trail; illustrations by Jon van Zyle. Walker & Co. 2002 unp il map hardcover o.p. pa $8.95

Grades: 3 4 5   **798.8**

1. Dogs 2. Alaska 3. Iditarod Trail Sled Dog Race, Alaska

ISBN 0-8027-8811-4; 0-8027-8812-2 (lib bdg); 0-8027-7723-2 (pa)   LC 2001-56777

The story of the heroic role played by sled dogs, including the Siberian husky Togo, in the delivery of antitoxin serum to those stricken with diphtheria in 1925 Nome. Includes historical notes about the event as well as about the Iditarod Sled Dog Race which commemorates it

"Zyle, official artist of the Iditarod and a musher himself, has created vivid, full-spread paintings to bring the story to life. . . . This is an excellent account told with lots of detail and drama." SLJ

Includes bibliographical references

Wood, Ted, 1965-

Iditarod dream; Dusty and his sled dogs compete in Alaska's Jr. Iditarod. Walker & Co. 1996 48p il map hardcover o.p. pa $8.95

Grades: 4 5 6 7   **798.8**

1. Sled dog racing

ISBN 0-8027-8406-2; 0-8027-7535-7 (pa)

LC 95-31084

This "photo essay follows 15-year-old Dusty Whittemore of Cantwell, AK, through the 1995 Jr. Iditarod Sled Dog Race—158 miles from Lake Lucille to Yentna and back." SLJ

"Clear, close-up color photographs portray every stage of the event and offer interesting information about the difficulties and hazards of this two-day competition." Booklist

800 LITERATURE, RHETORIC & CRITICISM

808 Rhetoric

Children's writer's & illustrator's market; edited by Alice Pope. Writer's Digest Books il $29.99

Grades: Adult Professional   **808**

1. Authorship—Handbooks, manuals, etc. 2. Publishers and publishing

ISSN 0897-9790

Annual. First published 1998

This reference includes listings of children's book publishers, magazines, agents, art reps, contests, clubs, conferences, awards, and grants with contact information, along with articles and interviews on a variety of subjects relating to children's writing, illustrating, and publishing

Includes bibliographical references

Christelow, Eileen, 1943-
What do authors do? Clarion Bks. 1995 32p il
hardcover o.p. pa $5.95 *
Grades: 1 2 3   **808**
1. Authorship 2. Authors 3. Illustrators 4. Publishers
and publishing
ISBN 0-395-71124-X; 0-395-86621-9 (pa)
LC 94-19725
Companion volume to What do illustrators do?
The author "follows two next-door neighbors as they
independently develop stories about their pets—the
scruffy sheepdog, Rufus; and Max, his energetic feline
adversary. Dialogue in cartoon balloons and brief text
describe the writing process and the mechanics of publishing." SLJ
"Christelow packs a great deal of humor as well as information into her attractive pages. Best of all, she infuses the whole with a sense of the zest and love that
writers feel for their work." Booklist

Fletcher, Ralph, 1953-
How to write your life story; [by] Ralph
Fletcher. Collins 2007 102p $15.99; pa $5.99 *
Grades: 5 6 7 8   **808**
1. Authorship 2. Autobiography—Authorship
ISBN 978-0-06-050770-1; 978-0-06-050769-5 (pa)
LC 2007010990
A guide to help write an autobiography
"Fletcher gives readers and educators many practical
and supportive tips. . . . Interspersed within the text are
interviews with Jack Gantos, Kathi Appelt, and Jerry
Spinelli, along with passages from the author's own
memoir." SLJ

Leedy, Loreen, 1959-
Look at my book; how kids can write &
illustrate terrific books; written and illustrated by
Loreen Leedy. Holiday House 2004 32p il $16.95
*
Grades: K 1 2 3   **808**
1. Authorship 2. Illustration of books 3. Bookbinding
ISBN 0-8234-1590-2   LC 2003-41713
Provides ideas and simple directions for writing, illustrating, designing, and binding books.
"Following the writing process fairly closely . . . [the
author] takes readers through a step-by-step formula that
almost guarantees a successful product. . . . Lively, colorful illustrations expand and interpret the text." SLJ

Mack, James, 1978-
Journals and blogging; [by] Jim Mack. Raintree
2009 32p il (Culture in action) $28.21; pa $7.99
Grades: 5 6 7 8   **808**
1. Diaries 2. Weblogs
ISBN   978-1-4109-3406-2;   1-4109-3406-3;
978-1-4109-3423-9 (pa); 1-4109-3423-3 (pa)
LC 2009000490
This "encourages readers to write as a way to express
their feelings. It describes different types of journals and
blogs. A page on Internet safety and the danger of
downloading material encourages adult supervision. . . .
Well organized and with bright, colorful photography,

[this] introductory [title gives] readers good basic knowledge." SLJ
Includes glossary and bibliographical references

Miles, Liz
Writing a screenplay. Raintree 2009 32p il
(Culture in action) $28.21; pa $7.99
Grades: 5 6 7 8   **808**
1. Drama—Technique
ISBN   978-1-4109-3407-9;   1-4109-3407-1;
978-1-4109-3424-6 (pa); 1-4109-3424-1 (pa)
This covers writing for "film and television. Plot, location, characters, dialogue, and mood are a few of the
components discussed. . . . Well organized and with
bright, colorful photography, [this] introductory [title
gives] readers good basic knowledge." SLJ
Includes glossary and bibliographical references

Rau, Dana Meachen, 1971-
Ace your creative writing project. Enslow
Elementary 2009 48p il (Ace it! information
literacy) lib bdg $23.93
Grades: 3 4 5   **808**
1. Creative writing
ISBN 978-0-7660-3395-5 (lib bdg); 0-7660-3395-3 (lib
bdg)   LC 2008024888
This describes where writers get their ideas, your sto-
ry's characters and setting, writing, revising, and present-
ing your writing
Includes bibliographical references

Ace your writing assignment. Enslow
Elementary 2009 48p il (Ace it! information
literacy) lib bdg $23.93
Grades: 3 4 5   **808**
1. English language—Composition and exercises
ISBN 978-0-7660-3394-8 (lib bdg); 0-7660-3394-5 (lib
bdg)   LC 2008024887
This describes how to make writing better and more
interesting
Includes bibliographical references

Rosinsky, Natalie M. (Natalie Myra)
Write your own biography; by Natalie M.
Rosinsky. Compass Point Books 2008 64p il
(Write your own) lib bdg $31.93
Grades: 5 6 7 8   **808**
1. Biography—Authorship
ISBN 978-0-7565-3366-3 (lib bdg); 0-7565-3366-X
(lib bdg)   LC 2007011471
"Rosinsky adroitly leads readers through the challeng-
ing process of researching and writing a biography.
Chapters include helpful suggestions, excerpts from pub-
lished works, and writing exercises. Full-color photos,
charts, and graphics break up the text." SLJ
Includes glossary and bibliographical references

Trueit, Trudi Strain

Keeping a journal; [by] Trudi Strain Trueit. F. Watts 2004 80p (Life balance) $20.50; pa $6.95

Grades: 5 6 7 8 **808**

1. Diaries 2. Authorship

ISBN 0-531-12262-X; 0-531-15581-1 (pa)

LC 2003-25290

Contents: Navigating the journey; Why journal?; Time travel; Getting started; Write now! A 30-day journal

"Trueit features examples . . . to spark the imaginations of young people eager to express their unique views. Tips on how to begin, exercises designed to help overcome writer's block, and a 30-day calendar of creative ideas to get started are included. . . . The enthusiastic tone, inspirational examples, and writing prompts will help even those reluctant to express themselves to pick up a pen or pencil." SLJ

Includes bibliographical references

808.1   Rhetoric of poetry

Poetry from A to Z; a guide for young writers; compiled by Paul B. Janeczko; illustrated by Cathy Bobak. Bradbury Press 1994 131p il $16.95

Grades: 5 6 7 8 9 10 **808.1**

1. Poetics 2. American poetry—Collections

ISBN 0-02-747672-3 LC 94-10528

"In his guide, Janeczko gives many examples and ideas to get young writers started writing poetry. The book is organized alphabetically with seventy-two poems on almost any topic you could imagine. In addition, fourteen exercises labeled 'Try This' explain how to write different types of poems and help a young writer get started." Voice Youth Advocates

Includes bibliographical references

Prelutsky, Jack

Pizza, pigs, and poetry; how to write a poem. Greenwillow Books 2008 191p il $16.99; pa $5.99 *

Grades: 4 5 6 **808.1**

1. Poetics

ISBN 978-0-06-143449-5; 0-06-143449-3; 978-0-06-143448-8 (pa); 0-06-143448-5 (pa)

LC 2007-36738

"Along with easy-to-follow tips for creating verse, haiku, and concrete poetry, the reigning Children's Poet Laureate offers insights into his own thought processes, . . . glimpses of his childhood, and personal anecdotes. . . . Prelutsky tucks in more than a dozen examples of his own work, plus 10 two-and-part-of-a-third line 'poem starts.'" Booklist

Wolf, Allan

Immersed in verse; an informative, slightly irreverent & totally tremendous guide to living the poet's life; [by] Allan Wolf; illustrated by Tuesday Mourning. Lark Books 2006 112p il $14.95

Grades: 5 6 7 8 **808.1**

1. Poetics

ISBN 1-57990-628-1 LC 2005024825

Contains advice, ideas, writing activities, and encouragement from a working poet for aspiring poets. Includes poems by a variety of poets from the unknown to the famous, including Langston Hughes, E.E. Cummings, Eve Merriam, and more

"This how-to guide—chock-full of examples—is sure to inspire and nurture young poets. The information is intensive without being overwhelming, wise without being didactic. Wolf's love of language is evident throughout." SLJ

Includes glossary and bibliographical references

808.3   Rhetoric of fiction

Bullard, Lisa, 1961-

You can write a story! a story-writing recipe for kids; by Lisa Bullard; illustrated by Deborah Haley Melmon. Two-Can 2007 47p il $16.95

Grades: 2 3 4 **808.3**

1. Fiction—Technique 2. Authorship 3. Creative writing

ISBN 978-1-58728-587-5; 1-58728-587-8

LC 2006016771

"Bullard takes a clever approach to teaching children the basic steps in story composition by treating the process as a cooking exercise. She begins with the basic ingredients of character, setting, and action, and then takes readers through the various ways they can add flavorings to their stories, including spicy settings, tempting titles, and the all-important taste test (revising). . . . The clear, engaging text speaks directly to a child. . . . Melmon's cartoon illustrations are bright, amusing, and strategically placed to add interest." Booklist

Includes bibliographical references

Hershenhorn, Esther, 1945-

S is for story; a writer's alphabet; written by Esther Hershenhorn; illustrated by Zachary Pullen. Sleeping Bear Press 2009 unp il $17.95; lib bdg $7.95

Grades: 3 4 5 6 **808.3**

1. Fiction—Technique 2. Authorship 3. Alphabet

ISBN 978-1-58536-439-8; 1-58536-439-8; 978-1-58536-511-1 (lib bdg); 1-58536-511-4 (lib bdg)

LC 2009005433

"This engaging, instructive introduction to writing stands out. The concepts paired with each letter cover elements of story (*plot, characters*); technique (*revision, journaling*); and basic practices for fostering creativity (*observe*). Short poems; clear, enthusiastic explanations; tips; and quotes from well-known children's authors appear on each page." Booklist

Levine, Gail Carson, 1947-

Writing magic; creating stories that fly. Collins 2006 167p $16.99; pa $5.99 *

Grades: 5 6 7 8 **808.3**

1. Fiction—Technique 2. Authorship 3. Creative writing

ISBN 978-0-06-051961-2; 0-06-051969-4; 978-0-06-051960-5 (pa); 0-06-051960-6 (pa)

LC 2006-00481

Levine, Gail Carson, 1947- —*Continued*

"Levine, best known for *Ella Enchanted* (1997), offers middle-graders ideas about making their own writing take flight. . . . Among the topics she covers are shaping character, beginnings and endings, revising, and finding ideas. . . . Each chapter concludes with writing exercises. . . . A terrific item to have on hand for writing groups or for individual young writers who want to improve." Booklist

Mazer, Anne, 1953-

Spilling ink; a young writer's handbook; by Anne Mazer and Ellen Potter; illustrated by Matt Phelan. Flash Point 2010 275p il $17.99; pa $9.99

Grades: 5 6 7 8   **808.3**

1. Fiction—Technique 2. Authorship 3. Creative writing

ISBN 978-1-59643-514-8; 1-59643-514-3; 978-1-59643-628-2 (pa); 1-59643-628-X (pa)

"Two fine writers put their heads together and come up with an equally fine guide to their craft for beginners. . . . Mazer speaks to beginnings . . . while Potter tackles endings; and both have diverting things to say about everything that happens in between, whether it's the narrative voice or (eek) writer's block. [They are] always agreeable, practical, and commonsensical in their approach. . . . Their text is enlivened with sidebar features, personal anecdotes, and suggestions to readers for exercising their new skills. . . . Such devices, along with the authors' unfailing good humor, will go a long way to convincing their audience that writing can actually be fun! A notion that is nicely underscored by Phelan's engaging and always appealing illustrations." Booklist

Otfinoski, Steven, 1949-

Extraordinary short story writing; by Steven Otfinoski. Franklin Watts 2005 128p il (F.W. prep) lib bdg $30.50; pa $9.95

Grades: 5 6 7 8   **808.3**

1. Fiction—Technique 2. Short story 3. Authorship 4. Creative writing

ISBN 0-531-16760-7 (lib bdg); 0-531-17578-2 (pa)
    LC 2005006650

"In this excellent resource, specific ways to write different types of stories, project ideas, and resources are presented in such a way as to make short story assignments enjoyable. Readers are given many tips and practice activities in chapters that progress from gathering ideas to the final revision. Each section includes quotes from wellknown authors such as Edgar Allan Poe, Richard Peck, and Louis Sachar." SLJ

Includes bibliographical references

808.5   Rhetoric of speech

Bullard, Lisa, 1961-

Ace your oral or multimedia presentation. Enslow Elementary 2009 48p il (Ace it! information literacy) lib bdg $23.93

Grades: 3 4 5   **808.5**

1. Public speaking 2. Multimedia

ISBN 978-0-7660-3391-7 (lib bdg); 0-7660-3391-0 (lib bdg)
    LC 2008024885

"Learn how to research, write, practice, and present an oral or multimedia presentation with confidence" Publisher's note

Includes bibliographical references

808.8   Literature—Collections

Bauer, Caroline Feller, 1935-

Celebrations; read-aloud holiday and theme book programs; drawings by Lynn Gates Bredeson. Wilson, H.W. 1985 301p il $85

Grades: Professional   **808.8**

1. Holidays 2. Literature—Collections 3. Books and reading 4. Children's libraries

ISBN 0-8242-0708-4   LC 85-714

"Aimed at librarians and other adults who work with middle-grade children, this book offers a potpourri of ideas and suggestions for planning holiday programs. Each chapter focuses on a holiday—some well known, some concocted by Bauer—and includes prose [and poetry] selections, activities, and a booklist." Booklist

Includes bibliographical references

The **big** book for toddlers; edited by Alice Wong & Lena Tabori. Welcome Books 2009 219p il $24.95

Grades: PreK K   **808.8**

1. Fairy tales 2. Nursery rhymes 3. Handicraft 4. Games

ISBN 978-1-59962-071-8; 1-59962-071-5

"Full-bleed vintage illustrations by Jessie Willcox Smith, Maxfield Parrish, Margaret Evans Price and others grace the pages of this cheerful . . . hardcover book, divided into five sections: arts and crafts activities, condensed fairy tales, songs, games and nursery rhymes. The projects are simple and have buoyant instructions, . . . songs such as 'Old MacDonald' and 'Ants Go Marching' include musical notation; and familiar stories and rhymes appear as well. The lively assemblage will appeal to toddlers, and the heirloom images should captivate them as well as nostalgic adults." Publ Wkly

Celebrate Cricket; 30 years of stories and art; edited by Marianne Carus. Cricket Bks. 2003 262p il $24.95

Grades: Professional   **808.8**

1. Cricket (Periodical) 2. Literature—Collections

ISBN 0-8126-2695-8   LC 2003-10284

A treasury of stories, poems, and illustrations from Cricket, along with reminiscences about the magazine and color reproductions of Cricket cover art

"The selections flow well, and most of them are enjoyable at least and remarkable at best. . . . This is primarily a book for adults, and it deserves a place in collections where there's an interest in children's literature." SLJ

Everything I need to know I learned from a children's book. Roaring Brook 2009 233p $29.99

Grades: Professional **808.8**

1. Children's literature—History and criticism

ISBN 978-1-59643-395-3; 1-59643-395-7

"Over 100 noteworthy figures, from Ursula K. Le Guin to Jay Leno, convey lessons learned from specific children's books in this affirming collaboration, which is divided into six thematic sections and features full-color images. For each selection, a contributor provides a brief essay about how the book influenced him or her, accompanied by an excerpt. . . . A moving patchwork message about the transformative powers of reading." Publ Wkly

Hudson, Wade

Powerful words; more than 200 years of extraordinary writing by African Americans; illustrated by Sean Qualls; foreword by Marian Wright Edelman. Scholastic Nonfiction 2004 178p il $19.95 *

Grades: 5 6 7 8 **808.8**

1. American literature—African American authors 2. African Americans—Biography 3. African Americans—History

ISBN 0-439-40969-1 LC 2003-42792

A collection of speeches and writings by African Americans, with commentary about the time period in which each person lived, information about the speaker/writer, and public response to the words.

"Short enough to hold attention, the selections . . . are also long enough to show the writers' tone and style. Many sensitive full-page portraits are included. . . . This well-designed volume will be an excellent addition to many library collections." Booklist

Includes bibliographical references

Julie Andrews' collection of poems, songs, and lullabies; edited by Julie Andrews and Emma Walton Hamilton; paintings by James McMullan. Little, Brown Books for Young Readers 2009 192p il $24.99

Grades: K 1 2 3 **808.8**

1. Poetry—Collections 2. Lullabies 3. Songs

ISBN 978-0-316-04049-5; 0-316-04049-5

LC 2009-5121

"Julie Andrews and her daughter's selection of material for children contains works by figures as diverse as Emily Dickinson, Langston Hughes, Rodgers and Hammerstein, A.A. Milne and Shel Silverstein, as well as offerings by Andrews and Hamilton. McMullan's paintings express the sometimes silly, sometimes melancholic temperaments of the pieces, which together form a tapestry of human emotions and experiences, grand and small. The broad potpourri of voices, given a modern yet comforting flair by the artwork, is bound to become a favorite. An audio CD with poems read by Andrews and Hamilton is included." Publ Wkly

The **Norton** anthology of children's literature; the traditions in English; Jack Zipes, general editor . . . [et al.] W.W. Norton 2005 xxxviii, 2471p il pa $65

Grades: Professional **808.8**

1. Literature—Collections 2. Children's literature—History and criticism

ISBN 0-393-97538-X LC 2004-54172

A collection of fairy tales, picture books, nursery rhymes, fantasy, alphabets, chapbooks, and comics published in English since 1659, representing 170 authors and illustrators, and including more than ninety complete works and excerpts from others

"The delights are abundant. . . . A mile wide and very deep, this is an invaluable resource for professionals, but fun for casual perusing, too." Publ Wkly

Includes bibliographical references

Spinelli, Eileen, 1942-

Today I will; a year of quotes, notes, and promises to myself; [by] Eileen & Jerry Spinelli; illustrated by Julia Rothman. Alfred A. Knopf 2009 unp il $15.99; lib bdg $18.99

Grades: 5 6 7 8 **808.8**

1. Conduct of life 2. Quotations 3. American literature—Collections

ISBN 978-0-375-84057-9; 0-375-84057-5; 978-0-375-96230-1 (lib bdg); 0-375-96230-1 (lib bdg)

LC 2008047869

"The Spinellis turn their skills to inspiring readers with quotes and promises for every day of the year. There is a single-page entry for each day, and each one begins with a quote from children's literature. . . . Each quote is followed by an explanatory note. Each note is then summarized into a short promise on which readers can reflect. . . . The book covers a vast array of topics and themes, from serious to silly, and is inspiring and helpful." SLJ

808.81 Poetry—Collections

A **children's** treasury of poems; illustrations by Linda Bleck. Sterling 2008 unp il $12.95

Grades: PreK K 1 2 **808.81**

1. Poetry—Collections

ISBN 978-1-4027-4498-3; 1-4027-4498-6

"This collection of 19 humorous poems includes Robert Louis Stevenson's 'Bed in Summer,' Vachel Lindsay's 'The Little Turtle,' Edward Lear's 'The Owl and the Pussycat,' and Gelett Burgess's 'The Purple Cow,' among other familiar verses. Playful, cartoonlike illustrations with cutout characters and details superimposed on sturdy pages give the book texture and help create a novel effect. Different ethnicities are represented in the illustrations, although most are of fanciful animals and fairies. Young children should find the childlike format appealing." SLJ

Driscoll, Michael, 1973-
A child's introduction to poetry; listen while you learn about the magic words that have moved mountains, won battles and made us laugh and cry; illustrated by Meredith Hamilton. Black Dog & Leventhal 2003 90p il $19.95 *
Grades: 4 5 6 7   808.81
1. Poetry—Collections 2. Poetry—History and criticism
ISBN 1-57912-282-5
"The first section discusses the different forms the genre takes: nursery rhyme, narrative verse, ballad, free verse, pastoral, etc. Driscoll offers a clear explanation of each type and defines any difficult, associated vocabulary. Commentary on each example and a note on where to find the recording on the accompanying CD is provided for each selection. The second section covers individual poets from Homer to Maya Angelou and offers at least one example or excerpt from each writer's work. The brief introductions to the forms and poets are lively and often amusing. Readers will find the varied layouts and warm cartoon watercolors inviting." SLJ
Includes glossary and bibliographical references

Eric Carle's animals, animals. Philomel Bks. 1989 87p $21.99; pa $7.99
Grades: 2 3 4 5   808.81
1. Animals—Poetry 2. Poetry—Collections
ISBN 0-399-21744-4; 0-698-11855-3 (pa)
       LC 88-31646
"Illustrations take center stage in *Eric Carle's Animals Animals* . . . compiled by Laura Whipple. The well-chosen poems are from a variety of sources—the Bible, Shakespeare, Japanese Haiku, Pawnee Indian, weather sayings and contemporary poets like Judith Viorst, Ogden Nash, and Jack Prelutsky. On many pages the poem may be only two or three lines but the pictures are full-page spreads in Mr. Carle's familiar vividly colored, collage style." Kobrin Letter

Eric Carle's dragons dragons and other creatures that never were. Philomel Bks. 1991 69p il $21.99; pa $12.99
Grades: 2 3 4 5   808.81
1. Mythical animals—Poetry 2. Poetry—Collections
ISBN 0-399-22105-0; 0-399-22837-3 (pa)
       LC 91-11986
An illustrated collection of poems about dragons and other fantastic creatures by a variety of authors
"The collection offers a sumptuous viewing of Carle's rich blend of tissue-paper and paint collages and a grand introduction to the imaginary beasts. Laura Whipple concludes this adroit compilation with a brief commentary on the fabulous animals as 'a magical part of our human heritage.'" Horn Book
Includes glossary

A **family** of poems; my favorite poetry for children; [selected by] Caroline Kennedy; paintings by Jon J. Muth. Hyperion Books for Children 2005 143p il $19.95
Grades: 3 4 5 6   808.81
1. Poetry—Collections
ISBN 0-7868-5111-2
An anthology of over 100 poems divided into categories such as "About Me," "Animals," "Adventure" and

"Bedtime," including works by such poets as A.A. Milne, Robert Louis Stevenson, Jack Prelutsky, Edward Lear, Robert Frost, William Wordsworth, T.S. Eliot, Carl Sandberg, William Shakespeare.
"From the cover photograph of Kennedy as a toddler reading to her teddy to the red linen-textured endpapers; from her thoughtful introduction and words of encouragement to children at the beginning of each section of carefully chosen poems to Muth's beautifully executed watercolors, this volume is a treasure." SLJ

A **foot** in the mouth; poems to speak, sing, and shout; [edited by Paul B. Janeczko; illustrated by Chris Raschka] Candlewick Press 2009 64p il $17.99 *
Grades: 4 5 6 7   808.81
1. Poetry—Collections
ISBN 978-0-7636-0663-3; 0-7636-0663-4
       LC 2008-935581
"The poems in Janeczko and Raschka's collection . . . are not complacent, although plenty are funny and some are familiar. . . . Punchy collages flutter across airy white pages in loose visual arrangements; torn scraps of origami paper layer with fluid lines in tart color. Janeczko introduces the collection with the idea that 'Poetry is sound,' a pleasure to vocalize and memorize. . . . Readers will be emboldened to join in the 'song.'" Publ Wkly

Index to children's poetry; a title, subject, author, and first line index to poetry in collections for children and youth; compiled by John E. and Sara W. Brewton. Wilson, H.W. 1942-1965 3v $115; first supplement $85; second supplement $85
Grades: Professional   808.81
1. Poetry—Indexes 2. Reference books
ISBN 0-8242-0021-7; 0-8242-0022-5 (first supplement); 0-8242-0023-3 (second supplement)
Basic volume published 1942; first supplement published 1954; second supplement published 1965
The main volume indexes 15,000 poems by 2,500 authors in 130 collections. The two supplements analyze another 15,000 poems by 2700 authors in 151 collections.
"This tool is an invaluable reference source." Peterson. Ref Books for Child

Index to poetry for children and young people; a title, subject, author, and first line index to poetry in collections for children and young people. Wilson, H.W. 1964-1998 6v 1964-1969 $105; 1970-1975 $105; 1976-1981 $105; 1982-1987 $110; 1988-1992 $110; 1993-1997 $115
Grades: Professional   808.81
1. Poetry—Indexes 2. Reference books
ISBN 0-8242-0435-2 (1964-1969); 0-8242-0621-5 (1970-1975); 0-8242-0681-9 (1976-1981); 0-8242-0773-4 (1982-1987); 0-8242-0861-7 (1988-1992); 0-8242-0939-7 (1993-1997)
A continuation of Index to children's poetry
The volume covering 1964-1969 published 1972 and compiled by John E. and Sara W. Brewton and G. Mere-

Index to poetry for children and young people—*Continued*

dith Blackburn III; 1970-1975 published 1978 compiled by John E. Brewton, G. Meredith Blackburn III and Lorraine A. Blackburn; 1976-1981 published 1984 compiled by John E. Brewton, G. Meredith Blackburn III and Lorraine A. Blackburn; 1982-1987 published 1989 compiled by G. Meredith Blackburn III and Lorraine A. Blackburn; 1988-1992 published 1994 compiled by G. Meredith Blackburn III ; 1993-1997 published 1998 compiled by G. Meredith Blackburn III

Each volume analyzes approximately 10,000 poems by some 2,000 authors in more than 110 collections. Over 2,000 subject headings are used in each volume.

The **Oxford** book of story poems; [compiled by] Michael Harrison and Christopher Stuart-Clark. Oxford University Press 2006 175p il pa $18.95
Grades: 5 6 7 8 **808.81**
1. Poetry—Collections
ISBN 978-0-19-276344-0 (pa); 0-19-276344-X (pa)
LC 2007282711

First published 1990

This anthology contains "narrative verse by British and American poets, from traditional ballads such as 'Sir Patrick Spens' to contemporary poems such as Judith Nicholls' 'Storytime.' . . . The poets include Carroll, Keats, de la Mare, Kennedy, Lear, Lindsay, Longfellow, Noyes, Poe, Southey, and Tolkien. . . . A handy collection of story poems for reading aloud or alone." Booklist [review of 1990 edition]

Poetry speaks: who I am; poems of discovery, inspiration, independence, and everything else. Sourcebooks Jabberwocky 2010 136p $19.99 *
Grades: 5 6 7 8 9 10 **808.81**
1. Poetry—Collections
ISBN 978-1-4022-1074-7; 1-4022-1074-4

This collection "aims at middle-grade readers with more than 100 strikingly diverse poems by writers including Poe, Frost, Nikki Giovanni, and Sandra Cisneros. The works are slotted together in mindful thematic order, beside occasional spot art. . . . Pairing a contemporary poem like Toi Derricotte's 'Fears of the Eighth Grade' alongside Keats's 'When I Have Fears That I May Cease to Be,' results in a refreshing lack of literary hierarchy that enables disparate works to build and reflect upon one another. An accompanying CD features recordings of 44 of the poems. . . . A sound and rewarding introduction to the joys of poetry." Publ Wkly

Rhymes round the world; [compiled by] Kay Chorao. Dutton Children's Books 2009 40p il $17.99
Grades: PreK K 1 **808.81**
1. Poetry—Collections
ISBN 978-0-525-47875-1; 0-525-47875-2
LC 2008013887

"These 40 poems and songs offer children a taste of many different cultures. Most are anonymous or traditional nursery rhymes; a few are by English or American poets. The tone is light and joyous. Sweet illustrations of babies and toddlers engaged in playful activities depict the universality of children everywhere." SLJ

River of words; young poets and artists on the nature of things; edited by Pamela Michael; introduced by Robert Hass. Milkweed Editions 2008 298p il hardcover o.p. pa $18 *
Grades: 4 5 6 7 8 9 **808.81**
1. Poetry—Collections 2. Nature poetry 3. Children's writings 4. Teenagers' writings 5. Children's art
ISBN 978-1-57131-685-1; 1-57131-685-X; 978-1-57131-680-6 (pa); 1-57131-680-9 (pa)

"In 1995 Michael and Hass . . . cofounded the River of Words project, designed to connect students' art and poetry education to the natural world immediately around them. . . . The poems and pictures in this handsomely designed volume have been culled from yearly contests. . . . The works are startling, many of them dislocating and highly complex." Publ Wkly

Sail away with me; old and new poems; selected and written by Jane Collins-Philippe; illustrated by Laura Beingessner. Tundra Books 2010 unp il $15.95
Grades: K 1 2 3 **808.81**
1. Poetry—Collections 2. Sea poetry
ISBN 978-0-88776-842-2; 0-88776-842-3

"Starting off with 'My Bonnie Lies Over the Ocean' and other folk-song favorites, this picture-book poetry collection celebrates the sea and sailing traditions. . . . The lively watercolor illustrations extend the images i the words. . . . Ranging in theme from adventure to nonsense, these poems will be fun for reading aloud." Booklist

Starry night, sleep tight; a bedtime book of lullabies; illustrated by Gail Yerrill. Tiger Tales 2009 unp il $12.95
Grades: PreK **808.81**
1. Poetry—Collections 2. Lullabies
ISBN 978-1-58925-844-0; 1-58925-844-4

"This collection of familiar lullabies and poems is enhanced by soft, dreamlike artwork and attractively designed, quiltlike borders. The classic verses and songs are coupled with soft and lovable illustrations of animals and sprinkled with a touch of glitter to make bedtime seem magical." SLJ

The **tree** that time built; a celebration of nature, science, and imagination; selected by Mary Ann Hoberman and Linda Winston; [illustrations by Barbara Fortin] Sourcebooks Jabberwocky 2009 209p il $19.99
Grades: 5 6 7 8 **808.81**
1. Nature poetry 2. Science—Poetry 3. Poetry—Collections
ISBN 978-1-4022-2517-8; 1-4022-2517-2
LC 2009032608

Includes CD

An anthology of more than 100 poems celebrating the wonders of the natural world and encouraging environmental awareness. Includes an audio CD that comprises readings of 44 of the poems, many performed by the poets themselves.

"Classic works by Walt Whitman, Emily Dickinson, Christina Rossetti, and the like, and selections from contemporary poets are included. . . . This handsome col-

The tree that time built—*Continued*

lection is especially appropriate for classroom use and instruction. . . . From the playful to the profound, the poems invite reflection and inspire further investigation." SLJ

Includes glossary and bibliographical references

War and the pity of war; edited by Neil Philip; illustrated by Michael McCurdy. Clarion Bks. 1998 96p il $20
Grades: 5 6 7 8 9 10   **808.81**
1. War poetry 2. Poetry—Collections
ISBN 0-395-84982-9   LC 97-32897
"The selections, covering conflicts from ancient Persia to modern-day Bosnia, are by a wide variety of poets, from the well known (Tennyson, Whitman, Sandburg, Auden), to the obscure (Anakreon from ancient Greece and 11th-century Chinese poet Bunno). . . . The stark and simple scratchboard drawings are reminiscent of the Ernie Pyle illustrations from World War II and are as memorable as the best propaganda." SLJ

Winter poems; selected by Barbara Rogasky; illustrated by Trina Schart Hyman. Scholastic 1994 40p il $15.95; pa $5.99 *
Grades: 3 4 5 6   **808.81**
1. Winter—Poetry 2. Poetry—Collections
ISBN 0-590-42872-1; 0-590-42873-X (pa)
     LC 91-24419
"Rogasky has selected a wide range of poems—25 in all—dating from 10th-century Japan to the contemporary U.S. The best of the ages is represented, with familiar favorites from Shakespeare, Thomas Hardy, Robert Frost, Emily Dickinson, Carl Sandburg, etc. . . . Hyman's illustrations perfectly capture the spirit of that season, with acrylics in deep, chilling shades. . . . A beautiful presentation of outstanding quality." SLJ

808.82   Drama—Collections

Play index. Wilson, H.W. 1953-2007 11v
Grades: 8 9 10 11 12 Adult Professional
     808.82
1. Reference books 2. Drama—Indexes
ISSN 0554-3037
Also available on-line version
1949-1952 edited by Dorothy Herbert West and Dorothy Margaret Peake $90; 1953-1960 $90 edited by Estelle A. Fidell and Dorothy Margaret Peake; 1961-1967 $90 edited by Estelle A. Fidell; 1968-1972 $90 edited by Estelle A. Fidell; 1973-1977 $90 edited by Estelle A. Fidell; 1978-1982 $90 edited by Juliette Yaakov; 1983-1987 $270 edited by Juliette Yaakov and John Greenfieldt; 1988-1992 $270 edited by Juliette Yaakov and John Greenfieldt; 1993-1997 $270 edited by Juliette Yaakov and John Greenfieldt $270; 1998-2002 edited by John Greenfieldt $270; 2003-2007 edited by John Greenfieldt $315
Play index indexes plays in collections and single plays; one-act and full-length plays; radio, television, and Broadway plays; plays for amateur production; plays for children, young adults, and adults. It is divided into four parts. Part I is an author, title, and subject index; the author or main entry includes the title of the play, brief

synopsis of the plot, number of acts and scenes, size of cast, number of sets, and bibliographic information. Part II is a list of collections indexed, and Part III, a cast analysis, lists plays by the type of cast and number of players required
"This index is an excellent source for locating published plays." Safford. Guide to Ref Materials for Sch Media Cent. 5th edition

808.88   Collections of miscellaneous writings

Alcorn, Stephen, 1958-
A gift of days; the greatest words to live by. Atheneum Books for Young Readers 2009 115p il $21.99
Grades: 5 6 7 8   **808.88**
1. Celebrities 2. Quotations
ISBN 978-1-4169-6776-7; 1-4169-6776-1
     LC 2007-48766
"Beautifully designed and imaginatively conceptualized, this volume presents 366 days and 366 quotations from famous people, tagged to the days they were born. Alcorn lays this out on each double-page spread with a stunning polychrome-relief block-print bordered with pattern on one leaf and, facing, a week of birthdays and quotes. These images are often brilliantly inventive. . . . Librarians, educators and historically minded kids will take much pleasure from looking up birthdays to see the associated wisdom from women and men across the ages." Kirkus

809   Literary history and criticism

Carpenter, Humphrey
The Oxford companion to children's literature; [by] Humphrey Carpenter and Mari Prichard. Oxford Univ. Press 1984 586p il hardcover o.p. pa $70
Grades: Adult Professional   **809**
1. Reference books 2. Children's literature—Dictionaries
ISBN 0-19-211582-0; 0-19-860228-6 (pa)
     LC 83-15130
"One volume work with brief critiques of authors, illustrators, books, characters, and radio and television programs. Largely British in coverage of materials but does include most Newbery winners as well as well-known American, Australian and Canadian authors. Contemporary and historical subjects related to children's literature are examined." N Y Public Libr. Ref Books for Child Collect. 2d edition

The **Oxford** encyclopedia of children's literature; Jack Zipes, editor in chief. Oxford University Press 2006 4v il set $495
Grades: Professional   **809**
1. Reference books 2. Children's literature—Encyclopedias
ISBN 978-0-19-514656-1; 0-19-514656-5
     LC 2005-34390

The Oxford encyclopedia of children's literature—*Continued*

"The 3200 signed articles in this set include brief discussions of the work of major writers, important trends, genres, characters, organizations, and noteworthy publications and people in the field. All of the alphabetical articles are clearly written and most include cross-references. . . . There is no comparable single work that brings together all aspects of the topic, making this a valuable resource." SLJ

Includes bibliographical references

809.1 Poetry—History and criticism

Bodden, Valerie

Concrete poetry. Creative Education 2010 32p il (Poetry basics) $28.50

Grades: 5 6 7 8   **809.1**
  1. Poetry—History and criticism
  ISBN 978-1-58341-775-1; 1-58341-775-3
                                            LC 2008009156

This book describes concrete poetry's "history, characteristics, and variations. Many examples are provided as well as ideas for how children can write their own pieces. The information is accessible, and the writing is sufficiently lively to engage readers. The well-designed pages feature a variety of art reproductions from different literary eras and some photographs." Horn Book Guide

Includes glossary and bibliographical references

Haiku. Creative Education 2010 32p il (Poetry basics) $19.95

Grades: 5 6 7 8   **809.1**
  1. Haiku
  ISBN 978-1-58341-776-8; 1-58341-776-1
                                            LC 2008-9158

Presents history and examples of the Japanese form of poetry called haiku.

"The information is accessible, and the writing is sufficiently lively to engage readers. The well-designed pages feature a variety of art reproductions from different literary eras and some photographs." Horn Book Guide

Includes glossary and bibliographical references

Limericks. Creative Education 2010 32p il (Poetry basics) $19.95

Grades: 5 6 7 8   **809.1**
  1. Limericks
  ISBN 978-1-58341-777-5; 1-58341-777-X
                                            LC 2008-9159

This describes limericks' "history, characteristics, and variations. Many examples are provided as well as ideas for how children can write their own pieces. The information is accessible, and the writing is sufficiently lively to engage readers. The well-designed pages feature a variety of art reproductions from different literary eras and some photographs." Horn Book Guide

Includes glossary and bibliographical references

810.3 American literature— Encyclopedias and dictionaries

McElmeel, Sharron L.

100 most popular picture book authors and illustrators; biographical sketches and bibliographies. Libraries Unlimited 2000 xxix, 579p (Popular authors series) $68

Grades: Adult Professional   **810.3**
  1. Reference books 2. Children's literature—Bio-bibliography
  ISBN 1-56308-647-6   LC 00-23181

The 100 profiles "are accompanied by photographs, reading lists, and lists of related information sources (such as Web pages). Contemporary authors and illustrators whose works are still in print provide the focus." Publisher's note

Includes bibliographical references

810.8 American literature— Collections

Dude!; stories and stuff for boys; edited by Sandy Asher and David Harrison. Dutton Childrens Books 2006 258p il $17.99

Grades: 4 5 6 7   **810.8**
  1. Boys 2. American literature—Collections
  ISBN 0-525-47684-9   LC 2005025060

"These 18 original stories, plays, and poems by prize-winning writers range from entertaining to challenging and offer an array of characters and experiences. In Bill C. Davis' intimate, thought-provoking 'Family Meeting,' a boy whose stepbrother committed suicide discovers the value of life. Jamie Adoff's 'Twelve' is a rap poem about experiencing violence but still retaining hope. Jose Cruz Gonzalez's play *Watermelon Kisses* is an amusing, credible portrayal of brotherly love and squabbles. The selections, which include many well-written gems, will resonate with and also amuse middle-grade boys." Booklist

Wáchale! poetry and prose on growing up Latino in America; edited by Ilan Stavans. Cricket Publs. 2001 146p $16.95 *

Grades: 5 6 7 8   **810.8**
  1. Hispanic Americans 2. American literature—Hispanic American authors—Collections 3. Bilingual books—English-Spanish
  ISBN 0-8126-4750-5   LC 2001-47189

A bilingual collection of poems, stories, and other writings which celebrates diversity among Latinos.

"This collection would make a fine classroom text, great for reading aloud and for stimulating students from everywhere to write about their roots and celebrate their shifting places across borders." Booklist

Includes glossary and bibliographical references

Yolen, Jane

Here there be dragons; illustrated by David Wilgus. Harcourt Brace & Co. 1993 149p il pa $10 hardcover o.p.

Grades: 5 6 7 8   **810.8**

1. Dragons—Fiction 2. American literature—Collections

ISBN 0-15-201705-4 (pa)   LC 92-23194

Includes the following stories: Great-Grandfather Dragon's tale; The dragon woke and stretched; "Story," the old man said; Cockfight; Dragonfield; The king's dragon; The dragon's boy; One Ox, Two Ox, Three Ox, and the Dragon King

"Yolen has compiled a collection of her poetry and prose about dragons of all sizes, shapes and dispositions. She introduces each piece with a brief description including the circumstances surrounding its writing. . . . The poetry, like the prose, varies in length but will enthrall readers. David Wilgus' pen and ink drawings further enhance the book." Book Rep

810.9   American literature—History and criticism

Wilkin, Binnie Tate, 1933-

African and African American images in Newbery Award winning titles; progress in portrayals. Scarecrow Press 2009 195p pa $40

Grades: Professional   **810.9**

1. Children's literature—History and criticism 2. African Americans in literature 3. Newbery Medal

ISBN 978-0-8108-6959-2 (pa); 0-8108-6959-4 (pa)

          LC 2009017726

"The author has exhaustively examined all books that have won the Newbery Medal and been cited as honor books since the award's creation in 1922. Her purpose is to evaluate the representation of Africans and African Americans, and to describe how these groups are portrayed in each title's historical context. . . . Books with the most positive images are awarded three pluses, while books with marginal African-American characters are indicated with an 'M.' . . . An essential volume for scholars, teachers, and librarians." SLJ

Includes bibliographical references

Wilkinson, Brenda Scott, 1946-

African American women writers; [by] Brenda Wilkinson. Wiley 2000 166p il (Black stars) $22.95

Grades: 4 5 6 7   **810.9**

1. Reference books 2. African American authors—Bio-bibliography

ISBN 0-471-17580-3   LC 99-25552

Discusses the lives and work of such notable African American women authors as: Phillis Wheatley, Ida B. Wells-Barnett, Zora Neale Hurston, Gwendolyn Brooks, Nikki Giovanni, and Terry McMillan

Includes bibliographical references

811   American poetry

Ada, Alma Flor, 1938-

Gathering the sun; an alphabet in Spanish and English; English translation by Rosa Zubizarreta; illustrated by Simón Silva. Lothrop, Lee & Shepard Bks. 1997 unp il $16.95; pa $6.99 *

Grades: 2 3 4   **811**

1. Mexican Americans—Poetry 2. Alphabet 3. Bilingual books—English-Spanish 4. Poetry—By individual authors

ISBN 0-688-13903-5; 0-688-17067-7 (pa)

"Using the Spanish alphabet as a template, Ada has written 27 poems that celebrate both the bounty of the harvest and the Mexican heritage of the farmworkers and their families. The poems, presented in both Spanish and English, are short and simple bursts of flavor. . . . Silva's sun-drenched gouache paintings are robust, with images sculpted in paint." Booklist

Adoff, Arnold, 1935-

Touch the poem; poems by Arnold Adoff; pictures by Lisa Desimini. Blue Sky Press (NY) 2000 unp il $16.95

Grades: K 1 2 3   **811**

1. Touch—Poetry 2. Poetry—By individual authors

ISBN 0-590-47970-9

A collection of poems about the sense of touch including a baby's foot in one's palm, peach fuzz on the lip, and the forehead against a cold window

"The solid imagery of Adoff's poetry takes on a visual dimension when paired with Desimini's bold photographs." Booklist

Agee, Jon

Orangutan tongs; poems to tangle your tongue. Hyperion Books for Children 2009 47p il $16.99 *

Grades: 2 3 4 5   **811**

1. Tongue twisters 2. Humorous poetry 3. Poetry—By individual authors

ISBN 978-1-4231-0315-8; 1-4231-0315-7

          LC 2008-13941

"This collection is loaded with tricky tongue-twisting rhymes that will challenge readers. . . . In addition to being just plain funny, Agee is a wordsmith and accomplished illustrator, factors that have produced another must-have winner from a comic master." SLJ

Ahlberg, Allan

Everybody was a baby once, and other poems; illustrator Bruce Ingman. Candlewick Press 2010 63p il $15.99

Grades: PreK K 1   **811**

1. Infants—Poetry 2. Poetry—By individual authors

ISBN 978-0-7636-4682-0; 0-7636-4682-2

"From the creators of The Pencil, these 19 poems cover whimsical territory and feature kids, angels, sausages, and monsters, rendered in kinetic, childlike sketches. A few poems strike nostalgic, melancholy notes . . . but

Ahlberg, Allan—*Continued*

most are upbeat, with gently jazzy rhythms. . . . The Lilliputian cast and memorable verse could make this a dog-eared favorite." Publ Wkly

Alarcón, Francisco X., 1954-

Animal poems of the Iguazu; [by] Francisco X. Alarcon; illustrations, Maya Christina Gonzalez. Children's Book Press 2008 30p il $16.95

Grades: 2 3 4 5   811

1. Animals—Poetry 2. Rain forests—Poetry 3. Nature poetry 4. Bilingual books—English-Spanish 5. Poetry—By individual authors

ISBN 978-0-89239-225-4; 0-89239-225-8

LC 2007-50011

"Two West Coast Chicano artists . . . celebrate Iguaz Falls, the immense rain forest waterfalls that lie between Argentina and Brazil. . . . Each of the 26 poems appears in both English and Spanish, with many explanatory footnotes; together with the dense illustrations, the effect of the pages duplicates that of the rain forest, jam-packed with things to look at." Publ Wkly

From the bellybutton of the moon and other summer poems; poems, Francisco X. Alarcón; illustrations, Maya Christina Gonzalez. Children's Bk. Press 1998 31p il hardcover o.p. pa $7.95 *

Grades: 2 3 4   811

1. Summer—Poetry 2. Bilingual books—English-Spanish 3. Poetry—By individual authors

ISBN 0-89239-153-7; 0-89239-201-0 (pa)

LC 97-37457

A bilingual collection of poems in which the renowned Mexican American poet revisits and celebrates his childhood memories of summers, Mexico, and nature

"Responding to and expanding on the poetry, Gonzalez's happy paintings weave rich waves of color in an exuberant dance between text and design." Booklist

Iguanas in the snow and other winter poems; poems, Francisco X. Alarcón; illustrations, Maya Christina Gonzalez. Children's Bk. Press 2001 31p il hardcover o.p. pa $7.95

Grades: 2 3 4   811

1. Winter—Poetry 2. Bilingual books—English-Spanish 3. Poetry—By individual authors

ISBN 0-89239-168-5; 0-89239-202-9 (pa)

LC 00-65667

Text and title page in English and Spanish

"Eighteen verses in Spanish and English offer homage not just to winter but to the year-round delights of San Francisco and the rest of northern California." Bull Cent Child Books

"Brief, zippy verses express delight in such simple things as a family frolic in the snow and the wonder of giant redwoods. . . . The selections are short of line and long on meter, with a rhythmic roll that begs reading aloud. . . . Gonzalez's illustrations are bright and busy, catching the playful cadence of the words." SLJ

Poems to dream together; Poemas para soñar juntos; illustrations by Paula Barragán. Lee & Low Books 2005 unp il $16.95 *

Grades: 3 4 5   811

1. Mexican Americans—Poetry 2. Bilingual books—English-Spanish 3. Poetry—By individual authors

ISBN 1-58430-233-X   LC 2004-20963

In a "bilingual collection of short poems, Alarcon shares his dreams of peace, community building, and a bright future for children of all cultures. . . . The rhythm and cadence work well in both the Spanish and the English entries, and Barragan's illustrations are a fine complement to the text. Flat, bright colors and simple shapes give them the look of classroom paper cutouts, but the compositions are as intricate as Mexican mural paintings." Booklist

Angelou, Maya

Amazing peace; a Christmas poem; by Maya Angelou; paintings by Steve Johnson and Lou Fancher. Schwartz & Wade Books 2008 unp il $17.99; lib bdg $20.99

Grades: 3 4 5   811

1. Christmas—Poetry 2. Poetry—By individual authors

ISBN 978-0-375-84150-7;   0-375-84150-4; 978-0-375-94327-0 (lib bdg); 0-375-94327-7 (lib bdg)

"This poem was largely inspired by the terrible natural disasters occurring throughout the world when Angelou was invited to read at the 2005 White House tree-lighting ceremony. Thus, the opening lines rumble and roil almost menacingly to illustrate the climate of doubt and anxiety into which the spirit of Christmas arrives. Hope enters as a whisper and grows until it is 'louder than the explosion of bombs.' . . . Johnson and Fancher's paintings, rendered in oil, acrylic, and fabric on canvas, elegantly depict a calm, snow-blanketed village where children play, families shop, and artisans ply their crafts. . . . This is a comforting book that gets to the heart of what Christmas should mean. As an added treat, Angelou reads the poem on the accompanying CD." SLJ

Maya Angelou; edited by Edwin Graves Wilson; illustrated by Jerome Lagarrigue. Sterling Pub. 2007 48p il (Poetry for young people) $14.95 *

Grades: 4 5 6 7   811

1. Poets, American 2. African American women 3. African Americans—Poetry 4. Poetry—By individual authors

ISBN 978-1-4027-2023-9; 1-4027-2023-8

LC 2006013803

"Wilson's introduction . . . addresses how Angelou's life has informed her imagination. . . . Twenty-five poems show her concern with the African-American experience. . . . Dignity, pride, and resiliency are at this collection's core. . . . Footnotes offer definitions of colloquialisms and difficult words. Lagarrigue's painterly artwork uses golds, greens, and violets to capture the luminescent quality of the poems. . . . This [is a] distinguished work." SLJ

Archer, Peggy

From dawn to dreams; poems for busy babies; illustrated by Hanako Wakiyama. Candlewick Press 2007 unp il $15.99

Grades: PreK   **811**

    1. Infants—Poetry 2. Poetry—By individual authors

    ISBN 978-0-7636-2467-5; 0-7636-2467-5

                     LC 2006051832

"15 poems cover the gamut of activities in which babies and toddlers participate: a first step, clomping around in adult shoes, exploring faces in a mirror, introducing oneself to the family cat, and so on. . . . The oil-on-paper illustrations are in a style reminiscent of art in the 1950s. On various pages, the text is surrounded by a zigzag frame that adds to the old-fashioned feel." SLJ

Name that dog! puppy poems from A to Z; illustrations by Stephanie Buscema. Dial Books for Young Readers 2010 unp il $16.99

Grades: PreK K 1 2 3   **811**

    1. Dogs—Poetry 2. Poetry—By individual authors

    ISBN 978-0-8037-3322-0; 0-8037-3322-4

                     LC 2009009286

"This picture book poetry collection presents a rogue's gallery of pooches in selections designed to help an unidentified dog owner name his or her new pet. . . . The poems, representing a variety of styles, read smoothly and are complemented by Buscema's energetic, stylized illustrations." Booklist

Argueta, Jorge

Sopa de frijoles = Bean soup; un poema para cocinar = a cooking poem. Groundwood Books/House of Anansi Press 2009 unp $18.95

Grades: 1 2 3   **811**

    1. Food—Poetry 2. Cooking—Poetry 3. Bilingual books—English-Spanish 4. Poetry—By individual authors

    ISBN 978-0-88899-881-1; 0-88899-881-3

"This free-verse cooking poem is more than a simple recipe for bean soup. Argueta's lyrical Spanish translated into its counterpart English is filled with visual and aromatic imagery that turns soup-making into art. . . . Yockteng's parallel earthy-toned paintings oppose each new instructive page. . . . Starred cues appropriately indicate adult help where needed in this eloquent rendering of a nutritious and delicious meal." Kirkus

Talking with Mother Earth; poems; illustrated by Lucia Angela Perez. Groundwood Books 2006 unp il $15.95

Grades: 3 4 5 6   **811**

    1. Nature poetry 2. Racism—Poetry 3. Pipil Indians—Poetry 4. Bilingual books—English-Spanish 5. Poetry—By individual authors

    ISBN 0-88899-626-8

This presents poems which explore a Pipil Nahua Indian boy's connection to Mother Earth and how it heals the wounds of racism.

"This literary offering stands out for its beauty and depth of expression. . . . Pérez's illustrations are colorful, detailed, and appealing, incorporating many indigenous icons." SLJ

Bagert, Brod, 1947-

School fever; by Brod Bagert; pictures by Robert Neubecker. Dial Books for Young Readers 2008 unp il $16.99

Grades: 1 2 3   **811**

    1. Schools—Poetry 2. Poetry—By individual authors

    ISBN 978-0-8037-3201-8; 0-8037-3201-5

                     LC 2007-9324

This is a book of "poems, most of which follow a basic rhyming pattern, [and] touch on a number subjects and school situations near and dear to children. . . . The fun illustrations, completed with ink and a computer, really capture the essence of the poems." Libr Media Connect

Beck, Carolyn

Buttercup's lovely day; illustrated by Andrea Beck. Orca Book Publishers 2008 unp il $19.95

Grades: 1 2 3 4   **811**

    1. Cattle—Poetry 2. Farm life—Poetry 3. Nature poetry 4. Poetry—By individual authors

    ISBN 978-1-55143-512-1; 1-55143-512-8

"Beginning with the rising sun and ending as she falls asleep at night, a Holstein waxes poetic about all the things she enjoys about her life. . . . The iambic rhythm makes the selections easy to read and recite aloud, and the poems would be wonderful additions to storytimes about cows, farms, or even during Valentine's Day programs. The cheery illustrations subtly reflect the changing light throughout Buttercup's day." SLJ

Behn, Harry

Halloween; illustrated by Greg Couch. North-South Bks. 2003 unp il $15.95; lib bdg $16.50

Grades: 1 2 3   **811**

    1. Halloween—Poetry 2. Poetry—By individual authors

    ISBN 0-7358-1609-3; 0-7358-1766-9 (lib bdg)

                     LC 2002-43238

"A Cheshire Studio book"

"A skeleton, a witch, and a devil go out to trick-or-treat, but are frightened by every sound they hear and everything they see. Larger-than-life, vivid illustrations bring this simple rhyming verse to life on each haunting spread." SLJ

Bernier-Grand, Carmen T.

César; si, se puede! yes, we can! illustrated by David Diaz. Marshall Cavendish 2004 48p il $16.95

Grades: 3 4 5 6   **811**

    1. Chavez, Cesar, 1927-1993 2. Mexican Americans—Poetry 3. Poetry—By individual authors

    ISBN 0-7614-5172-2   LC 2003-26866

Also available Spanish language edition

"A sequence of free-verse poems surveys the life and the work of Mexican-American activist Cesar Chavez." Bull Cent Child Books

"The lyrical language describes events and paints evocative pictures to which children will relate. Diaz's stylized, computer-drawn, folk-art illustrations capture the subject's private and public life." SLJ

Inlcudes glossary and bibliographical references

Blackaby, Susan

Nest, nook & cranny; poems by Susan Blackaby; illustrated by Jamie Hogan. Charlesbridge 2010 48p il $15.95

Grades: 3 4 5 6 **811**

1. Habitat (Ecology) 2. Animals—Poetry 3. Poetry—By individual authors

ISBN 978-1-58089-350-3; 1-58089-350-3

LC 2009004302

"This lively poetry collection pairs verse about animals with black-and-white drawings of creatures in their natural habitats. . . . The various settings, accompanied by notes on nature, will grab young conservationists. . . . Teachers will welcome the extensive final notes on animal habitats and poetic forms for science and creative-writing classes." Booklist

Brooks, Gwendolyn

Bronzeville boys and girls; illustrated by Faith Ringgold. newly illustrated ed. Amistad/HarperCollins Publishers 2007 c1956 41p il $16.99; lib bdg $18.89 *

Grades: K 1 2 3 **811**

1. African Americans—Poetry 2. Poetry—By individual authors

ISBN 978-0-06-029505-9; 0-06-029505-8; 978-0-06-029506-6 (lib bdg); 0-06-029506-6 (lib bdg)

LC 2006-01947

A newly illustrated edition of the title first published 1956

"Brooks's deceptively simple poems for children combined with Ringgold's vibrant illustrations help to rejuvenate this collection first published in 1956. . . . Each poem is tightly constructed, rhythmic and distinctive. . . . Ringgold's bold illustrations, outlined with her signature thick black lines, are among some of her best and most narrative works since *Tar Beach*." Publ Wkly

Brown, Calef

Flamingoes on the roof; poems and paintings by Calef Brown. Houghton Mifflin 2006 unp il $16 *

Grades: 3 4 5 6 **811**

1. Humorous poetry 2. Poetry—By individual authors

ISBN 0-618-56298-2 LC 2004-25125

"These 29 nonsense poems, written in a variety of rhymed meters, are deliciously loaded with alliterative and assonant sounds and filled with delightful doggerel. . . . Full-page, flat acrylic illustrations, most painted in harmonious jewel tones, face single-toned pages of text in a variety of colors." SLJ

Soup for breakfast; poems and pictures. Houghton Mifflin Co. 2008 unp il $16

Grades: K 1 2 3 **811**

1. Humorous poetry 2. Poetry—By individual authors

ISBN 978-0-618-91641-2; 0-618-91641-5

LC 2007047734

Brown's "fun-filled poems feature an unpredictable range of topics and imagery. . . . He offsets each poem with one of his flat, idiosyncratic paintings; with their oddball beasts and improbable color combinations, his pictures are somewhere between surreal and folk art." Publ Wkly

Brown, Margaret Wise, 1910-1952

Nibble nibble; [by] Margaret Wise Brown; paintings by Wendell Minor. HarperCollins 2007 unp il $16.99; lib bdg $17.89

Grades: PreK K 1 **811**

1. Rabbits—Poetry 2. Poetry—By individual authors

ISBN 978-0-06-059208-0; 0-06-059208-7; 978-0-06-059209-7 (lib bdg); 0-06-059209-5 (lib bdg)

LC 2006029869

A collection of poetry about rabbits

"Large, almost tactile paintings of birds, butterflies, and bunnies combine well with the flow of Brown's charming poems, originally published in 1959. . . . Onomatopoeic and motion words are reflected in the pictures with their ground-level perspective. These five beautifully and newly illustrated poems will enchant another generation of children." SLJ

Bruchac, Joseph, 1942-

Thirteen moons on a turtle's back; a Native American year of moons; by Joseph Bruchac and Jonathan London; illustrated by Thomas Locker. Philomel Bks. 1992 unp il $16.95; pa $5.99

Grades: K 1 2 3 4 **811**

1. Native Americans—Folklore 2. Native Americans—Poetry 3. Seasons—Poetry 4. Poetry—By individual authors

ISBN 0-399-22141-7; 0-698-11584-8 (pa)

LC 91-3961

"Native American stories are retold as poems that capture the cycles of the moon. Months slip by as the oil paintings show each moon in the shell of the turtle's back." Child Book Rev Serv

"Locker . . . has created a dramatic oil painting for each short tale. His artwork portrays seasonal changes in the land as well as the specific seasonal activities of humans and animals. The large format with minimal text will appeal to younger children, while the alternative calendar, based on changes in nature, will interest middle readers. An unusual, easy-to-use resource for librarians, teachers, and others wishing to incorporate multicultural activites throughout the year." Booklist

Bryan, Ashley, 1923-

Sing to the sun; poems and pictures by Ashley Bryan. HarperCollins Pubs. 1992 unp il pa $6.95

Grades: 2 3 4 5 **811**

ISBN 0-06-443437-0 LC 91-38359

A collection of poems and paintings celebrating the ups and downs of life

"With an energetic beat that's hard to resist, Bryan drums out poetry with a Caribbean sway. These short poems that sing the praises of everyday joys are further charged by the riotous primary colors Bryan splashes around." Booklist

Bulion, Leslie, 1958-

Hey there, stink bug! [by] Leslie Bulion; illustrated by Leslie Evans. Charlesbridge 2006 45p il $12.95

Grades: 4 5 6 **811**

1. Insects—Poetry 2. Poetry—By individual authors

ISBN 978-1-58089-304-6; 1-58089-304-X

LC 2005019627

Bulion, Leslie, 1958-—*Continued*

"The poems in this collection flit and buzz effortlessly from page to page as members of the insect world are showcased in a variety of poetic forms, from haiku to clerihew. . . . A brief annotation accompanies each poem, providing a few juicy factoids for budding entomologists while ever-present humor pulls in all fans of anything gross. . . . Evans's naturalistic block prints crawl playfully through the text, echoing the lighthearted tone." SLJ

Bunting, Eve, 1928-

Sing a song of piglets; a calendar in verse; pictures by Emily Arnold McCully. Clarion Bks. 2002 32p il $16 *

Grades: K 1 2   811
1. Pigs—Poetry 2. Months—Poetry 3. Poetry—By individual authors
ISBN 0-618-01137-4   LC 2001-55267

From skiing in January to surfing in July, two energetic piglets romp through the months of the years in this calendar in verse

"There's a delightful exuberance to the artwork, and children will enjoy looking at the pictures to catch more of the details. A charming choice, too, for beginning readers." Booklist

Burleigh, Robert, 1936-

Hoops; illustrated by Stephen T. Johnson. Harcourt Brace & Co. 1997 unp il hardcover o.p. pa $6 *

Grades: 6 7 8 9   811
1. Basketball—Poetry 2. Poetry—By individual authors
ISBN 0-15-201450-0; 0-15-216380-8 (pa)
                                              LC 96-18440

"Silver Whistle"

Illustrations and poetic text describe the movement and feel of the game of basketball

"Burleigh's staccato text is well matched by Johnson's dynamic pastels. Muted colors and a strong sense of motion as bodies leap and lift, pounce and poke, aptly complement the words." SLJ

Calmenson, Stephanie

Good for you! toddler rhymes for toddler times; original rhymes by Stephanie Calmenson; pictures by Melissa Sweet. HarperCollins Pubs. 2001 64p il $16.95; lib bdg $16.89 *

Grades: K 1   811
1. Poetry—By individual authors
ISBN 0-688-17737-9; 0-06-029811-1 (lib bdg)
                                              LC 00-40891

"This collection includes verses about colors, riddles about the playground, poems about manners, and bits on other topics of concern to toddlers. Sweet's vibrant illustrations with bright backgrounds pick up where the rhymes leave off, giving the audience a nice view of the diverse world of children." SLJ

Welcome, baby! baby rhymes for baby times; original rhymes by Stephanie Calmenson; pictures by Melissa Sweet. HarperCollins Pubs. 2002 64p il $16.99; lib bdg $18.89; pa $7.99 *

Grades: K 1   811
1. Infants—Poetry 2. Poetry—By individual authors
ISBN 0-688-17736-0; 0-06-000492-4 (lib bdg); 0-06-113610-8 (pa)   LC 2001-24634

Companion volume to Good for you!

This "offers very young children 33 short poems to match to their own perspective of the world. . . . Colorful and childlike Sweet's appealing artwork is a wonderful complement to the simple language and early childhood topics." Booklist

Ciardi, John, 1916-1986

You read to me, I'll read to you; drawings by Edward Gorey. Lippincott 1962 64p il pa $7.95 hardcover o.p. *

Grades: 1 2 3 4   811
1. Humorous poetry 2. Poetry—By individual authors
ISBN 0-06-446060-6 (pa)

Thirty-five "imaginative and humorous poems for an adult and a child to read aloud together. Written in a basic first-grade vocabulary, the poems to be read by the child alternate with poems to be read by the adult." Booklist

Clements, Andrew, 1949-

Dogku; [by] Andrew Clements; illustrations by Tim Bowers. Simon & Schuster Books for Young Readers 2007 unp il $16.99

Grades: 1 2 3 4   811
1. Haiku 2. Dogs—Poetry 3. Poetry—By individual authors
ISBN 978-0-689-85823-9; 0-689-85823-X
                                              LC 2006003691

"A stray dog's first day in a family's home is more or less a test of whether he'll get to stay. . . . [The author] tells the entire tale in haiku, a remarkably effective vehicle for delivering such a sweet and simple story. . . . While each haiku is typically spare, Bowers's vibrant illustrations are busy and bright, filling the pages with the same unbounded energy as the lovable pooch." SLJ

Cox, Kenyon, 1856-1919

Mixed beasts; or, A miscellany of rare and fantastic creatures; compiled by Professor Julius Duckworth O'Hare, Esq.; illustrations by Wallace Edwards; verses by Kenyon Cox. Kids Can Press 2005 unp il $17.95

Grades: 3 4 5   811
1. Nonsense verses 2. Animals—Poetry 3. Poetry—By individual authors
ISBN 1-55337-796-6

"Inspired by Kenyon Cox's Mixed beasts published in 1904"

"These original nonsense poems about a miscellany of odd beasts comprised of a mixture of two species, such as a Rhinocerostrich, a Bumblebeaver, a Kangarooster,

Cox, Kenyon, 1856-1919—*Continued*

and a Camelelephant, are clever and funny. Full-page, detailed illustrations of exotic flora and fauna as well as preposterous creatures are rendered in watercolor, colored pencil, and gouache. The humor of the selections is carried out in the art." SLJ

Dant, Traci

Some kind of love; a family reunion in poems; illustrated by Eric Velasquez. Marshall Cavendish Children 2010 unp il $17.99

Grades: K 1 2 3   **811**

1. Family reunions—Poetry 2. African Americans—Poetry 3. Poetry—By individual authors
ISBN 978-0-7614-5559-2; 0-7614-5559-0
LC 2008-20878

"'Must be some kind of love.' That is the refrain that starts off each moving poem in this picture book about an annual African American family reunion, told in free verse from the viewpoint of a nine-year-old boy. Handsome oil paintings show the 'giant sleepover,' with group pictures of multiple generations, as well as closeups of cousins sharing bikes, eating fried chicken, and sleeping four boys to a bed." Booklist

Dawes, Kwame Senu Neville, 1962-

I saw your face; [drawings by] Tom Feelings; text by Kwame Dawes; afterword by Jerry Pinkney. Dial Books 2004 unp il $16.99 *

Grades: 3 4 5   **811**

1. Blacks—Poetry 2. Face in art 3. Poetry—By individual authors
ISBN 0-8037-1894-2   LC 2004-00241

A poem and portraits of children illustrate the shared beauty and heritage of people of African descent living throughout the world.

"Accompanied by Dawes's celebratory verses, page after page of evocative drawings are set in Africa, the Caribbean, England, and the American South." Horn Book Guide

Dotlich, Rebecca Kai

Over in the pink house. Wordsong/Boyds Mills Press 2004 30p il $15.95 *

Grades: K 1 2 3   **811**

1. Jump rope rhymes 2. Poetry—By individual authors
ISBN 1-59078-027-2

"These 32 original rhymes are infused with fresh, colorful imagery and toe-tapping rhythm. Appropriate for reading or chanting aloud while jumping rope, each one has a lighthearted, whimsical quality. The vibrantly colored illustrations are equally playful." SLJ

Eliot, T. S. (Thomas Stearns), 1888-1965

Old Possum's book of practical cats; illustrated by Axel Scheffler. Harcourt Children's Books 2009 64p il $16 *

Grades: 3 4 5 6   **811**

1. Cats—Poetry 2. Poetry—By individual authors
ISBN 978-0-547-24827-1; 0-547-24827-X

"Scheffler brings his considerable illustrative talents to this new edition of Eliot's much-loved collection of cat whimsy, first published in 1939. Scheffler's cartoon felines, with their expressive eyes, are a deliciously animated cast. . . . These cats by turns baffle and delight the humans around them." SLJ

Esbensen, Barbara Juster

Swing around the sun; poems; art by Cheng-Khee Chee . . . [et al.] Carolrhoda Bks. 2003 unp il lib bdg $16.95 *

Grades: 2 3 4   **811**

1. Seasons—Poetry 2. Poetry—By individual authors
ISBN 0-87614-143-2   LC 2002-7980

A newly illustrated edition of the title first published 1965 by Lerner

A collection of poems that celebrates the seasons, with illustrations for each season by a different Minnesota artist

"A rich, vibrant reading and viewing experience. . . . The poetry's impact is heightened by masterful new illustrations from four distinguished artists. . . . Cheng-Khee Chee's textured watercolors sprout and bloom across the pages of 'Spring.' Janice Lee Porter's 'Summer' oil pastels hum with energetic color and sinuous shapes. Mary GrandPré ushers in fall with a warmer palette of pastels. . . . Finally, Stephen Gammell's snowscapes, spattered in icy grays and blue capture winter's wild spirit." SLJ

Fehler, Gene, 1940-

Change-up; baseball poems; illustrated by Donald Wu. Clarion Books 2009 48p il $16

Grades: 2 3 4 5   **811**

1. Baseball—Poetry 2. Poetry—By individual authors
ISBN 978-0-618-71962-4; 0-618-71962-8
LC 2008-21950

"Thirty-six brief poems follow a baseball player's year. . . . Fehler's verses offer simple images and the delights of the game's terse play-by-play. . . . Wu's comically exaggerated illustrations are done in acrylic and colored pencils. With its charming wordplay and humor, this book should win an audience." SLJ

Field, Eugene, 1850-1895

Wynken, Blynken, and Nod; written by Eugene Field; illustrated by Giselle Potter. Schwartz & Wade Books 2008 unp il $16.99; lib bdg $19.99

Grades: PreK K 1 2   **811**

1. Sleep—Poetry 2. Poetry—By individual authors
ISBN   978-0-375-84196-5;   0-375-84196-2;
978-0-375-94596-0 (lib bdg); 0-375-94596-2 (lib bdg)
LC 2007-09568

"Field's soothing lullaby of a poem (1889) is handsomely visualized via the classic device of translating the

Field, Eugene, 1850-1895—*Continued*
contents of a child's own room into the stuff of dreams.
Potter's appealing dreamlike art features a moon-faced
child and the three eponymous figures who are as like
him . . . as peas in a pod. . . . An idyllic and imaginative new look at an old favorite." Horn Book

Fisher, Aileen Lucia, 1906-2002
Do rabbits have Christmas? poems; by Aileen
Fisher; illustrated by Sarah Fox-Davies. Henry
Holt 2007 unp il $16.95
Grades: PreK K 1 2   **811**
1. Christmas—Poetry 2. Winter—Poetry 3. Nature poetry 4. Poetry—By individual authors
ISBN 978-0-8050-7491-8; 0-8050-7491-0
                              LC 2006030504
"This well-chosen verse collection features 15 short
poems culled from eight of Fisher's books. . . . Clean
and precise, the poems create indelible but often delicate images. Fox-Davies' endearing paintings reflect the
childlike tone and quiet appreciation of nature inherent in
the verse." Booklist

Fleischman, Paul
Big talk; poems for four voices; illustrated by
Beppe Giacobbe. Candlewick Press 2000 44p il
$17.99; pa $7.99 *
Grades: 4 5 6 7   **811**
1. Poetry—By individual authors
ISBN 0-7636-0636-7; 0-7636-3805-6 (pa)
                              LC 99-46882
A collection of poems to be read aloud by four people, with color-coded text to indicate which lines are
read by which readers
"Each poem is more demanding, and more rewarding,
than the last. Giacobbe highlights the humor in strips of
vignettes that run along the bottom of the page. This is
'toe-tapping, tongue-flapping fun.'" Horn Book Guide

I am phoenix: poems for two voices; illustrated
by Ken Nutt. Harper & Row 1985 51p il pa $5.99
hardcover o.p. *
Grades: 4 5 6 7   **811**
1. Birds—Poetry 2. Poetry—By individual authors
ISBN 0-06-446092-4 (pa)   LC 85-42615
"A Charlotte Zolotow book"
A collection of poems about birds to be read aloud by
two voices
"Devotés of the almost lost art of choral reading
should be among the first to appreciate this collection.
. . . Printed in script form, the selections . . . have a cadenced pace and dignified flow; their combination of
imaginative imagery and realistic detail is echoed by the
combination of stylized fantasy and representational
drawings in the black and white pictures, all soft line and
strong nuance." Bull Cent Child Books

Joyful noise: poems for two voices; illustrated
by Eric Beddows. Harper & Row 1988 44p il
$15.99; lib bdg $16.89; pa $5.99 *
Grades: 4 5 6 7   **811**
1. Insects—Poetry 2. Poetry—By individual authors
ISBN 0-06-021852-5; 0-06-021853-3 (lib bdg);
0-06-446093-2 (pa)   LC 87-45280

Awarded the Newbery Medal, 1989
"A Charlotte Zolotow book"
"This collection of poems for two voices explores the
lives of insects. Designed to be read aloud, the phrases
of the poems are spaced vertically on the page in two
columns, one for each reader. The voices sometimes alternate, sometimes speak in chorus, and sometimes echo
each other." Booklist
"There are fourteen poems in the handsomely designed volume, with stylish endpapers and wonderfully
interpretive black-and-white illustrations. Each selection
is a gem, polished perfection." Horn Book

Fletcher, Ralph, 1953-
A writing kind of day; poems for young poets;
illustrations by April Ward. Wordsong/Boyds Mills
Press 2005 32p il $17.95; pa $9.95
Grades: 3 4 5   **811**
ISBN 1-59078-276-3; 1-59078-353-0 (pa)
"A young writer's daily experiences and concerns are
folded into poems to which many readers can relate. . . .
Varied in mood and tone, the offerings entertain as they
celebrate words and language. . . . Ward's black-and-
white illustrations use a variety of mediums, including
pencil, photography, computer-generated images, and ink.
" SLJ

Florian, Douglas, 1950-
Autumnblings; poems and paintings by Douglas
Florian. Greenwillow Bks. 2003 48p il $15.99; lib
bdg $16.89 *
Grades: 2 3 4 5   **811**
1. Autumn—Poetry 2. Poetry—By individual authors
ISBN 0-06-009278-5; 0-06-009279-3 (lib bdg)
                              LC 2002-29780
A collection of poems that portray the essence of the
season between summer and winter
"Short verse lines make the entries particularly suitable for reading aloud or reciting. . . . The illustrations,
luminous watercolors touched with colored pencils, often
move beyond the decorative to witty visual commentary
or elegant, streamlined scenes." Bull Cent Child Books

Bing bang boing; poems and drawings by
Douglas Florian. Harcourt Brace & Co. 1994 144p
il hardcover o.p. pa $8 *
Grades: 2 3 4 5   **811**
1. Nonsense verses 2. Poetry—By individual authors
ISBN 0-15-233770-9; 0-15-205860-9 (pa)
                              LC 94-3894
Also available in paperback from Penguin Bks.
An illustrated collection of more than 150 nonsense
verses
"The author's spare, pen-and-ink drawings, like the
poems themselves, deftly explore the comic potential in
each combination of words. With a few clean lines, he
creates an original, funny vision." SLJ

Florian, Douglas, 1950-——*Continued*

Comets, stars, the Moon, and Mars; space poems and paintings. Harcourt 2007 45p il $16 *
Grades: 2 3 4 5   811
  1. Astronomy—Poetry 2. Poetry—By individual authors
  ISBN 978-0-15-205372-7; 0-15-205372-7
                        LC 2006-08274
This "book looks at astronomy through the magnifying, clarifying lens of poetry. Each double-page spread features a short, accessible poem about a subject such as the sun, each of its planets, a comet, a constellation, or the universe, set with an impressive painting." Booklist

Dinothesaurus; prehistoric poems and paintings; by Douglas Florian. Atheneum 2009 43p il $17.99 *
Grades: 2 3 4 5   811
  1. Dinosaurs—Poetry 2. Poetry—By individual authors
  ISBN 978-1-4169-7978-4; 1-4169-7978-6
"Florian's freeflowing, witty collection of poems and collages about dinosaurs is a giganotosaurus delight. . . . The poems marry facts with a poet's eye for detail. . . . The heart of the book is in its humor, the spontaneity of both illustrations and poems, and Florian's slightly askew view of the Mesozoic creatures." Publ Wkly
Includes glossary and bibliographical references

Handsprings; poems & paintings by Douglas Florian. Greenwillow Books 2006 48p il $15.99; lib bdg $16.89 *
Grades: 2 3 4 5   811
  1. Spring—Poetry 2. Poetry—By individual authors
  ISBN 0-06-009280-7; 0-06-009281-5 (lib bdg)
                        LC 2005-04567
A collection of short poems about spring
This includes "twenty-nine exuberant poems coupled with whimsical paintings distinguished for their warm colors, spare imagery, and a peculiar, sweet grace." Horn Book

Laugh-eteria; poems and drawings by Douglas Florian. Harcourt Brace & Co. 1999 157p $17; pa $8 *
Grades: 2 3 4 5   811
  1. Humorous poetry 2. Poetry—By individual authors
  ISBN 0-15-202084-5; 0-15-206148-7 (pa)
                        LC 98-20047
A collection of more than 100 humorous poems on such topics as ogres, pizza, fear, school, dragons, trees, and hair
"Florian's pithy poems echo playground chants (and sometimes, better yet, jeers) in their rhythmic recitability . . . and his focus on orality and absurdity makes them thematically irresistible. The line drawings have a sophisticated quirkiness." Bull Cent Child Books

Omnibeasts; animal poems and paintings by Douglas Florian. Harcourt 2004 95p il $18 *
Grades: 2 3 4 5   811
  1. Animals—Poetry 2. Poetry—By individual authors
  ISBN 0-15-205038-8   LC 2003-18823
A compilation of animal poems selected from the author's previously published collections

This "is a treasure chest of wit and charm. The author weaves information into each poem, combining fun and fact. Combined with Florian's signature watercolors . . . each short offering occupies its own spread. This book has enormous appeal for readers of many ages." SLJ

Poetrees. Beach Lane Books 2010 45p il $16.99 *
Grades: 3 4 5 6   811
  1. Trees—Poetry 2. Poetry—By individual authors
  ISBN 978-1-4169-8672-0; 1-4169-8672-3
                        LC 2009-03025
"Florian focuses on trees (seeds, bark, leaves, roots, and tree rings) and introduces readers to 13 species from around the world. An oversize, double-page illustration accompanies each poem. . . . The selections are accessible and concise, with child-friendly wordplay and artful design. . . . The primitive illustrations—crafted on 'primed paper bags' using mixed media including gouache watercolor paints, colored pencils, rubber stamps, oil pastels, and collage—range in nuance from whimsy to mystery and reverence." SLJ

Summersaults; poems & paintings by Douglas Florian. Greenwillow Bks. 2002 48p il $16.99; lib bdg $17.89 *
Grades: 2 3 4 5   811
  1. Summer—Poetry 2. Poetry—By individual authors
  ISBN 0-06-029267-9; 0-06-029268-7 (lib bdg)
                        LC 2001-23619
"Florian examines the joys of summer in twenty-eight brief verses." Bull Cent Child Books
"Florian ably captures the freedom and exuberance of the season in bright, new greens, sun-baked browns, and images of leaping, grinning figures. The gleeful puns, wordplay, and creative grammar will charm youngsters." Booklist

Winter eyes; poems & paintings by Douglas Florian. Greenwillow Bks. 1999 48p il $16 *
Grades: 2 3 4 5   811
  1. Winter—Poetry 2. Poetry—By individual authors
  ISBN 0-688-16458-7   LC 98-19483
A collection of poems about winter, including "Sled," "Icicles," and "Ice Fishing"
"The short rhyming lines are clear and will be easy to read aloud, and the softly toned watercolor-and-colored-pencil pictures show snowy winter scenes, some realistic, some playful." Booklist

Zoo's who; poems and paintings by Douglas Florian. Harcourt 2005 47p il $17 *
Grades: K 1 2 3   811
  1. Animals—Poetry 2. Poetry—By individual authors
  ISBN 0-15-204639-9   LC 2004-4576
A collection of short poems about animals
"There's plenty of humor throughout. . . . The artwork . . . always has unexpected bits. . . . The more astute the reader, the better the time he or she will have with this." Booklist

Frampton, David

Mr. Ferlinghetti's poem. Eerdmans Books for Young Readers 2006 unp $18 *

Grades: K 1 2 3   **811**
    1. Summer—Poetry 2. Fire fighters—Poetry 3. Brooklyn (New York, N.Y.)—Poetry 4. Poetry—By individual authors
    ISBN 0-8028-5290-4   LC 2005024287
"On a sweltering summer day in Brooklyn, the local firemen spray a group of bored city kids with cool water from their hoses." Publisher's note

"Frampton's exuberant pictures match well with an equally vivacious poem. . . . Frampton's signature woodcuts are wonderful, balancing cool and warm colors, and also managing to look both blocky and fluid at the same time." SLJ

Franco, Betsy

Bees, snails, and peacock tails shapes—naturally; [by] Betsy Franco; illustrated by Steve Jenkins. Margaret K. McElderry Books 2008 unp il $16.99 *

Grades: PreK K 1 2   **811**
    1. Nature poetry 2. Shape—Poetry 3. Poetry—By individual authors
    ISBN 978-1-4169-0386-4; 1-4169-0386-0
                    LC 2006-12094
"The pair behind *Birdsongs* tackles another science topic—geometry in the animal world. Whether addressing hexagonal beehive cells or a snail's spiral shell, brisk rhymes draw attention to nature's math. . . . Striking color combinations make the illustrations pop. This inviting book is bound to spark more careful observation of the shapes and colors in the reader's natural world." Publ Wkly

A curious collection of cats; concrete poems; illustrations by Michael Wertz. Tricycle Press 2009 unp il $16.99

Grades: PreK K 1 2 3   **811**
    1. Cats—Poetry 2. Poetry—By individual authors
    ISBN 978-1-58246-248-6; 1-58246-248-8
                    LC 2008-11359
"Thirty-two unusual, concrete poems, one per page with a single exception, are matched by Wertz's monoprints. The words move in several directions and sometimes inhabit multiple objects. The poems are so embedded within the illustrations that it is hard to imagine them without the artwork. . . . Cat lovers will recognize their felines stretching, purring, and napping." SLJ

Messing around on the monkey bars; illustrated by Jessie Hartland. Candlewick Press 2009 45p il $17.99

Grades: 3 4 5   **811**
    1. Poetry—By individual authors 2. Schools—Poetry
    ISBN 978-0-7636-3174-1; 0-7636-3174-4
"A cheeky romp through elementary schoolchildren's academic and social lives. Though readers could tackle the poems alone, differences in typeface cue the possibility for two readers to share the poems aloud. . . . Hartland's energetic gouache illustrations adopt a naive style that matches the playful spirit of the text while serving as a splendid complement to its evocation of children's voices." Kirkus

Frank, John

Keepers; treasure-hunt poems; by John Frank; photographs by Ken Robbins. Roaring Brook Press 2008 64p il $17.95

Grades: 3 4 5   **811**
    1. Collectors and collecting—Poetry 2. Poetry—By individual authors
    ISBN 978-1-59643-197-3; 1-59643-197-0
                    LC 2007013201

"A Neal Porter book"
This is a "collection of short poems about treasures, from geodes to baseball cards to costume jewelry. The verse is grouped thematically according to where the treasures might be found. . . . Writing with clarity and simplicity, Frank varies the rhythm and length of line and stanza from one poem to the next. . . . Though a few poems stand alone, most are illustrated with color photos that are as clear and straightforward as the verse." Booklist

Frost, Robert, 1874-1963

Birches; illustrated by Ed Young. Holt & Co. 1988 unp il pa $8.95 hardcover o.p.

Grades: 3 4 5   **811**
    1. Trees—Poetry 2. Poetry—By individual authors
    ISBN 0-8050-7230-6 (pa)   LC 86-4787
An illustrated version of the well-known poem written in 1916, about birch trees and the pleasures of climbing them

"The freedom called for in the sweep and depth of Frost's words should not be hemmed in by rigidly defined illustrations, and Young allows this license, giving the viewer ample opportunity to absorb and be absorbed by the imagery. The text is set two to three lines to a page, with the poem repeated in its entirety at the end." Booklist

Robert Frost; edited by Gary D. Schmidt; illustrated by Henri Sorensen. Sterling 1994 48p il (Poetry for young people) $14.95; pa $6.95 *

Grades: 4 5 6 7   **811**
    1. Poetry—By individual authors
    ISBN 0-8069-0633-2; 1-4027-5475-2 (pa)
                    LC 94-11161

"A Magnolia Editions book"
This volume "contains a three-page overview of the poet's life, 29 poems selected and arranged around the seasons of the year, brief and apt commentaries on each, and a useful index of titles and subject matter. The realistic watercolor illustrations capture the delicate beauty of a New England spring and the glory of fall while still suggesting the around-the-corner chill of winter, a disquiet echoing throughout much of Frost's poetry." SLJ

George, Kristine O'Connell

Fold me a poem; illustrated by Lauren Stringer. Harcourt 2005 unp il $16 *

Grades: K 1 2 3   **811**
    1. Origami—Poetry 2. Poetry—By individual authors
    ISBN 0-15-202501-4   LC 2003-19382
"George's 32 brief poems focus on a boy as he folds a series of origami animals and imagines their thoughts and possible activities. . . . The vividly colored acrylics

George, Kristine O'Connell—*Continued*

depict the boy actively engaged in play with his creations, and the details that Stringer provides infuse the verses with both energy and humor." SLJ

Includes bibliographical references

The great frog race and other poems; pictures by Kate Kiesler; with an introduction by Myra Cohn Livingston. Clarion Bks. 1997 40p il $15; pa $5.95 *

Grades: 3 4 5   **811**

1. Poetry—By individual authors

ISBN 0-395-77607-4; 0-618-60478-2 (pa)

LC 95-51090

A collection of poems about frogs and dragonflies, wind and rain, a visit to the tree farm, the garden hose, and other aspects of country life

"George's astute imagery pairs beautifully with Kiesler's rich, warm-toned oil paintings to impart a strong sense of the pleasures of rural landscape." Booklist

Little Dog and Duncan; poems by Kristine O'Connell George; illustrated by June Otani. Clarion Bks. 2002 40p il $12

Grades: K 1 2   **811**

1. Dogs—Poetry 2. Poetry—By individual authors

ISBN 0-618-11758-X   LC 2001-28481

"Little Dog hosts a sleepover when big dog Duncan, a rangy Irish wolfhound, comes for a visit. . . . The verses themselves could hardly be shorter, but they are just the right size for Litte Dog and little kids. The layout of the poems is harmoniously designed both for sense and for interplay with Otani's beguilingly casual watercolor sketches." Horn Book Guide

Little dog poems; illustrated by June Otani. Clarion Bks. 1999 40p il $12 *

Grades: K 1 2   **811**

1. Dogs—Poetry 2. Poetry—By individual authors

ISBN 0-395-82266-1   LC 97-46678

"Thirty short poems about a lively terrier, narrated by the dog's young mistress." SLJ

"The language is simple and concrete enough for the youngest listeners. Otani's pen and watercolor illustrations make a fine complement to the verse." Horn Book Guide

Old Elm speaks; tree poems; illustrated by Kate Kiesler. Clarion Bks. 1998 48p il $15; pa $5.95 *

Grades: 2 3 4   **811**

1. Trees—Poetry 2. Poetry—By individual authors

ISBN 0-395-87611-7; 0-618-75242-0 (pa)

LC 97-49333

A collection of short, simple poems which present images relating to trees in various circumstances and throughout the seasons

"George conveys a deep understanding of nature, here particularly of trees, in a way that is readily accessible to children. Kiesler's warm oil paintings beautifully complement the poems." Booklist

Toasting marshmallows; camping poems; illustrated by Kate Kiesler. Clarion Bks. 2001 48p il $15

Grades: 3 4 5   **811**

1. Camping—Poetry 2. Poetry—By individual authors

ISBN 0-618-04597-X   LC 00-56984

"Thirty poems, mostly unrhymed, treat the splendors of camping in the woods." Bull Cent Child Books

"All of the selections convey a child-focused sense of wonder. . . . The poems are varied and inventive, replete with marvelous images and universal truths. . . . Each one is accompanied by a well-executed and evocative acrylic painting." SLJ

Giovanni, Nikki

Spin a soft black song: poems for children; illustrated by George Martins. rev ed. Hill & Wang 1985 57p il pa $4.95 hardcover o.p. *

Grades: 3 4 5 6   **811**

1. African Americans—Poetry 2. Poetry—By individual authors

ISBN 0-374-46469-3 (pa)   LC 84-19287

First published 1971

A poetry collection which recounts the feelings of black children about their neighborhoods, American society, and themselves

"A beautifully illustrated book of poems about black children for children of all ages. . . . Simple in theme but a very moving collection nonetheless." Read Ladders for Hum Relat. 5th edition

The sun is so quiet; poems; illustrations by Ashley Bryan. Holt & Co. 1996 31p il $14.95 *

Grades: K 1 2 3   **811**

1. Nature poetry 2. Poetry—By individual authors

ISBN 0-8050-4119-2   LC 95-39357

A collection of poems primarily about nature and the seasons but also concerned with chocolate and scary movies

"Of the 13 poems presented here, 12 appeared in books published between 1973 and 1993. The new poem, entitled 'Connie,' represents the best of Giovanni: a series of quicksilver images that capture a mood to perfection. Painted in Bryan's signature style, the illustrations fill the pages with sunny colors and bold patterns." Booklist

Gottfried, Maya

Good dog; poems by Maya Gottfried; paintings by Robert Rahway Zakanitch. Alfred A. Knopf 2005 unp il $15.95; lib bdg $17.99; pa $6.99 *

Grades: K 1 2 3   **811**

1. Dogs—Poetry 2. Poetry—By individual authors

ISBN 0-375-83049-9; 0-375-93049-3 (lib bdg); 0-553-11383-6 (pa)   LC 2004-15098

In this "book, free-verse poems that present the inner musings of 16 dogs are combined with painterly, full-page portraits. The verses capture distinct canine personalities. . . . Pencil sketches of the canines are scattered around the text. On the facing pages, Zakanitch's stunning oil paintings of the pets are set against shiny black backgrounds." SLJ

Gottfried, Maya—*Continued*

Our farm; by the animals of Farm Sanctuary; [by] Maya Gottfried [and] Robert Rahway Zakanitch. Alfred A. Knopf 2010 unp il $17.99; lib bdg $20.99 *

Grades: PreK K 1 2 3   **811**

1. Farm Sanctuary Inc. 2. Animals—Poetry 3. Farm life—Poetry 4. Poetry—By individual authors

ISBN   978-0-375-86118-5;   0-375-86118-1; 978-0-375-96118-2 (lib bdg); 0-375-96118-6 (lib bdg)

LC 2009-14885

"This homage to the shelter for neglected and abused farm animals where Gottfried served as a volunteer is a book of poems and accompanying paintings that will raise awareness both of the Sanctuary and the sad reasons for which such a place exists. But it has more to recommend it. The poems are 'narrated' by some of the shelter's inhabitants. . . . There's a disarming innocence throughout, and the best of the selections are enchanting. Zakanitch's illustrations are superb. Each one is a collectible work of art, exhibiting a masterful technique, tenderness, subtlety, and humor." SLJ

Graham, Joan Bransfield

Flicker flash; poems by Joan Bransfield Graham; illustrated by Nancy Davis. Houghton Mifflin 1999 unp il $15; pa $6.95 *

Grades: K 1 2 3   **811**

1. Poetry—By individual authors

ISBN 0-395-90501-X; 0-618-31102-5 (pa)

LC 98-12956

A collection of poems celebrating light in its various forms, from candles and lamps to lightning and fireflies

"A vivid fusion of ingenious concrete poetry and boldly colored graphics." SLJ

Grandits, John, 1949-

Blue lipstick; concrete poems. Clarion Books 2007 unp il $15; pa $5.95 *

Grades: 5 6 7 8 9 10   **811**

1. Poetry—By individual authors

ISBN   978-0-618-56860-4;   0-618-56860-3; 978-0-618-85132-4 (pa); 0-618-85132-1 (pa)

LC 2006-23332

"This selection introduces readers to Jessie, who impulsively purchases blue lipstick, but later, regretfully decides to give it 'the kiss-off.' Jessie is big sister to Robert, who was featured in Grandits's *Technically, It's Not My Fault* (Clarion, 2004). As he did in that terrific collection, the author uses artful arrangements of text on the page, along with 54 different typefaces, to bring his images and ideas to life. . . . This irreverent, witty collection should resonate with a wide audience." SLJ

Technically, it's not my fault; concrete poems; by John Grandits. Clarion Books 2004 unp il $15; pa $5.95 *

Grades: 5 6 7 8   **811**

1. Poetry—By individual authors

ISBN 0-618-42833-X; 0-618-50361-7 (pa)

LC 2004-231

A collection of concrete poems on such topics as roller coasters, linguini, basketball, and sisters

"Grandits combines technical brilliance and goofy good humor to provide an accessible, fun-filled collection of poems, dramatically brought to life through a brilliant book design." SLJ

Grant, Shauntay

Up home; artwork by Susan Tooke; story by Shauntay Grant. Nimbus Publishing 2009 unp il $19.95

Grades: K 1 2 3   **811**

1. Nova Scotia—Poetry 2. African Americans—Poetry

ISBN 978-1-55109-660-5; 1-55109-660-9

This illustrated poem evokes the author's memories of growing up in the Canadian town of Preston, Nova Scotia.

"Deceptively simple, the poetic narrative vividly conveys an array of remembered images, sights, sounds, and emotions, all of which are brought to life in Tooke's realistic acrylic images." SLJ

Greenfield, Eloise, 1929-

Brothers & sisters; family poems; illustrated by Jan Spivey Gilchrist. Amistad 2009 32p il $17.99; lib bdg $18.89

Grades: K 1 2 3   **811**

1. Siblings—Poetry 2. African Americans—Poetry 3. Poetry—By individual authors

ISBN   978-0-06-056284-7;   0-06-056284-6; 978-0-06-056285-4 (lib bdg); 0-06-056285-4 (lib bdg)

LC 2008020209

"Greenfield's poetic observations and commentaries succinctly capture siblings at various ages and stages. . . . With only a few lines, the author grasps the love and admiration, the frustration and hurt, the fun and aggravation that they can engender. . . . The illustrator is equally as skillful in depicting the wide range of emotions and ages in the faces of the individual African Americans peopling the paintings. The realistic watercolors fit around and beside the poems, using the white space to highlight the art and give balance to the pages." SLJ

Honey, I love, and other love poems; pictures by Diane and Leo Dillon. Crowell 1978 unp il $14.95; pa $5.95 *

Grades: 2 3 4   **811**

1. African Americans—Poetry 2. Love poetry 3. Poetry—By individual authors

ISBN 0-690-01334-5; 0-06-443097-9 (pa)

LC 77-2845

"These 16 poems explore facets of warm, loving relationships with family, friends and schoolmates as experienced by a young Black girl. Central to the theme of the book is the idea that the child loves herself and is very confident in expressing that love." Interracial Books Child Bull

"The Dillons transform this quiet book into magic with soft, grey charcoal renderings of the young girl and her friends, overlaid with child-like brown scratchboard pictures embodying the images in the poems." SLJ

Greenfield, Eloise, 1929-—_Continued_

When the horses ride by; children in the times of war; poems by Eloise Greenfield; illustrations by Jan Spivey Gilchrist. Lee & Low Books 2006 unp il $17.95
Grades: 2 3 4 **811**
    1. War poetry 2. Poetry—By individual authors
    ISBN 978-1-58430-249-0; 1-58430-249-6
                         LC 2005015393
Collection of poems about children around the world, focusing on the children's perceptions of war and how the turmoil of war affects their lives.
"Combining 17 rhythmic poems with dramatic illustrations, this title addresses a complex topic. Greenfield's deceptively simple verses express universal truths about both conflict and childhood." SLJ

Grimes, Nikki

At Jerusalem's gate; poems of Easter; with woodcuts by David Frampton. Eerdmans Books for Young Readers 2005 unp il $20
Grades: 5 6 7 8 **811**
    1. Jesus Christ—Poetry 2. Easter—Poetry 3. Poetry—By individual authors
    ISBN 0-8028-5183-5   LC 2003-1089
A collection of poems which tells the story of the first Easter.
"Each poem is preceded by a brief synopsis of the event, often accompanied by the author's own musings and queries, which prompt readers to think and ask questions of their own. . . . Bold, handsome woodcuts reinforce the powerful drama depicted in poetry. An outstanding effort." SLJ

Meet Danitra Brown; illustrated by Floyd Cooper. Lothrop, Lee & Shepard Bks. 1994 unp il pa $6.99 hardcover o.p. *
Grades: 2 3 4 **811**
    1. African Americans—Poetry 2. Friendship—Poetry 3. Poetry—By individual authors
    ISBN 0-688-15471-9 (pa)   LC 92-43707
"A collection of 13 original poems that stand individually and also blend together to tell a story of feelings and friendship between two African-American girls. . . . Cooper's distinguished illustrations in warm dusty tones convey the feeling of closeness. The poignant text and lovely pictures are an excellent collaboration." SLJ
 Other titles about Danitra Brown are:
Danitra Brown, class clown (2005)
Danitra Brown leaves town (2002)

A pocketful of poems; illustrated by Javaka Steptoe. Clarion Bks. 2001 30p il $15 *
Grades: K 1 2 3 **811**
    1. City and town life—Poetry 2. Haiku 3. Poetry—By individual authors
    ISBN 0-395-93868-6   LC 00-24232
"Tiana has round glasses, a wide mouth, and long braids; she opens her hands full of letters and her pocket full of words. Each page has two facing poems, both in Tiana's voice: one is short and bracing, the other is a haiku in the standard five-seven-five syllable configuration. . . . The first poem in a pair is set in standard type;

the haiku usually floats or sways or sashays amidst the illustrations. . . . Steptoe is a fabulously inventive collagist. He does amazing things not only with cut and torn paper and string but also with drinking straws, aluminum plates, and stray beads." Booklist

Thanks a million; poems by Nikki Grimes; pictures by Cozbi A. Cabrera. Greenwillow Books 2006 31p il $15.99; lib bdg $16.89
Grades: K 1 2 3 **811**
    1. Poetry—By individual authors
    ISBN 0-688-17292-X; 0-688-17293-8 (lib bdg)
                       LC 2004-54158
"Sixteen thoughtful poems about being thankful for everyday things. Grimes uses a variety of forms that include haiku, a riddle, and a rebus in selections that speak directly to the experiences of young children. . . . Cabreras acrylic illustrations are distinctive, folksy, and effective." SLJ

What is goodbye? illustrations by Raúl Colón. Hyperion Books for Children 2004 unp il $15.99 *
Grades: 4 5 6 7 **811**
    1. Death—Poetry 2. Family life—Poetry 3. Poetry—By individual authors
    ISBN 0-7868-0778-4   LC 2002-72987
Alternating poems by a brother and sister convey their feelings about the death of their older brother and the impact it had on their family.
"Grimes handles these two voices fluently and lucidly, shaping her characters through her form. Colón's paintings in muted colors combine imagism with realism to create an emotional dreamscape on nearly every page." SLJ

When Gorilla goes walking; by Nikki Grimes; illustrated by Shane Evans. Orchard Books 2007 unp il $16.99 *
Grades: PreK K 1 2 **811**
    1. Cats—Poetry 2. African Americans—Poetry 3. Poetry—By individual authors
    ISBN 978-0-439-31770-2   LC 2006017194
"In interlinked poems, Cecilia, a young African American girl, introduces her 'cool cat'—a fierce, tailless, gray shorthair named Gorilla. . . . In spare, expressive lines and bold colors, Evans' dynamic paintings capture the messy intimacy of the cat and human bond." Booklist

Gutman, Dan

Casey back at bat; paintings by Steve Johnson and Lou Fancher. HarperCollins 2007 unp il $16.99; lib bdg $17.89 *
Grades: K 1 2 3 4 **811**
    1. Baseball—Poetry 2. Poetry—By individual authors
    ISBN   978-0-06-056025-6;   0-06-056025-8; 978-0-06-056026-3 (lib bdg); 0-06-056026-6 (lib bdg)
                       LC 2006029468
Sequel to Ernest Lawrence Thayer's Casey at the bat
"Gutman revisits and updates Thayer's classic baseball poem. This time around . . . Casey hits a fly ball that soars out of the park and keeps on going. It crosses the Atlantic Ocean and has an unfortunate encounter with a tower in Pisa before continuing on to the Sphinx in

Gutman, Dan—*Continued*

Egypt. . . . It passes dinosaurs . . . and astronauts before heading back to Earth. The ride is uproarious from start to finish, and Gutman's broadly humorous verse hits all the right notes. . . . Johnson and Fancher's paintings have a playfully nostalgic look, with a mix of textured papers and newsprint splashed across the surfaces of uniforms." SLJ

Harley, Avis

African acrostics; a word in edgeways; poems by Avis Harley; photographs by Deborah Noyes. Candlewick Press 2009 unp il $17.99 *

Grades: 4 5 6 7   **811**

1. Animals—Africa 2. Animals—Poetry 3. Acrostics 4. Poetry—By individual authors

ISBN 978-0-7636-3621-0; 0-7636-3621-5

LC 2008-17916

"Harley has written 18 poems, each one featuring a different animal. All are written as acrostics, with most of them based on the first letter of each line, but several with more unusual patterns. . . . Much of Harley's poetry consists of carefully crafted descriptive word imagery that is right on target. . . . Most of the full-page, full-color photos of the animals are perfect companions to the facing selections." SLJ

The monarch's progress; poems with wings; written and illustrated by Avis Harley. Wordsong 2008 32p il $16.95

Grades: 3 4 5   **811**

1. Butterflies—Poetry 2. Poetry—By individual authors

ISBN 978-1-59078-558-4

"This collection of 18 illustrated poems celebrates butterflies in general and monarchs in particular. Cleverly written with obvious attention to craft, the poetry varies in form from rhymed couplets to acrostic verse to haiku and explores topics such as the physical differences between the larval and adult stages, the way monarch wings look when magnified, and the usefulness of having taste sensors in one's feet. Accompanying each poem is a color-pencil drawing, often featuring precise lines and intense hues." Booklist

Sea stars; saltwater poems; [by] Avis Harley; photographs by Margaret Butschler. Wordsong 2006 35p il $16.95 *

Grades: 3 4 5   **811**

1. Marine animals—Poetry 2. Poetry—By individual authors

ISBN 978-1-59078-429-7; 1-59078-429-4

LC 2006000931

"Butschler's beautiful color photographs came first, and her visual images of creatures on the seashore and in the aquarium inspired Harley's brief, concrete poems—from haiku and tanka to rhyming couplets and nursery rhyme parody. The wordplay will grab readers . . . and so will the exquisite images in both words and pictures." Booklist

Harrison, David L. (David Lakin), 1937-

Bugs; poems about creeping things; [by] David L. Harrison; drawings by Rob Shepperson. Wordsong 2007 55p il $16.95

Grades: K 1 2 3   **811**

1. Insects—Poetry 2. Poetry—By individual authors

ISBN 978-1-59078-451-8   LC 2006011586

"This compact volume attempts to capture a variety of bugs for closer examination. The 40 small poems feature everything from a louse to a chocolate-covered grasshopper. Playful black-and-white cartoon illustrations and page layouts punch up the poetry's delicate silliness." SLJ

Vacation; we're going to the ocean; poems by David Harrison; illustrations by Rob Shepperson. Wordsong 2009 62p il $16.95

Grades: 2 3 4   **811**

1. Family life—Poetry 2. Ocean—Poetry 3. Vacations—Poetry 4. Poetry—By individual authors

ISBN 978-1-59078-568-3; 1-59078-568-1

LC 2008017718

"These delightful poems center on a family's trip to the ocean and are told from the perspective of young Sam. . . . This book, with its expressive art that expands on the humor in each poem, should have wide appeal." SLJ

Harrison, David Lee, 1937-

Pirates; poems by David L. Harrison; illustrations by Dan Burr. Wordsong 2008 unp il $17.95

Grades: 4 5 6   **811**

1. Pirates—Poetry 2. Poetry—By individual authors

ISBN 978-1-59078-455-6; 1-59078-455-3

LC 2007-52386

"Large realistic paintings work with 20 narrative poems to describe the nitty-gritty details of pirate life. Nothing is sugarcoated. One young man is shown tied to a post, subjected to a whipping. . . . Two pirates are shown in shackles, facing the hangman's noose. . . . Burr's illustrations do a fine job of conveying the emotions of each poem and of showing the details of dress and shipboard life. An afterword further explains the unromantic world of piracy." SLJ

Harvey, Sarah N., 1950-

The West is calling; imagining British Columbia; [by] Sarah N. Harvey & Leslie Buffam; illustrated by Dianna Bonder. Orca Book Publishers 2008 unp il $19.95

Grades: 1 2 3 4   **811**

1. British Columbia 2. Haiku 3. Poetry—By individual authors

ISBN 978-1-55143-936-5; 1-55143-936-0

"Though it includes a haiku on each page, this title is much more than simply a poetry book. It is a history lesson, a seek-and-find (objects to find on each spread are listed in the back), and a paean to British Columbia all rolled into one neatly designed package. Realistic paintings expand the essence of each haiku and are full of details that will hold readers' interest." SLJ

Havill, Juanita

I heard it from Alice Zucchini; poems about the garden; by Juanita Havill; illustrated by Christine Davenier. Chronicle Books 2006 29p il $15.95

Grades: K 1 2 3 4 **811**
1. Gardens—Poetry 2. Gardening—Poetry 3. Poetry—By individual authors
ISBN 978-0-8118-3962-4; 0-8118-3962-1
LC 2004013365

"Havill's collection of verse captures the science and backyard magic of growing things. . . . Davenier extends the fanciful imagery in scenes of lively, gossiping plants and animals, rendered in her signature watercolor-washed ink sketches." Booklist

Herrera, Juan Felipe, 1948-

Laughing out loud, I fly; poems in English and Spanish; drawings by Karen Barbour. HarperCollins Pubs. 1998 unp il $15.99 *

Grades: 6 7 8 9 **811**
1. Bilingual books—English-Spanish 2. Poetry—By individual authors 3. Mexican Americans—Poetry
ISBN 0-06-027604-5
LC 96-45476

"Joanna Cotler books"

A collection of poems in Spanish and English about childhood, place, and identity

"Barbour's black-and-white drawings accompany each poem, delicately underlining its images but allowing the strong sensuality of the words to seep into readers' minds." SLJ

Hines, Anna Grossnickle, 1946-

Pieces; a year in poems & quilts. Greenwillow Bks. 2001 unp il $15.95; lib bdg $15.89

Grades: K 1 2 3 **811**
1. Nature poetry 2. Quilts 3. Poetry—By individual authors
ISBN 0-688-16963-5; 0-688-16964-3 (lib bdg)
LC 99-86463

Poems about the four seasons, as reflected in the natural world, are accompanied by photographs of quilts made by the author

"An appendix explains Hines's meticulous quilting process. . . . Hines takes her quilter's stash of fabric swatches and her wordsmith's metaphors for memories of the seasons, and pieces together a unified, artistic whole. An outstanding book for aspiring quilters or anyone at all." Publ Wkly

Includes bibliographical references

Winter lights; a season in poems & quilts. Greenwillow Bks. 2005 unp il $16.99; lib bdg $17.89 *

Grades: K 1 2 3 **811**
1. Winter—Poetry 2. Holidays—Poetry 3. Quilts 4. Poetry—By individual authors
ISBN 0-06-000817-2; 0-06-000818-0 (lib bdg)

"Winter is the time of lights, and Hines celebrates the season in thoughtful poems and pictures of gorgeous quilts full of bright, beautiful colors. Christmas is only one of the light-producing celebrations that Hines illuminates. The feast of Santa Lucia, Hanukkah, Kwanzaa, and the Chinese New Year are spectacularly introduced with short bursts of poetry and quilts that capture the spirit of the day." Booklist

Hoberman, Mary Ann, 1930-

You read to me, I'll read to you; very short Mother Goose tales to read together; illustrated by Michael Emberley. Little, Brown 2005 32p il $16.99 *

Grades: K 1 2 3 **811**
1. Nursery rhymes—Fiction 2. Poetry—By individual authors
ISBN 0-316-14431-2
LC 2004-7569

"Megan Tingley books"

Contents: Humpty dumpty; Jack, be nimble; Jack and Jill; Jack Sprat; Little Boy Blue and Little Bo Peep; Little Jack Horner and Little Tommy Tucker; Little Miss Muffet; Old King Cole and The cat and the fiddle; Old Mother Hubbard; Peter, Peter, pumpkin eater; Pussycat, pussycat, where have you been?; Simple Simon

"Hoberman and Emberley introduce shared reading experiences that retell and elaborate on Mother Goose rhymes. Consisting of 14 short tales, each story is designed to be read by two voices that, at times, come together for shared lines. . . . Told in verse, these stories will appeal to readers who are familiar with the original rhymes. . . . The careful word choices are ideal for beginning and reluctant readers. . . . The bright and cheery artwork captures the humor." SLJ

You read to me, I'll read to you; very short stories to read together; illustrated by Michael Emberley. Little, Brown 2001 unp il $15.95 *

Grades: K 1 2 3 **811**
1. Poetry—By individual authors
ISBN 0-316-36350-2
LC 00-35230

"Megan Tingley books"

"Hoberman offers 13 rhymed variations on the theme of getting together to read. The short poems are designed to be read aloud by two voices, with occasional parts to share. . . . The energy never flags, neither in Hoberman's trademark bouncy rhythms nor in Emberley's exuberant illustrations, which picture a wonderful array of children and animals tumbling across the pages." Booklist

You read to me, I'll read to you: very short scary tales to read together; illustrated by Michael Emberley. Little, Brown 2007 32p il $16.99 *

Grades: K 1 2 3 **811**
1. Monsters—Poetry 2. Poetry—By individual authors
ISBN 978-0-316-01733-6

"The fourth uproarious poetry picture book in Hoberman and Emberley's popular You Read to Me, I'll Read to You series continues the pattern of simple, rhyming, illustrated stories for two voices. . . . The clear words with gorgeously gruesome, comic-style pictures tell of wild action and monster characters as lurid as they come." Booklist

Hoce, Charley

Beyond Old MacDonald; funny poems from down on the farm; illustrated by Eugenie Fernandes. Wordsong/Boyds Mills Press 2005 31p il $16.95

Grades: K 1 2 3 **811**

1. Farm life—Poetry 2. Poetry—By individual authors
ISBN 1-59078-312-3

"Hoce employs wordplay in many of these 30 selections. . . . The humor is age appropriate and poems about 'ants in my plants' and a hoarse horse will appeal to children who are beginning to enjoy playing with language. . . . This book is fun, but it's also excellent for classroom use; a 'Wordplay Guide' that indicates language skills, such as identifying homophones, personification, and idioms, is appended." SLJ

Hopkins, Lee Bennett, 1938-

City I love; by Lee Bennett Hopkins; illustrated by Marcellus Hall. Abrams Books for Young Readers 2009 unp il $16.95 *

Grades: K 1 2 3 4 **811**

1. City and town life—Poetry 2. Poetry—By individual authors
ISBN 978-0-8109-8327-4; 0-8109-8327-3

LC 2008008226

"A backpack-toting, humble hound with wanderlust and a winged companion tour several of the world's cities. Hopkins's 18 poems observe skyscrapers, hot-dog vendors, subways, taxis, bridges, bright lights, and the diversity of people and pigeons. . . . These polished poems are equally matched by Hall's graphic-style cartoons, which offer many added layers of narrative delight as well as beautiful colors and an eye-catching sense of design." SLJ

Hughes, Langston, 1902-1967

The dream keeper and other poems; including seven additional poems; [by] Langston Hughes; illustrated by Brian Pinkney. 75th anniversary ed. Alfred A. Knopf 2007 83p il $16.99 *

Grades: 4 5 6 7 **811**

1. African Americans—Poetry 2. Poetry—By individual authors
ISBN 978-0-679-84421-1

First published 1932; this is a reissue of the 1994 edition

A collection of sixty-six poems, selected by the author for young readers, including lyrical poems, songs, and blues, many exploring the black experience

"Black-and-white scratchboard illustrations in Pinkney's signature style express the emotion and beat of the poetry. . . . The poems are . . . colloquial and direct yet mysterious and complex." Booklist

Langston Hughes; edited by Arnold Rampersad & David Roessel; illustrations by Benny Andrews. Sterling Pub. 2006 48p il (Poetry for young people) $14.95 *

Grades: 5 6 7 8 **811**

1. African Americans—Poetry 2. Poetry—By individual authors
ISBN 1-4027-1845-4; 978-1-4027-1845-8

LC 2005025369

A brief profile of African American poet Langston Hughes accompanies some of his better known poems for children.

"This charming collection of 26 poems is vibrantly illustrated with depictions of African Americans in varied settings. . . . This will be a welcome introduction to Hughes's poetry for elementary students, and it includes sufficient detail to make it useful and enjoyable for older students." SLJ

My people; photographs by Charles R. Smith Jr. Atheneum Books for Young Readers 2009 unp il $17.99 *

Grades: K 1 2 3 **811**

1. African Americans—Poetry 2. Poetry—By individual authors
ISBN 978-1-4169-3540-7; 1-4169-3540-1

LC 2008025604

ALA EMIERT Coretta Scott King Illustrator Award (2010)

"ginee seo books"

"Introducing the poem two or three words at a time, Smith pairs each phrase with a portrait of one or more African Americans; printed in sepia, the faces of his subjects materialize on black pages. . . . Smith's faces emerge into the light, displaying the best that humanity has to offer—intelligence, wisdom, curiosity, love and joy." Publ Wkly

The Negro speaks of rivers; [by] Langston Hughes; with illustrations by E. B. Lewis. Disney Jump at the Sun Books 2009 unp il $16.99 *

Grades: K 1 2 3 **811**

1. African Americans—Poetry 2. Rivers—Poetry 3. Poetry—By individual authors
ISBN 978-0-7868-1867-9; 0-7868-1867-0

ALA EMIERT Coretta Scott King Illustrator Award Honor Book (2010)

"Rivers all over the world . . . become the stage for portraying the experiences of black people throughout history." Publ Wkly

Children will "easily connect with these luminous, soul-stirring pictures that honor both African American heritage and the whole human family. Transcendent images for a transcendent poem." Booklist

Iyengar, Malathi Michelle

Tan to tamarind; poems about the color brown; poems by Malathi Michelle Iyengar; illustrations by Jamel Akib. Children's Book Press 2009 30p il $16.95

Grades: K 1 2 3 **811**

1. Color—Poetry 2. Poetry—By individual authors
ISBN 978-0-89239-227-8; 0-89239-227-4

LC 2008022225

"Illustrated with pastel pictures in warm autumn colors, both dark and light, the simple poems celebrate the diversity and the connections in nature, culture, place, and language among blacks, Latinos, Indians, Native Americans, and many mixed-race kids. All the names for brown—from *tan* to *honey*, *beige*, and *ocher*—show the wonder of the senses." Booklist

Janeczko, Paul B., 1945-

Wing nuts; screwy haiku; by Paul B. Janeczko and J. Patrick Lewis; illustrated by Tricia Tusa. Little, Brown 2006 unp il $15.99 *

Grades: 2 3 4   **811**

    1. Poetry—By individual authors

    ISBN 0-316-60731-2   LC 2005-07970

"This book introduces senryu, a Japanese verse form that can involve the evasive, the punny, the parodic, and the slapstick. . . . The highly spirited verses feature witty wordplay and puns. . . . This book fulfills its purpose to revive and invigorate the language, and does so with humor. In her ink-and-watercolor cartoons, Tusa uses a soft palette, strong lines, and abundant white space to define the comical characters." SLJ

Johnson, Dinah

Hair dance! words by Dinah Johnson; photographs by Kelly Johnson. Henry Holt 2007 unp il $16.95

Grades: K 1 2   **811**

    1. Hair—Poetry 2. Girls—Poetry 3. African Americans—Poetry 4. Poetry—By individual authors

    ISBN 978-0-8050-6523-7; 0-8050-6523-7

                LC 2006-30616

"This vibrant offering pairs colorful photographs of African-American girls with upbeat verses. The youngsters are shown alone and together, and their moods and expressions vary from shy and pensive to bold and exuberant. They wear their hair loose and natural, and in barrettes, beads, Afro puffs, or braids that 'fly high into the sky.' . . . Most of the verses are short and rhythmic and read aloud like a jump-rope rhyme." SLJ

Includes bibliographical references

Johnston, Tony

Voice from afar; poems of peace; by Tony Johnston; paintings by Susan Guevara. Holiday House 2008 32p il $16.95

Grades: 5 6 7 8   **811**

    1. War poetry 2. Poetry—By individual authors

    ISBN 978-0-8234-2012-4; 0-8234-2012-4

                LC 2007031434

"Johnston offers thoughtful responses to war's senseless violence. Her free-verse word pictures call to mind scenes of terrible devastation. . . .Yet Johnston finds cause for hope amid the grimness. . . . Johnston adds her own voice, the sympathetic observer from afar, sending prayers for peace. Guevara's paintings, crafted with acrylic and oil paint with collage on textured canvas, feature subdued, neutral colors and haunting images." SLJ

Katz, Alan

Oops! poems by Alan Katz; drawings by Edward Koren. Margaret K. McElderry Books 2008 132p il $17.99

Grades: 3 4 5 6   **811**

    1. Humorous poetry 2. Poetry—By individual authors

    ISBN 978-1-4169-0204-1; 1-4169-0204-X

                LC 2005-32439

"This collection of more than 100 short, funny, rhyming poems never lags. It includes occasional (rather funny) potty humor. . . . Puns and other groaners abound and are sure to delight young readers, especially boys. . . . Koren's pen-and-ink cartoons resemble the art in Shel Silverstein's collections. The illustrations match the tone of the book and sometimes add extra interpretations of the poems. This is a great choice for reluctant poetry readers and aspiring class clowns." SLJ

Katz, Susan

Oh, Theodore! guinea pig poems; illustrated by Stacey Schuett. Clarion Books 2007 43p il $16

Grades: PreK K 1 2   **811**

    1. Guinea pigs—Poetry 2. Poetry—By individual authors

    ISBN 978-0-618-70222-0; 0-618-70222-9

                LC 2006-29205

"The young narrator badly wants a pet, but his mom says dogs are loud and snakes are too scary. So the boy reluctantly winds up with a guinea pig. Through short poems and free verse, the boy and readers get to know Theodore. . . . The Latino mother and son, along with Theodore himself, are attractively portrayed. . . . An oversize format with plenty of white space adds appeal, and the short text can be used with beginning readers." Booklist

Larios, Julie Hofstrand, 1949-

Imaginary menagerie; a book of curious creatures; poems by Julie Larios; [illustrated by] Julie Paschkis. Harcourt 2008 32p il $16 *

Grades: K 1 2 3   **811**

    1. Mythical animals—Poetry 2. Poetry—By individual authors

    ISBN 978-0-15-206325-2   LC 2006-37442

This is a collection of poems about "mythical creatures. . . . Working in a range of styles, Larios creates accessible, atmospheric poems full of sounds and rhythms that are best read aloud. . . . Paschkis' beautifully patterned pictures use motifs such as Nordic designs scrawled across the trolls' bridge to correspond to each creature's country of origin." Booklist

Yellow elephant; a bright bestiary; poems by Julie Larios; paintings by Julie Paschkis. Harcourt 2006 31p il $16 *

Grades: K 1 2 3   **811**

    1. Animals—Poetry 2. Color—Poetry 3. Poetry—By individual authors

    ISBN 0-15-205422-7   LC 2004-25163

"The animals featured in these well-crafted poems flash with color and emotion. Each spread features a picture of a brightly hued animal, and Larios' rhythms and sounds skillfully reinforce the memorable, evocative images. . . . Together with Paschkis' vibrant, patterned, gouache paintings, the poems beautifully show how color and sound create mood and imagery." Booklist

811   CHILDREN'S CORE COLLECTION
TWENTIETH EDITION

Lawrence, Jacob, 1917-2000

Harriet and the Promised Land. Simon & Schuster Bks. for Young Readers 1993 unp il $18; pa $6.99 *

Grades: 2 3 4 5   811

1. Tubman, Harriet, 1820?-1913—Poetry 2. Poetry—By individual authors

ISBN 0-671-86673-7; 0-689-80965-4 (pa)

LC 92-33740

A newly illustrated edition of the title first published 1968 by Windmill Books

"Simple rhymes tell the story of Harriet Tubman, the slave who led many of her people North to freedom." Adventuring with Books

"The strength of this volume is in the forceful, stylized paintings by the famous black artist, which capture the degradation of slavery." Brooklyn. Art Books for Child

Lawson, JonArno, 1968-

Black stars in a white night sky; [by] JonArno Lawson; illustrated by Sherwin Tjia. Wordsong 2008 c2006 118p il $16.95

Grades: 4 5 6 7   811

1. Humorous poetry 2. Poetry—By individual authors

ISBN 978-1-59078-521-8   LC 2007018927

First published 2006 in Canada

"This uproarious collection blends slapstick, puns, parodies, and sheer absurdity with lots of wry ideas. . . . Tjia's surreal art, in black-and-white silhouettes, is as rhythmic and absurd as the verse, which is perfect for reading aloud." Booklist

Levy, Debbie

Maybe I'll sleep in the bathtub tonight; and other funny bedtime poems; illustrated by Stephanie Buscema. Sterling Pub. 2010 24p il $14.95

Grades: PreK K 1 2   811

1. Bedtime—Poetry 2. Humorous poetry 3. Poetry—By individual authors

ISBN 978-1-4027-4944-5; 1-4027-4944-9

LC 2008-48826

"These cozy rhymes for sharing at bedtime have a lot of fun with wordplay, from the literal interpretations of sleepover, showing kids on a roof, and sleep tight (I unkinked myself and vowed: / Tonight I will sleep loose!), to a familiar nursery lullaby. . . . Young children with their caregivers will giggle at the humorous scenes, illustrated with colorful gouache pictures, which could make a good prelude to the usual soothing lullabies." Booklist

The year of goodbyes; a true story of friendship, family and farewells. Disney-Hyperion Books 2010 136p il $16.99 *

Grades: 5 6 7 8   811

1. Holocaust, 1933-1945—Poetry 2. Jews—Poetry 3. Poetry—By individual authors

ISBN 978-1-4231-2901-1; 1-4231-2901-6

LC 2009-18671

"Artfully weaving together her mother's *poesiealbum* (autograph/poetry album), diary, and her own verse, Levy crafts a poignant portrait of her Jewish mother's life in 1938 Nazi Germany that crackles with adolescent vitality." Publ Wkly

Lewin, Betsy, 1937-

Animal snackers; by Betsy Lewin. Henry Holt & Co. 2004 unp il $15.95

Grades: K 1 2 3   811

1. Animals—Poetry 2. Food—Poetry 3. Poetry—By individual authors

ISBN 0-8050-6748-5   LC 2003-22501

A revised and newly illustrated edition of the title first published 1980 by Dodd, Mead

Short poems describe the eating habits of gorillas, ostriches, koalas, tickbirds, sea otters, and other animals

"Lewin uses humor in language and large, loose ink and watercolor paintings to give preschoolers a first, very basic natural history lesson." Horn Book Guide

Lewis, J. Patrick

Birds on a wire; a Renga 'round town; [by] J. Patrick Lewis & Paul B. Janeczko; illustrations by Gary Lippincott. Wordsong 2008 unp il $17.95 *

Grades: 2 3 4   811

1. Renga 2. Poetry—By individual authors

ISBN 978-1-59078-383-2; 1-59078-383-2

LC 2006-11582

"In the Japanese verse form called *renga*, a cousin to the haiku, two or more poets take turns, each playing off the previous verse so that the narrative is propelled in constantly new and surprising directions. Lewis and Janeczko, both accomplished youth poets, prove just how compelling this form can be. . . . Mirroring the verse form, each of Lippincott's two-page spreads offers visual clues as to what the next will hold as well as echoes of the previous one. . . . This lovely picture book is an impeccable synthesis of text and image, each simultaneously playing off the other in ways insightful and visceral." Booklist

Blackbeard, the pirate king; several yarns detailing the legends, myths, and real-life adventures of history's most notorious seaman; told in verse by J. Patrick Lewis. National Geographic Society 2006 unp il map $16.95; lib bdg $25.90 *

Grades: 3 4 5   811

1. Blackbeard, 1680?-1718—Poetry 2. Pirates—Poetry 3. Poetry—By individual authors

ISBN 0-7922-5585-2; 0-7922-5586-0 (lib bdg)

LC 2005-29514

"Lewis crafts sophisticated verse around the few facts and many fictions told of Edward Teach, otherwise known as Blackbeard, the seventeenth century pirate king. In antique type, the poems are either set against parchment-style backgrounds or against one of the book's diverse images, which include paintings by N. C. Wyeth, and Caspar David Friedrich, as well as archival prints and striking modern paintings. Despite the broad range of art styles, the story flows cohesively throughout, vividly evoking the buccaneer's adventures in swashbuckling lines that read aloud well." Booklist

Lewis, J. Patrick—*Continued*

The brothers' war; Civil War voices in verse; including photographs by Civil War photographers. National Geographic 2007 31p il $17.95; lib bdg $20.90 *

Grades: 5 6 7 8 9 10   **811**
  1. United States—History—1861-1865, Civil War—Poetry 2. Poetry—By individual authors
  ISBN 978-1-4263-0036-3; 978-1-4263-0037-0 (lib bdg)   LC 2006-103275

"This heartrending collection of original poems paired with photographs by Civil War photographers makes real what statistics about war cannot—that the casualties of any war have human faces. Lewis . . . writes poignantly and lyrically. . . . An elegant design of gold, silver and black handsomely frames the text and photographs." Publ Wkly

Countdown to summer; a poems for every day of the school year; illustrations by Ethan Long. Little, Brown and Co. 2009 unp il $15.99

Grades: 4 5 6   **811**
  1. Schools—Poetry 2. Poetry—By individual authors
  ISBN 978-0-316-02089-3; 0-316-02089-3   LC 2008016772

"180 poems are here gathered to be enjoyed on a vitamin-like one-a-day basis. . . . Some verses are long, some short, some thought-provoking, some laugh-provoking. Long's penciled spot art provides an agreeable visual accompaniment." Kirkus

Doodle dandies; poems that take shape; J. Patrick Lewis, words; Lisa Desimini, images; with design and typography by Ann Bobco and Lisa Desimini. Atheneum Bks. for Young Readers 1998 unp il hardcover o.p. pa $7.99 *

Grades: 1 2 3 4   **811**
  1. Poetry—By individual authors
  ISBN 0-689-81075-X; 0-689-84889-7 (pa)   LC 96-1920

"An Anne Schwartz book"

A collection of poems each of which appears on the page in the shape of its subject so that the poem looks like whatever it's about

"Every page of this book is well designed, creating words and images that work together in harmony. . . . *Doodle Dandies* captures the joy that wordplay can bring." SLJ

The house; illustrated by Roberto Innocenti. Creative Editions 2009 unp il $19.95 *

Grades: 4 5 6 7   **811**
  1. Houses—Poetry 2. Poetry—By individual authors
  ISBN 978-1-56846-201-1; 1-56846-201-8

"The walls in a stone farmhouse literally talk in this first-person narrative that deals with the ravages of time and their effects on the structure and its inhabitants. After a brief history, the house (constructed in 1656, 'a plague year') fast forwards to the dawn of the 20th century, when children discover its ruins. The quatrains, one to a spread, alternate between an AABB and ABBA rhyme scheme, thus avoiding singsong predictability. . . . Children will pore over Innocenti's marvelously detailed spreads, composed in an oversize, vertical format

and set in an Italian hill town. . . . In the subset of books dealing intelligently with the effects of time on a single location, this is a provocative choice." SLJ

Monumental verses. National Geographic 2005 31p il $16.95; lib bdg $25.90 *

Grades: 5 6 7 8   **811**
  1. Monuments—Poetry 2. Poetry—By individual authors
  ISBN 0-7922-7135-1; 0-7922-7139-4 (lib bdg)

"Lewis offers 14 poems celebrating monumental structures. From the remnants of civilizations at Stonehenge, Easter Island, and Machu Picchu to the more modern achievements of the Taj Mahal, the Eiffel Tower, and the Statue of Liberty, the subjects are varied and the accompanying photos are striking." Booklist

Once upon a tomb; gravely humorous verses; illustrated by Simon Bartram. Candlewick 2006 unp il $16.99 *

Grades: 3 4 5   **811**
  1. Death—Poetry 2. Poetry—By individual authors
  ISBN 0-7636-1837-3

"Proving himself to be anything but a grave man, Lewis offers 22 irreverent epitaphs and other mortuary verses, each of which is paired with a large, polished portrait or burial scene created in richly hued acrylics. . . . This rare look at the lighter side of death should elicit plenty of surprised giggles from young audiences." Booklist

Please bury me in the library; illustrated by Kyle M. Stone. Harcourt 2005 32p il $16

Grades: 3 4 5   **811**
  1. Books and reading—Poetry 2. Poetry—By individual authors
  ISBN 0-15-216387-5   LC 2003-26983

"Gulliver books"

A "collection of 16 poems celebrating books, reading, language, and libraries. . . . The brief selections encompass various forms, from an eight-word acrostic to haiku to rhyming quatrains and couplets. . . . The poems are accompanied by richly dark artwork. The thickly applied acrylic paint and mixed-media illustrations . . . [have] a comically grotesque air, and add comprehension to the verses." SLJ

Spot the plot; a riddle book of book riddles; illustrated by Lynn Munsinger. Chronicle Books 2009 unp il $15.99

Grades: K 1 2 3   **811**
  1. Riddles 2. Books and reading—Poetry 3. Poetry—By individual authors
  ISBN 978-0-8118-4668-4; 0-8118-4668-7   LC 2008-03206

"Short poetic riddles are presented on spreads, each providing the clues in both text and illustrations of the plot of a well-known children's story. Two young detectives and their dog are looking at such activities as farm animals typing letters in a field (Click, Clack, Moo), a train running along snowy railway tracks (The Polar Express), or a pumpkin coach careening along as it's drawn by a bunch of rats (Cinderella). . . . This book is perfect for an interactive read-aloud." SLJ

Lewis, J. Patrick—*Continued*

Under the kissletoe; Christmastime poems; [by] J. Patrick Lewis; illustrations by Rob Shepperson. Wordsong 2007 32p il $16.95

Grades: 2 3 4 **811**

1. Christmas—Poetry 2. Poetry—By individual authors
ISBN 978-1-59078-438-9; 1-59078-438-3
LC 2006038984

"In Lewis's collection of poems . . . affable wit and infectious cadence bring fresh energy to traditional yuletide images. . . . Shepperson's brightly shaded, borderline cartoon-y illustrations balance humor with warmth." Horn Book

The underwear salesman; and other jobs for better or verse; [by] J. Patrick Lewis; illustrated by Serge Bloch. Atheneum Books for Young Readers 2009 unp il $16.99

Grades: 3 4 5 **811**

1. Occupations—Poetry 2. Work—Poetry 3. Poetry—By individual authors
ISBN 978-0-689-85325-8; 0-689-85325-4
LC 2008025884

"Puns are everywhere in this playful, rhyming survey of jobs, and the collage illustrations extend the verbal fun with wry, literal images." Booklist

The World's Greatest; poems; [written by] J. Patrick Lewis; [illustrated by Keith Graves] Chronicle Books 2008 33p il $16.99

Grades: K 1 2 3 **811**

1. World records—Poetry 2. Poetry—By individual authors
ISBN 978-0-8118-5130-5; 0-8118-5130-3
LC 2007-14717

At head of title: J. Patrick Lewis & Keith Graves present

"This sprightly, clever collection centers on facts found in various editions of the 'Guinness Book of Records.' . . . The droll, distinct illustrations created using acrylic paint and colored pencils capture perfectly the humor and vigor of the text. This attractive book is saturated with color and will charm children who understand its adroit wordplay." SLJ

Lobel, Arnold

The frogs and toads all sang; color by Adrianne Lobel. HarperCollinsPublishers 2009 29p il $16.99; lib bdg $17.89 *

Grades: PreK K 1 2 **811**

1. Frogs—Poetry 2. Toads—Poetry 3. Poetry—By individual authors
ISBN 978-0-06-180022-1; 978-0-06-180023-8 (lib bdg)
LC 2008051768

A collection of poems featuring frogs, toads, and polliwogs

"Originally created by the late Lobel as a handmade book for a fellow author, these poems and pencil sketches (skillfully given washes of color by his daughter, Adrianne) are the progenitors of Lobel's classic Frog and Toad series. But even kids who haven't spent much time with those amphibious friends will find plenty to enjoy. . . . The drawings of genteelly domesticated amphibians large and small bring to mind the spontaneity, intimacy and exuberance of the sketchpad." Publ Wkly

Odd owls & stout pigs; a book of nonsense; color by Adrianne Lobel. Harper 2009 31p il $15.99; lib bdg $16.89

Grades: PreK K 1 2 **811**

1. Humorous poetry 2. Owls—Poetry 3. Pigs—Poetry 4. Poetry—By individual authors
ISBN 978-0-06-180054-2; 0-06-180054-6; 978-0-06-180055-9 (lib bdg); 0-06-180055-4 (lib bdg)
LC 2009001406

Presents a linked collection of brief rhymes featuring owls and pigs

"This collection of nonsense rhymes and poems explodes with fun and frivolity. . . . The verses cover a wide variety of topics, and the words create sound patterns that will engage listeners. . . . Original illustrations were scanned and enhanced with oil pastels and colored pencils. They play buoyantly off Mr. Lobel's clever text and provide a breezy feel." SLJ

Longfellow, Henry Wadsworth, 1807-1882

Hiawatha; pictures by Susan Jeffers. Dial Bks. for Young Readers 1983 unp il pa $6.99 hardcover o.p. **811**

1. Native Americans—Poetry 2. Native Americans—Folklore 3. Poetry—By individual authors
ISBN 0-14-055882-9 (pa)
LC 83-7225

Verses excerpted from the poem first published 1855 with title: Song of Hiawatha

"Jeffers has captured the essence of this brief section from the classic poem. . . . The pale tints of the pictures are in complete harmony with nature and with the text and show in detail how Hiawatha might have seen his world. A fine first exposure to the poem for children and a beautiful artistic experience." SLJ

Low, Alice, 1926-

The fastest game on two feet and other poems about how sports began; illustrated by John O'Brien. Holiday House 2009 40p il $17.95

Grades: 3 4 5 6 **811**

1. Sports—Poetry 2. Poetry—By individual authors
ISBN 978-0-8234-1905-0; 0-8234-1905-3
LC 2007013441

"These 19 poems, each for a different sport, score a goal. Under the title, a short paragraph establishes a context for the origin of the sport. . . . The poems are tightly phrased and put a spin on the historical information of how the sport has evolved. O'Brien's signature style of dappled watercolors-over-ink comically underscores the theme that sports are fun." Kirkus

MacLachlan, Patricia, 1938-

Once I ate a pie; by Patricia MacLachlan and Emily MacLachlan Charest; illustrated by Katy Schneider. Joanna Cotler Books 2006 unp il $15.99; lib bdg $16.89; pa $6.99 *

Grades: K 1 2 3 **811**

1. Dogs—Poetry 2. Poetry—By individual authors
ISBN 978-0-06-073531-9; 0-06-073531-7; 978-0-06-073532-6 (lib bdg); 0-06-073532-5 (lib bdg); 978-0-06-073533-3 (pa); 0-06-073533-3 (pa)
LC 2004-22225

MacLachlan, Patricia, 1938—*Continued*

"Free-verse poems about 14 individual dogs sprawl across oversize spreads accompanied by large oil illustrations. The poems and paintings together delightfully capture each distinct personality in few words and with broad strokes of the brush." SLJ

Maddox, Marjorie, 1959-

Rules of the game; baseball poems; illustrated by John Sandford. Wordsong 2009 32p il $16.95
Grades: 5 6 7 8   811
1. Baseball—Poetry 2. Poetry—By individual authors
ISBN 978-1-59078-603-1; 1-59078-603-3
LC 2008-19018
"Sports fans will find themselves nodding in recognition of Maddox's sophisticated grasp of the game's intricacies, while language mavens will appreciate her joyous wordplay and dead-on command of poetic devices. . . . Sandford's charcoal pencil drawings, backed by sepia-toned pages . . . impart a classy timelessness to the book that's a nice match to its subject." Booklist

Mitton, Tony, 1951-

Gnash, gnaw, dinosaur! prehistoric poems with lift-the-flap surprises! written by Tony Mitton; illustrated by Lynne Chapman. Kingfisher 2009 unp il $12.99
Grades: PreK K 1 2 3   811
1. Dinosaurs—Poetry 2. Poetry—By individual authors
ISBN 978-0-7534-6226-3; 0-7534-6226-5
"Mitton's rhyming verses impart a fair amount of information about their dinosaur subjects, reflecting their behavior, food and eating habits and habitats. . . . Chapman's illustrations reflect the text's subtle fact-underneath-fun manner. . . . With great vocabulary, verses that scan well and a large trim size, this fits well into dinosaur-themed storytimes." Kirkus

Rumble, roar, dinosaur! more prehistoric poems with lift-the-flap surprises! written by Tony Mitton; illustrated by Lynne Chapman. Kingfisher 2010 unp il $12.95
Grades: PreK K 1 2 3   811
1. Dinosaurs—Poetry 2. Poetry—By individual authors
ISBN 978-0-7534-1932-8; 0-7534-1932-7
LC 2010007498
"With its expressive cartoon dinosaurs, this lift-the-flap poetry book . . . emphasizes fun over science. The rhymes have plenty of bounce." Publ Wkly

Moore, Clement Clarke, 1779-1863

The night before Christmas; retold and illustrated by Rachel Isadora. G. P. Putnam's Sons 2009 unp il $16.99
Grades: PreK K 1 2   811
1. Santa Claus—Poetry 2. Christmas—Poetry
3. Poetry—By individual authors
ISBN 978-0-399-25408-6; 0-399-25408-0
LC 2008053359
"Santa's Christmas Eve journey takes him to Africa in this charming version of the poem. Isadora uses collaged papers and oil paints to create a vibrant African village, dusted by snow. . . . Full of details, rich color, and an exuberant spirit, this book will provide opportunities for discussion as well as a new cultural landscape for the 'right jolly old elf.'" SLJ

The night before Christmas; illustrated by Richard Jesse Watson. HarperCollins Pubs. 2006 unp il $16.99; lib bdg $17.89 *
Grades: K 1 2 3   811
1. Santa Claus—Poetry 2. Christmas—Poetry
3. Poetry—By individual authors
ISBN 0-06-075741-8; 0-06-075742-6 (lib bdg)
"Watson presents a modern, hip, and playful version of the classic poem with Santa cruising in a rocket-ship-style sleigh into an ordinary American '50s town, dressed like a biplane aviator. Multicultural elves, including one with dreadlocks and carrying a boom box and another in an Asian jacket carrying an origami paper crane, decorate the text side of each spread. Watson's imaginative style, dynamic composition, and use of perspective are stunning and exciting." SLJ

Moore, Lilian, 1909-2004

Beware, take care; fun and spooky poems; by Lilian Moore; illustrated by Howard Fine. Henry Holt and Co. 2006 unp il $16.95 *
Grades: PreK K 1 2   811
1. Supernatural—Poetry 2. Monsters—Poetry
3. Fear—Poetry 4. Poetry—By individual authors
ISBN 978-0-8050-6917-4; 0-8050-6917-8
LC 2005020257
Poems first published in the author's *Spooky Rhymes and Riddles* (1973) and *See My Lovely Poison Ivy* (1975)
"The ghosts, monsters, and dragons are amusing and not the least bit scary in this congenial picture-book gathering of short verses. . . . Illustrated with humor and warmth, these poems are simple enough for independent readers and silly enough to evoke chuckles and giggles during read-aloud sharing." SLJ

Mural on Second Avenue, and other city poems; illustrated by Roma Karas. Candlewick Press 2005 unp il $16.99
Grades: K 1 2 3   811
1. City and town life—Poetry 2. Poetry—By individual authors
ISBN 0-7636-1987-6   LC 2002-73702
"These 17 poems, all but one of which were chosen from Moore's previous collections, celebrate life in the city. . . . The poems appear on pages covered in bright oil paintings. . . . These poems speak loudly to children." SLJ

Mora, Pat

Yum! mmmm! que rico! Americas' sproutings: haiku; illustrated by Rafael López. Lee & Low 2007 unp il map lib bdg $16.95 *
Grades: 1 2 3 4   811
1. Food—Poetry 2. Fruit 3. Vegetables 4. Haiku
5. Poetry—By individual authors
ISBN 978-1-58430-271-1 (lib bdg); 1-58430-271-2 (lib bdg)
LC 2006-38199

Mora, Pat—*Continued*
"This inventive stew of food haiku celebrates indigenous foods of the Americas. Each of the 13 poems appears on a gloriously colorful double-page spread, accompanied by a sidebar that presents information about the origin of the food. . . . The acrylic-on-wood-panel illustrations burst with vivid colors and stylized Mexican flair." Booklist
Includes bibliographical references

Mordhorst, Heidi
Pumpkin butterfly; poems from the other side of nature; illustrations by Jenny Reynish. Wordsong 2009 32p il $16.95
Grades: 3 4 5 6   **811**
    1. Nature poetry 2. Poetry—By individual authors
    ISBN 978-1-59078-620-8; 1-59078-620-3
                     LC 2009019918
"A collection of 23 nature poems cycles through the seasons, emphasizing the play between the outward and the hidden realms. The vocabulary and imagery stretch the maturing apprehension of young readers. . . . The use of contrasts . . . vividly convey an observant look at what is often overlooked. . . . Reynish's decorative illustrations reflect a thoughtful and purposeful artistic hand." Kirkus

Myers, Walter Dean, 1937-
Blues journey; illustrated by Christopher Myers. Holiday House 2003 unp il $18.95; pa $8.95 *
Grades: 4 5 6   **811**
    1. Blues music—Poetry 2. African Americans—Poetry 3. Poetry—By individual authors
    ISBN   978-0-8234-1613-4;   0-8234-1613-5; 978-0-8234-2079-7 (pa); 0-8234-2079-5 (pa)
                     LC 2001-16645
"In this picture book for older readers, Myers offers blues-inspired verse that touches on the black-and-blue moments of individual lives. . . . Much of Myers' poetry here is terrific, by turn, sweet, sharp, ironic, but it's the memorable collage artwork, executed in the bluest of blue ink and brown paper, that will draw readers first." Booklist

Harlem; a poem; pictures by Christopher Myers. Scholastic 1997 unp il $16.95 *
Grades: 5 6 7 8 9 10   **811**
    1. African Americans—Poetry 2. Harlem (New York, N.Y.)—Poetry 3. Poetry—By individual authors
    ISBN 0-590-54340-7   LC 96-8108
    A Caldecott Medal honor book, 1998
    A poem celebrating the people, sights, and sounds of Harlem
"Myers's paean to Harlem sings, dances, and swaggers across the pages, conveying the myriad sounds on the streets. . . . Christopher Myers's collages add an edge to his father's words, vividly bringing to life the sights and scenes of Lenox Avenue." Horn Book Guide

Jazz; illustrated by Christopher Myers. Holiday House 2006 unp il $18.95; pa $8.95 *
Grades: 4 5 6 7   **811**
    1. Jazz music—Poetry 2. Poetry—By individual authors
    ISBN   978-0-8234-1545-8;   0-8234-1545-7; 978-0-8234-2134-2 (pa); 0-8234-2173-2 (pa)
                     LC 2005-52639
Illustrations and poetry celebrate the roots of jazz music
"Walter Dean Myers infuses his lines . . . with so much savvy syncopation that readers can't help but be swept up in the rhythms. . . . Christopher Myers lays black-inked acetate over brilliant, saturated acrylics. The resulting chiaroscuro conjures the deep shadows and lurid reflections of low-lit after-dark jazz clubs." Publ Wkly

Nelson, Marilyn, 1946-
Sweethearts of rhythm; the story of the greatest all-girl swing band in the world; written by Marilyn Nelson; illustrated by Jerry Pinkney. Dial Books 2009 unp il $21.99 *
Grades: 4 5 6 7   **811**
    1. International Sweethearts of Rhythm 2. Jazz music—Poetry 3. Women musicians 4. Poetry—By individual authors
    ISBN 978-0-8037-3187-5; 0-8037-3187-6
                     LC 2008-46255
"Nelson's syncopated poetry jives perfectly with Pinkney's layered watercolors in this look at the famous all-girl African-American swing band that toured the U.S., breaking attendance records, from 1937 to 1946." SLJ
"On all fronts, a resonant performance." Publ Wkly

Nesbitt, Kenn, 1962-
My hippo has the hiccups; and other poems I totally made up; illustrated by Ethan Long. Sourcebooks Jabberwocky 2009 155p il $17.99
Grades: 2 3 4   **811**
    1. Poetry—By individual authors
    ISBN 978-1-4022-1809-5; 1-4022-1809-5
                     LC 2008-48478
    Includes audio CD
"This is a zany and at times challenging volume of more than 100 poems, 39 of which are read by the author on an accompanying CD. Nesbitt's consistent rhythms and unforced rhymes make these poems readable . . . [and] Long's spare line illustrations add humorous touches. This will be a popular addition to most collections." SLJ

Nye, Naomi Shihab, 1952-
Come with me; poems for a journey; images by Dan Yaccarino. Greenwillow Bks. 2000 32p il $15.95; lib bdg $15.89
Grades: 3 4 5 6   **811**
    1. Poetry—By individual authors
    ISBN 0-688-15946-X; 0-688-15947-8 (lib bdg)
                     LC 99-34164

Nye, Naomi Shihab, 1952-—*Continued*

"Sixteen poems depict different aspects of going places: subjects include imaginary voyages, the pace of travel, arrival in new places, the trajectory of words, and personal journeys of growth. . . . Nye uses sophisticated metaphor and oblique evocations of emotion in simple and concrete phraseology, making the poems conceptually challenging yet literarily accessible. The visuals are bold and dramatic, making excellent use of collage and mixed media." Bull Cent Child Books

O'Neill, Mary Le Duc, 1908-1990

Hailstones and halibut bones; adventures in color; newly illustrated by John Wallner. Doubleday 1989 unp il $15.95; pa $9.95
Grades: K 1 2 3   811
  1. Color—Poetry 2. Poetry—By individual authors
  ISBN   978-0-385-24484-8;   0-385-24484-3;
  978-0-385-41078-6 (pa); 0-385-41078-6 (pa)
                                              LC 88-484
A newly illustrated edition of the title first published 1961
Twelve poems reflect the author's feelings about various colors
"Wallner has created montages of each poem's images and colored them with various hues of the featured color. The results do complement the moods of the poems." SLJ

Paolilli, Paul

Silver seeds; a book of nature poems; by Paul Paolilli and Dan Brewer; paintings by Steve Johnson and Lou Fancher. Viking 2001 unp il $15.99; pa $6.99
Grades: K 1 2 3   811
  1. Nature poetry 2. Poetry—By individual authors
  ISBN 0-670-88941-5; 0-14-250010-0 (pa)
                                              LC 00-9469
"Paolilli and Brewer have selected 15 . . . words on which to build nature poems. The first letter of the first word in each line of a poem is part of another word that is the title (or subject) of the poem." Booklist

Park, Linda Sue, 1960-

Tap dancing on the roof; sijo (poems); illustrated by Istvan Banyai. Clarion Books 2007 unp il $16 *
Grades: 4 5 6   811
  1. Sijo 2. Poetry—By individual authors
  ISBN 978-0-618-23483-7; 0-618-23483-7
                                          LC 2006-24901
Park's "sijo skip lightly from breakfast . . . to bedtime . . . with excursions to the backyard, the classroom, and the beach. . . . The sijo's contours are clean and spare, qualities echoed in the blue-gray, black and white architecture and crisp shadows of Banyai's . . . digital illustrations." Publ Wkly

Patz, Nancy

Who was the woman who wore the hat? written and illustrated by Nancy Patz. Dutton 2003 unp il $14.99 *
Grades: 3 4 5   811
  1. Poetry—By individual authors
  ISBN 0-525-46999-0   LC 2003-545123
"When author Patz saw an unlabeled woman's hat in a glass case in the Jewish Historical Museum in Amsterdam, she wondered whose it could be. . . . She drew the hat in her sketchbook and eventually created this quiet tribute to the woman—any Jewish woman—who might have been forced to leave her home in Amsterdam for a cruel fate in the Nazi extermination camps. Patz combines an accessible prose poem . . . with collages that blend historical photographs with her own sketches. A chronology of the Holocaust completes the book." Booklist

Peters, Lisa Westberg

Earthshake; poems from the ground up; pictures by Cathie Felstead. Greenwillow Bks. 2003 32p il $16.99; lib bdg $17.89 *
Grades: 3 4 5   811
  1. Poetry—By individual authors
  ISBN 0-06-029265-2; 0-06-029266-0 (lib bdg)
                                          LC 2002-32177
Presents twenty-two poems about geology. End notes provide information about the earth's surface and interior, types of rocks, and how volcanoes, glaciers, and erosion modify the landscape
"Exuberant, silly, and serious by turns, the selections engage imagination with often-humorous wordplay. The simple yet clever collages, many of which incorporate clip-art elements, deepen the intellectual and emotional content, yet keep a light tone." SLJ

Volcano wakes up! illustrated by Steve Jenkins. Henry Holt and Company 2010 unp il $16.99
Grades: 2 3 4   811
  1. Volcanoes—Poetry 2. Hawaii—Poetry 3. Poetry—By individual authors
  ISBN 978-0-8050-8287-6; 0-8050-8287-5
                                          LC 2008-38225
"Personified features of a Hawaiian landscape speak in verse during a day in the life of a waking volcano, rendered in Jenkins's atmospheric trademark cut-paper collages. . . . A humorous, imaginative, and artful concept." Publ Wkly

Podwal, Mark H., 1945-

Jerusalem sky; stars, crosses, and crescents. Doubleday Book for Young Readers 2005 unp $15.95; lib bdg $17.99 *
Grades: 3 4 5   811
  1. Jerusalem—Poetry 2. Religious poetry 3. Poetry—By individual authors
  ISBN 0-385-74689-X; 0-385-90927-6 (lib bdg)
A series of illustrated poems about the city of Jerusalem and its importance to Jews, Christians, and Muslims
"With beautiful poems and vivid, impressionistic artwork, Podwal captures the hope and tears the city evokes among followers of the three monotheistic religions of the world." Booklist

Prelutsky, Jack

Awful Ogre running wild; by Jack Prelutsky; illustrations by Paul O. Zelinsky. Greenwillow Books 2008 40p il $17.99; lib bdg $18.89 *

Grades: 2 3 4 5   **811**

1. Monsters—Poetry 2. Poetry—By individual authors

ISBN   978-0-06-623866-1;   0-06-623866-8; 978-0-06-623867-8 (lib bdg); 0-06-623867-6 (lib bdg)

LC 2007027683

In a series of poems, Awful Ogre has a picnic with a lovely ogress, visits Grandma, exercises, paints a picture, enters a cook-off, attends a concert, causes a commotion, swims, goes through other activities

"Prelutsky shows his sure sense of rhythm and rhyme as well as his child-pleasing sense of humor in this series of 17 clearly written poems. Most appear on double-page spreads, accompanied by large ink-and-watercolor illustrations that reflect the tone of the verse." Booklist

Awful Ogre's awful day; poems by Jack Prelutsky; pictures by Paul O. Zelinsky. Greenwillow Bks. 2001 39p il $15.95; pa $6.99 *

Grades: 2 3 4 5   **811**

1. Monsters—Poetry 2. Poetry—By individual authors

ISBN 0-688-07778-1; 0-06-077459-2 (pa)

LC 99-54323

In a series of poems, Awful Ogre rises, grooms himself, dances, pens a letter, and goes through other activities as the day passes

"Awful Ogre proves an ideal agent for Prelutsky's oversize humor. . . . Zelinsky presents Awful Ogre as a grotesque but goofy innocent, sillier than he is sinister. . . . A virtuoso performance by two master funny-bone-ticklers." Publ Wkly

Be glad your nose is on your face and other poems; some of the best of Jack Prelutsky; illustrated by Brandon Dorman. Greenwillow Books 2008 194p il $22.99

Grades: PreK K 1 2 3   **811**

1. Poetry—By individual authors

ISBN 978-0-06-157653-9; 0-06-157653-0

LC 2008013371

"This fat, sunny volume brings together 112 of Prelutsky's poems. Most are old favorites from the past four decades, but 15 of them have never been published before. Kicking off with a letter from the poet, the book contains five sections, each concluding with a page of activities such as word games and drawing prompts. Digital illustrations with lavish details and colors stand out nicely from the ample white space. . . . A CD features the author reading 30 of the poems to a . . . musical accompaniment." SLJ

Behold the bold umbrellaphant; and other poems; illustrations by Carin Berger. Greenwillow Books 2006 31p il $16.99; lib bdg $17.89 *

Grades: 3 4 5 6   **811**

1. Humorous poetry 2. Poetry—By individual authors

ISBN   978-0-06-054317-4;   0-06-054317-5; 978-0-06-054318-1 (lib bdg); 0-06-054318-3 (lib bdg)

LC 2005-22185

Each poem in this collection "is about a creature that is part animal and part inanimate object. For instance, the Alarmadillos have alarm clocks for bodies, and the

Ballpoint Penguins can write with their beaks. The poems are full of fun and wit, with wordplay and meter that never miss a beat. The whimsical illustrations use cut-print media, old-fashioned print images, and a variety of paper textures to create a rich visual treat well suited to the poetry." SLJ

The dragons are singing tonight; pictures by Peter Sis. Greenwillow Bks. 1993 39p il $16; pa $6.95 *

Grades: 2 3 4 5   **811**

1. Poetry—By individual authors

ISBN 0-688-09645-X; 0-688-12511-5 (lib bdg); 0-688-16162-6 (pa)   LC 92-29013

"Dragons are verbally and visually portrayed in this collection with wonder, whimsy, and a touch of wistfulness. . . . The oil and gouache paintings on a gesso background have marvelous details and unexpected bursts of humor." SLJ

The frogs wore red suspenders; rhymes by Jack Prelutsky; pictures by Petra Mathers. Greenwillow Bks. 2002 63p il $16.95; lib bdg $16.89; pa $6.99 *

Grades: K 1 2 3   **811**

1. Nonsense verses 2. Nursery rhymes 3. Poetry—By individual authors

ISBN 0-688-16719-5; 0-688-16720-9 (lib bdg); 0-06-073776-X (pa)   LC 00-68128

A collection of 28 "lighthearted poems, many of which invoke place names in the United States. . . . The mild humor lies not in the action but in Prelutsky's deft use of language, particularly effective shared aloud. The result is enjoyable, but it is Petra Mathers's illustrations that make the book memorable. Demurely naive, her cheerful, delicately delineated human and animal characters focus on their activities with becoming modesty and grace." Horn Book

Good sports; illustrated by Chris Raschka. Alfred A. Knopf 2007 unp il $16.99; lib bdg $19.99 *

Grades: 2 3 4 5   **811**

1. Sports—Poetry 2. Poetry—By individual authors

ISBN 978-0-375-83700-5; 978-0-375-93700-2 (lib bdg)   LC 2006-05092

"This picture book uses poetry to express the physical sensations and wide-ranging emotions of participating in sports. Prelutsky's smoothly rhyming quatrains, ideal for recitation, cover team sports . . . as well as several individual ones and celebrate disciplined efforts as exuberantly as noncompetitive play. . . . Raschka's watercolors extend the high-energy verses without overwhelming them." Booklist

Includes bibliographical references

The Headless Horseman rides tonight; more poems to trouble your sleep; illustrated by Arnold Lobel. Greenwillow Bks. 1980 38p il pa $6.99 hardcover o.p. *

Grades: 2 3 4 5   **811**

1. Monsters—Poetry 2. Poetry—By individual authors

ISBN 0-688-11705-8 (pa)   LC 80-10372

Prelutsky, Jack—*Continued*

"In addition to the perambulating mummy, the author deals with, among others, a writhing specter on a misty moor, a zombie, a sorceress, a baleful banshee . . . the abominable snowman and a headless horseman." Horn Book

The author's "rhymes are as lethal, lithe, and literate as ever and Lobel wrings every atmospheric ounce out of them." SLJ

If not for the cat; haiku by Jack Prelutsky; paintings by Ted Rand. Greenwillow Books 2004 40p il $16.99; lib bdg $17.89
Grades: 1 2 3 4   **811**
1. Animals—Poetry 2. Haiku 3. Poetry—By individual authors
ISBN 0-06-059677-5; 0-06-059678-3 (lib bdg)
LC 2003-17064

"Each of the 17 haiku in this collection explores the essence of an animal, the words forming a sort of riddle answered in Rand's accompanying double-page illustration. . . . Prelutsky shows his command of word choice through a minimalist form that is perfectly matched by Rand's control of his mixed-media artwork to create a wonderful celebration of the art of haiku." SLJ

In Aunt Giraffe's green garden; pictures by Petra Mathers. Greenwillow Books 2007 63p il $16.99; lib bdg $17.89
Grades: K 1 2 3   **811**
1. Animals—Poetry 2. Poetry—By individual authors
ISBN   978-0-06-623868-5;   0-06-623868-4;
978-0-06-623869-2 (lib bdg); 0-06-623869-2 (lib bdg)
LC 2005035928

This is a "picture-book poetry collection of gleeful nonsense verse and captivating illustrations. . . . The bouncing, rhyming couplets are best read aloud. . . . Mathers' watercolor artwork greatly enhances each selection." Booklist

It's Christmas! by Jack Prelutsky; pictures by Marylin Hafner. HarperCollins Publishers 2008 46p il (I can read!) $16.99 *
Grades: K 1 2 3   **811**
1. Christmas—Poetry 2. Poetry—By individual authors
ISBN 978-0-06-053706-7; 0-06-053706-X
LC 2007040112

A newly illustrated edition of the title first published 1981 by Greenwillow Books

This collection of Christmas poems covers such topics as Christmas trees, mistletoe, Santa Claus, a Christmas play, and gifts.

"Hafner's line-and-watercolor pictures illustrate the bouncing, rhyming words in clear, playful holiday scenes." Booklist

It's snowing! it's snowing! winter poems; illustrated by Yossi Abolafia. HarperCollins Pubs. 2006 48p il (I can read book) $15.99; lib bdg $16.89 *
Grades: 1 2 3   **811**
1. Winter—Poetry 2. Poetry—By individual authors
ISBN 0-06-053715-9; 0-06-053716-7 (lib bdg)

A newly illustrated edition of the title first published 1984 by Greenwillow Bks.

A collection of short poems about winter

"The sounds of the rhyming words are as much fun as the snow action in these 16 poems . . . accompanied by exuberant line-and-watercolor illustrations that capture all the play in the cold." Booklist

It's Thanksgiving! by Jack Prelutsky; pictures by Marylin Hafner. HarperCollins 2007 44p il (I can read!) $15.99; lib bdg $16.89 *
Grades: 1 2 3   **811**
1. Thanksgiving Day—Poetry 2. Poetry—By individual authors
ISBN 978-0-06-053710-4; 978-0-06-053709-8 (lib bdg)
LC 2007014465

First published 1982 by Greenwillow Books

A collection of twelve Thanksgiving Day poems

It's Valentine's Day; pictures by Yossi Abolafia. Greenwillow Bks. 1983 47p il (Greenwillow read-alone books) pa $5.95 hardcover o.p. *
Grades: 1 2 3   **811**
1. Poetry—By individual authors
ISBN 0-688-14652-X (pa)   LC 83-1449

"The 14 poems here range from the genuine joy of 'It's Valentine's Day' . . . to the giddy goofiness of 'I love you more than applesauce' or 'Jelly Jill loves Weasel Will'. . . . The rhymes are generally simple but clever and the line drawings in red and blue, with their expressive faces and explanatory vignettes, add tremendously to the enjoyment of the poetry." SLJ

Monday's troll; poems by Jack Prelutsky; pictures by Peter Sís. Greenwillow Bks. 1996 39p il $16 paperback o.p. *
Grades: 2 3 4 5   **811**
1. Supernatural—Poetry 2. Poetry—By individual authors
ISBN 0-688-09644-1; 0-688-14373-3 (lib bdg); 0-688-17529-5 (pa)
LC 95-7085

A collection of seventeen poems about such unsavory characters as witches, ogres, wizards, trolls, giants, a yeti, and seven grubby goblins

This "collection overflows with energy, tongue-in-cheek wit, rich vocabulary, and rollicking rhyme and meter. The oil and gouache paintings on gesso backgrounds are equally playful, as each gold-bordered, double-page spread adds more layers of meaning to the words." SLJ

My dog may be a genius; poems; [drawings by James Stevenson] Greenwillow Books 2008 159p il $18.99; lib bdg $19.89 *
Grades: 2 3 4 5   **811**
1. Poetry—By individual authors
ISBN 978-0-06-623862-3; 978-0-06-623863-0 (lib bdg)
LC 2007-19462

"Prelutsky has created yet another volume of short poems with guaranteed child appeal. Again he has assembled a zany cast of imaginary creatures and machines. . . . Prelutsky plays with language and does not shy away from challenging vocabulary. . . . Stevenson's simple signature drawings capture the spirit of each poem with just the right amount of illustration." SLJ

Prelutsky, Jack—*Continued*

The new kid on the block: poems; drawings by James Stevenson. Greenwillow Bks. 1984 159p il $17.95; lib bdg $17.93 *

Grades: 3 4 5 6   **811**
   1. Humorous poetry 2. Poetry—By individual authors
   ISBN 0-688-02271-5; 0-688-02272-3 (lib bdg)
                                          LC 83-20621

"Most of the 100-plus poems here are mini-jokes, wordplay, and character sketches . . . with liberal doses of monsters and meanies as well as common, garden-variety child mischief." Booklist

"The author's rollicking, silly poems bounce and romp with fun; Stevenson's cartoon-like sketches capture the hilarity with equal skill. A book everyone will enjoy dipping into." Child Book Rev Serv

Nightmares: poems to trouble your sleep; illustrated by Arnold Lobel. Greenwillow Bks. 1976 38p il lib bdg $17.89 *

Grades: 2 3 4 5   **811**
   1. Monsters—Poetry 2. Poetry—By individual authors
   ISBN 0-688-84053-1   LC 76-4820

This "collection of poems is calculated to evoke icy apprehension, and the poems about wizards, bogeymen, ghouls, ogres (well, one poem apiece to each or to others of their ilk) are exaggerated just enough to bring simulta-neous grins and shudders. Prelutsky uses words with rel-ish and his rhyme and rhythm are, as usual, deft. Lobel's illustrations are equally adroit, macabre yet elegant." Bull Cent Child Books

A pizza the size of the sun; poems by Jack Prelutsky; drawings by James Stevenson. Greenwillow Bks. 1996 159p il $18; lib bdg $17.93 *

Grades: 3 4 5 6   **811**
   1. Humorous poetry 2. Poetry—By individual authors
   ISBN 0-688-13235-9; 0-688-13236-7 (lib bdg)
                                          LC 95-35930

This collection of humorous poems is "filled with zany people, improbable creatures, and rhythm and rhyme galore, all combining to celebrate the unusual, the mundane, and the slightly gruesome. . . . Each page is brimming with Stevenson's complementary, droll water-colors, reproduced here in black and white." SLJ

Ride a purple pelican; pictures by Garth Williams. Greenwillow Bks. 1986 64p il $17.95; pa $7.95 *

Grades: K 1 2 3   **811**
   1. Nonsense verses 2. Nursery rhymes 3. Poetry—By individual authors
   ISBN 0-688-04031-4; 0-688-15625-8 (pa)
                                          LC 84-6024

A collection of short nonsense verses and nursery rhymes

"Prelutsky has caught the rhythm and spirit of nursery rhymes in 29 short poems about drum-beating bunnies, bullfrogs on parade, Chicago winds, giant sequoias and other wondrous things. Many of these easy-to-remember poems are filled with delicious sounding American and Canadian place names. Garth Williams' full-color, full-page illustrations are good complements to the poems. Highly recommended." Child Book Rev Serv

Scranimals; poems by Jack Prelutsky; pictures by Peter Sís. Greenwillow Bks. 2002 40p il $16.99; lib bdg $18.89

Grades: 2 3 4 5   **811**
   1. Nonsense verses 2. Poetry—By individual authors
   ISBN 0-688-17819-7; 0-688-17820-0 (lib bdg)
                                          LC 2001-23620

"Prelutsky introduces the curious inhabitants of Scranimal Island through his . . . poems. The creatures, such as the Mangorilla and Orangutangerine, are each a cross between an animal and a fruit, vegetable, or flower, and behave accordingly." SLJ

"The verse sparkles with wit and mad invention. . . . Sís' art picks up on the strange and otherworldly aspects of the poems, evincing a surreal and haunting edge to its intricately lined visions." Bull Cent Child Books

Something big has been here; drawings by James Stevenson. Greenwillow Bks. 1990 160p il $17.95 *

Grades: 3 4 5   **811**
   1. Humorous poetry 2. Poetry—By individual authors
   ISBN 0-688-06434-5   LC 89-34773

An illustrated collection of humorous poems on a vari-ety of topics

"Puns and verbal surprises abound. Clever use of allit-eration and abundant variety in the sound and texture of words add to the pleasure. . . . Stevenson's small car-toons of snaggle-toothed animals and deadpan children extend and expand the mad humor of the poems, sup-porting but never overwhelming their good-natured fun. A fine prescription against the blues at any time of year." Horn Book

The swamps of Sleethe; poems from beyond the solar system; illustrated by Jimmy Pickering. Alfred A. Knopf 2009 unp il $16.99; lib bdg $19.99

Grades: 3 4 5 6   **811**
   1. Extrasolar planets—Poetry 2. Extraterrestrial be-ings—Poetry 3. Poetry—By individual authors
   ISBN   978-0-375-84674-8;   0-375-84674-3;
   978-0-375-94674-5 (lib bdg); 0-375-94674-8 (lib bdg)
                                          LC 2008006530

"Nineteen poems with jaunty rhythms lure readers to some very menacing planets. Almost all tell of the hor-rors to be found in worlds beyond our solar system. . . . Dark colors with sharp contrasts help define these worlds in mixed-media illustrations. Some of the unusual planet names are anagrams to solve with answers in the back of the book. Science-fiction and poetry lovers should unite over this slim and entertaining volume." SLJ

Tyrannosaurus was a beast; illustrated by Arnold Lobel. Greenwillow Bks. 1988 31p il hardcover o.p. pa $6.99 *

Grades: 2 3 4 5   **811**
   1. Dinosaurs—Poetry 2. Poetry—By individual authors
   ISBN 0-688-06443-4 (lib bdg); 0-688-11569-1 (pa)
                                          LC 87-25131

A collection of humorous poems about dinosaurs

"Fourteen dinosaurs meet their match in this outstand-ing author/illustrator team. While Prelutsky's short, pithy, often witty verses sum up their essential characters, Lobel's line and watercolor portraits bring the beasts to life, enormous yet endearingly vulnerable." Booklist

Prelutsky, Jack—*Continued*

What a day it was at school! poems by Jack Prelutsky; pictures by Doug Cushman. Greenwillow Books 2006 39p il $15.99; lib bdg $16.89 *
Grades: K 1 2 3   **811**
1. Schools—Poetry 2. Poetry—By individual authors
ISBN 978-0-06-082336-8; 0-06-082336-4; 978-0-06-082335-1 (lib bdg); 0-06-082335-6 (lib bdg)
LC 2005-48968
"Cushman has interpreted Prelutsky's school-aged protagonist as a cat. The feline's journal contains 17 poems about everyday joys and predicaments. . . . Lively and fun, with perfect meter and an abundance of interesting word choices, these poems beg to be read aloud. And they will be. Cushman has created an appealing school environment with a variety of colorful cartoon animal characters that are happily compatible with Prelutsky's silly and energetic verse." SLJ

Rammell, S. Kelly

City beats; a hip-hoppy pigeon poem; by S. Kelly Rammell; illustrated by Jeanette Canyon. Dawn Publications 2006 unp il $16.95; pa $8.95
Grades: K 1 2   **811**
1. Pigeons—Poetry 2. City and town life—Poetry 3. Poetry—By individual authors
ISBN 1-58469-076-3; 1-58469-077-1 (pa)
LC 2005028363
"A brief foreword gives some background information on pigeons, then asks, What do you think a day is like for a pigeon? The rest of the book is a hip-hop-style poem that answers that question, starting with sunrise and ending in the evening. . . . Most of the text has a good rhythmic beat. . . . Created with polymer clay and photographed, the vibrant spreads show delicately feathered figures and urban backdrops in an array of rainbow colors." SLJ

Rex, Adam

Frankenstein makes a sandwich. Harcourt 2006 40p il $16 *
Grades: 2 3 4 5   **811**
1. Monsters—Poetry 2. Poetry—By individual authors
ISBN 0-15-205766-8   LC 2005-13678
Companion volume to: Frankenstein takes the cake (2008)
A collection of humorous poems about monsters such as Frankenstein, The Creature from the Black Lagoon, Count Dracula, The Invisible Man, Godzilla, and The Phantom of the Opera
"Told with smooth, unstrained rhymes, each selection captures its subject's voice. Rex uses an impressive variety of techniques and media in the artwork while paying homage to famed illustrators. . . . The book is fresh, creative, and funny, with just enough gory detail to cause a few gasps." SLJ

Frankenstein takes the cake. Harcourt 2008 39p il lib bdg $16 *
Grades: 2 3 4 5   **811**
1. Monsters—Poetry 2. Poetry—By individual authors
ISBN 978-0-15-206235-4 (lib bdg); 0-15-206235-1 (lib bdg)
LC 2007-44634

Companion volume to: Frankenstein makes a sandwich (2006)
Frankenstein wants to marry his undead bride in peace, but his best man, Dracula, is freaking out about the garlic bread, and the Headless Horseman wishes everyone would stop drooling over his pumpkin head.
"With maniacal glee, Rex . . . delivers spot-on rhymes about B-movie monsters, loosely organized around the nuptials of Frankenstein and his bride. . . . Rex's eclectic imagery and freewheeling verse will have readers going back for seconds." Publ Wkly

Rockwell, Thomas, 1933-

Emily Stew; with some side dishes; illustrated by David McPhail. Roaring Brook Press 2010 43p il $16.99
Grades: 2 3 4 5   **811**
1. Poetry—By individual authors
ISBN 978-1-59643-336-6; 1-59643-336-1
This is "a wildly inventive poetic portrait of a riveting character who's made up—rather literally—of a stew of contradictions. Moody and prone to the most erratic behavior, Emily is depicted in these playful rhymed vignettes as an eccentric yet eminently recognizable and likable young creature. . . . McPhail's pen-and-ink spot art helps capture the defiant Emily as she asserts her individuality in scenes ranging from dancing with a fish to being eaten by a tiger." Kirkus

Rosen, Michael J., 1954-

The cuckoo's haiku; and other birding poems; illustrated by Stan Fellows. Candlewick Press 2009 unp il $17.99 *
Grades: 2 3 4   **811**
1. Birds—Poetry 2. Haiku 3. Poetry—By individual authors
ISBN 978-0-7636-3049-2; 0-7636-3049-7
LC 2008-21417
"A rare gift for young and old alike, this exquisite book about birds combines delicate verses and stunning watercolors that celebrate the natural world. Designed as if it were a birder's notebook, the book provides an intriguing haiku for each bird, dazzling paintings of the species in their habitats, as well as notes about their behaviors and traits." Publ Wkly

Ruddell, Deborah

A whiff of pine, a hint of skunk; a forest of poems; illustrated by Joan Rankin. Margaret K. McElderry Books 2009 unp il $16.99 *
Grades: 3 4 5   **811**
1. Nature poetry 2. Forest animals—Poetry 3. Poetry—By individual authors
ISBN 978-1-4169-4211-5; 1-4169-4211-4
LC 2007-38023
"Twenty-three evocative poems about forest animals, beautifully illustrated. Literary variety serves this collection well, with many different lengths, rhyme schemes and moods. The common elements in Ruddell's verse are economy and an observer's respect for her subjects. . . . Similarly, Rankin's watercolors show respect via their accuracy and detail, while still capturing the various flavors of the poems." Kirkus

Ryder, Joanne, 1946-

Toad by the road; a year in the life of these amazing amphibians; by Joanne Ryder; illustrations by Maggie Kneen. Henry Holt 2007 37p il $16.95

Grades: 2 3 4   **811**
1. Toads—Poetry 2. Poetry—By individual authors
ISBN 978-0-8050-7354-6; 0-8050-7354-X
LC 2006015361

"Dividing the year into seasons, Ryder offers a cycle of poetry reflecting the toad's experience. . . . In the quietly beautiful artwork, fine strokes and delicately mottled areas of color define the forms of toads and their surroundings. . . . Combining poetry and natural history, the book offers an impressive interpretation of a humble but amazing animal." Booklist

Rylant, Cynthia

Baby face; a book of love for baby; [by] Cynthia Rylant; illustrated by Diane Goode. Simon & Schuster Books for Young Readers 2008 unp il $16.99

Grades: PreK   **811**
1. Infants—Poetry 2. Poetry—By individual authors
ISBN 978-1-4169-4909-1; 1-4169-4909-7
LC 2007015817

"A Paula Wiseman Book"

"This collection of six poems celebrating universal moments in a baby's life (bathtime, first steps, a ride in the carriage) turns on the 'awww' factor. Rylant's rhyming verse offers numerous expressions of love. . . . A slightly oversize square format makes this an excellent choice for lap sharing. Goode . . . [offsets] the sentimentality of the poems with buoyant, energetic vignettes. She creates a sense of motion with watercolor spot illustrations that flow between the text on the ample white space." Publ Wkly

Sandburg, Carl, 1878-1967

Carl Sandburg; edited by Frances Schoonmaker Bolin; illustrated by Steve Arcella. Sterling 1995 48p il (Poetry for young people) $14.95; pa $6.95 *

Grades: 4 5 6 7   **811**
1. Poetry—By individual authors
ISBN 0-8069-0818-1; 1-4027-5471-X (pa)
LC 94-30777

"A Magnolia Editions book"

"The 33 poems in *Sandburg* vary in length and theme, but most are the staples of anthologies, e.g., 'Fog,' 'Arithmetic,' and 'We Must Be Polite.' The surrealistic illustrations, which appear to be rendered in pastels, are appealing; the soft edges and warm tones work well with Sandburg's imagery." SLJ

Rainbows are made: poems; selected by Lee Bennett Hopkins; wood engravings by Fritz Eichenberg. Harcourt Brace Jovanovich 1982 81p il pa $13 hardcover o.p.

Grades: 5 6 7 8   **811**
1. Poetry—By individual authors
ISBN 0-15-265481-X (pa)   LC 82-47934

This book "offers some 70 short poems by Carl Sandburg and groups them by theme: the seasons, the sea, the imaginative mind, etc. Each theme explores different aspects of poetic creativity as envisioned by Sandburg and illustrated by Fritz Eichenberg's wood engravings. Eichenberg has truly captured the power and vigorousness of Sandburg's verse." SLJ

Scanlon, Liz Garton

All the world; illustrated by Marla Frazee. Beach Lane Books 2009 unp il $17.99 *

Grades: PreK K 1   **811**
1. Poetry—By individual authors 2. Beaches—Poetry
3. Family life—Poetry
ISBN 978-1-4169-8580-8; 1-4169-8580-8
LC 2008-51057

ALA ALSC Caldecott Medal Honor Book (2010)

"Charming illustrations and lyrical rhyming couplets speak volumes in celebration of the world and humankind, combining to create a lovely book that will be appreciated by a wide audience. The pictures, made with black Prismacolor pencil and watercolors, primarily follow a multicultural family from a summer morning on the beach through a busy day and night." SLJ

Schertle, Alice, 1941-

Button up! [illustrations by] Petra Mathers. Harcourt 2009 33p il $16 *

Grades: PreK K 1 2   **811**
1. Animals—Poetry 2. Clothing and dress—Poetry
3. Poetry—By individual authors
ISBN 978-0-15-205050-4; 0-15-205050-7
LC 2007-42839

An illustrated collection of poetry features animals wearing an array of shoes, jackets, hats, and other fun attire to demonstrate their unique personalities.

"Mathers' charming watercolors show a variety of decked out animals in vignettes and double-page spreads that add to the humor. . . . The whimsical illustrations pair perfectly with the wittiness of the text, and the whole is a clever and original poetic treat." Booklist

Scieszka, Jon, 1954-

Truckery rhymes; written by Jon Scieszka; characters and environments developed by the Design Garage—David Shannon, Loren Long, David Gordon. Simon & Schuster Books for Young Readers 2009 57p il $17.99

Grades: PreK K 1 2 3   **811**
1. Nursery rhymes 2. Trucks—Poetry 3. Poetry—By individual authors
ISBN 978-1-4169-4135-4; 1-4169-4135-5
LC 2007037439

"This collection of lively truck-themed 'Mother Goose' rhymes is filled with humor. . . . The digital illustrations are colorful, energetic, and playful: the vehicles have personality plus. . . . This effervescent picture book will zoom off your shelves." SLJ

Service, Robert W., 1874-1958

The cremation of Sam McGee; by Robert W. Service; paintings by Ted Harrison; introduction by Pierre Berton. 20th anniversary ed. Kids Can Press 2006 unp il $17.95 *

Grades: 4 5 6 7   811
1. Yukon Territory—Poetry 2. Poetry—By individual authors
ISBN 978-1-55453-092-2; 1-55453-092-X

Text first published 1907. This is a reissue of the edition first published 1986 in Canada and 1987 in the United States by Greenwillow Bks.

"Pledged to cremate his friend Sam, the narrator tells how, after carting the frozen body for miles, he stuffs it into a ship's roaring furnace. To his surprise, when he later opens the door he discovers Sam alive . . . and warm for the first time 'since he left Tennessee.'" Publ Wkly

This poem "has gripped readers and listeners for decades. . . . [The illustrator] obviously appreciates the humor inherent in the text. . . . As Pierre Berton observes in his introduction, [Harrison's] 'style is unique: part Oriental, part native American, part Ted Harrison.'" Horn Book

Shange, Ntozake

We troubled the waters; poems by Ntozake Shange; paintings by Rod Brown. Amistad/Collins 2009 unp il $16.99; lib bdg $17.89 *

Grades: 4 5 6 7 8 9 10   811
1. African Americans—Civil rights—Poetry 2. Poetry—By individual authors
ISBN   978-0-06-133735-2;   0-06-133735-8;
978-0-06-133737-6 (lib bdg); 0-06-133737-4 (lib bdg)
LC 2008025360

"Each spread pairs a poem with blurred, expressive acrylic paintings, and the pages feature both well-known civil rights leaders and ordinary people who endured oppression. . . . The messages are haunting. . . . The colloquial lines, indelible images, and comparisons between then and now will keep readers talking." Booklist

Shannon, George, 1952-

Busy in the garden; poems by George Shannon; pictures by Sam Williams. Greenwillow Books 2006 36p il $15.99; lib bdg $16.89

Grades: K 1 2   811
1. Gardening—Poetry 2. Poetry—By individual authors
ISBN 0-06-000464-9; 0-06-000465-7 (lib bdg)
LC 2003-56863

A collection of short poems and riddles about planting seeds, watching garden vegetables dance, and growing jack-o-lanterns.

"The best selections are immediately accessible and bounce with humor and an irresistible beat. Williams' lively watercolor-and-pencil illustrations of children and animals digging in the rows shine with the colors of spring." Booklist

Chicken scratches; Grade A poultry poetry and rooster rhymes; by George Shannon & Lynn Brunelle; illustrated by Scott Menchin. Chronicle Books 2010 unp il $14.99

Grades: K 1 2 3   811
1. Chickens—Poetry
ISBN 978-0-8118-6648-4; 0-8118-6648-3

"This attractive volume features 16 wacky rhyming verses. The somewhat irreverent poems include odes to imagined daily lives of opera-singing and sumo-wrestling chickens to complex egg laying and eating. . . . Rendered in pen and colored digitally, the simple yet expressive cartoon illustrations really bring out the fun of the poetry." SLJ

Shapiro, Karen Jo, 1964-

I must go down to the beach again; [by] Karen Jo Shapiro; illustrated by Judy Love. Charlesbridge 2007 48p il $14.95; pa $5.95

Grades: 4 5 6 7   811
1. Parodies 2. Humorous poetry 3. Poetry—By individual authors
ISBN 978-158089-143-1 (lib bdg); 1-58089-143-8 (lib bdg); 978-158089-144-8 (pa); 1-58089-144-6 (pa)
LC 2006009029

"Shapiro offers parodies of 23 classic British and American poems. . . . It is clear in reading her selections that the author knows the sources through and through and that she is quite a good poet in her own right. . . . Love's black-and-white pen-and-ink drawings underscore the humor in each selection." SLJ

Shields, Carol Diggory

Almost late to school and more school poems; illustrated by Paul Meisel. Dutton Children's Bks. 2003 40p il $15.99; pa $6.99 *

Grades: 2 3 4   811
1. Schools—Poetry 2. Humorous poetry 3. Poetry—By individual authors
ISBN 0-525-45743-7; 0-14-240328-8 (pa)

Companion volume to Lunch money and other poems about school

"The 22 energetic selections reflect the typical day-to-day activities and problems including being late for school, the first day, having to go to the bathroom, fundraising, and other events. Shields utilizes a variety of forms including a concrete poem, poems for two voices, and a jump-rope rhyme. Meisel's vibrant cartoon illustrations are lively and fun and capture the poems' humor and insight." SLJ

English, fresh squeezed! 40 thirst-for-knowledge-quenching poems; by Carol Diggory Shields; illustrations by Tony Ross. Handprint Books 2004 80p il $14.95 *

Grades: 4 5 6 7   811
1. English language—Poetry 2. Poetry—By individual authors
ISBN 1-59354-053-1   LC 2004-53905

"Shields presents humorous poems both celebrating and bemoaning parts of speech, grammatical rules, and other annoyances of English class. Her rhyming verse is

Shields, Carol Diggory—*Continued*

generally snappy and pointed. . . . Ross's spot illustrations in black and white with a blue tone add visual amusement without overwhelming." SLJ

Someone used my toothbrush! and other bathroom poems; illustrated by Paul Meisel. Dutton Children's Books 2010 32p il $16.99

Grades: PreK K 1 2 3   **811**

1. Bathrooms—Poetry 2. Poetry—By individual authors

ISBN 978-0-525-47937-6; 0-525-47937-6

Comic, kid-centric poems about the bathroom.

"This collection of 21 short poems is right on target with its rhymed glimpses into the cheerful chaos of family life. . . . The colorful cartoons add just the right tone. They are light and funny, featuring a multicultural cast of characters. There's a lot to like in this clever and appealing collection." SLJ

Shore, Diane ZuHone

This is the dream; by Diane Z. Shore and Jessica Alexander; illustrated by James Ransome. HarperCollinsPublishers 2006 unp il $15.99; lib bdg $16.89 *

Grades: 2 3 4   **811**

1. African Americans—Civil rights—Poetry 2. Poetry—By individual authors

ISBN 0-06-055519-X; 0-06-055520-3 (lib bdg)

LC 2003-26554

"A chronicle of the Civil Rights movement presented through lyrical verses and distinguished illustrations. Ransome juxtaposes collaged archival photographs and newspaper clippings with his paintings. . . . Each succinct and evocative verse is accompanied by a double-page image." SLJ

Sidman, Joyce, 1956-

Butterfly eyes and other secrets of the meadow; written by Joyce Sidman; illustrated by Beth Krommes. Houghton Mifflin Co. 2006 unp il $16

Grades: 3 4 5 6   **811**

1. Animals—Poetry 2. Meadows—Poetry 3. Poetry—By individual authors

ISBN 0-618-56313-X   LC 2005-03921

"Eight pairs of 'poetry riddles' present such related elements as the spittlebug . . . and the xylem sap it sucks from its host plant. A spread giving answers to the riddle and adding specific details . . . follows each pair of poems. . . . Kromme's scratchboard illustrations are splendid. . . . An elegantly conceived, beautifully integrated volume." Horn Book

Dark Emperor and other poems of the night; illustrated by Rick Allen. Houghton Mifflin Harcourt 2010 il $16.99 *

Grades: 3 4 5 6   **811**

1. Forest animals—Poetry 2. Night—Poetry 3. Poetry—By individual authors

ISBN 978-0-547-15228-8; 0-547-15228-0

"This picture book combines lyrical poetry and compelling art with science concepts. . . . Poems about the

woods at night reveal exciting biology facts that are explained in long notes on each double-page spread. . . . In an opening note, Allen explains his elaborate, linoleum-block printmaking technique, and each atmospheric image shows the creatures and the dense, dark forest with astonishing clarity." Booklist

Eureka! poems about inventors; illustrated by K. Bennett Chavez. Millbrook Press 2002 48p il lib bdg $24.90 *

Grades: 4 5 6   **811**

1. Poetry—By individual authors

ISBN 0-7613-1665-5   LC 00-56620

"In 16 poems, mostly free verse, Sidman commemorates the best-known achievements of dozens of inventors, from the World Wide Web's Tim Berners-Lee to the prehistoric person—a woman, Sidman supposes—who first shaped clay into a bowl." Booklist

"Chavez's full-color, surrealistic illustrations add depth, character, and feeling to the selections. . . . The entire book reads beautifully." SLJ

Meow ruff; a story in concrete poetry; written by Joyce Sidman; illustrated by Michelle Berg. Houghton Mifflin 2006 unp il $16 *

Grades: 1 2 3   **811**

1. Cats—Poetry 2. Dogs—Poetry 3. Rain—Poetry 4. Poetry—By individual authors

ISBN 0-618-44894-2

"Sidman develops a simple tale about a cat and dog trapped in a rainstorm, coding much of the substance right into the physical landscape. . . . Berg, who created the pictures digitally and is also the book's graphic designer, intelligently showcases the concept of words as building blocks in a stylized landscape of flat colors, two-dimensional forms, and wildly mutating typefaces." Booklist

Song of the water boatman; & other pond poems; written by Joyce Sidman; illustrated by Beckie Prange. Houghton Mifflin 2005 unp il $16 *

Grades: 3 4 5   **811**

1. Ponds—Poetry 2. Poetry—By individual authors

ISBN 0-618-13547-2

A Caldecott Medal honor book, 2006

A collection of poems that provide a look at some of the animals, insects, and plants that are found in ponds, with accompanying information about each.

"In this strikingly illustrated collection, science facts combine with vivid poems about pond life through the seasons. . . . Throughout, plants and animals come alive in the bold woodcut prints." Booklist

This is just to say; poems of apology and forgiveness; by Joyce Sidman; illustrated by Pamela Zagarenski. Houghton Mifflin Co. 2007 47p il $16

Grades: 4 5 6   **811**

1. Poetry—By individual authors

ISBN 978-0-618-61680-0; 0-618-61680-2

LC 2006009820

"Mrs. Merz assigns her sixth-grade students to write poems of apology, and what emerges is a surprising ar-

Sidman, Joyce, 1956-—*Continued*

ray of emotions, poetic forms, and subjects. . . . Sidman's ear is keen, capturing many voices. Her skill as a poet accessible to young people is unmatched. Zagarenski's delicately outlined collage drawings and paintings are created on mixed backgrounds—notebook paper, paper bags, newspaper, graph paper, school supplies." SLJ

Ubiquitous; celebrating nature's survivors; poetry by Joyce Sidman; illustrated by Beckie Prange. Houghton Mifflin 2010 unp il $17 *

Grades: 2 3 4 5   **811**

1. Animals—Poetry 2. Poetry—By individual authors

ISBN 978-0-618-71719-4; 0-618-71719-6

Sidman and Prange "offer another winning blend of poetry, science, and art in this picture-book collection that celebrates the earth's most resilient and long-lived species. . . . Each dynamic spread features a poem, a prose paragraph, and a captivating illustration that work together to reinforce both the science concepts and the awe they inspire. Prange's watercolor-tinted linocut illustrations beautifully expand both the information and imagery in the words." Booklist

Siebert, Diane

Tour America; a journey through poems and art; by Diane Siebert; illustrated by Stephen T. Johnson. Chronicle Books 2006 unp il map $17.95 *

Grades: 3 4 5 6   **811**

1. United States—Poetry 2. Poetry—By individual authors

ISBN 978-0-8118-5056-8; 0-8118-5056-0

LC 2005027125

"This stunning tour of America highlights 26 of the poet's favorite sights . . . Siebert's striking word choices and images reflect the essence of each subject. . . . A double-page map at the beginning of the book alerts readers to the exciting destinations they will experience, and a smaller map and inset box of additional information for each sight increase the educational value. Johnson masterfully varies his medium and art style to reflect the mood of each locale. There are quiet watercolors . . . and dynamic collages . . . as well as pastels, oils, acrylics, and photos." SLJ

Sierra, Judy

Monster Goose; illustrated by Jack E. Davis. Harcourt 2001 unp il $17; pa $7 *

Grades: 2 3 4 5   **811**

1. Monsters—Poetry 2. Poetry—By individual authors

ISBN 0-15-202034-9; 0-15-205417-0 (pa)

LC 00-8808

"Gulliver books"

A collection of parodies of Mother Goose rhymes featuring monsters

"Davis, working in acrylics and colored pencil, crowds his illustrations with monsters, vermin and gross gags. . . . This volume strikes a nice balance between goofy and ghastly." Publ Wkly

Silverstein, Shel

Don't bump the glump and other fantasies; [by] Shel Silverstein. HarperCollins Publishers 2008 unp il $17.99; lib bdg $18.89 *

Grades: 3 4 5 6   **811**

1. Humorous poetry 2. Poetry—By individual authors

ISBN 978-0-06-149338-6; 978-0-06-149619-6 (lib bdg)   LC 2007036737

First published 1964 by Simon & Schuster with title: Uncle Shelby's zoo: don't bump the glump!

"This collection of 45 poems tours readers past imaginary creatures. . . . There's no question that the intensity of Silverstein's watercolor palette adds to the fun." Publ Wkly

Falling up; poems and drawings by Shel Silverstein. HarperCollins Pubs. 1996 171p il $17.99; lib bdg $18.89 *

Grades: 3 4 5 6   **811**

1. Humorous poetry 2. Nonsense verses 3. Poetry—By individual authors

ISBN 0-06-024802-5; 0-06-024803-3 (lib bdg)

LC 96-75736

This "collection includes more than 150 poems. . . . As always, Silverstein has a direct line to what kids like, and he gives them poems celebrating the gross, the scary, the absurd, and the comical. The drawings are much more than decoration. They often extend a poem's meaning and, in many cases, add some great comedy." Booklist

A light in the attic. Special edition. Harper 2009 185p il $18.99 *

Grades: 3 4 5 6   **811**

1. Humorous poetry 2. Nonsense verses 3. Poetry—By individual authors

ISBN 978-0-06-190585-8; 0-06-190585-2

First published 1981

This edition includes 12 new poems and drawings from the Silverstein Archives

This collection of more than one hundred poems "will delight lovers of Silverstein's raucous, rollicking verse and his often tender, whimsical, philosophical advice. . . . The poems are tuned in to kids' most hidden feelings, dark wishes and enjoyment of the silly. . . . The witty line drawings are a full half of the treat of this wholly satisfying anthology by the modern successor to Edward Lear and Hilaire Belloc." SLJ [review of 1981 edition]

Runny Babbit; a billy sook. HarperCollins Pub. 2005 89p il $17.99; lib bdg $18.89 *

Grades: 3 4 5 6   **811**

1. Humorous poetry 2. Poetry—By individual authors

ISBN 0-06-025653-2; 0-06-028404-8 (lib bdg)

In this book "readers are introduced to Runny Babbit and his friends . . . and are encouraged to plunge headlong into this phonemic flipflop world of funny poems. . . . Complete with signature comical bold line drawings that provide visual clues, the poems require concentration to translate the silly phrases. . . . Children will love these clever poems and without prompting will probably create their own." SLJ

Silverstein, Shel—*Continued*

Where the sidewalk ends; the poems & drawings of Shel Silverstein. 30th anniversary special ed. HarperCollins 2004 183p il $17.99; lib bdg $18.89 *

Grades: 3 4 5 6 7 8 9 10   **811**
    1. Humorous poetry 2. Nonsense verses 3. Poetry—By individual authors
    ISBN 0-06-057234-5; 0-06-058653-2 (lib bdg)
                       LC 2004-269335

First published 1974

This edition contains 12 new poems

"There are skillful, sometimes grotesque line drawings with each of the 127 poems, which run in length from a few lines to a couple of pages. The poems are tender, funny, sentimental, philosophical, and ridiculous in turn, and they're for all ages." Sat Rev

Singer, Marilyn, 1948-

Central heating; poems about fire and warmth; illustrated by Meilo So. Alfred A. Knopf 2005 41p il $15.95; lib bdg $17.99 *

Grades: 4 5 6 7   **811**
    1. Fire—Poetry 2. Heat—Poetry 3. Poetry—By individual authors
    ISBN 0-375-82912-1; 0-375-92912-6 (lib bdg)
                       LC 2004-4274

"The complicated nature of fire is explored in Singer's energetic short poems and So's deceptively simple single-color illustrations. . . . This title . . . belongs on library shelves everywhere." SLJ

First food fight this fall and other school poems; by Marilyn Singer; illustrated by Sachiko Yoshikawa. Sterling 2008 42p il $14.95

Grades: K 1 2 3 4   **811**
    1. Schools—Poetry 2. Poetry—By individual authors
    ISBN 978-1-4027-4145-6; 1-4027-4145-6
                       LC 2007043386

"Twenty-nine poems, in the voices of a dozen children who ride the school bus together, depict various activities that take place in and out of the classroom. Bright, cartoon illustrations in acrylics, pastels, and collage capture the youngsters' boundless energy. . . . These poems resonate with mischievous good cheer." SLJ

Mirror mirror; a book of reversible verse; illustrated by Josée Masse. Dutton Children's Books 2010 unp il $16.99 *

Grades: 3 4 5 6   **811**
    1. Fairy tales—Poetry 2. Poetry—By individual authors
    ISBN 978-0-525-47901-7; 0-525-47901-5
                       LC 2009-17917

A collection of short poems which, when reversed, provide new perspectives on the fairy tale characters they feature.

"This appealing collection . . . is a marvel to read. . . . The vibrant artwork is painterly yet unfussy and offers hints to the characters who are narrating the poems. An endnote shows children how to create a 'reverse' poem. This is a remarkably clever and versatile book." SLJ

Smith, Charles R.

Hoop kings; poems. Candlewick Press 2004 37p il $14.99; pa $5.99

Grades: 4 5 6 7   **811**
    1. Basketball—Poetry 2. Poetry—By individual authors
    ISBN 0-7636-1423-8; 0-7636-3560-X (pa)
                       LC 2003-55340

A collection of twelve poems that celebrate contemporary basketball stars, including Shaquille O'Neal, Allen Iverson, and Kobe Bryant

"Combining dynamic illustrations and full-bodied language, Smith's latest collection of poems enthusiastically conveys both love for and knowledge of the game. . . . This book will have enormous appeal for all ages; basketball fans will love it, but so will others who respond to color, lively language, and energy." SLJ

Hoop queens; poems. Candlewick Press 2003 35p il hardcover o.p. pa $5.99

Grades: 4 5 6 7   **811**
    1. Basketball—Poetry 2. Women athletes—Poetry 3. Poetry—By individual authors
    ISBN 0-7636-1422-X; 0-7636-3561-8 (pa)
                       LC 2002-41111

A collection of twelve poems that celebrate contemporary women basketball stars, including Yolanda Griffith, Chamique Holdsclaw, and Natalie Williams

"Action photos of the athletes are pasted large on colorful, dynamic backgrounds that barely hold the motion-filled poems to the page. Notes about each player and poem communicate the joy Smith finds both in watching the game and writing poetry. Pure pleasure for basketball fans and inspiration for kids who doubted poetry was alive." SLJ

Smith, Hope Anita

Mother poems; words and pictures by Hope Anita Smith. Henry Holt and Co. 2009 72p il $16.95 *

Grades: 4 5 6 7   **811**
    1. Mothers—Poetry 2. Bereavement—Poetry 3. Death—Poetry 4. African Americans—Poetry 5. Poetry—By individual authors
    ISBN 978-0-8050-8231-9; 0-8050-8231-X
                       LC 2008-18342

"Christy Ottaviano books"

"Smith writes about an African American child's grief at the sudden death of her mother. . . . Like the poetry, Smith's simple, torn-paper collages in a folk-art style show the close embraces and vignettes without overwhelming the words." Booklist

Soto, Gary

Canto familiar; [illustrated by Annika Nelson] Harcourt Brace & Co. 1995 79p il $18; pa $5.95

Grades: 4 5 6   **811**
    1. Mexican Americans—Poetry 2. Poetry—By individual authors
    ISBN   978-0-15-200067-7;   0-15-200067-4; 978-0-15-205885-2 (pa); 0-15-205885-0 (pa)
                       LC 94-24218

Soto, Gary—*Continued*

"This collection of simple free verse captures common childhood moments at home, at school, and in the street. Many of the experiences are Mexican American . . . and occasional Spanish words are part of the easy, colloquial, short lines. . . . The occasional full-page, richly colored woodcuts by Annika Nelson capture the child's imaginative take on ordinary things." Booklist

Neighborhood odes; illustrated by David Diaz. Harcourt Brace Jovanovich 1992 68p il hardcover o.p. pa $5.95 *
Grades: 4 5 6   **811**
  1. Hispanic Americans—Poetry 2. Poetry—By individual authors
  ISBN 0-15-256879-4; 0-15-205364-6 (pa)
                                       LC 91-20710
"Twenty-one poems, all odes, celebrate life in a Hispanic neighborhood. Other than the small details of daily life—peoples' names or the foods they eat—these poems could be about any neighborhood. With humor, sensitivity, and insight, Soto explores the lives of children. . . . David Diaz's contemporary black-and-white illustrations, which often resemble cut paper, effortlessly capture the varied moods—happiness, fear, longing, shame, and greed—of this remarkable collection. With a glossary of thirty Spanish words and phrases." Horn Book

Spinelli, Eileen, 1942-

Polar bear, arctic hare; poems of the frozen North; illustrations by Eugenie Fernandes. Wordsong 2007 32p il $16.95
Grades: K 1 2 3   **811**
  1. Arctic regions—Poetry 2. Animals—Poetry 3. Poetry—By individual authors
  ISBN 978-1-59078-344-3   LC 2006012623
In this "collection, 24 Arctic-inspired poems . . . are matched with 12 spreads of acrylic paintings of the region's flora and fauna. . . . Well paced, with a strong relationship between illustration and poetry, this book will help children understand this vital ecosystem and the beauty of its wildlife." SLJ

Stevenson, James, 1929-

Corn-fed; poems by James Stevenson; with illustrations by the author. Greenwillow Bks. 2002 48p il hardcover o.p. lib bdg $15.89 *
Grades: 2 3 4 5   **811**
  1. Poetry—By individual authors
  ISBN 0-06-000597-1; 0-06-000598-X (lib bdg)
                                       LC 2001-33261
A collection of short poems with such titles as "Coney Island movie," "Why bicycles are locked up," and "Aquarium"
"These musings are shot through with Stevenson's wry scrutiny of and appreciation for, the world around him. . . . Spare but appealing, these poetic ponderings render the ordinary fresh." Horn Book Guide

Popcorn; poems by James Stevenson; with illustrations by the author. Greenwillow Bks. 1998 64p il $16 *
Grades: 2 3 4 5   **811**
  1. Poetry—By individual authors
  ISBN 0-688-15261-9   LC 97-6320

A collection of short poems with such titles as "Popcorn," "Driftwood," and "My new bird book"
"With a physical immediacy and a casual voice, Stevenson's poems capture quiet, intensely moving moments of daily life in a small seaside town, and his exquisite, understated watercolors extend the concrete particulars of the words." Booklist

Sturges, Philemon

Down to the sea in ships; illustrated by Giles Laroche. Putnam's 2005 unp il $16.99
Grades: 3 4 5   **811**
  1. Boats and boating—Poetry 2. Poetry—By individual authors
  ISBN 0-399-23464-0   LC 2002-67957
Poems describe a variety of watercraft, from birch bark canoes to cruise ships, and reveal their impact on the world.
"A seamless collection of finely honed but telling histories of important ships in fully realized poems. . . . Laroche's boats, made of cut paper and paint, appear to lift from the waves and float in their pictorial waters. This author and illustrator work wonders together." SLJ

Thayer, Ernest Lawrence, 1863-1940

Casey at the bat; a ballad of the republic sung in the year 1888; [by] Ernest L. Thayer; illlustrated by C.F. Payne. Simon & Schuster Bks. for Young Readers 2003 unp il lib bdg $16.95 *
Grades: K 1 2 3   **811**
  1. Baseball—Poetry 2. Poetry—By individual authors
  ISBN 0-689-85494-3   LC 2002-3472
Poem first published 1888
A narrative poem about the celebrated baseball player who strikes out at the crucial moment of the game
"Payne's caricatures, rendered in a mix of acrylics, watercolor ink, oils, and colored pencils, are a marvel of texture and personality." SLJ

Ernest L. Thayer's Casey at the bat; a ballad of the Republic sung in the year 1888; reported by Ernest L. Thayer; illustrated by Christopher Bing. Handprint Books 2000 unp il $17.95
Grades: 3 4 5 6   **811**
  1. Baseball—Poetry 2. Poetry—By individual authors
  ISBN 1-929766-00-9   LC 00-37010
A Caldecott Medal honor book, 2001
"Thayer's classic poem of the 19th-century baseball legend has been revived for a new generation in this creatively designed package. . . . Bing has orchestrated every detail to great effect. Each double spread, rendered in ink and brush on scratchboard, is a scene from the poem. The multitude of lines adds energy; the multiple perspectives create interest." SLJ

Thomas, Joyce Carol

The blacker the berry; poems; illustrated by Floyd Cooper. HarperCollins 2008 unp il $16.99; lib bdg $17.89 *

Grades: PreK K 1 2   **811**
1. African Americans—Poetry 2. Poetry—By individual authors
ISBN   978-0-06-025375-2;   0-06-025375-4; 978-0-06-025376-9 (lib bdg); 0-06-025376-2 (lib bdg)
Coretta Scott King Award for illustration, 2009
"Joanna Cotler books"
"Black comes in all shades from dark to light, and each is rich and beautiful in this collection of simple, joyful poems and glowing portraits that show African American diversity and connections." Booklist

Brown honey in broomwheat tea; poems by Joyce Carol Thomas; illustrated by Floyd Cooper. HarperCollins Pubs. 1993 unp il $16.95; pa $6.99 *

Grades: K 1 2 3   **811**
1. African Americans—Poetry 2. Poetry—By individual authors
ISBN 0-06-021087-7; 0-06-443439-7 (pa)
LC 91-46043
"A dozen poems rooted in home, family, and the African American experience combine with a series of warm and evocative watercolors in this highly readable and attractive picture book." Booklist

Thomas, Patricia J., 1934-

Nature's paintbox; a seasonal gallery of art and verse; [by] Patricia Thomas; illustrated by Craig Orback. Millbrook Press, Inc. 2007 unp il lib bdg $16.95

Grades: 2 3 4   **811**
1. Seasons—Poetry 2. Poetry—By individual authors
ISBN 978-0-8225-6807-0   LC 2006035079
"The verse connects each season with the artist's medium, beginning with pen and ink for winter, then cycling through pastel chalk for springs, watercolor for summer, and oils for fall. . . . This picture book is both intriguing to look at and excellent for reading aloud." Booklist

Updike, John, 1932-2009

A child's calendar; illustrations by Trina Schart Hyman. Holiday House 1999 unp il $16.95 *

Grades: K 1 2 3   **811**
1. Months—Poetry 2. Poetry—By individual authors
ISBN 0-8234-1445-0   LC 98-46166
A Caldecott Medal honor book, 2000
A newly illustrated edition of the title first published 1965 by Knopf
"Hyman's colorful illustrations portray a multiracial family living in rural New Hampshire. . . . Each evocative illustration has its own story to tell, celebrating the small moments in children's lives with clarity and sensitivity, with empathy and joy." Booklist

Van Wassenhove, Sue, 1951-

The seldom-ever-shady glades; poems and quilts by Sue Van Wassenhove. Wordsong 2008 32p il $17.95

Grades: 3 4 5 6   **811**
1. Birds—Poetry 2. Everglades (Fla.)—Poetry 3. Nature poetry 4. Poetry—By individual authors
ISBN 978-1-59078-352-8   LC 2007018099
"Through exuberant poems and quilted illustrations . . . Van Wassenhove offers an unusual tour of the delicate Everglades habitat. . . . Van Wassenhove's creative application of quilting techniques to depict the rippled surfaces and shifting hues of a wetland environment will draw fascinated gazes." Booklist

Vardell, Sylvia M.

Poetry people; a practical guide to children's poets. Libraries Unlimited 2007 170p $50

Grades: Professional   **811**
1. Reference books 2. Children's literature—Bio-bibliography 3. Children's poetry 4. Poets 5. Poetry—By individual authors
ISBN 978-1-59158-443-8; 1-59158-443-4
LC 2007003329
This is "a comprehensive survey of 62 contemporary children's poets. Each of the one- to two-page entries begins with a brief biography and includes Web sites, bibliographies, suggestions for use and reading of specific poems, plus connections to other children's literature. . . . This book will be welcomed by all adults interested in connecting children with poetry." SLJ
Includes bibliographical references

Viorst, Judith

If I were in charge of the world and other worries; poems for children and their parents; illustrated by Lynne Cherry. Atheneum Pubs. 1981 56p il lib bdg $16.95; pa $4.95

Grades: 3 4 5 6   **811**
1. Humorous poetry 2. Poetry—By individual authors
ISBN 0-689-30863-9 (lib bdg); 0-689-70770-3 (pa)
LC 81-2342
"Forty-one lively, funny poems written from a wry, self-deprecating point of view. Some poems verge on adult feelings—such as a broken heart or a lyrical appreciation of spring—but most of them deal with children's worries, to which the author seems to be specially attuned." Horn Book

Walker, Alice, 1944-

There is a flower at the tip of my nose smelling me; by Alice Walker; illustrated by Stefano Vitale. HarperCollinsPublishers 2006 unp il $16.99; lib bdg $17.89

Grades: 2 3 4   **811**
1. Senses and sensation—Poetry 2. Poetry—By individual authors
ISBN   978-0-06-057080-4;   0-06-057080-6; 978-0-06-057081-1 (lib bdg); 0-06-057081-4 (lib bdg)
LC 2005014517
"Walker celebrates the beauty of the world and our connection to it through a series of short verses that

Walker, Alice, 1944-—*Continued*
praise the senses. . . . Vitale's vibrant, jewel-toned illustrations embolden the folk-art simplicity of each verse."
SLJ

Why war is never a good idea; illustrations by Stefano Vitale. HarperCollins Publishers 2007 unp il $16.99; lib bdg $17.89
Grades: 3 4 5   **811**
   1. War poetry 2. Poetry—By individual authors
   ISBN   978-0-06-075385-6;   0-06-075385-4;
   978-0-06-075386-3 (lib bdg); 0-06-075386-2 (lib bdg)
                      LC 2006036255
Simple, rhythmic text explores the wanton destructiveness of War, which has grown old but not wise, as it demolishes nice people and beautiful things with no consideration for the consequences
"A thought-provoking, eloquent poem and brilliant art combine to bring the abstract concept of war to a personal, immediate level." SLJ

Weatherford, Carole Boston, 1956-
Birmingham, 1963. Wordsong 2007 39p il $17.95 *
Grades: 3 4 5 6   **811**
   1. Bombings—Poetry 2. Birmingham (Ala.)—Race relations—Poetry 3. African Americans—Civil rights—Poetry 4. Poetry—By individual authors
   ISBN 978-1-59078-440-2; 1-59078-440-5
                      LC 2006038105
"In free verse, a fictional 10-year-old tells of actual events leading up to the Ku Klux Klan bombing of the Sixteenth Street Baptist Church on September 15, 1963, and of the four young girls who died in the explosion. On each double-page spread, a few lines of spare poetry . . . are placed opposite a stirring, unframed archival photograph. . . . The quiet yet arresting book design will inspire readers." Booklist

Remember the bridge; poems of a people; designed by Semador Megged. Philomel Bks. 2002 53p il $17.99
Grades: 5 6 7 8   **811**
   1. African Americans—Poetry 2. Poetry—By individual authors
   ISBN 0-399-23726-7   LC 2001-36161
"Twenty-nine poems trace African-American history and include observations about Harriet Tubman, Marian Anderson, and Martin Luther King, Jr." Horn Book Guide
"The author evokes imagined and actual individual experiences of the people . . . in the historical black-and-white photos, drawings, and etchings. . . . This celebratory, visually striking book will be appreciated in most collections." SLJ

Weinstock, Robert
Food hates you too; and other poems. Hyperion Books for Children 2009 26p il $15.99
Grades: 2 3 4 5   **811**
   1. Food—Poetry 2. Poetry—By individual authors
   ISBN 978-1-4231-1391-1; 1-4231-1391-8
"This hilarious collection of poems about food stretches the imagination and vocabulary. . . . Varying in

length and form, . . . the poetry is fresh, funny, and challenging. . . . Full-color and sometimes delightfully bizarre mixed-media illustrations offer clever asides . . . goofy perspectives, . . . and amusing visual scenarios." SLJ

Weisburd, Stefi, 1957-
Barefoot; poems for naked feet; [by] Stefi Weisburd; illustrations by Lori McElrath-Eslick. Wordsong 2008 32p il $16.95
Grades: K 1 2 3   **811**
   1. Foot—Poetry 2. Poetry—By individual authors
   ISBN 978-1-59078-306-1   LC 2006018011
Children "will recognize the delight of walking on the sandy beach as well as the dislike of . . . the . . . icky stuff no one wants to step on. The leap to metaphor imagines what feet feel like on an elephant, a butterfly, or a fly. . . . The watercolor illustrations extend the words and help explain them." Booklist

Whipple, Laura
If the shoe fits; voices from Cinderella; illustrations by Laura Beingessner. Margaret K. McElderry Bks. 2002 67p il $17.95 *
Grades: 5 6 7 8   **811**
   1. Cinderella—Poetry 2. Fairy tales—Poetry 3. Poetry—By individual authors
   ISBN 0-689-84070-5   LC 2001-30778
In this version of the fairy tale "the characters tell the story in blank verses. . . . The story unfolds just as it always does, but the multiple points of view—from Cinderella's to the prince's to the rat's to the queen's—enlarge and enrich the familiar tale to win a more sophisticated audience. . . . Paintings by Beingessner achieve just the right mixture of sorrow, beauty, and humor." Booklist

Whitehead, Jenny
Holiday stew; by Jenny Whitehead. Henry Holt & Co. 2007 64p il $17.95
Grades: 2 3 4   **811**
   1. Holidays—Poetry 2. Poetry—By individual authors
   ISBN 978-0-8050-7715-5; 0-8050-7715-4
                      LC 2006011144
This poetry collection is "a celebration of a year's worth of holidays. . . . The collection is organized by season, and each of the 78 original poems is accompanied by a richly detailed ink illustration. Neither the rhyme nor the meter is forced, and the poems remain rooted in child-based experiences." SLJ

Wilbur, Richard, 1921-
The disappearing alphabet; illustrated by David Diaz. Harcourt Brace & Co. 1998 unp il hardcover o.p. pa $7
Grades: 3 4 5   **811**
   1. Alphabet 2. Poetry—By individual authors
   ISBN 0-15-201470-5; 0-15-216362-X (pa)
                      LC 97-24617
A collection of twenty-six short poems pondering what the world would be like if any letters of the alpha-

Wilbur, Richard, 1921-—*Continued*

bet should disappear

"The poems presented here were first printed in *The Atlantic Monthly* magazine. A series of rhyming couplets of varying lengths, they range from the innocently whimsical to the cleverly sophisticated. Diaz uses computer-generated illustrations to add just the right touches to the verses; the images are lush and playful at the same time." SLJ

Willard, Nancy, 1936-

A visit to William Blake's inn; poems for innocent and experienced travelers; illustrated by Alice and Martin Provensen. Harcourt Brace Jovanovich 1981 44p il $16; pa $7 *

Grades: 2 3 4 5   811

1. Nonsense verses 2. Poetry—By individual authors
ISBN 0-15-293822-2; 0-15-293823-0 (pa)

LC 80-27403

Awarded the Newbery Medal, 1982; A Caldecott Medal honor book, 1982

This "collection of sixteen nonsense verses describes the lively goings-on among several incongruous travelers who put up at an imaginary inn run by the English poet William Blake." Child Book Rev Serv

"Nancy Willard's fantasy is pure pleasure, and her joy is expressed in the juxtaposition of sense and nonsense. . . . Done chiefly in glowing tawny colors, the pictures are highly decorative, and the whole book, printed on buff paper speckled to simulate an antique look, presents an elegant appearance." Horn Book

Williams, Vera B.

Amber was brave, Essie was smart; the story of Amber and Essie told here in poems and pictures by Vera B. Williams. Greenwillow Bks. 2001 unp il $15.95; lib bdg $15.89; pa $7.99

Grades: 3 4 5   811

1. Sisters—Poetry 2. Poetry—By individual authors
ISBN 0-06-029460-4; 0-06-029461-2 (lib bdg); 0-06-057182-9 (pa)   LC 00-48438

Two sisters help each other deal with life while their mother is working and their father has been sent to jail

"An engaging, affecting view of the bonds between sisters, this balances reality with hope and love as it shows how small moments tell a big story." Booklist

Wilson, Karma

What's the weather inside? poems by Karma Wilson; drawings by Barry Blitt. Margaret McElderry Books 2009 170p il $17.99

Grades: 2 3 4   811

1. Humorous poetry 2. Poetry—By individual authors
ISBN 978-1-4169-0092-4; 1-4169-0092-6

LC 2006-23623

"This collection of more than 100 poems features comical wordplay . . . as well as lots of fun riffs on Mother Goose rhymes and fairy tales. Many are about family, friends, and school. . . . Blitt's line drawings are a great match for the verses. They are funny, dynamic, and full of personality." SLJ

Wong, Janet S., 1962-

Knock on wood; poems about superstitions; written by Janet S. Wong; illustrated by Julie Paschkis. Margaret K. McElderry Bks. 2003 33p il $17.95

Grades: 3 4 5   811

1. Superstition—Poetry 2. Poetry—By individual authors
ISBN 0-689-85512-5   LC 2002-8319

Contents: Cat; Clover; Ears; Garlic; Hair; Hat; Horseshoe; Key; Ladder; Ladybug; Mirror; Potatoes; Rooster; Salt; Thirteen; Umbrellas; Wood

A collection of seventeen original poems about superstitions, including walking under a ladder, breaking a mirror, and knocking on wood. Includes notes about the superstitions

"Some selections are haunting, and some humorous. . . . Paschkis creates an exquisite backdrop for the verses. Presented on a panoramic spread, each poem and facing watercolor scene have matching frames, anchoring them as reflections of one another. . . . There is much to ponder in both words and pictures." SLJ

Twist; yoga poems; written by Janet S. Wong; illustrated by Julie Paschkis. Margaret K. McElderry Books 2007 39p il $17.99

Grades: 2 3 4 5   811

1. Yoga—Poetry 2. Poetry—By individual authors
ISBN 0-689-87394-8; 978-0-689-87394-2

LC 2005-15888

"This collection of 16 poems touches on the uplifting and emotional aspects of yoga, putting words to the spirit of the poses and evoking the energy and feelings of the practice. . . . Paschkis's watercolor paintings frame both the poem and a child performing the pose with colorful fauna, flora, and people that suggest India as well as that particular exercise." SLJ

Worth, Valerie

All the small poems and fourteen more; pictures by Natalie Babbitt. Farrar, Straus & Giroux 1994 194p il pa $6.95 hardcover o.p. *

Grades: 2 3 4 5   811

1. Poetry—By individual authors
ISBN 0-374-40345-7 (pa)   LC 94-8810

"As the title implies, all the original collaborations between this poet and artist are collected in this volume, which includes ninety-nine poems and an additional fourteen new ones. The earlier works have been widely praised, for good reason, and the new verses are every bit as worthy as their predecessors." Horn Book

Animal poems; pictures by Steve Jenkins. Farrar, Straus & Giroux 2007 unp il $17 *

Grades: 4 5 6   811

1. Animals—Poetry 2. Poetry—By individual authors
ISBN 0-374-38057-0; 978-0-374-38057-1

LC 2005-56812

A collection of twenty-three illustrated poems about animals

"This pairing of . . . Worth's exquisite poems with Jenkins's . . . extraordinary, cut-paper illustrations make this a volume to treasure. . . . Each poem in this handsome volume is a gem—full of crisp language, vivid images and thoughtful ideas." Publ Wkly

Worth, Valerie—*Continued*

Peacock and other poems; pictures by Natalie Babbitt. Farrar, Straus & Giroux 2002 40p il $15

Grades: 2 3 4 5   **811**

1. Poetry—By individual authors

ISBN 0-374-35766-8   LC 2001-23828

A collection of short blank verse about common sights and objects such as "umbrella," "pencil," "crayons"

"The illustrations, minimalist in form but not in impact, match the incisive delicacy of the poems, twenty-six in all—and each is a delight." Horn Book

Yolen, Jane

An egret's day; poems by Jane Yolen; photographs by Jason Stemple. Wordsong 2009 30p il $17.95

Grades: 3 4 5   **811**

1. Herons—Poetry

ISBN 978-1-59078-650-5; 1-59078-650-5

LC 2008051688

"Poetry and short informative paragraphs combine to celebrate both the elegance and the natural history of the American egret. Haiku, free verse, rhyming couplets and even a limerick are just some of the forms Yolen masterfully uses to engage readers on both aesthetic and scientific levels. Gorgeous photography completes this carefully designed literary science piece with scenes of the egret's daily life." Kirkus

A mirror to nature; poems about reflection; [by] Jane Yolen; photographs by Jason Stemple. Wordsong 2009 31p il $17.95

Grades: 3 4 5   **811**

1. Nature poetry 2. Poetry—By individual authors

ISBN 978-1-59078-624-6   LC 2008031760

"Water acts as a mirror in this picture book that combines short poems with full-page color photographs of animals in the wild. . . . The poetic forms are well matched to the mood in the pictures. . . . Drawn by the rich play in words and pictures, kids will see reflections, strange and beautiful, in the the natural world." Booklist

Young, Ed

Beyond the great mountains; a visual poem about China. Chronicle Books 2005 32p il $17.95 *

Grades: 4 5 6 7   **811**

1. China—Poetry 2. Poetry—By individual authors

ISBN 0-8118-4343-2

"The book is comprised of 14 lines, each of which is accompanied by its own double-page illustration, done in cut and torn-paper collage. Young also provides the ancient characters for the images he presents. . . . Designed to be read vertically, each page is flipped up to reveal the accompanying illustration. In this way, the entire book becomes a piece of art, a visual treat of sublime colors and textures that joins with text and characters to describe the vastness and beauty of China." SLJ

Zimmer, Tracie Vaughn

Steady hands; poems about work; by Tracie Vaughn Zimmer; illustrated by Megan Halsey and Sean Addy. Clarion Books 2009 48p il $16 *

Grades: 4 5 6   **811**

1. Work—Poetry 2. Occupations—Poetry 3. Poetry—By individual authors

ISBN 978-0-618-90351-1; 0-618-90351-8

LC 2007038848

"Inventive, complicated collages and well-crafted poems focus on the activities of working people in this eye-catching book. With an observant eye, Zimmer . . . captures different individuals performing work with 'steady hands.' . . . Halsey and Addy's . . . hip collages combine individual cut-outs of people along with drawings, photos, textured backgrounds and designs." Publ Wkly

Zobel, Allia

Smelly feet sandwich; and other silly poems; by Allia Zobel Nolan; illustrated by Kate Leake. Tiger Tales 2008 unp il $7.95

Grades: 1 2 3   **811**

1. Humorous poetry 2. Poetry—By individual authors

ISBN 978-1-58925-836-5; 1-58925-836-3

"This book, containing nine poems . . . will cause children to laugh out loud as they read them. The easy-to-read font will not intimidate students but will be a drawing point for them to want to pick up the book and read. Leake uses watercolor and pen-and-ink drawings to convey the message of each zany poem and bring it alive." Libr Media Connect

811.008   American poetry— Collections

The **20th** century children's poetry treasury; selected by Jack Prelutsky; illustrated by Meilo So. Knopf 1999 87p il $19.95 *

Grades: 3 4 5 6   **811.008**

1. American poetry—Collections

ISBN 0-679-89314-8; 0-679-99314-2 (lib bdg)

LC 99-23988

A collection of more than 200 poems by such modern poets as Nikki Grimes, John Ciardi, Karla Kuskin, Ted Hughes, e.e. cummings, Eve Merriam, Deborah Chandra, Arnold Adoff, and more than 100 others

"While all of these selections have been published elsewhere, the format and illustrations in this collection give them new life. . . . So's watercolor illustrations are, by turn, impressionistic, childlike, silly, and serious, as called for by the tone of the poems featured. . . . A splendid collection." SLJ

Amazing faces; edited by Lee Bennett Hopkins; illustrated by Chris Soentpiet. Lee & Low 2010 unp il $18.95

Grades: 2 3 4 5   **811.008**

1. American poetry—Collections

ISBN 978-1-60060-334-1; 1-60060-334-3

"Illustrated with large, handsome watercolor portraits, the 16 poems in this anthology celebrate the rich diversi-

Amazing faces—*Continued*

ty of American kids—what makes each one special and the connections between them. . . . A great collection for sharing at home and in the classroom." Booklist

America at war; poems; selected by Lee Bennett Hopkins; illlustrated by Stephen Alcorn. Margaret K. McElderry Books 2008 84p il $21.99 *

Grades: 5 6 7 8   **811.008**
1. War poetry 2. United States—History—Poetry 3. American poetry—Collections
ISBN 978-1-4169-1832-5; 1-4169-1832-9
                                    LC 2006-08723

"This handsome anthology, expressing Americans' varied experience during wartime, is a fine selection of poems accessible to children. . . . The poems will touch readers with their sharp poignancy and undeniable power. Throughout the well-designed book, the expressive watercolor artwork enhances the poetry." Booklist

Ashley Bryan's ABC of African-American poetry. Atheneum Bks. for Young Readers 1997 unp il hardcover o.p. pa $7.99 *

Grades: K 1 2 3   **811.008**
1. African Americans—Poetry 2. American poetry—African American authors—Collections 3. Alphabet
ISBN 0-689-81209-4; 0-689-84045-4 (pa)
                                    LC 96-25148

"A Jean Karl book"

Each letter of the alphabet is represented by a line from a poem by a different African American poet, describing an aspect of the black experience

This book is illustrated "by Bryan's vivid tempera and gouache paintings. . . . The selections . . . display a loving acquaintance with poets from James Weldon Johnson to Rita Dove. While there is a full range of emotions, joy and pride predominate." SLJ

The **Beauty** of the beast; poems from the animal kingdom; selected by Jack Prelutsky; illustrated by Meilo So; opening poems for each section especially written for this anthology by Jack Prelutsky. Knopf 1997 101p il $19.95 *

Grades: 4 5 6   **811.008**
1. Animals—Poetry 2. Poetry—Collections
ISBN 0-679-87058-X   LC 96-14423

This collection includes "more than 200 animal poems by twentieth-century writers, loosely arranged into five sections—insects and worms, fish, reptiles, birds, and mammals. . . . The poets include Hoberman, Lawrence, Worth, Jarrell, Roethke, and many more." Booklist

"Prelutsky has selected a remarkable array of poems full of movement and sound. . . . Each page has several poems and bright watercolors that writhe with texture." SLJ

Includes bibliographical references

Behind the museum door; poems to celebrate the wonders of museums; selected by Lee Bennett Hopkins; illustrated by Stacey Dressen-McQueen. Abrams Books for Young Readers 2007 unp il $16.95 *

Grades: 3 4 5   **811.008**
1. American poetry—Collections 2. Museums—Poetry 3. Art—Poetry
ISBN 978-0-8109-1204-5; 0-8109-1204-X
                                    LC 2006013576

"This collection of poems touches on the sights and sensations a group of children experience on a field trip. . . . Selections are by such poets as Lilian Moore, Jane Yolen, Alice Schertle, and Myra Cohn Livingston. . . . Each of Dressen-McQueen's folk-art-style 'exhibits,' carefully crafted in acrylic paint, oil pastel, and colored pencil, successfully captures and reinforces the mood of its accompanying poem." SLJ

The **Bill** Martin Jr. Big book of poetry; edited by Bill Martin Jr., with Michael Sampson; foreword by Eric Carle; afterword Steven Kellogg. Simon & Schuster Books for Young Readers 2008 175p $21 *

Grades: PreK K 1 2 3   **811.008**
1. American poetry—Collections
ISBN 978-1-4169-3971-9; 1-4169-3971-7

"The almost 200 selections in this big handsome anthology . . . have a singing beat. . . . The collection brings together poems from Robert Frost, Christina Rossetti, Langston Hughes, Nikki Grimes, Aliki, Jack Prelutsky, and many other well-known poets. Accompanying the poems are pictures from many of the best picture-book illustrators whose work . . . extends the words' lyrical rhythms and playfulness." Booklist

Carnival of the animals; poems inspired by Saint-Saëns' music; by James Berry . . . [et al.]; edited by Judith Chernaik; illustrated by Satoshi Kitamura. Candlewick Press 2006 unp il $16.99

Grades: K 1 2 3 4   **811.008**
1. Animals—Poetry 2. Music—Poetry 3. American poetry—Collections
ISBN 0-7636-2960-X   LC 2005-48445

"Chernaik commissioned 13 poets to respond to the musical animal portraits in Saint-Saens' kid-friendly *Carnival of the Animals* . . . Their concise, vibrant word painting will forge an instant connection with children. . . . The poems . . . can be appreciated with or without the accompanying 55-minute CD of music and readings. . . . Having said that, separating this from its inspirational basis would miss the point; children will find it fascinating to see how their own impressions of the original works match the poets'—not to mention illustrator Kitamura's, whose engaging watercolors shift fluidly among the poems' many moods while lending the whole a welcome cohesion." Booklist

Cool salsa; bilingual poems on growing up Latino in the United States; edited by Lori M. Carlson; introduction by Oscar Hijuelos. Holt & Co. 1994 xx, 123p il hardcover o.p. pa $6.99 *
Grades: 5 6 7 8 9 10   **811.008**
1. American poetry—Hispanic American authors—Collections 2. Bilingual books—English-Spanish
ISBN 0-8050-3135-9; 978-0-449-70436-3 (pa); 0-449-70436-X (pa)   LC 93-45798
"This collection presents poems by 29 Mexican-American, Cuban-American, Puerto Rican, and other Central and South American poets, including Sandra Cisneros, Luis J. Rodriguez, Pat Mora, Gary Soto, Ana Castillo, Oscar Hijuelos, Ed J. Vega, Judith Ortiz-Cofer, and other Latino writers both contemporary and historical. Brief biographical notes on the authors are provided. All the poems deal with experiences of teenagers." Book Rep

The **entrance** place of wonders; poems of the Harlem Renaissance; selected by Daphne Muse; illustrated by Charlotte Riley-Webb. Abrams 2006 unp il $15.95 *
Grades: 3 4 5   **811.008**
1. American poetry—African American authors—Collections 2. Harlem Renaissance
ISBN 0-8109-5997-6
"Twenty poems written during the Harlem Renaissance are perfectly paired with exuberant oil paintings. Familiar poets such as Countee Cullen, Langston Hughes, James Weldon Johnson, and Claude McKay are joined by less immediately recognized names such as Effie Lee Newsome, Dorothy Vena Johnson, and Gladys May Caseley-Hayford. Their collective work, firmly grounded in this exciting explosion of African-American culture, affirms the joy of life and of personal growth and discovery." SLJ

Every second something happens; poems for the mind and senses; selected by Christine San José and Bill Johnson; illustrations by Melanie Hall. Wordsong 2009 48p il $17.95
Grades: PreK K 1 2   **811.008**
1. American poetry—Collections
ISBN 978-1-59078-622-2; 1-59078-622-X
                    LC 2008024115
"Fun for reading aloud, the very short verses in this collection are easy, rhythmic, and immediate. Some are written by young kids and some by children's poets, and there are even a few lines from Shakespeare. . . . Hall's clear colorful illustrations never overwhelm the words as they show kids in action." Booklist

Falling down the page; [compiled] by Georgia Heard. Roaring Brook Press 2009 47p il $16.95
Grades: 3 4 5 6   **811.008**
1. American poetry—Collections
ISBN 978-1-59643-220-8; 1-59643-220-9
                    LC 2007-38870
"Thirty-two 'list' poems are presented in a dynamic design and trim size. . . . The accessible yet thought-provoking selections are from mostly well-known poets such as Marilyn Singer, Lee Bennett Hopkins and Rebecca Kai Dotlich, and include a couple from Heard. . . . The poems will spark imagination." Kirkus

For laughing out loud; poems to tickle your funnybone; selected by Jack Prelutsky; illustrated by Marjorie Priceman. Knopf 1991 84p il $17 *
Grades: 3 4 5 6   **811.008**
1. American poetry—Collections 2. Humorous poetry
ISBN 0-394-82144-0   LC 90-33010
A collection of humorous poems by writers including Ellen Raskin, Karla Kuskin, Ogden Nash, and Arnold Lobel
"These nonsense verses by a wide variety of poets combine the domestic and the gross, deadpan and slapstick, with a lilting rhythm and satisfying rhyme. . . . The design is ebullient, often with several poems appearing on a double-page spread surrounded by wildly energetic wash-and-line illustrations." Booklist

Got geography! poems; selected by Lee Bennett Hopkins; pictures by Philip Stanton. Greenwillow Books 2006 32p il $15.99; lib bdg $16.89
Grades: 3 4 5   **811.008**
1. Geography—Poetry 2. American poetry—Collections
ISBN 0-06-055601-3; 0-06-055602-1 (lib bdg)
                    LC 2004-59662
"Sixteen selections from a variety of poets explore the curiosity piqued by maps, globes, the land we live on, and places far away. The gentle, often-moving verses cover a wide spectrum of ways to explore the Earth from mapping the world to examining its surface to finding one's place within it. . . . The bright acrylic-and-watercolor illustrations bring energy to the pages and set the mood for each poem." SLJ

Hamsters, shells, and spelling bees; school poems; edited by Lee Bennett Hopkins; pictures by Sachiko Yoshikawa. HarperCollins 2008 46p il (I can read!) $16.99; lib bdg $17.89
Grades: PreK K 1 2   **811.008**
1. American poetry—Collections 2. Schools—Poetry
ISBN 978-0-06-074112-9; 0-06-074112-0; 978-0-06-074113-6 (lib bdg); 0-06-074113-9 (lib bdg)
                    LC 2007020881
"Contributed by well-known poets for young people (Jane Yolen, J. Patrick Lewis, Alice Schertle, among others), the poems in this bright compilation . . . describe a wide range of school experiences. . . . The selections range in style from haikus to free verse, although many poems follow a bouncy, rhyming structure. All are written in accessible words targeted straight to emerging readers. . . . [Illustrated with] jellybean-bright cartoon-style illustrations." Booklist

Hanukkah lights; holiday poetry; selected by Lee Bennett Hopkins; pictures by Melanie Hall. HarperCollins 2004 28p il (I can read book) $15.99; lib bdg $16.89 *
Grades: K 1 2 3   **811.008**
1. Hanukkah—Poetry 2. American poetry—Collections
ISBN 0-06-008051-5; 0-06-008052-3 (lib bdg)
                    LC 2003-18901
A collection of poems that celebrate the activities and experiences of Hanukkah

Hanukkah lights—*Continued*

"The poems are simple, evocative, and rhythmic without lapsing into a singsong cadence. Hall's expressive artwork creates an appealing contemporary tone with vivid pastels and a smattering of collage." SLJ

Heart to heart; new poems inspired by twentieth-century American art; edited by Jan Greenberg. Abrams 2001 80p il map $19.95 *
Grades: 5 6 7 8 9 10   811.008
1. American poetry—Collections 2. American art 3. Art—20th century
ISBN 0-8109-4386-7   LC 99-462335
Michael L. Printz Award honor book, 2002

A compilation of poems by Americans writing about American art in the twentieth century, including such writers as Nancy Willard, Jane Yolen, and X. J. Kennedy.

"From a tight diamante and pantoum to lyrical free verse, the range of poetic styles will speak to a wide age group. . . . Concluding with biographical notes on each poet and artist, this rich resource is an obvious choice for teachers, and the exciting interplay between art and the written word will encourage many readers to return again and again to the book." Booklist

Here's a little poem; a very first book of poetry; collected by Jane Yolen and Andrew Fusek Peters; illustrated by Polly Dunbar. Candlewick Press 2007 104p il $21.99 *
Grades: PreK   811.008
1. American poetry—Collections
ISBN 978-0-7636-3141-3; 0-7636-3141-8
LC 2006-40621

"This big, spacious anthology of more than 60 poems is a wonderful first book to read with babies and toddlers over and over again. . . . The clear, active, mixed-media illustrations show very young children outdoors and in; morning to bedtime; loving, teary, absurd, furious." Booklist

Hip hop speaks to children; a celebration of poetry with a beat; editor, Nikki Giovanni; advisory editors, Tony Medina, Willie Perdomo, Michele Scott; series editor, Dominique Raccah; illustrators, Kristen Balouch, Michele Noiset, Jeremy Tugeau, Alicia Vergel de Dios, and Damian Ward. Sourcebooks Jabberwocky 2008 72p il $19.99 *
Grades: 3 4 5 6   811.008
1. American poetry—Collections 2. American poetry—African American authors—Collections
ISBN 978-1-4022-1048-8; 1-4022-1048-5
LC 2008004627

"Editor Giovanni states, 'Poetry with a beat. That's hip hop in a flash,' and she goes on to link hip-hop to grand opera and present a capsule history of African American vernacular music. This features a wide-ranging selection of 51 entries, plus a CD with new or previously released recorded versions of 29, some with music. The poets range from Langston Hughes and W.E.B. DuBois to Kanye West, Mos Def, and Queen Latifah. . . . Although created by five illustrators, the art shares both vibrant colors and a dancing free-spirited look that matches the general tone of the poetry." Booklist

I am the darker brother; an anthology of modern poems by African Americans; edited and with an afterword by Arnold Adoff; drawings by Benny Andrews; introduction by Rudine Sims Bishop; foreword by Nikki Giovanni. rev ed. Simon & Schuster Bks. for Young Readers 1997 208p il hardcover o.p. pa $5.99 *
Grades: 6 7 8 9   811.008
1. American poetry—African American authors—Collections
ISBN 0-689-81241-8; 0-689-80869-0 (pa)
LC 97-144181

First published 1968

This anthology presents "the African-American experience through poetry that speaks for itself. . . . Because of the historical context of many of the poems, the book will be much in demand during Black History Month, but it should be used and treasured as part of the larger canon of literature to be enjoyed by all Americans at all times of the year. An indispensable addition to library collections." SLJ

I, too, sing America; three centuries of African American poetry; [selected and annotated by] Catherine Clinton; illustrated by Stephen Alcorn. Houghton Mifflin 1998 128p il $21 *
Grades: 6 7 8 9   811.008
1. African Americans—Poetry 2. American poetry—African American authors—Collections
ISBN 0-395-89599-5   LC 97-46137

"For each poet, Clinton provides a biography and a brief, insightful commentary on the poem(s) she has chosen, including a discussion of political as well as literary connections. Alcorn's dramatic, full-page, full-color illustrations opposite each poem evoke the quiltlike patterns and rhythmic figures of folk art." Booklist

In daddy's arms I am tall; African Americans celebrating fathers; illustrated by Javaka Steptoe. Lee & Low Bks. 1997 unp il $15.95; pa $6.95 *
Grades: K 1 2 3   811.008
1. African Americans—Poetry 2. Fathers—Poetry 3. American poetry—Collections
ISBN 1-880000-31-8; 1-58430-016-7 (pa)
LC 97-7311

Coretta Scott King Award for illustration

A collection of poems celebrating African-American fathers by Angela Johnson, E. Ethelbert Miller, Carole Boston Weatherford, and others

"Certain poems . . . elevate this collection above the mundane, but it is the illustrations that set this volume apart. Steptoe uses a variety of materials and techniques and art forms to enhance the language of the poems, including torn paper, collages, realia, paintings, and drawings." Horn Book

Incredible inventions; poems selected by Lee Bennett Hopkins; illustrations by Julia Sarcone-Roach. Greenwillow Books 2009 27p il $17.99; lib bdg $18.89

Grades: 1 2 3 4   **811.008**
1. Inventions—Poetry 2. American poetry—Collections
ISBN 978-0-06-087245-8; 0-06-087245-4; 978-0-06-087246-5 (lib bdg); 0-06-087246-2 (lib bdg)
LC 2008003830

"Ingenious inventions are the focus of this lively picture-book poetry collection. Contributed by both well-known and emerging poets, the selections represent a wide range of styles. . . . The subjects, drawn from a young person's everyday world, add to the poems' accessiblity. . . . The mixed-media artwork's well-designed compositions add energy without overwhelming the words." Booklist

It rained all day that night; autographs, rhymes & inscriptions; compiled by Lillian Morrison; illustrated by Christy Hale. August House 2003 80p il $16.95; pa $9.95

Grades: 3 4 5 6   **811.008**
1. American poetry—Collections
ISBN 0-87483-735-9; 0-87483-726-X (pa)
LC 2003-51987

An illustrated compilation of short poems and other inscriptions from autograph albums, arranged by such themes as friendship, school, and nonsense.

"Morrison has created a stunning collection of autograph verses. . . . Hale's ink-and-watercolor paintings dance across each page, extending the sentiment . . . implicit in each verse." SLJ

A **kick** in the head; selected by Paul B. Janeczko; illustrated by Chris Raschka. Candlewick Press 2005 61p il $17.99; pa $9.99 *

Grades: 4 5 6 7   **811.008**
1. American poetry—Collections
ISBN 978-0-7636-0662-6; 0-7636-0662-6; 978-0-7636-4132-0 (pa); 0-7636-4132-4 (pa)
LC 2004-48508

This collection offers examples of poetic forms "building from a couplet, tercet, and quatrain to the less familiar and more complex persona poem, ballad, and pantoum." SLJ

"Raschka's high-spirited, spare torn-paper-and-paint collages ingeniously broaden the poems' wide-ranging emotional tones. . . . Clear, very brief explanations of poetic forms . . . accompany each entry; a fine introduction and appended notes offer further information. . . . This is the introduction that will ignite enthusiasm." Booklist

Knock at a star; a child's introduction to poetry; [compiled by] X. J. Kennedy and Dorothy M. Kennedy; illustrated by Karen Lee Baker. rev ed. Little, Brown 1999 180p il hardcover o.p. pa $12.99

Grades: 3 4 5 6   **811.008**
1. American poetry—Collections 2. English poetry—Collections
ISBN 0-316-48436-9; 0-316-48800-3 (pa)
LC 98-21572

A revised and newly illustrated edition of the title first published 1982

An anthology of mostly very short poems by standard, contemporary, and anonymous poets, intended to stimulate interest in reading and writing poetry

"Karen Lee Baker's small, shaded-pencil drawings capture the many moods of the verse." Booklist

Lives: poems about famous Americans; selected by Lee Bennett Hopkins; illustrated by Leslie Staub. HarperCollins Pubs. 1999 31p il $15.99 *

Grades: 4 5 6 7   **811.008**
1. United States—Biography—Poetry 2. American poetry—Collections
ISBN 0-06-027767-X; 0-06-027768-8 (lib bdg)
LC 98-29851

A collection of poetic portraits of sixteen famous Americans from Paul Revere to Neil Armstrong, by such authors as Jane Yolen, Nikki Grimes, and X. J. Kennedy

"Hopkins's eloquent introduction praises the power of poetry. Concluding 'Notes on the Lives' give readers useful biographical information. Full-page portraits feature Staub's distinctive, flat, primitive style, and their backgrounds have details particular to the subject. . . . A winning combination of poems and illustrations." SLJ

Marvelous math; a book of poems; selected by Lee Bennett Hopkins; illustrated by Karen Barbour. Simon & Schuster Bks. for Young Readers 1997 31p il hardcover o.p. pa $6.99 *

Grades: 3 4 5   **811.008**
1. Mathematics—Poetry 2. American poetry—Collections
ISBN 0-689-80658-2; 0-689-84442-5 (pa)
LC 96-21597

Presents such poems as "Math Makes Me Feel Safe," "Fractions," "Pythagoras," and "Time Passes," by such writers as Janet S. Wong, Lee Bennett Hopkins, and Ilo Orleans

"Rhymed and open verse styles are represented, as are a variety of tones. . . . Barbour's lively illustrations dance and play around the poems. Her boldly outlined watercolor figures, often wearing ill-fitting hats, fill the pages with childlike whimsy." SLJ

More pocket poems; selected by Bobbi Katz; illustrated by Deborah Zemke. Dutton Children's Books 2009 28p il $17.99

Grades: K 1 2 3   **811.008**
1. American poetry—Collections
ISBN 978-0-525-42076-7; 0-525-42076-2
LC 2008013883

"This brightly illustrated anthology presents 44 short poems for children. . . . [It has a] thematic arrangement by season, cycling from spring to winter. . . . Writers represented include Eve Merriam, Emily Dickinson, Alan Benjamin, Langston Hughes, Arnold Lobel, Myra Cohn Livingston, Betsy Franco, Aileen Fisher, Jack Prelutsky, and John Ciardi. Lively, upbeat paintings illustrate each verse." Booklist

My America; a poetry atlas of the United States; selected by Lee Bennett Hopkins; illustrated by Stephen Alcorn. Simon & Schuster Bks. for Young Readers 2000 83p il $21.95 *

Grades: 4 5 6 7   **811.008**

1. United States—Poetry 2. American poetry—Collections

ISBN 0-689-81247-7   LC 98-47402

A collection of poems evocative of seven geographical regions of the United States, including the Northeast, Southeast, Great Lakes, Plains, Mountain, Southwest, and Pacific Coast States.

"Some poems are purposive, but the best . . . capture places and people in all their diversity. Stephen Alcorn's handsome, multi-textured pictures . . . avoid literal interpretation and capture the sweep of the land and the rhythm of the words." Booklist

The **Oxford** book of children's verse in America; edited by Donald Hall. Oxford University Press 1985 xxxviii, 319p $39.95; pa $19.95

Grades: 5 6 7 8 9 10 11 12 Adult

                         811.008

1. American poetry—Collections

ISBN 0-19-503539-9; 0-19-506761-4 (pa)

                         LC 84-20755

"Hall's intention, expressed in the introduction, is to create an anthology of American poetry actually written for or adopted by children during a particular historical period. The emphasis is on authenticity rather than personal taste." SLJ

"A fine and carefully winnowed collection of American poetry is gathered in a book that will interest students of children's literature and young people who simply enjoy browsing." Horn Book

The **Place** my words are looking for; what poets say about and through their work; selected by Paul B. Janeczko. Bradbury Press 1990 150p il $17.95 *

Grades: 4 5 6 7   **811.008**

1. American poetry—Collections 2. Poetics

ISBN 0-02-747671-5   LC 89-39331

"More than forty contemporary poets are included: Eve Merriam, X. J. Kennedy, Felice Holman, Gary Soto, Mark Vinz, Karla Kuskin, and John Updike, among others. Their contributions vary widely in theme and mood and style, though the preponderance of the pieces are written in modern idiom and unrhymed meter. The accompanying comments frequently are as insightful and eloquent as the poems themselves." Horn Book

Poetry speaks to children; editor, Elise Paschen; illustrators, Judy Love, Wendy Rasmussen, Paula Zinngrabe Wendland. Sourcebooks 2005 104p il $19.95

Grades: 3 4 5 6   **811.008**

1. American poetry—Collections

ISBN 1-4022-0329-2; 978-1-4022-0329-9

"A fine, basic collection. Approximately half of the 97 selections are read or performed on the accompanying CD. The book provides a mix of adult writers (Rita Dove, Seamus Heaney, and Billy Collins, among others) and those whose work is specifically for children, such as X. J. Kennedy and Mary Ann Hoberman. Topics include childhood, animals, nonsense poems, and humor. . . . The three illustrators have captured the different tones of the selections." SLJ

A **Poke** in the I; [selected by] Paul Janeczko; illustrated by Chris Raschka. Candlewick Press 2001 35p il $16.99; pa $7.99 *

Grades: 4 5 6 7 8 9   **811.008**

1. American poetry—Collections

ISBN 0-7636-0661-8; 0-7636-2376-8 (pa)

                         LC 00-33675

"Thirty concrete poems of all shapes and sizes are carefully laid on large white spreads, extended by Raschka's quirky watercolor and paper-collage illustrations. . . . Beautiful and playful, this title should find use in storytimes, in the classroom, and just for pleasure anywhere." SLJ

The **Random** House book of poetry for children; selected and introduced by Jack Prelutsky; illustrated by Arnold Lobel. Random House 1983 248p il $19.95; lib bdg $21.99 *

Grades: 3 4 5 6   **811.008**

1. American poetry—Collections 2. English poetry—Collections

ISBN 0-394-85010-6; 0-394-95010-0 (lib bdg)

                         LC 83-2990

Opening poems for each section especially written for this anthology by Jack Prelutsky

In this anthology emphasis "is placed on humor and light verse; but serious and thoughtful poems are also included. . . . Approximately two thirds of the selections were written within the past forty years—the splendid contributions of such writers as John Ciardi, Aileen Fisher, Dennis Lee, Myra Cohn Livingston, David McCord, Eve Merriam, and Lilian Moore. [There are] . . . samplings of earlier poets from Shakespeare and Blake to Emily Dickinson and Walter de la Mare." Horn Book

Read a rhyme, write a rhyme; poems selected by Jack Prelutsky; illustrated by Meilo So. Alfred A. Knopf 2005 23p il $16.95 *

Grades: 2 3 4   **811.008**

1. American poetry—Collections 2. Poetics

ISBN 0-375-82286-0   LC 2004-26501

"Prelutsky designed this collection to jumpstart children's creative juices. Three short poems are chosen for each theme: dogs, food, birthdays, bugs, cows, friends, snow, turtles, rain, and self. He also includes a poemstart: an unfinished verse, along with advice and lists of rhyming words, so that readers can complete the poem on their own. The compiler displays a fine sense for lighthearted, kid-friendly poetry. . . . So's watercolor-and-ink illustrations add playfully jumbled perspectives." SLJ

Salting the ocean; 100 poems by young poets; selected by Naomi Shihab Nye; pictures by Ashley Bryan. Greenwillow Bks. 2000 111p il $16.99

Grades: 4 5 6 7   **811.008**

1. Children's writings 2. American poetry—Collections

ISBN 0-688-16193-6   LC 99-30590

Salting the ocean—*Continued*
"These poems are divided into four topics: The Self and the Inner World, Where We Live, Anybody's Family, and the Wide Imagination." Horn Book Guide
"Nye presents the exceptional work of students in grades 1 through 12. . . . Illustrated with Ashley Bryan's signature bright-hued, bold-lined paintings and multicultural imagery, the poems are varied in both sophistication and subject." Booklist
Includes bibliographical references

Sharing the seasons; a book of poems; selected by Lee Bennett Hopkins; illustrated by David Diaz. Margaret K. McElderry Books 2010 83p il $21.99 *
Grades: 3 4 5   **811.008**
1. Seasons—Poetry 2. American poetry—Collections
ISBN 978-1-4169-0210-2; 1-4169-0210-4
LC 2009-19297
"This dynamic collection features 48 poems—12 for each of the seasons—mingling previously published poems by Carl Sandburg, Karla Kuskin, and others, with new works by several poets, including Hopkins. The diverse, accessible selections create a mosaic that stirs the senses. Diaz's ethereal silhouettes of animals and people, which resemble layered, cut-paper shadows, are ornately inlaid with nature motifs." Publ Wkly

She's all that! poems about girls; selected by Belinda Hollyer; illustrated by Susan Hellard. Kingfisher 2006 128p il $14.95
Grades: 4 5 6   **811.008**
1. Girls—Poetry 2. American poetry—Collections
ISBN 978-0-7534-5852-5; 0-7534-5852-7
"The poems, penned by famous poets and children's book authors, move from topics of racial identity and body image to love and sports. Lee Bennett Hopkins, Gertrude Stein, Roald Dahl, Russell Hoban, Douglas Florian, and Judith Viorst are among those included. The full-page and spot-art line drawings adorn the pages as doodles might decorate a journal." SLJ

Sky magic; poems; selected by Lee Bennett Hopkins; illustrated by Mariusz Stawarski. Dutton Children's Books 2009 31p il $17.99
Grades: 1 2 3   **811.008**
1. Sun—Poetry 2. Moon—Poetry 3. Stars—Poetry 4. American poetry—Collections
ISBN 978-0-525-47862-1; 0-525-47862-0
LC 2008034222
"Hopkins has gathered 14 poems about the sun, moon, and stars. Some are by well-known authors, like Carl Sandburg and Tennessee Williams, while others are less familiar. Almost all of the selections are short, wistful, free verse, and well crafted. The dreamlike tone is reflected in Stawarski's quasi-surrealistic illustrations." SLJ

Soul looks back in wonder; [illustrated by] Tom Feelings. Dial Bks. 1993 unp il hardcover o.p. pa $7.99 *
Grades: 4 5 6 7   **811.008**
1. American poetry—African American authors—Collections 2. African Americans—Poetry
ISBN 0-8037-1001-1; 0-14-056501-9 (pa)
LC 93-824
Coretta Scott King Award for illustration

Artwork and poems by such writers as Maya Angelou, Langston Hughes, and Askia Toure portray the creativity, strength, and beauty of their African American heritage
"This thoughtful collection of poetry is unique. . . . Feelings selected sketches done while he was in West Africa, South America, and at home in America. The original drawings were enhanced with colored pencils, colored papers, stencil cut-outs, and other techniques to give a collage effect. Marbled textures bring vibrancy to the work." Horn Book

Words with wings; a treasury of African-American poetry and art; selected by Belinda Rochelle. HarperCollins Pubs. 2001 unp il lib bdg $18.99 *
Grades: 4 5 6 7   **811.008**
1. American poetry—African American authors—Collections 2. African Americans in art 3. African Americans—Poetry
ISBN 0-688-16415-3   LC 00-26864
"Amistad"
Pairs twenty works of art by African-American artists such as Horace Pippin and Jacob Lawrence with twenty poems by African-American poets such as Langston Hughes, Countee Cullen, and Lucille Clifton
"Most of the combinations are stunning. . . . Short biographical paragraphs on each poet and artist round out this moving presentation." SLJ

812   American drama

Black, Ann N.
Readers theatre for middle school boys; investigating the strange and mysterious; illustrated by Cody Rust. Teachers Idea Press 2008 190p il (Readers theatre) pa $30
Grades: Professional   **812**
1. Drama—Collections 2. Readers' theater
ISBN 978-1-59158-535-0 (pa); 1-59158-535-X (pa)
LC 2007034923
"This book provides solid offerings of Readers Theater scripts for educators working with middle school boys. Selections include adaptations of such creepy classics as 'The Legend of Sleepy Hollow,' 'The Masque of the Red Death,' . . . and 'The Monkey's Paw.' The scripts have a new, fresh feel, and contain plenty of elements to capture and maintain adolescent males' attention." Libr Media Connect
Includes bibliographical references

Bruchac, Joseph, 1942-
Pushing up the sky: seven Native American plays for children; illustrated by Teresa Flavin. Dial Bks. for Young Readers 2000 94p il $21.99 paperback o.p.
Grades: 3 4 5   **812**
1. Native American drama 2. Drama—Collections
ISBN 0-8037-2168-4; 0-8037-2535-3 (pa)
LC 98-20483
Contents: Gluskabe and Old Man Winter; Star sisters; Possum's tail; Wihio's duck dance; Pushing up the sky; The cannibal monster; The strongest one

Bruchac, Joseph, 1942-—*Continued*

Uses drama to tell seven different stories from Native American traditions including the Abenaki, Ojibway, Cherokee, Cheyenne, Snohomish, Tlingit, and Zuni

"The short, simple scripts are accessible to young, inexperienced actors. . . . Suggestions are given for easy-to-make costumes, props, and scenery. A variety of pen-and-ink drawings illustrate the plays, as well as one lively gouache illustration per selection." SLJ

Includes bibliographical references

Dabrowski, Kristen

My first monologue book; 100 monologues for young children; by Kristen Dabrowski. Smith and Kraus 2006 112p (Young actors series) pa $11.95

Grades: 2 3 4 5 6   **812**

1. Monologues 2. Acting

ISBN 978-1-57525-533-0 (pa); 1-57525-533-2 (pa)

                                                   LC 2006938162

"A Smith and Kraus book"

"Dabrowski offers short, accessible selections on common topics such as games, families, food, friends, school, and wishes. The true-to-life experiences and emotions are delivered in a child's voice and run the gamut from funny to serious." SLJ

My second monologue book; famous and historical people: 101 monologues for young children. Smith and Kraus 2008 115p il (My first acting series) pa $11.95

Grades: 2 3 4 5 6   **812**

1. Monologues 2. Acting

ISBN 978-1-57525-601-6 (pa); 1-57525-601-0 (pa)

                                                   LC 2008927862

"A Smith and Kraus book"

Presents over a hundred monologues focusing on ordinary and famous people designed for use by children who are just starting with acting

"The monologues and activities will fire the imaginations of young students." SLJ

My third monologue book; places near and far: 102 monologues for young children. Smith and Kraus Publishers 2008 116p il (My first acting series) pa $11.95

Grades: 2 3 4 5 6   **812**

1. Monologues 2. Acting

ISBN 978-1-57525-602-3   LC 2008927864

"A Smith and Kraus book"

This collection of monologues is "divided into four parts: places you know (the woods, grandma's house), places in the United States (Laredo, TX; Flagstaff, AZ), foreign countries (Italy, Morocco), and imaginary and far-out places (Hogwarts, an alien world). . . . Concluding activities range from figuring out where the character is, to circling or underlining grammar clues, to completing a travel journal. [This is a] good [addition] as [it suggests] well-rounded activities for students to practice reading, writing, speaking, and both critical and imaginative thinking." SLJ

Fredericks, Anthony D.

African legends, myths, and folktales for readers theatre; illustrated by Bongaman. Teachers Idea Press 2008 xxiii, 166p il (Readers Theatre) pa $25

Grades: Professional   **812**

1. Folklore—Africa 2. Readers' theater 3. Drama—Collections

ISBN 978-1-59158-633-3 (pa); 1-59158-633-X (pa)

                                                   LC 2007044594

Author Tony Fredericks and illustrator, Bongaman, present readers theatre scripts based on traditional African folklore. Includes background information for teachers on each African country, as well as instruction and presentation suggestions, and additional resources for studies of African folklore

"For the most part, the stories . . . are short, lively, and often humorous. . . . A valuable volume." SLJ

Includes bibliographical references

Levine, Karen

Hana's suitcase on stage; original story by Karen Levine; play by Emil Sher. Second Story 2007 171p il (Holocaust remembrance book for young readers) pa $18.95 *

Grades: 5 6 7 8   **812**

1. Brady, Hana 2. Holocaust, 1933-1945—Drama

ISBN 978-1-89718-705-0 (pa); 1-89718-705-X (pa)

"Set in the Tokyo Holocaust Center, the two-act play opens with the woman and two of her student helpers questioning and searching for answers to the suitcase's history. . . . Act II blends characters of Ishioka and her students with Hana and her family, each group individually recounting their stories in alternating voices. As with the original book, this title succeeds in recreating a striking representation of one child's tragic and beautiful life in a terrifying world of hate and prejudice. This volume will serve as one of the most effective teaching models for Holocaust curriculums available. Photographs and facsimiles of Nazi documents are included." SLJ

Shepard, Aaron

Stories on stage; children's plays for reader's theater (or readers theatre), with 15 Play scripts from 15 authors. 2nd ed. Shepard 2005 160p pa $15 Grades: Professional   **812**

1. Readers' theater 2. Drama—Collections

ISBN 0-938497-22-7

First published 1993 in H. W. Wilson Co.

A collection of twenty-two plays adapted from folk tales, short stories, myths, and novels and intended for use in reader's theater programs

"With its mix of humor, fantasy, and multicultural tales . . . this book gives teachers both a fun and useful tool for bringing reading and literature to their students." SLJ

813.009 American fiction—History and criticism

Hamilton, Virginia, 1936-2002
Virginia Hamilton: speeches, essays, and conversations; edited by Arnold Adoff & Kacy Cook. Blue Sky Press 2010 368p $29.99 *
Grades: 8 9 10 11 12 Professional
813.009
1. Authorship 2. Children's literature—History and criticism
ISBN 978-0-439-27193-6; 0-439-27193-2
LC 2009031676
"A groundbreaking writer of children's fiction, folktales, biography, and picture books, Hamilton won every major award, and much of this book is made up of her acceptance speeches, including those for the Newbery, Hans Christian Andersen, and Coretta Scott King awards, as well as her Arbuthnot and Zena Sutherland lectures. Aimed at a general audience, the book employs a tone both scholarly and informal, as Hamilton talks about her career as a woman and a black writer in America and about the form and content of her work in general and with particular titles. . . . Many speeches include introductions by children's literature scholars and editors, who add perspective on Hamilton's lasting influence, while family members fill in biographical details. A must for YAs who love her books, this will also appeal to librarians, teachers, and children's literature students." Booklist
Includes bibliographical references

817 American humor and satire

Brewer, Paul
You must be joking! lots of cool jokes; compiled and illustrated by Paul Brewer; foreword by Kathleen Krull. Cricket Books 2003 107p il $16.95
Grades: 3 4 5 6
817
1. Jokes 2. Riddles 3. Wit and humor
ISBN 0-8126-2661-3
LC 2002-13926
A collection of over two hundred jokes and riddles, grouped by subject, plus tips on writing, learning, and telling jokes.
"The cartoon sketches scattered throughout the text add to the humor. A gem among joke books." SLJ

You must be joking, two! even cooler jokes, plus 11 1/2 tips for laughing yourself into your own stand-up comedy routine; written and illustrated by Paul Brewer. Cricket Books 2007 92p il $16.95
Grades: 3 4 5 6
817
1. Jokes 2. Riddles 3. Wit and humor
ISBN 978-0-8126-2752-7; 0-8126-2752-0
LC 2007014450
Includes riddles, jokes, and knock-knocks about monsters, aliens, cyberspace, school, pirates, animals, birds, and bugs
"An introduction plus the 11 ½ Tips will inspire readers to look at everyday events with an eye for humor and offer some suggestions on keeping children's attention, jokes to avoid, stage fright, and more. Black-and-white drawings introduce each chapter and spot art is sprinkled throughout the book. Most collections should make room for this one." SLJ

Cleary, Brian P., 1959-
The laugh stand; adventures in humor; by Brian P. Cleary; illustrated by J.P. Sandy. Millbrook Press 2008 48p il lib bdg $16.95
Grades: 4 5 6
817
1. Wit and humor 2. Word games
ISBN 978-0-8225-7849-9
LC 2007021889
Cleary "promotes fun with words in 13 small sections that toy with puns, anagrams, daffynitions, Tom Swifties, and more. . . . Sandy's ideally matched cartoons are a google-eyed cast that includes humans, animals, food items with faces, and societal icons. This team marries humor with sublime learning." SLJ
Includes bibliographical references

Knock, knock! [by] Saxton Freymann . . . [et al.] Dial Books for Young Readers 2007 unp il $16.99
Grades: K 1 2
817
1. Jokes
ISBN 978-0-8037-3152-3; 0-8037-3152-3
LC 2006-39463
"14 children's book artists . . . illustrate a different groan-inducing knock-knock joke in signature style. Saxton Freymann uses photos of lettuce ('Lettuce who?' 'Lettuce in!') made to look like pigs. Tomie de Paola creates two love-struck gorillas to illustrate 'Gorilla who?' 'Gorilla my dreams, I love you!' and so on. . . . The artwork is . . . just great and varied enough to keep children turning the pages." Booklist

Rosenthal, Amy Krouse
The wonder book; drawings by Paul Schmid. Harper 2010 79p il $17.99
Grades: 2 3 4
817
1. Wit and humor
ISBN 978-0-06-142974-3; 0-06-142974-0
LC 2008-939052
"Here is a joyous, totally original potpourri of stories, poems, lists, palindromes, visual jokes, and random observations about the universal delights and conundrums of childhood. Set squarely in the world of the 21st-century child . . . these varied musings nonetheless speak to everyone's inner child, young or old. . . . Simple, evocative, and childlike black-and-white line drawings, in concert with judicious and varied use of white space, perfectly capture the happy/sad/serious/silly moods of the selections." SLJ

818 American miscellany

Sandburg, Carl, 1878-1967
The Sandburg treasury; prose and poetry for young people; introduction by Paula Sandburg; illustrated by Paul Bacon. Harcourt Brace Jovanovich 1970 480p il pa $24 hardcover o.p.
Grades: 5 6 7 8 **818**
   1. American literature
   ISBN 0-15-202678-9 (pa)
   "Including, 'Rootabaga stories,' 'Early moon,' 'Wind song,' 'Abe Lincoln grows up,' 'Prairie-town boy.'" Title page
This volume brings together all of Sandburg's books for young people; his whimsical stories, two books of poetry, a version of his biography of Abraham Lincoln, and portions of his autobiography specially edited for children

820.8 English literature— Collections

Krull, Kathleen, 1952-
A pot o' gold; a treasury of Irish stories, poetry, folklore, and (of course) blarney; selected and adapted by Kathleen Krull; illustrated by David McPhail. Hyperion Books For Children 2004 181p il map hardcover o.p. pa $9.99 *
Grades: 3 4 5 6 **820.8**
   1. Irish literature 2. Folklore—Ireland
   ISBN 0-7868-0625-7; 1-4231-1752-2 (pa)
                  LC 2001-39058
A collection of stories, folklore, poetry, and songs from Ireland, including works by authors such as James Joyce and Oscar Wilde as well as classic myths, stories and poems about Finn McCool, fairies, leprechauns and saints Patrick and Bridget
"Children will love the limericks and the folk riddles. McPhail's signature full-color illustrations enliven the pages and add tremendous appeal for younger readers. The stunning cover and spine shimmer with the gold promised in the title and honor the intricate designs found in the Book of Kells. This is an eclectic grouping and an excellent introduction to the country's culture." SLJ
Includes bibliographical references

821 English poetry

Carroll, Lewis, 1832-1898
Jabberwocky; the classic poem from Lewis Carroll's Through the looking glass, and what Alice found there; reimagined and illustrated by Christopher Myers. Jump at the Sun/Hyperion Books for Children 2007 unp il $15.99 *
Grades: 4 5 6 7 **821**
   1. Nonsense verses 2. Poetry—By individual authors
   ISBN 978-1-4231-0372-1; 1-4231-0372-6
                  LC 2007-18337

"Myers cleverly translates Carroll's nonsense poem into a contemporary tale through sports imagery. . . . The spectacular paintings have silhouetted figures on vibrant backgrounds. . . . The jaunty text is in capital letters in an extra-large black font, with some words highlighted in color." SLJ

Cohen, Barbara, 1932-1992
Canterbury tales; [by] Geoffrey Chaucer; selected, translated, and adapted by Barbara Cohen; illustrated by Trina Schart Hyman. Lothrop, Lee & Shepard Bks. 1988 87p il $24.99 *
Grades: 4 5 6 7 **821**
   1. Chaucer, Geoffrey, d. 1400—Adaptations 2. Poetry—By individual authors 3. Middle Ages
   ISBN 0-688-06201-6   LC 86-21045
   Contents: The nun's priest's tale; The pardoner's tale; The wife of Bath's tale; The franklin's tale
"Cohen's evident love and respect for Chaucer's writing keep her close to the text. Her writing retains the flavor of the times and the spirit of Chaucer's words while her prose retelling, enriched by Hyman's lively full-color paintings, enhances the book's appeal to young people. . . . An excellent introduction to *The Canterbury Tales* for young readers." Booklist

Dahl, Roald
Vile verses. Viking 2005 191p il $25 *
Grades: 4 5 6 **821**
   1. Humorous poetry 2. Poetry—By individual authors
   ISBN 0-670-06042-9
A collection of Roald Dahl's poems, many previously published in his novels, such as *Charlie and the Chocolate Factory* and *James and the Giant Peach*, and illustrated by various artists such as Tony Ross, Lane Smith, Quentin Blake, and Chris Riddle
"This vivacious addition to poetry collections will amuse a broad audience." SLJ

Howitt, Mary Botham, 1799-1888
The spider and the fly; based on the poem by Mary Howitt; with illustrations by Tony DiTerlizzi. Simon & Schuster Bks. for Young Readers 2002 unp il $16.95
Grades: K 1 2 3 **821**
   1. Spiders—Poetry 2. Flies—Poetry 3. Poetry—By individual authors
   ISBN 0-689-85289-4   LC 2002-5760
An illustrated version of the well-known poem about a wily spider who preys on the vanity and innocence of a little fly
"Rendered in black-and-white gouache and pencil, then reproduced in silver-and-black duotone, the paintings have a spooky quality perfectly suited to retelling this melancholy tale. Ms. Fly, with her whimsical flower umbrella and Roaring '20s attire, captures the flavor of an old-time Hollywood heroine." SLJ

Hughes, Ted, 1930-1998

Collected poems for children; pictures by Raymond Briggs. Farrar, Straus and Giroux 2007 c2005 259p il $18

Grades: 3 4 5 6   **821**

1. Poetry—By individual authors

ISBN 978-0-374-31429-3; 0-374-31429-2

LC 2006-37437

First published 2005 in the United Kingdom

This is a "collection of 250 poems by the late English poet laureate Ted Hughes. . . . Children will love the sounds of the rhythmic lines, and Briggs' scattering of small black-and-white drawings perfectly captures the tiny details in the words." Booklist

Includes bibliographical references

Kipling, Rudyard, 1865-1936

If; a father's advice to his son; [by] Rudyard Kipling; photographs by Charles R. Smith. Atheneum Books for Young Readers 2007 unp il $14.99

Grades: 4 5 6   **821**

1. Poetry—By individual authors

ISBN 978-0-689-87799-5; 0-689-87799-4

LC 2006005312

"Kipling's powerful poem comes to life for a contemporary audience in atmospheric photographs that use the metaphor of sports. A lovely shot of a boy heading a soccer ball accompanies the opening couplet: 'If you can keep your head/when all about you/are losing theirs/and blaming it on you.' The mood and actions in most of the illustrations clearly invoke the verse." SLJ

Lear, Edward, 1812-1888

The complete verse and other nonsense; compiled and edited with an introduction and notes by Vivien Noakes. Penguin Bks. 2002 566p il pa $18

Grades: 4 5 6 7 8 9 10 11 12 Adult   **821**

1. Poetry—By individual authors 2. Nonsense verses

ISBN 0-14-200227-5   LC 2002-28998

This volume "presents all of Lear's verse and other nonsense writings, including stories, letters, and illustrated alphabets, as well as previously unpublished material, line drawings, and . . . [an] introduction by scholar Vivien Noakes." Publisher's note

Includes bibliographical references

Edward Lear; edited by Edward Mendelson; illustrated by Laura Huliska-Beith. Sterling 2002 c2001 48p il (Poetry for young people) $14.95 *

Grades: 4 5 6 7   **821**

1. Nonsense verses 2. Limericks 3. Poetry—By individual authors

ISBN 0-8069-3077-2   LC 2001-20112

"In an analytical introduction, Mendelson looks at Lear's serious and silly sides before selecting 15 limericks and 18 longer poems, all of which feature odd creatures adapting to, or reveling in, their differences. Sporting conical noses or other physical peculiarities, Huliska-Beith's smiling, rubber-limbed figures dance through vertiginously tilted, brightly colored minimalist settings. . . . Thought- and laugh-provoking." Booklist

Edward Lear's The duck & the kangaroo; illustrated by Jane Wattenberg. Greenwillow Books 2009 unp il $17.99 *

Grades: PreK K 1 2   **821**

1. Nonsense verses 2. Poetry—By individual authors 3. Ducks—Poetry 4. Kangaroos—Poetry

ISBN 978-0-06-136683-3; 0-06-136683-8

LC 2008024126

"Duck, envious of Kangaroo's hop . . . asks to ride upon the larger animal's back. Upon reflection, Kangaroo expresses his concern that Duck's wet and cold feet will give him rheumetism. Duck solves the problem by wearing beautifully knitted socks. . . . Wattenberg's quirky photo collages . . . are perfectly suited for Lear's nonsensical text." Booklist

The owl and the pussycat; by Edward Lear; illustrated by Anne Mortimer. Katherine Tegen Books 2006 unp il $15.99; lib bdg $16.89 *

Grades: K 1 2 3   **821**

1. Nonsense verses 2. Cats—Poetry 3. Owls—Poetry 4. Poetry—By individual authors

ISBN 0-06-027228-7; 0-06-027229-5 (lib bdg)

LC 2003015476

After a courtship voyage of a year and a day, Owl and Pussy finally buy a ring from Piggy and are blissfully married

"Lear's poem is beautifully illustrated with a mixture of elaborate, stylized borders and sumptuous portrayals of natural elements like verdant plant and tree leaves and colorful tropical flowers." SLJ

Milne, A. A. (Alan Alexander), 1882-1956

Now we are six; with decorations by Ernest H. Shepard. Dutton 1961 c1927 104p il $22.99; pa $4.99 *

Grades: K 1 2 3   **821**

1. Poetry—By individual authors

ISBN 0-525-44960-4; 0-14-0361234-3 (pa)

First published 1927. "Reprinted September 1961 in this completely new format designed by Warren Chappell." Verso of title page

"The boy or girl who has liked 'When were were very young' and 'Winnie-the-Pooh' will enjoy reading about Alexander Beetle who was mistaken for a match, the knight whose armor didn't squeak, and the old sailor who had so many things which he wanted to do. There are other entertaining poems, also, and many pictures as delightful as the verses." Pittsburgh

When we were very young; with decorations by Ernest H. Shepard. Dutton 1961 c1924 102p il $11.99; pa $6.99 *

Grades: K 1 2 3   **821**

1. Poetry—By individual authors

ISBN 0-525-44445-9; 0-14-036123-5 (pa)

First published 1924. "Reprinted September 1961 in this completely new format designed by Warren Chappell." Verso of title page

Verse "written for Milne's small son Christopher Robin, which for its bubbling nonsense, its whimsy, and the unexpected surprises of its rhymes and rhythms, furnishes immeasurable joy to children." Right Book for the

Milne, A. A. (Alan Alexander), 1882-1956—*Continued*

Right Child

"Mr. Milne's gay jingles have found a worthy accompaniment in the charming illustrations of Mr. Shepard." Saturday Rev

Stevenson, Robert Louis, 1850-1894

A child's garden of verses; by Robert Louis Stevenson; illustrated by Tasha Tudor. rev format ed. Simon & Schuster Books for Young Readers 1999 67p il $19.99 *

Grades: K 1 2 3   821

1. Poetry—By individual authors

ISBN 0-689-82382-7   LC 98-19561

"Verses known and loved by one generation after another. Among the simpler ones for preschool children are: Rain; At the Seaside; and Singing." Right Book for the Right Child

A child's garden of verses; by Robert Louis Stevenson; illustrated by Brian Wildsmith. Star Bright Books 2008 80p il $19.95

Grades: K 1 2 3   821

1. Poetry—By individual authors

ISBN 978-1-59572-057-3; 1-59572-057-X

LC 2007010085

A reissue of the edition published 1966 by Watts

Robert Louis Stevenson's classic poetry collection for children.

Williams, Marcia, 1945-

Chaucer's Canterbury Tales; retold and illustrated by Marcia Williams. Candlewick Press 2007 45p il $16.99 *

Grades: 4 5 6 7   821

1. Chaucer, Geoffrey, d. 1400—Adaptations 2. Middle Ages 3. Poetry—By individual authors

ISBN 978-0-7636-3197-0; 0-7636-3197-3

A retelling in comic strip form of Geoffrey Chaucer's famous work in which a group of pilgrims in fourteenth-century England tell each other stories as they travel on a pilgrimage to the cathedral at Canterbury

"Chaucer's pilgrims come to life in the energetic retelling of nine tales. . . . The watercolor-and-ink cartoon-art displayed in a comic-book format is a perfect match for the raucous and sometimes-raw humor." SLJ

821.008   English poetry—Collections

The **Barefoot** book of classic poems. Barefoot Books 2006 128p $19.99

Grades: 3 4 5 6   821.008

1. Poetry—Collections

ISBN 1-905236-56-5   LC 2005-30379

"An appealing assortment of 74 classic poems that touch on childhood, animals and the natural world, love, war, and the stages of life. The selections range from standard children's fare, such as Robert Louis Stevenson's 'Bed in Summer' and 'The Land of Counterpane,' to more mature works, such as John Donne's 'Meditation

XVII.' . . . This is a sumptuously packaged collection, with many large, double-paged illustrations. Morris's watercolors on hot-pressed paper are romantic and spirited." SLJ

Read-aloud rhymes for the very young; selected by Jack Prelutsky; illustrated by Marc Brown; with an introduction by Jim Trelease. Knopf 1986 98p il $19.95; lib bdg $21.99 *

Grades: K 1 2   821.008

1. English poetry—Collections 2. American poetry—Collections 3. Nursery rhymes

ISBN 0-394-87218-5; 0-394-97218-X (lib bdg)

LC 86-7147

"Prelutsky has selected and combined joyous, sensitive poems . . . by such traditional poets as Dorothy Aldis and A. A. Milne, as well as by more contemporary poets such as Karla Kuskin, Dennis Lee, and Prelutsky himself. All are lively, rhythmic poems that young children will enjoy. . . . Brown's bright pastel illustrations effectively use framing, action, and cheerful creatures to echo the light tone of the book. The poems are arranged with others of the same topic and include popular concerns of small children such as animals, bath time, dragons, and play. Teachers and librarians will appreciate poems about seasons, months, holidays, and special events that can be easily incorporated into story hours and classroom life." SLJ

822.3   William Shakespeare

Aliki

William Shakespeare & the Globe; written & illustrated by Aliki. HarperCollins Pubs. 1999 48p il hardcover o.p. lib bdg $15.89; pa $6.99 *

Grades: 4 5 6 7 8 9   822.3

1. Shakespeare, William, 1564-1616 2. Globe Theatre (London, England) 3. Shakespeare's Globe (London, England)

ISBN 0-06-027820-X; 0-06-027821-8 (lib bdg); 0-06-443722-1 (pa)   LC 98-7903

The "text describes Shakespeare's life, the Elizabethan world and entertainments, and the ups and downs of the theatrical industry . . . including tidbits such as the Burbage brothers' piece-by-piece theft of the original Globe Theatre. A fast-forward to the twentieth century then treats Sam Wanamaker's dream of making the Globe rise again." Bull Cent Child Books

"A logically organized and engaging text, plenty of detailed illustrations with informative captions, and a clean design provide a fine introduction to both bard and theater." Horn Book Guide

Chrisp, Peter

Welcome to the Globe; the story of Shakespeare's theater; written by Peter Chrisp. Dorling Kindersley 2000 48p il $12.95; pa $3.95

Grades: 1 2 3   822.3

1. Shakespeare, William, 1564-1616 2. Globe Theatre (London, England)

ISBN 0-7894-6641-4; 0-7894-6640-6 (pa)

LC 00-21931

"Dorling Kindersley readers"

Chrisp, Peter—*Continued*

Various characters, including a waterman, an actor, a gallant, and an apple seller, from Shakespeare's London describe the Globe Theatre from their own perspective

"Illustrations and photographs are excellent, showing details of the building and the people." SLJ

Includes glossary

Coville, Bruce

William Shakespeare's A midsummer night's dream. Dial Bks. 1996 unp $17.95; pa $7.99

Grades: 5 6 7 8 9   822.3

1. Shakespeare, William, 1564-1616—Adaptations
ISBN 0-8037-1784-9; 0-14-250168-9 (pa)

LC 94-12600

A simplified prose retelling of Shakespeare's play about the strange events that take place in a forest inhabited by fairies who magically transform the romantic fate of two young couples.

"Coville introduces the story and also conveys something of the poetry and drama. Nolan's framed graphite and watercolor paintings express the dreaminess and absurdity of the play, and the pictures have a theatrical flair." Booklist

William Shakespeare's Macbeth; retold by Bruce Coville; pictures by Gary Kelley. Dial Bks. 1997 unp il $18

Grades: 5 6 7 8 9   822.3

1. Shakespeare, William, 1564-1616—Adaptations
ISBN 0-8037-1899-3   LC 97-7582

A simplified prose retelling of Shakespeare's play about a man who kills his king after hearing the prophesies of three witches

"Kelley's framed pastel illustrations of the hideous hags will hold kids from the start, and Coville's dramatic narrative will keep them reading. . . . Words and pictures are true to the dark, brooding spirit of the play." Booklist

William Shakespeare's Romeo and Juliet; retold by Bruce Coville; pictures by Dennis Nolan. Dial Bks. 1999 unp il $16.99

Grades: 5 6 7 8 9   822.3

1. Shakespeare, William, 1564-1616—Adaptations
ISBN 0-8037-2462-4   LC 98-36178

A simplified prose retelling of Shakespeare's play about two young people who defy their warring families' prejudices and dare to fall in love

"Coville's treatment is generally faithful to the original and is nicely enhanced by Dennis Nolan's lushly romantic illustrations. . . . This is an accessible and enticing introduction to one of Shakespeare's most popular works." Booklist

William Shakespeare's Twelfth night; retold by Bruce Coville; illustrated by Tim Raglin. Dial Bks. 2003 unp il $16.99

Grades: 5 6 7 8 9   822.3

1. Shakespeare, William, 1564-1616—Adaptations
ISBN 0-8037-2318-0   LC 2001-28252

This "provides a short, prose version of Shakespeare's *Twelfth Night*. . . . Though simplified, the story is intact and bits of the original language are preserved. Large-

scale ink drawings, warmed with tints of color and shaded with cross-hatching, clearly depict the action." Booklist

Nettleton, Pamela Hill, 1955-

William Shakespeare; playwright and poet; by Pamela Hill Nettleton. Compass Point Books 2005 112p il map (Signature lives) lib bdg $30.60

Grades: 5 6 7 8   822.3

1. Shakespeare, William, 1564-1616
ISBN 0-7565-0816-9   LC 2004-23081

Contents: All the world's a stage; Shakespeare's time; Shakespeare as a boy; At school and beyond; Shakespeare in love; Shakespeare in London; Shakespeare's poems; Success as a playwrite; At the peak of his powers; The final years

Profiles the life and work of William Shakespeare

"This biography is one of the best available for younger students. Nettleton supplements what little is actually known about the bard's life with detailed and accurate information about everyday life in England during the period, the theater, and publishing practices of the time. The text is enhanced by full-color illustrations and black-and-white reproductions." SLJ

Includes bibliographical references

Packer, Tina, 1938-

Tales from Shakespeare; retold by Tina Packer; illustrated by Gail de Marcken . . . [et al.] Scholastic Press 2004 192p il $24.95 *

Grades: 5 6 7 8   822.3

1. Shakespeare, William, 1564-1616—Adaptations
ISBN 0-439-32107-7   LC 2003-42710

Tina Packer retells ten of Shakespeare's plays. The stories are illustrated by various artists: Macbeth by Barry Moser, The Tempest by Mark Teague, Othello by Kadir Nelson, Twelfth Night by Chesley McLaren, Romeo and Juliet by David Shannon, Much Ado About Nothing by Mary GrandPre, King Lear by Leo and Diane Dillon, As You Like It by Barbara McClintock, A Midsummer Night's Dream by Gail De Marcken, and Hamlet by P.J. Lynch

This is "a treasure trove of well-told tales. In these adaptations, Packer captures the essence of the playwright's words and ideas, placing them in concise and clearly told stories. . . . Each illustrator sets the appropriate tone for and conveys the mood of the tale, and the breadth of artistic interpretations gives the book appeal to a wide audience." SLJ

Stanley, Diane, 1943-

Bard of Avon: the story of William Shakespeare; by Diane Stanley and Peter Vennema; illustrated by Diane Stanley. Morrow Junior Bks. 1992 unp il hardcover o.p. pa $6.99 *

Grades: 4 5 6 7   822.3

1. Shakespeare, William, 1564-1616
ISBN 0-688-09108-3; 0-688-09109-1 (lib bdg);
0-688-16294-0 (pa)   LC 90-46564

A brief biography of the world's most famous playwright, using only historically correct information

"A remarkably rounded picture of Shakespeare's life

Stanley, Diane, 1943-—*Continued*

and the period in which he lived is presented . . . together with a thoughtful attempt to relate circumstances
in his personal life to the content of his plays. . . . The
text is splendidly supported by the illustrations, which
are stylized, yet recognizable, and present a clear view
of life in the late sixteenth century. A discerning, knowledgeable biography, rising far above the ordinary." Horn
Book

Includes bibliographical references

823.009   English fiction—History and criticism

Colbert, David

The magical worlds of Harry Potter. Updated
and complete ed. Berkley Books 2008 335p il pa
$14

Grades: 5 6 7 8   **823.009**

1. Rowling, J. K.—Characters 2. Fantasy fiction—History and criticism

ISBN 978-0-425-22318-5; 0-425-22318-3

First published 2001 in the United Kingdom; first
United States edition 2002

Explores the sources and meanings of aspects of the
literary world of Harry Potter within myths, legends, and
history.

"Long after the enthusiasm for Harry and friends has
abated, this small volume will serve as a resource to answer questions that may result from reading other stories
in the genre." SLJ [review of 2002 edition]

828   English miscellaneous writings

Thomas, Dylan, 1914-1953

A child's Christmas in Wales; illustrated by
Chris Raschka. Candlewick Press 2004 unp il
$17.99 *

Grades: 2 3 4 5 6 7 8 9   **828**

1. Christmas—Wales

ISBN 0-7636-2161-7   LC 2003-65274

The Welsh poet Dylan Thomas recalls the celebration
of Christmas with his family and the feelings it evoked
in him as a child.

"Applied to torn paper, the ink and watercolors spread
through the fibers, freely forming soft outlines and shadows. The result is an intriguing contemporary take on a
story that is by now part of the rather staid canon of
Christmas classics." N Y Times Book Rev

A child's Christmas in Wales; [by] Dylan
Thomas; illustrated by Trina Schart Hyman.
Holiday House 1985 47p il $16.95

Grades: 3 4 5 6   **828**

1. Christmas—Wales

ISBN 0-8234-0565-6   LC 85-766

A Welsh poet recalls the celebration of Christmas in
Wales and the feelings it evoked in him as a child.

841   French poetry

Cendrars, Blaise, 1887-1961

Shadow; translated and illustrated by Marcia
Brown from the French of Blaise Cendrars.
Scribner 1982 unp il $17; pa $6.99 *

Grades: 1 2 3   **841**

1. French poetry 2. Africa—Poetry 3. Shades and
shadows—Poetry 4. Poetry—By individual authors

ISBN 0-684-17226-7; 0-689-71875-6 (pa)

            LC 81-9424

Awarded the Caldecott Medal, 1983

Original text first published in France

This is the French poet's "version of a West African
folk tale about a spirit that is at once elusive and multi-
form." N Y Times Book Rev

"Inspired by the exotic atmosphere and the dramatic
possibilities of the text, Brown has choreographed a sequence of almost theatrical illustrations, placing human
and animal figures—and their shadows—against brilliant,
contrasting, always changing settings. Resplendent—yet
controlled—in color, texture, and form, the work is an
impressive, sophisticated example of the art of the picture book." Horn Book

861   Spanish poetry

Argueta, Jorge

A movie in my pillow; story by Jorge Argueta;
illustrations by Elizabeth Gómez. Children's Bk.
Press 2001 31p il $15.95 *

Grades: 3 4 5 6   **861**

1. Bilingual books—English-Spanish 2. Immigrants—
Poetry 3. Hispanic Americans—Poetry 4. Poetry—By
individual authors

ISBN 0-89239-165-0   LC 00-55582

Text and title page in English and Spanish

These poems recount Argueta's "childhood experiences of being an immigrant and having dual homelands,
with roots in El Salvador and a new life in San Francisco's Mission District." Booklist

"Gómez's rich and bright paintings fill every spread
with . . . joy and literal humor. . . . An excellent addition to any poetry collection." SLJ

Luján, Jorge

Colors! Colores! by Jorge Luján; illustrated by
Piet Grobler; translated by John Oliver Simon and
Rebecca Parfitt. Groundwood Books 2008 36p il
$17.95

Grades: K 1 2   **861**

1. Color—Poetry 2. Bilingual books—English-Spanish
3. Poetry—By individual authors

ISBN 978-0-88899-863-7; 0-88899-863-5

This is "a fully illustrated collection of 11 brief, free-
verse poems linked by a common theme: colors. Each
poem appears in English and then in Spanish on a double-page spread surrounded by white space and accompanied by an eye-catching watercolor painting. . . . Gobler
. . . interprets the verse through watercolor paintings that
are as spare and fanciful as the writing." Booklist

861.008 Spanish poetry—Collections

Messengers of rain and other poems from Latin America; edited by Claudia M. Lee; illustrated by Rafael Yockteng; translations by Andrew C. Leone . . . [et al.] Douglas & McIntyre 2002 80p il $18.95

Grades: 3 4 5 6 **861.008**
1. Spanish poetry—Collections
ISBN 0-88899-470-2

"A Groundwood book"

"The 64 poems from 19 countries include 20th-century classics and more recent selections, and represent women, indigenous writers, and widely published names such as Octavio Paz and Rafael Pombo. . . . Yockteng's fanciful watercolors head each section with a full-page spread, and spots brighten the pages between, here and there, without distracting from the poems." SLJ

883 Classical Greek epic poetry and fiction

Landmann, Bimba
The incredible voyage of Ulysses; text and illustrations by Bimba Landmann. Getty Publications 2010 unp il $19.95 *
Grades: 4 5 6 7 **883**
1. Homer—Adaptations
ISBN 978-1-60606-012-4; 1-60606-012-0

"With narrative restraint and illustrative power, Landmann's . . . retelling of Homer's *Odyssey* follows Ulysses as he battles frightening creatures and endures the treachery of the gods while sailing home to Ithaca. . . . The paintings, worked with swift, bold strokes, combine the solemn stiffness of Greek statuary with the prophetic sweep of William Blake's imaginings." Publ Wkly

895.6 Japanese literature

Kobayashi, Issa, 1763-1827
Today and today; by Kobayashi Issa; pictures by G. Brian Karas. Scholastic Press 2007 unp il $16.99 *
Grades: K 1 2 3 **895.6**
1. Haiku
ISBN 0-4395-9078-7 LC 2003-26684

"Karas uses the haiku of the eighteenth-century Japanese poet Issa to limn a gentle, understated tale of one family over a year. . . . The translations . . . are simply and clearly crafted. . . . Kara's art, using rice paper, paint, and pencil, is precise, enticing, and evocative." Booklist

896 African literatures

Talking drums; a selection of poems from Africa south of the Sahara; edited and illustrated by Véronique Tadjo. Bloomsbury Children's Books 2003 96p il map $15.95 *
Grades: 5 6 7 8 **896**
1. African poetry—Collections
ISBN 1-58234-813-8 LC 2003-52173

Contents: Our universe; The animal kingdom; Love and celebrations; People; Death; Pride and defiance; The changing times

A collection of traditional and twentieth-century poems from sub-Saharan Africa, written in or translated into English, that expresses the spirit and history of this region

"The contemporary and the traditional are both well represented in this lively anthology. . . . Illustrated with small, black-and-white folk-art drawings, the collection ranges widely, including poems of love, sorrow, and pride. . . . This [is a] fine resource for social studies and literature classes, which will also be great for reading aloud." Booklist

Includes glossary

897 Literatures of North American native languages

Dancing teepees: poems of American Indian youth; selected by Virginia Driving Hawk Sneve, with art by Stephen Gammell. Holiday House 1989 32p il $17.95; pa $8.95 *
Grades: 4 5 6 **897**
1. Native Americans—Poetry
ISBN 0-8234-0724-1; 0-8234-0879-5 (pa)
LC 88-11075

An illustrated collection of poems from the oral tradition of Native Americans

This is an "eclectic collection, drawn from a variety of tribal traditions. Printed on heavy paper, the book is illustrated with a catalogue of marvelously rendered designs and motifs, ranging from those of the Northwest Coast to the intricate beadwork patterns of the Great Lakes and the zigzag geometric borders of Southwestern pottery." N Y Times Book Rev

900 HISTORY

902 Miscellany of history

Timelines of history. Grolier 2005 10v il map set $339
Grades: 6 7 8 9 **902**
1. Historical chronology 2. Reference books
ISBN 0-7172-6002-X LC 2005040222

Contents: v1 The early empires, prehistory-500 B.C.; v2 The Classical Age, 500 B.C.-500 A.D.; v3 Raiders and conquerors, 500-1000 A.D.; v4 The fuedal era, 1000-1250; v5 The end of the Middle Ages. 1250-1500; v6 A wider world, 1500-1600; v7 Royalty and revolt, 1600-

Timelines of history—*Continued*
1700; v8 The Age of Reason, 1700-1800; v9 Industry and empire, 1800-1900; v10 The modern world, 1900-2000

"This set of 10 brief volumes presents an overview of world history from prehistory (6.8 million years ago) up until 2005. . . . The content consists of alternating types of two-page spreads: time-line pages and feature pages. . . . The feature pages highlight topics such as individuals, events, or a civilization presented in the time lines. . . . The narratives in the features are clear and simply written. . . . The design is clean and colorful and features hundreds of illustrations, including maps, on every page." Booklist

904   Collected accounts of events

Blackwood, Gary L.
Enigmatic events. Marshall Cavendish Benchmark 2005 72p il (Unsolved history) lib bdg $29.93
Grades: 4 5 6 7   **904**
1. History—Miscellanea 2. Disasters 3. Curiosities and wonders
ISBN 0-7614-1889-X   LC 2004-23755
Contents: The death of the dinosaurs; The lost colony; The Salem witch trials; *The Mary Celeste*; *The Maine*; The Tunguska event; *The Hindenburg*
Explores several events that have baffled scientists and historians for years, such as the demise of the dinosaurs, the "lost colony" of Roanoke, the sinking of the Main, and the Hindenberg disaster
This collection of "tidbits about lingering mysteries of the past . . . [offers] more substance than most. . . . [This offers] a full-page illustration opening each chapter; reproductions, many in color; and a generously spaced format." SLJ
Includes glossary and bibliographical references

Guiberson, Brenda Z., 1946-
Disasters; natural and man-made catastrophes through the centuries. Henry Holt and Company 2010 228p il $18.99
Grades: 5 6 7 8 9   **904**
1. Natural disasters 2. Disasters
ISBN 978-0-8050-8170-1; 0-8050-8170-4
LC 2009018908
"Christy Ottaviano books"
"The subtitle provides an accurate outline of the contents of this lively treatment of disasters from smallpox to Hurricane Katrina. In each chapter, Guiberson outlines the sources of the disaster, the results, and means of obviating the problems that caused these tragedies. For example, the chapter on the Great Chicago Fire begins with the construction of the city over unstable marshland. . . . This kind of exhaustive background serves to create an understanding of the contributory issues and demonstrates possible preventive steps. Guiberson's compellingly written exegesis is equally good in the other nine chapters. Well-placed, black-and-white reproductions and photos extend the text. A perfect example of solid historical research coupled with engaging writing." SLJ
Includes bibliographical references

909   World history

The **Kingfisher** history encyclopedia. rev ed. Kingfisher 2004 491p il map $24.95
Grades: 5 6 7 8   **909**
1. World history 2. Reference books
ISBN 0-7534-5784-9
First published 1999
A reference guide to world history, featuring a timeline, key date boxes, and biographies of historical figures
"Students will find this tool useful and engaging." Booklist

Knight, Margy Burns
Talking walls; illustrated by Anne Sibley O'Brien. Tilbury House 1992 unp il map hardcover o.p. pa $8.95
Grades: 3 4 5   **909**
1. Walls 2. World history
ISBN 0-88448-102-6; 0-88448-154-9 (pa)
LC 91-67867
An illustrated description of walls around the world and their significance
"A praiseworthy celebration of similarities and differences among the world's peoples. . . . Young readers will recognize such landmarks as the Great Wall of China, the cave walls of Lascaux, the Wailing Wall and the Vietnam Memorial. More surprising selections feature the work of Australian aborigines, Indian Hindus, Islamic Egyptians, Native Americans and Africans. The narrative is respectful and egalitarian, with the clear intent of valuing no one people over another. O'Brien's . . . well-designed and affecting pastels cover each spread." Publ Wkly

909.07   World history—ca. 500-1450/1500

Adams, Simon
The Kingfisher atlas of the medieval world. Kingfisher 2007 44p il map $15.95
Grades: 4 5 6 7   **909.07**
1. Medieval civilization 2. Historical geography 3. Reference books
ISBN 978-0-7534-5946-1; 0-7534-5946-9
LC 2006005554
"Sixteen colorful maps depict the world from A.D. 500 to 1500. A chronology appears in the right margin of the first map. Specific time lines for India, China, Japan and Korea, Southeast Asia, the Pacific Islands, the Vikings, Europe, African kingdoms, and North and Central America help students integrate the major historical events of the period. Topics include cathedrals and monasteries, Islamic culture, knights and castles, and the Aztec capital of Tenochtitlán." SLJ

909.8 World history—1800-

Adams, Simon
The Kingfisher atlas of the modern world; [by]
Simon Adams; illustrated by Kevin Maddison
2007 45p il map $15.95
Grades: 4 5 6 7   **909.8**
  1. World history—19th century 2. World history—
  20th century 3. Historical geography 4. Reference
  books
  ISBN 978-0-7534-6034-4
This atlas examines world history and geography
"from 1800 to the present. . . . Each map focuses on a
major region, exploring the conflicts, changes, and social
movements that took place during a specific period of
time. The subjects are arranged chronologically." Publisher's note

909.82 World history—20th century, 1900-1999

Feinstein, Stephen
Decades of the 20th Century [series] rev ed.
Enslow Pubs. 2006 10v il ea $27.93
Grades: 5 6 7 8   **909.82**
  1. World history—20th century
  First published 2001
Contents: The 1900s, from Teddy Roosevelt to flying
machines; The 1910s, from World War I to ragtime mu-
sic; The 1920s, from Prohibition to Charles Lindbergh;
The 1930s, from the Great Depression to the Wizard of
Oz; The 1940s, from World War II to Jackie Robinson;
The 1950s, from the Korean War to Elvis; The 1960s,
from the Vietnam War to Flower Power; The 1970s,
from Watergate to disco; The 1980s, from Ronald
Reagan to MTV; The 1990s, from the Persian Gulf War
to Y2K
  "Taking a popular-culture approach, each book begins
with a look at 'Lifestyles, Fashion, and Fads,' followed
by arts and entertainment, sports, and then politics, with
science, technology, and medicine coming last. . . . The
books are visually exciting, and the texts are clear and
vigorous." SLJ
  Includes bibliographical references

910 Geography & travel

Cunha, Stephen F.
National Geographic Bee; official study guide;
by Stephen F. Cunha; [foreword by Caitlin
Snaring] 3rd ed. National Geographic 2008 127p
il map $9.95
Grades: 4 5 6 7 8   **910**
  1. Geography
  ISBN 978-1-4263-0198-8; 1-4263-0198-7
                                        LC 2009293527
  First published 2002
This is a guide to prepare for the National Geographic
"annual geography competition. Featuring maps, photos,

graphs, and a variety of questions actually used in past
Bees, plus an extensive resource section, this guide not
only reviews geographic facts but also helps readers recognize themes, identify clues that lead to correct answers, and understand how geographers think." Publisher's note

Jenkins, Steve
Hottest, coldest, highest, deepest. Houghton
Mifflin 1998 unp il $16 *
Grades: K 1 2   **910**
  1. Geography
  ISBN 0-395-89999-0   LC 97-53080
Describes some of the remarkable places on earth, in-
cluding the hottest, coldest, windiest, snowiest, highest,
and deepest
  This book "uses striking colorful paper collage illus-
trations. . . . This eye-catching introduction to geography
will find a lot of use in libraries and classrooms." SLJ
  Includes bibliographical references

Rockwell, Anne F., 1934-
Our earth; written and illustrated by Anne
Rockwell. Harcourt Brace & Co. 1998 unp il
hardcover o.p. pa $6 *
Grades: K 1 2   **910**
  1. Geography
  ISBN 0-15-201679-1; 0-15-202383-6 (pa)
                                          LC 97-1247
A simple introduction to geography which explains
such things as how the earth was shaped, how islands are
born from volcanoes, and how gushing springs affect rivers
  "The watercolor-and-gouache illustrations are very accessible. The pictures should provoke questions; parents
and teachers can use the answers to provide kids with
more information." Booklist

Sepehri, Sandy
Continents; [by] Sandy Sepehri. Rourke Pub.
2008 32p il map (Landforms) lib bdg $28.50; pa
$7.95
Grades: 1 2 3 4   **910**
  1. Continents
  ISBN 978-1-60044-548-4 (lib bdg); 1-60044-548-9 (lib
  bdg); 978-1-60044-709-9 (pa); 1-60044-709-0 (pa)
                                        LC 2007012141
This introduces the seven continents of the world.
  "The illustrations and photographs are plentiful and
colorful. . . . The [volume is] well written and success-
fully [conveys] the basics of the topic." Sci Books Films
  Includes glossary and bibliographical references

910.3   Geography—Dictionaries, encyclopedias, concordnces, gazetteers

Gifford, Clive
The Kingfisher geography encyclopedia. Kingfisher 2003 488p il map $39.95
Grades: 4 5 6 7   910.3
1. Geography—Encyclopedias 2. Reference books
ISBN 0-7534-5591-9   LC 2003-47420
Contents: The physical earth; The Arctic; North America; Central America; The Caribbean; South America; Europe; Russian Federation; Asia; Indian subcontinent; Eastern Asia; Southeast Asia; Africa; Australasia; Oceania; Antarctica
Statistics, text, and color maps reveal the physical geography, peoples, politics, governments, languages, religions, and currencies of each nation of the world
"The arrangement is logical and the format accessible. . . . Striking color photographs and informative captions highlight the uniqueness of each locale." SLJ

Junior Worldmark encyclopedia of the nations; [edited by] Timothy L. Gall and Susan Bevan Gall. 5th ed. Thomson Gale 2007 10v il map set $546 *
Grades: 5 6 7 8   910.3
1. Geography—Encyclopedias 2. World history—Encyclopedias 3. Reference books
ISBN 978-1-4144-1095-1   LC 2007002388
First published 1996
This reference "profiles 194 countries worldwide. . . . Each country chapter includes 35 core headings that describe climate, population, labor, religion, housing, education, and other key data. Also included are brief biographical profiles of the countries' leaders, and charts, graphs, and tables that highlight the current economic conditions. . . . The encyclopedia also showcases color images of flags and coats of arms. . . . New to the 5th edition is information on each country's carbon dioxide emissions. . . . This resource incorporates a wealth of information into its chapters." Am Ref Books Annu, 2008
Includes bibliographical references

The **World** Book encyclopedia of people and places. World Bk. 6v il maps * set $329
Grades: 5 6 7 8   910.3
1. Reference books 2. Geography—Dictionaries
First published 1992. Revised annually
This set profiles close to 200 countries. Coverage of each country includes an overview of its history, geography, economy, people, culture and government; a physical/political map; a locator map; and fact box

910.4   Accounts of travel and facilities for travelers

Aronson, Marc
The world made new; why the Age of Exploration happened & how it changed the world; [by] Marc Aronson & John W. Glenn. National Geographic 2007 64p il map $17.95; lib bdg $27.90 *
Grades: 4 5 6 7   910.4
1. Exploration 2. Explorers
ISBN 978-0-7922-6454-5; 978-0-7922-6978-6 (lib bdg)   LC 2006022091
This provides an "account of the charting of the New World and the long-term effects of America's march into history." Publisher's note
"This highly pictorial, readable overview provides significant depth of coverage. . . . The illustrations, most in full color, make ample and appropriate use of period prints as well as contemporary illustrations and photographs. The result is a visual feast that fleshes out the . . . remarkably evenhanded narrative." SLJ
Includes glossary and bibliographical references

Brown, Don, 1949-
All stations! distress! April 15, 1912, the day the Titanic sank. Roaring Brook Press 2008 unp il $17.95 *
Grades: 2 3 4 5   910.4
1. Titanic (Steamship) 2. Shipwrecks
ISBN 978-1-59643-222-2; 1-59643-222-5
LC 2008-08934
"Don Brown recounts the complicated, compact last moments of the [Titanic's] only voyage. . . . The tale ends with something of the later lives of the survivors. . . . The glory of *All Stations! Distress!* is in Brown's moody watercolors done with a brush dipped in stardust and frozen mist." Horn Book

Butterfield, Moira
Pirates & smugglers; foreword by Captain Stephen Bligh. Kingfisher 2005 63p il map (Kingfisher knowledge) $12.95 *
Grades: 5 6 7 8   910.4
1. Pirates 2. Smuggling
ISBN 0-7534-5864-0
This is an "introduction to the highwaymen and women of the seas from the cruel Cilician pirates who terrorized the Mediterranean more than 2,000 years ago to the . . . modern-day buccaneers who target supertankers on the South China Sea and the loot they plunder and smuggle." Publisher's note
This offers "stunning illustrations and engaging text. . . . This book is fascinating. Photographs from the movies mix with drawings and reproductions to clarify the text." SLJ
Includes glossary

Cerullo, Mary M., 1949-

Shipwrecks; exploring sunken cities beneath the sea; [by] Mary M. Cerullo. Dutton Children's Books 2009 64p il $18.99 *

Grades: 5 6 7 8   910.4

1. Henrietta Marie (Ship) 2. Portland (Steamer) 3. Shipwrecks

ISBN 978-0-525-47968-0; 0-525-47968-6

LC 2008-48967

This focuses "on two wrecks: the *Henrietta Marie*, sunk in 1700 near the Florida Keys, and the *Portland*, sunk in 1898 off the coast of Massachusetts. The book makes the convincing case that these wrecks are important not only for historical reasons but also for the underwater ecosystems their structures now host. . . . This delivers both education and shivers." Booklist

Clifford, Barry

Real pirates; the untold story of the Whydah from slave ship to pirate ship; by Barry Clifford and Kenneth J. Kinkor with Sharon Simpson; photography by Kenneth Garrett. National Geographic 2008 c2007 175p il map $16.95

Grades: 4 5 6 7   910.4

1. Whidah (Ship) 2. Pirates 3. Shipwrecks 4. Slave trade 5. Archeology 6. Cape Cod (Mass.)

ISBN 978-1-4263-0279-4; 1-4263-0279-7

LC 2008299778

"Clifford, an underwater archaeological explorer, used research and the artifacts recovered from the *Whydah* to tell the story of its life as a slave galley and pirate ship. In the process, he dispels many myths about buccaneers. . . . Photographs of artifacts . . . and the recovery crew at work combine with large visually appealing paintings of dramatic battle, storm, and courtroom scenes. . . . The book is a fascinating blend of history, ocean-diving recovery, and archaeology, and demonstrates archaeology in action and the role artifacts play in informing us about the past." SLJ

Includes bibliographical references

Fritz, Jean

Around the world in a hundred years; from Henry the Navigator to Magellan; illustrated by Anthony Bacon Venti. Putnam 1994 128p il map hardcover o.p. pa $8.99

Grades: 4 5 6 7   910.4

1. Explorers

ISBN 0-399-22527-7; 0-698-11638-0 (pa)

LC 92-27042

"Fritz examines the voyages of ten explorers, acknowledging that their contributions, though deserving of recognition, were dearly bought. Opening and closing chapters summarize the fourteenth-century world view and indicate later expansion of geographic understanding. As always, Fritz tempers scholarship with humor in this brief volume—illustrated with drawings in pencil—which reads like an adventure story." Horn Book Guide

Includes bibliographical references

Gibbons, Gail

Sunken treasure. Crowell 1988 32p il hardcover o.p. pa $6.95 *

Grades: K 1 2 3   910.4

1. Nuestra Señora de Atocha (Ship) 2. Buried treasure 3. Shipwrecks

ISBN 0-690-04736-3 (lib bdg); 0-06-446097-5 (pa)

LC 87-30114

"Gibbons concentrates on the ancient Spanish galleon, the *Atocha*, which sank off the coast of Florida in 1662, describing under labeled headings the sinking, the search, the find, recording, salvage, restoration and preservation, cataloguing, and eventual distribution of the treasure. . . . A handsomely designed book, well organized, and easily accessible to younger readers." Horn Book

Jenkins, Martin

Titanic; [illustrated by] Brian Sanders. Candlewick Press 2008 31p il map $29.99

Grades: 4 5 6   910.4

1. Titanic (Steamship) 2. Shipwrecks

ISBN 978-0-7636-3795-8; 0-7636-3795-5

LC 2007-36029

This follows the Titanic's history from the shipyard to its tragic end.

"A series of vignettes and drawings depict the last moments of the tragedy and are helpful to those interested in details. Archival photographs, drawings, sidebars, and inserts extend and clarify the text." Horn Book Guide

Kentley, Eric

Story of the Titanic; illustrated by Steve Noon; written by Eric Kentley. DK Pub. 2001 32p il $17.95

Grades: 4 5 6 7   910.4

1. Titanic (Steamship) 2. Shipwrecks

ISBN 0-7894-7943-5   LC 2001-28432

"Each spread features one paragraph of text superimposed on a large, colorful drawing of the ill-fated luxury liner. The pictures detail the building of the ship through the rescue of its survivors. Borders contain facts and trivia and duplications of small scenes and figures from within each picture that readers can search for in the spread." SLJ

"This book, with its oversize format, brief, informative text, and large illustrations, will be a first choice for many children." Booklist

Includes glossary

Marschall, Ken

Inside the Titanic; illustrated by Ken Marschall; text by Hugh Brewster. Little, Brown 1997 32p il $19.95 *

Grades: 4 5 6 7   910.4

1. Titanic (Steamship) 2. Shipwrecks

ISBN 0-316-55716-1   LC 97-382

"A Madison Press book"

"Color cutaway paintings of the *Titanic* in this oversize book allow readers to view every deck as they follow two 12-year-old boys exploring the vessel, and to see how the liner struck the iceberg and sank." Booklist

Includes glossary and bibliographical references

O'Brien, Patrick, 1960-
The mutiny on the Bounty. Walker Books for
Young Readers 2007 unp il map $17.95; lib bdg
$18.85 *
Grades: 3 4 5 6   **910.4**
    1. Bligh, William, 1754-1817 2. Christian, Fletcher,
1764-1793 3. Bounty (Ship) 4. Ocean travel
    ISBN   978-0-8027-9587-8;   0-8027-9587-0;
978-0-8027-9588-5 (lib bdg); 0-8027-9588-9 (lib bdg)
                       LC 2006-10193
    "In flowing text, illustrated with striking single and
double-page paintings and smaller panels, O'Brien retells
the story of the Bounty's fateful voyage and William
Bligh, the ship's brilliant but harsh, unyielding captain.
. . . The handsome illustrations, done in watercolor and
gouache, are packed with details and action, and add to
the drama." SLJ
    Includes bibliographical references

Platt, Richard, 1953-
    Shipwreck;   written   by   Richard   Platt;
photographed by Alex Wilson and Tina Chambers.
rev ed. DK Pub. 2005 72p il (DK eyewitness
books) $15.99 *
Grades: 4 5 6 7   **910.4**
    1. Shipwrecks
    ISBN 0-7566-1089-3; 0-7566-1090-7 (lib bdg)
    First published 1997 by Knopf
    Describes the history of shipwrecks, famous wrecks,
causes, navigation and rescue techniques, and underwater
archeology and the exploration of wrecks.

Stefoff, Rebecca, 1951-
    Exploration. Benchmark Books 2004 c2005 48p
il map (World historical atlases) lib bdg $18.95
Grades: 5 6 7 8   **910.4**
    1. Exploration
    ISBN 0-7614-1640-4   LC 2003-12032
    Contents: A widening world: Ancient explorers; Chi-
nese travelers; Viking voyages; The journey of Marco
Polo; Ibn Battuta explores the Islamic world; The Great
Age of European exploration: The Portuguese navigators;
To the Indies; The unexpected Americas; Around the
World; Into the Pacific; Filling in the blanks: American
interiors; African riddles; Forbidden Asia; The frozen
north; Antarctica
    This "offers a brief overview of world exploration, be-
ginning with ancient Mediterranean travelers and closing
with the polar expeditions of Shackleton and Amundsen.
. . . Numerous maps depicting travelers' routes across
the globe are noteworthy, and the text provides a solid
starting place for further research." Booklist
    Includes glossary and bibliographical references

911   Historical geography

Adams, Simon
    The Kingfisher atlas of exploration & empires;
illustrated by Mark Bergin. Kingfisher 2007 44p il
$15.95
Grades: 4 5 6 7   **911**
    1. Historical geography 2. Exploration 3. Reference
books
    ISBN 978-0-7534-6033-7
    This atlas is "pictorial guide to the world in A.D.
1450–1800, the great age of conquest. Seventeen . . .
maps present the story of human civilization from continent to continent, featuring . . . tales of trade, war, innovation, and exploration." Publisher's note

Chrisp, Peter
    Atlas of ancient worlds; author, Peter Chrisp;
consultant, Philip Parker. DK Pub. 2009 96p il
map $21.99
Grades: 4 5 6 7 8   **911**
    1. Ancient   civilization   2.   Historical   atlases
3. Reference books
    ISBN 978-0-7566-4512-0; 0-7566-4512-3
    This atlas consists "of maps and illustrations accompa-
nied by extensive captions outlining the cultures of many
civilizations. Each section begins with a map of a continent and a table of contents detailing which peoples will
be discussed in it. Each civilization is covered in a chapter spread that includes a small map of the extent of each
empire and many photos, pictures, and captioned drawings. . . . The accompanying clip art CD contains images of many of the artifacts as well as of the maps
found in the book. . . . This atlas offers a wonderful introduction to [ancient civilizations] as well as solid geography basics." SLJ
    Includes glossary

Leacock, Elspeth, 1946-
    Places in time; a new atlas of American history;
[by] Elspeth Leacock and Susan Buckley;
illustrations by Randy Jones. Houghton Mifflin
2001 48p il $15; pa $6.95 *
Grades: 4 5 6 7   **911**
    1. United States—Historical geography 2. Reference
books
    ISBN 0-395-97958-7; 0-618-3113-0 (pa)
                       LC 00-59741
    This book presents "20 sites in American history at
the moment of their historical significance, beginning in
1200 (Cahokia) and ending in 1953. Places and times include New Plymouth—1627, Charlestown—1739, Saratoga—1777, Philadelphia—1787, Abilene—1871, and Chicago—1893. The detailed cutaway views of homes, forts,
and mills are impressive enough to keep readers looking
again and again. These fascinating slices of life stir the
imagination and lead to questions and further research."
SLJ
    Includes bibliographical references

912   Atlases. Maps

Adams, Simon

The most fantastic atlas of the whole wide world by the Brainwaves; illustrated by Lisa Swerling and Ralph Lazar; written by Simon Adams. DK Publishing 2008 61p il map (Brainwaves) $19.99 *

Grades: 3 4 5 6   912

1. Atlases 2. Reference books

ISBN 978-0-7566-4009-5; 0-7566-4009-1

"Presents information about the geographical features of each of the six continents and includes additional facts about the Earth's structure, oceans, climate, and weather, in a text with a gatefold for each continent." Publisher's note

"The combination of facts with highly detailed, humorous, and sometimes irreverent art makes this browsing item just right." SLJ

Includes glossary

Atlas of the world; [prepared by National Geographic Maps for the Book Division] 8th ed. National Geographic Society 2005 various paging il map $165 *

Grades: 5 6 7 8 9 10   912

1. Reference books 2. Atlases

ISBN 0-7922-7543-8   LC 2004-45002

First published 1963

At head of title: National Geographic

This edition features 60 political maps, 17 thematic maps, and 10 panoramic satellite views of the world. Also includes views of all five ocean floors and both polar regions, the latest imagery from the Hubble Space Telescope, and new information from Mars. A world-thematic section addressing such global concerns as biodiversity, the world economy, and terrorism is also provided. The Web site that accompanies the atlas includes interactive maps

For a review see: Booklist, Feb. 15, 2005

Baber, Maxwell

Map basics; [by] Maxwell Baber. Heinemann Library 2007 32p il map (Map readers) $27.07; pa $7.99 *

Grades: 4 5 6   912

1. Maps

ISBN 1-4034-6794-3; 1-4034-6801-X (pa)

LC 2006003351

"The book begins with a history of mapping, then goes on to discuss globes, with an explanation of hemispheres and meridians, and the international date line. Among the other topics covered are map projections, scale, keys, various types of maps and how to use them, and the future of mapping. The book concludes with map projects. . . . The illustrations are crisp and easy to use. A fine choice." Booklist

Includes bibliographical references

Beginner's United States atlas; a it's your country, be a part of it! National Geographic 2009 128p il map $18.95 *

Grades: 1 2 3 4   912

1. United States—Maps 2. Atlases 3. Reference books

ISBN 978-1-4263-0512-2; 1-4263-0512-5

Provides information about the United States, including state flags, birds, flowers, and capitals, as well as key points about the water, people, and physical features of each state

Britannica's student atlas. Encyclopaedia Britannica Inc. 2009 132p il map $29.95 *

Grades: 5 6 7 8   912

1. Atlases 2. Reference books

ISBN 978-1-59339-841-5; 1-59339-841-7

"This colorful, well-organized atlas is designed to appeal to the Google generation. It adopts the clean, graphics-heavy look of a good Web site. . . . 'About Our World' provides physical and political overviews and includes a staggering number of specialty maps that show everything from world forest cover to land use and from distributions of religions to major mineral deposits. Each continent receives its own series of more detailed presentations. . . . The real marvel of this information-packed resource is that its creators have managed to make it so accessible and visually interesting, while keeping the page count backpack-friendly." SLJ

Goode, J. Paul, 1862-1932

Goode's world atlas; Howard Veregin, editor. 21st ed. Rand McNally 2005 371p il map $49.95

Grades: 4 5 6 7 8 9 10 11 12 Adult   912

1. Reference books 2. Atlases

ISBN 0-528-85339-2

First published 1922 with title: Goode's school atlas

At head of title: Rand McNally

"Contains thematic maps and tables showing distribution of population, minerals, manufacturing, and other subjects. Also included are metropolitan-area maps, physical-political maps of regions, geographic tables, and ocean-floor maps showing earth movement. Pronouncing index included." N Y Public Libr Book of How & Where to Look It Up

Includes bibliographical references

Leedy, Loreen, 1959-

Mapping Penny's world. Holt & Co. 2000 unp il map $17; pa $7.95 *

Grades: 1 2 3   912

1. Maps

ISBN 0-8050-6178-9; 0-8050-7262-4 (pa)

LC 99-48327

After learning about maps in school, Lisa maps all the favorite places of her dog Penny

"The concepts are clear, and the digital-painting and photo-collage illustrations are uncluttered and ably clarify the text." SLJ

National Geographic beginner's world atlas. updated edition. National Geographic Society 2005 64p il map $17.95; lib bdg $27.90 *

Grades: K 1 2 3   912
1. Reference books 2. Atlases
ISBN 0-7922-4205-X; 0-7922-4211-4 (lib bdg)
First published 1999

This "starts by looking at a house, its street, and the surrounding neighborhood, showing how they appear on a map. In simple language, it explains what a physical map is and provides an example of one. Clear, full-color photographs offer views of what the different land features depicted on such a map might look like. The political map receives similar attention. For each continent, both types of maps are provided along with large, often stunning photos depicting landscapes, famous sites, and native peoples. Brief statements note the countries, cities, peoples, languages, and diversity within these areas. . . . High-quality illustrations and excellent maps characterize [thise title]. [It] will be [a] wonderful [resource] for novices and [an] excellent teaching [tool]." SLJ [review of 1999 editon]

National Geographic United States atlas for young explorers. 3rd ed. National Geographic 2008 175p il map $24.95 *

Grades: 4 5 6 7   912
1. Atlases 2. United States—Maps 3. Reference books
ISBN 978-1-4263-0255-8; 1-4263-0255-X
First published 1999

This atlas offers maps of each of the states in the United States, divided into five geographical regions, plus U.S. territories. Each state map indicates physical features such as mountains and rivers, national forests, cities, major interstate roads, and industries, and is accompanied by color photos and facts about the state. An introductory section describes how to use the companion web site for more information, maps of the United States biomes, climates, natural hazards, political states, population, ethnic diversity, and energy use.

National Geographic world atlas for young explorers. 3rd ed. National Geographic 2007 191p il map $24.95 *

Grades: 3 4 5 6   912
1. Reference books 2. Atlases
ISBN 978-1-4263-0088-2
First published 1998

This atlas includes photographs taken from space, political and physical maps, flags and statistics, and links to additional images and information on a companion website.

Rubel, David
Scholastic atlas of the United States. new and updated. Scholastic Reference 2003 144p il map hardcover o.p. pa $10.95 *

Grades: 4 5 6 7   912
1. United States—Maps 2. Atlases 3. Reference books
ISBN 0-439-55494-2; 0-439-47436-1 (pa)
"An Agincourt Press book"
First published 2000

This atlas "offers students a detailed map of each of the 50 states plus the District of Columbia and Puerto Rico. [It] also features an information page about each state that uses photos, graphics, . . . facts, and a brief essay to explain what makes each state unique." Publisher's note

Steele, Philip
Scholastic atlas of the world; [text by Philip Steele, Jane Walker] New and updated ed. Scholastic 2003 224p il map pa $12.95

Grades: 4 5 6 7   912
1. Atlases 2. Reference books
ISBN 0-439-52797-X
First published 2001

This world atlas includes "more than 80 maps, hundreds of color photographs, and thousands of statistics. . . . Topographical maps . . . locate important cities, mountains, deserts, and bodies of water, and indicate border countries and national capitals. Essays describing the culture and geography of each country are accompanied by photographs." Publisher's note

Student Atlas. 5th ed., rev. DK Pub. 2008 176p il map $19.95 *

Grades: 5 6 7 8   912
1. Atlases 2. Reference books
ISBN 978-0-7566-3818-4; 0-7566-3818-6
First published 1998

Maps, illustrations, and text describe various aspects of countries of the world including physical features, population, standards of living, natural resources, industries, environmental issues, and climate.

Wilkinson, Philip, 1955-
The Kingfisher student atlas. Kingfisher 2003 128p il map $24.95

Grades: 5 6 7 8   912
1. Reference books 2. Atlases
ISBN 0-7534-5589-7

This "volume presents maps of planet Earth, the poles, the oceans, North and South America, Europe, Africa, Asia, and Oceania. . . . Introductory material is provided on the solar system and on Earth's geological features, climate, and various habitats. Full-color photographs and maps give readers concrete examples of the facts given in the text. . . . A glossary, index, and a wall map of North America are appended, and a MAC or PC compatible CD that can be used to print more than 40 maps is housed in the front cover. This is an easy-to-use resource for home and classroom use." SLJ

917.3 Geography of and travel in the United States

Koehler-Pentacoff, Elizabeth, 1957-
Jackson and Bud's bumpy ride; America's first cross-country automobile trip; by Elizabeth Koehler-Pentacoff; illustrated by Wes Hargis. Millbrook Press 2009 unp il lib bdg $16.95
Grades: 1 2 3   **917.3**
1. Jackson, Horatio Nelson 2. United States—Description and travel 3. Automobile travel
ISBN 978-0-8225-7885-7 (lib bdg); 0-8225-7885-9 (lib bdg)   LC 2008012752
An account of the first cross-country automobile trip in the United States made in 1903 by Dr. Horatio Jackson, mechanic Sewall J. Crocker, and bulldog Bud
"Short sentences and readable prose capture much of the triumph and challenge of the 63-day trip. . . . The animated, cartoon illustrations are lighthearted and detailed, and add much to the narrative." SLJ
Includes bibliographical references

917.47 Geography of and travel in New York

Rubbino, Salvatore, 1970-
A walk in New York. Candlewick Press 2009 37p il map $16.99 *
Grades: 2 3 4   **917.47**
1. New York (N.Y.)—Description and travel
ISBN 978-0-7636-3855-9; 0-7636-3855-2
                                        LC 2008-20787
This follows a wide-eyed boy and his dad on their walk around Manhattan, from Grand Central Terminal to the top of the Empire State Building, from Greenwich Village to the Statute of Liberty. Includes lots of facts and trivia and a gatefold of the Empire State Building.
"The book's large trim size and the illustrator's perspective provide an entertaining and palpable sense of scale as the small boy marvels at skyscrapers and landmarks. . . . Neophytes and jaded residents alike will embrace this vibrant and enticing slice of the Big Apple." Pub Wkly

917.53 Geography of and travel in the District of Columbia (Washington)

Clark, Diane C.
A kid's guide to Washington, D.C.; [written by Diane C. Clark; illustrations and maps by Richard E. Brown] rev and updated ed., by Miriam Chernick. Harcourt, Inc. 2008 154p il map pa $14 *
Grades: 3 4 5 6   **917.53**
1. Washington (D.C.) 2. Children—Travel 3. Puzzles
ISBN 978-0-15-206125-8 (pa); 0-15-206125-8 (pa)
                                        LC 2007-015509
First published 1989

"Brimming with useful information in both text and sidebars, this sturdy, large-format guidebook covers a broad array of topics, everything from a brief history of Washington, D.C., to practical advice on how to get around the city. . . . The extensive appendix now lists 128 places to see and gives their locations in the city and online. Shades of blue and red add color to the pages, which usually include graphic elements such as photos and line drawings. An attractive, practical guide for young visitors to Washington." Booklist

919 Geography of and travel in other parts of world and on extraterrestrial worlds. Geography of and travel in Pacific Ocean Islands

O'Brien, Patrick, 1960-
You are the first kid on Mars. G.P. Putnam's Sons 2009 unp il $16.99 *
Grades: K 1 2 3   **919**
1. Mars (Planet)—Exploration 2. Life on other planets
ISBN 978-0-399-24634-0; 0-399-24634-7
                                        LC 2008-29486
"Answering the questions on many kids' minds when imagining life in space, this book 'will tell you what would happen, and what you would do, if you were the first kid on Mars.' . . . O'Brien then takes readers through every step of the four-month trip from Earth to Mars: aboard space elevators, orbital stations, transport rockets, landing modules, and more." Booklist
"This intriguing vision of space exploration should set imaginations soaring." Publ Wkly

920 Biography & genealogy

Books of biography are arranged as follows: 1. Biographical collections (920) 2. Biographies of individuals alphabetically by name of biographee (92)

Adler, David A., 1947-
Heroes for civil rights; by David A. Adler; illustrated by Bill Farnsworth. Holiday House 2007 32p il $16.95
Grades: 3 4 5   **920**
1. African Americans—Civil rights 2. African Americans—Biography
ISBN 978-0-8234-2008-7   LC 2006038185
"Adler presents biographical sketches of several individuals and the defining actions or events in their lives as they relate to the roles they played during the Civil Rights Movement. . . . The format is attractive, with the easy-to-read text facing a full-page illustration. Farnsworth's oil paintings complement the simple presentations by featuring a large portrait of each individual, with one or more smaller pictures of a significant moment superimposed on it." SLJ
Includes bibliographical references

Alegre, Cesar, 1967-
Extraordinary Hispanic Americans; by Cesar
Alegre. Children's Press 2007 288p il
(Extraordinary people) lib bdg $40; pa $16.95
Grades: 5 6 7 8   **920**
    1. Hispanic Americans—Biography
    ISBN 0-516-25343-3 (lib bdg); 978-0-516-25343-5 (lib
    bdg); 978-0-516-29846-7 (pa); 0-516-29846-1 (pa)
                              LC 2005031579
"This volume has short (two to three pages) biogra-
phies of more than 200 people, from historical figures to
those in present-day politics, entertainment, and sports.
The writing is energetic, interesting, and without bias.
. . . Black-and-white photographs appear throughout. A
good general reference source for reports." SLJ
    Includes bibliographical references

Altman, Susan
Extraordinary African-Americans. Children's
Press 2001 288p il (Extraordinary people)
hardcover o.p. pa $16.95 *
Grades: 5 6 7 8   **920**
    1. African Americans—Biography
    ISBN 0-516-22549-9 (lib bdg); 0-516-25962-8 (pa)
                               LC 00-52373
    First published 1988 with title: Extraordinary Black
Americans: from colonial to contemporary times
    This "profiles more than 100 African-American
achievers, including writers, artists, musicians, athletes,
activists, politicians, and others who have made headlines. It also includes descriptions of important periods in
African-American history, including the Harlem Renaissance, Reconstruction, the Great Northern Migration, and
the civil rights movement." SLJ
    "Perfect for quick reference, in an attractive layout
that will appeal to even the most reluctant researchers."
Voice Youth Advocates
    Includes bibliographical references

Bausum, Ann
Our country's first ladies; [by] Ann Bausum;
with a foreword by First Lady Laura Bush.
National Geographic 2007 127p il $19.95; lib bdg
$28.90 *
Grades: 5 6 7 8   **920**
    1. Presidents' spouses—United States
    ISBN 978-1-4263-0006-6; 978-1-4263-0007-3 (lib
    bdg)   LC 2006021284
    "A well-researched, thoughtfully written, attractive ac-
count. Fact boxes provide basic information such as birth
and death dates, marriage dates, and children's names; a
'Did You Know' section shares interesting personal tidbits. Periodic time lines help to place the women's lives
within the broader events of history. There is enough information here for simple reports. Interesting facts and
anecdotes will hold readers' attention. . . . An excellent
layout and clear, colorful photographs and reproductions
will further entice readers." SLJ
    Includes bibliographical references

Our country's presidents; all you need to know
about the presidents, from George Washington to
Barack Obama; [by] Ann Bausum; with a
foreword by President Barack Obama. 3rd ed.
National Geographic 2009 215p il map $24.95 *
Grades: 5 6 7 8   **920**
    1. Presidents—United States
    ISBN 978-1-4263-0375-3; 1-4263-0375-0
                             LC 2009290293
    First published 2001
    This profiles the United States Presidents from George
Washington to Barack Obama, and discusses such topics
as The White House, the Electoral College, past presidents as elder statesmen, presidential security, the First
Ladies, the Vice Presidents, children in the White House,
pollsters and polling, and the expanding global role of
the president.
    "This exceedingly attractive offering is . . . chock-full
of information, presented . . . in such an inviting manner
that children will enjoy paging through, even if there's
no school report looming. . . . Full of interesting tidbits
as well as solid information." Booklist
    Includes bibliographical references

Beccia, Carlyn
The raucous royals; test your royal wits: crack
codes, solve mysteries, and deduce which royal
rumors are true. Houghton Mifflin 2008 64p il $17
Grades: 4 5 6 7   **920**
    1. Kings and rulers 2. Nobility 3. Historiography
    ISBN 978-0-618-89130-6; 0-618-89130-7
                             LC 2008-298419
    "Thirteen beliefs about rulers receive an acerbic and
irreverent interrogation in this blend of royal-watching
and skeptical investigation. The royal rumors, arranged
chronologically, start with the real story behind Prince
Dracula and Richard III's murderous ways, stopping en
route at Napoleon's short stature and Marie Antoinette's
'let them eat cake' utterance, and finish up with Catherine the Great's death and King George's madness. . . .
The energy and gleefully gossipy nature makes this a
fine companion for Krull's Lives of . . . series, while its
verve particularly recommends it as an entreé into histo-
riography and critical thinking." Bull Cent Child Books
    Includes bibliographical references

Blackwood, Gary L.
Debatable deaths. Marshall Cavendish
Benchmark 2005 72p il (Unsolved history) lib bdg
$29.93
Grades: 4 5 6 7   **920**
    1. Death
    ISBN 0-7614-1888-1   LC 2004-22237
    Explores the mystery surrounding the deaths of vari-
ous historical figures: Tutankhamen, the English Princes
in the Tower, Christopher Marlowe, Mozart, Meriwether
Lewis, and Amelia Earhart
    This collection of "tidbits about lingering mysteries of
the past . . . [offers] more substance than most. . . . [It
offers] a full-page illustration opening each chapter; reproductions, many in color; and a generously spaced format." SLJ
    Includes glossary and bibliographical references

Bolden, Tonya

Portraits of African-American heroes; paintings by Ansel Pitcairn. Dutton Children's Books 2003 88p il $18.99; pa $11.99

Grades: 4 5 6 7   **920**

　1. African Americans—Biography

　ISBN 0-525-47043-3; 0-14-240473-X (pa)

　　　　　　　　　　　　　　　　LC 2002-75911

Contents: Frederick Douglass; Matthew Henson; W.E.B. DuBois; Mary McLeod Bethune; Bessie Coleman; Paul Robeson; Satchel Paige; Thurgood Marshall; Pauli Murray; Joe Louis; Gwendolyn Brooks; Jacob Lawrence; Dizzy Gillespie; Shirley Chisholm; Malcolm X; Martin Luther King, Jr.; Charlayne Hunter-Gault; Judith Jamison; Ruth Simmons; Ben Carson

"Bolden profiles 20 people, ranging from Matthew Henson, Thurgood Marshall, and Martin Luther King, Jr., to Paul Robeson, Ruth Simmons, Judith Jamison, and Charlayne Hunter-Gault." SLJ

"Each profile lists expected biographical information, but offers even more by way of keen insights into a subject's personality based on interviews and information drawn from personal memoirs. . . . Pitcairn's beautifully rendered sepia-toned portraits make each subject jump from the page, beckoning children to come ever closer and learn." Booklist

Colman, Penny

Adventurous women; eight true stories about women who made a difference; [by] Penny Colman. Henry Holt and Co. 2006 186p il map $18.95 *

Grades: 5 6 7 8   **920**

　1. Women—Biography

　ISBN 978-0-8050-7744-5; 0-8050-7744-8

　　　　　　　　　　　　　　　　LC 2005050311

"The eight individuals profiled are Louise Boyd, arctic explorer; Mary Gibson Henry, plant hunter and botanist; Juana Briones, a Hispanic landowner in early San Francisco; Alice Hamilton, a pioneer in industrial medicine; Mary McLeod Bethune, educator; Katharine Wormeley, nursing superintendent during the Civil War; Biddy Mason, humanitarian; and Peggy Hull, reporter. The chapters include black-and-white photos, and some have excerpts from diaries. . . . Libraries wanting readable, browsing nonfiction will want this book." SLJ

Includes bibliographical references

Cook, Michelle

Our children can soar; a celebration of Rosa, Barack, and the pioneers of change; illustrations by Cozbi A. Cabrera . . . [et al.]; foreword by Marian Wright Edelman. Bloomsbury 2009 unp il $16.99; lib bdg $17.89 *

Grades: K 1 2   **920**

　1. African Americans—Biography 2. African Americans—History

　ISBN 978-1-59990-418-4; 1-59990-418-7; 978-1-59990-419-1 (lib bdg); 1-59990-419-5 (lib bdg)

　　　　　　　　　　　　　　　　LC 2009-1730

"Taking its inspiration from the saying that emerged during the 2008 presidential campaign . . . this book takes readers step by step through American history from freed slaves in the Civil War to the future, touching on Hattie McDaniel, Ruby Bridges, Thurgood Marshall and other African-American 'Pioneers of Change' along the way." Kirkus

"The spreads understandably represent an array of artistic styles and media, yet they form a cohesive and affecting collective portrait. . . . Additional images from Leo and Diane Dillon, James Ransome, E.B. Lewis, Eric Velasquez and others, corroborate Children's Defense Fund founder Marian Wright Edelman's assertion, in the book's foreword, that African-American history is 'the story of hope.'" Publ Wkly

Cotter, Charis

Born to write; the remarkable lives of six famous authors. Annick Press 2009 167p il $24.95; pa $14.95

Grades: 5 6 7 8   **920**

　1. Authors

　ISBN 978-1-55451-192-1; 1-55451-192-5; 978-1-55451-191-4 (pa); 1-55451-191-7 (pa)

A collective biography of authors Lucy Maud Montgomery, Christopher Paul Curtis, C. S. Lewis, E.B. White, Madeleine L'Engle, and Philip Pullman

"Younger readers will find the presentation of the book appealing, with many colorful photographs and illustrations; however, more mature readers will gain the most enjoyment as they discover the backgrounds and inspirations of some of their favorite writers. . . . An excellent resource for reports and pleasure reading." SLJ

Kids who rule; the remarkable lives of five child monarchs. Annick Press 2007 120p il map $24.95; pa $14.95

Grades: 5 6 7 8   **920**

　1. Kings and rulers

　ISBN 978-1-55451-062-7; 1-55451-062-7; 978-1-55451-061-0 (pa); 1-55451-061-9 (pa)

This "book discusses five people who became monarchs as children: Tutankhamen of Egypt, Mary Queen of Scots, Queen Christina of Sweden, China's Emperor Puyi, and the fourteenth Dalai Lama. . . . The illustrations, many in color, include portrait paintings, engravings, and maps as well as photos of people, places, and artifacts. . . . This appealing collective biography presents five unusual children whose stories are well worth reading." Booklist

Cummins, Julie

Women daredevils; thrills, chills, and frills; illustrated by Cheryl Harness. Dutton Children's Books 2008 48p il $17.99 *

Grades: 3 4 5 6   **920**

　1. Stunt performers 2. Women—Biography

　ISBN 978-0-525-47948-2; 0-525-47948-1

　　　　　　　　　　　　　　　　LC 2007-18102

"Cummins introduces 10 women stunt performers, active from 1880 to 1929. . . . Each story includes broad historical context with facts about women's status and societal expectations. . . . Cummins' lively text provides a sense of each individual by including quotes and physical descriptions. . . . Harness' richly colored, detailed illustrations . . . are expressive, realistic, and filled with action." Booklist

Drucker, Malka, 1945-

Portraits of Jewish American heroes; by Malka Drucker; illustrated by Elizabeth Rosen. Dutton Children's Books 2008 96p il $22.99

Grades: 4 5 6   **920**

    1. Jews—United States—Biography

    ISBN 978-0-525-47771-6; 0-525-47771-3

                       LC 2007-028481

"From Albert Einstein and Bella Abzug to Ruth Bader Ginsburg, Hank Greenberg, and Steven Spielberg, this invitingly illustrated collective biography celebrates 20 Jewish American heroes in all their diversity. . . . The nicely designed volume includes full-page portraits of the subjects in various media. . . . Drucker's eloquent, chatty style opens up big issues about Judaism as a source of idealism and for a just, compassionate society." Booklist

Includes bibliographical references

Fortey, Jacqueline

Great scientists; written by Jacqueline Fortey. DK Pub. 2007 72p il map (DK eyewitness books) $15.99

Grades: 5 6 7 8   **920**

    1. Scientists

    ISBN 978-0-7566-2974-8; 0-7566-2974-8

                       LC 2007-298205

This introduces readers to the great scientists and their discoveries from ancient history to modern times.

"An accompanying CD provides clip art taken from the book; this art can prove invaluable to both teachers and students. . . . A very fine book for elementary and middle school students and those who teach them." Sci Books and Films

Fradin, Dennis B.

The founders; the 39 stories behind the U.S. Constitution; [by] Dennis Brindell Fradin; illustrated by Michael McCurdy. Walker & Co. 2005 162p il map $22.95; lib bdg $23.95

Grades: 4 5 6 7   **920**

    1. United States. Constitution 2. Statesmen—United States 3. United States—Politics and government—1783-1809

    ISBN 0-8027-8972-2; 0-8027-8973-0 (lib bdg)

"The makers of the U.S. Constitution are profiled in two or three pages each, in sections introduced by a brief note about their home states. McCurdy's black-and-white scratchboard illustrations are properly stately and engaging. Readers will find great nuggets of fact." Booklist

Includes bibliographical references

The signers; the fifty-six stories behind the Declaration of Independence; [by] Dennis Brindell Fradin; illustrations by Michael McCurdy. Walker & Co. 2002 164p il map $22.95; lib bdg $23.85 *

Grades: 4 5 6 7   **920**

    1. United States. Declaration of Independence 2. Statesmen—United States 3. United States—Politics and government—1775-1783, Revolution

    ISBN 0-8027-8849-1; 0-8027-8850-5 (lib bdg)

                       LC 2002-66364

Profiles each of the fifty-six men who signed the Declaration of Independence, giving historical information about the colonies they represented. Includes the text of the Declaration and its history

"Fradin gives brief, fascinating glimpses into the people who have been overlooked as well as those with whom readers might be familiar. . . . An excellent resource for report writing." SLJ

Includes bibliographical references

Freedman, Russell

Indian chiefs. Holiday House 1987 151p il $24.95; pa $14.95

Grades: 6 7 8 9   **920**

    1. Native Americans—Biography

    ISBN 0-8234-0625-3; 0-8234-0971-6 (pa)

                       LC 86-46198

This "book chronicles the lives of six renowned Indian chiefs, each of whom served as a leader during a critical period in his tribe's history. . . . The text relates information about the lives of each chief and aspects of Indian/white relationships that illuminate his actions. Interesting vignettes and quotations are well integrated into the narrative as are dramatic accounts of battles. While the tone of the text is nonjudgmental, an underlying sympathy for the Indians' situation is apparent." Horn Book

Includes bibliographical references

Funny business; conversations with writers of comedy; compiled and edited by Leonard S. Marcus. Candlewick Press 2009 214p il $21.99 *

Grades: 5 6 7 8 9 10   **920**

    1. Authors 2. Authorship 3. Wit and humor

    ISBN 978-0-7636-3254-0; 0-7636-3254-6

"In 12 entertaining interviews . . . Marcus's compilation explores the childhoods, writing processes and senses of humor of well-known writers for children, including Judy Blume, Beverly Cleary, Daniel Handler, Norton Juster and Jon Scieszka. Marcus's evident knowledge of his subjects' writing makes for some intriguing questions and answers. . . . Photographs, manuscript pages and even e-mail chains between the writers and their editors add fascinating tidbits." Publ Wkly

George-Warren, Holly

Honky-tonk heroes & hillbilly angels; the pioneers of country & western music; words by Holly George-Warren; pictures by Laura Levine. Houghton Mifflin 2006 32p il $16

Grades: 3 4 5 6   **920**

    1. Country music 2. Musicians

    ISBN 0-618-19100-3   LC 2003-5364

Profiles important and influential performers of country and western music, including the Carter Family, Roy Acuff, Gene Autry, Bill Monroe, Patsy Cline, and Loretta Lynn.

"Concise but thorough. . . . Colorful, stylized, folk art of the performers and/or their instruments is included." SLJ

George-Warren, Holly—*Continued*

Shake, rattle, & roll; the founders of rock & roll; words by Holly George-Warren; pictures by Laura Levine. Houghton Mifflin 2001 unp il hardcover o.p. pa $5.95

Grades: 3 4 5 6   **920**

1. Musicians 2. Rock music
ISBN 0-618-05540-1; 0-618-43229-9 (pa)
     LC 00-33480

"Brief profiles of 15 men and women whose music 'created a sound that changed our culture forever,' including Bill Haley, Fats Domino, Little Richard, Elvis Presley, Carl Perkins, Wanda Jackson and Ritchie Valens." N Y Times Book Rev

"A wonderfully entertaining browsing book that will also fill a gap in most music collections." SLJ

Gifford, Clive

10 inventors who changed the world; written by Clive Gifford; illustrated by David Cousens. Kingfisher 2009 63p il $14.99

Grades: 4 5 6 7   **920**

1. Inventors 2. Inventions
ISBN 978-0-7534-6259-1; 0-7534-6259-1

"The innovative efforts of nine men and one woman are presented here. Some of the names will be familiar (Galileo, Franklin, Edison, Curie) while others will prove less so (Isambard Kindgom Brunel, Glenn Curtiss, Sergei Korolev). Starting in ancient times with Archimedes, the chronology ends in modern times with Korolev, a Soviet-era rocket designer. Each section offers a succinct yet thorough biography of the inventors. Striking graphic-novel-style art is a visual aid to draw readers into each setting and era." SLJ

10 kings & queens who changed the world; written by Clive Gifford; illustrated by David Cousens. Kingfisher 2009 63p il map $14.99

Grades: 4 5 6 7   **920**

1. Kings and rulers
ISBN 978-0-7534-6252-2; 0-7534-6252-4

"In this look at ten royals, beginning with Queen Hatshepsut of Egypt and ending with Catherine the Great, each leader's biography is linked with another based on influences, events, and geography." Publisher's note

"Cousens' bright graphic novel-style artwork is the grabber here; he uses theatrical angles to portray each historical figure as a chiseled or beautiful adventurer. . . . The writing is clear, packed with information, and presented in agile paragraphs that twist around the scenes of war, plotting, and murder." Booklist

Haven, Kendall F.

Reluctant heroes; true five-minute-read adventure stories for boys. Libraries Unlimited 2008 169p pa $30

Grades: Professional   **920**

1. Heroes and heroines
ISBN 978-1-59158-749-1 (pa); 1-59158-749-2 (pa)
     LC 2008014017

"These 25 true stories are divided into three sections: 'Stories from History,' 'Stories from the Modern World,' and 'Stories from the Natural World.' Each one offers a short history or explanation to place events in context and concludes with suggestions for further reading. . . . Appropriate as partnered works to nonfiction topics, these brief entries create useful classroom writing prompts or simply entertaining read-alouds. Quick-moving action and dialogue place readers squarely in the midst of dangerous, momentous events." SLJ

Includes bibliographical references

Housel, Debra J., 1961-

Ecologists; from Woodward to Miranda. Compass Point Books 2009 40p il (Mission: science) lib bdg $26.60

Grades: 4 5 6   **920**

1. Environmentalists 2. Ecology
ISBN 978-0-7565-4076-0 (lib bdg); 0-7565-4076-3 (lib bdg)
     LC 2008-35733

Profiles ecologists John Woodward, Aldo Leopold, Rachel Carson, Ruth Patrick, Eugene Odum, Lan Lubchenco, and Neo Martinez

Includes glossary and bibliographical references

Jankowski, Connie

Astronomers; from Copernicus to Crisp. Compass Point Books 2009 40p il (Mission: science) lib bdg $26.60

Grades: 4 5 6   **920**

1. Astronomers
ISBN 978-0-7565-3965-8 (lib bdg); 0-7565-3965-X (lib bdg)
     LC 2008-8325

Explores the lives and discoveries of noted astronomers from the fifteenth to the twenty-first century.

Includes glossary and bibliographical references

Jones, Charlotte Foltz, 1945-

Westward ho! eleven explorers of the West; [by] Charlotte Foltz Jones. Holiday House 2005 233p bibl il map $22.95

Grades: 5 6 7 8   **920**

1. West (U.S.)—History 2. Explorers
ISBN 0-8234-1586-4   LC 2003-57004

Contents: Robert Gray (1755-1806); George Vancouver (1757-1798); Alexander Mackenzie (1764-1820); John Colter (1774 or 1775-1813); Zebulon Montgomery Pike (1779-1813); Stephen Harriman Long (1784-1864); James Bridger (1804-1881); Jedediah Smith (1799-1831); Joseph Reddeford Walker (1798-1876); John C. Fremont (1813-1890); John Wesley Powell (1834-1902)

A collective biography of eleven men who explored the American West in the 18th and 19th centuries, including ship's officers, fur traders, and Army officers

"Jones makes history a lively endeavor by writing vivid accounts of lives that were sometimes stranger, and nearly always more exciting, than fiction. . . . Black-and-white reproductions of period drawings, paintings, prints, and photos illustrate the text." Booklist

Includes bibliographical references

Kiernan, Denise

Signing our lives away; the fame and misfortune of the men who signed the Declaration of Independence; by Denise Kiernan & Joseph D'Agnese. Quirk 2009 255p $19.95 *

Grades: 5 6 7 8   920
1. United States. Declaration of Independence 2. Statesmen—United States 3. United States—Politics and government—1775-1783, Revolution
ISBN 978-1-59474-330-6; 1-59474-330-4

"Kiernan and D'Agnese present readers with astonishing individual portraits of all the signers [of the Declaration of Independence] in an attempt both to dispel some of the mythology surrounding the document as well as to establish a place in the historical discourse for those men not named Jefferson, Hancock, Franklin, or Adams. The marvelously arranged work lends itself to either straightforward reading or skipping around. . . . An entertaining and effective narrative of about three to five pages per individual is presented." SLJ

Includes bibliographical references

Kimmel, Elizabeth Cody

Ladies first; 40 daring American women who were second to none; [by] Elizabeth Cody Kimmel; foreword by Stacy Allison. National Geographic 2006 192p il $18.95

Grades: 5 6 7 8   920
1. Women—Biography 2. United States—Biography
ISBN 0-7922-5393-0   LC 2005005113

This offers "introductions to forty of America's most brilliant and courageous women. Each essay is three pages in length and includes a fourth full-page portrait of the woman being introduced. . . . The women chosen achieved greatness in a wide range of endeavors, from athletics to the arts to politics. . . . Students will find these excellent essays useful as an introduction to the women portrayed and as a good jumping off point for further research." Voice Youth Advocates

Includes bibliographical references

Krull, Kathleen, 1952-

The brothers Kennedy; John, Robert, Edward; illustrated by Amy June Bates. Simon & Schuster Books for Young Readers 2010 40p il $16.99

Grades: 2 3 4   920
1. Kennedy, John F. (John Fitzgerald), 1917-1963 2. Kennedy, Robert F., 1925-1968 3. Kennedy, Edward Moore, 1932-2009 4. Kennedy family 5. Statesmen 6. Brothers
ISBN 978-1-4169-9158-8; 1-4169-9158-1

"Focusing on John, Robert, and Edward, the book describes the Kennedys' early family life and highlights a pivotal event for each featured sibling. . . . The stylized artwork [is] rendered in pencil, watercolor, and gouache. . . . The likenesses are strong, and the images set a historic tone." Booklist

Includes bibliographical references

Lives of extraordinary women; rulers, rebels (and what the neighbors thought); written by Kathleen Krull; illustrated by Kathryn Hewitt. Harcourt 2000 95p il $21 *

Grades: 4 5 6 7   920
1. Women in politics 2. Women—Biography
ISBN 0-15-200807-1   LC 99-6840

"The subjects range from Cleopatra in ancient Egypt to contemporary activists Wilma Mankiller, Aung San Suu Kyi, and Rigoberta Menchu." Voice Youth Advocates

"Each entry offers a tightly written biography, often filled with delicious anecdote. . . . Each biographical essay is accompanied by one of Hewitt's full-page, full-color caricatures. Both artful and witty, the illustrations provide perfect accompaniments to the often breezy and accessible text." N Y Times Book Rev

Includes bibliographical references

Lives of the artists; masterpieces, messes (and what the neighbors thought); written by Kathleen Krull; illustrated by Kathryn Hewitt. Harcourt Brace & Co. 1995 96p il $21 *

Grades: 4 5 6 7   920
1. Artists
ISBN 0-15-200103-4   LC 94-35357

"Krull's brief biographies provide basic facts as well as intriguing details. The subjects chosen range from the famous (Michelangelo Buonarroti) to the infamous (Andy Warhol) to the less well known. Hewitt's caricaturelike illustrations reflect and extend the lively text." Horn Book Guide

Includes glossary and bibliographical references

Lives of the athletes; thrills, spills (and what the neighbors thought); written by Kathleen Krull; illustrated by Kathryn Hewitt. Harcourt Brace & Co. 1997 96p il $21 *

Grades: 4 5 6 7   920
1. Athletes
ISBN 0-15-200806-3   LC 95-50702

"Krull profiles twenty legendary athletes of the twentieth century who broke new ground in their sports and often broke through racial or gender barriers as well. . . . The brief biographies are enhanced by unusual details of personality and Hewitt's lively caricatures of the subjects." Horn Book

Includes bibliographical references

Lives of the musicians; good times, bad times (and what the neighbors thought); written by Kathleen Krull; illustrated by Kathryn Hewitt. Harcourt Brace Jovanovich 1993 96p il $21; pa $12 *

Grades: 4 5 6 7   920
1. Composers
ISBN 0-15-248010-2; 0-15-216436-7 (pa)
                LC 91-33497

"Twenty (including both Gilbert and Sullivan) composers, from Vivaldi to Gershwin, are here profiled in a series of irreverent, anecdotal vignettes, each stylishly illustrated with an elegant caricature." Bull Cent Child Books

Includes glossary and bibliographical references

Krull, Kathleen, 1952-—*Continued*

Lives of the presidents; fame, shame (and what the neighbors thought); written by Kathleen Krull; illustrated by Kathryn Hewitt. Harcourt Brace & Co. 1998 96p il $21 *

Grades: 4 5 6 7 **920**

1. Presidents—United States

ISBN 0-15-200808-X   LC 97-33069

Focuses on the lives of presidents as parents, husbands, pet-owners, and neighbors while also including humorous anecdotes about hairstyles, attitudes, diets, fears, and sleep patterns

"Packed with enough detail for brief reports, these articles are also just plain entertaining. . . . Hewitt's spirited watercolor cartoons add to the presentation immensely." SLJ

Includes bibliographical references

Lives of the writers; comedies, tragedies (and what the neighbors thought); written by Kathleen Krull; illustrated by Kathryn Hewitt. Harcourt Brace & Co. 1994 96p il *

Grades: 4 5 6 7 **920**

1. Authors

ISBN 0-15-248009-9   LC 93-32436

This offers "views of twenty writers . . . from various countries and historical periods. Included are William Shakespeare, Edgar Allan Poe, Mark Twain, Zora Neale Hurston, Isaac Bashevis Singer, and many others." Publisher's note

The "authors profiled are cleverly chosen. . . . Hewitt provides a full-page color portrait, part caricature, part realistic, for each, and Krull's text includes hard facts as well as enough lively anecdotes to make clear that the writers are human." Booklist

Includes glossary and bibliographical references

Major, John S., 1942-

Caravan to America; living arts of the Silk Road; [by] John S. Major and Betty J. Belanus. Cricket Bks. 2002 130p il map hardcover o.p. pa $15.95

Grades: 4 5 6 7 **920**

1. Arts

ISBN 0-8126-2666-4; 0-8126-2677-X (pa)

LC 2002-5477

"A Marcato book"

Contents: Qi Shu Fang: Peking opera performer; Doug Kim: Korean American martial artist; Yeshi Dorjee: Tibetan artist-monk; Abdul Khaliq Muradi: Turkmen rug restorer; Tamara Katayev: Bukharan singer; Najmieh Batmanglij: Iranian American cook; La Verne J. Magarian: Armenian American calligrapher and paper artist; Peter Kyvelos, Greek American oud maker

Profiles eight artists and artisans now living in America who are originally from the "Silk Road," an ancient network of caravan trails through which trade goods, ideas, and arts pass between Asia and the Mediterranean

"Full of colorful and informative archival and contemporary photographs and drawings. . . . Each person's story is told in an interesting manner, and information about their specialty and its history is woven throughout the text. . . . Not only is the work informative, but it is handsome as well." SLJ

Includes glossary and bibliographical references

Marcus, Leonard S., 1950-

Pass it down; five picture book families make their mark. Walker & Co. 2006 56p il $19.95; lib bdg $20.85

Grades: 4 5 6 **920**

1. Authors, American 2. Illustrators 3. Illustration of books

ISBN   978-0-8027-9600-4;   0-8027-9600-1; 978-0-8027-9601-1 (lib bdg); 0-8027-9601-X (lib bdg)

LC 2006-12288

"Marcus presents the events and circumstances that have resulted in five picture-book dynasties. Each chapter includes biographical information about the subjects that zeroes in on the salient pieces that nurtured artistic growth and includes numerous quotes from the authors/illustrators themselves. The featured families are Donald Crews, Ann Jonas, and Nina Crews; Clement and Edith Hurd and Thacher Hurd; Walter Dean Myers and Christopher Myers; Jerry Pinkney and Brian Pinkney; and Harlow and Anne Rockwell and Lizzy Rockwell. . . . Marcus's writing is . . . tight but lively, and each chapter is liberally laced with photographs, preliminary sketches, and final art." SLJ

Includes bibliographical references

Meltzer, Milton, 1915-2009

Ten kings; and the worlds they ruled; illustrated by Bethanne Andersen. Orchard Bks. 2002 132p il map $21.95 *

Grades: 5 6 7 8 **920**

1. Kings and rulers

ISBN 0-439-31293-0   LC 2001-33202

This "volume comprises biographies of ten legendary leaders, including Hammurabi, Alexander the Great, Attila, Kublai Khan, and Peter the Great. Meltzer's sources for discussing these lives and their cultural contexts are impeccable, and he writes knowledgeably and thoughtfully." Horn Book Guide

Includes bibliographical references

Ten queens; portraits of women of power; illustrated by Bethanne Andersen. Dutton Children's Bks. 1998 134p il map hardcover o.p. pa $14.99 *

Grades: 5 6 7 8 **920**

1. Queens

ISBN 0-525-45643-0; 0-525-47158-8 (pa)

LC 97-36428

"The 10 women Meltzer showcases are Esther, Cleopatra, Boudicca, Zenobia, Eleanor of Aquitaine, Isabella of Spain, Elizabeth I, Christine of Sweden, Maria Theresa, and Catherine the Great." Booklist

Meltzer "has a storyteller's flair and an eye for the small details and anecdotes that bring these queens to life. . . . Colorful expressionistic paintings, boldly stroked onto unframed panels, enrich the pages." SLJ

Includes bibliographical references

Nathan, Amy
Meet the dancers; from ballet, broadway, and beyond. Henry Holt 2008 231p il $18.95

Grades: 5 6 7 8   **920**
1. Dancers 2. Dance
ISBN 978-0-8050-8071-1; 0-8050-8071-6
                                     LC 2007-27589
"This collective biography reveals the paths that 16 diverse dancers followed to become professionals and to join prestigious companies. . . . The tone of the text is conversational. . . . The pictures dramatically capture how talented these performers are. Anyone, whether considering a career in dance or not, will be inspired and educated by these up-close-and-personal accounts." SLJ

Pinkney, Andrea Davis
Let it shine; stories of Black women freedom fighters; illustrated by Stephen Alcorn. Harcourt 2000 107p il $20 *

Grades: 4 5 6 7   **920**
1. African American women—Biography 2. African Americans—Civil rights 3. United States—Race relations
ISBN 0-15-201005-X   LC 99-42806
"Gulliver books"
This "collective biography tells of 10 extraordinary black women. From Sojourner Truth to Shirley Chisholm, this is also a view of African American history through individual lives. . . . Stephen Alcorn's allegorical oil portraits are dramatic and beautiful. . . . The immediacy of the text and the spacious design of the large volume make this a natural for reading aloud." Booklist
Includes bibliographical references

Piven, Hanoch, 1963-
What presidents are made of. Atheneum Bks. for Young Readers 2004 unp il $15.95

Grades: 2 3 4   **920**
1. Presidents—United States
ISBN 0-689-86880-4
"Piven presents the characters and interests of 17 U.S. presidents in text and collage portraits that make use of small toys and objects." Booklist
"This book exhibits Piven's flair for creativity and whimsy. . . . Children will be fascinated by the imaginative, humorous artwork and will appreciate the anecdotes." SLJ

Rappaport, Doreen, 1939-
We are the many; a picture book of American Indians; illustrated by Cornelius Van Wright and Ying-Hwa Hu. HarperCollins Pubs. 2002 28p il hardcover o.p. lib bdg $17.89 *

Grades: 2 3 4   **920**
1. Native Americans—Biography
ISBN 0-688-16559-1; 0-06-001139-4 (lib bdg)
                                     LC 2001-39820
"One incident from each person's life is re-created, giving a quick, snapshot-style view of the individual's contribution to the world. . . . The text is large, and sentences are accessible to emerging readers. . . . There is some fictionalizing . . . but it is limited and does not detract from the overall worth of the title." SLJ

Rivera, Raquel, 1966-
Arctic adventures; tales from the lives of Inuit artists; pictures by Jirina Marton. Groundwood Books/House of Anansi Press 2007 47p il $18.95

Grades: 3 4 5 6   **920**
1. Artists, Inuit 2. Inuit—Art
ISBN 978-0-88899-714-2; 0-88899-714-0
"This dynamic picture book draws on memoir, legend, art, and history to tell true dramatized events in the lives of four modern Inuit artists. . . . Beautiful illustrations in colored pencil and mixed media show the individual people and creatures in the Arctic landscape. . . . After each story, there is a brief, straightforward biography of the artist, a photo, and a reproduction of his or her work." Booklist
Includes glossary and bibliographical references

Roop, Connie, 1951-
Tales of famous Americans; [by] Connie and Peter Roop; illustrations by Charlie Powell. Scholastic Reference 2007 108p il $17.99

Grades: 3 4 5 6   **920**
1. United States—Biography
ISBN 978-0-439-64116-6; 0-439-64116-0
                                     LC 2007061714
"This gallery introduces readers to 19 renowned Americans—from Pocahontas and Davy Crockett to Mia Hamm and Yo-Yo Ma. Each sketch opens with a large, easily recognizable caricature by Powell superimposed on a photo of a significant locale. . . . The individuals here make up a truly diverse group; all are well worth knowing." Booklist

Rubel, David
Scholastic encyclopedia of the presidents and their times; with a foreword by James M. McPherson. updated. Scholastic Reference 2009 246p il map $21.99 *

Grades: 5 6 7 8   **920**
1. Presidents—United States
ISBN 978-0-545-10149-3; 0-545-10149-2
First published 1994
This reference "documents the tenure of each of the American presidents. It also includes information about the headlines, people, and fads that were defining America during each presidency. . . . Each profile includes a fact box that lists the president's birthday, birthplace, vice president, wife, children, and nickname." Publisher's note
"This is an attractive, inexpensive resource . . . providing concise information in an easy-to-read format." Booklist [review of 1997 edition]

Sinnott, Susan
Extraordinary Asian Americans and Pacific Islanders. rev ed. Children's Press 2003 288p il (Extraordinary people) lib bdg $39 paperback o.p. *

Grades: 5 6 7 8   **920**
1. Asian Americans—Biography
ISBN 0-516-22655-X (lib bdg); 0-516-29355-9 (pa)
                                     LC 2002-11220

Sinnott, Susan—*Continued*

First published 1993 with title: Extraordinary Asian-Pacific Americans

Biographical sketches of notable Asian Americans and Pacific Islander Americans, from the nineteenth century up to the present

"This well-written resource is accompanied by black-and-white photographs, and will be useful for both browsers and report writers." SLJ

Includes bibliographical references

Thimmesh, Catherine

Girls think of everything; illustrated by Melissa Sweet. Houghton Mifflin 2000 57p $16; pa $6.95 *

Grades: 5 6 7 8   **920**

1. Women inventors 2. Inventions

ISBN 0-395-93744-2; 0-618-19563-7 (pa)

LC 99-36270

"Ten women and two girls are given a few pages each. Included are Mary Anderson, who invented the windshield wiper (after she was told it wouldn't work); Ruth Wakefield, who, by throwing chunks of chocolate in her cookie batter, gave Toll House cookies to the world; and young Becky Schroeder, who invented Glo-paper because she wanted to write in the dark. The text is written in a fresh, breezy manner, but it is the artwork that is really outstanding." Booklist

Winter, Jonah

Peaceful heroes; illustrated by Sean Addy. Arthur A. Levine Books 2009 56p il $17.99

Grades: 4 5 6 7   **920**

1. Heroes and heroines 2. Peace

ISBN 978-0-439-62307-0; 0-439-62307-3

LC 2008-48311

Contents: Jesus of Nazareth; Mahatma Gandhi; Martin Luther King, Jr.; Sojourner Truth; Clara Barton; Corrie ten Boom; Ginetta Sagan; Abdul Ghaffar Khan; Oscar Romero; Paul Rusesabagina; Aung San Suu Kyi; Meena Keshwar Kamal; Marla Ruzicka; William Feehan

"Starting off with Jesus, Gandhi, King, and Sojourner Truth, this collective biography goes on to profile many less well-known peace activists across the world. . . . The detailed portraits never deny the horrifying realities that the peace-seeking leaders are fighting against. With the chatty interactive text, there are handsome full-page pictures of each activist, rendered in oil, acrylic, and collage in shades of red and brown." Booklist

Yolen, Jane

Sea queens; women pirates around the world; illustrated by Christine Joy Pratt. Charlesbridge 2008 103p il $18.95

Grades: 4 5 6 7   **920**

1. Women pirates 2. Women—Biography

ISBN 978-1-58089-131-8; 1-58089-131-4

LC 2007026983

This offers "12 portraits of sword-swinging, seafaring women throughout history, from Artemisia, in 500 B.C.E. Persia, to Madame Ching, an early nineteenth-century Chinese woman and named here as 'the most successful pirate in the world.' . . . The scratchboard illustrations work well as portraits. . . . The book is filled with fascinating, dramatically told stories and sidebars." Booklist

Includes bibliographical references

920.003 Dictionaries, encyclopedias, concordances of biography as a discipline

Biography for beginners: world explorers; Laurie Lanzen Harris, editor. Favorable Impressions 2003 xxi, 598p il maps $55

Grades: 3 4 5   **920.003**

1. Reference books 2. Explorers—Dictionaries

ISBN 1-931360-20-0   LC 2003-1942

Profiles 107 world explorers, from 500 B.C. when Carthaginian explorer Hanno colonized West Africa, to such present-day adventurers as astronaut Neil Armstrong and ocean explorer Sylvia Earle

"This title would be a useful addition in elementary-school libraries as well as in public libraries." Booklist

Eighth book of junior authors and illustrators; edited by Connie C. Rockman. Wilson, H.W. 2000 592p il $110 *

Grades: Professional   **920.003**

1. Authors—Dictionaries 2. Illustrators—Dictionaries 3. Children's literature—Bio-bibliography 4. Reference books

ISBN 0-8242-0968-0   LC 99-86615

This volume contains "information about 202 current authors and illustrators of books for children and young adults. In addition to the many fresh voices, the book contains revised entries on 15 artists and writers, such as Tom Feelings, Beverly Cleary, and Charlotte Zolotow, whose works continue to have an impact." SLJ

Includes bibliographical references

Favorite children's authors and illustrators; E. Russell Primm III, editor-in-chief. 2nd ed. Tradition Books 2006 8v set $368

Grades: Professional   **920.003**

1. Reference books 2. Authors—Dictionaries 3. Illustrators—Dictionaries

ISBN 978-1-59187-065-4 (set); 1-59187-065-8 (set)

LC 2006011358

First published 2003

"Nearly 300 well-known children's and young(er) adult authors are featured in this second edition. . . . It provides easy-to-read commentary on the author's personal and professional lives. . . . This set is an enjoyable introduction to mainstay children's authors and illustrators." Booklist

Includes bibliographical references

Murphy, Barbara Thrash

Black authors and illustrators of books for children and young adults; a biographical dictionary; foreword by E.J. Josey. 3rd ed. Garland 1999 xxiii, 513p il $95

Grades: Professional   **920.003**

1. Reference books 2. Children's literature—Bio-bibliography 3. Illustrators

ISBN 0-8153-2004-3   LC 98-42690

First published 1988 under the authorship of Barbara Rollock with title: Black authors and illustrators of children's books

This volume offers 274 biographical sketches. "Each entry ranges in length from a paragraph to two pages and includes such information as year and place of birth, influences, approaches to writing and or illustrating, achievements, awards, and a selected bibliography of works. Photographs of the authors or illustrators are included when available. An appendix of sample book covers and jackets is included, followed by an appendix listing books that have received awards or honors." Booklist

Includes bibliographical references

Ninth book of junior authors and illustrators; edited by Connie C. Rockman. Wilson, H.W. 2004 [i.e. 2005] 583p il $115 *

Grades: Professional   **920.003**

1. Authors—Dictionaries 2. Illustrators—Dictionaries 3. Children's literature—Bio-bibliography 4. Reference books

ISBN 0-8242-1043-3   LC 2004-61627

This volume covers some 200 authors and illustrators of books for children and young adults including Kate DiCamillo, Pura Belpré, Julia Alvarez and Kadir Nelson. For 20 authors and artists whose careers include significant new works and honors since their profile in earlier editions of the series, newly written entries are featured

This "offers solid and appealing information for students, librarians, and educators. . . . School and public libraries would be well served by this informative and easy-to-read text." Booklist

Rourke's complete history of our presidents encyclopedia. Rourke Pub. 2009 14v set $399.95

Grades: 3 4 5 6 7 8   **920.003**

1. Presidents—United States—Encyclopedias 2. Reference books

ISBN 978-1-6069-4293-2 (set); 1-6069-4293-X (set)
LC 2009000393

A revised edition of: The complete history of our presidents by Michael Weber, published 1997

"Fourteen slim volumes cover all of the U.S. presidents and their administrations. . . . Each individually paged volume begins with a description of the time, especially political and economic concerns. This is followed by profiles of three or four presidents in chronological order. . . . Each entry begins with a photograph or painting and describes the individual's early career, First Lady and family, election, important events during and after his administration, and death. A unique feature is the discussion of the impact of each. . . . The set is informative and contains many comparisons that make the articles relevant to life today. Attractively designed and illustrated." Booklist

Includes bibliographical references

Something about the author; facts and pictures about authors and illustrators of books for young people. Gale Res. il ea $140

Grades: Professional   **920.003**

1. Authors—Dictionaries 2. Illustrators—Dictionaries 3. Children's literature—Bio-bibliography 4. Reference books

ISSN 0276-816X

Also available Major authors and illustrators for children and young adults: a selection of sketches from Something about the author, 8 volume set $605 (ISBN 0-7876-1234-0)

First published 1971. Frequency varies

Editors vary

"This important series gives comprehensive coverage of the individuals who write and illustrate books for children. Each new volume adds about 100 profiles. Entries include career and personal data, a bibliography of the author's works, information on works in progress and references to further information." Safford. Guide to Ref Materials for Sch Libr Media Cent. 5th edition

Something about the author: autobiography series. Gale Res. il ea $149

Grades: Professional   **920.003**

1. Authors—Dictionaries 2. Illustrators—Dictionaries 3. Children's literature—Bio-bibliography 4. Reference books

ISSN 0885-6842

First published 1986

Editors vary

An "ongoing series in which juvenile authors discuss their lives, careers, and published works. Each volume contains essays by 20 established writers or illustrators (e.g., Evaline Ness, Nonny Hogrogian, Betsy Byars, Jean Fritz) who represent all types of literature, preschool to young adult. . . . Some articles focus on biographical information, while others emphasize the writing career. Most, however, address young readers and provide family background, discuss the writing experience, and cite some factors that influenced it. Illustrations include portraits of the authors as children and more recent action pictures and portraits. There are cumulative indexes by authors, important published works, and geographical locations mentioned in the essays." Safford. Guide to Ref Books for Sch Libr Media Cent. 5th edition

Tenth book of junior authors and illustrators; edited by Connie C. Rockman. Wilson, H.W. 2008 803p autog il por $120 *

Grades: Professional   **920.003**

1. Children's literature—Bio-bibliography 2. Authors—Dictionaries 3. Illustrators—Dictionaries 4. Reference books

ISBN 978-0-8242-1066-3; 0-8242-1066-2
LC 2008043312

This volume covers some 200 authors and illustrators of books for children and young adults including David Almond, Blue Balliett, Terry Pratchett, and Laura Vaccaro Seeger. For 17 authors and artists whose careers include significant new works and honors since their profile in earlier editions of the series, newly written entries are featured

"Standard resource for libraries serving young readers and students studying children's and young adult litera-

Tenth book of junior authors and illustrators—
Continued

ture." Booklist

Includes bibliographical references

92 Individual biography

Lives of individuals are arranged alphabetically under the name of the person written about. A number of subject headings have been added to the entries in this section to aid in curriculum work. It is not necessarily recommended that these subjects be used in the library catalog.

Aaron, Hank, 1934-

Golenbock, Peter. Hank Aaron; brave in every way; illustrated by Paul Lee. Harcourt 2001 unp il $16 *

Grades: 1 2 3   **92**

1. Baseball—Biography 2. African American athletes

ISBN 0-15-202093-4   LC 00-8855

A biography of the Hall of Fame baseball player who broke Babe Ruth's career home run record

"This richly illustrated biography . . . deftly tells the athlete's story. . . . Lee's strong, full-page acrylic illustrations in rich tones and textures work well and give the story depth and intensity." SLJ

Tavares, Matt. Henry Aaron's dream. Candlewick Press 2010 unp il $16.99 *

Grades: 3 4 5   **92**

1. Baseball—Biography 2. African American athletes

ISBN 978-0-7636-3224-3; 0-7636-3224-4

LC 2008037417

"This is a biography of Henry Aaron's young life — from his sandlot days through his time in the Negro Leagues to the day he played his first spring training game for the Braves." Publisher's note

"Well-written text and brilliantly composed art highlight the poignancy and triumph in Aaron's story. This rousing tribute should resonate with a wide audience." SLJ

Ada, Alma Flor, 1938-

Ada, Alma Flor. Under the royal palms; a childhood in Cuba. Atheneum Bks. for Young Readers 1998 85p il $15

Grades: 4 5 6 7   **92**

1. Authors, American 2. Women authors

ISBN 0-689-80631-0   LC 97-48887

Companion volume to Where the flame trees bloom (1994)

The author recalls her life and impressions growing up in Cuba

"The attention paid to small daily things as well as the occasional awareness of historical events will encourage readers to look for their own family stories." Booklist

Parker-Rock, Michelle. Alma Flor Ada; an author kids love. Enslow Publishers 2008 48p bibl il por (Authors kids love) lib bdg $23.93

Grades: 3 4 5   **92**

1. Authors, American 2. Women authors 3. Cuban Americans

ISBN 978-0-7660-2760-2 (lib bdg); 0-7660-2760-0 (lib bdg)   LC 2008004641

"A short biography of author Alma Flor Ada, including her life, how she became an author, her books, and her advice to young writers." Publisher's note

"The frequent use of direct quotes makes the [text] particularly enjoyable. . . . Kids will be fascinated with Ada's childhood home in Cuba. . . . Well written, interesting, and useful for reports." SLJ

Includes bibliographical references

Adams, Abigail, 1744-1818

Adler, David A. A picture book of John and Abigail Adams. See entry under Adams, John, 1735-1826

Wallner, Alexandra. Abigail Adams; written and illustrated by Alexandra Wallner. Holiday House 2001 unp il $17.95; pa $6.95

Grades: 1 2 3   **92**

1. Presidents' spouses—United States

ISBN 0-8234-1442-6; 0-8234-1942-8 (pa)

LC 00-23149

A biography of Abigail Adams, wife of second United States President John Adams, and a dedicated wife and mother who spoke up against slavery and for women's rights

"Full-page, colorful pictures in a folk-art style contribute greatly to the text, capturing the daily life, clothing, and household routines of the times." SLJ

Adams, John, 1735-1826

Adler, David A. A picture book of John and Abigail Adams; by David A. Adler and Michael S. Adler; illustrated by Ronald Himler. Holiday House 2010 unp il $17.95

Grades: 1 2 3   **92**

1. Adams, Abigail, 1744-1818 2. Presidents—United States 3. Presidents' spouses—United States

ISBN 978-0-8234-2007-0; 0-8234-2007-8

LC 2006050069

"This excellent picture-book biography introduces the childhoods, courtship, and family life of John and Abigail Adams as well as their years in public service. . . . Himler's graceful and well-composed drawings are brightened with luminous washes." Booklist

Includes bibliographical references

Harness, Cheryl. The revolutionary John Adams; written and illustrated by Cheryl Harness. National Geographic Soc. 2003 39p il map $17.95; pa $7.95

Grades: 3 4 5 6   **92**

1. Presidents—United States 2. United States—History—1775-1783, Revolution

ISBN 0-7922-6970-5; 0-7922-5491-0 (pa)

LC 2002-11271

Adams, John, 1735-1826—*Continued*
  A biography of John Adams with emphasis on his role
in the American Revolution
  "Harness' warm, friendly, mixed-media illustrations,
which range from full-color, double-page spreads to labeled diagrams to black-line silhouettes, will delight children, and quotes from Adams' letters, including many
letters to his wife, Abigail, are a bonus. A fascinating
book for young history buffs." Booklist
  Includes bibliographical references

  Mara, Wil. John Adams. Marshall Cavendish
Benchmark 2009 112p il (Presidents and their
times) lib bdg $23.95
Grades: 5 6 7 8   92
  1. Presidents—United States
  ISBN 978-0-7614-2840-4 (lib bdg); 0-7614-2840-2 (lib
  bdg)   LC 2007023410
  "Provides comprehensive information on President
John Adams and places him within his historical and cul-
tural context. Also explored are the formative events of
his times and how he responded." Publisher's note
  Includes glossary and bibliographical references

Adams, Samuel, 1722-1803
  Fradin, Dennis B. Samuel Adams; the father of
American Independence; [by] Dennis Brindell
Fradin. Clarion Bks. 1998 182p il $18 *
Grades: 6 7 8 9   92
  1. United States—History—1775-1783, Revolution
  ISBN 0-395-82510-5   LC 97-20027
  "Archival reproductions effectively complement a de-
scriptive and accurate narrative that imaginatively inte-
grates details of Adams's life with the social and politi-
cal milieu of the time." Horn Book Guide
  Includes bibliographical references

  Fritz, Jean. Why don't you get a horse, Sam
Adams? illustrated by Trina Schart Hyman 1974
47p il $15.99; pa $5.99 *
Grades: 2 3 4   92
  1. United States—History—1775-1783, Revolution
  ISBN 0-399-23401-2; 0-698-11416-7 (pa)
  "A piece of history far more entertaining and readable
than most fiction. . . . The author has humanized a figure of the Revolution: Adams emerges a marvelously
funny and believable man. The illustrations play upon his
foibles; they are, in fact, even more outrageously mock-
ing than the text. A tour de force, for both author and
illustrator." Horn Book

Albers, Josef, 1888-1976
  Wing, Natasha. An eye for color: the story of
Josef Albers; illustrated by Julia Breckenreid. Holt
& Co. 2009 unp il $16.99 *
Grades: 3 4 5 6   92
  1. Artists, German 2. Color in art
  ISBN 978-0-8050-8072-8; 0-8050-8072-4
                                        LC 2008038214
  "This creative biography explores how Albers, perhaps
best known for his paintings of squares in different color
combinations, 'saw art in the simplest things.' . . . After

visiting Mexico—Albers is shown climbing an abstract
templelike structure of colorful rectangles—he reflects on
the effects of combining different colors. . . . An accessible and lively introduction to this artist and to color
theory." Publ Wkly
  Includes glossary and bibliographical references

Alcott, Louisa May, 1832-1888
  McDonough, Yona Zeldis. Louisa; the life of
Louisa May Alcott; illustrated by Bethanne
Andersen. Henry Holt and Co. 2009 unp il $17.99
Grades: 2 3 4   92
  1. Authors, American 2. Women authors
  ISBN 978-0-8050-8192-3; 0-8050-8192-5
                                        LC 2008-38222
  "Christy Ottaviano books"
  "McDonough clearly lays out the essentials of Alcott's
life story. Often striking and occasionally memorable,
Andersen's gouache-and-pastel illustrations use strong
shapes and rich colors to create iconic images." Booklist
  Includes bibliographical references

Aldrin, Buzz
  Aldrin, Buzz. Reaching for the moon; paintings
by Wendell Minor. HarperCollins Children's
Books 2005 unp il $16.99; lib bdg $17.89; pa
$6.99 *
Grades: 2 3 4   92
  1. Astronauts
  ISBN 0-06-055445-2; 0-06-055446-0 (lib bdg);
  0-06-055447-7 (pa)   LC 2004-6247
  "In this picture book, Aldrin, the second man to step
foot on the moon, relates the life events that led him to
the space program and his assignment on Apollo 11. . . .
Minor's colorful and precisely rendered illustrations help
this effort really take off, especially in the images of Aldrin's space journeys." Booklist

Alexander, the Great, 356-323 B.C.
  Adams, Simon. Alexander; the boy soldier who
conquered the world. National Geographic 2005
64p il map (World history biographies) $17.95; lib
bdg $27.90
Grades: 4 5 6 7   92
  1. Ancient civilization
  ISBN 0-7922-3660-2; 0-7922-3661-0 (lib bdg)
  This describes the life and times of Alexander the
Great.
  This is a "handsomely designed [book]. . . . illustrated with maps and many color photographs of art and
sculpture that give substance to [the era]. . . . Adams
does not downplay Alexander's brutality or all-
consuming ambition and includes examples of both." SLJ
  Includes bibliographical references

Ali, Muhammad, 1942-

Bolden, Tonya. The champ! the story of Muhammad Ali; illustrated by R. Gregory Christie. Alfred A. Knopf 2004 unp il $17.95; lib bdg $19.99; pa $6.99 *

Grades: 2 3 4 5   **92**

   1. Boxing—Biography 2. African American athletes
   ISBN 0-375-82401-4; 0-375-92401-9 (lib bdg); 0-440-41782-1 (pa)   LC 2004-10082

A biography of the African American boxer

"In simple, clear, and lively text, Bolden introduces both Ali the fighter and Ali the activist. . . . The words interact well with Christie's sturdy acrylic paintings." Booklist

Myers, Walter Dean. Muhammad Ali; the people's champion; illustrated by Alix Delinois. Collins Amistad 2010 unp il $16.99; lib bdg $17.89

Grades: 1 2 3   **92**

   1. Boxing—Biography 2. African American athletes
   ISBN 978-0-06-029131-0; 0-06-029131-1; 978-0-06-029132-7 (lib bdg); 0-06-029132-X (lib bdg)   LC 2009-05326

"The curious mix of bravado and humility constituting the life of Muhammad Ali receives a sensitive exploration in this vibrantly illustrated biography. . . . Delinois is with Myers every step, using wild splotches of paint and scribbles of chalk not only to capture the velocity of a punch but also fill in contexual blanks. . . . Unexpectedly far reaching, this is a Muhammed Ali for the thinking child." Booklist

Smith, Charles R. Twelve rounds to glory: the story of Muhammad Ali; illustrated by Bryan Collier. Candlewick Press 2007 80p il $19.99 *

Grades: 5 6 7 8   **92**

   1. Boxing—Biography 2. African American athletes
   ISBN 978-0-7636-1692-2; 0-7636-1692-3   LC 2007-25998

"Rap-style cadences perfectly capture the drama that has always surrounded the boxer's life. . . . Collier's compelling watercolor collages with their brown overtones beautifully portray Ali's determination and strength." SLJ

Winter, Jonah. Muhammad Ali; champion of the world; written by Jonah Winter; illustrated by François Roca. Schwartz & Wade Books 2007 unp il $16.99; lib bdg $19.99

Grades: 2 3 4 5   **92**

   1. Boxing—Biography 2. African American athletes
   ISBN 978-0-375-83622-0; 0-375-83622-5; 978-0-375-93787-3 (lib bdg); 0-375-93787-0 (lib bdg)   LC 2006-101855

"Winter and Roca offer a rousing tribute to Ali's spirit, determination, and strength of will in this picture-book biography. . . . Winter's highly charged prose is well matched by Roca's eye-catching oil paintings, which vividly capture Ali's proud, defiant character and detail the racism he encountered and the hero worship he inspired." SLJ

Ali, Rubina

Ali, Rubina. Slumgirl dreaming; Rubina's journey to the stars; [by] Rubina Ali in collaboration with Anne Berthod and Divya Dugar. Delacorte Press 2009 187p il pa $9.99

Grades: 5 6 7 8   **92**

   1. Slumdog millionaire (Motion picture) 2. Actors 3. India
   ISBN 978-0-385-73908-5 (pa); 0-385-73908-7 (pa)   LC 2009029305

The young actress describes her life growing up in the slums of Mumbai, her experiences on the set of the film "Slumdog Millionaire," and how her life has changed as a result of her role in the film

"The writing here has a journalistic feel. It is not poetic or especially nuanced. But in a sea of cookie-cutter biography series, this book stands out. It has heart, and is aimed at an age group that will identify with Ali in essential ways." SLJ

Alvarez, Luis W., 1911-1988

Venezia, Mike. Luis Alvarez; wild idea man; written and illustrated by Mike Venezia. Children's Press 2010 32p il (Getting to know the world's greatest inventors and scientists) lib bdg $28; pa $6.95

Grades: 2 3 4   **92**

   1. Physicists
   ISBN 978-0-531-23703-8 (lib bdg); 0-531-23703-6 (lib bdg); 978-0-531-20777-2 (pa); 0-531-20777-3 (pa)   LC 2009-356

"Employing oversized font, judicious use of white space, and appealing illustrations . . . readers learn about physicist Luis Alvarez and his numerous contributions to early 20th-century science. . . . Student researchers will appreciate the glossary and index, since there are no chapter headings or subheadings. This title, . . . serves equally well for research assignments, biography units, or as engaging leisure reading for aspiring scientists." Libr Media Connect

   Includes glossary

Andersen, Hans Christian, 1805-1875

Varmer, Hjørdis. Hans Christian Andersen; his fairy tale life; illustrated by Lilian Brogger; translated by Tiina Nunnally. Groundwood Books 2005 111p il $19.95 *

Grades: 5 6 7 8   **92**

   1. Authors, Danish
   ISBN 0-88899-690-X

"Most of this book describes Andersen's childhood and belated schooling, showing his poverty and the grief he experienced over the death of his beloved father, as well as several horrifying events such as being forced by a teacher to witness the beheading of three young people. . . . The biography is divided into 11 chapters, set up as if they were stories. . . . The writing flows smoothly, with many details provided to help students picture the places and events. Brøgger's haunting, mixed-media illustrations add to the somber and at times surreal feeling of the text." SLJ

Andersen, Hans Christian, 1805-1875—*Continued*

Yolen, Jane. The perfect wizard; Hans Christian Andersen; illustrated by Dennis Nolan. Dutton Children's Books 2005 unp il $16.99 *
Grades: 2 3 4   92
1. Authors, Danish
ISBN 0-525-46955-9   LC 2003-55717
A biography of the famous Danish writer of fairy tales, interspersed with excerpts from his stories.
"This volume, with its patrician wallpaper and sepia-tinged pastel pictures framed with gentle arches, is handsome. . . . This is a carefully crafted, lovely, and loving tribute to the father of the modern fairy tale." SLJ

Anderson, Marian, 1897-1993

Freedman, Russell. The voice that challenged a nation; Marian Anderson and the struggle for equal rights. Clarion Books 2004 114p il $18 *
Grades: 5 6 7 8   92
1. African American singers 2. African American women—Biography 3. African Americans—Civil rights
ISBN 0-618-15976-2   LC 2003-19558
A Newbery Medal honor book, 2005
Contents: Easter Sunday, April 9, 1939; Twenty-five cents a song; A voice in a thousand four: Marian fever; Banned by the DAR; Singing to the nation; Breaking barriers; "What I had was singing."
In the mid-1930s, Marian Anderson was a famed vocalist who had been applauded by European royalty and welcomed at the White House. But, because of her race, she was denied the right to sing at Constitution Hall in Washington, D.C. This is the story of her resulting involvement in the civil rights movement of the time.
"In his signature prose, plain yet eloquent, Freedman tells Anderson's triumphant story, with numerous black-and-white photos and prints that convey her personal struggle, professional artistry, and landmark civil rights role." Booklist
Includes bibliographical references

Ryan, Pam Muñoz. When Marian sang: the true recital of Marian Anderson, the voice of a century; libretto by Pam Muñoz Ryan; staging by Brian Selznick. Scholastic Press 2002 unp il $16.95 *
Grades: 2 3 4   92
1. African American singers 2. African American women—Biography
ISBN 0-439-26967-9   LC 2001-49508
An introduction to the life of Marian Anderson, extraordinary singer and civil rights activist, who was the first African American to perform at the Metropolitan Opera, whose life and career encouraged social change
"This book masterfully distills the events in the life of an extraordinary musician. . . . Working with a sepia-toned palette, Selznick's paintings shimmer with emotion." Publ Wkly

Anderson, Walter Inglis, 1903-1965

Bass, Hester. The secret world of Walter Anderson; illustrated by E.B. Lewis. Candlewick Press 2009 unp il $17.99 *
Grades: 2 3 4 5   92
1. Artists—United States
ISBN 978-0-7636-3583-1; 0-7636-3583-9
                                    LC 2008029674
"This sensitive portrait of Anderson—'the most famous American artist you've never heard of'—paints him as a solitary man who kept a private room hidden from his wife and children and often took his rowboat to the Mississippi Gulf Coast's isolated Horn Island to glean inspiration. Subdued watercolors evoke the artist's love of the natural world. . . . A powerful tribute to the lengths artists will go for their passions." Publ Wkly

Andrews, Roy Chapman, 1884-1960

Bausum, Ann. Dragon bones and dinosaur eggs: a photobiography of Roy Chapman Andrews. National Geographic Soc. 2000 64p il map $17.95 *
Grades: 5 6 7 8   92
1. Fossils 2. Dinosaurs 3. Naturalists
ISBN 0-7922-7123-8   LC 99-38363
A biography of the great explorer-adventurer, who discovered huge finds of dinosaur bones in Mongolia, pioneered modern paleontology field research, and became the director of the American Museum of Natural History
"Bausum's account reads smoothly, and a layout dense with captioned sepia photographs and quotes from Andrews provides plenty of oases for readers as they follow him through the desert." Bull Cent Child Books
Includes bibliographical references

Anning, Mary, 1799-1847

Brown, Don. Rare treasure: Mary Anning and her remarkable discoveries. Houghton Mifflin 1999 unp il hardcover o.p. pa $5.95 *
Grades: K 1 2 3   92
1. Fossils
ISBN 0-395-92286-0; 0-618-31081-9 (pa)
                                    LC 98-32372
Describes the life of the English girl whose discovery of an Ichthyosaurus fossil led to a lasting interest in other prehistoric animals
"Brown dwells on Mary's self-determination, focusing on her adventurous spirit . . . and lifelong quest for knowledge in her chosen field of study. . . . The understated watercolors suit the mood. Their subdued palette (ocean blues, sand browns) and simple compositions are undistracting." Bull Cent Child Books

Appleseed, Johnny, 1774-1845

Kellogg, Steven. Johnny Appleseed; a tall tale retold and illustrated by Steven Kellogg. Morrow Junior Bks. 1988 unp il $16.95; lib bdg $16.89 *
Grades: K 1 2 3   92
1. Frontier and pioneer life
ISBN 0-688-06417-5; 0-688-06418-3 (lib bdg)
                                    LC 87-27317

Appleseed, Johnny, 1774-1845—*Continued*

"Oversize pages have given Kellogg a fine opportunity for pictures that are on a large scale, colorful and animated if often busy with details. His version of Chapman's life is more substantial than the subtitle (*A Tall Tale*) would indicate, since the text makes clear the difference between what Chapman really did and what myths grew up about his work, his life, his personality, and his achievements. There's some exaggeration, but on the whole the biography is factual and written with clarity." Bull Cent Child Books

Moses, Will. Johnny Appleseed; the story of a legend. Philomel Bks. 2001 unp il $16.99

Grades: 3 4 5 6   92

1. Frontier and pioneer life
ISBN 0-399-23153-6   LC 00-44600

This is a "picture-book biography of John Chapman, aka Johnny Appleseed. . . . Starting in 1774, the year of Chapman's birth, Moses briefly covers Chapman's early childhood, and then quickly moves on to his young adult years, when he leaves home for the frontier. The bulk of the book documents Chapman's rich adult life and celebrates his odd ways. . . . The paintings . . . are filled with rich detail and are unforgettable." Booklist

Includes bibliographical references

Worth, Richard. Johnny Appleseed; "select good seeds and plant them in good ground". Enslow Publishers 2010 128p il map (Americans: the spirit of a nation) $23.95

Grades: 4 5 6 7   92

1. Apples 2. Frontier and pioneer life
ISBN 978-0-7660-3352-8; 0-7660-3352-X
                                              LC 2008048701

"Discusses the life of Johnny Appleseed, including his childhood in colonial America, his moveable nursery, the real stories behind his folk legend, and the legacy he left on American history." Publisher's note

"This nicely illustrated and sourced [biography] . . . includes full-page sidebars." Booklist

Includes glossary and bibliographical references

Yolen, Jane. Johnny Appleseed; the legend and the truth; by Jane Yolen; illustrated by Jim Burke. HarperCollinsPublishers 2008 unp il $16.99; lib bdg $17.89

Grades: K 1 2 3   92

1. Apples 2. Frontier and pioneer life
ISBN   978-0-06-059135-9;   0-06-059135-8;
978-0-06-059136-6 (lib bdg); 0-06-059136-6 (lib bdg)
                                              LC 2005017789

"In this comely, homespun picture-book biography, Yolen assembles the fact and fiction surrounding America's favorite orchardist into a tale both substantive and lyrical. . . . Burke's striking paintings conform to a natural, yarn-dyed palette of apple reds, forest greens, meadow golds, and midnight blues." Booklist

Archimedes, ca. 287-212 B.C.

Hightower, Paul. The greatest mathematician; Archimedes and his eureka! moment. Enslow Publishers 2010 128p il (Great minds of ancient science and math) lib bdg $31.93

Grades: 5 6 7 8   92

1. Mathematicians 2. Greece—History
ISBN 978-0-7660-3408-2 (lib bdg); 0-7660-3408-9 (lib bdg)   LC 2008051818

"A biography of ancient Greek mathematician Archimedes, who invented the compound pulley and other machines. His contributions to mathematics included devising the formulas for the surface and volume of a sphere" Publisher's note

This biography is a "solid [choice], as . . . [it provides] a good overview of the cultural and political landscape of the times, as well as pictures." SLJ

Includes glossary and bibliographical references

Armstrong, John Barclay, 1850-1913

Alter, Judy. John Barclay Armstrong; Texas Ranger; by Judy Alter. Bright Sky Press 2007 59p il $14.95

Grades: 4 5 6 7   92

1. Texas Rangers 2. West (U.S.)—History
ISBN 978-1-931721-86-8

"Born in 1850 and raised in Tennessee, Armstrong went west to seek his fortune. At 25, he joined the Texas Rangers and soon came to embody the legendary qualities of these remarkable lawmen. He is an interesting character, and the author aptly tells his tale. The archival black-and-white photos add authenticity and help bring the man to life." SLJ

Armstrong, Louis, 1900-1971

Kimmel, Eric A. A horn for Louis; by Eric A. Kimmel; illustrated by James Bernardin. Random House 2005 86p il $11.95; lib bdg $13.99; pa $3.99 *

Grades: 2 3 4   92

1. Jazz musicians 2. African American musicians
ISBN 0-375-83252-1; 0-375-93252-6 (lib bdg); 978-0-375-84005-0 (pa)   LC 2005004151

"A Stepping Stone book"

"Adapted from an unpublished memoir, this beginning chapter book is an account of [Louis] Armstrong's youthful acquisition of his first true horn. . . . Kimmel's skilled narrative accentuates the diversity of the boys surroundings and the early influence of local music upon his innate gift. Bernardins dynamic black-and-white artwork captures the vivacious subject well and includes many period and cultural details." SLJ

Armstrong, Neil, 1930-

Brown, Don. One giant leap: the story of Neil Armstrong. Houghton Mifflin 1998 unp il hardcover o.p. pa $6.95 *

Grades: K 1 2 3   92

1. Astronauts
ISBN 0-395-88401-2; 0-618-15239-3 (pa)
                                              LC 97-42152

Armstrong, Neil, 1930-—*Continued*

Discusses the life and accomplishments of astronaut Neil Armstrong, from his childhood in Ohio to his famous moon landing

"The sense of Armstrong as a boy growing into his childhood dream is strong in the well-constructed text, and that feeling is extended through watercolors with an airy sense of lightness that suits the emotional tone." Bull Cent Child Books

Arn Chorn-Pond

Lord, Michelle. A song for Cambodia; by Michelle Lord; illustrated by Shino Arihara. Lee & Low 2008 unp il $16.95

Grades: 3 4 5   92

1. Cambodia 2. Musicians

ISBN 978-1-60060-139-2; 1-60060-139-1

LC 2007026248

A biography of Arn Chorn-Pond who, as a young boy in 1970s Cambodia, survived the Khmer Rouge killing fields because of his skill on the khim, a traditional instrument, and later went on to help heal others and revive Cambodian music and culture.

"Filled with drama and tragedy, this picture-book biography skillfully telescopes Arn's tumultuous boyhood. Realistic gouache illustrations depict the terrors of war but refrain from showing graphic violence. Amazing and inspiring." Booklist

Astaire, Adele, 1896-1981

Orgill, Roxane. Footwork. See entry under Astaire, Fred

Astaire, Fred

Orgill, Roxane. Footwork; the story of Fred and Adele Astaire; illustrated by Stephane Jorisch. Candlewick Press 2007 unp il $17.99 *

Grades: 2 3 4 5   92

1. Astaire, Adele, 1896-1981 2. Dancers

ISBN 978-0-7636-2121-6; 0-7636-2121-8

LC 2006-40068

The biography of Fred and Adele Astaire, from their humble beginnings to Broadway stars.

Orgill's text "brims with well-chosen biographical and period details, and . . . Jorisch's whisper-weight, line-and-watercolor drawings convey the fizz of the footwork and the gritty backdrop of steam trains and stage doors." Booklist

Includes bibliographical references

Atlas, Charles, 1893-1972

McCarthy, Meghan. Strong man: the story of Charles Atlas. Alfred A. Knopf 2007 unp il $15.99; lib bdg $18.99

Grades: 1 2 3   92

1. Bodybuilders

ISBN   978-0-375-82940-6;   0-375-82940-7; 978-0-375-92940-3 (lib bdg); 0-375-92940-1 (lib bdg)

LC 2006-23952

This is "the story of Charles Atlas, the man who would become 'the World's Most Perfectly Developed Man' and, with his fitness campaign, inspired the entire nation to get in shape, eat right, and take charge of our lives." Publisher's note

This offers "smoothly paced, concise text. . . . The artwork's cartoonish style—bug-eyed, thickly outlined characters in rich flat colors—echoes Atlas' larger-than-life, superhero persona." Booklist

Audubon, John James, 1785-1851

Davies, Jacqueline. The boy who drew birds: a story of John James Audubon; illustrated by Melissa Sweet. Houghton Mifflin Co. 2004 unp il map $15 *

Grades: 2 3 4   92

1. Artists—United States 2. Naturalists 3. Birds

ISBN 0-618-24343-7   LC 2004-971

This describes how John James Audubon studied and painted birds

"Sweet's mixed-media collage artwork includes sensitive pencil sketches and ink drawings washed with watercolors and gouache, as well as elements such as photos of bird nests and bones. . . . This handsome book makes a beguiling introduction to the painter." Booklist

Includes bibliographical references

Banneker, Benjamin, 1731-1806

Maupin, Melissa. Benjamin Banneker. Child's World 2010 39p il map (Journey to freedom) lib bdg $20.92

Grades: 3 4 5 6   92

1. Astronomers 2. African Americans—Biography

ISBN 978-1-60253-117-8 (lib bdg); 1-60253-117-X (lib bdg)   LC 2009003639

A biography of the African American scientist and mathematician

"Maupin has created an accessible account of Banneker's like and accomplishments. Short, uncomplicated text is interspersed with sepia-tone primary source photographs and documents." Booklist

Includes bibliographical references

Pinkney, Andrea Davis. Dear Benjamin Banneker; illustrated by Brian Pinkney. Harcourt Brace & Co. 1994 unp il hardcover o.p. pa $7 *

Grades: 2 3 4   92

1. Astronomers 2. African Americans—Biography

ISBN 0-15-200417-3; 0-15-201892-1 (pa)

LC 93-31162

"Gulliver books"

"The Pinkneys chronicle Banneker's work on his almanac and, most particularly, his letter to Thomas Jefferson, then secretary of state, protesting the country's—and Jefferson's—involvement in slavery." Bull Cent Child Books

This offers "lucid text and striking illustrations, rendered on scratchboard and colored with oil paint." Publ Wkly

Barnum, P. T. (Phineas Taylor), 1810-1891

Fleming, Candace. The great and only Barnum; the tremendous, stupendous life of showman P.T. Barnum; illustrated by Ray Fenwick. Schwartz & Wade Books 2009 151p il $18.99; lib bdg $21.99 *

Grades: 5 6 7 8   92
   1. Circus
   ISBN   978-0-375-84197-2;   0-375-84197-0; 978-0-375-94597-7 (lib bdg); 0-375-94597-0 (lib bdg)
                 LC 2008-45847

"In this sweeping yet cohesive biography, Fleming so finely tunes Barnum's legendary ballyhoo that you can practically hear the hucksterism and smell the sawdust. . . . The material is inherently juicy, but credit Fleming's vivacious prose, bountiful period illustrations, and copious source notes for fashioning a full picture on one of the forebearers of modern celebrity." Booklist

Includes bibliographical references

Barrie, J. M. (James Matthew), 1860-1937

Yolen, Jane. Lost boy; the story of the man who created Peter Pan; illustrated by Steve Adams. Dutton 2010 il $17.99

Grades: 2 3 4   92
   1. Authors, Scottish
   ISBN 978-0-525-47886-7; 0-525-47886-8

"This handsome picture-book biography presents the life of James Barrie, the creator of *Peter Pan.* . . . Adams' paintings provide evocative views of Barrie and his world. Yolen smoothly relates intriguing incidents from Barrie's childhood and adult life without making comments or drawing conclusions." Booklist

Barton, Clara, 1821-1912

Somervill, Barbara A. Clara Barton; founder of the American Red Cross. Compass Point Books 2007 112p bibl il por lib bdg $23.95

Grades: 5 6 7 8   92
   1. American Red Cross 2. Nurses
   ISBN 978-0-7565-1888-2 (lib bdg); 0-7565-1888-1 (lib bdg)
                 LC 2006027071

"With an open design, clear type, and period prints and photos on every double-page spread, this highly readable biography . . . does a great job of setting Barton's personal story within the history of her time." Booklist

Includes bibliographical references

Wade, Mary Dodson. Amazing civil war nurse Clara Barton. Enslow Publishers 2009 24p il (Amazing Americans) lib bdg $21.26

Grades: 1 2 3   92
   1. American Red Cross 2. Nurses
   ISBN 978-0-7660-3281-1 (lib bdg); 0-7660-3281-7 (lib bdg)
                 LC 2008-24889

"An entry-level biography of Clara Barton, and the American Red Cross." Publisher's note

"Colorful photos are found throughout, with a timeline, dictionary, websites concerning the topic, as well as an index making . . . [this] book a wonderful introduction to nonfiction features." Libr Media Connect

Includes glossary

Bates, Peg Leg, 1907-1998

Barasch, Lynne. Knockin' on wood; starring Peg Leg Bates; by Lynne Barasch. Lee & Low Books 2004 unp il $16.95 *

Grades: 2 3 4   92
   1. African American dancers 2. Tap dancing 3. Handicapped
   ISBN 1-58430-170-8   LC 2003-22905

A picture book biography of Clayton "Peg Leg" Bates, an African American who lost his leg in a factory accident at the age of twelve and went on to become a world-famous tap dancer

"Sprightly ink-and-watercolor art ably depicts both the poverty of Bates' early life and the colorful world of entertainment. . . . Barasch subtly sets the story against American racism." Booklist

Baum, L. Frank, 1856-1919

Krull, Kathleen. The road to Oz; twists, turns, bumps, and triumphs in the life of L. Frank Baum; illustrated by Kevin Hawkes. Alfred A. Knopf 2008 unp il $17.99; lib bdg $20.99

Grades: 2 3 4 5   92
   1. Authors, American
   ISBN   978-0-375-83216-1;   0-375-83216-5; 978-0-375-93216-8 (lib bdg); 0-375-93216-X (lib bdg)
                 LC 2007-41526

This picture-book biography of the author of *The Wonderful Wizard of Oz* "displays Krull's usual stylistic strengths: a conversational tone, well-integrated facts, vivid anecdotes, and sly asides. . . . Hawkes' ink-and-acrylic illustrations . . . support the sense of Baum as a multifaceted, fascinating individual." Booklist

Beebe, William, 1877-1962

Sheldon, David. Into the deep; the life of naturalist and explorer William Beebe. Charlesbridge 2009 unp il lib bdg $16.95

Grades: 2 3 4   92
   1. Zoologists 2. Explorers
   ISBN 978-1-58089-341-1 (lib bdg); 1-58089-341-4 (lib bdg)
                 LC 2008-25341

"This colorful introduction to Beebe's life for younger readers opens with his parents' encouragement of his interests in the natural world and his early work as a curator and collector of birds before he developed the idea of observing animals in their native habitat and began to focus on undersea life. . . . Sheldon's lush double-page paintings, in acrylic, gouache and India ink, show young Will surrounded by animals, alive and stuffed, and the older man at work in a variety of settings. . . . A fine offering for would-be explorers." Kirkus

Includes bibliographical references

Beethoven, Ludwig van, 1770-1827

Martin, Russell. The mysteries of Beethoven's hair; [by Russell Martin and Lydia Nibley] Charlesbridge 2009 120p il lib bdg $15.95

Grades: 5 6 7 8   92
   1. Composers
   ISBN 978-1-57091-714-1 (lib bdg); 1-57091-714-0 (lib bdg)
                 LC 2008-07257

Beethoven, Ludwig van, 1770-1827—*Continued*
"Based on Martin's adult book Beethoven's Hair: An Extraordinary Historical Odyssey and Scientific Mystery Solved (Broadway, 2000), this reworking for a young audience presents an intriguing interdisciplinary story. Martin and Nibley trace the labyrinthine journey of a lock of Beethoven's hair encased in a glass and wooden locket from the 18th century to the present. . . . This is a most unusual, thoroughly researched detective story written in a clearly accessible and lively tone. Black-and-white photos and reproductions appear throughout. . . . It is . . . an incredibly readable and absorbing selection that demonstrates the multidimensional nature of true scholarship." SLJ

Viegas, Jennifer. Beethoven's world; [by] Jennifer Viegas. Rosen Pub. Group 2008 64p il (Music throughout history) lib bdg $29.25
Grades: 5 6 7 8   92
1. Composers
ISBN 1-4042-0724-4 (lib bdg); 978-1-4042-0724-0 (lib bdg)   LC 2005028917
This "book begins with an introduction briefly addressing social issues of the day, historical background, or other significant information. . . . Successive chapters discuss the [man's] early [life], family background, social status, personality characteristics, musical training and education, obstacles or challenges, and influences. A chapter . . . focuses on the musician's well-known compositions, describing through lively and colorful language some of the musical elements employed . . . The format and layout are appealing and uncluttered." SLJ
Includes glossary and bibliographical references

Bell, Alexander Graham, 1847-1922
Carson, Mary Kay. Alexander Graham Bell; giving voice to the world; [by] Mary Kay Carson. Sterling 2007 124p il (Sterling biographies) lib bdg $12.95; pa $5.95
Grades: 6 7 8 9   92
1. Inventors
ISBN 978-1-4027-4951-3 (lib bdg); 1-4027-4951-1 (lib bdg); 1-4027-3230-9 (pa); 978-1-4027-3230-0 (pa)
                                                    LC 2007003502
"Carson introduces Bell's life, giving readers an excellent picture of why this man became so famous. . . . [The book provides] clear, concise information in an easy-to-follow format with captioned photographs and illustrations on most pages." SLJ
Includes glossary and bibliographical references

Garmon, Anita. Alexander Graham Bell invents; by Anita Garmon. National Geographic 2007 40p il (National Geographic history chapters) lib bdg $17.90
Grades: 2 3 4   92
1. Inventors
ISBN 978-1-4263-0189-6   LC 2007007828
This biography of the inventor is "nicely illustrated with photos, paintings, engravings, and facsimiles. [It is] just right for emerging chapter-book readers. . . . Useful for reports . . . and interesting pleasure reading." SLJ
Includes glossary and bibliographical references

Matthews, Tom L. Always inventing: a photobiography of Alexander Graham Bell. National Geographic Soc. 1999 64p il hardcover o.p. pa $7.95 *
Grades: 4 5 6 7   92
1. Inventors
ISBN 0-7922-7391-5; 0-7922-5932-7 (pa)
                                                    LC 98-27209
A biography, with photographs and quotes from Bell himself, which follows this well known inventor from his childhood in Scotland through his life-long efforts to come up with ideas that would improve people's lives
"Succinct, lively, and readable, the text is illustrated with many well-captioned period photographs of Bell, his family, his associate, and his inventions as well as a host of diagrams." Booklist
Includes bibliographical references

Benedict, Saint, Abbot of Monte Cassino
Norris, Kathleen. The holy twins: Benedict and Scholastica; written by Kathleen Norris; illustrated by Tomie De Paola. Putnam 2001 unp il $16.99 *
Grades: 3 4 5   92
1. Scholastica, Saint, 6th cent 2. Christian saints
ISBN 0-399-23424-1   LC 00-40294
"This fictionalized biography of Saints Benedict and Scholastica, twins who lived in sixth-century Italy, is told in a lively, authoritative manner. . . . dePaola's elegant, stylized artwork seems particularly well suited to the eternal quality of religious subjects. The framed spreads are painted in soft, warm acrylics on tea-stained watercolor paper, which gives the semblance of an old manuscript." SLJ

Bentley, Wilson Alwyn, 1865-1931
Martin, Jacqueline Briggs. Snowflake Bentley; illustrated by Mary Azarian. Houghton Mifflin 1998 unp il $16; pa $7.99 *
Grades: K 1 2 3   92
1. Snow 2. Scientists
ISBN 0-395-86162-4; 0-547-24829-6 (pa)
                                                    LC 97-12458
Awarded the Caldecott Medal, 1999
A biography of a self-taught scientist who photographed thousands of individual snowflakes in order to study their unique formations
"Azarian's woodblock illustrations, hand tinted with watercolors, blend perfectly with the text and recall the rural Vermont of Bentley's time. . . . The story of this man's life is written with graceful simplicity." SLJ

Black Elk, 1863-1950
Nelson, S. D. Black Elk's vision; a Lakota story. Abrams Books for Young Readers 2010 47p il $19.95 *
Grades: 5 6 7 8   92
1. Oglala Indians
ISBN 978-0-8109-8399-1; 0-8109-8399-0
                                                    LC 2009-9392
"This handsomely designed, large-format book tells the story of Black Elk (1863-1950), a Lakota man who

Black Elk, 1863-1950—*Continued*

saw many changes come to his people. . . . Often quoting from *Black Elk Speaks* (1932), Nelson makes vivid the painful ways life changed for the Lakotain in the 1800s. . . . Colorful, imaginative artwork, created using pencils and acrylic paints, is interspersed with nineteenth-century photos, underscoring that this dramatic account reflects the experiences of a man who witnessed history." Booklist

Blériot, Louis, 1872-1936

Provensen, Alice. The glorious flight: across the Channel with Louis Blériot, July 25, 1909; [by] Alice and Martin Provensen. Viking 1983 39p il pa $6.99 hardcover o.p.

Grades: 1 2 3 4   92

1. Air pilots 2. Airplanes—Design and construction
ISBN 0-14-050729-9 (pa)   LC 82-7034
Awarded the Caldecott Medal, 1984

This book "recounts the persistence of a Frenchman, Louis Blériot, to build a flying machine to cross the English Channel. For eight years (1901-1909) he tries and tries again to create a kind of contraption light enough to lift him off the ground and yet strong enough to keep from falling apart." SLJ

"A pleasing text recounts Bleriot's adventures with gentle humor and admiration for his earnest, if accident-prone, determination. Best of all, the pictures shine with the illustrator's delight in the wondrous flying machines themselves." Horn Book

Bly, Nellie, 1864-1922

Macy, Sue. Bylines: a photobiography of Nellie Bly; foreword by Linda Ellerbee. National Geographic 64p il map $19.95; lib bdg $28.90 *

Grades: 5 6 7 8   92

1. Women journalists
ISBN 978-1-4263-0513-9; 1-4263-0513-3; 978-1-4263-0514-6 (lib bdg); 1-4263-0514-1 (lib bdg)
LC 2008-52329

"This detailed biography of the trailblazing 19th-century journalist incorporates photographs of Bly and her subjects. The extensive text explores the details of a life spent seeking justice. . . . A thorough introduction to the life of a fascinating figure." Publ Wkly

Bonetta, Sarah Forbes, b. 1843?

Myers, Walter Dean. At her majesty's request; an African princess in Victorian England. Scholastic Press 1999 146p il map $17.95

Grades: 5 6 7 8   92

1. Africans
ISBN 0-590-48669-1   LC 98-7217

Biography of the African princess saved from execution and taken to England where Queen Victoria oversaw her upbringing and where she lived for a time before marrying an African missionary

"Myers tells an extraordinary tale which will intrigue young readers. . . . A fascinating narrative of a little-known facet of Victorian history, this book is rich with illustrations, including photographs, sketches, portraits, and maps." ALAN

Includes bibliographical references

Boone, Daniel, 1734-1820

Calvert, Patricia. Daniel Boone; beyond the mountains. Benchmark Bks. 2002 79p il (Great explorations) lib bdg $23.90

Grades: 5 6 7 8   92

1. West (U.S.)—Biography 2. Frontier and pioneer life—West (U.S.)
ISBN 0-7614-1243-3   LC 00-51902

A biography of the Western pioneer

This "well-researched [book] . . . will be useful to students writing reports." Horn Book Guide

Includes bibliographical references

Spradlin, Michael P. Daniel Boone's great escape; [by] Michael P. Spradlin; illustrated by Ard Hoyt. Walker & Co. 2008 unp il $16.95; lib bdg $17.85

Grades: K 1 2 3   92

1. Escapes 2. Shawnee Indians 3. Frontier and pioneer life 4. Explorers
ISBN 978-0-8027-9581-6; 0-8027-9581-1; 978-0-8027-9582-3 (lib bdg); 0-8027-9582-X (lib bdg)
LC 2007-50382

"Spradlin . . . and Hoyt . . . deliver a thrilling adventure about famed 18th-century frontiersman Daniel Boone. The storytelling is immediate and swift. . . . Gripping prose relates Boone's experiences as the Shawnee hold him captive from February to June in 1778, until he makes a daring escape to warn fellow settlers of an impending attack. Hoyt's skillful blend of closeups and eye-level perspectives pulls readers right into the action. Maintaining the tight-as-a drum tension, the watercolor-and-ink scenes show the escapee hightailing it through thick forests." Publ Wkly

Booth, Edwin, 1833-1893

Giblin, James. Good brother, bad brother. See entry under Booth, John Wilkes, 1838-1865

Booth, John Wilkes, 1838-1865

Giblin, James. Good brother, bad brother; the story of Edwin Booth and John Wilkes Booth. Clarion Books 2005 244p il $22 *

Grades: 5 6 7 8   92

1. Booth, Edwin, 1833-1893 2. Lincoln, Abraham, 1809-1865—Assassination 3. Actors 4. United States—History—1861-1865, Civil War 5. Brothers
ISBN 0-618-09642-6   LC 2004-21260

Giblin "frames the intertwined tale of two brothers with accounts of their families, friends, the Civil War, and nineteenth-century theater. . . . Alcoholism and depression afflicted the family, but Giblin is brilliant at showing that darkness was only one part of a life. . . . Giblin's book will engross readers until the very last footnote." Booklist

Includes bibliographical references

Braille, Louis, 1809-1852

Adler, David A. A picture book of Louis Braille; illustrated by John & Alexandra Wallner. Holiday House 1997 unp il $16.95; pa $6.95

Grades: 1 2 3   92

1. Blind—Books and reading
ISBN 0-8234-1291-1; 0-8234-1413-2 (pa)

                     LC 96-38453

Presents the life of the nineteenth-century Frenchman, accidentally blinded as a child, who originated the raised dot system of reading and writing used by the blind throughout the world

"The text is simple yet informative. . . . Adler sprinkles in interesting facts about early 19th-century France that help readers better grasp Braille's world. . . . Softly colored illustrations in line and watercolor add visual clues for younger children." SLJ

Freedman, Russell. Out of darkness: the story of Louis Braille; illustrated by Kate Kiesler. Clarion Bks. 1997 81p il $16.95; pa $7.95 *

Grades: 4 5 6 7   92

1. Blind—Books and reading
ISBN 0-395-77516-7; 0-395-96888-7 (pa)

                     LC 95-52353

This biography "tells about Braille's life and the development of his alphabet system for the blind." SLJ

"Without melodrama, Freedman tells the momentous story in quiet chapters in his best plain style, making the facts immediate and personal. . . . A diagram explains how the Braille alphabet works, and Kate Kessler's full-page shaded pencil illustrations are part of the understated poignant drama." Booklist

Breckinridge, Mary, 1881-1965

Wells, Rosemary. Mary on horseback; three mountain stories; pictures by Peter McCarty. Dial Bks. for Young Readers 1998 53p il $16.99; pa $4.99 *

Grades: 4 5 6 7   92

1. Nurses
ISBN 0-670-88923-7; 0-14-130815-X (pa)

                     LC 97-43409

Tells the stories of three families who were helped by the work of Mary Breckinridge, the first nurse to go into the Appalachian Mountains and give medical care to the isolated inhabitants. Includes an afterword with facts about Breckinridge and the Frontier Nursing Service she founded

"These beautifully written stories will remain with the reader long after the book is closed." Booklist

Bridges, Ruby

Bridges, Ruby. Through my eyes: the autobiography of Ruby Bridges; articles and interviews compiled and edited by Margo Lundell. Scholastic Press 1999 63p il $16.95 *

Grades: 4 5 6   92

1. African Americans—Civil rights 2. New Orleans (La.)—Race relations
ISBN 0-590-18923-9   LC 98-49242

Ruby Bridges recounts the story of her involvement, as a six-year-old, in the integration of her school in New Orleans in 1960

"Profusely illustrated with sepia photos—including many gritty journalistic reproductions—this memoir brings some of the raw emotions of a tumultuous period into sharp focus. . . . A powerful personal narrative that every collection will want to own." SLJ

Donaldson, Madeline. Ruby Bridges. Lerner Publications 2009 48p il (History maker bios) $27.93

Grades: 3 4 5   92

1. African Americans—Civil rights 2. School integration 3. New Orleans (La.)—Race relations
ISBN 978-0-7613-4220-5; 0-7613-4220-6

                     LC 2008046526

"Donaldson recounts the story of this young African American girl who, in 1960 at the age of six, integrated New Orleans' William Franz Elementary School. . . . Donaldson's book is illustrated will fill-color drawings and carefully chosen period photos. . . . The book . . . makes a good introduction for report writers too young for Bridges' own memoir, Through My Eyes (1999)." Booklist

Includes bibliographical references

Bridgman, Laura Dewey, 1829-1889

Alexander, Sally Hobart. She touched the world: Laura Bridgman, deaf-blind pioneer; by Sally Hobart Alexander and Robert Alexander. Clarion Books 2008 100p il $18

Grades: 5 6 7 8   92

1. Howe, Samuel Gridley, 1801-1876 2. Blind 3. Deaf
ISBN 978-0-618-85299-4; 0-618-85299-9

"At the age of three, in 1832, Laura Bridgman contracted scarlet fever and lost her sight, her hearing, her sense of smell, and much of her sense of taste. Her family sent her to Dr. Samuel [Gridley] Howe at the New England Institute for the Education of the Blind, and by the age of 10, Laura was world-famous for her accomplishments. . . . Alexander . . . presents a well-written and thoroughly researched biography of this remarkable woman, with numerous black-and-white photos." Booklist

Includes bibliographical references

Brown, Clara, 1800-1885

Lowery, Linda. Aunt Clara Brown; official pioneer; illustrations by Janice Lee Porter. Carolrhoda Bks. 1999 48p il (On my own biography) lib bdg $19.93; pa $5.95 *

Grades: 2 3 4   92

1. African American women—Biography 2. Frontier and pioneer life
ISBN 1-57505-045-5 (lib bdg); 1-57505-416-7 (pa)

                     LC 98-24259

A biography of the freed slave who made her fortune in Colorado and used her money to bring other former slaves there to begin new lives

"The well-defined primitivist shapes, canvas-y textures, and muted earth tones of the illustrations perfectly

Brown, Clara, 1800-1885—*Continued*

evoke the roughness of the terrain and the historical period, as well as the powerful basic emotions motivating the characters. The straightforward text allows the facts speak for themselves. . . . A good story and a solid resource." Bull Cent Child Books

Brown, John, 1800-1859

Hendrix, John. John Brown; his fight for freedom; written and illustrated by John Hendrix. Abrams Books for Young Readers 2009 39p il $18.95 *

Grades: 4 5 6 7   92

1. Abolitionists 2. Slavery—United States
ISBN 978-0-8109-3798-7; 0-8109-3798-0
LC 2008-45969

The author "traces how John Brown went from conducting slaves along the Underground Railroad to espousing violent insurrection as a means to end slavery. . . . Reinforcing Brown as a larger-than-life folk hero, the pictures are exhilarating. . . . By embracing Brown's complexity, especially in the well-argued afterword, Hendrix sows acres of fertile ground for discussion." Booklist

Bruchac, Joseph, 1942-

Parker-Rock, Michelle. Joseph Bruchac; an author kids love. Enslow Publishers, Inc. 2009 48p il (Authors kids love) lib bdg $23.93

Grades: 3 4 5   92

1. Authors, American
ISBN 978-0-7660-3160-9 (lib bdg); 0-7660-3160-8 (lib bdg)
LC 2008-33051

Based on a live interview with Joseph Bruchac on June 6, 2007

"Explores the life of author Joseph Bruchac, including his childhood and early career, his many books for kids, and tips he has for young, aspiring writers." Publisher's note

"Clearly written, [this] outstanding [biography provides] many interesting details about the [subject's] personal [life] and [includes] photos that enhance the [text]." SLJ

Includes glossary and bibliographical references

Bryan, Ashley, 1923-

Bryan, Ashley. Ashley Bryan; words to my life's song; with photographs by Bill McGuinness. Atheneum Books for Young Readers 2009 58p il $18.99 *

Grades: 3 4 5 6   92

1. Authors, American 2. African American authors 3. Illustrators 4. African American artists
ISBN 978-1-4169-0541-7; 1-4169-0541-3
LC 2008-14369

"In rich collages of words and pictures, this highly visual autobiography introduces artist Ashley Bryan's life and his vision of the world around him. . . . Photos of Bryan's world and reproductions of his often bright-hued and inherently vibrant artworks appear on every page. . . . They infuse the entire presentation with energy, color, and joy. . . . Beautifully designed, the book creates an original, stimulating, and inspiring portrait of the artist . . . as well as a celebration of his vision." Booklist

Burningham, John, 1936-

Burningham, John. John Burningham; preface by Maurice Sendak; commentary by Brian Alderson. Candlewick Press 2009 223p il $70

Grades: Professional   92

1. Illustrators 2. Authors, English
ISBN 978-0-7636-4434-5; 0-7636-4434-X

"The British author and illustrator has garnered an international reputation for combining imaginative, offbeat illustrations with highly funny, original stories for children. In this oversize, lavishly illustrated volume, Burningham relates his life story from his nonconformist schooling and his early meanderings around the world to his various artistic ventures, picture books being only one of his endeavors. . . . Students of children's literature will be intrigued by Maurice Sendak's short preface and by the six-page opening commentary by children's literature scholar Brian Alderson. A fascinating and insightful treat for Burningham aficionados." SLJ

Caesar, Julius, 100-44 B.C.

Galford, Ellen. Julius Caesar; the boy who conquered an empire; [by] Ellen Galford. National Geographic 2007 64p il map (World history biographies) $17.95; lib bdg $27.90

Grades: 5 6 7 8   92

1. Rome—History 2. Emperors—Rome
ISBN 978-1-4263-0064-6; 978-1-4263-0065-3 (lib bdg)
LC 2006020777

A biography of the Roman emperor

This "visually appealing [title is] packed with excellent photographs and reproductions, interesting sidebars, and [has] a time line running along the bottom of every page. . . . [This book is] useful, well-written." SLJ

Includes glossary and bibliographical references

Calder, Alexander, 1898-1976

Stone, Tanya Lee. Sandy's circus; a story about Alexander Calder; illustrated by Boris Kulikov. Viking 2008 unp il $16.99 *

Grades: 1 2 3   92

1. Circus in art 2. Sculptors 3. Artists—United States
ISBN 978-0-670-06268-3; 0-670-06268-5
LC 2008-08380

"This beautifully illustrated picture-book biography . . . [offers a] spare, direct story that focuses on Calder's youth and what are, perhaps, his most kid-accessible artworks: his wire sculptures of circus performers. . . . Kulikov's elegant, fanciful, multimedia collages extend the story." Booklist

Includes bibliographical references

Campanella, Roy, 1921-1993

Adler, David A. Campy; the Roy Campanella story; by David A. Adler; illustrated by Gordon C. James. Viking Penguin 2007 unp il $15.99

Grades: 2 3 4   92

1. Baseball—Biography 2. African American athletes
ISBN 0-670-06041-0   LC 2005023314

"Roy Campanella . . . was the second African American signed by Branch Rickey to play for the Brooklyn Dodgers. . . . Adler . . . capably reprises Campy's on-

Campanella, Roy, 1921-1993—*Continued*

field triumphs . . . and off-field tragedy (he was paralyzed in a car accident in 1958), while James delivers evocative illustrations in the soft-focus, pastel-heavy style that has become standard for baseball." nostalgia. Booklist

Includes bibliographical references

Carson, Kit, 1809-1868

Calvert, Patricia. Kit Carson; he led the way; [by] Patricia Calvert. Marshall Cavendish Benchmark 2006 c2007 96p il (Great explorations) lib bdg $32.79

Grades: 5 6 7 8   92
    1. Frontier and pioneer life—West (U.S.)
    ISBN 978-0-7614-2223-5 (lib bdg); 0-7614-2223-4 (lib bdg)   LC 2005037375
    "An examination of the life and frontier explorations of legendary trapper and Indian agent Christopher 'Kit' Carson." Publisher's note
    Includes bibliographical references

Carson, Rachel, 1907-1964

Ehrlich, Amy. Rachel; the story of Rachel Carson; illustrated by Wendell Minor. Silver Whistle/Harcourt 2003 unp il $16 *

Grades: 2 3 4   92
    1. Women scientists
    ISBN 0-15-216227-5   LC 00-13115
    This "anecdotal biography of nature writer and environmentalist Carson focuses on incidents that influenced Carson's thinking and career aspirations. . . . Minor's . . . impressively realistic watercolor and gouache paintings lend a pleasing cohesiveness to the volume." Publ Wkly

Gow, Mary. Rachel Carson; ecologist and activist. Enslow Pubs. 2005 128p il (Great minds of science) lib bdg $31.93

Grades: 5 6 7 8   92
    1. Women scientists
    ISBN 0-7660-2503-9
    A biography of the environmentalist and author of "Silent Spring."
    Includes glossary and bibliographical references

Scherer, Glenn. Who on earth is Rachel Carson? mother of the environmental movement; [by] Glenn Scherer and Marty Fletcher. Enslow Publishers 2009 112p il (Scientists saving the earth) lib bdg $31.93

Grades: 5 6 7 8   92
    1. Biologists 2. Environmentalists 3. Women scientists
    ISBN 978-1-59845-116-0 (lib bdg); 1-59845-116-2 (lib bdg)   LC 2008028498
    "Details the life of Rachel Carson, with chapters devoted to her early years, life, work, ecological writings, and legacy, as well as how children can follow in her footsteps" Publisher's note
    "The writing is clear and informative. . . . Color photographs are relevant and of good quality." SLJ
    Includes bibliographical references

Carver, George Washington, 1864?-1943

Bolden, Tonya. George Washington Carver. Abrams Books for Young Readers 2008 41p il $18.95 *

Grades: 3 4 5 6   92
    1. Scientists 2. African Americans—Biography
    ISBN 978-0-8109-9366-2; 0-8109-9366-X
                                        LC 2007-28069
    NCTE Orbis Pictus Award honor book (2009)
    This is a biography of "the slave-born black scientist. . . . Offering sourced quotations throughout, Bolden covers subtleties that simpler treatments tend to bypass. . . . Photos and reproductions, many of Carver's own paintings, are exceptional, and their arrangement in the style of an old-fashioned album lends the book a suitable gravitas. . . . [The book is] absorbing." Booklist
    Includes bibliographical references

Harness, Cheryl. The groundbreaking, chance-taking life of George Washington Carver and science & invention in America; by Cheryl Harness. National Geographic 2008 143p il map (Cherly Harness histories) $16.95; lib bdg $25.90

Grades: 4 5 6 7   92
    1. Scientists 2. African Americans—Biography
    ISBN   978-1-4263-0196-4;   1-4263-0196-0; 978-1-4263-0197-1 (lib bdg); 1-4263-0197-9 (lib bdg)   LC 2007029316
    "Harness presents Carver as a man who, regardless of constant hardship and racial prejudice, persevered to become a beloved teacher and devoted scientist. . . . The author raises challenging questions throughout. . . . The lively prose style conveys his sense of passion and adventure about the man and his intellectual pursuits, and the simple black-and-white drawings add a further sense of drama." SLJ
    Includes bibliographical references

Cassatt, Mary, 1844-1926

Casey, Carolyn. Mary Cassatt; the life of an artist. Enslow Publishers 2004 48p il (Artist biographies) lib bdg $23.93

Grades: 2 3 4   92
    1. Artists—United States 2. Women artists
    ISBN 978-0-7660-2093-1 (lib bdg); 0-7660-2093-2 (lib bdg)   LC 2003-17616
    Discusses the life and the work of the Impressionist painter Mary Cassatt
    Includes glossary and bibliographical references

Harris, Lois V. Mary Cassatt; impressionist painter; [by] Lois V. Harris. Pelican 2007 32p il $15.95

Grades: 2 3 4   92
    1. Artists—United States 2. Women artists
    ISBN 978-1-58980-452-4   LC 2007011755
    "With large, crisply reproduced, color artwork on nearly every page, this picture-book biography of American Impressionist Mary Cassatt will appeal to a broad age-range of readers." Booklist

Cézanne, Paul, 1839-1906

Burleigh, Robert. Paul Cezanne; a painter's journey. H.N. Abrams 2006 31p il $17.95

Grades: 4 5 6 7   92

1. Artists, French

ISBN 0-8109-5784-1   LC 2005011779

Published in association with the National Gallery of Art

"Burleigh offers brief insights into Cézanne's personal life, such as his relationship with his father, who did not support his sons interest in art. However, the emphasis is on interpreting some individual paintings and understanding the artist's various styles, including the impact of the Impressionists and his evolution to a freer and simpler manner of expression in his later years. . . . The high-quality reproductions demonstrate Burleigh's points. . . . A solid, lively introduction." SLJ

Chagall, Marc, 1887-1985

Markel, Michelle. Dreamer from the village; the story of Marc Chagall; illustrated by Emily Lisker. Henry Holt & Co. 2005 unp il $17.95 *

Grades: K 1 2 3   92

1. Artists, Russian 2. Jews—Biography

ISBN 978-0-8050-6373-8; 0-8050-6373-0

LC 2003-22498

"Opening with the artist's dramatic birth during a fire in a small Russian village, Markel describes Chagall's childhood and early career. The village, his extended family, and deep Jewish roots are all emphasized, elements that are central to understanding his art. . . . The language is often poetic. . . . The vivid illustrations are inspired by Chagall, but Lisker doesn't attempt to copy his style directly. . . . [This is] an excellent portrait of an artist that will open and expand children's minds." SLJ

Champlain, Samuel de, 1567-1635

Faber, Harold. Samuel de Champlain; explorer of Canada; Harold Faber. Benchmark Books 2005 80p il map (Great explorations) lib bdg $29.93

Grades: 5 6 7 8   92

1. Explorers 2. America—Exploration

ISBN 0-7614-1608-0   LC 2003-974

Contents: Growing up; First voyage to Canada; The fur trade; Founding of Quebec; The battle of Lake Champlain; More voyages to Canada; Disappointments; Governor of New France

"Faber draws on Champlain's own accounts to trace his exploration of and dogged determination to colonize Canada. . . . Illustrated with beautiful reproductions of period illustrations, paintings, and maps. . . . Well-written." SLJ

Includes bibliographical references

MacLeod, Elizabeth. Samuel de Champlain; written by Elizabeth MacLeod; illustrated by John Mantha. Kids Can Press 2008 32p il (Kids Can Read) $14.95; pa $3.95

Grades: 1 2 3   92

1. Explorers 2. America—Exploration

ISBN   978-1-55453-049-6;   1-55453-049-0; 978-1-55453-050-2 (pa); 1-55453-050-4 (pa)

A biography of the French explorer of Canada

This is a "fresh, short [biography] for newly independent readers. . . . The writing is clear if sedate, and the type is large. Abundant pen-and-ink illustrations are finely rendered and enhance [the] text." SLJ

Champollion, Jean François, 1790-1832

Rumford, James. Seeker of knowledge; the man who deciphered Egyptian hieroglyphs. Houghton Mifflin 2000 unp il $15; pa $6.95

Grades: 3 4 5   92

1. Hieroglyphics

ISBN 0-395-97934-X; 0-618-33345-2 (pa)

LC 99-37254

A biography of the French scholar whose decipherment of the Egyptian hieroglyphic language made the study of ancient Egypt possible

"Despite the book's traditional picture-book appearance, with a short text and nicely rendered watercolor art, the topic requires and gets sturdy treatment. . . . Those intrigued by hieroglyphs . . . will find this a useful introduction." Booklist

Chanel, Coco, 1883-1971

Matthews, Elizabeth. Different like Coco. Candlewick Press 2007 unp il $16.99 *

Grades: 2 3 4   92

1. Fashion designers

ISBN 978-0-7636-2548-1; 0-7636-2548-5

LC 2006-40622

"A celebration of the life of a major fashion designer and independent spirit. . . . The story is accompanied, appropriately, by elegant pen-and-ink and watercolor cartoons that capture her struggles as a young woman, as well as her innate sense of style." SLJ

Chaplin, Charlie, 1889-1977

Fleischman, Sid. Sir Charlie; Chaplin, the funniest man in the world. Greenwillow Books 2010 268p il $19.99; lib bdg $20.89 *

Grades: 5 6 7 8 9   92

1. Comedians 2. Motion pictures 3. Actors

ISBN   978-0-06-189640-8;   0-06-189640-3; 978-0-06-189641-5 (lib bdg); 0-06-189641-1 (lib bdg)

LC 2009019689

"This lively and engaging account of a poor Cockney boy who became the world's greatest silent-movie comedian is a must for biography collections. . . . Brief, easily digestible chapters, an extensive time line, and plenty of photos make the book's well-researched content accessible and appealing." SLJ

Chapman, Oscar L., 1896-1978

Hopkinson, Deborah. Sweet land of liberty; written by Deborah Hopkinson; illustrated by Leonard Jenkins. Peachtree 2007 unp il $16.95 *
Grades: K 1 2 3 4   92
1. Anderson, Marian, 1897-1993 2. United States—Race relations 3. African Americans—Civil rights 4. African Americans—Biography
ISBN 1-56145-395-1; 978-1-56145-395-5
LC 2006024331

"As Assistant Secretary of the Interior under President Franklin D. Roosevelt, Oscar Chapman played a vital role in securing Marian Anderson's use of the Lincoln Memorial as a venue for her free concert in 1939. Hopkinson ties incidents from Chapman's childhood to his efforts on Anderson's behalf. . . . The event was a blazing success and remains a touchstone of the Civil Rights Movement." Booklist

"Jenkins' powerful, bright, mixed-media collages show and tell the connections, past, present, and future." SLJ

Chavez, Cesar, 1927-1993

Krull, Kathleen. Harvesting hope; the story of Cesar Chavez; illustrated by Yuyi Morales. Harcourt 2003 unp il $17 *
Grades: 2 3 4   92
1. Mexican Americans—Biography 2. Migrant labor
ISBN 0-15-201437-3   LC 2002-5096

A biography of Cesar Chavez, from age ten when he and his family lived happily on their Arizona ranch, to age thirty-eight when he led a peaceful protest against California migrant workers' miserable working conditions

"The brief text creates a remarkably complex view of Chavez—his experiences and feelings. Krull's empathetic words are well paired with artist Yuyi Morales's mixed-media acrylic paintings, which are suffused with a variety of emotions. . . . The pictures glow with intense shades of gold, green, pink, and orange." Horn Book

Wadsworth, Ginger. Cesar Chavez; by Ginger Wadsworth; illustrations by Mark Schroder. Carolrhoda Books 2005 48p il (On my own biography) lib bdg $23.93; pa $5.95
Grades: 2 3 4   92
1. Mexican Americans—Biography 2. Migrant labor
ISBN 1-57505-652-6 (lib bdg); 1-57505-826-X (pa)
LC 2004-6571

Contents: Arizona; Hard times; Growing up; Action!; After the strike

This "picture book combines the history of the migrant farm workers' struggle with Chavez's personal story. The clear, direct text tells how Chavez . . . grew up to organize the first farm workers union with Dolores Huerta, and led a successful, five-year grape boycott in the 1960s. . . . Schroder's realistic color, often full-page illustrations show Chavez with his people, working in the fields and on the march. . . . A good way to introduce children to the hero and to the issues." Booklist

Clemente, Roberto, 1934-1972

Perdomo, Willie. Clemente! illustrated by Bryan Collier. Henry Holt & Co. 2010 unp il $16.99
Grades: 1 2 3   92
1. Baseball—Biography
ISBN 978-0-8050-8224-1; 0-8050-8224-7

"Perdomo's witty, passionate account of the beloved Puerto Rican baseball pioneer takes an unusual approach. The child narrator, whose father is president of the Roberto Clemente fan club, was named in honor of the great player, and little Clemente can tell you just about everything there is to know about the man. . . . Collier's kinetic artwork uses collage to explosive effect. . . . More than just a biography, this book warmly illustrates the parent-child bond that is one of the finer by-products of sports fandom." Booklist

Winter, Jonah. Roberto Clemente; pride of the Pittsburgh Pirates; illustrated by Raul Colón. Atheneum Books for Young Readers 2005 unp il $16.95 *
Grades: 2 3 4   92
1. Baseball—Biography 2. Puerto Ricans—Biography
ISBN 0-689-85643-1   LC 2003-25546

"An Anne Schwartz book"

"Winter tells the . . . story of how Clemente's passionate love of the game and unrivaled work ethic took him from poverty in Puerto Rico . . . to World Series triumph with the Pittsburgh Pirates and, later . . . to near-mythic status as a role model for young Latino ballplayers. Soaked in pastoral greens and browns, Colón's evocatively grainy, soft-focus illustrations, rendered with a mix of watercolors, colored pencils, and litho pencils, capture perfectly the worlds in which Clemente was most at home. . . . Baseball history brought vividly to life for a younger audience." Booklist

Cleopatra, Queen of Egypt, d. 30 B.C.

Blackaby, Susan. Cleopatra; Egypt's last and greatest queen. Sterling Pub. 2009 124p il (Sterling biographies) $12.95; pa $5.95
Grades: 5 6 7 8   92
1. Egypt—History 2. Queens
ISBN 978-1-4027-6540-7; 1-4027-6540-1; 978-1-4027-5710-5 (pa); 1-4027-5710-7 (pa)
LC 2008030146

"Villainess or goddess, a great queen or a selfish and overly ambitious woman—readers get to decide. They will be drawn into this biography by a description of a legendary magnificent banquet given by Mark Antony for Cleopatra. The lively narrative maintains interest from her birth in 69 BCE to her death in 31 BCE. . . . Sidebars, color photographs, and reproductions appear throughout. . . . This book leaves readers fascinated and eager to learn more about her time in history." SLJ

Includes glossary and bibliographical references

Stanley, Diane. Cleopatra; [by] Diane Stanley, Peter Vennema; illustrated by Diane Stanley. Morrow Junior Bks. 1994 unp il map hardcover o.p. pa $7.99 *
Grades: 4 5 6 7   92
1. Egypt—History 2. Queens
ISBN 0-688-10413-4; 0-688-10414-2 (lib bdg); 0-688-15480-8 (pa)   LC 93-27032

Cleopatra, Queen of Egypt, d. 30 B.C.—*Continued*

This is a biography of the ancient Egyptian queen

"Lucid writing combines with carefully selected anecdotes, often attributed to the Greek historian Plutarch to create an engaging narrative. . . . Stanley's stunning, full-color gouache artwork is arresting in its large, well-composed images executed in flat Greek style." SLJ

Includes bibliographical references

Cogswell, Alice

McCully, Emily Arnold. My heart glow: Alice Cogswell, Thomas Gallaudet and the birth of American sign language. See entry under Gallaudet, T. H. (Thomas Hopkins), 1787-1851

Coleman, Bessie, 1896?-1926

Grimes, Nikki. Talkin' about Bessie: the story of aviator Elizabeth Coleman; illustrated by E. B. Lewis. Orchard Bks. 2002 unp il $16.95 *
Grades: 3 4 5   92
1. Women air pilots 2. African American pilots
ISBN 0-439-35243-6
Coretta Scott King Award for illustration, 2003
"Following a brief introduction to Coleman's life, the story, couched in a fictional framework, opens in the parlor of a house in Chicago, where friends and relatives gather to mourn Bessie's death. Each spread features one person speaking about Bessie. . . . Lewis' paintings, subdued in tone and color, reflect the spirit of the verse through telling details and sensitive, impressionistic portrayals." Booklist

Includes bibliographical references

Coltrane, John, 1926-1967

Weatherford, Carole Boston. Before John was a jazz giant: a song of John Coltrane; [illustrated by] Sean Qualls. Henry Holt & Co. 2008 unp il $16.95
Grades: K 1 2 3   92
1. Jazz musicians 2. African American musicians
ISBN 978-0-8050-7994-4; 0-8050-7994-7
LC 2007-07196
Coretta Scott King honor book for illustration, 2009
"The beat of lyrical words and the rhythm of the beautiful illustrations express how, as a child, jazz-musician Coltrane heard music in the world around him. Vibrant with color and movement, double-page spreads in acrylic, collage, and pencil extend the images about the magical sounds of everyday things." Booklist

Columbus, Christopher

Collier, James Lincoln. Christopher Columbus; to the New World; [by] James Lincoln Collier. Marshall Cavendish Benchmark 2006 80p il map (Great explorations) lib bdg $32.79
Grades: 5 6 7 8   92
1. Explorers 2. America—Exploration
ISBN 978-0-7614-2221-1 (lib bdg); 0-7614-2221-8 (lib bdg)
An account of the life and times of the explorer credited with the European discovery of America
Includes bibliographical references

Fritz, Jean. Where do you think you're going, Christopher Columbus? pictures by Margot Tomes. Putnam 1980 80p il maps $15.99; pa $5.99
Grades: 2 3 4   92
1. Explorers 2. America—Exploration
ISBN 0-399-20723-6; 0-698-11580-5 (pa)
LC 80-11377
Discusses the voyages of Christopher Columbus who was determined to beat everyone in the race to the Indies

"Reducing a life as well-documented as Columbus's to 80 pages must result in some simplifications of fact or context, but in this case they are not readily apparent. Mrs. Fritz's breezy narrative gives us a highly individual Columbus. . . . Margot Tomes's three-color illustrations are attractive, amusing and informative." N Y Times Book Rev

Confucius

Freedman, Russell. Confucius; the golden rule; illustrated by Frédéric Clément. Levine Bks. 2002 48p il $17.99 *
Grades: 4 5 6 7   92
1. Philosophers
ISBN 0-439-13957-0   LC 2001-29372
This is a "biography of the 5th-century B.C. philosopher Confucius, whose teachings have influenced the development of modern government and education in both China and the West." Publ Wkly

"The fascinating narrative seamlessly intersperses stories from the *Analects* with Chinese history and biographical information about Confucius. . . . Clement's muted, elegant paintings of towns, temples, and the bucktoothed Confucius himself have a suitably ancient feel with jagged borders and fading colors." Booklist

Copernicus, Nicolaus, 1473-1543

Andronik, Catherine M. Copernicus; founder of modern astronomy. rev ed. Enslow Publishers 2009 128p bibl il (Great minds of science) lib bdg $31.93
Grades: 5 6 7 8   92
1. Astronomers
ISBN 978-0-7660-3013-8 (lib bdg); 0-7660-3013-X (lib bdg)   LC 2008-23940
First published 2002
"A highly readable book that presents a good balance between the biographical information needed to understand Copernicus as a man and the scientific explanations necessary to understand his work. . . . Good-quality, black-and-white reproductions, illustrations, and photo-

Copernicus, Nicolaus, 1473-1543—*Continued*
graphs add interest to the clearly written text." SLJ [review of 2002 edition]
Includes glossary and bibliographical references

Fradin, Dennis B. Nicolaus Copernicus; the earth is a planet; by Dennis Brindell Fradin; illustrated by Cynthia von Buhler. Mondo 2003 32p il $15.95 *
Grades: 3 4 5 6   92
   1. Astronomers
   ISBN 1-59336-006-1   LC 2003-56147
A biography of astronomer Nicolaus Copernicus, who challenged the belief of his age that Earth was the center of the universe and proved that it is, instead, a planet orbiting the Sun.
"The text is beautifully supported by dramatic oil-on-gesso artwork. . . . Von Buhler's style suggests the muted colors and two-dimensional quality of late-medieval illustration. . . . This is a useful and accessible introduction to Copernicus's life and works." SLJ

Corwin, Jeff
Corwin, Jeff. Jeff Corwin: a wild life; the authorized biography. Penguin Group 2009 100p il pa $6.99
Grades: 4 5 6 7   92
   1. Biologists
   ISBN 978-0-14-241403-3 (pa); 0-14-241403-4 (pa)
                 LC 2009008092
"The host of *Animal Planet* . . . and other popular TV programs blends his exciting adventure in the wild with his passionate call for conservation. . . . An insert of beautifully reproduced color photos from his global travels show him with a giraffe in Kenya, a moose in Alaska, and more. . . . The adventures are thrilling, and the messages are urgent." Booklist

Coup, W. C., 1857-1895
Covert, Ralph. Sawdust and spangles: the amazing life of W.C. Coup; [by] Ralph Covert, G. Riley Mills; illustrated by Giselle Potter. Abrams Books for Young Readers 2007 unp il $16.95
Grades: K 1 2 3   92
   1. Circus
   ISBN 978-0-8109-9351-8; 0-8109-9351-1
                 LC 2006031981
"As a boy, William Cameron Coup left home to run away with the circus. . . . He eventually became one of the industry's most successful and inventive entrepeneurs. This picture book biography relates Coup's story in an accessible . . . way. Potter's illustrations are beautifully rendered, interpreting Coup's life and world with quirky energy and imaginative color." Horn Book Guide

Cousteau, Jacques Yves, 1910-1997
Berne, Jennifer. Manfish: a story of Jacques Cousteau; illustrated by Eric Puybaret. Chronicle Books 2008 unp il $16.99 *
Grades: K 1 2 3   92
   1. Ocean 2. Skin diving 3. Scientists
   ISBN 978-0-8118-6063-5; 0-8118-6063-9
                 LC 2007-30513

"Writing in simple poetic language, both lyrical and concise . . . Berne offers a luminous picture-book biography of about Jacques Cousteau. . . . Puybaret's smooth-looking acrylic paintings extend the words' elegant simplicity and beautifully convey the sense of infinite, underwater space." Booklist

Yaccarino, Dan. The fantastic undersea life of Jacques Cousteau. Knopf 2009 unp il $16.99; lib bdg $19.99 *
Grades: K 1 2 3   92
   1. Ocean 2. Skin diving 3. Scientists
   ISBN 978-0-375-85573-3; 978-0-375-95573-0 (lib bdg)   LC 2008-04581
"Yaccarino deftly provides information about important events in Cousteau's life while conveying the excitement and wonder that the ocean explorer experienced. . . . Effective layout and page design plus colorful gouache illustrations result in a striking visual presentation." SLJ

Coville, Bruce
Parker-Rock, Michelle. Bruce Coville; by Michelle Parker-Rock. Enslow Publishers 2008 48p bibl il por (Authors kids love) lib bdg $23.93
Grades: 3 4 5   92
   1. Authors, American
   ISBN 978-0-7660-2755-8 (lib bdg); 0-7660-2755-4 (lib bdg)   LC 2006015873
A biography of the popular children's author, Bruce Coville, based on a interview.
The text is "interesting and conversational throughout. . . . [A] colorful [cover], family photos, and a font size that's not too intimidating all contribute to the [book's] appeal. . . . Suitable for reports or for pleasure reading." SLJ
Includes glossary and bibliographical references

Crandall, Prudence, 1803-1890
Jurmain, Suzanne. The forbidden schoolhouse; the true and dramatic story of Prudence Crandall and her students. Houghton Mifflin 2005 150p il $18 *
Grades: 5 6 7 8   92
   1. African Americans—Education 2. Educators 3. Abolitionists
   ISBN 0-618-47302-5
This is the story of Prudence Crandall, who, in 1831, opened a school for African American girls in Canterbury, Connecticut.
"A compelling, highly readable book. . . . Writing with a sense of drama that propels readers forward . . . Jurmain makes painfully clear what Crandall and her students faced. . . . Including a number of sepia-toned and color photographs as well as historical engravings, the book's look will draw in readers." Booklist
Includes bibliographical references

Crazy Horse, Sioux Chief, ca. 1842-1877

Brimner, Larry Dane. Chief Crazy Horse; following a vision. Marshall Cavendish Benchmark 2009 41p il (American heroes) lib bdg $20.95
Grades: 2 3 4   **92**
1. Native Americans—Biography
ISBN 978-0-7614-3061-2   LC 2008002868
A biography of Crazy Horse, warrior chief of the Oglala tribe of the Sioux nation
This "concise and well-written [title covers] key biographical facts without overwhelming young readers, and [includes] captioned illustrations and reproductions, most of which are in color. Text is large, and the layout is age-appropriate and attractive, with wide margins." SLJ
Includes glossary and bibliographical references

Freedman, Russell. The life and death of Crazy Horse; drawings by Amos Bad Heart Bull. Holiday House 1996 166p il maps $22.95 *
Grades: 5 6 7 8 9 10   **92**
1. Oglala Indians
ISBN 0-8234-1219-9   LC 95-33303
A biography of the Oglala Indian leader who relentlessly resisted the white man's attempt to take over Indian lands
This is "a compelling biography that is based on primary source documents and illustrated with pictographs by a Sioux band historian." Voice Youth Advocates
Includes bibliographical references

Crews, Donald

Crews, Donald. Bigmama's. Greenwillow Bks. 1991 unp il $16; lib bdg $15.93; pa $5.95 *
Grades: K 1 2 3   **92**
1. Authors, American 2. African Americans—Biography 3. Country life
ISBN 0-688-09950-5; 0-688-09951-3 (lib bdg); 0-688-15842-0 (pa)   LC 90-33142
Visiting Bigmama's house in the country, young Donald Crews finds his relatives full of news and the old place and its surroundings just the same as the year before
"This is an evocative celebration of the joy and wonder of childhood; would that every child had such a summer. The last page is a hauntingly lovely remembrance. The illustrations are perfect and make this a truly beautiful book." Child Book Rev Serv

Crum, George, fl. 1853

Taylor, Gaylia. George Crum and the Saratoga chip; illustrated by Frank Morrison. Lee & Low Books 2006 32p il $16.95
Grades: 2 3 4   **92**
1. Cooking 2. Racially mixed people 3. United States—Race relations
ISBN 978-1-58430-255-1; 1-58430-255-0
                                LC 2005015313
"Part Native American, part African American, George Crum coped with prejudice as a boy in New York State during the 1830s. As a young man, he became an excellent cook and was hired as a chef at a renowned restaurant in Saratoga Springs. . . . Once . . . Crum retrieved [a] dish of French fries, whittled them into very thin slices, and cooked them in hot oil, creating the forerunner of the potato chip. . . . This picture-book biography describes dramatic moments that reveal Crum's creativity, artistic temperament, and relentless pursuit of perfection. Buoyant acrylic illustrations accentuate the absurdity of situations, depicting the jaunty chef, all angles and energy." Booklist
Includes bibliographical references

Cruz, Celia, 1929-2003

Chambers, Veronica. Celia Cruz, Queen of salsa; illustrated by Julie Maren. Dial Books for Young Readers 2005 unp il $15.99
Grades: 2 3 4   **92**
1. Singers 2. Cuban Americans
ISBN 0-8037-2970-7   LC 2004-18960
"In this picture-book biography, Chambers offers a . . . tribute to salsa superstar Celia Cruz. Short paragraphs follow the vocalist from her Havana childhood . . . to her . . . emigration from Cuba and worldwide stardom. . . . Chambers' enthusiasm for her subject is contagious, and the bright, uncluttered paintings of rounded, stylized figures in saturated, tropical hues echo the energy in the words." Booklist

Curie, Marie, 1867-1934

Cregan, Elizabeth R. Marie Curie; pioneering physicist. Compass Point Books 2009 40p il map (Mission: Science) lib bdg $26.60
Grades: 4 5 6   **92**
1. Chemists 2. Women scientists
ISBN 978-0-7565-3960-3
This biography of the discoverer of radium "does a good job of connecting the scientist's work to our lives today. . . . [The] book has a variety of graphics including diagrams, photos, and reproductions of paintings and sketches. [This volume is] a definite plus for a school library or the juvenile collection in a public library." Libr Media Connect

Krull, Kathleen. Marie Curie; [illustrations by] Boris Kulikov. Viking 2007 128p il (Giants of science) $15.99 *
Grades: 5 6 7 8   **92**
1. Chemists 2. Women scientists
ISBN 978-0-670-05894-5; 0-670-05894-7
                                LC 2007-24251
A biography of "Marie Curie, the woman who coined the term radioactivity, [and who] won not just one Nobel prize but two—in physics and in chemistry." Publisher's note
"The compelling and conversational narrative (ably assisted by Kulikov's black-and-white drawings) portrays a brilliant . . . woman with plenty of idiosyncrasies, and the story of her discovery of radium . . . is as engaging as any of her personal dramas and challenges." Horn Book

McClafferty, Carla Killough. Something out of nothing; Marie Curie and radium. Farrar, Straus & Giroux 2006 134p il $18
Grades: 5 6 7 8 9 10   **92**
1. Chemists 2. Women scientists
ISBN 0-374-38036-8   LC 2004-56414

Curie, Marie, 1867-1934—*Continued*

This "biography examines Curie's life and work as a groundbreaking scientist and as an independent woman. . . . The groundbreaking science is as thrilling as the personal story. . . . The spacious design makes the text easy to read, and occasional photos . . . bring the story closer." Booklist

Steele, Philip. Marie Curie; the woman who changed the course of science. National Geographic 2006 64p il map (World history biographies) $17.95 *
Grades: 4 5 6 7   92
1. Chemists 2. Women scientists
ISBN 0-7922-5387-6
A biography of the French chemist famous for the discovery of radium
This "book is written in a clear, readable style. . . . It will be an excellent and accessible resource for libraries." Voice Youth Advocates
Includes glossary and bibliographical references

Curtis, Christopher Paul

Parker-Rock, Michelle. Christopher Paul Curtis; an author kids love. Enslow Publishers 2009 48p il (Authors kids love) lib bdg $23.93
Grades: 1 2 3   92
1. Authors, American 2. African American authors
ISBN 978-0-7660-3161-6 (lib bdg); 0-7660-3161-6 (lib bdg)   LC 2009022379
A biography of the author of the Newbery honor book *The Watsons Go to Birmingham—1963* and the Newbery winner *Bud, not Buddy*
Includes glossary and bibliographical references

Custer, George Armstrong, 1839-1876

Anderson, Paul Christopher. George Armstrong Custer; the Indian Wars and the Battle of the Little Bighorn; [by] Paul Christopher Anderson. PowerPlus Books 2004 112p il (Library of American lives and times) lib bdg $31.95
Grades: 4 5 6 7   92
1. Little Bighorn, Battle of the, 1876 2. Native Americans—Wars 3. Generals
ISBN 0-8239-6631-3   LC 2002-153404
Contents: Remembering Custer; The boy from New Rumley; School and skins; Autie Custer's first war; Wolverine in blue; A warrior without a war; Frustrated frontiersman; A life on the Plains; To the Little Bighorn and beyond; Heroes and history
A biography of the Civil War general who died at the Battle of the Little Bighorn
This "is not an apologia but a carefully measured analysis. . . . Stunning reproductions and photos provide a clear sense of the times and settings." SLJ
Includes bibliographical references

Dahl, Roald

Dahl, Roald. More about Boy; Roald Dahl's tales from childhood. Farrar, Straus, and Giroux 2009 c2008 229p il $16.99
Grades: 5 6 7 8   92
1. Authors, English
ISBN 978-0-374-35055-0; 0-374-35055-8
LC 2009016118
First published 2008 in the United Kingdom
"Containing the entire text and artwork from Dahl's 1984 autobiography Boy, this reworked and expanded version also incorporates previously unpublished materials from the Roald Dahl Museum and Story Centre in England, as well as excerpts that have appeared in earlier books. . . . Dahl's revealing writing, open and full of wicked humor, is certain to endear the beloved writer . . . to a new generation." Publ Wkly

Dalai Lama XIV, 1935-

Demi. The Dalai Lama; a biography of the Tibetan spiritual and political leader. Henry Holt & Co. 1998 unp il $18.95 *
Grades: 4 5 6 7   92
1. Buddhism 2. Tibet (China)
ISBN 0-8050-5443-X   LC 97-30654
In this biography of the Buddhist spiritual leader, Demi "uses straightforward prose and fluid, eastern-influenced art—small pen-and-ink and watercolor images with fine, intricate detail. . . . Told with respect and devotion, this is an inspirational picture-book biography." Horn Book

Kimmel, Elizabeth Cody. Boy on the lion throne; the childhood of the 14th Dalai Lama; with a foreword by His Holiness the Dalai Lama. Roaring Brook Press 2009 146p il map $18.95
Grades: 4 5 6 7   92
1. Buddhism 2. Tibet (China)
ISBN 978-1-59643-394-6; 1-59643-394-9
Follows the childhood of Lhamo Thondup, who was identified at the age of two as the fourteenth reincarnation of the Dalai Lama, describing the humble life he was born into and how his life changed after he was recognized
"Kimmel is reverent without being adulatory, and her explanation of the Dalai Lama's relationship with Maoist China is presented in simple, clear language. This is a strange and fascinating story told in an engaging style, and young readers will find lots to keep them turning the pages." Bull Cent Child Books
Includes bibliographical references

Danziger, Paula, 1944-2004

Reed, Jennifer. Paula Danziger; voice of teen troubles; [by] Jennifer Bond Reed. Enslow Publishers 2006 104p bibl il por (Authors teens love) lib bdg $31.93
Grades: 5 6 7 8   92
1. Women authors 2. Authors, American
ISBN 0-7660-2444-X   LC 2005030332
A biography of the author of *The Cat Ate My Gymsuit* and other books for young people.

Danziger, Paula, 1944-2004—*Continued*

Danziger's "many fans will be fascinated to learn how much of her lively, funny fiction draws on her own troubled childhood in a dysfunctional home." Booklist

Includes bibliographical references

Darwin, Charles, 1809-1882

Ashby, Ruth. Young Charles Darwin and the voyage of the Beagle; written by Ruth Ashby. Peachtree 2009 116p il map $12.95

Grades: 4 5 6   92

    1. Beagle Expedition (1831-1836) 2. Naturalists 3. Evolution

ISBN 978-1-56145-478-5; 1-56145-478-8

                    LC 2008-36747

"Beginning with the letter inviting him to sail aboard the Beagle, this traditional biography relates Darwin's life with an emphasis on the trip that led him to forge his theory about natural selection. Ashby makes good use of Darwin's own writing, sprinkling quotes throughout the text, which allow his adventures and opinions to come to life. . . . This biography will work well for book reports . . . providing accurate and readable information about the scientist and his journey." Booklist

Includes bibliographical references

Lasky, Kathryn. One beetle too many: the extraordinary adventures of Charles Darwin. Candlewick Press 2009 unp il $17.99 *

Grades: 3 4 5 6   92

    1. Beagle Expedition (1831-1836) 2. Naturalists 3. Evolution

ISBN 0-7636-1436-X; 978-0-7636-1436-2

                    LC 2002-71254

Describes the life and work of the renowned nineteenth-century biologist who transformed conventional Western thought with his theory of natural evolution.

"Distilling tough concepts into light, conversational prose, Lasky . . . gives middle-graders a just-right introduction to Charles Darwin. . . . Trueman . . . up-ends perspective with multilayed mixed-media illustrations; mostly paint, these also incorporate bits of flowers and weeds as well as string, paper, and fabric. . . . Highly accessible." Publ Wkly

Markle, Sandra. Animals Charles Darwin saw; an around-the-world adventure; illustrated by Zina Saunders. Chronicle Books 2009 45p il $16.99

Grades: 2 3 4 5   92

    1. Beagle Expedition (1831-1836) 2. Naturalists 3. Evolution 4. Animals

ISBN 978-0-8118-5049-0; 0-8118-5049-8

                    LC 2007-53058

Looks at the animals that Charles Darwin saw throughout his life, from his early explorations in local woods and fields to his travels on the HMS Beagle, and how they influenced his later thought.

"Sandra Markle tells Darwin's story in clear prose spiced with interesting vignettes, . . . and Zina Saunders brings the scenes alive with colorful woodcut illustrations." NY Times Book Rev

McGinty, Alice B. Darwin; illustrated by Mary Azarian. Houghton Mifflin Books for Children 2009 unp il $18 *

Grades: 1 2 3 4   92

    1. Beagle Expedition (1831-1836) 2. Naturalists 3. Evolution

ISBN 978-0-618-99531-8; 0-618-99531-5

                    LC 2008-33930

"After tracing Charles Darwin's youth and education, this fully illustrated biography focuses on his five-year voyage about the HMS *Beagle*. . . . Azarian . . . illustrates the book using handsome woodcut prints painted with watercolors. . . . The interplay of the clearly written third-person text with Darwin's own words and occasional quotes from his contemporaries creates a multifaceted view that leads to a broader understanding." Booklist

Schanzer, Rosalyn. What Darwin saw; the journey that changed the world. National Geographic 2009 47p il map $17.95; lib bdg $26.90 *

Grades: 3 4 5 6   92

    1. Beagle Expedition (1831-1836) 2. Naturalists 3. Evolution

ISBN   978-1-4263-0396-8;   1-4263-0396-3; 978-1-4263-0397-5 (lib bdg); 1-4263-0397-1 (lib bdg)

                    LC 2008-39809

"Schanzer uses Darwin's own words, taken from his journals, books, and letters, in the speech balloons of her graphic depiction of the voyage of the Beagle. This is not a full biography, but begins with Darwin's acceptance of the offer to sail on the expedition and ends with the presentation of his theory of evolution in 1860. Bright, watercolor cartoons accurately portray landscapes and specimens while also creating a vivid sense of adventure." SLJ

Includes bibligraphical references

Sís, Peter. The tree of life: a book depicting the life of Charles Darwin, naturalist, geologist & thinker. Frances Foster Bks./Farrar, Straus & Giroux 2003 unp il map $18 *

Grades: 4 5 6 7   92

    1. Naturalists

ISBN 0-374-45628-3   LC 2002-40706

Presents the life of the famous nineteenth-century naturalist using text from Darwin's writings and detailed drawings by Sís

"Muted tones of blue, green, and tan, and finely hatched drawings in the manner of old prints lend a period look to the pages. Beautifully conceived and executed, the presentation is a humorous and informative tour de force that will absorb and challenge readers." SLJ

David-Neel, Alexandra, 1868-1969

Brown, Don. Far beyond the garden gate: Alexandra David-Neel's journey to Lhasa. Houghton Mifflin 2002 unp il $16 *

Grades: 3 4 5   92

    1. Tibet (China) 2. Travelers 3. Buddhism

ISBN 0-618-08364-2   LC 2002-222

David-Neel, Alexandra, 1868-1969—*Continued*

Describes the life and travels of Alexandra David-Neel, who became a scholar of Buddhism and Tibet in the early twentieth century and trekked thousands of miles to reach Llasa, the Tibetan capital.

This "tells a fascinating tale. . . . David-Neel's vivid quotes are interspersed throughout the story. . . . The beiges, grays, and whites of Brown's palette capture the feeling of the unfamiliar world into which the woman and her companion ventured." SLJ

Includes bibliographical references

De Paola, Tomie, 1934-

De Paola, Tomie. 26 Fairmount Avenue; written and illustrated by Tomie dePaola. Putnam 1999 56p il $14.99; pa $6.99 *

Grades: 2 3 4   92

1. Authors, American 2. Illustrators

ISBN 0-399-23246-X; 0-698-11864-2 (pa)

LC 98-12918

A Newbery Medal honor book, 2000

Children's author-illustrator Tomie De Paola describes his experiences at home and in school when he was a boy

"A disarmingly unselfconscious reminiscence. . . . The immediacy of detail resists nostalgia, and dePaola is wise to what recent graduates of his picture books will find interesting. Neat sketches and silhouettes will draw browsers in to this satisfying easy chapter book." Horn Book Guide

Followed by Here we all are

De Paola, Tomie. Christmas remembered; [by] Tomie dePaola. G. P. Putnam's Sons 2006 86p il $19.99; pa $9.99

Grades: 5 6 7 8   92

1. Christmas 2. Authors, American 3. Illustrators

ISBN 0-399-24622-3; 0-14-241481-6 (pa)

LC 2005032658

The children's author and artist shares his love of Christmas in 15 memories, which span six decades

"Brightening the pages are illustrations in varied styles and media, from an intriguing portrait of dePaola's Italian grandmother to decorative paper collages to iconic paintings of great stillness and beauty. . . . Written with dialogue and humor as well as reflection." Booklist

De Paola, Tomie. For the duration; a 26 Fairmount Avenue book; the war years; written and illustrated by Tomie dePaola. Putnam's Sons 2009 99p il $15.99

Grades: 2 3 4   92

1. Authors, American 2. Illustrators 3. World War, 1939-1945

ISBN 978-0-399-25209-9; 0-399-25209-6

From gas rationing to air-raid drills, as long as the war lasts, life is going to be different for Tomie. And sometimes different is hard. Fortunately, Tomie still has school, his family, and the things he's good at to carry him through.

"DePaola's style and word choices are just right for his audience, and the point of view is consistently that of a second grader. Full-page and spot art black-and-white pencil drawings and silhouette art by the author illustrate this must-read title for fans of the series." SLJ

De Paola, Tomie. Here we all are; a 26 Fairmount Avenue book; written and illustrated by Tomie dePaola. Putnam 2000 26p il $13.99; pa $5.99

Grades: 2 3 4   92

1. Authors, American 2. Illustrators

ISBN 0-399-23496-9; 0-698-11909-6 (pa)

LC 99-46747

"Continuing the memoir begun in dePaola's Newbery Honor Book 26 *Fairmount Avenue* (1999), this short chapter book shows young Tomie as he takes tap dancing lessons, finds his way in kindergarten, and waits a seemingly interminable 10 days for his mother and new baby sister to come home from the hospital. . . . Another satisfying book in a warm episodic family story that makes writing autobiography look easy." Booklist

Followed by On my way

De Paola, Tomie. I'm still scared; a 26 Fairmount Avenue book, book 6; written and illustrated by Tomie dePaola. G. P. Putnam's Sons 2006 83p il $13.99; pa $5.99

Grades: 2 3 4   92

1. Authors, American 2. Illustrators 3. World War, 1939-1945—United States

ISBN 0-399-24502-2; 0-14-240826-3 (pa)

LC 2005-13500

"DePaola picks up his autobiographical series right where his last title, *Things Will Never Be the Same* (2003), left off: December, 7, 1941. Now in second grade, little Tomie describes the reactions to the Pearl Harbor bombings, first at home, then at church, and finally at school. . . . Once again, the warm, childlike narration captures both the specifics of the time and universal experiences that will connect with most children. The shaded, black-and-white sketches on each page extend the story's small, revealing moments." Booklist

Followed by Why?

De Paola, Tomie. On my way; a 26 Fairmount Avenue book; written and illustrated by Tomie dePaola. Putnam 2001 73p il $13.99; pa $6.99

Grades: 2 3 4   92

1. Authors, American 2. Illustrators

ISBN 0-399-23583-3; 0-698-11948-7 (pa)

LC 00-38229

"The saga of dePaola's early life related in 26 *Fairmount Avenue* . . . and *Here We All Are* . . . continues with this reminiscence of kindergarten and first grade. dePaola describes his baby sister Maureen's recovery from pneumonia, a family trip to the 1939 World's Fair, and his theatrical debut as the blushing bride in a 'Tiny Tot Bridal Party.' . . . The humor is clear and the selection of incidents indicates the author has a comfortable familiarity with the concerns of his audience." Bull Cent Child Books

Followed by What a year!

De Paola, Tomie. Things will never be the same; a 26 Fairmount Avenue book; written and illustrated by Tomie dePaola. Putnam 2003 69p il $13.99; pa $5.99

Grades: 2 3 4   92

1. Authors, American 2. Illustrators

ISBN 0-399-23982-0; 0-14-240155-2 (pa)

LC 2002-5995

De Paola, Tomie, 1934-—*Continued*

This fifth volume in DePaola's autobiographical 24 Fairmount Avenue series "takes the budding artist into his seventh year. . . . [This] re-creates the joys of sledding, the dangers of polio, and the glories of the Ferris wheel." Horn Book Guide

"Livening nearly every page with vignettes or larger drawings, the author again draws children into a vanished, but somehow universal, world with his youthful narration, convincingly childlike sensibility, and irrepressible spirit." Booklist

Followed by I'm still scared

De Paola, Tomie. What a year! a 26 Fairmount Avenue book; written and illustrated by Tomie dePaola. Putnam 2002 72p il $13.99; pa $5.99

Grades: 2 3 4   **92**
1. Authors, American 2. Illustrators
ISBN 0-399-23797-6; 0-14-250158-1 (pa)
LC 2001-19921

"The fourth volume in dePaola's autobiographical 24 Fairmont Avenue series opens with the beginning of first grade in September 1940 and ends on New Year's Eve. DePaola appears to remember his childhood in vivid detail. . . . Small silhouette drawings and paintings brighten nearly every page. Young readers will gain a sense of period and feel empathy with young Tomie in this appealing episodic chapter book." Booklist

Followed by Things will never be the same

De Paola, Tomie. Why? a 26 Fairmount Avenue book; written and illustrated by Tomie dePaola. G. P. Putnam's Sons 2007 85p il $14.99

Grades: 2 3 4   **92**
1. Authors, American 2. Illustrators
ISBN 978-0-399-24692-0   LC 2006011911

"This seventh installment in dePaola's autobiography covers New Year's Day through April 20, 1942. . . . Tomie overhears talk of rationing and hoarding, peeks out from behind blackout curtains, and notes that, due to the war, Fleer bubblegum will no longer be available. As ever, the author fills the story with authentically childlike details. . . . The black-and-white full-page and spot pictures convey emotions effectively." SLJ

Followed by For the duration

Degas, Edgar, 1834-1917

Cocca-Leffler, Maryann. Edgar Degas: paintings that dance; written and illustrated by Maryann Cocca-Leffler. Grosset & Dunlap 2001 unp il (Smart about art) hardcover o.p. pa $5.99

Grades: 2 3 4   **92**
1. Artists, French
ISBN 0-448-42520-3; 0-448-42520-3 (pa)
LC 2001-23149

Written in the format of a school report by a fictitious student named Kristin Cole, this recounts events in the life of the French artist Degas and offers insight into his work

Illustrated with "charming childlike drawings and reproductions of the artist's paintings in scrapbook-style layouts. . . . [This] is a successful blend of fact and humor that makes sophisticated concepts completely accessible and even entertaining." Booklist

Rubin, Susan Goldman. Degas and the dance; the painter and the petits rats, perfecting their art. Abrams 2002 31p il $17.95

Grades: 3 4 5 6   **92**
1. Artists, French 2. Ballet
ISBN 0-8109-0567-1   LC 2001-6580

"Degas depicted the young girls of the Paris Opéra corps over and over again in painting and sculpture from 1855 to 1905. This book traces that artistic involvement, discussing the hard life of the 'little rats' of the ballet and Degas' interest in various aspects of that life; it also addresses Degas' technique . . . and changing approach as his sight dimmed. . . . The art history is skillfully blended with the ballet interest . . . and Rubin's fluid text provides a measured and elegant entree to both." Bull Cent Child Books

Includes bibliographical references

Délano, Poli, 1936-

Délano, Poli. When I was a boy Neruda called me Policarpo; illustrated by Manuel Monroy. Groundwood Books/House of Anansi Press 2006 84p il $15.95 *

Grades: 5 6 7 8   **92**
1. Neruda, Pablo, 1904-1973 2. Poets, Chilean 3. Mexico
ISBN 0-88899-726-4

"Based on the author's childhood remembrances of when he and his diplomat parents lived with Tío Pablo [Neruda] in Mexico, these seven chapters reveal both the genius and the eccentricities of the Nobel Prize-winning Chilean poet. . . . The chapters are short, well written, and filled with interesting details that will open up a new and exotic world. . . . Monroy's pen-and-sepia-toned drawings are . . . at times humorous, at times dramatic, but always enticing." SLJ

Dickens, Charles, 1812-1870

Rosen, Michael. Dickens; his work and his world; illustrated by Robert Ingpen. Candlewick Press 2005 95p il $19.99

Grades: 5 6 7 8   **92**
1. Authors, English
ISBN 0-7636-2752-6   LC 2004-61847

"Opening with Dickens's touring life and final London performance, Rosen then turns to the writer's humble beginnings and nomadic childhood, paying particular attention to the people he met, the sights he saw, and the situations he endured—all of which were to find their way into his writings. The author looks at 1800s London, pointing out the societal changes that were to influence Dickens's progressive thinking." SLJ

"The art adds to the richness of a volume designed and written with care." Booklist

Douglass, Frederick, 1817?-1895

McKissack, Patricia C. Frederick Douglass; leader against slavery; [by] Patricia and Fredrick McKissack. rev ed. Enslow Pubs. 2002 32p il (Great African Americans) lib bdg $18.60

Grades: 2 3 4   **92**
1. Abolitionists 2. African Americans—Biography
ISBN 0-7660-1696-X   LC 00-12415

Douglass, Frederick, 1817?-1895—*Continued*
First published 1991
A biography of the African American abolitionist
This contains "many facts presented in a readable style. . . . Attractive." SLJ
Includes bibliographical references

Du Bois, W. E. B. (William Edward Burghardt), 1868-1963
Whiting, Jim. W.E.B. Du Bois; civil rights activist, author, historian. Mason Crest Publishers 2010 64p il (Transcending race in America: biographies of biracial achievers) $22.95; pa $9.95
Grades: 5 6 7 8   92
  1. African Americans—Biography 2. African Americans—Civil rights
  ISBN   978-1-4222-1618-7;   1-4222-1618-7;
  978-1-4222-1632-3 (pa); 1-4222-1632-2 (pa)
                                    LC 2009022049
"The author openly discusses Du Bois' political and ideological struggles, which concluded with his move to Ghana and admittance into the Communist Party. . . . The book . . . provides solid information about Du Bois." Booklist
Includes glossary and bibliographical references

Earhart, Amelia, 1898-1937
Adler, David A. A picture book of Amelia Earhart; illustrated by Jeff Fisher. Holiday House 1998 unp il $16.95; pa $6.95
Grades: 1 2 3   92
  1. Women air pilots
  ISBN 0-8234-1315-2; 0-8234-1517-1 (pa)
                                    LC 96-54854
Discusses the life of the pilot who was the first woman to cross the Atlantic by herself in a plane
This offers "a straightforward, informative text full of detail. The illustrations ably reflect both the humorous and more serious moments in the narrative." Horn Book Guide
Includes bibliographical references

Lauber, Patricia. Lost star: the story of Amelia Earhart. Scholastic 1988 106p il maps pa $4.50 hardcover o.p.
Grades: 5 6 7 8   92
  1. Women air pilots
  ISBN 0-590-41159-4 (pa)   LC 88-3043
"Earhart's early life is covered succinctly, including the family problems that resulted from her father's alcoholism. Close to half of the book is concerned with the details of the last flight around the world and the mysterious disappearance, sure to hold the attention of readers. Small but very clear black-and-white photographs are included." SLJ
Includes bibliographical references

Tanaka, Shelley. Amelia Earhart; the legend of the lost aviator; by Shelley Tanaka; illustrated by David Craig. Abrams Books for Young Readers 2008 48p il map $18.95 *
Grades: 3 4 5 6   92
  1. Women air pilots
  ISBN 978-0-8109-7095-3; 0-8109-7095-3
                                    LC 2007-39749
NCTE Orbis Pictus Award (2009)
This is an account of the life of aviator Amelia Earhart from her childhood up to the time she disappeared on a flight in 1937.
"This title is notable . . . for its smooth, powerful storytelling, ample gallery of well-chosen photographs, and nicely placed sidebar information on such topics as flight delays, navigation, and around-the-world flight records." Bull Cent Child Books
Includes bibliographical references

Earle, Sylvia A., 1935-
Reichard, Susan E. Who on earth is Sylvia Earle? undersea explorer of the ocean. Enslow Publishers 2009 112p il (Scientists saving the earth) $31.93
Grades: 5 6 7 8   92
  1. Underwater exploration 2. Marine biology 3. Women scientists
  ISBN 978-1-59845-118-4; 1-59845-118-9
                                    LC 2008032014
"Details Sylvia Earle's life, with chapters devoted to her early years, life, work, writings, and legacy" Publisher's note
"The writing is clear and informative. . . . Color photographs are relevant and of good quality." SLJ
Includes glossary and bibliographical references

Eastman, George, 1854-1932
Kulling, Monica. It's a snap! George Eastman's first photograph; illustrated by Bill Slavin. Tundra Books 2009 unp il (Great idea series, 1) $17.95
Grades: 2 3 4   92
  1. Photography—History 2. Inventors
  ISBN 978-0-88776-881-1; 0-88776-881-4
"This picture-book biography begins in 1877, in Rochester, NY, with Eastman buying his first camera. . . . The picture-taking process took too long and the bored townspeople headed home before he could develop the wet plate. Eastman was determined to make photography easier and more affordable for everyone. During the next eight years, he invented the dry plate, the first roll of film, and the Kodak camera, and started the Eastman Kodak Company. The book will entertain and inform readers. . . . Slavin's pen-and-ink and watercolor illustrations . . . complement the text." SLJ

Ederle, Gertrude, 1905-2003

Adler, David A. America's champion swimmer: Gertrude Ederle; written by David A. Adler; illustrated by Terry Widener. Harcourt 2000 unp il $16; pa $7

Grades: 2 3 4   92

1. Women athletes 2. Swimming

ISBN 0-15-201969-3; 0-15-205251-8 (pa)

           LC 98-54954

"Gulliver books"

Describes the life and accomplishments of Gertrude Ederle, the first woman to swim the English Channel and a figure in the early women's rights movement

This book "illustrated with richly colored acrylic paintings . . . captures the highlights of Ederle's life in evocative images and telling details that will appeal to children." N Y Times Book Rev

Edison, Thomas A. (Thomas Alva), 1847-1931

Brown, Don. A wizard from the start: the incredible boyhood & amazing inventions of Thomas Edison. Houghton Harcourt 2010 unp il $16 *

Grades: 2 3 4   92

1. Inventors

ISBN 978-0-547-19487-5; 0-547-19487-0

"Focusing on the great inventor's youth, roughly from age eight to mid-20s, this anecdotal picture-book biography is both engaging and accessible. . . . Youngsters will find much to relate to. . . . Brown's signature sketches combine digital imagery and watercolors and reflect the period costume and key moments in Edison's early life." SLJ

Carlson, Laurie M. Thomas Edison for kids; his life and ideas: 21 activities; [by] Laurie Carlson. Chicago Review Press 2006 147p il $14.95 *

Grades: 5 6 7 8   92

1. Inventors 2. Science—Experiments

ISBN 1-55652-584-2   LC 2005025659

"Part biography, part science activity book, this resource will appeal to casual researchers and novice inventors. It contains a wealth of full-page primary source archival photographs, sidebars, and short biographical profiles of Edison's contemporaries, in addition to short and straightforward experiments." Voice Youth Advocates

Includes bibliographical references

Delano, Marfe Ferguson. Inventing the future: a photobiography of Thomas Alva Edison. National Geographic Soc. 2002 64p il $18.95; pa $7.95 *

Grades: 5 6 7 8   92

1. Inventors

ISBN 0-7922-6721-4; 0-7922-5934-3 (pa)

           LC 2001-7357

Presents a biography of the tireless Thomas Edison, illustrated with many photos of his life and inventions

"Well-written and -illustrated. . . . This biography would inspire young people who are interested in experimenting with new ideas and methods." Libr Media Connect

Includes bibliographical references

Dooling, Michael. Young Thomas Edison. Holiday House 2005 unp il $16.95

Grades: 1 2 3   92

1. Inventors

ISBN 0-8234-1868-5   LC 2004-49345

"Dooling has brought Edison's boyhood into focus through careful attention to visual detail and a readable text. What emerges is a story of a determined, focused young man who, despite significant hearing loss and other setbacks, continued to experiment and create inventions that we still benefit from today. . . . Doolings somber oil-on-canvas illustrations use a dark palette and are extraordinarily beautiful." SLJ

Includes bibliographical references

Thomas Edison; a brilliant inventor; by the editors of Time for kids; with Lisa DeMauro. HarperCollins Pubs. 2005 44p (Time for kids biographies) $14.99

Grades: 2 3 4   92

1. Inventors

ISBN 0-06-057612-X

A brief illustrated biography of the inventor

This is "sure to be highly popular with students. . . . Pages feature eye-catching sidebars with . . . photographs and brightly colored drawings. . . . [It features] short lively [text]." Lib Media Connect

Venezia, Mike. Thomas Edison; inventor with a lot of bright ideas; written and illustrated by Mike Venezia. Children's Press 2008 c2009 32p il (Getting to know the world's greatest inventors and scientists) lib bdg $28; pa $6.95

Grades: 2 3 4   92

1. Inventors

ISBN 0-531-14978-1 (lib bdg); 978-0-531-14978-2 (lib bdg); 0-531-22209-8 (pa); 978-0-531-22209-6 (pa)

           LC 2008002306

In this biography of inventor Thomas Edison "the humor and silly scenarios depicted in the cartoon drawings will draw readers back into the smooth, straightforward language." Booklist

Einstein, Albert, 1879-1955

Brown, Don. Odd boy out: young Albert Einstein. Houghton Mifflin 2004 unp il $16 *

Grades: 2 3 4   92

1. Physicists

ISBN 0-618-49298-4   LC 2003-17701

An introduction to the work and early life of the twentieth-century physicist whose theory of relativity revolutionized scientific thinking.

"Brown's pen-and-ink and watercolor illustrations [are] rendered in a palette of dusky mauve and earthy brown. . . . Through eloquent narrative and illustration, Brown offers a thoughtful introduction to an enigmatic man." SLJ

Einstein, Albert, 1879-1955—*Continued*

Delano, Marfe Ferguson. Genius; a photobiography of Albert Einstein. National Geographic 2005 64p il $17.95; lib bdg $27.90; pa $7.95 *

Grades: 5 6 7 8   **92**
    1. Physicists
    ISBN 0-7922-9544-7; 0-7922-9545-5 (lib bdg); 1-4263-0294-0 (pa)   LC 2004-15001
    A biography of the German American physicist.
This "combines a solid text with a particularly attractive format. . . . Delano offers just enough information about Einstein's theories to give a sense of his work. . . . Oversize and filled with well-selected photographs, the book is very handsome." Booklist

Herweck, Don. Albert Einstein and his theory of relativity. Compass Point Books 2009 40p il (Mission: science) lib bdg $26.60

Grades: 4 5 6   **92**
    1. Relativity (Physics) 2. Physicists
    ISBN 978-0-7565-4072-2 (lib bdg); 0-7565-4072-0 (lib bdg)   LC 2008-35729
    An introduction to the life and career of the eminent German American physicist Albert Einstein
    Includes glossary

Krull, Kathleen. Albert Einstein; illustrated by Boris Kulikov. Viking 2009 141p il (Giants of science) $15.99 *

Grades: 5 6 7 8   **92**
    1. Physicists
    ISBN 978-0-670-06332-1; 0-670-06332-0   LC 2009-16037
    "Krull delivers a splendidly humane biography of that gold standard of brilliance, Albert Einstein. . . . Drawing extensively on Einstein's writings, she presents a fully rounded portrait of a man whose genius combined with a bad temper and arrogance, to the detriment of his own professional advancement, not to mention his relationships with women and his children. Using concrete examples, the author brings such mind-bending notions as his General Theory of Relativity within the grasp of child readers." Kirkus

MacLeod, Elizabeth. Albert Einstein; a life of genius; written by Elizabeth MacLeod. Kids Can Press 2003 32p il hardcover o.p. pa $6.95

Grades: 4 5 6 7   **92**
    1. Physicists
    ISBN 1-55337-396-0; 1-55337-397-9 (pa)
    A brief introduction to the life and work of the physicist
    "It looks like a scrapbook, with information offered in small bites accompanied by lots of small photos and illustrations, but this introduction to the life of Einstein is as informative as it is appealing. . . . This is concise, but there's still plenty here for students and browsers alike." Booklist

Meltzer, Milton. Albert Einstein. Holiday House 2008 32p il $16.95

Grades: 3 4 5   **92**
    1. Scientists
    ISBN 978-0-8234-1966-1; 0-8234-1966-5   LC 2006-43676

"Meltzer offers a sound, cogent introduction to Einstein in this attractive volume, which discusses the scientist's work and its significance within a lively account of his life. . . . Well-chosen black-and-white photos and a few documents illustrate the narrative that takes both its subject and its audience seriously." Booklist
    Includes bibliographical references

Venezia, Mike. Albert Einstein; universal genius; written and illustrated by Mike Venezia. Children's Press 2009 32p il (Getting to know the world's greatest inventors and scientists) lib bdg $28; pa $6.95

Grades: 2 3 4   **92**
    1. Physicists
    ISBN 978-0-531-14975-1 (lib bdg); 0-531-14975-7 (lib bdg); 978-0-531-22206-5 (pa); 0-531-22206-3 (pa)   LC 2008-2307
    This biography of the scientist is "super skinny and heavily illustrated, [has] jumbo-sized font and plenty of white space, and [includes] only three-to-five sentences per page. Even so, there's a satisfactory amount of substantive and accessible information contained in the standard overview of [Einstein's] life and accomplishments. . . . The text is enhanced by the period photographs and their helpful captions." SLJ
    Includes glossary

Eleanor, of Aquitaine, Queen, consort of Henry II, King of England, 1122?-1204

Kramer, Ann. Eleanor of Aquitaine; the queen who rode off to battle. National Geographic 2006 64p il map (World history biographies) $17.95; lib bdg $27.90

Grades: 5 6 7 8   **92**
    1. Queens 2. France—History—0-1328 3. Great Britain—History—1154-1399, Plantagenets
    ISBN 0-7922-5895-9; 0-7922-5896-7 (lib bdg)
    An illustrated biography of the medieval queen who traveled to the Crusades with her first husband King Louis VII of France and later married King Henry II of England.
    Includes glossary and bibliographical references

Elizabeth I, Queen of England, 1533-1603

Adams, Simon. Elizabeth I; the outcast who became England's queen; [by] Simon Adams. National Geographic 2005 64p il map (World history biographies) $17.95; lib bdg $27.90 *

Grades: 4 5 6 7   **92**
    1. Queens 2. Great Britain—Kings and rulers 3. Great Britain—History—1485-1603, Tudors
    ISBN 0-7922-3649-1; 0-7922-3654-8 (lib bdg)   LC 2005001359
    An illustrated introduction to the life and times of the 16th century queen of England
    "Accomplishments and hardships are clearly explained with supporting quotes and facts. . . . Beautifully illustrated and visually appealing." SLJ
    Includes glossary and bibliographical references

Elizabeth I, Queen of England, 1533-1603—
Continued

Stanley, Diane. Good Queen Bess: the story of Elizabeth I of England; by Diane Stanley and Peter Vennema; illustrated by Diane Stanley. HarperCollins Pubs. 2001 c1990 unp il $16.99 *

Grades: 4 5 6 7   92

1. Queens 2. Great Britain—Kings and rulers 3. Great Britain—History—1485-1603, Tudors

ISBN 0-688-17961-4   LC 00-47267

A reissue of the title first published 1990 by Four Winds Press

Follows the life of the strong-willed queen who ruled England in the time of Shakespeare and the defeat of the Spanish Armada

"The handsome illustrations . . . are worthy of their subject. Although the format suggests a picture-book audience, this biography needs to be introduced to older readers who have the background to appreciate and understand this woman who dominated and named an age." SLJ

Includes bibliographical references

Ellington, Duke, 1899-1974

Pinkney, Andrea Davis. Duke Ellington; the piano prince and his orchestra; illustrated by Brian Pinkney. Hyperion Bks. for Children 1998 unp il $15.95; pa $5.99 *

Grades: 2 3 4   92

1. Jazz musicians 2. African Americans—Biography

ISBN 0-7868-0178-6; 0-7868-1420-9 (pa)

     LC 96-46031

A Caldecott Medal honor book, 1999; Coretta Scott King honor book for illustration, 1999

A brief recounting of the career of this jazz musician and composer who, along with his orchestra, created music that was beyond category

This is "written in a folksy, colloquial style. . . . The warmly colored, exquisitely designed scratchboard illustrations have a grand time evoking the sounds of Ellington's music." Horn Book Guide

Includes bibliographical references

Stein, Stephanie. Duke Ellington; his life in jazz with 21 activities; [by] Stephanie Stein Crease. Chicago Review Press 2009 148p il $16.95

Grades: 4 5 6 7 8   92

1. Jazz musicians 2. African American musicians

ISBN 978-1-55652-724-1; 1-55652-724-1

     LC 2008023742

"This biography begins with a brief discussion of the lives of Ellington's parents and his childhood introduction to music and instruments. As each chapter introduces separate highlights of the man's life and musical growth, sidebar articles emphasize historical milestones in music . . . and the impact of individuals or events on his life. The book also features 21 interactive activities, each of which is positioned to provide a greater understanding of an instrument, performance, or music theory in jazz style. . . . Illustrations include performance photographs and portraits of notable names from the Big Band era." SLJ

Includes bibliographical references, discography, and filmography

Eratosthenes, 3rd cent. B.C.

Lasky, Kathryn. The librarian who measured the earth; illustrated by Kevin Hawkes. Little, Brown 1994 48p il $16.95 *

Grades: 2 3 4 5   92

1. Astronomers

ISBN 0-316-51526-4   LC 92-42656

Describes the life and work of Eratosthenes, the Greek geographer and astronomer who accurately measured the circumference of the Earth

"Illustrating the text with warmth and humor, Hawkes' acrylic paintings capture the period details of the setting and clarify the geometric concepts used in the measurement. The often dramatic compositions vary from page to page, while the sunlit reds, oranges, and yellows glow brightly against the cooler blues and greens. . . . Entertaining as well as instructional." Booklist

Includes bibliographical references

Farnsworth, Philo T., 1906-1971

Krull, Kathleen. The boy who invented TV: the story of Philo Farnsworth; illustrated by Greg Couch. Alfred A. Knopf 2009 unp il $16.99; lib bdg $19.99 *

Grades: 3 4 5   92

1. Inventors 2. Television

ISBN 978-0-375-84561-1; 0-375-84561-5; 978-0-375-94561-8 (lib bdg); 0-375-94561-X (lib bdg)

     LC 2008-35500

"This entertaining book explores the life of inventor Philo Farnsworth, who discovered how to transmit images electronically, leading to the first television. . . . Krull's substantial, captivating text is balanced by Couch's warm, mixed-media illustrations." Publ Wkly

Includes bibliographical references

Ferris, George Washington Gale, 1859-1896

Sneed, Dani. Ferris wheel!: George Ferris and his amazing invention; by Dani Sneed. Enslow 2008 32p il (Genius at work!: great inventor biographies) lib bdg $22.60

Grades: 4 5 6   92

1. Inventors 2. Ferris wheels

ISBN 978-0-7660-2834-0 (lib bdg); 0-7660-2834-8 (lib bdg)   LC 2007010605

"Though Ferris wheels are a staple at every fair and amusement park today, the man whose name they carry was at first ridiculed for proposing the idea for the World's Fair in Chicago in 1893. . . . Dani Sneed describes how the visionary George Ferris overcame great obstacles to build his dream." Publisher's note

"Color and black-and-white photos and color graphics add to the information on most pages. [This book is] easy to read and full of enough facts to make a solid basis for research." SLJ

Includes glossary and bibliographical references

Fibonacci, Leonardo, ca. 1170-ca. 1240

D'Agnese, Joseph. Blockhead; the life of Fibonacci; illustrated by John O'Brien. Henry Holt and Company 2010 40p il $16.99 *

Grades: 2 3 4 5   92

1. Mathematicians 2. Numbers
ISBN 978-0-8050-6305-9; 0-8050-6305-6
LC 2009005264

"D'Agnese's introduction to medieval Europe's greatest mathematician offers both a coherent biographical account—spun, with some invented details, from very sketchy historical records—and the clearest explanation to date for younger readers of the numerical sequence that is found throughout nature and still bears his name. O'Brien's illustrations place the prosperously dressed, woolly headed savant in his native Pisa and other settings." Booklist

Fillmore, Millard, 1800-1874

Gottfried, Ted. Millard Fillmore; by Ted Gottfried. Marshall Cavendish Benchmark 2007 96p il (Presidents and their times) lib bdg $22.95

Grades: 5 6 7 8   92

1. Presidents—United States
ISBN 978-0-7614-2431-4   LC 2006019707

This "explores the presidency of a man from humble beginnings who, throughout his presidency, battled the question of slavery and maintaining the unity of the nation." Publisher's note

"Primary-source materials and quotes, helpful insets, and carefully selected . . . reproductions bring history to life and help make [this] clearly written [biography] highly readable." SLJ

Includes glossary and bibliographical references

Fitzgerald, Ella

Orgill, Roxane. Skit-scat raggedy cat: Ella Fitzgerald; illustrated by Sean Qualls. Candlewick Press 2010 il $17.99

Grades: 2 3 4   92

1. African American singers 2. African American women—Biography
ISBN 978-0-7636-1733-2; 0-7636-1733-4
LC 2009047407

This is "a stylish portrayal of Ella Fitzgerald. . . . There's no question that Orgill and Qualls know what makes [jazz] so catchy: it's slinky, rhythmic, and joyful and on full display in both the lively text and swinging artwork." Booklist

Pinkney, Andrea Davis. Ella Fitzgerald; the tale of a vocal virtuosa; by Andrea Davis Pinkney with Scat Cat Monroe; illustrated by Brian Pinkney. Hyperion 2002 unp il $16.99 *

Grades: 2 3 4   92

1. African American singers 2. African American women—Biography
ISBN 0-7868-0568-4; 0-7868-2493-X (lib bdg)

"Scat Cat Monroe, a jazzy feline in a zoot suit, tells Fitzgerald's life story. . . . The general details of an extraordinary life—when, what, where, and how—are related in rhythmic, vivid language that matches the verve of the hand-colored scratchboard illustrations." Bull Cent Child Books

Fleischman, Sid, 1920-2010

Fleischman, Sid. The abracadabra kid; a writer's life. Greenwillow Bks. 1996 198p il $16.99 paperback o.p. *

Grades: 5 6 7 8   92

1. Authors, American
ISBN 0-688-14859-X; 0-688-15855-2 (pa)
LC 95-47382

This autobiography, "turns real life into a story complete with cliffhangers. And it's a classic *boy's* story, from card tricks and traveling magic shows to World War II naval experiences and screen-writing gigs for John Wayne movies. En route, we learn how Fleischman learned the craft of writing." Bull Cent Child Books

Includes bibliographical references

Parker-Rock, Michelle. Sid Fleischman; an author kids love. Enslow Publishers 2008 c2009 48p il por (Authors kids love) lib bdg $23.93

Grades: 3 4 5   92

1. Authors, American
ISBN 978-0-7660-2757-2 (lib bdg); 0-7660-2757-0 (lib bdg)   LC 2007046079

This a biography of the author of *By the Great Horn Spoon*, *The Whipping Boy*, the McBroom series, and other popular children's books, based on an interview.

"The frequent use of direct quotes makes the [text] particularly enjoyable. . . . Kids will be fascinated with . . . Fleischman's passion for magic. . . . Well written, interesting, and useful for reports." SLJ

Includes bibliographical references

Fleming, Alexander, 1881-1955

Tocci, Salvatore. Alexander Fleming; the man who discovered penicillin. Enslow Pubs. 2002 128p il (Great minds of science) lib bdg $26.60

Grades: 5 6 7 8   92

1. Penicillin 2. Bacteriologists
ISBN 0-7660-1998-5   LC 2001-3072

A biography of Alexander Fleming, the discoverer of penicillin

"Large type and lots of white space make this title accessible, and the black-and-white photographs enhance the well-written text. Activities for students reinforce the principles that are presented." SLJ

Includes glossary and bibliographical references

Fletcher, Ralph, 1953-

Fletcher, Ralph. Marshfield dreams; when I was a kid. Holt & Co. 2005 183p il $16.95

Grades: 4 5 6 7   92

1. Authors, American
ISBN 0-8050-7242-X   LC 2004-60746

"Fletcher reminisces about growing up in Marshfield, VT, recalling boyhood friendships, sibling attachments, and romps through the woods. . . . Written with sagacious eloquence and gentle humor, this work stands strong in the ranks of authors' memoirs and autobiographies." SLJ

Ford, Henry, 1863-1947

Mitchell, Don. Driven; a photobiography of Henry Ford; foreword by Lee Iacocca. National Geographic 2010 64p il map $18.95; lib bdg $27.90 *

Grades: 5 6 7 8   92

1. Automobile industry 2. Businessmen

ISBN   978-1-4263-0155-1;   1-4263-0155-3; 978-1-4263-0156-8 (lib bdg); 1-4263-0156-1 (lib bdg)

LC 2009-07136

"Mitchell introduces readers to the founder of the auto company. . . . Thoughts, feelings, and quotes abound, and they are well sourced. . . . The writing is clear, and the organization is chronological. . . . *Driven* combines fine photography and an inviting text to depict Ford's life and his impact on the world." SLJ

Includes bibliographical references

Forten, James, 1766-1842

Figley, Marty Rhodes. Prisoner for liberty; by Marty Rhodes Figley; illustrations by Craig Orback. Millbrook Press 2008 48p il (On my own history) lib bdg $25.26

Grades: 2 3 4   92

1. United States—History—1775-1783, Revolution 2. African Americans—Biography

ISBN 978-0-8225-7280-0 (lib bdg); 0-8225-7280-X (lib bdg)   LC 2006028582

"In dramatic words and vivid paintings, this [book] . . . celebrates the heroism of an African American teen in the Revolutionary War. Born free, 15-year-old James Forten joined the crew of the Royal Louis as a sailor. When the British captured the ship, he refused the chance to escape to help a sickly white friend. . . . This inspiring, personal story will help draw early readers into U.S. history." Booklist

Includes bibliographical references

Fortune, Amos, 1709 or 10-1801

Yates, Elizabeth. Amos Fortune, free man; illustrations by Nora S. Unwin. Dutton 1950 181p il hardcover o.p. pa $5.99

Grades: 4 5 6 7   92

1. African Americans—Biography 2. Slavery—United States

ISBN 0-525-25570-2; 0-14-034158-7 (pa)

Awarded the Newbery Medal, 1951

"Born free in Africa, Amos Fortune was sold into slavery in America in 1725. After more than 40 years of servitude Amos was able to purchase his freedom and, in time, that of several others. He died a tanner of enviable reputation, a landowner, and a respected citizen of his community. Based on fact, this is a . . . story of a life dedicated to the fight for freedom and service to others." Booklist

Fossey, Dian

Kushner, Jill Menkes. Who on earth is Dian Fossey? defender of the mountain gorillas. Enslow Publishers 2009 112p il (Scientists saving the earth) $31.93

Grades: 5 6 7 8   92

1. Women scientists 2. Gorillas

ISBN 978-1-59845-117-7; 1-59845-117-0

LC 2008029376

"Details Dian Fossey's life, with chapters devoted to her early years, life, work, writings, and legacy, as well as how children can follow in her footsteps" Publisher's note

"The book is filled with factual information, yet is written in a manner that makes both Fossey and her gorillas come to life for the reader." Sci Books Films

Includes glossary and bibliographical references

Frank, Anne, 1929-1945

Frank, Anne. The diary of a young girl: the definitive edition; edited by Otto H. Frank and Mirjam Pressler; translated by Susan Massotty. Doubleday 1995 340p $29.95; pa $6.99 *

Grades: 6 7 8 9   92

1. Jews—Netherlands 2. Holocaust, 1933-1945 3. World War, 1939-1945—Jews 4. Netherlands—History—1940-1945, German occupation

ISBN 0-385-47378-8; 0-553-57712-3 (pa)

LC 94-41379

"This new translation of Frank's famous diary includes material about her emerging sexuality and her relationship with her mother that was originally excised by Frank's father, the only family member to survive the Holocaust." Libr J

Hurwitz, Johanna. Anne Frank: life in hiding; illustrated by Vera Rosenberry. Jewish Publ. Soc. 1988 62p il map $13.95

Grades: 3 4 5   92

1. Jews—Netherlands 2. Holocaust, 1933-1945 3. World War, 1939-1945—Jews 4. Netherlands—History—1940-1945, German occupation

ISBN 0-8276-0311-8   LC 87-35263

The author "gives a concise explanation of the political and economic background to the Holocaust and provides a map of Europe and a chronology. She ably covers the events of Anne's life before, during, and after the period covered by the 'Diary of Anne Frank,' explaining the significance and importance of the 'Diary' throughout the world." SLJ

Metselaar, Menno. Anne Frank: her life in words and pictures; from the archives of The Anne Frank House; [by] Menno Metselaar and Ruud van der Rol; translated by Arnold J. Pomerans. Roaring Brook Press 2009 215p il map pa $12.99 *

Grades: 5 6 7 8   92

1. Jews—Netherlands 2. Holocaust, 1933-1945 3. World War, 1939-1945—Jews 4. Netherlands—History—1940-1945, German occupation

ISBN   978-1-59643-546-9;   1-59643-546-1; 978-1-59643-547-6 (pa); 1-59643-547-X (pa)

First published 2004 in the Netherlands with title: The story of Anne Frank

Frank, Anne, 1929-1945—*Continued*

"Beginning with a single photograph of the cover of Anne Frank's diary and the quote, 'One of my nicest presents,' this small, beautifully formatted book is accessible, compelling, and richly pictorial. . . . The book immediately immerses readers in the girl's life via a series of family photographs, many previously unpublished. Divided chronologically, the accompanying text is enhanced by diary entries, resulting in a historically succinct yet descriptive presentation. . . . Even for those collections where Anne Frank is well represented, this is a moving and valuable book." SLJ

Poole, Josephine. Anne Frank; illustrations by Angela Barrett. Knopf 2005 unp il $17.95 *
Grades: 2 3 4   92
    1. Jews—Netherlands 2. Holocaust, 1933-1945 3. World War, 1939-1945—Jews 4. Netherlands—History—1940-1945, German occupation
    ISBN 0-375-83242-4   LC 2004-15099
This biography "tells of Anne Frank's childhood up through the moment her family's hideout is raided by the Nazis." Publ Wkly
"The familiar yet compelling story is told with simple poignancy and dignity. . . . Both the text and illustrations quickly create a sense of foreboding. Spreads are dominated by Barrett's realistically rendered paintings done in subdued tones." SLJ

Rol, Ruud van der. Anne Frank, beyond the diary; a photographic remembrance; by Ruud van der Rol and Rian Verhoeven; in association with the Anne Frank House; translated by Tony Langham and Plym Peters; with an introduction by Anna Quindlen. Viking 1993 113p il map hardcover o.p. pa $10.99
Grades: 5 6 7 8   92
    1. Jews—Netherlands 2. Holocaust, 1933-1945 3. World War, 1939-1945—Jews 4. Netherlands—History—1940-1945, German occupation
    ISBN 0-670-84932-4; 0-14-036926-0 (pa)
                                        LC 92-41528
Original Dutch edition, 1992
Photographs, illustrations, and maps accompany historical essays, diary excerpts, and interviews, providing an insight to Anne Frank and the massive upheaval which tore apart her world
"Readers will become absorbed in the richness of the detail and careful explanation which revisit and expand the familiar, well-loved story." Horn Book

Franklin, Benjamin, 1706-1790

Adler, David A. B. Franklin, printer. Holiday House 2001 126p il lib bdg $19.95 *
Grades: 4 5 6 7   92
    1. Statesmen—United States
    ISBN 0-8234-1675-5   LC 2001-24535
This "surveys Benjamin Franklin's life as a printer, a scientist, an inventor, a writer, and a statesman. . . . Throughout the book, details, anecdotes, and quotations bring the man's portrait into clearer focus, while period illustrations . . . help readers envision the background of his times." Booklist
Includes bibliographical references

Fleming, Candace. Ben Franklin's almanac; being a true account of the good gentleman's life. Atheneum Bks. for Young Readers 2003 120p il $19.95
Grades: 5 6 7 8   92
    1. Statesmen—United States
    ISBN 0-689-83549-3   LC 2002-6136
"An Anne Schwartz book"
Brings together eighteenth century etchings, artifacts, and quotations to create the effect of a scrapbook of the life of Benjamin Franklin
"An authoritative work of depth, humor, and interest, presenting Franklin in all his complexity, ranging from the heroic to the vulgar, the saintly to the callous." SLJ

Fritz, Jean. What's the big idea, Ben Franklin? illustrated by Margot Tomes. Putnam Pub. Group 1976 46p il $15.99; pa $5.99 *
Grades: 2 3 4   92
    1. Statesmen—United States
    ISBN 0-399-23487-X; 0-698-11372-1 (pa)
The text "focuses on Franklin's multifaceted career but also gives personal details and quotes some of his pithy sayings. Enough background information about colonial affairs is given to enable readers to understand the importance of Franklin's contributions to the public good but not so much that it obtrudes on his life story. Although the text is not punctuated by references or footnotes, a page of notes (with numbers for pages referred to) is appended." Bull Cent Child Books

Harness, Cheryl. The remarkable Benjamin Franklin; written & illustrated by Cheryl Harness. National Geographic Society 2005 47p il $17.95 *
Grades: 2 3 4   92
    1. Statesmen—United States
    ISBN 0-7922-7882-8   LC 2004-20504
"Beginning with Franklin's birth, Harness explores the activities that filled his days from his quest to open his own print shop to his role in the American Revolution to his personal intrigues and inventions. Her conversational writing style and vivid illustrations will appeal to readers just becoming acquainted with this important figure." SLJ
Includes bibliographical references

McCurdy, Michael. So said Ben; drawings by Michael McCurdy. Creative Editions 2007 31p il $17.95
Grades: K 1 2 3   92
    1. Proverbs 2. Statesmen—United States
    ISBN 978-1-56846-147-2; 1-56846-147-X
                                        LC 2006027667
"Thirteen of Ben Franklin's pithy proverbs are introduced to young readers by author Michael McCurdy. . . . McCurdy weaves a vignette from Franklin's extraordinary life together with each proverb. Each proverb is illustrated with a woodblock pint incorporating the theme as well as social or historical elements. . . . Multiple reading and comprehension levels will find satisfaction—if not some wisdom—from this presentation of an American icon." Libr Media Connect

Franklin, Benjamin, 1706-1790—Continued

Miller, Brandon Marie. Benjamin Franklin, American genius; his life and ideas, with 21 activities. Chicago Review Press 2009 125p il pa $16.95

Grades: 4 5 6 7   92

1. Statesmen 2. Inventors 3. Scientists

ISBN 978-1-55652-757-9 (pa); 1-55652-757-8 (pa)

LC 2009012456

"Miller does an excellent job of presenting a synopsis of Franklin's life in a highly readable manner. . . . Imbedded in each chapter are asides that further elaborate on Franklin's life and activities that coordinate with the text or the historical facts presented. The directions are easy to follow and enhance the overall presentation, especially in terms of classroom connections. Illustrations accompany each project and reproductions of primary documents, renderings, and paintings provide added value." SLJ

Includes glossary and bibliographical references

Rushby, Pamela. Ben Franklin; printer, author, inventor, politician; by Pamela Rushby. National Geographic 2007 40p il (National Geographic history chapters) lib bdg $17.90

Grades: 2 3 4   92

1. Statesmen—United States

ISBN 978-1-4263-0191-9   LC 2007007896

This biography of Benjamin Franklin is "nicely illustrated with . . . paintings, engravings, and facsimiles. . . . [It is] just right for emerging chapter-book readers. . . . Useful . . . for reports . . . and interesting pleasure reading." SLJ

Includes glossary and bibliographical references

Freud, Sigmund, 1856-1939

Krull, Kathleen. Sigmund Freud; illustrated by Boris Kulikov. Viking 2006 144p il (Giants of science) $15.99 *

Grades: 5 6 7 8   92

1. Psychiatrists

ISBN 0-670-05892-0

"Krull unravels just how much the inventor of psychoanalysis and student of the human mind has shaped the way we think . . . while at the same time noting his personal and professional short-comings. . . . Illustrator Kulikov provides knowing and witty illustrations." Booklist

Includes bibliographical references

Fritz, Jean

Fritz, Jean. Homesick: my own story; illustrated with drawings by Margot Tomes and photographs. Putnam 1982 163p il $16.99; pa $5.99 *

Grades: 5 6 7 8   92

1. China 2. Women authors

ISBN 0-399-20933-6; 0-698-11782-4 (pa)

LC 82-7646

A Newbery Medal honor book, 1983

Companion volume to China homecoming

This is a somewhat fictionalized memoir of the author's childhood in China. "Born in Hankow, where her father was director of the YMCA, Jean loved the city. . . . But she knew she 'belonged on the other side of the world'—in Pennsylvania with her grandmother and her other relations." Horn Book

"The descriptions of places and the times are vivid in a book that brings to the reader, with sharp clarity and candor, the yearnings and fears and ambivalent loyalties of a young girl." Bull Cent Child Books

Fulton, Robert, 1765-1815

Herweck, Don. Robert Fulton; engineer of the steamboat. Compass Point Books 2009 40p il (Mission: Science) lib bdg $26.60

Grades: 4 5 6 7   92

1. Inventors 2. Steamboats

ISBN 978-0-7565-3961-0 (lib bdg); 0-7565-3961-7 (lib bdg)   LC 2008007728

Covers the life and accomplishments of American inventor and mechanic, Robert Fulton, who is best known for building the first successful steamboat

Gág, Wanda, 1893-1946

Ray, Deborah Kogan. Wanda Gag; the girl who lived to draw; [by] Deborah Kogan Ray. Viking Childrens Books 2008 unp il $16.99

Grades: 2 3 4   92

1. Illustrators 2. Women authors 3. Authors, American

ISBN 978-0-670-06292-8; 0-670-06292-8

LC 2008-13132

"This charming biography of the creator of *Millions of Cats* . . . shows how Gág's family and childhood inspired her lifelong pursuit of art. . . . Each page of text is introduced with a quote from the subject's diaries and letters, and faces a white-framed illustration reflecting the Old World charm of her childhood, which comes to life with Ray's evocative paintings." SLJ

Galilei, Galileo, 1564-1642

Panchyk, Richard. Galileo for kids; his life and ideas: 25 activities; foreword by Buzz Aldrin. Chicago Review Press 2005 166p il map pa $16.95 *

Grades: 5 6 7 8   92

1. Astronomers

ISBN 1-55652-566-4   LC 2004-22936

A biography of the Renaissance scientist and his times with related activities

"Clear . . . writing places Galileo squarely within the historical context of the turbulent Italian Renaissance. . . . Panchyk's title is a good choice for those interested in integrating history and science curriculums." SLJ

Includes bibliographical references

Sís, Peter. Starry messenger; a book depicting the life of a famous scientist, mathematician, astronomer, philosopher, physicist, Galileo Galilei; created and illustrated by Peter Sis. Farrar, Straus & Giroux 1996 unp il $18; pa $7.99 *

Grades: 2 3 4 5   92

1. Astronomers

ISBN 0-374-37191-1; 0-374-47027-8 (pa)

LC 95-44986

Galilei, Galileo, 1564-1642—*Continued*
A Caldecott Medal honor book, 1997

"Frances Foster books"

Describes the life and work of the man who changed the way people saw the galaxy, by offering objective evidence that the earth was not the fixed center of the universe

"Large, beautiful drawings reflect the ideas, events, books, maps, world view, and symbolism of the times. These intricate ink drawings, idiosyncratic in concept and beautifully tinted with delicate watercolor washes, are complemented by smaller drawings and prints that illustrate a side-text of significant dates, time lines, quotations, comments, and explanations. . . . Those drawn to the book will find that it works on many levels, offering not just facts but intuitive visions of another world." Booklist

Steele, Philip. Galileo; the genius who faced the Inquisition. National Geographic 2005 64p il (World history biographies) $17.95; lib bdg $27.90 *

Grades: 4 5 6 7   92
1. Astronomers
ISBN 0-7922-3656-4; 0-7922-3657-2 (lib bdg)
LC 2005-01357

An illustrated introduction to the 16th century astronomer and his times

"Accompliments and hardships are clearly explained with supporting quotes and facts. . . . Beautifully illustrated and visually appealing." SLJ

Gallaudet, T. H. (Thomas Hopkins), 1787-1851
McCully, Emily Arnold. My heart glow: Alice Cogswell, Thomas Gallaudet and the birth of American sign language. Hyperion Books for Children 2008 unp il $15.99 *
Grades: 2 3 4   92
1. Cogswell, Alice 2. Deaf 3. Sign language
ISBN 978-1-4231-0028-7; 1-4231-0028-X

This is the story of Thomas Gallaudet and his deaf neighbor, Alice Cogswell, and how Gallaudet established a school for the deaf in the United States and developed American Sign Language.

"Emily Arnold McCully's watercolor illustrations are beautifully rendered. . . . Not only does this book accurately present the engrossing story of Alice and Gallaudet, it is also an excellent resource for teaching diversity and encouraging empathy for others." Libr Media Connect

Gama, Vasco da, 1469-1524
Calvert, Patricia. Vasco da Gama; so strong a spirit; [by] Patricia Calvert. Benchmark Books 2005 96p il map (Great explorations) lib bdg $29.93 *
Grades: 5 6 7 8   92
1. Explorers
ISBN 0-7614-1611-0   LC 2003-22946

Recounts the voyages undertaken by fifteenth-century Portuguese explorer Vasco da Gama to strengthen his nation's power by establishing a sea trade route to India.

Includes bibliographical references

Goodman, Joan E. A long and uncertain journey: the 27,000 mile voyage of Vasco da Gama; by Joan Elizabeth Goodman; illustrated by Tom McNeely. Mikaya Press 2001 47p il map (Great explorers book) $22.95
Grades: 4 5 6 7   92
1. Explorers
ISBN 0-9650493-7-X   LC 00-63795

"Goodman reviews the accomplishments of 15th century Portuguese explorer Vasco da Gama and his role in the rise of the Portuguese Empire." Book Rep

"McNeely's full-page illustrations, which vibrate with life and action, lighten the format, and quotations from the diary of an anonymous sailor on the voyage add fascinating detail and vivid description. . . . A good resource for reports, but the book is also intelligently written and exciting." Booklist

Ganci, Peter J., 1946-2001
Ganci, Chris. Chief; the life of Peter J. Ganci, a New York City firefighter. Orchard Bks. 2003 unp il $16.95
Grades: 3 4 5 6   92
1. Fire fighters
ISBN 0-439-44386-5   LC 2002-72816

"The author describes his dad . . . [Peter J. Ganci, who] became a member of the FDNY in 1968 and, in 1999, became Chief of the New York City Fire Department. . . . He lost his life on September 11, 2001, saving countless others, inside the raging inferno at the World Trade Center. . . . The text is balanced with large and small photos, in color and black and white. . . . The narrative is compelling, and children are likely to add Chief Ganci to the top of their list of heroes." SLJ

Gandhi, Mahatma, 1869-1948
Demi. Gandhi. Margaret K. McElderry Bks. 2001 unp il $19.95 *
Grades: 3 4 5 6   92
1. India—Politics and government 2. Passive resistance
ISBN 0-689-84149-3   LC 00-32911
Maps on lining papers

"Beginning with Gandhi's failure as a student in India, this . . . biography traces Gandhi's life, from his first rallies against prejudice in South Africa to his remarkable victory over colonialism in India. . . . With extraordinarily detailed illustrations, decorated with gold leaf . . . and accessible, flowing text, veteran artist-author Demi reveals how a simple man who spun his own cloth became one of history's most important political and spiritual leaders." Booklist

Severance, John B. Gandhi, great soul. Clarion Bks. 1997 143p il map $18
Grades: 5 6 7 8   92
1. India—Politics and government 2. Passive resistance
ISBN 0-395-77179-X   LC 95-20887

Severance "begins with an introduction to Gandhi's message and gives a brief overview of the mahatma's personal evolution as well as India's external and internal struggles. He then chronicles Gandhi's life. . . . Sever-

Gandhi, Mahatma, 1869-1948—*Continued*
ance details Gandhi's philosophy of *satyagraha*, or peaceful resistance." Booklist

"It is not only Gandhi who comes alive in this considered, well-documented biography but the multifarious personalities and politics of his world." Horn Book Guide

Includes bibliographical references

Wilkinson, Philip. Gandhi; the young protester who founded a nation. National Geographic 2005 64p il (World history biographies) $17.95; lib bdg $27.90 *
Grades: 4 5 6 7   92
  1. India—Politics and government 2. Passive resistance
  ISBN 0-7922-3647-5; 0-7922-3648-3 (lib bdg)
"Double-page spreads describe phases in Gandhi's life, from childhood to his tragic death, detailed in Wilkinson's straightforward, succinct language and in anecdotes, which will capture young people's attention and also humanize the great leader." Booklist
Includes glossary and bibliographical references

Gantos, Jack
Parker-Rock, Michelle. Jack Gantos; an author kids love; [by] Michelle Parker-Rock. Enslow Publishers 2007 48p bibl il por (Authors kids love) lib bdg $23.93
Grades: 3 4 5   92
  1. Authors, American
  ISBN 978-0-7660-2756-5 (lib bdg); 0-7660-2756-2 (lib bdg)   LC 2006035563
This is a biography of the author of the children's book series' about Rotten Ralph, Joey Pigza, and Jack Henry.
"Invitingly designed with colorful pages, relatively large type, and photos of Gantos at different ages, this book serves up an intriguing and very readable introduction to a popular author." Booklist
Includes glossary and bibliographical references

García Márquez, Gabriel, 1928-
Brown, Monica. My name is Gabito: the life of Gabriel Garcia Márquez; by Monica Brown. Rising Moon 2007 unp il $15.95; bi-lingual edition (English and Spanish) $15.95 *
Grades: K 1 2 3   92
  1. Authors, Colombian 2. Bilingual books—English-Spanish
  ISBN   978-0-87358-934-5;   0-87358-934-3;
  978-0-87358-908-6 (bi-lingual edition (English and Spanish); 0-87358-908-4 (bi-lingual edition (English and Spanish)
A Pura Belpré Award illustrator honor book, 2008
A picture book about the childhood of the Colombian author
This offers "vivid, lyrical text. . . . Colón's artwork interprets the story with verve. Glowing with rich, subtle colors on rounded forms, the illustrations recreate real and imagined scenes with equal conviction." Booklist

Gaudí, Antoni, 1852-1926
Rodriguez, Rachel. Building on nature; the life of Antoni Gaudi; illustrated by Julie Paschkis. Henry Holt & Co. 2009 unp il $16.99 *
Grades: 1 2 3   92
  1. Architects
  ISBN 978-0-8050-8745-1; 0-8050-8745-1
                                         LC 2008-38213
This is a biography of "the Catalonian architect Antoni Gaudi. The immediacy of the present-tense narrative is simple, direct, and at times piercingly poetic. . . . Paschkis doesn't try to reproduce the delicate exoticism of Gaudi's buildings in a line-for-line manner but rather soaks up the wondrous strange oozing from his designs and renders their dreamlike qualities in pointed details and large-scale impressions." Booklist

Gee, Maggie
Moss, Marissa. Sky high: the true story of Maggie Gee; illustrated by Carl Angel. Tricycle Press 2009 unp il $16.99 *
Grades: 3 4 5   92
  1. World War, 1939-1945—Aerial operations
  2. Women air pilots
  ISBN 978-1-58246-280-6; 1-58246-280-1
                                         LC 2008042387
This is a biography of the Asian American World War II air pilot, Maggie Gee
"Based on interviews with Gee, this has a lovely, personal feel to it. And while some of the faces in the acrylic and colored-pencil illustrations are a bit stiff, the scenes themselves exude a panoramic joy." Booklist

Gehrig, Lou, 1903-1941
Adler, David A. Lou Gehrig; the luckiest man; illustrated by Terry Widener. Harcourt Brace & Co. 1997 unp il $17; pa $7
Grades: 2 3 4   92
  1. Baseball—Biography
  ISBN 0-15-200523-4; 0-15-202483-3 (pa)
                                         LC 95-7997
"Gulliver books"
Traces the life of the Yankees' star ballplayer, focusing on his character and his struggle with the terminal disease amyotrophic lateral sclerosis
"Adler's restrained tone makes his description of Gehrig's stoic and uncomplaining struggle all the more moving. The illustrations, meticulously detailed . . . also pack an emotional wallop." Horn Book Guide

Viola, Kevin. Lou Gehrig. LernerSports 2005 106p il (Sports heroes and legends) hardcover o.p. pa $9.95
Grades: 4 5 6 7   92
  1. Baseball—Biography
  ISBN 0-8225-1794-9 (lib bdg); 0-7607-5062-9 (pa)
                                         LC 2003-23649
Contents: Prologue: The luckiest man; Little Lou; Another Babe?; Lou Lewis; Earning his stripes; The greatest team of all time; Ups and downs; Love and marriage; Captain Lou; A new partner; The streak and the slump; Epilogue: The pride of the Yankees

Gehrig, Lou, 1903-1941—_Continued_

This "begins with the shy player's farewell at Yankee Stadium after being diagnosed with ALS. It then goes back to describe his early life as the son of German immigrants and how his enormous talent lifted his family from poverty. There is plenty of detail about the games he played and the records he broke, but the book also lends insight into the man himself." Booklist

Includes bibliographical references

Gehry, Frank

Bodden, Valerie. Frank Gehry. Creative Education 2009 48p il (Xtraordinary artists) lib bdg $32.80

Grades: 4 5 6 7   92

1. Architects
ISBN 978-1-58341-662-4 (lib bdg); 1-58341-662-5 (lib bdg)   LC 2007004201

This is a biography of architect Frank Gehry

This offers an "interesting [layout]; big, high-quality reproductions and photographs on heavy paper; insightful quotes from diverse sources; and . . . an excerpt from an essay about [Gehry] at the end of the book. Readers get a strong sense of [the] artist's personality along with an excellent survey of his work." SLJ

Includes bibliographical references

Genghis Khan, 1162-1227

Demi. Genghis Khan. Marshall Cavendish Children 2009 c1991 unp il $19.99 *

Grades: 4 5 6 7   92

1. Mongols 2. Kings and rulers
ISBN 978-0-7614-5547-9; 0-7614-5547-7
      LC 2008006001

A reissue of Chingis Khan, published 1991 by Henry Holt & Co.

A biography of the Mongol leader and military-strategist who, at the height of his power, was supreme master of the largest empire ever created in the lifetime of one man.

"Demi has managed to portray a fierce conqueror as a sympathetic character who follows a strict code that places loyalty, obedience, and discipline above all else. . . . The artist achieves a clever grandeur with the liberal use of iridescent gold and detailed scenes that spill out of their gilded borders and nearly off the pages. . . . This handsome biography is a feast for the eyes from cover to cover." Booklist

George III, King of Great Britain, 1738-1820

Fritz, Jean. Can't you make them behave, King George? pictures by Tomie de Paola. Putnam 1977 45p il $16.99; pa $6.99 *

Grades: 2 3 4   92

1. Great Britain—Kings and rulers
ISBN 0-399-23304-0; 0-698-11402-7 (pa)
      LC 75-33722

"As a boy, George is seen to have had struggles in deportment; as King George III, he is mystified that the colonists refuse to be taught. Bits of history, a sense of George's personality, and the loneliness of being king are all conveyed with good humor. The artist's drawings evoke more chuckles." LC. Child Books, 1977

George, Jean Craighead, 1919-

George, Jean Craighead. A tarantula in my purse; and 172 other wild pets; written and illustrated by Jean Craighead George. HarperCollins Pubs. 1996 134p il hardcover o.p. pa $5.99

Grades: 4 5 6   92

1. Women authors 2. Authors, American 3. Naturalists 4. Pets
ISBN 0-06-023626-4; 0-06-446201-3 (pa)
      LC 95-54151

"George tells of the many wild pets that lived with her family, particularly while her children were growing up. Each chapter describes a different animal or incident." Booklist

"Told in a casual and thoroughly engaging manner, the stories will enchant all animal lovers and even those who aren't." SLJ

Gibson, Althea, 1927-2003

Deans, Karen. Playing to win: the story of Althea Gibson; by Karen Deans; illustrated by Elbrite Brown. Holiday House 2007 unp il $16.95

Grades: 1 2 3 4   92

1. Tennis—Biography 2. African American athletes 3. Women athletes
ISBN 0-8234-1926-6   LC 2004052275

"Not only was Gibson a record-breaking tennis player, but she also played an important role in breaking down racial barriers. . . . The multimedia illustrations are well matched to the power and fluidity of the text, particularly in capturing the champion in action. . . . This well-written and attractive biography will be a popular addition to most collections." SLJ

Includes bibliographical references

Stauffacher, Sue. Nothing but trouble; the story of Althea Gibson; illustrated by Greg Couch. Alfred A. Knopf 2007 unp il $16.99; lib bdg $19.99 *

Grades: 2 3 4 5   92

1. Tennis—Biography 2. African American athletes 3. Women athletes
ISBN 978-0-375-83408-0; 978-0-375-93408-7 (lib bdg)   LC 2006-12605

A biography of the first African American tennis player to win at Wimbleton and Forest Hills in 1957 and 1958

"Couch's kinetic illustrations done in acrylic with digital imaging wonderfully enhance the text. Althea stands out in a blur of color against somber sepia, blue, and olive-drab backgrounds. The prose is rhythmic and has the cadence of the street, and it's a treat to read aloud." SLJ

Giff, Patricia Reilly

Giff, Patricia Reilly. Don't tell the girls; a family memoir; by Patricia Reilly Giff. Holiday House 2005 131p il $16.95

Grades: 4 5 6 7   92

1. Women authors 2. Authors, American
ISBN 0-8234-1813-8   LC 2004-47452

Giff, Patricia Reilly—*Continued*

"Giff reflects on her childhood and her family, going back through several generations. Spotlighting her two grandmothers, she lovingly relates remembered conversations and incidents involving the one she knew well before turning to the other grandmother, whom she never met. . . . This little book has much to offer thoughtful children. . . . With . . . sharply reproduced family photos and documents, this handsome book's small format reflects its intimate, conversational style." Booklist

Gillespie, Dizzy, 1917-1993

Winter, Jonah. Dizzy; [illustrated by] Sean Qualls. Arthur A. Levine Books 2006 48p il $16.99 *

Grades: K 1 2 3   92

1. African American musicians 2. Jazz musicians

ISBN 0-439-50737-5   LC 2005-24043

A picture book biography of the African American jazz musician who originated the style known as Bebop

"Through a powerful marriage of rhythmic text and hip and surprising illustrations, the unorthodox creator of Bebop comes to life. . . . Winter's lively writing pops with energy and begs to be read aloud. Qualls's acrylic, collage, and pencil illustrations swing across the large pages with unique, jazzy rhythms, varying type sizes and colors, and playful perspectives." SLJ

Glenn, John, 1921-

Ashby, Ruth. Rocket man; the Mercury adventure of John Glenn; written by Ruth Ashley; illustrated by Robert Hunt. Peachtree 2004 105p il $12.95

Grades: 4 5 6   92

1. Project Mercury 2. Astronauts 3. Statesmen—United States

ISBN 1-56145-323-4

A biography of astronaut and U.S. Senator John Glenn

"This book describes Glenn's life in a highly readable style. Ashby also skillfully includes historical events in the narrative." SLJ

Mitchell, Don. Liftoff; a photobiography of John Glenn. National Geographic Society 2006 64p il $17.95; lib bdg $27.90

Grades: 5 6 7 8   92

1. Astronauts 2. Statesmen—United States

ISBN 0-7922-5899-1; 0-7922-5900-9 (lib bdg)
                                                  LC 2005-30916

This is a biography of the American astronaut, pilot, and U.S. Senator from Ohio.

This is "well-written and well-illustrated." Sci Books Films

Includes bibliographical references

Gogh, Vincent van, 1853-1890

Bodden, Valerie. Vincent van Gogh. Creative Education 2009 48p il (Xtraordinary artists) lib bdg $32.80

Grades: 4 5 6 7   92

1. Artists, Dutch

ISBN 978-1-58341-663-1 (lib bdg); 1-58341-663-3 (lib bdg)   LC 2007002118

This biography of the artist offers an "interesting [layout]; big, high-quality reproductions and photographs on heavy paper; insightful quotes from diverse sources; and meaty selections of the artist's own writing . . . at the end of the book. Readers get a strong sense of [the] artist's personality along with an excellent survey of his work." SLJ

Includes bibliographical references

Goodall, Jane, 1934-

Jankowski, Connie. Jane Goodall; primatologist and animal activist. Compass Point Books 2009 40p il (Mission: science) lib bdg $26.60

Grades: 4 5 6   92

1. Women scientists 2. Chimpanzees 3. Gombe Stream National Park (Tanzania)

ISBN 978-0-7565-4054-8 (lib bdg); 0-7565-4054-2 (lib bdg)   LC 2008-37621

A biography of the woman whose childhood love of wildlife led her into the African bush to study chimpanzees and into later becoming a world-famous ethologist

Includes glossary

Grant, Ulysses S. (Ulysses Simpson), 1822-1885

Aronson, Billy. Ulysses S. Grant; [by] Billy Aronson. Marshall Cavendish Benchmark 2008 96p il (Presidents and their times) lib bdg $22.95

Grades: 5 6 7 8   92

1. Presidents—United States 2. Generals 3. United States—History—1861-1865, Civil War

ISBN 978-0-7614-2430-7 (lib bdg); 0-7614-2430-X (lib bdg)   LC 2006011087

A biography of the president and Civil War general

Includes bibliographical references

Sapp, Richard. Ulysses S. Grant and the road to Appomattox; [by] Richard Sapp. World Almanac Library 2006 64p il map (In the footsteps of American heroes) lib bdg $33.27; pa $11.95

Grades: 5 6 7 8   92

1. Presidents—United States 2. Generals 3. United States—History—1861-1865, Civil War

ISBN 0-8368-6431-X (lib bdg); 0-8368-6436-0 (pa)
                                                  LC 2005054471

"This smoothly written, informative book spotlights the life and accomplishments of Ulysses S. Grant. After conveying a vivid sense of Grant's personality in the opening sections, the focus shifts toward a more standard account of the strategy and the events of the Civil War. The closing chapter concerns Grant's troubled presidency and his lasting reputation." Booklist

Includes bibliographical references

Greenberg, Hank, 1911-1986

McDonough, Yona Zeldis. Hammerin' Hank; the life of Hank Greenberg; [by] Yona Zeldis McDonough; illustrations by Malcah Zeldis. Walker & Co. 2006 30p il $16.95

Grades: K 1 2 3   92

1. Baseball—Biography 2. Jews—Biography

ISBN 978-0-8027-8997-6; 0-8027-8997-8
                                                  LC 2005048639

Greenberg, Hank, 1911-1986—*Continued*

"The life of baseball star Hank Greenberg deserves to be celebrated, and this solid, chronological telling does just that, centering on Greenberg's religion and America's reaction to its first Jewish baseball star. . . . Zeldis' distinctive folk-art style works well here, especially in the action-filled baseball scenes. The neon colors and unusual design will attract children." Booklist

Includes glossary and bibliographical references

Greene, Charles Sumner, 1868-1957

Thorne-Thomsen, Kathleen. Greene & Greene for kids; art, architecture, activities. Gibbs Smith 2004 112p il $17.95

Grades: 5 6 7 8   92

1. Greene, Henry Mather, 1870-1954 2. Architecture 3. Handicraft

ISBN 1-58685-440-2

"Charlie and Henry Greene were born in Cincinnati, OH, during the late 19th century, a time period the author elucidates through full-color photographs and illustrations to make it more accessible to her audience. . . . The book [introduces] readers to their architecture after detailing a history of their ideas, concepts, and life experiences. . . . Thorne-Thomsen presents the history, culture, and art of Greene and Greene through clear descriptions, fun activities, and lots of pictures." SLJ

Greene, Henry Mather, 1870-1954

Thorne-Thomsen, Kathleen. Greene & Greene for kids. See entry under Greene, Charles Sumner, 1868-1957

Greene, Nathanael, 1742-1786

Mierka, Gregg A. Nathanael Greene; the general who saved the Revolution; [by] Gregg A. Mierka. OTTN Pub. 2007 88p il map (Forgotten heroes of the American Revolution) $23.95; pa $12.95

Grades: 5 6 7 8   92

1. Generals 2. Society of Friends 3. United States—History—1775-1783, Revolution

ISBN   978-1-59556-012-4;   1-59556-012-2; 978-1-59556-017-9 (pa); 1-59556-017-3 (pa)

LC 2006021044

"A biography of the general whose successful campaign in the South, in what seemed an impossible situation, turned the tide of the American Revolution and led to a Patriot victory." Publisher's note

"This lively profile combines an engrossing account of the Revolutionary War with healthy measures of images and passages drawn from primary—and sometimes previously unpublished—sources." Booklist

Includes bibliographical references

Grimm, Jacob, 1785-1863

Hettinga, Donald R. The Brothers Grimm; two lives, one legacy. Clarion Bks. 2001 180p il $22

Grades: 5 6 7 8   92

1. Grimm, Wilhelm, 1786-1859 2. Folklore—Germany

ISBN 0-618-05599-1   LC 00-65598

A biography of the brothers famous for collecting German folk tales

"No book for young readers presents the Grimms' intertwined lives against the larger background of early 19th-century Europe in such fascinating detail as this absorbing new biography. . . . Students will find it an excellent resource for term papers, yet it is written so clearly that it makes for enjoyable pleasure reading." SLJ

Includes bibliographical references

Grimm, Wilhelm, 1786-1859

Hettinga, Donald R. The Brothers Grimm. See entry under Grimm, Jacob, 1785-1863

Gross, Elly Berkovits, 1929-

Gross, Elly Berkovits. Elly; my true story of the Holocaust; [by] Elly Berkovits Gross. Scholastic Press 2009 125p il $14.99

Grades: 4 5 6 7   92

1. Holocaust survivors 2. Holocaust, 1933-1945—Personal narratives 3. Jews—Romania

ISBN 978-0-545-07494-0; 0-545-07494-0

Relates how the author was torn from her happy home and sent to Birkenau by the Nazis, describing how she worked long hours and fought for survival before being set free at the end of the war and beginning a new life in America.

"As a powerful reminder of man's capacity for inhumanity, this memoir is essential reading." Booklist

Guthrie, Woody, 1912-1967

Christensen, Bonnie. Woody Guthrie, poet of the people. Knopf 2001 unp il hardcover o.p. pa $7.99 *

Grades: 3 4 5 6   92

1. Singers

ISBN 0-375-81113-3; 0-375-91113-8 (lib bdg); 0-553-11203-1 (pa)   LC 00-65504

Christensen tells "the life story of American songwriter Woody Guthrie. . . . The book both describes Guthrie's personal involvement in historical events such as the Dust Bowl drought and the rise of unionism and demonstrates those connections with short excerpts from songs he wrote at the time." Bull Cent Child Books

"Christensen makes a fine union of a spirited, vibrant text and hand-colored woodcuts that are sinewy and emotionally compelling." Booklist

Hale, Bruce, 1957-

Parker-Rock, Michelle. Bruce Hale; an author kids love. Enslow Publishers 2008 48p bibl il por (Authors kids love) lib bdg $23.93

Grades: 3 4 5   92

1. Authors, American

ISBN 978-0-7660-2758-9 (lib bdg); 0-7660-2758-9 (lib bdg)   LC 2007029319

A biography of the author of the Chet Gecko mystery series for children, based on an interview

"The frequent use of direct quotes makes the [text] particularly enjoyable. . . . Kids will be fascinated with . . . Hale's hat collection and love of surfing. . . . Well written, interesting, and useful for reports." SLJ

Halvorsen, Gail

Tunnell, Michael O. Candy bomber; the story of the Berlin airlift's "chocolate pilot". Charlesbridge 2010 il $18.95 *

Grades: 4 5 6 7   **92**
    1. Air pilots 2. Berlin (Germany)—History—Blockade, 1948-1949
    ISBN 978-1-58089-336-7; 1-58089-336-8

"Curious about the city into which he ferried goods during the Berlin Airlift in 1948, pilot Gail Halvorsen stayed over to visit, met some children, and offered to drop candy and gum when he next flew over. This simple idea grew into a massive project with reverberations today. Tunnell tell this appealing story . . . clearly and chronologically, weaving just enough background for twenty-first century readers and illustrating almost every page with black-and-white photographs, many from Halvorsen's own collection." Booklist

Includes bibliographical references

Hancock, John, 1737-1793

Adler, David A. A picture book of John Hancock; by David A. Adler and Michael S. Adler; illustrated by Ronald Himler. Holiday House 2007 unp il $16.95

Grades: 1 2 3   **92**
    1. United States—History—1775-1783, Revolution
    ISBN 978-0-8234-2005-6; 0-8234-2005-1
                           LC 2005052649

"This biography begins with what is probably Hancock's most famous act, the signing of the Declaration of Independence. It then takes readers back to the beginning of his life to tell how he became such an important and influential part of America's Revolutionary War. . . . Himler's watercolors in muted tones offer visual guides to historical events. This title . . . is a solid addition to biography collections." SLJ

Includes bibliographical references

Fritz, Jean. Will you sign here, John Hancock? pictures by Trina Schart Hyman. Putnam Pub. Group 1976 47p il hardcover o.p. pa $5.99 *

Grades: 2 3 4   **92**
    1. United States—History—1775-1783, Revolution
    ISBN 0-399-23306-7; 0-698-11440-X (pa)

"A straightforward biography of the rich Boston dandy with the gigantic signature. When he signed the Declaration of Independence he quipped, 'There! George the Third can read "that" without his spectacles. Now he can double his reward for my head.'" Saturday Rev

"An affectionate look at a flamboyant, egocentric, but kindly, patriot, the book is a most enjoyable view of history. . . . The delightful illustrations exactly suit the times and the extraordinary character of John Hancock." Horn Book

Handel, George Frideric, 1685-1759

Anderson, M. T. Handel, who knew what he liked; illustrated by Kevin Hawkes. Candlewick Press 2001 unp il hardcover o.p. pa $6.99 *

Grades: 4 5 6   **92**
    1. Composers
    ISBN 0-7636-1046-1; 0-7636-2562-0 (pa)
                           LC 00-57210

In this biography Handel, who would later compose some of the world's most beautiful music, is shown as a stubborn little boy with a mind of his own

The author "infuses the composer's story with warmth and color, humor and humanity. . . . Relating pithy stories with plain words and short sentences, Anderson never forgets his audience in his enthusiasm for his subject." Booklist

Harrison, John, 1693-1776

Dash, Joan. The longitude prize; pictures by Dusan Petricic. Farrar, Straus and Giroux 1999 200p il $17

Grades: 5 6 7 8   **92**
    1. Longitude
    ISBN 0-374-34636-4   LC 97-44257

"Frances Foster books"

The story of John Harrison, inventor of watches and clocks, who spent forty years working on a time-machine which could be used to accurately determine longitude at sea

"Students looking for new subjects for reports will discover . . . an excellent resource on a topic seldom addressed in a book for youth. Charming ink drawings by Dusan Petricic illustrate. A glossary, an afterword, a time line, and a bibliography conclude." Booklist

Harvey, William, 1578-1657

Yount, Lisa. William Harvey; discoverer of how blood circulates; [by] Lisa Yount. rev ed. Enslow Publishers 2008 128p il map (Great minds of science) lib bdg $31.93

Grades: 5 6 7 8   **92**
    1. Blood—Circulation 2. Physicians
    ISBN 978-0-7660-3010-7 (lib bdg); 0-7660-3010-5 (lib bdg)   LC 2007020301

First published 1994

"A biography of the seventeenth-century English physician William Harvey and includes related activities for readers." Publisher's note

Includes glossary and bibliographical references

Haskell, Katharine Wright, 1874-1929

Maurer, Richard. The Wright sister; Katharine Wright and her famous brothers. Millbrook Press 2003 127p il $18.95; lib bdg $25.90 *

Grades: 5 6 7 8   **92**
    1. Wright, Wilbur, 1867-1912 2. Wright, Orville, 1871-1948 3. Air pilots
    ISBN 0-7613-1546-2; 0-7613-2564-6 (lib bdg)
                          LC 2002-151080

"Maurer chronicles the events surrounding Wilbur and Orville, while all along filling in the details of their younger sister's life and the relationship among the three." SLJ

"Quotations from diaries and letters bring the close-knit Wright family to life. . . . The layout is spacious, and the many well chosen, black-and-white photos help visualize the Wrights and their times." Booklist

Hatshepsut, Queen of Egypt

Galford, Ellen. Hatshepsut; the princess who became king. National Geographic 2005 64p il map (World history biographies) $17.95; lib bdg $27.90 *

Grades: 4 5 6 7   92

1. Egypt—History 2. Egypt—Civilization 3. Kings and rulers
ISBN 0-7922-3645-9; 0-7922-3646-7 (lib bdg)

This "presents the life of Queen Hatshepsut, who ruled Egypt as pharaoh during the New Kingdom, around 3500 years ago. Illustrated with clear, color photos of artifacts and sites as well as colorful maps, the text discusses aspects of Egyptian life such as education and religion in Hatshepsut's life. . . . With a clearly written text and many handsome photos, this provides an accessible introduction to Hatshepsut and her times." Booklist

Hawkins, Benjamin Waterhouse

Kerley, Barbara. The dinosaurs of Waterhouse Hawkins; an illuminating history of Mr. Waterhouse Hawkins, artist and lecturer; with drawings by Brian Selznick, many of which are based on the original sketches of Mr. Hawkins. Scholastic 2001 unp il $16.95 *

Grades: 3 4 5   92

1. Dinosaurs
ISBN 0-439-11494-2   LC 00-58376
A Caldecott Medal honor book, 2002

"A true dinosaur story—in three ages—from a childhood love of art, to the monumental dinosaur sculptures at the Crystal Palace in England, to the thwarted work in New York's Central Park . . . it's all here!" Title page

The true story of Victorian artist Benjamin Waterhouse Hawkins, who built life-sized models of dinosaurs in the hope of educating the world about these awe-inspiring ancient animals and what they were like

"Kerley suffuses her text with a sense of wonder and amazement, a tone well-matched by Selznick's lush, dramatic illustrations." Publ Wkly

Haydn, Joseph, 1732-1809

Norton, James R. Haydn's world; [by] James R. Norton. Rosen Pub. Group 2008 64p il (Music throughout history) lib bdg $29.25

Grades: 5 6 7 8   92

1. Composers
ISBN 978-1-4042-0727-1 (lib bdg); 1-4042-0727-9 (lib bdg)   LC 2007000907

This "book begins with an introduction briefly addressing social issues of the day, historical background, or other significant information. . . . Successive chapters discuss the [man's] early [life], family background, social status, personality characteristics, musical training and education, obstacles or challenges, and influences. A chapter . . . focuses on the musician's well-known compositions, describing through lively and colorful language some of the musical elements employed. . . . The format and layout are appealing and uncluttered." SLJ

Includes glossary and bibliographical references

Henry, John William, 1847?-ca. 1875

Nelson, Scott Reynolds. Ain't nothing but a man; my quest to find the real John Henry; [by] Scott Reynolds Nelson with Marc Aronson. National Geographic 2008 64p il $18.95; lib bdg $27.90 *

Grades: 4 5 6 7 8   92

1. African Americans—Biography 2. John Henry (Legendary character) 3. Railroads—History
ISBN   978-1-4263-0000-4;   1-4263-0000-X; 978-1-4263-0001-1 (lib bdg); 1-4263-0001-8 (lib bdg)   LC 2007-12446

This describes the author's research to find the real man who inspired the songs and legends about the African American steel-driving hero.

"The layout is attractive, with a sepia and beige background for the text and sepia-toned photographs. . . . This is an excellent example of how much detective work is needed for original research." SLJ

Includes bibliographical references

Henry, Patrick, 1736-1799

Fritz, Jean. Where was Patrick Henry on the 29th of May? illustrated by Margot Tomes. Putnam Pub. Group 1975 47p il $16.99; pa $6.99 *

Grades: 2 3 4   92

1. United States—History—1600-1775, Colonial period
ISBN 0-399-23305-9; 0-698-11439-6 (pa)

A "portrait of a founding father. Patrick Henry was born on May 29, and the author uses this date to focus on significant periods in his life. Henry's skill at oratory is shown in development as well as his anger at English laws, until they peak in his famous speech." Child Book Rev Serv

"The color pictures are artful evocations of the [18th] century in America and the text presents Patrick Henry as a human being—not a sterilized historic 'figure.'" Publ Wkly

Henson, Matthew Alexander, 1866-1955

Hopkinson, Deborah. Keep on! the story of Matthew Henson, co-discoverer of the North Pole; written by Deborah Hopkinson; illustrated by Stephen Alcorn. Peachtree Publishers 2009 unp il $17.95

Grades: 2 3 4   92

1. African Americans—Biography 2. Explorers 3. North Pole
ISBN 978-1-56145-473-0; 1-56145-473-7
                                       LC 2008031118

This tells the story of "Matthew Henson, the African-American explorer credited as being the 'co-discoverer' (along with Admiral Robert Peary) of the North Pole in 1909." Publ Wkly

"Written in articulate and straightforward prose, and accompanied by quotes from Henson, *Keep On!* tells the story of an inspiring and courageous figure and is enhanced by Alcorn's dramatic, sweeping scenes." SLJ

Henson, Matthew Alexander, 1866-1955—*Continued*

Johnson, Dolores. Onward; a photobiography of African-American polar explorer Matthew Henson. National Geographic 2006 64p il $17.95 *

Grades: 5 6 7 8   92

    1. Explorers 2. North Pole 3. African Americans—Biography

    ISBN 0-7922-7914-X   LC 2005-05837

"The quest to be the first to reach the North Pole is an exciting adventure story, and Henson got there first, as part of the ninth expedition led by Robert Peary in 1909. But Henson was African American, labeled as Peary's 'Negro manservant,' and he did not get full recognition until 2001. This . . . focuses on the physical details of the dangerous Arctic journeys . . . the repeated failures and the teamwork, as well as Henson's skills, stamina, and essential role in forging relationships with the Inuit. . . . The book design is beautiful: thick paper, spacious type, and stirring photos that capture the icy storms as well as the people involved in the history." Booklist

Herrera, Juan Felipe, 1948-

Herrera, Juan Felipe. The upside down boy; story by Juan Felipe Herrera; illustrations by Elizabeth Gómez. Children's Bk. Press 2000 31p il $15.95

Grades: K 1 2 3   92

    1. Poets 2. Mexican Americans—Biography 3. Bilingual books—English-Spanish

    ISBN 0-89239-162-6   LC 99-49113

    Title page and text in English and Spanish

The author recalls the year when his farm worker parents settled down in the city so that he could go to school for the first time

"Herrera's poetic prose sings with a unique voice in both languages, and Gómez's illustrations are colorful and ethereal." Horn book guide

Heschel, Abraham Joshua, 1907-1972

Michelson, Richard. As good as anybody: Martin Luther King Jr. and Abraham Joshua Heschel's amazing march toward freedom. See entry under King, Martin Luther, Jr., 1929-1968

Hildegard, von Bingen, Saint, 1098-1179

Winter, Jonah. The secret world of Hildegard; illustrated by Jeanette Winter. Arthur A. Levine Books 2007 unp il $16.99 *

Grades: 2 3 4   92

    1. Christian saints

    ISBN 0-439-50739-1; 978-0-439-50739-4

           LC 2006-15990

A picture book biography of Hildegard who, born in Germany in the Middle Ages, became "celebrated as a visionary and a woman beyond her times. . . . Narrated with elegant simplicity, the story also makes use of Hildegard's own words. . . . Jeanette Winter's artistic style is deceptively simple. Her images feature plainly drawn characters, yet surrounding Hildegard are mystical Hebrew letters, halos filled with stars and thorns, comprehensible symbols of ecstacy, and other pieces of religious iconography." Booklist

    Includes bibliographical references

Hillary, Sir Edmund

Coburn, Broughton. Triumph on Everest: a photobiography of Sir Edmund Hillary. National Geographic Soc. 2000 64p il map $17.95; pa $7.95

Grades: 4 5 6 7   92

    1. Mount Everest (China and Nepal) 2. Mountaineering

    ISBN 0-7922-7114-9; 0-7922-7932-8 (pa)

           LC 00-27009

A biography of Edmund Hillary, whose love of snow, mountains, and the outdoor life culminated in his conquering the highest peak in the world

"Threaded with quotes from Hillary's own writings, and full of fine, blue-toned photographs, the engrossing text presents the life of a reticent but world-renowned mountaineer, adventurer, and philanthropist." SLJ

    Includes bibliographical references

Hodgman, Ann

Hodgman, Ann. The house of a million pets; with illustrations by Eugene Yelchin. Henry Holt & Co. 2007 263p il $16.95

Grades: 3 4 5 6   92

    1. Pets

    ISBN 978-0-8050-7974-6; 0-8050-7974-2

           LC 2006-36447

Hodgman offers an "anecdotal memoir about her family and its myriad animal members. Owls, raccoons, hedgehogs, prairie dogs, sugar gliders, voles, and pygmy mice are among Hodgman's menagerie." Booklist

This is a "witty and personable narrative. . . . Yelchin's inky animal vignettes are inviting, with a cheerful impudence in their scrawled lines that perfectly matches the text." Bull Cent Child Books

Hokusai (Katsushika Hokusai), 1760-1849

Ray, Deborah Kogan. Hokusai; the man who painted a mountain. Foster Bks. 2001 unp il $18

Grades: 3 4 5 6   92

    1. Artists, Japanese

    ISBN 0-374-33263-0   LC 00-50395

"The life of the iconoclastic Japanese artist who produced more than thirty thousand works of art." Booklist

"The text and evocative artwork provide details and scenes of everyday Japanese life in the 19th century. The illustrations include accomplished soft watercolor and colored-pencil paintings, labeled Chinese characters, drawings from the artist's sketchbooks, and a reproduction of Hokusai's 'The Great Wave off Kanagawa.'" SLJ

    Includes bibliographical references

Honda, Sōichirō, 1906-1991

Weston, Mark. Honda; the boy who dreamed of cars; illustrated by Katie Yamasaki. Lee & Low Books 2008 unp il $17.95

Grades: 3 4 5   92

1. Automobile industry 2. Executives 3. Businesspeople

ISBN 978-1-60060-246-7; 1-60060-246-0

LC 2007049040

"A biography of Japanese businessman Soichiro Honda, founder of the Honda Motor Company, focusing on his early influences and later career as an innovative inventor and manufacturer of motorcyles and cars." Publisher's note

"Weston's writing is clear and accessible. . . . The book reads like a story, with fictionalization of Honda's thoughts and dialogue. . . . Yamasaki's acrylic illustrations dominate each page. At first glance they seem representational, but on closer inspection readers will find little men climbing on the engine parts, . . . [and] miniature cars going around a globe and down Honda's arm. . . . Yamasaki's creative composition makes the pictures interesting and dynamic." SLJ

Hopper, Edward, 1882-1967

Rubin, Susan Goldman. Edward Hopper; painter of light and shadow. Abrams Books for Young Readers 2007 47p il $18.95 *

Grades: 5 6 7 8   92

1. Artists—United States

ISBN 978-0-8109-9347-1; 0-8109-9347-3

LC 2006-31978

"On every page of this beautifully designed biography, readers will find a reproduction of Hopper's work, matched to clear, eloquent commentary. . . . Readers . . . will come back to read about the man and look at his art again and again." Booklist

Includes bibliographical references

Houdini, Harry, 1874-1926

Carlson, Laurie M. Harry Houdini for kids; his life and adventures with 21 magic tricks and illusions. Chicago Review Press 2009 136p il pa $16.95

Grades: 4 5 6 7   92

1. Magicians 2. Magic tricks

ISBN 978-1-55652-782-1 (pa); 1-55652-782-9 (pa)

LC 2008021404

"Reluctant readers (as well as budding troublemakers) will flock to this biography/handbook hybrid about one of the most famous magicians who ever lived. Even for those familiar with Houdini's fascinating story, Carlson's snappy writing gives it new life. . . . Nearly every page is enlivened with period photographs, boxed sections containing biographies and definitions, and, most important, 21 magic tricks that will have readers breaking out their deck of cards and practicing their sleight of hand." Booklist

Fleischman, Sid. Escape! the story of the great Houdini. Greenwillow Books 2006 210p il $18.99; lib bdg $19.89 *

Grades: 5 6 7 8   92

1. Magicians

ISBN 978-0-06-085094-4; 0-06-085094-9; 978-0-06-085095-1 (lib bdg); 0-06-0850957-1 (lib bdg)

LC 2005052631

"Fleischman looks at Houdini's life through his own eyes, as a fellow magician. . . . Fleischman's tone is lively and he develops a relationship with readers by revealing just enough truth behind Houdini's razzle-dazzle to keep the legend alive. . . . Engaging and fascinating." SLJ

Includes bibliographical references

Krull, Kathleen. Houdini; the world's greatest mystery man and escape king; in a production written by Kathleen Krull; and illustrated by Eric Velasquez. Walker & Co. 2005 unp il hardcover o.p. pa $6.95 *

Grades: 2 3 4   92

1. Magicians

ISBN 0-8027-8953-6; 0-8027-8954-4 (lib bdg); 0-8027-9646-X (pa)

LC 2004-49493

"Framed descriptions of some of Houdini's most famous stunts are interspersed within the overview of his life. The author's crisp narrative style and careful choice of detail are evident here. . . . Velasquez's impressive framed, posed oil paintings portray the magician's intensity and sense of showmanship." SLJ

Includes bibliographical references

MacLeod, Elizabeth. Harry Houdini; a magical life; written by Elizabeth MacLeod. Kids Can Press 2005 32p il $14.95

Grades: 4 5 6   92

1. Magicians

ISBN 1-55337-769-9

"The world's best-known magician began performing as an acrobat in his neighborhood at the age of nine to make money desperately needed by his family. MacLeod provides a straightforward history of her colorful subject. . . . Reproduced images of photos, handbills, and advertisements bring the text on each double-page spread to life." Booklist

Houston, Samuel, 1793-1863

Fritz, Jean. Make way for Sam Houston; illustrations by Elise Primavera. Putnam 1986 109p il map hardcover o.p. pa $5.99 *

Grades: 4 5 6   92

ISBN 0-399-21303-1; 0-698-11646-1 (pa)

LC 85-25601

This is a biography of the "lawyer, governor of Tennessee, general in the wars against Santa Anna, president of the Republic of Texas, and finally U.S. senator and governor of the state of Texas." Horn Book

"Artfully weaving the threads of fact, Fritz creates a biography that is both interesting and informative. Developing Houston as a human character that readers can identify with as well as admire, and drawing him against the scene of America's own political turmoil, Fritz gives

Houston, Samuel, 1793-1863—*Continued*
us a book to be read and to be felt." Voice Youth Advocates

Includes bibliographical references

Howard, Luke, 1772-1864
Hannah, Julie. The man who named the clouds; [by] Julie Hannah and Joan Holub; illustrations by Paige Billin-Frye. A. Whitman 2006 40p il $15.95
Grades: 2 3 4   92
1. Clouds
ISBN 978-0-8075-4974-2; 0-8075-4974-6
LC 2006-00002
"Born in England in 1772, Luke Howard began keeping a weather journal when he was 10 years old. . . . In 1802, he proposed a system of classifying clouds into seven types. . . . His system was adopted and, in adapted form, is still used today. This colorful book balances biographical and historical information with basic weather science. . . . An attractive combination of biographical narrative and weather science." Booklist
Includes bibliographical references

Hudson, Henry, d. 1611
Weaver, Janice. Hudson. Tundra Books 2010 il map $22.95 *
Grades: 3 4 5 6   92
1. Explorers 2. America—Exploration
ISBN 978-0-88776-814-9; 0-88776-814-8
"This dramatic picture-book biography about Henry Hudson, who discovered neither the new land nor the passage to Asia he sought, makes the explorer's lack of success a gripping read. . . . Weaver is clear about what is fact and what is supposition, and the tumultuous early-seventeenth-century history is meticulously documented. . . . Craig's glowing period portraits, landscapes, and watercolors of the ship in dangerous seas intensify the drama, and archival prints and maps add interest." Booklist

Hughes, Langston, 1902-1967
Cooper, Floyd. Coming home; from the life of Langston Hughes. Philomel Bks. 1994 unp il lib bdg $16.95; pa $6.99 *
Grades: K 1 2 3   92
1. Poets, American 2. African American authors
ISBN 0-399-22682-6 (lib bdg); 0-698-11612-7 (pa)
LC 93-36332
This "biography highlights pivotal events in Hughes's life, emphasizing his loneliness as a child and his development as a poet. . . . Cooper's hazy illustrations in gold, brown, and sepia tones reveal keen observations of people and neighborhood. The text and art combine to create a fine tribute and introduction to the writer's life." Horn Book
Includes bibliographical references

Walker, Alice. Langston Hughes, American poet; paintings by Catherine Deeter. HarperCollins Pubs. 2002 37p il hardcover o.p. pa $7.99
Grades: 2 3 4 5   92
1. Poets, American 2. African American authors
ISBN 0-06-021518-6; 0-06-021519-4 (lib bdg); 0-06-079889-0 (pa)   LC 92-28540

"Amistad"
A newly illustrated edition of the title first published 1974 by Crowell

An illustrated biography of the Harlem poet whose works gave voice to the joy and pain of the black experience in America

This "is an excellent introduction to Hughes, focusing mainly on his adolescence and early adulthood. . . . The engaging, anecdotal style is perfect for read-alouds, and the brief sentences and simple vocabulary make the book a good choice for beginning and struggling readers. Deeter's realistic paintings capture the text's pivotal moments." Booklist

Hunter, Clementine, 1886?-1988
Whitehead, Kathy. Art from her heart: folk artist Clementine Hunter; [illustrated by] Shane Evans. G.P. Putnam's Sons 2008 unp il $16.99 *
Grades: 4 5 6 7   92
1. African American artists 2. Women artists 3. Folk art
ISBN 978-0-399-24219-9; 0-399-24219-8
LC 2006-34458
A biography of "folk artist Clementine Hunter. Her paintings went from hanging on her clothesline to hanging in museums, yet because of the color of her skin, a friend had to sneak her in when the gallery was closed." Publisher's note
"Whitehead's lyrical text speaks of Hunter's perseverance and talent as well as of the simplicity, love of nature, and caring of friends and family that informed her work. Evans bolsters Whitehead's words with bold mixed-media illustrations that portray Hunter in hard times and in good." SLJ

Hurston, Zora Neale, 1891-1960
Miller, William. Zora Hurston and the chinaberry tree; illustrated by Cornelius Van Wright and Ying-hwa Hu. Lee & Low Bks. 1994 unp il $15.95; pa $6.95
Grades: K 1 2 3   92
1. African American authors 2. Women authors
ISBN 1-880000-14-8; 1-880000-33-4 (pa)
LC 94-1291
"This biography, which covers a brief period in Zora Neale Hurston's childhood, ends with the young girl grieving over her mother's death but finding inner power and strength from her mother's life." Horn Book
"Conveying the changing expressions on the face of the young Hurston as easily as they show the grandeur of the sky at nightfall, the versatile artists neatly capture the emotions in this lucidly told story." Publ Wkly

Porter, A. P. Jump at de sun: the story of Zora Neale Hurston; foreword by Lucy Ann Hurston. Carolrhoda Bks. 1992 95p il pa $6.95 hardcover o.p.
Grades: 4 5 6 7   92
1. African American authors 2. Women authors
ISBN 0-87614-546-2 (pa)   LC 91-37241
Follows the life of the African American writer known for her novels, plays, articles, and collections of folklore
This is "written in engagingly fresh prose and attrac-

Hurston, Zora Neale, 1891-1960—*Continued*
tively laid out in a large, clear type. . . . The well-chosen and appropriately placed black-and-white photographs serve not only to extend the text, but also to put faces on the many names that crop up in the story of Hurston's eventful life." SLJ

Includes bibliographical references

Hutchinson, Anne Marbury, 1591-1643
Atkins, Jeannine. Anne Hutchinson's way; [by] Jeannine Atkins; pictures by Michael Dooling. Farrar, Straus and Giroux 2007 unp il $17 *
Grades: 2 3 4   92
1. Massachusetts—History—1600-1775, Colonial period
ISBN 0-374-30365-7
"Anne Hutchinson arrives with her family in Massachusetts colony in 1634 and begins preaching scripture from her home after finding herself in disagreement with the minister's beliefs. . . . Atkins is able to take the issue of religious freedom and make it personal by telling the story through the eyes of Hutchinson's young daughter, Susanna. . . . A sense of sturdiness is everywhere here: in the story . . . and in Dooling's impressive artwork, plain in color but rugged in its portrayal of the demands of colony life. Illustrated in a photo-realistic style that makes the long-ago events seem close." Booklist

Huynh, Quang Nhuong
Huynh, Quang Nhuong. The land I lost: adventures of a boy in Vietnam; with pictures by Vo-Dinh Mai. Harper & Row 1982 115p il pa $4.99 hardcover o.p.
Grades: 5 6 7 8   92
1. Vietnam—Social life and customs
ISBN 0-06-440183-9 (pa)   LC 80-8437
"Each chapter in this book of reminiscence about the author's boyhood in a hamlet in the Vietnamese highlands, is a separate episode, although the same characters appear in many of the episodes. . . . The writing has an ingenuous quality that adds to the appeal of the strong sense of familial and communal ties that pervades the story." Bull Cent Child Books

Huynh, Quang Nhuong. Water buffalo days; growing up in Vietnam; pictures by Jean and Mou-sien Tseng. HarperCollins Pubs. 1997 116p il $13.95; pa $4.95
Grades: 3 4 5   92
1. Vietnam—Social life and customs 2. Water buffalo
ISBN 0-06-024957-9; 0-06-446211-0 (pa)
                                        LC 96-35058
The author describes his close relationship to his water buffalo, Tank, when he was growing up in a village in the central highlands of Vietnam
"Most of the incidents described are entertaining and readers will learn fascinating information about the importance of these animals in this culture. . . . The Tsengs' soft sketches show Tank, his young master, and the various villagers mentioned in the text." SLJ

Hypatia, ca. 370-415
Love, D. Anne. Of numbers and stars; the story of Hypatia; by D. Anne Love; illustrated by Pam Paparone. Holiday House 2006 unp il $16.95 *
Grades: 2 3 4   92
1. Women mathematicians 2. Philosophers
ISBN 0-8234-1621-6   LC 2003064725
"In fourth-century C.E. Egypt, women had few opportunities. How Hypatia, daughter of mathematician Theon, became one of the greatest philosophers of her day makes fascinating reading. . . . Attractive paintings add life to a clear and captivating text that offers a unique contribution to units about Egypt, philosophers, or women in history." SLJ

Includes bibliographical references

Ibn Battuta, 1304-1377
Rumford, James. Traveling man: the journey of Ibn Battuta, 1325-1354; written, illustrated, and illuminated by James Rumford. Houghton Mifflin 2001 unp il map hardcover o.p. pa $7.99
Grades: 3 4 5 6   92
1. Voyages and travels
ISBN 0-618-08366-9; 0-618-43233-7 (pa)
                                        LC 00-57257
This describes the "journey of Ibn Battuta, the celebrated 14th-century scholar and cultural geographer from Tangier who spent 29 years wandering through Africa, the Middle East and Asia." N Y Times Book Rev
"Rumford's presentation is lavish and undeniably impressive. Ibn Battuta's route snakes across the spreads to create an extended map, with text boxes serving as stopping points along the way. Lush watercolor scenes, awash in gold highlights, are frequently borded by equally lush calligraphy quotes, rendered in Arabic, Persian, or Chinese." Bull Cent Child Books
Includes glossary

Irving, Washington, 1783-1859
Harness, Cheryl. The literary adventures of Washington Irving; American storyteller; by Cheryl Harness. National Geographic Society 2008 43p il $17.95; lib bdg $27.90 *
Grades: 2 3 4 5   92
1. Authors, American
ISBN 978-1-4263-0438-5;   1-4263-0438-2;
978-1-4263-0439-2 (lib bdg); 1-4263-0439-0 (lib bdg)
                                        LC 2008024975
A biography of the American author of The adventures of Rip Van Winkle and The Legend of Sleepy Hollow.
"Pairing insightful text with paintings organized into comic-book-style frames, Harness captures with exuberance everything that made Irving's life so exciting." Booklist
Includes bibliographical references

Ives, Charles Edward, 1874-1954
Gerstein, Mordicai. What Charlie heard. Foster Bks. 2001 unp il $17
Grades: K 1 2 3   92
1. Composers
ISBN 0-374-38292-1   LC 00-25557

Ives, Charles Edward, 1874-1954—*Continued*

Describes the life of American composer Charles Ives, who wrote music which expressed all the sounds he heard in the world, but which was not well received during his lifetime

"Gerstein creates a rousing visual cacophony that echoes Ives's compositions in this inspired picture-book biography." Publ Wkly

Jackson, Stonewall, 1824-1863

Fritz, Jean. Stonewall; with drawings by Stephen Gammell. Putnam 1979 152p il map hardcover o.p. pa $5.99 *
Grades: 4 5 6 7   92
1. Generals 2. United States—History—1861-1865, Civil War
ISBN 0-399-20698-1; 0-698-11552-X (pa)
LC 79-12506
A biography of the brilliant southern general who gained the nickname Stonewall by his stand at Bull Run during the Civil War

"Fritz's trenchant, compassionate life of General Thomas Jonathan Jackson grips the reader and makes one understand why Stonewall is an honored legend in American history. . . . The tragic irony of his death at age 39 is movingly described." Publ Wkly
Includes bibliographical references

Jalāl al-Dīn Rūmī, Maulana, 1207-1273

Demi. Rumi; whirling dervish; written and illustrated by Demi. Marshall Cavendish Children 2009 31p il $19.99 *
Grades: 4 5 6 7   92
1. Persian poetry 2. Poets
ISBN 978-0-7614-5527-1; 0-7614-5527-2
LC 2008012920
"Demi presents this picture-book introduction to the thirteenth-century mystical poet. . . . Demi condenses her famous subject's life into a brief but substantive text. . . . She adds frequent excerpts from Rumi's poems and writings. . . . In an introductory note, Demi cites Turkish miniatures as her inspiration for the small-scale, elaborately patterned pictures, rendered in Turkish and Chinese inks with gold overlay. . . . The gilded, celebratory pictures create shimmering beauty from the smallest details." Booklist

Jefferson, Thomas, 1743-1826

Adler, David A. A picture book of Thomas Jefferson; illustrated by John & Alexandra Wallner. Holiday House 1990 unp il lib bdg $17.95; pa $6.95
Grades: 1 2 3   92
1. Presidents—United States
ISBN 0-8234-0791-8 (lib bdg); 0-8234-0881-7 (pa)
LC 89-20076
Traces the life and achievements of the architect, bibliophile, president, and author of the Declaration of Independence

"The book includes an amazing amount of material. An appealing package with simple language and detailed drawings." Horn Book

Jemison, Mae C.

Jemison, Mae C. Find where the wind goes; moments from my life; [by] Mae Jemison. Scholastic Press 2001 196p il $16.95 paperback o.p.
Grades: 5 6 7 8   92
1. Astronauts 2. African American women—Biography
ISBN 0-439-13195-2; 0-439-13196-0 (pa)
LC 00-41008
"Dr. Jemison, the first woman of color to travel in space, shares her life story in this autobiographical selection." Book Rep
"Jemison's vitality, intelligence, and humor shine through the book, and she has a fascinating and inspiring life story to tell." Booklist

Joan, of Arc, Saint, 1412-1431

Hodges, Margaret. Joan of Arc; the Lily Maid; illustrated by Robert Rayevsky. Holiday House 1999 unp il $16.95 *
Grades: 2 3 4   92
1. Christian saints 2. France—History—1328-1589, House of Valois
ISBN 0-8234-1424-8   LC 98-24260
A biography of the fifteenth-century peasant girl who led a French army to victory against the English, witnessed the crowning of King Charles VII, and was later burned at the stake for witchcraft

"Hodges tells Joan's story with simplicity, distilling the myriad events of bravery and betrayal down to their essence. . . . The pictures are full of action and naive charm, and they have the same strong simplicity as the text. Rayevsky incorporates medieval styles and techniques into his artwork, using two printmaking techniques: dry point and etching." Booklist

Stanley, Diane. Joan of Arc. Morrow Junior Bks. 1998 unp il hardcover o.p. pa $7.99 *
Grades: 4 5 6 7   92
1. Christian saints 2. France—History—1328-1589, House of Valois
ISBN 0-688-14329-6; 0-06-443748-5 (pa); 978-0-06-443748-6 (pa)   LC 97-45652
A biography of the fifteenth-century peasant girl who led a French army to victory against the English and was burned at the stake for witchcraft

Stanley "orchestrates the complexities of history into a gripping, unusually challenging story in this exemplary biography. . . . Judiciously chosen details build atmosphere in both the text and the artwork—painstakingly wrought, gilded paintings modeled after the illuminated manuscripts of Joan's day." Publ Wkly
Includes bibliographical references

Wilkinson, Philip. Joan of Arc; the teenager who saved her nation; [by] Philip Wilkinson. National Geographic Society 2007 64p il map (World history biographies) $17.95; lib bdg $27.90
Grades: 4 5 6 7   92
1. Christian saints 2. France—History—1328-1589, House of Valois
ISBN 978-1-4263-0116-2; 1-4263-0116-2; 978-1-4263-0117-9 (lib bdg); 1-4263-0117-0 (lib bdg)
LC 2006026106

Joan, of Arc, Saint, 1412-1431—*Continued*
A look at the life, death, and continuing influence of Joan of Arc.

This book is "attractively illustrated and pleasingly presented. . . . Dates, highlighted across the bottom of pages in a colorful band, note biographical points of reference and historical events. The writing is competent . . . and covers all the essentials." SLJ

Includes glossary and bibliographical references

Johnson, Jack, 1878-1946
Smith, Charles R. Black Jack; the ballad of Jack Johnson; [by] Charles R. Smith jr.; illustrated by Shane W. Evans. Roaring Brook Press unp il $16.99 *
Grades: K 1 2 3   92
1. Boxing 2. African American athletes
ISBN 978-1-59643-473-8; 1-59643-473-2
"A Neal Porter book"
A picture book biography in verse of boxer Jack Jackson, the first African American heavyweight champion of the world.

"The elegant simplicity and rat-a-tat rhythms land some stunners. . . . [The book is] enhanced by Evans' lithe and swaggering artwork, which lends a tremendous visual charisma, grace, and grandeur to the man." Booklist

Johnson, Lyndon B. (Lyndon Baines), 1908-1973
Gold, Susan Dudley. Lyndon B. Johnson. Marshall Cavendish Benchmark 2009 112p il (Presidents and their times) lib bdg $34.21
Grades: 5 6 7 8   92
1. Presidents—United States
ISBN 978-0-7614-2837-4 (lib bdg); 0-7614-2837-2 (lib bdg)   LC 2007038518
A biography of the thirty-sixth president of the United States discusses his personal life, education, and political career and covers the formative events of his time
Includes glossary and bibliographical references

Johnson, Mamie, 1935-
Green, Michelle Y. A strong right arm: the story of Mamie "Peanut" Johnson; introduction by Mamie Johnson. Dial Bks. for Young Readers 2002 111p il $15.99; pa $5.99 *
Grades: 4 5 6 7   92
1. Baseball—Biography 2. Women athletes 3. African American athletes
ISBN 0-8037-2661-9; 0-14-240072-6 (pa)
LC 2001-28616
"Johnson was a pitcher with the Negro Leagues' Indianapolis Clowns from 1953 to 1955. In the introduction, Johnson speaks directly and movingly to the reader about her meeting with author Green, who then lets the famous ballplayer tell her own story in a lively first-person narrative. Johnson's ebullient personality and determination fairly leap off the page." Booklist
Includes bibliographical references

Jones, John Paul, 1747-1792
Cooper, Michael L. Hero of the high seas; John Paul Jones and the American Revolution. National Geographic 2006 128p il map $21.95; lib bdg $32.90
Grades: 5 6 7 8   92
1. Admirals 2. United States—History—1775-1783, Revolution
ISBN 0-7922-5547-X; 0-7922-5548-8 (lib bdg)
LC 2005-36256
"Cooper charts his subject's life from a scandal-ridden Scottish captain on a trading ship to a man of self-invention who came to the American colonies to start a new life and became a naval hero. Jones is presented as a loyal captain, an arrogant leader, a determined sailor, and a flagrant social climber. The narrative style will appeal to reluctant readers, for it reads like a chronicle of thrilling naval adventures. . . . The text is clear and understandable." SLJ
Includes bibliographical references

Joseph, Nez Percé Chief, 1840-1904
Englar, Mary. Chief Joseph, 1840-1904; by Mary Englar. Blue Earth Books 2004 32p (American Indian biographies) lib bdg $23.93
Grades: 3 4 5   92
1. Nez Percé Indians
ISBN 0-7368-2444-8   LC 2003-11071
Contents: "I will fight no more forever"; Life in Wallowa Valley; The white men come; Joseph becomes chief; The Nez Perce war; Life after the war
A biography of the peace chief who ended the Nez Percé War by surrendering to United States soldiers in 1877, believing that he would be permitted lead his people back to their ancestral lands in Idaho. Includes a recipe for berry fritters and directions for "the stick game."
This "very accessible [title is] well illustrated with maps, photographs, and paintings, and [it offers] an introduction to American Indian history as well as specific information for reports." Booklist

Juana Inés de la Cruz, 1651-1695
Mora, Pat. A library for Juana: the world of Sor Juana Inés; illustrated by Beatriz Vidal. Knopf 2002 unp il $15.95 *
Grades: 2 3 4   92
1. Women authors 2. Authors, Mexican 3. Nuns
ISBN 0-375-80643-1   LC 2001-50851
A biography of the seventeenth-century Mexican poet, learned in many subjects, who became a nun later in life
"Mora's beautifully crafted text does credit to its subject. . . . The text is perfectly complemented by Vidal's brilliant, detailed illustrations that have the look and exactitude of Renaissance miniatures." SLJ
Includes glossary

Jumper, Betty Mae, 1923-

Annino, Jan Godown. She sang promise: the story of Betty Mae Jumper, Seminole tribal leader; illustrated by Lisa Desimini; afterword by Moses Jumper, Jr. National Geographic 2010 33p il map lib bdg $26.90

Grades: 1 2 3   92

    1. Seminole Indians

    ISBN 978-1-4263-0592-4; 1-4263-0592-3

                           LC 2009-16066

"Elected in 1967 as one of the first women tribal leaders in modern times, Seminole Betty Mae Tiger Jumper overcame oppression and prejudice, starting in her childhood. This picture-book biography tells her story in a dramatic present-tense narrative that blends details of her life with the historical struggle of her people. . . . The large collage paintings in bright colors blend old and new traditions, the natural world, and Seminole artwork." Booklist

Includes glossary and bibliographical references

Kahanamoku, Duke, 1890-1968

Crowe, Ellie. Surfer of the century; the life of Duke Kahanamoku; illustrations by Richard Waldrep. Lee & Low Books 2007 unp il map $18.95 *

Grades: 3 4 5 6   92

    1. Swimming 2. Surfing

    ISBN 978-1-58430-276-6   LC 2006036562

"A biography of Hawaiian Duke Kahanamoku, five-time Olympic swimming champion from the early 1900s who is also considered worldwide as the 'father of modern surfing.'" Publisher's note

"The text is concise and readable, ably supported by Waldrep's full-page color art on every spread. These vibrant, action-filled illustrations . . . add much to the book's overall appeal. Well researched and fact-filled." SLJ

Kahlo, Frida, 1907-1954

Frith, Margaret. Frida Kahlo; the artist who painted herself; written by Margaret Frith; illustrated by Tomie DePaola. Grosset & Dunlap 2003 unp il (Smart about art) hardcover o.p. pa $5.99 *

Grades: 2 3 4   92

    1. Artists, Mexican 2. Women artists

    ISBN 0-448-43239-0; 0-448-42677-3 (pa)

                           LC 2003-5221

Biography of Mexican artist Frida Kahlo, written as a child's school report

"Kahlo's story is clear, concise, and accessible. All of the basic facts are here, along with many personal details that enliven the narrative. . . . The well-written prose is beautifully complemented both by photos of Kahlo and of some of her best-known paintings and by dePaola's splendid trademark illustrations, all set against vividly colored backgrounds." SLJ

Sabbeth, Carol. Frida Kahlo and Diego Rivera: their lives and ideas; 24 activities; [by] Carol Sabbeth. Chicago Review Press 2005 147p il map pa $17.95 *

Grades: 5 6 7 8   92

    1. Rivera, Diego, 1886-1957 2. Artists, Mexican 3. Women artists

    ISBN 1-55652-569-9   LC 2004-24525

"An overview of two complicated and controversial figures whose personal affairs, political ideas and affiliations, and artworks were out of the mainstream, even radical. . . . The pages are colorfully designed with bright borders at the tops of the pages, colored sidebars, and appropriately placed photos and reproductions, including works by both artists. The 24 related activities range from artwork to cultural projects." SLJ

Includes bibliographical references

Winter, Jonah. Frida; illustrated by Ana Juan. Levine Bks. 2002 unp il $16.95; pa $5.99 *

Grades: K 1 2 3   92

    1. Artists, Mexican 2. Women artists

    ISBN 0-590-20320-7; 0-590-20321-5 (pa)

                           LC 00-51421

Also available Spanish language edition

This "illustrated short biography argues that the seeds of iconic painter Frida Kahlo's genius were planted during her childhood. . . . Winter consistently manages to convey much with a few well-chosen words, and the illustrations are appropriately awash with traditional Mexican folk art motifs and characters. Especially pleasing are Juan's surreal, Kahlo like touches." Horn Book

Kaiulani, Princess of Hawaii, 1875-1899

Stanley, Fay. The last princess: the story of Princess Ka'iulani of Hawai'i; illustrated by Diane Stanley. HarperCollins Pubs. 2001 40p il map $15.95 *

Grades: 4 5 6 7   92

    1. Princesses 2. Hawaii—History

    ISBN 0-688-18020-5   LC 00-32048

A reissue of the title first published 1991 by Four Winds Press

Recounts the story of Hawaii's last heir to the throne, who was denied her right to rule when the monarchy was abolished

"The princesses's story sheds new light on long-forgotten history; the vibrant, handsome gouache illustrations establish the lush Hawaiian background and provide historic detail." Horn Book

Includes bibliographical references

Kearton, Cherry

Bond, Rebecca. In the belly of an ox: the unexpected photographic adventures of Richard and Cherry Kearton. See entry under Kearton, Richard, 1862-1928

Kearton, Richard, 1862-1928

Bond, Rebecca. In the belly of an ox: the unexpected photographic adventures of Richard and Cherry Kearton; written and illustrated by Rebecca Bond. Houghton Mifflin Books for Children 2009 unp il $16 *
Grades: K 1 2 3   92
1. Kearton, Cherry 2. Photographers 3. Photography of birds 4. Birds—Nests 5. Naturalists
ISBN 978-0-547-07675-1; 0-547-07675-4
"In the late 19th century, these nature-loving brothers spent their youth navigating the British countryside. . . . When they were older, the boys devised a method to photograph wild birds in their nests. . . . Bond's graceful watercolors depict the brothers as they piece together their disguises and gain recognition for their innovative approach to photography. The brothers' dedication and ingenuity are especially resonant, and their elaborate costumes will amuse but also inspire." Publ Wkly

Keaton, Buster, 1895-1966

Brighton, Catherine. Keep your eye on the kid; the early years of Buster Keaton. Roaring Brook Press 2008 unp il $16.95 *
Grades: 3 4 5   92
1. Motion picture producers and directors 2. Actors
ISBN 978-1-59643-158-4; 1-59643-158-X
         LC 2007-16534
This is a first-person account of the early years of Buster Keaton, who started performing as a child with his parents in vaudeville and "grew up to become a famous movie producer and performer. . . . Brighton's cartoon drawings shaded in umber and gray tones have a graphic look quite appropriate to the comic subject. The account ends with a brief look at the elaborate stage falls typical of Keaton's movie humor, and a full-page author's note gives added information on his career." SLJ
Includes bibliographical references.

Keats, Ezra Jack, 1916-1983

Engel, Dean. Ezra Jack Keats; a biography with illustrations; [by] Dean Engel and Florence B. Freedman. Silver Moon Press 1995 81p il $24.95
Grades: 3 4 5   92
1. Authors, American 2. Illustrators
ISBN 1-881889-65-3   LC 94-34960
A "profile of a significant creator of twentieth-century children's books, this study of Ezra Jack Keats for young readers is based on reminiscences of conversations with and autobiographical essays by the subject. . . . The illustrations, most from published works, integrate Keats's persona with that of his characters." Horn Book
"This attractive, oversized volume is a must read for Keats's many fans and a marvelous way to introduce (or reintroduce) children to his work." SLJ

Keckley, Elizabeth, ca. 1818-1907

Jones, Lynda. Mrs. Lincoln's dressmaker: the unlikely friendship of Elizabeth Keckley and Mary Todd Lincoln; by Lynda D. Jones. National Geographic 2009 80p il $18.95; lib bdg $27.90 *
Grades: 5 6 7 8   92
1. Lincoln, Mary Todd, 1818-1882 2. African American women—Biography 3. Slavery—United States 4. Presidents' spouses—United States 5. Washington (D.C.)—Social life and customs 6. United States—Race relations
ISBN   978-1-4263-0377-7;   1-4263-0377-7; 978-1-4263-0378-4 (lib bdg); 1-4263-0378-5 (lib bdg)
         LC 2008-29314
"In 1868, a controversial tell-all called Behind the Scenes introduced readers to Elizabeth Hobbs Keckley. Mrs. Keckley was a former slave who had been Mary Todd Lincoln's dressmaker and friend during the White House years, and in the aftermath of President Lincoln's assassination." Publisher's note
"Readers may be familiar with the ups and downs of Lincoln's life, but details of Keckley's story . . . will give them new insights into the life of a slave, in this case, one who was educated and had a profession." Booklist
Includes bibliographical references

Kehret, Peg, 1936-

Kehret, Peg. Five pages a day; a writer's journey. Whitman, A. 2002 185p lib bdg $15.99
Grades: 4 5 6 7   92
1. Authors, American 2. Women authors
ISBN 0-8075-8650-1   LC 2002-16768
A biography of the author of numerous books for young people, describing her childhood bout with polio, how she became a writer, family relationships, and the importance of writing in her life
"With the same eye for well-chosen details that characterizes her other writing, [Kehret] mines her experiences for anecdotes young readers will appreciate." Booklist

Kehret, Peg. Small steps; the year I got polio. Anniversary ed. Albert Whitman 2006 205p il $15.95; pa $6.99 *
Grades: 4 5 6   92
1. Poliomyelitis 2. Authors, American 3. Women authors
ISBN   978-0-8075-7459-1;   0-8075-7459-7; 978-0-8075-7458-4 (pa); 0-8075-7458-9 (pa)
         LC 2006005136
First published 1996
This "memoir takes readers back to 1949 when the author, at age 12, contracted polio. . . . She describes her seven-month ordeal—her diagnosis and quarantine, her terrifying paralysis, her slow and difficult recuperation—and the people she encountered along the way." Booklist
Kehret "writes in an approachable, familiar way, and readers will be hooked from the first page on." SLJ
Includes bibliographical references

Keita, Soundiata, d. 1255

Wisniewski, David. Sundiata; lion king of Mali; story and pictures by David Wisniewski. Clarion Bks. 1992 unp il hardcover o.p. pa $5.95 *

Grades: 1 2 3 4   **92**

1. Mali—History

ISBN 0-395-61302-7; 0-395-76481-5 (pa)

LC 91-27951

The story of Sundiata, who overcame physical handicaps, social disgrace, and strong opposition to rule Mali in the thirteenth century

"Passed down through oral tradition, this historical account has the drama and depth of a folktale. The illustrations—elaborate collages inspired by the artifacts and culture of the Malinke—create a series of dramatic images. The intricacy of the paper-cuts and the richness of the colors and patterns give the artwork visual as well as narrative strength." Booklist

Keller, Helen, 1880-1968

Cline-Ransome, Lesa. Helen Keller; the world in her heart; [by] Lesa Cline-Ransome; illustrated by James Ransome. Collins 2008 unp il $16.99; lib bdg $17.89

Grades: PreK K 1 2   **92**

1. Sullivan, Anne, 1866-1936 2. Deaf 3. Blind

ISBN 978-0-06-057074-3; 0-06-057074-1; 978-0-06-057075-0 (lib bdg); 0-06-057075-X (lib bdg)

LC 2007025851

"Cline-Ransome wisely keeps her focus tight, showing the developing relationship between Keller and her teacher, Annie Sullivan. . . . Cline-Ransome is able to match the spirit of Keller's autobiographical writings. James Ransome cites John Singer Sargent as his inspiration for his bright, handsome paintings. An excellent, accessible introduction to a fascinating woman." SLJ

Delano, Marfe Ferguson. Helen's eyes. See entry under Sullivan, Anne, 1866-1936

Garrett, Leslie. Helen Keller. DK Publishing 2004 127p il (DK biography) hardcover o.p. pa $4.99

Grades: 5 6 7 8   **92**

1. Blind 2. Deaf

ISBN 0-7566-0488-5; 0-7566-0339-0 (pa)

LC 2004-8451

This is a "first look at the . . . woman, blind and deaf since childhood, who . . . learned to read and speak and traveled the world as an inspiring public speaker and political activist. The . . . illustration-rich page design works well . . . and the smooth [narrative is] broken up on every page with boxed facts and quotes as well as well-chosen, small color photos." Booklist

Includes bibliographical references

Lawlor, Laurie. Helen Keller: rebellious spirit. Holiday House 2001 168p il $22.95

Grades: 5 6 7 8   **92**

1. Blind 2. Deaf

ISBN 0-8234-1588-0   LC 00-36950

A "biography of the most famous deaf and blind person in history. Drawing on social and scientific studies of deafness and blindness as well as on American history

texts, Lawlor puts Keller's experiences in context. . . . At the same time, readers get a strong feel for Keller's personality and for the personalities of Annie Sullivan, Alexander Graham Bell, and other major figures in her life. Aided by numerous well-chosen photographs and excerpts from Keller's writings." Horn Book

Includes bibliographical references

Sullivan, George. Helen Keller; her life in pictures; foreword by Keller Johnson Thompson. Scholastic Nonfiction 2007 80p il $17.99

Grades: 4 5 6 7   **92**

1. Blind 2. Deaf

ISBN 0-439-91815-4; 978-0-439-91815-2

LC 2006-51401

"Accompanied by brief, simply phrased commentary from Sullivan, this suite of photos portrays Keller from early childhood into her 80s. . . . This profile will serve equally well as an introduction, or as supplementary reading for confirmed admirers." Booklist

Includes bibliographical references

Kellerman, Annette, 1888-1975

Corey, Shana. Mermaid Queen; the spectacular true story of Annette Kellerman, who swam her way to fame, fortune, & swimsuit history! illustrated by Edwin Fotheringham. Scholastic Press 2008 unp il $17.99

Grades: K 1 2 3   **92**

1. Swimming 2. Women athletes

ISBN 978-0-439-69835-1; 0-439-69835-9

LC 2007-52664

This is a picture book biography of "the swimmer Annette Kellerman (1886-1975). As a child in Australia, Kellerman had to wear leg braces for some unspecified illness; to strengthen her body, she swam—and grew up to become an endurance swimmer, to invent water ballet and introduce the modern bathing suit to horrified Americans and Europeans." Publ Wkly

"Fotheringham's glorious artwork is filled with period details and dress, high-dives and stunts, and priceless expressions on the faces of amazed audiences. . . . This well-written and brightly illustrated account is a perfect pearl." SLJ

Kennedy, John F. (John Fitzgerald), 1917-1963

Adler, David A. A picture book of John F. Kennedy; illustrated by Robert Casilla. Holiday House 1991 unp il $16.95; pa $6.95

Grades: 1 2 3   **92**

1. Presidents—United States

ISBN 0-8234-0884-1; 0-8234-0976-7 (pa)

LC 90-23589

Depicts the life and career of John F. Kennedy

"Adler presents a brief, clearly written text that provides basic information about his subject in an appealing format. . . . Casilla's watercolors are full-color copies of famous photographs." SLJ

Heiligman, Deborah. High hopes; a photobiography of John F. Kennedy. National Geographic 2003 63p il map $17.95 *

Grades: 4 5 6 7   **92**

1. Presidents—United States

ISBN 0-7922-6141-0   LC 2003-7819

Kennedy, John F. (John Fitzgerald), 1917-1963—*Continued*

Photographs and text trace the life of President John F. Kennedy.

The text "successfully captures the spirit that makes Kennedy an enduring figure in our history. . . . This well-designed book features large, well-chosen, black-and-white photographs." SLJ

Includes bibliographical references

Sommer, Shelley. John F. Kennedy; his life and legacy; introduction by Caroline Kennedy. HarperCollins Publishers 2005 152p il lib bdg $17.89

Grades: 5 6 7 8   **92**
1. Presidents—United States
ISBN 0-06-054135-0; 0-06-054136-9 (lib bdg)

A "portrait of our 35th president. In discussing his curious mind, his love of reading, and his sense of humor, Sommer creates an empathetic connection with readers early in the book. . . . In an easy-to-read style, Sommer does a fine job of painting an interesting and sympathetic picture of a leader who left his mark." SLJ

Includes bibliographical references

King, Coretta Scott, 1927-2006

Shange, Ntozake. Coretta Scott; poetry by Ntozake Shange; paintings by Kadir Nelson. Amistad/Katherine Tegen Books 2009 unp il $17.99; lib bdg $18.89 *

Grades: K 1 2 3   **92**
1. King, Martin Luther, Jr., 1929-1968 2. African American women—Biography 3. African Americans—Civil rights
ISBN 978-0-06-125364-5; 0-06-125364-2; 978-0-06-125365-2 (lib bdg); 0-06-125365-0 (lib bdg)
LC 2008-10486

Nelson's "jacket portrait of Coretta Scott, monumental and tender at the same time, sets the tone for this intimate picture biography. The artist's full-bleed paintings, powerfully molded and saturated with color, depict crucial moments in Scott's life. . . . Shange's . . . rhythmic lines and format syntax roll like waves . . . carrying readers on a soul-stirring ride." Publ Wkly

King, Martin Luther, Jr., 1929-1968

Farris, Christine. March on! the day my brother Martin changed the world; [by] Christine King Farris; illustrated by London Ladd. Scholastic Press 2008 unp il $17.99 *

Grades: 2 3 4   **92**
1. Farris, Christine 2. Civil rights demonstrations 3. African Americans—Civil rights
ISBN 978-0-545-03537-8; 0-545-03537-6
LC 2007038620

"Describing the 1963 March on Washington, Farris, the older sister of Martin Luther King Jr., maintains the deft touch that made My Brother Martin so moving. . . . Farris . . . effectively uses plain language and well-chosen facts to explain her brother's extraordinary achievements. . . . Ladd . . . demonstrates a rare talent for portraiture. . . . His King looks human—in other words, capable of inspiring the reader." Publ Wkly

Farris, Christine. My brother Martin; a sister remembers growing up with the Rev. Dr. Martin Luther King Jr.; by Christine King Farris; illustrated by Chris Soentpiet. Simon & Schuster Bks. for Young Readers 2003 35p il $17.95 *

Grades: K 1 2 3   **92**
1. African Americans—Biography 2. African Americans—Civil rights
ISBN 0-689-84387-9   LC 2001-44681

Looks at the early life of Martin Luther King, Jr., as seen through the eyes of his older sister.

"The warmth of the text is exquisitely echoed in Soentpiet's realistic, light-filled watercolor portraits. . . . This outstanding book belongs in every collection." SLJ

Marzollo, Jean. Happy birthday, Martin Luther King; illustrated by J. Brian Pinkney. Scholastic 1993 unp il $15.95; pa $6.99 *

Grades: K 1 2 3   **92**
1. African Americans—Biography 2. African Americans—Civil rights
ISBN 0-590-44065-9; 0-439-78224-4 (pa)
LC 91-42137

"This very easy biography of Martin Luther King is distinguished by its succinct explanations of King's achievements. . . . The narrative of King's life is smooth and accessible. Pinkney's scratchboard paintings are fluidly drawn, warm, and dignified." Bull Cent Child Books

Michelson, Richard. As good as anybody: Martin Luther King Jr. and Abraham Joshua Heschel's amazing march toward freedom; by Richard Michelson; illustrated by Raul Colón. Knopf 2008 unp il $16.99; lib bdg $19.99 *

Grades: 2 3 4   **92**
1. Heschel, Abraham Joshua, 1907-1972 2. African Americans—Biography 3. Jews—Biography 4. African Americans—Civil rights
ISBN 978-0-375-83335-9; 0-375-83335-8; 978-0-375-93335-6 (lib bdg); 0-375-93335-2 (lib bdg)

This is the story of how Abraham Joshua Heschel, a Polish rabbi who escaped the Holocaust, and Martin Luther King worked together for African American civil rights.

"Michelson writes in poetic language. . . . Also admirable is Michelson's ability to convey complex historical concepts . . . in clear, potent terms that will speak directly to readers. . . . In both palette and style, Colón's colored-pencil and watercolor art . . . suggests the past, but his themes carry into today's headlines." Booklist

Myers, Walter Dean. I've seen the promised land; the life of Dr. Martin Luther King, Jr.; illustrated by Leonard Jenkins. HarperCollins Publishers 2004 unp il $15.99; lib bdg $16.89 *

Grades: K 1 2 3   **92**
1. African Americans—Biography 2. African Americans—Civil rights
ISBN 0-06-027703-3; 0-06-027704-1 (lib bdg)
LC 2003-4098

Pictures and easy-to-read text introduce the life of civil rights leader Dr. Martin Luther King, Jr.

"This eloquent picture book presents a brief overview of King's life and accomplishments. . . . Jenkins's stunning collage artwork dramatically reflects the events described in the narrative." SLJ

King, Martin Luther, Jr., 1929-1968—*Continued*

Rappaport, Doreen. Martin's big words: the life of Dr. Martin Luther King, Jr.; illustrated by Bryan Collier. Hyperion Bks. for Children 2001 unp il $15.99; pa $6.99 *

Grades: K 1 2 3   92

1. African Americans—Biography 2. African Americans—Civil rights

ISBN 0-7868-0714-8; 1-4231-0635-0 (pa)

LC 00-40957

A Caldecott Medal honor book, 2002; A Coretta Scott King honor book for illustration, 2002

The author "has taken key phrases from King's early life and from his speeches, and used them as markers in telling a simplified story of his life." N Y Times Book Rev

"Rappaport's spare narrative captures the essentials of the man, the movement he led, and his policy of nonviolence. . . . Collier's collage art is glorious. Combining cut-paper, photographs, and watercolor he expresses his own Christian faith and King's power 'to make many different things one.'" Booklist

Knight, Margaret, 1838-1914

McCully, Emily Arnold. Marvelous Mattie; how Margaret E. Knight became an inventor. Farrar, Straus & Giroux 2006 unp il $16 *

Grades: K 1 2 3   92

1. Women inventors

ISBN 0-374-34810-3   LC 2004-56415

Margaret (or Mattie) "Knight's design for a safer loom saved textile workers from injuries and death. . . . She fought in court and won the right to patent her most famous invention, a machine that would make paper bags. Mattie's story is told in a style that is not only easy to understand, but that is also a good read-aloud. The watercolor-and-ink illustrations capture the spirited inventor and support the text in style and design." SLJ

Kobayashi, Issa, 1763-1827

Gollub, Matthew. Cool melons—turn to frogs!: the life and poems of Issa; story and Haiku translations by Matthew Gollub; illustrations by Kazuko G. Stone; calligraphy by Keiko Smith. Lee & Low Bks. 1998 unp il $16.95; pa $9.95 *

Grades: 3 4 5 6   92

1. Poets

ISBN 1-880000-71-7; 1-58430-241-0 (pa)

LC 98-13087

A biography and introduction to the work of the Japanese haiku poet whose love for nature finds expression in the more than thirty poems included in this book

This contains the life of the poet "told in simple language; lots of his exquisite and accessible haiku; limpid watercolor and colored pencil illustrations reminiscent of Japanese prints and drawings; and beautiful Japanese calligraphy." Booklist

Korczak, Janusz, 1878-1942

Bogacki, Tomek. The champion of children; the story of Janusz Korczak. Farrar Straus Giroux 2009 unp il $17.99 *

Grades: 1 2 3 4   92

1. Jews—Poland 2. Holocaust, 1933-1945

ISBN 978-0-374-34136-7; 0-374-34136-2

LC 2008-16188

"Frances Foster books"

This is a "picture-book biography of the Holocaust-era children's advocate and doctor. Early Polish childhood life and interests quickly move into the doctor's student days and expand to his renowned, democratically run orphanage. . . . He steadfastly stayed with his children during the Nazi invasion and deportation and ultimately perished with them at Treblinka. . . . Though this is a story that ends in dark despair, the author succeeds in creating a positive, upbeat atmosphere with his palette of muted reds, blues and greens." Kirkus

Koufax, Sandy, 1935-

Winter, Jonah. You never heard of Sandy Koufax!? illustrations by Andre Carrilho. Schwartz & Wade Books 2009 unp il $17.99; lib bdg $20.99 *   92

1. Los Angeles Dodgers (Baseball team) 2. Baseball—Biography 3. Jews—Biography

ISBN 978-0-375-83738-8;   0-375-83738-8; 978-0-375-93738-5 (lib bdg); 0-375-93738-2 (lib bdg)

LC 2007-41860

The author relates "the story of arguably the greatest left-handed pitcher in baseball history as if he were an unnamed teammate along for the ride. . . . Winter makes a point to emphasize that at the time, . . . Koufax was one of very few Jewish players, and he encountered his share of prejudice. . . . Carrilho's digitally enhanced graphite artwork, which resembles highly expressionistic cartoons, emphasizes movement, . . . with touches of deep gold and swift strokes of red against Dodger blue." Booklist

Includes glossary

La Salle, Robert Cavelier, sieur de, 1643-1687

Goodman, Joan E. Despite all obstacles: La Salle and the conquest of the Mississippi; by Joan Elizabeth Goodman; illustrated by Tom McNeely. Mikaya Press 2001 47p il map (Great explorers book) $19.95

Grades: 4 5 6 7   92

1. Explorers 2. Mississippi River valley

ISBN 1-931414-01-7   LC 2001-31732

A biography of the man who explored the St. Lawrence, Ohio, Illinois, and Mississippi rivers, and who claimed America's heartland for King Louis XIV and France

"Vivid color illustrations and Goodman's exciting writing style will attract both researchers and pleasure readers." Voice Youth Advocates

Lafayette, Marie Joseph Paul Yves Roch Gilbert du Motier, marquis de, 1757-1834

Fritz, Jean. Why not, Lafayette? illustrated by Ronald Himler. Putnam 1999 87p il $16.99; pa $5.99 *

Grades: 5 6 7 8   92
1. United States—History—1775-1783, Revolution
ISBN 0-399-23411-X; 0-698-11882-0 (pa)
LC 98-31417
Traces the life of the French nobleman who fought for democracy in revolutions in both the United States and France
This biography is "chock-full of quotes, anecdotes, and wry humor." Booklist
Includes bibliographical references

Lange, Dorothea, 1895-1965

Partridge, Elizabeth. Restless spirit: the life and work of Dorothea Lange. Viking 1998 122p il hardcover o.p. pa $12.99

Grades: 6 7 8 9   92
1. Women photographers
ISBN 0-670-87888-X; 0-14-230024-1 (pa)
LC 98-9807
A biography of Dorothea Lange, whose photographs of migrant workers, Japanese American internees, and rural poverty helped bring about important social reforms
"Generously placed throughout this accessibly written biography are the photographic images that make Lange a pre-eminent artist of the century. The book is elegantly designed and the photographic reproductions are excellent." Bull Cent Child Books
Includes bibliographical references

Law, Westley Wallace, 1923-2002

Haskins, James. Delivering justice; W.W. Law and the fight for civil rights; [by] Jim Haskins; illustrated by Benny Andrews. Candlewick Press 2005 unp il $16.99 *

Grades: 2 3 4   92
1. African Americans—Civil rights
ISBN 0-7636-2592-2   LC 2005-47114
A biography of Westley (W. W.) Law, a mail carrier who played a leading role in the civil rights movement
"With handsome, full-page illustrations in oil and collage, this picture-book biography tells the stirring story of a quiet hero." Booklist

Lawrence, Jacob, 1917-2000

Collard, Sneed B., III. Jacob Lawrence; a painter's story. Marshall Cavendish Benchmark 2009 41p bibl il por (American heroes) lib bdg $20.95

Grades: 2 3 4   92
1. African American artists 2. Artists—United States
ISBN 978-0-7614-4058-1 (lib bdg); 0-7614-4058-5 (lib bdg)   LC 2008034819
This introduces "young readers to one of the preeminent twentieth-century African American artists. Collard recounts a few important touchstones of Lawrence's life . . . but mostly frames the narrative around his works.

. . . The narrative is concise, but not to the point of simplicity. . . . Reproductions of paintings and period photos alternate each page of the text." Booklist
Includes glossary and bibliographical references

Duggleby, John. Story painter: the life of Jacob Lawrence. Chronicle Bks. 1998 55p il $16.95 *

Grades: 4 5 6 7   92
1. African American artists
ISBN 0-8118-2082-3   LC 98-4513
A biography of the African American artist who grew up in the midst of the Harlem Renaissance and became one of the most renowned painters of the life of his people
"Lawrence's expressionistic, stark paintings, in excellent full-page color reproduction . . . nicely complement Duggleby's measured account of a materially poor but culturally rich childhood and Lawrence's subsequent struggles and successes." Publ Wkly
Includes bibliographical references

Ledger, Heath, 1979-2008

Watson, Stephanie. Heath Ledger; talented actor. ABDO Pub. Company 2010 112p il (Lives cut short) lib bdg $32.79

Grades: 5 6 7 8   92
1. Actors
ISBN 978-1-60453-789-5 (lib bdg); 1-60453-789-2 (lib bdg)   LC 2009034353
This discusses Heath Ledger's "early life, providing details that give insight into later success and troubles and maintaining a laudatory tone that focuses on the individual's artistic achievements and hard work to achieve fame. Details [such as] explaining that Jack Nicholson warned Heath Ledger about the Joker role . . . are bound to resonate with readers. Numerous photos and sidebars appear throughout. [A] worthwhile [resource] for reports as well as popular reading." SLJ
Includes bibliographical references

Lee, Bruce, 1940-1973

Mochizuki, Ken. Be water, my friend; the early years of Bruce Lee; illustrated by Dom Lee. Lee & Low Books 2006 unp il $16.95

Grades: K 1 2 3   92
1. Martial arts 2. Actors
ISBN 1-58430-265-0
"A biography of Bruce Lee focusing on his early years in Hong Kong, where he discovered martial arts and began developing the physical and mental skills that led to his career as a . . . martial artist and film star." Publisher's note
"This distinctive-looking book offers a smoothly written text and many handsome, textured acrylic paintings done in tones of brown and cream." Booklist

Lee, Sammy, 1920-

Yoo, Paula. Sixteen years in sixteen seconds; the Sammy Lee story; illustrations by Dom Lee. Lee & Low Books 2005 unp il $16.95 *

Grades: 2 3 4   92
1. Diving 2. Korean Americans
ISBN 1-58430-247-X   LC 2004-20962

Lee, Sammy, 1920-—_Continued_

"Yoo introduces Sammy Lee, the son of Korean immigrants who overcame formidable odds to become an Olympic diving champion as well as a doctor. . . . Washed in nostalgic sepia tones, Dom Lee's acrylic-and-wax textured illustrations are reminiscent of his fine work in Ken Mochizuki's watershed _Baseball Saved Us_ (1993) and like Yoo's understated words, the uncluttered images leave a deep impression." Booklist

Lee, Stan

Miller, Raymond H. Stan Lee; creator of Spider-man; [by] Raymond H. Miller. KidHaven Press 2006 48p il (Inventors and creators) lib bdg $23.70

Grades: 4 5 6 7   92

1. Comic books, strips, etc.

ISBN 0-7377-3447-7   LC 2005026845

The author "tells how Lee came up with the idea of Spider-Man, and how the Depression, World War II, and immigration shaped his life. . . . The book also highlights The Hulk, Fantastic Four, and other major works. The photos are fun and engaging, and will make superhero fans want to read more." SLJ

Includes glossary and bibliographical references

Leeper, David Rohrer, 1832-1900

Leeper, David Rohrer. The diary of David R. Leeper; rushing for gold; edited by Connie and Peter Roop; illustrations and map by Laszlo Kubinyi. Benchmark Bks. 2001 78p il (In my own words) lib bdg $24.21

Grades: 4 5 6 7   92

1. Overland journeys to the Pacific 2. Frontier and pioneer life—West (U.S.) 3. California—Gold discoveries

ISBN 0-7614-1011-2   LC 00-23840

A young prospector describes his experiences traveling overland to the California gold fields and during the five years he spent digging for gold

"Leeper's story, taken from a book he published in 1894 . . . is a lively account of his life as forty-niner." Booklist

Includes glossary and bibliographical references

Lennon, John, 1940-1980

Anderson, Jennifer Joline. John Lennon; legendary musician & Beatle. ABDO 2010 112p il (Lives cut short) lib bdg $32.79

Grades: 5 6 7 8   92

1. Rock musicians

ISBN 978-1-60453-790-1 (lib bdg); 1-60453-790-6 (lib bdg)   LC 2009034354

This discusses the John Lennon's "early life, providing details that give insight into later success and troubles and maintaining a laudatory tone that focuses on the individual's artistic achievements and hard work to achieve fame. Details [such as] explaining that . . . John Lennon had no musical training . . . are bound to resonate with readers. Numerous photos and sidebars appear throughout. [A] worthwhile [resource] for reports as well as popular reading." SLJ

Includes glossary and bibliographical references

Rappaport, Doreen. John's secret dreams; the life of John Lennon; written by Doreen Rappaport; illustrated by Bryan Collier. Hyperion Books for Children 2004 unp il $16.99

Grades: 4 5 6 7   92

1. Beatles 2. Rock musicians

ISBN 0-7868-0817-9   LC 2003-57116

"Using a combination of simple prose, song lyrics, and illustration, this heartfelt picture-book biography traces Lennon's life from his childhood to his death. Striking in both its simplicity and complexity, it captures this enigmatic singer, artist, songwriter, and folk hero in a way that will move and fascinate those too young to remember the man but are surrounded by his music and myth." SLJ

Leonardo, da Vinci, 1452-1519

Anderson, Maxine. Amazing Leonardo da Vinci inventions you can build yourself. Nomad Press 2006 122p il map (Learn some hands-on history) pa $14.95

Grades: 5 6 7 8   92

1. Inventions 2. Handicraft 3. Artists, Italian 4. Scientists 5. Renaissance

ISBN 0-9749344-2-9

"Anderson has combined biography with doable activities that mirror ideas found in Leonardo's notebooks. Using common household objects (duct tape, foil, cereal boxes, paper-towel tubes, etc.), readers can make a parachute, hydrometer, invisible ink, walk-on-water shoes, etc. Anderson introduces each project with an explanation of why Leonardo came up with the idea and whether he created just the sketch or the sketch and the object. Detailed steps and illustrations provide clarity." SLJ

Byrd, Robert. Leonardo, beautiful dreamer. Dutton Children's Bks. 2003 unp il $17.99

Grades: 3 4 5 6   92

1. Artists, Italian

ISBN 0-525-47033-6   LC 2003-44860

Illustrations and text portray the life of Leonardo da Vinci, who gained fame as an artist through such works as the Mona Lisa, and as a scientist by studying various subjects including human anatomy and flight

"The brilliant, full-page ink-and-watercolor paintings characterize da Vinci's life in a cartoonlike manner. The animated artwork and lively text that brings together facts and anecdotes keep interest high." SLJ

Krull, Kathleen. Leonardo da Vinci; illustrated by Boris Kulikov. Viking 2005 128p il (Giants of science) $15.99 *

Grades: 5 6 7 8   92

1. Artists, Italian 2. Scientists 3. Renaissance

ISBN 0-670-05920-X

This is a "biography of Leonardo da Vinci that highlights his scientific approach to understanding the physical world. The first half of the book describes Leonardo's apprenticeship and his work as an artist in Milan. The second half relates events in his later life, emphasizing his observation and investigation of the human body and nature. . . . Six excellent ink drawings illustrate this attractive volume. A very readable, vivid portrait set against the backdrop of remarkable times."

Leonardo, da Vinci, 1452-1519—*Continued*
Booklist
Includes bibliographical references

O'Connor, Barbara. Leonardo da Vinci; Renaissance genius. Carolrhoda Bks. 2003 112p il (Trailblazer biography) lib bdg $27.93
Grades: 5 6 7 8   92
1. Artists, Italian 2. Scientists 3. Renaissance
ISBN 0-87614-467-9   LC 2001-6470
A biography of the notable Italian Renaissance artist, scientist, and inventor
"Outstanding writing and design result in a compelling and accessible portrait of this master artist." SLJ
Includes bibliographical references

Phillips, John. Leonardo da Vinci; the genius who defined the Renaissance. National Geographic 2006 64p bibl il (World history biographies) $17.95; lib bdg $27.90; pa $6.95
Grades: 5 6 7 8   92
1. Artists, Italian 2. Scientists 3. Renaissance
ISBN   978-0-7922-5385-3;   0-7922-5385-X; 978-0-7922-5386-0 (lib bdg); 0-7922-5386-8 (lib bdg); 978-1-4263-0248-0 (pa); 1-4263-0249-7 (pa)
Examines the life of Renaissance genius Leonardo da Vinci, discussing his inquiries and accomplishments in art and various fields of science
Includes bibliographical references

Stanley, Diane. Leonardo da Vinci. Morrow Junior Bks. 1996 unp il $16.95; lib bdg $15.93; pa $6.95 *
Grades: 4 5 6 7   92
1. Artists, Italian
ISBN 0-688-10437-1; 0-688-10438-X (lib bdg); 0-688-16155-3 (pa)   LC 95-35227
"Stanley begins with a brief introduction to the Italian Renaissance and then looks at the life of the artist. The text pages feature a series of sketches from Leonardo's notebooks. These vivid drawings, chosen to reflect ideas and events in the story, juxtapose well with the large illustrations created with colored pencil, gouache, and watercolors on the facing pages. . . . The craftsmanship that makes this biography so solid in concept, appealing in design, and accessible in presentation extends to the scholarship behind it, as glimpsed in the appended postscript and bibliographies." Booklist

Lester, Helen, 1936-
Lester, Helen. Author; a true story. Houghton Mifflin 1997 32p il $11
Grades: K 1 2 3   92
1. Women authors
ISBN 0-395-82744-2   LC 96-9645
An "autobiographical look at the evolution of a writer describes Lester's experiences—including her earliest three-year-old scribbles and the acceptance of her first manuscript (on the seventh try). Illustrated with Lester's own rather childlike illustrations, this lighthearted but realistic (and helpful) guide for the writer has lots of fresh tips for young authors-in-the-making." Horn Book Guide

Lewis, John, 1940-
Haskins, James. John Lewis in the lead; a story of the civil rights movement; [by] Jim Haskins and Kathleen Benson; illustrations by Benny Andrews. Lee & Low 2006 unp il $17.95 *
Grades: 3 4 5   92
1. African Americans—Civil rights
ISBN 1-58430-250-X   LC 2005-35472
"Born in a sharecropper family in the segregated South in 1940, John Lewis grew up to lead many protests for civil rights, and he has served in Congress for the last 20 years. In this handsome picture book for older readers, the authors blend information on Lewis' political contributions with the history of the civil rights struggle. . . . Andrews' dramatic, folk-art-style, color-saturated illustrations combine handsome individual portraits of Lewis with overviews of the horrific street violence by mobs, police, and troopers." Booklist

Li Cunxin
Li Cunxin. Dancing to freedom; the true story of Mao's last dancer; illustrated by Anne Spudvilas. Walker & Co. 2008 unp il $16.95; lib bdg $17.85
Grades: K 1 2 3   92
1. Ballet 2. China
ISBN   978-0-8027-9777-3;   0-8027-9777-6; 978-0-8027-9778-0 (lib bdg); 0-8027-9778-4 (lib bdg)
                                       LC 2007-37150
"A poignant memoir of a boy caught in the difficulties of life in Maoist China, this is the author's own story of how he was given a chance to break the bonds of his bleak life and become an international star. . . . [Li] was offered the chance to dance with the Houston Ballet, and his greatest dream was realized when his parents were finally able to come to the U.S. to see him perform. This fascinating, heartfelt story is perfectly matched by Spudvilas's masterful paintings." SLJ

Lichtenstein, Roy, 1923-1997
Rubin, Susan Goldman. Whaam!: the art & life of Roy Lichtenstein. Abrams 2008 47p il $18.95 *
Grades: 4 5 6 7   92
1. Artists—United States 2. Pop art
ISBN 978-0-8109-9492-8; 0-8109-9492-5
                                       LC 2007-42048
"Rubin presents an overview of a modern master with clear writing and an abundance of his eye-popping works, all framed on pages that mirror the artist's signature use of primary colors and Benday dots." Booklist

Limón, José, 1908-1972
Reich, Susanna. José! born to dance: the story of José Limón; illustrated by Raúl Colón. Simon & Schuster Books for Young Readers 2005 unp il $16.95 *
Grades: 2 3 4   92
1. Dancers 2. Choreographers 3. Mexican Americans—Biography
ISBN 0-689-86576-7   LC 2004-4776
"A Paula Wiseman book"

Limón, José, 1908-1972—*Continued*

"This picture-book biography tells the story of Jose Limon, who became a legendary figure in the history of American dance. . . . Sensitively written and beautifully illustrated, this picture book offers a soaring portrayal of achievement. Colon's distinctive watercolor-and-colored-pencil artwork includes many strong compositions that are fundamentally narrative yet emotionally resonate and often memorable." Booklist

Includes bibliographical references

Lincoln, Abraham, 1809-1865

Aylesworth, Jim. Our Abe Lincoln; an old tune with new lyrics; adapted by Jim Aylesworth; illustrated by Barbara McClintock. Scholastic Press 2009 unp il $16.99 *

Grades: PreK K 1 2   **92**

1. Presidents—United States 2. Songs
ISBN 978-0-439-92548-8; 0-439-92548-7
LC 2007-31060

"With a fresh approach to Lincoln that is both delightful and accurate, Aylesworth sets history to the tune of 'The Old Gray Mare' and the derivative song 'Our Abe Lincoln Came Out of the Wilderness,' which was popular during the 16th president's campaign. . . . McClintock captures the exuberance with charming visuals that outline significant aspects of the leader's life and lore. Scenes rendered in watercolor and pen and ink feature a multicultural cast." SLJ

Burleigh, Robert. Abraham Lincoln comes home; [by] Robert Burleigh; paintings by Wendell Minor. Henry Holt and Co. 2008 unp il $16.95

Grades: 2 3 4   **92**

1. Presidents—United States
ISBN 978-0-8050-7529-8; 0-8050-7529-1
LC 2007040030

"Following Lincoln's death, his body was taken back to Illinois for burial. Burleigh focuses on one boy's perceptions as he and his father travel through the night by horse-drawn carriage to see the funeral train pass. . . . Minor's gouache watercolors capture the prairie as well as multiple perspectives of the train, while Burleigh's prose is almost poetic." SLJ

Denenberg, Barry. Lincoln shot! a president's life remembered; chief writer, Barry Denenberg; artist, Christopher Bing. Feiwel and Friends 2008 40p il $24.95 *

Grades: 5 6 7 8   **92**

1. Presidents—United States 2. United States—History—1861-1865, Civil War
ISBN 978-0-312-37013-8; 0-312-37013-X
LC 2007-48851

"The concept is that this is a commemorative edition of 'The National News' published one year after Lincoln's death . . . Also included is an engaging, readable yet detailed account of Lincoln's life. . . . [This book] is an example of how high-quality bookmaking can turn a history lesson into an authentic experience." Booklist

Freedman, Russell. Lincoln: a photobiography. Clarion Bks. 1987 149p il $18; pa $7.95 *

Grades: 5 6 7 8 9 10   **92**

1. Presidents—United States 2. United States—History—1861-1865, Civil War
ISBN 0-89919-380-3; 0-395-51848-2 (pa)
LC 86-33379

Awarded the Newbery Medal, 1988

The author "begins by contrasting the Lincoln of legend to the Lincoln of fact. His childhood, self-education, early business ventures, and entry into politics comprise the first half of the book, with the rest of the text covering his presidency and assassination." SLJ

This is "a balanced work, elegantly designed and enhanced by dozens of period photographs and drawings, some familiar, some refreshingly unfamiliar." Publ Wkly

Includes bibliographical references

Harness, Cheryl. Abe Lincoln goes to Washington, 1837-1865; written and illustrated by Cheryl Harness. National Geographic Soc. 1997 unp il maps $18

Grades: 2 3 4   **92**

1. Presidents—United States
ISBN 0-7922-3736-6   LC 96-9587

Companion volume to Young Abe Lincoln: the frontier days, 1809-1837 (1996)

Portrays Lincoln's life as a lawyer in Springfield, a devoted husband and father, and president during the Civil War years

"The text gallops through years of history, with sudden stops for surprisingly vivid little scenes. . . . Filled with color and action, Harness' paintings and maps dominate the pages and provide a wealth of historical detail as well as a humanizing view of the Lincolns." Booklist

Includes bibliographical references

Herbert, Janis. Abraham Lincoln for kids; his life and times with 21 activities; [by] Janis Herbert. Chicago Review Press 2007 149p il pa $14.95

Grades: 4 5 6 7   **92**

1. Presidents—United States
ISBN 978-1-55652-656-5 (pa); 1-55652-656-3 (pa)
LC 2007009052

"This attractive biographical guide offers a good mixture of information, anecdotes, and activities, balancing facts about Lincoln's personal and family life with the record of his accomplishments as president and a broader view of his times." Booklist

Includes glossary and bibliographical references

Krull, Kathleen. Lincoln tells a joke; how laughter saved the President (and the country); [by] Kathleen Krull & Paul Brewer; illustrated by Stacy Innerst. Harcourt 2010 unp il $16 *

Grades: 2 3 4   **92**

1. Presidents—United States 2. Wit and humor
ISBN 978-0-15-206639-0; 0-15-206639-X
LC 2009-24197

"Moving through the sixteenth president's many challenges, from family deaths to lost elections to fighting slavery, the text emphasizes how Lincoln coped with a joke on his tongue and a smile on his lips. . . . Innerst's acrylic artwork feels homey and humorous." Booklist

Lincoln, Abraham, 1809-1865—*Continued*

Rappaport, Doreen. Abe's honest words; the life of Abraham Lincoln; [illustrated by] Kadir Nelson. Hyperion Books for Children 2008 44p il $16.99 *

Grades: 2 3 4   92
   1. Presidents—United States
   ISBN 1-4231-0408-0; 978-1-4231-0408-7
                     LC 2006-43608

"This collaboration between Rappaport and Nelson provides a sweeping arc of Lincoln's life. . . . Rappaport writes in the very free verse and on each page echoes her narrative with prescient samplings of Lincoln's words. In generously sized artwork . . . Nelson makes the familiar face . . . exciting again. . . . The exceptional art, along with Rappaport's and Lincoln's words, makes this a fine celebration of a man who needs little introduction." Booklist

   Includes bibliographical references

St. George, Judith. Stand tall, Abe Lincoln; [by] Judith St. George; illustrated by Matt Faulkner. Philomel Books 2007 unp il $16.99 *
Grades: 2 3 4   92
   1. Presidents—United States
   ISBN 978-0-399-24174-1   LC 2006024877

"This account of Lincoln's childhood is written in fast-paced short sentences. St. George . . . uses a folksy, conversational style. . . . Faulkner's humorous illustrations are a perfect match for the text. . . . The expressive images are done in a caricature style, with slightly exaggerated hands, feet, and heads." SLJ

   Includes bibliographical references

Sullivan, George. Abraham Lincoln. Scholastic Ref. 2000 128p il (In their own words) pa $4.99 hardcover o.p.
Grades: 4 5 6 7   92
   1. Presidents—United States 2. United States—History—1861-1865, Civil War
   ISBN 0-439-09554-9 (pa)   LC 99-33387

Presents a biography, including excerpts from his speeches, letters, and other writings, of the man who was President during the Civil War

This book features "black-and-white photos and reproductions, a useful index, a short bibliography of primary and secondary sources, and a short list of further readings, along with places to contact for further information." SLJ

   Includes bibliographical references

Thomson, Sarah L. What Lincoln said; by Sarah L. Thomson; art by James Ransome. Collins 2009 unp il $17.99; lib bdg $18.89 *
Grades: K 1 2 3   92
   1. Presidents—United States
   ISBN   978-0-06-084819-4;   0-06-084819-7;
   978-0-06-084820-0 (lib bdg); 0-06-084820-0 (lib bdg)
                     LC 2008020095

"By using Lincoln's own words, Thomson builds a portrait that relates his statements to significant events in his life. . . . Short descriptions of the circumstances and a related quote are set on bold, colorful spreads.

Ransome delivers a larger-than-life portrait of this homely president with acrylic, almost cartoonlike paintings. . . . An engaging overview, this is a worthy introduction to this famous president." SLJ

Turner, Ann Warren. Abe Lincoln remembers; [by] Ann Turner; pictures by Wendell Minor. HarperCollins Pubs. 2001 unp il hardcover o.p. pa $6.99
Grades: K 1 2 3   92
   1. Presidents—United States 2. United States—History—1861-1865, Civil War
   ISBN 0-06-027577-4; 0-06-027578-2 (lib bdg); 0-06-051107-9 (pa)   LC 98-50937

A simple description of the life of Abraham Lincoln, presented from his point of view

"Turner's free-verse reminiscence gracefully ties images and themes from Lincoln's youth to those of his adult years. . . . Minor's well-composed paintings, best seen from a little distance, effectively portray the man as he ages." Booklist

Lincoln, Mary Todd, 1818-1882

Jones, Lynda. Mrs. Lincoln's dressmaker: the unlikely friendship of Elizabeth Keckley and Mary Todd Lincoln. See entry under Keckley, Elizabeth, ca. 1818-1907

Lincoln, Tad, 1853-1871

Rabin, Staton. Mr. Lincoln's boys; being the mostly true adventures of Abraham Lincoln's trouble-making sons, Tad and Willie; by Staton Rabin; illustrated by Bagram Ibatoulline. Penguin Group 2008 unp il $16.99 *
Grades: 1 2 3   92
   1. Lincoln, Abraham, 1809-1865 2. Lincoln, William Wallace, 1850-1862 3. Lincoln family 4. Presidents—United States
   ISBN 978-0-670-06169-3; 0-670-06169-7
                     LC 2008-1774

"Tad and Willie, the mischievous sons of President Abraham Lincoln, scampered around the White House surprising and irritating almost everyone. Their pranks, however, delighted their father, who was faced with the grim realities of the Civil War. . . . Fictionalized dialogue throughout is believable. A large part of the appeal of this book can be credited to Ibatoulline's masterful illustrations. Evocative and detailed, they fill the pages with visual information and emotion. Readers will be intrigued by the antics of these famous children." SLJ

   Includes bibliographical references

Lincoln, William Wallace, 1850-1862

Rabin, Staton. Mr. Lincoln's boys. See entry under Lincoln, Abraham, 1809-1865

Lindbergh, Charles, 1902-1974

Burleigh, Robert. Flight: the journey of Charles Lindbergh; illustrated by Mike Wimmer; introduction by Jean Fritz. Philomel Bks. 1991 unp il hardcover o.p. pa $6.99
Grades: 2 3 4   92
   1. Aeronautics—Flights 2. Air pilots
   ISBN 0-399-22272-3; 0-698-11425-6 (pa)
                     LC 90-35401

Describes how Charles Lindbergh achieved the remarkable feat of flying nonstop and solo from New York to Paris in 1927

"Using Charles Lindbergh's autobiography, *The Spirit of St. Louis*, as the basis for his text, Burleigh vividly creates that first solo flight in words, while Wimmer fashions exhilarating pictures that are, above all else, emotional. . . . This artistic emotion . . . works terrifically with the terseness of the near-poetic text." Booklist

Linné, Carl von, 1707-1778

Anderson, Margaret Jean. Carl Linnaeus; father of classification; [by] Margaret J. Anderson. rev ed. Enslow Publishers 2009 128p il (Great minds of science) lib bdg $31.93
Grades: 5 6 7 8 9   92
   1. Naturalists
   ISBN 978-0-7660-3009-1 (lib bdg); 0-7660-3009-1 (lib bdg)   LC 2008-23941
   First published 1997

"A biography of eighteenth-century Swedish botanist Carl Linnaeus, who established the modern system of classifying plants and animals." Publisher's note

"Budding scientists will surely draw inspiration from this biography of Linnaeus. . . . Anderson creates a dramatic narrative fully capable of keeping readers enthralled." Kirkus

Includes glossary and bibliographical references

Livingstone, David, 1813-1873

Otfinoski, Steven. David Livingstone; deep in the heart of Africa. Marshall Cavendish Benchmark 2006 79p il map (Great explorations) lib bdg $32.79
Grades: 5 6 7 8   92
   1. Explorers 2. Africa—Exploration
   ISBN 978-0-7614-2226-6 (lib bdg); 0-7614-2226-9 (lib bdg)   LC 2005027930

"An examination of the life and accomplishments of the explorer and missionary who traveled southern Africa and was the first European to reach Victoria Falls." Publisher's note

This "appealing [title features] readable [text], solid research, and a variety of color illustrations." SLJ

Includes bibliographical references

Lockwood, Belva Ann, 1830-1917

Bardhan-Quallen, Sudipta. Ballots for Belva; the true story of a woman's race for the presidency; by Sudipta Bardhan-Quallen; illustrated by Courtney A. Martin. Abrams Books for Young Readers 2008 unp il $16.95
Grades: 2 3 4 5   92
   1. Women politicians 2. Feminism 3. Women lawyers
   ISBN 978-0-8109-7110-3; 0-8109-7110-0
                     LC 2007049842

"This picture-book biography introduces [Belva Ann Lockwood], the woman who ran for president more than a century ago. . . . She obtained a law degree, fought for equal rights, and ultimately became the first woman to receive certified votes during her 1884 presidential campaign. . . . Quotes from Lockwood and others enliven the text. . . . Handsome illustrations clearly set the time and place, and Lockwood's fortitude comes through in her posture and facial expressions." SLJ

Lomax, John Avery, 1867-1948

Hopkinson, Deborah. Home on the range; John A. Lomax and his cowboy songs; illustrated by S. D. Schindler. G. P. Putnam's Sons 2009 unp il $16.99 *
Grades: 2 3 4   92
   1. Ethnomusicologists 2. Folk songs—United States
   ISBN 978-0-399-23996-0; 0-399-23996-0
                     LC 2008-16802

This traces the early career of John A Lomax, the collector and recorder of American folk songs.

This a "colorful narrative. . . . Glimpses of his thoughts and emotions . . . as well as dialogue help personalize the story. . . . Schindler's . . . realistic illustrations, painted with a light touch in muted hues, ably capture the expressions of skeptical cowboys . . . or the eagerness with which Lomax goes about his work." Publ Wkly

Longworth, Alice Roosevelt, 1884-1980

Kerley, Barbara. What to do about Alice? how Alice Roosevelt broke the rules, charmed the world, and drove her father Teddy crazy! illustrated by Edwin Fotheringham. Scholastic Press 2008 unp il $16.99 *
Grades: K 1 2 3   92
   1. Roosevelt, Theodore, 1858-1919 2. Presidents—United States—Family
   ISBN 978-0-439-92231-9; 0-439-92231-3
                     LC 2006-38372
   Boston Globe-Horn Book Award honor book: Nonfiction (2008)

"The daughter of Theodore Roosevelt, . . . Alice had a joie de vivre that she called 'eating up the world.' . . . Kerley's text has the same rambunctious spirit as its subject. . . . The large format gives Fotheringhame . . . plenty of room for spectacular art, which includes use of digital media." Booklist

Lorenz, Konrad

Greenstein, Elaine. The goose man; the story of Konrad Lorenz. Clarion Books 2009 32p il $16

Grades: K 1 2 3   **92**

1. Scientists 2. Geese

ISBN 978-0-547-08459-6; 0-547-08459-5

LC 2008-44618

"From childhood, Konrad Lorenz was fascinated by ducks and geese, growing up to become a prizewinning scientist who offered new insights into animal behavior. This picture-book biography . . . summarizes his life's work with geese. . . . The pastel illustrations, in gouache, ink and colored pencil, use a technique that includes scratchboard effects and is childlike in style. . . . These pictures tell the story as clearly as the simple text, whose language and frequent repetition make this scientific biography easily accessible to beginning readers." Kirkus

Includes bibliographical references

Louis, Joe, 1914-1981

Adler, David A. Joe Louis; America's fighter; written by David A. Adler; illustrated by Terry Widener. Harcourt 2005 unp il $16

Grades: 2 3 4   **92**

1. Boxing—Biography 2. African American athletes

ISBN 0-15-216480-4   LC 2003-12817

"Gulliver books"

The life story of Joe Louis, heavyweight champion boxer, with the complete history of his career in the ring.

"This creative team's collaboration packs a powerful punch. . . . The action-packed acrylics capture the setting and emotions—Widener's signature muscular figures are particularly apt here." SLJ

Includes bibliographical references

Lowry, Lois

Lowry, Lois. Looking back; a book of memories. Houghton Mifflin 1998 181p il $17

Grades: 5 6 7 8   **92**

1. Authors, American 2. Women authors

ISBN 0-395-89543-X   LC 98-11376

Also available in paperback from Delacorte Press

"A Walter Lorraine book"

Using family photographs and quotes from her books, the author provides glimpses into her life

"A compelling and inspirational portrait of the author emerges from these vivid snapshots of life's joyful, sad and surprising moments." Publ Wkly

Lyons, Maritcha Rémond, 1848-1929

Bolden, Tonya. Maritcha; a nineteenth-century American girl. Abrams 2005 47p il $17.95 *

Grades: 4 5 6 7 8 9 10   **92**

1. African American women—Biography 2. New York (N.Y.)—Race relations 3. African Americans—New York (N.Y.)

ISBN 0-8109-5045-6   LC 2004-05849

This is a "life history of Maritcha Rémond Lyons, born a free black in 1848 in lower Manhattan. The author draws her biographical sketch primarily from Lyons's unpublished memoir, dated one year before her death in 1929. . . . One of the . . . sections of the book documents the Draft Riots . . . of July 1868, and the impact of them on Maritcha and other citizens." Publ Wkly

"The high quality of writing and the excellent documentation make this a first choice for all collections." SLJ

Maathai, Wangari, 1940-

Johnson, Jen Cullerton. Seeds of change; planting a path to peace; illustrated by Sonia Lynn Sadler. Lee & Low 2010 unp il $18.95

Grades: 2 3 4   **92**

1. Green Belt Movement (Kenya) 2. Environmentalists 3. Kenya

ISBN 978-1-60060-367-9; 1-60060-367-X

This picture biography "draws on Wangari Maathai's autobiographical writing to present an overview of the activist's life from childhood to the present. . . . Richer than other treatments of Maathai for children and more grounded in her work's implicit feminism, this details her education in Nairobi and the United States, her imprisonment for activism and her scientific and environmental work, resulting in the planting of 30,000,000 trees and economic empowerment for Kenyan women. Sadler's beautiful scratchboard illustrations incise white contoured line into saturated landscapes of lush green leaf patterns, brilliant-hued textiles and undulating, stylized hills. . . . Vibrant and accomplished." Kirkus

Napoli, Donna Jo. Mama Miti: Wangari Maathai and the trees of Kenya; illustrated by Kadir Nelson. Simon & Schuster Books for Young Readers 2010 unp il $16.99 *

Grades: K 1 2 3   **92**

1. Green Belt Movement (Kenya) 2. Kenya 3. Environmentalists

ISBN 978-1-4169-3505-6; 1-4169-3505-3

LC 2008-23604

"Napoli adopts a folkloric narrative technique to showcase the life work of Wangari Maathai, whose seminal role in Kenya's reforestation earned her the Nobel Peace Prize in 2004. When, one after the other, women journey to Maathai to seek counsel about scarce food, disappearing firewood and ailing animals, she tells them, 'Plant a tree.' . . . Nelson's pictures, a jaw-dropping union of African textiles collaged with oil paintings, brilliantly capture the villagers' clothing and the greening landscape. The richly modulated oils portray the dignified, intent gazes of Maathai and other Kenyans. . . . This is, in a word, stunning." Kirkus

Includes bibliographical references

Nivola, Claire A. Planting the trees of Kenya; the story of Wangari Maathai. Farrar, Straus & Giroux 2008 unp il $16.95 *

Grades: 2 3 4   **92**

1. Green Belt Movement (Kenya) 2. Environmentalists 3. Kenya

ISBN 978-0-374-39918-4; 0-374-39918-2

LC 2006038249

"Frances Foster books"

"Kenyan activist Wangari Maathai was awarded the Nobel Peace Prize in 2004 for her environmental and human rights achievements. Founder of the Green Belt

Maathai, Wangari, 1940---*Continued*

Movement, she has encouraged people to repair their economy, land, and health with simple, environmentally friendly acts, such as planting more trees. This beautiful picture-book biography echoes the potent simplicity of Maathai's message with direct, spare prose and bright, delicate watercolors." Booklist

Winter, Jeanette. Wangari's trees of peace; a true story from Africa. Harcourt 2008 unp il $17 *

Grades: K 1 2 3   92
   1. Green Belt Movement (Kenya) 2. Environmentalists 3. Kenya
   ISBN 978-0-15-206545-4; 0-15-206545-8
                     LC 2007-34810

"Wangari Maathai, the 2004 Nobel Peace Prize winner whose Green Belt Movement has planted 30 million trees in Kenya, is the subject of Winter's . . . eloquent picture biography. . . . The tightly focused text moves quickly without sacrificing impact. . . . Winter's images appear in framed, same-size squares on each page, creating a flat, frieze-like effect." Publ Wkly

Madison, Dolley, 1768-1849

Adler, David A. A picture book of Dolley and James Madison. See entry under Madison, James, 1751-1836

Brown, Don. Dolley Madison saves George Washington; written and illustrated by Don Brown. Houghton Mifflin Co. 2007 unp il $16 *
Grades: 1 2 3   92
   1. War of 1812 2. Washington (D.C.) 3. Presidents' spouses—United States
   ISBN 978-0-618-41199-3; 0-618-41199-2
                     LC 2006-09813

"While First Lady, [Dolley Madison] redecorated the President's Mansion, ensuring that Gilbert Stuart's portrait of George Washington was prominently displayed. However, it was during the War of 1812 that she earned the gratitude of her nation when, despite the fact that the 100 soldiers assigned to protect the mansion ran off, she bravely remained behind to make sure that the painting as well as important government documents were saved from otherwise certain destruction by British forces. Pen and ink and watercolors effectively depict the simplicity and roughness of Colonial life and convey with humor the spirit of the time and characters." SLJ

Madison, James, 1751-1836

Adler, David A. A picture book of Dolley and James Madison; by David A. Adler and Michael S. Adler; illustrated by Ronald Himler. Holiday House 2009 unp il $17.95
Grades: 1 2 3   92
   1. Madison, Dolley, 1768-1849 2. Presidents—United States 3. Presidents' spouses—United States
   ISBN 978-0-8234-2009-4; 0-8234-2009-4
                 LC 2007041178

"Adler's picture-book biography focuses mainly on the War of 1812, but also mentions Madison's contributions to the Constitution and the creation of the three branches of government. Although this is a biography of the couple, there is more specific information on James Madison than on Dolley. Still, readers do learn some interesting facts about her. . . . Adler's writing is clear yet not oversimplified, and is without fictionalization." SLJ
   Includes bibliographical references

Elish, Dan. James Madison; [by] Dan Elish. Marshall Cavendish Benchmark 2007 96p il (Presidents and their times) lib bdg $22.95
Grades: 5 6 7 8   92
   1. Presidents—United States
   ISBN 978-0-7614-2432-1   LC 2006036856

A biography of the fourth president of the United States.
"Primary-source materials and quotes, helpful insets, and carefully selected . . . reproductions bring history to life and help make [this] clearly written [biography] highly readable." SLJ
   Includes glossary and bibliographical references

Fritz, Jean. The great little Madison. Putnam 1989 159p il hardcover o.p. pa $6.99
Grades: 5 6 7 8   92
   1. Presidents—United States
   ISBN 0-399-21768-1; 0-698-11621-6 (pa)
                     LC 88-31584

"Small, soft-spoken, and by nature diffident, James Madison found it difficult to speak in the midst of controversy, but his zeal and his convictions in the struggle between Republicans and Federalists gave him confidence, and his successes brought him to the presidency. Fritz has given a vivid picture of the man and an equally vivid picture of the problems—especially the internal dissension—that faced the leaders of the new nation. . . . Notes by the author and a bibliography are appended." Bull Cent Child Books

Magellan, Ferdinand, 1480?-1521

Levinson, Nancy Smiler. Magellan and the first voyage around the world. Clarion Bks. 2001 132p il map $19
Grades: 5 6 7 8   92
   1. Explorers 2. Voyages around the world
   ISBN 0-395-98773-3   LC 00-52350

This "biography of the great explorer, navigator, and adventurer presents him as a man of action who overcame political, social, and financial obstacles to sail around the globe." Horn Book Guide
"This clearly written book shows through involving narrative and vivid detail what a monumental achievement the journey was. . . . A well-designed volume, useful for research and interesting as biography." Booklist
   Includes bibliographical references

Maiman, Theodore Harold, 1927-2007

Wyckoff, Edwin Brit. Laser man; Theodore H. Maiman and his brilliant invention; [by] Edwin Brit Wyckoff. Enslow Elementary 2008 32p il (Genius at work!: great inventor biographies) lib bdg $20.60

Grades: 4 5 6   92

1. Engineers 2. Lasers
ISBN 978-0-7660-2848-7 (lib bdg); 0-7660-2848-8 (lib bdg)   LC 2006034680
A biography of Theodore H. Maiman, the engineer who invented the laser
Includes glossary and bibliographical references

Malcolm X, 1925-1965

Myers, Walter Dean. Malcolm X; a fire burning brightly; illustrated by Leonard Jenkins. HarperCollins Pubs. 2000 unp il $15.95 *

Grades: 3 4 5 6   92

1. African Americans—Biography
ISBN 0-06-027707-6   LC 99-21527
This biography of the civil rights activist "combines quotes from interviews and speeches." Bull Cent Child Books
"Myers's spare and eloquent narrative makes the complexities of Malcolm X's story accessible without compromising its integrity. The book has appeal for reluctant teen readers as well as younger readers. The sophisticated paintings blend realism with abstraction to heighten the underlying emotional drama of scenes." Horn Book Guide

Mandela, Nelson

Cooper, Floyd. Mandela; from the life of the South African statesman; written and illustrated by Floyd Cooper. Philomel Bks. 1996 unp il hardcover o.p. pa $6.99

Grades: 2 3 4   92

1. South Africa—Race relations 2. South Africa—Politics and government
ISBN 0-399-22942-6; 0-698-11816-2 (pa)
LC 95-19639
In this biography "the author focuses more closely on Mandela's boyhood and schooling than on his adulthood as an anti-apartheid activist or his ascension to the presidency of South Africa." Publ Wkly
"Cooper's oil paintings are infused with golden light. Elegant composition and subtle shifts in perspective add emotional value to the carefully focused account." SLJ
Includes bibliographical references

Kramer, Ann. Mandela; the rebel who led his nation to freedom. National Geographic 2005 63p il (World history biographies) $17.95; lib bdg $27.90 *

Grades: 4 5 6 7   92

1. South Africa—Race relations 2. South Africa—Politics and government
ISBN 0-7922-3658-0; 0-7922-3659-9 (lib bdg)
"This biography introduces readers not only to Mandela, but also to the political turmoil that affected South Africa for over a century. It begins with his birth,

and covers his school years, his political ventures, imprisonment, release, presidency, Nobel Peace Prize, and retirement. Full-color photographs appear throughout and a time line runs along the bottom of each spread. . . . the book is well worth purchasing." SLJ
Includes glossary and bibliographical references

Mandela, Nelson. Nelson Mandela: long walk to freedom; abridged by Chris van Wyk; illustrated by Paddy Bouma. Roaring Book Press 2009 unp il $16 *

Grades: 2 3 4 5   92

1. South Africa—Politics and government 2. South Africa—Race relations
ISBN 978-1-59643-566-7; 1-59643-566-6
"Abridged from Mandela's 1994 autobiography, this picture book distills the basic facts of his childhood, his education, and the influences that led him to become one of the world's most renowned political activists. In a simple, yet effective manner, he describes the growing system of apartheid, and the unjust treatment of blacks in South Africa is made clear without horrifying details. . . . The writing is clear, providing chronological detail for even young students new to the concept and history of apartheid. Full-page, color paintings accompany the text on every spread and depict crucial moments from the narrative in a way that both complements and enhances the story." SLJ

McDonough, Yona Zeldis. Peaceful protest: the life of Nelson Mandela; illustrations by Malcah Zeldis. Walker & Co. 2002 unp il hardcover o.p. pa $8.95 *

Grades: 2 3 4 5   92

1. South Africa—Race relations 2. South Africa—Politics and government
ISBN 0-8027-8821-1; 0-8027-8823-8 (lib bdg); 0-8027-8948-X (pa)   LC 2002-23462
Map of South Africa on endpapers
A biography of the black South African leader who became a civil rights activist, political prisoner, and president of South Africa
This is an "easy-to-read but engaging biography. . . . Zeldis's brightly colored folk-art illustrations reflect her subject's life and struggle with candid simplicity." SLJ
Includes bibliographical references

Mantle, Mickey, 1931-1995

Marlin, John. Mickey Mantle; by John Marlin. LernerSports 2005 106p il (Sports heroes and legends) lib bdg $26.60

Grades: 4 5 6 7   92

1. Baseball—Biography
ISBN 0-8225-1796-5   LC 2003-22798
Contents: The "Washington Wallop;" Born for baseball; Close call; The windup; The waiting game; Too much, too soon; Turning point; Crown prince; Perfect game; The M&M boys; Hall of Famer
A biography of the Yankee baseball player known as the "Washington Wallop."
This is a "good, solid [biography]. . . . [The book is] engagingly written." Booklist
Includes bibliographical references

Marley, Bob

Medina, Tony. I and I; Bob Marley; illustrated by Jesse Joshua Watson. Lee & Low Books 2009 unp il $19.95 *

Grades: 4 5 6   92

    1. Singers 2. Jamaica

    ISBN 978-1-60060-257-3; 1-60060-257-6

                        LC 2008-33485

"A biography in verse about the Jamaican reggae musician Bob Marley, offering an overview of key events and themes in his life, including his biracial heritage, Rastafarian beliefs, and love of music. End notes on poems provide further biographical information." Publisher's note

"In the words and rhythms of Jamaican patois, Medina's lyrical, direct lines make the most sense when read in tandem with the extensive appended notes. . . . Like the words, Watson's beautifully expressive acrylic paintings evoke a strong sense of Marley's remarkable life and his Caribbean homeland." Booklist

Includes bibliographical references

Marshall, Thurgood, 1908-1993

Adler, David A. A picture book of Thurgood Marshall; illustrated by Robert Casilla. Holiday House 1997 unp il $16.95; pa $6.95

Grades: 1 2 3   92

    1. United States. Supreme Court 2. African Americans—Biography 3. Judges

    ISBN 0-8234-1308-X; 0-823-41506-6 (pa)

                        LC 96-37248

Follows the life of the first African American to serve as a judge on the United States Supreme Court

"Adler presents the high points of Marshall's life with enough detail to humanize the man. . . . Sensitive line-and-watercolor illustrations on every page add warmth to the story as they define people and settings." Booklist

Martini, Helen, 1912-

Lyon, George Ella. Mother to tigers; illustrations by Peter Catalanotto. Atheneum Bks. for Young Readers 2003 unp il $16.95 *

Grades: K 1 2 3   92

    1. Zoos

    ISBN 0-689-84221-X   LC 00-45375

"A Richard Jackson book"

"Helen Martini cared for both lion and tiger cubs in her New York City apartment before building the Bronx Zoo's first nursery back in 1944." SLJ

"Lyon's succinct, yet elegant, prose emphasizes Martini's dedication to the animals in her care. . . . Catalanotto's watercolor, charcoal, and torn-paper art is particularly effective here." Booklist

Matisse, Henri

Anholt, Laurence. Matisse; the king of color. Barron's 2007 unp il $14.99

Grades: 2 3 4 5   92

    1. Artists, French

    ISBN 0-7641-6047-8

"Anholt tells the story behind Matisse's final masterpiece—Chapelle du Rosaire. During a serious illness, the artist becomes friends with his nurse, Monique, and he draws and paints several pictures of her. When his health improves, she leaves the man who has been like a grandfather to her and joins a strict religious order. Years later, the two friends are reunited when Matisse moves into a villa close to the nunnery. As a final gift for Monique, now Sister Jacques-Marie, he designs a simple chapel for the nuns. . . . The bright and cheerful illustrations draw heavily on Matisse's drawings, paintings, and collages. Facts about the artist's life and style are also skillfully woven into the story and illustrations." SLJ

Welton, Jude. Henri Matisse. Watts 2002 46p il (Artists in their time) $22; pa $6.95

Grades: 5 6 7 8   92

    1. Artists, French

    ISBN 0-531-12228-X; 0-531-16621-X (pa)

                        LC 2002-69106

Discusses the life and career of this French artist, describing and giving examples of his work

This offers a "clear and lively [text]. . . . Captioned, full-color and black-and-white photographs and art reproductions are liberally scattered throughout." SLJ

Matzeliger, Jan, 1852-1889

Mitchell, Barbara. Shoes for everyone: a story about Jan Matzeliger; illustrations by Hetty Mitchell. Carolrhoda Bks. 1986 63p il (Carolrhoda creative minds book) hardcover o.p. pa $8.95

Grades: 3 4 5   92

    1. Shoe industry 2. African American inventors

    ISBN 0-87614-290-0; 0-87614-473-3 (pa)

                        LC 86-4157

A biography of the half-Dutch half-black Surinamese man who, despite the hardships and prejudice he found in his new Massachusetts home, invented a shoe-lasting machine that revolutionized the shoe industry in the late nineteenth century

This is "a compelling story of human endeavor. A clear text blessedly allows the extraordinary individual in focus, Jan Matzeliger, . . . to emerge without undue exclamatory adulation." Bull Cent Child Books

McCain, John S., 1936-

Wells, Catherine. John McCain. Morgan Reynolds Pub. 2007 112p il map (Political profiles) lib bdg $27.95

Grades: 5 6 7 8   92

    1. Statesmen—United States

    ISBN 978-1-59935-046-2 (lib bdg); 1-59935-046-7 (lib bdg)   LC 2007027133

A biography of the U.S. senator and candidate for president

"The key exciting portion of the book for most students will be the narrative of McCain's experiences as a fighter pilot and a prisoner of war in Vietnam. . . . [This book] should be painless, even enjoyable reading for reluctant readers." Voice Youth Advocates

Includes bibliographical references

McClintock, Barbara

Pasachoff, Naomi E. Barbara McClintock; genius of genetics; by Naomi Pasachoff. Enslow Publishers 2006 128p il (Great minds of science) lib bdg $31.93

Grades: 5 6 7 8   92

1. Genetics 2. Women scientists

ISBN 0-7660-2505-5   LC 2005014915

A biography of "a pioneering scientist in the field of genetics at a time when nearly all scientists were men. Her experiments with corn led to the . . . discovery that genes can move over generations from one place on the genome to another and even from one type of organism to another." Publisher's note

Includes glossary and bibliographical references

McKissack, Fredrick, 1939-

Parker-Rock, Michelle. Patricia and Fredrick McKissack. See entry under McKissack, Patricia C., 1944-

McKissack, Patricia C., 1944-

Parker-Rock, Michelle. Patricia and Fredrick McKissack; authors kids love; [by] Michelle Parker-Rock. Enslow Publishers 2008 48p il (Authors kids love) lib bdg $23.93

Grades: 3 4 5   92

1. McKissack, Fredrick, 1939- 2. Authors, American 3. African American authors

ISBN 978-0-7660-2759-6 (lib bdg); 0-7660-2759-7 (lib bdg)   LC 2008-1746

"A short biography of this husband and wife writing team, including their relationship, how they became authors, how they write together, and their advice for young, aspiring authors." Publisher's note

Includes glossary and bibliographical references

Menchú, Rigoberta

Menchú, Rigoberta. The girl from Chimel; [by] Rigoberta Menchú with Dante Liano; pictures by Domi; translated by David Unger. House of Anansi Press 2005 54p il $16.95

Grades: 4 5 6 7   92

1. Guatemala 2. Mayas

ISBN 0-88899-666-7

This is "Menchú's account of her childhood in the small village of Chimel, Guatamala. . . . Short sketches provide glimpses of Menchú's early years; lyrical language and repeated phrases such as 'when I was a girl in Chimel' link the text to oral storytelling. . . . Each chapter sports a vivid oil painting by Domi, featuring thick strokes of bright oranges, purples, greens, and reds and a naive approach that lends a folk-art feel, effectively capturing the action and emotion of the stories." Bull Cent Child Books

Mendel, Gregor, 1822-1884

Bardoe, Cheryl. Gregor Mendel; the friar who grew peas; illustrated by Jos. A. Smith. Abrams Books for Young Readers 2006 unp il $18.95

Grades: 2 3 4   92

1. Genetics 2. Scientists

ISBN 0-8109-5475-3   LC 2005-22957

"Published in association with the Field Museum."

A picture book biography of the scientist who became known as the father of genetics

"This slim, oversize volume is as much a treat for the eye as it is for the curious mind. Smith's crisp, realistic paintings, often flooded with the bright green of pea plants, accompany Bardoe's readable text." SLJ

Includes bibliographical references

Klare, Roger. Gregor Mendel; father of genetics. Enslow Pubs. 1997 128p il (Great minds of science) lib bdg $26.60

Grades: 5 6 7 8   92

1. Genetics

ISBN 0-89490-789-1   LC 96-35791

Examines the life and work of the nineteenth-century Austrian monk who discovered the laws of genetics

"Easy-to-understand explanations of groundbreaking discoveries. . . . An activity section encourages readers to try their hands at the techniques and principles under discussion. Black-and-white photos, reproductions, and diagrams enhance the [presentation]. Useful . . . especially for reports." SLJ

Includes bibliographical references

Van Gorp, Lynn. Gregor Mendel; genetics pioneer; science contributor, Sally Ride Science. Compass Point Books 2008 40p il (Mission: Science) lib bdg $26.60

Grades: 4 5 6   92

1. Genetics 2. Scientists

ISBN 978-0-7565-3963-4 (lib bdg); 0-7565-3963-3 (lib bdg)   LC 2008-07725

A biography of scientist Gregor Mendel, with an introduction to the principles of genetics

This "will entice students to become excited about an assignment or just satisfy their own curiosity. . . . The text . . . does a good job of connecting the scientist's work to our lives today. . . . [The] book has a variety of graphics including diagrams, [and] photos." Libr Media Connect

Merian, Maria Sibylla, 1647-1717

Engle, Margarita. Summer birds: the butterflies of Maria Merian; pictures by Julie Paschkis. Henry Holt & Co. 2010 unp il $16.99 *

Grades: K 1 2 3   92

1. Caterpillars 2. Butterflies 3. Women scientists 4. Women artists

ISBN 978-0-8050-8937-0; 0-8050-8937-3

LC 2009005267

"Born in Frankfurt in 1647, Maria Sibylla Marian disagreed with the conventional wisdom . . . that 'summer birds,' or butterflies, were 'beasts of the devil' that sprang alive from the mud . . . . Engle writes in the voice of Maria as a young teen, who carefully watches the slow transformation of caterpillars to winged adults,

Merian, Maria Sibylla, 1647-1717—*Continued*
painting everything that she sees. . . . In expertly pared-down language, the poetic lines deftly fold in basic science concepts about life cycles, along with biographical details that are further developed in an appended historical note. Paschkis' brilliantly colored and patterned paintings are an exuberant counterpoint to the minimal words." Booklist

Michelangelo Buonarroti, 1475-1564
Stanley, Diane. Michelangelo. HarperCollins Pubs. 2000 unp il $18.99; pa $6.99 *
Grades: 4 5 6 7   92
  1. Artists, Italian 2. Renaissance
  ISBN 0-688-15085-3; 0-06-052113-9 (pa)
  A biography of the Renaissance sculptor, painter, architect, and poet, well known for his work on the Sistine Chapel in Rome's St. Peter's Cathedral
  This is "as readable as it is useful. . . . Integrating Michelangelo's art with Stanley's watercolor, gouache, and colored-pencil figures and settings has the desired effect: readers will be dazzled with the master's ability, while at the same time pulled into his daily life and struggles." SLJ
  Includes bibliographical references

Wilkinson, Philip. Michelangelo; the young artist who dreamed of perfection. National Geographic 2006 64p il map (World history biographies) $17.95; lib bdg $27.09
Grades: 5 6 7 8   92
  1. Artists, Italian 2. Renaissance
  ISBN 0-7922-5533-X; 0-7922-5534-8 (lib bdg)
  An illustrated biography of Michelangelo, the Italian Renaissance painter and sculptor
  Includes glossary and bibliographical references

Miller, Norma, 1919-
Miller, Norma. Stompin' at the Savoy; the story of Norma Miller; collected and edited by Alan Govenar; illustrated by Martin French. Candlewick Press 2006 54p il $15.99
Grades: 3 4 5 6   92
  1. African American dancers 2. African American women—Biography
  ISBN 0-7636-2244-3   LC 2004-57916
  This is an autobiography of the African American jazz dancer of the Harlem Renaissance
  This "sizzles with spirit and swings with vitality. . . . Miller tells her story with humor and candor. . . . Stylized black-and-white illustrations, produced digitally and in mixed media, nearly swing right off the pages." SLJ

Mohapatra, Jyotirmayee, 1978-
Woog, Adam. Jyotirmayee Mohapatra; by Adam Woog. KidHaven Press 2006 48p il $24.95
Grades: 4 5 6 7   92
  1. Women—India 2. Social action
  ISBN 0-7377-3611-9   LC 2006009121
  "Mohapatra grew up in a rural village in India and became a leader in the fight for the rights of girls and women. . . . The power of one individual to inspire others to action is clearly expressed in this well-written profile. Full-color photos and a map enhance the presentation." SLJ
  Includes bibliographical references

Monet, Claude, 1840-1926
Kelley, True. Claude Monet: sunshine and waterlilies; written and illustrated by True Kelley. Grosset & Dunlap 2001 unp il (Smart about art) $14.89; pa $7.50
Grades: 2 3 4   92
  1. Artists, French
  ISBN 0-448-42613-7; 0-448-42522-X (pa)
                                        LC 2001-23147
  Written in the format of a school report by a fictitious student named Kristin Cole, this recounts the events in the life of the French artist and offers insight into his work
  Illustrated with "charming childlike drawings and reproductions of the artist's paintings in scrapbook-style layouts. . . . [This] is a successful blend of fact and humor that makes sophisticated concepts completely accessible and even entertaining." Booklist

Monroe, James, 1758-1831
Naden, Corinne J. James Monroe; [by] Corinne J. Naden and Rose Blue. Marshall Cavendish Benchmark 2009 96p il map (Presidents and their times) lib bdg $34.21
Grades: 5 6 7 8   92
  1. Presidents—United States
  ISBN 978-0-7614-2838-1 (lib bdg); 0-7614-2838-0 (lib bdg)   LC 2007-29480
  "Provides comprehensive information on President James Monroe and places him within his historical and cultural context. Also explored are the formative events of his times and how he responded." Publisher's note
  Includes glossary and bibliographical references

Montezuma, Carlos, 1866?-1923
Capaldi, Gina. A boy named Beckoning: the true story of Dr. Carlos Montezuma, Native American hero; adapted and illustrated by Gina Capaldi. Carolrhoda Books 2008 32p il lib bdg $16.95 *
Grades: 2 3 4   92
  1. Native Americans—Biography 2. Physicians
  ISBN 978-0-8225-7644-0   LC 2007021745
  "Capaldi uses Montezuma's own words to tell this gripping story of a Yavapai boy who was captured by the Pima in 1871 and grew up to become a prominent doctor and Native American spokesperson. Solidly researched, the well-written text follows Wassaja (later renamed Carlos Montezuma) as he was sold into slavery and purchased by a kind Italian photographer. . . . The illustrations are stunning, with multiple perspectives and rich gold and brown tones." SLJ
  Includes bibliographical references

Montgomery, L. M. (Lucy Maud), 1874-1942

Wallner, Alexandra. Lucy Maud Montgomery; the author of "Anne of Green Gables"; written and illustrated by Alexandra Wallner. Holiday House 2006 unp il $16.95

Grades: 2 3 4   **92**

1. Authors, Canadian 2. Women authors
ISBN 0-8234-1549-X   LC 2005-52638

This "chronicles the life of Lucy Maud Montgomery, the writer best known for *Anne of Green Gables* and its sequels. . . . Wallner's clean, spare paintings capture the writer's life and times in scenes created with a light palette and an innocent, folk-art look." Booklist

Moran, Thomas, 1837-1926

Judge, Lita. Yellowstone Moran; painting the American West. Viking 2009 unp il $16.99

Grades: K 1 2 3   **92**

1. Artists—United States 2. Yellowstone National Park 3. West (U.S.) in art
ISBN 978-0-670-01132-2; 0-670-01132-0
LC 2008049879

"In 1871, American artist Thomas Moran journeyed with a team of geologists through the Rocky Mountains to 'the land called the Yellowstone,' observing and sketching the landscape around him. Judge's watercolor illustrations capture the movement and pristine energy of the wilderness along with the team's arduous journey over rocks, ravines and woods." Publ Wkly

Includes bibliographical references

Morgan, Julia

Mannis, Celeste Davidson. Julia Morgan built a castle; by Celeste Mannis; illustrated by Miles Hyman. Viking 2006 unp il $17.99 *

Grades: 1 2 3 4   **92**

1. Women architects
ISBN 0-670-05964-1   LC 2004-17401

A picture book biography of "a groundbreaking female architect. Luminescent illustrations, created using soft pastels and pencils in a golden-peach palette, appear to glow with the light of California and France, both seminal locations in Morgan's life. . . . Filled with rich vocabulary, the narrative employs scrumptious architectural terms such as Baroque, flying buttresses, and teakwood cornice." SLJ

Morrison, Toni, 1931-

Haskins, James. Toni Morrison; the magic of words; [by] Jim Haskins. Millbrook Press 2001 48p il (Gateway biography) lib bdg $23.90

Grades: 4 5 6 7   **92**

1. Authors, American 2. African American authors 3. Women authors
ISBN 0-7613-1806-2   LC 00-32868

Haskins discusses Morrison's "childhood, her career as an editor . . . and he gives a very brief outline of each of her books and its critical reception, from *The Bluest Eye to Beloved*." Booklist

"This introductory biography is well organized, attractive, and inspiring." SLJ

Includes bibliographical references

Mozart, Wolfgang Amadeus, 1756-1791

Riggs, Kate. Wolfgang Amadeus Mozart. Creative Education 2009 48p il (Xtraordinary artists) lib bdg $32.80

Grades: 4 5 6 7   **92**

1. Composers
ISBN 978-1-58341-664-8 (lib bdg); 1-58341-664-1 (lib bdg)   LC 2007008963

This biography of the composer offers an "interesting [layout]; big, high-quality reproductions and photographs on heavy paper; insightful quotes from diverse sources; and meaty selections of the artist's own writing . . . at the end of the book. Readers get a strong sense of [Mozart's] personality along with an excellent survey of his work." SLJ

Includes bibliographical references

Sís, Peter. Play, Mozart, play! Greenwillow Books 2006 unp il $16.99 *

Grades: K 1 2   **92**

1. Composers
ISBN 0-06-112181-9   LC 2005-30152

"Recognizing his son's talent at a very young age, Mozart's stern father resolutely turned him into a child sensation!. . . . Illustrations give a hint of a unique boy who, despite a childhood of narrow restrictions, was released by the freedom he found in his music and his imagination. The clear, brief, readable text is augmented by a biographical afterword." SLJ

Stanley, Diane. Mozart, the wonder child; a puppet play in three acts. Collins 2009 unp il $17.99; lib bdg $18.89

Grades: 3 4 5   **92**

1. Puppets and puppet plays 2. Composers
ISBN 978-0-06-072674-4; 0-06-072674-1; 978-0-06-072676-8 (lib bdg); 0-06-072676-8 (lib bdg)
LC 2008-10487

"Stanley takes a look at one of the Western world's most celebrated prodigies, wee Wolfgang Mozart. . . . [Stanley] manages a neat overview of her subject's life in surprisingly few pages. . . . The illustrations treat the proceedings as a marionette show performed by the famous Salzberg Marionettes." Bull Cent Child Books

Includes bibliographical references

Weeks, Marcus. Mozart; the boy who changed the world with his music; [by] Marcus Weeks. National Geographic 2007 64p il map (World history biographies) $17.95; lib bdg $27.90

Grades: 5 6 7 8   **92**

1. Composers
ISBN 978-1-4263-0002-8; 1-4263-0002-6; 978-1-4263-0003-5 (lib bdg); 1-4263-0003-4 (lib bdg)
LC 2006020783

An introduction to the life and music of the composer and musician Mozart.

This "visually appealing [title is] packed with excellent photographs and reproductions, interesting sidebars, and have a time line running along the bottom of every page. . . . [The book is] useful, well-written." SLJ

Includes bibliographical references

Muir, John, 1838-1914

Lasky, Kathryn. John Muir; America's first environmentalist; illustrated by Stan Fellows. Candlewick Press 2006 41p il $16.99

Grades: 3 4 5   **92**

1. Naturalists

ISBN 0-7636-1957-4

A biography of John Muir, naturalist and founder of the Sierra Club, whose travels, speeches and writings led directly to the creation of the Yosemite National Park in 1890 and other national parks that followed.

"Lasky's clear prose quotes liberally from diary entries Muir recorded. . . . True to Muir's vision, Fellows' spacious double-page watercolors show the beauty of the wide landscapes in storm and sunshine as well as the tiny details in a single meadow." Booklist

Includes bibliographical references

Wadsworth, Ginger. Camping with the president. See entry under Roosevelt, Theodore, 1858-1919

Murphy, Isaac, 1861-1896

Trollinger, Patsi B. Perfect timing; how Isaac Murphy became one of the world's greatest jockeys; by Patsi B. Trollinger; paintings by Jerome Lagarrigue. Viking 2006 unp il $15.99

Grades: 2 3 4   **92**

1. Horse racing 2. African American athletes

ISBN 0-670-06083-6   LC 2005033855

"This picture-book biography describes how 12-year-old Murphy, the grandson of slaves, accepted a chance offer to ride a racehorse in 1873 in Lexington, KY, changing his life forever. He became one of the most successful jockeys in history. . . . Trollinger's prose style is clear but not oversimplified. . . . Lagarrigue's russet-hued oil paintings are vibrant and full of movement." SLJ

Naismith, James, 1861-1939

Wyckoff, Edwin Brit. The man who invented basketball: James Naismith and his amazing game. Enslow Publishers 2007 32p bibl il por (Genius at work!: great inventor biographies) lib bdg $22.60

Grades: 4 5 6   **92**

1. Basketball—History

ISBN 978-0-7660-2846-3 (lib bdg); 0-7660-2846-1 (lib bdg)   LC 2006018655

This "introduces the man behind one of today's most high-profile sports. . . . Young hoops devotees will enjoy the details of a favorite sport's infancy. . . . Crisp photos, illustrations, and a sidebar featuring Naismith's original 13 rules break up the accessible text." Booklist

Includes glossary and bibliographical references

Nakahama, Manjirō, 1827-1898

Blumberg, Rhoda. Shipwrecked!: the true adventures of a Japanese boy. HarperCollins Pubs. 2000 80p il map hardcover o.p. pa $7.99 *

Grades: 5 6 7 8   **92**

1. Survival after airplane accidents, shipwrecks, etc. 2. Japan—Foreign relations—United States 3. United States—Foreign relations—Japan 4. Japan—History

ISBN 0-688-17484-1; 0-688-17485-X (pa)

     LC 99-86664

In 1841, rescued by an American whaler after a terrible shipwreck leaves him and his four companions castaways on a remote island, fourteen-year-old Manjiro learns new laws and customs as he becomes the first Japanese person to set foot in the United States

"Exemplary in both her research and writing, Blumberg hooks readers with anecdotes that astonish without sensationalizing, and she uses language that's elegant and challenging, yet always clear. Particularly notable is the well-chosen reproductions of original artwork." Booklist

Includes bibliographical references

McCully, Emily Arnold. Manjiro; the boy who risked his life for two countries. Farrar, Straus & Giroux 2008 unp il $16.95

Grades: 2 3 4 5   **92**

1. Survival after airplane accidents, shipwrecks, etc. 2. Japan—Foreign relations—United States 3. United States—Foreign relations—Japan 4. Japan—History

ISBN 978-0-374-34792-5; 0-374-34792-1

     LC 2007-26929

"Manjiro was a 14-year-old Japanese fisherman when his boat was swept out to sea in 1841. At that time, the law threatened death to any citizen who returned after leaving Japan. A castaway on a rocky island, Manjiro was rescued by an American ship whose captain took the boy under his wing, taught him navigation and farming, sent him to school, and enabled him to realize his dream of returning home. . . . McCully's clearly written narrative portrays mid-nineteenth-century America as vividly as Manjiro's adventures, and both setting and characters come to life in this Caldecott-winning illustrator's dramatic paintings." Booklist

Includes bibliographical references

Napoleon I, Emperor of the French, 1769-1821

Burleigh, Robert. Napoleon; the story of the little corporal. Abrams Books for Young Readers 2007 43p il map $18.95

Grades: 4 5 6 7   **92**

1. France—History—1799-1815 2. France—Kings and rulers

ISBN 978-0-8109-1378-3; 0-8109-1378-X

     LC 2006-23610

"Published in association with the American Federation of Arts."

"Burleigh's straightforward style and clear focus make accessible this account of the rapid rise and fall of the skilled military leader and emperor of France. The period artwork, accompanied by helpful captions, enhances the cleanly designed presentation." Horn Book Guide

Neruda, Pablo, 1904-1973

Délano, Poli. When I was a boy Neruda called me Policarpo. See entry under Délano, Poli, 1936-

Ray, Deborah Kogan. To go singing through the world; the childhood of Pablo Neruda; [by] Deborah Kogan Ray. Farrar, Straus and Giroux 2006 unp il $17

Grades: 2 3 4   **92**

1. Poets, Chilean 2. Chile

ISBN 0-374-37627-1   LC 2005044317

Neruda, Pablo, 1904-1973—*Continued*

This picture book biography describes the childhood of Pablo Neruda in Temuco, Chile with excepts from his poetry and prose.

"The evocative art captures both the activity of the developing town and the tranquility of nature. An excellent introduction to the human face of poetry." SLJ

Includes bibliographical references

Newton, Sir Isaac, 1642-1727

Anderson, Margaret Jean. Isaac Newton; the greatest scientist of all time; [by] Margaret J. Anderson. rev ed. Enslow Publishers 2008 128p il (Great minds of science) lib bdg $31.93 *

Grades: 5 6 7 8   92

1. Scientists
ISBN 978-0-7660-2793-0 (lib bdg); 0-7660-2793-7 (lib bdg)   LC 2007-29382
First published 1996
This is a biography of the eighteenth-century English scientist

"The book is well illustrated. . . . A unique aspect of the volume is that it lists a series of experiments that students can perform to sharpen their understanding of a number of Newton's scientific theories." Sci Books Films

Includes glossary and bibliographical references

Hollihan, Kerrie Logan. Isaac Newton and physics for kids; his life and ideas with 21 activities. Chicago Review Press 2009 131p il map pa $16.95

Grades: 4 5 6 7   92

1. Scientists
ISBN 978-1-55652-778-4 (pa); 1-55652-778-0 (pa)   LC 2008048635

"Hollihan introduces readers to the scientific brilliance, as well as the social isolation, of this giant figure, blending a readable narrative with an attractive format that incorporates maps, diagrams, historical photographs, and physics activities." Booklist

Includes bibliographical references

Krull, Kathleen. Isaac Newton; illustrated by Boris Kulikov. Viking 2006 126p il (Giants of science) $15.99 *

Grades: 5 6 7 8   92

1. Scientists
ISBN 0-670-05921-8   LC 2005017741

This "profiles Sir Isaac Newton, the secretive, obsessive, and brilliant English scientist who invented calculus, built the first reflecting telescope, developed the modern scientific method, and discerned many of our laws of physics and optics. . . . The lively, conversational style will appeal to readers. . . . Kulikov's humorous pen-and-ink drawings complement the lighthearted text of this fascinating introduction." Booklist

Steele, Philip. Isaac Newton; the scientist who changed everything; [by] Philip Steele. National Geographic Society 2007 64p il map (World history biographies) $17.95; lib bdg $27.90

Grades: 4 5 6 7   92

1. Scientists
ISBN 978-1-4263-0114-8; 978-1-4263-0115-5 (lib bdg)   LC 2006020772

"The cradle-to-grave text includes vivid descriptions of Newton's youth. . . . The dynamic format is a draw; numerous mostly archival images . . . and a time-line border add interest and cultural context on each spacious page." Booklist

Includes bibliographical references

Nezahualcóyotl, King of Texcoco, 1402-1472

Serrano, Francisco. The poet king of Tezcoco; a great leader of Ancient Mexico; illustrated by Pablo Serrano; biography translated and adapted by Trudy Balch; poetry translated by Jo Anne Engelbert. Groundwood Books/House of Anansi Press 2007 35p il $18.95 *

Grades: 4 5 6 7   92

1. Aztecs 2. Mexico—History
ISBN 978-0-88899-787-6; 0-88899-787-6

"In the fifteenth century, the land where Mexico City now sprawls was a vast, green kingdom called Tezcoco. This . . . introduces one of Tezcoco's greatest rulers, a Toltec royal named Nezahualcoyotl. . . . The folk-art inspired illustrations echo the area's artistic traditions with beautiful patterning and symbolic imagery and flat, simplified characters reminiscent of hieroglyphics. Groundbreaking in its coverage of exciting history, this book offers details that are rarely presented to young people." Booklist

Nicholas, Saint, Bishop of Myra

Demi. The legend of Saint Nicholas. Margaret K. McElderry Bks. 2003 unp il $19.95

Grades: 3 4 5 6   92

1. Christian saints 2. Santa Claus
ISBN 0-689-84681-9   LC 2002-8426

Recounts pivotal events in the history and life of Saint Nicholas, including how he came to be associated with Christmas and Santa Claus

"The gilded paintings are full of absorbing . . . details. . . . The greatest strength of this book is its straightforward, affectionate depiction of a person who, by his deep love for the young and the needy, embodies the spirit of Christmas." SLJ

Nightingale, Florence, 1820-1910

Gorrell, Gena K. (Gena Kinton). Heart and soul: the story of Florence Nightingale. Tundra Bks. 2000 146p il map hardcover o.p. pa $11.95

Grades: 5 6 7 8   92

1. Nurses
ISBN 0-88776-494-0; 0-88776-703-6 (pa)
A biography of the 19th century English woman known as the founder of modern nursing

"This highly readable and well-researched biography does an excellent job of integrating the social and medical conditions of Nightingale's time. . . . Enlivening the narrative are black-and-white reproductions of drawings . . . and period photographs." SLJ

Includes bibliographical references

Nixon, Richard M. (Richard Milhous), 1913-1994

Aronson, Billy. Richard M. Nixon; [by] Billy Aronson. Marshall Cavendish Benchmark 2007 c2008 96p il (Presidents and their times) lib bdg $22.95 *

Grades: 5 6 7 8　　　　　　　　　　**92**
　　1. Presidents—United States
　　ISBN 978-0-7614-2428-4　　　　LC 2006013839

Aronson "is able to paint a picture so full that readers will come away feeling that they know the man and understand at least some of the forces that shaped him. . . . The narrative moves chronologically, marching through the war years, Nixon's tenure in Congress and as vice-president, his presidential loss to JFK, his successful efforts to remake himself as a politician, and his years as president. . . . The typeface is clear, the photographs are well chosen." Booklist

Includes glossary and bibliographical references

Noguchi, Isamu, 1904-1988

Hale, Christy. The East-West house; Noguchi's childhood in Japan. Lee & Low Books 2009 unp il $17.95 *

Grades: 3 4 5 6　　　　　　　　　　**92**
　　1. Japanese Americans 2. Sculptors
　　ISBN 978-1-60060-363-1; 1-60060-363-7
　　　　　　　　　　　　　　　　　　LC 2008053728

"A biography of Isamu Noguchi, Japanese American artist, sculptor, and landscape architect, focusing on his boyhood in Japan, his mixed heritage, and his participation in designing and building a home that fused Eastern and Western influences. Includes an afterword about Noguchi's adult life and works, plus photographs." Publisher's note

"The mixed-media collage illustrations reflect the blend of East and West. . . . Thoroughly documented and heavily reliant on primary sources. . . . An original and thought-provoking addition to biography or art collections." SLJ

Oakley, Annie, 1860-1926

Macy, Sue. Bulls-eye: a photobiography of Annie Oakley. National Geographic Soc. 2001 64p il $17.95; pa $7.95 *

Grades: 4 5 6 7　　　　　　　　　　**92**
　　1. Entertainers
　　ISBN　0-7922-7008-8;　978-0-7922-7008-9; 978-0-7922-5933-6 (pa); 0-7922-5933-5 (pa)
　　　　　　　　　　　　　　　　　　LC 2001-125

A biography of the woman born Phoebe Ann Moses, who, under the name Annie Oakley, became a famous sharpshooter touring with Buffalo Bill's Wild West Show

"This book is exemplary nonfiction: well documented, lots of period photos with credits, a resource list, and a chronology. Equally important is its engaging and well crafted account of this famous woman of the West." SLJ

Includes bibliographical references

Wills, Charles A. Annie Oakley: a photographic story of a life; [by] Chuck Wills. DK Pub. 2007 128p il (DK biography) $14.99

Grades: 4 5 6 7　　　　　　　　　　**92**
　　1. Entertainers
　　ISBN 978-0-7566-2986-1

A biography of the sharp-shooter in Buffalo Bill's Wild West Show, from her humble Quaker heritage, her childhood filled with poverty and abuse, to her rise to international fame.

"This highly readable book has a rich layout of photographs and illustrations on every spread." SLJ

Obama, Barack, 1961-

Abramson, Jill. Obama; the historic journey. Young reader's ed. Callaway 2009 94p il map $24.95

Grades: 5 6 7 8　　　　　　　　　　**92**
　　1. Presidents—United States 2. African Americans—Biography 3. Racially mixed people
　　ISBN 978-0-670-01208-4; 0-670-01208-4
　　　　　　　　　　　　　　　　　　LC 2009-5051

"This scaled down, teen-friendly version of The New York Times's adult biography is geared for middle school students. Containing many of the same photos, it provides a brief overview of the President's life, information that has been revealed over the election year and during his administration. . . . Its allure is in the many photographs with captions, sidebars, speech quotes, and charts. The book is nicely organized. The writing is direct and simple, explaining things such as convention delegates. . . . The book should entice young readers to explore his life further." Voice Youth Advocates

Feinstein, Stephen. Barack Obama. Enslow Publishers 2008 24p il map por (African-American heroes) lib bdg $21.26

Grades: K 1 2 3　　　　　　　　　　**92**
　　1. Presidents—United States 2. African Americans—Biography 3. Racially mixed people
　　ISBN 978-0-7660-2893-7 (lib bdg); 0-7660-2893-3 (lib bdg)　　　　　　　　　LC 2007036363

This is a "slim introduction to the [president] that begins with his childhood in Hawaii and Indonesia. Feinstein's upbeat text, divided into very short chapters, focuses on details that will capture kids' interest." Booklist

Includes bibliographical references

Grimes, Nikki. Barack Obama; son of promise, child of hope; illustrated by Bryan Collier. Simon & Schuster Books for Young Readers 2008 unp il $16.99

Grades: 1 2 3 4　　　　　　　　　　**92**
　　1. African Americans—Biography 2. Presidents—United States 3. Racially mixed people
　　ISBN 978-1-4169-7144-3; 1-4169-7144-0
　　　　　　　　　　　　　　　　　　LC 2008-06245

"With fast free verse . . . and big, handsome illustrations, Coretta Scott King Award winners Grimes and Collier tell the story of Obama's life." Booklist

Who Obama "is and where he comes from is conveyed in beautifully poetic language [and] . . . the illustrator's impressive interpretation of the author's text

Obama, Barack, 1961-—*Continued*
takes the story to a more meaningful visual level for younger readers." Libr Media Connect

Includes bibliographical references

Schuman, Michael. Barack Obama; "we are one people"; [by] Michael A. Schuman. rev & expanded. Enslow Publishers 2009 160p il (African-American biography library) lib bdg $34.60
Grades: 5 6 7 8   92
1. Presidents—United States 2. African Americans—Biography 3. Racially mixed people
ISBN 978-0-7660-3649-9 (lib bdg); 0-7660-3649-9 (lib bdg)   LC 2008-53678
First published 2008
"A biography of Barack Obama, the 44th president of the United States and the first African American to hold office." Publisher's note
"The text is straightforward and concise. . . . [The book is illustrated with] many color photos. . . . [This is a] timely, sturdy title." Booklist [review of 2008 edition]

Includes bibliographical references

Obama, Michelle
Brophy, David. Michelle Obama; meet the First Lady; by David Bergen Brophy. HarperCollins 2009 114p il $16.99; pa $6.99
Grades: 5 6 7 8   92
1. Presidents' spouses—United States 2. African American women—Biography
ISBN 978-0-06-177991-6; 0-06-177991-1; 978-0-06-177990-9 (pa); 0-06-177990-3 (pa)
A brief biography of Michelle Obama, wife of President Barack Obama
"The author . . . mixes personal data with information about the political process that brought the Obamas to the White House. . . . This biography is a must-have for all school libraries." Voice Youth Advocates

Includes glossary

Colbert, David. Michelle Obama; an American story. Houghton Mifflin Harcourt 2009 151p il $16
Grades: 5 6 7 8   92
1. Presidents' spouses—United States 2. African American women—Biography
ISBN 978-0-547-24941-4; 0-547-24941-1
This biography delves into "the subject of The First Lady's family roots. . . . It offers a strong sense of who Obama was as a child, her solid upbringing, and her adult choices, all bolstered with numerous quotes from Obama and those who know her best. . . . Two sections of color photos and appended source notes for direct quotes complete this timely, highly readable biography." Booklist

Hopkinson, Deborah. Michelle; illustrated by A.G. Ford. Katherine Tegen Books 2009 unp il $17.99; lib bdg $18.89
Grades: K 1 2 3   92
1. Presidents' spouses—United States 2. African American women—Biography
ISBN 978-0-06-182739-6; 0-06-182739-8; 978-0-06-182743-3 (lib bdg); 0-06-182743-6 (lib bdg)   LC 2009014551
This biography of the First Lady "touches on Michelle's childhood years in a loving working-class family, her academic accomplishments, courtship, marriage, careers and role as devoted mother and active supporter of her husband's presidential campaign. The straightforward, accessible text at times assumes dramatic overtones. . . . Ford's paintings offer likenesses of Michelle and her family, often capturing facial expressions and nuances of posture and gesture with uncanny realism. This warm, respectful portrait succeeds in presenting its subject as both inspirational and relatable." Publ Wkly

O'Keeffe, Georgia, 1887-1986
Bryant, Jennifer. Georgia's bones; [illustrated by] Bethanne Anderson. Eerdmans Books for Young Readers 2005 32p il $16
Grades: K 1 2 3   92
1. Women artists 2. Artists—United States
ISBN 0-8028-5217-3   LC 2004-6800
Artist Georgia O'Keeffe was interested in the shapes she saw around her, from her childhood on a Wisconsin farm to her adult life in New York City and New Mexico
"Bryant writes in spare, lyrical verse, honoring her subject's idiosyncratic impressions and precise observation of the natural world. . . . Cow skulls, southwestern landscapes, and oversize flowers are present and accounted for, but the swooping brushstrokes and earthy textures are unmistakably Andersen's own." Booklist

Rodriguez, Rachel. Through Georgia's eyes; illustrated by Julie Paschkis. Henry Holt and Co. 2006 unp il $16.95
Grades: K 1 2 3   92
1. Women artists 2. Artists—United States
ISBN 978-0-8050-7740-7; 0-8050-7740-5
LC 2005012479
"Rodríguez gently tells this inspirational artist's story . . . with quiet simplicity. . . . Using short, strong sentences and phrases, the author emphasizes the artist's creative force. Paschkis extends the words with the visual simplicity of colorful, cut-paper collages." SLJ

Winter, Jeanette. My name is Georgia; a portrait. Harcourt Brace & Co. 1998 unp il $16; pa $7 *
Grades: K 1 2 3   92
1. Women artists 2. Artists—United States
ISBN 0-15-201649-X; 0-15-204597-X (pa)
LC 97-7087
Presents, in brief text and illustrations, the life of the painter who drew much of her inspiration from nature
"Winter mirrors the artist's stark imagery and strong personality in spare, poetic text and folk art—inspired illustrations." Publ Wkly

Includes bibliographical references

Oppenheimer, J. Robert, 1904-1967

Allman, Toney. J. Robert Oppenheimer; theoretical physicist, atomic pioneer; [by] Toney Allman. Blackbirch Press 2005 64p il map (Giants of science) $24.95

Grades: 5 6 7 8   92

1. Physicists 2. Atomic bomb

ISBN 1-56711-889-5   LC 2004-11199

Subtitle on cover: Father of the atomic bomb

This is a biography of the nuclear physicist who was instrumental in the development of the atomic bomb in the United States

This is a "readable, inviting overview. . . . Full-color and black-and-white photographs and diagrams energize the text and clarify the complex ideas discussed." SLJ

Includes bibliographical references

Owens, Jesse, 1913-1980

Adler, David A. A picture book of Jesse Owens; [by] David Adler; illustrated by Robert Casilla. Holiday House 1992 unp il lib bdg $16.95; pa $6.95

Grades: 1 2 3   92

1. African American athletes 2. Track athletics

ISBN 0-8234-0966-X (lib bdg); 0-8234-1066-8 (pa)

LC 91-44735

A simple biography of the noted black track star who competed in the 1936 Berlin Olympics

"The portrait presented, although brief, is accurate and touches on the major events of the track-and-field champion's life. . . . Casilla contributes full-page watercolor paintings that nicely complement and expand the writing." SLJ

Weatherford, Carole Boston. Jesse Owens; the fastest man alive; [by] Carole Boston Weatherford; illustrations by Eric Velasquez. Walker & Company 2006 unp il $16.95; lib bdg $17.85

Grades: 2 3 4 5   92

1. Track athletics 2. African American athletes

ISBN 978-0-8027-9550-2; 0-8027-9550-1; 978-0-8027-9551-9 (lib bdg); 0-8027-9551-X (lib bdg)

LC 2006010187

"The year is 1936, and Owens is about to win an unprecedented four Olympic gold medals in Berlin, toppling Hitler's dream to showcase Aryan superiority. Written in second-person narration, the book focuses tightly on Owens's accomplishments, giving details about each of the four races and his role in uniting people across racial lines. Rich pastel illustrations, many of them based on historical photographs, make this title stand out." SLJ

Paganini, Nicolò, 1782-1840

Frisch, Aaron. Dark fiddler: the life and legend of Nicolo Paganini; [by] Aaron Frisch; illustrated by Gary Kelley. Creative Editions 2008 unp il lib bdg $17.95 *

Grades: 3 4 5 6   92

1. Violinists 2. Composers

ISBN 978-1-56846-200-4 (lib bdg); 1-56846-200-X (lib bdg)

"Readers may not be familiar with the name Paganini, but after one look at the dramatic cover, with the spectral violinist staring back, a slight smile on his lips, they will want to find out more. . . . The folksy tone of the narrative will draw kids close as the story of Paganini's life unfolds. All this is set against breathtaking, chalklike art." Booklist

Paige, Satchel, 1906-1982

Adler, David A. Satchel Paige; don't look back; written by David A. Adler; illustrated by Terry Widener. Harcourt 2006 c2007 unp il $16 *

Grades: K 1 2 3   92

1. Baseball—Biography 2. African American athletes

ISBN 978-0-15-205585-1; 0-15-205585-1

LC 2005026354

A brief illustrated biography of the baseball player who, after a long career in the Negro Leagues, joined the Cleveland Indians and became the first African American to pitch in the World Series.

"Widener's acrylic paintings elongate and exaggerate the figures, using a rubbery perspective and old-fashioned hues to great effect." Booklist

Includes bibliographical references

Cline-Ransome, Lesa. Satchel Paige; paintings by James E. Ransome. Simon & Schuster Bks. for Young Readers 2000 unp il hardcover o.p. pa $7.99 *

Grades: 2 3 4   92

1. Baseball—Biography 2. African American athletes

ISBN 0-689-81151-9; 0-689-85681-4 (pa)

LC 97-13790

Examines the life of the legendary baseball player, who was the first African-American to pitch in a Major League World Series

"Cline-Ransome plays up the mythic elements of the Paige story in her rollicking narrative, while Ransome's paintings jump off the page with bright colors and startling contrasts." Booklist

Includes bibliographical references

Park, Linda Sue, 1960-

Parker-Rock, Michelle. Linda Sue Park; an author kids love. Enslow Publishers 2009 48p il (Authors kids love) lib bdg $23.93

Grades: 3 4 5   92

1. Authors, American

ISBN 978-0-7660-3158-6 (lib bdg); 0-7660-3158-6 (lib bdg)

LC 2008-44549

"Discusses the life of children's author Linda Sue Park, including her childhood, her path to becoming an author, how she writes, and her advice for young au-

Park, Linda Sue, 1960-—*Continued*

thors." Publisher's note

"Clearly written, [this] outstanding [biography provides] many interesting details about the [subject's] personal [life] and [includes] photos that enhance the [text]." SLJ

Includes glossary and bibliographical references

Parker, John P., 1827-1900

Rappaport, Doreen. Freedom river; pictures by Bryan Collier. Jump at the Sun 2000 unp il map $14.99 *

Grades: 2 3 4 5   92

1. Underground railroad 2. Slavery—United States 3. African Americans—Biography

ISBN 0-7868-0350-9   LC 99-33438

Coretta Scott King honor book for illustration, 2001

Map on lining papers

Describes an incident in the life of John Parker, an ex-slave who became a successful businessman in Ripley, Ohio, and who repeatedly risked his life to help other slaves escape to freedom

This book "combines an exciting, heartrending narrative with dramatic collage and watercolor pictures." Booklist

Includes bibliographical references

Parkhurst, Charley, 1812-1879

Kay, Verla. Rough, tough Charley; by Verla Kay; illustrated by Adam Gustavson. Tricycle Press 2007 unp il $15.95

Grades: K 1 2 3   92

1. Frontier and pioneer life—California 2. Women—West (U.S.)

ISBN 978-1-58246-184-7; 1-58246-184-8

LC 2006026611

"Many folks thought they knew the real Charley Parkhurst (1812-1879): a scrappy orphan . . . who became one of the bravest, fastest, saltiest and most respected stagecoach drivers in Gold Country. . . . But everybody had Charley wrong, for . . . Charley had successfully disguised the fact that he was actually a woman. . . . Gustavson's . . . lush, realistic oil illustrations are a lavish counterpoint to Kay's spare verse, [and] are suffused with the romance and roughness of a bygone era." Publ Wkly

Parks, Rosa, 1913-2005

Giovanni, Nikki. Rosa; illustrated by Bryan Collier. Henry Holt 2005 32p il $16.95 *

Grades: 3 4 5   92

1. African American women—Biography 2. African Americans—Civil rights

ISBN 0-8050-7106-7

A Caldecott Medal honor book, 2006

A picture book biography of the Alabama black woman whose refusal to give up her seat on a bus helped establish the civil rights movement

"Paired very effectively with Giovanni's passionate, direct words, Collier's large watercolor-and-collage illustrations depict Parks as an inspiring force that radiates golden light, and also as part of a dynamic activist community." Booklist

Parks, Rosa. Rosa Parks: my story; by Rosa Parks with Jim Haskins. Dial Bks. 1992 192p il $17.99; pa $6.99 *

Grades: 5 6 7 8   92

1. African American women—Biography 2. African Americans—Civil rights 3. Montgomery (Ala.)—Race relations

ISBN 0-8037-0673-1; 0-14-130120-1 (pa)

LC 89-1124

Rosa Parks describes her early life and experiences with race discrimination, and her participation in the Montgomery bus boycott and the civil rights movement

"A remarkable story, a record of quiet bravery and modesty, a document of social significance, a taut drama told with candor." Bull Cent Child Books

Pasteur, Louis, 1822-1895

Smith, Linda Wasmer. Louis Pasteur; disease fighter. rev ed. Enslow Publishers 2007 c2008 128p bibl il por (Great minds of science) lib bdg $31.93

Grades: 5 6 7 8   92

1. Scientists

ISBN 978-0-7660-2792-3 (lib bdg); 0-7660-2792-9 (lib bdg)   LC 2006036434

First published 1997

A biography of the noted French scientist whose discoveries, including a rabies vaccine and the process of pasteurization, had important practical applications in both medicine and industry

Includes glossary and bibliographical references

Zamosky, Lisa. Louis Pasteur; founder of microbiology. Compass Point Books 2009 40p il map (Mission: Science) lib bdg $26.60

Grades: 4 5 6   92

1. Scientists

ISBN 978-0-7565-3962-7   LC 2008007726

This biography of the father of microbiology "does a good job of connecting the scientist's work to our lives today. . . . [The] book has a variety of graphics including diagrams, photos, and reproductions of paintings and sketches. [This volume is] a definite plus for a school library or the juvenile collection in a public library." Libr Media Connect

Includes glossary and bibliographical references

Patch, Sam, 1807-1829

Cummins, Julie. Sam Patch; daredevil jumper; [illustrated by Michael Allen Austin] Holiday House 2009 unp il $16.95

Grades: PreK K 1 2   92

1. Stunt performers

ISBN 978-0-8234-1741-4; 0-8234-1741-7

LC 2007-34624

This "chronicles the short life of early-19th-century stuntman Sam Patch. . . . The conversational style briskly moves the tale from Sam's childhood jumping exploits to the showstopping stunts of his brief but world-famous career. . . . Austin's . . . sepia-infused acrylics set a tone alternating between whimsical and haunting. The dynamic illustrations make exaggerated use of light and perspective." Publ Wkly

Patrick, Saint, 373?-463?

De Paola, Tomie. Patrick: patron saint of Ireland. Holiday House 1992 unp il lib bdg $16.95; pa $6.95

Grades: K 1 2 3   92

1. Christian saints

ISBN 0-8234-0924-4 (lib bdg); 0-8234-1077-3 (pa)

LC 91-19417

Relates the life and legends of Patrick, the patron saint of Ireland

"The combination of book design, text, and illustration is suitably reverent but never saccharine; the whole is a well-executed treatment of an appealing subject." Horn Book

Paul, Les, 1915-2009

Wyckoff, Edwin Brit. Electric guitar man: the genius of Les Paul; [by] Edwin Brit Wyckoff. Enslow Elementary 2008 32p il (Genius at work!: great inventor biographies) lib bdg $22.60

Grades: 4 5 6   92

1. Guitarists 2. Inventors

ISBN 978-0-7660-2847-0 (lib bdg); 0-7660-2847-X (lib bdg)   LC 2006034681

"Without the electronic guitar invented by Les Paul, music would never have been the same. In this biography of Paul's life and career, Edwin Brit Wyckoff shares how the rambunctious boy from Waukesha, Wisconsin, was propelled to stardom by his unrivaled playing ability and technological prowess." Publisher's note

Includes glossary and bibliographical references

Paulsen, Gary

Paulsen, Gary. Caught by the sea; my life on boats. Delacorte Press 2001 103p maps $15.95; pa $5.50 *

Grades: 5 6 7 8   92

1. Authors, American 2. Boats and boating 3. Ocean travel

ISBN 0-385-32645-9; 0-440-40716-8 (pa)

LC 2001-17336

"Paulsen traces his life at sea, from buying his first sailboat to getting lost in the Pacific to encountering sharks. . . . His sometimes comic, sometimes near-fatal sea-going errors make for absorbing, captivating reading." Booklist

Paulsen, Gary. How Angel Peterson got his name; and other outrageous tales about extreme sports. Wendy Lamb Bks. 2003 111p hardcover o.p. pa $5.99 *

Grades: 5 6 7 8   92

1. Authors, American

ISBN 0-385-72949-9; 0-385-90090-2 (lib bdg); 978-0-440-22935-3 (pa); 0-440-22935-9 (pa)

LC 2002-7668

Author Gary Paulsen relates tales from his youth in a small town in northwestern Minnesota in the late 1940s and early 1950s, such as skiing behind a souped-up car and imitating daredevil Evel Knievel

"Writing with humor and sensitivity, Paulsen shows boys moving into adolescence believing they can do any-thing. . . . None of them dies (amazingly), and even if Paulsen exaggerates the teensiest bit, his tales are side-splittingly funny and more than a little frightening." Booklist

Paulsen, Gary. My life in dog years; with drawings by Ruth Wright Paulsen. Delacorte Press 1998 137p il $15.95; pa $6.50 *

Grades: 4 5 6 7   92

1. Authors, American 2. Dogs

ISBN 0-385-32570-3; 0-440-41471-7 (pa)

LC 97-40254

The author describes some of the dogs that have had special places in his life, including his first dog, Snowball, in the Philippines; Dirk, who protected him from bullies; and Cookie, who saved his life

"Paulsen differentiates his canine friends beautifully, as only a keen observer and lover of dogs can. At the same time, he presents an intimate glimpse of himself, a lonely child of alcoholic parents, who drew strength and solace from his four-legged companions and a love of the great outdoors. Poignant but never saccharine, honest, and open." Booklist

Pavlov, Ivan Petrovich, 1849-1936

Saunders, Barbara R. Ivan Pavlov; exploring the mysteries of behavior. Enslow Publishers 2006 112p il por (Great minds of science) lib bdg $31.93

Grades: 5 6 7 8   92

1. Scientists 2. Behaviorism

ISBN 0-7660-2506-3   LC 2005031648

This is a biography of Russian scientist Ivan Pavlov, best known for his experiments with dogs, which were key to the development of behaviorism, and who won the 1904 Nobel Prize for his research on digestion

"The accessible [text has] an inviting, open format and [offers] many anecdotes. . . . Good-quality photos and illustrations complement the [narrative]." SLJ

Includes glossary and bibliographical references

Peary, Marie Ahnighito, 1893-1978

Kirkpatrick, Katherine A. Snow baby; the Arctic childhood of Admiral Robert E. Peary's daring daughter; [by] Katherine Kirkpatrick. Holiday House 2007 50p il map $16.95

Grades: 5 6 7 8   92

1. Peary, Robert Edwin, 1856-1920 2. Arctic regions 3. Explorers

ISBN 978-0-8234-1973-9; 0-8234-1973-8

LC 2006-02016

"Born north of the Arctic Circle in 1893, Marie Ahnighito Peary published her own version of her youth in 1934 (*The Snowbaby's Own Story*), on which this book is based. Kirkpatrick's engaging text captures the girl's adventurous spirit and the opportunities that her father's life as an explorer presented, as well as her love of the North and her Inuit friends." SLJ

Peary, Robert Edwin, 1856-1920

Calvert, Patricia. Robert E. Peary; to the top of the world. Benchmark Bks. 2002 80p il map (Great explorations) lib bdg $29.93 *

Grades: 5 6 7 8   92

1. Explorers 2. North Pole
ISBN 0-7614-1242-5   LC 00-51900

A biography of Admiral Robert Peary whose expedition reached the North Pole in 1909

"The well-researched [book] . . . will be useful to students writing reports. Maps and archival reproductions in both black and white and color extend the text." Horn Book Guide

Includes bibliographical references

Peet, Bill

Peet, Bill. Bill Peet: an autobiography. Houghton Mifflin 1989 190p il hardcover o.p. pa $15 *

Grades: 4 5 6 7   92

1. Walt Disney Productions 2. Authors, American 3. Illustrators
ISBN 0-395-50932-7; 0-395-68982-1 (pa)
                                            LC 88-37067

A Caldecott Medal honor book, 1990

This memoir "describes the life of the well-known children's book author who worked as an illustrator for Walt Disney from the making of 'Dumbo' until 'Mary Poppins.'" N Y Times Book Rev

"Every page of this oversized book is illustrated with Peet's unmistakable black-and-white drawings of himself and the people, places, and events described in the text. Familiar characters from his books and movies appear often." SLJ

Pelé, 1940-

Brown, Monica. Pele, king of soccer; illustrated by Rudy Gutierrez; translated by Fernando Gayesky. Rayo 2009 unp il $17.99

Grades: K 1 2 3   92

1. Soccer—Biography 2. Bilingual books—English-Spanish
ISBN 978-0-06-122779-0; 0-06-122779-X
                                            LC 2008-19125

This is a biography of the soccer champion, in English and Spanish

"Twisting multiple perspectives, adding swirls of color, and limning distorted figures with loose auras of yellow and blue, Gutiérrez creates high-energy, full-bleed illustrations." Booklist

Cline-Ransome, Lesa. Young Pelé; soccer's first star; illustrated by James E. Ransome. Schwartz & Wade Bks. 2007 unp il $16.99; lib bdg $19.99 *

Grades: K 1 2 3   92

1. Soccer—Biography
ISBN 978-0-375-83599-5; 0-375-83599-7; 978-0-375-93599-2 (lib bdg); 0-375-93599-1 (lib bdg)

"With handsome oil paintings and a stirring story, this picture-book biography will first grab children with its action. Just as exciting, though, is the account of Brazilian-born Pelé's personal struggle—his amazing rise from poverty to international soccer stardom." Booklist

Penn, William, 1644-1718

Kroll, Steven. William Penn; founder of Pennsylvania; illustrated by Ronald Himler. Holiday House 2000 unp il $16.95

Grades: 3 4 5   92

1. Society of Friends 2. Pennsylvania—History
ISBN 0-8234-1439-6   LC 98-18932

A biography of William Penn, founder of the Quaker colony of Pennsylvania, who struggled throughout his life for the freedom to practice his religion

"The watercolor, pencil, and gouache paintings light up the book with their mix of dramatic scenes and sensitive portraits. . . . This biographical picture book will be a useful and certainly a handsome addition to library collections." Booklist

Peter I, the Great, Emperor of Russia, 1672-1725

Stanley, Diane. Peter the Great. Morrow Junior Bks. 1999 32p il $16 *

Grades: 4 5 6 7   92

1. Russia—Kings and rulers
ISBN 0-688-16708-X   LC 98-45250

A reissue of the title first published 1986 by Four Winds Press

A biography of the tsar who began the transformation of Russia into a modern state in the late seventeenth-early eighteenth centuries

The author's "material is presented with a modicum of oversimplification and a plethora of details that are sure to fascinate children. But what really makes this biography shine are its breathtaking illustrations. The meticulously researched, vivid scenes of Russian life during Peter's reign—courts, countryside, architecture, costumes—are beautifully rendered." Publ Wkly

Phelps, Michael, 1985-

Torsiello, David P. Michael Phelps; swimming for Olympic gold. Enslow Publishers 2009 48p il (Hot celebrity biographies) lib bdg $23.93

Grades: 2 3 4   92

1. Athletes 2. Swimming
ISBN 978-0-7660-3591-1 (lib bdg); 0-7660-3591-3 (lib bdg)   LC 2008-48700

"A biography of American Olympic swimmer Michael Phelps. In 2008, he won eight gold medals at the Olympic Games in Beijing, breaking the record of most gold medals won at a single Olympics." Publisher's note

"Quality design, including an interesting color palette, distinguishes [this profile] . . . [which] is illustrated with large, recent color photos. The tone is light but not breathless; the writing is solid." SLJ

Includes glossary

Picasso, Pablo, 1881-1973

Hodge, Susie. Pablo Picasso; by Susie Hodge. new ed. World Almanac Library 2004 48p il (Lives of the artists) lib bdg $30; pa $11

Grades: 4 5 6 7   92

1. Artists, French
ISBN 0-8368-5601-5 (lib bdg); 0-8368-5606-6 (pa)
                                            LC 2003-67238

Original Italian edition 2003

Picasso, Pablo, 1881-1973—*Continued*

This discusses the life and work of the twentieth century artist

This is "concise and straightforward. . . . [It] includes remarkably accomplished sketches and paintings from the artist's childhood and adolescence." Booklist

Includes bibliographical references

Jacobson, Rick. Picasso; soul on fire; [by] Rick Jacobson; illustrated by Laura Fernandez & Rick Jacobson. Tundra Books 2004 unp il $15.95

Grades: 3 4 5   92

1. Artists, French

ISBN 0-88776-599-8

This is an introduction the life of the artist, exploring his influences, selected works, and his creative processes.

"Written in simple, clear language. . . . The softly radiant oil paintings are mostly full page and enhance the enjoyment of the book. . . . This eloquent tribute will serve as an introduction to Picasso and to an artist's inspirations." SLJ

Scarborough, Kate. Pablo Picasso. Watts 2002 46p il map (Artists in their time) lib bdg $22; pa $6.95

Grades: 5 6 7 8   92

1. Artists, French

ISBN 0-531-12229-8 (lib bdg); 0-531-16622-8 (pa)
LC 2002-27017

Discusses the life, art, and legacy of the artist Pablo Picasso. Includes a timeline linking the events in his life with world events

This offers a "clear and lively [text]. . . . Captioned, full-color and black-and-white photographs and art reproductions are liberally scattered throughout." SLJ

Includes glossary

Pickett, Bill, ca. 1860-1932

Pinkney, Andrea Davis. Bill Pickett, rodeo-ridin' cowboy; written by Andrea D. Pinkney; illustrated by Brian Pinkney. Harcourt Brace & Co. 1996 unp il hardcover o.p. pa $7 *

Grades: K 1 2 3   92

1. Cowhands 2. African Americans—Biography 3. Rodeos

ISBN 0-15-200100-X; 0-15-202103-5 (pa)
LC 95-35920

"Gulliver books"

Describes the life and accomplishments of the son of a former slave whose unusual bulldogging style made him a rodeo star

"The story is told with verve, relish, and just enough of a cowboy twang, with Pinkney giving an excellent overview of the history of rodeos and black cowboys in a closing note. Husband Brian Pinkney's pictures, in his typical scratchboard technique, are well suited to the story, their lines and colors swirling with movement and excitement on the deep black surface." Booklist

Includes bibliographical references

Pike, Zebulon Montgomery, 1779-1813

Calvert, Patricia. Zebulon Pike; lost in the Rockies; by Patricia Calvert. Benchmark Books 2005 96p il map (Great explorations) lib bdg $29.93

Grades: 5 6 7 8   92

1. Explorers 2. West (U.S.)—Exploration

ISBN 0-7614-1612-9   LC 2003-17583

This "discusses the explorer's military service, relationship with the corrupt general James Wilkinson, the historical speculation about his motives for his meandering expedition to the Spanish west, and his failure to climb the mountain named for him. . . . Illustrated with beautiful reproductions of period illustrations, paintings, and maps. . . . Well-written." SLJ

Includes bibliographical references

Pinchot, Gifford, 1865-1946

Hines, Gary. Midnight forests; a story of Gifford Pinchot and our national forests; illustrated by Robert Casilla. Boyds Mills Press 2005 unp il $16.95

Grades: 3 4 5   92

1. Conservationists 2. Forests and forestry

ISBN 1-56397-148-8   LC 2003-26876

"This picture-book biography introduces Gifford Pinchot, a wealthy young American who studied forestry in France and returned home to put his knowledge to good use in his own country. Appointed Secretary of Agriculture in 1898, he later joined forces with Theodore Roosevelt to turn 16 million acres into national forests. . . . Mirroring the quiet prose, the dignified pencil-and-watercolor illustrations depict Pinchot at work and in quiet contemplation." Booklist

Includes bibliographical references

Pinkwater, Daniel Manus, 1941-

McGinty, Alice B. Meet Daniel Pinkwater. PowerKids Press 2003 24p il (About the author) lib bdg $18.75

Grades: 1 2 3   92

1. Authors, American

ISBN 0-8239-6406-X   LC 2002-136

A short biography of the author of more than seventy books for children, Daniel Pinkwater

"Each spread has photographs and drawings on one side and text and a sidebar with interesting or fun facts on the other." SLJ

Includes glossary and bibliographical references

Pippin, Horace, 1888-1946

Venezia, Mike. Horace Pippin; written and illustrated by Mike Venezia. Children's Press 2008 32p il (Getting to know the world's greatest artists) lib bdg $28

Grades: 3 4 5   92

1. African American artists 2. Artists—United States

ISBN 978-0-531-18527-8 (lib bdg); 0-531-18527-3 (lib bdg)
LC 2007016127

A biography of the African American artist best known for his paintings of life in America during slavery

Pippin, Horace, 1888-1946—*Continued*
and the years of segregation.

"Though the [text is] simply written, [this title contains] a wealth of information. . . . [The book has] many reproductions of the [artist's] works as well as those of the masters who influenced [him]. To help illustrate his points, Venezia has incorporated his own cartoon-style illustrations." SLJ

Pitcher, Molly, 1754-1832
Rockwell, Anne F. They called her Molly Pitcher; by Anne Rockwell; illustrated by Cynthia von Buhler. Knopf 2002 unp il $16.95; lib bdg $17.99

Grades: 3 4 5   92
    1. United States—History—1775-1783, Revolution
    ISBN 0-679-89187-0; 0-679-99187-5 (lib bdg)
                  LC 2001-29422
A biography of the woman who was named a sergeant in the Continental Army by George Washington for her bravery in the Battle of Monmouth

"The language is inviting, the story, exciting. Von Buhler's illustrations, which appear crackled, as if they were painted during this period, make the book shine." SLJ

Pizarro, Francisco, ca. 1475-1541
Meltzer, Milton. Francisco Pizarro; the conquest of Peru; by Milton Meltzer. Benchmark Books 2005 80p il map (Great explorations) lib bdg $29.93

Grades: 5 6 7 8   92
    1. Explorers 2. America—Exploration
    ISBN 0-7614-1607-2   LC 2002-156000
Contents: Where Pizarro came from; The Spanish conquistadores; The business of conquest; A glimpse of gold; The Inca empire; Epidemics and civil wars; The decisive day; Turning an empire into a colony

Introduces the life of the explorer who was sent to Peru in the sixteenth century by the king of Spain to conquer the Incas and claim their land and wealth for the Spanish crown.

Includes bibliographical references

Planck, Max, 1858-1947
Weir, Jane. Max Planck; revolutionary physicist. Compass Point Books 2009 40p il (Mission: science) lib bdg $26.60

Grades: 4 5 6   92
    1. Physicists
    ISBN 978-0-7565-4073-9 (lib bdg); 0-7565-4073-9 (lib bdg)   LC 2008-37622
Biography of the physicist Max Planck
Includes glossary and bibliographical references

Pocahontas, d. 1617
Brimner, Larry Dane. Pocahontas; bridging two worlds. Marshall Cavendish Benchmark 2009 41p il (American heroes) lib bdg $20.95

Grades: 2 3 4   92
    1. Powhatan Indians 2. Virginia—History 3. United States—History—1600-1775, Colonial period
    ISBN 978-0-7614-3065-0
This traces the life of Pocahontas from her birth in about 1595 to her death and considers the impact her life had on American history

This "concise and well-written [title covers] key biographical facts without overwhelming young readers, and [includes] captioned illustrations and reproductions, most of which are in color. Text is large, and the layout is age-appropriate and attractive, with wide margins." SLJ

Krull, Kathleen. Pocahontas; princess of the New World; [by] Kathleen Krull; pictures by David Diaz. Walker 2007 unp il $16.95; lib bdg $17.85

Grades: K 1 2 3   92
    1. Powhatan Indians 2. Virginia—History 3. United States—History—1600-1775, Colonial period
    ISBN   978-0-8027-9554-0;   0-8027-9554-4; 978-0-8027-9555-7 (lib bdg); 0-8027-9555-2 (lib bdg)   LC 2006025723
This focuses on "the mischievous girl Matoaka, affectionately nicknamed Pocahontas. Primary sources provide the basic facts. . . . Diaz's cut-paper collage illustrations literally glow with vibrancy. He uses a palette of tropical colors—lemon yellow, lime green, ocean blue, and orange." SLJ

Pollock, Jackson, 1912-1956
Greenberg, Jan. Action Jackson; [by] Jan Greenberg and Sandra Jordan; illustrated by Robert Andrew Parker. Roaring Brook Press 2002 32p il hardcover o.p. pa $6.95 *

Grades: 3 4 5 6   92
    1. Artists—United States
    ISBN 0-7613-1682-5; 0-7613-2770-3 (lib bdg); 0-312-36751-1 (pa)   LC 2002-6211
Imagines Jackson Pollock at work during the creation of one of his paint-swirled and splattered canvasses

"Using spare, lyrical words, the authors layer the exciting story with deep observations about what art is and how it is made. . . . Parker's scribbly pen-and-watercolor illustrations get the mood just right; the loose lines have an improvised, energetic quality that echoes Pollock's painting." Booklist

Includes bibliographical references

Polo, Marco, 1254-1323?
Demi. Marco Polo; written and illustrated by Demi. Marshall Cavendish 2008 unp il map $19.99 *

Grades: 4 5 6 7   92
    1. Voyages and travels 2. Explorers
    ISBN 978-0-7614-5433-5; 0-7614-5433-0
"This elegant, scholarly picture-book biography brings the explorer's fantastic journey to life. . . . Demi weaves

Polo, Marco, 1254-1323?—*Continued*
her subject's own accounts into a seamless tale of wonder. . . . The delicately rendered illustrations, painted with Chinese inks and gold overlays . . . capture the exotic beauty of 13th-century China." SLJ

Freedman, Russell. The adventures of Marco Polo; with illustrations by Bagram Ibatoulline; accompanied by archival, period artwork. Arthur A. Levine Books 2006 63p il map $17.99 *
Grades: 5 6 7 8   92
  1. Voyages and travels 2. Explorers
  ISBN 0-439-52394-X   LC 2005-22791
"Using Polo's own descriptions (as told to a writer he met in prison) Freedman shepherds readers across deserts, down the Silk Road, and over mountains until the adventurer reaches the magnificent kingdom of Kublai Khan. Supporting Freedman's informative yet evocative prose are enchanting illustrations. Ibatoulline follows the follows the historic journey with are inspired by different periods. . . . This is a glorious piece of bookmaking." Booklist

Markle, Sandra. Animals Marco Polo saw; an adventure on the Silk Road; illustrated by Daniela Jaglenka Terrazzini. Chronicle Books 2009 45p il $16.99
Grades: 3 4 5 6   92
  1. Explorers 2. Voyages and travels 3. Asia—Description and travel 4. Animals—Asia
  ISBN 978-0-8118-5051-3; 0-8118-5051-X
                                        LC 2007053057
"This intriguing book discusses generally agreed-upon details of Marco Polo's explorations in Mongolia and the Far East, and speculates about the moths, jackals, van cats, zebu, oxen, Persian lions, snow cats, and camels he may have met along the way. . . . The text is enhanced by color, mixed-media illustrations that occupy one page or the top half of each spread. . . . A useful introduction to 13th-century history." SLJ

McCarty, Nick. Marco Polo; the boy who traveled the medieval world. National Geographic 2006 64p il map (World history biographies) $17.95; lib bdg $27.90
Grades: 5 6 7 8   92
  1. Voyages and travels 2. Explorers
  ISBN 0-7922-5893-2; 0-7922-5894-0 (lib bdg)
A biography of the Italian explorer who became famous for his travels in Asia
Includes glossary and bibliographical references

Otfinoski, Steven. Marco Polo; to China and back. Benchmark Bks. 2003 77p il map (Great explorations) lib bdg $19.95 *
Grades: 5 6 7 8   92
  1. Voyages and travels 2. Explorers
  ISBN 0-7614-1480-0   LC 2002-68
Contents: A distant world; A father's journey; Marco joins the adventure; Mountain and desert; In the court of Kublai Khan; A most trusted aide; Escort for a princess; Strange homecoming; A prisoner of war; Marco millions
This describes the life of the medieval explorer and his travels through Asia

"Maps, contemporary drawings and paintings, and diary excerpts reveal not only the complexities of Polo's groundbreaking adventures but also the awe and exhilaration they brought him." SLJ
Includes bibliographical references

Ponce de Leon, Juan, 1460?-1521
Otfinoski, Steven. Juan Ponce de Leon; discoverer of Florida; by Steven Otfinoski. Benchmark Books 2005 77p il map (Great explorations) lib bdg $29.93
Grades: 5 6 7 8   92
  1. Explorers 2. America—Exploration
  ISBN 0-7614-1610-2   LC 2003-17582
Contents: The soldier's way; Westward with Columbus; The Governor of Higuey; Father of Puerto Rico; The Fountain of Youth; An island called Florida; The King's favorite; At war with the Carib; To die in Florida
A biography of the Spanish explorer who was called the Father of Puerto Rico and who discovered Florida in his search for the Fountain of Youth.
Includes bibliographical references

Potter, Beatrix, 1866-1943
Winter, Jeanette. Beatrix: various episodes from the life of Beatrix Potter. Farrar, Straus & Giroux 2003 62p il $15 *
Grades: K 1 2 3   92
  1. Authors, English 2. Women authors 3. Women artists
  ISBN 0-374-30655-9   LC 2002-69724
"Frances Foster books"
This simple biography of Beatrix Potter, best known for writing *The Tale of Peter Rabbit*, includes excerpts from her published letters and journals and reveals why she drew and wrote about animals.
"The text is spare, just two to five sentences per page; the paintings, in Winter's characteristic muted tones and flat style, are delicately outlined in black ink. Brief as it is, the book successfully conveys Potter's life and personality." Booklist
Includes bibliographical references

Powell, Colin L., 1937-
Waxman, Laura Hamilton. Colin Powell; [by] Laura Hamilton Waxman. Lerner Publications Co. 2005 47p il (History maker bios) lib bdg $25.26
Grades: 2 3 4 5   92
  1. Generals 2. Statesmen 3. African Americans—Biography
  ISBN 0-8225-2433-3   LC 2004-2595
Contents: Growing up in the Bronx; Army life; Life in Washington, D.C; War with Iraq; Secretary of State
"This clearly written, interesting biography begins with Powell's childhood in the Bronx and focuses on the man's distinguished career in the military and in government, with additional information about how he was affected by discrimination and segregation. . . . Black-and-white and color photos are included." SLJ
Includes bibliographical references

Powell, John Wesley, 1834-1902

Ray, Deborah Kogan. Down the Colorado; John Wesley Powell, the one-armed explorer. Frances Foster Books/Farrar, Straus & Giroux 2007 unp il $17 *

Grades: 3 4 5   92
1. Explorers 2. Colorado River (Colo.-Mexico) 3. West (U.S.)—Exploration
ISBN 0-374-31838-7; 978-0-374-31838-3
                                 LC 2006-43994

"This picture-book biography traces the life of explorer John Wesley Powell, whose landmark journey in 1869 down the Colorado River made him a national hero. Each double-page spread combines text on one side describing an episode from Powell's life with a stunning, full-page illustration on the opposite side. . . . An exciting adventure story and an instructive account of the exploration of the West." Booklist

Pujols, Albert, 1980-

Needham, Tom. Albert Pujols; MVP on and off the field. Enslow Publishers 2007 128p bibl por (Sports stars with heart) lib bdg $23.95

Grades: 4 5 6 7   92
1. Baseball—Biography
ISBN 978-0-7660-2866-1 (lib bdg); 0-7660-2866-6 (lib bdg)   LC 2006031843

"Baseball fans know Pujols from his outstanding record: Rookie of the Year, a National League MVP, a team leader helping the St. Louis Cardinals win the World Series in 2006. However, with its combination of sharp writing, eye-catching design, and well-chosen photos, this . . . is so pleasing that even those who don't follow baseball will enjoy learning about Pujols." Booklist

Includes bibliographical references

Quan, Elizabeth, 1921-

Quan, Elizabeth. Once upon a full moon. Tundra Books 2007 48p il $19.95

Grades: 3 4 5   92
1. Chinese 2. China 3. Voyages and travels
ISBN 978-0-8876-813-2

Describes a trip that the author's family took back to China from Toronto, Canada, in the 1920s to visit a grandmother she had never met

"The watercolor illustrations offer windows on the world as seen through a child's eyes. . . . A fine memoir for middle-grade students." Booklist

Quezada, Juan, 1939-

Andrews-Goebel, Nancy. The pot that Juan built; pictures by David Diaz. Lee & Low Bks. 2002 unp il $16.95 *

Grades: K 1 2 3   92
1. Pottery
ISBN 1-58430-038-8   LC 2001-38139

A cumulative rhyme summarizes the life's work of renowned Mexican potter, Juan Quezada. Additional information describes the process he uses to create his pots after the style of the Casas Grandes people.

"This unusual book is set up to allow for differing levels of reading expertise. . . . One page contains a catchy cumulative rhyme modeled on 'This Is the House That Jack Built,' which outlines the process of making a pot. The facing page offers a clearly written prose presentation. . . . Diaz's arresting illustrations, rendered in Adobe Photoshop, use yellows, oranges, and reds in a layered effect that seems to glow with an inward light." SLJ

Quimby, Harriet, 1875-1912

Moss, Marissa. Brave Harriet; the first woman to fly the English Channel; illustrated by C.F. Payne. Silver Whistle Bks. 2001 unp il $16

Grades: K 1 2 3   92
1. Women air pilots
ISBN 0-15-202380-1   LC 99-50463

Harriet Quimby, the first American woman to have received a pilot's license, describes her April 1912 solo flight across the English Channel, the first such flight by any woman

"Moss writes effectively in first person, putting readers in touch with Quimby's dreams and determination through direct, vivid language. The mixed media artwork combines paints and pastels in a series of beautiful scenes." Booklist

Whitaker, Suzanne. The daring Miss Quimby; by Suzanne George Whitaker; illustrated by Catherine Stock. Holiday House 2009 unp il $16.95

Grades: 1 2 3   92
1. Women air pilots
ISBN 978-0-8234-1996-8; 0-8234-1996-7
                                 LC 2008022569

A biography of Harriet Quimby, who, in 1911 "became the first American woman to earn a pilot's license. . . . Whitaker's spare, engaging narrative and Stock's lively watercolors bring this little-known female adventurer to life." Booklist

Ramon, Ilan, 1954-2003

Stone, Tanya Lee. Ilan Ramon, Israel's first astronaut; by Tanya Lee Stone. Millbrook Press 2003 48p il lib bdg $16.70

Grades: 3 4 5   92
1. Astronauts 2. Space shuttles—Accidents
ISBN 0-7613-2888-2   LC 2003-9254

A biography of Israeli astronaut Ilan Ramon, who died in the explosion of the space shuttle Columbia on February 1, 2003

"The excellent-quality color photos show Ramon at work and in his private life, and the author's research is impeccably documented. Overall, an appealing and informative book." SLJ

Includes bibliographical references

Ream, Vinnie, 1847-1914

Fitzgerald, Dawn. Vinnie and Abraham; [by] Dawn Fitzgerald; illustrated by Catherine Stock. Charlesbridge 2007 unp il lib bdg $15.95 *

Grades: 2 3 4   92
1. Sculptors 2. Women artists
ISBN 978-1-57091-658-8 (lib bdg); 1-57091-658-6 (lib bdg)   LC 2006009033

Ream, Vinnie, 1847-1914—*Continued*

"This picture-book biography presents Vinnie Ream as a young woman who transcended the conventions of her time through determination and a remarkable talent for sculpture. . . . After Lincoln's assassination, Congress commissioned her to sculpt a marble statue of the late president, which is still on display in the Capital rotunda. Fitzgerald's clearly written narrative portrays Vinnie as a hardworking, resolute person who succeeded through her own gifts and the help of others who believed in her. Stock's watercolor paintings light up the pages." Booklist

Reeves, Bass, 1838-1910

Nelson, Vaunda Micheaux. Bad news for outlaws; the remarkable life of Bass Reeves, deputy U.S. Marshal; illustrations by R. Gregory Christie. Carolrhoda Books 2009 unp il lib bdg $17.95 *

Grades: 3 4 5   92

1. African Americans—Biography 2. Frontier and pioneer life 3. West (U.S.)—History 4. Law enforcement 5. Oklahoma

ISBN 978-0-8225-6764-6 (lib bdg); 0-8225-6764-4 (lib bdg)   LC 2008-01188

ALA EMIERT Coretta Scott King Author Award (2010)

"Kids will have no trouble loping into this picture-book biography. Born a slave, Reeves became one of the most feared and respected Deputy U.S. Marshals to tame the West. . . . The text, especially, gets into the tall-tale spirit of things. . . . An exciting subject captured with narrative panache and visual swagger." Booklist

Reinhardt, Django, 1910-1953

Christensen, Bonnie. Django. Roaring Brook Press 2009 unp il $17.99 *

Grades: 1 2 3 4   92

1. Jazz musicians 2. Guitarists

ISBN 978-1-59643-422-6; 1-59643-422-8

ALA Schneider Family Book Award (2010)

"Richly expressive paint and ink illustrations portray the hard-earned successes of Django Reinhardt, whose childhood was spent traveling with his impoverished gypsy family, where music was a constant and illuminating presence. . . . Christensen's soft, rhythmic prose echoes her evocative images as Django explores the music scene of 1920s Paris, before suffering serious burns on his hands and leg when his wagon catches fire. Despite his injuries, Reinhardt teaches himself to play again. . . . A sensuous tribute to an illustrious musician." Publ Wkly

Reiss, Johanna

Reiss, Johanna. The upstairs room. Crowell 1972 273p $19.99; pa $5.99 *

Grades: 5 6 7 8 9 10   92

1. World War, 1939-1945—Jews 2. Netherlands—History—1940-1945, German occupation 3. Jews—Netherlands 4. Holocaust, 1933-1945—Personal narratives

ISBN 0-690-85127-8; 0-06-440370-X (pa)

A Newbery Medal honor book, 1973

"In a vital, moving account the author recalls her experiences as a Jewish child hiding from the Germans occupying her native Holland during World War II. . . . Ten-year-old Annie and her twenty-year-old sister Sini, . . . are taken in by a Dutch farmer, his wife, and mother who hide the girls in an upstairs room of the farm house. Written from the perspective of a child the story affords a child's-eye-view of the war." Booklist

Followed by The journey back

Rembert, Winfred

Rembert, Winfred. Don't hold me back; my life and art; with Charles and Rosalie Baker. Cricket Books 2003 40p il $19.95

Grades: 4 5 6 7   92

1. African Americans—Biography 2. African American artists

ISBN 0-8126-2703-2   LC 2003-9980

"A Marcato book"

Through words and paintings, an artist tells about growing up on a cotton plantation in Cuthbert, Georgia, serving time in prison for his actions during a civil rights demonstration, and finding a purpose and direction in life.

"Rembert's unusual pictures are classified as 'outsider art.' . . . Each one is a piece of leather that has been carved, tooled, and dyed with rich colors. . . . This beautifully designed, very accessible book offers a vivid impression of an African American man's experiences in the mid-twentieth-century South." Booklist

Includes bibliographical references

Renoir, Auguste, 1841-1919

Somervill, Barbara A. Pierre-Auguste Renoir; [by] Barbara Somervill. Mitchell Lane 2007 48p il (Art profiles for kids) lib bdg $29.95

Grades: 5 6 7 8   92

1. Artists, French

ISBN 978-1-58415-566-9 (lib bdg); 1-58415-566-3 (lib bdg)   LC 2007000661

Profiles the famous French artist best known for his portraits and his paintings such as "The Luncheon of the Boating Party" that depict people enjoying themselves

"The glossy pages allow for good reproductions of paintings as well as a few photos. . . . Back matter includes a glossary, chronology, chapter notes for quotes, lists of books and Internet sites, and a Timeline in History . . . offers a concise, readable account of the artist's life." Booklist

Includes glossary and bibliographical references

Revere, Paul, 1735-1818

Fritz, Jean. And then what happened, Paul Revere? pictures by Margot Tomes. Coward, McCann & Geoghegan 1973 45p il $16.99; pa $5.99 *

Grades: 2 3 4   92

1. United States—History—1775-1783, Revolution

ISBN 0-399-23337-7; 0-698-11351-9 (pa)

This "description of Paul Revere's ride to Lexington is funny, fast-paced, and historically accurate; it is given added interest by the establishment of Revere's character:

Revere, Paul, 1735-1818—*Continued*
busy, bustling, versatile, and patriotic, a man who loved people and excitement. The account of his ride is preceded by a description of his life and the political situation in Boston, and it concludes with Revere's adventures after reaching Lexington." Bull Cent Child Books

Giblin, James. The many rides of Paul Revere; by James Cross Giblin. Scholastic Press 2007 85p il map $17.99
Grades: 4 5 6 7   92
    1. United States—History—1775-1783, Revolution
    ISBN 978-0-439-57290-3; 0-439-57290-8
                   LC 2006-38369
"This well-organized biography presents a lucid account of Revere's childhood, his limited education, his training in his father's workshop, his brief military career, and his adult life as a silversmith, family man, and Revolutionary War leader. . . . Giblin presents salient facts and intriguing details to create a well-rounded and credible image of the man. Among the many illustrations are period portraits, narrative paintings, engravings, drawings, and maps as well as photos of significant sites and artifacts." Booklist
Includes bibliographical references

Mortensen, Lori. Paul Revere's ride; illustrated by Craig Orback. Picture Window Books 2010 32p il map (Our American story) lib bdg $23.99
Grades: 2 3 4   92
    1. Statesmen—United States 2. United States—History—1775-1783, Revolution
    ISBN 978-1-4048-5537-3; 1-4048-5537-8
                   LC 2009-6893
Highlights the life and accomplishments of Paul Revere, including the events leading up to his famous ride to warn of the British attack on Concord.
This book is "illustrated with well-executed, full-page, color illustrations, maps, and photos. . . . [It has] accurate, clearly written information that students can use for either leisure reading or reports." SLJ
Includes glossary and bibliographical references

Rey, H. A. (Hans Augusto), 1898-1977
Borden, Louise. The journey that saved Curious George. See entry under Rey, Margret

Rey, Margret
Borden, Louise. The journey that saved Curious George; the true wartime escape of Margret and H. A. Rey; illustrated by Allan Drummond. Houghton Mifflin 2005 72p il $17 *
Grades: 3 4 5 6   92
    1. Rey, H. A. (Hans Augusto), 1898-1977 2. Authors, American 3. Jewish refugees
    ISBN 0-618-33924-8   LC 2004-01015
This "book tells the story of Margret and H. A. Rey. Part 1 concerns their childhoods in Germany, their lives together in Rio de Janeiro and Paris in the 1920s and 1930s, and the growing menace after war broke out in 1939. As German-born Jews, they were suspect in many quarters. Part 2 recalls the Reys' flight from Paris and the couple's escape to Lisbon, Rio, and finally New

York. They were carrying several illustrated manuscripts, including *The Adventures of FiFi*, later retitled *Curious George*. Photos, reproductions of documents, and artwork appear throughout the book, as do Drummond's spirited ink-and-watercolor illustrations, brimming with action and details. The text . . . reads well." Booklist

Ringgold, Faith
Venezia, Mike. Faith Ringgold; written and illustrated by Mike Venezia. Children's Press 2008 32p il (Getting to know the world's greatest artists) lib bdg $28
Grades: 3 4 5   92
    1. Artists—United States 2. African American artists 3. Women artists
    ISBN 978-0-531-18526-1 (lib bdg); 0-531-18526-5 (lib bdg)   LC 2007016125
This examines the work and life of Faith Ringgold, an African American artist who works in a variety of mediums including textiles, paintings, and prints, and is best known for her story quilts.
"Though the [text is] simply written, [this title contains] a wealth of information. . . . [The book has] many reproductions of the [artist's] works as well as those of the masters who influenced [her]. To help illustrate his points, Venezia has incorporated his own cartoon-style illustrations." SLJ

Rivera, Diego, 1886-1957
Rivera Marín, Guadalupe. My papa Diego and me; memories of my father and his art; recollections by Guadalupe Rivera Marín; artwork by Diego Rivera = reminiscencias de Guadalupe Rivera Marín; arte de Diego Rivera. Childrens Book Press 2009 29p il $17.95 *
Grades: K 1 2 3   92
    1. Rivera Marín, Guadalupe, 1924- 2. Artists, Mexican 3. Bilingual books—English-Spanish
    ISBN 978-0-89239-228-5; 0-89239-221-5
                   LC 2008053193
Parallel title in Spanish: Mi papá Diego y yo: recuerdos de mi padre y su arte
"Through bilingual commentaries on 13 of Rivera's paintings, the artist's daughter provides an anecdotal portrait of her childhood with her father. All of the works feature children and will give readers a sense of Rivera's range as an artist. . . . The personalities of father and daughter alike, as well as the vibrancy of Mexican culture, shine brightly in this personal, insightful book." Publ Wkly

Sabbeth, Carol. Frida Kahlo and Diego Rivera: their lives and ideas. See entry under Kahlo, Frida, 1907-1954

Winter, Jonah. Diego; concept and illustrations by Jeanette Winter; text by Jonah Winter; translated from the English by Amy Prince. Knopf 1991 unp il $15.99; pa $6.99
Grades: K 1 2 3   92
    1. Artists, Mexican 2. Bilingual books—English-Spanish
    ISBN 978-0-679-81987-5; 0-679-85617-X (pa)
                   LC 90-25923

Rivera, Diego, 1886-1957—*Continued*

This book "in both Spanish and English, chronicles the life of Mexican muralist Diego Rivera. . . . Jonah Winter's crisp text and Jeanette Winter's elaborately bordered, dynamic illustrations successfully convey the spirit of the man and his work." Publ Wkly

Rivera, Tomás

Medina, Jane. Tomás Rivera; [by] Jane Medina; illustrated by Edward Martinez. Harcourt 2004 unp il $12.95; pa $3.95

Grades: K 1 2 **92**

1. Authors, American 2. Mexican American authors 3. Mexican Americans—Biography

ISBN 0-15-205145-7; 0-15-205146-5 (pa)

LC 2003-17482

"Green light readers"

"This simple story recounts an incident from the childhood of Mexican American writer and educator Tomas Rivera and suggests its far-reaching effects on his life. After a day of hard work picking farm crops with his family in the 1940s, young Tomas enjoys hearing his grandfather tell stories. When Tomas confides that he wants to tell stories, too, Grandpa takes him to the library, and soon the boy begins writing stories of his own. When he becomes an adult, his stories are published and a library is named after him. . . . Medina's straightforward writing is enhanced by the warm depictions of Rivera and his family in the painterly illustrations." Booklist

Rivera Marín, Guadalupe, 1924-

Rivera Marín, Guadalupe. My papa Diego and me. See entry under Rivera, Diego, 1886-1957

Robeson, Paul, 1898-1976

Greenfield, Eloise. Paul Robeson; illustrated by George Ford. Lee & Low Books 2009 unp il $18.95; pa $9.95

Grades: 2 3 4 5 **92**

1. African Americans—Biography 2. Actors 3. Singers 4. Political activists

ISBN 978-1-60060-256-6; 1-60060-256-8; 978-1-60060-262-7 (pa); 1-60060-262-2 (pa)

LC 2008030420

First published 1975 by HarperCollins

"A biography of Paul Robeson, who overcame racial discrimination to become a world-famous African American athlete, actor, singer, and civil rights activist." Publisher's note

"Vibrant, monochromatic acrylic illustrations . . . use shading and depth to convey tremendous emotion. Powerful movements and vivid expressions enhance the narrative. . . . This book offers a fully developed portrayal of the man." SLJ

Robinson, Jackie, 1919-1972

Adler, David A. A picture book of Jackie Robinson; illustrated by Robert Casilla. Holiday House 1994 unp il $17.95; pa $6.95

Grades: 1 2 3 **92**

1. Baseball—Biography 2. African American athletes

ISBN 0-8234-1122-2; 0-8234-1304-7 (pa)

LC 93-27224

"A brief look at the life of baseball great Jackie Robinson. The subject's childhood, sporting accomplishments, and later endeavors are touched upon, as are the bigotry and prejudice he faced as the first African American to play in the major leagues. . . . Casilla's full-and double-page watercolors provide attractive backgrounds for the text. A sound introduction to a significant figure." SLJ

Burleigh, Robert. Stealing home; written by Robert Burleigh; illustrated by Mike Wimmer. Simon & Schuster Books for Young Readers 2007 unp il $16.99 *

Grades: 1 2 3 4 **92**

1. Baseball—Biography 2. African American athletes

ISBN 978-0-689-86276-2; 0-689-86276-8

LC 2006-01048

"A Paula Wiseman book"

"Burleigh employs two narrative voices, one a spare, lyrical moment-by-moment replay of [Jackie] Robinson's bold steal home from third base in the first game of the 1955 World Series against the New York Yankees. . . . Historical sidebars on each spread supplement this dramatic, immediate account, providing anecdotes about the era, Robinson's struggles . . . plus highlights of his baseball career . . . and personal life. Wimmer's textured, animated oil paintings depict the game action at close range and with lifelike clarity." Publ Wkly

Golenbock, Peter. Teammates; written by Peter Golenbock; designed and illustrated by Paul Bacon. Harcourt Brace Jovanovich 1990 unp il $16; pa $7

Grades: 1 2 3 4 **92**

1. Reese, Pee Wee, 1919-1999 2. Brooklyn Dodgers (Baseball team) 3. Baseball—Biography 4. African American athletes

ISBN 0-15-200603-6; 0-15-284286-1 (pa)

LC 89-38166

"Gulliver books"

Describes the racial prejudice experienced by Jackie Robinson when he joined the Brooklyn Dodgers and became the first black player in Major League baseball and depicts the acceptance and support he received from his white teammate Pee Wee Reese

"Golenbock's bold and lucid style distills this difficult issue, and brings a dramatic tale vividly to life. Bacon's spare, nostalgic watercolors, in addition to providing fond glimpses of baseball lore, present a haunting portrait of one man's isolation. Historic photographs of the major characters add interest and a touch of stark reality to an unusual story, beautifully rendered." Publ Wkly

Robinson, Jackie, 1919-1972—*Continued*

O'Sullivan, Robyn. Jackie Robinson plays ball; by Robyn O'Sullivan. National Geographic 2007 40p il (National Geographic history chapters) lib bdg $17.90

Grades: 2 3 4　　　　　　　　　　　　92
　　1. Baseball—Biography 2. African American athletes
　　ISBN 978-1-4263-0190-2　　　　LC 2007007893

This biography of Jackie Robinson is "nicely illustrated with photos. . . . [It is] just right for emerging chapter-book readers. . . . Useful . . . for reports . . . and interesting pleasure reading." SLJ

Includes glossary and bibliographical references

Robinson, Sharon. Promises to keep: how Jackie Robinson changed America. Scholastic 2004 64p il $16.95

Grades: 4 5 6 7　　　　　　　　　　92
　　1. Baseball—Biography 2. African American athletes
　　ISBN 0-439-42592-1　　　　LC 2003-42709

"Robinson's daughter, Sharon, describes her father's youth, his rise to become major-league baseball's first African American player, and his involvement in the civil rights movement. . . . Her private view of her father's accomplishments, placed within the context of American sports and social history, makes for absorbing reading. An excellent selection of family and team photographs and other materials . . . illustrate this fine tribute." Booklist

Robinson, Sharon. Testing the ice: a true story about Jackie Robinson; illustrated by Kadir Nelson. Scholastic Press 2009 unp il $16.99

Grades: 1 2 3 4　　　　　　　　　　92
　　1. African American athletes 2. Baseball—Biography
　　ISBN 978-0-545-05251-1; 0-545-05251-3
　　　　　　　　　　　　　　　LC 2008-38838

As a testament to his courage, Jackie Robinson's daughter shares memories of him, from his baseball career to the day he tests the ice for her, her brothers, and their friends.

"Robinson neatly sums up the significance of her father's achievements while depicting him as a loving family man. Nelson's large paintings, done in pencil, watercolor, and oils, dramatically convey Robinson's public persona, the intensely competitive athlete, and contrasts that with the relaxed, yet commanding father Sharon and her brothers knew." SLJ

Rockwell, Norman, 1894-1978

Gherman, Beverly. Norman Rockwell; storyteller with a brush. Atheneum Bks. for Young Readers 2000 57p il $19.95

Grades: 4 5 6 7　　　　　　　　　　92
　　1. Artists—United States
　　ISBN 0-689-82001-1　　　　LC 98-36546

Describes the life and work of the popular American artist who depicted both traditional and contemporary subjects, including children, family scenes, astronauts, and the poor

"The format of the biography is appealing and attractive. The pages are replete with color reproductions of Rockwell's paintings as well as photographs of the man and his family. The text is well researched and authentic;

the writing style is free-flowing and the words capture the naturalness of Rockwell's paintings." SLJ

Includes bibliographical references

Rogers, Will, 1879-1935

Keating, Frank. Will Rogers: an American legend; written by Frank Keating; illustrated by Mike Wimmer. Silver Whistle/Harcourt 2002 unp il $16

Grades: K 1 2 3　　　　　　　　　　92
　　1. Entertainers 2. Humorists
　　ISBN 0-15-202405-0　　　　LC 2001-5949

A biography of the man from Oklahoma, known for his wise and witty sayings

"The highly episodic text, presented in the form of typewritten pages to evoke Rogers' own typed newspaper columns, makes good use of quotations from its subject. . . . The adulatory, iconographic tone is reinforced by Wimmer's full-page oil paintings. Inarguably beautiful, accomplished, and occasionally witty." Booklist

Roosevelt, Eleanor, 1884-1962

Cooney, Barbara. Eleanor. Viking 1996 unp il $15.99; pa $6.99 *

Grades: K 1 2 3　　　　　　　　　　92
　　1. Presidents' spouses—United States
　　ISBN 0-670-86159-6; 0-14-055583-8 (pa)
　　　　　　　　　　　　　　　LC 96-7723

"Beginning the story with Eleanor Roosevelt's mother's disappointment at her birth, the author emphasizes the girl's lonely and often fearful childhood. . . . The book ends with Eleanor's public role still to come. A brief afterword provides information about her worldwide influence in her later life." SLJ

"There are many biographies of Eleanor Roosevelt but this one is special. Not only does it boast Cooney's artwork, but it also gets to the heart of a young girl, which in many ways is as interesting as Roosevelt's later, well-known accomplishments." Booklist

Fleming, Candace. Our Eleanor; a scrapbook look at Eleanor Roosevelt's remarkable life. Atheneum Books for Young Readers 2005 176p il $19.95

Grades: 5 6 7 8　　　　　　　　　　92
　　1. Presidents' spouses—United States
　　ISBN 0-689-86544-9　　　　LC 2004-22825

"An Anne Schwartz book"

Told in scrapbook style, this biography looks behind the politics to present First Lady Eleanor Roosevelt in her many roles: wife and mother, United Nations delegate, popular columnist, civil rights crusader, and champion of the underprivileged.

"Each of the seven chapters leads readers through the subject's busy life with short sections of text filled with well-documented first-person accounts and direct quotes. . . . Not a spread goes by without incredible archival photographs or reproductions, newspaper and magazine clippings, handwritten letters, and diary entries. . . . They all provide relevant and fascinating insight." SLJ

Roosevelt, Eleanor, 1884-1962—*Continued*

Freedman, Russell. Eleanor Roosevelt; a life of discovery. Clarion Bks. 1993 198p il $17.95; pa $11.95 *

Grades: 5 6 7 8 9 10   92

    1. Presidents' spouses—United States

    ISBN 0-89919-862-7; 0-395-84520-3 (pa)

                     LC 92-25024

A Newbery Medal honor book, 1994

This "traces the life of the former First Lady from her early childhood through the tumultuous years in the White House to her active role in the founding of the United Nations after World War II." Publisher's note

"This impeccably researched, highly readable study of one of this country's greatest First Ladies is nonfiction at its best. . . . Approximately 140 well-chosen black-and-white photos amplify the text." Publ Wkly

Includes bibliographical references

Koestler-Grack, Rachel A. The story of Eleanor Roosevelt. Chelsea Clubhouse 2004 32p il (Breakthrough biographies) lib bdg $14.95

Grades: 2 3 4   92

    1. Presidents' spouses—United States

    ISBN 0-7910-7313-0   LC 2003-269

Chronicles the life of Eleanor Roosevelt, from her privileged childhood, to her accomplishments as First Lady of the United States, to her work with the United Nations

"The style and design are just right for middle-graders. The type is spacious, illustrations appear on every page. . . . [This volume] will stimulate readers to find out more." Booklist

Includes glossary and bibliographical references

Rappaport, Doreen. Eleanor, quiet no more; written by Doreen Rappaport; illustrated by Gary Kelley. Hyperion 2009 unp il $16.99 *

Grades: 2 3 4 5   92

    1. Presidents' spouses—United States

    ISBN 978-0-7868-5141-6; 0-7868-5141-4

"The narrative moves swiftly through the important moments in [Eleanor] Roosevelt's life . . . but along with accomplishments, Rappaport does something more subtle—she shows the way Eleanor grew into herself. Crisp sentences focus the narrative and are bolstered by the quotes that end each page. . . . The accompanying art is composed of rich, beautifully crafted paintings that also catch Roosevelt's growing sense of purpose." Booklist

Roosevelt, Franklin D. (Franklin Delano), 1882-1945

Elish, Dan. Franklin Delano Roosevelt. Marshall Cavendish Benchmark 2009 96p il (Presidents and their times) $23.95

Grades: 5 6 7 8   92

    1. Presidents—United States 2. United States—Politics and government—1933-1945

    ISBN 978-0-7614-2841-1; 0-7614-2841-0

                     LC 2007-25619

"Provides comprehensive information on President Franklin Delano Roosevelt and places him within his his-torical and cultural context. Also explored are the formative events of his times and how he responded." Publisher's note

Includes glossary and bibliographical references

Freedman, Russell. Franklin Delano Roosevelt. Clarion Bks. 1990 200p il hardcover o.p. pa $9.95 *

Grades: 5 6 7 8 9 10   92

    1. Presidents—United States 2. United States—Politics and government—1933-1945

    ISBN 0-89919-379-X; 0-395-62978-0 (pa)

                     LC 89-34986

The author "traces the personal and public events in a life that led to the formation of one of the most influential and magnetic leaders of the twentieth century." Horn Book

"The carefully researched, highly readable text and extremely effective coordination of black-and-white photographs chronicle Roosevelt's priviledged youth, his early influences, and his maturation. . . . Even students with little or no background in American history will find this an intriguing and inspirational human portrait." SLJ

Includes bibliographical references

Panchyk, Richard. Franklin Delano Roosevelt for kids; his life and times with 21 activities; [by] Richard Panchyk. Chicago Review Press 2007 147p il pa $14.95

Grades: 4 5 6 7   92

    1. Presidents—United States 2. United States—Politics and government—1933-1945

    ISBN 978-1-55652-657-2 (pa); 1-55652-657-1 (pa)

                     LC 2007003484

"Franklin Delano Roosevelt's enduring legacy upon the history, culture, politics, and economics of the United States is introduced to children in this . . . activity book." Publisher's note

"There are many interesting photos . . . and they are all sufficiently captioned. . . . Information about the Roosevelts [is] presented in a lively, engaging manner." SLJ

Includes bibliographical references

St. George, Judith. Make your mark, Franklin Roosevelt; [by] Judith St. George; illustrated by Britt Spencer. Philomel Books 2007 unp il $16.99

Grades: 2 3 4   92

    1. Presidents—United States

    ISBN 978-0-399-24175-8; 0-399-24175-2

                     LC 2006008921

"This illustrated biography . . . explores . . . the influences that shaped Roosevelt's life with stories that will delight young readers. . . . Throughout, Spencer's spirited watercolor, gouache, and ink illustrations bring to life the culture and background of this American icon." SLJ

Includes bibliographical references

Roosevelt, Theodore, 1858-1919

Brown, Don. Teedie; the story of young Teddy Roosevelt. Houghton Mifflin Books for Children 2009 unp il $16 *

Grades: 2 3 4   92
    1. Presidents—United States
    ISBN 978-0-618-17999-2; 0-618-17999-2
                    LC 2008033879

"Teedie led a privileged life in one of New York City's wealthiest households, but was a sickly child. His asthma didn't stop him from being curious or from reading widely. . . . Teedie became Teddy when he entered Harvard University in 1876. After graduation, Roosevelt sought his own way. . . . He traveled, became an outdoorsman, a politician, and ultimately the youngest president of the United States. Line and wash illustrations add movement and a playful tone to the serious text, which generously incorporates quotes from Roosevelt." SLJ

Includes bibliographical references

Fritz, Jean. Bully for you, Teddy Roosevelt! illustrations by Mike Wimmer. Putnam 1991 127p il hardcover o.p. pa $5.99

Grades: 5 6 7 8   92
    1. Presidents—United States
    ISBN 0-399-21769-X; 0-698-11609-7 (pa)
                    LC 90-8142

Follows the life of the twenty-sixth president, discussing his conservation work, hunting expeditions, family life, and political career

"Jean Fritz gives a rounded picture of her subject and deftly blends the story of a person and a picture of an era." Bull Cent Child Books

Includes bibliographical references

Harness, Cheryl. The remarkable, rough-riding life of Theodore Roosevelt and the rise of empire America; painstakingly written and illustrated by Cheryl Harness. National Geographic 2007 144p il map $16.95; lib bdg $25.90

Grades: 4 5 6 7   92
    1. Presidents—United States
    ISBN   978-1-4263-0008-0;   1-4263-0008-5;
    978-1-4263-0009-7 (lib bdg); 1-4263-0009-3 (lib bdg)
                    LC 2006029039

"Animated writing and intricate black-and-white illustrations drive this biography of the ever-enthusiastic twenty-sixth president of the United States. An extensive running timeline at the bottom of the pages emphasizes the dramatic changes that occurred during Roosevelt's life. The book is jam-packed with information." Horn Book Guide

Includes bibliographical references

Keating, Frank. Theodore; illustrated by Mike Wimmer. Simon & Schuster Books for Young Readers 2006 unp il $16.95

Grades: K 1 2 3   92
    1. Presidents—United States
    ISBN 0-689-86532-5   LC 2003-17046

"A Paula Wiseman book"

A picture book biography of the 26th president of the United States

"This handsome, well-researched biography is as dignified as its subject. Using a spare, readable style, the author captures Roosevelt's spirit and determination." SLJ

Wade, Mary Dodson. Amazing president Theodore Roosevelt. Enslow Publishers 2009 24p il (Amazing Americans) lib bdg $21.26

Grades: 1 2 3   92
    1. Presidents—United States
    ISBN 978-0-7660-3284-2 (lib bdg); 0-7660-3284-1 (lib bdg)   LC 2008-24892

"Readers will find out about Roosevelt's life as a young boy through being president in this entry-level biography." Publisher's note

"Colorful photos are found throughout, with a timeline, dictionary, websites concerning the topic, as well as an index making . . . [this] book a wonderful introduction to nonfiction features." Libr Media Connect

Includes glossary

Wadsworth, Ginger. Camping with the president; illustrated by Karen Dugan. Calkins Creek 2009 32p il $16.95

Grades: 3 4 5   92
    1. Muir, John, 1838-1914 2. Yosemite National Park (Calif.)   3.   National   parks   and   reserves 4. Environmental movement 5. Presidents—United States
    ISBN 978-1-59078-497-6; 1-59078-497-9
                    LC 2008024155

"Inspired by conservationist John Muir's nature essays, President Theodore Roosevelt traveled west, visiting national parks and learing more about their resources. Wadsworth's well written, lively account highlights the pair's 1903 exploration of the Yosemite wilderness, as well as America's early conservation movement, in an accessible and engaging picture book for older readers. Dugan's abundant, intricately rendered watercolors portray the stunning vistas and wildlife and are set against white backgrounds." Booklist

Includes bibliographical references

Rowling, J. K.

Chippendale, Lisa A. Triumph of the imagination: the story of writer J.K. Rowling; introduction by James Scott Brady. Chelsea House 2002 112p il (Overcoming adversity) lib bdg $30

Grades: 5 6 7 8   92
    1. Authors, English 2. Women authors
    ISBN 0-7910-6312-7   LC 2001-47604

"This title blends biographical data, literary review, and the effects of the 'Harry Potter' books on the world, written at a reading level that is accessible to many of Rowling's fans." SLJ

Includes bibliographical references

Harmin, Karen Leigh. J. K. Rowling; author of Harry Potter; [by] Karen Leigh Harmin. Enslow Publishers 2006 128p bibl il por (People to know today) lib bdg $31.93

Grades: 4 5 6 7   92
    1. Women authors 2. Authors, English
    ISBN 0-7660-1850-4   LC 2005020400

Rowling, J. K.—*Continued*

This introduces the author of the Harry Potter book series.

"Well researched and clearly written. . . . Attactively designed, the book includes a number of excellent color photos as well as informative sidebars . . . Up-to-date and very readable." Booklist

Includes bibliographical references

Rudolph, Wilma, 1940-1994

Krull, Kathleen. Wilma unlimited: how Wilma Rudolph became the world's fastest woman; illustrated by David Diaz. Harcourt Brace & Co. 1996 unp il $17; pa $7 *

Grades: 2 3 4   92

1. African American athletes 2. Women athletes

ISBN 0-15-201267-2; 0-15-202098-5 (pa)

LC 95-32105

A biography of the African-American woman who overcame crippling polio as a child to become the first woman to win three gold medals in track in a single Olympics

"Brightly colored paintings contrast with sepia-toned photographic backgrounds, creating juxtapositions that extend both the text and the pictures in the foreground. Krull's understated conversational style is perfectly suited to Rudolph's remarkable and inspiring story." Horn Book Guide

Wade, Mary Dodson. Amazing Olympic athlete Wilma Rudolph. Enslow Publishers 2009 24p il (Amazing Americans) lib bdg $21.26

Grades: 1 2 3   92

1. African American athletes 2. Women athletes 3. Track athletics

ISBN 978-0-7660-3282-8 (lib bdg); 0-7660-3282-5 (lib bdg)   LC 2008-24890

This brief "biography describes how Wilma Rudolph overcame childhood polio and competed in the Olympics." Publisher's note

"The book features a design that is clear and inviting with a full-page photo on every double-page spread." Booklist

Includes glossary and bibliographical references

Rustin, Bayard, 1910-1987

Brimner, Larry Dane. We are one: the story of Bayard Rustin. Calkins Creek 2007 48p il $17.95 *

Grades: 5 6 7 8   92

1. African Americans—Civil rights 2. African Americans—Biography

ISBN 1-59078-498-7

"Brimner sets Rustin's personal story against the history of segregation in his time and focuses on his leadership role . . . in the struggle for civil rights. On each page, the clearly written, informal text is accompanied by eloquently captioned archival photos." Booklist

Includes bibliographical references

Sacagawea, b. 1786

Adler, David A. A picture book of Sacagawea; illustrated by Dan Brown. Holiday House 2000 unp il $16.95; pa $6.95

Grades: 1 2 3   92

, 1. Lewis and Clark Expedition (1804-1806) 2. Shoshoni Indians

ISBN 0-8234-1485-X; 0-8234-1665-8 (pa)

LC 99-37135

A biography of the Shoshone woman who joined the Lewis and Clark Expedition

"The narrative is clear, direct, and never fictionalized. . . . The soft watercolor art is more successful in depicting landscapes than human figures." Booklist

Includes bibliographical references

St. George, Judith. Sacagawea. Putnam 1997 115p maps $16.99

Grades: 4 5 6   92

1. Lewis and Clark Expedition (1804-1806) 2. Shoshoni Indians

ISBN 0-399-23161-7   LC 96-49311

Tells the story of the Shoshoni Indian girl who served as interpreter, peacemaker, and guide for the Lewis and Clark Expedition to the Northwest in 1805-1806

"In a well-written and well-researched account, St. George humanizes her subject. . . . Adventure lovers will find much to like in the book." Booklist

Includes bibliographical references

Sachar, Louis, 1954-

Greene, Meg. Louis Sachar. Rosen Pub. Group 2004 112p il (Library of author biographies) lib bdg $26.50

Grades: 5 6 7 8   92

1. Authors, American

ISBN 0-8239-4017-9   LC 2002-154252

Contents: Meet Louis Sachar; "Louis the yard teacher"; Success; From middle school to grade school; Holes; How does he do it?; Interview with Louis Sachar; Timeline

Discusses life and work of the popular children's author, including his writing process and methods, inspirations, a critical discussion of his books, biographical timeline, and awards

A "solid [introduction]. . . . Libraries looking to expand their biography section will be well served by [this] informative [title]." SLJ

Includes bibliographical references

Saint-Georges, Joseph Boulogne, chevalier de, 1745-1799

Brewster, Hugh. The other Mozart; the life of the famous Chevalier de Saint George; [by] Hugh Brewster; illustrated by Eric Velasquez. Abrams Books for Young Readers 2007 48p il $18.95

Grades: 4 5 6 7   92

1. Composers 2. Racially mixed people 3. Nobility

ISBN 0-8109-5720-5; 978-0-8109-5720-6

LC 2006-07488

"Born to a white plantation owner and a black slave in eighteenth-century Guadeloupe, Joseph Bologne grew up to become the Chevalier de Saint-George, one of

Saint-Georges, Joseph Boulogne, chevalier de, 1745-1799—*Continued*

France's most accomplished composers. In this picture-book biography for middle-graders, Brewster introduces his subject's fascinating life. . . . Archival images and Velasquez's arresting full-page portraits will captivate many young readers." Booklist

Saladin, Sultan of Egypt and Syria, 1137-1193

Geyer, Flora. Saladin; the Muslim Warrior who defended his people. National Geographic 2006 64p il map (World history biographies) $17.95; lib bdg $27.90

Grades: 4 5 6 7   92

1. Crusades 2. Kings and rulers
ISBN 0-7922-5535-6; 0-7922-5536-4 (lib bdg)
Presents an illustrated biography Saladin, from his birth into a prominent Kurdish family in Tikrit, Mesopotamia, in 1138, through his wars to regain holy lands in and around Jerusalem, to his death in Damascus on March 4, 1193.

Includes glossary and bibliographical references

Stanley, Diane. Saladin: noble prince of Islam. HarperCollins Pubs. 2002 unp il $16.99; lib bdg $18.89

Grades: 4 5 6 7   92

1. Crusades 2. Kings and rulers
ISBN 0-688-17135-4; 0-688-17136-2 (lib bdg)
LC 2001-24636
A biography of the Islamic leader who defended his people during the Crusades

The author demonstrates "her trademark ability to research and then distill complex topics in terms accessible to middle-graders. . . . Stanley's precise, detailed artwork pays homage to period architecture. She evokes the colors of Persian miniatures (and medieval stained glass) as her paintings incorporate the complex patterning associated with Islamic art." Publ Wkly

Includes glossary and bibliographical references

Salk, Jonas, 1914-1995

Tocci, Salvatore. Jonas Salk; creator of the polio vaccine. Enslow Pubs. 2003 128p il (Great minds of science) lib bdg $20.95

Grades: 5 6 7 8   92

1. Scientists 2. Poliomyelitis vaccine
ISBN 0-7660-2097-5   LC 2002-3888
Contents: Innocent victims; Survival and success; A change of plans; Relationships; His own project; His next project; The polio vaccine; The polio pioneers; An American hero
A biography of the American doctor and medical researcher who helped to develop successful influenza and polio vaccines, then turned his attention to vaccines for cancer and AIDS prevention

This is an "effective volume. . . . Tocci does a good job of showing how the fear of polio affected the public during the 1950s." Booklist

Includes glossary and bibliographical references

Sandburg, Carl, 1878-1967

Niven, Penelope. Carl Sandburg: adventures of a poet; with poems and prose by Carl Sandburg; illustrated by Marc Nadel. Harcourt 2003 unp il $17

Grades: 3 4 5 6   92

1. Poets, American
ISBN 0-15-204686-0   LC 2002-14592
Traces the life of the American poet, journalist, and historian who won the Pulitzer Prize for Poetry and the Pulitzer Prize for History

"Pairing readable, carefully selected biographical details with a specific poem or prose excerpt on facing pages, this book makes Sandburg accessible to young readers. . . . Nadel's masterful watercolor-and-crosshatch illustrations give additional visual information." SLJ

Sargent, John Singer, 1856-1925

Kreiter, Eshel. John Singer Sargent; the life of an artist; [by] Eshel Kreiter, Marc Zabludoff. Enslow Pubs. 2002 48p il (Artist biographies) $23.93

Grades: 2 3 4   92

1. Artists—United States
ISBN 0-7660-1879-2   LC 2001-1813
A biography of the late 19th and early 20th century American painter known for his portraits

"The use of full color, good paper, large type, and uncluttered design results in [a book] that [offers] several excellent reproductions of artworks, and the relatively simple [text respects] the capabilities of a young audience." SLJ

Includes glossary and bibliographical references

Sasaki, Sadako, 1943-1955

Coerr, Eleanor. Sadako; illustrated by Ed Young. Putnam 1993 unp il $17.95; pa $6.99

Grades: 1 2 3 4   92

1. Leukemia 2. Atomic bomb—Physiological effect
3. Hiroshima (Japan)—Bombardment, 1945
ISBN 0-399-21771-1; 0-698-11588-0 (pa)
LC 92-41483
"This is the same story as the author's *Sadako and the Thousand Paper Cranes*, told through an entirely new text. In this abbreviated version, the beautiful, limpid prose and crisp dialogue further telescope Sadako's fight with leukemia. . . . Young's pastels vividly capture all the moods of the narrative, place, and characters. . . . A masterful collaboration." SLJ

Coerr, Eleanor. Sadako and the thousand paper cranes; paintings by Ronald Himler. Putnam 1977 64p il $16.99; pa $5.99 *

Grades: 3 4 5 6   92

1. Leukemia 2. Atomic bomb—Physiological effect
3. Hiroshima (Japan)—Bombardment, 1945
ISBN 0-399-20520-9; 0-698-11802-2 (pa)
LC 76-9872
"A story about a young girl of Hiroshima who died from leukemia ten years after the dropping of the atom bomb. Her dreams of being an outstanding runner are dimmed when she learns she has the fatal disease. But her spunk and bravery, symbolized in her efforts to have faith in the story of the golden crane, are beautifully portrayed by the author." Babbling Bookworm

Satie, Erik, 1866-1925

Anderson, M. T. Strange Mr. Satie; illustrated by Petra Mathers. Viking 2003 unp il $16.99

Grades: 2 3 4   **92**

1. Composers

ISBN 0-670-03637-4   LC 2003-949

Introduces the life of the French composer, Erik Satie, who spent his entire career challenging established conventions in music

"A splendid alliance of topic, text, and illustration produces a hauntingly compelling biography. . . . Mathers's illustrations are superb in their crisp, colorful clarity." SLJ

Savage, Augusta Christine, 1892-1962

Schroeder, Alan. In her hands; the story of sculptor Augusta Savage; illustrated by JaeMe Bereal. Lee & Low Books 2009 unp il $19.95

Grades: 3 4 5 6   **92**

1. Sculptors 2. African American artists 3. Women artists 4. Harlem Renaissance

ISBN 978-1-60060-332-7; 1-60060-332-7

LC 2009003859

"A biography of African American sculptor Augusta Savage, who overcame many obstacles as a young woman to become a premier female sculptor of the Harlem Renaissance. Includes an afterword about Savage's adult life and works, plus photographs." Publisher's note

"Young readers will . . . find this a solid introduction to the art world and a daring but lesser-known African American artist. Bereal's . . . expansive, richly hued one and two-page spreads fit nicely with the text and deftly capture the emotions of the story." Booklist

Schaller, George B.

Turner, Pamela S. A life in the wild; George Schaller's struggle to save the last great beasts. Farrar, Straus and Giroux 2008 103p il map $21.95

Grades: 5 6 7 8   **92**

1. Zoologists 2. Wildlife conservation

ISBN 978-0-374-34578-5; 0-374-34578-3

LC 2007-42844

"Melanie Kroupa books"

"The author interviewed Schaller and had access to his photos, which allowed her to capture beautifully the spirit of Schaller's work. The book is organized chronologically, and each chapter covers a geographic area and the principal animals that Schaller studied there. . . . Animal lovers and conservation-minded students will enjoy this excellent introduction to Schaller and his ideals." Voice Youth Advocates

Includes bibliographical references

Schliemann, Heinrich, 1822-1890

Schlitz, Laura Amy. The hero Schliemann; the dreamer who dug for Troy; illustrated by Robert Byrd. Candlewick Press 2006 72p il $12.23 *

Grades: 4 5 6   **92**

1. Archeologists 2. Excavations (Archeology) 3. Troy (Extinct city)

ISBN 0-7636-2283-4   LC 2005046916

"In this slim biography, Schlitz introduces Heinrich Schliemann, a nineteenth-century 'storyteller, archaeologist, and crook,' who led a search for the lost cities of Homer's epic poems." Booklist

"This intriguing, well-documented biography is made more compelling by information boxes on history and such literary figures as Homer. Byrds ink-and-watercolor illustrations, both diminutive and full page, add to this captivating story." SLJ

Includes bibliographical references

Scholastica, Saint, 6th cent

Norris, Kathleen. The holy twins: Benedict and Scholastica. See entry under Benedict, Saint, Abbot of Monte Cassino

Schulz, Charles M.

Gherman, Beverly. Sparky: the life and art of Charles Schulz. Chronicle Books 2010 125p il $16.99

Grades: 5 6 7 8   **92**

1. Cartoonists

ISBN 978-0-8118-6790-0; 0-8118-6790-0

A look at the life and influences of Charles Schulz, creator of the beloved comic strip Peanuts.

"Gherman's clear and direct prose is just right for portraying the life of the famous cartoonist for young readers. The splashy, bright design, with multicolored pages and several of Schulz's cartoons included, makes this a cheery read that may well introduce the Peanuts comic strip to a new generation, who likely know Charlie Brown mostly through the holiday TV specials. An informative yet lighthearted look at the life of an American icon." Kirkus

Schumann, Clara, 1819-1896

Reich, Susanna. Clara Schumann; piano virtuoso. Clarion Bks. 1999 118p il $18; pa $9.95 *

Grades: 5 6 7 8   **92**

1. Pianists 2. Women composers

ISBN 0-395-89119-1; 0-618-55160-3 (pa)

LC 98-24510

Describes the life of the German pianist and composer who made her professional debut at age nine and who devoted her life to music and to her family

"This thoroughly researched book draws on primary sources, both Clara's own diaries and her voluminous correspondence with her husband. . . . Reich's lucid, quietly passionate biography is liberally illustrated with photographs and reproductions." Horn Book Guide

Scieszka, Jon, 1954-

Scieszka, Jon. Knucklehead; tall tales and mostly true stories of growing up Scieszka. Viking 2008 106p il $16.99; pa $12.99

Grades: 4 5 6 7   **92**

1. Authors, American

ISBN 978-0-670-01106-3; 0-670-01106-1; 978-0-670-01138-4 (pa); 0-670-01138-X (pa)

LC 2008-16870

Scieszka, Jon, 1954-—*Continued*

"Scieszka . . . has written an autobiography about boys, for boys and anyone else interested in baseball, fire and peeing on stuff. . . . The text is divided into two- to three- page nonsequential chapters and peppered with scrapbook snapshots and comic-book-ad reproductions. . . . By themselves, the chapters entertain with abrupt, vulgar fun. Taken together, they offer a look at the makings of one very funny author." Booklist

Scott, Wendell, 1921-1990

Weatherford, Carole Boston. Racing against the odds; the story of Wendell Scott, stock car racing's African-American champion; illustrated by Eric A. Velasquez. Marshall Cavendish Children 2009 unp il $17.99

Grades: 3 4 5   92

1. Automobile racing 2. African American athletes
ISBN 978-0-76145-465-6; 0-76145-465-9
                         LC 2008010711

"In this stirring biography of Scott, the only black race car driver to win a NASCAR race, Velasquez's expressive pastels showcase the driver's determination and resourcefulness. . . . With as much attention paid to Scott's life off the track as on, readers won't need to be racing fans to be drawn in." Publ Wkly

Selkirk, Alexander, 1676-1721

Kraske, Robert. Marooned; the strange but true adventures of Alexander Selkirk, the real Robinson Crusoe; illustrated by Robert Andrew Parker. Clarion Books 2005 120p il map $15 *

Grades: 5 6 7 8   92

1. Survival after airplane accidents, shipwrecks, etc.
ISBN 0-618-56843-3   LC 2004-28769

"In 1704, English sailing master Alexander Selkirk was marooned on Juan Fernandez, an isolated Pacific island. . . . In 1709, two English ships rescued him, hired him as a second mate, and later captured a Spanish treasure ship. . . . Kraske offers a well-focused look at life in several quite different settings during the early eighteenth century as well as an absorbing telling of Selkirk's story." Booklist

Includes glossary and bibliographical references

Sennett, Mack, 1880-1960

Brown, Don. Mack made movies. Roaring Brook Press 2003 unp il $16.95; lib bdg $23.90

Grades: 2 3 4   92

1. Motion picture producers and directors 2. Actors
ISBN 0-7613-1538-1; 0-7613-2504-2 (lib bdg)
                          LC 2002-6357

A simple biography of the director whose silent films immortalized such slapstick clowns as the Keystone Kops, Charlie Chaplin, Fatty Arbuckle, Mabel Normand, and Ben Turpin

This offers a "concise, brilliantly understated text. . . . Especially fine in conveying facial expression, Brown's spare, fluid sketches, softly washed in sepia and butterscotch tones, cunningly capture the look of the times." Booklist

Sequoyah, 1770?-1843

Dennis, Yvonne Wakim. Sequoyah, 1770?-1843; by Yvonne Wakim Dennis. Blue Earth Books 2004 32p il map (American Indian biographies) $23.93

Grades: 3 4 5 6   92

1. Cherokee Indians
ISBN 0-7368-2447-2   LC 2003-17584

Contents: A gift for the Cherokee; Growing up Cherokee; Inventor and soldier; Sequoyah seeks an answer; The syllabary spreads; A quiet ending

The story of Sequoyah's life is "told in easy-to-read prose that is amplified by handsome works of art . . . colorful and dramatic maps, and games and recipes." SLJ

Includes bibliographical references

Rumford, James. Sequoyah; the Cherokee man who gave his people writing. Houghton Mifflin 2004 unp il $16 *

Grades: 1 2 3 4   92

1. Cherokee Indians
ISBN 0-618-36947-3   LC 2004-00980

"Rumford presents the seminal events in Sequoyah's life, culminating in his invention of the Cherokee syllabary. The author writes with a concise eloquence that echoes the oral tradition and makes this one of those rare gems of read-aloud nonfiction. . . . Done in ink, watercolor, pastel, and pencil, the illustrations were adhered to a rough piece of wood, and its textures were highlighted through the use of chalk and colored pencil. . . . The parallel text in Cherokee . . . makes this beautiful book readily accessible to Cherokee children in their own language." SLJ

Wade, Mary Dodson. Amazing Cherokee writer Sequoyah. Enslow Publishers 2009 24p il (Amazing Americans) lib bdg $21.26

Grades: 1 2 3   92

1. Cherokee Indians
ISBN 978-0-7660-3285-9 (lib bdg); 0-7660-3285-X (lib bdg)   LC 2008-24893

"Readers will find out about Sequoyah's life, and how he created the Cherokee alphabet in this entry-level biography." Publsiher's note

"Colorful photos are found throughout, with a timeline, dictionary, websites concerning the topic, as well as an index making . . . [this] book a wonderful introduction to nonfiction features." Libr Media Connect

Includes glossary

Seuss, Dr.

Cohen, Charles D. The Seuss, the whole Seuss, and nothing but the Seuss; a visual biography of Theodor Seuss Geisel. Random House 2004 390p il $35; lib bdg $36.99

Grades: Professional   92

1. Authors, American 2. Illustrators
ISBN 0-375-82248-8; 0-375-92248-2 (lib bdg)
                          LC 2003-20526

This is a "profile of the creator of Horton, the Grinch, and the Cat in the Hat. . . . Crisp full-color illustrations on every page of the coffee-table volume will pull readers into Cohen's accessible recap of Theodore Geisel's career, which is enhanced with just enough personal in-

Seuss, Dr.—*Continued*
formation to bring everything together. . . . [The volume includes] clear reproductions of posters, book illustrations, newspaper cartoons, and book pages, with intriguing background information." Booklist

Krull, Kathleen. The boy on Fairfield Street: how Ted Geisel grew up to become Dr. Seuss; paintings by Steve Johnson and Lou Fancher; with decorative illustrations by Dr. Seuss. Random House 2004 43p il $16.95; lib bdg $18.99 *
Grades: K 1 2 3   92
   1. Authors, American 2. Illustrators
   ISBN 0-375-82298-4; 0-375-92298-9 (lib bdg)
                            LC 2003-1754
Introduces the life of renowned children's author and illustrator Ted Geisel, popularly known as Dr. Seuss, focusing on his childhood and youth in Springfield, Massachusetts
"Johnson and Fancher's lovely, full-page illustrations are supplemented by samples of Dr. Seuss's artwork. . . . Krull's work is a terrific look at the boyhood of one of the most beloved author/illustrators of the 20th century." SLJ

Sewall, May Wright, 1844-1920
Boomhower, Ray E. Fighting for equality; a life of May Wright Sewall; [by] Ray E. Boomhower. Indiana Historical Society Press 2007 160p il $17.95
Grades: 4 5 6   92
   1. Feminism 2. Reformers
   ISBN 978-0-87195-253-0; 0-87195-253-X
                            LC 2007008517
"This accessible volume tells of the life and work of suffragist and educator [May] Wright Sewall. . . . Archival black-and-white photos enhance the text." Horn Book Guide
Includes bibliographical references

Shackleton, Sir Ernest Henry, 1874-1922
Calvert, Patricia. Sir Ernest Shackleton; by endurance we conquer. Benchmark Bks. 2003 80p il map (Great explorations) lib bdg $19.95 *
Grades: 5 6 7 8   92
   1. Endurance (Ship) 2. Imperial Trans-Antarctic Expedition (1914-1917) 3. Antarctica—Exploration 4. Explorers
   ISBN 0-7614-1485-1   LC 2002-3784
Contents: A pig-headed, obstinate boy; Afraid of nothing; Don't expect a feather bed; No eagles in the barnyard; An old dog for the hard road; The long road home; He never spares himself; A lone star above the bay
Presents the life and Arctic explorations of Sir Ernest Shackleton
"This concise and straightforward account is enhanced by archival photos, reproductions, and maps." SLJ
Includes bibliographical references

Kostyal, K. M. Trial by ice: a photobiography of Sir Ernest Shackleton. National Geographic Soc. 1999 64p il map $17.95
Grades: 4 5 6 7   92
   1. Explorers 2. Antarctica—Exploration
   ISBN 0-7922-7393-1   LC 99-20980
Traces the adventurous life of the South Pole explorer whose ship, the Endurance, was frozen in ice and crushed, leaving the captain and crew to fight for survival
"The stunning, archival black-and-white photographs are this book's strength." SLJ
Includes bibliographical references

Shakur, Tupac
Harris, Ashley Rae. Tupac Shakur; multi-platinum rapper. ABDO Pub. Co. 2010 112p il (Lives cut short) lib bdg $32.79
Grades: 5 6 7 8   92
   1. Rap music 2. African American musicians
   ISBN 978-1-60453-791-8 (lib bdg); 1-60453-791-4 (lib bdg)
This discusses Tupac Shakur's early life, "providing details that give insight into later success and troubles and maintaining a laudatory tone that focuses on the individual's artistic achievements and hard work to achieve fame. Details [such as] explaining . . . that Tupac Shakur was a standout student in high school are bound to resonate with readers. Numerous photos and sidebars appear throughout. [A] worthwhile [resource] for reports as well as popular reading." SLJ

Shepard, Alan B., Jr.
Orr, Tamra. Alan Shepard; the first American in space; [by] Tamra B. Orr. Rosen Pub. Group 2004 112p il (Library of astronaut biographies) lib bdg $29.95
Grades: 4 5 6 7   92
   1. Astronauts
   ISBN 0-8239-4455-7   LC 2003-10703
Contents: A decade of contrasts; The launching of a future astronaut; The Mercury 7 astronauts; Freedom 7; The terror and triumph of Apollo; Into the business world; A quiet ending
This describes Alan Shepard's childhood, education, and training as an astronaut
"The writing is fast paced and lively. Many color photographs and occasional full-page sidebars enhance the [text]." SLJ
Includes glossary and bibliographical references

Sholem Aleichem, 1859-1916
Silverman, Erica. Sholom's treasure; how Sholom Aleichem became a writer; pictures by Mordicai Gerstein. Farrar, Straus and Giroux 2005 unp il $16
Grades: K 1 2 3   92
   1. Authors, Yiddish 2. Jews—Biography
   ISBN 0-374-38055-4   LC 2002-44672
Describes some events in the life of Sholem Aleichem, the Yiddish author who wrote stories about

Sholem Aleichem, 1859-1916—*Continued*
Jewish life in nineteenth-century Russia.
"Silverman keeps her focus on the things about
Aleichem's life that will appeal most to young readers.
. . . Gerstein's ink-and-watercolor paintings appear as
full-page art and strips of illustration, both of which are
equally adept at capturing the pathos and absurdities of
everyday life." Booklist

Shuster, Joe, 1914-1992
Nobleman, Marc Tyler. Boys of steel. See entry
under Siegel, Jerry, 1914-1996

Siegal, Aranka
Siegal, Aranka. Memories of Babi; stories.
Farrar, Straus & Giroux 2008 116p $16
Grades: 4 5 6 7   92
1. Jews—Biography 2. Grandmothers 3. Ukraine
4. Farm life
ISBN 978-0-374-39978-8; 0-374-39978-6
                                        LC 2007007002
Siegal's "*Upon the Head of the Goat*" (1981) is about
her childhood in Hungary as Hitler comes to power. In
this follow-up, written in nine wry sketches, she remembers the years before that—especially her close relationship with her Jewish grandmother, who lived on a small
farm just across the Hungarian border in Ukraine."
Booklist

Siegel, Jerry, 1914-1996
Nobleman, Marc Tyler. Boys of steel; the
creators of Superman; illustrated by Ross
MacDonald. Knopf 2008 unp il $16.99; lib bdg
$19.99 *
Grades: 1 2 3   92
1. Shuster, Joe, 1914-1992 2. Cartoonists
3. Superman (Fictional character)
ISBN   978-0-375-83802-6;   0-375-83802-3;
978-0-375-93802-3 (lib bdg); 0-375-93802-8 (lib bdg)
                                        LC 2007041606
"This book brings the young men behind the Man of
Steel to a picture-book audience. Along with the com-
pressed account of the partnership between nerdy high-
school outcasts Joe Shuster and Jerry Siegel, Nobleman
includes insights about superheroes' cultural significance
and the chord struck by Superman. . . . It's hard to
imagine a better sidekick for the text than MacDonald's
illustrations, which capture the look of 1930s comics
with their sepia-toned, stylized imagery." Booklist

Sís, Peter, 1949-
Sís, Peter. The wall; growing up behind the Iron
Curtain. Farrar, Straus and Giroux 2007 unp il $18
*
Grades: 4 5 6 7 8 9 10   92
1. Cold war 2. Prague (Czech Republic)
ISBN 978-0-374-34701-7; 0-374-34701-8
                                        LC 2006-49149
Boston Globe-Horn Book Award: Nonfiction (2008)
"Frances Foster books"

"The author pairs his remarkable artistry with journal
entries, historical context and period photography to
create a powerful account of his childhood in Cold War-
era Prague." Publ Wkly

Sitting Bull, Dakota Chief, 1831-1890
Bruchac, Joseph. A boy called Slow: the true
story of Sitting Bull; illustrated by Rocco Baviera.
Philomel Bks. 1994 unp il $16.99; pa $6.99
Grades: 1 2 3   92
1. Dakota Indians
ISBN 0-399-22692-3; 0-698-11616-X (pa)
                                        LC 93-21233
The author "recounts the early years of the young
Lakota boy who grows from an unprepossessing child
named 'Slow,' to a youth whose careful and deliberate
actions bring honor to the name, to a young warrior
whose courage in defeating the Crow earns him his father's vision name Tatan'ka Iyota'ke—Sitting Bull." Bull
Cent Child Books
"Baviera's darkly atmospheric, dramatic paintings frequently feature startling bits of bright color, as in the setting sun or a piece of sky visible through the smoke hole
of a family's tipi. The pictures evoke a sense of timelessness and distance, possessing an almost mythic quality
that befits this glimpse into history." Horn Book

Turner, Ann Warren. Sitting Bull remembers;
paintings   by   Wendell   Minor.
HarperCollinsPublishers 2007 unp il $16.99; lib
bdg $17.89
Grades: 3 4 5 6   92
1. Dakota Indians 2. Little Bighorn, Battle of the,
1876
ISBN   978-0-06-051399-3;   0-06-051399-3;
978-0-06-051400-6 (lib bdg); 0-06-051400-0 (lib bdg)
                                        LC 2006-29870
"In this first-person, fictionalized account, Sitting Bull
is living in captivity near the end of his life and remembering his past. . . . Turner's writing is lyrical, almost
poetic. The story is poignant and sympathetic to the
plight of the Native peoples who were driven from their
land and forced to live on tiny reservations. . . . The
well-crafted art adds drama and depth to the story." SLJ

Smalls, Robert, 1839-1915
Halfmann, Janet. Seven miles to freedom; the
Robert Smalls story; by Janet Halfmann; illustrated
by Duane Smith. Lee & Low Books 2008 unp il
$17.95
Grades: 3 4 5   92
1. Planter (Steamship) 2. African Americans—Biography 3. Slavery—United States 4. United States—History—1861-1865, Civil War 5. African Americans—
Civil rights
ISBN 978-1-60060-232-0; 1-60060-232-0
                                        LC 2007029274
"A biography of Robert Smalls who, during the Civil
War, commandeered the Confederate ship Planter to carry his family and twelve other slaves to freedom, and
went on to become a United States Congressman working toward African American advancement." Publisher's
note

Smalls, Robert, 1839-1915—*Continued*

This "will grab readers with exciting action. . . . Spacious, impressionistic oil paintings accompany [the] text." Booklist

Kennedy, Robert Francis. Robert Smalls; the boat thief; illustrations by Patrick Faricy. Hyperion Books for Children 2008 40p il map (Robert F. Kennedy Jr.'s American heroes) $16.99

Grades: 5 6 7 8   92

1. Planter (Steamship) 2. African Americans—Biography 3. Slavery—United States 4. United States—History—1861-1865, Civil War 5. African Americans—Civil rights

ISBN 978-1-4231-0802-3; 1-4231-0802-7

"Kennedy focuses not only on the daring escape Smalls made to freedom but also on Smalls as a political hero, especially his important role in the emancipation of slaves and in improving things for blacks during Reconstruction. . . . The volume features many illustrations—black-and-white portraits, and stirring, full-color scenes of ocean battles." Booklist

Smith, John, 1580-1631

Schanzer, Rosalyn. John Smith escapes again! National Geographic 2006 64p il map $16.95; lib bdg $25.90

Grades: 3 4 5   92

1. Explorers

ISBN 0-7922-5930-0; 0-7922-5931-9 (lib bdg)

LC 2006-01312

"The lore of Captain John Smith extends far beyond the familiar Pocahontas story, as Schanzer . . . attests in this vivid, extensively documented biography of the 17th-century explorer. . . . Schanzer offsets the formal borders with the cartoonlike artwork within. . . . Students of history will most appreciate the new light shed on this plucky voyager, but adventure fans will also be swept up in his escapades." Publ Wkly

Smith, Margaret Chase, 1897-1995

Plourde, Lynn. Margaret Chase Smith; a woman for president; illustrated by David McPhail. Charlesbridge 2008 unp il (Time line biography) $16.95; pa $7.95

Grades: 3 4 5   92

1. Women politicians

ISBN 978-1-58089-234-6; 978-1-58089-235-3 (pa)

LC 2007013549

"In 1964, Smith became the first woman from a major political party to run for President of the United States, and her career in politics featured other highlights as well. Clear, well-paced writing traces her eventful 97 years chronologically with two or three paragraphs of text per spread. . . . McPhail's warm pen-and-ink and watercolor illustrations feature Smith prominently and provide appealing visual references to the various stages of her life." SLJ

Snicket, Lemony, 1970-

Haugen, Hayley Mitchell. Daniel Handler; the real Lemony Snicket. Kidhaven Press 2005 48p il (Inventors and Creators) $23.70

Grades: 4 5 6 7   92

1. Authors, American

ISBN 0-7377-3117-6

In this biography of the author of the A Series on Unfortunate Events series "Haugen explains Handler's reasons for writing under a pen name. . . . He also explains Snicket's many interruptions, for vocabulary lessons, throughout the titles. A brief section presents some of the criticism of the series and Snicket's creative allusions to other literature and authors within his work. The full-color photos of Handler are sure to please the fans who've been longing for a glimpse. . . . This book will be read for reports and by adoring fans." SLJ

Snyder, Grace, 1882-1982

Warren, Andrea. Pioneer girl; a true story of growing up on the prairie; with a new afterword by the author. University of Nebraska Press 2009 104p il map pa $14.95

Grades: 5 6 7 8   92

1. Frontier and pioneer life

ISBN 978-0-8032-2526-8; 0-8032-2526-1

LC 2009-20883

First published 1998 by Morrow Junior Books

Biography of Nebraska homesteader, Grace McCance Snyder.

"This new edition offers an afterword that includes information about black homesteaders, Native Americans, and the specific tasks of women, especially quilting. . . . Although it is written for younger readers than a teen audience, readability and intense subject matter should make the book popular with those readers." Voice Youth Advocates

Includes bibliographical references

Sockalexis, Louis, 1871-1913

Wise, Bill. Louis Sockalexis; Native American baseball pioneer; by Bill Wise; illustrated by Bill Farnsworth. Lee & Low Books 2007 unp il $16.95

Grades: 2 3 4 5   92

1. Baseball—Biography 2. Native Americans—Biography

ISBN 978-1-58430-269-8   LC 2006017730

"This picture book offers a rousing introduction to the life of the first Native American to play major league baseball. . . . Wise and Farnsworth collaborate to great effect in rendering this story both informative and poignant. The color-drenched paintings do an excellent job of bringing this period to life and capturing the intense emotion of the ballpark drama." SLJ

Includes bibliographical references

Soto, Gary

Abrams, Dennis. Gary Soto; foreword by Kyle Zimmer. Chelsea House Pubs. 2008 120p bibl il por (Who wrote that?) $30

Grades: 5 6 7 8   92

1. Authors, American 2. Mexican Americans—Biography 3. Mexican American authors

ISBN 978-0-7910-9529-4; 0-7910-9529-0

LC 2007045509

A biography of the popular Mexican American author for children and young adults.

Includes bibliographical references

Sotomayor, Sonia, 1954-

McElroy, Lisa Tucker. Sonia Sotomayor; first Hispanic U.S. Supreme Court justice. Lerner 2010 il lib bdg $26.60

Grades: 5 6 7 8   92

1. Hispanic Americans—Biography 2. Judges 3. Women judges

ISBN 978-0-7613-5861-9; 0-7613-5861-7

LC 2009037703

"Well organized and straightforward, this biography is appealing with its bright photographs and bold, easy-to-read font. Starting with Sotomayor's childhood in the Bronx, the author covers the justice's life and career up to her nomination to the Supreme Court. . . . An informative, interesting, and, most of all, inspiring read." SLJ

Includes bibliographical references

Winter, Jonah. Sonia Sotomayor; a judge grows in the Bronx; illustrated by Edel Rodriguez. Atheneum Books for Young Readers 2009 unp il $16.99

Grades: K 1 2 3   92

1. Judges 2. Hispanic Americans—Biography 3. Women judges 4. Bilingual books—English-Spanish

ISBN 978-1-4424-0303-1; 1-4424-0303-9

LC 2009031659

A biography of the Bronx-born Latina Supreme Court justice.

"This timely, accessible picture-book biography, which features both English and Spanish text on every page, brings Sotomayer's exciting rags-to-riches story to young readers. . . . Winter lets the small details convey the drama, which is amplified in the mixed-media illustrations in warm shades of red and brown." Booklist

Spinelli, Jerry, 1941-

Spinelli, Jerry. Knots in my yo-yo string; the autobiography of a kid. Knopf 1998 148p il hardcover o.p. pa $10.95 *

Grades: 4 5 6 7   92

1. Authors, American

ISBN 0-679-98791-6; 0-679-88791-1 (pa)

LC 97-30827

This Italian-American Newbery Medalist presents a humorous account of his childhood and youth in Norristown, Pennsylvania

"There is an 'everyboy' universality to Spinelli's experiences, but his keen powers of observation and recall turn the story into a richly rewarding personal history." Horn Book Guide

Squires, Emily Swain, 19th cent.

Hailstone, Ruth. The white ox; the journey of Emily Swain Squires; [illustrations by] Dan Burr; [written by] Ruth Hailstone. Calkins Creek 2009 unp il $18.95

Grades: 2 3 4   92

1. Mormons 2. Immigrants 3. Frontier and pioneer life

ISBN 978-1-59078-555-3; 1-59078-555-X

LC 2008024154

Hailstone's "narrative describes the real-life journey of ten-year-old Emily Swain Squires (her great-great grandmother), who traveled ahead of her family from England to Salt Lake City around 1863. During the hardest part of the journey, walking across the plains, she befriended a weary white ox, which gave her enough strength to complete the long trek. Burr uses a digital version of oil painting in Photoshop, applied to a traditional surface, to create 15 stunning and dramatic spreads that appear historically accurate in every detail. Children will be swept up by the lovely art and the tale of Emily's remarkable journey." Kirkus

Standish, Myles, 1584?-1656

Harness, Cheryl. The adventurous life of Myles Standish; and the amazing-but-true survival story of Plymouth Colony; painstakingly written and illustrated by Cheryl Harness. National Geographic 2006 144p il map (Cheryl Harness history) $16.95; lib bdg $25.90

Grades: 4 5 6 7   92

1. Pilgrims (New England colonists) 2. Massachusetts—History—1600-1775, Colonial period

ISBN 978-0-7922-5918-3; 0-7922-5918-1; 978-0-7922-5919-0 (lib bdg); 0-7922-5919-X (lib bdg)

"Harness chronicles the history of the Plymouth Pilgrims from their troubles in England to their first years in North America, with the focus on Standish. Separating documented history from speculation, the narrative explains religious movements, introduces key figures, and gives a balanced account of Pilgrim-Indian relationships. . . . The tone is casual. . . . A reader-friendly approach to history." Booklist

Includes bibliographical references

Stanton, Elizabeth Cady, 1815-1902

Fritz, Jean. You want women to vote, Lizzie Stanton? illustrated by DyAnne DiSalvo-Ryan. Putnam 1995 88p il $16.99; pa $5.99

Grades: 2 3 4   92

1. Feminism 2. Women—Suffrage

ISBN 0-399-22786-5; 0-698-11764-6 (pa)

LC 94-30018

This is a biography of the 19th century feminist and advocate of women's suffrage

"With remarkable clarity, sensitivity, and momentum, Fritz has captured—but never imprisoned [Stanton's] spirit in an accessible, fascinating portrait." Horn Book

Includes bibliographical references

Stanton, Elizabeth Cady, 1815-1902—Continued

Stone, Tanya Lee. Elizabeth leads the way; Elizabeth Cady Stanton and the right to vote; illustrations by Rebecca Gibbon. Henry Holt & Co. 2008 unp il $16.95 *

Grades: 1 2 3   92

1. Suffragists 2. Women—Suffrage

ISBN 978-0-8050-7903-6; 0-8050-7903-3

LC 2007002833

This is "a short, incisive biography covering some of the high points of Stanton's life, beginning with her shocking realization about how unfairly the law treated women, which translated into Stanton's work for women's suffrage. . . . The child-pleasing artwork features characters a bit reminiscent of clothespin dolls, but the cameos of action, matched by full-page pictures, make the history accessible." Booklist

Stein, Gertrude, 1874-1946

Winter, Jonah. Gertrude is Gertrude is Gertrude is Gertrude; written by Jonah Winter; illustrated by Calef Brown. Atheneum Books for Young Readers 2009 unp il $16.99

Grades: K 1 2 3   92

1. Authors, American 2. Women authors

ISBN 978-1-4169-4088-3; 1-4169-4088-X

LC 2007-01447

Winter "crafts a Steinesque 'word portrait' of the modernist author. Stein wears a serene smile in Brown's . . . patchy acrylic images, and by her side is an enigmatic Alice B. Toklas. . . . Winter's nonlinear prose echoes *The Autobiography of Alice B. Toklas*, and his fugues suit a poet fond of repetition (and babble). Brown's idiosyncratic visuals and complementary palette . . . befit this impresario of experimental artists and writers on the Rive Gauche." Publ Wkly

Stevenson, Robert Louis, 1850-1894

Murphy, Jim. Across America on an emigrant train. Clarion Bks. 1993 150p il hardcover o.p. pa $10.95

Grades: 5 6 7 8   92

1. Authors, Scottish 2. Railroads—History 3. United States—Description and travel

ISBN 0-395-63390-7; 0-395-76483-1 (pa)

LC 92-38650

"Murphy presents a forthright and thoroughly engrossing history of the transcontinental railway, with entries from Robert Louis Stevenson's 1879 journal as he rode cross country. It's also an inviting introduction to Stevenson, with a romance in the bargain." SLJ

Includes bibliographical references

Stowe, Harriet Beecher, 1811-1896

Adler, David A. A picture book of Harriet Beecher Stowe; illustrated by Colin Bootman. Holiday House 2003 unp il $17.95; pa $6.95

Grades: K 1 2 3   92

1. Women authors 2. Authors, American 3. Abolitionists

ISBN 0-8234-1646-1; 0-8234-1878-2 (pa)

LC 2002-27626

Details the life and achievements of abolitionist Harriet Beecher Stowe whose book, Uncle Tom's Cabin, is said to have started the Civil War

"This biography offers easily accessible information supported by realistic, evocative oil paintings." SLJ

Includes bibliographical references

Fritz, Jean. Harriet Beecher Stowe and the Beecher preachers. Putnam 1994 144p il $15.99; pa $5.99

Grades: 5 6 7 8   92

1. Beecher family 2. Women authors 3. Authors, American 4. Abolitionists

ISBN 0-399-22666-4; 0-698-11660-7 (pa)

LC 93-6408

This is a biography of the abolitionist author of "Uncle Tom's Cabin" with an emphasis on the influence of her preacher father and her family on her life and work.

"Written with vivacity and insight, this readable and engrossing biography is an important contribution to women's history as well as to the history of American letters." Horn Book

Includes bibliographical references

Su, Shih, 1036 or 7-1101

Demi. Su Dongpo; Chinese genius. Lee & Low Books 2006 unp il map $24

Grades: 3 4 5 6   92

1. Authors, Chinese

ISBN 978-1-58430-256-8; 1-58430-256-9

LC 2005030437

"A biography of Su Dongpo, Chinese poet, civil engineer, and statesman, whose appreciation for nature and justice were evident in his works and led him to experience both triumph and adversity in 11th century China." Publisher's note

"Beautifully designed and produced, the book features delicately limned, brilliantly colored paintings of scenes from Su Dongpo's life, outlined in scarlet and bordered with thin bands of gold. A visually striking introduction to the man sometimes referred to as Su Shi or Su Tungpo." Booklist

Sullivan, Anne, 1866-1936

Delano, Marfe Ferguson. Helen's eyes; a photobiography of Annie Sullivan, Helen Keller's teacher; [foreword by Keller Johnson Thompson] National Geographic 2008 63p il map $17.95; lib bdg $27.90

Grades: 4 5 6 7   92

1. Keller, Helen, 1880-1968 2. Blind 3. Teachers

ISBN 978-1-4263-02-9-1; 1-4263-0209-6; 978-1-4263-0210-7 (lib bdg); 1-4263-0210-X (lib bdg)

"There are many biographies of Helen Keller and Annie Sullivan, but this one is very nicely done. . . . The book is honest in its portrayals, especially of Sullivan. . . . What makes this oversize book so appealing is the clean design, with large typeface. The many fascinating photographs are sometimes placed over historical documents." Booklist

Includes bibliographical references

Suzuki, Hiromi

Barasch, Lynne. Hiromi's hands. Lee & Low Books 2007 unp il $17.95 *

Grades: K 1 2 3   92

1. Cooking 2. Japanese Americans 3. Sex role
ISBN 978-1-58430-275-9   LC 2006017283

"A biography of Hiromi Suzuki, a Japanese American girl who, with her father's guidance, defies tradition and trains to become a sushi chef at her family's restaurant in New York City." Publisher's note

"Ink-and-watercolor scenes are rendered in salmon and grays; each childhood is captured in black-and-white snapshots. . . . An inspiring story." SLJ

Tallchief, Maria

Tallchief, Maria. Tallchief; America's prima ballerina; by Maria Tallchief with Rosemary Wells; illustrations by Gary Kelley. Viking 1999 unp il $15.99

Grades: 3 4 5   92

1. Ballet 2. Native American women
ISBN 0-670-88756-0   LC 98-35783

Ballerina Maria Tallchief describes her childhood on an Osage reservation, the development of her love of dance, and her rise to success in that field

"Through eloquent words, readers are immediately drawn into the first-person narrative. . . . As beautiful as the text is, so too are Kelley's pictures. The large illustrations, several covering double-page spreads, are rendered in soft pastels." SLJ

Tatum, Art, 1910-1956

Parker, Robert Andrew. Piano starts here: the young Art Tatum. Schwartz & Wade Books 2008 unp il $16.99; lib bdg $19.99 *

Grades: K 1 2 3   92

1. Jazz musicians 2. African American musicians 3. Pianists
ISBN   978-0-375-83965-8;   0-375-83965-8; 978-0-375-93965-5 (lib bdg); 0-375-93965-5 (lib bdg)
LC 2006-102105

This is a "a biography of famed jazz pianist Art Tatum. . . . A subtle sophistication shines through Parker's easygoing yet dynamic watercolors. . . . Parker's unhurried account could inspire visions of jazz greatness among young musicians." Publ Wkly

Includes bibliographical references

Taylor, Major, 1878-1932

Brill, Marlene Targ. Marshall "Major" Taylor; world champion bicyclist, 1899-1901; by Marlene Targ Brill. Twenty-First Century Books 2008 112p il (Trailblazer biography) lib bdg $31.93

Grades: 5 6 7 8   92

1. Bicycle racing 2. African American athletes
ISBN 978-0-8225-6610-6 (lib bdg); 0-8225-6610-9 (lib bdg)   LC 2006003883

"Marshall Taylor, an African American bicyclist who, despite facing prejudice in racing and in life, achieved world renown at the turn of the last century. . . . Brill's accessible, personable prose vividly relates Taylor's experiences." Booklist

Includes bibliographical references

Taylor, Mildred D.

Houghton, Gillian. Mildred Taylor. Rosen Pub. Group 2005 112p il (Library of author biographies) lib bdg $26.50

Grades: 5 6 7 8   92

1. Women authors 2. African American authors
ISBN 1-4042-0330-3

"Houghton presents readers with an understanding of Taylor's work as based on family stories and the history of African Americans in the United States. The result is a blend of history with the author's life and literature. . . . [This is] well-written." SLJ

Tecumseh, Shawnee Chief, 1768-1813

Collier, James Lincoln. The Tecumseh you never knew; [by] James Lincoln Collier; [illustrations by Greg Copeland] Children's Press 2004 80p il map lib bdg $25.95 *

Grades: 4 5 6 7   92

1. Shawnee Indians
ISBN 0-516-24426-4   LC 2003-28205

Contents: An Indian boy grows up; The war heats up; Rebuilding the confederacy; Tippecanoe; Triumph and tragedy

A biography of the Shawnee Indian chief who struggled to build a confederacy of Indians in order to thwart American expansionism after the Revolutionary war.

"A mix of realistic paintings and reproductions depict Tecumseh's life. Easy-to-read type on spacious white pages may tempt children into reading biographies." SLJ

Includes bibliographical references

Tenayuca, Emma, 1916-1999

Tafolla, Carmen. That's not fair! Emma Tenayuca's struggle for justice = No es justo!: la lucha de Emma Tenayuca por la justicia; written by Carmen Tafolla & Sharyll Teneyuca; illustrated by Terry Ybáñez; Spanish translation by Carmen Tafolla. Wings Press 2008 38p il $17.95

Grades: 2 3 4 5   92

1. Labor movement—History 2. Mexican Americans—Biography 3. Bilingual books—English-Spanish
ISBN 978-0-916727-33-8; 0-916727-33-5
LC 2007033343

Biography of Emma Tenayuca, who, in 1938, led 12,000 poor Mexican-American workers in a strike for better wages and living conditions

"Ybáñez's striking illustrations, framed by pecan-tree branches, are reflective of traditional Mexican mural art, with bold colors and simple shapes. An important book celebrating the struggle for justice and civil rights." SLJ

Tenzing Norgay, 1914-1986

Burleigh, Robert. Tiger of the snows; Tenzing Norgay; the boy whose dream was Everest; [by] Robert Burleigh and [illustrated by] Ed Young. Simon & Schuster 2006 unp il $16.95 *

Grades: 3 4 5 6   92

1. Mountaineering 2. Mount Everest (China and Nepal)
ISBN 0-689-83042-4   LC 2005-00469

Tenzing Norgay, 1914-1986—*Continued*

Presents the true story of Nepalese Sherpa Tenzing Norgay who, realizing his own dreams, helped Sir Edmund Hillary reach the summit of Mount Everest.

"Young's hauntingly beautiful illustrations capture the mystery and grandeur of these dangerously high peaks with somber-hued pastels, predominantly blues and purples, set against black backgrounds. . . . A stunning and lyrical ode to a contemplative man and his amazing achievement." SLJ

Thorpe, Jim, 1888-1953

Brown, Don. Bright path; young Jim Thorpe. Roaring Brook Press 2006 unp il $17.95 *
Grades: 2 3 4   92
1. Athletes 2. Native Americans—Biography
ISBN 978-1-59643-041-9; 1-59643-041-9
LC 2005-22029
A biography of Native American athlete Jim Thorpe, focusing on how his boyhood education set the stage for his athletic achievements which gained him international fame and Olympic gold medals.

"The legendary athlete gets an understated, humane treatment in Brown's latest outing, his characteristically soft palette perfect for both the Oklahoma prairies Thorpe called home and the government Indian schools he attended for most of his youth." Horn Book Guide
Includes bibliographical references

Thurman, Howard, 1900-1981

Jackson Issa, Kai. Howard Thurman's great hope; by Kai Jackson Issa; illustrated by Arthur L. Dawson. Lee & Low Books 2008 unp il $16.95
Grades: 2 3 4 5   92
1. Clergy
ISBN 978-1-60060-249-8; 1-60060-249-5
LC 2007050093
"A biography of Reverend Howard Thurman, who overcame adversity in his youth to pursue his dream of education and ultimately become a renowned African American theologian and civil rights leader." Publisher's note

"Reds, blues, and yellows pop against brown wood desks or whitewashed walls in vivid, realistic oil paintings. The author drew from Thurman's memoir and papers to create this accessible, engaging biography." SLJ

Tillage, Leon, 1936-

Tillage, Leon. Leon's story; [by] Leon Walter Tillage; collage art by Susan L. Roth. Farrar, Straus & Giroux 1997 107p il hardcover o.p. pa $6.95 *
Grades: 4 5 6 7 8 9 10   92
1. African Americans—Biography 2. North Carolina—Race relations
ISBN 0-374-34379-9; 0-374-44330-0 (pa)
LC 96-43544
The son of a North Carolina sharecropper recalls the hard times faced by his family and other African Americans in the first half of the twentieth century and the changes that the civil rights movement helped bring about

The author's "voice is direct, the words are simple. There is no rhetoric, no commentary, no bitterness. . . . This quiet drama will move readers of all ages . . . and may encourage them to record their own family stories." Booklist

Tingle, Tim

Tingle, Tim. Saltypie; a Choctaw journey from darkness into light; with illustrations by Karen Clarkson. Cinco Puntos Press 2010 40p il $17.95
Grades: 2 3 4 5   92
1. Choctaw Indians 2. Blind 3. Grandmothers
ISBN 978-1-933693-67-5; 1-933693-67-3
"Tingle tells his family's story from their origins in Oklahoma Choctaw country to their life in Texas. The account spans generations and weaves in ghosts from the past to the present day. . . . The author was six that he learned that his grandmother was blind. Tingle was a junior in college when he got word that Mawmaw was having surgery. As the family gathered at the hospital, they told stories about their past, and he heard about her days as an orphan at an Indian boarding school and the discrimination she encountered living in Texas. . . . The large, full-spread illustrations are vibrant and vital in moving the story along. A lovely piece of family history." SLJ

Toulouse-Lautrec, Henri de, 1864-1901

Burleigh, Robert. Toulouse-Lautrec; the Moulin Rouge and the City of Light. Abrams 2005 32p il $17.95
Grades: 3 4 5   92
1. Artists, French
ISBN 0-8109-5867-8
This "volume introduces the life and art of Toulouse-Lautrec. . . . Burleigh relates the facts in a way that is comprehensible to children, without talking down to them. . . . The book's format allows for many illustrations, including period photos and paintings of Paris by artists such as Pissarro and Renoir, which are cleverly mingled with reproductions of Toulouse-Lautrec's arresting drawings, paintings, and lithographs, many in color. . . . A beautifully designed book that provides a lively, accessible introduction to the artist's life and work." Booklist

Toussaint Louverture, 1743?-1803

Rockwell, Anne F. Open the door to liberty!: a biography of Toussaint L'Ouverture; illustrated by R. Gregory Christie. Houghton Mifflin Books for Children 2009 64p il $18 *
Grades: 5 6 7 8   92
1. Haiti—History 2. Slavery—West Indies 3. Blacks—Biography 4. Generals
ISBN 978-0-618-60570-5; 0-618-60570-3
LC 2007-25746
"In this eye-opening biography, Rockwell makes a strong case that Toussaint L'Ouverture is one of the most overlooked heroes of the eighteenth century. A freed slave of the French colony of St. Domingue (what we now know as Haiti), L'Ouverture was 48 when he was so inspired by his people's uprising against the French

Toussaint Louverture, 1743?-1803—*Continued*
that he joined them and, through his oratory and strategical skills, became their leader. In 1793, he led history's first triumphant slave rebellion, but the resulting freedom would not last long. . . . Evocative paintings in primary colors help tell the story." Booklist

Includes bibliographical references

Truth, Sojourner, d. 1883

Adler, David A. A picture book of Sojourner Truth; illustrated by Gershom Griffith. Holiday House 1994 unp il $17.95; pa $6.95

Grades: 1 2 3   92
1. African American women—Biography
2. Abolitionists 3. Feminism
ISBN 0-8234-1072-2; 0-8234-1262-8 (pa)
                            LC 93-7478

An introduction to the life of the woman born into slavery who became a well-known abolitionist and crusader for the rights of African Americans in the United States

The author "portrays his subject in a realistic manner, discussing slavery and other issues in an easy-to-read style. The quotes, while undocumented, are simple enough for the target audience and help to place events in context. Excellent-quality watercolor illustrations capture the action and provide effective representations and details of the time period." SLJ

Clinton, Catherine. When Harriet met Sojourner. See entry under Tubman, Harriet, 1820?-1913

Horn, Geoffrey. Sojourner Truth; speaking up for freedom; by Geoffrey M. Horn. Crabtree 2010 64p il (Voices for freedom: abolitionist heroes) lib bdg $22.95; pa $10.95

Grades: 4 5 6 7   92
1. African American women—Biography
2. Abolitionists 3. Feminism
ISBN 978-0-7787-4824-3 (lib bdg); 0-7787-4824-3 (lib bdg); 978-0-7787-4840-3 (pa); 0-7787-4840-5 (pa)

Examines the life of the woman born into slavery who became a wellknown abolitionist and crusader for the rights of African Americans in the United States

"Combining accessible, lively prose and abundant visuals, this title . . . offers an engaging, informative introduction to the early advocate for the rights of African Americans and women." Booklist

Includes glossary and bibliographical references

McKissack, Patricia C. Sojourner Truth; a voice for freedom; [by] Patricia and Fredrick McKissack. rev ed. Enslow Pubs. 2001 32p il (Great African Americans) lib bdg $18.60

Grades: 1 2 3   92
1. African American women—Biography
2. Abolitionists 3. Feminism
ISBN 0-7660-1693-5   LC 00-12420
First published 1992

Describes the life of the anti-slavery and women's rights activist, from her beginnings in slavery to her tireless campaign for the rights and welfare of the freedmen

"Short sentences, large, well-spaced text, and a blend of black-and-white photographs and sketches. . . . [This] will give an overview of that great woman's achieve-

ments." SLJ [review of 1992 edition]

Includes glossary and bibliographical references

Pinkney, Andrea Davis. Sojourner Truth's step-stomp stride; [by] Andrea Davis Pinkney & Brian Pinkney. Disney Jump at the Sun Books 2009 unp il $16.99 *

Grades: K 1 2 3   92
1. African American women—Biography
2. Abolitionists 3. Feminism
ISBN 978-0-7868-0767-3; 0-7868-0767-9

The Pinkneys "collaborate on an upbeat yet nuanced picture biography of Sojourner Truth, whose slave name was Isabella. . . . Andrea Davis Pinkney's narrative adopts a confidential, admiring tone, tracing Truth's years of enslaved toil, her subsequent escape, deep religious faith and narration of her life story to abolitionist Olive Gilbert. . . . Brian Pinkney's watercolors, in washes of ochre and slate blue contoured in inky black, utilize a dry-brush technique well suited for depicting Truth's hardscrabble youth and unyielding commitment to justice." Kirkus

Rockwell, Anne F. Only passing through: the story of Sojourner Truth; by Anne Rockwell; illustrated by Gregory Christie. Knopf 2000 unp il $16.95; lib bdg $18.99

Grades: 3 4 5   92
1. African American women—Biography
2. Abolitionists 3. Feminism
ISBN 0-679-89186-2; 0-679-99186-7 (lib bdg)
                          LC 00-35736

"Rockwell traces the life of 'Isabella,' who renamed herself Sojourner Truth when she began her journeys at the age of forty-six to speak out for the abolition of slavery." Horn Book

Rockwell's narrative "is both conversational and immediately riveting. . . . The semi-abstract paintings are inspirational rather than representational, their authority residing in the presence Christie imparts to this heroine." Bull Cent Child Books

Roop, Peter. Sojourner Truth; [by] Peter Roop and Connie Roop. Scholastic 2002 128p il (In their own words) pa $4.50

Grades: 3 4 5 6   92
1. African American women—Biography
2. Abolitionists 3. Feminism
ISBN 0-439-26323-9   LC 2001-32025

"The Roops make use of recollections, historical photos, letters, and newspaper articles to reveal the personality behind Truth's famous rousing oratory, 'Ain't I a Woman?' The biography covers the subjects birth into enslavement through her tireless travels across the country speaking out against slavery and fighting for social reforms, and her death at age 86 in 1883. . . . This book gives a complete picture, providing facts and insight into the woman's character and convictions." SLJ

Includes bibliographical references

Tubman, Harriet, 1820?-1913

Adler, David A. A picture book of Harriet Tubman; illustrated by Samuel Byrd. Holiday House 1992 unp il $17.95; pa $6.95

Grades: 1 2 3   92
1. African American women—Biography
2. Underground railroad
ISBN 0-8234-0926-0; 0-8234-1065-X (pa)
                                    LC 91-19628

Biography of the black woman who escaped from slavery to become famous as a conductor on the Underground Railroad

This book features "brief, easy-to-read text. . . . Byrd's appealing, colorful illustrations convey the quiet dignity of a brave heroine." Booklist

Clinton, Catherine. When Harriet met Sojourner; illustrated by Shane W. Evans. Katherine Tegen Books 2008 unp il $16.99; lib bdg $17.89

Grades: K 1 2 3   92
1. Truth, Sojourner, d. 1883 2. Slavery—United States 3. Abolitionists 4. African American women—Biography
ISBN 978-0-06-050425-0; 0-06-050425-0; 978-0-06-050426-7 (lib bdg); 0-06-050426-9 (lib bdg)
                                    LC 2006-19099

"Amistad"

"Clinton imagines what might have been said during a meeting between Harriet Tubman and Sojourner Truth, who both found themselves in Boston one day in October 1864. Their meeting is the climax of this picture book, which tells the stories of the two heroes in clear, simple words on alternating double-page spreads. Evans' dramatic collage-style illustrations evoke the quilts the women worked on, piecing together their history." Booklist

Turner, Glennette Tilley. An apple for Harriet Tubman; [by] Glennette Tilley Turner; illustrated by Susan Keeter. Albert Whitman & Co. 2006 unp il $15.95

Grades: 2 3 4   92
1. African American women—Biography 2. Slavery—United States 3. Apples
ISBN 978-0-8075-0395-9; 0-8075-0395-9
                                    LC 2005037360

"At age seven, Tubman's job was to care for the baby of an unkind white woman, who whipped her. Later, the overseer of an orchard lashes her for eating an apple. . . . Ketter's unframed, thickly painted pictures depict the slave child's cruel working conditions and her brave escape and rescue, culminating as Tubman buys a house and plants apple trees, which produce fruit for everyone to share. The story, with its concrete details, works as both fact and metaphor, bringing the transformation full circle—from the scars of suffering to the fruit of freedom." Booklist

Includes bibliographical references

Weatherford, Carole Boston. Moses; when Harriet Tubman led her people to freedom; illustrated by Kadir Nelson. Hyperion 2006 unp il $15.99 *

Grades: 2 3 4   92
1. African American women—Biography
2. Underground railroad
ISBN 0-7868-5175-9

A Caldecott Medal honor book, 2007

Describes Tubman's spiritual journey as she hears the voice of God guiding her north to freedom on that very first trip to escape the brutal practice of forced servitude.

This is a "handsome, poetic account. . . . Shifting perspectives and subtle details . . . underscore the narrative's spirituality. . . . Tubman's beautifully furrowed face is expressive and entrancing." SLJ

Tutankhamen, King of Egypt

Demi. Tutankhamun; written and illustrated by Demi. Marshall Cavendish Children 2009 unp il map $19.99

Grades: 4 5 6 7   92
1. Egypt—History 2. Kings and rulers
ISBN 978-0-7614-5558-5; 0-7614-5558-2
                                    LC 2008029313

"The unmistakable designs and opulent glitter of ancient Egyptian art gleam on every page of Demi's picture-book introduction to Tutankhamun. Beginning with King Tut's great-grandfather, Demi presents the broad historical context surrounding the young monarch's reign. . . . Demi's language, organized into brief but pithy paragraphs, is clear. . . . It's the beautiful illustrations that will attract and hold a young audience most, and as usual, Demi incorporates artistic motifs and materials appropriate to her subject." Booklist

Sabuda, Robert. Tutankhamen's gift; written and illustrated by Robert Sabuda. Atheneum Pubs. 1994 unp il $17; pa $6.99

Grades: K 1 2 3   92
1. Egypt—Antiquities
ISBN 0-689-31818-9; 0-689-81730-4 (pa)
                                    LC 93-5401

"His tutor foresees that little Tutankhamen's 'gift for the gods' will someday be revealed. That day comes sooner than expected, when the young boy becomes pharaoh after his brother's death and rebuilds the beautiful temples created by his father and destroyed by his brother. Bold pictures outlined in black against a background of painted, handmade Egyptian papyrus illustrate the book, and an afterword provides historical details." Horn Book Guide

Twain, Mark, 1835-1910

Brown, Don. American boy: the adventures of Mark Twain; written and illustrated by Don Brown. Houghton Mifflin 2003 unp il $16 *

Grades: 2 3 4   92
1. Authors, American
ISBN 0-618-17997-6   LC 2002-151177

Provides a brief biography of the noted American writer who was born Samuel Clemens

Twain, Mark, 1835-1910—*Continued*

"The boyhood of writer Samuel Clemens is irresistible, with much of his youth inspiring scenes in his works that have become folklore in their own right. Brown does a spirited job of telling some of those stories. . . . Brown's strengths as an artist, making evocative vistas and suggesting architecture and flora, are in evidence here." Booklist

Includes bibliographical references

Collier, James Lincoln. The Mark Twain you never knew; [by] James Lincoln Collier; [illustrations by Greg Copeland] Children's Press 2004 80p il lib bdg $25.50

Grades: 4 5 6 7   92

1. Authors, American
ISBN 0-516-24430-2   LC 2003-28305
Contents: A writer's boyhood; Earning a living; Roughing it; Writing the classics; The masterpiece

A biography of the American author.

"Excellent photographs bring . . . Twain to life. . . . [This offers] easy-to-read type on spacious white pages." SLJ

Includes bibliographical references

Fleischman, Sid. The trouble begins at 8; a life of Mark Twain in the wild, wild West. Greenwillow Books 2008 224p il $18.99; lib bdg $19.89 *

Grades: 5 6 7 8   92

1. Authors, American
ISBN 978-0-06-134431-2;   0-06-134431-1; 978-0-06-134432-9 (lib bdg); 0-06-134432-X (lib bdg)
      LC 2007-37891

"Fleischman writes a charming biography of Samuel Clemens before he became Mark Twain, the great American novelist. . . . Written with a sense of humor and wit that honors Twain, this book is sprinkled with famous Twain quotes, excerpts of his writing, and pictures of Twain and other primary documents from the era Clemens spent both on the Mississippi River and in the West." Voice Youth Advocates

Includes bibliographical references

Kerley, Barbara. The extraordinary Mark Twain (according to Susy); illustrated by Edwin Fotheringam. Scholastic Press 2010 unp il $17.99 *

Grades: 2 3 4 5   92

1. Clemens, Susy, 1872-1894 2. Authors, American 3. Authorship 4. Biography
ISBN 978-0-545-12508-6; 0-545-12508-1
      LC 2009-04752

"Wanting to present a portrait of her papa beyond that of just humorist and author, Mark Twain's 13-year-old daughter Susy spent a year chronicling her observations and reflections. . . . Kerley contextualizes the teenager's admiring musings with vivid familial backdrops. . . . Minibooklets titled 'Journal' appear in the fold of many spreads, containing excerpts from Susy's notebook. . . . Adding dynamic flair to the limited palettes of each digitally created scene are curlicues representing words, which emanate wildly from pen tips, pages, and mouths. Author notes about Susy and her father, a time line of Twain's life, and tips for writing an 'extraordinary biog-

raphy' complete this accessible and inventive vision of a American legend." Publ Wkly

Lasky, Kathryn. A brilliant streak: the making of Mark Twain; illustrated by Barry Moser. Harcourt Brace & Co. 1998 41p il $18 *

Grades: 4 5 6 7   92

1. Authors, American
ISBN 0-15-252110-0   LC 95-18479
An illustrated biography of young Samuel Clemens

"An obvious delight in her subject makes Lasky's biography an appealing choice, and a similar enthusiasm invests Moser's illustrations." Horn Book Guide

Includes bibliographical references

MacLeod, Elizabeth. Mark Twain; an American star; written by Elizabeth MacLeod. Kids Can Press 2008 32p il (Snapshots: Images of People and Places in History) $14.95; pa $6.95

Grades: 3 4 5 6   92

1. Authors, American
ISBN   978-1-55337-908-9;   1-55337-908-X; 978-1-55337-909-6 (pa); 1-55337-909-8 (pa)

"This large-format book offers double-page spreads presenting aspects of Twain's life in a chronological arrangement. Each left-hand page features paragraphs of text with a related quote and picture in the margin, while the facing page includes a scrapbook-like array of captioned images, such as period photos, drawings, artifacts, and documents. . . . Clearly written, this brief biography offers a very accessible introduction to the writer's life." Booklist

Valentine, Saint

Sabuda, Robert. Saint Valentine; retold and illustrated by Robert Sabuda. Atheneum Pubs. 1992 unp il $16.95; pa $5.99

Grades: 1 2 3   92

1. Christian saints
ISBN 0-689-31762-X; 0-689-82429-7 (pa)
      LC 91-25012

Recounts an incident in the life of St. Valentine, a physician who lived some 200 years after Christ, in which he treated a small child for blindness

"The fluid, straightforward retelling of the legend is accompanied by evocative, mosaiclike illustrations created from colored cut paper. Varying sizes of illustrations, careful page placement, and effective use of white space create the impression of the large-scale period mosaics. A fine melding of text and art." SLJ

Velázquez, Diego, 1599-1660

Venezia, Mike. Diego Velázquez; written and illustrated by Mike Venezia. Children's Press 2004 32p il (Getting to know the world's greatest artists) lib bdg $26; pa $6.95

Grades: K 1 2 3   92

1. Artists, Spanish
ISBN 0-516-22580-4 (lib bdg); 0-516-26980-1 (pa)
      LC 2003-4590

Describes the life and career of the seventeenth-century Spanish artist famous for his portraits of royalty.

Velázquez, Diego, 1599-1660—*Continued*

"The unusually abundant full-color reproductions more than justify this series' longevity, as do Venezia's light-hearted cartoons, which foster welcome associations between 'art appreciation' and 'fun.'" Booklist

Vivaldi, Antonio, 1678-1741

Shefelman, Janice Jordan. I, Vivaldi; written by Janice Shefelman; illustrated by Tom Shefelman. William B. Eerdmans Pub. Co. 2007 unp il $18
Grades: 3 4 5   92
  1. Composers
  ISBN 978-0-8028-5318-9; 0-8028-5318-8
                                                       LC 2006-20120
This is a picture book "biography of composer Antonio Vivaldi. . . . The first-person narration offers an accessible and personable view of Vivaldi's intense passion for music. . . . Stunning ink-and-watercolor scenes evoke the ornate, shadowy church interiors and gilded ornamentation of 17th century Venice." Publ Wkly

Wagner, Honus, 1874-1955

Yolen, Jane. All-star! Honus Wagner and the most famous baseball card ever; illustrated by Jim Burke. Philomel Books 2010 unp il $17.99 *
Grades: 2 3 4   92
  1. Pittsburgh Pirates (Baseball team) 2. Baseball—Biography 3. Baseball cards
  ISBN 978-0-399-24661-6; 0-399-24661-4
                                                       LC 2009-15066
Biography of Honus Wagner and an explanation of why his baseball card is worth almost $3 million.
"The treatment of Wagner's hardscrabble early years . . . is particularly masterful. . . . An eloquently understated tribute to that archetypal American combination of stoicism, decency, drive, and sheer talent." Publ Wkly

Waldman, Neil, 1947-

Waldman, Neil. Out of the shadows; an artist's journey. Boyds Mills Press 2006 144p il $21.95
Grades: 5 6 7 8   92
  1. Illustrators 2. Artists—United States 3. Jews—Biography
  ISBN 1-59078-411-1
Neil Waldman reveals how his passion for art emerged in the kitchen of his family's apartment, where he discovered the work of Vincent Van Gogh and the ability to use illustration as a means to escape the sadness that plagued his home.
"Young artists, as well as readers who wonder about the person behind the pictures they have seen, will appreciate every element of this book: well-constructed story, visual richness, and uncompromising honesty." Booklist

Walker, C. J., Madame, 1867-1919

Lasky, Kathryn. Vision of beauty: the story of Sarah Breedlove Walker; illustrated by Nneka Bennett. Candlewick Press 2000 unp il $16.99
Grades: 3 4 5   92
  1. African American businesspeople 2. African American women—Biography
  ISBN 0-7636-0253-1   LC 99-19594

A biography of Sarah Breedlove Walker who, though born in poverty, pioneered in hair and beauty care products for black women, and became a great financial success
"Lasky's engaging account moves smoothly through events in Walker's life. . . . The illustrations . . . are attractive and rich in historical detail." Booklist

McKissack, Patricia C. Madam C.J. Walker; self-made millionaire; [by] Patricia and Fredrick McKissack. rev ed. Enslow Pubs. 2001 32p il $18.60
Grades: 1 2 3   92
  1. African American businesspeople 2. African American women—Biography
  ISBN 0-7660-1682-X   LC 00-10055
  First published 1992
Describes the life of the black laundress who founded a cosmetics company and became the first female self-made millionaire in the United States

Walking Coyote

Bruchac, Joseph. Buffalo song; by Joseph Bruchac; illustrated by Bill Farnsworth. Lee & Low Books 2008 unp il $17.95 *
Grades: 1 2 3   92
  1. Kalispel Indians 2. Native Americans—Biography 3. Bison 4. Wildlife conservation
  ISBN 978-1-58430-280-3; 1-58430-280-1
                                                       LC 2007024912
"The story of the first efforts to save the vanishing bison (buffalo) herds from extinction in the United States in the 1870s and 1880s. Based on the true story of Samuel Walking Coyote, a Salish (Kalispel) Indian who rescued and raised orphaned buffalo calves." Publisher's note
This biography is "partly fictionalized. . . . Bruchac's long, eloquent afterword fills in the facts. . . . [It is illustrated with] Farnsworth's beautiful, full-bleed oil paintings." Booklist

Warhol, Andy, 1928?-1987

Rubin, Susan Goldman. Andy Warhol; pop art painter. H.N. Abrams 2006 48p il $18.95 *
Grades: 4 5 6 7   92
  1. Artists—United States 2. Pop art
  ISBN 0-8109-5477-X   LC 2005-13238
"Andy Warhol was a colorful figure who revolutionized how the world looks at art. Rubin's coherent and interesting narrative is filled with quotes by the artist and people who knew him. . . . Excellent-quality black-and-white and full-color photographs of Warhol and his family and reproductions of his paintings and those of others who influenced him appear throughout." SLJ

Washington, Booker T., 1856-1915

Brimner, Larry Dane. Booker T. Washington; getting into the schoolhouse. Marshall Cavendish Benchmark 2009 41p il (American heroes) lib bdg $20.95
Grades: 2 3 4   92
  1. Scientists 2. African Americans—Biography
  ISBN 978-0-7614-3063-6   LC 2008002870

Washington, Booker T., 1856-1915—*Continued*
A biography of Booker T. Washington, who rose from slavery to become a great African-American leader and educator
This "concise and well-written [title covers] key biographical facts without overwhelming young readers, and [includes] captioned illustrations and reproductions, most of which are in color. Text is large, and the layout is age-appropriate and attractive, with wide margins." SLJ
Includes glossary and bibliographical references

McKissack, Patricia C. Booker T. Washington; leader and educator; [by] Patricia and Fredrick McKissack. rev ed. Enslow Pubs. 2001 32p il $18.60
Grades: 1 2 3   **92**
1. Tuskegee Institute 2. African American educators
ISBN 0-7660-1679-X   LC 00-10056
First published 1992
A biography of the former slave who founded Tuskegee University and later became the most powerful African American leader at the turn of the century
This is a "solid, straightforward [biography]." Booklist

Washington, George, 1732-1799
Adler, David A. George Washington; an illustrated biography; by David A. Adler. Holiday House 2004 274p il map $24.95
Grades: 5 6 7 8   **92**
1. Presidents—United States
ISBN 0-8234-1838-3   LC 2003-67606
This "look at America's premier founding father literally spans his lifetime and attempts to focus . . . on how Washington's early character formation impacted his decisions as a military officer and later as president. . . . The illustrations are largely engravings from the late 19th century. . . . The writing style is accessible without ever falling prey to oversimplification." SLJ

Allen, Kathy. President George Washington; illustrated by Len Ebert. Picture Window Books 2010 32p il (Our American story) lib bdg $23.99
Grades: 2 3 4   **92**
1. Presidents—United States
ISBN 978-1-4048-5539-7; 1-4048-5539-4
     LC 2009-6894
Highlights the life and accomplishments of the Commander in Chief of the Continental Army and first president of the United States.
This title is "illustrated with well-executed, full-page, color illustrations, maps, and photos. . . . [It has] accurate, clearly written information that students can use for either leisure reading or reports." SLJ
Includes glossary and bibliographical references

Bial, Raymond. Where Washington walked; [by] Raymond Bial. Walker & Co. 2004 48p il $17.95; lib bdg $18.85
Grades: 3 4 5 6   **92**
1. Presidents—United States
ISBN 0-8027-8899-8; 0-8027-8900-5 (lib bdg)
     LC 2004-41931
"Bial briefly recounts the life of his subject with reference to the places he lived and worked." SLJ

"This well-designed book introduces George Washington through a clearly written biographical account of his life and achievements, illustrated with many sharply focused, well-composed photographs and a few reproductions of period paintings and prints." Booklist
Includes bibliographical references

Dolan, Edward F. George Washington; [by] Edward F. Dolan. Marshall Cavendish Benchmark 2008 96p il (Presidents and their times) lib bdg $32.79
Grades: 5 6 7 8   **92**
1. Presidents—United States
ISBN 978-0-7614-2427-7 (lib bdg); 0-7614-2427-X (lib bdg)   LC 2006037802
This biography of the first president of the United States "is illustrated with color photos and contains boxed descriptions of key historical events, artwork, and political concepts experienced during the time period. . . . This . . . will be of great use both for biographical research and for enriching the curriculum." Libr Media Connect
Includes glossary and bibliographical references

Harness, Cheryl. George Washington. National Geographic Soc. 2000 48p il $17.95
Grades: 3 4 5   **92**
1. Presidents—United States
ISBN 0-7922-7096-7   LC 99-29920
Presents the life of George Washington, focusing on the Revolutionary War years and his presidency
"Detailed paintings, full of action and rich with color, portray Washington as well as important moments in American history. . . . This heavily illustrated biography serves as a good introduction to Washington." Booklist
Includes bibliographical references

Jurmain, Suzanne. George did it; by Suzanne Tripp Jurmain; illustrated by Larry Day. Dutton Children's Books 2006 40p il $16.99
Grades: 2 3 4   **92**
1. Presidents—United States
ISBN 0-525-47560-5   LC 2004-25068
"This picture book focuses on George Washington as a reluctant first president. . . . The lively text follows Washington as friends such as Jefferson convince him to accept the challenge. . . . The text is studded with short quotes and memorable details. . . . Brightened with watercolor washes, Day's strong drawings illustrate the story with wit and finesse." Booklist
Includes bibliographical references

Miller, Brandon Marie. George Washington for kids; his life and times with 21 activities; [by] Brandon Marie Miller. Chicago Review Press 2007 130p il pa $14.95
Grades: 4 5 6 7   **92**
1. Presidents—United States
ISBN 1-55652-655-5 (pa); 978-1-55652-655-8 (pa)
This book covers Washington's life and includes 21 hands-on projects based on his experiences and the times in which he lived.
This is "accessible and absorbing . . . clearly written and informative. . . . Primary quotes are interposed throughout, and illustrations, photographs, and visual aids are plentiful and well placed." SLJ

Washington, George, 1732-1799—*Continued*

Rockwell, Anne F. Big George: how a shy boy became President Washington; [by] Anne Rockwell; illustrated by Matt Phelan. Harcourt 2009 unp il $17 *

Grades: K 1 2 3   92

    1. Presidents—United States

    ISBN 0-15-216583-5; 978-0-15-216583-3

                        LC 2002-4984

Portrays George Washington as a shy boy who wasn't afraid of anything except talking to people, but who grew up to lead an army against the British and serve as president of the new nation

This "adulatory biography offers plenty for contemporary kids to connect with. . . . But it's Phelan's . . . extraordinary artwork that cements the bond with readers. As his pencil-and-gouache scenes review Washington's life up to the presidency, his scenes bristle with immediacy, dramatic tension and emotional insight." Publ Wkly

Thomas, Peggy. Farmer George plants a nation; [by] Peggy Thomas; paintings by Layne Johnson. Calkins Creek 2008 40p il $17.95

Grades: 2 3 4   92

    1. Presidents—United States

    ISBN 978-1-59078-460-0   LC 2007-18449

"This picture-book biography focuses on George Washington's life as a farmer, inventor, and scientist; however, the author also draws many parallels between his role as farmer and as leader. . . . Thomas's enthusiasm for her subject is evident in her storytelling-style text. She not only used primary sources in her research, but also included several quotes from Washington's diaries and letters. . . . Johnson's oil paintings support the text while adding a feel of the 18th century." SLJ

Includes bibliographical references

Weber, EdNah New Rider

Weber, EdNah New Rider. Rattlesnake Mesa; stories from a native American childhood; by EdNah New Rider Weber; photographs by Richela Renkun. Lee & Low Books 2004 132p il $18.95

Grades: 4 5 6 7   92

    1. Native Americans—Biography

    ISBN 1-58430-231-3   LC 2004-2385

"Weber grew up in the early twentieth century on the Crown Point Navajo Reservation . . . and she attended a government boarding school for Native American children. She recounts childhood experiences in both places." Booklist

"Weber describes her experiences with warmth and affection in this unusually compelling memoir. Striking black-and-white photos . . . add to the book's appeal." Horn Book Guide

Wells-Barnett, Ida B., 1862-1931

Dray, Philip. Yours for justice, Ida B. Wells; the daring life of crusading journalist; written by Philip Dray; illustrated by Stephen Alcorn. Peachtree Publishers 2008 unp il $18.95

Grades: 2 3 4   92

    1. African American women—Biography 2. African Americans—Civil rights 3. United States—Race relations

    ISBN 978-1-56145-417-4; 1-56145-417-6

                      LC 2007-4016

"Dray introduces this civil rights crusader and journalist who campaigned tirelessly to end the practice of lynching. . . . Alcorn's ink-and-watercolor illustrations have a fluid quality, conveying both action within the story and movement from one scene to the next. . . . This makes a good choice for middle-grade readers." Booklist

Includes bibliographical references

Fradin, Dennis B. Ida B. Wells; mother of the civil rights movement; [by] Dennis Brindell Fradin and Judith Bloom Fradin. Clarion Bks. 2000 178p il $19

Grades: 5 6 7 8   92

    1. African American women—Biography 2. African Americans—Civil rights 3. United States—Race relations

    ISBN 0-395-89898-6   LC 99-37038

This "biography chronicles the life of teacher, writer, publisher and civil rights champion, Ida B. Wells." ALAN

"This stellar biography of one of history's most inspiring women offers an excellent overview of Wells's life and contributions. . . . Black-and-white photographs and reproductions enhance the clear, well-written text." SLJ

Includes bibliographical references

Myers, Walter Dean. Ida B. Wells; let the truth be told; illustrated by Bonnie Christensen. HarperCollinsPublishers 2008 37p il $16.99; lib bdg $17.89 *

Grades: 2 3 4 5   92

    1. African American women—Biography 2. African Americans—Civil rights 3. United States—Race relations

    ISBN 978-0-06-027705-5; 0-06-027705-X; 978-0-06-027706-2 (lib bdg); 0-06-027706-8 (lib bdg)

                    LC 2007-40107

"Myers deals with Wells-Barnett's career—from child of slaves, to teacher, to writer and organizer in the causes of anti-lynching and women's suffrage—in a style accessible to younger elementary audiences. . . . Each spread features a limited amount of text, and sourced quotations from Well-Barnett are frequently appended in red. Christensen's shaggy line and watercolor illustrations soften the rougher edges of the drama without straying into cartoonishness." Bull Cent Child Books

West, Benjamin, 1738-1820

Brenner, Barbara. The boy who loved to draw: Benjamin West; illustrated by Olivier Dunrea. Houghton Mifflin 1999 unp il $15; pa $6.99

Grades: K 1 2 3   92

1. Artists—United States

ISBN 0-395-85080-0; 0-618-31089-4 (pa)

LC 97-5183

Recounts the life story of the Pennsylvania artist who began drawing as a boy and eventually became well known on both sides of the Atlantic

"Naive in style and reminiscent of some colonial art, the illustrations present clear visual expressions of the activities and emotions related in the story. . . . A fascinating look at art in colonial times, and a likable portrait of the artist as a young boy." Booklist

Wheatley, Phillis, 1753-1784

Clinton, Catherine. Phillis's big test; written by Catherine Clinton; illustrated by Sean Qualls. Houghton Mifflin 2008 unp il $16

Grades: 1 2 3 4   92

1. Poets, American 2. African American authors 3. Women poets 4. Slavery—United States

ISBN 978-0-618-73739-0; 0-618-73739-1

LC 2007-13241

"This picture-book biography deals with a transformative moment in the life of Phillis Wheatley, the first African American to publish a book of poetry. In 1772, 18 members of the intelligentsia from the Massachusetts Bay Colony . . . gathered to question the 17-year-old slave to ascertain the authorship of the poems she claimed were her own. . . . Qualls's uncluttered acrylic and collage compositions employ strong diagonal lines, swirling ribbons of thought, and a combination of opaque images and outlined, transparent figures over washes of color to create visual interest. . . . A formal tone, an occasional quaint turn of phrase, and a typeface with an irregular impression create the flavor of a time past. Clinton and Qualls offer an elegant introduction to an important individual." SLJ

Lasky, Kathryn. A voice of her own: the story of Phillis Wheatley, slave poet; illustrated by Paul Lee. Candlewick Press 2003 unp il $17.99; pa $7.99

Grades: 3 4 5   92

1. Poets, American 2. African American authors 3. Women poets 4. Slavery—United States

ISBN 0-7636-0252-3; 0-7636-2878-6 (pa)

LC 2001-47139

A biography of an African girl brought to New England as a slave in 1761 who became famous on both sides of the Atlantic as the first Black poet in America

Written "in evocative language that's rich with historical detail. . . . This will serve as a good introduction to Wheatley's life and times for young children, who will appreciate Lee's full-page, historically accurate acrylics." Booklist

Whitfield, Simon, 1975-

Whitfield, Simon. Simon says gold: Simon Whitfield's pursuit of athletic excellence; by Simon Whitfield with Cleve Dheensaw. Orca Publishers 2009 118p il pa $14

Grades: 5 6 7 8   92

1. Athletes 2. Track athletics

ISBN 978-1-55469-141-8 (pa); 1-55469-141-9 (pa)

"In 2000, Whitfield won a gold medal in the inaugural triathlon race held in the Sydney Summer Olympics. . . . He tells his story with candor, and he sheds light on the dark side of early success and the pressures athletes face. Sidebars offer more information on the sport of triathlon, and scrapbook-style color photographs enliven the tale." SLJ

Whitman, Narcissa Prentiss, 1808-1847

Harness, Cheryl. The tragic tale of Narcissa Whitman and a faithful history of the Oregon Trail; written and illustrated by Cheryl Harness. National Geographic Society 2006 144p il map (Cheryl Harness history) $16.95; lib bdg $25.90

Grades: 4 5 6 7   92

1. Frontier and pioneer life 2. Overland journeys to the Pacific

ISBN 0-7922-5920-3; 0-7922-7890-9 (lib bdg)

LC 2005-30930

This "introduces a nineteenth-century pioneer and missionary. . . . [She and her husband Marcus Whitman] journeyed along the Oregon Trail to the Waiilatpu Mission, where they ministered to the Cayuse. . . . Harness' chatty, conversational style makes the pair accessible to modern readers, and frequent quotes from Narcissa's diaries and letters and a time line help to frame the story in light of world and national events. Harness' black-line illustrations . . . help to break up the text for younger readers." Booklist

Includes bibliographical references

Whitman, Walt, 1819-1892

Kerley, Barbara. Walt Whitman; words for America; illustrated by Brian Selznick. Scholastic Press 2004 unp il $16.95 *

Grades: 4 5 6 7   92

1. Poets, American

ISBN 0-439-35791-8   LC 2003-20085

A biography of the American poet whose compassion led him to nurse soldiers during the Civil War, to give voice to the nation's grief at Lincoln's assassination, and to capture the true American spirit in verse

"Delightfully old-fashioned in design, [the book's] oversized pages are replete with graceful illustrations and snippets of poetry. The brilliantly inventive paintings add vibrant testimonial to the nuanced text." SLJ

Wickenheiser, Hayley, 1978-

Etue, Elizabeth. Hayley Wickenheiser; born to play. Kids Can Press 2005 40p il pa $6.95

Grades: 4 5 6 7   92

1. Hockey 2. Women athletes
ISBN 1-55337-791-5

"The first woman to play professional hockey, Hayley Wickenheiser took up the sport in her family's backyard rink in a small Saskatchewan town at the age of three. . . . In 2003, Wickenheiser played professional hockey in a men's league in Finland. Fully illustrated with clear, colorful photos of Wickenheiser in action as well as posed shots off the ice, this appealing, large-format paperback offers a look at one woman's career in a 'man's' sport and shows the drive that propelled her to the top." Booklist

Wiesenthal, Simon

Rubin, Susan Goldman. The Anne Frank Case: Simon Wiesenthal's search for the truth; illustrated by Bill Farnsworth. Holiday House 2009 40p il $18.95 *

Grades: 4 5 6 7   92

1. Jews—Biography 2. Holocaust survivors 3. Holocaust, 1933-1945
ISBN 978-0-8234-2109-1; 0-8234-2109-0
LC 2007-28396

"In 1958, Holocaust deniers disrupted a theater performance of *The Diary of Anne Frank*. In response, the well-known Nazi hunter Simon Wiesenthal vowed to prove Anne's story true. . . . This 'hook' is the framing story for a picture-book biography chronicling Wiesenthal's experiences during World War II and illustrating the development of his unusual career." SLJ

"Even those who have heard of Wiesenthal will be thrilled by this account. . . . Farnsworth's stirring full-page oil paintings are filled with emotion." Booklist

Includes glossary and bibliographical references

Wild Boy of Aveyron, d. 1828

Gerstein, Mordicai. The wild boy; based on the true story of the Wild Boy of Aveyron. Foster Bks. 1998 39p il hardcover o.p. pa $6.95 *

Grades: K 1 2 3   92

1. Wild children
ISBN 0-374-38431-2; 0-374-48396-5 (pa)
LC 97-37246

"Frances Foster Books"

"Based on the true story of the Wild Boy of Aveyron"

Relates the story of a boy who grew up wild in the forests of France and was captured in 1800, studied and cared for and named Victor, but who never learned to speak

"Gerstein's prose finds power in its simplicity and emotional resonance in its declarative understatement. . . . The narrative strength and energy of the illustrations expand the inherent drama of Victor's situation. Together, Gerstein's text and pictures work to create an unforgettable story." Booklist

Wilder, Laura Ingalls, 1867-1957

Anderson, William T. Pioneer girl: the story of Laura Ingalls Wilder; by William Anderson; illustrated by Dan Andreasen. HarperCollins Pubs. 1998 unp il hardcover o.p. pa $6.99

Grades: 2 3 4   92

1. Authors, American 2. Frontier and pioneer life 3. Women authors
ISBN 0-06-027243-0; 0-06-027244-9 (lib bdg);
0-06-446234-X (pa)   LC 96-31203

Recounts the life story of the author of the "Little House" books, from her childhood in Wisconsin to her old age at Rocky Ridge Farm

"Laura Ingalls Wilder's many fans will delight in this inviting biographical overview in a picture-book format, graced by Andreasen's dreamy landscapes, glowing prairie skies and warm character portraits." Publ Wkly

Berne, Emma Carlson. Laura Ingalls Wilder; by Emma Carlson Berne. ABDO Pub. 2008 112p il map $22.95

Grades: 4 5 6 7   92

1. Authors, American 2. Frontier and pioneer life 3. Women authors
ISBN 978-1-59928-843-7; 1-59928-843-5
LC 2007012513

"Beginning in 1929 with the events that led up to the publication of Little House in the Big Woods, this readable biography further amplifies Wilder's life and correlates it with her books. . . . This volume is packed with relevant material, a time line, archival photographs, quotes from primary sources, and an official Web site." SLJ

Includes glossary and bibliographical references

Wilder, Laura Ingalls. A Little House traveler; writings from Laura Ingalls Wilder's journeys across America; by Laura Ingalls Wilder. HarperCollins 2006 344p il $16.99

Grades: 5 6 7 8   92

1. Authors, American 2. Women authors 3. United States—Description and travel
ISBN 978-0-06-072491-7   LC 2005014975

"This volume combines three Wilder travel diaries: *On the Way Home*, recounting the 1894 trip from South Dakota to Missouri, with husband Almanzo and daughter Rose; *West from Home*, featuring letters written by Laura to Almanzo during her 1915 solo visit to Rose in San Francisco; and *The Road Back*, highlighting Laura's previously unpublished record of a 1931 trip with Almanzo to De Smet, South Dakota, and the Black Hills. . . . This offers an amazing look at a beloved author, as well as a fascinating account of travel before interstate highways and air-conditioning." Booklist

Wilder, Laura Ingalls. West from home; letters of Laura Ingalls Wilder to Almanzo Wilder, San Francisco, 1915; edited by Roger Lea MacBride; historical setting by Margot Patterson Doss. Harper & Row 1974 124p il hardcover o.p. pa $5.99

Grades: 6 7 8 9   92

1. Women authors 2. Authors, American
ISBN 0-06-024110-1; 0-06-440081-6 (pa)
LC 73-14342

Wilder, Laura Ingalls, 1867-1957—*Continued*

This collection is "edited from letters sent to her beloved husband while Laura spent two months in late 1915 visiting their daughter and immersing herself in the sights of bustling San Francisco and the exciting Panama-Pacific Exposition. Wilder readers of all ages will lose themselves in this trip—the adults with nostalgia and wholesome pleasure, the youth with wonder and awe over the sights vividly described in her inimitable combination of homespun literary and journalistic styles." Child Book Rev Serv

Williams, J. W., 1929-

Barbour, Karen. Mr. Williams. Henry Holt and Co. 2005 29p il $16.95

Grades: K 1 2 3   **92**

1. African Americans 2. Louisiana 3. Country life

ISBN 0-8050-6773-6   LC 2004-22182

"Recounting stories told by J. W. Williams, a friend of her mother's, Barbour captures the essence of a black Louisiana farmer's life in the early 20th century. . . . The words are succinct but evocative of a larger picture. . . . The ink-and-gouache illustrations, punctuated with well-placed bits of fabric collage, are perfect." SLJ

Williams, Lindsey, 1987-

Houle, Michelle E. Lindsey Williams; gardening for impoverished families; [by] Michelle Houle. KidHaven Press 2008 48p il (Young heroes) lib bdg $27.45

Grades: 4 5 6 7   **92**

1. Food relief 2. Social action 3. Gardening

ISBN 978-0-7377-3867-4 (lib bdg); 0-7377-3867-7 (lib bdg)   LC 2007022923

This "introduces 20-year-old Lindsey Williams, who has won numerous awards, including the International Eco-Hero Award, for her groundbreaking work with agriculture and hunger issues. . . . Williams has developed growing techniques that produce more food using fewer natural resources. . . . The straightforward text, with many quotes from Williams, will draw children into the science and environmental issues." Booklist

Includes glossary and bibliographical references

Williams, Roger, 1604?-1683

Avi. Finding Providence: the story of Roger Williams; story by Avi; illustrations by James Watling. HarperCollins Pubs. 1997 46p il (I can read chapter book) hardcover o.p. pa $3.99

Grades: 2 3 4   **92**

1. United States—History—1600-1775, Colonial period 2. Rhode Island—History

ISBN 0-06-025179-4; 0-06-444216-0 (pa)

       LC 95-46360

After being forced to leave the Massachusetts Bay Colony, Roger Williams travels south and, with the help of the Narragansett Indians, founds Providence, Rhode Island

"Plentiful dialogue speeds the action along, and even the philosophical issues are cogently presented for young readers in the form of Williams' interrogation at the trial. Watling's watercolors have a roughhewn quality appropiate to the early colonies, and his grave figures are charged with tension." Bull Cent Child Books

Williams, Ted, 1918-2002

Bowen, Fred. No easy way; the story of Ted Williams and the last .400 season; illustrations by Charles S. Pyle. Dutton Children's Books 2010 unp il lib bdg $16.99

Grades: 1 2 3   **92**

1. Baseball—Biography

ISBN 978-0-525-47877-5 (lib bdg); 0-525-47877-9 (lib bdg)   LC 2009-17920

This recounts the 1941 baseball season in which Ted Williams hit .406 for the Boston Red Sox.

"Unlike many decades-old baseball stories, this one hasn't lost its appeal over the years, and Bowen makes the most of it in terms kids will understand. Pyle's illustrations, combined with vintage photographs, capture the drama of Williams at bat." Booklist

Williams, William Carlos, 1883-1963

Bryant, Jennifer. A river of words: the story of William Carlos Williams; written by Jen Bryant; illustrated by Melissa Sweet. Eerdmans Books for Young Readers 2008 unp il $17 *

Grades: 1 2 3 4   **92**

1. Poets, American 2. Physicians

ISBN 978-0-8028-5302-8; 0-8028-5302-1

       LC 2007-49347

A Caldecott Medal honor book, 2009

This picture book biography of William Carlos Williams traces childhood events that lead him to become a doctor and a poet.

Bryant's "simple, spare language matches her subject well. Sweet's mixed-media collages will draw varying age groups. . . . [This is an] inspiring title." Booklist

Winfrey, Oprah

Weatherford, Carole Boston. Oprah; the little speaker; illustrated by London Ladd. Marshall Cavendish Children 2010 unp il $17.99

Grades: K 1 2 3   **92**

1. Entertainers 2. African American women—Biography

ISBN 978-0-7614-5632-2; 0-7614-5632-5

       LC 2009006339

This picture book biography of Oprah Winfrey "focuses solely on her childhood. An author's note at the beginning sets the stage for the true rags-to-riches story about a poor girl on a Mississippi pig farm who became an entertainer, entrepreneur, and philanthropist. . . . The narrative portrays a bright, spunky child . . . while the soft-edged, acrylic illustrations paint a determined, soberfaced girl." Booklist

Westen, Robin. Oprah Winfrey; "I don't believe in failure.". Enslow Pubs. 2005 128p il (African-American biography library) lib bdg $31.93

Grades: 5 6 7 8   **92**

1. African American women—Biography 2. African American actors

ISBN 978-0-7660-2462-5 (lib bdg); 0-7660-2462-8 (lib bdg)   LC 2004016800

Winfrey, Oprah—*Continued*

A biography of the actress and TV personality

"Background information is included without being sensationalistic, yet it does not avoid controversy. . . . Students writing reports on modern-day African Americans will appreciate the presentation and content of this [book]." Voice Youth Advocates

Includes bibliographical references

Winkfield, Jimmy, 1882-1974

Hubbard, Crystal. The last Black king of the Kentucky Derby; the story of Jimmy Winkfield; by Crystal Hubbard; illustrated by Robert McGuire. Lee & Low Books 2008 unp il $17.95

Grades: 2 3 4   92

1. African American athletes 2. Horse racing

ISBN 978-1-58430-274-2; 1-58430-274-7

LC 2006039015

"A biography of Jimmy Winkfield, who battled racism and other obstacles on the road to becoming one of horseracing's best jockeys and, in 1902, the last African American to win the Kentucky Derby." Publisher's note

"Hubbard's text is richly informative and filled with exciting sensory details. . . . The stirring scenes of horses streaking down the track . . . will easily capture children's attention." Booklist

Wonder, Stevie

Troupe, Quincy. Little Stevie Wonder; by Quincy Troupe; illustrated by Lisa Cohen. Houghton Mifflin 2005 unp il $18

Grades: K 1 2 3   92

1. African American musicians 2. Blind

ISBN 0-618-34060-2   LC 2003-17703

Includes an audio CD with two songs

"This tribute introduces young readers to the life and music of . . . Stevie Wonder. Echoes from his song lyrics . . . highlight his early life and reveal the evolution of his musical genius. . . . The acrylic paintings perfectly match the joyful nature of the narrative." SLJ

Wong, Anna May, 1905-1961

Yoo, Paula. Shining star: the Anna May Wong story; by Paula Yoo; illustrated by Lin Wang. Lee & Low Books 2009 unp il $17.95

Grades: 2 3 4 5   92

1. Actors 2. Chinese Americans—Biography

ISBN 978-1-60060-259-7; 1-60060-259-2

LC 2008042673

"A biography of Chinese American film star Anna May Wong who, in spite of limited opportunities, achieved her dream of becoming an actress and worked to represent her race on screen in a truthful, positive manner." Publisher's note

"Lin Wang's . . . elegant paintings in muted hues capture the actress's emotions in her expressive eyes framed by dark bangs. . . . The conversational narrative uses many descriptive vignettes. . . . A fascinating account of the life of a determined actress." Publ Wkly

Wright, Orville, 1871-1948

Collins, Mary. Airborne: a photobiography of Wilbur and Orville Wright. National Geographic Soc. 2003 63p il maps $18.95

Grades: 4 5 6 7   92

1. Wright, Wilbur, 1867-1912 2. Aeronautics—History

ISBN 0-7922-6957-8   LC 2002-5279

Examines the lives of the Wright brothers and discusses their experiments and triumphs in the field of flight

"The well-chosen photos give readers a feel for Kitty Hawk—windy, sandy, solitary. This is an exceptionally well-informed picture of the Wright brothers and what their 100-year-old achievement really meant." SLJ

Dixon-Engel, Tara. The Wright brothers; first in flight; [by] Tara Dixon-Engel and Mike Jackson. Sterling 2007 128p il (Sterling biographies) $12.95; pa $5.95

Grades: 5 6 7 8   92

1. Wright, Wilbur, 1867-1912 2. Aeronautics—History

ISBN 978-1-4027-4954-4; 1-4027-4954-6; 978-1-4027-3231-7 (pa); 1-4027-3231-7 (pa)

LC 2007003631

This "follows the Wright brothers from their early lives through first diagrams to their historic flight. . . . [The book provides] clear, concise information in an easy-to-follow format with captioned photographs and illustrations on most pages." SLJ

Includes glossary and bibliographical references

Freedman, Russell. The Wright brothers: how they invented the airplane; with original photographs by Wilbur and Orville Wright. Holiday House 1991 129p il hardcover o.p. pa $14.95 *

Grades: 5 6 7 8 9 10   92

1. Wright, Wilbur, 1867-1912 2. Aeronautics—History

ISBN 0-8234-0875-2; 0-8234-1082-X (pa)

LC 90-48440

A Newbery Medal honor book, 1992

In this "combination of photography and text, Freedman reveals the frustrating, exciting, and ultimately successful journey of these two brothers from their bicycle shop in Dayton, Ohio, to their Kitty Hawk flights and beyond. . . . An essential purchase for younger YAs." Voice Youth Advocates

Includes bibliographical references

Old, Wendie. To fly: the story of the Wright brothers; illustrated by Robert Andrew Parker. Clarion Bks. 2002 48p il $17

Grades: 3 4 5   92

1. Wright, Wilbur, 1867-1912 2. Aeronautics—History

ISBN 0-618-13347-X   LC 2001-47219

Traces the work that the two Wright brothers did together to develop the first machine-powered aircraft

"Old writes in a clear, straightforward manner, using intriguing details to enliven the account. . . . The innocence and optimism reflected in illustrations catch the tone of the story." Booklist

Includes bibliographical references

Wright, Orville, 1871-1948—*Continued*

O'Sullivan, Robyn. The Wright brothers fly; by Robyn O'Sullivan. National Geographic 2007 40p il (National Geographic history chapters) lib bdg $17.90

Grades: 2 3 4   **92**

1. Wright, Wilbur, 1867-1912 2. Aeronautics—History
ISBN 978-1-4263-0188-9   LC 2007007895

This history of the Wright brothers is "nicely illustrated with photos. . . . [It is] just right for emerging chapter-book readers. . . . Useful . . . for reports . . . and interesting pleasure reading." SLJ

Includes glossary and bibliographical references

Wright, Patience Lovell, 1725-1786

Shea, Pegi Deitz. Patience Wright; America's first sculptor, and revolutionary spy; [by] Pegi Deitz Shea; illustrated by Bethanne Andersen. Henry Holt 2007 unp il $17.95 *

Grades: 4 5 6   **92**

1. Sculptors 2. Women artists 3. Spies 4. United States—History—1775-1783, Revolution
ISBN 978-0-8050-6770-5; 0-8050-6770-1
     LC 2005021696

A biography of Patience Wright, born in 1725, who became a sculptor and a spy for the American colonies

"Shea writes with a dynamic simplicity that brings Wright to life. At the same time, she seamlessly incorporates information about the war and events leading up to it into her text." Booklist

Wright, Wilbur, 1867-1912

Collins, Mary. Airborne: a photobiography of Wilbur and Orville Wright. See entry under Wright, Orville, 1871-1948

Dixon-Engel, Tara. The Wright brothers. See entry under Wright, Orville, 1871-1948

Freedman, Russell. The Wright brothers: how they invented the airplane. See entry under Wright, Orville, 1871-1948

Old, Wendie. To fly: the story of the Wright brothers. See entry under Wright, Orville, 1871-1948

O'Sullivan, Robyn. The Wright brothers fly. See entry under Wright, Orville, 1871-1948

Yep, Laurence

Yep, Laurence. The lost garden. Beech Tree Books 1996 116p il pa $5.99

Grades: 5 6 7 8   **92**

1. Authors, American 2. Chinese Americans—Biography
ISBN 0-688-13701-6   LC 95053801

First published 1991 by Julian Messner

The author describes how he grew up as a Chinese American in San Francisco and how he came to use his writing to celebrate his family and his ethnic heritage

"The writing is warm, wry, and humorous. . . . The Lost Garden will be welcomed as a literary autobiography for children and, more, a thoughtful probing into what it means to be an American." SLJ

Yolen, Jane

McGinty, Alice B. Meet Jane Yolen. PowerKids Press 2003 24p il (About the author) lib bdg $18.75

Grades: 1 2 3   **92**

1. Authors, American 2. Women authors
ISBN 0-8239-6407-8   LC 2002-116

A short biography of Jane Yolen, a prolific and well-known writer of juvenile literature

This "book is filled with vintage black-and-white and full-color photographs of . . . [Yolen] from early childhood to the present. Reprints of book covers, illustrations, and excerpts from the authors' works are also found throughout." SLJ

Includes glossary

York, ca. 1775-ca. 1815

Pringle, Laurence P. American slave, American hero; York of the Lewis and Clark Expedition; [by] Laurence Pringle; illustrations by Cornelius Van Wright and Ying-Hwa Hu. Calkins Creek Books 2005 40p il $17.95 *

Grades: 3 4 5   **92**

1. Lewis and Clark Expedition (1804-1806) 2. West (U.S.)—Exploration 3. Slavery—United States
ISBN 978-1-59078-282-8; 1-59078-282-8
     LC 2005037352

"With a detailed text and handsome watercolor paintings, this illustrated biography celebrates the heroic role of Clark's personal slave on the famous expedition out west in 1804, with the horror of slavery in the background." Booklist

Includes bibliographical references

Zaharias, Babe Didrikson, 1911-1956

Freedman, Russell. Babe Didrikson Zaharias; the making of a champion. Clarion Bks. 1999 192p il $18

Grades: 5 6 7 8 9 10   **92**

1. Women athletes
ISBN 0-395-63367-2   LC 98-50208

A biography of Babe Didrikson, who broke records in golf, track and field, and other sports, at a time when there were few opportunities for female athletes

"Freedman's measured yet lively style captures the spirit of the great athlete. . . . Plenty of black-and-white photos capture Babe's spirit and dashing good looks; the documentation . . . is impeccable." Horn Book

Includes bibliographical references

Zuckerberg, Mark

Woog, Adam. Mark Zuckerberg, Facebook creator. KidHaven Press 2009 48p il map (Innovators) $28.25

Grades: 4 5 6 7   **92**

1. Facebook Inc. 2. Businesspeople
ISBN 978-0-7377-4566-5; 0-7377-4566-5
     LC 2009013458

"This brisk, readable [biography the creator of Facebook] . . . presents an appealing picture of the shy, lonely future billionaire. . . This is fascinating and relevant stuff." Booklist

Includes bibliographical references

929 Genealogy, names, insignia

Taylor, Maureen, 1955-
Through the eyes of your ancestors. Houghton Mifflin 1999 86p il hardcover o.p. pa $8.95
Grades: 4 5 6 7 **929**
1. Genealogy
ISBN 0-395-86980-3; 0-395-86982-X (pa)
LC 98-8776
Discusses genealogy, the study of one's family, examining how such an interest develops, how to get started, how to use family stories and keepsakes, where to get help, and the positive effects of such study
"Motivated young researchers with adult help will find the book a good starting place." SLJ
Includes bibliographical references

929.9 Flags. Forms of insignia and identification

Allen, Kathy
The first American flag; illustrated by Siri Weber Feeney. Picture Window Books 2010 32p il map (Our American story) lib bdg $23.99
Grades: 2 3 4 **929.9**
1. Flags—United States
ISBN 978-1-4048-5541-0 (lib bdg); 1-4048-5541-6 (lib bdg)
LC 2009-6892
An introduction to the American flag and its symbolism discusses the features and history of early American flags
This title is "illustrated with well-executed, full-page, color illustrations, maps, and photos. . . . [It has] clearly written information that students can use for either leisure reading or reports." SLJ
Includes glossary and bibliographical references

Bateman, Teresa
Red, white, blue, and Uncle who? the stories behind some of America's patriotic symbols; illustrated by John O'Brien. Holiday House 2001 64p il $16.95; pa $6.95 *
Grades: 4 5 6 7 **929.9**
1. National emblems 2. National monuments
ISBN 0-8234-1285-7; 0-8234-1784-0 (pa)
LC 00-57258
This "volume presents 17 'patriotic symbols,' an umbrella term that encompasses everything from the flag to Uncle Sam, from Mount Rushmore to the Korean War Memorial. Bateman finds plenty of interesting information to share about each symbol or site, and browsers will be entertained by the many stories of origination, construction, and history." Booklist
Includes bibliographical references

Bednar, Sylvie
Flags of the world. Abrams Books for Young Readers 2009 187p il $19.95 *
Grades: 4 5 6 7 **929.9**
1. Flags 2. Geography
ISBN 978-0-8109-8010-5; 0-8109-8010-X
LC 2008-45923
"Organized by continent, this book takes a close look at the artwork and meaning of each country's flag. A large color image of the flag is accompanied by entries about the state's capital, currency, official language, area, and highest geographical point. More than 100 captioned illustrations add fascinating facts as well. . . . The consistent layout of the book and its accessible information will create an ease of both student use and comprehension." SLJ

Jackson, Donna M., 1959-
The name game; a look behind the labels; illustrated by Ted Stearn. Viking 2009 64p il $16.99
Grades: 4 5 6 7 8 **929.9**
1. Names
ISBN 978-0-670-01197-1; 0-670-01197-5
LC 2008-37705
"All kinds of entertaining and random facts are found in this quirky book. Tips for naming pets and companies are given, in a chapter each, along with hints for remembering people's names, explanations of conventions in other countries, and the system of choosing hurricane monikers. Sports, people, and geographic locations all have different sections. Black-and-white cartoons add a bit of humor. Students will navigate this book with ease." SLJ

World Book's encyclopedia of flags. World Book 2007 12v il map set $347
Grades: 4 5 6 7 **929.9**
1. Flags 2. Reference books
ISBN 978-0-7166-7901-1; 0-7166-7901-9
First published 2005
"This set includes articles on flags of every nation in the world as well as on historical flags and flags of organizations and political groups. . . . With more than 380 flags, this set would be a valuable resource for students in elementary and middle school." Booklist [review of 2005 edition]
Includes bibliographical references

930 History of ancient world (to ca.499)

Adams, Simon
The Kingfisher atlas of the ancient world; illustrated by Katherine Baxter. Kingfisher 2006 44p il $15.95
Grades: 4 5 6 7 **930**
1. Ancient civilization 2. Historical geography 3. Reference books
ISBN 978-0-7534-5914-0; 0-7534-5914-0
"Featuring seventeen . . . hand-illustrated maps and . . . with . . . information about ancient civilizations

Adams, Simon—*Continued*
and peoples, this is [a] . . . pictorial guide to what the
world was like between 10,000 B.C. and A.D. 1000.
Each . . . map shows the major sites from a particular
civilization or group of civilizations. . . . Feature spreads
use photographs of cultural and architectural artifacts, as
well as additional information, to focus in greater depth
on the key cultures of Egypt, Greece, and Rome." Publisher's note

Merrill, Yvonne Young
  Hands-on ancient people. Kits Pub. 2003-2004
2v il map pa ea $20
Grades: 5 6 7 8   **930**
  1. Ancient civilization 2. Handicraft
  ISBN 0-9643177-8-8 (v1); 0-9643177-9-6 (v2)
  Contents: v1 Art activities about Mesopotamia, Egypt,
and Islam; v2 Art activities about Minoans, Trojans, Ancient Greeks, Etruscans and Romans
  Each volume offers instructions for creating 60 objects
based on ancient artifacts such as a cardboard model of
the Parthenon, masks, Greek vases, war shields, mosaics,
toys, banners, tomb paintings, a wheel, board games, and
the ziggurat.
  "These exciting art projects are illustrated with dramatic full-page, full-color photographs. Each activity occupies an inviting spread with a list of materials, clear
instructions, and background information on the artifacts
and the culture they represent." SLJ [review of v2]
  Includes bibliographical references

930.1   Archaeology

Deem, James M.
  Bodies from the bog. Houghton Mifflin 1998
42p il hardcover o.p. pa $5.95 *
Grades: 4 5 6 7   **930.1**
  1. Mummies 2. Prehistoric peoples 3. Archeology
  ISBN 0-395-85784-8; 0-618-35402-6 (pa)
                                        LC 97-12010
  Describes the discovery of bog bodies in northern Europe and the evidence which their remains reveal about
themselves and the civilizations in which they lived
  "The text is engaging and accessible, and the starkly
dramatic photos are given dignity by the spacious and
understated page design." Horn Book Guide
  Includes bibliographical references

Getz, David, 1957-
  Frozen man; illustrated by Peter McCarty. Holt
& Co. 1994 68p il maps hardcover o.p. pa $10.99
*
Grades: 5 6 7 8   **930.1**
  1. Mummies 2. Prehistoric peoples 3. Archeology
  ISBN 0-8050-3261-4; 0-8050-4645-3 (pa)
                                        LC 94-9109
  "A Redfeather book"
  "This is an account of the mummified stone-age
corpse who was found in Austria in 1991. . . . Getz's
generally well-organized information and smooth exposi-
tion makes the effort to understand the Iceman, as this

book calls him, into an intriguing detective story. This
could well stimulate the interest of kids who didn't think
they liked science or archeology. Black-and-white drawings include useful maps and diagrams." Bull Cent Child
Books
  Includes glossary and bibliographical references

McIntosh, Jane
  Archeology; written by Jane McIntosh. Dorling
Kindersley 2000 63p il (DK eyewitness books)
$15.99; lib bdg $19.99
Grades: 4 5 6 7   **930.1**
  1. Archeology
  ISBN 0-7894-5864-0; 0-7894-6605-8 (lib bdg)
  First published 1994 by Knopf
  This book contains "photographs, illustrations, and
terms covering the specialized field of archeology. Inside
are a contents page, an index, and 26 sections of two to
three pages each, covering . . . the various techniques
used by archeologists and historians to learn about past
civilizations." Sci Books Films [review of 1994 edition]

Panchyk, Richard, 1970-
  Archaeology for kids; uncovering the mysteries
of our past: 25 activities. Chicago Review Press
2001 146p il map pa $14.95
Grades: 5 6 7 8   **930.1**
  1. Archeology 2. Ancient civilization 3. Antiquities
  ISBN 1-55652-395-5   LC 2001-42134
  Twenty five activities support an overview of the science of archaeology as well as some of the secrets it has
revealed from ancient civilizations throughout the world
  "Panchyk explains things clearly and vividly. . . . Illustrations are plentiful, and suggested activities are practical and illuminate the subject matter well." Booklist
  Includes bibliographical references

Peterson, Judy Monroe
  Digging up history; archaeologists; [by] Judy
Monroe Peterson. PowerKids Press 2009 24p il
(Extreme scientists) lib bdg $21.25 *
Grades: 2 3 4 5   **930.1**
  1. Archeology 2. Antiquities 3. Excavations (Archeology)
  ISBN 978-1-4042-4523-5 (lib bdg); 1-4042-4523-5 (lib
bdg)   LC 2008-6837
  Looks at the work of archaeologists, including their
working conditions and the scientific discoveries they
have made
  "The author does a great job of capturing the scope of
archeology digs, as well as introducing the job-related
jargon and vocabulary. . . . Every chapter is accompanied by a full-page color photo of an actual archeological
find or site, and each photo is topped off with an easy-
to-read caption that will draw the reader into going on
to the next find. . . . Both school and public libraries
should add this volume to their collections to complement career or science research by young readers." Libr
Media Connect
  Includes glossary

931 China to 420 A.D.

Ball, Jacqueline A.

Ancient China; archaeology unlocks the secrets of China's past; by Jacqueline Ball and Richard Levey, Robert Murowchick, consultant. National Geographic 2006 c2007 64p il (National Geographic investigates) $17.95; lib bdg $27.90 *

Grades: 5 6 7 8   **931**

    1. China—Antiquities 2. China—Civilization

    ISBN 978-0-7922-7783-5; 0-7922-7783-X; 978-0-7922-7858-6 (lib bdg); 0-7922-7856-9 (lib bdg)

"This volume spotlights archaeological finds from Ancient China. . . . While the discussions of archaeology will hold readers' interest, the accompanying illustrations steal the show." Booklist

Cole, Joanna

Ms. Frizzle's adventures: Imperial China; illustrated by Bruce Degen. Scholastic Press 2005 39p il $16.95; pa $6.99

Grades: 2 3 4   **931**

    1. China—Civilization 2. China—History

    ISBN 0-590-10822-0; 0-590-10823-9 (pa)

Ms. Frizzle and her tour group are transported to China 1000 years in the past, where they learn how rice, tea and silk are grown and harvested, and visit the Emperor in the Forbidden City

"Readers will savor sidebars touting Chinese contributions to society, pore over Degen's delightfully cluttered compositions and lovely chinoiserie embellishments." Booklist

Dean, Arlan

Terra-cotta soldiers; army of stone; [by] Arlan Dean. Children's Press 2005 48p il map (Digging up the past) lib bdg $23; pa $6.95

Grades: 4 5 6 7   **931**

    1. Ch'in Shih-huang, Emperor of China, 259-210 B.C.—Tomb 2. China—Antiquities

    ISBN 0-516-25124-4 (lib bdg); 0-516-25093-0 (pa)

    LC 2005002699

"Hi-lo interest books"

This "discusses ancient Chinese history, including the first emperor and his tomb, which was found to contain 8000 clay soldiers, made to protect him in his afterlife. Beliefs about life after death are explained. The author also discusses Qin Shi Huangdis role in creating the Great Wall." SLJ

This consists of "short chapters, with text sharing space with mostly snapshot-size photos. . . . Reluctant readers at ease with the High Interest series format may want to start with this." Booklist

Includes glossary and bibliographical references

O'Connor, Jane, 1947-

The emperor's silent army; terracotta warriors of Ancient China. Viking 2002 48p il $17.99 *

Grades: 4 5 6 7   **931**

    1. Ch'in Shih-huang, Emperor of China, 259-210 B.C.—Tomb 2. China—Antiquities

    ISBN 0-670-03512-2   LC 2001-46900

Describes the archaeological discovery of thousands of life-sized terracotta warrior statues in northern China in 1974, and discusses the emperor who had them created and placed near his tomb

"This intriguing book is enhanced by beautiful illustrations—pictures of stone engravings, colorful paintings, drawings, and maps—while numerous photographs show the clay soldiers from different perspectives. . . . The author's writing style is entertaining, yet informative." Book Rep

Includes bibliographical references

Schomp, Virginia, 1953-

The ancient Chinese; written by Virginia Schomp. Franklin Watts 2004 112p il map (People of the ancient world) $29.50; pa $9.95

Grades: 5 6 7 8   **931**

    1. China—Civilization

    ISBN 0-531-11817-7; 0-531-16737-2 (pa)

    LC 2004-2174

Contents: At the center of the world; Kings and emperors; Civil servants and nobles; Philosophers and holy men; Peasant farmers and soldiers; Artisans and silk makers; Merchants and traders; Inventors, scientists, and healers; Writers and artists; The legacy of ancient China

"Focusing mainly on the Shang, Zhou, Qin, and Han dynasties, this book explores ancient China through its social structure. It takes a look at its people and details the duties of an emperor, the activities of a merchant, and . . . more. It also describes some of the discoveries and writings that have led to our present-day understanding of this . . . civilization." Publisher's note

"Crisp reproductions of visuals, along with impressive ancilliary content. . . . help make [this title] among the best available on ancient [China]." Booklist

Includes bibliographical references

Shuter, Jane, 1955-

Ancient China; [by] Jane Shuter. Heinemann Library 2006 48p il map (Excavating the past) lib bdg $31.43

Grades: 4 5 6   **931**

    1. China—Civilization 2. China—Antiquities 3. Excavations (Archeology)—China

    ISBN 1-4034-5995-9   LC 2005009178

"Ancient China covers the region's history from the first single kingdom dynasty, Xia (2205 B.C.E. to 1700 B.C.E), to the conquering of China by Mongols in C.E.1279. Shuter includes a history of archaeology conducted by Westerners and by the Chinese government. Artifacts and a few well-preserved burial sites reveal lifestyles of the powerful and wealthy. Short chapters describe living conditions of the poor and of skilled workers as well." SLJ

Includes bibliographical references

932 Egypt to 640 A.D.

Adams, Simon
Ancient Egypt. Kingfisher 2006 53p il (Kingfisher voyages) $15.95
Grades: 4 5 6   **932**
1. Egypt—Civilization
ISBN 978-0-7534-6027-6; 0-7534-6027-0
      LC 2005033938
"Adams guides readers on a journey through this ancient civilization as seen through the eyes of Egyptologist Dr. Kent Weeks. Using clear language and a light, upbeat tone, the author explores the history of Egypt. . . . This . . . book incorporates visually appealing translucent overlays and foldout pages that highlight and help to explain some of the technical information." SLJ
Includes bibliographical references

Biesty, Stephen
Egypt in spectacular cross-section; text by Stewart Ross. Scholastic Nonfiction 2005 28p il $18.99 *
Grades: 4 5 6 7   **932**
1. Egypt—Antiquities 2. Egypt—Civilization
ISBN 0-439-74537-3   LC 2004-59185
"Employing his large, trademark cross-section or cutaway style illustrations that are full of detail and bustling small figures, Biesty, supported by Ross, uses the fictional construct of family members traveling to a wedding as a way of exploring various aspects of daily life in Egypt around the year 1230 B.C.E." SLJ
Includes glossary

Bolton, Anne
Pyramids and mummies. Simon & Schuster 2008 unp il map $21.99
Grades: 3 4 5 6   **932**
1. Mummies 2. Pyramids 3. Egypt
ISBN 978-1-4169-5873-4; 1-4169-5873-8
      LC 2008-299284
"Published in a triangle form"
"The illustrations are an alluring mix of gold, images from ancient walls, cutaway views, and dried-out bodies. Almost hidden beneath all the visual glamour is a . . . text that begins with the death(s) of Osiris, ends with a game of 'Asps and Ladders,' and in between touches on the preparation of mummies, the history and purposes of Egyptian pyramids, animal mummies, sphinxes, King Tut, and other related topics. All in all, an ephemeral but artfully designed showstopper." SLJ

Giblin, James, 1933-
Secrets of the Sphinx; by James Cross Giblin; illustrated by Bagram Ibatoulline. Scholastic Press 2004 47p il map $17.95 *
Grades: 4 5 6 7   **932**
1. Egypt—Antiquities 2. Egypt—Civilization
ISBN 0-590-09847-0   LC 2003-19666
Discusses some of Egypt's most famous artifacts and monuments, including the pyramids, the Rosetta Stone, and, especially, the Great Sphinx, presenting research and speculation about their origins and their future
"In his signature plain style the . . . author presents a wealth of scholarship. . . . He vividly conveys the drama of recent discoveries. . . . The photorealistic gouache and watercolor illustrations are beautiful." Booklist
Includes bibliographical references

Harris, Geraldine, 1951-
Ancient Egypt. 3rd ed. Chelsea House 2007 96p il map (Cultural atlas for young people) $35
Grades: 5 6 7 8   **932**
1. Egypt—Civilization 2. Egypt—Antiquities
ISBN 978-0-8160-6823-4; 0-8160-6823-2
First published 1990
Maps, charts, illustrations, and text explore the history and culture of ancient Egypt.
"Filled with excellent captioned, color maps, photographs, and illustrations of primary source materials. There are sidebars, gazetteers, and timelines of events in politics, war, art, technology, etc." Libr Media Connect
Includes glossary and bibliographical references

Hawass, Zahi A.
Curse of the pharaohs; my adventures with mummies. National Geographic Society 2004 144p il $19.95; lib bdg $29.90 *
Grades: 5 6 7 8   **932**
1. Egypt—Antiquities 2. Archeology
ISBN 0-7922-6963-2; 0-7922-6665-X (lib bdg)
      LC 2003-18813
"Hawass delineates and attempts to debunk the alleged curses attached to the entering of the pharaohs' tombs." Publ Wkly
"Hawass' writing is passionate, informative, and kid friendly. . . . Even so, what will probably most attract aspiring archeologists are the National Geographic-quality photographs, which lend tantalizing immediacy to real-life tales from the crypt." Booklist
Includes glossary and bibliographical references

Tutankhamun; the mystery of the boy king; by Zahi Hawass. National Geographic 2005 64p il $17.95; lib bdg $27.90 *
Grades: 3 4 5 6   **932**
1. Tutankhamen, King of Egypt 2. Egypt—Civilization 3. Egypt—History
ISBN 0-7922-8354-6; 0-7922-8355-4 (lib bdg)
      LC 2004-15002
Contents: The great discovery; Egypt before Tutankhamun; Tutankhamun, king of Egypt; The life of the boy king; Death and burial; After King Tut
"Hawass, director of excavations at the Giza pyramids and head of Egypt's archaeological council, . . . offers a solid summary . . . of the complex and controversial 18th dynasty in which Tut lived. . . . Black-and-white shots from the past join rich color photographs that almost glow. Especially marvelous is a stunning recreation, employing current reconstructive techniques, of what Tut might have looked like. . . . A first-rate investigation enriched by beautiful artwork." SLJ
Includes bibliographical references

Kennett, David, 1959-
Pharaoh; life and afterlife of a God. Walker & Company 2008 48p il map $18.95; lib bdg $19.85 *

Grades: 3 4 5 6   932
1. Egypt—Civilization 2. Egypt—Religion
ISBN   978-0-8027-9567-0;   0-8027-9567-6; 978-0-8027-9568-7 (lib bdg); 0-8027-9568-4 (lib bdg)
LC 2007-24236
"This extraordinarily handsome [book] delves deeply into the various roles of the pharoah, and, in the process, gives readers a much fuller understanding of Egyptian life. . . . One of the best things about this is the way the narrative moves simply and logically from topics such as flooding to farming and trading. But as fine as the text is, it more than meets its match in the masterful artwork. . . . There is much to see here, and children will want to look at the book again and again." Booklist

Langley, Andrew
Ancient Egypt; [by] Andrew Langley. Raintree 2005 48p il map (History in art) lib bdg $31.43
Grades: 4 5 6 7   932
1. Egyptian art 2. Egypt—Civilization
ISBN 978-1-4109-0518-5 (lib bdg); 1-4109-0518-7 (lib bdg)   LC 2004-7524
Contents: Art of ancient Egypt; Art as evidence; Beginnings; The old kingdom; The middle kingdom; The new kingdom; Land of the pharaohs; Building the pyramids; Trade and empire; The Valley of the Kings; Greeks and Romans; Homes and families; Eating and drinking; At work; Entertainment; Scribes and hieroglyphs; Gods and the afterlife; Mummification; Burial; Priests and rituals
This book has "a depth of content that is unusual in art-history books for this age group. . . . [It] is amply illustrated with full-color photographs and reproductions. . . . Well-written, informative." SLJ
Includes bibliographical references

Logan, Claudia
The 5,000-year-old puzzle; solving a mystery of Ancient Egypt; illustrated by Melissa Sweet. Farrar, Straus & Giroux 2001 41p il $17 *
Grades: 2 3 4   932
1. Reisner, George Andrew, 1867-1942 2. Egypt—Civilization 3. Excavations (Archeology)—Egypt
ISBN 0-374-32335-6   LC 00-60243
"Melanie Kroupa books"
With the cooperation of the Museum of Fine Arts, Boston
An account of Dr. George Reisner's 1925 discovery and excavation of a secret tomb in Giza, Egypt, based on archival documents and records, but told through the fictionalized experiences of a young boy named Will who accompanies his father on the dig.
"There's considerable value to the sidebar information . . . and the journal-style exposition of the excavation's painstaking pace. Snapshots and photographed artifacts from the expedition mingle with Sweet's golden acrylic and watercolor scenes, and readers who patiently sift through the fictional bits will be rewarded with an intriguing glimpse of an important excavation." Bull Cent Child Books

Perl, Lila
The ancient Egyptians; written by Lila Perl. Franklin Watts 2004 112p il map (People of the ancient world) $29.50; pa $9.95 *
Grades: 5 6 7 8   932
1. Egypt—Civilization
ISBN 0-531-12345-6; 0-531-16738-0 (pa)
LC 2004-1940
Contents: How we know about ancient Egypt; Farmers, bakers, and brewers; Priests and scribes; Kings, queens, and pharaohs; Builders in stone; Quarrymen and craft workers; Warriors and captives; Mummy makers; The legacy of ancient Egypt
"Crisp reproductions of visuals, along with impressive ancillary content. . . . help make [this title] among the best available on ancient [Egypt]." Booklist
Includes bibliographical references

Rubalcaba, Jill
Ancient Egypt; archaeology unlocks the secrets of Egypt's past; by Jill Rubalcaba. National Geographic 2007 64p il map (National Geographic investigates) $17.95; lib bdg $27.90 *
Grades: 5 6 7 8   932
1. Egypt—Civilization 2. Egypt—Antiquities 3. Excavations (Archeology)—Egypt
ISBN   0-7922-7784-8;   978-0-7922-7784-2; 0-7922-7857-7 (lib bdg); 978-0-7922-7857-3 (lib bdg)
LC 2006032111
This describes how archeologists have learned about Ancient Egypt.
This offers "the beautiful photography and illustrations characteristic of the National Geographic Society, [a] well-written [text] and sidebars, and information on recent archaeological finds." SLJ
Includes bibliographical references

Taylor, John H.
Mummy; the inside story. Abrams 2004 48p il map pa $14.95 *
Grades: 5 6 7 8   932
1. Mummies 2. Egypt—Antiquities
ISBN 0-8109-9181-0
Using non-invasive cutting-edge technology, this exhibit by the British Museum reveals the secrets of one mummy, the priest Nesperennub, while leaving him undisturbed.
"There are many excellent mummy books available, but this one explores the impact and potential of cutting-edge technology especially well." SLJ

Van Vleet, Carmella
Great Ancient Egypt projects you can build yourself. Nomad 2006 122p il (Build it yourself series) pa $14.95
Grades: 4 5 6   932
1. Egypt—Civilization 2. Handicraft
ISBN 0-9771294-5-4
"The fascinating text in this collection of 30 projects is supplemented by sepia-colored illustrations or photos on each page. . . . The projects are tied to many aspects

Van Vleet, Carmella—*Continued*
of this civilization, including the Nile River, agriculture, craftsmanship, pyramids, mummies, family, farming, bartering, the Egyptian calendar, Royal Library of Alexandria, temples, hieroglyphs, and more." SLJ

Includes bibliographical references

Weitzman, David L., 1936-
Pharaoh's boat; written and illustrated by David Weitzman. Houghton Mifflin Harcourt 2009 unp il map $17 *
Grades: 4 5 6 7   **932**
   1. Cheops, King of Egypt, fl. 2900-2877 B.C.
2. Ships 3. Egypt—Civilization
   ISBN 978-0-547-05341-7; 0-547-05341-X
                 LC 2008036081
"Weitzman recounts the construction of a boat made for the Pharaoh Cheops and discusses its rediscovery and restoration in the 20th century. He weaves the history, texts, mythology, and customs of ancient Egypt into an effective narrative. . . . The volume's stylized illustrations are inspired by the two-dimensional depictions from ancient Egyptian art. The paintings' earth tones, accentuated by bright greens and blues, are both appropriate for the subject matter and pleasing to the eye." SLJ

Whiting, Jim, 1943-
Threat to ancient Egyptian treasures; by Jim Whiting. Mitchell Lane Publishers 2007 32p il (On the verge of extinction: crisis in the environment) lib bdg $25.70
Grades: 3 4 5   **932**
   1. Egypt—Antiquities
   ISBN 978-1-58415-588-1   LC 2007000817
"A Robbie reader"
This describes dangers to ancient Egyptian archeological sites and artifacts, including sand storms, air pollution, flooding, and human activity.
"Short chapters, large font, and pronunciation guides to key words engage children doing research, but the depth of information is not compromised. . . . Colorful, up-close photographs are accompanied by satisfying explanatory captions." SLJ

Includes glossary and bibliographical references

934   India to 647 A.D.

Schomp, Virginia, 1953-
Ancient India; written by Virginia Schomp. Franklin Watts 2005 112p il map (People of the ancient world) lib bdg $30.50; pa $9.95
Grades: 5 6 7 8   **934**
   1. India—Civilization
   ISBN 0-531-12379-0 (lib bdg); 0-531-16846-8 (pa)
                 LC 2004-25156
Contents: Brahman priests; Kings, queens, and princes; Government leaders and warriors; Farmers and merchants; Servants, laborers, and craftspeople; Outcastes and slaves; Poets and playwrights
This examines the society of ancient India through its "literature, artifacts, and documents. Religion, farming,

levels of society, art, government, and fine arts are covered in [this] well-written and attractive [book]. . . . Quality full-color photos and reproductions on glossy pages will give readers insight into the daily lives, arts, and contributions of [this culture]." SLJ

Includes bibliographical references

935   Mesopotamia and Iranian Plateau to 637 A.D.

Gruber, Beth
Ancient Iraq; archaeology unlocks the secrets of Iraq's past; by Beth Gruber; Tony Wilkinson, consultant. National Geographic 2007 64p il map (National Geographic investigates) $17.95; lib bdg $27.90 *
Grades: 5 6 7 8   **935**
   1. Iraq—Antiquities 2. Excavations (Archeology)—Iraq 3. Iraq—Civilization
   ISBN 978-0-7922-5382-2; 978-0-7922-5383-9 (lib bdg)   LC 2006032109
This explores the "world of ancient Iraq, in the region once known as Mesopotamia, the cradle of civilization. Join scientists as they study the Citadel in northern Iraq; explore the ancient city of Nineveh; and see how ancient treasures help scientists reassemble the mosaic-like puzzle of Iraq's past." Publisher's note

Includes bibliographical references

Schomp, Virginia, 1953-
Ancient Mesopotamia; the Sumerians, Babylonians, and Assyrians; written by Virginia Schomp. Franklin Watts 2004 112p il map (People of the ancient world) lib bdg $30.50; pa $9.95
Grades: 5 6 7 8   **935**
   1. Iraq—Civilization
   ISBN 0-531-11818-5 (lib bdg); 0-531-16741-0 (pa)
                 LC 2004-1947
Contents: Cradle of civilization; The warrior-kings; Nobles, government officials, and priests; Merchants and traders; Artisans and artists; Peasant farmers; Soldiers and slaves; Doctors and scientists; Scribes and poets; The legacy of ancient Mesopotamia
"This book explores the cultures of ancient Mesopotamia through their social structure. It takes a look at the people and details the duties of a king, the activities of a peasant farmer, and . . . more. It also describes some of the discoveries and writings that have led to our present-day understanding of this . . . civilization." Publisher's note
"Crisp reproductions of visuals, along with impressive ancillary content . . . help make [this title] among the best available on ancient [Mesopotamia]." Booklist

Includes bibliographical references

Shuter, Jane, 1955-
Mesopotamia; [by] Jane Shuter. Heinemann Library 2006 48p il map (Excavating the past) lib bdg $31.43
Grades: 4 5 6   **935**
   1. Iraq—Antiquities 2. Sumerians 3. Excavations (Archeology)—Iraq
   ISBN 1-4034-5998-3   LC 2005009177

Shuter, Jane, 1955-—*Continued*

Contents: Archaeology and Mesopotamia; Rediscovering the Sumerians; The importance of writing; City-states; What was a city like?; Outside the city; Beliefs and burials; Temples; Burial and the afterlife; Royal tombs; Daily life; Skilled work; Travel and trade; Archaeology in modern Iraq

"Photos, maps, diagrams, and sidebars combine with an accessible text to demonstrate the roles of archaeological discoveries and scientific advancement in providing an accurate history of [this] ancient civilization." Horn Book Guide

936   Europe north and west of Italian peninsula to ca. 499 A.D.

Aronson, Marc

If stones could speak; unlocking the secrets of Stonehenge; by Marc Aronson with the generous cooperation of Mike Parker Pearson and the Riverside Project. National Geographic 2010 64p il map lib bdg $17.95 *

Grades: 4 5 6 7   936

1. Pearson, Mike Parker 2. Stonehenge (England) 3. Excavations (Archeology)—England 4. Archeology

ISBN 978-1-4263-0600-6; 1-4263-0600-8

"Aronson investigates the work of archaeologist Mike Parker Pearson and his controversial theory that Stonehenge is but one end of a memorial ritual pathway that would have had an equivalent wood structure at the other end. . . . Time lines, resource lists, and photos of researchers at work add even more value to this informative, thought-provoking study. A uniquely perceptive look at how real science works." Booklist

Includes bibliographical references

Calvert, Patricia, 1931-

The ancient Celts; written by Patricia Calvert. Watts 2005 112p il map (People of the ancient world) lib bdg $30.50; pa $9.95

Grades: 5 6 7 8   936

1. Celts

ISBN 0-531-12359-6 (lib bdg); 0-531-16845-X (pa)

This book portrays the lives of the ancient Celts "by examining their arts, culture, economy, government, religious beliefs, and societal [structure]. . . . Attractively designed and illustrated, the [book features] excellent color representations of architecture, artwork, and other cultural and historical artifacts." SLJ

Includes bibliographical references

Green, Jen

Ancient Celts; archaeology unlocks the secrets of the Celts' past; by Jen Green; Bettina Arnold, consultant. National Geographic 2008 64p il map (National Geographic investigates) $17.95; lib bdg $27.90 *

Grades: 4 5 6 7   936

1. Celts 2. Celtic civilization 3. Great Britain—Antiquities 4. Ireland—Antiquities 5. Excavations (Archeology)—Europe

ISBN 978-1-4263-0225-1; 1-4263-0225-8; 978-1-4263-0226-8 (lib bdg); 1-4263-0226-6 (lib bdg)

LC 2007047836

This describes ancient Celtic civilization and how archeologists have found out about it.

"With excellent-quality photographs and a well-written text, this is a thorough presentation of the most up-to-date knowledge about this ancient European culture." SLJ

Includes glossary and bibliographical references

936.1   British Isles to 410 A.D. Northern Britain and Ireland

Arnold, Caroline, 1944-

Stone Age farmers beside the sea; Scotland's prehistoric village of Skara Brae; photographs by Arthur P. Arnold. Clarion Bks. 1997 48p il map $15.95

Grades: 4 5 6 7   936.1

1. Scotland—Antiquities 2. Prehistoric peoples

ISBN 0-395-77601-5   LC 96-20021

Describes the Stone Age settlement preserved in the sand dunes on one of Scotland's Orkney Islands, telling how it was discovered and what it reveals about life in prehistoric times

Arnold "carefully distinguishes between what is known and what is surmised about the people who lived at Skara Brae. . . . The photos' clear images, subtle colors, and pleasing compositions give the book its pervasive sense of beauty." Booklist

Includes glossary

937   Roman Empire

Beller, Susan Provost, 1949-

Roman legions on the march; soldiering in the ancient Roman Army; by Susan Provost Beller. Twenty-First Century Books 2008 112p il map (Soldiers on the battlefront) lib bdg $33.26

Grades: 5 6 7 8   937

1. Soldiers—Rome 2. Rome—Civilization

ISBN 978-0-8225-6781-3   LC 2006037829

"In about 100 B.C., Gaius Marius took command of the Roman citizen army and created a professional fighting force—the Roman legions. . . . Author Susan Provost Beller describes how legionaries brought Roman ways to the local populations, influenced the creation of roads and buildings, and much more." Publisher's note

"The format is inviting with a variety of fonts at the

Beller, Susan Provost, 1949-—*Continued*
beginning of each chapter, quotations, and a multitude of
illustrations. . . . The text is clear and to the point, and
chapters are divided into short topics." SLJ
Includes bibliographical references

Biesty, Stephen
Rome: in spectacular cross section; text by
Andrew Solway. Scholastic Nonfiction 2003 29p il
$18.95 *
Grades: 4 5 6 7   937
1. Rome—Civilization 2. Rome—Social life and cus-
toms
ISBN 0-439-45546-4   LC 2002-70694
Detailed illustrations with explanatory captions and
narrative text survey some sites in ancient Rome, includ-
ing the house of a wealthy family, the Colosseum, the
Baths of Trajan, and the Temple of Jupiter
This "is a visually intriguing, reader-friendly introduc-
tion to ancient Rome." Booklist
Includes glossary

Bingham, Jane
How people lived in ancient Rome. The Rosen
Pub. Group's PowerKids Press 2009 30p il map
(How people lived) lib bdg $25.25
Grades: 4 5 6 7   937
1. Rome—Social life and customs
ISBN 978-1-4042-4432-0 (lib bdg); 1-4042-4432-8 (lib
bdg)   LC 2007-40221
Describes everyday life among the ancient Romans,
covering family life, marriage, leisure, education, cloth-
ing, food and drink, warfare, religion, and funerals
"Clear, readable narrative is supplemented by large
color and b&w reproductions of Roman art and artifacts.
. . . It will hold the attention of both readers and
reasearchers, and is a good choice for collections that
serve elementary and younger middle level students."
Libr Media Connect
Includes bibliographical references

Blacklock, Dyan, 1951-
The Roman Army; the legendary soldiers who
created an empire; illustrations by David Kennett.
Walker & Company 2004 48p il map $17.95; lib
bdg $18.85 *
Grades: 4 5 6 7   937
1. Rome—Military history
ISBN 0-8027-8896-3; 0-8027-8897-1 (lib bdg)
LC 2003-57574
An illustrated history of the Roman Army, including
information about its composition, organization, training,
methods, weapons, and campaigns.
"Blacklock's writing is clear and lively and the book,
packed with dramatic cartoon illustrations, will captivate
readers." SLJ
Includes bibliographical references

Deckker, Zilah
Ancient Rome; archaeology unlocks the secrets
of Rome's past; by Zilah Deckker; Robert Lindley
Vann, Consultant. National Geographic 2007 64p
il map (National Geographic investigates) $17.95;
lib bdg $27.90 *
Grades: 4 5 6 7   937
1. Rome—Civilization   2. Rome—Antiquities
3. Archeology
ISBN 978-1-4263-0128-5; 978-1-4263-0129-2 (lib
bdg)   LC 2007024795
This describes what archeologists have learned about
Ancient Rome
Includes glossary and bibliographical references

Deem, James M.
Bodies from the ash. Houghton Mifflin 2005
50p il $16 *
Grades: 4 5 6 7   937
1. Pompeii (Extinct city)
ISBN 0-618-47308-4   LC 2004-26553
"On August 24, 79 C.E., the long-silent Mt. Vesuvius
erupted, and volcanic ash rained down on the 20,000 residents of Pompeii. This photo-essay explains what happened when the volcano exploded—and how the results
of this disaster were discovered hundreds of years later.
. . . [This offers an] enormous amount of information.
. . . But the jewels here are the numerous . . . photographs, especially those featuring the plaster casts and
skeletons of people in their death throes. . . . Excellent
for browsers as well as researchers." Booklist

Hanel, Rachael
Gladiators. Creative Education 2008 48p il
(Fearsome fighters) lib bdg $31.35
Grades: 4 5 6   937
1. Gladiators 2. Rome—Civilization
ISBN 978-1-58341-535-1 (lib bdg); 1-58341-535-1 (lib
bdg)   LC 2006021842
This "recounts the brutality and cruelty of fighting for
sport celebrated during Roman times. . . . [The book
does] an adequate job of covering fighting techniques,
weapons, and history. Photographs and archival reproductions enhance the [presentation]; sidebars provide additional information." Horn Book Guide
Includes glossary and bibliographical references

James, Simon, 1957-
Ancient Rome; written by Simon James. rev ed.
DK Pub. 2008 72p il map (DK eyewitness books)
$15.99
Grades: 4 5 6 7   937
1. Rome—Civilization 2. Rome—Antiquities
ISBN 978-0-7566-3766-8; 0-7566-3766-X
LC 2008-276034
First published 1990 by Knopf
A photo essay documenting ancient Rome and the
people who lived there as revealed through the many ar-
tifacts they left behind, including shields, swords, tools,
toys, cosmetics, and jewelry
Includes glossary

Lassieur, Allison
The ancient Romans; written by Allison Lassieur. Franklin Watts 2004 112p il map (People of the ancient world) lib bdg $30.50; pa $9.95 *
Grades: 5 6 7 8   937
  1. Rome—Civilization
  ISBN 0-531-12338-3 (lib bdg); 0-531-16742-9 (pa)
                                      LC 2004-1955
  Contents: The rulers of Rome; Power and influence of the Roman senate; People of the Roman government; Scholars and writers; Soldiers and the Roman army; The lives of Roman women; Priests and the Roman religion; Architects and engineers; Working-class Romans; Slaves and slavery; Legacy of the Roman empire
  "This attractive, thorough, and comprehensible book . . . offers a stellar introduction to life in ancient Rome." Booklist
  Includes bibliographical references

Mann, Elizabeth, 1948-
The Roman Colosseum; with illustrations by Michael Racz. Mikaya Press 1998 45p il (Wonders of the world) $19.95 *
Grades: 4 5 6   937
  1. Colosseum (Rome, Italy) 2. Rome—Antiquities
  ISBN 0-9650493-3-7   LC 98-20060
  Describes the building of the Colosseum in ancient Rome, and tells how it was used
  This offers "a clear, well-written text and full-color drawings and paintings." SLJ
  Includes glossary

Murrell, Deborah Jane, 1963-
Gladiator; written by Deborah Murrell. QEB Pub. 2010 32p il map (QEB warriors) lib bdg $28.50
Grades: 4 5 6 7   937
  1. Gladiators
  ISBN 978-1-59566-736-6 (lib bdg); 1-59566-736-9 (lib bdg)   LC 2009-3540
  "Learn all about the devious tactics, wicked weapons, and courageous battles fought by gladiators." Publisher's note
  "Bold, comprehensible type and full-color and black-and-white illustrations; reproductions; and photographs will make this offering a hit with its target audience, including reluctant readers." SLJ
  Includes glossary

Osborne, Mary Pope, 1949-
Pompeii; lost & found; frescoes by Bonnie Christensen. Knopf 2006 unp il $16.95; lib bdg $18.99 *
Grades: 3 4 5   937
  1. Pompeii (Extinct city)
  ISBN 0-375-82889-3; 0-375-92889-8 (lib bdg)
                                      LC 2005-09331
  "After brief accounts of the events of 79 A.D. and the first archaeological investigations of the city that lay beneath the fields surrounding Mt. Vesuvius, Osborne's straightforward text focuses on the life at Pompeii at the time of the volcano's eruption. . . . Christensen's distinctive, haunting frescoes are reminiscent of the art found throughout the site. . . . Osborne's text . . . will serve as an enticing introduction to this legendary city frozen in time." SLJ

Park, Louise, 1961-
The Roman gladiators; by Louise Park and Timothy Love. Marshall Cavendish Benchmark 2009 32p il (Ancient and medieval people) $19.95
Grades: 4 5 6   937
  1. Gladiators 2. Rome—Social life and customs 3. Rome—History
  ISBN 978-0-7614-4443-5; 0-7614-4443-2
  "An introduction to the history and lifestyle of Roman gladiators." Publisher's note
  This title has "a simple and elegant design with the proper balance of quality writing and quantity of information. . . . Handy time lines, well-chosen photos of ruins and artifacts, quality illustrations, inset 'Quick Facts,' and 'What You Should Know About' features will grab reluctant readers and captivate even those with short attention spans." SLJ
  Includes glossary

Platt, Richard, 1953-
Pompeii; [by] Richard Platt. Kingfisher 2007 48p (Through time) $16.95 *
Grades: 2 3 4 5   937
  1. Pompeii (Extinct city)
  ISBN 978-0-7534-6044-3   LC 2007004851
  "Through the story of one house in one city, this handsome . . . book introduces young readers to Italy's tumultuous history, beginning in 750 CE. . . . Precise, detailed color illustrations dominate each spread. . . . [A] well-designed, captivating entry." Booklist

Sonneborn, Liz
Pompeii; by Liz Sonneborn. Twenty-First Century Books 2008 80p il map (Unearthing ancient worlds) lib bdg $30.60
Grades: 5 6 7 8   937
  1. Pompeii (Extinct city) 2. Excavations (Archeology)—Italy 3. Rome (Italy)—Antiquities
  ISBN 978-0-8225-7505-4 (lib bdg); 0-8225-7505-1 (lib bdg)   LC 2007022058
  This describes the excavation of the Roman city buried in lava and ash when the volcano Mount Vesuvius erupted in A.D. 79.
  This "clearly written [title is] illustrated with large photographs and period artwork, and the pages are broken up with text boxes featuring quotes and interesting anecdotes." SLJ
  Includes glossary and bibliographical references

Watkins, Richard Ross
Gladiator; by Richard Watkins. Houghton Mifflin 1997 80p il map hardcover o.p. pa $8.95
Grades: 4 5 6 7   937
  1. Gladiators 2. Rome—Social life and customs
  ISBN 0-395-82656-X; 0-618-07032-X (pa)
                                      LC 96-21107

Watkins, Richard Ross—*Continued*

Describes the history of gladiators, including types of armor, use of animals, amphitheaters, and how the practice fit into Roman society for almost 700 years

"In a balanced treatment of a potentially sensational topic, Watkins provides colorfully written, detailed accounts of the fights as well as pithy discussions of what gladiators meant to the Romans and what they tell us about Roman society. . . . The solid gray-and-white drawings illustrate the text effectively." Booklist

Includes glossary and bibliographical references

938   Greece to 323 A.D.

Hart, Avery

Ancient Greece! 40 hands-on activities to experience this wondrous age; [by] Avery Hart & Paul Mantell; illustrations by Michael Kline. Williamson 1999 104p il pa $12.95 *

Grades: 4 5 6 7   938

1. Greece—Civilization 2. Handicraft

ISBN 1-885593-25-2   LC 98-35762

"A Kaleidoscope Kids book"

Introduces the places, people, historical events, myths, culture, and philosophy of ancient Greece. Includes forty hands-on activities, such as making an early Greek theater, building an Ionic temple, and pressing olives for oil

This is "a clever title that encourages learning and creativity." SLJ

Includes bibliographical references

Lassieur, Allison

The ancient Greeks; written by Allison Lassieur. Franklin Watts 2004 112p il map (People of the ancient world) lib bdg $30.50; pa $9.95 *

Grades: 5 6 7 8   938

1. Greece—Civilization

ISBN 0-531-12339-1 (lib bdg); 0-531-16739-9 (pa)

LC 2004-1942

Contents: The people of the government; Scientists of Greece; Greek athletes and sport; Philosophers and thinkers; Priests, priestesses, and the Greek religion; Poets and playwrights; Artists and architects; Warriors; Slaves and workers; Legacy of the ancient Greeks

This title offers "useful information that would help report writers and would also engage interested readers." SLJ

Includes bibliographical references

McGee, Marni

Ancient Greece; archaeology unlocks the secrets of Greece's past; by Marni McGee; Michael Shanks, consultant. National Geographic 2007 64p il map (National Geographic investigates) $17.95; lib bdg $27.90 *

Grades: 5 6 7 8   938

1. Greece—Civilization 2. Greece—Antiquities 3. Excavations (Archeology)—Greece

ISBN   978-0-7922-7826-9;   0-7922-7826-7; 978-0-7922-7872-6 (lib bdg); 0-7922-7872-0 (lib bdg)

LC 2006032108

This describes how archeologists have found out about Ancient Greek civilization

This offers "the beautiful photography and illustrations characteristic of the National Geographic Society, [a] well-written [text] and sidebars, and information on recent archaeological finds." SLJ

Includes bibliographical references

Park, Louise, 1961-

The Spartan hoplites; by Louise Park and Timothy Love. Marshall Cavendish Benchmark 2009 32p il map (Ancient and medieval people) $19.95

Grades: 4 5 6   938

1. Sparta (Extinct city) 2. Soldiers 3. Athens (Greece)—History

ISBN 978-0-7614-4449-7; 0-7614-4449-1

LC 2008-55779

"An introduction to the history and lifestyle of Spartan hoplites." Publisher's note

This title has "a simple and elegant design with the proper balance of quality writing and quantity of information. . . . Handy time lines, well-chosen photos of ruins and artifacts, quality illustrations, inset 'Quick Facts', and 'What You Should Know About' features will grab reluctant readers and captivate even those with short attention spans." SLJ

Includes glossary

Pearson, Anne

Ancient Greece; written by Anne Pearson. rev ed. DK Pub. 2007 72p il (DK eyewitness books) $15.99; lib bdg $19.99

Grades: 4 5 6 7   938

1. Greece—Civilization

ISBN   978-0-7566-3002-7;   0-7566-3002-9; 978-0-7566-0648-0 (lib bdg); 0-7566-0648-9 (lib bdg)

LC 2007280849

First published 1992 by Knopf

Includes CD with clip-art and wall chart

Introduces the land, history, and civilization of ancient Greece, describing everyday life, religion, politics, farming, trade, art, sport, and warfare

Reynolds, Susan

The first marathon: the legend of Pheidippides; by Susan Reynolds; illustrated by Daniel Minter. Albert Whitman & Company 2006 unp il $16.95

Grades: 2 3 4   938

1. Pheidippides, fl. 490 B.C. 2. Marathon, Battle of, 490 B.C. 3. Marathon running

ISBN 978-0-8075-0867-1; 0-8075-0867-5

LC 2005024618

The author tells the "story of how the Greeks fought off the mighty Persian army on the plains of Marathon, and how the young long-distance runner Pheidippides ran 140 miles in 36 hours to Sparta to ask for help, then ran back without stopping, fought in the battle, ran to tell Athens of the victory, and died. Now marathons are named for his heroic run. The dramatic, full-color, double-page illustrations, with heavy black accents, show the strong, rhythmic movement of the brave young athlete, the battle scenes, and then runners across the world today." Booklist

Stefoff, Rebecca, 1951-
The ancient Mediterranean. Benchmark Books 2004 c2005 48p il map (World historical atlases) lib bdg $18.95
Grades: 5 6 7 8 **938**
    1. Mediterranean region—History 2. Greece—History—0-323 3. Rome—Civilization 4. Greece—Civilization
    ISBN 0-7614-1641-2   LC 2003-12027
    Contents: Greece: Bronze Age ancestors; The Dark Age; Greek civilization is born; The Persian wars; Athens against Sparta; Alexander's empire: Macedonian might; To rule the world; The Hellenistic age; Conquest by Rome; Rome: The Kingdom; The Republic; Conquest and war; The birth of an empire; East and West; An empire falls
    Text plus historical and contemporary maps provide a look at the history of cultures that flourished along the Mediterranean Sea
    The text is "clearly written and well organized. The [book includes] large, full-color photographs and illustrations reproduced from original pieces of art found in diverse national museums. Maps placed throughout clearly show the boundaries and areas of the empires. [This volume makes an] excellent [supplement] to history lessons and [a] good starting [point] for research." SLJ

939   Other parts of ancient world to ca. 640

Sherrow, Victoria
Ancient Africa; archaeology unlocks the secrets of Africa's past; by Victoria Sherrow; James Denbow, consultant. National Geographic Society 2007 64p il map (National Geographic investigates) $17.95 *
Grades: 4 5 6 7 **939**
    1. Africa—Civilization 2. Africa—Antiquities
    ISBN 978-0-7922-5384-6; 0-7922-5384-1
        LC 2007277594
    This describes archeological discoveries about ancient peoples of Africa including the Dogon people of Mali, the ancient city of Jenne-jeno, and the Kushite temples at Jebel Barkal.
    Includes bibliographical references

Sonneborn, Liz
The ancient Kushites. Franklin Watts 2005 112p il map (People of the ancient world) lib bdg $30.50; pa $9.95 *
Grades: 5 6 7 8 **939**
    1. Cushites
    ISBN 0-531-12380-4 (lib bdg); 0-531-16847-6 (pa)
        LC 2004-13908
    This book portrays the lives of the ancient Kushites "by examining their arts, culture, economy, government, religious beliefs, and societal [structure]. . . . Attractively designed and illustrated, the [book features] excellent color representations of architecture, artwork, and other cultural and historical artifacts." SLJ
    Includes bibliographical references

Stefoff, Rebecca, 1951-
The ancient Near East; [by] Rebecca Stefoff. Benchmark Books 2004 c2005 48p il map (World historical atlases) lib bdg $27.07
Grades: 5 6 7 8 **939**
    1. Middle East—History 2. Middle East—Civilization
    ISBN 0-7614-1639-0   LC 2003-12030
    Contents: Mesopotamia—Empires and invasions: Beginnings; The rise of city-states; Sumer and Akkad; Babylonia and Assyria; The Persian conquest; Anatolia—Cultures of the crossroads: Where three worlds meet; Early Anatolian states; Trade and war; The Hittite empire; Phrygia and Lydia; Egypt—Land of the river: Before the pharaohs; The old kingdom; The middle kingdom; The new kingdom; Foreign rulers
    Text plus historical and contemporary maps provide a look at the history of the Ancient Near East
    This is "clearly written and well organized. The [book includes] large, full-color photographs and illustrations reproduced from original pieces of art found in diverse national museums. . . . [This volume makes an] excellent [supplement] to history lessons and [a] good starting [point] for research." SLJ
    Includes bibliographical references

940   History of Europe

Foster, Karen, 1964-
Atlas of Europe. Picture Window Books 2008 32p il map (Picture Window Books world atlases) lib bdg $27.93
Grades: 2 3 4 **940**
    1. Europe
    ISBN 978-1-4048-3882-6 (lib bdg); 1-4048-3882-1 (lib bdg)
    This introduction to the geography of Europe offers maps and information about countries, landforms, bodies of water, climate, plants, animals, population, people and customs, places of interest, industries, transportation, and the Orient Express.
    Includes glossary

940.1   Europe—Early history to 1453

Adkins, Jan, 1944-
What if you met a knight? [by] Jan Adkins, scribe and illuminator. Roaring Brook Press 2006 32p il $16.95 *
Grades: 3 4 5 6 **940.1**
    1. Knights and knighthood 2. Medieval civilization
    ISBN 1-59643-148-2; 978-1-59643-148-5
        LC 2005-29163
    "Adkins sets out to debunk some common misconceptions about knights, and he does so with style and wit. . . . Light in approach but quite informative, the text ably explains the feudal system, the business of knighthood, and the origins of legends such as King Arthur and dragons, and also discusses castles, arms, and the Crusades. Throughout the book, colorful, detailed illustrations and captions provide information even as they open windows on the medieval world." Booklist

Aliki
A medieval feast; written and illustrated by
Aliki. Crowell 1983 unp il hardcover o.p. pa $6.95
*
Grades: 2 3 4 5   **940.1**
    1. Dining—History 2. Courts and courtiers
3. Medieval civilization 4. Festivals—History
    ISBN 0-690-04246-9 (lib bdg); 0-06-446050-9 (pa)
                             LC 82-45923
"In pictures of minute, charming detail and vibrant,
translucent colors, Aliki takes us through the ritual of
preparation and the enthusiastic consumption of a medieval feast served to a king and his retinue when they
stop for a few days at Camdenton Manor. Not to be out-
done by the art, the text has its own various facets.
There is the fictional story set in type outside the art and
there is within the paintings a collection of delightful historical, gastronomical, agricultural, and zoological facts
printed by hand. And throughout the spendid whole are
border decorations worthy of the great illuminated manuscripts." Child Book Rev Serv

Ashman, Linda, 1960-
Come to the castle! a visit to a castle in
thirteenth-century England; illuminated by S.D.
Schindler. Roaring Brook Press 2009 unp il $17.95
*
Grades: 3 4 5   **940.1**
    1. Stories in rhyme 2. Medieval civilization
3. Castles
    ISBN 978-1-59643-155-3; 1-59643-155-5
"Ashman offers voices of several characters within the
castle of a bumbling earl as he decrees that he will hold
a tournament and a banquet." SLJ
"Wit meets historical accuracy in a pitch-perfect mix
of laugh-out-loud text and entertaining image." Kirkus

Corbishley, Mike
The Middle Ages. 3rd ed. Chelsea House 2007
96p il map (Cultural atlas for young people) $35
Grades: 5 6 7 8   **940.1**
    1. Medieval civilization 2. Middle Ages
    ISBN 978-0-8160-6825-8; 0-8160-6825-9
    First published 1989
Maps, charts, illustrations, and text explore the history
and culture of the Middle Ages.
"The maps are excellent, precise, clear, and easy to
read and understand, and the illustrations, particularly
those of works of art, are wonderful. . . . This attractive
volume provides an intriguing cross-cultural look at the
medieval world. An excellent addition." SLJ
    Includes glossary and bibliographical references

Galloway, Priscilla, 1930-
Archers, alchemists, and 98 other medieval jobs
you might have loved or loathed; art by Martha
Newbigging. Annick Press 2003 96p il lib bdg
$24.95; pa $14.95 *
Grades: 3 4 5 6   **940.1**
    1. Medieval civilization
    ISBN 1-55037-811-2 (lib bdg); 1-55037-810-4 (pa)
"Galloway introduces medieval Europe from 1000 to
1500 not by recounting dates, wars, and rulers but by
discussing the occupations available in the society. . . .
The jaunty, cartoonlike ink drawings, brightened with
color washes, heighten the informal, upbeat tone of the
informative text." Booklist
    Includes bibliographical references

Gibbons, Gail
Knights in shining armor. Little, Brown 1995
unp il hardcover o.p. pa $7.99 *
Grades: K 1 2 3   **940.1**
    1. Knights and knighthood 2. Medieval civilization
    ISBN 0-316-30948-6 (lib bdg); 0-316-30038-1 (pa)
                             LC 94-35525
The author "covers tournaments, chivalry, and what
happened when a bad knight was caught. Legendary
knights such as Sir Gawain and the knights of the Round
Table are briefly described, as is St. George and the
dragon, and Gibbons also discusses present-day knights.
The watercolor-and-ink pictures are some of Gibbons'
liveliest and most attractive." Booklist

Gravett, Christopher, 1951-
Knight; written by Christopher Gravett;
photographed by Geoff Dann. rev ed. DK Pub.
2007 72p il (DK eyewitness books) $15.99; lib
bdg $19.99
Grades: 4 5 6 7   **940.1**
    1. Knights and knighthood 2. Medieval civilization
    ISBN   978-0-7566-3003-4;   0-7566-3003-7;
978-0-7566-0695-4 (lib bdg); 0-7566-0695-0 (lib bdg)
                            LC 2007281111
    First published 2004
    Includes CD with clip-art and wall chart
Examines the life of medieval knights, with color photographs depicting the weapons, clothing, armor, art, and
artifacts of the period

Hanel, Rachael
Knights. Creative Education 2008 48p il
(Fearsome fighters) lib bdg $31.35
Grades: 4 5 6   **940.1**
    1. Knights and knighthood 2. Medieval civilization
    ISBN 978-1-58341-536-8 (lib bdg); 1-58341-536-X
(lib bdg)   LC 2006021843
This "deals with the chivalry and battlefield encounters in medieval Europe. [The books does] an adequate
job of covering fighting techniques, weapons, and history. Photographs and archival reproductions enhance the
[presentation]; sidebars provide additional information."
Horn Book Guide
    Includes glossary and bibliographical references

Hart, Avery

Knights & castles; 50 hands-on activities to experience the Middle Ages; [by] Avery Hart & Paul Mantell. Williamson 1998 96p il pa $10.95 *

Grades: 4 5 6 7   **940.1**
1. Medieval civilization 2. Middle Ages 3. Knights and knighthood 4. Handicraft
ISBN 1-885593-17-1   LC 97-32863
"A Kaleidoscope Kids book"
Introduces the Middle Ages, including activities and crafts that are representative of medieval life, for example creating an hour glass, a catapult, a coat of arms, and a code of honor
"The text is written in a breezy tone and illustrated with a combination of line drawings and blue-or-purple-ink reproductions of medieval art and woodcuts." SLJ
Includes bibliographical references

Kroll, Steven

Barbarians! illustrated by Robert Byrd. Dutton Children's Books 2009 48p il $18.99 *
Grades: 3 4 5   **940.1**
1. Middle Ages 2. Goths 3. Mongols 4. Vikings 5. Huns
ISBN 978-0-525-47958-1; 0-525-47958-9
                                      LC 2008-39210
"Kroll introduces four notable groups referred to by their enermies as barbarians: the Goths, the Huns, the Vikings, and the Mongols. . . . Showing clear differences among the four groups, the many detailed, energetic ink-and-watercolor illustrations show the barbarians at home and at war. . . . This handsome volume will fill a collection gap while providing warrior-loving browsers with an informative and brightly illustrated book to enjoy." Booklist

Langley, Andrew

Medieval life; written by Andrew Langley; photographed by Geoff Brightling. rev ed. DK Pub. 2004 72p il (DK eyewitness books) $15.99; lib bdg $19.99
Grades: 4 5 6 7   **940.1**
1. Medieval civilization
ISBN 0-7566-0705-1; 0-7566-0704-3 (lib bdg)
First published 1996 by Knopf
An illustrated look at various aspects of life in medieval Europe, covering everyday life, religion, royalty, and more.

Park, Louise, 1961-

The medieval knights; by Louise Park and Timothy Love. Marshall Cavendish Benchmark 2009 32p il map (Ancient and medieval people) $19.95
Grades: 4 5 6   **940.1**
1. Knights and knighthood 2. Medieval civilization
ISBN 978-0-7614-4444-2; 0-7614-4444-0
                                      LC 2008-55777
"An introduction to the history and lifestyle of medieval knights." Publisher's note

This title has "a simple and elegant design with the proper balance of quality writing and quantity of information. . . . Handy time lines, well-chosen photos of ruins and artifacts, quality illustrations, inset 'Quick Facts', and 'What You Should Know About' features will grab reluctant readers and captivate even those with short attention spans." SLJ
Includes glossary

Ross, Stewart

Monarchs; [by] Stewart Ross. Lucent 2004 48p il map (Medieval realms) lib bdg $28.70
Grades: 5 6 7 8   **940.1**
1. Kings and rulers 2. Medieval civilization
ISBN 978-1-59018-535-3 (lib bdg); 1-59018-535-8 (lib bdg)   LC 2003-60387
This describes medieval kings and queens of Europe and their governments, courts, succession, relationships to the church, wars, the Crusades, and the beginnings of nations
This is "attractive, informative. . . . Well reproduced and mostly colorful, the illustrations include a great many reproductions of period paintings and prints, along with maps and a few photos." Booklist
Includes glossary and bibliographical references

Schlitz, Laura Amy

Good masters! Sweet ladies! voices from a medieval village; [by] Laura Amy Schlitz; illustrated by Robert Byrd. Candlewick Press 2007 85p il $19.99; pa $9.99 *
Grades: 5 6 7 8   **940.1**
1. Middle Ages—Drama 2. Monologues
ISBN 978-0-7636-1578-9; 0-7636-1578-1; 978-0-7636-4332-4 (pa); 0-7636-4332-7 (pa)
Awarded the Newbery Medal, 2008
A collection of short one-person plays featuring characters, between ten and fifteen years old, who live in or near a thirteenth-century English manor
"Designed for performance and excellent for use in interdisciplinary history classrooms, the book offers students an incredibly approachable format for learning about the Middle Ages that makes the period both realistic and relevant. . . . Byrd's illustrations evoke the era and give dramatists ideas for appropriate costuming and props." SLJ

940.3   World War I, 1914-1918

Adams, Simon

World War I; written by Simon Adams; photographed by Andy Crawford. rev ed. DK Pub. 2007 72p il (DK eyewitness books) $15.99; lib bdg $19.99
Grades: 4 5 6 7   **940.3**
1. World War, 1914-1918
ISBN 978-0-7566-3007-2; 0-7566-3007-X; 978-0-7566-0741-8 (lib bdg); 0-7566-0741-8 (lib bdg)   LC 2007279476
First published 2001
Includes CD with clip-art and wall chart
This look at World War I examines life in the trenches and the devastation of Europe by the Great War

940.4   Military history of World War I

Beller, Susan Provost, 1949-
The doughboys over there; soldiering in World War I; by Susan Provost Beller. Twenty-First Century Books 2008 112p il map (Soldiers on the battlefront) lib bdg $33.26
Grades: 5 6 7 8   **940.4**
1. World War, 1914-1918 2. Soldiers—United States
ISBN 978-0-8225-6295-5 (lib bdg); 0-8225-6295-2 (lib bdg)   LC 2006026249
The is an account of the U.S. soldiers who fought in Europe in the First World War.
"The format is inviting with a variety of fonts at the beginning of each chapter, quotations, and a multitude of illustrations. . . . The text is clear and to the point, and chapters are divided into short topics." SLJ
Includes bibliographical references

Burleigh, Robert, 1936-
Fly, Cher Ami, fly! the pigeon who saved the lost battalion; by Robert Burleigh; illustrated by Robert MacKenzie. Abrams Books for Young Readers 2008 unp il $16.95
Grades: K 1 2 3   **940.4**
1. Pigeons 2. World War, 1914-1918
ISBN 978-0-8109-7097-7; 0-8109-7097-X
"Burleigh tells the true story of the last flight of a U.S. Army Signal Corps carrier pigeon, which took place in France during World War I. Cher Ami was the last hope for the 'Lost Battalion' of the 77th Division in the Battle of Argonne. . . . Burleigh's short text clearly depicts the story's action, while MacKenzie's full-page golden-hued yet somber illustrations add to the account by showing the drama from a variety of perspectives." Booklist

Greenwood, Mark, 1958-
The donkey of Gallipoli; a true story of courage in World War I; [by] Mark Greenwood; illustrated by Frane Lessac. Candlewick Press 2008 unp il map $16.99
Grades: 2 3 4   **940.4**
1. Kirkpatrick, John Simpson, 1892-1915 2. World War, 1914-1918 3. Gallipoli campaign, 1915 4. Donkeys 5. Soldiers
ISBN 978-0-7636-3913-6; 0-7636-3913-3
                                            LC 2007032525
"When Jack Simpson was a boy in England, he loved leading donkeys along the beach for a penny a ride. So when he enlists as a stretcher bearer in World War I, his gentle way with those animals soon leads him to his calling. Braving bullets and bombs on the battlefields of Gallipoli, Jack brings a donkey to the aid of 300 Allied soldiers." Publisher's note
This is a "stirring picture book. . . . In folk-art style, the paintings, in shades that reflect the heat of a sandy landscape, show the heroic soldier and the gentle animal amid the slaughter of war." Booklist

Murphy, Jim, 1947-
Truce; the day the soldiers stopped fighting. Scholastic Press 2009 116p il map $19.99 *
Grades: 5 6 7 8   **940.4**
1. World War, 1914-1918
ISBN 978-0-545-13049-3; 0-545-13049-2
                                            LC 2008-40500
"By December 1918, the western front of World War I featured two parallel trenches stretching from the North Sea to the Alps. . . . On Christmas Day, an informal peace broke out in many locations along the front. . . . Murphy's excellent telling of this unusual war story begins with an account of the events that led to WWI and follows the shift in the soldiers' mind-sets. . . . Printed in tones of sepia, the illustrations in this handsome volume include many period photos as well as paintings and maps. . . . Well organized and clearly written, this presentation vividly portrays the context and events of the Christmas Truce." Booklist
Includes bibliographical references

Myers, Walter Dean, 1937-
The Harlem Hellfighters; when pride met courage; [by] Walter Dean Myers and Bill Miles. HarperCollins 2006 150p il map hardcover o.p. lib bdg $18.89 *
Grades: 5 6 7 8   **940.4**
1. World War, 1914-1918 2. African American soldiers
ISBN 0-06-001136-X; 0-06-001137-8 (lib bdg)
                                            LC 2005-08951
This is a "tribute to the 369th Infantry Regiment, comprised entirely of African American soldiers (many from Harlem), who fought in World War I. . . . The clear prose; effective use of white space; and numerous, often full-page black-and-white photographs will attract reluctant readers while enticing more dedicated history buffs." Booklist
Includes bibliographical references

940.53   World War II, 1939-1945

Adams, Simon
World War II; written by Simon Adams; photographed by Andy Crawford. rev ed. DK Pub. 2007 72p il (DK eyewitness books) $16.99
Grades: 4 5 6 7   **940.53**
1. World War, 1939-1945
ISBN 978-0-7566-3008-9; 0-7566-3008-8
                                            LC 2008273315
First published 2000
Includes CD with clip-art and wall chart
Provides a concise history of World War II including information about the Holocaust, the code-breaking Enigma, and the deadly V2 rocket

Adler, David A., 1947-

Hiding from the Nazis; illustrated by Karen Ritz. Holiday House 1997 unp il $15.95; pa $6.95

Grades: 2 3 4   **940.53**

1. Baer, Lore, 1938- 2. Holocaust, 1933-1945 3. World War, 1939-1945—Jews 4. Jews—Netherlands

ISBN 0-8234-1288-1; 0-8234-1666-6 (pa)

         LC 96-38451

The true story of Lore Baer who as a four-year-old Jewish child was placed with a Christian family in the Dutch farm country to avoid persecution by the Nazis

"Adler includes a lot of factual information about the history of the time and about the people in the story, before and after the war. Ritz's realistic watercolors in warm shades of brown focus on the small girl whose childhood games of hide-and-seek become a terrifying reality." Booklist

Ambrose, Stephen E.

The good fight; how World War II was won. Atheneum Bks. for Young Readers 2001 96p il maps $19.95 *

Grades: 5 6 7 8   **940.53**

1. World War, 1939-1945

ISBN 0-689-84361-5   LC 00-49600

"A Byron Preiss Visual Publications Inc. book"

"Beginning with an explanation of the origin of the war in Europe and Asia, the text moves on to Pearl Harbor through the major battles to the war-crimes trials and the Marshall Program." SLJ

"An excellent balance between the big picture and the humanizing details, well supported by fact boxes, tinted photographs, and battlefield maps that are both simple and clear. . . . Ambrose's style is authoritative and warm." Booklist

Includes glossary and bibliographical references

Bachrach, Susan D., 1948-

Tell them we remember; the story of the Holocaust. Little, Brown 1994 109p il maps pa $15.99 *

Grades: 5 6 7 8   **940.53**

1. United States Holocaust Memorial Museum 2. Holocaust, 1933-1945

ISBN 0-316-69264-6; 0-316-07484-5 (pa)

         LC 93-40090

"United States Holocaust Memorial Museum."

"Intended to extend the experience of the United States Holocaust Memorial Museum beyond its walls, this book reproduces some of its artifacts, photographs, maps, and taped oral and video histories. . . . Bachrach makes the victims of Hitler's cruelty immediate to readers, showing that, like readers, they were individuals with hobbies and desires, friends and families. . . . This is a very personal approach to Holocaust history and a very effective one." SLJ

Includes glossary and bibliographical references

Finkelstein, Norman H., 1941-

Remember not to forget; a memory of the Holocaust; [by] Norman H. Finkelstein; illustrated by Lois and Lars Hokanson. Jewish Publication Society 2004 31p il pa $9.95

Grades: 4 5 6 7   **940.53**

1. Holocaust, 1933-1945 2. Jews—History

ISBN 0-82760-770-9   LC 2004556462

A reissue of the title first published 1985 by Watts

"This spare, starkly illustrated book explains what the Holocaust was and how it is remembered on Yom Hashoa, Holocaust Remembrance Day. The explanation reaches back to the explusion of the Jews from Jerusalem in A.D. 70 and describes how Jews . . . became targets of anti-Semitism, which culminated in the systematic murder of six million by the Nazis in World War II. The tone is straightforward and matter-of-fact. Black-and-white woodcuts accompany the text with somber scenes reflective of the narrative." Booklist [review of 1985 edition]

Greenfeld, Howard

The hidden children. Ticknor & Fields Bks. for Young Readers 1993 118p il hardcover o.p. pa $9.99 *

Grades: 4 5 6 7   **940.53**

1. Holocaust, 1933-1945—Personal narratives 2. Jews—Europe

ISBN 0-395-66074-2; 0-395-86138-1 (pa)

         LC 93-20326

Describes the experiences of those Jewish children who were forced to go into hiding during the Holocaust and survived to tell about it

"Illustrated with black-and-white photographs, the moving stories and dramatic facts make inspiring, and often troubling, reading. A lovely, important book about heroism and survival." Horn Book Guide

Includes bibliographical references

Judge, Lita, 1968-

One thousand tracings; healing the wounds of World War II. Hyperion Books for Children 2007 unp il $15.99 *

Grades: 2 3 4 5   **940.53**

1. World War, 1939-1945—Civilian relief

ISBN 978-1-4231-0008-9; 1-4231-0008-5

         LC 2007-18282

"Judge's lyrical prose tells the true and poignant story of her grandmother and mother's endeavor to find shoes, clothing and foodstuffs for hundreds of Germans devastated by [World War II]. . . . Softly rendered watercolor bleeds portray the quiet emotions of mother and daughter." Publ Wkly

Kacer, Kathy, 1954-

Hiding Edith; a true story. Second Story 2006 120p (Holocaust remembrance book for young readers) pa $10.95

Grades: 4 5 6 7   **940.53**

1. Schwalb, Edith 2. Holocaust, 1933-1945 3. Jews—France

ISBN 1-897187-06-8

"Kacer recounts some extraordinary history: in Moissac, France, under Nazi occupation, a French Jewish couple hid 100 Jewish refugee children—with the support of the townspeople. Kacer, who based her account on interviews, tells the story of one child, Edith Schwalb. Captioned black-and-white photos on almost every page show Edith at home in Vienna before the war, then in Belgium, and then, separated from her parents, living with the rescuers." Booklist

Krinitz, Esther Nisenthal

Memories of survival; [by] Esther Nisenthal Krinitz & Bernice Steinhardt. Hyperion Books for Children 2005 63p il $15.99 *

Grades: 6 7 8 9   **940.53**

1. Holocaust, 1933-1945—Personal narratives 2. Jews—Poland

ISBN 0-7868-5126-0

"Krinitz set down the story of her Holocaust survival in a series of 36 exquisite, hand-embroidered fabric collages and hand-stitched narrative captions. For this picture-book presentation, Steinhardt, Krinitz's daughter, reproduced those panels, adding eloquent commentary to fill in the facts and the history. . . . The telling is quiet, and the hand-stitched pictures are incredibly detailed, with depth and color that will make readers look closely." Booklist

Levine, Karen

Hana's suitcase; a true story. Whitman, A. 2003 111p il lib bdg $15.95

Grades: 4 5 6 7   **940.53**

1. Brady, Hana 2. Holocaust, 1933-1945

ISBN 0-8075-3148-0   LC 2002-27439

Also available in paperback with CD-ROM from Second Story Press

First published 2002 in Canada

A biography of a Czech girl who died in the Holocaust, told in alternating chapters with an account of how the curator of a Japanese Holocaust center learned about her life after Hana's suitcase was sent to her

"The account, based on a radio documentary Levine did in Canada . . . is part history, part suspenseful mystery, and always anguished family drama, with an incredible climactic revelation." Booklist

Meltzer, Milton, 1915-2009

Never to forget: the Jews of the Holocaust. Harper & Row 1976 217p maps pa $9.99 hardcover o.p. *

Grades: 6 7 8 9   **940.53**

1. Holocaust, 1933-1945

ISBN 0-06-446118-1 (pa)

"The mass murder of six million Jews by the Nazis during World War II is the subject of this compelling history. Interweaving background information, chilling statistics, individual accounts and newspaper reports, it provides an excellent introduction to its subject." Interracial Books Child Bull

Includes bibliographical references

Rescue: the story of how Gentiles saved Jews in the Holocaust. Harper & Row 1988 168p maps hardcover o.p. pa $9.99 *

Grades: 6 7 8 9   **940.53**

1. Holocaust, 1933-1945 2. World War, 1939-1945—Jews—Rescue

ISBN 0-06-024210-8; 0-06-446117-3 (pa)

LC 87-47816

A recounting drawn from historic source material of the many individual acts of heroism performed by righteous gentiles who sought to thwart the extermination of the Jews during the Holocaust

"This is an excellent portrayal of a difficult topic. Meltzer manages to both explain without accusing, and to laud without glorifying. . . . The discussion of the complicated relations between countries are clear, but not simplistic. An impressive aspect of this book is its lack of didacticism." Voice Youth Advocates

Includes bibliographical references

Millman, Isaac, 1933-

Hidden child. Farrar, Straus and Giroux 2005 73p il $18 *

Grades: 4 5 6 7   **940.53**

1. Holocaust, 1933-1945—Personal narratives 2. Jews—France

ISBN 0-374-33071-9   LC 2003-60688

"Frances Foster books"

The author details his difficult experiences as a young Jewish child living in Nazi-occupied France during the 1940s.

"Millman tells his story in a straightforward, yet compelling voice. . . . Dense text pages—with occasional black-and-white photos—alternate with double-page montage paintings in which Millman presents images that emphasize his fears, emotions, and reactions to the events he describes. . . . An inspiring and powerful view of this tragic period in human history." SLJ

Mochizuki, Ken, 1954-

Passage to freedom; the Sugihara story; written by Ken Mochizuki; illustrated by Dom Lee; afterword by Hiroki Sugihara. Lee & Low Bks. 1997 unp il $15.95 *

Grades: 3 4 5 6   **940.53**

1. Sugihara, Sempo, 1900-1986 2. Holocaust, 1933-1945 3. World War, 1939-1945—Jews—Rescue

ISBN 1-880000-49-0   LC 96-35359

"The story of a Japanese diplomat who saved thousands of Jewish refugees in defiance of official government orders." SLJ

"Lee's stirring mixed-media illustrations in sepia shades are humane and beautiful. . . . The immediacy of the narrative will grab kids' interest and make them think." Booklist

Nicholson, Dorinda Makanaōnalani

Remember World War II; kids who survived tell their stories. National Geographic 2005 61p il map $17.95; lib bdg $27.90 *

Grades: 5 6 7 8   **940.53**

    1. World War, 1939-1945—Personal narratives

ISBN 0-7922-7179-3; 0-7922-7191-2 (lib bdg)

This book offers "views of the Second World War through the eyes of those who experienced it as children. . . . Providing enough background information to give a framework for the progression of the war as a whole and the particular conditions and events surrounding the interviewees' memories, Nicholson lets the first-person accounts bring the experiences to life. Photographs of these individuals as children, other period photos, excellent maps, and pictures of artifacts illustrate the text." Booklist

Includes bibliographical references

Perl, Lila

Four perfect pebbles; a Holocaust story; by Lila Perl and Marion Blumenthal Lazan. Greenwillow Bks. 1996 130p il $16.99; pa $5.99

Grades: 6 7 8 9   **940.53**

    1. Holocaust, 1933-1945—Personal narratives 2. Jews—Germany

ISBN 0-688-14294-X; 0-380-73188-6 (pa)

                LC 95-9752

"Starting with a description of one of the days that Marion Blumenthal Lazan survived in Bergen-Belsen, this chronicle of her experiences during the Holocaust then goes further back for a look at her family's secure prewar life in Germany." Bull Cent Child Books

"This book warrants attention both for the uncommon experiences it records and for the fullness of that record. . . . Quotes from Lazan's 87-year-old mother are invaluable—her memories of the family's experiences afford Marion's story a precision and wholeness rarely available to child survivors." Publ Wkly

Includes bibliographical references

Rosenberg, Maxine B., 1939-

Hiding to survive; stories of Jewish children rescued from the Holocaust. Clarion Bks. 1994 166p il hardcover o.p. pa $8.95

Grades: 5 6 7 8   **940.53**

    1. Holocaust, 1933-1945—Personal narratives 2. Jews—Europe

ISBN 0-395-65014-3; 0-395-90020-4 (pa)

               LC 93-28328

First person accounts of fourteen Holocaust survivors who as children were hidden from the Nazis by non-Jews

"Told in the plain, unvarnished language of childhood memories, these harrowing first-person accounts are particularly moving in their straightforward simplicity, and all are accompanied by photos of the survivors as children and as they are today." Voice Youth Advocates

Includes glossary and bibliographical references

Rubin, Susan Goldman, 1939-

The cat with the yellow star; coming of age in Terezin; [by] Susan Goldman Rubin, with Ela Weissberger. Holiday House 2006 40p il $16.95 *

Grades: 3 4 5 6   **940.53**

    1. Holocaust, 1933-1945 2. Jews—Czechoslovakia 3. Terezin (Czechoslovakia: Concentration camp)

ISBN 0-8234-1831-6   LC 2004-57582

"In 1942, at age 11, Ela Weissberger was transported with her Czech family to the Nazi concentration camp Terezin. She survived, and now, based on extensive personal interviews, Rubin tells Weissberger's story of being a Jewish child in that camp, including how the young prisoners rehearsed and performed the opera *Brundibar*." Booklist

"This finely tuned collaboration weaves together narrative and memories into one cohesive story of trauma, friendship, and survival. . . . Extensive use of historical photographs, drawings, and primary visual sources brings even greater depth to readers' understanding." SLJ

The flag with fifty-six stars; a gift from the survivors of Mauthausen; illustrated by Bill Farnsworth. Holiday House 2005 39p il $16.95

Grades: 3 4 5   **940.53**

    1. Holocaust, 1933-1945 2. World War, 1939-1945—Germany 3. Jews—Germany 4. Flags—United States

ISBN 0-8234-1653-4   LC 2004-47457

"In the spring of 1945, U.S. troops marched into the Mauthausen concentration camp in Austria to liberate surviving prisoners and were given an American flag that had been secretly made by a group of detainees there. This is an inspiring account of the camp, its survivors, and its liberators. . . . Nazi atrocities are muted here, but the sorrow, hunger, hopelessness, and, finally, optimism shine through in the pictures and in the text." SLJ

Includes bibliographical references

Ruelle, Karen Gray, 1957-

The grand mosque of Paris; a story of how Muslims saved Jews during the Holocaust; by Karen Gray Ruelle and Deborah Durland DeSaix. Holiday House 2009 40p il $17.95 *

Grades: 3 4 5 6   **940.53**

    1. World War, 1939-1945—Jews—Rescue 2. Holocaust, 1933-1945 3. World War, 1939-1945—France 4. France—History—1940-1945, German occupation 5. Muslims 6. Jewish-Arab relations

ISBN 978-0-8234-2159-6; 0-8234-2159-7

              LC 2008-17209

"During the Nazi occupation of Paris, no Jew was safe from arrest and deportation to a concentration camp. Few Parisians were willing to risk their own lives to help. Yet many Jews found refuge in an unlikely place—the sprawling complex of the Grand Mosque of Paris." Publisher's note

"Although few documents remain, substantial evidence supports this fascinating and courageous story. . . . Realistic oil paintings complement the lengthy text. . . . A must read." Kirkus

Russo, Marisabina, 1950-

Always remember me; how one family survived World War II; [by] Marisabina Russo. Atheneum Books for Young Readers 2005 unp il $16.95 *

Grades: 3 4 5   **940.53**

1. Jews—Germany 2. Holocaust, 1933-1945

ISBN 0-689-86920-7   LC 2004-4228

"Russo tells her Jewish family's story of Holocaust survival. She remembers herself as a small child visiting her grandmother, Oma, who tells Russo the family history with photos stretching back to Oma's youth and marriage before World War I. . . . Russo personalizes the history with photo-album entries printed on the endpapers, and her gouache illustrations, framed like photos, show the individuality and strength of family members." Booklist

Includes glossary

Talbott, Hudson

Forging freedom; a true story of heroism during the Holocaust. Putnam 2000 64p il $15.99

Grades: 4 5 6 7   **940.53**

1. Penraat, Jaap 2. World War, 1939-1945—Jews—Rescue 3. Holocaust, 1933-1945

ISBN 0-399-23434-9   LC 99-52551

"Talbott tells the story of his friend Jaap Penraat, who, as a young architectural student in Amsterdam under the Nazi occupation, saved hundreds of Jews from arrest, first by forging their ID cards, and then by devising an elaborate escape plan to smuggle them over the border to freedom." Booklist

Taylor, Peter Lane

The secret of Priest's Grotto; a Holocaust survival story; [by] Peter Lane Taylor with Christos Nicola. Kar-Ben Pub. 2007 64p il map lib bdg $10.95; pa $8.95

Grades: 5 6 7 8 9 10 11 12   **940.53**

1. Holocaust, 1933-1945 2. Jews—Ukraine 3. Caves

ISBN 978-1-58013-260-2 (lib bdg); 1-58013-260-X (lib bdg); 978-1-58013-261-9 (pa); 1-58013-261-8 (pa)
LC 2006-21709

"This volume relays the tale of 38 Ukrainian Jews who sought refuge in a local cave to escape the invading Nazis in fall of 1942 and remained there for 344 days. . . . At once sobering and uplifting, this is an astounding story of survival, powerfully told." Publ Wkly

Tunnell, Michael O.

The children of Topaz; the story of a Japanese-American internment camp; based on a classroom diary; by Michael O. Tunnell and George W. Chilcoat. Holiday House 1996 74p il $19.95

Grades: 5 6 7 8   **940.53**

1. Central Utah Relocation Center 2. Japanese Americans—Evacuation and relocation, 1942-1945 3. World War, 1939-1945—Children

ISBN 0-8234-1239-3   LC 95-49360

"Interned behind barbed wire in a desert relocation camp in Topaz, Utah, Japanese American teacher Lillian 'Anne' Yamauchi Hori kept a classroom diary with her third-grade class from May to August 1943. . . . Twenty of the small diary entries appear in this book, together with several black-and-white archival photos of the camps. Tunnell and Chilcoat provide a long historical introduction and then detailed commentary that puts each diary entry in the context of what was happening in the camp and in the country at war. . . . The primary sources have a stark authority; it's the very ordinariness of the children's concerns that grabs you." Booklist

Includes bibliographical references

Warren, Andrea

Surviving Hitler; a boy in the Nazi death camps. HarperCollins Pubs. 2001 146p il hardcover o.p. pa $6.99 *

Grades: 5 6 7 8   **940.53**

1. Mandelbaum, Jack 2. Holocaust, 1933-1945

ISBN 0-688-17497-3; 0-06-029218-0 (lib bdg); 0-06-000767-2 (pa)   LC 00-38899

"Jack Mandelbaum, a Polish Jew, had a happy family life until 1939, when Germany invaded Poland, beginning World War II. Fifteen-year-old Jack is sent to Nazi concentration camps. Despite fear, starvation, and other horrors, he survives." Voice Youth Advocates

"Simply told, Warren's powerful story blends the personal testimony of Holocaust survivor Jack Mandelbaum with the history of his time, documented by stirring photos from the archives of the U.S. Holocaust Memorial Museum. . . . An excellent introduction for readers who don't know much about the history." Booklist

Includes bibliographical references

Whiteman, Dorit Bader

Lonek's journey; the true story of a boy's escape to freedom. Star Bright Books 2005 142p il map $15.95

Grades: 5 6 7 8   **940.53**

1. Holocaust, 1933-1945 2. Jews—Poland 3. Jewish refugees

ISBN 1-59572-021-9   LC 2005010898

"Lonek is 11 when the Nazis invade his Polish hometown in 1939. First he hides in a hole under the stable of friendly neighbors; then his family makes the dangerous escape to Russian-occupied Poland, from where the family members are deported in a horrific three-week crossing to the harsh Siberian slave-labor camps. But following a deal with the British, Stalin lets them go, and for two years Lonek travels on foot, by train, and by ship, until, with 1,000 other orphans, he reaches safety in Palestine. . . . The story . . . is told in short, stark chapters, each ending on a note of mounting suspense. . . . With occasional black-and-white photos, clear maps, and extensive historical notes, this is an important addition to history collections." Booklist

940.54 Military history of World War II

Allen, Thomas B., 1929-

Remember Pearl Harbor; American and Japanese survivors tell their stories; foreword by Robert D. Ballard. National Geographic Soc. 2001 57p il maps $17.95 *

Grades: 5 6 7 8   **940.54**

1. Pearl Harbor (Oahu, Hawaii), Attack on, 1941 2. World War, 1939-1945—Personal narratives
ISBN 0-7922-6690-0   LC 2001-796

Personal accounts of the Japanese attack on Pearl Harbor, with background information.

"Eyewitness testimony of Japanese and American men and women from various backgrounds enriches this balanced treatment of World War II. . . . The first-person voices along with dozens of black-and-white photos and several full-color maps make this a draw for both browsers and World War II buffs." Booklist

Includes bibliographical references

Beller, Susan Provost, 1949-

Battling in the Pacific; soldiering in World War II; by Susan Provost Beller. Twenty-First Century Books 2007 112p il map (Soldiers on the battlefront) lib bdg $33.26

Grades: 5 6 7 8   **940.54**

1. World War, 1939-1945—Pacific Ocean 2. Soldiers—United States
ISBN 978-0-8225-6381-5 (lib bdg); 0-8225-6381-9 (lib bdg)   LC 2006028168

This is an account of the U.S. troops who fought in the Pacific during World War II.

"The format is inviting with a variety of fonts at the beginning of each chapter, quotations, and a multitude of illustrations. . . . The text is clear and to the point, and chapters are divided into short topics." SLJ

Includes bibliographical references

De Capua, Sarah

The Tuskegee airmen; by Sarah E. De Capua. Child's World 2009 32p il map (Journey to freedom) lib bdg $28.50

Grades: 4 5 6   **940.54**

1. World War, 1939-1945—Aerial operations 2. African American pilots
ISBN 978-1-60253-138-3 (lib bdg); 1-60253-138-2 (lib bdg)   LC 2008031939

Tuskegee "Airmen celebrates the pilots' extraordinary achievements by placing them within the context of their time, when segregation was common. . . . Personal accounts, historical photographs of training, news stories about the men's fighting ability, and records of successful missions help to explain the squadron's determination not only to fly but also to prove its proficiency and bravery. . . . The [book is] concise and direct, yet the writing remains sophisticated. Vibrant personal stories accompanied by striking photographs of historical figures and artifacts provide a sense of the subjects' hopes and dreams." SLJ

Includes glossary and bibliographical references

Drez, Ronald J.

Remember D-day; the plan, the invasion, survivor stories. National Geographic Books 2004 61p il map $17.95; lib bdg $27.90 *

Grades: 5 6 7 8   **940.54**

1. World War, 1939-1945—Campaigns—France
ISBN 0-7922-6666-8; 0-7922-6965-9 (lib bdg)
                             LC 2003-17733

Discusses the events and personalities involved in the momentous Allied invasion of France on June 6, 1944

"This well-organized, clearly written account provides a solid overview for readers unfamiliar with the subject. A first-rate purchase." SLJ

Includes bibliographical references

Hama, Larry

The battle of Iwo Jima; guerilla warfare in the Pacific; by Larry Hama; illustrated by Anthony Williams. Rosen Pub. 2007 48p il map (Graphic battles of World War II) lib bdg $29.25 *

Grades: 5 6 7 8 9   **940.54**

1. Iwo Jima, Battle of, 1945—Graphic novels 2. Graphic novels 3. World War, 1939-1945—Graphic novels
ISBN 978-1-4042-0781-3 (lib bdg); 1-4042-0781-3 (lib bdg)   LC 2006007645

"Using a graphic novel to introduce the battle for Iwo Jima makes it very accessible. Before the graphic-novel section of the book begins, Hama provides a short, informative background piece describing the run-up to World War II, the significance of the Japanese war machine, and the importance of the tiny island of Iwo Jima. Then the graphic novel, illustrated by Williams in camouflage colors, does a terrific job of examining the ups and downs of the battle as well as the horror of so many losses—on both sides." Booklist

Includes bibliographical references

Lawton, Clive, 1951-

Hiroshima; the story of the first atom bomb; [by] Clive A. Lawton. Candlewick Press 2004 48p il map $18.99

Grades: 5 6 7 8   **940.54**

1. Hiroshima (Japan)—Bombardment, 1945 2. Atomic bomb 3. World War, 1939-1945—Japan
ISBN 0-7636-2271-0   LC 2004-45166

The author "explores the politics and the science behind the military decision that began the nuclear arms race. . . . He investigates the events that led up to the disaster at Hiroshima in 1945 and discusses the consequences that we are still living with today." Publisher's note

"Engaging text and powerful photographs are intricately woven together to make a long-lasting impact on readers." Libr Media Connect

Manning, Mick

Tail-end Charlie; [by] Mick Manning and Brita Granström. Frances Lincoln Children's Books 2009 unp il $16.95

Grades: 3 4 5   **940.54**

   1. World War, 1939-1945—Aerial operations

   ISBN 978-1-84507-651-1; 1-84507-651-6

"The remembrances of Manning's father, a British Air Force gunner during World War II, are vividly presented through comic strips, watercolor-and-ink illustrations, and memorabilia such as ration books, postcards, and photographs. . . . Reluctant readers will be drawn to the graphic format and quickly engaged by the authentic voice." SLJ

Williams, Barbara

World War II, Pacific; by Barbara Williams. Lerner Publications 2005 96p il map (Chronicle of America's wars) lib bdg $27.93

Grades: 5 6 7 8   **940.54**

   1. World War, 1939-1945

   ISBN 0-8225-0138-4   LC 2004-3371

This chronicles World War II in the Pacific focusing on the war's impact on America and its people

"A precise, well-documented chronology of the major battles in the Pacific theater. Though the narration is brief, it is informative and avoids misconceptions." SLJ

Includes glossary and bibliographical references

941   British Isles

Bean, Rachel

United Kingdom; [by] Rachel Bean; Robert Bennett and Michael Dunford, consultants. National Geographic 2007 64p il map (Countries of the world) lib bdg $28.50 *

Grades: 4 5 6 7   **941**

   1. Great Britain 2. Northern Ireland

   ISBN 978-1-4263-0126-1 (lib bdg); 1-4263-0126-X (lib bdg)   LC 2007024750

This describes the geography, nature, history, people and culture, government and economy of the United Kingdom

"What helps [this book] stand out from the pack is [its] high-quality, rich photography. . . . The photos provide as much information as the [text]. . . . The writing is straightforward and solid." SLJ

Includes glossary and bibliographical references

Dunn, James

ABC UK; illustrated by Helen Bate. Frances Lincoln 2009 c2008 unp il $16.95

Grades: K 1 2 3   **941**

   1. Great Britain 2. Alphabet

   ISBN 978-1-84507-696-2; 1-84507-696-6

"Featuring historical and cultural highlights of Great Britain (Giant's Causeway, punk music, vindaloo), each letter of the alphabet gets a uniquely stylized treatment in Bate's mixed media art. . . . The diversity of subjects makes it a prime pick for Anglophiles of all ages." Publ Wkly

Gordon, Sharon

Great Britain. Benchmark Bks. 2003 c2004 48p il map (Discovering cultures) lib bdg $28.50

Grades: 2 3 4   **941**

   1. Great Britain

   ISBN 0-7614-1717-6   LC 2003-6956

Contents: Where in the world is Great Britain?; What makes Great Britain British?; Living in Great Britain; School days; Just for fun; Let's celebrate!

Highlights the geography, people, food, schools, recreation, celebrations, and language of Great Britain

Includes glossary and bibliographical references

941.1   Scotland

Levy, Patricia, 1951-

Scotland. Benchmark Bks. 2001 128p il map (Cultures of the world) lib bdg $42.79

Grades: 5 6 7 8   **941.1**

   1. Scotland

   ISBN 0-7614-1159-3   LC 00-39831

An illustrated look at the geography, history, government, politics, people, religion, language, food and culture of Scotland

Includes glossary and bibliographical references

Oxlade, Chris

A visit to Scotland; [by] Chris Oxlade and Anita Ganeri. Heinemann Lib. 2003 32p il map (Visit to) lib bdg $22.79

Grades: 1 2 3 4   **941.1**

   1. Scotland

   ISBN 1-4034-0966-8   LC 2002-7409

Contents: Scotland; Land; Landmarks; Homes; Food; Clothes; Work; Transportation; Language; School; Free time; Celebrations; The arts; Fact file

An introduction to the history, geography, and culture of Scotland

"Despite the simple language, the subject matter is not oversimplified and the [book is] jam-packed with interesting facts. Crisp, full-color photographs on every page add meaning to the ideas presented and provide visual treats." SLJ

Includes glossary and bibliographical references

941.5   Ireland

Levy, Patricia, 1951-

Ireland. 2nd ed. Benchmark Books 2004 144p il map (Cultures of the world) lib bdg $42.79

Grades: 5 6 7 8   **941.5**

   1. Ireland

   ISBN 0-7614-1784-2   LC 2004-12902

First published 1994

This describes the geography, history, government, economy, environment, lifestyle, religion, and culture of Ireland

Includes glossary and bibliographical references

McQuinn, Colm

Ireland; [by] Anna and Colm McQuinn; Elizabeth Malcolm and John McDonagh, consultants. National Geographic 2008 64p il map (Countries of the world) lib bdg $27.90 *

Grades: 4 5 6 7   **941.5**
    1. Ireland
    ISBN 978-1-4263-0299-2 (lib bdg); 1-4263-0299-1 (lib bdg)
    This describes the geography, nature, history, people and culture, government, and economy of Ireland.
    Includes glossary and bibliographical references

Murphy, Patricia J., 1963-

Ireland; by Patricia J. Murphy. Benchmark Bks. 2003 48p il map (Discovering cultures) lib bdg $28.50

Grades: 2 3 4   **941.5**
    1. Ireland
    ISBN 0-7614-1515-7   LC 2002-15303
    Contents: Where in the world is Ireland?; What makes Ireland Irish?; Living in Ireland; School days; Just for fun; Let's celebrate!
    Highlights the geography, people, food, schools, recreation, celebrations, and language of Ireland
    "Illustrated with clear color photos [and] simply written." Horn Book Guide
    Includes glossary and bibliographical references

942   England and Wales

Blashfield, Jean F.

England; by Jean F. Blashfield. rev ed. Children's Press 2007 144p il map (Enchantment of the world, second series) lib bdg $38

Grades: 5 6 7 8   **942**
    1. England
    ISBN 0-516-24869-3   LC 2005028213
    First published 1997
    Describes the geography, history, economy, language, religions, culture, people, plants, and animals of England
    Includes bibliographical references

Oxlade, Chris

A visit to England; [by] Chris Oxlade and Anita Ganeri. Heinemann Lib. 2003 32p il map (Visit to) lib bdg $22.79

Grades: 1 2 3 4   **942**
    1. England
    ISBN 1-4034-0965-X   LC 2002-7415
    Contents: England; Land; Landmarks; Homes; Food; Clothes; Work; Transportation; Language; School; Free time; Celebrations; The arts; Fact file
    An introduction to the land and culture of England
    This is "clear, concise, . . . reader-friendly, [and] informative. . . . Accurate, up-to-date material is supported by large, full-color photographs on each spread." SLJ
    Includes glossary and bibliographical references

942.1   London

Platt, Richard, 1953-

London; illustrated by Manuela Cappon. Kingfisher 2009 45p il (Through time) $16.95 *

Grades: 3 4 5   **942.1**
    1. London (England)—History
    ISBN 978-0-7534-6255-3; 0-7534-6255-9
    This "book explores the history of London from 'Neolithic camp' to the modern city it is today. . . . Cutaway views of various structures and concise but engaging text effectively capture the changing face of a city over time." Publ Wkly

Stacey, Gill

London; by Gill Stacey. World Almanac Library 2004 48p il map (Great cities of the world) lib bdg $31 paperback o.p.

Grades: 4 5 6 7   **942.1**
    1. London (England)
    ISBN 0-8368-5022-X (lib bdg); 0-8368-5182-X (pa)
                             LC 2003-49693
    Contents: Introduction; History of London; People of London; Living in London; London at work; London at play; Looking forward
    This "up-to-date, attractively formatted [title contains an] interesting, informative [text] set in an easy-to-read font. Well-chosen, excellent-quality color photos, quotations, and sidebars appear throughout." SLJ
    Includes bibliographical references

943   Central Europe. Germany

Fuller, Barbara, 1961-

Germany; [by] Barbara Fuller, Gabriele Vossmeyer. 2nd ed. Benchmark Bks. 2003 c2004 144p il map (Cultures of the world) lib bdg $42.79

Grades: 5 6 7 8   **943**
    1. Germany
    ISBN 0-7614-1667-6   LC 2003-8186
    First published 1993
    Explores the geography, history, government, economy, people, and culture of Germany
    Includes glossary and bibliographical references

Gordon, Sharon

Germany; by Sharon Gordon. Benchmark Books 2004 48p il map (Discovering cultures) lib bdg $28.50

Grades: 2 3 4   **943**
    1. Germany
    ISBN 0-7614-1792-3   LC 2004-6132
    Contents: Where in the world is Germany?; What makes Germany German?; Living in Germany; School days; Just for fun; Let's celebrate!
    An introduction to the geography, history, people, and culture of Germany
    Includes glossary and bibliographical references

Russell, Henry, 1954-
Germany; [by] Henry Russell; Benedict Kork and Antje Schlottmann, consultants. National Geographic 2007 64p il map (Countries of the world) lib bdg $27.90 *
Grades: 4 5 6 7   **943**
1. Germany
ISBN 978-1-4263-0059-2   LC 2007024677
Describes the geography, nature, history, people and culture, government and economy of Germany.
This "appealing [title has] wonderful photographs and maps. . . . The [book offers] reliable sources for country research, and the interesting and current material holds browsing potential as well." SLJ
Includes glossary and bibliographical references

943.6   Austria and Liechtenstein

Grahame, Deborah A.
Austria; [by] Deborah Grahame. Marshall Cavendish Benchmark 2007 48p il map (Discovering cultures) lib bdg $28.50
Grades: 2 3 4   **943.6**
1. Austria
ISBN 978-0-7614-1984-6 (lib bdg); 0-7614-1984-5 (lib bdg)   LC 2006011471
An introduction to the geography, history, people, and culture of Austria
Includes glossary and bibliographical references

Sheehan, Sean, 1951-
Austria. 2nd ed. Benchmark Bks. 2003 144p il map (Cultures of the world) lib bdg $42.79
Grades: 5 6 7 8   **943.6**
1. Austria
ISBN 0-7614-1497-5   LC 2002-11623
First published 1993
Presents the geography, history, economy, and social life and customs of Austria, the birthplace of such people as Kurt Waldheim, Wolfgang Amadeus Mozart, Sigmund Freud, and Arnold Schwarzenegger
Includes glossary and bibliographical references

943.7   Czech Republic and Slovakia

Sioras, Efstathia
Czech Republic; [by] Efstathia Sioras and Michael Spilling. Marshall Cavendish Benchmark 2010 144p il map (Cultures of the world) lib bdg $42.79
Grades: 5 6 7 8   **943.7**
1. Czech Republic
ISBN 978-0-7614-4476-3 (lib bdg); 0-7614-4476-9 (lib bdg)   LC 2009003185
This describes the geography, history, wildlife, governmental structure, economy, cultural diversity, peoples, religion, and culture of the Czech Republic
Includes glossary and bibliographical references

943.8   Poland

Deckker, Zilah
Poland; [by] Zilah Deckker; Richard Butterwick and Iwona Sagan, consultants. National Geographic 2008 64p il map (Countries of the world) lib bdg $27.90 *
Grades: 4 5 6 7   **943.8**
1. Poland
ISBN 978-1-4263-0201-5   LC 2007047823
This describes the geography, nature, history, people and culture, government, and economy of Poland.
Includes glossary and bibliographical references

Gordon, Sharon
Poland. Benchmark Bks. 2004 48p il map (Discovering cultures) lib bdg $28.50
Grades: 2 3 4   **943.8**
1. Poland
ISBN 0-7614-1724-9   LC 2003-19101
Contents: Where in the world is Poland?; What makes Poland Polish?; Living in Poland; School days; Just for fun; Let's celebrate!
An introduction to the geography, history, people, and culture of Poland
Includes glossary and bibliographical references

Heale, Jay
Poland; [by] Jay Heale & Pawel Grajnert. 2nd ed. Benchmark Books 2005 144p il map (Cultures of the world) lib bdg $42.79
Grades: 5 6 7 8   **943.8**
1. Poland
ISBN 0-7614-1847-4
First published 1994
Describes the geography, history, government, economy, environment, people, and culture of Poland
"Richly detailed and illustrated with numerous striking, full-color photographs. . . . [This is] well-organized, carefully researched, readable." SLJ
Includes glossary and bibliographical references

943.9   Hungary

Esbenshade, Richard S.
Hungary. 2nd ed. Benchmark Books 2005 144p il map (Cultures of the world) lib bdg $42.79
Grades: 5 6 7 8   **943.9**
1. Hungary
ISBN 0-7614-1846-6
First published 1994
Describes the geography, history, government, economy, environment, and culture of Hungary
Includes glossary and bibliographical references

944 France and Monaco

King, David C., 1933-
Monaco; [by] David C. King. Marshall Cavendish Benchmark 2008 144p il map (Cultures of the world) lib bdg $42.79
Grades: 5 6 7 8   **944**
1. Monaco
ISBN 978-0-7614-2567-0   LC 2006030238
This describes the geography, history, government, economy, environment, people, and culture of Monaco
Includes glossary and bibliographical references

NgCheong-Lum, Roseline, 1962-
France. Stevens, G. 1999 96p il (Countries of the world) lib bdg $30.60
Grades: 4 5 6 7   **944**
1. France
ISBN 978-0-8368-2260-1 (lib bdg); 0-8368-2260-9 (lib bdg)   LC 98-33770
An overview of France, discussing its history, geography, government, economy, culture, and relations with North America
"The full-color photos on every page are outstanding and the style of writing is graceful." SLJ
Includes glossary and bibliographical references

Tidmarsh, Celia, 1956-
France. Sea-to-sea Publications 2009 32p il map (Facts about countries) lib bdg $28.50
Grades: 3 4 5   **944**
1. France
ISBN 978-1-59771-115-9 (lib bdg); 1-59771-115-2 (lib bdg)
Describes the geography, history, industries, education, government, and cultures of France
"The attractive layout includes color photographs and charts of current statistics as well as maps illustrating main farming regions, natural resources, or the literacy rates of girls and boys. The [text is] clear and succinct." SLJ

944.04 France—Revolutionary period, 1789-1804

Riggs, Kate
The French Revolution. Creative Education 2009 48p il map (Days of change) lib bdg $32.80
Grades: 5 6 7 8   **944.04**
1. France—History—1789-1799, Revolution
ISBN 978-1-58341-734-8; 1-58341-734-6
          LC 2008009728
"With elegant design and mature prose, the Days of Change series is an ideal starting point for all manner of school projects. . . . The political pressures at the center of *The French Revolution* are difficult to dramatize, but Riggs carefully lays out the factions and civil disobedience that led to the Declaration of the Rights of Man and of The Citizen—and then the emperor's reign that overthrew everything." Booklist
Includes bibliographical references

945 Italian Peninsula and adjacent islands. Italy

Macaulay, David, 1946-
Rome antics. Houghton Mifflin 1997 79p il $18
Grades: 4 5 6 7   **945**
1. Rome (Italy)—Description and travel
ISBN 0-395-82279-3   LC 97-20941
"Modern Rome is seen through the skewed perspective of a homing pigeon's erratic flight through the city streets as she delivers a message to an artist in a garret. . . . Macaulay adds sly touches of humor to the pen-and-ink sketches. . . . The book includes a map of the city 'As the pigeon flies' with each structure numbered, and an addendum shows the 22 featured buildings with a paragraph or two of interesting facts about each one." SLJ

Malone, Margaret Gay
Italy. Benchmark Bks. 2002 c2003 48p il map (Discovering cultures) lib bdg $28.50
Grades: 2 3 4   **945**
1. Italy
ISBN 0-7614-1176-3   LC 2001-7458
Contents: Where in the world is Italy?; What makes Italy Italian?; Living in Italy; School days; Just for fun; Let's celebrate!
Highlights the geography, people, food, schools, recreation, celebrations, and language of Italy
Includes glossary and bibliographical references

Sheehan, Sean, 1951-
Malta. Benchmark Bks. 2000 128p il map (Cultures of the world) lib bdg $42.79
Grades: 5 6 7 8   **945**
1. Malta
ISBN 0-7614-0993-9   LC 99-53436
The text covers Malta's "government, economy, people, lifestyles, religion, language, arts and leisure, festivals, and food. . . . Copious colorful photographs and reproductions complement and reinforce the facts presented." SLJ
Includes glossary and bibliographical references

Winter, Jane Kohen, 1959-
Italy; [by] Jane Kohen Winter, Leslie Jermyn. 2nd ed. Benchmark Bks. 2003 144p il maps (Cultures of the world) lib bdg $42.79
Grades: 5 6 7 8   **945**
1. Italy
ISBN 0-7614-1500-9   LC 2002-11628
First published 1995
Describes the geography, history, government, economy, and culture of Italy
"Colorful photographs with informative captions decorate almost every page of [this book]." SLJ
Includes glossary and bibliographical references

946   Iberian Peninsula and adjacent islands. Spain

Augustin, Byron
   Andorra; by Byron D. Augustin. Marshall Cavendish Benchmark 2009 144p il map (Cultures of the world) lib bdg $42.79
   Grades: 5 6 7 8   **946**
      1. Andorra
      ISBN 978-0-7614-3122-0 (lib bdg); 0-7614-3122-5 (lib bdg)   LC 2007040356
   "Provides comprehensive information on the geography, history, governmental structure, economy, cultural diversity, peoples, religion, and culture of Andorra." Publisher's note
   Includes glossary and bibliographical references

Croy, Anita
   Spain. National Geographic 2010 64p il map (Countries of the world) lib bdg $27.90
   Grades: 4 5 6 7   **946**
      1. Spain
      ISBN 978-1-4263-0633-4; 1-4263-0633-4
   This describes the geography, nature, history, people and culture, government and economy of Spain.
   "The information is substantial but not overwhelming. The [text is] clear, and the discussion points are well chosen. . . . [The text is] complemented with stunning photographs." SLJ
   Includes glossary and bibliographical references

Kohen, Elizabeth, 1960-
   Spain; [by] Elizabeth Kohen, Marie Louise Elias. 2nd ed. Benchmark Bks. 2003 144p il maps (Cultures of the world) lib bdg $42.79
   Grades: 5 6 7 8   **946**
      1. Spain
      ISBN 0-7614-1501-7   LC 2002-11626
      First published 1996
   Introduces the geography, history, economy, culture, and people of Spain
   "Colorful photographs with informative captions decorate almost every page of [this book]." SLJ
   Includes glossary and bibliographical references

Parker, Lewis K.
   Spain. Benchmark Bks. 2003 48p il map (Discovering cultures) lib bdg $28.50
   Grades: 2 3 4   **946**
      1. Spain
      ISBN 0-7614-1520-3   LC 2002-15301
   Contents: Where in the world is Spain?; What makes Spain Spanish?; Living in Spain; School days; Just for fun; Let's celebrate!
   An introduction to Spain, highlighting the country's geography, people, foods, schools, recreation, celebrations, and language
   This title is "illustrated with clear color photos [and is] simply written." Horn Book Guide
   Includes glossary and bibliographical references

946.9   Portugal

Deckker, Zilah
   Portugal. National Geographic 2009 64p il map (Countries of the world) lib bdg $27.90 *
   Grades: 4 5 6 7   **946.9**
      1. Portugal
      ISBN 978-1-4263-0390-6 (lib bdg); 1-4263-0390-4 (lib bdg)   LC 2009275584
   This describes the geography, nature, history, people and culture, government and economy of Portugal
   Includes glossary and bibliographical references

Heale, Jay
   Portugal; [by] Jay Heale & Angeline Koh. 2nd ed. Marshall Cavendish Benchmark 2006 144p il map (Cultures of the world) lib bdg $42.79
   Grades: 5 6 7 8   **946.9**
      1. Portugal
      ISBN 0-7614-2053-3   LC 2005022922
      First published 1995
   Describes the geography, history, government, economy, culture, peoples, and religion of Portugal
   Includes glossary and bibliographical references

947   Eastern Europe. Russia

De Capua, Sarah
   Russia. Benchmark Bks. 2003 c2004 48p il map (Discovering cultures) lib bdg $28.50
   Grades: 2 3 4   **947**
      1. Russia
      ISBN 0-7614-1716-8   LC 2003-6957
   Contents: Where in the world is Russia?; What makes Russia Russian?; Living in Russia; School days; Just for fun; Let's celebrate!
   Highlights the geography, people, food, schools, recreation, celebrations, and language of Russia
   Includes glossary and bibliographical references

Russell, Henry, 1954-
   Russia; [by] Henry Russell; Laurie Bernstein and Ilya Utekhin, consultants. National Geographic 2008 64p il map (Countries of the world) lib bdg $27.90 *
   Grades: 4 5 6 7   **947**
      1. Russia
      ISBN 978-1-4263-0259-6 (lib bdg); 1-4263-0259-2 (lib bdg)
   This describes the geography, nature, history, people and culture, government, and economy of Russia.
   Includes glossary and bibliographical references

947.5 Caucasus

Beliaev, Edward
Dagestan; [by] Edward Beliaev & Oksana Buranbaeva. Marshall Cavendish Benchmark 2006 144p il map (Cultures of the world) lib bdg $42.79
Grades: 5 6 7 8   **947.5**
1. Dagestan (Russia)
ISBN 0-7614-2015-0   LC 2005013698
An exploration of the geography, history, government, economy, people, and culture of the former Soviet republic of Dagestan
Includes glossary and bibliographical references

Dhilawala, Sakina, 1964-
Armenia; [by] Sakina Dhilawala. 2nd ed. Marshall Cavendish Benchmark 2008 144p il map (Cultures of the world) lib bdg $39.93
Grades: 5 6 7 8   **947.5**
1. Armenia
ISBN 978-0-7614-2029-3   LC 2007014890
First published 1997
"Provides comprehensive information on the geography, history, wildlife, governmental structure, economy, cultural diversity, peoples, religion, and culture of Armenia." Publisher's note
Includes glossary and bibliographical references

King, David C., 1933-
Azerbaijan; [by] David C. King. Marshall Cavendish Benchmark 2006 144p il map (Cultures of the world) lib bdg $42.79
Grades: 5 6 7 8   **947.5**
1. Azerbaijan
ISBN 0-7614-2011-8   LC 2004028443
An overview of the history, culture, peoples, religion, government, and geography of Azerbaijan
Includes glossary and bibliographical references

Spilling, Michael
Georgia; [by] Michael Spilling & Winnie Wong. 2nd ed. Marshall Cavendish Benchmark 2008 c2009 144p il map (Cultures of the world) lib bdg $42.79
Grades: 5 6 7 8   **947.5**
1. Georgia (Republic)
ISBN 978-0-7614-3033-9 (lib bdg); 0-7614-3033-4 (lib bdg)   LC 2007050796
First published 1998
This describes the geography, nature, history, people and culture, government and economy of Georgia
Includes glossary and bibliographical references

947.6 Moldova

Sheehan, Patricia, 1954-
Moldova. Benchmark Bks. 2000 128p il map (Cultures of the world) lib bdg $42.79
Grades: 5 6 7 8   **947.6**
1. Moldova
ISBN 0-7614-0997-1   LC 99-53433
An illustrated look at the history and culture of the small landlocked country between Russia and the Ukraine that proclaimed its independence in August, 1991
Includes glossary and bibliographical references

947.7 Ukraine

Bassis, Volodymyr
Ukraine; [by] Volodymyr Bassis & Sakina Dhilawala. 2nd ed. Marshall Cavendish Benchmark 2008 144p il map (Cultures of the world) lib bdg $42.79
Grades: 5 6 7 8   **947.7**
1. Ukraine
ISBN 978-0-7614-2090-3   LC 2007019179
First published 1997
"Provides comprehensive information on the geography, history, wildlife, governmental structure, economy, cultural diversity, peoples, religion, and culture of Ukraine." Publisher's note
Includes glossary and bibliographical references

947.93 Lithuania

Kagda, Sakina, 1939-
Lithuania; [by] Sakina Kagda & Zawiah Abdul Latif. 2nd ed. Marshall Cavendish Benchmark 2008 144p il map (Cultures of the world) lib bdg $42.79
Grades: 5 6 7 8   **947.93**
1. Lithuania
ISBN 978-0-7614-2087-3   LC 2007016290
First published 1997
"Provides comprehensive information on the geography, history, wildlife, governmental structure, economy, cultural diversity, peoples, religion, and culture of Lithuania." Publisher's note
Includes glossary and bibliographical references

947.96 Latvia

Barlas, Robert
Latvia; [by] Robert Barlas and Winnie Wong. 2nd ed. Marshall Cavendish Benchmark 2010 144p il map (Cultures of the world) lib bdg $29.95
Grades: 5 6 7 8   **947.96**
1. Latvia
ISBN 978-0-7614-4857-0; 0-7614-4857-8
LC 2009046001

Barlas, Robert—*Continued*
First published 2000
This offers information on the geography, history, wildlife, governmental structure, economy, cultural diversity, peoples, religion, and culture of Latvia.
Includes glossary and bibliographical references

947.98   Estonia

Spilling, Michael
Estonia. 2nd ed. Marshall Cavendish Benchmark 2010 142p il map (Cultures of the world) lib bdg $42.79
Grades: 5 6 7 8   **947.98**
1. Estonia
ISBN 978-0-7614-4846-4; 0-7614-4846-2
LC 2009021201
First published 1999
This describes the geography, history, wildlife, governmental structure, economy, cultural diversity, peoples, religion, and culture of Estonia.
Includes glossary and bibliographical references

948   Scandinavia

Berger, Melvin, 1927-
The real Vikings; craftsmen, traders, and fearsome raiders; [by] Melvin and Gilda Berger. National Geographic Society 2003 55p il map $18.95 *
Grades: 4 5 6 7   **948**
1. Vikings
ISBN 0-7922-5132-6   LC 2002-154474
This book offers an "introduction to the Vikings, beginning with their attack on Lindisfarne in 793 and ending, in 1066, with William the Conqueror." SLJ
"The many illustrations include maps, drawings, prints, and paintings from many periods in addition to color photographs of Viking artifacts and sites. . . . Visually appealing and quite informative, the book will appeal to browsers as well as young researchers." Booklist

Park, Louise, 1961-
The Scandinavian Vikings; by Louise Park and Timothy Love. Marshall Cavendish Benchmark 2009 32p il map (Ancient and medieval people) $19.95
Grades: 4 5 6   **948**
1. Vikings 2. Scandinavia—Civilization
ISBN 978-0-7614-4445-9; 0-7614-4445-9
"An introduction to the history and lifestyle of Scandinavian Vikings." Publisher's note
This title has "a simple and elegant design with the proper balance of quality writing and quantity of information. . . . Handy time lines, well-chosen photos of ruins and artifacts, quality illustrations, inset 'Quick Facts', and 'What You Should Know About' features will grab reluctant readers and captivate even those with short attention spans." SLJ
Includes glossary

Schomp, Virginia, 1953-
The Vikings. Franklin Watts 2005 112p il map (People of the ancient world) lib bdg $30.50; pa $9.95
Grades: 5 6 7 8   **948**
1. Vikings
ISBN 0-531-12382-0 (lib bdg); 0-531-16849-2 (pa)
LC 2004-24311
Contents: Legends and history; Warrior kings; Upperclass men and women; Farmers and settlers; Artisans and artists; Merchants and traders; Warriors; Poets and rune masters; Slaves; The legacy of the Vikings
This examines the culture of the Vikings "through their literature, artifacts, and documents. Religion, farming, levels of society, art, government, and fine arts are covered in [this] well-written and attractive [book]." Booklist
Includes bibliographical references

948.1   Norway

Kagda, Sakina, 1939-
Norway; [by] Sakina Kagda & Barbara Cooke. 2nd ed. Marshall Cavendish Benchmark 2006 144p il map (Cultures of the world) lib bdg $42.79
Grades: 5 6 7 8   **948.1**
1. Norway
ISBN 978-0-7614-2067-5 (lib bdg); 0-7614-2067-3 (lib bdg)
First published 1995
This provides "information on the geography, history, governmental structure, economy, cultural diversity, peoples, religion, and culture of Norway." Publisher's note
"Organization is clear and user friendly. Fine-quality, full-color photographs and reproductions draw readers in and help to hold their interest." SLJ [review of 1995 edition]
Includes glossary and bibliographical references

948.5   Sweden

Gan, Delice, 1954-
Sweden; [by] Delice Gan, Leslie Jermyn. 2nd ed. Benchmark Bks. 2003 144p il maps (Cultures of the world) lib bdg $42.79
Grades: 5 6 7 8   **948.5**
1. Sweden
ISBN 0-7614-1502-5   LC 2002-152559
First published 1993 under the authorship of Delice Gan
Introduces the geography, history, economy, culture, and people of the fourth largest country in Europe
Includes glossary and bibliographical references

Grahame, Deborah A.
Sweden; [by] Deborah Grahame. Marshall Cavendish Benchmark 2007 48p il map (Discovering cultures) lib bdg $28.50
Grades: 2 3 4   **948.5**
1. Sweden
ISBN 978-0-7614-1985-3 (lib bdg); 0-7614-1985-3 (lib bdg)
LC 2006011474

Grahame, Deborah A.—*Continued*
An introduction to geography, history, government, and culture of Sweden
Includes glossary and bibliographical references

Phillips, Charles
Sweden; [by] Charles Phillips; Susan C. Brantly and Eric Clark consultants. National Geographic 2009 64p il map (Countries of the world) lib bdg $27.90 *
Grades: 4 5 6 7 **948.5**
1. Sweden
ISBN 978-1-4263-0389-0 (lib bdg); 1-4263-0389-0 (lib bdg) LC 2009275585
This describes the geography, nature, history, people & culture, and government & economy of Sweden
Includes glossary and bibliographical references

948.9 Denmark and Finland

Pateman, Robert, 1954-
Denmark; [by] Robert Pateman. 2nd ed. Marshall Cavendish Benchmark 2006 144p il map (Cultures of the world) lib bdg $42.79
Grades: 5 6 7 8 **948.9**
1. Denmark
ISBN 0-7614-2024-X LC 2005021610
First published 1995
Introduces the geography, history, economics, culture, and people of Denmark
Includes glossary and bibliographical references

948.97 Finland

Tan, Chung Lee, 1949-
Finland; [by] Tan Chung Lee. 2nd ed. Marshall Cavendish Benchmark 2007 144p il map (Cultures of the world) lib bdg $39.93 *
Grades: 5 6 7 8 **948.97**
1. Finland
ISBN 978-0-7614-2073-6 (lib bdg); 0-7614-2073-8 (lib bdg) LC 2006015897
First published 1996
This provides "information on the geography, history, governmental structure, economy, cultural diversity, peoples, religion, and culture of Finland." Publisher's note
Includes glossary and bibliographical references

949.12 Iceland

McMillan, Bruce
Going fishing; written and photo-illustrated by Bruce McMillan. Houghton Mifflin Co. 2005 32p il $16
Grades: 2 3 4 **949.12**
1. Iceland 2. Fishing
ISBN 0-618-47201-0 LC 2004-15506
"Walter Lorraine books"

"This narrative photo-essay follows a young boy from Reykjavik to the fishing village where his two grandfathers live. Each takes his grandson out on his own boat to catch a type of fish important to Iceland. . . . The clarity of the color photos brings the people, their surroundings, and the process of fishing sharply into focus. . . . A delightfully illustrated presentation of fishing, family, and, of course, Iceland." Booklist

Wilcox, Jonathan, 1960-
Iceland; [by] Jonathan Wilcox & Zawiah Abdul Latif. 2nd ed. Marshall Cavendish Benchmark 2007 144p il map (Cultures of the world) lib bdg $42.79
Grades: 5 6 7 8 **949.12**
1. Iceland
ISBN 978-0-7614-2074-3 (lib bdg); 0-7614-2074-6 (lib bdg) LC 2006047548
First published 1996
This provides "information on the geography, history, wildlife, governmental structure, economy, diversity, peoples, religion, and culture of Iceland." Publisher's note
Includes glossary and bibliographical references

949.2 Netherlands

Seward, Pat, 1939-
Netherlands; [by] Pat Seward & Sunandini Arora Lal. 2nd ed. Marshall Cavendish Benchmark 2006 144p il map (Cultures of the world) lib bdg $42.79
Grades: 5 6 7 8 **949.2**
1. Netherlands
ISBN 0-7614-2052-5 LC 2005019823
First published 1995
Describes the geography, history, government, economy, culture, peoples, and religion of the Netherlands
Includes glossary and bibliographical references

949.3 Southern Low Countries. Belgium

Pateman, Robert, 1954-
Belgium; [by] Robert Pateman & Mark Elliott. 2nd ed. Marshall Cavendish Benchmark 2006 144p il map (Cultures of the world) lib bdg $42.79
Grades: 5 6 7 8 **949.3**
1. Belgium
ISBN 978-0-7614-2059-0 (lib bdg); 0-7614-2059-2 (lib bdg)
First published 1995
This provides "information on the geography, history, governmental structure, economy, cultural diversity, peoples, religion, and culture of Belgium." Publisher's note
"Organization is clear and user friendly. Fine-quality, full-color photographs and reproductions draw readers in and help to hold their interest." SLJ [review of 1995 edition]
Includes glossary and bibliographical references

949.35 Luxembourg

Sheehan, Patricia, 1954-
Luxembourg; by Patricia Sheehan & Sakina Dhilawala. 2nd ed. Marshall Cavendish Benchmark 2008 144p il map (Cultures of the world) lib bdg $42.79
Grades: 5 6 7 8 **949.35**
   1. Luxembourg
   ISBN 978-0-7614-2088-0   LC 2007014891
   First published 1997
   Discusses the geography, history, government, economy, and customs of the smallest of the Benelux countries
   Includes glossary and bibliographical references

949.4 Switzerland

Harris, Pamela K., 1962-
Welcome to Switzerland; by Pamela K. Harris and Brad Clemmons. Child's World 2008 32p il map (Welcome to the world) lib bdg $27.07
Grades: 1 2 3 4 **949.4**
   1. Switzerland
   ISBN 978-1-59296-980-7 (lib bdg); 1-59296-980-1 (lib bdg)   LC 2007038146
   This briefly describes the geography, history, people, and culture of Switzerland.
   "Report writers and browsers will appreciate [this book]. . . . The captioned, color photographs have a balanced gender representation. Maps, fast facts, and recipes round out excellent offerings." SLJ
   Includes glossary and bibliographical references

Levy, Patricia, 1951-
Switzerland; [by] Patricia Levy & Richard Lord. 2nd ed. Benchmark Books 2005 144p il map (Cultures of the world) lib bdg $42.79
Grades: 5 6 7 8 **949.4**
   1. Switzerland
   ISBN 0-7614-1850-4
   First published 1994
   Describes the geography, history, government, economy, people, and culture of Switzerland
   Includes glossary and bibliographical references

949.5 Greece

DuBois, Jill, 1952-
Greece; [by] Jill Dubois, Xenia Skoura, Olga Gratsaniti. 2nd ed. Benchmark Bks. 2003 143p il maps (Cultures of the world) lib bdg $42.79
Grades: 5 6 7 8 **949.5**
   1. Greece
   ISBN 0-7614-1499-1   LC 2002-11625
   First published 1992 under the authorship of Jill Du-Bois
   Introduces the geography, history, economics, culture, and people of the Mediterranean country of Greece
   "An attractive, lively, and perceptive look at Greece." SLJ
   Includes glossary and bibliographical references

Gordon, Sharon
Greece. Benchmark Bks. 2004 48p il maps (Discovering cultures) lib bdg $28.50
Grades: 2 3 4 **949.5**
   1. Greece
   ISBN 0-7614-1718-4   LC 2003-8130
   Contents: Where in the world is Greece?; What makes Greece Greek?; Living in Greece; School days; Just for fun; Let's celebrate!
   An introduction to the history, geography, language, schools, and social life and customs of Greece
   Includes glossary and bibliographical references

Green, Jen
Greece; [by] Greg Anderson and Kostas Vlassopoulos, consultants. National Geographic 2009 64p il map (Countries of the world) lib bdg $27.90 *
Grades: 4 5 6 7 **949.5**
   1. Greece
   ISBN 978-1-4263-0470-5 (lib bdg); 1-4263-0470-6 (lib bdg)
   This describes the geography, nature, history, people and culture, government and economy of Greece
   Includes glossary and bibliographical references

949.6 Balkan Peninsula

Barber, Nicola
Istanbul; [by] Nicola Barber. World Almanac Library 2006 48p il map (Great cities of the world) lib bdg $31
Grades: 3 4 5 6 **949.6**
   1. Istanbul (Turkey)
   ISBN 0-8368-5050-5   LC 2005042112
   This describes the geography, culture, work, play, history, and religion of Istanbul, Turkey
   This is "attractive, informative . . . straightforward and objective." SLJ
   Includes bibliographical references

949.65 Albania

Knowlton, MaryLee, 1946-
Albania; by MaryLee Knowlton. Marshall Cavendish Benchmark 2005 144p il map (Cultures of the world) lib bdg $42.79
Grades: 5 6 7 8 **949.65**
   1. Albania
   ISBN 0-7614-1852-0   LC 2004-22236
   Contents: Geography; History; Government; Economy; Environment; Albanians; Lifestyle; Religion; Language; Arts; Leisure; Festivals; Food
   An overview of the history, culture, peoples, religion, government, and geography of Albania
   Includes glossary and bibliographical references

949.7 Serbia and Montenegro, Croatia, Slovenia, Bosnia and Hercegovina, Macedonia

Cooper, Robert, 1945-
Croatia. Benchmark Bks. 2001 128p il map (Cultures of the world) lib bdg $42.79
Grades: 5 6 7 8   **949.7**
1. Croatia
ISBN 0-7614-1156-9   LC 00-29510
"The initial chapters go over basic geography, history, and government, while the bulk of the book examines Croatia's culture and contemporary life. The short chapters are divided into highlighted segments of a page or two. This format allows easy access to information." SLJ
Includes glossary and bibliographical references

Halilbegovich, Nadja, 1979-
My childhood under fire; a Sarajevo diary. Kids Can Press 2006 120p il $14.95
Grades: 5 6 7 8   **949.7**
1. Yugoslav War, 1991-1995 2. Sarajevo (Bosnia and Hercegovina)
ISBN 1-55337-797-4
"In 1992, when the bombing started in Sarajevo, Halilbegovich, 12, kept a diary of her terrifying daily life under siege. Her terse vignettes replay the horror of her comfortable home torn apart." Booklist

King, David C., 1933-
Serbia and Montenegro; by David C. King. Benchmark Bks. 2005 144p il map (Cultures of the world) lib bdg $39.93
Grades: 5 6 7 8   **949.7**
1. Serbia 2. Montenegro
ISBN 0-7614-1855-5   LC 2004-22248
Contents: Geography; History; Government; Economy; Environment; Serbs and Montenegrins; Lifestyle; Religion; Language; Arts; Leisure; Festivals; Food
This offers "historical, geographical, and cultural information as well as observations about contemporary lifestyles and issues. In general the writing is clear; at times it is lively. . . . The photographs are excellent." SLJ
Includes glossary and bibliographical references

Knowlton, MaryLee, 1946-
Macedonia; by MaryLee Knowlton. Benchmark Books 2005 144p il map (Cultures of the world) lib bdg $42.79
Grades: 5 6 7 8   **949.7**
1. Macedonia (Republic)
ISBN 0-7614-1854-7   LC 2004-22735
Contents: Geography; History; Government; Economy; Environment; Macedonians; Lifestyle; Religion; Language; Arts; Leisure; Festivals; Food
Describes the geography, history, government, economy, people, and culture of Macedonia
Includes glossary and bibliographical references

950 History of Asia

Law, Felicia
Atlas of Southwest and Central Asia. Picture Window Books 2008 32p il map (Picture Window Books world atlases) lib bdg $27.93; pa $7.95
Grades: 2 3 4   **950**
1. Asia 2. Middle East
ISBN 978-1-4048-3884-0 (lib bdg); 1-4048-3884-8 (lib bdg); 978-1-4048-3892-5 (pa); 1-4048-3892-9 (pa)
This introduction to the geography of Southwest and Central Asia offers maps and information about countries, landforms, bodies of water, climate, plants, animals, population, people and customs, places of interest, industries, transportation, and Mount Everest
Includes glossary

Atlas of the Far East and Southeast Asia. Picture Window Books 2008 32p il map (Picture Window Books world atlases) lib bdg $27.93; pa $7.95
Grades: 2 3 4   **950**
1. Asia
ISBN 978-1-4048-3883-3 (lib bdg); 1-4048-3883-X (lib bdg); 978-1-4048-3891-8 (pa); 1-4048-3891-0 (pa)
This introduction to the geography of the Far East and Southeast Asia offers maps and information about countries, landforms, bodies of water, climate, plants, animals, population, people and customs, places of interest, industries, transportation, and the Pacific Islands
Includes glossary

Peoples of Western Asia. Marshall Cavendish 2007 11v il map set $359.80
Grades: 5 6 7 8   **950**
1. Asia 2. Reference books
ISBN 978-0-7614-7677-1; 0-7614-7677-6
Contents: v1 Afghanistan-Armenia; v2 Azerbaijan-Georgia; v3 Iran-Iraq; v4 Israel-Kazakhstan; v5 Kuwait-Lebanon; v6 Maldives-Pakistan; v7 Qatar-Russian Federation; v8 Saudi Arabia-Tajikistan; v9 Turkey-Turkmenistan; v10 United Arab Emirates-Yemen; v11 Index
This describes the cultures and histories of countries as far west as Turkey, Israel, and Saudi Arabia, and as far east as Kazakhstan, Kyrgyzstan, and the Siberian region of the Russian Federation
"All of the entries are clearly written. . . . The hundreds of photographs . . . are of high quality and invaluable as illustrations for the text." Booklist

951 China and adjacent areas

Asher, Sandy, 1942-
China. Benchmark Bks. 2003 48p il map (Discovering cultures) lib bdg $28.50
Grades: 2 3 4   **951**
1. China
ISBN 0-7614-1179-8   LC 2001-7293
Highlights the geography, people, food, schools, recreation, celebrations, and language of China
Includes glossary and bibliographical references

Ferroa, Peggy Grace, 1959-
China; [by] Peggy Ferroa, Elaine Chan. 2nd ed.
Benchmark Bks. 2002 144p il map (Cultures of
the world) lib bdg $42.79
Grades: 5 6 7 8   **951**
  1. China
  ISBN 0-7614-1474-6   LC 2002-19209
  First published 1991
  Describes the geography, history, government, econo-
my, environment, people, and culture of China
  Includes glossary and bibliographical references

Keister, Douglas, 1948-
To grandmother's house; a visit to old-town
Beijing. Gibbs Smith, Publisher 2008 unp $15.95
Grades: K 1 2 3 4   **951**
  1. Beijing (China) 2. China 3. Bilingual books—En-
glish-Chinese
  ISBN 978-1-4236-0283-5; 1-4236-0283-8
                 LC 2007033167
"Through an engaging bilingual narrative and lovely,
full-color photos, Zhang Yue gives readers a tour of her
hometown, beautiful and historic Beijing. She starts the
day with a visit to her grandmother in a hutong, or
neighborhood, in the old part of the city. Along the way
she introduces the sights and shops in a voice that is natural and interesting, inviting readers to experience all of
the little details that make Beijing unique. The photographs wonderfully capture the splendor of the major
monuments as well as the fascinating bustle of the outdoor markets." SLJ

Levy, Patricia, 1951-
Tibet; [by] Patricia Levy & Don Bosco. 2nd ed.
Marshall Cavendish Benchmark 2007 144p il map
(Cultures of the world) lib bdg $42.79
Grades: 5 6 7 8   **951**
  1. Tibet (China)
  ISBN 978-0-7614-2076-7 (lib bdg); 0-7614-2076-2 (lib
bdg)   LC 2006015826
  First published 1996
  This provides "information on the geography, history,
wildlife, governmental structure, economy, diversity, peo-
ples, religion, and culture of Tibet." Publisher's note
  Includes glossary and bibliographical references

Marx, Trish, 1948-
Elephants and golden thrones; inside China's
Forbidden City; written by Trish Marx;
photographs and photograph selection by Ellen B.
Senisi; foreword by Li Ji. Abrams Books for
Young Readers 2008 48p il $18.95
Grades: 4 5 6 7   **951**
  1. Forbidden City (Beijing, China) 2. China
  ISBN 978-0-8109-9485-0; 0-8109-9485-2
               LC 2007-022413
Introduces Beijing's Forbidden City, recounting some
of the most famous incidents from its past, and describ-
ing its rooms, their function, and some of the daily ritu-
als of palace life.
  The author "brings the Forbidden City to life by tell-
ing stories about six different royal inhabitants from

Zhengde, 'one of the worst emperors in Chinese history,'
to Puyi, who became a pawn of the invading Japanese.
. . . Beautiful drawings and photographs, some provided
by the Palace Museum and some taken for this book,
lend color and provide additional information. Of particular note are the photos of the interiors of buildings, a
number of which are not regularly open to the public."
Booklist
  Includes bibliographical references

Riehecky, Janet, 1953-
China; by Janet Riehecky. Lerner Publications
Company 2008 48p il (Country explorers) lib bdg
$27.93
Grades: 2 3 4   **951**
  1. China
  ISBN 978-0-8225-7129-2   LC 2006036731
  This introduction to China covers "all of the areas of
interest to students, including animals, sports, foods, celebrations, storytime, and even a few words in the country's native language. Small amounts of information are
surrounded by current photographs, maps, charts, and illustrations. . . . Sure to grab the attention of even reluctant readers." SLJ
  Includes glossary and bibliographical references

Sís, Peter, 1949-
Tibet; through the red box. Farrar, Straus &
Giroux 1998 unp il maps $25 *
Grades: 4 5 6 7   **951**
  1. Tibet (China)
  ISBN 0-374-37552-6   LC 97-50175
  A Caldecott Medal honor book, 1999
  "Frances Foster books"
  "When Sis opens the red lacquered box that has sat on
his father's table for decades, he finds the diary his father kept when he was lost in Tibet in the mid-1950s.
The text replicates the diary's spidery handwriting, while
the illustrations depict elaborate mazes and mandalas,
along with dreamlike spreads that are filled with frag-
mented details of the father's and son's lives. . . . Impeccably designed and beautifully made, the book has a
dreamlike quality that will keep readers of many ages
coming back to find more in its pages." Booklist

951.05   China—Period of People's Republic, 1949-

Chen, Jiang Hong, 1963-
Mao and me; the Little Red Guard; [by] Chen
Jiang Hong; [translated by Claudia Zoe Bedrick]
Enchanted Lion Books 2008 77p il $19.95
Grades: 3 4 5   **951.05**
  1. China—History—1949-1976—Personal narratives
  2. Children—China
  ISBN 978-1-59270-079-0; 1-59270-079-9
               LC 2008037650
  Originally published in French
  Chen's "picture book memoir of growing up during
the Cultural Revolution is not easy to read, but stands
out for its epic sweep and unflinching honesty. Rendered

Chen, Jiang Hong, 1963-—Continued

in large panels, his ink and wash paintings document everything from the making of dumplings to the public humiliation of cherished neighbors. . . . [This shows] excellence in representing political upheaval." Publ Wkly

Jiang, Ji-li

Red scarf girl; a memoir of the Cultural Revolution; foreword by David Henry Hwang. HarperCollins Pubs. 1997 285p $16.99; pa $6.99

Grades: 6 7 8 9   **951.05**

    1. China—History—1949-1976—Personal narratives

    ISBN 0-06-027585-5; 0-06-446208-0 (pa)

                   LC 97-5089

"This is an autobiographical account of growing up during Mao's Cultural Revolution in China in 1966. . . . Jiang describes in terrifying detail the ordeals of her family and those like them, including unauthorized search and seizure, persecution, arrest and torture, hunger, and public humiliation. . . . Her voice is that of an intelligent, confused adolescent, and her focus on the effects of the revolution on herself, her family, and her friends provides an emotional focal point for the book, and will allow even those with limited knowledge of Chinese history to access the text." Bull Cent Child Books

Zhang, Ange

Red land, yellow river; a story from the Cultural Revolution. Douglas & McIntyre 2004 55p il $16.95 *

Grades: 5 6 7 8   **951.05**

    1. China—History—1949-1976—Personal narratives

    ISBN 0-88899-489-3

"A Groundwood book"

"Zhang was a teen living in Beijing when Mao Zedong began the Cultural Revolution. In a youthful voice he records his experiences in the early years of that turbulent decade that began in 1966. . . . This moving account of a youngster swept up in the revolutionary fervor and then beginning to question its goals is accompanied by attractive, digitally rendered illustrations." SLJ

951.2   Taiwan, Hong Kong, Macau

Moiz, Azra, 1963-

Taiwan; [by] Azra Moiz & Janice Wu. 2nd ed. Marshall Cavendish Benchmark 2006 144p il map (Cultures of the world) lib bdg $42.79

Grades: 5 6 7 8   **951.2**

    1. Taiwan

    ISBN 978-0-7614-2069-9 (lib bdg); 0-7614-2069-X (lib bdg)

    First published 1995

This describes "the geography, history, government, economy, people, religion, food, and other facets of [Taiwan]. . . . Organization is clear and user friendly. Fine-quality, full-color photographs and reproductions draw readers in and help to hold their interest." SLJ [review of 1995 edition]

    Includes glossary and bibliographical references

951.25   Hong Kong

Kagda, Falaq

Hong Kong; [by] Falaq Kagda & Magdalene Koh. 2nd ed. Marshall Cavendish Benchmark 2008 c2009 144p il map (Cultures of the world) lib bdg $42.79

Grades: 5 6 7 8   **951.25**

    1. Hong Kong (China)

    ISBN 978-0-7614-3034-6 (lib bdg); 0-7614-3034-2 (lib bdg)   LC 2007048285

    First published 1998

Surveys the geography, history, government, economy, and culture of Hong Kong

    Includes glossary and bibliographical references

951.7   Mongolia

Lewin, Ted, 1935-

Horse song; the Naadam of Mongolia; [by] Ted and Betsy Lewin. Lee & Low Books 2008 unp il $19.95 *

Grades: 2 3 4 5   **951.7**

    1. Mongolia 2. Festivals 3. Horse racing 4. Nomads

    ISBN 978-1-58430-277-3; 1-58430-277-1

                LC 2007025899

"Ted and Betsy Lewin describe the landscapes, people, and activities they encounter during a trip to Mongolia for Naadam, the annual summer festival where child jockeys ride half-wild horses for miles across the Mongolian steppe." Publisher's note

"In simple, captivating language, the Lewins describe their long journey. . . . Throughout, clearly presented cultural specifics mix with vivid sensory perceptions . . . but it's the color-washed sketches and beautiful full-page spreads . . . that will truly capture readers' attention." Booklist

Pang, Guek-Cheng, 1950-

Mongolia. Marshall Cavendish Benchmark 2010 144p il map (Cultures of the world) lib bdg $42.79

Grades: 5 6 7 8   **951.7**

    1. Mongolia

    ISBN 978-0-7614-4849-5 (lib bdg); 0-7614-4849-7 (lib bdg)   LC 2009022643

This describes the geography, history, wildlife, governmental structure, economy, cultural diversity, peoples, religion, and culture of Mongolia

    Includes glossary and bibliographical references

951.9   Korea

Cheung, Hyechong
K is for Korea; [by] Hyechong Chung, Prodeepta Das. Frances Lincoln 2008 unp il $16.95
Grades: K 1 2 3   951.9
1. Korea 2. Alphabet
ISBN 978-1-84507-789-1; 1-84507-789-X
"This attractive book presents several aspects of Korea: its culture, traditional practices, national treasures, wildlife, food, and dress. Nicely designed pages showcase the excellent color photos. . . . Although other books speak more precisely of South Korea, North Korea, and the Korean peninsula, few are as accessible to primary-grade children as this one." Booklist

De Capua, Sarah
Korea. Benchmark Books 2004 c2005 48p il map (Discovering cultures) lib bdg $28.50
Grades: 2 3 4   951.9
1. Korea
ISBN 0-7614-1794-X   LC 2004-6140
Contents: Where in the world is Korea?; What makes Korea Korean?; Living in Korea; School days; Just for fun; Let's celebrate!
An introduction to the geography, history, people, and culture of Korea
Includes glossary and bibliographical references

DuBois, Jill, 1952-
Korea. 2nd ed. Benchmark Books 2004 144p il map (Cultures of the world) lib bdg $42.79
Grades: 5 6 7 8   951.9
1. Korea
ISBN 0-7614-1786-9   LC 2004-7678
First published 1994
Describes the geography, history, government, economy, environment, people, and culture of Korea
Includes glossary and bibliographical references

Feldman, Ruth Tenzer
The Korean War; by Ruth Tenzer Feldman. Lerner Publications Co. 2004 88p il map (Chronicle of America's wars) lib bdg $27.93
Grades: 5 6 7 8   951.9
1. Korean War, 1950-1953
ISBN 0-8225-4716-3   LC 2002-156557
Contents: Korea sometime in January 1951; Drawing the line; Storm!; Saving the South; North to the Yalu almost; "An entirely new war;" Setting limits; The talking war; Epilogue; Timeline
This "begins briefly with the events that led to Korea's division before focusing in greater detail on North Korea's invasion of South Korea. The author offers good overviews of the roles of the major players, and she outlines the significant battles and campaigns, and the lengthy negotiations that resulted in armistice. . . . [This is] abundantly illustrated with color and black-and-white photographs as well as maps." Booklist
Includes glossary and bibliographical references

Santella, Andrew
The Korean War; by Andrew Santella. Compass Point Books 2007 48p il map (We the people) lib bdg $25.26; pa $8.95
Grades: 4 5 6 7   951.9
1. Korean War, 1950-1953
ISBN 978-0-7565-2027-4 (lib bdg); 0-7565-2027-4 (lib bdg); 978-0-7565-2039-7 (pa); 0-7565-2039-8 (pa)
       LC 2006006767
This "begins by explaining how North and South Korea became divided; the involvement of the United Nations and the United States; conflict between President Harry Truman and General Douglas MacArthur; eventual peace talks; and the division still occurring today. Accessible and straightforward, this book is an excellent one for the intended audience." SLJ
Includes bibliographical references

951.93   North Korea (People's Democratic Republic of Korea)

Kummer, Patricia K.
North Korea; by Patricia K. Kummer. Children's Press 2008 144p il map (Enchantment of the world, second series) lib bdg $38
Grades: 5 6 7 8 9   951.93
1. Korea (North)
ISBN 978-0-531-18485-1 (lib bdg); 0-531-18485-4 (lib bdg)   LC 2007025693
In this introduction to North Korea "geography is the focus, but Kummer also discusses ancient and recent history, . . . the economy, religion, sports, education, and more. Without discounting the rich culture, the book doesn't shy away from more sensitive issues. . . . The open design will draw readers, with clear type on thick, high-quality paper; numerous maps and color photos and spacious back matter are also included." Booklist
Includes bibliographical references

951.95   South Korea (Republic of Korea)

Jackson, Tom, 1972-
South Korea; [by] Tom Jackson. National Geographic 2007 64p il map (Countries of the world) lib bdg $27.90 *
Grades: 4 5 6 7   951.95
1. Korea (South)
ISBN 978-1-4263-0125-4   LC 2007024663
This describes the geography, nature, history, people and culture, government, and economy of South Korea
Includes glossary and bibliographical references

Ryan, Patrick, 1948-
Welcome to South Korea; by Patrick Ryan. The Child's World 2008 32p il map (Welcome to the world) lib bdg $27.07
Grades: 1 2 3 4   951.95
1. Korea (South)
ISBN 978-1-59296-978-4 (lib bdg); 1-59296-978-X (lib bdg)   LC 2007036354

Ryan, Patrick, 1948-—*Continued*

This briefly describes the geography, history, people, and culture of South Korea.

"Report writers and browsers will appreciate [this book]. . . . The captioned, color photographs have a balanced gender representation. Maps, fast facts, and recipes round out excellent offerings." SLJ

Includes glossary and bibliographical references

952   Japan

Blumberg, Rhoda, 1917-

Commodore Perry in the land of the Shogun. Lothrop, Lee & Shepard Bks. 1985 144p il map $21.99; pa $8.99 *

Grades: 5 6 7 8   **952**
1. Perry, Matthew Calbraith, 1794-1858 2. United States Naval Expedition to Japan (1852-1854) 3. United States—Foreign relations—Japan 4. Japan—Foreign relations—United States 5. Japan—History

ISBN 0-688-03723-2; 0-06-008625-4 (pa)
LC 84-21800

A Newbery Medal honor book, 1986

This "is a well-written story of Matthew Perry's expedition to open Japan to American trade and whaling ports. The account is sensitive to the extreme cultural differences that both the Japanese and Americans had to overcome. Especially good are the chapters and paragraphs explaining Japanese feudal society and culture. The text is marvelously complemented by the illustrations, almost all reproductions of contemporary Japanese art." SLJ

Includes bibliographical references

Hanel, Rachael

Samurai. Creative Education 2008 48p il (Fearsome fighters) lib bdg $31.35

Grades: 4 5 6   **952**
1. Samurai 2. Japan—Civilization

ISBN 978-1-58341-538-2 (lib bdg); 1-58341-538-6 (lib bdg)   LC 2006023575

This "title explains the social conditions that led to the rise of [the Samurai] and describes the types of people who joined their ranks. Chapters detail the weapons, armor, and fighting techniques used. . . . The [book concludes] with a description of the social changes that led to a decline in the need for these warriors, but also [shows] how their legends have lived on in film and literature. . . . The [book is] well organized and clearly . . . written." SLJ

Includes glossary and bibliographical references

Phillips, Charles

Japan; [by] Charles Phillips; Gil Latz and Kyohei Shibata, consultants. National Geographic 2007 64p il map (Countries on the world) lib bdg $27.90 *

Grades: 4 5 6 7   **952**
1. Japan

ISBN 1-4263-0029-8 (lib bdg); 978-1-4263-0029-5 (lib bdg)   LC 2007296571

A basic overview of the history, geography, climate and culture of Japan.

This "clear, succinct [overview] will support assignments without overwhelming casual readers. . . . A good selection of recent, high quality color photographs gives the [book] visual appeal." SLJ

Includes glossary and bibliographical references

Reiser, Robert, 1941-

Japan. Benchmark Bks. 2003 48p il map (Discovering cultures) lib bdg $28.50

Grades: 2 3 4   **952**
1. Japan

ISBN 0-7614-1177-1   LC 2001-7459

Contents: Where in the world is Japan?; What makes Japan Japanese?; Living in Japan; School days; Just for fun; Let's celebrate!

An introduction to the geography, history, people, and culture of Japan

Includes glossary and bibliographical references

Takabayashi, Mari, 1960-

I live in Tokyo; written & illustrated by Mari Takabayashi. Houghton Mifflin 2001 unp il map $16 *

Grades: K 1 2 3   **952**
1. Tokyo (Japan) 2. Japan—Social life and customs

ISBN 0-618-07702-2   LC 00-5964

"Seven-year-old narrator Mimiko takes readers on a month-by-month tour of contemporary Tokyo, briefly describing one or two festivals, customs, or facets of life each month. The narrative remains consistently childlike throughout. . . . This book is a model of efficiency and elegance, cramming numerous details into a small space in a compact and attractive manner." Horn Book

Turnbull, Stephen R.

Real samurai; over 20 true stories about the knights of old Japan! by Stephen Turnbull; illustrated by James Field. Enchanted Lion 2007 48p il $15.95

Grades: 4 5 6   **952**
1. Samurai 2. Japan—History—0-1868

ISBN 1-59270-060-8

"A comprehensive, highly engaging introduction to the world of the samurai for young readers. Each spread focuses on a different subject, such as training practices, codes of honor, battle accounts, castles, weapons, and profiles of famous warriors." Booklist

953   Arabian Peninsula and adjacent areas

Foster, Leila Merrell

Oman. Children's Press 1999 144p il map (Enchantment of the world, second series) lib bdg $33

Grades: 5 6 7 8   **953**
1. Oman

ISBN 0-516-20964-7   LC 98-19572

Foster, Leila Merrell—*Continued*
Describes the geography, plants and animals, history, economy, language, religions, culture, and people of Oman, a small nation strategically located on the eastern part of the Arabian peninsula
Includes bibliographical references

King, David C., 1933-
The United Arab Emirates; [by] David C. King. 2nd ed. Marshall Cavendish Benchmark 2008 144p il map (Cultures of the world) lib bdg $42.79 *
Grades: 5 6 7 8   **953**
  1. United Arab Emirates
  ISBN 978-0-7614-2565-6   LC 2006030237
This describes the geography, history, government, economy, environment, people, and culture of the United Arab Emirates.
Includes glossary and bibliographical references

953.3   Yemen

Hestler, Anna
Yemen; by Anna Hestler and Jo-Ann Spilling. 2nd ed. Marshall Cavendish Benchmark 2010 144p il map (Cultures of the world) lib bdg $42.79
Grades: 5 6 7 8   **953.3**
  1. Yemen
  ISBN 978-0-7614-4850-1 (lib bdg); 0-7614-4850-0 (lib bdg)   LC 2009021200
First published 1999
This describes the geography, history, wildlife, governmental structure, economy, cultural diversity, peoples, religion, and culture of Yemen
Includes glossary and bibliographical references

953.6   Persian Gulf States

Orr, Tamra
Qatar; [by] Tamra Orr. Marshall Cavendish Benchmark 2008 144p il map (Cultures of the world) lib bdg $42.79
Grades: 5 6 7 8   **953.6**
  1. Qatar
  ISBN 978-0-7614-2566-3; 0-7614-2566-7
                                  LC 2006033626
This describes the geography, history, government, economy, environment, people, and culture of Qatar
Includes glossary and bibliographical references

953.67   Kuwait

O'Shea, Maria
Kuwait; by Maria O'Shea and Michael Spilling. 2nd ed. Marshall Cavendish Benchmark 2010 144p il map (Cultures of the world) lib bdg $42.79
Grades: 5 6 7 8   **953.67**
  1. Kuwait
  ISBN 978-0-7614-4479-4 (lib bdg); 0-7614-4479-3 (lib bdg)   LC 2009007069

First published 1999
Provides information on the geography, history, wildlife, governmental structure, economy, cultural diversity, peoples, religion, and culture of Kuwait
Includes glossary and bibliographical references

953.8   Saudi Arabia

Fazio, Wende
Saudi Arabia. Children's Press 1999 47p il map (True book) lib bdg $22; pa $6.95
Grades: 3 4 5   **953.8**
  1. Saudi Arabia
  ISBN 0-516-21190-0 (lib bdg); 0-516-26502-4 (pa)
                                    LC 98-12273
Provides an overview of the geography, history, and culture of the Kingdom of Saudi Arabia
"An informative text is coupled with crisp photographs." Horn Book Guide
Includes glossary and bibliographical references

954   South Asia. India

Apte, Sunita
India. Children's Press 2009 48p il map (True book) lib bdg $26
Grades: 3 4 5   **954**
  1. India
  ISBN 978-0-531-16890-5 (lib bdg); 0-531-16890-5 (lib bdg)   LC 2008014786
This "attractive [work covers] the geography, history, people, customs, and economy of [India]. . . . [The book has] large-size print and colorful pictures. [It] contains a section about current political challenges such as the recent terrorist attacks in Mumbai, India." SLJ
Includes glossary and bibliographical references

Arnold, Caroline, 1944-
Taj Mahal; by Caroline Arnold and Madeleine Comora; illustrated by Rahul Bhushan. Carolrhoda Books 2007 unp il lib bdg $17.95 *
Grades: 4 5 6 7   **954**
  1. Taj Mahal (Agra, India) 2. Mogul Empire
  ISBN 978-0-7613-2609-0 (lib bdg); 0-7613-2609-X (lib bdg)   LC 2001006685
Recounts the love story behind the building of the Taj Mahal in India, discussing how it was constructed and providing information on Indian culture.
"The small, detailed paintings are . . . set on beautifully constructed pages resembling those of illuminated manuscripts. . . . The book is sumptuous in appearance and presents a bit of history not often told for children." SLJ

Dalal, A. Kamala

India; [by] A. Kamala Dalal; Ramesh C. Dhussa and Pradyumna P. Karan, consultants. National Geographic 2007 64p il map (Countries of the world) lib bdg $27.90 *

Grades: 4 5 6 7   **954**

  1. India

  ISBN 978-1-4263-0127-8 (lib bdg); 1-4263-0127-8 (lib bdg)   LC 2007039552

  This describes the geography, nature, history, people and culture, government and economy of India

  "What helps [this book] stand out from the pack is [its] high-quality, rich photography. . . . The photos provide as much information as the [text]. . . . The writing is straightforward and solid." SLJ

  Includes glossary and bibliographical references

Guile, Melanie, 1949-

Culture in India; [by] Melanie Guile. Raintree 2005 32p il map lib bdg $29.29

Grades: 4 5 6 7   **954**

  1. India

  ISBN 1-4109-1134-9   LC 2004-16649

  Contents: Culture in India; Traditions and customs; Minority groups; Costume and clothing; Food; Performing arts; Literature; Film and television; Arts and crafts

  This "title includes a map and picture of the nation's flag as well as color photographs that bring to life the wide range of topics addressed. Two to four-page chapters briefly cover languages, history, people, religions, holidays and festivals, customs, minority groups, costumes and clothing, food, and arts and crafts, providing students with lots of cultural information. Text is well spaced in an overall neat and pleasing manner." SLJ

  Includes bibliographical references

Mann, Elizabeth, 1948-

Taj Mahal; a story of love and empire; by Elizabeth Mann; with illustrations by Alan Witschonke. Mikaya 2008 47p il (Wonders of the world) $22.95 *

Grades: 4 5 6 7   **954**

  1. Taj Mahal (Agra, India) 2. Mogul Empire

  ISBN 1-931414-20-3; 978-1-931414-20-3

         LC 2008060054

  This is a "dramatic retelling of the construction of the Taj Mahal. Mann begins with two pages of prose that relay the commonly told legend, but then proceeds to explode that legend with descriptive writing, colorful illustrations, ancient paintings, maps, and photographs." Booklist

  Includes bibliographical references

Murphy, Patricia J., 1963-

India; by Patricia J. Murphy. Benchmark Bks. 2003 48p il map (Discovering cultures) lib bdg $28.50

Grades: 2 3 4   **954**

  1. India

  ISBN 0-7614-1516-5   LC 2002-15306

Highlights the geography, people, food, schools, recreation, celebrations, and languages of the largest country in Southeast Asia

"Report writers will appreciate [this] simply written [volume]. . . . Illustrated with clear color photos." Horn Book Guide

Includes glossary and bibliographical references

Srinivasan, Radhika

India; [by] Radhika Srinivasan, Leslie Jermyn. 2nd ed. Benchmark Bks. 2002 144p il maps (Cultures of the world) lib bdg $42.79

Grades: 5 6 7 8   **954**

  1. India

  ISBN 0-7614-1354-5   LC 2001-28608

  First published 1990

  This describes the geography, history, government, economy, environment, people, and culture of India

  Includes glossary and bibliographical references

954.91   Pakistan

Sheehan, Sean, 1951-

Pakistan; by Sean Sheehan & Shahrezad Samiuddin. 2nd ed. Benchmark Books 2004 144p il map (Cultures of the world) lib bdg $42.79 *

Grades: 5 6 7 8   **954.91**

  ISBN 0-7614-1787-7   LC 2004-7677

  First published 1994

  Contents: Geography; History; Government; Economy; Environment; Pakistanis; Lifestyle; Religion; Language; Arts; Leisure; Festivals; Food

  An introduction to the geography, history, government, and culture of Pakistan

  "Excellent-quality, full-color photographs and sidebars highlight special information and make this book accessible and appealing. . . . A gold mine of information for reports." SLJ

  Includes glossary and bibliographical references

954.92   Bangladesh

March, Michael, 1946-

Bangladesh. Sea-to-sea Publications 2009 32p il map (Facts about countries) $28.50

Grades: 3 4 5   **954.92**

  1. Bangladesh

  ISBN 978-1-59771-113-5; 1-59771-113-6

  Describes the geography, history, industries, education, government, and cultures of Bangladesh

  "The attractive layout includes color photographs and charts of current statistics as well as maps illustrating main farming regions, natural resources, or the literacy rates of girls and boys. The [text is] clear and succinct." SLJ

  Includes glossary

Orr, Tamra
Bangladesh; by Tamra B. Orr. Children's Press 2007 144p il map (Enchantment of the world, second series) lib bdg $38
Grades: 5 6 7 8   954.92
1. Bangladesh
ISBN 978-0-516-25012-0 (lib bdg); 0-516-25012-4 (lib bdg)   LC 2006024160
Describes the geography, people, government, culture, history, religion, economy, and wildlife of Bagladesh
"The strong design features highly readable type and beautiful, color photos on almost every page. . . . Includes clear maps and useful end matter." Booklist
Includes bibliographical references

954.93   Sri Lanka

Wanasundera, Nanda P., 1932-
Sri Lanka; [by] Nanda Pethiyagoda Wanasundera. 2nd ed. Benchmark Bks. 2002 144p il maps (Cultures of the world) lib bdg $42.79
Grades: 5 6 7 8   954.93
1. Sri Lanka
ISBN 0-7614-1477-0   LC 2002-25980
First published 1990
Describes the geography, history, government, economy, social life and customs, religion, culture, and more of this island country in the Indian Ocean
Includes glossary and bibliographical references

954.96   Nepal

Burbank, Jon, 1951-
Nepal. 2nd ed. Benchmark Bks. 2002 144p il map (Cultures of the world) lib bdg $42.79
Grades: 5 6 7 8   954.96
1. Nepal
ISBN 0-7614-1476-2   LC 2002-25994
First published 1991
Describes the geography, history, government, economy, people, religion, language, and culture of Nepal, a predominantly Hindu country located north of India. Includes several recipes
Includes glossary and bibliographical references

Kalz, Jill
Mount Everest; by Jill Kalz. Creative Education 2004 32p il map (Natural wonders of the world) lib bdg $27.10
Grades: 4 5 6   954.96
1. Mount Everest (China and Nepal)
ISBN 1-58341-325-1   LC 2003-65232
This describes Mount Everest's "geological formation and climate, ecology and wildlife, and human inhabitants and expeditions. A final chapter is devoted to tourism. . . . The [text], sufficient in informational quantity and quality for short reports, [is] briskly and engagingly written. But the real selling point here is the gorgeous color photographs." SLJ

Taylor-Butler, Christine, 1959-
Sacred mountain; Everest. Lee & Low Books 2009 48p il $19.95
Grades: 5 6 7 8   954.96
1. Mount Everest (China and Nepal)
ISBN 978-1-60060-255-9; 1-60060-255-X
LC 2008-30423
"A cultural, geological, and ecological history of Mount Everest focusing on the indigenous Sherpa and their spiritual connection to the mountain, record-setting multinational climbing expeditions, and the effects of tourism on the environment. Illustrated with photographs, maps, diagrams, and timelines." Publisher's note
"The informative text is amply illustrated with well-chosen black-and-white and color photographs." SLJ
Includes glossary

955   Iran

Gray, Leon, 1974-
Iran; [by] Leon Gray; Edmund Herzig and Dorreh Mirheydar, consultants. National Geographic 2008 64p il map (Countries of the world) lib bdg $27.90 *
Grades: 4 5 6 7   955
1. Iran
ISBN 978-1-4263-0200-8   LC 2007047834
This describes the geography, nature, history, people and culture, government and economy of Iran
"With high-quality color photographs, archival art, and several excellent, full-page maps, this [is a] highly readable, detailed overview." Booklist
Includes glossary and bibliographical references

Mara, Wil
Iran; [by] Wil Mara. Marshall Cavendish Benchmark 2007 48p il map (Discovering cultures) lib bdg $28.50
Grades: 2 3 4   955
1. Iran
ISBN 978-0-7614-1986-0 (lib bdg); 0-7614-1986-1 (lib bdg)   LC 2006011476
An introduction to the geography, history, people, and culture of Iran
Includes glossary and bibliographical references

Rajendra, Vijeya, 1936-
Iran; [by] Vijeya Rajendra, Gisela Kaplan, Rudi Rajendra. 2nd ed. Benchmark Bks. 2003 c2004 144p il map (Cultures of the world) lib bdg $42.79
Grades: 5 6 7 8   955
1. Iran
ISBN 0-7614-1665-X   LC 2003-8257
First published 1993
Contents: Geography; History; Government; Economy; Environment; Iranians; Lifestyle; Religion; Language; Arts; Leisure; Festivals; Food
Explores the geography, history, government, economy, people, and culture of Iran
Includes glossary and bibliographical references

956 Middle East

Steele, Philip
Middle East; foreword by Paul Adams. Kingfisher 2006 63p il map (Kingfisher knowledge) $12.95
Grades: 5 6 7 8   956
1. Middle East
ISBN 978-0-7534-5984-3; 0-7534-5984-1
"A concise overview of the history and culture of the region, defined as the countries of Turkey, Syria, Lebanon, Israel, the Palestinian territories, Egypt, Jordan, Saudi Arabia, Yemen, Oman, the Gulf states, Iraq, Iran, and Afghanistan. The text is brief but informative, and current political controversies are touched on in an age-appropriate and evenhanded manner. . . . The real strength of this book is the appealing graphic design and the excellent-quality color photographs throughout." SLJ
Includes glossary and bibliographical references

956.04 Middle East—1945-1980

Marx, Trish, 1948-
Sharing our homeland; Palestinian and Jewish Children at summer Peace Camp; photographs by Cindy Karp. Lee & Low Books 2010 il $19.95
Grades: 3 4 5 6   956.04
1. Jewish-Arab relations 2. Israel 3. Palestinian Arabs
ISBN 978-158430260-5; 1584302607
"Alya, an Israeli Palestinian girl in a Muslim family, chooses to wear a hijab. Yuval, an Israeli Jewish boy, lives in a moshav farming community. In this picture-book photo-essay, crisp color images show the kids at home and then having fun at Peace Camp, where they swim, make arts and crafts, and do other universal summer-camp activities. Field trips introduce some kids to places they've never been, including a museum, a kibbutz, and an Arab village. . . . Marx weaves in detailed history of the Holy Land, from ancient times to 1948 and the establishment of the Jewish state and then the 1967 War. Throughout, she is frank about the continuing violence and conflict, and a contemporary image shows that the tall West Bank safety wall is also a divider between cultures. Realistic and upbeat, this moves beyond stereotypes and notions of the 'other.'" Booklist

Senker, Cath
The Arab-Israeli conflict; [by] Cath Senker. new ed. Arcturus Pub. 2008 48p il map (Timelines) lib bdg $32.80
Grades: 5 6 7 8   956.04
1. Israel-Arab conflicts
ISBN 978-1-84193-725-0 (lib bdg); 1-84193-725-8 (lib bdg)   LC 2007-7547
First published 2005 by Smart Apple Media
This describes current conditions in Israel and the occupied territories and includes a history of major events and political developments.
"A complex situation is clearly explained. . . . [This is] well-illustrated. . . . Throughout, the tone is nonjudgmental." SLJ [review of 2005 edition]
Includes bibliographical references

956.1 Turkey

Shields, Sarah D., 1955-
Turkey; [by] Sarah Shields. National Geographic 2009 64p il map (Countries of the world) lib bdg $27.90 *
Grades: 4 5 6 7   956.1
1. Turkey
ISBN 978-1-4263-0387-6 (lib bdg); 1-4263-0387-4 (lib bdg)   LC 2009275583
This describes the geography, nature, history, people and culture, government and economy of Turkey
Includes glossary and bibliographical references

956.7 Iraq

Falvey, David
Letters to a soldier; by First Lieutenant David Falvey and Mrs. Julie Hutt's fourth-grade class. Marshall Cavendish Children 2009 unp il $16.99
Grades: 3 4 5   956.7
1. Falvey, David—Correspondence. 2. Iraq War, 2003-—Personal narratives 3. Soldiers 4. Children's writings
ISBN 978-0-7614-5637-7; 0-7614-5637-6
LC 2008050268
"While serving in Iraq in 2008, First Lieutenant David Falvey received a packet of letters from Julie Hutt's fourth-grade class in Roslyn, NY. The children's correspondences and drawings, paired with Falvey's thoughtful answers and photographs from his deployment, are reproduced in an inviting, child-friendly format." SLJ

Hassig, Susan M., 1969-
Iraq; [by] Susan M. Hassig, Laith Muhmood Al Adely. 2nd ed. Benchmark Bks. 2003 144p il maps (Cultures of the world) lib bdg $42.79
Grades: 5 6 7 8   956.7
1. Iraq
ISBN 0-7614-1668-4   LC 2003-10082
First published 1993
Explores the geography, history, government, economy, people, and culture of Iraq

Samuels, Charlie, 1961-
Iraq; [by] Charlie Samuels; Sarah Shields and Shakir Mustafa, consultants. National Geographic 2007 64p il map (Countries of the world) lib bdg $27.90 *
Grades: 4 5 6 7   956.7
1. Iraq
ISBN 978-1-4263-0061-5   LC 2007024675
This describes the geography, nature, history, people and culture, government and economy of Iraq.
Includes glossary and bibliographical references

956.91   Syria

South, Coleman, 1948-
Syria; by Coleman South & Leslie Jermyn. 3rd ed. Marshall Cavendish Benchmark 2006 144p il map (Cultures of the world) lib bdg $42.79
Grades: 5 6 7 8   **956.91**
   1. Syria
   ISBN 0-7614-2054-1   LC 2005023848
   First published 1995
This describes the geography, history, government, economy, culture, peoples, and religion of Syria
"Straightforward, up-to-date . . . [and] well-written. . . . The attractive layout features a high-quality full-color photo on each page." SLJ
Includes glossary and bibliographical references

956.92   Lebanon

Boueri, Marijean
Lebanon A to Z; a Middle Eastern mosaic; [by] Marijean Boueri, Jill Boutros, Joanne Sayad; illustrations by Titiana Sabbagh. Publishing Works 2005 77p il map $25
Grades: 4 5 6   **956.92**
   1. Lebanon
   ISBN 0-9744803-4-7
Kareem, an eleven-year-old boy, provides an introduction to his country, describing its history, government, and culture.
"Written by three authors who obviously know and love the country, this lovely book is a wonderful introduction to Lebanon's history and culture. . . . Sabbagh's detailed, colorful paintings depicting everyday life are a blend of the traditional and the modern." SLJ

Sheehan, Sean, 1951-
Lebanon; [by] Sean Sheehan & Zawiah Abdul Latif. 2nd ed. Marshall Cavendish Benchmark 2008 144p il map (Cultures of the world) lib bdg $42.79
Grades: 5 6 7 8   **956.92**
   1. Lebanon
   ISBN 978-0-7614-2081-1 (lib bdg); 0-7614-2081-9 (lib bdg)   LC 2006101735
   First published 1997
"Provides comprehensive information on the geography, history, wildlife, governmental structure, economy, cultural diversity, peoples, religion, and culture of Lebanon." Publisher's note
Includes bibliographical references

956.93   Cyprus

Spilling, Michael
Cyprus; [by] Michael Spilling and Jo-Ann Spilling. 2nd ed. Marshall Cavendish Benchmark 2010 144p il map (Cultures of the world) lib bdg $29.95
Grades: 5 6 7 8   **956.93**
   1. Cyprus
   ISBN 978-0-7614-4855-6; 0-7614-4855-1   LC 2009045689
   First published 2000
This offers information on the geography, history, wildlife, governmental structure, economy, cultural diversity, peoples, religion, and culture of Cyprus.
Includes glossary and bibliographical references

956.94   Palestine. Israel

Bowden, Rob
Jerusalem; [by] Rob Bowden. World Almanac Library 2006 48p il map (Great cities of the world) lib bdg $31
Grades: 3 4 5 6   **956.94**
   1. Jerusalem
   ISBN 0-8368-5051-3   LC 2005043586
This describes the geography, cultures, work, play, history, and religions of Jerusalem
This is "attractive, informative . . . straightforward and objective." SLJ
Includes bibliographical references

DuBois, Jill, 1952-
Israel; by Jill DuBois, Mair Rosh. 2nd ed. Benchmark Bks. 2003 c2004 144p il map (Cultures of the world) lib bdg $42.79
Grades: 5 6 7 8   **956.94**
   1. Israel
   ISBN 0-7614-1669-2   LC 2003-10083
   First published 1993
Explores the geography, history, government, economy, people, and culture of Israel
Includes glossary and bibliographical references

Ellis, Deborah, 1960-
Three wishes; Palestinian and Israeli children speak. Groundwood Bks. 2004 110p il map hardcover o.p. pa $9.99
Grades: 5 6 7 8   **956.94**
   1. Israel-Arab conflicts 2. Palestinian Arabs
   ISBN 0-88899-608-X; 0-88899-645-4 (pa)
"Growing up separate and apart in a world of bombs, bullets, removals, checkpoints, and curfews, 20 Israeli and Palestinian young people talk about how the war has affected them." Booklist
"An excellent presentation of a confusing historic struggle, told within a palpable, perceptive and empathetic format." SLJ
Includes bibliographical references

Roy, Jennifer Rozines
Israel. Benchmark Bks. 2003 48p il maps (Discovering cultures) lib bdg $28.50
Grades: 2 3 4   **956.94**
1. Israel
ISBN 0-7614-1720-6   LC 2003-8127
Contents: Where in the world is Israel?; What makes Israel Israeli?; Living in Israel; School days; Just for fun; Let's celebrate!
Highlights the geography, people, food, schools, recreation, celebrations, and language of Israel
Includes glossary and bibliographical references

Young, Emma, 1973-
Israel; [by] Emma Young; Zvi Ben-Dor Benite, George Kanazi, and Aviva Halamish, consultants. National Geographic 2008 64p il map (Countries of the world) lib bdg $27.90 *
Grades: 4 5 6 7   **956.94**
1. Israel
ISBN 978-1-4263-0258-9 (lib bdg); 1-4263-0258-4 (lib bdg)
This describes the geography, nature, history, people and culture, government, and economy of Israel.
Includes glossary and bibliographical references

958.1   Afghanistan

Ali, Sharifah Enayat, 1943-
Afghanistan; by Sharifah Enayat Ali. 2nd ed. Marshall Cavendish Benchmark 2006 144p il map (Cultures of the world) lib bdg $42.79
Grades: 5 6 7 8   **958.1**
1. Afghanistan
ISBN 978-0-7614-2064-4 (lib bdg); 0-7614-2064-9 (lib bdg)   LC 2005034789
First published 1995
"Provides . . . information on the geography, history, governmental structure, economy, cultural diversity, peoples, religion, and culture of Afghanistan." Publisher's note
This is "well organized, informative, and entertaining. . . . Excellent-quality full-color photographs and reproductions show the people, landforms, buildings, and everyday activities of [Afghanistan]." SLJ [review of 1995 edtion]
Includes glossary and bibliographical references

O'Brien, Tony, 1971-
Afghan dreams; young voices of Afghanistan; by Tony O'Brien and Mike Sullivan; photographs by Tony O'Brien. Bloomsbury Children's Books 2008 69p il map $18.99; lib bdg $19.89 *
Grades: 3 4 5 6   **958.1**
1. Teenagers—Afghanistan 2. Children—Afghanistan 3. Afghanistan
ISBN   978-1-59990-287-6;   1-59990-287-7; 978-1-59990-321-7 (lib bdg); 1-59990-321-0 (lib bdg)
LC 2008-07004

"This handsome photo-essay features contemporary Afghan children ranging in age from 8 to 18 years. They were asked about their families, lives, and hopes for the future. The young people's straightforward statements tell much about the devastating effects of decades of war." SLJ

Whitfield, Susan
Afghanistan; [by] Susan Whitfield; Thomas Barfield and Maliha Zulfacar, consultants. National Geographic 2008 64p il map (Countries of the world) lib bdg $27.90
Grades: 4 5 6 7   **958.1**
1. Afghanistan
ISBN 978-1-4263-0256-5 (lib bdg); 1-4263-0256-8 (lib bdg)
This describes the geography, nature, history, people and culture, government, and economy of Aghanistan.
Includes glossary and bibliographical references

958.4   Turkestan

King, David C., 1933-
Kyrgyzstan; [by] David C. King. Marshall Cavendish Benchmark 2005 144p il map (Cultures of the world) lib bdg $42.79
Grades: 5 6 7 8   **958.4**
1. Kyrgyzstan
ISBN 0-7614-2013-4   LC 2005001314
Describes the geography, history, government, economy, people, and culture of Kyrgyzstan
Includes glossary and bibliographical references

958.5   Turkmenistan

Knowlton, MaryLee, 1946-
Turkmenistan; [by] MaryLee Knowlton. Marshall Cavendish Benchmark 2006 144p il map (Cultures of the world) lib bdg $42.79
Grades: 5 6 7 8   **958.5**
1. Turkmenistan
ISBN 0-7614-2014-2   LC 2005006455
Describes the geography, history, government, economy, people, and culture of Turkmenistan
Includes glossary and bibliographical references

958.6   Tajikistan

Abazov, Rafis, 1966-
Tajikistan; [by] Rafis Abazov. Marshall Cavendish Benchmark 2006 144p il map (Cultures of the world) lib bdg $42.79
Grades: 5 6 7 8   **958.6**
1. Tajikistan
ISBN 0-7614-2012-6   LC 2005001166
Describes the geography, history, government, economy, people, and culture of the former Soviet republic of Tajikistan
Includes glossary and bibliographical references

958.7   Uzbekistan

Knowlton, MaryLee, 1946-
Uzbekistan; [by] MaryLee Knowlton. Marshall Cavendish Benchmark 2005 144p il map (Cultures of the world) lib bdg $42.79
Grades: 5 6 7 8   **958.7**
  1. Uzbekistan
  ISBN 0-7614-2016-9   LC 2005016875
  An examination of the geography, history, government, economy, culture, and peoples of Uzbekistan
  Includes glossary and bibliographical references

959.3   Thailand

Goodman, Jim, 1947-
Thailand. 2nd ed. Benchmark Bks. 2003 144p il map (Cultures of the world) lib bdg $42.79
Grades: 5 6 7 8   **959.3**
  1. Thailand
  ISBN 0-7614-1478-9   LC 2002-25979
  First published 1990
  Describes the geography, history, government, economy, people, religion, language, and culture of Thailand, a predominantly Buddhist country located in Southeast Asia. Includes several recipes
  Includes glossary and bibliographical references

Morris, Ann
Tsunami; helping each other; by Ann Morris & Heidi Larson. Millbrook Press 2005 32p il map $15.95 *
Grades: 3 4 5   **959.3**
  1. Tsunamis 2. Indian Ocean earthquake and tsunami, 2004 3. Thailand
  ISBN 0-7613-9501-6   LC 2005-13616
  The story of how one family in Thailand survived the tsunami of December 26, 2004, and, with the help of others, began to rebuild their lives.
  "The brisk and straightforward text is enhanced by many excellent well-captioned color photos." Horn Book Guide

Rau, Dana Meachen, 1971-
Thailand; [by] Dana Meachen Rau. Marshall Cavendish Benchmark 2007 48p il map (Discovering cultures) lib bdg $28.50
Grades: 2 3 4   **959.3**
  1. Thailand
  ISBN 978-0-7614-1989-1 (lib bdg); 0-7614-1989-6 (lib bdg)   LC 2006011475
  An introduction to the geography, history, people, and culture of Thailand
  Includes glossary and bibliographical references

959.4   Laos

Dalal, A. Kamala
Laos; [by] A. Kamala Dalal. National Geographic 2009 64p il (Countries of the world) lib bdg $27.90 *
Grades: 4 5 6 7   **959.4**
  1. Laos
  ISBN 978-1-4263-0388-3 (lib bdg); 1-4263-0388-2 (lib bdg)
  This describes the geography, nature, history, people and culture, and govenment and economy of Laos
  Includes glossary and bibliographical references

Mansfield, Stephen
Laos; [by] Stephen Mansfield & Magdalene Koh. 2nd ed. Marshall Cavendish Benchmark 2008 c2009 144p il map (Cultures of the world) lib bdg $42.79
Grades: 5 6 7 8   **959.4**
  1. Laos
  ISBN 978-0-7614-3035-3 (lib bdg); 0-7614-3035-0 (lib bdg)   LC 2007048292
  First published 1998
  "Provides comprehensive information on the geography, history, wildlife, governmental structure, economy, cultural diversity, peoples, religion, and culture of Laos." Publisher's note
  Includes glossary and bibliographical references

959.5   Commonwealth of Nations territories. Malaysia

Guile, Melanie, 1949-
Culture in Malaysia; [by] Melanie Guile. Raintree 2005 32p il map lib bdg $29.29
Grades: 4 5 6 7   **959.5**
  1. Malaysia
  ISBN 1-4109-1133-0   LC 2004-16650
  Contents: Culture in Malaysia; Traditions and customs; Minority groups; Costume and clothing; Food; Performing arts; Folklore and literature; Film and television; Arts and crafts
  This "title includes a map and picture of the nation's flag as well as color photographs that bring to life the wide range of topics addressed. Two to four-page chapters briefly cover languages, history, people, religions, holidays and festivals, customs, minority groups, costumes and clothing, food, and arts and crafts, providing students with lots of cultural information. Text is well spaced in an overall neat and pleasing manner." SLJ
  Includes bibliographical references

Munan, Heidi
Malaysia; [by] Heidi Munan, Foo Yuk Yee. 2nd ed. Benchmark Bks. 2002 144p il map (Cultures of the world) lib bdg $42.79
Grades: 5 6 7 8   **959.5**
  1. Malaysia
  ISBN 0-7614-1351-0   LC 2001-25302

Munan, Heidi—*Continued*
First published 1990
This describes the geography, history, government, economy, environment, people and culture of Malaysia
Includes glossary and bibliographical references

959.57 Singapore

Layton, Lesley, 1954-
Singapore; [by] Lesley Layton, Pang Guek Cheng. 2nd ed. Benchmark Bks. 2002 144p il map (Cultures of the world) lib bdg $42.79
Grades: 5 6 7 8 **959.57**
1. Singapore
ISBN 0-7614-1352-9 LC 2001-25413
First published 1990
This describes the geography, history, government, economy, environment, people, and culture of Singapore
Includes glossary and bibliographical references

Rau, Dana Meachen, 1971-
Singapore. Benchmark Bks. 2004 48p il map (Discovering cultures) lib bdg $28.50
Grades: 2 3 4 **959.57**
1. Singapore
ISBN 0-7614-1727-3 LC 2003-19102
Contents: Where in the world is Singapore?; What makes Singapore Singaporean?; Living in Singapore; School days; Just for fun; Let's celebrate!
An introduction to the geography, history, people, and culture of Singapore
This book is "informative and balanced." SLJ
Includes glossary and bibliographical references

959.6 Cambodia

Sheehan, Sean, 1951-
Cambodia; [by] Sean Sheehan & Barbara Cooke. 2nd ed. Marshall Cavendish Benchmark 2007 144p il map (Cultures of the world) lib bdg $42.79
Grades: 5 6 7 8 **959.6**
1. Cambodia
ISBN 978-0-7614-2071-2 (lib bdg); 0-7614-2071-1 (lib bdg) LC 2006020818
First published 1996
This provides "information on the geography, history, governmental structure, economy, cultural diversity, peoples, religion, and culture of Cambodia." Publisher's note
Includes glossary and bibliographical references

959.7 Vietnam

Green, Jen
Vietnam; [by] Jen Green. National Geographic 2008 64p il map (Countries of the world) lib bdg $27.90
Grades: 4 5 6 7 **959.7**
1. Vietnam
ISBN 978-1-4263-0202-2
LC 2007047832

This describes the geography, nature, history, people and culture, government, and economy of Vietnam.
Includes glossary and bibliographical references

Guile, Melanie, 1949-
Culture in Vietnam; [by] Melanie Guile. Raintree 2005 32p il map lib bdg $29.29
Grades: 4 5 6 7 **959.7**
1. Vietnam
ISBN 1-4109-1135-7 LC 2004-16651
Contents: Culture in Vietnam; Traditions and customs; Minority groups; Costume and clothing; Food; Performing arts; Film and television; Literature; Arts and crafts
This "title includes a map and picture of the nation's flag as well as color photographs that bring to life the wide range of topics addressed. Two to four-page chapters briefly cover languages, history, people, religions, holidays and festivals, customs, minority groups, costumes and clothing, food, and arts and crafts, providing students with lots of cultural information. Text is well spaced in an overall neat and pleasing manner." SLJ
Includes bibliographical references

959.704 Vietnam—1949-

Seah, Audrey, 1958-
Vietnam; [by] Audrey Seah, Charissa M. Nair. 2nd ed. Benchmark Books 2004 144p il map (Cultures of the world) lib bdg $42.79
Grades: 5 6 7 8 **959.704**
1. Vietnam
ISBN 0-7614-1789-3 LC 2004-12903
First published 1994
Contents: Geography; History; Government; Economy; Environment; Vietnamese; Lifestyle; Religion; Language; Arts; Leisure; Festivals; Food
This describes the geography, history, government, economy environment, and culture of Vietnam
Includes glossary and bibliographical references

959.9 Philippines

Gordon, Sharon
Philippines. Benchmark Bks. 2003 48p il map (Discovering cultures) lib bdg $28.50
Grades: 2 3 4 **959.9**
1. Philippines
ISBN 0-7614-1518-1 LC 2002-15304
Highlights the geography, people, food, schools, recreation, celebrations, and languages of the Philippines
"Report writers will appreciate [this] simply written [volume]. . . . Illustrated with clear color photos." Horn Book Guide
Includes glossary and bibliographical references

Tope, Lily Rose R., 1955-

Philippines; [by] Lily Rose R. Tope; Detch P. Nonan-Mercado. 2nd ed. Benchmark Bks. 2002 144p il maps (Cultures of the world) lib bdg $42.79

Grades: 5 6 7 8   **959.9**
    1. Philippines
    ISBN 0-7614-1475-4   LC 2002-19725
    First published 1990

Discusses the geography, history, government, economy, people, and culture of the Philippines, an archipelago of many islands in the Western Pacific

Includes glossary and bibliographical references

960   History of Africa

Bowden, Rob

African culture; [by] Rob Bowden and Rosie Wilson. Heinemann Library 2009 48p il map (Africa focus) $30; pa $8.99 *

Grades: 4 5 6   **960**
    1. Africa—Social life and customs 2. Africa—Civilization
    ISBN 978-1-4329-2440-9; 1-4329-2440-0; 978-1-4329-2445-4 (pa); 1-4329-2445-1 (pa)
            LC 2008-48310

This book "presents a clear and timely overview of the diverse and complex continent. The full-color photographs are of exceptional quality. [The] book also includes interesting fact boxes, sidebars, maps, and a time line. [It] focuses on traditions and how they are relevant for today. Highlights include family and daily life; religion, beliefs, and customs; and the performing and visual arts." SLJ

Includes bibliographical references

Ancient Africa; [by] Rob Bowden and Rosie Wilson. Heinemann Library 2008 48p il map (Africa focus) $30; pa $8.99 *

Grades: 4 5 6   **960**
    1. Africa—History
    ISBN 978-1-4329-2439-3; 1-4329-2439-7; 978-1-4329-2444-7 (pa); 1-4329-2444-3 (pa)
            LC 2008-48306

This book "presents a clear and timely overview of the diverse and complex continent. The full-color photographs are of exceptional quality. [The] book also includes interesting fact boxes, sidebars, maps, and a time line. . . . [It] begins with the origin of humankind and continues through the beginning of the slave trade in Europe and America. Early civilizations such as Egypt, ancient Ghana, the Mali Empire, Great Zimbabwe, and Kongo are represented. Invasions and explorations are discussed, as is slavery and colonialism." SLJ

Includes bibliographical references

Changing Africa; [by] Rob Bowden and Rosie Wilson. Heinemann Library 2009 48p il map (Africa focus) $30; pa $8.99 *

Grades: 4 5 6   **960**
    1. Africa—Social conditions 2. Africa—Economic conditions
    ISBN 978-1-4329-2437-9; 1-4329-2437-0; 978-1-4329-2442-3 (pa); 1-4329-2442-7 (pa)
            LC 2008-48277

This book "presents a clear and timely overview of the diverse and complex continent. The full-color photographs are of exceptional quality. [The] book also includes interesting fact boxes, sidebars, maps, and a time line. . . . [It] presents recent positive and negative changes. The rise of poverty and slums is explored, as is the lowered life expectancy due to the spread of malaria and HIV/AIDS. Positive changes include the freedom that voting has brought." SLJ

Includes bibliographical references

Modern Africa; [by] Rosie Wilson and Rob Bowden. Heinemann Library 2009 48p il map (Africa focus) $30; pa $8.99 *

Grades: 4 5 6   **960**
    1. Africa
    ISBN 978-1-4329-2438-6; 1-4329-2438-9; 978-1-4329-2443-0 (pa); 1-4329-2443-5 (pa)

This book "presents a clear and timely overview of the diverse and complex continent. The full-color photographs are of exceptional quality. [The] book also includes interesting fact boxes, sidebars, maps, and a time line. . . . [It] chronicles the history of colonial Africa to independence, and the changes that have arisen and continue to manifest themselves. Topics include apartheid and recent and ongoing violence in Rwanda, Darfur, and the Congo. While corrupt leaders continue to hamper Africa's attempts at advancement, the exportation of oil as well as aid from missionaries and international organizations are presented as hopes for the future." SLJ

Mooney, Carla, 1970-

Amazing Africa; projects you can build yourself; illustrated by Megan Stearns. Nomad Press 2010 122p il (Build it yourself) pa $15.95

Grades: 4 5 6 7   **960**
    1. Africa 2. Handicraft
    ISBN 978-1-934670-41-5; 1-934670-41-3

"Casual and informative, this large, attractive, browsable paperback . . . offers a view of contemporary African life that reaches far beyond the usual scenery-and-wildlife tourists' perspective. Blending history, culture, and tradition with politics and life in both cities and rural areas, the chapters begin with a look at natural wonders and dangerous wildlife that will grab readers, then move on to historical discussions of humankind's birthplace and early civilizations. . . . The open design includes sketches on every page. . . . The craft projects [include making] your own Maasai beaded necklace, kente cloth, woven basket, galimoto doll, and . . . more." Booklist

Murray, Jocelyn, 1929-2001

Africa; updated by Brian A. Stewart. 3rd ed. Chelsea House 2007 96p il map (Cultural atlas for young people) $35

Grades: 5 6 7 8   **960**

1. Africa—History 2. Africa—Civilization
ISBN 978-0-8160-6826-5; 0-8160-6826-7
First published 1990
Presents information on the history and various regions and cultures of Africa.
Includes glossary and bibliographical references

Musgrove, Margaret, 1943-

Ashanti to Zulu: African traditions; pictures by Leo and Diane Dillon. Dial Bks. for Young Readers 1976 unp il $21.99; pa $6.99 *

Grades: 3 4 5 6   **960**

1. Africa—Social life and customs 2. Ethnology—Africa
ISBN 0-8037-0357-0; 0-14-054604-9 (pa)
Awarded the Caldecott Medal, 1977
"In brief texts arranged in alphabetical order, each accompanied by a large framed illustration, the author introduces 'the reader to twenty-six African peoples by depicting a custom important to each.' . . . In most of the paintings the artists 'have included a man, a woman, a child, their living quarters, an artifact, and a local animal' and have, in this way, stressed the human and the natural ambience of the various peoples depicted." Horn Book
"The writing is dignified and the material informative, but it is the illustrations that make the book outstanding." Bull Cent Child Books

961.1   Tunisia

Brown, Roslind Varghese

Tunisia; [by] Roslind Varghese Brown & Michael Spilling. 2nd ed. Marshall Cavendish Benchmark 2008 c2009 144p il map (Cultures of the world) lib bdg $42.79

Grades: 5 6 7 8   **961.1**

1. Tunisia
ISBN 978-0-7614-3037-7 (lib bdg); 0-7614-3037-7 (lib bdg)   LC 2007050798
First published 1998
"Provides comprehensive information on the geography, history, wildlife, governmental structure, economy, cultural diversity, peoples, religion, and culture of Tunisia." Publisher note
Includes glossary and bibliographical references

961.2   Libya

Malcolm, Peter, 1937-

Libya; [by] Peter Malcolm, Elie Losleben. 2nd ed. Benchmark Bks. 2004 144p il map (Cultures of the world) lib bdg $42.79

Grades: 5 6 7 8   **961.2**

1. Libya
ISBN 0-7614-1702-8   LC 2003-20887

First published 1993
Contents: Geography; History; Government; Economy; Environment; Libyans minority; Lifestyle; Religion; Language; Arts; Leisure; Festivals; Food
Examines the geography, history, government, economy, people, and culture of Libya
Includes glossary and bibliographical references

962   Egypt and Sudan

Bowden, Rob

The Nile; [by] Rob Bowden. Raintree Steck-Vaughn Publishers 2004 48p il map (River journey) lib bdg $29.93

Grades: 5 6 7 8   **962**

1. Nile River 2. Nile River valley
ISBN 0-7398-6072-0   LC 2002-155378
Contents: The source of the Nile; Calming the Nile; The rivers meet; The Nile cataracts; The Nile Valley; The Nile Delta
The author presents information about the Nile River "as though readers are taking a trip from the river's source to where it meets the sea. This approach works surprisingly well at drawing youngsters in. . . . The author presents an integrated view of the geological, economic, and cultural aspects of [The Nile], and does not shy away from realities, such as how thousands of people lose their homes when dams are built, or the pollution that threatens wildlife. Full-color photographs appear throughout." SLJ

Heinrichs, Ann

The Nile. Marshall Cavendish Benchmark 2008 96p il map (Nature's wonders) lib bdg $24.95

Grades: 5 6 7 8   **962**

1. Nile River 2. Nile River valley
ISBN 978-0-7614-2854-1   LC 2007019187
"Provides comprehensive information on the geography, history, wildlife, peoples, and environmental issues of the Nile River Basin." Publisher's note
"It's tough to make a river interesting, but this . . . does an admirable job of it. . . . Crisp, full-color photos and original artwork decorate nearly every page. . . . [This is a] well-thought-out natural history." Booklist
Includes glossary and bibliographical references

Parker, Lewis K.

Egypt. Benchmark Bks. 2003 48p il map (Discovering cultures) lib bdg $28.50

Grades: 2 3 4   **962**

1. Egypt
ISBN 0-7614-1519-X   LC 2002-15305
Highlights the geography, people, food, schools, recreation, celebrations, and language of Egypt
This "is written in simple prose and illustrated with appealing color photos. The emphasis is on child-friendly topics. . . . Helpful for school reports." Horn Book Guide
Includes glossary and bibliographical references

Pateman, Robert, 1954-
Egypt; [by] Robert Pateman, Salwa El-Hamamsy. 2nd ed. Benchmark Bks. 2003 144p il map (Cultures of the world) lib bdg $42.79
Grades: 5 6 7 8   962
1. Egypt
ISBN 0-7614-1670-6   LC 2003-9859
First published 1993
Contents: Geography; History; Government; Economy; Environment; Egyptians; Lifestyle; Religion; Language; Arts; Leisure; Festivals; Food; Map of Egypt; About the economy; About the culture
Explores the geography, history, government, economy, people, and culture of Egypt
Includes glossary and bibliographical references

962.4   Sudan

Levy, Patricia, 1951-
Sudan; [by] Patricia Levy and Zawiah Abdul Latif. 2nd ed. Marshall Cavendish Benchmark 2008 144p il map (Cultures of the world) lib bdg $42.79
Grades: 5 6 7 8   962.4
1. Sudan
ISBN 978-0-7614-2083-5 (lib bdg); 0-7614-2083-5 (lib bdg)   LC 2006101725
Describes the geography, history, government, economy, people, lifestyle, religion, language, arts, leisure, festivals, and food of Sudan
Includes bibliographical references

963   Ethiopia and Eritrea

Gish, Steven, 1963-
Ethiopia; [by] Steven Gish & Winnie Thay & Zawiah Abdul Latif. 2nd ed. Marshall Cavendish Benchmark 2007 144p il map (Cultures of the world) lib bdg $42.79
Grades: 5 6 7 8   963
1. Ethiopia
ISBN 978-0-7614-2025-5 (lib bdg); 0-7614-2025-8 (lib bdg)   LC 2006020819
First published 1996
This provides "information on the geography, history, governmental structure, economy, cultural diversity, peoples, religion, and culture of Ethiopia." Publisher's note
Includes glossary and bibliographical references

964   Northwest African coast and offshore islands. Morocco

Seward, Pat, 1939-
Morocco; [by] Pat Seward & Orin Hargraves. 2nd ed. Marshall Cavendish Benchmark 2006 144p il map (Cultures of the world) lib bdg $42.79
Grades: 5 6 7 8   964
1. Morocco
ISBN 0-7614-2051-7   LC 2005020782

First published 1995
Describes the geography, history, government, economy, people, and culture of Morocco
Includes glossary and bibliographical references

965   Algeria

Kagda, Falaq
Algeria; [by] Falaq Kagda & Zawiah Abdul Latif. 2nd ed. Marshall Cavendish Benchmark 2008 144p il map (Cultures of the world) lib bdg $42.79
Grades: 5 6 7 8   965
1. Algeria
ISBN 978-0-7614-2085-9 (lib bdg); 0-7614-2085-1 (lib bdg)   LC 2007014888
First published 1997
"Provides comprehensive information on the geography, history, wildlife, governmental structure, economy, cultural diversity, peoples, religion, and culture of Algeria." Publisher's note
Includes glossary and bibliographical references

966.1   Mauritania

Blauer, Ettagale
Mauritania; [by] Ettagale Blauer & Jason Lauré. Marshall Cavendish Benchmark 2009 144p il map (Cultures of the world) lib bdg $42.79
Grades: 5 6 7 8   966.1
1. Mauritania
ISBN 978-0-7614-3116-9
This describes the geography, history, government, economy, environment, people, and culture of Mauritania

966.2   Mali, Burkina Faso, Niger

Blauer, Ettagale
Mali; [by] Ettagale Blauer & Jason Lauré. 2nd ed. Marshall Cavendish Benchmark 2008 144p il map (Cultures of the world) lib bdg $42.79
Grades: 5 6 7 8   966.2
1. Mali
ISBN 978-0-7614-2568-7
First published 1997
This describes the geography, history, government, economy, environment, people, and culture of Mali
Includes glossary and bibliographical references

McKissack, Patricia C., 1944-
The royal kingdoms of Ghana, Mali, and Songhay; life in medieval Africa; [by] Patricia and Fredrick McKissack. Holt & Co. 1993 142p il maps pa $12.99 hardcover o.p.
Grades: 5 6 7 8   966.2
1. Ghana Empire 2. Songhai Empire 3. Mali—History
ISBN 0-8050-4259-8 (pa)   LC 93-4838

McKissack, Patricia C., 1944-—*Continued*

Examines the civilizations of the Western Sudan which flourished from 700 to 1700 A.D., acquiring such vast wealth that they became centers of trade and culture for a continent

"The McKissacks are careful to distinguish what is known from what is surmised; they draw on the oral tradition, eyewitness accounts, and contemporary scholarship; and chapter source notes discuss various conflicting views of events." Booklist

Includes bibliographical references

966.23   Mali

Brook, Larry

Daily life in ancient and modern Timbuktu; illustrations by Ray Webb. Runestone Press 1999 64p il (Cities through time) lib bdg $25.26 *

Grades: 4 5 6 7   966.23

1. Tombouctou (Mali)

ISBN 0-8225-3215-8   LC 98-18314

Examines the history of the city of Timbuktu, or Tombouctou, from its time as a camping site for nomadic Tuaregs through its prominence in the sixteenth century to the current decline it faces

"Brook presents the political and social history of the city known as the 'Pearl of Africa' in clean, engaging prose." Horn Book Guide

Includes bibliographical references

966.26   Niger

Seffal, Rabah

Niger. Benchmark Bks. 2001 128p il maps (Cultures of the world) lib bdg $42.79

Grades: 5 6 7 8   966.26

1. Niger

ISBN 0-7614-0995-5   LC 99-55064

A history and geography as well as a description of the government, economy, people, lifestyle, religion, language, arts, leisure time activities, festivals, and food of this landlocked West African country

Includes glossary and bibliographical references

966.3   Senegal

Berg, Elizabeth, 1953-

Senegal; by Elizabeth L. Berg and Ruth Lau. 2nd ed. Marshall Cavendish Benchmark 2009 144p il map (Cultures of the world) lib bdg $42.79

Grades: 5 6 7 8   966.3

1. Senegal

ISBN 978-0-7614-4481-7 (lib bdg); 0-7614-4481-5 (lib bdg)   LC 2009007067

First published 1999

Describes the geography, history, wildlife, governmental structure, economy, cultural diversity, peoples, religion, and culture of Senegal

Includes glossary and bibliographical references

966.4   Sierra Leone

LeVert, Suzanne

Sierra Leone; [by] Suzanne LeVert. Marshall Cavendish Benchmark 2007 144p il map (Cultures of the world) lib bdg $42.79

Grades: 5 6 7 8   966.4

1. Sierra Leone

ISBN 978-0-7614-2334-8 (lib bdg); 0-7614-2334-6 (lib bdg)   LC 2005035964

This provides "information on the geography, history, governmental structure, economy, cultural diversity, peoples, religion, and culture of Sierra Leone." Publisher's note

Includes glossary and bibliographical references

966.7   Ghana

Levy, Patricia, 1951-

Ghana; [by] Patricia Levy and Winnie Wong. 2nd ed. Marshall Cavendish Benchmark 2010 144p il map (Cultures of the world) lib bdg $42.79

Grades: 5 6 7 8   966.7

1. Ghana

ISBN 978-0-7614-4847-1; 0-7614-4847-0

First published 1999

Introduces the geography, history, government, economy, culture, and people of Ghana.

Includes glossary and bibliographical references

966.83   Benin

Kneib, Martha

Benin; [by] Martha Kneib. Marshall Cavendish Benchmark 2006 144p il map (Cultures of the world) lib bdg $42.79

Grades: 5 6 7 8   966.83

1. Benin

ISBN 978-0-7614-2328-7 (lib bdg); 0-7614-2328-1 (lib bdg)   LC 2005029052

This provides "information on the geography, history, wildlife, governmental structure, economy, diversity, peoples, religion, and culture of Benin." Publisher's note

Includes glossary and bibliographical references

966.9   Nigeria

Giles, Bridget

Nigeria; [by] Bridget Giles. National Geographic 2007 64p il map (Countries of the world) lib bdg $27.90 *

Grades: 4 5 6 7   966.9

1. Nigeria

ISBN 978-1-4263-0124-7   LC 2007024729

This describes the geography, nature, history, people and culture, government, and economy of Nigeria

"What helps [this book] stand out from the pack is

Giles, Bridget—*Continued*
[its] high-quality, rich photography. . . . The photos provide as much information as the [text]. . . . The writing is straightforward and solid." SLJ
Includes glossary and bibliographical references

Levy, Patricia, 1951-
Nigeria. 2nd ed. Benchmark Bks. 2004 144p il map (Cultures of the world) lib bdg $42.79
Grades: 5 6 7 8   **966.9**
1. Nigeria
ISBN 0-7614-1703-6   LC 2003-20886
First published 1993
Contents: Geography; History; Government; Economy; Environment; Nigerians; Lifestyle; Religion; Language; Arts; Leisure; Festivals; Food
Examines the geography, history, government, economy, people, and culture of Nigeria
Includes glossary and bibliographical references

Murphy, Patricia J., 1963-
Nigeria. Benchmark Books 2004 c2005 48p il map (Discovering cultures) lib bdg $28.50
Grades: 2 3 4   **966.9**
1. Nigeria
ISBN 0-7614-1795-8
An introduction to the geography, history, people, and culture of Nigeria
Includes glossary and bibliographical references

Oluonye, Mary N., 1955-
Nigeria; by Mary N. Oluonye. Lerner Publications Company 2007 c2008 48p il map (Country explorers) lib bdg $27.93; pa $8.95
Grades: 2 3 4   **966.9**
1. Nigeria
ISBN   978-0-8225-7131-5   (lib   bdg);
978-0-8225-8509-1 (pa)   LC 2006035846
"With short, chatty sentences and a lively, contemporary color photo on every page, this title . . . gives a brief overview of the history, geography, and culture of Nigeria. . . . The current information is not oversimplified." Booklist

Onyefulu, Ifeoma, 1959-
Ikenna goes to Nigeria. Frances Lincoln 2007 33p il map $16.95 paperback o.p.
Grades: K 1 2 3   **966.9**
1. Nigeria
ISBN   978-1-84507-585-9;   1-84507-585-4;
978-1-84507-960-4 (pa); 1-84507-960-4 (pa)
"Onyefulu delivers another photo-essay filled with vivid, colorful photographs, accompanied by brief, clear text about the land, people, and culture of her native Nigeria. The text is narrated by the author's son. . . . An outline map of the country shows the location of the cities/towns/villages that Ikenna will visit during the course of his trip. . . . The clear images contain a wealth of detail and provide valuable visual insight into the people and culture." SLJ

967 Central Africa and offshore islands

Haskins, James, 1941-2005
Africa; a look back; by James Haskins and Kathleen Benson. Marshall Cavendish Benchmark 2007 68p il map (Drama of African-American history) lib bdg $34.21
Grades: 5 6 7 8   **967**
1. Africa 2. Slavery 3. African Americans—History
ISBN 978-0-7614-2148-1 (lib bdg); 0-7614-2148-3 (lib bdg)   LC 2005030477
"Provides a history of the roots of African-American culture, going back to the period of the transatlantic slave trade and earlier. Much of the history is told through reminiscences of slaves or former slaves in their narratives." Publisher's note
Includes glossary and bibliographical references

967.3 Angola

Sheehan, Sean, 1951-
Angola; [by] Sean Sheehan and Jui Lin Yong. 2nd ed. Marshall Cavendish Benchmark 2010 144p il map (Cultures of the world) lib bdg $42.79
Grades: 5 6 7 8   **967.3**
1. Angola
ISBN 978-0-7614-4845-7; 0-7614-4845-4
LC 2009021203
"Provides comprehensive information on the geography, history, wildlife, governmental structure, economy, cultural diversity, peoples, religion, and culture of Angola." Publisher's note
Includes glossary and bibliographical references

967.43 Chad

Kneib, Martha
Chad; [by] Martha Kneib. Marshall Cavendish Benchmark 2007 144p il map (Cultures of the world) lib bdg $42.79
Grades: 5 6 7 8   **967.43**
1. Chad
ISBN 978-0-7614-2327-0 (lib bdg); 0-7614-2327-3 (lib bdg)   LC 2005027079
This provides "information on the geography, history, governmental structure, economy, cultural diversity, peoples, religion, and culture of Chad." Publisher's note
Includes glossary and bibliographical references

967.51 Democratic Republic of the Congo

Heale, Jay
Democratic Republic of the Congo; by Jay Heale and Yong Jui Lin. 2nd ed. Marshall Cavendish Benchmark 2009 144p il map (Cultures of the world) lib bdg $42.79
Grades: 5 6 7 8   967.51
  1. Congo (Republic)
  ISBN 978-0-7614-4478-7 (lib bdg); 0-7614-4478-5 (lib bdg)   LC 2009003195
  First published 1999
Describes the geography, history, government, economy, people, lifestyle, religion, languages, arts, leisure, festivals, and food of The Democratic Republic of the Congo
Includes glossary and bibliographical references

Willis, Terri
Democratic Republic of the Congo. Children's Press 2004 143p il map (Enchantment of the world, Second series) lib bdg $38
Grades: 5 6 7 8   967.51
  1. Congo (Republic)
  ISBN 0-516-24250-4   LC 2003-504
Contents: Collapsing under its weight; The country and the river; Congo's bountiful diversity; Kingdoms, colonies, and corruption; Moving toward freedom; Poverty amidst plenty; People of the Congo; Overlapping faiths; Expression through the arts; Life in Congo; Timeline; Fast facts
Discusses the geography and climate, history, wildlife, economy, government, people, religion, and culture of the Congo
This offers "lucid commentary, digestible quantities of facts and statistics, eye-catching color photos, and eminently useful back matter." Booklist
Includes bibliographical references

967.571 Rwanda

King, David C., 1933-
Rwanda; [by] David C. King. Marshall Cavendish Benchmark 2007 144p il map (Cultures of the world) lib bdg $42.79
Grades: 5 6 7 8   967.571
  1. Rwanda
  ISBN 978-0-7614-2333-1 (lib bdg); 0-7614-2333-8 (lib bdg)   LC 2005031817
This provides "information on the geography, history, governmental structure, economy, cultural diversity, peoples, religion, and culture of Rwanda." Publisher's note
Includes glossary and bibliographical references

967.61 Uganda

Barlas, Robert
Uganda; [by] Robert Barlas and Yong Jui Lin. 2nd ed. Marshall Cavendish Benchmark 2010 144p il map (Cultures of the world) lib bdg $29.95
Grades: 5 6 7 8   967.61
  1. Uganda
  ISBN 978-0-7614-4859-4; 0-7614-4859-4
                                  LC 2009046002
  First published 2000
This offers information on the geography, history, wildlife, governmental structure, economy, cultural diversity, peoples, religion, and culture of Uganda.
Includes glossary and bibliographical references

967.62 Kenya

Pateman, Robert, 1954-
Kenya; by Robert Pateman. 2nd ed. Benchmark Bks. 2004 144p il map (Cultures of the world) lib bdg $42.79
Grades: 5 6 7 8   967.62
  1. Kenya
  ISBN 0-7614-1701-X   LC 2003-20921
  First published 1993
Contents: Geography; History; Government; Economy; Environment; Kenyans; Lifestyle; Religion; Language; Arts; Leisure; Festivals; Foods
Examines the geography, history, government, economy, people, and culture of Kenya
Includes glossary and bibliographical references

967.73 Somalia

Hassig, Susan M., 1969-
Somalia; by Susan M. Hassig & Zawiah Abdul Latif. 2nd ed. Marshall Cavendish Benchmark 2008 144p il map (Cultures of the world) lib bdg $42.79
Grades: 5 6 7 8   967.73
  1. Somalia
  ISBN 978-0-7614-2082-8 (lib bdg); 0-7614-2082-7 (lib bdg)   LC 2006102270
  First published 1997
"Provides comprehensive information on the geography, history, wildlife, governmental structure, economy, cultural diversity, peoples, religion, and culture of Somalia." Publisher's note
Includes glossary and bibliographical references

967.8   Tanzania

Heale, Jay
Tanzania; by Jay Heale & Winnie Wong. 2nd
ed. Marshall Cavendish Benchmark 2009 144p il
map (Cultures of the world) lib bdg $42.79
Grades: 5 6 7 8   **967.8**
     1. Tanzania
     ISBN 978-0-7614-3417-7 (lib bdg); 0-7614-3417-8 (lib
bdg)   LC 2008028802
     First published 1998
     "Provides comprehensive information on the geography, history, wildlife, governmental structure, economy, cultural diversity, peoples, religion, and culture of Tanzania." Publisher's note
     Includes glossary and bibliographical references

967.9   Mozambique

King, David C., 1933-
Mozambique; [by] David C. King. Marshall
Cavendish Benchmark 2007 144p il map (Cultures
of the world) lib bdg $42.79
Grades: 5 6 7 8   **967.9**
     1. Mozambique
     ISBN 978-0-7614-2331-7 (lib bdg); 0-7614-2331-1 (lib
bdg)   LC 2006002302
     This provides "information on the geography, history, wildlife, governmental structure, economy, cultural diversity, peoples, religion, and culture of Mozambique." Publisher's note
     Includes glossary and bibliographical references

968   Southern Africa. Republic of South Africa

Mace, Virginia
South Africa; [by] Virginia Mace; Kate
Rowntree and Vukile Khumalo, consultants.
National Geographic 2008 64p il map (Countries
of the world) lib bdg $27.90 *
Grades: 4 5 6 7   **968**
     1. South Africa
     ISBN 978-1-4263-0203-9   LC 2007047835
     This describes the geography, nature, history, people and culture, government, and economy of South Africa.
     "Through its numerous maps and standout photographs, this book provides a general overview of South Africa that will satisfy the basic needs of upper-elementary research paper writers." Horn Book Guide
     Includes glossary and bibliographical references

Murphy, Patricia J., 1963-
South Africa. Benchmark Bks. 2004 48p il map
(Discovering cultures) lib bdg $28.50
Grades: 2 3 4   **968**
     1. South Africa
     ISBN 0-7614-1719-2   LC 2003-8129

An introduction to the history, geography, language, schools, and social life and customs of South Africa
     Includes glossary and bibliographical references

Rosmarin, Ike, 1915-
South Africa; [by] Ike Rosmarin, Dee Rissik.
2nd ed. Benchmark Bks. 2004 144p il map
(Cultures of the world) lib bdg $42.79
Grades: 5 6 7 8   **968**
     1. South Africa
     ISBN 0-7614-1704-4   LC 2003-20923
     First published 1993
     Contents: Geography; History; Government; Economy; Environment; South Africans; Lifestyle; Religion; Language; Arts; Leisure; Festivals; Food
     Examines the geography, history, government, economy, people, and culture of South Africa
     Includes glossary and bibliographical references

968.83   Botswana

LeVert, Suzanne
Botswana; [by] Suzanne LeVert. Marshall
Cavendish Benchmark 2007 144p il map (Cultures
of the world) lib bdg $42.79
Grades: 5 6 7 8   **968.83**
     1. Botswana
     ISBN 978-0-7614-2330-0 (lib bdg); 0-7614-2330-3 (lib
bdg)   LC 2005032575
     This offers "information on the geography, history, governmental structure, economy, cultural diversity, peoples, religion, and culture of Botswana." Publisher's note
     Includes glossary and bibliographical references

968.91   Zimbabwe

Sheehan, Sean, 1951-
Zimbabwe. 2nd ed. Benchmark Bks. 2004 144p
il map (Cultures of the world) lib bdg $42.79
Grades: 5 6 7 8   **968.91**
     1. Zimbabwe
     ISBN 0-7614-1706-0 (lib bdg); 978-0-7614-1706-4 (lib
bdg)   LC 2003-20883
     First published 1994
     Contents: Geography; History; Government; Economy; Environment; Zimbabweans; Lifestyle; Religion; Language; Arts; Leisure; Festivals; Foods
     Examines the geography, history, government, economy, people, and culture of Zimbabwe
     Includes glossary and bibliographical references

968.94   Zambia

Holmes, Timothy
Zambia; by Timothy Holmes & Winnie Wong. rev ed. Marshall Cavendish Benchmark 2008 c2009 144p il map (Cultures of the world) lib bdg $42.79
Grades: 5 6 7 8   **968.94**
  1. Zambia
  ISBN 978-0-7614-3039-1 (lib bdg); 0-7614-3039-3 (lib bdg)   LC 2007050794
  First published 1998
  Describes the geography, history, government, economy, people, lifestyle, religion, language, arts, leisure, festivals, and food of Zambia
  Includes glossary and bibliographical references

969.1   Madagascar

Heale, Jay
Madagascar; [by] Jay Heale & Zawiah Abdul Latif. 2nd ed. Marshall Cavendish Benchmark 2008 c2009 144p il map (Cultures of the world) lib bdg $42.79
Grades: 5 6 7 8   **969.1**
  1. Madagascar
  ISBN 978-0-7614-3036-0 (lib bdg); 0-7614-3036-9 (lib bdg)   LC 2007048288
  First published 1998
  "Provides comprehensive information on the geography, history, wildlife, governmental structure, economy, cultural diversity, peoples, religion, and culture of Madagascar." Publisher's note
  Includes glossary and bibliographical references

970   History of North America

Foster, Karen, 1964-
Atlas of North America. Picture Window Books 2008 32p il map (Picture Window Books world atlases) lib bdg $27.93; pa $7.95
Grades: 2 3 4   **970**
  1. North America
  ISBN 978-1-4048-3885-7 (lib bdg); 1-4048-3885-6 (lib bdg); 978-1-4048-3893-2 (pa); 1-4048-3893-7 (pa)
  This introduction to the geography of North America offers maps and information about countries, landforms, bodies of water, climate, plants, animals, population, people and customs, places of interest, industries, transportation, and the Mississippi River
  This book offers "well-organized, easy-to-access information. . . . Small photographs or colorful text boxes draw readers' attention to points of interest or fun facts. Maps and legends are simple, yet disseminate information clearly." SLJ
  Includes glossary

970.004   North American native peoples

Ancona, George, 1929-
Powwow; photographs and text by George Ancona. Harcourt Brace Jovanovich 1993 unp il hardcover o.p. pa $10
Grades: 3 4 5 6   **970.004**
  1. Crow Fair (Crow Agency, Mont.) 2. Native Americans—Rites and ceremonies
  ISBN 0-15-263268-9; 0-15-263269-7 (pa)
                                    LC 92-15912
  A photo essay on the pan-Indian celebration called a powwow, this particular one being held on the Crow Reservation in Montana
  The book is "illustrated with well-placed, full-color photos that clearly reflect the text. . . . An exquisite kaleidoscope of Native American music, customs, and crafts." SLJ

Andre, Julie-Ann
We feel good out here; by Julie-Ann Andre and Mindy Willett; photographs by Tessa Macintosh. Fitzhenry & Whiteside 2008 32p il (The land is our storybook) $16.95
Grades: 3 4 5 6   **970.004**
  1. Native Americans—Canada 2. Northwest Territories
  ISBN 978-1-89725-233-8; 1-89725-233-1
  This title focuses on the land and culture "of Canada's Northwest Territories and is replete with sharp and attractive full-color photographs. In [this book] a local woman describes her life with her husband and two daughters. Julie-Ann is a Canadian Ranger who studies business management but, more importantly, she is a student of Gwich'in language and culture. She was sent to a residential school at age seven and has spent the last 10 years reestablishing her people's traditional practices and beliefs. A boxed area, 'Our Words,' gives a few words in English and in Gwichya Gwich'in. . . . [This title provides] some useful information for reports and [is an] interesting [addition] for general reading." SLJ

Arnold, Caroline, 1944-
The ancient cliff dwellers of Mesa Verde; photographs by Richard Hewett. Clarion Bks. 1992 64p il hardcover o.p. pa $7.95 *
Grades: 4 5 6 7   **970.004**
  1. Pueblo Indians
  ISBN 0-395-56241-4; 0-618-05149-X (pa)
                                    LC 91-8145
  Discusses the native Americans known as the Anasazi, who migrated to southwestern Colorado in the first century A.D. and mysteriously disappeared in 1300 A.D. after constructing extensive dwellings in the cliffs of the steep canyon walls
  "A thorough and attractive introduction to the Anasazi people with outstanding photographs of the dramatic vistas and ceremonial chambers within this national park." SLJ
  Includes glossary

Baylor, Byrd, 1924-
When clay sings; illustrated by Tom Bahti. Scribner 1972 unp il hardcover o.p. pa $6.99 *
Grades: 1 2 3 4   **970.004**
  1. Native American art 2. Native Americans—Southwestern States 3. Pottery
  ISBN 0-684-18829-5; 0-689-71106-9 (pa)
  A Caldecott Medal honor book, 1973
  "A lyrical tribute to an almost forgotten time of the prehistoric Indian of the desert West presents broken bits of pottery from this ancient time. The designs and drawings, done in rich earth tones, are derived from prehistoric pottery found in the American Southwest." Read Ladders for Hum Relat. 6th edition

Bealer, Alex W.
Only the names remain; the Cherokees and the Trail of Tears; illustrated by Kristina Rodanas. Little, Brown 1996 79p il pa $6.99 hardcover o.p.
Grades: 4 5 6   **970.004**
  1. Cherokee Indians
  ISBN 0-316-08519-7 (pa)
  A reissue with new illustrations of the title first published 1972
  The author describes "the rise of the Cherokee Nation, with its written language, constitution, and republican form of government, and its tragic betrayal in the 1830s." Chicago Public Libr

Bjorklund, Ruth
The Hopi; by Ruth Bjorklund. Marshall Cavendish Benchmark 2009 48p il (First Americans) lib bdg $31.36
Grades: 2 3 4   **970.004**
  1. Hopi Indians
  ISBN 978-0-7614-3021-6 (lib bdg); 0-7614-3021-0 (lib bdg)   LC 2007-33676
  "Provides comprehensive information on the background, lifestyle, beliefs, and present-day lives of the Hopi people." Publisher's note
  Includes glossary and bibliographical references

A **Braid** of lives; Native American childhood; edited by Neil Philip. Clarion Bks. 2000 81p il $20 *
Grades: 4 5 6 7   **970.004**
  1. Native Americans
  ISBN 0-395-64528-X   LC 00-21343
  This "book presents the remembrances of 33 individuals from 22 different American Indian nations, ranging from anonymous men and women to such well-known figures as Black Elk and Sarah Winnemucca Hopkins." SLJ
  "This is an excellent choice for curriculum support and brief read-aloud material." Booklist
  Includes bibliographical references

Bruchac, Joseph, 1942-
The Trail of Tears; illustrated by Diana Magnuson. Random House 1999 46p il hardcover o.p. pa $3.99 *
Grades: 2 3 4   **970.004**
  1. Cherokee Indians
  ISBN 0-679-99052-6 (lib bdg); 0-679-89052-1 (pa)   LC 98-36199
  "Step into reading"
  Recounts how the Cherokees, after fighting to keep their land in the nineteenth century, were forced to leave and travel 1200 miles to a new settlement in Oklahoma, a terrible journey known as the Trail of Tears
  "Magnuson's colorful pictures, packed with people and action, are a little bright for the subject, but strong new readers will find that nonfiction can tell a powerful story." Booklist

Connolly, Sean, 1956-
The Americas and the Pacific. Zak Books 2009 48p il map (History of world) $34.25 *
Grades: 4 5 6 7 8   **970.004**
  1. Native Americans—History 2. Aboriginal Australians 3. Maoris
  ISBN 978-8-860981-61-5; 8-860981-61-1   LC 2008008404
  This is an "overview of the early history of American and Pacific peoples, including Native Americans, Maya, Aztecs, Inca, Aborigines, and the Maori, up to 1200 CE." Publisher's note
  "Artists' renderings show groups of people engaged in representative activities, but it's the reproductions of artifacts . . . that will pull readers and browsers most. . . . [This is an] engaging overview." Booklist
  Includes bibliographical references

De Capua, Sarah
The Cheyenne. Marshall Cavendish Benchmark 2007 47p il (First Americans) lib bdg $31.36
Grades: 2 3 4   **970.004**
  1. Cheyenne Indians
  ISBN 978-0-7614-2248-8 (lib bdg); 0-7614-2248-X (lib bdg)   LC 2006011967
  Provides information on the background, lifestyle, beliefs, and present-day lives of the Cheyenne people
  Includes glossary and bibliographical references

The Choctaw; by Sarah De Capua. Marshall Cavendish Benchmark 2009 48p il (First Americans) lib bdg $31.36
Grades: 2 3 4   **970.004**
  1. Choctaw Indians
  ISBN 978-0-7614-3018-6 (lib bdg); 0-7614-3018-0 (lib bdg)   LC 2007-33727
  "Provides comprehensive information on the background, lifestyle, beliefs, and present-day lives of the Choctaw people." Publisher's note
  Includes glossary and bibliographical references

The Comanche. Marshall Cavendish Benchmark 2007 47p il (First Americans) lib bdg $31.36
Grades: 2 3 4   **970.004**
  1. Comanche Indians
  ISBN 978-0-7614-2249-5 (lib bdg); 0-7614-2249-8 (lib bdg)   LC 2006011975

De Capua, Sarah—*Continued*

Provides information on the background, lifestyle, beliefs, and present-day lives of the Comanche people

Includes glossary and bibliographical references

The Menominee. Marshall Cavendish Benchmark 2009 48p il (First Americans) lib bdg $31.36

Grades: 2 3 4   **970.004**

1. Menominee Indians

ISBN 978-0-7614-4131-1 (lib bdg); 0-7614-4131-X (lib bdg)   LC 2008041999

Provides information on the background, lifestyle, beliefs, and present-day lives of the Menominee people

The Shawnee. Marshall Cavendish Benchmark 2007 48p il (First Americans) lib bdg $31.36

Grades: 2 3 4   **970.004**

1. Shawnee Indians

ISBN 978-0-7614-2682-0 (lib bdg); 0-7614-2682-5 (lib bdg)   LC 2006034117

Provides information on the background, lifestyle, beliefs, and present-day lives of the Shawnee people

Includes glossary and bibliographical references

The Shoshone. Marshall Cavendish Benchmark 2007 48p il (First Americans) lib bdg $31.36

Grades: 2 3 4   **970.004**

1. Shoshone Indians

ISBN 978-0-7614-2683-7 (lib bdg); 0-7614-2683-3 (lib bdg)   LC 2006034113

Provides information on the background, lifestyle, beliefs, and present-day lives of the Shoshone people

Includes glossary and bibliographical references

Dennis, Yvonne Wakim

Children of native America today; [by] Yvonne Wakim Dennis & Arlene Hirschfelder; with a foreword by Buffy Sainte-Marie. Charlesbridge Pub. 2003 64p il map lib bdg $19.95 *

Grades: 3 4 5 6   **970.004**

1. Native Americans

ISBN 1-57091-499-0   LC 2002-2272

"Shakti for children"

"This photo-essay features 25 of the more than 500 native cultures of the U.S. as well as a section on urban Indians. In this 'book of few words and many pictures,' the clear, captioned photographs speak eloquently of contemporary Native American young people. . . . An excellent resource for multicultural studies, this handsome album will also attract browsers." Booklist

Includes glossary and bibliographical references

A kid's guide to native American history; more than 50 activities; by Yvonne Wakim Dennis and Arlene Hirschfelder. Chicago Review Press 2009 226p il pa $16.95 *

Grades: 3 4 5 6   **970.004**

1. Native Americans—History 2. Handicraft 3. Cooking 4. Games

ISBN 978-1-55652-802-6 (pa); 1-55652-802-7 (pa)   LC 2009015832

"This two-in-one history and activity book does an excellent job of explaining Native American history in easy-to-understand language while stressing the differences between and diversity among tribes. The book is divided by region. . . . Activities are kid-friendly . . . and encourage exploration of the text. . . . Clear illustrations accompany each activity." SLJ

Includes glossary and bibliographical references

Ehrlich, Amy, 1942-

Wounded Knee: an Indian history of the American West; adapted for young readers by Amy Ehrlich from Dee Brown's Bury my heart at Wounded Knee. Holt & Co. 1974 202p il maps pa $13.95 hardcover o.p.

Grades: 6 7 8 9   **970.004**

1. Native Americans—West (U.S.) 2. Native Americans—Wars 3. West (U.S.)—History

ISBN 0-8050-2700-9 (pa)

This book traces the plight of the Navaho, Apache, Cheyenne and Sioux Indians in their struggles against the white man in the West between 1860 and 1890. It recounts battles and their causes, participants, and consequences during this era

"Some chapters [of the original] have been deleted, others condensed, and in some instances sentence structure and language have been simplified. The editing is good, and this version is interesting, readable, and smooth." SLJ

Includes bibliographical references

Flanagan, Alice K.

The Pueblos. Children's Press 1998 47p il maps lib bdg $25; pa $6.95

Grades: 2 3 4   **970.004**

1. Pueblo Indians

ISBN 0-516-20626-5 (lib bdg); 0-516-26383-8 (pa)   LC 97-12683

"A True book"

Examines the culture, history, and society of the Pueblos

Includes bibliographical references

The Zunis. Children's Press 1998 47p il lib bdg $25

Grades: 2 3 4   **970.004**

1. Zuni Indians

ISBN 0-516-20630-3   LC 97-6712

"A True book"

Examines the history, culture, and society of the Zuni Indians, one of the groups of Pueblo Indians living in New Mexico

Includes bibliographical references

Freedman, Russell

Buffalo hunt. Holiday House 1988 52p il lib bdg $24.95 paperback o.p. *

Grades: 4 5 6 7   **970.004**

1. Native Americans—Great Plains 2. Bison

ISBN 0-8234-0702-0 (lib bdg); 0-8234-1159-1 (pa)   LC 87-35303

Freedman, Russell—*Continued*

The author discusses the importance of the buffalo in the lore and day-to-day life of the Indian tribes of the Great Plains. He describes hunting methods, the uses found for each part of the animal, and the near disappearance of the buffalo as white hunters, traders and settlers moved west

"Freedman has hit his stride in terms of selection, style, and illustration: the color reproductions of historical art work form a stunning complement to the carefully researched, graceful presentation of information." Bull Cent Child Books

Goble, Paul

All our relatives; traditional Native American thoughts about nature; compiled and illustrated by Paul Goble. World Wisdom 2005 unp il $15.95
Grades: 5 6 7 8   **970.004**
1. Native Americans 2. Philosophy of nature
ISBN 0-941532-77-1; 978-0-941532-77-8
                        LC 2005004285
"The pages of this book are chock-full of quotations, songs, and brief stories that exemplify Native American attitudes toward nature. . . . Black Elk, Standing Bear, Brave Buffalo, and others observe the importance of various animals and the sacred qualities of all living things. . . . The spaces between text blocks are filled with Goble's familiar illustrations based on traditional Native American designs and colors." SLJ
Includes bibliographical references

Hicks, Terry Allan

The Chumash; by Terry Allan Hicks. Marshall Cavendish Benchmark 2008 48p il map (First Americans) lib bdg $29.93
Grades: 2 3 4   **970.004**
1. Chumash Indians
ISBN 978-0-7614-2678-3 (lib bdg); 0-7614-2678-7 (lib bdg)   LC 2006034101
This describes Chumash "history and culture, way of life, beliefs, present status, and future outlook. Colorful modern photographs appear throughout, as do paintings, photos, and maps. [The] volume includes a simple craft . . . as well as a Native recipe. . . . [The] book has a helpful, easy-to-read graphical time line. Clear writing and attractive [layout makes this book] accessible and appealing." SLJ
Includes glossary and bibliographical references

Hoyt-Goldsmith, Diane

Pueblo storyteller; photographs by Lawrence Migdale. Holiday House 1991 26p il $16.95; pa $6.95 *
Grades: 3 4 5   **970.004**
1. Pueblo Indians
ISBN 0-8234-0864-7; 0-8234-1080-3 (pa)
                        LC 90-46405
A young Cochiti Indian girl living with her grandparents in the Cochiti Pueblo near Santa Fe, New Mexico, describes her home and family and the day-to-day life and customs of her people
"The bright, crisp, almost shadowless photographs

smoothly integrate additional details into the lively text." Publ Wkly
Includes glossary

King, David C., 1933-

First people; an illustrated history of American Indians. DK Pub. 2008 192p il map $19.99
Grades: 5 6 7 8   **970.004**
1. Native Americans
ISBN 978-0-7566-4092-7; 0-7566-4092-X
"This rich pictorial work serves as an entertaining, informative, and visually appealing introduction to American Indian culture and history. Each of the seven chapters covers a different time period in chronological order. . . . The glossy photographs, colorful drawings, and easily accessible paragraphs . . . make for an easy-to-use overall package." SLJ

The Haida. Marshall Cavendish Benchmark 2007 48p il (First Americans) lib bdg $31.36
Grades: 2 3 4   **970.004**
1. Haida Indians
ISBN 978-0-7614-2250-1 (lib bdg); 0-7614-2250-1 (lib bdg)   LC 2006011969
Provides information on the background, lifestyle, beliefs, and present-day lives of the Haida people
Includes glossary and bibliographical references

The Huron. Marshall Cavendish Benchmark 2007 48p il (First Americans) lib bdg $31.36
Grades: 2 3 4   **970.004**
1. Huron Indians
ISBN 978-0-7614-2251-8 (lib bdg); 0-7614-2251-X (lib bdg)   LC 2006011970
Provides information on the background, lifestyle, beliefs, and present-day lives of the Huron people
Includes glossary and bibliographical references

The Inuit; [by] David C. King. Marshall Cavendish Benchmark 2008 48p il map (First Americans) lib bdg $31.36
Grades: 2 3 4   **970.004**
1. Inuit
ISBN 978-0-7614-2679-0 (lib bdg); 0-7614-2679-5 (lib bdg)   LC 2006034111
This describes Inuit "history and culture, way of life, beliefs, present status, and future outlook. Colorful modern photographs appear throughout, as do paintings, photos, and maps. . . . [It] includes a simple craft . . . (soapstone carving) as well as a Native recipe . . . (fish soup). . . . [It] has a helpful, easy-to-read graphical time line. Clear writing and attractive [layout makes this book] accessible and appealing." SLJ
Includes glossary and bibliographical references

The Mohawk. Marshall Cavendish Benchmark 2009 48p il (First Americans) lib bdg $31.36
Grades: 2 3 4   **970.004**
1. Mohawk Indians
ISBN 978-0-7614-4132-8 (lib bdg); 0-7614-4132-8 (lib bdg)   LC 2008042000
Provides information on the background, lifestyle, beliefs, and present-day lives of the Mohawk people.
Includes glossary and bibliographical references

King, David C., 1933-—*Continued*

The Nez Perce; by David C. King. Marshall Cavendish Benchmark 2008 48p il map (First Americans) lib bdg $31.36

Grades: 2 3 4   **970.004**
1. Nez Percé Indians
ISBN 978-0-7614-2680-6 (lib bdg); 0-7614-2678-7 (lib bdg)   LC 2006034114

This describes Nez Perce "history and culture, way of life, beliefs, present status, and future outlook. Colorful modern photographs appear throughout, as do paintings, photos, and maps. [The] volume includes a simple craft . . . as well as a Native recipe. . . . [The] book has a helpful, easy-to-read graphical time line. Clear writing and attractive [layout makes this book] accessible and appealing." SLJ

Includes glossary and bibliographical references

The Ojibwe. Marshall Cavendish Benchmark 2007 45p il (First Americans) lib bdg $31.36

Grades: 2 3 4   **970.004**
1. Ojibwa Indians
ISBN 978-0-7614-2252-5 (lib bdg); 0-7614-2252-8 (lib bdg)   LC 2006011971

Provides information on the background, lifestyle, beliefs, and present-day lives of the Ojibwe people

Includes glossary and bibliographical references

The Powhatan. Marshall Cavendish Benchmark 2007 48p il (First Americans) lib bdg $31.36

Grades: 2 3 4   **970.004**
1. Powhatan Indians
ISBN 978-0-7614-2681-3 (lib bdg); 0-7614-2681-7 (lib bdg)   LC 2006034115

Provides information on the background, lifestyle, beliefs, and present-day lives of the Powhatan people

Includes glossary and bibliographical references

The Seminole. Marshall Cavendish Benchmark 2007 48p il (First Americans) lib bdg $31.36

Grades: 2 3 4   **970.004**
1. Seminole Indians
ISBN 978-0-7614-2253-2 (lib bdg); 0-7614-2253-6 (lib bdg)   LC 2006011977

Provides information on the background, lifestyle, beliefs, and present-day lives of the Seminole people

Includes glossary and bibliographical references

King, Sandra

Shannon: an Ojibway dancer; photographs by Catherine Whipple; with a foreword by Michael Dorris. Lerner Publs. 1993 48p il map (We are still here) pa $6.95 hardcover o.p.

Grades: 3 4 5 6   **970.004**
1. Ojibwa Indians
ISBN 0-8225-9643-1 (pa)   LC 92-27261

Shannon, a twelve-year-old Ojibwa Indian living in Minneapolis, Minnesota, learns about her tribe's traditional costumes from her grandmother and gets ready to dance at a powwow

"Numerous, colorful photographs show Shannon's daily activities as well as the costumes and dances at the powwow. The photos combine with a contemporary focus and straightforward text to make the book an excellent choice for middle readers." Booklist

Includes glossary and bibliographical references

McLeod, Tom

The Delta is my home; by Tom McLeod and Mindy Willett; photographs by Tessa Macintosh. Fitzhenry & Whiteside 2008 26p il (The land is our storybook) $16.95

Grades: 4 5 6 7   **970.004**
1. Native Americans—Canada 2. Northwest Territories 3. Mackenzie River (N.W.T.)
ISBN 978-1-8972-5232-1; 1-8972-5232-3
Includes text in Gwich'in and Inuvialuktun.

"An 11-year-old boy who lives in the Mackenzie Delta region with his family tells about life there. His father is a renewable resource officer and has taught him how to hunt, fish, trap, and drive a boat. Readers also learn about his language, schooling, and clothing as well as the important role that storytelling plays in the culture. [This title provides] some useful information for reports and [is an] interesting [addition] for general reading." SLJ

McNeese, Tim

The fascinating history of American Indians; the age before Columbus. Enslow Publishers 2009 128p il map (America's living history) lib bdg $31.93

Grades: 5 6 7 8   **970.004**
1. Native Americans
ISBN 978-0-7660-2938-5 (lib bdg); 0-7660-2938-7 (lib bdg)

"This thorough discussion of Native American life prior to Columbus's arrival combines theories of archaeologists, anthropologists, historians, and scientists to provide an engaging portrayal of the daily experiences of regional tribes. Based mostly on archaeological discoveries, the accessible text is supported by archival photographs, maps, and sidebars." Horn Book Guide

Includes glossary and bibliographic references

Molin, Paulette Fairbanks

American Indian stereotypes in the world of children; a reader and bibliography. 2nd ed, by Arlene Hirschfelder, Paulette Fairbanks Molin, Yvonne Wakim. Scarecrow Press 1999 343p il hardcover o.p. pa $40.50

Grades: Professional   **970.004**
1. Native Americans 2. Race awareness
ISBN 0-8108-3612-2; 0-8108-3613-0 (pa)   LC 98-49654

First published 1982

"This volume presents a collection of . . . articles detailing uses and abuses of Native American symbols, images, ideas, and stories that are directed at youth in the mass media. Toys, cartoons, textbooks, general reading, media portrayals, sports, logos, nicknames and more are discussed in stand-alone articles." Voice Youth Advocates

Includes bibliographical references

Murdoch, David Hamilton, 1937-
North American Indian; written by David Murdoch; chief consultant, Stanley A. Freed; photographed by Lynton Gardiner. rev ed. DK Pubs. 2005 72p il (DK eyewitness books) $16.99; lib bdg $19.99
Grades: 4 5 6 7   **970.004**
1. Native Americans
ISBN 0-7566-1081-8; 0-7566-1082-6 (lib bdg)
First published 1995 by Knopf
Published in association with the American Museum of Natural History
This is a guide to the civilizations of North American Indians including full-color photographs of artifacts and descriptions ceremonies and customs.

Peters, Russell M.
Clambake; a Wampanoag tradition; photographs by John Madama; with a foreword by Michael Dorris. Lerner Publs. 1992 48p il (We are still here) hardcover o.p. pa $6.95
Grades: 3 4 5 6   **970.004**
1. Wampanoag Indians
ISBN 0-8225-2651-4 (lib bdg); 0-8225-9621-0 (pa)
LC 92-8423
Steven Peters, a twelve-year-old Wampanoag Indian in Massachusetts, learns from his grandfather how to prepare a clambake in the tradition of his people.
"The full-color photographs illustrate the clearly written text and portray real people who are part of the contemporary world, passing on old traditions to their children." SLJ
Includes glossary and bibliographical references

Roessel, Monty
Songs from the loom; a Navajo girl learns to weave; text and photographs by Monty Roessel. Lerner Publs. 1995 48p il (We are still here) lib bdg $21.27; pa $6.95
Grades: 3 4 5 6   **970.004**
1. Navajo Indians 2. Weaving
ISBN 0-8225-2657-3 (lib bdg); 0-8225-9712-8 (pa)
LC 94-48765
"Ten-year-old Jaclyn's grandmother teaches her the art of traditional Navajo rug-weaving. Jaclyn learns the songs and stories that invest the weaving with meaning, as well as the use of the proper tools and techniques. The color photographs of contemporary Navajo life are clear and engrossing, enhancing the solid text." Horn Book Guide
Includes glossary and bibliographical references

Terry, Michael Bad Hand
Daily life in a Plains Indian village, 1868. Clarion Bks. 1999 48p il map hardcover o.p. pa $9.95
Grades: 4 5 6 7   **970.004**
1. Native Americans—Great Plains
ISBN 0-395-94542-9; 0-395-97499-2 (pa)
LC 98-32382

Depicts the historical background, social organization, and daily life of a Plains Indian village in 1868, presenting interiors, landscapes, clothing, and everyday objects
"The author presents short paragraphs of fascinating information accompanied by visuals that explain even more than the text." SLJ
Includes glossary

Zoe, Therese
Living stories; [by] Therese Zoe, Philip Zoe and Mindy Willett; photographs by Tessa Macintosh. Fitzhenry & Whiteside 2009 32p il (The land is our storybook) $16.95
Grades: 3 4 5 6   **970.004**
1. Native Americans—Canada 2. Northwest Territories 3. Native Americans—Folklore
ISBN 978-1-89725-244-4; 1-89725-244-7
"Therese Zoe is a Tlicho woman from Gamèti in the Northwest Territories. . . . [In this book she] shares her love for her community and translates the sacred stories and traditional wisdom of her brother-in-law, Philip Zoe, and his sister, Elizabeth Chocolate. . . . Join Tlicho young people, Shelinda, Forest, and Bradley, as they learn about making dry-fish, bows and arrows, and birchbark baskets; the practices of old-time healers; as well as the sacred stories that tell the history of the Tlicho people." Publisher's note

970.01   North America—Early history to 1599

Bodden, Valerie
Columbus reaches the New World. Creative Education 2009 48p il (Days of change) lib bdg $32.80
Grades: 5 6 7 8   **970.01**
1. Columbus, Christopher 2. America—Exploration
ISBN 978-158341-732-4; 1-58341-732-X
LC 2008009163
"With elegant design and mature prose, the Days of Change series is an ideal starting point for all manner of school projects. . . . *Columbus Reaches the New World* intelligently explains the famous sailor's motivations for forging a new trade route. . . . Anti-Columbus Day sentiments are mostly relegated to sidebars, but Bodden doesn't surgarcoat the enslavement and death that followed discovery." Booklist
Includes bibliographical references

Englar, Mary
French colonies in America. Compass Point Books 2009 48p il (We the people) lib bdg $26.60
Grades: 4 5 6   **970.01**
1. France—Colonies 2. America—Exploration 3. French Canadians 4. French Americans
ISBN 978-0-7565-3839-2   LC 2008007209
This is a history of French exploration and colonization in North America.
This provides "solid background matter and [introduces] key people and vocabulary." SLJ

Hernández, Roger E.
Early explorations: the 1500s. Marshall Cavendish Benchmark 2009 79p il map (Hispanic America) lib bdg $34.21
Grades: 4 5 6 7   **970.01**
   1. America—Exploration 2. Southern States—History 3. Southwestern States—History 4. Explorers 5. Spain—Colonies
   ISBN 978-0-7614-2937-1 (lib bdg); 0-7614-2937-9 (lib bdg)
   "Provides comprehensive information on the history of Spanish exploration in the United States." Publisher's note
   Includes glossary and bibliographical references

Huey, Lois Miner
American archaeology uncovers the Vikings. Marshall Cavendish Benchmark 2009 c2010 64p il map (American archaeology) lib bdg $21.95
Grades: 4 5 6 7   **970.01**
   1. Vikings—North America 2. America—Exploration 3. America—Antiquities 4. Excavations (Archeology)—United States 5. Excavations (Archeology)—Canada
   ISBN 978-0-7614-4270-7 (lib bdg); 0-7614-4270-7 (lib bdg)   LC 2008050266
   This describes how archeologists have learned about the Vikings in America.
   This is "both intriguing and engaging for young readers. . . . A welcomed addition to classroom and school libraries." Libr Media Connect
   Includes glossary and bibliographical references

Lilly, Alexandra
Spanish colonies in America. Compass Point Books 2009 48p il map (We the people) lib bdg $26.60
Grades: 4 5 6   **970.01**
   1. America—Exploration 2. Spaniards—United States 3. Explorers 4. Spain—Colonies
   ISBN 978-0-7565-3840-8 (lib bdg); 0-7565-3840-8 (lib bdg)   LC 2008011727
   This is a history Spanish exploration, conquest, and colonization in North America.
   This provides "solid background matter and [introduces] key people and vocabulary." SLJ

Maestro, Betsy, 1944-
The discovery of the Americas; by Betsy and Giulio Maestro. Lothrop, Lee & Shepard Bks. 1990 48p il maps hardcover o.p. pa $6.95 *
Grades: 2 3 4   **970.01**
   1. America—Exploration
   ISBN 0-688-06837-5; 0-688-11512-8 (pa)
      LC 89-32375
   Discusses both hypothetical and historical voyages of discovery to America by the Phoenicians, Saint Brendan of Ireland, the Vikings, and such later European navigators as Columbus, Cabot, and Magellan
   "The dazzlingly clean and accurate prose and the exhilarating beauty of the pictures combine for an extraordinary achievement in both history and art." SLJ

Exploration and conquest; the Americas after Columbus, 1500-1620; [by] Betsy & Giulio Maestro. Lothrop, Lee & Shepard Bks. 1994 48p il maps hardcover o.p. pa $6.95 *
Grades: 2 3 4   **970.01**
   1. America—Exploration
   ISBN 0-688-09268-3 (lib bdg); 0-688-15474-3 (pa)
      LC 93-48618
   This is a "discussion of the European exploration and conquest of the 'New World.' The author carefully explains that, 'The great gain of one people was the great loss of another' and traces the disastrous effects that the Portuguese, Spanish, English, French, and Dutch had on the native peoples of the Americas, while acknowledging the benefits the Europeans enjoyed." SLJ
   "The book's most outstanding feature is its full-color artwork. Large, double-page spreads give scope to dramatic landscapes, while smaller pictures on every page show events, places, and maps pertinent to the text. . . . This book provides a useful overview of the period." Booklist

Mann, Charles C.
Before Columbus; the Americas of 1491. Atheneum Books for Young Readers 2009 117p il map $24.99 *
Grades: 5 6 7 8 9 10   **970.01**
   1. Native Americans—Origin 2. Native Americans—History 3. America—Antiquities
   ISBN 978-1-4169-4900-8; 1-4169-4900-3
      LC 2009007691
   "A Downtown Bookworks book"
   Adapted from 1491, published 2006 by Knopf for adults
   "Mann paints a superb picture of pre-Columbian America. In the process, he overturns the misconceived image of Natives as simple, widely scattered savages with minimal impact on their surroundings. Well-chosen, vividly colored graphics and photographs of mummies, pyramids, artifacts, and landscapes as well as the author's skillful storytelling will command the attention of even the most reluctant readers." SLJ
   Includes glossary and bibliographical references

Markle, Sandra, 1946-
Animals Christopher Columbus saw; an adventure in the New World; by Sandra Markle; illustrations by Jamel Akib. Chronicle Books 2008 46p il $16.99
Grades: 2 3 4   **970.01**
   1. Columbus, Christopher 2. America—Exploration 3. Animals—North America
   ISBN 978-0-8118-4916-6; 0-8118-4916-3
      LC 2006033623
   This "concentrates less on Christopher Columbus and more on the location, habitat, and fauna found during his discovery of the Americas." Publisher's note
   Includes glossary and bibliographical references

Wyatt, Valerie
Who discovered America? with illustrations by
Howie Woo. Kids Can Press 2008 40p il map
$17.95; pa $8.95 *
Grades: 4 5 6   **970.01**
1. America—Antiquities 2. America—Exploration
ISBN   978-1-55453-128-8;   1-55453-128-4;
978-1-55453-129-5 (pa); 1-55453-129-2 (pa)
"With interesting sidebars and engaging illustrations
and photos, this 'whodunit' of sorts describes, on a
spread each, evidence for the journeys of various groups
who discovered, or claimed to have discovered, [the
North American] continent. . . . Wyatt writes clearly
about how scientists unlock clues to how and when various groups could have made landfall. . . . Raising perhaps more questions than it answers, this book leaves it
to readers to decide the solution to the mystery." SLJ
Includes glossary

971   Canada

Bowers, Vivien, 1951-
Crazy about Canada! amazing things kids want
to know; illustrated by Dianne Eastman. Maple
Tree Press 2006 96p il map (Canadian geographic
kids) hardcover o.p. pa $18.95 *
Grades: 4 5 6   **971**
1. Canada
ISBN 1-897066-47-3; 1-897066-48-1 (pa)
"Organized into topical chapters dealing with animals,
landforms, and Canadians themselves, the book follows
two bespectacled cartoon researchers, Vivien and Morton,
as they encounter an assortment of creatures and experts
who help them answer their questions. Frequent clear,
full-color photographs, drawings, graphs, and sidebars
break up the text and flesh out the commentary."
Booklist

Harris, Tim
The Mackenzie River; by Tim Harris. Gareth
Stevens Pub. 2003 32p il map (Rivers of North
America) lib bdg $24.67
Grades: 5 6 7 8   **971**
1. Mackenzie River (N.W.T.)
ISBN 0-8368-3756-8   LC 2003-42741
Contents: River of the North; From source to mouth;
The life of the river; Northern people; Land of black
gold; Places to visit
This describes the longest river in Canada, which runs
from its source east of the Rocky Mountains in the
Northwest Territories to its mouth at the Arctic Ocean
This "clearly describes [the Mackenzie River's], colorful history, and strong impact on the development of
towns found along its banks. In well-organized fashion,
the [author delves] into wild life, environmental issues
facing [this region], and the people who live there. The
color photographs enhance the [text] nicely to enrich
readers' understanding." SLJ
Includes bibliographical references

Junior Worldmark encyclopedia of the Canadian
provinces; [Timothy L. Gall and Susan Bevan
Gall, editors] 5th ed. U.X.L 2007 294p il map
$70 *
Grades: 5 6 7 8 9 10   **971**
1. Canada 2. Reference books
ISBN 978-1-4144-1060-9; 1-4144-1060-3
LC 2007003908
First published 1997
"Arranged by 40 . . . subheadings . . . this . . . re-
source provides . . . information on all of Canada's
provinces and territories. [It includes] details on Canada's
arts, climate, government, health, languages, notable per-
sons, ethnic groups and . . . more." Publisher's note
Includes bibliographical references

Murphy, Patricia J., 1963-
Canada. Benchmark Bks. 2004 48p il map
(Discovering cultures) lib bdg $28.50
Grades: 2 3 4   **971**
1. Canada
ISBN 0-7614-1725-7   LC 2003-19098
Contents: Where in the world is Canada?; What makes
Canada Canadian?; School days; Just for fun; Let's cele-
brate!
An introduction to the geography, history, people, and
culture of Canada
This book is "informative and balanced." SLJ
Includes glossary and bibliographical references

Pang, Guek-Cheng, 1950-
Canada. 2nd ed. Benchmark Books 2004 144p
il map (Cultures of the world) lib bdg $42.79
Grades: 5 6 7 8   **971**
1. Canada
ISBN 0-7614-1788-5   LC 2004-8584
First published 1994
This describes the geography, history, government,
economy, environment, and culture of Canada
"There is excellent coverage of Canadian arts. . . .
Full-color photos appear throughout, and the maps are
current and easy to read." SLJ
Includes glossary and bibliographical references

Penn, Briony, 1960-
The kids book of Canadian geography; written
and illustrated by Briony Penn. Kids Can Press
2008 56p il map $19.95
Grades: 3 4 5 6   **971**
1. Canada
ISBN 978-1-55074-890-1; 1-55074-890-4
This "traces the continents' formation, touching on
Canada's ancient landscapes, evolving climate, continent
shaping and life on the land including human settlement,
plus a geographical coast to coast tour and much more."
Publisher's note

Rowe, Percy

Toronto; by Percy Rowe. World Almanac Library 2004 48p il map (Great cities of the world) lib bdg $31

Grades: 3 4 5 6   **971**

1. Toronto (Ont.)

ISBN 0-8368-5026-2   LC 2003-53477

Contents: History of Toronto; People of Toronto; Living in Toronto; Toronto at work; Toronto at play; The future of Toronto

This "provides a concise overview of the history, geography, economy, and population of [Toronto] as well as a good sense of the residents' lifestyles, including work, shopping, religion, and more. Useful maps and statistics are included, and clear, color photographs convey the city's flavor." SLJ

Williams, Brian, 1943-

Canada; [by] Brian Williams; Tom Carter and Ben Cecil, consultants. National Geographic 2007 64p il map (Countries of the world) lib bdg $27.90; pa $12.95 *

Grades: 4 5 6 7   **971**

1. Canada

ISBN   978-1-4263-0025-7   (lib   bdg); 978-1-4263-0573-3 (pa)   LC 2007296572

A basic overview of the history, geography, climate and culture of Canada

This "clear, succinct [overview] will support assignments without overwhelming casual readers. . . . A good selection of recent, high-quality color photographs gives the [book] visual appeal." SLJ

Includes glossary and bibliographical references

971.27   Manitoba

Kurelek, William, 1927-1977

A prairie boy's winter; paintings and story by William Kurelek. Houghton Mifflin 1973 unp il pa $8.95 hardcover o.p.

Grades: 3 4 5   **971.27**

1. Children—Canada 2. Farm life—Canada 3. Winter

ISBN 0-395-36609-7 (pa)

The author depicts the rigors and pleasures of boyhood winters on a Manitoba farm in the 1930's including hauling hay, playing hockey, and surviving a blizzard

971.3   Ontario

Greenwood, Barbara

A pioneer sampler; the daily life of a pioneer family in 1840; illustrated by Heather Collins. Ticknor & Fields Bks. for Young Readers 1995 240p il hardcover o.p. pa $15 *

Grades: 4 5 6 7   **971.3**

1. Frontier and pioneer life 2. Ontario

ISBN 0-395-71540-7; 0-395-88393-8 (pa)

LC 94-12829

First published 1994 in Canada with title: A pioneer story

"Using a combination of fiction and fact-filled supplementary commentary, with illustrations inspired by Garth Williams, the author tells the story of the Robertsons, a large, hardworking farm family. Good projects for school or home." N Y Times Book Rev

971.9   Northern territories of Canada

Baker, Stuart

In the Arctic. Marshall Cavendish Benchmark 2010 32p il map (Climate change) lib bdg $19.95

Grades: 5 6 7 8   **971.9**

1. Greenhouse effect 2. Arctic regions

ISBN 978-0-7614-4437-4; 0-7614-4437-8

LC 2009-5767

The book about climate change in the Arctic "is perfectly organized for students. . . . Unique layout features serve as signposts and will help focus readers' attention. . . . [The book] features an outstanding chart of possible effects of global warming on the area in question, listing 'Possible Event,' 'Predicted Result,' and 'Impact' in short, bulleted statements." SLJ

Includes glossary

Wallace, Mary, 1950-

Inuksuk journey; an artist at the top of the world. Maple Tree Press 2008 64p il $24.95

Grades: 5 6 7 8   **971.9**

1. Inuit 2. Arctic regions 3. Canada

ISBN 978-1-897349-26-7; 1-897349-26-2

"Nunavut, an Arctic territory in northern Canada, is a cold, open space where inuksuk, piles of stone in the shape of a person used to 'mark a family home, welcome guests, guide travelers, and ensure safe passage,' are commonly found. Wallace has developed a passion for these ancient messengers, and here she presents a journal of her weeklong trek to Inuksugassait, a place where countless numbers of the stone markers stand. . . . Wallace includes personal photos, sketches, and comments that give readers an intimate portrait of life in this place. Over a dozen vibrant oil paintings depicting scenes from her journey are scattered throughout. . . . Readers will be fascinated by this firsthand account of true adventure." SLJ

972   Middle America. Mexico

Apte, Sunita

The Aztec empire. Children's Press 2009 c2010 48p il map (True book) lib bdg $26; pa $6.95

Grades: 3 4 5   **972**

1. Aztecs

ISBN 978-0-531-25227-7 (lib bdg); 0-531-25227-2 (lib bdg); 978-0-531-24108-0 (pa); 0-531-24108-4 (pa)

LC 2009000299

In this book the Aztec empire is "outlined for young readers with care and precision. . . . Loaded with access points such as captions, pull-outs, a time line, and a map, and with better-than-usual reproductions of well-chosen

Apte, Sunita—*Continued*

primary sources and art, the [book sports] a bright, peppy design. . . . [This book is] rigorous in distinguishing fact from theory, and conscientious about presenting competing theories where they exist." SLJ

Includes glossary and bibliographical references

Cooke, Tim

Ancient Aztec; archaeology unlocks the secrets of Mexico's past. National Geographic 2007 64p il map (National Geographic investigates) $17.95; lib bdg $27.90 *

Grades: 4 5 6 7   972

1. Aztecs 2. Excavations (Archeology)—Mexico 3. Mexico—Antiquities

ISBN   978-1-4263-0072-1;   1-4263-0072-7; 978-1-4263-0073-8 (lib bdg); 1-4263-0073-5 (lib bdg)

LC 2007024813

This describes ancient Aztec origins, technology, major archeological sites, civilization, and connections to the present

"Pithy and appealing. . . . Aerial photos, time [line], informative sidebars, an interview with an archaeologist, and excellent maps augment rigorously supported [text] that [asks] and [answers] interesting questions." SLJ

Coulter, Laurie

Ballplayers and bonesetters; one hundred ancient Aztec and Maya jobs you might have adored or abhorred; [written] by Laurie Coulter; illustrated by Martha Newbigging. Annick Press 2008 96p il $25.95; pa $16.95 *

Grades: 4 5 6   972

1. Aztecs 2. Mayas

ISBN   978-1-55451-141-9;   1-55451-141-0; 978-1-55451-140-2 (pa); 1-55451-140-2 (pa)

"Following a readable and humorous overview of the highly developed Aztec and Maya civilizations, this lively text lists 100 jobs that a young person might have held or aspired to during the Late Postclassic period in Mesoamerica (1350 to 1521). . . . Taken as a whole, the descriptions of the vocations yield a rich view of the culture, and the breezy text makes this as much a browsing as a reference title. The colorful cartoon illustrations enhance the text, adding just the right artistic complement." SLJ

Gruber, Beth

Mexico; [by] Beth Gruber; Gary S. Elbow and Jorge Zamora, consultants. National Geographic 2007 64p il map (Countries of the world) lib bdg $27.90; pa $12.95 *

Grades: 4 5 6 7   972

1. Mexico

ISBN 0-7922-7669-8 (lib bdg); 1-4263-0566-4 (pa)

LC 2004026452

"This volume introduces Mexico's geography, history, wildlife, culture, and government. The many excellent color photos and maps are a striking feature of the series. . . . This will be a useful addition to many libraries." Booklist

Includes glossary and bibliographical references

Harris, Nathaniel

Ancient Maya; archaeology unlocks the secrets to the Maya's past; by Nathaniel Harris; Elizabeth Graham, consultant. National Geographic 2008 64p il map (National Geographic investigates) $17.95; lib bdg $27.90 *

Grades: 4 5 6 7   972

1. Mayas 2. Excavations (Archeology)—Mexico 3. Mexico—Antiquities

ISBN   978-1-4263-0227-5;   1-4263-0227-4; 978-1-4263-0228-2 (lib bdg); 1-4263-0228-2 (lib bdg)

LC 2007047837

This describes ancient Mayan civilization and how archeologists found out about it.

Includes glossary and bibliographical references

Junior Worldmark encyclopedia of the Mexican states; [Timothy L. Gall and Susan Bevan Gall, editors] 2nd ed. U.X.L,Thomson/Gale 2007 423p il map $70 *

Grades: 5 6 7 8 9 10   972

1. Mexico 2. Reference books

ISBN 978-1-4144-1112-5   LC 2007003906

First published 2004

"Arranged by 28 . . . subheadings . . . Junior Worldmark Encyclopedia of the Mexican States provides . . . information on each of Mexico's 31 states. Topics covered include climate, plants and animals, population and ethnic groups, religions, transportation, history, state and local governments, political parties, judicial system, economy, education, arts, media, tourism, sports, famous people and . . . more." Publisher's note

Includes bibliographical references

Kops, Deborah

Palenque; by Deborah Kops. Twenty-First Century Books 2008 80p il (Unearthing ancient worlds) lib bdg $30.60

Grades: 5 6 7 8   972

1. Palenque site (Mexico) 2. Mayas 3. Excavations (Archeology)—Mexico 4. Mexico—Antiquities

ISBN 978-0-8225-7504-7 (lib bdg); 0-8225-7504-3 (lib bdg)   LC 2007021323

This describes the discovery of the ancient Mayan site of Palenque in 1840 by John Stephens and Frederick Catherwood, and the mid-20th century excavations of the site by Alberto Ruz Lhuillier, who discovered the tomb of the Mayan king Pakal, who died in 683 A.D., inside a pyramid

This "clearly written [title is] illustrated with large photographs and period artwork, and the pages are broken up with text boxes featuring quotes and interesting anecdotes." SLJ

Includes glossary and bibliographical references

Lourie, Peter

Hidden world of the Aztec. Boyds Mills Press 2006 48p il map $17.95

Grades: 4 5 6 7   972

1. Aztecs 2. Excavations (Archeology)—Mexico

ISBN 978-1-59078-069-5; 1-59078-069-8

The author takes a "look at the Aztecs from the perspective of archaeological digs at the Great Temple in

Lourie, Peter—*Continued*

modern-day Mexico City and at the Pyramid of the Moon in Teotihuacan. . . . The writing style is clear, informative, and interesting." SLJ

Includes glossary and bibliographical references

Milord, Susan, 1954-

Mexico! 40 activities to experience Mexico past & present; illustrations by Michael Kline. Williamson 1998 96p il maps pa $10.95 *

Grades: 3 4 5   **972**

1. Mexico 2. Handicraft

ISBN 1-88559-322-8   LC 98-34153

"A Kaleidoscope kids book"

"Milord provides an amazing amount of information about Mexico, ranging from ancient history through the Spanish conquest to contemporary life. Activities include such standards as making an *Ojo de Dios* and a *piñata*, but there are also directions for creating marzipan skulls for the Day of the Dead celebration, as well as recipes for salsa, tortillas, and hot chocolate. . . . This is an excellent starting point for students investigating this culture." SLJ

Includes bibliographical references

Orr, Tamra

The Maya. Franklin Watts 2005 63p il map (Watts library) $25.50

Grades: 4 5 6 7   **972**

1. Mayas 2. Mexico—Antiquities

ISBN 978-0-531-12296-9; 0-531-12296-4

       LC 2004025232

"Large type, wide margins, and pronunciation assistance distinguish this history of the Maya. . . . Short sidebars, a good map, large color photos, and an excellent list of further resources give this book lots of chances to hook readers." SLJ

Includes bibliographical references

Perl, Lila

The ancient Maya. Franklin Watts 2005 112p il map (People of the ancient world) $29.50; pa $9.95 *

Grades: 5 6 7 8   **972**

1. Mayas

ISBN 0-531-12381-2; 0-531-16848-4 (pa)

This book portrays the lives of the ancient Maya "by examining their arts, culture, economy, government, religious beliefs, and societal structures. . . . Attractively designed and illustrated, the [book features] excellent color representations of architecture, artwork, and other cultural and historical artifacts." SLJ

Includes bibliographical references

Sonneborn, Liz

The ancient Aztecs; written by Liz Sonneborn. Franklin Watts 2005 112p il map (People of the ancient world) lib bdg $30.50; pa $9.95 *

Grades: 5 6 7 8   **972**

1. Aztecs

ISBN 0-531-12362-6 (lib bdg); 0-531-16844-1 (pa)

       LC 2004-13909

Contents: Introduction; Commoners, nobles, and rulers; Warriors; Priests and scholars; Merchants and craftspeople; Farmers; Conquest and survival

This examines ancient Aztec society "through their literature, artifacts, and documents. Religion, farming, levels of society, art, government, and fine arts are covered in [this] well-written and attractive [book]." SLJ

Includes bibliographical references

Stein, R. Conrad, 1937-

The Aztec empire. Benchmark Bks. 1996 80p il (Cultures of the past) lib bdg $34.21

Grades: 4 5 6 7   **972**

1. Aztecs

ISBN 0-7614-0072-9   LC 95-7333

An illustrated look at Aztec art, architecture, religion, mythology, government and society

Includes glossary and bibliographical references

Streissguth, Thomas, 1958-

Mexico; by Tom Streissguth. Lerner Publications Company 2008 48p il map (Country explorers) lib bdg $27.93; pa $8.95

Grades: 2 3 4   **972**

1. Mexico

ISBN   978-0-8225-7130-8   (lib   bdg); 978-0-8225-8508-4 (pa)   LC 2006036726

This introduction to Mexico covers "all of the areas of interest to students, including animals, sports, foods, celebrations, storytime, and even a few words in the country's native language. Small amounts of information are surrounded by current photographs, maps, charts, and illustrations. . . . Sure to grab the attention of even reluctant readers." SLJ

Includes glossary and bibliographical references

972.8   Central America

Shields, Charles J., 1951-

Central America: facts and figures. Mason Crest Pubs. 2003 63p il maps (Discovering Central America) lib bdg $19.95

Grades: 4 5 6 7   **972.8**

1. Central America

ISBN 1-59084-099-2   LC 2002-9194

This title "looks at the region as a whole, briefly reviewing geography and history and providing a glimpse of the area's peoples and cultures. . . . Tailored for the quick research needs of students, the . . . [title presents its] information smoothly and in well-organized fashion." Booklist

Includes glossary and bibliographical references

972.81   Guatemala

Croy, Anita
Guatemala. National Geographic 2009 64p il map (Countries of the world) lib bdg $27.90 *
Grades: 4 5 6 7   **972.81**
1. Guatemala
ISBN 978-1-4263-0471-2 (lib bdg); 1-4263-0471-4 (lib bdg)
This describes the geography, nature, history, people and culture, government and economy of Guatemala
Includes glossary and bibliographical references

Mann, Elizabeth, 1948-
Tikal; the center of the Maya world; with illustrations by Tom McNeely. Mikaya Press 2002 47p il map (Wonders of the world) $19.95 *
Grades: 4 5 6 7   **972.81**
1. Mayas—Antiquities
ISBN 1-931414-05-X   LC 2002-29599
A history of the Maya Indians in the city of Tikal, founded in 800 B.C.
"Mann's narrative flows smoothly, and frequent, full-color illustrations . . . help to clarify the details mentioned in the text." Booklist
Includes glossary

972.82   Belize

Shields, Charles J., 1951-
Belize. Mason Crest Pubs. 2003 63p il map (Discovering Central America) lib bdg $19.95
Grades: 4 5 6 7   **972.82**
1. Belize
ISBN 1-59084-092-5   LC 2002-8937
Contents: A warm, sultry land cooled by sea breezes; A history different from the rest of Central America; Careful land use strengthens the economy; A mosaic of backgrounds and languages; Communities and cultures clustered by districts; A calendar of Belizean festivals; Recipes
This describes the history, geography, and culture of Belize
"Tailored for the quick research needs of students, the . . . [title presents its] information smoothly and in well-organized fashion." Booklist
Includes glossary and bibliographical references

972.83   Honduras

McGaffey, Leta
Honduras; [by] Leta McGaffey and Michael Spilling. 2nd ed. Marshall Cavendish Benchmark 2010 144p il map (Cultures of the world) lib bdg $42.79
Grades: 5 6 7 8   **972.83**
1. Honduras
ISBN 978-0-7614-4848-8 (lib bdg); 0-7614-4848-9 (lib bdg)   LC 2009022642

"Provides comprehensive information on the geography, history, wildlife, governmental structure, economy, cultural diversity, peoples, religion, and culture of Honduras." Publisher's note
Includes glossary and bibliographical references

Shields, Charles J., 1951-
Honduras. Mason Crest Pubs. 2003 63p il map (Discovering Central America) lib bdg $19.95
Grades: 4 5 6 7   **972.83**
1. Honduras
ISBN 1-59084-096-8   LC 2002-9089
Contents: Honduras, the knee of Central America; Honduras becomes the "Banana Republic;" A fragile economy; The people of Honduras; Language, religion, and home life; A calendar of Honduran festivals; Recipes
This describes the history, geography, and culture of Honduras
This is "jam-packed with useful information. . . . [It contains] straightforward writing, clearly titled chapters, high quality color, and well-captioned photographs and graphics." Libr Media Connect
Includes glossary and bibliographical references

972.84   El Salvador

Foley, Erin, 1967-
El Salvador; [by] Erin Foley, Rafiz Hapipi. 2nd ed. Benchmark Bks. 2005 144p il map (Cultures of the world) lib bdg $42.79
Grades: 5 6 7 8   **972.84**
1. El Salvador
ISBN 0-7614-1967-5   LC 2005009360
First published 1994
This describes the geography, history, government, economy, environment, people, lifestyle, religion, language, arts, leisure, festivals, and food of El Salvador
Includes glossary and bibliographical references

972.85   Nicaragua

Kott, Jennifer, 1971-
Nicaragua; [by] Jennifer Kott, Kristi Streiffert. 2nd ed. Benchmark Bks. 2005 144p il map (Cultures of the world) lib bdg $42.79 *
Grades: 5 6 7 8   **972.85**
1. Nicaragua
ISBN 0-7614-1969-1   LC 2005009240
First published 1994
An illustrated overview of the geography, economy, history, government, politics, and culture of Nicaragua
Includes glossary and bibliographical references

972.86　Costa Rica

Foley, Erin, 1967-
Costa Rica; [by] Erin Foley and Barbara Cooke. 2nd ed. Marshall Cavendish Benchmark 2008 144p il map (Cultures of the world) lib bdg $42.79
Grades: 5 6 7 8　　　　**972.86**
1. Costa Rica
ISBN 978-0-7614-2079-8 (lib bdg); 0-7614-2079-7 (lib bdg)　　　　LC 2006101736
First published 1997
This offers "information on the geography, history, wildlife, governmental structure, economy, cultural diversity, peoples, religion, and culture of Costa Rica." Publisher's note
Includes glossary and bibliographical references

972.87　Panama

Hassig, Susan M., 1969-
Panama; [by] Susan Hassig & Lynette Quek. 2nd ed. Marshall Cavendish Benchmark 2007 144p il map (Cultures of the world) lib bdg $42.79
Grades: 5 6 7 8　　　　**972.87**
1. Panama
ISBN 978-0-7614-2028-6 (lib bdg); 0-7614-2028-2 (lib bdg)　　　　LC 2006020824
First published 1996
This provides "information on the geography, history, wildlife, governmental structure, economy, cultural diversity, peoples, religion, and culture of Panama." Publisher's note
Includes glossary and bibliographical references

972.9　West Indies (Antilles) and Bermuda

Karwoski, Gail, 1949-
Miracle; the true story of the wreck of the Sea Venture; by Gail Langer Karwoski. Darby Creek Pub. 2004 64p il map $28.95
Grades: 4 5 6　　　　**972.9**
1. Sea Venture (Ship) 2. Bermuda 3. Jamestown (Va.)—History
ISBN 1-58196-015-8
This is an "account of the 17th-century British sailing ship *Sea Venture*, flagship of nine vessels bound for the colony of Jamestown. A powerful hurricane forced it to break from the fleet. . . . Eventually [it ran] aground on the shores of the Bermuda islands. . . . Karwoski offers a wealth of historical information through a well-researched narrative. . . . [An] attractive, well-designed title." SLJ
Includes bibliographical references

972.91　Cuba

Gordon, Sharon
Cuba. Benchmark Bks. 2003 48p il map (Discovering cultures) lib bdg $28.50
Grades: 2 3 4　　　　**972.91**
1. Cuba
ISBN 0-7614-1517-3　　　　LC 2002-15302
Contents: Where in the world is Cuba?; What makes Cuba Cuban?; Living in Cuba; School days; Just for fun; Let's celebrate!
Highlights the geography, people, food, schools, recreation, celebrations, and language of Cuba
"Gordon includes lots of interesting specifics that convey a strong sense of daily life." Booklist
Includes glossary and bibliographical references

Green, Jen
Cuba; [by] Jen Green; Damián Fernández and Alejandro de la Fuente, consultants. National Geographic 2007 64p il map (Countries of the world) lib bdg $27.90 *
Grades: 4 5 6 7　　　　**972.91**
1. Cuba
ISBN 978-1-4263-0057-8　　　　LC 2007026468
This describes the geography, nature, history, people & culture, government & economy of Cuba.
Includes glossary and bibliographical references

Sheehan, Sean, 1951-
Cuba; [by] Sean Sheehan, Leslie Jermyn. 2nd ed. Benchmark Bks. 2005 144p il map (Cultures of the world) lib bdg $42.79
Grades: 5 6 7 8　　　　**972.91**
1. Cuba
ISBN 0-7614-1965-9　　　　LC 2005009362
First published 1994
This describes the geography, history, government, economy, population, lifestyle, religion, language, arts, leisure, festivals, and food of Cuba
Includes glossary and bibliographical references

Stein, R. Conrad, 1937-
Cuban Missile Crisis; in the shadow of nuclear war. Enslow Publishers 2009 128p il map (America's living history) lib bdg $31.93
Grades: 5 6 7 8　　　　**972.91**
1. Cuban Missile Crisis, 1962
ISBN 978-0-7660-2905-7 (lib bdg); 0-7660-2905-0 (lib bdg)　　　　LC 2008-4703
"Discusses the Cuban missile crisis, a thirteen-day struggle between the United States and the Soviet Union, including the causes of the conflict, the leaders faced with important decisions, and the final resolution to avoid nuclear war." Publisher's note
"This engaging account provides a thorough discussion of events. . . . Archival photographs, maps, sidebars, and many primary sources effectively depict key figures, political posturing, and the nation's anxiety." Horn Book Guide
Includes glossary and bibliographical references

972.92 Jamaica and Cayman Islands

Green, Jen
Jamaica; [by] Jen Green; David J. Howard and Joel Frater, consultants. National Geographic 2008 64p il map (Countries of the world) lib bdg $27.90 *

Grades: 4 5 6 7   972.92
1. Jamaica
ISBN 978-1-4263-0300-5 (lib bdg); 1-4263-0300-9 (lib bdg)
This describes the geography, nature, history, people and culture, government, and economy of Jamaica.
Includes glossary and bibligraphical references

Roy, Jennifer Rozines
Jamaica; [by] Jennifer Rozines Roy and Gregory Roy. Benchmark Books 2004 48p il map (Discovering cultures) lib bdg $25.64
Grades: 2 3 4   972.92
1. Jamaica
ISBN 0-7614-1793-1   LC 2004-6142
Contents: Where in the world is Jamaica?; What makes Jamaica Jamaican?; Living in Jamaica; School days; Just for fun; Let's celebrate!
An introduction to the geography, history, people, and culture of Jamaica
Includes bibliographical references

Sheehan, Sean, 1951-
Jamaica; [by] Sean Sheehan & Angela Black. 2nd ed. Benchmark Books 2004 144p il map (Cultures of the world) lib bdg $42.79
Grades: 5 6 7 8   972.92
1. Jamaica
ISBN 0-7614-1785-0   LC 2004-7676
First published 1996
Introduces the geography, history, religion, government, economy, and culture of Jamaica
"An informative book with captivating pictures, a visually attractive layout, and flowing text. . . . A well-balanced and interesting look at one country's culture." SLJ
Includes glossary and bibliographical references

972.93 Dominican Republic

De Capua, Sarah
Dominican Republic. Benchmark Bks. 2004 48p il map (Discovering cultures) lib bdg $25.64
Grades: 2 3 4   972.93
1. Dominican Republic
ISBN 0-7614-1722-2   LC 2003-19099
Contents: Where in the world is the Dominican Republic?; What makes the Dominican Republic Dominican?; Living in the Dominican Republic; School days; Just for fun; Let's celebrate!
An introduction to the geography, history, people, and culture of the Dominican Republic.
Includes glossary and bibliographical references

Foley, Erin, 1967-
Dominican Republic; [by] Erin Foley & Leslie Jermyn. 2nd ed. Marshall Cavendish Benchmark 2005 144p (Cultures of the world) lib bdg $42.79
Grades: 5 6 7 8   972.93
1. Dominican Republic
ISBN 0-7614-1966-7
First published 1995
"Explores the geography, history, government, economy, people, and culture of the Dominican Republic." Publisher's note
"The material is well organized in easily readable sections, accurately illustrated with well-placed, full-color photographs on every page." SLJ

972.94 Haiti

Cheong-Lum, Roseline Ng, 1962-
Haiti; [by] Roseline Ng Cheong-Lum & Leslie Jermyn. 2nd ed. Marshall Cavendish Benchmark 2005 144p il map (Cultures of the world) lib bdg $42.79
Grades: 5 6 7 8   972.94
1. Haiti
ISBN 0-7614-1968-3
First published 1995
Describes the geography, history, government, economy, culture, peoples, and religion of Haiti
Includes glossary and bibliographical references

Mara, Wil
Haiti; [by] Wil Mara. Marshall Cavendish Benchmark 2007 48p il map (Discovering cultures) lib bdg $28.50
Grades: 2 3 4   972.94
1. Haiti
ISBN 978-0-7614-1987-7 (lib bdg); 0-7614-1987-X (lib bdg)   LC 2006011473
An introduction to the geography, history, people, and culture of Haiti
Includes glossary and bibliographical references

972.95 Puerto Rico

Levy, Patricia, 1951-
Puerto Rico; [by] Patricia Levy & Nazry Bahrawi. 2nd ed. Marshall Cavendish Benchmark 2005 144p il map (Cultures of the world) lib bdg $42.79
Grades: 5 6 7 8   972.95
1. Puerto Rico
ISBN 0-7614-1970-5
First published 1995
This introduction to Puerto Rico "covers geography, history, government, economy, population, lifestyle, religion, language, arts, leisure, festivals, and food. . . . The material is well organized in easily readable sections, accurately illustrated with well-placed, full-color photographs on every page." SLJ
Includes glossary and bibliographical references

972.96 Bahama Islands

Barlas, Robert
Bahamas. Benchmark Bks. 2000 128p il map (Cultures of the world) lib bdg $42.79
Grades: 5 6 7 8   **972.96**
1. Bahamas
ISBN 0-7614-0992-0   LC 99-88028
Introduces the geography, history, government, economy, religion, language, arts, leisure activities, festivals, food, and people of this archipelago lying in the Atlantic Ocean off the coast of Florida
Includes bibliographical references

972.97 Leeward Islands

Kras, Sara Louise
Antigua and Barbuda; [by] Sara Louise Kras. Marshall Cavendish Benchmark 2008 144p il map (Cultures of the world) lib bdg $42.79
Grades: 5 6 7 8   **972.97**
1. Antigua and Barbuda
ISBN 978-0-7614-2570-0   LC 2006031537
This describes the geography, history, government, economy, environment, people, and culture of Antigua and Barbuda
Includes glossary and bibliographical references

972.98 Windward and other southern islands

Orr, Tamra
Saint Lucia; [by] Tamra Orr. 2nd ed. Marshall Cavendish Benchmark 2008 144p il map (Cultures of the world) lib bdg $42.79
Grades: 5 6 7 8   **972.98**
1. Saint Lucia
ISBN 978-0-7614-2569-4
First published 1997
This describes the geography, history, government, economy, environment, people, and culture of Saint Lucia
Includes glossary and bibliographical references

972.983 Trinidad and Tobago

Hernandez, Romel
Trinidad & Tobago. Mason Crest Pubs. 2003 63p il map (Discovering the Caribbean) lib bdg $19.95
Grades: 4 5 6 7   **972.983**
1. Trinidad and Tobago
ISBN 1-59084-304-5   LC 2002-75112
Presents the geography, history, economy, cities and communities, and people and culture of Trinidad and Tobago. Includes recipes, related projects, and a calendar of festivals

The author's "readable [style] will capture children's interest. . . . [The book is] illustrated with full-color photographs and include[s] quick-facts inserts, easy-to-prepare recipes . . . and useful project and report ideas." SLJ
Includes glossary and bibliographical references

973 United States

America the Beautiful, third series. Children's Press 2007-2009 52v il map lib bdg set $851.20
Grades: 4 5 6 7   **973**
1. United States
ISBN 978-0-531-20407-8 (lib bdg); 0-531-20407-3 (lib bdg)
Volumes also available separately, $38 each
Replaces America the Beautiful, second series, published 1998-2001; Original series published 1987-1992
Contents: Alabama by Barbara A. Somervill; Alaska by Tamra B. Orr; Arizona by Barbara A. Somervill; Arkansas by G. S. Prentzas; California by Tamra B. Orr; Colorado by Barbara A. Somervill; Connecticut by Zachary Kent; Delaware by Ann Heinrichs; Florida by Tamra B. Orr; Georgia by G. S. Prentzas; Hawai'i by Deborah Kent; Idaho by Deborah Kent; Illinois by Michael Burgan; Indiana by Darlene R. Stille; Iowa by Jean F. Blashfield; Kansas by Deborah Cannarella; Kentucky by Andrew Santella; Louisiana by Allison Lassieur; Maine by Ann Heinrichs; Maryland by Jean F. Blashfield; Massachusetts by Trudi Strain Trueit; Michigan by Lucia Raatma; Minnesota by Martin Hintz; Missouri by Jean F. Blashfield; Mississippi by Pamela Dell; Montana by R. Conrad Stein; Nebraska by Ann Heinrichs; Nevada by Ann Heinrichs; New Hampshire by Deborah Kent; New Jersey by Deborah Kent; New Mexico by Michael Burgan; New York by Barbara A. Somervill; North Carolina by Ann Heinrichs; North Dakota by Darlene R. Stille; Ohio by Darlene R. Stille; Oklahoma by Tamra B. Orr; Oregon by Deborah Kent; Pennsylvania by Barbara A. Somervill; Puerto Rico by Darlene R. Stille; Rhode Island by Michael Burgan; South Carolina by Barbara A. Somervill; South Dakota by Michael Burgan; Tennessee by Barbara A. Somerville; Texas by Barbara A. Somervill; Utah by Deborah Kent; Vermont by Ann Heinrichs; Virginia by Deborah Kent; Washington by R. Conrad Stein; Washington D. C. by Deborah Kent; West Virginia by Ann Heinrichs; Wisconsin by Jean F. Blashfield; Wyoming by G. S. Prentzas;
This series describes the geography, history, people, economy, and government of each state
"Most students should be able to satisfy their information needs with these polished new editions, and the copious extras and lively presentation will help keep them interested too." Booklist

Armstrong, Jennifer, 1961-
The American story; 100 true tales from American history; illustrated by Roger Roth. Alfred A. Knopf 2006 358p il map $34.95; lib bdg $39.99 *
Grades: 4 5 6 7   **973**
1. United States—History
ISBN 0-375-81256-3; 0-375-91256-8 (lib bdg)
                                                    LC 2005-34822

Armstrong, Jennifer, 1961-—*Continued*

"This large, fully illustrated compendium features 100 stories, familiar and lesser known, drawn from America's past and arranged in chronological order. . . . Thanks to writing that is consistently good and sometimes excellent, the tales will certainly hold readers' attention, and brightening nearly every page are lively drawings enhanced by watercolor washes." Booklist

Includes bibliographical references

Bockenhauer, Mark H.

Our fifty states; by Mark H. Bockenhauer and Stephen F. Cunha; foreword by former president Jimmy Carter. National Geographic Society 2004 239p il map $25.95; lib bdg $45.90 *

Grades: 4 5 6 7   973

1. United States 2. Reference books

ISBN 0-7922-6402-9; 0-7922-6992-6 (lib bdg)

LC 2004-1190

This "book is organized by regions: the Northeast, Southeast, Midwest, Southwest, and West, with a map of each region and a short history. Four pages are devoted to each state and include basic facts and a map. The full-color photographs are outstanding. Reproductions of archival illustrations depict four important events from each state's history. The final sections offer a paragraph about each of the territories and a page of facts and figures about the United States." SLJ

Includes bibliographical references

Buckley, Susan

Journeys for freedom; a new look at America's story; [by] Susan Buckley and Elspeth Leacock; illustrations by Rodica Prato. Houghton Mifflin Co. 2006 48p il map $17 *

Grades: 4 5 6 7   973

1. United States—History

ISBN 978-0-618-22323-7; 0-618-22323-1

LC 2004000974

This "history focuses on 20 individuals' quest for freedom across U.S. history. Some . . . will be familiar, but most will not. The stories, both varied and fascinating, often go beyond the personal. . . . Running along the bottom of each double-page spread is a pictorial map keyed to the text. . . . The authors make excellent use of primary sources. . . . As powerful as it is useful." Booklist

Kids make history; a new look at America's story; [by] Susan Buckley and Elspeth Leacock; Illustrations by Randy Jones. Houghton Mifflin 2006 48p il $17

Grades: 4 5 6 7   973

1. United States—History

ISBN 978-0-618-22329-9; 0-618-22329-0

LC 2005036309

"This book introduces 20 children in extraordinary times, starting in 1607 with Pocahontas and ending in 2001 with 9/11 as experienced by high school senior Jukay Hsu. Laura Ingalls Wilder; John Rankin, Jr.; and Susie Baker, a young slave celebrating her independence in 1863, are among those included. The text and the highly detailed watercolor illustrations are married with

numbers in small red boxes keyed to both elements for clarification. . . . A good browsing choice for children interested in American history." SLJ

Celebrate the states. 2nd ed. Marshall Cavendish Benchmark 2005-2009 52v il map Each group 5v set $213.93; each group 4v set $159.71 *

Grades: 4 5 6 7   973

1. United States

ISBN 978-0-7614-1733-0 (group 1); 978-0-7614-2017-0 (group 2); 978-0-7614-2150-4 (group 3); 978-0-7614-2347-8 (group 4); 978-0-7614-2557-1 (group 5); 978-0-7614-2714-8 (group 6); 978-0-7614-0668-6 (group 7); 978-0-7614-3395-8 (group 8); 978-0-7614-1061-4 (group 9); 978-0-7614-1066-9 (group 10); 978-0-7614-1310-3 (group 11)

Also available separate volumes $39.93 each

Replaces the set published 1996-2001

Contents: Group 1: California by Linda Jacobs Altman; Illinois by Marlene Targ Brill; New York by Virginia Schomp; Texas by Carmen Bredeson and Mary Dodson Wade; Virginia by Tracy Barrett; Group 2: Colorado by Eleanor Ayer and Dan Elish; Indiana by Marlene Targ Brill; Louisiana by Suzanne LeVert; Oregon by Rebecca Stefoff; Vermont by Dan Elish; Group 3: Alaska by Rebecca Stefoff; Connecticut by Victoria Sherrow; South Dakota by Melissa McDaniel; Tennessee by Tracy Barrett; Wisconsin by Karen Zeinert and Joyce Hart; Group 4: Florida by Perry Chang and Joyce Hart; Hawaii by Jake Goldberg and Joyce Hart; Iowa by Polly Morrice and Joyce Hart; Michigan by Marlene Targ Brill; Washington, D.C. by Dan Elish; Group 5: Minnesota by Martin Schwabacher and Patricia K Kummer; Ohio by Victoria Sherrow; Rhode Island by Ted Klein; Washington by Rebecca Stefoff; West Virginia by Nancy Hoffman and Joyce Hart; Group 6: Kentucky by Tracy Barrett; Mississippi by David Shirley & Patricia K. Kummer; New Hampshire by Steve Otfinoski; New Mexico by Melissa McDaniel, Ettagale Blauer & Jason Lauré; Wyoming by Guy Baldwin & Joyce Hart; Group 7: Arkansas by Linda Jacobs Altman, Ettagale Blauer, and Jason Lauré; Idaho by Rebecca Stefoff; Maryland by Leslie Pietrzyk and Martha Kneib; Massachusetts by Suzanne LeVert and Tamra B. Orr; New Jersey by Wendy Moragne and Tamra B. Orr; Group 8: Alabama by David Shirely and Joyce Hart; Arizona by Melissa McDaniel and Wendy Mead; Delaware by Michael Schuman and Marlee Richards; Kansas by Ruth Bjorklund and Trudi Strain Trueit; Pennsylvania by Stephen Peters and Joyce Hart; Group 9: Georgia by Steve Otfinoski; Oklahoma by Guy Baldwin; South Carolina by Nancy Hoffman; Utah by Rebecca Stefoff; Group 10: Maine by Margaret Dornfeld; Missouri by Michelle Bennett; Nevada by Rebecca Stefoff; North Carolina by David Shirley; Group 11: Montana by Clayton Bennett; Nebraska by Ruth Bjorklund; North Dakota by Melissa McDaniel; Puerto Rico by Martin Schwabacher

"These titles cover standard facts: geography, history, government, economy, landmarks, and regions. They are attractively illustrated with clear maps, charts, and pie graphs. Photos and reproductions of original documents add to overall effectiveness. . . . Excellent additions for reports or general interest." SLJ

Croy, Elden
United States. National Geographic 2010 64p il map (Countries of the world) lib bdg $27.90
Grades: 4 5 6 7 **973**
1. United States
ISBN 978-1-4263-0632-7; 1-4263-0632-6
This describes the geography, nature, history, people and culture, government and economy of the United States.
"The information is substantial but not overwhelming. The [text is] clear, and the discussion points are well chosen. . . . [The text is] complemented with stunning photographs." SLJ

Hoose, Phillip M., 1947-
We were there, too! young people in U.S. history; [by] Phillip Hoose. Farrar, Straus & Giroux 2001 264p il $28 *
Grades: 5 6 7 8 **973**
1. United States—History 2. Children 3. Youth
ISBN 0-374-38252-2 LC 99-89052
"Melanie Kroupa books"
Biographies of dozens of young people who made a mark in American history, including explorers, planters, spies, cowpunchers, sweatshop workers, and civil rights workers
"A treasure chest of history come to life, this is an inspired collection. . . . Because the book is packed with historical documents, evocatively illustrated . . . and full of eyewitness quotations, it should prove valuable to young historians and researchers." SLJ
Includes bibliographical references

It's my state! [series] Benchmark Bks. 2003-2007 52v il map * lib bdg ea $27.07
Grades: 3 4 5 **973**
1. United States
Contents: Alabama by J. Hart; Alaska by R. Bjorklund; Arizona by K. Derzipilski; Arkansas by D. C. King; California by M. Burgan; Colorado by L. J. Altman; Connecticut by M. Burgan; Delaware by D. C. King; Florida by D. Hess; Georgia by K. Haywood; Hawaii by A. G. Gaines; Idaho by D. Sanders; Illinois by C. Price-Groff; Indiana by K. Gerzipilski; Iowa by D. C. King; Kansas by D. C. King; Kentucky by A. G. Gaines; Louisiana by R. Bjorklund; Maine by T. A. Hicks; Maryland by S. Otfinoski; Massachusetts by R. Bjorklund; Michigan by J. Haney; Minnesota by M. T. Brill; Mississippi by A. Gaines; Missouri by S. Sanders; Montana by R. Bjorklund; Nebraska by D. Sanders; Nevada by T. Allan Hicks; New Hampshire by T. A. Hicks; New Jersey by D. C. King; New Mexico by R. Bjorklund; New York by D. Elish; North Carolina by A. G. Gaines; North Dakota by D. Sanders; Ohio by J. Hart; Oklahoma by D. Sanders; Oregon by J. Hart; Pennsylvania by J. Hart; Puerto Rico by R. Bjorklund; Rhode Island by S. Petreycik; South Carolina by D. Hess; South Dakota by R. Bjorkland; Tennessee by R. Petreycik; Texas by L. J. Altman; Utah by D. Sanders; Vermont by M. Dornfeld; Virginia by D. C. King; Washington by S. Otfinoski; Washington D. C. by T. A. Hicks; West Virginia by R. Petreycik; Wisconsin by M. Dornfeld; Wyoming by Rick Petreycki

Each book in the series covers "the state's topography, climate, and wildlife; history; lifestyle and population; government; and major industries and resources. Several spreads offer quick reference for state facts, such as the state flower, flag, and seal; famous residents; etc. The texts are basic and informative, providing solid insight into local life and culture." Booklist

Johnston, Robert D. (Robert Dougall)
The making of America; the history of the United States from 1492 to the present; with a foreword by Laura Bush. National Geographic Soc. 2002 240p il maps $29.95
Grades: 5 6 7 8 **973**
1. United States—History
ISBN 0-7922-6944-6 LC 2002-4825
Contents: A new world from many old worlds: beginnings to 1763; A revolutionary age: 1763-1789; The new republic: 1789-1848; A new birth of freedom: Civil War and Reconstruction, 1848-1877; Industry and empire: 1876-1900; Progressivism and the New Deal, 1900-1941; War, prosperity, and social change: 1941-1968; The age of conservatism: 1969-present
This is a "narrative of American history from Columbus through the terrorist attacks on Sept. 11, 2001." Libr Media Connect
"Johnston takes on an enormous, complex topic and presents an excellent overview for young people. . . . This well-written book does a particularly good job of balancing political and social history." Booklist
Includes bibliographical references

Junior state maps on file. Facts on File 2002 unp il loose-leaf $185
Grades: Professional **973**
1. United States—Maps
ISBN 0-8160-4752-9
Also available CD-ROM version
"This title offers more than 400 reproducible state maps and fact sheets in a looseleaf, three-ring binder format. . . . After a general section on the United States and its regions, the maps are arranged by geographic region. . . . Five maps and a fact sheet are provided for each state: major cities, outline map, physical features, industry, agriculture and state facts and flag. . . . This is an excellent U.S. geography resource for school and public libraries that do not subscribe to the online version." Am Ref Books Annu, 2003

Kuntz, Lynn, 1953-
Celebrate the USA; hands-on history activities for kids; [by] Lynn Kuntz; illustrated by Mark A. Hicks. Gibbs Smith, Publisher 2007 c2006 80p il map pa $7.95 *
Grades: 3 4 5 **973**
1. United States—History
ISBN 978-1-58685-846-9 (pa); 1-58685-846-7 (pa)
LC 2006021953
This is a "fact-filled, fun-to-read compendium of American history and 25 related activities. . . . Many topics and fascinating facts are covered in brief, sometimes humorous explanations. Coverage includes the early immigrants, how America got its name, Native Americans, the 13 colonies, currency, songs, and holidays." SLJ

Leacock, Elspeth, 1946-

Journeys in time; a new atlas of American history; [by] Elspeth Leacock and Susan Buckley; illustrations by Rodica Prato. Houghton Mifflin 2001 48p il maps $15; pa $6.95 *
Grades: 4 5 6 7   973
1. United States—History 2. United States—Historical geography
ISBN 0-395-97956-0; 0-618-31114-9 (pa)
                                              LC 00-40803
Each double-page spread of this book "takes an individual who was part of a historic movement (such as the Underground Railroad or immigration) and gives a brief narrative outlining his or her circumstances. Added to the text are sequential numbers that indicate major events in each of the twenty journeys. A double-page location map traces the routes each took, using illustrative vignettes marked with corresponding numbers that reference the text." Horn Book

Leedy, Loreen, 1959-

Celebrate the 50 states; written and illustrated by Loreen Leedy. Holiday House 1999 32p il maps hardcover o.p. pa $6.95
Grades: K 1 2 3   973
1. United States
ISBN 0-8234-1431-0; 0-8234-1631-3 (pa)
                                              LC 99-10986
Introduces statistics, emblems, notable cities, products, and other facts about the fifty states, United States territories, and Washington, D.C.
"Brightly colored and amusingly designed, this is a simple yet winning introduction to the U.S." Booklist

Sís, Peter, 1949-

The train of states; [by] Peter Sís. Greenwillow Books 2004 unp il $17.99; lib bdg $18.89 *
Grades: 2 3 4   973
1. United States
ISBN 0-06-057838-6; 0-06-057839-4 (lib bdg)
                                              LC 2003-56826
"Using the motif of a circus train, Sís has designed a different car for each state in the Union and a caboose for Washington, DC. . . . The cars are lined up chronologically according to their date of statehood and are decorated with the state flag, nickname, motto, bird, tree, and animal as well as important people or sites." SLJ
"The wagons—with their rococo embellishments and glorious gallimaufry of visual factoids, trivia, hoopla, and American hyperbole . . . command attention and invite endless, wondering reexamination." Booklist

Smith, David J.

If America were a village; a book about the people of the United States; written by David J. Smith; illustrated by Shelagh Armstrong. Kids Can Press 2009 32p il $18.95 *
Grades: 3 4 5   973
1. United States
ISBN 978-1-55453-344-2; 1-55453-344-9
This "offers a thought-provoking perspective on the people who make up America. Organized by overarching questions such as 'Where do we come from?' and 'What do we use?' the text illustrates the ethnic divisions, income levels and material consumption (among other categories) of Americans—were a theoretical village containing only 100 people. . . . Armstrong's cheerful, smudgy paintings balance the text's heaviness." Publ Wkly

St. George, Judith, 1931-

So you want to be president? by Judith St. George; illustrated by David Small. Updated and rev ed. Philomel Books 2004 52p il $17.99 *
Grades: 3 4 5 6   973
1. Presidents—United States
ISBN 0-399-24317-8   LC 2004-4464
2000 edition awarded the Caldecott Medal, 2001
First published 2000
This book presents an assortment of facts about the qualifications and characteristics of U.S. presidents, from George Washington to George W. Bush.
This book "is easy enough to read even for children in the lower grades, but like many such books it is ideally enjoyed by a child with an adult. That way, its rich anecdotes provoke questions, answers, definitions, recollections and more anecdotes." NY Times Book Rev [review of 2000 edition]

Talbott, Hudson

United tweets of America; 50 state birds; their stories, their glories; [by] Hudson Talbott. G.P. Putnam's Sons 2008 unp il $17.99 *
Grades: 3 4 5   973
1. United States 2. State birds
ISBN 978-0-399-24520-6; 0-399-24520-0
                                              LC 2007019419
"In this sly, comic, and irreverent book, loaded with hilarious puns and parodies about our 50 state birds, words and images deliver bits of history, folklore, and geography about each state. . . . Talbott's colored pencil and mixed-media illustrations ably combine the cartoon uproar with a sense of the individuality of the feathered creatures. . . . Clever, refeshing, and fun." Booklist

World Almanac Library of the States series. World Almanac 2002-2003 52v il map each $30, pa $11.95; set $1560, pa $569.40
Grades: 4 5 6 7   973
1. United States
Contents: Alabama by Michael A. Martin; Alaska by Isaac Seder; Arizona by Michael A. Martin; Arkansas by Darice Bailer; California by Scott Ingram; Colorado by Megan Elias; Connecticut by Darice Bailer; Delaware by

World Almanac Library of the States series—
Continued

Justine Fontes; Florida by Patricia Chui; Georgia by Eric Siegfried Holtz; Hawaii by Robin S. Doak; Idaho by Karen Edwards; Illinois by Kathleen Feeley; Indiana by Lynn Brunelle; Iowa by Michael E. Martin; Kansas by Scott Ingram; Kentucky by Miriam Heddy Pollack; Louisiana by Leslie S. Gildart; Maine by Deborah H. DeFord; Maryland by Michael A. Martin; Massachusetts by Rachel Barenblat; Michigan by Rachel Barenblat; Minnesota by Miriam Heddy Pollack; Mississippi by Acton Figueroa; Missouri by Scott Ingram; Montana by Kris Hirschmann; Nebraska by Michael Flocker; Nevada by Jon Hana; New Hampshire by Joanne Mattern; New Jersey by Eric Siegfried Holtz; New Mexico by Michael Burgan; New York by Jacqueline A. Ball; North Carolina by Sarah Rafle; North Dakota by Justine Fontes; Ohio by Michael A. Martin; Oklahoma by Michael A. Martin; Oregon by Scott Ingram; Pennsylvania by Scott Ingram; Puerto Rico and other outlying areas by Michael Burgan; Rhode Island by Joanne Mattern; South Carolina by Ann Volkwein; South Dakota by Kris Hirschmann; Tennessee by Barbara Peck; Texas by Rachel Barenblat; Utah by Kris Hirschmann; Vermont by Michael Flocker; Virginia by Pamela Pollack; Washington by Rachel Barenblat; Washington D.C. by Acton Figueroa; West Virginia by Justine Fontes; Wisconsin by Rachel Barenblat; Wyoming by Justine Fontes

Each of these "titles briefly outlines the state's history, politics, government, culture, etc., and includes numerous colorful sidebars, charts, graphs, maps, and photographs that illustrate or supplement the texts. An introductory 'Almanac' lists state emblems and provides an assortment of facts. A time line presents state events. . . . Brief biographical sketches of notable native sons and daughters are included. . . . Most libraries will want to consider adding these books." SLJ

Yaccarino, Dan

Go, go America. Scholastic Press 2008 71p il map $17.99

Grades: 1 2 3 4 **973**

1. United States
ISBN 0-439-70338-7; 978-0-439-70338-3
LC 2007-05733

"Readers accompany the fabulous Farley Family on their circuitous car and plane trip across the U.S., from Maine to Hawaii. Mom, Dad, Freddie, Fran, and Fido appear on each pastel-colored page chronicling the fun-filled activities available in each state and learning unusual facts. . . . Each fact is presented in a separate area of the page, with accompanying cartoon art, resulting in a busy but energetic layout. . . . The concluding pages list the states in alphabetical order and give their capitals, dates of statehood, rank in entering the Union, area, bird, flower, insect, tree, motto, and nickname. This book is loads of fun and is certain to stimulate interest in the U.S." SLJ

Yorinks, Adrienne

Quilt of states; quilts by Adrienne Yorinks; written by Adrienne Yorinks and 50 librarians from across the nation; librarian contributions compiled and edited by Jeanette Larson. National Geographic 2005 122p il $19.95

Grades: 5 6 7 8 **973**

1. United States—History
ISBN 0-7922-7285-4 LC 2004-17796

"The United States is stitched together chronologically in this stunning book that features a quilted spread for each state. Yorinks enlisted a librarian from each state to contribute a short entry to point up a few significant facts that add to the tapestry of the emerging nation. . . . The quilted representations are not only artistically intricate and beautiful, but also informative. A handsome book to linger over and learn from." SLJ

973.03 United States—History—Encyclopedias and dictionaries

Brownstone, David M.

Frontier America; [by] David M. Brownstone, Irene M. Franck. Grolier 2004 10v il map set $369 *

Grades: 5 6 7 8 **973.03**

1. Reference books 2. United States—History—Encyclopedias
ISBN 0-7172-5990-0 LC 2004-42445

Contents: v1 A new world; v2 West to the Pacific; v3 Acadia-Butterfield Overland Stage; v4 Cabeza de Vaca-Custer; v5 Delaware-Homestead Act; v6 Horses-Louisiana Purchase; v7 Mail-Northwest Territory; v8 Oakley-Roanoke Island; v9 Rocky Mountains-Turnpike; v10 Utah-Young

"The first two volumes present the overall history of the American frontier, with volume 2 containing a chronology of key events and a map of the lower 48 states. Volumes 3 through 10 offer alphabetically organized articles on events, people, and places. . . . The writing style is brisk and engaging enough to hold the attention of younger researchers. Coverage is evenhanded." Booklist

Junior Worldmark encyclopedia of the states; [Timothy L. Gall and Susan Bevan Gall, editors] 5th ed. Thomson Gale 2007 4v il map set $235 *

Grades: 5 6 7 8 9 10 **973.03**

1. United States—Encyclopedias 2. Reference books
ISBN 978-1-4144-1106-4 (set); 1-4144-1106-5 (set)
LC 2007003910

First published 1996

Contents: v1 Alabama to Illinois; v2 Indiana to Nebraska; v3 Nevada to South Dakota; v4 Tennessee to Wyoming, Washington, D.C., Puerto Rico, U.S. Pacific and Caribbean dependencies and U.S. overview

This reference "includes facts and details on every state in the U.S., including the District of Columbia and U.S. dependencies. Entries cover the geography, history, politics, economy and other facts about each state. Alphabetically arranged entries feature . . . subheadings for each state. . . . An index of people, places and subjects [is included]." Publisher's note

Includes bibliographical references

King, David C., 1933-
Children's encyclopedia of American history.
DK Pub. 2003 304p il map $29.99 *
Grades: 5 6 7 8   **973.03**
　　1.　United　States—History—Encyclopedias
2. Reference books
　　ISBN 0-7894-8330-0   LC 2002-73388
Full-color maps, photographs, and paintings illustrate
a comprehensive reference guide to American history
　"A visually enticing and textually fascinating survey."
SLJ

The **student** encyclopedia of the United States.
Kingfisher 2005 776p il map $29.95
　　Grades: 5 6 7 8   **973.03**
　　1. Reference books 2. United States—Encyclopedias
　　ISBN 0-7534-5925-6
"Designed to be a starting place for young researchers
and browsers alike, this reference tool explains topics relating to the 'people, places, and events that have shaped
the United States.' . . . More than 1,200 entries are arranged alphabetically and range in length from one paragraph to two pages. Entries are illustrated throughout
with more than 2,000 full-color photographs, illustrations,
diagrams, charts, time lines, and maps. . . . Students will
find this tool useful, and school and public libraries will
want to purchase both reference and circulating copies."
Booklist

973.1　United States—Early history to 1607

Hernández, Roger E.
New Spain: 1600-1760s. Marshall Cavendish
Benchmark 2009 79p il map (Hispanic America)
lib bdg $34.21
Grades: 4 5 6 7   **973.1**
　　1. Southwestern States—History 2. Southern States—
History 3. Spaniards—United States
　　ISBN 978-0-7614-2936-4 (lib bdg); 0-7614-2936-0 (lib
bdg)
"Provides comprehensive information on the history of
Spanish exploration in the United States." Publisher's
note
　Includes glossary and bibliographical references

973.2　United States—Colonial period, 1607-1775

Colonial America and the Revolutionary War; the
story of the people of the colonies, from early
settlers to revolutionary leaders; Laurie Lanzen
Harris, editor. Favorable Impressions 2009 399p
il map (Biography for beginners) $49 *
Grades: 2 3 4 5   **973.2**
　　1. United States—History—1775-1783, Revolution
2. United States—History—1600-1775, Colonial period 3. United States—Biography 4. Reference books
　　ISBN 978-1-931360-34-0; 1-931360-34-0
　　　　　　　　　　　　　　　LC 2008-49193

This "volume provides a brief general introduction and
three chronological sections: 'Colonial America,' 'The
Revolutionary War,' and 'Biographical Profiles.' The
first section includes chapters on regions from New England to Georgia, and on various social groups. Discussion is centered on issues concerning daily life and topics
such as representative government, Native Americans,
and slavery. Part two traces the origins of the conflict,
from the French and Indian War to the outbreak of hos-
tilities at Lexington and Concord, terminating at the
adoption of the U.S. Constitution and the Bill of Rights.
The 28 brief, illustrated biographical sketches cover perennial research favorites such as Benjamin Franklin,
Thomas Jefferson, George Washington, Abigail Adams,
Dolley Madison, and Phillis Wheatley." SLJ
　"This volume is highly recommended for public and
school library collections. The affordable price, well-
organized basic information, and user-friendly format
make it a valuable resource for young researchers."
Booklist
　Includes glossary

Fishkin, Rebecca Love, 1972-
English colonies in America. Compass Point
Books 2009 48p il map (We the people) lib bdg
$26.60
Grades: 4 5 6   **973.2**
　　1. United States—History—1600-1775, Colonial peri-
od
　　ISBN 978-0-7565-3838-5   LC 2008007210
This is a history of English colonies in North Ameri-
ca.
　This provides "solid background matter and introduce
key people and vocabulary." SLJ
　Includes glossary and bibliographical references

Huey, Lois Miner
American archaeology uncovers the earliest
English colonies. Marshall Cavendish Benchmark
2009 64p il map (American archaeology) lib bdg
$31.36
Grades: 4 5 6 7   **973.2**
　　1. America—Antiquities 2. Excavations (Archeology)—United States 3. Great Britain—Colonies—
America 4. America—Exploration
　　ISBN 978-0-7614-4264-6 (lib bdg); 0-7614-4264-2 (lib
bdg)   LC 2008050259
This describes how archeologists have learned about
the history of early English colonists in America at
Jamestown, Popham Colony, and Roanoke
　"Huey enthusiastically brings . . . [this era] to life
through artifacts and field research. . . . [The volume
begins with an] introduction that defines 'historical archaeology' and explains its value in terms simple enough
for lower-elementary readers to comprehend, yet detailed
enough for older children to enjoy, an approach followed
in the remaining chapters. . . . Huey's focus on American history, which is broken down into small, manageable chunks, is sure to entice budding historians." SLJ
　Includes glossary and bibliographical references

King, David C., 1933-
Colonial days; discover the past with fun projects, games, activities, and recipes; Illustrations by Bobbie Moore. Wiley 1998 118p il (American kids in history) pa $12.95
Grades: 3 4 5 6   973.2
 1. United States—Social life and customs—1600-1775, Colonial period
 ISBN 0-471-16168-3   LC 97-16083
 "A Roundtable Press book"
Discusses colonial life in America, depicts a year in the life of a fictional colonial family, and presents projects and activities, such as butter churning, candle dipping, baking bread, and playing colonial games
 "Explanatory text alternates with instructions and other sidebars that provide brief history lessons. The materials needed are readily accessible in grocery, hobby, or craft stores. The line drawings are clear and helpful." SLJ
 Includes glossary and bibliographical references

Maestro, Betsy, 1944-
The new Americans; colonial times, 1620-1689; illustrated by Giulio Maestro. Lothrop, Lee & Shepard Bks. 1998 48p il map hardcover o.p. pa $7.99 *
Grades: 2 3 4   973.2
 1. United States—History—1600-1775, Colonial period 2. Canada—History—0-1763 (New France)
 ISBN 0-688-13448-3; 0-06-57572-7 (pa)
                                  LC 95-19636
Traces the competition among the American Indians, French, English, Spanish, and Dutch for land, furs, timber, and other resources of North America
 This is "accessibly written and meticulously illustrated. . . . Giulio Maestro's carefully detailed watercolor and color-pencil art includes maps, closely focused spot illustrations and dramatic spreads, which together provide a vivid picture of the century's pivotal events." Publ Wkly

Struggle for a continent; the French and Indian Wars, 1689-1763; illustrated by Giulio Maestro. HarperCollins Pubs. 2000 48p il maps (American story series) $18.99 hardcover o.p. *
Grades: 3 4 5 6   973.2
 1. United States—History—1600-1775, Colonial period 2. United States—History—1755-1763, French and Indian War
 ISBN 0-688-13450-5; 0-688-13451-3 (lib bdg)
                                  LC 99-11500
Discusses the relations between the European colonists and the Native Americans, the disputes between settlers from France, England, and Spain, and the role these conflicts played in the history of North America
 "The text is a model of clarity, balance, and nuance. . . . A wide variety of beautifully delineated pictures—maps, townscapes, seascapes, battlefields, and portraits—add to the spirited sweep of the text. A fine resource." Booklist

Tunis, Edwin, 1897-1973
Colonial living; written and illustrated by Edwin Tunis. Johns Hopkins Univ. Press 1999 155p il pa $18.95 *
Grades: 5 6 7 8   973.2
 1. United States—Social life and customs—1600-1775, Colonial period
 ISBN 0-8018-6227-2   LC 99-22591
 A reprint of the title first published 1957 by World Pub. Co.
 "Common everyday aspects of colonial living from 1564-1770 are highlighted by the detailed descriptions and numerous black and white illustrations of items such as tools, home furnishings, clothing, etc." N Y Public Libr. Ref Books for Child Collect

Voices from colonial America [series] National Geographic 2005-2007 18v il map ea $21.95
Grades: 5 6 7 8   973.2
 1. United States—History—1600-1775, Colonial period
Contents: California 1542-1850 by Robin Doak with Andrés Reséndez; Connecticut 1614-1776 by Michael Burgan; Delaware 1638-1776 by Karen Hossel with Karin Wulf; Florida 1513-1821 by Matthew C. Cannavale; Georgia 1521-1776 by Robin Doak; Louisiana 1682-1803 by Richard Worth; Maryland 1634-1776 by Robin S. Doak; Massachusetts 1620-1776 by Michael Burgan; New France 1534-1763 by Richard Worth; New Hampshire 1603-1776 by Scott Auden; New Jersey 1609-1776 by Robin Doak with Brendan McConville; New York 1609-1776 by Michael Burgan; North Carolina 1524-1776 by Matthew C. Cannavale; Pennsylvania 1643-1776 by Lisa Trumbauer; Rhode Island 1636-1776 by Jesse McDermott; South Carolina by Robin Doak; Texas 1527-1836 by Michael Teitelbaum; Virginia 1607-1776 by Sandy Pobst
 Each volume in this series describes the colonial history of a state illustrated with historical maps and reprints of period artwork, and includes excerpts from first-person accounts.
 "Presented in clear, succinct text . . . this resource, containing a great deal of information, will be a welcome addition to history classes and a great source for report writers." Booklist [review of New Jersey volume]
 Includes bibliographical references

973.3 United States—Periods of Revolution and Confederation, 1775-1789

Allen, Thomas B., 1929-
Remember Valley Forge; patriots, Tories, and Redcoats tell their stories; [by] Thomas B. Allen. National Geographic 2007 61p il map $17.95; lib bdg $27.90
Grades: 5 6 7 8   973.3
 1. Washington, George, 1732-1799 2. Valley Forge (Pa.)—History 3. United States—History—1775-1783, Revolution
 ISBN 978-1-4263-0149-0; 978-1-4263-0150-6 (lib bdg)   LC 2007024821

Allen, Thomas B., 1929——*Continued*

The author "recounts here the activities of Washington and his soldiers during the winter of 1777-8, spent regrouping at Valley Forge, Pennsylvania. . . . Allen's strength is his attention to military details and strategies, but his account is clearly presented and succinctly written as well. . . . Illustrated with reproductions of period artwork, drawings, maps, and a few contemporary photographs." Booklist

Anderson, Laurie Halse, 1961-

Independent dames; what you never knew about the women and girls of the American Revolution; by Laurie Halse Anderson; illustrated by Matt Faulkner. Simon & Schuster Books for Young Readers 2008 37p il $16.99 *

Grades: 3 4 5   **973.3**

1. United States—History—1775-1783, Revolution 2. Women—United States—History

ISBN 978-0-689-85808-6; 0-689-85808-6

LC 2007042643

"The stories of 22 'Revolutionary Grandmothers' take center stage in this well-illustrated volume. . . . Faulkner's ink-and-watercolor illustrations are exuberant, often amusing, and filled with crosshatching and dialogue balloons. The spreads are busy and information-packed, and readers will be both engaged by and educated about this critical period." SLJ

Includes bibliographical references

Bobrick, Benson, 1947-

Fight for freedom; the American Revolutionary War. Atheneum Books for Young Readers 2004 96p il map $22.95 *

Grades: 5 6 7 8   **973.3**

1. United States—History—1775-1783, Revolution

ISBN 0-689-86422-1   LC 2003-25548

"This large-format volume profiles significant individuals and discusses the progress of the Revolutionary War. . . . Printed in color, most of the illustrations are period paintings and prints. . . . Students will find the book a well-organized and clearly written introduction to the war." Booklist

Includes glossary and bibliographical references

Brenner, Barbara, 1925-

If you were there in 1776. Bradbury Press 1994 136p il $17.95 *

Grades: 3 4 5 6   **973.3**

1. United States. Declaration of Independence 2. United States—Social life and customs

ISBN 0-02-712322-7   LC 93-24060

Demonstrates how the concepts and principles expressed in the Declaration of Independence were drawn from the experiences of living in America in the late eighteenth century, with emphasis given to how children lived on a New England farm, a Southern plantation, and the frontier

"The author's inclusion of details of how peoples' lives began to change as a result of the Revolution and her accessible style are the selling points here. Both budding historians and report writers will find this title worth their time." SLJ

Includes bibliographical references

Brown, Don, 1949-

Let it begin here! April 19, 1775, the day the American Revolution began. Roaring Brook Press 2008 unp il $17.95 *

Grades: 2 3 4   **973.3**

1. United States—History—1775-1783, Revolution 2. Lexington (Mass.), Battle of, 1775 3. Concord (Mass.), Battle of, 1775

ISBN 978-1-59643-221-5; 1-59643-221-7

LC 2008-11221

"Brown distills the fairly complex story of the beginning of the American Revolution in a manner that deftly balances information and intrigue. . . . Equally impressive and vital to the success of this picture book are Brown's compositions which sometimes dramatically, sometimes whimsically intersect with the text. . . . [This is] rousing, accessible, and splendidly executed." Booklist

Decker, Timothy

For liberty; the story of the Boston Massacre. Calkins Creek 2009 unp il $17.95

Grades: 4 5 6   **973.3**

1. Boston Massacre, 1770

ISBN 978-1-59078-608-6; 1-59078-608-4

"This handsomely designed picture book begins the story of the Boston Massacre by filling in the background. . . . The book concludes with the soldiers' trial and their lawyer, John Adams, reflecting on the protection of liberty. . . . The book does quite a good job of conveying how the actions and emotions of those on both sides escalated toward violence and death. Using parallel lines, crosshatching, and other texturing effects, the black-and-white drawings hold attention. . . . A fine, balanced look at an important event." Booklist

Fleming, Thomas J., 1927-

Everybody's revolution; a new look at the people who won America's freedom; [by] Thomas Fleming. Scholastic Nonfiction 2006 96p il $19.99

Grades: 4 5 6 7   **973.3**

1. United States—History—1775-1783, Revolution

ISBN 0-439-63404-0   LC 2005051814

A history of the American Revolution, focusing on the roles played by women, young people, and various ethnic groups.

"With an open layout and clean typeface, this clearly written title is attractive and inviting. . . . Fleming's sound offering is an excellent starting point for discussions of the implications of the Revolutionary War in terms of freedom for all people." SLJ

Includes glossary and bibliographical references

Fradin, Dennis B.

The Boston Tea Party; [by] Dennis Brindell Fradin. Marshall Cavendish Benchmark 2007 45p il map (Turning points in U.S. history) lib bdg $31.36

Grades: 3 4 5   **973.3**

1. Boston Tea Party, 1773

ISBN 978-0-7614-2035-4   LC 2006025344

Fradin, Dennis B.—*Continued*

Beginning with British debt for its colonial wars and ending with the battles of Lexington and Concord, this is an account of the American colonists' rebellion against taxes on British tea

Includes glossary and bibliographical references

The Declaration of Independence; [by] Dennis Brindell Fradin. Marshall Cavendish Benchmark 2007 45p il map (Turning points in U.S. history) lib bdg $31.36

Grades: 3 4 5   **973.3**

1. United States. Declaration of Independence 2. United States—Politics and government—1775-1783, Revolution

ISBN 978-0-7614-2129-0 (lib bdg); 0-7614-2129-7 (lib bdg)   LC 2005016023

This "describes the unrest that led up to the signing of the famous document, how Jefferson composed it, and the uncertainty surrounding the vote for independence. . . . The clear, concise, and dynamic style of writing simplifies the information without dumbing it down. . . . The photos, paintings, and maps . . . add a wealth of information." SLJ

Includes glossary and bibliographical references

Let it begin here! Lexington & Concord: first battles of the American Revolution; [by] Dennis Brindell Fradin; illustrations by Larry Day. Walker & Co. 2005 unp il maps $16.95; lib bdg $17.85

Grades: 2 3 4   **973.3**

1. Lexington (Mass.), Battle of, 1775 2. Concord (Mass.), Battle of, 1775

ISBN 0-8027-8945-5; 0-8027-8946-3 (lib bdg)
LC 2004-49473

This is an "account of Paul Revere's actions on the night of April 18, 1775, and the battles in Lexington and Concord on the following day. . . . Well-composed double-page illustrations, ink drawings with watercolor and gouache, highlight the human drama implicit in the text." Booklist

Includes bibliographical references

Freedman, Russell

Give me liberty! the story of the Declaration of Independence. Holiday House 2000 90p il $24.95; pa $14.95 *

Grades: 5 6 7 8 9   **973.3**

1. United States. Declaration of Independence 2. United States—Politics and government—1775-1783, Revolution

ISBN 0-8234-1448-5; 0-8234-1753-0 (pa)
LC 99-57513

Describes the events leading up to the Declaration of Independence as well as the personalities and politics behind its framing

"Handsomely designed with a generous and thoughtful selection of period art, the book is dramatic and inspiring." Horn Book

Includes bibliographical references

Washington at Valley Forge. Holiday House 2008 100p il map $24.95 *

Grades: 5 6 7 8 9   **973.3**

1. Washington, George, 1732-1799 2. Valley Forge (Pa.)—History 3. Pennsylvania—History 4. United States—History—1775-1783, Revolution

ISBN 978-0-8234-2069-8; 0-8234-2069-8
LC 2007-52467

NCTE Orbis Pictus Award honor book (2009)

This is an "account of the survival of American soldiers while camped at Valley Forge during a crucial period in the American Revolution." Publisher's note

"With his usual clarity of focus and keen eye for telling quotations, Freedman documents how Washington struggled to maintain morale despite hunger, near-nakedness, and freezing conditions. . . . Throughout, high-quality reproductions depict Washington among the men, and with the numerous other influential people who played crucial roles." Booklist

Herbert, Janis, 1956-

The American Revolution for kids; a history with 21 activities. Chicago Review Press 2002 139p il pa $14.95 *

Grades: 4 5 6   **973.3**

1. United States—History—1775-1783, Revolution

ISBN 1-55652-456-0   LC 2002-7938

Discusses the events of the American Revolution, from the hated Stamp Act and the Boston Tea Party to the British surrender at Yorktown and the writing of the Constitution. Activities include making a tricorn hat and discovering local history

"Achieving a good balance between textual material, illustration, and projects, the book immerses children in the milieu of these years. . . . The directions are detailed enough and adequately illustrated with pencil drawings to make them exciting and easy to follow." SLJ

Includes glossary and bibliographical references

Jules, Jacqueline, 1956-

Unite or die; how thirteen states became a nation; illustrated by Jef Czekaj. Charlesbridge 2009 48p il $16.95; pa $7.95

Grades: 2 3 4 5   **973.3**

1. United States—History—1783-1809

ISBN 978-1-58089-189-9; 1-58089-189-6; 978-1-58089-190-5 (pa); 1-58089-190-X (pa)
LC 2008-07229

"This presentation is written as if it were a school play about the 13 colonies becoming a nation. Told through colorful comic-book illustrations, it stars students dressed as states humorously explaining the path to the writing of the Constitution. The brief text is accompanied by speech balloons expressing the states' multiple, often competing, views. . . . The vividly colored spreads will hold the interest of even middle school students and would be useful to introduce how our form of government was created." SLJ

Includes bibliographical references

Kostyal, K. M., 1951-

1776; a new look at revolutionary Williamsburg; by K.M. Kostyal with the Colonial Williamsburg Foundation; photographs by Lori Epstein. National Geographic 2009 48p il $17.95; lib bdg $27.90

Grades: 4 5 6   **973.3**
    1. Colonial Williamsburg (Williamsburg, Va.)
    2. United States—History—1775-1783, Revolution
    ISBN   978-1-4263-0517-7;   1-4263-0517-6;
    978-1-4263-0518-4 (lib bdg); 1-4263-0518-4 (lib bdg)
                                        LC 2009-18002

"Clear, distinctive photos add visual appeal to this short history of the American Revolution, written from the point of view of those living in Williamsburg, Virginia's capital in 1776. Kostyal blends political and social history into a readable account of the period, bolstered by informative sidebars, a chronology, and a closing note about the restoration of colonial Williamsburg. . . . The increasing inclusion of nonwhite colonists in the illustrations as well as the text is a welcome trend." Booklist

    Includes bibliographical references

Leavitt, Amie Jane

The Declaration of Independence in translation; what it really means; by Amie Jane Leavitt. Capstone Press 2009 32p il (Fact finders. Kids' translations) lib bdg $23.93; pa $7.95

Grades: 3 4 5   **973.3**
    1. United States. Declaration of Independence
    2. United States—Politics and government—1775-1783, Revolution
    ISBN 978-1-4296-1929-5 (lib bdg); 1-4296-1929-5 (lib bdg); 978-1-4296-2844-0 (pa); 1-4296-2844-8 (pa)
                                        LC 2008-3229

"Presents the Declaration of Independence in both its original version and in a translated version using everyday language. Describes the events that led to the creation of the document and its significance through history." Publisher's notes

    Provides "a nearly line-by-line translation that makes . . . the written word accessible and meaningful." SLJ

    Includes glossary and bibliographical references

Maestro, Betsy, 1944-

Liberty or death; the American Revolution, 1763-1783; illustrated by Giulio Maestro. HarperCollins 2005 64p il map (American story series) $15.99; lib bdg $16.89

Grades: 3 4 5 6   **973.3**
    1. United States—History—1775-1783, Revolution
    ISBN 0-688-08802-3; 0-688-08803-1 (lib bdg)
                                        LC 00-54042

The author and illustrator describe "the 20 years leading up to, and fighting, the American Revolution. A simple narrative, largely from the Colonists' perspective, touches on the major events, players, and ideas of the times, beginning with the Stamp Act and ending with Yorktown and the subsequent peace treaty. . . . Full-color ink, colored-pencil, and watercolor illustrations . . . grace the page in a pleasing, uncluttered way. . . . This book serves as a good introductory overview." SLJ

A new nation; the United States, 1783-1815; illustrated by Giulio Maestro. HarperCollins Publishers 2009 64p il map (American story series) $17.99; lib bdg $18.89

Grades: 3 4 5 6   **973.3**
    1. United States—History—1783-1865
    ISBN   978-0-688-16015-9;   0-688-16015-8;
    978-0-688-16016-6 (lib bdg); 0-688-16016-6 (lib bdg)
                                        LC 2008-26947

"The Maestros . . . cover a jam-packed 32 years that saw the country more than double in population and, with the Lousiana Purchase, double in size. . . . The abundant pastel artwork breaks up the pages and provides nifty images of the times. . . . Interesting for history buffs, useful for researchers." Booklist

Micklos, John, 1956-

The brave women and children of the American Revolution; [by] John Micklos, Jr. Enslow Publishers 2008 48p il (The Revolutionary War library) lib bdg $17.95

Grades: 3 4 5 6   **973.3**
    1. United States—History—1775-1783, Revolution
    2. Women—United States—History 3. Children—United States
    ISBN 978-0-7660-3019-0 (lib bdg); 0-7660-3019-9 (lib bdg)   LC 2007048510

This describes the roles of women and children in the American Revolution, at home, in business, as spies and messengers, and on the battlefield.

This is "illustrated with historical engravings and photographs. . . . The many sidebars are informative. . . . The well-written text is studded with footnotes, and the appended time line is helpful." Booklist

    Includes glossary and bibliographical references

Miller, Brandon Marie

Declaring independence; life during the American Revolution; by Brandon Marie Miller. Lerner Publications Co. 2005 112p il map (People's history) lib bdg $31.93

Grades: 5 6 7 8   **973.3**
    1. United States—History—1775-1783, Revolution
    2. United States—Social conditions
    ISBN 0-8225-1275-0   LC 2004-17917

    Contents: The people are ripe for mischief; They feel their importance; You are now my enemy; Free and independent states; The ragged lousey naked regiment; Where God can we fly from danger; The revolution just accomplished

This describes the lives of American colonists in the late 1700s and the fight for independence from Great Britain with emphasis on "firsthand accounts, contemporary writings, and official documents. Miller does a good job of chronicling the history, presenting the information in a clear, concise, and well-organized manner." SLJ

    Includes bibliographical references

Miller, Brandon Marie—*Continued*

Growing up in revolution and the new nation, 1775 to 1800. Lerner Publs. 2003 59p il map (Our America) $26.60

Grades: 5 6 7 8   **973.3**

1. United States—History—1775-1783, Revolution 2. United States—Social life and customs 3. Children—United States

ISBN 0-8225-0078-7   LC 2001-4654

Presents details of daily life of American children during the period from 1775 to 1800

The author "does a good job presenting this information by using quotes from primary sources, historical photographs, and artwork from this time period." Libr Media Connect

Includes bibliographical references

Minor, Wendell

Yankee Doodle America; the spirit of 1776 from A to Z; [by] Wendell Minor. G.P. Putnam's Sons 2006 unp il $16.99

Grades: 2 3 4   **973.3**

1. United States—History—1775-1783, Revolution 2. Alphabet

ISBN 0-399-24003-9   LC 2005025174

"In colonial America, the public houses served as the news hubs of their surrounding areas. . . . Using hand-carved replicas of the signs for these inns and taverns to share facts about the American Revolution, Minor, in concert with master woodworker John Reichling, has created an unusual alphabet book. . . . The factual material is correct, clearly stated, and intriguing." SLJ

Includes bibliographical references

Murphy, Jim, 1947-

A young patriot; the American Revolution as experienced by one boy. Clarion Bks. 1996 101p il maps $16; pa $7.95 *

Grades: 5 6 7 8   **973.3**

1. Martin, Joseph Plumb, 1760-1850 2. United States—History—1775-1783, Revolution

ISBN 0-395-60523-7; 0-395-90019-0 (pa)

LC 93-38789

"Using Joseph Plumb Martin's first person account of his participation in the Revolutionary War as primary source material, Murphy intertwines this story of one teenager's life as a soldier with broader information about the Revolution, to put Martin's story in context. The handsome, informative, and fascinating look at American history is illustrated with many period reproductions." Horn Book Guide

Includes bibliographical references

Otfinoski, Steven, 1949-

The new republic: 1760-1840s. Marshall Cavendish Benchmark 2009 79p il map (Hispanic America) lib bdg $23.95

Grades: 4 5 6 7   **973.3**

1. Hispanic Americans 2. Spaniards—United States 3. United States—History—1775-1783, Revolution 4. Florida—History 5. Mexico—History

ISBN 978-0-7614-2938-8 (lib bdg); 0-7614-2938-7 (lib bdg)   LC 2007-45958

"Provides comprehensive information on the history of the Spanish exploring the United States." Publisher's note

Includes glossary and bibliographical references

Rappaport, Doreen, 1939-

Victory or death! eight stories of the American Revolution; by Doreen Rappaport and Joan Verniero; illustrated by Greg Call. HarperCollins 2003 120p il map $16.99; lib bdg $17.89 *

Grades: 4 5 6   **973.3**

1. United States—History—1775-1783, Revolution

ISBN 0-06-029515-5; 0-06-029516-3 (lib bdg)

LC 2002-12837

Contents: The soldier with the pen: Peter Brown; The oath: Francis Salvador; "Yours, Portia": Abigail Adams; The decision: George Washington; Tarnation Sybil!: Sybil Ludington; A question of justice: Grace Growden Galloway; The spy: James Armistead; The recruit: Robert Shurtliff

This tells the stories of eight people who displayed courage during the American Revolution

"A well-researched and thoroughly engaging approach to history." SLJ

Sanders, Nancy I., 1960-

America's black founders; revolutionary heroes & early leaders with 21 activities. Chicago Review Press 2010 150p il $16.95

Grades: 4 5 6 7   **973.3**

1. United States—History—1775-1783, Revolution 2. African Americans—History

ISBN 978-1-55652-811-8; 1-55652-811-6

"This activity-based guide reveals how African Americans played crucial roles in helping the United States gain its independence. Sanders includes well-known figures such as Phillis Wheatley, Crispus Attucks, and James Forten in her narrative, but also enriches traditional accounts of the period by explaining the contributions of lesser-known patriots. . . . Most of the activities help make this period real to young people. . . . Sanders makes excellent use of primary sources." SLJ

Schanzer, Rosalyn

George vs. George; the American Revolution as seen from both sides. National Geographic 2004 60p il maps $16.95 *

Grades: 3 4 5 6   **973.3**

1. Washington, George, 1732-1799 2. George III, King of Great Britain, 1738-1820 3. United States—History—1775-1783, Revolution

ISBN 0-7922-7349-4   LC 2003-20843

Explores how the characters and lives of King George III of England and George Washington affected the progress and outcome of the American Revolution

"A carefully researched, evenhanded narrative with well-crafted, vibrant, watercolor illustrations. . . . This is a lovely book, showing historical inquiry at its best." SLJ

Includes bibliographical references

Sheinkin, Steve, 1968-

King George: what was his problem? everything your schoolbooks didn't tell you about the American Revolution. Roaring Brook Press 2008 195p il map $19.95 *

Grades: 4 5 6   **973.3**
    1. United States—History—1775-1783, Revolution
    ISBN 978-1-59643-319-9; 1-59643-319-1
                                  LC 2007-39999

First published 2005 in paperback by Summer Street Press, in series Storyteller's History, with title: The American Revolution

This history of the American Revolution "features many droll line drawings that suit the tone of the writing and source notes for the extensive quotes. Sheinkin clearly conveys the gravity of events during the Revolutionary period, but he also has the knack of bringing historical people to life and showing what was at stake for them as individuals as well as for the new nation. . . . Vivid storytelling makes this an unusually readable history book." Booklist

Includes bibliographical references

St. George, Judith, 1931-

The journey of the one and only Declaration of Independence; illustrated by Will Hillenbrand. Philomel Books 2005 unp il $16.99 *

Grades: 2 3 4   **973.3**
    1. United States. Declaration of Independence
    2. United States—Politics and government—1775-1783, Revolution
    ISBN 0-399-23738-0   LC 2004-13567

This decribes how the Declaration of Independence was written and how the document was preserved and displayed throughout American history

"Readers will learn fascinating details. . . . Hillenbrand's lively mixed-media illustrations are a perfect match for the text, filling the pages with visual energy and humor. . . . This well-researched, readable, and well-illustrated book belongs on the shelves of all public and school libraries." SLJ

Includes bibliographical references

Winters, Kay

Colonial voices; hear them speak; [by] Kay Winters; illustrated by Larry Day. Dutton Children's Books 2008 unp il map $17.99 *

Grades: 3 4 5 6   **973.3**
    1. Boston Tea Party, 1773 2. Boston (Mass.)—History
    3. United States—History—1775-1783, Revolution
    ISBN 978-0-525-47872-0; 0-525-47872-8
                                  LC 2007-28480

"Colonial Bostonians introduce themselves through free-verse vignettes that describe their work and their feelings about the current political situation. As errand boy Ethan moves about the city, he links the people together. . . . The watercolor and ink illustrations add humor and drama through shifting perspectives and well-detailed settings full of period details. . . . A unique presentation for all libraries." SLJ

Includes bibliographical references

973.4   United States—Constitutional period, 1789-1809

Fradin, Dennis B.

Duel! Burr and Hamilton's deadly war of words; by Dennis Brindell Fradin; illustrated by Larry Day. Walker & Co. 2008 unp il $16.95; lib bdg $17.85 *

Grades: 3 4 5 6   **973.4**
    1. Burr, Aaron, 1756-1836 2. Hamilton, Alexander, 1757-1804
    ISBN   978-0-8027-9583-0;   0-8027-9583-8;
    978-0-8027-9584-7 (lib bdg); 0-8027-9584-6 (lib bdg)
                                  LC 2007-37994

"Even children who don't know much about Aaron Burr . . . and Alexander Hamilton . . . will be hooked by this dramatic picture-book account of their deadly quarrel. . . . When Fradin deals with the divisive politics, Day's ink, watercolor, and gouache illustrations ably show the body language as the enemies furiously confront one another. . . . The words and art humanize the history for children." Booklist

Schlaepfer, Gloria G.

The Louisiana Purchase; [by] Gloria G. Schlaepfer. Franklin Watts 2005 63p il map (Watts library) lib bdg $25.50

Grades: 5 6 7 8   **973.4**
    1. Louisiana Purchase
    ISBN 0-531-12300-6   LC 2005001465

"Schlaepfer tells the story of 'the greatest land deal in American history.'. . . Black-and-white and color illustrations, maps, sidebars, and time lines enhance the well-organized [text]." SLJ

Includes bibliographical references

973.5   United States—1809-1845

Childress, Diana

The War of 1812; [by] Diana Childress. Lerner Publications Co. 2004 80p il map (Chronicle of America's wars) lib bdg $27.93

Grades: 5 6 7 8   **973.5**
    1. War of 1812
    ISBN 0-8225-0800-1   LC 2003-18805

Contents: The road to war; Losses on land, victories at sea; The pattern changes; A new front and a victory in the Northwest; The Creek vanquished, the last invasion; The British counterattack; A dramatic end

This describes the events of the War of 1812 and focusing on the impact the war had on America and its people.

Includes glossary and bibliographical references

Edelman, Rob

The War of 1812; by Rob Edelman and Audrey Kupferberg. Blackbirch Press 2005 48p il map (People at the center of) lib bdg $23.70

Grades: 5 6 7 8   **973.5**
    1. War of 1812
    ISBN 1-56711-926-3   LC 2004-16944

Edelman, Rob—*Continued*

This profiles 15 people connected with the War of 1812 such as Thomas Jefferson, Tecumseh, Jean Laffite, Francis Scott Key, William Henry Harrison, and Oliver Hazard Perry

Includes bibliographical references

973.6   United States—1845-1861

Feldman, Ruth Tenzer

The Mexican-American War; [by] Ruth Tenzer Feldman. Lerner Publications Co. 2004 88p il map (Chronicle of America's wars) lib bdg $27.93

Grades: 5 6 7 8   **973.6**

1. Mexican War, 1846-1848

ISBN 0-8225-0831-1   LC 2003-23395

Contents: Bordering on war; Manifest destiny; Rough and ready; Continuing conflict; Conquering peace; March to Mexico City; The struggle for peace; Two nations, one border

This chronicles the events of the Mexican War of 1846-1848 focusing the impact the war had on America and its people.

Includes glossary and bibliographical references

973.7   United States—Administration of Abraham Lincoln, 1861-1865. Civil War

Anderson, Dale, 1953-

World Almanac library of the Civil War [series] World Almanac Library 2004 8v il map * set $180; pa $87.60

Grades: 4 5 6   **973.7**

1. United States—History—1861-1865, Civil War

Also available as separate volumes ea $30; pa $11.95

Contents: The aftermath of the Civil War; The causes of the Civil War; The Civil War at sea; The Civil War in the East (1861-July 1863); The Civil War in the West (1861-July 1863); The home fronts in the Civil War; A soldier's life in the Civil War; The Union victory (July 1863-1865)

"While series on the Civil War are rather common, this one stands apart by presenting a wide breadth of topics in a concise way. These . . . titles offer accessible overviews for students just becoming acquainted with this period in American history. . . . Clear maps and extremely helpful photographs, illustrations, and reproductions are everywhere, many in full color." SLJ

Includes bibliographical references

Beller, Susan Provost, 1949-

Billy Yank and Johnny Reb; soldiering in the Civil War. Twenty-First Century Books 2008 112p il map (Soldiers on the battlefront) lib bdg $33.26

Grades: 5 6 7 8   **973.7**

1. Soldiers—United States 2. United States—History—1861-1865, Civil War

ISBN 978-0-8225-6803-2 (lib bdg); 0-8225-6803-9 (lib bdg)   LC 2006010240

First published 2000

Describes military life for the average soldier in the Civil War, including camp life, diseases, and conditions for the wounded and prisoners of war. Includes excerpts from first-person accounts, letters, and diaries

The author "presents a good deal of solid information in an interesting manner. . . . Good black-and-white reproductions, mainly of photographs from the 1860s, appear throughout the book." Booklist [review of 2000 ed]

Includes bibliographical references

Bolotin, Norm, 1951-

Civil War A to Z; a young readers' guide to over 100 people, places, and points of importance; [by] Norman Bolotin. Dutton Children's Bks. 2002 148p il map $19.99 *

Grades: 4 5 6 7   **973.7**

1. United States—History—1861-1865, Civil War

ISBN 0-525-46268-6   LC 2001-33370

Alphabetically arranged articles present over 100 people, places, and points of importance of the Civil War

"Bolotin has a good eye for what students need to understand about the war and provides a great deal of information, skillfully whittled down to its most salient points. . . . The format is attractive, with numerous photographs." Booklist

Includes glossary and bibliographical references

The **Civil** War. Grolier 2004 10v il map set $309

Grades: 5 6 7 8   **973.7**

1. United States—History—1861-1865, Civil War
2. Reference books

ISBN 0-7172-5883-1   LC 2003-49315

Contents: v1 Abolition-Camp followers; v2 Camp life-Custer, George A.; v3 Daily life-Flags; v4 Florida-Hill, Ambrose P.; v5 Home Front, Confederacy-Legacy of the Civil War; v6 Lincoln, Abraham-Mobile Bay, Battle of; v7 Money and banking-Politics, Confederate; v8 Politics, Union-Shenandoah Valley; v9 Sheridan, Philip H.-Trade; v10 Training-Zouaves

This set "features detailed multipage articles that address significant individuals, battles, events, and conditions of the American Civil War." Booklist

"The variety of topics addressed in this set will give students a wide perspective on the conflict. . . . The clearly written, objective entries, ranging in length from one to six pages, all offer basic analysis." SLJ

Clinton, Catherine, 1952-

Hold the flag high; illustrated by Shane W. Evans. Katherine Tegen Books 2005 unp il $15.99; lib bdg $16.89 *

Grades: 2 3 4   **973.7**

1. Carney, William, 1840-1908 2. United States—History—1861-1865, Civil War 3. African American soldiers

ISBN 0-06-050428-5; 0-06-050429-3 (lib bdg)   LC 2003-11956

"Amistad"

Describes the Civil War battle of Morris Island, South Carolina, during which Sargeant William H. Carney became the first African American to earn a Congressional Medal of Honor

Clinton, Catherine, 1952-—*Continued*

"The story captures the fear and horror of battle as well as the bravery of the soldiers. . . . Evans' paintings convey the emotions of the characters as well as their actions." Booklist

Includes bibliographical references

Friedman, Robin, 1968-

The silent witness; a true story of the Civil War; illustrated by Claire A. Nivola. Houghton Mifflin Co. 2005 unp il $16

Grades: K 1 2 3   973.7

1. McLean family 2. United States—History—1861-1865, Civil War 3. Virginia—History

ISBN 0-618-44230-8   LC 2004-1013

"Young Lula McLean watched the Civil War begin and end: General Beauregard used her family's Virginia home as his headquarters, and Lee surrendered at their second home. The finely executed, primitive-like paintings accentuate the idea that this war was an intimate part of everyday life in the South, and the small telling details show a personal side of the war." Horn Book Guide

Hernández, Roger E.

The Civil War, 1840s-1890s. Marshall Cavendish Benchmark 2008 80p il map (Hispanic America) lib bdg $34.21

Grades: 4 5 6 7   973.7

1. Hispanic Americans 2. United States—Ethnic relations 3. United States—History—1861-1865, Civil War

ISBN 978-0-7614-2939-5 (lib bdg); 0-7614-2939-5 (lib bdg)   LC 2007049525

Discusses Hispanic participation during the Civil War

Includes glossary and bibliographical references

Holzer, Harold

The president is shot! the assassination of Abraham Lincoln. Boyds Mills Press 2004 181p il $17.95

Grades: 5 6 7 8   973.7

1. Lincoln, Abraham, 1809-1865—Assassination

ISBN 1-56397-985-3

This is a "description of the violent end to Lincoln's life. Holzer provides the Civil War context of the event and then details April 14 and 15, 1865." SLJ

"A page-turner of a text, a fascinating array of photos and archival illustrations, and an event that changed the course of history: all these elements combine in this strong, highly readable book." Booklist

Includes bibliographical references

Huey, Lois Miner

American archaeology uncovers the Underground Railroad. Marshall Cavendish Benchmark 2009 c2010 64p il map (American archaeology) lib bdg $21.95

Grades: 4 5 6 7   973.7

1. Underground railroad 2. Slavery—United States 3. Abolitionists 4. Excavations (Archeology)—United States

ISBN 978-0-7614-4267-7 (lib bdg); 0-7614-4267-7 (lib bdg)   LC 2009003168

This describes how archeologists have learned about the history of the Underground Railroad.

This is "both intriguing and engaging for young readers. . . . A welcomed addition to classroom and school libraries." Libr Media Connect

Includes glossary and bibliographical references

Jordan, Anne Devereaux, 1943-

The Civil War; by Anne Devereaux Jordan; with Virginia Schomp. Marshall Cavendish Benchmark 2007 72p il (Drama of African-American history) lib bdg $34.21

Grades: 5 6 7 8   973.7

1. United States—History—1861-1865, Civil War 2. African Americans—History

ISBN 978-0-7614-2179-5 (lib bdg); 0-7614-2179-3 (lib bdg)   LC 2006012472

Describes the role of African Americans during the Civil War (1861-1865)

Includes glossary and bibliographical references

Landau, Elaine

Fleeing to freedom on the Underground Railroad; the courageous slaves, agents, and conductors. Twenty-First Century Books 2006 88p il map (People's history) lib bdg $26.60

Grades: 5 6 7 8   973.7

1. Underground railroad 2. Slavery—United States 3. Abolitionists

ISBN 978-0-8225-3490-7 (lib bdg); 0-8225-3490-8 (lib bdg)   LC 2005020358

"Landau discusses the history of slavery in the United States, slave life, the Underground Railroad, and the leaders, both black and white, of antislavery organizations. Three chapters outline specifics of slaves' escapes. . . . An outstanding feature of this book is the use of primary sources and quotes from former slaves, contemporary newspaper accounts, and reminiscences of escaped slaves. . . . Excellent historical photographs and illustrations enhance the text." SLJ

Includes bibliographical references

McKissack, Patricia C., 1944-

Days of Jubilee; the end of slavery in the United States; [by] Patricia C. & Fredrick L. McKissack. Scholastic Press 2003 134p il $18.95 *

Grades: 5 6 7 8   973.7

1. Slavery—United States 2. African Americans—History 3. United States—History—1861-1865, Civil War

ISBN 0-590-10764-X   LC 2001-57568

McKissack, Patricia C., 1944-—*Continued*

Uses slave narratives, letters, diaries, military orders, and other documents to chronicle the various stages leading to the emancipation of slaves in the United States

"The balanced perspective, vivid telling, and well-chosen details give this book an immediacy that many history books lack." Booklist

McPherson, James M.

Fields of fury; the American Civil War. Atheneum Bks. for Young Readers 2002 96p il map $22.95 *

Grades: 5 6 7 8   973.7

1. United States—History—1861-1865, Civil War
ISBN 0-689-84833-1   LC 2001-46048

"A Byron Preiss Visual Publications, Inc. book"

Examines the events and effects of the American Civil War

"McPherson writes with authority, offering a broad overview as well as many details and anecdotes that give his account a human dimension. . . . The many fine illustrations include period photographs, paintings, prints, some excellent maps." Booklist

Includes glossary and bibliographical references

Murphy, Jim, 1947-

The boys' war; Confederate and Union soldiers talk about the Civil War. Clarion Bks. 1990 110p il hardcover o.p. pa $8.95 *

Grades: 5 6 7 8 9 10   973.7

1. United States—History—1861-1865, Civil War
ISBN 0-89919-893-7; 0-395-66412-8 (pa)
LC 89-23959

This book includes diary entries, personal letters, and archival photographs to describe the experiences of boys, sixteen years old or younger, who fought in the Civil War.

"An excellent selection of more than 45 sepia-toned contemporary photographs augment the text of this informative, moving work." SLJ

Includes bibliographical references

The long road to Gettysburg. Clarion Bks. 1992 116p il maps $17; pa $7.95 *

Grades: 5 6 7 8 9 10   973.7

1. Gettysburg (Pa.), Battle of, 1863
ISBN 0-395-55965-0; 0-618-05157-0 (pa)
LC 90-21881

Describes the events of the Battle of Gettysburg in 1863 as seen through the eyes of two actual participants, nineteen-year-old Confederate lieutenant John Dooley and seventeen-year-old Union soldier Thomas Galway. Also discusses Lincoln's famous speech delivered at the dedication of the National Cemetery at Gettysburg

The author "uses all of his fine skills as an information writer—clarity of detail, conciseness, understanding of his age group, and ability to find the drama appealing to readers—to frame a well-crafted account of a single battle in the war." Horn Book

Includes bibliographical references

Rappaport, Doreen, 1939-

United no more! stories of the Civil War; by Doreen Rappaport and Joan Verniero; illustrated by Rick Reeves. HarperCollinsPublishers 2006 132p il map $15.99; lib bdg $16.89 *

Grades: 4 5 6 7   973.7

1. United States—History—1861-1865, Civil War
ISBN 0-06-050599-0; 0-06-050600-8 (lib bdg)
LC 2005005724

"An interesting and readable introduction to the Civil War. Drawn from primary sources, the seven short narratives reflect the experiences of people on both sides of the conflict. . . . Maps and occasional black-and-white, pen-and-ink drawings add detail and drama to the narratives." SLJ

Includes bibliographical references

Rossi, Ann

Freedom struggle; the anti-slavery movement in America 1830-1865. National Geographic 2005 40p il (Crossroads America) $12.95; lib bdg $21.90

Grades: 4 5 6   973.7

1. Slavery—United States 2. Abolitionists
ISBN 0-7922-7828-3; 0-7922-8061-X (lib bdg)
LC 2003-19824

Contents: America in 1860; Slavery, right or wrong?; The Underground Railroad; Slavery divides the nation; Should slavery be abolished?; The Path to War; Uncle Tom's Cabin; Fighting for freedom

This discusses the Abolitionist Movement in the United States, profiling some of its leaders and its role in the Civil War.

"Period photographs, drawings, and cartoons; primary-source material; and biographical content make [this] introductory [title] interesting and accessible." SLJ

Includes glossary

Sheinkin, Steve, 1968-

Two miserable presidents; everything your schoolbooks didn't tell you about the Civil War; illustrated by Tim Robinson. Roaring Brook Press 2008 246p il $19.95 *

Grades: 4 5 6 7   973.7

1. United States—History—1861-1865, Civil War
ISBN 978-1-59643-320-5; 1-59643-320-5
LC 2007-33115

"Chatty and accessible, this book does double duty: it introduces Civil War history for readers who don't know much about it and supplies browsable commentary for those familiar with the big picture. . . . [Sheinkin's] fast-paced narrative is broken into short, tersely titled vignettes." Booklist

Includes bibliographical references

Stanchak, John E.

Civil War; written by John Stanchak. Dorling Kindersley 2000 64p il map (DK eyewitness books) $15.99; lib bdg $19.99

Grades: 4 5 6 7   973.7

1. United States—History—1861-1865, Civil War
ISBN 0-7894-6302-4; 0-7894-6988-X (lib bdg)
LC 00-20431

Stanchak, John E.—*Continued*

Examines many aspects of the Civil War, including the issue of slavery, secession, the raising of armies, individual battles, the commanders, Northern life, Confederate culture, the surrender of the South, and the aftermath

This "offers a stunning array of reproductions and photographs of the sites, people, and artifacts associated with the war. . . . A paragraph of text introduces each topic and informative, often lengthy, captions accompany the numerous black-and-white and full-color illustrations." SLJ

Stark, Ken

Marching to Appomattox; the footrace that ended the Civil War; [by] Ken Stark. G.P. Putnam's Sons 2009 unp il $17.99

Grades: 3 4 5   **973.7**

1. Lee, Robert E. (Robert Edward), 1807-1870 2. Grant, Ulysses S. (Ulysses Simpson), 1822-1885 3. Appomattox Campaign, 1865 4. United States—History—1861-1865, Civil War

ISBN 978-0-399-24212-0; 0-399-24212-0

LC 2008012551

"The beginning of April 1865 was a pivotal time in the Civil War. Following a defeat at Richmond, VA, the Confederate forces tried to outrun the Union troops and get to waiting reinforcements in North Carolina. Instead, Lee's men ended up trapped by General Grant's army. The week culminated with Lee's surrender at Appomattox Court House. Stark frames this war vignette effectively for young readers. . . . The illustrations are a great strength. Rendered in watercolor, the inclusion of gouache and casein gives the hues a vividness and depth not always associated with the medium." SLJ

Includes bibliographical references

Williams, Carla, 1965-

The Underground Railroad. Child's World 2009 32p il (Journey to freedom) lib bdg $28.50

Grades: 4 5 6   **973.7**

1. Underground railroad 2. Slavery—United States

ISBN 978-1-60253-139-0 (lib bdg); 1-60253-139-0 (lib bdg)   LC 2008031946

"*Underground Railroad* describes how this secret system worked and introduces key figures. Williams discusses relevant laws and amendments as well as the advent and conclusion of the Civil War. The facts, presented through stories, historical news accounts, and biographical sketches of Harriet Tubman and Levi Weeks, capture the desperation of the enslaved as well as the abolitionists' commitment to them. The [book is] concise and direct, yet the writing remains sophisticated. Vibrant personal stories accompanied by striking photographs of historical figures and artifacts provide a sense of the subjects' hopes and dreams." SLJ

Includes glossary and bibliographical references

973.8   United States—Reconstruction period, 1865-1901

Custer, Elizabeth Bacon, 1842-1933

The diary of Elizabeth Bacon Custer; on the plains with General Custer; edited by Nancy Plain; illustrations and map by Laszlo Kubinyi. Benchmark Bks. 2004 95p il map (In my own words) lib bdg $18.95

Grades: 5 6 7 8   **973.8**

1. Custer, George Armstrong, 1839-1876 2. Native Americans—Wars

ISBN 0-7614-1647-1   LC 2003-1432

Presents the diary of the wife of General George Armstrong Custer, focusing on their life on the Great Plains from 1873 to 1876, when Custer and his Seventh Cavalry were clearing the way for the Northern Pacific Railroad and battling Native Americans

This offers "an engaging history lesson." Horn Book Guide

Includes glossary and bibliographical references

January, Brendan, 1972-

Little Bighorn, June 25, 1876. Enchanted Lion Books 2004 32p il map (American battlefields) $14.95

Grades: 5 6 7 8   **973.8**

1. Little Bighorn, Battle of the, 1876 2. Native Americans—Great Plains

ISBN 1-59270-028-4   LC 2003-64300

This "describes the Native American and U.S. Cavalry clashes at Little Bighorn: the history, the leaders and their actions on that day, and the aftermath of the battle. . . . The [text is] well written. . . . The books' many illustrations . . . include excellent reproductions of period photos, drawings, engravings, and paintings, along with clearly drawn maps and a few photos of sites." Booklist

Includes glossary and bibliographical references

Kupferberg, Audrey E.

The Spanish-American War; by Audrey Kupferberg. Blackbirch Press 2005 48p il (People at the center of) lib bdg $23.70

Grades: 5 6 7 8   **973.8**

1. Spanish-American War, 1898

ISBN 1-56711-924-7

This profiles 15 people connected with the Spanish-American War, such as Grover Cleveland, Clara Barton, Mark Twain, Theodore Roosevelt, and William McKinley

Stroud, Bettye, 1939-

The Reconstruction era; by Bettye M. Stroud with Virginia Schomp. Marshall Cavendish Benchmark 2007 70p il (Drama of African-American history) lib bdg $34.21

Grades: 5 6 7 8   **973.8**

1. Reconstruction (1865-1876) 2. African Americans—History

ISBN 978-0-7614-2181-8 (lib bdg); 0-7614-2181-5 (lib bdg)   LC 2006012149

Stroud, Bettye, 1939-—*Continued*

"Traces the history of Reconstruction, from the end of the Civil War in 1865 to 1877, when federal troops were removed from the South." Publisher's note

Includes glossary and bibliographical references

Uschan, Michael V., 1948-

The Battle of the Little Bighorn. World Almanac 2002 48p il map (Landmark events in American history) hardcover o.p. pa $11.95

Grades: 5 6 7 8   973.8

1. Custer, George Armstrong, 1839-1876 2. Little Bighorn, Battle of the, 1876

ISBN 0-8368-5338-5; 0-8368-5352-0 (pa)

LC 2002-24632

Describes the causes, events, and aftermath of the fateful encounter at the Little Bighorn River on June 25, 1876, between the Seventh Cavalry troops commanded by Lieutenant Colonel Custer and the Cheyenne and Lakota Sioux led by Chiefs Sitting Bull and Crazy Horse

The "design is attractive, with drawings, maps, paintings, and photos; primary sources, such as excerpts from diaries, letters, and newspapers, support and enhance the [text]." Booklist

Includes glossary and bibliographical references

Walker, Paul Robert

Remember Little Bighorn; Indians, soldiers, and scouts tell their stories; [by] Paul Robert Walker; [foreword by John A. Doerner] National Geographic Society 2006 61p il map $17.95; lib bdg $27.90 *

Grades: 5 6 7 8   973.8

1. Little Bighorn, Battle of the, 1876

ISBN 0-7922-5521-6; 0-7922-5522-4 (lib bdg)

LC 2005030929

This "volume gives an almost blow-by-blow account of the famous battle that came to be known as Custer's Last Stand. Walker concentrates on the battle itself, fought on the Great Plains in 1876, and the book includes diagrams of each side's tactics. . . . Walker's exhaustive research . . . [brings] together the conflicting viewpoints of the whites and the Lakota Sioux, Cheyenne, and Arapaho fighters, documenting everything in source notes. The handsome book design, with thick paper, clear type, maps, stirring photos, and archival images, will attract readers to the battle story and then start them thinking about lasting historical issues." Booklist

Includes bibliographical references

973.9 United States—1901-

Sandler, Martin W.

The Dust Bowl through the lens; how photography revealed and helped remedy a national disaster. Walker & Co. 2008 96p il map $15.99; lib bdg $20.89 *

Grades: 5 6 7 8   973.9

1. Dust storms 2. Great Plains—History 3. Documentary photography

ISBN 978-0-8027-9547-2; 0-8027-9547-1; 978-0-8027-9548-9 (lib bdg); 0-8027-9548-X (lib bdg)

LC 2008-55979

"This excellent photo-essay traces the history of the Dust Bowl from its causes to its resolution. In tandem, Sandler treats the role of the budding field of photojournalism. Forty-four spreads feature a page of clear, direct text with a large, well-reproduced image, many of which are set on color pages. . . . Seldom has the connection between the arts and the general quality of life been made so clear. The text deals equally with those who fled the decimated Bread Basket for California and those who waited out the devastation and dust. Throughout, the use of primary sources is superb, with quotations from affected citizens, the photojournalists themselves, political and entertainment figures, and writers, giving a multifaceted picture of a seminal time in United States history." SLJ

973.91 United States—1901-1953

Stanley, George Edward, 1942-

An emerging world power (1900-1929); [by] George E. Stanley. World Almanac Library 2005 48p il (Primary source history of the United States) lib bdg $30

Grades: 5 6 7 8   973.91

1. United States—Politics and government—1919-1933 2. United States—History—1919-1933 3. United States—Foreign relations

ISBN 0-8368-5828-X   LC 2004-61501

The author describes United States politics and foreign relations in the 1920s.

"Stanley explains and connects events utilizing clear language and a blending of text, images, and primary accounts. . . . Well-organized, highly attractive." SLJ

Includes bibliographical references

973.917 United States—Administration of Franklin D. Roosevelt, 1933-1945

Cooper, Michael L., 1950-

Dust to eat; drought and depression in the 1930's. Clarion Books 2004 81p il map $15 *

Grades: 4 5 6 7   973.917

1. Great Depression, 1929-1939 2. Migrant labor 3. Droughts

ISBN 0-618-15449-3   LC 2003-17807

Contents: The "Okie" problem; The dirty thirties; "Dust to eat, dust to breathe, dust to drink"; California-bound; Harvest gypsies; Crisis in the valley; World War II ends the Depression

This is a history of the Great Depression and the Dust Bowl drought of the 1930s that drove desperate families to California in search of work.

This includes "lots of stunning black-and-white archival photos and a clear, spacious text that draws on eloquent eyewitness reports—including comments from John Steinbeck and Woody Guthrie. . . . This is an excellent historical account." Booklist

Includes bibliographical references

973.92   United States—1953-2001

Anderson, Dale, 1953-
The Cold War years. Raintree Steck-Vaughn
Pubs. 2001 96p il (Making of America) lib bdg
$35.64
Grades: 5 6 7 8   **973.92**
1. Cold war 2. United States—History—1945-
3. United States—Social conditions
ISBN 0-8172-5711-X   LC 00-62827
This discusses factors that led to the Cold War and
the formation of alliances in reaction to it, as well as domestic issues such as the demand for equality for women
and African Americans
"Written in a clear and concise fashion [this book pro-
vides] . . . enough details to give a taste for the era
without overwhelming students." SLJ
Includes bibliographical references

Stanley, George Edward, 1942-
America in today's world (1969-2004); by
George E. Stanley. World Almanac Library 2005
48p il (Primary source history of the United
States) lib bdg $30; pa $14.05
Grades: 5 6 7 8   **973.92**
1. United States—Politics and government—1945-
2. United States—History—1945- 3. Presidents—United States
ISBN 0-8368-5831-X (lib bdg); 0-8368-5839-5 (pa)
This "covers the end of the Vietnam War through the
2004 presidential election. The terms of Presidents Nixon
through George W. Bush are highlighted through brief
but evenhanded descriptions of the major events of each
administration. . . . Well-organized, highly attractive."
SLJ
Includes bibliographical references

973.922   United States— Administration of John F. Kennedy, 1961-1963

Hampton, Wilborn
Kennedy assassinated! the world mourns: a
reporter's story. Candlewick Press 1997 96p il
$17.99 paperback o.p. *
Grades: 5 6 7 8 9   **973.922**
1. Kennedy, John F. (John Fitzgerald), 1917-1963—
Assassination 2. Journalism
ISBN 1-56402-811-9; 0-7636-1564-1 (pa)
                                        LC 96-25801
This is the author's "account of November 22, 1963,
when, as a cub reporter for UPI in Dallas, he was drafted
to cover JFK's assassination. His personal response to
the tragedy is fluidly juxtaposed with the nuts and bolts
of scooping the story in this insider's view of one of the
most pivotal events of our nation's recent history." Publ
Wkly
Includes bibliographical references

973.931   United States— Administration of George W. Bush, 2001-2009

Fradin, Dennis B.
September 11, 2001; by Dennis Brindell Fradin.
Marshall Cavendish Benchmark 2009 c2010 47p il
map (Turning points in U.S. history) lib bdg
$21.95
Grades: 3 4 5   **973.931**
1. September 11 terrorist attacks, 2001 2. War on terrorism 3. United States—Politics and government—
2001- 4. United States—Social conditions
ISBN 978-0-7614-4259-2 (lib bdg); 0-7614-4259-6 (lib
bdg)   LC 2008038267
"Covers the 9/11 terrorist attacks as a watershed event
in U.S. history, influencing social, economic, and political policies that shaped the nation's future." Publisher's
note
This book provides "accurate, nonsensationalized information in [a] well-organized, clearly written, and politically neutral [text]. The photos are crisp, and, due to
the subject matter, heartrending." SLJ
Includes glossary and bibliographical references

973.932   United States— Administration of Barack Obama, 2009-

Weatherford, Carole Boston, 1956-
First pooch; the Obamas pick a pet; Illustrated
by Amy Bates. Marshall Cavendish 2009 unp il
$16.99
Grades: PreK K 1 2   **973.932**
1. Obama, Barack, 1961- 2. Dogs 3. Presidents—United States—Family
ISBN 978-0-7614-5636-0; 0-7614-5636-8
                                   LC 2009006117
"This brief, lighthearted chronicle of the Obama family's search for a suitable puppy to fulfill candidate
Obama's promise to his daughters focuses on Malia and
Sasha. But it also brings in information about promises
made by previous presidents, various breeds of dogs that
lived in the White House, whimsical duties of a first
dog. . . . Lively watercolor, pencil, and gouache illustrations featuring a smiling Obama family happy in their
endeavors, portraits of select past presidents, and a lineup
of adorable potential first pooches add to the telling."
Booklist

974   Northeastern United States

Rylant, Cynthia
Appalachia; the voices of sleeping birds;
illustrated by Barry Moser. Harcourt Brace
Jovanovich 1991 21p il $17; pa $6 *
Grades: 4 5 6 7   **974**
1. Appalachian region
ISBN 0-15-201605-8; 0-15-201893-X (pa)
                                    LC 90-36798

Rylant, Cynthia—*Continued*

"This is a running narrative description of the dogs, people, houses, seasons, and lifestyles of Appalachia." Bull Cent Child Books

"Taking her subtitle from a passage by James Agee, the author conveys with a marvelous economy of words the essence of the very special part of America where she was raised. A poetic text projects emotion as well as information. . . . Moser's watercolors capture the scene perfectly. . . . The book is a treasure—simply a beautiful combination of text and art." Horn Book

974.4   Massachusetts

Armentrout, David, 1962-

The Mayflower Compact; [by] David & Patricia Armentrout. Rourke Pub. 2005 48p il map (Documents that shaped the nation) $29.93 paperback o.p.

Grades: 4 5 6 7   **974.4**
  1. Mayflower (Ship) 2. Pilgrims (New England colonists) 3. Massachusetts—History—1600-1775, Colonial period
  ISBN 1-59515-229-6; 1-59515-334-9 (pa)
                                        LC 2004-14413
Contents: The Pilgrims; Before the Pilgrims; The Church of England; The Scrooby separatists; William Bradford; Escape; Life in Holland; Choosing America; Merchant adventurers; Saints and strangers; A leaky mess; The Mayflower; Life at sea; Land!; The Mayflower Compact; A new settlement

The book introduces "the cultural and political factors that lead to the creation of [The Mayflower Compact], admirably distilling pertinent events into simple language that still manages to explain the complex issues and connections. . . . A wide mix of archival etchings, portraits, maps, and other images illustrate the [text]." Booklist

Includes glossary and bibliographical references

Fritz, Jean

Who's that stepping on Plymouth Rock? illustrated by J. B. Handelsman. Coward, McCann & Geoghegan 1975 30p il hardcover o.p. pa $6.99 *

Grades: 2 3 4   **974.4**
  1. Plymouth Rock
  ISBN 0-698-20325-9; 0-698-11681-X (pa)
An "account of the Rock which is visited yearly by about one and a half million people. It stands now under a monument on the waterfront of Plymouth, Massachusetts, sacred to the memory of the First Comers (Pilgrims) but it has figured in many adventures since the Pilgrims did—or did not—step upon it in 1620." Publ Wkly

"Both a delightful story and a perceptive commentary on how the mythmaking process works in American history." N Y Times Book Rev

Krensky, Stephen, 1953-

What's the big idea? four centuries of innovation in Boston; [by] Stephen Krensky. Charlesbridge 2008 64p il lib bdg $18.95; pa $9.95

Grades: 4 5 6   **974.4**
  1. Boston (Mass.)—History
  ISBN 978-1-58089-310-7 (lib bdg); 1-58089-310-4 (lib bdg); 978-1-58089-311-4 (pa); 1-58089-311-2 (pa)
                                        LC 2006021255
This "title combines a short history of Boston with brief biographies of some of the city's major figures in diverse fields. . . . Each page includes a well-captioned illustration, many in color, and the book is effectively laid out, making for pleasant browsing. . . . Teachers and students . . . will find some well-presented and useful information here." Booklist

Includes bibliographical references

Sewall, Marcia, 1935-

The pilgrims of Plimoth; written and illustrated by Marcia Sewall. Atheneum Pubs. 1986 48p il hardcover o.p. pa $6.99 *

Grades: 3 4 5 6   **974.4**
  1. Pilgrims (New England colonists)
  2. Massachusetts—History—1600-1775, Colonial period
  ISBN 0-689-31250-4; 0-689-80861-5 (pa)
                                        LC 86-3362
The author provides a "first-person narrative account of the Mayflower voyage of 1620 and the early years of the Plymouth colony. This is not the personal diary of an individual, but rather a journal of the community." Booklist

"Translating narrative and descriptive details into visual images, the illustrations accompany every page of text, occasionally overspreading double pages for panoramic effects. Combining subtle, modulating color with a spiritual as well as an actual luminosity, the paintings—done in gouache—are vibrant with the daily pulse of life among an energetic, enterprising people." Horn Book

Waters, Kate

Sarah Morton's day; a day in the life of a pilgrim girl; photographs by Russ Kendall. Scholastic 1989 32p il hardcover o.p. pa $5.99

Grades: 2 3 4   **974.4**
  1. Pilgrims (New England colonists)
  2. Massachusetts—History—1600-1775, Colonial period
  ISBN 0-590-42634-6; 0-590-47400-6 (pa)
                                        LC 88-35581
Text and photographs of Plimoth Plantation follow a pilgrim girl through a typical day as she milks the goats, cooks and serves meals, learns her letters, and adjusts to her new stepfather

Includes glossary

Yero, Judith Lloyd
The Mayflower Compact. National Geographic
2006 40p il (American documents) $15.95; lib bdg
$23.90
Grades: 3 4 5 6   **974.4**
   1. Mayflower Compact (1620) 2. Pilgrims (New England colonists) 3. Massachusetts—History—1600-
1775, Colonial period
   ISBN 0-7922-5891-6; 0-7922-5892-4 (lib bdg)
"Yero gently strips away layers of myth about the
landfall of the *Mayflower* and that first Thanksgiving. At
the same time, she provides a stirring account of what
did happen, and some of the consequences. . . .
Sidebars, period images, and photographs add interest to
an already compelling narrative." Booklist

974.7   New York

Bauer, Marion Dane, 1938-
The Statue of Liberty; illustrated by John
Wallace. Aladdin 2007 32p il (Ready-to-read:
Wonders of America) lib bdg $13.89; pa $3.99 *
Grades: K 1 2   **974.7**
   1. Statue of Liberty (New York, N.Y.)
   ISBN 978-1-4169-3480-6 (lib bdg); 1-4169-3480-4 (lib
bdg); 978-1-4169-3479-0 (pa); 1-4169-3479-0 (pa)
                LC 2006036917
"The story of how the Statue of Liberty came to the
United States, who constructed it, and how
schoolchildren throughout America contributed to the
building of its foundation is told in easy-to-read sentences. Some sophisticated vocabulary . . . may challenge readers, but unfussy watercolor illustrations support
the text with picture clues." Horn Book Guide

Bial, Raymond
Tenement; immigrant life on the Lower East
Side. Houghton Mifflin 2002 48p il $16 *
Grades: 4 5 6 7   **974.7**
   1. Poor 2. Immigrants—United States 3. Lower East
Side (New York, N.Y.)
   ISBN 0-618-13849-8   LC 2002-00407
Presents a view of New York City's tenements during
the peak years of foreign immigration, discussing living
conditions, laws pertaining to tenements, and the occupa-
tions of their residents
"The writing is particularly clear and sharp. Calling
upon and quoting the writing of reformer Jacob Riis (and
featuring his compelling photographs), Bial explains simply, yet engagingly, what tenement life was like. . . .
Along with Riis' photographs, Bial provides some of his
own, taken at the Lower East Side Tenement Museum in
New York City." Booklist
   Includes bibliographical references

Curlee, Lynn, 1947-
Liberty. Atheneum Bks. for Young Readers
2000 41p hardcover o.p. pa $7.99
Grades: 3 4 5 6   **974.7**
   1. Bartholdi, Frédéric Auguste, 1834-1904 2. Statue of
Liberty (New York, N.Y.)
   ISBN 0-689-82823-3; 0-689-85683-0 (pa)
                LC 98-44732

The author narrates the "story of Liberty's creation,
from its conception by French professor Édouard de
Laboulaye (who proposed the idea at a dinner party attended by young sculptor Frédéric-Auguste Bartholdi) to
the fulfillment of Bartholdi's obsession to create a monument to liberty that would rival the Colossus of Rhodes."
Horn Book
"Curlee's illustrations—bold, bright full-page acrylic
paintings, most dramatically composed—are helpful in
conveying technical details and in portraying the various
stages in the creation of the statue. But they are also
quite beautiful, for they communicate not just information but also excitement and sentiment." N Y Times
Book Rev
   Includes bibliographical references

Englar, Mary
Dutch colonies in America. Compass Point
Books 2009 48p il map (We the people) lib bdg
$26.60
Grades: 4 5 6   **974.7**
   1. New York (State)—History—1600-1775, Colonial
period 2. Dutch Americans
   ISBN 978-0-7565-3837-8   LC 2008007211
This is a history of Dutch exploration and colonization
in North America.
"This provides "solid background matter and [intro-
duces] key people and vocabulary." SLJ
   Includes glossary and bibliographical references

Glaser, Linda
Emma's poem; the voice of the Statue of
Liberty; with paintings by Claire A. Nivola.
Houghton Mifflin Books for Children 2010 unp il
$16 *
Grades: K 1 2 3   **974.7**
   1. Lazarus, Emma, 1849-1887 2. Statue of Liberty
(New York, N.Y.) 3. Immigrants—United States
   ISBN 978-0-5471-7184-5; 0-5471-7184-6
"The art and words are moving in this picture book,
which pairs free verse with detailed, full-page paintings
in watercolor, ink, and gouache to tell the history behind
Lazarus' famous inscription on the Statue of Liberty."
Booklist

Hopkinson, Deborah
Shutting out the sky; life in the tenements of
New York, 1880-1924. Orchard Bks. 2003 134p il
$17.95 *
Grades: 5 6 7 8 9 10   **974.7**
   1. Poor 2. Immigrants—United States 3. Lower East
Side (New York, N.Y.)
   ISBN 0-439-37590-8   LC 2002-44781
   Contents: Coming to the golden land; Tenements:
shutting out the sky; Settling in: greenhorns and board-
ers; Everyone worked on; On the streets: pushcarts, pick-
les and play; A new language, a new life; Looking to the
future: will it ever be different?
Photographs and text document the experiences of five
individuals who came to live in the Lower East Side of
New York City as children or young adults from
Belarus, Italy, Lithuania, and Romania at the turn of the

Hopkinson, Deborah—*Continued*

twentieth century.

"The text is supported by numerous tinted archival photos of living and working conditions. Although this book will appeal to students looking for material for projects, the writing lends immediacy and vivid images make it simply a fascinating read." SLJ

Includes bibliographical references

Huey, Lois Miner

American archaeology uncovers the Dutch colonies. Marshall Cavendish Benchmark 2009 c2010 64p il map (American archaeology) lib bdg $21.95

Grades: 4 5 6 7   **974.7**

    1. Netherlands—Colonies—America 2. Dutch Americans 3. America—Antiquities 4. Excavations (Archeology)—United States

    ISBN 978-0-7614-4263-9 (lib bdg); 0-7614-4263-4 (lib bdg)   LC 2008050187

This describes how archeologists have learned about the history of Dutch settlers in America

"The text is quite chatty in this attractive title. . . . An inviting design with clear type includes several paintings of the period by a modern artist as well as maps and photos of excavation sites." Booklist

Includes glossary and bibliographical references

Kalman, Maira

Fireboat; the heroic adventures of the John J. Harvey. Putnam 2002 unp il $16.99 *

Grades: K 1 2 3   **974.7**

    1. John J. Harvey (Fireboat) 2. September 11 terrorist attacks, 2001

    ISBN 0-399-23953-7   LC 2002-2423

A fireboat, launched in 1931, is retired after many years of fighting fires along the Hudson River, but is saved from being scrapped and then called into service again on September 11, 2001

"Among the many literary tributes to 9-11 heroism, Kalman's is particularly exciting, uplifting, and child-sensitive." Bull Cent Child Books

Maestro, Betsy, 1944-

The story of the Statue of Liberty; [by] Betsy & Giulio Maestro. Lothrop, Lee & Shepard Bks. 1986 39p il pa $5.95 hardcover o.p.

Grades: K 1 2 3   **974.7**

    1. Bartholdi, Frédéric Auguste, 1834-1904 2. Statue of Liberty (New York, N.Y.)

    ISBN 0-688-08746-9 (pa)   LC 85-11324

"Although Maestro simplifies the story—including only the most important people's names, for example—she still presents an accurate account of what happened. The exceptional drawings are visually delightful—primarily in the blue-green range, although they are in full color—and cover most of every page. Human figures—workers, tourists—are included in many drawings, indicating the statue's tremendous scale. Further, the drawings involve viewers through the use of unusual perspectives and angles and by placing the statue in scenes of city life." SLJ

Includes bibliographical references

Matsen, Bradford

Go wild in New York City; [by] Brad Matsen; illustrations by Paul Corio; scientific illustration by Kate Lake. National Geographic 2005 79p il map $16.95

Grades: 4 5 6 7   **974.7**

    1. Natural history 2. New York (N.Y.)

    ISBN 0-7922-7982-4

This is a "picture-book tour through New York City's 'true wildness,' with chapters that cover the area's water, rocks, air, plants, and animals as well as a closing section about food production and waste removal. . . . Packed with color photographs, cartoons, diagrams, and numerous sidebars. . . . There's an impressive array of basic science here, described mostly in accessible, enthusiastic text. Students will find enough to support reports, and the open format will attract browsers." Booklist

Melmed, Laura Krauss

New York, New York; the Big Apple from A to Z; illustrated by Frané Lessac. HarperCollins Pub. 2005 unp il $16.99; lib bdg $17.89; pa $6.99

Grades: K 1 2 3   **974.7**

    1. New York (N.Y.) 2. Alphabet

    ISBN 0-06-054674-6; 0-06-054876-2 (lib bdg); 0-06-054877-0 (pa)

"From the American Museum of Natural History to the Bronx Zoo, each letter is accompanied by a peppy eight-line poem as well as multiple sidebars, factoids, and tidbits about the sights described. Melmed brilliantly touches on all the major sights of NYC." SLJ

Rappaport, Doreen, 1939-

Lady Liberty; a biography; illustrated by Matt Tavares. Candlewick Press 2008 unp il $17.99 *

Grades: 2 3 4 5   **974.7**

    1. Statue of Liberty (New York, N.Y.)

    ISBN 978-0-7636-2530-6; 0-7636-2530-2

    LC 2007-40723

This presents the story of the Statue of Liberty including "its conception and construction in France, the efforts to raise funds on both sides of the Atlantic, preparations for her arrival in New York, and the celebration culminating in her unveiling in 1886. Rappaport tells the story in a series of free-verse poems representing the reflections of individuals. . . . The first-person narratives effectively convey the personal significance the statue has had for many people. Large in scale and monumental in effect, the watercolor, ink, and pencil illustrations . . . offer often beautiful views of her many-faceted story." Booklist

Includes bibliographical references

Shea, Pegi Deitz, 1960-

Liberty rising; the story of the Statue of Liberty; illustrated by Wade Zahares. Henry Holt 2005 unp il $17.95 *

Grades: 2 3 4   **974.7**

    1. Bartholdi, Frédéric Auguste, 1834-1904 2. Statue of Liberty (New York, N.Y.)

    ISBN 0-8050-7220-9   LC 2004-24279

Shea, Pegi Deitz, 1960-—*Continued*

In this account of the building of the Statue of Liberty "Shea introduces the size and scale of creating such a large object. . . . Each step in the process . . . is told in simple text. . . . The book is easy to read, with three-quarter spreads of illustration and single columns of text. The stylized graphic art is fairly realistic with bold colors and unusual angles to create a sense of excitement." SLJ

Includes bibliographical references

Talbott, Hudson

River of dreams; the story of the Hudson River. G. P. Putnam's Sons 2009 unp il map $17.99 *

Grades: 4 5 6 7   974.7

1. Hudson River (N.Y. and N.J.)

ISBN 978-0-399-24521-3; 0-399-24521-9

Talbott offers a "compelling blend of political and natural history in this beautifully illustrated celebration of the Hudson River. Combining delicate watercolor-and-pencil illustrations with accessible text, the spreads move briskly through the Hudson's River's history." Booklist

Vila, Laura

Building Manhattan. Viking 2008 unp il $16.99 *

Grades: K 1 2 3   974.7

1. Manhattan (New York, N.Y.) 2. New York (N.Y.)—History

ISBN 978-0-670-06284-3; 0-670-06284-7

LC 2007-38119

"Tracing the growth of Manhattan from a time 'before maps or words were used' to the present day, . . . author/artist Vila employs many lenses—geography, sociology, politics, ethnography. Likewise, her radiantly dramatic mural-like paintings present a wide range of visual styles and approaches. . . . While her paintings are lavish, it takes her only one pithy sentence on each spread to convey both a specific moment and a sense of history and human ambitions." Publ Wkly

974.8   Pennsylvania

Magaziner, Henry J.

Our Liberty Bell; by Henry Jonas Magaziner; illustrated by John O'Brien. Holiday House 2007 32p il $15.95; pa $5.95 *

Grades: 2 3 4   974.8

1. Liberty Bell

ISBN   978-0-8234-1892-3;   0-8234-1892-8; 978-0-8234-2081-0 (pa); 0-8234-2081-7 (pa)

LC 2004054196

This is the "story of the Liberty Bell—from its humble beginnings to its prominence as a lasting symbol of American freedom." Publisher's note

"Written with clarity and verve. . . . O'Brien's imaginative and sometimes witty ink drawings illustrate with finesse." Booklist

Includes glossary and bibliographical references

Staton, Hilarie

Independence Hall. Chelsea Clubhouse 2010 48p il (Symbols of American freedom) $30

Grades: 3 4 5   974.8

1. Independence Hall (Philadelphia, Pa.) 2. United States—Politics and government—1775-1783, Revolution 3. United States—Politics and government—1783-1809 4. Philadelphia (Pa.)

ISBN 978-1-60413-521-3; 1-60413-521-2

LC 2009-12824

This book about Independence Hall in Philedelphia "provides nearly as much information as a guided tour by a park ranger. [It begins] with the story of how the place came to be, and where it fits into U.S. history. Information boxes offer additional background and some surprising facts. . . . The final chapter shows the landmark today and includes maps and photographs of the visitors' center and some of the things individuals might see or do while visiting the site. Much information is packed into [this] slim [book]. Excellent . . . for state reports or to complement U.S. history units." SLJ

Includes glossary

975.3   District of Columbia (Washington)

Ashabranner, Brent K., 1921-

No better hope; what the Lincoln Memorial means to America; [by] Brent Ashabranner; photographs by Jennifer Ashabranner. 21st Cent. Bks. (Brookfield) 2001 64p il (Great American memorials) lib bdg $25.90 *

Grades: 4 5 6 7   975.3

1. Lincoln, Abraham, 1809-1865 2. Lincoln Memorial (Washington, D.C.)

ISBN 0-7613-1523-3   LC 00-61546

"Seven brief chapters review Lincoln's presidency, discuss preliminary plans for a permanent memorial, describe the processes by which architect Henry Bacon and sculptor Daniel French developed and executed their creation, and suggest how the site has 'become a symbol of the 'patient confidence' that Lincoln had in the wisdom and courage of the common people.'" Bull Cent Child Books

A "well-designed volume. . . . Excellent color photographs by Jennifer Ashabranner appear throughout the book." Booklist

Includes bibliographical references

Curlee, Lynn, 1947-

Capital. Atheneum Bks. for Young Readers 2003 40p il map hardcover o.p. pa $7.99 *

Grades: 3 4 5 6   975.3

1. National monuments 2. Washington (D.C.)

ISBN 0-689-84947-8; 1-4169-1801-9 (pa)

LC 2001-56083

Provides a history of Washington, D.C., focusing on the National Mall, its monuments and surrounding buildings

"Curlee brings history to life with small details and historical incidents. . . . With clean lines, muted colors, dramatic lighting, and dignified compositions, Curlee's

Curlee, Lynn, 1947-—*Continued*

acrylic art faithfully represents these structures, while placing them within a human context." Booklist

Includes bibliographical references

Grace, Catherine O'Neill, 1950-

The White House; an illustrated history. Scholastic 2003 144p il $19.95

Grades: 3 4 5 6   **975.3**

1. White House (Washington, D.C.)

ISBN 0-439-42971-4   LC 2002-30603

Explores the history, architecture, and symbolism of the White House, which serves as a museum, office, ceremonial site, and a home to presidents and their families.

"Published in cooperation with the White House Historical Association, this is a fascinating and beautifully produced gem. . . . This accessible volume is filled with many interesting facts, and is a handsomely designed tribute." SLJ

Includes bibliographical references

Our White House; looking in, looking out; created by The National Children's Book and Literacy Alliance; introduction by David McCullough. Candlewick Press 2008 241p il $29.99 *

Grades: 5 6 7 8   **975.3**

1. White House (Washington, D.C.)

ISBN 978-0-7636-2067-7; 0-7636-2067-X

"The White House is the focus of this handsome, large-format compendium of writings, both factual and fictional, and illustrations. . . . Poems and essays, stories and memoirs—all combine to create a mosaic of impressions of the house's residents and visitors and of the important events that occurred there. . . . The often-spectacular, beautifully reproduced on glossy paper, is particularly striking." Booklist

Rinaldo, Denise

White House Q & A. Smithsonian/Collins 2008 47p il (Smithsonian Q & A) lib bdg $16.99; pa $7.99

Grades: 3 4 5   **975.3**

1. White House (Washington, D.C.) 2. Presidents—United States 3. Washington (D.C.)

ISBN 978-0-06-089966-0 (lib bdg); 0-06-089966-2 (lib bdg); 978-0-06-089965-3 (pa); 0-06-089965-4 (pa)

LC 2006102994

"The history and functions of the presidential residence are unveiled in the typical series format. The questions are organized so that the story of the White House unfolds logically—first with a definition of what it is, how it came to be, some of its history, how to visit, special rooms, and, of course, a look at how the first families live. Anecdotes are plentiful and child-centered. . . . The elegant page layout includes full-color, full-bleed illustrations from Smithsonian archives and some presidential libraries." SLJ

Includes glossary and bibliographical references

975.5   Virginia

Chorao, Kay, 1936-

D is for drums; a Colonial Williamsburg ABC; [by] Kay Chorao. Harry N. Abrams 2004 unp il $16.95

Grades: K 1 2 3   **975.5**

1. Colonial Williamsburg (Williamsburg, Va.) 2. Alphabet

ISBN 0-8109-4927-X   LC 2003-25793

"Chorao has created a large, visually charming, and fact-rich look at Colonial Williamsburg. Endpaper maps of the city's streets show everything from a shoemaker's shop to the Governor's Palace. Each page in between displays a huge capital letter decorated with drawings that showcase an alliterative list of words. . . . Chorao selected items to foster chuckles and amazement. Her pen-and-ink and watercolor drawings of children and animals add energy to the stunning layouts." SLJ

Lange, Karen E.

1607; a new look at Jamestown; photography by Ira Block. National Geographic 2007 48p il $17.95; lib bdg $27.90 *

Grades: 3 4 5 6   **975.5**

1. Jamestown (Va.)—History 2. Virginia—History 3. United States—History—1600-1775, Colonial period

ISBN 1-4263-0012-3; 1-4263-0013-1 (lib bdg)

LC 2006-05824

"In 1994, scientists unearthed important new evidence about the original Jamestown fort. The work . . . has changed many established ideas about the early settlers. *1607* incorporates these findings and offers a fascinating look at archaeology in action. Color photographs of costumed interpreters and recreated buildings from the Jamestown Settlement living-history museum depict both English and Native American ways of life." SLJ

Richards, Norman, 1932-

Monticello. Children's Press 1995 30p il (Cornerstones of freedom) lib bdg $20.50; pa $5.95

Grades: 4 5 6   **975.5**

1. Jefferson, Thomas, 1743-1826—Homes and haunts

ISBN 0-516-06695-1 (lib bdg); 0-516-46695-X (pa)

LC 94-35654

A revised and newly illustrated edition of The story of Monticello, published 1970

The construction and furnishing of the home of Thomas Jefferson "are described as they relate to the events of Jefferson's life and to the founding of our country. The well-written text is handsomely enhanced by full-color and black-and-white photographs and illustrations of the house, gardens, and Jefferson's inventions. His beliefs and feelings about slavery are briefly discussed." SLJ

Rosen, Daniel

New beginnings; Jamestown and the Virginia Colony, 1607-1699; [by] Daniel Rosen. National Geographic 2005 40p il map (Crossroads America) $12.95; lib bdg $21.90 *

Grades: 4 5 6   **975.5**
    1. Jamestown (Va.)—History 2. Virginia—History 3. United States—History—1600-1775, Colonial period
    ISBN 0-7922-8277-9; 0-7922-8335-7 (lib bdg)
                                    LC 2004007101
First published 2004 with title: Jamestown and the Viriginia Colony

This describes colonial Virginia, from the founding of Jamestown to the building of Williamsburg

This "solid [title] for report writers may even pull in a few curious browsers because of [its] plentiful, full-color photos and reproductions. The [layout is] inviting, and the [text is] clear, informative, and readable." SLJ
    Includes glossary

Sewall, Marcia, 1935-

James Towne: struggle for survival; written and illustrated by Marcia Sewall. Atheneum Bks. for Young Readers 2001 40p il $16

Grades: 3 4 5   **975.5**
    1. Jamestown (Va.)—History 2. Virginia—History 3. United States—History—1600-1775, Colonial period
    ISBN 0-689-81814-9   LC 99-32167
"The story of the first permanent English settlement in North America is narrated here by an 18-year-old carpenter who in 1607, along with 104 other Englishmen established the colony of Jamestown, Virginia." Booklist

"Sewall's art . . . is subtle, thoughtful, and dignified. It appeals to the intellect, not to raw emotion, yet is moving and evocative—like the text." Horn Book
    Includes glossary and bibliographical references

975.6   North Carolina

Fritz, Jean

The Lost Colony of Roanoke; illustrated by Hudson Talbott. G.P. Putnam's Sons 2004 58p il map $16.99 *

Grades: 3 4 5 6   **975.6**
    1. Roanoke Island (N.C.)—History
    ISBN 0-399-24027-6   LC 2002-152000
Describes the English colony of Roanoke, which was founded in 1585, and discusses the mystery of its disappearance.

"Talbott's softly colored watercolor illustrations . . . are at once detailed and impressionistic. Clever touches of humor abound. . . . Fritz has scored again, making history breathe while showing both historians and archaeologists at their reconstructive best." SLJ

Miller, Lee

Roanoke; the mystery of the Lost Colony. Scholastic Nonfiction 2007 112p il map $18.99

Grades: 4 5 6 7   **975.6**
    1. Roanoke Island (N.C.)—History 2. United States—History—1600-1775, Colonial period
    ISBN 0-439-71266-1; 978-0-439-71266-8
                                    LC 2005-51820
"Miller, author of *Roanoke: solving the mystery of the Lost Colony* (2001), here reprises for a young audience her historical theory that a certain man sabotaged the expedition eventually known as the Lost Colony. . . . Miller does an exceptional job of preseneting the Native American culture and viewpoint. . . . This handsomely designed book features one or two illustrations on each spread, many in color, including reproductions or period drawings, paintings, and maps, as well as modern photos of sites and wildlife." Booklist
    Includes bibliographical references

Reed, Jennifer

Cape Hatteras National Seashore; adventure, explore, discover; [by] Jennifer Reed. MyReportLinks.com Books 2008 128p il map (America's national parks) lib bdg $33.27

Grades: 5 6 7 8   **975.6**
    1. National parks and reserves—United States 2. Cape Hatteras National Seashore (N.C.)
    ISBN 978-1-59845-086-6 (lib bdg); 1-59845-086-7 (lib bdg)   LC 2006102321
This "informative, well-written book contains a physical description of the park; a summary of its history including the Native peoples of the area; activities such as hiking trails, campsites, and visitor centers; information about the park's plants, animals, and weather; full-color photographs; and numerous approved links available through the publisher's Web page. . . . Thorough, useful, and appealing, this . . . is a great update for collections." SLJ
    Includes glossary and bibliographical references

975.9   Florida

George, Jean Craighead, 1919-

Everglades; paintings by Wendell Minor. HarperCollins Pubs. 1995 unp il hardcover o.p. pa $6.95 *

Grades: 2 3 4   **975.9**
    1. Everglades (Fla.)
    ISBN 0-06-021228-4; 0-06-446194-7 (pa)
                                    LC 92-9517
"Though structured as a tale told to five children whom a storyteller has poled into the Everglades, the narrative focuses on the history of that unusual ecosystem. The narrator tells how the Everglades became 'a living kaleidoscope of color and beauty,' filled with plants and animals, and how human involvement has changed the ecology, devastating the area. . . . When the children ask about what happened to the orchids, egrets, and alligators, the storyteller suggests that they can make a happy ending to the story when they grow up." Booklist

"The story and the art create a mystical tale that flows from a serene start to a powerful conclusion." SLJ

Jankowski, Susan

Everglades National Park; adventure, explore, discover; [by] Susan Jankowski. MyReportLinks.com Books 2009 128p il map (America's national parks) lib bdg $33.27

Grades: 5 6 7 8   **975.9**

1. National parks and reserves—United States 2. Everglades National Park (Fla.)

ISBN 978-1-59845-091-0 (lib bdg); 1-59845-091-3 (lib bdg)   LC 2007-38262

This "informative, well-written book contains a physical description of the park; a summary of its history including the Native peoples of the area; activities such as hiking trails, campsites, and visitor centers; information about the park's plants, animals, and weather; full-color photographs; and numerous approved links available through the publisher's Web page. . . . Thorough, useful, and appealing, this . . . is a great update for collections." SLJ

Includes glossary and bibliographical references

976.4   Texas

Fradin, Dennis B.

The Alamo; [by] Dennis Brindell Fradin. Marshall Cavendish Benchmark 2007 45p il map (Turning points in U.S. history) lib bdg $29.93

Grades: 3 4 5   **976.4**

1. Alamo (San Antonio, Tex.) 2. Texas—History

ISBN 978-0-7614-2127-6 (lib bdg); 0-7614-2127-0 (lib bdg)   LC 2005016022

This "includes the background to the battle, as well as an account of its aftermath and some information on famous combatants. . . . The clear, concise, and dynamic style of writing simplifies the information without dumbing it down. . . . The photos, paintings, and maps . . . add a wealth of information." SLJ

Includes glossary and bibliographical references

Lourie, Peter

Rio Grande; from the Rocky Mountains to the Gulf of Mexico. Boyds Mills Press 1999 46p il $17.95; pa $9.95

Grades: 4 5 6 7   **976.4**

1. Rio Grande valley

ISBN 1-56397-706-0; 1-56397-896-2 (pa)   LC 97-77907

The author "reports on his 1,900-mile journey down the Rio Grande, from its headwaters near a former silver town in Colorado to its inconspicuous outlet into the Gulf. In dramatic prose . . . he not only describes the passing scenery but also evokes some of its colorful history. . . . Unusually well-chosen photographs enhance the connections between the river's past and present with a mix of historical shots, new portraits, and landscapes in sharp color, and even a satellite picture." Booklist

Melmed, Laura Krauss

Heart of Texas; a Lone Star ABC; Illustrated by Frané Lessac. Collins 2009 unp il $17.99; lib bdg $18.89

Grades: 1 2 3 4   **976.4**

1. Texas 2. Alphabet

ISBN 978-0-06-114283-3; 0-06-114283-2; 978-0-06-114285-7 (lib bdg); 0-06-114285-9 (lib bdg)   LC 2008026948

"From Alamo to Ziller Park, Melmed and Lessac provide a tour of places to visit, people to know, and historic events to remember about Texas. Each entry begins with an eight-line poem with an impeccable rhythmic beat that slips off the tongue for reading aloud. . . . [Lessac's] detailed and colorful folk art perfectly conveys the multicultural panorama of the second-largest state." Booklist

Spradlin, Michael P.

Texas Rangers; legendary lawmen; [by] Michael P. Spradlin; illustrations by Roxie Munro. Walker & Co. 2008 unp il $16.95; lib bdg $17.85

Grades: 2 3 4   **976.4**

1. Texas Rangers 2. West (U.S.)—History 3. Texas—History 4. Frontier and pioneer life

ISBN 978-0-8027-8096-6; 0-8027-8096-2; 978-0-8027-8097-3 (lib bdg); 0-8027-8097-0 (lib bdg)   LC 2007020139

"This picture-book account of the nearly 200-year history of the Texas Rangers begins in 1823. . . . The bulk of the book covers the 1800s, when the Rangers fought Indian tribes; participated in the war against Mexico; and defended settlers from bank robbers, cattle rustlers, and horse thieves. . . . There is a brief section on modern Rangers. . . . Munro's colorful illustrations provide a look at the lawmen, depict the action and locales, and portray the changing times. They're sure to entice youngsters and keep them turning the pages." SLJ

Walker, Paul Robert

Remember the Alamo; Texians, Tejanos, and Mexicans tell their stories; by Paul Robert Walker. National Geographic 2007 61p il map $17.95; lib bdg $27.90 *

Grades: 5 6 7 8   **976.4**

1. Alamo (San Antonio, Tex.) 2. Texas—History

ISBN 978-1-4263-0010-3; 978-1-4263-0011-0 (lib bdg)   LC 2006034497

"Opening with clear context about why tensions between Texas residents and the Mexican government were brought to a head, the book then chronicles events directly leading to the siege of the Alamo and its immediate aftermath, following up with an epilogue on the decisive battle of San Jacinto 10 months later. Bringing the history to life is a healthy selection of dramatic, modern paintings along with plenty of archival drawings, maps, and old photos." Booklist

Includes bibliographical references

976.8   Tennessee

Graham, Amy
Great Smoky Mountains National Park; adventure, explore, discover; [by] Amy Graham. MyReportLinks.com Books 2009 128p il map (America's national parks) lib bdg $33.27
Grades: 5 6 7 8   **976.8**
  1. National parks and reserves—United States 2. Great Smoky Mountains National Park (N.C. and Tenn.)
  ISBN 978-1-59845-093-4 (lib bdg); 1-59845-093-X (lib bdg)   LC 2007-13456
This "informative, well-written book contains a physical description of the park; a summary of its history including the Native peoples of the area; activities such as hiking trails, campsites, and visitor centers; information about the park's plants, animals, and weather; full-color photographs; and numerous approved links available through the publisher's Web page. . . . Thorough, useful, and appealing, this . . . is a great update for collections." SLJ
Includes glossary and bibliographical references

977   North Central United States. Lake states

Kummer, Patricia K.
The Great Lakes; [by] Patricia K. Kummer. Marshall Cavendish Benchmark 2008 c2009 96p il map (Nature's wonders) lib bdg $35.64
Grades: 5 6 7 8   **977**
  1. Great Lakes
  ISBN 978-0-7614-2853-4 (lib bdg); 0-7614-2853-4 (lib bdg)   LC 2007019728
"Provides comprehensive information on the geography, history, wildlife, peoples, and environmental issues of the Great Lakes." Publisher's note
Includes glossary and bibliographical references

977.3   Illinois

Hurd, Owen
Chicago history for kids; triumphs and tragedies of the Windy city, includes 21 activities; [by] Owen Hurd. Chicago Review Press 2007 182p il map $14.95
Grades: 5 6 7 8   **977.3**
  1. Chicago (Ill.)—History
  ISBN 978-1-55652-654-1; 1-55652-654-7
                       LC 2006031807
"This attractive overview begins with geography and moves to the colorful stories that characterize the city. Hurd tapped local experts and collections, using primary and secondary sources and the responses of young readers to craft this engaging resource. . . . Excellent-quality photos, maps, illustrations, or boxed facts appear on every page." SLJ
Includes bibliographical references

Murphy, Jim, 1947-
The great fire. Scholastic 1995 144p il maps $16.95 *
Grades: 5 6 7 8 9 10   **977.3**
  1. Fires—Chicago (Ill.)
  ISBN 0-590-47267-4   LC 94-9963
  Newbery honor book, 1996
"Firsthand descriptions by persons who lived through the 1871 Chicago fire are woven into a gripping account of this famous disaster. Murphy also examines the origins of the fire, the errors of judgment that delayed the effective response, the organizational problems of the city's firefighters, and the postfire efforts to rebuild the city. Newspaper lithographs and a few historical photographs convey the magnitude of human suffering and confusion." Horn Book Guide
Includes bibliographical references

977.8   Missouri

Bullard, Lisa, 1961-
The Gateway Arch. Lerner Publications 2010 32p il map (Lightning Bolt Books. Famous places) lib bdg $25.26
Grades: 2 3 4   **977.8**
  1. Gateway Arch (Saint Louis, Mo.) 2. Monuments
  ISBN 978-0-8225-9406-2; 0-8225-9406-4
                       LC 2008-30640
Discusses the history, design, and construction of the Gateway Arch in Saint Louis, Missouri.
This book uses "high-quality photos, illustrations, maps, and diagrams. . . . Readers will enjoy learning about [the Gateway Arch] . . . and the challenges of building and maintaining large structures." SLJ
Includes glossary and bibliographical references

978   Western United States

Bial, Raymond
Ghost towns of the American West. Houghton Mifflin 2001 48p il $16 *
Grades: 3 4 5 6   **978**
  1. Ghost towns 2. West (U.S.)—History
  ISBN 0-618-06557-1   LC 00-31895
"This photo-essay offers views of America's ghost towns and discusses their place in history. Several period photographs from the 1800s show these communities while they flourished, but the book's most effective illustrations are the evocative color photos of ghost towns today." Booklist
Includes bibliographical references

Blumberg, Rhoda, 1917-

York's adventures with Lewis and Clark; an African-American's part in the great expedition. HarperCollins 2004 88p il map lib bdg $18.89; pa $7.99

Grades: 5 6 7 8   **978**

1. York, ca. 1775-ca. 1815 2. Lewis and Clark Expedition (1804-1806) 3. West (U.S.)—Exploration 4. African Americans—Biography

ISBN 0-06-009112-6 (lib bdg); 0-06-009113-4 (pa)
LC 2003-9425

Relates the adventures of York, a slave and "body servant" to William Clark, who journeyed west with the Lewis and Clark Expedition of 1804-1806

"This well-researched selection helps to round out the study of an amazing event in our country's history. . . . Meticulously documented and illustrated with black-and-white photos and reproductions, this is a solid purchase for all collections." SLJ

Includes bibliographical references

Burgan, Michael

The Arapaho. Marshall Cavendish Benchmark 2009 48p il map (First Americans) lib bdg $31.36

Grades: 2 3 4   **978**

1. Arapaho Indians

ISBN 978-0-7614-3017-9 (lib bdg); 0-7614-3017-2 (lib bdg)   LC 2007-33675

Provides information on the background, lifestyle, beliefs, and present-day lives of the Arapaho people

Includes glossary and bibliographical references

Calabro, Marian

The perilous journey of the Donner Party. Clarion Bks. 1999 192p il maps $20 *

Grades: 5 6 7 8   **978**

1. Donner party 2. Frontier and pioneer life—West (U.S.) 3. Overland journeys to the Pacific

ISBN 0-395-86610-3   LC 98-29610

Uses materials from letters and diaries written by survivors of the Donner Party to relate the experiences of that ill-fated group as they endured horrific circumstances on their way to California in 1846-47

"Calabro's offering is a fine addition to the Donner Party canon and particularly well suited to its young audience, for whom the story of hardship and survival will be nothing short of riveting. . . . From the haunting cover with its lonely campfire to the recounting of a survivors' reunion, this is a page-turner." Booklist

Includes bibliographical references

Croy, Anita

Ancient Pueblo; archaeology unlocks the secrets of America's past; by Anita Croy; J. Jefferson Reid, consultant. National Geographic 2007 64p il map (National Geographic investigates) $17.95; lib bdg $27.90

Grades: 4 5 6 7   **978**

1. Pueblo Indians 2. Archeology 3. Southwestern States—Antiquities

ISBN 978-1-4263-0130-8; 978-1-4263-0131-5 (lib bdg)   LC 2007024800

This describes the prehistoric sites of the American Southwest, and what archeologists have learned from them about the lives of ancient Pueblo peoples.

Includes glossary and bibliographical references

Faber, Harold

Lewis and Clark; from ocean to ocean. Benchmark Bks. 2002 80p il map (Great explorations) lib bdg $29.93

Grades: 5 6 7 8   **978**

1. Lewis, Meriwether, 1774-1809 2. Clark, William, 1770-1838 3. Lewis and Clark Expedition (1804-1806) 4. West (U.S.)—Exploration

ISBN 0-7614-1241-7   LC 00-51898

This "discusses the 1804 expedition that set out to explore the American continent. . . . Supplementing Faber's account are journal quotations that offer firsthand reportage of events, conditions, and reflections about the journey. The last chapter tells what happened to significant members of the expedition and includes information on the Lewis and Clark Trail. . . . The colorful and sometimes quite beautiful illustrations include paintings, drawings, and prints, as well as a few photographs of sites and artifacts." Booklist

Includes bibliographical references

Freedman, Russell

Children of the wild West. Clarion Bks. 1983 104p il map $18; pa $6.95 *

Grades: 4 5 6 7   **978**

1. Children—West (U.S.) 2. Frontier and pioneer life—West (U.S.) 3. West (U.S.)—History

ISBN 0-89919-143-6; 0-395-54785-7 (pa)
LC 83-5133

"A smooth narrative and numerous historical photographs combine for an intriguing backward look at how children fared in pioneer times." Booklist

An Indian winter; paintings and drawings by Karl Bodmer. Holiday House 1992 88p il $21.95; pa $12.95 *

Grades: 6 7 8 9   **978**

1. Wied, Maximilian, Prinz von, 1782-1867 2. Native Americans—Missouri River valley 3. Missouri River valley

ISBN 0-8234-0930-9; 0-8234-1158-3 (pa)
LC 91-24205

Relates the experiences of a German prince, his servant, and a young Swiss artist as they traveled through the Missouri River Valley in 1833 learning about the territory and its inhabitants and recording their impressions in words and pictures

"The pictures are particularly effective in presenting rich details of village life, clothing, ceremonies, and customs. Both the book's specific information about native peoples and its use of primary-source material make it a valuable creation." Horn Book

Includes bibliographical references

Friedman, Mel, 1946-
The Oregon Trail. Children's Press 2010 il map (True book) lib bdg $26; pa $6.95
Grades: 3 4 5   **978**
1. Oregon Trail 2. Frontier and pioneer life 3. Overland journeys to the Pacific
ISBN   978-0-531-20584-6;   0-531-20584-3; 978-0-531-21247-9 (pa); 0-531-21247-5 (pa)
LC 2009014186
This introduction to the Oregon Trail provides "readers with clear explanations, maps, illustrations, time lines, and engaging reproductions of primary resources. [This] volume contains eye-catching quick facts; illustrations and photographs are representative of regional Native Americans, pioneers, and explorers. This is ideal material for reports on the Westward expansion." SLJ
Includes bibliographical references

Galford, Ellen
The trail West; exploring history through art; [by] Ellen Galford. Two-Can Pub. 2005 64p il (Picture that!) $19.95
Grades: 5 6 7 8   **978**
1. West (U.S.)—History 2. West (U.S.) in art
ISBN 1-58728-442-1   LC 2004-8334
This examines pioneer life in the American West through the works of such artists as Wislow Homer, Eastman Johnson, George Catlin, and George Caleb Bingham
"Art and history meld with entertaining and successful results. . . . [This] unique, well-thought-out [title is] good for reports, and browsers would enjoy [it], too." SLJ

Grupper, Jonathan
Destination: Rocky Mountains. National Geographic Soc. 2001 31p il $16.95
Grades: 3 4 5 6   **978**
1. Rocky Mountains
ISBN 0-7922-7722-8   LC 00-55926
"A hypothetical trek up the Rocky Mountains provides the framework for . . . information about its animals and the vegetation that sustains them at elevations beyond fourteen thousand feet. Each animal—from huge grizzly bear to tiny pika—has a double-page spread, lavishly illustrated with well-chosen color photographs. The text and graphics work well together." Horn Book Guide

Huey, Lois Miner
American archaeology uncovers the westward movement. Marshall Cavendish Benchmark 2009 c2010 64p il map (American archaeology) lib bdg $21.95
Grades: 4 5 6 7   **978**
1. United States—Territorial expansion 2. West (U.S.)—History 3. Frontier and pioneer life—West (U.S.) 4. Historical geography 5. Excavations (Archeology)—United States
ISBN 978-0-7614-4265-3 (lib bdg); 0-7614-4265-0 (lib bdg)   LC 2009003167
This describes how archeologists have learned about the history of the American West.

"The visually pleasing . . . [book is] replete with maps, paintings, and photographs, all appropriately placed and thoughtfully captioned. . . . Huey's focus on American history, which is broken down into small, manageable chunks, is sure to entice budding historians." SLJ
Includes glossary and bibliographical references

Josephson, Judith Pinkerton
Growing up in pioneer America, 1800 to 1890. Lerner Publs. 2003 64p il map (Our America) lib bdg $26.60 *
Grades: 5 6 7 8   **978**
1. Frontier and pioneer life—West (U.S.) 2. West (U.S.)—History
ISBN 0-8225-0659-9   LC 2001-6825
Describes what life was like for young people moving to and living on the western frontier
"Primary-source materials including selections from letters and diaries join numerous reproductions and archival photos to deliver a clear picture of the varied experiences of children living in the U.S. during the 1800s. Accessible, attractive, and useful." SLJ
Includes bibliographical references

Katz, William Loren
Black women of the Old West. Atheneum Bks. for Young Readers 1995 84p il $19.95
Grades: 5 6 7 8 9   **978**
1. African American women 2. Frontier and pioneer life—West (U.S.) 3. West (U.S.)—History
ISBN 0-689-31944-4   LC 95-9969
This work contains "vignettes and photographs of dozens of women, some famous, others unknown outside their own family circles, who lived across the West in the 19th and early 20th centuries." N Y Times Book Rev
"Katz succeeds in establishing that women of color were an important, if unsung, presence on the westward-shifting frontier." Bull Cent Child Books

King, David C., 1933-
Pioneer days; discover the past with fun projects, games, activities, and recipes. Wiley 1997 118p il (American kids in history) pa $12.95 *
Grades: 3 4 5 6   **978**
1. Frontier and pioneer life—West (U.S.) 2. West (U.S.)—Social life and customs
ISBN 0-471-16169-1   LC 96-37495
This book is an "assortment of history, culture, crafts, and stories to teach about the daily life of the pioneers. . . . [Crafts and recipes include] air-dried flowers, toys and games, homemade soda pop, johnny-cakes, and various holiday ornaments. The author's research is evident, and the presentation of the activities and recipes is so engaging that the book will appeal to a wide audience." SLJ
Includes glossary and bibliographical references

Olson, Tod, 1962-

How to get rich on a Texas cattle drive; afterword by Marc Aronson; illustrations by Scott Allred & Gregory Proch. National Geographic 2010 47p il map $18.95

Grades: 4 5 6 7   **978**

1. Cowhands 2. Frontier and pioneer life—West (U.S.) 3. West (U.S.)—History

ISBN 978-1-4263-0524-5; 1-4263-0524-9

"This book provides one of the better true-to-life insider accounts of what happens on a cattle drive: why the cattle are being driven, where they're being driven to and from, and the multitude of daily chores and unforeseen obstacles along the way. Period photos and artwork, as well as original drawings, make for a lively design, and an ongoing ledger keeps track of the main character's mostly modest finances." Booklist

How to get rich on the Oregon Trail; my adventures among cows, crooks & heroes on the road to fame and fortune; [illustrations by Scott Allred & Gregory Proch; afterword by Marc Anonson] National Geographic 2009 47p il (How to get rich) $18.95; lib bdg $27.90 *

Grades: 4 5 6 7   **978**

1. Frontier and pioneer life 2. Oregon Trail 3. Overland journeys to the Pacific 4. West (U.S.)—History

ISBN 978-1-4263-0412-5; 1-4263-0412-9; 978-1-4263-0413-2 (lib bdg); 1-4263-0413-7 (lib bdg)

"The action follows young Will Reed and his family as they set off from Illinois to find their fortune along the 2,000-mile Oregon Trail. . . . Informing Will's impish sketches and wry journal entries is a wealth of information about life along the trail. . . . An ongoing ledger calculates the family's balance as it fluctuates from $10.70 to $3,021.70, but it's clear that this journey is more about survival than riches. The illustrations, historical anecdotes, and run-ins with everyone from the Mormons to escaped slaves to Abraham Lincoln form a perfect blend of history and humbuggery." Booklist

Patent, Dorothy Hinshaw

Animals on the trail with Lewis and Clark; photographs by William Muñoz. Clarion Bks. 2002 118p il map $18

Grades: 4 5 6 7   **978**

1. Lewis and Clark Expedition (1804-1806) 2. Animals—United States 3. West (U.S.)—Exploration

ISBN 0-395-91415-9   LC 2001-42200

Retraces the Lewis and Clark journey and blends their observations of previously unknown animals with modern information about those same animals

"The spacious page layouts, beautiful illustrations, and well-written text help ensure that this historically significant story will be read and enjoyed." Booklist

Includes bibliographical references

The buffalo and the Indians; a shared destiny; photographs by William Muñoz. Clarion Books 2006 85p il $18

Grades: 5 6 7   **978**

1. Native Americans—Great Plains 2. Bison 3. West (U.S.)—History

ISBN 0-618-48570-8; 978-0-618-48570-3

Provides a review of the bond between Native Americans and buffalos throughout history and examines how European settlers disrupted nature's balance and nearly caused the extinction of an animal so highly respected by the native tribes

"Patent's narrative is clear and her writing is almost lyrical. Muñoz's breathtaking color photos of bison, landscapes, and artifacts are mixed with reproductions of period art and illustrations." SLJ

Includes bibliographical references

Plants on the trail with Lewis and Clark; photographs by William Muñoz. Clarion Bks. 2003 104p il map $18

Grades: 4 5 6 7   **978**

1. Lewis and Clark Expedition (1804-1806) 2. Plants—United States 3. West (U.S.)—Exploration

ISBN 0-618-06776-0   LC 2002-10383

Contents: Jefferson, Lewis, and plants; The importance of trees; Plants as food; Wildflowers and their uses; The fate of Lewis's specimens

Describes the journey of Lewis and Clark through the western United States, focusing on the plants they cataloged, their uses for food and medicine, and the plant lore of Native American people

"Good-quality, full-color photos and reproductions clearly extend the text. . . . The author's knowledge of and keen interest in her subject matter is very evident in this fascinating account." SLJ

Includes bibliographical references

Perritano, John, 1962-

The Lewis and Clark Expedition. Children's Press 2010 48p il (True book) lib bdg $26; pa $6.95

Grades: 3 4 5   **978**

1. Lewis, Meriwether, 1774-1809 2. Clark, William, 1770-1838 3. Lewis and Clark Expedition (1804-1806) 4. West (U.S.)—Exploration 5. Explorers

ISBN 978-0-531-20582-2 (lib bdg); 0-531-20582-7 (lib bdg); 978-0-531-21245-5 (pa); 0-531-21245-9 (pa)

LC 2009014183

This introduction to the Lewis and Clark Expedition provides "elementary readers with clear explanations, maps, illustrations, time lines, and engaging reproductions of primary resources. [This] volume contains eye-catching quick facts; illustrations and photographs are representational of regional Native Americans, pioneers, and explorers. This is ideal material for reports on the Westward expansion." SLJ

Includes bibliographical references

Schanzer, Rosalyn

How we crossed the West; the adventures of Lewis & Clark. National Geographic Soc. 1997 unp il hardcover o.p. pa $7.95 *

Grades: 3 4 5   **978**

1. Lewis, Meriwether, 1774-1809 2. Clark, William, 1770-1838 3. Lewis and Clark Expedition (1804-1806)

ISBN 0-7922-3738-2; 0-7922-6726-5 (pa)

LC 96-6585

This "account of the 1804-1805 journey [has]. . . . a text composed of brief excerpts drawn from the actual journals and letters written by Lewis and Clark and members of the expedition." SLJ

"Pithy and sometimes humorous, the text tells of contacts with Native Americans, encounters with wildlife . . . and the hardships of the trail. Warm in color and accessible in style, the acrylic paintings have a folk-art inspiration." Booklist

Scott, Ann Herbert, 1926-

Cowboy country; pictures by Ted Lewin. Clarion Bks. 1993 unp il hardcover o.p. pa $6.95 *

Grades: K 1 2 3   **978**

1. Cowhands 2. West (U.S.)

ISBN 0-395-57561-3; 0-395-76482-3 (pa)

LC 92-24499

An "old buckaroo" tells how he became a cowboy, what the work was like in the past, and how this life has changed

The author "succinctly captures the laconic speaking rhythms and distinctive jargon of her subject. . . . Lewin's . . . well-lit watercolors suggest the affability of the weathered narrator and the awe of the boy with him." Publ Wkly

Sheinkin, Steve, 1968-

Which way to the wild West? everything your schoolbooks didn't tell you about America's westward expansion; illustrated by Tim Robinson. Roaring Brook Press 2009 260p il map $19.95 *

Grades: 5 6 7 8   **978**

1. Frontier and pioneer life—West (U.S.) 2. West (U.S.)—History 3. United States—Territorial expansion

ISBN 978-1-59643-321-2; 1-59643-321-3

Presents the greatest adventures of America's Westward expansion, from the Louisiana Purchase and the gold rush to the Indian wars and life of the cowboy, as well as the everyday happenings that defined living on the frontier

"An engaging storyteller, the author uses humor and little-known anecdotes to make such subjects as Manifest Destiny, the Mexican-American War, the Gold Rush and Custer's Last Stand entertaining for readers. His chatty, informal style . . . will appeal to young readers turned off to history by stale textbooks. Robinson's cartoons complement the text. . . . An accessible and engaging historical overview." Kirkus

Includes bibliographical references

Sonneborn, Liz

The Mormon Trail; [by] Liz Sonneborn. Franklin Watts 2005 63p il (Watts library) $25.50

Grades: 5 6 7 8   **978**

1. Mormons 2. Frontier and pioneer life—West (U.S.)

ISBN 0-531-12317-0   LC 2005001466

This "title tells how in the 19th century Mormons traveled west to establish a community where they could practice their religion without fear of persecution. Black-and-white and color illustrations, maps, sidebars, and time lines enhance the well-organized [text]." SLJ

Includes bibliographical references

Steele, Christy

Cattle ranching in the American West; by Christy Steele. World Almanac Library 2005 48p il map (America's westward expansion) lib bdg $30; pa $11.95

Grades: 5 6 7 8   **978**

1. Ranch life 2. Cattle 3. West (U.S.)—History

ISBN 0-8368-5787-9 (lib bdg); 0-8368-5794-1 (pa)

LC 2004-56769

This volume describing Western cattle ranching is "richly illustrated with historical photographs, illustrations, maps, and quotes from primary sources presented in sidebars." SLJ

Includes bibliographical references

Famous wagon trails; by Christy Steele. World Almanac Library 2005 48p il map (America's westward expansion) lib bdg $30; pa $11.95

Grades: 5 6 7 8   **978**

1. Frontier and pioneer life 2. West (U.S.)—History 3. Overland journeys to the Pacific

ISBN 0-8368-5788-7 (lib bdg); 0-8368-5795-X (pa)

LC 2004-57822

This description of famous wagon trails in the West is "richly illustrated with historical photographs, illustrations, maps, and quotes from primary sources presented in sidebars." SLJ

Includes bibliographical references

Pioneer life in the American West; by Christy Steele. World Almanac Library 2005 48p il map (America's westward expansion) lib bdg $30; pa $11.95

Grades: 5 6 7 8   **978**

1. Frontier and pioneer life 2. West (U.S.)—History

ISBN 0-8368-5790-9 (lib bdg); 0-8368-5797-6 (pa)

LC 2004-56772

This description of pioneer life in the American West is "richly illustrated with historical photographs, illustrations, maps, and quotes from primary sources presented in sidebars." SLJ

Includes bibliographical references

Waldman, Stuart, 1941-
The last river; John Wesley Powell & the Colorado River Exploration Expedition; by Stuart Waldman; illustrated by Gregory Manchess. Mikaya Press 2005 47p il map (Great explorers book) $19.95
Grades: 3 4 5 6   **978**
    1. Powell, John Wesley, 1834-1902 2. Colorado River (Colo.-Mexico) 3. West (U.S.)—Exploration
    ISBN 1-931414-09-2   LC 2005041580
"In 1869 the Colorado River Exploring Expedition set forth from Green River City led by John Wesley Powell, a one-armed explorer who was determined to reach the Colorado's canyons to study their geology. . . . Waldman relates their story clearly in the main text, while occasional sidebars carry short excerpts from the men's journals and letters. Illustrations include clear nineteenth-century photos as well as handsome full and double-page paintings. . . . Rich in color, strong in composition, and beautifully executed, these often-dramatic paintings bring the story to life." Booklist
Includes bibliographical references

978.3   South Dakota

Thomas, William, 1948-
Mount Rushmore; by William David Thomas. Chelsea Clubhouse 2010 48p il (Symbols of American freedom) $30
Grades: 3 4 5   **978.3**
    1. Mount Rushmore National Memorial (S.D.)
    ISBN 978-1-60413-515-2; 1-60413-515-8
               LC 2009-13027
This book about Mount Rushmore "provides nearly as much information as a guided tour by a park ranger. [It begins] with the story of how the place came to be, and where it fits into U.S. history. Information boxes offer additional background and some surprising facts, such as . . . the origin of the name of Mount Rushmore. The final chapter shows the landmark today and includes maps and photographs of the visitors' center and some of the things individuals might see or do while visiting the site. Much information is packed into [this] slim [book]. Excellent . . . for state reports or to complement U.S. history units." SLJ
Includes glossary

978.8   Colorado

Quigley, Mary, 1963-
Mesa Verde; [by] Mary Quigley. Heinemann Library 2006 48p il (Excavating the past) lib bdg $31.43
Grades: 4 5 6   **978.8**
    1. Native Americans—Antiquities 2. Excavations (Archeology)—United States 3. Mesa Verde National Park (Colo.)
    ISBN 1-4034-5997-5   LC 2005009179
"*Mesa Verde* explains how these ancient people reached North and South America using the land bridge and settled down to farm in the Four Corners area.

Quigley uses the term Ancestral Puebloans rather than the sometimes derogatory Anasazi and explains why. She describes the daily lives of the people and includes current theories about why they may have abandoned this site. Activities and discoveries by the Wetherill brothers and other archaeologists as well as cultural information from modern-day people bring knowledge about the ancients up to date. This [is an] excellent title." SLJ
Includes bibliographical references

979.4   California

Jaskol, Julie, 1958-
City of angels; in and around Los Angeles; by Julie Jaskol & Brian Lewis; illustrated by Elisa Kleven. Dutton Children's Bks. 1999 47p il $16.99
Grades: 2 3 4   **979.4**
    1. Los Angeles (Calif.)
    ISBN 0-525-46214-7   LC 99-35233
Surveys the history, historic sites, ethnic neighborhoods, festivals, and culture of the Los Angeles area
This offers "bright, exuberant collages filled with fascinating, minute details and a few paragraphs of text equally jam-packed with tidbits of information." SLJ

Murphy, Claire Rudolf
Children of Alcatraz; growing up on the rock. Walker & Co. 2006 64p il map $17.95; lib bdg $18.85 *
Grades: 5 6 7 8   **979.4**
    1. Alcatraz Island (Calif.)
    ISBN 0-8027-9577-3; 978-0-8027-9577-9; 0-8027-9578-1 (lib bdg); 978-0-8027-9578-1 (lib bdg)
               LC 2006-10588
"Murphy's clearly written history starts with the island's use by Native Americans in the pre-Colonial era and continues through its various incarnations as a lighthouse, military post, and then prison. She follows the federal penitentiary years, the island's rearming during World War II, the Native American occupation of 1969-71, and the island's current incarnation as a National Historical Park. . . . Liberally illustrated with black-and-white archival photographs, the book also includes print, AV, and Internet resources. While useful for reports, this title will appeal to general readers." SLJ
Includes bibliographical references

O'Donnell, Kerri, 1972-
The gold rush; a primary source history of the search for gold in California. Rosen Central Primary Source 2003 64p il maps (Primary sources in American history) lib bdg $29.25
Grades: 4 5 6 7   **979.4**
    1. California—Gold discoveries 2. Frontier and pioneer life—California
    ISBN 0-8239-3682-1   LC 2002-1367
    Contents: El Dorado; Timeline; The great discovery; Gold fever; To California by sea; The Overlanders; Life in the mines; The lawless West
Uses primary source documents, narrative, and illustrations to recount how the mid-nineteenth century Cali-

O'Donnell, Kerri, 1972-—*Continued*
fornia gold rush affected Americans and immigrants and
how it shaped history

This "will be extremely effective when introducing
students to primary source material." Libr Media Connect

Includes glossary and bibliographical references

Olson, Tod, 1962-
How to get rich in the California Gold Rush; an
adventurer's guide to the fabulous riches
discovered in 1848 . . .; illustrations by Scott
Allred; afterword by Marc Aronson. National
Geographic 2008 47p il map (How to get rich)
$16.95; lib bdg $25.90 *

Grades: 4 5 6 7   **979.4**

1. California—Gold discoveries 2. Frontier and pioneer life—California 3. Gold mines and mining
ISBN   978-1-4263-0315-9;   1-4263-0315-7;
978-1-4263-0316-6 (lib bdg); 1-4263-0316-5 (lib bdg)
            LC 2008-19601

The fictional Thomas Hartley gives readers a historical
portrait of life in the California gold fields

This "deftly blends story with history to not only give
readers an understanding of a gold rush but also to provide a lighthearted and engaging entry point into frontier
life. . . . Period lithographs are reproduced alongside
original illustrations. . . . A ledger on each page tracks
the young men's finances in a genuinely exciting way,
adding a sly element of math to this well-conceived and
compulsively appealing book." Booklist

Includes bibliographical references

Ryan, Pam Muñoz
Our California; by Pam Munoz Ryan; illustrated
by Rafael Lopez. Charlesbridge 2008 unp il
$17.95; pa $7.95

Grades: PreK K 1 2   **979.4**

1. California
ISBN 978-1-58089-116-5; 978-1-58089-117-2 (pa)

"A whirlwind loop tour whisks readers through the
Golden State, starting with the beaches of San Diego,
heading up to L.A. and beyond to Gold Country, then
swinging down through Yosemite (depicted in a stunning
nighttime vertical spread) and Death Valley before ending up poolside at Palm Springs. . . . López's illustrations, paintings rendered on wood and sometimes distressed, remain fresh and surprising as he finds ways to
express wonder and affection. . . . This title is virtually
certain to inspire California dreamin' in readers of all
ages." Publ Wkly

Zuehlke, Jeffrey, 1968-
The Golden Gate Bridge. Lerner Publications
2010 32p il map (Lightning bolt books. Famous
places) lib bdg $25.26

Grades: 2 3 4   **979.4**

1. Golden Gate Bridge (San Francisco, Calif.)
ISBN 978-0-8225-9407-9; 0-8225-9407-2
            LC 2008-30641

Describes the Golden Gate Bridge that connects Marin
County to the city of San Francisco, including information about its history, design, and construction.

This book uses "high-quality photos, illustrations,
maps, and diagrams. . . . Readers will enjoy learning
about [the Golden Gate Bridge] . . . and the challenges
of building and maintaining large structures." SLJ

Includes glossary and bibliographical references

979.7   Washington

Jankowski, Susan
Olympic National Park; adventure, explore,
discover; [by] Susan Jankowski.
MyReportLinks.com Books 2009 128p il map
(America's national parks) lib bdg $33.27

Grades: 5 6 7 8   **979.7**

1. National parks and reserves—United States
2. Olympic National Park (Wash.)
ISBN 978-1-59845-092-7 (lib bdg); 1-59845-092-1 (lib
bdg)   LC 2007-17341

This "informative, well-written book contains a physical description of the park; a summary of its history including the Native peoples of the area; activities such as
hiking trails, campsites, and visitor centers; information
about the park's plants, animals, and weather; full-color
photographs; and numerous approved links available
through the publisher's Web page. . . . Thorough, useful, and appealing, this . . . is a great update for collections." SLJ

Includes glossary and bibliographical references

979.8   Alaska

Miller, Debbie S.
Big Alaska; journey across America's most
amazing state; illustrations by Jon Van Zyle.
Walker 2006 unp il map $17.95; lib bdg $18.85

Grades: 2 3 4   **979.8**

1. Alaska
ISBN   978-0-8027-8069-0;   0-8027-8069-5;
978-0-8027-8070-6 (lib bdg); 0-8027-8070-9 (lib bdg)
            LC 2005-24086

"Miller's text follows a bald eagle's flight across
Alaska, beginning with Admiralty Island and circling
back to the Chilkat Bald Eagle Preserve. . . . Zyle's
acrylic paintings perfectly suit the grandeur of the subject. . . . Back matter includes Alaska Facts, State Symbols, Climate Records, and Alaska's Special Places,
which has additional information on the locations described in the text. . . . The book . . . is a special treasure both for readers already interested in the subject and
newcomers." SLJ

Includes bibliographical references

980 History of South America

Foster, Karen, 1964-
Atlas of South America. Picture Window books 2008 32p il map (Picture Window Books world atlases) lib bdg $27.93
Grades: 2 3 4   **980**
1. South America
ISBN 978-1-4048-3887-1 (lib bdg); 1-4048-3887-2 (lib bdg)
This introduction to the geography of South America offers maps and information about countries, landforms, bodies of water, climate, plants, animals, population, people and customs, places of interest, industries, transportation, and Lake Titicaca.
Includes glossary

Gorrell, Gena K. (Gena Kinton), 1946-
In the land of the jaguar; South America and its people; illustrated by Andrej Krystoforski. Tundra Books 2007 149p il $22.95 *
Grades: 5 6 7 8 9   **980**
1. South America
ISBN 978-0-88776-756-2
"This beautifully designed volume, with an engaging narrative, combines a highly informative overview of the continent with country-by-country detail. . . . The spacious design includes big maps, clear type on thick paper, and small, beautiful, fully captioned illustrations."
Booklist

981 Brazil

Berkenkamp, Lauri
Discover the Amazon; the world's largest rainforest; illustrated by Blair Shedd. Nomad Press 2008 90p il map pa $16.95
Grades: 4 5 6 7   **981**
1. Amazon River valley
ISBN 978-1-9346702-7-9 (pa); 1-9346702-7-8 (pa)
"Berkenkamp's introduction to the [Amazon] river basin incorporates maps, drawings, and photos in various shades of green and brown on recycled paper. . . . The conversational style provides a 'you are there' feeling, conveying information and anecdotes while stressing outdoor survival skills. . . . Even readers who never travel to Amazonia will appreciate the region's complexity and significance after perusing this book." SLJ

Deckker, Zilah
Brazil; [by] Zilah Deckker; David Robinson and Joao Cezar de Castro Rocha, consultants. National Geographic 2008 64p il (Countries of the world) lib bdg $27.90 *
Grades: 4 5 6 7   **981**
1. Brazil
ISBN 978-1-4263-0298-5 (lib bdg); 1-4263-0298-3 (lib bdg)
This describes the geography, nature, history, people and culture, government, and economy of Brazil.
Includes glossary and bibliographical references

Fitzpatrick, Anne, 1978-
Amazon River; [by] Anne Fitzpatrick. Creative Education 2004 c2005 32p il map (Natural wonders of the world) lib bdg $27.10
Grades: 4 5 6   **981**
1. Amazon River 2. Amazon River valley
ISBN 1-58341-322-7   LC 2003-62574
The describes the Amazon River's "geological formation and climate, ecology and wildlife, and human inhabitants and expeditions. A final chapter is devoted to tourism. . . . The [text], sufficient in informational quantity and quality for short reports, [is] briskly and engagingly written. But the real selling point here is the gorgeous color photographs." SLJ

Reiser, Robert, 1941-
Brazil. Benchmark Bks. 2003 48p il map (Discovering cultures) lib bdg $28.50
Grades: 2 3 4   **981**
1. Brazil
ISBN 0-7614-1180-1   LC 2001-7292
Contents: Where in the world is Brazil?; What makes Brazil Brazilian?; Living in Brazil; School days; Just for fun; Let's celebrate!
An introduction to the geography, history, people, and culture of Brazil
Includes glossary and bibliographical references

Richard, Christopher, 1959-
Brazil; [by] Christopher Richard, Leslie Jermyn. 2nd ed. Benchmark Bks. 2002 144p il map (Cultures of the world) lib bdg $42.79
Grades: 5 6 7 8   **981**
1. Brazil
ISBN 0-7614-1359-6   LC 2001-47263
First published 1991
Presents the geography, history, government, economy, and social life and customs of the South American country of Brazil
Includes glossary and bibliographical references

Walters, Tara, 1973-
Brazil. Children's Press 2008 48p il map (True book) lib bdg $26; pa $6.95
Grades: 2 3 4   **981**
1. Brazil
ISBN 978-0-531-16851-6 (lib bdg); 0-531-16851-4 (lib bdg); 978-0-531-20725-3 (pa); 0-531-20725-0 (pa)
Examines the country of Brazil, including its history, geography, people, arts, religion, language, festivals, and recreation
"Page layout is appealing, with a variety of bright, clear, captioned color photos." SLJ

982 Argentina

Gofen, Ethel, 1937-
Argentina; by Ethel Caro Gofen, Leslie Jermyn. 2nd ed. Benchmark Bks. 2002 144p il map (Cultures of the world) lib bdg $42.79
Grades: 5 6 7 8　　　　　　　　982
1. Argentina
ISBN 0-7614-1358-8　　　　LC 2001-47759
First published 1991
Presents the history, geography, government, economy, people, and social life and customs of Argentina
Includes glossary and bibliographical references

Gordon, Sharon
Argentina. Benchmark Bks. 2004 48p il map (Discovering cultures) lib bdg $28.50
Grades: 2 3 4　　　　　　　　982
ISBN 0-7614-1723-0　　　　LC 2003-19097
Contents: Where in the world is Argentina?; What makes Argentina Argentinean?; Living in Argentina; School days; Just for fun; Let's celebrate!
An introduction to the geography, history, people, and culture of Argentina
Includes glossary and bibliographical references

Lourie, Peter
Tierra del Fuego; a journey to the end of the earth. Boyds Mills Press 2002 47p il map $19.95
Grades: 4 5 6 7　　　　　　　　982
1. Tierra del Fuego (Argentina and Chile)
ISBN 1-56397-973-X　　　　LC 2001-96395
The author describes his travels in Tierra del Fuego and provides historical background on the area
"Lourie's smooth, first-person narrative mixes history, adventure, and personal insights, while glorious photographs of the remarkable land at the southernmost point of the world enhance his travelogue. . . . Highly informative for reports, this fascinating account will also appeal to young readers with wanderlust." SLJ

983 Chile

Rau, Dana Meachen, 1971-
Chile. Marshall Cavendish Benchmark 2007 48p il map (Discovering cultures) lib bdg $28.50
Grades: 2 3 4　　　　　　　　983
1. Chile
ISBN 978-0-7614-1988-4 (lib bdg); 0-7614-1988-8 (lib bdg)
An introduction to the geography, history, people, and culture of Chile
Includes glossary and bibliographical references

Winter, Jane Kohen, 1959-
Chile; by Jane Kohen Winter, Susan Roraff. 2nd ed. Benchmark Bks. 2002 144p il map (Cultures of the world) lib bdg $42.79
Grades: 5 6 7 8　　　　　　　　983
1. Chile
ISBN 0-7614-1360-X　　　　LC 2001-47827

First published 1991
Introduces the history, geography, culture, and lifestyles of Chile
Includes glossary and bibliographical references

984 Bolivia

Pateman, Robert, 1954-
Bolivia; [by] Robert Pateman & Marcus Cramer. 2nd ed. Marshall Cavendish Benchmark 2006 144p il map (Cultures of the world) lib bdg $42.79
Grades: 5 6 7 8　　　　　　　　984
1. Bolivia
ISBN 978-0-7614-2066-8 (lib bdg); 0-7614-2066-5 (lib bdg)　　　　LC 2006002425
First published 1995
This provides "information on the geography, history, governmental structure, economy, cultural diversity, peoples, religion, and culture of Bolivia." Publisher's note
This is "well organized, informative, and entertaining. . . . Excellent-quality full-color photographs and reproductions show the people, landforms, buildings, and everyday activities." SLJ
Includes bibliographical references

985 Peru

Calvert, Patricia, 1931-
The ancient Inca; written by Patricia Calvert. Franklin Watts 2004 128p il (People of the ancient world) lib bdg $30.50; pa $9.95 *
Grades: 5 6 7 8　　　　　　　　985
1. Incas
ISBN 0-531-12358-8 (lib bdg); 0-531-16740-2 (pa)
LC 2004-1956
Contents: The science of the past: why it matters; Before the Inca; Children of the sun; Life in a highland family; Growing up among the Inca; Medicine, magic, and death; The top of the Inca pyramid; Warriors, war, and keeping the peace; Buildings, bridges, and roads; The war of two brothers; Suncasapa, the bearded one; The aftermath of conquest
This "well-written, attractive [title has] extensive collections of quality color photographs of ruins and artifacts." SLJ
Includes bibliographical references

De Capua, Sarah
Peru; by Sarah De Capua. Benchmark Books 2004 48p il map (Discovering cultures) lib bdg $28.50
Grades: 2 3 4　　　　　　　　985
1. Peru
ISBN 0-7614-1796-6　　　　LC 2004-6125
Contents: Where in the world is Peru?; What makes Peru Peruvian?; Living in Peru; School days; Just for fun; Let's celebrate!
An introduction to the geography, history, people, and culture of Peru
Includes glossary and bibliographical references

Falconer, Kieran, 1970-
Peru; [by] Kieran Falconer & Lynette Quek. 2nd ed. Marshall Cavendish Benchmark 2006 144p il map (Cultures of the world) lib bdg $42.79
Grades: 5 6 7 8   **985**
1. Peru
ISBN 978-0-7614-2068-2 (lib bdg); 0-7614-2068-1 (lib bdg)
First published 1995
This provides "information on the geography, history, governmental structure, economy, cultural diversity, peoples, religion, and culture of Peru." Publisher's note
Includes glossary and bibliographical references

Gruber, Beth
Ancient Inca; archaeology unlocks the secrets of the Inca's past; by Beth Gruber; Johan Reinhard, consultant. National Geographic 2007 64p il map (National Geographic investigates) $17.95; lib bdg $27.90 *
Grades: 5 6 7 8   **985**
1. Incas 2. Excavations (Archeology)—Peru 3. Peru—Antiquities
ISBN 978-0-7922-7827-6; 978-0-7922-7873-3 (lib bdg)   LC 2006032104
This describes how archeologists have found out about ancient Incan civilization.
This offers "the beautiful photography and illustrations characteristic of the National Geographic Society, [a] well-written [text] and sidebars, and information on recent archaeological finds." SLJ
Includes bibliographical references

Krebs, Laurie
Up and down the Andes; a Peruvian festival tale; [by] Laurie Krebs, Aurelia Fronty. Barefoot Books 2008 unp il $16.99
Grades: K 1 2 3   **985**
1. Inti Raymi Festival 2. Native Americans—Peru 3. Peru—Social life and customs 4. Festivals—Peru 5. Andes
ISBN 978-1-84686-203-8; 1-84686-203-5
LC 2008020722
This is a "picture book about the Peruvian Inti Raymi Festival as children travel from all over southern Peru, by bus, train, boat, mule, and truck, to the city of Cusco to celebrate with feasting and fun in their traditional costumes. The simply rhyming text and the bright, clear, beautiful unframed acrylic paintings express a strong sense of the rich traditions that are still part of contemporary life." Booklist

Lewin, Ted, 1935-
Lost city; the discovery of Machu Picchu. Philomel Bks. 2003 unp il $16.99 *
Grades: 2 3 4   **985**
1. Machu Picchu (Peru)
ISBN 0-399-23302-4   LC 2002-4461
In 1911, Yale professor Hiram Bingham discovers a lost Incan city with the help of a young Peruvian boy
"The language is graceful and uncomplicated, weaving in bits of background history along the way. . . . Full-page watercolors spreads of the stunning vistas and thick forests contrast with dark, intimate views of Bingham inside homes and walking along walled city streets. . . . An exciting, eye-catching story." Booklist

Newman, Sandra, 1965-
The Inca empire. Children's Press 2009 c2010 48p il map (True book) lib bdg $26; pa $6.95
Grades: 3 4 5   **985**
1. Incas
ISBN 978-0-531-25228-4 (lib bdg); 0-531-25228-0 (lib bdg); 978-0-531-24109-7 (pa); 0-531-24109-2 (pa)
LC 2009000293
In this book the Inca civilization is "outlined for young readers with care and precision. . . . Loaded with access points such as captions, pull-outs, a time line, and a map, and with better-than-usual reproductions of well-chosen primary sources and art, the [book sports] a bright, peppy design. . . . [This book is] rigorous in distinguishing fact from theory, and conscientious about presenting competing theories where they exist." SLJ

986.1   Colombia

Croy, Anita
Colombia; [by] Anita Croy; Ulrich Oslender and Mauricio Pardo, consultants. National Geographic 2008 64p il map (Countries of the world) lib bdg $27.90 *
Grades: 4 5 6 7   **986.1**
1. Colombia
ISBN 978-1-4263-0257-2 (lib bdg); 1-4263-0257-6 (lib bdg)
This describes the geography, nature, history, people and culture, government, and economy of Colombia
Includes glossary and bibliographical references

De Capua, Sarah
Colombia. Benchmark Bks. 2004 48p il maps (Discovering cultures) lib bdg $28.50
Grades: 2 3 4   **986.1**
1. Colombia
ISBN 0-7614-1715-X   LC 2003-8128
Contents: Where in the world is Colombia?; What makes Colombia Colombian?; Living in Colombia; School days; Just for fun; Let's celebrate!
Highlights the geography, people, food, schools, recreation, celebrations, and language of Colombia
Includes glossary and bibliographical references

DuBois, Jill, 1952-
Colombia; by Jill DuBois, Leslie Jermyn. 2nd ed. Benchmark Bks. 2002 144p il map (Cultures of the world) lib bdg $42.79
Grades: 5 6 7 8   **986.1**
1. Colombia
ISBN 0-7614-1361-8   LC 2001-47264
First published 1991
Presents the geography, history, government, economy, and social life and customs of the country of Colombia
Includes glossary and bibliographical references

986.6 Ecuador

Foley, Erin, 1967-
Ecuador; [by] Erin L. Foley & Leslie Jermyn. 2nd ed. Marshall Cavendish Benchmark 2006 144p il map (Cultures of the world) lib bdg $42.79
Grades: 5 6 7 8   986.6
1. Ecuador
ISBN 0-7614-2050-9   LC 2005022671
First published 1995
This briefly describes Ecuador's "history, government, economy, and geography. . . . Particularly useful is the information on religion, the arts, food, leisure activities, and social roles. The [book has] great visual appeal with excellent full-color photographs on every page. [It] is especially successful in explaining social and economic hierarchies within the country." SLJ
Includes glossary and bibliographical references

Kras, Sara Louise
The Galapagos Islands; [by] Sara Louise Kras. Marshall Cavendish Benchmark 2008 c2009 96p il map (Nature's wonders) lib bdg $35.64
Grades: 5 6 7 8   986.6
1. Galapagos Islands
ISBN 978-0-7614-2856-5 (lib bdg); 0-7614-2856-9 (lib bdg)   LC 2007020416
"Provides comprehensive information on the geography, history, wildlife, peoples, and environmental issues of the Galapagos Islands." Publisher's note
Includes glossary and bibliographical references

987 Venezuela

Winter, Jane Kohen, 1959-
Venezuela; [by] Jane Kohen Winter, Kitt Baguley. 2nd ed. Benchmark Bks. 2002 144p il map (Cultures of the world) lib bdg $42.79
Grades: 5 6 7 8   987
1. Venezuela
ISBN 0-7614-1362-6   LC 2001-53877
First published 1990
Presents the geography, history, economy, and social life and customs of Venezuela
Includes glossary and bibliographical references

988.1 Guyana

Jermyn, Leslie
Guyana. Benchmark Bks. 2000 128p il map (Cultures of the world) lib bdg $42.79
Grades: 5 6 7 8   988.1
1. Guyana
ISBN 0-7614-0994-7   LC 99-55063
Examines the geography, history, government, economy, people, and culture of Guyana
Includes glossary and bibliographical references

989.2 Paraguay

Jermyn, Leslie
Paraguay; [by] Leslie Jermyn and Yong Jui Lin. 2nd ed. Marshall Cavendish Benchmark 2011 144p il map (Cultures of the world) lib bdg $29.95
Grades: 5 6 7 8   989.2
1. Paraguay
ISBN 978-0-7614-4858-7; 0-7614-4858-6
                    LC 2009046495
First published 2000
This offers information on the geography, history, wildlife, governmental structure, economy, cultural diversity, peoples, religion, and culture of Paraguay.
Includes glossary and bibliographical references

989.5 Uruguay

Jermyn, Leslie
Uruguay; by Leslie Jermyn and Winnie Wong. 2nd ed. Marshall Cavendish Benchmark 2009 144p il map (Cultures of the world) lib bdg $42.79
Grades: 5 6 7 8   989.5
1. Uruguay
ISBN 978-0-7614-4482-4 (lib bdg); 0-7614-4482-3 (lib bdg)   LC 2009007127
First published 1999
Provides information on the geography, history, wildlife, governmental structure, economy, cultural diversity, peoples, religion, and culture of Uruguay
Includes glossary and bibliographical references

993 New Zealand

Jackson, Barbara
New Zealand; [by] Barbara Jackson; Vaughan Wood and Simon Milne, consultants. National Geographic 2008 64p il map (Countries of the world) lib bdg $27.90 *
Grades: 4 5 6 7   993
1. New Zealand
ISBN 978-1-4263-0301-2 (lib bdg); 1-4263-0301-7 (lib bdg)
This describes the geography, nature, history, people and culture, government, and economy of New Zealand.

Smelt, Roselynn
New Zealand; by Roselynn Smelt. 2nd ed. Marshall Cavendish Benchmark 2009 128p il map (Cultures of the world) lib bdg $42.79
Grades: 5 6 7 8   993
1. New Zealand
ISBN 978-0-7614-3415-3 (lib bdg); 0-7614-3415-1 (lib bdg)   LC 2008028792
First published 1998
"Provides comprehensive information on the geography, history, wildlife, governmental structure, economy, cultural diversity, peoples, religion, and culture of New Zealand." Publisher's note
Includes glossary and bibliographical references

994   Australia

Arnold, Caroline, 1944-

Uluru, Australia's Aboriginal heart; photographs by Arthur Arnold. Clarion Books 2003 64p il $16 *

Grades: 5 6 7 8   **994**

   1. Aboriginal Australians 2. Australia 3. Uluru-Kata Tjuta National Park (Australia)

   ISBN 0-618-18181-4   LC 2002-15542

Describes Uluru, formerly known as Ayers Rock, in Australia's Uluru-Kata Tjuta National Park, its plant and animal life, and the country's Aboriginal people for whom the site is sacred

   "The book's greatest accomplishment . . . is to give readers a sense of the ongoing spiritual importance of Uluru to the Anangu, who have lived around it for 10,000 years. Clear, colorful photos of Uluru and its surroundings appear on nearly every page, illustrating the text with beauty and finesse." Booklist

Foster, Karen, 1964-

Atlas of Australia. Picture Window Books 2008 32p il map (Picture Window Books world atlases) lib bdg $27.93

Grades: 2 3 4   **994**

   1. Australia

   ISBN 978-1-4048-3881-9 (lib bdg); 1-4048-3881-3 (lib bdg)

This introduction to the geography of Australia offers maps and information about landforms, bodies of water, climate, plants, animals, population, people and customs, places of interest, industries, transportation, and the Great Barrier Reef.

   This book offers "well-organized, easy-to-access information. . . . Small photographs or colorful text boxes draw readers' attention to points of interest or fun facts. Maps and legends are simple, yet disseminate information clearly." SLJ

   Includes glossary

Gordon, Sharon

Australia. Benchmark Books 2004 c2005 48p il map (Discovering cultures) lib bdg $28.50

Grades: 2 3 4   **994**

   1. Australia

   ISBN 0-7614-1791-5   LC 2004-6136

   An introduction to the geography, history, people, and culture of Australia

   Includes glossary and bibliographical references

Lewin, Ted, 1935-

Top to bottom down under; [by] Ted and Betsy Lewin. HarperCollins Pub. 2005 40p il $15.99; lib bdg $16.89 *

Grades: 2 3 4   **994**

   1. Australia 2. Animals—Australia 3. Natural history—Australia

   ISBN 0-688-14113-7; 0-688-14114-5 (lib bdg)

                       LC 2003-26934

"The Lewins share their . . . journey to the land down under in a fresh, funny, fact-filled travelogue that meanders from Kakadu National Park to Kangaroo Island. Striking, realistic watercolor landscapes are juxtaposed with comical sketches and circa-1900 spot illustrations of Aboriginals killing snakes and riding on paperbark rafts. The pictures catch attention, and the text is intelligently written." Booklist

Rajendra, Vijeya, 1936-

Australia; [by] Vijeya & Sundran Rajendra. 2nd ed. Benchmark Bks. 2002 143p il map (Cultures of the world) lib bdg $42.79

Grades: 5 6 7 8   **994**

   1. Australia

   ISBN 0-7614-1473-8   LC 2002-19206

   First published 1990

Presents the history, geography, government, economy, environment, religion, people, and social life and customs of the island continent of Australia

   Includes glossary and bibliographical references

Rau, Dana Meachen, 1971-

Australia. Sea-to-Sea Publications 2009 32p il map (Facts about countries) lib bdg $28.50

Grades: 3 4 5   **994**

   1. Australia

   ISBN 978-1-59771-112-8 (lib bdg); 1-59771-112-8 (lib bdg)   LC 2008004630

Describes the geography, history, industries, education, government, and cultures of Australia

   "The attractive layout includes color photographs and charts of current statistics as well as maps illustrating main farming regions, natural resources, or the literacy rates of girls and boys. The [text is] clear and succinct." SLJ

   Includes glossary

Turner, Kate

Australia; [by] Kate Turner; Elaine Stratford and Joseph Powell, consultants. National Geographic 2007 64p il map (Countries of the world) lib bdg $27.90 *

Grades: 4 5 6 7   **994**

   1. Australia

   ISBN 978-1-4263-0055-4

Describes the geography, nature, history, people and culture, government and economy of Australia

   This "appealing [title has] wonderful photographs and maps. . . . [This book is a] reliable [source] for country research, and the interesting current material hold browsing potential as well." SLJ

   Includes glossary and bibliographical references

995.3   Papua New Guinea. New Guinea region

Gascoigne, Ingrid
Papua New Guinea; [by] Ingrid Gascoigne. 2nd ed. Marshall Cavendish Benchmark 2009 144p il map (Cultures of the world) lib bdg $42.79
Grades: 5 6 7 8   **995.3**
  1. Papua New Guinea
  ISBN 978-0-7614-3416-0 (lib bdg); 0-7614-3416-X (lib bdg)   LC 2008028794
  First published 1998
  "Provides comprehensive information on the geography, history, wildlife, governmental structure, economy, cultural diversity, peoples, religion, and culture of Papua New Guinea." Publisher's note
  Includes glossary and bibliographical references

996   Other parts of Pacific. Polynesia

Arnold, Caroline, 1944-
Easter Island; giant stone statues tell of a rich and tragic past; text and photographs by Caroline Arnold. Clarion Bks. 2000 48p il map hardcover o.p. pa $5.95 *
Grades: 5 6 7 8   **996**
  1. Easter Island
  ISBN 0-395-87609-5; 0-618-48605-4 (pa)
                                LC 99-27189
  Describes the formation, geography, ecology, and inhabitants of the isolated Easter Island in the Pacific Ocean
  This is a "straightforward account of what archaeologists have determined about the history of the Rapanui people and their monuments. The clearly written text is accompanied by breathtaking color photographs that show the beauty of the island and its rich collection of archaeological features." Horn Book
  Includes bibliographical references

NgCheong-Lum, Roseline, 1962-
Tahiti; [by] Roseline NgCheong-Lum. 2nd ed. Marshall Cavendish Benchmark 2008 144p il map (Cultures of the world) lib bdg $42.79
Grades: 5 6 7 8   **996**
  1. Tahiti (French Polynesia)
  ISBN 978-0-7614-2089-7   LC 2007014901
  "Provides comprehensive information on the geography, history, wildlife, governmental structure, economy, cultural diversity, peoples, religion, and culture of Tahiti." Publisher's note
  Includes glossary and bibliographical references

Webster, Christine
Polynesians; [by] Christine Webster. Weigl Publishers 2004 32p il map (Indigenous peoples) lib bdg $26
Grades: 3 4 5   **996**
  1. Polynesians
  ISBN 1-59036-123-7   LC 2003-3963

Contents: Where in the world?; Stories and legends; Out of the past; Social structures; Communication; Law and order; Celebrating cultures; Art and design; Dressing up; Food and fun; Great ideas; At issue; Into the future; Fascinating facts
  This discusses the history, social structure, language, culture, and current issues facing the Polynesian people.
  This provides "a wealth of information. . . . The well-designed pages provide a mixture of vivid color photographs, historical drawings, and eye-catching graphics." SLJ
  Includes bibliographical references

996.9   North Central Pacific Islands. Hawaii

Feeney, Stephanie
Sun and rain; exploring seasons in Hawaii. University of Hawaii Press 2008 unp il $13.95
Grades: K 1 2 3   **996.9**
  1. Sun 2. Rain 3. Hawaii 4. Seasons
  ISBN 978-0-8248-3088-5; 0-8248-3088-1
                                LC 2008272547
  "A Latitude 20 book"
  "Readers learn that Hawaii has only two seasons: wet and dry. Easy-to-read text and large, inviting photographs show the changing seasons and explain how humans, animals, and plants are affected. . . . Back matter includes additional information for adults." Horn Book Guide

998   Arctic islands and Antarctica

Beattie, Owen
Buried in ice; by Owen Beattie and John Geiger with Shelley Tanaka. Scholastic 1992 64p il maps (Time quest book) pa $6.95 hardcover o.p.
Grades: 4 5 6 7   **998**
  1. Franklin, Sir John, 1786-1847 2. Arctic regions
  ISBN 0-590-43849-2 (pa)   LC 91-23897
  "A Scholastic/Madison Press book"
  Probes the tragic and mysterious fate of Sir John Franklin's failed expedition to the Arctic to find the Northwest Passage in 1845
  "The narrative is interspersed with an imaginative section that relates the story of the expedition from the point of view of 19-year-old Luke, a member of the crew. While the text is exciting, the book's greatest strength is its superb illustrations: drawings, paintings, and historic and present day photographs are used to enrich each page." SLJ
  Includes glossary and bibliographical references

Bledsoe, Lucy Jane
How to survive in Antarctica; written and photographed by Lucy Jane Bledsoe. Holiday House 2006 101p il map $16.95 *
Grades: 5 6 7 8   **998**
  1. Antarctica
  ISBN 0-8234-1890-1   LC 2004-60639

Bledsoe, Lucy Jane—*Continued*

"Bledsoe, who made three trips to study Antarctica, bases her informal, chatty narrative on her thrilling adventure, bringing close the amazing science and geography as well as the gritty facts of human survival in the frigid environment. . . . Bledsoe's own black-and-white photos . . . will grab students across the curriculum." Booklist

Includes glossary

Foster, Karen, 1964-

Atlas of the Poles and Oceans. Picture Window Books 2008 32p il map (Picture Window Books world atlases) lib bdg $27.93

Grades: 2 3 4   **998**
1. Antarctica 2. Arctic regions 3. Ocean
ISBN 978-1-4048-3886-4 (lib bdg); 1-4048-3886-4 (lib bdg)
This introduction to the geography of the Arctic, Antarctic, and the oceans offers maps and information about plants, animals, people, and protecting the environment.
Includes glossary

Goodman, Susan, 1952-

Life on the ice; [by] Susan E. Goodman; with photographs by Michael J. Doolittle. Millbrook Press 2006 32p il lib bdg $22.60 *

Grades: 3 4 5   **998**
1. Polar regions
ISBN 978-0-7613-2775-2 (lib bdg); 0-7613-2775-4 (lib bdg)   LC 2005-06141
"This fully illustrated book introduces a few aspects of the Earth's polar regions. Topics presented include the difficulties of flying to and landing at the poles, scientific research done at each pole, and the challenge of human survival in the extreme cold." Booklist

"Excellent photos, often captioned with fascinating facts . . . accompany this text." Horn Book Guide

Kimmel, Elizabeth Cody

Ice story; Shackleton's lost expedition. Clarion Bks. 1999 120p il maps $18 *

Grades: 4 5 6 7   **998**
1. Shackleton, Sir Ernest Henry, 1874-1922
2. Endurance (Ship) 3. Imperial Trans-Antarctic Expedition (1914-1917) 4. Antarctica—Exploration
ISBN 0-395-91524-4   LC 98-29956
Describes the events of the 1914 Shackleton Antarctic expedition, when the ship the Endurance was crushed in a frozen sea and the men made the perilous journey across ice and stormy seas to reach inhabited land

"The amazing story is well served in this account, which includes photos by expedition photographer Frank Hurley." Horn Book Guide

Includes bibliographical references

Levinson, Nancy Smiler, 1938-

North Pole, South Pole; illustrated by Diane Dawson Hearn. Holiday House 2002 40p il $14.95 *

Grades: K 1 2 3   **998**
1. North Pole 2. South Pole
ISBN 0-8234-1737-9   LC 2001-59419

An introduction to the geography, climate, and inhabitants of the polar regions at the top and the bottom of the earth where the North Pole and the South Pole are located

"Beginning readers can find a clear and concise discussion of the differences between the poles. . . . Hearn's colorful illustrations in white, blue, and teal green depict a number of the animal inhabitants, all identified." SLJ

Lourie, Peter

Arctic thaw; the people of the whale in a changing climate. Boyds Mills Press 2007 47p il map $17.95

Grades: 5 6 7 8   **998**
1. Inupiat 2. Human ecology 3. Whaling 4. Alaska
5. Greenhouse effect
ISBN 978-1-59078-436-5; 1-59078-436-7
                                         LC 2006-20045
"A somewhat sobering, yet upbeat examination of the probable effects of global warming on the culture of the Iñupiaq whale hunters of Alaska's North Slope. . . . [Lourie's] lively, straightforward text describes the mixture of traditional and modern ways of the present-day Iñupiaq, as well as the work of [Paul] Shepson and his team to record weather and climate changes and to predict what effect they will have locally and globally." SLJ

Includes bibliographical references

Love, Ann, 1947-

The kids book of the Far North; written by Ann Love & Jane Drake; illustrated by Jocelyne Bouchard. Kids Can Press 2000 48p il hardcover o.p. pa $14.95

Grades: 3 4 5 6   **998**
1. Arctic regions
ISBN 1-55074-563-8; 1-55453-258-2 (pa)
"The book introduces the Arctic's landscape and rigorous climate, natural resources, early human settlement, European exploration, and the life ways of its peoples, both traditional and contemporary." Booklist

"The information will encourage meaningful discussions of topics often glossed over in other books about the Arctic. . . . An up-to-date, accessible overview." SLJ

Lynch, Wayne

Arctic; text and photographs by Wayne Lynch; assisted by Aubrey Lang. NorthWord Books for Young Readers 2007 64p il map (Our wild world: ecosystems) hardcover o.p. pa $8.95

Grades: 4 5 6 7   **998**
1. Arctic regions 2. Animals—Arctic regions
ISBN 978-1-55971-960-5; 978-1-55971-961-2 (pa)
                                         LC 2006021920
"With accessible first-person writing, Lynch describes the Arctic ecosystem, discussing both the high and low Arctic. . . . Stunning photographs include close-ups and more expansive views." Horn Book Guide

Includes bibliographical references

Markle, Sandra, 1946-
Animals Robert Scott saw; an adventure in Antarctica. Chronicle Books 2008 45p il (Explorers) $16.99
Grades: 2 3 4 5   **998**
1. Scott, Robert Falcon, 1868-1912 2. Explorers 3. Antarctica—Exploration 4. Animals—Antarctica
ISBN 978-0-8118-4918-0; 0-8118-4918-X
LC 2006-20920
"Well illustrated with acrylic paintings and archival photos, this volume . . . traces the two Antarctic expeditions of English explorer Robert Falcon Scott, who reached the South Pole with his companions in 1912, 35 days after Amundsen's Norwegian expedition. The story may be Scott's, but the focus continually turns to animals. . . . Children fascinated by both explorers and animals are the natural audience for this." Booklist
Includes glossary and bibliographical references

Martin, Jacqueline Briggs, 1945-
The lamp, the ice, and the boat called Fish; based on a true story; pictures by Beth Krommes. Houghton Mifflin 2001 unp il $15 *
Grades: 3 4 5 6   **998**
1. Karluk (Ship) 2. Canadian Arctic Expedition (1913-1918) 3. Inuit 4. Arctic regions
ISBN 0-618-00341-X   LC 99-35303
"Trapped and drifting amid the ice floes, the 1913 Canadian Arctic Expedition aboard the *Karluk* may well have been doomed, save for the resilience of her crew and the particular resourcefulness of the Inupiat who were hired as provisioners and guides. . . . Martin recounts their frigid adventures." Bull Cent Child Books
"The quiet, intriguing language, with a poet's attention to sound, will lull young ones into the story's drama, as will Beth Krommes' captivating scratchboard illustrations." Booklist

Scott, Elaine, 1940-
Poles apart; why penguins and polar bears will never be neighbors. Viking 2004 63p il maps $17.99 *
Grades: 5 6 7 8   **998**
1. Arctic regions 2. Antarctica
ISBN 0-670-05925-0   LC 2004-4270
Contents: Drifting apart: Gondwanaland and Eurasia; Poles apart: summer and winter; Mutual attraction: the magnetic poles; The people: Inuit and None; Never neighbors: penguins in the south; Never neighbors: polar bears in the north; Great races: first to see them; Great races: first to claim them; The poles today: lessons from the ice
This "book introduces the North and South Poles: their origins, seasons, composition, magnetism, people, animals, exploration, and recent changes. . . . The many excellent color illustrations include clear photographs of wildlife and mysterious, beautiful shots of the northern lights as well as maps and period photos. Scott writes well, never talking down to her audience but making scientific and historical information understandable." Booklist

Thompson, Gare
Roald Amundsen and Robert Scott race to the South Pole; by Gare Thompson. National Geographic 2007 48p il (National Geographic history chapters) lib bdg $17.90
Grades: 2 3 4   **998**
1. Amundsen, Roald, 1872-1928 2. Scott, Robert Falcon, 1868-1912 3. Antarctica—Exploration 4. South Pole
ISBN 978-1-4263-0187-2   LC 2007007898
This "presents the dramatic, tragic story of the South Pole's dueling explorers. . . . Crisp, informatively captioned photographs, some presumably taken by the doomed men, lend immediacy to the facts." Booklist

Fic   FICTION

A number of subject headings have been added to the books in this section to aid in curriculum work. It is not necessarily recommended that these subjects be used in the library catalog.

Abbott, Tony
Firegirl. Little, Brown 2006 145p $15.99; pa $5.99
Grades: 5 6 7 8   **Fic**
1. School stories 2. Burns and scalds—Fiction
ISBN   978-0-316-01171-6;   0-316-01171-1; 978-0-316-01170-9 (pa); 0-316-01170-3 (pa)
LC 2005-07964
A middle school boy's life is changed when Jessica, a girl disfigured by burns, starts attending his Catholic school while receiving treatment at a local hospital.
"Through realistic settings and dialogue, and believable characters, readers will be able to relate to the social dynamics of these adolescents who are trying to handle a difficult situation." SLJ

Kringle; illustrated by Greg Call. Scholastic Press 2005 324p il $14.99
Grades: 5 6 7 8   **Fic**
1. Santa Claus—Fiction 2. Fantasy fiction 3. Orphans—Fiction
ISBN 0-439-74942-5   LC 2005-12697
In the fifth century A.D., as order retreats from Britain with the departing Roman Army, orphaned, twelve-year-old Kringle determines to rescue his beloved guardian from the evil goblins who terrorize the countryside by kidnapping and enslaving humans and, in the process, with the help of elves and others along the way, discovers his true destiny.
"The enticing premise, appealing young hero, and nonstop action will appeal to many fantasy lovers." Booklist

The postcard. Little, Brown 2008 358p il $15.99; pa $5.99
Grades: 5 6 7 8   **Fic**
1. Mystery fiction 2. Grandmothers—Fiction 3. Florida—Fiction 4. Books and reading—Fiction
ISBN   978-0-316-01172-3;   0-316-01172-X; 978-0-316-01173-0 (pa); 0-316-01173-8 (pa)
LC 2007-31074

Abbott, Tony—*Continued*

While in St. Petersburg, Florida, to help clean out his recently-deceased grandmother's house, thirteen-year-old Jason finds an old postcard which leads him on an adventure that blends figures from an old, unfinished detective story with his family's past.

"Mystery fans will appreciate the depth and intrigue of the dual level mysteries, and will also enjoy the wit and banter of the main characters." Libr Media Connect

Abraham, Susan Gonzales, 1951-

Cecilia's year; by Susan Gonzales Abraham & Denise Gonzales Abraham. Cinco Puntos Press 2004 210p il $16.95; pa $11.95

Grades: 4 5 6 7   **Fic**
1. Poverty—Fiction 2. Sex role—Fiction 3. Hispanic Americans—Fiction 4. New Mexico—Fiction
ISBN 978-0-938317-87-6; 0-938317-87-3; 978-1-933693-02-6 (pa); 1-933693-02-9 (pa)
LC 2004-13374

Nearly fourteen and poor, Ceclia Gonzales wants desperately to go to high school and become a teacher until her mother's old-fashioned ideas about a woman's place threaten her dreams

"The cultural details are vivid and integrated into the story, providing a rich context and a snapshot of an entire community. . . . This fictionalized biography succeeds on several levels." SLJ

Another title about Cecilia is:
Surprising Cecilia (2005)

Ackerman, Karen, 1951-

The night crossing; illustrated by Elizabeth Sayles. Knopf 1994 56p il pa $4.99 hardcover o.p.

Grades: 3 4 5   **Fic**
1. Holocaust, 1933-1945—Fiction 2. Jews—Fiction
ISBN 0-679-87040-7 (pa)   LC 94-10805

In 1938, having begun to feel the persecution that all Jews are experiencing in their Austrian city, Clara and her family escape over the mountains into Switzerland

"Ackerman's writing is clear and direct; despite its simplicity, it is never banal. This is an excellent fictional introduction to the Holocaust." SLJ

Adams, Richard, 1920-

Watership Down. Scribner classics ed. Scribner 1996 c1972 429p $30; pa $15 *

Grades: 6 7 8 9   **Fic**
1. Rabbits—Fiction 2. Allegories
ISBN 0-684-83605-X; 0-7432-7770-8 (pa)

First published 1972 in the United Kingdom; first United States edition 1974 by Macmillan

"Faced with the annihilation of its warren, a small group of male rabbits sets out across the English downs in search of a new home. Internal struggles for power surface in this intricately woven, realistically told adult adventure when the protagonists must coordinate tactics in order to defeat an enemy rabbit fortress. It is clear that the author has done research on rabbit behavior, for this tale is truly authentic." Shapiro Fic for Youth. 3d edition

Adler, C. S. (Carole S.), 1932-

One unhappy horse. Clarion Bks. 2000 156p $16

Grades: 5 6 7 8   **Fic**
1. Horses—Fiction 2. Friendship—Fiction
ISBN 0-618-04912-6   LC 00-25907

Things are difficult for twelve-year-old Jan and her mother after her father's death, and when it turns out that her beloved horse needs an operation, Jan reluctantly gets money from an elderly woman whom she has befriended

"A well-paced story with interesting and mostly sympathetic characters." SLJ

Adler, David A., 1947-

Cam Jansen and the mystery of the stolen diamonds; illustrated by Susanna Natti. Viking 1980 58p il $13.99 paperback o.p. *

Grades: 2 3 4   **Fic**
1. Mystery fiction
ISBN 0-670-20039-5; 0-14-034670-8 (pa)
LC 79-20695

Easy-to-read titles about Cam Jansen are also available

Cam Jansen, a fifth-grader with a photographic memory, and her friend Eric help solve the mystery of the stolen diamonds

This is a "fast-action uncomplicated adventure . . . [with] a touch of humor, a breezy writing style, and some very enjoyable pen-and-ink drawings." Booklist

Other titles about Cam Jansen are:
Cam Jansen and the barking treasure mystery (1999)
Cam Jansen and the birthday mystery (2000)
Cam Jansen and the catnapping mystery (1998)
Cam Jansen and the chocolate fudge mystery (1993)
Cam Jansen and the first day of school mystery (2002)
Cam Jansen and the ghostly mystery (1996)
Cam Jansen and the mystery at the haunted house (1992)
Cam Jansen and the mystery at the monkey house (1985)
Cam Jansen and the mystery of Flight 54 (1989)
Cam Jansen and the mystery of the Babe Ruth baseball (1982)
Cam Jansen and the mystery of the carnival prize (1984)
Cam Jansen and the mystery of the circus clown (1983)
Cam Jansen and the mystery of the dinosaur bones (1981)
Cam Jansen and the mystery of the gold coins (1982)
Cam Jansen and the mystery of the monster movie (1984)
Cam Jansen and the mystery of the stolen corn popper (1986)
Cam Jansen and the mystery of the television dog (1981)
Cam Jansen and the mystery of the UFO (1980)
Cam Jansen and the scary snake mystery (1997)
Cam Jansen and the school play mystery (2001)
Cam Jansen and the Secret Service mystery (2006)
Cam Jansen and the snowy day mystery (2004)
Cam Jansen and the Sports Day mysteries (2009)
Cam Jansen and the summer camp mysteries (2007)
Cam Jansen and the tennis trophy mystery (2003)
Cam Jansen and the Triceratops Pops mystery (1995)
Cam Jansen and the Valentine baby mystery (2005)

Adler, David A., 1947-—*Continued*
Don't talk to me about the war. Viking 2008
216p $15.99; pa $6.99
Grades: 4 5 6 7   **Fic**
  1. Bronx (New York, N.Y.)—Fiction 2. Family life—
Fiction 3. Friendship—Fiction 4. World War, 1939-
1945—Fiction
  ISBN   978-0-670-06307-9;   0-670-06307-X;
978-0-14-241372-2 (pa); 0-14-241372-0 (pa)
                                  LC 2007-17889
  In 1940, thirteen-year-old Tommy's routine of school,
playing stickball in his Bronx, New York, neighborhood,
talking with his friend Beth, and listening to Dodgers
games on the radio changes as his mother's illness and
his increasing awareness of the war in Europe transform
his world.
  "An engaging and very accessible historical novel."
Booklist

Aguiar, Nadia
The lost island of Tamarind; [by] Nadia Aguiar.
Feiwel and Friends 2008 437p il map (The Book
of Tamarind) $17.95
Grades: 5 6 7 8   **Fic**
  1. Adventure fiction 2. Islands—Fiction 3. Magic—
Fiction 4. Siblings—Fiction 5. Pirates—Fiction
6. Giants—Fiction 7. War stories
  ISBN 978-0-312-38029-8; 0-312-38029-1
                                  LC 2008-5623
  Thirteen-year-old Maya, who has spent her life at sea
with her marine biologist parents, yearns for a normal
life, but when a storm washes her parents overboard, life
becomes anything but normal for Maya, her younger
brother and baby sister, as they land at a mysterious, un-
charted island filled with danger.
  "Each detail of this fantasy is crafted with care; readers will be drawn into this dangerous, magical world
where anything is possible and nothing can be fully explained." SLJ

Aiken, Joan, 1924-2004
The wolves of Willoughby Chase; illustrated by
Pat Marriott. Delacorte Press 2000 c1962 181p il
hardcover o.p. pa $6.50 *
Grades: 5 6 7 8   **Fic**
  1. Great Britain—Fiction
  ISBN 0-385-32790-0; 0-440-49603-9 (pa)
  First published 1962 in the United Kingdom; first
United States edition 1963 by Doubleday
  "In this burlesque of a Victorian melodrama, two Lon-
don children are sent to a country estate while their par-
ents are away. Here they outwit a wicked governess, es-
cape from packs of hungry wolves, and restore the estate
to its rightful owner." Hodges. Books for Elem Sch Libr
  "Plot, characterization, and background blend perfectly
into an amazing whole. . . . Highly recommended." SLJ
  Other titles in this series are:
Black hearts in Battersea (1964)
Cold Shoulder Road (1996)
The cuckoo tree (1971)
Dangerous games (1999)
Is underground (1993)
Midwinter nightingale (2003)
The stolen lake (1981)
The witch of Clatteringshaws (2005)

Alcott, Louisa May, 1832-1888
Little women; illustrated by Scott McKowen.
Sterling Pub. 2004 525p il $9.95
Grades: 5 6 7 8   **Fic**
  1. Sisters—Fiction 2. Family life—Fiction 3. New En-
gland—Fiction
  ISBN 978-1-4027-1458-0; 1-4027-1458-0
                                  LC 2004-15669
  First published 1868
  Chronicles the joys and sorrows of the four March sis-
ters as they grow into young women in mid-nineteenth-
century New England.
  Other titles about members of the March family are:
Eight cousins (1875)
Jo's boys (1886)
Little men (1871)
Rose in bloom (1876)

Alexander, Lloyd, 1924-2007
The book of three. rev ed. Holt & Co. 1999
190p (Chronicles of Prydain) $19.95; pa $6.99 *
Grades: 5 6 7 8   **Fic**
  1. Fantasy fiction
  ISBN   978-0-8050-6132-1;   0-8050-6132-0;
978-0-8050-8048-3 (pa); 0-8050-8048-1 (pa)
                                  LC 98-40901
  First published 1964
  "The first of five books about the mythical land of
Prydain finds Taran, an assistant pig keeper, fighting
with Prince Gwydion against the evil which theatens the
kingdom." Hodges. Books for Elem Sch Libr
  "Related in a simple, direct style, this fast-paced tale
of high adventure has a well-balanced blend of fantasy,
realism, and humor." SLJ
  Other titles about the mythical land of Prydain are:
The black cauldron (1965)
The castle of Llyr (1966)
The foundling and other tales of Prydain (1999)
The high king (1968)
Taran Wanderer (1967)

The golden dream of Carlo Chuchio. Henry Holt
& Co. 2007 306p il $16.95
Grades: 5 6 7 8 9   **Fic**
  1. Fantasy fiction 2. Buried treasure—Fiction
3. Middle East—Fiction 4. Voyages and travels—Fiction
  ISBN 978-0-8050-8333-0; 0-8050-8333-2
                                  LC 2006-49710
  Naive and bumbling Carlo, his shady camel-puller
Baksheesh, and Shira, a girl determined to return home,
follow a treasure map through the deserts and cities of
the infamous Golden Road, as mysterious strangers try in
vain to point them toward real treasures
  This "is an exuberant and compassionate tale of adventure." Publ Wkly

The Illyrian adventure. Dutton 1986 132p pa
$5.99 hardcover o.p.
Grades: 5 6 7 8   **Fic**
  1. Adventure fiction
  ISBN 0-14-130313-1 (pa)   LC 85-30762
  "Sixteen-year-old Vesper Holly drags her long-
suffering guardian, Brinnie, off to Illyria to vindicate her

Alexander, Lloyd, 1924-2007—*Continued*

late father's reputation as a scholar. With humor, beguiling charm, and intelligence she manages to find a treasure, thwart a conspiracy to murder Illyria's King Osman, and guide two rival factions to the peace table." Wilson Libr Bull

"Alexander's archeological mystery has intricate plotting and witty wording." Bull Cent Child Books

Other adventure titles featuring Vesper Holly are:
The Drackenberg adventure (1988)
The El Dorado adventure (1987)
The Jedera adventure (1989)
The Philadelphia adventure (1990)
The Xanadu adventure (2005)

The iron ring. Dutton Children's Bks. 1997 283p pa $5.99 hardcover o.p.
Grades: 5 6 7 8   **Fic**
  1. Adventure fiction 2. India—Fiction
  ISBN 0-14-130348-4 (pa)   LC 96-29730
"Young Tamar, ruler of a small Indian kingdom, wagers with a visiting king and loses his kingdom and his freedom. Traveling to the king's land to make good on his debt, he collects quite an entourage and eventually overcomes his enemies with his friends' help. This tale offers delightful characters, a philosophical interest in the meaning of life, a thoughtful look at the caste system, and a clever use of Indian animal folktales." Horn Book Guide

The remarkable journey of Prince Jen. Dutton Children's Bks. 1991 273p pa $6.99 hardcover o.p.
Grades: 5 6 7 8   **Fic**
  1. Adventure fiction 2. China—Fiction
  ISBN 0-14-240225-7 (pa)   LC 91-13720
Bearing six unusual gifts, young Prince Jen in Tang Dynasty China embarks on a perilous quest and emerges triumphantly into manhood
"Alexander satisfies the taste for excitement, but his vivid characters and the food for thought he offers will nourish long after the last page is turned." SLJ

The rope trick. Dutton Children's Bks. 2002 195p $16.99; pa $5.99
Grades: 4 5 6 7   **Fic**
  1. Magicians—Fiction 2. Adventure fiction 3. Italy—Fiction
  ISBN 0-525-47020-4; 0-14-240119-6 (pa)
      LC 2002-67497
Motivated by her quest to learn a legendary rope trick, the magician Princess Lidi and her troupe embark on a journey through Renaissance Italy that intertwines adventure, love, and mystery
"Even as the outsize characterizations and rollicking adventure amuse, the compassionate vision of life's possibilities is likely to bring a lump to the throat." Publ Wkly

Westmark. Dutton 1981 184p pa $5.99 hardcover o.p.
Grades: 5 6 7 8   **Fic**
  1. Adventure fiction
  ISBN 0-14-131068-5 (pa)
A boy fleeing from criminal charges falls in with a charlatan, his dwarf attendant, and an urchin girl, travels

with them about the kingdom of Westmark, and ultimately arrives at the palace where the king is grieving over the loss of his daughter

The author "peoples his tale with a marvelous cast of individuals, and weaves an intricate story of high adventure that climaxes in a superbly conceived conclusion, which, though predictable, is reached through carefully built tension and subtly added comic relief." Booklist

Other titles in this series are:
The Beggar Queen (1984)
The Kestrel (1982)

Allison, Jennifer

Gilda Joyce, psychic investigator. Sleuth/Dutton 2005 321p $13.99; pa $6.99 *
Grades: 5 6 7 8   **Fic**
  1. Mystery fiction 2. Cousins—Fiction
  ISBN   978-0-525-47375-6;   0-525-47375-0;
  978-0-14-240698-4 (pa); 0-14-240698-8 (pa)
      LC 2004-10834
During the summer before ninth grade, intrepid Gilda Joyce invites herself to the San Francisco mansion of distant cousin Lester Splinter and his thirteen-year-old daughter, where she uses her purported psychic abilities and detective skills to solve the mystery of the mansion's boarded-up tower.

"Allison pulls off something special here. She not only offers a credible mystery . . . but also . . . provides particularly strong characterizations." Booklist

Other titles about Gilda Joyce are:
Gilda Joyce: the Ladies of the Lake (2006)
Gilda Joyce: the ghost sonata (2007)
Gilda Joyce: the dead drop (2009)

Almond, David, 1951-

The boy who climbed into the moon; illustrated by Polly Dunbar. Candlewick Press 2010 117p il $15.99
Grades: 3 4 5   **Fic**
  1. Adventure fiction 2. Moon—Fiction 3. Great Britain—Fiction
  ISBN 978-0-7636-4217-4; 0-7636-4217-7
      LC 2009-11158
Helped by a very long ladder, some unusual acquaintances, two rather worried parents, and a great deal of community spirit, a young English boy makes an astonishing discovery when he embarks on a mission to prove that the moon is nothing but a big hole in the sky

"Almond employs all manners of amusements . . . while never losing sight of some refreshing realities: Paul's parents are a real presence, and the city feels appropriately dense. . . . Dunbar's full-color illustrations . . . nimbly dodge the prose." Booklist

Heaven Eyes. Delacorte Press 2001 c2000 233p hardcover o.p. pa $5.50
Grades: 5 6 7 8   **Fic**
  1. Orphans—Fiction 2. Adventure fiction
  ISBN 0-385-32770-6; 0-440-22910-3 (pa)
      LC 00-31798
First published 2000 in the United Kingdom
Having escaped from their orphanage on a raft, Erin, January, and Mouse float down into another world of

Almond, David, 1951-—*Continued*

abandoned warehouses and factories, meeting a strange old man and an even stranger girl with webbed fingers and little memory of her past

"The ambiguous and surreal setting and the lyricism of the metaphor-laden prose make this a compelling and original novel." SLJ

My dad's a birdman; illustrated by Polly Dunbar. Candlewick Press 2008 115p il $15.99

Grades: 4 5 6   **Fic**

1. Fathers—Fiction 2. Flight—Fiction
ISBN 978-0-7636-3667-8; 0-7636-3667-3

In a rainy town in the north of England, there are strange goings-on. Dad is building a pair of wings, eating flies, and feathering his nest. Lizzie is missing her Mom and looking after Dad by letting him follow his new-found whimsy. What's behind it all? It's the great human bird competition.

"Handsomely produced, the book is printed in varying size typefaces and enhanced by Dunbar's pencil, water-color, and collage illustrations interspersed throughout the text. Casual yet evocative, they perfectly interpret Al-mond's broadly sketched characters. A fine read-aloud." SLJ

Skellig. 10th anniversary ed. Delacorte Press 2009 c1998 182p $16.99; pa $6.99 *

Grades: 5 6 7 8 9 10   **Fic**

1. Fantasy fiction
ISBN 978-0-385-32653-7; 0-385-32653-X; 978-0-440-41602-9 (pa); 0-440-41602-7 (pa)

Michael L. Printz Award honor book

First published 1998 in the United Kingdom; first United States edition 1999

Unhappy about his baby sister's illness and the chaos of moving into a dilapidated old house, Michael retreats to the garage and finds a mysterious stranger who is something like a bird and something like an angel.

"The plot is beautifully paced and the characters are drawn with a graceful, careful hand. . . . A lovingly done, thought-provoking novel." SLJ

Alvarez, Julia, 1950-

How Tía Lola came to visit/stay. Knopf 2001 147p $15.95; pa $5.50 *

Grades: 4 5 6 7   **Fic**

1. Aunts—Fiction 2. Dominican Americans—Fiction
3. Divorce—Fiction 4. Vermont—Fiction
ISBN 0-375-80215-0; 0-440-41870-4 (pa)
                                        LC 00-62932

On title page "visit" is crossed out

Although ten-year-old Miguel is at first embarrassed by his colorful aunt, Tia Lola, when she comes to Ver-mont from the Dominican Republic to stay with his mother, his sister, and him after his parents' divorce, he learns to love her

"Readers will enjoy the funny situations, identify with the developing relationships and conflicting feelings of the characters, and will get a spicy taste of Caribbean culture in the bargain." SLJ

Return to sender. Alfred A. Knopf 2009 325p $16.99; lib bdg $19.99 *

Grades: 4 5 6 7   **Fic**

1. Farm life—Fiction 2. Friendship—Fiction
3. Migrant labor—Fiction 4. Illegal aliens—Fiction
5. Vermont—Fiction
ISBN 978-0-375-85838-3; 0-375-85838-5; 978-0-375-95838-0 (lib bdg); 0-375-95838-X (lib bdg)
                                        LC 2008-23520

Awarded the Belpre Author Medal (2010)

After his family hires migrant Mexican workers to help save their Vermont farm from foreclosure, eleven-year-old Tyler befriends the oldest daughter, but when he discovers they may not be in the country legally, he real-izes that real friendship knows no borders.

"Readers will be moved by small moments. . . . A tender, well-constructed book." Publ Wkly

Amato, Mary, 1961-

Stinky and successful; the Riot brothers never stop; illustrated by Ethan Long. Holiday House 2007 152p il (The Riot Brothers) $16.95; pa $7.95

Grades: 2 3 4   **Fic**

1. Brothers—Fiction
ISBN 978-0-8234-2100-8; 0-8234-2100-7; 978-0-8234-2196-1 (pa); 0-8234-2196-1 (pa)
                                        LC 2007013366

Wilbur and Orville Riot "set out to rescue a damsel in distress, . . . trick their mother on April Fools' Day, and become mad scientists. . . . Plenty of wordplay; fast-paced, episodic chapters; and lively cartoon illustra-tions will keep readers engaged." SLJ

Other titles in this series are:
Snarf attack, underfoodle, and the secret of life (2004)
Drooling and dangerous (2006)
Take the mummy and run (2009)

Anaya, Rudolfo A.

The first tortilla; a bilingual story; [by] Rudolfo Anaya; illustrated by Amy Cordova; translated into Spanish by Enrique R. Lamadrid. University of New Mexico 2007 unp il $16.95

Grades: 2 3 4   **Fic**

1. Mexico—Fiction 2. Bilingual books—English-Spanish
ISBN 978-0-8263-4214-0

Guided by a blue hummingbird, Jade brings an offer-ing to the Mountain Spirit who lives near her village in Mexico, and asks if he will send rain to end the drought that threatens the people.

"Anaya has retold a Mexican legend and made it his own with his spiritual prose. . . . Córdova's rich acrylic paintings lend a traditional feel to the setting while main-taining the tale's mystical elements. A beautifully written and illustrated title." SLJ

Andersen, Hans Christian, 1805-1875

The little match girl; illustrated by Rachel Isadora. Putnam 1987 30p il $16.99

Grades: 3 4 5   **Fic**

ISBN 0-399-21336-8   LC 85-30082

Andersen, Hans Christian, 1805-1875—Continued

The wares of the poor little match girl illuminate her cold world, bringing some beauty to her brief, tragic life
"Isadora follows Andersen's lead, neither sensationalizing nor apologizing for the tale's potentially sentimental plot. . . . A moving, original picture-book interpretation of the classic tale." Booklist

The princess and the pea; illustrated by Dorothée Duntze. North-South Bks. 1985 unp il $16.95; pa $7.95
Grades: K 1 2 3   Fic
1. Fairy tales
ISBN 1-55858-034-4; 1-55858-381-5 (pa)
LC 85-7199
A young girl feels a pea through twenty mattresses and twenty featherbeds and proves she is a real princess
"This classic Andersen fairy tale is presented in simple text and with elaborate illustrations. . . . Duntze appears to set the story during the Renaissance, and her illustrations are precise, intricate and detailed." SLJ

Anderson, Janet, 1946-

The last treasure; [by] Janet S. Anderson. Dutton 2003 257p il hardcover o.p. pa $6.99
Grades: 5 6 7 8   Fic
1. Family life—Fiction 2. Buried treasure—Fiction
ISBN 0-525-46919-2; 0-14-240217-6 (pa)
LC 2002-74143
Thirteen-year-old Ellsworth leaves his father to visit the relatives he has never met and eventually joins forces with Jess, his distant cousin, to uncover family secrets and search for their ancestor's hidden treasure
"Anderson has conjured up a fascinating read for puzzle lovers while sandwiching in an important message about intergenerational relationships." SLJ

Anderson, Jodi Lynn

May Bird and The Ever After; book one; illustrations by Leonid Gore. Atheneum Books for Young Readers 2005 317p il $17.99; pa $5.99
Grades: 5 6 7 8   Fic
1. Fantasy fiction
ISBN 978-0-689-86923-5; 0-689-86923-1; 978-1-4169-0607-0 (pa); 1-4169-0607-X (pa)
LC 2004-17829
Lonely and shy, ten-year-old May Ellen Bird has no idea what awaits her when she falls into the lake and enters The Ever After, home of ghosts and the Bogeyman.
"Anderson sets the unsettling, nightmarish tone of her offbeat fantasy in the first paragraph, then compounds the horror chapter after scary chapter. . . . The first of a trilogy, this book leaves loads of tantalizing, unanswered questions." Booklist
Other titles in this series are:
May Bird among the stars (2006)
May Bird, warrior princess (2007)

Anderson, Laurie Halse, 1961-

Chains; seeds of America. Simon & Schuster Books for Young Readers 2008 316p $16.99; pa $6.99 *
Grades: 6 7 8 9 10   Fic
1. United States—History—1775-1783, Revolution—Fiction 2. Slavery—Fiction 3. African Americans—Fiction 4. Spies—Fiction 5. New York (N.Y.)—Fiction
ISBN 978-1-4169-0585-1; 1-4169-0585-5; 978-1-4169-0586-8 (pa); 1-4169-0586-3 (pa)
LC 2007-52139
After being sold to a cruel couple in New York City, a slave named Isabel spies for the rebels during the Revolutionary War.
"This gripping novel offers readers a startlingly provocative view of the Revolutionary War. . . . [Anderson's] solidly researched exploration of British and Patriot treatment of slaves during a war for freedom is nuanced and evenhanded, presented in service of a fast-moving, emotionally involving plot." Publ Wkly

Fever, 1793. Simon & Schuster Bks. for Young Readers 2000 251p $17.99; pa $6.99
Grades: 5 6 7 8   Fic
1. Yellow fever—Fiction 2. Epidemics—Fiction 3. Philadelphia (Pa.)—Fiction
ISBN 978-0-689-83858-3; 0-689-83858-1; 978-0-689-84891-9 (pa); 0-689-84891-9 (pa)
LC 00-32238
ALA YALSA Margaret A. Edwards Award (2009)
In 1793 Philadelphia, sixteen-year-old Matilda Cook, separated from her sick mother, learns about perseverance and self-reliance when she is forced to cope with the horrors of a yellow fever epidemic.
"A vivid work, rich with well-drawn and believable characters. Unexpected events pepper the top-flight novel that combines accurate historical detail with a spellbinding story line." Voice Youth Advocates

Anderson, M. T., 1968-

The Game of Sunken Places; [by] M. T. Anderson. Scholastic Press 2004 260p $16.95; pa $5.99
Grades: 5 6 7 8   Fic
1. Games—Fiction 2. Vermont—Fiction
ISBN 0-439-41660-4; 0-439-41661-2 (pa)
LC 2003-20055
When two boys stay with an eccentric relative at his mansion in rural Vermont, they discover an old-fashioned board game that draws them into a mysterious adventure.
"Deliciously scary, often funny, and crowned by a pair of deeply satisfying surprises, this tour de force leaves one marveling at Anderson's ability to slip between genres as fluidly as his middle-grade heroes straddle worlds." Booklist
Followed by: The suburb beyond the stars (2010)

Whales on stilts; illustrations by Kurt Cyrus. Harcourt 2005 188p il $15; pa $5.95 *
Grades: 4 5 6 7   Fic
1. Science fiction
ISBN 0-15-205340-9; 0-15-205394-8 (pa)
LC 2004-17754

Anderson, M. T., 1968-—*Continued*

Racing against the clock, shy middle-school student Lily and her best friends, Katie and Jasper, must foil the plot of her father's conniving boss to conquer the world using an army of whales.

"A story written with the author's tongue shoved firmly into his cheek. . . . It's full of witty pokes at other series novels and Jasper's nutty inventions." SLJ

Other titles about Lily, Kate, and Jasper are:

The clue of the linoleum lederhosen (2006)
Jasper Dash and the Flame-pits of Delaware (2009)

Angle, Kimberly Greene

Hummingbird; [by] Kimberly Greene Angle. Farrar Straus Giroux 2008 243p $16.95

Grades: 5 6 7 8   **Fic**

1. Bereavement—Fiction 2. Death—Fiction 3. Family life—Fiction 4. Farm life—Fiction 5. Georgia—Fiction 6. Grandmothers—Fiction

ISBN 978-0-374-33376-8; 0-374-33376-9

LC 2007-9156

In spite of a busy life on the family pumpkin and watermelon farm in Jubilee, Georgia, twelve-year-old March Anne Tanner feels that something is missing, and when Grenna, the grandmother who has helped raise her since her mother died when she was three, also passes on, March Anne finds that she must act on her feelings of loss.

"The novel is a call to notice nature's bounty as well as the story of a search for identity; and it reveals much about the hard work and simple life on a farm in rural Georgia. Charmingly told, the pace is slow but as compelling as the return of spring." KLIATT

Appelbaum, Susannah

The Hollow Bettle; illustrated by Jennifer Taylor. Alfred A. Knopf 2009 399p il (The Poisons of Caux) $16.99; lib bdg $19.99

Grades: 4 5 6 7   **Fic**

1. Poisons and poisoning—Fiction 2. Uncles—Fiction 3. Fantasy fiction

ISBN 978-0-375-85173-5; 0-375-85173-9; 978-0-375-95173-2 (lib bdg); 0-375-95173-3 (lib bdg)

LC 2008-22626

Eleven-year-old Ivy Manx sets out with her new friend, a young "taster," to find her missing uncle, an outlawed healer, in the dangerous kingdom of Caux where magic, herbs, and poisons rule.

This "is a deeply satisfying, humor-laced quest with elements of wizardry and herbology, deeds of a dastardly nature, and, ultimately, redemption." Booklist

Appelt, Kathi, 1954-

Keeper; illustrated by August Hall. Atheneum Books for Young Readers 2010 il $16.99

Grades: 5 6 7 8   **Fic**

1. Sailing—Fiction 2. Ocean—Fiction 3. Mermaids and mermen—Fiction 4. Mother-daughter relationship—Fiction

ISBN 978-1-4169-5060-8; 1-4169-5060-5

LC 2010000795

On the night of the blue moon when mermaids are said to gather on a sandbar in the Gulf of Mexico, ten-year-old Keeper sets out in a small boat, with her dog BD and a seagull named Captain, determined to find her mother, a mermaid, as Keeper has always believed, who left long ago to return to the sea.

"Deftly spinning together mermaid lore, local legend and natural history, this stunning tale proves 'every landscape has its magical beings,' and the most unlikely ones can form a perfect family. Hall's black-and-white illustrations lend perspective and immediacy. Beautiful and evocative—an absolute 'keeper.' " Kirkus

The underneath; illustrated by David Small. Atheneum Books for Young Readers 2008 313p il $16.99; pa $7.99 *

Grades: 3 4 5 6   **Fic**

1. Dogs—Fiction 2. Cats—Fiction

ISBN 978-1-4169-5058-5; 1-4169-5058-3; 978-1-4169-5059-2 (pa); 1-4169-5059-1 (pa)

LC 2007031969

A Newbery Medal honor book, 2009

An old hound that has been chained up at his hateful owner's run-down shack, and two kittens born underneath the house, endure separation, danger, and many other tribulations in their quest to be reunited and free.

"Well realized in Small's excellent full-page drawings, this fine book is most of all distinguished by the originality of the story and the fresh beauty of its author's voice." Horn Book

Applegate, Katherine

Home of the brave. Feiwel & Friends 2007 249p $16.95

Grades: 5 6 7 8   **Fic**

1. Immigrants—Fiction 2. Refugees—Fiction 3. Africans—Fiction 4. Cattle—Fiction 5. Minnesota—Fiction 6. Novels in verse

ISBN 0-312-36765-1; 978-0-312-36765-7

LC 2006-32053

Kek, an African refugee, is confronted by many strange things at the Minneapolis home of his aunt and cousin, as well as in his fifth grade classroom, and longs for his missing mother, but finds comfort in the company of a cow and her owner.

"This beautiful story of hope and resilience is written in free verse." Voice Youth Advocates

Armstrong, Alan, 1939-

Looking for Marco Polo; illustrated by Tim Jessell. Random House 2009 286p $16.99

Grades: 4 5 6 7   **Fic**

1. Polo, Marco, 1254-1323?—Fiction 2. Missing persons—Fiction 3. Venice (Italy)—Fiction

ISBN 978-0-375-83321-2; 0-375-83321-8

When they lose touch with his father's Gobi Desert expedition, eleven-year-old Mark accompanies his mother to Venice, Italy, and there, while waiting for news of his father, learns about the legendary Marco Polo and his adventures in the Far East.

"Armstrong ably conjures up the atmosphere of damp, foggy Venice in late December while blowing some dust off of the accounts of Marco Polo's travels with his live-

Armstrong, Alan, 1939-—*Continued*

ly storytelling. . . . Whether or not readers know the specifics of Marco Polo's voyages, they will enjoy this entertaining blend of contemporary and historical adventure." Booklist

Raleigh's page; illustrated by Tim Jessell. Random House 2007 328p il $16.99; lib bdg $19.99

Grades: 4 5 6 7   **Fic**

1. Raleigh, Sir Walter, 1552?-1618—Fiction 2. Great Britain—History—1485-1603, Tudors—Fiction 3. Virginia—Fiction 4. Native Americans—Fiction 5. Adventure fiction

ISBN 978-0-375-83319-9; 978-0-375-93319-6 (lib bdg)   LC 2006-08434

In the late 16th century, fifteen-year-old Andrew leaves school in England and must prove himself as a page to Sir Walter Raleigh before embarking for Virginia, where he helps to establish relations with the Indians.

Armstrong "weaves a richly detailed historical narrative. . . . Historical figures such as Raleigh, Thomas Harriot, and Manteo mix with fictional characters in an adventure that makes for compelling reading. Illustrated with expressive pencil drawings." Booklist

Whittington; illustrated by S. D. Schindler. Random House 2005 191p il $14.95; lib bdg $16.99; pa $6.50 *

Grades: 4 5 6   **Fic**

1. Cats—Fiction 2. Domestic animals—Fiction

ISBN 0-375-82864-8; 0-375-92864-2 (lib bdg); 0-375-82865-6 (pa)   LC 2004-05789

A Newbery Medal honor book, 2006

Whittington, a feline descendant of Dick Whittington's famous cat of English folklore, appears at a rundown barnyard plagued by rats and restores harmony while telling his ancestor's story.

"The story works beautifully, both as historical fiction about medieval street life and commerce and as a witty, engaging tale of barnyard camaraderie and survival." Booklist

Armstrong, William Howard, 1914-1999

Sounder; [by] William H. Armstrong; illustrations by James Barkley. Harper & Row 1969 116p il $15.99; pa $5.99 *

Grades: 5 6 7 8   **Fic**

1. Dogs—Fiction 2. African Americans—Fiction 3. Family life—Fiction

ISBN 0-06-020143-6; 0-06-440020-4 (pa)

Awarded the Newbery Medal, 1970

"Set in the South in the era of sharecropping and segregation, this succinctly told tale poignantly describes the courage of a father who steals a ham in order to feed his undernourished family; the determination of the eldest son, who searches for his father despite the apathy of prison authorities; and the devotion of a coon dog named Sounder." Shapiro. Fic for Youth. 3d edition

Arnosky, Jim

The pirates of Crocodile Swamp. G. P. Putnam's Sons 2009 230p il $15.99

Grades: 3 4 5 6   **Fic**

1. Adventure fiction 2. Brothers—Fiction 3. Runaway children—Fiction 4. Florida—Fiction 5. Wetlands—Fiction

ISBN 978-0-399-25068-2; 0-399-25068-9

Kidnapped by their father, two boys escape into the mangrove swamps of Key Largo, Florida, where they learn to live on their own among the wildlife.

This "is an exciting story, with plenty of Arnosky's trademark insight into the delights and dangers of the natural (and human) world. The prose is direct and gripping, the characterization strong, and the story includes just enough of the author's illustrations to enrich the fast-moving tale." SLJ

Asch, Frank

Star jumper; journal of a cardboard genius. Kids Can Press 2006 128p $14.95; pa $5.95

Grades: 3 4 5   **Fic**

1. Inventors—Fiction 2. Brothers—Fiction 3. Space vehicles—Fiction

ISBN 978-1-55337-886-0; 1-55337-886-5; 978-1-55337-887-7 (pa); 1-55337-887-3 (pa)

"Using his astounding scientific ability . . . Alex designs the Star Jumper. This advanced cardboard spacecraft will take him across the galaxy to a brother-free planet—if only he can keep the first grader out of the way until liftoff. The first-person narration is lively and realistic." SLJ

Other titles about Alex and his brother are:

Gravity buster (2007)
Time twister (2008)

Atkinson, Elizabeth

From Alice to Zen and everyone in between; a novel. Carolrhoda Books 2008 247p $16.95

Grades: 5 6 7   **Fic**

1. Popularity—Fiction 2. School stories 3. Eccentrics and eccentricities—Fiction 4. Moving—Fiction 5. Family life—Fiction 6. Massachusetts—Fiction

ISBN 978-0-8225-7271-8; 0-8225-7271-0
                                                                                                  LC 2007-9659

Upon moving from Boston to the suburbs, eleven-year-old tomboy Alice meets Zen, a very strange neighbor who is determined to help her become popular when they both begin middle school, although he himself is a loner.

"Atkinson describes Alice's ethical development credibly and engagingly." Booklist

Atwater, Richard Tupper, 1892-1948

Mr. Popper's penguins; [by] Richard and Florence Atwater; illustrated by Robert Lawson. Little, Brown 1988 138p il $18.99; pa $6.99 *

Grades: 3 4 5   **Fic**

1. Penguins—Fiction

ISBN 0-316-05842-4; 0-316-05843-2 (pa)

A Newbery Medal honor book, 1939

Reissue first published in 1938

Atwater, Richard Tupper, 1892-1948—*Continued*

When Mr. Popper, a mild little painter and decorator with a taste for books and movies on polar explorations, was presented with a penguin, he named it Captain Cook. From that moment on life was changed for the Popper family

"To the depiction of the penguins in all conceivable moods Robert Lawson [the] artist has brought not only his skill but his individual humor, and his portrayal of the wistful Mr. Popper is memorable." N Y Times Book Rev

Auch, Mary Jane

A dog on his own. Holiday House 2008 153p $16.95; pa $6.95

Grades: 3 4 5   **Fic**
1. Dogs—Fiction
ISBN   978-0-8234-2088-9;   0-8234-2088-4;
978-0-8234-2243-2 (pa); 0-8234-2243-7 (pa)
                                    LC 2008-15963
After a daring escape from the animal shelter, Pearl, Peppy, and K-10—so named because he is one step above all the other canines—explore the outside world while moving from one adventure to another.

"This is a compelling, affectionate story of opening not just one's home, but also one's heart." Booklist

I was a third grade science project; illustrated by Herm Auch. Holiday House 1998 96p il $15.95

Grades: 2 3 4   **Fic**
1. School stories 2. Hypnotism—Fiction
ISBN 0-8234-1357-8   LC 97-41996
While trying to hypnotize his dog for the third grade science fair, Brian accidentally makes his best friend Josh think he's a cat

"Auch's wisecracking third-graders and superb comic timing will have readers rolling on the floor." Booklist
Other titles about Brian are:
I was a third grade bodyguard (2003)
I was a third grade spy (2001)

Journey to nowhere. Holt & Co. 1997 202p pa $4.99 hardcover o.p.

Grades: 4 5 6 7   **Fic**
1. Frontier and pioneer life—Fiction 2. New York (State)—Fiction
ISBN 0-440-41491-1 (pa)   LC 96-42249
This is the first title in the Genesee trilogy. In 1815, while traveling by covered wagon to settle in the wilderness of western New York, eleven-year-old Mem experiences a flood and separation from her family

"A well-written, realistic, and thoroughly researched novel." Booklist
Other titles in the Genesee trilogy are;
Frozen summer (1998)
The road to home (2000)

One-handed catch; [by] MJ Auch. Henry Holt and Co. 2006 248p $16.95; pa $6.99 *

Grades: 4 5 6   **Fic**
1. Handicapped—Fiction 2. Family life—Fiction
ISBN   978-0-8050-7900-5;   0-8050-7900-9;
978-0-312-53575-9 (pa); 0-312-53575-9 (pa)
                                    LC 2006-00370

After losing his hand in an accident in his father's butcher shop in 1946, sixth-grader Norman uses hard work and humor to learn to live with his disability and to succeed at baseball, art, and other activities.

"Loosely based on childhood experiences of the author's husband, this story offers both inspiration and useful information, deftly wrapped in an engaging narrative." Booklist

Wing nut; [by] MJ Auch. Henry Holt & Co. 2005 231p $16.95

Grades: 5 6 7 8   **Fic**
1. Moving—Fiction 2. Birds—Fiction 3. Old age—Fiction
ISBN 0-8050-7531-3   LC 2004-54046
When twelve-year-old Grady and his mother relocate yet again, they find work taking care of an elderly man, who teaches Grady about cars, birds, and what it means to have a home

"Auch's story . . . is engaging. . . . What will attract readers . . . is the author's careful integration of bird lore and the unusual challenges of creating and maintaining a purple martin colony." Booklist

Avi, 1937-

The barn. Orchard Bks. 1994 106p hardcover o.p. pa $4.99

Grades: 4 5 6 7   **Fic**
1. Farm life—Fiction 2. Frontier and pioneer life—Fiction 3. Father-son relationship—Fiction
ISBN 0-531-06861-7; 978-0-380-72562-5 (pa)
                                    LC 94-6920
"A Richard Jackson book"
In an effort to fulfill their dying father's last request, nine-year-old Ben and his brother and sister construct a barn on their land in the Oregon Territory in the 1850s

"While focusing mainly on his characters, Avi presents a vivid picture of the time and place, including fairly involved details about how the barn is constructed. This novel . . . is a thought-provoking and engaging piece of historical fiction." SLJ

Blue heron. Avon Bks. 1993 186p pa $6.99

Grades: 5 6 7 8   **Fic**
1. Family life—Fiction 2. Herons—Fiction
ISBN 978-0-380-72043-9 (pa); 0-380-72043-4 (pa)
First published 1992 by Bradbury Press
While spending the month of August on the Massachusetts shore with her father, stepmother, and their new baby, almost thirteen-year-old Maggie finds beauty in and draws strength from a great blue heron, even as the family around her unravels

"Maggie emerges as a sensitive heroine whose perceptions are genuine as well as compelling. Reflecting the complexity of people and their emotions, this novel explores rather than solves the conflicts introduced." Pub Wkly

Avi, 1937-—*Continued*

The Book Without Words; a fable of medieval magic. Hyperion Books for Children 2005 203p hardcover o.p. pa $5.99

Grades: 5 6 7 8 **Fic**

1. Supernatural—Fiction 2. Magic—Fiction 3. Middle Ages—Fiction 4. Great Britain—History—0-1066—Fiction

ISBN 0-7868-0829-2; 0-7868-1659-7 (pa)

"At the dawning of the Middle Ages, Thorston, an old alchemist, works feverishly to create gold and to dose himself with a concoction that will enable him to live forever. The key to his success lies in a mysterious book with blank pages that can only be read by desperate, green-eyed people. . . . Avi's compelling language creates a dreary foreboding. . . . Clearly this is a story with a message, a true fable. Thoughtful readers will devour its absorbing plot and humorous elements, and learn a 'useful truth' along the way." SLJ

Crispin: the cross of lead. Hyperion Bks. for Children 2002 $15.99; pa $6.99 *

Grades: 5 6 7 8 **Fic**

1. Orphans—Fiction 2. Middle Ages—Fiction 3. Great Britain—History—1154-1399, Plantagenets—Fiction

ISBN 0-7868-0828-4; 0-7868-1658-9 (pa)

LC 2001-51829

Awarded the Newbery Medal, 2001

Falsely accused of theft and murder, an orphaned peasant boy in fourteenth-century England flees his village and meets a larger-than-life juggler who holds a dangerous secret

This "book is a page-turner from beginning to end. . . . A meticulously crafted story, full of adventure, mystery, and action." SLJ

Other titles in this series are:

Crispin at the edge of the world (2006)

Crispin: the end of time (2010)

Don't you know there's a war on? HarperCollins Pubs. 2001 200p hardcover o.p. pa $5.99

Grades: 4 5 6 7 **Fic**

1. World War, 1939-1945—Fiction 2. Teachers—Fiction 3. Brooklyn (New York, N.Y.)—Fiction

ISBN 0-380-97863-6; 0-380-81544-3 (pa)

LC 00-46102

In wartime Brooklyn in 1943, eleven-year-old Howie Crispers mounts a campaign to save his favorite teacher from being fired

"The 1943 Brooklyn setting is well evoked in Howie's lively, slang-spangled narration. The novel's uncomplicated, compact structure invites reading aloud." Horn Book Guide

The end of the beginning; being the adventures of a small snail (and an even smaller ant); with illustrations by Tricia Tusa. Harcourt 2004 143p il $14.95; pa $6.95

Grades: 3 4 5 **Fic**

1. Snails—Fiction 2. Ants—Fiction

ISBN 0-15-204968-1; 0-15-205532-0 (pa)

LC 2004-2696

Avon the snail and Edward, a take-charge ant, set off together on a journey to an undetermined destination in search of unspecified adventures.

"Whimsical pen-and-ink sketches add much to this wise little book. It's perfect for reading and discussing." SLJ

Another title about Avon the snail and Edward the ant is:

A beginning, a muddle, and an end (2008)

The fighting ground. Lippincott 1984 157p hardcover o.p. lib bdg $16.89; pa $5.99

Grades: 5 6 7 8 **Fic**

1. United States—History—1775-1783, Revolution—Fiction

ISBN 0-397-32073-6; 0-397-32074-4 (lib bdg); 0-06-440185-5 (pa) LC 82-47719

"It's April 1776, and the fighting ground is both the farm country of Pennsylvania and the heart of a boy which is 'wonderful ripe for war.' Twenty-four hours transform Jonathan from a cocky 13-year-old, eager to take on the British, into a young man who now knows the horror, the pathos, the ambiguities of war." Voice Youth Advocates

The author "has written a taut, fast-paced novel that builds to a shattering climax. His protagonist's painful, inner struggle to understand the intense and conflicting emotions brought on by a war that spares no one is central to this finely crafted novel." ALAN

The good dog. Atheneum Bks. for Young Readers 2001 243p $16; pa $5.99

Grades: 4 5 6 **Fic**

1. Dogs—Fiction 2. Wolves—Fiction

ISBN 0-689-83824-7; 0-689-83825-5 (pa)

LC 00-53600

"A Richard Jackson book"

McKinley, a malamute, is torn between the domestic world of his human family and the wild world of Lupin, a wolf that is trying to recruit dogs to replenish the dwindling wolf pack

"Falling somewhere between a naturalistic account of animal life and a fantasy, the strongest parts of the book depict the communication gap between McKinley and the human family with whom he resides." Horn Book Guide

Hard gold; The Colorado gold rush of 1859. Hyperion Books for Children 2008 224p map (I witness) $15.99

Grades: 5 6 7 8 **Fic**

1. Colorado—Gold discoveries—Fiction 2. Uncles—Fiction

ISBN 978-1-4231-0519-0; 1-4231-0519-2

Early Whitcomb, whose family's farm in Iowa is failing due to drought, is enticed by his uncle Jesse to go west and dig for gold to help prevent foreclosure, but during their adventure, Jesse gets into trouble, and Early makes hard decisions while trying to find his relative and the riches that lay hidden in the mountains.

"The chapters are short and broken up into diary format so as to mimic travel journals of the early wagon train adventurers. A rewarding addition." SLJ

Includes glossary and bibliographical references

Avi, 1937-—_Continued_

Iron thunder; the battle between the Monitor and the Merrimac, a civil war novel. Hyperion 2007 205p il $15.99; pa $5.99

Grades: 4 5 6   **Fic**
   1. United States—History—1861-1865, Civil War—Fiction 2. Ships—Fiction 3. Brooklyn (New York, N.Y.)—Fiction
   ISBN   978-1-4231-0446-9;   1-4231-0446-3; 978-1-4231-0518-3 (pa); 1-4231-0518-4 (pa)
   "This fascinating adventure taken from U.S. history begins in Brooklyn in 1862, when Tom Carroll, 13, is hired at the Iron Works in Greenpoint for a secret project, derisively known around the borough as Ericsson's Folly. John Ericsson, a Swedish inventor, is trying to build an ironclad ship that can battle the _Merrimac_, a Confederate ship being outfitted with metal plates in Virginia. . . . Illustrated with period engravings, this is gripping historical fiction from a keenly imagined perspective." Publ Wkly

Midnight magic. Scholastic Press 1999 249p hardcover o.p. pa $5.99

Grades: 5 6 7 8   **Fic**
   1. Magicians—Fiction 2. Renaissance—Fiction 3. Italy—Fiction
   ISBN 0-590-36035-3; 0-439-24219-3 (pa)
                              LC 98-50192
   In Italy in 1491, Mangus the magician and his apprentice are summoned to the castle of Duke Claudio to determine if his daughter is indeed being haunted by a ghost.
   An "entertaining tale of mystery and intrigue." SLJ
   Another title about Mangus and Fabrizio is:
   Murder at midnight (2009)

Never mind! a twin novel; [by] Avi and Rachel Vail. HarperCollins 2004 200p hardcover o.p. lib bdg $16.89; pa $5.99

Grades: 5 6 7 8   **Fic**
   1. Twins—Fiction 2. New York (N.Y.)—Fiction
   ISBN 0-06-054314-0; 0-06-054315-9 (lib bdg); 0-06-054316-7 (pa)   LC 2003-21439
   Twelve-year-old New York City twins Meg and Edward have nothing in common, so they are just as shocked as everyone else when Meg's hopes for popularity and Edward's mischievous schemes coincidentally collide in a hilarious showdown.
   "The dialogue is great, especially the conversations that reveal how hard it is to listen and to say what you mean. . . . The wit and slapstick carry the story, which has moments of sadness that raise serious issues everyone will recognize. Best of all is the message: laugh at yourself." Booklist

Poppy; [by] Avi; illustrated by Brian Floca. Revised Harper Trophy ed. HarperTrophy 2005 156p il pa $5.99 *

Grades: 3 4 5   **Fic**
   1. Mice—Fiction 2. Owls—Fiction 3. Animals—Fiction
   ISBN 978-0-380-72769-8 (pa); 0-380-72769-2 (pa)
                        LC 2005281589
   First published 1995 by Orchard Books

Poppy the deer mouse urges her family to move next to a field of corn big enough to feed them all forever, but Mr. Ocax, a terrifying owl, has other ideas
   "This exciting story is richly visual, subtly humorous, and skillfully laden with natural-history lessons. The anthropomorphism is believable and the characters are memorable." SLJ
   Other titles in this series are:
Poppy and Rye (1998)
Ragweed (1999)
Ereth's birthday (2000)
Poppy's return (2005)
Poppy and Ereth (2009)

Prairie school; story by Avi; pictures by Bill Farnsworth. HarperCollins Pubs. 2001 47p il (I can read chapter book) hardcover o.p. pa $3.99

Grades: 2 3 4   **Fic**
   1. Books and reading—Fiction 2. Aunts—Fiction 3. Frontier and pioneer life—Fiction 4. Physically handicapped—Fiction
   ISBN 0-06-027664-9; 0-06-051318-7 (pa)
                        LC 00-38834
   In 1880, Noah's aunt teaches the reluctant nine-year-old how to read as they explore the Colorado prairie together, Noah pushing Aunt Dora in her wheelchair
   "Warm, soft-edged illustrations capture the intimacy of the loving family relationships and the vastness of the landscape. . . . This gentle story with a great message . . . would make a pleasant read-aloud as well as a good addition to easy chapter-book collections." SLJ

S.O.R. losers. Avon Bks. 1986 c1984 90p pa $4.99

Grades: 5 6 7 8   **Fic**
   1. Soccer—Fiction 2. School stories
   ISBN 978-0-380-69993-3 (pa); 0-380-69993-1 (pa)
   First published 1984 by Bradbury Press
   Each member of the South Orange River seventh-grade soccer team has qualities of excellence, but not on the soccer field
   "Short, pithy chapters highlighting key events maintain the pace necessary for successful comedy. . . . The style is vivid, believably articulate." Horn Book

The secret school. Harcourt 2001 153p $16; pa $5.95

Grades: 4 5 6 7   **Fic**
   1. School stories 2. Colorado—Fiction
   ISBN 0-15-216375-1; 0-15-204699-2 (pa)
                        LC 2001-629
   In 1925, fourteen-year-old Ida Bidson secretly takes over as the teacher when the one-room schoolhouse in her remote Colorado area closes unexpectedly
   "This carefully plotted, enjoyable, old-fashioned tale of children taking control of a bad situation is a welcome addition to the literature of empowerment." SLJ

The seer of shadows. HarperCollinsPublishers 2008 202p $16.99; lib bdg $17.89; pa $6.99 *

Grades: 4 5 6 7   **Fic**
   1. Photography—Fiction 2. Ghost stories 3. Swindlers and swindling—Fiction 4. New York (N.Y.)—Fiction
   ISBN   978-0-06-000015-8;   0-06-000015-5; 978-0-06-000016-5 (lib bdg); 0-06-000016-3 (lib bdg); 978-0-06-000017-2 (pa); 0-06-000017-1 (pa)
                        LC 2007-10891

Avi, 1937-—*Continued*

In New York City in 1872, fourteen-year-old Horace, a photographer's apprentice, becomes entangled in a plot to create fraudulent spirit photographs, but when Horace accidentally frees the real ghost of a dead girl bent on revenge, his life takes a frightening turn.

"Fast-paced yet haunting. . . . This engaging novel has great immediacy and strong narrative drive." Booklist

Traitor's gate. Atheneum Books for Young Readers 2007 351p $17.99

Grades: 5 6 7 8   **Fic**
1. London (England)—Fiction 2. Spies—Fiction 3. Family life—Fiction 4. Poverty—Fiction
ISBN 0-689-85335-1

When his father is arrested as a debtor in 1849 London, fourteen-year-old John Huffman must take on unexpected responsibilities, from asking a distant relative for help to determining why people are spying on him and his family.

"With plenty of period detail, this action-packed narrative of twists, turns, and treachery is another winner from a master craftsman." SLJ

The true confessions of Charlotte Doyle. Orchard Books 2003 c1990 215p il hardcover o.p. pa $5.99 *

Grades: 6 7 8 9   **Fic**
1. Sea stories
ISBN 0-439-32731-8; 0-380-72885-0 (pa)

A Newbery Medal honor book, 1991

First published 1990

"Includes a new preface from Avi and a discussion guide."

As the only passenger, and the only female, on a transatlantic voyage in 1832, thirteen-year-old Charlotte finds herself caught between a murderous captain and a mutinous crew

The author has "fashioned an intriguing, suspenseful, carefully crafted tale, with nonstop action on the high seas." Booklist

Ayres, Katherine

Macaroni boy. Delacorte Press 2003 182p hardcover o.p. pa $5.99

Grades: 5 6 7 8   **Fic**
1. School stories 2. Great Depression, 1929-1939—Fiction
ISBN 0-385-73016-0; 0-440-41884-4 (pa)
LC 2002-6768

In Pittsburgh in 1933, sixth-grader Mike Costa notices a connection between several strange occurrences, but the only way he can find out the truth about what's happening is to be nice to the class bully. Includes historical facts

"Actual places and events are interwoven with a heartwarming story of a close-knit family facing difficult times." Voice Youth Advocates

Babbitt, Natalie

The eyes of the Amaryllis. Farrar, Straus & Giroux 1977 127p pa $6.99 hardcover o.p.

Grades: 5 6 7 8   **Fic**
1. Sea stories 2. Grandmothers—Fiction
ISBN 0-312-37008-3 (pa)   LC 77-11862

"The sea holds countless mysteries and gives up very few secrets; when she does, it is truly a remarkable event, an event that eleven-year-old Geneva Reade experiences when she visits her grandmother who lives in a house by the water's edge. Sent for to tend her Gran through a broken leg, Jenny is put to work, at once, combing the beach for a sign from her grandfather, a captain lost at sea with his ship and crew thirty years ago." Child Book Rev Serv

"The book succeeds as a well-wrought narrative in which a complex philosophical theme is developed through the balanced, subtle use of symbol and imagery. It is a rare story." Horn Book

Kneeknock Rise; story and pictures by Natalie Babbitt. Farrar, Straus & Giroux 1970 117p il pa $6.99 hardcover o.p.

Grades: 4 5 6   **Fic**
1. Allegories 2. Superstition—Fiction
ISBN 0-312-37009-1 (pa)

A Newbery Medal honor book, 1971

"Did you ever meet a Megrimum? There is one in KneeKnock Rise, and on stormy nights the villagers of Instep tremble in delicious delight as its howls echo over the Mammoth Mountains. Egan learns a lesson when he climbs to meet and conquer the Megrimum." Best Sellers

"An enchanting tale imbued with a folk flavor, enlivened with piquant imagery and satiric wit." Booklist

The search for delicious. Farrar, Straus & Giroux 1969 167p il hardcover o.p. pa $6.99

Grades: 5 6 7 8   **Fic**
1. Fantasy fiction
ISBN 0-374-36534-2; 0-312-36982-4 (pa)

"An Ariel book"

The Prime Minister is compiling a dictionary and when no one at court can agree on the meaning of delicious, the King sends his twelve-year-old messenger to poll the country

"The theme, foolish arguments can lead to great conflict, may not be clear to all children who will enjoy this fantasy." Best Sellers

Tuck everlasting. Farrar, Straus & Giroux 1975 139p $16; pa $6.99 *

Grades: 5 6 7 8   **Fic**
1. Fantasy fiction
ISBN 0-374-37848-7; 0-312-36981-6 (pa)

The Tuck family is confronted with an agonizing situation when they discover that a ten-year-old girl and a malicious stranger now share their secret about a spring whose water prevents one from ever growing any older

"The story is macabre and moral, exciting and excellently written." N Y Times Book Rev

Baccalario, Pierdomenico

The door to time; illustrations by Iacopo Bruno. Scholastic 2006 222p il (Ulysses Moore) $12.99

Grades: 4 5 6   **Fic**
1. Twins—Fiction 2. Adventure fiction 3. Mystery fiction
ISBN 0-439-77438-1

Original Italian edition 2004

Baccalario, Pierdomenico—*Continued*

After moving from London to an old mansion on the English coast, eleven-year-old twins Jason and Julia discover that their new home has twisting tunnels, strange artifacts from around the world, and a mysterious, locked door

"The book offers a well-paced adventure story, attractive line drawings, and the promise of many time-travel fantasies to come in the series." Booklist

Another title in this series is:

The long-lost map (2006)

Ring of fire; translated by Leah D. Janeczko; illustrations by Iacopo Bruno. Random House 2009 293p il $16.99; lib bdg $19.99

Grades: 5 6 7 8   **Fic**
1. Good and evil—Fiction 2. Rome (Italy)—Fiction 3. Italy—Fiction
ISBN   978-0-375-85895-6;   0-375-85895-4;
978-0-375-95895-3 (lib bdg); 0-375-95895-9 (lib bdg)
                                           LC 2009-08204

Original Italian edition, 2006

Four seemingly unrelated children are brought together in a Rome hotel where they discover that they are destined to become involved in a deep and ancient mystery involving a briefcase full of artifacts that expose them to great danger

"There are some genuinely exciting moments and the premise is intriguing." Publ Wkly

Baggott, Julianna

The   Prince   of   Fenway   Park. HarperCollinsPublishers 2009 322p $16.99; lib bdg $17.89

Grades: 4 5 6 7   **Fic**
1. Boston Red Sox (Baseball team)—Fiction 2. Fenway Park (Boston, Mass.)—Fiction 3. Baseball—Fiction 4. Orphans—Fiction 5. Father-son relationship—Fiction 6. Supernatural—Fiction
ISBN   978-0-06-087242-7;   0-06-087242-X;
978-0-06-087243-4 (lib bdg); 0-06-087243-8 (lib bdg)
                                           LC 2008-19666

In the fall of 2004, twelve-year-old Oscar Egg is sent to live with his father in a strange netherworld under Boston's Fenway Park, where he joins the fairies, pooka, banshee, and other beings that are trapped there, waiting for someone to break the eighty-six-year-old curse that has prevented the Boston Red Sox from winning a World Series

"Both whimsical and provocative (the 'N' word crops up in some historical references), this story will engage readers who like clever tales, and also those who enjoy chewing over controversial themes." SLJ

Baker, Deirdre F., 1955-

Becca at sea. Groundwood 2007 165p $16.95

Grades: 4 5 6   **Fic**
1. Islands—Fiction 2. Grandmothers—Fiction 3. Family life—Fiction 4. British Columbia—Fiction
ISBN 978-0-88899-737-1

After Becca's mom becomes pregnant, Becca visits her grandmother at her rustic cabin by the sea alone, and although she dreads it at first, she finds adventures and friendship and returns to the island again and again.

"Each episode enriches the portrait of Becca's memorable extended family with delightfully preposterous, yet insightful detail. . . . This funny, endearing book should find a wide audience." Horn Book

Baker, Olaf

Where the buffaloes begin; illustrated by Stephen Gammell. Puffin Bks. 1985 c1981 unp il pa $6.99

Grades: 2 3 4   **Fic**
1. Native Americans—Fiction 2. Bison—Fiction
ISBN 0-14-050560-1   LC 85-5682

A Caldecott Medal honor book, 1982

First published in book form 1981 by Warne

"Originally published in 1915 in 'St. Nicholas Magazine,' the story tells in four short chapters of the adventure of Little Wolf, a ten-year-old Indian boy. He was fascinated by a tribal legend about a lake to the south, a sacred spot where the buffaloes were said to originate. . . . Narrated in cadenced prose rich in images, the story evokes the Plains Indians' feelings of reverence for the buffalo. Magnificent full- and double-page pencil drawings . . . capture the immensity of the prairie and the mighty strength of the awesome beasts." Horn Book

Balliett, Blue, 1955-

Chasing Vermeer; illustrated by Brett Helquist. Scholastic Press 2004 254p il $16.95 *

Grades: 5 6 7 8   **Fic**
1. Vermeer, Johannes, 1632-1675—Fiction 2. Mystery fiction 3. Art—Fiction
ISBN 0-439-37294-1   LC 2002-152106

When seemingly unrelated and strange events start to happen and a precious Vermeer painting disappears, eleven-year-olds Petra and Calder combine their talents to solve an international art scandal.

Balliett's purpose "seems to be to get children to think—about relationships, connections, coincidences, and the subtle language of artwork. . . . [This is] a book that offers children something new upon each reading. . . . Helquist . . . outdoes himself here, providing an interactive mystery in his pictures." Booklist

Other titles about Petra and Calder are:

The Wright 3 (2006)

The Calder game (2008)

Banerjee, Anjali

Looking for Bapu. Wendy Lamb Books 2006 162p hardcover o.p. pa $6.50 *

Grades: 4 5 6 7   **Fic**
1. East Indians—United States—Fiction 2. Hindus—Fiction 3. Grandfathers—Fiction 4. Bereavement—Fiction
ISBN   978-0-385-74657-1;   0-385-90894-6;
978-0-553-49425-9 (pa); 0-553-49425-2 (pa)
                                           LC 2006-02021

When his beloved grandfather dies, eight-year-old Anu feels that his spirit is near and will stop at nothing to bring him back, including trying to become a Hindu holy man.

Banerjee, Anjali—*Continued*

"With episodes that ring true to a boy's perspective, Banerjee's novel provides discussable issues and multicultural insights as well as humor and emotion. An excellent read aloud." Booklist

Seaglass summer. Wendy Lamb Books 2010 163p il $15.99; lib bdg $18.99

Grades: 4 5 6 **Fic**
    1. East Indian Americans—Fiction 2. Uncles—Fiction 3. Veterinarians—Fiction 4. Washington (State)—Fiction
    ISBN   978-0-385-73567-4;   0-385-73567-7; 978-0-385-90555-8 (lib bdg); 0-385-90555-6 (lib bdg)
LC 2009-25468

"Eleven-year-old Poppy wants to be a veterinarian like her uncle Sanjay. So while her parents are in India visiting relatives, she spends several weeks with him on Nisqually Island, Washington, helping out at his Furry Friends Animal Clinic. Episodic chapters focus on the people and animals that Poppy meets, [and] her efforts to do a good job. . . . There are many moving events here. . . . Sometimes amusing, sometimes gross, and always true to itself, this should find a wide readership. Pencil illustrations enliven the chapter headings." Booklist

Banks, Kate, 1960-

Dillon Dillon. Foster Bks. 2002 150p hardcover o.p. pa $5.95

Grades: 4 5 6 7 **Fic**
    1. Family life—Fiction 2. Adoption—Fiction 3. Loons—Fiction 4. New Hampshire—Fiction
    ISBN 0-374-31786-0; 0-374-41715-6 (pa)
LC 2001-33207

During the summer that he turns ten years old, Dillon Dillon learns the surprising story behind his name and develops a relationship with three loons, living on the lake near his family's New Hampshire cabin, that help him make sense of his life

This "succeeds as an emotionally intricate, quietly well-observed, symbolically charged novel." Horn Book

Lenny's space. Farrar, Straus and Giroux 2007 151p $16

Grades: 4 5 6 **Fic**
    1. Friendship—Fiction 2. School stories 3. Leukemia—Fiction
    ISBN 978-0-374-34575-4; 0-374-34575-9
LC 2006-37384

"Frances Foster books"

Nine-year-old Lenny gets in trouble and has no friends because he cannot control himself in school and his interests are not like those of his classmates, until he starts visiting Muriel, a counselor, and meets Van, a boy his age who has leukemia.

This is an "exceptional portrait. . . . [with] steady character development and precise turns in . . . plot." Publ Wkly

Banks, Lynne Reid, 1929-

The Indian in the cupboard; illustrated by Brock Cole. Doubleday 1980 181p il $16.95; pa $6.99 *

Grades: 5 6 7 8 **Fic**
    1. Fantasy fiction
    ISBN 0-385-17051-3; 0-375-84753-7 (pa)
LC 79-6533

A nine-year-old boy receives a plastic Indian, a cupboard, and a little key for his birthday and finds himself involved in adventure when the Indian comes to life in the cupboard and befriends him

Other titles in this series are:
The key to the Indian (1998)
The mystery of the cupboard (1993)
The return of the Indian (1986)
The secret of the Indian (1989)

Barber, Tiki, 1975-

Go long! [by] Tiki and Ronde Barber with Paul Mantell. Simon & Schuster Books for Young Readers 2008 153p $15.99

Grades: 4 5 6 7 **Fic**
    1. Football—Fiction 2. Twins—Fiction 3. Brothers—Fiction
    ISBN 978-1-4169-3619-0; 1-4169-3619-X
LC 2007045843

"A Paula Wiseman book"

When Coach Spangler leaves at the start of their second year of junior high school, thirteen-year-old twins Tiki and Ronde wonder if his replacement, history teacher Mr. Wheeler, can coach the Eagles to another winning football season

"Football fans will find the on-field action scenes and even the coaching sessions very readable." Booklist
Other titles about Tiki and Ronde are:
Kickoff (2007)
Wild card! (2009)

Barker, M. P., 1960-

A difficult boy. Holiday House 2008 298p $16.95; pa $7.95

Grades: 5 6 7 8 **Fic**
    1. Contract labor—Fiction 2. Irish Americans—Fiction 3. Massachusetts—Fiction 4. Swindlers and swindling—Fiction
    ISBN   978-0-8234-2086-5;   0-8234-2086-8; 978-0-8234-2244-9 (pa); 0-8234-2244-5 (pa)
LC 2007-37059

In Farmington, Massachusetts, in 1839, nine-year-old Ethan experiences hardships as an indentured servant of the wealthy Lyman family alongside Daniel, a boy scorned simply for being Irish, and the boys bond as they try to right a terrible wrong.

"A memorable tale of friendship and a fascinating glimpse into mid-19th-century Massachusetts." SLJ

Barnett, Mac

The case of the case of mistaken identity; illustrations by Adam Rex. Simon & Schuster Books for Young Readers 2009 179p il (The Brixton Brothers) $14.99 * **Fic**

1. Books and reading—Fiction 2. Librarians—Fiction 3. Police—Fiction 4. Quilts—Fiction 5. Mystery fiction

ISBN 978-1-4169-7815-2; 1-4169-7815-1

LC 2008-43305

When twelve-year-old Steve Brixton, a fan of Bailey Brothers detective novels, is mistaken for a real detective, he must elude librarians, police, and the mysterious Mr. E as he seeks a missing quilt containing coded information.

The book provides "action and adventure but adds a level of humor that will sometimes have readers laughing out loud. Similarly, Rex's illustrations have a mid-twentieth-century look, and in an accomplished, deadpan manner, offer one of the book's funniest moments." Booklist

Barrett, Tracy, 1955-

The 100-year-old secret; by Tracy Barrett. Henry Holt and Co. 2008 157p (The Sherlock files) $15.95

Grades: 4 5 6 7 **Fic**

1. Great Britain—Fiction 2. Siblings—Fiction 3. Mystery fiction

ISBN 978-0-8050-8340-8; 0-8050-8340-5

LC 2007034004

Xena and Xander Holmes, an American brother and sister living in London for a year, discover that Sherlock Holmes was their great-great-great grandfather when they are inducted into the Society for the Preservation of Famous Detectives and given his unsolved casebook, from which they attempt to solve the case of a famous missing painting

"The main characters are observant, bright, and gifted with powers of deduction." SLJ

Other titles in this series are:

The beast of Blackslope (2009)

The case that time forgot (2010)

Cold in summer. Holt & Co. 2003 203p $16.95

Grades: 5 6 7 8 **Fic**

1. Ghost stories 2. Tennessee—Fiction

ISBN 0-8050-7052-4 LC 2002-67888

At the beginning of seventh grade, Ariadne moves to a Tennessee town near a former farming community submerged under a man-made lake and meets the ghost of a girl from the past

"This is a straightforward ghost tale with a doughty main character, a strong sense of history, and solid secondary players." Bull Cent Child Books

On Etruscan time. Henry Holt and Co. 2005 172p $16.95

Grades: 5 6 7 8 **Fic**

1. Archeology—Fiction 2. Etruscans—Fiction 3. Italy—Fiction

ISBN 0-8050-7569-0 LC 2004-52341

While spending the summer on an archaeological dig near Florence, Italy, with his mother, eleven-year-old Hector meets an Etruscan boy who needs help to foil his treacherous uncle's plan to make him a human sacrifice-1,000 years in the past

"Barrett's accurate description of the archaeological dig and the details of Etruscan daily life are well researched and interesting. The plot holds excitement and suspense." SLJ

Barrie, J. M. (James Matthew), 1860-1937

Peter Pan; the complete and unabridged text; by J. M. Barrie; illustrated by Scott Gustafson. Viking 1991 184p il $24.99

Grades: 3 4 5 6 **Fic**

1. Fairy tales

ISBN 0-670-84180-3 LC 91-50392

The adventures of the three Darling children in Neverland with Peter Pan, the boy who would not grow up.

"Gustafson's artwork opens doors to glimpses of old friends and to new interpretations. Fifty oil paintings reveal expressive, changing characters." SLJ

Barron, T. A.

The lost years of Merlin. Philomel Bks. 1996 326p $19.99; pa $7.99 *

Grades: 5 6 7 8 **Fic**

1. Merlin (Legendary character)—Fiction 2. Fantasy fiction

ISBN 978-0-399-23018-1; 978-0-441-00668-7 (pa)

LC 96-33920

"A boy, hurled on the rocks by the sea, regains consciousness unable to remember anything—not his parents, not his own name. He is sure that the secretive Branwen is not his mother, despite her claims, and that Emrys is not his real name. The two soon find themselves feared because of Branwen's healing abilities and Emrys' growing powers. . . . Barron has created not only a magical land populated by remarkable beings but also a completely magical tale, filled with ancient Celtic and Druidic lore, that will enchant readers." Booklist

Other titles in this series are:

The fires of Merlin (1998)

The mirror of Merlin (1999)

The seven songs of Merlin (1997)

The wings of Merlin (2000)

Barrows, Annie

Ivy + Bean; written by Annie Barrows; illustrated by Sophie Blackall. Chronicle Books 2006 113p il $14.95; pa $5.99 *

Grades: 1 2 3 **Fic**

1. Friendship—Fiction

ISBN 978-0-8118-4903-6; 0-8118-4903-1; 978-0-8118-4909-8 (pa); 0-8118-4909-0 (pa)

LC 2005023944

When seven-year-old Bean plays a mean trick on her sister, she finds unexpected support for her antics from Ivy, the new neighbor, who is less boring than Bean first suspected.

"The deliciousness here is in the details, with both girls drawn distinctly and with flair. . . . Even with all the text's strong points, what takes the book to a higher level is Blackall's artwork, which captures the girls' spirit." Booklist

Barrows, Annie—*Continued*

Other titles about Ivy and Bean are:
Ivy + Bean and the ghost that had to go (2006)
Ivy + Bean break the fossil record (2007)
Ivy + Bean take care of the babysitter (2008)
Ivy + Bean: bound to be bad (2009)
Ivy + Bean: doomed to dance (2009)

The magic half. Bloomsbury Children's Books
2008 211p $15.95; pa $6.99
Grades: 3 4 5   **Fic**
    1. Twins—Fiction 2. Sisters—Fiction
    ISBN   978-1-59990-132-9;   1-59990-132-3;
    978-1-59990-358-3 (pa); 1-59990-358-X (pa)
                                    LC 2007-23551
Eleven-year-old Miri Gill feels left out in her family,
which has two sets of twins and her, until she travels
back in time to 1935 and discovers Molly, her own lost
twin, and brings her back to the present day.
    "Readers will savor the author's lively observations
. . . while the heroine's adaptability and independent
thinking endow her with the appeal of a Ramona
Quimby or a Clementine." Publ Wkly

Barry, Dave

Peter and the starcatchers; by Dave Barry and
Ridley Pearson; illustrations by Greg Call.
Hyperion 2004 451p il $17.99; pa $7.99 *
Grades: 5 6 7 8   **Fic**
    1. Adventure fiction 2. Fairy tales 3. Pirates—Fiction
    ISBN 0-7868-5445-6; 0-7868-4907-X (pa)
                                    LC 2004-55275
Soon after Peter, an orphan, sets sail from England on
the ship Never Land, he befriends and assists Molly, a
young Starcatcher, whose mission is to guard a trunk of
magical stardust from a greedy pirate and the native inhabitants of a remote island
    "The authors plait multiple story lines together in
short, fast-moving chapters. . . . Capitalizing on familiar
material, this adventure is carefully crafted to set the
stage for Peter's later exploits. This smoothly written
page-turner just might send readers back to the original."
SLJ
    Other titles in this series are:
Peter and the shadow thieves (2006)
Peter and the secret of Rundoon (2007)
Peter and the Sword of Mercy (2009)

Barshaw, Ruth McNally

Ellie McDoodle: have pen, will travel; written
and illustrated by Ruth McNally Barshaw.
Bloomsbury Children's Books 2007 170p il
$11.95; pa $5.99
Grades: 2 3 4 5   **Fic**
    1. Camping—Fiction 2. Cousins—Fiction
    ISBN   978-1-58234-745-5;   1-58234-745-X;
    978-1-59990-276-0 (pa); 1-59990-276-1 (pa)
                                    LC 2006-28424
Eleven-year-old Ellie McDoodle illustrates her sketchbook with chronicles of her adventures and mishaps
while camping with her cousins, aunt, and uncle.
    "The engaging text reflects a contemporary preadoles-
cent sensibility and is chock-full of clean, distinguished
line drawings on each spread." SLJ

Another title about Ellie McDoodle is:
Ellie McDoodle: new kid in school (2008)

Bartek, Mary

Funerals & fly fishing; [by] Mary Bartek. H.
Holt 2004 148p $16.95; pa $6.99
Grades: 4 5 6 7   **Fic**
    1. Grandfathers—Fiction 2. Funeral rites and ceremo-
    nies—Fiction 3. Pennsylvania—Fiction
    ISBN 0-8050-7409-0; 0-312-56124-5 (pa)
                                    LC 2003-57046
The summer after sixth grade, Brad Stanislawski trav-
els to Pennsylvania by himself to visit the grandfather he
has never met before, and overcomes some of the pre-
conceived ideas he has gotten from his mother
    "The characters are believable and well developed.
. . . There is enough action to keep children's attention."
SLJ

Bartoletti, Susan Campbell, 1958-

The boy who dared. Scholastic Press 2008 202p
$16.99 *
Grades: 5 6 7 8   **Fic**
    1.   Hübener,   Helmuth,   1925-1942—Fiction
    2. Courage—Fiction 3. National socialism—Fiction
    4. Germany—History—1933-1945—Fiction
    ISBN 978-0-439-68013-4; 0-439-68013-1
                                    LC 2007014166
In October, 1942, seventeen-year-old Helmuth
Hübener, imprisoned for distributing anti-Nazi leaflets,
recalls his past life and how he came to dedicate himself
to bringing the truth about Hitler and the war to the German people.
    Bartoletti "does and excellent job of conveying the po-
litical climate surrounding Hitler's ascent to power,
seamlessly integrating a complex range of socioeconomic
conditions into her absorbing drama." Publ Wkly

Base, Graeme, 1958-

Enigma; a magical mystery; [by] Graeme Base.
Abrams Books for Young Readers 2008 36p il
$19.95
Grades: 3 4 5   **Fic**
    1.   Stories   in   rhyme   2.   Magicians—Fiction
    3.   Grandfathers—Fiction   4.   Badgers—Fiction
    5. Rabbits—Fiction 6. Ciphers—Fiction 7. Picture
    puzzles
    ISBN 978-0-8109-7245-2; 0-8109-7245-X
                                    LC 2007042397
When Bertie the badger visits his grandfather at a retirement home for magicians, he learns that his grandfather's rabbit, Enigma, has disappeared along with everyone's magical things, and the reader is invited to help
break a code to find the items hidden throughout the
book. Includes a built-in decoder.
    "Readers could simply hunt for the missing objects,
which Base conceals within elaborately detailed paintings, but then they would miss out on the tricky fun of
mastering several codes also embedded in the book. . . .
A set of bonus challenges will keep kids (and older siblings) poring closely over the pages for weeks, enthralled." Publ Wkly

Baskin, Nora Raleigh, 1961-

Anything but typical. Simon & Schuster Books for Young Readers 2009 195p il $15.99 *

Grades: 4 5 6 7   **Fic**

1. Autism—Fiction 2. School stories 3. Family life—Fiction 4. Authorship—Fiction

ISBN 978-1-4169-6378-3; 1-4169-6378-2

LC 2008-20994

ALA Schneider Family Book Award Honor Book (2010)

Jason, a twelve-year-old autistic boy who wants to become a writer, relates what his life is like as he tries to make sense of his world

"This is an enormously difficult subject, but Baskin, without dramatics or sentimentality, makes it universal." Booklist

The truth about my Bat Mitzvah. Simon & Schuster Books for Young Readers 2008 138p $15.99; pa $5.99

Grades: 5 6 7 8   **Fic**

1. Jews—Fiction 2. Bat mitzvah—Fiction 3. Grandmothers—Fiction

ISBN 978-1-4169-3558-2; 1-4169-3558-4; 978-1-4169-7469-7 (pa); 1-4169-7469-5 (pa)

LC 2007-01248

After her beloved grandmother, Nana, dies, non-religious twelve-year-old Caroline becomes curious about her mother's Jewish ancestry.

"Readers will identify with Caroline and her preoccupations. . . . This quick read will be a hit with preteens contemplating their own identities." Booklist

What every girl (except me) knows; a novel. Little, Brown 2001 213p hardcover o.p. pa $4.99

Grades: 4 5 6 7   **Fic**

1. Mothers—Fiction 2. Friendship—Fiction 3. Death—Fiction

ISBN 0-316-07021-1; 0-440-41852-6 (pa)

LC 00-40557

"Twelve-year-old Gabby feels like she's speeding into womanhood without a map, since her mother died when she was small. . . . She's convinced that girls with mothers have knowledge to which she's not privy, and one of the benefits of her friendship with new girl Taylor is a helpful dose of female camaraderie. . . . The book's depiction of Gabby's family dynamics . . . is perceptive and sympathetic." Bull Cent Child Books

Bateman, Colin, 1962-

Running with the Reservoir Pups; [by] Colin Bateman. Delacorte Press 2005 c2003 263p (Eddie & the gang with no name) hardcover o.p. lib bdg $17.99

Grades: 5 6 7 8   **Fic**

1. Gangs—Fiction 2. Divorce—Fiction 3. Northern Ireland—Fiction

ISBN 0-385-73244-9; 0-385-90268-9 (lib bdg)

LC 2004-43912

First published 2003 in the United Kingdom

When his parents divorce and his mother moves with him to Belfast, Northern Ireland, twelve-year-old Eddie contends with the Reservoir Pups, a gang of children who rule his neighborhood.

This "author's hilarious, dark Northern Irish wit, penchant for action-packed mayhem, sense of irony, and snappy dialogue are all evident in this [book]." SLJ

Another title about Eddie is:

Bring me the head of Oliver Plunkett (2005)

Bateson, Catherine, 1960-

Being Bee. Holiday House 2007 126p il $16.95; pa $7.95

Grades: 4 5 6   **Fic**

1. Family life—Fiction 2. Father-daughter relationship—Fiction 3. Guinea pigs—Fiction 4. Australia—Fiction

ISBN 978-0-8234-2104-6; 0-8234-2104-X; 978-0-8234-2208-1 (pa); 0-8234-2208-9 (pa)

LC 2006-101561

Bee faces friction at home and at school when her widowed father begins seriously dating Jazzi, who seems to take over the house and their lives, but as shared secrets and common interests finally begin to draw them together, Jazzi accidentally makes a terrible mistake.

"Bee's emotions are perspectives are honest and clearly presented. . . . She is a likable, believable character." SLJ

Magenta McPhee. Holiday House 2010 c2009 171p $16.95

Grades: 4 5 6 7   **Fic**

1. Father-daughter relationship—Fiction 2. Authorship—Fiction 3. Dating (Social customs)—Fiction 4. Single parent family—Fiction 5. Australia—Fiction

ISBN 978-0-8234-2253-1; 0-8234-2253-4

LC 2009-10854

First published 2009 in Australia

Thinking her father needs a new interest in his life after he is laid-off of work, teenaged Magenta, who envisions herself as a future fantasy author, decides to dabble in matchmaking which brings unexpected results.

"With a personality as colorful as her name, Bateson's . . . eponymous heroine has a narrative voice that is smart, wry, and down-to-earth. . . . This [is a] real and ultimately reassuring story." Publ Wkly

Stranded in Boringsville. Holiday House 2005 138p $16.95; pa $6.95

Grades: 5 6 7 8   **Fic**

1. Moving—Fiction 2. Divorce—Fiction 3. Friendship—Fiction 4. Australia—Fiction

ISBN 0-8234-1969-X; 0-8234-2113-9 (pa)

First published 2002 in Australia with title: Rain May and Captain Daniel

"Twelve year-old Rain's parents have separated. Her father has moved in with his trendy, younger girlfriend, and her mother has turned in her business suits for yoga and a simpler life in 'Boringsville,' tiny Clarkson, Central Victoria. . . . Her neighbor Daniel is almost 12, . . . and, as Rain learns, cruelly bullied at school. In alternating chapters, . . . Bateson deftly allows Rain and Daniel to chronicle their budding friendship. . . . Readers will ache for the kids, whose conflicted feelings seem all too real." Booklist

Bauer, A. C. E.

No castles here. Random House 2007 270p
$15.99; lib bdg $18.99

Grades: 4 5 6 7 **Fic**
1. New Jersey—Fiction 2. City and town life—Fiction
3. Books and reading—Fiction 4. Choirs (Music)—
Fiction 5. Magic—Fiction
ISBN 978-0-375-83921-4; 978-0-375-93921-1 (lib
bdg) LC 2006023601

Eleven-year-old Augie Boretski dreams of escaping
his rundown Camden, New Jersey, neighborhood, but
things start to turn around with help from a Big Brother,
a music teacher, and a mysterious bookstore owner, so
when his school is in trouble, he pulls the community together to save it

This is a "heartwarming novel." Booklist

Bauer, Marion Dane, 1938-

A bear named Trouble. Clarion Books 2005
120p $15

Grades: 3 4 5 6 **Fic**
1. Bears—Fiction 2. Zoos—Fiction 3. Alaska—Fiction
ISBN 0-618-51738-3 LC 2004-21259

In Anchorage, Alaska, two lonely boys make a connection—a brown bear injured just after his mother sends
him out on his own, and a human whose father is a new
keeper at the Alaska Zoo and whose mother and sister
are still in Minnesota.

"With a strong plot, well-developed characters, and an
engaging writing format, this book is a great choice for
young readers." SLJ

The blue ghost; illustrated by Suling Wang.
Random House 2005 85p il $11.95; lib bdg
$13.99; pa $3.99 *

Grades: 2 3 4 **Fic**
1. Ghost stories
ISBN 0-375-83179-7; 0-375-93179-1 (lib bdg);
0-375-83339-0 (pa)

"A Stepping Stone book"

At her grandmother's log cabin, nine-year-old Liz is
led to make contact with children she believes may be
her ancestors.

"This gentle ghost story, written in simple prose,
blends mild suspense with a look at how the past connects to and influences the present. Mystery fans will enjoy the spooky premise, and Wang's softly rendered
black-and-white drawings increase the ghostly atmosphere." Booklist

Other titles in this series are:
The green ghost (2008)
The red ghost (2008)

The double-digit club. Holiday House 2004
118p $15.95

Grades: 3 4 5 **Fic**
1. Friendship—Fiction
ISBN 0-8234-1805-7 LC 2003-047862

Nine-year-old Sarah is excited about summer vacation,
but she faces unexpected crises when her best friend
Paige becomes old enough to join a local girls' clique,
and when she makes choices which affect her relationship with an elderly blind neighbor.

"While many of the story elements will be familiar to

readers, they are presented here in a meaningful and
thoughtful way." SLJ

On my honor. Clarion Bks. 1986 90p $15 *
Grades: 4 5 6 7 **Fic**
1. Accidents—Fiction
ISBN 0-89919-439-7 LC 86-2679

A Newbery Medal honor book, 1987

When his best friend drowns while they are both
swimming in a treacherous river that they had promised
never to go near, Joel is devastated and terrified at having to tell both sets of parents the terrible consequences
of their disobedience

"Bauer's association of Joel's guilt with the smell of
the polluted river on his skin is particularly noteworthy.
Its miasma almost rises off the pages. Descriptions are
vivid, characterization and dialogue natural, and the style
taut but unforced. A powerful, moving book." SLJ

Runt. Clarion Bks. 2002 138p $14
Grades: 4 5 6 7 **Fic**
1. Wolves—Fiction
ISBN 0-618-21261-2 LC 2002-3965

Runt, the smallest wolf cub in the litter, seeks to
prove himself to his father King and the rest of the pack
and to earn a new name

The author's "passion for the animals is evident
throughout this compelling, poignant story." Booklist

The secret of the painted house; illustrated by
Leonid Gore. Random House 2007 96p il
hardcover o.p. lib bdg $14.99; pa $3.99

Grades: 2 3 4 **Fic**
1. Ghost stories 2. Moving—Fiction 3. Illinois—Fiction
ISBN 978-0-375-84079-1; 0-375-84079-6;
978-0-375-94079-8 (lib bdg); 0-375-94079-0 (lib bdg);
978-0-375-84080-7 (pa); 0-375-84080-X (pa)
LC 2006-24829

"A Stepping Stone book"

When her family moves from Chicago to the country,
nine-year-old Emily is drawn to a mysterious playhouse
she finds in the woods and soon meets its sad, lonely inhabitant.

"This short, accessible chapter book depicts characters
with swift, sure strokes and places them in an intriguing
situation." Booklist

Baum, L. Frank, 1856-1919

The Wizard of Oz; illustrated by Lisbeth
Zwerger. North-South Books 1996 103p il $19.95

Grades: 3 4 5 6 **Fic**
1. Fantasy fiction
ISBN 1-55858-638-5 LC 96-21733

"A Michael Neugebauer book"

First published 1900 with title: The wonderful Wizard
of Oz

After being transported by a cyclone to the land of
Oz, Dorothy and her dog are befriended by a scarecrow,
a tin man, and a cowardly lion, who accompany her to
the Emerald City to look for a wizard who can help Dorothy return home to Kansas

This edition is "a beauty. . . . Zwerger's characters
are completely original. Dorothy is diminutive and femi-

Baum, L. Frank, 1856-1919—*Continued*

nine with straight, cropped hair. The rotund Scarecrow is dressed in an enormous blue overcoat. . . . The pages are a tour de force of design." SLJ

The Wizard of Oz; illustrated by Charles Santore; with an introduction by Michael Patrick Hearn. Sterling 2009 96p il $16.95

Grades: 3 4 5   **Fic**
    1. Fantasy fiction
    ISBN 978-1-4027-6625-1; 1-4027-6625-4
                        LC 2008046862

A reissue of the edition first published 1991 by Random House

After a cyclone transports her to the land of Oz, Dorothy must seek out the great Wizard in order to return to Kansas

"This edition has been skillfully condensed for those not ready for the longer original work. Santore's many paintings, including spot art and full- and double-page spreads, add a successful dose of drama to the classic fantasy." Horn Book Guide

The wonderful Wizard of Oz; with pictures by W. W. Denslow. 100th anniversary ed. HarperCollins Publishers 2000 267p $24.99 *

Grades: 3 4 5 6   **Fic**
    1. Fantasy fiction
    ISBN 0-06-029323-3   LC 2001-265945
    "Books of Wonder"
    First published 1900

After a cyclone transports her to the land of Oz, Dorothy must seek out the great wizard in order to return to Kansas.

"For those who want the look and feel of the 1900 publication, this fills the bill. It's a very handsome facsimile, printed on high-quality paper and containing all of W. W. Denslow's 24 original colorplates and 130 two-color drawings." Booklist

Bawden, Nina, 1925-

Granny the Pag. Clarion Bks. 1996 184p $16

Grades: 4 5 6 7   **Fic**
    1. Grandmothers—Fiction 2. Parent-child relationship—Fiction
    ISBN 0-395-77604-X   LC 95-38191
    First published 1995 in the United Kingdom

Originally abandoned by her actor parents who later attempt to gain custody, Cat wages a spirited campaign to decide her own fate and remain with her grandmother

"Bawden has created some enormously appealing characters in this funny and very touching novel." SLJ

Beard, Darleen Bailey, 1961-

Annie Glover is not a tree lover; pictures by Heather Maione. Farrar Straus Giroux 2009 120p il $15.99

Grades: 3 4 5   **Fic**
    1. Trees—Fiction 2. Environmental protection—Fiction 3. Grandmothers—Fiction
    ISBN 978-0-374-30351-8; 0-374-30351-7
                        LC 2008043418

When her grandmother chains herself to the tree across from the school to save it from being cut down, fourth-grader Annie wants to die of humiliation, but when she dicovers the town's history, her attitude changes.

"Light fun, with a save-the-planet message, Beard's fast-paced plot accompanied by Maione's comic illustrations will have plenty of fans, including reluctant readers." SLJ

Operation Clean Sweep; [by] Darleen Bailey Beard. Farrar Straus Giroux 2004 151p $16

Grades: 3 4 5 6   **Fic**
    1. Women—Suffrage—Fiction 2. Elections—Fiction 3. Oregon—Fiction
    ISBN 0-374-38034-1   LC 2003-49430

In 1916, just four years after getting the right to vote, the women of Umatilla, Oregon band together to throw the mayor and other city officials out of office, replacing them with women

"Beard's story, based on real events, features believable characters, strong local color, and a plot that gently makes its point without offending anyone." Booklist

Bearn, Emily

Tumtum & Nutmeg; adventures beyond Nutmouse Hall; stories by Emily Bearn; with pictures by Nick Price. Little, Brown Books for Young Readers 2009 504p il $16.99 *

Grades: 4 5 6   **Fic**
    1. Mice—Fiction 2. Siblings—Fiction
    ISBN 978-0-316-02703-8; 0-316-02703-0
                        LC 2008-45294

Contents: Tumtum & Nutmeg; Great escape; Pirate's treasure

Wealthy, married mice Tumtum and Nutmeg find adventure when they secretly try to help two human siblings who live in a tumbledown cottage with their absent-minded inventor father.

"The stories are filled with descriptions of good food, cheering fires and warm beds. Price's black-and-white line drawings have a scratchy, comic air that brings a welcome edge to the gentle storytelling. . . . The sympathetic characters, enchanting setting and quickly paced plots will hold readers' interest." Publ Wkly

Beaty, Andrea

Cicada summer. Amulet Books 2008 167p $15.95

Grades: 4 5 6 7   **Fic**
    1. Siblings—Fiction 2. Bereavement—Fiction 3. Illinois—Fiction
    ISBN 978-0-8109-9472-0; 0-8109-9472-0
                        LC 2007-22266

Twelve-year-old Lily mourns her brother, and has not spoken since the accident she feels she could of prevented but the summer Tinny comes to town she is the only one who realizes Lily's secret.

"This is compelling fiction that will be a hit with young readers. . . . Rich and thought-provoking and yet . . . accessible." Horn Book

Beck, Ian

The secret history of Tom Trueheart. Greenwillow Books 2007 341p il hardcover o.p. lib bdg $17.89; pa $6.99

Grades: 4 5 6 7   **Fic**

1. Storytelling—Fiction 2. Fairy tales 3. Brothers—Fiction

ISBN 978-0-06-115210-8; 0-06-115210-2; 978-0-06-115211-5 (lib bdg); 0-06-115211-0 (lib bdg); 978-0-06-115212-2 (pa); 0-06-115212-9 (pa)

LC 2006043362

When young Tom Trueheart's seven older brothers all go missing during their adventures in the Land of Stories, he embarks on a perilous mission to save them and to capture the rogue story-writer who wants to do away with the heroes.

This "is a charming twist on fairy tales. . . . Silhouette drawings interspersed throughout add a wonderfully nostalgic touch." SLJ

Another title about Tom Trueheart is:
Tom Trueheart and the Land of Dark Stories (2008)

Becker, Bonny

Holbrook; a lizard's tale; by Bonny Becker; illustrated by Abby Carter. Clarion Books 2006 150p il $15

Grades: 3 4 5   **Fic**

1. Lizards—Fiction 2. Artists—Fiction 3. City and town life—Fiction

ISBN 978-0-618-71458-2; 0-618-71458-8

LC 2006-03962

Holbrook the lizard has an artist's soul, but when his paintings are ridiculed by the owls, geckoes, and other creatures in his desert town, he decides to seek his fortune in the big city, unaware of the dangers of urban life.

"The story moves along quickly, enlivened by dramatic situations, dry wit, and dynamic full-page illustrations. An enjoyable romp." Booklist

The magical Ms. Plum; illustrated by Amy Portnoy. Alfred A. Knopf 2009 104p il $12.99; lib bdg $15.99

Grades: 2 3 4   **Fic**

1. Teachers—Fiction 2. School stories 3. Magic—Fiction

ISBN 978-0-375-85637-2; 0-375-85637-4; 978-0-375-95637-9 (lib bdg); 0-375-95637-9 (lib bdg)

LC 2008-42682

The students in Ms Plum's third grade class soon learn that there is something very special about their teacher and her classroom's mysterious supply closet.

"Readers will relate to the youngsters' problems and enjoy their magical resolutions. Illustrated with delightful black-and-white drawings and filled with clever and short vignettes, this fast-paced story is a good choice for struggling readers." SLJ

Beha, Eileen

Tango; the tale of an island dog. Bloomsbury 2009 244p $15.99

Grades: 4 5 6   **Fic**

1. Dogs—Fiction 2. Abandoned children—Fiction 3. Foxes—Fiction 4. Country life—Fiction 5. Prince Edward Island—Fiction 6. Canada—Fiction

ISBN 978-1-59990-262-3; 1-59990-262-1

LC 2008046184

Lost at sea while sailing with his wealthy owners, a Yorkshire terrier washes up, nearly dead, in a village on Prince Edward Island where he is nursed back to health by a lonely widow and is befriended by a fox and an abandoned waif who is also struggling to find a home for herself somewhere

"The anthropomorphized characters are well crafted. . . . The human characters are are empathetic and interesting as well. . . . The themes of loyalty, courage, and belonging are effectively woven throughout the exciting plot twists." SLJ

Behrens, Andy

The fast and the furriest. Alfred A. Knopf 2010 247p $15.99; lib bdg $18.99

Grades: 2 3 4 5   **Fic**

1. Dogs—Fiction 2. Football—Fiction 3. Obesity—Fiction

ISBN 978-0-375-85922-9; 0-375-85922-5; 978-0-375-95922-6 (lib bdg); 0-375-95922-X (lib bdg)

LC 2009018365

The overweight and unathletic son of a famous former football star discovers that his equally fat and lazy dog is unexpectedly—and obsessively—interested in competing in dog agility contests.

"Behrens's engaging style will appeal to children. Students will relate to likable Kevin's self-deprecating humor, and Cromwell's perseverance gives anyone with an unrealized dream a glimmer of hope." SLJ

Beil, Michael D.

The Red Blazer Girls: the ring of Rocamadour. Alfred A. Knopf 2009 299p $15.99; lib bdg $18.99 *

Grades: 5 6 7 8   **Fic**

1. Puzzles—Fiction 2. Friendship—Fiction 3. School stories 4. Mystery fiction

ISBN 978-0-375-84814-8; 0-375-84814-2; 978-0-375-94814-5 (lib bdg); 0-375-94814-7 (lib bdg)

LC 2008-25254

Catholic-schooled seventh-graders Sophie, Margaret, Rebecca, and Leigh Ann help an elderly neighbor solve a puzzle her father left for her estranged daughter twenty years ago.

"The dialogue is fast and funny, the clues are often solvable." Booklist

Bell, Joanne, 1956-

Breaking trail. Groundwood Books/House of Anansi Press 2005 135p $15.95; pa $6.95

Grades: 5 6 7 8   **Fic**
1. Yukon River valley (Yukon and Alaska)—Fiction 2. Sled dog racing—Fiction 3. Depression (Psychology)—Fiction

ISBN 0-88899-630-6; 0-88899-662-4 (pa)

"Becky has always lived with her family in a log cabin in the Yukon, but when the fur market dwindled away, her father, a dog musher and trapper, had to quit trapping and her family moved into town. Now her father is depressed. . . . [Becky's plan is] to train her own dog team to race in the Junior Quest, a challenging five-day dog race across Alaska, in hopes of making her father happy." Publisher's note

"Although there are no easy solutions to the difficulties that confront this family, their love and support for one another are touching and believable." SLJ

Bell, Krista, 1950-

If the shoe fits; [illustrated by] Craig Smith. Charlesbridge 2008 60p il $14.95; pa $5.95

Grades: 2 3 4   **Fic**
1. Dance—Fiction

ISBN   978-1-58089-338-1;   1-58089-338-4; 978-1-58089-339-8 (pa); 1-58089-339-2 (pa)

                   LC 2007027022

First published 2006 in Australia

Cassie wants to be a dancer when she grows up but is afraid to dance in front of anyone outside her family, until the day of her first jazz performance arrives and her mother and a new friend help her to gain confidence.

"The text tells a believable story in a straightforward way, and readers will empathize with the characters. Scribbly pencil drawings reflect Cassie's inner turmoil." Horn Book Guide

Bellairs, John

The curse of the blue figurine. Dial Bks. for Young Readers 1983 200p hardcover o.p. pa $5.99 *

Grades: 5 6 7 8   **Fic**
1. Mystery fiction

ISBN 0-8446-7138-4; 0-14-240258-3 (pa)

                  LC 82-73217

Also available Brad Strickland's titles based on John Bellairs characters; Hardcover available from P. Smith

"The terror for young Johnny Dixon begins when cranky eccentric Professor Childermass tells him that St. Michael's Church is haunted by Father Baart, an evil sorcerer who mysteriously disappeared years ago. When Johnny finds a blue Egyptian figurine hidden in the church basement, he takes it home in spite of the warning note from Father Baart threatening harm to anyone who removes it from the church." SLJ

The author "intertwines real concerns with sorcery in a seamless fashion, bringing dimension to his characters and events with expert timing and sharply honed atmosphere." Booklist

Other titles about Johnny Dixon and Professor Childermass are:

The chessmen of doom (1989)
The eyes of the killer robot (1986)

The mummy, the will and the crypt (1983)
The revenge of the wizard's ghost (1985)
The secret of the underground room (1990)
The spell of the sorcerer's skull (1984)
The trolley to yesterday (1989)

The house with a clock in its walls; pictures by Edward Gorey. Dial Bks. for Young Readers 1973 179p il pa $5.99 *

Grades: 5 6 7 8   **Fic**
1. Witchcraft—Fiction

ISBN 0-14-240257-5

Also available Brad Strickland's titles based on John Bellair's characters

In 1948, Lewis, a ten-year-old orphan, goes to New Zebedee, Michigan with his warlock Uncle Jonathan, who lives in a big mysterious house and practices white magic. Together with their neighbor, Mrs. Zimmerman, a witch, they search to find a clock that is programmed to end the world and has been hidden in the walls of the house by the evil Isaac Izard

"Bellairs's story and Edward Gorey's pictures are satisfyingly frightening." Publ Wkly

Other titles about Lewis are:

The doom of the haunted opera (1995)
The figure in the shadows (1975)
The ghost in the mirror (1993)
The letter, the witch, and the ring (1976)
The vengeance of the witch-finder (1993)

Belton, Sandra, 1939-

The tallest tree. Amistad/Greenwillow Books 2008 154p $16.99; lib bdg $17.89

Grades: 3 4 5   **Fic**
1. Robeson, Paul, 1898-1976—Fiction 2. African Americans—Fiction

ISBN   978-0-06-052749-5;   0-06-052749-8; 978-0-06-052750-1 (lib bdg); 0-06-052750-1 (lib bdg)

                 LC 2007-22476

When a group of young African-American children learn about Paul Robeson from one of the neighborhood "elders," they decide to reclaim the town theater in order to celebrate Robeson's life

"A realistic hopeful story of finding one's roots. . . . What will grab readers is the portrait of Robeson, a towering 'inspiring' figure." Booklist

Benedictus, David, 1938-

Return to the Hundred Acre Wood; in which Winnie-the-Pooh enjoys further adventures with Christopher Robin and his friends; decorations by Mark Burgess. Dutton Children's Books 2009 201p il map lib bdg $19.99

Grades: 1 2 3 4   **Fic**
1. Animals—Fiction 2. Short stories

ISBN 978-0-525-42160-3 (lib bdg); 0-525-42160-2 (lib bdg)

Collects the further stories of Christopher Robin and his imaginary animal friends in the Hundred Acre Wood, where the animals anticipate Christopher Robin's return, meet a new friend, and solve the mystery of missing bees.

"The book is surprisingly deft at evoking the sensibili-

Benedictus, David, 1938-—*Continued*

ties of its predecessors, with the whimsy generally bounded by solid affection. . . . Burgess' art, line and watercolor thoughout, definitely echoes Shepard's. . . . Those who come out of curiosity will want to stay for the pleasing revisit with beloved old friends." Bull Cent Child Books

Berkeley, Jon

The hidden boy. Katherine Tegen Books 2010 262p (Bell Hoot fables) $16.99

Grades: 3 4 5 6   **Fic**

1. Adventure fiction 2. Missing children—Fiction 3. Siblings—Fiction

ISBN   978-0-06-168758-7;   0-06-168758-8; 978-0-06-168759-4 (lib bdg); 0-06-168759-6 (lib bdg)

LC 2009-12272

When Bea and her family are transported aboard an underwater bus to a strange land, her younger brother Theo is lost during the voyage, and somehow it falls to Bea to find out what has become of him.

"Berkeley's arch writing and his characters' hilarious, pathos-inspiring temperaments and abilities make this magical stew both compelling and delightful." Booklist

The Palace of Laughter; illustrated by Brandon Dorman. HarperCollins Pub. 2006 427p il (The Wednesday tales) hardcover o.p. pa $7.99

Grades: 4 5 6 7   **Fic**

1. Orphans—Fiction 2. Circus—Fiction 3. Adventure fiction

ISBN   0-06-075507-5;   978-0-06-075507-2; 978-0-06-075509-6 (pa); 0-06-075509-1 (pa)

LC 2005-22801

"The Julie Andrews collection"

Orphaned eleven-year-old Miles Wednesday and his companion, a Song Angel named Little, are helped by a talking tiger as they set off to find a missing Storm Angel and Miles's beloved stuffed bear, ending up in a peculiar circus where the audience cannot stop laughing.

"The story is filled with captivating and ingenious descriptive passages. . . . The lively plot and colorful supporting cast are enough to hold readers' attention." SLJ

Other titles in this series are:

The tiger's egg (2007)
The lightning key (2009)

Berlin, Eric

The puzzling world of Winston Breen; the secret in the box. Putnam 2007 215p il $16.99; pa $7.99 *

Grades: 4 5 6 7   **Fic**

1. Siblings—Fiction 2. Puzzles—Fiction 3. Mystery fiction

ISBN   978-0-399-24693-7;   0-399-24693-2; 978-0-14-241388-3 (pa); 0-14-241388-7 (pa)

LC 2006-20531

Puzzle-crazy, twelve-year-old Winston and his ten-year-old sister Katie find themselves involved in a dangerous mystery involving a hidden ring. Puzzles for the reader to solve are included throughout the text

"A delightfully clever mystery. . . . There is plenty of suspense to engage readers." SLJ

Followed by: The potato chip puzzles (2009)

Berryhill, Shane

Chance Fortune and the Outlaws; [by] Shane Berryhill. Starscape 2006 269p (The adventures of Chance Fortune) $17.95; pa $5.99

Grades: 4 5 6 7   **Fic**

1. Science fiction 2. Adventure fiction

ISBN 0-7653-1468-1; 0-7653-5354-7 (pa)

LC 2005036400

"A Tom Doherty Associates book"

"Josh Blevins, resident of a planet almost but not quite like earth, has only one dream. He longs to attend the Burlington Academy for the Superhuman. . . . His application is rejected because he has no superpowers, but he reapplies and gets admitted as Chance Fortune, claiming the power of unnaturally good luck. . . . Berryhill blends elements of space opera, comic book adventure, [and] classic horror literature . . . into a lively and engrossing tale that neither takes itself too seriously nor underestimates its readers." Voice Youth Advocates

Another title about Chance Fortune is:

Chance Fortune in the shadow zone (2008)

Betancourt, Jeanne, 1941-

Ava Tree and the wishes three. Feiwel and Friends 2009 130p il $14.99

Grades: 2 3 4   **Fic**

1. Wishes—Fiction 2. Birthdays—Fiction 3. Parties—Fiction 4. Orphans—Fiction 5. Siblings—Fiction

ISBN 978-0-312-37760-1; 0-312-37760-6

LC 2008015265

"Waking up on her eighth birthday, Ava tears up thinking about her parents, who died in a car accident. . . . She now lives with her 22-year-old brother, Jack. . . . Struggling to clean her pet rabbit's litter box, Ava wishes it 'would use the toilet like a person' and when it suddenly does, Ava and Jack wonder if it could be a birthday gift from their mother, who had been a magician. Ava's 'wishing power' seems to continue, though some of her wishes—that her parents weren't dead—go unanswered. . . . Kids will embrace this bighearted novel and its thoughtful, resilient narrator." Publ Wkly

My name is brain Brian. Scholastic 1993 128p pa $4.99 hardcover o.p.

Grades: 4 5 6   **Fic**

1. Dyslexia—Fiction 2. School stories 3. Friendship—Fiction

ISBN 0-590-44922-2 (pa)   LC 92-16513

On title page the word "brain" appears with an "X" through it

Although he is helped by his new sixth grade teacher after being diagnosed as dyslexic, Brian still has some problems with school and with people he thought were his friends

"Betancourt's depiction of Brian's emotional and psychological growth is believable and involving." Booklist

Bianco, Margery Williams, 1881-1944

The velveteen rabbit; or, How toys become real; by Margery Williams; with illustrations by William Nicholson. Doubleday 1991 33p il $13.95 *

Grades: 2 3 4   **Fic**

1. Toys—Fiction 2. Rabbits—Fiction 3. Fairy tales

ISBN 0-385-07725-4   LC 90-25339

Bianco, Margery Williams, 1881-1944—*Continued*

First published 1922 by Doran

By the time the velveteen rabbit is dirty, worn out, and about to be burned, he has almost given up hope of ever finding the magic called Real.

"Quiet, graceful illustrations accentuate the classic tale's nostalgic tone." Publ Wkly

Billingsley, Franny, 1954-

The Folk Keeper. Atheneum Bks. for Young Readers 1999 162p hardcover o.p. pa $4.99

Grades: 5 6 7 8   **Fic**

1. Fantasy fiction

ISBN 0-689-82876-4; 0-689-84461-1 (pa)

                                    LC 98-48778

"A Jean Karl book"

Orphan Corinna disguises herself as a boy to pose as a Folk Keeper, one who keeps the Evil Folk at bay, and discovers her heritage as a seal maiden when she is taken to live with a wealthy family in their manor by the sea

"The intricate plot, vibrant characters, dangerous intrigue, and fantastical elements combine into a truly remarkable novel steeped in atmosphere." Horn Book

Well wished. Atheneum Bks. for Young Readers 1997 170p hardcover o.p. pa $4.99

Grades: 4 5 6   **Fic**

1. Wishes—Fiction 2. Magic—Fiction 3. Fantasy fiction

ISBN 0-689-81210-8; 0-689-83255-9 (pa)

                                    LC 96-24511

"A Jean Karl book"

"In Nuria's town, a magical wishing well grants individuals one wish per lifetime, but if possible, twists the requests to produce a ruinous outcome. When Nuria wishes that her crippled friend 'had a body just like mine,' the girls switch bodies. Fantasy elements play a pivotal role in the plot, but keen character development leaves the strongest impression in this well-constructed, thought-provoking first novel." Horn Book Guide

Binding, Tim

Sylvie and the songman; with illustrations by Angela Barrett. Random House 2009 339p il $15.99; lib bdg $18.99 *

Grades: 5 6 7 8   **Fic**

1. Fantasy fiction

ISBN 978-0-385-75157-5; 0-385-75159-1; 978-0-385-75159-9 (lib bdg); 0-385-75159-1 (lib bdg)

"Sylvie's composer father . . . goes missing and that's the first odd thing that interrupts her happy routine. Next, the animals seem to have lost their voices. The third is the arrival of the eerie, malevolent Woodpecker Man. . . . The dense narrative is packed with surreal imagery. . . . It's a testament to Binding's assured writing that the abstractions become visceral thrills, like a dream you just can't shake. . . . An unforgettable tale." Booklist

Birdsall, Jeanne

The Penderwicks; a summer tale of four sisters, two rabbits, and a very interesting boy. Knopf 2005 262p $15.95; lib bdg $17.77; pa $6.99 *

Grades: 3 4 5 6   **Fic**

1. Sisters—Fiction 2. Single parent family—Fiction

ISBN 0-375-83143-6; 0-375-93143-0 (lib bdg); 0-440-42047-4 (pa)   LC 2004-20364

While vacationing with their widowed father in the Berkshire Mountains, four lovable sisters, ages four through twelve, share adventures with a local boy, much to the dismay of his snobbish mother.

"This comforting family story . . . [offers] . . . four marvelously appealing sisters, true childhood behavior . . ., and a writing style that will draw readers close." Booklist

Another title about the Penderwicks is:

The Penderwicks on Gardam Street (2008)

Birdseye, Tom, 1951-

A tough nut to crack. Holiday House 2006 113p $16.95

Grades: 5 6 7 8   **Fic**

1. Farm life—Fiction 2. Family life—Fiction 3. Kentucky—Fiction

ISBN 978-0-8234-1967-8; 0-8234-1967-3

                                    LC 2006-24887

Raised in Portland, Oregon, Cassie adapts quickly when an emergency brings her family to her grandfather's Kentucky farm, where she feels the spirits of her mother and grandmother as she tries to heal the rift between her father and grandfather.

"The novel's simplicity, humor, action, and warmth will appeal to a broad range of readers." SLJ

Birney, Betty G., 1947-

The princess and the Peabodys. HarperCollinsPublishers 2007 249p $15.99; lib bdg $16.89

Grades: 5 6 7 8   **Fic**

1. Princesses—Fiction 2. School stories 3. Family life—Fiction

ISBN 0-06-084720-4; 978-0-06-084720-3; 978-0-06-084721-0 (lib bdg); 0-06-084721-2 (lib bdg)

                                    LC 2006-100447

When a medieval princess named Eglantine (Egg for short) appears out of a rusty box bought at a yard sale, fourteen-year-old tomboy Casey Peabody and her family are stuck with her royal snobbiness until the young wizard who had trapped her there figures out the spell to send her home.

"Eglantine and Casey . . . make terrific narrative foils for eachother. . . . Their eventual warm and lasting friendship is all the more satisfying because it is so realistically hard-won." Bull Cent Child Books

The seven wonders of Sassafras Springs; written by Betty Birney; illustrated by Matt Phelan. Atheneum Books for Young Readers 2005 210p il $16.95; pa $6.99

Grades: 3 4 5 6   **Fic**

1. Country life—Fiction 2. Family life—Fiction

ISBN 0-689-87136-8; 1-4169-3489-8 (pa)

                                    LC 2004-11399

Birney, Betty G., 1947-—*Continued*

Eben McAllister searches his small town to see if he can find anything comparable to the real Seven Wonders of the World

"Black-and-white sketches enhance the text and its folksy character. Perfect for reading aloud." SLJ

The world according to Humphrey. G. P. Putnam's Sons 2004 124p $14.99; pa $5.99
Grades: 2 3 4 **Fic**
   1. Hamsters—Fiction 2. School stories
   ISBN 978-0-399-24198-7; 0-399-24198-1; 978-0-14-240352-5 (pa); 0-14-240352-0 (pa)
                  LC 2003-5974

Humphrey, pet hamster at Longfellow School, learns that he has an important role to play in helping his classmates and teacher.

The "lively, first-person narrative, filled with witty commentary on human and hamster behavior, makes for an engaging, entertaining read." Booklist

Other titles about Humphrey are:
Friendship according to Humphrey (2005)
Trouble according to Humphrey (2007)
Surprises according to Humphrey (2008)
Adventure according to Humphrey (2009)
Summer according to Humphrey (2010)

Blackwood, Gary L.

Second sight; [by] Gary Blackwood. Dutton 2005 279p hardcover o.p. pa $6.99
Grades: 5 6 7 8 **Fic**
   1. Lincoln, Abraham, 1809-1865—Fiction 2. United States—History—1861-1865, Civil War—Fiction 3. Washington (D.C.)—Fiction 4. Clairvoyance—Fiction
   ISBN 0-525-47481-1; 0-14-240747-X (pa)

In Washington, D.C., during the last days of the Civil War, a teenage boy who performs in a mind reading act befriends a clairvoyant girl whose frightening visions foreshadow an assassination plot.

"This is a well-researched, engrossing story grounded in historical detail." SLJ

The Shakespeare stealer; [by] Gary Blackwood. Dutton Children's Bks. 1998 216p $15.99; pa $5.99 *
Grades: 5 6 7 8 **Fic**
   1. Shakespeare, William, 1564-1616—Fiction 2. Theater—Fiction 3. Orphans—Fiction 4. Great Britain—History—1485-1603, Tudors—Fiction
   ISBN 0-525-45863-8; 0-14-130595-9 (pa)
                  LC 97-42987

A young orphan boy is ordered by his master to infiltrate Shakespeare's acting troupe in order to steal the script of "Hamlet," but he discovers instead the meaning of friendship and loyalty

"Wry humor, cliffhanger chapter endings, and a plucky protagonist make this a fitting introduction to Shakespeare's world." Horn Book

Other titles in this series are:
Shakespeare's scribe (2000)
Shakespeare's spy (2003)

Bledsoe, Lucy Jane

Cougar canyon. Holiday House 2001 130p $16.95
Grades: 4 5 6 7 **Fic**
   1. Pumas—Fiction 2. Wildlife conservation—Fiction 3. Mexican Americans—Fiction
   ISBN 0-8234-1599-6   LC 2001-16718

After hearing that people are planning to kill a mountain lion in the wilds near her neighborhood, twelve-year-old Izzie decides that it is her duty to protect the animal

"An entertaining adventure story with fast-paced action and a strong female protagonist." SLJ

Block, Francesca Lia

House of dolls; illustrated by Barbara McClintock. Harper 2010 61p il $15.99 *
Grades: 3 4 5 6 **Fic**
   1. Dolls—Fiction 2. Fantasy fiction
   ISBN 978-0-06-113094-6; 0-06-113094-X

"Young Madison is growing tired of her dollhouse and its residents. . . . Increasingly abandoned by her mother, Madison begins exercising a capacious cruelty [to the dolls]. . . . The reality/unreality of any of this is a tightrope Block toes with precision. . . . What at first seems to be about the perennial war between familial generations is expanded into a message about the global forces of pride and avarice that plunge innocents into devastation. This is powerful, haunting, and—just when you don't think it's possible—inspiring too." Booklist

Blos, Joan W., 1928-

A gathering of days: a New England girl's journal, 1830-32; a novel. Scribner 1979 144p $16.95; pa $4.99 *
Grades: 6 7 8 9 **Fic**
   1. New Hampshire—Fiction
   ISBN 0-684-16340-3; 0-689-71419-X (pa)
                  LC 79-16898

Awarded the Newbery Medal, 1980

The journal of a 14-year-old girl, kept the last year she lived on the family farm, records daily events in her small New Hampshire town, her father's remarriage, and the death of her best friend

"The 'simple' life on the farm is not facilely idealized, the larger issues of the day are felt . . . but it is the small moments between parent and child, friend and friend that are at the fore, and the core, of this low-key, intense, and reflective book." SLJ

Letters from the corrugated castle; a novel of gold rush California, 1850-1852. Atheneum Books for Young Readers 2007 310p $17.99; pa $5.99
Grades: 5 6 7 8 **Fic**
   1. Frontier and pioneer life—Fiction 2. Mother-daughter relationship—Fiction 3. Gold mines and mining—Fiction 4. Mexican Americans—Fiction 5. California—Fiction
   ISBN 978-0-689-87077-4; 0-689-87077-9; 978-0-689-87078-1 (pa); 0-689-87078-7 (pa)
                  LC 2007-02673

"Ginee Seo books."

Blos, Joan W., 1928-—*Continued*

A series of letters and newspaper articles reveals life in California in the 1850s, especially for thirteen-year-old Eldora, who was raised in Massachusetts as an orphan only to meet her influential mother in San Francisco, and Luke, who hopes to find a fortune in gold.

"It is Blos' sturdy characters, whose experiences reveal the complexity of human relationships and wisdom about 'the salt and the sweet of life,' who will make this last." Booklist

Blume, Judy

Are you there God?, it's me, Margaret. rev format ed. Atheneum 2001 c1970 149p $17.95

Grades: 5 6 7 8   **Fic**

1. Religion—Fiction

ISBN 0-689-84158-2

Also available in paperback from Dell

A reissue of the title first published 1970 by Bradbury Press

A "story about the emotional, physical, and spiritual ups and downs experienced by 12-year-old Margaret, child of a Jewish-Protestant union." Natl Counc of Teach of Engl. Adventuring with Books. 2d edition

"The writing style is lively, the concerns natural, and the problems are treated with both humor and sympathy, but the story is intense in its emphasis on the four girls' absorption in, and discussions of, menstruation and brassieres." Bull Cent Child Books

Freckle juice; illustrated by Sonia O. Lisker. Four Winds Press 1971 40p il lib bdg $17.95

Grades: 2 3 4   **Fic**

ISBN 0-02-711690-5

Also available in paperback from Dell

"A gullible second-grader pays 50¢ for a recipe to grow freckles." Best Books for Child

"Spontaneous humor, sure to appeal to the youngest reader." Horn Book

Otherwise known as Sheila the Great. Dutton Children's Books 2002 c1972 138p $16.99; pa $5.99

Grades: 4 5 6   **Fic**

1. Fear—Fiction 2. Vacations—Fiction

ISBN   978-0-525-46928-5;   0-525-46928-1; 978-0-14-240879-7 (pa); 0-14-240879-4 (pa)

A reissue of the title first published 1972

A summer in Tarrytown, N.Y., is a lot of fun for ten-year-old Sheila even though her friends make her face up to some self-truths she doesn't want to admit.

"An unusual and merry treatment of the fears of a young girl. . . . This is a truly appealing book in which the author makes her points without a single preachy word." Publ Wkly

Soupy Saturdays with The Pain and The Great One; illustrations by James Stevenson. Delacorte Press 2007 108p il $12.99; lib bdg $16.99

Grades: 1 2 3   **Fic**

1. Siblings—Fiction

ISBN   978-0-385-73305-2;   0-385-73305-4; 978-0-385-90324-0 (lib bdg); 0-385-90324-3 (lib bdg)

LC 2006-26892

"Third-grader Abigail calls her little brother 'The Pain' because he causes so much trouble. Jake is in first grade and calls his older sister 'The Great One' because she thinks so highly of herself. The book . . . is a series of vignettes in which the children continually clash and then reconcile. . . . The stories are sweet and accurately depict the growing pains of childhood. Stevenson's black-and-white ink illustrations are entertaining." SLJ

Other titles about the The Pain and The Great One are:

Cool zone with The Pain and The Great One (2008)

Going, going, gone! with The Pain and The Great One (2008)

Friend or fiend? with The Pain and The Great One (2009)

Tales of a fourth grade nothing. Dutton Children's Books 2002 c1972 120p $15.99; pa $5.99 *

Grades: 3 4 5 6   **Fic**

1. Brothers—Fiction 2. Family life—Fiction

ISBN 0-525-46931-1; 0-14-240881-6 (pa)

A reissue of the title first published 1972

"Jacket illustration c2002 by Peter Reynolds."

This story describes the trials and tribulations of nine-year-old Peter Hatcher who is saddled with a pesky two-year-old brother named Fudge who is constantly creating trouble, messing things up, and monopolizing their parents' attention. Things come to a climax when Fudge gets at Peter's pet turtle

"The episode structure makes the book a good choice for reading aloud." Saturday Rev

Other titles about Peter and Fudge are:

Double Fudge (2002)

Fudge-a-mania (1990)

Superfudge (1980)

Blume, Lesley M. M.

Cornelia and the audacious escapades of the Somerset sisters. Knopf 2006 264p $15.95; pa $5.99

Grades: 4 5 6   **Fic**

1. Storytelling—Fiction 2. Friendship—Fiction 3. Sisters—Fiction

ISBN 0-375-83523-7; 0-440-42110-1 (pa)

LC 2005-18295

Cornelia, eleven-years-old and lonely, learns about language and life from an elderly new neighbor who has many stories to share about the fabulous adventures she and her sisters had while traveling around the world

This "is a fabulous read that will enchant its audience with the magic to be found in everyday life." SLJ

The rising star of Rusty Nail; [by] Lesley M.M. Blume. Alfred A. Knopf 2007 270p $15.99; lib bdg $18.99; pa $6.50

Grades: 4 5 6   **Fic**

1. Pianists—Fiction 2. Musicians—Fiction 3. Russian Americans—Fiction 4. Minnesota—Fiction

ISBN 978-0-375-83524-7; 978-0-375-93524-4 (lib bdg); 978-0-440-42111-5 (pa)   LC 2006024252

In the small town of Rusty Nail, Minnesota, in the early 1950s, musically talented ten-year-old Franny wants to take advanced piano lessons from newcomer Olga Malenkov, a famous Russian musician suspected of being a

Blume, Lesley M. M.—*Continued*

communist spy by gossipy members of the community

"Blume has skillfully combined humor, history, and music to create an enjoyable novel that builds to a surprising crescendo." SLJ

Tennyson. Alfred A. Knopf 2008 288p $15.99; lib bdg $18.99; pa $6.99

Grades: 6 7 8 9 10 11 12   **Fic**

1. Great Depression, 1929-1939—Fiction 2. Family life—Fiction 3. New Orleans (La.)—Fiction

ISBN 978-0-375-84703-5; 978-0-375-94703-2 (lib bdg); 978-0-440-24061-7 (pa)   LC 2007-25983

After their mother abandons them during the Great Depression, eleven-year-old Tennyson Fontaine and her little sister Hattie are sent to live with their eccentric Aunt Henrietta in a decaying plantation house

"Many readers will respond to this novel's Southern gothic sensibility, especially Blume's beautiful, poetic writing about how the past resonates through the generations." Booklist

Bode, N. E.

The Anybodies. HarperCollins 2004 276p il $15.99; pa $6.99

Grades: 5 6 7 8   **Fic**

1. Magic—Fiction

ISBN 0-06-055735-4; 0-06-055737-0 (pa)

After learning that she is not the biological daughter of boring Mr. and Mrs. Drudger, Fern embarks on magical adventures with her real father and finally finds "a place that feels like home."

"The writing is fluid, the characters are multifaceted, and the situations range from poignant to gloriously silly. Eye-catching, black-and-white sketches echo the story's nuances and add to the atmosphere. There's laugh-out-loud humor, fantasy, mystery, real-life family drama." SLJ

Other titles in this series are:

The nobodies (2005)

The somebodies (2006)

The slippery map; by N.E. Bode; illustrated by Brandon Dorman. HarperCollinsPublishers 2007 273p il $16.99; lib bdg $17.89

Grades: 4 5 6   **Fic**

1. Adventure fiction 2. Imagination—Fiction 3. Parents—Fiction 4. Baltimore (Md.)—Fiction

ISBN 978-0-06-079108-7; 0-06-079108-X; 978-0-06-079109-4 (lib bdg); 0-06-079109-8 (lib bdg)   LC 2007010900

Oyster R. Motel, a lonely boy raised as a foundling in a Baltimore nunnery, travels through a portal to the imaginary world of his parents, where he heroically confronts the villainous Dark Mouth

The author "effortlessly renders an expansive, entertainingly quirky cast of creatures benign and malevolent. Her snappy prose makes the case for the story's explicit messages about the value of unbridled imagination." Publ Wkly

Boie, Kirsten, 1950-

The princess plot; translated by David Henry Wilson. Scholastic 2009 378p $17.99

Grades: 5 6 7 8   **Fic**

1. Princesses—Fiction 2. Conspiracies—Fiction

ISBN 978-0-545-03220-9; 0-545-03220-2   LC 2008-24403

Original German edition, 2005

Believing that she is on a film set after auditioning and winning the role of a princess, fourteen-year-old Jenna becomes the unsuspecting pawn in a royal conspiracy

"This novel takes simple, straightforward writing and layers it with kidnappings, political intrigue, and an abundance of secret plots. Readers will enjoy leisurely uncovering the mystery of Jenna's heritage, right along with Jenna herself." Booklist

Another title about Jenna is:

The princess trap (2010)

Boles, Philana Marie

Little divas. Amistad 2006 164p $15.99; lib bdg $16.89; pa $5.99

Grades: 5 6 7 8   **Fic**

1. African Americans—Fiction 2. Father-daughter relationship—Fiction 3. Divorce—Fiction 4. Cousins—Fiction

ISBN 0-06-073299-7; 0-06-073300-4 (lib bdg); 0-06-073301-2 (pa)

"Amistad"

The summer before seventh grade, Cassidy Carter must come to terms with living with her father, practically a stranger, as well as her relationships with her cousins, all amidst the overall confusion of adolescence.

"Boles portrays this variable age well, and readers will feel for Cassidy's trials." SLJ

Bolger, Kevin

Zombiekins; illustrated by Aaron Blecha. Razor Bill 206p il $10.99

Grades: 4 5 6   **Fic**

1. Zombies—Fiction 2. Monsters—Fiction 3. Toys—Fiction 4. School stories

ISBN 978-1-59514-177-4; 1-59514-177-4

During a "yard sale, Stanley Nudelman . . . buys Zombiekins, an adorable yet repulsive stuffed bunnybear . . . and ignores the Widow's entreaty to read the instructions. When Stanley takes Zombiekins to school, the moonlight from a science movie awakens it, and its bite starts a zombie plague." Kirkus

"Offering a thoroughly accessible introduction to verbal, situational and dramatic irony, this generously illustrated chapter book mines multiple veins of humor, from witty turns of phrase and metafictional intrusions, send-ups of conventional story expectations, surprise reversals, horror-genre allusions, and physical slapstick to good, old-fashioned grossout fare; certainly, it's a contemporary riff on Dahl, but perhaps, even funnier." Bull Cent Child Books

Boling, Katharine
January 1905. Harcourt 2004 170p $16; pa $5.95
Grades: 4 5 6 7   **Fic**
1. Twins—Fiction 2. Sisters—Fiction 3. Child labor—Fiction
ISBN 0-15-205119-8; 0-15-205121-X (pa)
LC 2003-24470
In a 1905 mill town, eleven-year-old twin sisters, Pauline, who goes to work with the rest of the family, and Arlene, whose crippled foot keeps her home doing the cooking, cleaning, and washing, are convinced that the other sister has an easier life until a series of incidents helps them see each other in a new light.
"This vivid account will draw readers into the period." Horn Book Guide

Bond, Michael, 1926-
A bear called Paddington; with drawings by Peggy Fortnum. Houghton Mifflin 1998 c1958 128p il $15; pa $4.95 *
Grades: 2 3 4 5   **Fic**
1. Bears—Fiction 2. Great Britain—Fiction
ISBN 0-395-92951-2; 0-618-15071-4 (pa)
Picture books about Paddington for younger readers are also available
First published 1958 in the United Kingdom; first United States edition 1960
"Mr. and Mrs. Brown first met Paddington on a railway platform in London. Noticing the sign on his neck reading 'Please look after this bear. Thank you,' they decided to do just that. From there on home was never the same though the Brown children were delighted." Publ Wkly
Other titles about Paddington Bear are:
More about Paddington
Paddington abroad
Paddington at large
Paddington at work
Paddington goes to town
Paddington here and now
Paddington helps out
Paddington marches on
Paddington on screen
Paddington on stage
Paddington on top
Paddington takes the air
Paddington takes the test
Paddington takes to TV
Paddington treasury

Bond, Nancy, 1945-
A string in the harp. Atheneum Pubs. 1976 370p il $19.95; pa $6.99
Grades: 6 7 8 9   **Fic**
1. Taliesin—Fiction 2. Fantasy fiction 3. Wales—Fiction
ISBN 0-689-50036-X; 1-4169-2771-9 (pa)
LC 75-28181
A Newbery Medal honor book, 1977
"A Margaret K. McElderry book"
"Present-day realism and the fantasy world of sixth-century Taliesin meet in an absorbing novel set in Wales. The story centers around the Morgans—Jen, Peter,

Becky, and their father—their adjustment to another country, their mother's death, and especially, Peter's bitter despair, which threatens them all." LC. Child Books, 1976

Bondoux, Anne-Laure
Vasco leader of the tribe; [by] Anne-Laure Bondoux; translated from the French by Y. Maudet. Delacorte Press 2007 336p $15.99; lib bdg $18.99; pa $6.99
Grades: 3 4 5 6   **Fic**
1. Rats—Fiction 2. Voyages and travels—Fiction
ISBN 978-0-385-73363-2; 978-0-385-90378-3 (lib bdg); 978-0-440-42153-5 (pa)
Following his dreams of finding a safe haven in a new place, Vasco leads a motley group of rats out of the city, through a dangerous sea voyage, and finally to a forest where the rats, now a true tribe, can make a fresh start.
"Bondoux does an excellent job of setting the story firmly and believably in the rodent world while imbuing the characters with enough human qualities to allow young readers to relate to them." SLJ

Boniface, William
The hero revealed; [by] William Boniface; illustrations by Stephen Gilpin. HarperCollins Pub. 2006 294p il (The extraordinary adventures of Ordinary Boy) $15.99; lib bdg $16.89; pa $6.99
Grades: 4 5 6 7   **Fic**
1. Superheroes—Fiction
ISBN   978-0-06-077464-6;   0-06-077464-9; 978-0-06-077465-3 (lib bdg); 0-06-077465-7 (lib bdg); 978-0-06-077466-0 (pa); 0-06-077466-5 (pa)
LC 2005018676
Ordinary Boy, the only resident of Superopolis without a superpower, uncovers and foils a sinister plot to destroy the town
"This first book in a new series is great fun. . . . Boniface wields a cynical, but definitely kid-friendly, sense of humor, and Gilpin's illustrations are sharp and witty." SLJ
Other titles in this series are:
The return of Meteor Boy? (2007)
The great powers outage (2008)

Bonners, Susan, 1947-
Edwina victorious; story and pictures by Susan Bonners. Farrar, Straus & Giroux 2000 131p il $16
Grades: 3 4 5   **Fic**
1. Letter writing—Fiction 2. Political activists—Fiction
ISBN 0-374-31968-5   LC 00-24229
Edwina follows in the footsteps of her namesake great-aunt when she begins to write letters to the mayor about community problems and poses as Edwina the elder
"Occasional soft cartoon drawings bring the characters and town to life. This charming tale is an easy fit for lessons on social activism, letter writing, and even plagiarism." SLJ

Borden, Louise, 1949-

Across the blue Pacific; a World War II story; illustrated by Robert Andrew Parker. Houghton Mifflin 2006 unp il $17

Grades: 2 3 4 5 **Fic**

1. World War, 1939-1945—Fiction

ISBN 0-618-33922-1 LC 2004-9206

A woman reminisces about her neighbor's son who was the object of a letter writing campaign by some fourth-graders when he went away to war in 1943.

"Beautifully written in an understated tone, the story offers a believable picture of life during the war. . . . Restrained yet expressive, the artwork conveys moods and mindsets as well as a strong sense of the time and place." Booklist

The greatest skating race; a World War II story from the Netherlands; illustrated by Niki Daly. Margaret K. McElderry Books 2004 44p il $18.95

Grades: 2 3 4 5 **Fic**

1. World War, 1939-1945—Fiction 2. Netherlands—Fiction 3. Ice skating—Fiction

ISBN 0-689-84502-2 LC 2002-12040

During World War II in the Netherlands, a ten-year-old boy's dream of skating in a famous race allows him to help two children escape to Belgium by ice skating past German soldiers and other enemies.

"Told with immediacy and suspense. . . . The gorgeously detailed watercolor illustrations capture a sense of the time. The subdued, winter hues of brown and smoky gray are those often found in the oil paintings of Dutch and Flemish masters and match the quiet tone of the text." SLJ

The last day of school; written by Louise Borden; illustrated by Adam Gustavson. Margaret K. McElderry Books 2005 unp il $15.95

Grades: 2 3 4 **Fic**

1. School stories 2. Gifts—Fiction

ISBN 0-689-86869-3 LC 2003025124

Matthew Perez, the official timekeeper of Mrs. Mallory's third-grade class, has a special goodbye gift for her

"Varied sizes of colorful oil illustrations accompany the tale of Matts patient delivery of the perfect gift. True to a childs remembrance of final school days, each page recalls memorable moments for students and teachers." SLJ

The lost-and-found tooth; [by] Louise Borden; illustrated by Adam Gustavson. Margaret K. McElderry Books 2008 unp il $16.99

Grades: K 1 2 **Fic**

1. Teeth—Fiction 2. School stories 3. Lost and found possessions—Fiction

ISBN 978-1-4169-1814-1; 1-4169-1814-0

LC 2006028761

A special calendar hangs in Mr. Reilly's second grade classroom, and Lucy Webb impatiently awaits the day when she can add her name for losing a tooth, but when her time arrives something unexpected happens

"The low-key story is nicely illustrated with watercolors and is well suited to either independent reading or classroom sharing." Booklist

Bosch, Pseudonymous

The name of this book is secret; by Pseudonymous Bosch; illustrations by Gilbert Ford. Little, Brown & Co. 2007 360p il $16.99; pa $5.99

Grades: 4 5 6 7 **Fic**

1. Adventure fiction 2. Immortality—Fiction

ISBN 978-0-316-11366-3; 0-316-11366-2; 978-0-316-11369-4 (pa); 0-316-11369-7 (pa)

LC 2007021909

Two eleven-year-old misfits try to solve the mystery of a dead magician and stop the evil Dr. L and Ms. Mauvais, who are searching for the secret of immortality

This "is equal parts supernatural whodunit, suspense-filled adventure and evocative coming-of-age tale." Publ Wkly

Other titles in this series are:

If you're reading this, it's too late (2008)

This book is not good for you (2009)

Boston, L. M. (Lucy Maria), 1892-1990

The children of Green Knowe; illustrated by Peter Boston. Harcourt 2002 c1954 183p il hardcover o.p. pa $6

Grades: 4 5 6 **Fic**

1. Fantasy fiction 2. Great Britain—Fiction

ISBN 0-15-202462-X; 0-15-202468-9 (pa)

LC 2001-51806

First published 1954 in the United Kingdom

"An Odyssey/Harcourt young classic"

Tolly comes to live with his great-grandmother at the ancient house of Green Knowe and becomes friends with three children who lived there in the seventeenth century.

"A special book for the imaginative child, in which mood predominates and fantasy and realism are skillfully blended." Booklist

Other titles about Green Knowe are:

An enemy of Green Knowe (c1976)

The river of Green Knowe (c1959)

A stranger of Green Knowe (c1961)

The treasure of Green Knowe (c1958)

Bouwman, H. M.

The remarkable and very true story of Lucy and Snowcap; [by] H.M. Bouwman. Marshall Cavendish 2008 270p $16.99

Grades: 5 6 7 8 **Fic**

1. Adventure fiction 2. Magic—Fiction 3. Infants—Fiction 4. Islands—Fiction

ISBN 978-0-7614-5441-0; 0-7614-5441-1

LC 2008003180

In 1788, thirteen years after English convicts are shipwrecked on the magical islands of Tathenland, two twelve-year-old girls, one a native Colay, the other the child-governor of the English, set out on a journey to stop the treachery from which both peoples are suffering

"The page-turning adventure fronts for a subtle moral tale about loyalty, perseverance, and the power of finding one's own particular gifts. . . . The combination of historical and fantasy elements gives Lucy and Snowcap's quest folkloric as well as dramatic appeal." Bull Cent Child Books

Bowe, Julie, 1962-
My last best friend. Harcourt 2007 146p $16; pa $5.95
Grades: 2 3 4   **Fic**
1. Friendship—Fiction 2. School stories
ISBN 978-0-15-205777-0; 978-0-15-206197-5 (pa)
LC 2006009244
After her best friend moves away, fourth-grader Ida May is determined not to make another best friend, despite the efforts of a new girl in her class
"Delightful details enhance this friendship story that develops realistically." SLJ
Other titles about Ida May are:
My new best friend (2008)
My best frenemy (2010)

Bowen, Fred, 1953-
Touchdown trouble; written by Fred Bowen. Peachtree Publishers 2009 123p pa $5.95
Grades: 3 4 5   **Fic**
1. Football—Fiction
ISBN 978-1-5614-5497-6; 1-5614-5497-4
LC 2008054867
Sam is proud that his touchdown in the final play of a game left his football team undefeated, but when a videorecording of the game reveals that the touchdown was scored illegally, he and the other Cowboys must decide whether to reveal the truth. Includes facts about a similar situation faced by Cornell University's team after a game with Dartmouth in 1940.
This book is "a great choice to hand off to reader's who'd rather be tossing pigskins that flipping pages." Booklist

Bracegirdle, P. J.
Fiendish deeds. Margaret K. McElderry Books 2008 215p (The joy of Spooking) $15.99
Grades: 4 5 6   **Fic**
1. Marshes—Fiction 2. Endangered species—Fiction 3. Siblings—Fiction 4. Mystery fiction
ISBN 978-1-4169-3416-5; 1-4169-3416-2
LC 2007-23826
As eleven-year-old Joy Wells, proud resident of the nearly-abandoned town of Spooking, tries to stop construction of a water park in a bog she believes is home to a monster and the setting of her favorite horror story, a man with his own mysterious connection to Spooking will do anything to stop her.
"The themes of conformity and environmentalism versus business opportunity are explored with sophistication. This novel is for fans of black humor and real horror, perfect for those looking for a more literary R.L. Stine." SLJ

Bradford, Chris
Young samurai: the way of the warrior. Hyperion Books for Children 2009 359p $16.99 *
Grades: 4 5 6 7   **Fic**
1. Samurai—Fiction 2. Martial arts—Fiction 3. Adventure fiction 4. Japan—Fiction
ISBN 978-1-4231-1871-8; 1-4231-1871-5
LC 2008-46180
First published 2008 in the United Kingdom

Orphaned by a ninja pirate attack off the coast of Japan in 1611, twelve-year-old English lad Jack Fletcher is determined to prove himself, despite the bullying of fellow students, when the legendary sword master who rescued him begins training him as a samurai warrior.
"Jack's story alone makes for a page-turner, but coupling it with intriguing bits of Japanese history and culture, Bradford produces an adventure novel to rank among the genre's best." Publ Wkly
Includes bibliographical references
Followed by: Young samurai: the way of the sword (2010)

Bradley, Kimberly Brubaker
The lacemaker and the princess. Margaret K. McElderry Books 2007 199p $16.99; pa $6.99
Grades: 4 5 6 7 8   **Fic**
1. Marie Antoinette, Queen, consort of Louis XVI, King of France, 1755-1793—Fiction 2. France—History—1789-1799, Revolution—Fiction 3. Friendship—Fiction 4. Lace and lace making—Fiction
ISBN 978-1-4169-1920-9;   1-4169-1920-1; 978-1-4169-8583-9 (pa); 1-4169-8583-2 (pa)
In 1788, eleven-year-old Isabelle, living with her lacemaker grandmother and mother near the palace of Versailles, becomes close friends with Marie Antoinette's daughter, Princess Therese, and finds their relationship complicated not only by their different social class but by the growing political unrest and resentment of the French people.
"Skillfully integrated historical facts frame this engrossing, believable story." Booklist

The President's daughter; [by] Kimberly Brubaker Bradley. Delacorte Press 2004 166p hardcover o.p. lib bdg $17.99; pa $5.50
Grades: 3 4 5   **Fic**
1. Derby, Ethel Roosevelt, 1891-1977—Fiction 2. Roosevelt, Theodore, 1858-1919—Fiction 3. Presidents—Fiction
ISBN 0-385-73147-7; 0-385-90179-8 (lib bdg); 0-440-41995-6 (pa)   LC 2003-19018
A fictionalized account of ten-year-old Ethel Roosevelt's early experiences in the White House after her father, Theodore Roosevelt, becomes president in 1901.
"Loaded with historical details . . . the novel rings true and the people come to life." SLJ

Bragg, Georgia
Matisse on the loose. Delacorte Press 2009 149p $16.99; lib bdg $19.99
Grades: 4 5 6   **Fic**
1. Matisse, Henri. Portrait of Pierre Matisse—Fiction 2. Family life—Fiction 3. Artists—Fiction 4. Art museums—Fiction
ISBN 978-0-385-73570-4;   0-385-73570-7; 978-0-385-90559-6 (lib bdg); 0-385-90559-9 (lib bdg)
LC 2008019624
An aspiring artist's daily routine of being embarrassed by his eccentric family is interrupted when he finds himself in the middle of an art museum fiasco involving Matisse's 1909 portrait of his son Pierre.
"Bragg creates plenty of suspenseful, often comedic scenarios. . . . Readers will enjoy the diverse, memorable characters." Booklist

Brandeis, Gayle, 1968-
My life with the Lincolns. Holt & Co. 2010
248p $16.99
Grades: 4 5 6 7   **Fic**
1. Family life—Fiction 2. Race relations—Fiction
3. African Americans—Fiction
ISBN 978-0-8050-9013-0; 0-8050-9013-4
"Twelve-year-old Mina Edelman is convinced that her
family members are the Lincolns reincarnate, and she has
many coincidences to back her up. . . . The strong
theme of social justice creates a unifying thread in this
informative, clear, personal, and passionate novel."
Booklist

Branford, Henrietta, 1946-
Fire, bed, & bone. Candlewick Press 1998 122p
hardcover o.p. pa $5.99
Grades: 5 6 7 8   **Fic**
1. Dogs—Fiction 2. Middle Ages—Fiction 3. Great
Britain—History—1154-1399, Plantagenets—Fiction
ISBN 0-7636-0338-4; 0-7636-2992-8 (pa)
                                    LC 97-17491
In 1381 in England, a hunting dog recounts what hap-
pens to his beloved master Rufus and his family when
they are arrested on suspicion of being part of the peas-
ants' rebellion led by Wat Tyler and the preacher John
Ball
"The dog's observant eye, sympathetic personality,
and courageous acts hook the reader into what is both ir-
resistible adventure and educational historical fiction."
Booklist

Breathed, Berke
Flawed dogs; the untold account of the shocking
attack on Westminster. Philomel Books 2009 216p
il $16.99
Grades: 4 5 6   **Fic**
1. Dogs—Fiction
ISBN 978-0-399-25218-1; 0-399-25218-5
                                    LC 2009-2638
After being framed by a jealous poodle, a dachshund
is left for dead, but comes back with a group of mutts
from the National Last Ditch Dog Depository to disrupt
the prestigious Westminster Kennel Club dog show and
exact revenge on Cassius the poodle.
"Dramatically lit and featuring comically exaggerated
characters (human and canine alike), Berkeley's b&w
artwork augments the story's drama and humor. A moving tale about the beauty of imperfections and the capacity for love." Publ Wkly

Bredsdorff, Bodil
The Crow-girl; translated from the Danish by
Faith Ingwersen. Farrar Straus Giroux 2004 155p
map (The children of Crow Cove series) $16
Grades: 4 5 6   **Fic**
1. Orphans—Fiction 2. Grandmothers—Fiction
3. Denmark—Fiction
ISBN 0-374-31247-8   LC 2003-49310
Original Danish editon, 1993
After the death of her grandmother, a young orphaned
girl leaves her house by the cove and begins a journey

which leads her to people and experiences that exemplify
the wisdom her grandmother had shared with her
"Touching on universal themes, this quiet adventure
story has the depth and flavor of a tale from long ago
and far away." SLJ

Eidi; translated from the Danish by Kathryn
Mahaffy. Farrar Straus Giroux 2009 138p (The
children of Crow Cove series) $16.99 *
Grades: 4 5 6   **Fic**
1. Orphans—Fiction 2. Denmark—Fiction
ISBN 978-0-374-31267-1; 0-374-31267-2
                                    LC 2008-26052
Awarded the Batchelder Award Honor Book (2010)
Eidi leaves her mother and stepfather in Crow Cove
to live in a nearby village, where she meets the much
younger Tink and rescues him from the abusive man he
has been living with
"This unassuming yet compelling story is notable for
the simplicity and power of the storytelling, the clarity of
description and characterization, and the humanity of the
ideas at the novel's heart." Booklist

Breen, M. E.
Darkwood. Bloomsbury 2009 273p il $16.99
Grades: 5 6 7 8   **Fic**
1. Adventure fiction 2. Orphans—Fiction 3. Sisters—
Fiction 4. Wolves—Fiction 5. Fantasy fiction
ISBN 978-1-59990-259-3; 1-59990-259-1
                                    LC 2008-44413
A clever and fearless orphan endures increasing danger while trying to escape from greedy, lawless men and
elude the terrifying "kinderstalks"—animals who steal
children—before discovering her true destiny.
"Breen's finely tuned storytelling—pithy description,
quick and keen emotion, broad trust of readers' intelligence—offers equal gratification whether readers spot
clues and connections early or late. Both grounded and
wondrous." Kirkus

Brewster, Hugh
Carnation, Lily, Lily, Rose; the story of a
painting; by Hugh Brewster; with paintings by
John Singer Sargent. Kids Can Press 2007 48p il
$17.95
Grades: 3 4 5   **Fic**
1. Sargent, John Singer, 1856-1925—Fiction
2. Artists—Fiction
ISBN 978-1-55453-137-0; 1-55453-137-3
This volume "introduces a true episode from nine-
teenth-century art history, delivering facts about John
Singer Sargent and his luminous masterwork, *Carnation,
Lily, Lily, Rose*, through the imagined words of a child
present during its creation. . . . Widely accessible are
the profuse visuals, including some of Sargent's sketchbook doodles and real photos of the featured family."
Booklist

Brink, Carol Ryrie, 1895-1981

Caddie Woodlawn; illustrated by Trina Schart Hyman. Macmillan 1973 275p il $17.95; pa $6.99 *

Grades: 4 5 6   Fic
1. Frontier and pioneer life—Fiction 2. Wisconsin—Fiction
ISBN 0-02-713670-1; 1-4169-4028-6 (pa)
Awarded the Newbery Medal, 1936
A newly illustrated edition of the title first published 1935

Caddie Woodlawn was eleven in 1864. Because she was frail, she had been allowed to grow up a tomboy. Her capacity for adventure was practically limitless, and there was plenty of adventure on the Wisconsin frontier in those days. The story covers one year of life on the pioneer farm, closing with the news that Mr. Woodlawn had inherited an estate in England, and the unanimous decision of the family to stay in Wisconsin. Based upon the reminiscences of the author's grandmother

The typeface "is eminently clear and readable, and the illustrations in black and white . . . are attractive and expressive." Wis Libr Bull

Brittain, Bill

The wish giver; three tales of Coven Tree; drawings by Andrew Glass. Harper & Row 1983 181p il $16.89; pa $5.99

Grades: 5 6 7 8   Fic
1. Wishes—Fiction 2. Magic—Fiction
ISBN 0-06-020687-X; 0-06-440168-5 (pa)
                                              LC 82-48264
A Newbery Medal honor book, 1984

"Witchy and devilish things happen in Coven Tree, New England, and their chronicler is Stew Meat, proprietor of the Coven Tree store. . . . Stew relates the King Midas luck that came to three young people, each of whom had a wish fulfilled, and each of whom rued that fulfillment." SLJ

"Captivating, fresh, and infused with homespun humor." Horn Book

Other titles about Coven Tree are:
Dr. Dredd's wagon of wonders (1987)
Professor Popkin's prodigious polish (1990)

Brittney, L.

Dangerous times; the first Nathan Fox mission; [by] L. Brittney. Feiwel & Friends 2008 283p (Nathan Fox) $16.95

Grades: 5 6 7 8   Fic
1. Walsingham, Sir Francis, 1530?-1590—Fiction
2. Shakespeare, William, 1564-1616—Fiction
3. Spies—Fiction 4. Adventure fiction 5. Actors—Fiction 6. Great Britain—History—1485-1603, Tudors—Fiction
ISBN 978-0-312-36962-0; 0-312-36962-X

"The setting is Elizabethan England, and young Nathan Fox is an actor who works with the likes of Will Shakespeare. Because of his many talents, he is recruited by the Queen's spymaster, the all-powerful Sir Francis Walsingham. . . . Nathan is in the thick of much action in the Eastern Mediterranean, accompanying the Venetian general Othello on the way to gaining back Cyprus for the Venetians. . . . There is no question that it is cleverly written by Brittney, and we look forward to more tales about Nathan." KLIATT

Broach, Elise, 1963-

Masterpiece; illustrated by Kelly Murphy. Henry Holt & Co. 2008 292p il $16.95

Grades: 4 5 6 7   Fic
1. Artists—Fiction 2. Mystery fiction 3. Beetles—Fiction 4. New York (N.Y.)—Fiction
ISBN 978-0-8050-8270-8; 0-8050-8270-0
"Christy Ottaviano books"

After Marvin, a beetle, makes a miniature drawing as an eleventh birthday gift for James, a human with whom he shares a house, the two new friends work together to help recover a Durer drawing stolen from the Metropolitan Museum of Art.

Broach "packs this fast-moving story with perennially seductive themes: hidden lives and secret friendships, miniature worlds lost to disbelievers. . . . Loosely implying rather than imitating the Old Masters they reference, the finely hatched drawings depict the settings realistically and the characters, especially the beetles, with joyful comic license." Publ Wkly

Shakespeare's secret; [by] Elise Broach. Henry Holt 2005 250p il $16.95; pa $5.99

Grades: 5 6 7 8   Fic
1. Mystery fiction
ISBN 0-8050-7387-6; 0-312-37132-2 (pa)
                                              LC 2004-54020
Named after a character in a Shakespeare play, misfit sixth-grader Hero becomes interested in exploring this unusual connection because of a valuable diamond supposedly hidden in her new house, an intriguing neighbor, and the unexpected attention of the most popular boy in school.

"The mystery alone will engage readers. . . . The main characters are all well developed, and the dialogue is both realistic and well planned." SLJ

Brockmeier, Kevin

Grooves; a kind of mystery; [by] Kevin Brockmeier. Katherine Tegen Books 2006 199p $15.99; lib bdg $16.89

Grades: 4 5 6 7   Fic
1. Jeans (Clothing)—Fiction 2. Factories—Fiction 3. Mystery fiction
ISBN 0-06-073691-7; 0-06-073692-5 (lib bdg)
                                              LC 2004-22683
After seventh-grader Dwayne Ruggles discovers that the grooves in his Thigpen-brand blue jeans are encoded with a cry for help, he sets out to save the factory workers from greedy entrepreneur Howard Thigpen

"Brockmeier constructs a frothy, fanciful, and entertaining blend of science fiction and mystery." Booklist

Brooks, Bruce, 1950-

Everywhere. Harper & Row 1990 70p lib bdg $16.89

Grades: 4 5 6 7   Fic
1. Grandfathers—Fiction 2. Death—Fiction
ISBN 0-06-020729-9   LC 90-4073

Brooks, Bruce, 1950-—*Continued*

Afraid that his beloved grandfather will die after suffering a heart attack, a nine-year-old boy agrees to join ten-year-old Dooley in performing a mysterious ritual called soul switching

"Echoes of the great Southern writers with their themes of loneliness and faith can be heard in this masterly novella. . . . Brooks's precise use of language is a tour de force." Horn Book

Brown, Jackie

Little Cricket. Hyperion Bks. for Children 2004 252p $15.99

Grades: 4 5 6 **Fic**

1. Hmong (Asian people)—Fiction 2. Immigrants—Fiction 3. Minnesota—Fiction

ISBN 0-7868-1852-2

After the upheaval of the Vietnam War reaches them, twelve-year-old Kia and her Hmong family flee from the mountains of Laos to a refugee camp in Thailand and eventually to the alien world of Saint Paul, Minnesota

"Brown's debut is both a gripping survival story and a gentle, heart-wrenching portrait of an immigrant family." Booklist

Brown, Jason Robert

13; [by] Jason Robert Brown & Dan Elish. Laura Geringer Books 2008 201p il $15.99; lib bdg $16.89

Grades: 5 6 7 8 **Fic**

1. Jews—Fiction 2. Bar mitzvah—Fiction 3. Divorce—Fiction 4. School stories 5. Indiana—Fiction

ISBN 978-0-06-078749-3; 0-06-078749-X; 978-0-06-078750-9 (lib bdg); 0-06-078750-3 (lib bdg)

LC 2008000777

Almost thirteen-year-old Evan Goldman learns what it means to be a man when his parents separate and he and his mother move from New York City to Appleton, Indiana, right before his bar mitzvah.

"This quick read, accented with humor, takes up a vast array of themes while hewing rather closely to the strand of finding oneself. . . . A fine school story with characters that are limned with enough thoroughness to make them real." Booklist

Brown, Susan Taylor, 1958-

Hugging the rock; [by] Susan Taylor Brown; [cover illustration by Michael Morgenstern] Tricycle Press 2006 170p $14.95; pa $6.95

Grades: 5 6 7 8 **Fic**

1. Divorce—Fiction 2. Mother-daughter relationship—Fiction 3. Father-daughter relationship—Fiction

ISBN 978-1-58246-180-9; 1-58246-180-5; 978-1-58246-236-3 (pa); 1-58246-236-4 (pa)

LC 2006005738

Through a series of poems, Rachel expresses her feelings about her parents' divorce, living without her mother, and her changing attitude towards her father

"This is a poignant character study of a dysfunctional family. . . . Written in straightforward language, the text clearly reveals Rachel's emotions, describing moments both painful and reassuring." SLJ

Bruchac, Joseph, 1942-

The arrow over the door; pictures by James Watling. Dial Bks. for Young Readers 1998 89p il hardcover o.p. pa $4.99

Grades: 4 5 6 **Fic**

1. Native Americans—Fiction 2. Society of Friends—Fiction 3. United States—History—1775-1783, Revolution—Fiction

ISBN 0-8037-2078-5; 0-14-130571-1 (pa)

LC 96-36701

"In this fictionalized account of a Quaker assembly's encounter with a band of Indian scouts in service to King George's Loyalists, Bruchac alternates the viewpoints of fourteen-year-old Samuel Russell and his Abenaki counterpart, Stands Straight." Bull Cent Child Books

"Bruchac's elegant and powerful writing fills in much of the fascinating detail of this serendipitous wartime friendship. . . . Watling's rugged, textured pen-and-ink drawings provide an atmospheric backdrop." Publ Wkly

Bearwalker; [by] Joseph Bruchac; illustrations by Sally Wern Comport. HarperCollinsPublishers 2007 208p il $15.99; lib bdg $16.89

Grades: 5 6 7 8 **Fic**

1. Camping—Fiction 2. Bears—Fiction 3. Mohawk Indians—Fiction 4. Adirondack Mountains (N.Y.)—Fiction

ISBN 978-0-06-112309-2; 0-06-112309-9; 978-0-06-112311-5 (lib bdg); 0-06-112311-0 (lib bdg)

LC 2006-30420

Although the littlest student in his class, thirteen-year-old Baron Braun calls upon the strength and wisdom of his Mohawk ancestors to face both man and beast when he tries to get help for his classmates, who are being terrorized during a school field trip in the Adirondacks.

"This exciting horror story, illustrated with b/w drawings, is based on Native American folklore." Kliatt

Children of the longhouse. Dial Bks. for Young Readers 1996 150p hardcover o.p. pa $5.99

Grades: 4 5 6 7 **Fic**

1. Mohawk Indians—Fiction 2. Siblings—Fiction 3. Twins—Fiction

ISBN 0-8037-1793-8; 0-14-038504-5 (pa)

LC 95-11344

Eleven-year-old Ohkwa'ri and his twin sister Otsi:stia must make peace with a hostile gang of older boys in their Mohawk village during the late 1400s

"This is a fascinating story that will leave the middle-grade reader with an appreciation for Mohawk culture." Book Rep

The dark pond; illustrations by Sally Wern Comport. HarperCollins 2004 142p il hardcover o.p. pa $6.99 *

Grades: 5 6 7 8 **Fic**

1. Ponds—Fiction 2. Monsters—Fiction 3. Shawnee Indians—Fiction

ISBN 0-06-052995-4; 0-06-052998-9 (pa)

LC 2003-22212

After he feels a mysterious pull drawing him toward a dark, shadowy pond in the woods, Armie looks to old Native American tales for guidance about the dangerous monster lurking in the water

Bruchac, Joseph, 1942-—*Continued*
"Effectively illustrated by Comport, this eerie story skillfully entwines Native American lore, suspense, and the realization that people and things are not always what they seem to be on the surface. . . . A perfect choice for reluctant readers." SLJ

Night wings; illustrations by Sally Wern Comport. HarperCollins 2009 194p $15.99; lib bdg $16.89
Grades: 5 6 7 8   **Fic**
1. Abnaki Indians—Fiction 2. Monsters—Fiction 3. New Hampshire—Fiction
ISBN   978-0-06-112318-4;   0-06-112318-8; 978-0-06-112319-1 (lib bdg); 0-06-112319-6 (lib bdg)
LC 2008032096
After being taken captive by a band of treasure seekers, thirteen-year-old Paul and his Abenaki grandfather must face a legendary Native American monster at the top of Mount Washington.
"The intriguing Native lore, the realistic teen narrative, and cliffhanger sentences that build suspense at the end of each chapter are signature Bruchac and will captivate readers." SLJ

Skeleton man. HarperCollins Pubs. 2001 114p il $15.99; pa $4.99 *
Grades: 4 5 6 7   **Fic**
1. Kidnapping—Fiction 2. Mohawk Indians—Fiction
ISBN 0-06-029075-7; 0-06-440888-4 (pa)
LC 00-54345
After her parents disappear and she is turned over to the care of a strange "great-uncle," Molly must rely on her dreams about an old Mohawk story for her safety and maybe even for her life
"The mix of traditional and contemporary cultural references adds to the story's haunting appeal, and the quick pace and suspense . . . will likely hold the interest of young readers." Publ Wkly
Another title about Skeleton man is:
The return of Skeleton man (2006)

Whisper in the dark; illustrations by Sally Wern Comport. HarperCollins Pub. 2005 174p il $15.99; pa $5.99
Grades: 5 6 7 8   **Fic**
1. Narragansett Indians—Fiction 2. Traffic accidents—Fiction 3. Horror fiction 4. Rhode Island—Fiction
ISBN 0-06-058087-9; 0-06-058089-5 (pa)
LC 2004-22561
An ancient and terrifying Narragansett native-American legend begins to come true for a teenage long-distance runner, whose recovery from the accident that killed her parents has stunned everyone, including her guardian aunt in Providence, Rhode Island
"This fast-paced, macabre novel is perfect for reluctant readers." SLJ

The winter people. Dial Bks. 2002 168p $16.99; pa $5.99
Grades: 5 6 7 8   **Fic**
1. Abnaki Indians—Fiction 2. United States—History—1755-1763, French and Indian War—Fiction
ISBN 0-8037-2694-5; 0-14-240229-X (pa)
LC 2002-338

As the French and Indian War rages in October of 1759, Saxso, a fourteen-year-old Abenaki boy, pursues the English rangers who have attacked his village and taken his mother and sisters hostage
"The narrative itself is thrilling, its spiritual aspects enlightening." Booklist

Buckingham, Royce
Demonkeeper. G. P. Putnam's Sons 2007 216p hardcover o.p. pa $7.99
Grades: 4 5 6 7   **Fic**
1. Horror fiction 2. Supernatural—Fiction
ISBN   978-0-399-24649-4;   0-399-24649-5; 978-0-14-241166-7 (pa); 0-14-241166-3 (pa)
LC 2006-26541
When Nat, the weirdest boy in Seattle, leaves for a date with the plainest girl in town, chaos breaks out in the houseful of demons of which he is the sole guardian.
"This is horror on the mild side. . . . The easygoing, breezy humor adds appeal to an already engaging premise." Bull Cent Child Books

Buckley, Michael
The fairy-tale detectives; pictures by Peter Ferguson. Amulet Books 2005 284p il (The sisters Grimm) $15.95
Grades: 4 5 6   **Fic**
1.   Sisters—Fiction   2.   Orphans—Fiction 3. Grandmothers—Fiction 4. Monsters—Fiction 5. Fairy tales
ISBN 0-8109-5925-9   LC 2005011784
"After the mysterious disappearance of their parents, Sabrina and Daphne Grimm spend a year and a half as victims of New York's foster care system until a woman claiming to be their long-dead grandmother comes to claim them. . . . Granny reveals to the girls that they are descendants of the Brothers Grimm, and the fairy tales that the brothers wrote are actually a history of the magical people known as 'Everafters.' . . . Sabrina and Daphne are intrepid heroines, and the modern interpretations of familiar fairy-tale characters are often truly hilarious." Voice Youth Advocates
Other titles in this series are:
The usual suspects (2005)
The problem child (2006)
Once upon a crime (2007)
Magic and other misdemeanors (2007)
Tales from the hood (2008)
The Everafter War (2009)
The inside story (2010)

NERDS; National Espionage, Rescue, and Defense Society. Amulet Books 2009 306p il (NERDS) $14.95
Grades: 4 5 6 7   **Fic**
1. Spies—Fiction 2. School stories
ISBN 978-0-8109-4324-7; 0-8109-4324-7
LC 2009-15484
While running a spy network from their elementary school, five unpopular misfits combine their talents and use cutting-edge gadgetry to fight evil around the world.
"An action-packed, tongue-in-cheek take on the world of superheroes and villains. . . . Funny, clever, and thoroughly entertaining." SLJ

Buckley-Archer, Linda

Gideon the cutpurse; being the first part of the Gideon trilogy. Simon & Schuster Books for Young Readers 2006 404p (Gideon trilogy) $17.95; pa $7.99

Grades: 5 6 7 8   **Fic**

1. Science fiction 2. Thieves—Fiction 3. Great Britain—History—1714-1837—Fiction

ISBN   978-1-4169-1525-6;   1-4169-1525-7; 978-1-4169-1526-3 (pa); 1-4169-1526-5 (pa)

LC 2006-42204

Ignored by his father and sent to Derbyshire for the weekend, twelve-year-old Peter and his new friend, Kate, are accidentally transported back in time to 1763 England where they are befriended by a reformed cutpurse

"This wonderfully rich and complex novel, written in lyrical and vivid language, is destined to be a classic." SLJ

Other titles in this series are:

The time thief (2007)

The time quake (2009)

Bulion, Leslie, 1958-

The trouble with rules; [by] Leslie Bulion. Peachtree 2008 137p $14.95

Grades: 3 4 5   **Fic**

1. Friendship—Fiction 2. School stories 3. Family life—Fiction

ISBN 978-1-56145-440-2; 1-56145-440-0

LC 2007039687

Now that she is in fourth grade and is not supposed to be friends with boys anymore, Nadie must hide her friendship with Nick, her neighbor and lifelong best friend, but when a new girl arrives who believes that some rules need to be broken, Nadie learns a lot from her

"Nadie is caught up in feelings and social situations that will seem real to kids her age. . . . Adults include an inspiring teacher and a supportive, at-home father." SLJ

Bulla, Clyde Robert, 1914-2007

The Paint Brush Kid; illustrated by Ellen Beier. Random House 1999 64p il pa $3.99

Grades: 2 3 4   **Fic**

1. Artists—Fiction 2. Mexican Americans—Fiction

ISBN 0-679-89282-6 (pa)   LC 97-51153

"A Stepping Stone book"

Nine-year-old Gregory paints pictures representing the life of the Mexican American old man known as Uncle Pancho and attempts to save him from losing his house

"The conclusion is realistic—satisfying, yet containing some unresolved conflict." Horn Book Guide

Bunting, Eve, 1928-

Blackwater. HarperCollins Pubs. 1999 146p hardcover o.p. pa $5.99

Grades: 5 6 7 8   **Fic**

1. Death—Fiction 2. Guilt—Fiction

ISBN 0-06-027843-9 (lib bdg); 0-06-440890-6 (pa)

LC 99-24895

"Joanna Cotler books"

When a boy and girl are drowned in the Blackwater River, thirteen-year-old Brodie must decide whether to confess that he may have caused the accident

"Bunting's thought-provoking theme, solid characterization and skillful juggling of suspense and pathos make this a top-notch choice." Publ Wkly

The man with the red bag. HarperCollins 2007 230p hardcover o.p. lib bdg $16.89

Grades: 5 6 7 8   **Fic**

1. Terrorism—Fiction 2. Travel—Fiction 3. Mystery fiction

ISBN   978-0-06-081828-9;   0-06-081828-X; 978-0-06-081835-7 (lib bdg); 0-06-081835-2 (lib bdg)

LC 2006-103558

In the months following the September 11, 2001 terrorist attacks, twelve-year-old Kevin, an aspiring mystery writer traveling cross-country with his grandmother on a sightseeing trip to various national parks and monuments, suspects a sinister-looking man in his tour group of carrying a bomb

"Bunting writes an effective psychological thriller." Voice Youth Advocates

Nasty, stinky sneakers. HarperCollins Pubs. 1994 105p hardcover o.p. lib bdg $15.89; pa $4.99

Grades: 4 5 6   **Fic**

ISBN 0-06-024236-1; 0-06-024237-X (lib bdg); 0-06-440507-9 (pa)   LC 93-34641

Will ten-year-old Colin find his missing stinky sneakers in time to enter The Stinkiest Sneakers in the World contest?

"A fast-paced, funny book that should elicit some delighted groans." Horn Book Guide

Some frog! illustrated by Scott Medlock. Harcourt Brace & Co. 1998 unp il hardcover o.p. pa $6

Grades: 2 3 4   **Fic**

1. Father-son relationship—Fiction 2. Divorce—Fiction

ISBN 0-15-277082-8; 0-15-216384-0 (pa)

LC 96-24844

Billy is disappointed when his father doesn't show up to help him catch a frog for the frog-jumping competition at school, but the one he and his mother catch wins the championship and Billy begins to accept his father's absence

"The author does an excellent job of presenting a realistic situation and its resolution in straightforward yet eloquent prose. Medlock's bright oil illustrations appear on almost every page, adroitly mirroring the child's emotions and the contest events." SLJ

Spying on Miss Müller. Clarion Bks. 1995 179p $15; pa $6.99

Grades: 5 6 7 8   **Fic**

1. World War, 1939-1945—Fiction 2. School stories 3. Ireland—Fiction

ISBN 0-395-69172-9; 0-449-70455-6 (pa)

LC 94-15003

At Alveara boarding school in Belfast at the start of World War II, thirteen-year-old Jessie must deal with her suspicions about a teacher whose father was German and with her worries about her own father's drinking problem

Bunting, Eve, 1928-—*Continued*

"A thoughtful, moving coming-of-age novel. Jessie and her world . . . are portrayed with page-turning immediacy." Horn Book

Burch, Robert, 1925-

Ida Early comes over the mountain. Viking 1980 145p pa $4.99 hardcover o.p.

Grades: 4 5 6 7   **Fic**

1. Great Depression, 1929-1939—Fiction 2. Country life—Fiction 3. Georgia—Fiction

ISBN 0-14-034534-5 (pa)   LC 79-20532

"Set in the mountains of rural Georgia during the Depression. Ida Early arrives one day to the motherless Sutton family of four children. Mr. Sutton agrees to hire her as a temporary housekeeper." Interracial Books Child Bull

"The book works on two levels—the hilarious account of Ida Early's exotic housekeeping in which real cleverness and skill is as effective and amazing as any fantasy magic, and the gentle, touching story of an ungainly woman's longing for beauty and femininity. . . . [A] fine book." SLJ

Another title about Ida Early is:
Christmas with Ida Early (1983)

Queenie Peavy; illustrated by Jerry Lazare. Viking 1966 159p il pa $5.99 hardcover o.p.

Grades: 5 6 7 8   **Fic**

1. Georgia—Fiction

ISBN 0-14-032305-8 (pa)

"Defiant, independent and intelligent, 13-year-old Queenie idolized her father who was in jail and was neglected by her mother who had to work all the time. Growing up in the [Depression] 1930's in Georgia, Queenie eventually understands her father's real character, herself and her relationships to those about her." Wis Libr Bull

"Queenie is so real that the reader becomes deeply involved in everything that concerns her." Horn Book

Burnett, Frances Hodgson, 1849-1924

A little princess; illustrated by Tasha Tudor. HarperCollins 1999 245p il (Illustrated junior library) $17.99; pa $6.99

Grades: 4 5 6   **Fic**

1. School stories 2. Great Britain—Fiction

ISBN   978-0-3973-0693-0;   0-3973-06938; 978-0-06-440187-6 (pa); 0-06-440187-1 (pa)

First American edition published 1892 by Scribner in shorter form with title: Sara Crewe

The story of Sara Crewe, a girl who is sent from India to a boarding school in London, left in poverty by her father's death, and rescued by a mysterious benefactor

"The story is inevitably adorned with sentimental curlicues but the reader will hardly notice them since the story itself is such a satisfying one. Tasha Tudor's gentle, appropriate illustrations make this a lovely edition." Publ Wkly

The secret garden; illustrated by Inga Moore. Candlewick Press 2008 278p il $21.99 *

Grades: 3 4 5 6   **Fic**

1. Orphans—Fiction 2. Gardens—Fiction 3. Great Britain—Fiction

ISBN 0-7636-3161-2; 978-0-7636-3161-1

LC 2006051838

First published 1911

A ten-year-old orphan comes to live in a lonely house on the Yorkshire moors where she discovers an invalid cousin and the mysteries of a locked garden.

"Burnett's tale . . . is presented in an elegant, oversize volume and handsomely illustrated with Moore's detailed ink and watercolor paintings. Cleanly laid-out text pages are balanced by artwork ranging from delicate spot images to full-page renderings." SLJ

Burns, Khephra

Mansa Musa; the lion of Mali; illustrated by Leo & Diane Dillon. Harcourt 2001 unp il $18

Grades: 4 5 6 7   **Fic**

1. Musa, d. 1337—Fiction 2. Mali—Fiction

ISBN 0-15-200375-4   LC 97-50559

"Gulliver books"

A fictional account of the nomadic wanderings of the boy who grew up to become Mali's great fourteenth-century leader, Mansa Musa

This is "part coming-of-age tale, part cautionary tale, and part fairy tale. . . . Burn's story moves in a languid magical atmosphere beautifully supported by the Dillons' jewel-like illustrations and stylized text ornaments, which, together with parchment-colored pages, give the impression of an illuminated manuscript." Horn Book

Butler, Dori Hillestad

The case of the lost boy; pictures by Jeremy Tugeau. Albert Whitman 2010 123p il (The Buddy files) $14.99

Grades: 1 2 3   **Fic**

1. Dogs—Fiction 2. Missing children—Fiction 3. Mystery fiction

ISBN 978-0-8075-0910-4; 0-8075-0910-8

LC 2009-23763

While searching for his mysteriously lost human family, King the dog detective is adoped by another family, who names him Buddy.

"The type is large, the text is easy, and the occasional black-and-white illustrations complement the text well. The clues are unique and true to the fact that a dog is telling the story." SLJ

The truth about Truman School; by Dori Hillestad Butler. Albert Whitman 2008 170p $15.95; pa $7.99

Grades: 5 6 7 8   **Fic**

1. School stories 2. Bullies—Fiction 3. Newspapers—Fiction 4. Journalism—Fiction

ISBN   978-0-8075-8095-0;   0-8075-8095-3; 978-0-8075-8096-7 (pa); 0-8075-8096-1 (pa)

LC 2007-29977

Tired of being told what to write by the school newspaper's advisor, Zibby and her friend Amr start an underground newspaper online where everyone is free to

Butler, Dori Hillestad—*Continued*

post anything, but things spiral out of control when a cyberbully starts using the site to harrass one popular girl.

"The story moves at a good pace and the timely subject of cyberbullying will be relevant to readers. The language is accessible and the students' voices ring true." SLJ

Butterworth, Oliver, 1915-1990

The enormous egg; illustrated by Louis Darling. Little, Brown 1956 187p il pa $6.99 hardcover o.p. *

Grades: 4 5 6 7   **Fic**
1. Dinosaurs—Fiction
ISBN 0-316-11920-2 (pa)

"Up in Freedom, New Hampshire, one of the Twitchell's hens laid a remarkable egg. . . . Six weeks later when a live dinosaur hatched from the egg, the hen was dazed and upset, the Twitchells dumbfounded, and the scientific world went crazy. Twelve-year-old Nate who had taken care of the egg and made a pet out of the triceratops tells of the hullabaloo." Booklist

This story is "great fun. . . . And if you have any trouble visualizing a Triceratops moving placidly through the twentieth-century world you need only turn to Louis Darling's illustrations to believe." NY Times Book Rev

Byars, Betsy Cromer, 1928-

Boo's dinosaur; illustrated by Erik Brooks. Henry Holt 2006 41p il $15.95 *
Grades: 1 2 3   **Fic**
1. Dinosaurs—Fiction
ISBN 978-0-8050-7958-6; 0-8050-7958-0
LC 2006-00726

"An early chapter book"

When young Boo is followed home by a dinosaur that only she can see, it causes a bit of trouble for her older brother, Sammy.

This is a "charming early chapter book. . . . Brooks's illustrations show the action as well as Boo's flights of fancy. Byars takes full advantage of short words and sentences." SLJ

Followed by: Boo's surprise (2009)

The burning questions of Bingo Brown; [by] Betsy Byars. Viking 1988 166p pa $5.99 hardcover o.p. *
Grades: 4 5 6 7   **Fic**
1. School stories
ISBN 0-14-032479-8 (pa)   LC 87-21022

A boy is puzzled by the comic and confusing questions of youth and worried by disturbing insights into adult conflicts

"A fully worked out novel. . . . Readers will recognize the pitfalls, agonies, and joys of elementary school life in this book. . . . The short chapters and comic style are designed to appeal to young readers and to move them right into other books." Christ Sci Monit

Other titles about Bingo Brown are:

Bingo Brown and the language of love (1989)
Bingo Brown, gypsy lover (1990)
Bingo Brown's guide to romance (1992)

Cracker Jackson; [by] Betsy Byars. Viking Kestrel 1985 147p hardcover o.p. pa $5.99
Grades: 5 6 7 8   **Fic**
1. Wife abuse—Fiction 2. Child abuse—Fiction
ISBN 0-670-80546-7; 0-14-031881-X (pa)
LC 84-24684

"Young Jackson discovers that his ex-baby sitter has been beaten by her husband; and, spurred by affection for her, the boy enlists his friend Goat to help drive her to a home for battered women. The pathetic story of Alma, with her adored baby, tidy home, and treasured collection of Barbie dolls, is relieved by flashbacks to the two boys' antics at school and by their hilarious, if potentially lethal, attempt to drive her to safety." Horn Book

"Suspense, danger, near-tragedy, heartbreak and tension-relieving, unwittingly comic efforts at seriously heroic action mark this as the best of middle-grade fiction to highlight the problems of wife-battering and child abuse." SLJ

The Cybil war; [by] Betsy Byars; illustrated by Gail Owens. Viking 1981 126p il pa $5.99 hardcover o.p.
Grades: 4 5 6   **Fic**
1. Friendship—Fiction
ISBN 0-14-034356-3 (pa)   LC 80-26912

"Simon is deeply smitten by Cybil, a fourth-grade classmate, and just as deeply angered by his once-closest friend Tony, a blithely inventive liar who persists in telling fibs to and about Cybil to strengthen his cause: Tony is also smitten by Cybil." Bull Cent Child Books

"In her gently comic style, Byars presents Simon and the other people in her . . . story (even nasty Tony) as subteens who are people dealing with real problems. . . . Owens has illustrated sympathetically, making up a book that readers will take to their hearts." Publ Wkly

The dark stairs; a Herculeah Jones mystery; by Betsy Byars. Viking 1994 130p hardcover o.p. pa $5.99 *
Grades: 4 5 6   **Fic**
1. Mystery fiction
ISBN 0-670-85487-5; 0-14-240592-2 (pa)
LC 94-14012

The intrepid Herculeah Jones helps her mother, a private investigator, solve a puzzling and frightening case

"There is plenty to laugh at in this book, including classic chapter headings guaranteed to cause shivers for the uninitiated; practiced mystery readers may feel that they are in on a bit of a joke and appreciate the hint of parody. This is a page-turner that is sure to entice the most reluctant readers." SLJ

Other titles about Herculeah Jones are:

The black tower (2006)
Dead letter (1996)
Death's door (1997)
Disappearing acts (1998)
King of murder (2006)
Tarot says beware (1995)

Byars, Betsy Cromer, 1928-—_Continued_

The keeper of the doves; by Betsy Byars. Viking 2002 121p $14.99; pa $5.99

Grades: 4 5 6 7   **Fic**
    1. Sisters—Fiction 2. Family life—Fiction
3. Kentucky—Fiction
    ISBN 0-670-03576-9; 0-14-240063-7 (pa)
                                    LC 2002-9283

In the late 1800s in Kentucky, Amie McBee and her four sisters both fear and torment the reclusive and seemingly sinister Mr. Tominski, but their father continues to provide for his needs

"This is Byars at her best—witty, appealing, thought-provoking." Horn Book

Little Horse; [by] Betsy Byars; illustrated by David McPhail. Holt & Co. 2001 45p il $15.95

Grades: 1 2 3   **Fic**
    1. Horses—Fiction
    ISBN 0-8050-6413-3   LC 00-40983
    "An Early chapter book"

Little Horse falls into the stream and is swept away into a dangerous adventure and a new life

"Byars deftly combines crisp action with a lyrically evoked setting. Language is simple, but not simplistic; uncommon terms are clearly defined in the text and the soft black-and-white art." Horn Book Guide

Another title about Little Horse is:
Little Horse on his own (2004)

The not-just-anybody family; [by] Betsy Byars. Holiday House 2008 176p pa $6.95

Grades: 5 6 7 8   **Fic**
    1. Siblings—Fiction 2. Family life—Fiction
    ISBN 978-0-8234-2145-9 (pa); 0-8234-2145-7 (pa)
                                  LC 2007-42253

First published 1986 by Delacorte Press

With a young brother in the hospital, a grandfather in jail, and their mother traveling with a rodeo, Maggie and Vern try to settle family problems

"The story of the pathetically self-reliant, eccentric, but deeply loving family makes a book that is funny and sad, warm and wonderful." [review of 1986 edition] Horn Book

Other titles about the Blossom family are:
A Blossom promise (1987)
The Blossoms and the Green Phantom (1987)
The Blossoms meet the Vulture Lady (1986)
Wanted-Mud Blossom (1991)

The pinballs; [by] Betsy Byars. Harper & Row 1977 136p lib bdg $16.89; pa $5.99 *

Grades: 5 6 7 8   **Fic**
    1. Foster home care—Fiction 2. Friendship—Fiction
    ISBN 0-06-020918-6 (lib bdg); 0-06-440198-7 (pa)

"Pinballs go where they're pushed—and life's 'tilts' have thrown together three misfits. Suddenly finding themselves in a warm, loving foster home are Thomas J., eight, who is homeless now that his octogenarian twin guardians are hospitalized; Harvey, 13, whose mother ran off to a commune and whose hard-drinking father ran over him in a car; and Carlie, 15, who cannot get along with a succession of stepfathers—or the rest of the world, for that matter." SLJ

"A deceptively simple, eloquent story, its pain and ac-

rimony constantly mitigated by the author's light, offhand style and by Carlie's wryly comic view of life." Horn Book

The SOS file; [by] Betsy Byars, Betsy Duffey, Laurie Myers; illustrated by Arthur Howard. Henry Holt 2004 71p il $15.95

Grades: 3 4 5   **Fic**
    1. School stories
    ISBN 0-8050-6888-0   LC 2003-18240

The students in Mr. Magro's class submit stories for the SOS file about their biggest emergencies, and then they read them aloud for extra credit

"Some tales are poignant, others are humorous; all are as credible as the characters sketched. . . . Lighthearted sketches enhance characterization. . . . [An] engaging, plausible, and highly readable collection of anecdotes." SLJ

The summer of the swans; [by] Betsy Byars; illustrated by Ted CoConis. Viking 1970 142p il $15.99; pa $5.99 *

Grades: 5 6 7 8   **Fic**
    1. Mentally handicapped children—Fiction
2. Siblings—Fiction
    ISBN 0-670-68190-3; 0-14-031420-2 (pa)
    Awarded the Newbery Medal, 1971

"The thoughts and feelings of a young girl troubled by a sense of inner discontent which she cannot explain are tellingly portrayed in the story of two summer days in the life of fourteen-year-old Sara Godfrey. Sara is jolted out of her self-pitying absorption with her own inadequacies by the disappearance of her ten-year-old retarded brother who gets lost while trying to find the swans he had previously seen on a nearby lake. Her agonizing, albeit ultimately successful, search for Charlie and the reactions of others to this traumatic event help Sara gain a new perspective on herself and life." Booklist

Tornado; by Betsy Byars; illustrations by Doron Ben-Ami. HarperCollins Pubs. 1996 49p il lib bdg $15.89; pa $4.99

Grades: 2 3 4   **Fic**
    1. Dogs—Fiction 2. Tornadoes—Fiction
    ISBN 0-06-026452-7 (lib bdg); 0-06-442063-9 (pa)
                                  LC 95-41584

As they wait out a tornado in their storm cellar, a family listens to their farmhand tell stories about the dog that was blown into his life by another tornado when he was a boy

"The handsome illustrations by Doron Ben-Ami give the volume a more distinguished, less juvenile look than the typical chapter book and convey the story's drama, warmth, and occasional humor. Parents and teachers will find this an excellent book to read aloud, and dog lovers of any age will find it irresistible." Booklist

Byrd, Tim

Doc Wilde and the frogs of doom. G. P. Putnam's Sons 2009 186p il $15.99

Grades: 4 5 6 **Fic**

1. Adventure fiction 2. Missing persons—Fiction 3. Frogs—Fiction 4. Rain forests—Fiction 5. Extraterrestrial beings—Fiction 6. South America—Fiction

ISBN 978-0-399-24783-5; 0-399-24783-1

LC 2008-32493

Twelve-year-old Brian, ten-year-old Wren, and their father, Doc Wilde, risk their lives in a South American rainforest as they seek the eldest member of their famous family of adventurers, Grandpa, amidst a throng of alien frogs.

"The book's small format, breakneck pacing, and broad humor will appeal to middle-grade adventure fans." SLJ

Cabot, Meg, 1967-

Moving day. Scholastic Press 2008 228p (Allie Finkle's rules for girls) $15.99; pa $5.99

Grades: 3 4 5 **Fic**

1. Moving—Fiction 2. Friendship—Fiction 3. Family life—Fiction 4. School stories

ISBN 978-0-545-03947-5; 0-545-03947-9; 978-0-545-04041-9 (pa); 0-545-04041-8 (pa)

LC 2007-27836

Nine-year-old Allie Finkle has rules for everything and is even writing her own rule book, but her world is turned upside-down when she learns that her family is moving across town, which will mean a new house, school, best friend, and plenty of new rules.

Cabot's "trademark frank humor makes for compulsive reading—as always. . . . Allie is funny, believable and plucky . . . but most of all, and most interestingly, Allie is ambivalent." Publ Wkly

Other titles in this series are:
The new girl (2008)
Best friends and drama queens (2009)
Stage fright (2009)
Glitter girls and the great fake out (2010)

Cameron, Ann, 1943-

Colibri. Farrar, Straus & Giroux 2003 227p $17; pa $5.99

Grades: 5 6 7 8 **Fic**

1. Kidnapping—Fiction 2. Mayas—Fiction

ISBN 0-374-31519-1; 0-440-42052-0 (pa)

LC 2002-192542

"Frances Foster books"

Kidnapped when she was very young by an unscrupulous man who has forced her to lie and beg to get money, a twelve-year-old Mayan girl endures an abusive life, always wishing she could return to the parents she can hardly remember

"The taut, chilling suspense and search for riches will keep readers flying through the pages. But it's Cameron's beautiful language and Rosa's larger identity quest that make this novel extraordinary." Booklist

Gloria's way; pictures by Lis Toft. Farrar, Straus & Giroux 2000 96p il hardcover o.p. pa $4.99

Grades: 2 3 4 **Fic**

1. Friendship—Fiction 2. Family life—Fiction 3. African Americans—Fiction

ISBN 0-374-32670-3; 0-14-230023-3 (pa)

LC 99-12104

Also available in paperback from Puffin Bks.

"Frances Foster books"

This companion volume to the series featuring Julian and Huey centers on their friend Gloria. Gloria shares special times with her mother and father and with her friends

"Lis Toft's shaded pencil drawings portray these African American characters and their predicaments with warmth and humor." Booklist

Another title about Gloria is:
Gloria rising (2002)

The stories Julian tells; illustrated by Ann Strugnell. Pantheon Bks. 1981 71p il pa $4.99 hardcover o.p. *

Grades: 2 3 4 **Fic**

1. Family life—Fiction 2. African Americans—Fiction

ISBN 0-394-82892-5 (pa)

LC 80-18023

"When seven-year-old Julian tells his little brother, Huey, that cats come from catalogues, Huey believes him. But when he flips the pages of the catalogue and doesn't find any cats, he begins to cry and Julian has some fast explaining to do. . . . A loving family is the center for six happy stories about catalog cats, strange teeth, a garden, a birthday fig tree and a new friend." West Coast Rev Books

"Strugnell's delightful drawings depict Julian, his little brother Huey and their parents as black, but they could be members of any family with a stern but loving and understanding father." Publ Wkly

Other titles about Julian and his family are:
Julian, dream doctor (1990)
Julian, secret agent (1988)
Julian's glorious summer (1987)
More stories Huey tells (1997)
More stories Julian tells (1986)
The stories Huey tells (1995)

Cameron, Eleanor, 1912-1996

The wonderful flight to the Mushroom Planet; [by] Eleanor Cameron; with illustrations by Robert Henneberger. Little, Brown 1954 214p il pa $7.99 hardcover o.p.

Grades: 4 5 6 **Fic**

1. Science fiction

ISBN 0-316-12540-7 (pa)

"An Atlantic Monthly Press book"

Two boys help a neighbor build a space ship in answer to an ad and take off for the dying planet of Basidium. There they help the inhabitants to restore an essential food to their diets and thereby save the life of the planet

"Scientific facts are emphasized in this well-built story. Since they are necessary to the development of the story the reader absorbs them naturally as he soars with the boys on the mission." N Y Times Book Rev

Carbone, Elisa Lynn, 1954-

Blood on the river; James Town 1607; [by] Elisa Carbone. Viking 2006 237p $16.99; pa $6.99

Grades: 5 6 7 8   **Fic**
1. Jamestown (Va.)—History—Fiction 2. Powhatan Indians—Fiction 3. United States—History—1600-1775, Colonial period—Fiction
ISBN 0-670-06060-7; 0-14-240932-4 (pa)
                                        LC 2005023646
Traveling to the New World in 1606 as the page to Captain John Smith, twelve-year-old orphan Samuel Collier settles in the new colony of James Town, where he must quickly learn to distinguish between friend and foe.
"A strong, visceral story of the hardship and peril settlers faced, as well as the brutal realities of colonial conquest." Booklist

Storm warriors; [by] Elisa Carbone. Knopf 2001 168p hardcover o.p. pa $6.50

Grades: 4 5 6 7   **Fic**
1. United States. Life-Saving Service—Fiction 2. African Americans—Fiction 3. North Carolina—Fiction
ISBN 0-375-80664-4; 0-440-41879-8 (pa)
                                        LC 00-59924
In 1895, after his mother's death, twelve-year-old Nathan moves with his father and grandfather to Pea Island off the coast of North Carolina, where he hopes to join the all-black crew at the nearby lifesaving station, despite his father's objections
"This thoughtfully crafted first-person narrative combines historical figures with created characters in the best traditions of the historical novel." Horn Book Guide

Carlson, Drew

Attack of the Turtle; a novel; by Drew Carlson; illustrations by David A. Johnson. Eerdmans Books for Young Readers 2007 149p il hardcover o.p. pa $8

Grades: 4 5 6 7   **Fic**
1. Bushnell, David, 1742-1824—Fiction 2. United States—History—1775-1783, Revolution—Fiction 3. Submarines—Fiction 4. Inventors—Fiction
ISBN 978-0-8028-5308-0; 0-8028-5308-0; 978-0-8028-5338-7 (pa); 0-8028-5338-2 (pa)
                                        LC 2005032068
During the Revolutionary War, fourteen-year-old Nathan joins forces with his older cousin, the inventor David Bushnell, to secretly build the first submarine used in naval warfare.
"Though Nate makes for a sympathetic character and the plot is well constructed, the actual tale of the *Turtle* is quite involving, too." Booklist

Carlson, Natalie Savage, 1906-

The family under the bridge; pictures by Garth Williams. Harper & Row 1958 99p il lib bdg $16.89; pa $5.99

Grades: 3 4 5   **Fic**
1. Tramps—Fiction 2. Christmas—Fiction 3. Paris (France)—Fiction
ISBN 0-06-020991-7 (lib bdg); 0-06-440250-9 (pa)
A Newbery Medal honor book, 1959

"Old Armand, a Parisian hobo, enjoyed his solitary, carefree life. . . . Then came a day just before Christmas when Armand, who wanted nothing to do with children because they spelled homes, responsibility, and regular work, found that three homeless children and their working mother had claimed his shelter under the bridge. How the hobo's heart and life become more and more deeply entangled with the little family and their quest for a home is told." Booklist
"Garth Williams' illustrations are perfect for this thoroughly delightful story of humor and sentiment." Libr J

Carman, Patrick

The Dark Hills divide; [by] Patrick Carman. Orchard Books 2005 253p (The land of Elyon) $11.95

Grades: 4 5 6 7   **Fic**
1. Fantasy fiction
ISBN 0-439-70093-0   LC 2004-16312
When she finds the key to a secret passageway leading out of the walled city of Bridewell, twelve-year-old Alexa realizes her lifelong wish to explore the mysterious forests and mountains that lie beyond the wall
"Narrator Aasne Vigesaa clearly portrays Alexa's thoughtful, inquisitive nature and unsettled feelings. . . . Vigesaa's excellent use of pace, pitch, and tone help differentiate each character." SLJ
Other titles in this series are:
Beyond the Valley of Thorns (2005)
The tenth city (2006)
Into the mist (2007)
Stargazer (2008)

The house of power. Little, Brown & Co. 2007 330p il (Atherton) $16.99; pa $5.99

Grades: 5 6 7 8   **Fic**
1. Social classes—Fiction 2. Friendship—Fiction 3. Earthquakes—Fiction 4. Orphans—Fiction 5. Science fiction
ISBN 978-0-316-16670-6; 0-316-16670-7; 978-0-316-16671-3 (pa); 0-316-16671-5 (pa)
                                        LC 2006025976
Edgar, an eleven-year-old orphan, finds a book that reveals significant secrets about Atherton, the strictly divided world on which he lives, even as geological changes threaten to shift the power structure that allows a select few to live off the labor of others.
This "is a fast-paced novel with a unique setting, fascinating plot, and cliffhanger ending. It shines because of the author's imagination and skill." SLJ
Other titles about Edgar are:
Rivers of fire (2008)
Dark planet (2009)

Carmichael, Clay

Wild things; [written and illustrated by Clay Carmichael] Front Street 2009 248p il $18.95 *

Grades: 5 6 7 8   **Fic**
1. Family life—Fiction 2. Orphans—Fiction 3. Uncles—Fiction 4. Artists—Fiction 5. Cats—Fiction
ISBN 978-1-59078-627-7; 1-59078-627-0
                                        LC 2007-49911

Carmichael, Clay—*Continued*

Stubborn, self-reliant, eleven-year-old Zoe, recently orphaned, moves to the country to live with her prickly half-uncle, a famous doctor and sculptor, and together they learn about trust and the strength of family

"Carmichael gives a familiar plot a fresh new life in this touching story with a finely crafted sense of place." Booklist

Carris, Joan Davenport, 1938-

Welcome to the Bed & Biscuit; [by] Joan Carris; illustrated by Noah Jones. Candlewick Press 2006 116p il $15.99; pa $5.99 *

Grades: 2 3 4   Fic

1. Veterinarians—Fiction 2. Animals—Fiction

ISBN 0-7636-2151-X; 0-7636-4621-0 (pa)

LC 2004062857

The family animals at the Bed & Biscuit begin to feel slighted when Dr. Bender returns from a fire with something that occupies the time usually reserved for them.

"This is a small, remarkably sweet beginning chapter book with more than its fair share of amusing illustrations and gentle humor." SLJ

Another title about the Bed & Biscuit is:

Wild times at the Bed & Biscuit (2009)

Carroll, Lewis, 1832-1898

Alice through the looking glass; illustrated by Helen Oxenbury. Candlewick Press 2005 224p il $24.99; pa $14.99 *

Grades: 4 5 6 7   Fic

1. Fantasy fiction

ISBN 978-0-7636-2892-5; 0-7636-2892-1; 978-0-7636-4262-4 (pa); 0-7636-4262-2 (pa)

First published 1871 with title: Through the looking-glass and what Alice found there

In this edition of Lewis Carroll's classic which follows Alice in Wonderland, Alice "steps through the looking glass and into a world depicted in warm watercolors, sepia-toned illustrations, and line drawings. Not a word of the original tale has been altered. The artwork echoes the whimsy of the language." SLJ

Alice's adventures in Wonderland; by Lewis Carroll; with forty-two illustrations by John Tenniel. Books of Wonder 1992 196p il $16.99

Grades: 4 5 6 7   Fic

1. Fantasy fiction

ISBN 0-688-11087-8   LC 91-31482

First published 1865

A little girl falls down a rabbit hole and discovers a world of nonsensical and amusing characters

Alice's adventures in Wonderland; [by] Lewis Carroll; illustrated by Helen Oxenbury. Candlewick Press 1999 206p il hardcover o.p. pa $12.99 *

Grades: 4 5 6 7   Fic

1. Fantasy fiction

ISBN 0-7636-0804-1; 0-7636-2049-1 (pa)

LC 99-28788

A little girl falls down a rabbit hole and discovers a world of nonsensical and amusing characters.

"Oxenbury presents the unforgettable characters in a winning combination of black-and-white drawings and her recognizable softly shaded watercolors. Hers is a thoroughly modern Alice clad in a blue jumper and sneakers. . . . Despite the contemporary twists, Oxenbury's droll, understated humor captures the essence of Carroll's fantasy world." SLJ

Alice's adventures in Wonderland; illustrated by Alison Jay. Dial Books for Young Readers 2006 203p il $25.99

Grades: 4 5 6 7   Fic

1. Fantasy fiction

ISBN 0-8037-2940-5

Alice falls down a rabbit hole and discovers a world of nonsensical and amusing characters.

"Heavy white pages and spacious book design showcase Jay's distinctive paintings. Combining elegance with innocence, the artwork features rounded forms of people, trees, and animals that are each a little apart from the others, isolated in a splendid but strange dream world. . . . The paintings glow with color under the crackle-glaze textured varnish." Booklist

Alice's adventures in Wonderland; with illustrations by Robert Ingpen. Sterling 2009 191p il $19.95

Grades: 4 5 6 7   Fic

1. Fantasy fiction

ISBN 978-1-4027-6835-4; 1-4027-6835-4

Alice falls down a rabbit hole and discovers a world of nonsensical and amusing characters.

"Carroll's unabridged text is accompanied by abundant illustrations that draw readers into the tale. . . . Filled with soft textures and dramatic shadowing, Ingpen's artwork blends realism and whimsy. . . . An inviting layout and plentiful artwork make this book a good choice for independent readers who may need a bit of encouragement, as well as for one-on-one sharing with younger children." SLJ

Lewis Carroll's Alice in Wonderland; illustrated by Rodney Matthews. Candlewick Press 2009 95p il $24.99

Grades: 4 5 6 7   Fic

1. Fantasy fiction

ISBN 978-0-7636-4568-7; 0-7636-4568-0

On a hot summer day, a little girl sitting by her sister on the bank, having nothing to do, begins to let her imagination grow. Her curiosity and hatred of logic cause her to dream of a nonsensical world filled with amusing characters

Matthews' illustrations "have an imagination-stretching, otherworldly veneer. . . . The cartoon artwork portrays Alice with a somewhat angular face and straight blond hair. The depictions of the other characters are fresh and creative. . . . The small-size type, which may demand more accomplished or patient readers, and the sophisticated visual tone make this volume appropriate for older Alice fans." SLJ

Casanova, Mary

The klipfish code; by Mary Casanova. Houghton Mifflin Company 2007 227p map $16

Grades: 4 5 6 7   **Fic**

1. Norway—Fiction 2. World War, 1939-1945—Norway—Fiction 3. World War, 1939-1945—Underground movements—Fiction 4. Family life—Fiction

ISBN 978-0-618-88393-6; 0-618-88393-2

LC 2007012752

Sent with her younger brother to Godøy Island to live with her aunt and grandfather after Germans bomb Norway in 1940, ten-year-old Merit longs to join her parents in the Resistance and when her aunt, a teacher, is taken away two years later, she resents even more the Nazis' presence and her grandfather's refusal to oppose them.

"Casanova spins an adventure-filled and harrowing story." SLJ

Includes glossary and bibliographical references

Cassidy, Cathy, 1962-

Dizzy; a novel; by Cathy Cassidy. Viking 2004 247p hardcover o.p. pa $6.99

Grades: 5 6 7 8   **Fic**

1. Mother-daughter relationship—Fiction 2. Great Britain—Fiction

ISBN 0-670-05936-6; 0-14-240474-8 (pa)

LC 2004-1642

After an eight-year absence, Dizzy's "New Age traveler" mother suddenly shows up on her twelfth birthday and whisks her away to a series of festivals throughout Scotland in her rattletrap van.

"The eclectic characters and their lifestyle are presented as captivating yet questionable in the girl's first-person narrative, and the well-developed plot fosters concern for Dizzy from the beginning. A unique, satisfying story." SLJ

Indigo Blue. Viking 2005 215p hardcover o.p. pa $6.99

Grades: 5 6 7 8   **Fic**

1. Moving—Fiction 2. Abused women—Fiction 3. Great Britain—Fiction

ISBN 0-670-05927-7; 0-14-240703-8 (pa)

Eleven-year-old Indigo, her mother, and her toddler sister have to move out of their apartment because of troubles with Mum's boyfriend, while Indie is also having best friend problems at school, leaving her stressed, confused, and lonely.

"This British story of domestic abuse is firmly child-centered, and Indigo's confusion and fear . . . are sensitively portrayed. . . . The hopeful ending rings true." Booklist

Scarlett; [by] Cathy Cassidy. Viking 2006 261p $16.99

Grades: 5 6 7 8   **Fic**

1. Stepfamilies—Fiction 2. Country life—Fiction 3. Ireland—Fiction

ISBN 0-670-06068-2   LC 2006001029

After being expelled from yet another school in London, twelve-year-old Scarlett is sent by her exasperated mother to live with her father, stepmother, and stepsister in Ireland, where, with the help of a mysterious boy, she eventually overcomes her anger and resentment and feels part of a family again.

"Infused with a bit of fairy-tale magic, this is a fast-paced yet thoughtful story. The heroine is feisty and troublesome, yet quirky and lovable." SLJ

Catalanotto, Peter

No more pumpkins; [by] Peter Catalanotto and Pamela Schembri. Henry Holt 2007 62p (2nd-grade friends) $15.95

Grades: 1 2 3   **Fic**

1. School stories 2. Friendship—Fiction 3. Pumpkin—Fiction

ISBN 978-0-8050-7839-8; 0-8050-7839-8

LC 2006035464

Second-grader Emily is tired of pumpkins being at the center of every lesson in school, but she is not prepared when a jealous friend damages the jack-o-lantern portrait Emily made for Open House

"The black-and-white illustrations are well done and expressive. Fans of Barbara Park's 'Junie B. Jones' series and Patricia Reilly Giff's 'Polk Street School' books . . . will enjoy this beginning chapter book." SLJ

Other titles in this series are:

The secret lunch special (2006)

The Veteran's Day visitor (2008)

Catanese, P. W., 1961-

Happenstance found. Aladdin 2009 342p il (The books of Umber) $16.99

Grades: 5 6 7 8   **Fic**

1. Adventure fiction 2. Magic—Fiction 3. Fantasy fiction

ISBN 978-1-4169-7519-9; 1-4169-7519-5

LC 2008-45966

A boy awakens, blindfolded, with no memory of even his name, but soon meets Lord Umber, an adventurer and inventor, who calls him Happenstance and tells him that he has a very important destiny—and a powerful enemy.

"Catanese packs a lot into the book: rich characterizations, . . . well-choreographed action sequences and genuinely surprising twists at the end." Publ Wkly

Followed by: Dragon games (2010)

Chabon, Michael

Summerland. Hyperion Bks. for Children 2002 500p hardcover o.p. pa $8.95

Grades: 5 6 7 8   **Fic**

1. Fantasy fiction 2. Baseball—Fiction 3. Magic—Fiction

ISBN 0-7868-0877-2; 0-7868-1615-5 (pa)

LC 2002-27497

Ethan Feld, the worst baseball player in the history of the game, finds himself recruited by a 100-year-old scout to help a band of fairies triumph over an ancient enemy

"Much of the prose is beautifully descriptive as Chabon navigates vividly imagined other worlds and offers up some timeless themes." Horn Book

Chang, Margaret Scrogin
Celia's robot; by Margaret Chang. Holiday House 2009 211p $16.95
Grades: 4 5 6 **Fic**
1. Robots—Fiction 2. Family life—Fiction 3. Friendship—Fiction 4. Racially mixed people—Fiction 5. Chinese Americans—Fiction
ISBN 978-0-8234-2181-7; 0-8234-2181-3
LC 2009-07555
Surprised by her scientist father's gift of a robot for her birthday, ten-year-old Celia comes to appreciate its help in organizing her chaotic day-to-day life until it suddenly mysteriously disappears.
"A bit of mystery plus solidly believable, complex friend-family relationships and a smart girl who's fearless about technology make for an appealing light read." Kirkus

Chatterton, Martin
The Brain finds a leg. Peachtree Publishers 2009 212p $16.95
Grades: 4 5 6 **Fic**
1. Mystery fiction 2. Intellect—Fiction 3. Animals—Fiction 4. Inventions—Fiction 5. School stories 6. Australia—Fiction
ISBN 978-1-56145-503-4; 1-56145-503-2
LC 2009-00304
First published 2007 in Australia
In Farrago Bay, Australia, thirteen-year-old Sheldon is recruited by a new student, Theo Brain, to help investigate a murder, which is tied not only to bizzare animal behavior but also to a diabolical plot to alter human intelligence.
"Several deaths in the story war against the comedy but the laughs win. Readers shouldn't expect anything remotely realistic and instead surrender themselves to the industrial-strength zaniness." Kirkus

Cheaney, J. B.
The middle of somewhere. Alfred A. Knopf 2007 218p $15.99; lib bdg $18.99; pa $6.50
Grades: 5 6 7 8 **Fic**
1. Automobile travel—Fiction 2. Siblings—Fiction 3. Attention deficit disorder—Fiction 4. Grandfathers—Fiction 5. Kansas—Fiction
ISBN 978-0-375-83790-6; 978-0-375-93790-3 (lib bdg); 978-0-440-42165-8 (pa) LC 2006-29202
Twelve-year-old Ronnie loves organization, especially because her brother has attention-deficit hyperactivity disorder, but traveling with their grandfather who is investigating wind power in Kansas brings some pleasant, if chaotic, surprises.
"The main characters are particularly well drawn and believable, and readers will root for both children as they attempt to overcome the obstacles placed in front of them." Booklist

My friend, the enemy. Knopf 2005 266p hardcover o.p. pa $6.50
Grades: 5 6 7 8 **Fic**
1. Japanese Americans—Fiction 2. Friendship—Fiction 3. World War, 1939-1945—Fiction
ISBN 0-375-81432-9; 0-440-42102-0 (pa)
LC 2004-26927

During World War II, a twelve-year-old girl becomes friends with a young Japanese-American boy she discovers being sheltered and hidden by her neighbor.
"Written in first person, this novel offers quiet but finely tuned portrayal of the stresses that changed life on the home front and one child's attempts to cope with it all." Booklist

Chen, Pauline, 1966-
Peiling and the chicken-fried Christmas; [by] Pauline Chen. Bloomsbury Children's Books 2007 133p $15.95
Grades: 4 5 6 **Fic**
1. Taiwanese Americans—Fiction 2. Christmas—Fiction
ISBN 978-1-59990-122-0; 1-59990-122-6
LC 2006102095
Fifth-grader Peiling Wang wants to celebrate "a real American Christmas," much to the displeasure of her traditional, Taiwanese-born father
"Peiling makes an appealingly levelheaded protagonist, and . . . [Chen] doesn't miss much in this often-amusing picture of the Wang family working at fitting its new and old cultures together." Booklist

Cheng, Andrea, 1957-
The bear makers. Front Street 2008 170p $16.95
Grades: 5 6 7 8 **Fic**
1. Hungary—Fiction 2. Family life—Fiction
ISBN 978-1-59078-518-8; 1-59078-518-5
LC 2007049005
In post-World War II Budapest, a young girl and her family struggle against the oppressive Hungarian Worker's Party policies and try to find a way to a better life
"Cheng has crafted a cast of characters and palpable setting that are vivid and compelling, and she offers a glimpse into history that many children will find easy to relate to and powerfully affecting." Booklist

Brushing Mom's hair; illustrations by Nicole Wong. Wordsong 2009 59p il $17.95
Grades: 4 5 6 7 **Fic**
1. Novels in verse 2. Cancer—Fiction 3. Sick—Fiction 4. Mother-daughter relationship—Fiction
ISBN 978-1-59078-599-7; 1-59078-599-1
LC 2009021965
A fourteen-year-old girl, whose mother's breast cancer diagnosis and treatment have affected every aspect of their lives, finds release in ballet and art classes.
"With one or two words on each line, the poems are a fast read, but the chatty voice packs in emotion. . . . Wong's small black-and-white pencil drawings on every page extend the poetry through the characters' body language." Booklist

Eclipse. Front Street 2006 129p $16.95
Grades: 4 5 6 7 **Fic**
1. Immigrants—Fiction 2. Hungarian Americans—Fiction 3. Ohio—Fiction
ISBN 978-1-932425-21-5; 1-932425-21-7
LC 2006-00785
In Cincinnati, Ohio, in the summer of 1952, eight-year-old Peti gives up his room to his Hungarian rela-

Cheng, Andrea, 1957-—*Continued*

tives, including a twelve-year-old cousin who bullies him, and worries about his grandfather who cannot escape from behind the Iron Curtain.

"The pain of the immigrant experience . . . is compellingly captured in this spare, unsentimental novel." Booklist

Honeysuckle house. Front Street 2004 136p $16.95; pa $10.95

Grades: 3 4 5   **Fic**
1. Friendship—Fiction 2. Chinese Americans—Fiction 3. Immigrants—Fiction

ISBN 1-886910-99-5; 1-59078-632-7 (pa)

An all-American girl with Chinese ancestors and a new immigrant from China find little in common when they meet in their fourth grade classroom, but they are both missing their best friends and soon discover other connections

"Told in first person in alternating chapters, the narratives balance well between large issues . . . and more intimate ones. . . . With a smoothly drawn and interesting plot, strong characters, and graceful writing, the story has more immediacy than much realistic contemporary fiction." SLJ

The lace dowry. Front Street 2005 113p $16.95

Grades: 4 5 6 7   **Fic**
1. Friendship—Fiction 2. Sex role—Fiction 3. Hungary—Fiction

ISBN 1-932425-20-9   LC 2004-21186

In Hungary in 1933, a twelve-year-old from Budapest befriends the Halas village family of lacemakers hired to stitch her dowry.

"Cheng tells a familiar story of children discovering empathy across class and cultural divides, enriching the theme with a vivid historical setting and Juli's strong narration, which is written in spare language and a believable voice." Booklist

Only one year; illustrations by Nicole Wong. Lee & Low Books 2010 97p il $16.95

Grades: 2 3 4   **Fic**
1. Family life—Fiction 2. Chinese Americans—Fiction 3. Siblings—Fiction

ISBN 978-1-60060-252-8; 1-60060-252-5

LC 201044

"Although she sometimes finds him troublesome, fourth-grader Sharon can't bear the idea that her two-year-old brother, Di Di, will spend a whole school year with relatives in China while she and her first-grade sister, Mary, go to school and her parents work. . . . Supportive black-and-white illustrations and a glossary/pronunciation guide for the occasional Chinese words and phrases complete the appealing package of this gentle family story." Booklist

Shanghai messenger; illustrated by Ed Young. Lee & Low 2005 unp il $18.95

Grades: 3 4 5 6   **Fic**
1. Chinese Americans—Fiction 2. China—Fiction 3. Novels in verse

ISBN 1-58430-238-0   LC 2004-4025934

A free-verse novel about eleven-year-old Xiao Mei's visit with her extended family in China, where the Chinese-American girl finds many differences but also the similarities that bind a family together.

"Cheng does an admirable job of capturing this experience from the perspective of a child, and each free-verse chapter is brief but satisfying. . . . Young's illustrations delicately intertwine with the text, gently supporting each vignette. This is a superb book." SLJ

Where the steps were. Front Street 2008 143p il $16.95

Grades: 3 4 5 6   **Fic**
1. School stories 2. Teachers—Fiction 3. Friendship—Fiction 4. Novels in verse

ISBN 978-1-932425-88-8; 1-932425-88-8

LC 2007-18787

Verse from the perspectives of five students in Miss D.'s third grade class details the children's last year together before their inner city school is to be torn down

This is "a spare, eloquent novel in verse illustrated in [the author's] own bold block prints." Publ Wkly

Cheshire, Simon

The curse of the ancient mask and other case files; pictures by R. W. Alley. Roaring Book Press 2009 c2007 169p il (Saxby Smart, private detective) $13.95 *

Grades: 3 4 5   **Fic**
1. Lost and found possessions—Fiction 2. Mystery fiction

ISBN 978-1-59643-474-5; 1-59643-474-0

First published 2007 in the United Kingdom

Case file one: the curse of the ancient mask; Case file two: the mark of the purple homework; Case file three: the clasp of doom

"Saxby Doyle Christie Chandler Ellin Allan Smart wants to be a detective as good as the greats. . . . In the first of three 'case files,' . . . Saxby . . . discovers that [an ancient] mask's real curse is a case of competitive sabotage. [In the] second case file . . . Saxby uncovers the secret behind the appearance of purple goo on his classmates' projects. In the third mystery, Saxby sets out to find the thief of a valuable coat clasp. . . . The stories are liberally illustrated with Alley's homey sketches plus representations of Saxby's notebooks. While each short mystery is involving, the distinguishing aspect of this series opener is Saxby's enthusiastic invitations to readers to participate in the sleuthing." Kirkus

Another title in this series is:
The treasure of Dead Man's Lane and other case files (2010)

Chick, Bryan

The secret zoo. Greenwillow Books 2010 295p $16.99

Grades: 4 5 6   **Fic**
1. Fantasy fiction 2. Mystery fiction 3. Zoos—Fiction 4. Animals—Fiction 5. Siblings—Fiction

ISBN 978-0-06-198750-2; 0-06-198750-6

First published 2007 by Second Wish Press

Noah and his friends follow a trail of mysterious clues to uncover a secret behind the walls of the Clarksville City Zoo—a secret that must be protected at all costs.

"Chick debuts with an action-packed and breathless story about teamwork. . . . The story should appeal both

Chick, Bryan—_Continued_

to animal-lovers and a broader audience. While many threads are resolved, Chick lays the groundwork for later books." Publ Wkly

Child, Lauren, 1965-

Clarice Bean spells trouble; [by] Lauren Child. Candlewick Press 2005 189p il $15.99; pa $5.99
Grades: 3 4 5   **Fic**
1. Authorship—Fiction 2. Friendship—Fiction
ISBN 0-7636-2813-1; 0-7636-2903-0 (pa)
Picture book titles about Clarice Bean also available
Clarice Bean, aspiring actress and author, unsuccessfully tries to avoid getting into trouble as she attempts to help a friend in need by following the rules of the fictional spy, Ruby Redfort.
This is written "with fresh, childlike turns of phrase and a hyperawareness of words. . . . With a sprinkling of small, childlike line drawings, a few other illustrations, and some creative typography, this entertaining chapter book will please readers." Booklist
Other titles about Clarice Bean are:
Clarice Bean, don't look now (2007)
Utterly me, Clarice Bean (2003)

Choldenko, Gennifer, 1957-

Al Capone does my shirts. G.P. Putnam's Sons 2004 225p il $15.99; pa $6.99 *
Grades: 5 6 7 8   **Fic**
1. Alcatraz Island (Calif.)—Fiction 2. Autism—Fiction 3. Siblings—Fiction
ISBN 0-399-23861-1; 0-14-240370-9 (pa)
                                    LC 2002-31766
A Newbery Medal honor book, 2005
A twelve-year-old boy named Moose moves to Alcatraz Island in 1935 when guards' families were housed there, and has to contend with his extraordinary new environment in addition to life with his autistic sister.
"With its unique setting and well-developed characters, this warm, engaging coming-of-age story has plenty of appeal, and Choldenko offers some fascinating historical background on Alcatraz Island in an afterword." Booklist
Followed by: Al Capone shines my shoes (2009)

If a tree falls at lunch period. Harcourt Children's Books 2007 216p $17; pa $6.99
Grades: 5 6 7 8   **Fic**
1. School stories 2. Race relations—Fiction 3. Obesity—Fiction
ISBN   978-0-15-205753-4;   0-15-205753-6; 978-0-15-206644-4 (pa); 0-15-206644-6 (pa)
                                    LC 2006-28664
Kirsten and Walk, seventh-graders at an elite private school, alternate telling how race, wealth, weight, and other issues shape their relationships as they and other misfits stand up to a mean but influential classmate, even as they are uncovering a long-kept secret about themselves.
"The sparkling characterization and touches of humor are real pluses." SLJ

Notes from a liar and her dog. Putnam 2001 216p hardcover o.p. pa $5.99
Grades: 5 6 7 8   **Fic**
1. Family life—Fiction 2. Truthfulness and falsehood—Fiction
ISBN 0-399-23591-4; 0-14-250068-2 (pa)
                                    LC 00-55354
Eleven-year-old Ant, stuck in a family that she does not like, copes by pretending that her "real" parents are coming to rescue her, by loving her dog Pistachio, by volunteering at the zoo, and by bending the truth and telling lies
"Choldenko's writing is snappy and tender, depicting both Ant's bravado and her isolation with sympathy." Bull Cent Child Books

Christopher, John, 1922-

The White Mountains. 35th anniversary ed. Simon & Schuster Bks. for Young Readers 2003 c1967 164p hardcover o.p. pa $5.99
Grades: 5 6 7 8   **Fic**
1. Science fiction
ISBN 0-689-85504-4; 0-689-85672-5 (pa)
                                    LC 2002-70808
A reissue of the title first published 1967 by Macmillan
Young Will Parker and his companions make a perilous journey toward an outpost of freedom where they hope to escape from the ruling Tripods, who capture mature human beings and make them docile, obedient servants
This "remarkable story . . . belongs to the school of science-fiction which puts philosophy before technology and is not afraid of telling an exciting story." Times Lit Suppl
Other titles about the Tripods are:
The city of gold and lead (2003 c1967)
The pool of fire (2003 c1968)
When the Tripods came (2003 c1988)

Clark, Clara Gillow, 1951-

Hill Hawk Hattie. Candlewick Press 2003 159p hardcover o.p. pa $6.99
Grades: 4 5 6 7   **Fic**
1. Father-daughter relationship—Fiction 2. Death—Fiction 3. Sex role—Fiction
ISBN 0-7636-1963-9; 0-7636-2559-0 (pa)
                                    LC 2002-73740
Angry and lonely after her mother dies, eleven-year-old Hattie pretends to be a boy and joins her father on an adventure-filled rafting trip down the Delaware River in the late 1800s to transport logs from New York to Philadelphia.
"With beautiful rhythmic sentences, the simple first-person narrative captures [Hattie's] rustic innocence, the thrilling rafting adventure, and the heartfelt struggle of a tough girl who feels useful to her father only in the role of a boy." Booklist
Other titles about Hattie are:
Hattie on her way (2005)
Secrets of Greymoor (2009)

Cleary, Beverly

Dear Mr. Henshaw; illustrated by Paul O. Zelinsky. Morrow 1983 133p il $15.99; lib bdg $16.89; pa $5.99 *

Grades: 4 5 6 7   **Fic**
1. Divorce—Fiction 2. Parent-child relationship—Fiction 3. School stories
ISBN 0-688-02405-X; 0-688-02406-8 (lib bdg); 0-380-70958-9 (pa)   LC 83-5372
Awarded the Newbery Medal, 1984

"Leigh Botts started writing letters to his favorite author, Boyd Henshaw, in the second grade. Now, Leigh is in the sixth grade, in a new school, and his parents are recently divorced. This year he writes many letters to Mr. Henshaw, and also keeps a journal. Through these the reader learns how Leigh adjusts to new situations, and of his triumphs." Child Book Rev Serv

"The story is by no means one of unrelieved gloom, for there are deft touches of humor in the sentient, subtly wrought account of the small triumphs and tragedies in the life of an ordinary boy." Horn Book

Followed by: Strider (1991)

Ellen Tebbits; illustrated by Louis Darling. Morrow 1951 160p il $15.99; pa $5.99

Grades: 3 4 5   **Fic**
1. School stories
ISBN 0-688-21264-6; 0-380-70913-9 (pa)

"Ellen Tebbits is eight years old, takes ballet lessons, wears bands on her teeth, and has a secret—she wears woolen underwear. But she finds a friend in Austine, a new girl in school, who also wears woolen underwear. They have the usual troubles that beset 'best friends' in grade school plus some that are unusual." Carnegie Libr of Pittsburgh

"Their experiences in the third grade are comical and very appealing to children in the middle grades." Hodges. Books for Elem Sch Libr

Henry Huggins; illustrated by Louis Darling. HarperCollins Pubs. 2000 155p il $15.99; pa $5.99 *

Grades: 3 4 5   **Fic**
1. Family life—Fiction 2. School stories
ISBN 0-688-21385-5; 0-380-70912-0 (pa)   LC 00-27567
A reissue of the title first published 1950 by Morrow

"Henry Huggins is a typical small boy who, quite innocently, gets himself into all sorts of predicaments—often with the very apt thought, 'Won't Mom be surprised.' There is not a dull moment but some hilariously funny ones in the telling of Henry's adventures at home and at school." Booklist

Other titles about Henry Huggins are:
Henry and Beezus (1952)
Henry and Ribsy (1954)
Henry and the clubhouse (1962)
Henry and the paper route (1957)
Ribsy (1964)

Mitch and Amy; illustrated by Bob Marstall. Morrow Junior Bks. 1991 222p il $16.99
Grades: 3 4 5   **Fic**
1. Twins—Fiction 2. School stories
ISBN 0-688-10806-7   LC 91-25657
Also available in paperback from Avon Bks.

A newly illustrated edition of the title first published 1967

"The twins Mitch and Amy are in the fourth grade. Mitch is plagued by a bully and by reading difficulties, Amy struggles with multiplication tables, and their patient mother mediates their squabbles." SLJ

"The writing style and dialogue, the familial and peer group relationships, the motivations and characterizations all have the ring of truth. Written with ease and vitality, lightened with humor, the story is perhaps most appealing because it is clear that the author respects children." Bull Cent Child Books

The mouse and the motorcycle; illustrated by Louis Darling. Morrow 1965 158p il $16; pa $5.99
Grades: 3 4 5   **Fic**
1. Mice—Fiction
ISBN 0-688-21698-6; 0-380-70924-4 (pa)

"A fantasy about Ralph, a mouse, who learns to ride a toy motorcycle and goes on wild rides through the corridors of the hotel where he lives. Keith, the boy to whom the motorcycle belongs, becomes fast friends with Ralph and defends him when danger threatens." Hodges. Books for Elem Sch Libr

"The author shows much insight into the thoughts of children. She carries the reader into an imaginative world that contains many realistic emotions." Wis Libr Bull

Other titles about Ralph are:
Ralph S. Mouse (1982)
Runaway Ralph (1970)

Muggie Maggie; illustrated by Kay Life. Morrow Junior Bks. 1990 70p il $15.99; pa $5.99 *
Grades: 2 3 4   **Fic**
1. Handwriting—Fiction 2. School stories
ISBN 0-688-08553-9; 0-380-71087-0 (pa)   LC 89-38959
Maggie resists learning cursive writing in the third grade, until she discovers that knowing how to read and write cursive promises to open up an entirely new world of knowledge for her

"This deceptively simple story is accessible to primary-grade readers able to read longhand, as some of the text is in script. . . . Everything in this book rings true, and Cleary has created a likable, funny heroine about whom readers will want to know more." SLJ

Otis Spofford; illustrated by Louis Darling. Morrow 1953 191p il $16.99; pa $5.99
Grades: 3 4 5   **Fic**
1. School stories
ISBN 0-688-21720-6; 0-380-70919-8 (pa)

"Otis, a mischievous, fun loving boy, is always getting in and out of trouble. His mother, a dancing teacher, is busy and often leaves Otis on his own. This book tells of several episodes in Otis's life—from his sneaking vitamins to a white rat to 'disprove' a diet experiment, to getting his final 'come-uppance' when a trick on Ellen Tebbits backfires." Read Ladders for Hum Relat. 6th edition

"This writer has her elementary school down pat, and manages to report her growing boys, teachers, and P.T.A. meetings so that parents chuckle and boys laugh out loud." N Y Her Trib Books

Cleary, Beverly—*Continued*

Ramona the pest; illustrated by Louis Darling. Morrow 1968 192p il $16.99; pa $5.99 *

Grades: 3 4 5   **Fic**

1. Kindergarten—Fiction 2. School stories

ISBN 0-688-21721-4; 0-380-70954-6 (pa)

"Ramona Quimby comes into her own. Beezus keeps telling her to stop acting like a pest, but Ramona is five now, and she is convinced that she is 'not' a pest; she feels very mature, having entered kindergarten, and she immediately becomes enamoured of her teacher. Ramona's insistence on having just the right kind of boots, her matter-of-fact interest in how Mike Mulligan got to a bathroom, her determination to kiss one of the boys in her class, and her refusal to go back to kindergarten because Miss Binney didn't love her any more—all of these incidents or situations are completely believable and are told in a light, humorous, zesty style." Bull Cent Child Books

Other titles about Ramona are:

Beezus and Ramona (1955)

Ramona and her father (1977)

Ramona and her mother (1979)

Ramona, forever (1984)

Ramona Quimby, age 8 (1981)

Ramona the brave (1975)

Ramona's world (1999)

Socks; illustrated by Beatrice Darwin. Morrow 1973 156p il $16.99; pa $5.99

Grades: 3 4 5   **Fic**

1. Cats—Fiction 2. Infants—Fiction

ISBN 0-688-20067-2; 0-380-70926-0 (pa)

"The Brickers' kitten, Socks, is jealous when they bring a baby home from the hospital. How he copes with this rivalry makes an amusing story true to cat nature." Cleveland Public Libr

"Not being child-centered, this may have a smaller audience than earlier Cleary books, but it is written with the same easy grace, the same felicitous humor and sharply observant eye." Bull Cent Child Books

Strider; illustrated by Paul O. Zelinsky. Morrow Junior Bks. 1991 179p il hardcover o.p. lib bdg $16.89; pa $5.99

Grades: 4 5 6 7   **Fic**

1. Dogs—Fiction 2. Divorce—Fiction

ISBN 0-688-09900-9; 0-688-09901-7 (lib bdg); 0-380-71236-9 (pa)   LC 90-6608

Sequel to Dear Mr. Henshaw

In a series of diary entries, Leigh tells how he comes to terms with his parents' divorce, acquires joint custody of an abandoned dog, and joins the track team at school

"The development of the narrative is vintage Beverly Cleary, an inimitable blend of comic and poignant moments." Horn Book

Cleaver, Vera

Where the lillies bloom; [by] Vera & Bill Cleaver; illustrated by Jim Spanfeller. Lippincott 1969 174p il hardcover o.p. pa $5.99

Grades: 5 6 7 8   **Fic**

1. Orphans—Fiction 2. Siblings—Fiction 3. Appalachian region—Fiction

ISBN 0-397-31111-7; 0-06-447005-9 (pa)

Mary Call Luther is "fourteen years old and made of granite. When her sharecropper father dies, Mary Call becomes head of the household, responsible for a boy of ten and a retarded, gentle older sister. Mary and her brother secretly bury their father so they can retain their home [in the Appalachian hills]; tenaciously she fights to keep the family afloat by selling medicinal plants and to keep them together by fending off [Kiser Pease, their landlord], who wants to marry her sister." Saturday Rev

"The setting is fascinating, the characterization good, and the style of the first-person story distinctive." Bull Cent Child Books

Followed by Trial Valley (1977)

Clements, Andrew, 1949-

Extra credit; illustrations by Mark Elliott. Atheneum Books for Young Readers 2009 183p il $16.99

Grades: 4 5 6   **Fic**

1. Letters—Fiction 2. Family life—Fiction 3. Afghanistan—Fiction 4. Illinois—Fiction

ISBN 978-1-4169-4929-9; 1-4169-4929-1

LC 2008-42877

As letters flow back and forth—between the prairies of Illinois and the mountains of Afghanistan, across cultural and religious divides—sixth-grader Abby and eleven-year-old Sadeed begin to speak and listen to each other.

Clements "successfully bridges two cultures in this timely and insightful dual-perspective story." Publ Wkly

Frindle; [by] Andrew Clements; pictures of Brian Selznick. Simon & Schuster Books for Young Readers 2006 c1996 105p il $15.95 *

Grades: 4 5 6   **Fic**

1. School stories

ISBN 978-0-689-80669-8; 0-689-80669-8

A reissue of the title first published 1996

When he decides to turn his fifth grade teacher's love of the dictionary around on her, clever Nick Allen invents a new word and begins a chain of events that quickly moves beyond his control.

"Sure to be popular with a wide range of readers, this will make a great read-aloud as well." Booklist

The janitor's boy; a novel; by the best-selling author of Frindle. Simon & Schuster Bks. for Young Readers 2000 140p $15.95; pa $5.99

Grades: 4 5 6   **Fic**

1. Father-son relationship—Fiction 2. School stories

ISBN 0-689-81818-1; 0-689-83585-X (pa)

LC 99-47457

Fifth grader Jack finds himself the target of ridicule at school when it becomes known that his father is one of the janitors, and he turns his anger onto his father

"Clements' strength is his realistic depiction of public

Clements, Andrew, 1949-—*Continued*

schools. . . . Jack's antics and those of his classmates ring true, as do the behaviors of the teachers and administrators." Booklist

The Landry News; illustrations by Salvatore Murdocca. Simon & Schuster Bks. for Young Readers 1999 123p il $15.95; pa $5.99

Grades: 4 5 6   Fic
  1. Newspapers—Fiction 2. Teachers—Fiction
3. School stories
  ISBN 0-689-81817-3; 0-689-82868-3 (pa)
                     LC 98-34376

A fifth-grader starts a newspaper with an editorial that prompts her burnt-out classroom teacher to really begin teaching again, but he is later threatened with disciplinary action as a result

"The text flows effortlessly yet explores thought-provoking issues such as intellectual freedom that are likely to engender further exploration." Horn Book Guide

Lost and found; illustrations by Mark Elliott. Atheneum Books for Young Readers 2008 161p il $16.99

Grades: 4 5 6   Fic
  1. Twins—Fiction 2. Brothers—Fiction 3. School stories 4. Moving—Fiction 5. Ohio—Fiction
  ISBN 978-1-4169-0985-9; 1-4169-0985-0
                     LC 2008-07018

Twelve-year-old identical twins Jay and Ray have long resented that everyone treats them as one person, and so they hatch a plot to take advantage of a clerical error at their new school and pretend they are just one

"This slim story has all the elements readers have come to expect from Clements . . . : a school setting, likable secondary characters, supportive adults and a challenge to the audience to see things from a different perspective." Publ Wkly

Lunch money; illustrations by Brian Selznick. Simon & Schuster Books for Young Readers 2005 222p il $15.95; pa $5.99

Grades: 4 5 6   Fic
  1. Money-making projects for children—Fiction
2. School stories
  ISBN 0-689-86683-6; 0-689-86685-2 (pa)
                     LC 2005-00061

Twelve-year-old Greg, who has always been good at moneymaking projects, is surprised to find himself teaming up with his lifelong rival, Maura, to create a series of comic books to sell at school.

"The characters are rich with interesting quirks and motivations. . . . Along with providing a fast-paced and humorous story line, the author examines concepts of true wealth, teamwork, community mindedness, and the value of creative expression. Selznick's pencil sketches add comic touches throughout." SLJ

No talking; illustrations by Mark Elliott. Simon & Schuster Books for Young Readers 2007 146p il $15.99; pa $5.99 *

Grades: 3 4 5 6   Fic
  1. School stories
  ISBN   978-1-4169-0983-5;   1-4169-0983-4;
978-1-4169-0984-2 (pa); 1-4169-0984-2 (pa)
                     LC 2006-31883

The noisy fifth grade boys of Laketon Elementary School challenge the equally loud fifth grade girls to a "no talking" contest.

"This is an interesting and thought-provoking book. . . . The plot quickly draws readers in and keeps them turning pages. . . . The black-and-white pencil drawings add immediacy to the story." SLJ

The report card. Simon & Schuster Books for Young Readers 2004 173p $15.95; pa $5.99

Grades: 4 5 6   Fic
  1. School stories
  ISBN 0-689-84515-4; 0-689-84524-3 (pa)
                     LC 2003-7384

Fifth-grader Nora Rowley has always hidden the fact that she is a genius from everyone because all she wants is to be normal, but when she comes up with a plan to prove that grades are not important, things begin to get out of control.

"Clements has . . . built a solid story around a controversial issue for which there is no easy answer, and to his credit, he never tries to offer one. . . . A novel sure to generate strong feelings and discussion." Booklist

Room one; a mystery or two; illustrations by Chris Blair. Simon & Schuster Books for Young Readers 2006 162p il $15.95; pa $5.99

Grades: 3 4 5   Fic
  1. School stories 2. Homeless persons—Fiction
3. Mystery fiction 4. Nebraska—Fiction
  ISBN 0-689-86686-9; 0-689-86687-9 (pa)

Ted Hammond, the only sixth grader in his small Nebraska town's one-room schoolhouse, searches for clues to the disappearance of a homeless family.

"There is a good balance of seriousness and humor with brisk, realistic dialogue and observations. Small black-and-white illustrations emphasize key points in the plot. Clements's usual excellent sense of character is evident." SLJ

The school story; illustrated by Brian Selznick. Simon & Schuster Bks. for Young Readers 2001 196p il $16; pa $5.99

Grades: 4 5 6 7   Fic
  1. Authorship—Fiction 2. Publishers and publishing—Fiction
  ISBN 0-689-82594-3; 0-689-85186-3 (pa)
                     LC 00-49683

After twelve-year-old Natalie writes a wonderful novel, her friend Zoe helps her devise a scheme to get it accepted at the publishing house where Natalie's mother works as an editor

"The girls are believable characters. . . . Selznick's black-and-white illustrations add humorous details. A comic novel that's a sure winner." SLJ

We the children; illustrated by Adam Stower. Atheneum Books for Young Readers 2010 142p il (Benjamin Pratt and the Keepers of the School) $14.99

Grades: 4 5 6   Fic
  1. School stories 2. Massachusetts—Fiction
3. Mystery fiction 4. Adventure fiction
  ISBN 978-1-4169-3886-6; 1-4169-3886-9
                     LC 2009-36428

Clements, Andrew, 1949—*Continued*

"Sixth-grader Ben Pratt is thrust into a mystery-adventure when his school's janitor shoves a gold coin in his hand, passing on the responsibility to save Oakes School from developers. Captain Oakes gave the school to the community back in 1783; its original building overlooks the Massachusetts town's harbor. But the land has been sold, and buildings will be razed to make way for a theme park. . . . Clements ably sets up his planned six-volume series with topical problems, convincing, likable characters and intriguing extra details." Kirkus

Clifford, Eth, 1915-

Help! I'm a prisoner in the library; illustrated by George Hughes. Houghton Mifflin 1979 105p il $16; pa $5.95

Grades: 3 4 5   Fic

1. Libraries—Fiction 2. Blizzards—Fiction

ISBN 0-395-28478-3; 0-618-49482-0 (pa)

LC 79-14447

Also available in paperback from Scholastic

"Caught in a blinding snowstorm with their car out of gas, Mary Rose and Jo-Beth are told to stay put while their father finds fuel for the stalled vehicle. Jo-Beth, however, develops 'an emergency' and Mary Rose takes her to a nearby library to find a restroom. . . . Without warning the girls find themselves locked in when the building closes early. As the storm worsens, the lights and telephone go out and a series of flying objects, creaking noises, and moaning sounds thoroughly frighten the girls. . . . Clifford uses a light touch while evoking a pleasingly scary atmosphere that children will enjoy. Spirited dialogue and swift pace are an additional plus." Booklist

Coatsworth, Elizabeth Jane, 1893-1986

The cat who went to heaven; [by] Elizabeth Coatsworth; illustrated by Lynd Ward. Macmillan 1958 62p il $17.95; pa $4.99

Grades: 4 5 6 7   Fic

1. Cats—Fiction 2. Japan—Fiction

ISBN 0-02-719710-7; 1-4169-4973-9 (pa)

LC 58-10917

First published 1930. The 1958 edition is a reprint with new illustrations of the book which won the Newbery Medal award in 1931

"Watched by his little cat, Good Fortune, a Japanese artist paints a picture of the Buddha receiving homage from the animals. By tradition the cat should not be among them, but the artist risks his reputation by adding Good Fortune and is vindicated by a miracle." Hodges. Books for Elem Sch Libr

"Into this lovely and imaginative story the author has put something of the serenity and beauty of the East and of the gentleness of a religion that has a place even for the humblest of living creatures." N Y Times Book Rev

Cochran, Thomas, 1955-

Running the dogs. Farrar, Straus & Giroux 2007 153p $16

Grades: 4 5 6 7   Fic

1. Dogs—Fiction 2. Louisiana—Fiction

ISBN 978-0-374-36360-4; 0-374-36360-9

LC 2006-46515

When an unexpected snowstorm hits his part of Louisiana, ten-year-old Tal demonstrates his determination and responsibility after his hunting dogs become lost in the woods

"Cochran's greatest strength lies in evoking hushed yet intense moods; his light-handed conjuration of rural Louisiana is also admirable." Horn Book Guide

Cockcroft, Jason

Counter clockwise. HarperCollins Publishers 2009 202p il $15.99; lib bdg $16.89

Grades: 5 6 7 8   Fic

1. Fantasy fiction 2. Time travel—Fiction 3. Father-son relationship—Fiction 4. London (England)—Fiction

ISBN 978-0-06-125554-0;   0-06-125554-8; 978-0-06-125555-7 (lib bdg); 0-06-125555-6 (lib bdg)

With the aid of Bartleby, an enormous Tower of London guard known as a Beefeater, Nathan travels through time to stop his father from changing the past.

"Cockcroft employs a cleverness that keeps the story fresh. . . . [This book] should appeal to fantasy fans." Voice Youth Advocates

Cody, Matthew

Powerless. Alfred A. Knopf 2009 279p $15.99; lib bdg $18.99

Grades: 5 6 7 8   Fic

1. Supernatural—Fiction 2. Bullies—Fiction 3. Moving—Fiction 4. School stories 5. Family life—Fiction 6. Pennsylvania—Fiction 7. Superheroes—Fiction

ISBN 978-0-375-85595-5;   0-375-85595-5; 978-0-375-95595-2 (lib bdg); 0-375-95595-X (lib bdg)

LC 2008-40885

Soon after moving to Noble's Green, Pennsylvania, twelve-year-old Daniel learns that his new friends have super powers that they will lose when they turn thirteen, unless he can use his brain power to protect them.

"This first novel has an intriguing premise, appealing characters, and a straightforward narrative arc with plenty of action as well as some serious moments." Booklist

Cohagan, Carolyn

The lost children. Aladdin 2010 313p $16.99

Grades: 4 5 6   Fic

1. Time travel—Fiction 2. Voyages and travels—Fiction 3. Friendship—Fiction

ISBN 978-1-4169-8616-4; 1-4169-8616-2

LC 2009-16608

When twelve-year-old Josephine falls through a wormhole in her garden shed into another time and place, she realizes the troubles she has at home are minor compared to what she has to tackle now in the world where she has landed.

"The main characters are well developed, particularly the spunky and plain-spoken Ida, the laconic but loyal Fargus, and Josephine." Booklist

Cohen, Barbara, 1932-1992

Thank you, Jackie Robinson; drawings by Richard Cuffari. Lothrop, Lee & Shepard Bks. 1974 125p il pa $4.99 hardcover o.p.

Grades: 4 5 6   **Fic**
1. Baseball—Fiction 2. Friendship—Fiction 3. African Americans—Fiction

ISBN 0-688-15293-7 (pa)

"When 60-year-old Davey (Black) comes to work at the inn for Sam's mother, Sam (Jewish and fatherless) gains a friend. Davey takes Sam to see the Brooklyn Dodgers (circa 1945), and an avid, statistic-spouting Dodger fan is born. When Davey becomes ill, Sam gets Jackie Robinson and his teammates to autograph a ball for Davey." Child Book Rev Serv

"Cohen's characters have unusual depth and her story succeeds as a warm, understanding consideration of friendship and, finally, death." Booklist

Cohen, Miriam, 1926-

Mimmy and Sophie all around the town; pictures by Thomas F. Yezerski. Farrar, Straus and Giroux 2004 68p il $16

Grades: 2 3 4   **Fic**
1. Sisters—Fiction 2. Brooklyn (New York, N.Y.)—Fiction

ISBN 0-374-34989-4   LC 2003-48059

Features the same characters as the picture book Mimmy & Sophie (1999)

"Frances Foster books"

Describes the experiences of two sisters growing up in Brooklyn in the time of Shirley Temple movies and trolleys

"With plenty of dialogue and straightforward action, this charming story is just right for newly independent readers. Yezerski's black-and-white drawings illustrate the era, while conveying all of the energy of the characters." SLJ

Cohen, Tish, 1963-

The invisible rules of the Zoë Lama. Dutton 2007 247p $15.99

Grades: 4 5 6 7   **Fic**
1. School stories 2. Grandmothers—Fiction 3. Mother-daughter relationship—Fiction 4. Alzheimer's disease—Fiction

ISBN 978-0-525-47810-2

Twelve-year-old Zoë, famous for advising other people using her unwritten rules, has her hands full with chairing a school dance committee, training a new student to fit in, keeping her grandmother out of a nursing home, and trying to find a husband for her mother.

"Periodic cartoon drawings and scanned cookie images add whimsy and visual interest. An entertaining read." Booklist

Followed by: The one and only Zoe Lama (2008)

Cohn, Rachel

The Steps. Simon & Schuster Bks. for Young Readers 2003 137p hardcover o.p. pa $4.99

Grades: 5 6 7 8   **Fic**
1. Stepfamilies—Fiction 2. Family life—Fiction 3. Australia—Fiction

ISBN 978-0-689-84549-9; 0-689-84549-9; 978-0-689-87414-7 (pa); 0-689-87414-6 (pa)

LC 2001-57566

Over Christmas vacation, Annabel goes from her home in Manhattan to visit her father, his new wife, and her half- and step-siblings in Sydney, Australia

"Packed with humorous incident, life lessons learned, Australian travel tidbits, and a litany of preteen-girl touchstones." Horn Book

Another title about this family is:
Two steps forward (2006)

Cole, Henry

A nest for Celeste; a story about art, inspiration, and the meaning of home; [written and illustrated by] Henry Cole. Katherine Tegen Books 2010 342p il $16.99; lib bdg $17.89

Grades: 4 5 6   **Fic**
1. Mason, Joseph, 1807-1883—Fiction 2. Audubon, John James, 1785-1851—Fiction 3. Mice—Fiction 4. Artists—Fiction 5. Home—Fiction 6. New Orleans (La.)—Fiction

ISBN 978-0-06-170410-9; 0-06-170410-5; 978-0-06-170411-6 (lib bdg); 0-06-170411-3 (lib bdg)

LC 2009-11813

Celeste, a mouse longing for a real home, becomes a source of inspiration to teenaged Joseph, assistant to the artist and naturalist John James Audubon, at a New Orleans, Louisiana, plantation in 1821

"Evocative illustrations, compelling characters, and thoughtful reflections on the nature of home combine to powerful effect." Publ Wkly

Cole, Stephen, 1971-

Z. Rex; [by] Steve Cole. Philomel Books 2009 245p (The hunting) $16.99; pa $7.99

Grades: 5 6 7 8   **Fic**
1. Dinosaurs—Fiction 2. Virtual reality—Fiction 3. Father-son relationship—Fiction 4. New Mexico—Fiction 5. Scotland—Fiction 6. Science fiction

ISBN 978-0-399-25253-2; 0-399-25253-3; 978-0-14-241712-6 (pa); 0-14-241712-2 (pa)

LC 2009-6637

From Santa Fe, New Mexico, to Edinburgh, Scotland, thirteen-year-old Adam Adlar must elude police while being hunted by a dinosaur come-to-life from a virtual reality game invented by his father, who has gone missing.

"Cole has created a likable character who manages to come out on top in an extraordinary situation. The science aspects offer an interesting perspective and dilemma for a discussion on genetic engineering. In addition, the adventure, video gaming, and the perilous, sometimes bloody scenes will capture reluctant readers who may not normally devour their reading materials." SLJ

Colfer, Eoin, 1965-

Airman; [by] Eoin Colfer. Hyperion Books for Children 2008 412p $17.99; pa $7.99 *

Grades: 5 6 7 8 9   **Fic**

1. Airplanes—Fiction 2. Prisoners—Fiction 3. Adventure fiction 4. Inventors—Fiction 5. Ireland—Fiction

ISBN 978-1-4231-0750-7; 1-4231-0750-0; 978-1-4231-0751-4 (pa); 1-4231-0751-9 (pa)

LC 2007-38415

In the late nineteenth century, when Conor Broekhart discovers a conspiracy to overthrow the king, he is branded a traitor, imprisoned, and forced to mine for diamonds under brutal conditions while he plans a daring escape from Little Saltee prison by way of a flying machine that he must design, build, and, hardest of all, trust to carry him to safety.

This is "polished, sophisticated storytelling. . . . A tour de force." Publ Wkly

Artemis Fowl. Hyperion Bks. for Children 2001 277p $16.95; pa $7.99 *

Grades: 5 6 7 8   **Fic**

1. Fairies—Fiction 2. Fantasy fiction

ISBN 0-7868-0801-2; 1-4231-2452-9 (pa)

LC 2001-16632

When a twelve-year-old evil genius tries to restore his family fortune by capturing a fairy and demanding a ransom in gold, the fairies fight back with magic, technology, and a particularly nasty troll

"Colfer's antihero, techno fantasy is cleverly written and filled to the brim with action, suspense, and humor." SLJ

Other titles in this series are:
Artemis Fowl: the Arctic incident (2002)
Artemis Fowl: the Eternity code (2003)
Artemis Fowl: the lost colony (2006)
Artemis Fowl: the Opal deception (2005)
Artemis Fowl: the time paradox (2008)

Benny and Omar. Miramax Books/Hyperion Books for Children 2007 280p hardcover o.p. pa $7.95

Grades: 5 6 7 8   **Fic**

1. Friendship—Fiction 2. Hurling (Game)—Fiction 3. Tunisia—Fiction

ISBN 978-1-4231-0281-6; 1-4231-0281-9; 978-1-4231-0282-3 (pa); 1-4231-0282-7 (pa)

LC 2006-100644

First published 1998 in Ireland

Twelve-year-old Benny, a hurling fanatic, moves to Tunisia, North Africa, when his father is transferred and has a hard time adjusting to the new land until he meets Omar.

"Colfer does such a masterful job of mixing humor and tragedy with Benny's smart-alecky remarks that youngsters will like him in spite of themselves. This is a funny, fast-paced read." SLJ

Another title about Benny is:
Benny and Babe (2007)

Half-Moon investigations. Miramax Books/Hyperion Books for Children 2006 290p $16.95; pa $7.99

Grades: 4 5 6 7   **Fic**

1. Mystery fiction

ISBN 0-7868-4957-6; 0-7868-4960-6 (pa)

"Diminutive Fletcher Moon may not be the most popular 12-year-old in his Irish town but he's proud . . . of the badge that he constantly flashes to let everyone know that he's an online graduate of a private detective academy in Washington, DC. . . . But when . . . April Devereux hires him to find a lock of a pop star's hair that she claims was stolen . . . everything starts going wrong for Fletcher." SLJ

"The private-eye lingo has a great, comical grade-school snap, and . . . the kid's goofy charm and stubborn dedication to crime solving will win him a hefty, enthusiastic following." Booklist

Collard, Sneed B., III

Double eagle. Peachtree 2009 245p $15.95

Grades: 4 5 6 7   **Fic**

1. Coins—Fiction 2. Buried treasure—Fiction 3. Hurricanes—Fiction 4. Alabama—Fiction

ISBN 978-1-56145-480-8; 1-56145-480-X

LC 2008036746

In 1973, Michael and Kyle's discovery of a rare Confederate coin near an old Civil War fort turns into a race against time as the boys try to find more coins before a hurricane hits Alabama's Gulf coast.

"Mike's narrative moves quickly with likable and believable characters. The story will have particular appeal to readers with an interest in historical places and artifacts." SLJ

Includes bibliographical references

Collier, James Lincoln, 1928-

The dreadful revenge of Ernest Gallen; [by] James Lincoln Collier. Bloomsbury Children's Books 2008 232p $16.95 *

Grades: 5 6 7 8   **Fic**

1. Supernatural—Fiction 2. Great Depression, 1929-1939—Fiction 3. Horror fiction

ISBN 978-1-59990-220-3; 1-59990-220-6

LC 2007044453

When Eugene starts hearing a voice inside his head telling him to do awful things, it leads him to look into his small town's past before the Depression, and to discover long-hidden secrets about his neighbors and his town

"Collier has written an eerily weird and strangely believable historical mystery. . . . A complex, spooky page-turner." Booklist

The empty mirror. Bloomsbury 2004 192p $16.95; pa $6.95

Grades: 5 6 7 8   **Fic**

1. Ghost stories 2. Influenza—Fiction 3. Orphans—Fiction

ISBN 1-58234-949-5; 1-58234-904-5 (pa)

"Nick's an admitted troublemaker, but when his mysterious doppelganger starts committing increasingly sinister crimes, his small New England town is ready to

Collier, James Lincoln, 1928-—_Continued_
string Nick up. The secret of this ghostly presence might
lie in the recent influenza epidemic of 1918. . . . Collier's challenging novel effectively combines historical
fiction with a genuinely spooky supernatural tale." Horn
Book Guide

Jump ship to freedom; [by] James Lincoln
Collier, Christopher Collier. Delacorte Press 1981
198p pa $5.99 hardcover o.p.
Grades: 6 7 8 9   **Fic**
  1. United States—History—1783-1809—Fiction
  2. Slavery—Fiction 3. African Americans—Fiction
  ISBN 0-440-44323-7 (pa)   LC 81-65492
Companion volume to War comes to Willy Freeman
and Who is Carrie?
  In 1787 Dan Arabus, a fourteen-year-old slave, anxious to buy freedom for himself and his mother, escapes
from his dishonest master and tries to find help in cash-
ing the soldier's notes received by his father, Jack
Arabus, for fighting in the Revolution
  "The period seems well researched, and the speech
has an authentic ring without trying to imitate a dialect."
SLJ

Me and Billy; [by] James Lincoln Collier.
Marshall Cavendish 2004 185p $15.95
Grades: 5 6 7 8   **Fic**
  1. Swindlers and swindling—Fiction 2. Orphans—Fiction 3. Friendship—Fiction
  ISBN 0-7614-5174-9   LC 2003-26865
  After escaping the orphanage where they have spent
their lives together, two boys become assistants to a con
artist, and while Possum objects to the lying, stealing,
and cheating, Billy only cares about making money and
taking life easy
  "A small gem. . . . The book's momentum is sustained by the author's wonderful use of vernacular and
the friendship/tension between the boys." SLJ

My brother Sam is dead; by James Lincoln
Collier and Christopher Collier. Four Winds Press
1985 c1974 216p $17.95 *
Grades: 6 7 8 9   **Fic**
  1. United States—History—1775-1783, Revolution—
Fiction
  ISBN 0-02-722980-7   LC 84-28787
  Also available in paperback from Scholastic
  A Newbery Medal honor book, 1975
  A reissue of the title first published 1974
  "In 1775 the Meeker family lived in Redding, Con-
necticut, a Tory community. Sam, the eldest son, allied
himself with the Patriots. The youngest son, Tim,
watched a rift in the family grow because of his broth-
er's decision. Before the war was over the Meeker fami-
ly had suffered at the hands of both the British and the
Patriots." Shapiro. Fic for Youth. 3d edition

War comes to Willy Freeman; [by] James
Lincoln Collier, Christopher Collier. Delacorte
Press 1983 178p pa $5.99 hardcover o.p.
Grades: 6 7 8 9   **Fic**
  1. United States—History—1775-1783, Revolution—
Fiction 2. African Americans—Fiction 3. Slavery—
Fiction
  ISBN 0-440-49504-0 (pa)   LC 82-70317

This deals with events prior to those in Jump ship to
freedom, and involves members of the same family.
"Willy is thirteen when she begins her story, which takes
place during the last two years of the Revolutionary War;
her father, a free man, has been killed fighting against
the British, her mother has disappeared. Willy makes her
danger-fraught way to Fraunces Tavern in New York,
her uncle, Jack Arabus, having told her that Mr.
Fraunces may be able to help her. She works at the tavern until the war is over, goes to the Arabus home to
find her mother dying, and participates in the trial (historically accurate save for the fictional addition of Willy)
in which her uncle sues for his freedom and wins." Bull
Cent Child Books

Collins, Ross
  Medusa Jones. Arthur A. Levine Books 2008
134p il $16.99
Grades: 3 4 5   **Fic**
  1. Classical mythology—Fiction 2. Medusa (Greek
mythology)—Fiction
  ISBN 978-0-439-90100-0; 0-439-90100-6
                                    LC 2007-17199
  In ancient Greece, Medusa Jones, a gorgon, and her
friends, a minotaur and a centaur, are mocked and
sneered at by the other Acropolis Academy children
whose parents are kings and gods, but when they go on
a school camping trip together, the "freaks" become true
heroes.
  This is a "witty romp through Greek mythology. . . .
Imaginatively laid out pages that incorporate energetic
b&w illustrations of varying size welcome readers." Publ
Wkly

Collins, Suzanne
  Gregor the Overlander. Scholastic Press 2003
311p (Underland chronicles) $16.95; pa $5.99 *
Grades: 4 5 6 7   **Fic**
  1. Fantasy fiction
  ISBN 0-439-43536-6; 0-439-67813-7 (pa)
                                    LC 2002-155865
  When eleven-year-old Gregor and his two-year-old
sister are pulled into a strange underground world, they
trigger an epic battle involving men, bats, rats, cock-
roaches, and spiders while on a quest foretold by ancient
prophecy
  "Collins creates a fascinating, vivid, highly original
world and a superb story to go along with it." Booklist
  Other titles in this series are:
Gregor and the prophecy of Bane (2004)
Gregor and the curse of the warmbloods (2005)
Gregor and the marks of secret (2006)
Gregor and the code of claw (2007)

Collodi, Carlo, 1826-1890
  The adventures of Pinocchio; [by] Carlo
Collodi; illustrated by Roberto Innocenti; designed
by Rita Marshall. Creative Editions 2005 191p il
$24.95 *
Grades: 3 4 5 6   **Fic**
  1. Puppets and puppet plays—Fiction 2. Fairy tales
  ISBN 1-56846-190-9   LC 2003-62740

Collodi, Carlo, 1826-1890—_Continued_

A wooden puppet full of tricks and mischief, with a talent for getting into and out of trouble, wants more than anything else to become a real boy

Innocenti's illustrations have a "19th-century European setting, and the careful composition, use of perspective, and dark earth tones are an apt visual expression of this complex moral tale." SLJ

Coman, Carolyn

What Jamie saw. Front Street 1995 126p $13.95; pa $9.95

Grades: 5 6 7 8   **Fic**

1. Child abuse—Fiction

ISBN 1-886910-02-2; 1-59078-639-4 (pa)

LC 95-23545

A Newbery Medal honor book, 1996

Having fled to a family friend's hillside trailer after his mother's boyfriend tried to throw his baby sister against a wall, nine-year-old Jamie finds himself living an existence full of uncertainty and fear

"Shocking in its simple narration and child's-eye view, _What Jamie Saw_ is a bittersweet miracle in understated language and forthright hopelessness." SLJ

Comerford, Lynda B.

Rissa Bartholomew's declaration of independence. Scholastic Press 2009 250p $16.99

Grades: 4 5 6 7   **Fic**

1. Friendship—Fiction 2. Illinois—Fiction 3. School stories

ISBN 978-0-545-05058-6; 0-545-05058-8

LC 2008-26618

Having told off all of her old friends at her eleventh birthday party, Rissa starts middle school determined to make new friends while being herself, not simply being part of a herd.

"Rissa's troubles are ones that many middle-schoolers will identify with: new schools, shifting allegiances, new feelings, and changing bodies. First-time novelist Comerford gives her readers an appealing heroine who, despite her flaws and quirks, finds herself along the way." Booklist

Compestine, Ying Chang

Revolution is not a dinner party; a novel. Henry Holt and Company 2007 256p map $16.95; pa $7.99

Grades: 5 6 7 8   **Fic**

1.   China—History—1949-1976—Fiction 2. Communism—Fiction 3. Persecution—Fiction

ISBN   978-0-8050-8207-4;   0-8050-8207-7; 978-0-312-58149-7 (pa); 0-312-58149-1 (pa)

LC 2006035465

Starting in 1972 when she is nine years old, Ling, the daughter of two doctors, struggles to make sense of the communists' Cultural Revolution, which empties stores of food, homes of appliances deemed "bourgeois," and people of laughter.

"Readers should remain rapt by Compestine's storytelling throughout this gripping account of life during China's Cultural Revolution." Publ Wkly

Conford, Ellen

Annabel the actress starring in "Gorilla my dreams"; illustrated by Renée Williams-Andriani. Simon & Schuster Bks. for Young Readers 1999 64p il hardcover o.p. pa $3.99 *

Grades: 2 3 4   **Fic**

1. Actors—Fiction 2. Parties—Fiction

ISBN 0-689-81404-6; 0-689-83883-2 (pa)

LC 97-39449

Though a little disappointed that her first acting part is to be a gorilla at a birthday party, Annabel determines to really get into the role

"The vocabulary is appropriate for those graduating from easy-readers, but the language is never stilted. Amusing pen-and-ink illustrations appear on almost every page." SLJ

Other titles about Annabel are:

Annabel the actress starring in "Hound of the Barkervilles" (2002)

Annabel the actress, starring in "Camping it up" (2004)

Annabel the actress, starring in "Just a little extra" (2000)

A case for Jenny Archer; illustrated by Diane Palmisciano. Little, Brown 1988 61p il pa $4.99 hardcover o.p. *

Grades: 2 3 4   **Fic**

1. Mystery fiction

ISBN 0-316-01486-9 (pa)   LC 88-14169

"A Springboard book"

After reading three mysteries in a row, Jenny becomes convinced that the neighbors across the street are up to no good and decides to investigate

"This lots-of-fun advanced easy reader contains eight chapters, all about three pages long, with large, clear print, and lots of white space. . . . The children here are lively, the adults funny, wise, and supportive." SLJ

Other titles about Jenny Archer are:

Can do, Jenny Archer (1991)

Get the picture, Jenny Archer (1994)

Jenny Archer, author (1989)

Jenny Archer to the rescue (1990)

A job for Jenny Archer (1988)

Nibble, nibble, Jenny Archer (1993)

What's cooking, Jenny Archer (1989)

Conly, Jane Leslie

Crazy lady! HarperCollins Pubs. 1993 180p lib bdg $18.89; pa $5.99

Grades: 5 6 7 8   **Fic**

1.   Prejudices—Fiction   2.   Death—Fiction 3. Alcoholism—Fiction 4. Mentally handicapped—Fiction

ISBN 0-06-021360-4 (lib bdg); 0-06-440571-0 (pa)

LC 92-18348

A Newbery Medal honor book, 1994

"A Laura Geringer book"

As he tries to come to terms with his mother's death, Vernon finds solace in his growing relationship with the neighborhood outcasts, an alcoholic and her retarded son

The narration "is fast and blunt, and the conversations are lively and true." Bull Cent Child Books

Connor, Leslie

Crunch. Katherine Tegen Books 2010 330p
$16.99; lib bdg $17.89

Grades: 5 6 7 8   **Fic**
1. Family life—Fiction 2. Bicycles—Fiction
3. Siblings—Fiction 4. New England—Fiction
5. Business enterprises—Fiction 6. Energy conservation—Fiction
ISBN   978-0-06-169229-1;   0-06-169229-8;
978-0-06-169233-8 (lib bdg); 0-06-169233-6 (lib bdg)
This novel concerns "the trials and tribulations of 14-
year-old Dewey Mariss and his family. His parents are
away from home, unable to return because of a gasoline
shortage. Running their small family business, the Bike
Barn, with his younger brother and helping older sister
Lil look after the five-year-old twins keeps Dewey plenty
busy. . . . Characters are colorful but believable, dialogue crisp and amusing. The New England setting is attractively realized, and the underlying energy crisis treated seriously but not sensationally." Kirkus

Waiting for normal. Katherine Tegen Books
2008 290p $16.99; lib bdg $17.89 *

Grades: 5 6 7 8   **Fic**
1. Family life—Fiction 2. Mothers—Fiction 3. New
York (State)—Fiction
ISBN   978-0-06-089088-9;   0-06-089088-6;
978-0-06-089089-6 (lib bdg); 0-06-089089-4 (lib bdg)
                                        LC 2007-06881
Twelve-year-old Addie tries to cope with her mother's
erratic behavior and being separated from her beloved
stepfather and half-sisters when she and her mother go
to live in a small trailer by the railroad tracks on the outskirts of Schenectady, New York.
"Connor . . . treats the subject of child neglect with
honesty and grace in this poignant story. . . . Characters
as persuasively optimistic as Addie are rare, and readers
will gravitate to her." Publ Wkly

Conrad, Pam, 1947-1996

My Daniel. Harper & Row 1989 137p pa $5.99
*

Grades: 5 6 7 8   **Fic**
1. Nebraska—Fiction
ISBN 0-06-440309-2 (pa)   LC 88-19850
"When she's 80 years old, Julia Summerwaithe decides to visit her grandchildren, Ellie and Stevie, in New
York City, for the first time. She has something important to show them; in the Natural History Museum is the
dinosaur she and her brother discovered on their farm in
Nebraska when they were young. But even more important to Julia than seeing the dinosaur is sharing her memories of the discovery and excavation with her
grandchildren." SLJ
"Rendering scenes from both the past and the present
with equal skill, Conrad is at the peak of her storytelling
powers." Publ Wkly

Conway, Celeste

The goodbye time. Delacorte Press 2008 98p
$14.99; lib bdg $17.99

Grades: 4 5 6   **Fic**
1. Friendship—Fiction 2. New York (N.Y.)—Fiction
ISBN   978-0-385-73555-1;   0-385-73555-3;
978-0-385-90540-4 (lib bdg); 0-385-90540-8 (lib bdg)
                                        LC 2008-35675
The close friendship of two eleven-year-old girls, who
live in New York City, begins to unravel as each struggles to deal with a brother who is leaving home.
"The writing is simple and clear, and gently delivers
the message that growing up is inextricably linked with
change." Publ Wkly

Cook, Kacy

Nuts. Marshall Cavendish 2010 155p $16.99

Grades: 4 5 6   **Fic**
1. Squirrels—Fiction 2. Pets—Fiction 3. Family life—
Fiction 4. Ohio—Fiction
ISBN 978-0-7614-5652-0; 0-7614-5652-X
                                        LC 2009004354
When eleven-year-old Nell finds a tiny baby squirrel
on the ground in her yard, she begs her parents to let her
raise it as a pet, even after the research she does shows
that this is not a good idea.
"Cook does a nice job of taking a seemingly innocent
plot and almost sneaking in (a little like pureed vegetables) much weightier themes of love, honesty and death.
. . . The straightforward, upbeat prose consistently engages readers, and her characters are dead on. There's
more here than meets the eye." Kirkus

Coombs, Kate

The runaway princess. Farrar, Straus and Giroux
2006 279p $17

Grades: 5 6 7 8   **Fic**
1. Fairy tales 2. Princesses—Fiction 3. Dragons—Fiction
ISBN 0-374-35546-0   LC 2005-51225
Fifteen-year-old Princess Meg uses magic and her wits
to rescue a baby dragon and escape the unwanted atten-
tions of princes hoping to gain her hand in marriage
through a contest arranged by her father, the king.
"This witty, humorous tale will be popular with fantasy buffs who enjoy takeoffs on fairy tales." Booklist
Another title about Princess Meg is:
The runaway dragon (2009)

Cooper, Ilene, 1948-

Look at Lucy! illustrated by David Merrell.
Random House 2009 102p il lib bdg $11.99; pa
$4.99

Grades: 2 3 4   **Fic**
1. Anxiety—Fiction 2. Contests—Fiction 3. School
stories 4. Dogs—Fiction
ISBN 978-0-375-95558-7 (lib bdg); 0-375-95558-5 (lib
bdg); 978-0-375-85558-0 (pa); 0-375-85558-0 (pa)
                                        LC 2008-36312
"A Stepping Stone Book"
Entering his beagle, Lucy, in a contest to be
"spokespet" for Pet-O-Rama helps shy, nine-year-old

Cooper, Ilene, 1948——*Continued*
Bobby get over his anxiety about speaking in front of groups of people, from his third-grade classmates to the contest judges.

"This beginning chapter book has realistic characters that readers can identify with and root for. . . . The action and suspense will keep children engaged. The occasional drawings lend graphic support." SLJ

Other titles about Lucy and Bobby are:
Absolutely Lucy (2000)
Lucy on the loose (2007)

Cooper, Susan, 1935-
The Boggart. Margaret K. McElderry Bks. 1993 196p hardcover o.p. pa $5.99 *
Grades: 4 5 6 7 **Fic**
1. Supernatural—Fiction 2. Scotland—Fiction 3. Canada—Fiction
ISBN 0-689-50576-0; 0-689-86930-4 (pa)
LC 92-15527
After visiting the castle in Scotland which her family has inherited and returning home to Canada, twelve-year-old Emily finds that she has accidentally brought back with her a boggart, an invisible and mischievous spirit with a fondness for practical jokes

"Using both electronics and theater as metaphors for magic, Cooper has extended the world of high fantasy into contemporary children's lives through scenes superimposing the ordinary and the extraordinary." Bull Cent Child Books

Another title about the Boggart is:
The Boggart and the monster (1997)

The grey king; illustrated by Michael Heslop. Atheneum Pubs. 1975 208p il $18.95; pa $8.99 *
Grades: 5 6 7 8 **Fic**
1. Wales—Fiction 2. Good and evil—Fiction 3. Fantasy fiction
ISBN 0-689-50029-7; 1-4169-4967-4 (pa)
Awarded the Newbery Medal, 1976
"A Margaret K. McElderry book"

"In the fourth of Cooper's Arthurian fantasies, Will Stanton, last and youngest of the Old Ones, the strange Welsh boy, Bran, and the sheep dogs and ghostly gray foxes of the mountains are drawn into the epic struggles of a world beyond time." SLJ

"So well-crafted that it stands as an entity in itself, the novel . . . is nevertheless strengthened by its relationship to the preceding volumes—as the individual legends within the Arthurian cycles take on deeper significance in the context of the whole. A spellbinding tour de force." Horn Book

King of shadows. Margaret K. McElderry Bks. 1999 186p $16; pa $4.99 *
Grades: 5 6 7 8 **Fic**
1. Shakespeare, William, 1564-1616—Fiction 2. Globe Theatre (London, England)—Fiction 3. Actors—Fiction
ISBN 0-689-82817-9; 0-689-84445-X (pa)
LC 98-51127
While in London as part of an all-boy acting company preparing to perform in a replica of the famous Globe Theatre, Nat Field suddenly finds himself transported

back to 1599 and performing in the original theater under the tutelage of Shakespeare himself

"Cleverly explicating old and new acting and performance techniques, Susan Cooper entertains her contemporary readers while giving them a first-rate theatrical education." N Y Times Book Rev

The magician's boy; illustrated by Serena Riglietti. Margaret K. McElderry Bks. 2005 100p il $15.95; pa $7.95
Grades: 2 3 4 **Fic**
1. Fairy tales 2. Magicians—Fiction
ISBN 0-689-87622-X; 1-4169-1555-9 (pa)
A boy who works for a magician meets familiar fairy tale characters when he is transported to the Land of Story in search of a missing puppet

"Fanciful and mildly amusing, the dreamlike story flows along smoothly through a strange yet vaguely familiar wonderland. Riglietti contributes a series of expressive, stylized illustrations." Booklist

Over sea, under stone; illustrated by Margery Gill. Harcourt Brace Jovanovich 1966 c1965 252p il $18; pa $4.99 *
Grades: 5 6 7 8 **Fic**
1. Fantasy fiction 2. Good and evil—Fiction 3. Great Britain—Fiction
ISBN 0-15-259034-X; 0-689-84035-7 (pa)
Also available in paperback from Simon & Schuster
First published 1965 in the United Kingdom
Three children on a holiday in Cornwall find an ancient manuscript which sends them on a dangerous quest for a grail that would reveal the true story of King Arthur and that entraps them in the eternal battle between the forces of the Light and the forces of the Dark.

"The air of mysticism and the allegorical quality of the continual contest between good and evil add much value to a fine plot, setting, and characterization." Horn Book

Other titles in this series are:
The dark is rising (1973)
Greenwitch (1974)
The grey king (1975)
Silver on the tree (1977)

Victory. Margaret K. McElderry Books 2006 196p il $16.95; pa $6.99
Grades: 5 6 7 8 **Fic**
1. Nelson, Horatio Nelson, Viscount, 1758-1805—Fiction 2. Sea stories 3. Great Britain—Fiction
ISBN 1-4169-1477-3; 1-4169-1478-1 (pa)
LC 2005-16747
Alternating chapters follow the mysterious connection between a homesick English girl living in present-day America and an eleven-year-old boy serving in the British Royal Navy in 1803, aboard the H.M.S. Victory, commanded by Admiral Horatio Nelson.

"Seamlessly weaving details of period seamanship into the narrative, Cooper offers a vivid historical tale within the framework of a compelling modern story." Booklist

Corbett, Sue

Free baseball; [by] Sue Corbett. Dutton Children's Books 2006 152p $15.99; pa $5.99

Grades: 5 6 7 8   **Fic**

1. Baseball—Fiction 2. Cuban Americans—Fiction 3. Florida—Fiction

ISBN 0-525-47120-0; 0-14-241080-2 (pa)

         LC 2005004792

Angry with his mother for having too little time for him, eleven-year-old Felix takes advantage of an opportunity to become bat boy for a minor league baseball team, hoping to someday be like his father, a famous Cuban outfielder. Includes glossaries of baseball terms and Spanish words and phrases

"An engaging, well-written story with a satisfying ending." SLJ

The last newspaper boy in America. Dutton Childrens Books 2009 199p $16.99

Grades: 4 5 6 7   **Fic**

1. Newspaper carriers—Fiction 2. Mystery fiction

ISBN 978-0-525-42205-1; 0-525-42205-6

When the newspaper company cancels his route, Wil David is prepared to fight to get his job back, but his focus changes when he stumbles upon a carnival mystery and a plot by a con man that could destroy the town.

"Corbett's graceful dialogue, lovingly drawn characters and clever plot form a timely and refreshing tale." Publ Wkly

Corder, Zizou

Lionboy. Dial Books 2004 275p il hardcover o.p. pa $6.99

Grades: 4 5 6 7   **Fic**

1. Kidnapping—Fiction 2. Lions—Fiction 3. Circus—Fiction 4. Voyages and travels—Fiction

ISBN 0-8037-2982-0; 0-14-240226-5 (pa)

In the near future, Charlie Ashanti, a boy who can speak the language of cats, sets out from London to find his kidnapped parents and finds himself on a Paris-bound circus ship learning to train lions

This is a "fast-paced, original adventure." Voice Youth Advocates

Other titles in this series are:

Lionboy: the chase (2004)

Lionboy: the truth (2005)

Cornwell, Nicki

Christophe's story; [by] Nicki Cornwell; illustrated by Karin Littlewood. Frances Lincoln Children's 2007 74p il $14.95; pa $7.95

Grades: 2 3 4   **Fic**

1. Rwanda—Fiction 2. School stories 3. Refugees—Fiction 4. Immigrants—Fiction

ISBN 978-1-84507-765-5; 1-84507-765-2; 978-1-84507-521-7 (pa); 1-84507-521-8 (pa)

Coping with a new country, a new school and a new language, Christophe wants to tell everyone why he had to leave Rwanda.

"The book succeeds, giving insight into the refugee experience and a glimpse of the horrors in Rwanda that will not overwhelm young readers." Booklist

Correa, Shan

Gaff; written by Shan Correa. Peachtree 2010 212p $15.95

Grades: 4 5 6 7   **Fic**

1. Hawaii—Fiction 2. Animal welfare—Fiction 3. Roosters—Fiction

ISBN 978-1-56145-526-3; 1-56145-526-1

In Hawaii, thirteen-year-old Paul Silva is determined to find a way to get his family out of the illegal cockfighting business.

"Correa's debut evokes the lush melange of sights, sounds and smells in 13-year-old Paulie's multicultural neighborhood in Hawaii. . . . Also woven into this ethical debate, rooted in economics and traditions, is Hawaiian pidgin English, which may challenge even experienced readers. . . . A fascinating look at the United States most mainlanders have never seen." Kirkus

Corriveau, Art

How I, Nicky Flynn, finally get a life (and a dog); a novel. Amulet Books 2010 249p $16.95

Grades: 4 5 6 7   **Fic**

1. Divorce—Fiction 2. Moving—Fiction 3. Runaway children—Fiction 4. Dogs—Fiction 5. Father-son relationship—Fiction 6. Boston (Mass.)—Fiction

ISBN 978-0-8109-8298-7; 0-8109-8298-6

"Since his parents' recent divorce, Nicky, 11, has moved with Mom into a rundown Boston city neighborhood. . . . Then Mom brings home a guide dog, Reggie, who was trained to lead the blind before he was dumped at the pound. Nicky bonds with his new pet, and together they run away. . . . The characters are vividly drawn without sentimentality. . . . More than independence, it is Nicky's blindness about Dad's rejection that is the powerful theme." Booklist

Cotten, Cynthia

Fair has nothing to do with it. Farrar, Straus and Giroux 2007 153p $16

Grades: 4 5 6 7   **Fic**

1. Bereavement—Fiction 2. Grandfathers—Fiction 3. Drawing—Fiction

ISBN 0-374-39935-2; 978-0-374-39935-1

         LC 2006-45170

When Michael's beloved grandfather dies, he has a hard time admitting how much it hurts and allowing himself to trust anyone again.

"The dramatic portrayal of Michael's grief, true to the child's viewpoint, is far from sentimental. . . . A excellent book for discussion." Booklist

Cottrell Boyce, Frank

Cosmic. Walden Pond Press 2010 311p $16.99; lib bdg $17.89 *

Grades: 4 5 6 7   **Fic**

1. Outer space—Exploration—Fiction 2. Size—Fiction

ISBN 978-0-06-183683-1; 0-06-183683-4; 978-0-06-183686-2 (lib bdg); 0-06-183686-9 (lib bdg)

         LC 2008277816

"Liam has always felt a bit like he's stuck between two worlds. This is primarily because he's a twelve-year-old kid who looks like he's about thirty. . . . Liam cons

Cottrell Boyce, Frank—*Continued*

his way onto the first spaceship to take civilians into space, a special flight for a group of kids and an adult chaperone, and he is going as the adult chaperone." Publisher's note

Boyce "knows how to tell a compellingly good story. But in his latest extravagantly imaginative and marvelously good-natured novel he has also written one that is bound to win readers' hearts." Booklist

Framed. HarperCollins 2006 306p $16.99; lib bdg $17.89; pa $6.99

Grades: 5 6 7 8   Fic

1. Automobiles—Fiction 2. Art—Fiction 3. Business enterprises—Fiction 4. Family life—Fiction 5. Wales—Fiction

ISBN 0-06-073402-7; 0-06-073403-5 (lib bdg); 0-06-073404-3 (pa)   LC 2006-00557

Dylan and his sisters have some ideas about how to make Snowdonia Oasis Auto Marvel into a more profitable business, but it is not until some strange men arrive in their small town of Manod, Wales with valuable paintings, and their father disappears, that they consider turning to crime.

"The colorful characters steal the show—even the secondary players are cleverly drawn. But it is Dylan's narrative voice . . . that is truly a masterpiece." SLJ

Millions. HarperCollins 2004 247p $15.99; lib bdg $16.89; pa $6.99

Grades: 5 6 7 8   Fic

1. Money—Fiction 2. Great Britain—Fiction

ISBN 0-06-073330-6; 0-06-073331-4 (lib bdg); 0-06-073332-2 (pa)

After their mother dies, two brothers find a huge amount of money which they must spend quickly before England switches to the new European currency, but they disagree on what to do with it.

"The humor, the strong family story, and Damian's narrative voice make this satisfying novel succeed on several levels." SLJ

Couloumbis, Audrey

Getting near to baby. Putnam 1999 211p $17.99; pa $5.99 *

Grades: 5 6 7 8   Fic

1. Sisters—Fiction 2. Death—Fiction 3. Aunts—Fiction

ISBN 0-399-23389-X; 0-698-11892-8 (pa)
                                          LC 99-18191

A Newbery Medal honor book, 2000

Although thirteen-year-old Willa Jo and her Aunt Patty seem to be constantly at odds, staying with her and Uncle Hob helps Willa Jo and her younger sister come to terms with the death of their family's baby

"Couloumbis's writing is strong; she captures wonderfully the Southern voices of her characters and conveys with great depth powerful emotions. . . . A compelling novel." SLJ

Love me tender. Random House 2008 209p $16.99; lib bdg $19.99; pa $6.50

Grades: 5 6 7 8   Fic

1. Family life—Fiction 2. Pregnancy—Fiction 3. Grandmothers—Fiction 4. Memphis (Tenn.)—Fiction

ISBN 978-0-375-83839-2; 0-375-83839-2; 978-0-375-93839-9 (lib bdg); 0-375-93839-7 (lib bdg); 978-0-375-83840-8 (pa); 0-375-83840-6 (pa)
                                          LC 2006033162

Thirteen-year-old Elvira worries about her future when, after a fight, her father heads to Las Vegas for an Elvis impersonator competition and her pregnant mother takes her and her younger sister to Memphis to visit a grandmother the girls have never met.

"Tart characterizations, lively dialogue and Elvira's frank narration keep this perceptive novel both credible and buoyant." Publ Wkly

The misadventures of Maude March; or, Trouble rides a fast horse; [by] Audrey Couloumbis. Random House 2005 295p hardcover o.p. lib bdg $17.99; pa $7.50 *

Grades: 5 6 7 8   Fic

1. Frontier and pioneer life—Fiction 2. Orphans—Fiction 3. Adventure fiction

ISBN 0-375-83245-9; 0-375-93245-3 (lib bdg); 0-375-83247-5 (pa)   LC 2004-16464

After the death of the stern aunt who raised them since they were orphaned, eleven-year-old Sallie and her fifteen-year-old sister escape their self-serving guardians and begin an adventure resembling those in the dime novels Sallie loves to read.

"Sallie's narration is delightful, with understatements that are laugh-out-loud hilarious. . . . Hard to put down, and a fun read-aloud." SLJ

Another title about Maude March is:

Maude March on the run! (2007)

War games; a novel based on a true story; [by] Audrey Couloumbis & Akila Couloumbis. Random House Children's Books 2009 232p $16.99; lib bdg $19.99

Grades: 5 6 7 8   Fic

1. World War, 1939-1945—Underground movements—Fiction 2. Greece—Fiction 3. Brothers—Fiction 4. Cousins—Fiction

ISBN 978-0-375-85628-0; 0-375-85628-5; 978-0-375-95628-7 (lib bdg); 0-375-95628-X (lib bdg)
                                          LC 2008-46784

What were once just boys' games become matters of life and death as Petros and his older brother Zola each wonder if, like their resistance-fighter cousin, they too can make a difference in a Nazi-occupied Greece.

"The climactic violence is believable, and the resolution—though it takes place offstage—is deeply satisfying. Memorable." SLJ

Coville, Bruce

Aliens ate my homework; illustrated by Katherine Coville. Pocket Bks. 1993 179p il pa $5.99 hardcover o.p. *

Grades: 4 5 6   Fic

1. Science fiction 2. Extraterrestrial beings—Fiction

ISBN 1-4169-3883-4 (pa)   LC 93-3945

Coville, Bruce—*Continued*

"A Minstrel book"

Rod is surprised when a miniature spaceship lands in his school science project and reveals five tiny aliens, who ask his help in apprehending an interstellar criminal

"A funny and suspenseful romp, with appealing illustrations throughout." Horn Book Guide

Other titles in this series are:

Aliens stole my body (1998)

I left my sneakers in dimension X (1994)

The search for Snout (1995)

Jennifer Murdley's toad; a magic shop book; illustrated by Gary A. Lippincott. Harcourt 2002 c1992 159p il $17; pa $5.95 *

Grades: 4 5 6   **Fic**

1. Toads—Fiction 2. Fantasy fiction

ISBN 0-15-204613-5; 0-15-206246-7 (pa)

LC 2002-24107

A reissue of the title first published 1992

When an ordinary-looking fifth grader purchases a talking toad, she embarks on a series of extraordinary adventures

"This light, fast-paced fantasy has touches of humor (at times low comedy), an implicit moral, and a hint that Jennifer may be in for more adventures." Booklist

Jeremy Thatcher, dragon hatcher; a magic shop book; illustrated by Gary A. Lippincott. Harcourt 2002 c1991 151p il $17; pa $5.95 *

Grades: 4 5 6   **Fic**

1. Dragons—Fiction 2. Fantasy fiction

ISBN 0-15-204614-3; 0-15-206252-1 (pa)

LC 2002-68714

A reissue of the title first published 1991

Small for his age but artistically talented, twelve-year-old Jeremy Thatcher unknowingly buys a dragon's egg

This is "right on target. Not only is the story involving but the reader can really get a feeling for Jeremy as a person. Coville's technique of combining the real world with a fantasy one works well in this story." Voice Youth Advocates

Juliet Dove, Queen of Love; a magic shop book. Harcourt 2003 190p $17; pa $5.95 *

Grades: 4 5 6   **Fic**

1. Magic—Fiction 2. Classical mythology—Fiction

ISBN 0-15-204561-9; 0-15-205217-8 (pa)

LC 2003-11846

A shy twelve-year-old girl must solve a puzzle involving characters from Greek mythology to free herself from a spell which makes her irresistible to boys

"Although humorous, the story has surprising depth. . . . Coville capably interweaves mythological characters with realistic modern ones, keeping readers truly absorbed." SLJ

The skull of truth; a magic shop book; illustrated by Gary A. Lippincott. Harcourt 2002 c1997 194p il $17 *

Grades: 4 5 6   **Fic**

1. Truthfulness and falsehood—Fiction 2. Fantasy fiction

ISBN 0-15-204612-7   LC 2002-24244

A reissue of the title first published 1997

Charlie, a sixth-grader with a compulsion to tell lies, acquires a mysterious skull that forces its owner to tell only the truth, causing some awkward moments before he understands its power

"Coville has structured the story very carefully, with a great deal of sensitivity to children's thought processes and emotions. The mood shifts from scary to funny to serious are fused with understandable language and sentence structures." SLJ

Thor's wedding day; by Thialfi, the goat boy; as told to and translated by Bruce Coville; illustrations by Matthew Cogswell. Harcourt 2005 137p il $15; pa $5.95

Grades: 4 5 6 7   **Fic**

1. Norse mythology—Fiction 2. Giants—Fiction

ISBN 0-15-201455-1; 0-15-205872-9 (pa)

LC 2004-29580

Thialfi, the Norse thunder god's goat boy, tells how he inadvertently helped the giant Thrym to steal Thor's magic hammer, the lengths to which Thor must go to retrieve it, and his own assistance along the way.

"Coville takes a Norse poem called the Thrymskvitha and turns it into a delightful prose romp. . . . Throughout, he injects a modern sensibility while keeping the feel of the original myth." Booklist

Cowley, Joy

Chicken feathers; [by] Joy Cowley; with illustrations by David Elliot. Philomel Books 2008 149p il $15.99 *

Grades: 3 4 5   **Fic**

1. Chickens—Fiction 2. Farm life—Fiction 3. Family life—Fiction

ISBN 978-0-399-24791-0; 0-399-24791-2

LC 2007-38635

Relates the story of the summer Josh spends while his mother is in the hospital awaiting the birth of his baby sister, and his pet chicken Semolina, who talks but only to him, is almost killed by a red fox.

"Elliott's personality-laden pencil illustrations extend readers' sense of Cowley's characters. . . . Original, well-crafted, and touching." SLJ

Snake and Lizard; [written by] Joy Cowley; [illustrated by] Gavin Bishop. Kane Miller Pub. 2008 85p il $14.95

Grades: 2 3 4   **Fic**

1. Snakes—Fiction 2. Lizards—Fiction 3. Friendship—Fiction

ISBN 978-1-933605-83-8; 1-933605-83-9

"Snake and Lizard were born to squabble. . . . Each argument begins in misunderstanding and ends in companionable accord; yet their disagreements spring so obviously from their natures, and their repartee is so comical—snappy, ludicrous yet logical—that the salutary message is absorbed with delight. . . . Bishop's art (apparently pen-and-ink, with cheery watercolor added) enlivens almost every spread of this attractive small volume, capturing each interaction with wit and affection." Horn Book

Cowley, Marjorie, 1925-

The golden bull. Charlesbridge 2008 206p lib bdg $15.95

Grades: 5 6 7 8   **Fic**

1. Iraq—Fiction 2. Siblings—Fiction 3. Goldwork—Fiction 4. Apprentices—Fiction 5. Slavery—Fiction

ISBN 978-1-58089-181-3 (lib bdg); 1-58089-181-0 (lib bdg)   LC 2007-42620

During a severe drought in Mesopotamia in 2600 B.C., when their parents can no longer support them, Jomar and his sister Zefa are sent to the city of Ur, where Jomar is apprenticed to a goldsmith and Zefa must try to find a way to keep from becoming a slave. Includes author's note on the history of the region.

"Pulsating action, suspenseful dilemmas, and well-chosen details of gold-smithing and Mesopotamian justice add up to a fine tale that entertains as it reveals the sophistication of society in the cradle of civilization." Booklist

Cox, Judy, 1954-

Butterfly buddies; illustrated by Blanche Sims. Holiday House 2001 86p il $15.95

Grades: 2 3 4   **Fic**

1. School stories 2. Friendship—Fiction 3. Butterflies—Fiction

ISBN 0-8234-1654-2   LC 2001-16720

Third grader Robin has a series of mishaps and learns the value of honesty as she tries to become best friends with Zoey, her partner for a class project on raising butterflies. Includes butterfly care tips

"Written in simple, highly descriptive language that brings settings and characters alive, and sprinkled with lively drawings, this warmhearted friendship story is a good choice for readers transitioning to chapter books." Booklist

The case of the purloined professor; with illustrations by Omar Rayyan. Marshall Cavendish 2009 245p il $16.99

Grades: 3 4 5   **Fic**

1. Adventure fiction 2. Kidnapping—Fiction 3. Rats—Fiction 4. Mystery fiction

ISBN 978-0-7614-5544-8; 0-7614-5544-2
                                        LC 2008000293

Rat brothers Frederick and Ishbu again escape the comfort of their fifth-grade classroom to go on an adventure, this time to help their friend, Natasha, seek her missing father, who is a specialist in the biochemistry of domestic animals

"This fast-paced story has lovable characters, humor, and unique plot twists." SLJ

Another title about Frederick and Ishbu is:
The mystery of the Burmese bandicoot (2007)

Puppy power; illustrated by Steve Björkman. Holiday House 2008 91p il $15.95; pa $6.95

Grades: 2 3 4   **Fic**

1. Dogs—Fiction 2. School stories

ISBN 978-0-8234-2073-5; 0-8234-2073-6; 978-0-8234-2210-4 (pa); 0-8234-2210-0 (pa)
                                        LC 2007-28395

Boisterous third-grader Fran has trouble controlling herself, but learning how to train her gigantic Newfoundland puppy helps her gain enough self-control to win the part of princess in the class play. Includes instructions on puppy training.

This is an "entertaining novel full of believable kids with recognizable problems. . . . With a brisk plot, short chapters, and frequent pen-and-ink illustrations, this story is a choice selection." Booklist

Coy, John, 1958-

Top of the order. Feiwel and Friends 2009 182p $16.99

Grades: 3 4 5 6   **Fic**

1. Baseball—Fiction 2. Friendship—Fiction 3. School stories 4. Sex role—Fiction 5. Divorce—Fiction 6. Family life—Fiction

ISBN 978-0-312-37329-0; 0-312-37329-5
                                        LC 2008-28551

Ten-year-old Jackson lives for baseball, but becomes distracted by the approach of middle school, his mother's latest boyfriend, and the presence of a girl—his good friend's sister—on his team.

"Coy effortlessly captures the voices of boys on the verge of adolescence. Jackson and his friends are fully developed. . . . Gripping play-by-play and a fast-moving plot will appeal to sports enthusiasts and reluctant readers." SLJ

Another title about Jackson is:
Eyes on the goal (2010)

Crabtree, Julie

Discovering pig magic. Milkweed Editions 2008 184p $16.95; pa $6.95

Grades: 5 6 7 8   **Fic**

1. Friendship—Fiction 2. Magic—Fiction 3. School stories

ISBN 978-1-57131-683-7; 1-57131-683-3; 978-1-57131-684-4 (pa); 1-57131-684-1 (pa)
                                        LC 2008-00625

After three sixth-grade best friends perform a "magic" ritual, they experience what they think are unintended consequences of their wishes and they must all find ways to deal with their lives—with or without magic.

"Crabtree's portrayals both of the charm and power of friendship and of the internal emotional life of a young teen are deft and complex, and her confident pacing never drags." Kirkus

Creech, Sharon

Absolutely normal chaos. HarperCollins Pubs. 1995 c1990 230p $16.99; pa $5.99 *

Grades: 5 6 7 8   **Fic**

1. Family life—Fiction

ISBN 0-06-026989-8; 0-06-440632-6 (pa)
                                        LC 95-22448

First published 1990 in the United Kingdom

"Mary Lou Finney's summer journal describes family life in a high-spirited household in Ohio that includes five children." N Y Times Book Rev

"Those in search of a light, humorous read will find it; those in search of something a little deeper will also be rewarded." SLJ

Creech, Sharon—*Continued*

Bloomability. HarperCollins Pubs. 1998 273p
hardcover o.p. pa $5.99 *

Grades: 5 6 7 8   **Fic**

1. School stories 2. Switzerland—Fiction

ISBN 0-06-026993-6; 0-06-440823-X (pa)

                   LC 98-14601

"Joanna Cotler books"

When her aunt and uncle take her from New Mexico
to Lugano, Switzerland, to attend an international school,
thirteen-year-old Dinnie discovers her world expanding

"As if fresh, smart characters in a picturesque setting
weren't engaging enough, Creech also poses an array of
knotty questions, both personal and philosophical. . . . A
story to stimulate both head and heart." Booklist

Chasing Redbird. HarperCollins Pubs. 1997
261p hardcover o.p. pa $5.99

Grades: 5 6 7 8   **Fic**

1. Family life—Fiction 2. Kentucky—Fiction

ISBN 0-06-026987-1; 0-06-440696-2 (pa)

                   LC 96-44128

"Joanna Cotler books"

Thirteen-year-old Zinnia Taylor uncovers family secrets and self truths while clearing a mysterious settler
trail that begins on her family's farm in Kentucky

"With frequent flashbacks, the narrative makes clear
the complexities of the story, while the unsolved puzzles
lead the reader on to the end. The writing is laced with
figurative language and folksy comments that intensify
both atmosphere and emotion." Horn Book Guide

Granny Torrelli makes soup; drawings by Chris
Raschka. HarperCollins Pubs. 2003 141p il $15.99;
lib bdg $16.89; pa $5.99 *

Grades: 4 5 6   **Fic**

1. Grandmothers—Fiction

ISBN 0-06-029290-3; 0-06-029291-1 (lib bdg);
0-06-440960-0 (pa)   LC 2002-152662

With the help of her wise old grandmother, twelve-
year-old Rosie manages to work out some problems in
her relationship with her best friend, Bailey, the boy next
door who is blind

"This gets high marks for its unique voice (make that
voices) and for the way the subtleties that are woven into
the story." Booklist

Heartbeat. HarperCollins 2004 180p $15.99; lib
bdg $16.89; pa $5.99

Grades: 4 5 6 7   **Fic**

1. Friendship—Fiction 2. Grandfathers—Fiction
3. Pregnancy—Fiction 4. Running—Fiction

ISBN 0-06-054022-2; 0-06-054023-0 (lib bdg);
0-06-054024-9 (pa)   LC 2003-7832

"Joanna Cotler books"

Twelve-year-old Annie ponders the many rhythms of
life the year that her mother becomes pregnant, her
grandfather begins faltering, and her best friend (and running partner) becomes distant

"A tenderhearted story told in spare, free-verse poems.
. . . This is vintage Creech, and its richness lies in its
sheer simplicity." SLJ

Love that dog. HarperCollins Pubs. 2001 86p
$15.99; lib bdg $14.89; pa $5.99

Grades: 4 5 6 7   **Fic**

1. Poetry—Fiction 2. School stories

ISBN 0-06-029287-3; 0-06-029289-X (lib bdg);
0-06-440959-7 (pa)   LC 00-54233

"Joanna Cotler books"

"Jack's free-verse journal charts his evolution from
doubt to delight in poetry. His teacher, Miss
Stretchberry, introduces him to poetry, serves as an advocate for his writing, and flatters him into believing he's
a poet." Horn Book

"Creech has created a poignant, funny picture of a
child's encounter with the power of poetry. . . . This
book is a tiny treasure." SLJ

Another title about Jack is:

Hate that cat (2008)

Ruby Holler. HarperCollins Pubs. 2002 310p
hardcover o.p. pa $5.99 *

Grades: 4 5 6 7   **Fic**

1. Orphans—Fiction 2. Twins—Fiction 3. Country
life—Fiction

ISBN 0-06-027732-7; 0-06-056015-0 (pa)

                   LC 00-66371

"Joanna Cotler books"

Thirteen-year-old fraternal twins Dallas and Florida
have grown up in a terrible orphanage but their lives
change forever when an eccentric but sweet older couple
invites them each on an adventure, beginning in an almost magical place called Ruby Holler

"This poignant story evokes a feeling as welcoming as
fresh-baked bread. . . . The novel celebrates the healing
effects of love and compassion." Publ Wkly

The unfinished angel. Joanna Cotler Books 2009
164p $15.99; lib bdg $16.89

Grades: 4 5 6   **Fic**

1. Angels—Fiction 2. Orphans—Fiction 3. Villages—
Fiction 4. Switzerland—Fiction

ISBN   978-0-06-143095-4;   0-06-143095-1;
978-0-06-143096-1 (lib bdg); 0-06-143096-X (lib bdg)

                   LC 2009-02796

In a tiny village in the Swiss Alps, an angel meets an
American girl named Zola who has come with her father
to open a school, and together Zola and the angel rescue
a group of homeless orphans, who gradually change everything.

"Some books are absolute magic, and this is one of
them. . . . Creech's protagonist is hugely likable. . . .
Creech's offering deserves to be read out loud and more
than once to truly enjoy the angel's hilarious malaprop-
isms and outright invented words, and to appreciate the
book's tender, comical celebration of the human spirit."
SLJ

Walk two moons. HarperCollins Pubs. 1994
280p $16.99; lib bdg $17.89; pa $6.99 *

Grades: 6 7 8 9   **Fic**

1. Death—Fiction 2. Grandparents—Fiction 3. Family
life—Fiction 4. Friendship—Fiction

ISBN 0-06-023334-6; 0-06-023337-0 (lib bdg);
0-06-440517-6 (pa)   LC 93-31277

Awarded the Newbery Medal, 1995

Creech, Sharon—*Continued*

After her mother leaves home suddenly, thirteen-year-old Sal and her grandparents take a car trip retracing her mother's route. Along the way, Sal recounts the story of her friend Phoebe, whose mother also left

"An engaging story of love and loss, told with humor and suspense. . . . A richly layered novel about real and metaphorical journeys." SLJ

The Wanderer; drawings by David Diaz. HarperCollins Pubs. 2000 305p il $16.99 paperback o.p.; lib bdg $17.89

Grades: 5 6 7 8   **Fic**
1. Sailing—Fiction 2. Family life—Fiction 3. Sea stories
ISBN 0-06-027730-0; 0-06-027731-9 (lib bdg); 0-06-076673-5 (pa)   LC 99-42699
A Newbery Medal honor book, 2001
"Joanna Cotler books"

Thirteen-year-old Sophie and her cousin Cody record their transatlantic crossing aboard the Wanderer, a forty-five foot sailboat, which, along with uncles and another cousin, is en route to visit their grandfather in England

"The story is exciting, funny, and brimming with life. . . . This is a beautifully written and imaginatively constructed novel." SLJ

Crowley, Suzanne, 1963-

The very ordered existence of Merilee Marvelous. Greenwillow 2007 380p $16.99; lib bdg $17.89; pa $7.99

Grades: 5 6 7 8   **Fic**
1. Asperger's syndrome—Fiction 2. Family life—Fiction 3. Texas—Fiction
ISBN 0-06-123197-5; 0-06-123198-3 (lib bdg); 0-06-123199-1 (pa)   LC 2006-50983

In the small town of Jumbo, Texas, thirteen-year-old Merilee, who has Asperger's Syndrome, tries to live a "Very Ordered Existence," but disruptions begin when a boy and his father arrive in town and the youngster makes himself a part of the family.

This is "a beautifully crafted story that will give children much to talk about." Booklist

Cuffe-Perez, Mary, 1946-

Skylar; a story; illustrated by Renata Liwska. Philomel Books 2008 138p il $14.99

Grades: 3 4 5   **Fic**
1. Geese—Fiction 2. Birds—Migration—Fiction
ISBN 978-0-399-24543-5; 0-399-24543-X
                                   LC 2007-20437

Skylar, who claims he was once wild, leads four pond geese in their first attempt at migration when an injured heron asks their help in reaching Lost Pond, where the annual Before the Migration Convention is about to be held.

"Nature imagery and extensive information on the migratory habits of Canada geese infuse a text, punctuated by occasional soft, black-and-white full-page illustrations. . . . The pace quickens when the geese talk with each other, their near constant bickering adding a dose of humor." Booklist

Cummings, Mary, 1951-

Three names of me; illustrated by Lin Wang. Albert Whitman 2006 unp il $15.95

Grades: 3 4 5   **Fic**
1. Personal names—Fiction 2. Adoption—Fiction 3. Chinese Americans—Fiction
ISBN 978-0-8075-7903-9; 0-8075-7903-3
                                   LC 2006-04725

A girl adopted from China explains that her three names—one her birth mother whispered in her ear, one the babysitters at her orphanage called her, and one her American parents gave her—are each an important part of who she is. Includes scrapbooking ideas for other girls adopted from China.

"Simple, lyrical text enhances the quiet tone of the story. Soft and delicate, the realistic illustrations capture the mood of the story and reveal Ada's thoughts about who she is and where she came from." SLJ

Curry, Jane Louise, 1932-

The Black Canary. Margaret K. McElderry Books 2005 279p $16.95

Grades: 5 6 7 8   **Fic**
1. Essex, Robert Devereux, 2nd Earl of, 1566-1601—Fiction 2. Racially mixed people—Fiction 3. Singers—Fiction 4. London (England)—Fiction 5. Great Britain—History—1485-1603, Tudors—Fiction
ISBN 0-689-86478-7   LC 2003-26150

As the child of two musicians, twelve-year-old James has no interest in music until he discovers a portal to seventeenth-century London in his uncle's basement, and finds himself in a situation where his beautiful voice and the fact that he is biracial might serve him well.

"A genuinely good story that conveys a sense of darkness and mystery in the textured backdrop of a storied time and place." Booklist

Curtis, Christopher Paul

Bucking the Sarge. Wendy Lamb Books 2004 259p $15.95; lib bdg $17.99; pa $6.99

Grades: 5 6 7 8   **Fic**
1. Mothers—Fiction 2. Fraud—Fiction 3. African Americans—Fiction
ISBN 0-385-32307-7; 0-385-90159-3 (lib bdg); 0-440-41331-1 (pa)

Deeply involved in his cold and manipulative mother's shady business dealings in Flint, Michigan, fourteen-year-old Luther keeps a sense of humor while running the Happy Neighbor Group Home For Men, all the while dreaming of going to college and becoming a philosopher.

This is a "hilarious, anguished novel. . . . There are some real surprises in plot and character. . . . The farce and the failure tell the truth in this gripping story." Booklist

Bud, not Buddy. Delacorte Press 1999 245p $16.95; pa $6.50 *

Grades: 4 5 6 7   **Fic**
1. Orphans—Fiction 2. African Americans—Fiction 3. Great Depression, 1929-1939—Fiction
ISBN 0-385-32306-9; 0-440-41328-1 (pa)
                                   LC 99-10614

Curtis, Christopher Paul—*Continued*

Awarded the Newbery Medal, 2000

Ten-year-old Bud, a motherless boy living in Flint, Michigan, during the Great Depression, escapes a bad foster home and sets out in search of the man he believes to be his father—the renowned bandleader, H. E. Calloway of Grand Rapids

"Curtis says in a afterword that some of the characters are based on real people, including his own grandfathers, so it's not surprising that the rich blend of tall tale, slapstick, sorrow, and sweetness has the wry, teasing warmth of family folklore." Booklist

Elijah of Buxton. Scholastic 2007 341p $16.99; pa $7.99 *

Grades: 5 6 7 8   **Fic**

1. Slavery—Fiction 2. Canada—Fiction
ISBN   0-439-02344-0;   978-0-439-02344-3; 0-439-02345-9 (pa); 978-0-439-02345-0 (pa)

LC 2007-05181

A Newbery Medal honor book, 2008

In 1859, eleven-year-old Elijah Freeman, the first free-born child in Buxton, Canada, which is a haven for slaves fleeing the American south, uses his wits and skills to try to bring to justice the lying preacher who has stolen money that was to be used to buy a family's freedom.

"Many readers drawn to the book by humor will find themselves at times on the edges of their seats in suspense and, at other moments, moved to tears." Booklist

Mr. Chickee's funny money. Wendy Lamb Books 2005 151p il (Flint future detective series) $15.95; pa $6.50

Grades: 3 4 5 6   **Fic**

1. Mystery fiction 2. African Americans—Fiction
ISBN 0-385-32772-2; 0-440-22919-7 (pa)

LC 2004-30863

Flint Future Detective Club members Steven Carter, his friend Russell, and Russell's huge dog Zoopy solve the mystery of a quadrillion-dollar bill with the image of James Brown on it.

"A humorous and exciting tall tale. . . . Curtis piles the laughs on in this fast-paced mystery." SLJ

Another title about the Flint Future Detective Club is: Mr. Chickee's messy mission (2007)

The Watsons go to Birmingham—1963; a novel. Delacorte Press 1995 210p $16.95; pa $6.50 *

Grades: 4 5 6 7   **Fic**

1. African Americans—Fiction 2. Family life—Fiction
3. Prejudices—Fiction
ISBN 0-385-32175-9; 0-440-41412-1 (pa)

LC 95-7091

A Newbery Medal honor book, 1996

The ordinary interactions and everyday routines of the Watsons, an African American family living in Flint, Michigan, are drastically changed after they go to visit Grandma in Alabama in the summer of 1963

"Curtis's ability to switch from fun and funky to pinpoint-accurate psychological imagery works unusually well. . . . Ribald humor, sly sibling digs, and a totally believable child's view of the world will make this book an instant hit." SLJ

Cushman, Karen, 1941-

Alchemy and Meggy Swann. Clarion Books 2010 167p $16 *

Grades: 5 6 7 8   **Fic**

1. Handicapped—Fiction 2. Alchemy—Fiction
3. Poverty—Fiction 4. Father-daughter relationship—Fiction 5. London (England)—Fiction 6. Great Britain—History—1485-1603, Tudors—Fiction
ISBN 978-0-547-23184-6; 0-547-23184-9

LC 2009-16387

In 1573, the crippled, scorned, and destitute Meggy Swann goes to London, where she meets her father, an impoverished alchemist, and eventually discovers that although her legs are bent and weak, she has many other strengths.

"Writing with admirable economy and a lively ability to recreate the past believably, Cushman creates a memorable portrayal of a troubled, rather mulish girl who begins to use her strong will in positive ways." Booklist

The ballad of Lucy Whipple. Clarion Bks. 1996 195p $15

Grades: 5 6 7 8   **Fic**

1. Frontier and pioneer life—Fiction 2. Family life—Fiction 3. California—Gold discoveries—Fiction
ISBN 0-395-72806-1   LC 95-45257

Also available in paperback from HarperCollins

In 1849, twelve-year-old California Morning Whipple, who renames herself Lucy, is distraught when her mother moves the family from Massachusetts to a rough California mining town

"Cushman's heroine is a delightful character, and the historical setting is authentically portrayed." SLJ

Catherine, called Birdy. Clarion Bks. 1994 169p $16 *

Grades: 6 7 8 9   **Fic**

1. Middle Ages—Fiction 2. Great Britain—Fiction
ISBN 0-395-68186-3   LC 93-23333

Also available in paperback from HarperCollins

A Newbery Medal honor book, 1995

The fourteen-year-old daughter of an English country knight keeps a journal in which she records the events of her life, particularly her longing for adventures beyond the usual role of women and her efforts to avoid being married off

"In the process of telling the routines of her young life, Birdy lays before readers a feast of details about medieval England. . . . Superb historical fiction." SLJ

Matilda Bone. Clarion Bks. 2000 167p $15; pa $5.99

Grades: 5 6 7 8   **Fic**

1. Physicians—Fiction 2. Middle Ages—Fiction
3. Great Britain—Fiction
ISBN 0-395-88156-0; 0-440-41822-4 (pa)

LC 00-24032

Fourteen-year-old Matilda, an apprentice bonesetter and practitioner of medicine in a village in medieval England, tries to reconcile the various aspects of her life, both spiritual and practical

"A fascinating glimpse into the colorful life and times of the 14th century. . . . Cushman's character descriptions are spare, with each word carefully chosen to paint wonderful pictures." SLJ

Includes bibliographical references

Cushman, Karen, 1941-—*Continued*

The midwife's apprentice. Clarion Bks. 1995
122p $12; pa $5.99 *
Grades: 6 7 8 9   **Fic**
    1. Middle Ages—Fiction 2. Midwives—Fiction
3. Great Britain—Fiction
    ISBN 0-395-69229-6; 0-06-440630-X (pa)
                       LC 94-13792
Awarded the Newbery Medal, 1996
In medieval England, a nameless, homeless girl is tak-
en in by a sharp-tempered midwife, and in spite of obstacles and hardship, eventually gains the three things she
most wants: a full belly, a contented heart, and a place
in this world
"Earthy humor, the foibles of humans both high and
low, and a fascinating mix of superstition and genuinely
helpful herbal remedies attached to childbirth make this
a truly delightful introduction to a world seldom seen in
children's literature." SLJ

Rodzina. Clarion Bks. 2003 215p $16; pa $6.50
*
Grades: 5 6 7 8   **Fic**
    1. Polish Americans—Fiction 2. Orphans—Fiction
    ISBN 0-618-13351-8; 0-440-41993-X (pa)
                      LC 2002-15976
A twelve-year-old Polish American girl is boarded
onto an orphan train in Chicago with fears about traveling to the West and a life of unpaid slavery
"The story features engaging characters, a vivid setting, and a prickly but endearing heroine. . . . Rodzina's
musings and observations provide poignancy, humor, and
a keen sense of the human and topographical landscape."
SLJ

Includes bibliographical references

Cutler, Jane
Rats! pictures by Tracey Campbell Pearson.
Farrar, Straus & Giroux 1996 114p il hardcover
o.p. pa $5.95
Grades: 3 4 5   **Fic**
    1. Brothers—Fiction 2. Family life—Fiction
    ISBN 0-374-36181-9; 0-374-46203-8 (pa)
                      LC 95-22953
Fourth-grader Jason and his younger brother Edward
shop for school clothes, get ready for Halloween, acquire
a couple of pet rats, and deal with not-birthday presents
from Aunt Bea
"The brothers, alternately squabbling and supporting
each other, are convincing in this lighthearted episodic
novel." Horn Book Guide
 Other titles about Jason and Edward are:
'Gator aid (1999)
Leap, frog (2002)
No dogs allowed (1992)

D'Adamo, Francesco
Iqbal; a novel; written by Francesco D'Adamo;
translated by Ann Leonori. Atheneum Bks. for
Young Readers 2003 120p $15.95; pa $4.99
Grades: 5 6 7 8   **Fic**
    1. Masih, Iqbal, d. 1995—Fiction 2. Child labor—Fic-
tion 3. Pakistan—Fiction
    ISBN 0-689-85445-5; 1-4169-0329-1 (pa)
                    LC 2002-153498
Original Italian edition, 2001
A fictionalized account of the Pakistani child who escaped from bondage in a carpet factory and went on to
help liberate other children like him before being gunned
down at the age of thirteen
"The situation and setting are made clear in this novel.
Readers cannot help but be moved by the plight of these
youngsters. . . . This readable book will certainly add
breadth to most collections." SLJ

Dahl, Michael, 1954-
The man behind the mask; written by Michael
Dahl; illustrated by Dan Schoening; Batman
created by Bob Kane. Stone Arch Books 2010 48p
il (DC super heroes. Batman) lib bdg $25.32; pa
$5.95
Grades: 3 4 5   **Fic**
    1. Superheroes—Fiction 2. Batman (Fictional charac-
ter)
    ISBN 978-1-4342-1563-5 (lib bdg); 1-4342-1563-6 (lib
bdg); 978-1-4342-1730-1 (pa); 1-4342-1730-2 (pa)
                    LC 2009006303
"Many years after the death of his parents, Bruce
Wayne comes face to face with their murderer, Joe Chill.
While chasing down this cold-blooded crook, Bruce recalls the story of his own past and the evolution of his
alter ego Batman." Publisher's note
This "full-color chapter [book is] fast moving and entertaining. . . . The story serves as a nice starting point
for readers unfamiliar with the character. . . . The retro
comic-book illustrations . . . appear every few pages,
adding a vibrant visual element to the proceedings.
Sound effects are displayed in large, expressive fonts and
colors, capturing the feel of comics." SLJ

Dahl, Roald
The BFG; pictures by Quentin Blake. Farrar,
Straus & Giroux 1982 219p il $18
Grades: 4 5 6   **Fic**
    1. Giants—Fiction 2. Orphans—Fiction
    ISBN 0-374-30469-6   LC 82-15548
Also available in paperback from Penguin Bks.
Kidsnatched from her orphanage by a BFG (Big
Friendly Giant), who spends his life blowing happy
dreams to children, Sophie concocts with him a plan to
save the world from nine other man-gobbling cannybull
giants
This "is a book not all adults will like, but most kids
will. . . . Highly unusual, often hilarious, and occasionally vulgar, even grisly." Booklist

Dahl, Roald—*Continued*

Charlie and the chocolate factory; illustrated by Quentin Blake. rev ed. Knopf 2001 162p il $15.95; lib bdg $17.99 *

Grades: 4 5 6 7   **Fic**

1. Conduct of life—Fiction
ISBN 0-375-81526-0; 0-375-91526-5 (lib bdg)
LC 2001-29461

A newly illustrated edition of the title first published 1964

Each of five children lucky enough to discover an entry ticket into Mr. Willy Wonka's mysterious chocolate factory takes advantage of the situation in his own way

"Blake's energetic black-and-white illustrations enliven and update Dahl's cautionary rags-to-riches story. . . . The slapdash effect of the whimsical drawings matches Wonka's hyperactive speech and the generally frenetic narrative." Horn Book Guide

The enormous crocodile; illustrated by Quentin Blake. Knopf 2000 c1978 unp il pa $7.99 hardcover o.p.

Grades: 2 3 4   **Fic**

1. Crocodiles—Fiction 2. Animals—Fiction
ISBN 0-14-241453-0 (pa)

A reissue of the title first published 1978

"'For my lunch today,' says the crocodile, 'I would like a nice juicy little child.' To this end, he sets off from the muddy river to go to town. On his way he meets Humpy Rumpy the hippo, Trunky the elephant, Muggle-Wump the monkey, and the Roly-Poly bird, all of whom are horrified by his quest. Each in turn manages to foil one of his attempts on unsuspecting children." SLJ

"Mr. Dahl's gift for sonorous and inventive language carries the story along merrily . . . and Quentin Blake's squidgy jungle and scaly villain, colorful crowds and righteous elephant couldn't be improved upon." N Y Times Book Rev

James and the giant peach; a children's story; illustrated by Lane Smith. Knopf 1996 126p il $16; lib bdg $17.99 *

Grades: 4 5 6   **Fic**

1. Fantasy fiction
ISBN 0-679-88090-9; 0-679-98090-3 (lib bdg)
LC 91-33489

Also available in paperback from Penguin Bks.

A newly illustrated edition of the title first published 1961

After the death of his parents, little James is forced to live with Aunt Sponge and Aunt Spike, two cruel old harpies. A magic potion causes the growing of a giant-sized peach on a puny peach tree. James sneaks inside the peach and finds a new world of insects. With his new family, James heads for many adventures

"A 'juicy' fantasy, 'dripping' with humor and imagination." Commonweal

The magic finger; illustrated by Quentin Blake. Viking 1995 62p il hardcover o.p. pa $5.99

Grades: 2 3 4   **Fic**

1. Hunting—Fiction 2. Magic—Fiction
ISBN 0-670-85252-X; 0-14-241385-2 (pa)
LC 92-31443

A newly illustrated edition of the title first published 1966 by Harper & Row

Angered by a neighboring family's sport hunting, an eight-year-old girl turns her magic finger on them

This is an "original and intriguing fantasy." Booklist

Matilda; illustrations by Quentin Blake. Viking Kestrel 1988 240p il $16.99; pa $6.99

Grades: 4 5 6   **Fic**

1. School stories
ISBN 0-670-82439-9; 0-14-241037-3 (pa)
LC 88-40312

"Matilda knows how to be extremely and creatively naughty—lining her father's hat with super glue, putting her mother's hair bleach in her father's hair tonic bottle, for example. This streak of imaginative wickedness not only allows her to make a loyal friend, Lavender, but also to wreak revenge on her unloving parents, defeat the fiendish headmistress, Miss Turnbull, and return her victimized teacher, the enchanting Miss Honey, to her rightful place in the world." N Y Times Book Rev

"Dahl has written another fun and funny book with a child's perspective on an adult world. As usual, Blake's comical sketches are the perfect complement to the satirical humor." SLJ

Dahlberg, Maurine F., 1951-

The story of Jonas; [by] Maurine F. Dahlberg. Farrar, Straus Giroux 2007 148p $16

Grades: 4 5 6 7   **Fic**

1. Slavery—Fiction 2. African Americans—Fiction
ISBN 0-374-37264-0   LC 2006041344

In the mid-1800s, a slave boy dreams of escaping to freedom while on a journey from Missouri to the gold fields of Kansas Territory with his master's n'er-do-well son

This is a "well-crafted, engaging novel appropriate for a middle-grade audience." Booklist

Dakin, Glenn, 1960-

The Society of Unrelenting Vigilance; [illustrations by Greg Swearingen] Egmont 2009 300p il (Candle Man) $15.99; lib bdg $18.99

Grades: 4 5 6 7   **Fic**

1. Adventure fiction 2. Superheroes—Fiction
ISBN 978-1-60684-015-3; 1-60684-015-0; 978-1-60684-047-4 (lib bdg); 1-60684-047-9 (lib bdg)
LC 2009-14035

Thirteen-year-old Theo, who has lived in seclusion his entire life, discovers he is the descendant of the Candle Man, a Victorian vigilante with the ability to melt criminals with a single touch.

This is a "lighthearted, action-driven adventure. . . . With the help of a cast of appealing characters, the non-stop action rolls to a satisfying conclusion." SLJ

Daley, Michael J.

Space station rat; by Michael J. Daley. Holiday House 2005 181p $15.95; pa $6.99

Grades: 4 5 6   **Fic**

1. Rats—Fiction 2. Space stations—Fiction 3. Science fiction
ISBN 0-8234-1866-9; 0-8234-2151-1 (pa)
LC 2004-40534

Daley, Michael J.—*Continued*

A lavender rat that has escaped from a laboratory, and Jeff, a lonely boy whose parents are scientists, meet on an orbiting space station, communicate by email, and ultimately find themselves in need of each other's help and friendship

"The point of view shifts between Jeff and Rat. . . . The developing interspecies communication raises interesting questions about the nature of intelligence and individuality. A thoughtful and satisfying adventure." SLJ

Another title about Jeff and Rat is:

Rat trap (2008)

Dalgliesh, Alice, 1893-1979

The bears on Hemlock Mountain; illustrated by Helen Sewell. Scribner 1990 c1952 unp il pa $4.99 hardcover o.p.

Grades: 1 2 3 4   Fic

1. Bears—Fiction

ISBN 0-689-71604-4 (pa)

A Newbery Medal honor book, 1953

First published 1952

"This is the story of a little boy sent by his mother to borrow an iron from an aunt who lived on the other side of Hemlock Mountain—really only a hill. Jonathan's mother did not believe that there were bears on Hemlock Mountain but Jonathan did. . . . The two-color, somewhat stylized illustrations seem right for the story." Booklist

"Jonathan's adventure is a tall tale passed down in Pennsylvania, which might have happened to a pioneer boy almost anywhere. Full of suspense and humor, it will make good reading aloud." N Y Her Trib Books

Daly, Niki, 1946-

Bettina Valentino and the Picasso Club. Farrar, Straus and Giroux 2009 103p il $16 *

Grades: 4 5 6   Fic

1. Art—Fiction 2. Teachers—Fiction 3. School stories

ISBN 978-0-374-30753-0; 0-374-30753-9

LC 2008-03827

A controversial new teacher at Bayside Preparatory School introduces the exciting world of art to aspiring artist Bettina Valentino and her fifth-grade classmates, encouraging them to see everyday life in a different way.

"If the story's execution wasn't delightful enough (it is), Daly provides wonderful ink-and-wash drawings . . . that up the amusing ante. Not only are the cast's eccentricities on display, but Daly sometimes draws on the styles of famous artists." Booklist

Daneshvari, Gitty

School of Fear; illustrated by Carrie Gifford. Little, Brown Books for Young Readers 2009 339p il $15.99

Grades: 4 5 6   Fic

1. Phobias—Fiction 2. School stories

ISBN 978-0-316-03326-8; 0-316-03326-X

LC 2008051309

Twelve-year-olds Madeleine, Theo, and Lulu, and thirteen-year-old Garrison, are sent to a remote Massachusetts school to overcome their phobias, but tragedy

strikes and the quartet must work together—with no adult assistance—to face their fears.

This is "tautly paced, spine-tingling and quite funny." Publ Wkly

Danneberg, Julie, 1958-

Family reminders; illustrated by John Shelley. Charlesbridge 2009 105p il $14.95

Grades: 3 4 5   Fic

1. Family life—Fiction 2. Frontier and pioneer life—Fiction 3. Colorado—Fiction

ISBN 978-1-58089-320-6; 1-58089-320-1

In 1890s Cripple Creek, Colorado, when young Mary McHugh's father loses his leg in a mining accident, she tries to help, both by earning money and by encouraging her father to go back to carving wooden figurines and playing piano.

"Shelley's India ink and pen illustrations add to the historical feel of this gentle, yet gripping story. This is a heartwarming novel about overcoming hardship." SLJ

Danziger, Paula, 1944-2004

Amber Brown is not a crayon; illustrated by Tony Ross. Putnam 1994 80p il $15.99; pa $4.99
*

Grades: 2 3 4   Fic

1. Friendship—Fiction 2. Moving—Fiction 3. School stories

ISBN 0-399-22509-9; 0-14-240619-8 (pa)

LC 92-34678

Also available easy-to-read titles about Amber Brown in series: A is for Amber

The year she is in the third grade is a sad time for Amber because her best friend Justin is getting ready to move to a distant state

"Ross's black-and-white sketches throughout add humor and keep the pages turning swiftly. Danziger reaches out to a younger audience in this funny, touching slice of third-grade life, told in the voice of a feisty, lovable heroine." SLJ

Other titles about Amber Brown are:

Amber Brown goes fourth (1995)

Amber Brown is feeling blue (1998)

Amber Brown is green with envy (2003)

Amber Brown sees red (1997)

Amber Brown wants extra credit (1996)

Forever Amber Brown (1996)

I, Amber Brown (1999)

You can't eat your chicken pox, Amber Brown (1995)

The cat ate my gymsuit; [by] Paula Danziger. 30th anniversary edition. G.P. Putnam's Sons 2004 c1974 151p $15.99; pa $5.99

Grades: 4 5 6 7   Fic

1. School stories 2. Teachers—Fiction

ISBN 0-399-24307-0; 0-14-240654-6 (pa)

LC 2004001892

A reissue of the title first published 1974 by Delacorte Press

When the unconventional English teacher who helped her conquer many of her feelings of insecurity is fired, thirteen-year-old Marcy Lewis uses her new found courage to campaign for the teacher's reinstatement.

Danziger, Paula, 1944-2004—*Continued*

"Paula Danziger's compassionate and accurate portrayal of a young girl struggling to find her own voice rings as true today as it did 30 years ago. A full cast brings this modern American classic of teenage angst to life with humor and pathos." SLJ

P.S. Longer letter later; [by] Paula Danziger & Ann M. Martin. Scholastic 1998 234p hardcover o.p. pa $4.99

Grades: 5 6 7 8   **Fic**
   1. Friendship—Fiction 2. Letters—Fiction
   ISBN 0-590-21310-5; 0-590-21311-3 (pa)
                                          LC 97-19120
Companion volume to Snail mail no more

Twelve-year-old best friends Elizabeth and Tara-Starr continue their friendship through letter-writing after Tara-Starr's family moves to another state

"The authenticity of the well-drawn characters gives life and vitality to the story. . . . Readers will thoroughly enjoy this fast-paced read." SLJ

Snail mail no more; [by] Paula Danziger & Ann M. Martin. Scholastic Press 2000 307p hardcover o.p. pa $5.99

Grades: 5 6 7 8   **Fic**
   1. Friendship—Fiction 2. Letters—Fiction
   ISBN 0-439-06335-3; 0-439-06336-1 (pa)
                                          LC 99-33593
Companion volume to P.S. Longer letter later

Now that they live in different cities, thirteen-year-old Tara and Elizabeth use e-mail to "talk" about everything that is occurring in their lives and to try to maintain their closeness as they face big changes

"A funny, thought-provoking page-turner that will delight readers and leave them ready for more messages." Booklist

There's a bat in bunk five. Delacorte Press 1980 150p il pa $5.99 hardcover o.p.

Grades: 4 5 6 7   **Fic**
   1. Camps—Fiction
   ISBN 0-14-240681-3 (pa)   LC 80-15581

"A thinner Marcy than appeared in 'The Cat Ate My Gymsuit' here eagerly accepts an invitation from Ms. Finney, her favorite teacher, to work as a counselor-in-training at a summer camp. Though wanting to do a good job, particularly in reaching the abrasive and uncooperative Ginger, Marcy also indulges in a romance with fellow camper Ted and spends time sorting out her own inner conflicts." Booklist

"In some ways this is the usual camping story of pranks, bunkmates, adjustment to separation from parents, etc. This doesn't, however, follow a formula plot; it has depth in the relationships and characterizations; and it's written with vigor and humor." Bull Cent Child Books

David, Peter

Mascot to the rescue! drawings by Colleen Doran. Laura Geringer Books 2008 232p il $15.99

Grades: 4 5 6   **Fic**
   1. Superheroes—Fiction 2. Comic books, strips, etc.—Fiction 3. Imagination—Fiction 4. Single parent family—Fiction
   ISBN 978-0-06-134911-9;   0-06-134911-9;
   978-0-06-134913-3 (lib bdg); 0-06-134913-5 (lib bdg)
                                          LC 2007-25906

Twelve-year-old Josh, who feels connected to the comic book superhero, Mascot, sets out on an odyssey to discover the comic's creator when he learns that the fictional Mascot is going to die.

"This novel . . . offers plenty of humor, action, and comic-style dramatics to keep readers enthralled." Bull Cent Child Books

Davies, Jacqueline

The lemonade war; by Jacqueline Davies. Houghton Mifflin Company 2007 173p $16; pa $6.99

Grades: 3 4 5   **Fic**
   1. Siblings—Fiction 2. Money-making projects for children—Fiction
   ISBN 978-0-618-75043-6;   0-618-75043-6;
   978-0-547-23765-7 (pa); 0-547-23765-0 (pa)
                                          LC 2006026076

Evan and his younger sister, Jesse, react very differently to the news that they will be in the same class for fourth grade and as the end of summer approaches, they battle it out through lemonade stands, each trying to be the first to earn 100 dollars. Includes mathematical calculations and tips for running a successful lemonade stand.

The author "does a good job of showing the siblings' strengths, flaws, and points of view in this engaging chapter book." Booklist

Davis, Katie

The curse of Addy McMahon. Greenwillow Books 2008 271p $16.99; lib bdg $17.89

Grades: 4 5 6   **Fic**
   1. Authorship—Fiction 2. Cartoons and caricatures—Fiction 3. Bereavement—Fiction 4. Family life—Fiction 5. Friendship—Fiction
   ISBN 978-0-06-128711-4;   0-06-128711-3;
   978-0-06-128712-1 (lib bdg); 0-06-128712-1 (lib bdg)
                                          LC 2007041154

After her father's death, aspiring sixth-grade writer Addy McMahon feels like she is cursed with bad luck, and when she temporarily loses her best friend, and is forced to admit that her mother is dating again, she vows she will never write another word

"Peppered with authentic preteen conversations, the novel combines traditional narrative with graphic-novel stories, emails, and IMs. . . . The book is a fast-paced and interesting read." SLJ

Davis, Tony, 1961-

Roland Wright: future knight. Delacorte Press 2009 c2007 129p il $12.99; lib bdg $15.99

Grades: 2 3 4   **Fic**

1. Knights and knighthood—Fiction 2. Middle Ages—Fiction

ISBN 978-0-385-73800-2; 0-385-73800-5; 978-0-385-90706-4 (lib bdg); 0-385-90706-0 (lib bdg)

LC 2008053074

First published 2007 in the United Kingdom

In 1409, skinny, clumsy Roland, the ten-year-old son of a blacksmith, pursues his dream of becoming a knight.

"This engaging book, the first in a series, has accurate details about the Middle Ages and a feisty, persevering hero. . . . Rogers's charming pen-and-ink illustrations enhance the story and may also make it more appealing to reluctant readers." SLJ

Day, Karen

Tall tales. Wendy Lamb Books 2007 229p $15.99; lib bdg $18.99; pa $6.50

Grades: 4 5 6 7   **Fic**

1. Alcoholism—Fiction 2. Family life—Fiction 3. Friendship—Fiction 4. Indiana—Fiction

ISBN 978-0-375-83773-9; 0-375-83773-6; 978-0-375-93773-6 (lib bdg); 0-375-93773-0 (lib bdg); 978-0-375-83774-6 (pa); 0-375-83774-4 (pa)

LC 2006-35242

Sixth-grader Meg Summers and her family move to a new state every few years as her alcoholic father tries to get a fresh start, but when they land in Indiana and Meg finally makes a real friend and begins to talk about her family's problems, they all find the strength to try to change their destiny.

"Although there is no fairy-tale ending, the story is realistic and hopeful with discussable issues appropriate for a wide audience." SLJ

De Angeli, Marguerite Lofft, 1889-1987

The door in the wall; by Marguerite de Angeli. Doubleday 1989 c1949 120p il hardcover o.p. pa $4.99

Grades: 4 5 6   **Fic**

1. Physically handicapped children—Fiction 2. Great Britain—Fiction 3. Middle Ages—Fiction

ISBN 0-385-07283-X; 0-440-22779-8 (pa)

Awarded the Newbery Medal, 1950

First published 1949

Robin, a crippled boy in fourteenth-century England, proves his courage and earns recognition from the King

"An enthralling and inspiring tale of triumph over handicap. Unusually beautiful illustrations, full of authentic detail, combine with the text to make life in England during the Middle Ages come alive." N Y Times Book Rev

Thee, Hannah! written and illustrated by Marguerite de Angeli. Herald Press 2000 99p il pa $15.99

Grades: 3 4 5   **Fic**

1. Society of Friends—Fiction 2. Philadelphia (Pa.)—Fiction

ISBN 0-8361-9106-4   LC 99-52422

A reissue of the title first published 1940 by Doubleday

Nine-year-old Hannah, a Quaker living in Philadelphia just before the Civil War, longs to have some fashionable dresses like other girls but comes to appreciate her heritage and its plain dressing when her family saves the life of a runaway slave

"Hannah and the other children are very real and, in addition to the [author's] lovely pictures that follow the story, the street cries of old Philadelphia are effectively introduced and illustrated at the beginning of each chapter." Libr J

De Guzman, Michael

Finding Stinko. Farrar, Straus and Giroux 2007 136p $16 *

Grades: 5 6 7 8   **Fic**

1. Foster home care—Fiction 2. Ventriloquism—Fiction 3. Dolls—Fiction 4. Runaway children—Fiction

ISBN 0-374-32305-4; 978-0-374-32305-9

LC 2006-40859

Having spent his life trying to escape the foster care system, eventually becoming mute to keep out of trouble, twelve-year-old Newboy finally hits the streets, where a discarded ventriloquist's dummy gives him back his voice and his hope.

This is a "gritty, engagingly offbeat page-turner. . . . Readers will be riveted." Booklist

Henrietta Hornbuckle's circus of life. Farrar, Straus and Giroux 2010 152p $16.99

Grades: 4 5 6   **Fic**

1. Clowns—Fiction 2. Circus—Fiction 3. Family life—Fiction 4. Death—Fiction 5. Bereavement—Fiction

ISBN 978-0-374-33513-7; 0-374-33513-3

LC 2009-13602

Twelve-year-old Henrietta Hornbuckle and her parents perform as clowns in a tiny, ramshackle traveling circus until a family tragedy jeopardizes Henrietta's whole offbeat world

"The writing is worthy of a tall tale, but the details are all realistic. A simple and satisfying story with a likable, unusual star." Booklist

De Mari, Silvana, 1953-

The last dragon; translated from the Italian by Shaun Whiteside. Miramax Books/Hyperion Books for Children 2006 361p $16.95; pa $6.99 *

Grades: 5 6 7 8   **Fic**

1. Dragons—Fiction 2. Fantasy fiction

ISBN 0-7868-3636-9; 1-4231-0405-6 (pa)

"In a post-apocalyptic world . . . a young elf named Yorsh struggles to survive. When his village is destroyed by the torrential waters, Yorsh finds himself suddenly orphaned and alone–the earth's last elf. But soon Yorsh discovers he is part of a powerful prophecy: when the last dragon and the last elf break the circle, the past and the future will meet, and the sun of a new summer will shine in the sky." Publisher's note

"With its combination of humor and deeply felt emotion, *The Last Dragon* . . . will leave readers enthralled." Horn Book

Dee, Barbara

Solving Zoe. Margaret K. McElderry Books 2009 230p $15.99

Grades: 4 5 6 7   **Fic**

1. School stories 2. Cryptography—Fiction 3. Family life—Fiction 4. Gifted children—Fiction 5. Brooklyn (New York, N.Y.)—Fiction

ISBN 978-1-4169-6128-4; 1-4169-6128-3

LC 2008-06217

Zoe's sixth-grade year at a Brooklyn school for gifted students is marked by changing relationships with her fellow students and teachers, recognition of her talent for cryptography, and a greater awareness of her passion.

"The novel realistically portrays Zoe's general unhappiness and her pain at losing a close friend while it shows her finding a way out of the emotional tangle. . . . This vivid middle-school novel offers readers plenty to think about." Booklist

Deedy, Carmen Agra

The yellow star; the legend of King Christian X of Denmark; illustrated by Henri Sørensen. Peachtree Pubs. 2000 unp il $16.95

Grades: 3 4 5   **Fic**

1. Christian X, King of Denmark, 1870-1947—Fiction 2. Denmark—Fiction 3. World War, 1939-1945—Fiction 4. Holocaust, 1933-1945—Fiction

ISBN 1-56145-208-4   LC 00-20602

Retells the story of King Christian X and the Danish resistance to the Nazis during World War II

"Deedy's language is simple and rhythmic. . . . This is an interesting and thought-provoking piece of work." SLJ

DeFelice, Cynthia C.

Bringing Ezra back. Farrar, Straus & Giroux 2006 147p $16

Grades: 4 5 6 7   **Fic**

1. Frontier and pioneer life—Fiction 2. Voyages and travels—Fiction

ISBN 0-374-39939-5   LC 2005-49763

In the mid-1800s, twelve-year-old Nathan journeys from his farm on the Ohio frontier to Western Pennsylvania to rescue a friend held captive by the owners of a freak show.

"Told in Nathan's voice, this adventure treats readers to a double-dip cliff-hanging plot and heart-searing maturation." SLJ

Sequel to Weasel (1990)

The ghost of Fossil Glen; [by] Cynthia DeFelice. Farrar, Straus & Giroux 1998 167p $16 *

Grades: 4 5 6   **Fic**

1. Ghost stories

ISBN 0-374-31787-9   LC 97-33230

Also available in paperback from Avon Bks.

"Sixth-grader Allie Nichols encounters the ghost of Lucy Stiles and becomes involved with Lucy's unsolved death, eventually finding proof that Lucy was murdered." Horn Book Guide

"A supernatural cliff-hanger with breathless chases and riveting suspense." SLJ

Other titles in this series are:

The ghost and Mrs. Hobbs (2001)
The ghost of Cutler Creek (2004)
The ghost of Poplar Point (2007)

The missing manatee; [by] Cynthia DeFelice. Farrar, Straus and Giroux 2005 181p $16; pa $6.95

Grades: 5 6 7 8   **Fic**

1. Fishing—Fiction 2. Mystery fiction 3. Florida—Fiction

ISBN 0-374-31257-5; 0-374-40020-2 (pa)

LC 2004-50633

While coping with his parents' separation, eleven-year-old Skeet spends most of Spring Break in his skiff on a Florida river, where he finds a manatee shot to death and begins looking for the killer

"DeFelice offers a realistic adventure story that is fast paced and full of drama. . . . The characters are multifaceted and well developed, and the story should prompt readers to think about cause and effect." SLJ

Signal. Farrar, Straus and Giroux 2009 151p $16.99 *

Grades: 5 6 7 8   **Fic**

1. Friendship—Fiction 2. Loneliness—Fiction 3. Child abuse—Fiction 4. Moving—Fiction 5. Country life—Fiction

ISBN 978-0-374-39915-3; 0-374-39915-8

LC 2008-09278

After moving with his emotionally distant father to the Finger Lakes region of upstate New York, twelve-year-old Owen faces a lonely summer until he meets an abused girl who may be a space alien.

"Well-drawn secondary characters create a threatening backdrop to the developing mystery, while Owen's poignant relationship with his work-driven father elicits sympathy. The tension builds on several fronts to a gripping climax and satisfying conclusion. Owen's likable voice, the plot's quick pace and the science fiction overtones make this a winner." Publ Wkly

Weasel; [by] Cynthia DeFelice. Avon Books 1990 119p pa $4.99

Grades: 4 5 6 7   **Fic**

1. Frontier and pioneer life—Fiction 2. Ohio—Fiction

ISBN 978-0-380-71358-5 (pa); 0-380-71358-6 (pa)

"An Avon Camelot book"

First published 1990 by Macmillan

Alone in the frontier wilderness in the winter of 1839 while his father is recovering from an injury, eleven-year-old Nathan runs afoul of the renegade killer known as the weasel and makes a surprising discovery about the concept of revenge

"A masterfully told, riveting tale sure to inspire strong discussion about moral choices." SLJ

DeGross, Monalisa

Donavan's double trouble; [by] Monalisa DeGross; illustrated by Amy Bates. Amistad 2008 180p il $15.99; lib bdg $17.89

Grades: 2 3 4   **Fic**

1. Amputees—Fiction 2. Uncles—Fiction 3. School stories 4. African Americans—Fiction

ISBN 978-0-06-077293-2; 978-0-06-077294-9 (lib bdg)   LC 2007011244

DeGross, Monalisa—*Continued*

Fourth-grader Donavan is sensitive about the problems he has understanding math, and then when his favorite uncle, a former high school basketball star, returns from National Guard duty an amputee, Donavan's problems get even worse as he struggles to accept this "new" Uncle Vic.

"The fast, funny dialogue between friends and the warm family relationships will draw readers to the realistic story." Booklist

Another title about Donavan is:
Donavan's word jar (1994)

DeJong, Meindert, 1906-1991

The house of sixty fathers; pictures by Maurice Sendak. Harper & Row 1956 189p il lib bdg $15.89; pa $5.39

Grades: 4 5 6   **Fic**
1. Sino-Japanese Conflict, 1937-1945—Fiction
2. China—Fiction
ISBN 0-06-021481-3 (lib bdg); 0-06-440200-2 (pa)
A Newbery Medal honor book, 1957
This story is set in "China during the early days of the Japanese invasion. Tien Pao, a small Chinese boy, and his family fled inland on a sampan when the Japanese attacked their coastal village, but Tien Pao was separated from his parents during a storm and swept back down the river on the sampan. . . . [The author paints] starkly realistic word pictures that give the reader the full impact of the terror, pain, hunger and finally the joy that Tien Pao knew during his search for his family." Bull Cent Child Books

The wheel on the school; pictures by Maurice Sendak. Harper & Row 1954 298p il $18.95; pa $6.95

Grades: 4 5 6   **Fic**
1. Netherlands—Fiction 2. Storks—Fiction 3. School stories
ISBN 0-06-021585-2; 0-06-021586-0 (lib bdg); 0-06-440021-2 (pa)
Awarded the Newbery Medal, 1955
"Six Dutch children encouraged by a sensitive schoolmaster search for a wheel to place on the schoolhouse roof as a nesting place for storks. Their efforts and ultimate success lead to better understanding among the children and closer ties to older members of the community." Read Ladders for Hum Relat

"This author goes deeply into the heart of childhood and has written a moving story, filled with suspense and distinguished for the quality of its writing." Child Books Too Good To Miss

DeLaCroix, Alice, 1940-

The best horse ever; illustrated by Ronald Himler. Holiday House 2010 74p il $15.95

Grades: 3 4 5   **Fic**
1. Horses—Fiction 2. Friendship—Fiction
ISBN 978-0-8234-2254-8; 0-8234-2254-2
                                    LC 2009-25542
"Abby gets her heart's desire: her parents purchase Griffin, the gentle horse she has grown to love during her riding lessons. But when her best friend, Devon, can't get past her fear of the horse to share Abby's excitement, they quarrel. . . . Although girls who love horses are the obvious audience, other readers will also enjoy this appealing chapter book with its simple plot and subtly drawn characters. . . . Himler contributes shaded pencil drawings that capture the actions and emotions of the characters." Booklist

Delaney, Joseph, 1904-1991

Revenge of the witch; illustrations by Patrick Arrasmith. Greenwillow Bks. 2005 344p il (The last apprentice) $14.99; lib bdg $15.89; pa $7.99 *

Grades: 5 6 7 8   **Fic**
1. Supernatural—Fiction 2. Witches—Fiction
ISBN 0-06-076618-2; 0-06-076619-0 (lib bdg); 0-06-076620-4 (pa)   LC 2004-54003
Young Tom, the seventh son of a seventh son, starts work as an apprentice for the village spook, whose job is to protect ordinary folk from "ghouls, boggarts, and all manner of wicked beasties"

"Delaney grabs readers by the throat and gives them a good shake in a smartly crafted story. . . . This is a gristly thriller. . . . Yet the twisted horror is amply buffered by an exquisitely normal young hero, matter-of-fact prose, and a workaday normalcy." Booklist

Other titles in this series are:
Curse of the bane (2006)
Night of the soul-stealer (2007)
Attack of the fiend (2008)
Wrath of the Bloodeye (2008)
Clash of the demons (2009)

Delton, Judy, 1932-2001

Angel's mother's wedding; illustrated by Margot Apple. Houghton Mifflin 1987 166p il $16; pa $4.95

Grades: 3 4 5   **Fic**
1. Weddings—Fiction 2. Family life—Fiction
ISBN 0-395-44470-5; 0-618-11118-2 (pa)
                                    LC 87-16937
"Angel's capacity for worry, added to her friend Edna's knowledge of how a wedding should be properly organized, leads to confusions and misunderstandings that reach almost epic proportions. . . . Humor, affection, and action narrowly skirting disaster mark each chapter in the progress from bridal shower to wedding march. Angel, her family, and friends are all pleasantly ordinary folk with a singular capacity to bring near-chaos into the normally quiet routines and celebrations of their daily life." Horn Book

Other titles about Angel are:
Angel bites the bullet (2000)
Angel in charge (1985)
Angel spreads her wings (1999)
Angel's mother's baby (1989)
Angel's mother's boyfriend (1986)
Back yard Angel (1983)

Derby, Sally, 1934-

Kyle's island. Charlesbridge 2010 191p $16.95

Grades: 5 6 7 8   **Fic**

1. Siblings—Fiction 2. Lakes—Fiction 3. Islands—Fiction 4. Family life—Fiction 5. Michigan—Fiction

ISBN 978-1-58089-316-9; 1-58089-316-3

LC 2009-17581

Kile, almost thirteen, spends much of the summer yearning to explore a nearby island, striving to be a good brother, fishing with an elderly neighbor, and fuming at his parents over their separation that is forcing his mother to sell the family's cabin on a Michigan lake.

"Derby writes a subtle coming-of-age novel that is engaging from start to finish. Kyle's character is so well developed that many readers will be able to understand the realistic emotions and situations taking place." Libr Media Connect

Deriso, Christine Hurley, 1961-

The Right-Under Club; [by] Christine Hurley Deriso. Delacorte Press 2007 195p $15.99; lib bdg $18.99

Grades: 5 6 7 8   **Fic**

1. Stepfamilies—Fiction 2. Friendship—Fiction

ISBN 978-0-385-73334-2; 978-0-385-90351-6 (lib bdg)   LC 2006019768

Over the summer, five middle school girls form a club based on the fact that they all feel neglected and misunderstood by their blended families

"In this timely novel, Deriso introduces solid characters. . . . The changing voices are easy to navigate and lend charm to the narrative." SLJ

Talia Talk. Delacorte Press 2009 184p $15.99; lib bdg $18.99

Grades: 4 5 6 7   **Fic**

1. Mother-daughter relationship—Fiction 2. Friendship—Fiction 3. School stories 4. Television programs—Fiction

ISBN 978-0-385-73620-6; 0-385-73620-7; 978-0-385-90592-3 (lib bdg); 0-385-90592-0 (lib bdg)

LC 2007-50556

Trying to fit in despite having a loud, embarrassing best friend, eleven-year-old Talia becomes a commentator on her middle school's closed-circuit television program and turns the tables on her mother, a talk show host who has been revealing Talia's most humiliating experiences for years.

This is "breezy, readable, and full of gentle insight." Bull Cent Child Books

Diamand, Emily

Raiders' ransom. Chicken House/Scholastic 2009 334p map $17.99 *

Grades: 4 5 6 7   **Fic**

1. Science fiction 2. Adventure fiction 3. Environmental degradation—Fiction 4. Pirates—Fiction 5. Kidnapping—Fiction 6. Great Britain—Fiction

ISBN 978-0-545-14297-7; 0-545-14297-0

LC 2008-43692

It's the 22nd century and, because of climate change, much of England is underwater. Poor Lilly is out fishing with her trusty sea-cat when greedy raiders pillage the town—and kidnap the prime minister's daughter. Her village blamed, Lilly decides to find the girl.

This is a "captivating story. . . . A well-drawn world, plot twists galore and spunky characters make this one a true page-turner." Kirkus

DiCamillo, Kate, 1964-

Because of Winn-Dixie. Candlewick Press 2000 182p $15.99; pa $6.99 *

Grades: 4 5 6 7   **Fic**

1. Dogs—Fiction 2. Florida—Fiction

ISBN 978-0-7636-0776-0; 0-7636-0776-2; 978-0-7636-4432-1 (pa); 0-7636-4432-3 (pa)

LC 99-34260

A Newbery honor book, 2001

Ten-year-old India Opal Buloni describes her first summer in the town of Naomi, Florida, and all the good things that happen to her because of her big ugly dog Winn-Dixie

"This well-crafted, realistic, and heartwarming story will be read and reread as a new favorite deserving a long-term place on library shelves." SLJ

The magician's elephant; illustrated by Yoko Tanaka. Candlewick Press 2009 201p il $16.99 *

Grades: 4 5 6 7   **Fic**

1. Orphans—Fiction 2. Missing children—Fiction 3. Elephants—Fiction 4. Adventure fiction 5. Siblings—Fiction

ISBN 978-0-7636-4410-9; 0-7636-4410-2

LC 2009-07359

When ten-year-old orphan Peter Augustus Duchene encounters a fortune teller in the marketplace one day and she tells him that his sister, who is presumed dead, is in fact alive, he embarks on a remarkable series of adventures as he desperately tries to find her.

"The profound and deeply affecting emotions at work in the story are bouyed up by the tale's succinct, lyrical text; gentle touches of humor; and uplifting message." Booklist

Mercy Watson to the rescue; illustrated by Chris Van Dusen. Candlewick Press 2005 68p il $12.99 *

Grades: K 1 2 3   **Fic**

1. Pigs—Fiction

ISBN 0-7636-2270-2   LC 2004-51896

After Mercy the pig snuggles to sleep with the Watsons, all three awaken with the bed teetering on the edge of a big hole in the floor.

"Appropriate as both a picture book and a beginning reader, this joyful story combines familiar elements . . . with a raucous telling that lets readers in on the joke. . . . The gouache illustrations are polished to a sheen and have plenty of heft." Booklist

Other titles about Mercy Watson are:

Mercy Watson fights crime (2006)

Mercy Watson goes for a ride (2006)

Mercy Watson: princess in disguise (2007)

Mercy Watson thinks like a pig (2008)

Mercy Watson: something wonky this way comes (2009)

DiCamillo, Kate, 1964-—*Continued*

The miraculous journey of Edward Tulane; illustrated by Bagram Ibatoulline. Candlewick Press 2006 198p il $18.99; pa $6.99 *

Grades: 3 4 5 6   **Fic**

1. Toys—Fiction 2. Rabbits—Fiction

ISBN 0-7636-2589-2; 0-7636-4367-X (pa)

LC 2004-56129

Edward Tulane, a coldhearted and proud toy rabbit, loves only himself until he is separated from the little girl who adores him and travels across the country, acquiring new owners and listening to their hopes, dreams, and histories.

"This achingly beautiful story shows a true master of writing at her very best. . . . Ibatoulline's lovely sepia-toned gouache illustrations and beautifully rendered color plates are exquisite." SLJ

The tale of Despereaux; being the story of a mouse, a princess, some soup, and a spool of thread; illustrated by Timothy Basil Ering. Candlewick Press 2003 267p il $17.99; pa $7.99 *

Grades: 3 4 5 6   **Fic**

1. Fairy tales 2. Mice—Fiction

ISBN 0-7636-1722-9; 0-7636-2529-9 (pa)

LC 2002-34760

Awarded the Newbery Medal, 2004

The adventures of Despereaux Tilling, a small mouse of unusual talents, the princess that he loves, the servant girl who longs to be a princess, and a devious rat determined to bring them all to ruin

"Forgiveness, light, love, and soup. These essential ingredients combine into a tale that is as soul stirring as it is delicious. . . . Ering's soft pencil illustrations reflect the story's charm." Booklist

Dickens, Charles, 1812-1870

A Christmas carol; [by] Charles Dickens; [illustrated by] Brett Helquist; [abridged by Josh Greenhut] HarperCollins 2009 unp il $17.99; lib bdg $18.89 *

Grades: 3 4 5 6   **Fic**

1. Christmas—Fiction 2. Ghost stories 3. Great Britain—History—19th century—Fiction

ISBN 978-0-06-165099-4; 0-06-165099-4; 978-0-06-165100-7 (lib bdg); 0-06-165100-1 (lib bdg)

LC 2008044031

A miser learns the true meaning of Christmas when three ghostly visitors review his past and foretell his future.

"Sacrificing none of Dickens's rich language, this retelling reads beautifully. The artist uses watercolor, pencil, and pastel to create cinematic artwork that contains amusing details; additionally, there are a number of pen-and-ink vignettes that help set the scenes. A winning combination of sparkling prose and exciting art." SLJ

DiSalvo, DyAnne, 1960-

The sloppy copy slipup; [by] DyAnne DiSalvo. Holiday House 2006 103p il $16.95; pa $6.95

Grades: 2 3 4   **Fic**

1. School stories 2. Authorship—Fiction

ISBN 0-8234-1947-9; 0-8234-2189-9 (pa)

Fourth-grader Brian Higman worries about how his teacher Miss Fromme—nicknamed The General—will react when he fails to hand in a writing assignment, but he ends up being able to tell his story, after all

"DiSalvo combines spot-on humor, vivid classroom scenes, and tension that builds from the first page, and Brian's story . . . will keep children eagerly engaged." Booklist

DiTerlizzi, Tony

Kenny & the dragon; [by] Tony DiTerlizzi. Simon & Schuster Books for Young Readers 2008 151p $15.99

Grades: 4 5 6 7   **Fic**

1. Dragons—Fiction 2. Knights and knighthood—Fiction 3. Rabbits—Fiction

ISBN 978-1-4169-3977-1; 1-4169-3977-6

LC 2008-7309

Book-loving Kenny the rabbit has few friends in his farming community, so when one, bookstore owner George, is sent to kill another, gentle dragon Grahame, Kenny must find a way to prevent their battle while satisfying the dragon-crazed townspeople.

"DiTerlizzi's novel is lighthearted and his informal pencil sketches enhance the creative interpretation of what would otherwise be a simple animal story." Publ Wkly

The Nixie's song; [by] Tony DiTerlizzi and Holly Black. Simon & Schuster 2007 162p (Beyond The Spiderwick Chronicles) $10.99

Grades: 3 4 5 6   **Fic**

1. Fantasy fiction 2. Florida—Fiction

ISBN 978-0-689-87131-3

"Eleven-year-old Nicholas Vargas only thinks his life has been turned upside down after his developer father remarries and moves his new wife and daughter into the soon-to-be completed Mangrove Hollow. But an 'expedition' to a nearby lake turns up a little nixie with a giant problem." Publisher's note

"Fans of *The Spiderwick Chronicles*, rejoice! The saga continues, brimming with the same sly humor . . . that marked the original series." Booklist

Divakaruni, Chitra Banerjee, 1956-

The conch bearer. Roaring Brook Press 2003 265p (Brotherhood of the conch) $16.95; lib bdg $23.90

Grades: 5 6 7 8   **Fic**

1. Magic—Fiction 2. India—Fiction

ISBN 978-0-7613-1935-1; 0-7613-1935-2; 978-0-7613-2793-6 (lib bdg); 0-7613-2793-2 (lib bdg)

LC 2003-8578

"A Neal Porter book"

In India, a healer invites twelve-year-old Anand to join him on a quest to return a magical conch to its safe and rightful home, high in the Himalayan mountains

"Divakaruni keeps her tale fresh and riveting." Publ Wkly

Divakaruni, Chitra Banerjee, 1956-—*Continued*
Other titles in this series are:
The mirror of fire and dreaming (2005)
Shadowland (2009)

Doder, Joshua, 1968-
A dog called Grk. Delacorte Press 2007 249p
hardcover o.p. pa $6.50
Grades: 5 6 7   **Fic**
1. Dogs—Fiction 2. Adventure fiction
ISBN   978-0-385-73359-5;   0-385-73359-3;
978-0-440-42147-4 (pa); 0-440-42147-0 (pa)
LC 2006-46258
A British schoolboy finds adventure when he travels
to a dangerous foreign country to return a small dog to
its rightful owner.
"This is fast-paced and entertaining." Booklist
Other titles about Grk are:
Grk and the Pelotti gang (2007)
Grk and the hot dog trail (2008)
Grk: Operation Tortoise (2009)
Grk smells a rat (2009)

Dodge, Mary Mapes, 1830-1905
Hans Brinker, or, The silver skates; [by] Mary
Mapes Dodge. Aladdin Paperbacks 2002 381p pa
$4.99
Grades: 4 5 6   **Fic**
1. Ice skating—Fiction 2. Netherlands—Fiction
ISBN 0-689-84909-5   LC 2001092790
"Aladdin classics"
First published 1865
A new friend gives Hans and his sister Gretel enough
money for one pair of ice skates, so Hans insists that
Gretel enter the grand competition for silver skates,
while he seeks the great Doctor who consents to try to
restore their father's memory

Doherty, Berlie
The goblin baby; [illustrated by Lesley Harker]
Random House 2009 128p il (Stepping stone
book) lib bdg $11.99; pa $4.99
Grades: 2 3 4   **Fic**
1. Fantasy fiction 2. Fairies—Fiction
ISBN 978-0-375-95841-0 (lib bdg); 0-375-95841-X
(lib bdg); 978-0-375-85841-3 (pa); 0-375-85841-5 (pa)
LC 2008-37097
First published 2004 in the United Kingdom with title:
The starburster
After nine-year-old Tam's baby sister is stolen away
by faeries and replaced by a goblin baby, he must journey to the land of the faeries to retrieve her and bring
her back home.
"Simple but engaging line drawings bring the characters and the trials Tam must face to life. A well-told tale
worth sharing." SLJ

Donofrio, Beverly
Thank you, Lucky Stars; [by] Beverly Donofrio.
Schwartz & Wade 2008 234p $16.99; lib bdg
$19.99
Grades: 4 5 6   **Fic**
1. Friendship—Fiction 2. Bullies—Fiction 3. School
stories
ISBN   978-0-375-83964-1;   0-375-83964-X;
978-0-375-93964-8 (lib bdg); 0-375-93964-4 (lib bdg)
LC 2007-00853
Ally has looked forward to a new school year, especially since she and her best friend, Betsy, have planned
since kindergarten to sing in the fifth grade talent show,
but Betsy has a new best friend and Ally, shy and prone
to cry, is targeted by bullies and a strange new student
who is looking for a friend.
"Young readers with friendship issues of their own
may find it easy to identify with shy Ally and rejoice at
her final performance, while the bittersweet ending may
come as a surprise." Booklist

Donovan, Gail, 1962-
In loving memory of Gorfman T. Frog;
[illustrated by Janet Pedersen] Dutton Children's
Books 2009 180p il $15.99
Grades: 3 4 5   **Fic**
1. Frogs—Fiction 2. School stories 3. Family life—
Fiction
ISBN 978-0-525-42085-9; 0-525-42085-1
LC 2008-13897
When irrepressible fifth-grader Josh finds a five-
legged frog in his backyard pond, it leads to him learn-
ing a lot about amphibians—and himself.
"Pedersen's full-page illustrations ramp up the comedy
and action, and Donovan ably shows how the school
world of kids is separate and little understood by adults."
Booklist

Dorris, Michael
Morning Girl. Hyperion Bks. for Children 1992
74p pa $4.99 hardcover o.p.
Grades: 4 5 6 7   **Fic**
1. Taino Indians—Fiction 2. America—Exploration—
Fiction
ISBN 0-7868-1358-X (pa)   LC 92-52989
Twelve year old Morning Girl, a Taino Indian who
loves the day, and her younger brother Star Boy, who
loves the night, take turns describing their life on a Ba-
hamian island in 1492; in Morning Girl's last narrative,
she witnesses the arrival of the first Europeans to her
world
"The author uses a lyrical, yet easy-to-follow, style to
place these compelling characters in historical context.
. . . Dorris does a superb job of showing that family dynamics are complicated, regardless of time and place.
. . . A touching glimpse into the humanity that connects
us all." Horn Book

Sees Behind Trees. Hyperion Bks. for Children
1996 104p pa $4.99 hardcover o.p.
Grades: 4 5 6 7   **Fic**
1. Native Americans—Fiction 2. Vision disorders—
Fiction
ISBN 0-7868-1357-1 (pa)   LC 96-15859

Dorris, Michael—*Continued*

"For the partially sighted Walnut, it is impossible to prove his right to a grown-up name by hitting a target with his bow and arrow. With his highly developed senses, however, he demonstrates that he can do something even better: he can see 'what cannot be seen' which earns him the name Sees Behind Trees. . . . Set in sixteenth-century America, this richly imagined and gorgeously written rite-of-passage story has the gravity of legend. Moreover, it has buoyant humor and the immediacy of a compelling story that is peopled with multidimensional characters." Booklist

Dowd, Siobhan

The London Eye mystery. David Fickling Books 2008 c2007 322p $15.99; lib bdg $18.99; pa $7.50 *

Grades: 5 6 7 8   Fic
1. Asperger's syndrome—Fiction 2. Missing children—Fiction 3. Siblings—Fiction 4. Cousins—Fiction 5. Mystery fiction 6. London (England)—Fiction
ISBN   978-0-375-84976-3;   0-375-84976-9; 978-0-375-94976-0 (lib bdg); 0-375-84976-3 (lib bdg); 978-0-385-75184-1 (pa); 0-385-75184-2 (pa)
LC 2007-15119
First published 2007 in the United Kingdom
When Ted and Kat's cousin Salim disappears from the London Eye ferris wheel, the two siblings must work together—Ted with his brain that is "wired differently" and impatient Kat—to try to solve the mystery of what happened to Salim.
"Everything rings true here, the family relationships, the quirky connections of Ted's mental circuitry, and . . . the mystery. . . . A page turner with heft." Booklist

Dowell, Frances O'Roark

Chicken boy. Atheneum Books for Young Readers 2005 201p $15.95; pa $5.99 *
Grades: 4 5 6 7   Fic
1. Chickens—Fiction 2. Friendship—Fiction 3. Family life—Fiction
ISBN 0-689-85816-7; 1-4169-3482-0 (pa)
LC 2004-10928
Since the death of his mother, Tobin's family life and school life have been in disarray, but after he starts raising chickens with his seventh-grade classmate, Henry, everything starts to fall into place.
"There is no glib resolution, here. But the strong narration and the child's struggle with forgiveness make for poignant, aching drama." Booklist

Dovey Coe. Atheneum Bks. for Young Readers 2000 181p $16; pa $5.99 *
Grades: 5 6 7 8   Fic
1. Mountain life—Fiction 2. North Carolina—Fiction
ISBN 0-689-83174-9; 0-689-84667-3 (pa)
LC 99-46870
When accused of murder in her North Carolina mountain town in 1928, Dovey Coe, a stronged-willed twelve-year-old girl, comes to a new understanding of others, including her deaf brother
"Dowell has created a memorable character in Dovey, quick-witted and honest to a fault. . . . This is a delightful book, thoughtful and full of substance." Booklist

Falling in. Atheneum Books for Young Readers 2010 245p il $16.99 *
Grades: 4 5 6 7   Fic
1. Fantasy fiction
ISBN 978-1-4169-5032-5; 1-4169-5032-X
LC 2009-10412
Middle-schooler Isabelle Bean follows a mouse's squeak into a closet and falls into a parallel universe where the children believe she is the witch they have feared for years, finally come to devour them.
"This perfectly paced story has enough realistic elements to appeal even to nonfantasy readers." Booklist

The kind of friends we used to be. Atheneum Books for Young Readers 2009 234p $16.99
Grades: 5 6 7 8   Fic
1. Friendship—Fiction 2. School stories
ISBN 978-1-4169-5031-8; 1-4169-5031-1
LC 2008-22245
Sequel to: The secret language of girls (2004)
Twelve-year-olds Kate and Marylin, friends since preschool, draw further apart as Marylin becomes involved in student government and cheerleading, while Kate wants to play guitar and write songs, and both develop unlikely friendships with other girls and boys.
"Dowell gets middle-school dynamics exactly right, and while her empathetic portraits of Kate and Marylin are genuine and heartfelt, even secondary characters are memorable. A realistic and humorous look at the trials and tribulations of growing up and growing independent." SLJ

Phineas L. Macguire erupts! the first experiment. Atheneum Books for Young Readers 2006 167p il (From the highly scientific notebooks of Phineas L. MacGuire) $15.95; pa $4.99
Grades: 2 3 4   Fic
1. School stories 2. Science—Experiments—Fiction
ISBN   978-1-4169-0195-2;   1-4169-0195-7; 978-1-4169-4734-9 (pa); 1-4169-4734-5 (pa)
LC 2005-12605
Fourth-grade science whiz Phineas MacGuire is forced to team up with the new boy in class on a science fair project, but the boy's quirky personality causes Phineas to wonder if they have any chance of winning.
"The type is large and well spaced, and black-and-white art playfully captures the characters. . . . Budding scientists will find instructions for their own experiments at the end of the book." Booklist
Other titles in this series are:
Phineas L. MacGuire . . . gets slimed! (2007)
Phineas L. MacGuire . . . blasts off! (2008)

The secret language of girls. Atheneum Books for Young Readers 2004 247p $15.95; pa $5.99
Grades: 5 6 7 8   Fic
1. Friendship—Fiction 2. School stories
ISBN 0-689-84421-2; 978-1-4169-0717-6 (pa)
LC 2003-12026
Marylin and Kate have been friends since nursery school, but when Marylin becomes a middle school cheerleader and Kate begins to develop other interests, their relationship is put to the test.
"Excellent characterization, an accurate portrayal of the painful and often cruel machinations of preteens, and

Dowell, Frances O'Roark—*Continued*

evocative dialogue will make this tale resonate with most readers." SLJ

Followed by: The kind of friends we used to be (2009)

Shooting the moon. Atheneum Books for Young Readers 2008 163p $16.99; pa $5.99 *

Grades: 4 5 6 7   **Fic**

1. Vietnam War, 1961-1975—Fiction 2. Soldiers—Fiction 3. Family life—Fiction

ISBN   978-1-4169-2690-0;   1-4169-2690-9; 978-1-4169-7986-9 (pa); 1-4169-7986-7 (pa)

LC 2006-100347

Boston Globe-Horn Book Award honor book: Fiction and Poetry (2008)

When her brother is sent to fight in Vietnam, twelve-year-old Jamie begins to reconsider the army world that she has grown up in.

"The clear, well-paced first-person prose is perfectly matched to this novel's spare setting and restrained plot. . . . This [is a] thoughtful and satisfying story. . . . Readers will find beauty in its resolution, and will leave this eloquent heroine reluctantly." SLJ

Where I'd like to be. Atheneum Bks. for Young Readers 2003 232p hardcover o.p. pa $5.99

Grades: 4 5 6 7   **Fic**

1. Foster home care—Fiction 2. Tennessee—Fiction 3. Friendship—Fiction

ISBN 0-689-84420-4; 0-689-87067-1 (pa)

LC 2002-2183

"When a new girl moves into the East Tennessee Children's Home, her charisma has an immediate effect on Maddie, the story's narrator. Maddie's scrapbooks filled with pictures of the houses she dreams of living in serve as a catalyst for Murphy, as she gathers a fledgling group of unlikely friends around her. . . . The foster children's backgrounds are believable, diverse, and engaging, and readers familiar with eastern Tennessee will appreciate the references to real towns and cities that are sprinkled throughout the text." SLJ

Downer, Ann, 1960-

Hatching magic. Atheneum Bks. for Young Readers 2003 242p $16.95; pa $5.99 *

Grades: 4 5 6 7   **Fic**

1. Dragons—Fiction 2. Magic—Fiction

ISBN 0-689-83400-4; 0-689-87057-4 (pa)

LC 00-56570

When a thirteenth-century wizard confronts twenty-first century Boston while seeking his pet dragon, he is followed by a rival wizard and a very unhappy demon, but eleven-year-old Theodora Oglethorpe may hold the secret to setting everything right

"With likable characters, and laced with plenty of humor and adventure, Downer's fantasy will have solid appeal for young genre fans." Booklist

Another title about Theodora is:

The dragon of never-was (2006)

Draanen, Wendelin van

Flipped. Knopf 2001 212p $14.95; pa $8.95

Grades: 6 7 8 9   **Fic**

ISBN 0-375-81174-5; 0-375-82544-4 (pa)

LC 2001-29238

In alternating chapters, eighth-graders Juli and Bryce describe how their feelings about themselves, each other, and their families have changed over the years

"There's lots of laugh-out-loud egg puns and humor in this novel. There's also, however, a substantial amount of serious social commentary woven in, as well as an exploration of the importance of perspective in relationships." SLJ

Sammy Keyes and the hotel thief. Knopf 1998 163p il hardcover o.p. pa $6.50 *

Grades: 4 5 6 7   **Fic**

1. Mystery fiction

ISBN 978-0-679-88839-0; 0-679-89264-8 (pa)

LC 97-40776

Thirteen-year-old Sammy's penchant for speaking her mind gets her in trouble when she involves herself in the investigation of a robbery at the "seedy" hotel across the street from the seniors' building where she is living with her grandmother

"This is a breezy novel with vivid characters." Bull Cent Child Books

Other titles about Sammy Keyes are:

Sammy Keyes and the art of deception (2003)
Sammy Keyes and the cold hard cash (2008)
Sammy Keyes and the curse of Moustache Mary (2000)
Sammy Keyes and the dead giveaway (2005)
Sammy Keyes and the Hollywood mummy (2001)
Sammy Keyes and the psycho Kitty Queen (2004)
Sammy Keyes and the runaway elf (1999)
Sammy Keyes and the search for snake eyes (2002)
Sammy Keyes and the Sisters of Mercy (1999)
Sammy Keyes and the skeleton man (1998)
Sammy Keyes and the wild things (2007)

Shredderman: Secret identity; illustrated by Brian Biggs. Knopf 2004 138p il $12.95; pa $5.99 *

Grades: 3 4 5   **Fic**

1. School stories 2. Superheroes—Fiction

ISBN 0-375-82351-4; 0-440-41912-3 (pa)

LC 2003-17856

Fifth-grader Nolan Byrd, tired of being called names by the class bully, has a secret identity—Shredderman!

"This entertaining story . . . will keep even reluctant readers laughing and wanting more stories about this cyber superhero. Droll, black-and-white cartoons are a perfect accompaniment to the clever text." SLJ

Other titles about Shredderman are:

Shredderman: Attack of the tagger (2004)
Shredderman: Enemy spy (2005)
Shredderman: Meet the gecko (2005)

Drake, Salamanda

Dragonsdale; illustrations by Gilly Marklew. Chicken House/Scholastic 2007 269p il (Dragonsdale) $16.99 *

Grades: 3 4 5   **Fic**

1. Dragons—Fiction 2. Fantasy fiction
ISBN 978-0-439-87173-0; 0-439-87173-5

LC 2006-32890

Cara yearns to ride her beloved Skydancer, a rare Goldenbrow dragon, but her father refuses to permit her to fly and she must be content with mucking out stalls and helping raise young dragons at the famed stud and training farm known as Dragonsdale.

"This will delight precisely the audience it's meant to—young girls who find tame dragons captivating." Booklist

Followed by: Riding the storm (2008)

Draper, Sharon M., 1948-

Little Sister is not my name. Scholastic Press 2009 102p (Sassy) $14.99

Grades: 3 4 5   **Fic**

1. Size—Fiction 2. Family life—Fiction 3. African Americans—Fiction
ISBN 978-0-545-07151-2; 0-545-07151-8

LC 2008-15634

Fashion-savy Sassy does not like being the smallest student in her fourth-grade class, until a family emergency calls for a pint-sized hero.

"Draper hits her middle-grade target in this cheerful yet reflective novel about feeling appreciated and finding one's place. . . . Filled with energy and opinion, Sassy more than lives up to her name." Publ Wkly

Other titles in this series are:
The birthday storm (2009)
The silver secret (2010)

Out of my mind. Atheneum 2010 295p $16.99 *

Grades: 5 6 7 8   **Fic**

1. Cerebral palsy—Fiction
ISBN 978-1-4169-7170-2; 1-4169-7170-X

LC 2009-18404

"Fifth-grader Melody has cerebral palsy, a condition that affects her body but not her mind. Although she is unable to walk, talk, or feed or care for herself, she can read, think, and feel. A brilliant person is trapped inside her body, determined to make her mark in the world despite her physical limitations. . . . Told in Melody's voice, this highly readable, compelling novel quickly establishes her determination and intelligence and the almost insurmountable challenges she faces. . . . Uplifting and upsetting." Booklist

Du Bois, William Pène, 1916-1993

The twenty-one balloons; written and illustrated by William Pène Du Bois. Viking 1947 179p il $16.99; pa $5.99

Grades: 5 6 7 8   **Fic**

1. Balloons—Fiction
ISBN 0-670-73441-1; 0-14-032097-0 (pa)
Awarded the Newbery Medal, 1948

"Professor Sherman set off on a flight across the Pacific in a giant balloon, but three weeks later the headlines read 'Professor Sherman in wrong ocean with too many balloons.' This book is concerned with the professor's explanation of this phenomenon. His account of his one stopover on the island of Krakatoa which blew up with barely a minute to spare to allow time for his escape, is the highlight of this hilarious narrative." Ont Libr Rev

Dudley, David L.

The bicycle man. Clarion Books 2005 249p $16

Grades: 4 5 6   **Fic**

1. Country life—Fiction 2. African Americans—Fiction 3. Georgia—Fiction
ISBN 0-618-54233-7   LC 2005-06409

In poor, rural Georgia in 1927, twelve-year-old Carrisa and her suspicious mama take in an elderly drifter with a shiny bicycle, never expecting how profoundly his wise and patient ways will affect them.

Readers "will find complex characters and rich themes. . . . There is much here to digest and a wealth of material for book discussions." SLJ

Duey, Kathleen

Lara and the gray mare; by Kathleen Duey. Dutton Children's Books 2005 140p (Hoofbeats) hardcover o.p. pa $4.99

Grades: 4 5 6   **Fic**

1. Horses—Fiction 2. Ireland—Fiction
ISBN 0-525-47332-7; 0-14-240230-3 (pa)

LC 2004-53521

While her father is away fighting the Normans and other Irish clans, nine-year-old Lara works hard to help harvest food and also cares for the pregnant gray mare that she loves

"Writing with a keen appreciation for everyday goings-on in thirteenth-century Ireland and an unusual ability to bring the past to life, Duey creates a convincing setting, a thoroughly likable heroine, and a strong narrative." Booklist

Other titles in the Hoofbeats series are:
Lara and the Moon-colored filly (book two) (2005)
Lara at Athnery Castle (book three) (2005)
Lara at the silent place (book four) (2005)
Silence and Lily (2007)

Dunn, Mark, 1956-

The age altertron. MacAdam/Cage 2009 149p (The calamitous adventures of Rodney and Wayne, cosmic repairboys) $12.95

Grades: 4 5 6 7   **Fic**

1. Time travel—Fiction 2. Science—Experiments—Fiction 3. Scientists—Fiction 4. Twins—Fiction 5. Brothers—Fiction
ISBN 978-1-59692-345-4; 1-59692-345-8

In a small, mid-twentieth century town that is secretly being used as a laboratory, thirteen-year-old twins Rodney and Wayne and their physicist friend, Professor Johnson, face a series of calamities including a time experiment that sends the boys from infancy to old age in just a few days.

"The boys are fun heroes, and the nutty, eccentric pro-

Dunn, Mark, 1956-—*Continued*

fessor is what one would expect in a madcap world. The story's tongue-in-cheek absurdity is charming, and competent readers will love the zany adventures that evolve from a world turned upside down." SLJ

Dunrea, Olivier, 1953-

Hanne's quest; [by] Olivier Dunrea. Philomel Books 2005 95p il $16.99

Grades: 3 4 5   **Fic**

1. Fairy tales 2. Chickens—Fiction 3. Scotland—Fiction

ISBN 0-399-24216-3   LC 2004-9091

On an island off the coast of Scotland, a young hen must prove herself pure, wise, and brave in a quest to help her beloved owner, Mem Pocket, from losing her family's farm.

"Beautifully composed and often darkly atmospheric, the handsome full-page paintings rival . . . those in the best picture books. This handsome, well-written book will find a rapt audience amoung children who prefer sturdy, homespun fairy tales." Booklist

DuPrau, Jeanne, 1944-

The city of Ember. Random House 2003 270p (Books of Ember) $15.95; lib bdg $17.99; pa $6.99

Grades: 5 6 7 8   **Fic**

1. Science fiction

ISBN 0-375-82273-9; 0-375-92274-1 (lib bdg); 0-385-73628-2 (pa)   LC 2002-10239

"More than 200 years after an unspecified holocaust, the residents of Ember have lost all knowledge of anything beyond the area illuminated by the floodlamps on their buildings. . . . Food and other supplies are running low, and the power failures that plunge the town into impenetrable darkness are becoming longer and more frequent. Then Lina, a young foot messenger, discovers a damaged document from the mysterious Builders that hints at a way out." SLJ

"The writing and storytelling are agreeably spare and remarkably suspenseful." Horn Book

Other titles in this series are:

The people of Sparks (2004)
The prophet of Yonwood (2006)
The diamond of Darkhold (2008)

Durand, Hallie

Dessert first; illustrations by Christine Davenier. Atheneum Books for Young Readers 2009 153p il $14.99

Grades: 3 4 5   **Fic**

1. School stories 2. Restaurants—Fiction 3. Family life—Fiction

ISBN 978-1-4169-6385-1; 1-4169-6385-5

LC 2008-11390

Third-grader Dessert's love of treats leads to a change in her large family's dinner routine, then an awful mistake, and later a true sacrifice after her teacher, Mrs. Howdy Doody, urges students to march to the beat of their own drums

"Experiences are delightfully imagined through Des-

sert's realistic, child-centered perspective. Short chapters interspersed with Davenier's pen-and-ink washes add immediacy to the text." Kirkus

Durango, Julia, 1967-

The walls of Cartagena; by Julia Durango; illustrated by Tom Pohrt. Simon & Schuster Books for Young Readers 2008 152p il $15.99

Grades: 5 6 7 8   **Fic**

1. Slavery—Fiction 2. Leprosy—Fiction 3. Catholic Church—Fiction 4. Colombia—Fiction

ISBN 978-1-4169-4102-6; 1-4169-4102-9

LC 2007041861

Thirteen-year-old Calepino, an African slave in the seventeenth-century Caribbean city of Cartagena, works as a translator for a Jesuit priest who tends to newly-arrived slaves and, after working for a Jewish doctor in a leper colony and helping an Angolan boy and his mother escape, he realizes his true calling

"Illustrated with occasional small ink sketches, the ultimate rescue adventure is gripping, but more compelling is the authentic history of people desperate and brave." Booklist

Durbin, William, 1951-

Blackwater Ben. Wendy Lamb Bks. 2003 199p hardcover o.p. pa $5.99

Grades: 5 6 7 8   **Fic**

1. Lumber and lumbering—Fiction 2. Father-son relationship—Fiction 3. Frontier and pioneer life—Fiction 4. Minnesota—Fiction

ISBN 0-385-72928-6; 0-440-42008-3 (pa)

LC 2002-155586

In the winter of 1898, a seventh-grade boy drops out of school to work with his father, the cook at Blackwater Logging Camp in Minnesota

"Lively details about logging add depth to this warm, colorful historical novel." Booklist

Dutton, Sandra

Mary Mae and the gospel truth. Houghton Mifflin Books for Children 2010 $15

Grades: 4 5 6   **Fic**

1. Family—Fiction 2. Mother-daughter relationship—Fiction 3. Christian life—Fiction 4. School stories 5. Creationism—Fiction 6. Ohio—Fiction

ISBN 978-0-547-24966-7; 0-547-24966-7

LC 2009-49706

Ten-year-old Mary Mae, living with her parents in fossil-rich southern Ohio, tries to reconcile, despite her mother's strong disapproval, her family's Creationist beliefs with the prehistoric fossils she studies in school.

"Very few books for this age group tackle religious subjects as this one does, in a way that shows respect for all sides. Dutton allows Mary Mae to retain both her questions and her faith; instead of a definitive answer, she shows evolutionists and creationists working to find a small, shared piece of middle ground. Mary Mae is a memorable character-spunky but not defiant-whose search for truth drives the narrative." Kirkus

Dyer, Heather, 1970-

Ibby's magic weekend; illustrated by Peter Bailey. Chicken House 2008 140p il $16.99

Grades: 2 3 4 5   **Fic**

1. Magic—Fiction 2. Magicians—Fiction 3. Cousins—Fiction

ISBN 0-545-03209-1; 978-0-545-03209-4

While visiting her two troublemaking cousins, Ibby learns about a magic box the boys found in the attic in their country home. She soon stumbles upon the strange tale of Uncle Godfrey, a professional magician who mysteriously vanished many years ago.

"This action-filled story is just right for beginning chapter book readers, who will be fascinated with the magic as well as the personalities. Bailey's black-and-white line drawings help make the book accessible to reluctant readers." SLJ

Eager, Edward, 1911-1964

Half magic; illustrated by N.M. Bodecker; introduction by Jack Gantos. 50th anniversary ed. Harcourt 2004 c1954 217p il $18.95 *

Grades: 4 5 6   **Fic**

1. Fantasy fiction

ISBN 0-15-205302-6

A reissue with a new introduction of the title first published 1954

Faced with a dull summer in the city, Jane, Mark, Katharine, and Martha suddenly find themselves involved in a series of extraordinary adventures after Jane discovers an ordinary-looking coin that seems to grant wishes

"Entertaining and suspenseful fare for readers of make-believe." Booklist

Other titles in this series are:

Knight's castle (1956)

Magic by the lake (1957)

The time garden (1958)

Magic or not? illustrated by N.M. Bodecker. Harcourt Brace & Co. 1999 c1959 197p il hardcover o.p. pa $5.40

Grades: 4 5 6   **Fic**

1. Fantasy fiction

ISBN 0-15-202081-0; 0-15-202080-2 (pa)

LC 99-22566

A reissue of the title first published 1959

"An Odyssey/Harcourt Brace young classic."

When the family moves to Connecticut, twins James and Laura make new friends and begin a series of unusual adventures after discovering an old well that seems to be magic in their backyard

"The children are lifelike and likable, their doings are entertaining." Booklist

Another title in this series is:

The well-wishers (1960)

Seven-day magic; illustrated by N.M. Bodecker. Harcourt Brace & Co. 1999 190p il hardcover o.p. pa $6 *

Grades: 4 5 6   **Fic**

1. Fantasy fiction

ISBN 0-15-202079-9; 0-15-202078-0 (pa)

LC 99-22563

A reissue of the title first published 1962

"Five children find a magic book that describes themselves, and realize that they can create their own magic by wishing with the book. . . . The children are lively and a bit precocious. . . . [The book has] humor, and some fresh and imaginative situations." Bull Cent Child Books

Easton, Kelly, 1960-

The outlandish adventures of Liberty Aimes; illustrated by Greg Swearingen. Wendy Lamb Books 2009 214p il $15.99; lib bdg $18.99

Grades: 3 4 5 6   **Fic**

1. Runaway children—Fiction 2. Family life—Fiction 3. Inventors—Fiction 4. Adventure fiction

ISBN 978-0-375-83771-5; 0-375-83771-X; 978-0-375-93771-2 (lib bdg); 0-375-93771-4 (lib bdg)

LC 2008-22119

Ten-year-old Libby Aimes escapes her prison-like home by using a strange concoction of her father's, then tries to make her way to the boarding school of her dreams, aided by various people and animals.

"The understated humor and friendly, imperturbable tone of the narration bring to mind the fantasies of Eva Ibbotson. The charming illustrations sprinkled throughout add immense appeal to this warm, delightfully odd fantasy." SLJ

Eboch, Chris

The ghost on the stairs. Aladdin 2009 169p (Haunted) pa $5.99

Grades: 4 5 6   **Fic**

1. Ghost stories 2. Siblings—Fiction 3. Television programs—Fiction 4. Colorado—Fiction 5. Mystery fiction

ISBN 978-1-4169-7548-9 (pa); 1-4169-7548-9 (pa)

"Thirteen-year-old Jon and 11-year-old Tania's mother works for a ghost-hunting television show and is married to the producer. When the siblings travel to Colorado with the show, Tania is shocked to discover that she can see the ghost of a sad young bride floating down the hotel stairs. Tania convinces her brother to assist her in solving the mystery of the dead woman's origins. . . . [This] is a fun read with some thrills and chills and has the added bonus of some genuine, compassionate personalities." SLJ

Other titles in this series are:

The riverboat phantom (2009)

The knight in the shadows (2009)

Eckert, Allan W., 1931-

Incident at Hawk's Hill; with illustrations by John Schoenherr. Little, Brown 1998 173p il hardcover o.p. pa $5.95

Grades: 6 7 8 9   **Fic**

1. Badgers—Fiction 2. Wilderness survival—Fiction 3. Saskatchewan—Fiction

ISBN 0-316-21905-3; 0-316-20948-1 (pa)

A Newbery Medal honor book, 1972

First published 1971

This account of an actual incident in Saskatchewan at the turn of the century tells of six-year-old Ben Macdonald, more attuned to animals than to people, who gets

Eckert, Allan W., 1931-—*Continued*
lost on the prairie and is nurtured by a female badger for
two months before being found. Although a strange bond
continues between the boy and the badger, the parents'
understanding of their son and his communication with
them improve as a result of the bizarre experience
"A very deeply moving, well written book." Jr Bookshelf
Followed by Return to Hawk's Hill (1998)

Edwards, Michelle
The talent show. Harcourt 2002 56p il hardcover
o.p. pa $5.95 *
Grades: 1 2 3   Fic
1. School stories
ISBN 0-15-216403-0; 0-15-205760-9 (pa)
LC 2001-1227
"A Jackson friends book"
Second-grader Howardina Geraldina Paulina Maxina
Gardenia Smith is sure she will be the star of the talent
show, but when she gets up to sing at the dress rehears-
al, she gets stage fright
"This combines strong characterizations with a heart-
felt story that touches on real emotions. The pen-and-ink
and watercolor-and-gouache artwork is very imagina-
tive." Booklist
Other titles in the Jackson friends series are:
Pa Lia's first day (1999)
Stinky Stern forever (2005)
Zero grandparents (2001)

Ehrlich, Amy, 1942-
The Snow Queen; [by] Hans Christian
Andersen; retold by Amy Ehrlich; [illustrated by]
Susan Jeffers. Dutton Children's Books 2006 40p
il $16.99 *
Grades: 2 3 4   Fic
1. Andersen, Hans Christian, 1805-1875—Adaptations
2. Fairy tales
ISBN 0-525-47694-6   LC 2006004415
A revised reissue of the edition published 1982 by
Dial Books
The strength of a little girl's love enables her to over-
come many obstacles and free a boy from the Snow
Queen's spell

Elish, Dan, 1960-
The attack of the frozen woodchucks; by Dan
Elish; illustrations by Greg Call. Laura Geringer
Books 2008 247p il $16.99; lib bdg $17.89; pa
$6.99
Grades: 4 5 6   Fic
1. Extraterrestrial beings—Fiction 2. Marmots—Fic-
tion 3. New York (N.Y.)—Fiction 4. Science fiction
ISBN 978-0-06-113870-6; 0-06-113870-3;
978-0-06-113871-3 (lib bdg); 0-06-113871-1 (lib bdg);
978-0-06-113872-0 (pa); 0-06-113872-X (pa)
LC 2006-102962
When extraterrestrial woodchucks attack, ten-year-old
Jimmy, his two-and-a-half-year-old sister, friend William,
and an eccentric classmate who has built a flying saucer
in her Manhattan brownstone, join forces to save the uni-

verse.
"This is ridiculous, over-the-top fun all the way. . . .
Science fiction fans who welcome absurdity as much as
planet-hopping in their reads will find this an ideal balance of both." Bull Cent Child Books

Elliott, Laura
Give me liberty; [by] L. M. Elliott. Katherine
Tegen Books 2006 376p $16.99; lib bdg $17.89;
pa $7.99
Grades: 5 6 7 8   Fic
1. United States—History—1775-1783, Revolution—
Fiction 2. Virginia—Fiction
ISBN 0-06-074421-9; 0-06-074422-7 (lib bdg);
0-06-074423-5 (pa)
Follows the life of thirteen-year-old Nathaniel Dunn,
from May 1774 to December 1775, as he serves his
indentureship with a music teacher in Williamsburg, Virginia, and witnesses the growing rift between patriots
and loyalists, culminating in the American Revolution.
"Elliott packs a great deal of historical detail into a
novel already filled with action, well-drawn characters,
and a sympathetic understanding of many points of
view." Booklist

Ellis, Deborah, 1960-
I am a taxi. Groundwood Books/House of
Anansi Press 2006 205p (The cocalero novels)
$16.95; pa $9.95
Grades: 5 6 7 8   Fic
1. Bolivia—Fiction 2. Cocaine—Fiction
ISBN 978-0-88899-735-7; 0-88899-735-3;
978-0-88899-736-4 (pa); 0-88899-736-1 (pa)
"Diego, 12, lives in prison in the city of Cochabamba,
Bolivia, stuck there with his parents, who have been
falsely arrested for smuggling drugs. He attends school
and works as a 'taxi,' running errands for the inmates in
the great street market. Then his friend, Mando, persuades him to make big money, and the boys find themselves stomping coca leaves in cocaine pits in the jungle.
. . . Readers will be caught up by the nonstop action in
the prison, and also in the jungle survival adventure."
Booklist
Followed by Sacred leaf (2007)

Ellis, Sarah, 1952-
The several lives of Orphan Jack; pictures by
Bruno St-Aubin. Douglas & McIntyre 2003 84p il
hardcover o.p. pa $7.95
Grades: 3 4 5 6   Fic
1. Orphans—Fiction 2. Adventure fiction
ISBN 0-88899-529-6; 0-88899-618-7 (pa)
"A Groundwood book"
When, at the age of twelve, he is sent out from the
Opportunities School for Orphans and Foundlings to be
a bookkeeper's apprentice, Jack finds his heretofore pre-
dictable life full of unusual adventures.
"Ellis has created a small gem here, with messages
about following your heart tucked into the sentences,
phrases, thoughts, and ideas that she seamlessly weaves
together." Booklist

Ellison, Elizabeth Stow, 1970-

Flight. Holiday House 2008 245p $16.95

Grades: 4 5 6 7   **Fic**

1. Siblings—Fiction 2. Learning disabilities—Fiction
3. Literacy—Fiction

ISBN 978-0-8234-2128-2; 0-8234-2128-7

LC 2008-9372

Twelve-year-old Samantha struggles with how to best
help her artistic older brother and parents who will not
have him tested for a learning disability.

"Readers will appreciate the gently hinted-at optimistic
ending. . . . An obvious choice for a classroom read-
aloud or as a discussion opener on a topic uncomfortable
for many families." SLJ

Emerson, Kevin

Carlos is gonna get it; [by] Kevin Emerson.
Arthur A. Levine Books 2008 291p $16.99 *

Grades: 4 5 6 7   **Fic**

1. School stories 2. African Americans—Fiction
3. Boston (Mass.)—Fiction 4. New Hampshire—Fiction

ISBN 978-0-439-93525-8; 0-439-93525-3

LC 2007037088

Recounts the events that occur at the end of seventh
grade, when a group of friends plan to trick Carlos, an
annoying "problem" student who says he is visited by
aliens, while they are on a field trip in the mountains of
New Hampshire.

This is a "gripping story. . . . The dialogue is right
on, as is the hurt of betrayal and the guilt that cannot be
resolved." Booklist

English, Karen

Francie. Farrar, Straus & Giroux 1999 199p $17
paperback o.p.

Grades: 5 6 7 8   **Fic**

1. African Americans—Fiction 2. Race relations—Fiction 3. Alabama—Fiction

ISBN 0-374-32456-5; 0-374-42459-4 (pa)

LC 98-53047

Coretta Scott King honor book for text, 2000

"The best student in her small, all-black school in
preintegration Alabama, 12-year-old Francie hopes for a
better life. . . . When Jessie, an older school friend who
is without family, is forced on the run by a racist employer, Francie leaves her mother's labeled canned food
for him in the woods. Only when the sheriff begins
searching their woods . . . does she realize the depth of
the danger she may have brought to her family. Francie's
smooth-flowing, well-paced narration is gently assisted
by just the right touch of the vernacular. Characterization
is evenhanded and believable, while place and time en-
velop readers." SLJ

Nikki & Deja; [illustrated by] Laura Freeman.
Clarion Books 2007 80p il $15; pa $3.99

Grades: 2 3 4   **Fic**

1. Friendship—Fiction 2. School stories 3. African
Americans—Fiction

ISBN 978-0-618-75238-6; 0-618-75238-2;
978-0-547-13362-1 (pa); 0-547-13362-6 (pa)

LC 2006-30974

When an arrogant new girl comes to school, third-
graders and best friends Nikki and Deja decide to form
a club that would exclude her but find the results not
what they expected.

"More probing than many chapter books, this title delivers the satisfaction of a full-length novel." Publ Wkly

Other titles about Nikki and Deja are:

Nikki & Deja: birthday blues (2009)

Nikki & Deja: the newsy news newsletter (2010)

Enright, Elizabeth, 1909-1968

Gone-Away Lake; illustrated by Beth and Joe
Krush. Harcourt 2000 c1957 256p il hardcover o.p.
pa $6

Grades: 4 5 6   **Fic**

ISBN 0-15-202274-0; 0-15-202272-4 (pa)

LC 99-55281

A Newbery Medal honor book, 1958

"An Odyssey/Harcourt young classic"

A reissue of the title first published 1957

Portia and her cousin Julian discover adventure in a
hidden colony of forgotten summer houses on the shores
of a swampy lake

"Excellent writing, clear in setting of scene and details
of nature, and strong in appeal for children." Horn Book

Another title about Gone-Away Lake is:

Return to Gone-Away Lake (1961)

Ensor, Barbara

Thumbelina; tiny runaway bride; based on the
fairy tale by Hans Christian Andersen. Schwartz &
Wade Books 2008 140p $12.99; lib bdg $15.99

Grades: 2 3 4   **Fic**

1. Andersen, Hans Christian, 1805-1875—Adaptations
2. Fairy tales

ISBN   978-0-375-83960-3;   0-375-83960-7;
978-0-375-93960-0 (lib bdg); 0-375-93960-1 (lib bdg)

LC 2007015684

In this expanded version of the Andersen fairy tale, a
tiny girl no bigger than a thumb becomes separated from
her overprotective mother, has adventures with various
animals, and records her feelings in a diary as she gains
self-reliance and searches for someone to love

"In this light, charming retelling of Andersen's classic
fairy tale, Ensor focuses on Thumbelina's engagements,
with an alternative ending that many girls will relish.
. . . Black-and-white paper-cut illustrations, like those
Andersen himself made, and Thumbelina's diary entries
round out this satisfying addition to the retold fairy-tale
genre." Booklist

Erdrich, Louise

The birchbark house. Hyperion Bks. for
Children 1999 244p il hardcover o.p. pa $6.99 *

Grades: 5 6 7 8   **Fic**

1. Ojibwa Indians—Fiction

ISBN 0-7868-0300-2; 0-7868-1454-3 (pa)

LC 98-46366

Omakayas, a seven-year-old Native American girl of
the Ojibwa tribe, lives through the joys of summer and
the perils of winter on an island in Lake Superior in
1847.

Erdrich, Louise—*Continued*

"Erdrich crafts images of tender beauty while weaving Ojibwa words seamlessly into the text. Her gentle spot art throughout complements this first of several projected stories that will 'attempt to retrace [her] own family's history.'" Horn Book Guide

Followed by: The game of silence (2004)

The game of silence; [by] Louise Erdrich. HarperCollins 2004 256p $15.99; lib bdg $16.89; pa $5.99 *

Grades: 5 6 7 8   **Fic**
1. Ojibwa Indians—Fiction
ISBN 0-06-029789-1; 0-06-029790-5 (lib bdg); 0-06-441029-3 (pa)   LC 2004-6018

Sequel to: The birchbark house (1999)

Nine-year-old Omakayas, of the Ojibwa tribe, moves west with her family in 1849

"Erdrich's captivating tale of four seasons portrays a deep appreciation of our environment, our history, and our Native American sisters and brothers." SLJ

Followed by: The porcupine year (2008)

The porcupine year. HarperCollinsPublishers 2008 193p $15.99; lib bdg $16.89 *

Grades: 5 6 7 8   **Fic**
1. Ojibwa Indians—Fiction 2. Family life—Fiction 3. Voyages and travels—Fiction
ISBN 978-0-06-029787-9; 0-06-029787-5; 978-0-06-029788-6 (lib bdg); 0-06-029788-3 (lib bdg)   LC 2008000757

Sequel to: The game of silence (2004)

In 1852, forced by the United States government to leave their beloved Island of the Golden Breasted Woodpecker, fourteen-year-old Omokayas and her Ojibwe family travel in search of a new home.

"Based on Erdrich's own family history, this celebration of life will move readers with its mischief, its anger, and its sadness. What is left unspoken is as powerful as the story told." Booklist

Erskine, Kathryn

Mockingbird. Philomel Books 2010 235p $15.99 *

Grades: 4 5 6   **Fic**
1. Asperger's syndrome—Fiction 2. School stories 3. Bereavement—Fiction 4. Siblings—Fiction 5. Father-daughter relationship—Fiction
ISBN 978-0-399-25264-8; 0-399-25264-9   LC 2009-06741

After her brother is killed in a school shooting, ten-year-old Caitlyn, who has Asperger's Syndrome, struggles to understand emotions, show empathy, and make friends at school, while at home she seeks closure by working on a project with her father.

"The sharp insights into Caitlyn's behavior enhance this fine addition to the recent group of books with narrators with autism and Asbergers." Booklist

Estes, Eleanor, 1906-1988

The Alley; illustrated by Edward Ardizzone. Harcourt 2003 c1964 283p il hardcover o.p. pa $5.95

Grades: 4 5 6   **Fic**
1. Brooklyn (New York, N.Y.)—Fiction 2. Mystery fiction
ISBN 0-15-204917-7; 0-15-204918-5 (pa)   LC 2003-45290

"An Odyssey/Harcourt young classic"

A reissue of the title first published 1964

Ten-year-old Connie, who lives in the Brooklyn neigborhood called The Alley, investigates a burglary with her friend Billy Maloon

"Even the minor characters are deftly drawn. A book with substance and a great deal of humor." Horn Book

Followed by The tunnel of Hugsy Goode

Ginger Pye; with illustrations by the author. Harcourt 2000 c1951 306p il $17; pa $6

Grades: 4 5 6   **Fic**
1. Dogs—Fiction
ISBN 0-15-202499-9; 0-15-202505-7 (pa)   LC 00-26700

Awarded the Newbery Medal, 1952

"An Odyssey/Harcourt young classic"

A reissue of the title first published 1951

The disappearance of a new puppy named Ginger and the appearance of a mysterious man in a mustard yellow hat bring excitement into the lives of the Pye children

Estes' drawings are "vivid, amusing sketches that point up and confirm the atmosphere of the story. It is a book to read and reread." Saturday Rev

Another title about the Pye family is:
Pinky Pye (1958)

The hundred dresses; illustrated by Louis Slobodkin. New ed. Harcourt 2004 c1944 80p il $16; pa $7

Grades: 4 5 6   **Fic**
ISBN 0-15-205170-8; 0-15-205260-7 (pa)   LC 2003-57037

A Newbery honor book, 1945

A reissue of the title first published 1944

"The 100 dresses are just dream dresses, pictures Wanda Petronski has drawn, but she describes them in self-defense as she appears daily in the same faded blue dress. Not until Wanda, snubbed and unhappy, moves away leaving her pictures at school for an art contest, do her classmates realize their cruelty." Books for Deaf Child

"Written with great simplicity it reveals, in a measure, the pathos of human relationships and the suffering of those who are different. Mr. Slobodkin's watercolors interpret the mood of the story and fulfill the quality of the text." N Y Public Libr

The Moffats; illustrated by Louis Slobodkin. Harcourt 2001 c1941 290p il $17; pa $6 *

Grades: 4 5 6   **Fic**
1. Family life—Fiction
ISBN 0-15-202535-9; 0-15-202541-3 (pa)   LC 00-39726

"An Odyssey/Harcourt young classic"

A reissue of the title first published 1941

Estes, Eleanor, 1906-1988—*Continued*

Relates the adventures and misadventures of the four Moffat children living with their widowed mother in a yellow house on New Dollar Street in the small town of Cranbury, Connecticut

"A captivating family story with highly individual characters. Each chapter is a separate episode, suitable for reading aloud." Hodges. Books for Elem Sch Libr

Other titles about the Moffats are:

The middle Moffat (1942)

The Moffat Museum (1983)

Rufus M. (1943)

The witch family; illustrated by Edward Ardizzone. Harcourt 2000 223p il hardcover o.p. pa $6 *

Grades: 4 5 6   **Fic**

1. Witches—Fiction

ISBN 0-15-202604-5; 0-15-202610-X (pa)

LC 99-89152

"An Odyssey/Harcourt young classic"

A reissue of the title first published 1960

"The Old Witch, the Little Witch Girl and Witch Baby are all the creations of crayons wielded by Amy and Clarissa. . . . As their imaginations run riot, the witches take on an independent life of their own, and the two groups mix and mingle." Libr J

"A very special book that is certain to give boundless pleasure." Horn Book

Estevis, Anne

Chicken Foot Farm; by Anne Estevis. Pinata Books 2008 154p pa $10.95

Grades: 5 6 7 8   **Fic**

1. Mexican Americans—Fiction 2. Ranch life—Fiction 3. Family life—Fiction 4. Texas—Fiction

ISBN 978-1-55885-505-2 (pa); 1-55885-505-X (pa)

LC 2007048338

Alejandro grows from ten years old to the age of seventeen, learning about life from his extended Mexican American family on a small ranch in 1940s South Texas.

"The vignettes are filled with nostalgia and range in tone from funny and tender to tragic and wistful. . . . The emotional intimacy and deep love between its characters is *Chicken Foot Farm's* greatest charm." SLJ

Etchemendy, Nancy, 1952-

The power of Un. Front St./Cricket Bks. 2000 148p $16.95; pa $4.99

Grades: 4 5 6 7   **Fic**

1. Fantasy fiction

ISBN 0-8126-2850-0; 0-439-31331-7 (pa)

LC 99-58281

When he is given a device that will allow him to "undo" what has happened in the past, Gib Finney is not sure what event from the worst day in his life he should change in order to keep his sister from being hit by a truck

The author has a "knack for writing hilarious dialogue that perfectly paints the funny, poignant, and altogether unpredictable world of eleven and twelve year olds. . . . A unique, thought-provoking book." Voice Youth Advocates

Fagan, Deva

Fortune's folly. Henry Holt 2009 260p $17.95

Grades: 5 6 7 8   **Fic**

1. Fairy tales 2. Prophecies—Fiction 3. Adventure fiction

ISBN 978-0-8050-8742-0; 0-8050-8742-7

LC 2008-36780

Ever since her mother died and her father lost his shoemaking skills, Fortunata has survived by pretending to tell fortunes, but when she is tricked into telling the fortune of a prince, she is faced with the impossible task of fulfilling her wild prophecy to save her father's life.

"Fagan's language evokes images of fairy tales and legends, and the protagonist's first-person narrative sparkles with humor. In this book, words are powerful, impressive, mystical, and, sometimes, downright silly." SLJ

The magical misadventures of Prunella Bogthistle. Henry Holt and Company 2010 263p $17.99

Grades: 5 6 7 8   **Fic**

1. Witches—Fiction 2. Magic—Fiction

ISBN 978-0-8050-8743-7; 0-8050-8743-5

The personal quests of a young witch who aspires to be a villain and a young thief who's determined to become a hero intersect in a swampy bog.

"This colorful, fast-paced fantasy is recommended for fans of funny, fairy-tale-inspired stories." SLJ

Falls, Kat

Dark life. Scholastic Press 2010 297p $16.99

Grades: 4 5 6 7   **Fic**

1. Science fiction 2. Ocean—Fiction

ISBN 978-0-545-17814-3; 0-545-17814-2; 978-0-545-17815-0 (pa); 0-545-17815-0 (pa)

LC 2009-24907

"Ty has lived subsea his entire life. His family members moved below the water to make a better life for themselves. In this future, the climate changes on Earth have been so drastic that hardly any solid ground exits anymore. . . . This book will appeal to middle grade readers, who will enjoy the novel's mystery and suspense. It is a definite must-read for SF fans." Voice Youth Advocates

Fardell, John, 1967-

The 7 professors of the Far North. G. P. Putnam's Sons 2005 217p il hardcover o.p. pa $6.99

Grades: 4 5 6 7   **Fic**

1. Adventure fiction 2. Arctic regions—Fiction 3. Science fiction

ISBN 0-399-24381-X; 0-14-240735-6 (pa)

Eleven-year-old Sam finds himself involved in a dangerous adventure when he and his new friends, brother and sister Ben and Zara, set off for the Arctic to try and rescue the siblings' great-uncle and five other professors from the mad scientist holding them prisoner.

"Action is nonstop and very exciting. This inventive, funny, suspenseful, and exciting book will appeal to most readers." SLJ

Followed by: The flight of the Silver Turtle (2006)

Farley, Walter, 1915-1989

The Black Stallion; by Walter Farley; illustrated by Keith Ward. Random House 2008 c1941 275p il $15.99; lib bdg $18.99

Grades: 4 5 6 7   **Fic**

1. Horses—Fiction

ISBN   978-0-375-85582-5;   0-375-85582-3; 978-0-375-95578-5 (lib bdg); 0-375-95578-X (lib bdg)

A reissue of the title first published 1941

Young Alec Ramsay is shipwrecked on a desert island with a horse destined to play an important part in his life. Following their rescue their adventure continues in America.

Other titles in this series are:

The Black Stallion and Flame (1960)

The Black Stallion and the shape-shifter (2008) by Steven Farley

The Black Stallion returns (1945)

The Black Stallion's ghost (1969)

The Black Stallion's shadow (1996) by Steven Farley

The Black Stallion's steeplechaser (1997) by Steven Farley

Son of the Black Stallion (1947)

The young Black Stallion (1989)

Farmer, Nancy, 1941-

Clever Ali; illustrated by Gail De Marcken. Orchard Books 2006 unp il $17.99 *

Grades: 2 3 4   **Fic**

1. Pigeons—Fiction 2. Egypt—Fiction 3. Kings and rulers—Fiction 4. Cherries—Fiction

ISBN 0-439-37014-0   LC 2005-27133

When seven-year-old Ali's greedy pet steals cherries from the wicked Sultan for whom his father keeps carrier pigeons, Ali is given three days to find 600 new cherries or his father will be thrown into the deep, dark oubliette

"Farmer presents an imaginative tale based on a true story about a 12th-century Egyptian ruler, Al-Azeez. . . . Vivid watercolors depict the characters and the setting and lend atmosphere to the action." SLJ

The Ear, the Eye, and the Arm; a novel. Puffin Books 1995 c1994 311p pa $6.99 *

Grades: 6 7 8 9   **Fic**

1. Science fiction 2. Zimbabwe—Fiction

ISBN 978-0-14-131109-8 (pa); 0-14-131109-6 (pa)
                                        LC 95019982

A Newbery Medal honor book, 1995

First published 1994 by Orchard Books

In 2194 in Zimbabwe, General Matsika's three children are kidnapped and put to work in a plastic mine while three mutant detectives use their special powers to search for them

"Throughout the story, it's the thrilling adventure that will grab readers, who will also like the comic, tender characterizations." Booklist

A girl named Disaster. Orchard Bks. 1996 309p $19.95; pa $7.99 *

Grades: 6 7 8 9   **Fic**

1. Supernatural—Fiction 2. Adventure fiction 3. Mozambique—Fiction 4. Zimbabwe—Fiction

ISBN 0-531-09539-8; 0-14-038635-1 (pa)
                                        LC 96-15141

A Newbery Medal honor book, 1997

"A Richard Jackson book"

While journeying from Mozambique to Zimbabwe to escape an arranged marriage, eleven-year-old Nhamo struggles to escape drowning and starvation and in so doing comes close to the luminous world of the African spirits

"This story is humorous and heartwrenching, complex and multilayered." SLJ

The Sea of Trolls. Atheneum Books for Young Readers 2004 459p $17.95; pa $9.99 *

Grades: 5 6 7 8   **Fic**

1. Norse mythology—Fiction 2. Druids and Druidism—Fiction 3. Vikings—Fiction 4. Fantasy fiction

ISBN 0-689-86744-1; 0-689-86746-8 (pa)
                                        LC 2003-19091

"A Richard Jackson book"

After Jack becomes apprenticed to a Druid bard, he and his little sister Lucy are captured by Viking Berserkers and taken to the home of King Ivar the Boneless and his half-troll queen, leading Jack to undertake a vital quest to Jotunheim, home of the trolls.

"This exciting and original fantasy will capture the hearts and imaginations of readers." SLJ

Other titles in this series are:

The Land of the Silver Apples (2007)

The Islands of the Blessed (2009)

Includes bibliographical references

Fawcett, Katie Pickard

To come and go like magic. Alfred A. Knopf 2010 263p $16.99; lib bdg $19.99

Grades: 5 6 7 8   **Fic**

1. Country life—Fiction 2. Family life—Fiction 3. Kentucky—Fiction

ISBN   978-0-375-85846-8;   0-375-85846-6; 978-0-375-95846-5 (lib bdg); 0-375-95846-0 (lib bdg)
                                        LC 2008-52188

In the 1970s, twelve-year-old Chili Sue Mahoney longs to escape her tiny Kentucky home town and see the world, but she also learns to recognize beauty in the people and places around her.

"Chili's first-person narrative stretches from poetic thoughts . . . to more down-to-earth observations. Her insights are absorbing and her setbacks heartbreaking, as she weighs the only home she's ever known against the possibilities that loom farther afield." Publ Wkly

Feiffer, Jules

A room with a zoo. Hyperion Books for Children 2005 182p il hardcover o.p. pa $7.99

Grades: 3 4 5   **Fic**

1. Pets—Fiction 2. Family life—Fiction

ISBN 0-7868-3702-0; 0-7868-3703-9 (pa)
                                        LC 2005-922875

"Michael di Capua books"

Nine-year-old Julie loves animals. So much it seems that she's assembling a zoo in her room. But, what she really wants is a dog.

"This is briskly written with lots of amusing moments. . . . Feiffer's distinctive drawings delectably capture the rousing events." Booklist

Feiffer, Kate

The problem with the Puddles; illustrated by Tricia Tusa. Simon & Schuster Books for Young Readers 2009 193p il $16.99

Grades: 3 4 5   **Fic**

1. Dogs—Fiction 2. Lost and found possessions—Fiction 3. Family life—Fiction
ISBN 978-1-4169-4961-9; 1-4169-4961-5

LC 20080-51388

"A Paula Wiseman book"

The Puddle parents cannot seem to agree about anything, but when their dogs go missing the whole family embarks on an unlikely quest that eventually answers many unasked questions.

"The kid-friendly humor . . . the full cast of eccentric characters and Tusa's . . . lively b&w spot art should readily win fans for the Puddle family." Publ Wkly

Fein, Eric

My frozen valentine; illustrated by Gregg Schigiel and Lee Loughridge; Batman created by Bob Kane. Stone Arch Books 2010 49p il (DC superheroes. Batman) lib bdg $25.32; pa $5.95

Grades: 3 4 5   **Fic**

1. Superheroes—Fiction 2. Batman (Fictional character) 3. Valentine's Day—Fiction
ISBN 978-1-4342-1564-2 (lib bdg); 1-4342-1564-4 (lib bdg); 978-1-4342-1731-8 (pa); 1-4342-1731-0 (pa)

LC 2009006302

"It's Valentine's Day in Gotham, but not everyone is celebrating. Victor Fries (aka Mr. Freeze) has never gotten over the death of his wife, Nora, and he's not about to let anyone enjoy this painful holiday. Only Batman can stop the coldhearted criminal before Victor refrigerates the entire city." Publisher's note

This " full-color chapter [book is] fast moving and entertaining. . . . The retro comic-book illustrations . . . appear every few pages, adding a vibrant visual element to the proceedings. Sound effects are displayed in large, expressive fonts and colors, capturing the feel of comics." SLJ

Fellowes, Julian, 1950-

The curious adventures of the abandoned toys; based on an idea by Shirley-Anne Lewis; pictures by S. D. Schindler. Henry Holt 2007 60p il $17.95 *

Grades: 3 4 5   **Fic**

1. Teddy bears—Fiction 2. Toys—Fiction
ISBN 978-0-8050-7526-7; 0-8050-7526-7

LC 2006-31375

When Doc the bear arrives at the dump from his former home, he isn't sure about what awaits him but his new friends are determined to make his new home a welcoming one.

"Fellowes exhibits a wonderful flair for both dialogue and characterization, and his descriptive narrative, touched with wit, echoes with the drama and poignancy of classic animal tales. Schindler's enchanting, intricate artwork . . . sympathetically captures the characters' feelings." Booklist

Fenner, Carol

Snowed in with Grandmother Silk; illustrated by Amanda Harvey. Dial Books for Young Readers 2003 75p il hardcover o.p. pa $6.99

Grades: 2 3 4   **Fic**

1. Grandmothers—Fiction 2. Snow—Fiction
ISBN 0-8037-2857-3; 0-14-240472-1 (pa)

LC 2002-152296

Ruddy is disappointed when his parents go on a cruise and he must stay with his fussy grandmother for a whole week, but an unexpected snowstorm reveals a surprising side of Grandmother Silk

"Harvey's pencil-and-watercolor artwork extends the warmth and gentle humor in this chapter book, which will be a good choice for beginning readers as well as for reading aloud." Booklist

Yolonda's genius. Margaret K. McElderry Bks. 1995 211p $18.95; pa $5.99

Grades: 4 5 6   **Fic**

1. Siblings—Fiction 2. Musicians—Fiction 3. African Americans—Fiction
ISBN 0-689-80001-0; 0-689-81327-9 (pa)

LC 94-46962

A Newbery Medal honor book, 1996

After moving from Chicago to Grand River, Michigan, fifth grader Yolonda, big and strong for her age, determines to prove that her younger brother is not a slow learner but a true musical genius

"In this brisk and appealing narrative, readers are introduced to a close-knit, middle-class African-American family. . . . [This novel] is suffused with humor and spirit." Horn Book

Ferber, Brenda A., 1967-

Jemma Hartman, camper extraordinaire. Farrar, Straus and Giroux 2009 215p $16.95

Grades: 3 4 5 6   **Fic**

1. Camps—Fiction 2. Friendship—Fiction 3. Sailing—Fiction
ISBN 978-0-374-33672-1; 0-374-33672-5

LC 2008-26049

Spending the summer after fifth grade at Camp Star Lake in Wisconsin, Jemma discovers the joy of sailing and learns a lesson about friendship.

"The plot moves along swiftly, and Jemma's first-person narrative rings true, as do the issues and the camp experience." SLJ

Ferraiolo, Jack D.

The big splash; by Jack D. Ferraiolo. Amulet Books 2008 277p $15.95

Grades: 4 5 6 7   **Fic**

1. School stories 2. Mystery fiction
ISBN 978-0-8109-7067-0; 0-8109-7067-8

LC 2007-49978

Matt Stevens, an average middle schooler with a glib tongue and a knack for solving crimes, uncovers a mystery while working with "the organization," a mafia-like syndicate run by seventh-grader Vincent "Mr. Biggs" Biggio, specializing in forged hall passes, test-copying rings, black market candy selling, and taking out hits with water guns.

Ferraiolo, Jack D.—*Continued*

This "novel delivers plenty of laughs, especially in the opening chapters, and fans of private-eye spoofs will enjoy this entertaining read." Booklist

Ferrari, Michael

Born to fly. Delacorte Press 2009 212p $15.99; lib bdg $18.99

Grades: 4 5 6   **Fic**
    1. Air pilots—Fiction 2. Family life—Fiction 3. Friendship—Fiction 4. Sex role—Fiction 5. World War, 1939-1945—Fiction 6. Rhode Island—Fiction
    ISBN   978-0-385-73715-9;   0-385-73715-7; 978-0-385-90649-4 (lib bdg); 0-385-90649-8 (lib bdg)
                                          LC 2008035664
In 1942, an eleven-year-old girl who longs to be a pilot and her family try to manage their lives in Rhode Island when the father goes to fight in World War II.
    "Ferrari's fast-paced plot and well-developed characters will keep readers engaged until the last page." Booklist

Ferris, Jean, 1939-

Much ado about Grubstake. Harcourt 2006 265p $17

Grades: 5 6 7 8   **Fic**
    1. Gold mines and mining—Fiction 2. Orphans—Fiction 3. City and town life—Fiction 4. Colorado—Fiction
    ISBN 0-15-205706-4
When two city folks arrive in the depressed mining town of Grubstake, Colorado in 1888, sixteen-year-old orphaned Arley tries to discover why they want to buy the supposedly worthless mines in the area
    "Ferris combines adventure, love, and off-the-wall characters in a page-turning story full of good laughs and common sense messages." Voice Youth Advocates

Field, Rachel, 1894-1942

Hitty: her first hundred years; [by] Rachel Field; with illustrations by Dorothy P. Lathrop. Macmillan 1929 207p il $19.99; pa $6.99

Grades: 4 5 6 7   **Fic**
    1. Dolls—Fiction
    ISBN 0-02-734840-7; 0-689-82284-7 (pa)
    Awarded the Newbery Medal, 1930
"Hitty, a doll of real character carved from a block of mountain ash, writes a story of her eventful life from the security of an antique-shop window which she shares with Theobold, a rather over-bearing cat. . . . The illustrations by Dorothy P. Lathrop are the happiest extension of the text." Cleveland Public Libr

Fields, Bryan W.

Lunchbox and the aliens; illustrated by Kevan Atteberry. Henry Holt & Co. 2006 183p il $16.95; pa $6.99

Grades: 3 4 5 6   **Fic**
    1. Dogs—Fiction 2. Extraterrestrial beings—Fiction 3. Science fiction
    ISBN 0-8050-7995-5; 0-312-56115-6 (pa)
Lunchbox is an ordinary basset hound until he is abducted by aliens, zapped by a mental enhancer, and sent back to convert Earth's garbage into food—a task that would be easier if he had opposable thumbs, or at least tentacles
    "The author weaves a delightful story. . . . The pencil-drawn cartoons throughout enhance the fun. . . . The fast-moving plot and satisfying conclusion make this a good choice for reluctant readers, science-fiction fans, or any child who enjoys a good book about a boy and his dog." SLJ
    Another title about Lunchbox is:
Froonga planet (2008)

Fine, Anne

The diary of a killer cat; [by] Anne Fine; pictures by Steve Cox. Farrar, Straus and Giroux 2006 c1994 58p il $15

Grades: 2 3 4   **Fic**
    1. Cats—Fiction
    ISBN 0-374-31779-8   LC 2004-56212
    First published 2001 in the United Kingdom
Tuffy the pet cat tries to defend himself against accusations of terrifying other animals and murdering the neighbor's rabbit
    "The book is funny throughout. . . . The black-and-white sketches, some full page, bring movement and personality to the characters." SLJ
    Another title about the killer cat is:
The return of the killer cat (2007)

Jamie and Angus together; illustrated by Penny Dale. Candlewick Press 2007 102p il $15.99

Grades: PreK K 1 2   **Fic**
    1. Toys—Fiction 2. Friendship—Fiction 3. Play—Fiction
    ISBN 978-0-7636-3374-5; 0-7636-3374-7
                                          LC 2007-25166
    Best friends Jamie and his toy Highland bull Angus tackle a lively playmate, become muddled by a pretend game, and discover that playing is not fun unless they are doing it together.
    "Fine renders another pitch-perfect transitional chapter book. . . . Spare yet vivid language captures Jamie's perspective while supplying humor for adult readers. . . . Soft pencil illustrations . . . capture Jamie's loving family and convey his deep friendship with Angus." Booklist
    Another title about Jamie and Angus is:
The Jamie and Angus stories (2002)

Notso hotso; [by] Anne Fine; pictures by Tony Ross. Farrar, Straus and Giroux 2006 c2001 92p il $15

Grades: 2 3 4   **Fic**
    1. Dogs—Fiction
    ISBN 0-374-35550-9   LC 2004-56282
    First published 2001 in the United Kingdom

Fine, Anne—*Continued*

Anthony, a neglected pet dog, develops an irritating skin condition and has most of his hair shaved off, which embarrasses him greatly until he realizes he now looks like a lion and can frighten other animals and people

"Ross' line drawings, full of action and expression, effectively capture the transformation. [This book] will be great for reading aloud and reading alone." Booklist

Fireside, Bryna J.

Private Joel and the Sewell Mountain seder; by Bryna J. Fireside; illustrations by Shawn Costello. Kar-Ben Pub. 2008 47p il lib bdg $16.95; pa $6.95

Grades: 2 3 4   **Fic**
1. Passover—Fiction 2. Jews—United States—Fiction 3. United States—History—1861-1865, Civil War—Fiction
ISBN 978-0-8225-7240-4 (lib bdg); 0-8225-7240-0 (lib bdg); 978-0-8225-9050-7 (pa); 0-8225-9050-6 (pa)
LC 2007005275
A group of Jewish soldiers, and three freed slaves, have a Passover seder in 1862 on the battlefields of the Civil War

The book is based "on a true story. . . . Costello's impressionistic artwork seems well suited to this nostalgic story. Although respectful in tone, the illustrations also pick up on occasional humor." Booklist

Fisher, Dorothy Canfield, 1879-1958

Understood Betsy; with new illustrations by Kimberly Bulcken Root. Holt & Co. 1999 229p il $17.95

Grades: 4 5 6   **Fic**
1. Farm life—Fiction 2. Vermont—Fiction
ISBN 0-8050-6073-1   LC 99-25265
A newly illustrated edition of the title first published 1917

Timid and small for her age, nine-year-old Elizabeth Ann discovers her own abilities and gains a new perception of the world around her when she goes to live with relatives on a farm in Vermont

"Kimberly Bulcken Root's inviting, unaffected pencil drawings have a cozy feel to them. . . . 'Understood Betsy' is sure to delight a new generation." N Y Times Book Rev

Fitzgerald, Dawn

Soccer chick rules. Roaring Brook Press 2006 150p $16.95

Grades: 5 6 7 8   **Fic**
1. School stories 2. Soccer—Fiction 3. Politics—Fiction
ISBN 1-59643-137-7
"A Deborah Brodie book"
While trying to focus on a winning soccer season, thirteen-year-old Tess becomes involved in local politics when she learns that all sports programs at her school will be stopped unless a tax levy is passed.

This is "a fast-moving, true-to-life, amusing take on school life. The dialogue is especially spot-on." Booklist

Fitzgerald, John D., 1907-1988

The Great Brain; illustrated by Mercer Mayer. Dial Bks. for Young Readers 1967 175p il $17.99; pa $5.99 *

Grades: 4 5 6 7   **Fic**
1. Utah—Fiction
ISBN 0-8037-2590-6; 0-14-240058-0 (pa)
"The Great Brain was Tom Dennis ('T.D.') Fitzgerald, age ten, of Adenville, Utah; the time, 1896. . . . This autobiographical yarn is spun by his brother John Dennis ('J.D.'), age seven . . . who can tell stories about himself and his family with enough tall-tale exaggeration to catch the imagination." Horn Book
Other titles about the Great Brain are:
The Great Brain at the academy (1972)
The Great Brain does it again (1975)
The Great Brain is back (1995)
The Great Brain reforms (1973)
Me and my little brain (1971)
More adventures of the Great Brain (1969)
The return of the Great Brain (1974)

Fitzhugh, Louise, 1928-1974

Harriet, the spy; written and illustrated by Louise Fitzhugh. Delacorte Press 2000 c1964 300p il $15.95 *

Grades: 4 5 6 7   **Fic**
1. School stories
ISBN 0-385-32783-8   LC 00712298
A reissue of the title first published 1964 by Harper & Row

Eleven-year-old Harriet keeps notes on her classmates and neighbors in a secret notebook, but when some of the students read the notebook, they seek revenge.

"A very, very funny and a very, very affective story; the characterizations are marvelously shrewd, the pictures of urban life and of the power structure of the sixth grade class are realistic." Bull Cent Child Books
Another title about Harriet is:
The long secret (1965)

Fitzmaurice, Kathryn

The year the swallows came early. Bowen Press 2009 277p $16.99; lib bdg $17.89 *

Grades: 4 5 6   **Fic**
1. Father-daughter relationship—Fiction 2. Prisoners—Fiction
ISBN 978-0-06-162497-1; 0-06-162497-7; 978-0-06-162499-5 (lib bdg); 0-06-162499-3 (lib bdg)
LC 2008-20156
After her father is sent to jail, eleven-year-old Groovy Robinson must decide if she can forgive the failings of someone she loves.

This "novel is peopled with three-dimensional characters whose imperfections make them believable and interesting. . . . The well-structured plot is underscored by clear writing and authentic dialogue." SLJ

Flake, Sharon G.

The broken bike boy and the Queen of 33rd Street. Jump at the Sun/Hyperion Books for Children 2007 132p il $15.99; pa $5.99 *

Grades: 4 5 6 7   **Fic**

1. Friendship—Fiction 2. School stories 3. African Americans—Fiction

ISBN   978-1-4231-0032-4;   1-4231-0032-8; 978-1-4231-0035-5 (pa); 1-4231-0035-2 (pa)

LC 2006-35590

Ten-year-old Queen, a spoiled and conceited African American girl who is disliked by most of her classmates, learns a lesson about friendship from an unlikely "knight in shining armor."

"Complex intergenerational characters and a rich urban setting defy stereotyping. . . . Infrequent detailed pencil illustrations . . . add a welcome dimension." Horn Book

Flanagan, John

The ruins of Gorlan. Philomel Books 2005 249p (Ranger's apprentice) $15.99; pa $7.99 *

Grades: 5 6 7 8   **Fic**

1. Fantasy fiction

ISBN 0-399-24454-9; 0-14-240663-5 (pa)

When fifteen-year-old Will is rejected by battleschool, he becomes the reluctant apprentice to the mysterious Ranger Halt, and winds up protecting the kingdom from danger.

"Flanagan concentrates on character, offering readers a young protagonist they will care about and relationships that develop believably over time." Booklist

Other titles in this series are:

The burning bridge (2006)
The icebound land (2007)
The battle for Skandia (2008)
The socerer of the north (2008)
The siege of Macindaw (2009)
Erak's ransom (2010)
The kings of Clonmel (2010)

Fleischman, Paul

Bull Run; woodcuts by David Frampton. HarperCollins Pubs. 1993 104p il pa $4.99

Grades: 6 7 8 9   **Fic**

1. Bull Run, 1st Battle of, 1861—Fiction 2. United States—History—1861-1865, Civil War—Fiction

ISBN 0-06-440588-5 (pa)   LC 92-14745

"A Laura Geringer book"

"In a sequence of sixty one- to two-page narratives, fifteen fictional characters (and one real general) recount their experiences during the Civil War. A few encounter each other, most meet unawares or not at all, but they have in common a battle, Bull Run, that affects—and sometimes ends—their lives." Bull Cent Child Books

"Abandoning the conventions of narrative fiction, Fleischman tells a vivid, many-sided story in this original and moving book. An excellent choice for readers' theater in the classroom or on stage." Booklist

The dunderheads; illustrated by David Roberts. Candlewick Press 2009 54p il $16.99 *

Grades: 2 3 4 5   **Fic**

1. Teachers—Fiction 2. School stories

ISBN 978-0-7636-2498-9; 0-7636-2498-5

When Miss Breakbone confiscates Junkyard's crucial find, Wheels, Pencil, Spider, and the rest of the Dunderheads plot to teach her a lesson.

"Roberts's quirky watercolor and ink interpretations of Fleischman's deadpan humor and impeccable pacing produce hilarious results." SLJ

The Half-a-Moon Inn; illustrated by Kathy Jacobi. Harper & Row 1980 88p il pa $4.99 hardcover o.p. *

Grades: 4 5 6   **Fic**

1. Kidnapping—Fiction 2. Physically handicapped children—Fiction 3. Hotels and motels—Fiction

ISBN 0-06-440364-5 (pa)   LC 79-2010

"A mute boy, Aaron, leaves the cottage he shares with his mother to search for her when she is days late returning from market. Lost in a blizzard, he seeks shelter at the Half-A-Moon Inn. Here the evil crone Miss Grackle, who owns the place, forces Aaron to abet her thieving. The boy tries to warn guests against Miss Grackle but none of them can read his hastily written notes. . . . The ending is a terrific twist." Publ Wkly

"Despite the grimness of Aaron's predicament, accentuated by dark scratch drawings of figures in grotesque proportion, the story's tone is hopeful and its style concrete and brisk. Elements of folklore exist in the story's characterization, structure, and narration." SLJ

Seedfolks; illustrations by Judy Pedersen. HarperCollins Pubs. 1997 69p $14.99; lib bdg $15.89; pa $4.99 *

Grades: 4 5 6 7   **Fic**

1. Gardens—Fiction 2. City and town life—Fiction

ISBN 0-06-027471-9; 0-06-027472-7 (lib bdg); 0-06-447207-8 (pa)   LC 96-26696

"Joanna Cotler books"

This "novel tells about an urban garden started by a child and nurtured by people of all ages and ethnic and economic backgrounds. Each of the thirteen chapters is narrated by a different character, allowing the reader to watch as a community develops out of disconnected lives and prior suspicions." Horn Book Guide

"The characters' vitality and the sharply delineated details of the neighborhood make this not merely an exercise in craftsmanship or morality but an engaging, entertaining novel as well." Booklist

Fleischman, Sid, 1920-2010

The 13th floor; a ghost story; illustrations by Peter Sis. Greenwillow Bks. 1995 134p il $15.99; pa $5.99

Grades: 4 5 6   **Fic**

1. Fantasy fiction 2. Pirates—Fiction

ISBN 0-688-14216-8; 0-06-134503-2 (pa)

LC 94-42806

When his older sister disappears, twelve-year-old Buddy Stebbins follows her back in time and finds himself aboard a seventeenth-century pirate ship captained by a distant relative

Fleischman, Sid, 1920-2010—*Continued*

"Liberally laced with dry wit and thoroughly satisfying. . . . Readers could hardly ask for more." Publ Wkly

Bandit's moon; illustrations by Jos. A. Smith. Greenwillow Bks. 1998 136p il $16.99; pa $6.99

Grades: 4 5 6   **Fic**

1. Murieta, Joaquín, d. 1853—Fiction 2. Thieves—Fiction 3. California—Gold discoveries—Fiction 4. Adventure fiction

ISBN 0-688-15830-7; 0-06-145096-0 (pa)

LC 97-36197

Twelve-year-old Annyrose relates her adventures with Joaquin Murieta and his band of outlaws in the California gold-mining region during the mid-1800s

"A quick read, with lots of twists, wonderful phrasing, historical integrity, and a bit of the tall tale thrown in." SLJ

Bo & Mzzz Mad. Greenwillow Bks. 2001 103p hardcover o.p. pa $4.99

Grades: 5 6 7 8   **Fic**

1. Family life—Fiction 2. Gold mines and mining—Fiction 3. Orphans—Fiction 4. Mojave Desert (Calif.)—Fiction

ISBN 0-06-029397-7; 0-06-440972-4 (pa)

LC 00-56198

When his father dies, Bo Gamage warily moves to the Mojave Desert home of his distant and estranged relatives, the Martinkas, and finds that "Mad" lives up to her name, PawPaw despises him, and Aunt Juna hopes he'll help search for the gold mine that started a family feud

"Fleischman does a first-rate job, using some clever twists and snappy repartee. . . . Add to that a shot of genuine suspense, and you have a quick, enjoyable read that will fly off the shelves." Booklist

By the Great Horn Spoon! illustrated by Eric von Schmidt. Little, Brown 1963 193p il hardcover o.p. pa $6.99 *

Grades: 4 5 6   **Fic**

1. California—Gold discoveries—Fiction

ISBN 0-316-28577-3; 0-316-28612-5 (pa)

"An Atlantic Monthly Press book"

"Jack and his aunt's butler, Praiseworthy, stow away on a ship bound for California. Here are their adventures aboard ship and in the Gold Rush of '49." Publ Wkly

The dream stealer; pictures by Peter Sís. Greenwillow Books 2009 89p il $16.99; lib bdg $17.89 *   **Fic**

1. Dreams—Fiction 2. Mythical animals—Fiction 3. Mexico—Fiction

ISBN 978-0-06-175563-7; 0-06-175563-X; 978-0-06-175564-4 (lib bdg); 0-06-175564-8 (lib bdg)

LC 2008-47694

A plucky Mexican girl tries to recover her dream from the Dream Stealer who takes her to his castle where countless dreams and even more adventures await

"The range of imaginative inventions . . . will delight children, as will the narrator's expertly modulated storyteller's cadence." Booklist

The ghost on Saturday night; illustrated by Laura Cornell. Greenwillow Bks. 1997 53p il hardcover o.p. pa $4.99

Grades: 3 4 5   **Fic**

1. Ghost stories 2. West (U.S.)—Fiction 3. Thieves—Fiction

ISBN 0-688-14919-7; 0-688-14920-0 (pa)

LC 96-43551

A newly illustrated edition of the title first published 1974 by Little, Brown

When Professor Pepper gives Opie tickets to a ghost-raising instead of a nickel in payment for being guided through the dense fog, Opie manages to make money anyway by helping to thwart a bank robbery

"This story is filled with the hyperbole, piquant phrasing, and bravura that make Fleischman's books so much fun to read." Horn Book Guide

The Giant Rat of Sumatra; [illustrations by] John Hendrix. Greenwillow Books 2005 194p il hardcover o.p. lib bdg $16.89; pa $5.99

Grades: 4 5 6 7   **Fic**

1. Pirates—Fiction 2. Mexican War, 1846-1848—Fiction 3. California—Fiction 4. Adventure fiction

ISBN 0-06-074238-0; 0-06-074239-9 (lib bdg); 0-06-074240-2 (pa)   LC 2004-42457

"First shipwrecked and then captured by pirates, young Edmund Amos Peters winds up in sunny San Diego. . . . The year is 1846, and the U.S. is at war with Mexico, which puts Edmund, an American, once more in jeopardy. . . . Fleischman has written another tale that seamlessly blends rousing adventure and good humor." Booklist

Here comes McBroom! three more tall tales; illustrated by Quentin Blake. Greenwillow Bks. 1992 79p il pa $4.95 hardcover o.p. *

Grades: 3 4 5   **Fic**

1. Farm life—Fiction 2. Tall tales

ISBN 0-688-16364-5 (pa)   LC 91-32689

The stories were originally published separately by Grosset and Dunlap

Contents: McBroom the rainmaker (c1973); McBroom's ghost (c1971); McBroom's zoo (c1972)

The tall tale adventures of a farm family

Fleischman's "humor is still as fresh as ever, and Quentin Blake's illustrations continue to delight." Booklist

Other titles about McBroom are:

McBroom tells a lie (1976)

McBroom tells the truth (1981)

McBroom's wonderful one-acre farm: three tall tales (1992)

The midnight horse; illustrations by Peter Sis. Greenwillow Bks. 1990 84p il hardcover o.p. pa $4.99

Grades: 3 4 5 6   **Fic**

1. Magicians—Fiction 2. Ghost stories 3. Orphans—Fiction

ISBN 0-688-09441-4; 0-06-072216-9 (pa)

LC 89-23441

Touch enlists the help of The Great Chaffalo, a ghostly magician, to thwart his great-uncle's plans to put

Fleischman, Sid, 1920-2010—*Continued*
Touch into the orphan house and swindle The Red Raven Inn away from Miss Sally

"The prose is colorful and earthy. . . . Good and bad are clearly defined, a happy ending is never in doubt, and the reader must accept in good faith the capricious appearances of a deceased but still-practicing magician." Horn Book

The whipping boy; illustrations by Peter Sis. Greenwillow Bks. 1986 90p il $16.99; pa $5.99 *
Grades: 5 6 7 8   **Fic**
   1. Thieves—Fiction 2. Adventure fiction
   ISBN 0-688-06216-4; 0-06-052122-8 (pa)
                          LC 85-17555
   Awarded the Newbery Medal, 1987

"A round tale of adventure and humor, this follows the fortunes of Prince Roland (better known as Prince Brat) and his whipping boy, Jemmy, who has received all the hard knocks for the prince's mischief. . . . There's not a moment's lag in pace, and the stock characters, from Hold-Your-Nose Billy to Betsy's dancing bear Petunia, have enough inventive twists to project a lively air to it all." Bull Cent Child Books

The white elephant; [illustrated by] Robert McGuire. Greenwillow Books 2006 95p il $15.99; lib bdg $16.89 *
Grades: 3 4 5   **Fic**
   1. Elephants—Fiction 2. Thailand—Fiction
   ISBN 978-0-06-113136-3; 0-06-113136-9; 978-0-06-113137-0 (lib bdg); 0-06-113137-7 (lib bdg)
                        LC 2005-46793

In old Siam, young elephant trainer Run-Run and his old charge, Walking Mountain, must deal with the curse of a sacred white elephant.

"Fleischman successfully immerses readers in this ancient culture, creating clever and believable plot twists that bring the story to a satisfying but open-ended conclusion." SLJ

Fleming, Candace
Lowji discovers America. Atheneum Books for Young Readers 2005 152p $15.95; pa $5.99
Grades: 3 4 5   **Fic**
   1. Moving—Fiction 2. East Indians—United States—Fiction 3. Immigrants—Fiction
   ISBN 0-689-86299-7; 1-4169-5832-0 (pa)
                        LC 2004-6899
   "An Anne Schwartz book"

A nine-year-old East Indian boy tries to adjust to his new life in suburban America

"Fleming tells a gentle, effective story about the loneliness and bewilderment that come with moving, and her brisk, lively sentences make this a good choice for readers gaining confidence with chapter books." Booklist

Fletcher, Charlie
Stoneheart. Hyperion Books for Children 2007 450p (Stoneheart trilogy) $16.99; pa $7.99
Grades: 5 6 7 8   **Fic**
   1. Fantasy fiction
   ISBN 978-1-4231-0175-8; 1-4231-0175-8; 978-1-4231-0176-5 (pa); 1-4231-0176-6 (pa)
                        LC 2007-01138

When twelve-year-old George accidentally decapitates a stone statue in London, England, he falls into a parallel dimension where he must battle ancient "live" statues and solve a dangerous riddle.

"This "is an action-packed fantasy filled with battles, chases, and an intriguing variety of characters." SLJ
   Other titles in this series are:
Ironhand (2008)
Silvertongue (2009)

Fletcher, Ralph, 1953-
Fig pudding. Clarion Bks. 1995 136p $15
Grades: 4 5 6 7   **Fic**
   1. Family life—Fiction 2. Death—Fiction
   ISBN 0-395-71125-8   LC 94-3654

"Twelve-year-old Cliff, the oldest of six children . . . recalls the past year in episodes focusing on his brothers and his sister. . . . There were good times, but there were also ones he'd like to forget—among them, the death of one brother." Booklist

"Written with humor, perception, and clarity of language, the book resonates with laughter and sorrow." SLJ

Flying solo. Clarion Bks. 1998 138p $15; pa $5.99 *
Grades: 5 6 7 8   **Fic**
   1. School stories 2. Death—Fiction
   ISBN 0-395-87323-1; 0-547-07652-5 (pa)
                        LC 98-10775

Rachel, having chosen to be mute following the sudden death of a classmate, shares responsibility with the other sixth-graders who decide not to report that the substitute teacher failed to show up

"Fletcher expertly balances a wide variety of emotions, giving readers a story that is by turns sad, poignant, and funny." Booklist

Fletcher, Susan, 1951-
Shadow spinner. Atheneum Bks. for Young Readers 1998 219p hardcover o.p. pa $4.99
Grades: 6 7 8 9   **Fic**
   1. Storytelling—Fiction 2. Physically handicapped—Fiction 3. Iran—Fiction
   ISBN 0-689-81852-1; 0-689-83051-3 (pa)
                        LC 97-37346
   "A Jean Karl book"

When Marjan, a thirteen-year-old crippled girl, joins the Sultan's harem in ancient Persia, she gathers for Shahrazad the stories which will save the queen's life

"An elegantly written novel that will delight and entertain even as it teaches." SLJ

Flores-Galbis, Enrique, 1952-
90 miles to Havana. Roaring Brook Press 2010 $17.99
Grades: 5 6 7 8   **Fic**
   1. Cuban refugees—Fiction 2. Cuba—Fiction 3. Florida—Fiction
   ISBN 978-1-59643168-3; 1-59643168-7

"Drawing on his own experience as a child refugee from Cuba, Flores-Galbis offers a gripping historical

Flores-Galbis, Enrique, 1952-—*Continued*
novel about children who were evacuated from Cuba to
the U.S. during Operation Pedro Pan in 1961. Julian, a
young Cuban boy, experiences the violent revolution and
watches mobs throw out his family's furniture and move
into their home. For his safety, his parents send him to
a refugee camp in Miami. . . . This is a seldom-told refugee story that will move readers with the first-person,
present-tense rescue narrative, filled with betrayal, kindness, and waiting for what may never come." Booklist

Fogelin, Adrian, 1951-
The sorta sisters; [by] Adrian Fogelin. Peachtree
2007 279p il $14.95
Grades: 5 6 7 8   **Fic**
1. Friendship—Fiction 2. Foster home care—Fiction
3. Single parent family—Fiction 4. Alcoholism—Fiction 5. Letters—Fiction 6. Florida—Fiction
ISBN 978-1-56145-424-2; 1-56145-424-9
LC 2007011735
In Florida, Anna Casey lives with what she hopes is
the last in a long line of foster mothers, and Mica Delano lives with her father on their small boat, and when
the two of them begin corresponding, they discover they
have a lot in common.
This is written "with insight and compassion. . . .
Lovely sepia drawings by the author depict wildlife and
the packages that the girls send to each other throughout
the novel." Booklist

Fombelle, Timothée de, 1973-
Toby alone; translated by Sarah Ardizzone;
illustrated by François Place. Candlewick Press
2009 384p il $17.99
Grades: 5 6 7 8   **Fic**
1. Trees—Fiction 2. Fantasy fiction
ISBN 978-0-7636-4181-8; 0-7636-4181-2
Original French edition 2006
Toby is just one and a half millimeters tall, and he's
the most wanted person in his world of the great oak
Tree. When Toby's father discovers that the Tree is
alive, he realizes that exploiting it could do damage to
their world. Refusing to reveal the secret to an enraged
community, Toby's parents have been imprisoned. Only
Toby has managed to escape, but for how long?
"The impressive debut novel from French playwright
de Fombelle deftly weaves mature political commentary,
broad humor and some subtle satire into a thoroughly enjoyable adventure." Publ Wkly

Forester, Victoria
The girl who could fly. Feiwel and Friends 2008
329p $16.95 *
Grades: 4 5 6 7   **Fic**
1. Science fiction 2. Flight—Fiction 3. School stories
ISBN 978-0-312-37462-4; 0-312-37462-3
LC 2008-06882
When homeschooled farm girl Piper McCloud reveals
her ability to fly, she is quickly taken to a secret government facility to be trained with other exceptional children, but she soon realizes that something is very wrong
and begins working with brilliant and wealthy Conrad to

escape.
"The story soars, just like Piper, with enough loop-de-
loops to keep kids uncertain about what will come next.
. . . Best of all are the book's strong, lightly wrapped
messages about friendship and authenticity and the difference between doing well and doing good." Booklist

Fox, Helen
Eager. Wendy Lamb Books 2004 280p
hardcover o.p. pa $6.50 *
Grades: 5 6 7 8   **Fic**
1. Robots—Fiction 2. Science fiction
ISBN 0-385-74672-5; 0-553-48795-7 (pa)
LC 2003-19489
Unlike Grumps, their old-fashioned robot, the Bell
family's new robot, Eager, is programmed to not merely
obey but to question, reason, and exercise free will.
"There is a lot of warmth and humor in this engaging
. . . novel. . . . The characters are well developed and
the action moves quickly. The author also raises thought-
provoking questions about what it means to be human,
the dangers of technology, and the concept of free will."
SLJ
Another title about Eager is:
Eager's nephew (2006)

Fox, Paula
The slave dancer. Atheneum 2001 c1973 176p
$18.99; pa $6.99 *
Grades: 5 6 7 8   **Fic**
1. Slave trade—Fiction 2. Sea stories
ISBN   978-0-689-84505-5;   0-689-84505-7;
978-1-4169-7139-9 (pa); 1-4169-7139-4 (pa)
Awarded the Newbery Medal, 1974
"Richard Jackson books"
A reissue of the title first published 1973 by Bradbury
Press
"Thirteen-year-old Jessie Bollier is kidnapped from
New Orleans and taken aboard a slave ship. Cruelly tyr-
annized by the ship's captain, Jessie is made to play his
fife for the slaves during the exercise period into which
they are forced in order to keep them fit for sale. When
a hurricane destroys the ship, Jessie and Ras, a young
slave, survive. They are helped by an old black man who
finds them, spirits Ras north to freedom, and assists Jessie to return to his family." Shapiro. Fic for Youth. 3d
edition

The stone-faced boy. Front Street 2005 83p pa
$8.95
Grades: 4 5 6   **Fic**
1. Dogs—Fiction 2. Siblings—Fiction 3. Family life—
Fiction
ISBN 978-1-932425-42-0 (pa); 1-932425-42-X (pa)
LC 2005-12056
First published 1968 by Bradbury Press
Only his strange great-aunt seems to understand the
thoughts behind a young boy's expressionless face as he
returns on an eerie, snowy night from rescuing a dog that
dislikes him

Frazier, Sundee Tucker, 1968-

Brendan Buckley's universe and everything in it; [by] Sundee Frazier. Delacorte Press 2007 198p $14.99; pa $6.50

Grades: 4 5 6 **Fic**

1. Racially mixed people—Fiction 2. Rocks—Fiction 3. Grandfathers—Fiction 4. Family life—Fiction 5. Washington (State)—Fiction

ISBN 978-0-385-73439-4; 978-0-440-42206-8 (pa)

LC 2006034041

Brendan Buckley, a biracial ten-year-old, applies his scientific problem-solving ability and newfound interest in rocks and minerals to connect with his white grandfather, the president of Puyallup Rock Club, and to learn why he and Brendan's mother are estranged

"Frazier writes affectingly about what being biracial means in 21st century America." SLJ

Frederick, Heather Vogel

The voyage of Patience Goodspeed. Simon & Schuster Bks. for Young Readers 2002 219p hardcover o.p. pa $4.99

Grades: 5 6 7 8 **Fic**

1. Seafaring life—Fiction 2. Whaling—Fiction 3. Navigation—Fiction

ISBN 0-689-84851-X; 0-689-84869-2 (pa)

LC 2001-49039

Following their mother's death in Nantucket, Captain Goodspeed brings twelve-year-old Patience and six-year-old Tad aboard his whaling ship, where a new crew member incites a mutiny and Patience puts her mathematical ability to good use

"This is an exciting voyage of peril and self-discovery." N Y Times Book Rev

Another title about Patience is:
The education of Patience Goodspeed (2004)

Freeman, Martha, 1956-

The trouble with cats; illustrated by Cat Bowman Smith. Holiday House 2000 77p il $15.95

Grades: 2 3 4 **Fic**

1. School stories 2. Stepfathers—Fiction 3. Cats—Fiction 4. San Francisco (Calif.)—Fiction

ISBN 0-8234-1479-5 LC 99-29291

After a difficult first week of third grade, Holly begins to adjust to her new school and living in her new stepfather's tiny apartment with his four cats

"Bowman contributes pen-and-ink drawings with lines that quiver with energy. . . . Freeman has a knack for wholesome, undemanding fiction . . . with enough action and humor to carry the plot." Bull Cent Child Books

Other titles about Holly are:
The trouble with babies (2002)
The trouble with twins (2007)

Who stole Halloween? Holiday House 2005 232p il (The Chickadee Court mysteries) $16.95; pa $7.95

Grades: 4 5 6 **Fic**

1. Mystery fiction 2. Cats—Fiction 3. Halloween—Fiction

ISBN 0-8234-1962-2; 0-8234-2170-8 (pa)

When nine-year-old Alex and his friend Yasmeen investigate the disappearance of cats in their neighborhood, they stumble onto a larger mystery involving a haunted house and a ghostly cat

"The story unfolds to a satisfying resolution . . . Characters are well drawn, and the book will entice even reluctant readers with its action and humor." SLJ

Other titles about Alex and Yasmeen are:
Who is stealing the 12 days of Christmas (2003)
Who stole Uncle Sam? (2008)
Who stole Grandma's million-dollar pumpkin pie? (2009)

French, Jackie, 1950-

Rover. HarperCollins Publishers 2007 283p $16.99 *

Grades: 5 6 7 8 **Fic**

1. Freydis Eriksdottir, ca. 971-ca. 1010—Fiction 2. Vikings—Fiction 3. Slavery—Fiction 4. Dogs—Fiction 5. Sex role—Fiction

ISBN 978-0-06-085078-4; 0-06-085078-7

LC 2006-19545

Captured by Vikings, young Hekja is taken as a slave to Greenland by the daughter of Erik the Red, and accompanied by no one from her homeland but her loyal dog, shares adventures with her new mistress.

"In French's accessible, historically accurate telling, Hekja both suffers and profits from her experiences. . . . French has created compelling, fully realized characters." Booklist

Friedman, Laurie B., 1964-

Campfire Mallory; by Laurie Friedman; illustrations by Jennifer Kalis. Carolrhoda Books 2008 175p il lib bdg $15.95; pa $5.95

Grades: 2 3 4 **Fic**

1. Camps—Fiction 2. Friendship—Fiction

ISBN 978-0-8225-7657-0 (lib bdg); 0-8225-7657-0 (lib bdg); 978-1-58013-841-3 (pa); 1-58013-841-1 (pa)

LC 2007022218

Nine-and-a-half-year-old Mallory's trepidation about going to sleepaway camp is multiplied when she and her best friend are assigned to different cabins, and a new "friend" seems determined to get Mallory in trouble

"The plot is believable, and the language is well suited to the intended audience. Mallory's diary entries and black-and-white cartoons appear throughout. The action is well paced. . . . A lighthearted, enjoyable read." SLJ

Other titles about Mallory are:
Back to school Mallory (2004)
Mallory on the move (2004)
Mallory vs. Max (2005)
Happy birthday, Mallory (2005)
Happy New Year, Mallory (2009)
In business with Mallory (2006)
Heart-to-heart with Mallory (2006)

Friedman, Laurie B., 1964-—*Continued*
Mallory on board (2007)
Honestly, Mallory (2007)
Step fourth, Mallory (2008)
Red, white & true blue Mallory (2009)
Mallory goes green (2010)

Fritz, Jean
The cabin faced west; illustrated by Feodor
Rojankovsky 1958 124p il hardcover o.p. pa $6.99
Grades: 3 4 5 6   **Fic**
1. Scott, Ann Hamilton—Fiction 2. Frontier and pio-
neer life—Fiction 3. Pennsylvania—Fiction
ISBN 0-698-20016-0; 0-698-11936-3 (pa)
"Ann is unhappy when her family moves from Gettys-
burg to the Pennsylvania frontier, but she soon finds
friends and begins to see that there is much to enjoy
about her new home—including a visit from General
Washington." Hodges. Books for Elem Sch Libr

Frost, Helen, 1949-
Spinning through the universe; a novel in poems
from room 214. Farrar, Straus and Giroux 2004
93p $16
Grades: 4 5 6 7   **Fic**
1. School stories 2. Poetry
ISBN 0-374-37159-8   LC 2003-48056
"Frances Foster books"
A collection of poems written in the voices of Mrs.
Williams of room 214, her students, and a custodian
about their interactions with each other, their families,
and the world around them. Includes notes on the poetic
forms represented
"Interwoven dramatic stories and interesting poetic
patterns give this book extra appeal. A boon for poetry
classes." SLJ

Funke, Cornelia Caroline
Dragon rider; [by] Cornelia Funke; translated by
Anthea Bell. Scholastic 2004 523p il $12.95 *
Grades: 5 6 7 8   **Fic**
1. Dragons—Fiction 2. Fantasy fiction
ISBN 0-439-45695-9   LC 2004-45419
Original German edition 1997
After learning that humans are headed toward his hidden home, Firedrake, a silver dragon, is joined by a
brownie and an orphan boy in a quest to find the legendary valley known as the Rim of Heaven, encountering
friendly and unfriendly creatures along the way, and
struggling to evade the relentless pursuit of an old enemy.
"Funke proves she knows how to tickle the imaginations of younger readers. . . . This is a good, old-
fashioned ensemble-cast quest." Booklist

Igraine the brave; [by] Cornelia Funke; with
illustrations by the author; translated from the
German by Anthea Bell. Chicken House/Scholastic
2007 212p il $16.99 *
Grades: 4 5 6   **Fic**
1. Knights and knighthood—Fiction 2. Magic—Fiction
3. Fantasy fiction
ISBN 978-0-439-90379-0; 0-439-90379-3
                                LC 2006032672

The daughter of two magicians, twelve-year-old
Igraine wants nothing more than to be a knight, and
when their castle is attacked by a treacherous neighbor
bent on stealing their singing magic books, Igraine has
an opportunity to demonstrate her bravery.
"Funke's inventive re-imagining of the knight-in-
shining-armor story benefits from its playful details. . . .
The author . . . provides her own line drawings, witty
images of the singing books . . . and atmospheric
spreads with inset text." Publ Wkly

Inkheart; [by] Cornelia Funke; translated from
the German by Anthea Bell. Scholastic 2003 534p
$19.95; pa $9.99 *
Grades: 5 6 7 8   **Fic**
1. Books and reading—Fiction 2. Fantasy fiction
ISBN 0-439-53164-0; 0-439-70910-5 (pa)
                                LC 2003-45844
"The Chicken House"
Twelve-year-old Meggie learns that her father, who repairs and binds books for a living, can "read" fictional
characters to life when one of those characters abducts
them and tries to force him into service.
The author "proves the power of her imagination;
readers will be captivated by the chilling and thrilling
world she has created here." Publ Wkly
Other titles in this series are:
Inkspell (2005)
Inkdeath (2008)

Fuqua, Jonathon Scott
Darby. Candlewick Press 2002 242p hardcover
o.p. pa $6.99
Grades: 4 5 6 7   **Fic**
1. Race relations—Fiction 2. African Americans—Fic-
tion 3. South Carolina—Fiction
ISBN 0-7636-1417-3; 0-7636-2290-7 (pa)
                                LC 2001-35061
In 1926, nine-year-old Darby Carmichael stirs up trou-
ble in Marlboro County, South Carolina, when she writes
a story for the local newspaper promoting racial equality
"Darby's voice, rich with Southern idiom, rings true."
Horn Book Guide

Gaiman, Neil, 1960-
Coraline; [by] Neil Gaiman; with illustrations by
Dave McKean. HarperCollins Pubs. 2002 162p il
$15.99; pa $5.99 *
Grades: 5 6 7 8   **Fic**
1. Supernatural—Fiction 2. Horror fiction
ISBN 0-380-97778-8; 0-380-80734-3 (pa)
                                LC 2002-18937
Looking for excitement, Coraline ventures through a
mysterious door into a world that is similar, yet
disturbingly different from her own, where she must
challenge a gruesome entity in order to save herself, her
parents, and the souls of three others
"Gaiman twines his taut tale with a menacing tone
and crisp prose fraught with memorable imagery . . . yet
keeps the narrative just this side of terrifying." Publ
Wkly

Gaiman, Neil, 1960-—*Continued*

The graveyard book; with illustrations by Dave McKean. HarperCollins 2008 312p il $17.99; lib bdg $18.89 *

Grades: 5 6 7 8 9 10   **Fic**

1. Death—Fiction 2. Supernatural—Fiction 3. Cemeteries—Fiction

ISBN   978-0-06-053092-1;   0-06-053092-8; 978-0-06-053093-8 (lib bdg); 0-06-053093-6 (lib bdg)

LC 2008-13860

Awarded the Newbery Medal (2009)

Nobody Owens is a normal boy, except that he has been raised by ghosts and other denizens of the graveyard

"Gaiman writes with charm and humor, and again he has a real winner." Voice Youth Advocates

Odd and the Frost Giants; illustrated by Brett Helquist. HarperCollinsPublishers 2009 117p il $14.99

Grades: 3 4 5 6   **Fic**

1. Norse mythology—Fiction

ISBN 978-0-06-167173-9; 0-06-167173-8

LC 2009014574

An unlucky twelve-year-old Norwegian boy named Odd leads the Norse gods Loki, Thor, and Odin in an attempt to outwit evil Frost Giants who have taken over Asgard.

"Along with Gaiman's deft humor, lively prose, and agile imagination, a few unexpected themes—the double-edged allure of beauty, the value of family—sneak into this slim tale with particular appeal to kids drawn to Norse mythology, but suitable for any readers of light fantasy." Booklist

Galante, Cecilia, 1971-

Hershey herself; [by] Cecilia Galante. Aladdin Mix 2008 330p pa $5.99

Grades: 5 6 7 8   **Fic**

1. Music—Fiction 2. Friendship—Fiction 3. Abused women—Fiction

ISBN 978-1-4169-5463-7 (pa); 1-4169-5463-5 (pa)

"When twelve-year-old Hershey must run away with her mother to a women's shelter, she wonders how, among other things, she'll compete in the town talent show with her best friend, Phoebe." Publisher's note

"Subplots with multiple themes of self-respect, abuse, poverty, friendship, music, depression and dreams are all skillfully blended into an engaging novel for middle school readers." Libr Media Connect

Willowood. Simon & Schuster 2010 265p $16.99

Grades: 4 5 6 7   **Fic**

1. Moving—Fiction 2. Single parent family—Fiction 3. Geckos—Fiction 4. Friendship—Fiction

ISBN 978-1-4169-8022-3; 1-4169-8022-9

Eleven-year-old Lily has trouble leaving her best friend behind and moving to the city when her mother changes jobs, but she makes some very unlikely friends that soon become like family members.

"The characters . . . are fully realized individuals. . . . [This book has a] finely tuned plot and poetic language. . . . Children will enjoy the story of Lily's first few months in the big city." SLJ

Gannett, Ruth Stiles, 1923-

My father's dragon; story by Ruth Stiles Gannett; illustrations by Ruth Chrisman Gannett. 60th anniversary edition. Random House 2008 c1948 86p il $16.99; lib bdg $19.99

Grades: 1 2 3 4   **Fic**

1. Dragons—Fiction 2. Fantasy fiction 3. Animals—Fiction

ISBN   978-0-375-85610-5;   0-375-85610-2; 978-0-375-95610-2 (lib bdg); 0-375-95610-7 (lib bdg)

A Newbery Medal honor book, 1949

A reissue of the title first published 1948

This describes the adventures of a small boy, Elmer Elevator, who befriended an old alley cat and in return heard the story of the captive baby dragon on Wild Island. Right away Elmer decided to free the dragon. The tale of Elmer's voyage to Tangerina and his arrival on Wild Island, his encounters with various wild animals, and his subsequent rescue of the dragon follows

Other titles in this series are:

The dragons of Blueland (1951)

Elmer and the dragon (1950)

Gantos, Jack

Heads or tails; stories from the sixth grade. Farrar, Straus Giroux 1994 151p il $16; pa $4.95 *

Grades: 5 6 7 8   **Fic**

1. Diaries—Fiction 2. Family life—Fiction 3. School stories

ISBN 0-374-32909-5; 0-374-42923-5 (pa)

LC 93-43117

"Jack is trying to survive his sixth-grade year, and he narrates, through a series of short-stories-cum-chapters, his difficulties in dodging the obstacles life throws in his path. . . . The writing is zingy and specific, with snappily authentic dialogue and a vivid sense of juvenile experience. . . . Jack and his family have a recognizably thorny relationship. This is a distinctive and lively sequence of everyday-life stories." Bull Cent Child Books

Other titles about Jack are:

Jack adrift (2003)

Jack on the tracks (1999)

Jack's black book (1997)

Jack's new power (1995)

Joey Pigza swallowed the key. Farrar, Straus & Giroux 1998 153p $16.99 *

Grades: 5 6 7 8   **Fic**

1. Attention deficit disorder—Fiction 2. School stories

ISBN 0-374-33664-4   LC 98-24264

Also available in paperback from HarperCollins

To the constant disappointment of his mother and his teachers, Joey has trouble paying attention or controlling his mood swings when his prescription meds wear off and he starts getting worked up and acting wired

This "frenetic narrative pulls at heartstrings and tickles funny bones." SLJ

Other titles about Joey Pigza are:

Joey Pigza loses control (2000)

What would Joey do? (2002)

I am not Joey Pigza (2007)

García, Cristina, 1958-

I wanna be your shoebox. Simon & Schuster Books for Children 2008 198p $16.99; pa $6.99 *
Grades: 4 5 6 7   **Fic**

1. Racially mixed people—Fiction 2. Grandfathers—Fiction 3. Jews—Fiction 4. Cuban Americans—Fiction 5. Family life—Fiction 6. California—Fiction
ISBN   978-1-4169-3928-3;   1-4169-3928-8; 978-1-4169-7904-3 (pa); 1-4169-7904-2 (pa)

Thirteen-year-old, clarinet-playing, Southern California surfer, Yumi Ruiz-Hirsch, comes from a complex family—her father is Jewish-Japanese, her mother is Cuban, and her parents are divorced—and when her grandfather Saul is diagnosed with terminal cancer, Yumi asks him to tell her his life story, which helps her to understand her own history and identity.

"García's . . . exceptional ability to channel a range of voices lights up her first children's novel. . . . The large personalities propel the story and bring tenderness and credibility to a classic message about change." Publ Wkly

Gardiner, John Reynolds, 1944-2006

Stone Fox; illustrated by Marcia Sewall. Crowell 1980 81p il $15.99; lib bdg $16.89; pa $5.50
Grades: 2 3 4 5   **Fic**

1. Sled dog racing—Fiction 2. Dogs—Fiction
ISBN 0-690-03983-2; 0-690-03984-0 (lib bdg); 0-06-440132-4 (pa)   LC 79-7895

"When his usually spry grandfather won't get out of bed Willy searches for a remedy. Back taxes are the problem and the only way to get the money is to win the dogsled race. Stone Fox, a towering Indian who has never lost a race, is primary competition. Both want the prize money for the government—Willy for taxes and Stone Fox to buy his native land back." SLJ

This story "is rooted in a Rocky Mountain legend, a locale faithfully represented in Sewall's wonderful drawings. . . . In Gardiner's bardic chronicle, the tension is teeth rattling, with the tale flying to a conclusion that is almost unbearably moving, one readers won't soon forget." Publ Wkly

Gardner, Lyn

Into the woods; pictures by Mini Grey. David Fickling Books 2007 427p il $16.99; lib bdg $19.99; pa $7.50 *
Grades: 5 6 7 8   **Fic**

1. Sisters—Fiction 2. Fantasy fiction
ISBN   978-0-385-75115-5;   0-385-75115-X; 978-0-385-75116-2 (lib bdg); 0-385-75116-8 (lib bdg); 978-0-440-42223-5 (pa); 0-440-42223-X (pa)
LC 2006-24350

Pursued by the sinister Dr. DeWilde and his ravenous wolves, three sisters—Storm, the inheritor of a special musical pipe, the elder Aurora, and the baby Any—flee into the woods and begin a treacherous journey filled with many dangers as they try to find a way to defeat their pursuer and keep him from taking the pipe and control of the entire land.

"Gardner's fast-paced fantasy-adventure cleverly borrows from well-known fairy tales, and astute readers will enjoy identifying the many folkloric references. . . . Grey's appealing black-and-white illustrations add humor and detail to the story." Booklist

Followed by: Out of the woods (2010)

Garza, Xavier, 1968-

Lucha libre: the Man in the Silver Mask; a bilingual cuento; written & illustrated by Xavier Garza. Cinco Puntos Press 2005 unp il $17.95 *
Grades: 2 3 4 5   **Fic**

1. Uncles—Fiction 2. Wrestling—Fiction 3. Mexico—Fiction 4. Bilingual books—English-Spanish
ISBN 0-938317-92-X   LC 2004-29756

When Carlitos attends a wrestling match in Mexico City with his father, his favorite masked-wrestler has eyes that are strangely familiar.

"Smoothly integrated information in fluid colloquial English and Spanish combines with grainy graphic-novel-style illustrations executed in acrylic to create an oddly compelling and sophisticated package. An informative endnote, in English only, presents a brief but engrossing history of lucha libre." SLJ

Gates, Doris, 1901-1987

Blue willow; illustrated by Paul Lantz. Viking 1940 172p il pa $5.99 hardcover o.p.
Grades: 4 5 6 7   **Fic**

1. Migrant labor—Fiction 2. California—Fiction
ISBN 0-14-030924-1 (pa)

"Having to move from one migrant camp to another intensifies Janey Larkin's desire for a permanent home, friends, and school. The only beautiful possession the family has is a blue willow plate handed down from generation to generation. It is a reminder of happier days in Texas and represents dreams and promises for a better future. Reading about this itinerant family's ways of life, often filled with despair and yet always hopeful, leaves little room for the reader's indifference." Read Ladders for Hum Relat. 6th edition

Gauch, Patricia Lee

This time, Tempe Wick? illustrated by Margot Tomes. Boyds Mills Press 2003 c1974 43p il $16.95 paperback o.p. *
Grades: 3 4 5   **Fic**

1. United States—History—1775-1783, Revolution—Fiction
ISBN 1-59078-179-1; 1-59078-185-6 (pa)

A reissue of the title first published 1974 by Coward, McCann & Geoghegan

Everyone knows Tempe Wick is a most surprising girl, but she exceeds even her own reputation when two mutinous Revolutionary soldiers try to steal her beloved horse.

"The writing is the perfect vehicle for the illustrations—in the artist's inimitable style—which capture the down-to-earth, unpretentious, and humorous quality of the storytelling." Horn Book

Gauch, Patricia Lee—_Continued_

Thunder at Gettysburg; drawings by Stephen Gammell. Boyds Mills Press 2003 c1975 46p il $16.95; pa $9.95

Grades: 3 4 5   **Fic**

1. Gettysburg (Pa.), Battle of, 1863—Fiction

ISBN 1-59078-180-5; 1-59078-186-4 (pa)

A reissue of the title first published 1975 by Coward, McCann & Geoghegan

Fourteen-year-old Tillie becomes involved in the tragic battle of July 13, 1863

"Gauch has drawn on the experiences of a real person, in this case Tillie Pierce Alleman, whose 1889 book 'At Gettysburg' provided the basis of the story. Gammell's thorough pencilled scenes are full of atmosphere and acute emotion, their escalating drama effectively congruent with that of the story." Booklist

Gauthier, Gail, 1953-

A girl, a boy, and three robbers; illustrated by Joe Cepeda. G.P. Putnam's Sons 2008 87p il $14.99

Grades: 2 3 4   **Fic**

1. Play—Fiction 2. Imagination—Fiction 3. Cats—Fiction

ISBN 978-0-399-24690-6; 0-399-24690-8

LC 2007-23967

Sequel to: A girl, a boy, and a monster cat (2007)

Three afternoons a week, Brandon reluctantly stays with his imaginative classmate, Hannah, and her oversized cat, Buttercup, playing games, but their adventures really begin when the dreaded Sunderland triplets from next door try to steal Buttercup.

"Filled with comic moments and realistic escapades, this short chapter book is laugh-out-loud funny. The characters fairly jump off the pages." SLJ

Geisert, Bonnie, 1943-

Prairie summer; illustrated by Arthur Geisert. Houghton Mifflin 2002 113p il $15

Grades: 4 5 6   **Fic**

1. Farm life—Fiction 2. Family life—Fiction 3. South Dakota—Fiction

ISBN 0-618-21293-0   LC 2001-4176

Ten-year-old Rachel demonstrates the maturity gained from her experiences growing up with three sisters on a farm in South Dakota

"Geisert skillfully uses the plot and the setting to reveal the relationships and develop the characters. . . . A poignant family story that's true to a child's point of view." SLJ

Other titles about Rachel are:

Lessons (2005)

Prairie winter (2009)

George, Jean Craighead, 1919-

The cats of Roxville Station; illustrated by Tom Pohrt. Dutton Children's Books 2009 163p il $16.99

Grades: 4 5 6   **Fic**

1. Cats—Fiction

ISBN 978-0-525-42140-5; 0-525-42140-8

LC 2008034217

Thrown into a river by a cruel human, a young tiger-striped cat fights to survive amid feral cats and other creatures near Roxville train station, aided by Mike, an eleven-year-old foster boy who is not allowed to have a pet.

"George packs a lot of natural information on species from mosquitoes to owls in this slim volume. There is no anthropomorphization of the cats; when Ratchet and the other cats 'talk' it is with scent and body language. Pohrt's line drawings complement the text nicely." Kirkus

Charlie's raven; written and illustrated by Jean Craighead George. Dutton Children's Books 2004 190p il hardcover o.p. pa $6.99

Grades: 5 6 7 8   **Fic**

1. Ravens—Fiction 2. Grandfathers—Fiction 3. Naturalists—Fiction

ISBN 0-525-47219-3; 0-14-240547-7 (pa)

Charlie's friend, Singing Bird, a Teton Sioux, tells him that ravens have curing powers, so Charlie steals a baby bird from its nest, hoping to heal his ailing Granddad, a retired naturalist.

"The story is technically accurate and offers a vivid sense of place and a window into Native American beliefs through storytelling." SLJ

Julie; illustrated by Wendell Minor. HarperCollins Pubs. 1994 226p il hardcover o.p. pa $5.99

Grades: 6 7 8 9   **Fic**

1. Inuit—Fiction 2. Arctic regions—Fiction 3. Wolves—Fiction

ISBN 0-06-023528-4; 0-06-440573-7 (pa)

LC 93-27738

This sequel to Julie of the wolves "details Julie's adjustment to family and modernization after returning home. Her father's musk oxen enterprise depicts the problems inherent to environment-versus-economics issues as Julie struggles to save her wolf friends." Sci Child

Followed by Julie's wolf pack

Julie of the wolves; pictures by John Schoenherr. Harper & Row 1972 170p il $15.99; lib bdg $16.89; pa $5.99 *

Grades: 6 7 8 9   **Fic**

1. Inuit—Fiction 2. Arctic regions—Fiction 3. Wilderness survival—Fiction 4. Wolves—Fiction

ISBN 0-06-021943-2; 0-06-021944-0 (lib bdg); 0-06-440058-1 (pa)

Awarded the Newbery Medal, 1973

"Lost in the Alaskan wilderness, thirteen-year old Miyax [Julie in English], an Eskimo girl, is gradually accepted by a pack of Arctic wolves that she comes to love." Booklist

"The superb narration includes authentic descriptions and details of the Eskimo way-of-life and of Eskimo rituals. . . . The whole book has a rare, intense reality which the artist enhances beautifully with animated drawings." Horn Book

Followed by Julie

George, Jean Craighead, 1919-—*Continued*

My side of the mountain trilogy; written and illustrated by Jean Craighead George. Dutton Children's Books 2000 177, 170, 258p il $24.99 *

Grades: 5 6 7 8   **Fic**
1. Wilderness survival—Fiction 2. Falcons—Fiction 3. New York (State)—Fiction
ISBN 0-525-46269-4   LC 00-712305

Also available in paperback from Puffin as separate volumes

My side of the mountain was a Newbery honor book, 1960

Originally published as three separate volumes, 1959, 1990, and 1999 respectively

Contents: My side of the mountain; On the far side of the mountain; Frightful's mountain

In *My Side of the Mountain* Sam Gribley tells of his year in the wilderness of the Catskill Mountains. In *On the Far Side of the Mountain* Sam's peaceful existence in his wilderness home is disrupted when his sister runs away and his pet falcon is confiscated by a conservation officer. In *Frightful's Mountain* Sam's pet falcon must learn to live as a wild bird

There's an owl in the shower; illustrated by Christine Herman Merrill. HarperCollins Pubs. 1995 133p il hardcover o.p. pa $5.99
Grades: 3 4 5   **Fic**
1. Owls—Fiction 2. Endangered species—Fiction
ISBN 0-06-024891-2; 0-06-440682-2 (pa)
                                    LC 94-38893

Because protecting spotted owls has cost Borden's father his job as a logger in the old growth forest of northern California, Borden intends to kill any spotted owl he sees, until he and his father find themselves taking care of a young owlet

"George's writing skill and knowledge of animal behavior turn what could have been nothing but a message into an absorbing story that shows both sides of the controversy. . . . Merrill's drawings perfectly capture the engaging bird and the family's affection for it." SLJ

Gephart, Donna

As if being 12 3/4 isn't bad enough, my mother is running for president! by Donna Gephart. Delacorte Press 2008 227p $15.99; lib bdg $18.99
Grades: 4 5 6   **Fic**
1. Politics—Fiction 2. Mother-daughter relationship—Fiction 3. School stories 4. Florida—Fiction
ISBN 978-0-385-73481-3; 978-0-385-90479-7 (lib bdg)   LC 2007027601

Preparing for spelling bees, having a secret admirer, and waiting for her chest size to catch up with her enormous feet are pressure enough, but twelve-year-old Vanessa must also deal with loneliness and very real fears as her mother, Florida's Governor, runs for President of the United States.

"Gephart creates a likable protagonist. . . . Vanessa's emotional and social life . . . will keep readers engaged, and also the kid's-eye view of a candidate's campaigning." Booklist

How to survive middle school. Delacorte Press 2010 247p $15.99; lib bdg $18.99 *
Grades: 5 6 7 8   **Fic**
1. School stories 2. Family life—Fiction
ISBN   978-0-385-73793-7;   0-385-73793-9; 978-0-385-90701-9 (lib bdg); 0-385-90701-X (lib bdg)
                                    LC 2009-21809

When thirteen-year-old David Greenberg's best friend makes the start of middle school even worse than he feared it could be, David becomes friends with Penny, who shares his love of television shows and posts one of their skits on YouTube, making them wildly popular—online, at least.

"Gephart crafts for her likable protagonist an engaging, feel-good transition into adolescence that's well stocked with tears and laughter." Booklist

Gervay, Susanne

I am Jack; illustrations by Cathy Wilcox. Tricycle Press 2009 126p il $14.99
Grades: 3 4 5   **Fic**
1. Bullies—Fiction 2. School stories
ISBN 978-1-58246-286-8; 1-58246-286-0

"Eleven-year-old Jack has a problem, and his name is George Hamel, the school bully. George has targeted Jack for teasing and name-calling, and soon other kids are accosting and harassing him, too. . . . This story is a good portrayal of a young boy facing a situation that comes out of nowhere and affects his entire life. It is a solid addition to the growing collection of books about bullying." SLJ

Giblin, James, 1933-

The boy who saved Cleveland; based on a true story; [by] James Cross Giblin; illustrated by Michael Dooling. Henry Holt and Company 2006 64p il $15.95
Grades: 3 4 5   **Fic**
1. Frontier and pioneer life—Fiction 2. Epidemics—Fiction 3. Malaria—Fiction 4. Ohio—Fiction
ISBN 0-8050-7355-8; 978-0-8050-7355-3
                                    LC 2005021695

During a malaria epidemic in late eighteenth-century Cleveland, Ohio, ten-year-old Seth Doan surprises his family, his neighbors, and himself by having the strength to carry and grind enough corn to feed everyone.

"Young readers will enjoy the clear writing and plot-driven pace. Dooling's full-page pencil-on-paper illustrations convey the time period as well as the emotional tone. A solid choice for those seeking pioneer fiction and strong characters." Booklist

Did Fleming rescue Churchill? a research puzzle; by James Cross Giblin; illustrated by Erik Brooks. Henry Holt 2008 64p il $16.95
Grades: 3 4 5   **Fic**
1. Fleming, Alexander, 1881-1955—Fiction 2. Research—Fiction 3. School stories
ISBN 978-0-8050-8183-1; 0-8050-8183-6
                                    LC 2007-27568

Ten-year-old Jason uses everything he knows about research, including how to separate fact from fiction when using the Internet, to make the deadline for his his-

Giblin, James, 1933-—*Continued*

tory paper on scientist Alexander Fleming—the discoverer of penicillin. Includes research tips, emphasizing the
importance of accuracy

"Giblin turns a potentially dull subject into a good
story. Expressive pen drawings illustrate this appealing
chapter book." Booklist

Includes bibliographical references

Gifaldi, David

Listening for crickets. Henry Holt 2008 178p
$16.95

Grades: 3 4 5   **Fic**
1. Family life—Fiction 2. Storytelling—Fiction
3. Siblings—Fiction
ISBN 978-0-8050-7385-0; 0-8050-7385-X
                           LC 2007-27574

With parents that fight all the time, ten-year-old Jake
finds comfort and escape in the stories he creates for
himself and his little sister.

"The dialogue is lively and realistic, and each character is conveyed compassionately. . . . This short novel
finishes with just enough resolution to be believable but
not overly tidy." Horn Book

Giff, Patricia Reilly

All the way home. Delacorte Press 2001 169p
hardcover o.p. pa $5.99

Grades: 4 5 6 7   **Fic**
1. Poliomyelitis—Fiction 2. Apples—Fiction
3. Friendship—Fiction 4. Brooklyn (New York,
N.Y.)—Fiction
ISBN 0-385-32209-7; 0-440-41182-3 (pa)
                           LC 2001-28174

In 1941, circumstances bring together Brick, a boy
from New York's apple country, and Mariel, a young
girl made shy by her bout with polio, and the two make
a journey from Brooklyn back to help Brick's elderly
neighbors save their apple crop and to help Mariel learn
about her past

"A compelling story of two unforgettable youngsters,
their strength, and their friendship." SLJ

Eleven. Wendy Lamb Books 2008 164p $15.99;
lib bdg $18.99; pa $6.50

Grades: 4 5 6 7   **Fic**
1. Kidnapping—Fiction 2. Friendship—Fiction
3. Learning disabilities—Fiction 4. Woodwork—Fiction
ISBN 978-0-385-73069-3; 978-0-385-90098-0 (lib
bdg); 978-0-440-23802-7 (pa)   LC 2007-12638

When Sam, who can barely read, discovers an old
newspaper clipping just before his eleventh birthday, it
brings forth memories from his past, and, with the help
of a new friend at school and the castle they are building
for a school project, his questions are eventually answered.

This is an "exquisitely rendered story of self-
discovery." Publ Wkly

A house of tailors. Wendy Lamb Books 2004
148p $15.95; pa $5.50

Grades: 5 6 7 8   **Fic**
1. Immigrants—Fiction 2. German Americans—Fiction
3. Brooklyn (New York, N.Y.)—Fiction
ISBN 0-385-73066-7; 0-440-23800-5 (pa)
                         LC 2003-26103

When thirteen-year-old Dina emigrates from Germany
to America in 1871, her only wish is to return home as
soon as she can, but as the months pass and she survives
a multitude of hardships living with her uncle and his
young wife and baby, she finds herself thinking of
Brooklyn as her home.

"This novel is rich with believable, endearing characters as well as excitement and emotion." SLJ

Kidnap at the Catfish Cafe; illustrated by Lynne
Cravath. Viking 1998 73p il pa $4.99

Grades: 3 4 5   **Fic**
1. Mystery fiction
ISBN 0-14-130821-4 (pa)   LC 98-5711

Assisted by her cat Max, sixth grader Minnie starts up
her new detective agency by investigating a kidnapping
and a thief who will steal anything, even a hot stove

"Young mystery lovers will enjoy the witty story with
its standout characters." Booklist

Another title about Minnie and Max is:
Mary Moon is missing (1998)

Lily's crossing. Delacorte Press 1997 180p
$15.95; pa $6.50

Grades: 4 5 6 7   **Fic**
1. World War, 1939-1945—Fiction 2. Friendship—
Fiction
ISBN 0-385-32142-2; 0-440-41453-9 (pa)
                          LC 96-23021

A Newbery Medal honor book, 1998

During a summer spent at Rockaway Beach in 1944,
Lily's friendship with a young Hungarian refugee causes
her to see the war and her own world differently

"Gentle elements of danger and suspense . . . keep
the plot moving forward, while the delicate balance of
characters and setting gently coalesces into an emotional
whole that is fully satisfying." Bull Cent Child Books

Nory Ryan's song. Delacorte Press 2000 148p
hardcover o.p. pa $5.99

Grades: 5 6 7 8   **Fic**
1. Ireland—Fiction 2. Famines—Fiction
ISBN 0-385-32141-4; 0-440-41829-1 (pa)
                         LC 00-27690

When a terrible blight attacks Ireland's potato crop in
1845, twelve-year-old Nory Ryan's courage and ingenuity help her family and neighbors survive

"Giff brings the landscape and the cultural particulars
of the era vividly to life and creates in Nory a heroine
to cheer for. A beautiful, heart-wrenching novel that
makes a devastating event understandable." Booklist

Another title about Nory is:
Maggie's door (2003)

Giff, Patricia Reilly—*Continued*

Pictures of Hollis Woods. Wendy Lamb Bks. 2002 166p $15.95; pa $6.50

Grades: 5 6 7 8   **Fic**

1. Artists—Fiction 2. Foster home care—Fiction 3. Old age—Fiction

ISBN 0-385-32655-6; 0-440-41578-0 (pa)

LC 2002-426

A Newbery Medal honor book, 2003

"She was named for the place where she was found as an abandoned baby. Twelve-year-old Hollis Woods has been through many foster homes—and she runs away, every time. In her latest placement, with an artist named Josie, the tightly wound Hollis begins to relax ever so slightly. . . . But Josie is slowly slipping into dementia, and Hollis knows that she'll be taken away from her if Josie is found out. . . . Giff has a sure hand with language, and the narrative is taut and absorbing." Booklist

Water Street. Wendy Lamb Books 2006 164p $15.95; lib bdg $17.99; pa $6.50

Grades: 5 6 7 8   **Fic**

1. Irish Americans—Fiction 2. Brooklyn (New York, N.Y.)—Fiction 3. Family life—Fiction

ISBN 978-0-385-90097-3; 0-385-73068-3; 978-0-385-90097-3 (lib bdg); 0-385-90097-X (lib bdg); 978-0-440-41921-1 (pa); 0-440-41921-2 (pa)

LC 2006-02024

In the shadow of the construction of the Brooklyn Bridge, eighth-graders and new neighbors Bird Mallon and Thomas Neary make some decisions about what they want to do with their lives.

"Continuing the Irish American immigration story begun in *Nory Ryan's Song* (2000) and *Maggie's Door* (2003), [this] novel, set in 1875, is about the next generation. . . . A poignant immigration story of friendship, work, and the meaning of home." Booklist

Wild girl. Wendy Lamb Books 2009 147p $15.99; lib bdg $18.99

Grades: 3 4 5 6   **Fic**

1. Horses—Fiction 2. Family life—Fiction 3. Immigrants—Fiction 4. Brazilian Americans—Fiction 5. New York (State)—Fiction

ISBN 978-0-375-83890-3; 0-375-83890-2; 978-0-375-93890-0 (lib bdg); 0-375-93890-7 (lib bdg)

LC 2008-47733

When twelve-year-old Lydie leaves Brazil to join her father and brother on a horse ranch in New York, she has a hard time adjusting to her changed circumstances, as does a new horse that has come to the ranch.

"Readers who choose the book because of the horse on the jacket will find a satisfying girl-meets-horse story. Those looking for a convincing, sometimes moving immigrant story will find it here as well." Booklist

Willow run. Wendy Lamb Bks. 2005 149p $15.95; pa $5.99

Grades: 4 5 6 7   **Fic**

1. World War, 1939-1945—Fiction

ISBN 0-385-73067-5; 0-440-23801-3 (pa)

LC 2004-24541

During World War II, after moving with her parents to Willow Run, Michigan, when her father gets a job in the B24 bomber-building factory, eleven-year-old Meggie learns about different kinds of bravery from all of the people around her.

"Giff artfully carves the sentiments so prevalent in times of war—anxiety, inspiration, boredom—into sharp relief while creating a cast of finely drawn characters." Booklist

Gifford, Peggy Elizabeth, 1952-

Moxy Maxwell does not love Stuart Little. Schwartz & Wade Books 2007 91p il $12.99; lib bdg $15.99; pa $5.50 *

Grades: 2 3 4   **Fic**

1. Books and reading—Fiction 2. Summer—Fiction 3. Family life—Fiction

ISBN 0-375-83915-1; 978-0-375-83915-3; 0-375-93915-6 (lib bdg); 978-0-375-93915-0 (lib bdg); 978-0-440-42230-3 (pa); 0-440-42230-2 (pa)

LC 2006-16869

With summer coming to an end, about-to-be-fourth-grader Moxy Maxwell does a hundred different things to avoid reading her assigned summer reading book.

"Moxy is funny. . . . A dryly observant narration, clever chapter titles, and the spot-on illustrations provide added lift to the story." SLJ

Other titles about Moxy Maxwell are:

Moxy Maxwell does not love writing thank-you notes (2008)

Moxy Maxwell does not love practicing the piano (2009)

Gilman, Laura Anne

Grail quest: the Camelot spell; book one. HarperCollins 2006 291p $10.99; lib bdg $14.89

Grades: 5 6 7 8   **Fic**

1. Arthur, King—Fiction 2. Knights and knighthood—Fiction 3. Middle Ages—Fiction 4. Magic—Fiction

ISBN 0-06-077279-4; 0-06-077280-8 (lib bdg)

Three teenagers living in Camelot are forced to undertake a dangerous mission when King Arthur's court falls under a mysterious enchantment on the eve of the quest for the Holy Grail.

"The believable dialogue, succint plot, and uncomplicated references to court life will appeal to middle graders who are beginning to explore Aurthurian legend." Voice Youth Advocates

Other titles in this series are:

Grail quest: Morgain's revenge (2006)

Grail quest: The shadow companion (2006)

Gilson, Jamie, 1933-

4B goes wild; illustrated by Linda Strauss Edwards. Lothrop, Lee & Shepard Bks. 1983 160p il lib bdg $16 *

Grades: 4 5 6   **Fic**

1. Camping—Fiction 2. School stories

ISBN 0-688-02236-7   LC 83-948

"Hobie Hanson, a sensitive fourth grader, tells of the time two fourth grade classes went on a three day camping trip." Child Book Rev Serv

"The writing style is breezy and comic . . . The dialogue is natural." Bull Cent Child Books

Other titles about Hobie Hanson are:

Gilson, Jamie, 1933-—*Continued*
Double dog dare (1988)
Hobie Hanson, you're weird (1987)
Thirteen ways to sink a sub (1982)

Bug in a rug; illustrated by Diane deGroat.
Clarion Books 1998 69p il $15 paperback o.p.
Grades: 2 3 4   **Fic**
  1. School stories 2. Clothing and dress—Fiction
  3. Uncles—Fiction
  ISBN 0-395-86616-2; 0-618-31670-1
                                          LC 97-16437
Seven-year-old Richard is self-conscious when he re-
ceives a pair of purple pants from his aunt and uncle and
has to wear them to school, but he is even more worried
when his uncle shows up for a visit to his classroom
  "Gilson captures the thoughts and fears of second
graders through authentic dialogue and solid characteriza-
tion." SLJ
  Other titles about Richard are:
Chess! I love it, I love it, I love it! (2008)
Gotcha! (2006)
It goes Eeeeeeeeeeeee! (1994)
Itchy Richard (1991)

Gipson, Frederick Benjamin, 1903-1973
Old Yeller; [by] Fred Gipson; drawings by Carl
Burger. Harper & Row 1956 158p il $23; pa $5.99
Grades: 6 7 8 9   **Fic**
  1. Dogs—Fiction 2. Texas—Fiction 3. Frontier and pioneer life—Fiction
  ISBN 0-06-011545-9; 0-06-440382-3 (pa)
                                          LC 56-8780
  A Newbery Medal honor book, 1957
"Travis at fourteen was the man of the family during
the hard summer of 1860 when his father drove his herd
of cattle from Texas to the Kansas market. It was the
summer when an old yellow dog attached himself to the
family and won Travis' reluctant friendship. Before the
summer was over, Old Yeller proved more than a match
for thieving raccoons, fighting bulls, grizzly bears, and
mad wolves. This is a skillful tale of a boy's love for a
dog as well as a description of a pioneer boyhood and
it can't miss with any dog lover." Horn Book

Glaser, Linda
Bridge to America; based on a true story.
Houghton Mifflin Co. 2005 200p $16
Grades: 4 5 6   **Fic**
  1. Immigrants—Fiction 2. Jews—Fiction
  ISBN 0-618-56301-6
Eight-year-old Fivel narrates the story of his family's
Atlantic Ocean crossing to reunite with their father in the
United States, from its desperate beginning in a shtetl in
Poland in 1920 to his stirrings of identity as an Ameri-
can boy.
  "Even reluctant readers will enjoy this riveting ac-
count and sensitive portrayal of what it means to be an
immigrant." SLJ

Glatstein, Jacob, 1896-1971
Emil and Karl; by Yankev Glatshteyn; translated
by Jeffrey Shandler. Roaring Brook Press 2006
194p $17.95; pa $6.99
Grades: 5 6 7 8   **Fic**
  1. Holocaust, 1933-1945—Fiction 2. Jews—Fiction
  3. Vienna (Austria)—Fiction 4. Friendship—Fiction
  ISBN 1-59643-119-9; 0-312-37387-2 (pa)
                                          LC 2005-26800
  Original Yiddish edition 1940
A story about the dilemma faced by two young
boys—one Jewish, the other not—when they suddenly
find themselves without homes or families in Vienna on
the eve of World War II.
  "The fast-moving prose is stark and immediate.
Glatshteyn was, of course, writing about what was happening to children in his time. . . . The translation, 65
years after the novel's original publication, is nothing
short of haunting." Booklist

Glatt, Lisa, 1963-
Abigail Iris: the one and only. Walker & Co.
2009 148p $14.99
Grades: 2 3 4   **Fic**
  1. Family life—Fiction 2. Friendship—Fiction
  3. Siblings—Fiction
  ISBN 978-0-8027-9782-7; 0-8027-9782-2
                                          LC 2008007391
Abigail Iris thinks she would rather be an only child
but after going on vacation with her best friend, who is
an "Only," she realizes there are benefits of being one of
many.
  "Told in the first person from Abigail Iris' point of
view, this chapter book comes to life through her ingenuous voice and reflections. Appealing black-and-white
drawings show the characters' personalities, attitudes, and
emotions." Booklist
  Another title about Abigail Iris is:
Abigail Iris: the pet project (2010)

Glickman, Susan, 1953-
Bernadette and the lunch bunch. Second Story
Press 2008 123p il pa $6.95
Grades: 2 3 4   **Fic**
  1. School stories 2. Friendship—Fiction
  ISBN 978-1-897187-51-7 (pa); 1-897187-51-3 (pa)
  After her best friend moves away, Bernadette is dread-
ing the new school year, but things improve after she
discovers a group of new friends and they form the
Lunch Bunch
  "This curious girl is an engaging and quirky character.
. . . Written with light humor throughout, the story un-
folds nicely. . . . This is a fun read with accessible language and appeal for early chapter-book readers." SLJ

Gliori, Debi

Pure dead frozen. Alfred A. Knopf 2007 311p $15.99; pa $6.50

Grades: 4 5 6 7   **Fic**

1. Magic—Fiction 2. Witches—Fiction 3. Scotland—Fiction

ISBN   978-0-375-83317-5;   0-375-83317-X; 978-0-440-42075-0 (pa); 0-440-42075-X (pa)

First published 2006 in the United Kingdom with title: Deep fear

The Strega-Borgias make one last stand to defend their home against invaders who seek the Chronostone—and one little baby who may not be what he appears.

"Gliori clearly delights in word play and elicits laughter with her descriptions of characters, both good and evil. Playful language and inept evildoers make this book a fun but not scary read." Voice Youth Advocates

Other titles in this series are:

Pure dead magic (2001)
Pure dead wicked (2002)
Pure dead brilliant (2004)
Pure dead trouble (2005)
Pure dead batty (2006)

Goble, Paul

Beyond the ridge; story and illustrations by Paul Goble. Bradbury Press 1989 unp il pa $6.99 hardcover o.p.

Grades: 2 3 4   **Fic**

1. Native Americans—Fiction

ISBN 0-689-71731-8 (pa)   LC 87-33113

At her death an elderly Plains Indian woman experiences the afterlife believed in by her people, while the surviving family members prepare her body according to their custom

"Goble's illustrations—in a double spread of gray rocks, smoothly surfaced in a skyscape of flying vultures—make a dignified context for a moving, direct discussion of death." Bull Cent Child Books

Godden, Rumer, 1907-1998

The doll's house; illustrated by Tasha Tudor. Viking 1962 c1947 136p il pa $5.99 hardcover o.p.

Grades: 2 3 4   **Fic**

1. Dollhouses—Fiction 2. Dolls—Fiction

ISBN 0-14-030942-X (pa)

First published 1947 in the United Kingdom; first United States edition illustrated by Dana Saintsbury published 1948

Adventures of a brave little hundred-year-old Dutch farthing doll, her family, their Victorian dollhouse home and the two little English girls to whom they all belonged. Tottie's great adventure was when she went to the exhibition, Dolls through the ages, and was singled out for notice by the Queen who opened the exhibition

"Each doll has a firmly drawn, recognizably true character; the children think and behave convincingly. . . . The story is enthralling, and complete in every detail." Spectator

Godwin, Jane, 1964-

Falling from Grace; [by] Jane Godwin. Holiday House 2007 187p $16.95

Grades: 5 6 7 8   **Fic**

1. Missing children—Fiction 2. Sisters—Fiction 3. Australia—Fiction

ISBN 978-0-8234-2105-3; 0-8234-2105-8

LC 2006101432

Relates, from varying points of view, events surrounding the search for a twelve-year-old girl lost during a storm off the coast of Australia.

"Readers of all abilities will appreciate the short, descriptive chapters; teachers and librarians will value the possibilities for discussion in this unusual mystery that's sure to prompt readers to examine the consequences of their choices." SLJ

Going, K. L.

The garden of Eve. Harcourt 2007 234p $17; pa $6.99

Grades: 4 5 6 7   **Fic**

1. Magic—Fiction   2. Death—Fiction 3. Bereavement—Fiction 4. New York (State)—Fiction

ISBN   978-0-15-205986-6;   0-15-205986-5; 978-0-15-206614-7 (pa); 0-15-206614-4 (pa)

LC 2007-05074

Eve gave up her belief in stories and magic after her mother's death, but a mysterious seed given to her as an eleventh-birthday gift by someone she has never met takes her and a boy who claims to be a ghost on a strange journey, to where their supposedly cursed town of Beaumont, New York, flourishes.

"Believably and with delicacy, Going paints a suspenseful story suffused with the poignant questions of what it means to be alive, and what might await on the other side." Horn Book

Goscinny, 1926-1977

Nicholas; [by] Rene Goscinny & [illustrated by] Jean-Jacques Sempe; translated by Anthea Bell. Phaidon 2005 126p il $19.95

Grades: 4 5 6   **Fic**

1. School stories

ISBN 0-7148-4529-9

"This classic book about a mischievous schoolboy and his friends, originally published in French in 1959, is now available in English. The expertly translated text is enlivened by artwork by a New Yorker cartoonist to create the unforgettable milieu of Nicholas and his rowdy friends. A collection of 19 escapades, the stories introduce the protagonist and his cohorts as they wreak havoc out of simple, everyday situations at school, on the playground, and at home." SLJ

Other titles about Nicholas are:

Nicholas again (2006)
Nicholas on vacation (2007)

Goto, Scott

The perfect sword. Charlesbridge 2008 unp il lib bdg $15.95

Grades: 3 4 5   **Fic**

1. Japan—Fiction 2. Samurai—Fiction 3. Sword—Fiction

ISBN 978-1-57091-697-7 (lib bdg); 1-57091-697-7 (lib bdg)   LC 2007017184

After a Japanese master swordmaker and his apprentice craft the perfect sword, they search high and low for someone worthy of it.

"Goto inserts his readers directly into late-1500s Japan, giving them a feel for the culture and history. His vibrant oil paintings are detailed enough to keep readers poring over them, but large enough for group sharing. . . . This book is sure to attract browsers with its excellent illustrations and hold readers with its simple story, beautifully told." SLJ

Grabenstein, Chris

The crossroads. Random House 2008 325p $16.99; lib bdg $19.99; pa $6.99

Grades: 5 6 7 8   **Fic**

1. Ghost stories 2. Stepmothers—Fiction 3. Connecticut—Fiction

ISBN 978-0-375-84697-7; 0-375-84697-2; 978-0-375-94697-4 (lib bdg); 0-375-94697-7 (lib bdg); 978-0-375-84698-4 (pa); 0-375-84698-0 (pa)   LC 2007024803

When eleven-year-old Zack Jennings moves to Connecticut with his father and new stepmother, they must deal with the ghosts left behind by a terrible accident, as well as another kind of ghost from Zack's past

"An absorbing psychological thriller . . . as well as a rip-roaring ghost story, this switches points of view among humans, trees, and ghosts with astonishing élan." Booklist

Grabien, Deborah

Dark's tale. Egmont USA 2010 300p $15.99

Grades: 4 5 6   **Fic**

1. Cats—Fiction 2. Animals—Fiction 3. Parks—Fiction 4. San Francisco (Calif.)—Fiction

ISBN 978-1-60684-037-5; 1-60684-037-1

"Dark, a house cat abandoned in San Francisco's Golden Gate Park, must learn to survive in her new habitat. Befriended by a raccoon, she learns to recognize park inhabitants she must fear, like the 'crazybad' people, and those she can trust, including a wise owl named Memorie and a magical woman in rags who calls herself Streetwise Sal. . . . Written in first person from Dark's point of view, the novel creates a believable natural world, where predators hunt smaller animals and a cat must rely on her senses, her skills, and her friends for survival." Booklist

Graff, Lisa, 1981-

The life and crimes of Bernetta Wallflower; a novel. Laura Geringer Books 2008 250p $15.99; lib bdg $17.89

Grades: 4 5 6   **Fic**

1. Swindlers and swindling—Fiction 2. Magic tricks—Fiction 3. Money-making projects for children—Fiction 4. School stories

ISBN 978-0-06-087592-3; 0-06-087592-5; 978-0-06-087593-0 (lib bdg); 0-06-087593-3 (lib bdg)   LC 2006-103470

After her supposed best friend implicates her in a cheating and blackmail scam, twelve-year-old Bernie loses her private school scholarship but, with the help of a new friend, spends the summer using her knowledge of magic and sleight-of-hand both to earn the $9,000 in tuition money and to get revenge.

"The characters are well drawn, and Bernetta's growing qualms of conscience are believable. Readers will appreciate the well-constructed plot and intriguing snippets of magic slipped in here and there." SLJ

The thing about Georgie; a novel; by Lisa Graff. Laura Geringer Books 2006 220p $15.99; lib bdg $16.89; pa $5.99

Grades: 3 4 5 6   **Fic**

1. Dwarfism—Fiction 2. Family life—Fiction 3. Friendship—Fiction 4. School stories

ISBN 978-0-06-087589-3; 0-06-087589-5; 978-0-06-087590-9 (lib bdg); 0-06-087590-9 (lib bdg); 978-0-06-087591-6 (pa); 0-06-087591-7 (pa)   LC 2006000393

Georgie's dwarfism causes problems, but he could always rely on his parents, his best friend, and classmate Jeanie the Meanie's teasing, until a surprising announcement, a new boy in school, and a class project shake things up

"An upbeat and sensitive look at what it's like to be different, this novel will spark discussion." Booklist

Umbrella summer. Laura Geringer Books 2009 235p $15.99

Grades: 4 5 6   **Fic**

1. Death—Fiction 2. Bereavement—Fiction 3. Worry—Fiction

ISBN 978-0-06-143187-6; 0-06-143187-7   LC 2008-26015

After her brother Jared dies, ten-year-old Annie worries about the hidden dangers of everything, from bug bites to bicycle riding, until she is befriended by a new neighbor who is grieving her own loss.

"Annie's story deals with death with sensitivity, love, and understanding." SLJ

Grahame, Kenneth, 1859-1932

The reluctant dragon; by Kenneth Grahame; illustrated by Ernest H. Shepard. Holiday House 1989 unp il $15.95 *

Grades: 3 4 5   **Fic**

1. Dragons—Fiction 2. Fairy tales

ISBN 0-8234-0093-X   LC 89-1658

This chapter from Dream days was first published 1938

Grahame, Kenneth, 1859-1932—*Continued*

The boy who finds the dragon in the cave knows it is a kindly, harmless one, but how can he convince the frightened villagers and especially St. George the dragon killer that there is no cause for concern?

The wind in the willows; [by] Kenneth Grahame; abridged and illustrated by Inga Moore. Candlewick Press 2003 180p il (Candlewick illustrated classics) $21.99; pa $12.99

Grades: 3 4 5 6 **Fic**

1. Animals—Fiction

ISBN 978-0-7636-2242-8; 0-7636-2242-7; 978-0-7636-4211-2 (pa); 0-7636-4211-8 (pa)

LC 2003044001

This edition first published 2000 by Walker Books

The escapades of four animal friends who live along a river in the English countryside—Toad, Mole, Rat, and Badger.

"Previously published in two volumes, *The River Bank* (1996) and *The Adventures of Mr. Toad* (1998), Moore's intelligently abridged edition of Grahame's classic is now available in a single large-format volume. The relatively large print, the wide margins, and the beautiful ink-and-pastel artwork on nearly every page make this version a good choice for middle-grade independent readers put off by the original or for parents in search of a pleasing edition to read aloud to younger children." Booklist

The wind in the willows; illustrated by Robert Ingpen. Palazzo Editions 2008 224p il $19.95

Grades: 3 4 5 6 **Fic**

1. Animals—Fiction

ISBN 978-0-9553046-3-7; 0-9553046-3-6

First published 1908

The escapades of four animal friends, Toad, Mole, Rat, and Badger, who live along a river in the English countryside.

"This handsomely illustrated, unabridged edition celebrates the 100th anniversary of Grahame's classic animal fantasy. Ingpen's detailed paintings blend earthy tones with firelit highlights to create a warm mood. . . . Both the woodland scenes and animal abodes are charmingly depicted, and the characters, costumed in 19th-century garb, have loads of personality." SLJ

The wind in the willows; by Kenneth Grahame; illustrated in color and black and white by Ernest H. Shepard. 75th anniversary ed. Scribner 1983 244p il $15.96 *

Grades: 3 4 5 6 **Fic**

1. Animals—Fiction

ISBN 0-684-17957-1

First published 1908

In this fantasy "the characters are Mole, Water Rat, Mr. Toad, and other small animals, who live and talk like humans but have charming individual animal characters. The book is a tender portrait of the English countryside." Reader's Ency

Gratz, Alan, 1972-

The Brooklyn nine; a novel in nine innings. Dial Books 2009 299p $16.99 *

Grades: 5 6 7 8 **Fic**

1. Baseball—Fiction 2. Brooklyn (New York, N.Y.)—Fiction 3. Family life—Fiction 4. United States—History—Fiction 5. German Americans—Fiction

ISBN 978-0-8037-3224-7; 0-8037-3224-4

LC 2008-21263

Follows the fortunes of a German immigrant family through nine generations, beginning in 1845, as they experience American life and play baseball.

Gratz "builds this novel upon a clever . . . conceit . . . and executes it with polish and precision." Booklist

Green, Tim

Baseball great. HarperCollinsPublishers 2009 250p $16.99; lib bdg $17.89

Grades: 5 6 7 8 **Fic**

1. Baseball—Fiction 2. Father-son relationship—Fiction 3. School stories

ISBN 978-0-06-162686-9; 0-06-162686-4; 978-0-06-162687-6 (lib bdg); 0-06-162687-2 (lib bdg)

LC 2008051778

All twelve-year-old Josh wants to do is play baseball but when his father, a minor league pitcher, signs him up for a youth championship team, Josh finds himself embroiled in a situation with potentially illegal consequences.

"Issues of peer and family pressure are well handled, and the short, punchy chapters and crisp dialogue are likely to hold the attention of young baseball fans." SLJ

Followed by: Rivals (2010)

Football genius. HarperCollinsPublishers 2007 244p $16.99; lib bdg $17.89; pa $6.99

Grades: 5 6 7 8 **Fic**

1. Football—Fiction 2. Atlanta (Ga.)—Fiction

ISBN 978-0-06-112270-5; 0-06-112270-X; 978-0-06-112272-9 (lib bdg); 0-06-112272-6 (lib bdg); 978-0-06-112273-6 (pa); 0-06-112273-4 (pa)

LC 2006-29470

Troy, a sixth-grader with an unusual gift for predicting football plays before they occur, attempts to use his ability to help his favorite team, the Atlanta Falcons, but he must first prove himself to the coach and players.

The author "imparts many insider details that football fans will love. Green makes Troy a winning hero, and he ties everything together with a fast-moving plot." Booklist

Followed by: Football champ (2009)

Football hero. HarperCollinsPublishers 2008 297p $16.99; lib bdg $17.89; pa $6.99

Grades: 5 6 7 8 **Fic**

1. Football—Fiction 2. Mafia—Fiction 3. New Jersey—Fiction

ISBN 978-0-06-112274-3; 0-06-112274-2; 978-0-06-112275-0 (lib bdg); 0-06-112275-0 (lib bdg); 978-0-06-112276-7 (pa); 0-06-112276-9 (pa)

LC 2007-24184

When twelve-year-old Ty's brother Thane is recruited out of college to play for the New York Jets, their Uncle Gus uses Ty to get insider information for his gambling

Green, Tim—*Continued*

ring, landing Ty and Thane in trouble with the Mafia.

"The novel is briskly paced and undemanding, and might be a good bet for sports-minded reluctant readers." SLJ

Greene, Bette, 1934-

Philip Hall likes me, I reckon maybe; pictures by Charles Lilly. Dial Bks. for Young Readers 1974 135p il pa $5.99 hardcover o.p. *

Grades: 4 5 6   **Fic**

1. Friendship—Fiction 2. African Americans—Fiction 3. Arkansas—Fiction

ISBN 0-14-130312-3 (pa)

A Newbery Medal honor book, 1975

Eleven-year-old Beth, an African American girl from Arkansas, thinks that Philip Hall likes her, but their on-again, off-again relationship sometimes makes her wonder

"The action is sustained; . . . the illustrations are excellent black-and-white pencil sketches." Read Teach

Other titles about Beth and Philip Hall are:

Get out of here, Philip Hall (1981)

I've already forgotten your name, Philip Hall (2004)

Summer of my German soldier. Dial Books 2003 230p $18.99; pa $6.99 *

Grades: 6 7 8 9   **Fic**

1. World War, 1939-1945—Fiction 2. German prisoners of war—Fiction 3. Arkansas—Fiction

ISBN   978-0-8037-2869-1;   0-8037-2869-7; 978-0-14-240651-9 (pa); 0-14-240651-1 (pa)

LC 2002-9548

First published 1973

When German prisoners of war are brought to her Arkansas town during World War II, twelve-year-old Patty, a Jewish girl, befriends one of them and must deal with the consequences of that friendship.

Followed by: Morning is a long time coming (1978)

Greene, Jacqueline Dembar

The secret shofar of Barcelona; illustrated by Doug Chayka. Kar-Ben 2009 unp il lib bdg $17.95

Grades: 2 3 4 5   **Fic**

1. Jews—Spain—Fiction 2. Musicians—Fiction 3. Rosh ha-Shanah—Fiction 4. Spain—Fiction

ISBN 978-0-8225-9915-9 (lib bdg); 0-8225-9915-5 (lib bdg)   LC 2008031197

In the late 1500s, while the conductor of the Royal Orchestra of Barcelona prepares for a concert to celebrate Spain's colonies in the New World, his son secretly practices playing the Shofar to help Jews, who must hide their faith from the Inquisition, to celebrate Rosh Hashanah. Includes historical facts and glossary

"Based on a legend, this intriguing slice of converso life offers a thoughtful hero and a suspenseful plot. The warm opaque paintings are expressive and create a strong sense of place." SLJ

Greene, Stephanie

Moose's big idea; illustrated by Joe Mathieu. Marshall Cavendish 2005 51p il (Moose and Hildy) $14.95

Grades: 1 2 3   **Fic**

1. Moose—Fiction 2. Pigs—Fiction

ISBN 0-7614-5212-5   LC 2004-22536

"Moose is sad upon losing his very large antlers, but cheers up a bit when his pig friend, Hildy, is now able to observe his pretty eyes and muscular legs. . . . In the next chapter, he stays inside during hunting season. . . . When cabin fever ensues, Moose gets the idea to sell doughnuts, coffee, and original artwork to hunters. . . . making a sale to a naive hunter. In another chapter, this same man finds Moose's old antlers but won't give them back. Finally, Moose's new antlers begin to grow. . . . Readers stepping up to chapter books will laughingly turn these pages and clamor for more. Mathieu's frequent black-and-white illustrations expand on the fun." SLJ

Other titles about Moose and Hildy are:

Moose crossing (2005)

Pig pickin' (2006)

The show-off (2007)

Owen Foote, frontiersman; illustrated by Martha Weston. Clarion Bks. 1999 88p il $14; pa $4.95 *

Grades: 2 3 4   **Fic**

1. Outdoor life—Fiction

ISBN 0-395-61578-X; 0-618-24620-7 (pa)

LC 98-44843

Second grader Owen Foote is looking forward to spending time with his friend Joseph in their tree fort, until some bullies visiting his neighbor, Mrs. Gold, threaten to wreck the fort

"Real-boy characters with an appealingly loyal friendship, a good balance of narrative and dialogue, and an honestly childlike sense of the way the world works." Horn Book

Other titles about Owen Foote are:

Owen Foote, mighty scientist (2004)

Owen Foote, money man (2000)

Owen Foote, second grade strongman (1997)

Owen Foote, super spy (2001)

Owen Foote, soccer star (1998)

Princess Posey and the first grade parade; illustrated by Stephanie Roth Sisson. G.P. Putnam's Sons 2010 83p il $12.99

Grades: K 1 2   **Fic**

1. Fear—Fiction 2. School stories

ISBN 978-0-399-25167-2; 0-399-25167-7

LC 2009-12471

Posey's fear of starting first grade is alleviated when her teacher invites the students to wear their most comfortable clothes to school on the first day.

"Emergent readers can be anxious as they make the transition from easy readers to early chapter books and, like Posey, can be overwhelmed by new challenges. Short sentences, a generous font, ample white space and Sisson's charming, expressive black-and-white illustrations make this sweet story just right for them." Kirkus

Greenfield, Eloise, 1929-

The friendly four; illustrations by Jan Spivey Gilchrist. HarperCollins/Amistad 2006 47p il $16.99; lib bdg $17.89 *

Grades: 2 3 4   **Fic**

1. Friendship—Fiction 2. African Americans—Fiction 3. Summer—Fiction

ISBN 978-0-06-000759-1; 0-06-000759-1; 978-0-06-000760-7 (lib bdg); 0-06-000760-5 (lib bdg)

LC 2005-18588

"Free-verse poems tell the story of a group of children who find each other during one otherwise lonely summer. . . . The African-American friends all bond, play, and build and paint an elaborate cardboard town they call Goodsummer. The simple watercolors work well at setting scenes of tidy streets lined with homes and lots of backyards and parks. Gilchrist's talent shows in her use of color, splashed with light. . . . For a younger audience than most novels-in-verse, this accessible and well-written book has a nostalgic tone." SLJ

Sister; drawings by Moneta Barnett. Crowell 1974 83p il hardcover o.p. pa $4.99

Grades: 4 5 6 7   **Fic**

1. Sisters—Fiction 2. Single parent family—Fiction 3. African Americans—Fiction

ISBN 0-690-00497-4; 0-06-440199-5 (pa)

A 13-year-old black girl whose father is dead watches her 16-year-old sister drifting away from her and her mother and fears she may fall into the same self-destructive behavior herself. While waiting for her sister's return home, she leafs through her diary, reliving both happy and unhappy experiences while gradually recognizing her own individuality

"The book is strong . . . strong in perception, in its sensitivity, in its realism." Bull Cent Child Books

Greenwald, Lisa

My life in pink and green. Amulet Books 2009 267p $16.95; pa $6.95

Grades: 4 5 6 7   **Fic**

1. Mother-daughter relationship—Fiction 2. Cosmetics—Fiction 3. Environmental protection—Fiction

ISBN 978-0-8109-8352-6; 0-8109-8352-4; 978-0-8109-8984-9 (pa); 0-8109-8984-0 (pa)

LC 2008025577

When the family's drugstore is failing, seventh-grader Lucy uses her problem solving talents to come up with solution that might resuscitate the business, along with helping the environment.

"Greenwald deftly blends eco-facts and makeup tips, friendship dynamics, and spot-on middle-school politics into a warm, uplifting story." Booklist

Greenwald, Sheila, 1934-

Rosy Cole's worst ever, best yet tour of New York City. Farrar, Straus & Giroux 2003 121p il $16 *

Grades: 3 4 5   **Fic**

1. Cousins—Fiction 2. Family life—Fiction 3. New York (N.Y.)—Fiction

ISBN 0-374-36349-8   LC 2002-192526

"Melanie Kroupa books"

Rosy plans to show her small-town cousin all the amazing sights that make New York City such a great place to live, but things do not go as she had hoped

"Expressive ink drawings reflect the story's energy and humor." Booklist

Other titles about Rosy Cole are:

Give us a great big smile, Rosy Cole (1981)

Here's Hermione: a Rosy Cole production (1991)

Rosy Cole discovers America! (1992)

Rosy Cole: she grows and graduates (1997)

Rosy Cole: she walks in beauty (1994)

Rosy Cole's great American guilt club (1985)

Rosy Cole's memoir explosion (2006)

Rosy's romance (1989)

Write on, Rosy! (a young author in crisis (1988)

Valentine Rosy (1984)

Watch out world, Rosy Cole is going green! (2010)

Gregory, Kristiana

Bronte's book club; by Kristiana Gregory. Holiday House 2008 160p $16.95; pa $7.95

Grades: 3 4 5 6   **Fic**

1. Books and reading—Fiction 2. California—Fiction

ISBN 978-0-8234-2136-7; 0-8234-2136-8; 978-0-8234-2209-8 (pa); 0-8234-2209-7 (pa)

LC 2007036806

When twelve-year-old Bronte moves to a small California beach town, her idea to form a book club in order to make friends turns out to be a good one, after a rocky start

"Back matter includes suggestions for starting a book group; but more than just about creating a club, this book shows how talking about a great story can spark connections." Booklist

My darlin' Clementine. Holiday House 2009 206p $16.95

Grades: 5 6 7 8   **Fic**

1. Frontier and pioneer life—Fiction 2. Family life—Fiction 3. Sisters—Fiction 4. Sex role—Fiction 5. Miners—Fiction 6. Idaho—Fiction

ISBN 978-0-8234-2198-5; 0-8234-2198-8

LC 2008-39203

Expands on the folk song to tell of seventeen-year-old Clementine, whose dream of being a doctor is complicated by her drunken, gambling father, the lawlessness of 1866 Idaho Territory, and the affections of handsome Boone Reno.

"Clem is an inspiring character, and Gregory provides plenty of cliff-hangers and historical background to keep avid fans of the author, or the genre, reading." SLJ

Gregory, Nan, 1944-

I'll sing you one-o. Clarion Books 2006 220p $16

Grades: 5 6 7 8   **Fic**

1. Foster home care—Fiction 2. Siblings—Fiction 3. Twins—Fiction 4. Family life—Fiction

ISBN 978-0-618-60708-2; 0-618-60708-0

LC 2005-32709

Reunited with her long-lost twin brother, twelve-year-old Gemma constantly tests the boundaries of acceptable behavior while relying on angels to help her connect with her new family

Gregory, Nan, 1944-—_Continued_

"Fine characterization provides a broad cast. . . . The child's enormous need to verify her birth mother's love for her is achingly real." SLJ

Griffin, Peni R.

The ghost sitter. Dutton Children's Bks. 2001 131p $14.99; pa $5.99

Grades: 4 5 6 7 **Fic**

1. Ghost stories

ISBN 0-525-46676-2; 0-14-230216-3 (pa)

LC 00-65859

When she realizes that her new house is haunted by the ghost of a ten-year-old girl who used to live there, Charlotte tries to help her find peace

"Griffin's book has several strong appeals: new best friends solving a mystery together, a just-scary-enough ghost girl, and a deathless bond between sisters that provides the book with its resoundingly satisfying conclusion and bang-up last sentence." Horn Book

Grimes, Nikki

Make way for Dyamonde Daniel; illustrated by R. Gregory Christie. G.P. Putnam's Sons 2009 74p il $10.99

Grades: 2 3 4 **Fic**

1. Moving—Fiction 2. Friendship—Fiction 3. African Americans—Fiction

ISBN 978-0-399-25175-7; 0-399-25175-8

LC 2008-26788

Spunky third-grader Dyamonde Daniel misses her old neighborhood, but when she befriends a boy named Free, another new student at school, she finally starts to feel at home.

"Dyamonde . . . is a memorable main character. . . . Her actions and feelings ring true. Christie's illustrations flesh out the characters, and along with patterned page borders, contribute child appeal." SLJ

Another title about Dyamonde Daniel is:

Rich (2009)

The road to Paris. G. P. Putnam's Sons 2006 153p $15.99; pa $6.99

Grades: 4 5 6 7 **Fic**

1. Foster home care—Fiction 2. Racially mixed people—Fiction 3. Siblings—Fiction

ISBN 0-399-24537-5; 978-0-399-24537-4; 978-0-14-241082-0 (pa); 0-14-241082-9 (pa)

LC 2005-28920

Inconsolable at being separated from her older brother, eight-year-old Paris is apprehensive about her new foster family but just as she learns to trust them, she faces a life-changing decision.

"In clear, short chapters, Grimes tells a beautiful story of family, friendship, and faith from the viewpoint of a child in search of home in a harsh world." Booklist

Grindley, Sally, 1953-

Dear Max; by D. J. Lucas a.k.a. Sally Gindley; [illustrated by Tony Ross] Margaret K. McElderry Books 2006 c2004 140p il $14.95; pa $4.99

Grades: 2 3 4 **Fic**

1. Authorship—Fiction 2. Friendship—Fiction 3. Letters—Fiction

ISBN 978-1-4169-0392-5; 1-4169-0392-5; 978-1-4169-3443-1 (pa); 1-4169-3443-X (pa)

First published 2004 in the United Kingdom

As Max—who is almost ten—and his favorite author, D.J. Lucas, exchange letters, the two writers help each other with their new books and develop a special friendship

This "is a charming story full of likable, multidimensional characters that will inspire young writers and satisfy readers. . . . Ross' line drawings add to the fun." Booklist

Another title about Max is:

Bravo, Max! (2007)

Gunderson, Jessica, 1976-

The emperor's painting; a story of ancient China; by Jessica Gunderson; illustrated by Caroline Hu. Picture Window Books 2009 64p il (Read-it! chapter books: historical tales) lib bdg $21.26

Grades: 2 3 4 **Fic**

1. China—Fiction 2. Artists—Fiction 3. Poets—Fiction

ISBN 978-1-4048-4734-7 (lib bdg); 1-4048-4734-0 (lib bdg)

LC 2008006305

"Han Li thinks he is the smartest poet and most talented painter in China. His master, Lin Cho, tries to warn him about his arrogance, but Han Li does not listen. When Lin Cho becomes ill before he can finish his painting for the emperor, Han Li must decide what to do." Publisher's note

"Sassy, graphic-novel-style illustrations give [this] great little first chapter [book] extra appeal. . . . [This is a] wonderful [introduction] to historical fiction." SLJ

The jade dragon; a story of ancient China; by Jessica Gunderson; illustrated by Caroline Hu. Picture Window Books 2009 64p il (Read-it! chapter books: historical tales) lib bdg $21.26; pa $5.99

Grades: 2 3 4 **Fic**

1. China—Fiction 2. Brothers—Fiction

ISBN 978-1-4048-4735-4 (lib bdg); 1-4048-4735-9 (lib bdg); 978-0-7636-4061-3 (pa); 0-7636-4061-1 (pa)

LC 2008006306

"Zhou never seems to beat his brother, Cheng, at anything. But when Zhou finds a jade dragon, his luck changes. Soon, Zhou is beating Cheng at everything." Publisher's note

"Sassy, graphic-novel-style illustrations give [this] great little first chapter [book] extra appeal. . . . [This is a] wonderful [introduction] to historical fiction." SLJ

Gunderson, Jessica, 1976-—*Continued*

Stranger on the silk road; a story of ancient China; by Jessica Gunderson; illustrated by Caroline Hu. Picture Window Books 2009 64p il (Read-it! chapter books: historical tales) lib bdg $21.26

Grades: 2 3 4   **Fic**
    1. China—Fiction 2. Silk—Fiction
    ISBN 978-1-4048-4736-1 (lib bdg); 1-4048-4736-7 (lib bdg)   LC 2008006308
Song Sun likes to talk but never listens. After talking too much to a stranger, Song Sun accidentally gives away the Chinese secret of silk making
    "Sassy, graphic-novel-style illustrations give [this] great little first chapter [book] extra appeal. . . . [This is a] wonderful [introduction] to historical fiction." SLJ

The terracotta girl; a story of ancient China; by Jessica Gunderson; illustrated by Caroline Hu. Picture Window Books 2009 64p il (Read-it! chapter books: historical tales) lib bdg $21.26

Grades: 2 3 4   **Fic**
    1. China—Fiction 2. Sex role—Fiction 3. Orphans—Fiction
    ISBN 978-1-4048-4737-8 (lib bdg); 1-4048-4737-5 (lib bdg)   LC 2008006309
"After Yung-lu's father dies of mercury poisoning, the young girl leaves for Chang'an. She is determined to take her father's place as a warrior. When Yung-lu arrives, she is met with two big surprises. The emperor is taking mercury, and the army is not what she had imagined." Publisher's note
    "Sassy, graphic-novel-style illustrations give [this] great little first chapter [book] extra appeal. . . . [This is a] wonderful [introduction] to historical fiction." SLJ

Guo Yue, 1958-

Little Leap Forward; a boy in Beijing; by Guo Yue and Clare Farrow; illustrated by Helen Cann. Barefoot Books 2008 126p il $16.99 *

Grades: 3 4 5 6   **Fic**
    1.   China—History—1949-1976—Fiction
    2. Friendship—Fiction 3. Family life—Fiction
    4. Communism—Fiction
    ISBN 978-1-84686-114-7; 1-84686-114-4
                                  LC 2007-42676
In Communist China in 1966, eight-year-old Leap Forward learns about freedom while flying kites with his best friend, by trying to get a caged wild bird to sing, and through the music he is learning to play on a bamboo flute. Includes author's notes on his childhood in Beijing, life under Mao Zedong, and the Cultural Revolution.
    "The simple prose is quiet and physical. . . . The beautifully detailed, clear illustrations in ink and brilliant watercolors combine realistic group scenes with spare, individual portraits." Booklist

Gutman, Dan

The Christmas genie; illustrated by Dan Santat. Simon & Schuster Books for Young Readers 2009 150p il $15.99

Grades: 3 4 5   **Fic**
    1. Wishes—Fiction 2. School stories 3. Christmas—Fiction 4. Meteorites—Fiction
    ISBN 978-1-4169-9001-7; 1-4169-9001-1
                                  LC 2009017765
When a meteorite crashes into a fifth-grade classroom at Lincoln School in Oak Park, Illinois, the genie inside agrees to grant the class a Christmas wish—if they can agree on one within an hour.
    This is "lively, thought-provoking, and hilarious. . . . Gutman packs plenty of history, science, and ethics lessons in this fun, well-paced fantasy." SLJ

Coach Hyatt is a riot! pictures by Jim Paillot. HarperTrophy 2009 106p il $15.89; pa $3.99

Grades: 3 4 5   **Fic**
    1. Football—Fiction 2. School stories
    ISBN   978-0-06-155408-7;   0-06-155408-1;
    978-0-06-155406-3 (pa); 0-06-155406-5 (pa)
                                  LC 2008031421
A new football coach arrives at school and, with help from an unexpected new team member, the Moose win a game.
    "There is some graphic support for younger readers in the kooky black-and-white cartoon illustrations scattered throughout. Even the most reluctant reader will be drawn in by the humor and repetitive silliness." SLJ

The homework machine. Simon & Schuster Books for Young Readers 2006 146p $15.95; pa $5.99

Grades: 4 5 6   **Fic**
    1. School stories
    ISBN 0-689-87678-5; 0-689-87679-3 (pa)
                                  LC 2005-19785
Four fifth-grade students—a geek, a class clown, a teacher's pet, and a slacker—as well as their teacher and mothers, each relate events surrounding a computer programmed to complete homework assignments.
    "This fast-paced, entertaining book has something for everyone: convincing characters deftly portrayed . . . ; points of discussion on ethics and student computer use; and every child's dream machine." Booklist
    Followed by: Return of the homework machine (2009)

Shoeless Joe & me; a baseball card adventure. HarperCollins Pubs. 2002 163p (Baseball card adventures) hardcover o.p. lib bdg $17.89; pa $5.99

Grades: 4 5 6 7   **Fic**
    1. Jackson, Joe, 1888-1951—Fiction 2. Baseball—Fiction
    ISBN 0-06-029253-9; 0-06-029254-7 (lib bdg); 0-06-447259-0 (pa)   LC 2001-24638
Joe Stoshack travels back to 1919, where he meets Shoeless Joe Jackson and tries to prevent the fixing of the World Series in which Jackson was wrongly implicated
    "Shoeless Joe is compelling, and Joe's adventures are exciting." Voice Youth Advocates
    Other titles in the Baseball card adventures series are:

Gutman, Dan—*Continued*
Abner & me (2005)
Babe & me (2000)
Honus & me (1997)
Jackie & me (1999)
Jim & me (2008)
Mickey & me (2003)
Ray & me (2009)
Roberto & me (2010)
Satch & me (2006)

Gwaltney, Doris
Homefront. Simon & Schuster Books for Young Readers 2006 310p $16.99; pa $6.99
Grades: 5 6 7 8 **Fic**
1. Family life—Fiction 2. World War, 1939-1945—Fiction 3. Virginia—Fiction
ISBN 0-689-86842-1; 1-4169-9572-2 (pa)
LC 2006-283492
"As Margaret Ann Motley looks forward to seventh grade, the only changes she sees on the horizon are her sister's leaving for college and, immediately afterwards, moving . . . into her sister's old room. With the U.S. on the brink of World War II, though, greater changes are in store. . . . Gwaltney provides vivid character portrayals. . . . Well grounded in the Tidewater area of Virginia, the novel's social context is made real." Booklist

Haas, Jessie
Birthday pony; pictures by Margot Apple. Greenwillow Books 2004 80p il hardcover o.p. lib bdg $15.89 *
Grades: 2 3 4 **Fic**
1. Horses—Fiction 2. Horsemanship—Fiction 3. Grandmothers—Fiction
ISBN 0-06-057359-7; 0-06-057360-0 (lib bdg)
LC 2003-57286
Grandma Aggie tries to help her granddaughter Jane and the independent pony Popcorn, who were born on the same day, become riding partners
"Sentences are short and prose style and vocabulary are accessible to youngsters who are making the transition from beginning readers to chapter books. This delightful story is enhanced by Apple's black-and-white pencil drawings." SLJ

Chase. Greenwillow Books 2007 250p $16.99; lib bdg $17.89
Grades: 5 6 7 8 **Fic**
1. Coal mines and mining—Fiction 2. Irish Americans—Fiction 3. Pennsylvania—Fiction
ISBN 978-0-06-112850-9; 0-06-112850-3; 978-0-06-112851-6 (lib bdg); 0-06-112851-1 (lib bdg)
LC 2006-41240
In the coal mining region of mid-nineteenth century eastern Pennsylvania, Phin witnesses a murder and runs for his life, pursued by a mysterious man and a horse with the instincts of a bloodhound.
"This exciting story is soaked in historical detail and psychological credibility." Booklist

Jigsaw pony; pictures by Ying-hwa Hu. Greenwillow Books 2005 128p il $15.99; lib bdg $16.89 *
Grades: 2 3 4 **Fic**
1. Horses—Fiction 2. Twins—Fiction 3. Sisters—Fiction
ISBN 0-06-078245-5; 0-06-078250-1 (lib bdg)
LC 2004-60724
Twins Kiera and Fran have never agreed on anything but when their dream comes true and their father surprises them with a pony, they must learn to work together to care for their new pet
This is "a very pleasing tale . . . with large, easy-to-read type and a spacious layout that make it ideal for readers new to chapter books." Booklist

Haddix, Margaret Peterson, 1964-
Dexter the tough; [by] Margaret Peterson Haddix; illustrated by Mark Elliott. Simon & Schuster Books for Young Readers 2007 141p il $15.99; pa $4.99
Grades: 2 3 4 **Fic**
1. School stories 2. Authorship—Fiction
ISBN 978-1-4169-1159-3; 1-4169-1159-6; 978-1-4169-1170-8 (pa); 1-4169-1170-7 (pa)
LC 2006-09403
A sympathetic teacher and her writing assignment help fourth-grader Dexter deal with being the new kid in school after he punches a kid on the first day.
"Haddix does an excellent job of capturing the voice of a fourth-grade boy. Dexter is a multifaceted character." SLJ

Found. Simon & Schuster Books for Young Readers 2008 314p (The missing) $15.99; pa $6.99 *
Grades: 5 6 7 8 **Fic**
1. Adoption—Fiction 2. Science fiction
ISBN 978-1-4169-5417-0; 1-4169-5417-1; 978-1-4169-5421-7 (pa); 1-4169-5421-X (pa)
LC 2007-23614
When thirteen-year-olds Jonah and Chip, who are both adopted, learn they were discovered on a plane that appeared out of nowhere, full of babies with no adults on board, they realize that they have uncovered a mystery involving time travel and two opposing forces, each trying to repair the fabric of time.
This is "a tantalizing opener to a new series. . . . Readers will be hard-pressed to wait for the next installment." Publ Wkly
Followed by: Sent (2009)

Haddon, Mark
Boom! David Fickling Books 2010 194p $15.99; lib bdg $18.99
Grades: 4 5 6 7 **Fic**
1. Interplanetary voyages—Fiction 2. Extraterrestrial beings—Fiction 3. Science fiction 4. Great Britain—Fiction
ISBN 978-0-385-75187-2; 0-385-75187-7; 978-0-385-75188-9 (lib bdg); 0-385-75188-5 (lib bdg)
First published 1992 in the United Kingdom with title: Gridzbi spudvetch

Haddon, Mark—*Continued*

When Jim and Charlie overhear two of their teachers talking in a secret language and the two friends set out to solve the mystery, they do not expect the dire consequences of their actions.

"Adventure and quirky humor keep the pages turning, and readers will connect to Jimbo with little difficulty. If they can overcome some of the cultural differences, they will appreciate the simple and engaging tale." SLJ

Hahn, Mary Downing, 1937-

All the lovely bad ones; a ghost story. Clarion Books 2008 182p $16; pa $5.99

Grades: 4 5 6 7   **Fic**
1. Ghost stories 2. Siblings—Fiction 3. Hotels and motels—Fiction 4. Vermont—Fiction
ISBN 978-0-618-85467-7; 978-0-547-24878-3 (pa)
LC 2007-37932

While spending the summer at their grandmother's Vermont inn, two prankster siblings awaken young ghosts from the inn's distant past who refuse to "rest in peace."

"In addition to crafting some genuinely spine-chilling moments, the author takes a unique approach to a well-traversed genre." Publ Wkly

Anna all year round; illustrated by Diane deGroat. Clarion Bks. 1999 133p il $15

Grades: 3 4 5   **Fic**
1. Family life—Fiction 2. Baltimore (Md.)—Fiction
ISBN 0-395-86975-7   LC 98-19985

Eight-year-old Anna experiences a series of episodes, some that are funny, others sad, involving friends and family during a year in Baltimore just before World War I

"Based on the childhood of the author's mother. . . . Hahn's use of the present tense helps keep nostalgia at bay, as does the energetic, just-dashed-off quality of deGroat's rough pencil sketches." Horn Book Guide

Another title about Anna is:
Anna on the farm (2001)

Closed for the season; a mystery story. Clarion Books 2009 182p $16

Grades: 5 6 7 8   **Fic**
1. Mystery fiction 2. Homicide—Fiction 3. Friendship—Fiction 4. Virginia—Fiction
ISBN 978-0-547-08451-0; 0-547-08451-X
LC 2008046846

When thirteen-year-old Logan and his family move into a run-down old house in rural Virginia, he discovers that a woman was murdered there and becomes involved with his neighbor Arthur in a dangerous investigation to try to uncover the killer

"This is an enjoyable mystery with just the right amount of frightening and dangerous elements to entice readers. Logan is a sympathetic character." SLJ

Deep and dark and dangerous; a ghost story. Clarion Books 2007 187p $16; pa $5.99

Grades: 5 6 7 8   **Fic**
1. Ghost stories 2. Mother-daughter relationship—Fiction 3. Cousins—Fiction
ISBN 978-0-618-66545-7; 0-618-66545-5; 978-0-547-07645-4 (pa); 0-547-07645-2 (pa)
LC 2006-25652

When thirteen-year-old Ali spends the summer with her aunt and cousin at the family's vacation home, she stumbles upon a secret that her mother and aunt have been hiding for over thirty years

"Hahn weaves into the story some classic mystery elements such as a torn photograph, a waterlogged doll, dense fog, and an empty grave, all of which add to the suspense and keep the well-plotted story moving along to a satisfying conclusion." SLJ

The doll in the garden; a ghost story. Clarion Bks. 1989 128p $15; pa $5.95

Grades: 4 5 6   **Fic**
1. Space and time—Fiction 2. Ghost stories
ISBN 0-89919-848-1; 0-618-87315-5 (pa)
LC 88-20365

Also available in paperback from Avon Bks.

After Ashley and Kristi find an antique doll buried in old Miss Cooper's garden, they discover that they can enter a ghostly turn-of-the-century world by going through a hole in the hedge

"Hahn's elegant use of language, as well as her ability to probe complex emotions at a child's level, elevates this above-the-ordinary ghost tale into a story with universal themes." Booklist

Hear the wind blow. Clarion Bks. 2003 212p $15 *

Grades: 5 6 7 8   **Fic**
1. United States—History—1861-1865, Civil War—Fiction 2. Siblings—Fiction
ISBN 0-618-18190-3   LC 2002-15977

With their mother dead and their home burned, a thirteen-year-old boy and his little sister set out across Virginia in search of relatives during the final days of the Civil War

The author "gives readers an entertaining and thought-provoking combination: a strong adventure inextricably bound to a specific time and place, but one that resonates with universal themes." Horn Book

The old Willis place; a ghost story. Clarion Books 2004 199p $16; pa $6.99

Grades: 5 6 7 8   **Fic**
1. Ghost stories
ISBN 0-618-43018-0; 0-618-89741-0 (pa)
LC 2004-2345

Tired of the rules that have bound them ever since "the bad thing happened," twelve-year-old Diana ignores her brother's warnings and befriends the daughter of the new caretaker, setting in motion events that lead to the release of the spirit of an evil, crazy woman who once ruled the old Willis place

"The story is taut, spooky, and fast-paced with amazingly credible, memorable characters." SLJ

Stepping on the cracks. Clarion Bks. 1991 216p $16; pa $6.99

Grades: 5 6 7 8   **Fic**
1. World War, 1939-1945—Fiction
ISBN 0-395-58507-4; 0-547-07660-6 (pa)
LC 91-7706

In 1944, while her brother is overseas fighting in World War II, eleven-year-old Margaret gets a new view of the school bully Gordy when she finds him hiding his

Hahn, Mary Downing, 1937-—*Continued*
own brother, an army deserter, and decides to help him
 "Well-drawn characters and a satisfying plot. . . .
There is plenty of action and page-turning suspense to
please those who want a quick read, but there is much
to ponder and reflect on as well." SLJ

Time for Andrew; a ghost story. Clarion Bks.
1994 165p hardcover o.p. pa $5.95
Grades: 5 6 7 8   **Fic**
 1. Ghost stories 2. Space and time—Fiction
 ISBN 0-395-66556-6; 0-618-87316-3 (pa)
                                           LC 93-2877
Also available in paperback from Avon Bks.

When he goes to spend the summer with his great-
aunt in the family's old house, eleven-year-old Drew is
drawn eighty years into the past to trade places with his
great-great-uncle who is dying of diphtheria
 "There's plenty to enjoy in this delightful time-slip
fantasy: a fascinating premise, a dastardly cousin, some
good suspense, and a roundup of characters to care
about." Booklist

Wait till Helen comes; a ghost story. Clarion
Bks. 1986 184p $15; pa $5.95 *
Grades: 4 5 6   **Fic**
 1. Ghost stories 2. Stepchildren—Fiction
 ISBN 0-89919-453-2; 0-547-02864-4 (pa)
                                           LC 86-2648
Also available in paperback from Avon Bks.

Molly and Michael dislike their spooky new stepsister
Heather but realize that they must try to save her when
she seems ready to follow a ghost child to her doom
 "Intertwined with the ghost story is the question of
Molly's moral imperative to save a child she truly dis-
likes. Though the emotional turnaround may be a bit
quick for some, this still scores as a first-rate thriller."
Booklist

Witch catcher. Clarion Books 2006 236p $16 *
Grades: 3 4 5 6   **Fic**
 1. Witches—Fiction 2. Fairies—Fiction
 3. Father-daughter relationship—Fiction 4. West Virginia—Fiction
 ISBN 0-618-50457-5   LC 2005-24795
Having just moved into the West Virginia home they
inherited from a distant relative, twelve-year-old Jen is
surprised that her father is already dating a local antiques
dealer, but more surprised by what the spooky woman
really wants.
 "A fast-paced, suspenseful fantasy in which an appealing heroine stands against forces seemingly beyond her
control." Booklist

Haig, Matt, 1975-
Samuel Blink and the forbidden forest. Putnam
2007 316p il hardcover o.p. pa $7.99
Grades: 4 5 6 7   **Fic**
 1. Siblings—Fiction 2. Magic—Fiction 3. Dogs—Fiction 4. Orphans—Fiction 5. Norway—Fiction
 ISBN 978-0-399-24739-2; 978-0-14-241191-9 (pa)
                                       LC 2006024827
Accompanied by his aunt's Norwegian elkhound, Ib-
sen, twelve-year-old Samuel ventures into a weird forest
filled with strange and dangerous creatures to rescue his
younger sister, Martha, who has been mute since their
parents' recent death.
 "Crisp dialogue, fast-paced action, short chapters, and
a wry narrative voice bring this tale to life." SLJ
Followed by: Samuel Blink and the runaway troll
(2008)

Hale, Bruce, 1957-
From Russia with lunch. Harcourt 2009 112p il
(Chet Gecko mystery) $15
Grades: 3 4 5   **Fic**
 1. Geckos—Fiction 2. Animals—Fiction 3. School sto-
 ries 4. Inventions—Fiction 5. Mystery fiction
 ISBN 978-0-15-205488-5; 0-15-205488-X
                                       LC 2008004261
Detectives Chet Gecko and his partner Natalie Attired
try to solve the mystery of why Emerson Hicky Elemen-
tary school students have suddenly started acting strange-
ly.
 "Chet's nonstop wisecracks and sidekick Natalie's
jokes are . . . giggle- (and groan-) inducing. Black-and-
white illustrations display the animal cast's antics." Horn
Book Guide
 Other titles in this series are:
The chameleon wore chartreuse (2000)
The mystery of Mr. Nice (2000)
Farewell my lunchbag (2001)
The big nap (2001)
The hamster of the Baskervilles (2002)
The gum for hire (2002)
Trouble is my beeswax (2003)
The malted falcon (2003)
Give my regrets to Broadway (2004)
Murder my tweet (2004)
Key Lardo (2006)
The possum always rings twice (2006)
Hiss me deadly (2007)
Dial M for mongoose (2009)

Hale, Marian
The truth about sparrows. Henry Holt & Co.
2004 260p $16.95; pa $6.99
Grades: 5 6 7 8   **Fic**
 1. Friendship—Fiction 2. Moving—Fiction 3. Great
 Depression, 1929-1939—Fiction
 ISBN 0-8050-7584-4; 0-312-37133-0 (pa)
                                       LC 2003-56981
Twelve-year-old Sadie promises that she will always
be Wilma's best friend when their families leave
drought-stricken Missouri in 1933, but once in Texas,
Sadie learns that she must try to make a new home—and
new friends, too
 "Rich with social history, this first novel is informative, enjoyable, and evocative." SLJ

Hall, Teri
The Line. Dial Books 2010 219p $16.99
Grades: 5 6 7 8   **Fic**
 1. Science fiction
 ISBN 978-0-8037-3466-1; 0-8037-3466-2
                                       LC 2009-12301

Hall, Teri—*Continued*

Rachel thinks that she and her mother are safe working for Ms. Moore at her estate close to The Line, an invisible border of the Unified States, but when Rachel has an opportunity to Cross into the forbidden zone, she is both frightened and intrigued

This "sets readers up for a series about another world that might have come from situations too close to our own." Libr Media Connect

Halpern, Jake, 1975-

Dormia; written by Jake Halpern & Peter Kujawinski. Houghton Mifflin Harcourt 2009 506p il $17

Grades: 4 5 6   **Fic**

1. Sleep—Fiction 2. Fantasy fiction

ISBN 978-0-547-07665-2; 0-547-07665-7

LC 2008-36108

After learning of his ancestral ties to Dormia, a hidden kingdom in the Ural Mountains whose inhabitants possess the ancient power of 'wakeful sleeping,' twelve-year-old Alfonso sets out on a mission to save the kingdom from destruction, discovering secrets that lurk in his own sleep.

This "is old-fashioned storytelling, ably done, where action supports story development rather than substituting for it. This fantasy is a wonderful intergenerational read-along and is a strong choice for readers still mourning the end of the Harry Potter books." Booklist

Hamilton, Virginia, 1936-2002

The bells of Christmas. Harcourt Brace Jovanovich 1989 59p hardcover o.p. pa $10

Grades: 4 5 6   **Fic**

1. Christmas—Fiction 2. Family life—Fiction 3. African Americans—Fiction 4. Ohio—Fiction

ISBN 0-15-206450-8; 0-15-201550-7 (pa)

LC 89-7468

"On Christmas Day, 1890, in Ohio, the Bell family comes along the National Road to spend the holiday with Jason and his family. The gentle story is stuffed like a proper plum pudding with specific details of rural life almost a century ago." N Y Times Book Rev

Drylongso; illustrated by Jerry Pinkney. Harcourt Brace Jovanovich 1992 54p il pa $10 hardcover o.p.

Grades: 3 4 5   **Fic**

1. Droughts—Fiction 2. Farm life—Fiction 3. African Americans—Fiction

ISBN 0-15-201587-6 (pa)   LC 91-25575

As a great wall of dust moves across their drought-stricken farm, a family's distress is relieved by a young man called Drylongso, who literally blows into their lives with the storm

"In an understand story of drought and hard times and longing for rain, a great writer and a great artists have pared down their rich, exuberant styles to something quieter but no less intense." Booklist

The house of Dies Drear; illustrated by Eros Keith. Macmillan 1968 246p il hardcover o.p. pa $5.99 *

Grades: 5 6 7 8   **Fic**

1. African Americans—Fiction 2. Mystery fiction 3. Ohio—Fiction

ISBN 0-02-742500-2; 1-4169-1405-6 (pa)

"A hundred years ago, Dies Drear and two slaves he was hiding in his house, an Underground Railroad station in Ohio, had been murdered. The house, huge and isolated, was fascinating, Thomas thought, but he wasn't sure he was glad Papa had bought it—funny things kept happening, frightening things." Bull Cent Child Books

"The answer to the mystery comes in a startling dramatic dénouement that is pure theater. This is gifted writing; the characterization is unforgettable, the plot imbued with mounting tension." Saturday Rev

Followed by The mystery of Drear House (1987)

M.C. Higgins, the great. 25th anniversary ed. Simon & Schuster 1999 c1974 232p $18; pa $5.99 *

Grades: 5 6 7 8   **Fic**

1. African Americans—Fiction 2. Family life—Fiction 3. Appalachian region—Fiction

ISBN 0-689-83074-2; 1-4169-1407-2 (pa)

LC 99014288

Awarded the Newbery Medal, 1975

"A reissue of the title first published 1974 by Macmillan"

As a slag heap, the result of strip mining, creeps closer to his house in the Ohio hills, fifteen-year-old M.C. is torn between trying to get his family away and fighting for the home they love

"This is a deeply involving story possessing a folkorish quality." Child Book Rev Serv

The planet of Junior Brown. Macmillan 1971 210p hardcover o.p. pa $5.99

Grades: 6 7 8 9   **Fic**

1. Friendship—Fiction 2. African Americans—Fiction

ISBN 0-689-71721-0; 1-4169-1410-2 (pa)

A Newbery Medal honor book, 1972

"This is the story of a crucial week in the lives of two black, eighth-grade dropouts who have been spending their time with the school janitor. Each boy is presented as a distinct individual. Jr. is a three-hundred pound musical prodigy as neurotic as his overprotective mother. Buddy has learned to live by his wits in a world of homeless children. Buddy becomes Jr. Brown's protector and says to the other boys, 'We are together because we have to learn to live for each other.'" Read Ladders for Hum Relat. 6th edition

Zeely. Macmillan 1967 122p il hardcover o.p. pa $5.99

Grades: 4 5 6 7   **Fic**

1. African Americans—Fiction

ISBN 0-02-742470-7; 1-4169-1413-7 (pa)

"Imaginative eleven-year-old Geeder is stirred when she sees Zeely Tayber, who is dignified, stately, and six-and-a-half feet tall. Geeder thinks Zeely looks like the magazine picture of the Watusi queen. Through meeting Zeely personally and getting to know her, Geeder finally returns to reality." Read Ladders for Hum Relat. 5th edition

Hannigan, Katherine

Emmaline and the bunny. Greenwillow Books 2009 94p il $14.99 *

Grades: 1 2 3   Fic
1. Cleanliness—Fiction 2. Loneliness—Fiction
3. Rabbits—Fiction
ISBN 978-0-06-162654-8; 0-06-162654-6
LC 2008012639

Everyone and everything in the town of Neatasapin is tidy, except Emmaline who likes to dig dirt and jump in puddles, and wants to adopt an untidy bunny.

"Told in very short chapters and using language in unusual ways, this is a small delight, cunningly illustrated by Hannigan's own sweet watercolors." Booklist

Ida B; —and her plans to maximize fun, avoid disaster, and (possibly) save the world. Greenwillow Books 2004 246p $15.99; pa $6.99

Grades: 4 5 6   Fic
1. Cancer—Fiction 2. Family life—Fiction 3. School stories 4. Wisconsin—Fiction
ISBN 0-06-073024-2; 0-06-073026-9 (pa)
LC 2003-25625

In Wisconsin, fourth-grader Ida B spends happy hours being home-schooled and playing in her family's apple orchard, until her mother begins treatment for breast cancer and her parents must sell part of the orchard and send her to public school

"Through a masterful use of voice, Hannigan's first-person narration captures an unforgettable heroine with intelligence, spirit, and a unique imagination." SLJ

Hanson, Mary Elizabeth

How to save your tail; if you are a rat nabbed by cats who really like stories about magic spoons, wolves with snout-warts, big hairy chimney trolls . . . and cookies too; illustrated by John Hendrix. Schwartz & Wade Books 2007 93p il $15.99; lib bdg $18.99; pa $5.50

Grades: 2 3 4 5   Fic
1. Storytelling—Fiction 2. Rats—Fiction 3. Cats—Fiction 4. Fairy tales
ISBN 978-0-375-83755-5; 0-375-83755-8;
978-0-375-93755-2 (lib bdg); 0-375-93755-2 (lib bdg);
978-0-440-42228-0 (pa); 0-440-42228-0 (pa)
LC 2006-03833

When he is captured by two of the queen's cats, Bob the rat prolongs his life by sharing fresh-baked cookies and stories of his ancestors, whose escapades are remarkably similar to those of well-known fairy tale heroes

"Clever wordplay and large doses of humor make this a most enjoyable selection that has great potential as a read-aloud. The black-and-white cartoon-style illustrations add to the fun." SLJ

Haptie, Charlotte

Otto and the flying twins; the first book of the Karmidee; [by] Charlotte Haptie. Holiday House 2004 304p il $17.95

Grades: 4 5 6 7   Fic
1. Fantasy fiction 2. Magic—Fiction
ISBN 0-8234-1826-X   LC 2003-57135
First published 2002 in the United Kingdom

Young Otto comes to the rescue when he discovers that his family and city are the last remnants of an ancient magical world now under threat from the Normal Police

"The amazing oddities and quirks of this world and its residents are described with delicious nonchalance. . . . The characters are equally surprising and unpredictable. . . . The writing is as fresh and invigorating as the setting." SLJ

Another title about Otto is:
Otto and the bird charmers (2005)

Hardinge, Frances

Fly by night. HarperCollinsPublishers 2006 487p hardcover o.p. lib bdg $17.89; pa $7.99 *

Grades: 5 6 7 8   Fic
1. Fantasy fiction
ISBN   978-0-06-087627-2;   0-06-087627-1;
978-0-06-087629-6 (lib bdg); 0-06-087629-8 (lib bdg);
978-0-06-087630-2 (pa); 0-06-087630-1 (pa)
LC 2005-20598

First published 2005 in the United Kingdom

Mosca Mye and her homicidal goose, Saracen, travel to the city of Mandelion on the heels of smooth-talking con-man, Eponymous Clent.

"Through rich, colorful language and a sure sense of plot and pacing, Hardinge has created a distinctly imaginative world full of engaging characters, robust humor, and true suspense." SLJ

Well witched. HarperCollins Publishers 2008 390p $16.99; lib bdg $17.89; pa $7.99 *

Grades: 5 6 7 8   Fic
1. Witches—Fiction   2.   Magic—Fiction
3. Friendship—Fiction 4. Great Britain—Fiction
ISBN   978-0-06-088038-5;   0-06-088038-4;
978-0-06-088039-2 (lib bdg); 0-06-088039-2 (lib bdg);
978-0-06-088040-8 (pa); 0-06-088040-6 (pa)
LC 2007020877

Three friends fall prey to the demands of the Well Witch when they trespass in her wishing well and steal some coins.

"This novel is alive with quirky, idiosyncratic characters. . . . There is no doubt that the book's hypnotic cover and inventive plot will attract many readers." Voice Youth Advocates

Hardy, Janice

The shifter. Balzer + Bray 2009 370p (The Healing Wars, 1) $16.99

Grades: 5 6 7 8   Fic
1. Fantasy fiction 2. Sisters—Fiction 3. Orphans—Fiction 4. War stories
ISBN 978-0-06-174704-5; 0-06-174704-1
LC 2008-47673

Nya is an orphan struggling for survival in a city crippled by war. She is also a Taker—with her touch, she can heal injuries, pulling pain from another person into her own body. But unlike her sister, Tali, and the other Takers who become Healers' League apprentices, Nya's skill is flawed: She can't push that pain into pynvium, the enchanted metal used to store it. All she can do is shift it into another person

"The ethical dilemmas raised . . . provide thoughtful

Hardy, Janice—*Continued*

discussion material and also make the story accessible to more than just fantasy readers." Booklist

Harlow, Joan Hiatt

Secret of the night ponies; [by Joan Hiatt Harlow] Margaret K. McElderry Books 2009 323p $16.99

Grades: 4 5 6 7   **Fic**

1. Horses—Fiction 2. Child abuse—Fiction 3. Dogs—Fiction 4. Newfoundland—Fiction

ISBN 978-1-4169-0783-1; 1-4169-0783-1

"Strong-willed and compassionate Jessie, 13, loves her island home of Newfoundland. With the help of Blizzard, her dependable dog, she and her family rescue three shipwreck victims. The survivors repay her later on with their friendship and support when she befriends an abused child, and when she devises a daring and dangerous plan to save some wild ponies from being rounded up for the slaughterhouse. . . . Harlow captures the rigors and rewards of island life . . . with interesting characters, an empathetic heroine, and a fast-paced plot." SLJ

Star in the storm. Margaret K. McElderry Bks. 2000 150p $16; pa $4.99   **Fic**

1. Dogs—Fiction 2. Newfoundland—Fiction

ISBN 0-689-82905-1; 0-689-84621-5 (pa)

LC 99-20416

In 1912, fearing for the safety of her beloved Newfoundland dog Sirius because of a new law outlawing non-sheepherding dogs in her Newfoundland village, twelve-year-old Maggie tries to save him by keeping him hidden

"Containing many authentic details of life in a remote region in days gone by, this story is educational as well as exciting." Booklist

Harper, Charise Mericle

Just Grace. Houghton Mifflin 2007 138p il $15; pa $4.99

Grades: 2 3 4   **Fic**

1. School stories

ISBN   978-0-618-64642-5;   0-618-64642-6; 978-0-547-01440-1 (pa); 0-547-01440-6 (pa)

LC 2006-17062

Misnamed by her teacher, seven-year-old Just Grace prides herself on being empathetic, but when she tries to help a neighbor feel better, her good intentions backfire.

"Grace is a funny, mischievous protagonist who should easily find a place in the pantheon of precocious third graders." SLJ

Other titles about Just Grace are:

Still Just Grace (2007)

Just Grace walks the dog (2008)

Just Grace goes green (2009)

Just Grace and the snack attack (2009)

Harper, Jessica, 1949-

Uh-oh, Cleo; illustrated by Jon Berkeley. G. P. Putnam's Sons 2008 58p il $14.99 *

Grades: K 1 2 3   **Fic**

1. Wounds and injuries—Fiction 2. Medical care—Fiction 3. Siblings—Fiction 4. Twins—Fiction 5. Family life—Fiction 6. Illinois—Fiction

ISBN 978-0-399-24671-5; 0-399-24671-1

LC 2007027507

What starts out as a perfectly ordinary day in the Small house turns into Stiches Saturday when Cleo gets a cut on the head after her twin brother, Jack, accidentally pulls down their "Toy House."

This is an "engaging early chapter book. . . . The story is studded with observations, incidents, and conversations that reflect true-to-life sibling relationships and realistic individual foibles. . . . Large type, spacious design, and appealing drawings add to the accessiblity." Booklist

Other titles about Cleo re:

Underpants on my head (2009)

I barfed on Mrs. Kenly (2010)

Harris, Lewis, 1964-

A taste for red. Clarion Books 2009 169p $16

Grades: 4 5 6   **Fic**

1. Vampires—Fiction 2. Missing children—Fiction 3. Friendship—Fiction

ISBN 978-0-547-14462-7; 0-547-14462-8

LC 2008-25318

When some of her classmates disappear, sixth-grader Svetlana, along with her new friends go in search of the missing students using her newfound ability as an Olfactive, one who has heightened smell, hearing, and the ability to detect vampires.

"Svetlana comes across as a strong character. . . . Her first-person narrative is fast-paced and witty, and her mild scorn for everything she encounters at school will appeal to angst-ridden tweens. Sure to be a crowd-pleaser." SLJ

Harrison, Michelle

13 treasures. Little, Brown Books for Young Readers 2010 355p il $15.99 *

Grades: 5 6 7 8   **Fic**

1. Fairies—Fiction 2. Grandmothers—Fiction 3. Great Britain—Fiction 4. Mystery fiction

ISBN 978-0-316-04148-5; 0-316-04148-3

LC 2008-45511

Bedeviled by evil fairies that only she can see, thirteen-year-old Tanya is sent to stay with her cold and distant grandmother at Elvesden Manor, where she and the caretaker's son solve a disturbing mystery that leads them to the discovery that Tanya's life is in danger.

"Harrison writes with great assurance, creating a seductive setting and memorable, fully developed characters. . . . It's an excellent choice for fans of the Spiderwick Chronicles and other modern-day fairy tales." Publ Wkly

Hartnett, Sonya, 1968-

The silver donkey; illustrated by Don T. Powers. Candlewick Press 2006 266p il $15.99; pa $7.99 *

Grades: 5 6 7 8   **Fic**
1. World War, 1914-1918—Fiction 2. France—Fiction 3. Soldiers—Fiction
ISBN   978-0-7636-2937-3;   0-7636-2937-5; 978-0-7636-3681-4 (pa); 0-7636-3681-9 (pa)
LC 2006-42582
First published 2004 in Australia
In France during World War I, four French children learn about honesty, loyalty, and courage from an English army deserter who tells them a series of stories related to his small, silver donkey charm

"Occasional full-page black-and-white art deftly suggests setting and mood without intruding on readers' imaginations. Provocative, timely, and elegantly honed." Horn Book

Hartry, Nancy

Watching Jimmy. Tundra Books 2009 152p $16.95

Grades: 5 6 7 8   **Fic**
1. Brain—Wounds and injuries—Fiction 2. Child abuse—Fiction
ISBN 978-0-88776-871-2; 0-88776-871-7
In Canada, in 1958, 11-year-old Carolyn secretly witnessed the abuse of her friend, Jimmy, at the hands of his drunken Uncle Ted, which caused Jimmy's severe brain damage. Now Jimmy's mother can't afford health insurance and is struggling to survive, and Carolyn is trying to protect Jimmy.

"Like a steady beat that pulses louder and louder, the story unfolds against a backdrop of postwar social and political concerns and Remembrance Day. Carolyn is a passionate and feisty character, delineated with love and precision, and readers will be drawn to her. A compelling and satisfying novel." SLJ

Haven, Paul

Two hot dogs with everything. Random House 2006 307p il hardcover o.p. lib bdg $17.89; pa $6.50

Grades: 4 5 6 7   **Fic**
1. Baseball—Fiction 2. Superstition—Fiction
ISBN 0-375-83348-X; 0-375-93348-4 (lib bdg); 0-375-83349-8 (pa)   LC 2005-08344
Although everyone credits him and his superstitions for the Slugger's first winning streak in 108 baseball seasons, eleven-year-old Danny Gurkin believes that his discovery of a secret from the team's past may be the real reason behind the ball club's success.

"Haven's first novel will delight readers with its whimsically exaggerated detail. . . . The intricate plot . . . will keep readers on the edge of their seats." SLJ

Haydon, Elizabeth

The Floating Island; the lost journals of Ven Polypheme; illustrated by Brett Helquist. Starscape 2006 368p il $17.95; pa $5.99

Grades: 5 6 7 8   **Fic**
1. Fantasy fiction
ISBN 0-7653-0867-3; 0-7653-4772-5 (pa)
LC 2006005768
"A Tom Doherty Associates book"
Ven, the youngest son of a long line of famous shipwrights, dreams of sailing to far-off lands where magic thrives. He gets his chance when he is chosen to direct the Inspection of his family's latest ship and sets sail on the journey of a lifetime

The author's "world building is as successful as her characters, with Helquist's occasional loose sketches providing some visual distraction and additional atmosphere. A delightful epic fantasy." Booklist
Followed by The Thief Queen's daughter (2007)

Hayter, Rhonda

The witchy worries of Abbie Adams. Dial Books for Young Readers 2010 242p $16.99

Grades: 4 5 6   **Fic**
1. Witches—Fiction   2. Magic—Fiction 3. Friendship—Fiction 4. Family life—Fiction
ISBN 978-0-8037-3468-5; 0-8037-3468-9
LC 2009-16743
Fifth-grader Abbie, descended from a long line of witches, tries to keep her family's magic powers secret from everyone she knows until her father brings home a kitten with some very unusual characteristics.

"Abby's breezy, personable narrative incorporates droll asides and references to [Thomas] Edison's and to famous literature. . . . Abbie is an appealing, peppy protagonist." Booklist

Hazen, Lynn E.

The amazing trail of Seymour Snail; illustrated by Doug Cushman. Henry Holt and Co. 2009 64p il $16.95

Grades: 1 2 3   **Fic**
1. Snails—Fiction 2. Artists—Fiction 3. New York (N.Y.)—Fiction
ISBN 978-0-8050-8698-0; 0-8050-8698-6
LC 2008036939
Hoping to become a famous artist one day, Seymour Snail takes a job in a New York City art gallery, where everyone is buzzing about a "magnificent mystery artist."

"With only a few sentences and at least one illustration per page, this title is perfect for students transitioning to chapter books. . . . Cushman's black-and-white cartoons delineate the characters and add humor and perspective." SLJ

Cinder Rabbit; [by] Lynn E. Hazen; illustrated by Elyse Pastel. Holt 2008 64p il $15.95

Grades: K 1 2   **Fic**
1. Rabbits—Fiction 2. School stories 3. Theater—Fiction
ISBN 978-0-8050-8194-7; 0-8050-8194-1
LC 2007027318

Hazen, Lynn E.—*Continued*

Zoe is chosen for the role of Cinder Rabbit in her school play and is also supposed to lead the class in the Bunny Hop at the end, but ever since wicked Winifred laughed at her for landing in a mud puddle, Zoe has forgotten how to hop

"This simple, sweet beginning chapter book contains the right amount of story for children just starting to read longer books; and the charming black-and-white illustrations, decorating every page, will engage kids." Booklist

Heide, Florence Parry, 1919-

The shrinking of Treehorn; drawings by Edward Gorey. Holiday House 1971 unp il lib bdg $16.95; pa $6.95

Grades: 2 3 4 5   **Fic**
ISBN 0-8234-0189-8 (lib bdg); 0-8234-0975-9 (pa)

Treehorn spends an unhappy day and night shrinking. Yet when he tells his mother, father, teacher and principal of his problem they're all too busy to do anything about it. To Treehorn's great relief he finally discovers a magical game that restores him to his natural size, but then he starts turning green!

This "is an imaginative little whimsy, whose sly humor and macabre touches are perfectly matched in Edward Gorey's illustrations." Book World

Heldring, Thatcher

Roy Morelli steps up to the plate. Delacorte Press 2010 229p $15.99; lib bdg $18.99

Grades: 5 6 7 8   **Fic**
1. Baseball—Fiction 2. School stories 3. Divorce—Fiction
ISBN 978-0-385-73391-5; 0-385-73391-7; 978-0-385-90406-3 (lib bdg); 0-385-90406-1 (lib bdg)
LC 2009033845

When eighth-grader Roy Morelli's divorced parents find out he is failing history, they ban him from playing on his beloved all-star baseball team, and, even worse, he winds up being tutored by his father's new girlfriend.

"The novel features good characterization and some sizzling dialogue. . . . The game action is fast paced and exciting, the depiction of middle school dynamics rings true, and the main character shows genuine emotional growth over the course of the novel." SLJ

Helgerson, Joseph

Crows & cards; a novel; written with diligence by Mr. Joseph Helgerson; to which are added fine illustrations by Mr. Peter Desève; also included is Dictionarium Americannicum; being the words herein most arcane and alien and their definitions. Houghton Mifflin Harcourt 2009 344p il $16

Grades: 4 5 6 7   **Fic**
1. Apprentices—Fiction 2. Gambling—Fiction 3. Slavery—Fiction 4. Native Americans—Fiction 5. Saint Louis (Mo.)—Fiction
ISBN 978-0-618-88395-0; 0-618-88395-9
LC 2008013308

In 1849, Zeb's parents ship him off to St. Louis to become an apprentice tanner, but the naive twelve-year-old rebels, casting his lot with a cheating riverboat gambler,

while a slave and an Indian medicine man try to get Zeb back on the right path. Includes historical notes, glossary, and bibliographical references

"Helgerson surrounds Zeb with a lively cast. . . . A solid choice for fans fo high-spun yarns and not-too-tall tales." Booklist

Horns & wrinkles. Houghton Mifflin 2006 357p il $16; pa $4.95 *

Grades: 4 5 6 7   **Fic**
1. Magic—Fiction 2. Trolls—Fiction 3. Bullies—Fiction 4. Mississippi River—Fiction
ISBN 0-618-61679-9; 0-618-98178-0 (pa)
LC 2005025448

Along a magic-saturated stretch of the Mississippi River near Blue Wing, Minnesota, twelve-year-old Claire and her bullying cousin Duke are drawn into an adventure involving Bodacious Deepthink the Great Rock Troll, a helpful fairy, and a group of trolls searching for their fathers.

"Tongue-in-cheek humor brings a delightful zing to the playfully inventive storytelling and fast-paced plot. Enchanting sketches foreshadow each chapter, adding to the wonder." SLJ

Hemingway, Edith Morris, 1950-

Road to Tater Hill; [by] Edith M. Hemingway. Delacorte Press 2009 213p map $16.99; lib bdg $19.99

Grades: 5 6 7 8   **Fic**
1. Bereavement—Fiction 2. Friendship—Fiction 3. Depression (Psychology)—Fiction 4. Grandparents—Fiction 5. Mountain life—Fiction 6. North Carolina—Fiction
ISBN 978-0-385-73677-0; 0-385-73677-0; 978-0-385-90627-2 (lib bdg); 0-385-90627-7 (lib bdg)
LC 2008-24906

At her grandparents' North Carolina mountain home during the summer of 1963, eleven-year-old Annie Winters, grief-stricken by the death of her newborn sister and isolated by her mother's deepening depression, finds comfort in holding an oblong stone 'rock baby' and in the friendship of a neighbor boy and a reclusive mountain woman with a devastating secret.

"Drawing on the author's childhood roots, the heart of this first novel is the sense of place, described in simple lyrical words. . . . True to Annie's viewpoint, the particulars tell a universal drama of childhood grief, complete in all its sadness, anger, loneliness, and healing." Booklist

Hemphill, Helen, 1955-

The adventurous deeds of Deadwood Jones. Front Street 2008 228p $16.95

Grades: 5 6 7 8   **Fic**
1. Cowhands—Fiction 2. African Americans—Fiction 3. Race relations—Fiction 4. Cousins—Fiction 5. West (U.S.)—Fiction
ISBN 978-1-59078-637-6; 1-59078-637-8
LC 2008005422

Thirteen-year-old Prometheus Jones and his eleven-year-old cousin Omer flee Tennessee and join a cattle drive that will eventually take them to Texas, where Prometheus hopes his father lives, and they find adventure

Hemphill, Helen, 1955-—_Continued_

and face challenges as African Americans in a land still recovering from the Civil War.

"Prometheus is an always sympathetic and engaging character, and the dangers and misadventures he encounters . . . make for compelling reading." Booklist

Hemphill, Michael

Stonewall Hinkleman and the Battle of Bull Run; [by] Michael Hemphill and Sam Riddleburger. Dial Books for Young Readers 2009 168p $16.99

Grades: 4 5 6   **Fic**

1. Bull Run, 1st Battle of, 1861—Fiction 2. United States—History—1861-1865, Civil War—Fiction 3. Time travel—Fiction

ISBN 978-0-8037-3179-0; 0-8037-3179-5

LC 2008-15795

While participating in a reenactment of the Battle of Bull Run, twelve-year-old Stonewall Hinkleman is transported back to the actual Civil War battle by means of a magic bugle.

This is a "well-paced time-travel novel. . . . Stonewall is a likable character whose attitude changes for the better in the story. . . . A good choice for historical fiction fans." SLJ

Heneghan, Judith, 1965-

The magician's apprentice. Holiday House 2008 c2005 168p $16.95

Grades: 4 5 6 7   **Fic**

1. Swindlers and swindling—Fiction 2. Adventure fiction 3. Magicians—Fiction 4. Orphans—Fiction 5. Great Britain—History—19th century—Fiction

ISBN 978-0-8234-2150-3; 0-8234-2150-3

LC 2007-35186

First published 2005 in the United Kingdom with title: Stonecipher

In 1874 Winchester, England, Jago Stonecipher, magician's assistant to his unscrupulous uncle, becomes involved in a series of plots and deceits revolving around a lady's maid and her employer's family, and finally escapes to sea, where the trouble follows him, even aboard ship.

"The complex plot is full of unexpected twists and hairbreadth escapes, and the dialogue rings true to the period. An exciting choice for historical fiction fans." SLJ

Henham, R. D.

The red dragon codex. Mirrorstone 2008 244p il map (Dragon condices) pa $9.95

Grades: 4 5 6   **Fic**

1. Dragons—Fiction 2. Fantasy fiction

ISBN 978-0-7869-4925-0 (pa); 0-7869-4925-2 (pa)

LC 2007014679

Mudd must seek a silver dragon's help to rescue Shemnara, an old woman who is practically his mother, when she is kidnapped by a red dragon.

"Inventive details, dimensional characterizations, and fast-paced action make this a good introduction to the fantasy genre." Booklist

Henkes, Kevin, 1960-

Bird Lake moon. Greenwillow Books 2008 179p $15.99; lib bdg $16.89; pa $5.99 *

Grades: 4 5 6 7   **Fic**

1. Divorce—Fiction 2. Bereavement—Fiction 3. Lakes—Fiction 4. Friendship—Fiction 5. Family life—Fiction 6. Wisconsin—Fiction

ISBN 978-0-06-147076-9; 0-06-147076-7; 978-0-06-147078-3 (lib bdg); 0-06-147078-3 (lib bdg); 978-0-06-147079-0 (pa); 0-06-147079-1 (pa)

LC 2007-36564

Twelve-year-old Mitch and his mother are spending the summer with his grandparents at Bird Lake after his parents separate, and ten-year-old Spencer and his family have returned to the lake where Spencer's little brother drowned long ago, and as the boys become friends and spend time together, each of them begins to heal

"Characters are gently and believably developed as the story weaves in and around the beautiful Wisconsin setting. The superbly crafted plot moves smoothly and unhurriedly, mirroring a slow summer pace." SLJ

The birthday room. Greenwillow Bks. 1999 152p $15.99; pa $5.99 *

Grades: 5 6 7 8   **Fic**

1. Family life—Fiction 2. Uncles—Fiction

ISBN 0-688-16733-0; 0-06-443828-7 (pa)

LC 98-39887

"For his twelfth birthday, Ben Hunter receives a room that he can use as an art studio and a letter from his uncle—the one responsible for the loss of Ben's little finger when Ben was a toddler. . . . Mrs. Hunter, who has been angry at her brother since the accident, reluctantly agrees to go to Oregon with Ben." Booklist

"Told in spare, unobtrusive prose, a story that helps us see our own chances for benefiting from mutual tolerance, creative conflict resolution, and other forms of good will." Horn Book

Olive's ocean. Greenwillow Bks. 2003 217p $15.99; pa $6.99 *

Grades: 5 6 7 8   **Fic**

1. Grandmothers—Fiction 2. Family life—Fiction

ISBN 0-06-053543-1; 0-06-053545-8 (pa)

LC 2002-29782

A Newbery Medal honor book, 2004

On a summer visit to her grandmother's cottage by the ocean, twelve-year-old Martha gains perspective on the death of a classmate, on her relationship with her grandmother, on her feelings for an older boy, and on her plans to be a writer.

"Rich characterizations move this compelling novel to its satisfying and emotionally authentic conclusion." SLJ

Protecting Marie. Greenwillow Bks. 1995 195p $18.99; pa $5.99 *

Grades: 5 6 7 8   **Fic**

1. Father-daughter relationship—Fiction 2. Dogs—Fiction

ISBN 0-688-13958-2; 0-06-053545-8 (pa)

LC 94-16387

Also available in paperback from Puffin Bks.

Relates twelve-year-old Fanny's love-hate relationship with her father, a temperamental artist, who has given Fanny a new dog

Henkes, Kevin, 1960-—*Continued*
"The characters ring heartbreakingly true in this quiet, wise story; they are complex and difficult—like all of us—and worthy of our attention." Horn Book

Sun & Spoon. Greenwillow Bks. 1997 135p $15.99; pa $5.99 *
Grades: 4 5 6 7   **Fic**
1. Grandmothers—Fiction 2. Death—Fiction
ISBN 0-688-15232-5; 0-06-128875-6 (pa)
LC 96-46259
Also available in paperback from Puffin Bks.
"Spoon, 10, spends his summer trying to reconfigure his world, which seems strangely out of kilter since his grandmother's death." SLJ
"Sensitively placed metaphors enrich the narrative, embuing its perceptive depictions of grief with a powerful message of affirmation." Publ Wkly

Words of stone. Greenwillow Bks. 1992 152p $18.99; pa $6.99
Grades: 5 6 7 8   **Fic**
1. Friendship—Fiction
ISBN 0-688-11356-7; 0-06-078230-7 (pa)
LC 91-28543
Busy trying to deal with his many fears nd his troubled feelings for his dead mother, ten-year-old Blaze has his life changed when he meets the boisterous and irresistible Joselle
"A story rich in characterization, dramatic subplots, and some very creepy moments." SLJ

Hennesy, Carolyn, 1962-
Pandora gets jealous. Bloomsbury Children's Books 2008 264p $14.95; pa $6.99
Grades: 4 5 6 7   **Fic**
1. Pandora (Legendary character)—Fiction
2. Classical mythology—Fiction
ISBN 978-1-59990-196-1; 1-59990-196-X; 978-1-59990-291-3 (pa); 1-59990-291-5 (pa)
LC 2007-23975
Thirteen-year-old Pandy is hauled before Zeus and given six months to gather all of the evils that were released when the box she brought to school as her annual project was accidentally opened.
"Hennesy's Hollywood comedian background shows in her witty juxtapositions of modern popular culture and classical Greek legend. . . . Accurate where it counts, this loosely interpreted myth rarely misses a comic twist." Publ Wkly
Other titles in this series are:
Pandora gets vain (2008)
Pandora gets lazy (2009)

Henry, Marguerite, 1902-1997
Brighty of the Grand Canyon; illustrated by Wesley Dennis. Macmillan 1991 222p il hardcover o.p. pa $3.95
Grades: 4 5 6 7   **Fic**
1. Donkeys—Fiction 2. Grand Canyon (Ariz.)—Fiction
ISBN 0-02-743664-0; 0-689-71485-8 (pa)
LC 90-28636
First published 1953 by Rand McNally

Drawn from a real-life incident, this is the story of "Brighty, the shaggy little burro who roamed the canyons of the Colorado River {and} had a will of his own. He liked the old prospector and Uncle Jim and he helped solve a mystery, but chiefly he was the freedom loving burro." Chicago Public Libr
"Only those who are unfamiliar with the West would say it is too packed with drama to be true. And the author's understanding warmth for all of God's creatures still shines through her superb ability as a story teller making this a vivid tale." Christ Sci Monit

Justin Morgan had a horse; illustrated by Wesley Dennis. Simon & Schuster Bks. for Young Readers 2002 c1954 169p il $17.95; pa $5.99
Grades: 4 5 6 7   **Fic**
1. Horses—Fiction 2. Vermont—Fiction
ISBN 0-689-85279-7; 1-4169-2785-9 (pa)
A Newbery Medal honor book, 1946
A reissue of the edition first published 1954 by Rand McNally; an expanded version of the book first published 1945 by Wilcox & Follett
An unusual work horse raised in Vermont and known originally as [Little Bub] becomes the sire of a famous American breed and takes the name of his owner, Justin Morgan
A horse story "in a book that is rich in human values—the sort of book that makes you proud and sometimes brings a lump to your throat." Book Week

King of the wind; illustrated by Wesley Dennis. Macmillan 1991 172p il $18.95; pa $5.99 *
Grades: 4 5 6 7   **Fic**
1. Horses—Fiction
ISBN 0-02-743629-2; 0-689-71486-6 (pa)
LC 91-13474
Awarded the Newbery Medal, 1949
A reissue of the title first published 1948 by Rand McNally
"A beautiful, sympathetic story of the famous [ancestor of a line of great thoroughbred horses] . . . and the little mute Arabian stable boy who accompanies him on his journey across the seas to France and England [in the eighteenth century]. The lad's fierce devotion to his horse and his great faith and loyalty are skillfully woven into an enthralling tale which children will long remember. The moving quality of the writing is reflected in the handsome illustrations." Wis Libr Bull

Misty of Chincoteague; illustrated by Wesley Dennis. Macmillan 1991 173p il hardcover o.p. pa $5.99 *
Grades: 4 5 6 7   **Fic**
1. Horses—Fiction 2. Chincoteague Island (Va.)—Fiction
ISBN 0-02-743622-5; 1-4169-2783-2 (pa)
LC 90-27237
A Newbery Medal honor book, 1948
First published 1947 by Rand McNally
"The islands of Chincoteague and Assateague, just off the coast of Virginia, are the setting. . . . Two children have their hearts set on owning a wild pony and her colt, descendants, so legend says, of the Moorish ponies who were survivors of a Spanish galleon wrecked there long ago." Booklist

Henry, Marguerite, 1902-1997—*Continued*

"The beauty and pride of the wild horses is the highpoint in the story, and skillful drawings of them reveal their grace and swiftness." Ont Libr Rev

Other titles about the ponies of Chincoteague Island are:
Sea star, orphan of Chincoteague (1949)
Stormy, Misty's foal (1963)

Henson, Heather

Here's how I see it, here's how it is. Atheneum Books for Young Readers 2009 270p $16.99

Grades: 5 6 7   **Fic**

1. Theater—Fiction 2. Actors—Fiction 3. Asperger's syndrome—Fiction

ISBN 978-1-4169-4901-5; 1-4169-4901-1

LC 2008-22213

At almost-thirteen, Junebug has never felt right except as stagehand at her father's summer theater, but after her parents separate and an irritating intern takes over her responsibilities, she discovers how hard life can be without a script to follow.

"Henson . . . creates a funny, bittersweet story filled with colorful personalities and plenty of backstage detail and drama." Publ Wkly

Hermes, Patricia, 1936-

Emma Dilemma and the new nanny. Marshall Cavendish 2006 106p il $15.95

Grades: 2 3 4   **Fic**

1. Family life—Fiction

ISBN 0-7614-5286-9; 978-0-7614-5286-7

LC 2005024668

Emma tries to help her parents understand that, although their beloved new nanny has made a few mistakes, no one can behave perfectly responsibly all the time

"The tumult in a family with five preteen children, several pets, and two working parents provides a lively setting, and the author lightly but effectively conveys the ideas that adults aren't perfect and that admitting mistakes is often the first step toward solutions that leave everyone pleased." Booklist

Other titles about Emma are:
Emma Dilemma and the two nannies (2007)
Emma Dilemma and the soccer nanny (2008)
Emma Dilemma and the camping nanny (2009)
Emma Dilemma, the nanny, and the secret ferret (2010)

Herrick, Steven, 1958-

Naked bunyip dancing; pictures by Beth Norling. Front Street 2008 c2005 201p il $16.95

Grades: 3 4 5 6   **Fic**

1. Teachers—Fiction 2. School stories 3. Australia—Fiction 4. Novels in verse

ISBN 978-1-59078-499-0   LC 2007-18353

First published 2005 in Australia

This novel in verse follows the school year of Australian students in classroom 6C, as their unconventional teacher encourages them to discover their own strengths and talents and perform in a memorable concert.

"The novel captures the humor and unpredictability of 11 and 12-year-olds. . . . The terse free verse, in short

clear lines, is easily accessible. Funny, with some touches of poignancy. . . . The childlike, black-and-white illustrations are reminiscent of the drawings of Shel Silverstein and complement the narrative." SLJ

Hershey, Mary

10 lucky things that have happened to me since I nearly got hit by lightning. Wendy Lamb Books 2008 230p $15.99; lib bdg $18.99

Grades: 3 4 5   **Fic**

1. Friendship—Fiction 2. Priests—Fiction 3. School stories

ISBN 978-0-385-73541-4; 0-385-73541-3; 978-0-385-90522-0 (lib bdg); 0-385-90522-X (lib bdg)

LC 2007-030939

Sequel to: My big sister is so bossy she says you can't read this book (2005)

Even though her father is in prison for embezzlement, ten-year-old Effie considers herself pretty lucky until her mother's old friend, Father Frank, comes to stay with them, Effie's friend Aurora decides to quit their Catholic school to attend public school, and her contrary sister begins to transform herself into "Saint Maxey."

"Humor, warmth, and Effie's Catholic values shine through in this entertaining story." Booklist

Followed by: Love and pollywogs from Camp Calamity (2010)

Hesse, Karen

Brooklyn Bridge; a novel. Feiwel and Friends 2008 229p il map $17.95 *

Grades: 5 6 7 8 9 10   **Fic**

1. Family life—Fiction 2. Social classes—Fiction 3. Homeless persons—Fiction 4. Immigrants—Fiction 5. Russian Americans—Fiction 6. Brooklyn (New York, N.Y.)—Fiction

ISBN 978-0-312-37886-8; 0-312-37886-6

LC 2008-05624

In 1903 Brooklyn, fourteen-year-old Joseph Michtom's life changes for the worse when his parents, Russian immigrants, invent the teddy bear and turn their apartment into a factory, while nearby the glitter of Coney Island contrasts with the dismal lives of children dwelling under the Brooklyn Bridge.

Hesse "applies her gift for narrative voice to this memorable story. . . . The novel explodes with dark drama before its eerie but moving resolution." Publ Wkly

Just Juice. Scholastic 1998 138p il hardcover o.p. pa $4.99 *

Grades: 3 4 5   **Fic**

1. Literacy—Fiction 2. Family life—Fiction 3. Poverty—Fiction

ISBN 0-590-03382-4; 0-590-03383-2 (pa)

LC 98-13375

Realizing that her father's lack of work has endangered her family, nine-year-old Juice decides that she must return to school and learn to read in order to help their chances of surviving and keeping their house

"Hesse's plain, beautiful words tell of the harsh dailiness of poverty through the eyes of a child." Booklist

Hesse, Karen—*Continued*

Letters from Rifka. Holt & Co. 1992 148p
$16.95; pa $6.99 *
Grades: 5 6 7 8   **Fic**
   1. Immigrants—Fiction 2. Jews—Fiction 3. Letters—
Fiction
   ISBN 0-8050-1964-2; 0-312-53561-9 (pa)
                          LC 91-48007
In letters to her cousin, Rifka, a young Jewish girl,
chronicles her family's flight from Russia in 1919 and
her own experiences when she must be left in Belgium
for a while when the others emigrate to America
   "Based on the true story of the author's great-aunt, the
moving account of a brave young girl's story brings to
life the day-to-day trials and horrors experienced by
many immigrants as well as the resourcefulness and
strength they found within themselves." Horn Book

Out of the dust. Scholastic 1997 227p $16.95;
pa $6.99 *
Grades: 5 6 7 8   **Fic**
   1. Dust storms—Fiction 2. Farm life—Fiction
3. Great Depression, 1929-1939—Fiction
4. Oklahoma—Fiction 5. Novels in verse
   ISBN 0-590-36080-9; 0-590-37125-8 (pa)
                          LC 96-40344
Awarded the Newbery Medal, 1998
   "After facing loss after loss during the Oklahoma Dust
Bowl, Billie Jo begins to reconstruct her life." SLJ
   "Hesse's writing transcends the gloom and transforms
it into a powerfully compelling tale of a girl with enormous strength, courage, and love. The entire novel is
written in very readable blank verse." Booklist

Stowaway; with drawings by Robert Andrew
Parker. Margaret K. McElderry Bks. 2000 319p il
$17.95; pa $6.99
Grades: 5 6 7 8   **Fic**
   1. Cook, James, 1728-1779—Fiction 2. Voyages
around the world—Fiction 3. Sea stories
   ISBN 0-689-83987-1; 0-689-83989-8 (pa)
                          LC 00-56976
A fictional journal relates the experiences of Nicholas,
a young stowaway, from 1768 to 1771 aboard the Endeavor which sailed around the world under Captain
James Cook
   "Hesse is a master storyteller who gives Nicholas an
authentic voice. . . . The author's subtle yet thorough attention to detail creates a memorable tale that is a virtual
encyclopedia of life in the days when England ruled the
seas." SLJ

Witness. Scholastic Press 2001 161p $16.95; pa
$5.99 *
Grades: 6 7 8 9   **Fic**
   1. Ku Klux Klan—Fiction 2. Prejudices—Fiction
3. Vermont—Fiction 4. Novels in verse
   ISBN 0-439-27199-1; 0-439-27200-9 (pa)
                          LC 00-54139
A series of poems express the views of eleven people
in a small Vermont town, including a young black girl
and a young Jewish girl, during the early 1920s when the
Ku Klux Klan is trying to infiltrate the town
   "The story is divided into five acts, and would lend itself beautifully to performance. The plot unfolds smooth-

ly, and the author creates multidimensional characters."
SLJ

Hest, Amy

Remembering Mrs. Rossi; [illustrated by]
Heather Maione. Candlewick Press 2007 184p il
$14.99 *
Grades: 3 4 5   **Fic**
   1. Death—Fiction 2. Mothers—Fiction 3. Teachers—
Fiction 4. Father-daughter relationship—Fiction
5. New York (N.Y.)—Fiction
   ISBN 978-0-7636-2163-6; 0-7636-2163-3
                        LC 2006-41649
Although she loves her father, their home in New
York City, and third-grade teacher Miss Meadows, Annie
misses her mother who died recently
   "Hest imbues her characters with warmth, humor, and
realistic imperfections. . . . Maione's ink sketches highlight the tender affections." Booklist

Hiaasen, Carl, 1953-

Flush. Knopf 2005 263p $16.95; lib bdg $18.99;
pa $8.99 *
Grades: 5 6 7 8   **Fic**
   1. Environmental protection—Fiction 2. Florida—Fiction 3. Boats and boating—Fiction
   ISBN 0-375-82182-1; 0-375-92182-6 (lib bdg);
0-375-84185-7 (pa)   LC 2005-05259
With their father jailed for sinking a river boat, Noah
Underwood and his younger sister, Abbey, must gather
evidence that the owner of this floating casino is emptying his bilge tanks into the protected waters around their
Florida Keys home
   "This quick-reading, fun, family adventure harkens
back to the Hardy Boys in its simplicity and quirky characters." SLJ

Hoot. Knopf 2002 292p $15.95; pa $8.95 *
Grades: 5 6 7 8   **Fic**
   1. Owls—Fiction 2. Environmental protection—Fiction
3. Florida—Fiction
   ISBN 0-375-82181-3; 0-375-82916-4 (pa)
                          LC 2002-25478
A Newbery Medal honor book, 2003
Roy, who is new to his small Florida community, becomes involved in another boy's attempt to save a colony of burrowing owls from a proposed construction site
   "The story is full of offbeat humor, buffoonish yet
charming supporting characters, and genuinely touching
scenes of children enjoying the wildness of nature."
Booklist

Scat. Knopf 2009 371p $16.99; lib bdg $19.99;
pa $8.99 *
Grades: 5 6 7 8   **Fic**
   1. Teachers—Fiction 2. Missing persons—Fiction
3. Wildlife conservation—Fiction 4. Florida—Fiction
   ISBN 978-0-375-83486-8; 0-375-83486-9;
978-0-375-93486-5 (lib bdg); 0-375-93486-3 (lib bdg);
978-0-375-83487-5 (pa); 0-375-83487-7 (pa)
                        LC 2008-28266
Nick and his friend Marta decide to investigate when
a mysterious fire starts near a Florida wildlife preserve

Hiaasen, Carl, 1953-—_Continued_
and an unpopular teacher goes missing.

"Once again, Hiaasen has written an edge-of-the-seat eco-thriller. . . . From the first sentence, readers will be hooked. . . . This well-written and smoothly plotted story, with fully realized characters, will certainly appeal to mystery lovers." SLJ

Hicks, Betty
Basketball Bats; illustrated by Adam McCauley. Roaring Brook Press 2008 55p il (Gym shorts) $15.95
Grades: 2 3 4   **Fic**
1. Basketball—Fiction
ISBN 978-1-59643-243-7; 1-59643-243-8
                                    LC 2007-019501
Henry and his basketball teammates, the Bats, take on the Tigers, and Henry learns a lesson about working as a team.

"Hicks finds just the right balance between story line, play-by-play action, and wry humor. . . . Nearly every double-page spread includes a droll illustration by McCauley, the illustrator of Scieszka's Time Warp Trio series." Booklist
Other titles in this series are:
Goof-off goalie (2008)
Swimming with sharks (2008)
Scaredy-cat catcher (2009)
Track attack (2009)
Doubles troubles (2010)

Out of order. Roaring Brook Press 2005 169p $15.95; pa $6.99 *
Grades: 4 5 6   **Fic**
1. Stepfamilies—Fiction
ISBN 1-59643-061-3; 0-312-37355-4 (pa)
                                    LC 2004-30107
"A Deborah Brodie book."
Four youngsters, ages nine to fifteen, narrate one side of the story of their newly blended family's adjustment, interwoven with grief and loss.

"Hicks provides readers with a fresh look at blended families, offering much food for thought and several multilayered characters." SLJ

Higgins, F. E.
The Black Book of Secrets. Feiwel and Friends 2007 273p $14.95 *
Grades: 4 5 6 7   **Fic**
1. Pawnbrokers—Fiction 2. Apprentices—Fiction
ISBN 978-0-312-36844-9; 0-312-36844-5
                                    LC 2007-32559
Companion volume to: The bone magician (2008)
When Ludlow Fitch runs away from his thieving parents in the City, he meets up with the mysterious Joe Zabbidou, who calls himself a secret pawnbroker, and who takes Ludlow as an apprentice to record the confessions of the townspeople of Pagus Parvus, where resentments are many and trust is scarce.

This is "an intriguing blend of adventure and historical fiction spiced with a light touch of the fantastic." Voice of Youth Advocates

The bone magician. Feiwel and Friends 2008 272p $14.95
Grades: 4 5 6 7   **Fic**
1. Magicians—Fiction 2. Undertakers and undertaking—Fiction 3. Mystery fiction
ISBN 978-0-312-36845-6; 0-312-36845-3
                                    LC 2008-6777
Companion volume to: Black book of secrets (2007)
With his father, a fugitive, falsely accused of multiple murders and the real serial killer stalking the wretched streets of Urbs Umida, Pin Carpue, a young undertaker's assistant, investigates and soon discovers that all of the victims may have attended the performance of a stage magician who claims to be able to raise corpses and make the dead speak.

This offers "no end of picaresque charms, creepy turns, and beguiling cast members." Booklist

Hill, Kirkpatrick, 1938-
The year of Miss Agnes. Margaret K. McElderry Bks. 2000 115p $16; pa $5.99
Grades: 3 4 5   **Fic**
1. School stories 2. Teachers—Fiction 3. Athapascan Indians—Fiction 4. Alaska—Fiction
ISBN 0-689-82933-7; 0-689-85124-3 (pa)
                                    LC 99-46912
Ten-year-old Fred (short for Frederika) narrates the story of school and village life among the Athapascans in Alaska during 1948 when Miss Agnes arrived as the new teacher

"Hill has created more than just an appealing cast of characters; she introduces readers to a whole community and makes a long-ago and faraway place seem real and very much alive. This is an inspirational story." SLJ

Hirahara, Naomi, 1962-
1001 cranes. Delacorte Press 2008 230p $15.99; lib bdg $18.99; pa $6.50
Grades: 5 6 7 8   **Fic**
1. Japanese Americans—Fiction 2. Family life—Fiction 3. Grandparents—Fiction
ISBN 978-0-385-73556-8; 0-385-73556-1; 978-0-385-90541-1 (lib bdg); 0-385-90541-6 (lib bdg); 978-0-440-42234-1 (pa); 0-440-42234-5 (pa)
                                    LC 2007-27655
With her parents on the verge of separating, Angela, a twelve-year-old Japanese American girl, spends the summer in Los Angeles with her grandparents, where she folds paper cranes into wedding displays, becomes involved with a young skateboarder, and learns how complicated relationships can be.

Angela's "colorful, bold voice captures the excitement of her first love as well as the anxiety of not understanding the many secrets of the adults around her. By experiencing her family's support, by learning about her Japanese heritage, and by acknowledging the various ways that love is expressed, Angela emerges into a strong, caring person." SLJ

Hobbs, Valerie, 1941-

Defiance. Farrar, Straus and Giroux 2005 116p
$16; pa $7.99

Grades: 5 6 7 8   Fic

1. Cancer—Fiction 2. Death—Fiction 3. Country
life—Fiction

ISBN 0-374-30847-0; 0-312-53581-3 (pa)

LC 2004-61524

"Frances Foster books."

While vacationing in the country, eleven-year-old
Toby, a cancer patient, learns some important lessons
about living and dying from an elderly poet and her cow.

"Spare, graceful writing, with just enough detail to
bring the characters and setting to life, skillfully paces
the action and keeps the focus on Toby's conflicted feelings. . . . A quiet, yet resonant story." SLJ

The last best days of summer. Frances Foster
Books 2010 197p $16.99 *

Grades: 5 6 7 8   Fic

1. Popularity—Fiction 2. Grandmothers—Fiction
3. Old age—Fiction 4. Down syndrome—Fiction
5. Artists—Fiction

ISBN 978-0-374-34670-6; 0-374-34670-4

LC 2008-47145

During a summer visit, twelve-year-old Lucy must
come to terms with both her grandmother's failing memory and how her mentally-challenged neighbor will impact her popularity when both enter the same middle
school in the fall.

"The story's finely tuned realism is refreshing, particularly in Lucy's yearning for social acceptance and in the
fully drawn and wholly memorable characters." Booklist

Sheep. Farrar, Straus and Giroux 2006 115p
$16; pa $6.99

Grades: 3 4 5   Fic

1. Dogs—Fiction 2. Sheep—Fiction

ISBN 0-374-36777-9; 0-312-56116-4 (pa)

LC 2005-46356

"Frances Foster books"

After a fire destroys the farm where he was born, a
young border collie acquires a series of owners and
learns about life as he seeks a home and longs to fulfill
his life's purpose of shepherding sheep.

"The classic foundling story is beautifully told in the
dog's simple, first-person voice." Booklist

Hobbs, Will

Crossing the wire. HarperCollins 2006 216p
$15.99; lib bdg $16.89; pa $5.99

Grades: 5 6 7 8   Fic

1. Illegal aliens—Fiction 2. Mexicans—Fiction

ISBN   978-0-06-074138-9;   0-06-074138-4;
978-0-06-074139-6 (lib bdg); 0-06-074139-2 (lib bdg);
978-0-06-074140-2 (pa); 0-06-074140-6 (pa)

LC 2005-19697

Fifteen-year-old Victor Flores journeys north in a desperate attempt to cross the Arizona border and find work
in the United States to support his family in central Mexico.

This is "an exciting story in a vital contemporary setting." Voice Youth Advocates

Jason's gold. Morrow Junior Bks. 1999 221p
$16.99; pa $5.99 *

Grades: 5 6 7 8   Fic

1. Klondike River Valley (Yukon)—Gold discoveries—Fiction 2. Voyages and travels—Fiction
3. Orphans—Fiction

ISBN 0-688-15093-4; 0-380-72914-8 (pa)

LC 99-17973

When news of the discovery of gold in Canada's Yukon Territory in 1897 reaches fifteen-year-old Jason, he
embarks on a 10,000-mile journey to strike it rich

"The successful presentation of a fascinating era, coupled with plenty of action, makes this a good historical
fiction choice." SLJ

Followed by Down the Yukon (2001)

Hoberman, Mary Ann, 1930-

Strawberry Hill; illustrated by Wendy Anderson
Halperin. Little, Brown Books for Young Readers
2009 230p il $15.99 *

Grades: 3 4 5   Fic

1. Moving—Fiction 2. Country life—Fiction
3. Friendship—Fiction 4. Great Depression, 1929-
1939—Fiction 5. Jews—United States—Fiction

ISBN 978-0-316-04136-2; 0-316-04136-X

LC 2008045300

Ten-year-old Allie's family moves from urban New
Haven to rural Stamford, Connecticut, in the midst of the
Great Depression.

This "is a small yet highly evocative story. . . . [This
offers] story lines that are simple but never simplistic
and perfectly drafted chapters in which the ordinary has
the opportunity to become special." Booklist

Hoeye, Michael, 1947-

Time stops for no mouse; a Hermux Tantamoq
adventure. Putnam 2002 250p $14.99 paperback
o.p. *

Grades: 5 6 7 8   Fic

1. Mice—Fiction 2. Animals—Fiction 3. Mystery fiction

ISBN 0-399-23878-6; 0-698-11991-6 (pa)

LC 2001-48486

First published 2000 by Terfle Bks.

When Linka Perflinger, a jaunty mouse, brings a
watch into his shop to be repaired and then disappears,
Hermux Tantamoq is caught up in a world of dangerous
search for eternal youth as he tries to find out what happened to her

"The snappy, sophisticated writing makes this adventure a delight from start to finish. The city of Pinchester
comes alive brilliantly with its multispecies population of
rats, mice, gophers, and other small furry folk. . . . A
delightful romp for imaginative readers and fantasy
fans." Voice Youth Advocates

Other titles in this series are:
No time like show time (2004)
The sands of time (2002)
Time to smell the roses (2007)

Hof, Marjolijn, 1956-

Against the odds; translated by Johanna H. Prins and Johanna W. Prins. Groundwood Books/House of Anansi Press 2009 124p $17.95

Grades: 3 4 5   **Fic**

1. Physicians—Fiction 2. Fathers—Fiction 3. War stories 4. Worry—Fiction

ISBN 978-0-88899-935-1; 0-88899-935-6

"Kiki's father is traveling to a war zone as a doctor, and the child and her mother worry that he won't return. As soon as he leaves, Kiki starts planning to increase the odds that he will be safe. . . . The language and writing style are a bit old-fashioned, yet comforting. The story is engaging and gives readers a chance to develop empathy." SLJ

Hoffman, Mary, 1945-

Starring Grace; pictures by Caroline Binch. Fogelman Pub. 2000 95p il hardcover o.p. pa $4.99 *

Grades: 3 4 5   **Fic**

1. African Americans—Fiction 2. Grandmothers—Fiction

ISBN 0-8037-2559-0; 0-14-230022-5 (pa)

Picture book titles about Grace are also available

Grace and her friends have all sorts of adventures during their summer vacation—going to the circus, taking an imaginary safari, making friends with an elderly neighbor, pretending to be astronauts, and calling the paramedics when her grandmother has an accident

"Hoffman's text reads easily and is filled with humor and the wide-eyed innocence of young children at play." SLJ

Other chapter-book titles about Grace are:

Bravo Grace! (2005)
Encore Grace! (2003)

Hoffmann, E. T. A. (Ernst Theodor Amadeus), 1776-1822

Nutcracker; pictures by Maurice Sendak; translated by Ralph Manheim. Crown 1984 102p il $40

Grades: 4 5 6 7   **Fic**

1. Fairy tales 2. Christmas—Fiction

ISBN 0-609-61049-X   LC 83-25266

This "book stems from Sendak's costume and set designs for the Pacific Northwest Ballet's 1981 production. That production, and this volume, differ from the traditional ballet as they are based on Hoffmann's original 1816 long short story, rather than a French version of Hoffmann's tale." SLJ

"The smooth, elegant, new translation re-creates the flavor of the period and does justice to the story. . . . The occasional quirkiness of the pictures . . . eerily reflect the mysterious story. Altogether a magnificent, splendid combination of talents." Horn Book

Holling, Holling C., 1900-1973

Paddle-to-the-sea; written and illustrated by Holling Clancy Holling. Houghton Mifflin 1941 unp il lib bdg $20; pa $11.95

Grades: 4 5 6   **Fic**

1. Great Lakes region—Fiction

ISBN 0-395-15082-5 (lib bdg); 0-395-29203-4 (pa)

A Caldecott Medal honor book, 1942

A toy canoe with a seated Indian figure is launched in Lake Nipigon by the Indian boy who carved it and in four years travels through all the Great Lakes and the St. Lawrence River to the Atlantic. An interesting picture of the shore life of the lakes and the river with striking full page pictures in bright colors and marginal pencil drawings

"The canoe's journey is used to show the flow of currents and of traffic, and each occurrence is made to seem plausible. . . . There are also diagrams of a sawmill, a freighter, the canal locks at the Soo, and Niagara Falls." Libr J

Hollyer, Belinda

River song; by Belinda Hollyer. Holiday House 2008 170p $16.95

Grades: 4 5 6 7   **Fic**

1. Mother-daughter relationship—Fiction 2. Grandmothers—Fiction 3. Maoris—Fiction

ISBN 978-0-8234-2149-7; 0-8234-2149-X

      LC 2007035995

First published 2007 in the United Kingdom

Jessye loves living with her grandmother in a traditional Maori village, but when her free-wheeling mother comes back into her life, Jessye must decide whether to stay or move to the city

"The natural-sounding first-person narrative draws readers into a story of a girl learning to make sense of all the strands that make up her life and heritage." SLJ

Holm, Jennifer L.

Middle school is worse than meatloaf; a year told through stuff; by Jennifer L. Holm; pictures by Elicia Castaldi. Atheneum Books for Young Readers 2007 unp il $12.99 *

Grades: 5 6 7 8   **Fic**

1. School stories 2. Family life—Fiction

ISBN 0-689-85281-9

"Ginny Davis begins seventh grade with a list of items to accomplish. This list, along with lots of other 'stuff'—including diary entries, refrigerator notes, cards from Grandpa, and IM screen messages—convey a year full of ups and downs. Digitally rendered collage illustrations realistically depict the various means of communication, and the story flows easily from one colorful page to the next. . . . The story combines honesty and humor to create a believable and appealing voice." SLJ

Our only May Amelia. HarperCollins Pubs. 1999 253p il hardcover o.p. pa $5.99 *

Grades: 5 6 7 8   **Fic**

1. Frontier and pioneer life—Fiction 2. Family life—Fiction 3. Finnish Americans—Fiction 4. Washington (State)—Fiction

ISBN 0-06-027822-6; 0-06-440856-6 (pa)

      LC 98-47504

Holm, Jennifer L.—*Continued*

A Newbery Medal honor book, 2000

As the only girl in a Finnish American family of seven brothers, May Amelia Jackson resents being expected to act like a lady while growing up in Washington State in 1899

"The voice of the colloquial first-person narrative rings true and provides a vivid picture of frontier and pioneer life. . . . An afterword discusses Holm's research into her own family's history and that of other Finnish immigrants." Horn Book Guide

Penny from heaven. Random House 2006 274p il $15.95; lib bdg $17.99; pa $6.99 *

Grades: 5 6 7 8   **Fic**

1. Family life—Fiction 2. New Jersey—Fiction 3. Italian Americans—Fiction

ISBN 0-375-83687-X; 0-375-93687-4 (lib bdg); 0-375-83689-6 (pa)   LC 2005-13896

A Newbery Medal honor book, 2007

As she turns twelve during the summer of 1953, Penny gains new insights into herself and her family while also learning a secret about her father's death.

"Holm impressively wraps pathos with comedy in this coming-of-age story, populated by a cast of vivid characters." Booklist

Turtle in paradise. Random House 2010 191p $16.99; lib bdg $19.99 *

Grades: 3 4 5   **Fic**

1. Cousins—Fiction 2. Family life—Fiction 3. Adventure fiction 4. Florida—Fiction 5. Great Depression, 1929-1939—Fiction

ISBN 978-0-375-83688-6; 0-375-83688-8; 978-0-375-93688-3 (lib bdg); 0-375-93688-2 (lib bdg)   LC 2009-19077

In 1935, when her mother gets a job housekeeping for a woman who does not like children, eleven-year-old Turtle is sent to stay with relatives she has never met in far away Key West, Florida.

"Holm's voice for Turtle is winning and authentic—that of a practical, clear-eyed observer—and her nimble way with dialogue creates laugh-out-loud moments. Sweet, funny and superb." Kirkus

Holmes, Elizabeth Ann, 1957-

Tracktown summer; [by] Elizabeth Holmes. Dutton Children's Books 2009 248p $16.99

Grades: 5 6 7 8   **Fic**

1. Father-son relationship—Fiction 2. Lakes—Fiction 3. Mental illness—Fiction

ISBN 978-0-525-47946-8; 0-525-47946-5   LC 2008-34223

Spending the summer with his father at a run-down house between a railroad track and a polluted section of a lake, twelve-year-old Jake gets involved with a fourteen-year-old neighbor who is hiding a secret within his home.

"Holmes' ever-graceful style captures the shifting moods of summer. Without melodrama, she subtly presents Jake's complex emotions, as he tries to resolve problems of friendship, separated parents, and a distant father. Readers will welcome this quiet, realistic story." Booklist

Holmes, Sara Lewis

Operation Yes. Arthur A. Levine Books 2009 234p $16.99 *

Grades: 5 6 7 8   **Fic**

1. Teachers—Fiction 2. Acting—Fiction 3. Military bases—Fiction 4. School stories 5. Cousins—Fiction

ISBN 978-0-545-10795-2; 0-545-10795-4; 978-0-545-10796-9 (pa); 0-545-10796-2 (pa)   LC 2008053732

In her first ever teaching job, Miss Loupe uses improvisational acting exercises with her sixth-grade students at an Air Force base school, and when she experiences a family tragedy, her previously skeptical class members use what they have learned to help her, her brother, and other wounded soldiers

"Quick, funny, sad, full of heart, and irresistibly absorbing." Booklist

Holt, K. A.

Mike Stellar: nerves of steel. Random House 2009 262p $15.99; lib bdg $18.99

Grades: 4 5 6 7   **Fic**

1. Space flight to Mars—Fiction 2. Space colonies—Fiction 3. Family life—Fiction 4. Science fiction

ISBN 978-0-375-84556-7; 0-375-84556-9; 978-0-375-94556-4 (lib bdg); 0-375-94556-3 (lib bdg)   LC 2008027272

Mike is suspicious when his family joins an expedition to Mars at the last minute, and his fears are confirmed when all of the adults on the colonizing mission, including his parents, begin to act strangely.

This "whizzes by at warp speed—the suspenseful plot and the precocious yet complex hero combine for a fun ride with a satisfying resolution." Publ Wkly

Holt, Kimberly Willis

Dancing in Cadillac light. Putnam 2001 167p hardcover o.p. pa $5.99 *

Grades: 5 6 7 8   **Fic**

1. Grandfathers—Fiction 2. Old age—Fiction 3. Texas—Fiction

ISBN 0-399-23402-0; 0-698-11970-3 (pa)   LC 00-40267

In 1968, eleven-year-old Jaynell's life in the town of Moon, Texas, is enlivened when her eccentric Grandpap comes to live with her family

"This nostalgic parable about loss and redemption is at once gritty and poetic, stark and sentimental, howlingly funny and depressingly sad, but it is a solid page-turner." SLJ

Piper Reed, Navy brat. Henry Holt 2007 146p il $14.95; pa $6.99

Grades: 3 4 5   **Fic**

1. Family life—Fiction 2. Moving—Fiction 3. Florida—Fiction

ISBN 978-0-8050-8197-8; 0-8050-8197-6; 978-0-312-38020-5 (pa); 0-312-38020-8 (pa)   LC 2006-35467

Piper is sad about leaving her home and friends behind when her father, a Navy aircraft mechanic, is transferred yet again, but with help from her often-annoying sisters and a surprise from their parents, she finds happi-

Holt, Kimberly Willis—*Continued*
ness in their new home in Pensacola, Florida.

"Holt tells a lively family story. . . . Davenier's occasional black-and-white pictures capture the daily family dramas." Booklist

Other titles about Piper Reed are:
Piper Reed, the great gypsy (2008)
Piper Reed gets a job (2009)

When Zachary Beaver came to town. Holt & Co. 1999 227p $17.99 *
Grades: 5 6 7 8   **Fic**
1. Obesity—Fiction 2. Friendship—Fiction 3. Texas—Fiction
ISBN 0-8050-6116-9   LC 99-27998

During the summer of 1971 in a small Texas town, thirteen-year-old Toby and his best friend Cal meet the star of a sideshow act, 600-pound Zachary, the fattest boy in the world

"Holt writes with a subtle sense of humor and sensitivity, and reading her work is a delightful experience." Voice Youth Advocates

Holub, Joan, 1956-
Bed, bats, and beyond; by Joan Holub; illustrated by Mernie Gallagher-Cole. Darby Creek Pub. 2008 64p il $14.95
Grades: 1 2 3   **Fic**
1. Bats—Fiction 2. Bedtime—Fiction 3. Storytelling—Fiction
ISBN 978-1-58196-077-8; 1-58196-077-8

It's dawn and time for bats to go to bed, but Fang's brother Fink can't sleep. Soon the whole family tries different bedtime stories to lull Fink to sleep

"The narrative as a whole feels satisfying. . . . Gallagher-Cole's illustrations add humorous details. . . . With no more than 15 lines per page and illustrations on every spread, the story is ideal for students who have just graduated to chapter books. Charming and full of humor." SLJ

Hopkinson, Deborah
Birdie's lighthouse; written by Deborah Hopkinson; illustrated by Kimberly Bulcken Root. Atheneum Bks. for Young Readers 1997 unp il hardcover o.p. pa $6.99
Grades: 1 2 3   **Fic**
1. Lighthouses—Fiction 2. Maine—Fiction
ISBN 0-689-81052-0; 0-689-83529-9 (pa)
                                        LC 94-24097
"An Anne Schwartz book"

Written in diary form, this "book tells the story of Birdie Holland, daughter of a lighthouse keeper on a tiny island off the Maine coast in 1855. Her brother helps their father in the lighthouse until he becomes a fisherman and leaves the island. Then Birdie must take his place. When her father becomes ill during a severe northeaster, she must carry out the duties alone." SLJ

"With an exemplary assemblage of genre paintings perfectly attuned to the flow of the text, the whole is restrained yet charged with emotion." Horn Book

Into the firestorm; a novel of San Francisco, 1906. Alfred A. Knopf 2006 200p hardcover o.p. pa $5.99
Grades: 5 6 7 8   **Fic**
1. San Francisco (Calif.)—Fiction 2. Earthquakes—Fiction 3. Orphans—Fiction
ISBN 0-375-83652-7; 0-440-42129-2 (pa)
                                        LC 2005-37189

Days after arriving in San Francisco from Texas, eleven-year-old orphan Nicholas Dray tries to help his new neighbors survive the 1906 San Francisco earthquake and the subsequent fires.

"The terror of the 1906 disaster is brought powerfully alive in this fast-paced tale. . . . Nick is a thoroughly developed protagonist, as are the supporting characters." SLJ

Includes bibliographical references

Horowitz, Anthony, 1955-
Public enemy number two; a Diamond brothers mystery. Philomel Books 2004 c1997 190p $16.99; pa $5.99 *
Grades: 5 6 7 8   **Fic**
1. Mystery fiction
ISBN 0-399-24154-X; 0-14-240218-4 (pa)
                                        LC 2004-10418

When thirteen-year-old Nick is framed for a jewel robbery, he and his brother, the bumbling detective Tim Diamond, attempt to clear his name by capturing the master criminal known as the Fence.

"Horowitz has a knack for puns and humor, and he successfully combines it with a nonstop action mystery that has everything from hydraulically controlled buses to secret caverns. A readable and exciting adventure." SLJ

Other titles in the Diamond Brothers Mystery series are:
The falcon's Maltester (2004)
South by southeast (2005)
Three of Diamonds (2005)
The Greek who stole Christmas (2008)

Stormbreaker. Philomel Bks. 2001 c2000 192p (Alex Rider) $17.99; pa $7.99 *
Grades: 5 6 7 8   **Fic**
1. Spies—Fiction 2. Terrorism—Fiction 3. Orphans—Fiction 4. Great Britain—Fiction
ISBN 0-399-23620-1; 0-14-240611-2 (pa)
                                        LC 00-63683
First published 2000 in the United Kingdom

After the death of the uncle who had been his guardian, fourteen-year-old Alex Rider is coerced to continue his uncle's dangerous work for Britain's intelligence agency, MI6

"Horowitz thoughtfully balances Alex's super-spy finesse with typical teen insecurities to create a likable hero living a fantasy come true. An entertaining, nicely layered novel." Booklist

Other titles about Alex Rider are:
Alex Rider, the gadgets (2006)
Ark angel (2006)
Crocodile tears (2009)
Eagle strike (2004)
Point blank (2002)
Scorpia (2005)
Skeleton key (2003)
Snakehead (2007)

Horowitz, Anthony, 1955-—_Continued_

The switch; [by] Anthony Horowitz. Philomel Books 2009 162p $16.99

Grades: 5 6 7 8   **Fic**
1. Supernatural—Fiction 2. Criminals—Fiction
3. Wealth—Fiction 4. Great Britain—Fiction
ISBN 978-0-399-25062-0; 0-399-25062-X
LC 2008-32380

When wealthy, spoiled, thirteen-year-old Tad Spencer wishes he were someone else, he awakens as Bob Snarby, the uncouth, impoverished son of carnival workers, and as he is drawn into a life of crime he begins to discover truths about himself and his family.

"A fun, tongue-in-cheek read that will captivate children who like adventure and mystery." SLJ

Horvath, Polly

Everything on a waffle. Farrar, Straus & Giroux 2001 149p $16 paperback o.p.

Grades: 4 5 6 7   **Fic**
1. Uncles—Fiction 2. British Columbia—Fiction
ISBN 0-374-32236-8; 0-374-42208-7 (pa)
LC 00-35399

A Newbery Medal honor book, 2002

Eleven-year-old Primrose living in a small fishing village in British Columbia recounts her experiences and all that she learns about human nature and the unpredictability of life in the months after her parents are lost at sea

"The story is full of subtle humor and wisdom, presented through the eyes of a uniquely appealing young protagonist." SLJ

My one hundred adventures. Schwartz & Wade Books 2008 260p $16.99; lib bdg $19.99; pa $7.99 *

Grades: 4 5 6 7   **Fic**
1. Siblings—Fiction 2. Single parent family—Fiction
3. Summer—Fiction 4. Beaches—Fiction
5. Babysitters—Fiction
ISBN 978-0-375-84582-6; 0-375-84582-8; 978-0-375-95582-2 (lib bdg); 0-375-95582-8 (lib bdg); 978-0-375-85526-9 (pa); 0-375-85526-2 (pa)
LC 2008-02243

Twelve-year-old Jane, who lives at the beach in a run-down old house with her mother, two brothers, and sister, has an eventful summer accompanying her pastor on bible deliveries, meeting former boyfriends of her mother's, and being coerced into babysitting for a family of ill-mannered children.

"With writing as foamy as waves, as gritty as sand, or as deep as the sea, this book may startle readers with the freedom given the heroine. . . . Unconventionality is Horvath's stock and trade, but here the high quirkiness quotient rests easily against Jane's inner story with its honest, childlike core." Booklist

Followed by: Northward to the Moon (2010)

The Pepins and their problems; pictures by Marylin Hafner. Farrar Straus Giroux 2004 179p il $16; pa $6.99

Grades: 3 4 5 6   **Fic**
1. Family life—Fiction
ISBN 0-374-35817-6; 0-312-37751-7 (pa)
LC 2003-60196

"Portions of this work originally appeared in somewhat different form in Cricket magazine" T.p. verso.

The reader is invited to help solve the Pepin family's unusual problems, which include having a cow who creates lemonade rather than milk and having to cope with a competitive neighbor

"Horvath spins a delightful yarn. . . . Absurd characters and situations and witty repartee are Horvath's strengths, and . . . the wordplay is a great argument for reading this aloud." Booklist

Hostetter, Joyce

Blue; [by] Joyce Moyer Hostetter. Boyds Mills Press 2005 197p $16.95

Grades: 5 6 7 8   **Fic**
1. Poliomyelitis—Fiction 2. North Carolina—Fiction
ISBN 1-59078-389-1   LC 2005033570

"Calkins Creek books"

"Thirteen-year-old Ann Fay contracts polio after her brother dies from it. Set in North Carolina during the polio epidemic of 1944, Hostetter's novel examines the complexities of the disease and its effect on the nation. The characters' authentic reactions result in a compelling story." Horn Book Guide

Followed by: Comfort (2009)

House, Silas, 1971-

Eli the Good. Candlewick Press 2009 295p $16.99 *

Grades: 5 6 7 8   **Fic**
1. Family life—Fiction 2. Post-traumatic stress disorder—Fiction 3. Friendship—Fiction 4. Veterans—Fiction 5. Aunts—Fiction
ISBN 978-0-7636-4341-6; 0-7636-4341-6
LC 2009004589

In the summer of 1976, ten-year-old Eli Book's excitement over Bicentennial celebrations is tempered by his father's flashbacks to the Vietnam War and other family problems, as well as concern about his tough but troubled best friend, Edie.

"House writes beautifully, with a gentle tone. He lays out Eli's world in exquisite detail. . . . The story flows along as steadily as a stream. . . . Eli is good company and children will enjoy accompanying him on his journey." SLJ

Howard, Ellen

The crimson cap. Holiday House 2009 177p $16.95

Grades: 5 6 7 8   **Fic**
1. La Salle, Robert Cavelier, sieur de, 1643-1687—Fiction 2. Explorers—Fiction 3. Native Americans—Fiction 4. Texas—Fiction 5. America—Exploration—Fiction
ISBN 978-0-8234-2152-7; 0-8234-2152-X
LC 2009-25551

In 1684, wearing his father's faded cap, eleven-year-old Pierre Talon joins explorer Rene-Robert Cavelier on an ill-fated expedition to seek the Mississippi River, but after the expedition falls apart Pierre, deathly ill, is taken in by Hasinai Indians. Includes historical facts.

"A riveting adventure that will prove to be hard to put

Howard, Ellen—*Continued*

down. Howard's fast-paced writing brings the story to life. This solid coming-of-age story is based on real events and historical figures." SLJ

The gate in the wall. Atheneum Bks. for Young Readers 1999 148p il hardcover o.p. pa $9.95
Grades: 5 6 7 8   **Fic**
1. Canals—Fiction 2. Orphans—Fiction 3. Great Britain—Fiction 4. Child labor—Fiction
ISBN 0-689-82295-2; 1-4169-6796-6 (pa)
                LC 98-22250
"A Jean Karl book"
In nineteenth-century England, ten-year-old Emma, accustomed to long working hours at the silk mill and the poverty and hunger of her sister's house, finds her life completely changed when she inadvertently gets a job on a canal boat carrying cargoes between several northern towns
"Howard has given her story a highly interesting venue and has created a cast of characters who are fully dimensional and engaging." Horn Book Guide

Howe, Deborah, 1946-1978

Bunnicula; a rabbit-tale of mystery; by Deborah and James Howe; illustrated by Alan Daniel. 25th anniversary edition. Atheneum Books for Young Readers 2004 c1979 92p il $16.95 *
Grades: 4 5 6   **Fic**
1. Animals—Fiction 2. Mystery fiction
ISBN 0-689-86775-1
A reissue of the title first published 1979
Other books about Bunnicula by James Howe
Though scoffed at by Harold the dog, Chester the cat tries to warn his human family that their foundling baby bunny must be a vampire
This book is "blithe, sophisticated, and distinguished for the wit and humor of the dialogue." Bull Cent Child Books

Howe, James, 1946-

Bunnicula meets Edgar Allan Crow; illustrated by Eric Fortune. 1st ed. Atheneum Books for Young Readers 2006 138p il $15.95; pa $5.99
Grades: 4 5 6   **Fic**
1. Pets—Fiction 2. Authors—Fiction 3. Crows—Fiction
ISBN 978-1-4169-1458-7; 1-4169-1458-7; 978-1-4169-1473-0 (pa); 1-4169-1473-0 (pa)
                LC 2006000574
Another title in the author's series about Bunnicula
"Ginee Seo books"
An overly-alarmed Chester the cat predicts a gruesome fate for the pets in the Monroe household when a writer of juvenile horror fiction and his bird companion stay overnight
"The writing style is a mixture of chills and chuckles, and the black-and-white pencil drawings are appropriately eerie." SLJ

Dew drop dead; a Sebastian Barth mystery. Atheneum Pubs. 1990 156p hardcover o.p. pa $4.99 *
Grades: 4 5 6   **Fic**
1. Mystery fiction 2. Homeless persons—Fiction
ISBN 0-689-31425-6; 0-689-80760-0 (pa)
                LC 89-34697
"A Jean Karl book"
"Sebastian Barth and his friends Corrie and David discover what appears to be a dead body in the long-abandoned Dew Drop Inn. But when they return with the police, the body has vanished. Police theory—that the 'body' was a homeless man passed-out drunk—is refuted when the kids find the body again in the woods, undeniably dead and possibly murdered." SLJ
"The story is well crafted and has substance beyond escapist fare as a result of Howe's inclusion of secondary storylines involving the homeless and Sebastian's own worries about his father's pending job loss." Booklist
Other titles about Sebastian Barth are:
Eat your poison, dear (1986)
Stage fright (1986)
What Eric knew (1985)

Howe, Peter, 1942-

Waggit's tale; drawings by Omar Rayyan. HarperCollinsPublishers 2008 288p il $16.99; lib bdg $17.89; pa $6.99
Grades: 5 6 7 8   **Fic**
1. Dogs—Fiction
ISBN 978-0-06-124261-8; 0-06-124261-6; 978-0-06-124262-5 (lib bdg); 0-06-124262-4 (lib bdg); 978-0-06-124263-2 (pa); 0-06-124263-2 (pa)
                LC 2007020878
Followed by: Waggit again (2009)
When Waggit is abandoned by his owner as a puppy, he meets a pack of wild dogs who become his friends and teach him to survive in the city park, but when he has a chance to go home with a kind woman who wants to adopt him, he takes it
"The novel celebrates the wild freedom of the feral dog pack, while also emphasizing the many hazards of urban life for homeless companion animals." Voice Youth Advocates

Hughes, Pat

Seeing the elephant; a story of the Civil War; [by] Pat Hughes; pictures by Ken Stark. Farrar, Straus and Giroux 2007 unp il $16
Grades: 2 3 4 5   **Fic**
1. United States—History—1861-1865, Civil War—Fiction 2. Soldiers—Fiction 3. Brothers—Fiction
ISBN 978-0-374-38024-3; 0-374-38024-4
                LC 2005052753
Ten-year-old Izzie wants to join the war like his older brothers and go into battle against the Confederate Army, but when he meets a Rebel soldier in a hospital, he begins to see things differently
"Presented in a clear and direct writing style, the story has an emotional power. . . . Stark's realistic paintings are remarkable both for their artistry and their meticulous attention to historical accuracy." SLJ

Hughes, Ted, 1930-1998

The iron giant; a story in five nights; illustrated by Andrew Davidson. Knopf 1999 79p il pa $4.99 hardcover o.p. *

Grades: 4 5 6   **Fic**

    1. Science fiction

    ISBN 0-375-80153-7 (pa)   LC 98-41368

A newly illustrated edition of the title first published 1968 by Harper & Row; published in the United Kingdom with title: The iron man

This is the story of an Iron Giant "who appears from nowhere and stalks the earth, devouring tractors and barbed wire for his supper. . . . But in the end he has to save the world from a creature from Outer Space." NY Times Book Rev

Hulme, John, 1970-

The glitch in sleep; [by] John Hulme and Michael Wexler; illustrations by Gideon Kendall. Bloomsbury Children's Books 2007 277p il (The Seems) $16.95; pa $7.99 *

Grades: 4 5 6 7   **Fic**

    1. Sleep—Fiction 2. Science fiction

    ISBN   978-1-59990-129-9;   1-59990-129-3;
    978-1-59990-298-2 (pa); 1-59990-298-2 (pa)
                       LC 2007-2598

When twelve-year-old Becker Drane is recruited by The Seems, a parallel universe that runs everything in The World, he must fix a disastrous glitch in the Department of Sleep that threatens everyone's ability to ever fall asleep again

"The story is upbeat and full of humor. . . . Dynamic full-page illustrations appear throughout." SLJ

Another title in this series is:

The split second (2008)

Hunt, Irene, 1907-2001

Across five Aprils. Berkley Jam Books 2002 212p pa $5.99

Grades: 5 6 7 8   **Fic**

    1. United States—History—1861-1865, Civil War—Fiction 2. Illinois—Fiction 3. Farm life—Fiction

    ISBN 978-0-425-18278-9; 0-425-18278-9

    A Newbery Medal honor book, 1965

    First published 1964 by Follett

Young Jethro Creighton grows from a boy to a man when he is left to take care of the family farm in Illinois during the difficult years of the Civil War.

"Authentic background, a feeling for the people of that time, and a story that never loses the reader's interest." Wilson Libr Bull

Hurst, Carol Otis

You come to Yokum; with illustrations by Kay Life. Houghton Mifflin Co. 2005 137p il $15

Grades: 3 4 5   **Fic**

    1. Women—Suffrage—Fiction 2. Family life—Fiction 3. Feminism—Fiction 4. Massachusetts—Fiction

    ISBN 0-618-55122-0

    "Walter Lorraine books"

Twelve-year-old Frank witnesses his mother's struggles to muster support for women's right to vote even as the family's life is transformed by a year running a lodge in western Massachusetts in the early 1920s.

"With mostly short chapters and charming black-and-white illustrations, this is a satisfying read." SLJ

Hurwitz, Johanna

The adventures of Ali Baba Bernstein; illustrated by Gail Owens. Morrow 1985 82p il hardcover o.p. pa $5.99 *

Grades: 2 3 4   **Fic**

    1. Personal names—Fiction

    ISBN 0-688-04161-2; 0-380-72349-2 (pa)

                       LC 84-27387

"Tired of his ordinary name, David Bernstein, age eight, decides he wants to be called Ali Baba, and he has a series of . . . adventures, culminating in a birthday party to which he invites every David Bernstein in the Manhattan telephone directory. That's when he realizes how different people with the same name can be, and he decides that some day he might go back to calling himself David." Bull Cent Child Books

"Hurwitz' characters, as always, are believable, the situations realistic and the plot well developed." SLJ

Another title about Ali Baba Bernstein is:

Hurray for Ali Baba Bernstein (1989)

Baseball fever; illustrated by Ray Cruz. Morrow 1981 128p il pa $4.99 hardcover o.p. *

Grades: 3 4 5   **Fic**

    1. Baseball—Fiction 2. Father-son relationship—Fiction

    ISBN 0-380-73255-6 (pa)   LC 81-5633

"Ten-year-old Ezra suffers from 'Baseball Fever' and a father who has no interest in the sport. Mr. Feldman is constantly nagging Ezra to show an interest in chess. A weekend trip that takes the pair to Cooperstown and the Hall of Fame sets the stage for father-and-son rapprochement." SLJ

"A brisk, breezy story about a believable family is told with warmth and humor." Bull Cent Child Books

Class clown; illustrated by Sheila Hamanaka. Scholastic 1988 c1987 98p il pa $3.99 *

Grades: 2 3 4   **Fic**

    1. School stories

    ISBN 978-0-590-41821-8 (pa); 0-590-41821-1 (pa)

    "A Little Apple paperback"

    First published 1987 by Morrow

Lucas Cott, the most obstreperous boy in the third grade, finds it hard to turn over a new leaf when he decides to become the perfect student.

"There are some very funny moments here, as well as some gentle and touching ones. . . . This [is] a fine choice for children just beginning chapter books." SLJ [review from 1987 edition published by Morrow]

Other titles in this series are:

Class president (1990)

Fourth-grade fuss (2004)

School spirit (1994)

School's out (1990)

Spring break (1997)

Teacher's pet (1988)

Hurwitz, Johanna—*Continued*

Mostly Monty. Candlewick Press 2007 86p il $15.99; pa $5.99

Grades: 1 2 3   **Fic**
1. Asthma—Fiction 2. Friendship—Fiction
ISBN   978-0-7636-2831-4;   0-7636-2831-X;
978-0-7636-4062-0 (pa); 0-7636-4062-X (pa)
                      LC 2006-49024

Because he suffers from asthma, six-year-old Monty is nervous about starting first grade but he soon learns to cope with his illness and use his special talents to make friends.

"Watercolor illustrations . . . appear every few pages, breaking up the text with pictures of cheerful button-nose children. More reserved children . . . will appreciate seeing themselves reflected in this gently funny story about learning to like oneself." Booklist

Another title about Monty is:
Mighty Monty (2008)

Rip-roaring Russell; illustrated by Lillian Hoban. Morrow 1983 80p il pa $4.95 hardcover o.p. *

Grades: 2 3 4   **Fic**
1. Family life—Fiction 2. School stories
ISBN 0-688-16664-4 (pa)   LC 83-1019

Russell "faces the challenges of growing up in his own inimitable way. . . . Being a big brother disturbs him because baby Elisa takes altogether too much of his mother's time, but by the book's end, he decides that it isn't so bad." SLJ

"The action is low-keyed. . . . This is both realistic and sunny, with good adult-child relationships, the appeal of everyday life experiences, and a light, humorous treatment." Bull Cent Child Books

Other titles about Russell and Elisa are:
E is for Elisa (1991)
Elisa in the middle (1995)
Elisa Michaels, bigger and better (2003)
Ever clever Elisa (1997)
Make room for Elisa (1993)
Russell and Elisa (1989)
Russell rides again (1985)
Russell sprouts (1987)
Russell's secret (2001)
Summer with Elisa (2000)

Squirrel world; illustrated by Kathi McCord. Chronicle Books 2007 124p il (Park pals adventure) $14.95

Grades: 2 3 4   **Fic**
1. Squirrels—Fiction 2. New York (N.Y.)—Fiction
ISBN 978-0-8118-5660-7; 0-8118-5660-7
                      LC 2006-26714

When Lexi the squirrel and his cousin Lenox leave Central Park to find the New York City streets for which they were named, they discover that the human world is wilder—and more dangerous—than they had ever imagined.

"This solidly written, charmingly illustrated book will appeal to readers clamoring for animal tales." Booklist

Other titles about PeeWee and Lexi are:
PeeWee's tale (2000)
Lexi's tale (2001)
PeeWee & Plush (2002)

Ibbotson, Eva

The beasts of Clawstone Castle; illustrated by Kevin Hawkes. Dutton Children's Books 2006 243p il hardcover o.p. pa $6.99

Grades: 4 5 6   **Fic**
1. Ghost stories 2. Castles—Fiction 3. Cattle—Fiction
4. Great Britain—Fiction
ISBN 0-525-47719-5; 0-14-240931-6 (pa)
                      LC 2005-29188

While spending the summer with elderly relatives at Clawstone Castle in northern England, Madlyn and her brother Rollo, with the help of several ghosts, attempt to save the rare cattle that live on the castle grounds.

"Ibbotson's charismatic ghosts are great. . .—as human as they are horrific—and there's plenty of quirky humor in this energetic, diverting read, loaded with charm." Booklist

Dial-a-ghost. Dutton Children's Bks. 2001 195p hardcover o.p. pa $5.99

Grades: 4 5 6   **Fic**
1. Orphans—Fiction 2. Ghost stories 3. Great Britain—Fiction
ISBN 0-525-46693-2; 0-14-250018-6 (pa)
                      LC 00-52287

A family of nice ghosts protects a British orphan from the diabolical plans of his evil guardians

"The book is filled with a large and delightful cast of characters. . . . The black-and-white illustrations have an eerie charm." SLJ

Another title about the nice ghosts is:
The great ghost rescue (2002)

The dragonfly pool; illustrated by Kevin Hawkes. Dutton Children's Books 2008 377p il $17.99; pa $7.99 *

Grades: 5 6 7 8   **Fic**
1. World War, 1939-1945—Fiction 2. School stories
ISBN   978-0-525-42064-4;   0-525-42064-9;
978-0-14-241486-6 (pa); 0-14-241486-7 (pa)

"At first Tally doesn't want to go to the boarding school called Delderton. But she soon discovers that it is a wonderful place. . . . Tally organizes a ragtag dance troupe so the school can participate in an international folk dancing festival in Bergania in the summer of 1939. There she befriends Karil, the crown prince. . . . When Karil's father is assassinated, it is up to Tally and her friends to help Karil escape the Nazis and the bleak future he has inherited." Publisher's note

"Ibbotson's trademark eccentric characters and strongly contrasted principles of right and wrong brighten and broaden this uplifting tale." Booklist

The secret of platform 13; illustrated by Sue Porter. Dutton Children's Bks. 1998 c1994 231p il hardcover o.p. pa $5.99 *

Grades: 5 6 7 8   **Fic**
1. Fantasy fiction
ISBN 0-525-45929-4; 0-14-130286-0 (pa)
                      LC 97-44601

First published 1994 in the United Kingdom

Odge Gribble, a young hag, accompanies an old wizard, a gentle fey, and a giant ogre on their mission through a magical tunnel from their Island to London to rescue their King and Queen's son who had been stolen

Ibbotson, Eva—*Continued*

as an infant

"Lively, funny fantasy with a case of mistaken identity and a cast of eccentric characters." SLJ

The star of Kazan; illustrated by Kevin Hawkes. Dutton 2004 405p il $16.99; pa $7.99 *

Grades: 5 6 7 8   Fic

1. Vienna (Austria)—Fiction 2. Germany—Fiction
3. Mystery fiction

ISBN 0-525-47347-5; 0-14-240582-5 (pa)

LC 2004-45455

After twelve-year-old Annika, a foundling living in late nineteenth-century Vienna, inherits a trunk of costume jewelry, a woman claiming to be her aristocratic mother arrives and takes her to live in a strangely decrepit mansion in Germany

"This is a rich saga . . . full of stalwart friends, sly villains, a brave heroine, and good triumphing over evil. . . . An intensely satisfying read." SLJ

Iggulden, Conn, 1971-

Tollins; explosive tales for children; illustrated by Lizzy Duncan. Harper 2009 172p il $16.99 *

Grades: 3 4 5 6   Fic

1. Fantasy fiction

ISBN 978-0-06-173098-6; 0-06-173098-X

"Tollins are tiny, nectar-eating woodland creatures with elf ears and wings but bigger than the fairies they casually use as handkerchiefs. They enjoy an idyllic existance until a fireworks factory is built in the village of Chorleywood. . . . The men of the village hunt the Tollins down to use as fodder for their fireworks. . . . Duncan's full-color illustrations and maps bring the world to witty life. A note at the end likens the Tollin's fate to child labor during the Industrial Revolution. There is much to think about and love in this beautifully realized world." Booklist

Ignatow, Amy

The popularity papers; research for the social improvement and general betterment of Lydia Goldblatt & Julie Graham-Chang. Amulet Books 204p il $15.95

Grades: 3 4 5 6   Fic

1. School stories 2. Popularity—Fiction

ISBN 978-0-8109-8421-9; 0-8109-8421-0

LC 2009-39741

"Before they leave elementary school behind, two fifth-grade best friends are determined to uncover the secrets of popularity by observing, recording, discussing, and replicating the behaviors of the cool girls. . . . In a notebook format, this heavily illustrated title shows their research in dramatic, alternating, handwritten entries and colorful, hilarious drawings. . . . Ignatow offers a quick, fun, well-developed story that invites repeated readings." Booklist

Irving, Washington, 1783-1859

The Legend of Sleepy Hollow; illustrated by Gris Grimly. Atheneum Books for Young Readers 2007 unp il $16.99

Grades: 4 5 6   Fic

1. New York (State)—Fiction 2. Ghost stories

ISBN 1-4169-0625-8; 978-1-4169-0625-4

LC 2005-27502

A superstitious schoolmaster, in love with a wealthy farmer's daughter, has a terrifying encounter with a headless horseman.

"The tale, . . . slightly condensed but with language and ambiguities intact, is reimagined here with humor, vigor, [and] clarity. . . . Irving's language is challenging . . . but Grimly's numerous Halloween-hued panel and spot illustrations . . . parse it into comprehensible tidbits. The comically amplified emotions and warm yellow and orange tones balance the horror aspects of the text." Horn Book

Washington Irving's Rip van Winkle; illustrated by Arthur Rackham. Dover Publications 2005 19p pa $12.95

Grades: 5 6 7 8   Fic

1. Catskill Mountains (N.Y.)—Fiction

ISBN 0-486-44242-X   LC 2004063543

A reissue of the edition first published 1905 by Doubleday

Rip Van Winkle "is based on a folk tale. Henpecked Rip and his dog Wolf wander into the Catskill mountains before the Revolutionary War. There they meet a dwarf, whom Rip helps to carry a keg. They join a group of dwarfs playing ninepins. When Rip drinks from the keg, he falls asleep and wakes 20 years later, an old man. Returning to his town, he discovers his termagant wife dead, his daughter married, and the portrait of King George replaced by one of George Washington. Irving uses the folk tale to present the contrast between the new and old societies." Reader's Ency. 3d edition

Ives, David

Scrib; some characters, adventures, letters and conversations from the year 1863, including a deadly chase in the wilderness of the Fearsome Canyon, all as told by Billy Christmas, who was there; a novel. HarperCollins 2005 188p $15.99

Grades: 5 6 7 8   Fic

1. West (U.S.)—Fiction 2. United States—History—1861-1865, Civil War—Fiction 3. Adventure fiction

ISBN 0-06-059841-7   LC 2004-12483

In 1863, a sixteen-year-old boy nicknamed Scrib travels around the West making his living writing and delivering letters, an occupation that leads to him nearly getting killed, being jailed as a criminal, joining up with the notorious Crazy James Kincaid, and delivering a letter from President Abraham Lincoln to a Paiute Indian.

"Ives's witty wordplay is lively and the plot is fast and funny in this great read-aloud." Horn Book Guide

Jackson, Alison, 1953-

Rainmaker. Boyds Mills Press 2005 192p $16.95

Grades: 5 6 7 8   **Fic**

1. Droughts—Fiction 2. Great Depression, 1929-1939—Fiction 3. Florida—Fiction

ISBN 1-59078-309-3

"For 13-year-old Pidge Martin, the summer of 1939 brings changes and challenges. Her town, Frostfree, Florida, faces its longest drought in 40 years, and if it doesn't rain soon, area families . . . may lose their farms. A miracle is in order, and Pidge's father hopes a rainmaker can provide one. . . . Pidge is a well-characterized, sympathetic protagonist that readers will connect with." Booklist

Jacobson, Jennifer, 1958-

Andy Shane and the very bossy Dolores Starbuckle; [by] Jennifer Richard Jacobson; illustrated by Abby Carter. Candlewick Press 2005 56p il $13.99; pa $4.99

Grades: 1 2 3   **Fic**

1. School stories 2. Grandmothers—Fiction

ISBN 0-7636-1940-X; 0-7636-3044-6 (pa)

LC 2004-57040

Andy Shane hates school, mainly because of a tattle-tale know-it-all named Dolores Starbuckle, but Granny Webb, who has taken care of him all his life, joins him in class one day and helps him solve the problem

"The characters are complex and realistic. . . . The narrative voice is fresh and whimsical. . . . The pen-and-ink illustrations effectively depict Andy's frustration, Dolores's temper, and Granny's zany self-assuredness." SLJ

Other titles about Andy Shane are:

Andy Shane and the pumpkin trick (2006)

Andy Shane and the Queen of Egypt (2008)

Andy Shane is NOT in love (2008)

Andy Shane and the barn sale mystery (2009)

Andy Shane, hero at last (2010)

Winnie (dancing) on her own; by Jennifer Richard Jacobson; illustrated by Alissa Imre Geis. Houghton Mifflin 2001 105p il hardcover o.p. pa $5.95

Grades: 2 3 4   **Fic**

1. Friendship—Fiction 2. Ballet—Fiction

ISBN 0-618-13287-2; 0-618-36921-X (pa)

LC 00-53929

Winnie is worried when her best friends Zoe and Vanessa enroll her in ballet classes with them, since she would rather go to the library and read like they always do

"Geis's uncomplicated pencil drawings capture the girls' energy and personalities. . . . A good title for those who are just beginning to read chapter books." SLJ

Other titles about Winnie are:

Truly Winnie (2003)

Winnie at her best (2006)

Jacques, Brian

Redwall; illustrated by Gary Chalk. 20th anniversary ed. Philomel 2007 351p il $23.99; pa $7.99 *

Grades: 5 6 7 8 9   **Fic**

1. Mice—Fiction 2. Animals—Fiction 3. Fantasy fiction

ISBN 978-0-399-24794-1; 0-399-24794-7; 978-0-441-00548-2 (pa); 0-441-00548-9 (pa)

First published 1986

"Only the lost sword of Martin the Warrior can save Redwall Abbey from the evil rat Cluny and his greedy horde. The young mouse Matthias (formerly Redwall's most awkward novice) vows to recover the legendary weapon." Publ Wkly

"Thoroughly engrossing, this novel captivates despite its length. . . . The theme will linger long after the story is finished." Booklist

Other titles in this series are:

The Bellmaker (1995)

Doomwyte (2008)

Eulalia! (2007)

High Rhulain (2005)

The legend of Luke (2000)

Loamhedge (2003)

The long patrol (1998)

Lord Brocktree (2000)

Mariel of Redwall (1992)

Marlfox (1998)

Martin the Warrior (1994)

Mattimeo (1990)

Mossflower (1998)

The outcast of Redwall (1996)

Pearls of Lutra (1997)

Rakkety Tam (2004)

Sable Quean (2009)

Salamandastron (1993)

Taggerung (2001)

Triss (2002)

Jansson, Tove, 1914-2001

Moominsummer madness; translated by Thomas Warburton. Farrar, Straus & Giroux 1991 c1955 159p il hardcover o.p. pa $5.95

Grades: 4 5 6   **Fic**

1. Fantasy fiction

ISBN 0-374-35039-6; 0-374-45310-1 (pa)

LC 90-56150

Original Swedish edition 1954; this translation first published 1955 in the United Kingdom; first United States edition 1961 by Henry Z. Walck

A flood hits Moomin Valley and triggers a series of adventures for the Moomins

"Newcomers to the long-established Moominvalley series might first glance at the simple, playfully illustrated appendix—'Moomin Gallery'—to acquaint themselves with the host of Moomin-species that adorn the plot. Once initiated, it's difficult not to be drawn in by the inventive adventures of Moomintroll and his family." Publ Wkly

Other titles about the Moomintrolls are:

Comet in Moominland (1968)

Finn Family Moomintroll (1965)

Moominland midwinter(1967)

Moominpapa at sea (1967)

Jansson, Tove, 1914-2001—*Continued*
Moominpapa's memoirs (1994)
Moominvalley in November (1971)
Tales from Moominvalley (1964)

Jaramillo, Ann, 1949-
La linea. Roaring Brook Press 2006 131p
$16.95; pa $7.99
Grades: 5 6 7 8   **Fic**
1. Siblings—Fiction 2. Immigrants—Fiction
3. Mexicans—Fiction
ISBN 1-59643-154-7; 0-312-37354-6 (pa)
                                    LC 2005-20133
"A Deborah Brodie book"
When fifteen-year-old Miguel's time finally comes to
leave his poor Mexican village, cross the border illegally,
and join his parents in California, his younger sister's determination to join him soon imperils them both.
"A gripping contemporary survival adventure, this
spare first novel is also a heart-wrenching family story
of courage, betrayal, and love." Booklist

Jarrell, Randall, 1914-1965
The animal family; decorations by Maurice
Sendak. HarperCollins Pubs. 1996 179p il $16.99;
pa $8.95 *
Grades: 4 5 6 7   **Fic**
1. Animals—Fiction 2. Fantasy fiction
ISBN 0-06-205088-5; 0-06-205904-1 (pa)
                                    LC 94-76270
"Michael di Capua books"
A reissue of the title first published 1965 by Pantheon
Bks.
A lonely hunter living in the wilderness beside the sea
gains a family made up of a mermaid, a bear, a lynx,
and a boy
This story is "sensitively related with touches of hu-
mor and wisdom. A delight for the imaginative reader."
Booklist

The bat-poet; pictures by Maurice Sendak.
HarperCollins Pubs. 1996 42p il $15.95; pa $7.95
Grades: 2 3 4   **Fic**
1. Bats—Fiction 2. Poetry—Fiction
ISBN 0-06-205084-2; 0-06-205905-X (pa)
                                    LC 94-76271
"Michael di Capua books"
A reissue of the title first published 1964 by MacMil-
lan
A bat who can't sleep days makes up poems about the
woodland creatures he now perceives for the first time
"A lovely book, perfectly illustrated—one well worth
a child's attention and affection." Publ Wkly

Jarvis, Robin
The alchemist's cat; book one of the Deptford
histories. Seastar Books 2004 304p hardcover o.p.
pa $6.95 *
Grades: 5 6 7 8   **Fic**
1. Witchcraft—Fiction 2. Horror fiction 3. London
(England)—Fiction
ISBN 1-58717-257-7; 0-8118-5450-7 (pa)
Prequel to the Deptford mice trilogy that includes The
dark portal, The crystal prison, and The final reckoning

First published 1989 in the United Kingdom
When Will Godwin, assistant to a wicked alchemist in
1664 London, takes in a mother cat and her kittens, a
story of villainy unfolds which reveals how Jupiter, Lord
of Darkness, became so evil and powerful
"Jarvis delivers a vivid tale of treachery, cruelty, and
sorcery, leavened only by Will's innate goodness. It's
also a real page-turner." Booklist
Other titles in the Deptford histories series are:
The oaken throne (2005)
Thomas (2006)

The Whitby witches; book one of the Whitby
witches trilogy; [by] Robin Jarvis; illustrated by
Jeff Petersen. Chronicle Books 2006 295p il
$17.95 *
Grades: 5 6 7 8   **Fic**
1. Orphans—Fiction 2. Witches—Fiction
3. Supernatural—Fiction 4. Great Britain—Fiction
ISBN 978-0-8118-5413-9; 0-8118-5413-2
                                    LC 2005026778
First published 1991 in the United Kingdom
Ben and Jennet, an orphaned brother and sister, are
taken in by an old woman in the quaint fishing village
of Whitby, where they soon learn of the town's ancient
lore and become involved in an epic struggle between
good and evil.
This "is a dark but delightful read. . . . There is just
the right amount of suspense to make the book creepy,
but not enough to make it truly scary for younger readers." SLJ

Jenkins, Emily, 1967-
Toys go out; being the adventures of a
knowledgeable Stingray, a toughy little Buffalo,
and someone called Plastic; illustrated by Paul O.
Zelinsky. Schwartz & Wade Bks. 2006 116p il
$16.95; lib bdg $18.99; pa $5.99 *
Grades: 1 2 3   **Fic**
1. Toys—Fiction 2. Friendship—Fiction
ISBN 0-375-83604-7; 0-375-93604-1 (lib bdg);
0-385-73661-4 (pa)
"For beginning chapter-book readers, this . . . relates
the experiences of three engaging toy best friends:
Lumphy the buffalo, plush StingRay, and Plastic. . . .
The simple prose is clever and often hilarious, incorporating dialogue and musings that ring kid-perspective
true, and Zelinsky's charming black-and-white illustrations, wonderfully detailed and textured, expressively
portray character situations and feelings." Booklist
Another title about Lumphy, StingRay, and Plastic is:
Toy dance party (2008)

Jenkins, Martin
Don Quixote; [by] Miguel de Cervantes; retold
by Martin Jenkins; illustrated by Chris Riddell.
Candlewick Press 2009 347p il $27.99
Grades: 5 6 7 8   **Fic**
1. Knights and knighthood—Fiction 2. Spain—Fiction
ISBN 978-0-7636-4081-1; 0-7636-4081-6
                                    LC 2008026500
An illustrated retelling of the exploits of an idealistic
Spanish country gentleman and his shrewd squire who

Jenkins, Martin—*Continued*

set out, as knights of old, to search for adventure, right wrongs, and punish evil

"Jenkins' rendition is faithful almost to a fault. . . . The book does a fine job of capturing the sly satire and the duo's slapstick schtick. The chapter headings are especially mirthful. . . . Jenkins' always impressive and expressive artwork—characters are both gnarled and caricaturish—is an ideal medium in which to mix the tale's deadpan silliness with Quixote's unhinged fantasies." Booklist

Jennings, Patrick, 1962-

Out standing in my field. Scholastic Press 2005 165p hardcover o.p. pa $5.99

Grades: 4 5 6   **Fic**
    1. Baseball—Fiction 2. Father-son relationship—Fiction
    ISBN 0-439-46581-8; 0-439-48749-8 (pa)
                                        LC 2004-41619

Although fifth-grader Ty Cutter is named after baseball great Ty Cobb, he is the worst player on the Brewer's team—which happens to be coached by his overly-competitive father

"The book is funny, poignant, and deeper than one might think at first glance." SLJ

We can't all be rattlesnakes. HarperCollins Pubs. 2009 121p $15.99

Grades: 3 4 5 6   **Fic**
    1. Snakes—Fiction 2. Pets—Fiction
    ISBN 978-0-06-082114-2; 0-06-082114-0
                                        LC 2008-07118

When Crusher the snake is captured, her only thought is to escape but as time goes by and she befriends the other inmates of the "zoo," she realizes that freedom also means leaving companions behind

"Crusher is a compelling narrator, her voice dripping with sarcasm. . . . [Kids will enjoy] Crusher's commentary on human habits and absorbing the facts about snakes that are seamlessly integrated into the narrative." SLJ

The weeping willow; an Ike and Mem story; illustrated by Anna Alter. Holiday House 2002 56p il $15.95 *

Grades: 2 3 4   **Fic**
    1. Siblings—Fiction 2. Friendship—Fiction
    ISBN 0-8234-1671-2   LC 2002-20544

While trying to build a tree house for guys, Ike and his best friend Buzzy argue so much that Ike builds his sister Mem a play house instead, but still misses his friend

"Sentences are short, and the vocabulary is simple and descriptive. There are also touches of humor throughout the story. . . . A well-written, perceptive story with likable characters." Booklist

Other titles about Ike and Mem are:
The bird shadow (2001)
The ears of corn (2003)
The lightning bugs (2003)
The tornado watches (2002)

Jennings, Richard W., 1945-

Orwell's luck; [by] Richard Jennings. Houghton Mifflin 2000 146p $15; pa $6.95 *

Grades: 5 6 7 8   **Fic**
    1. Rabbits—Fiction 2. Magic—Fiction
    ISBN 0-618-03628-8; 0-618-69335-1 (pa)
                                        LC 99-33501

"Walter Lorraine books"

While caring for an injured rabbit which becomes her confidant, horoscope writer, and source of good luck, a thoughtful seventh grade girl learns to see things in more than one way

"This absolutely captivating tale is about everyday magic . . . filled with quiet humor and seamless invention. The characters . . . are the sort that readers fall in love with." Booklist

Jocelyn, Marthe, 1956-

Mable Riley; a reliable record of humdrum, peril, and romance. Candlewick Press 2004 279p $15.99; pa $6.99 *

Grades: 5 6 7 8   **Fic**
    1. Teachers—Fiction 2. Women's rights—Fiction
    3. Canada—Fiction
    ISBN 0-7636-2120-X; 0-7636-3287-2 (pa)
                                        LC 2003-55322

In 1901, fourteen-year-old Mable Riley dreams of being a writer and having adventures while stuck in Perth County, Ontario, assisting her sister in teaching school and secretly becoming friends with a neighbor who holds scandalous opinions on women's rights.

"This book is a funny and inspiring tale of a young girl finding her voice and the courage to make it heard." Voice Youth Advocates

Johnson, Angela, 1961-

Bird. Dial Books 2004 133p $15.99; pa $5.99

Grades: 5 6 7 8   **Fic**
    1. Runaway teenagers—Fiction 2. Stepfathers—Fiction
    3. African Americans—Fiction 4. Alabama—Fiction
    ISBN 0-8037-2847-6; 0-14-240544-2 (pa)
                                        LC 2003-22793

Devastated by the loss of a second father, thirteen-year-old Bird follows her stepfather from Cleveland to Alabama in hopes of convincing him to come home, and along the way helps two boys cope with their difficulties

"Johnson writes with a poet's knowledge of rhythm and knows how to use the space between words. . . . Johnson also creates a visceral sense of each character's search for love and connection." Booklist

A cool moonlight. Dial Bks. 2003 133p hardcover o.p. pa $6.99 *

Grades: 4 5 6   **Fic**
    1. Skin—Diseases—Fiction
    ISBN 0-8037-2846-8; 0-14-240284-2 (pa)
                                        LC 2002-31521

Nine-year-old Lila, born with xeroderma pigmentosum, a skin disease that make her sensitive to sunlight, makes secret plans to feel the sun's rays on her tenth birthday

"The book's real magic resides in the spell cast by Johnson's spare, lucid, lyrical prose. Using simple words and vivid sensory images, she creates Lila's inner world as a place of quiet intensity." Booklist

Johnson, Gillian

Thora; written and illustrated by Gillian Johnson. Katherine Tegen Books 2005 c2003 229p il $12.99; lib bdg $15.89

Grades: 4 5 6   **Fic**

1. Mermaids and mermen—Fiction 2. Magic—Fiction
ISBN 0-06-074378-6; 0-06-074379-4 (lib bdg)

LC 2004-14904

First published 2003 in Australia

Ten-year-old Thora, daughter of a mermaid mother and a human father, has many adventures at sea until she must return to the English seaside town of Grimli and save her mother who has been captured by the greedy real estate developer, Frooty de Mare.

"This entertaining fantasy will charm children who like their magic with its feet on the ground. . . . Lively, witty line drawings illustrate the action." Booklist

Another title about Thora is: Thora and the green sea-unicorn (2007)

Johnston, Julie

A very fine line. Tundra Books 2006 198p $18.95; pa $10.95

Grades: 5 6 7 8   **Fic**

1. Clairvoyance—Fiction 2. Canada—Fiction
ISBN 978-0-88776-746-3; 0-88776-746-X; 978-0-88776-829-3 (pa); 0-88776-829-6 (pa)

Then thirteen-year-old Rosalind's "aunt informs her that as the seventh daughter of a seventh daughter, she can . . . see glimpses of the future, she balks. . . . The story begins in Kepston, Ontario, in 1941. . . . Readers who come to the book intrigued by the idea of clairvoyance will fine much more: several vivid characters, a well-realized setting, and a sensitively nuanced resolution." Booklist

Johnston, Tony

Any small goodness; a novel of the barrio; illustrations by Raúl Colón. Blue Sky Press (NY) 2001 128p il $16.95; pa $4.99

Grades: 4 5 6 7   **Fic**

1. Mexican Americans—Fiction 2. Los Angeles (Calif.)—Fiction
ISBN 0-439-18936-5; 0-439-23384-4 (pa)

LC 99-59877

Arturo and his family and friends share all kinds of experiences living in the barrio of East Los Angeles—reclaiming their names, playing basketball, championing the school librarian, and even starting their own gang

"The characters are likable and warm. . . . The message is positive and the episodes, while occasionally serious, are more often humorous and gratifying." SLJ

The spoon in the bathroom wall. Harcourt 2005 134p $16; pa $5.95

Grades: 3 4 5   **Fic**

1. Magic—Fiction 2. Fantasy fiction
ISBN 0-15-205292-5; 0-15-205625-4 (pa)

LC 2004-17415

Living in the boiler room of the school where her father is janitor seems normal to fourth grader Martha Snapdragon, until she has experiences with an evil principal, the class bully, and a mysterious giant spoon, all

reminiscent of the Arthurian legends.

"This delightful story is filled with humor, wisdom, and wonderful sayings." Lib Media Connect

Jonell, Lynne, 1956-

Emmy and the incredible shrinking rat. Henry Holt 2007 346p il $16.95; pa $6.99 *

Grades: 4 5 6   **Fic**

1. Rats—Fiction
ISBN 978-0-8050-8150-3; 0-8050-8150-X; 978-0-312-38460-9 (pa); 0-312-38460-2 (pa)

LC 2006-35461

Followed by: Emmy and the Home for Troubled Girls (2008)

When Emmy discovers that she and her formerly loving parents are being drugged by their evil nanny with rodent potions that can change people in frightening ways, she and some new friends must try everything possible to return things to normal.

"This tale turns smoothly on its fanciful premise and fabulous characters." Booklist

The secret of zoom. Henry Holt 2009 291p $16.99 *

Grades: 4 5 6   **Fic**

1. Adventure fiction 2. Orphans—Fiction 3. Energy resources—Fiction
ISBN 978-0-8050-8856-4; 0-8050-8856-3

LC 2008-50276

Ten-year-old Christina lives a sheltered life until she discovers a secret tunnel, an evil plot to enslave orphans, and a mysterious source of energy known as zoom.

"This exciting tale, with just a touch of fantasy and humor, is a winner. . . . Complete with a cast of clearly drawn characters, the adventure proceeds at a breakneck pace until all is resolved and a happy ending completes the picture." SLJ

Jones, Diana Wynne

Castle in the air. Greenwillow Bks. 1991 199p hardcover o.p. pa $6.99 *

Grades: 6 7 8 9   **Fic**

1. Fantasy fiction
ISBN 0-688-09686-7; 0-06-447345-7 (pa)

LC 90-30266

In this "follow-up to *Howl's Moving Castle* . . . the protagonist is a young carpet merchant called Abdullah, who spends much of his time creating a richly developed daydream in which he is the long-lost son of a great prince, kidnapped as a child by a villainous bandit. . . . Feisty Sophie and the Wizard Howl (from *Howl's Moving Castle* do not become apparent till late in the story, but their fortunes do link up with those of Abdullah and his love. Jones maintains both suspense and wit throughout, demonstrating once again that frequently nothing is what it seems to be." Booklist

Jones, Diana Wynne—*Continued*

House of many ways. Greenwillow Books 2008
404p $17.99; lib bdg $18.89; pa $8.99

Grades: 5 6 7 8 **Fic**

1. Houses—Fiction 2. Magic—Fiction 3. Uncles—Fiction 4. Fantasy fiction

ISBN 978-0-06-147795-9; 0-06-147795-8;
978-0-06-147796-6 (lib bdg); 0-06-147796-6 (lib bdg);
978-0-06-147797-3 (pa); 0-06-147797-4 (pa)

LC 2007036147

Sequel to: Howl's moving castle (1986)

When Charmain is asked to housesit for Great Uncle
William, the Royal Wizard of Norland, she is ecstatic to
get away from her parents, but finds that his house is
much more than it seems.

This is "a buoyantly entertaining read. . . . [Jones']
comic pacing and wit are amply evident." Horn Book

Howl's moving castle. Greenwillow Books 1986
212p hardcover o.p. pa $6.99 *

Grades: 5 6 7 8 **Fic**

1. Fantasy fiction

ISBN 0-688-06233-4; 978-0-06-147878-9 (pa);
0-06-147878-4 (pa) LC 85-21981

"When the wicked Witch of the Waste turns Sophie
Hatter into an ugly crone, the girl seeks refuge in Wizard
Howl's moving castle. To her surprise and dismay, she
finds herself embroiled in a contest between the witch
and the wizard, in the tangled love affairs of the wizard,
and in a perplexing mystery." Child Book Rev Serv

"Satisfyingly, Sophie meets a fate far exceeding her
dreary expectations. This novel is an exciting, multifaceted puzzle, peopled with vibrant, captivating characters. A generous sprinkling of humor adds potency to
this skillful author's spell." Voice Youth Advocates

Followed by: House of many ways (2008)

Jones, Kimberly K., 1957-

Sand dollar summer. Margaret K. McElderry
Books 2006 206p $15.95; pa $5.99

Grades: 5 6 7 8 **Fic**

1. Islands—Fiction 2. Maine—Fiction 3. Family life—Fiction

ISBN 978-1-4169-0362-8; 1-4169-0362-3;
978-1-4169-5834-5 (pa); 1-4169-5834-7 (pa)

LC 2005012740

When twelve-year-old Lise spends the summer on an
island in Maine with her self-reliant mother and bright—
but oddly mute—younger brother, her formerly safe
world is complicated by an aged Indian neighbor, her
mother's childhood friend, and a hurricane.

"The drama in [the] smart, tough, first-person narrative is understated; the spaces between the words are as
eloquent as what is said. . . . The family story . . . is
exquisitely told." Booklist

Jones, Marcia Thornton, 1958-

Ratfink; with illustrations by C. B. Decker.
Dutton Children's Books 2010 216p il $16.99 *

Grades: 3 4 5 **Fic**

1. Grandfathers—Fiction 2. Friendship—Fiction
3. School stories

ISBN 978-0-525-42066-8; 0-525-42066-5

Creative, impulsive Logan vows to turn over a new
leaf in fifth grade so his parents will let him have a pet,
but when a competitive new girl arrives at school and his
forgetful and embarrassing grandfather takes over the
basement of Logan's house, doing the right thing becomes harder than it has ever been.

"Told in rapid dialogue, this novel's gripping conflicts
about loyalty, betrayal, and kindness are never simplistic,
and the standoffs with family, friends, and enemies are
realistic and dramatic. . . . Hilarious and heartbreaking."
Booklist

Jordan, Rosa, 1939-

Lost Goat Lane. Peachtree Publisher 2004 197p
$14.95

Grades: 5 6 7 8 **Fic**

1. Goats—Fiction 2. Race relations—Fiction
3. African Americans—Fiction 4. Florida—Fiction

ISBN 1-56145-325-0 LC 2004-5343

Two families—one white, one black—living near one
another in rural Florida overcome their suspicions of
each other and find ways to work together, with the help
of their children and a few goats

"The fully realized characters and the warmth of the
story make up for the small sermons. A tender, satisfying
offering." SLJ

Other titles in this series are:
The goatnappers (2007)
The last wild place (2008)

Joseph, Lynn

The color of my words. HarperCollins Pubs.
2000 138p hardcover o.p. pa $5.99

Grades: 5 6 7 8 **Fic**

1. Family life—Fiction 2. Siblings—Fiction
3. Dominican Republic—Fiction

ISBN 0-06-028232-0; 0-06-447204-3 (pa)

LC 00-22440

"Joanna Cotler books"

When life gets difficult for Ana Rosa, a twelve-year-
old would-be writer living in a small village in the Dominican Republic, she can depend on her older brother
to make her feel better—until the life-changing events on
her thirteenth birthday

"A finely crafted novel, lovely and lyrical." SLJ

Jukes, Mavis

Smoke. Farrar, Straus and Giroux 2009 164p
$16.95

Grades: 5 6 7 8 **Fic**

1. Single parent family—Fiction 2. Cats—Fiction
3. Lost and found possessions—Fiction 4. California—
Fiction

ISBN 978-0-374-37085-5; 0-374-37085-0

LC 2008-07157

Jukes, Mavis—*Continued*

Twelve-year-old Colton and his mother move to a farm in California, away from his grandfather and his rodeo-champion father in Idaho, and after his cat Smoke goes missing, Colt feels even more lonely for his old life.

"Jukes's prose is straightforward and unadorned, with strong dialogue and an abundance of exclamation points. It's a tender, audience-appropriate story that subtly handles themes of home, family and community." Kirkus

Juster, Norton, 1929-

The phantom tollbooth; illustrated by Jules Feiffer. Random House 1961 255p il $19.95; pa $6.50 *

Grades: 5 6 7 8 **Fic**

1. Fantasy fiction

ISBN 0-394-81500-9; 0-394-82037-1 (pa)

"Milo, a boy who receives a surprise package which, when put together, is a toll-booth, goes off in a toy automobile on a tour of an imaginary country." Bull Cent Child Books

"It's all very clever. The author plays most ingeniously on words and phrases . . . and on concepts of averages and infinity and such . . . while the pictures are even more diverting than the text, for they add interesting details." N Y Her Trib Books

Kadohata, Cynthia

Cracker! the best dog in Vietnam. Atheneum Books for Young Readers 2007 312p $16.99; pa $7.99 *

Grades: 5 6 7 8 **Fic**

1. Dogs—Fiction 2. Vietnam War, 1961-1975—Fiction

ISBN 978-1-4169-0637-7; 1-4169-0637-1; 978-1-4169-0638-4 (pa); 1-4169-0638-X (pa)

LC 2006-22022

The author "tells a stirring, realistic story of America's war in Vietnam, using the alternating viewpoints of an army dog named Cracker and her 17-year-old handler, Rick Hanski. . . . The heartfelt tale explores the close bond of the scout-dog team." Booklist

Kira-Kira. Atheneum Bks. for Young Readers 2004 244p $15.95; pa $6.99 *

Grades: 5 6 7 8 **Fic**

1. Sisters—Fiction 2. Japanese Americans—Fiction 3. Death—Fiction 4. Georgia—Fiction

ISBN 0-689-85639-3; 0-689-85640-7 (pa)

Awarded the Newbery Medal, 2005

Chronicles the close friendship between two Japanese-American sisters growing up in rural Georgia during the late 1950s and early 1960s, and the despair when one sister becomes terminally ill.

"This beautifully written story tells of a girl struggling to find her own way in a family torn by illness and horrendous work conditions. . . . All of the characters are believable and well developed." SLJ

A million shades of gray. Atheneum Books for Young Readers 2010 216p $16.99 *

Grades: 5 6 7 8 **Fic**

1. Vietnam—Fiction 2. Elephants—Fiction 3. Wilderness survival—Fiction

ISBN 978-1-4169-1883-7; 1-4169-1883-3

LC 2009-33307

In 1975 after American troops pull out of Vietnam, a thirteen-year-old boy and his beloved elephant escape into the jungle when the Viet Cong attack his village.

"Kadohata delves deep into the soul of her protagonist while making a faraway place and stark consequences of war seem very near." Publ Wkly

Outside beauty. Atheneum Books for Young Readers 2008 265p $16.99; pa $8.99

Grades: 5 6 7 8 **Fic**

1. Sisters—Fiction 2. Father-daughter relationship—Fiction 3. Mother-daughter relationship—Fiction 4. Japanese Americans—Fiction

ISBN 978-0-689-86575-6; 0-689-86575-9; 978-1-4169-9818-1 (pa); 1-4169-9818-7 (pa)

LC 2007-39711

Thirteen-year-old Shelby and her three sisters must go to live with their respective fathers while their mother, who has trained them to rely on their looks, recovers from a car accident that scarred her face

Kadohata's "gifts for creating and containing drama and for careful definition of character prove as powerful as ever in this wise, tender and compelling novel." Publ Wkly

Weedflower. Atheneum Books for Young Readers 2006 260p $16.95; pa $5.99 *

Grades: 5 6 7 8 **Fic**

1. Japanese Americans—Evacuation and relocation, 1942-1945—Fiction 2. World War, 1939-1945—Fiction 3. Arizona—Fiction

ISBN 0-689-86574-0; 1-4169-7566-7 (pa)

LC 2004-24912

After twelve-year-old Sumiko and her Japanese-American family are relocated from their flower farm in southern California to an internment camp on a Mojave Indian reservation in Arizona, she helps her family and neighbors, becomes friends with a local Indian boy, and tries to hold on to her dream of owning a flower shop.

Sumiko "is a sympathetic heroine, surrounded by well-crafted, fascinating people. The concise yet lyrical prose conveys her story in a compelling narrative." SLJ

Karr, Kathleen

Fortune's fool. Alfred A. Knopf 2008 201p $15.99; lib bdg $18.99; pa $6.50

Grades: 5 6 7 8 **Fic**

1. Middle Ages—Fiction 2. Fools and jesters—Fiction 3. Germany—History—0-1517—Fiction

ISBN 978-0-375-84816-2; 0-375-84816-9; 978-0-375-94816-9 (lib bdg); 0-375-84816-3 (lib bdg); 978-0-375-84307-5 (pa); 0-375-84307-8 (pa)

LC 2007-49034

In medieval Germany, fifteen-year-old Conrad, a court jester, and his beloved Christa, a servant girl, escape from a cruel master and journey through the countryside on a quest to find a kind lord who will give them sanctu-

Karr, Kathleen—*Continued*
ary.

"Karr does an splendid job of recreating the medieval milieu, especially the life of a professional entertainer with all of its challenges and hardships." Booklist

Keehn, Sally M., 1947-
Gnat Stokes and the Foggy Bottom Swamp Queen; [by] Sally M. Keehn. Philomel Books 2005 152p $16.99
Grades: 5 6 7 8   **Fic**
1. Magic—Fiction 2. Tennessee—Fiction
ISBN 0-399-24287-2   LC 2003-26635
In Mary's Cove, Tennessee, in 1869, twelve-year-old Gnat Stokes decides to prove she's not just a trouble maker by rescuing a boy who was spirited away seven years earlier by the evil Swamp Queen of Foggy Bottom
"Keehn's tale is by turns, creepy, laugh-aloud funny, touching, and utterly satisfying. Her voice is sassy and straight out of the Tennessee hills." Booklist

Kehret, Peg, 1936-
Abduction! Dutton Children's Books 2004 215p $16.99; pa $6.99
Grades: 5 6 7 8   **Fic**
1. Kidnapping—Fiction
ISBN 0-525-47294-0; 0-14-240617-1 (pa)
                                        LC 2003-63531
Thirteen-year-old Bonnie has a feeling of foreboding on the very day that her six-year-old brother Matt and their dog Pookie are abducted, and she becomes involved in a major search effort as well as a frightening adventure
"This novel has enough suspense to keep children interested, and it will also appeal to reluctant readers." SLJ

Don't tell anyone. Dutton Children's Bks. 2000 137p hardcover o.p. pa $5.99
Grades: 5 6 7 8   **Fic**
1. Cats—Fiction 2. Criminals—Fiction
ISBN 0-525-46388-7; 0-14-230031-4 (pa)
                                        LC 99-89605
Twelve-year-old Megan does not realize that feeding a group of feral cats living in a field near her house will involve her as a witness to a traffic accident and in the dangerous plan of an unstable criminal
"There are subplots galore in this quick read . . . but they all hang together, and thanks to Kehret's even tone, the scary aspects won't frighten younger readers." Booklist

The ghost's grave. Dutton Children's Books 2005 210p $16.99; pa $5.99
Grades: 5 6 7 8   **Fic**
1. Ghost stories 2. Coal miners—Fiction 3. Washington (State)—Fiction
ISBN 0-525-46162-0; 0-14-240819-0 (pa)
                                        LC 2004-22064
Apprehensive about spending the summer in Washington State with his Aunt Ethel when his parents get an overseas job, twelve-year-old Josh soon finds adventure when he meets the ghost of a coal miner.
"This fast-paced and engaging book should be a hit with fans of ghost stories. Josh is a rich character to whom readers can relate." SLJ

Keith, Harold, 1903-1998
Rifles for Watie. Crowell 1957 332p lib bdg $16.89; pa $5.99
Grades: 6 7 8 9   **Fic**
1. Watie, Stand, 1806-1871—Fiction 2. United States—History—1861-1865, Civil War—Fiction
ISBN 0-690-04907-2 (lib bdg); 0-06-447030-X (pa)
Awarded the Newbery Medal, 1958
"Young Jeff Bussey longs for the life of a Union soldier during the Civil War, but before long he realizes the cruelty and savagery of some men in the army situation. The war loses its glamor as he sees his very young friends die. When he is made a scout, his duties take him into the ranks of Stand Watie, leader of the rebel troops of the Cherokee Indian Nation, as a spy." Stensland. Lit By & About the Am Indian

Kelly, Jacqueline
The evolution of Calpurnia Tate. Henry Holt and Co. 2009 340p $16.99 *
Grades: 4 5 6 7   **Fic**
1. Nature—Fiction 2. Family life—Fiction 3. Grandfathers—Fiction 4. Naturalists—Fiction 5. Texas—Fiction
ISBN 978-0-8050-8841-0; 0-8050-8841-5
                                        LC 2008-40595
A Newbery Medal honor book (2010)
In central Texas in 1899, eleven-year-old Callie Vee Tate is instructed to be a lady by her mother, learns about love from the older three of her six brothers, and studies the natural world with her grandfather, the latter of which leads to an important discovery.
"Callie is a charming, inquisitive protagonist; a joyous, bright, and thoughtful creation. . . . Several scenes . . . mix gentle humor and pathos to great effect." SLJ

Kelly, Katy
Lucy Rose, here's the thing about me; illustrated by Adam Rex. Delacorte Press 2004 137p il hardcover o.p. pa $5.99
Grades: 2 3 4   **Fic**
1. Moving—Fiction 2. Family life—Fiction 3. School stories 4. Washington (D.C.)—Fiction
ISBN 0-385-73203-1; 0-440-42026-1 (pa)
                                        LC 2003-20754
Eight-year-old Lucy Rose keeps a diary of her first year in Washington, D.C., her home since her parents separation, where she spends time with her grandparents, makes new friends, and longs to convince her teacher to let her take care of the class pet during a holiday
"There's something especially endearing about Lucy Rose, and her interactions with her parents, grandparents, teacher, and friends seem believable and comfortable." Booklist
Other titles about Lucy Rose are:
Lucy Rose, big on plans (2005)
Lucy Rose, busy like you can't believe (2006)
Lucy Rose, working myself to pieces and bits (2007)

Kelly, Katy—*Continued*

Melonhead; illustrated by Gillian Johnson. Delacorte Press 2009 209p il $12.99; lib bdg $15.99

Grades: 3 4 5   **Fic**

1. Inventors—Fiction 2. Washington (D.C.)—Fiction
ISBN   978-0-385-73409-7;   0-385-73409-3; 978-0-385-90426-1 (lib bdg); 0-385-90426-6 (lib bdg)
LC 2007-46076

In the Washington, D.C. neighborhood of Capitol Hill, Lucy Rose's friend Adam "Melonhead" Melon, a budding inventor with a knack for getting into trouble, enters a science contest that challenges students to recycle an older invention into a new invention.

This is "laugh-out-loud funny. . . . The capital setting and a unique cast of characters round out this strong chapter-book offering." SLJ

Another title about Melonhead is:
Melonhead and the big stink (2010)

Kelsey, Marybeth

A recipe 4 robbery. Greenwillow Books 2009 282p $16.99; lib bdg $17.89

Grades: 4 5 6   **Fic**

1. Mystery fiction
ISBN   978-0-06-128843-2;   0-06-128843-8; 978-0-06-128845-6 (lib bdg); 0-06-128845-4 (lib bdg)
LC 2008-29145

An unsupervised goose, missing family heirlooms, and some suspicious characters turn the annual cucumber festival into a robbery investigation for three sixth-grade friends.

"The novel is full of likable characters and fun twists and turns. The plot moves quickly, and Kelsey writes with wit and verve." SLJ

Tracking Daddy down. Greenwillow Books 2008 292p $16.99; lib bdg $17.89 *

Grades: 4 5 6   **Fic**

1. Father-daughter relationship—Fiction 2. Stepfathers—Fiction 3. Cousins—Fiction 4. Family life—Fiction 5. Thieves—Fiction 6. Indiana—Fiction
ISBN   978-0-06-128842-5;   0-06-128842-X; 978-0-06-128841-8 (lib bdg); 0-06-128841-1 (lib bdg)
LC 2008003828

Daredevil eleven-year-old Billie has an exciting summer, in spite of her overprotective stepfather, when she figures out where her father and uncle are hiding after robbing a bank and enlists her cousin's help in convincing them to surrender

"A riveting opening sentence pulls readers into this unusual story. . . . This multifaceted story of adventure, family, love, and trust is a testament to how strong a child's need for fatherly attention and love can be." SLJ

Kendall, Carol

The Gammage Cup; a novel of the Minnipins; illustrated by Erik Blegvad. Harcourt 2000 c1959 283p il hardcover o.p. pa $6

Grades: 5 6 7 8   **Fic**

1. Fantasy fiction
ISBN 0-15-202487-5; 0-15-202493-X (pa)
LC 99-55279

A Newbery Medal honor book, 1960

"An Odyssey/Harcourt young classic"
A reissue of the title first published 1959

A handful of Minnipins, a sober and sedate people, rise up against the Periods, the leading family of an isolated mountain valley, and are exiled to a mountain where they discover that the ancient enemies of their people are preparing to attack

"An original and wholly delightful tale." Booklist
Another title about the Minnipins is:
The whisper of Glocken (1965)

Kennedy, Marlane, 1962-

The dog days of Charlotte Hayes. Greenwillow Books 2009 233p $15.99; lib bdg $16.89

Grades: 4 5 6   **Fic**

1. Family life—Fiction 2. Dogs—Fiction 3. Old age—Fiction 4. West Virginia—Fiction
ISBN   978-0-06-145241-3;   0-06-145241-6; 978-0-06-145242-0 (lib bdg); 0-06-145242-4 (lib bdg)
LC 2008-07507

Eleven-year-old Charlotte is not a dog person but does not like that the rest of her family neglects their Saint Bernard puppy, and so with a lot of determination and a little sneakiness, she works on finding a good home for the gentle giant.

This is a "gentle, appealing story. . . . The familiar family and friendship issues and satisfying resolution make this an agreeable read." Booklist

Me and the pumpkin queen. Greenwillow Books 2007 181p $15.99; lib bdg $16.89; pa $5.99

Grades: 3 4 5   **Fic**

1. Pumpkin—Fiction 2. Gardening—Fiction 3. Aunts—Fiction 4. Bereavement—Fiction
ISBN   978-0-06-114022-8;   0-06-114022-8; 978-0-06-114023-5 (lib bdg); 0-06-114023-6 (lib bdg); 978-0-06-114024-2 (pa); 0-06-114024-4 (pa)
LC 2006-20019

Although Aunt Arlene tries to interest her in clothing and growing up, ten-year-old Mildred is entirely focused on growing a pumpkin big enough to win the annual Circleville, Ohio, contest, as her mother dreamed of doing before she died.

"The author combines the art and science of horticulture with a gentle family story, a feel for a child in mourning, and just the right amount of humor and tension to keep the plot moving along." SLJ

Kennemore, Tim, 1957-

Alice's birthday pig; written by Tim Kennemore; illustrated by Mike Spoor. Eerdmans Books for Young Readers 2008 54p il $12

Grades: 2 3 4   **Fic**

1. Birthdays—Fiction 2. Family life—Fiction 3. Siblings—Fiction 4. Pigs—Fiction
ISBN 978-0-8028-5335-6; 0-8028-5335-8
LC 2007-25460

First published 2005 in the United Kingdom

Alice's brother teases her mercilessly because she cannot say the word "animal" correctly, but she gets her revenge on her birthday.

"The story contends with typical family and sibling issues. . . . Black-and-white illustrations keep things light." Horn Book Guide

Other titles in this series are:

Kennemore, Tim, 1957-—*Continued*
Alice's world record (2008)
Alice's shooting star (2009)

Kent, Rose
Kimchi & calamari. HarperCollinsPublishers
2007 220p $15.99; lib bdg $16.89
Grades: 4 5 6 7   **Fic**
1. Korean Americans—Fiction 2. Italian Americans—
Fiction 3. Adoption—Fiction
ISBN   978-0-06-083769-3;   0-06-083769-1;
978-0-06-083770-9 (lib bdg); 0-06-083770-5 (lib bdg)
                                   LC 2006-20041
"Fourteen-year-old Korean adoptee Joseph Calderaro
is stumped when his social studies teacher assigns an ancestry essay. . . . Kent's debut novel humorously captures the feelings of a young teen who thoroughly enjoys
his Italian-American family but still wonders about his
birth parents." Booklist

Kerley, Barbara
Greetings from planet Earth. Scholastic Press
2007 246p $16.99
Grades: 5 6 7 8   **Fic**
1. Father-son relationship—Fiction 2. Vietnam War,
1961-1975—Fiction 3. Family life—Fiction
ISBN 0-439-80203-2; 978-0-439-80203-1
                                   LC 2006-11300
In 1977, as twelve-year-old Theo struggles with a science class project on space exploration, questions emerge
about why his father never returned from Vietnam and
why Theo's mother has been keeping secrets for many
years.
"The novel convincingly portrays a family overshadowed by secrets." Booklist

Kerrin, Jessica Scott
Martin Bridge: ready for takeoff! written by
Jessica Scott Kerrin; illustrated by Joseph Kelly.
Kids Can Press 2005 120p il $14.95; pa $4.95 *
Grades: 2 3 4   **Fic**
ISBN 1-55337-688-9; 1-55337-772-9 (pa)
"Martin Bridge usually has a scheme or project under
way. In the three school and home stories presented in
this beginning chapter book, he sees how a happy surprise intended for one person makes a positive difference
for another, figures out what to say to a little girl whose
hamster has died, and suffers the consequences of jealousy. . . . [Martin's] responses are on target for a third
grader. Kerrin relates the episodes in a straightforward
way that incorporates rich language. Kelly's full-page illustrations and spot art follow the narrative closely
enough to support the newly independent readers for
whom this book is written." SLJ
 Other titles about Martin Bridge are:
Martin Bridge on the lookout! (2005)
Martin Bridge blazing ahead! (2006)
Martin Bridge out of orbit! (2007)
Martin Bridge sound the alarm (2007)
Martin Bridge in high gear! (2008)
Martin Bridge: the sky's the limit (2008)
Martin Bridge: onwards and upwards! (2009)

Kessler, Liz
Philippa Fisher's fairy godsister; illustrated by
Katie May. Candlewick Press 2008 274p il $15.99;
pa $6.99
Grades: 3 4 5   **Fic**
1. Fairies—Fiction 2. Magic—Fiction 3. Wishes—Fiction 4. Fantasy fiction
ISBN   978-0-7636-4070-5;   0-7636-4070-0;
978-0-7636-4596-0 (pa); 0-7636-4596-6 (pa)
"Philippa Fisher's life is a disaster. Her parents em-
barrass her in front of her friends; they are party entertainers and drive a bright yellow VW camper with pictures of clowns and jesters and rabbits painted on the
side. Then her best friend moves away and she feels totally alone. She is so miserable, in fact, that the ATC
(Above the Clouds) sends her a fairy godmother from
3WD (the Three Wishes Department). . . . It is her
choices and the consequences that make this story so
moving. Equally as charming is the way fairy magic has
been modernized with MagiCell messaging and a fairy
facing her own trials and errors." SLJ
Followed by: Philippa Fisher and the dream-maker's
daughter (2009)

Ketchum, Liza, 1946-
Newsgirl. Viking 2009 327p $16.99 *
Grades: 4 5 6 7   **Fic**
1. Frontier and pioneer life—Fiction 2. Sex role—Fiction 3. San Francisco (Calif.)—Fiction 4. Adventure
fiction
ISBN 978-0-670-01119-3; 0-670-01119-3
In 1851 twelve-year-old Amelia and her friend Estelle
come to San Francisco, where Amelia disguises herself
as a boy and sells newspapers, becomes trapped in a hot
air balloon, and has an adventure in the gold fields
"Ketchum nicely interweaves actual events into this
engaging story. She also covers the topics of discrimination and same-sex couples with aplomb. Amelia is a
well-rounded character." SLJ

Where the great hawk flies. Clarion Books 2005
264p $16
Grades: 5 6 7 8   **Fic**
1. Prejudices—Fiction 2. Pequot Indians—Fiction
3. Vermont—Fiction
ISBN 0-618-40085-0   LC 2004-29832
Years after a violent New England raid by the Redcoats and their Revolutionary War Indian allies, two
families, one that suffered during that raid and one with
an Indian mother and Patriot father, become neighbors
and must deal with past trauma and prejudices before
they can help each other in the present. Based on the author's family history. Includes historical notes and notes
on the Pequot Indians.
The author writes "in prose as sturdy and well crafted
as a cedar-frame wigwam or hand-pegged pine barn."
Booklist

Key, Watt, 1970-

Alabama moon. Farrar, Straus & Giroux 2006 294p $16; pa $6.99

Grades: 5 6 7 8 **Fic**

1. Orphans—Fiction 2. Wilderness survival—Fiction 3. Alabama—Fiction

ISBN 0-374-30184-0; 0-312-38428-9 (pa)

LC 2005-40165

After the death of his father, ten-year-old Moon leaves their forest shelter home and is sent to an Alabama institution, becoming entangled in the outside world he has never known and making good friends, a relentless enemy, and finally a new life

"The book is well written with a flowing style, plenty of dialogue, and lots of action. The characters are well drawn and three-dimensional." SLJ

Followed by: Dirt road home (2010)

Kilworth, Garry

Attica. Little, Brown 2009 334p pa $11.95

Grades: 5 6 7 8 **Fic**

1. Fantasy fiction 2. Stepfamilies—Fiction

ISBN 978-1-904233-56-5 (pa); 1-904233-56-2 (pa)

"New stepsiblings Jordy, Chloe and Alex move into a duplex landlorded by initially crotchety Mr. Grantham. When the children venture into the attic to find Grantham's pocket watch, they find a vast world that they dub Attica." Kirkus

"The children have distinct personalities and react to Attica in realistic ways, finding their own strengths in this exhilarating, unpredictable environment. This book is a rare find." Booklist

Kimmel, Elizabeth Cody

The reinvention of Moxie Roosevelt. Dial Books for Young Readers 2010 256p $16.99

Grades: 4 5 6 7 **Fic**

1. School stories

ISBN 978-0-8037-3303-9; 0-8037-3303-8

LC 2009-37939

On her first day of boarding school, a thirteen-year-old girl who feels boring and invisible decides to change her personality to match her unusual name.

"Kimmel's sharply observed novel reflects a keen understanding of the agony of self-definition that is adolescence. Readers will cheer for Moxie as she charts her path toward self-acceptance." Kirkus

School spirit. Little, Brown and Co. 2008 316p (Suddenly supernatural) $15.99

Grades: 5 6 7 8 **Fic**

1. Clairvoyance—Fiction 2. Ghost stories 3. Mother-daughter relationship—Fiction 4. Popularity—Fiction 5. School stories

ISBN 978-0-316-06683-9; 0-316-06683-4

LC 2007-031542

Like her mother, a professional medium, Kat has been able to see dead people since turning thirteen, and although they would prefer to be normal, Kat and her best friend come to terms with their own talents while helping free the spirit of a girl trapped at their middle school.

"This delightfully fun and well-written story is a fast, clean read. . . . Its nice blend of supernatural and reality will attract fantasy and non-fantasy readers alike." Voice Youth Advocates

Other titles in this series are:
Scaredy Kat (2009)
Unhappy medium (2009)

Kimmel, Eric A.

A picture for Marc; illustrated by Matthew Trueman. Random House 2007 101p il $11.99; lib bdg $13.99; pa $4.99

Grades: 3 4 5 **Fic**

1. Chagall, Marc, 1887-1985—Fiction 2. Artists—Fiction 3. Russia—Fiction

ISBN 978-0-375-83253-6; 978-0-375-93253-3 (lib bdg); 978-0-375-85225-1 (pa) LC 2006029617

Marc, an imaginative Russian boy, discovers his talent for drawing and, with the encouragement of a friend and an art teacher, decides to become an artist. Based loosely on the childhood of Marc Chagall

"The author skillfully weaves actual events into the narrative. The black-and-white illustrations contain vivid details and add depth to the story." SLJ

King, Thomas, 1943-

A Coyote solstice tale; pictures by Gary Clement. Groundwood Books 2009 unp il $14.95

Grades: 1 2 3 4 **Fic**

1. Coyotes—Fiction 2. Animals—Fiction 3. Shopping—Fiction 4. Winter solstice—Fiction 5. Stories in rhyme

ISBN 978-0-88899-929-0; 0-88899-929-1

ALA America Indian Library Association American Indian Youth Literature Award (2010)

"Coyote is expecting Beaver, Bear, Otter, and Moose for a solstice dinner at his small house in the woods but a little girl in a reindeer costume shows up first. When the friends follow her tracks to discover where she came from, they discover a huge and frenzied mall just beyond the woods, where Coyote goes wild shopping until he discovers that he has to pay for the stuff. The humor is dry and affectionate, the rhyming text delights with sly turns of phrase, the watercolor cartoons are whimsical, and the small size of the book (a bit bigger than a DVD case) adds to the charm." SLJ

King-Smith, Dick, 1922-

Babe; the gallant pig; illustrated by Maggie Kneen. Twentieth anniversary edition. Knopf 2005 130p il $16.95 *

Grades: 3 4 5 **Fic**

1. Pigs—Fiction

ISBN 0-375-82970-9 LC 2004-5832

First published 1983 in the United Kingdom with title: The sheep-pig; first United States edition 1985 by Crown

A piglet destined for eventual butchering arrives at the farmyard, is adopted by an old sheep dog, and discovers a special secret to success

"Mary Rayner's engaging black-and-white drawings capture the essence of Babe and the skittishness of sheep and enhance this splendid book-which should once and for all establish the intelligence and nobility of pigs." Horn Book

King-Smith, Dick, 1922-—*Continued*

The Catlady; illustrated by John Eastwood. Knopf 2006 c2004 71p il hardcover o.p. pa $5.50

Grades: 2 3 4   **Fic**
1. Cats—Fiction 2. Great Britain—Fiction
ISBN 0-375-82985-7; 0-440-42031-8 (pa)
                                     LC 2005009507
First published 2004 in the United Kingdom

Muriel Ponsonby, the Catlady, lives with dozens of cats, many of whom she believes are reincarnated friends, relatives, and even royalty

"Creating setting and characters in a few sure strokes, King-Smith sets the story in motion and carries his readers along in a quietly engaging way. . . . Illustrated with many appealing ink drawings." Booklist

Clever duck; illustrated by Nick Bruel. Roaring Brook Press 2008 85p il $15.95

Grades: 1 2 3   **Fic**
1. Ducks—Fiction 2. Pigs—Fiction 3. Farm life—Fiction
ISBN 978-1-59643-327-4; 1-59643-327-2
                                     LC 2008-11138
First published 1996 in the United Kingdom

When the pigs start picking on all the other farm animals, Damaris, who is a very clever duck, and her best friend, Rory the sheepdog, find a way to exact revenge, only to find their plot backfiring.

"Engaging characters fill this wonderfully wacky farm. Humorous black-and-white illustrations add even more personality to the already exuberant animals." Horn Book Guide

Dinosaur trouble; [by] Dick King-Smith; illustrated by Nick Bruel. Roaring Brook Press 2008 118p il $14.95

Grades: 2 3 4   **Fic**
1. Dinosaurs—Fiction
ISBN 978-1-59643-324-3; 1-59643-324-8
Young dinosaurs Nosy, a pterodactyl, and Banty, an apatosaurus, become friends, despite their parents' prejudices

"Much of the book's humor relies on wordplay and the juxtaposition of the clever mothers next to their dim-witted husbands. Frequent black-and-white cartoon illustrations . . . enliven the text and add a light comic touch." Booklist

Funny Frank; illustrated by John Eastwood. Knopf 2002 c2001 108p il hardcover o.p. pa $5.50

Grades: 3 4 5   **Fic**
1. Chickens—Fiction 2. Ducks—Fiction
ISBN 0-375-81460-4; 0-440-41880-1 (pa)
                                     LC 2001-29539
First published 2001 in the United Kingdom

Gertie the hen is appalled when her son Frank wants to swim with the ducks, but Jemima and her mother, the farmer's wife, make him a special outfit so that his dream can come true

"Illustrated with comic line drawings, the short chapter book is entertaining and easy to read." Horn Book Guide

The golden goose; illustrated by Ann Kronheimer. Knopf 2005 c2003 113p il hardcover o.p. pa $5.50

Grades: 2 3 4   **Fic**
1. Geese—Fiction 2. Farm life—Fiction
ISBN 0-375-82984-9; 0-440-4203-0X (pa)
                                     LC 2004-40842
First published 2003 in the United Kingdom

Farmer Skint and his family on Woebegone Farm have fallen on hard times, but their luck changes with the arrival of a special golden goose

"The novel's breezy premise, Kronheimer's simple and appealing halftone illustrations, the text's relatively large typeface and brief chapters make this perhaps best suited to those just embarking on chapter books, but reluctant readers will also take a fancy to it. And all will be tickled by the uplifting conclusion that caps this engaging story." Publ Wkly

Lady Lollipop; illustrated by Jill Barton. Candlewick Press 2001 120p il $14.99; pa $6.99

Grades: 3 4 5   **Fic**
1. Princesses—Fiction 2. Pigs—Fiction
ISBN 0-7636-1269-3; 0-7636-2181-1 (pa)
                                     LC 00-58498
A quick-witted swineherd and a pig named Lollipop are royally rewarded after they reform a spoiled princess

"The short chapters and the book's open, lively design and engaging pencil illustrations add to this amusing book's appeal." Horn Book Guide

Another title about Lollipop is:
Clever Lollipop (2003)

The mouse family Robinson; [by] Dick King-Smith; illustrated by Nick Bruel. Roaring Brook Press 2008 71p il $15.95

Grades: 3 4 5   **Fic**
1. Mice—Fiction 2. Family life—Fiction
ISBN 978-1-59643-326-7; 1-59643-326-4
                                     LC 2008011139
After a close call with the cat who stalks the hallways, a family of wild mice, including adventurous, young Beaumont and elderly Uncle Brown, emigrates to a more mouse-friendly house down the block

"The lively, often droll narrative, divided into short chapters, and the many captivating illustrations . . . provide an accessible, engaging read filled with everyday details of imagined mouse life and appealing characters." Booklist

The nine lives of Aristotle; illustrated by Bob Graham. Candlewick Press 2003 75p il $14.99

Grades: 2 3 4   **Fic**
1. Cats—Fiction 2. Witches—Fiction
ISBN 0-7636-2260-5   LC 2003-40942
Aristotle, a little white kitten, goes to live with a witch in an old cottage, where he finds so many opportunities for risky adventures that he soon has only one life left

"With winsome watercolor-and-ink illustrations, this short, lighthearted fantasy will appeal to beginning chapter-book readers." SLJ

Kingfisher, Rupert

Madame Pamplemousse and her incredible edibles; [by] Rupert Kingfisher; illustrated by Sue Hellard. Bloomsbury Children's Books 2008 138p il $15.99

Grades: 2 3 4   **Fic**

1. Food—Fiction 2. Restaurants—Fiction 3. Paris (France)—Fiction

ISBN 978-1-59990-306-4; 1-59990-306-7

LC 2008-10409

Forced to work in her unpleasant uncle's horrible restaurant, a Parisian girl finds comfort and companionship in a shop nearby that sells otherworldly foods prepared by a mysterious cook and her cat

"Kingfisher writes in whimsical, humorous prose, creating vivid scenarios and intriguing characters. . . . This droll title is sprinkled with fanciful line drawings and topped with a moral about the magical power and rewards of following one's heart." Booklist

Kinney, Jeff

Diary of a wimpy kid: Greg Heffley's journal. Amulet Books 2007 217p pa $14.95 *

Grades: 5 6 7 8   **Fic**

1. Friendship—Fiction 2. School stories

ISBN 978-0-8109-9313-6 (pa); 0-8109-9313-9 (pa)

LC 2006-31847

Greg records his sixth grade experiences in a middle school where he and his best friend, Rowley, undersized weaklings amid boys who need to shave twice daily, hope just to survive, but when Rowley grows more popular, Greg must take drastic measures to save their friendship

"Kinney's background as a cartoonist is apparent in this hybrid book that falls somewhere between traditional prose and graphic novel. . . . The pace moves quickly. The first of three installments, it is an excellent choice for reluctant readers, but more experienced readers will also find much to enjoy and relate to." SLJ

Other titles about Greg are:

Diary of a wimpy kid: Rodrick rules (2008)

Diary of a wimpy kid: the last straw (2009)

Diary of a wimpy kid: dog days (2009)

Kinsey-Warnock, Natalie

Lumber camp library; illustrated by James Bernardin. HarperCollins Pubs. 2002 87p il hardcover o.p. pa $4.99

Grades: 3 4 5   **Fic**

1. Books and reading—Fiction 2. Lumber and lumbering—Fiction 3. Blind—Fiction

ISBN 0-06-029321-7; 0-06-444292-6 (pa)

LC 2001-39684

Ruby wants to be a teacher, but after her father's death in a logging accident she must quit school to care for her ten brothers and sisters, until a chance meeting with a lonely old blind woman transforms her life

"Kinsey-Warnock's likable characters work hard to overcome the obstacles life has dealt them. The simple, direct language and short, accessible chapters will appeal to beginning chapter-book readers." Booklist

Kipling, Rudyard, 1865-1936

The elephant's child; [by] Rudyard Kipling; illustrations by Lorinda Bryan Cauley. Harcourt Brace Jovanovich 1983 unp il hardcover o.p. pa $6

Grades: 2 3 4 5   **Fic**

1. Elephants—Fiction

ISBN 0-15-225385-8 (lib bdg); 0-15-225386-6 (pa)

LC 82-21266

Originally published 1902 as part of Kipling's Just so stories

Because of his "satiable curtiosity" about what the crocodile has for dinner, the elephant's child and all elephants thereafter have long trunks

Kirk, Daniel

The low road. Amulet Books 2008 498p il (Elf Realm) $18.95; pa $8.95 *

Grades: 5 6 7 8   **Fic**

1. Fantasy fiction 2. Fairies—Fiction 3. Magic—Fiction

ISBN 978-0-8109-7069-4; 0-8109-7069-4; 978-0-8109-4084-0 (pa); 0-8109-4084-1 (pa)

LC 2007039751

When Matt and his family move to a new development, they stumble into the middle of massive upheaval in the Fairy world, and as the elves' territory disintegrates and dark factions try to seize control, an apprentice mage sees in Matt the key to saving the realms from destruction.

"The complex, suspense-filled plot pits humans against elves and elves against elves. Highly imaginative, intricately described, and filled with a wide cast of memorable characters, this is a thoroughly engaging fantasy that never lags." Booklist

Followed by: Elf realm: the high road (2009)

Kirov, Erica

Magickeepers: the eternal hourglass. Sourcebooks Jabberwocky 2009 231p $16.99

Grades: 5 6 7 8   **Fic**

1. Magic—Fiction 2. Magicians—Fiction 3. Good and evil—Fiction 4. Russia—Fiction 5. Las Vegas (Nev.)—Fiction

ISBN 978-1-4022-1501-8; 1-4022-1501-0

LC 2008-47718

Living in Las Vegas with his unsuccessful father, Nick Rostov learns on his thirteenth birthday that he is descended from a powerful line of Russian Magickeepers on his dead mother's side, and that the equally powerful but evil Shadowkeepers will stop at nothing to get an ancient relic that his grandfather gave him.

"The intricate, well-paced plot involves ancient spells and riddles, historical figures including Rasputin and Harry Houdini, and sinister Shadowkeepers seeking precious talismans. . . . Kirov's story feels plenty original, and kids will be charmed by her brand of magic." Publ Wkly

Kladstrup, Kristin

The book of story beginnings. Candlewick Press 2006 360p $15.99; pa $7.99

Grades: 4 5 6 7   **Fic**

1. Authorship—Fiction 2. Storytelling—Fiction 3. Magic—Fiction 4. Space and time—Fiction

ISBN 0-7636-2609-0; 0-7636-3419-0 (pa)

                    LC 2005054262

After moving with her parents to Iowa, twelve-year-old Lucy discovers a mysterious notebook that can bring stories to life and which has a link to the 1914 disappearance of her great uncle.

"Kladstrup's first novel offers mystery, adventure, and fantasy, as well as reflections on family dynamics, time travel, and the structure of stories." Booklist

Klages, Ellen, 1954-

The green glass sea. Viking 2006 321p $16.99; pa $7.99 *

Grades: 5 6 7 8   **Fic**

1. Scientists—Fiction 2. Atomic bomb—Fiction 3. World War, 1939-1945—Fiction 4. New Mexico—Fiction

ISBN 0-670-06134-4; 0-14-241149-3 (pa)

It is 1943, and 11-year-old Dewey Kerrigan is traveling west on a train to live with her scientist father—but no one will tell her exactly where he is. When she reaches Los Alamos, New Mexico, she learns why: he's working on a top secret government program.

"Many readers will know as little about the true nature of the project as the girls do, so the gradual revelation of facts is especially effective, while those who already know about Los Alamos's historical significance will experience the story in a different, but equally powerful, way." SLJ

Followed by: White sands, red menace (2008)

Klass, David, 1960-

Stuck on Earth. Farrar Straus & Giroux 2010 227p $16.99

Grades: 4 5 6 7   **Fic**

1. Science fiction 2. Extraterrestrial beings—Fiction 3. Bullies—Fiction

ISBN 978-0-374-39951-1; 0-374-39951-4

                  LC 2008--48133

"Frances Foster books"

On a secret mission to evaluate whether the human race should be annihilated, a space alien inhabits the body of a bullied fourteen-year-old boy.

"Klass's . . . thoughtful, often wrenching book offers plenty to think about, from what's really going on in Tom's head to questions about human responsibility to the planet and each other. It takes 'alienation' to a whole new level." Publ Wkly

Klimo, Kate

The dragon in the sock drawer; with illustrations by John Schroades. Random House Childrens Books 2008 159p il (Dragon keepers) $14.99; lib bdg $17.99

Grades: 3 4 5   **Fic**

1. Dragons—Fiction 2. Cousins—Fiction 3. Eggs—Fiction

ISBN   978-0-375-85587-0;   0-375-85587-4; 978-0-375-95587-7 (lib bdg); 0-375-95587-9 (lib bdg)

                  LC 2007-42306

Cousins Jesse and Daisy always knew they would have a magical adventure, but they are not prepared when the "thunder egg" Jesse has found turns out to be a dragon egg that is about to hatch.

"Illustrated with small black-and-white drawings to introduce each of the 11 chapters, this novel, with its unique and modern twists, is a great addition to the dragon genre for younger readers." SLJ

other titles in this series are:

The dragon in the driveway (2009)

The dragon in the library (2010)

Kline, Suzy, 1943-

Herbie Jones; illustrated by Richard Williams. Putnam 1985 95p il hardcover o.p. pa $4.99 *

Grades: 3 4 5   **Fic**

1. School stories

ISBN 0-399-21183-7; 0-698-11939-8 (pa)

                  LC 84-24915

Herbie's experiences in the third grade include finding bones in the boy's bathroom, wandering away from his class on their field trip, and being promoted to a higher reading group

This is "filled with light humor in its accounts of classroom incidents." Bull Cent Child Books

Other titles about Herbie Jones are:

Herbie Jones and Hamburger Head (1989)

Herbie Jones and the birthday showdown (1993)

Herbie Jones the the class gift (1987)

Herbie Jones and the dark attic (1992)

Herbie Jones and the monster ball (1988)

Herbie Jones and the second grade slippers (2006)

Herbie Jones moves on (2003)

Herbie Jones sails into second grade (2006)

What's the matter with Herbie Jones? (1986)

Horrible Harry in room 2B; pictures by Frank Remkiewicz. Viking Kestrel 1988 56p il pa $3.99 hardcover o.p. *

Grades: 2 3 4   **Fic**

1. School stories

ISBN 0-14-038552-5 (pa)   LC 88-14204

Harry "is the devilish second grader who plays pranks and gets into mischief but can still end up a good friend. In a series of brief scenes, children meet Harry as he shows a garter snake to Song Lee and later ends up being a snake himself for Halloween. His trick to make scary people out of pencil stubs backfires when no one is scared, and his budding romance with Song Lee goes nowhere on the trip to the aquarium. . . . This story should prove to be popular with those just starting chapter books." SLJ

Other titles about Horrible Harry and Song Lee are:

Kline, Suzy, 1943-—*Continued*

Horrible Harry and the ant invasion (1989)
Horrible Harry and the Christmas surprise (1991)
Horrible Harry and the dragon war (2002)
Horrible Harry and the Drop of Doom (1998)
Horrible Harry and the dungeon (1996)
Horrible Harry and the goog (2005)
Horrible Harry and the green slime (1989)
Horrible Harry and the holidaze (2003)
Horrible Harry and the kickball wedding (1992)
Horrible Harry and the locked closet (2004)
Horrible Harry and the mud gremlins (2003)
Horrible Harry and the purple people (1997)
Horrible Harry and the triple revenge (2006)
Horrible Harry at Halloween (2000)
Horrible Harry bugs the three bears (2008)
Horrible Harry goes to the moon (2000)
Horrible Harry moves up to third grade (1998)
Horrible Harry takes the cake (2006)
Horrible Harry's secret (1990)
Song Lee and Leech Man (1995)
Song Lee and the hamster hunt (1994)
Song Lee and the "I hate you" notes (1999)
Song Lee in room 2B (1993)

Klise, Kate

Dying to meet you; illustrated by M. Sarah Klise. Harcourt 2009 147p il (43 Old Cemetery Road) $15

Grades: 3 4 5 6   **Fic**

1. Authors—Fiction 2. Ghost stories 3. Letters—Fiction

ISBN 978-0-15-205727-5; 0-15-205727-7

LC 2007-28534

In this story told mostly through letters, children's book author, I. B. Grumply, gets more than he bargained for when he rents a quiet place to write for the summer.

"This first title in a new series will appeal to readers, especially reluctant ones, as it moves quickly and leaves its audience eager for book two, which is announced in this ghastly and fun tale." SLJ

Another title in this series is:
Over my dead body (2009)

Regarding the sink; where, oh where, did Waters go? illustrated by M. Sarah Klise. Harcourt 2004 127p il $15

Grades: 4 5 6 7   **Fic**

1. School stories

ISBN 0-15-205019-1   LC 2003-26560

A series of letters reveals the selection of the famous fountain designer, Florence Waters, to design a new sink for the Geyser Creek Middle School cafeteria, her subsequent disappearance, and the efforts of a class of sixth-graders to find her

"Piecing the story and clues together is satisfying. Introduce this book to savvy readers who are ready for the jump to a clever, unconventional reading experience." SLJ

Other titles in this series are:
Regarding the bathrooms (2006)
Regarding the bees (2007)
Regarding the fountain (1998)
Regarding the trees (2005)

Knight, Joan

Charlotte in Giverny; by Joan MacPhail Knight; watercolor illustrations by Melissa Sweet. Chronicle Bks. 2000 unp il $16.95; pa $6.95

Grades: 3 4 5   **Fic**

1. Artists—Fiction 2. France—Fiction

ISBN 0-8118-2383-0; 0-8118-5803-0 (pa)

LC 99-6878

While living in France in 1892, Charlotte, a young American girl, writes a journal of her experiences including those among the Impressionist painters at the artist colony of Giverny. Includes profiles of artists who appear in the journal and a glossary of French words

"The profuse illustrations, a mix of 1890s postcards and other memorabilia, reproductions of (mostly) impressionistic paintings by the mentioned artists, and Melissa Sweet's delicately drawn vignettes of vegetables and other items, lay an air of sunny, well-bred tranquility over the scene." Booklist

Other titles in this series are:
Charlotte in New York (2006)
Charlotte in Paris (2003)
Charlotte in London (2009)

Knight, Richard John, 1966-

Winter Shadow; [text by] Richard Knight; [illustrations by] Richard Johnson. Barefoot Books 2009 79p il $16.99

Grades: 2 3 4   **Fic**

1. Wolves—Fiction 2. Villages—Fiction 3. Grandfathers—Fiction

ISBN 978-1-84686-116-1; 1-84686-116-0

LC 2008028092

In an isolated mountain village, nine-year-old Maria and her grandfather rescue and raise a wolf cub, Shadow, and when Shadow eventually leaves to join his own kind, a stranger's words help Maria to accept that this is for the best

"The plot moves steadily and gracefully, presenting enjoyment at face value or taken deeper as comprehension allows. Johnston's soft, whimsical illustrations enhance a text that explores the issues of responsibility of humans to their environment in a subtle, thought-provoking style." SLJ

Knudsen, Michelle

The dragon of Trelian. Candlewick Press 2009 407p $16.99

Grades: 4 5 6 7   **Fic**

1. Fantasy fiction 2. Dragons—Fiction 3. Princesses—Fiction 4. Magic—Fiction

ISBN 978-0-7636-3455-1; 0-7636-3455-7

LC 2008025378

A mage's apprentice, a princess, and a dragon combine their strength and magic to bring down a traitor and restore peace to the kingdom of Trelian.

"Knudsen does a fantastic job of creating sympathetic and realistic characters that really drive the story. The tale is adventurous and exciting with many twists and turns along the way." SLJ

Knudson, Mike, 1965-

Raymond and Graham rule the school; by Mike Knudson and Steve Wilkinson; illustrated by Stacy Curtis. Viking Childrens Books 2008 136p il $14.99; pa $6.99

Grades: 2 3 4   **Fic**
1. School stories 2. Theater—Fiction 3. Friendship—Fiction
ISBN   978-0-670-01101-8;   0-670-01101-0;
978-0-14-241426-2 (pa); 0-14-241426-3 (pa)
                                    LC 2007033350

Best friends Raymond and Graham have looked forward to being the "oldest, coolest, toughest" boys at East Millcreek Elementary School, but from the start of fourth grade everything goes wrong, from getting the scary teacher to not getting the lead in the school play

"This story is filled with nonstop action and kid-friendly humor. Done in an exaggerated cartoon style, Curtis's occasional black-and-white illustrations perfectly suit the tone of the text." SLJ

Other titles about Raymond and Graham are:
Raymond and Graham, dancing dudes (2008)
Raymond and Graham: bases loaded (2010)
Raymond and Graham: cool campers (2010)

Konigsburg, E. L.

From the mixed-up files of Mrs. Basil E. Frankweiler. Atheneum Pubs. 1967 162p il $16; pa $9.99 *

Grades: 4 5 6   **Fic**
1. Metropolitan Museum of Art (New York, N.Y.)—Fiction
ISBN 0-689-20586-4; 1-4169-4975-5 (pa)
Also available in paperback from Dell
Awarded the Newbery Medal, 1968

"Claudia, feeling misunderstood at home, takes her younger brother and runs away to New York where she sets up housekeeping in the Metropolitan Museum of Art, making ingenious arrangements for sleeping, bathing, and laundering. She and James also look for clues to the authenticity of an alleged Michelangelo statue, the true story of which is locked in the files of Mrs. Frankweiler, its former owner. Claudia's progress toward maturity is also a unique introduction to the Metropolitan Museum." Moorachian. What is a City?

Jennifer, Hecate, Macbeth, William McKinley, and me, Elizabeth. Atheneum Pubs. 1967 117p il $16; pa $5.99

Grades: 4 5 6   **Fic**
1. Friendship—Fiction 2. Witchcraft—Fiction 3. African Americans—Fiction
ISBN 0-689-30007-7; 1-4169-3396-4 (pa)
Also available in paperback from Dell
A Newbery Medal honor book, 1968

"Two fifth grade girls, one of whom is the first black child in a middle-income suburb, play at being apprentice witches in this amusing and perceptive story." NY Public Libr. Black Exper in Child Books

The mysterious edge of the heroic world. Atheneum Books for Young Readers 2007 244p $16.99; pa $5.99

Grades: 5 6 7 8   **Fic**
1. Friendship—Fiction 2. Art museums—Fiction 3. Florida—Fiction
ISBN   978-1-4169-4972-5;   1-4169-4972-0;
978-1-4169-5353-1 (pa); 1-4169-5353-1 (pa)

"Amedeo Kaplan (son of characters met in *The Outcasts of 19 Schuyler Place*) has just moved to coastal Florida and made friends with William Wilcox, son of an estate sale manager. . . . As the boys help William's mother pack up the palatial home of Amedeo's next-door neighbor, a larger-than-life retired opera singer, Amedeo finds a signed Modigliani drawing. . . . Amedeo is primed to uncover the history behind the drawing—a dark provenance that links the retired opera singer, the Vanderwaals and the Nazi occupation of Amsterdam." Publ Wkly

"This humorous, poignant, tragic, and mysterious story has intertwining plots that peel away like the layers of an onion." SLJ

A proud taste for scarlet and miniver. Atheneum Pubs. 1973 201p il $18.95; pa $5.99

Grades: 5 6 7 8   **Fic**
1. Eleanor, of Aquitaine, Queen, consort of Henry II, King of England, 1122?-1204—Fiction
ISBN 0-689-30111-1; 0-689-84624-X (pa)
Also available in paperback from Aladdin Bks.

This is an historical novel about the 12th century queen, Eleanor of Aquitaine, wife of kings of France and England and mother of King Richard the Lion Hearted and King John. Impatiently awaiting the arrival of her second husband, King Henry II, in heaven, she recalls her life with the aid of some contemporaries

The author "has succeeded in making history amusing as well as interesting. . . . The characterization is superb. . . . The black-and-white drawings are skillfully as well as appropriately modeled upon medieval manuscript illuminations and add their share of joy to the book." Horn Book

Up from Jericho Tel. Atheneum Pubs. 1986 178p hardcover o.p. pa $4.99

Grades: 5 6 7 8   **Fic**
1. Actors—Fiction 2. Mystery fiction
ISBN 0-689-31194-X; 0-689-82332-0 (pa)
                                    LC 85-20061

"Jeanmarie and Malcolm are both unpopular, both bossy, both latchkey children; both live in a trailer park, and both want to be famous. Jeanmarie knows that she will be a famous actress and that Malcolm will one day be a famous scientist. These two friends embark on a series of adventures encouraged by the spirit of the long dead actress, Tallulah. Yes, presumably 'the' Tallulah! Tallulah, as a ghost, has the ability to make them invisible, and in that state the kids are sent to find the missing Regina Stone." Voice Youth Advocates

"Konigsburg always provides fresh ideas, tart wit and humor, and memorable characters. As for style, she is a natural and gifted storyteller. . . . This is a lively, clever, and very funny book." Bull Cent Child Books

Konigsburg, E. L.—*Continued*

The view from Saturday. Atheneum Bks. for Young Readers 1996 163p $16.95; pa $5.99 *

Grades: 4 5 6 7 **Fic**

1. School stories 2. Friendship—Fiction 3. Physically handicapped—Fiction

ISBN 0-689-80993-X; 0-689-81721-5 (pa)

LC 95-52624

Awarded the Newbery Medal, 1997

"A Jean Karl book"

Four students, with their own individual stories, develop a special bond and attract the attention of their teacher, a paraplegic, who choses them to represent their sixth-grade class in the Academic Bowl competition

"Glowing with humor and dusted with magic. . . . Wrought with deep compassion and a keen sense of balance." Publ Wkly

Koppe, Susanne

The Nutcracker; [by] E. T. A. Hoffmann; illustrated by Lisbeth Zwerger; retold by Susanne Koppe; translated from the German by Anthea Bell; North-South Books 2004 unp il $15.95; lib bdg $16.50

Grades: 3 4 5 **Fic**

1. Fairy tales 2. Christmas—Fiction

ISBN 0-7358-1733-2; 0-7358-1734-0 (lib bdg)

In this retelling of the original 1816 German story, Godfather Drosselmeier gives young Marie a nutcracker for Christmas, and she finds herself in a magical realm where she saves a boy from an evil curse

"This version features somewhat surreal, almost theatrically presented tableaux, delicately and darkly rendered in pen and ink and watercolor. . . . Koppe's retelling is . . . accessible and detailed." SLJ

Korman, Gordon, 1963-

The sixth grade nickname game. Hyperion Bks. for Children 1998 154p hardcover o.p. pa $5.99

Grades: 4 5 6 7 **Fic**

1. Nicknames—Fiction 2. School stories

ISBN 0-7868-0432-7; 0-7868-5190-2 (pa)

LC 98-12343

Eleven-year-old best friends Jeff and Wiley, who like to give nicknames to their classmates, try to find the right one for the new girl Cassandra, while adjusting to the football coach who has become their new teacher

"This is a funny, fast-paced grade-school romp." Bull Cent Child Books

Swindle. Scholastic Press 2008 252p $16.99; pa $6.99

Grades: 3 4 5 6 **Fic**

1. Swindlers and swindling—Fiction 2. Baseball cards—Fiction

ISBN 978-0-439-90344-8; 0-439-90344-0; 978-0-439-90345-5 (pa); 0-439-90345-9 (pa)

LC 2007-17225

After unscrupulous collector S. Wendell Palamino cons him out of a valuable baseball card, sixth-grader Griffin Bing puts together a band of misfits to break into Palomino's heavily guarded store and steal the card back, planning to use the money to finance his father's failing invention, the SmartPick fruit picker.

"The plot is the main attraction, and its clever intricacies—silly, deceptively predictable, and seasoned with the occasional unexpected twist—do not disappoint." Booklist

Another title about Griffin Bing is:

Zoobreak (2009)

Kornblatt, Marc, 1954-

Izzy's place. Margaret K. McElderry Bks. 2003 118p $16.95

Grades: 4 5 6 **Fic**

1. Death—Fiction

ISBN 0-689-84639-8 LC 2002-6185

While spending the summer at his grandmother's Indiana home, ten-year-old Henry Stone gets help from a new friend in coping with the recent death of his grandfather and the possibility of his parents getting divorced

"In straightforward language, Kornblatt writes a realistic, affecting account of the challenges of coming to terms with grief and family difficulties and the process of acceptance and healing." Booklist

Koss, Amy Goldman, 1954-

The girls. Dial Bks. for Young Readers 2000 121p $16.99; pa $5.99

Grades: 5 6 7 8 **Fic**

1. Friendship—Fiction

ISBN 0-8037-2494-2; 0-14-230033-0 (pa)

LC 99-19318

"One Saturday morning a girl finds out that her group of friends, for reasons unknown, has decided to exclude her. As the short novel moves over the course of the weekend, five girls narrate in turns, each moving the story forward as well as providing sometimes unwitting commentary on her friends' versions of events." Horn Book Guide

"This provocative page-turner will be passed from one girl to the next." SLJ

The not-so-great depression. Roaring Brook Press 2010 266p pa $9.99

Grades: 5 6 7 8 **Fic**

1. Recessions—Fiction 2. Unemployment—Fiction 3. Mother-daughter relationship—Fiction

ISBN 978-1-59643-613-8; 1-59643-613-1

Jacki's ninth–grade teacher is always going on about the unemployment index and the recession, but nothing sinks in until her mom is laid off and everything seems to cost more than they can afford.

"Koss makes the economic reality accessible while giving readers a character with whom they can either identify or relate to a friend they might know. . . . Koss' writing is smooth, and the dialogue keeps things moving briskly." Booklist

Krensky, Stephen, 1953-

Dangerous crossing; the revolutionary voyage of John Quincy Adams; by Stephen Krensky; illustrated by Greg Harlin. Dutton Children's Books 2005 unp il $16.99

Grades: 2 3 4   **Fic**
   1. Adams, John Quincy, 1767-1848—Fiction 2. Adams, John, 1735-1826—Fiction 3. Voyages and travels—Fiction 4. United States—History—1775-1783, Revolution—Fiction
   ISBN 0-525-46966-4   LC 2003-40852
In 1778, ten-year-old Johnny Adams and his father make a dangerous midwinter voyage from Massachusetts to Paris in hopes of gaining support for the colonies during the American Revolution
   "Harlin's richly atmospheric paintings dramatize scene after scene with subtle hues and lighting effects. . . . The story offers a stirring account of life aboard ship, spiced with details from the voyage. An appended author's note comments on the story's source and the illustrious careers of the two Adamses." Booklist

Kress, Adrienne

Alex and the Ironic Gentleman. Weinstein Books 2007 310p $16.95; pa $6.99

Grades: 4 5 6 7   **Fic**
   1. Pirates—Fiction 2. Buried treasure—Fiction 3. Adventure fiction
   ISBN 978-1-60286-005-6; 1-60286-005-X; 978-1-60286-025-4 (pa); 1-60286-025-4 (pa)
   Companion novel to: Timothy and the dragon's gate (2008)
   "Alex, who lives with her uncle in the flat above their doorknob shop, is dreading the sixth grade . . . but on the first day she learns that a new teacher has been installed—the young Mr. Underwood. . . . He turns out to be a descendant of a famous pirate, and soon three vicious men turn up in town, looking for a map to a fabled family treasure. . . . Kress has a delightfully simple, observational prose style. . . . This inspired book should hold up to many re-readings." Publ Wkly

Krieg, Jim

Griff Carver, hallway patrol. Razorbill 2010 224p $15.99

Grades: 4 5 6 7   **Fic**
   1. Counterfeits and counterfeiting—Fiction 2. School stories
   ISBN 978-1-59514-276-4; 1-59514-276-2
                   LC 2009032553
Legendary Griff Carver joins the Rampart Middle School Hallway Patrol and, with the help of his friend Tommy, Griff solves the case of counterfeit hall passes.
   "With comically over-the-top cop lingo . . . Griff and Tommy tell their stories through incident reports and interviews, adding drama and humor to the most mundane aspects of school. . . . Krieg will keep readers chuckling through the hilarious but action-packed showdown." Publ Wkly

Krull, Kathleen, 1952-

Fartiste; [by] Kathleen Krull and Paul Brewer; illustrated by Boris Kulikov. Simon & Schuster Books for Young Readers 2008 unp il $16.99

Grades: 3 4 5   **Fic**
   1. Pujol, Joseph, 1857-1945—Fiction 2. Entertainers—Fiction 3. Paris (France)—Fiction 4. Stories in rhyme
   ISBN 978-1-4169-2828-7; 1-4169-2828-6
                   LC 2007-37526
In nineteenth-century France, Joseph Pujol, a little boy who can control his farts, grows up to become Le Petomaine, making audiences laugh at the Moulin Rouge in Paris with his animal noises, songs, and other sounds. Includes facts about Joseph Pujol and life in turn-of-the-century Paris.
   "Written in well-rhymed couplets, this gleefully tasteless tale reads easily. Kulikov's illustrations allude to the age of vaudevillian stage performance, painted playbills, and fire-hazard footlights that bronzed everything nearest them in golden warmth." SLJ

Krumgold, Joseph, 1908-1980

Onion John; illustrated by Symeon Shimin. Crowell 1959 248p il lib bdg $15.89; pa $5.95

Grades: 5 6 7 8   **Fic**
   1. Friendship—Fiction
   ISBN 0-690-04698-7 (lib bdg); 0-06-440144-8 (pa)
   Awarded the Newbery Medal, 1960
   The story "of Andy Rusch, twelve, and European-born Onion John, the town's odd-jobs man and vegetable peddler who lives in a stone hut and frequents the dump. Andy . . . tells of their . . . friendship and of how he and his father, as well as Onion John, are affected when the Rotary Club, at his father's instigation, attempts to transform Onion John's way of life." Booklist
   "The writing has dignity and strength. There is conflict, drama, and excellent character portrayal." SLJ

Kuhlman, Evan

The last invisible boy; written by Evan Kuhlman; illustrated by J. P. Coovert. Atheneum Books for Young Readers 2008 233p il $16.99; pa $5.99

Grades: 4 5 6 7   **Fic**
   1. Bereavement—Fiction 2. Father-son relationship—Fiction 3. Family life—Fiction 4. School stories 5. Ohio—Fiction
   ISBN 978-1-4169-5797-3; 1-4169-5797-9; 978-1-4169-6089-8 (pa); 1-4169-6089-9 (pa)
                   LC 2007-40258
   "Ginee Seo books"
In the wake of his father's sudden death, twelve-year-old Finn feels he is becoming invisible as his hair and skin become whiter by the day, and so he writes and illustrates a book to try to understand what is happening and to hold on to himself and his father
   "Vivid details . . . add depth to the characterizations and grow in meaning as the story progresses. . . . Finn's distinct narrative voice, and the sweet precision with which the story unfolds, give this title a touching resonance." Booklist

Kuijer, Guus, 1942-

The book of everything; a novel; translated by John Nieuwenhuizen. Arthur A. Levine Books 2006 101p $16.99 paperback o.p.

Grades: 5 6 7 8   **Fic**

1. Christian life—Fiction 2. Family life—Fiction 3. Netherlands—Fiction

ISBN 0-439-74918-2; 0-439-74919-0 (pa)

LC 2005-18717

Nine-year-old Thomas receives encouragement from many sources, including candid talks with Jesus, to help him tolerate the strict family life dictated by his deeply-religious father.

"Set in Amsterdam in 1951, this slender Dutch novel is filled with quirky characters, frightening family confrontations, and laugh-out-loud moments. Dark humor and a wry, ironic tone . . . give the story a sharp edge." Booklist

Kurtz, Jane

The storyteller's beads. Harcourt Brace & Co. 1998 154p $15

Grades: 5 6 7 8   **Fic**

1. Friendship—Fiction 2. Prejudices—Fiction 3. Blind—Fiction 4. Ethiopia—Fiction

ISBN 0-15-201074-2   LC 97-42312

"Gulliver books"

During the political strife and famine of the 1980's, two Ethiopian girls, one Christian and the other Jewish and blind, struggle to overcome many difficulties, including their prejudices about each other, as they make the dangerous journey out of Ethiopia

"The novel presents an involving portrait of Ethiopian culture through the eyes of two well-defined characters." Horn Book Guide

Kushner, Ellen, 1955-

The golden dreydl; [by] Ellen Kushner; illustrations by Ilene Winn-Lederer. Charlesbridge 2007 126p il $15.95

Grades: 3 4 5   **Fic**

1. Hanukkah—Fiction 2. Jews—Fiction 3. Magic—Fiction

ISBN 978-1-58089-135-6   LC 2006021257

After receiving a magic dreydl at Aunt Leah's Chanukah party, Sara is catapulted into an alternate world of demons, fools, sorcerers, and sages

"The chatty storytelling is fast, furious, and sometimes funny, . . . and scattered throughout are delicate black-and-white illustrations that capture the magical realism." Booklist

La Fevers, R. L.

Flight of the phoenix; illustrated by Kelly Murphy. Houghton Mifflin Books for Children 2009 137p il (Nathaniel Fludd, Beastologist) $16

Grades: 3 4 5   **Fic**

1. Adventure fiction 2. Phoenix (Mythical bird)—Fiction 3. Mythical animals—Fiction 4. Cousins—Fiction 5. Bedouins—Fiction 6. Orphans—Fiction 7. Middle East—Fiction

ISBN 978-0-547-23865-4; 0-547-23865-7

LC 2009-28799

In 1928, when timid ten-year-old Nate learns that his parents have been lost at sea, he joins his father's cousin on a flight to Arabia where they must oversee the death and rebirth of the phoenix, thus beginning his training as a "beastologist."

"This is a solid start to a new series. . . . The story is packed with adventure and mythological creatures. Children who love fantasy, myth, exotic settings, and even a little dose of history will relate to Nate." SLJ

Another title in this series is:

The basilisk's lair (2010)

Theodosia and the Serpents of Chaos; illustrated by Yoko Tanaka. Houghton Mifflin 2007 343p il $16; pa $6.99

Grades: 4 5 6 7   **Fic**

1. Adventure fiction 2. Museums—Fiction 3. Magic—Fiction 4. Egypt—Fiction 5. London (England)—Fiction

ISBN 978-0-618-75638-4; 0-618-75638-8; 978-0-618-99976-7 (pa); 0-618-99976-0 (pa)

LC 2006-34284

Set in 1906 London and Cairo, this mystery adventure introduces an intrepid heroine—Theodosia Throckmorton, who is thrust into the heart of a mystery when she learns an ancient Egyptian amulet carries a curse that threatens to crumble the British Empire

"It's the delicious, precise, and atmospheric details (nicely extended in Tanaka's few, stylized illustrations) that will capture and hold readers." Booklist

Another title about Theodosia is:

Theodosia and the Staff of Osiris (2008)

LaFaye, A., 1970-

Water steps. Milkweed Editions 2009 175p $16.95; pa $6.95

Grades: 4 5 6 7   **Fic**

1. Phobias—Fiction 2. Water—Fiction 3. Irish Americans—Fiction

ISBN 978-1-57131-687-5; 1-57131-687-6; 978-1-57131-686-8 (pa); 1-57131-686-8 (pa)

LC 2008011684

Eleven-year-old Kyna, terrified of water since her family drowned in a storm that nearly took her life as well, works to overcome her phobia when her adoptive parents, Irish immigrants with a mysterious past, rent a cabin on Lake Champlain for the summer.

"The language is almost poetic with its use of sensory detail, alliteration, and precise word choices. A satisfying story of overcoming one's fears and discovering secrets." SLJ

Worth. Simon & Schuster Books for Young Readers 2004 144p $15.95; pa $5.99

Grades: 5 6 7 8   **Fic**

1. Frontier and pioneer life—Fiction 2. Orphans—Fiction 3. Nebraska—Fiction

ISBN 0-689-85730-6; 1-4169-1624-5 (pa)

LC 2003-8101

After breaking his leg, eleven-year-old Nate feels useless because he cannot work on the family farm in nineteenth-century Nebraska, so when his father brings home an orphan boy to help with the chores, Nate feels even worse.

"This short tale has a quietly epic sweep." Horn Book Guide

LaFleur, Suzanne M., 1983-

Love, Aubrey. Wendy Lamb Books 2009 262p $15.99; lib bdg $18.99 *

Grades: 5 6 7 8   **Fic**

1. Abandoned children—Fiction 2. Bereavement—Fiction 3. Grandmothers—Fiction 4. Letters—Fiction 5. Friendship—Fiction 6. School stories 7. Depression (Psychology)—Fiction 8. Vermont—Fiction

ISBN   978-0-385-73774-6;   0-385-73774-2; 978-0-385-90686-9 (lib bdg); 0-385-90686-2 (lib bdg)

LC 2008-31742

While living with her Gram in Vermont, eleven-year-old Aubrey writes letters as a way of dealing with losing her father and sister in a car accident, and then being abandoned by her grief-stricken mother.

Aubrey's "detailed progression from denial to acceptance makes her both brave and credible in this honest and realistic portrayal of grief." Kirkus

Lairamore, Dawn

Ivy's ever after. Holiday House 2010 311p $16.95

Grades: 5 6 7 8   **Fic**

1. Fairy tales 2. Dragons—Fiction 3. Princesses—Fiction

ISBN 978-0-8234-2261-6; 0-8234-2261-5

LC 2009-43288

Fourteen-year-old Ivy, a most unroyal princess, befriends Elridge, the dragon sent to keep her in a tower, and together they set out on a perilous quest to find Ivy's fairy godmother, who may be able to save both from their dire fates.

"Ivy is an engaging alternative to the standard damsel-in-distress figure, and with a lushly vivid setting, witty dialogue, and lots of adventure, this well-plotted first novel will appeal to fans of Vivian Vande Velde's A Hidden Magic (1985) and A Well-Timed Enchantment (1990)." Booklist

Lake, A. J.

The coming of dragons. Bloomsbury 2006 239p (Darkest age) $16.95; pa $7.99

Grades: 5 6 7 8   **Fic**

1. Magic—Fiction 2. Dragons—Fiction 3. Great Britain—Fiction 4. Fantasy fiction

ISBN   978-1-58234-965-7;   1-58234-965-7; 978-1-58234-902-2 (pa); 1-58234-902-9 (pa)

LC 2005030623

Two eleven-year-olds named Edmund and Elspeth discover that they have been given fantastic gifts to use against the ancient and evil forces that have been awakened by powerful magic during the Dark Ages in Great Britain

"This early medieval tale that blends adventure, suspense, friendship, and magic as well as the savage world of wild boars, malevolent knights, dragons, and ancient evil will appeal to boys and girls alike." Voice Youth Advocates

Landy, Derek

Skulduggery Pleasant. HarperCollinsPublishers 2007 392p $17.99; lib bdg $18.89; pa $7.99 *

Grades: 4 5 6 7   **Fic**

1. Magic—Fiction 2. Fantasy fiction

ISBN   978-0-06-123115-5;   0-06-123115-0; 978-0-06-123116-2 (lib bdg); 0-06-123116-9 (lib bdg); 978-0-06-123117-9 (pa); 0-06-123117-7 (pa)

LC 2006-29403

When twelve-year-old Stephanie inherits her weird uncle's estate, she must join forces with Skulduggery Pleasant, a skeleton mage, to save the world from the Faceless Ones

This "is a rich fantasy that is as engaging in its creative protagonists and villains as it is in the lightning-paced plot and sharp humor." Bulletin Cent Child Books

Other titles in this series are:
Playing with fire (2008)
The faceless ones (2009)

Lane, Kathleen, 1967-

Nana cracks the case! concept by Cabell Harris; illustrated by Sarah Horne. Chronicle Books 2009 112p il $14.99

Grades: 2 3 4   **Fic**

1. Grandmothers—Fiction 2. Candy—Fiction 3. Mystery fiction

ISBN 978-0-8118-6258-5; 0-8118-6258-5

LC 2007037929

Eufala and Bog's very feisty grandmother takes a job with the Crispy County Police Department, searching for a candy thief.

"The many quirky text asides and black-and-white illustrations add to an already funny and kid-friendly premise." Horn Book Guide

Langston, Laura

The trouble with Cupid; [by] Laura Langston. Fitzhenry & Whiteside 2009 251p pa $11.95

Grades: 5 6 7 8   **Fic**

1. School stories 2. Dogs—Fiction

ISBN 978-1-55455-059-3 (pa); 1-55455-059-9 (pa)

All Erin has to do is train the school mascot to perform on cue, and she will be a hero. But none of her dog-training experience has prepared Erin for Cupid, the laziest, most unlovable dog that ever woofed

"The story is a quick and entertaining read with believable characters. Although lighthearted, the plot introduces the themes of animal exploitation and the importance of standing up for one's principles." SLJ

Langton, Jane

The fledgling. Harper & Row 1980 182p il lib bdg $15.89; pa $5.95

Grades: 5 6 7 8   **Fic**

1. Geese—Fiction 2. Fantasy fiction

ISBN 0-06-023679-5 (lib bdg); 0-06-440121-9 (pa)

LC 79-2008

A Newbery Medal honor book, 1981
"An Ursula Nordstrom book"
"Quiet, introspective Georgie . . . yearns to fly. An encounter with a large, old Canadian goose, which stops

Langton, Jane—*Continued*

at Walden Pond on its migratory journey south, brings her that chance. . . . Then neighboring Mr. Preek, who tries to save Georgie from what he thinks is an attacking predator, and Miss Prawn, who sees the girl's feat as a saintly sign, interfere." Booklist

"The writing is alternately solemn and funny, elevated and colloquial. It is mythic, almost sacred, in passages involving Georgie and the goose; it is satiric, almost irreverent, when it relates to Mr. Preek and Miss Prawn." Horn Book

Lasky, Kathryn

Broken song. Viking 2005 154p hardcover o.p. pa $6.99

Grades: 5 6 7 8   **Fic**
1. Jews—Fiction 2. Russia—Fiction 3. Violinists—Fiction
ISBN 0-670-05931-5; 0-14-240741-0 (pa)
LC 2004-17741

In 1897, fifteen-year-old Reuven Bloom, a Russian Jew, must set aside his dreams of playing the violin in order to save himself and his baby sister after the rest of their family is murdered

"Through rich prose filled with imagery, distinct characterization, and historical research, Lasky breathes life into the horrific history of anti-Semitism in Russia in the late-19th and early-20th centuries." SLJ

Dancing through fire. Scholastic Inc. 2005 172p (Portraits) $9.99

Grades: 4 5 6   **Fic**
1. Ballet—Fiction 2. Paris (France)—Fiction
ISBN 0-439-71009-X

Sylvie dreams of being a prima ballerina. When the Franco-Prussian war begins in 1870, Sylvie is thrown into turmoil and tragedy. Sylvie must rely on the strength that ballet gives her in order to survive and acheive her goal.

"Though readers may be unfamiliar with this historical period, they will be swept along by the strong story line. Young dancers will particularly enjoy the evocative passages when Sylvie is on stage or in class." Booklist

Elizabeth I; red rose of the House of Tudor. Scholastic 1999 237p il (Royal diaries) $10.95

Grades: 4 5 6 7   **Fic**
1. Elizabeth I, Queen of England, 1533-1603—Fiction 2. Great Britain—History—1485-1603, Tudors—Fiction
ISBN 0-590-68484-1   LC 99-11178

In a series of diary entries, Princess Elizabeth, the eleven-year-old daughter of King Henry VIII, celebrates holidays and birthdays, relives her mother's execution, revels in her studies, and agonizes over her father's health

"Well written and captivating." Voice Youth Advocates

Felix takes the stage; illustrated by Stephen Gilpin. Scholastic Press 2010 142p il (The Deadlies) $15.99

Grades: 4 5 6   **Fic**
1. Spiders—Fiction 2. Moving—Fiction
ISBN 978-0-545-11681-7; 0-545-11681-3

Having been discovered, a family of poisonous but friendly brown recluse spiders must flee their cozy home in a symphony hall and go searching for a new place to live.

"Humor and action seamlessly blend as these arachnids struggle for survival against the scary E-Men who threaten them with extermination. Vivid characters, from the theatrical godspider Fat Cat to the pompous orb weaver Oliphant Uxbridge, make up the clever supporting cast. Genuinely funny dialogue helps move the brief chapters along, and Gilpin's lively black-and-white drawings provide an animated accompaniment." Kirkus

Lone wolf. Scholastic Press 2010 219p il map (Wolves of the Beyond, 1) $16.99

Grades: 5 6 7 8   **Fic**
1. Wolves—Fiction 2. Fantasy fiction
ISBN 978-0-545-09310-1; 0-545-09310-4
LC 2009-17007

Abandoned by his pack, a baby wolf with a mysterious mark on his deformed paw survives and embarks on a journey that will change the world of the wolves of the Beyond.

"Lasky merges anthropomorphic fantasy with realistic details about wolves and bears to produce an almost plausible emotional narrative, complete with dialogue and personalities. . . . The author builds a captivating world of forest, snow and volcanoes populated by intelligent animals and weaves a compelling story sure to bring readers back for the second installment." Kirkus

The night journey; [by] Kathryn Lasky. Viking 2005 151p $15.99; pa $5.99

Grades: 4 5 6 7   **Fic**
1. Jews—Fiction 2. Russia—Fiction
ISBN 0-670-05963-3; 0-14-240322-9 (pa)
LC 2005276376

A reissue of the title first published 1981 by Warne

Rachel ignores her parents' wishes and persuades her great-grandmother to relate the story of her escape from czarist Russia.

"The novel shifts back and forth from the dangerous journey out of Russia to Rachel's own casual, secure life at home and school. These transitions are handled with a smoothness that doesn't break the intrinsic tension of the story, and the contrast between the two lives demonstrates with poignant clarity the real meaning of freedom." SLJ

Two bad pilgrims; illustrated by John Manders; color work by Vince Dorse. Viking 2009 unp il $16.99

Grades: 2 3 4   **Fic**
1. Billington, John, d. 1630—Fiction 2. Billington family—Fiction 3. Pilgrims (New England colonists)—Fiction
ISBN 978-0-670-06168-6; 0-670-06168-9
LC 2008-37645

Lasky, Kathryn—*Continued*

Brothers Francis and Johnny Billington take issue with history's account of their troublemaking ways aboard the Mayflower and in the New World, as they tell their side of the story to Standish Brewster, professor of Pilgrimology at Plimouth University.

"The comic-book style of the artwork cartoony characters, speech balloons, and action broken up into panels will help attract kids who may be resistant to history books. . . . This book does a solid job of showing, rather than just telling, that history can be more lively than it may seem. A fine author's note separates fact from fancy." Booklist

Latham, Irene

Leaving Gee's Bend. G.P. Putnam's Sons 2010 230p $16.99

Grades: 5 6 7 8   Fic
1. Quilts—Fiction 2. African Americans—Fiction 3. Alabama—Fiction
ISBN 978-0-399-25179-5; 0-399-25179-0
                                    LC 2009-08732

Ludelphia Bennett, a determined, ten-year-old African American girl in 1932 Gee's Bend, Alabama, leaves home in an effort to find medical help for her sick mother, and she recounts her ensuing adventures in a quilt she is making.

"Ludelphia's voice is authentic and memorable, and Latham captures the tension of her dangerous journey and the racism she encounters." Booklist

Law, Ingrid, 1970-

Savvy. Dial Books for Young Readers 2008 342p $16.99 *

Grades: 4 5 6 7   Fic
1. Magic—Fiction 2. Family life—Fiction 3. Voyages and travels—Fiction
ISBN 978-0-8037-3306-0; 0-8037-3306-2
                                    LC 2007-39814

A Newbery Medal honor book, 2009

Recounts the adventures of Mississippi (Mibs) Beaumont, whose thirteenth birthday has revealed her "savvy"—a magical power unique to each member of her family—just as her father is injured in a terrible accident.

"Short chapters and cliffhangers keep the pace quick, while the mix of traditional language and vernacular helps the story feel both fresh and timeless. . . . [This is] a vibrant and cinematic novel that readers are going to love." Publ Wkly

Lawlor, Laurie

He will go fearless; [by] Laurie Lawlor. Simon & Schuster Books for Young Readers 2006 210p $15.95

Grades: 5 6 7 8   Fic
1. Father-son relationship—Fiction 2. United States—History—1865-1898—Fiction 3. Overland journeys to the Pacific—Fiction
ISBN 0-689-86579-1   LC 2005-06129

With the Civil War ended and Reconstruction begun, fifteen-year-old Billy resolves to make the dangerous and challenging journey West in search of real fortune – his

true father.

"Danger, adventure, and survival combine to make this a richly detailed story." SLJ

The school at Crooked Creek; illustrated by Ronald Himler. Holiday House 2004 83p il map $15.95

Grades: 3 4 5   Fic
1. Frontier and pioneer life—Fiction 2. School stories 3. Indiana—Fiction
ISBN 0-8234-1812-X   LC 2003-56759

Living on the nineteenth-century Indiana frontier with his parents and irritable older sister Louise, six-year-old Beansie dreads his first day of school, but his resilience surprises even his sister.

"The book is rich with colloquial language, superstitions, and information about the lifestyle of this pioneer family. Nicely done shaded, pencil drawings help set the tone." SLJ

Lawrence, Iain, 1955-

The convicts; [by] Iain Lawrence. Delacorte Press 2005 198p hardcover o.p. pa $5.99 *

Grades: 5 6 7 8   Fic
1. Prisoners—Fiction 2. Adventure fiction
ISBN 0-385-73087-X; 0-440-41932-8 (pa)
                                    LC 2004-14968

His efforts to avenge his father's unjust imprisonment force thirteen-year-old Tom Tin into the streets of nineteenth-century London, but after he is convicted of murder, Tom is eventually sent to Australia where he has a surprise reunion.

"The story abounds in terrifying villains, grime, misery, and cruelty. Yet it also serves up a fair share of optimism. . . . This book is . . . action packed and . . . thoroughly researched. . . . Give it to reluctant readers who are looking for an exciting adventure." SLJ

Other titles in this series are:
The cannibals (2005)
The castaways (2007)

The giant-slayer. Delacorte Press 2009 292p $16.99 *

Grades: 5 6 7 8   Fic
1. Poliomyelitis—Fiction 2. Storytelling—Fiction 3. Imagination—Fiction 4. Medical care—Fiction 5. Father-daughter relationship—Fiction
ISBN 978-0-385-73376-2; 0-385-73376-3
                                    LC 2008-35409

When her eight-year-old neighbor is stricken with polio in 1955, eleven-year-old Laurie discovers that there is power in her imagination as she weaves a story during her visits with him and other patients confined to iron lung machines.

This is "compelling. . . . This effectively shows how children face life-changing challenges with incredible determination." Booklist

Lord of the nutcracker men. Delacorte Press 2001 212p map hardcover o.p. pa $5.99

Grades: 5 6 7 8   Fic
1. World War, 1914-1918—Fiction
ISBN 0-385-72924-3; 0-440-41812-7 (pa)
                                    LC 2001-17254

Lawrence, Iain, 1955- —*Continued*

Johnny, a ten year old English boy, comes to believe that the battles he enacts with his toy soldiers control the war his father is fighting on the front in World War I

"There's realism in the grief of the village people and also in Dad's poignant letters. . . . This will be a fine introduction to World War I, both for personal interest and for curriculum use." Booklist

The wreckers. Delacorte Press 1998 196p hardcover o.p. pa $5.99 *

Grades: 5 6 7 8   **Fic**

1. Shipwrecks—Fiction 2. Adventure fiction 3. Great Britain—History—1714-1837—Fiction

ISBN 0-385-32535-5; 0-440-41545-4 (pa)

LC 97-31625

"In 1799 fourteen-year-old John Spencer survives a shipwreck on the coast of Cornwall. To his horror, he soon learns that the villagers are not rescuers, but pirates who lure ships ashore in order to plunder their cargoes. . . . Lawrence creates an edge-of-the-chair survival/mystery story. Fast-moving, mesmerizing." Horn Book Guide

Other titles in this series are:

The buccaneers (2001)
Ghost boy (2000)
The smugglers (1999)

Lawson, Robert, 1892-1957

Ben and me; a new and astonishing life of Benjamin Franklin, as written by his good mouse Amos; lately discovered, edited and illustrated by Robert Lawson. Little, Brown 1939 113p il hardcover o.p. pa $5.95

Grades: 5 6 7 8   **Fic**

1. Franklin, Benjamin, 1706-1790—Fiction 2. Mice—Fiction

ISBN 0-316-51732-1; 0-316-51730-5 (pa)

"How Amos, a poor church mouse, oldest son of a large family, went forth into the world to make his living, and established himself in Benjamin Franklin's old fur cap, 'a rough frontier-cabin type of residence,' and made himself indispensable to Ben with his advice and information, and incidentally let himself in for some very strange experiences is related here in a merry compound of fact and fancy." Bookmark

"The sophisticated and clever story is illustrated by even more sophisticated and clever line drawings." Roundabout of Books

Mr. Revere and I; set down and embellished with numerous drawings by Robert Lawson. Little, Brown 1953 152p il pa $5.95 hardcover o.p.

Grades: 5 6 7 8   **Fic**

1. Revere, Paul, 1735-1818—Fiction 2. Horses—Fiction 3. United States—History—1775-1783, Revolution—Fiction

ISBN 0-316-51729-1 (pa)

"Being an account of certain episodes in the career of Paul Revere, Esq., as recently revealed by his horse, Scheherazade, late pride of His Royal Majesty's 14th Regiment of Foot." Subtitle

"A delightful tale which is perfect for reading aloud to the whole family. The make-up is excellent, illustra-

tions are wonderful, and the reader will get a very interesting picture of the American Revolution." Libr J

Rabbit Hill. Viking 1944 127p il lib bdg $16.99; pa $5.99

Grades: 3 4 5 6   **Fic**

1. Rabbits—Fiction 2. Animals—Fiction

ISBN 0-670-58675-7 (lib bdg); 0-14-240796-8 (pa)

Awarded the Newbery Medal, 1945

"Story of the great rejoicing among the wild creatures when the news goes round that new people are coming to live in the big house. For people in the big house will mean a garden and a garden means food. Their hopes are rewarded. The new people are 'planting folks' and the garden is big enough to provide for all." Wis Libr Bull

"Robert Lawson, because he loves the Connecticut country and the little animals of field and wood and looks at them with the eye of an artist, a poet and a child, has created for the boy and girl, indeed for the sensitive reader of any age, a whole, fresh, lively, amusing world." N Y Times Book Rev

Followed by The tough winter (1954)

Le Guin, Ursula K., 1929-

Catwings; illustrations by S. D. Schindler. Orchard Bks. 1988 39p il pa $3.99 hardcover o.p.

Grades: 2 3 4   **Fic**

1. Cats—Fiction 2. Fantasy fiction

ISBN 0-439-55189-7 (pa)   LC 87-33104

"A Richard Jackson book"

"When four kittens with wings are born in a rough city neighborhood, their mother nurtures and protects them as they grow and learn to fly. At her urging they soon escape the dangerous streets and alleys, flying to a forest where they find more enemies but, finally, new friends." Booklist

"Le Guin's adroit writing style, the well-observed feline detail, the thematic concern for natural victims of human environment, and the gentle humor make this a prime choice for reading aloud, although one would not want children to miss the fine-line hatch drawings that further project the satisfying sense of reality." Bull Cent Child Books

Other titles about Catwings are:

Catwings return (1989)
Jane on her own (1999)
Wonderful Alexander and the Catwings (1994)

Leach, Sara

Jake Reynolds: chicken or eagle? Orca Book Publishers 2009 101p (Orca young readers) pa $7.95

Grades: 3 4 5   **Fic**

1. Wolves—Fiction 2. Courage—Fiction 3. Fear—Fiction 4. Islands—Fiction

ISBN 978-1-55469-145-6; 1-55469-145-1

Jake dreams of being a superhero, but he's not exactly brave, especially when it comes to wolves living on the island where he and his family are staying.

"The theme of confronting fear is made vivid in this chapter book. . . . [The book offers] a heart-pounding climax and a very satisfying resolution." Booklist

Leck, James

The adventures of Jack Lime; written by James Leck. Kids Can Press 2010 126p $16.95; pa $8.95

Grades: 5 6 7 8   **Fic**

1. Mystery fiction 2. Narcolepsy—Fiction

ISBN   978-1-55453-364-0;   1-55453-364-3; 978-1-55453-365-7 (pa); 1-55453-365-1 (pa)

"Jack Lime is the guy the come to if you've got a problem. . . . He'll find out what needs finding out. . . . This slim volume contains three cases. In the first, Jack susses out the whereabouts of a missing bike. In the second, he shakes down a hamster-napping and blackmail scheme. And in the final, he recounts his first case on the job. . . . All the touchstones that make for great noir are translated for kids. . . . The lingo that makes hard-boiled reading so much fun is here, but never schticky, and Leck knows that a great hero needs a debilitating flaw: for Jack, it's his narcolepsy." Booklist

Lee, Milly

Landed; [by] Milly Lee; pictures by Yangsook Choi. Farrar, Straus & Giroux 2006 unp il $16

        Fic

1. Immigrants—Fiction 2. Chinese Americans—Fiction 3. San Francisco (Calif.)—Fiction

ISBN 0-374-34314-4   LC 2004-47216

"Frances Foster books."

After leaving his village in southeastern China, twelve-year-old Sun is held at Angel Island, San Francisco, before being released to join his father, a merchant living in the area. Includes historical notes

"The story is told with quiet restraint. . . . Choi's beautiful, full-page oil paintings, in sepia tones and shades of green, are quiet and packed with feeling." Booklist

L'Engle, Madeleine, 1918-2007

Meet the Austins. Farrar, Straus & Giroux 1997 216p hardcover o.p. pa $6.99

Grades: 5 6 7 8   **Fic**

1. Family life—Fiction 2. Orphans—Fiction

ISBN 0-374-34929-0; 0-312-37931-5 (pa)

                LC 96-27655

ALA YALSA Margaret A. Edwards Award (1998)

A revised edition of the title first published 1960 by Vanguard Press

This edition includes a "chapter titled 'The Anti-Muffins,' which deals with being concerned for others and true to oneself." Book Rep

A "story of the family of a country doctor, told by the twelve-year-old daughter, during a year in which a spoiled young orphan, Maggy, comes to live with them. . . . [This is an] account of the family's adjustment to Maggy and hers to them." Horn Book

Other titles about the Austins are:

The moon by night (1963)

A ring of endless light (1980)

Troubling a star (1994)

A wrinkle in time. Farrar, Straus & Giroux 1962 211p $17; pa $7.99 *

Grades: 5 6 7 8 9 10   **Fic**

1. Fantasy fiction

ISBN 0-374-38613-7; 0-312-36754-6 (pa)

ALA YALSA Margaret A. Edwards Award (1998)

"A brother and sister, together with a friend, go in search of their scientist father who was lost while engaged in secret work for the government on the tesseract problem. A tesseract is a wrinkle in time. The father is a prisoner on a forbidding planet, and after awesome and terrifying experiences, he is rescued, and the little group returns safely to Earth and home." Child Books Too Good to Miss

"It makes unusual demands on the imagination and consequently gives great rewards." Horn Book

Followed by A wind in the door (1973)

Lennon, Joan, 1953-

Questors. Margaret K. McElderry Books 2007 358p $16.99

Grades: 5 6 7 8   **Fic**

1. Fantasy fiction

ISBN 978-1-4169-3658-9; 1-4169-3658-0

                LC 2006-28895

Three confused children are brought together then, with little training, sent off to save three worlds that were held in perfect balance until a cataclysmic disruption in the space-time continuum threatened their existence, which is just what their enemy desires.

"Fantasy fans . . . will be enthralled by the complex plot set in this strange multilayered world." Bull Cent Child Books

Leonard, Elmore, 1925-

A coyote's in the house. HarperEntertainment 2004 149p il $15.95

Grades: 5 6 7 8   **Fic**

1. Dogs—Fiction 2. Coyotes—Fiction 3. Hollywood (Calif.)—Fiction

ISBN 0-06-054404-X   LC 2003-71050

"Hip coyote Antwan . . . is foraging for garbage when he makes the acquaintance of German shepherd Buddy, a retired film star. Buddy is bored and has decided he'd like the freedom of the coyote's life in the wild, while Antwan . . . is interested in getting to know Miss Betty, a prizewinning poodle who lives with Buddy's family. . . . The story is good fun, but the real pleasure here . . . lies in listening to the characters banter with one another. . . . A poignant ending gives the tale just the right edge." Booklist

Lester, Julius

The old African; illustrated by Jerry Pinkney. Dial Bks. 2005 79p il $19.99 *

Grades: 3 4 5 6   **Fic**

1. Slavery—Fiction 2. African Americans—Fiction 3. Extrasensory perception—Fiction

ISBN 0-8037-2564-7   LC 2003-15671

An elderly slave uses the power of his mind to ease the suffering of his fellow slaves and eventually lead them back to Africa.

"The stirring illustrations, glowing with color and swirling with action, beautifully depict the dramatic escape fantasy (which is based on legend), but they never deny the horror." Booklist

Levine, Gail Carson, 1947-

Dave at night. HarperCollins Pubs. 1999 281p hardcover o.p. pa $5.99

Grades: 5 6 7 8   Fic

    1. Orphans—Fiction 2. Jews—Fiction 3. African Americans—Fiction 4. New York (N.Y.)—Fiction

    ISBN 0-06-028154-5; 0-06-440747-0 (pa)

                      LC 98-50069

When orphaned Dave is sent to the Hebrew Home for Boys where he is treated cruelly, he sneaks out at night and is welcomed into the music- and culture-filled world of the Harlem Renaissance

    "The magic comes from Levine's language and characterization. This novel will provide inspiration for all children while offering a unique view of a culturally diverse New York City." SLJ

    Ella enchanted. HarperCollins Pubs. 1997 232p $16.99; lib bdg $17.89; pa $6.50 *

Grades: 5 6 7 8   Fic

    1. Fantasy fiction

    ISBN 0-06-027510-3; 0-06-027511-1 (lib bdg); 0-06-440705-5 (pa)   LC 96-30734

    A Newbery Medal honor book, 1998

In this novel based on the story of Cinderella, Ella struggles against the childhood curse that forces her to obey any order given to her

    "As finely designed as a tapestry, Ella's story both neatly incorporates elements of the original tale and mightily expands them." Booklist

    Ever. HarperCollinsPublishers 2008 256p $16.99; lib bdg $17.89 *

Grades: 5 6 7 8   Fic

    1. Fate and fatalism—Fiction 2. Gods and goddesses—Fiction 3. Winds—Fiction 4. Immortality—Fiction

    ISBN 978-0-06-122962-6; 0-06-122962-8; 978-0-06-122963-3 (lib bdg); 0-06-122963-6 (lib bdg)

                LC 2007-32289

Fourteen-year-old Kezi and Olus, Akkan god of the winds, fall in love and together try to change her fate—to be sacrificed to a Hyte god because of a rash promise her father made—through a series of quests that might make her immortal.

    "Levine conducts a riveting journey, offering passion and profound pondering along the way." Publ Wkly

    The two princesses of Bamarre. HarperCollins Pubs. 2001 241p $15.99; pa $5.99

Grades: 5 6 7 8   Fic

    1. Fantasy fiction 2. Sisters—Fiction 3. Princesses—Fiction

    ISBN 0-06-029315-2; 0-06-440966-X (pa)

                LC 00-47953

With her adventurous sister, Meryl, suffering from the Gray Death, meek and timid Princess Addie sets out to find a cure

    "A lively tale with vivid characters and an exciting plot." Book Rep

Levine, Kristin, 1974-

The best bad luck I ever had. Putnam 2009 266p $16.99 *

Grades: 5 6 7 8   Fic

    1. Race relations—Fiction 2. Prejudices—Fiction 3. Friendship—Fiction 4. Country life—Fiction 5. Family life—Fiction 6. Alabama—Fiction

    ISBN 978-0-399-25090-3; 0-399-25090-5

                LC 2008-11570

In Moundville, Alabama, in 1917, twelve-year-old Dit hopes the new postmaster will have a son his age, but instead he meets Emma, who is black, and their friendship challenges accepted ways of thinking and leads them to save the life of a condemned man.

    "Tension builds just below the surface of this energetic, seamlessly narrated . . . novel. . . . Levine handles the setting with grace and nuance." Publ Wkly

Levitin, Sonia, 1934-

Journey to America; illustrated by Charles Robinson. Atheneum Pubs. 1993 c1970 150p il pa $4.99 hardcover o.p.

Grades: 4 5 6 7   Fic

    1. World War, 1939-1945—Fiction 2. Jewish refugees—Fiction 3. Family life—Fiction

    ISBN 0-689-71130-1 (pa)   LC 93-163980

    A reissue of the title first published 1970

    "In a strong immigration story, Lisa Platt, the middle daughter, tells how her family is forced to leave Nazi Germany and make a new life in the United States. First their father leaves, then the others escape to Switzerland, where they endure harsh conditions. After months of separation, the family is reunited in New York." Rochman. Against borders

    Followed by Silver days (1989) and Annie's promise (1993)

Levy, Elizabeth, 1942-

My life as a fifth-grade comedian. HarperCollins Pubs. 1997 184p hardcover o.p. pa $4.95

Grades: 4 5 6   Fic

    1. School stories

    ISBN 0-06-026602-3; 0-06-440723-3 (pa)

                 LC 97-3842

    "Bobby loves to joke around, but his constant misbehavior in class is about to land him in the School for Intervention. That's where his older brother went before he got kicked out of school and out of the house. Bobby's last chance to prove himself to his teacher, the principal, and his sarcastic father is to organize a school-wide stand-up comedy contest." Publisher's note

    "Levy incorporates a cornucopia of jokes and a wealth of subtle advice on becoming a comic. There is great pleasure in seeing Bobby and his father's earlier sarcasm and angry dialogue transformed by a turn of attitude into universal, and really funny comedy." SLJ

Lewis, C. S. (Clive Staples), 1898-1963

The lion, the witch, and the wardrobe; illustrated by Pauline Baynes. HarperCollins Pubs. 1994 189p il $16.99; lib bdg $17.89; pa $7.99 *

Grades: 4 5 6 7   **Fic**

1. Fantasy fiction
ISBN 0-06-023481-4; 0-06-023482-2 (lib bdg); 0-06-440499-4 (pa)   LC 93-8889

A reissue of the title first published 1950 by Macmillan

Four English schoolchildren find their way through the back of a wardrobe into the magic land of Narnia and assist Aslan, the golden lion, to triumph over the White Witch, who has cursed the land with eternal winter

This begins "the 'Narnia' stories, outstanding modern fairy tales with an underlying theme of good overcoming evil." Child Books Too Good to Miss

Other titles about Narnia are:
The horse and his boy (1954)
The last battle (1956)
The magician's nephew (1956)
Prince Caspian (1951)
The silver chair (1953)
The voyage of the Dawn Treader (1952)

Lewis, Elizabeth Foreman, 1892-1958

Young Fu of the upper Yangtze; [by] Elizabeth Foreman Lewis; illustrations by William Low. 75th anniversary ed. Henry Holt 2007 xii, 302p il $17.95; pa $7.99

Grades: 4 5 6   **Fic**

1. City and town life—Fiction 2. China—Fiction
ISBN   978-0-8050-8113-8;   0-8050-8113-5; 978-0-312-38007-6 (pa); 0-312-38007-0 (pa)
                                         LC 2006049633

Awarded the Newbery Medal, 1933

A newly illustrated edition of the title first published 1932 by The John C. Winston Company

In the 1920's, a Chinese youth from the country comes to Chungking with his mother where the bustling city offers adventure and his apprenticeship to a coppersmith brings good fortune

This edition "features a foreword by Katherine Paterson, extensive end-notes comparing China then and now, and new, atmospheric black-and-white illustrations." Horn Book Guide

Lewis, Maggie

Morgy makes his move; illustrated by Michael Chesworth. Houghton Mifflin 1999 74p il $15; pa $4.95 *

Grades: 2 3 4   **Fic**

1.   Moving—Fiction   2.   School   stories 3. Massachusetts—Fiction
ISBN 0-395-92284-4; 0-618-19680-3 (pa)
                                           LC 98-43245

When third-grader Morgy MacDougal-MacDuff moves from California to Massachusetts with his parents, he has a lot of new things to get used to before he feels comfortable

"Heavy issues are handled lightly; language is simple and straightforward; Michael Chesworth's illustrations are funny and exaggerated." Booklist

Other titles about Morgy are:

Morgy coast to coast (2005)
Morgy's musical summer (2008)

Lin, Grace, 1974-

Where the mountain meets the moon. Little, Brown and Co. 2009 278p il $16.99 *

Grades: 4 5 6 7   **Fic**

1. Fairy tales 2. Dragons—Fiction 3. Moon—Fiction
ISBN 978-0-316-11427-1; 0-316-11427-8
                                         LC 2008-32818

ALA ALSC Newbery Medal Honor Book (2010)

Minli, an adventurous girl from a poor village, buys a magical goldfish, and then joins a dragon who cannot fly on a quest to find the Old Man of the Moon in hopes of bringing life to Fruitless Mountain and freshness to Jade River.

"With beautiful language, Lin creates a strong, memorable heroine and a mystical land. . . . Children will embrace this accessible, timeless story about the evil of greed and the joy of gratitude." Booklist

The Year of the Dog; a novel. Little, Brown 2006 134p il $14.99; pa $5.99 *

Grades: 3 4 5   **Fic**

1. Taiwanese Americans—Fiction 2. Chinese New Year—Fiction
ISBN 0-316-06000-3; 0-316-06002-X (pa)
                                         LC 2005-02586

Frustrated at her seeming lack of talent for anything, Pacy, a young Taiwanese American girl, sets out to apply the lessons of the Chinese Year of the Dog, those of making best friends and finding oneself, to her own life.

"The story . . . is entertaining and often illuminating. Appealing, childlike decorative drawings add a delightful flavor to a gentle tale full of humor." Horn Book

Another title about Pacy is:
The Year of the Rat (2008)

Lindgren, Astrid, 1907-2002

Pippi Longstocking; [by] Astrid Lindgren; translated by Tiina Nunnally; illustrated by Lauren Child. Viking Children's Books 2007 207p il $25 *

Grades: 3 4 5 6   **Fic**

1. Sweden—Fiction
ISBN 978-0-670-06276-8
Original Swedish edition, 1945

Escapades of a lucky little girl who lives with a horse and a monkey—but without any parents—at the edge of a Swedish village.

"This oversize edition of the classic story has much to offer a new generation of readers. It has full-color illustrations . . . and a new translation. . . . Nunnally's language flows naturally and gives a fresh, modern feel to the line drawings, filled with color and pattern." SLJ

Other titles about Pippi Longstocking are:
Pippi goes on board (1957)
Pippi in the South Seas (1959)

Lindgren, Astrid, 1907-2002—*Continued*

Ronia, the robber's daughter; translated by Patricia Crampton. Viking 1983 176p hardcover o.p. pa $5.99

Grades: 4 5 6   **Fic**

1. Thieves—Fiction 2. Middle Ages—Fiction

ISBN 0-670-60640-5; 0-14-031720-1 (pa)

LC 82-60081

Original Swedish edition, 1981

Ronia, who lives with her father and his band of robbers in a castle in the woods, causes trouble when she befriends the son of a rival robber chieftain

"The book is full of high adventure, hairsbreadth escapes, droll earthy humor, and passionate emotional energy; and cast over the whole narrative is a primitive, ecstastic respones to the changing seasons and the wonders of nature." Horn Book

Lindo, Elvira, 1962-

Manolito Four-Eyes; illustrated by Emilio Urberuaga; translated by Joanne Moriarity. Marshall Cavendish Children 2008 144p il (Manolito Four-Eyes) $15.99

Grades: 4 5 6   **Fic**

1. Family life—Fiction 2. Grandfathers—Fiction 3. School stories 4. Spain—Fiction

ISBN 978-0-7614-5303-1; 0-7614-5303-2

Original Spanish edition 2003

Recounts the exploits of the irrepressible Manolito as he navigates the world of his small Madrid neighborhood, along with his grandpa, his little brother, and his school friends.

"The protagonist is a wild, spunky, dramatic, comical sort of character sure to be popular with children, who will probably find him, in Manolito's own inimitable words, a 'whole lotta cool.' Lively cartoon illustrations are scattered throughout." SLJ

Other titles about Manolito are:

Manolito Four-Eyes: the 2nd volume of the great encyclopedia of my life (2009)

Manolito Four-Eyes: the 3rd volume of the great encyclopedia of my life (2010)

Lisle, Holly, 1960-

The Ruby Key. Orchard Books 2008 361p (Moon & sun) $16.99; pa $7.99

Grades: 5 6 7 8   **Fic**

1. Fantasy fiction 2. Siblings—Fiction

ISBN 978-0-545-00012-3;   0-545-00012-2; 978-0-545-00013-0 (pa); 0-545-00013-0 (pa)

LC 2007-30217

In a world where an uneasy peace binds Humans and Nightlings, fourteen-year-old Genna and her twelve-year-old brother Dan learn of their uncle's plot to gain immortality in exchange for human lives, and the two strike their own bargain with the Nightling lord, which sets them on a dangerous journey along the Moonroads in search of a key.

"Lisle's fertile imagination provides the nightworlds with monsters . . . but it is her clever plotting in this . . . fantasy, leading up to a thrilling finish . . . That will bewitch her audience." Horn Book

Followed by: The silver door (2009)

Lisle, Janet Taylor, 1947-

Afternoon of the elves. Orchard Bks. 1989 122p hardcover o.p. pa $6.99

Grades: 4 5 6   **Fic**

1. Friendship—Fiction 2. Mentally ill—Fiction

ISBN 0-531-05837-9; 0-698-11806-5 (pa)

LC 88-35099

A Newbery Medal honor book, 1990

"Nine-year-old Hillary has a happy home, all the material possessions she wants, and plenty of friends at school. Eleven-year-old Sara-Kate is an outcast, thin, poorly dressed, with failing grades, a decrepit house, and a weedy yard adjoining Hillary's neat garden. But Sara-Kate has an elf village, and with it she hooks Hillary into a friendship that thrives on elf stories but suffers from Sara-Kate's stormy moods and prickly pride. It is for Hillary to discover that Sara-Kate alone is caring for a mother who is mentally ill, penniless, and unable to provide the most basic physical or emotional necessities." Bull Cent Child Books

"'Afternoon of the elves' is a distinctive portrayal of the way children figure out ways to inhabit the world when there aren't any adults around." N Y Times Book Rev

The art of keeping cool. Atheneum Bks. for Young Readers 2000 207p hardcover o.p. pa $4.99 *

Grades: 5 6 7 8   **Fic**

1. World War, 1939-1945—Fiction 2. Rhode Island—Fiction

ISBN 0-689-83787-9; 0-689-83788-7 (pa)

LC 00-32778

"A Richard Jackson book"

In 1942, Robert and his cousin Elliot uncover long-hidden family secrets while staying in their grandparents' Rhode Island town, where they also become involved with a German artist who is suspected of being a spy

"Lisle develops an unforgettable cast of characters placed against a fully realized setting. Engrossing, challenging, and well paced." Horn Book

Highway cats; illustrated by David Frankland. Philomel Books 2008 118p il $14.99; pa $6.99

Grades: 4 5 6 7   **Fic**

1. Cats—Fiction

ISBN   978-0-399-25070-5;   0-399-25070-0; 978-0-14-241485-9 (pa); 0-14-241485-9 (pa)

LC 2008-17165

A hard-bitten group of mangy highway cats is changed forever after the mysterious arrival of three kittens.

"Lisle shows that she can create and develop animal characters that are just as convincing as the humans in her past works. . . . Deftly written and attractively illustrated with chapter-opening silhouettes by Frankland, this is a treat for any reader and would be a delight to read aloud." Booklist

Littman, Sarah

Confessions of a closet Catholic; [by] Sarah Darer Littman. Dutton Children's Books 2005 193p hardcover o.p. pa $5.99

Grades: 5 6 7 8   **Fic**

1. Jews—Fiction 2. Catholics—Fiction

ISBN 0-525-47365-3; 0-14-240597-3 (pa)

LC 2004-10829

To be more like her best friend, eleven-year-old Justine decides to give up Judaism to become Catholic, but after her beloved, religious grandmother dies, she realizes that she needs to seek her own way of being Jewish.

"The novel is injected with humor throughout and written with the voice of a contemporary adolescent. Readers can't help but laugh and cry with this winning protagonist." SLJ

Llewellyn, Sam, 1948-

The well between the worlds. Orchard Books 2009 339p (Lyonesse) $17.99

Grades: 5 6 7 8   **Fic**

1. Arthur, King—Fiction 2. Fantasy fiction

ISBN 978-0-439-93469-5; 0-439-93469-9

LC 2008-20075

Eleven-year-old Idris Limpet, living with his family in the once noble but now evil and corrupt island country of Lyonesse, finds his life taking a dramatic turn when, after a near-drowning incident, he is accused of being allied to the feared sea monsters and is rescued from a death sentence by a mysterious and fearsome stranger.

"Seldom does one find a new fantasy that is so richly textured, so original in concept, and with such a wonderfully interesting story. . . . Fantasy lovers will be impatient to find out where their paths take them." Voice Youth Advocates

Followed by: Darksolstice (2010)

Lloyd, Alison, 1966-

Year of the tiger. Holiday House 2010 c2008 194p $16.95

Grades: 5 6 7 8   **Fic**

1. Archery—Fiction 2. Social classes—Fiction 3. Adventure fiction 4. China—Fiction

ISBN 978-0-8234-2277-7; 0-8234-2277-1

LC 2009033651

First published 2008 in Australia

In ancient China, Hu and Ren forge an unlikely alliance in an effort to become expert archers and, ultimately, to save their city from invading barbarians.

"Brimming with details of daily life in the Han Dynasty, this fast-paced story alternates in the third person between Hu and Ren." Kirkus

Lobel, Arnold

Fables; written and illustrated by Arnold Lobel. Harper & Row 1980 40p il $16.99; lib bdg $18.89; pa $6.99 *

Grades: 3 4 5   **Fic**

1. Animals—Fiction

ISBN 0-06-023973-5; 0-06-023974-3 (lib bdg); 0-06-443046-4 (pa)   LC 79-2004

Awarded the Caldecott Medal, 1981

"Short, original fables, complete with moral, poke subtle fun at human foibles through the antics of 20 memorable animal characters. . . . Despite the large picture-book format, the best audience will be older readers who can understand the innuendos and underlying messages. Children of all ages, however, will appreciate and be intrigued by the artist's fine, full-color illustrations. Tones are deftly blended to luminescent shadings, and the pictorial simplicity of ideas, droll expressions, and caricature of behavior work in many instances as complete and humorous stories in themselves." Booklist

Lofting, Hugh, 1886-1947

The voyages of Doctor Dolittle; told by Hugh Lofting; illustrated by Michael Hague; edited with a foreword by Patricia C. McKissack and Fredrick L. McKissack; afterword by Peter Glassman. HarperCollins Pubs. 2001 355p il $22.95

Grades: 4 5 6 7   **Fic**

1. Animals—Fiction 2. Fantasy fiction

ISBN 0-688-14002-5

Awarded the Newbery Medal, 1923

"Books of wonder"

A newly illustrated and revised edition of the title first published 1922 by Stokes

When his colleague Long Arrow disappears, Dr. Dolittle sets off with his assistant, Tommy Stubbins, his dog, Jip, and Polynesia the parrot on an adventurous voyage over tropical seas to floating Spidermonkey Island

Loizeaux, William

Clarence Cochran, a human boy; pictures by Anne Wilsdorf. Farrar, Straus and Giroux 2009 152p il $16

Grades: 4 5 6   **Fic**

1. Cockroaches—Fiction 2. Toleration—Fiction 3. Environmental protection—Fiction

ISBN 978-0-374-31323-4; 0-374-31323-7

LC 2007-35358

"Melanie Kroupa books"

With the threat of extermination looming, a cockroach who has been transformed into a tiny human learns to communicate with his human hosts, leading to an agreement both sides can live with, and a friendship between Clarence and ten-year-old Mimi, a human environmentalist.

"There's a serious message here about environmentalism and the power of words, and the action and suspense make this a good read-aloud or classroom-discussion choice." SLJ

Wings; pictures by Leslie Bowman. Farrar, Straus & Giroux 2006 138p il $16 *

Grades: 4 5 6   **Fic**

1. Birds—Fiction 2. Loss (Psychology)—Fiction

ISBN 978-0-374-34802-2; 0-374-34802-2

"Melanie Kroupa Books"

Ten-year-old Nick, who misses his father, finds companionship after rescuing an injured baby mockingbird.

"Shaded pencil drawings illustrate this graceful story with sensitivity and subtlety." Booklist

Lombard, Jenny

Drita, my homegirl. G. P. Putnam's Sons 2006 135p $15.99; pa $5.99 *

Grades: 3 4 5   **Fic**

1. Refugees—Fiction 2. Albanians—Fiction
3. African Americans—Fiction 4. Friendship—Fiction
5. New York (N.Y.)—Fiction

ISBN 0-399-24380-1; 0-14-240905-7 (pa)

LC 2005-13501

When ten-year-old Drita and her family, refugees from Kosovo, move to New York, Drita is teased about not speaking English well, but after a popular student named Maxine is forced to learn about Kosovo as a punishment for teasing Drita, the two girls soon bond.

"Maxie's attempts to help Drita understand American ways are touching, and Drita's understanding of her friend's loss is a testament to the emotional intelligence of children." SLJ

Look, Lenore

Alvin Ho: allergic to girls, school, and other scary things; pictures by LeUyen Pham. Schwartz & Wade Books 2008 170p il $15.99; lib bdg $18.99 *

Grades: 2 3 4 5   **Fic**

1. Fear—Fiction 2. Chinese Americans—Fiction
3. Massachusetts—Fiction

ISBN 978-0-375-83914-6; 0-375-83914-3; 978-0-375-93914-3 (lib bdg); 0-375-93914-8 (lib bdg)

LC 2007-029456

A young boy in Concord, Massachusetts, who loves superheroes and comes from a long line of brave Chinese farmer-warriors, wants to make friends, but first he must overcome his fear of everything.

Look's "intuitive grasp of children's emotions is rivaled only by her flair for comic exaggeration." Publ Wkly

Another title about Alvin Ho is:

Alvin Ho: allergic to camping, hiking, and other natural disasters (2009)

Ruby Lu, brave and true; illustrated by Anne Wilsdorf. Atheneum Books for Young Readers 2004 105p il $15.95; pa $3.99 *

Grades: 1 2 3   **Fic**

1. Chinese Americans—Fiction

ISBN 0-689-84907-9; 1-4169-1389-0 (pa)

LC 2003-3605

"An Anne Schwartz book"

"Almost-eight-year-old" Ruby Lu spends time with her baby brother, goes to Chinese school, performs magic tricks and learns to drive, and has adventures with both old and new friends.

This is a "funny and charming chapter book. . . . [It offers] generous font, ample white space, and animated and active illustrations rendered in India ink." SLJ

Another title about Ruby Lu is:

Ruby Lu, empress of everything (2006)

Lopez, Diana

Confetti girl. Little, Brown and Company 2009 198p $15.99

Grades: 4 5 6 7   **Fic**

1. Father-daughter relationship—Fiction 2. Mexican Americans—Fiction 3. School stories 4. Friendship—Fiction 5. Bereavement—Fiction 6. Texas—Fiction

ISBN 978-0-316-02955-1; 0-316-02955-6

LC 2008032819

After the death of her mother, Texas sixth-grader Lina's grades and mood drop as she watches her father lose himself more and more in books, while her best friend uses Lina as an excuse to secretly meet her boyfriend.

"Lopez effectively portrays the Texas setting and the characters' Latino heritage. . . . This . . . novel puts at its center a likable girl facing realistic problems on her own terms." Booklist

Lord, Bette Bao

In the Year of the Boar and Jackie Robinson; illustrations by Marc Simont. Harper & Row 1984 169p il lib bdg $15.89; pa $4.95

Grades: 4 5 6   **Fic**

1. Chinese Americans—Fiction 2. School stories

ISBN 0-06-024004-0 (lib bdg); 0-06-440175-8 (pa)

LC 83-48440

"In a story based in part on the author's experience as an immigrant, Shirley Temple Wong . . . arrives in Brooklyn and spends her first year in public school." Bull Cent Child Books

"Warm-hearted, fresh, and dappled with humor, the episodic book, which successfully encompasses both Chinese dragons and the Brooklyn Dodgers, stands out in the bevy of contemporary problem novels. And the unusual flavor of the text infiltrates the striking illustrations picturing the pert, pigtailed heroine making her way in 'Mei Guo'—her new 'Beautiful Country.'" Horn Book

Lord, Cynthia

Rules; [by] Cynthia Lord. Scholastic Press 2006 200p $15.99; pa $6.99 *

Grades: 4 5 6 7   **Fic**

1. Autism—Fiction 2. Siblings—Fiction
3. Handicapped—Fiction

ISBN 0-439-44382-2; 0-439-44383-0 (pa)

LC 2005017519

A Newbery Medal honor book, 2007

Frustrated at life with an autistic brother, twelve-year-old Catherine longs for a normal existence but her world is further complicated by a friendship with an young paraplegic

"The details of autistic behavior are handled well, as are depictions of relationships. . . . A heartwarming first novel." Booklist

Love, D. Anne, 1949-

Semiprecious. Margaret K. McElderry Books 2006 293p $16.95; pa $6.99

Grades: 5 6 7 8   **Fic**

1. Family life—Fiction 2. Oklahoma—Fiction

ISBN 978-0-689-85638-9; 0-689-85638-5; 978-0-689-87389-8 (pa); 0-689-87389-1 (pa)

LC 2005-14906

Love, D. Anne, 1949-—*Continued*

Uprooted and living with an aunt in 1960s Oklahoma, thirteen-year-old Garnet and her older sister Opal brave their mother's desertion and their father's recovery from an accident, learning that "the best home of all is the one you make inside yourself"

"An involving novel of hurt, healing, and adjustment." Booklist

Lovelace, Maud Hart, 1892-1980

Betsy-Tacy; illustrated by Lois Lenski. HarperCollins Pubs. 1994 c1940 112p il hardcover o.p. pa $5.99

Grades: 2 3 4 **Fic**

1. Friendship—Fiction 2. Minnesota—Fiction

ISBN 0-06-024415-1; 0-06-440096-4 (pa)

A reissue of the title first published 1940 by Crowell

Betsy and Tacy (short for Anastacia) were two little five-year-olds, such inseparable friends that they were regarded almost as one person. This is the story of their friendship in a little Minnesota town in the early 1900's

The author "has written a story of real literary merit as well as one with good story interest." Libr J

Other titles about Betsy through adolescence and young womanhood with reading levels to grade 5 and up are:

Betsy and Joe (1948)

Betsy and Tacy go downtown (1943)

Betsy and Tacy go over the big hill (1942)

Betsy and the great world (1952)

Betsy in spite of herself (1946)

Betsy, Tacy and Tib (1941)

Betsy was a junior (1947)

Betsy's wedding (1955)

Heavens to Betsy (1945)

Lowry, Lois

Anastasia Krupnik. Houghton Mifflin 1979 113p $16 *

Grades: 4 5 6 **Fic**

1. Family life—Fiction

ISBN 0-395-28629-8

Anastasia's 10th year has some good things like falling in love and really getting to know her grandmother and some bad things like finding out about an impending baby brother

"Anastasia's father and mother—an English professor and an artist—are among the most humorous, sensible, and understanding parents to be found in . . . children's fiction, and Anastasia herself is an amusing and engaging heroine." Horn Book

Other titles about Anastasia Krupnik and her family are:

All about Sam (1988)

Anastasia, absolutely (1995)

Anastasia again! (1981)

Anastasia, ask your analyst (1984)

Anastasia at this address (1991)

Anastasia at your service (1982)

Anastasia has the answers (1986)

Anastasia on her own (1985)

Anastasia's chosen career (1987)

Attaboy Sam! (1992)

See you around Sam! (1996)

Zooman Sam (1999)

Autumn Street. Houghton Mifflin 1980 188p $16 *

Grades: 4 5 6 7 **Fic**

1. World War, 1939-1945—Fiction 2. Friendship—Fiction

ISBN 0-395-27812-0 LC 80-376

"Elizabeth, the teller of the story, feels danger around her when her father goes to fight in World War II. She, her older sister, and her pregnant mother go to live with her grandparents on Autumn Street. Tatie, the black cook-housekeeper, and her street-wise grandson Charley love Elizabeth and reassure her during this difficult time." Child Book Rev Serv

"Characters, dialogue, believable plot combine in this well written story to capture the mind and heart of all who read this memorable and touching book." Voice Youth Advocates

Birthday ball; illustrations by Jules Feiffer. Houghton Mifflin Harcourt 2010 186p il $16 *

Grades: 4 5 6 **Fic**

1. Princesses—Fiction 2. Birthdays—Fiction 3. School stories

ISBN 978-0-547-23869-2; 0-547-23869-X

LC 2009-32966

When a bored Princess Patricia Priscilla makes her chambermaid switch identities with her so she can attend the village school, her attitude changes and she plans a new way to celebrate her sixteenth birthday.

"Lowry uses her knack for cleverly turning familiar stories on their heads . . . in this tale about a princess who's utterly bored with privileged palace life. . . . Feiffer's wiry ink illustrations paint the characters in offhand caricatures, adding to the merriment. Employing elements from the 'Prince and the Pauper' as well as ample doses of humor and slapstick, Lowry sets the stage for a rowdy denouement." Publ Wkly

The giver. Houghton Mifflin 1993 180p $17; pa $8.95 *

Grades: 6 7 8 9 **Fic**

1. Science fiction

ISBN 0-395-64566-2; 0-385-73255-4 (pa)

LC 92-15034

Awarded the Newbery Medal, 1994

Given his lifetime assignment at the Ceremony of Twelve, Jonas becomes the receiver of memories shared by only one other in his community and discovers the terrible truth about the society in which he lives.

"A riveting, chilling story that inspires a new appreciation for diversity, love, and even pain. Truly memorable." SLJ

Gooney Bird Greene; illustrated by Middy Thomas. Houghton Mifflin 2002 88p il $15

Grades: 2 3 4 **Fic**

1. Storytelling—Fiction 2. School stories

ISBN 0-618-23848-4 LC 2002-1478

"Walter Lorraine books"

A most unusual new student who loves to be the center of attention entertains her teacher and fellow second graders by telling absolutely true stories about herself, including how she got her name

"Lowry's masterful writing style reaches directly into her audience, managing both to appeal to young listeners and to engage older readers." Bull Cent Child Books

Lowry, Lois—*Continued*

Other titles about Gooney Bird are:
Gooney Bird and the room mother (2005)
Gooney the fabulous (2007)
Gooney Bird is so absurd (2009)

Number the stars. Houghton Mifflin 1989 137p
$16 *

Grades: 4 5 6 7   **Fic**
1. World War, 1939-1945—Fiction 2. Jews—Fiction
3. Friendship—Fiction 4. Denmark—Fiction
ISBN 0-395-51060-0   LC 88-37134
Awarded the Newbery Medal, 1990

In 1943, during the German occupation of Denmark,
ten-year-old Annemarie learns how to be brave and courageous when she helps shelter her Jewish friend from
the Nazis

"The appended details the historical incidents upon
which Lowry bases her plot. . . . The whole work is
seamless, compelling, and memorable." Horn Book

Stay! Keeper's story. Houghton Mifflin 1997
127p il $15

Grades: 5 6 7 8   **Fic**
1. Dogs—Fiction
ISBN 0-395-87048-8   LC 97-1569

"The canine narrator is a mongrel with class, a poetically inclined, refined animal of good upbringing if not
bloodlines. He leaves the relative safety of his first home
(an alley outside a French restaurant) for the perils of the
wide world in search of a human friend." Bull Cent
Child Books

"The author proves she is as well versed in animal behavior as in human sensibilities. Her warm sense of humor and vivid imagination . . . accentuate Keeper's unorthodox perceptions of the world." Publ Wkly

A summer to die; illustrated by Jenni Oliver.
Houghton Mifflin 1977 154p il $16
Grades: 5 6 7 8   **Fic**
1. Sisters—Fiction 2. Death—Fiction
ISBN 0-395-25338-1   LC 77-83

"Meg, 13, envies her older sister's popularity and prettiness and finds it difficult to cope with Molly's degener-
ating illness and eventual death." Booklist

"As told by Meg, the chronicle of this experience is
a sensitive exploration of the complex emotions underlying the adolescent's first confrontation with human mor-
tality; the author suggests nuances of contemporary conversation and situations without sacrificing the finesse
with which she limns her characters." Horn Book

The Willoughbys; nefariously written and
ignominiously illustrated by the author. Houghton
Mifflin 2008 174p $16
Grades: 4 5 6   **Fic**
1. Orphans—Fiction 2. Siblings—Fiction 3. Family
life—Fiction
ISBN 978-0-618-97974-5; 0-618-97974-3
                                        LC 2007-21550
"Walter Lorraine books"

In this tongue-in-cheek take on classic themes in children's literature, the four Willoughby children set about
to become "deserving orphans" after their neglectful parents embark on a treacherous around-the-world adven-

ture, leaving them in the care of an odious nanny.

This is "particularly inventive and wickedly amusing.
. . . Great fun." Booklist

Lubar, David, 1954-

My rotten life. Starscape 2009 160p (Nathan
Abercrombie, accidental zombie) $16.99; pa $5.99
Grades: 4 5 6   **Fic**
1. Popularity—Fiction 2. School stories 3. Zombies—
Fiction
ISBN   978-0-7653-2508-2;   0-7653-2508-X;
978-0-7653-1634-9 (pa); 0-7653-1634-X (pa)
                                        LC 2008-35762
"A Tom Doherty Associates Book"

Tired of continually having his feelings hurt by popular students and bullies, fifth-grader Nathan agrees to try
an experimental formula, Hurt-Be-Gone, and becomes a
half-dead zombie, a condition which, he soon discovers,
has some real advantages

"Lubar has a fine time inventing gross-outs, but he
also knows how to incorcorpate believable character motivation and work the heck out of a metaphor." Booklist

Lunn, Janet Louise Swoboda, 1928-

Laura Secord: a story of courage; [by] Janet
Lunn; illustrated by Maxwell Newhouse. Tundra
Bks. 2001 unp il maps $16.95
Grades: 3 4 5   **Fic**
1. Secord, Laura, d. 1868—Fiction 2. War of 1812—
Fiction
ISBN 0-88776-538-6

This is the fictionalized story of Laura "Secord's 19-
mile journey to inform British Lieutenant FitzGibbon of
the American plan for a surprise attack during the War
of 1812." SLJ

"The folkloric rhythm of the tale is underscored in the
dramatically colored, naively rendered illustrations."
Horn Book Guide

Lupica, Mike

The batboy. Philomel Books 2010 247p $17.99
Grades: 5 6 7 8   **Fic**
1. Detroit Tigers (Baseball team)—Fiction
2. Baseball—Fiction 3. Detroit (Mich.)—Fiction
4. Mother-son relationship—Fiction
ISBN 978-0-399-25000-2; 0-399-25000-X
                                        LC 2009015067
Even though his mother feels baseball ruined her marriage to his father, she allows fourteen-year-old Brian to
become a bat boy for the Detroit Tigers, who have just
drafted his favorite player back onto the team.

Lupica gives "his readers a behind-the-scenes look at
major league sports. In this this novel, he adds genuine
insights into family dynamics and the emotional state of
his hero." Booklist

Heat. Philomel Books 2006 220p $16.99; pa
$7.99
Grades: 5 6 7 8   **Fic**
1. Baseball—Fiction 2. Orphans—Fiction 3. Illegal
aliens—Fiction 4. Cubans—Fiction
ISBN 0-399-24301-1; 0-14-240757-7 (pa)
                                        LC 2005-13521

Lupica, Mike—*Continued*

Pitching prodigy Michael Arroyo is on the run from social services after being banned from playing Little League baseball because rival coaches doubt he is only twelve years old and he has no parents to offer them proof.

"The dialogue crackles, and the rich cast of supporting characters' . . . nearly steals the show. Topnotch entertainment." Booklist

Hot hand; [by] Mike Lupica. Philomel Books 2007 165p (Comeback kids) $9.99; pa $6.99

Grades: 3 4 5   **Fic**
1. Basketball—Fiction 2. Father-son relationship—Fiction 3. Bullies—Fiction
ISBN 978-0-399-24714-9; 978-0-14-241441-5 (pa)
                                            LC 2006034562

In the wake of his parents' separation, ten-year-old Billy seems to have continual conflicts with his father, who is also his basketball coach, but his quiet, younger brother Ben, a piano prodigy, is having even more trouble adjusting, and only Billy seems to notice.

"The characters . . . are always sympathetic . . . and the adults have complexity and depth. . . . The strongest point . . . is the quality of the sports play-by-play; Lupica portrays the action clearly and vividly." SLJ

Other titles in this series are:

Two-minute drill (2007)
Safe at home (2008)
Long shot (2008)
Shoot-out (2010)

Ly, Many

Home is east; [by] Many Ly. Delacorte Press 2005 294p hardcover o.p. pa $6.50

Grades: 5 6 7 8   **Fic**
1. Cambodian Americans—Fiction 2. Divorce—Fiction 3. Moving—Fiction 4. California—Fiction
ISBN 0-385-73222-8; 0-440-23900-1 (pa)
                                            LC 2004-14969

After her mother moves out, Amy, a Cambodian American girl, and her old-fashioned father leave their home in Florida to begin a new life in San Diego, experiencing turmoil and change as they slowly adjust to their new circumstances.

"Amy's narration is convincingly plainspoken, believable in its limitations but subtle in its understandings, and she's joined by a cast of compelling supporting characters." Bull Cent Child Books

Lynch, Chris

Cyberia; [by] Chris Lynch. Scholastic Press 2008 158p $16.99

Grades: 4 5 6 7   **Fic**
1. Technology and civilization—Fiction 2. Animals—Fiction 3. Science fiction
ISBN 978-0-545-02793-9; 0-545-02793-4
                                            LC 2008-05388

In a future where electronic surveillance has taken the place of love, a veterinarian is putting computer chips in animals to control them, and those creatures choose young Zane, who understands their speech, to release captives and bring them to a technology-free safety zone.

"This very funny book occasionally strikes notes of unexpected poignancy." Booklist

Another title in this series is:
Monkey see, monkey don't (2009)

Lyons, Mary E.

Letters from a slave girl; the story of Harriet Jacobs. Scribner 1992 146p il hardcover o.p. pa $5.99

Grades: 6 7 8 9   **Fic**
1. Jacobs, Harriet A., 1813-1897—Fiction 2. Slavery—Fiction 3. African Americans—Fiction 4. Letters—Fiction
ISBN 0-684-19446-5; 1-4169-3637-8 (pa)
                                            LC 91-45778

A fictionalized version of the life of Harriet Jacobs, told in the form of letters that she might have written during her slavery in North Carolina and as she prepared for escape to the North in 1842

This "is historical fiction at its best. . . . Mary Lyons has remained faithful to Jacobs's actual autobiography throughout her readable, compelling novel. . . . Her observations of the horrors of slavery are concise and lucid. The letters are written in dialect, based on Jacobs's own writing and on other slave narrations of the period." Horn Book

MacDonald, Alan, 1958-

Trolls go home! [by] Alan MacDonald; illustrations by Mark Beech. Bloomsbury Children's Books 2007 124p il $14.95; pa $5.95

Grades: 2 3 4 5   **Fic**
1. Trolls—Fiction
ISBN 978-1-59990-077-3; 1-59990-077-7; 978-1-59990-078-0 (pa); 1-59990-078-5 (pa)
                                            LC 2006-49887

When the Trolls move next door to the Priddles, both families find the other strange, which causes many misunderstandings.

"MacDonald includes deliciously silly vocabulary; . . . inventive details about the Troll lifestyle; and fractured-fairy-tale references to the Billy Goats Gruff. Beech's scribbly line drawings turn up the humor." Booklist

MacDonald, Amy

Too much flapdoodle! [illustrations by Cat Bowman Smith] Farrar Straus Giroux 2008 182p il $16.95

Grades: 3 4 5 6   **Fic**
1. Aunts—Fiction 2. Uncles—Fiction 3. Country life—Fiction 4. Farm life—Fiction
ISBN 978-0-374-37671-0; 0-374-37671-9
                                            LC 2007033273

"Melanie Kroupa books"

Twelve-year-old Parker reluctantly goes to spend the summer with his eccentric great-aunt and great-uncle on their dilapidated farm, where he discovers that there is more to life than the latest game system and the coolest cell phone

"Hilarious antics ensue as the boy matures and realizes that there is more to life than the latest video game. Black-and-white line drawings enhance the lighthearted text." SLJ

Other titles about these characters are:

MacDonald, Amy—*Continued*

No more nice (1996)

No more nasty (2001)

MacDonald, Bailey

Wicked Will. Aladdin 2009 201p $16.99

Grades: 5 6 7   **Fic**

1. Shakespeare, William, 1564-1616—Fiction
2. Theater—Fiction 3. Orphans—Fiction 4. Great Britain—History—1485-1603, Tudors—Fiction
5. Mystery fiction

ISBN 978-1-4169-8660-7; 1-4169-8660-X

LC 2008-50818

Performing in the English town of Stratford-on-Avon in 1576, Viola, a young actress (disguised as a boy) and a local lad named Will Shakespeare uncover a murder mystery.

"The chapters themselves logically reveal the twists and turns of the plot in concise, readable prose. The realistic details put flesh on the bones of not only the primary characters, but also of the secondary personages as well." SLJ

MacDonald, George, 1824-1905

The light princess; with pictures by Maurice Sendak. Farrar, Straus & Giroux 1969 110p il pa $5.95 hardcover o.p.

Grades: 3 4 5 6   **Fic**

1. Fairy tales

ISBN 0-374-44458-7 (pa)

This fairy story originally appeared 1864 in the author's novel Adela Cathcart and was reprinted in his 1867 story collection Dealings with the fairies

"The problems of the princess who had been deprived, as an infant, of her gravity and whose life hung in the balance when she grew up are amusing as ever and the sweet capitulation to love that brings her (literally) to her feet, just as touching. All of the best of Macdonald is reflected in the Sendak illustrations: the humor and wit, the sweetness and tenderness, and the sophistication—and they are beautiful." Sutherland. The Best in Child Books

Mack, Tracy, 1968-

The fall of the Amazing Zalindas; casebook no. 1; by Tracy Mack and Michael Citrin; illustrations by Greg Ruth. Orchard Books 2006 259p il (Sherlock Holmes and the Baker Street irregulars) $16.99; pa $6.99

Grades: 4 5 6 7   **Fic**

1. Mystery fiction 2. Circus—Fiction 3. Great Britain—Fiction

ISBN 0-439-82836-8; 0-545-06939-4 (pa)

LC 2005-34000

The ragamuffin boys known as the Baker Street Irregulars help Sherlock Holmes solve the mysterious deaths of a family of circus tightrope walkers.

"Colorful, well-defined characters . . . and plenty of historical detail, Cockney slang . . . and Sherlockian references bring Victorian England to life. Vintage-style design elements and evocative black-and-white illustrations further the effect." Booklist

Mackel, Kathy

MadCat; [by] Kathy Mackel. HarperCollins 2005 185p hardcover o.p. lib bdg $16.89

Grades: 5 6 7 8   **Fic**

1. Softball—Fiction 2. Friendship—Fiction 3. Women athletes—Fiction

ISBN 0-06-054869-X; 0-06-054870-3 (lib bdg)

LC 2004-6618

Fast-pitch softball catcher MadCat Campione's love for the sport—and her relationship with her best friends—is strained when her team competes on a national level

"With a credible plot, a distinct narrative voice, and sparky dialogue, this is a winner in any league." Booklist

MacLachlan, Patricia, 1938-

The facts and fictions of Minna Pratt. Harper & Row 1988 136p pa $4.95

Grades: 4 5 6 7   **Fic**

1. Musicians—Fiction

ISBN 0-06-440265-7 (pa)   LC 85-45388

"A Charlotte Zolotow book"

"Minna Pratt plays the cello and wishes she would get her vibrato. She wishes someone would answer her questions about herself and life and love. . . . Then she meets Lucas Ellerby. His life seems so perfect and he has a vibrato. As their friendship develops Minna finds that life is not always as it seems and even when you think you know someone or something there may be a hidden side that will surprise you." Voice Youth Advocates

"Ms. MacLachlan's skillful handling of her subject, and above all her vivid characterization . . . place her story in the ranks of outstanding middle-grade fiction." N Y Times Book Rev

Sarah, plain and tall. Harper & Row 1985 58p $14.99; lib bdg $15.89; pa $4.99 *

Grades: 3 4 5   **Fic**

1. Stepmothers—Fiction 2. Frontier and pioneer life—Fiction

ISBN 0-06-024101-2; 0-06-024102-0 (lib bdg); 0-06-440205-3 (pa)   LC 83-49481

Awarded the Newbery Medal, 1986

"A Charlotte Zolotow book"

When their father invites a mail-order bride to come live with them in their prairie home, Caleb and Anna are captivated by their new mother and hope that she will stay

"It is the simplest of love stories expressed in the simplest of prose. Embedded in these unadorned declarative sentences about ordinary people, actions, animals, facts, objects and colors are evocations of the deepest feelings of loss and fear, love and hope." N Y Times Book Rev

Other titles in this series are:

Caleb's story (2001)

Grandfather's dance (2006)

More perfect than the moon (2004)

Skylark (1994)

Seven kisses in a row; pictures by Maria Pia Marrella. Harper & Row 1983 56p il pa $4.95

Grades: 2 3 4   **Fic**

1. Aunts—Fiction 2. Uncles—Fiction 3. Family life—Fiction

ISBN 0-06-440231-2 (pa)   LC 82-47718

MacLachlan, Patricia, 1938-—*Continued*

"A Charlotte Zolotow book"

"How different life is for Emma and Zachary when Aunt Evelyn and Uncle Elliott babysit for them while their parents attend an 'eyeball meeting'! No seven kisses before breakfast or divided grapefruit with cherry. Nevertheless both learn from the others—Emma learns to eat broccoli and her aunt and uncle learn about babies and what they do." Child Book Rev Serv

"The brief understated story makes few demands on the reader, but it is full of humor and the warmth of family caring and mutual affection. Informal, offhand pen-and-ink drawings reflect the tone of both story and style." Horn Book

The true gift; a Christmas story; illustrated by Brian Floca. Atheneum Books for Young Readers 2009 81p il $12.99

Grades: 2 3 4   **Fic**

1. Siblings—Fiction 2. Cattle—Fiction 3. Books and reading—Fiction   4.   Grandparents—Fiction 5. Christmas—Fiction 6. Farm life—Fiction

ISBN 978-1-4169-9081-9; 1-4169-9081-X

LC 2009-375

While spending Christmas at their grandparents' farm, Lily becomes convinced that her younger brother Liam is right about White Cow being lonely and helps him seek a companion for her, leaving little time for Christmas preparations or reading.

"With MacLachlan's well-drawn characters and Floca's simple pencil and graphite drawings, it's a poignant story with a a classic feel." Publ Wkly

Word after word after word. HarperCollins lib bdg $15.89 *

Grades: 2 3 4 5   **Fic**

1. Poetry—Fiction   2.   Authorship—Fiction 3. Mother-daughter relationship—Fiction 4. Cancer—Fiction 5. School stories

ISBN 978-0-06-027971-4; 0-06-027971-0

"Katherine Tegan books"

"Mrs. Mirabel, a visiting poet, works with a fourth-grade class over several weeks as they first discuss why people write poetry and then attempt to express themselves in verse. . . . Narrator Lucy, whose mother is recovering from cancer treatments, often meets her friends to talk about their hopes, their fears, their families, and their charismatic mentor. . . . Showing great respect for both her readers and her craft, . . . MacLachlan makes every word count in Lucy's smooth-flowing economical narrative." Booklist

Madden, Kerry

Gentle's Holler; by Kerry Madden. Viking 2005 237p $16.99; pa $6.99

Grades: 5 6 7 8   **Fic**

1. Family life—Fiction 2. Poverty—Fiction 3. North Carolina—Fiction

ISBN 0-670-05998-6; 0-14-240751-8 (pa)

LC 2004-18424

In the early 1960s, twelve-year-old songwriter Livy Two Weems dreams of seeing the world beyond the Maggie Valley, North Carolina, holler where she lives in poverty with her parents and eight brothers and sisters,

but understands that she must put family first.

"Livy's narration rings true and is wonderfully voiced, and Madden's message about the importance of forgiveness will be well received." SLJ

Other titles in this series are:

Louisiana's song (2007)

Jessie's mountain (2008)

Madison, Alan

100 days and 99 nights; illustrated by Julia Denos. Little, Brown 2008 137p il $14.99; pa $5.99

Grades: 3 4 5   **Fic**

1. Father-daughter relationship—Fiction 2. Soldiers—Fiction 3. Toys—Fiction 4. Imagination—Fiction 5. Virginia—Fiction

ISBN   978-0-316-11354-0;   0-316-11354-9; 978-0-316-11798-2 (pa); 0-316-11798-6 (pa)

As Esme introduces her stuffed animal collection that is alphabetically arranged from Alvin the aardvark to Zelda the zebra she also relates her family's military life and her father's deployment

"In this moving debut novel, wordplay is part of every chapter. . . . This is a mix of hilarious language and one child's terror that there could be bad news." Booklist

Maguire, Gregory

Seven spiders spinning; illustrated by Dirk Zimmer. Clarion Bks. 1994 132p il $16

Grades: 4 5 6   **Fic**

1. Spiders—Fiction 2. School stories

ISBN 0-395-68965-1   LC 93-30478

Seven prehistoric spiders that had been trapped in ice for thousands of years bring excitement to rural Vermont and briefly unite two rival clubs at a local elementary school

"There is quite a bit of tongue-in-cheek humor here. . . . Characters are almost caricatures. . . . Yet, somehow it all comes together to create a funny, shivery story." SLJ

Other titles in this series are:

A couple of April fools (2004)

Five alien elves (1998)

Four stupid Cupids (2000)

One final firecracker (2005)

Six haunted hairdos (1997)

Three rotten eggs (2002)

Mahy, Margaret

Maddigan's Fantasia. Margaret K. McElderry Books 2007 499p $15.99

Grades: 4 5 6 7   **Fic**

1. Circus—Fiction 2. Magic—Fiction 3. Fantasy fiction

ISBN 1-4169-1812-4; 978-1-4169-1817-7

LC 2006-15512

In a world made uncertain by "the Chaos," two time-traveling boys, fifteen-year-old Timon and eleven-year-old Eden, seek to protect a magic talisman, aided by twelve-year-old Garland, a member of a traveling circus known as Maddigan's Fantasia.

"A well-drawn character, Garland resembles other Mahy protagonists—cranky, assertive and filled with self-doubt—and her adventures are invariably exciting." Publ Wkly

Malaghan, Michael

Greek ransom. Andersen Press 2010 264p pa $9.99

Grades: 5 6 7 8   **Fic**
    1. Greece—Fiction 2. Kidnapping—Fiction
3. Siblings—Fiction 4. Adventure fiction
    ISBN 978-184270-786-9; 1-84270-786-8

"Nick and Callie Latham are on the Greek island of Theta with their archaeologist parents for a working vacation. Then the children discover that Mum and Dad have lost the family's money in a reckless bid to locate the lost treasure of King Akanon. A shifty businessman kidnaps the couple in order to acquire it for himself. After Nick and Callie barely escape capture themselves, it's up to them to find a way to free their parents. . . . Readers will be on the edge of their seats throughout to see what happens next. . . . The relationship between Nick and Callie is spot-on, and kids will enjoy this high-spirited tale." SLJ

Marino, Nan

Neil Armstrong is my uncle; & other lies Muscle Man McGinty told me. Roaring Brook Press 2009 154p $16.95 *

Grades: 3 4 5 6   **Fic**
    1. Foster home care—Fiction 2. Bullies—Fiction
3. Friendship—Fiction 4. Long Island (N.Y.)—Fiction
    ISBN 978-1-59643-499-8; 1-59643-499-6

"It's the summer of 1969, when astronauts land on the moon, and Tamara Ann Simpson is not having a good time. Foster child and best friend Kebsie has suddenly moved away and now Douglas McGinty is in her spot with Mrs. Kutchner. Tammy dubs him 'Muscle Man' after one outrageous lie. . . . Fierce and plaintive, Tammy's voice crackles with originality and yet is completely childlike. The '60s setting comes to life with sharply honed details. . . . The authenticity of the time and the voice combine with a poignant plot to reveal a depth unusual in such a straightforward first-person narrative." Kirkus

Marsden, Carolyn, 1950-

The Buddha's diamonds; [by] Carolyn Marsden and Thay Phap Niem. Candlewick Press 2008 97p $14.99

Grades: 4 5 6   **Fic**
    1. Fishing—Fiction 2. Vietnam—Fiction
3. Buddhism—Fiction
    ISBN 978-0-7636-3380-6; 0-7636-3380-1
    LC 2007023025

As a storm sweeps in, Tinh's father tells him to tie up their fishing boat but the storm scares him and he runs away, but when the damage to the boat is discovered, Tinh realizes what he must do.

"Buddhist concepts are gently introduced and explained in the context of the story, but, more importantly, they are reflected in the tone and style. . . . Cultural references are beautifully integrated into this lovely coming-of-age story." SLJ

The gold-threaded dress. Candlewick Press 2002 73p hardcover o.p. pa $5.99 *

Grades: 3 4 5   **Fic**
    1. Thai Americans—Fiction 2. Prejudices—Fiction
3. School stories
    ISBN 0-7636-1569-2; 0-7636-2993-6 (pa)
    LC 2001-25132

When Oy and her Thai American family move to a new neighborhood, her third-grade classmates tease and exclude her because she is different

"Marsden writes with keen observation and finesse about the social dynamics of the classroom and with simplicity reveals the layers of emotion experienced by Oy." Booklist

Another title about Oy is:
The Quail Club (2006)

Moon runner; [by] Carolyn Marsden. Candlewick Press 2005 97p hardcover o.p. pa $5.99

Grades: 3 4 5   **Fic**
    1. Friendship—Fiction 2. Running—Fiction
    ISBN 0-7636-2117-X; 0-7636-3304-6 (pa)
    LC 2004-58143

When Mina discovers that she can run faster than her athlete friend, Ruth, she thinks she must choose between running and friendship

"A quiet, lyrical story that sensitively explores issues of friendship and being true to oneself. . . . The lucid prose is full of haunting metaphors. " SLJ

Silk umbrellas; [by] Carolyn Marsden. Candlewick Press 2004 134p $15.99; pa $5.99 *

Grades: 3 4 5 6   **Fic**
    1. Thailand—Fiction 2. Family life—Fiction
3. Artists—Fiction
    ISBN 0-7636-2257-5; 0-7636-3376-3 (pa)
    LC 2003-55323

Eleven-year-old Noi worries that she will have to stop painting the silk umbrellas her family sells at the market near their Thai village and be forced to join her older sister in difficult work at a local factory instead.

"In simple, lucid prose, Marsden tells a story that is foreign in detail and texture but universal in appeal. . . . This gracefully told story will resonate with many young readers." Booklist

Take me with you. Candlewick Press 2010 160p $14.99

Grades: 4 5 6 7   **Fic**
    1. Orphans—Fiction 2. Italy—Fiction 3. Racially mixed people—Fiction 4. Friendship—Fiction
    ISBN 978-0-7636-3739-2; 0-7636-3739-4
    LC 2009-38053

This story is set in "Italy after World War II. Pina and Susanna have lived at their Naples orphanage since they were babies. . . . Pina, pretty and blonde, . . . is sure the nuns tell prospective parents she is bad. Susanna is the daughter of an Italian woman and a black American solider. . . ; no one looks like her. Then two very different parents come into the girls' lives. . . . Both satisfy the girls' dreams in unexpected ways. Marsden often puts crafts like sewing or crocheting into her stories, and in many ways she is like a master craftsman, using words instead of stitches for her deceptively simple design." Booklist

Marsden, Carolyn, 1950-—*Continued*

When heaven fell. Candlewick Press 2007 183p
$15.99; pa $8.99
Grades: 4 5 6   **Fic**
    1. Aunts—Fiction   2. Family life—Fiction
3. Vietnam—Fiction
    ISBN   978-0-7636-3175-8;   0-7636-3175-2;
978-0-7636-4381-2 (pa); 0-7636-4381-5 (pa)
                              LC 2006-51712
When her grandmother reveals that the daughter that
she had given up for adoption is coming from America
to visit her Vietnamese family, nine-year-old Binh is
convinced that her newly-discovered aunt is wealthy and
will take care of all the family's needs.
    "Marsden sensitively portrays expectations and disap-
pointments on both sides. . . . An unusually accessible
introduction to the culture of modern Vietnam." Booklist

Martin, Ann M., 1955-
Belle Teal. Scholastic Press 2001 214p
hardcover o.p. pa $5.99 *
Grades: 4 5 6 7   **Fic**
    1. School stories 2. Race relations—Fiction
    ISBN 0-439-09823-8; 0-439-09824-6 (pa)
                              LC 00-136292
Belle Teal Harper is from a poor family in the country, and beginning fifth-grade is a challenge as her
grandmother's memory is slipping away, her brother and
father are fighting again, and she becomes involved with
the two new African American children in her class.
    "This is a solid piece of work with an absorbing plot."
SLJ

A corner of the universe. Scholastic Press 2002
189p $15.95; pa $5.99 *
Grades: 5 6 7 8   **Fic**
    1. Uncles—Fiction 2. Mentally handicapped—Fiction
3. Friendship—Fiction
    ISBN 0-439-38880-5; 0-439-38881-3 (pa)
                              LC 2001-57611
A Newbery Medal honor book, 2003
The summer that Hattie turns twelve, she meets the
childlike uncle she never knew and becomes friends with
a girl who works at the carnival that comes to Hattie's
small town
    "Martin delivers wonderfully real characters and an
engrossing plot through the viewpoint of a girl who tries
so earnestly to connect with those around her." SLJ

The doll people; by Ann M. Martin and Laura
Godwin; with pictures by Brian Selznick.
Hyperion Bks. for Children 2000 256p il $15.99;
pa $6.99
Grades: 3 4 5   **Fic**
    1. Dolls—Fiction
    ISBN 0-7868-0361-4; 0-7868-1240-0 (pa)
                              LC 98-12344
A family of porcelain dolls that has lived in the same
house for one hundred years is taken aback when a new
family of plastic dolls arrives and doesn't follow The
Doll Code of Honor
    "Superbly nuanced drawings echo the action that
breathes life into these extraordinary playthings." SLJ
    Other titles about the doll family are:

The meanest doll in the world (2003)
The runaway dolls (2008)

Martin, Patricia
Lulu Atlantis and the quest for true blue love;
[by] Patricia Martin. Schwartz & Wade Books
2008 228p il $15.99; lib bdg $18.99
Grades: 3 4 5   **Fic**
    1. Siblings—Fiction 2. Imaginary playmates—Fiction
3. Spiders—Fiction
    ISBN   978-0-375-84016-6;   0-375-84016-8;
978-0-375-94016-3 (lib bdg); 0-375-94016-2 (lib bdg)
                            LC 2007002082
Lulu Atlantis is peeved when her mother brings home
little brother Sam, and she turns to her imaginary friend,
Harry the daddy longlegs spider, for comfort, companionship, help, and advice as she is getting used to the addition to the family
    "The scenarios are whimsical; the emotions run true."
Publ Wkly

Martínez, Arturo O., 1933-
Pedrito's world. Texas Tech University Press
2007 131p il pa $16.95
Grades: 4 5 6   **Fic**
    1. Farm life—Fiction 2. Mexican Americans—Fiction
3. Texas—Fiction
    ISBN 978-0-89672-600-0 (pa); 0-89672-600-2 (pa)
                              LC 2006-21628
In southern Texas in 1941, six-year-old Pedrito holds
onto his hope for a better future as he helps to grow watermelons on his parents' farm and sell them in San Antonio, and attends school five miles from home.
    "Readers will be moved . . . through clean writing
and well-chosen details that breathe life into the characters and give heft to the setting." Booklist

Mason, Simon, 1962-
The Quigleys; illustrated by Helen Stephens.
David Fickling Books 2002 148p il hardcover o.p.
pa $4.99 *
Grades: 2 3 4   **Fic**
    1. Family life—Fiction 2. Great Britain—Fiction
    ISBN 0-385-75006-4; 0-440-41898-4 (pa)
                              LC 2002-20665
    "Each of four chapters is devoted to a different mem-
ber of the Quigley family. Dad baby-sits for neighbors
and manages to 'lose' one of the children temporarily,
headstrong Lucy appears as a junior bridesmaid in a self-
made bee costume, Lucy and Will guiltily try to make up
for being beastly on Mum's birthday, and Will finally
gets the pet he wants. Children will enjoy the plentiful
dialogue, likable family, mixture of low-key and over-
the-top humor, and occasional black-line illustrations."
SLJ
Other titles in this series are:
The Quigleys at large (2003)
The Quigleys not for sale (2004)
The Quigleys in a spin (2006)

Mason, Timothy

The last synapsid. Delacorte Press 2009 311p il
$16.99; lib bdg $19.99

Grades: 5 6 7 8   **Fic**

1. Prehistoric animals—Fiction 2. Time travel—Fiction
3. Space and time—Fiction 4. Colorado—Fiction
ISBN   978-0-385-73581-0;   0-385-73581-2;
978-0-385-90567-1 (lib bdg); 0-385-90567-X (lib bdg)
LC 2008-35678

On a mountain near their tiny town of Faith, Colorado, best friends Rob and Phoebe discover a squat, drooly
creature from thirty million years before the dinosaurs,
that needs their help in tracking down a violent carnivore
that must be returned to its proper place in time, or humans will never evolve.

"Mason has written a highly engaging fantasy that includes something for all readers. . . . Readers will find
it difficult to put this book down until they have reached
the last page." Libr Media Connect

Mass, Wendy, 1967-

11 birthdays. Scholastic Press 2009 267p
$16.99; pa $6.99

Grades: 4 5 6   **Fic**

1. Birthdays—Fiction   2.   Time—Fiction
3. Friendship—Fiction
ISBN   978-0-545-05239-9;   0-545-05239-4;
978-0-545-05240-5 (pa); 0-545-05240-8 (pa)
LC 2008-09784

After celebrating their first nine same-day birthdays
together, Amanda and Leo, having fallen out on their
tenth and not speaking to each other for the last year,
prepare to celebrate their eleventh birthday separately but
peculiar things begin to happen as the day of their birthday begins to repeat itself over and over again.

"From the double-entendre title to the solid character
portrayals to the clarity and wit of the writing, this novel
offers a fresh twist on the familiar themes of middle-
grade family and school dynamics." Booklist

Followed by: Finally (2010)

Every soul a star; a novel. Little, Brown and
Co. 2008 322p $15.99; pa $6.99 *

Grades: 5 6 7 8   **Fic**

1. Solar eclipses—Fiction 2. Friendship—Fiction
ISBN   978-0-316-00256-1;   0-316-00256-9;
978-0-316-00257-8 (pa); 0-316-00257-7 (pa)
LC 2008009259

Ally, Bree, and Jack meet at the one place the Great
Eclipse can be seen in totality, each carrying the burden
of different personal problems, which become dim when
compared to the task they embark upon and the friendship they find.

Mass "combines astronomy and storytelling for a well-
balanced look at friendships and the role they play in
shaping identity. . . . Information about solar eclipses
and astronomy is carefully woven into the plot to build
drama and will almost certainly intrigue readers." Publ
Wkly

Includes bibliographical references

Jeremy Fink and the meaning of life. Little,
Brown 2006 289p $15.99; pa $6.99

Grades: 5 6 7 8   **Fic**

1. Conduct of life—Fiction 2. Father-son relationship—Fiction
ISBN   978-0-316-05829-2;   0-316-05829-7;
978-0-316-05849-0 (pa); 0-316-05849-1 (pa)
LC 2005037291

Just before his thirteenth birthday, Jeremy Fink receives a keyless locked box—set aside by his father before his death five years earlier—that purportedly contains the meaning of life.

"Mass fashions an adventure in which both journey
and destination are worth the trip." Horn Book

Mathews, Ellie

The linden tree; [by] Ellie Mathews. Milkweed
Editions 2007 195p hardcover o.p. pa $6.95

Grades: 3 4 5 6   **Fic**

1. Bereavement—Fiction 2. Family life—Fiction
3. Farm life—Fiction 4. Aunts—Fiction 5. Iowa—Fiction
ISBN   978-1-57131-673-8;   1-57131-673-6;
978-1-57131-674-5 (pa); 1-57131-674-4 (pa)
LC 2006-38831

In 1948, nine-year-old Katy Sue's mother dies suddenly, and she and her family spend the next year trying to
recover from their loss, assisted by her Aunt Katherine,
who quits her teaching job to help out on their Iowa
farm

Matthews "tells a timeless, heartfelt story of family,
loss, and love." Booklist

Matthews, L. S.

A dog for life; [by] L.S. Matthews. Delacorte
Press 2006 144p $14.95; lib bdg $16.99; pa $5.99
*

Grades: 4 5 6 7   **Fic**

1. Dogs—Fiction 2. Runaway children—Fiction
3. Great Britain—Fiction
ISBN   978-0-385-73366-3;   0-385-73366-6;
978-0-385-90381-3 (lib bdg); 0-385-90381-2 (lib bdg);
978-0-440-42157-3 (pa); 0-440-42157-8 (pa)
LC 2006-45664

When John, who has a special ability to communicate
with animals, finds that his dog, Mouse, is scheduled to
go to the pound, he and Mouse decide to run away and
find his uncle who may be able to help them.

"Although John and Mouse encounter some disturbing
situations, the childlike tone and magical elements of the
narrative keep it age appropriate. . . . Highly enjoyable."
SLJ

Matthews, Tom L., 1949-

Danger in the dark; a Houdini & Nate mystery;
[by] Tom Lalicki; pictures by Carlyn Cerniglia.
Farrar, Straus and Giroux 2006 186p il $14.95

Grades: 4 5 6 7   **Fic**

1. Houdini, Harry, 1874-1926—Fiction 2. Magicians—
Fiction 3. Spiritualism—Fiction 4. Mystery fiction
ISBN 0-374-31680-5   LC 2005052111

Matthews, Tom L., 1949-—*Continued*

Thirteen-year-old Nathaniel, aided by the famous magician Harry Houdini, plots to unmask a phony spirit advisor attempting to relieve the boy's great-aunt of her fortune.

"The action is nonstop, and even a flurry of enormous coincidences won't spoil enthusiasm for this entertaining story." Booklist

Other titles in this series are:

Shots at sea (2007)

Frame-up on the Bowery (2009)

Mazer, Norma Fox, 1931-2009

Ten ways to make my sister disappear. Arthur A. Levine Books 2007 148p $16.99

Grades: 3 4 5 6   **Fic**

1. Sisters—Fiction   2. Family life—Fiction   3. Friendship—Fiction

ISBN 0-439-83983-1; 978-0-439-83983-9

LC 2007-09784

Ten-year-old Sprig no longer gets along with her twelve-year-old sister, Dakota, but the two pull together during their father's extended business trip to Afghanistan, sharing concerns about his safety, an elderly neighbor's health, fights with their best friends, and boys.

"The author excels at depicting the complexity of preteens' emotions and relationships, especially sibling relationships; many readers will recognize their own feelings here." Publ Wkly

McCaughrean, Geraldine, 1951-

The death-defying Pepper Roux. Harper 2010 328p $16.99; lib bdg $17.89 *

Grades: 5 6 7 8   **Fic**

1. Adventure fiction 2. Fate and fatalism—Fiction 3. France—Fiction

ISBN 978-0-06-183665-7;   0-06-183665-6;
978-0-06-183666-4 (lib bdg); 0-06-183666-4 (lib bdg)

LC 2009-39665

Having been raised believing he will die before he reaches the age of fourteen, Pepper Roux runs away on his fourteenth birthday in an attempt to elude his fate, assumes another identity, and continues to try to outrun death, no matter the consequences.

"McCaughrean's exuberant prose and whirling humor animate an unforgettable cast of characters." Booklist

The kite rider; a novel. HarperCollins Pubs. 2002 272p maps hardcover o.p. pa $6.99

Grades: 5 6 7 8   **Fic**

1. Kublai Khan, 1216-1294—Fiction 2. China—Fiction 3. Kites—Fiction

ISBN 0-06-623874-9; 0-06-441091-9 (pa)

LC 2001-39522

In thirteenth-century China, after trying to save his widowed mother from a horrendous second marriage, twelve-year-old Haoyou has life-changing adventures when he takes to the sky as a circus kite rider and ends up meeting the great Mongol ruler Kublai Khan

"The story is a genuine page-turner. . . . McCaughrean fully immerses her memorable characters in the culture and lore of the ancient Chinese and Mongols, which make this not only a solid adventure story but also a window to a fascinating time and place." Booklist

Peter Pan in scarlet; by Geraldine McCaughrean; illustrations by Scott M. Fischer. Margaret K. McElderry Books 2006 309p il $17.99; pa $6.99

Grades: 4 5 6 7   **Fic**

1. Fairy tales

ISBN   976-1-4169-1808-0;   1-4169-1808-6;
978-1-4169-1809-7 (pa); 1-4169-1809-4 (pa)

In the 1930s, all is not well. Nightmares are leaking out of Neverland. Fearing for Peter Pan's life, Wendy and the Lost Boys go back to Neverland with the help of the fairy Fireflyer only to discover their worst nightmares coming true!

"McCaughrean's story, with its picaresque descriptions, faithfully rekindled characters and an ending that leaves room for sequels, will keep the pages turning." Publ Wkly

McCloskey, Robert, 1914-2003

Homer Price. Viking 1943 149p il $16.99; pa $5.99 *

Grades: 4 5 6   **Fic**

ISBN 0-670-37729-5; 0-14-240415-2 (pa)

Six "stories about the exploits of young Homer Price, who divides his time between school and doing odd jobs at his father's filling station and in his mother's tourist lunchroom two miles outside of Centerburg." Bookmark

"Text and pictures are pure Americana, hilarious and convincing in their portrayal of midwestern small-town life." Child Books Too Good to Miss

Another title about Homer Price is:

Centerburg tales (1951)

McCully, Emily Arnold

The bobbin girl. Dial Bks. for Young Readers 1996 unp il $15.99

Grades: 3 4 5   **Fic**

1. Strikes—Fiction 2. United States—History—1815-1861—Fiction   3.   Massachusetts—Fiction 4. Factories—Fiction

ISBN 0-8037-1827-6   LC 95-6997

Rebecca, a ten-year-old bobbin girl working in a textile mill in Lowell, Massachusetts, in the 1830s, must make a difficult decision—will she participate in the first workers' strike in Lowell?

"McCully weaves historical facts and fictional characters into an intriguing story. The author's note details the background, incidents, and people who inspired the book. Beautifully composed watercolor paintings give a vivid impression of America in the 1830s and bring the period to life." Booklist

McDonald, Megan, 1959-

Judy Moody; illustrated by Peter Reynolds. Candlewick Press 2000 160p il $15.99; pa $5.99 *

Grades: 2 3 4   **Fic**

1. School stories

ISBN 0-7636-0685-5; 0-7636-1231-6 (pa)

LC 99-13464

Third grader Judy Moody is in a first day of school bad mood until she gets an assignment to create a collage all about herself and begins creating her master-

McDonald, Megan, 1959-—*Continued*

piece, the Me collage.

"This beginning chapter book features large type; simple, expressive prose and dialogue; and plenty of child-appealing humor." Booklist

Other titles about Judy Moody are:
Judy Moody & Stink: the holly joliday (2007)
Judy Moody: around the world in 8 1/2 days (2006)
Judy Moody declares independence (2005)
Judy Moody gets famous (2001)
Judy Moody goes to college (2008)
Judy Moody M.D., the doctor is in (2004)
Judy Moody predicts the future (2003)
Judy Moody saves the world (2002)

Stink: the incredible shrinking kid; illustrated by Peter H. Reynolds. Candlewick Press 2005 102p il $12.99 *

Grades: 2 3 4   **Fic**

1. School stories
ISBN 0-7636-2025-4   LC 2003-65246

The shortest kid in the second grade, James Moody, also known as Stink, learns all about the shortest president of the United States, James Madison, when they celebrate Presidents' Day at school

"Delightful full-page and spot-art cartoons and playful language in large type bring the child's adventures to life." SLJ

Other titles about Stink are:
Judy Moody & Stink: the holly joliday (2007)
Stink and the great Guinea Pig Express (2008)
Stink and the incredible super-galactic jawbreaker (2006)
Stink and the world's worst super-stinky sneakers (2007)
Stink: solar system superhero (2010)

McDonough, Yona Zeldis

The doll shop downstairs; illustrated by Heather Maione. Viking 2009 118p il $14.99

Grades: 2 3 4 5   **Fic**

1. Dolls—Fiction 2. Family life—Fiction 3. Immigrants—Fiction 4. Jews—United States—Fiction 5. World War, 1914-1918—Fiction 6. New York (N.Y.)—Fiction
ISBN 978-0-670-01091-2; 0-670-01091-X
    LC 2009-01934

When World War I breaks out, nine-year-old Anna thinks of a way to save her family's beloved New York City doll repair shop. Includes brief author's note about the history of the Madame Alexander doll, a glossary, and timeline.

"Anna's first person narrative creates convincing portrayals of her sisters and parents as well as her personal ups and downs. . . . Pleasant black-and-white pictures illustrate the action while helping children to visualize the period setting." Booklist

The doll with the yellow star; illustrated by Kimberly Bulcken Root. H. Holt 2005 90p il $16.95 *

Grades: 3 4 5   **Fic**

1. Holocaust, 1933-1945—Fiction 2. Dolls—Fiction 3. Jews—Fiction
ISBN 0-8050-6337-4   LC 2002-27554

When France falls to Germany at the start of World War II, nine-year-old Claudine must leave her beloved parents and friends to stay with relatives in America, accompanied by her doll, Violette

"This fiction book is informative, enjoyable, and passionately written." Libr Media Connect

McDowell, Marilyn Taylor

Carolina Harmony. Delacorte 2009 288p $16.99; lib bdg $19.99 *

Grades: 4 5 6 7   **Fic**

1. Orphans—Fiction 2. Farm life—Fiction 3. Blue Ridge Mountains region—Fiction
ISBN   978-0-385-73590-2;   0-385-73590-1; 978-0-385-90575-6 (lib bdg); 0-385-90575-0 (lib bdg)

"After Carolina's beloved Auntie Shen suffers a stroke, Carolina escapes from an unpleasant foster placement. The orphaned 10-year-old finds love at Harmony Farm, but the web of lies she spins almost leads to losing that home too. . . . This third-person narrative unwinds leisurely, with plenty of backtracking to fill in details of Carolina's life and the glories of her world in the Blue Ridge Mountains. . . . McDowell reveals her love for this part of the world, savoring the language, the environment, and the traditions of mountain culture." Booklist

McGhee, Alison, 1960-

Julia Gillian (and the art of knowing); pictures by Drazen Kozjan. Scholastic Press 2008 280p il $15.99 *

Grades: 3 4 5   **Fic**

1. Dogs—Fiction 2. Fear—Fiction 3. Family life—Fiction 4. Minnesota—Fiction
ISBN 978-0-545-03348-0; 0-545-03348-9
    LC 2007024898

Nine-year-old Julia Gillian learns a lot about facing fear as she and her St. Bernard, Bigfoot, take long walks through their Minneapolis neighborhood one hot summer, and she seeks the courage to finish a book that could have an unhappy ending.

"Julia Gillian's fears and their ultimate resolution are very relatable. The book is well paced, laced with line drawings that capture Julia Gillian's slightly whimsical personality." Publ Wkly

Other titles in this series are:
Julia Gillian (and the quest for joy) (2009)
Julia Gillian (and the dream of the dog) (2010)

Snap; a novel. Candlewick Press 2004 129p $15.99

Grades: 5 6 7 8   **Fic**

1. Friendship—Fiction 2. Grandmothers—Fiction 3. Death—Fiction
ISBN 0-7636-2002-5   LC 2002-34998

Eleven-year-old Edwina confronts old and new challenges when her longtime best friend Sally faces the inevitable death of the grandmother who raised her.

This "features memorable characters and a tolerance for eccentricity, emotional subtlety and complexity, themes of acceptance of death and love, and a spare and poetic text that begs to be reread and savored." SLJ

McGraw, Eloise Jarvis, 1915-2000

The moorchild; [by] Eloise McGraw. Margaret K. McElderry Bks. 1996 241p $17; pa $5.99

Grades: 4 5 6 7   Fic
    1. Fantasy fiction 2. Fairies—Fiction
    ISBN 0-689-80654-X; 1-4169-2768-9 (pa)
                                          LC 95-34107

A Newbery Medal honor book, 1997

"Saaski, a half-human, half-Moorfolk child, is banished from the Mound and placed as a changeling in a human village, where she is regarded with suspicion and treated with scorn." Horn Book Guide

"Incorporating some classic fantasy motifs and icons, McGraw . . . conjures up an appreciably familiar world that, as evidence of her storytelling power, still strikes an original chord." Publ Wkly

McKay, Hilary, 1959-

Dog Friday. Margaret K. McElderry Bks. 1995 135p hardcover o.p. pa $4.99

Grades: 4 5 6   Fic
    1. Dogs—Fiction 2. Great Britain—Fiction
    ISBN 0-689-80383-4; 0-689-81765-7 (pa)
                                          LC 95-4446

First published 1994 in the United Kingdom

Ten-year-old Robin Brogan is determined to keep the dog he finds abandoned on the beach from being impounded by the police

"The sharply realized characters, fast-paced story, and witty dialogue make this English novel both distinctive and refreshing." Booklist

Other titles about the Brogan family and their friends are:

The amber cat (1997)
Dolphin luck (1999)

Saffy's angel. Margaret K. McElderry Bks. 2002 152p $16; pa $4.99 *

Grades: 5 6 7 8   Fic
    1. Family life—Fiction 2. Adoption—Fiction 3. Great Britain—Fiction
    ISBN 0-689-84933-8; 0-689-84934-6 (pa)
                                          LC 2001-44110

First published 2001 in the United Kingdom

After learning that she was adopted, thirteen-year-old Saffron's relationship with her eccentric, artistic family changes, until they help her go back to Italy where she was born to find a special momento of her past

"Like the Casson household itself, the plot is a chaotic whirl that careens off in several directions simultaneously. But McKay always skillfully draws each clearly defined character back into the story with witty, well-edited details; rapid dialogue; and fine pacing." Booklist

Other titles in this series are:

Indigo's star (2004)
Permanent Rose (2005)
Caddy ever after (2006)
Forever Rose (2008)

McKinnon, Hannah Roberts

Franny Parker. Farrar Straus Giroux 2009 149p $16 *

Grades: 5 6 7 8   Fic
    1. Family life—Fiction 2. Droughts—Fiction 3. Violence—Fiction 4. Oklahoma—Fiction
    ISBN 978-0-374-32469-8; 0-374-32469-7
                                          LC 2008-01702

Through a hot, dry Oklahoma summer, twelve-year-old Franny tends wild animals brought by her neighbors, hears gossip during a weekly quilting bee, befriends a new neighbor who has some big secrets, and learns to hope.

"Franny is a relatable and consistent narrator, the homey rural setting is thoughtfully rendered and the easy prose should appeal to reluctant readers." Publ Wkly

McKissack, Patricia C., 1944-

Abby takes a stand; illustrated [by] Gordon C. James. Viking 2005 104p il (Scraps of time) $14.99; pa $4.99

Grades: 2 3 4   Fic
    1. Civil rights demonstrations—Fiction 2. African Americans—Fiction 3. Tennessee—Fiction
    ISBN 0-670-06011-9; 0-14-240687-2 (pa)
                                          LC 2004-21641

Gee recalls for her grandchildren what happened in 1960 in Nashville, Tennessee, when she, aged ten, passed out flyers while her cousin and other adults held sit-ins at restaurants and lunch counters to protest segregation.

"Although short and simply told, the book gives readers a kid's-eye view of important happenings and reminds them that history is something that is always in the making. Fine black-and-white art adds to the ambience of the time." Booklist

Other titles in this series are:

Away west (2006)
A song for Harlem (2007)
The homerun king (2008)

Let my people go; Bible stories told by a freeman of color to his daughter, Charlotte, in Charleston, South Carolina, 1806-16; by Patricia and Fredrick McKissack; illustrated by James Ransome. Atheneum Bks. for Young Readers 1998 134p il $20 *

Grades: 4 5 6 7   Fic
    1. African Americans—Fiction 2. Bible stories 3. Slavery—Fiction
    ISBN 0-689-80856-9   LC 97-19983

"An Anne Schwartz book"

Charlotte, the daughter of a free black man who worked as a blacksmith in Charleston, South Carolina, in the early 1800s recalls the stories from the Bible that her father shared with her, relating them to the experiences of African Americans

"The poignant juxtaposition of the Biblical characters and Charlotte's personal narrative is authentic and moving. . . . The occasional illustrations are powerful oil paintings in rich colors, emotional and evocative." SLJ

Includes bibliographical references

McKissack, Patricia C., 1944-—*Continued*

Stitchin' and pullin'; a Gee's Bend quilt; illustrated by Cozbi A. Cabrera. Random House 2008 unp il $17.99; lib bdg $20.99

Grades: 2 3 4 5   **Fic**
1. Quilts—Fiction 2. African Americans—Fiction 3. Family life—Fiction 4. Alabama—Fiction 5. Novels in verse
ISBN   978-0-375-83163-8;   0-375-83163-0; 978-0-375-93163-5 (lib bdg); 0-375-93163-5 (lib bdg)
LC 2007011066

As a young African American girl pieces her first quilt together, the history of her family, community, and the struggle for justice and freedom in Gee's Bend, Alabama unfolds.

"Rich naif-style paintings in a warm, deep palette bring the poems to life and reflect their tone and spirit. . . . It's marvelously clear that McKissack understands the creative pulse of the quilter and artist." Horn Book

Tippy Lemmey; illustrated by Susan Keeter. Simon & Schuster 2003 59p il pa $3.99 *

Grades: 2 3 4   **Fic**
1. Dogs—Fiction 2. African Americans—Fiction 3. Tennessee—Fiction
ISBN 0-689-85019-0

"Ready-for-chapters"

"In 1951, in Templeton, TN, Leanne Martin and her friends Paul and Jeannie are at war with Tippy Lemmey, a dog that frightens them. . . . The kids learn that Tippy is simply a puppy who wants to play, and that his owner is fighting in Korea. Leanne remains unconvinced about the dog's good intentions, but when the friends see thieves stealing him and other neighborhood dogs to sell across state, they rescue the animals and are rewarded when Tippy gets them out of a dangerous situation. . . . This charming and humorous story moves along at a fast pace, making it perfect for readers just venturing into chapter-book territory." SLJ

McMullan, Margaret

How I found the Strong; a Civil War story. Houghton Mifflin 2004 136p $15

Grades: 5 6 7 8   **Fic**
1. United States—History—1861-1865, Civil War—Fiction 2. Mississippi—Fiction 3. Slavery—Fiction
ISBN 0-618-35008-X   LC 2003-12294

Frank Russell, known as Shanks, wishes he could have gone with his father and brother to fight for Mississippi and the Confederacy, but his experiences with the war and his changing relationship with the family slave, Buck, change his thinking.

"The crisply written narrative is full of regional speech and detail, creating a vivid portrait." Voice Youth Advocates

When I crossed No-Bob. Houghton Mifflin Company 2007 209p $16

Grades: 5 6 7 8   **Fic**
1. Farm life—Fiction 2. Mississippi—Fiction 3. Abandoned children—Fiction 4. Reconstruction (1865-1876)—Fiction 5. Race relations—Fiction
ISBN 978-0-618-71715-6; 0-618-71715-3
LC 2007-12753

Ten years after the Civil War's end, twelve-year-old Addy, abandoned by her parents, is taken from the horrid town of No-Bob by schoolteacher Frank Russell and his bride, but when her father returns to claim her she must find another way to leave her O'Donnell past behind.

"The simple prose can be pure poetry. . . . Readers will be drawn by the history close-up and by the elemental moral choice." Booklist

McSwigan, Marie, 1907-1962

Snow treasure; [by] Marie McSwigan; illustrated by Mary Reardon. Dutton's Children's Books 2005 c1942 196p il $10.99; pa $5.99 *

Grades: 3 4 5 6   **Fic**
1. World War, 1939-1945—Fiction 2. Norway—Fiction
ISBN 0-525-47626-1; 0-14-240224-9 (pa)
LC 2005042108

A reissue of the title first published 1942

In 1940, when the Nazi invasion of Norway reaches their village in the far north, twelve-year-old Peter and his friends use their sleds to transport nine million dollars worth of gold bullion past the German soldiers to the secret harbor where Peter's uncle keeps his ship ready to take the gold for safekeeping in the United States.

"A dramatic reconstruction of an actual happening. . . . Well written." Booklist

Mead, Alice, 1952-

Junebug. Farrar, Straus & Giroux 1995 101p hardcover o.p. pa $6.99 *

Grades: 3 4 5   **Fic**
1. African Americans—Fiction 2. Sailing—Fiction
ISBN 0-374-33964-3; 0-312-56126-1 (pa)
LC 95-5421

"Junebug approaches his tenth birthday with fear because he knows he'll be forced by the older boys in his housing project to join a gang. On his birthday, with luck and persistence, Junebug realizes his secret dream of one day sailing a boat. The novel contains vivid descriptions of the grim realities of inner-city life but also demonstrates that strong convictions and warm hearts can bring about change." Horn Book Guide

Other titles about Junebug are:
Junebug and the Reverend (1998)
Junebug in trouble (2003)

Meddaugh, Susan

Lulu's hat. Houghton Mifflin 2002 74p il $15; pa $6.95

Grades: 3 4 5   **Fic**
1. Magicians—Fiction
ISBN 0-618-15277-6; 0-618-77127-1 (pa)
LC 2001-16787

"Walter Lorraine books"

"Lulu is adopted and thought to be unable to inherit her family's magic abilities. But when she finds a hat at the bottom of her magician uncle's truck, it allows her to do magic after all—even if it's somewhat unpredictable." Horn Book Guide

"With plot twists, cliff-hanger chapter endings, a large

Meddaugh, Susan—*Continued*

dose of originality, sparkling humor, and even an epilogue, this witty chapter book will hold readers' attention." SLJ

Meehl, Brian

Out of Patience. Delacorte Press 2006 292p hardcover o.p. lib bdg $17.99; pa $6.50

Grades: 5 6 7 8   **Fic**

1. Family life—Fiction 2. Kansas—Fiction
ISBN 0-385-73299-6; 0-385-90320-0 (lib bdg); 0-440-42090-3 (pa)   LC 2005-13873

Twelve-year-old Jake Waters cannot wait to escape the small town of Patience, Kansas, until the arrival of a cursed toilet plunger causes him to reevaluate his feelings toward his family and its history.

This includes "well-drawn characters, page-turning action, and lively prose peppered with dry humor." Bull Cent Child Books

Menotti, Gian Carlo, 1911-2007

Amahl and the night visitors; illustrated by Michèle Lemieux. Morrow 1986 64p il $21

Grades: 2 3 4   **Fic**

1. Jesus Christ—Fiction 2. Magi—Fiction
ISBN 0-688-05426-9   LC 84-27196

Relates how a crippled young shepherd comes to accompany the three Kings on their way to pay hommage to the newborn Jesus

"Some of the pictures, which are dominated by reddish brown, have rich tension and composition, as in the one of Amahl's mother contemplating theft, or in the portrait of Melchior describing the Christ child. . . . There is a great deal to look at, and the story, popular since the opera's 1951 debut, has sentimental appeal, humor, and some commanding moments." Bull Cent Child Books

Merrill, Jean, 1923-

The pushcart war; by Jean Merrill; with illustrations by Ronni Solbert. Bantam Doubleday Dell Books for Young Readers 1987 222p il pa $6.50 *

Grades: 5 6 7 8   **Fic**

1. Trucks—Fiction 2. New York (N.Y.)—Fiction
ISBN 0-440-47147-8

A reissue of the title first published 1964 by W. R. Scott

The outbreak of a war between truck drivers and pushcart peddlers brings the mounting problems of traffic to the attention of both the city of New York and the world.

"A book that is both humorous and downright funny. . . . Such a lively book will need little introducing." Horn Book

The toothpaste millionaire; by Jean Merrill; prepared by the Bank Street College of Education. 35th anniversary ed. Houghton Mifflin 2006 129p il $16; pa $5.95

Grades: 4 5 6   **Fic**

1. Business enterprises—Fiction 2. Mathematics—Fiction 3. Cleveland (Ohio)—Fiction
ISBN   978-0-618-75924-8;   0-618-75924-7; 978-0-618-75925-5 (pa); 0-618-75925-5 (pa)

"Bank Street"

A reissue of the title first published 1972

Includes an exclusive interview with the author and a reader's guide.

A young girl describes how her school friend made over a million dollars by creating and marketing a cheaper and better toothpaste

"The illustrations are engaging, the style is light, the project interesting (with more than a few swipes taken at advertising and business practices in our society) and Rufus a believable genius." Bull Cent Child Books

Miles, Miska, 1899-1986

Annie and the Old One; illustrated by Peter Parnall. Little, Brown 1971 44p il lib bdg $16.95; pa $7.95

Grades: 1 2 3 4   **Fic**

1. Navajo Indians—Fiction 2. Death—Fiction
ISBN 0-316-57117-2 (lib bdg); 0-316-57120-2 (pa)

A Newbery Medal honor book, 1972

"An Atlantic Monthy Press book"

"Annie, a young Navajo girl, struggles with the realization that her grandmother, the Old One, must die. Slowly and painfully, she accepts the fact that she cannot change the cyclic rhythms of the earth to which the Old One has been so sensitively attuned." Wis Libr Bull

This is "a poignant, understated, rather brave story of a very real child, set against a background of Navajo traditions and contemporary Indian life. Fine expressive drawings match the simplicity of the story." Horn Book

Milford, Kate

The Boneshaker; [illustrations by Andrea Offermann] Clarion Books 2010 372p il $17

Grades: 5 6 7 8   **Fic**

1. Supernatural—Fiction 2. Bicycles—Fiction 3. Demonology—Fiction 4. Missouri—Fiction
ISBN 978-0-547-24187-6; 0-547-24187-9

                                        LC 2009-45350

When Jake Limberleg brings his traveling medicine show to a small Missouri town in 1913, thirteen-year-old Natalie senses that something is wrong and, after investigating, learns that her love of automata and other machines make her the only one who can set things right.

"Natalie is a well-drawn protagonist with sturdy supporting characters around her. The tension built into the solidly constructed plot is complemented by themes that explore the literal and metaphorical role of crossroads and that thin line between good and evil." Kirkus

Millard, Glenda

The naming of Tishkin Silk; illustrated by Patrice Barton. Farrar, Straus and Giroux 2009 c2003 101p il $15.99

Grades: 3 4 5   **Fic**

1. Personal names—Fiction 2. Family life—Fiction 3. Death—Fiction 4. Friendship—Fiction 5. Australia—Fiction

ISBN 978-0-374-35481-7; 0-374-35481-2

LC 2008-16796

First published 2003 in Australia

Griffin Silk feels responsible for the absence of his mother and baby sister, but he and his new friend Layla find the perfect way to make everyone feel a little bit better.

"Illustrated with softly rendered black-and-white drawings, the gentle, descriptive narrative [is] touched with droll humor . . . and features a likable protagonist and other appealing, diverse characters." Booklist

Followed by: Layla, Queen of Hearts (2010)

Miller, Kirsten, 1963-

Kiki Strike: inside the shadow city; [by] Kirsten Miller. Bloomsbury Children's Books 2006 387p $16.95

Grades: 5 6 7 8   **Fic**

1. Mystery fiction 2. New York (N.Y.)—Fiction

ISBN 978-1-58234-960-2; 1-58234-960-6

LC 2005030945

Life becomes more interesting for Ananka Fishbein when, at the age of twelve, she discovers an underground room in the park across from her New York City apartment and meets a mysterious girl called Kiki Strike who claims that she, too, wants to explore the subterranean world

"If a 12-year-old can be a hardboiled detective, Ananka Fishbein is one. Her narration is fresh and funny, and the author's unadorned, economical, yet descriptive style carries her character through with verve." SLJ

Another title about Kiki Strike is:

Kiki Strike: The empress's tomb (2007)

Mills, Claudia, 1954-

7 x 9 = trouble! pictures by G. Brian Karas. Farrar, Straus & Giroux 2002 103p il $15; pa $6.95 *

Grades: 2 3 4   **Fic**

1. School stories 2. Mathematics—Fiction

ISBN 0-374-36746-9; 0-374-46452-9 (pa)

LC 2001-16028

Third-grader Wilson struggles with his times-tables in order to beat the class deadline

"Mills' sympathetic and detailed treatment of Wilson's travails makes this both a suspenseful and satisfying beginning chapter book." Bull Cent Child Books

Being Teddy Roosevelt; pictures by R.W. Alley. Farrar, Straus and Giroux 2007 89p il $16

Grades: 2 3 4   **Fic**

1. School stories

ISBN 978-0-374-30657-1; 0-374-30657-51

LC 2006-48978

When he is assigned Teddy Roosevelt as his biography project in school, fourth-grader Riley finds himself inspired by Roosevelt's tenacity and perseverance and resolves to find a way to get what he most wants—a saxophone and music lessons

"Lots of funny lines and comical situations enliven the simple story, which is also enriched by its portrait of grade-school friendships and goofy classroom happenings, depicted in Alley's appealing spot drawings." Booklist

How Oliver Olson changed the world; pictures by Heather Maione. Farrar, Straus and Giroux 2009 103p il $15.95 *

Grades: 2 3 4   **Fic**

1. Solar system—Fiction 2. Science projects—Fiction 3. School stories 4. Colorado—Fiction

ISBN 978-0-374-33487-1; 0-374-33487-0

LC 2007-48846

Afraid he will always be an outsider like ex-planet Pluto, nine-year-old Oliver finally shows his extremely overprotective parents that he is capable of doing great things without their help while his class is studying the solar system.

"An engaging and thought-provoking chapter book." Booklist

The totally made-up Civil War diary of Amanda MacLeish. Farrar, Straus and Giroux 2008 197p $16

Grades: 3 4 5   **Fic**

1. Family life—Fiction 2. United States—History—1861-1865, Civil War—Fiction 3. Maryland—Fiction 4. School stories

ISBN 978-0-374-37696-3; 0-374-37696-4

LC 2007-09162

While dealing with her parents' separation and her best friend's distance, Amanda is able to work out some of her anxiety through her fifth-grade project—writing a diary from the point of view of a ten-year-old girl whose brothers fight on opposite sides in the Civil War.

"Mills handles the MacLeish family's separation realistically. . . . Subplots provide the novel's lighter moments. . . . This makes a good choice for Mills' many fans, as well as for children in search of a satisfying family story." Booklist

Milne, A. A. (Alan Alexander), 1882-1956

The House at Pooh Corner; with decorations by Ernest H. Shepard. Dutton c1928 180p il $9.95; pa $4.99 *

Grades: 1 2 3 4   **Fic**

1. Bears—Fiction 2. Animals—Fiction 3. Toys—Fiction

ISBN 0-525-32302-3; 0-14-036122-7 (pa)

First published 1928

"Pooh and Piglet built a house for Eeyore at Pooh Corner. They called it that because it was shorter and sounded better than did Poohanpiglet Corner. Christopher Robin, Rabbit, and other old acquaintances of 'Winnie-the-Pooh' appear, and a new friend, Tigger, is introduced." Carnegie Libr of Pittsburgh

"It is hard to tell what Pooh Bear and his friends would have been without the able assistance of Ernest H. Shepard to see them and picture them so cleverly. . . . They are, and should be, classics." N Y Times Book Rev

Milne, A. A. (Alan Alexander), 1882-1956—Continued

Winnie-the-Pooh; illustrated by Ernest H. Shepard, colored by Hilda Scott. Dutton 1974 c1926 161p il $10.99; pa $4.99 *
Grades: 1 2 3 4   Fic
  1. Bears—Fiction 2. Animals—Fiction 3. Toys—Fiction
  ISBN 0-525-44443-2; 0-14-036121-9 (pa)
  First published 1926
  "The kindly, lovable Pooh is one of an imaginative cast of animal characters which includes Eeyore, the wistfully gloomy donkey, Tigger, Piglet, Kanga, and Roo, all living in a fantasy world presided over by Milne's young son, Christopher Robin. Many of the animals are drawn from figures in Milne's life, though each emerges as a universally recognizable type." Reader's Ency

Mitchell, Stephen, 1943-

The nightingale; [by] Hans Christian Andersen; retold by Stephen Mitchell; illustrated by Bagram Ibatoulline. Candlewick Press 2002 unp il hardcover o.p. pa $6.95
Grades: 2 3 4   Fic
  1. Andersen, Hans Christian, 1805-1875—Adaptations 2. Fairy tales 3. Nightingales—Fiction
  ISBN 0-7636-1521-8; 0-7636-2406-3 (pa)
                    LC 2001-25144
  Though the emperor banishes the nightingale in preference of a jeweled mechanical imitation, the little bird remains faithful and returns years later when the emperor is near death and no one else can help him
  "This is an elegant piece of bookmaking. Mixed-media illustrations (ink, gouache, watercolor) based on Chinese art and costume are rendered in a ceremonial, fairy-tale style." Bull Cent Child Books

The tinderbox; [by] Hans Christian Andersen; retold by Stephen Mitchell; illustrated by Bagram Ibatoulline. Candlewick Press 2007 unp il $17.99
Grades: 2 3 4 5   Fic
  1. Andersen, Hans Christian, 1805-1875—Adaptations 2. Fairy tales
  ISBN 978-0-7636-2078-3; 0-7636-2078-5
                    LC 2006-47554
  With the help of a magic tinderbox, a soldier finds a fortune and pursues a princess imprisoned in a castle.
  "The soldier may be handsome and the princess lovely, but the old witch and the three giant dogs along with the beautifully developed settings really create the superb fairy-tale ambience of this robust telling of Andersen's tale. Ibatoulline's finely hatched pen drawings, washed in muted tones, resemble lithographs." SLJ

Mohr, Nicholasa, 1935-

Going home. Dial Bks. for Young Readers 1986 192p pa $4.95 hardcover o.p.
Grades: 4 5 6   Fic
  1. Puerto Rico—Fiction
  ISBN 0-14-130644-0 (pa)   LC 85-20621

Feeling like an outsider when she visits her relatives in Puerto Rico for the first time, eleven-year-old Felita tries to come to terms with the heritage she always took for granted
  "This is a convincing story that captures the universality of preteen relationships." Rochman. Against borders
  Another title about Felita is:
Felita (1979)

Moloney, James, 1954-

The Book of Lies. HarperCollinsPublishers 2007 360p $16.99; lib bdg $17.89
Grades: 5 6 7 8   Fic
  1. Magic—Fiction 2. Orphans—Fiction 3. Fantasy fiction
  ISBN   978-0-06-057842-8;   0-06-057842-4; 978-0-06-057843-5 (lib bdg); 0-06-057843-2 (lib bdg)
                    LC 2006-29874
  On the night he was brought to an orphanage, Marcel's memories were taken by a sorceror and replaced with new ones by his Book of Lies, but Bea, a girl with the ability to make herself invisible, was watching and is determined to help him discover his true identity.
  "Readers who enjoy the mixture of mystery, riddles, action, and camaraderie will be pleased that the open-ended conclusion leads to a planned sequel." Booklist

Morey, Walt, 1907-1992

Gentle Ben; illustrated by John Schoenherr. Dutton 1965 191p il pa $6.99 hardcover o.p.
Grades: 5 6 7 8   Fic
  1. Bears—Fiction 2. Alaska—Fiction
  ISBN 0-14-240551-5 (pa)
  Set in Alaska before statehood, this is the story of 13-year-old Mark Anderson who befriends a huge brown bear which has been chained in a shed since it was a cub. Finally Mark's father buys the bear, but Orca City's inhabitants eventually insist that the animal, named Ben, be shipped to an uninhabited island. However, the friendship of Mark and Ben endures
  The author "has written a vivid chronicle of Alaska, its people and places, challenges and beauties. Told with a simplicity and dignity which befits its characters, human and animal, [it] is a memorable reading experience." SLJ

Morgan, Nicola, 1961-

Chicken friend; [by] Nicola Morgan. Candlewick Press 2005 148p $15.99
Grades: 5 6 7 8   Fic
  1. Diabetes—Fiction 2. Country life—Fiction 3. Friendship—Fiction 4. Great Britain—Fiction
  ISBN 0-7636-2735-6   LC 2004-54608
  When her parents decide to move their family to the English countryside, homeschool their children, and raise chickens, Becca tries to make friends with her new neighbors by hiding her diabetes and throwing a twelfth birthday party for herself
  "The girl is believable and likable as both character and narrator, which turns an apparently simple story into one that is funny, insightful, and moving." SLJ

Morgenstern, Susie Hoch

A book of coupons; by Susie Morgenstern; illustrated by Serge Bloch; translated by Gill Rosner. Viking 2001 62p il $12.99 *

Grades: 3 4 5   **Fic**

1. Teachers—Fiction 2. School stories
ISBN 0-670-89970-4   LC 00-11940
Original French edition, 1999

Elderly Monsieur Noel, the very unconventional new teacher, gives coupon books for such things as dancing in class and sleeping late, which are bound to get him in trouble with the military discipline of Principal Incarnation Perez

"Morgenstern's witty and poignant tribute to great teachers everywhere proclaims what education should be about. Her message may be pointed, but no reader will be unmoved." Horn Book Guide

Morpurgo, Michael

Kensuke's kingdom. Scholastic Press 2003 c1999 164p hardcover o.p. pa $5.99 *

Grades: 4 5 6 7   **Fic**

1. Survival after airplane accidents, shipwrecks, etc.—Fiction
ISBN 0-439-38202-5; 0-439-59181-3 (pa)
      LC 2002-9078
First published 1999 in the United Kingdom

When Michael is swept off his family's yacht, he washes up on a desert island, where he struggles to survive—until he finds he is not alone

This is "highly readable. . . . The end is bittersweet but believable, and the epilogue is a sad commentary on the long-lasting effects of war." Booklist

On angel wings; illustrated by Quentin Blake. Candlewick 2007 unp il $8.99 *

Grades: 3 4 5   **Fic**

1. Jesus Christ—Nativity 2. Angels—Fiction 3. Shepherds—Fiction
ISBN 0-7636-3466-2

Grandpa tells "of his boyhood recollection of being with the adult shepherds when the angel Gabriel . . . told them of the Baby Jesus's birth. . . . The adults follow and leave the boy behind to tend the sheep. Gabriel then reappears and offers to fly him to the stable to see the baby for himself." SLJ

"Morpurgo's tone blends reverence with wit, a combination matched in Blake's pen-and-ink and watercolor cartoons." Publ Wkly

Waiting for Anya. Viking 1991 c1990 172p hardcover o.p. pa $4.99

Grades: 5 6 7 8   **Fic**

1. World War, 1939-1945—Fiction 2. Jews—Fiction 3. France—Fiction
ISBN 0-670-83735-0; 0-14-038431-6 (pa)
      LC 90-50560
First published 1990 in the United Kingdom

"A World War II adventure story set in Vichy, France, this centers on a young shepherd, Jo, who becomes involved in smuggling Jewish children across the border from his mountain village to Spain. Morpurgo has injected the basic conventions of heroism and villainy with some complexities of character. . . . Independent

readers will appreciate the simple, clear style and fast-paced plot of the book, which will also hold up well in group read-alouds, commanding attention to ethics as well as action." Bull Cent Child Books

War horse; by Michael Morpurgo. Scholastic 2007 165p $16.99

Grades: 5 6 7 8   **Fic**

1. Horses—Fiction 2. World War, 1914-1918—Fiction
ISBN 978-0-439-79663-7; 0-439-79663-6
      LC 2006044368
First published 1982 in the United Kingdom

Joey the horse recalls his experiences growing up on an English farm, his struggle for survival as a cavalry horse during World War I, and his reunion with his beloved master

"At times deeply affecting, the story balances the horror with moments of respite and care." Horn Book Guide

Morris, Gerald, 1963-

The adventures of Sir Lancelot the Great; illustrated by Aaron Renier. Houghton Mifflin Company 2008 92p il (The knights' tales) $15; pa $4.99

Grades: 3 4 5 6   **Fic**

1. Arthur, King—Fiction 2. Lancelot (Legendary character)—Fiction 3. Knights and knighthood—Fiction 4. Great Britain—History—0-1066—Fiction
ISBN 978-0-618-77714-3; 0-618-77714-8; 978-0-547-23756-5 (pa); 0-547-23756-1 (pa)
      LC 2007-41167

This novel relates the story of Sir Lancelot, the bravest knight in King Arthur's court.

"This trim novel, with simple vocabulary and brief, witty chapters, is an ideal fit for early readers. . . . Fans of the legendary characters may find particular delight in this irreverent and unabashedly silly exploration of Arthur's court and his most influential knight. . . . Frequent black-and-white illustrations supplement the text, highlighting (and in most cases, exaggerating) elements from humorous passages." Bull Cent Child Books

Another title in this series is:
The adventures of Sir Givret the Short (2008)

Morris, Taylor

Total knockout; tale of an ex-class president. Aladdin Mix 2008 265p pa $5.99

Grades: 5 6 7 8   **Fic**

1. School stories 2. Politics—Fiction 3. Boxing—Fiction 4. Family life—Fiction
ISBN 978-1-4169-3599-5; 1-4169-3599-1

"After winning the class-president election for an unprecedented third straight time, Lucia has ambitious plans for her eighth-grade year. Along with her prestigious office, she has a reliable best friend, an unthreatening vice president, and a cool hobby: boxing. Her orderly world unravels, though, when her reckless scheme to purchase new vending machines backfires and she faces possible impeachment. . . . The well-paced plot balances Lucia's inner turmoil with interesting episodes involving school politics, friendships, and family relationships." SLJ

Morrison, P. R.

Wind tamer. Bloomsbury Children's Books 2006 335p $16.95

Grades: 4 5 6   Fic

1. Courage—Fiction 2. Hurricanes—Fiction 3. Winds—Fiction

ISBN 1-58234-781-6

Archie learns on his tenth birthday that he is about to inherit the family curse of cowardice unless he fights the powerful hurricane that will take his bravery.

"The fantasy atmosphere is well defined, with intriguing characters and imaginative magical elements." SLJ

Moses, Shelia P.

Sallie Gal and the Wall-a-kee man; illustrated by Niki Daly. Scholastic 2007 152p il $15.99 *

Grades: 3 4 5   Fic

1. African Americans—Fiction 2. Family life—Fiction 3. North Carolina—Fiction

ISBN 978-0-439-90890-0; 0-439-90890-6

LC 2006033171

More than anything, Sallie Gal wants pretty ribbons to wear in her hair, but she knows that they cannot afford them and Momma has too much dignity to accept charity.

"Appealing black-and-white illustrations in various sizes embellish the text. Moses takes a fond look at strong family ties and the values of honesty and hard work. Short paragraphs and peppy dialogue make this easy chapter book a candidate for reading aloud." SLJ

Moss, Jenny, 1958-

Winnie's war. Walker & Co. 2009 178p $16.99

Grades: 5 6 7 8   Fic

1. Influenza—Fiction 2. Epidemics—Fiction 3. Family life—Fiction 4. Texas—Fiction

ISBN 978-0-8027-9819-0; 0-8027-9819-5

LC 2008-23233

Living in the shadow of a Texas cemetery, twelve-year-old Winnie Grace struggles to keep the Spanish influenza of 1918 from touching her family—her coffin-building father, her troubled mother, and her two baby sisters.

"The small town of Coward Creek comes to life in Moss's writing. . . . Winnie and the others populate a solid plot, but it is the setting and the characters that will make this book last as a popular favorite with a space on shelves well into the future." Voice Youth Advocates

Moss, Marissa

Alien Eraser to the rescue. Candlewick Press 2009 52p il (Max Disaster) $16.99; pa $6.99

Grades: 3 4 5   Fic

1. Extraterrestrial beings—Fiction

ISBN 978-0-7636-3577-0; 0-7636-3577-4; 978-0-7636-4407-9 (pa); 0-7636-4407-2 (pa)

Welcome to Max's book of inventions, experiments, comic strips, and random thoughts about school, pimply older brothers, mutant marshmallows, erasers and good parents who get into bad fights.

"Moss is a master at verbalizing kids' anxieties and channeling their astute observations of family life—both as it breaks apart and begins to mend." Publ Wkly

Other titles in the Max Disaster series are:
Alien Eraser unravels the mystery of the pyramids (2009)
Alien Eraser reveals the secrets of evolution (2009)

Amelia's 6th-grade notebook; [by] Marissa Moss. Simon & Schuster Books for Young Readers 2005 unp il $9.95 *

Grades: 4 5 6   Fic

1. School stories

ISBN 0-689-87040-X   LC 2004-45309

"A Paula Wiseman book"

Problems arise for Amelia when she starts sixth grade at the same middle school where her older sister Cleo is an eighth-grader, and she gets the school's meanest teacher for three of her classes

"Both insightful and entertaining, Amelia's first-person narrative rings true. . . . [This] features a handwritten format; colorful, cartoonlike illustrations; and charming doodles with descriptive asides." Booklist

Other titles about Amelia are:
The all-new Amelia (1999)
Amelia hits the road (1997)
Amelia lends a hand (2002)
Amelia takes command (1998)
Amelia works it out (2000)
Amelia writes again (1996)
Amelia's are-we-there-yet longest ever car trip (1997)
Amelia's book of notes & note passing (2006)
Amelia's boredom survival guide (1999)
Amelia's bully survival guide (1998)
Amelia's family ties (2000)
Amelia's 5th-grade notebook (2003)
Amelia's guide to gossip (2006)
Amelia's itchy-twitchy, lovey-dovey summer at Camp Mosquito (2008)
Amelia's longest, biggest, most-fights-ever family reunion (2006)
Amelia's most unforgettable embarrassing moments (2005)
Amelia's must-keep resolutions for the best year ever! (2007)
Amelia's notebook (1995)
Amelia's school survival guide (2002)
Luv, Amelia luv, Nadia (1999)
Oh boy, Amelia! (2001)
Vote 4 Amelia (2007)
Amelia's science fair diaster (2009)

Mould, Chris

The wooden mile. Roaring Brook Press 2008 176p il (Something wickedly weird) $9.95 *

Grades: 3 4 5 6   Fic

1. Supernatural—Fiction 2. Pirates—Fiction 3. Werewolves—Fiction

ISBN 978-1-59643-383-0; 1-59643-383-3

LC 2008011258

First published 2007 in the United Kingdom

Eleven-year-old Stanley Buggle, happily anticipating a long summer vacation in the house he inherits from his great-uncle, discovers, soon after arriving in the seemingly peaceful village of Crampton Rock, that along with the house he has also inherited some sinister neighbors, a talking stuffed fish, and a host of mysteries surrounding his great-uncle's death.

"With its fairly easy text, many black-and-white illus-

Mould, Chris—*Continued*

trations, and a dramatic scene silhouetted on the cover, this chapter book will appeal to young readers who like their fiction fast-paced and a bit scary. Mould's richly atmospheric ink drawings capture the rather macabre tone of the story." Booklist

Other titles in this series are:
The icy hand (2008)
The darkling curse (2009)
Smugglers' mine (2010)

Mourlevat, Jean-Claude

The pull of the ocean; [by] Jean-Claude Mourlevat; translated from the French by Y. Maudet. Delacorte Press 2006 190p hardcover o.p. lib bdg $17.99; pa $6.50 *

Grades: 5 6 7   **Fic**
1. Size—Fiction 2. Brothers—Fiction 3. Twins—Fiction 4. France—Fiction
ISBN 978-0-385-73348-9; 0-385-73348-8; 978-0-385-90364-6 (lib bdg); 0-385-90364-2 (lib bdg); 978-0-385-73666-4 (pa); 0-385-73666-5 (pa)
        LC 2006001802

Loosely based on Charles Perrault's "Tom Thumb," seven brothers in modern-day France flee their poor parents' farm, led by the youngest who, although mute and unusually small, is exceptionally wise.

This "is a memorable novel that readers will find engaging and intellectually satisfying." SLJ

Murphy, Jim, 1947-

Desperate journey. Scholastic Press 2006 278p il map $16.99

Grades: 5 6 7 8   **Fic**
1. Erie Canal (N.Y.)—Fiction 2. Family life—Fiction
ISBN 0-439-07806-7   LC 2006-02526

In the mid-1800s, with both her father and her uncle in jail on an assault charge, Maggie, her brother, and her ailing mother rush their barge along the Erie Canal to deliver their heavy cargo or lose everything.

This is a "gripping novel." Booklist

Murphy, Pat, 1955-

The wild girls. Viking 2007 288p $16.99; pa $7.99

Grades: 5 6 7 8   **Fic**
1. Authorship—Fiction 2. Friendship—Fiction 3. School stories
ISBN 978-0-670-06226-3; 978-0-14-241245-9 (pa)
        LC 2007-14830

When thirteen-year-old Joan moves to California in 1972, she becomes friends with Sarah, who is timid at school but an imaginative leader when they play in the woods, and after winning a writing contest together they are recruited for an exclusive summer writing class that gives them new insights into themselves and others.

"Supporting characters are fully formed and intriguing. Murphy evokes her setting with skill and plays out themes of creativity and self-expression with grace and intensity." SLJ

Murphy, Rita

Bird. Delacorte Press 2008 151p $15.99; lib bdg $18.99

Grades: 5 6 7 8   **Fic**
1. Houses—Fiction 2. Supernatural—Fiction 3. Flight—Fiction 4. Kites—Fiction 5. Vermont—Fiction
ISBN 978-0-385-73018-1; 0-385-73018-7; 978-0-385-90557-2 (lib bdg); 0-385-90557-2 (lib bdg)
        LC 2008-04690

Miranda, a small, delicate girl easily carried off by the wind, lands at Bourne Manor on the coast of Lake Champlain and is raised by the dour Wysteria Barrows, but she begins to believe rumors that the Manor is cursed and, aided by a new friend and kites secreted in an attic, seeks to escape.

"This enchanting novel is well written with lyrical text and beautiful descriptions. . . . Good for middle school students, this book will make a nice addition to school and public libraries alike." Libr Media Connect

Myers, Laurie

Lewis and Clark and me; a dog's tale; illustrations by Michael Dooling. Holt & Co. 2002 64p il $16.95 *

Grades: 3 4 5 6   **Fic**
1. Lewis, Meriwether, 1774-1809—Fiction 2. Clark, William, 1770-1838—Fiction 3. Lewis and Clark Expedition (1804-1806)—Fiction 4. Dogs—Fiction
ISBN 0-8050-6368-4   LC 00-47298

Seaman, Meriwether Lewis's Newfoundland dog, describes Lewis and Clark's expedition, which he accompanied from St. Louis to the Pacific Ocean

"Myers is a dog lover, and that respect comes through in the dignified portrayal of Seaman. Attractive, realistic paintings illustrate the book, giving a feel for the period and, most importantly, a visual personality to Seaman." SLJ

Includes bibliographical references

Myers, Walter Dean, 1937-

Three swords for Granada; illustrated by John Speirs. Holiday House 2002 154p il $15.95

Grades: 3 4 5 6   **Fic**
1. Cats—Fiction 2. Dogs—Fiction 3. Fantasy fiction 4. Spain—Fiction
ISBN 0-8234-1676-3   LC 2001-59357

In 1420 Spain, three young cat friends join the warrior cats as they struggle to save their beloved Granada from the vicious dogs of the Fidorean Guard

"The snappy dialogue, flashing swords, and daring action, as well as the charming ink-and-wash drawings, will appeal to readers who enjoy high adventure laced with a touch of whimsy." SLJ

Myracle, Lauren, 1969-

Eleven. Dutton Children's Books 2004 201p (The Winnie years) $16.99; pa $6.99

Grades: 4 5 6 7   **Fic**
1. Friendship—Fiction 2. Family life—Fiction
ISBN 0-525-47165-0; 0-14-240346-6 (pa)
        LC 2003-49076

Myracle, Lauren, 1969-—*Continued*

The year between turning eleven and turning twelve bring many changes for Winnie and her friends

"The inclusion of details about the everyday lives of these girls . . . will make this novel enjoyable, even for reluctant readers. However, it's the book's occasional revelation of harder truths that lifts it out of the ordinary." SLJ

Other titles in this series are:

Twelve (2007)

Thirteen (2008)

Thirteen plus one (2010)

Luv ya bunches. Amulet Books 2009 335p $15.95 *

Grades: 4 5 6   **Fic**

1. Friendship—Fiction 2. School stories

ISBN 978-0-8109-4211-0; 0-8109-4211-9

LC 2009012585

Four friends—each named after a flower—navigate the ups and downs of fifth grade. Told through text messages, blog posts, screenplay, and straight narrative

Myracle "displays a shining awareness of and sensitivity to the highly textured society of tween girls. . . . This is a fun, challenging, and gently edifying story." Booklist

Nagda, Ann Whitehead, 1945-

The perfect cat-sitter; illustrated by Stephanie Roth. Holiday House 2007 104p il $15.95

Grades: 2 3 4   **Fic**

1. Cats—Fiction 2. School stories

ISBN 978-0-8234-2112-1; 0-8234-2112-0

LC 2007-18301

When her friend Rana goes to India, Susan volunteers to take care of her cat and her sister's fish, but the job turns out to be much more difficult than she expected.

"Humor infuses the story. . . . Classroom dynamics and school friendships are well rendered, as are all sides of Susan's perfectionism. . . . Soft black-and-white illustrations capture Susan's emotions throughout her escapades." Booklist

Tarantula power! by Ann Whitehead Nagda; illustrated by Stephanie Roth. Holiday House 2007 93p il $15.95

Grades: 2 3 4   **Fic**

1. School stories 2. Tarantulas—Fiction 3. Bullies—Fiction

ISBN 978-0-8234-1991-3; 0-8234-1991-6

Forced to work with the class bully on a project to design a new breakfast cereal, Richard also tries to stop him from picking on second-graders by using tarantula power.

"The convincing dialogue is crammed with interesting facts. . . . The characters and plot develop at a quick and mostly believable pace. Black-and-white wash illustrations match the action." SLJ

Naidoo, Beverley

Journey to Jo'burg; a South African story; illustrations by Eric Velasquez. Lippincott 1986 80p il pa $4.99 hardcover o.p. *

Grades: 5 6 7 8   **Fic**

1. South Africa—Race relations—Fiction

ISBN 0-06-440237-1 (pa)   LC 85-45508

"This touching novel graphically depicts the plight of Africans living in the horror of South Africa. Thirteen-year-old Maledi and her 9-year-old brother leave their small village, take the perilous journey to the city, and encounter, firsthand, the painful struggle for justice, freedom, and dignity in the 'City of Gold.' A provocative story with a message readers will long remember." Soc Educ

Followed by Chain of fire (1990)

Namioka, Lensey

Yang the youngest and his terrible ear; illustrated by Kees de Kiefte. Little, Brown 1992 134p il pa $4.50 hardcover o.p. *

Grades: 4 5 6   **Fic**

1. Chinese—United States—Fiction 2. Family life—Fiction

ISBN 0-440-40917-9 (pa)   LC 91-30345

"Joy Street books"

Recently arrived in Seattle from China, musically untalented Yingtao is faced with giving a violin performance to attract new students for his father when he would rather be working on friendships and playing baseball

"Namioka explores issues of diversity, self-realization, friendship, and duty with sensitivity and a great deal of humor." Horn Book

Other titles about the Yang family are:

Yang the eldest and his odd jobs (2000)

Yang the second and her secret admirers (1998)

Yang the third and her impossible family (1995)

Napoli, Donna Jo, 1948-

The king of Mulberry Street; [by] Donna Jo Napoli. Wendy Lamb Books 2005 245p lib bdg $17.99$15.95; pa $6.50 *

Grades: 5 6 7 8   **Fic**

1. Immigrants—Fiction 2. Italian Americans—Fiction 3. Jews—Fiction

ISBN 0-385-90890-3 (lib bdg); 0-553-49416-3 (pa)

LC 2004-30860

In 1892, Dom, a nine-year old Jewish stowaway from Naples, Italy, arrives in New York and must learn to survive the perils of street life in the big city

"The characters are drawn with depth . . . and the unsentimental story is honest about the grinding poverty and the prejudice among various immigrant groups." Booklist

The prince of the pond; otherwise known as De Fawg Pin; illustrated by Judy Schachner. Dutton Children's Bks. 1992 151p il hardcover o.p. pa $4.99

Grades: 4 5 6   **Fic**

1. Frogs—Fiction

ISBN 0-525-44976-0; 0-14-037151-6 (pa)

LC 91-40340

Napoli, Donna Jo, 1948-—*Continued*

This story based on the frog prince motif is "told from the point of view of Jade, a female frog. . . . Pin (as the Prince calls himself, hampered in his speech by a long, fat tongue attached at the front of his mouth) is handsome, but strangely ignorant of everything . . . so Jade must teach him the ropes. . . . Eventually, when the opportunity of kissing a princess represents itself, Pin leaps at it and disappears from Jade's life forever." Booklist

"An animal fantasy that fairy tale readers will relish. . . . Schachner's numerous ink-and-wash drawings go far in supporting the characterization." Bull Cent Child Books

Sly the Sleuth and the pet mysteries; by Donna Jo Napoli and Robert Furrow; illustrated by Heather Maione. Dial Books for Young Readers 2005 96p il $15.99 *

Grades: 2 3 4   **Fic**

1. Mystery fiction 2. Pets—Fiction
ISBN 0-8037-2993-6   LC 2003-24090

Contents: Case #1: Sly and the fat cat; Case #2: Sly and the Wish Fish; Case #3: Sly and the third case

Sly the Sleuth, also known as Sylvia, solves three mysteries for her friends and neighbors, all involving pets, through her detective agency, Sleuth for Hire.

"The stories are easy to read and engaging, the pen-and-ink illustrations convey the light tone of the adventures, and Sly's first-person narration is convincing." Horn Book Guide

Other titles about Sly the Sleuth are:
Sly the Sleuth and the sports mysteries (2006)
Sly the Sleuth and the food mysteries (2007)
Sly the Sleuth and the code mysteries (2009)

Stones in water. Dutton Children's Bks. 1997 209p hardcover o.p. pa $5.99

Grades: 5 6 7 8   **Fic**

1. World War, 1939-1945—Fiction
ISBN 0-525-45842-5; 0-14-130600-9 (pa)
         LC 97-14253

After being taken by German soldiers from a local movie theater along with other Italian boys including his Jewish friend, Roberto is forced to work in Germany, escapes into the Ukrainian winter, before desperately trying to make his way back home to Venice

This is a "gripping, meticulously researched story (loosely based on the life of an actual survivor)." Publ Wkly

Naylor, Phyllis Reynolds, 1933-

Emily's fortune; illustrated by Ross Collins. Delacorte Press 2010 147p il $14.99 *

Grades: 3 4 5 6   **Fic**

1. Orphans—Fiction 2. Voyages and travels—Fiction 3. Inheritance and succession—Fiction 4. Uncles—Fiction 5. West (U.S.)—Fiction
ISBN 978-0-385-73616-9; 0-385-73616-9
         LC 2009013096

While traveling to her aunt's home in Redbud by train and stagecoach, quiet young Emily and her turtle, Rufus, team up with Jackson, fellow orphan and troublemaker extraordinaire, to outsmart mean Uncle Victor, who is after Emily's inheritance.

"The local vernacular is lively and fun and the characters are well developed. Cliff-hangers between chapters are written in large boldface to keep readers hooked. . . . Simple, black-and-white illustrations complement the unfolding story. A rip-roaring good time." SLJ

Faith, hope, and Ivy June. Delacorte Press 2009 280p $16.99; lib bdg $19.99

Grades: 5 6 7 8   **Fic**

1. School stories 2. Kentucky—Fiction 3. Appalachian region—Fiction
ISBN 978-0-385-73615-2; 0-385-73615-0; 978-0-385-90588-6 (lib bdg); 0-385-90588-2 (lib bdg)
         LC 2008-19625

During a student exchange program, seventh-graders Ivy June and Catherine share their lives, homes, and communities, and find that although their lifestyles are total opposites they have a lot in common.

"This finely crafted novel . . . depicts a deep friendship growing slowly through understanding. As both girls wait out tragedies at the book's end, they cling to hope—and each other—in a thoroughly real and unaffected way. Naylor depicts Appalachia with sympathetic realism." Kirkus

The grand escape; illustrated by Alan Daniel. Atheneum Pubs. 1993 148p il hardcover o.p. pa $5.50

Grades: 4 5 6   **Fic**

1. Cats—Fiction 2. Adventure fiction
ISBN 0-689-31722-0; 0-689-87407-3 (pa)
         LC 91-40816

After years of being strictly house cats, Marco and Polo escape into the wonderful, but dangerous outside world and are sent on three challenging adventures by a group of cats known as the Club of Mysteries

"While Naylor's feline explorers are amusing and lovable, their behavior is always catlike, and their interpretation of human foibles is often hilarious." Booklist

Other titles Marco and Polo are:
Carlotta's kittens and the Club of Mysteries (2000)
The healing of Texas Jake (1997)
Polo's mother (2005)

Patches and scratches; by Phyllis Reynolds Naylor; illustrated by Marcy Ramsey. Marshall Cavendish Children 2007 74p il (Simply Sarah) $14.99

Grades: 2 3 4   **Fic**

1. Cats—Fiction 2. Pets—Fiction 3. Friendship—Fiction
ISBN 978-0-7614-5347-5; 0-7614-5347-4
         LC 2006026564

Sarah, who is very good at solving problems, tries to help her friend Peter find a pet that he and his grandmother both like

"The plot twists and turns, the dialogue is fast and easy, and the adult characters . . . are as much fun as the kids and their beloved animals. Ink-and-wash illustrations showing a multiracial neighborhood add a pleasing shine to the story." Booklist

Other titles in this series are:
Anyone can eat squid (2005)
Cuckoo feathers (2006)
Eating enchiladas (2008)

Naylor, Phyllis Reynolds, 1933-—*Continued*

Roxie and the Hooligans; with illustrations by Alexandra Boiger. Atheneum Books for Young Readers 2006 115p il $15.95; pa $4.99 *

Grades: 3 4 5   **Fic**
  1. Adventure fiction
  ISBN 1-4169-0243-0; 1-4169-0244-9 (pa)
                                    LC 2004-24645
  "Ginee Seo books."

Roxie Warbler, the niece of a famous explorer, follows Uncle Dangerfoot's advice on how to survive any crisis when she becomes stranded on an island with a gang of school bullies and a pair of murderous bank robbers.

This "mixes fantasy, absurdity, and reality in a way that never diminishes or overwhelms the story's heart. Boiger's black-and-white illustrations catch the energy of Naylor's over-the-top yet sympathetically portrayed characters." Booklist

Shiloh. Atheneum Pubs. 1991 144p $15; pa $6.99 *

Grades: 4 5 6   **Fic**
  1. Dogs—Fiction 2. West Virginia—Fiction
  ISBN 0-689-31614-3; 0-689-83582-5 (pa)
                                    LC 90-603
  Also available Shiloh trilogy as a boxed set $35; pa $14.99 (ISBN 0-689-82327-4; 0-689-01525-9 pa)

  Awarded the Newbery Medal, 1992

When he finds a lost beagle in the hills behind his West Virginia home, Marty tries to hide it from his family and the dog's real owner, a mean-spirited man known to shoot deer out of season and to mistreat his dogs

"A credible plot and characters, a well-drawn setting, and nicely paced narration combine in a story that leaves the reader feeling good." Horn Book

  Other titles about Shiloh are:
  Saving Shiloh (1997)
  Shiloh season (1996)

Starting with Alice. Atheneum Bks. for Young Readers 2002 181p hardcover o.p. pa $4.99 *

Grades: 3 4 5 6   **Fic**
  1. Family life—Fiction 2. Friendship—Fiction 3. School stories
  ISBN 0-689-84395-X; 0-689-84396-8 (pa)
                                    LC 2001-53610

This, the first of three prequels to the series about Alice, is written for younger readers. After she, her older brother, and their father move from Chicago to Maryland, Alice has trouble fitting into her new third grade class, but with the help of some new friends and her own unique outlook, she survives

"New characters and realistic third-grade situations are explored, but young Alice's humor and earnestness are refreshingly the same." Horn Book

  Other prequels to the Alice series are:
  Alice in Blunderland (2003)
  Lovingly Alice (2004)

Nelson, Nina

Bringing the boy home; by N.A. Nelson. HarperCollinsPublishers 2008 211p $15.99; lib bdg $16.89

Grades: 5 6 7 8   **Fic**
  1. Senses and sensation—Fiction 2. Extrasensory perception—Fiction 3. Rain forests—Fiction 4. Amazon River valley—Fiction
  ISBN 978-0-06-088698-1;   0-06-088698-6; 978-0-06-088699-8 (lib bdg); 0-06-088699-4 (lib bdg)
                                    LC 2007-31702

As two Takunami youths approach their thirteenth birthdays, Luka reaches the culmination of his mother's training for the tribe's manhood test while Tirio, raised in Miami, Florida, by his adoptive mother, feels called to begin preparations to prove himself during his upcoming visit to the Amazon rain forest where he was born.

"The vivid setting, imagined cultural particulars . . . and magical realism will captivate readers." Booklist

Neri, Greg

Chess rumble; by G. Neri; art by Jesse Joshua Watson. Lee & Low Books 2007 64p il $18.95

Grades: 5 6 7 8   **Fic**
  1. Chess—Fiction 2. African Americans—Fiction
  ISBN 978-1-58430-279-7   LC 2007010772

Branded a troublemaker due to his anger over everything from being bullied to his sister's death a year before, Marcus begins to control himself and cope with his problems at home and at his inner-city school when an unlikely mentor teaches him to play chess

"Neri expertly captures Marcus's voice and delicately teases out his alternating vulnerability and rage. The cadence and emotion of the verse are masterfully echoed through Watson's expressive acrylic illustrations." SLJ

Nesbit, E. (Edith), 1858-1924

The enchanted castle; illustrated by Paul O. Zelinsky; afterword by Peter Glassman. Morrow Junior Bks. 1992 292p il lib bdg $22.95 *

Grades: 4 5 6   **Fic**
  1. Fantasy fiction 2. Great Britain—Fiction
  ISBN 0-688-05435-8   LC 91-46267

  First published 1907 in the United Kingdom; first United States edition 1908 by Harper & Brothers

Four English children find a wonderful world of magic through an enchanted wishing ring

"With fine, cross-hatched lines tinted in luminous colors, Zelinsky's artwork is as lively as the story and very much of the period." Booklist

Five children and it; illustrated by H.R. Millar; with an introduction by Laurel Snyder. Random House 2010 255p il (Looking Glass library) $9.99; lib bdg $12.99 *

Grades: 4 5 6   **Fic**
  1. Fairies—Fiction 2. Wishes—Fiction 3. Siblings—Fiction 4. Great Britain—Fiction
  ISBN 978-0-375-86336-3;   0-375-86336-2; 978-0-375-96336-0 (lib bdg); 0-375-96336-7 (lib bdg)
                                    LC 2008-54569

  First published 1902 in the United Kingdom; first United States edition 1905 by Dodd, Mead & Co.

Nesbit, E. (Edith), 1858-1924—*Continued*

When four brothers and sisters discover a Psammead, or sand-fairy, in the gravel pit near the country house where they are staying, they have no way of knowing all the adventures its wish-granting will bring them

Other titles in this series are:

The Phoenix and the carpet (1904)

The story of the amulet (1907)

Nesbø, Jo, 1960-

Doctor Proctor's fart powder; illustrated by Mike Lowery. Aladdin 2010 265p il $14.99

Grades: 4 5 6   Fic

1. Inventors—Fiction 2. Eccentrics and eccentricities—Fiction 3. Friendship—Fiction 4. Bullies—Fiction 5. Norway—Fiction

ISBN 978-1-4169-7972-2; 1-4169-7972-7

LC 2009-27204

New friends Nilly and Lisa help eccentric professor Doctor Proctor to develop his latest invention, a powder that makes one fart, making them very popular at school, but someone is planning to steal the industrial-strength formula for evil purposes.

"Nesbo tells his fantastical story in a matter-of-fact, deadpan style, and Lowery's simple illustrations match the dry, comedic tone well." Booklist

Neville, Emily Cheney, 1919-

It's like this, Cat; [by] Emily Neville; illustrated by Emil Weiss. Harper & Row 1963 180p il $16.99; lib bdg $17.89; pa $5.99

Grades: 5 6 7 8   Fic

1. Cats—Fiction 2. New York (N.Y.)—Fiction

ISBN 0-06-024390-2; 0-06-024391-0 (lib bdg); 0-06-440073-5 (pa)

Awarded the Newbery Medal, 1964

This is the "story of a fourteen-year-old growing up in the neighborhood of Gramercy Park in New York City. He tells of life in the city and his relationships with his parents, neighbors, and friends. It is his pet, a stray tom cat whom he adopts, that brings him two new friends, one a troubled boy and the other his first girl." Wis Libr Bull

"A story told with a great amount of insight into human relationships. . . . This all provides a wonderfully real picture of a city boy's outlets and of one likable adolescent's inner feelings. An exceedingly fresh, honest, and well-rounded piece of writing." Horn Book

Newbery, Linda, 1952-

At the firefly gate. David Fickling Books 2007 152p hardcover o.p. pa $6.50

Grades: 5 6 7 8   Fic

1. Supernatural—Fiction 2. World War, 1939-1945—Fiction 3. Great Britain—Fiction

ISBN 978-0-385-75113-1; 978-0-440-42188-7 (pa)

LC 2006-01796

After moving with his parents from London to Suffolk near a former World War II airfield, Henry sees the shadowy image of a man by the orchard gate and feels an unusual affinity with an elderly woman who lives next door

"This is a well-written book, with an old-fashioned tone, that emphasizes character and feelings over plot. It's for thoughtful readers who appreciate a book that lingers in their minds." SLJ

Lost boy. David Fickling Books 2008 194p $15.99; lib bdg $18.99

Grades: 4 5 6 7   Fic

1. Mystery fiction 2. Ghost stories 3. Traffic accidents—Fiction 4. Wales—Fiction

ISBN 978-0-375-84574-1; 978-0-375-93617-3 (lib bdg)   LC 2007-15041

First published 2005 in the United Kingdom

After Matt moves to Hay-on-Wye in Wales, a boy his age who bears the same initials and was killed in a car accident many years earlier, appears to Matt.

"With its imaginative melding of present-day concerns, good storytelling, lush descriptions of the landscape and even a faithful dog, this novel will ensnare readers." Publ Wkly

Newman, Lesléa

Hachiko waits; illustrated by Machiyo Kodaira. H. Holt 2004 96p il $15.95; pa $6.99 *

Grades: 3 4 5   Fic

1. Dogs—Fiction 2. Japan—Fiction

ISBN 0-8050-7336-1; 0-312-55806-6 (pa)

LC 2003-68589

Professor Ueno's loyal Akita, Hachiko, waits for him at the train station every afternoon, and even after the professor has a fatal heart attack while at work, Hachiko faithfully continues to await his return until the day the dog dies. Based on a true story.

"Yasuo brings a childhood focus to the poignant story . . . and Kodaira's soft, black-and-white sketches help to break up the chapters for younger readers and add interest to the story." Booklist

Nicholls, Sally, 1983-

Ways to live forever; [by] Sally Nicholls. Arthur A. Levine Books 2008 212p il $16.99 *

Grades: 4 5 6 7   Fic

1. Leukemia—Fiction 2. Authorship—Fiction 3. Family life—Fiction 4. Death—Fiction

ISBN 978-0-545-06948-9; 0-545-06948-3

LC 2007047341

Eleven-year-old Sam McQueen, who has leukemia, writes a book during the last three months of his life, in which he tells about what he would like to accomplish, how he feels, and things that have happened to him.

This "skirts easy sentiment to confront the hard questions head-on, intelligently and realistically and with an enormous range of feeling." Publ Wkly

Nielsen, Susin

Word nerd. Tundra Books 2008 248p $18.95; pa $12.95 *

Grades: 5 6 7 8   **Fic**

1. Friendship—Fiction 2. Mother-son relationship—Fiction 3. Scrabble (Game)—Fiction

ISBN 978-0-88776-875-0; 0-88776-875-X; 978-0-88776-990-0 (pa); 0-88776-990-X (pa)

"Twelve-year-old Ambrose Bukowski and his widowed, overprotective mother . . . move frequently. When he almost dies after he bites into a peanut that bullies put in his sandwich, just to see if he is really allergic, Irene . . . decides to homeschool him. . . . Ambrose gets to know 25-year-old-Cosmo, recently released from jail and the son of the Bukowskis' . . . landlords. . . . Ambrose . . . talks Cosmo into taking him to a Scrabble Club. . . . This is a tender, often funny story with some really interesting characters. It will appeal to word nerds, but even more to anyone who has ever longed for acceptance or had to fight unreasonable parental restrictions." SLJ

Nigg, Joe

How to raise and keep a dragon; by John Topsell; executive editor, Joseph Nigg; illustrations, Dan Malone. Barron's 2006 128p il $18.99

Grades: 5 6 7 8   **Fic**

1. Dragons—Fiction

ISBN 0-7641-5920-8

"Posing as dragon-breeder John Topsell . . . Nigg instructs readers in selecting and caring for a breed of dragon suited for them. . . . While not intended as a serious book on mythology, Nigg does share many bits of real dragon lore while spinning out details of what it might be like to live in a world where people breed, register, and show these creatures. Malone's full-color illustrations on every page offer fans many cool pictures to copy or sketch. With its tongue firmly in cheek, this book is a lot of lighthearted fun." SLJ

Nimmo, Jenny, 1944-

Midnight for Charlie Bone. Orchard Bks. 2003 c2002 401p (Children of the Red King) $12.99

Grades: 5 6 7 8   **Fic**

1. Magic—Fiction 2. School stories 3. Great Britain—Fiction

ISBN 978-0-439-47429-0; 0-439-47429-9

LC 2002-30738

First published 2002 in the United Kingdom

Charlie Bone's life with his widowed mother and two grandmothers undergoes a dramatic change when he discovers that he can hear people in photographs talking.

"This marvelous fantasy is able to stand on its own despite inevitable comparisons to the students of Hogwarts." Voice Youth Advocates

Other titles in this series are:

Charlie Bone and the time twister (2003)
Charlie Bone and the invisible boy (2004)
Charlie Bone and the castle of mirrors (2005)
Charlie Bone and the hidden king (2006)
Charlie Bone and the beast (2007)
Charlie Bone and the shadow (2008)
Charlie Bone and the Red Knight (2010)

The snow spider; [by] Jenny Nimmo. Orchard Books 2006 146p (Magician trilogy) $9.99 *

Grades: 4 5 6 7   **Fic**

1. Magic—Fiction 2. Father-son relationship—Fiction 3. Wales—Fiction

ISBN 978-0-439-84675-2; 0-439-84675-7

LC 2006009445

A reissue of the title first published 1987 by Dutton

Gifts from Gwyn's grandmother on his ninth birthday open up a whole new world to him, as he discovers he has magical powers that help him heal the breach with his father that has existed ever since his sister's mysterious disappearance four years before

"The narration is paced well and builds in excitement along with the tale." SLJ

Other titles in this series are:

Emlyn's moon (2007)
Chestnut solider (2007)

Nixon, Joan Lowery, 1927-2003

A family apart. Bantam Bks. 1987 162p (Orphan train) hardcover o.p. pa $6.50 *

Grades: 5 6 7 8   **Fic**

1. Foster home care—Fiction

ISBN 0-553-05432-5; 0-440-22676-7 (pa)

LC 87-12563

"The first volume in the *Orphan Train* series, this is based on a real program, the Children's Aid Society's placement of orphans who travelled from New York City to the West to be adopted by residents there. In this story, set in 1860, widowed Mrs. Kelley realizes she cannot support her six children and gives them up for adoption. The protagonist is the oldest girl, Frances, who disguises herself as a boy so that she can be paired with her baby brother for adoption, and they are indeed taken together by a very nice family." Bull Cent Child Books

"The plot is rational and well paced; the characters are real and believable; the time setting important to U.S. history, and the values all that anyone could ask for." Voice Youth Advocates

Other titles in the Orphan train series are:

Caught in the act (1988)
Circle of love (1997)
A dangerous promise (1994)
In the face of danger (1988)
Keeping secrets (1995)
A place to belong (1989)

Laugh till you cry. Delacorte Press 2004 99p hardcover o.p. lib bdg $17.99

Grades: 5 6 7 8   **Fic**

1. Moving—Fiction 2. Family life—Fiction 3. School stories

ISBN 0-385-73027-6; 0-385-90186-0 (lib bdg)

LC 2004-9557

Thirteen years old and a budding comedian, Cody has little to laugh about after he and his mother move from California to Texas to help his sick grandmother and he finds himself framed by his jealous cousin for calling in bomb threats to their school.

"The pacing of the story, Cody's humorous side, and the book's length make this mystery ideal for reluctant readers." SLJ

Nolan, Lucy A.

On the road; by Lucy Nolan; illustrated by Mike Reed. Marshall Cavendish 2005 54p il (Down Girl and Sit) $14.95 *

Grades: 1 2 3   **Fic**

1. Dogs—Fiction

ISBN 0-7614-5234-6; 978-0-7614-5234-8

LC 2004-27511

A dog who thinks her name is Down Girl goes on a car ride to the beach, goes camping in the woods, and reluctantly pays a visit to the vet with her master, Rruff.

"Narrated from a dog's point of view, this easy chapter book covers the hilarious antics of two canine friends. . . . A small black-and-white illustration appears on almost every page, supporting the text's humor." SLJ

Other titles in this series are:

Smarter than squirrels (2005)

Bad to the bone (2008)

Home on the range (2010)

Norton, Mary, 1903-1992

Bed-knob and broomstick; illustrated by Erik Blegvad. Harcourt 2000 227p il hardcover o.p. pa $6

Grades: 3 4 5 6   **Fic**

1. Fantasy fiction 2. Witchcraft—Fiction

ISBN 0-15-202450-6; 0-15-202456-5 (pa)

LC 99-89153

"An Odyssey/Harcourt young classic"

A combined edition of The magic bed-knob (1943) and Bonfires and broomsticks (1947); present title is a reissue of the 1957 edition

With the powers they acquire from a spinster who is studying to be a witch, three English children have a series of exciting and perilous adventures traveling on a flying bed that takes them to a London police station, a tropical island, and back in time to the seventeenth century

Nuzum, K. A.

The leanin' dog. Joanna Cotler Books 2008 250p $15.99; lib bdg $16.89

Grades: 4 5 6 7   **Fic**

1. Dogs—Fiction 2. Bereavement—Fiction 3. Colorado—Fiction 4. Winter—Fiction

ISBN 978-0-06-113934-5; 0-06-113934-3; 978-0-06-113935-2 (lib bdg); 0-06-113935-1 (lib bdg)

LC 2008-11855

In wintry Colorado during the 1930s, eleven-year-old Dessa Dean mourns the death of her beloved mother, but the arrival of an injured dog and the friendship they form is just what they need to change their lives forever.

"Nuzum's pacing and spare, poetic narrative create something quite wonderful. . . . This is a beautiful story in which friendship and the power of being needed trump despair." SLJ

O'Brien, Robert C., 1918-1973

Mrs. Frisby and the rats of NIMH; [by] Robert C. O'Brien; illustrated by Zena Bernstein. Atheneum Books for Young Readers 2006 c1971 233p il $18; pa $6.99 *

Grades: 4 5 6 7   **Fic**

1. Mice—Fiction 2. Rats—Fiction

ISBN 978-0-689-20651-1; 0-689-20651-8; 978-0-689-71068-1 (pa); 0-689-71068-2 (pa)

Awarded the Newbery Medal, 1972

A reissue of the title first published 1971

Having no one to help her with her problems, a widowed mouse visits the rats whose former imprisonment in a laboratory made them wise and long lived.

"The story is fresh and ingenious, the style witty, and the plot both hilarious and convincing." Saturday Rev

O'Connell, Rebecca, 1968-

Penina Levine is a hard-boiled egg; [by] Rebecca O'Connell; illustrated by Majella Lue Sue. Roaring Brook Press 2007 163p il $16.95; pa $6.99

Grades: 4 5 6   **Fic**

1. Jews—Fiction 2. Easter—Fiction 3. Passover—Fiction 4. School stories

ISBN 978-1-59643-140-9; 1-59643-140-7; 978-0-312-55026-4 (pa); 0-312-55026-X (pa)

LC 2006016677

"A Deborah Brodie book"

"Penina Levine's new teacher has given an assignment to send cards as the Easter Bunny to kindergartners at a neighboring school, and the sixth grader is uncomfortable with it because she is Jewish. . . . The story moves along at an entertaining pace. . . . Penina is a feisty and thoroughly enjoyable heroine. . . . O'Connell's artful weaving of Jewish traditions and history throughout the novel makes it all the richer, and the occasional illustrations complement the dynamic humor." SLJ

Another title about Penina Levine is:

Penina Levine is a potato pancake (2008)

O'Connor, Barbara

Fame and glory in Freedom, Georgia. Farrar, Straus & Giroux 2003 104p $16; pa $6.95 *

Grades: 4 5 6 7   **Fic**

1. School stories 2. Contests—Fiction

ISBN 0-374-32258-9; 0-374-40018-0 (pa)

LC 2002-190212

"Frances Foster books"

Unpopular sixth-grader Burdette Bird Weaver persuades the new boy at school, whom everyone thinks is mean and dumb, to be her partner for a spelling bee that might win her everything she's ever wanted

"An idiosyncratic group of characters play out this touching and well-paced story about friendship, family, and connection." Horn Books

How to steal a dog; a novel. Farrar, Straus & Giroux 2007 170p $16; pa $6.99 *

Grades: 4 5 6   **Fic**

1. Homeless persons—Fiction 2. Siblings—Fiction 3. Dogs—Fiction

ISBN 978-0-374-33497-0; 0-374-33497-8; 978-0-312-56112-3 (pa); 0-312-56112-1 (pa)

LC 2005-40166

O'Connor, Barbara—*Continued*

"Frances Foster books"

Living in the family car in their small North Carolina town, Georgina persuades her younger brother to help her in an elaborate scheme to get money by stealing a dog and then claiming the reward that the owners are bound to offer

This is told "in stripped-down, unsentimental prose. . . . The myriad effects of homelessness and the realistic picture of a moral quandary will surely generate discussion." Booklist

The small adventure of Popeye and Elvis. Farrar, Straus and Giroux 2009 149p $16.99 *

Grades: 3 4 5 6   **Fic**

1. Friendship—Fiction 2. Adventure fiction 3. Grandmothers—Fiction 4. Dogs—Fiction 5. South Carolina—Fiction

ISBN 978-0-374-37055-8; 0-374-37055-9

                 LC 2008-24145

"Frances Foster books"

In Fayette, South Carolina, the highlight of Popeye's summer is learning vocabulary words with his grandmother until a motor home gets stuck nearby and Elvis, the oldest boy living inside, joins Popeye in finding the source of strange boats floating down the creek.

"Elvis and Popeye's journey reminds readers to look for and enjoy the small treasures in their lives. Save a spot on your shelves for this small adventure with a grand heart." SLJ

O'Dell, Kathleen

Agnes Parker . . . girl in progress. Dial Bks. 2003 156p hardcover o.p. pa $6.99

Grades: 4 5 6 7   **Fic**

1. Friendship—Fiction 2. School stories

ISBN 0-8037-2648-1; 0-14-240228-1 (pa)

                 LC 2001-58256

As she starts in the sixth grade, Agnes faces challenges with her old best friend, a longtime bully, a wonderful new classmate and neighbor, and herself

"This is a thoughtful, gently humorous, and resonant cusp-of-coming-of-age novel." Horn Book Guide

Other titles about Agnes Parker are:

Agnes Parker . . . Happy camper? (2005)

Agnes Parker . . . Keeping cool in middle school (2007)

O'Dell, Scott, 1898-1989

The black pearl; illustrated by Milton Johnson. Houghton Mifflin 1967 140p il $17

Grades: 6 7 8 9   **Fic**

1. Pearl fisheries—Fiction 2. Baja California (Mexico: Peninsula)—Fiction

ISBN 0-395-06961-0

Also available in paperback from Dell

A Newbery Medal honor book, 1968

In claiming as his own the magnificent black pearl he finds, sixteen-year-old Ramón Salazar enrages El Manta Diablo, the sea devil, who legend says is its owner.

"The stark simplicity of the story and the deeper significance it holds in the triumph of good over evil add importance to the book, but even without that the book would be enjoyable as a rousing adventure tale with supernatural overtones." Bull Cent Child Books

Island of the Blue Dolphins; illustrated by Ted Lewin. Houghton Mifflin 1990 181p il $22 *

Grades: 5 6 7 8   **Fic**

1. Native Americans—Fiction 2. Wilderness survival—Fiction 3. San Nicolas Island (Calif.)—Fiction

ISBN 0-395-53680-4   LC 90-35331

Also available in paperback from Dell

Awarded the Newbery Medal, 1961

A reissue with new illustrations of the title first published 1960

"Unintentionally left behind by members of her California Native American tribe who fled a tragedy-ridden island, young Karana must construct a life for herself. Without bitterness or self-pity, she is able to extract joy and challenge from her eighteen years of solitude." Shapiro. Fic for Youth. 2d edition

Followed by Zia

The King's fifth; decorations and maps by Samuel Bryant. Houghton Mifflin 1966 264p $17; pa $6.95

Grades: 5 6 7 8   **Fic**

1. Estevan, d. 1539—Fiction 2. Mexico—Fiction

ISBN 0-395-06963-7; 0-618-74783-4 (pa)

A Newbery Medal honor book, 1967

"Fifteen-year-old Esteban sailed with Admiral Alarcon as a cartographer; carrying supplies for Coronado, the expedition went astray and a small group was put ashore to find Coronado's camp. Thus begins a harrowing story of the exciting and dangerous journey in search of the fabled gold of Cibola." Sutherland. The Best in Child Books

Sing down the moon. Houghton Mifflin 1970 137p $18

Grades: 5 6 7 8   **Fic**

1. Navajo Indians—Fiction

ISBN 0-395-10919-1

Also available in paperback from Laurel Leaf

A Newbery Medal honor book, 1971

This story is told "through the eyes of a young Navaho girl as she sees the rich harvest in the Canyon de Chelly in 1864 destroyed by Spanish slavers and the subsequent destruction by white soldiers which forces the Navahos on a march to Fort Sumner." Publ Wkly

"There is a poetic sonority of style, a sense of identification, and a note of indomitable courage and stoicism that is touching and impressive." Saturday Rev

Streams to the river, river to the sea; a novel of Sacagawea. Houghton Mifflin 1986 191p $16; pa $6.99

Grades: 5 6 7 8   **Fic**

1. Sacagawea, b. 1786—Fiction 2. Lewis and Clark Expedition (1804-1806)—Fiction 3. Native Americans—Fiction

ISBN 0-395-40430-4; 0-618-96642-0 (pa)

                 LC 86-936

This novel "tells the story of the Lewis and Clark expedition through the eyes of the young Shoshone woman who served as interpreter and, often, guide." Soc Educ

"An informative and involving choice for American history students and pioneer-adventure readers." Bull Cent Child Books

Oppel, Kenneth

Silverwing. Simon & Schuster Bks. for Young
Readers 1997 217p hardcover o.p. pa $6.99

Grades: 5 6 7 8   **Fic**

  1. Bats—Fiction

  ISBN 0-689-81529-8; 1-4169-4998-4 (pa)

                   LC 97-10977

When a newborn bat named Shade but sometimes
called "Runt" becomes separated from his colony during
migration, he grows in ways that prepare him for even
greater journeys

"Oppel's bats are fully developed characters who, if
not quite cuddly, will certainly earn readers' sympathy
and respect. In *Silverwing* the author has created an intriguing microcosm of rival species, factions, and religions." Horn Book

Other titles in this series are:

Firewing (2003)

Sunwing (2000)

Darkwing (2007)

Orlev, Uri, 1931-

The man from the other side; translated from
the Hebrew by Hillel Halkin. Puffin Books 1995
186p pa $6.99

Grades: 5 6 7 8   **Fic**

  1. World War, 1939-1945—Fiction 2. Holocaust,
1933-1945—Fiction 3. Jews—Poland—Fiction

  ISBN 0-14-037088-9; 978-0-14-037088-1

                   LC 94-30189

Living on the outskirts of the Warsaw Ghetto during
World War II, fourteen-year-old Marek and his grandparents shelter a Jewish man in the days before the Jewish
uprising

"This is a story of individual bravery and national
shame that highlights just how hopeless was the fate of
the Warsaw Jews as they fought alone and heroically
against the Nazi war machine." SLJ

The song of the whales; translated by Hillel
Halkin. Houghton Mifflin Books for Children 2010
108p $16 *

Grades: 5 6 7 8   **Fic**

  1. Grandfathers—Fiction 2. Dreams—Fiction 3. Old
age—Fiction 4. Family life—Fiction 5. Jews—Fiction
6. Jerusalem—Fiction 7. Israel—Fiction

  ISBN 978-0-5472-5752-5; 0-5472-5752-X

                  LC 2009049720

At age eight, Mikha'el knows he is different from other boys, but over the course of three years as he helps
his parents care for his elderly grandfather in Jerusalem,
Grandpa teaches Mikha'el to use the gift they share of
making other people's dreams sweeter.

This is "the sort of story that operates on many different levels. . . . With a clean sense that less is more,
Orlev has crafted a sweetly mysterious and quietly moving read." Booklist

Orr, Wendy, 1953-

Mokie & Bik; [by] Wendy Orr; illustrations by
Jonathan Bean. Henry Holt 2007 72p il $15.95

Grades: 2 3 4   **Fic**

  1. Twins—Fiction 2. Siblings—Fiction 3. Boats and
boating—Fiction

  ISBN 978-0-8050-7979-1; 0-8050-7979-3

                  LC 2006011150

For two rambunctious twins, living on a boat means
always being underfoot or overboard

"Orr's colorful use of language brings energy to the
story. The many crosshatch drawings . . . are often
graceful and always appealing." Booklist

Another title about Mokie & Bik is:

Mokie & Bik go to sea (2008)

Oswald, Nancy, 1950-

Nothing here but stones; a Jewish pioneer story;
[by] Nancy Oswald. H. Holt 2004 215p $16.95

Grades: 5 6 7 8   **Fic**

  1. Jews—Fiction 2. Frontier and pioneer life—Fiction
3. Colorado—Fiction 4. Immigrants—Fiction

  ISBN 0-8050-7465-1   LC 2003-56969

In 1882, ten-year-old Emma and her family, along
with other Russian Jewish immigrants, arrive in Coto-
paxi, Colorado, where they face inhospitable conditions
as they attempt to start an agricultural colony, and lonely
Emma is comforted by the horse whose life she saved

"This well-paced, vivid account should capture readers' attention." SLJ

Palatini, Margie

Geek Chic; the Zoey zone. Katherine Tegen
Books 2008 184p $10.99; lib bdg $14.89

Grades: 3 4 5   **Fic**

  1. School stories

  ISBN   978-0-06-113898-0;   0-06-113898-3;
978-0-06-113899-7 (lib bdg); 0-06-113899-1 (lib bdg)

A contemporary Cinderella story about Zoey, 10, who
desperately needs a fairy godmother to give her a
makeover and teach her about style if she is ever going
to make it into the cool crowd in the lunchroom.

"This amalgamation of graphic novel and chapter
book cleverly integrates wrinkled-looking notes, varied
typefaces, wacky line drawings, and movie countdowns
with straightforward prose to tell the funny if farfetched
tale." SLJ

Palmer, Robin, 1969-

Yours truly, Lucy B. Parker: girl vs. superstar.
G. P. Putnam's Sons 2010 $15.99; pa $6.99

Grades: 4 5 6 7   **Fic**

  1. Celebrities—Fiction 2. Stepfamilies—Fiction

  ISBN   978-0-399-25489-5;   0-399-25489-7;
978-0-14-241500-9 (pa); 0-14-241500-6 (pa)

"Lucy B. Parker, 12, is having a difficult time. Her
best friend dumps her, she still hasn't gotten her period,
and her mom insists that she wear a bra. Just when
things can't get any worse, her mom announces that
she's going to marry the father of Laurel Moses, a TV-
music-movie star . . . who happens to hate Lucy's guts.
. . . Readers will relate to the lessons learned, but they

Palmer, Robin, 1969-—*Continued*

aren't preachy or in-your-face. The writing is easy to follow, and this book will definitely be enjoyed by preteens who long for Laurel's glamorous life, while also appreciating with Lucy's stable home." SLJ

Papademetriou, Lisa

Chasing normal; [by] Lisa Papademetriou. Hyperion Books for Children 2008 193p $15.99; pa $5.99

Grades: 3 4 5 6   **Fic**

1. Cousins—Fiction 2. Grandmothers—Fiction
3. Family life—Fiction 4. Houston (Tex.)—Fiction
ISBN   978-1-4231-0340-0;   1-4231-0340-8;
978-1-4231-0341-7 (pa); 1-4231-0341-6 (pa)
                                        LC 2007022418

When her mean, grouchy grandmother in Texas has a heart attack and she and father go to help, twelve-year-old Mieka meets her cousins' family and wishes for their "normal" type of life.

This "is solid fare for readers looking for a family-centered story and a protagonist who is smart, funny, and instantly recognizable." Booklist

Paratore, Coleen, 1958-

Sunny Holiday; [by] Coleen Murtagh Paratore. Scholastic Press 2009 160p $15.99; pa $5.99

Grades: 2 3 4   **Fic**

1. Mother-daughter relationship—Fiction 2. African Americans—Fiction
ISBN   978-0-545-07579-4;   0-545-07579-3;
978-0-545-07588-6 (pa); 0-545-07588-2 (pa)
                                        LC 2008009786

Spunky third-grader Sunny Holiday tries to make the best out of every situation, and even though her father is in prison, she and her mother count their blessings and manage to find joy in every day

"Difficult situations are handled gently, but realistically. . . . The text is not difficult and includes some fun images for abstract ideas." SLJ

Follwed by: Sweet and sunny (2010)

Park, Barbara, 1947-

Junie B. Jones and her big fat mouth; illustrated by Denise Brunkus. Random House 1993 69p il lib bdg $11.99; pa $3.99 *

Grades: 2 3 4   **Fic**

1. School stories
ISBN 0-679-94407-9 (lib bdg); 0-679-84407-4 (pa)
                                        LC 92-50957

"A First stepping stone book"

When her kindergarten class has Job Day, Junie B. goes through much confusion and excitement before deciding on the "bestest" job of all

"Brunkus' energetic drawings pick up the slapstick action and the spunky comic hero." Booklist

Other titles about Junie B. Jones are:

Junie B. Jones and a little monkey business (1993)
Junie B. Jones and some sneaky peeky spying (1994)
Junie B. Jones and that meanie Jim's birthday (1996)
Junie B. Jones and the mushy gushy valentine (1999)
Junie B. Jones and the stupid smelly bus (1992)

Junie B. Jones and the yucky blucky fruitcake (1995)
Junie B. Jones, first grader: Aloha-ha-ha (2006)
Junie B. Jones, first grader (at last!) (2001)
Junie B. Jones, first grader: boo . . . and I mean it! (2003)
Junie B. Jones, first grader: boss of lunch (2002)
Junie B. Jones, first grader: cheater pants (2003)
Junie B. Jones, first grader: jingle bells, Batman smells! (p.s. so does May) (2005)
Junie B. Jones, first grader: one-man band (2003)
Junie B. Jones, first grader: shipwrecked (2003)
Junie B. Jones, first grader: toothless wonder (2002)
Junie B. Jones has a monster under her bed (1997)
Junie B. Jones has a peep in her pocket (2000)
Junie B. Jones is a beauty shop guy (1998)
Junie B. Jones is a graduation girl (2001)
Junie B. Jones is a party animal (1997)
Junie B. Jones is (almost) a flower girl (1999)
Junie B. Jones is Captain Field Day (2000)
Junie B. Jones is not a crook (1997)
Junie B. Jones loves handsome Warren (1996)
Junie B. Jones smells something fishy (1998)

Mick Harte was here. Apple Soup Bks. 1995 89p hardcover o.p. pa $4.99

Grades: 4 5 6   **Fic**

1. Siblings—Fiction 2. Death—Fiction
ISBN 0-679-87088-1; 0-679-88203-0 (pa)
                                        LC 94-27272

Thirteen-year-old Phoebe recalls her younger brother Mick and his death in a bicycle accident

"The author is adept at portraying the stages of grief and the effects of this sudden tragedy on the family. The book's tone of sadness is mitigated by humor, reassurance, and hope." SLJ

Park, Linda Sue, 1960-

Project Mulberry; a novel. Clarion 2005 225p $16; pa $6.99

Grades: 5 6 7 8   **Fic**

1. Korean Americans—Fiction
ISBN 0-618-47786-1; 0-440-42163-2 (pa)
                                        LC 2004-18159

While working on a project for an afterschool club, Julia, a Korean American girl, and her friend Patrick learn not just about silkworms, but also about tolerance, prejudice, friendship, patience, and more. Between the chapters are short dialogues between the author and main character about the writing of the book

"The unforgettable family and friendship story, the quiet, almost unspoken racism, and the excitement of the science make this a great cross-curriculum title." Booklist

A single shard. Clarion Bks. 2001 152p $15; pa $6.99 *

Grades: 5 6 7 8   **Fic**

1. Pottery—Fiction 2. Korea—Fiction
ISBN 0-395-97827-0; 0-440-41851-8 (pa)
                                        LC 00-43102

Awarded the Newbery Medal, 2002

Tree-ear, a thirteen-year-old orphan in medieval Korea, lives under a bridge in a potters' village, and longs to learn how to throw the delicate celadon ceramics himself

"This quiet, but involving, story draws readers into a

Park, Linda Sue, 1960-—*Continued*

very different time and place. . . . A well-crafted novel with an unusual setting." Booklist

When my name was Keoko. Clarion Bks. 2002 199p $16; pa $6.99 *

Grades: 5 6 7 8   Fic

  1. Korea—Fiction 2. World War, 1939-1945—Fiction

  ISBN 0-618-13335-6; 0-440-41944-1 (pa)

                    LC 2001-32487

With national pride and occasional fear, a brother and sister face the increasingly oppressive occupation of Korea by Japan during World War II, which threatens to suppress Korean culture entirely

  "Park is a masterful prose stylist, and her characters are developed beautifully. She excels at making traditional Korean culture accessible to Western readers." Voice Youth Advocates

  Includes bibliographical references

Parker, Marjorie Hodgson

David and the Mighty Eighth; a British boy and a Texas airman in World War II; by Marjorie Hodgson Parker; illustrated by Mark Postlethwaite. Bright Sky Press 2007 176p il $17.95

Grades: 4 5 6 7   Fic

  1. World War, 1939-1945—Fiction 2. Great Britain—Fiction

  ISBN 978-1-931721-93-6; 1-931721-93-9

                    LC 2007025999

When, during the London Blitz, he and his older sister are evacuated to go live on their grandparents' East Anglia farm, a young English boy finds it difficult to adjust to his new life until the arrival of the pilots and crews of the U.S. Eight Air Force at nearby airfields brings excitement, friendship, and hope for the future.

  This is an "exciting novel, based on a true story. . . . The story is framed by extensive historical notes. . . . Spacious type, thick paper, and an occasional black-and-white drawings make this an appealing package all around." Booklist

Parkinson, Siobhán

Blue like Friday. Roaring Brook Press 2008 160p $16.95

Grades: 4 5 6 7   Fic

  1. Family life—Fiction 2. Missing persons—Fiction 3. Synesthesia—Fiction 4. Ireland—Fiction

  ISBN 978-1-59643-340-3; 1-59643-340-X

When Olivia helps her quirky friend Hal, whose synesthesia causes him to experience everything in colors, with a prank intended to get rid of Hal's potential stepfather, there are unexpected consequences, including the disappearance of Hal's mother.

  "Parkinson creates a warm, moving story of real families facing real problems. . . . The economy of her prose is admirable; all the characters are well drawn." Booklist

Paros, Jennifer

Violet Bing and the Grand House. Viking Childrens Books 2007 105p il $14.99

Grades: 1 2 3 4   Fic

  1. Aunts—Fiction 2. Houses—Fiction 3. Friendship—Fiction

  ISBN 978-0-670-06151-8; 0-670-06151-4

                    LC 2006-10199

Very definite in her likes and dislikes, seven (nearly eight) year-old Violet Bing goes to stay with her unusual Great-aunt Astrid in the Grand House

  "The writing is exquisitely understated. . . . The author's pen-and-ink illustrations complement this fine, subtle early chapter book perfectly." SLJ

Parry, Rosanne

Heart of a shepherd; [by] Rosanne Parry. Random House Children's Books 2009 161p $15.99; lib bdg $18.99 *

Grades: 4 5 6 7   Fic

  1. Ranch life—Fiction 2. Family life—Fiction 3. Christian life—Fiction 4. Iraq War, 2003-—Fiction 5. Oregon—Fiction

  ISBN 978-0-375-84802-5; 0-375-84802-9; 978-0-375-94802-2 (lib bdg); 0-375-94802-3 (lib bdg)

                    LC 2007-48094

Ignatius 'Brother' Alderman, nearly twelve, promises to help his grandparents keep the family's Oregon ranch the same while his brothers are away and his father is deployed to Iraq, but as he comes to accept the inevitability of change, he also sees the man he is meant to be

  There is "more action than introspection afoot, with sibling tensions, a wildfire, and the grandfather's death along the journey. It's refreshing . . . to find a protagonist with his eyes and heart open to positive adult examples . . . and who matches his mettle to theirs." Bull Cent Child Books

Paterson, Katherine

Bread and roses, too. Clarion Books 2006 275p $16; pa $6.99 *

Grades: 5 6 7 8   Fic

  1. Strikes—Fiction 2. Immigrants—Fiction 3. United States—History—1898-1919—Fiction 4. Lawrence (Mass.)—Fiction

  ISBN 978-0-618-65479-6; 0-618-65479-8; 978-0-547-07651-5 (pa); 0-547-07651-7 (pa)

                    LC 2005-31702

Jake and Rosa, two children, form an unlikely friendship as they try to survive and understand the 1912 Bread and Roses strike of mill workers in Lawrence, Massachusetts.

  "Paterson has skillfully woven true events and real historical figures into the fictional story and created vivid settings, clearly drawn characters, and a strong sense of the hardship and injustice faced by the mostly immigrant mill workers." SLJ

Paterson, Katherine—*Continued*

Bridge to Terabithia; illustrated by Donna Diamond. Crowell 1977 128p il $15.99; lib bdg $16.89; pa $5.99 *

Grades: 4 5 6 7   **Fic**
   1. Friendship—Fiction 2. Death—Fiction 3. Virginia—Fiction
   ISBN 0-690-01359-0; 0-690-04635-9 (lib bdg); 0-06-440184-7 (pa)   LC 77-2221
   Awarded the Newbery Medal, 1978
   The life of Jess, a ten-year-old boy in rural Virginia expands when he becomes friends with a newcomer who subsequently meets an untimely death trying to reach their hideaway, Terabithia, during a storm
   "Jess and his family are magnificently characterized; the book abounds in descriptive vignettes, humorous sidelights on the clash of cultures, and realistic depictions of rural school life." Horn Book

Come sing, Jimmy Jo. Lodestar Bks. 1985 193p hardcover o.p. pa $5.99

Grades: 5 6 7 8   **Fic**
   1. Country music—Fiction 2. Family life—Fiction
   ISBN 0-525-67167-6; 0-14-037397-7 (pa)   LC 84-21123
   When his family becomes a successful country music group and makes him a featured singer, eleven-year-old James has to deal with big changes in all aspects of his life, even his name
   "What Katherine Paterson does so well is catch the cadence of the locale without sounding fake. There isn't a false note in her diction. She has created a West Virginian world that is entirely believable: homely, honest, goodhearted. . . . This book is James's personal inward journey, and it is deeply felt." Christ Sci Monit

The great Gilly Hopkins. Crowell 1978 148p $15.99; lib bdg $16.89; pa $5.99 *

Grades: 5 6 7 8   **Fic**
   1. Foster home care—Fiction
   ISBN 0-690-03837-2; 0-690-03838-0 (lib bdg); 0-06-440201-0 (pa)   LC 77-27075
   A Newbery Medal honor book, 1979
   "Cool, scheming, and deliberately obstreperous, 11-year-old Gilly is ready to be her usual obnoxious self when she arrives at her new foster home. . . . But Gilly's old tricks don't work against the all-encompassing love of the huge, half-illiterate Mrs. Trotter. . . . Determined not to care she writes a letter full of wild exaggerations to her real mother that brings, in return, a surprising visit from an unknown grandmother." Booklist
   "A well-structured story, [this] has vitality of writing style, natural dialogue, deep insight in characterization, and a keen sense of the fluid dynamics in human relationships." Bull Cent Child Books

Jip; his story. Lodestar Bks. 1996 181p hardcover o.p. pa $6.99

Grades: 5 6 7 8   **Fic**
   1. Slavery—Fiction 2. African Americans—Fiction 3. Vermont—Fiction 4. Racially mixed people—Fiction
   ISBN 0-525-67543-4; 0-14-240411-X (pa)   LC 96-2680

While living on a Vermont poor farm during 1855 and 1856, Jip learns that his mother was a runaway slave, and that his father, the plantation owner, plans to reclaim him as property

"This historically accurate story is full of revelations and surprises, one of which is the return appearance of the heroine of *Lyddie*. . . . The taut, extremely readable narrative and its tender depictions of friendship and loyalty provide first-rate entertainment." Publ Wkly

Lyddie. Lodestar Bks. 1991 182p $17.99; pa $6.99 *

Grades: 5 6 7 8 9   **Fic**
   1. United States—History—1815-1861—Fiction 2. Massachusetts—Fiction 3. Factories—Fiction
   ISBN 0-525-67338-5; 0-14-240254-0 (pa)   LC 90-42944
   Impoverished Vermont farm girl Lyddie Worthen is determined to gain her independence by becoming a factory worker in Lowell, Massachusetts, in the 1840s
   "Not only does the book contain a riveting plot, engaging characters, and a splendid setting, but the language—graceful, evocative, and rhythmic—incorporates the rural speech patterns of Lyddie's folk, the simple Quaker expressions of the farm neighbors, and the lilt of fellow mill girl Bridget's Irish brogue. . . . A superb story of grit, determination, and personal growth." Horn Book

Park's quest. Lodestar Bks. 1988 148p pa $5.99 hardcover o.p. *

Grades: 5 6 7 8   **Fic**
   1. Farm life—Fiction 2. Vietnamese Americans—Fiction
   ISBN 0-14-034262-1 (pa)   LC 87-32422
   Eleven-year-old Park makes some startling discoveries when he travels to his grandfather's farm in Virginia to learn about his father who died in the Vietnam War and meets a Vietnamese-American girl named Thanh
   The author "confronts the complexity, the ambiguity, of the war and the emotions of those it involved with an honesty that young readers are sure to recognize and appreciate." N Y Times Book Rev

The same stuff as stars. Clarion Bks. 2002 242p $15

Grades: 5 6 7 8   **Fic**
   ISBN 0-618-24744-0   LC 2002-3967
   When Angel's self-absorbed mother leaves her and her younger brother with their poor great-grandmother, the eleven-year-old girl worries not only about her mother and brother, her imprisoned father, the frail old woman, but also about a mysterious man who begins sharing with her the wonder of the stars
   "Paterson's deft hand at characterization, her insight into the human soul, and her glorious prose make this book one to rejoice over." Voice Youth Advocates

Patneaude, David, 1944-

A piece of the sky; [by] David Patneaude; [cover illustration by Layne Johnson] Albert Whitman 2007 178p il $15.95

Grades: 5 6 7 8   **Fic**
   1. Meteorites—Fiction 2. Mountaineering—Fiction 3. Oregon—Fiction
   ISBN 978-0-8075-6536-0   LC 2006023529

Patneaude, David, 1944-—*Continued*

Fourteen-year-old Russell, his friend Phoebe, and her brother Isaac must find a legendary meteor in the Oregon mountains before it is exploited

"This old-fashioned adventure story has contemporary appeal." Booklist

Patron, Susan

The higher power of Lucky; with illustrations by Matt Phelan. Atheneum Books for Young Readers 2006 134p il $16.95; pa $6.99 *

Grades: 4 5 6   **Fic**

1. Runaway children—Fiction

ISBN 978-1-4169-0194-5; 1-4169-0194-9; 978-1-4169-7557-1 (pa); 1-4169-7557-8 (pa)

LC 2005-21767

Awarded the Newbery Medal, 2007

"A Richard Jackson book"

Fearing that her legal guardian plans to abandon her to return to France, ten-year-old aspiring scientist Lucky Trimble determines to run away while also continuing to seek the Higher Power that will bring stability to her life

"Patron's plotting is as tight as her characters are endearing. Lucky is a true heroine." Booklist

Followed by: Lucky breaks (2009)

Maybe yes, maybe no, maybe maybe; illustrated by Abigail Halpin. Aladdin Paperbacks 2009 107p il pa $5.99

Grades: 3 4 5   **Fic**

1. Moving—Fiction 2. Sisters—Fiction

ISBN 978-1-4169-6176-5 (pa); 1-4169-6176-3 (pa)

First published 1993 by Orchard Books

When her hardworking mother decides to move, eight-year-old PK uses her imagination and storytelling to help her older and younger sisters adjust

Patt, Beverly

Best friends forever; a World War II scrapbook; with illustrations by Shula Klinger. Marshall Cavendish 2009 92p il $17.99 *

Grades: 5 6 7 8   **Fic**

1. Puyallup Assembly Center (Wash.)—Fiction 2. Japanese Americans—Evacuation and relocation, 1942-1945—Fiction 3. World War, 1939-1945—Fiction 4. Friendship—Fiction 5. Washington (State)—Fiction

ISBN 978-0-7614-5577-6; 0-7614-5577-9

LC 2008020875

Fourteen-year-old Louise keeps a scrapbook detailing the events in her life after her best friend, Dottie, a Japanese-American girl, and her family are sent to a relocation camp during World War II.

"If the drama of the girls separation isn't enough, a romantic subplot and the antics of Dottie's goofy dog (living with Louise in her absence) will surely keep young readers interested. This heartwarming tale of steadfast friendship makes a wonderful access point for learning more about World War II and Japanese internment." SLJ

Includes bibliographical references

Patterson, Nancy Ruth, 1944-

The winner's walk; pictures by Thomas F. Yezerski. Farrar, Straus and Giroux 2006 114p il $16

Grades: 3 4 5   **Fic**

1. Dogs—Fiction 2. Family life—Fiction

ISBN 978-0-374-38445-6; 0-374-38445-2

LC 2005-49461

Surrounded by a multitalented family, nine-year-old Case Callahan feels driven to succeed, but his failed attempts at various competitions discourage him until he finds a stray dog with a surprising past

"With short, action-packed chapters, frequent full-page pencil illustrations, and interesting information about service dogs, this solid book will appeal to young animal lovers." Horn Book

Paulsen, Gary

The amazing life of birds; the twenty-day puberty journal of Duane Homer. Wendy Lamb Books 2006 84p $13.95; pa $6.50

Grades: 5 6 7 8   **Fic**

1. Puberty—Fiction 2. Boys—Fiction 3. Birds—Fiction

ISBN 0-385-74660-1; 0-553-49428-7 (pa)

As twelve-year-old Duane endures the confusing and humiliating aspects of puberty, he watches a newborn bird in a nest on his windowsill begin to grow and become more independent, all of which he records in his journal.

The author "has captured a very uncomfortable time of life amazingly well. . . . Paulsen's writing is beautiful." Voice Youth Advocates

Lawn Boy. Wendy Lamb Books 2007 88p $12.99; lib bdg $15.99; pa $6.50 *

Grades: 4 5 6 7   **Fic**

1. Business enterprises—Fiction 2. Summer employment—Fiction

ISBN 978-0-385-74686-1; 978-0-385-90923-5 (lib bdg); 978-0-553-49465-5 (pa)   LC 2006-39731

Things get out of hand for a twelve-year-old boy when a neighbor convinces him to expand his summer lawn mowing business

"This rags-to-riches success story has colorful characters, a villain, and enough tongue-in-cheek humor to make it an enjoyable selection for the whole family." SLJ

Followed by: Lawn Boy returns (2010)

The legend of Bass Reeves; being the true and fictional account of the most valiant marshal in the West. Wendy Lamb Books 2006 137p $15.95; pa $6.50 *

Grades: 5 6 7 8   **Fic**

1. Reeves, Bass, 1838-1910—Fiction 2. African Americans—Fiction 3. Slavery—Fiction 4. West (U.S.)—Fiction

ISBN 0-385-74661-X; 0-553-49429-5 (pa)

LC 2006-11492

"This engrossingly told tale fills in the unrecorded youth of an unjustly obscure historical figure who was born a slave, became a successful rancher, then later in his long life went on to play an integral role in taming

Paulsen, Gary—*Continued*

the rough-hewn Oklahoma Territory. . . . A stirring tale of adventure." Booklist

Mr. Tucket. Delacorte Press 1994 166p hardcover o.p. pa $4.50 *

Grades: 5 6 7 8   **Fic**
  1. Frontier and pioneer life—Fiction 2. West (U.S.)—Fiction
  ISBN 0-385-31169-9; 0-440-41133-5 (pa)
                                            LC 93-31180

In 1848, while on a wagon train headed for Oregon, fourteen-year-old Francis Tucket is kidnapped by Pawnee Indians and then falls in with a one-armed trapper who teaches him how to live in the wild

"Superb characterizations, splendidly evoked setting and thrill-a-minute plot make this book a joy to gallop through." Publ Wkly

  Other titles about Francis Tucket are:
Call me Francis Tucket (1995)
Tucket's gold (1999)
Tucket's home (2000)
Tucket's ride (1997)

Mudshark. Wendy Lamb Books 2009 83p $12.99; lib bdg $15.99

Grades: 3 4 5 6   **Fic**
  1. Lost and found possessions—Fiction 2. School stories
  ISBN   978-0-385-74685-4;   0-385-74685-7;
  978-0-385-90922-8 (lib bdg); 0-385-90922-5 (lib bdg)
                                           LC 2008033271

Principal Wagner confidently deals with a faculty washroom crisis, a psychic parrot, and a terrorizing gerbil, but when sixty-five erasers go missing, he enlists the help of the school's best problem solver and locator of lost items, twelve-year-old Lyle Williams, aka Mudshark.

"Diversions . . . keep this compact story quick and light. Yet . . . Paulsen . . . delves deeper, shaping Mudshark as a credible and compassionate protagonist." Publ Wkly

Notes from the dog. Wendy Lamb Books 2009 133p $15.99; lib bdg $18.99

Grades: 5 6 7 8   **Fic**
  1. Cancer—Fiction 2. Gardening—Fiction
  ISBN   978-0-385-73845-3;   0-385-73845-5;
  978-0-385-90730-9 (lib bdg); 0-385-90730-3 (lib bdg)
                                           LC 2009-13300

When Johanna shows up at the beginning of summer to house-sit next door to Finn, he has no idea of the profound effect she will have on his life by the time summer vacation is over.

"The plot is straightforward, but Paulsen's thoughtful characters are compelling and their interactions realistic. This emotional, coming-of-age journey about taking responsibilty for one's own happiness and making personal connections will not disappoint." Publ Wkly

The winter room. Orchard Bks. 1989 103p $16.95; pa $5.99 *

Grades: 5 6 7 8   **Fic**
  1. Farm life—Fiction 2. Minnesota—Fiction
  ISBN 0-531-05839-5; 0-545-08534-9 (pa)
                                           LC 89-42541

A Newbery Medal honor book, 1990

"A Richard Jackson book"

A young boy growing up on a northern Minnesota farm describes the scenes around him and recounts his old Norwegian uncle's tales of an almost mythological logging past

"While this seems at first to be a collection of anecdotes organized around the progression of the farm calendar, Paulsen subtly builds a conflict that becomes apparent in the last brief chapters, forceful and well-prepared. . . . Lyrical and only occasionally sentimental, the prose is clean, clear, and deceptively simple." Bull Cent Child Books

Paver, Michelle

Wolf brother. HarperCollins 2005 c2004 295p (Chronicles of ancient darkness) $16.99; lib bdg $17.89; pa $6.99

Grades: 5 6 7 8   **Fic**
  1. Prehistoric peoples—Fiction 2. Wolves—Fiction 3. Demoniac possession—Fiction 4. Bears—Fiction
  ISBN 0-06-072825-6; 0-06-072826-4 (lib bdg); 0-06-072827-2 (pa)   LC 2004-8857

First published 2004 in the United Kingdom

6,000 years in the past, twelve-year-old Tarak and his guide, a wolf cub, set out on a dangerous journey to fulfill an oath the boy made to his dying father—to travel to the Mountain of the World Spirit seeking a way to destroy a demon-possessed bear that threatens all the clans

"Paver's depth of research into the spiritual world of primitive peoples makes this impressive British import, slated to be the first in a six-book series, intriguing and believable." SLJ

  Other titles in this series are:
Spirit walker (2006)
Soul eater (2007)
Outcast (2008)
Oath breaker (2009)
Ghost hunter (2010)

Payne, C. C.

Something to sing about; written by C. C. Payne. Eerdmans Books for Young Readers 2008 167p pa $8.50

Grades: 4 5 6   **Fic**
  1. Fear—Fiction 2. Bees—Fiction 3. Family life—Fiction 4. Christian life—Fiction 5. Choirs (Music)—Fiction 6. Singing—Fiction 7. Kentucky—Fiction
  ISBN 978-0-8028-5344-8 (pa); 0-8028-5344-7 (pa)
                                           LC 2008006100

Ten-year-old Jamie Jo's fear of bees keeps her inside most of the time, but a series of events that begins when her mother is excluded from the church choir brings about many changes, including new friendships and greater trust in God

"The word *wholesome* sometimes gets a bad rap, but here it's leavened by gentle humor and considerable insight, and it fits this book just fine." Booklist

Pearce, Emily Smith, 1975-

Isabel and the miracle baby; [by] Emily Smith Pearce. Front Street 2007 125p $15.95

Grades: 2 3 4 5   **Fic**

1. Mother-daughter relationship—Fiction 2. Infants—Fiction 3. Cancer—Fiction 4. Family life—Fiction

ISBN 978-1-932425-44-4   LC 2006101750

Eight-year-old Isabel feels her mother no longer cares about her because she has no time or energy even to listen when Isa tries to share her sadness about being unpopular, her jealousy over her new baby sister, and, most importantly, her fear that her mother's cancer will come back

"Pearce gets into the mind and soul of a child. . . . [The child's] struggle is what sets this book apart from the dozens of others with the new-sibling theme." SLJ

Pearce, Philippa, 1920-2006

A finder's magic; illustrated by Helen Craig. Candlewick Press 2009 119p il $15.99

Grades: 3 4 5   **Fic**

1. Lost and found possessions—Fiction 2. Magic—Fiction

ISBN 978-0-7636-4072-9; 0-7636-4072-7

After a mysterious stranger offers to help Till find his dog, they embark on a magical quest, interviewing various witnesses including a heron, a mole, a riddling cat, and Miss Mousey, whose sketch of a peaceful riverbank offers a vital clue.

"The posthumous publication by classic author Pearce envinces her usual gift for blending reality and fantasy in plain and approachable style. . . . Younger readers who crave gentle shivers without terrors will appreciate this cozy fantasy quest to find a lost pet." Bull Cent Child Books

Tom's midnight garden; illustrated by Susan Einzig. Lippincott 1959 c1958 229p il hardcover o.p. pa $5.95 *

Grades: 4 5 6 7   **Fic**

1. Fantasy fiction 2. Space and time—Fiction

ISBN 0-397-30477-3; 0-06-440445-5 (pa)

First published 1958 in the United Kingdom

"Daytime life for Tom at his aunt's home in England is dull, but each night he participates through fantasy in the lives of the former inhabitants of the interesting old house in which he is spending an enforced vacation. The book is British in setting and atmosphere. The element of mystery is well sustained, and the reader is left to make his own interpretation of the reality of the story." Adventuring with Books

Pearsall, Shelley

All of the above; a novel; illustrations by Javaka Steptoe. Little, Brown 2006 234p il hardcover o.p. pa $5.99

Grades: 5 6 7 8   **Fic**

1. School stories 2. City and town life—Fiction

ISBN 0-316-11524-X; 978-0-316-11524-7; 978-0-316-11526-1 (pa); 0-316-11526-6 (pa)

LC 2005-33109

Five urban middle school students, their teacher, and other community members relate how a school project to build the world's largest tetrahedron affects the lives of everyone involved.

"Pearsall's novel, based on a real event in 2002—is a delightful story about the power of a vision and the importance of a goal. The authentic voices of the students and the well-intentioned, supportive adults surrounding them illustrate all that is good about schools, family, friendship, and community." Booklist

Crooked river; [by] Shelley Pearsall. Knopf 2005 249p $15.95; lib bdg $17.99; pa $6.50

Grades: 5 6 7 8   **Fic**

1. Ojibwa Indians—Fiction 2. Frontier and pioneer life—Fiction 3. Ohio—Fiction

ISBN 0-375-82389-1; 0-375-92389-6 (lib bdg); 0-440-42101-2 (pa)   LC 2004-10310

When twelve-year old Rebecca Carter's father brings a Native American accused of murder into their 1812 Ohio settlement town, Rebecca, witnessing the town's reaction to the Indian, struggles with the idea that an innocent man may be convicted and sentenced to death

"Pearsall quickly engages readers with her captivating tale of fear, ignorance, and bravery. . . . Packed with believable characters wrapped in a thoroughly researched plot." SLJ

Peck, Richard, 1934-

Fair weather; a novel. Dial Bks. 2001 130p il $16.99; pa $5.99

Grades: 5 6 7 8   **Fic**

1. Buffalo Bill, 1846-1917—Fiction 2. Russell, Lillian, 1861-1922—Fiction 3. Family life—Fiction 4. Chicago (Ill.)—Fiction

ISBN 0-8037-2516-7; 0-14-250034-8 (pa)

LC 00-55561

In 1893, thirteen-year-old Rosie and members of her family travel from their Illinois farm to Chicago to visit Aunt Euterpe and attend the World's Columbian Exposition which, along with an encounter with Buffalo Bill and Lillian Russell, turns out to be a life-changing experience for everyone

"Peck's unforgettable characters, cunning dialogue and fast-paced action will keep readers in stitches." Publ Wkly

Here lies the librarian. Dial Books 2006 145p $16.99; pa $6.99

Grades: 4 5 6   **Fic**

1. Automobiles—Fiction 2. Librarians—Fiction 3. Country life—Fiction 4. Indiana—Fiction

ISBN 0-8037-3080-2; 0-14-240908-1 (pa)

LC 2005-20279

Fourteen-year-old Eleanor "Peewee" McGrath, a tomboy and automobile enthusiast, discovers new possibilities for her future after the 1914 arrival in her small Indiana town of four young librarians.

"Another gem from Peck, with his signature combination of quirky characters, poignancy, and outrageous farce." SLJ

Peck, Richard, 1934-—*Continued*

A long way from Chicago; a novel in stories. Dial Bks. for Young Readers 1998 148p $15.99; pa $5.99 *

Grades: 5 6 7 8　　　　　　　　　　　　**Fic**
1. Grandmothers—Fiction 2. Great Depression, 1929-1939—Fiction
ISBN 0-8037-2290-7; 0-14-240110-2 (pa)
　　　　　　　　　　　　　　　　LC 98-10953
A Newbery Medal honor book, 1999

Joe recounts his annual summer trips to rural Illinois with his sister during the Great Depression to visit their larger-than-life grandmother

"The novel reveals a strong sense of place, a depth of characterization, and a rich sense of humor." Horn Book

Followed by A year down yonder (2000)

On the wings of heroes. Dial Books 2007 148p $16.99; pa $6.99 *

Grades: 4 5 6 7　　　　　　　　　　　　**Fic**
1. World War, 1939-1945—Fiction 2. Illinois—Fiction
ISBN 0-8037-3081-0; 0-14-241204-X (pa)
　　　　　　　　　　　　　　　LC 2006011906
A boy in Illinois remembers the homefront years of World War II, especially his two heroes, his brother in the Air Force and his father, who fought in the previous war.

"Peck's masterful, detail-rich prose describes wartime in the United States. . . . Peck's characters are memorable. . . . This book is an absolute delight." SLJ

A season of gifts. Dial Books for Young Readers 2009 156p $16.99 *

Grades: 5 6 7 8　　　　　　　　　　　　**Fic**
1. Moving—Fiction 2. Illinois—Fiction
ISBN 978-0-8037-3082-3; 0-8037-3082-9
　　　　　　　　　　　　　　　LC 2008-48050
A companion novel to: A long way from Chicago (1998) and A year down yonder (2000)

Relates the surprising gifts bestowed on twelve-year-old Bob Barnhart and his family, who have recently moved to a small Illinois town in 1958, by their larger-than-life neighbor, Mrs. Dowdel.

"The type of down-home humor and vibrant characterizations Peck fans have come to adore re-emerge in full as Peck resurrects Mrs. Dowdel, the irrepressible, self-sufficient grandmother featured in *A Year Down Yonder* and *A Long Way from Chicago*." Publ Wkly

The teacher's funeral; a comedy in three parts. Dial Books 2004 190p $16.99; pa $6.99 *

Grades: 5 6 7 8　　　　　　　　　　　　**Fic**
1. Teachers—Fiction 2. Indiana—Fiction 3. Country life—Fiction
ISBN 0-8037-2736-4; 0-14-240507-8 (pa)
　　　　　　　　　　　　　　　LC 2004-4361
In rural Indiana in 1904, fifteen-year-old Russell's dream of quitting school and joining a wheat threshing crew is disrupted when his older sister takes over the teaching at his one-room schoolhouse after mean, old Myrt Arbuckle "hauls off and dies."

"The dry wit and unpretentious tone make the story's events comical, its characters memorable, and its conclusion unexpectedly moving." Booklist

A year down yonder. Dial Bks. for Young Readers 2000 130p $16.99; pa $5.99 *

Grades: 5 6 7 8　　　　　　　　　　　　**Fic**
1. Grandmothers—Fiction 2. Great Depression, 1929-1939—Fiction
ISBN 0-8037-2518-3; 0-14-230070-5 (pa)
　　　　　　　　　　　　　　　LC 99-43159
Awarded the Newbery Medal, 2001

This sequel to A long way from Chicago "tells the story of Joey's younger sister, Mary Alice, 15, who spends the year of 1937 back with Grandma Dowdel in a small town in Illinois." Booklist

"Peck has created a delightful, insightful tale that resounds with a storyteller's wit, humor, and vivid description." SLJ

Peet, Mal

Cloud Tea monkeys; by Mal Peet & Elspeth Graham; illustrated by Juan Wijngaard. Candlewick Press 2010 unp il lib bdg $15.99

Grades: 1 2 3 4　　　　　　　　　　　　**Fic**
1. Tea—Fiction 2. Monkeys—Fiction 3. Mother-daughter relationship—Fiction
ISBN 978-0-7636-4453-6 (lib bdg); 0-7636-4453-6 (lib bdg)　　　　　　　　　　　　　LC 2009-11868
When her mother becomes too ill to harvest tea on the nearby plantation, Shenaz is too small to fill in, but when she tells the monkeys she has befriended why she is sad, they bring her a basket filled with rare and valuable wild tea.

"The tale has the feel of a time-honed fable—simple, elegant, and moving—which is especially well complemented by Wijngaard's sumptuous illustrations." Booklist

Peirce, Lincoln

Big Nate; in a class by himself. Harper 2010 214p $12.99

Grades: 3 4 5　　　　　　　　　　　　**Fic**
1. School stories
ISBN 978-0-06-194434-5; 0-06-194434-3; 978-0-06-194435-2 (lib bdg); 0-06-194435-1 (lib bdg)
　　　　　　　　　　　　　　　LC 2009-39668
The author "uses a mix of prose and cartoons to tell a quick story about a day in the life of an extroverted, impish kid. . . . Nate, has been the star of a long-running daily comic strip. . . . He wakes up feeling fine, sweats a bit about an upcoming test, then opens a fortune cookie at school that reads, 'Today you will surpass all others.' . . . The cartoons provide plenty of gags at the expense of various adults and classmates, and Nate's persistent good cheer and moxie make him a likable new proxy for young misfits." Booklist

Pennypacker, Sara, 1951-

Clementine; [illustrated by] Marla Frazee. Hyperion Books for Children 2006 144p il $14.99; pa $4.99 *

Grades: 2 3 4　　　　　　　　　　　　**Fic**
1. Friendship—Fiction 2. Family life—Fiction 3. School stories
ISBN 0-7868-3882-5; 0-7868-3883-3 (pa)
　　　　　　　　　　　　　　　LC 2005-50458

Pennypacker, Sara, 1951-—_Continued_

While sorting through difficulties in her friendship with her neighbor Margaret, eight-year-old Clementine gains several unique hairstyles while also helping her father in his efforts to banish pigeons from the front of their apartment building.

"Humorous scenarios tumble together, blending picturesque dialogue with a fresh perspective. . . . Frazee's engaging pen-and-ink drawings capture the energy and fresh-faced expressions of the irrepressible heroine." SLJ

Other titles about Clementine are:

The talented Clementine (2007)

Clementine's letter (2008)

Pérez, Amada Irma

My diary from here to there; story, Amada Irma Pérez; illustrations, Maya Christina Gonzalez. Children's Bk. Press 2002 unp il $16.95

Grades: 2 3 4   Fic

1. Mexican Americans—Fiction 2. Immigrants—Fiction 3. Bilingual books—English-Spanish

ISBN 0-89239-175-8   LC 2001-58251

Text and title page in English and Spanish

A young girl describes her feelings when her father decides to leave their home in Mexico to look for work in the United States

"The diary entries, written in conversational English and Spanish, resonate with the tensions of the experience. . . . The full-page, bright acrylic paintings complement the text, with the blocky primitive forms adding a reassuring note to the whole." SLJ

Perkins, Lynne Rae

All alone in the universe. Greenwillow Bks. 1999 140p il hardcover o.p. pa $5.99

Grades: 5 6 7 8   Fic

1. Friendship—Fiction

ISBN 0-688-16881-7; 0-380-73302-1 (pa)

LC 98-50093

Debbie is dismayed when her best friend Maureen starts spending time with ordinary, boring Glenna

"A poignant story written with sensitivity and tenderness." SLJ

Criss cross. Greenwillow Books 2005 337p $16.99; lib bdg $17.89; pa $6.99 *

Grades: 6 7 8 9   Fic

ISBN 0-06-009272-6; 0-06-009273-4 (lib bdg); 0-06-009274-2 (pa)   LC 2004-54023

Awarded the Newbery Medal, 2006

Teenagers in a small town in the 1960s experience new thoughts and feelings, question their identities, connect, and disconnect as they search for the meaning of life and love.

"Debbie . . . and Hector . . . narrate most of the novel. Both are 14 years old. Hector is a fabulous character with a wry humor and an appealing sense of self-awareness. . . . The descriptive, measured writing includes poems, prose, haiku, and question-and-answer formats. There is a great deal of humor in this gentle story." SLJ

Perkins, Mitali, 1963-

Bamboo people. Charlesbridge 2010 $16.95

Grades: 5 6 7 8   Fic

1. Myanmar—Fiction 2. Wilderness survival—Fiction

ISBN 978-1-58089-328-2; 1-58089-328-7

LC 2009005495

Two Burmese boys, one a Karenni refugee and the other the son of an imprisoned Burmese doctor, meet in the jungle and in order to survive they must learn to trust each other.

"Perkins seamlessly blends cultural, political, religious, and philosophical context into her story, which is distinguished by humor, astute insights into human nature, and memorable characters." Publ Wkly

Rickshaw girl; illustrated by Jamie Hogan. Charlesbridge 2007 91p il lib bdg $13.95 *

Grades: 3 4 5   Fic

1. Painting—Fiction 2. Sex role—Fiction 3. Bangladesh—Fiction

ISBN 978-1-58089-308-4   LC 2006-09031

In her Bangladesh village, ten-year-old Naimi excels at painting designs called alpanas, but to help her impoverished family financially she would have to be a boy—or disguise herself as one

"This short chapter book tells a realistic story with surprises that continue until the end. Hogan's bold black-and-white sketches show the brave girl, the beautiful traditional alpana painting and rickshaw art, and the contemporary changes in the girl's rural home." Booklist

Petersen, P. J., 1941-

Wild river. Delacorte Press 2009 120p $14.99; lib bdg $17.99

Grades: 4 5 6 7   Fic

1. Wilderness survival—Fiction 2. Kayaks and kayaking—Fiction 3. Brothers—Fiction

ISBN 978-0-385-73724-1; 0-385-73724-6; 978-0-385-90656-2 (lib bdg); 0-385-90656-0 (lib bdg)

LC 2008-24921

Considered lazy and unathletic, twelve-year-old Ryan discovers a heroic side of himself when a kayak trip with his older brother goes horribly awry.

"The compelling first-person narration sets this apart from other adventure stories. . . . With sharp pacing, short sentences, and an unintimidating length, this is a strong, accessible choice for younger readers." Booklist

Philbrick, W. R. (W. Rodman)

The mostly true adventures of Homer P. Figg; [by] Rodman Philbrick. Blue Sky Press 2009 224p $16.99 *

Grades: 5 6 7 8   Fic

1. Adventure fiction 2. Orphans—Fiction 3. Brothers—Fiction 4. United States—History—1861-1865, Civil War—Fiction

ISBN 978-0-439-66818-7; 0-439-66818-2

LC 2008-16925

ALA ALSC Newbery Medal Honor Book (2010)

Twelve-year-old Homer, a poor but clever orphan, has extraordinary adventures after running away from his evil uncle to rescue his brother, who has been sold into service in the Civil War.

Philbrick, W. R. (W. Rodman)—*Continued*
"The book wouldn't be nearly as much fun without Homer's tall tales, but there are serious moments, too, and the horror of war and injustice of slavery ring clearly above the din of playful exaggerations." Publ Wkly

The young man and the sea; [by] Rodman Philbrick. Blue Sky Press 2004 192p $16.95; pa $4.99 *

Grades: 5 6 7 8   **Fic**
1. Fishing—Fiction
ISBN 0-439-36829-4; 0-439-36830-8 (pa)
         LC 2003-050233
After his mother's death, twelve-year-old Skiff Beaman decides that it is up to him to earn money to take care of himself and his father, so he undertakes a dangerous trip alone out on the ocean off the coast of Maine to try to catch a hugh bluefin tuna
"This excellent maritime bildungsroman has all of the makings of a juvenile classic: wide-open adventure, heart-pounding suspense, and just the right amount of tear-jerking pathos, all neatly wrapped up in an ending that . . . is purely triumphant." SLJ

Pierce, Tamora, 1954-
Magic steps; book one of the Circle opens quartet. Scholastic Press 2000 264p pa $5.99 hardcover o.p. *

Grades: 5 6 7 8   **Fic**
1. Fantasy fiction
ISBN 0-590-39605-6 (pa)   LC 99-31943
Based on characters in the author's Circle of Magic quartet
Sandry "is a 'stitch witch' who can weave magic as well as cloth. She reluctantly takes on twelve-year-old Pasco as a student, and the plot revolves around her struggles as a first-time teacher and her involvement in investigating a series of vicious murders." Horn Book Guide
"Using descriptive, personable prose, Pierce combines dimensional characters, intricate details, plot twists, and alternating story lines for a gripping read. . . . There is some vivid violence." Booklist
Other titles in this series are:
Cold fire (2002)
Shatterglass (2003)
Street magic (2001)

Pinkney, Jerry, 1939-
The nightingale; [by] Hans Christian Andersen; adapted and illustrated by Jerry Pinkney. Phyllis Fogelman Bks. 2002 unp il $16.99 *

Grades: 2 3 4   **Fic**
1. Andersen, Hans Christian, 1805-1875—Adaptations
2. Fairy tales 3. Nightingales—Fiction
ISBN 0-8037-2464-0   LC 2001-47601
Despite being neglected by the emperor for a jewel-studded bird, the little nightingale revives the dying ruler with its beautiful song. A retelling set in Morocco
This "is a pleasing version of the classic, fresh in its interpretation but true to the spirit of the original. . . . Each double-page spread is illuminated by artwork that glows with rich colors and teems with lively details.

Done in graphic, gouache, and watercolor, the large, gracefully composed illustrations feature a profusion of patterns." Booklist

Pinkwater, Daniel Manus, 1941-
The Hoboken chicken emergency; by Daniel Pinkwater; illustrated by Tony Auth. Atheneum Books for Young Readers 2007 101p il $16.99; pa $4.99 *

Grades: 3 4 5 6   **Fic**
1. Chickens—Fiction
ISBN 978-1-4169-2809-6; 1-4169-2809-X; 978-1-4169-2810-2 (pa); 1-4169-2810-3 (pa)
         LC 2006101544
First published 1977 by Simon & Schuster
Arthur goes to pick up the turkey for Thanksgiving dinner but comes back with a 266-pound chicken.
"A contemporary tall tale that will stretch middle graders' imagination, sense of humor, and enthusiasm for reading." Booklist
Other titles about Henrietta the chicken are:
The Artsy Smartsy Club (2005)
Looking for Bobowicz (2004)

The Neddiad; how Neddie took the train, went to Hollywood, and saved civilization; by Daniel Pinkwater; illustrations by Calef Brown. Houghton Mifflin 2007 307p il $16

Grades: 5 6 7 8   **Fic**
1. Turtles—Fiction 2. Los Angeles (Calif.)—Fiction
ISBN 978-0-618-59444-3; 0-618-59444-2
         LC 2006033944
Followed by: The Yggyssey (2009)
When shoelace heir Neddie Wentworthstein and his family take the train from Chicago to Los Angeles in the 1940s, he winds up in possession of a valuable Indian turtle artifact whose owner is supposed to be able to prevent the impending destruction of the world, but he is not sure exactly how.
"A bright and breezy adventure with a smart and funny narrator. . . . [This is a] goofy and lovingly nostalgic historical fantasy." SLJ

The Yggyssey; how Iggy wondered what happened to all the ghosts, found out where they went, and went there; illustrations by Calef Brown. Houghton Mifflin Co. 2009 245p il $16

Grades: 4 5 6   **Fic**
1. Ghost stories 2. Hotels and motels—Fiction
3. Hollywood (Calif.)—Fiction
ISBN 978-0-618-59445-0; 0-618-59445-0
         LC 2008-01874
Sequel to: The Neddiad
In the mid-1950s, Yggdrasil Birnbaum and her friends, Seamus and Neddie, journey to Old New Hackensack, which is on another plane, to try to learn why ghosts are disappearing from the Birnbaum's hotel and other Hollywood, California, locations.
"Once again, Pinkwater combines a goofy plot, myth and fairy tale references, and an obvious affection for yesteryear Los Angeles in a supernaturally funny read." Booklist

Pitchford, Dean

Captain Nobody. G.P. Putnam's Sons 2009 195p $16.99; pa $6.99

Grades: 3 4 5 6   **Fic**
1. Halloween—Fiction   2. Brothers—Fiction 3. Costume—Fiction
ISBN   978-0-399-25034-7;   0-399-25034-4; 978-0-14-241667-9 (pa); 0-14-241667-3 (pa)
       LC 2008-27733

When ten-year-old Newton dresses up as an unusual superhero for Halloween, he decides to keep wearing the costume after the holiday to help save townspeople and eventually his injured brother.

The author "builds suspense adeptly. . . . The young narrator's earnest voice—and his raw sense of helplessness—are real and affecting." Publ Wkly

Place, François

The old man mad about drawing; a tale of Hokusai; translated from the French by William Rodarmor. David R. Godine 2004 105p il $19.95
Grades: 3 4 5 6   **Fic**
1. Hokusai (Katsushika Hokusai), 1760-1849—Fiction 2. Japan—Fiction 3. Artists—Fiction
ISBN 1-56792-260-0   LC 2003-13521

Tojiro, a young seller of rice cakes in the Japanese capital of Edo, later known as Tokyo, is amazed to discover that the grumpy and shabby old man who buys his cakes is a famous artist renowned for his sketches, prints, and paintings of flowers, animals, and landscapes.

This book "features fine reproductions of Hokusai's work, as well as Rodarmore's elegant detailed sketches of the quiet studio and crowded streets." Booklist

Platt, Randall Beth, 1948-

Hellie Jondoe; [by] Randall Platt. Texas Tech University Press 2009 216p pa $16.95
Grades: 5 6 7 8   **Fic**
1. Orphans—Fiction 2. Oregon—Fiction
ISBN 978-0-89672-663-5 (pa); 0-89672-663-0 (pa)
       LC 2009-21514

In 1918, as the Great War ends and the Spanish influenza pandemic begins, thirteen-year-old Hellie Jondoe survives on the streets of New York as a beggar and pickpocket until she boards the orphan train to Oregon, where she learns about loyalty, honesty, and the meaning of family

"This is solid historical fiction with a scrappy heroine who is genuinely tough and a true survivor. Irrepressible and irreverent." Kirkus

Poblocki, Dan

The stone child. Random House 2009 274p $15.99; lib bdg $18.99
Grades: 5 6 7 8   **Fic**
1. Authors—Fiction 2. Books and reading—Fiction 3. Supernatural—Fiction 4. Monsters—Fiction
ISBN   978-0-375-84254-2;   0-375-84254-3; 978-0-375-94254-9 (lib bdg); 0-375-94254-8 (lib bdg)
       LC 2008-21722

When friends Eddie, Harris, and Maggie discover that the scary adventures in their favorite author's fictional books come true, they must find a way to close the portal that allows evil creatures and witches to enter their hometown of Gatesweed.

"The creep factor is high but not graphic, and the kids act and react like real kids. . . . This briskly paced novel is sure to be popular with fans of scary stuff." SLJ

Pogue, David

Abby Carnelia's one and only magical power. Roaring Brook Press 2010 277p $15.99
Grades: 3 4 5   **Fic**
1. Magic—Fiction   2. Camps—Fiction 3. Connecticut—Fiction
ISBN 978-1-59643-384-7; 1-59643-384-1
       LC 2009-46619

After eleven-year-old Abby discovers that she has a completely useless magical power, she finds herself at a magic camp where her hope of finding others like herself is realized, but when a select group is taken to a different camp, a sinister plot comes to light.

"This book is a whimsical feast for children. The characters are well developed; the story is magical and reminiscent of Eva Ibbotsen's wonderful books. The chapters are short and move the plot along quickly. It is an adventure from beginning to end and a plain good story." Libr Media Connect

Polacco, Patricia

The butterfly. Philomel Bks. 2000 unp il $16.99; pa $7.99
Grades: 2 3 4   **Fic**
1. Jews—Fiction 2. World War, 1939-1945—Fiction 3. France—Fiction
ISBN 0-399-23170-6; 0-14-241306-2 (pa)
       LC 99-30038

During the Nazi occupation of France, Monique's mother hides a Jewish family in her basement and tries to help them escape to freedom

"Polacco's use of color has never been more effective. . . . The bold pattern and heightened color of the insect provides a counterpoint to the equally dynamic black-on-red swastikas. Convincing in its portrayal of both the disturbing and humanitarian forces of the time." SLJ

January's sparrow. Philomel Books 2009 94p il $21.99 *
Grades: 4 5 6   **Fic**
1. Underground railroad—Fiction 2. Slavery—Fiction 3. Family life—Fiction 4. African Americans—Fiction
ISBN 978-0-399-25077-4; 0-399-25077-8
       LC 2008-52726

After a fellow slave is beaten to death, Sadie and her family flee the plantation for freedom through the Underground Railroad.

"The illustrations, which include scenes of a bloody whipping and a heavily scarred back, have an urgent, unsettled look that fully captures the sharply felt danger and terror of Sadie's experiences. . . . This moving account effectively highlights a significant instance of nonviolent community resistance to injustice." SLJ

Polacco, Patricia—*Continued*

The junkyard wonders. Philomel 2010 unp il $17.99

Grades: 2 3 4 5   **Fic**
  1. School stories 2. Special education—Fiction
3. Airplanes—Models—Fiction 4. Teachers—Fiction
ISBN 978-0-399-25078-1; 0-399-25078-6

"Looking forward to a fresh start at a new school, Trisha is crestfallen when she is assigned to a special class with children who are different. Their teacher, Mrs. Peterson, proudly calls them the junkyard and takes them to an actual junkyard, which she describes as a place of wondrous possibilities. . . . Reclaiming and rebuilding an old model plane they intend to send to the moon, Trisha's tribe manages a triumphant launch. Illustrations, rendered in pencil and marker, portray children in saddle oxfords and poodle skirts brimming with energy and excitement, guided by a model teacher. Based on her own childhood, Polacco's inspiring story will touch children and teachers alike." Booklist

When lightning comes in a jar. Philomel Bks. 2002 unp il $16.99; pa $6.99

Grades: 2 3 4   **Fic**
  1. Family reunions—Fiction 2. Grandmothers—Fiction
3. Family life—Fiction
ISBN 0-399-23164-1; 0-14-240350-4 (pa)
         LC 2001-45925

A young girl describes the family reunion at her grandmother's house, from the food and baseball and photos to the flickering fireflies on the lawn

"The watercolor-and-pencil illustrations, skillfully composed on the pages, expressively sketch the characters. . . . This autobiographical story will convey the joys of family." Booklist

Polikoff, Barbara Garland

Why does the coqui sing? Holiday House 2004 213p $16.95

Grades: 5 6 7 8   **Fic**
  1. Puerto Ricans—Fiction 2. Puerto Rico—Fiction
3. Moving—Fiction
ISBN 0-8234-1817-0   LC 2003-56776

When thirteen-year-old Luz and her family move from Chicago to her stepfather's native home of Puerto Rico, she and her brother Rome struggle to adjust and to decide where it is they really belong

"Luz, an aspiring poet, beautifully describes the pain of leaving and resettling in a sensitive, sometimes lyrical voice that's always true to her age." Booklist

Porter, Tracey

Billy Creekmore. Joanna Cotler Books 2007 305p $16.99; lib bdg $17.89; pa $6.99 *

Grades: 5 6 7 8   **Fic**
  1. Orphanages—Fiction 2. Coal mines and mining—Fiction 3. Circus—Fiction 4. West Virginia—Fiction
ISBN   978-0-06-077570-4;   0-06-0-77570-X;
978-0-06-077571-1 (lib bdg); 0-06-077571-8 (lib bdg);
978-0-06-077572-8 (pa); 0-06-077572-6 (pa)
         LC 2007-00001

In 1905, ten-year-old Billy is taken from an orphanage to live with an aunt and uncle he never knew he had,

and he enjoys his first taste of family life until his work in a coal mine and involvement with a union brings trouble, then he joins a circus in hopes of finding his father.

"Porter's writing is strong, and the story, told in Billy's steadfast yet child-true voice, makes the shocking history about the lives of children at the turn of the last century come alive for today's readers." Booklist

Potter, Ellen, 1963-

Olivia Kidney; illustrated by Peter Reynolds. Philomel Bks. 2003 155p il $15.99; pa $5.99 *

Grades: 3 4 5 6   **Fic**
  1. Apartment houses—Fiction 2. New York (N.Y.)—Fiction
ISBN 0-399-23850-6; 0-14-240234-6 (pa)
         LC 2002-3660

Twelve-year-old Olivia explores her new apartment building and finds a psychic, talking lizards, a shrunken ex-pirate, an exiled princess, ghosts, and other unusual characters

"Potter has written a first-rate novel to be enjoyed on many levels. Its plot is so tightly woven that it's difficult to separate the mystical from the fantastical. Occasional full-page illustrations add another dimension to this narrative, which is wonderful medicine for the lonely." SLJ
Other titles about Olivia Kidney are:
Olivia Kidney and the Exit Academy (2005)
Olivia Kidney and the secret beneath the city (2007)

Slob. Philomel Books 2009 199p $16.99

Grades: 5 6 7 8   **Fic**
  1. Obesity—Fiction   2. Bereavement—Fiction
3. Siblings—Fiction   4. Inventions—Fiction
5. Orphans—Fiction 6. New York (N.Y.)—Fiction
ISBN 978-0-399-24705-7; 0-399-24705-X
         LC 2008-40476

Picked on, overweight genius Owen tries to invent a television that can see the past to find out what happened the day his parents were killed.

"An intriguingly offbeat mystery, . . . at turns humorous, suspenseful and poignant." Kirkus

Pratchett, Terry

Only you can save mankind. HarperCollins 2005 c1992 207p hardcover o.p. lib bdg $16.89; pa $6.99 *

Grades: 5 6 7 8   **Fic**
  1. Computer games—Fiction 2. War stories
ISBN 0-06-054185-7; 0-06-054186-5 (lib bdg);
0-06-054187-3 (pa)
First published 1992 in the United Kingdom

Twelve-year-old Johnny endures tensions between his parents, watches television coverage of the Gulf War, and plays a computer game called Only You Can Save Mankind, in which he is increasingly drawn into the reality of the alien ScreeWee

This is "a wild ride, full of Pratchett's trademark humor; digs at primitive, low-resolution games . . . ; and some not-so-subtle philosophy about war and peace." Booklist
Other titles in this trilogy are:
Johnny and the dead (2006)
Johnny and the bomb (2006)

Preller, James, 1961-

Six innings; a game in the life. Feiwel and Friends 2008 147p $16.95 *

Grades: 4 5 6 7   **Fic**

1. Baseball—Fiction 2. Cancer—Fiction
ISBN 978-0-312-36763-3; 0-312-36763-5

LC 2007-32846

Earl Grubb's Pool Supplies plays Northeast Gas & Electric in the Little League championship game, while Sam, who has cancer and is in a wheelchair, has to call the play-by-play instead of participating in the game.

"The outcome is predictable but the journey is nailbitingly tense. Kids will be nodding in agreement at the truths laid bare." Publ Wkly

Prévost, Guillaume, 1964-

The book of time; [by] Guillaume Prévost; translated by William Rodarmor. Arthur A. Levine Books 2007 213p $16.99; pa $6.99

Grades: 5 6 7 8   **Fic**

1. Science fiction 2. Missing persons—Fiction
ISBN   978-0-439-88375-7;   0-439-88375-X; 978-0-439-88379-5 (pa); 0-439-88379-2 (pa)

LC 2006-38446

Original French edition 2006

Sam Faulkner travels back in time to medieval Ireland, ancient Egypt and Renaissance Bruges in search of his missing father

"The appeal of the novel . . . comes from both well-drawn characters and a swiftly moving story." Booklist

Other titles in this series are:
The gate of days (2008)
The circle of gold (2009)

Priestley, Chris, 1958-

Tales of terror from the Black Ship; by Chris Priestley; illustrated by David Roberts. Bloomsbury Children's Books 2008 243p il $12.99

Grades: 5 6 7 8   **Fic**

1. Siblings—Fiction 2. Storytelling—Fiction 3. Sea stories 4. Cornwall (England)—Fiction 5. Great Britain—Fiction 6. Horror fiction
ISBN 978-1-59990-290-6; 1-59990-290-7

LC 2008-10408

One stormy night, in their family's otherwise deserted Cornwall inn, twelve-year-old Ethan and his sister Cathy shelter a mysterious guest who indulges their love of the macabre by telling horror stories of the sea

"Priestley and Roberts, whose Gorey-esque line illustrations can distill spirits from a nightmare, understand full well what kids want to read under the covers by flashlight." Bull Cent Child Books

Prineas, Sarah

The magic thief; illustrations by Antonio Javier Caparo. HarperCollins Pubs. 2008 419p il map $16.99; lib bdg $17.89; pa $6.99 *

Grades: 4 5 6 7   **Fic**

1.   Magic—Fiction   2.   Thieves—Fiction 3. Apprentices—Fiction 4. Fantasy fiction
ISBN   978-0-06-137587-3;   0-06-137587-X; 978-0-06-137588-0 (lib bdg); 0-06-137588-8 (lib bdg); 978-0-06-137590-3 (pa); 0-06-137590-X (pa)

LC 2007-31704

"Conn is a thief but, through desire and inevitability, becomes a wizard . . . This evolution begins when Conn picks the pocket of the wizard Nevery. . . . What works wonderfully well here is the boy's irresistable voice." Booklist

Other titles in this series are:
Lost (2009)
Found (2010)

Pullman, Philip, 1946-

Clockwork; or, All wound up; with illustrations by Leonid Gore. Levine Bks. 1998 c1996 112p il hardcover o.p. pa $4.99 *

Grades: 4 5 6 7   **Fic**

1. Supernatural—Fiction
ISBN 0-590-12999-6; 0-590-12998-8 (pa)

LC 97-27458

First published 1996 in the United Kingdom

Long ago in Germany, a storyteller's story and an apprentice clockwork-maker's nightmare meet in a menacing, lifelike figure created by the strange Dr. Kalmenius

"Pullman laces his tale with subtle humor while maintaining the suspense until the end. Misty, moody, and atmospheric black-and-white drawings by Leonid Gore make a perfect fit for this gothic gem." Voice Youth Advocates

I was a rat! illustrated by Kevin Hawkes. Knopf 2000 164p il $15.95; pa $4.99 *

Grades: 4 5 6 7   **Fic**

1. Fantasy fiction
ISBN 0-375-80176-6; 0-440-41661-2 (pa)

LC 99-31806

First published 1999 in the United Kingdom with illustrations by Peter Bailey

"Pullman tells what happens to Cinderella's rat-turned-pageboy, who, busily sliding down banisters at the palace, misses the pumpkin-coach ride home and gets trapped in boy form. Young readers will find the story completely entertaining, whether or not they appreciate the playful spoofing of sensational news stories, mob mentality, and the royal family." Horn Book Guide

Quattlebaum, Mary, 1958-

Jackson Jones and Mission Greentop. Delacorte Press 2004 101p hardcover o.p. pa $5.50

Grades: 3 4 5   **Fic**

1. Gardens—Fiction 2. African Americans—Fiction
ISBN 0-385-73114-0; 0-440-41957-3 (pa)

LC 2003-11823

His plot in a community garden brings 10-year-old Jackson Jones more zucchini than he cares to see and the unwanted attention of a bully, but when a company plans to destroy the garden, Jackson turns his attention to trying to save it.

"Quattlebaum's talent for depicting a lively, diverse neighborhood and funny interchanges between kids remains strong, as does her gift for simple conversational writing." Horn Book Guide

Other titles about Jackson Jones are:
Jackson Jones and the curse of the outlaw rose (2006)
Jackson Jones and the puddle of thorns (1995)

Railsback, Lisa

Noonie's masterpiece; art by Sarajo Frieden. Chronicle Books 2010 208p il $18.99

Grades: 4 5 6 7   **Fic**

1. Artists—Fiction 2. Eccentrics and eccentricities—Fiction 3. Family life—Fiction 4. Father-daughter relationship—Fiction 5. School stories
ISBN 978-0-8118-6654-5; 0-8118-6654-8

LC 2008-26831

Upon learning that her deceased mother, an artist, went through a "Purple Period," ten-year-old Noonie decides to do the same, hoping that this will bring her archaeologist father home to see her win a school art contest and that the aunt, uncle, and cousin she lives with will come to understand her just a little.

"Noonie may be an unreliable and even unlikable narrator at times, but her pain and vulnerability are as evident as her belief in herself as an artist, and by the end of the story, she'll have readers in her corner. The ink-and-watercolor illustrations, appearing throughout the book, have a 1960s-retro look." Booklist

Ramthun, Bonnie

The White Gates; by Bonnie Ramthun. Random House 2008 242p $16.99; lib bdg $19.99; pa $7.99

Grades: 4 5 6 7   **Fic**

1. Snowboarding—Fiction 2. Physicians—Fiction 3. Mother-son relationship—Fiction 4. Ute Indians—Fiction 5. Colorado—Fiction 6. Mystery fiction
ISBN   978-0-375-84554-3;   0-375-84554-2; 978-0-375-94554-0 (lib bdg); 0-375-94554-7 (lib bdg); 978-0-375-84555-0 (pa); 0-375-84555-0 (pa)

LC 2007-12800

When his mother becomes the doctor in Snow Park, Colorado, twelve-year-old Tor learns of a curse placed on the town's doctors many years before by an eccentric Ute woman, but suspects that a modern-day villain is hiding behind that curse.

"Solutions to puzzles come as swiftly and dramatically as an avalanche that nearly takes Tor's life, but the distinctive location and thrilling snowboard scenes overcome improbabilities in the denouement." Publ Wkly

Ransom, Candice F., 1952-

Finding Day's Bottom. Carolrhoda Books 2006 176p lib bdg $15.95

Grades: 4 5 6   **Fic**

1. Bereavement—Fiction 2. Grandfathers—Fiction 3. Country life—Fiction 4. Virginia—Fiction
ISBN 1-57505-933-9

After her father dies, eleven-year-old Jane-Ery slowly finds healing through her relationship with her grandfather and their rural Virginia home.

"This affecting first-person novel is an involving story of loss, pain, healing, and family love." Booklist

Rappaport, Doreen, 1939-

Freedom ship. Hyperion Books for Children 2006 unp il $15.99

Grades: 3 4 5 6   **Fic**

1. Smalls, Robert, 1839-1915—Fiction 2. African Americans—Fiction 3. Slavery—Fiction 4. United States—History—1861-1865, Civil War—Fiction
ISBN 0-7868-0645-1

"Jump at the Sun"

"In 1862, Robert Smalls, 23, a black wheelman on the Confederate steamship *Planter*, and other members of the ship's slave crew, seized the ship and delivered it to the Union Army. Five black women and three children escaped to freedom with the crew, and Rappaport uses the fictionalized viewpoint of one of the children to tell her story. . . . Though personal narrative gives the story immediacy, and the handsome illustrations show the strong child and his proud, smiling family standing tall, Rappaport's lengthy note about Smalls is even more exciting than the fiction." Booklist

Raskin, Ellen, 1928-1984

The mysterious disappearance of Leon (I mean Noel). Dutton 1971 149p il pa $5.99 hardcover o.p.

Grades: 4 5 6 7   **Fic**

1. New York (N.Y.)—Fiction 2. Mystery fiction
ISBN 0-14-032945-5 (pa)

"Wed at the age of five to a seven-year-old husband (it solved a business difficulty for their two families), the very young Mrs. Leon Carillon immediately loses her spouse, who is sent off to boarding school. This is the hilarious account of her search for Leon, aided by adopted twins, when she is older. With clever clues to stimulate the reader's participation, the story is a bouquet of wordplay garnished with jokes, sly pokes at our society, daft characters, and soupcon of slapstick. Fresh and funny, it's the kind of book that passes from child to child." Saturday Rev

The Westing game. Dutton Children's Books 2003 182p $16.99; pa $5.99 *

Grades: 5 6 7 8   **Fic**

1. Mystery fiction
ISBN 0-525-47137-5; 0-14-240120-X (pa)

LC 2004-268658

Awarded the Newbery Medal, 1979

First published 1978

"This mystery puzzle . . . centers on the challenge set forth in the will of eccentric multimillionaire Samuel Westing. Sixteen heirs of diverse backgrounds and ages are assembled in the old 'Westing house', paired off, and given clues to a puzzle they must solve—apparently in order to inherit." SLJ

"The rules of the game make eight pairs of the players; each oddly matched couple is given a ten thousand dollar check and a set of clues. The result is a fascinating medley of word games, disguises, multiple aliases and subterfuges—in a demanding but rewarding book." Horn Book

Rawlings, Marjorie Kinnan, 1896-1953

The yearling; with pictures by N. C. Wyeth. Scribner 1985 c1938 400p il hardcover o.p. pa $5.95

Grades: 5 6 7 8   **Fic**

    1. Florida—Fiction 2. Deer—Fiction

    ISBN 0-684-18461-3; 0-02-044931-3 (pa)

                     LC 85-40301

    Reissue of the title first published 1938; awarded Pulitzer Prize, 1939

    "Young Jody Baxter lives a lonely life in the scrub forest of Florida until his parents unwillingly consent to his adopting an orphan fawn. The two become inseparable until the fawn destroys the meager crops. Then Jody realizes that this situation offers no compromise. In the sacrifice of what he loves best, he leaves his own yearling days behind." Read Ladders for Hum Relat. 5th edition

    "With its excellent descriptions of Florida scrub landscapes, its skillful use of native vernacular, its tender relation between Jody and his pet fawn, The Yearling is a simply written, picturesque story of boyhood." Time

Rawls, Wilson, 1913-1984

Where the red fern grows; the story of two dogs and a boy. Bantam Bks. 1996 212p $16.95; pa $5.99 *

Grades: 4 5 6 7   **Fic**

    1. Dogs—Fiction 2. Ozark Mountains—Fiction

    ISBN 0-385-32330-1; 0-440-41267-6 (pa)

    First published 1961 by Doubleday

    "Looking back more than 50 years to his boyhood in the Ozarks, the narrator, recalls how he achieved his heart's desire in the ownership of two redbone hounds, how he taught them all the tricks of hunting, and how they won the championship coon hunt before Old Dan was killed by a mountain lion and Little Ann died of grief. Although some readers may find this novel hackneyed and entirely too sentimental, others will enjoy the fine coonhunting episodes and appreciate the author's feelings for nature." Booklist

Ray, Delia

Ghost girl; a Blue Ridge Mountain story. Clarion Bks. 2003 216p il $15

Grades: 5 6 7 8   **Fic**

    1. Hoover, Herbert, 1874-1964—Fiction 2. Hoover, Lou Henry, 1874-1944—Fiction 3. School stories 4. Teachers—Fiction 5. Virginia—Fiction

    ISBN 0-618-33377-0   LC 2003-4115

    Eleven-year-old April is delighted when President and Mrs. Hoover build a school near her Madison County, Virginia, home but her family's poverty, grief over the accidental death of her brother, and other problems may mean that April can never learn to read from the wonderful teacher, Miss Vest

    "This excellent portrayal of four important years in a girl's life rises to the top. Based on a real school and teacher, this novel seamlessly incorporates historical facts into the narrative." SLJ

Singing hands. Clarion Books 2006 248p il $16

Grades: 4 5 6 7   **Fic**

    1. Deaf—Fiction 2. Family life—Fiction 3. Clergy—Fiction 4. Alabama—Fiction

    ISBN 0-618-65762-2   LC 2005-22972

    In the late 1940s, twelve-year-old Gussie, a minister's daughter, learns the definition of integrity while helping with a celebration at the Alabama School for the Deaf—her punishment for misdeeds against her deaf parents and their boarders.

    "While the portrayal of a signing household is natural and convincing, the focus is on Gussie's rebellion and growth, the real heart of the story." Horn Book Guide

Reeder, Carolyn, 1937-

Across the lines. Atheneum Bks. for Young Readers 1997 220p hardcover o.p. pa $5.99

Grades: 5 6 7 8   **Fic**

    1. United States—History—1861-1865, Civil War—Fiction 2. African Americans—Fiction 3. Race relations—Fiction

    ISBN 0-689-81133-0; 0-380-73073-1 (pa)

                     LC 96-31068

    Available in paperback from HarperCollins

    Edward, the son of a white plantation owner, and his black house servant and friend Simon witness the siege of Petersburg during the Civil War

    "Told in the alternating voices of Edward and Simon, this thoughtful Civil War story resonates with authenticity." Horn Book Guide

Reeve, Philip, 1966-

Larklight; or, The revenge of the white spiders!, or To Saturn's rings and back!: a rousing tale of dauntless pluck in the farthest reaches of space; as chronicl'd by Art Mumby, with the aid of Philip Reeve; and decorated throughout by David Wyatt. Bloomsbury 2006 399p il $16.95; pa $7.95

Grades: 5 6 7 8   **Fic**

    1. Science fiction

    ISBN 1-59990-020-3; 1-59990-145-5 (pa)

    In an alternate Victorian England, young Arthur and his sister Myrtle, residents of Larklight, a floating house in one of Her Majesty's outer space territories, uncover a spidery plot to destroy the solar system

    "This wildly imaginative sci-fi pirate adventure has tongue-in-cheek humor and social commentary on accepting those who are different, among other things." SLJ

    Other titles about the Mumby family are:

Starcross (2007)

Mothstorm (2008)

Reiche, Dietlof, 1941-

I, Freddy; book one in the golden hamster saga; translated from the German by John Brownjohn; illustrated by Joe Cepeda. Scholastic Press 2003 201p il hardcover o.p. pa $4.99 *

Grades: 3 4 5   **Fic**

    1. Hamsters—Fiction

    ISBN 0-439-28356-6; 0-439-28357-4 (pa)

                     LC 2002-6981

Reiche, Dietlof, 1941-—_Continued_

Freddy, a remarkably intelligent golden hamster, learns how to read and how to write on a computer and escapes captivity to become an independent and civilized creature

"Illustrated with amusing black-ink sketches, this engaging story will appeal to fans of animal fantasies." SLJ

Other titles about Freddy are:

Freddy in peril (2004)
Freddy to the rescue (2005)
The haunting of Freddy (2006)
Freddy's final quest (2007)

Resau, Laura

Star in the forest. Delacorte Press 2010 149p il $14.99; lib bdg $17.99 *

Grades: 4 5 6   **Fic**

1. Illegal aliens—Fiction 2. Fathers—Fiction 3. Dogs—Fiction 4. Friendship—Fiction 5. Mexican Americans—Fiction

ISBN 978-0-385-73792-0; 0-385-73792-0; 978-0-385-90700-2 (lib bdg); 0-385-90700-1 (lib bdg)

LC 2009-03898

After eleven-year-old Zitlally's father is deported to Mexico, she takes refuge in her trailer park's forest of rusted car parts, where she befriends a spunky neighbor and finds a stray dog that she nurses to health and believes she must keep safe so that her father will return.

"Resau has woven details of immigrant life into a compelling story. . . . This is a well-told and deeply satisfying read." SLJ

What the moon saw; a novel. Delacorte Press 2006 258p $15.95; pa $5.99 *

Grades: 5 6 7 8   **Fic**

1. Mexico—Fiction 2. Country life—Fiction 3. Grandparents—Fiction

ISBN 0-385-73343-7; 0-440-23957-5 (pa)

LC 2006-04571

Fourteen-year-old Clara Luna spends the summer with her grandparents in the tiny, remote village of Yucuyoo, Mexico, learning about her grandmother's life as a healer, her father's decision to leave home for the United States, and her own place in the world.

This is an "exquisitely crafted narrative. . . . The characters are well developed. . . . Resau does an exceptional job of portraying the agricultural society sympathetically and realistically." SLJ

Rex, Adam

The true meaning of Smekday. Hyperion Books for Children 2007 423p il $16.99; pa $6.99 *

Grades: 5 6 7 8   **Fic**

1. End of the world—Fiction 2. Science fiction 3. Extraterrestrial beings—Fiction

ISBN 0-7868-4900-2; 978-0-7868-4900-0; 0-7868-4901-0 (pa); 978-0-7868-4901-7 (pa)

When her mother is abducted by aliens on Christmas Eve (or "Smekday" Eve since the Boov invasion), 11 year-old Tip hops in the family car and heads south to find her and meets an alien Boov mechanic who agrees to help her and save the planet from disaster.

"Incorporating dozens of his weird and wonderful illustrations and fruitfully manipulating the narrative structure, Rex skewers any number of subjects." Publ Wkly

Richter, Jutta, 1955-

Beyond the station lies the sea; translated from the German by Anna Brailovsky. Milkweed Editions 2009 81p $14

Grades: 4 5 6 7   **Fic**

1. Homeless persons—Fiction 2. Angels—Fiction

ISBN 978-1-57131-690-5; 1-57131-690-6

LC 2009018135

Trying to get to the beach where it is warm, two homeless boys enlist the aid of a rich woman who gives them money in exchange for a guardian angel.

"Richter presents a darkly poetic, masterfully crafted view of life on the streets." Publ Wkly

Riddell, Chris, 1962-

Ottoline and the yellow cat. HarperCollinsPublishers 2008 171p il $10.99; lib bdg $14.89; pa $6.99 *

Grades: 2 3 4 5   **Fic**

1. Mystery fiction 2. Dogs—Fiction 3. Cats—Fiction

ISBN 978-0-06-144879-9; 0-06-144879-6; 978-0-06-144880-5 (lib bdg); 0-06-144880-X (lib bdg); 978-0-06-144881-2 (pa); 0-06-144881-8 (pa)

"While her parents are off traveling the world collecting 'interesting things,' Ottoline Brown lives in an elaborate apartment in Big City with her best friend, guardian, and accomplice in forming clever plans. He is called Mr. Monroe and is a silent creature from Norway. . . . Ottoline solves a mystery involving a cat burglar, who is actually a cat, and the missing lapdogs of well-to-do women. The story is told through the text and the detailed line drawings that appear on each page. Done in black and white with red highlighting a quirky detail or two, the illustrations add humor, depth, and momentum to the narrative. The quickly moving plot is grounded in real emotion." SLJ

Another title about Ottoline is:

Ottoline goes to school (2009)

Riddleburger, Sam

The strange case of Origami Yoda; [by] Tom Angleberger. Amulet Books 2010 141p il $12.95

Grades: 4 5 6 7   **Fic**

1. Puppets and puppet plays—Fiction 2. Origami—Fiction 3. Eccentrics and eccentricities—Fiction 4. School stories

ISBN 978-0-8109-8425-7; 0-8109-8425-3

LC 2009-39748

Sixth-grader Tommy and his friends describe their interactions with a paper finger puppet of Yoda, worn by their weird classmate Dwight, as they try to figure out whether or not the puppet can really predict the future. Includes instructions for making Origami Yoda.

"The situations that Yoda has a hand in are pretty authentic, and the setting is broad enough to be any school. The plot is age-old but with the twist of being presented on crumpled pages with cartoon sketches, supposed hand printing, and varying typefaces. Kids should love it." SLJ

Riordan, Rick

The maze of bones. Scholastic 2008 220p il (The 39 clues) $12.99 *

Grades: 4 5 6 7 **Fic**

1. Ciphers—Fiction 2. Family—Fiction

ISBN 978-0-545-06039-4; 0-545-06039-7

At the reading of their grandmother's will, Dan and Amy Cahill are given the choice of receiving a million dollars or uncovering the 39 clues hidden around the world that will lead to the source of the family's power, but by taking on the clues, they end up in a dangerous race against their own family members.

"Adeptly incorporating a genuine kids' perspective, the narrative unfolds like a boulder rolling downhill and keeps readers glued to the pages. . . . The book dazzles with suspense, plot twists, and snappy humor." SLJ

Other titles in this series are:

One false note by Gordon Korman (2008)

The sword thief by Peter Lerangis (2009)

The black circle by Patrick Carman (2009)

Beyond the grave by Jude Watson (2009)

In too deep by Jude Watson (2010)

The viper's nest by Peter Lerangis (2010)

The emperor's code by Gordon Korman (2010)

Storm warning by Linda Sue Park (2010)

The red pyramid. Hyperion Books for Children 2010 516p (Kane chronicles) $17.99 *

Grades: 4 5 6 7 **Fic**

1. Siblings—Fiction 2. Egypt—Fiction 3. Secret societies—Fiction 4. Voyages and travels—Fiction 5. Gods and goddesses—Fiction

ISBN 978-1-4231-1338-6; 1-4231-1338-1

After their father's research experiment at the British Museum unleashes the Egyptian god Set, Carter and Sadie Kane embark on a dangerous journey across the globe—a quest which brings them ever closer to the truth about their family, and their links to a secret order that has existed since the time of the pharaohs.

"The first-person narrative shifts between Carter and Sadie, giving the novel an intriguing dual perspective made more complex by their biracial heritage and the tension between the siblings. . . . This fantasy adventure delivers . . . young protagonists with previously unsuspected magical powers, a riveting story marked by headlong adventure, a complex background rooted in ancient mythology, and wry, witty twenty-first-century narration." Booklist

Riskind, Mary, 1944-

Apple is my sign. Houghton Mifflin 1981 146p hardcover o.p. pa $5.95

Grades: 5 6 7 8 **Fic**

1. Deaf—Fiction

ISBN 0-395-30852-6; 0-395-65747-4 (pa)

"The story is set in Pennsylvania at the time of the first horseless carriages . . . in a school for the deaf. Ten-year-old Harry is at first homesick, but he soon makes friends, becomes excited about learning to draw and learning to talk. Aware that his father is ashamed of his own deafness (both parents are deaf) and that his mother is not, Harry learns to accept his situation." Bull Cent Child Books

"In a lengthy note the author explains that she had deaf parents and learned sign language before she learned to speak. She also explores some characteristics of sign language, which has been translated into print via sentence syntax and spelling. A warm, unpretentious story." Booklist

Roberts, Ken

Thumb on a diamond; illustrated by Leanne Franson. Groundwood Books/House of Anansi Press 2006 128p il $15.95; pa $6.95

Grades: 3 4 5 **Fic**

1. Baseball—Fiction 2. British Columbia—Fiction

ISBN 0-88899-629-2; 0-88899-705-1 (pa)

The kids from New Auckland are dying to see something outside of their little villiage. Then, Thumb comes up with a plan to form a baseball team so the kids can go to the big tournament in Vancouver, but there are a few problems with their plan. There is no grass in New Auckland, no baseball diamond and no place large enough to put one. Also, none of the kids have ever played baseball before.

"The characters are appealing and the plot unfolds naturally to create a satisfying and plausible story." SLJ

Others titles about Thumb and his friends are:

Thumb in the box (2001)

Thumb and the bad guys (2009)

Roberts, Marion, 1966-

Sunny side up. Wendy Lamb Books 2009 c2008 244p il $15.99; lib bdg $18.99

Grades: 4 5 6 7 **Fic**

1. Family life—Fiction 2. Friendship—Fiction 3. Australia—Fiction

ISBN 978-0-385-73672-5; 0-385-73672-X; 978-0-385-90624-1 (lib bdg); 0-385-90624-2 (lib bdg)

LC 2008-08633

First published 2008 in Australia

As the hot Australian summer draws to an end, eleven-year-old Sunny, content to be an only child with amicably divorced parents, finds her life getting much too complicated when her mother's boyfriend moves in with his two children, her best friend begins to develop an interest in boys, and she is contacted by her long-estranged grandmother.

"Character development is strong, as the girl is quick to observe and comment on the people in her life, and the setting forms an interesting backdrop. Small black-and-white photos are liberally scattered throughout." SLJ

Roberts, Willo Davis, 1928-2004

The kidnappers. Atheneum Bks. for Young Readers 1998 137p hardcover o.p. pa $4.99

Grades: 4 5 6 7 **Fic**

1. Kidnapping—Fiction 2. Wealth—Fiction 3. New York (N.Y.)—Fiction

ISBN 0-689-81394-5; 0-689-81393-7 (pa)

LC 96-53677

"A Jean Karl book"

No one believes eleven-year-old Joey, who has a reputation for telling tall tales, when he claims to have witnessed the kidnapping of the class bully outside their expensive New York City private school

"The combination of a witty narrative and a suspenseful plot makes this a good page-turner that will leave even the most reluctant readers glued to their seats." Booklist

Roberts, Willo Davis, 1928-2004—*Continued*

The one left behind; [by] Willo Davis Roberts. Atheneum Books for Young Readers 2006 139p $16.95; pa $5.99

Grades: 5 6 7 8   **Fic**
  1. Sisters—Fiction 2. Twins—Fiction 3. Bereavement—Fiction 4. Kidnapping—Fiction
  ISBN 978-0-689-85075-2; 0-689-85075-1; 978-0-689-85083-7 (pa); 0-689-85083-2 (pa)
                      LC 2005018196

"Since losing her vivacious twin sister, Angel, nearly a year ago, . . . 11-year-old [Mandy] drifts through the days, aching for her dead sister's company. But when someone breaks into the house and steals food, Mandy snaps into action and investigates what might be going on. . . . The suspense mounts to a desperate climax before all is resolved safely. An introspective page-turner." Booklist

The view from the cherry tree. Atheneum Pubs. 1975 181p hardcover o.p. pa $5.99 *

Grades: 5 6 7 8   **Fic**
  1. Mystery fiction
  ISBN 0-689-30483-8; 0-689-71784-9 (pa)

"Thoroughly disgruntled by the furor which accompanies his sister's wedding, eleven-year-old Rob Mallory retires to his favorite perch in the cherry tree. There, he is a horrified witness to the murder of an unpleasant neighborhood recluse. Because of the wedding preparations and the arrival of hordes of relatives, no adult will believe Rob's story. Soon, he finds that someone knows—and is trying to kill him, too." Child Book Rev Serv

"Although written in a direct and unpretentious style, this is essentially a sophisticated story, solidly constructed, imbued with suspense, evenly paced, and effective in conveying the atmosphere of a household coping with the last-minute problems and pressures of a family wedding." Bull Cent Child Books

Robertson, Keith, 1914-1991

Henry Reed, Inc.; illustrated by Robert McCloskey. Viking 1958 239p il pa $4.99 hardcover o.p. *

Grades: 4 5 6   **Fic**
  ISBN 0-14-034144-7 (pa)

"Henry Reed, on vacation from the American School in Naples, keeps a record of his research into the American free-enterprise system, to be used as a school report on his return. With a neighbor, Midge Glass, he starts a business in pure and applied research, which results in some very free and widely enterprising experiences, all recorded deadpan in his journal. Very funny and original escapades." Hodges. Books for Elem Sch Libr

 Another title about Henry Reed is:
Henry Reed's babysitting service (1966)

Robinet, Harriette Gillem, 1931-

Forty acres and maybe a mule. Atheneum Bks. for Young Readers 1998 132p hardcover o.p. pa $4.99 *

Grades: 4 5 6 7   **Fic**
  1. African Americans—Fiction 2. Reconstruction (1865-1876)—Fiction 3. United States—History—1865-1898—Fiction
  ISBN 0-689-82078-X; 0-689-83317-2 (pa)
                      LC 97-39169

"A Jean Karl book"

Born with a withered leg and hand, Pascal, who is about twelve years old, joins other former slaves in a search for a farm and the freedom which it promises

"Robinet skillfully balances her in-depth historical knowledge with the feelings of her characters, creating a story that moves along rapidly and comes to a bittersweet conclusion." Booklist

Walking to the bus-rider blues. Atheneum Bks. for Young Readers 2000 146p hardcover o.p. pa $4.99

Grades: 5 6 7 8   **Fic**
  1. African Americans—Fiction 2. Race relations—Fiction
  ISBN 0-689-83191-9; 0-689-83886-7 (pa)
                      LC 99-29054

"A Jean Karl book"

Twelve-year-old Alfa Merryfield, his older sister, and their grandmother struggle for rent money, food, and their dignity as they participate in the Montgomery, Alabama bus boycott in the summer of 1956

"Ingredients of mystery, suspense, and humor enhance and personalize this well-constructed story that offers insight into a troubled era." SLJ

Robinson, Barbara

The best Christmas pageant ever; pictures by Judith Gwyn Brown. Harper & Row 1972 80p il $15.99; lib bdg $16.89; pa $5.99 *

Grades: 4 5 6   **Fic**
  1. Christmas—Fiction 2. Pageants—Fiction
  ISBN 0-06-025043-7; 0-06-025044-5 (lib bdg); 0-06-440275-4 (pa)

In this story the six Herdmans, "absolutely the worst kids in the history of the world," discover the meaning of Christmas when they bully their way into the leading roles of the local church nativity play

The story "romps through the festive preparations with comic relish, and if the Herdmans are so gauche as to seem exaggerated, they are still enjoyable, as are the not-so-subtle pokes at pageant-planning in general." Bull Cent Child Books

 Other titles about the Herdmans are:
The best Halloween ever (2004)
The best school year ever (1994)

Robinson, Sharon, 1950-

Safe at home. Scholastic Press 2006 151p $16.99; pa $5.99

Grades: 4 5 6   **Fic**
  1. African Americans—Fiction 2. Baseball—Fiction 3. New York (N.Y.)—Fiction
  ISBN 0-439-67197-3; 0-439-67198-1 (pa)
                      LC 2005-50250

Robinson, Sharon, 1950-—_Continued_

After the death of his father, Elijah Breeze, a ten-year-old African American boy, moves back to New York City with his mother and attends a summer baseball camp as he tries to make new friends and adapt to urban ways.

The author "has created two intriguing protagonists and a group of equally colorful secondary characters. . . . Regardless of their interest in baseball, readers will identify with these youngsters and appreciate the simple story." SLJ

Another title about Elijah Breeze is:
Slam dunk! (2007)

Rockliff, Mara

The case of the stinky socks; illustrated by Amy Wummer. Kane Press 2009 94p il (Milo & Jazz mysteries) $22.60; pa $6.95

Grades: 1 2 3 4   Fic
1. Clothing and dress—Fiction 2. Baseball—Fiction 3. Mystery fiction
ISBN   978-1-57565-288-7;   1-57565-288-9;
978-1-57565-285-6 (pa); 1-57565-285-4 (pa)
                              LC 2008027536
Detectives-in-training Milo and Jazz join forces to tackle their first big case—finding out who stole the lucky socks from the high school baseball team's star pitcher.

This book "gets it just right: a fun, easy-to-solve mystery, readily identifiable young detectives, and some extras readers will enjoy. . . . The short chapters, written in a large typeface, are punctuated by pen-and-ink illustrations of better quality than those often seen in series books." Booklist

Other titles in this series are:
The case of the poisoned pig (2009)
The case of the haunted haunted house (2009)
The case of the Amazing Zelda (2009)

Rockwell, Thomas, 1933-

How to eat fried worms; pictures by Emily McCully. Watts 1973 115p il lib bdg $29 *
Grades: 3 4 5 6   Fic
1. Worms—Fiction
ISBN 0-531-02631-0
"The stakes are high when Alan bets $50 that his friend Billy can't eat 15 worms (one per day). . . . Billy's mother, instead of upchucking, comes to her son's aid by devising gourmet recipes like Alsatian Smothered Worm. Alan wants to win as desperately as Billy, who is itching to buy a used minibike, and few holds are barred in the contest." SLJ

"A hilarious story that will revolt and delight bumptious, unreachable, intermediate-grade boys and any other less particular mortals that read or listen to it. . . . The characters and their families and activities are natural to a T, and this juxtaposed against the uncommon plot, makes for some colorful, original writing in a much-needed comic vein." Booklist

Rodda, Emily, 1948-

The key to Rondo. Scholastic Press 2008 342p $16.99; pa $6.99 *
Grades: 5 6 7 8   Fic
1. Fantasy fiction 2. Cousins—Fiction 3. Magic—Fiction
ISBN   0-545-03535-X;   978-0-545-03535-4;
0-545-03536-8 (pa); 978-0-545-03536-1 (pa)
                              LC 2007-16873
Through an heirloom music box, Leo, a serious, responsible boy, and his badly-behaved cousin Mimi enter the magical world of Rondo to rescue Mimi's dog from a sorceress, who wishes to exchange him for the key that allows free travel between worlds.

"Rodda fills the cousins' quest with image-rich prose and compelling action." Bull Cent Child Books

Another title about Rondo is:
The Wizard of Rondo (2009)

Rowan of Rin. Greenwillow Bks. 2001 c1993 151p il hardcover o.p. pa $5.99 *
Grades: 4 5 6   Fic
1. Fantasy fiction
ISBN 0-06-029707-7; 0-06-056071-1 (pa)
                              LC 00-63619
First published 1993 in Australia

Because only he can read the magical map, young, weak and timid Rowan joins six other villagers to climb a mountain and try to restore their water supply, as fears of a dragon and other horrors threaten to drive them back

The author has created "a fully conceived fantasy world complete with its own flora and fauna, a well-developed back story, and fascinating characters." Booklist

Other titles about Rowan are:
Rowan and the Ice creepers (2003)
Rowan and the Keeper of the Crystal (2002)
Rowan and the travelers (2001)
Rowan and the Zebak (2002)

Rodgers, Mary, 1931-

Freaky Friday. Harper & Row 1972 145p hardcover o.p. lib bdg $16.89; pa $5.99 *
Grades: 4 5 6 7   Fic
1. Mother-daughter relationship—Fiction
ISBN 0-06-025048-8; 0-06-025049-6 (lib bdg);
0-06-057010-5 (pa)
"'When I woke up this morning, I found I'd turned into my mother.' So begins the most bizarre day in the life of 13-year-old Annabel Andrews, who discovers one Friday morning she has taken on her mother's physical characteristics while retaining her own personality. Readers will giggle in anticipation as Annabel plunges madly from one disaster to another trying to cope with various adult situations." Publ Wkly

"A fresh, imaginative, and entertaining story." Bull Cent Child Books

Rodman, Mary Ann

Jimmy's stars. Farrar, Straus & Giroux 2008 257p $16.95 *

Grades: 5 6 7 8   **Fic**

1. World War, 1939-1945—Fiction 2. Siblings—Fiction 3. Soldiers—Fiction 4. Family life—Fiction 5. Pittsburgh (Pa.)—Fiction

ISBN 978-0-374-33703-2; 0-374-33703-9

LC 2007-05091

In 1943, eleven-year-old Ellie is her brother Jimmy's "best girl," and when he leaves Pittsburgh just before Thanksgiving to fight in World War II, he promises he will return, asks her to leave the Christmas tree up until he does, and reminds her to "let the joy out."

Rodman "finds beauty in every emotional nuance. . . . The lively spirit of working-class Pittsburgh . . . extends Ellie's person story with a broader sense of home-front life." Booklist

Yankee girl. Farrar, Straus and Giroux 2004 219p $17; pa $7.99

Grades: 4 5 6 7   **Fic**

1. Race relations—Fiction 2. School stories 3. Mississippi—Fiction

ISBN 0-374-38661-7; 0-312-53576-7 (pa)

LC 2003-49048

When her FBI-agent father is transferred to Jackson, Mississippi, in 1964, eleven-year-old Alice wants to be popular but also wants to reach out to the one black girl in her class in a newly-integrated school.

"Rodman shows characters grappling with hard choices, sometimes courageously, sometimes willfully, sometimes inconsistently, but invariably believably." Publ Wkly

Rodowsky, Colby F., 1932-

The next-door dogs; [by] Colby Rodowsky; pictures by Amy June Bates. Farrar, Straus & Giroux 2005 103p il $15

Grades: 2 3 4   **Fic**

1. Dogs—Fiction 2. Fear—Fiction

ISBN 0-374-36410-9   LC 2004-43333

Although terrified of dogs, nine-year-old Sara forces herself to face a labrador retriever and a dalmatian when she must help her next-door neighbor, who has fallen and broken her leg

"Rodowsky makes Sara's fear palpable and her eventual recovery believable. Plentiful pencil illustrations add to the book's accessibility." Horn Book Guide

Rogan, S. Jones

The daring adventures of Penhaligon Brush; pictures by Christian Slade. Alfred A. Knopf 2007 230p il $15.99; pa $6.50

Grades: 4 5 6   **Fic**

1. Foxes—Fiction 2. Animals—Fiction 3. Adventure fiction

ISBN 978-0-375-84344-0; 978-0-440-42208-2 (pa); 0-375-84344-2; 0-440-42208-6 (pa)

LC 2006-35566

When Penhaligon Brush the fox is summoned by his stepbrother to the seaside town of Porthleven, he finds immediately upon arrival that his brother is incarcerated in the dungeon at Ferball Manor.

This is a "swift-paced, large-scale adventure. . . . Slade's halftone art . . . [represents] these robust characters in theatrical costume and with plenty of personality." Publ Wkly

Another title about Penhaligon Brush is:

The curse of the Romany wolves (2009)

Rollins, James, 1961-

Jake Ransom and the Skull King's shadow. HarperCollins 2009 399p il map $16.99; lib bdg $17.89; pa $7.99

Grades: 5 6 7 8   **Fic**

1. Adventure fiction 2. Mayas—Fiction 3. Archeology—Fiction 4. Siblings—Fiction

ISBN 978-0-06-147379-1; 0-06-147379-0; 978-0-06-147380-7 (lib bdg); 0-06-147380-4 (lib bdg); 978-0-06-147381-4 (pa); 0-06-147381-2 (pa)

LC 2009-14570

Connecticut middle-schooler Jake and his older sister Kady are transported by a Mayan artifact to a strange world inhabited by a mix of people from long-lost civilizations who are threatened by prehistoric creatures and an evil alchemist, the Skull King.

This is an "exciting time-travel adventure. . . . Rollins . . . presents a wide range of interesting historical information while telling a rollicking good story that should please a wide range of readers." Publ Wkly

Rosen, Michael J., 1954-

Elijah's angel; a story for Chanukah and Christmas; illustrated by Aminah Brenda Lynn Robinson. Harcourt Brace Jovanovich 1992 unp il pa $6 hardcover o.p.

Grades: 2 3 4   **Fic**

1. Pierce, Elijah, 1892-1984—Fiction 2. Artists—Fiction 3. Jews—Fiction 4. Christmas—Fiction 5. Hanukkah—Fiction

ISBN 0-15-201556-2 (pa)   LC 91-37552

At Christmas-Hanukkah time, Elijah Pierce, a black Christian woodcarver gives a carved angel to Michael, a young Jewish friend, who struggles with accepting the Christmas gift until he realizes that friendship means the same thing in any religion

"Perhaps because it's based on reality, Michael and Elijah's relationship rings sweetly true. The naive-style paintings, done in house paint on scrap rags, boldly simulate woodcuts, and though the artwork is not pretty, it, too, has the feel of reality." Booklist

Roy, James, 1968-

Max Quigley; technically not a bully; written and illustrated by James Roy. Houghton Mifflin Harcourt 2009 202p il $12.95

Grades: 4 5 6   **Fic**

1. Bullies—Fiction 2. Friendship—Fiction

ISBN 978-0-547-15263-9; 0-547-15263-9

LC 2008-36110

First published 2007 in Australia

After playing a prank on one of his "geeky" classmates, sixth-grader Max Quigley's punishment is to be tutored by him.

Roy, James, 1968-—*Continued*

"Straightforward chronology, believable dialogue, self-contained chapters, and plenty of humor make this accessible to reluctant readers and particularly appealing to boys who may see a bit of themselves in this realistic school story." Booklist

Roy, Jennifer Rozines

Yellow star; by Jennifer Roy. Marshall Cavendish 2006 227p $16.95

Grades: 5 6 7 8   Fic

1. Holocaust, 1933-1945—Fiction 2. Jews—Fiction 3. Poland—Fiction

ISBN 978-0-7614-5277-5; 0-7614-5277-X

LC 2005-50788

From 1939, when Syvia is four and a half years old, to 1945 when she has just turned ten, a Jewish girl and her family struggle to survive in Poland's Lodz ghetto during the Nazi occupation.

"In a thoughtful, vividly descriptive, almost poetic prose, Roy retells the true story of her Aunt Syvia's experiences. . . . This book is a standout in the genre of Holocaust literature." SLJ

Ruby, Laura

The chaos king. Eos 2007 325p $16.99; lib bdg $17.89

Grades: 5 6 7 8   Fic

1. Orphans—Fiction 2. Fantasy fiction 3. New York (N.Y.)—Fiction

ISBN 978-0-06-075258-3; 0-06-075258-0; 978-0-06-075259-0 (lib bdg); 0-06-075259-9 (lib bdg)

LC 2007-08621

Sequel to: The Wall and the Wing (2006)

Thirteen-year-old Georgie and Bug, a year older, have been pulled apart by the demands of their newfound fame and fortune, but join forces again when a punk, vampires, a giant sloth, and other creatures come after them on the streets of a New York City of the future.

This "is a wonderful story about how being different can be infinitely preferable to being ordinarily beautiful or talented, and Ruby's off-the-wall writing style and infinite imagination make the lesson fun to learn." Kliatt

Lily's ghosts. HarperCollins Pubs. 2003 258p hardcover o.p. pa $5.99 *

Grades: 5 6 7 8   Fic

1. Ghost stories

ISBN 0-06-051829-4; 0-06-051831-6 (pa)

LC 2002-154315

Strange goings-on at her great-uncle's summer home in Cape May, New Jersey, draw Lily and a new friend into a mystery involving lost treasure, a fake medium, and ghosts of all sizes, shapes, and dispositions

"Ruby doesn't horrify so much as she insinuates, in gracefully nuanced language that provides chilling support for the action." Bull Cent Child Books

The Wall and the Wing; [by] Laura Ruby. Eos 2006 327p $16.99; pa $6.99

Grades: 5 6 7 8   Fic

1. Orphans—Fiction 2. Fantasy fiction 3. New York (N.Y.)—Fiction

ISBN 978-0-06-075255-2; 0-06-075255-6; 978-0-06-075257-6 (pa); 0-06-075257-2 (pa)

LC 2005-23170

In a future New York where most people can fly and cats are a rarity, a nondescript resident of Hope House for the Homeless and Hopeless discovers that although she is shunned as a "leadfoot," she has the surprising ability to become invisible

"This poor-little-rich-girl story is packed with wildly eccentric characters. . . . All of this fast-paced wackiness is told with humor, often black, that will have young readers giggling." SLJ

Followed by The Chaos King

Runholt, Susan, 1948-

The mystery of the third Lucretia. Viking Childrens Books 2008 288p $16.99; pa $6.99

Grades: 5 6 7 8   Fic

1. Art—Fiction 2. Europe—Fiction 3. Friendship—Fiction 4. Mystery fiction

ISBN 978-0-670-06252-2; 0-670-06252-9; 978-0-14-241338-8 (pa); 0-14-241338-0 (pa)

LC 2007-24009

While traveling in London, Paris, and Amsterdam, fourteen-year-old best friends Kari and Lucas solve an international art forgery mystery.

"There are enough artistic details for fans of art mysteries and enough spying and fleeing for fans of detective adventure." Bull Cent Child Books

Another title about Kari and Lucas is:
Rescuing Seneca Crane (2009)

Rupp, Rebecca

Sarah Simpson's Rules for Living. Candlewick Press 2008 84p $13.99 *

Grades: 4 5 6   Fic

1. Remarriage—Fiction 2. Family life—Fiction 3. School stories 4. Vermont—Fiction

ISBN 978-0-7636-3220-5   LC 2007-34214

In a journal, twelve-year old Sarah Simpson records important lists and the daily events of her life at home and in school, beginning one year after her father moved from Vermont to California to divorce her mother and marry someone else.

"Although Sarah's tone ranges widely, from resentful to full-out funny, . . . her vulnerable yet take-charge personality comes through." Publ Wkly

Ruskin, John, 1819-1900

The king of the Golden River; [by] John Ruskin; illustrated by Iassen Ghiuselev. Simply Read Books 2005 65p il $19.95

Grades: 3 4 5   Fic

1. Fairy tales

ISBN 978-1-8949-6515-6; 1-8949-6515-9

Written 1841

Ruskin, John, 1819-1900—*Continued*

After Gluck's cruel and greedy older brothers refuse hospitality to a mysterious visitor, their prosperous farm fails and one by one each brother makes the perilous journey to find treasure in the nearby Golden River

"Exquisite drawings by Bulgarian artist Ghiuselev illustrate this . . . edition of Ruskin's classic fairy tale. . . . A well-designed and very handsome edition of the timeless tale." Booklist

Russell, Ching Yeung, 1945-

Tofu quilt. Lee & Low Books 2009 125p il $16.95 *

Grades: 4 5 6   **Fic**
1. Hong Kong (China)—Fiction 2. Novels in verse 3. Authorship—Fiction 4. Sex role—Fiction
ISBN 978-1-60060-423-2; 1-60060-423-4
                  LC 2009-16903
Growing up in 1960s Hong Kong, a young girl dreams of becoming a writer in spite of conventional limits placed on her by society and family.

"The story is revealed through Russell's tender poems that beautifully describe Yeung Ying's surroundings, her home life, her family, and her inner thoughts. The poems are simple, yet filled with images and language that create an atmosphere that brings the child's early years to light." SLJ

Russell, Christopher, 1947-

Dogboy. Greenwillow Books 2006 259p $15.99; lib bdg $16.89

Grades: 5 6 7 8   **Fic**
1. Knights and knighthood—Fiction 2. Orphans—Fiction 3. Dogs—Fiction 4. Hundred Years' War, 1339-1453—Fiction 5. Middle Ages—Fiction
ISBN 0-06-084116-8; 978-0-06-084116-4; 0-06-084117-6 (lib bdg); 978-0-06-084117-1 (lib bdg)
                  LC 2005-08525
First published 2005 in the United Kingdom
In 1346, twelve-year-old Brind, an orphaned kennel boy raised with hunting dogs at an English manor, accompanies his master, along with half of the manor's prized mastiffs, to France, where he must fend for himself when both his master and the dogs are lost at the decisive battle of Crécy.

"The action is fast-paced with narrow escapes at every turn and elements of dry humor at the most unlikely times." SLJ

Followed by Hunted (2007)

Hunted; [by] Christopher Russell. Greenwillow Books 2007 254p hardcover o.p. lib bdg $16.89

Grades: 5 6 7 8   **Fic**
1. Plague—Fiction 2. Dogs—Fiction 3. Great Britain—History—1154-1399, Plantagenets—Fiction 4. Middle Ages—Fiction
ISBN 978-0-06-084119-5; 0-06-084119-2; 978-0-06-084120-1 (lib bdg); 0-06-084120-6 (lib bdg)
                  LC 2006000946
First published 2006 in the United Kingdom with title: Brind: the plague sorcerer

Sequel to: Dogboy (2006)

When the landlord's wife dies of the Plague, he banishes his foster daughter, Aurélie, along dogboy Brind, from the manor. The pair take along two dogs in search of a safe haven, only to discover that sickness and death are everywhere

"The story is action driven, enhanced by the well-characterized dog companions. . . . An entertaining romp through the Middle Ages." SLJ

Rutkoski, Marie

The Cabinet of Wonders; [by] Marie Rutkoski. Farrar Straus Giroux 2008 258p (The Kronos Chronicles) $16.95; pa $6.99 *

Grades: 5 6 7 8   **Fic**
1. Magic—Fiction 2. Princes—Fiction 3. Gypsies—Fiction 4. Fantasy fiction
ISBN 978-0-374-31026-4; 0-374-31026-2; 978-0-312-60239-0 (pa); 0-312-60239-1 (pa)
                  LC 2007037702
Twelve-year-old Petra, accompanied by her magical tin spider, goes to Prague hoping to retrieve the enchanted eyes the Prince of Bohemia took from her father, and is aided in her quest by a Roma boy and his sister.

"Add this heady mix of history and enchantment to the season's list of astonishingly accomplished first novels. . . . Infusions of folklore (and Rutkowski's embellishments of them) don't slow the fast plot but more deeply entrance readers." Publ Wkly

Followed by: The Celestial Globe (2009)

Ryan, Pam Muñoz

Becoming Naomi León; [by] Pam Muñoz Ryan. Scholastic Press 2004 246p $16.95; pa $6.99 *

Grades: 5 6 7 8   **Fic**
1. Mexican Americans—Fiction 2. Mexico—Fiction 3. Family life—Fiction
ISBN 0-439-26969-5; 0-439-26997-0 (pa)
                  LC 2004-346
When Naomi's absent mother resurfaces to claim her, Naomi runs away to Mexico with her great-grandmother and younger brother in search of her father

"Ryan has written a moving book about family dynamics. . . . All of the characters are well drawn." SLJ

The dreamer; drawings by Peter Sís. Scholastic Press 2010 372p il $17.99 *

Grades: 4 5 6 7   **Fic**
1. Poets—Fiction 2. Father-son relationship—Fiction
ISBN 978-0-439-26970-4; 0-439-2-970-9
Neftali finds beauty and wonder everywhere. He loves to collect treasures, daydream, and write—pastimes his authoritarian father thinks are for fools. Against all odds, Neftali prevails against his father's cruelty and his own crippling shyness to become one of the most widely read poets in the world, Pablo Neruda.

"Ryan loads the narrative with vivid sensory details. And although it isn't poetry, it eloquently evokes the sensation of experiencing the world as someone who savors the rhythms of words and gets lost in the intricate surprises of nature. The neat squares of Sis' meticulously stippled illustrations, richly symbolic in their own right, complement and deepen the lyrical quality of the book." Booklist

Ryan, Pam Muñoz—*Continued*
Esperanza rising. Scholastic Press 2000 262p
$15.95; pa $4.99 *
Grades: 5 6 7 8   **Fic**
 1. Mexican Americans—Fiction 2. Agricultural laborers—Fiction 3. California—Fiction
ISBN 0-439-12041-1; 0-439-12042-X (pa)
                                        LC 00-24186
Esperanza and her mother are forced to leave their life
of wealth and privilege in Mexico to go work in the labor camps of Southern California, where they must adapt
to the harsh circumstances facing Mexican farm workers
on the eve of the Great Depression
 "Ryan writes movingly in clear, poetic language that
children will sink into, and the [book] offers excellent
opportunities for discussion and curriculum support."
Booklist

Rylant, Cynthia
 A blue-eyed daisy. Bradbury Press 1985 99p
hardcover o.p. pa $6.99
Grades: 5 6 7 8   **Fic**
 1. Family life—Fiction 2. West Virginia—Fiction
ISBN 0-02-777960-2; 0-689-84495-6 (pa)
                                        LC 84-21554
This story "describes a year in a child's life. . . .
Ellie is eleven, youngest of five girls. She wishes her father didn't drink but understands his frustration. . . . It
is a bond between them when they acquire a hunting
dog. . . . She also acquires a best friend during the year,
gets her first kiss (and is surprised to see that she enjoys
it) and adjusts to the fact that some of the events in her
life will be sad ones." Bull Cent Child Books
 "Episodic in nature, the story captures, as if in a frozen frame, the brief moments between childhood and adolescence." Horn Book

 A fine white dust. Simon & Schuster 2000
c1986 106p $25; pa $4.99 *
Grades: 5 6 7 8   **Fic**
 1. Religion—Fiction 2. Friendship—Fiction 3. Family
life—Fiction
ISBN   978-0-689-84087-6;   0-689-84087-X;
978-1-4169-2769-3 (pa); 1-4169-2769-7 (pa)
 A Newbery Medal honor book, 1987
 A reissue of the title first published 1986 by Bradbury
Press
 The visit of the traveling Preacher Man to his small
North Carolina town gives new impetus to thirteen-year-
old Peter's struggle to reconcile his own deeply felt religious belief with the beliefs and non-beliefs of his family
and friends
 "Blending humor and intense emotion with a poetic
use of language, Cynthia Rylant has created a taut, finely
drawn portrait of a boy's growth from seeking for belief,
through seduction and betrayal, to a spiritual acceptance
and a readiness 'for something whole.'" Horn Book

 Missing May. Orchard Bks. 1992 89p hardcover
o.p. pa $5.99 *
Grades: 5 6 7 8   **Fic**
 1. Death—Fiction 2. West Virginia—Fiction
ISBN 0-531-05996-0; 0-439-61383-3 (pa)
                                        LC 91-23303
 Awarded the Newbery Medal, 1993

 "A Richard Jackson book"
 After the death of the beloved aunt who has raised
her, twelve-year-old Summer and her uncle Ob leave
their West Virginia trailer in search of the strength to go
on living
 "There is much to ponder here, from the meaning of
life and death to the power of love. That it all succeeds
is a tribute to a fine writer who brings to the task a natural grace of language, an earthly sense of humor, and a
well-grounded sense of the spiritual." SLJ

Sachar, Louis, 1954-
 Holes; [by] Louis Sachar. 10th anniversary ed.
Farrar, Straus and Giroux 2008 c1998 265p $18 *
Grades: 5 6 7 8   **Fic**
 1. Juvenile delinquency—Fiction 2. Homeless per-
sons—Fiction 3. Friendship—Fiction 4. Buried trea-
sure—Fiction
ISBN 978-0-374-33266-2; 0-374-33266-5
                                        LC 2007045430
 Awarded the Newbery Medal, 1999
 "Frances Foster books"
 A reissue of the title first published 1998. Includes additional information about the author and his Newbery
acceptance speech
 As further evidence of his family's bad fortune which
they attribute to a curse on a distant relative, Stanley
Yelnats is sent to a hellish correctional camp in the Texas desert where he finds his first real friend, a treasure,
and a new sense of himself
 "This delightfully clever story is well-crafted and
thought-provoking, with a bit of a folklore thrown in for
good measure." Voice Youth Advocates

 Marvin Redpost, kidnapped at birth? illustrated
by Neal Hughes. Random House 1992 68p il
$11.99; pa $3.99 *
Grades: 2 3 4   **Fic**
ISBN 0-679-91946-5; 0-679-81946-0 (pa)
                                        LC 91-51105
 "A First Stepping Stone book"
 Red-haired Marvin is convinced that the reason he
looks different from the rest of his family is that he is
really the lost prince of Shampoon
 "Written almost completely in dialogue, the story is
fast paced, easy to read, and full of humor." SLJ
 Other titles about Marvin Redpost are:
Marvin Redpost, a flying birthday cake (1999)
Marvin Redpost, a magic crystal (2000)
Marvin Redpost, alone in his teacher's house (1994)
Marvin Redpost, class president (1999)
Marvin Redpost, is he a girl? (1993)
Marvin Redpost, superfast, out of control (2000)
Marvin Redpost, why pick on me? (1993)

 Wayside School gets a little stranger; illustrated
by Joel Schick. Morrow Junior Bks. 1995 168p il
$15.99; pa $4.95
Grades: 3 4 5 6   **Fic**
 1. School stories
ISBN 0-688-13694-X; 0-380-72381-6 (pa)
                                        LC 94-25448
 This is "about the zany goings-on in [an] unorthodox
30-story-tall school. . . . The narrative revolves around

Sachar, Louis, 1954-—*Continued*

the wacky substitute teachers who take Mrs. Jewls's place when she is on maternity leave." Publ Wkly

"Sachar's offering contains hilarity, malevolence, romance, relentless punning, goofiness, inspiration, revenge, and poignancy." SLJ

Other titles about Wayside School are:
Sideways stories from Wayside School (1978)
Wayside School is falling down (1989)

Sage, Angie

Magyk; Septimus Heap, book one; illustrations by Mark Zug. Katherine Tegen Books 2005 576p il $16.99; lib bdg $17.89; pa $7.99 *

Grades: 5 6 7 8   **Fic**
1. Fantasy fiction 2. Magic—Fiction
ISBN 0-06-057731-2; 0-06-057732-0 (lib bdg);
0-06-057733-9 (pa)   LC 2003-28185

After learning that she is the Princess, Jenna is whisked from her home and carried toward safety by the Extraordinary Wizard, those she always believed were her father and brother, and a young guard known only as Boy 412, pursued by agents of those who killed her mother ten years earlier.

"Youngsters will lose themselves happily in Sage's fluent, charismatic storytelling, which enfolds supportive allies and horrific enemies, abundant quirky details, and poignant moments of self-discovery." Booklist

Other titles in this series are:
Flyte (2006)
Physik (2007)
Queste (2008)
Syren (2009)

My haunted house; as told to Angie Sage; illustrated by Jimmy Pickering. Katherine Tegen Books 2006 132p il (Araminta Spookie) $8.99; lib bdg $14.89; pa $4.99

Grades: 3 4 5   **Fic**
1. Ghost stories
ISBN 978-0-06-077481-3; 0-06-077481-9;
978-0-06-077482-0 (lib bdg); 0-06-077482-7 (lib bdg);
978-0-06-077483-7 (pa); 0-06-077483-5 (pa)
                                       LC 2005-23815

Araminta enlists the help of several ghosts in an attempt to stop her Aunt Tabby from selling Spook House.

This is a "humorous, fast-paced . . . caper. . . . Pickering's quirky art adds to the kooky—and in spots somewhat spooky—fun." Publ Wkly

Other titles in this series are:
The sword in the grotto (2006)
Frognapped (2007)
Vampire brat (2007)
Ghostsitters (2008)

Saint-Exupéry, Antoine de, 1900-1944

The little prince; written and illustrated by Antoine de Saint-Exupéry; translated from the French by Richard Howard. Harcourt 2000 83p il $18; pa $12 *

Grades: 4 5 6 7 8 9 10 11 12 Adult   **Fic**
1. Fantasy fiction 2. Air pilots—Fiction 3. Princes—Fiction 4. Extraterrestrial beings—Fiction
ISBN 0-15-202398-4; 0-15-601219-7 (pa)
                                       LC 99-50439

A new translation of the title first published 1943 by Reynal & Hitchcock

"This many-dimensional fable of an airplane pilot who has crashed in the desert is for readers of all ages. The pilot comes upon the little prince soon after the crash. The prince tells of his adventures on different planets and on Earth as he attempts to learn about the universe in order to live peacefully on his own small planet. A spiritual quality enhances the seemingly simple observations of the little prince." Shapiro. Fic for Youth. 3d edition

The little prince: deluxe pop-up book; unabridged text; translated from the French by Richard Howard. Houghton Mifflin Harcourt 2009 60p il $35

Grades: 4 5 6   **Fic**
1. Fantasy fiction 2. Air pilots—Fiction 3. Princes—Fiction 4. Extraterrestrial beings—Fiction 5. Pop-up books
ISBN 978-0-547-26069-3; 0-547-26069-5

An aviator whose plane is forced down in the Sahara Desert encounters a little prince from a small planet who relates his adventures in seeking the secret of what is important in life

This "volume is a beautiful piece of bookmaking that actually extends the classic story. In 3-D form, the original artwork feels new, and inventive design elements . . . add whimsy while focusing even more attention on the images." Booklist

Salisbury, Graham, 1944-

Calvin Coconut: trouble magnet; illustrated by Jacqueline Rogers. Wendy Lamb Books 2009 152p il $12.99; lib bdg $15.99; pa $6.99

Grades: 3 4 5   **Fic**
1. Family life—Fiction 2. School stories 3. Bullies—Fiction 4. Hawaii—Fiction
ISBN 978-0-385-73701-2; 0-385-73701-7;
978-0-385-90639-5 (lib bdg); 0-385-90639-0 (lib bdg);
978-0-375-84600-7 (pa); 0-375-84600-X (pa)
                                       LC 2008-1415

Nine-year-old Calvin catches the attention of the school bully on the day before he starts fourth grade, while at home, the unfriendly, fifteen-year-old daughter of his mother's best friend has taken over his room

"The familial relationships among Calvin and his sister, their mom and her boyfriend are touching, realistically tempered with moments of frustration. Rogers's lively ink-and-wash drawings augment the story and evoke a playful feel." Kirkus

Other titles about Calvin are:
Calvin Coconut: The zippy fix (2009)
Calvin Coconut: dog heaven (2010)

Salisbury, Graham, 1944-—*Continued*

Lord of the deep. Delacorte Press 2001 182p hardcover o.p. pa $7.99

Grades: 5 6 7 8   **Fic**

1. Fishing—Fiction 2. Stepfathers—Fiction 3. Hawaii—Fiction

ISBN 0-385-72918-9; 0-440-22911-1 (pa)

LC 00-60280

Working for Bill, his stepfather, on a charter fishing boat in Hawaii teaches thirteen-year-old Mikey about fishing, and about taking risks, making sacrifices, and facing some of life's difficult choices

"With its vivid Hawaiian setting, this fine novel is a natural for book-discussion groups that enjoy pondering moral ambiguity. Its action-packed scenes will also lure in reluctant readers." SLJ

Night of the howling dogs; a novel. Wendy Lamb Books 2007 191p $16.99; lib bdg $19.99; pa $6.50 *

Grades: 5 6 7 8   **Fic**

1. Boy Scouts of America—Fiction 2. Earthquakes—Fiction 3. Tsunamis—Fiction 4. Survival after airplane accidents, shipwrecks, etc.—Fiction 5. Camping—Fiction 6. Hawaii—Fiction

ISBN 978-0-385-73122-5; 978-0-385-90146-8 (lib bdg); 978-0-440-23839-3 (pa)   LC 2007-07054

In 1975, eleven Boy Scouts, their leaders, and some new friends camping at Halape, Hawaii, find their survival skills put to the test when a massive earthquake strikes, followed by a tsunami.

This is a "vivid adventure. . . . Salisbury weaves Hawaiian legend into the modern-day narrative to create a haunting, unusual novel." Booklist

Salten, Felix, 1869-1945

Bambi; a life in the woods; [by] Felix Salten; illustrated by Barbara Cooney. Pocket Books 1988 190p il pa $5.99

Grades: 4 5 6   **Fic**

1. Deer—Fiction

ISBN 978-0-671-66607-1 (pa); 0-671-66607-X (pa)

Original German edition 1923; first United States edition published 1928 by Simon & Schuster

Describes the life of a deer in the forest as he grows into a beautiful stag

Sanchez, Anita, 1956-

The invasion of Sandy Bay; [by] Anita Sanchez. Calkins Creek 2008 147p $16.95

Grades: 5 6 7 8   **Fic**

1. War of 1812—Fiction 2. Massachusetts—Fiction 3. Adventure fiction

ISBN 978-1-59078-560-7; 1-59078-560-6

LC 2007051224

In 1814, as the War of 1812 rages, twelve-year-old Lemuel Brooks tries to save the sleepy fishing village of Sandy Bay, Massachussetts, where he, himself, is an outsider, from bumbling British invaders. Includes historical notes

"Clearly Sanchez has researched the period well, but the history never overwhelms the narrative. . . . History buffs will enjoy reading a war story that is so well grounded in actual events." Booklist

Includes bibliographical references

Sanderson, Brandon, 1975-

Alcatraz versus the evil Librarians. Scholastic Press 2007 308p $16.99; pa $6.99 *

Grades: 4 5 6 7   **Fic**

1. Librarians—Fiction 2. Grandfathers—Fiction 3. Fantasy fiction

ISBN 0-439-92550-9; 978-0-439-92550-1; 0-439-92552-5 (pa); 978-0-439-92552-5 (pa)

LC 2006-38378

On his thirteenth birthday, foster child Alcatraz Smedry receives a bag of sand which is immediately stolen by the evil Librarians who are trying to take over the world. Soon, Alcatraz is introduced to his grandfather and his own special talent, and told that he must use it to save civilization.

"Readers whose sense of humor runs toward the subversive will be instantly captivated. . . . This nutty novel isn't for everyone, but it's also sure to win passionate fans." Publ Wkly

Other titles about Alcatraz are:

Alcatraz versus the scrivener's bones (2008)

Alcatraz versus the Knights of Crystallia (2009)

Santopolo, Jill

The Niña, the Pinta, and the vanishing treasure; illustrations by C.B. Canga. Orchard Books 2008 183p il (Alec Flint, super sleuth) $15.99; pa $5.99

Grades: 3 4 5   **Fic**

1. Museums—Fiction 2. Theft—Fiction 3. Missing persons—Fiction 4. Mystery fiction

ISBN 978-0-439-90352-3; 0-439-90352-1; 978-0-439-90353-0 (pa); 0-439-90353-X (pa)

LC 2007-30218

When the entire Christopher Columbus exhibit disappears from the local museum, fourth-grade sleuth-in-training Alec Flint investigates, aided by his new classmate and potential partner, Gina, who wants his help looking into the disappearance of a teacher.

"Smartly combining a crime drama with some American history, this book succeeds in being both entertaining and informative." Horn Book Guide

Another title in this series is:

The ransom note blues (2009)

Sawyer, Ruth, 1880-1970

Roller skates; written by Ruth Sawyer and illustrated by Valenti Angelo. Viking 1995 c1936 186p il hardcover o.p. pa $5.99 *

Grades: 4 5 6   **Fic**

1. New York (N.Y.)—Fiction

ISBN 0-670-60310-4; 0-14-030358-8 (pa)

LC 85-43418

Awarded the Newbery Medal, 1937

A reissue of the title first published 1936

"For one never-to-be forgotten year Lucinda Wyman (ten years old) was free to explore New York on roller skates. She made friends with Patrick Gilligan and his hansom cab, with Policeman M'Gonegal, with the fruit vendor, Vittore Coppicco and his son Tony, and with many others. All Lucinda's adventures are true and happened to the author herself as is borne out by the occasional pages of Lucinda's diary which are a part of the story." Horn Book

Schirripa, Steven R.

Nicky Deuce; welcome to the family; [by] Steven R. Schirripa & Charles Fleming. Delacorte Press 2005 167p $15.95; pa $5.99 *

Grades: 4 5 6   Fic

1. Italian Americans—Fiction 2. Grandmothers—Fiction 3. Uncles—Fiction 4. Brooklyn (New York, N.Y.)—Fiction

ISBN 0-385-73257-0; 0-440-42053-9 (pa)

LC 2004-28810

While his parents are on a cruise, twelve-year-old Nicholas spends his summer in Brooklyn with his grandmother and uncle and learns, with unintended results, about his Italian-American heritage.

The authors "have created a warm, funny story with memorable characters and enough shady intrigue to keep readers turning the pages." Booklist

Another title about Nicky Deuce is:

Nicky Deuce: home for the holidays (2007)

Schlitz, Laura Amy

A drowned maiden's hair; a melodrama. Candlewick Press 2006 389p $15.99 *

Grades: 5 6 7 8   Fic

1. Orphans—Fiction 2. Spiritualism—Fiction

ISBN 978-0-7636-2930-4; 0-7636-2930-8

LC 2006-49056

At the Barbary Asylum for Female Orphans, eleven-year-old Maud is adopted by three spinster sisters moonlighting as mediums who take her home and reveal to her the role she will play in their seances.

"Filled with heavy atmosphere and suspense, this story recreates life in early-20th-century New England. . . . Maud is a charismatic, three-dimensional character." SLJ

The night fairy; illustrated by Angela Barrett. Candlewick Press 2010 117p il lib bdg $16.99 *

Grades: 4 5 6   Fic

1. Fairies—Fiction 2. Magic—Fiction 3. Friendship—Fiction 4. Adventure fiction

ISBN 978-0-7636-3674-6 (lib bdg); 0-7636-3674-6 (lib bdg)   LC 2008-27659

When Flory the night fairy's wings are accidentally broken and she cannot fly, she has to learn to do everything differently.

"Schlitz writes with strength of vision and delicate precision of word choice. . . . Beautifully composed, the artwork combines subtle use of color with a keen observation of nature. . . . This finely crafted and unusually dynamic fairy story is a natural for reading aloud." Booklist

Schmidt, Gary D.

The Wednesday wars. Clarion Books 2007 264p $16; pa $6.99 *

Grades: 5 6 7 8   Fic

1. Shakespeare, William, 1564-1616—Fiction 2. School stories

ISBN 978-0-618-72483-3; 0-618-72483-4; 978-0-547-23760-2 (pa); 0-547-23760-X (pa)

LC 2006-23660

A Newbery Medal honor book, 2008

During the 1967 school year, on Wednesday afternoons when all his classmates go to either Catechism or Hebrew school, seventh-grader Holling Hoodhood stays in Mrs. Baker's classroom where they read the plays of William Shakespeare and Holling learns much of value about the world he lives in.

"The serious issues are leavened with ample humor, and the supporting cast . . . is fully dimensional. Best of all is the hero." Publ Wkly

Schneider, Robyn, 1986-

Knightley Academy; by Violet Haberdasher. Aladdin 2010 469p $15.99

Grades: 5 6 7 8   Fic

1. Orphans—Fiction 2. Knights and knighthood—Fiction 3. School stories

ISBN 978-1-4169-9143-4; 1-4169-9143-3

In an alternate Victorian England, fourteen-year-old orphan Henry Grim, a maltreated servant at an exclusive school for the "sons of Gentry and Quality," begins a new life when he unexpectedly becomes the first commoner to be accepted at Knightley Academy, a prestigious boarding school for knights.

"Robyn Schneider . . . writing as the pseudonymous Haberdasher, delivers a cute novel that balances its simple plot with a solid lead character, witty dialogue, and a jaunty narrative voice. . . . The nebulous historical setting and focus on military training and chivalry are a welcome change of pace from fictional academies that revolve around magic." Publ Wkly

Schulman, Janet, 1933-

The nutcracker; [by] E.T.A. Hoffmann; adapted by Janet Schulman; illustrated by Renée Graef; audio CD narrated by Claire Bloom with music by Peter Ilyich Tchaikovsky. HarperCollins Pubs. 1999 34p il $19.95 *

Grades: 4 5 6 7   Fic

1. Fairy tales 2. Christmas—Fiction

ISBN 0-06-027814-5   LC 97-22346

This adaptation of the Nutcracker with illustrations by Kay Chorao was published 1979 by Dutton

One Christmas after hearing how the toy nutcracker made by her godfather got his ugly face, a little girl helps break the spell and watches him change into a handsome prince

"Graef's illustrations are floridly old-fashioned, with careful attention to period detail." Booklist

Schur, Maxine, 1948-

Gullible Gus; by Maxine Rose Schur; illustrated by Andrew Glass. Clarion Books 2009 45p il $16

Grades: 2 3 4 5   Fic

1. Tall tales 2. Cowhands—Fiction 3. Texas—Fiction

ISBN 978-0-618-92710-4; 0-618-92710-7

LC 2008-10477

Tired of the teasing he gets for being the most gullible man in Texas, Cowboy Gus goes to Fibrock to find the biggest liar there in hopes of hearing a tall tale that is impossible for anyone—even him—to believe.

"The stories are filled with exaggeration and alliteration. A Western twang is used to create mood. Readers

Schur, Maxine, 1948-—*Continued*
will laugh out loud and share passages with friends. . . . Glass's bright oil crayon cartoons fit the exaggerated storytelling style to a tee." SLJ

Schwabach, Karen
The Hope Chest. Random House 2008 274p $16.99
Grades: 4 5 6 7   **Fic**
1. Women—Suffrage—Fiction 2. Sisters—Fiction 3. Tennessee—Fiction
ISBN 978-0-375-84095-1; 0-375-84095-8
LC 2006-36692
When eleven-year-old Violet runs away from home in 1920 and takes the train to New York City to find her older sister who is a suffragist, she falls in with people her parents would call "the wrong sort," and ends up in Nashville, Tennessee, where "Suffs" and "Antis" are gathered, awaiting the crucial vote on the nineteenth amendment.
This confronts "heavy issues such as racism and sexism, but the narrative is leavened with humor. The story is packed with period details . . . but Schwabach's attention to character and plotting ensures that it never bogs down." SLJ

A pickpocket's tale. Random House 2006 225p $15.95; lib bdg $17.99; pa $6.50
Grades: 5 6 7 8   **Fic**
1. Orphans—Fiction 2. Contract labor—Fiction 3. Jews—Fiction 4. New York (N.Y.)—Fiction
ISBN   978-0-375-83379-3;   0-375-83379-X; 978-0-375-93379-0 (lib bdg); 0-375-93379-4 (lib bdg); 978-0-375-83380-9 (pa); 0-375-83380-3 (pa)
When Molly, a ten-year-old orphan, is arrested for picking pockets in London in 1731, she is banished to America and serves as an indentured servant for a New York City family that expects her to follow their Jewish traditions.
"Written in vividly detailed prose, this debut novel introduces an engaging protagonist. . . . Enjoyable and sometimes thought-provoking historical fiction." Booklist

Schwartz, Ellen, 1949-
Stealing home. Tundra Books 2006 217p pa $8.95 *
Grades: 5 6 7 8   **Fic**
1. Orphans—Fiction 2. Racially mixed people—Fiction 3. Family life—Fiction 4. Jews—Fiction
ISBN 978-0-88776-765-4 (pa); 0-88776-765-6 (pa)
"Joey, an orphaned, mixed-race 10-year-old isn't the only one who has to make adjustments after he's taken in by Jewish relatives he never knew he had. Wondering why his mother never told him about her side of the family, Joey moves to Brooklyn—to find a warm welcome from Aunt Frieda, an instant ally in baseball-loving cousin Bobbie, and a decidedly cold shoulder from his grandfather. . . . Keenly felt internal conflicts, lightened by some sparky banter, put this more than a cut above the average." Booklist

Scieszka, Jon, 1954-
Knights of the kitchen table; illustrated by Lane Smith. Viking 1991 55p il (Time Warp Trio) $14.99; pa $4.99 *
Grades: 3 4 5   **Fic**
1. Fantasy fiction
ISBN 0-670-83622-2; 0-14-240043-2 (pa)
LC 90-51009
"Transported to the Middle Ages, three friends save themselves from a dragon and a giant through quick thinking. The tongue-in-cheek narrative makes for laugh-out-loud enjoyment, and the easy-to-read sentences and zany dialogue perfectly suit the breathless pace." SLJ
Other titles about The Time Warp Trio are:
2095 (1995)
Da wild, da crazy, da Vinci (2004)
The good, the bad, and the goofy (1992)
Hey kid, want to buy a bridge? (2002)
It's all Greek to me (1999)
Marco? Polo! (2006)
The not-so-jolly Roger (1991)
Oh say I can't see (2005)
Sam Samurai (2001)
See you later, gladiator (2000)
Summer reading is killing me! (1998)
Tut, tut (1996)
Viking it & liking it (2002)
Your mother was a Neanderthal (1993)

Seen Art? [by] Jon Scieszka and Lane Smith. Viking 2005 unp il $16.99
Grades: 4 5 6 7   **Fic**
1. Museum of Modern Art (New York, N.Y.)—Fiction 2. Art appreciation—Fiction
ISBN 0-670-05986-2
While looking for his friend Art, a boy wanders through the Museum of Modern Art and is amazed by what he discovers there.
"The unusually long and narrow shape of the book and the stylized characters echo the modern-art theme while the muted background tones are an effective foil for the well-reproduced if sometimes diminutive artwork. . . . For anyone planning a trip to MoMA with a youngster, this is a provocative read." SLJ

Spaceheadz; [by] Jon Scieszka with Francesco Sedita; illustrated by Shane Prigmore. Simon & Schuster Books for Young Readers 2010 il (SPHDZ) $14.99
Grades: 3 4 5   **Fic**
1. Extraterrestrial beings—Fiction 2. School stories 3. Spies—Fiction 4. Moving—Fiction 5. Family life—Fiction 6. Brooklyn (New York, N.Y.)—Fiction
ISBN 978-1-416-97951-7; 1-416-97951-4
LC 2010001983
On his first day at Brooklyn's P.S. 858, fifth-grader Michael K. is teamed with two very strange students, and while he gradually comes to believe they are aliens who need his help, he has trouble convincing anyone else of the truth.
This is "fun enough to become the next big word-of-mouth, multiplatform attention suck." Booklist

Scott, Elaine, 1940-
Secrets of the Cirque Medrano. Charlesbridge 2008 216p lib bdg $15.95

Grades: 4 5 6 7 **Fic**
1. Picasso, Pablo, 1881-1973—Fiction 2. Paris (France)—Fiction 3. Restaurants—Fiction 4. Circus—Fiction 5. Orphans—Fiction
ISBN 978-1-57091-712-7 (lib bdg); 1-57091-712-4 (lib bdg) LC 2007-2329

In the Paris village of Montmartre in 1904, fourteen-year-old Brigitte works long hours in her aunt's cafe, where she serves such regular customers as the young artist Pablo Picasso, encounters Russian revolutionaries, and longs to attend the exciting circus nearby. Includes author's note on the Picasso painting "Family of Saltimbanques"

This "places an interesting historical moment within the grasp of middle-schoolers." Kirkus

Seabrooke, Brenda, 1941-
Wolf pie; illustrated by Liz Callen. Clarion Books 2010 46p il $16

Grades: 1 2 3 **Fic**
1. Wolves—Fiction 2. Pigs—Fiction 3. Friendship—Fiction
ISBN 978-0-547-04403-3; 0-547-04403-8 LC 2009-15820

When Wilfong the wolf fails to blow down the house of the Pygg brothers, he stays outside their door all winter learning their games and listening to their jokes and stories, but although he claims to be reformed, the pigs are reluctant to offer friendship.

"Callen's humorous, vibrant multimedia art deftly matches the tone of Seabrooke's amusing tale, resulting in a winning collaboration for independent readers ready to move on to meatier texts." Kirkus

Sebestyen, Ouida, 1924-
Words by heart. Little, Brown 1979 162p pa $5.50 *

Grades: 5 6 7 8 **Fic**
1. African Americans—Fiction 2. Race relations—Fiction 3. Family life—Fiction
ISBN 0-440-22688-0 LC 78-27847

"An Atlantic Monthly Press book"

"It is 1910, and Lena's family is the only black family in her small Southwestern town. When Lena wins a scripture reciting contest that a white boy is supposed to win, her family is threatened. Lena's father tries to make her understand that by hating the people who did this, the problems that cause their behavior are not solved. Only more hatred and violence cause Lena and the village to understand the words of her father." ALAN

Followed by On fire (1985)

Seidler, Tor, 1952-
Brainboy and the Deathmaster. Laura Geringer Bks. 2003 311p $16.99; lib bdg $17.89

Grades: 5 6 7 8 **Fic**
1. Orphans—Fiction 2. Video games—Fiction 3. Science fiction
ISBN 0-06-029181-8; 0-06-029182-6 (lib bdg) LC 2002-33918

When Darryl, a twelve-year-old orphan, is adopted by a technology genius, he finds himself the star of his very own life-threatening video game

"A fast-paced, science-fiction adventure. . . . Seidler has created empathetic characters and writes at a level that is accessible even to readers not usually drawn to this genre." SLJ

The dulcimer boy; illustrations by Brian Selznick. Laura Geringer Bks. 2003 153p il hardcover o.p. pa $6.99

Grades: 4 5 6 7 **Fic**
1. Twins—Fiction 2. Brothers—Fiction 3. New England—Fiction
ISBN 0-06-623609-6; 0-06-441048-X (pa) LC 2001-23875

A newly illustrated edition of the title first published 1979 by Viking Press

"Tracing the footsteps of musically gifted William Carbuncle from his arrival on his uncaring uncle's doorstep in a box containing him, his brother, and a silver-stringed dulcimer, the story follows William's escape and journey south. . . . Seidler's simple yet eloquent prose likens William's plight to a caged songbird. . . . Selznick's detailed sense of light and shadow shines as his soft-textured acrylic paintings not only echo the novel's overall poetic melancholy, but also serve as integral pieces of the plot itself." SLJ

Gully's travels; pictures by Brock Cole. Michael di Capua Books 2008 173p il $16.95 *

Grades: 4 5 6 **Fic**
1. Dogs—Fiction 2. New York (N.Y.)—Fiction 3. Voyages and travels—Fiction
ISBN 978-0-545-02506-5; 0-545-02506-0

Gulliver leads a life of luxury with his master. But when his master falls in love with a woman who is allergic to dogs, Gulliver is sent to a new home. He finds himself with a family of raucous human beings and three mutts. But just as Gulliver begins to make a grudging peace with his new reality, he gets swept up in a harrowing new adventure.

"Gulliver is a character readers won't forget. . . . Seidler vividly evokes each setting. . . . Cole's expressive, scribbled sketches of interesting characters appear on almost every page." Booklist

The Wainscott weasel; illustrated by Fred Marcellino. HarperCollins Pubs. 1993 193p il pa $11.95

Grades: 4 5 6 **Fic**
1. Weasels—Fiction 2. Animals—Fiction
ISBN 0-06-205911-4 (pa) LC 92-54526

"The weasels' summer begins with the visiting Wendy being charmed by both Zeke and Bagley Jr. . . . But Bagley pines for Bridget, a beautiful fish who lives in the nearby brook. . . . When Bridget's life is in danger, Bagley learns he can be a hero." Child Book Rev Serv

"Seidler's pacing is superb; he builds a solid structure within each chapter. A dry wit inspires his characterizations. . . . Marcellino enhances and even extends the beguiling ambiance with his exceptionally expressive art." Publ Wkly

Selden, George, 1929-1989

The cricket in Times Square; illustrated by Garth Williams. Farrar, Straus & Giroux 1960 151p il $16; pa $6.99 *

Grades: 3 4 5 6   **Fic**

1. Cats—Fiction 2. Crickets—Fiction 3. Mice—Fiction 4. New York (N.Y.)—Fiction

ISBN 0-374-31650-3; 0-312-38003-8 (pa)

Also available in paperback from Dell

A Newbery Medal honor book, 1961

"An Ariel book"

"A touch of magic comes to Times Square subway station with Chester, a cricket from rural Connecticut. He is introduced to the distinctive character of city life by three friends: Mario Bellini, whose parents operate a newsstand; Tucker, a glib Broadway mouse; and Harry, a sagacious cat. Chester saves the Bellinis' business by giving concerts from the newsstand, bringing to rushing commuters moments of beauty and repose. This modern fantasy shows that, in New York, anything can happen." Moorachian. What is a City?

Other titles about Chester and his friends are:

Chester Cricket's new home (1983)

Chester Cricket's pigeon ride (1981)

Harry Cat's pet puppy (1974)

Harry Kitten and Tucker Mouse (1986)

The old meadow (1987)

Tucker's countryside (1969)

Selfors, Suzanne, 1963-

Fortune's magic farm; illustrated by Catia Chien. Little, Brown 2009 264p il $14.99; pa $5.99

Grades: 4 5 6   **Fic**

1. Orphans—Fiction 2. Magic—Fiction 3. Farms—Fiction

ISBN 978-0-316-01818-0; 0-316-01818-X; 978-0-316-01819-7 (pa); 0-316-01819-8 (pa)

LC 2008-12493

Rescued from a rainy, boggy town where she works in a dismal factory, ten-year-old orphan Isabelle learns that she is the last surviving member of a family that tends the world's only remaining magic-producing farm.

"Readers will cozy up to the tale's quirky characters and enjoy the many twists and turns of this magical adventure." Kirkus

To catch a mermaid; illustrated by Catia Chien. Little, Brown 2007 245p il hardcover o.p. pa $5.99

Grades: 4 5 6   **Fic**

1. Mermaids and mermen—Fiction 2. Siblings—Fiction

ISBN 978-0-316-01816-6; 0-316-01816-3; 978-0-316-01817-3 (pa); 0-316-01817-1 (pa)

LC 2007-22700

When twelve-year-old Boomerang Broom discovers a wish-granting baby mermaid, he takes her home and his little sister begs to keep her, with unexpected consequences.

"This amusing story has lots of kid appeal. Selfors has conjured up great characters and settings, and her narrative voice never falters." SLJ

Selzer, Adam, 1980-

I put a spell on you; from the files of Chrissie Woodward, spelling bee detective. Delacorte Press 2008 247p $15.99; lib bdg $18.99

Grades: 4 5 6 7   **Fic**

1. Spelling bees—Fiction 2. School stories 3. Mystery fiction

ISBN 978-0-385-73504-9; 0-385-73504-9; 978-0-385-90498-8 (lib bdg); 0-385-90498-3 (lib bdg)

LC 2008035673

When Gordon Liddy Community School's resident tattletale-detective, Chrissie Woodward, realizes that the adults are out to fix the big spelling bee, she transfers her loyalty to her fellow students and starts collecting evidence. Told through in-class letters, administrative memos, file notes from Chrissie's investigation, and testimony from spelling bee contestants

"The wit in this school story is directed almost entirely against the grownups in a scathingly funny indictment of a shady principal and insanely competitive parents." Horn Book

Selznick, Brian

The Houdini box. Atheneum Books for Young Readers 2008 unp il $17.99; pa $6.99

Grades: 3 4 5   **Fic**

1. Houdini, Harry, 1874-1926—Fiction 2. Magicians—Fiction

ISBN 978-1-4169-6878-8; 1-4169-6878-4; 978-0-689-84451-5 (pa); 0-689-84451-4 (pa)

LC 2008024693

A reissue of the title first published 1991 by Knopf

A chance encounter with Harry Houdini leaves a small boy in possession of a mysterious box—one that might hold the secrets to the greatest magic tricks ever performed.

"In this new edition, Selznick follows his intriguing tale with bonus material: a biographical note on Houdini, an illustrated magic trick, research notes on the writing of the book, and early sketches for the artwork. . . . It is sure to intrigue youngsters, particularly those interested in magic." SLJ

The invention of Hugo Cabret; a novel in words and pictures. Scholastic Press 2007 533p il $22.95 *

Grades: 4 5 6 7   **Fic**

1. Méliès, Georges, 1861-1938—Fiction 2. Robots—Fiction 3. Orphans—Fiction 4. Motion pictures—Fiction 5. Paris (France)—Fiction

ISBN 0-439-81378-6   LC 2006-07119

Awarded the Caldecott Medal, 2008

When twelve-year-old Hugo, an orphan living and repairing clocks within the walls of a Paris train station in 1931, meets a mysterious toyseller and his goddaughter, his undercover life and his biggest secret are jeopardized.

"With characteristic intelligence, exquisite images, and a breathtaking design, Selznick shatters conventions related to the art of bookmaking." SLJ

Sendak, Maurice

Higglety pigglety pop! or, There must be more to life; story and pictures by Maurice Sendak. HarperCollins Pubs. c1967 69p il $14.95; pa $8.95 *

Grades: 2 3 4   **Fic**
  1. Dogs—Fiction
  ISBN 0-06-028479-X; 0-06-443021-9 (pa)

In this modern fairy tale "Jennie, the Sealyham terrier, leaves home because 'there must be more to life than having everything.' When she applies for a job as the leading lady of the World Mother Goose Theater, she discovers that what she lacks is experience. What follows are her adventures and her gaining of experience; finally Jennie becomes the leading lady of the play." Wis Libr Bull

"The story has elements of tenderness and humor; it also has . . . typically macabre Sendak touches. . . . The illustrations are beautiful, amusing, and distinctive." Sutherland. The Best in Child Books

Sensel, Joni, 1962-

The Farwalker's quest. Bloomsbury U.S.A Children's Books 2009 372p $16.99

Grades: 5 6 7 8   **Fic**
  1. Fantasy fiction
  ISBN 978-1-59990-272-2; 1-59990-272-9
                                      LC 2008-30523

When twelve-year-old Ariel and her friend Zeke find a mysterious artifact the like of which has not been seen in a long time, it proves to be the beginning of a long and arduous journey that will untimately reveal to them their true identities.

"This is a solid and well-paced fantasy in which the journey is more important than the conclusion." SLJ

Followed by: The timekeeper's moon (2010)

The timekeeper's moon. Bloomsbury 2010 339p il $16.99

Grades: 5 6 7 8   **Fic**
  1. Fantasy fiction
  ISBN 978-1-59990-457-3; 1-59990-457-8
                                      LC 2009-16690

Sequel to: The Farwalker's quest (2009)

Summoned by the moon to embark on a dangerous journey, thirteen-year-old Ariel Farwalker, knowing she must obey or risk destruction, sets out with her guardian, Scarl, to follow a mysterious map to an unknown entity called "Timekeeper."

"Vivid world building and tight pacing mark this sequel . . . further distinguished by rich characters with believable relationships." Booklist

Seredy, Kate, 1899-1975

The Good Master; written and illustrated by Kate Seredy. Viking 1935 210p il pa $4.99 hardcover o.p.

Grades: 4 5 6   **Fic**
  1. Farm life—Fiction 2. Hungary—Fiction
  ISBN 0-14-030133-X

A Newbery Medal honor book, 1936

Into this story of Jancsi, a ten-year-old Hungarian farm boy and his little hoyden of a cousin Kate from Bu-

dapest, is woven a description of Hungarian farm life, fairs, festivals, and folk tales. Under the tutelage of Jancsi's kind father, called by the neighbors The Good Master, Kate calms down and becomes a more docile young person

"The steady warm understanding of the wise father, the Good Master, is a shining quality throughout." Horn Book

Followed by The singing tree (1939)

The white stag; written and illustrated by Kate Seredy. Viking 1937 94p il pa $4.99 hardcover o.p.

Grades: 4 5 6   **Fic**
  1. Hungary—Fiction
  ISBN 0-14-031258-7 (pa)

Awarded the Newbery Medal, 1938

"Striking illustrations interpret this hero tale of the legendary founding of Hungary, when a white stag and a red eagle led the people to their promised land." Hodges. Books for Elem Sch Libr

Sewell, Anna, 1820-1878

Black Beauty; the autobiography of a horse; by Anna Sewell; text illustrated by Fritz Eichenberg. Grosset & Dunlap 1995 301p il $17.99 *

Grades: 4 5 6   **Fic**
  1. Horses—Fiction 2. Great Britain—Fiction
  ISBN 0-448-40942-9   LC 94040990

"Illustrated junior library"

First published 1877 in the United Kingdom; first United States edition, 1891

A horse in nineteenth-century England recounts his experiences with both good and bad masters.

Shafer, Audrey

The mailbox. Delacorte Press 2006 178p $15.95; lib bdg $17.99; pa $6.50

Grades: 5 6 7 8   **Fic**
  1. Foster home care—Fiction 2. Uncles—Fiction
  ISBN   978-0-385-73344-1;   0-385-73344-5;
  978-0-385-90361-5 (lib bdg); 0-385-90361-8 (lib bdg);
  978-0-440-42134-4 (pa); 0-440-42134-9 (pa)
                                      LC 2006-04572

When twelve-year-old Gabe tries to hide his uncle's death from the local authorities, he is not prepared for what happens when this secret is discovered.

"Complex and believably imperfect characters emerge from the first page to the last in this debut novel. . . . Warm and moving." SLJ

Shearer, Alex

Canned. Scholastic Press 2008 237p $16.99

Grades: 4 5 6 7   **Fic**
  1. Collectors and collecting—Fiction 2. Great Britain—Fiction 3. Mystery fiction
  ISBN 0-439-90309-2   LC 2007-09815

Fergal Banfield, an eccentric lad who collects cans, is surprised to find some unexpected—and even alarming—things in a few of his treasures, and when he meets Charlotte, another collector, they begin an investigation that leads them into dangerous territory.

Shearer, Alex—*Continued*

"Quirky and original, funky and totally gross, this fast-paced novel blends several genres: crime, horror, mystery, and fantasy. Its black humor, balanced by a serious look at forced child labor, will keep readers hooked from the beginning." SLJ

Shefelman, Janice Jordan, 1930-

Anna Maria's gift; by Janice Shefelman; illustrated by Robert Papp. Random House 2010 104p il $12.99; lib bdg $15.99

Grades: 2 3 4   Fic

1. Vivaldi, Antonio, 1678-1741—Fiction 2. Violinists—Fiction 3. Orphans—Fiction 4. School stories 5. Venice (Italy)—Fiction 6. Italy—Fiction

ISBN 978-0-375-85881-9; 0-375-85881-4; 978-0-375-95881-6 (lib bdg); 0-375-95881-9 (lib bdg)

LC 2009004553

"A Stepping Stone book"

In 1715 Italy, eight-year-old Anna Maria Lombardini arrives at a Venice orphanage with little but the special violin her father made for her, but when her teacher, Antonio Vivaldi, favors her over a fellow student, the beloved instrument winds up in a canal. Includes glossary and historical note.

"Strong emotions . . . lie at the heart of the story. . . . [This is a] short, appealing historical novel." Booklist

Sherlock, Patti

Letters from Wolfie. Viking 2004 232p $16.99; pa $6.99

Grades: 5 6 7 8   Fic

1. Dogs—Fiction 2. Vietnam War, 1961-1975—Fiction

ISBN 0-670-03694-3; 0-14-240358-X (pa)

LC 2003-24316

Certain that he is doing the right thing by donating his dog, Wolfie, to the Army's scout program in Vietnam, thirteen-year-old Mark begins to have second thoughts when the Army refuses to say when and if Wolfie will ever return.

"In this topnotch novel, Sherlock weaves together numerous threads of emotion, information, and plot so seamlessly that readers will be surprised by how much they've learned by the time they finish this deceptively simple story." SLJ

Sherman, Delia

Changeling. Viking 2006 292p $16.99; pa $8.99

Grades: 5 6 7 8   Fic

1. Fantasy fiction 2. New York (N.Y.)—Fiction

ISBN 0-670-05967-6; 0-14-241188-4 (pa)

"Neef is a changeling, a human baby stolen by fairies. She lives in 'New York Between,' an invisible parallel city, and she was raised under the protection of her godmother (a white rat) and the Green Lady of Central Park. . . . After breaking Fairy Law, Neef is expelled, and she must complete a heroic quest . . . in order to regain entry to her community. . . . Silly, profound, and lightning paced all at once, this novel will please adventure fans and fantasy readers alike." Bull Cent Child Books

Another title about Neef is:

The Magic Mirror of the Mermaid Queen (2009)

Sherrard, Valerie, 1957-

Tumbleweed skies. Fitzhenry & Whiteside 2010 pa $11.95 *

Grades: 3 4 5 6   Fic

1. Grandmothers—Fiction 2. Saskatchewan—Fiction

ISBN 978-1-5545-5113-2; 1-5545-5113-7

"In the summer of 1954, Ellie's grandma reluctantly agrees to look after 10-year-old Ellie in Saskatchewan so that her dad can take a job as a traveling salesman. Ellie's mother died on the day that Ellie was born, and Grandma blames Ellie for her death. . . . Many kids will recognize the sorrow and difficulty of living with a hostile, bitter relative. . . . The girl next door, a spoiled, bossy brat, offers some levity, but true to Ellie's viewpoint, the spare first-person narrative tells a heartbreaking family story with no mushy reconciliation." Booklist

Sheth, Kashmira

Blue jasmine; [by] Kashmira Sheth. Hyperion Books for Children 2004 186p $15.99; pa $5.99

Grades: 5 6 7 8   Fic

1. Immigrants—Fiction 2. East Indians—Fiction 3. India—Fiction

ISBN 0-7868-1855-7; 0-7868-5565-7 (pa)

LC 2003-50818

When twelve-year-old Seema moves to Iowa City with her parents and younger sister, she leaves friends and family behind in her native India but gradually begins to feel at home in her new country

"Seema's story, which articulates the ache for distant home and family, will resonate with fellow immigrants and enlighten their classmates." Booklist

Boys without names. Balzer & Bray 2010 316p $15.99

Grades: 4 5 6 7   Fic

1. India—Fiction 2. Child labor—Fiction 3. Slavery—Fiction 4. Missing persons—Fiction

ISBN 978-0-06-185760-7; 0-06-185760-2

LC 2009-11747

Eleven-year-old Gopal and his family leave their rural Indian village for life with his uncle in Mumbai, but when they arrive his father goes missing and Gopal ends up locked in a sweatshop from which there is no escape.

"Readers quickly come to care for this clever, perceptive boy who tries hard to do the right thing. . . . The author includes more about child labor at the end of this well-told survival story with a social conscience." SLJ

Shimko, Bonnie

The private thoughts of Amelia E. Rye. Farrar, Straus Giroux 2010 234p $16.99 *

Grades: 5 6 7 8   Fic

1. Mother-daughter relationship—Fiction 2. Friendship—Fiction 3. New York (State)—Fiction

ISBN 978-0-374-36131-0; 0-374-36131-2

LC 2008048092

"Melanie Kroupa books"

Growing up in a small town in upstate New York during the 1960s, 13-year-old Amelia E. Ryel, unwanted by her mother, searches for love and acceptance.

"The book is peopled with believable, multilayered characters. . . . Shimko's . . . story is original, and

Shimko, Bonnie—*Continued*

Amelia's distinctive voice and likable nature will have readers rooting for her in times of trouble and cheering her ultimate good fortune." Publ Wkly

Shreve, Susan Richards

The flunking of Joshua T. Bates; [by] Susan Shreve; illustrated by Diane de Groat. Knopf 1984 82p il pa $4.99 hardcover o.p. *

Grades: 3 4 5   **Fic**

1. School stories 2. Teachers—Fiction 3. Family life—Fiction

ISBN 0-679-84187-3 (pa)   LC 83-19636

Driving home from the beach on Labor Day, Joshua receives some shocking news from his mother: he must repeat third grade.

"In addition to the warm depiction of a teacher-pupil relationship, the story has other relationships, astutely drawn: Joshua's parents, the former classmate who teases Joshua, the best friend who stoutly defends him. The dialogue is particularly good, often contributing to characterization, just as often crisply humorous." Bull Cent Child Books

Other titles about Joshua are:

Joshua T. Bates in trouble again (1997)

Joshua T. Bates takes charge (1993)

Under the Watsons' porch; [by] Susan Shreve. Alfred A. Knopf 2004 199p hardcover o.p. pa $4.99 *

Grades: 5 6 7 8   **Fic**

1. Friendship—Fiction

ISBN 0-375-82630-0; 0-440-41969-7 (pa)

                                LC 2003-61383

Twelve-year-old Ellie's boring summer becomes exciting when she develops a crush on her new next-door neighbor, an older boy with a troubled past, whom her parents have forbidden her to see.

"Ellie's first-person narration is utterly and immediately believable. . . . Shreve imagines a troubled kid with unusual sensitivity and depth, and this novel will be treasured by readers." Booklist

Siebold, Jan

My nights at the Improv; by Jan Siebold. Albert Whitman & Co. 2005 98p $14.95

Grades: 4 5 6 7   **Fic**

1. Moving—Fiction 2. Acting—Fiction 3. School stories

ISBN 0-8075-5630-0   LC 2005004590

"Lizzie, an eighth-grader struggling with a move to a new town, feels as though her voice is on 30-second delay. . . . She learns to confront her fear of speaking out by secretly observing a community-education class on improvisational-drama techniques. . . . Improvisational theater is a fascinating topic that is not often represented in fiction for this age group; the concept is well covered in this high-interest novel." SLJ

Simmons, Jane

Beryl; a pig's tale. Little, Brown Books for Young Readers 2010 $14.99

Grades: 2 3 4 5   **Fic**

1. Pigs—Fiction 2. Toleration—Fiction 3. Family—Fiction 4. Adventure fiction

ISBN 978-0-316-04410-3; 0-316-04410-5

                                 LC 2009-3800

Tired of being mistreated and cooped up, Beryl the piglet escapes her farm and meets a group of wild pigs, whose settlement splits up over the decision of whether to let her stay, and with her new "family" she sets out to find a new home.

"Simmons interjects humorous episodes through her colorful cast of animal characters, providing a rich contrast to the serious topics she explores. Before the hopeful ending is neatly resolved, Beryl and her cohorts face cruelty and despair. Vivid black-and-white drawings convey a range of emotion by varying shade and light. Expressive faces highlight a wealth of feeling." SLJ

Simon, Francesca

Horrid Henry; illustrated by Tony Ross. Sourcebooks 2009 90p il pa $4.99

Grades: 2 3 4   **Fic**

ISBN 978-1-4022-1775-3 (pa); 1-4022-1775-7 (pa)

First published 1994 in the United Kingdom

"Four short chapters follow Henry as he tries to have a perfect day (and upstages his brother, Perfect Peter), disrupts a dance recital with his imitation of a pterodactyl, meets his piratical match in neighbor Moody Margaret, and sabotages a family camping vacation. . . . Short, easy-to-read chapters will appeal to early readers, who will laugh at Henry's exaggerated antics and relate to his rambunctious personality. . . . Ross's comical illustrations perfectly complement the [text]." SLJ

Other titles in this series are:

Horrid Henry and the mega-mean time machine (2009)

Horrid Henry and the scary sitter (2009)

Horrid Henry tricks the tooth fairy (2009)

Horrid Henry's Christmas (2009)

Horrid Henry's stinkbomb (2009)

Singh, Vandana

Younguncle comes to town; illustrated by B.M. Kamath. Viking 2006 c2004 153p il $14.99 *

Grades: 3 4 5   **Fic**

1. Uncles—Fiction 2. India—Fiction

ISBN 0-670-06051-8   LC 2005-14146

First published 2004 in India

In a small town in northern India, three siblings await their father's youngest brother, Younguncle, who is said to be somewhat eccentric.

"Singh's prose is humorous and delightfully understated." SLJ

Skelton, Matthew

Endymion Spring. Delacorte Press 2006 392p il $17.95; lib bdg $19.99; pa $9.99 *

Grades: 5 6 7 8   **Fic**

1. Gutenberg, Johann, 1397?-1468—Fiction 2. Magic—Fiction 3. Books and reading—Fiction 4. Great Britain—Fiction
ISBN 0-385-73380-1; 0-385-90397-9 (lib bdg); 0-385-73456-5 (pa)   LC 2006-46259

Having reluctantly accompanied his academic mother and pesky younger sister to Oxford, twelve-year-old Blake Winters is at loose ends until he stumbles across an ancient and magical book, secretly brought to England in 1453 by Gutenberg's mute apprentice to save it from evil forces, and which now draws Blake into a dangerous and life-threatening quest

"This book is certain to reach an audience looking for a page-turner, and it just might motivate readers to explore the . . . facts behind the fiction." SLJ

The story of Cirrus Flux. Delacorte Press 2010 288p il $17.99; lib bdg $20.99

Grades: 4 5 6 7   **Fic**

1. Orphans—Fiction 2. Supernatural—Fiction 3. Adventure fiction 4. London (England)—Fiction 5. Great Britain—History—1714-1837—Fiction
ISBN 978-0-385-73381-6; 0-385-73381-X; 978-0-385-90398-1 (lib bdg); 0-385-90398-7 (lib bdg)   LC 2009-18987

In 1783 London, the destiny of an orphaned boy and girl becomes intertwined as the boy, Cirrus Flux, is pursued by a sinister woman mesmerist, a tiny man with an all-seeing eye, and a skull-collecting scoundrel, all of whom believe that he possesses an orb containing a divine power.

Skelton "neatly weaves touches of fantasy into a late-eighteenth century London setting. . . . His literary sensibility and grubby atmospherics are strong enough to carry the tale." Booklist

Slade, Arthur G., 1967-

Jolted; Newton Starker's rules for survival; [by] Arthur Slade. Wendy Lamb Books 2009 227p $15.99; lib bdg $18.99

Grades: 5 6 7 8   **Fic**

1. Lightning—Fiction 2. School stories
ISBN 978-0-385-74700-4; 0-385-74700-4; 978-0-385-90944-0 (lib bdg); 0-385-90944-6 (lib bdg)   LC 2008-8632

First published 2008 in Canada

Many of Newton Starker's ancestors, including his mother, have been killed by lightning strikes, so when he enrolls at the eccentric Jerry Potts Academy of Higher Learning and Survival in Moose Jaw, Saskatchewan, he tries to be a model student so that he can avoid the same fate.

"The premise will snag readers immediately [and] . . . Slade's portrayal of Newton's sweep of emotions as he deals with his perceived fate–fear, fury, dogged determination–is especially convincing." Publ Wkly

Sleator, William

The boxes. Dutton Children's Bks. 1998 196p hardcover o.p. pa $4.99

Grades: 6 7 8 9   **Fic**

1. Science fiction
ISBN 0-525-46012-8; 0-14-130810-9 (pa)   LC 98-9285

When she opens two strange boxes left in her care by her mysterious uncle, fifteen-year-old Annie discovers a swarm of telepathic creatures and unleashes a power capable of slowing down time

"Sleator has written a page-turner. . . . His writing is crisp and clean, letting the story speak for itself." Voice Youth Advocates

Interstellar pig. Dutton 1984 197p pa $6.99 hardcover o.p.

Grades: 5 6 7 8   **Fic**

1. Science fiction
ISBN 0-14-037595-3 (pa)   LC 84-4132

Barney's boring seaside vacation suddenly becomes more interesting when the cottage next door is occupied by three exotic neighbors who are addicted to a game they call "Interstellar Pig."

The author "draws the reader in with intimations of danger and horror, but the climactic battle is more slapstick than horrific, and the victor's prize could scarcely be more ironic. Problematic as straight science fiction but great fun as a spoof on human-alien contact." Booklist

Another title about Barney is:
Parasite Pig (2002)

Slote, Alfred

Finding Buck McHenry. HarperCollins Pubs. 1991 250p pa $4.95 *

Grades: 4 5 6   **Fic**

1. Baseball—Fiction 2. African Americans—Fiction
ISBN 0-06-440469-2 (pa)   LC 90-39190

Eleven-year-old Jason, believing the school custodian Mack Henry to be Buck McHenry, a famous pitcher from the old Negro League, tries to enlist him as a coach for his Little League team by revealing his identity to the world

"Slote skillfully blends comedy, suspense and baseball in a highly entertaining tale." Publ Wkly

Smiley, Jane, 1949-

The Georges and the Jewels; with illustrations by Elaine Clayton. Alfred A. Knopf 2009 232p il $16.99; lib bdg $19.99

Grades: 4 5 6 7   **Fic**

1. Horses—Fiction 2. Ranch life—Fiction 3. California—Fiction 4. Christian life—Fiction
ISBN 978-0-375-86227-4; 0-375-86227-7; 978-0-375-96227-1 (lib bdg); 0-375-96227-1 (lib bdg)   LC 2009-06241

Seventh-grader Abby Lovitt grows up on her family's California horse ranch in the 1960s, learning to train the horses her father sells and trying to reconcile her strict religious upbringing with her own ideas about life.

"As might be expected from the skilled hands of Smiley . . . there are synchronous storylines . . . [and] many will find it difficult to say goodbye to Abby, Jack and especially to Ornery George." Publ Wkly

Smith, Cynthia Leitich

Indian shoes; illustrated by Jim Madsen. HarperCollins Pubs. 2002 66p il $15.95

Grades: 3 4 5 **Fic**

1. Grandfathers—Fiction 2. Native Americans—Fiction

ISBN 0-06-029531-7 LC 2001-39510

Together with Grampa, Ray Halfmoon, a Seminole-Cherokee boy, finds creative and amusing solutions to life's challenges

"The writing is warm and lively; the situations are sometimes humorous, sometimes poignant; and Ray and Grampa's loving relationship is depicted believably and without sentimentality." Horn Book Guide

Smith, Doris Buchanan

A taste of blackberries; illustrated by Charles Robinson. Crowell 1973 58p il lib bdg $14.89; pa $4.95 *

Grades: 4 5 6 **Fic**

1. Death—Fiction 2. Friendship—Fiction

ISBN 0-690-80512-8 (lib bdg); 0-06-440238-4 (pa)

"While gathering Japanese beetles to help a neighbor, Jamie is stung by a bee and falls screaming and writhing to the ground. His best friend (never named) disgustedly stalks off, only to find later that Jamie is dead of the bee sting." SLJ

"A difficult and sensitive subject, treated with taste and honesty, is woven into a moving story about a believable little boy. The black-and-white illustrations are honest, affective, and sensitive." Horn Book

Smith, Hope Anita

Keeping the night watch; with illustrations by E.B. Lewis. Henry Holt 2008 73p il $18.95 *

Grades: 4 5 6 7 **Fic**

1. Family life—Fiction 2. Fathers—Fiction 3. African Americans—Fiction 4. Novels in verse

ISBN 978-0-8050-7202-0; 0-8050-7202-0

LC 2007-12372

Coretta Scott King honor book for text, 2009

Sequel to: The way a door closes (2003)

A thirteen-year-old African American boy chronicles what happens to his family when his father, who temporarily left, returns home and they all must deal with their feelings of anger, hope, abandonment, and fear.

"The words are simple . . . and the beautiful watercolor pictures of the African American family have the same quiet intensity as pictures in the first book. . . . Although mainly in free verse, there's also a sonnet." Booklist

The way a door closes; [by] Hope Anita Smith; with illustrations by Shane W. Evans. Holt & Co. 2003 52p il $18.95

Grades: 4 5 6 7 **Fic**

1. Fathers—Fiction 2. Family life—Fiction 3. African Americans—Fiction 4. Novels in verse

ISBN 0-8050-6477-X LC 2002-67884

In this novel in verse "readers are drawn into the thoughts and feelings of a 13-year-old African American as he tries to understand and cope with a parent's departure from the family. . . . In carefully chosen, straight-

forward language, Smith conveys the boy's roller-coaster emotions with pinpoint accuracy. The results are poems that are heartbreaking, angry, and tender. Done in warm shades of mostly brown, blue, and gold, Evans's color spot and full-page paintings have a realistic, slightly sculptural appearance and are a perfect complement to the poems." SLJ

Followed by Keeping the night watch (2008)

Smith, Icy, 1966-

Half spoon of rice; a survival story of the Cambodian genocide; written by Icy Smith; illustrated by Sopaul Nhem. East West Discovery Press 2010 42p il $19.95

Grades: 5 6 7 8 **Fic**

1. Genocide—Fiction 2. Cambodia—Fiction

ISBN 978-0-9821675-8-8; 0-9821675-8-X

LC 2009002973

Nine-year-old Nat and his family are forced from their home on April 17, 1975, marched for many days, separated from each other, and forced to work in the rice fields, where Nat concentrates on survival. Includes historical notes and photographs documenting the Cambodian genocide

"Bold, impressionistic oil paintings, mainly full page but some full spreads, speak volumes, and archival photographs are appended. This powerful child's eye view of war is harsh and realistic—like its subject—though accessible and thought-provoking." SLJ

Smith, Robert Kimmel, 1930-

Chocolate fever; illustrated by Gioia Fiammenghi. Putnam 1989 c1972 93p il $14.99; pa $4.99 *

Grades: 4 5 6 **Fic**

1. Chocolate—Fiction

ISBN 978-0-399-24355-4; 0-399-24355-0; 978-0-14-240595-6 (pa); 0-14-240595-7 (pa)

LC 88-23508

A reissue of the title first published 1972 by Coward-McCann

"You've heard of too much of a good thing? You've never heard of it the way it happens to Henry Green. Henry's a chocolate maven, first class. No, that's too mild. Henry's absolutely freaky over chocolate, loco over cocoa. He can't get enough, until—aaarrrfh! Brown spots, brown bumps all over Henry. It's (gulp) 'Chocolate Fever.'" N Y Times Book Rev

"It's all quite preposterous and lots of laughs, and so are the cartoon illustrations." Publ Wkly

Smith, Roland, 1951-

Cryptid hunters. Hyperion Books for Children 2005 348p $15.99; pa $5.99

Grades: 5 6 7 8 **Fic**

1. Twins—Fiction 2. Congo (Republic)—Fiction 3. Adventure fiction

ISBN 0-7868-5161-9; 0-7868-5162-7 (pa)

Twins, Grace and Marty, along with a mysterious uncle, are dropped into the middle of the Congolese jungle in search of their missing photojournalist parents.

"The action is nonstop in this well-paced jungle ad-

Smith, Roland, 1951-—*Continued*

venture, and Smith adds a deeper layer in scenes of Marty and Grace discovering truths about their complicated family relationships." Booklist

Followed by: Tentacles (2009)

I, Q.: book one, Indepedence Hall. Sleeping Bear Press 2008 302p pa $8.95

Grades: 5 6 7 8   **Fic**

1. Terrorism—Fiction 2. Spies—Fiction 3. Adventure fiction

ISBN 978-1-58536-325-4 (pa); 1-58536-325-1 (pa)

In Philadelphia, Angela realizes she's being followed, and Q soon learns the secret about Angela's real mother, a former Secret Service agent.

"Adventure, suspense, humor, fascinating characters, and plot twists galore will draw middle-graders to this series starter." Booklist

Followed by: I, Q.: book two, The White House (2009)

Smith, Yeardley, 1964-

I, Lorelei; by Yeardley Smith. Laura Geringer Books 2009 339p il $16.99; lib bdg $17.89

Grades: 4 5 6   **Fic**

1. Divorce—Fiction 2. Diaries—Fiction 3. Family life—Fiction

ISBN 978-0-06-149344-7; 0-06-149344-9; 978-0-06-149345-4 (lib bdg); 0-06-149345-7 (lib bdg)

In letters to her recently deceased cat Mud, eleven-year-old Lorelei chronicles the ups and downs of her sixth-grade year, during which her parents separate, she gets a part in the school play, and she becomes friends with the cutest boy in her grade.

"Lorelei's authentic and endearing voice provide a richly layered reading experience. This funny, poignant story of self-centered parents and appealing, resilient children is a winner." SLJ

Sneve, Virginia Driving Hawk

Lana's Lakota moons. University of Nebraska Press 2007 116p pa $12.95

Grades: 3 4 5   **Fic**

1. Teton Indians—Fiction 2. Cousins—Fiction 3. Hmong (Asian people)—Fiction 4. Death—Fiction 5. Cancer—Fiction

ISBN 978-0-8032-6028-3 (pa); 0-8032-6028-8 (pa)

LC 2007-05469

Cousins Lori and Lana, Lakota Indians who have a close but competitive relationship, learn about their heritage and culture throughout the year, and when a Laotian-Hmong girl comes to their school, they make friends with her and "adopt" her as one of their own

This is an "unassuming yet potent chronicle. . . . This novel repays readers with its portraits of the sisters and their living heritage." Publ Wkly

Snicket, Lemony, 1970-

The bad beginning; illustrations by Brett Helquist. HarperCollins Pubs. 1999 162p il (A series of unfortunate events) $11.99; pa $6.99 *

Grades: 4 5 6   **Fic**

1. Orphans—Fiction

ISBN 0-06-440766-7; 0-06-114630-7 (pa)

LC 99-14750

After the sudden death of their parents, the three Baudelaire children must depend on each other and their wits when it turns out that the distant relative who is appointed their guardian is determined to use any means necessary to get their fortune

"While the misfortunes hover on the edge of being ridiculous, Snicket's energetic blend of humor, dramatic irony, and literary flair makes it all perfectly believable. . . . Excellent for reading aloud." SLJ

Other titles about the Baudelaire children are:

The austere academy (2000)

The carnivorous carnival (2003)

The end (2006)

The ersatz elevator (2000)

The grim grotto (2004)

The hostile hospital (2001)

The miserable mill (2000)

The penultimate peril (2005)

The reptile room (1999)

The slippery slope (2003)

The vile village (2001)

The wide window (2000)

Lemony Snicket: the unauthorized autobiography. HarperCollins Pubs. 2002 212p il $11.99; pa $6.99

Grades: 4 5 6 7   **Fic**

ISBN 0-06-000719-2; 0-06-056225-0 (pa)

LC 2001-51745

A fictitious autobiography of the author of a series of novels about the Baudelaire children

"The story of the fictitious Lemony Snicket and how he has dedicated his life to the case of the orphaned Baudelaire children. . . . Snicket tells you what he cannot tell you and then tells you, but what he tells you makes no sense. . . . [A] hilarious and clever book. . . . Lemony Snicket fans will love it, and new readers will laugh so much that they will want to read the series." Voice Youth Advocates

Sniegoski, Tom

Billy Hooten, Owlboy; by Thomas E. Sniegoski; illustrated by Eric Powell. Yearling 2007 242p il lib bdg $11.99; pa $5.99

Grades: 3 4 5 6   **Fic**

1. Superheroes—Fiction

ISBN 978-0-385-90402-5 (lib bdg); 978-0-440-42180-1 (pa)   LC 2007001552

Unassuming twelve-year-old Billy Hooten, who loves reading superhero comic books, suddenly learns that he has been chosen to become the next Owlboy, whose destiny it is to save the inhabitants of Monstros, a city underneath the cemetery next to Billy's house

"This lively tale should be a hit, especially with reluctant readers. A few black-and-white sketches appear throughout." SLJ

Others title about Owlboy are:

Sniegoski, Tom—*Continued*

Billy Hooten, Owlboy: the girl with the destructo touch (2007)

Billy Hooten, Owlboy: the flock of fury (2008)

Billy Hooten, Owlboy: tremble at the terror of Zis-boom-bah (2008)

Snow, Alan

Here be monsters! an adventure involving magic, trolls, and other creatures; written and illustrated by Alan Snow. Atheneum Books for Young Readers 2006 529p il (The Ratbridge chronicles) $17.95; pa $8.99

Grades: 4 5 6 7   **Fic**

1. Fantasy fiction 2. Monsters—Fiction

ISBN   978-0-689-87047-7;   0-689-87047-7; 978-0-689-87048-4 (pa); 0-689-87048-5 (pa)

LC 2005-24438

While gathering food to bring to his grandfather, young Arthur becomes trapped in the city of Ratbridge, where he and some new friends try to stop a plot to shrink the monsters of Arthur's home, the Underworld, for a nefarious purpose

"Helpful in creating the settings and bringing the more fantastic characters to life, the illustrations, which are often amusing, also make the book accessible to younger children who like lengthy books. Snow's inventive fantasy . . . combines stout hearts, terrible troubles, and inspired lunacy." Booklist

Snow, Maya

Sisters of the sword. HarperCollins 2008 275p (Sisters of the sword) $16.99; lib bdg $17.89; pa $6.99

Grades: 5 6 7 8   **Fic**

1. Samurai—Fiction 2. Sex role—Fiction 3. Sisters—Fiction 4. Japan—Fiction

ISBN   978-0-06-124387-5;   0-06-124387-6; 978-0-06-124388-2 (lib bdg); 0-06-124388-4 (lib bdg); 978-0-06-124389-9 (pa); 0-06-124389-2 (pa)

LC 2007-029610

Two aristocratic sisters in ancient Japan disguise themselves as samurai warriors to take revenge on the uncle who betrayed their family.

"This rousing new series . . . starts off with a bang, or more accurately, the silent thrust of a sword." Booklist

Other titles in this series are:

Chasing the secret (2009)

Journey through fire (2009)

Snyder, Laurel

Any which wall; drawings by LeUyen Pham. Random House 2009 242p il $16.99; lib bdg $19.99

Grades: 4 5 6 7   **Fic**

1. Magic—Fiction 2. Wishes—Fiction 3. Space and time—Fiction 4. Siblings—Fiction 5. Iowa—Fiction

ISBN   978-0-375-85560-3;   0-375-85560-2; 978-0-375-95560-0 (lib bdg); 0-375-95560-7 (lib bdg)

LC 2008-22605

In the middle of an Iowa cornfield, four children find a magic wall that enables them to travel through time

and space.

"Snyder's fresh, down-to-earth voice is complemented by Pham's energetic illustrations, which seem at once retro and modern. Fantasy fans will enjoy this novel, but so will readers who like stories about ordinary kids." SLJ

Snyder, Zilpha Keatley

The bronze pen. Atheneum Books for Young Readers 2008 200p $16.99; pa $5.99

Grades: 4 5 6   **Fic**

1. Authorship—Fiction 2. Magic—Fiction 3. Family life—Fiction

ISBN   978-1-4169-4201-6;   1-4169-4201-7; 978-1-4169-4208-5 (pa); 1-4169-4208-4 (pa)

LC 2006-102314

With her father's failing health and the family's shaky finances, twelve-year-old Audrey's dreams of becoming a writer seem very impractical until she is given a peculiar bronze pen that appears to have unusual powers.

"Snyder knows just how to allow magical elements to swell gradually from whispers to shouts, and how to open her characters' minds to uncanny possibilities." Booklist

The Egypt game; drawings by Alton Raible. Atheneum Books for Young Readers 2007 c1995 215p il $16.99; pa $6.99 *

Grades: 5 6 7 8   **Fic**

1. Imagination—Fiction 2. Egypt—Fiction 3. Games—Fiction

ISBN   978-1-4169-6065-2;   1-4169-6065-1; 978-1-4169-9051-2 (pa); 1-4169-9051-8 (pa)

A Newbery Medal honor book, 1968

First published 1967

A group of children, entranced with the study of Egypt, play their own Egypt game, are visited by a secret oracle, become involved in a murder, and befriend the Professor before they move on to new interests, such as Gypsies.

The headless cupid; illustrated by Alton Raible. Atheneum Books for Young Readers 2009 219p il $16.99; pa $6.99 *

Grades: 5 6 7 8   **Fic**

1. Occultism—Fiction

ISBN   978-1-4169-9532-6;   1-4169-9532-3; 978-1-4169-9052-9 (pa); 1-4169-9052-6 (pa)

A Newbery Medal honor book, 1972

A reissue of the title first published 1971

Life is never quite the same again for eleven-year-old David after the arrival of his new stepsister, a student of the occult.

"The author portrays children with acute understanding, evident both in her delineation of Amanda and David and of the distinctively different younger children. Good style, good characterization, good dialogue, good story." Sutherland. The Best in Child Books

William S. and the great escape. Atheneum Books for Young Readers 2009 214p $16.99

Grades: 5 6 7 8   **Fic**

1. Siblings—Fiction 2. Acting—Fiction

ISBN 978-1-4169-6763-7; 1-4169-6763-X

LC 2008-10377

Snyder, Zilpha Keatley—*Continued*

In 1938, twelve-year-old William has already decided to leave home when his younger sister informs him that she and their brother and sister are going too, and right away, but complications arise when an acquaintance decides to "help" them.

"Wit and pluck are rewarded in this quick-paced, high-drama adventure, which may also whet young appetites for Shakespeare." Publ Wkly

The witches of Worm; illustrated by Alton Raible. Atheneum Books for Young Readers 2009 183p il $16.99; pa $6.99

Grades: 5 6 7 8   **Fic**
  1. Witchcraft—Fiction 2. Cats—Fiction
  ISBN 978-1-4169-9531-9; 1-4169-9531-5; 978-1-4169-9053-6 (pa); 1-4169-9053-4 (pa)
  A Newbery Medal honor book, 1973
  A reissue of the title first published 1972

Lonely, twelve-year-old Jessica is convinced that the cat she finds is possessed by a witch and is responsible for her own strange behavior.

"This is a haunting story of the power of mind and ritual, as well as of misunderstanding, anger, loneliness and friendship. It is written with humor, pace, a sure feeling for conversation and a warm understanding of human nature." Commonweal

Sobol, Donald J., 1924-

Encyclopedia Brown, boy detective; illustrated by Leonard Shortall. Dutton Children's Bks. 1963 88p il pa $4.99 hardcover o.p. *

Grades: 3 4 5   **Fic**
  1. Mystery fiction
  ISBN 978-0-14-240888-9; 0-14-240888-3
  First published by Thomas Nelson

"Leroy Brown earns his nickname by applying his encyclopedic learning to community mysteries. The reader is asked to anticipate solutions before checking them in the back of the book." Natl Counc of Teach of Engl. Adventuring with Books. 2d edition

"The answers are logical; some are tricky, but there are no trick questions, and readers who like puzzles should enjoy the . . . challenge. The episodes are lightly humorous, brief, and simply written." Bull Cent Child Books

Other titles about Encyclopedia Brown are:
Encyclopedia Brown and the case of the dead eagles (1975)
Encyclopedia Brown and the case of the disgusting sneakers (1990)
Encyclopedia Brown and the case of the jumping frogs (2003)
Encyclopedia Brown and the case of the midnight visitor (1977)
Encyclopedia Brown and the case of the mysterious handprints (1985)
Encyclopedia Brown and the case of Pablo's nose (1996)
Encyclopedia Brown and the case of the secret pitch (1965)
Encyclopedia Brown and the case of the sleeping dog (1998)
Encyclopedia Brown and the case of the slippery salamander (1999)
Encyclopedia Brown and the case of the treasure hunt (1988)
Encyclopedia Brown and the case of the two spies (1994)
Encyclopedia Brown finds the clues (1966)
Encyclopedia Brown gets his man (1967)
Encyclopedia Brown keeps the peace (1969)
Encyclopedia Brown lends a hand (1974)
Encyclopedia Brown saves the day (1970)
Encyclopedia Brown sets the pace (1982)
Encyclopedia Brown shows the way (1972)
Encyclopedia Brown solves them all (1968)
Encyclopedia Brown: super sleuth (2009)
Encyclopedia Brown takes the cake! (1983)
Encyclopedia Brown takes the case (1973)
Encyclopedia Brown tracks them down (1971)
Encyclopedia Brown cracks the case (2007)

Sonnenblick, Jordan

After ever after. Scholastic Press 2010 260p $16.99 *

Grades: 5 6 7 8   **Fic**
  1. Cancer—Fiction 2. Friendship—Fiction 3. Family life—Fiction 4. School stories
  ISBN 978-0-439-83706-4; 0-439-83706-5
  Companion volume to: Drums, girls, & dangerous pie (2005)

Jeffery's cancer is in remission but the chemotherapy and radiation treatments have left him with concentration problems, and he worries about school work, his friends, his family, and a girl who likes him.

"Sonneblick imbues Jeffrey with a smooth, likable, and unaffected voice. . . . As hilarious as it is tragic, and as honest as it is hopeful . . . [this book is] irresistable reading." Booklist

Zen and the art of faking it. Scholastic Press 2007 264p $16.99; pa $7.99

Grades: 5 6 7 8   **Fic**
  1. School stories 2. Zen Buddhism—Fiction 3. Asian Americans—Fiction 4. Pennsylvania—Fiction
  ISBN 978-0-439-83707-1; 0-439-83707-3; 978-0-439-83709-5 (pa); 0-439-83709-X (pa)
                                            LC 2006-28841

When thirteen-year-old San Lee moves to a new town and school for the umpteenth time, he is looking for a way to stand out when his knowledge of Zen Buddhism, gained in his previous school, provides the answer—and the need to quickly become a convincing Zen master.

The author gives readers "plenty to laugh at. . . . Mixed with more serious scenes, . . . lighter moments take a basic message about the importance of honesty and forgiveness and treat it with panache." Publ Wkly

Soto, Gary

The skirt; illustrated by Eric Velasquez. Delacorte Press 2008 c1992 74p il $14.99; lib bdg $17.99; pa $5.99

Grades: 1 2 3   **Fic**
  1. Clothing and dress—Fiction 2. Lost and found possessions—Fiction 3. Mexican Americans—Fiction
  ISBN 978-0-385-30665-2; 0-385-30665-2; 978-0-385-90534-3 (lib bdg); 0-385-90534-3 (lib bdg); 978-0-440-40924-3 (pa); 0-440-40924-1 (pa)
  A reissue of the title first published 1992

Soto, Gary—*Continued*

When Miata leaves on the school bus the skirt that she is to wear in a dance performance, she needs all her wits to get it back without her parents' finding out that she has lost something yet again.

"This is a light, engaging narrative that successfully combines information on Hispanic culture with familiar and recognizable childhood themes. . . . A fine read-aloud and discussion starter, this story blends cultural differences with human similarities to create both interest and understanding." SLJ

Taking sides. Harcourt Brace Jovanovich 1991 138p hardcover o.p. pa $5.95 *

Grades: 5 6 7 8   **Fic**

1. Hispanic Americans—Fiction 2. Basketball—Fiction
ISBN 0-15-284076-1; 0-15-204694-1 (pa)

LC 91-11082

Fourteen-year-old Lincoln Mendoza, an aspiring basketball player, must come to terms with his divided loyalties when he moves from the Hispanic inner city to a white suburban neighborhood

This is a "light but appealing story. . . . Because of its subject matter and its clear, straightforward prose, it will be especially good for reluctant readers." SLJ

Includes glossary

Soup, Cuthbert

A whole nother story; illustrations by Jeffrey Stewart Timmins. Bloomsbury 2010 264p il $16.99

Grades: 3 4 5 6   **Fic**

1. Inventions—Fiction 2. Spies—Fiction 3. Family life—Fiction 4. Moving—Fiction 5. Automobile travel—Fiction
ISBN 978-1-59990-435-1; 1-59990-435-7

LC 2009-21998

Ethan Cheeseman and his children, ages eight, twelve, and fourteen, hope to settle in a nice small town, at least long enough to complete work on a time machine, but spies and goverment agents have been pursuing them for two years and are about to catch up.

"The storytelling, which merges deadpan narration with an absurdist sense of humor, is the real star of this fast-paced adventure." Publ Wkly

Speare, Elizabeth George, 1908-1994

The bronze bow. Houghton Mifflin 1961 255p $16; pa $6.95

Grades: 6 7 8 9   **Fic**

1. Jesus Christ—Fiction 2. Christianity—Fiction 3. Palestine—Fiction
ISBN 0-395-07113-5; 0-395-13719-5 (pa)
Awarded the Newbery Medal, 1962

"Daniel had sworn vengence against the Romans who had killed his parents, and he had become one of a band of outlaws. . . . Each time he saw the Rabbi Jesus, the youth was drawn to his cause; at last he resolved his own conflict by giving up his hatred and, as a follower of the Master, accepting his enemies. The story has drama and pace, fine characterization, and colorful background detail." Bull Cent Child Books

The sign of the beaver. Houghton Mifflin 1983 135p $16

Grades: 5 6 7 8   **Fic**

1. Frontier and pioneer life—Fiction 2. Native Americans—Fiction 3. Friendship—Fiction
ISBN 0-395-33890-5   LC 83-118
A Newbery Medal honor book, 1984

Left alone to guard the family's wilderness home in eighteenth-century Maine, Matt is hard-pressed to survive until local Indians teach him their skills

Matt "begins to understand the Indians' ingenuity and respect for nature and the devastating impact of the encroachment of the white man. In a quiet but not unsuspenseful story . . . the author articulates historical facts along with the adventures and the thoughts, emotions, and developing insights of a young adolescent." Horn Book

The witch of Blackbird Pond. Houghton Mifflin 1958 249p $17 *

Grades: 6 7 8 9   **Fic**

1. Connecticut—History—1600-1775, Colonial period—Fiction 2. Witchcraft—Fiction 3. Puritans—Fiction
ISBN 0-395-07114-3   LC 58-11063
Awarded the Newbery Medal, 1959

"Headstrong and undisciplined, Barbados-bred Kit Tyler is an embarrassment to her Puritan relatives, and her sincere attempts to aid a reputed witch soon bring her to trial as a suspect." Child Books Too Good to Miss

Sperry, Armstrong, 1897-1976

Call it courage. Simon & Schuster Books for Young Readers 1968 c1940 95p il $17.99; pa $5.99

Grades: 5 6 7 8   **Fic**

1. Courage—Fiction 2. Polynesia—Fiction 3. Wilderness survival—Fiction
ISBN 978-0-027-86030-6; 0-02-786030-2; 978-1-4169-5368-5 (pa); 1-4169-5368-X (pa)
Awarded the Newbery medal, 1941
First published 1940 by Macmillan

"Because he fears the ocean, a Polynesian boy is scorned by his people and must redeem himself by an act of courage. His lone journey to a sacred island and the dangers he faces there earn him the name Mafatu, 'Stout Heart.' Dramatic illustrations add atmosphere and mystery." Hodges. Books for Elem Sch Libr

Spinelli, Eileen, 1942-

The Dancing Pancake; illustrated by Joanne Lew-Vriethoff. Alfred A. Knopf 2010 248p il $12.99; lib bdg $15.99

Grades: 3 4 5   **Fic**

1. Novels in verse 2. Divorce—Fiction 3. Restaurants—Fiction
ISBN 978-0-375-85870-3; 0-375-85870-9; 978-0-375-95870-0 (lib bdg); 0-375-95870-3 (lib bdg)

"Bindi's life is pretty normal. She loves to read and has good friends and a loving extended family. This normalcy ends when her parents announce that they are separating and that her father is moving to another city to look for a job. Told entirely in verse, the story relates

Spinelli, Eileen, 1942-—_Continued_

the sixth grader's experiences, her feelings, and snippets of her daily life. . . . The poetic structure of this novel succeeds in capturing the child's voice and deepest feelings. The verse also provides sound development of secondary characters. Lew-Vriethoff's lively pen-and-ink illustrations add texture to the story and offer touches of humor." SLJ

Where I live; illustrated by Matt Phelan. Dial Books 2007 unp il $16.99 *

Grades: 1 2 3 4   **Fic**
   1. Moving—Fiction 2. Family life—Fiction 3. Novels in verse
   ISBN 978-0-8037-3122-6; 0-8037-3122-1
                          LC 2006-30971

In a series of poems, Diana writes about her life, both before and after her father loses his job and she and her family move far away to live with Grandpa Joe.

"Spinelli crafts a reassuring and engaging story in verse. . . . Phelan's charming pencil drawings are a perfect complement to this heartfelt tale." SLJ

Spinelli, Jerry, 1941-

Crash. Knopf 1996 162p hardcover o.p. lib bdg $17.99; pa $6.99

Grades: 5 6 7 8   **Fic**
   1. Football—Fiction 2. Grandfathers—Fiction 3. Friendship—Fiction
   ISBN 0-679-87957-9; 0-679-97957-3 (lib bdg); 0-440-23857-9 (pa)   LC 95-30942

"Crash is a star football player. He torments Penn, a classmate who is everything Crash is not—friendly, small, and a pacifist. When his beloved grandfather comes to live with his family and suffers a debilitating stroke, Crash begins to see value in many of the things he has scorned." Horn Book Guide

"Readers will devour this humorous glimpse at what jocks are made of while learning that life does not require crashing helmet-headed through it." SLJ

Loser. HarperCollins Pubs. 2002 218p $15.99; lib bdg $16.89; pa $5.99

Grades: 4 5 6 7   **Fic**
   1. School stories 2. Family life—Fiction
   ISBN 0-06-000193-3; 0-06-000483-5 (lib bdg); 0-06-054074-5 (pa)   LC 2001-47484
   "Joanna Cotler books"

Even though his classmates from first grade on have considered him strange and a loser, Daniel Zinkoff's optimism and exuberance and the support of his loving family do not allow him to feel that way about himself

"This novel is an offbeat, affectionate, colorful, and melancholy work." Voice Youth Advocates

Maniac Magee; a novel. Little, Brown 1990 184p $16.99; pa $6.99 *

Grades: 5 6 7 8   **Fic**
   1. Orphans—Fiction 2. Homeless persons—Fiction 3. Race relations—Fiction
   ISBN 0-316-80722-2; 0-316-80906-3 (pa)
                          LC 89-27144

Awarded the Newbery Medal, 1991

"Orphaned at three, Jeffery Lionel Magee, after eight unhappy years with relatives, one day takes off running. A year later, he ends up 200 miles away in Two Mills, a highly segregated community. Part tall tale and part contemporary realistic fiction, this unusual novel magically weaves timely issues of homelessness, racial prejudice, and illiteracy into an energetic story that bursts with creativity, enthusiasm, and hope for the future. In short, it's a celebration of life." Booklist

There's a girl in my hammerlock. Simon & Schuster Bks. for Young Readers 1991 199p pa $5.99 hardcover o.p.

Grades: 5 6 7 8   **Fic**
   1. Wrestling—Fiction 2. Sex role—Fiction 3. School stories
   ISBN 1-4169-3937-7 (pa)   LC 91-8765

Thirteen-year-old Maisie joins her school's formerly all-male wrestling team and tries to last through the season, despite opposition from other students, her best friend, and her own teammates

The author "tackles a meaty subject—traditional gender roles—with his usual humor and finesse. The result, written in a breezy, first-person style, is a rattling good sports story that is clever, witty and tightly written." Publ Wkly

Wringer. HarperCollins Pubs. 1997 228p $16.99; lib bdg $16.89; pa $6.50

Grades: 4 5 6 7   **Fic**
   1. Courage—Fiction 2. Violence—Fiction 3. Pigeons—Fiction
   ISBN 0-06-024913-7; 0-06-024914-5 (lib bdg); 0-06-440578-8 (pa)   LC 96-37897

A Newbery Medal honor book, 1998
"Joanna Cotler books"

"During the annual pigeon shoot, it is a town tradition for 10-year-old boys to break the necks of wounded birds. In this riveting story told with verve and suspense, Palmer rebels." SLJ

Springer, Nancy

The case of the missing marquess; an Enola Holmes mystery. Philomel Books 2006 216p $10.99; pa $6.99 *

Grades: 5 6 7 8   **Fic**
   1. Mystery fiction 2. London (England)—Fiction 3. Missing persons—Fiction
   ISBN 0-399-24304-6; 0-14-240933-2 (pa)

Enola Holmes, much younger sister of detective Sherlock Holmes, must travel to London in disguise to unravel the disappearance of her missing mother.

"Enola's loneliness, intelligence, sense of humor, and sheer pluck make her an extremely appealing heroine." SLJ

 Other titles about Enola Holmes are:
The case of the left-handed lady (2007)
The case of the bizarre bouquets (2008)
The case of the peculiar pink fan (2008)
The case of the cryptic crinoline (2009)
The case of the gypsy good-bye (2010)

Springer, Nancy—*Continued*

Dusssie. Walker & Co. 2007 176p $16.95

Grades: 5 6 7 8   **Fic**
  1. Classical mythology—Fiction 2. Mother-daughter
  relationship—Fiction 3. Snakes—Fiction 4. New York
  (N.Y.)—Fiction 5. Artists—Fiction
  ISBN 0-8027-9649-4; 978-0-8027-9649-3

At age thirteen Dusie makes the horrifying discovery
that she, like her New York artist mother, is a Gorgon—
a Greek mythological monster sprouting snakes from her
head and capable of turning humans into stone with one
angry look.

This "is an enjoyable read, fast paced and fun, with
a smart, likable character." SLJ

Rowan Hood, outlaw girl of Sherwood Forest.
Philomel Bks. 2001 170p hardcover o.p. pa $5.99
*

Grades: 4 5 6 7   **Fic**
  1. Robin Hood (Legendary character)—Fiction
  2. Middle Ages—Fiction 3. Adventure fiction
  ISBN 0-399-23368-7; 0-698-11972-X (pa)
                                       LC 00-63694

In her quest to connect with Robin Hood, the father
she has never met, thirteen-year-old Rosemary disguises
herself as a boy, befriends a half-wolf, half-dog, a runaway princess, and an overgrown boy whose singing is
hypnotic, and makes peace with her elfin heritage

"This tale is a charmer, filled with exciting action,
plenty of humor, engaging characters, and a nice fantasy
twist." Booklist

Other titles about Rowan Hood are:

Lionclaw (2002)

Outlaw princess of Sherwood (2003)

Rowan Hood returns (2005)

Wild boy (2004)

Spyri, Johanna, 1827-1901

Heidi; by Johanna Spyri; illustrated by Jessie
Willcox Smith. Morrow/Books of Wonder 1996
383p il $24.99 *

Grades: 4 5 6   **Fic**
  1. Orphans—Fiction 2. Switzerland—Fiction 3. Alps—
  Fiction
  ISBN 0-688-14519-1
  First published 1880

A Swiss orphan is heartbroken when she must leave
her beloved grandfather and their happy home in the
mountains to go to school and to care for an invalid girl
in the city.

St. Anthony, Jane

The summer Sherman loved me; [by] Jane St.
Anthony. Farrar, Straus & Giroux 2006 136p $16

Grades: 5 6 7 8   **Fic**
  1. Family life—Fiction 2. Mother-daughter relationship—Fiction 3. Friendship—Fiction
  ISBN 0-374-37289-6   LC 2005046361

In addition to coping with her changing relationship
with her mother, twelve-year-old Margaret spends her
summer trying to sort out her feelings for the boy next
door who claims to love her

"This fluidly told, well-paced novel is set in a more

innocent time. . . . The emotions experienced by the
well-drawn characters, however, remain universal. A
fresh and refreshing coming-of-age story." SLJ

St. John, Lauren, 1966-

The white giraffe; illustrated by David Dean.
Dial Books for Young Readers 2007 180p il
$16.99; pa $6.99

Grades: 4 5 6 7   **Fic**
  1. Mythical animals—Fiction 2. Giraffes—Fiction
  3. Orphans—Fiction 4. South Africa—Fiction
  ISBN 978-0-8037-3211-7;   0-8037-3211-2;
  978-0-14-241152-0 (pa); 0-14-241152-3 (pa)
                                     LC 2006-21323

After a fire kills her parents, eleven-year-old Martine
must leave England to live with her grandmother on a
wildlife game reserve in South Africa, where she befriends a mythical white giraffe

"The story is captivating and well spun." SLJ

Other titles in this series are:

Dolphin song (2008)

Last leopard (2009)

Stadler, Alexander

Julian Rodriguez: episode one, Trash crisis on
earth. Scholastic Press 2008 123p $15.99; pa $5.99
*

Grades: 2 3 4   **Fic**
  1. Extraterrestrial beings—Fiction 2. Science fiction
  ISBN 978-0-439-91966-1;   0-439-91966-5;
  978-0-439-91970-8 (pa); 0-439-91970-3 (pa)

"Julian Rodriguez is on a mission for the Mothership.
He's been sent to Earth to study human lifeforms and
their bizarre habits. . . . When Julian's Maternal Unit assigns a hideous task, it's nearly too much for the har-
dened space veteran to bear—but he finds his courage at
last." Publisher's note

"This hybrid of fiction and graphic novel dusts off a
favorite conceit with a slick swipe of edgy visuals and
tart commentary. . . . It's impossible to read this without
laughing." Publ Wkly

Another title in this series is:

Julian Rodgriguez: episode two, Invasion of the relatives
  (2009)

Stanley, Diane, 1943-

Bella at midnight; illustrated by Bagram
Ibatoulline. HarperCollins Pubs. 2006 278p il
$15.99; lib bdg $16.89; pa $6.99 *

Grades: 5 6 7 8   **Fic**
  1. Knights and knighthood—Fiction 2. Fairy tales
  ISBN 978-0-06-077573-5;   0-06-077573-4;
  978-0-06-077574-2 (lib bdg); 0-06-077574-2 (lib bdg);
  978-0-06-077575-9 (pa); 0-06-077575-0 (pa)
                                     LC 2005-05906

Raised by peasants, Bella discovers that she is actually
the daughter of a knight and finds herself caught up in
a terrible plot that will change her life and the kingdom
forever

"What raises this above other recreated fairy tales is
the quality of the writing, dotted with jeweled description
and anchored by the strong values—loyalty, truth, hon-
or." Booklist

Stanley, Diane, 1943-—*Continued*

The mysterious matter of I.M. Fine. HarperCollins Pubs. 2001 201p hardcover o.p. pa $5.99

Grades: 4 5 6 7   **Fic**
 1. Magic—Fiction 2. Books and reading—Fiction 3. Mystery fiction
 ISBN 0-688-17546-5; 0-380-73327-7 (pa)
                                    LC 00-54040
Noticing that a popular series of horror novels is having a bizarre effect on the behavior of its readers, Franny and Beamer set out to find the mysterious author
 "The solidly constructed mystery, well-rounded characters, and playful jab at wildly successful horror writers go down a treat." Horn Book Guide
 Another title about Franny and her friends is:
The mysterious case of the Allbright Academy (2008)

Roughing it on the Oregon Trail; illustrated by Holly Berry. HarperCollins Pubs. 2000 unp il (Time-traveling twins) hardcover o.p. pa $7.99 *
Grades: 2 3 4   **Fic**
 1. Oregon Trail—Fiction 2. Overland journeys to the Pacific—Fiction 3. Frontier and pioneer life—Fiction
 ISBN 0-06-027065-9; 0-06-449006-8 (pa)
                                    LC 98-41711
"Joanna Cotler Books"
Twins Liz and Lenny, along with their time-traveling grandmother, join a group of pioneers journeying west on the Oregon Trail in 1843
 "An engaging trip and a painless history lesson." SLJ
 Other titles in this series are:
Joining the Boston Tea Party (2001)
Thanksgiving on Plymouth Plantation (2004)

Saving Sky. Harper 2010 $15.99 *
Grades: 5 6 7 8   **Fic**
 1. Terrorism—Fiction 2. Prejudices—Fiction 3. Immigrants—Fiction 4. Family life—Fiction 5. Ranch life—Fiction 6. New Mexico—Fiction
 ISBN 978-0-06-123905-2; 0-06-123905-4
                                    LC 2010009393
In an America that has suffered continual terrorist attacks since 9/11, seventh-grader Sky stands up for what is right and helps a classmate of Middle Eastern descent, although doing so places her and her family at great risk.
 "Readers will have much to discuss after finishing this beautifully written, disturbing book." Booklist

Staples, Suzanne Fisher

The green dog; a mostly true story. Farrar, Straus & Giroux 2003 119p $16
Grades: 4 5 6   **Fic**
 1. Dogs—Fiction 2. Summer—Fiction
 ISBN 0-374-32779-3   LC 2002-26575
"Frances Foster books"
During the summer before fifth grade, Suzanne, a daydreaming loner who likes to fish and walk through the woods, acquires a canine companion. Based on the author's childhood in northeastern Pennsylvania
 The author's "writing is rich and descriptive, yet clear and simple." SLJ

Starke, Ruth, 1946-

Noodle pie. Kane Miller 2010 il $15.99
Grades: 4 5 6 7   **Fic**
 1. Vietnamese—Fiction 2. Vietnam—Fiction
 ISBN 978-1-935279-25-9; 1-935279-25-4
"Eleven-year-old Andy's first trip to Vietnam with his father, a 'Viet Kieu' (someone born in Vietnam who now lives overseas), exposes him to internalized prejudices about his heritage. . . . Andy distinguishes himself from his pushy relatives by emphasizing his Australian citizenship and criticizing customs that seem unfair. . . . This humorous, touching novel is a delicious cross-cultural treat, and includes an appendix of Vietnamese recipes." Publ Wkly

Stauffacher, Sue, 1961-

Donuthead. Knopf 2003 144p hardcover o.p. pa $5.99 *
Grades: 4 5 6   **Fic**
 1. Fear—Fiction 2. Friendship—Fiction
 ISBN 0-375-82468-5; 0-440-41934-4 (pa)
                                    LC 2003-40073
Franklin Delano Donuthead, a fifth-grader obsessed with hygiene and safety, finds an unlikely friend and protector in Sarah Kervick, the tough new student who lives in a dirty trailer, bonds with his mother, and is as "irregular" as he is
 "It's refreshing for a novel with problem situations to be so light and funny. An appealing story with some memorable characters and a lot of heart." SLJ
 Another title about Franklin is:
Donutheart (2006)

Gator on the loose! illustrated by Priscilla Lamont. Alfred A. Knopf 2010 149p il (Animal rescue team) $12.99; lib bdg $15.99
Grades: 4 5 6   **Fic**
 1. Alligators—Fiction 2. Family life—Fiction 3. Racially mixed people—Fiction
 ISBN 978-0-375-85847-5; 0-375-85847-4; 978-0-375-95847-2 (lib bdg); 0-375-95847-9 (lib bdg)
                                    LC 2009018340
Chaos ensues when Keisha's father brings an escaped alligator home to Carter's Urban Rescue, but it gets out of the bathroom while Grandma is guarding it.
 "Situational comedy, appealing spot art, and a personable protagonist will give this series broad appeal." Booklist
 Other titles about Keisha and the Carter family are:
Hide and seek (2010)
Show time (2011)
Special delivery (2010)

Harry Sue. Knopf 2005 288p hardcover o.p. lib bdg $17.99; pa $6.50 *
Grades: 5 6 7 8   **Fic**
 1. Prisoners—Fiction 2. Handicapped—Fiction 3. Mother-daughter relationship—Fiction
 ISBN 0-375-83274-2; 0-375-93274-7 (lib bdg); 0-440-42064-4 (pa)   LC 2004-16945
Although tough-talking Harry Sue would like to start a life of crime in order to be "sent up" and find her incarcerated mother, she must first protect the children at her neglectful grandmother's home day care center and

Stauffacher, Sue, 1961-—*Continued*

befriend a paralyzed boy.

"This is a riveting story, dramatically and well told, with characters whom readers won't soon forget." SLJ

Stead, Rebecca

First light. Wendy Lamb Books 2007 328p $15.99; lib bdg $18.99; pa $6.99

Grades: 5 6 7 8   **Fic**

1. Greenland—Fiction 2. Greenhouse effect—Fiction 3. Supernatural—Fiction

ISBN 978-0-375-84017-3; 0-375-84017-6; 987-0-375-094017-0 (lib bdg); 0-375-94017-0 (lib bdg); 978-0-440-42222-8 (pa); 0-440-42222-1 (pa)

LC 2006-39733

"The father of 12-year-old Peter is a glaciologist, his mother, a genetic scientist. Peter is thrilled when his father decides to take the family on his latest excursion to Greenland to study the effects of global warming. Fourteen-year-old Thea lives in a secret society called Gracehope under the Greenland ice. After finding a map that leads her to the surface, she becomes obsessed with seeing the sun and bringing her people back above ground. Peter and Thea accidentally meet on the surface and discover, through a secret kept by Peter's mother, that their destinies are unexpectedly joined." Booklist

This "novel is an exciting, engaging mix of science fiction, mystery, and adventure. . . . Peter and Thea are fully developed main characters." SLJ

When you reach me. Wendy Lamb Books 2009 199p $15.99; lib bdg $18.99 *

Grades: 5 6 7 8   **Fic**

1. Space and time—Fiction 2. New York (N.Y.)—Fiction

ISBN 978-0-385-73742-5; 0-385-73742-4; 978-0-385-90664-7 (lib bdg); 0-385-90664-1 (lib bdg)

LC 2008-24998

ALA ALSC Newbery Medal (2010)

As her mother prepares to be a contestant on the 1980s television game show, "The $20,000 Pyramid," a twelve-year-old New York City girl tries to make sense of a series of mysterious notes received from an anonymous source that seems to defy the laws of time and space.

"The '70s New York setting is an honest reverberation of the era; the mental gymnastics required of readers are invigorating; and the characters . . . are honest bits of humanity." Booklist

Steele, William Owen, 1917-

The perilous road; [by] William O. Steele; with an introduction by Jean Fritz. Harcourt 2004 c1958 156p $17; pa $5.95

Grades: 5 6 7 8   **Fic**

1. United States—History—1861-1865, Civil War—Fiction 2. Tennessee—Fiction

ISBN 0-15-205203-8; 0-15-205204-6 (pa)

A Newbery Medal honor book, 1959

"An Odyssey/Harcourt young classic"

A reissue of the title first published 1958

Fourteen-year-old Chris, bitterly hating the Yankees for invading his Tennessee mountain home, learns a difficult lesson about the waste of war and the meaning of tolerance and courage when he reports the approach of a Yankee supply troop to the Confederates, only to learn that his brother is probably part of that troop.

"Mr. Steele makes the tensions and excitements of the Brother's War very real, and customs of the mountain people, the speech and setting are well integrated into the narrative." NY Times Book Rev

Steer, Dugald

The dragon diary; [by] Dugald A. Steer; illustrated by Douglas Carrel. Candlewick Press 2009 248p il (Dragonology chronicles) $16.99

Grades: 5 6 7 8   **Fic**

1. Dragons—Fiction 2. Siblings—Fiction 3. Fantasy fiction

ISBN 978-0-7636-3425-4; 0-7636-3425-5

LC 2009005795

Apprentice dragonologists Daniel and Beatrice Cook's mentor is called away at a crucial time, leaving the brother and sister alone to search for an ancient diary that could cure some gravely ill dragons

"This fast-paced fantasy features sibling rivalry, multitudes of dragons, and mid-air heroics." Horn Book Guide

Steig, William, 1907-2003

Abel's island. Farrar, Straus & Giroux 1976 117p il $15; pa $5.99 *

Grades: 3 4 5   **Fic**

1. Mice—Fiction 2. Survival after airplane accidents, shipwrecks, etc.—Fiction

ISBN 0-374-30010-0; 0-312-37143-8 (pa)

A Newbery Medal honor book, 1977

Castaway on an uninhabited island, Abel, a very civilized mouse, finds his resourcefulness and endurance tested to the limit as he struggles to survive and return to his home.

"The line drawings washed with gray faithfully and delightfully record not only the rigors of Abel's experiences but the refinement of his domestic existence." Horn Book

Dominic; story and pictures by William Steig. Farrar, Straus & Giroux 1972 145p il pa $5.99 hardcover o.p.

Grades: 3 4 5   **Fic**

1. Dogs—Fiction

ISBN 0-312-37144-6 (pa)

Dominic, a gregarious dog, sets out on the high road one day, going no place in particular, but moving along to find whatever he can. And that turns out to be plenty, including an invalid pig who leaves Dominic his fortune; a variety of friends and adventures; and even—in the end—his life's companion

"A singular blend of naiveté and sophistication, comic commentary and philosophizing, the narrative handles situation clichés with humor and flair—perhaps because of the author's felicitous turn of phrase, his verbal cartooning, and his integration of text and illustrations. A chivalrous and optimistic tribute to gallantry and romance." Horn Book

Steig, William, 1907-2003—*Continued*

The real thief; story and pictures by William Steig. Farrar, Straus & Giroux 1973 58p il pa $5.99 hardcover o.p. *

Grades: 3 4 5   **Fic**
1. Animals—Fiction 2. Thieves—Fiction
ISBN 0-312-37145-4 (pa)

"Proud of his job as guard to the Royal Treasury, loyal to his king (Basil the bear) Gawain the goose is baffled by the repeated theft of gold and jewels from the massive building to which only Gawain and Basil have keys. He is heartsick when the king dismisses him publicly and calls him a disgrace to the kingdom. Sentenced to prison, the goose flies off to isolation. The true thief, a mouse, is penitent and decides that he will go on stealing so that the king will know Gawain is innocent." Bull Cent Child Books

"Steig's gray line-and-wash drawings provide a charming accompaniment to a wholly winning story." SLJ

Steinhöfel, Andreas

An elk dropped in; [by] Andreas Steinhofel; pictures by Kerstin Meyer; translated by Alissa Jaffa. Front Street 2006 78p il $16.95

Grades: 2 3 4   **Fic**
1. Elk—Fiction 2. Santa Claus—Fiction 3. Christmas—Fiction
ISBN 1-932425-80-2; 978-1-932425-80-2
                                      LC 2006-00804

While on a pre-Christmas trial run for the famous man in red, an elk named Mr. Moose crashes through the roof of a house and, while recuperating from a sprain, regales Billy Wagner and his family with stories.

"Winsome watercolor illustrations, droll details, and a young narrator who relates both wild and everyday details in the same matter-of-fact tone combine to create a charming, if offbeat, Christmas fantasy." SLJ

Stellings, Caroline, 1961-

The contest. Seventh Generation 2009 123p pa $9.95

Grades: 4 5 6 7   **Fic**
1. Contests—Fiction 2. Friendship—Fiction 3. Books and reading—Fiction 4. Poverty—Fiction 5. Racially mixed people—Fiction 6. Canada—Fiction
ISBN 978-0-9779183-5-5 (pa); 0-9779183-5-1 (pa)
                                      LC 2009-20294

"A Gutsy girl book"

Rosy, a poor, eleven-year-old, half-Mohawk girl from Hamilton, Ontario, Canada enters an Anne of Green Gables look-alike contest in hopes of winning a set of Anne books, and gains a new friend and deeper understanding of Anne's character

"Readers will enjoy Rosy and her spunky attitude. . . . Some readers will finish this book and go seeking the Anne series to read, and those already familiar with the Anne books will enjoy the connection." Libr Media Connect

Stevenson, Robert Louis, 1850-1894

Treasure Island; illustrated by John Lawrence. Candlewick Press 2009 269p il $24.99

Grades: 5 6 7 8 9 10 11 12 Adult   **Fic**
1. Buried treasure—Fiction 2. Pirates—Fiction 3. Adventure fiction
ISBN 978-0-7636-4445-1; 0-7636-4445-5
                                      LC 2009007338

First published in 1883

While going through the possessions of a deceased guest who owed them money, the mistress of the inn and her son find a treasure map that leads them to a notorious pirate's fortune

"Lawrence evokes the essence of classic adventure stories with his vinyl-cut illustrations, as thick black shapes are tempered by muted tones of blue, gold and green. . . . Readers will feel they've discovered a true relic with this edition." Publ Wkly

Treasure Island; illustrated by N.C. Wyeth. Scribner 1981 273p il hardcover o.p. pa $6.99

Grades: 7 8 9 10 11 12 Adult   **Fic**
1. Buried treasure—Fiction 2. Pirates—Fiction
ISBN 0-684-17160-0; 0-689-83212-5 (pa)
                                      LC 81-8788

First published 1882

Young Jim Hawkins discovers a treasure map in the chest of an old sailor who dies under mysterious circumstances at his mother's inn. He shows it to Dr. Livesey and Squire Trelawney who agree to outfit a ship and sail to Treasure Island. Among the crew is the pirate Long John Silver and his followers who are in pursuit of the treasure

Stewart, Paul, 1955-

Beyond the Deepwoods; [by] Paul Stewart, Chris Riddell. David Fickling Bks. 2004 c1998 276p il (Edge chronicles) $12.95; lib bdg $14.99; pa $6.99 *

Grades: 4 5 6   **Fic**
1. Fantasy fiction
ISBN 0-385-75068-4; 0-385-75069-2 (lib bdg); 0-440-42087-3 (pa)

First published 1998 in the United Kingdom

Thirteen-year-old Twig, having always looked and felt different from his woodtroll family, learns that he is adopted and travels out of his Deepwoods home to find the place where he belongs

"Those with hearty appetites for adventure (and strong stomachs) will find this a tremendously exciting fantasy. Riddell's wonderfully detailed ink drawings, on nearly every page, create a strong sense of the believable, well-imagined otherworld and bring its strange creatures to life." Booklist

Other titles in The Edge Chronicles series are:
Clash of the sky galleons (2007)
The curse of the Gloamglozer (2005)
Freeglader (2006)
The last of the sky pirates (2005)
Midnight over Sanctaphrax (2004)
Stormchaser (2004)
VOX (2005)
The winter knights (2007)

Stewart, Paul, 1955-—*Continued*

The curse of the night wolf; [by] Paul Stewart and Chris Riddell; illustrated by Chris Riddell. David Fickling Books 2008 204p il (Barnaby Grimes) $15.99; lib bdg $18.99

Grades: 4 5 6 7   Fic

1. Physicians—Fiction 2. Werewolves—Fiction 3. London (England)—Fiction 4. Great Britain—History—19th century—Fiction 5. Mystery fiction

ISBN 978-0-385-75125-4; 0-385-75125-7; 978-0-385-75126-1 (lib bdg); 0-385-75126-5 (lib bdg)

LC 2008-01697

Soon after Victorian messenger Barnaby Grimes is attacked by a huge beast while crossing London's rooftops, he becomes entangled in a mystery involving patent medicine, impoverished patients, and very expensive furs.

"Moody, highly detailed pen-and-ink drawings provide ornamentation throughout, lending a classic Victorian feel to help punctuate the drama. . . . Possessing an easy confidence and quick wit . . . Barnaby is an appealing character." Booklist

Other titles in this series are:
Return of the emerald skull (2009)
Legion of the Dead (2010)

Fergus Crane; [by] Paul Stewart & Chris Riddell. David Fickling Books 2006 214p (Far-flung adventures) $14.95 *

Grades: 3 4 5   Fic

1. Adventure fiction

ISBN 0-385-75088-9   LC 2005018478

Nine-year-old Fergus Crane's life is filled with classes on the school ship Betty Jeanne, interesting neighbors, and helping with his mother's work until a mysterious box flies into his window and leads him toward adventure

"With a simple plot, a few hints of mystery, and many intriguing details, this story will quickly hook readers. Riddell's expressive ink drawings make the fantastic elements more believable and add enormously to the book's appeal." Booklist

Other titles in this series are:
Corby Flood (2006)
Hugo Pepper (2007)

Stewart, Trenton Lee, 1970-

The mysterious Benedict Society; illustrated by Carson Ellis. Little, Brown 2007 485p il $16.99; pa $6.99 *

Grades: 5 6 7 8   Fic

1. Adventure fiction 2. Science fiction

ISBN 978-0-316-05777-6; 0-316-05777-0; 978-0-316-00395-7 (pa); 0-316-00395-6 (pa)

LC 2006-09925

After passing a series of mind-bending tests, four children are selected for a secret mission that requires them to go undercover at the Learning Institute for the Very Enlightened, where the only rule is that there are no rules

"Stewart's unusual characters, threatening villains, and dramatic plot twists will grab and hold readers' attention." SLJ

Other titles about the Benedict Society are:

The mysterious Benedict Society and the perilous journey (2008)
The mysterious Benedict Society and the prisoner's dilemma (2009)

Stier, Catherine

The terrible secrets of the Tell-All Club. Albert Whitman & Co. 2009 125p $14.99

Grades: 4 5 6   Fic

1. Friendship—Fiction 2. Clubs—Fiction 3. School stories

ISBN 978-0-8075-7798-1; 0-8075-7798-7

LC 2008055704

When four fifth-grade friends complete a "tell-all" survey, tensions arise and come to a head during an overnight class trip

"Told in the four voices of the club members, the story shows the characters' insecurities and the family issues they face. Reluctant readers will find it fast paced, easy to follow, and populated with likable personalities." SLJ

Stockton, Frank, 1834-1902

The bee-man of Orn; [by] Frank R. Stockton; illustrated by P.J. Lynch. Candlewick Press 2003 unp il $17.99

Grades: 2 3 4   Fic

1. Fairy tales

ISBN 0-7636-2239-7   LC 2003-48454

Story first published in St. Nicholas magazine 1883

When a Sorcerer tells him that he has been transformed from another sort of being, the Beeman sets out to discover what he was in his earlier incarnation. Story is accompanied by a DVD which provides a behind-the-scenes look at the illustrator at work.

"Lynch's spirited artwork, richly detailed and darkly atmospheric, provides a series of imaginative settings and creates a romantic and broadly appealing vision of this original fairy tale. . . . This edition is a read-aloud treasure for good listeners." Booklist

Stone, Phoebe, 1947-

Deep down popular; a novel; by Phoebe Stone. Arthur A. Levine Books 2008 280p $16.99; pa $4.99

Grades: 4 5 6 7   Fic

1. Friendship—Fiction 2. School stories 3. Country life—Fiction 4. Family life—Fiction 5. Virginia—Fiction

ISBN 978-0-439-80245-1; 0-439-80245-8; 978-0-439-80244-4 (pa); 0-439-80244-X (pa)

LC 2007017198

In a small Virginia town, sixth-grader Jessie Lou Ferguson has a crush on the hugely popular Conrad Parker Smith, and when he suddenly develops a medical problem and the teacher asks Jessie Lou to help him, they become friends, to her surprise

"Jessie Lou tells her tale with the strong, rough-edged purity of a young poet, which she is; equally strong are the story's underpinnings, longing and laughter, and a willingness to believe in something despite the facts." Booklist

Stout, Shawn K.

Fiona Finkelstein, big-time ballerina! illustrated by Angela Martini. Aladdin 2009 166p il $14.99

Grades: 2 3 4 **Fic**

1. Worry—Fiction 2. Family life—Fiction 3. Ballet—Fiction 4. Weather forecasting—Fiction 5. Maryland—Fiction

ISBN 978-1-4169-7927-2; 1-4169-7927-1

LC 2009022593

Nine-year-old Marylander Fiona Finkelstein tries to deal with stage-fright, missing her mother who is an actress in California, and hoping that her father, a television meteorologist, does not get in trouble when she antagonizes the anchorman.

"This novel is light and fun, with just enough wit and sass to keep young readers entertained. . . . The story maintains a fast pace throughout, and the illustrations give Fiona and company a sweet look that is simple and charming." SLJ

Strickland, Brad

The sign of the sinister sorcerer; [by] Brad Strickland. Dial Books for Young Readers 2008 168p $16.99

Grades: 4 5 6 7 **Fic**

1. Magic—Fiction 2. Supernatural—Fiction 3. Uncles—Fiction 4. Witches—Fiction 5. Orphans—Fiction 6. Michigan—Fiction 7. Mystery fiction

ISBN 978-0-8037-3151-6; 0-8037-3151-5

LC 2008007698

Continues John Bellairs' series about Lewis Barnavelt

Based on the characters of John Bellairs

In Michigan in the mid-1950s, Lewis Barnavelt is convinced that the series of accidents he and his uncle are experiencing are the result of a curse by a mysterious, hooded figure that may be part of his uncle's past.

"For readers who enjoy trying to solve the mystery as they read, there are abundant clues including an anagram. A quick, exciting read." SLJ

Other titles about Lewis Barnavelt by Brad Strickland are:

The beast under the wizard's bridge (2000)

The house where nobody lived (2006)

The spector from the magician's museum (1998)

The tower at the end of the world (2001)

The whistle, the grave, and the ghost (2003)

Stringer, Helen

Spellbinder. Feiwel and Friends 2009 372p $17.99 *

Grades: 5 6 7 8 **Fic**

1. Ghost stories 2. Dead—Fiction 3. Great Britain—Fiction

ISBN 978-0-312-38763-1; 0-312-38763-6

LC 2008-28552

Twelve-year-old Belladonna Johnson, who lives with the ghosts of her parents in the north of England, teams up with an always-in-trouble classmate to investigate why all of the ghosts in the world have suddenly disappeared.

"Magical creatures, amulets, and verses are all a part of this delightful tale. . . . Stringer maintains the humor and logic of preteens who are awkwardly coming into their magical destinies." SLJ

Stuchner, Joan Betty

Honey cake; illustrated by Cynthia Nugent. Random House 2008 c2007 101p il $11.99; lib bdg $14.99; pa $4.99

Grades: 3 4 5 **Fic**

1. Holocaust, 1933-1945—Fiction 2. Denmark—Fiction 3. Jews—Fiction

ISBN 978-0-375-85189-6; 0-375-85189-5; 978-0-375-95189-3 (lib bdg); 0-375-95189-X (lib bdg); 978-0-375-85190-2 (pa); 0-375-85190-9 (pa)

LC 2007-11501

"A Stepping Stone book"

First published 2007 in the United Kingdom and Canada

David and his family live in Denmark during the Nazi occupation, until September 1943 when their neighbors help smuggle them to Sweden to escape Hitler's orders to send the Danish Jews to concentration camps. Includes a recipe for honey cake, typically made to celebrate the Jewish New Year.

"The simply told story and black-and-white illustrations convey tension, fear, and hope." Horn Book Guide

Swinburne, Stephen R.

Wiff and Dirty George: the Z.E.B.R.A. Incident. Boyds Mills Press 2010 167p il $17.95

Grades: 4 5 6 7 **Fic**

1. Great Britain—Fiction

ISBN 978-1-59078-755-7; 1-59078-755-2

"London in 1969 was a trippy place, no doubt, but it's made even more psychodelic with the adventures of Wiff and Dirty George, two twelve-year-olds who follow their noses into a world of trouble. While on a morning train, the boys are slightly horrified when everyone's pants fall down, but instead of worrying overmuch about their own embarrassment, they take off after the large white rabbit who seems to be the instigator of the mass humiliation. . . . The humor is more situational than verbal; the characters are all comedic straight men in a twisted, absurd world. . . . Delightfully daft 'clues' precede each chapter, and a glossary of Britishisms will help young Yanks navigate the dialect." Bull Cent Child Books

Tacang, Brian

Bully-be-gone; [by] Brian Tacang. HarperCollins 2006 216p (Misadventures of Millicent Madding) $15.99

Grades: 3 4 5 6 **Fic**

1. Bullies—Fiction 2. Inventions—Fiction 3. Friendship—Fiction

ISBN 0-06-073911-8 LC 2005-07777

Budding-inventor Millicent Madding launches her latest invention to disastrous results, and she has only days to create an antidote before the local bullies wreak havoc and her dearest friendships are destroyed forever

"The book has zippy dialogue and brilliant use of alliteration. . . . The eccentric characters are fun, and the silly but substantive plot will surely appeal to children." SLJ

Tarshis, Lauren

Emma-Jean Lazarus fell out of a tree. Dial
Books for Young Readers 2007 199p $16.99 *

Grades: 5 6 7   **Fic**
1. Friendship—Fiction 2. School stories
ISBN 978-0-8037-3164-6; 0-8037-3164-7
LC 2006-18428

A quirky and utterly logical seventh-grade girl named
Emma-Jean Lazarus discovers some interesting results
when she gets involved in the messy everyday problems
of her peers.

"Readers will be fascinated by Emma-Jean's emotion-
less observations and her adult-level vocabulary. Tarshis
pulls off a balancing act, showing the child's detachment
yet making her a sympathetic character. Exceptionally
fleshed-out secondary characters add warmth to the story." SLJ

Followed by: Emma-Jean Lazarus fell in love (2009)

Tate, Eleanora E., 1948-

Celeste's Harlem Renaissance. Little, Brown
2007 279p $15.99; pa $5.99

Grades: 4 5 6 7   **Fic**
1. Aunts—Fiction 2. Harlem Renaissance—Fiction
3. African Americans—Fiction 4. Harlem (New York,
N.Y.)—Fiction
ISBN 978-0-316-52394-3; 978-0-316-11362-5 (pa)

In 1921, thirteen-year-old Celeste leaves North Carolina to stay with her glamorous Aunt Valentina in Harlem,
New York, where she discovers the vibrant Harlem Renaissance in full swing, even though her aunt's life is not
exactly what she was led to believe.

"Both sobering and inspiring, Tate's novel is a moving portrait of growing up black and female in 1920s
America." Booklist

Tate, Lindsey

Kate Larkin, bone expert; [by] Lindsey Tate;
illustrated by Diane Palmisciano. Henry Holt 2008
72p il $16.95

Grades: 1 2 3 4   **Fic**
1. Bones—Fiction 2. Family life—Fiction
ISBN 978-0-8050-7901-2; 0-8050-7901-7
LC 2007027588

When Kate breaks her arm, she learns all about bones,
from how x-rays work to how bones heal, and by the
time she gets her cast removed at the end of the summer,
she is an expert. Includes related activities and glossary

"The format is appealing: large type, short chapters,
and black-and-white illustrations generously dispersed
throughout. . . . This is a solid choice for newly independent readers or for science-minded children looking
for some fiction." SLJ

Taylor, Mildred D.

The friendship; pictures by Max Ginsburg. Dial
Bks. for Young Readers 1987 53p il $15.99; pa
$4.99 *

Grades: 4 5 6 7   **Fic**
1. African Americans—Fiction 2. Race relations—Fiction 3. Mississippi—Fiction
ISBN 0-8037-0417-8; 0-14-038964-4 (pa)
LC 86-29309

Coretta Scott King Award for text

This "story about race relations in rural Mississippi
during the Depression focuses on an incident between an
old Black man, Mr. Tom Bee, and a white storekeeper,
Mr. John Wallace. Indebted to Tom for saving his life as
a young man, John had promised they would always be
friends. But now, years later, John insists that Tom call
him 'Mister' and shoots the old man for defiantly—and
publicly—calling him by his first name. Narrator Cassie
Logan and her brothers . . . are verbally abused by Wallace's villainous sons before witnessing the encounter."
Bull Cent Child Books

The gold Cadillac; pictures by Michael Hays.
Dial Bks. for Young Readers 1987 43p il $16.99;
pa $4.99 *

Grades: 4 5 6 7   **Fic**
1. African Americans—Fiction 2. Prejudices—Fiction
3. Race relations—Fiction
ISBN 0-8037-0342-2; 0-14-038963-6 (pa)
LC 86-11526

"The shiny gold Cadillac that Daddy brings home one
summer evening marks a stepping stone in the lives of
Wilma and [Lois,] two black sisters growing up in Ohio
during the fifties. At first neighbors and relatives shower
them with attention. But when the family begins the long
journey to the South to show off the car to their Mississippi relatives, the girls, for the first time, encounter the
undisguised ugliness of racial prejudice." Horn Book

"Full-page sepia paintings effectively portray the characters, setting, and mood of the story events as Hays
ably demonstrates his understanding of the social and
emotional environments which existed for blacks during
this period." SLJ

Let the circle be unbroken. Dial Bks. for Young
Readers 1981 394p $17.99; pa $7.99 *

Grades: 4 5 6 7   **Fic**
1. African Americans—Fiction 2. Mississippi—Fiction
3. Great Depression, 1929-1939—Fiction
ISBN 0-8037-4748-9; 0-14-034892-1 (pa)
LC 81-65854

Sequel to Roll of thunder, hear my cry

This novel featuring the Logans covers "a series of
tangential events so that it is a family record, a picture
of the depression years in rural Mississippi, and an indictment of black-white relations in the Deep South. A
young friend is convicted of a murder of which he is innocent, a pretty cousin is insulted by some white boys
and her father taunted because he married a white woman, an elderly neighbor tries to vote, the government
pays farmers to plow their crops under, etc." Bull Cent
Child Books

The author "provides her readers with a literal sense
of witnessing important American history. . . . Moreover, [she] never neglects the details of her volatile 9-
year-old heroine's interior life. The daydreams, the jealousy, the incredible ardor of that age come alive." N Y
Times Book Rev

Mississippi bridge; by Mildred Taylor; pictures
by Max Ginsburg. Dial Bks. for Young Readers
1990 62p il pa $4.99 hardcover o.p. *

Grades: 4 5 6 7   **Fic**
1. Race relations—Fiction 2. African Americans—Fiction 3. Prejudices—Fiction 4. Mississippi—Fiction
ISBN 0-14-130817-6 (pa)   LC 89-27898

Taylor, Mildred D.—*Continued*

In this story featuring the children of Mississippi's Logan family, "Jeremy Simms, a 10-year-old white neighbor, describes a harrowing incident after the Logans and other blacks are ordered off the weekly bus in a foggy rainstorm." N Y Times Book Rev

"Taylor has shaped this episode into a haunting meditation that will leave readers vividly informed about segregation practices and the unequal rights that prevailed in that era. . . . The incident and its context constitute a telling piece of social history." Booklist

The road to Memphis; by Mildred Taylor. Dial Bks. 1989 290p $18.99; pa $6.99 *

Grades: 4 5 6 7   **Fic**
  1. Race relations—Fiction 2. African Americans—Fiction 3. Mississippi—Fiction
  ISBN 0-8037-0340-6; 0-14-036077-8 (pa)
           LC 88-33654

Coretta Scott King Award for text

Sadistically teased by two white boys in 1940's rural Mississippi, Cassie Logan's friend, Moe, severely injures one of the boys with a tire iron and enlists Cassie's help in trying to flee the state

"Taylor's continued smooth, easy language provides readability for all ages, with a focus on universal human pride, worthy values, and individual responsibility. This action-packed drama is highly recommended." Voice Youth Advocates

Roll of thunder, hear my cry. 25th anniversary ed. Phyllis Fogelman Books 2001 276p $17.99; pa $7.99 *

Grades: 4 5 6 7 8 9   **Fic**
  1. African Americans—Fiction 2. Mississippi—Fiction
  ISBN 0-8037-2647-3; 0-14-240112-9 (pa)
           LC 00-39378

Also available in paperback from Puffin Bks.

Awarded the Newbery Medal, 1977

First published 1976 by Dial Press

"The time is 1933. The place is Spokane, Mississippi where the Logans, the only black family who own their own land, wage a courageous struggle to remain independent, displeasing a white plantation owner bent on taking their land. But this suspenseful tale is also about the story's young narrator, Cassie, and her three brothers who decide to wage their own personal battles to maintain the self-dignity and pride with which they were raised. . . . Ms. Taylor's richly textured novel shows a strong, proud black family . . . resisting rather than succumbing to oppression." Child Book Rev Serv

Song of the trees; pictures by Jerry Pinkney. Dial Bks. for Young Readers 1975 48p il hardcover o.p. pa $5.99

Grades: 4 5 6 7   **Fic**
  1. African Americans—Fiction 2. Great Depression, 1929-1939—Fiction 3. Mississippi—Fiction
  ISBN 0-8037-5452-3; 0-14-250075-5 (pa)

Eight-year-old Cassie Logan tells how her family "leaving Mississippi during the Depression was cheated into selling for practically nothing valuable and beautiful giant old pines and hickories, beeches and walnuts in the forest surrounding their house." Adventuring with Books

The well; David's story. Dial Bks. for Young Readers 1995 92p hardcover o.p. pa $5.99 *

Grades: 4 5 6 7   **Fic**
  1. African Americans—Fiction 2. Race relations—Fiction 3. Mississippi—Fiction
  ISBN 0-8037-1802-0; 0-14-038642-4 (pa)
           LC 94-25360

"David Logan (Cassie's father) tells this story from his childhood. . . . There's a drought, and the Logans possess the only well in the area that has not gone dry. Black and white alike come for water freely given by the family, but the Simms boys can't seem to stand the necessary charity, and their resentment explodes when David's big brother Hammer beats Charlie Simms after Charlie hits David." Bull Cent Child Books

This story "delivers an emotional wallop in a concentrated span of time and action. . . . This story reverberates in the heart long after the final paragraph is read." Horn Book

Taylor, Sydney, 1904-1978

All-of-a-kind family; illustrations by Helen John. Delacorte Press 2005 c1951 188p il hardcover o.p. pa $5.99 *

Grades: 4 5 6   **Fic**
  1. Jews—Fiction 2. New York (N.Y.)—Fiction
  ISBN 0-385-73295-3; 0-440-40059-7 (pa)
  First published 1951 by Follett

"Five little Jewish girls grow up in New York's lower east side in a happy home atmosphere before the first World War." Carnegie Libr of Pittsburgh

"A genuine and delightful picture of a Jewish family . . . with an understanding mother and father, rich in kindness and fun though poor in money. The important part the public library played in the lives of these children is happily evident; and the Jewish holiday celebrations are particularly well described." Horn Book

  Other titles about this family are:
All-of-a-kind family downtown (1957)
All-of-a-kind family uptown (1957)
Ella of all-of-a-kind family (1978)
More all-of-a-kind family (1954)

Taylor, Theodore, 1921-2006

The cay. Delacorte Press 1987 c1969 137p $16.95; pa $5.50 *

Grades: 5 6 7 8   **Fic**
  1. Race relations—Fiction 2. Caribbean region—Fiction 3. Survival after airplane accidents, shipwrecks, etc.—Fiction 4. Blind—Fiction
  ISBN 0-385-07906-0; 0-440-22912-X (pa)
  A reissue of the title first published 1969

When the freighter on which they are traveling is torpedoed by a German submarine during World War II, Phillip, an adolescent white boy blinded by a blow on the head, and Timothy, an old black man, are stranded on a tiny Caribbean island where the boy acquires a new kind of vision, courage, and love from his old companion

"Starkly dramatic, believable and compelling." Saturday Rev

Followed by Timothy of the cay

Taylor, Theodore, 1921-2006—*Continued*
  Ice drift; [by] Theodore Taylor. Harcourt 2005
224p $16; pa $5.95
  Grades: 4 5 6 7   **Fic**
    1. Inuit—Fiction 2. Brothers—Fiction 3. Arctic re-
  gions—Fiction
    ISBN 0-15-205081-7; 0-15-205550-9 (pa)
                              LC 2003-27783
  Two Inuit brothers must fend for themselves while
stranded on an ice floe that is adrift in the Greenland
Strait.
  This is "a masterful and detailed look into a culture
unfamiliar to most Americans, a gripping adventure, and
a moving depiction of brotherly love." SLJ

  Teetoncey. Harcourt 2004 c1974 208p hardcover
o.p. pa $5.95 *
  Grades: 5 6 7 8   **Fic**
    1. Amnesia—Fiction 2. North Carolina—Fiction
    ISBN 0-15-205298-4; 0-15-205294-1 (pa)
                              LC 2003-67745
  "An Odyssey/Harcourt young classic"
  A reissue of the title first published 1974 by
Doubleday
  In this first novel of the Cape Hatteras trilogy, eleven-
year-old Ben rescues an English girl from a shipwreck
off the Outer Banks of North Carolina; and, though she
becomes part of his family, she never speaks.
  "The novel is rich with details of of local geography,
history, and folklore." Horn Book
  Other titles in the Cape Hatteras trilogy are:
The odyssey of Ben O'Neal (2004 c1977)
Teetoncey and Ben O'Neal (2004 c1975)

  Timothy of the cay. Harcourt Brace & Co. 1993
161p hardcover o.p. pa $5.95
  Grades: 5 6 7 8   **Fic**
    1. Race relations—Fiction 2. Caribbean region—Fic-
  tion 3. Survival after airplane accidents, shipwrecks,
  etc.—Fiction 4. Blind—Fiction
    ISBN 0-15-288358-4; 0-15-206320-X (pa)
                              LC 93-7898
  Sequel to The cay
  Having survived being blinded and shipwrecked on a
tiny Caribbean island with the old black man Timothy,
twelve-year-old white Phillip is rescued and hopes to regain his sight with an operation. Alternate chapters follow the life of Timothy from his days as a young cabin
boy
  "Somewhat more thoughtful than its well-loved ante-
cedent, this boldly drawn novel is no less commanding."
Publ Wkly

  The trouble with Tuck. Doubleday 1981 110p
hardcover o.p. pa $4.50
  Grades: 5 6 7 8   **Fic**
    1. Dogs—Fiction 2. Blind—Fiction
    ISBN 0-385-17774-7; 0-440-41696-5 (pa)
                              LC 81-43139
  Helen trains her blind dog Tuck to follow and trust a
seeing-eye companion dog
  This is "a touching dog story, written with good flow,
pace, and structure." Bull Cent Child Books
  Another title about Helen and Tuck is:
Tuck triumphant (1991)

Teague, Mark, 1963-
  The doom machine; a novel. Blue Sky Press
2009 376p $17.99 *
  Grades: 4 5 6 7   **Fic**
    1. Extraterrestrial beings—Fiction 2. Space and time—
  Fiction 3. Science fiction
    ISBN 978-0-545-15142-9; 0-545-15142-2
                              LC 2009-14262
  When a spaceship lands in the small town of Vern
Hollow in 1956, juvenile delinquent Jack Creedle and
prim, studious Isadora Shumway form an unexpected alliance as they try to keep a group of extraterrestrials
from stealing eccentric Uncle Bud's space travel machine.
  "This book is filled with humor and dramatic figurative language that makes the setting completely approachable. It is a great fit for science fiction, humor,
and adventure genre fans." Voice Youth Advocates

Tellegen, Toon, 1941-
  Letters to anyone and everyone; translated from
the Dutch by Martin Cleaver; illustrated by Jessica
Ahlberg. Boxer Books; distributed by Sterling
2010 il lib bdg $12.95
  Grades: 2 3 4 5   **Fic**
    1. Animals—Fiction 2. Letters—Fiction
    ISBN 978-1-906250-95-9; 1-906250-95-2
  "In this novel, snails, elephants, bears, and ants write
letters to one another, to the Sun, and to other letter writers. . . . Every brief missive is written in a distinct
voice, and the complete collection reveals Tellegen's
richly imagined world in which the creatures reside. The
book was originally published in Holland, and Cleaver's
smooth English translation retains humor and charm."
SLJ

Teplin, Scott, 1973-
  The clock without a face; a Gus Twintig
mystery; [by Scott Teplin, Mac Barnett & Eli
Horowitz; plus faces by Adam Rex & numbers by
Anna Sheffield] McSweeney's 2010 unp il $19.95
  Grades: 4 5 6 7   **Fic**
    1. Theft—Fiction 2. Clocks and watches—Fiction
  3. Apartment houses—Fiction 4. Picture puzzles
  5. Mystery fiction
    ISBN 978-1-934781-71-5; 1-934781-71-1
  Narrator Gus Twintig and Roy Dodge "are summoned
to a 13-story apartment building to investigate a string of
robberies: the emerald-encrusted numbers have been
stolen from a clock belonging to owner Bevel Ternky,
and his 12 tenants have also been burgled. . . . The right
side of each spread is an overhead cutaway view of each
apartment, ostensibly drawn by Twintig. Given the potential of discovering clues to where the actual bejeweled
numbers . . . have been hidden, kids should be plenty
motivated to pore over each scene." Publ Wkly

Testa, Maria
  Almost forever. Candlewick Press 2003 69p
$14.99; pa $5.99
  Grades: 3 4 5   **Fic**
    1. Vietnam War, 1961-1975—Fiction
    ISBN 0-7636-1996-5; 0-7636-3366-6 (pa)
                              LC 2002-34757

Testa, Maria—*Continued*

In free verse, a young girl describes what she, her brother, and their mother do during the year that her doctor father is serving in the Army in Vietnam

This is "sensitive and moving. . . . Testa's poems give her young speaker a believable, sympathetic voice." Publ Wkly

Thomas, Jane Resh, 1936-

Blind mountain. Clarion Books 2006 117p $15

Grades: 4 5 6   **Fic**

1. Wilderness survival—Fiction 2. Father-son relationship—Fiction 3. Mountaineering—Fiction 4. Montana—Fiction

ISBN 978-0-618-64872-6; 0-618-64872-0

LC 2005-34512

Unsure of himself and annoyed at having to spend a day climbing a Montana mountain with his bossy father, twelve-year-old Sam must become the guide on their perilous journey down when his carelessness temporarily blinds his father

"Thomas' wilderness knowledge comes through vividly here, particularly in the survival details, and the subplot involving the cougar will have great appeal." Booklist

Thomason, Mark

Moonrunner. Kane/Miller 2009 c2008 217p $15.95

Grades: 4 5 6 7   **Fic**

1. Australia—Fiction 2. Horses—Fiction

ISBN 978-1-935279-03-7; 1-935279-03-3

First published 2008 in Australia

"In the 1890s, Casey and his parents immigrate to Australia, to a homestead that they inherited from his grandfather. The 12-year-old finds the change difficult. He is bullied at school, and he misses his baseball team in Montana and his horse. Then he happens upon a magnificent wild stallion, and he is determined to befriend the brumby, whom he names Moonrunner. . . . This well-paced story effectively portrays the family's struggles. Casey is a strong, engaging protagonist whose interactions with the other characters are believable and interesting." SLJ

Thompson, Colin

Good neighbors; by Colin Thompson; illustrated by Crab Scrambly. HarperCollinsPublishers 2008 214p il (The Floods) lib bdg $16.89; pa $5.99

Grades: 3 4 5 6   **Fic**

1. Witches—Fiction 2. Magic—Fiction

ISBN 978-0-06-113199-8 (lib bdg); 0-06-113196-2 (lib bdg); 978-0-06-113197-4 (pa); 0-06-113197-0 (pa)

A family of wizards and witches living in an ordinary neighborhood in an ordinary town decides that they have had enough of the noisy family living next-door and makes them disappear.

The author "careens wildly from one extreme scenario to the next, letting the Floods get away with everything—despite their appearances, they're the good guys. Kids can enjoy the prankishness; adults can rest easy given the conventional underpinnings." Publ Wkly

Another title in this series is:

School plot (2008)

Thompson, Kate

Highway robbery; illustrated by Jonny Duddle and Robert Dress. Greenwillow Books 2009 118p il $15.99

Grades: 3 4 5 6   **Fic**

1. Turpin, Richard, 1706-1739—Fiction 2. Adventure fiction 3. Horses—Fiction 4. Thieves—Fiction 5. Great Britain—History—1714-1837—Fiction

ISBN 978-0-06-173034-4; 0-06-173034-3

LC 2008-27720

On a cold day in eighteenth-century England, a poor young boy agrees to watch a stranger's fine horse for a golden guinea but soon finds himself in a difficult situation when the king's guard appears and wants to use him as bait in their pursuit of a notorious highwayman

"It's a suspenseful and tautly written story as is, and Thompson's sly twist makes it all the richer." Publ Wkly

Thomson, Melissa

Keena Ford and the second-grade mixup; pictures by Frank Morrison. Dial Books for Young Readers 2008 102p il $14.99

Grades: 1 2 3   **Fic**

1. School stories 2. African Americans—Fiction 3. Diaries—Fiction

ISBN 978-0-8037-3263-6; 0-8037-3263-5

LC 2007-43749

Keena Ford chronicles her many mishaps as she begins second grade.

"Thomson, a former teacher, skillfully zeroes in on an eight-year-old s anxieties and creates a vivid sense of Keena s world, both at school and at home. . . . Morrison's full-page pencil sketches extend both the comedy and the emotions, particularly Keena's sense that she is accepted and loved, even as she clears up mistakes with family and friends." Booklist

Another title about Keena Ford is:

Keena Ford and the field trip mix-up (2009)

Thomson, Sarah L.

Dragon's egg; by Sarah L. Thomson. Greenwillow Books 2007 267p $16.99; lib bdg $17.89

Grades: 3 4 5 6   **Fic**

1. Dragons—Fiction 2. Fantasy fiction

ISBN 978-0-06-128848-7; 978-0-06-128847-0 (lib bdg)

LC 2007009145

Mella, a young girl trained as a dragon keeper, learns that the legends of old are true when she is entrusted with carrying a dragon's egg to the fabled Hatching Grounds, a dangerous journey on which she is assisted by a knight's squire

This is a "lively adventure. . . . Thomson's richly descriptive writing creates a fantasy world readers will want to revisit." Booklist

Thor, Annika, 1950-

A faraway island; translated from the Swedish by Linda Schenck. Delacorte Press 2009 247p map $16.99; lib bdg $19.99 *

Grades: 4 5 6 7   **Fic**

1. World War, 1939-1945—Fiction 2. Refugees—Fiction 3. Sisters—Fiction 4. Jews—Fiction 5. Islands—Fiction 6. Sweden—Fiction

ISBN   978-0-385-73617-6;   0-385-73617-7; 978-0-385-90590-9 (lib bdg); 0-385-90590-4 (lib bdg)
                                          LC 2009-15420

ALA ALSC Batchelder Award (2010)

In 1939 Sweden, two Jewish sisters wait for their parents to flee the Nazis in Austria, but while eight-year-old Nellie settles in quickly, twelve-year-old Stephie feels stranded at the end of the world, with a foster mother who is as cold and unforgiving as the island on which they live.

"Children will readily empathize with Stephie's courage. Both sisters are well-drawn, likable characters. This is the first of four books Thor has written about the two girls." SLJ

Tilly, Meg

Porcupine. Tundra Books 2007 233p $15.95

Grades: 5 6 7 8   **Fic**

1. Newfoundland—Fiction 2. Bereavement—Fiction 3. Family life—Fiction

ISBN 978-0-88776-810-1

"When Jacqueline Cooper's father is killed in Afghanistan, her mother goes to pieces and takes her three children to live on a farm with a strict great-grandmother they didn't know they had. After she leaves, the 12-year-old make it her job to keep her family together and safe. . . . A very satisfying read." SLJ

Timberlake, Amy

That girl Lucy Moon. Hyperion 2006 294p $15.99; pa $5.99

Grades: 5 6 7 8   **Fic**

1. Social action—Fiction 2. School stories 3. Sledding—Fiction

ISBN 0-7868-5298-4; 0-7868-5299-2 (pa)
                                          LC 2005-55105

"Life has changed for injustice-fighting Lucy Moon. Not only is junior high less accepting than elementary school of her activism . . . but there are also those annoying boys. . . . To top it off, the town's richest citizen, Miss Wiggins, has fenced off her beloved sledding hill. True to form, Lucy organizes a Free Wiggins Hill campaign. . . . Timberlake develops her feisty character through believable dialogue. . . . The carefully crafted plot moves through most of the school year." SLJ

Tingle, Tim

Crossing Bok Chitto; a Choctaw tale of friendship & freedom; illustrated by Jeanne Rorex Bridges. Cinco Puntos Press 2006 unp il $17.95; pa $8.95 *

Grades: 2 3 4 5   **Fic**

1. Choctaw Indians—Fiction 2. Slavery—Fiction 3. Friendship—Fiction 4. African Americans—Fiction 5. Mississippi—Fiction

ISBN   978-0-938317-77-7;   0-938317-77-6; 978-1-933693-20-0 (pa); 1-933693-20-7 (pa)
                                          LC 2005-23612

In the 1800s, a Choctaw girl becomes friends with a slave boy from a plantation across the great river, and when she learns that his family is in trouble, she helps them cross to freedom

The "text has the rhythm and grace of . . . oral tradition. It will be easily and effectively read aloud. The paintings are dark and solemn, and the artist has done a wonderful job of depicting all of the characters as individuals." Booklist

Tocher, Timothy

Bill Pennant, Babe Ruth, and me. Cricket Books 2009 178p $16.95

Grades: 5 6 7 8   **Fic**

1. Ruth, Babe, 1895-1948—Fiction 2. McGraw, John Joseph, 1873-1934—Fiction 3. New York Giants (Baseball team)—Fiction 4. New York Yankees (Baseball team)—Fiction. 5. Baseball—Fiction

ISBN 978-0-8126-2755-8; 0-8126-2755-5
                                          LC 2008026829

In 1920, sixteen-year-old Hank finds his loyalties divided when he is assigned to care for the Giants' mascot, a wildcat named Bill Pennant, as well as keep an eye on Babe Ruth in Ruth's first season with the New York Yankees.

The author "seamlessly blends fact and fiction. He recreates the era with scrupulous attention to its syntax and slang, as well as details of daily life. Ruth, McGraw and the other historical figures come alive for readers, and the fictional Hank is a sympathetic, fully developed character." Kirkus

Toksvig, Sandi

Hitler's canary. Roaring Brook Press 2007 191p $16.95 *

Grades: 5 6 7 8   **Fic**

1. World War, 1939-1945—Fiction 2. Denmark—Fiction 3. Jews—Fiction

ISBN 978-1-59643-247-5; 1-59643-247-0
                                          LC 2006-16607

"A Deborah Brodie book"

Ten-year-old Bamse and his Jewish friend Anton participate in the Danish Resistance during World War II.

"Though . . . suspenseful episodes will thrill readers, it is Bamse's growing courage and deepening understanding that drive the story." Booklist

Tolan, Stephanie S., 1942-

Listen! HarperCollins Publishers 2006 197p
$15.99; lib bdg $16.89; pa $5.99

Grades: 4 5 6 7   **Fic**
1. Dogs—Fiction 2. Bereavement—Fiction
3. Wounds and injuries—Fiction
ISBN 978-0-06-057935-7; 0-06-057935-8;
978-0-06-057936-4 (lib bdg); 0-06-057936-6 (lib bdg);
978-0-06-057937-1 (pa); 0-06-057937-4 (pa)
LC 2005-17792

During her solitary convalescence from a crippling accident, twelve-year-old Charley finds a wild dog, and the arduous process of training him leads her to explore her feelings about her mother's death two years earlier.

"This is a sweet, gentle story of healing and the strong bond that can develop between humans and animals. The lovely imagery and involving plot should appeal to more than just animal lovers." SLJ

Surviving the Applewhites. HarperCollins Pubs.
2002 216p $15.99; lib bdg $17.89; pa $5.99

Grades: 5 6 7 8   **Fic**
1. Eccentrics and eccentricities—Fiction 2. Theater—Fiction 3. Family life—Fiction
ISBN 0-06-623602-9; 0-06-623603-7 (lib bdg);
0-06-441044-7 (pa)   LC 2002-1474

A Newbery Medal honor book, 2003

Jake, a budding juvenile delinquent, is sent for home schooling to the arty and eccentric Applewhite family's Creative Academy, where he discovers talents and interests he never knew he had

This is a "thoroughly enjoyable book with humor, well-drawn characters, and a super cover." Voice Youth Advocates

Wishworks, Inc.; illustrated by Amy June Bates.
Arthur A. Levine Books 2009 146p il $15.99

Grades: 3 4 5   **Fic**
1. Imagination—Fiction 2. Wishes—Fiction 3. Dogs—Fiction 4. Friendship—Fiction 5. Divorce—Fiction 6. Moving—Fiction
ISBN 978-0-545-03154-7; 0-545-03154-0
LC 2008-42694

When he is granted his wish for a dog from Wishworks, Inc., third-grader Max is disappointed to find that his new pet is nothing like the dog of his imagination.

"Tolan's vivid, clean writing is deceptively uncomplicated and the many issues touched upon are handled well." SLJ

Tolkien, J. R. R. (John Ronald Reuel), 1892-1973

The hobbit, or, There and back again. Houghton Mifflin 2001 330p il $18; pa $10 *
Grades: 5 6 7 8 9 10 11 12 Adult   **Fic**
1. Fantasy fiction
ISBN 0-618-16221-6; 0-618-26030-7 (pa)
LC 2001276594

A reissue of the title first published 1938

"Text of this edition is based on that first published in Great Britain by Collins Modern Classics in 1998 . . . corrections have been made to that setting"—T.p. verso

"This fantasy features the adventures of hobbit Bilbo Baggins, who joins a band of dwarves led by Gandalf the Wizard. Together they seek to recover the stolen treasure that is hidden in Lonely Mountain and guarded by Smaug the Dragon. This book precedes the Lord of the Rings trilogy." Shapiro. Fic for Youth. 3d edition

Followed by The lord of the rings trilogy: The fellowship of the ring; The two towers; The return of the king

Townley, Rod

The blue shoe; a tale of thievery, villainy, sorcery, and shoes; by Roderick Townley; illustrated by Mary GrandPré. Alfred A. Knopf 2009 254p il $16.99; lib bdg $19.99

Grades: 4 5 6 7   **Fic**
1. Fables 2. Fairy tales
ISBN 978-0-375-85600-6; 0-375-85600-5;
978-0-375-95600-3 (lib bdg); 0-375-95600-X (lib bdg)
LC 2008-43851

A mysterious stranger commissions a single, valuable shoe from a humble cobbler, changing the cobbler's life and the life of his young apprentice forever.

This is a "fun, whimsical fairy tale. . . . The good-versus-evil plotline, dynamic cast of characters, . . . light romance between Hap and Sophia, and copious amounts of magic and intrigue will be a hit with a wide range of readers." Booklist

Tracy, Kristen, 1972-

Camille McPhee fell under the bus. Delacorte Press 2009 293p $16.99; lib bdg $19.99 *
Grades: 3 4 5   **Fic**
1. School stories 2. Friendship—Fiction 3. Family life—Fiction 4. Idaho—Fiction
ISBN 978-0-385-73687-9; 0-385-73687-8;
978-0-385-90633-3 (lib bdg); 0-385-90633-1 (lib bdg)
LC 2008-24903

Ten-year-old Camille McPhee relates the ups and downs of her fourth-grade year at her Idaho elementary school as she tries to adjust to the absence of her best friend, maintain control of her low-blood sugar, cope with the intensifying conflict between her parents, and understand the importance of honesty and fairness.

"The lively, first-person narrative moves readers through possibly banal or overly traumatic episodes with a gentleness and humor that has them rooting for Camille." SLJ

Travers, P. L. (Pamela L.), 1899-1996

Mary Poppins; illustrated by Mary Shepard. rev ed. Harcourt Brace & Co. 1997 c1981 202p il $12.95; pa $6 *
Grades: 4 5 6   **Fic**
1. Fantasy fiction
ISBN 0-15-205810-9; 0-15-201717-8 (pa)
LC 97-223987

First published 1934; this is a reissue of the 1981 revised edition

An extraordinary English nanny blows in on the East Wind with her parrot-headed umbrella and magic carpet-bag and introduces her charges, Jane and Michael Banks, to some delightful people and experiences

Travers, P. L. (Pamela L.), 1899-1996—*Continued*

"The chapter 'Bad Tuesday,' in which Mary and the Banks children travel to the four corners of the earth and meet the inhabitants, has been criticized for portraying minorities in an unfavorable light. . . . [In] the revised edition . . . the entourage meet up with a polar bear, macaw, panda, and dolphin instead of Eskimos, Africans, Chinese, and American Indians." Booklist

Other titles about Mary Poppins are:
Mary Poppins comes back (1935)
Mary Poppins in the kitchen (1975)
Mary Poppins in the park (1952)
Mary Poppins opens the door (1943)

Treviño, Elizabeth Borton de, 1904-

I, Juan de Pareja. Farrar, Straus & Giroux 1965 180p $17; pa $6.99

Grades: 6 7 8 9   **Fic**
1. Juan, de Pareja—Fiction 2. Velázquez, Diego, 1599-1660—Fiction 3. Artists—Fiction 4. Spain—Fiction 5. Slavery—Fiction
ISBN 0-374-33531-1; 0-312-38005-4 (pa)
                                              LC 65-19330
Awarded the Newbery Medal, 1966
"Bell books"

The black slave boy, Juan de Pareja, "began a new life when he was taken into the household of the Spanish painter, Velázquez. As he worked beside the great artist learning how to grind and mix colors and prepare canvases, there grew between them a warm friendship based on mutual respect and love of art. Created from meager but authentic facts, the story, told by Juan, depicts the life and character of Velázquez and the loyalty of the talented seventeenth-century slave who eventually won his freedom and the right to be an artist." Booklist

Tripp, Jenny

Pete & Fremont; [by] Jenny Tripp; with illustrations by John Manders. Harcourt, Inc. 2007 180p il $16; pa $5.95

Grades: 2 3 4   **Fic**
1. Circus—Fiction 2. Bears—Fiction 3. Dogs—Fiction
ISBN 978-0-15-205629-2; 0-15-205629-7; 978-0-15-206238-5 (pa); 0-15-206238-6 (pa)
                                              LC 2006008757
When circus owner Mike decides Pete the poodle has grown too old to continue as the starring act, Pete forms an unlikely alliance with a young grizzly bear, who only wants to go home to the woods.

"Manders's busy, freewheeling illustrations add an appropriate and enticing touch to this entertaining chapter book." SLJ

Another title about Pete is:
Pete's disappearing act (2009)

Trueit, Trudi Strain

No girls allowed (dogs okay); [illustrated by Jim Paillot] Aladdin Paperbacks 2009 128p il (Secrets of a lab rat) $14.99; pa $4.99

Grades: 2 3 4   **Fic**
1. Twins—Fiction 2. Siblings—Fiction 3. School stories
ISBN 978-1-4169-7592-2; 1-4169-7592-6; 978-1-4169-6111-6 (pa); 1-4169-6111-9 (pa)
                                              LC 2008-22329
Fearless nine-year-old 'Scab' McNally tries to get his twin sister's help in convincing their parents to let them get a dog, but when he embarrasses her in school with a particularly obnoxious invention, it looks like he has lost her cooperation forever.

"Scab is a likable, freethinking boy who is full of charm and humor. . . . His many tips, diagrams, and facts scattered throughout are entertaining, as are the numerous comical black-and-white illustrations." SLJ

Another title in this series is:
Mom, there's a dinosaur in Beeson's Lake (2010)

Trueman, Terry

Hurricane; a novel. HarperCollins 2008 137p $15.99; lib bdg $16.89

Grades: 5 6 7   **Fic**
1. Hurricanes—Fiction 2. Honduras—Fiction 3. Survival after airplane accidents, shipwrecks, etc.—Fiction
ISBN 978-0-06-000018-9; 0-06-000018-X; 978-0-06-000019-6 (lib bdg); 0-06-000019-8 (lib bdg)
                                              LC 2007-02990
A revised edition of Swallowing the sun, published 2004 in the United Kingdom

"Thirteen-year-old Jose lives with his family in Honduras. A hurricane hits, causing the recently clear-cut hillside adjacent to his village to become a mudslide that smothers and kills most of its fifty inhabitants. . . . Jose quickly takes charge and becomes a resourceful member of his ailing community. This survival tale is concise but engaging. Trueman's descriptions of the village buried in mud and of the difficulties it creates for the survivors are vivid." Voice Youth Advocates

Tunis, John R., 1889-1975

The Kid from Tomkinsville; illustrated by Jay Hyde Barnum. Harcourt 1940 355p il pa $5.95 hardcover o.p.

Grades: 5 6 7 8   **Fic**
1. Baseball—Fiction
ISBN 0-15-205641-6 (pa)
As the newest addition to the Brooklyn Dodgers, young Roy Tucker's pitching helps pull the team out of a slump; but, when a freak accident ends his career as a pitcher, he must try to find another place for himself on the team

Other titles about Roy Tucker and the Brooklyn Dodgers are:
Keystone kids (1943)
The kid comes back (1946)
Rookie of the year (1944)
World Series (1941)

Turner, Ann Warren, 1945-

Grasshopper summer. Macmillan 1989 166p pa $4.99 hardcover o.p.

Grades: 4 5 6 **Fic**

1. Frontier and pioneer life—Fiction 2. South Dakota—Fiction

ISBN 0-689-83522-1 (pa) LC 88-13847

In 1874 eleven-year-old Sam and his family move from Kentucky to the southern Dakota Territory, where harsh conditions and a plague of hungry grasshoppers threaten their chances for survival

"Carefully selected details, skillfully woven into the story line, evoke a sense of place and time. . . . Both a family story and an account of pioneer living, the book is accessible as well as informative." Horn Book

Twain, Mark, 1835-1910

The adventures of Tom Sawyer; illustrated by Barry Moser; afterword by Peter Glassman. Books of Wonder 1989 261p il $24.99 *

Grades: 5 6 7 8 **Fic**

1. Mississippi River—Fiction 2. Missouri—Fiction

ISBN 0-688-07510-X

Other editions also available

First published 1876

The adventures and pranks of a mischievous boy growing up in a Mississippi River town on the early nineteenth century.

Uchida, Yoshiko, 1921-1992

A jar of dreams. Atheneum Pubs. 1981 131p hardcover o.p. pa $4.99 *

Grades: 5 6 7 8 **Fic**

1. Japanese Americans—Fiction 2. Family life—Fiction 3. Prejudices—Fiction 4. California—Fiction

ISBN 0-689-50210-9; 0-689-71672-9 (pa)

LC 81-3480

"A Margaret K. McElderry book"

"A story of the Depression Era is told by eleven-year-old Rinko, the only girl in a Japanese-American family living in Oakland and suffering under the double burden of financial pressure and the prejudice that had increased with the tension of economic competition. Into the household comes a visitor who is a catalyst for change." Bull Cent Child Books

"Rinko in her guilelessness is genuine and refreshing, and her worries and concerns seem wholly natural, honest, and convincing." Horn Book

Other titles about Rinko Tsujimura and her family are:
The best bad thing (1983)
The happiest ending (1985)

Journey to Topaz; a story of the Japanese-American evacuation; illustrated by Donald Carrick. Heyday Books 2005 149p il pa $9.95 *

Grades: 5 6 7 8 **Fic**

1. Japanese Americans—Evacuation and relocation, 1942-1945—Fiction 2. World War, 1939-1945—Fiction

ISBN 1-89077-191-0; 978-1-89077-191-1

LC 2004-16537

First published 1971 by Scribner

After the Pearl Harbor attack an eleven-year-old Japanese-American girl and her family are forced to go to an aliens camp in Utah

Followed by: Journey home (1978)

Umansky, Kaye

Clover Twig and the magical cottage; illustrated by Johanna Wright. Roaring Brook 2009 297p il $16.99

Grades: 4 5 6 **Fic**

1. Witches—Fiction 2. Magic—Fiction

ISBN 978-1-59643-507-0; 1-59643-507-0

"Sensible, orderly Clover Twig enjoys her new job cleaning and helping out at Mrs. Eckles' cottage, even if the ramshackle place is full of magic and the woman is a witch. There, Clover has a room and even a bed of her own, and plenty to eat. But when Mrs. Eckles leaves for the Palsworthy Fayre, her grasping sister witch, Mesmeranza, steals the cottage." Booklist

"British author Umansky's giggle-worthy characterizations and dialogue make this winsome read-aloud stand out from the pack." Kirkus

Urban, Linda

A crooked kind of perfect. Harcourt 2007 213p $16; pa $5.95 *

Grades: 4 5 6 **Fic**

1. Organ (Musical instrument)—Fiction 2. Musicians—Fiction 3. Family life—Fiction 4. School stories

ISBN 978-0-15-206007-7; 0-15-206007-3; 978-0-15-206608-6 (pa); 0-15-206608-X (pa)

LC 2006-100622

Ten-year-old Zoe Elias, who longs to play the piano but must resign herself to learning the organ, instead, finds that her musicianship has a positive impact on her workaholic mother, her jittery father, and her school social life.

"An impressive and poignant debut novel. . . . The refreshing writing is full of pearls of wisdom, and readers will relate to this fully developed character. The sensitive story is filled with hope and humor." SLJ

Vail, Rachel

Justin Case; school, drool, and other daily disasters; illustrated by Matthew Cordell. Feiwel and Friends 2010 245p il $16.99

Grades: 3 4 5 **Fic**

1. School stories 2. Family life—Fiction

ISBN 978-0-312-53290-1; 0-312-53290-3

"Justin K. (for Krzeszewski), nicknamed Justin Case, has fairly standard third-grade worries (former best friends, rope climbing in gym) and pretty typical joys (current best friends, making it to the top of the rope). He expresses all of these in diary form throughout a school year, and his traditional nuclear family, which celebrates both Jewish and Christian holidays, supports him during all of the multiplication tables, violin lessons, soccer games, and dog messes." Booklist

"Honest and full of heart, Justin Case is a story for an oft-ignored segment of kids: the sensitive, introverted, and observant." SLJ

Van Cleve, Kathleen

Drizzle. Dial Books for Young Readers 2010 358p il $16.99 *

Grades: 4 5 6   **Fic**

1. Magic—Fiction 2. Farms—Fiction 3. Rain—Fiction 4. Droughts—Fiction

ISBN 978-0-8037-3362-6; 0-8037-3362-3

LC 2009-23819

When a drought threatens her family's magical rhubarb farm, eleven-year-old Polly tries to find a way to make it rain again

"Van Cleve's debut is emotionally subtle and action packed with a highly memorable setting." Publ Wkly

Van Leeuwen, Jean

Bound for Oregon; pictures by James Watling. Dial Bks. for Young Readers 1994 167p il map pa $5.99 hardcover o.p. *

Grades: 4 5 6   **Fic**

1. Todd, Mary Ellen, 1843-1924—Fiction 2. Overland journeys to the Pacific—Fiction 3. Oregon Trail—Fiction

ISBN 0-14-038319-0 (pa)   LC 93-26709

A fictionalized account of the journey made by nine-year-old Mary Ellen Todd and her family from their home in Arkansas westward over the Oregon Trail in 1852

"The appealing narrator, the forthright telling, and the concrete details of life along the Oregon Trail will draw readers into the story." Booklist

Cabin on Trouble Creek. Dial Books for Young Readers 2004 119p $16.99; pa $6.99

Grades: 4 5 6 7   **Fic**

1. Frontier and pioneer life—Fiction 2. Brothers—Fiction 3. Ohio—Fiction

ISBN 0-8037-2548-5; 0-14-241164-7 (pa)

LC 2003-14151

In 1803 in Ohio, two young brothers are left to finish the log cabin and guard the land while their father goes back to Pennsylvania to fetch their mother and younger siblings.

"Excellent pacing is what makes this novel work so well. . . . The suspense builds consistently. The boys' struggle is portrayed realistically, without sugarcoating nature's harshness." SLJ

Vande Velde, Vivian, 1951-

Smart dog. Harcourt Brace & Co. 1998 145p hardcover o.p. pa $5.95

Grades: 4 5 6   **Fic**

1. Dogs—Fiction

ISBN 0-15-201847-6; 0-15-206172-X (pa)

LC 98-4771

Fifth grader Amy finds her life growing complicated when she meets and tries to hide an intelligent, talking dog who has escaped from a university lab

"The accessible vocabulary, quick-moving plot, and humor make the novel appealing for reluctant readers as well as a good choice for reading aloud." Horn Book

There's a dead person following my sister around. Harcourt Brace & Co. 1999 143p hardcover o.p. pa $5.95

Grades: 4 5 6 7   **Fic**

1. Ghost stories 2. Slavery—Fiction 3. Underground railroad—Fiction

ISBN 0-15-202100-0; 0-15-206467-2 (pa)

LC 99-11462

Also available in paperback from Puffin Bks.

Ted becomes concerned and intrigued when his five-year-old sister Vicki begins receiving visits from the ghosts of two runaway slaves

"There is sufficient humor, action, and scariness to keep readers engaged." SLJ

Three good deeds. Harcourt 2005 147p $16; pa $5.95

Grades: 3 4 5   **Fic**

1. Geese—Fiction 2. Witches—Fiction

ISBN 0-15-205382-4; 0-15-205455-3 (pa)

LC 2004-29578

Caught stealing some goose eggs from a witch, Howard is cursed for his heartlessness and turned into a goose himself, and he can only become human again by performing three good deeds.

"With well-spaced print, plenty of dialogue, a strong dose of humor, and more invention than many books written at this level, this goose tale is a nicely accomplished, entertaining read." Booklist

Wizard at work; a novel in stories. Harcourt 2003 134p $16; pa $5.95

Grades: 3 4 5 6   **Fic**

1. Magic—Fiction 2. Princesses—Fiction

ISBN 0-15-204559-7; 0-15-205309-3 (pa)

LC 2002-68665

A young wizard, who runs a school to teach wizards, looks forward to a quiet summer off but is drawn into adventures with princesses, unicorns, and ghosts instead

"A lot of fairy-tale conventions are turned on their heads. . . . The language sparkles with sunny good humor. . . . Lighthearted and sly." Booklist

Vaupel, Robin

The rules of the universe by Austin W. Hale. Holiday House 2007 265p $16.95

Grades: 4 5 6 7   **Fic**

1. Science fiction 2. Grandfathers—Fiction 3. Death—Fiction

ISBN 978-0-8234-1811-4; 0-8234-1811-1

LC 2003-56751

Thirteen-year-old Austin Hale, an aspiring scientist and disciple of his grandfather, a Nobel Prize-winning molecular physicist, finds himself in control of a powerful energy force that can turn back time and turn his orbit upside down

"The captivating blend of scientific research and magic is effectively balanced against the stark realism of a boy facing his first significant losses; the overall tone is one of cautious optimism." Bull Cent Child Books

Venuti, Kristin Clark

Leaving the Bellweathers. Egmont USA 2009 242p $15.99; lib bdg $18.99

Grades: 4 5 6   **Fic**

1. Household employees—Fiction 2. Eccentrics and eccentricities—Fiction 3. Family life—Fiction 4. Authorship—Fiction 5. Lighthouses—Fiction

ISBN   978-1-60684-006-1;   1-60684-006-1; 978-1-60684-050-4 (lib bdg); 1-60684-050-9 (lib bdg)

LC 2009016244

In Eel-Smack-by-the-Bay, put-upon butler Tristan Benway writes a memoir of his years spent working for the chaotic and eccentric Bellweather family in their lighthouse, as he prepares for his long-awaited departure from indentured servitude

"Venuti's entertaining and humorous debut features an eccentric cast, absurdities, and droll details. . . . Readers will find much amusement in the quirky characters and scenarios touched with heart." Booklist

Verne, Jules, 1828-1905

20,000 leagues under the sea; illustrated by the Dillons; translated by Anthony Bonner. Books of Wonder 2000 394p il $21.95 *

Grades: 5 6 7 8 9 10 11 12 Adult   **Fic**

1. Science fiction 2. Submarines—Fiction

ISBN 0-688-10535-1   LC 00-24336

Original French edition, 1870

Retells the adventures of a French professor and his two companions as they sail above and below the world's oceans as prisoners on the fabulous electric submarine of the deranged Captain Nemo

Verrillo, Erica F.

Elissa's quest; [by] Erica Verrillo. Random House 2007 336p (Phoenix rising) $16.99; pa $6.99

Grades: 5 6 7 8   **Fic**

1. Magic—Fiction 2. Father-daughter relationship—Fiction 3. Fantasy fiction

ISBN   978-0-375-83946-7;   0-375-83946-1; 978-0-375-83947-4 (pa); 0-375-83947-X (pa)

LC 2006-14436

Thirteen-year-old Elissa knows nothing of her origins until her father comes and takes her to the Citadel of the evil Khan, in exchange for soldiers to protect the kingdom that will one day be hers, but upon discovering her power, she chooses to follow her own destiny.

This is a "charming and elegant story. Elissa emerges as a thoroughly lovable heroine." Publ Wkly

Other titles is this series are:

Elissa's odyssey (2008)

World's end (2009)

Vining, Elizabeth Gray, 1902-1999

Adam of the road; illustrated by Robert Lawson. Viking 1942 317p il $19.99; pa $6.99

Grades: 5 6 7 8   **Fic**

1. Minstrels—Fiction 2. Middle Ages—Fiction 3. Great Britain—Fiction

ISBN 0-670-10435-3; 0-14-240659-7 (pa)

Awarded the Newbery Medal, 1943

Tale of a minstrel and his son Adam, who wandered through southeastern England in the thirteenth century. Adam's adventures in search of his lost dog and his beloved father led him from St. Alban's Abbey to London, and thence to Winchester, back to London, and then to Oxford where the three were at last reunited

Voake, Steve

Daisy Dawson is on her way! illustrated by Jessica Meserve. Candlewick Press 2008 98p il $14.99; pa $5.99

Grades: 2 3 4   **Fic**

1. Animals—Fiction 2. Dogs—Fiction

ISBN   978-0-7636-3740-8;   0-7636-3740-8; 978-0-7636-4294-5 (pa); 0-7636-4294-0 (pa)

LC 2007-23150

One day when Daisy is late for school, an encounter with a butterfly leaves her suddenly able to communicate with animals, and when Boom, a stray dog, is caught by the pound, she enlists the help of a host of other animals to rescue him.

"Sprightly illustrations in a variety of shapes appear throughout. First in a series, this charmer, long on whimsy and adventure, is sure to appeal to newly independent and reluctant readers." SLJ

Another title about Daisy Dawson is:

Daisy Dawson and the secret pond (2009)

Voigt, Cynthia

Dicey's song. Atheneum Pubs. 1982 196p $17.95; pa $6.99

Grades: 5 6 7 8   **Fic**

1. Grandmothers—Fiction 2. Siblings—Fiction

ISBN 0-689-30944-9; 0-689-86362-4 (pa)

LC 82-3882

Awarded the Newbery Medal, 1983

Sequel to Homecoming

Dicey "had brought her siblings to the grandmother they'd never seen when their mother (now in a mental institution) had been unable to cope. This is the story of the children's adjustment to Gram (and hers to them) and to a new school and a new life—but with some of the old problems." Bull Cent Child Books

"The vividness of Dicey is striking; Voigt has plumbed and probed her character inside out to fashion a memorable protagonist." Booklist

Wait, Lea, 1946-

Finest kind. Margaret K. McElderry Books 2006 246p $16.95

Grades: 4 5 6 7   **Fic**

1. Family life—Fiction 2. Cerebral palsy—Fiction 3. Maine—Fiction

ISBN 978-1-4169-0952-1; 1-4169-0952-4

LC 2005-25422

When his father's Boston bank fails in 1838, causing his family to relocate to a small Maine town, twelve-year-old Jake Webber works to prepare the family for the harsh winter while also keeping the existence of his disabled younger brother a secret.

"Wait's prose is straightforward, the story is filled with diverse characters and period details, and Jake is an appealing, dimensional protagonist." Booklist

Waite, Michael P., 1960-

The witches of Dredmoore Hollow; by Riford McKenzie; with illustrations by Peter Ferguson. Marshall Cavendish Children 2008 264p il $16.99

Grades: 4 5 6 7   **Fic**

1. Witches—Fiction 2. Aunts—Fiction 3. New England—Fiction

ISBN 978-0-7614-5458-8; 0-7614-5458-6

LC 2007-29781

Strange things begin happening at Elijah's New England home just before his twelfth birthday in 1927, especially after two aunts he had never met whisk him away to Moaning Marsh, where he realizes that they are witches who need something from him in order to remove a curse.

"The book has continuous action and piles of demonic atmosphere." SLJ

Walden, Mark

H.I.V.E; The Higher Institute of Villainous Education. Simon & Schuster Books for Young Readers 2007 309p $15.99; pa $6.99

Grades: 5 6 7 8   **Fic**

1. Criminals—Fiction

ISBN 1-4169-3571-1; 978-1-4169-3571-1; 978-1-4169-3572-8 (pa); 1-4169-3572-X (pa)

LC 2007-16205

"H.I.V.E. is operated on a volcanic island in a distant ocean by G.L.O.V.E., a shadowy organization of worldwide wickedness. And, as 13-year-old master of mischief Otto Malpense soon discovers, here the slickest of young tricksters, thieves, and hackers have been brought against their will to be trained as the next generation of supervillains. . . . [This] novel is a real page-turner; those who love superhero stories will eat it up." SLJ

Another title about H.I.V.E. is:

H.I.V.E.: the Overlord protocol (2008)

Walker, Kate, 1950-

I hate books! [by] Kate Walker; illustrated by David Cox. Cricket Books 2007 78p il $16.95

Grades: 2 3 4 5   **Fic**

1. Books and reading—Fiction 2. Brothers—Fiction 3. School stories

ISBN 978-0-8126-2745-9; 0-8126-2745-8

LC 2006-36492

Although he is a great storyteller and good at art, Hamish cannot read, even with remedial classes, but his brother Nathan finally comes up with a way to teach him

"This is a warm and fast-paced story. . . . Witty black-and-white line drawings enhance the narrative." SLJ

Wallace, Bill, 1947-

The legend of thunderfoot. Simon & Schuster Books for Young Readers 2006 150p $15.95; pa $5.99

Grades: 3 4 5 6   **Fic**

1. Roadrunners—Fiction

ISBN 978-1-4169-0691-9; 1-4169-0691-6; 978-1-4169-0692-6 (pa); 1-4169-0692-4 (pa)

"After a young roadrunner is bitten by a rattlesnake, his feet swell to an enormous size. At first this seems to be a handicap. . . . After taking the advice of a wise old tortoise, though, the roadrunner, now called Thunderfoot, undergoes an exercise program. . . . The newly pumped-up Thunderfoot . . . winds up his days as a legendary figure in the animal world. Wallace creates a lively fantasy, with a cliff-hanging closing for nearly every chapter." Booklist

Skinny-dipping at Monster Lake. Simon & Schuster Bks. for Young Readers 2003 212p hardcover o.p. pa $5.99 *

Grades: 4 5 6 7   **Fic**

ISBN 0-689-85150-2; 0-689-85151-0 (pa)

LC 2002-152820

When twelve-year-old Kent helps his father in a daring underwater rescue, he wins the respect he has always craved.

"This old-fashioned adventure has wide appeal, and the youngsters' games and camaraderie will hook even reluctant readers." SLJ

Walliams, David, 1971-

The boy in the dress; illustrated by Quentin Blake. Razorbill 2009 231p il $15.99 *

Grades: 4 5 6 7   **Fic**

1. Transvestites—Fiction 2. Soccer—Fiction 3. School stories 4. Great Britain—Fiction

ISBN 978-1-59514-299-3; 1-59514-299-1

"Dennis is a bit surprised—but not terribly nonplussed—to discover that he enjoys wearing dresses. The 12-year-old does, however, realize this is not the kind of revelation he wants to share with his truck-driving dad, his older brother, or his mates on the school football team, where he is the star player. . . . Williams . . . has written a witty, high-spirited, and, well, sensible story about cross-dressing and other real-life issues." Booklist

Walter, Mildred Pitts, 1922-

Justin and the best biscuits in the world; with illustrations by Catherine Stock. Lothrop, Lee & Shepard Bks. 1986 122p il $16; pa $7.99 *

Grades: 3 4 5 6   **Fic**

1. Sex role—Fiction 2. Grandfathers—Fiction 3. Family life—Fiction 4. African Americans—Fiction

ISBN 0-688-06645-3; 0-06-195891-3 (pa)

LC 86-7148

Coretta Scott King Award for text

"Justin can't seem to do anything right at home. His sisters berate his dishwashing and his mother despairs of his ever properly tidying his room. As for Justin, he angrily rejects the tasks as 'women's work.' Enter now Justin's widowed grandfather, who sizes up the situation, invites Justin for a visit to his ranch, and through daily routines quietly shows Justin that 'it doesn't matter who does the work, man or woman, when it needs to be done.'" Booklist

"The strong, well-developed characters and humorous situations in this warm family story will appeal to intermediate readers; the large print will draw slow or reluctant readers." SLJ

Warner, Sally

It's only temporary; written and illustrated by Sally Warner. Viking Childrens Books 2008 182p il $15.99

Grades: 4 5 6 7   **Fic**

1. Siblings—Fiction 2. Bullies—Fiction 3. Brain—Wounds and injuries—Fiction 4. Grandmothers—Fiction

ISBN 978-0-670-06111-2; 0-670-06111-5

LC 2007-038220

When Skye's older brother comes home after a devastating accident, she moves from Albuquerque, New Mexico, to California to live with her grandmother and attend middle school, where she somewhat reluctantly makes new friends, learns to stand up for herself and those she cares about, and begins to craft a new relationship with her changed brother.

"Warner deftly handles Skye's anger toward her brain-injured brother, also infusing her with a convincingly developed sense of compassion. Witty line art decorates some pages." Horn Book Guide

Only Emma; illustrated by Jamie Harper. Viking 2004 115p il $14.99; pa $5.99 *

Grades: 2 3 4   **Fic**

ISBN 0-670-05979-X; 0-14-240711-9 (pa)

LC 2004-12478

Third-grader Emma's peaceful life as an only child is disrupted when she has to temporarily share her tidy bedroom with four-year-old Anthony Scarpetto.

"The black-and-white illustrations are charming, and thumbnail sidebars present fun scientific facts about animals mentioned in the story. . . . Emma is a likable character whose feelings and behaviors are common to many children." SLJ

Other titles about Emma are:

Not-so-weird Emma (2005)

Super Emma (2006)

Best friend Emma (2007)

Excellent Emma (2009)

This isn't about the money. Viking 2002 209p $15.99

Grades: 5 6 7 8   **Fic**

1. Death—Fiction 2. Orphans—Fiction 3. California—Fiction

ISBN 0-670-03574-2   LC 2001-56797

Twelve-year-old Janey tries to adjust in the aftermath of an automobile accident that kills her parents, severely injures her face, and forces her and her younger sister to move from Arizona to California to live with their grandfather and great-aunt

"Warner's dialog and characterization are rich and real." Booklist

Waters, Zack C., 1946-

Blood moon rider; [by] Zack C. Waters. Pineapple Press 2006 126p $13.95

Grades: 5 6 7 8   **Fic**

1. Grandfathers—Fiction 2. World War, 1939-1945—Fiction 3. Ranch life—Fiction 4. Florida—Fiction

ISBN 978-1-56164-350-9; 1-56164-350-5

LC 2005030749

After his father's death in World War II, fourteen-year-old Harley Wallace tries to join the Marines but is, instead, sent to live with his grandfather in Peru Landing, Florida, where he soon joins a covert effort to stop Nazis from destroying a secret airbase on Tampa Bay

This is "an adventure filled with unexpected kindnesses and the irrepressibility of family ties, as well as a brush with espionage and a couple of suspenseful shoot'em-up scenes. A colorful cast of characters and a nod to teenage romance help make this a good choice for middle school boys." SLJ

Watkins, Yoko Kawashima

My brother, my sister, and I. Bradbury Press 1994 275p hardcover o.p. pa $5.99

Grades: 6 7 8 9   **Fic**

1. World War, 1939-1945—Fiction 2. Japan—Fiction 3. Korea—Fiction

ISBN 0-02-792526-9; 0-689-80656-6 (pa)

LC 93-23535

"The author continues her autobiographical account begun in *So Far from the Bamboo Grove* with the story of how the two sisters, Ko and Yoko, now reunited with their brother Hideyo, try to survive in postwar Japan." Horn Book

"Watkins's first-person narrative is beautifully direct and emotionally honest." Publ Wkly

So far from the bamboo grove. Lothrop, Lee & Shepard Bks. 1986 183p map pa $5.99 hardcover o.p. *

Grades: 6 7 8 9   **Fic**

1. World War, 1939-1945—Fiction 2. Korea—Fiction 3. Japan—Fiction

ISBN 0-688-13115-8 (pa)   LC 85-15939

A fictionalized autobiography in which eight-year-old Yoko escapes from Korea to Japan with her mother and sister at the end of World War II

"An admirably told and absorbing novel." Horn Book

Followed by My brother, my sister and I

Watson, Stephanie Elaine, 1979-

Elvis & Olive; by Stephanie Watson. Scholastic Press 2008 230p $15.99

Grades: 3 4 5   **Fic**

1. Friendship—Fiction

ISBN 978-0-545-03183-7; 0-545-03183-4

LC 2007023924

In spite of their differences, Natalie Wallis and Annie Beckett become friends and decide to spend their summer spying on their neighbors

This is an "accomplished first novel." Publ Wkly

Another title about Elvis & Olive is:

Elvis & Olive: super detectives (2010)

Watts, Frances

Extraordinary Ernie and Marvelous Maud; illustrated by Judy Watson. Eerdmans Books for Young Readers 2010 66p il pa $5.99

Grades: 2 3 4   **Fic**

1. Superheroes—Fiction 2. Sheep—Fiction

ISBN 978-0-8028-5363-9 (pa); 0-8028-5363-3 (pa)

Ten-year-old Ernie is thrilled when he wins a contest to be trained as a superhero, and although he is disappointed that his sidekick is a talking sheep, just looking at his costume makes him feel heroic

"The action is tame . . . but the slapstick premise and banter between superhero and sidekick save the day. The brevity, spry pace, and humorous line art make Watts's . . . story a good choice for kids." Publ Wkly

Weatherford, Carole Boston, 1956-

Dear Mr. Rosenwald; by Carole Boston Weatherford; illustrated by Gregory Christie. Scholastic Press 2006 unp il $16.99

Grades: 2 3 4   **Fic**

1. Rosenwald, Julius, 1862-1932—Fiction 2. African Americans—Fiction 3. School stories 4. Segregation in education—Fiction

ISBN 0-439-49522-9   LC 2005-27971

Young Ovella rejoices as her community comes together to raise money and build a much-needed school in the 1920s, with matching funds from Julius Rosenwald, the president of Sears, Roebuck, and Company

"Christie's gouache and colored-pencil illustrations have the variegated look and stylized layout of collage art—a good complement to the child's rough-around-the-edges narration. An afterword explains Rosenwald's impact on thousands of poor black communities. An uplifting and inspiring story." SLJ

Weber, Elka, 1968-

The Yankee at the seder; illustrated by Adam Gustavson. Tricycle Press 2009 unp il $16.99 *

Grades: 2 3 4 5   **Fic**

1. Passover—Fiction 2. Jews—Fiction 3. Soldiers—Fiction 4. United States—History—1861-1865, Civil War—Fiction

ISBN 978-1-58246-256-1; 1-58246-256-9

LC 2008-11229

As a Confederate family prepares for Passover the day after the Civil War has ended, a Yankee arrives on their Virginia doorstep and is invited to share their meal, to the dismay of ten-year-old Jacob. Includes historical notes about Corporal Myer Levy, on whom the story is based, and his prominent Philadelphia family.

"With a cinematic flair and rich, realist oils, Gustavson . . . depicts how a détente between North and South is forged—albeit tenuously—by the timeless values of faith, civility and chicken soup. Basing her writing on a historical incident, Weber makes an impressive debut. . . . Sensitively written and beautifully illustrated." Publ Wkly

Wedekind, Annie

A horse of her own; by Annie Wedekind. Feiwel and Friends 2008 275p $16.95; pa $7.99

Grades: 5 6 7 8   **Fic**

1. Horses—Fiction 2. Horsemanship—Fiction 3. Camps—Fiction 4. Kentucky—Fiction

ISBN 978-0-312-36927-9; 0-312-36927-1; 978-0-312-58146-6 (pa); 0-312-58146-7 (pa)

LC 2007032769

At summer camp Jane feels like an outsider among the cliquish rich girls who board their horses at Sunny Acres farm, and when the horse she has been riding is sold to another camper, she feels even worse until her teacher asks her to help train a beautiful but skittish new horse, and the experience brings out the best in her.

"Tenacious and thoughtful, Jane is an appealing protagonist who gradually recognizes that being accepted no longer matters to her. The plot . . . has enough twists, including a hint of romance, to sustain readers' interest." SLJ

Wild Blue; the story of a mustang Appaloosa. Feiwel and Friends 2009 124p (Breyer horse collection) $16.99; pa $5.99

Grades: 3 4 5   **Fic**

1. Horses—Fiction

ISBN 978-0-312-38424-1; 0-312-38424-6; 978-0-312-59917-1 (pa); 0-312-59917-X (pa)

LC 2008-34742

After being captured by men, Blue the Appaloosa grabs a chance at freedom and tries to find her way home.

"A modern-day adventure that reads like an exuberant nature journal, this novel will grip readers from start to finish." SLJ

Weeks, Sarah

Jumping the scratch; a novel. Laura Geringer Books 2006 167p il $15.99; pa $5.99

Grades: 5 6 7 8   **Fic**

1. Child sexual abuse—Fiction 2. Memory—Fiction 3. Aunts—Fiction

ISBN 978-0-06-054109-5; 0-06-054109-1; 978-0-06-054110-1 (pa); 0-06-054111-3 (pa)

LC 2005-17776

After moving with his mother to a trailer park to care for an injured aunt, eleven-year-old Jamie Reardon struggles to cope with a deeply buried secret

"Weeks alludes to sexual abuse, but with a broad brush and no graphic details. . . . Weeks perfectly captures not only the guilt, shame, and pain of the abused boy but also the tenor of a fifth-grade classroom from the point of view of a new student who is friendless, targeted, and belittled by an insensitive teacher. Touches of humor ameliorate the pain and poignancy." SLJ

Oggie Cooder. Levithan/Scholastic Press 2008 172p il $16.99; pa $5.99

Grades: 3 4 5   **Fic**

1. Eccentrics and eccentricities—Fiction 2. Friendship—Fiction 3. School stories

ISBN 978-0-439-92791-8; 0-439-92791-9; 978-0-439-92794-9 (pa); 0-439-92794-3 (pa)

LC 2007-18645

Weeks, Sarah—*Continued*

Quirky fourth-grader Oggie Cooder goes from being shunned to everyone's best friend when his uncanny ability to chew slices of cheese into the shapes of states wins him a slot on a popular television talent show, but he soon learns the perils of being a celebrity—and having a neighbor girl as his manager.

The author "delivers a funny, fast-paced story, with the likable Oggie at its center." Booklist

Followed by: Oggie Cooder, party animal (2009)

Regular Guy. HarperCollins Pubs. 1999 120p hardcover o.p. pa $4.99 *

Grades: 4 5 6   **Fic**

1. Parent-child relationship—Fiction

ISBN 0-06-028367-X; 0-06-440782-9 (pa)

               LC 99-12118

"A Laura Geringer book"

Because he is so different from his eccentric parents, twelve-year-old Guy is convinced he has been switched at birth with a classmate whose parents seem more normal

"Weeks treats the situation with wild exaggeration, a farcical plot, and just a touch of tenderness. . . . Many middle-graders will enjoy the gross humor (lots of snot and clatter and fishy smells) as much as the view of embarrassing adults who love you even though they drive you nuts." Booklist

Other titles about Guy are:

Guy time (2000)

Guy wire (2002)

My Guy (2001)

So B. it; a novel. Laura Geringer Books 2004 245p $15.99; pa $6.99 *

Grades: 5 6 7 8   **Fic**

1. Mentally handicapped—Fiction 2. Mental illness—Fiction

ISBN 0-06-623622-3; 0-06-441047-1 (pa)

               LC 2003-15643

After spending her life with her mentally retarded mother and agoraphobic neighbor, twelve-year-old Heidi sets out from Reno, Nevada, to New York to find out who she is.

"This is lovely writing—real, touching, and pared cleanly down to the essentials." Booklist

Wells, Rosemary, 1943-

Lincoln and his boys; illustrated by P.J. Lynch. Candlewick Press 2009 96p il $16.99

Grades: 3 4 5 6   **Fic**

1. Lincoln, Abraham, 1809-1865—Fiction 2. Lincoln, William Wallace, 1850-1862—Fiction 3. Lincoln, Tad, 1853-1871—Fiction 4. Presidents—Fiction 5. Father-son relationship—Fiction

ISBN 978-0-7636-3723-1; 0-7636-3723-8

               LC 2008-21418

"Inspired by a 200-word essay by Willie Lincoln, Wells offers a fictional account of Lincoln and his boys. Written first from Willie's point of view, then Tad's after Willie dies, it's a touching account of Lincoln as a patient and loving father. . . . Lynch captures the people and the warmth of their interactions in carefully researched oil paintings that reflect his mastery with light, perspective, and portraiture." SLJ

Westera, Marleen, 1962-

Sheep and Goat; by Marleen Westera; illustrations by Sylvia van Ommen; translation by Nancy Forest-Flier. Front Street 2006 99p il $16.95 *

Grades: 1 2 3   **Fic**

1. Sheep—Fiction 2. Goats—Fiction 3. Friendship—Fiction

ISBN 978-1-932425-81-9   LC 2006000793

Follows the daily activities of Sheep and Goat who, despite often being grouchy or grumpy, are always there for one another when it counts

"Told with a subtle and consistent undercurrent of wit, these 18 short stories are pleasant bedtime reading. . . . The occasional pen-and-ink drawings are pitch perfect and more than a little extraordinary. They convey the low-key humor exquisitely." SLJ

Weston, Carol

The diary of Melanie Martin; or, How I survived Matt the Brat, Michelangelo, and the Leaning Tower of Pizza. Knopf 2000 144p hardcover o.p. pa $5.50

Grades: 3 4 5 6   **Fic**

1. Voyages and travels—Fiction 2. Family life—Fiction 3. Italy—Fiction

ISBN 0-375-80509-5; 0-440-41667-1 (pa)

               LC 99-53384

Fourth-grader Melanie Martin writes in her diary, describing her family's trip to Italy and all that she learned

"Sections of the book are laugh-out-loud funny and Weston's descriptions will have readers wanting to see the country for themselves. An enjoyable read." SLJ

Other titles about Melanie Martin are:

Melanie in Manhattan (2005)

Melanie Martin goes Dutch (2002)

With love from Spain, Melanie Martin (2005)

Weston, Robert Paul

Zorgamazoo. Razorbill 2008 281p il $15.99 *

Grades: 4 5 6 7   **Fic**

1. Novels in verse 2. Imagination—Fiction 3. Adventure fiction

ISBN 978-1-59514-199-6; 1-59514-199-5

               LC 2007-51682

Imaginative and adventurous Katrina eludes her maniacal guardian to help Morty, a member of a vanishing breed of zorgles, with his quest to uncover the fate of the fabled zorgles of Zorgmazoo as well as of other creatures that seem to have disappeared from the earth.

"This book is a natural descendant to the works of Dr. Seuss and Roald Dahl." Booklist

Wharton, Thomas, 1963-

The shadow of Malabron. Candlewick Press 2009 382p (The perilous realm) $16.99

Grades: 5 6 7 8   **Fic**

1. Fantasy fiction

ISBN 978-0-7636-3911-2; 0-7636-3911-7

               LC 2009-7768

When Will, a rebellious teen, stumbles from the present into the realm where stories come from, he learns he

Wharton, Thomas, 1963——*Continued*

has a mission concerning the evil Malabron and, aided by some of the story folk, he faces a host of perils while seeking the gateless gate that will take him home.

"Lush descriptive prose, cleverly sustained suspense, a sprinkling of humor and an exciting climax will keep readers riveted to the story, while those who know their folklore will be delighted by Wharton's twisting of the tropes and tales of myth and legend." Kirkus

Whelan, Gloria

Homeless bird. HarperCollins Pubs. 2000 216p $15.95; pa $5.99 *

Grades: 6 7 8 9   **Fic**

1. Women—India—Fiction 2. India—Fiction

ISBN 0-06-028454-4; 0-06-440819-1 (pa)

LC 99-33241

When thirteen-year-old Koly enters into an ill-fated arranged marriage, she must either suffer a destiny dictated by India's tradition or find the courage to oppose it

"This beautifully told, inspiring story takes readers on a fascinating journey through modern India and the universal intricacies of a young woman's heart." Booklist

Listening for lions. HarperCollins 2005 194p $15.99; lib bdg $16.89; pa $5.99 *

Grades: 5 6 7 8   **Fic**

1. Orphans—Fiction 2. East Africa—Fiction 3. Physicians—Fiction 4. Great Britain—Fiction

ISBN 0-06-058174-3; 0-06-058175-1 (lib bdg); 0-06-058176-X (pa)

Left an orphan after the influenza epidemic in British East Africa in 1918, thirteen-year-old Rachel is tricked into assuming a deceased neighbor's identity to travel to England, where her only dream is to return to Africa and rebuild her parents' mission hospital.

"In a straightforward, sympathetic voice, Rachel tells an involving, episodic story." Booklist

The locked garden. HarperCollins Children's Books 2009 168p $15.99 *

Grades: 4 5 6 7   **Fic**

1. Psychiatric hospitals—Fiction 2. Mental illness—Fiction 3. Family life—Fiction 4. Michigan—Fiction

ISBN 978-0-06-079094-3; 0-06-079094-6

LC 2008-24637

After their mother dies of typhoid, Verna and her younger sister Carlie move with their father, a psychiatrist, and stern Aunt Maude to an asylum for the mentally ill in early-twentieth-century Michigan, where new ideas in the treatment of mental illness are being proposed, but old prejudices still hold sway.

"Whelan establishes a strong sense of time, unusual setting and characters. . . . This convincing melodrama portrays an atypical attitude toward treating mental illness." Kirkus

White, E. B. (Elwyn Brooks), 1899-1985

Charlotte's web; pictures by Garth Williams. Harper & Row 1952 184p il $16.95; lib bdg $16.89; pa $5.95 *

Grades: 3 4 5 6   **Fic**

1. Pigs—Fiction 2. Spiders—Fiction

ISBN 0-06-026385-7; 0-06-026386-5 (lib bdg); 0-06-440055-7 (pa)

Also available Spanish language edition

A Newbery Medal honor book, 1953

The story of a little girl who could talk to animals, but especially the story of the pig, Wilbur, and his friendship with Charlotte, the spider, who could not only talk but write as well

"Illustrated with amusing sketches . . . [this] story is a fable for adults as well as children and can be recommended to older children and parents as an amusing story and a gentle essay on friendship." Libr J

Stuart Little; pictures by Garth Williams. Harper & Row 1945 131p il $16.95; lib bdg $16.89; pa $5.95 *

Grades: 3 4 5 6   **Fic**

1. Mice—Fiction

ISBN 0-06-026395-4; 0-06-026396-2 (lib bdg); 0-06-440056-5 (pa)

Also available Spanish language edition

This is "the story of a 'Tom Thumb'-like child born to a New York couple who is to all intents and purposes a mouse. . . . The first part of the book explores, with dead-pan humour, the advantages and disadvantages of having a mouse in one's family circle. Then Stuart sets out on a quest in search of his inamorata, a bird named Margalo, and the story ends in mid-air. The book is outstandingly funny and sometimes touching." Oxford Companion to Child Lit

The trumpet of the swan; illustrated by Fred Marcellino. HarperCollins Pubs. 2000 251p il $16.95; pa $5.95 *

Grades: 3 4 5 6   **Fic**

1. Swans—Fiction

ISBN 0-06-028935-X; 0-06-440867-1 (pa)

LC 99-44250

Also available Spanish language edition

A newly illustrated edition of the title first published 1970

Louis, a voiceless Trumpeter swan, finds himself far from his wilderness home when he determines to communicate by learning to play a stolen trumpet

The author "deftly blends true birdlore with fanciful adventures in a witty, captivating fantasy." Booklist

White, Ruth

Belle Prater's boy. Farrar, Straus & Giroux 1996 196p $17 *

Grades: 5 6 7 8   **Fic**

1. Cousins—Fiction 2. Virginia—Fiction 3. Appalachian region—Fiction

ISBN 0-374-30668-0   LC 94-43625

Also available in paperback from Random House

A Newbery Medal honor book, 1997

White, Ruth—Continued

"Gypsy and her cousin Woodrow become close friends after Woodrow's mother disappears. Both sixth-graders feel deserted by their parents—Gypsy discovers that her father committed suicide—and need to define themselves apart from these tragedies. White's prose evokes the coal mining region of Virginia and the emotional quality of her characters' transformations." Horn Book Guide

Another title about Belle Prater is:
The search for Belle Prater (2005)

Little Audrey. Farrar, Straus & Giroux 2008 145p $16 *
Grades: 5 6 7 8   **Fic**
1. Country life—Fiction 2. Virginia—Fiction 3. Coal miners—Fiction 4. Death—Fiction
ISBN 978-0-374-34580-8; 0-374-34580-5
LC 2007-29310

In 1948, eleven-year-old Audrey lives with her father, mother, and three younger sisters in Jewell Valley, a coal mining camp in Southwest Virginia, where her mother still mourns the death of a baby, her father goes on drinking binges on paydays, and Audrey tries to recover from the scarlet fever that has left her skinny and needing to wear glasses.

"The setting is perfectly portrayed and the characterizations ring true." Voice Youth Advocates

Way Down Deep. Farrar, Straus and Giroux 2007 197p $16 *
Grades: 5 6 7 8   **Fic**
1. Orphans—Fiction 2. West Virginia—Fiction
ISBN 0-374-38251-4; 978-0-374-38251-3
LC 2006-46324

In the West Virginia town of Way Down Deep in the 1950s, a foundling called Ruby June is happily living with Miss Arbutus at the local boarding house when suddenly, after the arrival of a family of outsiders, the mystery of Ruby's past begins to unravel.

This is "a story as tender as a breeze and as sharp as a tack. . . . At the heart of the story are profound questions that readers will enjoy puzzling out." Booklist

White, T. H. (Terence Hanbury), 1906-1964

The sword in the stone; with illustrations by Dennis Nolan. Putnam 1993 256p il $24.99 *
Grades: 4 5 6 7   **Fic**
1. Arthur, King—Fiction 2. Merlin (Legendary character)—Fiction
ISBN 0-399-22502-1   LC 92-24808
Also available in paperback from Dell

A newly illustrated edition of the title first published 1938 in the United Kingdom; first United States edition 1939 by G.P Putnam's Sons

"In White's classic story about the boyhood of King Arthur, Wart—unaware of his true identity—is tutored by Merlyn, who occasionally transform the young boy into various animals as part of his schooling. Contemporary children will still enjoy the text, which is both fantastical and down-to-earth." Horn Book Guide

Whittenberg, Allison

Sweet Thang. Delacorte Press 2006 149p $15.95
Grades: 5 6 7 8   **Fic**
1. African Americans—Fiction 2. Family life—Fiction 3. School stories
ISBN 0-385-73292-9   LC 2005-03809

In 1975, life is not fair for fourteen-year-old Charmaine Upshaw, who shares a room with her brother, tries to impress a handsome classmate, and acts as caretaker for a rambunctious six-year-old cousin who has taken over the family.

"Whittenberg has created a refreshing cast and a good read." SLJ

Another title about the Upshaw family is:
Hollywood & Maine (2009)

Wilder, Laura Ingalls, 1867-1957

Little house in the big woods; illustrated by Garth Williams. newly illustrated, uniform ed. Harper & Row 1953 237p il $16.95; lib bdg $16.89; pa $6.99 *
Grades: 4 5 6   **Fic**
1. Frontier and pioneer life—Fiction 2. Wisconsin—Fiction
ISBN 0-06-026430-6; 0-06-026431-4 (lib bdg); 0-06-440001-8 (pa)
First published 1932

This book "tells the story of the author's earliest days 'in the Big Woods of Wisconsin, in a little grey house made of logs.' The style of narrative is simple, almost naive, but the pioneer life is described unsqueamishly, with attention to such details as the butchering of the family hog. As in later books, the author refers to herself in the third person as 'Laura.' The record of daily life far from any town is punctuated with stories told in the evenings by Pa, who is also a great singer of folk-songs." Oxford Companion to Child Lit

Other titles in the Little House series are:
By the shores of Silver Lake (1939)
Farmer boy (1933)
The first four years (1971)
Little house on the prairie (1935)
Little town on the prairie (1941)
The long winter (1940)
On the banks of Plum Creek (1937)
These happy golden years (1943)

Wiles, Deborah

The Aurora County All-Stars. Harcourt 2007 242p il $16; pa $5.99 *
Grades: 4 5 6   **Fic**
1. Baseball—Fiction 2. Death—Fiction 3. Race relations—Fiction 4. Mississippi—Fiction
ISBN   978-0-15-206068-8;   0-15-206068-5; 978-0-15-206626-0 (pa); 0-15-206626-8 (pa)
LC 2006-102551

In a small Mississippi town, after the death of the old man to whom twelve-year-old star pitcher House Jackson has been secretly reading for a year, House uncovers secrets about the man and the history of baseball in Aurora County.

"Quotations from Walt Whitman's poetry, baseball players and Aurora County news dispatches pepper the story and add color. . . . A home run for Wiles." Publ Wkly

Wiles, Deborah—*Continued*

Countdown. Scholastic 2010 377p il $17.99 *
Grades: 4 5 6 7   **Fic**
1. Cuban Missile Crisis, 1962—Fiction 2. Family
life—Fiction 3. Cold war—Fiction
ISBN 978-0-545-10605-4; 0-545-10605-2

It's 1962, and it seems everyone is living in fear.
Twelve-year-old Franny Chapman lives with her family
in Washington, DC, during the days surrounding the Cuban Missile Crisis. Amidst the pervasive threat of nuclear
war, Franny must face the tension between herself and
her younger brother, figure out where she fits in with her
family, and look beyond outward appearances.

"Wiles skillfully keeps many balls in the air, giving
readers a story that appeals across the decades as well as
offering enticing paths into the history." Booklist

Love, Ruby Lavender. Harcourt 2001 188p il
$16; pa $5.95
Grades: 4 5 6   **Fic**
1. Grandparents—Fiction 2. Mississippi—Fiction
ISBN 0-15-202314-3; 0-15-205478-2 (pa)
                                   LC 00-11159
"Gulliver books"

When her quirky grandmother goes to Hawaii for the
summer, nine-year-old Ruby learns to survive on her
own in Mississippi by writing letters, befriending chickens as well as the new girl in town, and finally coping
with her grandfather's death

"The engaging narrative . . . is witty and fast paced
and the quirky, diverse cast of human and poultry characters is colorful and spirited, if not totally realistic." SLJ

Williams, Dar

Amalee; by Dar Williams. Scholastic 2004 180p
$16.95; pa $5.99
Grades: 5 6 7 8   **Fic**
1. Single parent family—Fiction 2. Friendship—Fiction 3. Sick—Fiction
ISBN 0-439-39563-1; 0-439-39564-X (pa)

Amalee is being raised by her single father and his
group of eccentric friends, and when he becomes seriously ill everyone pitches in to try to cope with the ensuing
fear and chaos.

"Readers will be charmed by Williams' eccentric, lovable characters and her sharp observations about the
world of both middle-schoolers and adults." Booklist

Another title about Amalee is:
Lights, camera, Amalee (2006)

Williams, Laura E.

Slant; [by] Laura E. Williams. Milkweed
Editions 2008 149p $16.95; pa $6.95
Grades: 5 6 7 8 9   **Fic**
1. Prejudices—Fiction   2.   Mothers—Fiction
3. Adoption—Fiction 4. Korean Americans—Fiction
5. Friendship—Fiction 6. Plastic surgery—Fiction
ISBN   978-1-57131-681-3;   1-57131-681-7;
978-1-57131-682-0 (pa); 1-57131-682-5 (pa)
                                 LC 2008007093
Thirteen-year-old Lauren, a Korean-American adoptee,
is tired of being called "slant" and "gook," and longs to

have plastic surgery on her eyes, but when her father
finds out about her wish—and a long-kept secret about
her mother's death is revealed—Lauren starts to question
some of her own assumptions

"The characters are exceptionally well drawn, and the
friendship between Julie and Lauren is not only believable, featuring humor, conflict, and true wit, but also
captures both girls' gains in maturity." SLJ

Williams, Maiya

The Fizzy Whiz kid. Amulet Books 2010 273p
$16.95
Grades: 5 6 7 8   **Fic**
1. Moving—Fiction 2. Hollywood (Calif.)—Fiction
3. Advertising—Fiction
ISBN 978-0-8109-8347-2; 0-8109-8347-8

Moving to Hollywood with his academic parents,
eleven-year-old Mitch feels like an outsider in his school
where everyone has connections to the powerful and famous in the entertainment industry, until he is cast in a
soda commercial that launches a popular catchphrase.

"Williams' breezy tale is as addictive and bubbly as
a Fizzy Whiz itself, and her experience in the entertainment industry packs real value into her descriptions of
auditions, movie sets, and agent negotiations. . . . Mitchell's realization that he is a product being assembled is
both goofy and poignant." Booklist

Williams, Marcia, 1945-

Archie's war; my scrapbook of the First World
War, 1914-1918. Candlewick Press 2007 45p il
$17.99
Grades: 3 4 5 6   **Fic**
1. World War, 1914-1918—Fiction 2. Great Britain—
Fiction
ISBN 978-0-7636-3532-9; 0-7636-3532-4
                                 LC 2007-23012
Companion to: My secret war diary, by Flossie Al-
bright: my history of the Second World War, 1939-1945
(2008)

When Archie is given a scrapbook for his tenth birthday in 1914, he chronicles the next four years of his life
using documents, artifacts, and comic strips

"The large-format pages, jam-packed with tiny colored-pencil drawings with extensive captions, detailed
sidebars, and pasted-in letters and postcards, flesh out the
story and characters. . . . This imaginative presentation
of historical fiction puts them in context and provides a
highly visual experience that readers will pore over again
and again." SLJ

My secret war diary, by Flossie Albright; my
history of the Second World War, 1939-1945.
Candlewick Press 2008 141p il lib bdg $21.99
Grades: 3 4 5 6   **Fic**
1. World War, 1939-1945—Fiction 2. Diaries—Fiction
ISBN 978-0-7636-4111-5 (lib bdg); 0-7636-4111-1 (lib
bdg)
Companion volume to: Archie's war: my scrapbook of
the First World War, 1914-1918 (2007)

Marcia Williams uses her own childhood momentos to
create a diary of a nine-year-old girl in Britain during
World War II

Williams, Marcia, 1945-—*Continued*

"Children will quickly come to enjoy Flossie's energetic delivery and endless doodling. They will love poring over the extras-asides, sidebars, and letters found under flaps and in envelopes, that Williams has compiled to give the book the feel that one has stumbled into a real girl's private keepsake. . . . Children who enjoy history will be fascinated by Flossie and will undoubtedly be inspired to learn more about the events she describes." SLJ

Williams, Mary

Brothers in hope; the story of the Lost Boys of Sudan; illustrated by R. Gregory Christie. Lee & Low Books 2005 unp il $17.95

Grades: 3 4 5   **Fic**

1. Refugees—Fiction 2. Sudan—Fiction 3. War stories

ISBN 1-58430-232-1   LC 2004-20965

Eight-year-old Garang, orphaned by a civil war in Sudan, finds the inner strength to help lead other boys as they trek hundreds of miles seeking safety in Ethiopia, then Kenya, and finally in the United States.

"Christie's distinctive acrylic illustrations, done in broad strokes of predominantly green, yellow, and burnt orange, are arresting in their combination of realism and the abstract. . . . This important profile in courage is one that belongs in most collections." SLJ

Williams, Tad

The dragons of Ordinary Farm; by Tad Williams and Deborah Beale; pictures by Greg Swearingen. Harper 2009 412p il $16.99

Grades: 4 5 6 7   **Fic**

1. Farms—Fiction 2. Mythical animals—Fiction 3. Supernatural—Fiction 4. Uncles—Fiction 5. Siblings—Fiction

ISBN 978-0-06-154345-6; 0-06-154345-4

LC 2008035298

When their great-uncle Gideon invites Tyler and Lucinda to his farm for the summer, they discover his animals are extremely unusual.

"Williams and Beale have created a gripping fantasy with realistic but appealing characters as well as scientific magic that explains the appearance of legendary creatures." SLJ

Williams-Garcia, Rita

One crazy summer. Amistad 2010 218p $15.99; lib bdg $16.89 *

Grades: 4 5 6 7   **Fic**

1. Black Panther Party—Fiction. 2. Sisters—Fiction 3. Mothers—Fiction 4. Poets—Fiction 5. African Americans—Civil rights—Fiction

ISBN 978-0-06-076088-5; 0-06-076088-5; 978-0-06-076089-2 (lib bdg); 0-06-076089-3 (lib bdg)

LC 2009-09293

In the summer of 1968, after travelling from Brooklyn to Oakland, California, to spend a month with the mother they barely know, eleven-year-old Delphine and her two younger sisters arrive to a cold welcome as they discover that their mother, a dedicated poet and printer, is resentful of the intrusion of their visit and wants them to at-

tend a nearby Black Panther summer camp.

"Delphine's growing awareness of injustice on a personal and universal level is smoothly woven into the story in poetic language that will stimulate and move readers." Publ Wkly

Willner-Pardo, Gina

Figuring out Frances. Clarion Bks. 1999 134p $14

Grades: 4 5 6   **Fic**

1. Friendship—Fiction 2. Grandmothers—Fiction 3. Alzheimer's disease—Fiction

ISBN 0-395-91510-4   LC 98-50082

Ten-year-old Abigail's neighbor Travis, her best friend although he is at a different school, upsets her when he transfers to her school, ignores her, and laughs at her grandmother's Alzheimer's along with his new friends

"The writing is witty, sincere, and insightful. This is a gem of a book." SLJ

Wilson, Jacqueline

Best friends. Roaring Brook Press 2008 229p $15.95; pa $7.99

Grades: 4 5 6 7   **Fic**

1. Friendship—Fiction 2. School stories 3. Scotland—Fiction

ISBN 978-1-59643-278-9; 1-59643-278-0; 978-0-312-58144-2 (pa); 0-312-58144-0 (pa)

LC 2006-39716

"A Deborah Brodie book."

Rambunctious and irrepressible Gemma has been best friends with Alice ever since they were born on the same day, so when Alice moves miles away to Scotland, Gemma is distraught over the idea that Alice might find a new best friend.

"Believable, sympathetic characters; recognizable home and school situations; and plenty of humor . . . will ensure that this becomes . . . a popular read for middle-grade girls." Booklist

Candyfloss; [illustrated by] Nick Sharratt. Roaring Brook Press 2007 339p il $14.95; pa $6.99

Grades: 4 5 6   **Fic**

1. Divorce—Fiction 2. Father-daughter relationship—Fiction 3. Friendship—Fiction 4. Great Britain—Fiction

ISBN 978-1-59643-241-3; 1-59643-241-1; 978-0-312-38418-0 (pa); 0-312-38418-1 (pa)

LC 2006-19923

When her mother plans to move to Australia with her new husband and baby, Floss must decide whether her loyalties lie with her mother or her father, while at the same time, her best friend begins to make fun of her and reject her.

This is "a novel that contains many compelling, sometimes gritty, elements." Publ Wkly

Wilson, Jacqueline—*Continued*
Cookie; illustrated by Nick Sharratt. Roaring Brook Press 2009 320p il $16.99
Grades: 4 5 6 7   **Fic**
1. Father-daughter relationship—Fiction 2. Friendship—Fiction
ISBN 978-1-59643-534-6; 1-59643-534-8
Cookie is plain and shy, not the confident, popular girl her father wanted when he named her Beauty Cookson. Her mother helps her cook up a clever scheme to change her image—but, as usual, Dad doesn't approve, and this time his anger reaches frightening new heights
"Wilson's talent shows again in this novel with strong, compelling characters and a plot that makes the book hard to put down." SLJ

The illustrated Mum; [by] Jacqueline Wilson. Delacorte Press 2005 282p hardcover o.p. pa $5.50
Grades: 5 6 7 8   **Fic**
1. Manic-depressive illness—Fiction 2. Mother-daughter relationship—Fiction 3. Sisters—Fiction 4. Tattooing—Fiction
ISBN 0-385-73237-6; 0-440-42043-1 (pa)
LC 2003-70123
First published 1999 in the United Kingdom
Ten-year-old Dolphin is determined to stay with her family, no matter what, but when her sister goes to live with her newly-discovered father, sending their mother further into manic-depression, Dolphin's life takes a turn for the better.
"Dolphin is a sympathetic character and the relationship between the sisters is realistically portrayed, as is Marigold's mental illness." SLJ

Wilson, Nancy Hope, 1947-
Mountain pose. Farrar, Straus & Giroux 2001 233p $17
Grades: 5 6 7 8   **Fic**
1. Grandmothers—Fiction 2. Diaries—Fiction 3. Vermont—Fiction
ISBN 0-374-35078-7   LC 00-57269
When twelve-year-old Ellie inherits an old Vermont farm from her cruel and heartless grandmother Aurelia, she reads a set of diaries written by an ancestor and discovers secrets from the past
"Beautifully written and suspenseful, this novel explores the many emotions associated with the tragedy of spousal and child abuse." Voice Youth Advocates

Wilson, Nathan D.
100 cupboards; [by] N.D. Wilson. Random House 2007 289p $16.99; lib bdg $19.99; pa $6.99
Grades: 5 6 7 8   **Fic**
1. Magic—Fiction 2. Cousins—Fiction 3. Kansas—Fiction
ISBN 978-0-375-83881-1; 978-0-375-93881-8 (lib bdg); 978-0-375-83882-8 (pa)   LC 2007-00164
After his parents are kidnapped, timid twelve-year-old Henry York leaves his sheltered Boston life and moves to small-town Kansas, where he and his cousin Henrietta discover and explore hidden doors in his attic room that seem to open onto other worlds.
"There's an appealing blend of genuine creepiness and kindly domesticity here." Bull Cent Child Books

Other titles in this series are:
Dandelion Fire (2008)
The Chestnut King (2010)

Leepike Ridge; [by] N.D. Wilson. Random House 2007 224p $15.99; lib bdg $18.99; pa $6.99
*
Grades: 4 5 6 7   **Fic**
1. Missing persons—Fiction 2. Caves—Fiction 3. Adventure fiction 4. Mother-son relationship—Fiction
ISBN 978-0-375-83873-6; 0-375-83873-2; 978-0-375-93873-3 (lib bdg); 0-375-93873-7 (lib bdg); 978-0-375-83874-3 (pa); 0-375-83874-0 (pa)
LC 2006-13352
While his widowed mother continues to search for him, eleven-year-old Tom, presumed dead after drifting away down a river, finds himself trapped in a series of underground caves with another survivor and a dog, and pursued by murderous treasure-hunters.
"While *Leepike Ridge* is primarily an adventure story involving murder, treachery, and betrayal, Wilson's rich imagination and his quirky characters are a true delight." SLJ

Winerip, Michael
Adam Canfield of the Slash. Candlewick Press 2005 326p $15.99; pa $6.99
Grades: 5 6 7 8   **Fic**
1. Journalism—Fiction 2. School stories
ISBN 0-7636-2340-7; 0-7636-2794-1 (pa)
While serving as co-editors of their school newspaper, middle-schoolers Adam and Jennifer uncover fraud and corruption in their school and in the city's government.
"This is a deceptively fun read that somehow manages to present kids with some of the most subtle social and ethical questions currently shaping their futures." SLJ
Other titles about Adam Canfield are:
Adam Canfield, watch you back! (2007)
Adam Canfield, the last reporter (2009)

Winterson, Jeanette, 1959-
Tanglewreck. Bloomsbury Children's Books 2006 414p $16.95; pa $6.95
Grades: 5 6 7 8   **Fic**
1. Science fiction 2. Space and time—Fiction 3. Clocks and watches—Fiction
ISBN 978-1-58234-919-0; 1-58234-919-3; 978-1-59990-081-0 (pa); 1-59990-081-5 (pa)
LC 2005-30630
Eleven-year-old Silver sets out to find the Timekeeper—a clock that controls time—and to protect it from falling into the hands of two people who want to use the device for their own nefarious ends
"Winterson seamlessly combines rousing adventure with time warps, quantum physics, and a few wonderfully hapless flunkies." Booklist

Winthrop, Elizabeth

Counting on Grace. Wendy Lamb Books 2006 232p $15.95; lib bdg $17.99; pa $6.99

Grades: 5 6 7 8   **Fic**

1. Hine, Lewis Wickes, 1874-1940—Fiction 2. Child labor—Fiction 3. Factories—Fiction 4. Photographers—Fiction 5. Vermont—Fiction

ISBN 0-385-74644-X; 0-385-90878-4 (lib bdg); 0-553-48783-3 (pa)

It's 1910 in Pownal, Vermont. At 12 Grace and her best friend Arthur must go to work in the mill, helping their mothers work the looms. Together Grace and Arthur write a secret letter to the Child Labor Board about underage children working in the mill. A few weeks later, Lewis Hine, a famous reformer, arrives undercover to gather evidence. Grace meets him and appears in some of his photographs, changing her life forever.

"Much information on early photography and the workings of the textile mills is conveyed, and history and fiction are woven seamlessly together in this beautifully written novel." SLJ

Wise, William, 1923-

Christopher Mouse; the tale of a small traveler; illustrations by Patrick Benson. Bloomsbury Children's Books 2004 152p il $15.95; pa $5.95

Grades: 3 4 5   **Fic**

1. Mice—Fiction

ISBN 1-58234-878-2; 1-58234-708-5 (pa)

LC 2003-56393

After being sold to an unscrupulous pet store owner, a young mouse lives with several owners and has many adventures, before ending up with an appreciative family.

"The writing is nicely mannered but very accessible, making the book not only a winner for reading aloud but also a delightful offering for children moving past beginning readers. The ink illustrations and the enticing cover will help them along." Booklist

Wiseman, David, 1916-

Jeremy Visick. Houghton Mifflin 1981 170p pa $5.95 hardcover o.p.

Grades: 5 6 7 8   **Fic**

1. Space and time—Fiction 2. Supernatural—Fiction 3. Great Britain—Fiction 4. Miners—Fiction

ISBN 0-618-34514-0 (pa)   LC 80-28116

Twelve-year-old Matthew is drawn almost against his will to help a boy his own age who was lost in a mining disaster a century before.

"This story blends the mystery and awe of the supernatural with the real terror and peril of descending the shaft of an 1850 Cornish copper mine." SLJ

Wittlinger, Ellen, 1948-

This means war! Simon & Schuster Books for Young Readers 2010 224p $16.99

Grades: 5 6 7 8   **Fic**

1. Friendship—Fiction 2. Fear—Fiction 3. Contests—Fiction

ISBN 978-1-4169-97101-6; 1-4169-7101-7

LC 2008-32586

In 1962, when her best friend Lowell begins to hang around new friends who think girls are losers, Juliet, a fearful fifth-grader, teams up with bold, brave Patsy who challenges the boys to a series of increasingly dangerous contests

"Wittlinger latches on to a poignant metaphor for war in the lively and readable tale set against the backdrop of the 1962 Cuban missile crisis." Booklist

Wojciechowska, Maia, 1927-2002

Shadow of a bull; drawings by Alvin Smith. Atheneum Pubs. 1964 165p il $16; pa $5.99

Grades: 6 7 8 9   **Fic**

1. Spain—Fiction 2. Bullfights—Fiction

ISBN 0-689-30042-5; 1-4169-3395-6 (pa)

Awarded the Newbery Medal, 1965

"Manolo was the son of the great bullfighter Juan Olivar. Ever since his father's death the town of Arcangel [Spain] has waited for [the time] when Manolo would be twelve and face his first bull." Publ Wkly

"In spare, economical prose [the author] makes one feel, see, smell the heat, endure the hot Andalusian sun and shows one the sand and glare of the bullring. Above all, she lifts the veil and gives glimpses of the terrible loneliness in the soul of a boy. . . . Superbly illustrated." N Y Times Book Rev

Wolf, Joan M., 1966-

Someone named Eva. Clarion Books 2007 200p $16; pa $6.99 *

Grades: 5 6 7 8   **Fic**

1. World War, 1939-1945—Fiction 2. National socialism—Fiction 3. Europe—History—1918-1945—Fiction 4. School stories

ISBN 0-618-53579-9; 0-547-23766-9 (pa)

LC 2006-26070

From her home in Lidice, Czechoslovakia, in 1942, eleven-year-old Milada is taken with other blond, blue-eyed children to a school in Poland to be trained as "proper Germans" for adoption by German families, but all the while she remembers her true name and history.

"This amazing, eye-opening story, masterfully written, is an essential part of World War II literature and belongs on the shelves of every library." SLJ

Wolf-Morgenlander, Karl

Ragtag. Clarion Books 2009 225p il $16

Grades: 3 4 5 6   **Fic**

1. Birds—Fiction 2. Fantasy fiction 3. War stories 4. Boston (Mass.)—Fiction

ISBN 978-0-547-07424-5; 0-547-07424-7

LC 2008025319

A young swallow leads a band of birds against an empire of raptors that has invaded Boston

"This novel opens up the world of these lively feathered creatures and their way of life. The story line moves quickly." SLJ

Wolfson, Jill

Home, and other big, fat lies. Henry Holt 2006 281p $16.95

Grades: 5 6 7 8 **Fic**

1. Foster home care—Fiction 2. Nature—Fiction 3. Environmental protection—Fiction

ISBN 978-0-8050-7670-7; 0-8050-7670-0

LC 200035843

Eleven-year-old Termite, a foster child with an eye for the beauty of nature and a talent for getting into trouble, takes on the loggers in her new home town when she tries to save the biggest tree in the forest.

"Written with humor and sensitivity." Voice Youth Advocates

What I call life. Holt & Co. 2005 270p $16.95; pa $6.99

Grades: 5 6 7 8 **Fic**

1. Foster home care—Fiction

ISBN 0-8050-7669-7; 0-312-37752-5 (pa)

Placed in a group foster home, eleven-year-old Cal Lavender learns how to cope with life from the four other girls who live there and from their storytelling guardian, the Knitting Lady.

"Wolfson paints her characters with delightful authenticity. Her debut novel is a treasure of quiet good humor and skillful storytelling that conveys subtle messages about kindness, compassion, and the gift of family regardless of its configuration." Booklist

Wong, Janet S., 1962-

Minn and Jake; [by] Janet Wong; pictures by Geneviève Côté. Farrar, Straus & Giroux 2003 146p il $16; pa $6.95

Grades: 3 4 5 **Fic**

1. Friendship—Fiction 2. School stories 3. Novels in verse

ISBN 0-374-34987-8; 978-0-374-34987-5; 978-0-374-40021-7 (pa); 0-374-40021-0 (pa)

LC 2002-35421

"Frances Foster books"

Fifth-grader Minn, the tallest girl in school, begins a rocky friendship with Jake, a new student who is not only very short, but is also afraid of the worms and lizards that Minn likes to collect

"This breezy free-verse novel introduces memorable characters in recognizable situations. . . . [Côté's] b&w illustrations achieve unusual dimension. Incorporating what seem to be collage elements, her strikingly graphic compositions mirror the deceptive ease of the verse narration." Publ Wkly

Another title about Minn and Jake is:

Minn and Jake's almost terrible summer (2008)

Wood, Maryrose

The mysterious howling; illustrated by Jon Klassen. Balzer & Bray 2010 267p il (The incorrigible children of Ashton Place) $15.99 *

Grades: 4 5 6 **Fic**

1. Wild children—Fiction 2. Christmas—Fiction 3. Orphans—Fiction

ISBN 978-0-06-179105-5; 0-06-179105-9

Fifteen-year-old Miss Penelope Lumley, a recent graduate of the Swanburne Academy for Poor Bright Fe-

males, is hired as governess to three young children who have been raised by wolves and must teach them to behave in a civilized manner quickly, in preparation for a Christmas ball.

"Smartly written with a middle-grade audience in mind, this is both fun and funny and sprinkled with dollops of wisdom." Booklist

Woodruff, Elvira

Fearless. Scholastic Press 2008 224p il $16.99

Grades: 5 6 7 8 **Fic**

1. Winstanley, Henry, 1644-1703—Fiction 2. Orphans—Fiction 3. Adventure fiction 4. Lighthouses—Fiction 5. Great Britain—History—1603-1714, Stuarts—Fiction

ISBN 978-0-439-67703-5; 0-439-67703-3

LC 2006-10137

In late seventeenth-century England, eleven-year-old Digory, forced to leave his hometown after his father is lost at sea, becomes an apprentice to the architect Henry Winstanley, who built a lighthouse on the treacherous Eddystone Reef—the very rocks that sank Digory's grandfather's ship years before.

"This fascinating, well-written story is closely based on the life of the real Henry Winstanley. . . . The characters are finely drawn and the action is nonstop." SLJ

The Ravenmaster's secret. Scholastic Press 2003 225p $15.95; pa $5.99

Grades: 5 6 7 8 **Fic**

1. Tower of London (England)—Fiction 2. Great Britain—History—1714-1837—Fiction 3. Ravens—Fiction 4. London (England)—Fiction

ISBN 0-439-28133-4; 0-439-28134-2 (pa)

LC 2002-15963

The eleven-year-old son of the Ravenmaster at the Tower of London befriends a Jacobite rebel being held prisoner there.

"An absorbing historical adventure with a unique and colorful setting. . . . The novel can be read for its exciting plot and sympathetic characters, but readers will also sense its underlying theme of courage." Booklist

Woods, Brenda

My name is Sally Little Song. G.P. Putnam's Sons 2006 182p $15.99; pa $5.99

Grades: 4 5 6 7 **Fic**

1. Slavery—Fiction 2. African Americans—Fiction 3. Seminole Indians—Fiction 4. Georgia—Fiction 5. Florida—Fiction

ISBN 0-399-24312-7; 0-14-240943-X (pa)

LC 2005-32651

When their owner plans to sell one of them in 1802, twelve-year-old Sally and her family run away from their Georgia plantation to look for both freedom from slavery and a home in Florida with the Seminole Indians.

"Based on historical accounts, this novel provides readers with an alternative view of the realities of slavery—an escape to the South rather than North. . . . This accessible tale will prove a rich resource for study and discussion." SLJ

Woods, Brenda—_Continued_

The red rose box. Putnam 2002 136p $16.99; pa
$5.99

Grades: 5 6 7 8   **Fic**
1. African Americans—Fiction 2. Louisiana—Fiction
3. Los Angeles (Calif.)—Fiction
ISBN 0-399-23702-X; 0-14-250151-4 (pa)
                                          LC 2001-18354
In 1953, Leah Hopper dreams of leaving the poverty
and segregation of her home in Sulphur, Louisiana, and
when Aunt Olivia sends train tickets to Los Angeles as
part of her tenth birthday present, Leah gets a first taste
of freedom
"In language made musical with southern phrases, this
. . . novel shapes the era and characters with both well-
chosen particulars and universal emotions." Booklist

Woodson, Jacqueline

Feathers. G.P. Putnam's Sons 2007 118p
$15.99; pa $6.99 *

Grades: 4 5 6 7   **Fic**
1. Race relations—Fiction 2. African Americans—Fic-
tion 3. Religion—Fiction
ISBN   978-0-399-23989-2;   0-399-23989-8;
978-0-14-241198-8 (pa); 0-14-241198-1 (pa)
                                          LC 2006-24713
A Newbery Medal honor book, 2008
When a new, white student nicknamed "The Jesus
Boy" joins her sixth grade class in the winter of 1971,
Frannie's growing friendship with him makes her start to
see some things in a new light.
"Woodson creates in Frannie a strong protagonist who
thinks for herself and recognizes the value and meaning
of family. The story ends with hope and thoughtfulness
while speaking to those adolescents who struggle with
race, faith, and prejudice." SLJ

Locomotion. Putnam 2003 100p $17.99; pa
$5.99 *

Grades: 4 5 6 7   **Fic**
1. African Americans—Fiction 2. Foster home care—
Fiction 3. Novels in verse
ISBN   978-0-399-23115-53;   0-399-23115-3;
978-0-14-241552-8 (pa); 0-14-241552-9 (pa)
                                          LC 2002-69779
In a series of poems, eleven-year-old Lonnie writes
about his life, after the death of his parents, separated
from his younger sister, living in a foster home, and
finding his poetic voice at school
"In a masterful use of voice, Woodson allows Lonnie's poems to tell a complex story of loss and grief and
to create a gritty, urban environment. Despite the spare
text, Lonnie's foster mother and the other minor characters are three-dimensional, making the boy's world a
convincingly real one." SLJ

Peace, Locomotion. G.P. Putnam's Sons 2009
134p $15.99; pa $7.99 *

Grades: 4 5 6 7   **Fic**
1. Foster home care—Fiction 2. Siblings—Fiction
3. Orphans—Fiction 4. African Americans—Fiction
5. Letters—Fiction
ISBN   978-0-399-24655-5;   0-399-24655-X;
978-0-14-241512-2 (pa); 0-14-241512-X (pa)
                                          LC 2008-18583

Companion volume to: Locomotion (2003)
Through letters to his little sister, who is living in a
different foster home, sixth-grader Lonnie, also known as
"Locomotion," keeps a record of their lives while they
are apart, describing his own foster family, including his
foster brother who returns home after losing a leg in the
Iraq War
"Woodson creates a full-bodied character in kind, sensitive Lonnie. Readers will understand his quest for
peace, and appreciate the hard work he does to find it."
Publ Wkly

Wrede, Patricia C., 1953-

Dealing with dragons. Harcourt Brace
Jovanovich 1990 212p pa $5.95 *

Grades: 6 7 8 9   **Fic**
1. Fairy tales 2. Dragons—Fiction
ISBN 0-15-222900-0; 0-15-204566-X (pa)
                                          LC 89-24599

"Jane Yolen books"
Bored with traditional palace life, a princess goes off
to live with a group of dragons and soon becomes involved with fighting against some disreputable wizards
who want to steal away the dragons' kingdom
"A decidedly diverting novel with plenty of action and
many slightly skewed fairy-tale conventions that add to
the laugh-out-loud reading pleasure and give the story a
wide appeal. The good news is that this is book one in
the Enchanted Forest Chronicles." Booklist
Other titles in the Enchanted Forest Chronicles are:
Calling on dragons (1993)
Searching for dragons (1991)
Talking to dragons (1993)

Wright, Betty Ren

The dollhouse murders. Holiday House 1983
149p $17.95; pa $7.95

Grades: 4 5 6 7   **Fic**
1. Mystery fiction
ISBN 0-8234-0497-8; 0-8234-2172-4 (pa)
                                          LC 83-6147
A dollhouse filled with a ghostly light in the middle
of the night and dolls that have moved from where she
last left them lead Amy and her retarded sister to unravel
the mystery surrounding grisly murders that took place
years ago
"More than just a mystery, this offers keen insight
into the relationship between handicapped and
nonhandicapped siblings and glimpses into the darker
adult emotions of guilt and anger. A successful, full-
bodied work." Booklist

Princess for a week; illustrated by Jacqueline
Rogers. Holiday House 2006 105p il $16.95; pa
$6.95

Grades: 2 3 4   **Fic**
1. Ghost stories 2. Mystery fiction
ISBN 0-8234-1945-2; 0-8234-2111-2 (pa)
                                          LC 2005-50288
When a confident girl named Princess arrives to spend
a week at Roddy's house, she encourages him to help
her investigate the suspicious activities happening at a
supposedly haunted house.

Wright, Betty Ren—*Continued*
"The story moves quickly and is excellently paced.
. . . The full-page illustrations add realism and depth to
the story." SLJ

Wyatt, Leslie J.
Poor is just a starting place; by Leslie J. Wyatt.
Holiday House 2005 196p $16.95
Grades: 5 6 7 8   **Fic**
1. Great Depression, 1929-1939—Fiction 2. Poverty—
Fiction 3. Kentucky—Fiction
ISBN 0-8234-1884-7   LC 2004-47451
During the Great Depression, twelve-year-old Artie
Wilson, determined to escape plowing and planting the
fields and milking the cow on her family's farm, longs
to leave Buck Creek, Kentucky, and her life of poverty
"Written with spare beauty, this first novel tells a
moving story." Booklist

Wynne-Jones, Tim
Rex Zero and the end of the world. Farrar,
Straus & Giroux 2007 86p $16 *
Grades: 4 5 6   **Fic**
1. Moving—Fiction 2. Family life—Fiction
3. Canada—Fiction 4. Cold war—Fiction
ISBN 0-374-33467-6; 978-0-374-33467-3
LC 2006-45172
In the summer of 1962 with everyone nervous about
a possible nuclear war, ten-nearly-eleven-year-old Rex,
having just moved to Ottawa from Vancouver with his
parents and five siblings, faces his own personal challenges as he discovers new friends and a new understanding of the world around him.
"Despite the weighty themes, Wynne-Jones writes
with a light, often humorous touch and maintains a perspective true to an 11-year-old's perspective." Publ Wkly
Another title about Rex Zero is:
Rex Zero, king of nothing (2008)

Wyss, Johann David, 1743-1818
The Swiss family Robinson; by Johann Wyss;
edited by William H. G. Kingston; illustrated by
Lynd Ward. Grosset & Dunlap 1999 388p il
$18.99
Grades: 5 6 7 8   **Fic**
1. Survival after airplane accidents, shipwrecks, etc.—
Fiction
ISBN 0-448-06022-1
"Illustrated junior library"
Originally published 1812-1813 in Switzerland
When a Swiss couple and their four sons are ship-
wrecked on an isolated island, they adapt to their "New
Switzerland" using many imaginative methods of farming
and animal taming.

Wyss, Thelma Hatch
Bear dancer; the story of a Ute girl. Margaret K.
McElderry Books 2005 181p il $15.95
Grades: 5 6 7 8   **Fic**
1. Ute Indians—Fiction
ISBN 1-4169-0285-6   LC 2005-40620

In late nineteenth-century Colorado, Elk Girl, sister of
Ute chief Ouray, is captured by Cheyenne and Arapaho
warriors, rescued by the white "enemy," and finally re-
turned to her home. Includes historical notes.
"This fascinating story is based on a real person. . . .
An excellent addition to historical-fiction collections."
SLJ

A tale of gold; [by] Thelma Hatch Wyss.
Margaret K. McElderry Books 2007 152p $15.99
Grades: 4 5 6   **Fic**
1. Friendship—Fiction 2. Orphans—Fiction 3. Gold
mines and mining—Fiction 4. Klondike River Valley
(Yukon)—Gold discoveries—Fiction
ISBN 978-1-4169-4212-2; 1-4169-4212-2
LC 2006037545
Orphaned fourteen-year-old James decides to join the
"stampeders" heading to the Yukon gold rush, and along
the way joins up with two unusual partners who share a
common bond of wanting to strike it rich
"Filled with interesting characters and fast-paced action, the book is well worth reading on a number of
levels." SLJ

Yee, Lisa
Bobby vs. girls (accidentally); illustrated by Dan
Santat. Arthur A. Levine Books 2009 170p il
$15.99; pa $5.99
Grades: 4 5 6   **Fic**
1. Friendship—Fiction 2. School stories
ISBN   978-0-545-05592-5;   0-545-05592-X;
978-0-545-05593-2 (pa); 0-545-05593-8 (pa)
When Bobby inadvertently gets into a fight with his
best friend Holly, their disagreement develops into a
boys versus girls war involving their whole fourth-grade
class.
"Yee really understands children's thought processes
and presents them with tact and good humor. . . .
Santat's drawings manage the fine line between cartoon
and realism and add dimension to the events. Readers
will recognize themselves and learn some gentle lessons
about relationships while they are laughing at the antics."
Kirkus

Millicent Min, girl genius. Arthur A. Levine
Books 2003 248p $16.95; pa $4.99
Grades: 5 6 7   **Fic**
1. Gifted children—Fiction 2. School stories
3. Chinese Americans—Fiction
ISBN 0-439-42519-0; 0-439-42520-4 (pa)
LC 2003-3747
"At the tender age of eleven, Millicent Min has completed her junior year of high school. Summer school is
Millie's idea of fun, so she is excited that her parents are
allowing her to take a college poetry course. . . . The
tension between Millie's formal, overly intellectual way
of expressing herself and her emotional immaturity
makes her a very funny narrator. . . . Readers considerably older than Millicent's eleven years will enjoy this
strong debut novel." Voice Youth Advocates
Other titles about Millicent Min and her friends are:
Stanford Wong flunks big-time (2005)
So totally Emily Ebers (2007)

Yep, Laurence

City of fire. Tom Doherty Associates 2009 320p $15.99

Grades: 5 6 7 8   **Fic**

1. Fantasy fiction 2. Magic—Fiction 3. Dragons—Fiction 4. Hawaii—Fiction

ISBN 978-0-7653-1924-1; 0-7653-1924-1

LC 2009016737

"A Starscape book"

Twelve-year-old Scirye and her companions travel to Houlani, a new Hawaiian island created by magic, where they enlist the help of volcano goddess Pele in an attempt to stop an evil dragon and a mysterious man from altering the universe.

"Readers will be on tenterhooks awaiting the next episode of this exhilarating chase." Booklist

The dragon's child; a story of Angel Island; [by] Laurence Yep, with Kathleen S. Yep. HarperCollinsPublishers 2008 133p $15.99; lib bdg $16.89 *

Grades: 3 4 5 6   **Fic**

1. California—Fiction 2. China—Fiction 3. Chinese Americans—Fiction 4. Immigrants—Fiction

ISBN 978-0-06-027692-8; 0-06-027692-4; 978-0-06-027693-5 (lib bdg); 0-06-027693-2 (lib bdg)

LC 2007-18373

"In a dramatic blend of fact and fiction, Laurence Yep and his niece draw on family stories, immigration records, and memories of Laurence's own conversations to tell his dad's story of coming to America at age 10 with *his* Chinese American dad. . . . With family photos, a historical note, and a long bibliography, this stirring narrative will spark readers' own search for roots." Booklist

The magic paintbrush; drawings by Suling Wang. HarperCollins Pubs. 2000 89p il hardcover o.p. pa $5.99

Grades: 3 4 5   **Fic**

1. Chinese Americans—Fiction 2. Magic—Fiction

ISBN 0-06-028199-5; 0-06-440852-3 (pa)

LC 99-34959

A magic paintbrush transports Steve and his elderly caretakers from their drab apartment in Chinatown to a world of adventures

"Yep's crisp style keeps the pages turning, and he leavens his story with snappy dialogue, realistic characters and plenty of wise humor." Publ Wkly

Mia; by Laurence Yep. American Girl Pub. 2008 130p il pa $6.95

Grades: 2 3 4 5   **Fic**

1. Ice skating—Fiction

ISBN 978-1-59369-409-8 (pa); 1-59369-409-1 (pa)

Mia has grown up playing ice hockey with her three older brothers and has the skills she needs to become a star hockey player. But she's tired of skating in her brothers' shadows and has decided to pursue her passion for figure skating instead. With the help of a new coach, Mia finds out whether she has what it takes to grow and compete as a figure skater.

"Readers . . . get a closer look into the world of competitive figure skating. Illustrations . . . look like digitized photos and are mostly of Mia with her family or free skating. . . . Well written and fun." SLJ

Another title about Mia is:

Bravo, Mia! (2008)

The traitor; Golden Mountain chronicles, 1885. HarperCollins Pubs. 2003 310p hardcover o.p. pa $6.99 *

Grades: 5 6 7 8   **Fic**

1. Prejudices—Fiction 2. Friendship—Fiction 3. Chinese Americans—Fiction

ISBN 0-06-027522-7; 0-06-000831-8 (pa)

LC 2002-22534

Sequel to Dragon's gate

In 1885, a lonely illegitimate American boy and a lonely Chinese American boy develop an unlikely friendship in the midst of prejudices and racial tension in their coal mining town of Rock Springs, Wyoming

"The short chapters read quickly, and readers will become involved through the first-person voices that capture each boy's feelings of being an outsider and a traitor." Booklist

When the circus came to town; drawings by Suling Wang. HarperCollins Pubs. 2002 113p il hardcover o.p. pa $5.99

Grades: 3 4 5   **Fic**

1. Frontier and pioneer life—Fiction 2. Chinese New Year—Fiction 3. Circus—Fiction 4. Chinese Americans—Fiction

ISBN 0-06-029325-X; 0-06-440965-1 (pa)

LC 2001-39290

An Asian cook and a Chinese New Year celebration help ten-year-old Ursula at a Montana stage coach station to regain her confidence after smallpox scars her face

"Yep has based his novel on a true story, and his writing is, by turns, direct, humorous, and poignant." Booklist

Ylvisaker, Anne

Little Klein. Candlewick Press 2007 186p $15.99; pa $6.99

Grades: 3 4 5 6   **Fic**

1. Size—Fiction 2. Brothers—Fiction 3. Dogs—Fiction 4. Family life—Fiction

ISBN 978-0-7636-3359-2; 0-7636-3359-3; 978-0-7636-4338-6 (pa); 0-7636-4338-6 (pa)

LC 2007-24189

Harold "Little" Klein is so much smaller than his three older brothers, a boisterous gang held together by bighearted Mother Klein, that he often feels small and left out but when disaster strikes, it is up to Harold and LeRoy, the stray dog he has adopted, to save the day.

"Ylvisaker's pleasing text is rich with wit and flows seamlessly; her knack for capturing a character's essence is remarkable." Voice Youth Advocates

Yohalem, Eve

Escape under the forever sky; a novel. Chronicle Books 2009 220p $16.99 *

Grades: 4 5 6 7   **Fic**

1. Wilderness survival—Fiction 2. Kidnapping—Fiction 3. Mother-daughter relationship—Fiction 4. Ethiopia—Fiction

ISBN 978-0-8118-6653-8; 0-8118-6653-X

LC 2008-19565

Yohalem, Eve—*Continued*

As a future conservation zoologist whose mother is the United States Ambassador to Ethiopia, thirteen-year-old Lucy uses her knowledge for survival when she is kidnapped and subsequently escapes.

"Lucy's past and present are gracefully woven together, through well-integrated flashbacks, into a powerful picture of the life of a foreigner in Ethiopia. The story should appeal to all with a sense of adventure." Publ Wkly

Young, Judy, 1956-

Minnow and Rose; an Oregon trail story; written by Judy Young; illustrated by Bill Farnsworth. Sleeping Bear Press 2009 unp il (Tales of young Americans) $17.95

Grades: 3 4 5   **Fic**

1. Frontier and pioneer life—Fiction 2. Native Americans—Fiction 3. Friendship—Fiction

ISBN 978-1-58536-421-3; 1-58536-421-5

                                  LC 2008024768

Traveling west with her pioneer family in a wagon train, Rose meets Minnow, who lives in a native American village along the banks of a river.

"Beautiful oil paintings . . . lend additional action and understanding to the story." SLJ

Zahler, Diane

The thirteenth princess. Harper 2009 243p $15.99; lib bdg $16.89

Grades: 4 5 6 7   **Fic**

1. Fairy tales 2. Princesses—Fiction 3. Sisters—Fiction 4. Household employees—Fiction 5. Father-daughter relationship—Fiction 6. Magic—Fiction

ISBN 978-0-06-182498-2; 0-06-182498-4; 978-0-06-182499-9 (lib bdg); 0-06-182499-2 (lib bdg)

                                  LC 2009-14575

Zita, cast aside by her father and raised as a kitchen maid, learns when she is nearly twelve that she is a princess and that her twelve sisters love her, and so when she discovers they are victims of an evil enchantment, she desperately tries to save them. Inspired by the Grimm fairy tale, "The twelve dancing princesses."

Zahler "deftly and thoughtfully embellishes the tale's classic elements. . . . Zahler takes a light story and gives it gratifying depth, rounding out the characters and their motivations without betraying the source material and wrapping it all together in a graceful and cohesive romantic drama." Publ Wkly

Zalben, Jane Breskin

Brenda Berman, wedding expert; illustrated by Victoria Chess. Clarion Books 2009 48p il lib bdg $16

Grades: 2 3 4   **Fic**

1. Weddings—Fiction 2. Uncles—Fiction 3. Friendship—Fiction

ISBN 978-0-618-31321-1 (lib bdg); 0-618-31321-4 (lib bdg)   LC 2006-34851

When Brenda's favorite uncle decides to marry, Brenda sees visions of a gold lame flower-girl's outfit, until

Uncle Harry and his bride-to-be show up with her niece. Includes cake recipe.

"Brenda's robust personality drives the narrative as well as the art, as Chess's folksy watercolors capture the girl's expressions, which vacillate wildly between outrage and exhilaration." Publ Wkly

Zimmer, Tracie Vaughn

42 miles; illustrated by Elaine Clayton. Clarion Books 2008 73p il $16

Grades: 4 5 6   **Fic**

1. Divorce—Fiction 2. Family life—Fiction 3. Farm life—Fiction 4. City and town life—Fiction 5. Novels in verse

ISBN 978-0-618-61867-5; 0-618-61867-8

                                  LC 2007-31032

As her thirteenth birthday approaches, JoEllen decides to bring together her two separate lives—one as Joey, who enjoys weekends with her father and other relatives on a farm, and another as Ellen, who lives with her mother in an apartment near her school and friends.

"Using free verse, Zimmer shows the richness in both places, while black-and-white composit illustrations bright the bits and pieces together." Booklist

The floating circus; by Tracie Vaughn Zimmer. Bloomsbury Children's Books 2008 198p $15.99

Grades: 4 5 6   **Fic**

1. Abandoned children—Fiction 2. Circus—Fiction 3. Boats and boating—Fiction

ISBN 978-1-59990-185-5; 1-59990-185-4

                                  LC 2007038998

In 1850s Pittsburgh, thirteen-year-old Owen leaves his younger brother and sneaks aboard a circus housed in a riverboat, where he befriends a freed slave, learns to work with elephants, and finally comes to terms with the choices he has made in his difficult life

This is a "lively historical novel. Readers will be hooked from the start by the voice of the narrator. . . . Bittersweet and satisfying." Publ Wkly

Sketches from a spy tree; poems by Tracie Vaughn Zimmer; illustrated by Andrew Glass. Clarion Books 2005 63p il $16

Grades: 3 4 5 6   **Fic**

1. Twins—Fiction 2. Sisters—Fiction 3. Divorce—Fiction 4. Stepfamilies—Fiction

ISBN 0-618-23479-9   LC 2003-27768

In a series of poems, narrator Anne Marie paints pictures of family life from grief to hope after her father abandons his "four girls" Anne Marie and her mother and twin and baby sister.

"The writing is lyrical yet fresh. . . . Glass's remarkable watercolors, sketches, photographs, and collages bring Anne Marie's experiences to life." SLJ

Zucker, Naomi Flink

Callie's rules; by Naomi Zucker. Egmont USA 2009 240p $15.99; lib bdg $18.99 *

Grades: 4 5 6 7   **Fic**

1. Family life—Fiction 2. School stories 3. New Jersey—Fiction 4. Halloween—Fiction

ISBN 978-1-60684-027-6; 1-60684-027-4; 978-1-60684-052-8 (lib bdg); 1-60684-052-5 (lib bdg)

                                  LC 2009-15419

Zucker, Naomi Flink—*Continued*

Eleven-year-old Callie Jones tries to keep track of all the rules for fitting in that other middle schoolers seem to know, but when the town decides to replace Halloween with an Autumn Festival, Callie leads her large family in an unusual protest.

"Callie herself is both funny and resourceful. Worthwhile and entertaining." Kirkus

S C STORY COLLECTIONS

Books in this class include collections of short stories by one author and collections by more than one author. Folk tales are entered in class 398.2. Collections of general literature, American literature, English literature, etc.—which may include but are not limited to short stories—are entered in classes 808.8, 810.8, 820.8, etc.

Aiken, Joan, 1924-2004

Shadows and moonshine; stories; illustrations by Pamela Johnson. Godine 2001 171p il hardcover o.p. pa $10.95

Grades: 4 5 6 7   S C

1. Fantasy fiction 2. Short stories
ISBN 1-56792-167-1; 1-56792-346-1 (pa)
LC 2001-23830

Contents: Gift pig; Rocking donkey; Cooks and prophecies; Lilac in the lake; Harp of fishbones; Small pinch of weather; King who stood all night; Cat's cradle; Moonshine in the mustard pot; Wolves and the mermaids; John Sculpin and the witches; Night the stars were gone; Boy with a wolf's foot

This is a collection 13 stories about such things as witches, enchanted pigs, mermaids, and dragons, selected from the author's earlier anthologies

"Whether scary, satiric, or poetic, Aiken's tales have strong settings, memorable characters, insight, and humor." SLJ

Alexander, Lloyd, 1924-2007

The foundling and other tales of Prydain. rev & expanded ed. Holt & Co. 1999 98p hardcover o.p. pa $5.99 *

Grades: 5 6 7 8   S C

1. Fantasy fiction 2. Short stories
ISBN 0-8050-6130-4; 0-8050-8053-8 (pa)
LC 98-42807

First published 1973; this revised and expanded edition includes two additional stories Coll and his white pig and The truthful harp, first published separately 1965 and 1967 respectively

Contents: The foundling; The stone; The true enchanter; The rascal crow; The sword; The smith, the weaver, and the harper; Coll and his white pig; The truthful harp

Eight short stories dealing with events that preceded the birth of Taran, the Assistant Pig-Keeper and key figure in the author's five works on the Kingdom of Prydain which began with The book of three

"The stories are written with vivid grace and humor." Chicago. Children's Book Center [review of 1973 edition]

Andersen, Hans Christian, 1805-1875

Hans Christian Andersen's Fairy Tales; selected and illustrated by Lisbeth Zwerger; translated by Anthea Bell. Minedition 2006 c1991 104p il $19.99 *

Grades: 4 5 6 7   S C

1. Fairy tales 2. Short stories
ISBN 0-698-40035-6

A reissue of the edition first published 1991

Contents: The sandman; The jumpers Thumbeline; The tinderbox; The rose tree regiment; The naughty boy; The swineherd; The emperor's new clothes; The princess and the pea; The nightingale; The little match girl

"This collection of . . . tales includes relatively unknown stories, such as 'The Rose Tree Regiment,' along with such familiar favorites as 'The Princess & the Pea.' Bell's finesse in writing is well matched by Zwerger's delicate, understated approach in the illustrations, which are introspective rather than dramatic. Sophisticated in design, the book features fluid watercolors and wide-bordered text on tall, white pages." Booklist

Avi, 1937-

Strange happenings; five tales of transformation. Harcourt 2006 147p $15; pa $5.95

Grades: 5 6 7 8   S C

1. Supernatural—Fiction 2. Short stories
ISBN 0-15-205790-0; 0-15-206461-3 (pa)
LC 2004-29579

Contents: Bored Tom; Babette the beautiful; Curious; The shoemaker and Old Scratch; Simon

"In this short story collection, Avi offers five fantastical tales, set in both contemporary and fairy-tale lands, that explore the notion of transformation. . . . The pieces are vividly imagined and shot through with a captivating, edgy spookiness, which, along with their brevity and some droll, crackling dialogue, makes them great choices for sharing aloud in class or as inspiration in creative-writing units." Booklist

What do fish have to do with anything? and other stories; illustrated by Tracy Mitchell. Candlewick Press 1997 202p il hardcover o.p. pa $6.99

Grades: 4 5 6 7   S C

1. Short stories
ISBN 0-7636-0329-5; 0-7636-2319-9 (pa)
LC 97-1354

Contents: What do fish have to do with anything?; The goodness of Matt Kaizer; Talk to me; Teacher tamer; Pets; What's inside; Fortune cookie

"Willie believes a homeless man possesses a cure for unhappiness. A minister dares his devilish son to be good. Pet-obsessed Eve receives visitations from two deceased cats. . . . These are among seven . . . stories dealing with communication in troubled relationships." Publisher's note

"While Avi's endings are not tidy, they are effective: each story brings its protagonist beyond childhood self-absorption to the realization that one is an integral part of a bigger picture." Horn Book

Babbitt, Natalie

The Devil's storybook; stories and pictures by Natalie Babbitt. Farrar, Straus & Giroux 1974 101p il pa $3.95 hardcover o.p.

Grades: 4 5 6   S C
1. Devil—Fiction 2. Short stories
ISBN 0-374-41708-3 (pa)

Contents: Wishes; The very pretty lady; The harps of Heaven; The imp in the basket; Nuts; A palindrome; Ashes; Perfection; The rose and the minor demon; The power of speech

Ten "stories about the machinations of the Devil to increase the population of his realm. He is not always successful and, despite his clever ruses, meets frustration as often as his intended victims do." Horn Book

"Twists of plot within traditional themes and a briskly witty style distinguish this book, illustrated amusingly with black-and-white line drawings." Booklist

Baseball crazy: ten short stories that cover all the bases; edited by Nancy E. Mercado. Dial Books for Young Readers 2008 191p $16.99; pa $6.99 *

Grades: 4 5 6 7   S C
1. Baseball—Fiction 2. Short stories
ISBN   978-0-8037-3162-2;   0-8037-3162-0; 978-0-14-241371-5 (pa); 0-14-241371-2 (pa)

LC 2007-26649

Contents: The great Gus Zernial and me by Jerry Spinelli; Mark Pang and the impossible square by Frank Portman; Fall ball by Sue Corbett; Great moments in baseball by Paul Acampora; Riding the pine: a play by Ron Koertge; Tomboy forgiveness by David Rice; Just like Grampy by Charles Smith, Jr.; Smile like Jeter by Maria Testa; Baseball crazy by John H. Ritter; Ball hawk by Joseph Bruchac

"There's no shortage of great writing in this collection of 10 stories. Baseball unifies the entries, but there the similarities end. . . . Readers will be drawn in by the masterful storytelling." Publ Wkly

Best shorts; favorite short stories for sharing; selected by Avi; assisted by Carolyn Shute; afterword by Katherine Paterson; [illustrations by Chris Raschka] Houghton Mifflin 2006 342p $16.95 *

Grades: 5 6 7 8   S C
1. Short stories
ISBN 978-0-618-47603-9; 0-618-47603-2

LC 2006011535

Contents: Rogue wave by Theodore Taylor; The caller by Robert D. San Souci; Scout's honor by Avi; The dog of Pompeii by Louis Untermeyer; LAFFF by Lensey Namioka; Rip Van Winkle by Washington Irving; Nuts by Natalie Babbitt; Flight of the swan by Marian Flandrick Bray; Ho-ichi the Earless by Rafe Martin; The lady who put salt in her coffee by Lucretia P. Hale; The town cats by Lloyd Alexander; Zlateh the goat by Isaac Bashevis Singer; To starch a spook by Andrew Benedict; The night of the pomegranate by Tim Wynne-Jones; The librarian and the robbers by Margaret Mahy; The woman in the snow by Patricia McKissack; The binnacle boy by Paul Fleischman; The baby in the night deposit box by Megan Whalen Turner; The circuit by Francisco Jiménez; The Widow Carey's chickens by Gerald Hausman;

The special powers of Blossom Culp by Richard Peck; A white heron by Sarah Orne Jewett; Jimmy takes vanishing lessons by Walter R. Brooks; The lady or the tiger? by Frank Stockton

"There is no integrating theme in the 24 short stories included here—just fine writing, cultural diversity, and timeless creativity. With such strong writers as Richard Peck, Natalie Babbitt, Lloyd Alexander, and Rafe Martin, one would expect nothing less." SLJ

The **Book** of dragons; selected and illustrated by Michael Hague. Morrow 1995 146p il hardcover o.p. pa $10.99

Grades: 5 6 7 8   S C
1. Dragons—Fiction 2. Fantasy fiction 3. Short stories
ISBN 0-688-10879-2; 0-06-075968-2 (pa)

LC 94-42958

Contents: The dragon and the enchanted filly retold by Italo Calvino; The adventures of Eustace by C.S. Lewis; Perseus and Andromeda by Padraic Colum; The reluctant dragon by Kenneth Grahame; The flower queen's daughter retold by Andrew Lang; Li Chi slays the serpent by Kan Pao; Bilbo Baggins and Smaug by J.R.R. Tolkien; Uncle Lubin and the dragon by W. Heath Robinson; The deliverers of their country by E. Nesbit; The devil and his grandmother by the Brothers Grimm; Sigurd and Fafnir retold by Andrew Lang; The story of Wang Li by Elizabeth Coatsworth; St. George and the dragon retold by William H.G. Kingston; Stan Bolovan retold by Andrew Lang; The good sword retold by Ruth Bryan Owen; The dragon of Wantley; The dragon tamers by E. Nesbit

"Excerpts from classic novels such as J. R. R. Tolkien's *The Hobbit*, C. S. Lewis's *Voyage of the Dawn Treader*, and short stories such as Kenneth Grahame's 'The Reluctant Dragon' are included. In addition, there are folktales from China, Italy, and Germany. Most of the heroes are men, but occasionally children are the only ones who can outsmart the dragon. . . . Hague's beautiful full-page watercolors reflect the different moods of the stories and the temperaments of the dragons depicted." SLJ

Byars, Betsy Cromer, 1928-

Cat diaries; secret writings of the MEOW Society; [by] Betsy Byars, Betsy Duffey, Laurie Myers; illustrated by Erik Brooks. Henry Holt and Company 2010 80p il $15.99

Grades: 2 3 4   S C
1. Cats—Fiction 2. Short stories
ISBN 978-0-8050-8717-8; 0-8050-8717-6

LC 2009-18877

On one night every year, cats in the MEOW Society, which stands for "Memories Expressed In Our Writing," gather to read from their diaries, hearing stories of a gypsy cat, a Caribbean pirate cat, a library cat, and many others.

"This is a solid collection of stories that young readers will enjoy." Libr Media Connect

Byars, Betsy Cromer, 1928-—_Continued_

Dog diaries; secret writings of the WOOF Society; [by] Betsy Byars, Betsy Duffey, Laurie Myers; illustrated by Erik Brooks. Henry Holt 2007 72p il $15.95

Grades: 2 3 4 **S C**
1. Dogs—Fiction 2. Storytelling—Fiction 3. Short stories
ISBN 978-0-8050-7957-9; 0-8050-7957-2
LC 2006011634
At the first annual meeting of WOOF—Words of Our Friends—assorted dogs preserve their heritage by sharing tales of canines throughout history, including Abu, who ruled all of Egypt except for one pesky cat, and Zippy, who simply must find the squeaky toy
"This collection of short stories combines the bedrocks of mass appeal: dogs, humor, and short chapters brimming with illustrations. . . . Expressive, energetic pencil illustrations adorn nearly every page." Booklist

Conrad, Pam, 1947-1996

Our house; pictures by Brian Selznick. 10th anniversary ed. Scholastic Press 2005 c1995 130p il $16.99 *

Grades: 4 5 6 7 **S C**
1. Short stories 2. Levittown (N.Y.)—Fiction
ISBN 0-439-74508-X LC 2004065082
A reissue of the title first published 1995. Includes a new artist's note by Brian Selznick
Six stories, one from each decade from the 1940s to the 1990s, about children growing up in Levittown, New York
"Vivid descriptions and poignant observations leave indelible impressions. . . . Conrad's fresh, imaginative approach to the concept of 'home' makes this an ideal starting point for discussion, creative writing, and other class activities." Booklist

Del Negro, Janice

Passion and poison; tales of shape-shifters, ghosts, and spirited women. Marshall Cavendish 2007 64p il $16.99 *

Grades: 5 6 7 8 **S C**
1. Ghost stories 2. Supernatural—Fiction 3. Short stories
ISBN 978-0-7614-5361-1; 0-7614-5361-X
LC 2007-07237
Contents: The bargain; Rosie Hopewell; Skulls and bones, ghosts and gold; The severed hand; Rubies; Seachild; Hide and seek
"Including both original tales and retellings, this collection of seven stories . . . features diverse female protagonists facing challenges and perils—from human bullies to ghosts. More eerie than scary, the tales of bravery, revenge, grief, and redemption share a gothic sensibility. . . . The black-and-white illustrations . . . evoke bygone times." Booklist

Delacre, Lulu, 1957-

Salsa stories; stories and linocuts by Lulu Delacre. Scholastic Press 2000 105p il $16.99 paperback o.p. *

Grades: 4 5 6 **S C**
1. Latin America—Fiction 2. Family life—Fiction 3. Short stories
ISBN 0-590-63118-7; 0-590-63121-7 (pa)
LC 99-25534
Contents: New Years Day; A carpet for Holy Week; At the beach; The night of San Juan; Teatime; Birthday piñata; The Lord of Miracles; Aguinaldo; Carmen Teresa's gift
A collection of stories within the story of a family celebration where the guests relate their memories of growing up in various Latin American countries. Also contains recipes
"Kids will respond to both the warmth and the anxiety of the family life described in the vivid writing, and in Delacre's nicely composed linocuts." Booklist

Delaney, Joseph, 1945-

The Spook's tale and other horrors; illustrations by Patrick Arrasmith. Greenwillow Books 2009 166p il (The last apprentice) $10.95; lib bdg $14.89

Grades: 5 6 7 8 **S C**
1. Supernatural—Fiction 2. Witches—Fiction 3. Short stories
ISBN 978-0-06-173028-3; 0-06-173028-9; 978-0-06-173030-6 (lib bdg); 0-06-173030-0 (lib bdg)
LC 2008042235
Contents: Horrors begin; Spook's tale: Dead apprentice; Witch's lair; Spook's bones; Blood dish; Silver chain; Alice's tale: Mouldheels and maggots; Grimalkin's tale: Witch assassin; Gallery of villains
As sixty-year-old John Gregory reflects on the past, he reveals how the world of ghosts, ghasts, witches, and boggarts was exposed to him and he later became the Spook, even though his first intention had been to join the priesthood
"These short stories are narrated by secondary characters from the popular series, giving insight into some of Tom Ward's well-known companions. A 'Gallery of Villains' section identifies additional characters and gives a citation to the novels. . . . This book would be perfect for pulling reluctant readers into the series. The occasional black-and-white illustrations add a creepy, atmospheric touch." SLJ

Fleischman, Paul

Graven images; three stories; by Paul Fleischman; illustrations by Bagram Ibatoulline. Candlewick Press 2006 116p il $16.99; pa $5.99

Grades: 5 6 7 8 **S C**
1. Supernatural—Fiction 2. Short stories
ISBN 0-7636-2775-5; 0-7636-2984-7 (pa)
LC 2005054283
A Newbery Medal honor book, 1983
A newly illustrated edition with a new afterword of the title first published 1982 by Harper & Row
Contents: The binnacle boy; Saint Crispin's follower; The man of influence

Fleischman, Paul—*Continued*

A collection of three stories about a child who reads the lips of those who whisper secrets into a statue's ear; a daydreaming shoemaker's apprentice who must find ways to make the girl he loves notice him; and a stone carver who creates a statue of a ghost.

"Readers will be delighted with the return to print of [this title] with haunting new acrylic gouache illustrations . . . evoking the spinetingling aspects of this trio of tales. . . . Via a new afterword, the author explains the stories' inspiration and describes this book's significance early in his career." Publ Wkly

Friends; stories about new friends, old friends, and unexpectedly true friends; edited by Ann M. Martin and David Levithan. Scholastic Press 2005 185p $16.95

Grades: 5 6 7 8   **S C**

1. Friendship—Fiction 2. Short stories

ISBN 0-439-72991-2   LC 2004-27758

Contents: The friend who changed my life by Pam Muñoz Ryan; My best friend by Jennifer L. Holm; Connie Hunter Williams, psychic teacher by Meg Cabot; Squirrel by Ann M. Martin; Smoking lessons by Patricia McCormick; Shashikala: a brief history of love and khadi by Tanuja Desai Hidier; The Wild Prince by Brian Selznick; Flit by Patrick Jennings; The Justice League by David Levithan; Minka and Meanie by Rachel Cohn; Doll by Virginia Euwer Wolff

"This collection of stories by well-known authors spans a broad definition of the term 'friend,' and also approaches the topic from a wide variety of viewpoints. . . . The selections by Ann M. Martin, Pam Muñoz Ryan, Rachel Cohn, David Levithan, and Patricia McCormick are among the more outstanding entries. . . . It is also likely that every reader will find at least one that hits home." SLJ

Give me shelter; stories about children who seek asylum; edited by Tony Bradman. Frances Lincoln 2007 220p $16.95

Grades: 5 6 7 8   **S C**

1. Refugees—Fiction 2. Short stories

ISBN 978-1-84507-522-4; 1-84507-522-6

Contents: Baa and the angels by Nicki Cornwell; Only up from here by Sulaiman Addonia; Samir Hakkim's healthy eating diary by Miriam Halahmy; A nice quiet girl by Gaye Hicyilmaz; Little fish by Kim Kitson; Give me shelter by Solomon Gebremedhin; Cherry studel by Leslie Wilson; Writing to the president by Kathleen McCreery; Beans for tea by Lucy Henning and Saeda Elmi; A place to hide by Rob Porteous; Final border by Lily Hyde

This is a "moving collection of 11 powerful narratives, quite different in their particulars but astonishingly similar in their sense of loss and loneliness. . . . While most of the stories focus on current asylum-seekers in Britain, one looks back to a Vietnamese child's trip to Australia, and another is set in an unnamed Eastern European country." SLJ

Half-minute horrors; edited by Susan Rich. HarperCollinsPublishers 2009 141p il $12.99

Grades: 5 6 7 8   **S C**

1. Short stories 2. Horror fiction

ISBN 978-0-06-183379-3; 0-06-183379-7

LC 2009-18293

An anthology of very short, scary stories by an assortment of authors and illustrators including Chris Raschka, Joyce Carol Oates, Neil Gaiman, Jack Gantos, and Lane Smith.

"This collection of more than 70 chilling snippets is ideal for campfires and car trips. The stories—some a couple sentences, some a few pages—range from darkly humorous . . . to outright creepy. . . . These are inherently quick reads, but with enough plot and detail to encourage further imagining." Publ Wkly

Hawes, Louise, 1943-

Black pearls; a faerie strand; by Louise Hawes; illustrations by Rebecca Guay. Houghton Mifflin Company 2008 211p il $16

Grades: 5 6 7 8 9 10 11 12   **S C**

1. Fairy tales 2. Short stories

ISBN 978-0-618-74797-9; 0-618-74797-4

LC 2007-41166

Contents: Dame Nigran's tower; Pipe dreams; Mother love; Ashes; Evelyn's song; Diamonda; Naked

"Seven gems based on traditional fairy tales make up this collection of unique short stories. . . . Each contains enough clues to guide teens back to the familiar and sometimes innuendo-laden classic fairy tales of their childhoods, and Guay's fantastical pencil drawings . . . enhance the sense of character and magic. Twisted, clever, and artfully written." Booklist

Hearne, Betsy Gould, 1942-

The canine connection: stories about dogs and people; [by] Betsy Hearne. Margaret K. McElderry Bks. 2003 113p hardcover o.p. pa $8.95

Grades: 5 6 7 8   **S C**

1. Dogs—Fiction 2. Short stories

ISBN 0-689-85258-4; 1-4169-6817-2 (pa)

LC 2001-58991

Contents: Lab; Restaurant; Room 313; Cargo; The drive; A grave situation; Fiona and Tim; The nose; Nameless creek; The canine connection; The boss; Bones

Twelve short stories that reflect the varied ways that dogs and humans relate

"The emotions and dialogue are pitch perfect. . . . A rewarding collection that will stay with readers." Booklist

Hauntings, and other tales of danger, love, and sometimes loss. Greenwillow Books 2007 211p $15.99; lib bdg $16.89 *

Grades: 5 6 7 8   **S C**

1. Ghost stories 2. Death—Fiction 3. Supernatural—Fiction 4. Short stories

ISBN   978-0-06-123910-6;   0-06-123910-0; 978-0-06-123911-3 (lib bdg); 0-06-123911-9 (lib bdg)

LC 2006033711

Contents: Rys; Fortress; Lost; Hauntings; Coins; Nurse's fee; The crossing; The letter; Fall; Loose chippings; Angel; Unnatural guests; Secret trees; Light; The devil and the dog

Ten stories of death and hauntings, set in the past, the present, and the afterlife.

"The settings of these 15 stories are painted with sure, deft, and simple strokes that use both action and mood to focus the reader's imagination." Booklist

Heyman, Alissa

The big book of horror; 21 tales to make you tremble; [adaptation and abridgement by Alissa Heyman]; illustrated by Pedro Rodriguez. Sterling 2006 108p il $12.95

Grades: 4 5 6   S C

1. Horror fiction 2. Short stories

ISBN 978-1-4027-3860-9

Contents: Signalman by Charles Dickens; Green eyes by Gustavo Adolfo Becquer; Vampire by John William Polidori; Murders in the rue morgue by Edgar Allen Poe; Bodysnatcher by Robert Louis Stevenson; Hand by Guy de Maupassant; Fall the of the House of Usher by Edgar Allan Poe; Torture by hope by Villiers de Isle Adam; He? by Guy de Maupassant; Pit and the pendulum by Edgar Allan Poe; Outsider by H.P. Lovecraft; Power of mind Morella by Edgar Allen Poe; House of the nightmare by Edward Lucas White; Magnetism by Guy de Maupassant; Facts in the case of M. Valdemar by Edgar Allan Poe; Sir Dominick's bargain by Sheridan Le Fanu; Green monster 88 by Gerard de Nerval; Tropical horror 92 by William Hope Hodgson; Black cat by Edgar Allan Poe; Werewolf by Eugene Field

Presents abridged and adapted versions of twenty-one horror stories, including Charles Dickens' "The Signalman" and Edgar Allan Poe's "The Black Cat."

"These simplified stories read smoothly, and children will find this collection of 21 horror tales quite engaging. . . . Unusually well designed for a collection of scary stories, this large-format volume features dramatically composed illustrations using unusual but effective color combinations and a fine sense of the macabre." Booklist

Horse tales; collected by June Crebbin; illustrated by Inga Moore. Candlewick Press 2005 148p il $18.99

Grades: 4 5 6 7   S C

1. Horses—Fiction 2. Short stories

ISBN 0-7636-2657-0   LC 2004-51897

Contents: Orange pony by Wendy Douthwaite; Snow pony by Alison Lester; Bucephalus: a king's horse by Alice Gall & Fleming Crew; Mud pony retold by Caron Lee Cohen; Gift horse by June Crebbin; Christmas pony by Lincoln Steffens; War horse by Michael Morpurgo; Black Beauty by Anna Sewell; I rode a horse of milk white jade by Diane Lee Wilson; Misty of Chincoteague by Marguerite Henry; Pony in the dark by K.M. Peyton; Unicorn by Peter Dickinson; Chestnut gray retold by Helen Cooper; The gray palfrey retold by Barbara Leonie Pickard

In these "short stories, the remarkable nature of the horse is revealed. . . . The offerings excerpted from novels work well as short stories here and may inspire readers to look for the full-length books. . . . This is an excellently conceived and executed collection with wonderful art." SLJ

I fooled you; ten stories of tricks, jokes, and switcheroos; collected and edited by Johanna Hurwitz. Candlewick Press 2010 174p il $16.99; pa $6.99

Grades: 4 5 6   S C

1. Short stories

ISBN 978-0-7636-3789-7; 0-7636-3789-0; 978-0-7636-4877-0 (pa); 0-7636-4877-9 (pa)

LC 2009-26017

Contents: Tall tale by Douglas Florian; Judy Moody, Stink, and the super-sneaky switcheroo by Megan McDonald; I'm not James by David A. Adler; Big Z, Cammi, and me by Carmela A. Martino; Poetice justice by Eve B. Feldman; April thirty-first by Johanna Hurwitz; Sam and Pam by Matthew Holm; Sweetie bird by Barbara Ann Porte; The bridge to Highlandsville by Michelle Knudsen; The prince of humbugs by Ellen Klages

"Hurwitz asked 10 authors to write a piece with the tagline of the title. . . . Megan McDonald uses her familiar characters, Judy Moody and Stink. . . . Douglas Florian's poem is distinctively in his style, but contains unexpected elements, nonetheless. . . . Michelle Knudsen's 'The Bridge to Highlandsville' is absolutely logical yet lacks the ending most would expect. Matthew Holm's almost wordless 'Sam and Pam' . . . adds a nice graphic-novel-style component to the package. Most readers will likely find something that they appreciate and something that they don't—which may be the best indication of the range of depth and complexity in this collection." SLJ

Kimmel, Eric A.

The jar of fools: eight Hanukkah stories from Chelm; illustrated by Mordicai Gerstein. Holiday House 2000 56p il $18.95

Grades: 4 5 6 7   S C

1. Hanukkah—Fiction 2. Short stories 3. Jews—Fiction

ISBN 0-8234-1463-9   LC 99-57823

Contents: The jar of fools; How they play dreidel in Chelm; Sweeter than honey, purer than oil; The Knight of the Golden Slippers; Silent Samson, the Maccabee; The magic spoon; The soul of a menorah; Wisdom for sale

Drawing on traditional Jewish folklore, these Hanukkah stories relate the antics of the people of Chelm, thought—perhaps incorrectly—to be a town of fools

"Kimmel gets the shtetl setting, the humanity, and the farce. . . . Gerstein's detailed ink-on-oil paint artwork, one full-page picture per story, captures the intricate silliness and slapstick." Booklist

Kipling, Rudyard, 1865-1936

A collection of Rudyard Kipling's Just so stories. Candlewick Press 2004 127p il $22.99 *

Grades: 3 4 5 6   S C

1. Animals—Fiction 2. India—Fiction 3. Short stories

ISBN 0-7636-2629-5   LC 2004-45858

Contents: How the whale got his throat illustrated by Peter Sis; How the camel got his hump illustrated by Clare Melinsky; How the rhinoceros got his skin illustrated by Christopher Corr; How the leopard got his spots illustrated by Cathie Felstead; The elephant's child illustrated by Louise Voce; The sing-song of Old Man Kangaroo illustrated by Jeff Fisher; The beginning of the armadillos illustrated by Jane Ray; The cat that walked by himself illustrated by Satoshi Kitamura

"This colorful collection of eight tales distinguishes itself with its range of artwork. Well-known children's book artists, including Peter Sis, Jane Ray, and Satoshi Kitamura, contributed the art, each one illustrating a different story. The vibrant mix of styles and materials adds new dimension to favorite stories. . . . A lively, accessible edition." Booklist

Kipling, Rudyard, 1865-1936—*Continued*

The jungle book: Mowgli's story; [illustrated by] Nicola Bayley. Candlewick Press 2005 151p il $19.99

Grades: 4 5 6 7   **S C**
1. Animals—Fiction 2. India—Fiction 3. Short stories
ISBN 0-7636-2317-2

Contents: Mowgli's brothers; Kaa's hunting; "Tiger! tiger!"

"Three stories–'Mowgli's Brothers,' 'Kaa's Hunting,' and 'Tiger! Tiger!'–and six of the poetic songs from Kipling's classic work are accompanied by painterly illustrations. . . . A combination of detailed miniature drawings and small framed paintings is strategically placed throughout the text. . . . The masterful use of light, detail, rich color, and texture creates striking and evocative visual effects." SLJ

The jungle book: the Mowgli stories; illustrated by Jerry Pinkney; afterword by Peter Glassman. Morrow 1995 258p il $22.95 *

Grades: 4 5 6 7   **S C**
1. Animals—Fiction 2. India—Fiction 3. Short stories
ISBN 0-688-09979-3   LC 92-1415

Contents: Mowgli's brothers; Hunting song of the Seeonee Pack; Kaa's hunting; Road song of the bandar-log; How fear came; The law of the jungle; "TigerTiger!"; Mowglie's song; Letting in the jungle; Mowglie's song gainst people; The king's ankus; The song of the little hunter; Red dog; Chil's song; The spring running; The outsong; "Rikkitikkitavi"; Darzee's chant

Selected stories from Kipling's two "Jungle Books" chronicle the adventures of Mowgli, the boy reared by a pack of wolves in an Indian jungle. Also includes "Rikki-Tikki-Tavi"

"The handsome illustrations in dappled watercolors show to admiration the lush jungle growth, the watchful animals, and Mowgli himself. A glorious pairing of text and illustration." Horn Book

Just so stories; illustrated by Barry Moser; afterword by Peter Glassman. Morrow 1996 148p il $24.99

Grades: 3 4 5 6   **S C**
1. Animals—Fiction 2. India—Fiction 3. Short stories
ISBN 0-688-13957-4   LC 95-13714

First published 1902

Contents: How the whale got his throat; How the camel got his hump; How the rhinoceros got his skin; How the leopard got his spots; The elephant's child; The sing-song of old man kangaroo; The beginning of the armadilloes; How the first letter was written; How the alphabet was made; The crab that played with the sea; The cat that walked by himself; The butterfly that stamped

A set of tales that "give far-fetched humorous explanations of the chief physical characteristics of certain animals." Oxford Companion to Child Lit

Lay-ups and long shots; an anthology of short stories; by Joseph Bruchac . . . [et al.] Darby Creek Pub. 2008 112p il $15.95

Grades: 4 5 6   **S C**
1. Sports—Fiction 2. Short stories
ISBN 978-1-58196-078-5; 1-58196-078-6

Contents: SWISH: a basketball story by Joseph Bruchac; Fat girls don't run by Lynea Bowdish; Bounceback by David Lubar; H-O-R-S-E by Terry Trueman; Amazing dirt girl rides again by C.S. Perryess; Riding the wave by Dorian Cirrone; Red shorts, white water by Jamie McEwan; Big foot by Max Elliot Anderson; Song of hope by Peggy Duffy

"These nine new short stories feature tweens or teens who, despite lack of skill or other obstacles, engage in athletic pursuits. Some . . . have autobiographical elements. . . . Consistently readable and engaging, the collection should have as much appeal for geeks as it does for jocks." Booklist

Marcantonio, Patricia Santos
Red ridin' in the hood; and other cuentos; pictures by Renato Alarcão. Farrar, Straus & Giroux 2005 181p il $16

Grades: 3 4 5   **S C**
1. Fairy tales 2. Hispanic Americans—Fiction 3. Short stories
ISBN 0-374-36241-6

"The fractured fairy tale gets cool Latino flavor in this lively collection of 11 fresh retellings, with witty reversals of class and gender roles and powerful, full-page pictures that set the drama in venues ranging from the desert and the barrio to a skyscraper." Booklist

Marshall, James, 1942-1992
Rats on the roof, and other stories. Dial Bks. for Young Readers 1991 79p il hardcover o.p. pa $4.99

Grades: 2 3 4   **S C**
1. Animals—Fiction 2. Short stories
ISBN 0-8037-0835-1; 0-14-038646-7 (pa)
                    LC 90-44084

Contents: Rats on the roof; A sheepish tale; The mouse who got married; Eat your vegetables; Swan song; Ooh-la-la; Miss Jones

An illustrated collection of seven stories about various animals, including a frog with magnificent legs, a hungry brontosaurus, and a mouse who gets married

"Marshall's fertile imagination gets lots of exercise here as does his sardonic wit, and he's included plenty of expressive illustrations, all done in his signature style." Booklist

McKissack, Patricia C., 1944-
The dark-thirty; Southern tales of the supernatural; illustrated by Brian Pinkney. Knopf 1992 122p il $18.95; lib bdg $20.99; pa $6.50 *

Grades: 4 5 6 7   **S C**
1. Ghost stories 2. African Americans—Fiction 3. Short stories
ISBN 0-679-81863-4; 0-679-91853-9 (lib bdg); 0-679-89006-8 (pa)   LC 92-3021

Coretta Scott King Award for text, 1993; A Newbery honor book, 1993

McKissack, Patricia C., 1944-—Continued

Contents: The legend of Pin Oak; We organized; Justice; The 11:59; The sight; The woman in the snow; The conjure brother; Boo Mama; The gingi; The chickencoop monster

A collection of ghost stories with African American themes, designed to be told during the Dark Thirty—the half hour before sunset—when ghosts seem all too believable

"Strong characterizations are superbly drawn in a few words. The atmosphere of each selection is skillfully developed and sustained to the very end. Pinkney's stark scratchboard illustrations evoke an eerie mood, which heightens the suspense of each tale." SLJ

Porch lies; tales of slicksters, tricksters, and other wily characters; [by] Patricia C. McKissack; illustrated by André Carrilho. Schwartz & Wade Books 2006 146p il $18.95; lib bdg $22.99 *
Grades: 4 5 6 7   S C
1. African Americans—Fiction 2. Short stories
ISBN 0-375-83619-5; 0-375-93619-X (lib bdg)
LC 2005-22048

Contents: When Pete Bruce came to town; Change; The devil's guitar; Aunt Gran and the outlaws; By the weight of a feather; A grave situation; The best lie ever told; The earth bone and the King of the Ghosts; Cake: Norris lives on, Part one; Cake: Norris lives on, Part two

The "original tales in this uproarious collection draw on African American oral tradition and blend history and legend with sly humor, creepy horror, villainous characters, and wild farce. McKissack based the stories on those she heard as a child while sitting on her grandparents' porch. . . . Carrilho's full-page illustrations—part cartoon, part portrait in silhouette—combine realistic characters with scary monsters." Booklist

Naidoo, Beverley

Out of bounds: seven stories of conflict and hope. HarperCollins Pubs. 2003 c2001 175p $16.99; pa $5.99
Grades: 5 6 7 8   S C
1. South Africa—Race relations—Fiction 2. Short stories
ISBN 0-06-050799-3; 0-06-050801-9 (pa)
LC 2002-68901

First published 2001 in the United Kingdom

Contents: The dare; The noose; One day, Lily, one day; The typewriter; The gun; The playground; Out of bounds

Seven stories, spanning the time period from 1948 to 2000, chronicle the experiences of young people from different races and ethnic groups as they try to cope with the restrictions placed on their lives by South Africa's apartheid laws

"Naidoo's book reveals our humanity and inhumanity with starkness and precision. . . . She honors her country's past, present, and future with these brave tales." Horn Book

Nix, Garth, 1963-

One beastly beast; (two aliens, three inventors, four fantastic tales); illustrated by Brian Biggs. HarperCollinsPublishers 2007 158p il $15.99; lib bdg $16.89
Grades: 3 4 5   S C
1. Fantasy fiction 2. Short stories
ISBN 0-06-084319-5; 0-06-084320-9 (lib bdg)
LC 2006-27916

Contents: Blackbread the pirate; The princess and the beastly beast; Bill the inventor; Serena and the sea serpent

A collection of four fantasy tales in which a boy joins a strange navy in pursuit of video pirates, a neglected princess seeks adventure, an orphaned inventor seeks the perfect parents, and a genius girl faces a sea serpent.

"Black-and-white cartoon illustrations complement the lighthearted tone. The positive message and amusing stories make this a good choice for younger fantasy fans." SLJ

Priestley, Chris, 1958-

Uncle Montague's tales of terror; [by] Chris Priestley; illustrations by David Roberts. Bloomsbury Children's Books 2007 238p il $12.95
Grades: 5 6 7 8 9   S C
1. Horror fiction 2. Uncles—Fiction 3. Storytelling—Fiction 4. Short stories
ISBN 978-1-59990-118-3; 1-59990-118-8

"Ghosts, demons, jinns, and deadly trees populate these 10 chilly short stories set in the late 19th century, with the language and black-and-white illustrations capturing the feel of Victorian times. Young Edgar hears these tales while visiting his eccentric Uncle Montague, and each one is connected to a strange object in his uncle's study. . . . An enjoyable collection with enough creepy atmosphere (and some gruesome action) to hold readers' attention." SLJ

The **Random** House book of bedtime stories; illustrated by Jane Dyer. Random House 2007 c2004 137p il $21.99
Grades: K 1 2 3 4   S C
1. Short stories 2. Folklore
ISBN 978-0-679-80832-9

A reissue of the title first published 1994

Contents: How the camel got his hump by Rudyard Kipling; The lion and the mouse by Aesop; The tale of Peter Rabbit by Beatrix Potter; The selfish giant by Oscar Wilde; Grumley the grouch by Marjorie Weinman Sharmat; The baker's cat by Joan Aiken; The lad who went to the north wind by Anne Rockwell; Under the moon by Joanne Ryder; Young Kate by Eleanor Farjeon; Follow the wind by Alvin Tresselt; The gingerbread boy, a folk tale retold by Gillian Kelly; The golden goose by the Brothers Grimm retold by Sue Kassirer; The three billy goats gruff, a Norwegian folk tale retold by Sue Kassirer; The little snow maiden, a Russian folk tale retold by Sue Kassirer; The Bremen town musicians by Walter de la Mare retold by Deborah Hautzig; The little red hen, an English folk tale retold by Gillian Kelly; The hare and the hedgehog by Walter de la Mare retold by Deborah Hautzig; Goldilocks and the three bears retold by Gillian Kelly; The man who had no dream by Ade-

The Random House book of bedtime stories—
Continued

laide Holl; The dreaming bunny by Margaret Wise Brown; Snow White and Rose Red by the Brothers Grimm retold by Rose Dobbs

"The 21 lyrically told stories include many European folktales and fairy tales . . . as well as childhood classics. . . . Dyer's brightly colored, precisely detailed illustrations are warm and gentle, with an old-fashioned, affectionate character. . . . . A fine collection to read at bedtime or any time, these are stories every child should know." Booklist

Reichenstetter, Friederun, 1940-

Andersen's fairy tales; retold by Friederun Reichenstetter; illustrated by Silke Leffler. North-South 2007 92p il $19.95

Grades: 4 5 6   S C

1. Andersen, Hans Christian, 1805-1875—Adaptations
2. Fairy tales
ISBN 0-7358-2141-0

Translated from the German

Contents: The princess and the pea; The Emperor's new clothes; The tinderbox; The ugly duckling; The traveling companion; There is no doubt; The little match girl; The swineherd; Thumbeline; The sweethearts; The steadfast tin soldier; The flying trunk; Jack the Dullard

"Thirteen tales . . . are adapted from excellent translations by Anthea Bell and H. P. Paul. . . . Leffler's often-humorous painted folk-art illustrations show cute little people with chubby line-drawn faces dressed in clothing of 18th-century style. . . . The volume . . . is quite handsome." SLJ

Root, Phyllis, 1949-

Aunt Nancy and the bothersome visitors; illustrated by David Parkins. Candlewick Press 2007 57p il $16.99

Grades: 1 2 3 4   S C

1. Cousins—Fiction 2. Aunts—Fiction
ISBN 978-0-7636-3074-4; 0-7636-3074-8
                                              LC 2007-60856

Includes two stories previously published separately in picture book format: Aunt Nancy and Old Man Trouble (1996) and Aunt Nancy and Cousin Lazybones (1998)

Contents: Aunt Nancy and Old Man Trouble; Aunt Nancy and Cousin Lazybones; Aunt Nancy and Old Woeful; Aunt Nancy and Mister Death

Clever Aunt Nancy manages to foil all those who try to get the better of her.

"Root's folksy style shines in every sentence. . . . Parkins provides full-color paintings to introduce each story, but his wit really shows itself in the droll silhouettes that milk body language for all it's worth." Horn Book

Rowling, J. K.

The tales of Beedle the Bard; translated from the ancient runes by Hermione Granger; commentary by Albus Dumbledore; introduction, notes, and illustrations by J.K. Rowling. Arthur A. Levine 2008 111p il $12.99

Grades: 5 6 7 8 9 10 11 12   S C

1. Fairy tales 2. Magic—Fiction 3. Short stories
ISBN 978-0-545-12828-5; 0-545-12828-5

Contents: The wizard and the hopping pot; The fountain of fair fortune; The warlock's hairy heart; Babbitty Rabbitty and her cackling stump; The tale of the three brothers

A collection of tales from the world of Harry Potter.

"The introduction is captivating . . . [and] the tales themselves are entertaining. . . . Rowling is at the top of her game as a superb storyteller, providing her legions of fans with an enchanting collection of wizard folklore." Voice Youth Advocates

San Souci, Robert, 1946-

Dare to be scared; thirteen stories to chill and thrill; illustrations by David Ouimet. Cricket Bks. 2003 159p il $15.95 *

Grades: 4 5 6 7   S C

1. Horror fiction 2. Short stories
ISBN 0-8126-2688-5   LC 2002-152827

Contents: Nighttown; The dark dark house; The caller; The double dare; Space is the place; Ants; The Halloween spirit; The Bald Mountain monster; Playland; Smoke; Mrs. Moonlight (Senora de Luna); Hungry ghosts; Bakotahl

"From a horrible dream a boy can't wake up from to an alien-driven bus to an eerie house with an alarming inhabitant, these stories cover the gamut of scary themes." SLJ

"With crisp, straightforward delivery and some intriguing endings, these 13 tales are great fun for young readers who like to be spooked." Booklist

Dare to be scared 4; thirteen more tales of terror; [by] Robert D. San Souci; illustrations by David Ouimet. Cricket Books 2009 275p il $17.95

Grades: 4 5 6 7   S C

1. Horror fiction 2. Short stories
ISBN 978-0-8126-2754-1; 0-8126-2754-7
                                              LC 2009018490

Contents: Heading home; Lich gate; Principal's office; Woody; Snow day; Fairy godmother; Violet; A really scary story; Witch; Red rain; Cabin 13; Smoke hands; Moonrise

"These deliciously shivery tales are perfect for campfire spookiness or as Halloween read-alouds. As in the previous books in the series, San Souci relies heavily on folklore and urban legends, giving the stories an even more chilling impact. . . . Strong themes such as death and murder are prevalent throughout. Ouimet's dark illustrations are paired perfectly with this creepy collection." SLJ

San Souci, Robert, 1946-—*Continued*

Double-dare to be scared: another thirteen chilling tales; [by] Robert D. San Souci; illustrated by David Ouimet. Cricket Books 2004 170p il $15.95
Grades: 4 5 6 7 **S C**
1. Horror fiction 2. Short stories
ISBN 0-8126-2716-4   LC 2003-26610
Companion volume to Dare to be scared (2003)
Contents: Campfire tale; Best friends; The quilt; Circus dreams; Rosalie; Mountain childers; Class cootie; Half-past midnight; Laughter; Click-clack; Daddy Boogey; Grey; "Gulp!"

This is a "collection of 13 tales. . . . Most of the main characters are menaced by a variety of scary, unexpected threats: a madman in the woods, a giant spider, unforgiving leprechauns, and exceptionally hungry Appalachian children." Booklist
"San Souci uses elements of urban legend and folklore to weave powerful and suspenseful yet age-appropriate stories that youngsters will revisit, finding new meaning with each reading." SLJ

Triple-dare to be scared; thirteen further freaky tales; [by] Robert D. San Souci; illustrations by David Ouimet. Cricket Books 2007 229p il $16.95
Grades: 4 5 6 7 **S C**
1. Horror fiction 2. Short stories
ISBN 978-0-8126-27497; 0-8126-2749-0
    LC 2006025899
Contents: Second childhood; They bite, too!; Plat-eye; Tour de force; Underwater; Far site; Field of nightmares; The double; John Mouldy; Green thumb; El arroyo de los fantasmas; Bookworm; Rain

"San Souci serves up 13 more spooky tales, and Ouimet's macabre black-and-white illustrations are a perfect complement to each one. The selections are short enough for read-alouds or for independent readers to complete in one sitting." SLJ

Sandburg, Carl, 1878-1967

Rootabaga stories; illustrated by Maud and Miska Petersham. Harcourt 2003 c1922 176p il hardcover o.p. pa $5.95 * **S C**
1. Fairy tales 2. Short stories
ISBN 0-15-204709-3; 0-15-204714-X (pa)
    LC 2002-191949
Newly illustrated edition of Rootabaga stories. Two volume edition by Michael Hague published 1988-1989 available
"An Odyssey/Harcourt young classic"
First published 1922; previously published as: Rootabaga stories, part one
Contents: How they broke away to go to the Rootabaga Country; How they bring back the Village of Cream Puffs when the wind blows it away; How the five rusty rats helped find a new village; The Potato Face Blind Man who lost the diamond rabbit on his gold accordion; How the Potato Face Blind Man enjoyed himself on a fine spring morning; Poker Face the Baboon and Hot Dog the Tiger; The Toboggan-to-the-Moon dream of the Potato Face Blind Man; How Gimme the Ax found out about the Zigzag Railroad and who made it zigzag; The story of Blixie Bimber and the power of the gold buckskin whincher; The story of Jason Squiff and why he had a popcorn hat, popcorn mittens and popcorn shoes; The story of Rags Habakuk, the two blue rats, and the circus man who came with spot cash money; The wedding procession of the Rag Doll and the Broom Handle and who was in it; How the hat ashes shovel helped Snoo Foo; Three boys with jugs of molasses and secret ambitions; How Bimbo the Snip's thumb stuck to his nose when the wind changed; The two skyscrapers who decided to have a child; The dollar watch and the five jack-rabbits; The wooden Indian and the Shaghorn Buffalo; The White Horse Girl and Blue Wind Boy; What six girls with balloons told the Gray Man on Horseback; How Henry Haggleyhoagly played the guitar with his mittens on; Never kick a slipper at the moon; Sand flat shadows; How to tell corn fairies if you see 'em; How the animals lost their tails and got them back traveling from Philadelphia to Medicine Hat
A selection of tales from Rootabaga Country peopled with such characters as the Potato Face Blind Man, the Blue Wind Boy, and many others

Shelf life: stories by the book; edited by Gary Paulsen. Simon & Schuster Bks. for Young Readers 2003 173p $16.95 *
Grades: 5 6 7 8 **S C**
1. Books and reading—Fiction 2. Short stories
ISBN 0-689-84180-9   LC 2002-66901
Contents: In your hat, by E. Conford; Escape, by M. P. Haddix; Follow the water, by J. L. Holm; Testing, testing 1 . . . 2 . . . 3, by A. La Faye; Tea party ends in bloody massacre, film at 11, by G. Maguire; What's a fellow to do, by K. Karr; Wet hens, by E. Wittlinger; The good deed, by M. D. Bauer; Bacarole for paper and bones, by M. T. Anderson; Clean sweep, by J. Bauer

Ten short stories in which the lives of young people in different circumstances are changed by their encounters with books
"Covering almost every genre of fiction, including mystery, SF, fantasy and realism, these well-crafted stories by familiar authors offer sharply drawn characterizations and intriguing premises." Publ Wkly

Shusterman, Neal

Darkness creeping; twenty twisted tales. Puffin Books 2007 291p pa $7.99
Grades: 5 6 7 8 **S C**
1. Horror fiction 2. Short stories
ISBN 0-14-240721-6
Contents: Catching cold; Who do we appreciate?; Soul survivor; Black box; Resting deep; Security blanket; Same time next year; River tour; Flushie; Monkeys tonight; Screaming at the wall; Growing pains; Alexander's skull; Connecting flight; Ralphy Sherman's root canal; Ear for music; Riding the raptor; Trash day; Crystalloid; Shadows of doubt

"The author takes a walk on the dark side in this collection of spooky stories, some old, some new, all delightfully creepy. He knows his audience, providing enough horrific touches to appeal to the most challenging readers—those hard-to-reach middle school boys. Each story is introduced with a brief statement describing where he got the idea." Voice Youth Advocates

Singer, Isaac Bashevis, 1904-1991

Stories for children. Farrar, Straus & Giroux 1984 337p hardcover o.p. pa $14

Grades: 4 5 6 7   S C

1. Jews—Fiction 2. Short stories

ISBN 0-374-37266-7; 0-374-46489-8 (pa)

LC 84-13612

Contents: The elders of Chelm & Genendel's key; A tale of three wishes; The extinguished lights; Mazel & Shlimazel; Why Noah chose the dove; Zlateh the goat; A Hanukkah Eve in Warsaw; The fools of Chelm & the stupid carp; The wicked city; Rabbi Leib & the witch Cunegunde; The parakeet named Dreidel; Lemel & Tzipa; The day I got lost; Menashe & Rachel; Shlemiel the businessman; Joseph & Koza; A Hanukkah evening in my parents' house; Tsirtsur & Peziza; Naftali the storyteller & his horse, Sus; Hershele & Hanukkah; When Shlemiel went to Warsaw; Elijah the slave; The power of light; Growing up; The Lantuch; Utzel & his daughter, Poverty; The squire; Ole & Trufa; Dalfunka, where the rich live forever; Topiel & Tekla; Hanukkah in the poorhouse; Shrewd Todie & Lyzer the miser; The fearsome inn; The cat who thought she was a dog & the dog who thought he was a cat; Menaseh's dream; Tashlik

This collection of thirty-six stories includes "parables, beast fables, allegories and reminiscences. Some stories are silly and charming, while others are wildly fantastic, dealing with savagery and miracles in mythical, medieval Poland. Frequently they are about scary situations, but all tend to end happily, with an edifying idea. Most appealing is the Nobel Prize winner's sheer story-telling power. In this respect, he has no equal among contemporaries." N Y Times Book Rev

Smith, Charles R.

Winning words; sports stories and photographs; [by] Charles R. Smith. Candlewick Press 2008 70p il $17.99

Grades: 5 6 7 8   S C

1. Sports—Fiction 2. Short stories

ISBN 978-0-7636-1445-4; 0-7636-1445-9

Contents: Don't say it; Stuffed eagles; I'm open; Crack-crack-crunch; A mountain of wood; Makes me wanna holla

In this collection of short stories and photographs, Charles R. Smith Jr. shows young athletes overcoming their fears and challenging themselves to do their best.

"This outstanding collection consists of six readable and engaging stories. . . . Smith does a fine job of evoking the action and character of the games, in words and in closeup photos." SLJ

Soto, Gary

Baseball in April, and other stories. 10th anniversary ed. Harcourt Brace Jovanovich 2000 c1990 111p $16; pa $6 *

Grades: 5 6 7 8   S C

1. Mexican Americans—Fiction 2. California—Fiction 3. Short stories

ISBN 0-15-202573-1; 0-15-202567-7 (pa)

A reissue of the title first published 1990

Contents: Broken chain; Baseball in April; Two dreamers; Barbie; The no-guitar blues; Seventh grade; Mother and daughter; The Karate Kid; La Bamba; The marble champ; Growing up

A collection of eleven short stories focusing on the everyday adventures of Hispanic young people growing up in Fresno, California

Each story "gets at the heart of some aspect of growing up. The insecurities, the embarrassments, the triumphs, the inequities of it all are chronicled with wit and charm. Soto's characters ring true and his knowledge of, and affection for, their shared Mexican-American heritage is obvious and infectious." Voice Youth Advocates

Facts of life; stories. Harcourt 2008 176p $16

Grades: 5 6 7 8   S C

1. Mexican Americans—Fiction 2. California—Fiction 3. Short stories

ISBN 978-0-15-206181-4; 0-15-206181-9

LC 2007-35765

Contents: The babysitter; Capturing the moment; Citizen of the world; D in English; The ideal city; Identity theft; Seeing the future; Where did I go wrong;? Wise Uncle Joe; You decide

"Pivitol moments in the lives of California Latino teens and tweens provide the starting points for Soto's collection of 10 . . . stories. For Letty, it's the realization that her boyfriend loves her money more than he does her; for Hector, it's the announcement of his parents' plan to divorce. . . . Soto's affection and concern for his characters is evident throughout." Booklist

Local news. Harcourt Brace Jovanovich 1993 148p hardcover o.p. pa $5.95

Grades: 5 6 7 8   S C

1. Mexican Americans—Fiction 2. California—Fiction 3. Short stories

ISBN 0-15-248117-6; 0-15-204695-X (pa)

LC 92-37905

Contents: Blackmail; Trick-or-treating; First job; El radio; Pushup; The school play; The Raiders jacket; The challenge; Nacho loco; The squirrels; The mechanical mind; Nickel-a-pound plane ride; New Year's Eve

A collection of thirteen short stories about the everyday lives of Mexican American young people in California's Central Valley

"These stories resonate with integrity, verve, and compassion." Horn Book

Petty crimes. Harcourt Brace & Co. 1998 157p $16; pa $6.99

Grades: 5 6 7 8   S C

1. Mexican Americans—Fiction 2. Short stories

ISBN 0-15-201658-9; 0-15-205437-5 (pa)

LC 97-37114

Contents: La güera; Mother's clothes; Try to remember; The boxing lesson; Your turn, Norma; The funeral suits; Little scams; If the shoe fits; Frankie the rooster; Born worker

A collection of short stories about Mexican American youth growing up in California's Central Valley

"A sense of family strength relieves the under-current of sadness in these raw stories." Horn Book Guide

Spinelli, Jerry, 1941-

The library card. Scholastic 1997 148p pa $4.99

Grades: 4 5 6 7   S C

1. Books and reading—Fiction 2. Short stories

ISBN 0-590-38633-6   LC 96-18412

Spinelli, Jerry, 1941-—*Continued*

Contents: Mongoose; Brenda; Sonseray; April Mendez

"A library card is the magical object common to each of these four stories in which a budding street thug, a television addict, a homeless orphan, and a lonely girl are all transformed by the power and the possibilities that await them within the walls of the public library. Spinelli's characters . . . are unusual and memorable; his writing both humorous and convincing." Horn Book Guide

Sports shorts. Darby Creek Pub. 2005 127p il $15.99; pa $4.99

Grades: 5 6 7 8   **S C**

1. Sports—Fiction 2. Short stories

ISBN 1-58196-040-9; 1-58196-058-1 (pa)

Contents: Bombardment by Joseph Bruchac; Two left feet, two left hands, and too left on the bench by David Lubar; First position by Marilyn Singer; Finishing blocks and deadly hook shots by Terry Trueman; Finding high-jump fame by Dorian Cirrone; Line drive by Tanya West; Riding the century by Alexandra Siy; On being written in by Jamie McEwan.

A collection of eight semi-autobiographical stories about the authors' experiences with sports while growing up.

"Some of the vignettes are laugh-out-loud funny. . . . The book's smaller-than-standard trim size and inviting page design will help attract readers to this rewarding collection." Booklist

Stine, R. L., 1943-

The haunting hour. HarperCollins Pubs. 2001 153p il $11.95; pa $5.99

Grades: 4 5 6 7   **S C**

1. Horror fiction 2. Short stories

ISBN 0-06-623604-5; 0-06-441045-5 (pa)

LC 2001-39142

"A Parachute Press book"

Contents: The Halloween dance; The bad baby-sitter; Revenge of the snowman; How to bargain with a dragon; The mummy's dream; Are we there yet?; Take me with you; My imaginary friend; Losers; Can you draw me?

A collection of ten short horror stories featuring a ghoulish Halloween party, a long, mysterious car trip, and a very dangerous imaginary friend. Each story includes drawings by a different illustrator

"The predictability of the stories and the unsophisticated storytelling won't keep Stine fans old and new from swallowing this down in one big gulp." Bull Cent Child Books

Troll's eye view; a book of villainous tales. Viking 2009 200p $16.99 *

Grades: 5 6 7 8   **S C**

1. Fairy tales 2. Short stories

ISBN 978-0-670-06141-9; 0-670-06141-7

Contents: Wizard's apprentice by Delia Sherman; An unwelcome guest by Garth Nix; Faery tales by Wendy Froud; Rags and riches by Nina Kiriki Hoffman; Up the down beanstalk: a wife remembers by Peter S. Beagle; The shoes that were danced to pieces by Ellen Kushner; Puss in boots, the sequel by Joseph Stanton; The boy who cried wolf by Holly Black; Troll by Jane Yolen; Castle Othello by Nancy Farmer; 'Skin by Michael

Cadnum; Delicate architecture by Catherynne M. Valente; Molly by Midori Snyder; Observing the formalities by Neil Gaiman; The Cinderella game by Kelly Link

Everyone thinks they know the real story behind the villains in fairy tales—evil, no two ways about it. But the villains themselves beg to differ. In this anthology for younger readers, you'll hear from the Giant's wife (from Jack and the Beanstalk), Rumpelstiltskin, the oldest of the Twelve Dancing Princesses, and more.

"A mixed bag of funny, quirky, and downright creepy entries. . . . The collection is largely accessible and very enjoyable." Booklist

E EASY BOOKS

This section consists chiefly of fiction books that would interest children from pre-school through third grade. Easy books that have a definite nonfiction subject content are usually classified with other nonfiction books. Easy books listed here include:

1. Picture books, whether fiction or nonfiction, that the young child can use independently

2. Fiction books with very little or scattered text, with large print and with vocabulary suitable for children with reading levels of grades 1-3

3. Picture storybooks with a larger amount of text to be used primarily by or with children in pre-school through grade 3

Ackerley, Sarah, 1981-

Patrick the somnambulist; written and illustrated by Sarah Ackerley. Blooming Tree Press 2008 unp il $14.95

Grades: PreK K 1   **E**

1. Sleep disorders—Fiction 2. Penguins—Fiction

ISBN 978-1-933831-07-7; 1-933831-07-3

LC 2007-31619

Patrick is a perfectly normal penguin, except for the fact that he walks in his sleep.

"This original take on the it's-okay-to-be-different story features an expressive protaganist doing his own (often weird) thing." Horn Book Guide

Ackerman, Karen, 1951-

Song and dance man; illustrated by Stephen Gammell. Knopf 1988 unp il lib bdg $17.99; pa $6.99

Grades: K 1 2 3   **E**

1. Entertainers—Fiction 2. Grandfathers—Fiction

ISBN 0-394-99330-6 (lib bdg); 0-679-81995-9 (pa)

LC 87-3200

Awarded the Caldecott Medal, 1989

"Grandpa takes three grandchildren up to the attic, where he arranges lights and gives a performance that enchants his audience. They tell him they wish they could have seen him dance in 'the good old days' but he says he wouldn't trade a million good old days for the time he spends with the narrators." Bull Cent Child Books

The illustrator "captures all the story's inherent joie de vivre with color pencil renderings that fairly leap off the pages." Booklist

Acosta Gonzalez, Ada

Mayte and the Bogeyman. Pinata Books 2006
32p il $14.95   **E**
1. Fear—Fiction 2. Bilingual books—English-Spanish
ISBN 1-55885-442-8

"Mayte enjoys interacting with all of the colorful
street vendors who ply their wares in her town. . . . All
are friendly, kind, and interesting in various ways, except
for the sour and bad-tempered ice-cream man. . . .
Mayte comes to believe that he is the Bogeyman (el
Cuco) who kidnaps bad children and eats them or sells
them at market. When she and her friend Pepito see the
man walking down the street with a squirming bag slung
over his shoulder, they assume the worst. . . . This fun
story has an interesting enough plotline to satisfy even
reluctant readers. . . . The smoothly rendered text in
both English and Spanish appears on the lefthand pages
facing a full-bleed painting on the right." SLJ

Adams, Diane, 1960-

I can do it myself! written by Diane Adams;
illustrated by Nancy Hayashi. Peachtree Publishers
2009 unp il $15.95
Grades: PreK K   **E**
1. Stories in rhyme 2. Bedtime—Fiction
ISBN 978-1-56145-471-6; 1-56145-471-0
                                    LC 2008031117
Emily Pearl is a big girl who insists on doing everything for herself until evening, when having someone
help her get ready for bed is nice

"Hayashi's cheerful watercolors vary in size from
spreads to small vignettes and help give the story just the
right pace. . . . This tale is told in a fresh, yet familiar
way." SLJ

Addasi, Maha, 1968-

The white nights of Ramadan; [by] Maha
Addasi; illustrated by Ned Gannon. Boyds Mills
Press 2008 unp il $16.95
Grades: 1 2 3 4   **E**
1.   Ramadan—Fiction   2.   Muslims—Fiction
3. Kuwait—Fiction
ISBN 978-1-59078-523-2; 1-59078-523-1
                                    LC 2008002637
"This story is centered around *Girgian*, a Muslim celebration observed mostly in the Arabian Gulf states during the middle of the month of Ramadan. When Noor,
who lives in Kuwait, sees the almost-full moon rise, she
knows it's time to prepare for the festival. The family
makes candy from honey, sugar, and nuts to share with
the children in the neighborhood, wrapping it with cellophane and colorful bows. . . . Shimmering with moonlit
hues, the attractive illustrations are done in a style that
reflects one of many Muslim cultures. A helpful author's
note and glossary are appended. An excellent choice for
units on diversity and multiculturalism." SLJ

Addy, Sharon, 1943-

Lucky Jake; illustrated by Wade Zahares.
Houghton Mifflin 2006 unp il $17
Grades: PreK K 1 2   **E**
1. Pigs—Fiction 2. Gold mines and mining—Fiction
ISBN 0-618-47286-X; 978-0-618-47286-4
                                    LC 2005-03917

While panning for gold with his Pa, Jake adopts a pig
that he names Dog.

"Using pastels in deep and heavy hues, solid shapes,
and unusual perspectives, he provides images that roll
breathtakingly across the pages. . . . An intriguing mix
of old-fashioned storytelling and cutting-edge art."
Booklist

Adler, David A., 1947-

The Babe & I; written by David A. Adler;
illustrated by Terry Widener. Harcourt Brace &
Co. 1999 unp il $17; pa $7
Grades: K 1 2 3   **E**
1. Ruth, Babe, 1895-1948—Fiction 2. Great Depres-
sion, 1929-1939—Fiction
ISBN 0-15-201378-4; 0-15-205026-4 (pa)
                                    LC 97-37580
"Gulliver books"
While helping his family make ends meet during the
Depression by selling newspapers, a boy meets Babe
Ruth

"Widener's illustrations evoke the ambiance of the period in this book that is carefully paced and remarkable
for its unified focus." Horn Book Guide

It's time to sleep, it's time to dream; illustrated
by Kay Chorao. Holiday House 2009 unp il
$16.95
Grades: PreK K   **E**
1. Seasons—Fiction 2. Bedtime—Fiction
ISBN 978-0-8234-1924-1; 0-8234-1924-X
                                    LC 2008022570
A parent lulls a child to sleep with visions of soft
spring breezes, lazy summer days, cool autumn winds,
and moon-lit winter nights

"Chorao's gouache-and-watercolor illustrations lend a
new-fashioned slant to a bedtime book. . . . The softly
infused color pictures pair well with the spare text. . . .
Kids will be drawn to the comforting cover image of a
cute tyke cuddling his toy bunny." Booklist

Young Cam Jansen and the dinosaur game;
illustrated by Susanna Natti. Viking 1996 32p il
(Viking easy-to-read) $13.99; pa $3.99 *
Grades: K 1 2 3   **E**
1. Mystery fiction
ISBN 0-670-86399-8; 0-14-037779-4 (pa)
                                    LC 95-46463
Titles about Cam Jansen for older readers are also
available

"A Viking easy-to-read"
"At Jane's birthday party, everyone guesses the number of toy dinosaurs in a big jar. Jennifer 'the Camera'
Jansen's photographic memory helps her nab Robert,
who has cheated in order to win all the dinosaurs. Observant readers can follow Cam's reasoning and solve the
mystery, too." Horn Book Guide

Other easy-to-read titles about Cam Jansen are:
Young Cam Jansen and the 100th day of school mystery
  (2009)
Young Cam Jansen and the baseball mystery (1999)
Young Cam Jansen and the double beach mystery (2002)
Young Cam Jansen and the ice skate mystery (1998)
Young Cam Jansen and the library mystery (2001)

Adler, David A., 1947-—*Continued*

Young Cam Jansen and the lions' lunch mystery (2007)
Young Cam Jansen and the lost tooth (1997)
Young Cam Jansen and the Molly shoe mystery (2008)
Young Cam Jansen and the missing cookie (1996)
Young Cam Jansen and the new girl mystery (2004)
Young Cam Jansen and the pizza shop mystery (2000)
Young Cam Jansen and the speedy car mystery (2010)
Young Cam Jansen and the substitute mystery (2005)
Young Cam Jansen and the zoo note mystery (2003)

Adler, Victoria

All of baby, nose to toes; pictures by Hiroe Nakata. Dial Books for Young Readers 2009 unp il $14.99 *

Grades: PreK   E
  1. Infants—Fiction 2. Stories in rhyme
  ISBN 978-0-8037-3217-9; 0-8037-3217-1
                            LC 2008-30971

Rhyming text celebrates everything about a beloved baby, from eyes to toes

"Adler's sunny poem and Nakata's ebullient watercolors demonstrate not only a baby's exploratory joy but also the palpable delight a baby brings to a family." Publ Wkly

Adoff, Arnold, 1935-

Black is brown is tan; pictures by Emily Arnold McCully. HarperCollins Pubs. 2002 unp il $17.99; pa $6.99 *

Grades: PreK K 1 2   E
  1. Racially mixed people—Fiction 2. Family life—Fiction
  ISBN 0-06-028776-4; 0-06-443644-6 (pa)
                            LC 00-44864

A newly illustrated edition of the title first published 1973

Describes in verse a family with a brown-skinned mother, white-skinned father, two children, and their various relatives

"Children everywhere will love the simple, joyful rhythmic words in Adoff's signature 'shaped speech' style, with McCully's beautiful dancing watercolors." Booklist

Agee, Jon

Milo's hat trick; story and pictures by Jon Agee. Hyperion Bks. for Children 2001 unp il $15.95

Grades: PreK K 1 2   E
  1. Magicians—Fiction 2. Bears—Fiction
  ISBN 0-7868-0902-7

"Michael di Capua books"

In the busy city, there are lots of people with hats. But there is only one guy with a bear in his hat. That's Milo The Magician

"Agee's bold, angular pencil-and-paint illustrations drive this warm story about perseverance, luck, and courage." Booklist

Nothing. Hyperion Books for Children 2007 unp il $16.99

Grades: K 1 2 3   E
  ISBN 978-0-7868-3694-9; 0-7868-3694-6
                            LC 2007-25191

When Suzie Gump, the richest lady in town, walks into Otis's empty antique shop and insists on buying nothing, she starts a fad that has everyone buying nothing and emptying their homes and stores to make room for it—until Suzie realizes things have gone too far.

"In illustrations that possess a timeless air, Agee contrasts cluttered, patterned spaces with airy rooms, outlines chunky, geometric areas with firm charcoal lines and tints broad surfaces with transparent watercolor wash. . . . This timely parable is certainly something worth having." Publ Wkly

The retired kid. Hyperion Books for Children 2008 unp il $16.99

Grades: K 1 2 3   E
  1. Retirement—Fiction 2. Florida—Fiction 3. Old age—Fiction
  ISBN 978-1-4231-0314-1; 1-4231-0314-9
                            LC 2007-41998

Although he enjoys some aspects of his retirement, eight-year-old Brian gains a new perspective on his job of being a child after spending time in Florida's Happy Sunset Retirement Community

"Agee's gentle story about juvenile job dissatisfaction is filled with witty verbal and visual flourishes . . . that will have kids—and their grandparents—chuckling from start to finish." Booklist

Terrific; story and pictures by Jon Agee. Hyperion Books for Children 2005 unp il $15.95 *

Grades: PreK K 1 2   E
  1. Shipwrecks—Fiction 2. Parrots—Fiction
  ISBN 0-7868-5184-8   LC 2004-117133

"Michael di Capua books"

"Terrific," says Eugene when he wins an all-expenses-paid cruise to Bermuda. "I'll probably get a really nasty sunburn." But Eugene's luck is much worse than that. His ship sinks, and he ends up stranded on a tiny island with a talking parrot.

"With pithy humor and a knack for comic timing, Agee has created a character who will endear himself to readers despite his curmudgeonly exterior and posturing. . . . The cartoon illustrations feature strong lines and soft colors that contrast wonderfully with the story line." SLJ

Z goes home. Hyperion Bks. for Children 2003 unp il $16.95 *

Grades: PreK K 1 2   E
  1. Alphabet
  ISBN 0-7868-1987-1   LC 2002-114205

"Michael di Capua books"

"The letter Z abandons its allotted spot in the City Zoo sign and heads off in Agee's innovative alphabet book. Children can track the red Z's journey past an Alien, over a Bridge, into some Cake, and over Hurdles until the red-letter moment when it finally finds its way to its similarly colored friends. . . . Each letter is exemplified by a noun . . . but to make matters more interesting, the object is also shaped like the letter. . . . Bold shapes and lines create a clean, comical look." Booklist

Ahlberg, Allan

The baby in the hat; written by Allan Ahlberg; illustrations by Andre Amstutz. Candlewick Press 2008 unp il $16.99 *

Grades: K 1 2   **E**
1. Seafaring life—Fiction 2. Great Britain—History—19th century—Fiction
ISBN 978-0-7636-3958-7; 0-7636-3958-3
                              LC 2007-52029

Catching a baby in his hat sets off a series of adventures for a young nineteenth-century English boy as he becomes a sea captain and finds a surprising mate.

"Ahlberg and Amstutz . . . overlook few opportunities for humor in this tall tale. . . . Witty, detailed gouaches dotted with dialogue balloons lend a theatricality to the picaresque tale." Publ Wkly

The pencil; [illustrated by] Bruce Ingman. Candlewick Press 2008 unp il $16.99 *

Grades: PreK K 1 2   **E**
1. Drawing—Fiction
ISBN 978-0-7636-3894-8; 0-7636-3894-3
                              LC 2007-51885

A lonely pencil timidly draws a boy, a dog, and other items but soon faces a problem as his creations begin demanding changes, and when he draws an eraser to make them happy, the real trouble begins.

"Both clever and suspenseful, this surefire delight tells the story of a pencil who must deal with the consequences of his inventions. . . . The book's comical, unexpected plot and wry narrator keep the story fresh throughout." Publ Wkly

Previously; [by] Allan Ahlberg; [illustrated by] Bruce Ingman. Candlewick Press 2007 unp il $16.99

Grades: PreK K 1 2   **E**
1. Fairy tales
ISBN 978-0-7636-3542-8; 0-7636-3542-1
                              LC 2006-51831

The adventures of various nursery rhyme and fairy tale characters are retold in backward sequence with each tale interrelated to the other. Includes Goldilocks, Jack and the beanstalk, Jack and Jill, the frog prince, Cinderella, and the gingerbread man.

"The jazzy, colorful pictures display substantive variety. . . . Children will delight in this energetic, amusing, and very approachable tale." SLJ

The runaway dinner; [by] Allan Ahlberg and [illustrated by] Bruce Ingman. Candlewick Press 2006 unp il $15.99; pa $6.99

Grades: PreK K 1 2   **E**
1. Dining—Fiction
ISBN 978-0-7636-3142-0;   0-7636-3142-6;
978-0-7636-3893-1 (pa); 0-7636-3893-5 (pa)
                              LC 2005058126

A young boy named Banjo Cannon always eats a sausage for dinner, until the night that his sausage—and the rest of his meal—runs away

"With a plot timed faster than fast food and illustrations that keep pace, this picture book about a dinner that literally runs away is a comic treat." Publ Wkly

The shopping expedition; illustrated by André Amstutz. Candlewick Press 2005 unp il $16.99

Grades: PreK K 1   **E**
1. Imagination—Fiction 2. Shopping—Fiction
ISBN 0-7636-2586-8   LC 2003-69674

A routine shopping trip becomes a grand adventure in the eyes of a little girl

"Amstutz's richly colored illustrations have a painterly look, often with visible brush strokes, that really suits the imaginative subject matter. The repetitive phrase keeps the pace of the story going and works well for reading aloud." SLJ

Ahlberg, Janet

The jolly postman; or other people's letters; [by] Janet and Allan Ahlberg. Little, Brown Books for Young Readers 2001 c1986 unp il $17.99

Grades: PreK K 1 2   **E**
1. Postal service—Fiction 2. Letters—Fiction 3. Fairy tales 4. Stories in rhyme
ISBN 978-0-316-12644-1; 0-316-12644-6

A reissue of the title first published 1986

A Jolly Postman delivers letters to several famous fairy-tale characters such as the Big Bad Wolf, Cinderella, and the Three Bears. Each letter may be removed from its envelope page and read separately.

"The story of the postman's travels is told in charming verse; the pictures are delightful, full of clever detail; and the results are frequently hilarious." Publ Wkly

Alalou, Elizabeth

The butter man; [by] Elizabeth Alalou and Ali Alalou; illustrated by Julie Klear Essakalli. Charlesbridge 2008 unp il lib bdg $14.95

Grades: K 1 2 3   **E**
1. Morocco—Fiction
ISBN 978-1-58089-127-1 (lib bdg); 1-58089-127-6 (lib bdg)   LC 2007-02278

While Nora waits for the couscous her father is cooking to be finished, he tells her a story about his youth in the High Atlas Mountains of Morocco. Includes author's note and glossary

The authors "write in descriptive language that speaks directly to children. . . . The folk-art paintings, created by a textile designer, feature whimsical characters and cozy domestic scenes, while the ochre, gold, and rust palette evokes the feeling of the dusty, sunlit landscape." Booklist

Alborough, Jez, 1959-

Duck in the truck. HarperCollins Pubs. 2000 unp il hardcover o.p. pa $7.95; bd bk $8.99 *

Grades: PreK K 1   **E**
1. Ducks—Fiction 2. Animals—Fiction 3. Stories in rhyme
ISBN 0-06-028685-7;   1-933605-76-6   (pa);
978-1-929132-83-6 (bd bk); 1-929132-83-2 (bd bk)
                              LC 99-60934

"A rhyming text relates the troubles of a duck whose truck gets stuck in the muck. . . . The art makes the most of the story's physical comedy, with exaggerated humor and an engaging animal cast, including a frog, a sheep, and a goat who all come to help out." Horn Book Guide

Alborough, Jez, 1959-—*Continued*

Other titles about Duck are:

Captain Duck (2003)

Duck's key, where can it be (2005)

Fix-it Duck (2002)

Hit the ball Duck (2006)

Super Duck (2009)

Some dogs do. Candlewick Press 2003 unp il
$15.99

Grades: PreK K 1 2   E

1. Dogs—Fiction 2. Stories in rhyme

ISBN 0-7636-2201-X   LC 2002-41760

When Sid tries to convince his doggy classmates that
he flew to school, they do not believe him.

"Done in gouache, the illustrations glow with bright
colors. . . . A wonderful addition to any library and a
great choice for storytime." SLJ

Tall. Candlewick Press 2005 unp il $15.99

Grades: PreK K 1 2   E

1. Chimpanzees—Fiction 2. Size—Fiction

ISBN 0-7634-2784-4   LC 2004-062941

Illustrations and just a few words depict how various
jungle animals help Bobo the chimp to feel that he is
tall.

"Bobo embodies an impressive range of identifiable
emotions. Alborough's adept pen-and-gouache illustrations make each feeling and point of view crystal clear.
. . . A must-have title for any children who have ever
felt less than enchanted with their diminutive status."
SLJ

Other titles about Bobo the chimp are:

Hug (2000)

Yes (2006)

Where's my teddy? Candlewick Press 1992 unp
il hardcover o.p. pa $6.99

Grades: PreK K   E

1. Bears—Fiction 2. Teddy bears—Fiction 3. Stories
in rhyme

ISBN 1-5640-2048-7; 1-5640-2280-3 (pa)

When a small boy named Eddie goes searching for his
lost teddy in the dark woods, he comes across a gigantic
bear with a similar problem.

"Alborough's verse adroitly employs kid-pleasing
rhythms and repetitions, while his watercolor, crayon and
pencil drawings underscore the broad comedy of this perfectly satisfying scenario of scary fun." Publ Wkly

Alda, Arlene, 1933-

Did you say pears? Tundra Books 2006 31p il
$16.95

Grades: K 1 2 3   E

1. English language—Homonyms

ISBN 0-88776-739-7

"A marvelously imaginative pairing (sorry) of homonyms (words that sound alike but have different meanings and the same spelling) and homophones (words that
sound alike but have different meanings and different
spellings), wrapped up in a rhyme of amazingly few
words and terrific offbeat photographs." Booklist

Hello, good-bye. Tundra Books 2009 unp il
$16.95

Grades: PreK K   E

1. Opposites

ISBN 978-0-88776-900-9; 0-88776-900-4

"Exceptionally fine color photographs bring clarity as
well as beauty to this book of opposites. Alda . . .
creates images that are striking in themselves and meaningful when paired with their opposites. . . . This offers
plenty of opportunities for interaction between young
children and those reading to them." Booklist

Here a face, there a face. Tundra 2008 unp il
$14.95

Grades: PreK K 1 2 3   E

1. Face 2. Stories in rhyme

ISBN 0-88776-845-8; 978-0-88776-845-3

"A simple rhyming text leads children from page to
page and photo to photo in the discovery of 'faces' in
ordinary objects. Each page has a short line of the verse
and a color photograph of a manmade or natural object
with facial characteristics. The photographs are clearly
focused and cropped so that viewers can zoom in on the
countenance. The subjects include buildings, a kitchen
pot, a tree, mailboxes, and more. Youngsters will delight
in finding the eyes, noses, and mouths." SLJ

Iris has a virus; [by] Arlene Alda; illustrated by
Lisa Desimini. Tundra Books 2008 unp il $18.95

Grades: PreK K 1 2   E

1. Sick—Fiction 2. Viruses—Fiction

ISBN 978-0-88776-844-6; 0-88776-844-X

"Iris finds out that having a stomach virus is exhausting, especially when her brother, Doug, lets her know
that she always gets sick at the wrong time." Publisher's
note

"Alda sensitively captures a kid's viewpoint on illness.
. . . The straightforward text is enlivened with occasional . . . rhyming couplets. . . . The colorful paper-collage
illustrations incorporate whimsical perspectives and scenarios." Booklist

Alderson, Brian

Thumbelina; [by] Hans Christian Andersen;
retold by Brian Alderson; illustrated by Bagram
Ibatoulline. Candlewick Press 2009 unp il $17.99

Grades: 1 2 3 4   E

1. Andersen, Hans Christian, 1805-1875—Adaptations
2. Fairy tales

ISBN 978-0-7636-2079-0; 0-7636-2079-3

LC 2008-27721

A tiny girl no bigger than a thumb is stolen by a great
ugly toad and subsequently has many adventures and
makes many animal friends, before finding the perfect
mate in a warm and beautiful southern land.

"This retelling of Andersen's classic tale remains close
to the original. . . . Alderson retells these adventures and
misadventures with a wry wit, moving the plot quickly
through each scene. . . . Ibatoulline's illustrations are
lavishly composed in watercolor and gouache." Bull Cent
Child Books

Alexander, Claire

Lucy and the bully; by Claire Alexander. Albert Whitman & Co. 2008 unp il $16.99 *

Grades: PreK K 1 2   **E**

1. Bullies—Fiction 2. School stories 3. Animals—Fiction

ISBN 978-0-8075-4786-1; 0-8075-4786-7

LC 2008001340

When a mean classmate in preschool wrecks Lucy's artwork, she discovers that they can be friends once he stops being jealous of her.

"Alexander's child-friendly watercolors beautifully convey a range of emotions. An excellent note to parents and teachers discusses bullying and ways to combat it." Booklist

Small Florence, piggy pop star. Albert Whitman & Co. 2010 unp il $16.99

Grades: PreK K 1   **E**

1. Pigs—Fiction 2. Sisters—Fiction 3. Shyness—Fiction 4. Singers—Fiction

ISBN 978-0-8075-7455-3; 0-8075-7455-4

LC 2009-23624

Florence, a young pig, is too shy to sing in front of her sisters but gathers her courage at a singing competition when they lose their nerve.

"Working mostly in midnight blues and spotlight yellows—and piggy pink, of course—Alexander's . . . spots, multiple panels, and three-quarter page spreads add flash to the pages. . . . Many laughs will find Florence lots of fans." Publ Wkly

Alexander, Lloyd, 1924-2007

The fortune-tellers; illustrated by Trina Schart Hyman. Dutton Children's Bks. 1992 unp il hardcover o.p. pa $6.99

Grades: K 1 2 3   **E**

1. Fortune telling—Fiction 2. Cameroon—Fiction

ISBN 0-525-44849-7; 0-14-056233-8 (pa)

LC 91-30684

A carpenter goes to a fortune teller and finds the predictions about his future coming true in an unusual way

"Alexander's rags-to-riches story combines universal elements of the trickster character and the cumulative disaster tale. Hyman's pictures set it all in a vibrant community in Cameroon, West Africa. . . . The energetic, brilliantly colored paintings are packed with people and objects that swirl around the main characters. . . . With its ups and downs, this is a funny, playful story that evokes the irony of the human condition." Booklist

Alexander, Martha G.

Max and the dumb flower picture; [by] Martha Alexander with James Rumford. Charlesbridge 2009 unp il $9.95

Grades: PreK K 1 2   **E**

1. School stories 2. Artists—Fiction 3. Mother's Day—Fiction

ISBN 978-1-58089-156-1; 1-58089-156-X

LC 2008007251

Despite his teacher's entreaties that it would be perfect for Mother's Day, Max refuses to color in the same flower picture as the rest of the class

"Before her death in 2006, Alexander . . . left her manuscript and sketches in the hands of James Rumford. . . . The tender result honors both Alexander and the children for whom she wrote for 40 years. . . . The soft sketches are color washed digitally and by hand, and with Rumford's collaboration, still bear Alexander's simple, expressive style." Publ Wkly

Aliki

All by myself! written and illustrated by Aliki. HarperCollins Pubs. 2000 unp il $14.95; lib bdg $14.89; pa $6.99

Grades: K 1 2 3   **E**

ISBN 0-06-028929-5; 0-06-028930-9 (lib bdg); 0-06-446253-2 (pa)

LC 99-51672

A child shows all the things he has learned to do all on his own

"Aliki's colorful illustrations closely match the moods and energy levels of a five- or six-year-old. . . . The text has a hand-printed appearance, large and easy to read. . . . A good choice for story-hours and beginning readers." SLJ

Painted words: Marianthe's story one. Greenwillow Bks. 1998 unp il $16.99; lib bdg $17.89 *

Grades: K 1 2 3   **E**

1. School stories 2. Immigrants—Fiction

ISBN 0-688-15661-4; 0-688-15662-2 (lib bdg)

LC 97-34653

Bound back to back with: Spoken memories: Marianthe's story two

Two separate stories, the first telling of Mari's starting school in a new land, and the second describing village life in her country before she and her family left in search of a better life

"In simple, understated language, Aliki has captured the emotions and experiences of many of today's children. Colored-pencil and crayon illustrations in soft primary and secondary colors reinforce the mood of the text." SLJ

A play's the thing; written and illustrated by Aliki. HarperCollins 2005 32p il $16.99; lib bdg $17.89 *

Grades: K 1 2 3   **E**

1. School stories 2. Theater—Fiction

ISBN 0-06-074355-7; 0-06-074356-5 (lib bdg)

LC 2004-22101

"When Miss Brilliant's class decides to put on a fractured version of [Mary Had a Little Lamb], José must learn to work with his classmates and overcome his antisocial tendencies. . . . This is . . . the type of work that children will be drawn to again and again because they recognize their world so aptly captured in both word and art. Each time they revisit, they will find something new in the colorful cartoon illustrations." SLJ

Push button. Greenwillow Books 2010 unp il $16.99; lib bdg $17.89 *

Grades: PreK   **E**

1. Play—Fiction 2. Stories in rhyme

ISBN 978-0-06-167308-5; 0-06-167308-0; 978-0-06-167309-2 (lib bdg); 0-06-167309-9 (lib bdg)

LC 2008047690

Aliki—*Continued*

A little boy who loves pushing buttons of all kinds ends up with such a sore finger that he must play with other things.

"Against the clean white backgrounds, Aliki's familiar style of mixing pencils, watercolors, ink, and markers give the tousle-headed protagonist a vivid, crayon-colored expressiveness. . . . Rhyming text and sound effects add wry touches." Booklist

Quiet in the garden; written and illustrated by Aliki. Greenwillow Books 2009 unp il $17.99; lib bdg $18.89

Grades: PreK K   E
   1. Gardens—Fiction 2. Animals—Fiction
   ISBN   978-0-06-155207-6;   0-06-155207-0;
   978-0-06-155208-3 (lib bdg); 0-06-155208-9 (lib bdg)
                                   LC 2008-12641

Sitting quietly in his garden, a little boy observes the eating habits of birds, bugs, butterflies, and other small animals. Includes instructions on how to make your own garden and a detailed illustration of plants typically found in a garden.

"With spare words and a balance of line and color against white backgrounds framed with lacey branches, Aliki deftly portrays the benefits of observing nature." SLJ

The two of them; written and illustrated by Aliki. Greenwillow Bks. 1979 unp il pa $6.99 hardcover o.p.

Grades: PreK K 1 2   E
   1. Grandfathers—Fiction 2. Death—Fiction
   ISBN 0-688-07337-9 (pa)   LC 79-10161

Describes the relationship of a grandfather and his granddaughter from her birth to his death

"The eloquent illustrations in muted full color and the smaller soft-pencil drawings show the life the two shared as well as the tenderness and pure pleasure implicit in their relationship." Horn Book

We are best friends. Greenwillow Bks. 1982 unp il $16.99; pa $5.99

Grades: PreK K 1 2   E
   1. Friendship—Fiction
   ISBN 0-688-00822-4; 0-688-07037-X (pa)
                                   LC 81-6549

When Robert's best friend Peter moves away, both are unhappy, but they learn that they can make new friends and still remain best friends

"Brightly lit pictures in cheerful primary colors portray with just a stroke of the pen the misery of losing a friend who must move away and the tentative beginnings of a new companionship. . . . Details of school and home abound in the lively pictures." Horn Book

  Another title about Robert and Peter is:

Best friends together again (1995)

Allard, Harry, 1928-

Miss Nelson is missing! [by] Harry Allard, James Marshall. Houghton Mifflin 1977 32p il $16; pa $5.95 *

Grades: PreK K 1 2   E
   1. School stories 2. Teachers—Fiction
   ISBN 0-395-25296-2; 0-395-40146-1 (pa)
                                   LC 76-55918

"The kids in room 207 were so fresh and naughty that they lost their sweet-natured teacher, the blonde Miss Nelson, and got in her place the sour-souled Miss Swamp." N Y Times Book Rev

"Humor and suspense fill the pages of [this book]." Christ Sci Monit

  Other titles about Miss Nelson are:

Miss Nelson has a field day (1985)

Miss Nelson is back (1982)

Allen, Debbie

Dancing in the wings; pictures by Kadir Nelson. Dial Bks. for Young Readers 2000 unp il $16.99; pa $6.99

Grades: PreK K 1 2   E
   1. Ballet—Fiction 2. African Americans—Fiction
   ISBN 0-8037-2501-9; 0-14-250141-7 (pa)
                                   LC 99-462181

Sassy tries out for a summer dance festival in Washington, D.C., despite the other girls' taunts that she is much too tall

"Allen's dialogue is realistic, and Nelson's illustrations of the predominantly African-American cast ably capture Sassy's love of dance and her lively personality." Horn Book Guide

Allen, Jonathan, 1957-

The little rabbit who liked to say moo. Boxer Books 2008 unp il $14.95

Grades: PreK K 1   E
   1. Rabbits—Fiction 2. Animals—Fiction 3. Sound—Fiction
   ISBN 978-1-905417-78-0; 1-905417-78-0

"Little Rabbit likes to say 'moo,' because rabbits don't have a big noise. The little creature also likes to say 'baa,' 'oink,' 'heehaw,' and 'quack,' and gets the other young farm animals to join the refrain until a surprise ending reveals the bunny's favorite sound. The illustrations are large, uncluttered, simple, and bold, made of black lines and computer air-brushed color. . . . With its large print and natural repetition, this cumulative tale will be useful for building early literacy skills." SLJ

Alter, Anna, 1974-

Abigail spells. Alfred A. Knopf 2009 unp il $16.99; lib bdg $19.99

Grades: K 1 2   E
   1. Friendship—Fiction 2. Spelling bees—Fiction
   ISBN   978-0-375-85617-4;   0-375-85617-X;
   978-0-375-95617-1 (lib bdg); 0-375-95617-4 (lib bdg)
                                   LC 2008024529

George helps his best friend Abigail practice for the city spelling bee, then cheers her up when she makes a mistake.

Alter, Anna, 1974-—_Continued_

"Alter's folk-style acrylics done in warm, muted shades beautifully complement this steady-paced, conversational story." SLJ

Altman, Alexandra

Waiting for Benjamin; a story about autism; by Alexandra Jessup Altman; illustrated by Susan Keeter. Albert Whitman & Co. 2008 unp il lib bdg $15.95

Grades: 1 2 3 4   E

1. Autism—Fiction 2. Brothers—Fiction

ISBN 978-0-8075-7364-8 (lib bdg); 0-8075-7364-7 (lib bdg)   LC 2007-24248

Alexander experiences feelings of disappointment, anger, embarrassment, and jealousy when his younger brother is diagnosed with autism

"Realistic illustrations depict the characters and their emotions. . . . The book may be useful as an introduction for young children who have a sibling with this condition." SLJ

Alvarez, Julia, 1950-

A gift of gracias; the legend of Altagracia; written by Julia Alvarez; illustrated by Beatriz Vidal. Knopf 2005 unp il $15.95; lib bdg $17.99

Grades: K 1 2 3   E

1. Oranges—Fiction 2. Dominican Republic—Fiction 3. Saints—Fiction

ISBN 0-375-82425-1; 0-375-92425-6 (lib bdg)

Maria's family is almost forced to leave their farm on the new island colony, until a mysterious lady appears in Maria's dream

"Rich in cultural authenticity and brimming with the magical realism that is characteristic of Hispanic literature, this elegantly woven tale introduces the legend of Our Lady of Altagracia, the patron saint of the Dominican Republic. . . . With an exquisite use of watercolor and gouache, Vidal has painted colorful, yet warm illustrations that add depth to the story." SLJ

Amado, Elisa

Tricycle; [by] Elisa Amado; [illustrated by] Alfonso Ruano. Groundwood Books/House of Anansi Press 2007 unp il $17.95

Grades: 1 2 3 4   E

1. Friendship—Fiction 2. Social classes—Fiction 3. Theft—Fiction 4. Truthfulness and falsehood—Fiction

ISBN 978-0-88899-614-5; 0-88899-614-4

"This book tells of rich and poor from the viewpoint of young Margarita, who climbs a tree on her rich family's estate and sees the shacks on the other side of the hedge, where her friend Rosario lives. Margarita watches as Rosario and her brother take her tricycle, but she doesn't say anything about it, even when her mother's lunch guests spew prejudice. . . . The text is spare, and the richly colored acrylic art . . . is just on the edge of magical realism. Although there is no overt message, there is much to talk about." Booklist

Amato, Mary, 1961-

The chicken of the family; illustrated by Delphine Durand. G.P. Putnam's Sons 2007 unp il $16.99

Grades: PreK K 1 2   E

1. Sisters—Fiction 2. Chickens—Fiction

ISBN 0-399-24196-5; 978-0-399-24196-3

LC 2006-03606

When her older sisters tease her into believing that she is actually a chicken, Henrietta runs off to a farm to be among her own kind.

The "storytelling is set off brilliantly by Durand's . . . off-kilter, kid-like cartooning. Packed with funny details and small plots . . . the art, like the story, delivers grade-AA comedy." Publ Wkly

American babies; developed by the Global Fund for Children. Charlesbridge 2010 unp il $6.95

Grades: PreK   E

1. Infants 2. Board books for children

ISBN 978-1-58089-280-3; 1-58089-280-9

"This appealing board book offers 17 closeup photos of babies. . . . [It] has a brief text, really a single sentence divided into phrases. . . . From the Hawaiian child on the cover to the African-American girl on the last page, all the babies pictured are beyond early infancy. Their expressive faces and emotions are as varied as their family backgrounds, surroundings, and activities. . . . The pleasing layout places each colorful, full-page photo opposite a page with a slightly smaller photo and large-type text on its bright, solid-color border." Booklist

Ander, 1967-

Me and my bike; [written & illustrated by] Ander. Heryin Books 2008 unp il $16.95

Grades: 2 3 4 5   E

1. Bicycles—Fiction 2. Wishes—Fiction

ISBN 978-0-9787550-2-7; 0-9787550-2-2

LC 2007005817

A child wants nothing more than a new bicycle, and it seems the wish might come true with some help from the magic lamp that once made Grandpa grow up really fast

"The book has the feel of a graphic novel. The sketchy cartoon illustrations done on heavy stock are full of movement and changes in perspective, and they carry much of the storytelling and humor. This is a beautifully understated, often amusing meditation on being resilient, appreciating what you have, and still sustaining hope for something better." SLJ

Andersen, Hans Christian, 1805-1875

The emperor's new clothes; designed and illustrated by Virginia Lee Burton. Houghton Mifflin 2004 c1949 44p il $16

Grades: K 1 2 3   E

1. Fairy tales

ISBN 0-618-34421-7

A reissue of the edition first published 1949

Weavers convince the vain emperor that the clothing they make for him can only be seen by those who are not fools, but only the child recognizes the truth

"Burton's sense of pageantry sets forth in beautiful

Andersen, Hans Christian, 1805-1875—_Continued_

colors the magnificence of the Emperor's domain and entourage; her sense of humor brings out rightly the ridiculous situation with all its implications." Horn Book Guide

Thumbeline; illustrated by Lisbeth Zwerger; translated by Anthea Bell. North-South Bks. 2000 unp il hardcover o.p. pa $6.95 *

Grades: K 1 2 3   E

1. Fairy tales

ISBN 0-7358-1213-6; 0-7358-2236-0 (pa)

LC 99-57073

"A Michael Neugebauer book"

A reissue of 1985 edition published by Picture Book Studio

The adventures of a tiny girl no bigger than a thumb and her many animal friends

"The book's squarish design . . . draws the reader's attention to the exceptional art. Lovely, lean, lithe lines combine with a palette of tawny earth tones to create a minimalist world redolent with grace and rich with imagination." Horn Book Guide

The ugly duckling; [illustrated by] Pirkko Vainio. NorthSouth 2009 unp il $16.95

Grades: PreK K 1 2   E

1. Fairy tales 2. Ducks—Fiction 3. Swans—Fiction

ISBN 978-0-7358-2226-9; 0-7358-2226-3

"Andersen's timeless story is lovingly revisited in this modest yet engaging retelling. With the sound and feel of a classic in the very best sense, the familiar tale has been reworked but not oversimplified, making it particularly appealing for children who might be too young for some of the harsher elements of the original. But what makes this version particularly appealing is the lovely watercolor artwork, which, like the text, exudes a feeling of tradition and familiarity." SLJ

Anderson, Laurie Halse, 1961-

The hair of Zoe Fleefenbacher goes to school; illustrated by Ard Hoyt. Simon & Schuster Books for Young Readers 2009 unp il $16.99

Grades: K 1 2   E

1. Hair—Fiction 2. School stories

ISBN 978-0-689-85809-3; 0-689-85809-4

LC 2007045161

A young girl's talented but untamed tresses do not impress her strict first-grade teacher, who has rules for everything, including hair.

"Anderson's narrative sparkles with exuberant language and exaggerated humor. Hoyt's buoyant cartoons, done in pen and ink and watercolors, are filled with flowing lines and comical touches." SLJ

Anderson, Peggy Perry

Chuck's truck; by Peggy Perry Anderson. Houghton Mifflin 2006 unp il $16

Grades: PreK K 1 2   E

1. Trucks—Fiction 2. Domestic animals—Fiction 3. Stories in rhyme

ISBN 0-618-66836-5; 978-0-618-66836-6

LC 2005020870

"Walter Lorraine books"

When too many barnyard friends climb in to go to town, Chuck's truck breaks down, but Handyman Hugh knows just what to do.

"Filled with rhyming language, this story will be a boon for beginning readers who will easily identify the rhyming words. . . . Anderson uses a crayon-resist technique to great effect, and the pictures are filled with dimension and texture. The bright colors are vibrant and energetic." SLJ

Another title about Chuck is:

Chuck's band (2008)

Joe on the go; [by] Peggy Perry Anderson. Houghton Mifflin 2007 32p il $16

Grades: PreK K 1 2   E

1. Family reunions—Fiction 2. Play—Fiction 3. Frogs—Fiction 4. Stories in rhyme

ISBN 978-0-618-77331-2; 0-618-77331-2

LC 2006009771

"Walter Lorraine books"

Joe the frog wants to be on the go, but even at a family reunion he is out of luck, as everyone says they are too busy, or he is too fast, too slow, too big, or too small to go with them, until Grandma invites him to go with her on a special outing.

"Illustrated with bright, boisterous line-and-watercolor pictures, the simple rhyming text . . . will draw story hour listeners as well as beginning readers to a scenario they may recognize." Booklist

Other titles about Joe the frog are:

Time for bed, the babysitter said (1987)

To the tub (1996)

Out to lunch (1998)

Let's clean up (2002)

Anderson, Sara

A day at the market. Handprint Books 2006 unp il $14.95

Grades: PreK K 1 2   E

1. Pike Place Market (Seattle, Wash.)—Fiction 2. Markets—Fiction 3. Seattle (Wash.)—Fiction 4. Stories in rhyme 5. Board books for children

ISBN 1-59354-149-X

A visit to Pike Place Market in Seattle, Washington, a working market where local residents purchase their food and flowers at farmers' stalls and merchant shops galore.

"In this oversize board book, Anderson takes readers on an exquisite visual tour. . . . A lively and lovely offering that children will find exhilarating." SLJ

Andreasen, Dan

The baker's dozen; [by] Dan Andreasen. Henry Holt 2007 unp il $16.95

Grades: PreK K   E

1. Baking—Fiction 2. Counting 3. Stories in rhyme

ISBN 978-0-8050-7809-1; 0-8050-7809-6

LC 2006031372

The reader is invited to count from one to thirteen as a jolly baker makes delectable treats from one mouthwatering eclair to twelve luscious cupcakes, and serves them to invited guests

This offers "a simple rhyme and clear, mouthwatering illustrations." Booklist

Andreasen, Dan—*Continued*

The giant of Seville; a "tall" tale based on a true story. Abrams Books for Young Readers 2007 unp il $15.95

Grades: K 1 2 3   E
1. Bates, Martin Van Buren, 1837-1919 2. Giants
ISBN 978-0-8109-0988-5; 0-8109-0988-X
LC 2006-13579

"Seville, Ohio, is so quiet that you can 'hear the corn grow' until a giant comes to town. Nearly eight feet tall, Captain Martin Van Buren is searching for a friendly community in which to settle down. Seville's residents welcome him, but accommodating a guest of his stature proves difficult. . . . An endnote introduces the historical people and events that inspired the story, and Andreasen extends the tale's old-fashioned feel in detailed, color-washed ink drawings of townspeople in nineteenth-century dress." Booklist

The treasure bath. Henry Holt and Co. 2009 unp il $16.99

Grades: PreK   E
1. Baths—Fiction 2. Imagination—Fiction 3. Stories without words
ISBN 978-0-8050-8686-7; 0-8050-8686-2
LC 2008-38224

"Christy Ottaviano books"

A wordless picture book in which a young boy explores a creature-filled world beneath the bubbles in his bathtub

"Andreasen borrows motifs from comic-book art—extra gleam on objects, squared-off, blunt-cut hair and the humans' doll-like postures—and combines them with Disney-esque cheer to create amiable scenarios with just a hint of irony." Publ Wkly

Andrews, Julie, 1935-

The very fairy princess; by Julie Andrews & Emma Walton Hamilton; [illustrations by Christine Davenier] Little, Brown Books for Young Readers 2010 unp il $16.99

Grades: K 1 2   E
1. Princesses—Fiction
ISBN 978-0-316-04050-1; 0-316-04050-9
LC 2009-19307

Despite her scabby knees and dirty fingernails, Geraldine knows that she is a princess inside and shows it through her behavior at home and in school.

"Davenier's whimsical ink-and-colored-pencil illustrations enchant. . . . The mother-daughter team successfully demonstrates an understanding of that magical stage of childhood in which determination, desire and dreams can transform reality." Kirkus

Anholt, Laurence

Cézanne and the apple boy. Barron's 2009 unp il $14.99

Grades: PreK K 1   E
1. Cézanne, Paul, 1839-1906—Fiction 2. Artists—Fiction 3. Father-son relationship—Fiction
ISBN 978-0-7641-6282-4; 0-7641-6282-9

Paul's father, the artist Paul Cézanne has been away from home for so long that the boy hardly recognizes his father when he returns. But the two soon become fast friends. The local townspeople laugh at the artist's pictures. But young Paul likes the art. An influential art dealer comes from Paris the lives of the artist and his son change dramatically.

"Evocative, realistic illustrations mix with reproductions of Cézanne works and, along with the young character, will draw kids into this enjoyable, informative portrayal of Cézanne as both a father and an influential artist." Booklist

Anno, Mitsumasa, 1926-

Anno's counting book. Crowell 1977 c1975 unp il $17.99; lib bdg $18.89; pa $6.99 *

Grades: PreK K 1   E
1. Counting 2. Seasons—Fiction 3. Stories without words
ISBN 0-690-01287-X; 0-690-01288-8 (lib bdg); 0-06-443123-1 (pa)
LC 76-28977

Original Japanese edition, 1975

"A distinctive, beautifully conceived counting book in which twelve full-color doublespreads show the same village and surrounding countryside during different hours (by the church clock) and months. Both the seasons and community changes are studied, as such components of the scene as flowers, trees, animals, people, and buildings increase from one to twelve." LC. Child Books, 1977

Appelt, Kathi, 1954-

Bats around the clock; illustrated by Melissa Sweet. HarperCollins Pubs. 2000 unp il $15.99; lib bdg $16.89 *

Grades: PreK K 1 2   E
1. Bats—Fiction 2. Rock music—Fiction 3. Stories in rhyme
ISBN 0-688-16469-2; 0-688-16470-6 (lib bdg)
LC 99-15502

Click Dark hosts a special twelve-hour program of American Bat Stand where the bats rock and roll until the midnight hour ends.

"The rhymes are delightful and the narrative jives right along." SLJ

Other titles about the bats are:
The bat jamboree (1996)
Bats on parade (1999)

Brand-new baby blues; words by Kathi Appelt; illustrations by Kelly Murphy. HarperCollins Publishers 2010 unp il $16.99

Grades: PreK K 1 2   E
1. Stories in rhyme 2. Infants—Fiction 3. Siblings—Fiction
ISBN 978-0-06-053233-8; 0-06-053233-5; 978-0-06-053234-5 (lib bdg); 0-06-053234-3 (lib bdg)
LC 2008-05796

The arrival of a new little brother has his big sister singing the blues.

"Funny and concise, the rollicking rhyme bounces along, accepting the frustration natural to the situation, while gently allowing the girl's love of and appreciation for her brother. . . . The process is complemented by the illustrations, which modulate in palette from angry blues

Appelt, Kathi, 1954-—*Continued*

and greens to sunny yellows, while serene compositions replace off-kilter ones. Older brothers and sisters will easily identify with this jaunty heroine and profit from her realizations—an excellent choice for a new older sibling." Kirkus

Bubba and Beau, best friends; [illustrated by] Arthur Howard. Harcourt 2002 unp il $16; pa $6
Grades: PreK K 1 2   E
   1. Infants—Fiction 2. Dogs—Fiction
   ISBN 0-15-202060-8; 0-15-205580-0 (pa)
                                        LC 2001-1987
When Mamma Pearl washes their favorite blanket it's a sad day for best friends Bubba and Beau, but it gets worse when she decides the baby boy and his puppy need baths, too.

"Appelt's snappy text is a readaloud romp, and Howard's equally snappy watercolors provide an offbeat, slyly funny subtext. Uncluttered compositions, a clean pastel palette, solid drafting, and terrifically expressive faces combine with the conversational, cheeky text." Bull Cent Child Books

Other titles about Bubba and Beau are:
Bubba and Beau go night-night (2003)
Bubba and Beau meet the relatives (2004)

Oh my baby, little one; pictures by Jane Dyer. Harcourt Brace & Co. 2000 unp il $16; pa $3.99
Grades: PreK K   E
   1. Mother-child relationship—Fiction 2. Stories in rhyme
   ISBN 0-15-200041-0; 0-15-206031-6 (pa)
                                        LC 99-6363
"An exploration of the love that exists between mother and child, even when Mama Bird must leave her baby at nursery school. Told in rhyming verse, each four-line stanza is a reassurance that mama's love will permeate all areas of Baby Bird's day." SLJ

"The light, bright pictures will charm young listeners, who will find this book best enjoyed while cuddled up next to Mama." Booklist

Applegate, Katherine

The buffalo storm; illustrated by Jan Ormerod. Clarion Books 2007 32p il $16
Grades: 2 3 4   E
   1. Overland journeys to the Pacific—Fiction
   2. Frontier and pioneer life—Fiction
   3. Grandmothers—Fiction 4. Fear—Fiction
   ISBN 978-0-618-53597-2; 0-618-53597-7
                                        LC 2006-15661
When Hallie and her parents join a wagon train to Oregon and leave her grandmother behind, Hallie must learn to face the storms that frighten her so, as well as other, newer fears, with just her grandmother's quilt to comfort her.

"Ormerod's . . . textured watercolors and pastels employ billowy swaths of color to suggest the vastness of the setting. . . . Vivid imagery makes this lyrical tale an accessible, fresh addition to the children's pioneer genre as it tackles themes of change, courage and home." Publ Wkly

Argueta, Jorge

Moony Luna; story, Jorge Argueta; illustrations, Elizabeth Gómez. Children's Book Press 2005 31p il $16.95
Grades: PreK K 1 2   E
   1. School stories 2. Bilingual books—English-Spanish
   ISBN 0-89239-205-3   LC 2004-56047
"This bilingual picture book presents . . . the fears five-year-old Luna experiences as she faces her first day of school. The little girl gives shape to her anxiety by visualizing it as the monster from a book her mother read to her the night before. The Spanish text . . . has a pleasing poetic structure and a comforting rhythm that will reassure young listeners. . . . The illustrations, well matched to the story, have the flat perspective and the vibrant colors of contemporary Latin American art." Booklist

Armstrong, Jennifer, 1961-

Magnus at the fire; illustrated by Owen Smith. Simon & Schuster Books for Young Readers 2005 unp il $15.95
Grades: PreK K 1 2   E
   1. Horses—Fiction 2. Fire fighting—Fiction
   ISBN 0-689-83922-7   LC 2004-11487
When the Broadway Fire House acquires a motorized fire engine, Magnus the fire horse is not ready to retire.

A "stirring historical story. . . . Impressive oil paintings in vibrant colors capture the drama of firefighting in the 1800s." SLJ

Once upon a banana; illustrated by David Small. Simon & Schuster Books for Young Readers 2006 unp il $16.95 *
Grades: PreK K 1 2   E
   1. City and town life—Fiction 2. Stories without words
   ISBN 0-689-84251-1; 978-0-689-84251-1
                                        LC 2005-08567
"A street juggler's pet monkey runs off and steals a deli's outdoor stall. . . . The monkey tosses the banana peel on the sidewalk, thus triggering a book-long, slapstick-rich chase that covers an entire city center and ensnares a cavalcade of characters. . . . Small's loose yet precise ink lines and watercolor wash seem ideal for these crowded streets where anarchy abounds. . . . The pages overflow with enough pratfalls and comic asides to reward many readings." Publ Wkly

Arnold, Caroline, 1944-

Wiggle and Waggle; [by] Caroline Arnold; illustrated by Mary Peterson. Charlesbridge 2007 48p il lib bdg $12.95; pa $5.95
Grades: K 1 2   E
   1. Worms—Fiction 2. Friendship—Fiction
   3. Gardens—Fiction
   ISBN 978-1-58089-306-0 (lib bdg);
   978-1-58089-307-4 (pa)   LC 2006020948
Two worms who are best friends have fun together as they tunnel their way through a garden. Includes facts on how worms help plants grow

"The artwork, done in earth tones, of course, features two goofy, google-eyed worms. Good quality paper and an attractive design add to the book's pick-me-up quotient." Booklist

Arnold, Marsha Diane, 1948-

Heart of a tiger; pictures by Jamichael Henterly. Dial Bks. for Young Readers 1995 unp il $16.99

Grades: PreK K 1 2   E

1. Cats—Fiction 2. Tigers—Fiction 3. India—Fiction

ISBN 0-8037-1695-8   LC 94-17126

"Small kitten Number Four must find a name for himself for his naming day. Not wanting to be called Smallest of All, he searches out Bengal, the beautiful tiger whose ways he greatly admires. He learns much from the big cat, and when he saves the tiger's life, he earns the name Heart of a Tiger. Arnold's original story has the feel of an oft-told tale, and Henterly's watercolors reward a lingering look." Horn Book Guide

Prancing, dancing Lily; pictures by John Manders. Dial Books for Young Readers 2004 unp il $16.99

Grades: PreK K 1 2   E

1. Cattle—Fiction 2. Dance—Fiction

ISBN 0-8037-2823-9   LC 2002-5852

Lily will someday be the "bell cow," leading her herd, but because her prancing and dancing only disrupts their order, she travels the world looking for the right place and dance for her

"Arnold's amusing characters and clever text come to life through Manders's comical cartoon illustrations." SLJ

Arnold, Tedd, 1949-

Green Wilma, frog in space. Dial Books for Young Readers 2009 unp il $16.99

Grades: K 1 2   E

1. Stories in rhyme 2. Extraterrestrial beings—Fiction 3. Space flight—Fiction 4. Frogs—Fiction

ISBN 978-0-8037-2698-7; 0-8037-2698-8

       LC 2008039497

Green Wilma the frog is mistaken for an alien child and taken on a trip through space.

This is written "in perfect rhyme. . . . The illustrations explode across the pages with frantic innocence. . . . To say that the pictures complement the text is like declaring that the Sun complements the Earth. Children will adore *Wilma*." SLJ

Another title about Green Wilma is:
Green Wilma (1993)

Hi, Fly Guy! Scholastic 2005 30p il $5.99; pa $3.99

Grades: PreK K 1 2   E

1. Flies—Fiction 2. Pets—Fiction

ISBN   978-0-439-63903-3;   0-439-63903-4; 978-0-439-85311-8 (pa); 0-439-85311-7 (pa)

       LC 2004-20553

"Cartwheel books"

When Buzz captures a fly to enter in The Amazing Pet Show, his parents and the judges tell him that a fly cannot be a pet, but Fly Guy proves them wrong.

"Suitably wacky cartoon art accompanies the text, which is simple enough for beginning readers." Publ Wkly

Other titles in this series are:
Super Fly Guy (2006)
Shoo Fly Guy (2006)

There was an old lady who swallowed Fly Guy (2007)
Fly high, Fly Guy (2008)
Hooray for Fly Guy! (2008)
I spy Fly Guy! (2009)
Fly Guy meets Fly Girl! (2010)

The twin princes; [by] Tedd Arnold. Dial Books for Young Readers 2006 unp il $16.99

Grades: K 1 2   E

1. Chickens—Fiction 2. Twins—Fiction 3. Princes—Fiction

ISBN 0-8037-2696-1   LC 2005013300

Two chicken princes who are twins take part in a contest to determine which one will inherit the throne.

"With his signature verve [Arnold] . . . folds a satisfying brainteaser into an original folktale. . . . The problem and its solution are clearly presented, and there are plenty of clever touches to engage kids and grownups alike." Booklist

Arnosky, Jim

Babies in the bayou; [by] Jim Arnosky. G. P. Putnam's Sons 2007 unp il $16.99 *

Grades: PreK K   E

1. Wetlands 2. Animal babies

ISBN 978-0-399-22653-3; 0-399-22653-2

       LC 2006011910

There are many babies in the bayou, and even though they might have sharp white teeth, hard shells, webbed feet, or quick claws, their mothers still need to protect them.

"This is a wonderful resource to use with children to illuminate the ways of nature; it's economical and rhythmic in text, and beautifully and clearly illustrated. Arnosky uses simple language and a repeated refrain to describe the animals that live in a lush Southern environment." SLJ

Dolphins on the sand; by Jim Arnosky. G.P. Putnam's Sons 2008 unp il $16.99

Grades: PreK K 1 2   E

1. Dolphins—Fiction 2. Wildlife conservation—Fiction

ISBN 978-0-399-24606-7; 0-399-24606-1

       LC 2007045384

A dozen dolphins, led by their eldest member and her youngster, become stranded on a sandbar and must be helped to safety by humans.

This "juxtaposes a straightforward narrative with particularly colorful paintings. . . . Arnosky reflects the simple beauty of the dolphins of the dolphins' happy existance in tropical pinks, oranges, and aquas, moving to a more somber palette of grays and blacks as danger sets in. He includes all manner of flora and fauna in his illustrative arc." Booklist

Gobble it up! a fun song about eating. Scholastic Press 2008 unp il $16.99

Grades: PreK K 1 2   E

1. Animals—Fiction 2. Food—Fiction 3. Stories in rhyme 4. Animals—Songs 5. Food—Songs

ISBN 978-0-439-90362-2; 0-439-90362-9

       LC 2007-29510

"This book takes a direct look at different animals and what they eat. It works well as a picture book, telling

Arnosky, Jim—*Continued*

readers that if they were wild raccoons, or crocodiles, or great white sharks, they would 'gobble up' crawdads, or ducklings, or fishes. The catchy song sung by the author on the accompanying CD adds the element of fun that's advertised. Recognizable, true-to-life acrylic illustrations . . . fill the spreads." SLJ

Grandfather Buffalo; [by] Jim Arnosky. G.P. Putnam's Sons 2006 unp il $16.99

Grades: PreK K 1 2   E

1. Bison—Fiction 2. Old age—Fiction

ISBN 0-399-24169-8   LC 2005003535

When Grandfather Buffalo, the oldest bull of the herd, trails behind the group, he finds that he is joined by a newborn calf.

"Arnosky's signature artwork, which beautifully evokes the western landscape, is especially effective showing the buffalo closeup, and the writer-artist's respect for nature is clearly reflected in the simple, poignant story." Booklist

I'm a turkey! Scholastic Press 2009 unp il $16.99

Grades: PreK K 1   E

1. Stories in rhyme 2. Turkeys—Fiction

ISBN 978-0-439-90364-6; 0-439-90364-5

LC 2008-38335

"In spoken-word song with rhyming text, a turkey describes his life in a large flock, always looking out for other creatures that might find him tasty. (Internet component includes downloadable song)." Publisher's note

"Arnosky's illustrations manage to be both autumnal and bright. . . . Arnosky gives [the birds] personality and charm." Booklist

Slow down for manatees. G. P. Putnam's Sons 2009 unp il $16.99

Grades: PreK K 1   E

1. Manatees—Fiction

ISBN 978-0-399-24170-3; 0-399-24170-1

LC 2008-47983

Injured by a passing motorboat, a pregnant manatee is rescued and taken to an aquarium to recover and have her baby in a safe environment.

"Text and art work in tandem to present a portrait of a gentle, innocent creature. . . . A solid addition to naturalist Arnosky's oeuvre." Publ Wkly

Turtle in the sea. Putnam 2002 unp il $16.99

Grades: PreK K 1 2   E

1. Sea turtles—Fiction

ISBN 0-399-22757-1   LC 2001-48123

A sea turtle "escapes from a shark, a boat, a waterspout, and a fisherman's net to drag her scarred body onto a beach to lay her eggs. Arnosky has chosen clear, candy colors for his illustrations—pink, lavender, turquoise—all surrounded by a sunny lemon yellow. . . . The text is often lyrical." SLJ

Arrigan, Mary, 1943-

Mario's Angels; a story about the artist Giotto; written by Mary Arrigan; illustrated by Gillian McClure. Frances Lincoln 2006 unp il $15.95 *

Grades: PreK K 1 2   E

1. Giotto, di Bondone, 1266?-1337—Fiction 2. Artists—Fiction 3. Italy—Fiction 4. Angels—Fiction

ISBN 1-84507-404-1

"Mario, an exuberant boy, visits the artist [Giotto] as he works on his fresco *Nativity* in Padua. . . . When the artist is at a loss about how to fill the sky, Mario suggests angels. . . . The gentle text is matched by light, airy colors and feathery movement in the art. The cherubic Mario is full of life and will seem very real to readers." SLJ

Aruego, Jose

The last laugh; [by] Jose Aruego & Ariane Dewey. Dial Books for Young Readers 2006 unp il $12.99 *

Grades: PreK K 1 2   E

1. Snakes—Fiction 2. Ducks—Fiction 3. Stories without words

ISBN 0-8037-3093-4   LC 2005-48461

A wordless tale in which a clever duck outwits a bullying snake

"In comic-strip panels, Aruego and Deweys signature pen-and-ink and gouache art is droll and accessible. . . . Young readers will find the format and the karmic justice of this story appealing." SLJ

Asch, Frank

Baby Bird's first nest. Harcourt Brace & Co. 1999 unp il $15

Grades: PreK K   E

1. Birds—Fiction 2. Frogs—Fiction

ISBN 0-15-201726-7   LC 97-32653

"Gulliver books"

When Baby Bird takes a tumble from her mama's nest in the middle of the night, she finds a friend in Little Frog.

"A satisfying read-aloud with just enough adventure, wit, and common sense to engage listeners and vocabulary easy enough for beginning readers. . . . Asch's trademark pen-and-ink drawings have been 'colorized' in Adobe Photoshop. The technique is very effective with deep, rich color fading to lighter shades." SLJ

Happy birthday, Moon. Simon & Schuster Books for Young Readers 2000 unp il pa $6.99

Grades: PreK K 1   E

1. Bears—Fiction 2. Moon—Fiction 3. Birthdays—Fiction

ISBN 978-0-689-83544-5; 0-689-83544-2

First published 1982 by Prentice Hall

Bear travels to the highest mountaintop to find out what to give the Moon for its birthday and discovers a delightful surprise—the Moon has the same birthday as Bear. Or so it seems.

Other titles in this series are:

Mooncake (1983)

Moongame (1984)

Moonbear's shadow (1985)

Asch, Frank—*Continued*

Like a windy day; [by] Frank Asch & Devin Asch. Harcourt 2002 unp il $16; pa $7
Grades: PreK K   E
  1. Winds—Fiction
  ISBN 0-15-216376-X; 0-15-206403-6 (pa)
                          LC 2001-5260
"Gulliver books"
A young girl discovers all the things the wind can do, by playing and dancing along with it
Written "in a poetic text. . . . The brief story is filled with action verbs. . . . The exciting pen-and-ink illustrations were colorized in Adobe Photoshop. Broad and sweeping spreads are filled with movement." SLJ

Mrs. Marlowe's mice; written by Frank Asch; illustrated by Devin Asch. Kids Can Press 2007 unp il $17.95
Grades: 2 3 4   E
  1. Cats—Fiction 2. Mice—Fiction
  ISBN 978-1-55453-022-9
Mrs. Marlowe, a cat, secretly cares for the large family of mice who live with her, until one day, suspicious officers from the Department of Catland Security search the premises.
"Carefully detailed period dress and furnishings add a genteel air to the digital picture-book art. . . . Children will have a quiet, compassionate new hero." Booklist

The sun is my favorite star. Harcourt 2001 unp il $15; pa $7
Grades: PreK K 1   E
  1. Sun—Fiction
  ISBN 0-15-202127-2; 0-15-206397-8 (pa)
                          LC 98-46383
"Gulliver books"
Celebrates a child's love of the sun and the wondrous ways in which it helps the earth and the life upon it
"Asch strikes just the right tone for his audience. . . . With colors as warm as a summer day, he creates a series of large-scale illustrations that reflect the direct unaffected tone of the writing." Booklist

Ashburn, Boni
Over at the castle; illustrated by Kelly Murphy. Abrams 2010 unp il $15.95
Grades: PreK K 1 2   E
  1. Dragons—Fiction 2. Castles—Fiction 3. Middle Ages—Fiction 4. Counting 5. Stories in rhyme
  ISBN 978-0-8109-8414-1; 0-8109-8414-8
"The familiar rhythm of the folk song Over in the Meadow finds a new setting as over at the castle, on the hill in the sun, an old mother dragon tries to teach her little dragon patience as they laze about near a castle. . . . Richly textured paintings in subtle hues that fit the medieval period convey the chores of the occupants of the castle, and comedic touches throughout . . . deepen the story and will have children flipping back through the pages." Booklist

Asher, Sandy, 1942-
Here comes Gosling! illustrations by Keith Graves. Philomel Books 2009 unp il $16.99
Grades: PreK K   E
  1. Infants—Fiction 2. Geese—Fiction 3. Animals—Fiction
  ISBN 978-0-399-25085-9; 0-399-25085-9
                         LC 2008032613
Froggie and Rabbit host a picnic for Goose and Gander's new baby, but when the guest of honor starts to cry, Froggie finds a way to cheer her up
"Graves's quirky cartoon illustrations, created in bold-colored acrylic, ink, and pencil, combine full-bleed spreads with spot illustrations, keeping the story flowing. . . . The characters are oddly appealing with their expressive faces, long necks, and short, round bodies. Asher perfectly captures her young protagonist's emotions, and preschoolers will easily empathize with him." SLJ

Ashman, Linda, 1960-
Babies on the go; illustrated by Jane Dyer. Harcourt 2003 unp il $16 *
Grades: PreK K 1   E
  1. Animal babies 2. Animal locomotion
  ISBN 0-15-201894-8   LC 2002-6310
Illustrations and rhyming text show how different animals carry their babies when they are on the move
"The large, soft watercolor illustrations and rhyming text make this celebration of parent/child love a natural for toddler storytime, and it's also perfect for one-on-one sharing." SLJ

Castles, caves, and honeycombs; illustrated by Lauren Stringer. Harcourt 2001 unp il $16
Grades: PreK K 1   E
  1. Home 2. Animals—Habitations 3. Stories in rhyme
  ISBN 0-15-202211-2   LC 99-50801
Describes some of the unique places where animals build their homes such as in a heap of twigs, on a castle tower, in a cave, or in the hollow space inside a tree
"The concise text and womb-like illustrations convey the feelings of love, safety, and security that a home should have." Horn Book Guide

Creaky old house; A topsy-turvy tale of a real fixer-upper; illustrated by Michael Chesworth. Sterling 2009 unp il $14.95
Grades: K 1   E
  1. Stories in rhyme 2. Houses—Fiction 3. Family life—Fiction
  ISBN 978-1-4027-4461-7; 1-4027-4461-7
                         LC 2008037836
A large family gets into an increasingly complicated home repair situation when the doorknob falls off a door
"The clever, rhyming text bounces along with a perfect cadence. The ink, watercolor, and pencil illustrations enhance the telling, and readers will take great pleasure in poring over the many amusing details." SLJ

M is for mischief; an A to Z of naughty children; illustrated by Nancy Carpenter. Dutton Children's Books 2008 unp il $16.99
Grades: K 1 2   E
  1. Alphabet 2. Stories in rhyme
  ISBN 978-0-525-47564-4; 0-525-47564-8
                         LC 2007-28491

Ashman, Linda, 1960-—_Continued_

A rhyme for each letter of the alphabet describes the misbehavior of a child, from Angry Abby to Zany Zelda.

"Each eight-line rhyme in this energetic title has fun with the sounds of words, as well as their slapstick meaning. . . . Though the words are the wonderful winners here, Carpenter's rambunctious watercolor-and-collage pictures provide excellent comedic support." Booklist

Mama's day; [illustrated by] Jan Ormerod. Simon & Schuster Books for Young Readers 2006 unp il $15.95 *
Grades: PreK K 1   E
1. Mother-child relationship—Fiction 2. Stories in rhyme
ISBN 0-689-83475-6   LC 00-45063
In rhyming text, mothers and their babies are described sharing in a variety of activities, from playing at the ocean to reading books and taking a bath

"Ashman's skillful verse and Ormerod's cozy ink-and-gouache artwork improve upon many other picture-book fulminations on mother love. A lilting line of verse appears on each spread, illustrated by a neatly framed scene of a different mother-child pair (including a demure image of breastfeeding) as well as a crew of charming, multicultural babies." Booklist

Stella, unleashed; notes from the doghouse; illustrated by Paul Meisel. Sterling Pub. Co. 2008 40p il $14.95
Grades: K 1 2   E
1. Dogs—Fiction 2. Family life—Fiction 3. Stories in rhyme
ISBN 978-1-4027-3987-3; 1-4027-3987-7
                                        LC 2007036499
The family dog describes her life in a series of rhymes.

"Ashman aptly captures life with a pup, balancing the sweet (lap naps) with the sour (shedding). . . . Meisel's realistic acrylic, gouache, and pencil illustrations are filled with a variety of people and pups. . . . This collection of rhymes is ideal for family read-alouds." SLJ

To the beach! illustrated by Nadine Bernard Westcott. Harcourt 2005 unp il $16
Grades: PreK K 1 2   E
1. Family life—Fiction 2. Beaches—Fiction
ISBN 0-15-216490-1   LC 2003-19444
A family keeps forgetting the things they need to take to the beach

"Rhyming text and bouncy and boldly colored illustrations in acrylic on watercolor paper capture the frenzy surrounding this hilarious . . . family. A rip-roaring fun read-aloud." SLJ

When I was king; by Linda Ashman; illustrated by David McPhail. HarperCollins 2008 unp il $16.99; lib bdg $17.89
Grades: PreK K 1   E
1. Infants—Fiction 2. Brothers—Fiction 3. Stories in rhyme
ISBN   978-0-06-029051-1;   0-06-029051-X;
978-0-06-029052-8 (lib bdg); 0-06-029052-8 (lib bdg)
                                        LC 2005017868

A young boy describes how he is no longer "king" now that there is a new baby in the house, but then his family helps him enjoy the change

This is an "expertly rhymed story. . . . McPhail's charming illustrations perfectly capture the narrator's mood in his facial expressions and body language. Ashman's verses, lettered in a child-friendly font that varies in size, are perfect for reading aloud." SLJ

Aston, Dianna Hutts, 1964-

Moon over Star; pictures by Jerry Pinkney. Dial Books for Young Readers 2008 unp il $17.99 *
Grades: PreK K 1 2 3   E
1. Apollo 11 (Spacecraft)—Fiction 2. Space flight to the moon—Fiction 3. Farm life—Fiction 4. African Americans—Fiction
ISBN 978-0-8037-3107-3; 0-8037-3107-8
                                        LC 2007050703
Coretta Scott King honor book for illustration, 2009

On her family's farm in the town of Star, eight-year-old Mae eagerly follows the progress of the 1969 Apollo 11 flight and moon landing and dreams that she might one day be an astronaut, too.

"Spaced vertically in phrases like free verse alongside the large illustrations, the text combines dignity and immediacy in a clean, spare telling of events. Pinkney's evocative artwork, created using graphite, ink, and watercolor, depicts a black family captivated, and perhaps subtly changed, by the moon landing in 1969." Booklist

Not so tall for six; [by] Dianna Hutts Aston; illustrated by Frank Dormer. Charlesbridge 2008 unp il lib bdg $14.95; pa $6.95
Grades: K 1 2   E
1. Size—Fiction 2. Bullies—Fiction 3. School stories
ISBN 978-1-57091-705-9 (lib bdg); 1-57091-705-1 (lib bdg); 978-1-57091-706-6 (pa); 1-57091-706-X (pa)
                                        LC 2007002279
Six-year-old Kylie Bell comes from a long line of not-so-tall people, but she remembers the family motto—"Brave and smart and big at heart"—which helps her to treat the class bully with kindness

This "manages to charm thanks to quirkily descriptive language with a southwest slant . . . and Kylie's genuine spunk and integrity. Equally winning are Dormer's line-and-watercolor illustrations, washed in a desert-hued palette of rusts and golds." Booklist

An orange in January; [by] Dianna Hutts Aston; illustrated by Julie Maren. Dial Books for Young Readers 2007 unp il $16.99
Grades: PreK K 1   E
1. Oranges—Fiction
ISBN 978-0-8037-3146-2   LC 2006014488
An orange begins its life as a blossom where bees feast on the nectar, and reaches the end of its journey, bursting with the seasons inside it, in the hands of a child.

This is a "poetic tale. . . . Like the text, the glowing acrylic paintings are artfully simple and make beautiful use of color." SLJ

Auch, Mary Jane

Beauty and the beaks; a Turkey's cautionary tale; [by] Mary Jane and Herm Auch. Holiday House 2007 unp il $16.95; pa $6.95

Grades: K 1 2 3   E

1. Turkeys—Fiction 2. Chickens—Fiction 3. Thanksgiving Day—Fiction

ISBN 978-0-8234-1990-6; 0-8234-1990-8; 978-0-8234-2164-0 (pa); 0-8234-2164-3 (pa)

LC 2006049468

When Lance, a very pretentious turkey, arrives on the farm and boasts that he is the only bird invited to a special feast, no hen is impressed, but when Beauty learns that Lance is the main course, she convinces the others to save him

"Wonderfully creative handmade characters and sets are the highlight of this over-the-top chicken tale. . . . The author made chicken mannequins with polymer eyes, beaks, and shoes, as well as wool wings and yarn feathers. Her husband designed the sets, built them, and photographed the images, adjusting their size. A humorous story about dressing a turkey, but not in the usual manner." SLJ

Peeping Beauty; written and illustrated by Mary Jane Auch. Holiday House 1993 unp il $16.95; pa $6.95

Grades: PreK K 1 2   E

1. Chickens—Fiction 2. Ballet—Fiction

ISBN 0-8234-1001-3; 0-8234-1170-2 (pa)

LC 92-16374

Poulette the dancing hen falls into the clutches of a hungry fox, who exploits her desire to become a great ballerina

"The language is lively, and filled with witty phrases and ballet references. Using bright colors and just enough detail, Auch sets her cast of characters against a simple backdrop." SLJ

Another title about Poulette is:

Hen Lake (1995)

The plot chickens; by Mary Jane and Herm Auch. Holiday House 2009 unp il $16.95

Grades: PreK K 1 2   E

1. Chickens—Fiction 2. Authorship—Fiction 3. Books and reading—Fiction

ISBN 978-0-8234-2087-2; 0-8234-2087-6

LC 2007011234

Henrietta the chicken loves to read so much that she decides to write a book herself, but first no one will publish a book written by a chicken, and then, when she publishes it herself and it gets a terrible review in "The Corn Book," Henrietta is devastated

"The illustrations, a combination of oil paints and digital technology, are bold and colorful. . . . A droll chicken with a repeating line adds to the humor. This offering works on two levels. It's a funny picture book that could be used as a manual on writing." SLJ

Averbeck, Jim

In a blue room; [by] Jim Averbeck; illustrated by Trica Tusa. Harcourt 2008 unp il $16 *

Grades: PreK K 1 2   E

1. Bedtime—Fiction 2. Color—Fiction 3. Mother-daughter relationship—Fiction

ISBN 978-0-15-205992-7; 0-15-205992-X

LC 2006034453

Alice wants everything in her bedroom to be blue before she falls asleep

"Prose and pictures partner each other effortlessly all the way to the last page." Publ Wkly

Avi, 1937-

Silent movie; Avi, the author; C.B. Mordan, the illustrator. Atheneum Bks. for Young Readers 2002 unp il $16.95

Grades: K 1 2 3   E

1. Immigrants—Fiction

ISBN 0-689-84145-0   LC 2001-33025

"An Anne Schwartz book"

In the early years of the twentieth century, a Swedish family encounters separation and other hardships upon immigrating to New York City until the son is cast in a silent movie, in a picture book that evokes an actual silent movie

"Clear, beautiful ink-on-clayboard illustrations; white type on thick, glossy black paper; and cinematic lighting effects combine to evoke the historical period." Booklist

Avraham, Kate Aver

What will you be, Sara Mee? illustrated by Anne Sibley O'Brien. Charlesbridge 2010 unp il $16.95; pa $7.95

Grades: PreK K 1   E

1. Birthdays—Fiction 2. Parties—Fiction 3. Siblings—Fiction 4. Korean Americans—Fiction

ISBN 978-1-58089-210-0; 1-58089-210-8; 978-1-58089-211-7 (pa); 1-58089-211-6 (pa)

LC 2009-1708

At her Tol, the first birthday party, Sara Mee plays the traditional Korean prophecy game—Toljabee—while her extended family and friends watch.

"The illustrations are ink brush line with watercolor and done in vibrant colors. The love among family and friends is evident in these pictures, depicting their joy about this important event." SLJ

Aylesworth, Jim, 1943-

The full belly bowl; illustrated by Wendy Halperin. Atheneum Bks. for Young Readers 1998 unp il $16.95 *

Grades: K 1 2 3   E

1. Fairy tales

ISBN 0-689-81033-4   LC 98-14052

In return for the kindness he showed a wee small man, a very old man is given a magical bowl that causes problems when it is not used properly

"From the dainty pictures on the endpapers to the stunning artwork inside, this book is a feast for the eyes. The story . . . is just as good, smoothly blending folktale conventions with touches of magic and a dusting of comedy." Booklist

Aylesworth, Jim, 1943—*Continued*

Little Bitty Mousie; [by] Jim Aylesworth; illustrated by Michael Hague. Walker 2007 unp il $16.95; lib bdg $17.85

Grades: PreK K 1   E

1. Mice—Fiction 2. Alphabet 3. Stories in rhyme
ISBN   978-0-8027-9637-0;   0-8027-9637-0; 978-0-8027-9638-7 (lib bdg); 0-8027-9638-9 (lib bdg)
LC 2007002366

Little Bitty Mousie sneaks into a house one night and discovers many tantalizing new things, as well as one very scary thing.

"The alphabet-related words are in boldface, the bouncy rhymes are fun, and the cute periodic refrain . . . will encourage listener participation. . . . Enchanting, vividly colored pictures, created in pencil and then digitally colored, set the sweet miss mouse in the middle of realistic, detailed close-ups of familiar household objects." Booklist

Old black fly; illustrations by Stephen Gammell. Holt & Co. 1992 unp il $16.95; pa $6.95

Grades: K 1 2 3   E

1. Flies—Fiction 2. Alphabet 3. Stories in rhyme
ISBN 0-8050-1401-2; 0-8050-3924-4 (pa)
LC 91-26825

Rhyming text and illustrations follow a mischievous old black fly through the alphabet as he has a very busy bad day landing where he should not be

Aylesworth's "snappy couplets constitute a waggish presentation of a basic concept. . . . Gammell's paintings are exuberant splashes of mayhem—rainbows of splattered hues from which truly memorable characters emerge. His appropriately bug-eyed (and cross-eyed) fly and gap-toothed humans sporting crazy hairdos provide a level of dementia that children will relish." Publ Wkly

Ayres, Katherine

Up, down, and around; [by] Katherine Ayres; illustrated by Nadine Bernard Westcott. Candlewick Press 2007 unp il $16.99

Grades: PreK K 1   E

1. Gardening—Fiction 2. Stories in rhyme
ISBN 978-0-7636-2378-4; 0-7636-2378-4
LC 2006049576

"This picture book depicts a bustling kitchen garden. Two children help a man with planting, watering, and harvesting vegetables, while a dog, a cat, and a rabbit observe the fun. All around them, snails, caterpillars, birds, bugs, and worms creep, crawl, fly, climb, dig, and generally cavort about. . . . The ink-and-watercolor illustrations offer plenty of details for children to explore. . . . The short verses create a quick pace and an upbeat tempo throughout." Booklist

Baasansuren, Bolormaa

My little round house; adapted by Helen Mixter. Groundwood Books 2009 unp il $18.95

Grades: K 1 2 3   E

1. Mongolia—Fiction 2. Infants—Fiction 3. Family life—Fiction
ISBN 978-0-88899-934-4; 0-88899-934-8

"The little round house of the title is a large tent, or ger, home to the nomadic people of Mongolia. In a spare first-person narrative, baby Jilu recounts his first year and introduces readers to the rhythm of his loving family's nomadic life. . . . Attractive full-page gouache illustrations by the Mongolian writer/illustrator Baasansuren show the round house's interior as well as the characters' clothes, including elaborate details such as painted woodwork, embroidery, and the texture of fabrics." SLJ

Babin, Claire

Gus is a fish; by Claire Babin; illustrated by Olivier Tallec; [translated by Claudia Bedrick] Enchanted Lion Books 2008 unp il $14.95

Grades: K 1 2   E

1. Baths—Fiction 2. Fishes—Fiction 3. Ponds—Fiction 4. Imagination—Fiction
ISBN 978-1-59270-101-8; 1-59270-101-9
LC 2007049454

"While playing in the tub, Gus pokes his head underwater and discovers that he can breathe comfortably there. It seems that he is no longer a boy in a tub at all, but a fish in a lively pond filled with wonders. Tallec's depiction of this underwater world is breathtaking; he seamlessly integrates photographs of reeds, water lilies, frogs, and ducks with his original artwork. Each page has depth, light, color, and density." SLJ

Another title about Gus is:
Gus is a tree (2008)

Bachelet, Gilles

My cat, the silliest cat in the world; written and illustrated by Gilles Bachelet. Abrams 2006 unp il $16.95

Grades: PreK K 1 2   E

1. Cats—Fiction 2. Elephants—Fiction
ISBN 0-8109-4913-X; 978-0-8109-4913-3
LC 2005-27837

"While the text is a completely conventional list of a cat's habits, the very, very, large cat in the pictures is, in fact, an elephant. The straight-faced humor becomes all the funnier because Bachelet captures a cat's peculiar postures and behavior exactly. The paintings are filled with visual wit." Horn Book Guide

Another title about the silliest cat is:
When the silliest cat was small (2007)

Baddiel, Ivor

Cock-a-doodle quack! quack! written by Ivor Baddiel and Sophie Jubb; illustrated by Ailie Busby. David Fickling Books 2007 unp il $15.99; lib bdg $18.99

Grades: PreK K   E

1. Sounds—Fiction 2. Roosters—Fiction 3. Animals—Fiction 4. Farm life—Fiction
ISBN 0-385-75104-4; 0-385-75105-2 (lib bdg)
LC 2005-34590

Baddiel, Ivor—*Continued*

A baby rooster learns through trial and error what sounds he must crow in the morning to wake up the rest of the farm

"Busby's full-page cartoons in colorful acrylics light-heartedly reflect the buoyant text." SLJ

Bae, Hyun-Joo

New clothes for New Year's Day. Kane/Miller 2007 unp il $15.95 *

Grades: K 1 2 3   E

1. Korea—Fiction 2. Clothing and dress—Fiction 3. New Year—Fiction

ISBN 978-1-933605-29-6

A young Korean girl describes the new clothes that she will be wearing to celebrate the new year.

"Simple words and inventively composed pictures depict each step in donning the elaborate, traditional costume. . . . Bae's delicate illustrations move smoothly between depictions of mishaps as the child wrestles with troublesome accessories and grand, wordless portraits." Booklist

Baehr, Patricia Goehner

Boo Cow; illustrated by Margot Apple. Charlesbridge 2010 unp il $14.95

Grades: K 1 2   E

1. Cattle—Fiction 2. Chickens—Fiction 3. Ghost stories 4. Farm life—Fiction

ISBN 978-1-58089-108-0; 1-58089-108-X

LC 2008-25333

When Mr. and Mrs. Noodleman start a chicken farm, they are terrorized by a ghostly cow that seems to be keeping the hens from laying any eggs, but upon further investigation they discover the real culprit.

"A mix of mystery and hilarity, Baehr's . . . story is made far from frightening by Apple's . . . soft pencil illustrations, as well as an ending that will leave children assured of Boo Cow's gentle nature." Publ Wkly

Baek, Matthew J., 1971-

Panda and polar bear; by Matthew J. Baek. Dial Books for Young Readers 2009 unp il $16.95

Grades: PreK   E

1. Giant panda—Fiction 2. Polar bear—Fiction 3. Bears—Fiction 4. Friendship—Fiction

ISBN 978-0-8037-3359-6; 0-8037-3359-3

LC 2008046231

Curious to know what lies beyond his wintry world, a polar bear goes exploring, falls into a mud puddle, and is mistaken for a panda by a new playmate

"The simple, lively text folds in light humor as it delivers a positive message about appreciating differences and finding commonalities, themes that are reflected in the soft watercolor illustrations." Booklist

Baicker-McKee, Carol, 1958-

Mimi. Bloomsbury 2008 unp il $15.95; lib bdg $16.85

Grades: PreK K   E

1. Lost and found possessions—Fiction 2. Pets—Fiction 3. Lice—Fiction 4. Pigs—Fiction

ISBN 978-1-59990-065-0; 1-59990-065-3; 978-1-59990-281-4 (lib bdg); 1-59990-281-8 (lib bdg)

LC 2007-50756

Mimi the pig and her bunny spend a very busy day at the library, the park, and home, but all the while she is thinking of her pet roly-poly bug, Frank, who has been missing since breakfast.

"A satisfying plot, whimsical illustrations and a beguiling main character add up to a delightful treat that even younger preschoolers will enjoy." Kirkus

Baker, Barbara, 1947-

Digby and Kate and the beautiful day; pictures by Marsha Winborn. Dutton Children's Bks. 1998 48p il hardcover o.p. pa $3.99 *

Grades: PreK K 1 2   E

1. Dogs—Fiction 2. Cats—Fiction

ISBN 0-525-45855-7; 0-14-240035-4 (pa)

Digby the dog and Kate the cat disagree about many things but they remain best friends

"The artwork . . . together with the cheerful stories make up good, light fare for beginning readers." Horn Book Guide

Other titles about Digby and Kate are:

Digby and Kate (1988)

Digby and Kate 1 2 3 (2004)

Digby and Kate again (1989)

One Saturday evening; pictures by Kate Duke. Dutton Children's Books 2007 48p il $13.99 hardcover o.p.

Grades: K 1 2 3   E

1. Family life—Fiction 2. Bears—Fiction

ISBN 978-0-525-47103-5; 0-525-47103-0

LC 2006-24785

On a Saturday evening, the members of a bear family busy themselves with cleaning up the kitchen, taking baths, and reading.

"The chapter structure and short, basic sentences are well tuned to newly confident readers, and the reassuringly familiar scenarios, nicely extended in Duke's expressive ink-and-watercolor pictures, will draw children into the cozy nighttime mayhem." Booklist

Another title about the bear family is:

One Saturday morning (1994)

Baker, Jeannie

Home. Greenwillow Books 2004 unp il $15.99

Grades: PreK K 1 2   E

1. Stories without words 2. City and town life

ISBN 0-06-623935-4   LC 2003-49287

A wordless picture book that observes the changes in a neighborhood from before a girl is born until she is an adult, as it first decays and then is renewed by the efforts of the residents

"Baker uses natural materials to create detailed, arresting collages that tell a story in which words are superfluous. Children can pore over these pages again and again and make fresh discoveries with each perusal." SLJ

Baker, Jeannie—*Continued*

Where the forest meets the sea; story and pictures by Jeannie Baker. Greenwillow Bks. 1988 c1987 unp il $16

Grades: PreK K 1 2   E

1. Australia—Fiction 2. Rain forests—Fiction

ISBN 0-688-06363-2   LC 87-7551

First published 1987 in the United Kingdom

On a camping trip in an Australian rain forest with his father, a young boy thinks about the history of the plant and animal life around him and wonders about their future

The illustrations "are relief collages 'constructed from a multitude of materials, including modeling clay, papers, textured materials, preserved natural materials, and paints.' Integrated by the artist's vision, the collages create three-dimensional effects on two-dimensional pages drawing the reader into each scene as willing observer and explorer." Horn Book

Window. Greenwillow Bks. 1991 unp il lib bdg $17.89

Grades: PreK K 1 2   E

1. Stories without words 2. Human ecology—Fiction 3. Australia—Fiction

ISBN 0-688-08918-6   LC 90-3922

"The story in this wordless book is told through the outdoor scene viewed over time from one child's bedroom window. Initially, a mother holding her infant son gazes out at the lush Australian bush; as the boy gets older, civilization swallows up the wilderness." Horn Book Guide

"Filled with marvelous detail, the textured collages make an affecting statement about the erosion of the planet Earth." SLJ

Baker, Keith, 1953-

Hickory dickory dock; [by] Keith Baker. Harcourt 2007 unp il $16

Grades: PreK K 1 2   E

1. Clocks and watches—Fiction 2. Animals—Fiction 3. Stories in rhyme

ISBN 978-0-15-205818-0; 0-15-205818-4

LC 2006003257

"The nursery rhyme 'Hickory Dickory Dock' gets new life as it goes through 12 hours of the day. . . . As each hour chimes, another creature appears, often completing an action initiated in the previous spread. . . . With a bouncy, easy-to-enjoy text and child-appealing collage-style pictures, this is a book that will work well one-on-one or with groups." Booklist

Just how long can a long string be!? Arthur A. Levine Books 2009 unp il $16.99 paperback o.p.

Grades: PreK K 1 2   E

1. Ants—Fiction 2. Birds—Fiction 3. Stories in rhyme

ISBN 978-0-545-08661-5; 0-545-08661-2; 978-0-545-08662-2 (pa); 0-545-08662-0 (pa)

LC 2008027344

Be it tied to a balloon, or kite, or hanging a picture, or stringing a banjo or a mop, a bird explains to an ant how long a string needs to be

"By using pale overlapping images, Baker creates a sense of movement in many of the illustrations. A palette of pastels captures the beauty of spring. . . . [This is a] lovely book . . . for a fine spring storytime." SLJ

LMNO peas. Beach Lane Books 2010 unp il $16.99 *

Grades: PreK K 1 2   E

1. Stories in rhyme 2. Occupations—Fiction 3. Alphabet

ISBN 978-1-4169-9141-0; 1-4169-9141-7

LC 2009012672

Busy little peas introduce their favorite occupations, from astronaut to zoologist.

"With its digital illustrations' luminous colors, buoyant spirit, and engaging characters, this handsome picture book is definitely worth a second look, even in the overcrowded field of alphabet books." Booklist

Meet Mr. and Mrs. Green. Harcourt 2004 71p il hardcover o.p. pa $5.95 *

Grades: K 1 2   E

1. Alligators—Fiction

ISBN 0-15-204954-1; 0-15-204955-X (pa)

LC 2001-1955

First published 2002

A loving alligator couple enjoy going camping, eating pancakes, and visiting the county fair

"The acrylic illustrations have a loud, oversized presence that is complemented by the strong text." SLJ

Other titles about Mr. and Mrs. Green are:

Lucky days with Mr. and Mrs. Green (2005)

More Mr. and Mrs. Green (2004)

On the go with Mr. and Mrs. Green (2006)

Potato Joe; [by] Keith Baker. Harcourt 2008 unp il $16

Grades: PreK K 1   E

1. Nursery rhymes 2. Counting—Fiction

ISBN 978-0-15-206230-9; 0-15-206230-0

LC 2007005930

Potato Joe leads the other spuds from the familiar nursery rhyme, "One Potato, Two Potato," in various activities, from a game of tic-tac-toe to a rodeo.

"The fuzzy-edged, childlike illustrations were done in Adobe Photoshop and complement the bouncy tone of the text. This will be fun to share, and even young children will soon have the rhyme committed to memory." SLJ

Quack and count. Harcourt Brace & Co. 1999 unp il $15; pa $6

Grades: PreK K 1   E

1. Addition 2. Ducks 3. Counting

ISBN 0-15-292858-8; 0-15-205025-6 (pa)

LC 98-7924

"Seven uniquely marked ducklings slide, chase bees, and play peekaboo as they group on double-spread pages to illustrate ways to add up to their sum. . . . Jaunty scenes in cut-paper collage with a gracious array of colors offer plenty of extras." SLJ

Balian, Lorna

Humbug witch; [by] Lorna Balian. Star Bright Books 2003 c1965 unp il $12.95

Grades: PreK K 1 2   E

1. Witches—Fiction

ISBN 1-932065-32-6   LC 2003-16979

A reissue of the title first published 1965 by Abingdon Press

Despite looking the part, a little witch cannot seem to do the things that witches are supposed to do.

This is a "warm-hearted, conversational story. . . . [Illustrated with] friendly ink drawings in black, red, and yellow." Horn Book Guide

Bang, Molly, 1943-

All of me! a book of thanks. Blue Sky Press 2009 unp il $16.99

Grades: PreK K   E

1. Human body—Fiction

ISBN 978-0-545-04424-0; 0-545-04424-3

LC 2008-49692

A celebration of how the body's parts work together, from hands and eyes to lips and heart, allowing one to exist in the wondrous universe. Includes instructions for making a book.

"Bang's artwork incorporates cut paper and fabric, photographed elements, red crayon, and paints. . . . Unusual, uneven, creative, and challenging." Booklist

The paper crane. Greenwillow Bks. 1985 unp il $16.99; pa $6.99 *

Grades: K 1 2 3   E

ISBN 0-688-04108-6; 0-688-07333-6 (pa)

LC 84-13546

"Bang gives a modern setting and details to the consoling story of a good man, deprived by unlucky fate of his livelihood, whose act of kindness and generosity is repaid by the restoration of his fortunes, through the bringing to life of a magical animal—the paper crane." SLJ

"Every detail of the restaurant interior, from the strawberries on the cake to the floral centerpieces, is a delight to the eye and imagination. . . . The book successfully blends Asian folklore themes with contemporary Western characterization." Horn Book

Ten, nine, eight. Greenwillow Bks. 1983 unp il $16.99; lib bdg $17.89; pa $6.99; bd bk $6.99 *

Grades: PreK K 1   E

1. Bedtime—Fiction 2. Counting

ISBN 0-688-00906-9; 0-688-00907-7 (lib bdg); 0-688-10480-0 (pa); 0-688-14901-4 (bd bk)

LC 81-20106

A Caldecott Medal honor book, 1984

"In countdown style, the text of this counting book begins with '10 small toes all washed and warm,' and ends with '1 big girl all ready for bed.' The captions rhyme . . . and the pictures—warm, bright paintings—show a black father and child snuggling in a chair, the child yawning, and the child hugging her toy bear after some loving good night kisses." Bull Cent Child Books

When Sophie gets angry—really, really angry. Blue Sky Press (NY) 1999 unp il $16.99; pa $6.99 *

Grades: PreK K 1   E

1. Anger—Fiction

ISBN 0-590-18979-4; 0-439-59845-1 (pa)

LC 97-42209

A Caldecott Medal honor book, 2000

"Sophie loses a tug-of-war altercation with her sister over a stuffed monkey, and her anger propels her out of the house and into an anger-reducing run. After running, crying, climbing a tree, and being soothed by the breeze, Sophie feels better and goes home, where everyone is happy to see her." Bull Cent Child Books

"The text is appropriately brief, for it is Bang's double-page illustrations, vibrating with saturated colors, that reveal the drama of the child's emotions." SLJ

Banks, Kate, 1960-

And if the moon could talk; pictures by Georg Hallensleben. Foster Bks. 1998 unp il $15 *

Grades: PreK K 1 2   E

1. Bedtime—Fiction 2. Night—Fiction 3. Moon—Fiction

ISBN 0-374-30299-5   LC 97-29770

"Originally published in France"—page facing t.p

As evening progresses into nighttime, the moon looks down on a variety of nocturnal scenes, including a child getting ready for bed

"The deeply saturated tones of the lovely, impressionistic oil paintings perfectly match the somnolent feeling of the text." SLJ

Baboon; pictures by Georg Hallensleben. Farrar, Straus & Giroux 1997 unp il $14

Grades: PreK K 1 2   E

1. Baboons—Fiction

ISBN 0-374-30474-2   LC 96-20888

"Frances Foster books"

Original French edition, 1994

"A baby baboon sees a forest and concludes that the world is green, but then his mother takes him farther afield. . . . Everything he encounters expands his understanding, and when night falls, he has seen with his own eyes that the world is a big and varied place." Publisher's note

"Visible brush-strokes give texture to the impressionistic paintings, and adept lighting evokes sunlight and shadow. The simple, eloquent text is as subtly understated." Horn Book Guide

The cat who walked across France; pictures by Georg Hallensleben. Farrar, Straus and Giroux 2004 unp il $16

Grades: PreK K 1 2   E

1. Cats—Fiction 2. France—Fiction

ISBN 0-374-39968-9   LC 2002-25091

"Frances Foster Books"

After his owner dies, a cat wanders across the countryside of France, unable to forget the home he had in the stone house by the edge of the sea

"Banks uses simple, lovely words to tell the elemental story of an outcast's journey home. . . . The paintings are exquisite . . . but what kids will like best is the cat's adventure and the loving welcome he receives." Booklist

Banks, Kate, 1960-—*Continued*

Close your eyes; pictures by Georg Hallensleben. Foster Bks. 2002 unp il $16 *

Grades: PreK K 1   E

1. Tigers—Fiction 2. Dreams—Fiction 3. Sleep—Fiction

ISBN 0-374-31382-2   LC 99-46430

A mother tiger entices her child to sleep by telling of all that can been seen with one's eyes closed

"Banks' language will delight young children with its delicious rhythms, patterned sounds, and the mystery in the poetic imagery. . . . Hallensleben's thick, expressive brush strokes occasionally blur shapes and details, but the vividly colored dreamscapes . . . will capture young imaginations and reassure children who . . . harbor secret fears of falling asleep." Booklist

The eraserheads; pictures by Boris Kulikov. Farrar, Straus and Giroux 2010 unp il $16.99

Grades: PreK K 1 2   E

1. Drawing—Fiction 2. Adventure fiction

ISBN 978-0-374-39920-7; 0-374-39920-4

LC 2008024144

"Frances Foster books"

Three eraserheads that live with a boy in the land of pencils, paper, rulers, numbers, letters, and drawings become trapped in one of his pictures while trying to correct mistakes

"Kulikov combines loving attention to detail . . . with beguiling portraits of the erasers in various attitudes of dismay and distress. In the story's dueling realities, the 'real life' sections of the spreads feature three-dimensional figures, while the boy's drawings are done in gawky crayon." Publ Wkly

Fox; pictures by Georg Hallensleben. Farrar, Straus and Giroux 2007 unp il $16

Grades: PreK K 1 2   E

1. Foxes—Fiction

ISBN 0-374-39967-0; 978-0-374-39967-2

LC 2005-47701

"Frances Foster books"

A baby fox anticipates the time when he can go out alone, but first his parents must teach him the ways of the wilderness.

"Hallensleben handles outdoor scenes with finesse, and his signature scuffled layers of brushwork mesh with Banks's evocative prose." Publ Wkly

A gift from the sea; pictures by Georg Hallensleben. Foster Bks. 2001 unp il $16

Grades: K 1 2 3   E

1. Rocks—Fiction

ISBN 0-374-32566-9   LC 00-26503

Unaware of its eons-old history, a boy finds a rock and takes it home to a shelf beside his sea glass and starfish

"Banks uses graceful and rhythmic language that hums with the sense and sound of the words." Booklist

Max's words; by Kate Banks; pictures by Boris Kulikov. Farrar, Straus and Giroux 2006 unp il $16 *

Grades: PreK K 1 2   E

1. English language—Fiction 2. Collectors and collecting—Fiction 3. Storytelling—Fiction

ISBN 978-0-374-39949-8; 0-374-39949-2

"Frances Foster Books"

When Max cuts out words from magazines and newspapers, collecting them the way his brothers collect stamps and coins, they all learn about words, sentences, and storytelling

"Imaginative, softly colored illustrations reveal the gathered words scattered all over the pages. . . . This tale pays homage to the written word and may get children thinking about cutting and pasting their own stories or creating concrete poetry." SLJ

Another title about Max is:

Max's dragon (2008)

Monkeys and the universe; pictures by Tomek Bogacki. Farrar, Straus & Giroux 2009 48p il (Monkey reader) $14.95

Grades: K 1 2   E

1. Astronomy—Fiction 2. Brothers—Fiction 3. Monkeys—Fiction

ISBN 978-0-374-35028-4; 0-374-35028-0

LC 2006048401

"Frances Foster Books"

Max and his older brother Pete learn about stars, planets, and galaxies when their father takes them to an astronomical observatory.

"Bogacki's illustrations, with soft colors and blurry lines, convey gentle feelings even amidst brotherly discord. Banks does a fine job combining facts with story." Horn Book Guide

Another title about Max and Pete is:

Monkeys and dog days (2008)

The night worker; pictures by Georg Hallensleben. Farrar, Straus & Giroux 2000 unp il $16 *

Grades: PreK K 1 2   E

1. Night—Fiction 2. Work—Fiction 3. Building—Fiction

ISBN 0-374-35520-7   LC 99-27595

"Frances Foster books"

Alex wants to be a "night worker" like his father who goes to work at a construction site after Alex goes to bed

"Banks' elegant, simple words and poetic images and rhythms evoke the book's exciting activity and the secure comfort Alex feels with his father. With thick brush strokes and deep, satisfying primary and earth colors, Hallensleben's paintings extend the story's balance of exhilarating intensity and reassuring calm." Booklist

That's Papa's way; pictures by Lauren Castillo. Farrar, Straus and Giroux 2009 unp il $16.95

Grades: PreK K 1   E

1. Father-daughter relationship—Fiction 2. Fishing—Fiction

ISBN 978-0-374-37445-7; 0-374-37445-7

LC 2007045475

"Frances Foster books"

Banks, Kate, 1960-—*Continued*

When a father and daughter go fishing together, each does certain things his own way, and both have a wonderful day.

"The illustrations in pastel and ink are perfect for conveying the sense of calm that the story requires. The full-bleed spreads show the expanse of the water and the pines, and the depiction of the wildlife is just detailed enough to be naturalistic." SLJ

What's coming for Christmas? pictures by Georg Hallensleben. Farrar, Straus and Giroux 2009 unp il $15.99

Grades: PreK K 1   E

1. Domestic animals—Fiction 2. Christmas—Fiction

ISBN 978-0-374-39948-1; 0-374-39948-4

LC 2008-20753

"Frances Foster books"

While a farm family bustles about, preparing for the arrival of Christmas, they do not notice the great anticipation spreading among the animals, who know that something very special is on its way.

"The muted colors and quality of Hallensleben's illustrations create a dreamlike feeling, matched by the quiet, lyrical text, with its simple, repeated refrains that create a mounting sense of mysterious expectation." Kirkus

Bannerman, Helen, 1862 or 3-1946

The story of Little Babaji; illustrated by Fred Marcellino. HarperCollins Pubs. 1996 unp il $16.99; pa $7.95 *

Grades: PreK K 1 2   E

1. India—Fiction 2. Tigers—Fiction

ISBN 0-06-205064-8; 0-06-008093-0 (pa)

"Michael di Capua books"

In this edition of the Story of Little Black Sambo, originally published 1899, the characters have been given Indian names

Babaji gives his new clothing to tigers who threaten to eat him, but they chase one another around a tree until they turn to butter

"Marcellino has set the story of Little Black Sambo in India. . . . Except for a change of names . . . Bannerman's text is essentially unaltered, retaining the narrative rhythm that has always paced a tightly patterned plot. Marcellino's watercolor paintings project a toy-like quality that emphasizes humor over suspense." Bull Cent Child Books

Bansch, Helga, 1957-

I want a dog! North-South 2009 unp il $16.95

Grades: K 1 2   E

1. Dogs—Fiction

ISBN 978-0-7358-2255-9; 0-7358-2255-7

"A dog is all young Lisa yearns for, but whether wheedles or tantrums, the parental answer is the same: 'Our apartment is still too small for a dog.' Finally, the clever girl puts up signs in the park asking for a dog to borrow, whereupon Mr. Lewis shows up at her door with sausagy hound Rollo. . . . Bausch writes with a dry humor even as the text effectively conveys Lisa's longing, and the solution is both a reasonable and creative one." Bull Cent Child Books

Bányai, István, 1949-

The other side. Chronicle Books 2005 unp il $15.95

Grades: K 1 2 3   E

1. Stories without words

ISBN 0-8118-4608-3   LC 2004-63448

"Banyai explores the concept of 'the other side' through visual vignettes offering contrasting perspectives on dreamlike scenarios, often revealing previously hidden information that significantly alters how a scene is perceived." Booklist

"This is a challenging book, one that allows for creative speculation. The graphite-rendered artwork is quirky as well as infinitely interesting." SLJ

Zoom. Viking 1995 unp il $16.99; pa $6.99

Grades: K 1 2 3   E

1. Stories without words

ISBN 0-670-85804-8; 0-14-055774-1 (pa)

LC 94-33181

Also available Re-zoom (1995)

A wordless picture book presents a series of scenes, each one from farther away, showing, for example, a girl playing with toys which is actually a picture on a magazine cover, which is part of a sign on a bus, and so on

"If the concept is not wholly new, the execution is superior. Readers are in for a perpetually surprising—and even philosophical—adventure." Publ Wkly

Barasch, Lynne, 1939-

First come the zebra. Lee & Low Books 2009 unp il $18.95   E

1. Masai (African people)—Fiction 2. Kikuyu (African people)—Fiction 3. Kenya—Fiction

ISBN 978-1-60060-365-5; 1-60060-365-3

LC 2008053717

When two young Kenyan boys, one Maasai and one Kikuyu, first meet, they are hostile toward each other based on traditional rivalries, but after they suddenly have to work together to save a baby in danger, the boys begin to discover what they have in common

"Heartfelt storytelling and strong research combine to offer a universal message with a unique setting. The clear, light-filled illustrations are expressive and create a sense of place. A lovely, hopeful story that manages to convey its message with minimal didacticism." SLJ

Includes bibliographical references

Barclay, Jane, 1957-

Proud as a peacock, brave as a lion; illustrated by Renné Benoit. Tundra Books 2009 unp il $18.95

Grades: PreK K 1 2   E

1. Veterans—Fiction 2. Grandfathers—Fiction 3. World War, 1939-1945—Fiction 4. Memory—Fiction

ISBN 978-0-88776-951-1; 0-88776-951-9

"A small boy has fun with his grandfather as they page through an old photo album, and Poppa tells how, at age 17, he lied about his age so that he could join the army. Small photos in sepia shades evoke the past. . . . Opposite the wartime photos, large, bright, unframed pictures in watercolor and gouache show the boy and Poppa

Barclay, Jane, 1957-—*Continued*

in the present, talking about the soldier's feelings—proud as a peacock, pretending to be brave as a lion—and the lively animal images in the words are also part of the pictures. . . . The blend of grim reality, heroic battle, and playful fantasy will speak to kids." Booklist

Bardhan-Quallen, Sudipta

The hog prince; illustrated by Jason Wolff. Dutton Children's Books 2009 unp il $16.99

Grades: K 1 2   E

1. Fairy tales 2. Pigs—Fiction

ISBN 978-0-525-47900-0; 0-525-47900-7

LC 2008-13888

On the advice of a mixed-up fairy, Eldon the hog tries to achieve his princely ambitions by kissing the perfect mate.

"The large acrylic illustrations are perfect for the story. The animal faces are expressive and the backgrounds are lush. This is a great read-aloud that cheerfully fractures many fairy tales all at once." SLJ

Barner, Bob

Bears! bears! bears! Chronicle Books 2010 unp il $14.99

Grades: PreK K 1   E

1. Bears—Fiction

ISBN 978-0-8118-7057-3; 0-8118-7057-X

"Collages rendered in vibrant hues lead youngsters through a fanciful expedition. The colorful spreads and rhyming text will entertain children as they discover the variety of bears found around the world. . . . Two concluding spreads contain facts about bears and ursine habitats. . . . Beginning readers might like to attempt this one on their own." SLJ

Bug safari. Holiday House 2004 unp il $16.95
*

Grades: PreK K 1 2   E

1. Insects—Fiction 2. Ants—Fiction

ISBN 0-8234-1707-7   LC 2003-56619

"A young explorer describes his experiences as he tracks an army of ants through 'a bug-infested jungle,' observing their progress through a magnifying glass." SLJ

"The bright, cut-paper collages will appeal to the youngest bug lovers, but the funny, dramatically told story is tailored to a more sophisticated young entomologist." Booklist

Fish wish. Holiday House 2000 unp il $16.95; pa $6.95

Grades: PreK K 1 2   E

1. Coral reefs and islands—Fiction

ISBN 0-8234-1482-5; 0-8234-1663-1 (pa)

LC 99-44491

A young boy's dream sends him on an underwater journey through a coral reef. Includes factual information on coral reefs and the animals that live in them

"The impressive collage illustrations combine pieces of torn, cut, and sometimes painted papers with found objects and bits of fabric. Bold forms and striking color combinations give the double-page spreads a vibrant sense of place and motion." Booklist

Barnett, Mac

Guess again! illustrated by Adam Rex. Simon & Schuster Books for Young Readers 2009 unp il $16.99

Grades: 1 2 3 4   E

1. Stories in rhyme

ISBN 978-1-4169-5566-5; 1-4169-5566-6

LC 2008-12882

"A rhymed text joins with hinting illustrations to encourage readers to fill in the last word of the verse. A page turn, however, unveils an answer that's an absurd breach of expectation. . . . The confounding of expectations is pleasingly goofy. . . . Rex partners the rhyme with robust and solid gouache scenes that are comedic in their own right. . . . This would be particularly useful as a quick pick for reluctant readers, who'll warm to the combination of corniness and sophistication in the satirically unguessable guessing game." Bull Cent Child Books

Oh no!, or, How my science project destroyed the world; written by Mac Barnett; illustrated by Dan Santat. Disney Hyperion Books 2010 unp il $16.99

Grades: K 1 2   E

1. Robots—Fiction 2. Science projects—Fiction

ISBN 978-1-4231-2312-5; 1-4231-2312-3

LC 2010004516

After winning the science fair with the giant robot she has built, a little girl realizes that there is a major problem.

"Santat's brilliantly hued digital illustrations are the perfect foil for Barnett's almost-wordless tale of a science project gone awry. . . . Comic-book, picture-book and movie styles come together in a well-designed package that includes a movie poster on the reverse side of the jacket, an old-time computation book as the inside cover and detailed scientific drawings on the endpapers. . . . A must-have." Kirkus

Barracca, Debra

The adventures of Taxi Dog; by Debra and Sal Barracca; pictures by Mark Buehner. Dial Bks. for Young Readers 1990 30p il $16.99; pa $5.99 *

Grades: PreK K 1 2   E

1. Dogs—Fiction 2. Taxicabs—Fiction 3. Stories in rhyme

ISBN 0-8037-0671-5; 0-14-056665-1 (pa)

LC 89-1056

"In snappy, rhymed lines, Maxi recalls his days as a stray and his adoption by taxi-driving Jim. Applying oil paint over acrylics, Buehner creates color with lush character. The hues' intense depth, coupled with the artist's finesse with perspective, will draw readers into the action." Booklist

Other titles about Maxi, the Taxi Dog are:

Maxi, the hero (1991)

Maxi, the star (1993)

A Taxi Dog Christmas (1994)

Barrett, Judi, 1941-

Cloudy with a chance of meatballs; written by Judi Barrett and drawn by Ron Barrett. Aladdin Paperbacks 1982 c1978 unp il pa $6.99

Grades: PreK K 1 2   E
   1. Food—Fiction 2. Weather—Fiction
   ISBN 0-689-70749-5   LC 87-29643
   First published 1978

Life is delicious in the town of Chewandswallow where it rains soup and juice, snows mashed potatoes, and blows storms of hamburgers—until the weather takes a turn for the worse.

Never take a shark to the dentist and other things not to do; [by] Judi Barrett; illustrated by John Nickle. Atheneum Books for Young Readers 2007 unp il $16.99 *

Grades: PreK K 1 2   E
   1. Animals—Fiction
   ISBN 978-1-4169-0724-4; 1-4169-0724-6
                  LC 2006000153

A list of things one should not do with various animals, such as "hold hands with a lobster"

"Nickle, working in hyper-detailed acrylics, enhances the comical phrases with surreal imagery. . . . Kids will revel in the absurd humor." Publ Wkly

Barry, Frances

Duckie's ducklings; a one-to-ten counting book. Candlewick 2005 unp il $7.99

Grades: PreK K   E
   1. Counting 2. Ducks—Fiction
   ISBN 0-7636-2514-0

Duckie is ready to take the family for a swim. But where are her ducklings? Turn the shaped pages to find out!

"Barry's uncluttered paper collages are excellent. The elemental shapes and vivid, saturated colors nicely fit the book's handsome design." Booklist

Bartlett, T. C.

Tuba lessons; illustrated by Monique Felix. Creative Editions 2009 unp il $25.65

Grades: PreK K 1   E
   1. Animals—Fiction 2. Musical instruments—Fiction
   3. Stories without words
   ISBN 978-1-56846-209-7; 1-56846-209-3
                 LC 2009-3834
   First published 1997 by Harcourt, Brace and Company

While walking through the woods on his way to his tuba lesson, a boy becomes sidetracked by all the animals that want to hear him play.

"This text is not only for storytimes, but can be used as a catalyst to get young readers and writers to create their own words to enhance the imaginative, playful illustrations. Friendship, music and the journey are the themes in this picture tale." Libr Media Connect

Barton, Byron

Bones, bones, dinosaur bones. Crowell 1990 unp il $16.99 *

Grades: PreK K   E
   1. Dinosaurs—Fiction 2. Fossils—Fiction
   ISBN 0-690-04825-4   LC 89-71306

"From the field search for dinosaur bones to reconstructed skeletons for museum display, paleontology as process is revealed in simple text, bold print, and flat illustrations with heavy, black outlines. Includes labeled illustrations of eight dinosaurs." Sci Child

Dinosaurs, dinosaurs. Crowell 1989 unp il $16.99; lib bdg $17.89; pa $6.99; bd bk $7.99 *

Grades: PreK K   E
   1. Dinosaurs—Fiction
   ISBN 0-694-00269-0; 0-690-04768-1 (lib bdg);
   0-06-443298-X (pa); 0-694-400625-4 (bd bk)
                 LC 88-22938

This book examines the many different kinds of dinosaurs, big and small, those with spikes and those with long, sharp teeth

"Barton conveys the primordial sense of excitement that draws children to these beasts. . . . The endpapers identify the creatures by scientific name and pronunciation. Barton wisely keeps his text simple, describing dinosaurs only by size and physical features." SLJ

My car. Greenwillow Bks. 2001 unp il $14.95; pa $6.99; bd bk $7.99 *

Grades: PreK K   E
   1. Automobiles—Fiction
   ISBN 0-06-029624-0; 0-06-029625-9 (lib bdg);
   0-06-058940-X (pa); 0-06-056045-2 (bd bk)
                 LC 00-50334

Sam describes in loving detail his car and how he drives it

"The chunky blocks of color and minimalist text will withstand countless readings." Publ Wkly

Barton, Chris

Shark vs. train; by Chris Barton & [illustrated by] Tom Lichtenheld. Little, Brown 2010 unp il $16.99 *

Grades: PreK K 1   E
   1. Sharks—Fiction 2. Railroads—Fiction
   ISBN 978-0-316-00762-7; 0-316-00762-5
                 LC 2009-17961

A shark and a train compete in a series of contests on a seesaw, in hot air balloons, bowling, shooting baskets, playing hide-and-seek, and more.

"This is a genius concept. . . . Lichtenheld's . . . watercolor cartoons have a fluidity and goofy intensity that recalls *Mad* magazine, while Barton . . . gives the characters snappy dialogue throughout." Publ Wkly

Bartone, Elisa

Peppe the lamplighter; illustrations by Ted Lewin. Lothrop, Lee & Shepard Bks. 1993 unp il $17.99; pa $6.99 *

Grades: K 1 2 3   E
   1. Italian Americans—Fiction 2. New York (N.Y.)—Fiction
   ISBN 0-688-10268-9; 0-688-15469-7 (pa)
                 LC 92-1397

A Caldecott Medal honor book, 1994

Peppe's father is upset when he learns that Peppe has taken a job lighting the gas street lamps in his New York City neighborhood

Bartone, Elisa—*Continued*

"Peppe's quiet quest for familial respect and pleasure in his work is touching and rhythmically written. The early-American city scenes are dark but have a nice period luminescence in the myriad street and table lamps, and the earth-toned watercolors lend the bustling streets and interiors of Little Italy an air both somber and lively." Bull Cent Child Books

Bartram, Simon

Bob's best ever friend. Templar Books 2009 unp il $16.99

Grades: K 1 2   E

1. Astronauts—Fiction 2. Moon—Fiction 3. Dogs—Fiction 4. Friendship—Fiction

ISBN 978-0-7636-4425-3; 0-7636-4425-0

"Bob, an astronaut who travels daily from Earth to the Moon to entertain tourists, is lonely: there are no visitors this Tuesday and his friends have gone off to Pluto. The next day, he begins to look for a 'best-ever friend' and decides that it could be a pet. One day he sees something amazing pop out of a crater: a dog. Bartram's detailed acrylics give readers comic relief while Bob is on his quest. . . . The artwork is reminiscent of books from the 1950s and is done in electric blues, yellows, and reds." SLJ

Another title about Bob is:
Man on the moon (2002)

Baruzzi, Agnese

The true story of Little Red Riding Hood; [by] Agnese Baruzzi and Sandro Natalini. Templar Books 2009 unp il $14.99

Grades: K 1 2 3   E

1. Fairy tales 2. Pop-up books

ISBN 978-0-7636-4427-7

"In this fractured fairy tale, the wolf asks for help rehabilitating his reputation. Little Red Riding Hood's advice (become a vegetarian) works—for a while. The book overflows with lift-the-flaps; envelopes with tiny letters inside and a fabric shower curtain and apron are also included. The boldly colored naive-style paintings are enhanced by collage elements, including rickrack borders." Horn Book Guide

Base, Graeme, 1958-

Uno's garden. Abrams Books for Young Readers 2006 unp il $19.95

Grades: 2 3 4   E

1. Nature—Fiction 2. Pollution—Fiction 3. Counting

ISBN 978-0-8109-5473-1; 0-8109-5473-7

LC 2006-13208

Uno builds a home and garden in the magnificent forest among the playful puddlebuts and feathered frinklepods, but as the place becomes more and more popular, it is overtaken by tourists and buildings until the forest and animals seem to disappear altogether.

"Providing plenty of opportunity for seek-and-find fun, the vibrant art also visually reinforces the progressive change. . . .This is both a visual treasure trove and a cautionary yet hopeful tale of environmental awareness and responsibility." Booklist

Bass, L. G.

Boom boom go away! by Laura Geringer; illustrated by Bagram Ibatoulline. Atheneum 2010 unp il $15.99

Grades: PreK K 1   E

1. Bedtime—Fiction 2. Music—Fiction 3. Toys—Fiction

ISBN 978-0-689-85093-6; 0-689-85093-X

"Each time a parent tells a boy to go to bed, the toys in his room delay the process by playing their instruments and saying they can't be disturbed. . . . The rhythmical text has an appealing cadence and a catchy refrain. Ibatoulline's watercolor and acrylic-gouache spreads of the child's room are wonderfully designed." SLJ

Bataille, Marion, 1963-

ABC3D. Roaring Brook Press 2008 unp il $19.95 *

Grades: 1 2 3 4 5   E

1. Alphabet 2. Pop-up books

ISBN 978-1-59643-425-7; 1-59643-425-2

LC 2008-08933

"From the lenticular cover to the jazzy use of a red, white and black color scheme, this hand-size French alphabet book is as stylish as a pop-up can be. Letters here not only pop up, they move and transform. . . . Many letters are three-dimensional (i.e., the legs of H are hollow paper rectangles), and gain extra glamour from high-contrast backgrounds (white on black; red or black on white). A-plus for drama and innovation." Publ Wkly

Bateman, Teresa

April foolishness; illustrated by Nadine Bernard Westcott. Albert Whitman & Co. 2004 unp il $15.95

Grades: PreK K 1 2   E

1. April Fools' Day—Fiction 2. Farm life—Fiction 3. Stories in rhyme

ISBN 0-8075-0404-1   LC 2004-825

"Grandpa thinks he's wise to his grandchildren's April Fools' Day tricks and ignores their warnings of animals run amok." SLJ

"Bateman's verse prances along in a pleasing way, never sounding a false note or tripping over its metric feet. Bright with colorful washes, Westcott's ink drawings illustrate the action with equal lightness and grace. . . . Zany and inventive, the artwork amplifies the story's humor." Booklist

The Bully Blockers Club; illustrated by Jackie Urbanovic. Albert Whitman & Co. 2004 unp il hardcover o.p. pa $6.95

Grades: PreK K 1 2   E

1. School stories 2. Bullies—Fiction

ISBN 0-8075-0918-3; 0-8075-0919-1 (pa)

LC 2004-524

When Lottie is bothered by a bully at school, she helps start a club where everyone is welcome

"Although this story is purposeful, it is told with humor and drama. The illustrations are colorful and engaging." SLJ

Bateman, Teresa—*Continued*

Harp o' gold; illustrated by Jill Weber. Holiday House 2001 unp il $16.95

Grades: K 1 2 3   E
1. Fairy tales 2. Harp—Fiction 3. Musicians—Fiction
ISBN 0-8234-1523-6   LC 99-18821

A poor musician who dreams of riches and fame trades his beloved but worn harp for one made of gold, but when he becomes famous he finds that something is missing

"Acrylic paintings rendered in a blue-green palette with flat tilty perspectives complement this bittersweet cautionary tale set in an Irish-looking countryside." Horn Book Guide

Keeper of soles; illustrated by Yayo. Holiday House 2006 unp il $16.95 *

Grades: K 1 2 3   E
1. Shoemakers—Fiction 2. Shoes—Fiction 3. Death—Fiction
ISBN 0-8234-1734-4   LC 2004-52297

When Death comes for a shoemaker's soul, he outwits him by making shoes for him, giving him soles instead of souls.

"Bateman pairs the cadences of a traditional folktale with contemporary humor. The scenes are imbued with suspense without being macabre. Yayo's full-bleed acrylics provide large expanses of rich, layered colors as foils for the smaller, whimsical details." SLJ

Bates, Katharine Lee, 1859-1929

America the beautiful; illustrated by Chris Gall. Little, Brown 2004 unp il $16.95 *

Grades: K 1 2 3   E
1. United States—Poetry 2. Songs—United States
ISBN 0-316-73743-7   LC 2003-54552
"Megan Tingley books"

Four verses of the nineteenth-century poem later set to music, illustrated by the author's great-great-grandnephew

"Children will be stirred by Gall's pictures. Using hand engraving on clay-covered board and enhancing elements such as color with a computer, he offers a series of pictures resembling woodcuts in form and WPA paintings in style." Booklist

Battut, Eric

The fox and the hen. Boxer 2010 unp il $16.95 *

Grades: PreK K   E
1. Foxes—Fiction 2. Eggs—Fiction 3. Domestic animals—Fiction
ISBN 978-1-907152-02-3; 1-907152-02-4

"Henrietta Hen lays her first egg and innocently trades it to Red Fox for a worm. The other farm animals quickly tell her that she must get her precious egg back and go with her to make the trade. . . . Each time Red Fox refuses and thinks of a new way to eat the egg. . . . Henrietta finds an enormous stone that her friends paint white, and Red Fox eagerly trades her egg for this bigger one. . . . The animals are outlined in thick, black line and dabs of white highlight the vibrant red and orange palette. . . . With great economy, Battut gives each animal an expressive face and moves the story to a satisfying conclusion." SLJ

Bauer, Marion Dane, 1938-

The longest night; illustrated by Ted Lewin. Holiday House 2009 unp il $17.95

Grades: K 1 2 3   E
1. Night—Fiction 2. Winter—Fiction 3. Animals—Fiction
ISBN 978-0-8234-2054-4; 0-8234-2054-X
     LC 2008022575

One very long night, a crow, a moose, and a fox all claim they can bring back the sun, but the wind knows that only one little creature has what is needed to end the darkness.

"This stunningly crafted tale, written in the language of the storyteller, realistically pictures, in both words and paintings, the phenomenon that is the winter solstice. . . . There is plenty of moonlight in Lewin's watercolor paintings created with just blue, brown, and green." SLJ

One brown bunny; text by Marion Dane Bauer; illustrated by Ivan Bates. Orchard Books 2009 32p il $14.99

Grades: PreK K   E
1. Rabbits—Fiction 2. Animals—Fiction 3. Play—Fiction 4. Friendship—Fiction 5. Stories in rhyme
ISBN 978-0-439-68010-3; 0-439-68010-7
     LC 2006102289

"A bright-eyed little bunny looks for playmates to share a sunny day in this engaging, energetic counting rhyme. Coupled with Bates's bright, dynamic illustrations that place a curious, slightly rumpled protagonist in an inviting forest landscape, the text bounces along cheerfully." Kirkus

Thank you for me! illustrated by Kristina Stephenson. Simon & Schuster Books for Young Readers 2010 unp il $14.99

Grades: PreK K 1   E
1. Human body—Fiction
ISBN 978-0-689-85788-1; 0-689-85788-8
     LC 2006023872

Rhythmic text enumerates what various body parts can do, including hands to clap and a body to twirl, then expresses thanks for each of those parts—and for the whole.

"Bauer's lilting text matches the jubilant energy in Stephenson's watercolor rainbow palette." SLJ

Bayer, Jane, d. 1985

A my name is Alice; pictures by Steven Kellogg. Dial Bks. for Young Readers 1984 unp il $16.99; pa $6.99

Grades: PreK K 1 2   E
1. Stories in rhyme 2. Alphabet
ISBN 0-8037-0123-3; 0-14-054668-5 (pa)
     LC 84-7059

"Each page contains (in the border above the illustration) the name of an animal ('A my name is Alice') and its spouse ('and my husband's name is Alex.'), their locale ('We come from Alaska') and occupation ('and we sell ants.'). Two sentences appear beneath the illustrations on each page identifying the kind of animals in the verse (Alice is an 'Ape.' Alex is an 'Anteater.')." SLJ

"It is a superlative blend of visual and textual nonsense because the visual surprises keep the repetitive pat-

Bayer, Jane, d. 1985—*Continued*

tern in the text from becoming tedious. The verbal parts gradually expand in their ludicrousness, in their cataloging of zany characters and occupations." Wilson Libr Bull

Bean, Jonathan, 1979-

At night. Farrar, Straus and Giroux 2007 unp il $15 *

Grades: PreK K 1   E

1. Night—Fiction 2. Sleep—Fiction 3. City and town life—Fiction

ISBN 0-374-30446-7; 978-0-374-30446-1

LC 2006-48403

Boston Globe-Horn Book Award: Picture Book (2008)

A sleepless city girl imagines what it would be like to get away from snoring family members and curl up alone with one's thoughts in the cool night air under wide-open skies.

"The artist supplies luminous aerial scenes of the roof garden amid a friendly, well-lit cityscape. . . . The story breathes reassurance and adventure at the same time." Publ Wkly

Beard, Darleen Bailey, 1961-

Twister; pictures by Nancy Carpenter. Farrar, Straus & Giroux 1999 unp il $16; pa $5.95

Grades: K 1 2 3   E

1. Tornadoes—Fiction 2. Siblings—Fiction

ISBN 0-374-37977-7; 0-374-48014-1 (pa)

LC 95-13862

"Lucille and her little brother, Natt, are partaking in the idle pleasures of summer when a storm blows up; when the storm throws a funnel cloud, Mama commands her brood out of their mobile home to safety in the storm cellar . . . while she goes in search of an elderly neighbor. . . . Lucille's present-tense first-person narration is unforcedly full of telling details that make the account immediate. . . . Carpenter's thick, smudgy pastels deftly convey the viscousness of summer air before a storm and the weight of the threatening skies and the inky cellar dark." Bull Cent Child Books

Beaty, Andrea

Doctor Ted; [illustrated by] Pascal Lemaitre. Atheneum Books for Young Readers 2008 32p il $14.99

Grades: PreK K 1   E

1. Physicians—Fiction 2. Imagination—Fiction 3. Bears—Fiction

ISBN 978-1-4169-2820-1; 1-4169-2820-0

LC 2006-03191

After bumping his knee one morning, Ted the bear cub decides to become a doctor, but he has only one problem—he has no patients!

This is "a breezy story about pretend play that's laugh-out-loud funny. . . . The pictures' chunky ink lines and almost neon-like digital colors give every page plenty of punch." Publ Wkly

Another title about Ted is:

Firefighter Ted (2009)

When giants come to play; written by Andrea Beaty; illustrated by Kevin Hawkes. Abrams Books for Young Readers 2006 unp il $16.95

Grades: PreK K 1 2   E

1. Giants—Fiction 2. Play—Fiction

ISBN 0-8109-5759-0   LC 2005-32243

"A perfect summer day in Anna's comfortable world transpires when two playmates, who just happen to be giants, join her to play." Booklist

"A delightful romp, full of imagination, told in lyrical prose. . . . Large, full-page illustrations in charcoal pencils and acrylics depict the oversize, affable playmates and diminutive girl." SLJ

Beaumont, Karen

Baby danced the polka; pictures by Jennifer Plecas. Dial Books for Young Readers 2004 unp il $12.99 *

Grades: PreK K 1 2   E

1. Infants—Fiction

ISBN 0-8037-2587-6

"Mama and Papa put their baby down for a nap, but the youngster feels like dancing. Each time the adults set out to do a chore, Baby escapes the crib and boogie-woogies, cha-chas, or shooby-doobies with a different stuffed-animal companion." SLJ

"What a happy, rollicking baby. And what a rolling, rhythmic text. . . . The sprightly pen-and-watercolor artwork bears a very strong resemblance to the work of Helen Oxenbury." Booklist

Doggone dogs! pictures by David Catrow. Dial Books for Young Readers 2008 unp il $16.99

Grades: PreK K   E

1. Dogs—Fiction 2. Counting 3. Stories in rhyme

ISBN 978-0-8037-3157-8; 0-8037-3157-4

LC 2007008620

Ten unruly dogs get loose at obedience school, and when they are captured by the dog-catcher, they work together to effect their escape and return home.

"The minimal rhyming text is paired with Catrow's exuberant, comic, pencil and watercolor illustrations. The frenetic, goofy-looking dogs of various sizes and breeds romping through the park are sure to bring smiles to young faces." SLJ

Duck, duck, goose! a coyote's on the loose! illustrated by Jose Aruego and Ariane Dewey. HarperCollins Pubs. 2004 unp il $15.95; lib bdg $16.89

Grades: PreK K 1 2   E

1. Animals—Fiction 2. Stories in rhyme

ISBN 0-06-050802-7; 0-06-050804-3 (lib bdg)

LC 2003-8734

Several farm animals try to evade a coyote that they think is dangerous

"Aruego and Dewey use bold paints as varied as a child's imagination to color their comically rendered farmyard animals. A suspenseful romp that will strike a chord with children." SLJ

Beaumont, Karen—*Continued*

I ain't gonna paint no more! illustrated by David Catrow. Harcourt 2005 unp il $16 *
Grades: PreK K 1 2   E
1. Painting—Fiction 2. Stories in rhyme
ISBN 0-15-202488-3   LC 2003-27739
"To the tune of 'It Ain't Gonna Rain No More,' one creative kid floods his world with color, painting first the walls, then the ceiling, then HIMSELF!" Publisher's note
"Catrow splashes color all over, uses white space cleverly, and includes playful flourishes. . . . Elongated figures and exaggerated expressions match the silly tone of the story. . . . With rhymes that invite audience participation and scenes that draw the eye, this is a strong storytime choice." SLJ

Move over, Rover; [by] Karen Beaumont; illustrated by Jane Dyer. Harcourt 2006 unp il $16
Grades: PreK K 1 2   E
1. Dogs—Fiction 2. Animals—Fiction 3. Rain—Fiction 4. Stories in rhyme
ISBN 978-0-15-201979-2; 0-15-201979-0
     LC 2005014557
When a storm comes, Rover expects to have his doghouse all to himself but finds that various other animals, including a skunk, come to join him.
This offers "marvelously textured watercolor-and-acrylic illustrations. . . . The repetition of key phrases, the rhythmic text, and the cumulative structure of the narrative make this book an ideal read-aloud." SLJ

Who ate all the cookie dough? [by] Karen Beaumont; illustrated by Eugene Yelchin. Henry Holt and Company 2008 unp il $16.95
Grades: PreK K 1   E
1. Lost and found possessions—Fiction 2. Animals—Fiction 3. Stories in rhyme
ISBN 978-0-8050-8267-8; 0-8050-8267-0
     LC 2007012733
Kanga and her friends try to discover who ate all of her cookie dough
"Infectious repetitive rhyming verse, eye-catching gouache illustrations with ample white space, and a lift-the-flap surprise combine to create a joyful tale." Horn Book Guide

Bechtold, Lisze

Sally and the purple socks; [by] Lisze Bechtold. Philomel Books 2008 unp il $15.99
Grades: PreK K 1   E
1. Clothing and dress—Fiction 2. Size—Fiction
ISBN 978-0-399-24734-7; 0-399-24734-3
     LC 2007023649
When her tiny purple socks start to expand, Sally turns them into a scarf and then curtains, but things soon get out of hand.
"The quirky, playful, and ultimately warm illustrations, coupled with the simple text and a plot with just the right amount of suspense, make the book spot-on for sharing with young audiences." Booklist

Beck, Andrea, 1956-

Pierre Le Poof! written and illustrated by Andrea Beck. Orca Book Publishers 2009 unp il $19.95
Grades: PreK K 1 2   E
1. Dogs—Fiction
ISBN 978-1-55469-028-2; 1-55469-028-5
"Lapdog Pierre Le Poof, 'a pedigreed pooch,' lives a pampered life with Miss Murphy but longs to frolic with the dogs in the park. At a practice session for a dog championship, Pierre makes his escape . . . but soon longs for the comforts of home. . . . Dog and owner bear a strong resemblance to each other in airy ink-and-watercolor pictures that delightfully go for the laughs." Booklist

Beck, Scott

Monster sleepover! Abrams Books for Young Readers 2009 unp il $14.95
Grades: K 1 2   E
1. Parties—Fiction 2. Monsters—Fiction
ISBN 978-0-8109-4059-8; 0-8109-4059-0
     LC 2009-00317
Doris throws a slumber party for Ben and her other monster friends, complete with games, snacks, and an effort to stay up all night.
"Bright, acrylic paintings enhance the lively tone. Beck's silly sense of humor will delight young readers." SLJ

Becker, Bonny

A visitor for Bear; [by] Bonny Becker; illustrated by Kady MacDonald Denton. Candlewick Press 2008 unp il $16.99
Grades: PreK K 1 2   E
1. Bears—Fiction 2. Mice—Fiction 3. Friendship—Fiction
ISBN 978-0-7636-2807-9; 0-7636-2807-7
     LC 2006-51850
Bear's efforts to keep out visitors to his house are undermined by a very persistent mouse.
This offers "watercolor, ink and gouache illustrations in a soft color palette. . . . The characters are highly expressive . . . and the dramatic text will lend itself to reading aloud." Booklist
Another title about Bear is:
A birthday for Bear (2009)

Becker, Suzy

Manny's cows; the Niagara Falls tale; written and illustrated by Suzy Becker. HarperCollins 2006 unp il lib bdg $16.89 *
Grades: PreK K 1 2   E
1. Cattle—Fiction 2. Vacations—Fiction 3. Niagara Falls (N.Y. and Ont.)—Fiction
ISBN   978-0-06-054152-1;   0-06-054152-0; 978-0-06-054153-8 (lib bdg); 0-06-054153-9 (lib bdg)
     LC 2005-14508
For his summer vacation, Manny takes his five hundred cows to Niagara Falls.
"The over-the-top story, full of fun and laced with amusing visual and verbal details, . . . is accompanied

Becker, Suzy—*Continued*

by occasional sidebar facts about dairy cattle. The cows' outrageous comments and antics are bolstered by free-spirited ink drawings brightened with color." Booklist

Bedford, David, 1969-

The way I love you. Simon & Schuster Books for Young Readers 2005 unp il $12.95

Grades: PreK K   E

1. Dogs—Fiction

ISBN 0-689-87625-4   LC 2004-3964

First published 2004 in Australia with title: I love

A little girl celebrates all of the ways she loves her puppy.

"Loose charcoal lines provide texture and motion, while splashes of pastel-hued watercolors keep the pictures warm and cozy. . . . The simple language and clean, colorful artwork make this book just right for the youngest pet lovers." SLJ

Bee, William

And the train goes. . . Candlewick Press 2007 unp il $15.99

Grades: PreK K   E

1. Railroads—Fiction 2. Parrots—Fiction 3. Sounds—Fiction

ISBN 978-0-7636-3248-9; 0-7636-3248-1

LC 2006-43857

As assorted passengers comment on their train ride, and the train itself goes "Clickerty click, clickerty clack," the station parrot is carefully listening to every sound

"Filled with sound effects galore, this rollicking read-aloud is perfect for transportation storytimes. . . . The train and the characters' clothing are depicted in glossy colors and covered with flat floral patterns and other graphic designs. . . . There are many details for children to pore over." SLJ

Beil, Karen Magnuson, 1950-

Jack's house; illustrated by Mike Wohnoutka. Holiday House 2008 unp il $16.95

Grades: PreK K 1 2   E

1. House construction—Fiction 2. Dogs—Fiction

ISBN 978-0-8234-1913-5; 0-8234-1913-4

LC 2007014978

Cumulative text reveals who was really responsible for the house that Jack claims to have built, and all of the trucks involved, from the bulldozer used to clear the land to the van that brought a hammock for the back yard

"A wonderful twist on an age-old rhyme. . . . Wohnoutka's full-page acrylic paintings are large scale, but are also full of small details for readers to enjoy. . . . This beguiling book will be a hit both at storytimes and in circulating collections." SLJ

Beiser, Tim, 1959-

Bradley McGogg, the very fine frog; illustrated by Rachel Berman. Tundra Books 2009 c2008 unp il $19.99

Grades: PreK K 1 2   E

1. Frogs—Fiction 2. Food—Fiction 3. Stories in rhyme

ISBN 978-0-88776-864-4; 0-88776-864-4

Bradley McGogg the frog "discovers that his cupboard is empty and goes in search of something for lunch. Miss Mousie offers him rye crackers and cheese, while Herr Bear and Herr Hare invite him to dine on carrots covered in honey. . . . Unable to accept the other animals' favorite foods and still hungry, Brad drags himself back home. To his delight, he discovers an infestation of bugs in his hollowed-out log and sits down to a delectable feast. . . . The sophisticated rhyming text is accompanied by subdued watercolor and gouache illustrations. . . . Each animal's face is imbued with character and personality." SLJ

Bell, Cece

Itty bitty. Candlewick Press 2009 unp il $9.99

Grades: PreK K 1   E

1. Dogs—Fiction 2. Size—Fiction

ISBN 978-0-7636-3616-6; 0-7636-3616-9

"Where does a tiny dog find just the right decor for his hollowed-out-bone house? Why, the 'teeny-weeny department' at a huge store downtown, of course! Such is the premise of this sweet and silly picture book that introduces a sunny pup of small size but big personality. . . . Bell's . . . crisp acrylic and ink artwork features blocks of color and simple stylized shapes on grainy, speckled backgrounds." Publ Wkly

Belton, Sandra, 1939-

Beauty, her basket; illustrated by Cozbi A. Cabrera. Greenwillow Books 2004 unp il $15.99; lib bdg $16.89 *

Grades: K 1 2 3   E

1. Gullahs—Fiction 2. African Americans—Fiction 3. Baskets—Fiction

ISBN 0-688-17821-9; 0-688-17822-7 (lib bdg)

LC 2003-40599

While visiting her grandmother in the Sea Islands, a young girl hears about her African heritage and learns to weave a sea grass basket.

"Fullbleed illustrations in darkly brilliant acrylics float and swirl across the page, complementing the lush, evocative tone of the text." SLJ

Bemelmans, Ludwig, 1898-1962

Madeline; story and pictures by Ludwig Bemelmans. Viking 1985 c1939 unp il $17.99; pa $7.99 *

Grades: PreK K 1 2   E

1. Paris (France)—Fiction 2. Stories in rhyme

ISBN 0-670-44580-0; 0-14-056439-X (pa)

A Caldecott Medal honor book, 1940

A reissue of the title first published 1939 by Simon & Schuster

Bemelmans, Ludwig, 1898-1962—_Continued_

"Madeline is a nonconformist in a regimented world—a Paris convent school. This rhymed story tells how she made an adventure out of having appendicitis." Hodges. Books for Elem Sch Libr

Other titles about Madeline are:

Madeline and the bad hat (1957)

Madeline and the gypsies (1959)

Madeline in London (1961)

Madeline's Christmas (1985)

Madeline's rescue (1985)

Benchley, Nathaniel, 1915-1981

A ghost named Fred; pictures by Ben Shecter. Harper & Row 1968 unp il lib bdg $17.89 *

Grades: K 1 2   E

1. Ghost stories

ISBN 0-06-020474-5

"An I can read mystery"

"George, an imaginative child used to playing alone, went into an empty house to get out of the rain; there he met an absent-minded ghost named Fred, who knew there was a treasure but had forgotten where. Only when Fred opened an umbrella for George's homeward journey did the treasure materialize." Bull Cent Child Books

"More humorous than scary . . . this is a pleasing and acceptable ghost story for beginning readers." Booklist

Bennett, Kelly

Dad and Pop; an ode to fathers & stepfathers; illustrated by Paul Meisel. Candlewick Press 2010 unp il $15.99

Grades: PreK K 1 2   E

1. Fathers—Fiction 2. Stepfathers—Fiction 3. Father-daughter relationship—Fiction

ISBN 978-0-7636-3379-0; 0-7636-3379-8

"A cheerful girl explains that Dad and Pop are different in many ways, but the same in their love for her. . . . Dad is the girl's biological father and . . . Pop is her step-father. . . . This is a positive and playful portrayal of a blended family. . . . Expressive faces and gentle humor add charm to the pictures." SLJ

Your daddy was just like you; illustrated by David Walker. G. P. Putnam's Sons 2010 unp il $16.99

Grades: PreK K 1   E

1. Fathers—Fiction 2. Grandmothers—Fiction

ISBN 978-0-399-24798-9; 0-399-24798-X

LC 2008053644

A grandmother describes to her grandson how his father was just like him when he was a child, never wanting to take a bath, fearing the dark, and swooping through the house in a cape and mask.

"Characters' facial expressions and body language successfully capture emotions, actions, and reactions. . . . The humorous text is in perfect sync with the simple illustrations." SLJ

Berenzy, Alix, 1957-

Sammy the classroom guinea pig. Henry Holt 2005 unp il $16.95 *

Grades: PreK K 1 2   E

1. Guinea pigs—Fiction 2. School stories

ISBN 0-8050-4024-2   LC 2004-10136

Ms. B. and her students try to understand what is bothering Sammy, the classroom guinea pig

"The pastel-and-colored-pencil illustrations are very successful in depicting the characters, particularly the endearing little animal with a variety of facial expressions. . . . Through simple text and engaging artwork, Berenzy shows the proper setup of a guinea-pig cage, what foods are best for these creatures, and how responsive they are to humans." SLJ

Berger, Carin

Forever friends. Greenwillow Books 2010 unp il $16.99; lib bdg $17.89

Grades: PreK K   E

1. Friendship—Fiction 2. Birds—Fiction 3. Rabbits—Fiction 4. Seasons—Fiction

ISBN 978-0-06-191528-4; 0-06-191528-9; 978-0-06-191529-1 (lib bdg); 0-06-191529-7 (lib bdg)

LC 2009-18758

In the spring, a blue bird awakens a rabbit and invites him to play, and they enjoy every day together until it is time for the bird to fly south for the winter, with a promise to return again next spring.

"Berger's superb, stylized cut-paper collage illustrations, constructed from lined and graph paper and magazines, depict sylvan landscapes with graceful curves and airy compositions that echo the simplicity and gentleness of the tale. A reassuring, poetic story that will give young children much to ponder any time of the year." Booklist

The little yellow leaf. Greenwillow Books 2008 unp il $16.99; lib bdg $17.89

Grades: PreK K 1 2   E

1. Trees—Fiction 2. Leaves—Fiction 3. Autumn—Fiction

ISBN 978-0-06-145223-9; 0-06-145223-8; 978-0-06-145224-6 (lib bdg); 0-06-145224-6 (lib bdg)

LC 2007-39191

A yellow leaf is not ready to fall from the tree when autumn comes, but finally, after finding another leaf still on the tree, the two let go together.

"In Berger's eye-catching collage illustrations, pieced background papers in shades of yellow, green, blue, and beige show off stylized forms of naked tree branches, leaves, and sun created by clipping and pasting (sometimes tiny) segments of various papers—faded, lined ledger, and graph paper; colored and printed magazine pages—and adding touches of paint." SLJ

OK go. Greenwillow Books 2009 unp il $17.99; lib bdg $18.89 *

Grades: K 1 2 3   E

1. Environmental protection—Fiction 2. Automobiles—Fiction

ISBN 978-0-06-157666-9; 0-06-157666-2; 978-0-06-157669-0 (lib bdg); 0-06-157669-7 (lib bdg)

LC 2008-14681

Berger, Carin—*Continued*

In this almost wordless picture book, car drivers stuck in traffic under smoggy skies seek "greener" alternatives to driving, including riding bicycles, walking, and playing

"Berger's simple environmental message is delivered through clever, innovative illustrations that make her point without being didactic. Idiosyncratic creatures decked out in fabric pieces, buttons, and tall imaginative hats sail along in even more idiosyncratic vehicles that are variously colored and decorated with stickers and decals." SLJ

Berger, Joe, 1970-

Bridget Fidget and the most perfect pet! Dial Books for Young Readers 2009 unp il $16.99

Grades: PreK K   E

1. Pets—Fiction 2. Ladybugs—Fiction

ISBN 978-0-8037-3405-0; 0-8037-3405-0

LC 2009011528

First published 2008 in the United Kingdom with title: Bridget Fidget

Bridget has always wanted a pet unicorn named Thunderhooves, so when a box is delivered to her door she is sure that is what is inside.

"Bridget Fidget is the timeless cartoon poppet, dreaming, dashing, fussing, laughing, dragging her remarkably expressive stuffed animal everywhere. . . . The cartoon illustrations . . . are so joyfully kinetic that viewers are left breathless." SLJ

Berger, Lou

The elephant wish; by Lou Berger; illustrated by Ana Juan. Schwartz & Wade Books 2008 unp il $16.99; lib bdg $19.99

Grades: PreK K 1 2   E

1. Wishes—Fiction 2. Elephants—Fiction 3. Family life—Fiction

ISBN   978-0-375-83962-7;   0-375-83962-3; 978-0-375-93962-4 (lib bdg); 0-375-93962-8 (lib bdg)

LC 2007034329

Soon after wishing that an elephant will come and take her away from her too-busy parents, Eliza's fondest desire comes true but her journey is observed by ninety-seven-year-old Adelle, who once made the same wish

"Berger threads shimmers of lighthearted whimsy through this obscure tale, creating a fantasy with deep resonance. Juan matches the slightly melancholic tone with dark, swirly images that are dense and dreamy." Booklist

Berger, Samantha, 1969-

Martha doesn't say sorry! illustrated by Bruce Whatley. Little, Brown and Co. 2009 unp il $15.99

Grades: PreK K 1 2   E

1. Otters—Fiction

ISBN 978-0-316-06682-2; 0-316-06682-6

LC 2008-16769

Young Martha learns that she must apologize for her bad behavior if she wants people to cooperate with her.

"The watercolor and colored pencil artwork encapsu-

lates Martha's girliness, her better-than-thou attitude and her internal struggle with her conscience. Whatley's representation of body language and facial expression powerfully complement the text. An enjoyable introduction to what could be a new beloved character." Kirkus

Bergman, Mara

Snip snap! what's that? illustrated by Nick Maland. Greenwillow Books 2005 unp il $15.99

Grades: PreK K 1 2   E

1. Alligators—Fiction

ISBN 0-06-077754-0   LC 2004-13420

Three siblings are frightened by the wide mouth, long teeth, and strong jaws of the alligator that has crept up the stairs—until they decide they have had enough

"Using elements of rhythm and rhyme as well as an enjoyably predictable question-and-answer refrain, the text maintains a playful tone beneath the scary details. . . . Expressive line drawings, brightened with watercolor washes, illustrate the story with wit and style." Booklist

Yum yum! What fun! written by Mara Bergman; illustrated by Nick Maland. Greenwillow Books 2009 unp il $17.99

Grades: PreK K 1 2   E

1. Animals—Fiction 2. Stories in rhyme

ISBN 978-0-06-168860-7; 0-06-168860-6

LC 2008012640

A series of animals sneaks into the house, looking for something to eat

"Enticing rhymes and onomatopoeia make each animal intruder's entrance the read-aloud equivalent of a star turn. . . . Treats usually disappear quickly, but this one will last through repeated readings." Publ Wkly

Bergren, Lisa Tawn

God found us you; art by Laura J. Bryant. HarperCollins Children's Books 2009 unp il $10.99

Grades: PreK K 1   E

1. Foxes—Fiction 2. Adoption—Fiction 3. Christian life—Fiction

ISBN 978-0-06-113176-9; 0-06-113176-8

LC 2008016216

When Little Fox asks his mother to tell his favorite story, Mama Fox recounts the day he arrived in her life, from God to her arms

"Bryant's delicate illustrations in pastel shades augment the heartfelt message of Bergren's simple story. . . . This woodland tale answers many questions adopted children may ask their parents." SLJ

Bergstein, Rita M.

Your own big bed; by Rita M. Bergstein; illustrated by Susan Kathleen Hartung. Viking 2008 unp il $15.99

Grades: PreK K 1   E

1. Growth—Fiction 2. Beds—Fiction

ISBN 978-0-670-06079-5; 0-670-06079-8

LC 2007-17902

Bergstein, Rita M.—_Continued_

Introduces how different animals and even human babies grow from being newly-hatched or born, through being carried everywhere, to having their own special place to sleep.

"The absence of the anxiety, whining, or excuses common to books of this ilk is refreshing. . . . This sweet book provides a gentle, matter-of-fact introduction to a sometimes-difficult transition." SLJ

Berkes, Marianne Collins, 1939-

Over in the jungle; a rainforest rhyme; by Marianne Berkes; illustrated by Jeanette Canyon. Dawn Publications 2007 unp il $16.95; pa $8.95

Grades: PreK K 1 2 3   E

1. Rain forest animals 2. Counting

ISBN 1-58469-091-7; 1-58469-092-5 (pa)

LC 2006030962

"Another variation on the familiar song, this one enumerates some of the unusual fauna of the rain forest. It not only spotlights some of the animals . . . but also offers pertinent information on the habitat. Berkes describes the different layers of the rainforest and its importance to our global ecology, and suggests movement activities for children to act out the rhyme. The unusual and colorful illustrations are made with polymer clay and then photographed, giving them a three-dimensional look." SLJ

Berner, Rotraut Susanne, 1948-

In the town all year 'round. Chronicle Books 2008 unp il $16.99

Grades: PreK K 1 2   E

1. City and town life—Fiction 2. Seasons—Fiction 3. Year—Fiction 4. Stories without words

ISBN 978-0-8118-6474-9; 0-8118-6474-X

LC 2008012860

Originally published in German in 4 vols.

"This oversize identification book . . . opens by introducing a cast of characters for children to find as they explore eight different scenes throughout each of the seasons. Myriad details of people, places, and events, colorfully drawn in cartoon style, will have youngsters examining the pages for hours." Booklist

Bernheimer, Kate

The girl in the castle inside the museum; [illustrated by] Nicoletta Ceccoli. Schwartz & Wade Books 2008 unp il $16.99; lib bdg $19.99

Grades: K 1 2 3   E

1. Castles—Fiction 2. Museums—Fiction

ISBN 978-0-375-83606-0; 978-0-375-83606-7 (lib bdg)   LC 2006-101854

"In an eclectic toy museum, children are drawn to a snow globe where it is said that, if they look hard enough, they can see the little girl who lives in the castle therein. To their delight, she is visible, as is her entire enchanted world. The girl is lonely when the museum empties, and she dreams of other children visiting her. . . . Using media as varied as clay sculpture and photography, Ceccoli has created a world that beckons young readers inside. . . . This unusual book will jump-start the imaginations of all who are lucky enough to enter it." SLJ

Berry, Lynne

Duck skates; illustrated by Hiroe Nakata. Henry Holt and Co. 2005 unp il $15.95 *

Grades: PreK K   E

1. Ducks—Fiction 2. Snow—Fiction 3. Stories in rhyme

ISBN 978-0-8050-7219-8; 0-8050-7219-5

LC 2004-22176

Five little ducks skate, romp, and play in the snow

"The illustrations follow the text exactly, allowing children to count the ducks engaged in each activity. The watercolor-and-ink pictures convey the playfulness in warm, cozy tones, and a surprising amount of expression is conveyed in simple lines." SLJ

Other titles about these ducks are:

Duck dunks (2008)

Duck tents (2009)

Berry, Matt

Up on Daddy's shoulders; by Matt Berry; illustrated by Lucy Corvino. Scholastic 2006 unp il $6.99

Grades: PreK K 1 2   E

1. Father-son relationship—Fiction 2. Size—Fiction

ISBN 0-439-67045-4   LC 2005023626

"Cartwheel books"

While riding on his father's shoulders, a young boy feels taller than everything in his house, his neighborhood, and the world.

"Corvino's sunny paintings fill each double-page spread. . . . Easy on the eyes and ears, this title's rhythm and attractiveness make it a fine read-aloud choice." Booklist

Bertrand, Lynne

Granite baby; pictures by Kevin Hawkes. Farrar, Straus and Giroux 2005 unp il $16 *

Grades: PreK K 1 2   E

1. Infants—Fiction 2. New Hampshire—Fiction 3. Tall tales

ISBN 0-374-32761-0   LC 2002-192882

"Melanie Kroupa books"

Five talented New Hampshire sisters try to care for a baby that one of them has carved out of granite.

"Together with Bertrand's rollicking text, Hawkes' broad double-page paintings make this ideal for sharing with groups." Booklist

Best, Cari, 1951-

Are you going to be good? pictures by G. Brian Karas. Farrar, Straus and Giroux 2005 unp il $16

Grades: PreK K 1 2   E

1. Parties—Fiction 2. Etiquette—Fiction 3. Old age—Fiction

ISBN 0-374-30394-0   LC 2004-46945

"Melanie Kroupa books"

While attending his first "night party" to celebrate Great-Gran Sadie's 100th birthday, Robert's manners disappoint family members and relatives but please the guest of honor who loves his dance steps

"Karas's spirited color illustrations portray the family gathering from a child's view. . . . Attempts to meet adults' expectations will resonate with most readers." SLJ

Best, Cari, 1951-—*Continued*

Easy as pie; [pictures by Melissa Sweet] Farrar, Straus and Giroux 2010 unp il $16.99
Grades: K 1 2 3   E
   1. Pies—Fiction 2. Baking—Fiction
   ISBN 978-0-374-39929-0; 0-374-39929-8
                                LC 2008-16803
   "Melanie Kroupa books"
Jacob watches his favorite television show, "Baking with Chef Monty," and bakes a beautiful peach pie, which he gives to his parents for their anniversary.
   "With pencil and watercolor illustrations done in a palette of soft colors, Sweet captures the warmth and security Jacob feels in the kitchen. . . . Important themes abound—love, security, cooperation, warmth, respect—and somehow all are tied to the simple acts of cooking and eating together. A delicious book for all collections." SLJ

Goose's story; pictures by Holly Meade. Farrar, Straus & Giroux 2002 unp il hardcover o.p. pa $6.99
Grades: PreK K 1 2   E
   1. Geese—Fiction
   ISBN 0-374-32750-5; 0-374-40032-6 (pa)
                                LC 2001-27285
   "Melanie Kroupa books"
A young girl finds a Canada goose with a badly injured foot and looks for her each day to see how she is doing
   "Holly Meade's animated paper collage enhances Best's poignant story. . . . Best tells the story from the girl's point of view, and her language is appropriately childlike and empathetic." Horn Book

Sally Jean, the Bicycle Queen; pictures by Christine Davenier. Farrar, Straus and Giroux 2005 unp il $16 *
Grades: PreK K 1 2   E
   1. Bicycles—Fiction 2. Cycling—Fiction
   ISBN 0-374-36386-2   LC 2004-40461
When Sally Jean outgrows her beloved bicycle, Flash, she experiments with various ideas for acquiring a new, bigger one.
   "Davenier's ink-and-watercolor illustrations are light and airy and convey a variety of emotions and delightful details. Sally Jean is a real charmer, and children will appreciate her resourcefulness and tenacity." SLJ

Shrinking Violet; illustrated by Giselle Potter. Farrar, Straus & Giroux 2001 unp il $16
Grades: PreK K 1 2   E
   1. School stories 2. Theater—Fiction
   ISBN 0-374-36882-1   LC 99-88966
   "Melanie Kroupa books"
Violet, who is very shy and hates for anyone to look at her in school, finally comes out of her shell when she is cast as Lady Space in a play about the solar system and saves the production from disaster
   "In wry, well-paced prose, Best . . . tells a good-natured story. . . . Potter's charming, signature-style illustrations, filled with wacky angles and proportions, rich colors, and slightly nostalgic details, extend the story's drama and warmth." Booklist

Three cheers for Catherine the Great! illustrated by Giselle Potter. Sunburst ed. Farrar, Straus and Giroux 2003 unp il pa $7.99 *
Grades: PreK K 1 2   E
   1. Grandmothers—Fiction 2. Birthdays—Fiction 3. Parties—Fiction 4. Gifts—Fiction 5. Russian Americans—Fiction
   ISBN 0-374-47551-2   LC 2002040804
   First published 1999 by DK Pub.
Sara's Russian grandmother has requested that there be no presents at her seventy-eighth birthday party so Sara must think of a gift from her heart.
   "In lively, lyrical prose, Best celebrates a special family relationship, and conveys the unique challenges and joys of an immigrant's new life. . . . Potter's festive, whimsical artwork is an irresistible play of vibrant colors and patterns, filled with rich detail and diverse, expressive characters." Booklist
   Another title about Sara and her grandmother is:
When Catherine the Great and I were eight! (2003)

What's so bad about being an only child? [by] Cari Best; pictures by Sophie Blackall. Farrar, Straus and Giroux 2007 unp il $16
Grades: PreK K 1 2   E
   1. Only child—Fiction 2. Pets—Fiction
   ISBN 0-374-39943-3; 978-0-374-39943-6
                                LC 2005-51232
Rosemary Emma Angela Lynette Isabel Iris Malone grows tired of being an only child, but eventually finds a way to feel less alone.
   "Kids should applaud this self-reliant, spunky heroine." Publ Wkly

Bevis, Mary Elizabeth, 1939-

Wolf song; [by] Mary Bevis; illustrated by Consie Powell. Raven Productions 2007 unp il $18.95; pa $12.95
Grades: K 1 2 3   E
   1. Wolves—Fiction 2. Uncles—Fiction
   ISBN 978-0-9794202-0-7; 978-0-9794202-1-4 (pa)
                                LC 2007027953
At twilight, Nell and her Uncle Walter go into the north woods, hoping to hear—and join—the howling of the wolves. Includes facts about wolves and howling expeditions.
   "The text and illustrations both convey the wonder and mystery of nature." SLJ

Bildner, Phil

The greatest game ever played; a football story; by Phil Bildner; illustrated by Zachary Pullen. Putnam's Sons 2006 unp il $16.99
Grades: K 1 2 3   E
   1. Father-son relationship—Fiction 2. Football—Fiction
   ISBN 0-399-24171-X   LC 2005025177
   "The New York Giants are Sam and his father's favorite baseball team until they move west. Sam misses the team, but most of all he misses spending time with Pop, who has forsaken sports—despite Sam's breathless discovery of a football team with the same name. When

Bildner, Phil—*Continued*
Sam is given tickets to the 1958 NFL championship game, he and Pop go together. . . . The father-son relationship . . . is realistically portrayed. . . . The energy of the paintings perfectly matches Bildner's lively text." Booklist

The Hallelujah Flight; illustrated by John Holyfield. G.P. Putnam's Sons 2010 unp il $16.99 *
Grades: K 1 2 3   E
1. Banning, Herman, d. 1933—Fiction 2. Allen, Thomas—Fiction 3. Air pilots—Fiction 4. Flight—Fiction 5. African Americans—Fiction
ISBN 978-0-399-24789-7; 0-399-24789-0
LC 2009-10362
In 1932, James Banning, along with his co-pilot Thomas Allen, make history by becoming the first African Americans to fly across the United States, relying on the generosity of people they meet in the towns along the way who help keep their 'flying jalopy' going.
"Based on both fictional and nonfiction sources, the story is briskly told in Allen's voice, with plenty of imagined dialogue. Holyfield's gorgeous . . . paintings are done on textured backgrounds in a palette of blues and browns." Kirkus

Shoeless Joe & Black Betsy; illustrated by C.F. Payne. Simon & Schuster Bks. for Young Readers 2002 unp il $17 *
Grades: K 1 2 3   E
1. Jackson, Joe, 1888-1951—Fiction 2. Baseball—Fiction
ISBN 0-689-82913-2   LC 99-40563
Shoeless Joe Jackson, said by some to be the greatest baseball player ever, goes into a hitting slump just before he is to start his minor league career, so he asks his friend to make him a special bat to help him hit
This is "told in a folksy, Southern voice, with many of the stylistic elements of a tall tale. . . . The mixed-media illustrations are layered and rich in texture, qualities that add depth and drama." SLJ

Turkey Bowl; [by] Phil Bildner; illustrated by C.F. Payne. Simon & Schuster Books for Young Readers 2008 unp il $15.99
Grades: 1 2 3   E
1. Thanksgiving Day—Fiction 2. Family life—Fiction 3. Football—Fiction 4. Snow—Fiction
ISBN 9780-689-87896-1; 0-689-87896-6
LC 2005020139
Ethan looks forward to the Thanksgiving Day when he and his friends are finally old enough to play in the annual family football game, but that day arrives full of snow and icy roads
"Payne's muted, full-color illustrations capture the disappointment and joy the characters experience and feature plenty of gridiron action. Perfect for reading aloud at holiday time, this lively story will resonate year-round with sports fans." SLJ

Billingsley, Franny, 1954-
Big Bad Bunny; story by Franny Billingsley; art by G. Brian Karas. Atheneum Books for Young Readers 2008 unp il $16.99 *
Grades: PreK K 1   E
1. Mice—Fiction 2. Mother-child relationship—Fiction
ISBN 978-1-4169-0601-8; 1-4169-0601-0
LC 2006-32754
"Richard Jackson book"
When Baby Boo-Boo, a mouse dressed in a bunny suit, becomes lost in the forest, his mother follows the sound of his cries to locate him.
Billingsley "extends her plot with satisfying onomatopoeia; the oversize format, too, marks this for a readaloud. Karas . . . strategically deploys mixed-media to render the id-gone-wild scenes with comic abandon." Publ Wkly

Billout, Guy, 1941-
The frog who wanted to see the sea. Creative Editions 2007 unp il $17.95
Grades: 1 2 3 4   E
1. Frogs—Fiction
ISBN 978-1-56846-188-5   LC 2005-51898
Feeling adventurous one day, a frog leaves her pond and sets out to visit the great sea she has heard so much about.
The illustrations "often employ tricks of scale and perspective, along with large expanses of deceptively flat color, compositions that resolve in witty visual jokes while tapping deeper currents of unease. . . . [The] story unfolds simply, with grace, nuance and high style." NY Times Book Rev

Birtha, Becky, 1948-
Grandmama's pride; illustrated by Colin Bootman. Albert Whitman 2005 unp il $16.95 *
Grades: K 1 2 3   E
1. Grandmothers—Fiction 2. African Americans—Fiction 3. Segregation—Fiction
ISBN 0-8075-3028-X   LC 2005003991
While on a trip in 1956 to visit her grandmother in the South, six-year-old Sarah Marie experiences segregation for the first time, but discovers that things have changed by the time she returns the following year.
"The strong, sensitive writing is enhanced by beautiful watercolor paintings filled with chips of light." SLJ

Lucky beans; illustrated by Nicole Tadgell. Albert Whitman 2010 unp il $16.99
Grades: 1 2 3   E
1. Great Depression, 1929-1939—Fiction 2. African Americans—Fiction 3. Mathematics—Fiction 4. Beans—Fiction
ISBN 978-0-8075-4782-3; 0-8075-4782-4
During the Great Depression, an African American boy named Marshall uses lessons learned in arithmetic class to figure out how many beans are in a jar to win his mother a sewing machine.
"Math and wry comedy mix in this lively historical story. . . . The expressive watercolor paintings show both the racism that Marshall and his family endure as well as his final triumph, and Tadgell folds in humor." Booklist

Black, Michael Ian

Chicken cheeks; illustrated by Kevin Hawkes. Simon & Schuster Books for Young Readers 2009 unp il $15.99

Grades: PreK K 1 2   E

1. Animals—Fiction 2. Stories in rhyme

ISBN 978-1-4169-4864-3; 1-4169-4864-3

LC 2007-16872

This "features the hind quarters of animals, complete with silly names for them. . . . The closeup, color-saturated illustrations—which are at the same time obviously hilarious and sneakily deadpan—tell a story. A brown bear stands poised atop a ladder, gazing thoughtfully up the skinny trunk of a tall, branch-free tree. He grabs a duck and sets it on his head. . . . Sixteen animals later, children can only laugh helplessly at the absurd ladder of animals balanced parallel to the tree trunk. . . . Filled with visual jokes and amusing details, *Chicken Cheeks* is a lot more than a list of words for kids to snicker at." SLJ

The purple kangaroo; illustrated by Peter Brown. Simon & Schuster Books for Young Readers 2010 unp il $16.99

Grades: PreK K 1 2   E

1. Imagination—Fiction 2. Telepathy—Fiction

ISBN 978-1-4169-5771-3; 1-4169-5771-5

LC 2008003534

After asking the reader to think of something spectacular, the narrator sets out to prove his ability to read minds by describing a preposterous situation and characters.

"The engaging artwork features muted acrylic paintings punctuated by the computer-generated monkey narrating each page. A silly, fun romp that kids will ask for again and again." SLJ

Blackford, Harriet

Elephant's story; illustrated by Manya Stojic. Boxer 2008 unp il $14.95

Grades: PreK K 1 2   E

1. Elephants—Fiction

ISBN 978-1-905417-75-9; 1-905417-75-6

LC 2007-213162

"Elephant enjoys her youth amid the shelter of the protective herd, learning the daily skills of elephant life; when Elephant becomes a big sister, she watches over the new baby. . . . The book covers some important details about wild elephant life. . . . The paintings are appealingly textured, with brushwork overlaying the planes of solid color to give a soft wispiness." Bull Cent Child Books

Tiger's story; written by Harriet Blackford; illustrated by Manya Stojic. Boxer Books 2007 unp il $12.95

Grades: PreK K   E

1. Tigers—Fiction

ISBN 978-1-905417-39-1; 1-905417-39-X

LC 2007-06854

Tiger is "growing up in the Indian forest. He spends his days playing with his sisters and learning to catch prey, becoming increasingly independent as he matures. Eventually he strikes out on his own. . . . Stojic's paint-

erly landscapes make Tiger's world soft, fuzzy, and inviting, with tigerish rust and complementary grass green prodominating." Bull Cent Child Books

Blackstone, Stella

My granny went to market; a round-the-world counting rhyme; written by Stella Blackstone; illustrated by Christopher Corr. Barefoot Books 2005 unp il $16.99

Grades: PreK K 1 2   E

1. Voyages and travels—Fiction 2. Grandmothers—Fiction 3. Counting 4. Stories in rhyme

ISBN 1-84148-792-9   LC 2004-17394

A child's grandmother travels around the world, buying things in quantities that illustrate counting from one to ten.

"The brightly colored gouache illustrations have the feel of Mexican folk art, and endpaper maps route Granny's travels, with a one-page legend showing her purchases—from one carpet to 10 llamas. A cheery, global shopping trip, fun to read alone and also useful in the classroom." Booklist

Octopus opposites; written by Stella Blackstone; illustrated by Stephanie Bauer. Barefoot Books 2010 unp il $16.99   E

1. Stories in rhyme 2. Opposites 3. Animals—Fiction

ISBN 978-1-84686-328-8; 1-84686-328-7

LC 2008051071

Creatures big and small introduce pairs of opposites.

"The text is accompanied by vivid, appealing acrylic drawings surrounded by textured borders, with backgrounds painted in thick strokes. An attractive, useful concept book." SLJ

Secret seahorse; written by Stella Blackstone; illustrated by Clare Beaton. Barefoot Books 2004 unp il $15.99; pa $7.99; bd bk $6.99

Grades: PreK K 1 2   E

1. Sea horses—Fiction 2. Coral reefs and islands—Fiction 3. Stories in rhyme

ISBN   1-84148-704-X;   1-84148-937-9   (pa); 1-905236-15-8 (bd bk)   LC 2003-19085

A sea horse leads the reader past coral reefs and underwater creatures to a sea horse family hidden in a cave. Includes notes on coral reefs and various marine animals

"The involving quest and appealing fabric collages make this rhyming hide-and-seek tale great for reading together or enjoying alone." Booklist

Blackwood, Gary L.

The just-so woman; story by Gary Blackwood; pictures by Jane Manning. HarperCollins Pubs. 2006 45p il (I can read book) $15.99; lib bdg $16.89

Grades: K 1 2   E

1. Farm life—Fiction

ISBN   978-0-06-057727-8;   0-06-057727-4; 978-0-06-057728-5 (lib bdg); 0-06-057728-2 (lib bdg)

LC 2005-28667

"An I can read book"

Blackwood, Gary L.—*Continued*

The Just-so Woman "has no butter for her morning bread, the stool is broken so she can't milk the cow, her cat licks the spoon she is using, and she is out of soap for washing. Since everything in her life must be 'just-so,' she ends up eating nothing until suppertime, when her neighbor, the AnyWay Man, convinces her to simply enjoy her bread without butter, dipped in tea." SLJ

Blake, Robert J.

Little devils. Philomel Books 2009 unp il $16.99

Grades: PreK K 1 2   E

1. Tasmanian devils—Fiction 2. Australia—Fiction

ISBN 978-0-399-24322-6; 0-399-24322-4

LC 2008048106

When their mother fails to return one night, three Tasmanian Devil cubs venture out of their den in search of food and, by doing what Tasmanian Devils are supposed to do, manage to save their mother from a trap.

"Blake loads his light-filled paintings with natural details and realistic expressions. . . . He makes the story heartwarming and accessible without anthropomorphizing the animals." SLJ

Togo. Philomel Bks. 2002 unp il $16.99 *

Grades: K 1 2 3   E

1. Dogs—Fiction 2. Alaska—Fiction

ISBN 0-399-23381-4   LC 2001-45926

In 1925, Togo, a Siberian husky who loves being a sled dog, leads a team that rushes to bring diphtheria antitoxin from Anchorage to Nome, Alaska

The author "paints a vivid word-picture of bitter, deadly conditions and the grueling effort required to surmount them, reinforcing it with dramatic art." Booklist

Blake, Stephanie

I don't want to go to school! written and illustrated by Stephanie Blake. Random House 2009 unp il $12.99; lib bdg $15.99

Grades: PreK K   E

1. Rabbits—Fiction 2. School stories

ISBN   978-0-375-85688-4;   0-375-85688-9; 978-0-375-95688-1 (lib bdg); 0-375-95688-3 (lib bdg)

LC 2008011256

Original French edition 2007

Simon the rabbit does not want to go to his first day of school, but by the time his mother comes to take him home, he is having such a good time that he does not want to leave

"This title has a standard premise that is instantly understandable and reassuring, and the naive-style art, rendered in bold outlines and primary colors, is appealing and expressive." Booklist

Blessing, Charlotte

New old shoes; written by Charlotte Blessing; illustrated by Gary R. Phillips. Pleasant St. Press 2009 unp il $16.95

Grades: K 1 2   E

1. Shoes—Fiction 2. Africa—Fiction

ISBN 978-0-9792035-6-5; 0-9792035-6-2

"This story is narrated by a pair of red sneakers and follows their journey from their first home with a young boy in America to children in Africa. . . . The color-saturated illustrations provide a vibrant background to this touching story." SLJ

Bley, Anette

And what comes after a thousand? Kane/Miller 2007 unp il $15.95

Grades: PreK K 1 2   E

1.   Death—Fiction   2.   Bereavement—Fiction 3. Friendship—Fiction

ISBN 978-1-933605-27-2

"This tender tale about intergenerational friendship, love, and loss tells of the cozy relationship between a young girl and an old, hard-of-hearing man. . . . After he dies, she must learn to deal with her pain and feelings of abandonment. The closeness of the characters is portrayed in heartwarming illustrations. . . . This universal story will speak to many readers." SLJ

Bloch, Serge

Butterflies in my stomach and other school hazards; by Serge Bloch. Sterling Pub. Co. 2008 unp il $12.95

Grades: PreK K 1 2   E

1. English language—Idioms—Fiction 2. School stories

ISBN 978-1-4027-4158-6; 1-4027-4158-8

LC 2007-43372

On the first day of school, a student is confused by many of the phrases that are used, such as when the librarian says not to open a can of worms, or when the teacher says he expects the class to be busy bees doing their homework.

"Bloch's simple though imaginative pictures and clean visual style invite discussion of the deeper meanings of these oft-used phrases, making this an ideal book for the classroom or for one-on-one sharing." SLJ

Blomgren, Jennifer, 1954-

Where do I sleep? a Pacific Northwest lullabye; illustrated by Andrea Gabriel. Sasquatch Bks. 2001 unp il $15.95

Grades: PreK K 12   E

1. Animals—Fiction 2. Sleep—Fiction 3. Pacific Northwest—Fiction 4. Stories in rhyme

ISBN 1-57061-258-7   LC 2001-20940

Rhyming text describes some of the young animals—from a gray wolf pup and a horned puffin to a cougar kit and a small brown bat—as they settle down to sleep

"Kids get an opportunity to practice map skills, learn about new animals, find out why Alaska's summer days are so long, and add such unfamiliar words as *tundra* to their vocabulary. . . . Gabriel's gorgeous artwork reflects the beauty and diversity of the wildlife and landscape." Booklist

Bloom, Suzanne, 1950-

A mighty fine time machine. Boyds Mills Press 2009 unp il $16.95

Grades: PreK K 1   E

1. Boxes—Fiction 2. Imagination—Fiction 3. Play—Fiction 4. Animals—Fiction

ISBN 978-1-59078-527-0; 1-59078-527-4

LC 2008-28043

An aardvark, an anteater, and an armadillo attempt to travel back in time when they turn a big box into a time machine.

"The colored pencil-and-gouache illustrations add warmth and humor to the story. Bloom's whimsical word choice will further draw children into the story and have them rooting for the friends' success." Booklist

A splendid friend, indeed; written and illustrated by Suzanne Bloom. Boyds Mills Press 2005 unp il $15.95 *

Grades: PreK K 1   E

1. Polar bear—Fiction 2. Geese—Fiction 3. Friendship—Fiction

ISBN 1-59078-286-0   LC 2004-10780

When a studious polar bear meets an inquisitive goose, they learn to be friends.

"The cool palette of the pastel illustrations, consisting of shades of blue and white and touches of violet, sets a quiet, friendly tone, and the animals' priceless expressions tell all. The gentle humor will elicit giggles." SLJ

Other titles about Bear and Goose are:

Treasure (2007)
What about Bear? (2010)

Blue, Rose

Ron's big mission; [by] Rose Blue and Corinne J. Naden; illustrated by Don Tate. Dutton Childrens Books 2009 unp il $16.99

Grades: K 1 2 3   E

1. McNair, Ronald E.—Fiction 2. Segregation—Fiction 3. Libraries—Fiction 4. Books and reading—Fiction 5. African Americans—Fiction 6. South Carolina—Fiction

ISBN 978-0-525-47849-2; 0-525-47849-3

LC 2007050563

One summer day in 1959, nine-year-old Ron McNair, who dreams of becoming a pilot, walks into the Lake City, South Carolina, public library and insists on checking out some books, despite the rule that only white people can have library cards. Includes facts about McNair, who grew up to be an astronaut

"Vibrant illustrations portray a cozy small town. . . . Tate's figures feature oversized heads with very expressive faces that vividly convey well-meant kindness and the frustrations of injustice. . . . This will make a good choice for reading aloud and discussing." Booklist

Bluemle, Elizabeth

Dogs on the bed; illustrated by Anne Wilsdorf. Candlewick Press 2008 unp il $15.99

Grades: PreK K 1 2   E

1. Dogs—Fiction 2. Bedtime—Fiction 3. Family life—Fiction

ISBN 978-0-7636-2608-2; 0-7636-2608-2

"As bedtime begins . . . everyone—Mom, Dad, two kids, and six dogs—falls asleep in the same big bed. Throughout the night, the pets do what they do best: sleep sideways, bark at things no one else can hear, and whine to go out, and then in. . . . The exuberant, rhyming text delights the ear as the hilarious illustrations engage the eye in this kid and dog-friendly tale." SLJ

How do you wokka-wokka? illustrated by Randy Cecil. Candlewick Press 2009 unp il $15.99 *

Grades: PreK K 1   E

1. Stories in rhyme 2. Dance—Fiction

ISBN 978-0-7636-3228-1; 0-7636-3228-7

LC 2008-27715

A young boy who likes to "wokka-wokka, shimmy-shake, and shocka-shocka" gathers his neighbors together for a surprise celebration.

"The sketchy, full-color oil illustrations in muted colors feature cartoon children cavorting alternately against stark white backgrounds or cityscapes as they join a giant block party. This bouncy book is a joy as a read-aloud." SLJ

Blume, Judy

The Pain and the Great One; illustrations by Irene Trivas. rev format ed. Atheneum Books for Young Readers 2002 c1984 unp il $17.95; pa $6.99 *

Grades: K 1 2 3   E

1. Siblings—Fiction

ISBN 0-689-85507-9; 0-440-40967-5 (pa)

First published 1984 by Bradbury Press

A six-year-old (The Pain) and his eight-year-old sister (The Great One) see each other as troublemakers and the best-loved in the family

"Young readers, depending on their position within the family, will readily identify with either character and may learn empathy for the other. Used in a group, this will provide much healthy discussion. . . . Trivas' vibrant colors add depth and humor to a valuable book on sibling relationships." SLJ

Bodeen, S. A., 1965-

Elizabeti's doll; illustrated by Christy Hale. Lee & Low Bks. 1998 unp il $15.95 *

Grades: K 1 2 3   E

1. Siblings—Fiction 2. Tanzania—Fiction

ISBN 1-880000-70-9   LC 98-13086

When a young Tanzanian girl gets a new baby brother, she finds a rock, which she names Eva, and makes it her baby doll

"Vibrant patterns and soft watercolor backgrounds evoke a sense of place and familial love." SLJ

Other titles about Elizabeti are:

Elizabeti's school (2002)
Mama Elizabeti (2000)

Bodeen, S. A., 1965-—*Continued*

A small, brown dog with a wet, pink nose; by Stephanie Stuve-Bodeen; [illustrations by Linzie Hunter] Little Brown Books for Young Readers 2009 unp il $16.99

Grades: K 1 2   E
   1. Dogs—Fiction 2. Parent-child relationship—Fiction
   ISBN 978-0-316-05830-8; 0-316-05830-0
                                              LC 2008039298
Amelia will stop at nothing to convince her parents to let her adopt a very special dog.
   "The concepts are complicated but clear, and Hunter's patterned illustrations are appropriately unpredictable, with nearly every page design different from the last. Plenty for kids to pore over." Booklist

Boelts, Maribeth, 1964-
Before you were mine; story by Maribeth Boelts; pictures by David Walker. Putnam 2007 unp il $15.99

Grades: PreK K 1 2   E
   1. Dogs—Fiction
   ISBN 978-0-399-24526-8; 0-399-24526-X
                                              LC 2006-20525
A young boy imagines what his rescued dog's life might have been like before he adopted him.
   "Cozy, soft-edged pictures of an adorable dog characterize this warmhearted book. . . . The pastel illustrations use a variety of layouts to infuse the story with emotion." Booklist

Dogerella; illustrated by Donald Wu. Random House 2008 48p il (Step into reading) lib bdg $11.99; pa $3.99

Grades: 1 2 3   E
   1. Fairy tales 2. Dogs—Fiction
   ISBN 978-0-375-93393-6 (lib bdg); 0-375-93393-X (lib bdg); 978-0-375-83393-9 (pa); 0-375-83393-5 (pa)
                                              LC 2007-15229
With the help of her fairy dogmother, Dogerella attends Princess Bea's ball where she competes with other dogs to become the princess's royal pet
   "The combination of dozens of dogs, an earnest princess and a touch of magic add up to a charming whole." Kirkus

Those shoes; [by] Maribeth Boelts; illustrated by Noah Z. Jones. Candlewick Press 2007 unp il $15.99; pa $6.99

Grades: K 1 2 3   E
   1. Shoes—Fiction 2. Grandmothers—Fiction
   ISBN   978-0-7636-2499-6;   0-7636-2499-3; 978-0-7636-4284-6 (pa); 0-7636-4284-3 (pa)
                                              LC 2006-51839
Jeremy, who longs to have the black high tops that everyone at school seems to have but his grandmother cannot afford, is excited when he sees them for sale in a thrift shop and decides to buy them even though they are the wrong size.
   "Jones mixed-media, digitally assembled pictures cleverly capture how thoroughly the shoe craze permeates every aspect of Jeremy's life. . . . Boelts and Jones create a work with broad appeal." Bull Cent Child Books

Bogan, Paulette, 1960-
Goodnight Lulu. Bloomsbury Children's Bk. 2003 unp il hardcover o.p. pa $6.95 *

Grades: PreK K 1 2   E
   1. Chickens—Fiction 2. Bedtime—Fiction
   ISBN 1-58234-803-0; 1-58234-983-5 (pa)
                                              LC 2002-27825
When her mother tucks her in for the night, Lulu the chicken worries what would happen if a bear or a tiger or an alligator should come in during the night
   This is a "funny, original, and reassuring tale. . . . The saturated watercolor and ink spreads deftly capture the night's ominous as well as cozy qualities." Horn Book Guide
   Another title about Lulu is:
Lulu the big little chick (2009)

Bogart, Jo Ellen
Big and small, room for all; illustrated by Gillian Newland. Tundra Books 2009 unp il $18.95

Grades: PreK K 1 2   E
   1. Size—Fiction
   ISBN 978-0-88776-891-0; 0-88776-891-1
   "A young girl sitting on a low tree branch views the vast mountains, sky, and fields around her. As the book progresses, realistic watercolor illustrations show the universe, the solar system, and a mountain range, as the spare text labels each concept in comparison to the size of the one before it. . . . Youngsters will delight in the awe-inspiring illustrations. . . . Word choice is highly suitable for the earliest independent readers." SLJ

Bond, Rebecca, 1971-
The great doughnut parade; written and illustrated by Rebecca Bond. Houghton Mifflin 2007 unp il $17

Grades: PreK K 1 2   E
   1. Parades—Fiction 2. Stories in rhyme
   ISBN 978-0-618-77705-1; 0-618-77705-9
                                              LC 2006026315
When Billy buys a doughnut and ties it to his belt with a string while walking down Main Street, he unwittingly sets off a chain of events that amazes and delights the entire town.
   "The poetic text reads well aloud . . . and the watercolor figures are fluid and dynamic." SLJ

Bonsall, Crosby Newell, 1921-1995
The case of the hungry stranger; by Crosby Bonsall. HarperCollins Pubs. 1992 64p il (I can read book) hardcover o.p. pa $3.99 *

Grades: K 1 2 3   E
   1. Mystery fiction
   ISBN 0-06-020571-7 (lib bdg); 0-06-444026-5 (pa)
                                              LC 91-13345
A reissue of the title first published 1963. This edition has full color illustrations
   Wizard and his friends are clueless when they are sent on the trail of a blueberry pie thief, until Wizard hits on a plan that is sure to nab the sweet-toothed pilferer
   This offers "suspense and humor." Horn Book
   Other titles in this series are:

Bonsall, Crosby Newell, 1921-1995—*Continued*
The case of the cat's meow (1965)
The case of the double cross (1980)
The case of the dumb bells (1966)
The case of the scaredy cats (1971)

The day I had to play with my sister; story and pictures by Crosby Bonsall. newly il ed. HarperCollins Pubs. 1999 32p il hardcover o.p. pa $3.99 *
Grades: K 1 2   E
  1. Siblings—Fiction
  ISBN 0-06-028181-2; 0-06-444253-5 (pa)
                                        LC 98-20342
"My first I can read book"
A newly illustrated edition of the title first published 1972
A young boy becomes very frustrated when he tries to teach his little sister to play hide-and-seek
"The extremely simple text . . . is one with which children can readily identify. . . . The realistic atmosphere makes Bonsall's book an excellent addition to the very early reading shelves." SLJ

Mine's the best. newly il ed. HarperCollins Pubs. 1996 32p il lib bdg $16.89; pa $3.99 *
Grades: K 1 2   E
  1. Friendship—Fiction 2. Balloons—Fiction
  ISBN 0-06-027091-8 (lib bdg); 0-06-444213-6 (pa)
                                        LC 95-12405
"My first I can read book"
A newly illustrated edition of the title first published 1973
Two little boys meet at the beach, each sure that his balloon is better
"The playful illustrations tell their own story; the extremely brief text (not to mention the head start provided by the two initial wordless spreads) will give new readers a sense of accomplishment." Horn Book Guide

Who's afraid of the dark? by Crosby Bonsall. Harper & Row 1980 32p il lib bdg $16.89; pa $3.99 *
Grades: K 1 2   E
  1. Night—Fiction 2. Fear—Fiction
  ISBN 0-06-020599-7 (lib bdg); 0-06-444071-0 (pa)
                                        LC 79-2700
"An Early I can read book"
"A little boy describes to a friend the nighttime fears of his dog Stella. Stella shivers in the dark, he claims; she sees shapes and hears scary sounds. The doubting but sympathetic friend offers a suggestion—hug Stella in the night and comfort her until her fears go away. . . . The illustrations in shades of light blue and brown are filled with as much life and warmth as ever." Horn Book

Bootman, Colin
Steel pan man of Harlem. Carolrhoda Books 2009 unp il lib bdg $16.95
Grades: K 1 2 3   E
  1. Rats—Fiction 2. Steel drum (Musical instrument)—Fiction 3. Harlem (New York, N.Y.)—Fiction
  ISBN 978-0-8225-9026-2 (lib bdg); 0-8225-9026-3 (lib bdg)
                                        LC 2008039654

A mysterious man appears in Harlem and promises to rid the city of its rats by playing the steel pan drum
Bootman "triumphs with this gorgeously moody, thoroughly cinematic retelling of the Pied Piper of Hamelin. . . . The oil paintings conjure up a gritty, workaday world where magic has taken hold." Publ Wkly

Borden, Louise, 1949-
The A+ custodian; illustrated by Adam Gustavson. Margaret K. McElderry Books 2004 unp il $15.95
Grades: K 1 2 3   E
  1. School stories 2. Janitors—Fiction
  ISBN 0-689-84995-8   LC 2002-12029
The students and teachers at Dublin Elementary School make banners, posters, and signs for their school custodian to show how much they appreciate him and all the work he does
"The simple, unrhymed poetic words and the realistic oil paintings create a strong sense of a diverse school community and a man in flannel shirt and worn leather shoes." Booklist

A. Lincoln and me; illustrated by Ted Lewin. Scholastic 1999 unp il pa $5.99 hardcover o.p.
Grades: K 1 2 3   E
  1. Lincoln, Abraham, 1809-1865—Fiction
  ISBN 0-590-45714-4 (pa)   LC 98-51921
With the help of his teacher, a young boy realizes that he not only shares his birthday and similar physical appearance with Abraham Lincoln, but that he is like him in other ways as well
"Borden's text flows nicely, creating imagery of the physical presence of the man. Lewin's distinctive watercolors lend style and substance to the book, producing a treat for the eyes." SLJ

Good luck, Mrs. K! written by Louise Borden; illustrated by Adam Gustavson. Margaret K. McElderry Bks. 1999 unp il hardcover o.p. pa $6.99
Grades: K 1 2 3   E
  1. Teachers—Fiction 2. Cancer—Fiction 3. School stories
  ISBN 0-689-82147-6; 0-689-85119-7 (pa)
                                        LC 97-50553
"Ann loves her third-grade teacher, who makes every child feel special and who introduces subjects with great zest. When Mrs. K. has cancer surgery the students are sad, but they (and their teacher) survive the year to return in the fall." Horn Book Guide
"A truly endearing story. Gustavson's watercolor illustrations exude all of the warmth and vibrancy of Borden's words." SLJ

The John Hancock Club; written by Louise Borden; illustrated by Adam Gustavson. Margaret K. McElderry Books 2007 unp il $16.99
Grades: 1 2 3   E
  1. Handwriting—Fiction 2. School stories
  ISBN 1-4169-1813-2   LC 2005033171
Third-grader Sean McFerrin wants to be part of the good penmanship club, but it all depends on how well he learns the new cursive writing

Borden, Louise, 1949-—*Continued*

"Gustavson's expressive paintings underscore the individuality of the characters and create a realistic school setting for the story. A fine picture book on a childhood rite of passage." Booklist

The little ships; the heroic rescue at Dunkirk in World War II; illustrated by Michael Foreman. Margaret K. McElderry Bks. 1997 unp il hardcover o.p. pa $6.99

Grades: K 1 2 3   E

1. Dunkerque (France), Battle of, 1940—Fiction
2. World War, 1939-1945—Fiction

ISBN 0-689-80827-5; 0-689-85396-3 (pa)

LC 95-52557

A young English girl and her father take their sturdy fishing boat and join the scores of other civilian vessels crossing the English Channel in a daring attempt to rescue Allied and British troops trapped by Nazi soldiers at Dunkirk

"Borden's descriptive style is potent, and Foreman's watercolors perfectly express the dulled and watery scenes of devastation, the exhausted and hopeful soldiers awaiting rescue." Horn Book Guide

Off to first grade; illustrated by Joan Rankin. Margaret K. McElderry Books 2008 unp il $16.99

Grades: PreK K 1   E

1. School stories

ISBN 978-0-689-87395-9; 0-689-87395-6

LC 2005-02320

Each member of a first grade class, as well as their teacher, principal, and a bus driver, expresses excitement, worry, or hope as the first day of school begins.

"The sequence is gentle yet genuinely perceptive in its documentation of the varying responses to the dramatic transition from home to school." Bull Cent Child Books

Boswell, Addie K.

The rain stomper. Marshall Cavendish 2008 unp il $16.99

Grades: PreK K 1 2   E

1. Rain—Fiction 2. Parades—Fiction

ISBN 978-0-7614-5393-2; 0-7614-5393-8

When it begins to rain and storm on the day of her big parade, Jazmin stomps, shouts, and does all she can think of to drive the rain away.

"Velasquez's large oils impart a sense of the girl's disappointment as well as the feel of a driving rain and eventual pleasure. Large letters in white, black, or red and in different sizes emphasize the sounds and rhythm of the rain and thunder. . . . A delightful read-aloud that deals with making the best of a disappointing situation." SLJ

Bottner, Barbara, 1943-

Bootsie Barker bites; illustrated by Peggy Rathmann. Putnam 1992 unp il $17.99; pa $5.99

Grades: K 1 2 3   E

1. Bullies—Fiction

ISBN 0-399-22125-5; 0-698-11427-2 (pa)

LC 91-12182

"When Bootsie comes to play, she casts herself as a dinosaur, and the intimidated narrator as a turtle or salamander to be eaten. The girl dreams that her enemy will go away on her own, but faced with a possible sleepover, she uses her wits to make Bootsie-the-dinosaur a thing of the past." Publisher's note

"Bottner's tone is a model of simplicity and matter-of-factness, sometimes droll but never coy. Rathmann's neon-bright, full-color artwork extends the emotional tenor and the humor of the text." Booklist

Another title about Bootsie is:
Bootsie Barker ballerina (1997)

Miss Brooks loves books (and I don't); story by Barbara Bottner; illustrations by Michael Emberley. Alfred A. Knopf 2010 unp il $17.99; lib bdg $20.99 *

Grades: PreK K 1 2   E

1. Books and reading—Fiction 2. Librarians—Fiction
3. School stories

ISBN 978-0-375-84682-3; 0-375-84682-4; 978-0-375-94682-0 (lib bdg); 0-375-94682-9 (lib bdg)

LC 2009-02305

A first-grade girl who does not like to read stubbornly resists her school librarian's efforts to convince her to love books until she finds one that might change her mind.

"Children will delight in Emberley's spirited watercolor and ink renderings of literary favorites. . . . Bottner's deadpan humor and delicious prose combine with Emberley's droll caricatures to create a story sure to please those who celebrate books—and one that may give pause to those who don't (or who work with the latter)." SLJ

Raymond and Nelda; written by Barbara Bottner; illustrated by Nancy Hayashi. Peachtree 2007 unp il $15.95

Grades: PreK K 1   E

1. Friendship—Fiction

ISBN 1-56145-394-3   LC 2006024277

Raymond and Nelda have always been the very best of friends, and when they have a falling out they are both so miserable that Florence, their mail carrier, helps them get past their pride and hurt feelings to make up

"In Hayashi's clear watercolor, pen, and colored-pencil illustrations, the plump, awkward characters wear clothes and act like children, their body language as expressive of their anger and longing as their words." Booklist

Bourguignon, Laurence

Heart in the pocket; by Laurence Bourguignon; illustrated by Valerie d'Heur. Eerdmans Books for Young Readers 2008 unp il $16.50

Grades: PreK K 1 2   E

1. Kangaroos—Fiction 2. Mother-child relationship—Fiction

ISBN 978-0-8028-5343-1; 0-8028-5343-9

LC 2007049348

A baby kangaroo is reluctant to leave the comfort of his mother's pocket, where he is safe and warm and can always hear her heartbeat, until he finds out that her heart is not actually in her pocket.

Bourguignon, Laurence—*Continued*

"The gentle, well-crafted text is sweet, but not overly so. The watercolor illustrations have a soft palette dominated by yellowish tans and light blues, and expressively portray a wise and loving mother with her shy, slightly fearful child." SLJ

Boutignon, Beatrice

Not all animals are blue; a big book of little differences. Kane/Miller 2009 unp il $15.95
Grades: PreK K 1 2   E
1. Animals
ISBN 978-1-933605-96-8; 1-933605-96-0

Boutignon "invites readers to examine five animals on one side of the spread, read five descriptive sentences on the other, and determine which sentence describes which animal. Working in pencil and watercolor, Boutignon confers on her creatures an elegance that they maintain even when they are wearing flippers or their umbrellas are being blown inside-out. . . . Children won't have any trouble matching words to pictures." Publ Wkly

Bowen, Anne, 1952-

The great math tattle battle; [by] Anne Bowen; illustrated by Jaime Zollars. A. Whitman 2006 unp il $15.95
Grades: 1 2 3   E
1. School stories 2. Mathematics—Fiction
ISBN 978-0-8075-3163-1; 0-8075-3163-4
LC 2005026192

Harley Harrison, the biggest tattletale and best math student in second grade, meets his match in both areas when Emma Jean Smith joins him Mr. Hall's class.

"The striking color cartoon art in soft pastel tones depicts children with expressive faces. The math is cleverly woven into the story and used effectively." SLJ

I know an old teacher; story by Anne Bowen; pictures by Stephen Gammell. Carolrhoda Books 2008 unp il lib bdg $16.95
Grades: K 1 2 3   E
1. Stories in rhyme 2. Teachers—Fiction 3. School stories 4. Pets—Fiction
ISBN 978-0-8225-7984-7; 0-8225-7984-7
LC 2007-42631

In this take on the well-known cumulative rhyme, a teacher inadvertently swallows a flea, then follows it with an assortment of classroom pets while her students look on in surprise.

"Bowen's rhymes will have kids rolling in the aisles between their desks, and Gammell's spiky mixed-media illustrations are fittingly absurd." Horn Book Guide

Boyle, Bob

Hugo and the really, really, really long string. Random House 2010 unp il $15.99; lib bdg $18.99
Grades: PreK K 1 2   E
1. Animals—Fiction 2. Stories in rhyme
ISBN   978-0-375-83423-3;   0-375-83423-0;
978-0-375-93423-0 (lib bdg); 0-375-93423-5 (lib bdg)
LC 2006016303

Hugo follows a mysterious red string through his town, collecting a series of new friends along the way, all of them knowing that something special must be at the end of the string.

"This is a great story that can lead to a discussion of friends and neighborhoods. Written in rhyme, it is an entertaining story. The geometric style used in the artwork will be familiar to students as Boyle is the author/illustrator who created the Nick Jr. television show, WOW! WOW! Wubbzy!" Libr Media Connect

Bradby, Marie

Momma, where are you from? illustrated by Chris K. Soentpiet. Orchard Bks. 2000 unp il $16.95 *
Grades: K 1 2 3   E
1. African Americans—Fiction 2. Mother-daughter relationship—Fiction
ISBN 0-531-30105-2   LC 99-23068

Momma describes the special people and surroundings of her childhood, in a place where the edge of town met the countryside, in a time when all the children at school were brown.

"Soentpiet's detailed, beautifully lit paintings freeze the mother's vivid memories, culminating in a dreamy, gray-toned montage of all the previous scenes. Children will be inspired by the mother's eloquent, proud answer to her daughter's essential question." Booklist

More than anything else; story by Marie Bradby; pictures by Chris K. Soentpiet. Orchard Bks. 1995 unp il $15.95 *
Grades: K 1 2 3   E
1. Washington, Booker T., 1856-1915—Fiction 2. African Americans—Fiction 3. Books and reading—Fiction
ISBN 0-531-09464-2   LC 94-48804

"A Richard Jackson book"

Nine-year-old Booker works with his father and brother at the saltworks, but dreams of the day when he'll be able to read.

"An evocative text combines with well-crafted, dramatic watercolors to provide a stirring, fictionalized account of the early life of Booker T. Washington." Horn Book

Bradley, Kimberly Brubaker

Ballerino Nate; illustrated by R.W. Alley. Dial Books for Young Readers 2006 unp il $16.99
Grades: PreK K 1 2   E
1. Ballet—Fiction 2. Sex role—Fiction
ISBN 0-8037-2954-5   LC 2004-17822

After seeing a ballet performance, Nate decides he wants to learn ballet but he has doubts when his brother Ben tells him that only girls can be ballerinas.

"Bradley writes smoothly and insightfully about Nate's experiences. . . . Alley's watercolor-and-pencil contributions, portraying an entirely canine universe, capture both the warm family dynamics and Nate's zooming, irrepressible energy. " Booklist

Bradley, Kimberly Brubaker—*Continued*

The perfect pony; [by] Kimberly Brubaker Bradley; pictures by Shelagh McNicholas. Dial Books for Young Readers/Penguin Group 2007 unp il $16.99

Grades: K 1 2　　　　　　　　　　　　E
1. Horses—Fiction
ISBN 0-8037-2851-4; 978-0-8037-2851-6
LC 2004024071

While searching for a sleek, fast, and spirited pony to own, a young girl comes to realize that the "perfect" pony is actually very different.

"McNicholas' realistic watercolor illustrations are completely in step with the understated text and the experience itself." Booklist

Bradman, Tony

Daddy's lullaby; illustrated by Jason Cockcroft. Margaret K. McElderry Bks. 2002 c2001 unp il $16.95 *

Grades: PreK K 1　　　　　　　　　　　E
1. Fathers—Fiction 2. Infants—Fiction
ISBN 0-689-84295-3　　　　　　LC 2001-31280
First published 2001 in the United Kingdom

A father takes his baby on a midnight stroll through the house, trying to get the baby to sleep

"This slice of life is simply told and depicted in softly rendered, realistic paintings across spreads that capture the quiet of a sleeping household and a father's tenderness." SLJ

Braeuner, Shellie

The great dog wash; illustrated by Robert Neubecker. Simon & Schuster Books for Young Readers 2009 unp il $15.99

Grades: PreK K 1　　　　　　　　　　　E
1. Dogs—Fiction 2. Cats—Fiction 3. Stories in rhyme
ISBN 978-1-4169-7116-0; 1-4169-7116-5

Rhyming text welcomes the reader to a dog wash that goes awry when someone brings their cat.

"Braeuner's sprightly, humorous rhymes are well paired with Neubecker's unfussy black-outlined digital illustrations." Horn Book Guide

Brallier, Jess M.

Tess's tree; pictures by Peter H. Reynolds. Harper 2009 unp il $16.99

Grades: PreK K 1　　　　　　　　　　　E
1. Trees—Fiction 2. Bereavement—Fiction
ISBN 978-0-06-168752-5; 0-06-168752-9
LC 2009014580

When nine-year-old Tess invites her friends, family, and neighbors to celebrate her beloved maple tree's life before it must be cut down, she learns that it has meant a lot to other people, as well.

"Reynolds's soft watercolor vignettes extend the quiet story. Wispy lines portray a subtle vulnerability; washes of muted blue effectively provide emotional depth as Tess survives grief's powerful storm." Kirkus

Brannen, Sarah S.

Uncle Bobby's wedding; [by] Sarah S. Brannen. G. P. Putnam's Sons 2008 32p il $15.99

Grades: PreK K 1 2　　　　　　　　　　E
1. Homosexuality—Fiction 2. Uncles—Fiction 3. Weddings—Fiction 4. Guinea pigs—Fiction
ISBN 978-0-399-24712-5; 0-399-24712-2
LC 2007-16550

Chloë the guinea pig is jealous and sad when her favorite uncle announces that he will be getting married, but as she gets to know Jamie better and becomes involved in planning the wedding, she discovers that she will always be special to Uncle Bobby—and to Uncle Jamie, too.

"Warmly affectionate watercolor and graphite illustrations accompany this genial story of same-sex marriage." Horn Book Guide

Braun, Sebastien

Back to bed, Ed! Peachtree Publishers 2010 unp il $15.95 *

Grades: PreK K 1　　　　　　　　　　　E
1. Bedtime—Fiction 2. Mice—Fiction 3. Sleep—Fiction 4. Parent-child relationship—Fiction
ISBN 978-1-56145-518-8; 1-56145-518-0
First published 2009 in the United Kingdom

Ed the mouse will not sleep in his own bed, until eventually his exasperated and tired parents find a way to keep him from joining them in the middle of the night.

"Braun's clean illustrations in India ink with markers and colored pencils are bright and bold. . . . They show all the emotions of the characters and many interesting details. . . . The simple text works in tandem with the illustrations to produce a great story that's fun to read." SLJ

Meeow and the big box. Boxer Books 2009 unp il lib bdg $12.95

Grades: PreK　　　　　　　　　　　　E
1. Cats—Fiction 2. Imagination—Fiction 3. Play—Fiction
ISBN 978-1-906250-86-7 (lib bdg); 1-906250-86-3 (lib bdg)

"Braun shows a wide-eyed black cat in a red scarf playing with a box. The omniscient narrator carries on a one-way dialogue, describing imaginative Meeow's actions and intentions as he transforms the box into a bright red fire engine. . . . The book is simple and direct, and pulls together all the ingredients (box, red paint, green scissors) in the same methodical way that toddlers hard at work would. Uncluttered pages and primary colors make this a highly attractive book, as does the tactile jacket that allows readers to stroke fuzzy Meeow." SLJ

Other titles about Meeow are:
Meeow and the little chairs (2009)
Meeow and the pots and pans (2010)

On our way home. Boxer 2009 unp il $14.95

Grades: PreK K　　　　　　　　　　　E
1. Father-child relationship—Fiction 2. Bears—Fiction
ISBN 978-1-906250-59-1; 1-906250-59-6

"Daddy Bear and Baby Bear walk through the forest, racing and resting and gazing at wonderful things on the

Braun, Sebastien—*Continued*

way: golden leaves falling from the trees, the big yellow sun going down, and beautiful stars twinkling overhead." Publisher's note

"With unadorned, heartfelt prose and idyllic images, Braun . . . conveys just how wonderful it feels to spend a day alone with Daddy. . . . Braun's acrylic pictures strike a lovely balance, as he places his genial, naïf-styled characters within majestically scaled landscapes." Publ Wkly

The ugly duckling. Boxer Books; distributed by Sterling 2010 il (A Story House book) lib bdg $16.95

Grades: PreK K   E

1. Andersen, Hans Christian, 1805-1875—Adaptations 2. Fairy tales 3. Ducks—Fiction 4. Swans—Fiction

ISBN 978-1-907152-04-7; 1-907152-04-0

A retelling of Hans Christian Andersen's tale of the ugly little duckling who grows up to become a beautiful swan.

"This text presents the highlights of the story in a straightforward fashion that perserves the formal feel of the original. . . . The expressive pictures, though rendered with ink and colored pencil, have the careful lines and bold edges that give them the feel of woodcuts. . . . The large format, combined with bright, bold illustrations and simplified language, makes this ideal for storytime sharing." SLJ

Braun, Trudi

My goose Betsy; illustrated by John Bendall-Brunello. Candlewick Press 1999 unp il hardcover o.p. pa $6.99

Grades: PreK K 1 2   E

1. Geese—Fiction

ISBN 0-7636-0449-6; 0-7636-1714-8 (pa)

LC 98-3456

Betsy the goose makes a cozy nest, lays her eggs, and tends to them until her little goslings are hatched. Includes a section with facts about geese

"Down-to-earth language, a minimum of detail, and an abundance of large yet cozy illustrations make this just right for the intended audience." Horn Book Guide

Breathed, Berke

Pete & Pickles; [by] Berkeley Breathed. Philomel Books 2008 unp il $17.99

Grades: 2 3 4   E

1. Friendship—Fiction 2. Pigs—Fiction 3. Elephants—Fiction

ISBN 978-0-399-25082-8; 0-399-25082-4

LC 2007-50044

When Pickles the elephant turns his life upside-down, Pete the pig comes to realize that a perfectly predictable, practical, and uncomplicated life is not always preferable.

"This heartwarming tale is packed with adventure, imagination, and the all-important message of accepting differences. The illustrations alternate from naturalistic renderings of fantastical scenarios to flat compositions reminiscent of traditional comic strips." SLJ

Breen, Steve

Stick; [by] Steve Breen. Dial Books For Young Readers 2007 unp il $16.99

Grades: PreK K 1 2 3   E

1. Frogs—Fiction 2. Dragonflies—Fiction

ISBN 978-0-8037-3124-0   LC 2006046318

An independent young frog goes on a wild adventure when he accidentally gets carried away by a dragonfly.

"Breen generates plenty of fun and suspense in the skillfully rendered, animated pictures." Booklist

Violet the pilot; [by] Steve Breen. Dial Books for Young Readers 2008 unp il $16.99

Grades: K 1 2 3   E

1. Air pilots—Fiction 2. Dogs—Fiction

ISBN 978-0-8037-3125-7   LC 2007022367

Young Violet's only friend is her dog, Orville, until one of her homemade flying machines takes her to the rescue of a Boy Scout troop in trouble.

"An engaging story of a spunky girl who follows her dreams. . . . Done in watercolors, acrylics, and Photoshop, the lively cartoon artwork evokes a nostalgic setting. Violet's various inventions are clever and amusing." SLJ

Brendler, Carol

Winnie Finn, worm farmer. Farrar Straus Giroux 2009 unp il $15.99

Grades: PreK K 1 2   E

1. Worms—Fiction

ISBN 978-0-374-38440-1; 0-374-38440-1

LC 2008004255

Winnie Finn raises earthworms, which help her neighbors win prizes at the county fair. Includes instructions on making a worm farm.

"Nimble lines and cool colors depict the energy of the active outdoor scenes. Humorous details abound through animated expressions. . . . Winnie's spunky, good-natured heart anchors a gentle and entertaining read." SLJ

Includes bibliographical references

Brennan-Nelson, Denise, 1960-

Willow; written by Denise Brennan Nelson and Rosemarie Brennan; illustrated by Cyd Moore. Sleeping Bear Press 2008 unp il $16.95

Grades: K 1 2 3   E

1. Art—Fiction 2. Painting—Fiction 3. Imagination—Fiction

ISBN 978-1-58536-342-1; 1-58536-342-1

LC 2007034588

In art class, neatness, conformity, and imitation are encouraged, but when Willow brings imagination and creativity to her projects, even straight-laced Miss Hawthorn is influenced

"Soft-toned watercolors contrast colorful, autumn trees with all-the-same green ones. . . . Expressive faces show wonderment and joy as teacher and students discover . . . the intese power of imagination." SLJ

Brenner, Barbara, 1925-

Good morning, garden; illustrated by Denise Ortakales. Northword Press 2004 unp il $15.95

Grades: K 1 2 3   E

1. Gardens—Fiction 2. Stories in rhyme

ISBN 1-55971-888-9

Upon entering a garden one morning, a child greets the flowers, plants, insects, and animals there.

"The alliterative tone and subtle rhyme scheme continue throughout this joyful celebration. . . . Ortakales works with sculpted paper to convey the depth and detail of a garden replete with luscious plants and friendly creatures." SLJ

Wagon wheels; story by Barbara Brenner; pictures by Don Bolognese. newly il ed. HarperCollins Pubs. 1993 64p il pa $3.99 hardcover o.p. *

Grades: K 1 2   E

1. Frontier and pioneer life—Fiction 2. African Americans—Fiction

ISBN 0-06-444052-4 (pa)   LC 92-18780

"An I can read book"

A newly illustrated edition of the title first published 1978

Shortly after the Civil War a black family travels to Kansas to take advantage of the free land offered through the Homestead Act

"The based-on-fact story . . . is as fascinating as ever. Beautifully narrated with sensitivity, compassion, and just the right amount of suspense, and featuring new full-color illustrations." Horn Book Guide

Brenner, Tom

And then comes Halloween; illustrated by Holly Meade. Candlewick Press 2009 unp il $16.99

Grades: PreK K 1 2   E

1. Halloween—Fiction 2. Autumn—Fiction

ISBN 978-0-7636-3659-3; 0-7636-3659-2

"When autumn arrives, a group of suburban children and their parents rake leaves, carve pumpkins, decorate yards and porches, and make Halloween costumes. The big day comes at last, and the children go trick-or-treating. . . . The descriptions beautifully evoke the feeling of fall. . . . The watercolor and collage art contributes to the autumnal mood, and the varied perspectives and page design make the story more dynamic. The text and illustrations are a perfect complement to one another." SLJ

Brett, Jan, 1949-

The Easter egg. G.P. Putnam's Sons 2010 unp il $17.99

Grades: PreK K   E

1. Eggs—Fiction 2. Easter—Fiction 3. Contests—Fiction 4. Rabbits—Fiction

ISBN 978-0-399-25238-9; 0-399-25238-X

LC 2009-08234

Hoppi the bunny wants to win the egg-decorating contest so the Easter Bunny will choose him to help distribute Easter eggs, but instead, while everyone else is working on their decorations, he finds himself guarding an egg that has fallen from a robin's nest.

"Brett's large watercolors include a few visual puns . . . and lots of woodland detail. . . . A satisfying, gentle tale whose text and images can be enjoyed multiple times over." Booklist

Gingerbread friends; [by] Jan Brett. G.P. Putnam's Sons 2008 unp il $17.99

Grades: PreK K 1 2   E

1. Friendship—Fiction 2. Cookies—Fiction

ISBN 978-0-399-25161-0; 0-399-25161-8

LC 2007042829

Lonely Gingerbread Baby, having set out to find a friend, enters a bakery where he tries to talk to different cookies and other figures, but winds up leading a crowd back to his house on a chase similar to the one in the familiar tale.

"Brett's highly detailed, luscious illustrations do a fine job telling this story for nonreaders, while readers and listeners will enjoy Gingerbread Baby's energy and enthusiasm." SLJ

The hat. Putnam 1997 unp il $16.95 *

Grades: PreK K 1 2   E

1. Hedgehogs—Fiction 2. Animals—Fiction 3. Clothing and dress—Fiction

ISBN 0-399-23101-3   LC 96-54015

When Lisa hangs her woolen clothes in the sun to air them out for winter, the hedgehog, to the amusement of the other animals, ends up wearing a stocking on his head

This story "has charm and humor. . . . The setting is the Danish countryside (detailed down to the moss on a tree) on a day when the first snow begins to fall, and Brett conveys the season with such loving spirit that children will almost wish for winter." Booklist

Honey . . . honey . . . lion! a story from Africa. G.P. Putnam's Sons 2005 unp il $16.99 *

Grades: PreK K 1 2   E

1. Badgers—Fiction 2. Honeyguides (Birds)—Fiction 3. Africa—Fiction

ISBN 0-399-24463-8   LC 2005-00449

After working together to obtain honey, the African honey badger always shares it with his partner, the honeyguide bird, until one day when the honey badger becomes greedy and his feathered friend decides to teach him a lesson.

"Brett has created another lush winner with beautifully detailed illustrations of the animals and a clear, fast-paced story." SLJ

On Noah's ark. Putnam 2003 unp il $16.99

Grades: K 1 2 3   E

1. Noah's ark—Fiction

ISBN 0-399-24028-4   LC 2003-1281

Noah's granddaughter helps him bring the animals onto the ark, calm them down, and get them to sleep

"The words are basic and effective; it's the detailed watercolors of the animals that are the real attraction here. In precise brushstrokes and vivid colors, Brett creates incredibly textured feathers and fur." Booklist

Breznak, Irene

Sneezy Louise; written by Irene Breznak; illustrated by Janet Pedersen. Random House 2009 unp il $15.99; lib bdg $18.99

Grades: PreK K 1   E

1. Sneezing—Fiction

ISBN   978-0-375-85169-8;   0-375-85169-0;
978-0-375-95169-5 (lib bdg); 0-375-95169-5 (lib bdg)
LC 2007026720

When Louise wakes up with itchy eyes, a wheezy throat, and a sneezy nose, she just knows it is not going to be a very good day

"Breezy watercolors with lots of free-flowing lines and action not only set the tone but also add energetic zest to this story." Booklist

Briant, Ed

Don't look now. Roaring Brook Press 2009 unp il $16.95

Grades: PreK K 1   E

1. Brothers—Fiction

ISBN 978-1-59643-345-8; 1-59643-345-0
LC 2008-49330

"A Neal Porter book"

"For two young brothers, playtime in the backyard quickly becomes rivalry time. . . . As the conflict rises, so do the boys, literally, and they sail skyward into a fantasy land. . . . Escape requires working together creatively. . . . The story's real and fantasy worlds come to life in vibrant illustrations, laid out in detailed panels and full-page pictures, peppered with occasional word and thought bubbles. Clever, fast paced, and entertaining." Booklist

If you lived here you'd be home by now. Roaring Brook Press 2009 unp il $17.99

Grades: PreK K 1 2   E

1. Stories without words 2. Leaves—Fiction
3. Animals—Fiction

ISBN 978-1-59643-420-2; 1-59643-420-1

"A Neal Porter Book"

In this "wordless tale, a nature-loving boy visits a city park to look for animals. When he jumps into a pile of leaves, he discovers an enormous, friendly creature made entirely of leaves, who takes the wide-eyed child to see a menagerie of woodland animals, as well as a crew felling trees for a new construction project. The story then fast forwards a few decades to a future filled with flying cars. The now adult boy's son finds a leaf that his father had long ago pressed inside a book, inspiring a trip to the same park, which is now a commercial strip. . . . Father and son travel to a patch of forest where they camp out overnight and encounter wildlife—including the elusive leaf creature." Publ Wkly

"Crisp colors and bold outlines make the illustrations sing, and tell the story without any words. The linear time line is easy to follow." SLJ

Bridges, Shirin Yim

Ruby's wish; illustrated by Sophie Blackall. Chronicle Bks. 2002 unp il $15.95 *

Grades: K 1 2 3   E

1. Sex role—Fiction 2. Education—Fiction 3. China—Fiction

ISBN 0-8118-3490-5   LC 2001-7406

In China, at a time when few girls are taught to read or write, Ruby dreams of going to the university with her brothers and male cousins

"This true story about Bridges' own grandmother has a gentle momentum. . . . Blackall's gouache illustrations have a quietly historical air, their palette subtly shaded with smoky inks and highlighted with touches of brilliant red." Bull Cent Child Books

The Umbrella Queen; illustrations by Taeeun Yoo. Greenwillow Books 2008 unp il $16.99; lib bdg $17.89

Grades: K 1 2 3   E

1. Umbrellas and parasols—Fiction 2. Painting—Fiction 3. Thailand—Fiction

ISBN   978-0-06-075040-4;   0-06-075040-5;
978-0-06-075041-1 (lib bdg); 0-06-075041-3 (lib bdg)
LC 2005-35730

In a village in Thailand where everyone makes umbrellas, young Noot dreams of painting the most beautiful one and leading the annual parade as Umbrella Queen, but her unconventional designs, depicting elephants instead of flowers and butterflies, displease her parents.

"Yoo's orange, green, and black colored linoleum prints wonderfully establish the tone for the story, which is related through gracefully told text." SLJ

Briggs, Raymond, 1934-

The snowman. Random House 1978 unp il $17; pa $6.99; bd bk $4.99 *

Grades: PreK K 1 2   E

1. Stories without words 2. Dreams—Fiction
3. Snow—Fiction

ISBN   0-394-83973-0;   0-394-88466-3   (pa);
0-375-81067-6 (bd bk)   LC 78-55904

A "wordless picture book about a small boy who expertly fashions a snowman and then dreams that his splendid creation comes alive. Affably greeting the child, the snowman enters the house and is introduced to the delights and dangers of gadgetry. . . . Finally, no longer earthbound, the two friends go soaring over city and countryside, magical in their snowy beauty." Horn Book

"The pastel-toned pencil-and-crayon pictures in their neat rectangular frames will hold the attention of primary 'readers.'" SLJ

Brisson, Pat

I remember Miss Perry; illustrated by Stéphane Jorisch. Dial Books for Young Readers 2006 unp il $16.99

Grades: K 1 2 3   E

1. School stories 2. Teachers—Fiction 3. Death—Fiction 4. Bereavement—Fiction

ISBN 0-8037-2981-2   LC 2004-24070

When his teacher, Miss Perry, is killed in a car accident, Stevie and his elementary school classmates take turns sharing memories of her, especially her fondest wish for each day.

"The delicate pen-and-ink, watercolor, and gouache illustrations reflect the varied emotions evoked by this treasured individual." SLJ

Brisson, Pat—*Continued*

Tap-dance fever; illustrated by Nancy Cote. Boyds Mills Press 2004 unp il $15.95

Grades: K 1 2 3   E

1. Tap dancing—Fiction

ISBN 1-59078-290-9   LC 2004-14575

Annabelle Applegate will not stop tap-dancing no matter what the frustrated citizens of Fiddlers Creek do to make her quit

"A deliciously tall tale with an appealing young heroine, the story of Annabelle's troubles and triumph reads aloud well. Just as amusing are Cote's fanciful watercolor-and-gouache paintings of a multicultural, rural community." Booklist

Broach, Elise, 1963-

Gumption! with pictures by Richard Egielski. Atheneum Books for Young Readers 2010 unp il $16.99

Grades: PreK K   E

1. Uncles—Fiction 2. Africa—Fiction 3. Jungles—Fiction 4. Animals—Fiction

ISBN 978-1-4169-1628-4; 1-4169-1628-8

       LC 2008-49048

"Peter is thrilled when his uncle Nigel invites him on an expedition in search of a rare African gorilla, but making it through the jungle involves lots of challenges. Nigel leads the way, surmounting each obstacle . . . but Egielski's ink-and-watercolor illustrations show a parallel story. As Nigel charges ahead, Peter is swept along by a succession of wild animals. . . . Egielski plays up the comedy with clever, small details, and Broach's repetitive text, with its occasionally vocabulary, is well suited for dramatic read-alouds." Booklist

When dinosaurs came with everything; written by Elise Broach; illustrated by David Small. Atheneum Books for Young Readers 2006 unp il $16.99

Grades: PreK K 1 2   E

1. Dinosaurs—Fiction 2. Mother-son relationship—Fiction

ISBN 978-0-689-86922-8; 0-689-86922-3

       LC 2005-11612

"A Junior Library Guild book."

Although his mother is a little worried, a young boy is delighted to discover that every shop in town is giving away real dinosaurs to their customers.

"Small's sketchy, tongue-in-cheek watercolor-and-ink artwork perfectly captures the boy's exuberance, the dinosaurs' mass, and the hubbub that a city full of these reptiles would create." SLJ

Brown, Jeff, 1926-2003

Flat Stanley; by Jeff Brown; illustrated by Scott Nash. HarperCollins Pubs. 2006 unp il $16.99 *

Grades: K 1 2 3   E

ISBN 978-0-06-112904-9; 0-06-112904-6

       LC 2006019547

"Based on the original *Flat Stanley* by Jeff Brown c1964"

A bulletin board falls on Stanley while he is sleeping, and he finds that being flat has its advantages

"Full-page, cartoon illustrations in watercolor and crayon enhance the story while remaining true to the original. This version of an old favorite will introduce a beloved character to a new generation of younger children." SLJ

Brown, Ken

The scarecrow's hat; written and illustrated by Ken Brown. Peachtree Pubs. 2001 unp il $15.95

Grades: PreK K 1 2   E

1. Chickens—Fiction 2. Scarecrows—Fiction

ISBN 1-56145-240-8   LC 00-46957

First published 2000 in the United Kingdom

Chicken thinks Scarecrow's hat will make a nice nest, but first she must swap with Badger, Crow, Sheep, Owl, and Donkey

"Realistic watercolors greatly enhance this plucky, humorous tale." Booklist

Brown, Lisa, 1972-

How to be. HarperCollins Pubs. 2006 unp il $15.99

Grades: PreK K 1   E

1. Animals—Fiction 2. Conduct of life—Fiction

ISBN 0-06-054635-2   LC 2005-15147

"A girl and a younger boy take turns imitating different animals, including a bear, a snake, and a dog. . . . The final chapter, How to be a PERSON, shows both children embodying all the positive characteristics of the critters with the animals shadowing their actions. . . . The spare text matches the black-and-white drawings, supplemented with well-placed smatterings of bright paint." SLJ

Brown, Marc Tolon

Arthur's nose; 25th aniversary limited edition; [by] Marc Brown. Little, Brown and Company 2001 unp il $15.95 *

Grades: PreK K 1 2   E

1. Nose—Fiction 2. Aardvark—Fiction

ISBN 0-316-11884-2   LC 00-106832

Books about Arthur are also available in other formats including board books, easy-to-read books, and chapter books

A reissue of the title first published 1976

Unhappy with his nose, Arthur the aardvark visits the rhinologist to get a new one. In this edition "Brown shows the evolution of his drawings of Arthur from 1976 to the present, along with a sidebar of 'Fun Facts,' . . . followed by a photo gallery of Brown's family with some pretty clear correlations between the author's relatives and Arthur's. Aspiring writers and artists also get a peek at the original manuscript and sketches for Arthur's Nose." Publ Wkly

Other titles about Arthur are:

Arthur babysits (1992)

Arthur goes to camp (1982)

Arthur, it's only rock 'n roll (2002)

Arthur meets the president (1991)

Arthur writes a story (1996)

Arthur's April Fool (1983)

Arthur's baby (1987)

Brown, Marc Tolon—*Continued*
Arthur's birthday (1989)
Arthur's chicken pox (1994)
Arthur's Christmas (1985)
Arthur's computer disaster (1997)
Arthur's eyes (1979)
Arthur's family vacation (1993)
Arthur's first sleepover (1994)
Arthur's Halloween (1982)
Arthur's new puppy (1993)
Arthur's perfect Christmas (2000)
Arthur's pet business (1990)
Arthur's teacher trouble (1986)
Arthur's Thanksgiving (1983)
Arthur's tooth (1985)
Arthur's TV trouble (1995)
Arthur's underwear (1999)
Arthur's valentine (1980)

D.W. all wet; [by] Marc Brown. Little, Brown 1988 unp il hardcover o.p. pa $5.95 *
Grades: PreK K 1 2   E
   1. Beaches—Fiction   2. Siblings—Fiction 3. Aardvark—Fiction
   ISBN 0-316-11268-2; 0-316-11077-9 (pa)
                                     LC 87-15752
"Joy Street books"
Arthur the Aardvark's little sister D.W. "announces 'I don't like the beach, and I don't like to get wet.' She asks to leave the minute she arrives, she won't play and she's afraid of getting sunburned. It's Arthur who helps change D.W.'s mind about the beach by unexpectedly tossing her into very shallow water." Publ Wkly
   "A simple, even predictable vignette, but entertaining nonetheless because of Brown's warm pictures." Booklist
 Other titles about D.W. are:
D.W. flips (1987)
D.W. go to your room! (1999)
D.W. rides again (1993)
D.W. the picky eater (1995)
D.W. thinks big (1993)
D.W.'s guide to perfect manners (2006)
D.W.'s guide to preschool (2003)
D.W.'s library card (2001)
D.W.'s lost blankie (1998)

Brown, Margaret Wise, 1910-1952
   Another important book; pictures by Chris Raschka. HarperCollins Pubs. 1999 unp il $15.99; lib bdg $16.89 *
Grades: PreK K 1   E
   1. Growth—Fiction 2. Counting 3. Stories in rhyme
   ISBN 0-06-026282-6; 0-06-026283-4 (lib bdg)
                                       LC 98-7212
"Joanna Cotler books"
Illustrations and simple rhyming text describe how a child grows from ages one through six
   "Raschka assigns each age group a geometric shape: a simple circle represents age one, pairs of stacked squares indicate two, a five-pointed star signifies five and so on. . . . It's a pleasure to hear the organic rhythms of Brown's prose . . . and Raschka paints in boisterous surprises." Publ Wkly

Big red barn; pictures by Felicia Bond. newly il ed. Harper & Row 1989 unp il $16.99; lib bdg $17.89; bd bk $7.99
Grades: PreK K 1 2   E
   1. Animals—Fiction 2. Farm life—Fiction 3. Stories in rhyme
   ISBN 0-06-020748-5; 0-06-020749-3 (lib bdg); 0-694-00624-6 (bd bk)   LC 85-45814
A newly illustrated edition of the title first published 1956
Rhymed text and illustrations introduce the many different animals that live in the big red barn
   "The large illustrations are somewhat stylized, but still have a strong sense of detail and reality. The bright colors will attract young readers. The short text on each page is superimposed on the picture, but always in a way that is easy to read. Children will enjoy studying each of the pages as the day progresses from early morning to night." SLJ

A child's good morning book; illustrated by Karen Katz. newly illustrated ed. HarperCollins 2009 unp il $17.99; lib bdg $18.89
Grades: PreK   E
   1. Morning—Fiction 2. Animals—Fiction
   ISBN 978-0-06-128864-7; 0-06-128864-0; 978-0-06-128861-6 (lib bdg); 0-06-128861-6 (lib bdg)
                                   LC 2008000786
A newly illustrated edition of the title first published 1952
As the sun rises, birds, horses, rabbits, flowers, bugs, and finally children get up to start their day.
   "Katz has reinterpreted the text in her warm and rounded style. . . . Brightly colored patterns and use of collage add interest to each page. This book has been popular over the years." SLJ

The fierce yellow pumpkin; story by Margaret Wise Brown; pictures by Richard Egielski. HarperCollins Pubs. 2003 unp il $15.99; lib bdg $16.89 *
Grades: PreK K 1   E
   1. Pumpkin—Fiction
   ISBN 0-06-024479-8; 0-06-024481-X (lib bdg)
                                     LC 2002-8338
A little pumpkin dreams of the day when he will be a big, fierce, yellow pumpkin who frightens away the field mice as the scarecrow does
   "Egielski's artwork features subtle shadings and interesting juxtapositions of colors. . . . The story rolls along smoothly with a clear plot line and some nice phrasing." Booklist

Goodnight moon; by Margaret Wise Brown; pictures by Clement Hurd. rev ed. HarperCollins Publishers 2005 c1947 unp il $17.99 *
Grades: PreK K   E
   1. Bedtime—Fiction 2. Rabbits—Fiction 3. Stories in rhyme
   ISBN 978-0-06-077585-8; 0-06-077585-8
                                   LC 2005281602
A reissue of the title first published 1947
A little bunny bids goodnight to all the objects in his room before falling asleep

Brown, Margaret Wise, 1910-1952—*Continued*

"Rhythmic, gently lulling words combined with warm and equally lulling pictures make this beloved classic an ideal bedtime book." Christ Sci Monit

The little island; with illustrations by Leonard Weisgard. Doubleday Bks. for Young Readers 2003 c1946 unp il $14.95
Grades: PreK K 1 2   E
1. Islands—Fiction
ISBN 0-385-74640-7
Awarded the Caldecott Medal, 1947
A reissue of the title first published 1946 under the pseudonym Golden MacDonald
There was a little island in the ocean and his book is about how the seasons and the storm and the day and night changed it, how the lobsters and seals and gulls and everything else lived on it, and what the kitten who came to visit found out about it

The little scarecrow boy; pictures by David Diaz. newly il ed. HarperCollins Pubs. 1998 unp il $15.99; lib bdg $16.89; pa $6.99
Grades: PreK K 1 2   E
1. Scarecrows—Fiction
ISBN 0-06-026284-2; 0-06-026290-7 (lib bdg); 0-06-77891-1 (pa)   LC 97-32558
"Joanna Cotler books"
Early one morning, a little scarecrow whose father warns him that he is not fierce enough to frighten a crow goes out into the cornfield alone
"Diaz provides wonderful illustrations for a story Brown wrote in the 1940s. . . . Brown's masterful use of repetition and rhythm creates a fine read-aloud story. The warm watercolor illustrations incorporate straw and patchwork." SLJ

The runaway bunny; pictures by Clement Hurd. HarperCollins Publishers 2005 c1942 unp il $16.99; lib bdg $17.89 *
Grades: PreK K   E
1. Rabbits—Fiction
ISBN 0-06-077582-3; 0-06-077583-1 (lib bdg)
A reissue, with some illustrations redrawn, of the title first published 1942
"Within a framework of mutual love, a bunny tells his mother how he will run away and she answers his challenge by indicating how she will catch him." SLJ
"The text has the simplicity of a folk tale and the illustrations are black and white or double page drawings in startling colour." Ont Libr Rev

Two little trains; pictures by Leo and Diane Dillon. HarperCollins Pubs. 2001 unp il $15.95; lib bdg $15.89; pa $6.99 *
Grades: PreK K 1 2   E
1. Railroads—Fiction
ISBN 0-06-028376-9; 0-06-028377-7 (lib bdg); 0-06-443568-7 (pa)   LC 00-40798
A newly illustrated edition of the title first published 1949 by Scott
Two little trains, one streamlined, the other old-fashioned, puff, puff, puff, and chug, chug, chug, on their way West

"The rhythms, the word sounds and the resonant echo of folk song set up a veritable hypnotic chant. . . . [The] soft-grained paintings . . . are beautifully composed in both form and color. A handsome reinterpretation." Booklist

Where have you been? pictures by Leo and Diane Dillon. HarperCollins 2004 unp il $15.99; lib bdg $16.89 *
Grades: PreK K 1   E
1. Animals—Fiction 2. Stories in rhyme
ISBN 0-06-028378-5; 0-06-028379-3 (lib bdg)   LC 2003-49981
A newly illustrated edition of the title first published 1952 by Crowell
In rhyming verse, various animals tell where they have been.
"Children fond of call-and-response will enjoy this humorous nursery rhyme. . . . The illustrations are as lively as they are charming, and have enough detail to keep children interested." SLJ

Brown, Monica, 1969-

Chavela and the Magic Bubble; illustrated by Magaly Morales. Clarion Books 2010 unp il $16
Grades: K 1 2 3   E
1. Chewing gum—Fiction 2. Magic—Fiction 3. Grandmothers—Fiction 4. Mexican Americans—Fiction
ISBN 978-0-547-24197-5; 0-547-24197-6   LC 2009015819
When Chavela blows a bubble with a strange new gum, she floats away to Mexico, where her great-grandfather once worked harvesting the tree sap that makes gum chewy.
"Kids will want to chew their own bubblegum as they listen to this exciting, magical journey, handsomely illustrated in brilliantly colored double-page spreads." Booklist

Brown, Peter, 1979-

Chowder; [by] Peter Brown. Little, Brown 2006 unp il $15.99
Grades: PreK K 1 2   E
1. Dogs—Fiction
ISBN 978-0-316-01180-8; 0-316-01180-0   LC 2005035616
Chowder the bulldog has never fit in with the other neighborhood canines, but he sees a chance to make friends with the animals at the local petting zoo
"The tongue-in-cheek humor melds delightfully with Brown's distinctive acrylic-and-pencil artwork." Booklist
Another title about Chowder is:
The fabulous bouncing Chowder (2007)

The curious garden. Little, Brown 2009 unp il $16.99 *
Grades: K 1 2 3   E
1. Gardens—Fiction 2. City and town life—Fiction
ISBN 978-0-316-01547-9; 0-316-01547-4   LC 2008-29165
Liam discovers a hidden garden and with careful tending spreads color throughout the gray city.

Brown, Peter, 1979——*Continued*

This "is a quiet but stirring fable of urban renewal, sure to capture imaginations. . . . In Brown's utopian vision, the urban and the pastoral mingle to joyfully harmonious effect." Publ Wkly

Brown, Ruth

A dark, dark tale; story and pictures by Ruth Brown. Dial Bks. for Young Readers 1981 unp il pa $6.99 hardcover o.p. *

Grades: PreK K 1 2   E

  1. Cats—Fiction

  ISBN 0-14-054621-9 (pa)

In a "style used by storytellers of ghostly tales, Brown begins 'Once upon a time there was a dark, dark moor' and goes on to describe the 'dark, dark wood' on the moor, the 'dark, dark house' in the wood and the stygian rooms in the huge place. A nimble black cat accompanies explorers of the mansion and leaps with them in gleeful terror when the final 'dark, dark thing' is discovered." Publ Wkly

"The book's mysterious power is engendered by the illustrations of weed-choked gardens and abandoned, echoing halls, of mullioned windows and blowing curtains." Time

The old tree. Candlewick Press 2007 unp il $16.99

Grades: PreK K 1 2   E

  1. Trees—Fiction 2. Animals—Fiction 3. Pop-up books

  ISBN 0-7636-3461-1

The animals who live in the Old Tree must band together when their home is threatened.

This is a "well-written story. . . . [illustrated with] beautiful acrylic-and-watercolor paintings . . . [and] a single, spectacular pop-up on the last spread." SLJ

Browne, Anthony

Little Beauty. Candlewick Press 2008 unp il $16.99

Grades: PreK K 1 2 3   E

  1. Gorillas—Fiction 2. Cats—Fiction 3. Sign language—Fiction 4. Zoos—Fiction

  ISBN 978-0-7636-3959-4; 0-7636-3959-1

                    LC 2007051887

When a gorilla who knows sign language tells his keepers that he is lonely, they bring him a small kitten and he names her Beauty

Browne "tells a picture-book story with exquisitely detailed art that blends magic and realism." Booklist

My brother; [by] Anthony Browne. Farrar, Straus & Giroux 2007 unp il $16 *

Grades: PreK K 1   E

  1. Brothers—Fiction

  ISBN 978-0-374-35120-5; 0-374-35120-1

                    LC 2006050262

"To the younger brother, the older one is coolness personified. . . . Browne . . . takes this universal theme of sibling idolatry and interprets it visually with economy and verve." Booklist

My dad. Farrar, Straus & Giroux 2001 c2000 unp il $16 *

Grades: PreK K 1 2   E

  1. Fathers—Fiction

  ISBN 0-374-35101-5   LC 00-37951

First published 2000 in the United Kingdom

A child describes the many wonderful things about "my dad," who can jump over the moon, swim like a fish, and be as warm as toast

"The offhand affection is genuinely moving as well as funny." Booklist

My mom. Farrar, Straus & Giroux 2005 unp il $16; pa $6.95 *

Grades: PreK K 1 2   E

  1. Mothers—Fiction

  ISBN 0-374-35098-1; 0-374-40026-1 (pa)

                    LC 2004-47173

A child describes the many wonderful things about "my mom," who can make anything grow, roar like a lion, and be as comfy as an armchair

"Browne's paintings hold attention, whether depicting images true to life or flights of fancy, and the honesty of the narrator's emotions and Mom's devotion shine through." Booklist

Piggybook. Knopf 1986 unp il pa $7.99 hardcover o.p.

Grades: PreK K 1 2   E

  1. Mothers—Fiction 2. Family life—Fiction

  ISBN 0-679-80837-X (pa)   LC 86-3008

When Mrs. Piggott unexpectedly leaves one day, her demanding family begins to realize just how much she did for them

"As in most of Browne's art, there is more than a touch of irony and visual humor here, bringing off the didactic with a light touch and turning the lesson into satire." Bull Cent Child Books

Silly Billy. Candlewick Press 2006 unp il $15.99

Grades: PreK K 1 2   E

  1. Worry—Fiction 2. Dolls—Fiction

  ISBN 0-7636-3124-8   LC 2005-55305

To help with his anxiety, Billy uses the worry dolls his grandmother recommends, but he finds that they do not quite solve his problem.

"The pictures are amazing. In counterpoint to the monochromatic worry scenes are pictures so vivid and colorful they ease concern and spread cheer with each turn of the page." Booklist

Voices in the park. DK Ink 1998 unp il pa $7.99 hardcover o.p. *

Grades: PreK K 1 2   E

  1. Gorillas—Fiction

  ISBN 978-0-7894-8191-7 (pa); 978-0-7894-2522-5

                    LC 97-48730

"A simple outing is described by two parents and two children, each with a different point of view and emotional outlook. Intriguing illustrations of the gorilla characters and surreal touches add layers of visual humor." SLJ

Browning, Diane

Signed, Abiah Rose; written and illustrated by Diane Browning. Tricycle Press 2010 il $15.99 *
Grades: 1 2 3   E

1. Artists—Fiction 2. Frontier and pioneer life—Fiction 3. Sex role—Fiction
ISBN 978-1-58246-311-7; 1-58246-311-5
LC 2009022172

In pioneer days, a young girl who is a talented artist is encouraged to paint portraits, Bible scenes, and other pictures, but told never to sign her work, either because it would be a sign of pride or because artists are expected to be men.

"In an engaging narrative, Abiah Rose tells of her experiences. . . . In Browning's pleasing colored-pencil-and-acrylic illustrations, the formal composition and decorative elements are reminiscent of folk art, while the softer, more natural depiction of the characters is all her own." Booklist

Broyles, Anne, 1953-

Priscilla and the hollyhocks; [by] Anne Broyles; illustrated by Anna Alter. Charlesbridge 2008 unp il $15.95
Grades: 2 3 4   E

1. African Americans—Fiction 2. Native Americans—Fiction 3. Slavery—Fiction
ISBN 978-1-57091-675-5   LC 2007002281

A young African American girl is sold away from her mother as a slave, and then later is sold to a Cherokee Indian, but eventually she is bought by a white man who not only sets her free, but adopts her into his family of fifteen children. Based on a true story; includes instructions for making a hollyhock doll.

"Told in descriptive language accompanied by engaging acrylic paintings, this fictionalized story about a real child . . . offers a unique perspective on slavery." SLJ

Bruchac, Joseph, 1942-

Crazy Horse's vision; illustrated by S.D. Nelson. Lee & Low Bks. 2000 unp il $16.95
Grades: K 1 2 3   E

1. Crazy Horse, Sioux Chief, ca. 1842-1877—Fiction 2. Oglala Indians—Fiction
ISBN 1-880000-94-6   LC 99-47451

A story based on the life of the dedicated young Lakota boy who grew up to be one of the bravest defenders of his people.

"Bruchac has created a memorable tale about Crazy Horse's childhood. . . . In beautiful illustrations inspired by the ledger book style of the Plains Indians, Sioux artist Nelson fills the pages with both action and quiet drama." Booklist

My father is taller than a tree; illustrated by Wendy Halperin. Dial Books for Young Readers 2010 unp il $16.99
Grades: PreK K 1   E

1. Stories in rhyme 2. Father-son relationship—Fiction
ISBN 978-0-803-73173-8; 0-803-73173-6
LC 2009-3608

Describes, in rhyming text and illustrations, the many different ways fathers and sons interact with one another.

"Short, simple rhymes are highlighted by Halperin's wonderfully expressive, soft yet colorful crayon and pencil drawings. . . . A charming celebration of fathers, dads, pops, papas, and pas." SLJ

Bruel, Nick

Bad Kitty. Roaring Brook 2005 unp il $15.95 *
Grades: 2 3 4   E

1. Cats—Fiction 2. Alphabet
ISBN 1-59643-069-9; 978-1-59643-069-3
LC 2004-24456

"A Neal Porter book"

"After Kitty discovers that the only food in the house consists of 26 kinds of vegetables (asparagus, beets, cauliflower and on through zucchini), her mood turns blacker than her scraggly fur coat. She unleashes her own alphabet of woe that will have youngsters howling with laughter. . . . Even readers who've mastered their ABCs will laugh at Bruel's gleefully composed litanies and the can-you-top-this spirit that animates every page." Publ Wkly

Other titles about Bad Kitty are:
Bad Kitty gets a bath (2008)
Happy birthday, Bad Kitty (2009)

Boing! Roaring Brook Press 2004 unp il $15.95; lib bdg $22.90
Grades: PreK K 1   E

1. Kangaroos—Fiction
ISBN 0-7613-2428-3; 0-7613-3412-2 (lib bdg)
LC 2003-18135

A mother kangaroo and various woodland animals coach her joey as she attempts her first jump.

"Told mainly through bright, cheerful pictures that are enhanced by bits of dialogue and pertinent sound effects, this simple story will make children smile." SLJ

Little red bird; by Nick Bruel. Roaring Brook Press 2008 unp il $16.95
Grades: PreK K 1 2   E

1. Birds—Fiction 2. Stories in rhyme
ISBN 978-1-59643-339-7; 1-59643-339-6
LC 2007-13198

"A Neal Porter book"

After escaping from her cage to see the world, a little red bird finds it difficult to decide whether to stay free or to go home and never fly again.

"The rhyming narrative, . . . is appealingly bouncy and will draw children through the small hero's exciting peregrinations until the final page, which hints at a satisfying conclusion while leaving room to wonder." Booklist

Bruel, Robert O.

Bob and Otto; pictures by Nick Bruel. Roaring Brook Press 2007 unp il $15.95
Grades: PreK K 1 2   E

1. Worms—Fiction 2. Caterpillars—Fiction 3. Friendship—Fiction 4. Butterflies—Fiction
ISBN 978-1-59643-203-1; 1-59643-203-9
LC 2006012008

"A Neal Porter book"

Bruel, Robert O.—*Continued*

Otto the worm is shocked to discover that his best friend Bob is actually a caterpillar who emerges one day as a butterfly.

"Along with the engaging story, the science in the illustrations and text is quite accurate; there are rich, not-to-be missed visual details." Horn Book

Bruins, David

The legend of Ninja Cowboy Bear; illustrated by Hilary Leuny. Kids Can Press 2009 unp il $16.95

Grades: PreK K 1 2   E

1. Ninja—Fiction 2. Cowhands—Fiction 3. Bears—Fiction

ISBN 978-1-55453-486-9; 1-55453-486-0

The ninja, the cowboy and the bear do everything together. But when a contest among themselves leads to resentment, they soon learn that the only way to stop disagreeing is to be considerate of their differences and appreciate one another.

"Readers can take the story a step further with the Ninja Cowboy Bear Game, which is strongly reminiscent of Rock Paper Scissors. The digital-cartoon illustrations are set in comic panels; the art and the occasional Japanese word bubble give the story an anime feel. A fun purchase with a solid message." SLJ

Brun-Cosme, Nadine

Big Wolf & Little Wolf; illustrated by Olivier Tallec. Enchanted Lion Books 2009 unp il $16.95 *

Grades: PreK K 1   E

1. Wolves—Fiction 2. Loneliness—Fiction

ISBN 978-1-5927-0084-4; 1-5927-0084-5

LC 2008054040

ALA ALSC Batchelder Award Honor Book (2010)

Big Wolf has always lived alone at the top of a hill under a tree, so when a little wolf suddenly arrives one day, he does not know what to think.

"Tallec's colorful illustrations play off the quiet dignity of the text, revealing emotion through the characters' stances and expressions, employing a sketchy painting style that brims with light." SLJ

No, I want daddy! illustrated by Michel Backès. Clarion Books 2004 unp il $14

Grades: PreK K 1   E

1. Mother-daughter relationship—Fiction 2. Foxes—Fiction

ISBN 0-618-38157-0   LC 2003-1165

Anna the fox is unhappy when her tired mother says no to all of her after-school plans but after an evening of letting only Daddy do things for her, Anna cannot go to sleep until she and Mama make up

"Simple sentences tell this universal story and make it ring true. The illustrations feature thick black lines and an earthy palette of tans, greens, and a foxlike reddish brown." SLJ

Brunhoff, Jean de, 1899-1937

The story of Babar, the little elephant; translated from the French by Merle S. Haas. Random House 1937 c1933 47p il $15.95; lib bdg $17.99 *

Grades: PreK K 1 2   E

1. Elephants—Fiction

ISBN 0-394-80575-5; 0-394-90575-X (lib bdg)

Additional titles about Babar by Laurent de Brunhoff are available

Original French edition, 1931; this is a reduced format version of the 1933 United States edition

"Babar runs away from the jungle and goes to live with an old lady in Paris, where he adapts quickly to French amenities. Later he returns to the jungle and becomes king. Much of the charm of the story is contributed by the author's gay pictures." Hodges. Books for Elem Sch Libr

Other titles about Babar are:

Babar and Father Christmas (1940)

Babar and his children (1938)

Babar the king (1935)

Bonjour, Babar (2000)

Travels of Babar (1934)

Bruss, Deborah

Book! book! book! illustrated by Tiphanie Beeke. Levine Bks. 2001 unp il $15.95

Grades: PreK K 1   E

1. Domestic animals—Fiction 2. Libraries—Fiction 3. Books and reading—Fiction

ISBN 0-439-13525-7   LC 99-59758

When the children go back to school, the animals on the farm are bored, so they go into the library in town trying to find something to do

"Soft, naive watercolor paintings illustrate the satisfying story, which, with its witty conclusion, will be a sure winner at story time." Horn Book Guide

Bryant, Jennifer

Abe's fish; a boyhood tale of Abraham Lincoln; by Jen Bryant; illustrated by Amy June Bates. Sterling 2009 unp il $15.95

Grades: PreK K 1 2   E

1. Presidents—United States—Fiction

ISBN 978-1-4027-6252-9; 1-4027-6252-6

LC 2008028597

Young Abe Lincoln learns the meaning of selflessness and freedom when he encounters a soldier on a country road and gives up his prized possession: a fish he caught for the family's evening meal. Includes author's note on the early life of the sixteenth president.

"Bates's lively watercolors have rich detail, depicting Abe as a boy in a coonskin hat, still too small to lift his father's ax. The full-spread, sepia-toned paintings capture his rustic lifestyle, the Kentucky landscape, and the reactions of Abe's family to his generosity." SLJ

Includes bibliographical references

Buckley, Helen E. (Helen Elizabeth), 1918-

Grandfather and I; [illustrated by] Jan Ormerod. Lothrop, Lee & Shepard Bks. 1994 unp il hardcover o.p. pa $6.99

Grades: PreK K 1 2   **E**

    1. Grandfathers—Fiction

ISBN 0-688-12533-6; 0-688-17526-0 (pa)

                          LC 93-22936

A newly illustrated edition of the title first published 1959

A child considers how Grandfather is the perfect person to spend time with because he is never in a hurry

"Ormerod's full-color paintings teem with the warmth of a loving intergenerational family and fairly burst from the pages." SLJ

Grandmother and I; [illustrated by] Jan Ormerod. Lothrop, Lee & Shepard Bks. 1994 unp il hardcover o.p. lib bdg $15.89; pa $7.99

Grades: PreK K 1 2   **E**

    1. Grandmothers—Fiction

ISBN 0-688-12531-X; 0-688-12532-8 (lib bdg);
0-688-17525-2 (pa)   LC 93-22937

A newly illustrated edition of the title first published 1961

A child considers how Grandmother's lap is just right for those times when lightning is coming in the window or the cat is missing

"The watercolor art, done mostly in earth tones, varies from soft to sassy, but most of all, it is honest. Any child who has shared the unconditional love of a grandparent will see that love reflected here." Booklist

Buehner, Caralyn

Fanny's dream; pictures by Mark Buehner. Dial Bks. for Young Readers 1996 unp il $16.99; pa $6.99

Grades: K 1 2 3   **E**

    1. Marriage—Fiction 2. Farm life—Fiction

ISBN 0-8037-1496-3; 0-14-250060-7 (pa)

                          LC 94-31910

Fanny Agnes is a sturdy farm girl who dreams of marrying a prince, but when her fairy godmother doesn't show up, she decides on a local farmer instead

"Fanny Agnes is a delight: a feminist with a wry sense of humor, she balances her dreams with common sense and a loving heart. What's more, there's plenty for youngsters to enjoy in the robust, bucolic pictures, which seem almost to jump off the page." Booklist

I did it, I'm sorry; pictures by Mark Buehner. Dial Bks. for Young Readers 1998 unp il hardcover o.p. pa $6.99

Grades: PreK K 1 2   **E**

    1. Animals—Fiction

ISBN 0-8037-2010-6; 0-14-056722-4 (pa)

                          LC 97-10216

Ollie Octopus, Bucky Beaver, Howie Hogg, and other animal characters encounter moral dilemmas involving such virtues as honesty, thoughtfulness, and trustworthiness. The reader is invited to select the appropriate behavior from a series of choices, and the letter for the correct answer is hidden in the pictures

The artist has "concealed bumblebees, cats, rabbits

and dinosaurs, among other things, in each of his lush and expressive oil-and-acrylic paintings. . . . Caralyn Buehner's snappy, alliterative text makes for an exuberant read-aloud." Publ Wkly

Snowmen at night; pictures by Mark Buehner. Phyllis Fogelman Bks. 2002 unp il $15.99 *

Grades: PreK K 1 2   **E**

    1. Snow—Fiction 2. Stories in rhyme

ISBN 0-8037-2550-7   LC 2001-33517

Snowmen play games at night when no one is watching

The "text has bouncy rhymes, but it's the artwork that is spectacular. Acrylic-over-oil paintings feature fat, happy snowpeople who practically jump—or sled—off the pages." Booklist

Another title about the snowmen is:
Snowmen at Christmas (2005)

Superdog; the heart of a hero; illustrated by Mark Buehner. HarperCollins 2004 unp il $15.99; lib bdg $16.89 *

Grades: PreK K 1 2   **E**

    1. Dogs—Fiction

ISBN 0-06-623620-7; 0-06-623621-5 (lib bdg)

                         LC 2002-3540

Tired of being overlooked because he is so small, a big-hearted dog named Dexter transforms himself into a superhero

"Solid shapings, surprising perspectives, and thick paints in dynamic colors combine for artwork that practically jumps off the page. There's plenty of wit, too." Booklist

Buell, Janet, 1945-

Sail away, Little Boat; by Janet Buell; illustrations by Jui Ishida. Carolrhoda Books 2006 unp il lib bdg $16.95

Grades: PreK K 1 2   **E**

    1. Boats and boating—Fiction 2. Toys—Fiction
3. Stories in rhyme

ISBN 978-1-57505-821-4 (lib bdg); 1-57505-821-9 (lib bdg)   LC 2005015003

A toy sailboat encounters a variety of animals as it journeys down a brook, to the river, and finally to the ocean

"Ishida's brilliantly colored spreads, done in mixed media, cast a swirling, whirling spell of balanced design. . . . Delightful sounds, rich language, imagery, and buoyant verse characterize the writing." SLJ

Buhler, Cynthia von

But who will bell the cats? Houghton Mifflin Books for Children 2009 unp il $16

Grades: K 1 2   **E**

    1. Mice—Fiction 2. Bats—Fiction 3. Cats—Fiction
4. Princesses—Fiction

ISBN 978-0-618-99718-3; 0-618-99718-0

                        LC 2008050165

While a princess spoils her eight cats, a mouse and his friend, a brown bat, live on scraps in the castle cellar, but Mouse decides to place bells on the cats necks so that he and Brown Bat might live comfortably, as well.

Buhler, Cynthia von—*Continued*
Includes the Aesop fable on which the story is based.
"Dark, complicated mixed-media illustrations bring a humorously creepy feel to the tale." Horn Book

Bulla, Clyde Robert, 1914-2007
The chalk box kid; illustrated by Thomas B. Allen. Random House 1987 unp il hardcover o.p. pa $3.99 *
Grades: K 1 2 3   E
   ISBN 0-394-99102-8; 0-394-89102-3 (pa)
                              LC 87-4683
"Gregory's family moves to a smaller house in a poorer part of town; the father has lost his factory job. There is no yard at the new house in which to play, but Gregory explores a nearly burnt-out building that formerly was a chalk factory. Gregory finds plenty of chalk in the debris as he cleans up, and the artist in him soars." Publ Wkly
"Bulla manages a poignant depth within the confines of simple style and narrative. Understated and easy to read, this nevertheless tackles problems that are not easy to solve without exercising the imagination." Bull Cent Child Books

Daniel's duck; pictures by Joan Sandin. Harper & Row 1979 60p il hardcover o.p. pa $3.99
Grades: K 1 2   E
   1. Wood carving—Fiction
   ISBN 0-06-020909-7 (lib bdg); 0-06-444031-1 (pa)
                             LC 77-25647
"An I can read book"
Daniel "carved a duck with its head looking backward. At the fair, people laughed when they saw the carving, and Daniel thought his work was being ridiculed: but he was more than consoled by a famous local wood-carver, who not only praised Daniel's duck but offered to buy it. The easy-to-read story and the simple format are excellently served by the subdued three-color illustrations, which round out the account of a traditional Appalachian family." Horn Book

Bunting, Eve, 1928-
Baby can; [by] Eve Bunting; illustrated by Maxie Chambliss. Boyds Mills Press 2007 unp il $15.95
Grades: PreK   E
   1. Infants—Fiction 2. Brothers—Fiction 3. Growth—Fiction
   ISBN 978-1-59078-322-1   LC 2006011485
Every time his family gets excited over something Baby James can do, big brother Brendan demonstrates that he can do even better, from burping to rolling over to walking
"The watercolor illustrations match the light touch of the spare text." Booklist

The Banshee; illustrated by Emily Arnold McCully. Clarion Books 2009 unp il $16
Grades: K 1 2 3   E
   1. Superstition—Fiction 2. Fear—Fiction 3. Family life—Fiction 4. Ireland—Fiction
   ISBN 978-0-618-82162-4; 0-618-82162-7
                          LC 2008-14581

When Terry wakes up in the middle of the night to horrible screeching, he thinks the Banshee has come to pay his family a visit.
"This picture book creates a convincing story of bravery in the face of vividly imagined danger. Not a word is wasted in the first-person text, and the ink-and-watercolor illustrations show Terry's emotions with clarity and sensitivity." Booklist

The bones of Fred McFee; illustrated by Kurt Cyrus. Harcourt 2002 unp il hardcover o.p. pa $6 *
Grades: K 1 2 3   E
   1. Halloween—Fiction 2. Stories in rhyme
   ISBN 0-15-202004-7; 0-15-205423-5 (pa)
                           LC 2001-2414
A toy skeleton at Halloween provides menace and mystery
"The story, told in rhyme keeps readers on the edge of their seats. . . . Cyrus's detailed, realistic illustrations, done in scratchboard and watercolor, are appropriately dark and are a perfect complement to the subtly scary mood of the text." SLJ

Butterfly house; illustrated by Greg Shed. Scholastic Press 1999 unp il $17.99
Grades: K 1 2 3   E
   1. Butterflies—Fiction 2. Grandfathers—Fiction 3. Stories in rhyme
   ISBN 0-590-84884-4   LC 98-16349
With the help of her grandfather, a little girl makes a house for a larva and watches it develop before setting it free, and every summer after that butterflies come to visit her
"Shed's gouache-on-canvas paintings evoke feelings of warmth and nostalgia suited to the quiet story. Earth tones predominate, especially the browns and oranges found in this species. Appended with directions for raising a butterfly." Booklist

Cheyenne again; illustrated by Irving Toddy. Clarion Bks. 1995 unp il $16; pa $5.95
Grades: K 1 2 3   E
   1. Cheyenne Indians—Fiction 2. School stories
   ISBN 0-395-70364-6; 0-618-19465-7 (pa)
                         LC 94-43287
Young Bull, "a young Cheyenne boy tells how he's taken from his parents on the reservation in the late 1880s and sent to a boarding school, where he's forced to learn white ways. . . . This is a picture book for older readers, a grim story of painful separation and forced assimilation. . . . The short, spare lines of free verse are illustrated by double-page-spread oil and acrylic paintings that contrast the open landscape with the stiffness of figures forced into uniform and regimentation." Booklist

Christmas cricket; illustrated by Timothy Bush. Clarion Bks. 2002 32p il $15
Grades: K 1 2 3   E
   1. Crickets—Fiction 2. Christmas—Fiction
   ISBN 0-618-06554-7   LC 2001-55266
On Christmas Eve, a little cricket finds its way into a house where its singing is thought to be the voice of an angel
"Bush's watercolor pictures celebrate the story's

Bunting, Eve, 1928-—*Continued*
cheerful warmth while their varying sizes and shapes
create a cinematic effect that cleverly captures both the
rhythm of the text and a cricket's kinetic spirit." Booklist

Dandelions; illustrated by Greg Shed. Harcourt
Brace & Co. 1995 unp hardcover o.p. pa $7
Grades: K 1 2 3   E
1. Frontier and pioneer life—Fiction 2. Family life—
Fiction 3. Nebraska—Fiction
ISBN 0-15-200050-X; 0-15-202407-7 (pa)
                            LC 94-27104
"Like the dandelions she plants on the roof of their
Nebraska soddie, Zoe believes that the transplanting of
her family will 'take,' despite the difficult transition.
Young Zoe's narration conveys both youthful confidence
and fear as the family work to adjust to their new life.
Gouache illustrations effectively portray the vast, sun-
drenched prairie and complement the text." Horn Book
Guide

Flower garden; written by Eve Bunting;
illustrated by Kathryn Hewitt. Harcourt Brace &
Co. 1994 unp il $16; pa $7; bd bk $10.95 *
Grades: K 1 2 3   E
1. Flowers—Fiction 2. Birthdays—Fiction 3. Stories in
rhyme
ISBN   0-15-228776-0;   0-15-202372-0   (pa);
0-15-206516-4 (bd bk)   LC 92-25766
"The young narrator has, with the help of her father,
assembled a 'garden in a shopping cart' to take home
and plant in a window box high above the city as a
birthday gift for her mother." Horn Book Guide
"The simple rhymed verse, which skips along in pace
with the child's anticipation, is smoothly integrated with
the vibrant, lifelike paintings." Booklist

Fly away home; illustrated by Ronald Himler.
Clarion Bks. 1991 32p il $16; pa $6.99 *
Grades: K 1 2 3   E
1. Homeless persons—Fiction 2. Airports—Fiction
ISBN 0-395-55962-6; 0-395-66415-2 (pa)
                            LC 90-42353
A homeless boy who lives in an airport with his father, moving from terminal to terminal and trying not to
be noticed, is given hope when he sees a trapped bird
find its freedom
"Himler's quiet paintings echo the economy and the
touching quality of the story, which is all the more effective in depicting the plight of the homeless because it is
so low-keyed." Bull Cent Child Books

Girls A to Z; illustrated by Suzanne Bloom.
Boyds Mills Press 2002 unp il $15.95
Grades: PreK K 1 2   E
1. Occupations 2. Alphabet
ISBN 1-56397-147-X
Girls with names ranging from Aliki to Zoe imagine
themselves in various fun and creative professions
"Bunting has created a winning alphabet book that is
playful, inventive, and (coincidentally) politically correct.
Accompanied by Bloom's exuberant watercolor por-
traits." SLJ

How many days to America? a Thanksgiving
story; illustrated by Beth Peck. Clarion Bks. 1988
unp il lib bdg $16; pa $5.95 *
Grades: K 1 2 3   E
1. Refugees—Fiction 2. Thanksgiving Day—Fiction
ISBN 0-89919-521-0 (lib bdg); 0-395-54777-6 (pa)
                            LC 88-2590
Refugees from an unnamed Caribbean island embark
on a dangerous boat trip to America where they have a
special reason to celebrate Thanksgiving
"Bunting's simple tale focuses on the hardships of the
journey and on the American ideals of freedom and safety. She wisely leaves aside the issues of politics in the
homeland or in this country. Her prose is poetically
spare. . . . Peck's richly colored crayon drawings yield
added enjoyment. . . . A poignant story and a thought-
provoking discussion starter." SLJ

Hurry! hurry! illustrated by Jeff Mack. Harcourt
2007 unp il $16
Grades: PreK K 1   E
1. Domestic animals—Fiction 2. Eggs—Fiction
3. Chickens—Fiction
ISBN 978-0-15-205410-6; 0-15-205410-3
                           LC 2005021120
All the animals of the barnyard community hurry to
greet their newest member, who is just pecking his way
out of an egg
"The sweet story is filled with movement and excitement. . . . Acrylic spreads are bright and cheerful." SLJ

Jin Woo; illustrated by Chris K. Soentpiet.
Clarion Bks. 2001 30p il $16
Grades: K 1 2 3   E
1. Adoption—Fiction 2. Brothers—Fiction 3. Korean
Americans—Fiction
ISBN 0-395-93872-4   LC 00-38408
Davey is dubious about having a new adopted brother
from Korea, but when he finds out that his parents still
love him, he decides that having a baby brother will be
fine
"Soentpiet's watercolors are suffused with light and
perfectly capture the characters' expressions. . . . The
story's emotional veracity will speak to any new sibling." SLJ

Little Bear's little boat; illustrated by Nancy
Carpenter. Clarion Bks. 2003 32p il $12
Grades: PreK K 1 2   E
1. Growth—Fiction 2. Bears—Fiction
ISBN 0-395-97462-3   LC 2001-37233
When Little Bear can no longer fit into his boat he
finds someone else who can use it
"This is a sensitive, affecting story about growing up
and leaving favorite things behind, with charming ink-
and-paint illustrations that echo the spare clarity of the
words." Booklist

The memory string; pictures by Ted Rand.
Clarion Bks. 2000 32p il $15
Grades: K 1 2 3   E
1. Memory—Fiction 2. Stepmothers—Fiction
ISBN 0-395-86146-2   LC 99-42771
While still grieving for her mother and unable to ac-
cept her stepmother, Laura clings to the memories repre-

Bunting, Eve, 1928-—*Continued*

sented by forty-three buttons on a string

"Rand's realistic artwork concentrates on the faces of the family and the emotions that cross them. Some children will find this touches them very deeply." Booklist

Mouse island; [by] Eve Bunting; illustrated by Dominic Catalano. Boyds Mills Press 2008 unp il $15.95

Grades: PreK K 1 2   E

    1. Cats—Fiction 2. Islands—Fiction 3. Mice—Fiction

    ISBN 978-1-59078-447-1; 1-59078-447-2

                             LC 2007-17558

Mouse enjoys living on his island but feels that something is missing from his life until the day he performs a daring rescue and acquires an unlikely friend.

"Illustrations in grays, greens, and blues, sometimes stormy, sometimes placid, provide the backdrop for this tale of camaraderie." Horn Book Guide

My robot; by Eve Bunting; illustrated by Dagmar Fehlau. Harcourt, Inc. 2006 unp il $12.95; pa $3.95

Grades: K 1 2   E

    1. Robots—Fiction

    ISBN 0-15-205593-2; 0-15-205617-3 (pa)

                             LC 2005006936

"Green light readers"

Cecil the robot is good at playing tag, leading the school band, and performing tricks with the dog, but there is one important thing he does best of all.

"Fehlau's bright, stylized illustrations have a festive feel and infuse the fantastical situations with lighthearted fun." Booklist

My special day at Third Street School; illustrated by Suzanne Bloom. Boyds Mills Press 2004 unp il $15.95; pa $9.95

Grades: K 1 2 3   E

    1. Authors—Fiction 2. School stories

    ISBN 1-59078-745-5; 1-59078-745-5 (pa)

A school visit from children's book author Amanda Drake brings a day full of fun.

"Just as Bunting's writing captures the action and the children's emotions in a convincing way, Bloom's gouache, colored pencil, and crayon artwork illustrates the contemporary classroom setting and the children's body language to perfection." Booklist

One candle; illustrated by K. Wendy Popp. HarperCollins Pubs. 2002 unp il hardcover o.p. pa $6.99

Grades: K 1 2 3   E

    1. Hanukkah—Fiction 2. Holocaust, 1933-1945—Fiction 3. Jews—Fiction

    ISBN 0-06-028115-4; 0-06-028116-2 (lib bdg); 0-06-008560-6 (pa)   LC 2001-47205

"Joanna Cotler books"

Every year a family celebrates Hanukkah by retelling the story of how Grandma and her sister managed to mark the day while in a German concentration camp

"Popp invests her art with all the emotion of Bunting's heartfelt text. . . . A gentle but forthright opening for discussion about the Holocaust." Booklist

One green apple; illustrated by Ted Lewin. Clarion Books 2006 unp il $16 *

Grades: K 1 2 3   E

    1. Immigrants—Fiction 2. Apples—Fiction 3. Muslims—Fiction 4. School stories

    ISBN 0-618-43477-1   LC 2005011378

While on a school field trip to an orchard to make cider, a young immigrant named Farah gains self-confidence when the green apple she picks perfectly complements the other students' red apples

"Young readers will respond as much to Bunting's fine first-person narrative as to Lewin's double-page, photorealistic watercolors." Booklist

Our library; by Eve Bunting; illustrated by Maggie Smith. Clarion Books 2008 32p il $16

Grades: K 1 2   E

    1. Libraries—Fiction 2. Books and reading—Fiction 3. Raccoons—Fiction 4. Animals—Fiction

    ISBN 978-0-618-49458-3; 0-618-49458-8

                             LC 2006009519

A raccoon and his friends go to great lengths to make sure they will always have a library from which to borrow books.

"Bunting's style has a graceful simplicity, descriptive enough to be evocative without overwhelming. . . . Smith's watercolor and acrylic illustrations are charming and should have most children longing to enter the buttercup-yellow library with the grass-green door. An excellent vehicle for discussing the importance of libraries, books, reading, and teamwork." SLJ

A picnic in October; illustrated by Nancy Carpenter. Harcourt Brace & Co. 1999 unp il $16; pa $6

Grades: K 1 2 3   E

    1. Statue of Liberty (New York, N.Y.)—Fiction 2. Immigrants—Fiction 3. Italian Americans—Fiction

    ISBN 0-15-201656-2; 0-15-205065-5 (pa)

                             LC 98-20044

A boy finally comes to understand why his grandmother insists that the family come to Ellis Island each year to celebrate Lady Liberty's birthday

"The talented Bunting makes this into a real story with characters that ring true. Carpenter's art, vibrant with sea and sky blues, has the same realistic feel." Booklist

Pop's bridge; written by Eve Bunting; illustrated by C. F. Payne. Harcourt, Inc. 2006 unp il $17 *

Grades: 1 2 3 4   E

    1. Golden Gate Bridge (San Francisco, Calif.)—Fiction 2. Fathers—Fiction 3. San Francisco (Calif.)—Fiction

    ISBN 0-15-204773-5   LC 2004-23774

Robert and his friend Charlie are proud of their fathers, who are working on the construction of San Francisco's Golden Gate Bridge.

"Distinguished by its lovely, understated text and Payne's lavish and affectionate mixed-media pictures, this picture book does a quietly successful job of humanizing one of the most important feats of civil engineering in American history." Booklist

Bunting, Eve, 1928-—*Continued*

Secret place; illustrated by Ted Rand. Clarion Bks. 1996 26p il $16

Grades: K 1 2 3   E

1. City and town life—Fiction 2. Nature—Fiction

ISBN 0-395-64367-8   LC 95-20466

"A little boy learns that the city, with all its grime and smoke and noise, can also be home for wildlife, when he discovers a 'secret place' in a river flowing between concrete walls. . . . Bunting's prose is evocative . . . and Rand's paintings vividly convey both the grayness of the city and the colors of the graceful wild creatures." Booklist

Smoky night; written by Eve Bunting; illustrated by David Diaz. Harcourt Brace & Co. 1994 unp il $17; pa $7 *

Grades: K 1 2 3   E

1. Riots—Fiction 2. Los Angeles (Calif.)—Fiction 3. African Americans—Fiction 4. Korean Americans—Fiction

ISBN 0-15-269954-6; 0-15-201884-0 (pa)

                                   LC 93-14885

Awarded the Caldecott Medal, 1995

When the Los Angeles riots break out in the streets of their neighborhood, Daniel and his mother, African Americans, make friends with Mrs. Kim, a Korean grocer from across the street

"Thick black lines border vibrant acrylic paintings. . . . Diaz places these dynamic paintings on collages of real objects that, for the most part, reinforce the narrative action. . . . Both author and illustrator insist on a headlong confrontation with the issue of rapport between different races, and the result is a memorable, thought-provoking book." Horn Book

So far from the sea; illustrated by Chris K. Soentpiet. Clarion Bks. 1998 30p il $16; pa $7.99

Grades: K 1 2 3   E

1. Japanese Americans—Evacuation and relocation, 1942-1945—Fiction

ISBN 0-395-72095-8; 0-547-23752-9 (pa)

                                   LC 97-28176

When seven-year-old Laura and her family visit Grandfather's grave at the Manzanar War Relocation Center, the Japanese American child leaves behind a special symbol

"Soentpiet's impressionistic watercolors perfectly complement Bunting's evocative text." SLJ

Someday a tree; illustrated by Ronald Himler. Clarion Bks. 1993 unp il hardcover o.p. pa $6.95

Grades: K 1 2 3   E

1. Trees—Fiction 2. Pollution—Fiction

ISBN 0-395-61309-4; 0-395-76478-5 (pa)

                                   LC 92-24074

Alice, her parents, and their neighbors try to save an old oak tree that has been poisoned by pollution

"Himler's soft, realistic watercolors spread over double pages and complement the sensitive, poetic mood of the story." SLJ

That's what leprechauns do; illustrated by Emily Arnold McCully. Clarion Books 2005 32p il $16

Grades: K 1 2 3   E

1. Leprechauns—Fiction 2. Ireland—Fiction

ISBN 0-618-35410-7

When leprechauns Ari, Boo, and Col need to place the pot of gold at the end of the rainbow, they cannot help getting into mischief along the way.

"McCully graces this lighthearted story with her characteristically expressive and charming watercolors that eloquently capture the verdant beauty of the Irish countryside and the irrepressible personalities." SLJ

Walking to school; by Eve Bunting; illustrated by Michael Dooling. Clarion Books 2008 32p il $16

Grades: 2 3 4   E

1. Prejudices—Fiction 2. Belfast (Northern Ireland)—Fiction

ISBN 978-0-618-26144-4; 0-618-26144-3

"Walking to school can be hard if you live in Belfast, Northern Ireland. It's downright dangerous if you're a Catholic, like Allison, and the shortest route to your school goes through a Protestant neighborhood." Publisher's note

"The book does an excellent job of presenting the situation from a child's perspective without demonizing either side. . . . Dooling's oil-on-canvas illustrations are realistic enough to resemble stills from documentary footage." SLJ

The Wall; illustrated by Ronald Himler. Clarion Bks. 1990 unp il $16; pa $5.95 *

Grades: K 1 2 3   E

1. Vietnam Veterans Memorial (Washington, D.C.)—Fiction

ISBN 0-395-51588-2; 0-395-62977-2 (pa)

                                   LC 89-17429

"A father and his young son come to the Vietnam Veterans Memorial to find the name of the grandfather the boy never knew. This moving account is beautifully told from a young child's point of view; the watercolors capture the impressive mass of the wall of names as well as the poignant reactions of the people who visit there." Horn Book Guide

The Wednesday surprise; illustrated by Donald Carrick. Clarion Bks. 1989 unp il lib bdg $16; pa $5.95

Grades: K 1 2 3   E

1. Grandmothers—Fiction 2. Reading—Fiction

ISBN 0-89919-721-3 (lib bdg); 0-395-54776-8 (pa)

                                   LC 88-12117

This "first-person account tells of the special gift that seven-year-old Anna and her grandmother have planned for her dad's birthday: secretly, the two read books together until finally, the grandmother has learned to read." SLJ

"Bunting's writing is simple and warm and direct. . . . Carrick's pictures echo the warmth, especially in the faces of the family, painted in realistically detailed watercolors with a careful attention to familial resemblance. A gentle charmer." Bull Cent Child Books

Bunting, Eve, 1928-—*Continued*

You were loved before you were born; [by] Eve Bunting & [illustrated by] Karen Barbour. Blue Sky Press 2008 unp il $16.99

Grades: PreK   E

1. Love—Fiction 2. Family life—Fiction

ISBN 978-0-439-04061-7; 0-439-04061-2

LC 2007-9703

A mother shares with her child all the ways in which family members and friends were loving and welcoming before the child was even born

"A marvelous integration of color, image and verbal rhythm sure to delight and to become a must-purchase for newborns and their parents." Kirkus

Burell, Sarah

Diamond Jim Dandy and the sheriff; illustrated by Bryan Langdo. Sterling Pub. 2010 unp il $14.95

Grades: K 1 2   E

1. Rattlesnakes—Fiction 2. Infants—Fiction 3. West (U.S.)—Fiction

ISBN 978-1-4027-5737-2; 1-4027-5737-9

LC 2008013767

When a friendly and talented rattlesnake slithers into Dustpan, Texas, he must prove his value to the residents of the town before the sheriff will allow him to stay.

"This charming tale has bright, appealing, kid-friendly illustrations. The lively dialogue combined with the satisfying ending will serve as an excellent storytime read-aloud." SLJ

Burgess, Mark

Where teddy bears come from; written by Mark Burgess; illustrated by Russell Ayto. Peachtree 2009 unp il $16.95

Grades: PreK K 1 2   E

1. Wolves—Fiction 2. Teddy bears—Fiction

ISBN 978-1-56145-487-7; 1-56145-487-7

LC 2008052705

When Little Wolf cannot fall asleep, he decides that he needs a teddy bear and goes into the woods to see if he can find out where to get one.

"This charming story plays with the conventions of familiar nursery tales. . . . With its lively, bold watercolors filled with humorous details, this tale is likely to be a storytime hit." SLJ

Burleigh, Robert, 1936-

Clang-clang! Beep-beep! listen to the city; illustrated by Beppe Giacobbe. Simon & Schuster Books for Young Readers 2009 unp il $14.99

Grades: PreK K 1   E

1. Stories in rhyme 2. Noise—Fiction 3. Sound—Fiction 4. City and town life—Fiction

ISBN 978-1-4169-4052-4; 1-4169-4052-9

LC 2007-45844

"A Paula Wiseman book"

From morning until night, a city is filled with such sounds as the roars and snores of a subway ride, the flutters and coos of pigeons, and the shouts and beeps of drivers in traffic

"The rhymes that accompany the story are short but evocative. . . . The artist uses a vivid mix of primary and secondary colors to set the stage." SLJ

Good-bye, Sheepie; illustrated by Peter Catalanotto. Marshall Cavendish 2010 unp il $16.99

Grades: K 1 2   E

1. Death—Fiction 2. Dogs—Fiction 3. Father-son relationship—Fiction

ISBN 978-0-7614-5598-1; 0-7614-5598-1

LC 2009-5955

A father teaches his young son about death and remembrance as he buries their beloved dog.

"Catalanotto's gentle watercolor-and-gouache paintings give off a yellow glow suggestive of warm sunshine on an autumn day, and are well suited to Burleigh's quiet text." Booklist

Home run; the story of Babe Ruth; illustrated by Mike Wimmer. Harcourt Brace & Co. 1998 unp il hardcover o.p. pa $7 *

Grades: K 1 2 3   E

1. Ruth, Babe, 1895-1948—Fiction 2. Baseball—Fiction

ISBN 0-15-200970-1; 0-15-204599-6 (pa)

LC 95-10038

"A Silver Whistle book"

A poetic account of the legendary Babe Ruth as he prepares to make a home run

"With a flowing minimal text, Burleigh brings the Babe to life through the moment of one at bat. . . . Wimmer's sprawling, photorealistic oil paintings depict the larger-than-life figure and his surroundings with folksy Norman Rockwell-like charm." SLJ

Burningham, John, 1936-

Edwardo; the horriblest boy in the whole wide world. Alfred A. Knopf 2006 unp il $16.99; lib bdg $19.99

Grades: PreK K 1 2 3   E

ISBN 978-0-375-84053-1; 0-375-84053-2; 978-0-375-94053-8 (lib bdg); 0-375-94053-7 (lib bdg)

LC 2006-03681

Each time he does something a little bit bad, Edwardo is told that he is very bad and soon his behavior is awful, but when he accidentally does good things and is complimented, he becomes much, much nicer.

"Fans of Burningham will delight in his witty, winsome pictures, so full of animation and expression." SLJ

It's a secret. Candlewick Press 2009 unp il $16.99 *

Grades: PreK K 1   E

1. Cats—Fiction 2. Night—Fiction

ISBN 978-0-7636-4275-4; 0-7636-4275-4

"Marie Elaine wonders what her cat, Malcolm, does at night that causes him to sleep all day. When she goes down to the kitchen late one night and finds him all dressed up to go out, she asks to come along. . . . He takes her and her neighbor Norman to a secret cat party on the rooftops, where they dance, feast, and meet the queen of the cats. Burningham's signature sketchy mixed-media illustrations are a good fit for the dreamlike story, as is the off-kilter logic of the text." SLJ

Burningham, John, 1936-—*Continued*

John Patrick Norman McHennessy; the boy who was always late. Alfred A. Knopf 2008 unp il $16.99

Grades: PreK K 1 2   E
 1. School stories 2. Teachers—Fiction 3. Truthfulness and falsehood—Fiction
 ISBN 978-0-375-85220-6; 0-375-85220-4
 First published 1987 by Crown Publishers

A teacher regrets his decison to disbelieve a student's outlandish excuses for being tardy.
 "Burningham uses mixed media here to create boldly-colored illustrations which do a marvelous job of reinforcing the text. The storyline is a simple one, but it is filled with irony." SLJ

Mr. Gumpy's outing. Holt & Co. 1971 c1970 unp il $17.95; pa $7.99; bd bk $6.95 *

Grades: PreK K 1 2   E
 1. Animals—Fiction
 ISBN 0-8050-0708-3; 0-8050-1315-6 (pa);
0-8050-6629-2 (bd bk)
 First published 1970 in the United Kingdom

"Mr. Gumpy is about to go off for a boat ride and is asked by two children, a rabbit, a cat, a dog, and other animals if they may come. To each Mr. Gumpy says yes, if—if the children don't squabble, if the rabbit won't hop, if the cat won't chase the rabbit or the dog tease the cat, and so on. Of course each does exactly what Mr. Gumpy forbade, the boat tips over, and they all slog home for tea in friendly fashion." Sutherland. The Best in Child Books
 Another title about Mr. Gumpy is:
Mr. Gumpy's motor car (1976)

Burton, Virginia Lee, 1909-1968

Katy and the big snow; story and pictures by Virginia Lee Burton. Houghton Mifflin 1943 32p il $16; pa $6.95

Grades: PreK K 1   E
 1. Tractors—Fiction 2. Snow—Fiction
 ISBN 0-395-18155-0; 0-395-18562-9 (pa)

"Katy was a beautiful red crawler tractor. In summer she wore a bulldozer to push dirt with. In winter she wore a snowplow. She was big and strong and the harder the job the better she liked it. When the Big Snow covered the city of Geoppolis like a thick blanket, Katy cleared the city from North to South and East to West." Ont Libr Rev

The little house; story and pictures by Virginia Lee Burton. Houghton Mifflin 1942 40p il $14.95; pa $5.95 *

Grades: PreK K 1   E
 1. Houses—Fiction 2. City and town life—Fiction
 ISBN 0-395-18156-9; 0-395-25938-X (pa)
 Awarded the Caldecott Medal, 1943

"The little house was very happy as she sat on the quiet hillside watching the changing seasons. As the years passed, however, tall buildings grew up around her, and the noise of city traffic disturbed her. She became sad and lonely until one day someone who understood her need for twinkling stars overhead and dancing apple blossoms moved her back to just the right little hill." Child Books Too Good to Miss

Mike Mulligan and his steam shovel; story and pictures by Virginia Lee Burton. Houghton Mifflin 1939 unp il $16; pa $6.95 *

Grades: PreK K 1   E
 1. Steam-shovels—Fiction
 ISBN 0-395-16961-5; 0-395-25939-8 (pa)

"Mike Mulligan remains faithful to his steam shovel, Mary Anne, against the threat of the new gas and Diesel-engine contraptions and digs his way to a surprising and happy ending." New Yorker
 "One of the most convincing personifications of a machine ever written. Lively pictures, dramatic action, and a satisfying conclusion." Adventuring with Books. 2d edition

Butler, Dori Hillestad

My grandpa had a stroke; written by Dori Hillestad Butler; illustrated by Nicole Wong. Magination Press 2007 31p il $14.95; pa $8.95

Grades: K 1 2   E
 1. Stroke—Fiction 2. Grandfathers—Fiction
3. Fishing—Fiction
 ISBN 978-1-59147-806-5; 1-59147-806-5;
978-1-59147-807-2 (pa); 1-59147-807-3 (pa)
         LC 2006034528

"Ryan loves spending Saturdays fishing with his grandfather. But when Grandpa suffers a stroke, everything changes. . . . The book, illustrated in soft-edged watercolors, ends on a hopeful note. . . . With quiet prose, this covers most of the emotional and practical hurdles faced by both patient and child." Booklist

Butler, John, 1952-

Bedtime in the jungle; [written and illustrated by John Butler] Peachtree 2009 unp il $16.95

Grades: PreK K   E
 1. Stories in rhyme 2. Bedtime—Fiction 3. Animals—Fiction 4. Counting
 ISBN 978-1-56145-486-0; 1-56145-486-9
         LC 2008040592

As dusk falls in the jungle, animal babies and their parents prepare for bedtime
 "What distinguishes this title is its stunning illustrations. . . . The animals are depicted in their natural settings in soothing shades that are sure to bring about the calm that encourages sleep. A lovely addition." SLJ

Buxton, Jane, 1947-

The littlest llama; by Jane Buxton; illustrated by Jenny Cooper. Sterling 2008 unp il $9.95

Grades: K 1 2   E
 1. Llamas—Fiction 2. Play—Fiction 3. Andes—Fiction 4. Stories in rhyme
 ISBN 978-1-4027-5277-3; 1-4027-5277-6
         LC 2007036396

High in the Andes Mountains, the littlest llama wants to play but his mother, sisters, gran, and aunt are busy, and so he leaves the herd to seek a playmate and finds

Buxton, Jane, 1947-—_Continued_

adventure, instead.

"The descriptive rhyming text will make a lively read-aloud, while the beautiful, intricately detailed color illustrations extend each scenario." Booklist

Buzzeo, Toni, 1951-

Adventure Annie goes to work; illustrated by Amy Wummer. Dial 2009 unp il lib bdg $16.99

Grades: PreK K 1   E

1. Superheroes—Fiction 2. Lost and found possessions—Fiction

ISBN 978-0-8037-3233-9; 0-8037-3233-3

When she goes to work with her mother on a Saturday, Adventure Annie uses her own special methods to help find a missing report.

"The bright, full-color pencil and watercolor pictures are set against ample white space and show the warm relationship between mother and daughter. This is an office adventure that children will want to experience and a heroine they'll love meeting." SLJ

Another title about Adventure Annie is:

Adventure Annie goes to kindergarten (2010)

Dawdle Duckling; illustrated by Margaret Spengler. Dial Bks. for Young Readers 2003 unp il $15.99

Grades: PreK K   E

1. Ducks—Fiction

ISBN 0-8037-2731-3   LC 2001-49913

Mama Duck tries to keep Dawdle Duckling together with his siblings, but he wants to dawdle and dream, preen and play, splash and spin

"The smile-provoking pastel illustrations put the characters front and center. . . . The repetitive text will hold children's attention, and the bit of tension at the book's conclusion adds sparkle." Booklist

Another title about Dawdle Duckling is:

Ready or not, Dawdle Ducking (2005)

The sea chest; illustrated by Mary GrandPré. Dial Bks. for Young Readers 2002 unp il $16.99

Grades: K 1 2 3   E

1. Lighthouses—Fiction 2. Islands—Fiction 3. Sisters—Fiction 4. Maine—Fiction

ISBN 0-8037-2703-8   LC 2001-28255

A young girl listens as her great-aunt, a lighthouse keeper's daughter, tells of her childhood living on a Maine island, and of the infant that washed ashore after a storm

"GrandPré's oil paintings create the dramatic effects of the story. . . . This lovely book has an intimacy that is enhanced by reading it aloud." SLJ

Byars, Betsy Cromer, 1928-

The Golly sisters go West; by Betsy Byars; pictures by Sue Truesdell. Harper & Row 1986 c1985 64p il lib bdg $16.89; pa $3.99 *

Grades: K 1 2   E

1. Entertainers—Fiction 2. Frontier and pioneer life—Fiction 3. West (U.S.)—Fiction

ISBN 0-06-020884-8 (lib bdg); 0-06-444132-6 (pa)

      LC 84-48474

"An I can read book"

May-May and Rose, the singing, dancing Golly sisters, travel west by covered wagon, entertaining people along the way

"The dialogue and antics are convincingly like those of rivalrous young siblings anywhere on the block. The story lines are cleverer than much easy-to-read fare, and the old-West setting adds flair. The accompanying watercolors, too, add a generous dollop of humor." Bull Cent Child Books

Other titles about the Golly sisters are:

The Golly sisters ride again (1994)

Hooray for the Golly sisters! (1990)

Bynum, Eboni

Jamari's drum; [by] Eboni Bynum and Roland Jackson; pictures on glazed tiles by Baba Wagué Diakité. Groundwood Books 2004 unp il $16.95

Grades: K 1 2 3   E

1. Drums—Fiction 2. Africa—Fiction 3. Volcanoes—Fiction

ISBN 0-88899-531-8

When Jamari forgets to heed Baba Mdogo's warning to play the drum in the village every day, he narrowly averts disaster from a volcano.

"The beautifully executed, folk-style artwork swirls with bold lines and bright patterns, incorporating backgrounds that blend earth tones with the blues and purples of the sky. . . . This book makes an excellent read-aloud." SLJ

Bynum, Janie

Kiki's blankie. Sterling Pub. 2009 unp il $14.95

Grades: PreK   E

1. Blankets—Fiction 2. Monkeys—Fiction 3. Lost and found possessions—Fiction

ISBN 978-1-4027-5910-9; 1-4027-5910-X

      LC 2008-26837

Kiki the monkey has many daring adventures with her polka-dot 'blankie,' but when it sails away without her and lands above a sleeping crocodile, she may not be brave enough to come to the rescue.

"Brightly colored, uncluttered illustrations are set on large areas of white space, making the objects and action easy for young children to find and follow. Preschoolers will relate to Kiki, her blankie attachment, and to her energy and creative play." SLJ

Cabral, Olga, 1909-

The seven sneezes; illustrated by Bruce Ingman. Golden Books 2009 unp il $15.99

Grades: PreK K 1 2   E

1. Animals—Fiction 2. Sneezing—Fiction

ISBN 978-0-375-83594-0; 0-375-83594-6

A newly illustrated edition of the title first published 1948

What happens when the local rag man sneezes? The kitten's ears end up on the bunny. The bunny's ears end up on the kitten. The dog meows, the cat barks. But with a little concentration—and a lot of pepper—the rag man tries to sneeze everything right

"At the conclusion of this sweet tale, one feels fully satisfied, as a topsy-turvy situation is resolved and order is regained. First published in 1948, this version pre-

Cabral, Olga, 1909——*Continued*

serves the original charm of Cabral's text and introduces Ingman's fresh illustrations, which combine splashes of bright color with simple line drawings." SLJ

Cabrera, Jane, 1968-

If you're happy and you know it. Holiday House 2005 unp il hardcover o.p. board book $7.95 *

Grades: PreK K   E
1. Songs 2. Animals—Fiction
ISBN 0-8234-1881-2; 978-0-8234-2227-2 (board book)
LC 2004-47264

An elephant, a monkey, and a giraffe join other animals to sing different verses of this popular song that encourages everyone to express their happiness through voice and movement.

"Cheerful painterly pictures in a kaleidoscope of colors enhance the jovial mood of the song." SLJ

Kitty's cuddles. Holiday House 2007 26p il $16.95

Grades: PreK   E
1. Cats—Fiction 2. Animals—Fiction
ISBN 978-0-8234-2066-7

Cat tries out hugs from all different animals but finds he likes the hug from his baby brother the best

"Cabrera's trademark eye-catching, lush colors are used to full advantage on every page. . . . Youngsters will be riveted by the bold pictures and find comfort in Kitty's predictable exploits." SLJ

Mommy, carry me please! Holiday House 2006 unp il $16.95 *

Grades: PreK K   E
1. Mother-child relationship—Fiction 2. Animals—Fiction
ISBN 0-8234-1935-5   LC 2004048862

"On each spread of this warm lapsit book, a baby animal asks its mother to carry me please. Each mother accommodates by transporting the youngster in that animals special way: lemur under its belly, kangaroo in a pouch, tiger in its mouth, crocodile in teeth, penguin on its feet, and so on until the cozy ending when a human child is carried in the mothers arms. The art features Cabrera's trademark breezy, blocky, and bold animals in bright and energetic colors that focus childrens eye and attention." SLJ

One, two, buckle my shoe. Holiday House 2009 unp il $16.95

Grades: PreK   E
1. Stories in rhyme 2. Birthdays—Fiction 3. Parties—Fiction 4. Animals—Fiction 5. Counting
ISBN 978-0-8234-2230-2; 0-8234-2230-5
LC 2008055303

Four chicks have fun hiding while Rabbit and Mommy Hen prepare a party for the little pigs' birthday.

Cabrera's "version of this familiar schoolyard song takes readers all the way up through the number 20. . . . The lively images, thick with paint strokes, create a cheerful atmosphere. Additionally, the opening challenge to find four small chicks on each spread will keep readers entertained as they read along." Publ Wkly

Cadena, Beth

Supersister; illustrated by Frank W. Dormer. Clarion Books 2009 unp il $16

Grades: K 1 2   E
1. Pregnancy—Fiction 2. Mother-daughter relationship—Fiction
ISBN 978-0-547-01006-9; 0-547-01006-0
LC 2008-11618

A young girl does all kinds of things around the house to help her pregnant mother, proud that when the new baby comes she is going to be 'a super sister.'

"Lively yet thoughtful text and bright, funny illustrations combine beautifully to settle into a pleasing conclusion: a supersister dream that features a superbrother. Highly recommended for children with siblings on the way." Kirkus

Cadow, Kenneth M.

Alfie runs away; pictures by Lauren Castillo. Frances Foster Books 2010 unp il $16.99

Grades: PreK K   E
1. Runaway children—Fiction 2. Mother-son relationship—Fiction
ISBN 978-0-374-30202-3; 0-374-30202-2
LC 2008024146

Told he must give up his favorite, now too-small, shoes, Alfie leaves home, but not before his mother persuades him to take all of the things he might need while he is gone

"Castillo's . . . spreads, comfortingly rendered in muted colors, are just right for Cadow's even-tempered narration." Publ Wkly

Calhoun, Mary, 1926-

Cross-country cat; illustrated by Erick Ingraham. Morrow 1979 unp il hardcover o.p. pa $6.99 *

Grades: K 1 2 3   E
1. Cats—Fiction
ISBN 0-688-22186-6; 0-698-06519-8 (pa)
LC 78-31718

When he becomes lost in the mountains, Henry, a cat with the unusual ability of walking on two legs finds his way home on cross-country skis

"Only the careful blending of skills by a talented author and illustrator could turn such a farfetched plot into a warm, rich, and rewarding story. The realistic illustrations seem to be enveloped in a glowing light and invite the reader to step right into the story." Child Book Rev Serv

Other titles about Henry the cat are:
Blue-ribbon Henry (1999)
Henry the Christmas cat (2004)
Henry the sailor cat (1994)
High-wire Henry (1991)
Hot-air Henry (1981)

Cali, Davide, 1972-

The enemy; a book about peace; written by Davide Cali and illustrated by Serge Bloch. Schwartz & Wade Books 2009 unp il $15.99; lib bdg $18.99

Grades: 1 2 3 4   E

  1. Soldiers—Fiction 2. War stories

  ISBN   978-0-375-84500-0;   0-375-84500-3; 978-0-375-93752-1 (lib bdg); 0-375-93752-8 (lib bdg)

                         LC 2007047974

After watching an enemy for a very long time during an endless war, a soldier finally creeps out into the night to the other man's hole and is surprised by what he finds there.

"Bloch pairs pen-and-ink cartoons with collage elements like family photos, and gives readers a bird's-eye view from which to observe the men's similarities. The point will not be lost on readers." Publ Wkly

I love chocolate; illustrated by Evelyn Daviddi. Tundra Books 2009 unp il $12.95

Grades: PreK K   E

  1. Chocolate—Fiction

  ISBN 978-0-88776-912-2; 0-88776-912-8

  Original Italian edition 2001

"'Why do I love chocolate?' a boy asks as he is about to take a colossal bite of a candy bar. He then lists all the reasons: it crunches and melts, and it can make bad times better. . . . The text captures the essence of chocolate—its varying incarnations and textures—and it will leave everyone salivating. In addition to being a great candidate for programs, the book has potential as an easy reader as well. The art has a European flair." SLJ

Calmenson, Stephanie

Jazzmatazz! by Stephanie Calmenson; illustrated by Bruce Degen. HarperCollinsPublishers 2008 unp il $16.99; lib bdg $17.89

Grades: PreK K 1   E

  1. Animals—Fiction 2. Jazz music—Fiction 3. Mice—Fiction 4. Musicians—Fiction 5. Stories in rhyme

  ISBN   978-0-06-077289-5;   0-06-077289-1; 978-0-06-077290-1 (lib bdg); 0-06-077290-5 (lib bdg)

                         LC 2007009133

When a mouse scurries into a house and starts to play jazz music, other animals join in, one by one, each using his or her own particular talent

"This cheerful book . . . is full of color and sound. . . . Degen fills the white space . . . with colorful zigzags, curlicues, stars, and other patterns to show how the music is connecting and joining all of the characters together." SLJ

Late for school! by Stephanie Calmenson; illustrated by Sachiko Yoshikawa. Carolrhoda Books 2008 unp il lib bdg $16.95

Grades: K 1 2   E

  1.   Teachers—Fiction   2.   School   stories 3. Transportation—Fiction 4. Stories in rhyme

  ISBN 978-1-57505-935-8 (lib bdg); 1-57505-935-5 (lib bdg)   LC 2007034776

When Mr. Bungles the teacher oversleeps, he goes to great lengths, trying every form of transportation he can find to get to school on time.

"Cartoon characters in scenes of collage and mixed media follow Mr. Bungles's efforts to watch the clock and avoid breaking his own rule, 'Never, ever, ever be late for school!' A colorful selection for all libraries." SLJ

Calvert, Pam, 1966-

Multiplying   menace;   the   revenge   of Rumpelstiltskin; illustrated by Wayne Geehan. Charlesbridge Pub. 2006 32p il $16.95; pa $6.95

Grades: 3 4 5 6   E

  1. Multiplication—Fiction 2. Fairy tales

  ISBN 1-57091-889-9; 1-57091-890-2 (pa)

                         LC 2004-23072

Ten years after being tricked, Rumpelstiltskin returns to the royal family to wreak vengeance using multiplication. Includes nonfiction math notes about multiplying by whole numbers and by fractions.

"Calvert has created an interesting vehicle for teaching children about the differences between multiplying with whole numbers and multiplying with fractions. . . . Calvert has written an enjoyable teaching tool, and Geehan's luminous and expressive paintings are perfect for this fairy-tale world." SLJ

Princess Peepers; illustrated by Tuesday Mourning. Marshall Cavendish 2008 unp il $16.99

Grades: K 1 2 3   E

  1. Eyeglasses—Fiction 2. Princesses—Fiction

  ISBN 978-0-7614-5437-3; 0-7614-5437-3

                         LC 2007022134

When the other princesses make fun of her for wearing glasses, Princess Peepers vows to go without, but after several mishaps—one of which is especially coincidental—she admits that she really does need them if she wants to see.

"Mourning's graphite and digital/collage illustrations combine figures in traditional costumes from different eras with lush backgrounds. The palette of pinks keeps the emphasis on sweet, even when some of the characters are not. Princess Peepers will circulate well and bring laughs during storytimes." SLJ

Campbell, Bebe Moore

Sometimes my mommy gets angry; illustrated by E. B. Lewis. Putnam 2003 unp il hardcover o.p. pa $5.99

Grades: PreK K 1   E

  1. Mother-child relationship—Fiction 2. Mentally ill—Fiction 3. African Americans—Fiction

  ISBN 0-399-23972-3; 0-14-240359-8 (pa)

                         LC 2003-1279

Annie copes with her mother's mental illness, with the help of her grandmother and friends

"Lewis makes excellent use of light and shadow in his watercolors. . . . The multicultural cast is depicted with realistic sensitivity. . . . A skillful treatment of a troubling subject." SLJ

Campbell, Bebe Moore—*Continued*
Stompin' at the Savoy; [by] Bebe Moore Campbell; illustrated by Richard Yarde. Philomel Books 2006 unp il $16.99
Grades: K 1 2 3   E
1. Jazz music—Fiction 2. Dance—Fiction 3. African Americans—Fiction 4. Harlem (New York, N.Y.)—Fiction
ISBN 0-399-24197-3   LC 2005025044
On the night of her jazz dance recital Mindy feels too nervous to go, until a magical drum whisks her away to the Savoy Ballroom in Harlem where she finds her "happy feet"
"Rhythmic gouache and pastel paintings depicting swinging dancers and jiving musicians perfectly complement the lyrical energy and magical realism of the cadenced prose." SLJ

Campbell, Nicola I.
Shi-shi-etko; pictures by Kim La Fave. Groundwood Books 2005 unp il $16.95
Grades: K 1 2 3   E
1. Native Americans—Fiction 2. Canada—Fiction
ISBN 0-88899-659-4
"This is a moving story set in Canada about the practice of removing Native children from their villages and sending them to residential schools to learn the English language and culture. . . . Shi-shi-etko counts down her last four days before going away. . . . The vivid, digital illustrations rely on a red palette, evoking not only the land but also the sorrow of the situation and the hope upon which the story ultimately ends." SLJ

Campbell, Rod, 1945-
Dear zoo; a pop-up book. Little Simon 2005 c1982 unp il $12.95
Grades: PreK K   E
1. Animals—Fiction 2. Pop-up books
ISBN 0-689-87751-X
First published as a board book in the United Kingdom 1982; first published as a pop-up book 2004 in the United Kingdom
Each animal arriving from the zoo as a possible pet fails to suit its prospective owner, until just the right one is found.

Cannon, Janell, 1957-
Crickwing; written and illustrated by Janell Cannon. Harcourt 2000 unp il $16 *
Grades: K 1 2 3   E
1. Cockroaches—Fiction 2. Ants—Fiction
ISBN 0-15-201790-9   LC 99-50456
A lonely cockroach named Crickwing has a creative idea that saves the day for the leaf-cutter ants when their fierce forest enemies attack them
"An amusing tale lightly rooted in natural history. . . . Cannon's illustrations skillfully blur the line between fact and fancy." Publ Wkly

Stellaluna. Harcourt Brace Jovanovich 1993 unp il $17 *
Grades: K 1 2 3   E
1. Bats—Fiction
ISBN 0-15-280217-7   LC 92-16439

After she falls headfirst into a bird's nest, a baby bat is raised like a bird until she is reunited with her mother
"Cannon's delightful story is full of gentle humor. . . . [She] provides good information about bats in the story, amplifying it in two pages of notes at the end of the book. Her full-page colored-pencil-and-acrylic paintings fairly glow." Booklist

Caple, Kathy
Duck & company. Holiday House 2007 32p il $14.95; pa $4.95
Grades: K 1 2   E
1. Ducks—Fiction 2. Rats—Fiction 3. Booksellers and bookselling—Fiction
ISBN 978-0-8234-1993-7; 0-8234-1993-2; 978-0-8234-2125-1 (pa); 0-8234-2125-2 (pa)
                                          LC 2006-12118
Rat and Duck run a bookshop and work to find the right book for each of their customers.
"There are tons of visual clues embedded in the ink and goauche illustrations to help burgeoning readers. . . .Young readers will appreciate both the humor and the diversity of the five included tales." Bull Cent Child Books

The friendship tree. Holiday House 2000 48p il lib bdg $15.95
Grades: K 1 2   E
1. Sheep—Fiction 2. Trees—Fiction 3. Friendship—Fiction
ISBN 0-8234-1376-4   LC 98-39043
"A Holiday House reader"
This book "includes four little stories about trees. Best friends Blanche and Otis are sheep who live next door to each other and share their sorrows and joys. . . . The line-and-watercolor illustrations reflect the sweet, gentle tone of the text with the soft, pastel shades." Booklist

Capucilli, Alyssa, 1957-
Biscuit's new trick; story by Alyssa Satin Capucilli; pictures by Pat Schories. HarperCollins Pubs. 2000 24p il $12.95; lib bdg $15.89; pa $3.99 *
Grades: PreK K 1 2   E
1. Dogs—Fiction
ISBN 0-06-028067-0; 0-06-028068-9 (lib bdg); 0-06-444308-6 (pa)   LC 99-23004
Also available board books about Biscuit
"My first I can read book"
"While his owner tries to teach him to fetch a ball, Biscuit the dog chews his bone or chases the cat—that is, until the ball lands in a mud puddle. . . . The simple language . . . and playful watercolor illustrations make this an appealing choice for beginning readers." Horn Book Guide
Other titles about Biscuit are:
Bathtime for Biscuit (1998)
Biscuit (1996)
Biscuit and the baby (2005)
Biscuit finds a friend (1997)
Biscuit goes to school (2002)
Biscuit visits the big city (2006)
Biscuit wants to play (2001)

Capucilli, Alyssa, 1957-—*Continued*
Biscuit wins a prize (2004)
Biscuit's big friend (2003)
Biscuit's day at the farm (2007)
Biscuit's new trick (2000)
Biscuit's picnic (1998)
Happy birthday, Biscuit! (1999)
Hello, Biscuit! (1998)

Katy duck is a caterpillar; by Alyssa Satin Capucilli; illustrated by Henry Cole. Simon & Schuster 2009 unp il $14.99
Grades: PreK K 1 2   E
   1. Ducks—Fiction 2. Dance—Fiction 3. Caterpillars—Fiction
   ISBN 978-1-4169-6061-4; 1-4169-6061-9
Katy Duck is disappointed when she is cast as a caterpillar in the Spring dance recital.
"Cole's illustrations aptly convey Katy's expressions of joy and disappointment, as well as her exuberant energy." SLJ

Pedro's burro; story by Alyssa Satin Capucilli; pictures by Pau Estrada. HarperCollinsPublishers 2007 32p il (I can read!) $15.99; lib bdg $16.89
Grades: PreK K 1   E
   1. Donkeys—Fiction 2. Mexico—Fiction
   ISBN   978-0-06-056031-7;   0-06-056031-2;
978-0-06-056032-4 (lib bdg); 0-06-056032-0 (lib bdg)
                          LC 2006036323
Pedro and his papa go to the market to look for the perfect burro.
"This winning story is enhanced by Estrada's colorful, inviting illustrations. . . . Featuring repetition and humor, the simple story is set in large type with ample white space." SLJ

Carbone, Elisa Lynn, 1954-
Night running; how James escaped with the help of his faithful dog; based on a true story; [by] Elisa Carbone; illustrated by E.B. Lewis. Alfred A. Knopf 2008 unp il $16.99; lib bdg $19.99 *
Grades: 2 3 4   E
   1. Slavery—Fiction 2. Dogs—Fiction 3. African Americans—Fiction
   ISBN   0-375-82247-X;   978-0-375-82247-6;
0-375-92247-4 (lib bdg); 978-0-375-92247-3 (lib bdg)
                          LC 2003014502
A runaway slave makes a daring escape to freedom with the help of his faithful hunting dog, Zeus. Based on the true story of James Smith's journey from Virginia to Ohio in the mid-1800s.
"The watercolor paintings beautifully evoke the sun-drenched cotton fields. Deep purples and rich, dark greens capture the moonlit night. . . . A vividly realized narrative, based on a true story." SLJ

Carle, Eric
10 little rubber ducks. HarperCollins 2005 unp il $21.99; bd bk $11.99 *
Grades: PreK K 1 2   E
   1. Toys—Fiction 2. Counting
   ISBN 0-06-074075-2; 0-06-074078-7 (bd bk)
                           LC 2004-1420

When a storm strikes a cargo ship, ten rubber ducks are tossed overboard and swept off in ten different directions. Based on a factual incident
"Carle's signature cut-paper collages burst with color, texture, light, and motion, delighting the eye and bringing out the text's nuances." SLJ

Do you want to be my friend? Crowell 1971 unp il $17.99; lib bdg $18.89; pa $6.99; bd bk $7.99 *
Grades: PreK K   E
   1. Mice—Fiction 2. Stories without words
   ISBN 0-690-24276-X; 0-690-01137-7 (lib bdg); 0-06-443127-4 (pa); 0-694-00709-9 (bd bk)
"The only text is the title question at the start and a shy 'Yes' at the close. The pictures do the rest, as the hopeful mouse overtakes one large creature after another. With each encounter, the mouse sees (on the right-hand page) an interesting tail. Turn the page, and there is a huge lion, or a malevolent fox, or a peacock, and then, at last another wee mouse." Saturday Rev
"Good material for discussion and guessing games. . . . The pictures tell an amusing story and they are good to look at as well." Times Lit Suppl

Does a kangaroo have a mother, too? HarperCollins Pubs. 2000 unp il $16.99; lib bdg $18.89; pa $6.99; bd bk $7.99 *
Grades: PreK K 1   E
   1. Animals
   ISBN 0-06-028768-3; 0-06-028767-5 (lib bdg); 0-06-443642-X (pa); 0-694-01456-7 (bd bk)
                           LC 99-36147
"The repetitious text is perfect for the toddler set. 'Does a lion have a mother, too? Yes! A lion has a mother. Just like me and you.' The text is repeated on every spread as the author showcases a dozen different animal mothers and their babies. . . . The vibrant artwork is classic Carle and should delight its audience." SLJ

The grouchy ladybug. HarperCollins Pubs. 1996 unp il $17.99; lib bdg $18.89; pa $7.99; bd bk $8.99 *
Grades: PreK K 1   E
   1. Ladybugs—Fiction
   ISBN 0-06-027087-X; 0-06-027088-8 (lib bdg); 0-06-443450-8 (pa); 0-694-01320-X (bd bk)
                           LC 95-26581
A reissue of the title first published 1977 by Crowell
A grouchy ladybug, looking for a fight, challenges everyone she meets regardless of their size or strength
"The finger paint and collage illustrations—as bold as the feisty hero—are satisfyingly placed on pages sized to suit the successive animals that appear. . . . Tiny clocks show the time of each enjoyable encounter, with the sun rising and setting as the action proceeds." SLJ

A house for Hermit Crab. Picture Bk. Studio 1988 c1987 unp il $18.99; pa $7.99; bd bk $8.99 *
Grades: PreK K 1   E
   1. Crabs—Fiction
   ISBN   0-88708-056-1;   0-689-84894-3   (pa);
0-689-87064-7 (bd bk)   LC 87-29261

Carle, Eric—*Continued*

"Hermit Crab, having outgrown his old shell, sets out to find a new one. He's a bit frightened at first, but over the course of the next year acquires not only a shell, but also an array of sea creatures to decorate, clean, and protect his new home. The story ends with him once again outgrowing his shell." SLJ

"The bright illustrations in Carle's familiar style, which seems particularly suited to undersea scenes, and the cumulative story are splendid." Horn Book

Mister Seahorse. Philomel Books 2004 unp il $17.99 *

Grades: PreK K 1   E

1. Sea horses—Fiction 2. Fishes—Fiction 3. Fathers—Fiction

ISBN 0-399-24269-4   LC 2003-17125

After Mrs. Seahorse lays her eggs on Mr. Seahorse's belly, he drifts through the water, greeting other fish fathers who are taking care of their eggs

"With each encounter comes a delightful surprise: an acetate overlay camouflages the sea creatures as Mister Seahorse passes by. . . . Awash with the wonders of undersea life, this is a stunning, ingeniously conceived lesson in nature as well as a celebration of fatherly affection." Booklist

The mixed-up chameleon. Crowell 1984 unp il $17.99; lib bdg $18.89; pa $6.99; bd bk $8.99 *

Grades: PreK K 1   E

1. Chameleons—Fiction

ISBN 0-690-04396-1; 0-690-04397-X (lib bdg); 0-06-443162-2 (pa); 0-694-01147-9 (bd bk)

     LC 83-45950

A revised and newly illustrated edition of the title first published 1975

"A chameleon goes to a zoo where it wishes it could become like the different animals it sees. It does, but then isn't happy until it wishes it could be itself again." Child Book Rev Serv

The author "has replaced the heavy-lined, childlike, scrawled colors with crisp, appealing collages and has streamlined the text. The cutaway pages have been retained, and none of the humor has been lost. The simpler text results in a smoother flow, and children will enjoy the resulting repetition." Booklist

Papa, please get the moon for me. Simon & Schuster Books for Young Readers 1991 c1986 unp il $6.99

Grades: PreK K 1   E

1. Moon—Fiction

ISBN 0-8870-8177-0   LC 91014561

First published 1986 by Picture Book Studio

Monica's father fulfills her request for the moon by taking it down after it is small enough to carry, but it continues to change in size. Some pages fold out to display particularly large pictures.

This is "drawn in thick, brilliant brushstrokes of blues and greens and reds that dazzle the eye. . . . A splendid introduction to the monthly lunar cycle, this is also a wondrous work of art that will stand up to countless readings." Publ Wkly

"Slowly, slowly, slowly," said the sloth. Philomel Bks. 2002 unp il $16.99; pa $7.99 *

Grades: PreK K 1   E

1. Sloths—Fiction 2. Animals—Fiction

ISBN 0-399-23954-5; 0-14-240847-6 (pa)

     LC 2002-16057

Challenged by the other jungle animals for its seemingly lazy ways, a sloth living in a tree explains the many advantages of his slow and peaceful existence

"Carle's art is at its best with a brightly colored selection of painted tissue-paper collage that captures 25 rainforest denizens." SLJ

The very busy spider. Philomel Bks. 1984 unp il $21.99 paperback o.p.; bd bk $11.99 *

Grades: PreK K 1   E

1. Spiders—Fiction

ISBN 0-399-21166-7; 0-399-21592-1 (pa); 0-399-22919-1 (bd bk)   LC 84-5907

The farm animals try to divert a busy little spider from spinning her web, but she persists and produces a thing of both beauty and usefulness

This book "has a disarming ingenuousness and a repetitive structure that will capture the response of preschool audiences. Of special note is the book's use of raised lines for the spider, its web, and an unsuspecting fly. Both sighted and blind children will be able to follow the action with ease." Booklist

The very clumsy click beetle. Philomel Bks. 1999 unp il $22.99 *

Grades: PreK K 1   E

1. Beetles—Fiction 2. Animals—Fiction

ISBN 0-399-23201-X   LC 97-33417

A clumsy young click beetle learns to land on its feet with encouragement from various animals and a wise old beetle. An electronic chip with a built-in battery creates clicking sounds to accompany the story

"Done in colored tissue-paper collage, the illustrations burst from the pages and are charmingly rendered. . . . A well-crafted story, joyfully illustrated." SLJ

The very hungry caterpillar. Philomel Bks. 1981 c1970 unp il $21.99; bd bk $10.99 *

Grades: PreK K 1   E

1. Caterpillars—Fiction

ISBN 0-399-20853-4; 0-399-22690-7 (bd bk)

Also available Pop-Up edition

First published 1970 by World Publishing Company

"This caterpillar is so hungry he eats right through the pictures on the pages of the book—and after leaving many holes emerges as a beautiful butterfly on the last page." Best Books for Child, 1972

The very lonely firefly. Philomel Bks. 1995 unp il $22.99; bd bk $11.99 *

Grades: PreK K 1   E

1. Fireflies—Fiction

ISBN 0-399-22774-1; 0-399-23427-6 (bd bk)

     LC 94-27827

A lonely firefly goes out into the night searching for other fireflies

"The illustrations are painted cut-paper collages, designed to draw the eye to the page. This is a compelling accomplishment." SLJ

Carle, Eric—*Continued*

The very quiet cricket. Philomel Bks. 1990 unp il $22.99; bd bk $12.99 *

Grades: PreK K 1   E

1. Crickets—Fiction

ISBN 0-399-21885-8; 0-399-22684-7 (bd bk)

LC 89-78317

A very quiet cricket who wants to rub his wings together and make a sound as do so many other animals finally achieves his wish

"The text is skillfully shaped; the illustrations convey energy and immediacy; and, in a surprise ending, a microchip inserted in the last page replicates the cricket's chirp." Horn Book Guide

Where are you going? To see my friend! [by] Eric Carle & Kazuo Iwamura. Orchard Bks. 2003 c2001 unp il $19.95 *

Grades: PreK K 1   E

1. Animals—Fiction 2. Friendship—Fiction 3. Bilingual books—English-Japanese

ISBN 0-439-41659-0   LC 2002-70396

Original Japanese edition, 2001

This "bilingual picture book is told in dialogue, with rebuslike symbols used to identify speakers. It details an energetic romp with a dog, cat, rooster, goat, rabbit, and a child, all of whom become friends. Carle's familiar collage technique is employed in the book's first half, while Iwamura's gentle watercolor illustrations, combined with the Japanese text, make up the second half. . . . An irresistible, spirited ode to friendship." SLJ

Carling, Amelia Lau, 1949-

Mama & Papa have a store; story and pictures by Amelia Lau Carling. Dial Bks. for Young Readers 1998 unp il $16.99

Grades: K 1 2 3   E

1. Retail trade—Fiction 2. Chinese—Fiction 3. Guatemala—Fiction

ISBN 0-8037-2044-0   LC 97-10217

A little girl describes what a day is like in her parents' Chinese store in Guatemala City

"Carling's lovingly detailed watercolors in candy-box colors illustrate [the author's] memories. . . . A pleasant family story that should enrich library collections, especially those looking for multicultural themes." SLJ

Carlson, Nancy L., 1953-

Get up and go! by Nancy Carlson. Viking 2006 unp il $15.99 *

Grades: PreK K   E

1. Pigs—Fiction 2. Rabbits—Fiction 3. Exercise

ISBN 0-670-05981-1   LC 2005003864

Text and illustrations encourage readers, regardless of shape or size, to turn off the television and play games, walk, dance, and engage in sports and other forms of exercise.

"Bright and sassy, the clearly delineated drawings with vivid washes provide a light, sometimes-comical tone that makes the lessons easier to take. With a short, simple text and a cheerful look, this will suit preschool and kindergarten teachers looking for an accessible book on exercise." Booklist

Harriet and the roller coaster. 20th anniversary ed. Carolrhoda Books 2003 unp il $15.95; pa $6.95

Grades: PreK K 1 2   E

1. Dogs—Fiction 2. Rabbits—Fiction 3. Roller coasters—Fiction

ISBN 1-57505-053-6; 1-57505-202-4 (pa)

LC 2002-13922

A reissue of the title first published 1982

Harriet accepts her friend George's challenge to ride the frightening roller coaster, and finds out that she is the brave one

"This emotionally satisfying story is illustrated with simple colorful art. This edition is slightly larger than the original but otherwise unchanged." Horn Book Guide

Henry and the Valentine surprise; [by] Nancy Carlson. Viking 2008 unp il $15.99

Grades: PreK K 1 2   E

1. Valentine's Day—Fiction 2. Teachers—Fiction 3. School stories 4. Mice—Fiction 5. Animals—Fiction

ISBN 978-0-670-06267-6; 0-670-06267-7

LC 2008001283

When Henry the mouse and his first-grade classmates notice a heart-shaped box on their teacher's desk the day before Valentine's Day, they try to find out if he has a girlfriend.

"Told with mounting suspense, this mystery has a delightful and satisfying conclusion. Brightly colored comic illustrations portray the excitement at school as the special day approaches." SLJ

Other titles about Henry are:

Henry's show and tell (2004)

Henry's 100 days of kindergarten (2005)

Henry's amazing imagination! (2008)

Start saving, Henry! (2009)

Henry and the bully (2010)

Hooray for Grandparent's Day; [by] Nancy Carlson. Viking 2000 unp il $15.99

Grades: PreK K 1 2   E

1. Grandparents—Fiction 2. School stories

ISBN 0-670-88876-1   LC 99-46237

Arnie doesn't have grandparents to come to school on Grandparent's Day, but it turns out he has a lot of people who can substitute

"Bright, cheery, cartoonlike illustrations of the animal characters carry out the upbeat tone of the story." SLJ

I like me! [by] Nancy Carlson. Viking Kestrel 1988 unp il lib bdg $16.99; pa $6.99

Grades: PreK K 1   E

1. Pigs—Fiction

ISBN 0-670-82062-8 (lib bdg); 0-14-050819-8 (pa)

LC 87-32616

By admiring her finer points and showing that she can take care of herself and have fun even when there's no one else around, a charming pig proves the best friend you can have is yourself

This book is "visually interesting, with sturdy animals drawn in a deliberately artless style. Simple shapes, strong lines, and clear colors, with lots of pattern mixing, show what is not described in the minimal text. The text is hand-lettered." SLJ

Another title about this pig is:

Carlson, Nancy L., 1953-—*Continued*
ABC I like me! (1997)

Carlstrom, Nancy White, 1948-
It's your first day of school, Annie Claire. Abrams Books for Young Readers 2009 unp il $15.95
Grades: PreK K   E
1. Stories in rhyme 2. School stories 3. Mother-daughter relationship—Fiction 4. Dogs—Fiction
ISBN 978-0-8109-4057-4; 0-8109-4057-4
LC 2009-2124
Annie Claire the puppy, excited but nervous about her first day of school, is reassured by her mother, whose love always goes with her.
"Sweet, gentle illustrations pair with reassuring text." Booklist

Jesse Bear, what will you wear? illustrations by Bruce Degen. Macmillan 1986 unp il $16.95; pa $6.99; bd bk $7.99 *
Grades: PreK K   E
1. Bears—Fiction 2. Stories in rhyme
ISBN 0-02-717350-X; 0-689-80623-X (pa); 0-689-80930-1 (bd bk)   LC 85-10610
"The happy, singsong verse of the title follows Jesse Bear through the changes of clothes and activities of his day, even to bath and bed." N Y Times Book Rev
"The big, cheerful watercolor paintings show the baby bear in loving relation to his family and world. Without crossing the line into sentimentality, this offers a happy, humorous soundfest that will associate reading aloud with a sense of play." Bull Cent Child Books
Other titles about Jesse Bear are:
Better not get wet, Jesse Bear (1988)
Climb the family tree, Jesse Bear (2004)
Guess who's coming, Jesse Bear (1998)
Happy birthday, Jesse Bear (1994)
How do you say it today, Jesse Bear? (1992)
It's about time, Jesse Bear, and other rhymes (1990)
Let's count it out, Jesse Bear (1996)
What a scare, Jesse Bear! (1999)
Where is Christmas, Jesse Bear? (2000)

Carluccio, Maria
The sounds around town; by Maria Carluccio. Barefoot Books 2008 unp il $16.99
Grades: PreK   E
1. Sound—Fiction 2. Day—Fiction 3. City and town life—Fiction 4. Stories in rhyme
ISBN 978-1-905236-28-2; 1-905236-28-X
LC 2007025044
Reveals many things a child might hear during the day, from the singing of birds at dawn to the soft sounds of sleep.
"The text is alive with onomatopoeia, and the visually stimulating cut-paper collages provide myriad sources of the sounds to share and enjoy." Horn Book Guide

Carr, Jan, 1953-
Greedy Apostrophe; a cautionary tale; by Jan Carr; illustrated by Ethan Long. Holiday House 2007 unp il $16.95
Grades: K 1 2 3   E
1. Punctuation—Fiction
ISBN 978-0-8234-2006-3; 0-8234-2006-X
LC 2006012114
"All the punctuation marks stumble into the Hiring Hall one morning, sipping cocoa and discussing their job prospects. Each receives an important assignment, even Greedy Apostrophe, who has a well-deserved reputation for his bad attitude. . . . Students are asked to be vigilant and to take Greedy away from all the places where he inserts himself but doesn't really belong. With jazzy colors and cartoon-style characters, the upbeat artwork gives personality to the inanimate while underscoring the witty, vivacious tone of the text." Booklist

Carrick, Carol
Mothers are like that; illustrated by Paul Carrick. Clarion Bks. 2000 unp il $15; pa $5.95
Grades: PreK K   E
1. Mother-child relationship—Fiction 2. Animals—Fiction
ISBN 0-395-88351-2; 0-618-75241-2 (pa)
LC 99-16587
A simple description of animal and human mothers caring for their young
"The text in this gentle, lulling bedtime story of maternal love is brief but complete. The acrylic paintings . . . brim with child-appealing, close-up portraits of mother animals and their babies." Horn Book Guide

Patrick's dinosaurs; pictures by Donald Carrick. Clarion Bks. 1983 unp il lib bdg $16; pa $5.95 *
Grades: PreK K 1 2   E
1. Dinosaurs—Fiction 2. Brothers—Fiction
ISBN 0-89919-189-4 (lib bdg); 0-89919-402-8 (pa)
LC 83-2049
When his older brother talks about dinosaurs during a visit to the zoo, Patrick is afraid, until he discovers they all died millions of years ago.
"The Carricks do a particularly good job of creating an impressive array of creatures both in text and illustrations—realistic pencil drawings washed in muted greens, browns and oranges." SLJ
Other titles about Patrick's dinosaurs are:
Patrick's dinosaurs on the Internet (1999)
What happened to Patrick's dinosaurs? (1986)

Carryl, Charles E., 1841-1920
The camel's lament; a poem by Charles Edward Carryl; illustrated by Charles Santore. Random House 2004 unp il $16.95; lib bdg $18.99
Grades: K 1 2 3   E
1. Camels—Poetry 2. Animals—Poetry
ISBN 0-375-81426-4; 0-375-91426-9 (lib bdg)
LC 2003-22271
A poem in which a camel compares his life with that of other animals of the world
This poem "has all the hallmarks of child-friendly verse: a clever idea, humor, and a sprightly rhyme. . . .

Carryl, Charles E., 1841-1920—*Continued*

But it's really Santore's fabulous artwork that will cata-pult this into kids' eager hands. . . . Richly colored and intensely detailed . . . the closeup art, set against crisp white backgrounds, will be fun to look at by individuals or in groups." Booklist

Carter, David A.

600 black spots. Little Simon 2007 unp il $19.99

Grades: 2 3 4 5 6   E

1. Counting 2. Puzzles 3. Pop-up books
ISBN 1-4169-4092-8; 978-1-4169-4092-0

"A Classic collectible pop-up"

In this pop-up book, readers are encouraged to search for the black spots throughout the pages

"This is both simple and stunning. . . . It takes a so-phisticated artistic taste to appreciate the modern-art-style creations. . . . Older children will have an interesting time interpreting the artwork and marveling at the skill involved in the construction." Booklist

Blue 2; a pop-up book for children of all ages. Little Simon 2006 unp il $10.95

Grades: 2 3 4 5 6   E

1. Puzzles 2. Pop-up books
ISBN 1-4169-1781-0

"A Classic collectible pop-up"

Each page contains an original piece of artwork that challenges the reader to find the a blue 2.

"Mobiles pop from the pages and readers spin pin-wheels and pull tabs to find each elusive numeral two. Another enchanting creation from the inventive paper en-gineer." Publ Wkly

One red dot; a pop-up book for children of all ages. Little Simon 2005 unp il $19.95 *

Grades: 2 3 4 5 6   E

1. Counting 2. Puzzles 3. Pop-up books
ISBN 0-689-87769-2

"A Classic collectible pop-up"

Original Italian edition 2004

"A graphically bold pop-up book that entices readers to find the one red dot that is hidden on each paper sculpture. Going from 1 to 10, Carter creates a visual hide-and-seek game, ranging from flip-flop flaps to flut-tering flicker clickers that really click to orbs that tower above the page. Bold primary colors and a silver-black text give the book a very slick, modern feel." SLJ

White noise; a pop-up book for children of all ages. Little Simon 2009 unp il $22.99

Grades: 2 3 4 5 6   E

1. Noise—Fiction 2. Pop-up books
ISBN 978-1-4169-4094-4; 1-4169-4094-4

"A Classic collectible pop-up"

"Each spread, designed to make crackly, crinkly, creaky, tinkling or snapping noises as the pages are turned, evokes children's construction-paper cutouts. . . . Carter's creations are akin to fireworks displays, each building in pyrotechnical intensity until the most impres-sive burst at the end." NY Times Book Rev

Yellow square; a pop-up book for children of all ages. Little Simon 2008 unp il $19.99

Grades: 2 3 4 5 6   E

1. Pop-up books
ISBN 978-1-4169-4093-7; 1-4169-4093-6

"A Classic collectible pop-up"

"A yellow square hides in plain sight in or within the paper engineering on each spread; sometimes, the cre-ation of the yellow square is entirely up to the reader. On the first spread, for example, that square exists only when the reader peers through a die-cut while holding the book at the correct angle-in other words, perspective is everything. Captions are variously enigmatic . . . or childlike. . . . Carter confines himself to primary colors, black and white; even with this palette, he alludes to a number of artists, among them Agam, . . . Christo, . . . Miro, and Calder. . . . Not all the spreads are equally impressive, but the best are dazzlers." Publ Wkly

Carville, James

Lu and the swamp ghost; [by] James Carville with Patricia C. McKissack; illustrated by David Catrow. Atheneum Books for Young Readers 2004 unp il $17.95

Grades: K 1 2 3   E

1. Great Depression, 1929-1939—Fiction
2. Friendship—Fiction 3. Louisiana—Fiction
ISBN 0-689-86560-0   LC 2003-14679

"An Anne Schwartz book"

During the Depression in the Louisiana bayou, a curi-ous young girl helps the "Swamp Ghost" that her cousins warned her about and finds herself with one good friend

"Carville tells this humorous . . . story . . . with gus-to. Catrow's wildly bright watercolor-and-pencil illustra-tions fill the pages with wonderful swamp critters and an indomitable red-haired heroine." SLJ

Casanova, Mary

Some dog! pictures by Ard Hoyt. Farrar, Straus & Giroux 2007 unp il $16

Grades: PreK K 1 2   E

1. Dogs—Fiction
ISBN 0-374-37133-4; 978-0-374-37133-3
LC 2004053262

"Melanie Kroupa books"

A stray dog moves into George's formerly peaceful home, dazzling the man and woman of the house with lively tricks and antics that just leave George exhausted

"The watercolor-and-pencil illustrations perfectly cap-ture the exuberance and spirit of this tale." SLJ

Utterly otterly day; by Mary Casanova; illustrated by Ard Hoyt. Simon & Schuster Books for Young Readers 2008 unp il $16.99

Grades: PreK K 1   E

1. Otters—Fiction 2. Stories in rhyme
ISBN 978-1-4169-0868-5; 1-4169-0868-4
LC 2007041428

After a day out on his own, Little Otter realizes that he still needs his family no matter how big he grows

"The pen-and-ink-and-watercolor illustrations . . . em-phasize the quick, exciting movement of the forest's ani-mals, while the text hops with made-up rhyming words. . . . The adventurous otter and his caring family prove fairly irresistible." Booklist

Case, Chris, 1976-
Sophie and the next-door monsters. Walker 2008 unp il $15.99; lib bdg $16.89
Grades: PreK K 1 2   E
    1. Monsters—Fiction
    ISBN   978-0-8027-9756-8;   0-8027-9756-3; 978-0-8027-9757-5 (lib bdg); 0-8027-9757-1 (lib bdg)
                          LC 2007-49133
When new neighbors move in next door to Sophie, she is startled—and afraid—to discover that they are monsters.
"This is an offbeat delight. The humans matter-of-factness about the monsters' monstrousness intensifies the humor, and the lively text begs to be read aloud. Case layers colors and uses lots of scratchy hatchwork lines and brushwork to accent the figures and objects in his ink, watercolor, and gouache art." Bull Cent Child Books

Caseley, Judith, 1951-
On the town; a community adventure. Greenwillow Bks. 2002 unp il $15.95; lib bdg $15.89 *
Grades: PreK K 1 2   E
    1. Community life—Fiction
    ISBN 0-06-029584-8; 0-06-029585-6 (lib bdg)
                          LC 2001-23896
Charlie and his mother walk around the neighborhood doing errands so that Charlie can write in his notebook about the people and places that make up his community
"Written from a child's perspective, the story has a cheerful tone and enough variety to keep the expedition interesting. The lively ink, watercolor, and colored-pencil illustrations are full of intriguing details." Booklist

Castañeda, Omar S., 1954-1997
Abuela's weave; illustrated by Enrique O. Sanchez. Lee & Low Bks. 1993 unp il $17.95; pa $8.95
Grades: K 1 2 3   E
    1. Grandmothers—Fiction 2. Guatemala—Fiction 3. Weaving—Fiction
    ISBN 1-880000-00-8; 1-880000-20-2 (pa)
                          LC 92-71927
A young Guatemalan girl and her grandmother grow closer as they weave some special creations and then make a trip to the market in hopes of selling them
"Castañeda affectingly portrays the loving rapport between a child and her grandmother, as well as the beauty of his homeland's cultural traditions. Sanchez's bright, richly grained acrylic-on-canvas paintings bring dimension to the characters and authenticity to the setting." Publ Wkly

Castella, Krystina
Discovering nature's alphabet; [by] Krystina Castella and Brian Boyl. Heyday Books 2005 unp il $15.95
Grades: 1 2 3 4   E
    1. Alphabet 2. Natural history
    ISBN 1-59714-021-X   LC 2005017857

"Castella and Boyl have assembled a portfolio of photographs of natural objects that form individual letters of the alphabet. From beaches to deserts, they discovered letters large and small in vines and flowers, tree trunks and seedpods. The minimal text urges readers to undertake such explorations to find their own hidden patterns." SLJ
Includes bibliographical references

Catalanotto, Peter
Emily's art. Atheneum Bks. for Young Readers 2001 unp il $16
Grades: PreK K 1   E
    1. Artists—Fiction 2. Contests—Fiction
    ISBN 0-689-83831-X   LC 00-29293
"A Richard Jackson book"
Emily paints four pictures and enters one in the first-grade art contest, but the judge interprets Emily's entry as a rabbit instead of a dog
"Filled with touches of humor and authentically childlike emotions, this book explores the subjectivity of opinion and the importance of personal conviction." Horn Book Guide

Cate, Annette LeBlanc
The magic rabbit; [by] Annette LeBlanc Cate. Candlewick Press 2007 unp il $15.99
Grades: K 1 2 3   E
    1.   Lost   and   found   possessions—Fiction 2. Magicians—Fiction 3. Rabbits—Fiction
    ISBN 978-0-7636-2672-3; 0-7636-2672-4
                          LC 2007022789
When Bunny becomes separated from Ray, a magician who is his business partner and friend, he follows a crowd to a park where he has a lovely afternoon, and after the people leave and darkness falls, the lonely and frightened Bunny finds a glittering trail of hope
"Embellished only with the gold of 'glittering stars,' Cate's black-and-white drawings perfectly evoke an urban setting in this tale of lost and found." SLJ

Cates, Karin
The Secret Remedy Book; a story of comfort and love; illustrated by Wendy Anderson Halperin. Orchard Bks. 2003 unp il $16.95 *
Grades: K 1 2 3   E
    1. Aunts—Fiction
    ISBN 0-439-35226-6   LC 2002-35475
Although Lolly loves to visit her Auntie Zep's house, she feels homesick when she actually gets there, and so Auntie Zep retrieves the Secret Remedy Book from an old trunk
"This wonderfully warm and satisfying story is paired with Halperin's lovely illustrations. Her trademark details and patterns abound, with softened edges, muted colors, and quiet landscapes." SLJ

Catrow, David

Dinosaur hunt. Orchard Books 2009 unp il (Max Spaniel) $6.99

Grades: PreK K 1   E

    1. Dogs—Fiction 2. Dinosaurs—Fiction

    ISBN 978-0-545-05748-6; 0-545-05748-5

                                   LC 2008-30144

Max Spaniel searches for dinosaurs in his back yard.

"Washed with colors, the exaggerated, cartoonlike drawings create a zany mood that energizes and extends the deadpan text." Booklist

Catusanu, Mircea

The strange case of the missing sheep. Viking 2009 unp il $16.99

Grades: PreK K 1   E

    1. Dogs—Fiction 2. Sheep—Fiction 3. Wolves—Fiction 4. Superheroes—Fiction

    ISBN 978-0-670-01131-5; 0-670-01131-2

                                   LC 2009-12358

When ten sheep go missing in the Dark Forest, Super Sheep Dog Doug comes to the rescue.

"Catusanu's cracked sense of humor and accomplished skills as an illustrator make for a strong authorial debut—readers won't be able to stop giggling." Publ Wkly

Cauley, Lorinda Bryan, 1951-

Clap your hands. Putnam 1992 unp il hardcover o.p. pa $6.99; bd bk $7.99

Grades: PreK K   E

    1. Animals—Fiction 2. Stories in rhyme

    ISBN 0-399-22118-2; 0-698-11428-0 (pa); 0-399-237100 (bd bk)   LC 91-12863

Rhyming text instructs the listener to find something yellow, roar like a lion, give a kiss, tell a secret, spin in a circle, and perform other playful activities along with the human and animal characters pictured

"The illustrations feature glowing colors and make good use of Cauley's gift for characterization. . . . Some parts of the book would be fun as action rhymes for preschool story time." Booklist

Cave, Kathryn, 1948-

One child, one seed; a South African counting book; photographs by Gisèle Wulfsohn. Holt & Co. 2003 unp il $16.95

Grades: PreK K 1 2   E

    1. Counting 2. Pumpkin 3. South Africa—Social life and customs

    ISBN 0-8050-7204-7   LC 2002-24098

"Children count from 1 to 10 with Nothando as she plants a pumpkin seed that grows to bear fruit for a delicious stew. . . . In a harmonious partnership of narrative and crisp, beautifully composed photographs that show the individuality of each person, readers get a glimpse into the life of an extended family living in a rural South African community. . . . The recipe for *isijingi*, the pumpkin stew, is included as are some basic geographical facts and a simple map. The writing has good rhythm, and reads aloud well." SLJ

Cazet, Denys, 1938-

Elvis the rooster almost goes to heaven. HarperCollins Pubs. 2003 48p il (I can read book) lib bdg $16.89

Grades: K 1 2   E

    1. Roosters—Fiction

    ISBN 978-0-06-000501-6; 0-06-000501-7

                                   LC 2002-14416

Elvis the rooster thinks he has died when he fails to crow at the rising of the sun but the chickens find a way to restore his cluck

"Cazet's writing is filled with quirky characters, simple wordplay, and gentle humor. The cartoon artwork perfectly reflects the tone of the text." SLJ

Another title about Elvis the rooster is:

Elvis the rooster and the magic words (2004)

Minnie and Moo, wanted dead or alive. HarperCollinsPublishers 2006 47p il hardcover o.p. lib bdg $16.89; pa $3.99 *

Grades: 1 2 3   E

    1. Cattle—Fiction 2. Thieves—Fiction

    ISBN 0-06-073010-2; 978-0-06-073010-9; 0-06-073011-0 (lib bdg); 978-0-06-073011-6 (lib bdg); 978-0-06-073012-3 (pa); 0-06-073012-9 (pa)

                                   LC 2005-14526

"An I can read book"

Trying to help Mr. Farmer with his finances, Minnie and Moo go to the bank to ask for money and are mistaken for the Bazooka sisters, dangerous outlaws.

"Cazet's watercolor illustrations of cows dressed as gangsters and cows driving a tractor extend the story's absurd humor and will help move emerging readers through eight chapters of text." Booklist

Other titles about Minnie and Moo are:

Minnie and Moo and the haunted sweater (2007)

Minnie and Moo and the potato from Planet X (2002)

Minnie and Moo meet Frankenswine (2001)

Minnie and Moo: the attack of the Easter bunnies (2004)

Minnie and Moo: the case of the missing jelly donut (2005)

Minnie and Moo: the night of the living bed (2003)

Minnie and Moo: will you be my Valentine? (2003)

The octopus; Grandpa Spanielson's Chicken pox stories, story #1. HarperCollins 2005 46p il $15.99; lib bdg $16.89 *

Grades: PreK K 1 2   E

    1. Octopuses—Fiction 2. Dogs—Fiction 3. Chickenpox—Fiction

    ISBN 0-06-051088-9; 0-06-051089-7 (lib bdg)

                                   LC 2003-26557

Grandpa Spanielson helps his favorite grandpup to avoid scratching his chicken pox by telling how he once had to fight off an octopus during a terrible storm.

"Beginning readers will love the humor, action, and compassion in this story, brought to life in the fun-filled text and superb cartoon illustrations." SLJ

Other titles in Grandpa Spanielson's Chicken pox stories series are:

A snout for chocolate (2006)

The shrunken head (2007)

Cazet, Denys, 1938-—*Continued*

Will you read to me? story and pictures by Denys Cazet. Atheneum Books for Young Readers 2007 unp il $16.99 *

Grades: PreK K 1 2   E

1. Pigs—Fiction 2. Books and reading—Fiction

ISBN 978-1-4169-0935-4; 1-4169-0935-4

LC 2005024144

"A Richard Jackson book"

Hamlet enjoys reading books and writing poetry, not playing in the mud and fighting over supper like the other pigs, but he finally finds someone who appreciates him just as he is

"Kids will enjoy the uproarious pigsty scenes. . . . But Cazet's simple poetry and soft-toned watercolor-and-colored-pencil spreads also show the beauty of the quiet night . . . and the farm community in solitude. This is not only a celebration of reading but also a moving story about not fitting in, even at home." Booklist

Cech, John

The nutcracker; based on the story by E.T.A. Hoffmann; retold by John Cech; illustrated by Eric Puybaret. Sterling 2009 unp il $17.95

Grades: 2 3 4 5   E

1. Fairy tales 2. Christmas—Fiction

ISBN 978-1-4027-5562-0; 1-4027-5562-7

LC 2008043084

In this retelling of the original 1816 German story, Godfather Drosselmeier gives young Marie a nutcracker for Christmas, and she finds herself in a magical realm where she saves a boy from an evil curse

"This beautifully illustrated rendition . . . is wordier than some picture-book adaptations. . . . The language is accessible, though, and lustrous, richly colored paintings cover half, sometimes more, of nearly every spread, providing valuable visual breaks." Booklist

The princess and the pea; by Hans Christian Andersen; retold by John Cech; illustrated by Bernhard Oberdieck. Sterling Pub. 2007 unp il $14.95

Grades: K 1 2 3   E

1. Andersen, Hans Christian, 1805-1875—Adaptations 2. Fairy tales

ISBN 978-1-4027-3065-8; 1-4027-3065-9

LC 2006007033

A girl proves that she is a real princess by feeling a pea through twenty mattresses and twenty featherbeds. Includes historical notes about Hans Christian Anderson and the original fairy tale.

"Cech's fluid text sparkles in this well-crafted retelling. . . . The illustrations, created with colored pencils, pastels, and acrylics, glow with lustrous yellow-gold, blue, and green tones." SLJ

Cecil, Randy

Duck; [by] Randy Cecil. Candlewick Press 2008 unp il $15.99

Grades: PreK K 1   E

1. Ducks—Fiction

ISBN 978-0-7636-3072-0   LC 2007040407

Companion volume to: Gator (2007)

Duck happily raises a duckling that has wandered into the amusement park where she is a carousel animal, but finds that she cannot teach what she herself has always longed to do—fly—and sets out to find real ducks to instruct him

"Cecil's illustrations . . . are done in oils. Duck, with her bright, striped scarf, stands out against soft green and gold hues. Many of the paintings are in circles of various sizes on a white background with a gold frame. . . . A beautifully realized friendship story with a happy ending." SLJ

Celenza, Anna Harwell

Gershwin's Rhapsody in Blue; [by] Anna Harwell Celenza; illustrated by JoAnn E. Kitchel. Charlesbridge 2006 unp il $19.95

Grades: 1 2 3 4   E

1. Gershwin, George, 1898-1937—Fiction 2. Composers—Fiction 3. Music—Fiction

ISBN 978-1-57091-556-7; 1-57091-556-3

LC 2005006009

In January of 1924, a twenty-six-year-old pianist, George Gershwin, finds himself slated to compose, in only five weeks, a concerto that defines "American music," and the result is his masterpiece, Rhapsody in Blue.

"Celenza's tale, complete with invented dialogue, brings the composer to life. . . . An author's note contains Gershwin's words describing the rhythm of the train ride that freed his mental block. . . . Kitchel's sensitivity to this source material is especially evident in her spread of multifaceted patterns and images. . . . An accompanying CD features Gershwin himself (courtesy of a piano roll)." SLJ

Chaconas, Dori, 1938-

Cork & Fuzz; illustrated by Lisa McCue. Viking 2005 32p il $13.99 *

Grades: K 1 2   E

1. Opossums—Fiction 2. Muskrats—Fiction 3. Friendship—Fiction

ISBN 0-670-03602-1   LC 2004-13613

"A Viking easy-to-read"

A possum and a muskrat become friends despite their many differences.

"The story's repeated words and entire sentences will help beginning readers feel successful. McCue's endearing drawings add personality and humor to the animals' faces. An excellent addition to easy-reader collections." SLJ

Other titles about Cork & Fuzz are:

Cork & Fuzz: short and tall (2006)

Cork & Fuzz: good sports (2007)

Cork & Fuzz: the collectors (2008)

Cork & Fuzz: finder's keepers (2009)

Cork & Fuzz: the babysitters (2010)

Mousie love; illustrated by Josee Masse. Bloomsbury U.S.A. Children's Books 2009 unp il $16.99; lib bdg $17.89

Grades: K 1 2   E

1. Mice—Fiction 2. Love—Fiction

ISBN 978-1-59990-111-4; 1-59990-111-0; 978-1-59990-368-2 (lib bdg); 1-59990-368-7 (lib bdg)

LC 2008-39888

Chaconas, Dori, 1938-—_Continued_

After falling in love at first sight, Tully the mouse strives to prove his devotion to Frill every day—while avoiding the cat—but never gives her a chance to respond to his marriage proposal

"Masse's bright, cheerful acrylic-and-gel illustrations complement the text . . . [and] courtship vignettes alternate with humorous, action-packed chase scenes from a mouse-eye perspective. Mousie love triumphs through adversity in this fetching little romance." Kirkus

Chall, Marsha Wilson

One pup's up; illustrated by Henry Cole. Margaret K. McElderry Books 2010 unp il $16.99
Grades: PreK K   E
  1. Stories in rhyme 2. Dogs—Fiction 3. Counting
ISBN 978-1-416-97960-9; 1-416-97960-3
                                    LC 2009003172
Rhyming text counts off ten puppies as they awaken one by one, chase and bounce around the house, eat kibble and get washed, then fall back to sleep.

"With its lively tone and large-scale art that, thanks to ample white space, focuses exclusively on the dogs, this is a winning choice for reading aloud at story hour or lap time." Publ Wkly

Chamberlain, Margaret, 1954-

Please don't tease Tootsie. Dutton 2008 unp il $16.99
Grades: PreK K 1 2   E
  1. Pets—Fiction 2. Stories in rhyme
ISBN 978-0-525-47982-6; 0-525-47982-1
"Tootsie, a disgruntled red cat, is arching her back and glowering at the little girl who is cheerfully threatening to spray her with a hose. On succeeding pages, readers meet a number of animals under siege by naughty preschoolers. The text consists of brief, alliterative entreaties to mend their ways. . . . The illustrations are droll and stylized, featuring expressive cartoon animals on fields of bright color or flamboyant Art Nouveau patterns." SLJ

Chandra, Deborah

George Washington's teeth; written by Deborah Chandra & Madeleine Comora; pictures by Brock Cole. Farrar, Straus & Giroux 2003 unp il $16 *
Grades: PreK K 1 2   E
  1. Washington, George, 1732-1799 2. Teeth
ISBN 0-374-32534-0   LC 2002-25086
A rollicking rhyme portrays George Washington's lifelong struggle with bad teeth. A timeline taken from diary entries and other nonfiction sources follows

This is written "with wit, verve, and a generous amount of sympathy for poor Washington and his dental woes. . . . Illustrator Cole is at his absolute best here, totally at ease with human gesture and expression." Booklist

Chapra, Mimi

Sparky's bark; El ladrido de Sparky; by Mimi Chapra; illustrated by Vivi Escrivá. Katherine Tegen Books 2006 unp il hardcover o.p. lib bdg $17.89
Grades: PreK K 1 2   E
  1. Latin Americans—Fiction 2. Dogs—Fiction 3. Bilingual books—English-Spanish
ISBN 0-06-053172-X; 0-06-053173-8 (lib bdg)
                                    LC 2004-12411
When young Lucy travels from Latin America to visit relatives in Ohio, she is very homesick until she realizes that the only way to communicate with her cousin's frisky dog is to learn to speak English

"The English and Spanish appear separately on the same page, but some intermingling of the two occurs occasionally without being intrusive. Escrivá's watercolor illustrations are delightful and detailed, complementing the story well." SLJ

Charles, Veronika Martenova

The birdman; illustrated by Annouchka Gravel Galouchko & Stéphan Daigle. Tundra Books 2006 unp il $17.95
Grades: K 1 2 3   E
  1. India—Fiction 2. Birds—Fiction 3. Bereavement—Fiction
ISBN 978-0-88776-740-1; 0-88776-740-0
"In the crowded streets of Calcutta, Nobi, a tailor, works hard to support his family. Then his wife and children are killed. . . . After weeks of immobilizing anguish, Nobi buys some caged birds at the market, sets them free, and finds some of his weighty sorrow released. . . . Charles, who based her vivid, poetic text on a true story (explained in a lengthy afterword), is frank about the pain of loss, but focuses on the uplifting message that acts of kindness can ease grief. The illustrators extend the story's spirit-healing themes in vibrant folk-art paintings, gloriously patterned with flowers, Hindu symbols, and soaring birds." Booklist

Charlip, Remy

Fortunately; written and illustrated by Remy Charlip. Aladdin Books 1993 unp il pa $6.99
Grades: PreK K 1   E
  1. Chance—Fiction 2. Travel—Fiction
ISBN 0-689-71660-5; 978-0-689-71660-7
                                    LC 92-22794
First published 1964 by Four Winds Press
Good and bad luck accompany Ned from New York to Florida on his way to a surprise party.

A perfect day; [by] Remy Charlip. Greenwillow Books 2007 unp il $16.99; lib bdg $17.89 *
Grades: PreK K 1 2   E
  1. Father-son relationship—Fiction 2. Stories in rhyme
ISBN 0-06-051972-X; 0-06-051973-8 (lib bdg)
                                    LC 2004-52350
A father and son's "perfect day consists of doing ordinary things—going for a walk, picnicking with friends, watching the clouds, reading books. . . . The simple illustrations resemble something a youngster might draw, and the palette of soft pastel colors supports the story's

Charlip, Remy—*Continued*

comforting atmosphere and the love between these two.
. . . Charlip has crafted a cozy story that is a perfect example of parent and child bonding." SLJ

Chen, Chih-Yuan

Guji Guji. Kane/Miller 2004 unp il $15.95 *

Grades: PreK K 1 2   E

1. Ducks—Fiction 2. Crocodiles—Fiction

ISBN 1-929132-67-0

Crocodile Guji Guji, who was raised by a family of ducks, meets three crocodiles who tell him that he was not a duck. When the crocodiles ask Guji Guji to help them trap the ducks he saves the duck family.

"This beautifully written story has much to say about appreciating families and differences. . . . Chen's unique illustrations are compelling. . . . The rich blues and earth tones and dramatic page layouts create moving scenes, but the quirky details and characters' expressions are hilarious." SLJ

On my way to buy eggs; written and illustrated by Chih-Yuan Chen. Kane/Miller 2003 unp il hardcover o.p. pa $7.99

Grades: PreK K 1 2   E

ISBN 1-929132-49-2; 1-933605-41-3 (pa)

LC 2002-117381

First published 2001 in Taiwan

"A young girl's errand to the store turns into a sensory adventure. . . . After a make-believe game with the shopkeeper and more adventures along the way, Shau-yu returns home to her loving dad. The story is basic, but the simple words and phrases easily show Shau-yu's delight in transforming small things. The earth-tone colors in the crisp paper-and-pencil collages are as quiet as the story." Booklist

Chen, Yong, 1963-

A gift. Boyds Mills Press 2009 unp il $16.95

Grades: K 1 2 3   E

1. Aunts—Fiction 2. Uncles—Fiction 3. Chinese Americans—Fiction 4. Chinese New Year—Fiction 5. China—Fiction

ISBN 978-1-59078-610-9; 1-59078-610-6

LC 2009012794

Amy receives a gift for the Chinese New Year from her aunt and uncles who live far away in China.

"Chen's text is spare but, combined with her luscious watercolors, evokes a vivid portrait of rural Chinese culture." SLJ

Cherry, Lynne, 1952-

The great kapok tree; a tale of the Amazon rainforest. Harcourt Brace Jovanovich 1990 unp il $16; pa $7 *

Grades: K 1 2 3   E

1. Rain forests—Fiction

ISBN 0-15-200520-X; 0-15-202614-2 (pa)

LC 89-2208

"Gulliver books"

The many different animals that live in a great kapok tree in the Brazilian rainforest try to convince a man with an ax of the importance of not cutting down their home

"A carefully researched picture book. . . . Cherry captures the Amazonian proportions of the plants and animals that live there by using vibrant colors, intricate details, and dramatic perspectives. . . . The writing is simple and clear." Booklist

How Groundhog's garden grew. Blue Sky Press (NY) 2003 unp il $15.95

Grades: PreK K 1 2   E

1. Marmots—Fiction

ISBN 0-439-32371-1   LC 2002-3428

Squirrel teaches Little Groundhog how to plant and tend a vegetable garden

The author "tells a charming and also informative story about plants, gardening, and environmental respect. Her beautiful, full-color illustrations—realistic and wonderfully detailed—often incorporate spot-art borders of labeled seedlings and plants, highlighting a diverse array of wildlife." Booklist

The sea, the storm, and the mangrove tangle. Farrar, Straus and Giroux 2004 unp il $16

Grades: K 1 2 3   E

1. Wetlands—Fiction 2. Ecology—Fiction 3. Marine animals—Fiction 4. Caribbean region—Fiction

ISBN 0-374-36482-6   LC 2002-29705

A seed from a mangrove tree floats on the sea until it comes to rest on the shore of a faraway lagoon where, over time, it becomes a mangrove island that shelters many birds and animals, even during a hurricane.

"Cherry paints lustrous, detailed scenes that, together with her accessible narrative, will spark children's interest in a magnificent, endangered ecosystem." Booklist

Chessa, Francesca

Holly's red boots; [by] Francesca Chessa. Holiday House 2008 unp il $16.95

Grades: PreK K 1   E

1. Shoes—Fiction 2. Color—Fiction 3. Snow—Fiction

ISBN 978-0-8234-2158-9; 0-8234-2158-9

LC 2007-35516

Holly wants to play in the snow and needs her red books, so she and her cat Jasper search the house for anything red.

"The bright, childlike art uses multiple perspectives and bold swatches of color to portray the freckled preschooler, her patient mom, and the chaotic house search." SLJ

Chichester-Clark, Emma, 1955-

Little Miss Muffet counts to ten. Andersen Press 2010 unp il pa $9.99

Grades: K 1 2   E

1. Nursery rhymes—Fiction 2. Counting 3. Animals—Fiction 4. Stories in rhyme

ISBN 978-1-84270-955-9; 1-84270-955-0

"In the nursery rhyme, the spider frightened Miss Muffet away. Well, not this time. The spider asks her to stay, and politely she does. Then come the animals: two, three, four, five—bearing gifts, and delicacies, and decorations." Publisher's note

Chichester-Clark, Emma, 1955-—*Continued*

"The text is spot-on as Clark keeps the rhyming pattern of the original nursery rhyme and makes it her own. . . . The whimsical illustrations show plenty of activity as the number of characters increases, but they never descend into overwhelming busyness and many invite closer inspection. Perfect for storytime or individual sharing." SLJ

Melrose and Croc: an adventure to remember. Walker & Co. 2008 unp il $16.95; lib bdg $17.85
Grades: PreK K 1 2   E
   1.   Birthdays—Fiction   2.   Dogs—Fiction
3. Crocodiles—Fiction
   ISBN   978-0-8027-9774-2;   0-8027-9774-1;
978-0-8027-9775-9 (lib bdg); 0-8027-9775-X (lib bdg)
                        LC 2007-037146
A friendly crocodile receives the best birthday present ever when he rescues his dear companion, Melrose the dog, during a storm at sea
"This simple story, set in a European seaside village, celebrates two caring individuals who think only of one another. Its gentle, affectionate message and expressive illustrations are a wonderful, reassuring way to lull any child into a peaceful sleep in which all is right with the world." SLJ
  Other titles about Melrose and Croc are:
Melrose and Croc: a Christmas to remember (2006)
Melrose and Croc beside the sea (2009)
Melrose and Croc find a smile (2009)
Melrose and Croc: friends for life (2009)
Melrose and Croc go to town (2009)

Piper; [written and illustrated by] Emma Chichester Clark. Eerdmans Books for Young Readers 2007 unp il $17
Grades: PreK K 1 2   E
   1. Dogs—Fiction
   ISBN 978-0-8028-5314-1   LC 2006008548
A young dog runs away from its cruel master, but finds a new home after saving the life of an old woman
"Both honorable and adorable, Piper will inspire strong reactions from kids, and Clark's always-impressive watercolors effectively capture both the happy and the dark moments of the tale." Booklist

Child, Lauren, 1965-

I am too absolutely small for school. Candlewick 2004 unp il $16.99; pa $6.99 *
Grades: PreK K 1 2   E
   1. School stories 2. Siblings—Fiction
   ISBN 0-7636-2403-9; 0-7636-2887-5 (pa)
                        LC 2003-65576
Board books about Lola and Charlie are also available
When Lola is worried about starting school, her older brother Charlie reassures her
"The children's relationship is refreshingly noncombative. . . . Incorporating photos, fabric, and appealingly childlike cartoon renderings of the siblings, the mixed-media illustrations are a visual treat of color and texture." SLJ
  Other titles about Lola and Charlie are:
But excuse me that is my book (2006)
I am not sleepy and I will not go to bed (2001)

I will never not eat a tomato (2000)
Say cheese (2007)
Snow is my favorite and my best (2006)

Who wants to be a poodle I don't. Candlewick Press 2009 unp il $16.99
Grades: PreK K 1 2   E
   1. Dogs—Fiction
   ISBN 978-0-7636-4610-3; 0-7636-4610-5
                        LC 2009003659
Tired of being a pampered poodle dressed in a little pink poncho, Trixie Twinkle Toes sets off in search of dangerous and daring adventures.
"Young readers will sympathize with Trixie and savor the details of her posh urban existence. . . . Child's . . . collages contain all the action Trixie's life lacks, sizzling with dizzying colors and patterns; her sentences lead adventurous lives of their own, curlicuing, shrinking, growing and spiraling into muddy puddles." Publ Wkly

Chinn, Karen, 1959-

Sam and the lucky money; illustrated by Cornelius Van Wright, and Ying-Hwa Hu. Lee & Low Bks. 1995 unp il hardcover o.p. pa $7.95
Grades: PreK K 1 2   E
   1. Chinese New Year—Fiction 2. Chinese Americans—Fiction
   ISBN 1-880000-13-X; 1-880000-53-9 (pa)
                        LC 94-11766
This is a "tale of a young boy eager to spend his 'lucky money' on Chinese New Year day. As Sam searches the streets of Chinatown for ways to spend his four dollars, he stumbles upon a stranger in need. After he decides to give, rather than spend, his money, Sam realizes that he's 'the lucky one.'" Horn Book Guide
"The illustrators masterfully combine Chinatown's exotic setting with the universal emotions of childhood through expressive portraits of the characters." SLJ

Chocolate, Debbi, 1954-

El barrio; illustrated by David Diaz. Henry Holt 2009 unp il $16.95
Grades: PreK K 1 2   E
   1. Hispanic Americans—Fiction 2. City and town life—Fiction 3. Community life—Fiction
   ISBN 978-0-8050-7457-4; 0-8050-7457-0
                        LC 2008013422
A young boy explores his vibrant Latino neighborhood, with its vegetable gardens instead of lawns, Nativity parades, quinceanera parties, and tejana and salsa music.
"Thick lines surround the woodcut-like artwork imbued with a rainbow of glowing colors. Fascinating mixed-media collages (toy skulls, rocks, beads, shells) border each spread. The whole is an exuberant cacophony of colors and sights." Booklist

Chodos-Irvine, Margaret

Best best friends; [by] Margaret Chodos-Irvine. Harcourt 2006 unp il $16
Grades: PreK K 1   E
   1.   Friendship—Fiction   2.   Birthdays—Fiction
3. School stories
   ISBN 0-15-205694-7   LC 2005002251

Chodos-Irvine, Margaret—*Continued*

Mary and Clare do everything together at preschool, but Mary's birthday celebration puts a strain on the girls' friendship.

"In spot-on words and crisp, gaily patterned prints, the [author-illustrator] captures the unselfconscious affection and quicksilver shifts in mood that characterize preschool friendships." Booklist

Ella Sarah gets dressed. Harcourt 2003 unp il $16; bd bk $10.95 *

Grades: PreK K 1   E

1. Clothing and dress—Fiction

ISBN 0-15-216413-8; 0-15-206486-9 (bd bk)
LC 2002-5097

A Caldecott Medal honor book, 2004

Despite the advice of others in her family, Ella Sarah persists in wearing the striking and unusual outfit of her own choosing

"With minimal words and her signature art marked by bright, bold prints, Chodos-Irvine perfectly captures a universal childhood struggle." Booklist

Choi, Sook Nyul

Halmoni and the picnic; illustrated by Karen Milone. Houghton Mifflin 1993 31p il $16

Grades: K 1 2 3   E

1. Korean Americans—Fiction 2. Grandmothers—Fiction

ISBN 0-395-61626-3   LC 91-34121

A third grade class helps Halmoni, Yunmi's newly arrived Korean grandmother, feel more comfortable with her life in the United States

This book is "is pleasing . . . thanks to the lovely bordered watercolor art and the subtle text, both of which display a fine sensitivity." Booklist

Another title about Yunmi and Halmoni is:
Yunmi and Halmoni's trip (1997)

Choi, Yangsook

Behind the mask. Farrar, Straus and Giroux 2006 unp il $16

Grades: PreK K 1 2   E

1. Halloween—Fiction 2. Masks (Facial)—Fiction 3. Korean Americans—Fiction 4. Grandfathers—Fiction

ISBN 0-374-30522-6   LC 2005-45950

"Frances Foster books"

Kimin, a young Korean-American boy, has trouble deciding on a Halloween costume, but as he looks through an old trunk of his grandfather's things, he suddenly unlocks a childhood mystery

"Quiet and well-crafted, the story manages some subtle emotional shifts as well as the smooth weaving of one tradition with another." Booklist

Choldenko, Gennifer, 1957-

Louder, Lili; [by] Gennifer Choldenko; illustrated by S.D. Schindler. G.P. Putnam's Sons 2007 unp il $16.99

Grades: PreK K 1 2   E

1. School stories 2. Friendship—Fiction

ISBN 978-0-399-24252-6   LC 2007007511

Lili is so shy that her voice is never heard in class until the day a good friend needs her help

"This engaging story is well written and even poetic. Lili is a well-developed character, and her growth is believable. The warm, energetic illustrations highlight the elements of humor in the story." SLJ

Choung, Euh-Hee

Minji's salon. Kane Miller 2008 unp il $15.95

Grades: PreK   E

1. Beauty shops—Fiction 2. Dogs—Fiction

ISBN 978-1-933605-67-8; 1-933605-67-7

"When Minji's mother heads to the beauty salon, Minji pretends to be her dog's hairdresser. . . . The simply charming story of a young girl using her imagination is accompanied by delightful artwork." Booklist

Christelow, Eileen, 1943-

Five little monkeys jumping on the bed; retold and illustrated by Eileen Christelow. Clarion Bks. 1989 unp il $15; pa $5.95; bd bk $11.99 *

Grades: PreK K 1 2   E

1. Monkeys—Fiction 2. Counting

ISBN   0-89919-769-8;   0-395-55701-1   (pa);
0-547-13176-3 (bd bk)   LC 88-22839

A counting book in which one by one the five little monkeys jump on the bed only to fall off and bump their heads

"Squiggling, swirling lines of color capture the sense of unbridled motion as the monkeys bounce and, one by one, topple from the bed. After all five bandaged youngsters finally fall asleep, a relaxed mama gratefully retires to her room . . . to bounce on 'her' bed. An amusingly presented counting exercise." Booklist

Other titles about the five little monkeys are:
Don't wake up Mama! (1992)
Five little monkeys go shopping (2007)
Five little monkeys play hide and seek (2004)
Five little monkeys sitting in a tree (1991)
Five little monkeys wash the car (2000)
Five little monkeys with nothing to do (1996)

Letters from a desperate dog; [by] Eileen Christelow. Clarion Books 2006 32p il $16

Grades: PreK K 1 2   E

1. Dogs—Fiction

ISBN 978-0-618-51003-0; 0-618-51003-6
LC 2005032744

Feeling misunderstood and unappreciated by her owner, Emma the dog asks for advice from the local canine advice columnist.

"This is a delightful romp, and Christelow shows Emma's story off to great advantage in an oversize format with comic-book-style watercolor art." Booklist

Church, Caroline

Digby takes charge; written and illustrated by Caroline Jayne Church. Margaret K. McElderry Books 2007 unp il $14.99

Grades: PreK K 1   E

1. Dogs—Fiction 2. Sheep—Fiction 3. Animals—Fiction

ISBN 978-1-4169-3441-7; 1-4169-3441-3
LC 2006023973

Church, Caroline—*Continued*

Digby is a very good sheepdog, but when faced with six unruly sheep who ignore him even when he goes to extremes to make them obey, the farm's cows and pigs give him some sage advice

"Using acrylic paint, textured papers, and collage, Church creates landscapes and characters with expressive lines and some unusual but effective color combinations. Simple, satisfying, and sometimes amusing as well." Booklist

One smart goose; [by] Caroline Jayne Church. Orchard Books 2005 c2003 unp il $16.95
Grades: PreK K 1 2   E
  1. Geese—Fiction 2. Foxes—Fiction
  ISBN 0-439-68765-9
First published 2003 in the United Kingdom

A goose who likes to wash in a muddy pond is teased by the other geese, until they realize that he is the only one not chased by the fox

"The clever story will hold the attention of young children, but the illustrations are the book's most striking feature. Bold black lines define the forms of the geese, the fox, and the setting, while textured papers, buts of smudgy print, and collage elements enrich the simple compositions." Booklist

Claflin, Willy, 1944-

The uglified ducky; a Maynard Moose tale; [by] Willy Claflin; illustrated by James Stimson. August House/LittleFolk 2008 unp il $18.95
Grades: K 1 2 3   E
  1. Fairy tales
  ISBN 978-0-87483-858-9; 0-87483-858-4
                      LC 2008000974

Resets Hans Christian Andersen's tale, The ugly duckling, in the Northern Piney Woods of Alaska, where a baby moose is raised by a family of ducks who try to teach him to waddle, quack, and fly but cannot see his true beauty.

"Stimson's colorful illustrations are a riot, featuring stylized shapes, funny expressions, and animated scenes. A CD of the story performed hilariously by Claflin is delightful. This fresh, lively story is laugh-out-loud funny." SLJ

Clarke, J. (Jane), 1954-

Stuck in the mud; [by] Jane Clarke; illustrations by Garry Parsons. Walker Pub. Co. 2008 unp il $16.95
Grades: PreK K 1   E
  1. Chickens—Fiction 2. Domestic animals—Fiction 3. Stories in rhyme
  ISBN 978-0-8027-9758-2; 0-8027-9758-X
                      LC 2007032179

"One morning, a hen awakens to find a chick missing from her brood. She spots him in the middle of a patch of 'mucky mud,' assumes he is trapped, and clucks hysterically until her friends come to help pull him out. One by one, the rescuers also become mired in the muck. . . . Bright paintings in solid colors and simple, yet expressive cartoon animals are well suited to very young listeners." SLJ

Cleary, Beverly

The hullabaloo ABC; illustrated by Ted Rand. rev ed. Morrow Junior Bks. 1998 unp il $17.99
Grades: PreK K 1 2   E
  1. Noise—Fiction 2. Farm life—Fiction 3. Stories in rhyme 4. Alphabet
  ISBN 0-688-15182-5   LC 97-6457
A revised and newly illustrated edition of the title first published 1960 by Parnassus Press

An alphabet book in which two children demonstrate all the fun that is to be had by making and hearing every kind of noise as they dash about on the farm

"Rand's expert watercolor illustrations on crisp white backgrounds bring the action to life with just the slightest touch of nostalgia." SLJ

Clement, Nathan, 1966-

Drive; [by] Nathan Clement. Front Street 2008 unp il $16.95 *
Grades: PreK K   E
  1. Fathers—Fiction 2. Trucks—Fiction
  ISBN 978-1-59078-517-1   LC 2007037469
In brief text with illustrations, a boy describes his father's work as a truck driver

"Working in big, streamlined shapes; flat, bright colors; and shiny, airbrushed-like surfaces, [Clement] evokes a deco-esque world. . . . Unusual and often cinematic perspectives . . . plunge readers into the action and give the compositions a red-blooded energy." Publ Wkly

Clements, Andrew, 1949-

Circus family dog; illustrated by Sue Truesdell. Clarion Bks. 2000 32p il $16
Grades: PreK K 1 2   E
  1. Dogs—Fiction 2. Circus—Fiction
  ISBN 0-395-78648-7   LC 99-52657
Grumps is content to do his one trick in the center ring at the circus, until a new dog shows up and steals the show—temporarily

"The combination of Clements's impeccable storyteller pacing and Truesdell's creative and whimsical cartoons create a reading and visual experience second only to actually being at the circus. The illustrator uses a mixture of watercolors with pen and ink to bring the action to life in vibrant colors." SLJ

The handiest things in the world; photographs by Raquel Jaramillo. Atheneum 2010 unp il $16.99
Grades: PreK K 1 2   E
  1. Hand—Fiction 2. Stories in rhyme
  ISBN 978-1-416-96166-6; 1-416-96166-6
"This unusual concept book looks at all the things that hands can do and the tools that help do them better. On a typical double-page spread, two short rhyming sentences are paired with photos. The first shows a child's hands performing a job, while the next shows them using a tool. . . . In the first picture, a girl untangles her hair with her fingers; in the next, with a comb. . . . Excellent color photos of different children engaged in everyday activities enhance the book's appeal." Booklist

Cocca-Leffler, Maryann, 1958-
Jack's talent. Farrar, Straus & Giroux 2007 unp
il $16
Grades: PreK K 1 2   E
    1. School stories
    ISBN 0-374-33681-4; 978-0-374-33681-3
                           LC 2006048951
On the first day of school, as the children in Miss Lucinda's class introduce themselves and name their special
talent, Jack wonders if he is good at anything.
"With simple, short sentences, Jack's feelings and
worries are sympathetically portrayed in this supportive,
positive read. Animated, expressive cartoon-style art,
with colorful texture and detail, depicts the diverse characters and their various activities." Booklist

Princess K.I.M. and the lie that grew. Albert
Whitman & Co. 2009 32p il $16.99
Grades: PreK K 1 2   E
    1. Truthfulness and falsehood—Fiction
    ISBN 978-0-8075-4178-4; 0-8075-4178-8
                           LC 2008-28056
After new girl Kim tells her classmates she is from a
royal family, her lie grows and grows.
"The brightly colored artwork brings the story to life.
. . . Varying layouts effectively convey the action." SLJ

Cochran, Bill, 1966-
The forever dog; by Bill Cochran; illustrated by
Dan Andreasen. HarperCollins 2007 unp il $15.99;
lib bdg $16.89
Grades: K 1 2 3   E
    1. Dogs—Fiction 2. Death—Fiction 3. Bereavement—
Fiction
    ISBN   978-0-06-053939-9;   0-06-053939-9;
978-0-06-053940-5 (lib bdg); 0-06-053940-2 (lib bdg)
                           LC 2006002501
Mike and his dog Corky plan to be best friends forever, so when Corky becomes sick and dies, Mike is angry
about the broken promise
"Andreasen's soft illustrations portray a heartwarming
relationship and capture the changing mood of the story
from joy and exhilaration to sadness and back again to
a subdued happiness and understanding." SLJ

My parents are divorced, my elbows have
nicknames, and other facts about me; illustrated by
Steve Björkman. HarperCollins 2009 unp il
$17.99; lib bdg $18.89
Grades: K 1 2 3   E
    1. Divorce—Fiction
    ISBN   978-0-06-053942-9;   0-06-053942-9;
978-0-06-053943-6 (lib bdg); 0-06-053943-7 (lib bdg)
While describing his not-so-weird life with his divorced parents, a young boy also describes some other
things about himself that could be considered weird.
"This story uses humor to help children cope with the
issue of divorce. . . . Ted has a believable voice that
children will recognize. . . . The colorful cartoons add to
the upbeat nature of the story and make a serious subject
a little easier to swallow." SLJ

Coerr, Eleanor, 1922-
The big balloon race; pictures by Carolyn Croll.
Harper & Row 1981 62p il pa $3.99 hardcover
o.p.
Grades: K 1 2   E
    1. Balloons—Fiction
    ISBN 0-06-444053-2 (pa)   LC 80-8368
"An I can read book"
The author "recounts the winning of a hydrogen balloon race by Carlotta Myers, a famous aeronaut, and her
stowaway daughter Ariel. Balloon facts are slipped naturally and painlessly into the story, which moves cogently
along. The novel subject matter, straightforward mother-
daughter relationship, and clear composition of the orange, blue and gray illustrations . . . make for a highflying new look at a piece of the past." SLJ

Chang's paper pony; pictures by Deborah Kogan
Ray. Harper & Row 1988 64p il pa $3.99
hardcover o.p.
Grades: K 1 2   E
    1. Chinese Americans—Fiction 2. Horses—Fiction
3. Gold mines and mining—Fiction
    ISBN 0-06-044163-6 (pa)   LC 87-45679
"An I can read book"
In San Francisco during the 1850's gold rush, Chang,
the son of Chinese immigrants, wants a pony but cannot
afford one until his friend Big Pete finds a solution
"Ray's forceful drawings support the text well and
firmly establish the dusty mining-town environment. She
is particularly adept at showing the vulnerability of children, as well as the ways in which large and small joys
affect them." Publ Wkly

The Josefina story quilt; pictures by Bruce
Degen. Harper & Row 1986 64p il hardcover o.p.
pa $3.99
Grades: K 1 2 3   E
    1. Quilts—Fiction 2. Overland journeys to the Pacif-
ic—Fiction
    ISBN 0-06-021348-5; 0-06-444129-6 (pa)
                           LC 85-45260
"An I can read book"
While traveling west with her family in 1850, a young
girl makes a patchwork quilt chronicling the experiences
of the journey and reserves a special patch for her pet
hen Josefina
"The story makes the history go down easily, and an
author's note at the end fills in facts about the western
trip and the place of quilts as pioneer diaries. The charcoal and blue/yellow wash illustrations are clear and natural. . . . A good introduction to historical fiction that
children can read for themselves." SLJ

Coffelt, Nancy
Dogs in space. Harcourt Brace Jovanovich 1993
unp il hardcover o.p. pa $7 *
Grades: PreK K 1 2   E
    1. Planets—Fiction 2. Solar system—Fiction
3. Dogs—Fiction
    ISBN 0-15-200440-8; 0-15-201004-1 (pa)
                           LC 91-29036
"Gulliver books"

Coffelt, Nancy—*Continued*

Dogs in space visit each of the planets in the solar system, finding no one at home anywhere, and return to Earth

"The bright oil pastels against velvety black backgrounds are delightful and, science notwithstanding, make for an exciting visual journey." SLJ

Fred stays with me; illustrated by Tricia Tusa. Little, Brown 2007 unp il $16.99 *

Grades: PreK K 1 2   E

1. Dogs—Fiction 2. Divorce—Fiction

ISBN 0-316-88269-0   LC 2005-07973

Boston Globe-Horn Book Award honor book: Picture Book (2008)

A child describes how she lives sometimes with his mother and sometimes with his father, but his dog is his constant companion.

"Coffelt and Tusa have teamed up to create a charming book that meshes text and illustrations seamlessly. . . . Tusa uses gold and brown hues with occasional splashes of red to create a warm tone." SLJ

Cohen, Barbara, 1932-1992

Molly's pilgrim; illustrated by Daniel Mark Duffy. Lothrop, Lee & Shepard Bks. 1998 unp il $17.99; pa $3.95 *

Grades: K 1 2 3   E

1. Jews—Fiction 2. School stories 3. Thanksgiving Day—Fiction 4. Immigrants—Fiction

ISBN 0-688-16279-7; 0-688-16280-0 (pa)

LC 98-9227

A newly illustrated edition of the title first published 1983

Told to make a Pilgrim doll for the Thanksgiving display at school, Molly is embarassed when her mother tries to help her out by creating a doll dressed as she herself was dressed before leaving Russia to seek religious freedom

Cohen, Deborah Bodin, 1968-

Nachshon, who was afraid to swim; a Passover story; by Deborah Bodin Cohen; illustrations by Jago. Kar-Ben Pub. 2009 unp il lib bdg $17.95; pa $8.95

Grades: 1 2 3 4   E

1. Slavery—Fiction 2. Courage—Fiction 3. Fear—Fiction 4. Passover—Fiction 5. Jews—Fiction

ISBN 978-0-8225-8764-4 (lib bdg); 0-8225-8764-5 (lib bdg); 978-0-8225-8765-1 (pa); 0-8225-8765-3 (pa)

LC 2007048359

When the Israelites flee Egypt, Nachshon exhibits great courage by being the first to step into the Red Sea, even though he cannot swim.

"The digitally prepared, mixed-media illustrations utilize muted yellow, orange, and brown tones to depict the sweltering heat of the desert and bright blue and green tones to illustrate the celebration of freedom. They complement and enhance the text marvelously. A wonderful, unique addition." SLJ

Cohen, Miriam, 1926-

First grade takes a test; by Miriam Cohen; illustrated by Ronald Himler. Star Bright Books 2006 unp il $15.95; pa $5.95 *

Grades: PreK K 1 2   E

1. School stories 2. Examinations—Fiction

ISBN 978-1-59572-054-2; 1-59572-054-5; 978-1-59572-055-9 (pa); 1-59572-055-3 (pa)

LC 2006020488

A revised and newly illustrated edition of the title first published 1980 by Greenwillow Bks.

"One day the first-graders are given a special multiple-choice test by the principal. Some kids find the questions puzzling. Then, suddenly, time's up. Anna Maria announces, 'That was easy.' But many kids are confused and upset, and 'You're a dummy!' echoes through the class, which only settles down when the kindly teacher reminds the children of all the things they do understand. . . . Cohen's sensitivity to children's feelings and reactions really shows here. . . . Himler's loose-lined, pencil-and-watercolor pictures skillfully use body language and facial expressions to chart the children's emotional highs and lows." Booklist

Jim's dog Muffins; illustrated by Ronald Himler. Star Bright Books 2007 unp il $15.95; pa $5.95

Grades: K 1 2   E

1. Death—Fiction 2. Bereavement—Fiction 3. School stories

ISBN 978-1-59572-099-3; 1-59572-099-5; 978-1-59572-100-6 (pa); 1-59572-100-2 (pa)

LC 2007-33696

First published 1984 by Greenwillow Books

When Jim's dog is killed, the other first graders experience with him his natural reactions to death.

"The issues raised are true and honest. Himler's softly colored illustrations sensitively capture the nuances of classroom life." Booklist

My big brother; art by Ronald Himler. Star Bright 2005 unp il $15.95

Grades: K 1 2 3   E

1. Brothers—Fiction 2. Family life—Fiction 3. Soldiers—Fiction

ISBN 1-59572-007-3   LC 2004-16056

When his big brother leaves to become a soldier, a boy does what he can to take his place in the family.

"This quiet picture book packs a strong emotional wallop. Himler's artwork, pencil with watercolor washes, sensitively depicts each character's emotions through body language and facial expressions." Booklist

Will I have a friend? by Miriam Cohen; illustrated by Ronald Himler. Star Bright Books 2009 unp il $15.95 *

Grades: PreK K 1   E

1. School stories 2. Friendship—Fiction

ISBN 978-1-59572-069-6; 1-59572-069-3

LC 2008036957

A newly illustrated edition of the title first published 1967 by Macmillan

Jim's anxieties on his first day of school are happily forgotten when he makes a new friend.

The art is "fresh and new. . . . Himler's soft water-

Cohen, Miriam, 1926-—*Continued*
colors are . . . contemporary in look, with touches like
a recycle mark on the trash bin. . . . Great for combating new-kid-in-school blues." Booklist

Cohn, Diana
Namaste! illustrated by Amy Cordova; with an
Afterward by Ang Rita Sherpa of the Mountain
Institute. SteinerBooks 2009 unp il $17.95
Grades: K 1 2   E
   1. Nepal—Fiction
ISBN 978-0-88010-625-2; 0-88010-625-5
                LC 2009003216
   Whenever Nima meets someone on her long walk to
the market village in Nepal, she brings her hands together with her fingers almost touching her chin, bows her
head slightly, and says "Namaste," which means "the
light in me meets the light in you." Includes information
on the geography, culture, and people of Nepal
   "The vibrant folk-art illustrations showing the details
of Nima's life in her village support the simple story
perfectly. This beautiful book will appeal to primary
readers and make an ideal addition to multicultural collections." SLJ

Colato Laínez, René
My shoes and I; illustrations by Fabricio
Vanden Broeck. Boyds Mills Press 2010 unp il
$16.95
Grades: K 1 2 3   E
   1. Travel—Fiction 2. Immigrants—Fiction 3. Shoes—
Fiction 4. Father-son relationship—Fiction 5. Central
America—Fiction
ISBN 978-1-59078-385-6; 1-59078-385-9
                LC 2008-30003
   As Mario and his Papa travel from El Salvador to the
United States to be reunited with Mama, Mario's won-
derful new shoes help to distract him from the long and
difficult journey.
   "Vanden Broeck's color-drenched illustrations on
weathered backgrounds add immediacy and detail. This
moving, heartfelt tale of courage and perseverance will
be embraced by a wide audience of readers, young and
old." SLJ

Playing loteria; illustrated by Jill Arena. Luna
Rising 2005 unp il hardcover o.p. pa $6.95
Grades: PreK K 1 2   E
   1. Grandmothers—Fiction 2. Mexican Americans—
Fiction 3. Mexico—Fiction 4. Games—Fiction
5. Bilingual books—English-Spanish
ISBN 0-87358-881-9; 978-0-87358-919-2 (pa);
0-87358-919-X (pa)
   A boy has a good time attending a fair with his grand-
mother in San Luis de La Paz, Mexico, as she teaches
him Spanish words and phrases and he teaches her En-
glish.
   "This is a warm and reassuring story of a boy's in-
volvement not only with his family but also his culture.
The prose flows easily in both English and Spanish.
[This is illustrated with] spirited primitive acrylics." SLJ

The Tooth Fairy meets El Ratón Pérez;
illustrations by Tom Lintern. Tricycle Press 2010
unp il $15.99; lib bdg $18.99
Grades: PreK K 1   E
   1. Teeth—Fiction 2. Mexican Americans—Fiction
3. Fairies—Fiction 4. Mice—Fiction
ISBN   978-1-58246-296-7;   1-58246-296-8;
978-1-58246-342-1 (lib bdg); 1-58246-342-5 (lib bdg)
                LC 2009-16782
   When Miguel loses a tooth, two legendary characters
come to claim it—one who is responsible for collecting
teeth in the United States and one who has collected the
teeth of the boy's parents and grandparents.
   "Lainez's creative story approaches the topic of cultural identity with humor and grace, while newcomer
Lintern's colored pencil illustrations give it a sense of
nocturnal whimsy." Publ Wkly

Cole, Barbara Hancock
Anna & Natalie; by Barbara H. Cole; illustrated
by Ronald Himler. Star Bright Books 2007 unp il
$16.95
Grades: K 1 2 3   E
   1. Blind—Fiction 2. Guide dogs—Fiction 3. School
stories 4. Washington (D.C.)—Fiction
ISBN 978-1-59572-105-1; 1-59572-105-3
                LC 2006036456
   Anna and her seeing-eye dog Natalie are chosen by
Anna's teacher to participate in the wreath-laying cere-
mony at the Tomb of the Unknown Soldier at Arlington
National Cemetary.
   "Pen and ink and watercolor artwork dramatically fills
the spreads." SLJ

Cole, Brock, 1938-
Buttons. Farrar, Straus & Giroux 2000 unp il
$16 paperback o.p. *
Grades: K 1 2 3   E
   1. Father-daughter relationship—Fiction
ISBN 0-374-31001-7; 0-374-41013-5 (pa)
                LC 99-27162
   When their father eats so much that he pops the buttons off his britches, each of his three daughters tries a
different plan to find replacements
   "A delectable tall tale. . . . Cole's narrative has a humorous lilt that's as much fun as his rollicking illustrations." Horn Book Guide

Good enough to eat. Farrar, Straus & Giroux
2007 unp il $16 *
Grades: K 1 2 3   E
   1. Orphans—Fiction 2. Homeless persons—Fiction
3. Fairy tales
ISBN 978-0-374-32737-8; 0-374-32737-8
                LC 2006-37368
   When an Ogre comes to town demanding a bride, the
mayor sacrifices the homeless girl with no name that everyone thinks is a pest and a bother, but she finds a way
to outwit them all.
   The illustrations offer "lively line and delicate use of
color. The cadenced language and blithe illustrations
work perfectly together. . . . With the structure of a
fairy tale and the freshness of an original story, *Good
Enough to Eat* is satisfying fare indeed." Horn Book

Cole, Brock, 1938-—*Continued*

Larky Mavis. Farrar, Straus & Giroux 2001 unp il $16 *
Grades: K 1 2 3   E
  1. Infants—Fiction
  ISBN 0-374-34365-9   LC 00-51419
Having found a tiny baby in a peanut shell, Larky Mavis calls him Heart's Delight and carries him around as he grows bigger, to the confusion and anger of the adults around her
"The prose is lyrical, peppered with quaint speech patterns and lively dialogue that is a delight to read aloud. . . . The rumpled, animated line-and-watercolor illustrations extend the charming story beyond his tightly constructed prose." SLJ

Cole, Henry

I took a walk. Greenwillow Bks. 1998 unp il $16.99
Grades: PreK K 1 2   E
  1. Animals—Fiction 2. Nature—Fiction
  ISBN 0-688-15115-9   LC 97-6692
A visit to woods, pasture, and pond brings encounters with various birds, insects, and other creatures of nature. Flaps fold out to reveal the animals hidden on each two-page spread
"Executed in acrylic paint, the realistic nature scenes invite close and careful inspection." Horn Book Guide

On Meadowview Street; [by] Henry Cole. Greenwillow Books 2007 unp il $17.99; lib bdg $18.89 *
Grades: K 1 2 3   E
  1. Meadows—Fiction 2. Nature—Fiction 3. Suburban life—Fiction
  ISBN 978-0-06-056481-0; 0-06-056481-4; 978-0-06-056482-7 (lib bdg); 0-06-056482-2 (lib bdg)
                                LC 2006023761
Upon moving to a new house, young Caroline and her parents encourage wildflowers to grow and birds and animals to stay in their yard, which soon has the whole suburban street living up to its name
"Cole's understated watercolors match the tale's gentle tone." Booklist

On the way to the beach. Greenwillow Bks. 2003 unp il $16.99
Grades: PreK K 1 2   E
  1. Nature—Fiction 2. Ecology—Fiction 3. Senses and sensation—Fiction
  ISBN 0-688-17515-5   LC 2002-23537
On a walk through the woods and a marsh to the seashore, the reader is encouraged to notice all sorts of plants, animals, insects, and shells
"Each locale . . . is gloriously depicted in a three-page foldout that is entered through a die-cut. . . . The outstanding realistic acrylic illustrations depict the scenes in an almost three-dimensional perspective. . . . This beautiful, interactive book encourages discussion, develops observation skills, and provides a learning experience that will bring children closer to nature." SLJ

Trudy. Greenwillow Books 2009 unp il $17.99; lib bdg $18.89
Grades: PreK K 1 2   E
  1. Goats—Fiction 2. Snow—Fiction
  ISBN 978-0-06-154267-1; 0-06-154267-9; 978-0-06-154268-8 (lib bdg); 0-06-154268-7 (lib bdg)
                                LC 2007-47641
It seems as though Trudy the goat knows when to expect snow, but it turns out that she is really expecting something completely different.
"Cole's acrylic paintings are rounded and soft. They juxtapose muted, earth-toned colors of the environment with the bright, primary colors of manmade objects. . . . The steady pace of the text combined with its loosely repetitive structure creates a calm, reassuring mood, making the book an excellent bedtime read." SLJ

Collard, Sneed B., III

Butterfly count; illustrated by Paul Kratter. Holiday House 2002 unp il $16.95
Grades: K 1 2 3   E
  1. Butterflies—Fiction 2. Wildlife conservation—Fiction 3. Prairies—Fiction
  ISBN 0-8234-1607-0   LC 2001-24114
Amy and her mother look for a very special butterfly while attending the annual Fourth of July Butterfly Count at a prairie restoration site. Includes factual information about butterflies and how to attract and watch them
"A gentle family story with an environmental message. . . . Soft watercolor illustrations of prairie grasses, plants, and butterflies quietly illuminate this tranquil tale." SLJ

Collier, Bryan

Uptown. Holt & Co. 2000 unp il $16.95 *
Grades: K 1 2 3   E
  1. African Americans—Fiction 2. Harlem (New York, N.Y.)—Fiction
  ISBN 0-8050-5721-8   LC 99-31774
  Coretta Scott King Award for illustration
A tour of the sights of Harlem, including the Metro-North Train, brownstones, shopping on 125th Street, a barber shop, summer basketball, the Boy's Choir, and sunset over the Harlem River
"Collier's evocative watercolor-and-collage illustrations create a unique sense of mood and place. Bold color choices for text as well as background pages complement engagingly detailed pictures of city life." SLJ

Collins, Ross

Dear Vampa; written and illustrated by Ross Collins. Katherine Tegen Books 2009 unp il $16.99
Grades: K 1 2   E
  1. Vampires—Fiction 2. Letters—Fiction
  ISBN 978-0-06-135534-9; 0-06-135534-8
                                LC 2008-22631
A young vampire writes a letter to his grandfather bemoaning his new neighbors
"Collins's . . . black, angular vampires lace the comedy with a drop of real creepiness. . . . Young vampire fans will enjoy (and perhaps be secretly relieved by) the vampires' beleaguered state." Publ Wkly

Compestine, Ying Chang

Boy dumplings; illustrated by James Yamasaki. Holiday House 2009 unp il $16.95 *

Grades: PreK K 1 2   E

1. Ghost stories 2. Cooking—Fiction 3. China—Fiction

ISBN 978-0-8234-1955-5; 0-8234-1955-X

           LC 2006050064

When a hungry ghost threatens to gobble up a plump little boy, the boy tricks the ghost by convincing him to prepare an elaborate recipe first.

"In keeping with the tale's brisk pacing and light tone, Yamasaki depicts the beaming, succulent boy and the menacing but increasingly beleaguered ghost with particularly comical faces in his cartoon illustrations. . . . [This is a] crowd-pleaser." Booklist

The runaway rice cake; pictures by Tungwai Chau. Simon & Schuster Bks. for Young Readers 2001 unp il $16.95 *

Grades: K 1 2 3   E

1. Chinese New Year—Fiction 2. China—Fiction

ISBN 0-689-82972-8   LC 99-462168

After chasing the special rice cake, Nian Gao, that their mother has made to celebrate the Chinese New Year, three poor brothers share it with an elderly woman and have their generosity richly rewarded

"Compestine's engaging tale brims with intriguing details of the traditions that surround the holiday. . . . Chau makes a splash with vibrant acrylics whose textured surface and controlled, sophisticated blending of shades mimic the look of pastels." Publ Wkly

Connor, Leslie

Miss Bridie chose a shovel; illustrated by Mary Azarian. Houghton Mifflin 2004 unp il $16

Grades: K 1 2 3   E

1. Immigrants—Fiction

ISBN 0-618-30564-5   LC 2003-12290

Miss Bridie emigrates to America in 1856 and chooses to bring a shovel, which proves to be a useful tool throughout her life.

"Azarian's sturdy woodcuts are an excellent choice to illustrate daily life in mid-nineteenth-century America, and her pictures catch some of the emotions that the text shies away from. . . . This is a simple pleasure that will be truly appreciated by those old enough to understand the message." Booklist

Conover, Chris, 1950-

Over the hills & far away; retold and with pictures by Chris Conover. Farrar, Straus and Giroux 2004 unp il $16

Grades: K 1 2 3   E

1. Musicians—Fiction 2. Stories in rhyme 3. Animals—Fiction

ISBN 0-374-38043-0   LC 2003-54878

"This version of the nursery rhyme 'Tom, the Piper's Son' features a bright-eyed otter pup. . . . He and his bagpipes encourage the woodland animals to drop their cares and dance. . . . The text remains true in spirit to the original. The detailed illustrations are a joy to behold. . . . Done in muted earth tones, the . . . paintings are festive, yet serene." SLJ

Conway, David, 1970-

The great nursery rhyme disaster; illustrated by Melanie Williamson. Tiger Tales 2009 unp il $15.95

Grades: PreK K 1 2   E

1. Nursery rhymes—Fiction

ISBN 978-1-58925-080-2; 1-58925-080-X

First published 2008 in the United Kingdom

Little Miss Muffet is bored. So she goes off to find a new nursery rhyme to be in. No rhyme seems quite right for Little Miss Muffet. Suddenly life with a scary little spider doesn't seem so bad after all.

"Witty prose and updated interpretations are complemented by Williamson's exuberant illustrations. Colorful, comical, and energetic, the characters race through the pages to the story's end." SLJ

Lila and the secret of rain; [by] David Conway; illustrated by Jude Daly. Frances Lincoln Children's 2007 unp il $16.95

Grades: PreK K 1 2   E

1. Droughts—Fiction 2. Kenya—Fiction 3. Rain—Fiction

ISBN 978-1-84507-407-4; 1-84507-407-6

Lila's village in Kenya is experiencing a terrible drought. When Lila's grandfather tells her the secret of rain, she sets off on her own to save her village.

"This quiet story offers inspiration and hope. . . . The illustrations are quite lovely. A huge orange sun in a brilliant blue sky dominates most pages. The prominence of the brown baked earth intensifies the unwanted result of the lack of rain. . . . This story will work well both as a read-aloud and for sharing one-on-one." SLJ

The most important gift of all; illustrated by Karin Littlewood. Gingham Dog Press 2006 unp il $15.95

Grades: K 1 2 3   E

1. Love—Fiction 2. Infants—Fiction 3. Siblings—Fiction 4. Kenya—Fiction

ISBN 0-7696-4618-2

"Ama is excited when her baby brother is born, and like all the people of her Kenyan village, she wants to bring him a gift. Because Grandma tells her that love is the most important gift of all, the small girl goes in search of it. . . . The beautiful blend of the traditional storytelling pattern and contemporary realism is expressed in Littlewood's double-page spreads." Booklist

Cooke, Trish, 1962-

Full, full, full of love; illustrated by Paul Howard. Candlewick Press 2003 unp il hardcover o.p. pa $3.99

Grades: PreK K 1   E

1. Grandmothers—Fiction 2. African Americans—Fiction

ISBN 0-7636-1851-9; 0-7636-3883-8 (pa)

           LC 2001-43761

For young Jay Jay, Sunday dinner at Gran's house is full of hugs and kisses, tasty dishes, all kinds of fishes, happy faces, and love

"Howard's generous, full-bleed illustrations capture the loving, bountiful spirit of a big family meal with a colorful palette and expressive eyes and smiles." Booklist

Coombs, Kate

The secret-keeper; story by Kate Coombs; paintings by Heather M. Solomon. Atheneum Books for Young Readers 2006 unp il $16.95
Grades: 1 2 3 4   E

1. Fairy tales

ISBN 0-689-83963-4   LC 2003-24695

The people of Maldinga and the surrounding area bring their deep, dark secrets to Kalli, who keeps them all safe until they become too much for her to bear.

"This original fairy tale is elegantly and tenderly told. . . . Solomon's watercolor and oil paintings are lushly colored. . . . The intricate details . . . slow and eye and invite repeated viewings." Bull Cent Child Books

Cooney, Barbara, 1917-2000

Chanticleer and the fox; adapted and illustrated by Barbara Cooney. Crowell 1958 unp il $16.99; lib bdg $17.89; pa $7.99
Grades: K 1 2 3   E

1. Chaucer, Geoffrey, d. 1400—Adaptations 2. Fables 3. Foxes—Fiction

ISBN 0-690-18561-8; 0-690-18562-6 (lib bdg); 0-06-443087-1 (pa)

Awarded the Caldecott Medal, 1959

"Adaptation of the 'Nun's Priest's Tale' from the Canterbury Tales." Verso of title page

"Chanticleer, the rooster, learns the pitfalls of vanity, while the fox who captures, then loses him, learns the value of self-control." Books for Deaf Child

This adaptation "retains the spirit of the original in its telling and in the beautiful, strongly colored illustrations softened by detailed lines. . . . [It] will be excellent for reading aloud to children." Libr J

Cooper, Elisha

Beach. Orchard Books 2006 unp il $16.99 *
Grades: PreK K 1 2   E

1. Beaches—Fiction 2. Seashore—Fiction

ISBN 0-439-68785-3   LC 2005-20195

Women, men, boys, and girls spend a day at the beach enjoying a variety of activities on the sand and in the water.

"Cooper opens with a gorgeous stretch of sand in sun-flecked, amber-white watercolors. . . . His fondness for his subject is evident and infectious." SLJ

Bear dreams. Greenwillow Books 2006 unp il $16.99; lib bdg $17.89
Grades: PreK K 1 2   E

1. Bears—Fiction 2. Sleep—Fiction

ISBN 0-06-087428-7; 0-06-087429-5 (lib bdg)

After a bear cub persuades his friends to play with him instead of hibernating, he gets very tired and falls asleep

"The watercolor-and-pencil illustrations softly portray the transition from fall to winter as well as from wakefulness to slumber. . . . This quiet book with its dreamlike quality is ideal for bedtime sharing." SLJ

Beaver is lost. Schwartz & Wade Books 2010 unp il $17.99; lib bdg $20.99
Grades: PreK K 1   E

1. Beavers—Fiction

ISBN 978-0-375-85765-2; 0-375-85765-6; 978-0-375-95765-9 (lib bdg); 0-375-95765-0 (lib bdg)
LC 2009-24915

A lost beaver looks for the way home.

"Beaver's saga unfolds entirely through Cooper's splendid watercolor-and-pencil illustrations. . . . Stunning in their simplicity, these pictures speak a thousand words." Kirkus

Farm. Orchard Books 2010 unp il $17.99
Grades: K 1 2 3   E

1. Farm life—Fiction

ISBN 978-0-545-07075-1; 0-545-07075-9
LC 2009004342

Describes the activities on a busy family farm from the spring when preparations for planting begin to the autumn when the cats grow winter coats and the cold rains begin to fall.

"Working in his signature style of loosely rendered figures and simple compositions in pencil and watercolor, Cooper combines beautiful expansive views of the farm . . . with small, individual images. . . . Filled with sensory details, the brief text has a poetic, stripped-down simplicity that matches the stark images and will read aloud well." Booklist

A good night walk. Orchard Books 2005 unp il $16.99
Grades: PreK K 1 2   E

1. Bedtime—Fiction 2. Walking—Fiction

ISBN 0-439-68783-7   LC 2004-23571

The reader is taken on a journey through a neighborhood and shown the sights, sounds, and smells as evening approaches.

"The clear, unfussy compositions echo the poetic words' soothing, elemental sounds . . . which beautifully capture the soft, slowdown rhythms of dusk. Children will find much that's cozy, reassuring, and familiar in the scenes, . . . depicted in luminous watercolors and firmly penciled shapes" Booklist

Magic thinks big. Greenwillow Books 2004 unp il $14.99; lib bdg $15.89 *
Grades: PreK K 1 2   E

1. Cats—Fiction

ISBN 0-06-058164-6; 0-06-058165-4 (lib bdg)
LC 2003-12566

A cat sits in the doorway and tries to decide whether to go inside where he might get fed again, go outside where he might have an adventure, or stay where he is.

"The simple text is full of dry humor and whimsy. The dreamy pencil-and-watercolor illustrations are a pleasing mixture of soft colors and thick lines." SLJ

Cooper, Floyd

Willie and the All-Stars; [by] Floyd Cooper. Philomel Books 2008 unp il $16.99 *
Grades: PreK K 1   E

1. Baseball—Fiction 2. African Americans—Fiction 3. Race relations—Fiction 4. Chicago (Ill.)—Fiction

ISBN 978-0-399-23340-1; 0-399-23340-7
LC 2007042101

Cooper, Floyd—*Continued*

In 1934 Chicago, Willie sees a game between the Negro League All-Star team and the Major League All-Stars, and realizes that his dream of becoming a professional baseball player could come true.

"By looking at race relations through the prism of baseball, Cooper will draw readers. . . . The soft-focus sepia-touched artwork, vintage Cooper, is a nice mix of action and nostalgia." Booklist

Cooper, Helen, 1963-

Dog biscuit. Farrar Straus Giroux 2009 unp il $16 *

Grades: PreK K 1   E

1. Dogs—Fiction 2. Imagination—Fiction

ISBN 978-0-374-31812-3; 0-374-31812-3

         LC 2008-24124

"One day, while Bridget is at Mrs. Blair's house being looked after, she eats a biscuit she finds in the shed—a dog biscuit. Mrs. Blair jokes that she will 'go bowwow and turn into a dog,' and Bridget begins to believe it. . . . A handsome and thoughtfully done layout uses different fonts and sizes for the text, and Cooper's illustrations alternate quiet, ordinary scenes with wild scenes of Bridget's imagination. . . . This is a beautiful and imaginative book for anyone who loves a good story." SLJ

Pumpkin soup. Farrar, Straus & Giroux 1999 c1998 unp il hardcover o.p. pa $6.95 *

Grades: PreK K 1 2   E

1. Cats—Fiction 2. Squirrels—Fiction 3. Ducks—Fiction 4. Cooking—Fiction

ISBN 0-374-36164-9; 0-374-46031-0 (pa)

         LC 98-18677

First published 1998 in the United Kingdom

The Cat and the Squirrel come to blows with the Duck in arguing about who will perform what duty in preparing their pumpkin soup, and they almost lose the Duck's friendship when he decides to leave them

"Cooper serves up a well-rounded tale told with storyteller's cadences. . . . Rich autumn colors and enchanting details on large spreads and spot illustrations embellish characterizations and setting." SLJ

Other titles about Cat, Squirrel and Duck are:

A pipkin of pepper (2005)

Delicious! (2007)

Cooper, Ilene, 1948-

The golden rule; by Ilene Cooper; illustrated by Gabi Swiatowska. Abrams Books for Young Readers 2007 unp il $16.95

Grades: K 1 2 3   E

1. Conduct of life—Fiction

ISBN 978-0-8109-0960-1; 0-8109-0960-X

         LC 2006013333

Grandpa explains that the golden rule is a simple statement on how to live that can be practiced by people of all ages and faiths, then helps his grandson figure out how to apply the rule to his own life.

"The rich, golden paintings and large format reinforce the importance of the topic. . . . Swirling patterns of animal shapes and symbols from various traditions are reminders that the topic is as abstract as the art, with much

room for interpretation. This is less a story than a discussion starter, and teachers, parents, and religious leaders will welcome it as a clear introduction to an important subject." SLJ

Copp, Jim, 1913-1999

Jim Copp, will you tell me a story? three uncommonly clever tales; as told by Jim Copp; illustrated by Lindsay duPont. Harcourt 2008 54p il $17.95

Grades: 2 3 4   E

1. Stories in rhyme 2. Short stories

ISBN 978-0-15-206331-3; 0-15-206331-5

         LC 2007033969

Contents: Kate Higgins; Miss Goggins and the gorilla; Martha Matilda O'Toole

"This collection contains three short stories that were originally recordings by Copp, who died in 1999. The humorous tales, some rhyming, have definite kid appeal. In the first, feisty Kate Higgins refuses to take her medicine and suffers the consequences in the morning. . . . [In] 'Miss Goggins and the Gorilla,' . . . a fourth-grade class is saved from a cruel teacher by a visitor in a gorilla suit. In the last story, forgetful Martha Matilda O'Toole has to keep returning home to get school supplies she's left behind—until her teacher reminds her that it is Sunday. . . . DuPont's pen-and-ink and watercolor illustrations are a perfect match for the quirky stories. . . . Copp's narration on the accompanying CD are a refreshing contrast to the commercialized sound of much of today's children's music." SLJ

Cordell, Matthew, 1975-

Trouble gum. Feiwel & Friends 2009 unp il $16.99

Grades: K 1 2 3   E

1. Pigs—Fiction 2. Brothers—Fiction 3. Chewing gum—Fiction

ISBN 978-0-312-38774-7; 0-312-38774-1

Playing indoors with his little brother on a rainy day, a rambunctious young pig causes a ruckus and then breaks his mother's three chewing gum rules.

"The simple story line and liberal use of white space open plenty of opportunities for Cordell's winsome art to generate laughs. Even better are the sound effects bouncing around each page." Booklist

Cordsen, Carol Foskett

Market day; illustrated by Douglas B. Jones. Dutton Children's Books 2008 unp il $16.99 *

Grades: PreK K 1   E

1. Markets—Fiction 2. Cattle—Fiction 3. Farm life—Fiction 4. Stories in rhyme

ISBN 978-0-525-47883-6; 0-525-47883-3

         LC 2007-28489

The Benson family is so busy preparing for their day at a farmers' market that they not only forget to feed the cow, they leave the farmyard gate open and the hungry cow follows them, making a mess of the market.

"It's not often that words and art mesh as well as they do here. . . . The retro-style artwork . . . mixes striking compositions with tints of glowing peach, vegetable green, honey yellow, and other luscious colors. A delightful read-aloud." Booklist

Cordsen, Carol Foskett—*Continued*

The milkman; illustrated by Douglas Jones. Dutton Children's Books 2005 unp il $15.99

Grades: PreK K 1   E

1. Stories in rhyme

ISBN 0-525-47208-8   LC 2004-21459

In the early, early morning, the milkman makes his rounds, helping his neighbors in a variety of ways.

"Cordsen tells the story in laconic phrases that read aloud well, but this picture book's most distinctive feature is its appealing, retro artwork." Booklist

Corey, Shana, 1974-

Monster parade; a sticker reader; illustrated by Will Terry. Random House 2009 24p il (Step into reading) lib bdg $11.99; pa $3.99

Grades: PreK K 1   E

1. Stories in rhyme 2. Halloween—Fiction 3. Monsters—Fiction

ISBN 978-0-375-95638-6 (lib bdg); 0-375-95638-7 (lib bdg); 978-0-375-85638-9 (pa); 0-375-85638-2 (pa)

LC 2008009718

Children dressed in monster costumes attend a community party, march in a Halloween parade, and go trick-or-treating.

"The bouncy rhymes, featuring kid-pleasing monster noises, encourage participation. With soft, friendly illustrations showing rounded, silly costumes, this is a decidedly non-scary holiday celebration." Horn Book Guide

Players in pigtails; illustrated by Rebecca Gibbon. Scholastic Press 2003 unp il $16.95

Grades: K 1 2 3   E

1. All-American Girls Professional Baseball League—Fiction 2. Baseball—Fiction 3. Sex role—Fiction

ISBN 0-439-18305-7   LC 2002-3445

Katie Casey, a fictional character, helps start the All-American Girls Professional Baseball League, which gave women the opportunity to play professional baseball while America was involved in World War II

"Kids, both girls and boys, will revel in the energy and joy Corey packs into her story. Gibbon's pictures look straight out of the 1940s, with vintage details and an evocative color palette. They also possess a winsome charm that plays nicely with the text." Booklist

Cosentino, Ralph

Batman: the story of the Dark Knight; written and illustrated by Ralph Cosentino; Batman created by Bob Kane. Viking Childrens Books 2008 32p il $15.99

Grades: 1 2 3   E

1. Superheroes—Fiction 2. Batman (Fictional character)

ISBN 978-0-670-06255-3; 0-670-06255-3

LC 2007044682

Wealthy Bruce Wayne relates how he became the costumed avenger known as Batman.

"The artwork enthralls but does not overwhelm. The text . . . is both hard-boiled and reassuring. . . . This is a gripping, sensitive celebration of superherodom." Publ Wkly

Superman: the story of the man of steel; written and illustrated by Ralph Cosentino; Superman created by Jerry Siegel & Joe Shuster. Viking 2010 33p il $16.99

Grades: 1 2 3   E

1. Superman (Fictional character) 2. Superheroes—Fiction

ISBN 978-0-670-06285-0; 0-670-06285-5

"Cosentino acquaints the youngest readers with a comic-book legend. . . . Cosentino presents snapshots that provide a groundwork for understanding Supe's endless print, TV, and movie iterations. Thick-lined new-retro cartoon art in startling primary colors sets off the . . . block-jawed hero. . . . A flashback follows his escape from Krypton, and his boyhood with the Kents features many beloved touchstones. . . . The lineup of his Daily Planet cohorts . . . is followed by the evildoers, who get one double-page spread apiece: Luthor, Metallo, Braniac, and Bizarro." Booklist

Costello, David

I can help; [by] David Hyde Costello. Farrar Straus Giroux 2010 unp il $12.99

Grades: PreK   E

1. Helping behavior—Fiction 2. Animals—Fiction

ISBN 978-0-374-33526-7; 0-374-33526-5

LC 2005044321

When a duck gets lost and a monkey helps him find his way, it starts a chain reaction in which all the young animals help each other solve their problems.

"The ink-and-watercolor artwork features simply drawn, brightly colored focal characters set against landscaped backgrounds. . . . Spare, repetitive text and attractive artwork make this an ideal story hour choice for even the squirmiest group." Booklist

Côté, Geneviève

Me and you. Kids Can Press 2009 unp il $16.95

Grades: PreK K   E

1. Pigs—Fiction 2. Rabbits—Fiction

ISBN 978-1-55453-446-3; 1-55453-446-1

"A rabbit and a pig decide they want to trade places with one another, so they use art supplies and other items at hand to transform themselves accordingly. . . . Children will identify with the animals' playful, imaginative antics. . . . Fans of dress up and creative play, especially, will relate to the story. Moreover, the mixed-media artwork evokes children's drawings and paintings." SLJ

Cote, Nancy

Jackson's blanket. G.P. Putnam's Sons 2008 unp il $16.99

Grades: PreK K   E

1. Stories in rhyme 2. Blankets—Fiction 3. Cats—Fiction

ISBN 978-0-399-24694-4; 0-399-24694-0

LC 2007-42339

A little boy is not ready to give up his beloved blanket until he finds a tiny kitten who needs it more than he does.

"The streamlined text and realistic watercolor illustra-

Cote, Nancy—*Continued*

tions come together to show how a boy grows up just a bit when the time is right. A great addition to most collections." SLJ

Cotten, Cynthia

Rain play; [by] Cynthia Cotten; illustrated by Javaka Steptoe. Henry Holt & Co. 2008 unp il $16.95

Grades: PreK K 1 2   E
   1. Play—Fiction 2. Rain—Fiction 3. African Americans—Fiction 4. Stories in rhyme
   ISBN 978-0-8050-6795-8; 0-8050-6795-7
                       LC 2007012734

Most people leave the park when rain begins to fall, while others enjoy the sights, sounds, and feel of the cool water—until thunder and lightening come near

"The text is written in rhythmic two-line rhymes. . . . Steptoe's cut-paper collages are filled with texture and motion. Facial features rendered in paint show the joy that the youngsters feel. . . . These African-American kids exuberantly jump, splash, run, and puddle-stomp all around the playground." SLJ

This is the stable; illustrated by Delana Bettoli. Holt 2006 unp il lib bdg $16.95

Grades: PreK K 1 2   E
   1. Jesus Christ—Nativity 2. Stories in rhyme
   ISBN 0-8050-7556-9   LC 2005-19904

Recalls, in rhyming text and illustrations, the Nativity story, from the brown and dusty stable to the star shining brightly above.

"This lovely picture book combines beautiful artwork and a seamless, thoughtful . . . style. . . . The rhyme is sweet but never forced. Bettoli uses a mixture of pastels, primary colors, and earth tones." SLJ

Cottin, Menena

The black book of colors; by Menena Cottin and Rosana Faria; translated by Elisa Amado. Groundwood/Anansi Books 2008 unp il $17.95 *

Grades: 1 2 3 4   E
   1. Blind—Fiction 2. Color—Fiction
   ISBN 978-0-88899-873-6; 0-88899-873-2
   Original Spanish edition 2006

"With entirely black pages and a bold white text, this is not your typical color book. Meant to be experienced with the fingers instead of the eyes, this extraordinary book allows sighted readers to experience colors the way blind people do: through the other senses. The text, in both print and Braille, presents colors through touch . . . taste . . . smell . . . and sound. . . . Faría's distinctive illustrations present black shapes embossed on a black background for readers to feel instead of see. . . . Fascinating, beautifully designed, and possessing broad child appeal, this book belongs on the shelves of every school or public library committed to promoting disability awareness and accessibility." SLJ

Cottringer, Anne, 1952-

Eliot Jones, midnight superhero; illustrated by Alex T. Smith. Tiger Tales 2009 unp il $15.95; pa $7.95

Grades: PreK K 1 2   E
   1. Superheroes—Fiction
   ISBN 978-1-58925-083-3;   1-58925-083-4;
   978-1-58925-416-9 (pa); 1-58925-416-3 (pa)

"By day, Eliot is a quiet boy who likes to read, but when the clock strikes midnight, he becomes a superhero. . . . Eliot's adventures are fast-paced and exciting. A variety of fonts are used, making the text feel integrated into the action-packed illustrations. Done in vibrant pastel hues, the collage-style spreads match the tone of each adventure and include many details that youngsters will enjoy exploring." SLJ

Cousins, Lucy

Hooray for fish! Candlewick Press 2005 unp il $14.99 *

Grades: PreK K 1   E
   1. Fishes—Fiction
   ISBN 0-7636-0274-1

Little Fish has all sorts of fishy friends in his underwater home, but loves one of them most of all

"This winning title . . . features . . . bright hues and cheerful, childlike creatures. The stars here are fish, and Cousins matches a gloriously decorated assortment of them with rhyming text that encourages children to look carefully and think about similarities and differences." Booklist

I'm the best. Candlewick Press 2010 unp il $14.99 *

Grades: PreK K 1   E
   1. Dogs—Fiction 2. Animals—Fiction 3. Friendship—Fiction
   ISBN 978-0-7636-4684-4; 0-7636-4684-9

When Dog's constant boasting makes his friends sad, they find a way to teach him what it means to be a good friend.

"The book's large format gives plenty of range for Cousins' naive, expressive pencil-and-ink illustrations. From the exuberant text to the bold, colorful artwork, a joyous spirit pervades this picture book and its fallible yet lovable protagonist." Booklist

Maisy goes to preschool. Candlewick Press 2009 unp il $12.99

Grades: PreK   E
   1. School stories 2. Mice—Fiction
   ISBN 978-0-7636-4254-9; 0-7636-4254-1

"Maisy is confident and acquainted with the routines of preschool. She clearly has no separation issues. She hangs up her coat, joins in making music, listens to a story, and so on. Throughout the day, the young mouse and her friends have a good time. As always, Cousins's bright color illustrations are simple and appealing." SLJ

Other titles about Maisy are:

Doctor Maisy (2001)
Happy birthday Maisy (2008)
Maisy at the beach (2001)
Maisy at the fair (2001)
Maisy at the farm (2008)

Cousins, Lucy—*Continued*

Maisy bakes a cake (2009)
Maisy big, Maisy small (2007)
Maisy, Charlie, and the wobbly tooth (2009)
Maisy cleans up (2002)
Maisy dresses up (1999)
Maisy drives the bus (2000)
Maisy goes camping (2005)
Maisy goes shopping (2001)
Maisy goes swimming (1990)
Maisy goes to school (2008)
Maisy goes to the hospital (2007)
Maisy goes to the library (2005)
Maisy goes to the museum (2009)
Maisy loves you (2000)
Maisy makes lemonade (2002)
Maisy takes a bath (2000)
Maisy's ABC (2008)
Maisy's amazing book of big words (2007)
Maisy's animals (2007)
Maisy's bedtime (1999)
Maisy's big flap book (2007)
Maisy's book of things that go (2010)
Maisy's Christmas day (2008)
Maisy's favorite animals (2001)
Maisy's morning on the farm (2001)
Maisy's nature walk (1999)
Maisy's pool (2008)
Sweet dreams, Maisy (2007)
Vroom, vroom Maisy (2008)
What are you doing, Maisy? (2003)
Where are Maisy's friends? (2000)
Where is Maisy? (2007)

Coville, Bruce

Hans Brinker; inspired by the novel by Mary Mapes Dodge; retold by Bruce Coville; illustrated by Laurel Long. Dial Books for Young Readers 2007 unp il $16.99

Grades: 3 4 5   E
   1. Netherlands—Fiction 2. Siblings—Fiction 3. Ice skating—Fiction
   ISBN 978-0-8037-2868-4   LC 2006027109

A Dutch brother and sister work toward two goals, finding the doctor who can restore their father's memory and winning the competition for the silver skates.

"The story's climax . . . is unglamorous yet satisfying. . . . The book's highlight is Long's glowing oil paintings, which are equally effective in illustrating Holland's snowy, glittering landscape and the story's warmer, more intimate family moments." Horn Book

Cowell, Cressida, 1966-

That rabbit belongs to Emily Brown; written by Cressida Cowell; illustrated by Neal Layton. Hyperion Books for Children 2006 unp il $16.99 *

Grades: PreK K 1 2   E
   1. Toys—Fiction 2. Rabbits—Fiction 3. Play—Fiction
   ISBN 978-1-4231-0645-0; 1-4231-0645-8
                 LC 2006-49046

Emily defends her stuffed rabbit from the naughty queen who is determined to acquire it any way she can

"The wacky illustrations, done in collage, pen and ink,

and watercolor, perfectly depict the joy and energy of the companions' playtime activities. The exuberant text makes use of various fonts and cartoon-bubble dialogue." SLJ

Cowley, Joy

Red-eyed tree frog; story by Joy Cowley; illustrated with photographs by Nic Bishop. Scholastic Press 1999 unp il $16.95 *

Grades: PreK K 1 2   E
   1. Frogs—Fiction 2. Rain forests—Fiction
   ISBN 0-590-87175-7   LC 98-15674

This frog found in the rain forest of Central America spends the night searching for food while also being careful not to become dinner for some other animal

"Stunning color photographs and a gripping interactive text." Booklist

Where horses run free; a dream for the American mustang; paintings by Layne Johnson. Boyds Mills Press 2003 unp il $15.95

Grades: K 1 2 3   E
   1. Horses—Fiction
   ISBN 1-59078-062-0

When a cowboy comes across a penned-up herd of wild horses, he vows to find a home where horses can run free.

"Readers come away with a feeling of overwhelming optimism shown by one man's ability to correct an injustice. The illustrations superbly convey the magnificence of the wilderness and the adaptation of rejuvenated, galloping residents to it." SLJ

Cox, Judy, 1954-

Go to sleep, Groundhog! illustrated by Paul Meisel. Holiday House 2004 unp il $16.95

Grades: PreK K 1 2   E
   1. Marmots—Fiction 2. Groundhog Day—Fiction
   ISBN 0-8234-1645-3   LC 2002-24124

When Groundhog is unable to sleep, he experiences autumn and winter holidays he never knew about, and then he finally falls asleep before Groundhog Day

"An endnote discussing the tradition of using critters as meteorologists makes this a useful as well as a charming answer to the scarcity of engaging material on Groundhog Day." Booklist

My family plays music; illustrated by Elbrite Brown. Holiday House 2003 unp il $17.95

Grades: PreK K 1 2 3   E
   1. Musicians—Fiction 2. Musical instruments—Fiction 3. Family life—Fiction
   ISBN 0-8234-1591-0   LC 00-44903

A musical family with talents for playing a variety of instruments enjoys getting together to celebrate

"The paper-cut illustrations vibrate with color and—almost—with sound. The multiracial family with its rainbow of skin tones is not only a lovely multicultural statement but also a vivid reflection of contemporary families and musical tastes." Booklist

Cox, Judy, 1954-—*Continued*

One is a feast for Mouse; a Thanksgiving tale; illustrated by Jeffrey Ebbeler. Holiday House 2008 unp il $16.95; pa $6.95

Grades: PreK K 1 2   **E**

1. Mice—Fiction 2. Cats—Fiction 3. Thanksgiving Day—Fiction

ISBN 978-0-8234-1977-7; 0-8234-1977-0; 978-0-8234-2231-9 (pa); 0-8234-2231-3 (pa)

LC 2007-13972

On Thanksgiving Day while everyone naps, Mouse spots one pea, a perfect feast, but he cannot help adding all of the fixings—until Cat spots him

"Whimsical, large-scale illustrations drawn in acrylics, pastels, and colored pencils are a perfect complement to the story. Plenty of action and humor as well as a thoroughly satisfying ending make this a wonderful holiday read-aloud." SLJ

Another title about Mouse is: Cinco de Mouse-O! (2010)

Coy, John

Strong to the hoop; illustrations by Leslie Jean-Bart. Lee & Low Bks. 1999 unp il hardcover o.p. pa $8.95 *

Grades: 2 3 4 5   **E**

1. Basketball—Fiction

ISBN 1-880000-80-6; 1-58430-178-3 (pa)

LC 98-33264

Ten-year-old James tries to hold his own and prove himself on the basketball court when the older boys finally ask him to join them in a game

"Coy's text moves with all the free-wheeling speed of playground ball. . . . Best of all, though, are Jean-Bart's collage-style illustrations, produced by combining Polaroid photographs and scratchboard drawings." Booklist

Craig, Lindsey

Dancing feet! illustrations by Marc Brown. Knopf 2010 unp il $16.99

Grades: PreK   **E**

1. Dance—Fiction 2. Animals—Fiction 3. Stories in rhyme

ISBN 978-0-375-86181-9; 0-375-86181-5

"Children are asked to guess who's dancing across a spread by looking at clues in the artwork and listening to the rhymes. . . . Brown uses hand-painted paper collage and primary shapes to create all of the happy dancers. A surprise pairing of partners ends this cheerful story and acts as a motivator to get children moving." SLJ

Crews, Donald

Harbor. Greenwillow Bks. 1982 unp il hardcover o.p. pa $6.99 *

Grades: PreK K 1   **E**

1. Harbors 2. Ships

ISBN 0-688-00862-3 (lib bdg); 0-688-07332-8 (pa)

LC 81-6607

"Liners, tankers, barges, and freighters move in and out. Ferryboats shuttle from shore to shore. Busiest of all are the tugboats as they push and tow the big ships to their docks. The New York harbor is full of action."

Publisher's note

This book "is an exciting, educational and beautiful show-and-tell. . . . The full-page, full-color paintings will delight children." Publ Wkly

Night at the fair; pictures and words by Donald Crews. Greenwillow Bks. 1998 unp il $17.99 *

Grades: PreK K 1 2   **E**

1. Fairs—Fiction

ISBN 0-688-11483-0   LC 96-48780

Nighttime is a wonderful time to enjoy the lights, the games, and the rides at a fair

"Each borderless double-page spread bursts with color and light and action and noise. . . . A minimal text acts for the most part as captioning or clues us in to what's coming next in this truly spectacular visual experience." Horn Book Guide

Parade. Greenwillow Bks. 1983 unp il hardcover o.p. pa $6.99 *

Grades: PreK K 1   **E**

1. Parades

ISBN 0-688-01996-X (lib bdg); 0-688-06520-1 (pa)

LC 82-20927

Illustrations and brief text present the various elements of a parade-the spectators, street vendors, marchers, bands, floats, and the cleanup afterwards.

The author/illustrator's "refined poster-art approach to evoking an event works again here. . . . A polished assembly of crisp shapes, effective compositions, and pure, bright color." Booklist

Sail away. Greenwillow Bks. 1995 unp il $17.99; pa $6.99 *

Grades: PreK K 1   **E**

1. Sailing—Fiction

ISBN 0-688-11053-3; 0-688-17517-1 (pa)

LC 94-6004

A family takes an enjoyable trip in their sailboat and watches the weather change throughout the day

"To read any Crews book is to be immersed in sights and sounds vividly rendered and perfectly phrased, and this book proves no exception. The paintings move and swell; the words are haiku-like in their efficiency and implication." Horn Book

School bus. Greenwillow Bks. 1984 unp il $16.99; lib bdg $17.89; pa $6.99; bd bk $7.99 *

Grades: PreK K 1   **E**

1. School stories 2. Buses—Fiction

ISBN 0-688-02807-1; 0-688-02808-X (lib bdg); 0-688-12267-1 (pa); 0-694-01690-X (bd bk)

LC 83-18681

Follows the progress of school buses as they take children to school and bring them home again

"The author-artist cleverly avoids monotony in his subject matter by using different size buses and a pleasing variety of background, perspectives, and the directions in which they travel. . . . The . . . yellow of the buses provides both a unifying element and a contrast for the cheerful colors of the children's clothing and for the bustle of city streets." Horn Book

Crews, Donald—*Continued*

Shortcut. Greenwillow Bks. 1992 unp il $17.99; lib bdg $18.89; pa $6.99 *

Grades: K 1 2   E

1. Railroads—Fiction 2. African Americans—Fiction

ISBN 0-688-06436-1; 0-688-06437-X (lib bdg); 0-688-813576-5 (pa)   LC 91-36312

Children taking a shortcut by walking along a railroad track find excitement and danger when a train approaches

"The story . . . is a perfect foil for the artist's masterful renderings of trains. . . . Scenes portraying the frightened children are equally effective in this out of the ordinary drama set forth with uncommon artistry." Publ Wkly

Ten black dots. rev ed. Greenwillow Bks. 1986 unp il $16.99; lib bdg $17.89; pa $6.99; bd bk $7.99   E

1. Counting 2. Stories in rhyme

ISBN 0-688-06067-6; 0-688-06068-4 (lib bdg); 0-688-13574-9 (pa); 978-0-06-185779-9 (bed bk)   LC 85-14871

A revision of the title first published 1968

"In this basic counting book . . . large black dots appear as an integral part of each illustrated subject. For example, 'Five dots can make buttons on a coat . . . or the port-holes of a boat.' This simple concept succeeds admirably through the bold, flat colors and briskly delineated graphics of Crews' illustrations." Booklist

Truck. Greenwillow Bks. 1980 unp il $16.99; lib bdg $17.89; pa $6.99; bd bk $7.99 *

Grades: PreK K 1   E

1. Trucks—Fiction 2. Stories without words

ISBN 0-688-80244-3; 0-688-84244-5 (lib bdg); 0-688-10481-9 (pa); 0-688-15597-9 (bd bk)   LC 79-19031

A Caldecott Medal honor book, 1981

A bright red tractor-trailer truck "pushes its way across the United States to deliver its prized cargo of tricycles." Christ Sci Monit

"Although there is no text, the story is far from wordless; trucks, buses, and vans are emblazoned with letters and emblems, the streets are lined with familiar traffic signs, and a truck stop is festooned with advertisements in neon lights. . . . [This is] an imaginative, almost pop-art view of mobile America." Horn Book

Crews, Nina

Below. Henry Holt 2006 unp il $16.95

Grades: PreK K 1 2   E

1. Toys—Fiction 2. Imagination—Fiction

ISBN 0-8050-7728-6; 978-0-8050-7728-5   LC 2005-12128

"Crews uses digitally manipulated photos and line drawings along with brief text to relate the adventures of Jack and his action-figure toy, Guy. . . . One day Guy falls through a hole in the stairs. . . . The child uses his crane and other action figures to effect a rescue. . . . This story . . . will surely inspire young readers to see everyday objects in a new light." SLJ

Another title about Guy is:

Sky-high Guy (2010)

Cronin, Doreen

Click, clack, moo; cows that type; pictures by Betsy Lewin. Simon & Schuster Bks. for Young Readers 2000 unp il $15 *

Grades: PreK K 1 2   E

1. Cattle—Fiction 2. Farm life—Fiction

ISBN 0-689-83213-3   LC 97-29718

A Caldecott Medal honor book, 2001

When Farmer Brown's cows find a typewriter in the barn they start making demands, and go on strike when the farmer refuses to give them what they want

"A laugh-out-loud look at life on a very funny farm. . . . Lewin's hilarious cartoons deftly capture the farmer's exasperation and the animals' sheer determination." SLJ

Other titles about Farmer Brown's animals are:

Giggle, giggle, quack (2002)

Click, clack, quackity quack (2005)

Click, clack, splish, splash (2006)

Dooby, dooby, moo (2006)

Thump, quack, moo (2008)

Diary of a fly; pictures by Harry Bliss. Joanna Cotler Books 2007 unp il $15.99; lib bdg $16.89 *

Grades: PreK K 1 2   E

1. Flies—Fiction

ISBN 978-0-06-000156-8; 0-06-000156-9; 978-0-06-000157-5 (lib bdg); 0-06-000157-7 (lib bdg)   LC 2006-36064

A young fly discovers, day by day, that there is a lot to learn about being an insect, including the dangers of flyswatters and that heroes come in all shapes and sizes.

"The attention to detail . . . and a lively layout that has a comic-book vibe are sure to appeal." SLJ

Diary of a spider; pictures by Harry Bliss. Joanna Cotler Books 2005 unp il $15.99; lib bdg $16.89 *

Grades: PreK K 1 2   E

1. Spiders—Fiction

ISBN 0-06-000153-4; 0-06-000154-2 (lib bdg)   LC 2004-11549

A young spider discovers, day by day, that there is a lot to learn about being a spider, including how to spin webs and avoid vacuum cleaners.

"The amusing pen-and-ink and watercolor cartoons, complete with funny asides in dialogue balloons, expand the sublime silliness of some of the scenarios." SLJ

Diary of a worm; pictures by Harry Bliss. HarperCollins Pubs. 2003 unp il $15.99; lib bdg $16.89 *

Grades: PreK K 1 2   E

1. Worms—Fiction

ISBN 0-06-000150-X; 0-06-000151-8 (lib bdg)   LC 2002-7949

A young worm discovers, day by day, that there are some very good and some not so good things about being a worm in this great big world

"Bliss's droll watercolor illustrations are a marvel. He gives each worm an individual character with a few deft lines. . . . Inventive and laugh-out-loud funny, this worm's-eye view of the world will be a sure-fire hit." Publ Wkly

Cronin, Doreen—*Continued*

Duck for President; illustrated by Betsy Lewin. Simon & Schuster Books for Young Readers 2004 unp il $15.95 *

Grades: PreK K 1 2   E

1. Ducks—Fiction 2. Elections—Fiction

ISBN 0-689-86377-2   LC 2003-21923

Companion volume to Click, clack, moo and Giggle, giggle, quack

When Duck gets tired of working for Farmer Brown, his political ambition eventually leads to his being elected President.

"Lewin's characteristic humorous watercolors with bold black outlines fill the pages with color and jokes. Cronin's text is hilarious for kids and adults and includes a little math and quite a bit about the electoral process." SLJ

Wiggle; art by Scott Menchin. Atheneum Books for Young Readers 2005 unp il $12.95 *

Grades: PreK K 1   E

1. Dogs—Fiction 2. Stories in rhyme

ISBN 0-689-86375-6   LC 2004-3326

"A spotted dog on the cover, vigorously working a hula hoop, leads children through a wiggling world. . . . The delightful cartoon-style, ink-and-watercolor artwork is highlighted by tidbits of collage. . . . Every candy-colored page features the funny, frenetic dog involved in some furious activity, and the sense of motion and movement is palpable each time." Booklist

Other titles about this dog are:

Bounce (2007)

Stretch (2009)

Crow, Kristyn

Bedtime at the swamp. HarperCollins Children's 2008 unp il $16.99

Grades: PreK K 1 2   E

1. Monsters—Fiction 2. Wetlands—Fiction 3. Bedtime—Fiction 4. Mothers—Fiction

ISBN 978-0-06-083952-9; 0-06-083952-X

It's bedtime at the swamp—except somebody's not ready. Somebody's still splashing in the water and the mud. Is there a monster on the loose?

"Lively, colorful cartoon characters set in inky black or deep blue moonlit scenes and offset by crisp, white pages add energy and suspense to the story. The repetitive chorus, a simple rhyming story line that will draw readers in, and the perennial appeal of books that are just 'scary' enough make this title an appropriate addition." SLJ

Cool Daddy Rat; [by] Kristyn Crow; illustrated by Mike Lester. Putnam 2008 unp il $16.99 *

Grades: PreK K 1 2   E

1. Jazz music—Fiction 2. Musicians—Fiction 3. Rats—Fiction 4. New York (N.Y.)—Fiction 5. Stories in rhyme

ISBN 978-0-399-24375-2; 0-399-24375-5

LC 2006020533

A young rat hides in his father's bass case and tags along as he plays and scats around the big city.

This "hip ode to jazz (and scat in particular) will sweep up its audience in its catchy beat as kinetic car-

toon art adds verve and wit. . . . Lester's . . . computer-assisted watercolor illustrations in a heady palette show characters seemingly in perpetual motion." Publ Wkly

The middle-child blues; illustrated by David Catrow. G.P. Putnam's Sons 2009 unp il $16.99

Grades: K 1 2   E

1. Stories in rhyme 2. Birth order—Fiction 3. Siblings—Fiction 4. Blues music—Fiction

ISBN 978-0-399-24735-4; 0-399-24735-1

LC 2008-30591

A boy named Lee sings about all the miserable aspects of being a middle child.

"Catrow's trademark pencil and watercolor illustrations are perfect for this story. Heads are oversized, and facial expressions exaggerated. The colorful illustrations dance all over the pages. This book is a winner." SLJ

Crowe, Carole

Turtle girl; [by] Carole Crowe; illustrated by Jim Postier. Boyds Mills Press 2007 unp il $16.95

Grades: K 1 2 3   E

1. Sea turtles—Fiction 2. Grandmothers—Fiction 3. Bereavement—Fiction

ISBN 978-1-59078-262-0   LC 2006037948

"With her grandmother on their island home, Magdalena watches sea turtles come ashore to dig their nests and lay their eggs. . . . When grandma dies, Magdalena feels hurt and angry, but somehow Grandma seems with her as she and her mother protect the new hatchlings. . . . The quiet, dramatic narrative and bright acrylic double-page spreads blend panoramic scenes of the big beach and ocean with the wonder of the small turtles." Booklist

Crowley, Ned

Nanook & Pryce; gone fishing; pictures by Larry Day. HarperCollinsPublishers 2009 unp il $16.99

Grades: PreK K 1 2   E

1. Stories in rhyme 2. Marine animals—Fiction 3. Voyages and travels—Fiction 4. Adventure fiction 5. Friendship—Fiction

ISBN   978-0-06-133641-6;   0-06-133641-6; 978-0-06-133642-3 (lib bdg); 0-06-133642-4 (lib bdg)

LC 2008032095

Parka-clad friends Nanook and Pryce and their dog Yukon encounter many different types of ocean life and adventure on an unexpected voyage.

"Crowley's perfectly rhymed narrative about an accidental adventure is both minimal and evocative, and Day's watercolor and line illustrations turn some very funny text into a hilarious book." SLJ

Crowther, Robert

Opposites. Candlewick Press 2005 unp il $12.99 *

Grades: PreK K 1   E

1. Opposites

ISBN 0-7636-2783-6

"Each page features a word and readers must take some action—pulling a tab or turning a wheel—to dis-

Crowther, Robert—*Continued*

cover its opposite. The pictures incorporate easy-to-understand examples in creative ways. . . . Warmly colored backgrounds and simply rendered images keep kids' attention focused on the task at hand, and the volume's sturdy pages and reinforced tabs will survive lots of use." SLJ

Croza, Laurel

I know here; pictures by Matt James. Groundwood Books 2010 unp il $18.95

Grades: K 1 2 3   E

1. Saskatchewan—Fiction 2. Moving—Fiction
ISBN 978-0-88899-923-8; 0-88899-923-2
Boston Globe-Horn Book Award honor book: Picture Book (2010)

A tale about a young girl whose family moves from the forests of northeastern Saskatchewan to a strange new place called "Toronto."

"James's vividly colored, naive-style scenes capture the bright intensity of the child's inner and outer landscapes and also the unaffected way in which she observes them. Good for sharing." Kirkus

Cruise, Robin, 1951-

Bartleby speaks! pictures by Kevin Hawkes. Farrar, Straus and Giroux 2009 unp il $16.99

Grades: PreK K 1   E

1. Growth—Fiction 2. Grandfathers—Fiction
3. Family life—Fiction
ISBN 978-0-374-30514-7; 0-374-30514-5
                                  LC 2008-17235
"Melanie Kroupa books"

As he grows from infancy to three-years of age, Bartleby Huddle remains quiet, not speaking a word, until the day Grampy Huddle arrives and discovers the solution

"Hawkes accompanies Cruise's gently pointed text with characteristically comic line-and-color cartoons, varying vignettes with full and double-page spreads that focus readers' attention exactly where it needs to be, modulating noise and silence through artful pacing. A sweetly underscored paean to the beauty of quiet." Kirkus

Little Mama forgets; illustrated by Stacey Dressen-McQueen. Farrar, Straus and Giroux 2006 32p il $16

Grades: PreK K 1 2   E

1. Grandmothers—Fiction 2. Memory—Fiction
3. Mexican Americans—Fiction 4. Family life—Fiction
ISBN 0-374-34613-5   LC 2004-40462
"Melanie Kroupa books"

Although her Mexican-American grandmother now forgets many things, Luciana finds that she still remembers the things that are important to the two of them. Includes glossary of Spanish words used

"The story is bittersweet, but Lucy's ability to look on the bright side, and the obvious love that she and Little Mama share, wrap the events in affection and warmth. Dressen-McQueen's artwork is outstanding. . . . The Mexican family . . . comes alive in pictures that show the vibrancy of the happy household." Booklist

Only you; [by] Robin Cruise; pictures by Margaret Chodos-Irvine. Harcourt 2006 unp il $16

Grades: PreK   E

1. Parent-child relationship—Fiction 2. Love—Fiction
ISBN 0-15-216604-5   LC 2005026895

"The narrator (in some pictures, a mom; in others, a dad) notes everything lovable about the child: a nose, a kiss, a small hand to hold." Booklist

"The sparse, rhyming text is evocative and affirming. . . . The art complements the text beautifully. Chodos-Irvine uses a combination of printmaking techniques to produce a soothing mix of patterns and textures." SLJ

Crum, Shutta

Thunder-Boomer! illustrated by Carol Thompson. Clarion Books 2009 32p il $16 *

Grades: PreK K 1 2   E

1. Thunderstorms—Fiction 2. Farm life—Fiction
3. Family life—Fiction
ISBN 978-0-618-61865-1; 0-618-61865-1
                                  LC 2008-10478

A farm family scurries for shelter from a violent thunderstorm that brings welcome relief from the heat and also an unexpected surprise.

"Thompson's illustrations, done in pastels, ink, and watercolor, are full of motion and capture the sensations. . . . The free-verse storytelling is light, airy, and perfectly matched to the drawings." SLJ

Crumpacker, Bunny

Alexander's pretending day; illustrated by Dan Andreasen. Dutton Children's Books 2005 unp il $15.99

Grades: PreK K   E

1. Mother-child relationship—Fiction 2. Imagination—Fiction
ISBN 0-525-46936-2   LC 2004-12094

When Alexander asks his mother questions, they use their imaginations to play together

"Andreasen's feathery, soft-tone paintings of a shape-shifting Alexander extend the humor and affection in the rhythmic words." Booklist

Cummings, Pat, 1950-

Harvey Moon, museum boy; written and illustrated by Pat Cummings. HarperCollinsPublishers 2008 unp il $16.99; lib bdg $17.89

Grades: PreK K 1 2   E

1. Museums—Fiction 2. Lizards—Fiction 3. African Americans—Fiction 4. Stories in rhyme
ISBN 978-0-688-17889-5; 0-688-17889-8;
978-0-06-057861-9 (lib bdg); 0-06-057861-0 (lib bdg)
                                  LC 2004030056

When Harvey and his pet lizard Zippy go on a school field trip, Zippy gets loose in the museum and they have a harrowing adventure

"A lively read-aloud." Booklist

Another title about Harvey Moon is:
Clean your room, Harvey Moon (1991)

Cummings, Phil, 1957-

Boom bah! Kane Miller 2010 unp il $15.99

Grades: PreK K   E

1. Orchestra—Fiction 2. Music—Fiction 3. Domestic animals—Fiction

ISBN 978-1-935279-22-8; 1-935279-22-X

First published 2008 in Australia

After a tiny mouse taps a cup with a spoon and creates a noise, everyone wants to join in. Follow the band as it gathers and grows from a solo perfomance to an explosive, full-scale orchestra.

"Cummings's minimal text moves along in clipped phrases, punctuated by onomatopoeic effects, creating a splendid read-aloud chant. Rycroft's buoyant watercolors, arranged gracefully against expansive white space, add zest. Even the youngest readers should be able to handle the simple text and catch the rhythm." Kirkus

Cummings, Troy

The eensy weensy spider freaks out (big time!); written and illustrated by Troy Cummings. Random House 2010 unp il $16.99; lib bdg $19.99

Grades: 1 2 3   E

1. Spiders—Fiction 2. Ladybugs—Fiction 3. Fear—Fiction

ISBN   978-0-375-86582-4;   0-375-86582-9; 978-0-375-96582-1 (lib bdg); 0-375-96582-3 (lib bdg)

Frightened after the scary waterspout incident, the Eensy Weensy Spider needs some encouragement from her friend the ladybug before she will try climbing again.

"The lively text and whimsical, cartoon-style illustrations include periodic word balloons . . . that advance the story line. The vibrant settings and expressive insects have a retro flair, while the varying perspectives add to the fun." Booklist

Cumpiano, Ina

Quinito's neighborhood; story Ina Cumpiano; illustrations by José Ramirez. Children's Book Press 2005 22p il $16.95

Grades: PreK K 1 2   E

1. Occupations—Fiction 2. Bilingual books—English-Spanish

ISBN 0-89239-209-6

Quinito not only knows everyone in his neighborhood, he also knows that each person in his community has a different, important occupation

"Ramírez's vibrant acrylic-on-canvas paintings bring this community to life, the primitive forms fairly bursting from the book's pages with their deep hues and sense of emotional warmth. The simple text, equally good in both English and Spanish, is in a font that resembles a child's printing." SLJ

Another title about Quinito is:

Quinito, day and night (2008)

Cunnane, Kelly

For you are a Kenyan child; [by] Kelly Cunnane; art by Ana Juan. Atheneum Books for Young Readers 2005 unp il $16.95 *

Grades: PreK K 1 2   E

1. Kenya—Fiction

ISBN 0-689-86194-X   LC 2004-17060

"An Anne Schwartz book"

From rooster crow to bedtime, a Kenyan boy plays and visits neighbors all through his village, even though he is supposed to be watching his grandfather's cows.

This story is told "through vivid, descriptive text. . . . The brilliant, colorful, and humorous illustrations stand out against the white backgrounds and are large enough for group viewing. A gentle story about family, responsibility, and a curious little boy." SLJ

Curtis, Carolyn, 1958-

I took the moon for a walk; written by Carolyn Curtis; illustrated by Alison Jay. Barefoot Books 2004 unp il lib bdg $16.99; bd bk $14.99

Grades: PreK K 1 2   E

1. Moon—Fiction 2. Stories in rhyme

ISBN 1-84148-611-6 (lib bdg); 1-84686-200-0 (bd bk)

LC 2003-19087

"A young boy takes the moon on a stroll around his neighborhood. Curtis' rhyming text is rich with descriptive language and images. . . . Jay's surreal . . . illustrations not only greatly enhance the dreamlike quality of the text but also provide visual images for some of the unfamiliar words and unusual phrasings." Booklist

Curtis, Gavin, 1965-

The bat boy & his violin; illustrated by E.B. Lewis. Simon & Schuster Bks. for Young Readers 1998 unp il hardcover o.p. pa $7.99 *

Grades: K 1 2 3   E

1. Violinists—Fiction 2. Baseball—Fiction 3. Father-son relationship—Fiction 4. African Americans—Fiction

ISBN 0-689-80099-1; 0-689-84115-9 (pa)

LC 97-25417

Reginald is more interested in practicing his violin than in his father's job managing the worst team in the Negro Leagues, but when Papa makes him the bat boy and his music begins to lead the team to victory, Papa realizes the value of his son's passion

"Lewis's soft watercolor illustrations portray the characters with depth and beauty, resulting in a very special book." SLJ

Curtis, Jamie Lee

Big words for little people; illustrated by Laura Cornell. Joanna Cotler Books 2008 unp il $16.99; lib bdg $17.89 *

Grades: PreK K 1   E

1. Stories in rhyme 2. Conduct of life—Fiction

ISBN   978-0-06-112759-5;   0-06-112759-0; 978-0-06-112760-1 (lib bdg); 0-06-112760-4 (lib bdg)

LC 2008011856

A big sister teaches her younger siblings some important words, like "responsibility," "perseverance," and "respect"

"Curtis once again demonstrates her trademark sensibility for childhood's simultaneously awkward and silly moments while focusing on the positive values learned from these experiences. Cornell keeps the tone ever lighthearted with her charmingly busy illustrations." SLJ

Curtis, Jamie Lee—*Continued*

I'm gonna like me; letting off a little self-esteem; illustrated by Laura Cornell. HarperCollins Pubs. 2002 unp il $16.99; lib bdg $17.89 *

Grades: PreK K 1 2   E

1. Stories in rhyme
ISBN 0-06-028761-6; 0-06-028762-4 (lib bdg)
LC 2002-1300

"Joanna Cotler books"

"In rhyming text, a boy and a girl describe how they will like themselves whether things are going right or wrong." SLJ

"Though the message is both catchy and effective in its delivery, it's Cornell's humorous, detailed, ink-and-watercolor illustrations that give this volume true pizzazz." Publ Wkly

Is there really a human race? illustrated by Laura Cornell. Joanna Cotler Books 2006 unp il $16.99; lib bdg $17.89 *

Grades: PreK K 1 2   E

1. Conduct of life—Fiction 2. Stories in rhyme
ISBN 978-0-06-075346-7; 0-06-075346-3; 978-0-06-075348-1 (lib bdg); 0-06-075348-X (lib bdg)
LC 2006-00274

While thinking about life as a race, a child wonders whether it is most important to finish first or to have fun along the way.

"Curtis writes so very well, in infectious toe-tapping poetic form, of the inner thoughts and worries that children struggle with all too frequently. . . . Cornell's ink-and-color wash cartoons are a perfect match to Curtis's lilting text." SLJ

Tell me again about the night I was born; illustrated by Laura Cornell. HarperCollins Pubs. 1996 unp il $16.99; pa $5.99; bd bk $7.99 *

Grades: PreK K 1 2   E

1. Adoption—Fiction 2. Infants—Fiction
ISBN 0-06-024528-X; 0-06-443581-4 (pa); 0-694-01215-7 (bd bk)
LC 95-5412

"Joanna Cotler books"

"The young female narrator asks her adoptive parents to 'tell me again' the story of her birth and introduction into the family she is now a part of. . . . The humorous, cartoon-style pictures by Laura Cornell . . . are a perfect visual counterpart to the text." Horn Book

Cushman, Doug

Dirk Bones and the mystery of the haunted house; story and pictures by Doug Cushman. HarperCollinsPublishers 2006 31p il $15.99; lib bdg $16.89

Grades: K 1 2   E

1. Ghost stories 2. Mystery fiction
ISBN 978-0-06-073764-1; 0-06-073764-6; 978-0-06-073765-8 (lib bdg); 0-06-073765-4 (lib bdg)
LC 2005019484

"An I can read book"

"Daily Tombs" newspaper reporter Dirk Bones, who also happens to be a skeleton, investigates when a family of ghosts fears that they are being haunted.

"Cushman's illustrations are delightfully silly and spirited; his hilarious plot will please youngsters who often claim that they want horror but are relieved to get humor instead." SLJ

Another title about Dirk Bones is:
Dirk Bones and the mystery of the missing books (2009)

Inspector Hopper; story and pictures by Doug Cushman. HarperCollins Pubs. 2000 64p il hardcover o.p. pa $3.99 *

Grades: K 1 2   E

1. Insects—Fiction 2. Mystery fiction
ISBN 0-06-028382-3; 0-06-028383-1 (lib bdg); 0-06-444260-8 (pa)
LC 99-30878

"An I can read book"

Inspector Hopper and his perpetually hungry assistant McBugg solve three mysteries for their insect friends

"Beginning readers will find a familiar structure, natural language, compelling plot, supporting illustrations, and engaging characters. . . . The light watercolors define the characters as soft-boiled while slyly playing on stereotypes out of film noir." Horn Book Guide

Another title about Inspector Hopper is:
Inspector Hopper's mystery year (2003)

Mystery at the Club Sandwich; written and illustrated by Doug Cushman. Clarion Books 2004 unp il $15

Grades: K 1 2 3   E

1. Mystery fiction 2. Elephants—Fiction 3. Animals—Fiction
ISBN 0-618-41969-1
LC 2004-537

When Lola, famous singer at the Club Sandwich, loses her lucky marbles, elephant detective Nick Trunk, lover of peanut butter, takes the case

"Readers will guess the villain early on but that won't interfere with their enjoyment of the droll story, which is greatly enhanced by delightful illustrations. Cushman uses black watercolor washes, colored pencil, and pastel against a stark white background, suggesting the silver nitrate photographs and popular black-and-white movies of the gumshoe era." SLJ

Cutbill, Andy

The cow that laid an egg; [by] Andy Cutbill; illustrated by Russell Ayto. HarperCollins Publishers 2008 unp il $16.99

Grades: PreK K 1 2   E

1. Cattle—Fiction 2. Eggs—Fiction 3. Chickens—Fiction
ISBN 978-0-06-137295-7; 0-06-137295-1

First published 2006 in the United Kingdom

Marjorie the cow "has no special talents like the rest of the herd, so the chickens hatch a plan. One morning, Marjorie shrieks, 'I've laid an egg!' . . . The bovine endures the taunts of the suspicious cows and the support of the ever-present, silent chickens, until the egg finally hatches a chick with an astonishing 'moo' voice. Cutbill's writing is spare and amusing, and Ayto's goofy, mixed-media collages are a perfect match." SLJ

Another title about Marjorie the cow is:
The cow that was the best moo-ther (2009)

Cutler, Jane

Guttersnipe; pictures by Emily Arnold McCully. Farrar Straus Giroux 2009 unp il $16.95

Grades: K 1 2 3   E

1. Immigrants—Fiction 2. Poverty—Fiction 3. Jews—Fiction 4. Canada—Fiction

ISBN 978-0-374-32813-9; 0-374-32813-7

LC 2007034417

In Canada early in the twentieth century, Ben, the youngest in a family of Jewish immigrants struggling to make ends meet, decides to help out but when a hat maker gives him a chance, disaster strikes and Ben nearly loses hope.

"Detailed watercolors reflect Ben's exhilaration and evoke the early-twentieth-century setting of this unusual story based on true events." Horn Book Guide

Rose and Riley; pictures by Thomas F. Yezerski. Farrar Straus Giroux 2005 48p il $15 *

Grades: PreK K 1 2   E

1. Friendship—Fiction

ISBN 0-374-36340-4   LC 2003-54887

Together, Rose, a vole, and Riley, a groundhog, figure out how to prepare for the possibility of rain, how to celebrate un-birthdays, and what to do with worries.

"Soft pastel illustrations add to the warmth of the text while repetition eases the decoding. A sweet, thoughtful offering with two memorable characters." SLJ

Another title about Rose and Riley is:
Rose and Riley come and go (2005)

Cuyler, Margery

100th day worries; illustrated by Arthur Howard. Simon & Schuster Bks. for Young Readers 2000 unp il $16

Grades: K 1 2   E

1. School stories 2. Worry—Fiction 3. Counting

ISBN 0-689-82979-5   LC 98-52887

Jessica worries about collecting 100 objects to take to class for the 100th day of school

"Energetic pen-and-ink squiggles and bright watercolors fill the pages with round-eyed figures and striped, dotted, and floral patterns as the groups of objects are described and counted." Booklist

Other titles about Jessica are:
Stop, drop, and roll (2001)
Hooray for Reading Day! (2008)
Bullies never win (2009)

The bumpy little pumpkin; illustrated by Will Hillenbrand. Scholastic Press 2005 unp il $15.95

Grades: PreK K 1 2   E

1. Pumpkin—Fiction

ISBN 0-439-52835-6   LC 2004-12179

Little Nell chooses an unusual pumpkin for her Halloween jacko-lantern, despite her big sisters' criticisms

"Cuyler's infectious, repetitive text, with its recurrent use of BIG, is perfectly paced for participatory read-alouds, and Hillenbrand's cheery, whimsical mixed-media illustrations show Little Nell's perspective." Booklist

Another title about Little Nell is:
The biggest, best snowman (1998)

The little dump truck; illustrated by Bob Kolar. Henry Holt and Co. 2009 unp il $12.99

Grades: PreK K 1   E

1. Stories in rhyme 2. Trucks—Fiction

ISBN 978-0-8050-8281-4; 0-8050-8281-6

LC 2008036811

"Christy Ottaviano books"

A happy little dump truck, driven by Hard Hat Pete, hauls stones, rocks, and debris from a construction site to a landfill.

"The digital artwork will appeal to young children, who will look for the face depicted on each of the various trucks. The endpapers show all of the vehicles that play a part in the illustrations. The heavy-duty pages are perfect for curious youngsters. Preschoolers will love this book." SLJ

Monster mess! [by] Margery Cuyler; illustrated by S.D. Schindler. Margaret K. McElderry Books 2008 40p il $14.99

Grades: PreK K 1   E

1. Monsters—Fiction 2. Cleanliness—Fiction 3. Stories in rhyme

ISBN 0-689-86405-1; 978-0-689-86405-6

LC 2005-012762

A monster sneaks into a boy's room and cleans up while the boy is asleep.

"The watercolor illustrations at times show only part of the creature as its head or other body parts extend off the page. . . . Rhyming, repetitive text and whimsical images whirl on the pages, making this a fun read-aloud." SLJ

Princess Bess gets dressed; illustrated by Heather Maione. Simon & Schuster Books for Young Readers 2009 unp il $15.99

Grades: PreK K 1   E

1. Clothing and dress—Fiction 2. Princesses—Fiction 3. Stories in rhyme

ISBN 978-1-4169-3833-0; 1-4169-3833-8

LC 2007-25915

A fashionably dressed princess reveals her favorite clothes at the end of a busy day.

This "story brims over with little-girl appeal. Princess Bess [is] depicted in debut artist Maione's zesty ink-and-watercolor art. . . . The well-crafted rhymes roll easily off the tongue; Maione's droll pictures, balancing fashion-loving detail with Bess's brio, are a skillful accompaniment." Publ Wkly

Skeleton hiccups; illustrated by S.D. Schindler. Margaret K. McElderry Books 2002 unp il $14.95; pa $6.99

Grades: PreK K 1   E

1. Skeleton—Fiction 2. Hiccups—Fiction 3. Ghost stories

ISBN 0-689-84770-X; 1-4169-0276-7 (pa)

LC 2001-44121

Ghost tries to help Skeleton get rid of the hiccups

"This simple story begs to be read aloud. . . . Schindler's gouache, watercolor, and ink pictures make the most out of each situation, instilling humor in every scene." SLJ

Cyrus, Kurt, 1954-

Big rig bugs. Walker 2010 unp il $16.99; lib bdg $17.89

Grades: PreK K 1   E

1. Insects—Fiction 2. Construction workers—Fiction 3. Stories in rhyme

ISBN 978-0-8027-8674-6; 0-8027-8674-X; 978-0-8027-8688-3 (lib bdg); 0-8027-8688-X (lib bdg)

"Digital illustrations explore perspective as a crew of insects joins together to clean up a construction worker's littered tuna-fish sandwich. Rhymed couplets . . . feature creatures such as an ant, a weevil, a pickleworm, an earwig, and a dragonfly. The oversize views of bugs will delight many children, as will the construction analogy." SLJ

Tadpole Rex; by Kurt Cyrus. Harcourt 2008 unp il $16 *

Grades: K 1 2 3   E

1. Frogs—Fiction 2. Dinosaurs—Fiction 3. Growth—Fiction 4. Stories in rhyme

ISBN 978-0-15-205990-3; 0-15-205990-3

LC 2006033825

A tiny primordial tadpole grows into a frog, feeling just as strong and powerful as the huge tyrannosaurus rex that stomps through the mud

"The rhyming text is image-rich, informational, and fun to read aloud. . . . Cyrus's oversize artwork conveys information spectacularly. . . . Created in scratchboard and then colored digitally, the illustrations are luminous and striking." SLJ

Czekaj, Jef

Hip & Hop, don't stop. Disney/Hyperion 2010 unp il $16.99

Grades: K 1 2   E

1. Rap music—Fiction 2. Contests—Fiction 3. Rabbits—Fiction 4. Turtles—Fiction

ISBN 978-1-4231-1664-6; 1-4231-1664-X

LC 2009-20022

A fast rabbit named Hip and a slow turtle named Hop defy convention when they team up to win a rap music contest in spite of their differences.

"Speech balloons and short rhymes are seamlessly incorporated into the story line. Red text means read fast and green text means read slowly. . . . The bright colors and engaging characters will grab children's attention." SLJ

Da Costa, Deborah

Hanukkah moon; [illustrated by] Gosia Mosz. Kar-Ben Pub. 2007 unp il lib bdg $17.95; pa $7.95

Grades: PreK K 1 2   E

1. Hanukkah—Fiction 2. Jews—Fiction 3. Mexican Americans—Fiction 4. Aunts—Fiction 5. Rosh Hodesh—Fiction 6. Moon—Fiction

ISBN 978-1-58013-244-2 (lib bdg); 1-58013-244-8 (lib bdg); 978-1-58013-245-9 (pa); 1-58013-245-6 (pa)

LC 2006-27430

When Isobel visits her Aunt Luisa, who has just arrived from Mexico, she celebrates Hanukkah with a dreidel-shaped piñata and learns how to celebrate Rosh Hodesh, the women's holiday of the new moon

This is "a valuable contribution to the canon of holiday literature. . . . Mosz's mixed-media pictures . . . feature a cast of doe-eyed, stylized characters golden as Hanukkah lights against the deep purple of moonless night." Bull Cent Child Books

Daddo, Andrew, 1967-

Goodnight, me; [by] Andrew Daddo; illustrations by Emma Quay. Bloomsbury Children's Books 2007 unp il $11.95

Grades: PreK   E

1. Orangutan—Fiction 2. Bedtime—Fiction

ISBN 978-1-59990-153-4; 1-59990-153-6

LC 2007002613

A baby orangutan says goodnight to each and every part of himself until sleep finally comes

"This delightful book has a quiet cadence. . . . Using a mix of pencil, acrylic paints, and watercolors, Quay has created uncluttered spreads that focus on the highlighted body parts. The colors are as soothing as the gentle text." SLJ

Daly, Niki, 1946-

Pretty Salma; a Red Riding Hood story from Africa. Clarion Books 2007 29p $16 *

Grades: K 1 2 3   E

1. Ghana—Fiction 2. Fairy tales

ISBN 978-0-618-72345-4; 0-618-72345-5

LC 2006-04249

In this version of "Little Red Riding Hood," set in Ghana, a young girl fails to heed Granny's warning about the dangers of talking to strangers.

"The cartoon-style paintings capture the sights and flavor of the setting and add dimension and humorous details to this modern version of a timeless tale." SLJ

Ruby sings the blues; story and pictures by Niki Daly. Bloomsbury Children's Books 2005 unp il $16.95

Grades: K 1 2 3   E

1. Jazz music—Fiction 2. Singers—Fiction

ISBN 1-58234-995-9   LC 2004-54457

Ruby's loud voice annoys everyone around her, until she learns to control her volume with the help of her new jazz musician friends.

"The nicely paced, rhythmic text will read well to a crowd, and the lyrical descriptions of what Ruby learns to do . . . will introduce children to the musicianship and emotion singers bring to their work. Daly's mixed-media illustrations showcase a cast of urban hipsters wearing patterned outfits that extend the rhythms in the story." Booklist

Welcome to Zanzibar Road; story and pictures by Niki Daly. Clarion Books 2006 31p il $16 *

Grades: PreK K 1 2   E

1. Elephants—Fiction 2. Chickens—Fiction 3. Africa—Fiction

ISBN 0-618-64926-3   LC 2005021758

After moving into the house on Zanzibar Road that her neighbors helped her build, Mama Jumbo the elephant decides to share it with Little Chico the chicken.

Daly, Niki, 1946-—*Continued*

"Through his warm, expressive watercolors, Daly teaches readers about some of the important things in life—friendship, family, and how to make a house into a home. Details abound, and the animals' patterned clothing adds texture and variety to the pages." SLJ

D'Amico, Carmela

Ella the Elegant Elephant; by Carmela & Steven D'Amico. Arthur A. Levine Books 2004 unp il $16.95

Grades: PreK K 1 2   E
1. Hats—Fiction 2. School stories 3. Elephants—Fiction
ISBN 0-439-62792-3   LC 2003-28081

Ella is nervous about the first day of school in her new town, but wearing her grandmother's good luck hat makes her feel better—until the other students tease her and call her names.

"Combining a fairy-tale quality with elements in story and setting that will be familiar to children, this has a charming protagonist, as well as lovely, whimsical art, in a soft rich palette. . . . The text is simple, descriptive, and often lively, making a good read-aloud." Booklist

Other titles about Ella are:
Ella takes the cake (2005)
Ella sets the stage (2006)
Ella sets sail (2008)

Danziger, Paula, 1944-2004

It's Justin Time, Amber Brown; illustrated by Tony Ross. Putnam 2001 48p il (A is for Amber) $12.99; pa $3.99 *

Grades: K 1 2 3   E
1. Clocks and watches—Fiction 2. Time—Fiction 3. Birthdays—Fiction
ISBN 0-399-23470-5; 0-698-11907-X (pa)
LC 99-89396

This Amber Brown easy reader features the protagonist at a younger age than Amber Brown is not a crayon and others in that series

Unlike her best friend Justin, Amber Brown loves to measure time and hopes to receive a watch on her seventh birthday

"The illustrations capture the mood of the story, which is playful and spirited. Beginning readers will enjoy sharing Amber's pre-birthday anticipation and older readers may want to go back and see the early years of the characters they know and love." SLJ

Other easy-to-read titles about Amber Brown are:
Get ready for second grade, Amber Brown (2002)
It's a fair day, Amber Brown (2002)
Orange you glad it's Halloween, Amber Brown (2005)
Second grade rules, Amber Brown (2004)
What a trip, Amber Brown (2001)

Darbyshire, Kristen

Put it on the list. Dutton Children's Books 2009 unp il $16.99

Grades: PreK K 1   E
1. Memory—Fiction 2. Shopping—Fiction 3. Family life—Fiction 4. Week—Fiction
ISBN 978-0-525-47906-2; 0-525-47906-6
LC 2007-28490

"A family of anthropomorphized chickens keeps running out of household staples. Mom tells everyone to put the needed items on the shopping list that's posted on the refrigerator, but they ignore the directive and just complain when supplies run out. . . . The chickens are depicted as stick figures with large round heads. The gouache illustrations are spare, with ink outlines and solid-colored backgrounds. An amusing cautionary tale for families everywhere." SLJ

Daugherty, James Henry, 1889-1974

Andy and the lion; by James Daugherty. Viking 1938 unp il pa $6.99 hardcover o.p. *

Grades: PreK K 1 2   E
1. Lions—Fiction
ISBN 0-14-050277-7 (pa)

A Caldecott Medal honor book, 1939

A modern picture story of Androcles and the lion in which Andy, who read a book about lions, was almost immediately plunged into action. The next day he met a circus lion with a thorn in his paw. Andy removed the thorn and earned the lion's undying gratitude

"This is a tall tale for little children. It is typically American in its setting and its fun. The large full page illustrations are in yellow, black and white and the brief, hand-lettered text on the opposite page is clear and readable." Libr J

D'Aulaire, Ingri, 1904-1980

Foxie; the singing dog; [by] Ingri and Edgar Parin d'Aulaire. New York Review Books 2007 unp il (New York Review Books children's collection) $14.95

Grades: K 1 2   E
1. Dogs—Fiction
ISBN 978-1-59017-264-3; 1-59017-264-7
LC 2007-27028

First published 1949

A lost dog's luck makes him fat and famous, but when given a chance he proves he still thinks there is no place like home.

"Foxie's adventures are illustrated in delightful color." Horn Book Guide

The two cars; [by] Ingri & Edgar Parin d'Aulaire. New York Review Books 2007 unp il (The New York Review children's collection) $14.95

Grades: PreK K 1   E
1. Automobiles—Fiction 2. Fables
ISBN 978-1-59017-234-6; 1-59017-234-5
LC 2007-2636

First published 1955 by Doubleday

On a magic moonlit night, the sleek, shiny automatic new car and the beat-up old car with many miles on its speedometer go for a drive to see which car is the best.

"A modern adaptation of The Tortoise and the Hare, in which safe and courteous driving wins the day. Delicate pencil illustrations and a plot delivered at a pace fit for a turnpike should prove as enchanting to today's automotively inclined children as when the book was first published in 1955." Pub Wkly

Davies, Jacqueline

The night is singing; illustrations by Kyrsten Brooker. Dial Books for Young Readers 2006 unp il $16.99

Grades: PreK K 1   E

1. Night—Fiction 2. Sound—Fiction 3. Stories in rhyme

ISBN 0-8037-3004-7; 978-0-8037-3004-5

LC 2004-14161

Rhyming text tells of lullabies that can be heard in the sounds of the night, such as a radiator's hiss, a cat's shadowboxing, and a rainstorm's drumming

This is a "perfect bedtime read. . . . Attractive, full-page folk-art illustrations that combine collage and oil paint on gessoed watercolor paper lend an old-fashioned charm." SLJ

Tricking the Tallyman; illustrated by S. D. Schindler. Alfred A. Knopf 2009 unp il $17.99; lib bdg $20.99 *

Grades: 1 2 3 4   E

1. Census—Fiction 2. Vermont—Fiction 3. United States—History—1783-1809—Fiction

ISBN 978-0-375-83909-2; 0-375-83909-7; 978-0-375-93909-9 (lib bdg); 0-375-93909-1 (lib bdg)

LC 2007-45488

In 1790, the suspicious residents of a small Vermont town try to trick the man who has been sent to count their population for the first United States Census.

"This lively, engaging picture book is an outstanding introduction to the concept of census taking and its role in the implementation of the new United States Constitution. . . . Schindler's exceptional illustrations, mainly in earth tones, depict indoor and outdoor scenes that are full of activity. . . . Charming and humorous." SLJ

Davies, Nicola, 1958-

Bat loves the night; illustrated by Sarah Fox-Davies. Candlewick Press 2001 28p il hardcover o.p. pa $6.99 *

Grades: PreK K 1 2   E

1. Bats—Fiction

ISBN 0-7636-1202-2; 0-7636-2438-1 (pa)

LC 00-66681

Bat wakes up, flies into the night, uses the echoes of her voice to navigate, hunts for her supper, and returns to her roost to feed her baby

"An enticing picture book . . . that blends story with fact. . . . Lovely, atmospheric watercolor-and-pencil illustrations show surprising detail and succeed in making an oft-maligned animal appear realistically fuzzy and appealing." Booklist

White owl, barn owl; illustrated by Michael Foreman. Candlewick Press 2007 29p il $16.99; pa $6.99 *

Grades: PreK K 1 2 3   E

1. Owls—Fiction

ISBN 978-0-7636-3364-6; 0-7636-3364-X; 978-0-7636-4143-6 (pa); 0-7636-4143-X (pa)

"Simple facts about the hunting and nesting habits of barn owls intertwine with the story of two humans who put a nesting box for them high in a tree. Narrated by a girl whose grandfather explains owl behavior as the two watch for avian visitors in the evenings, the story also contains insets of information bits. Well-chosen design elements move both fiction and fact along with clarity and ease. . . . Foreman's artwork includes lovely watercolor and pastel paintings of the birds." SLJ

Davis, Jill

The first rule of little brothers; illustrated by Sarah McMenemy. Alfred A. Knopf 2008 unp il $16.99; lib bdg $19.99

Grades: PreK K 1   E

1. Brothers—Fiction

ISBN 978-0-375-84046-3; 0-375-84046-X; 978-0-375-94046-0 (lib bdg); 0-375-94046-4 (lib bdg)

LC 2007-44314

A young boy learns that, while his little brother's constant mimicking may be annoying, it is also a sign of admiration.

"Davis makes her point—siblings can drive eachother crazy but also have fun together—credibly and sympathetically with plenty of humor as well. . . . McMenemy's mixed-media art (which looks to incorporate watercolor, ink, and torn paper collage) is sunny and vivid, with lots of crisp white space surrounding the brightly colored figures and backgrounds." Bull Cent Child Books

Davis, Nancy, 1949-

A garden of opposites. Schwartz & Wade Books 2009 unp il $10.95

Grades: PreK K   E

1. Opposites 2. Gardens—Fiction

ISBN 978-0-375-85666-2; 0-375-85666-8

LC 2008022766

Opposites abound in a colorful garden, including a closed bud, an open blossom, a short caterpillar, and a long snake

"Bright, crisp childlike illustrations, with one simple object and one word per page, result in a clean, uncluttered design. An attractive concept book for the very young." SLJ

Day, Alexandra

Carl's sleepy afternoon. Farrar, Straus and Giroux 2005 unp il $12.95 *

Grades: PreK K 1   E

1. Dogs—Fiction

ISBN 0-374-31088-2

Carl's owners have many errands to do and expect Carl to sleep the entire afternoon. Instead, Carl the rottweiler roams the town assisting many people in their daily chores

"The entertaining story is told through the gently detailed, warmly realistic paintings." SLJ

Other titles about Carl are:

Carl goes shopping (1990)

Carl goes to daycare (1993)

Carl makes a scrapbook (1994)

Carl's afternoon in the park (1991)

Carl's birthday (1995)

Carl's Christmas (1990)

Carl's masquerade (1992)

Day, Alexandra—*Continued*
Carl's snowy afternoon (2009)
Carl's summer vacation (2008)
Follow Carl (1998)
Good dog, Carl (1985)

De Groat, Diane
Trick or treat, smell my feet. Morrow Junior
Bks. 1998 unp il hardcover o.p. pa $4.95 *
Grades: K 1 2 3   E
1. Halloween—Fiction 2. Siblings—Fiction
ISBN 0-688-15766-1; 0-688-15767-X (lib bdg);
0-688-17061-7 (pa)   LC 97-32916
"When Gilbert and his sister accidentally bring each
other's costumes to school for the annual Halloween pa-
rade, Gilbert ends up donning a ballerina outfit." Publ
Wkly
"De Groat's funny watercolor pictures capture the var-
ious animal creatures' very human expressions and body
language." Booklist
Other titles about Gilbert are:
April fool!, watch out at school! (2009)
Brand-new pencils, brand-new books (2005)
Good night, sleep tight, don't let the bedbugs bite!
(2002)
Happy birthday to you, you belong in the zoo (1999)
Jingle, bells, homework smells (2000)
Last one in is a rotten egg! (2007)
Liar, liar, pants on fire (2003)
Mother, you are the best! (2008)
No more pencils, no more books, no more teacher's dirty
looks! (2006)
Roses are pink, your feet really stink (1996)
We gather together—now please get lost! (2001)

De Paola, Tomie, 1934-
The art lesson; written and illustrated by Tomie
dePaola. Putnam 1989 unp il hardcover o.p. pa
$5.99
Grades: PreK K 1 2   E
1. Art—Fiction
ISBN 0-399-21688-X; 0-698-11572-4 (pa)
LC 88-27617
Having learned to be creative in drawing pictures at
home, young Tommy is dismayed when he goes to
school and finds the art lesson there much more regimented
This is "engrossing reading. DePaola's characteristic
bright illustrations complement and enliven his tale of
growing up." Horn Book

The baby sister; written and illustrated by
Tomie dePaola. Putnam 1996 unp il $16.99; pa
$5.99
Grades: PreK K 1 2   E
1. Infants—Fiction   2.   Siblings—Fiction
3. Grandmothers—Fiction
ISBN 0-399-22908-6; 0-698-11773-5 (pa)
LC 94-37218
"Tommy's mother is expecting a baby. Tommy helps
get the baby's room ready and longs for a sister with a
red ribbon in her hair. He's thrilled when the baby is a
girl, but while his mother is away in the hospital, his

Italian grandmother comes to stay, and he finds it hard
to get along with her. . . . Simple lines and warm colors
convey the affection in the extended family and the special closeness between Tommy and his parents." Booklist

Four friends at Christmas. Aladdin 2009 c1977
unp il $12.99
Grades: PreK K 1 2   E
1. Christmas—Fiction 2. Frogs—Fiction 3. Animals—
Fiction 4. Friendship—Fiction
ISBN 978-1-4169-9175-5; 1-4169-9175-1
A reissue of the edition published 2002; previously
published 1977, in different form, as the chapter entitled
"Winter" in *Four Stories for Four Seasons*
Mister Frog has slept through Christmas every year
and is determined to celebrate this one with his three
best friends. But when he takes a short nap that turns
into a very long sleep, he wakes up late on Christmas
Eve, and there's no one to celebrate with!
"The tale of Frog's first Christmas is charming in its
simplicity. The four animal friends' unique personalities
come through in dePaola's trademark cozy illustrations."
Horn Book Guide

Guess who's coming to Santa's for dinner?
written and illustrated by Tomie dePaola. Putnam's
2004 unp il $16.99 *
Grades: PreK K 1 2   E
1. Christmas—Fiction 2. Santa Claus—Fiction
3. Family life—Fiction
ISBN 0-399-24271-6   LC 2003-26638
A houseful of relatives turns "Mrs. C." and Santa's
Christmas into a string of surprises, from the arrival of
a pet polar bear to Cousin James B.'s flaming plum pudding.
"The part comic strip-style format cleverly reflects the
busy, everyone-talk-at-once hum of a big family gathering and serves up plenty of funny asides. Warm and
wonderful as Christmas cake fresh out of the oven,
dePaola's softly hued, rounded illustrations shine with
holiday spirit." Booklist

Jamie O'Rourke and the pooka. Putnam 2000
unp il $16.99; pa $6.99 *
Grades: PreK K 1 2 3   E
1. Ireland—Fiction
ISBN 0-399-23467-5; 0-698-11974-X (pa)
LC 99-22469
While his wife is away, lazy Jamie O'Rourke relies on
a pooka to clean up the messes that he and his friends
make
"DePaola's cozy, colorful illustrations are a good
match for the lighthearted, rhythmic text." Horn Book
Guide

Meet the Barkers; Morgan and Moffat go to
school; written and illustrated by Tomie dePaola.
Putnam 2001 unp il $13.99; pa $5.99
Grades: PreK K 1 2   E
1. School stories 2. Twins—Fiction 3. Dogs—Fiction
ISBN 0-399-23708-9; 0-14-250083-6 (pa)
LC 00-55355
Bossy Moffie (a dog) and her quiet twin brother
Morgie both enjoy starting school, especially getting gold
stars and making new friends

De Paola, Tomie, 1934-—*Continued*

"Genuinely expressive, lovable characters, depicted in warm tones on handmade watercolor paper, make this a great read-aloud." SLJ

Other titles about the Barkers are:

Boss for a day (2001)

Hide-and-seek all week (2001)

A new Barker in the house (2002)

Trouble in the Barkers' class (2003)

Nana Upstairs & Nana Downstairs; written and illustrated by Tomie dePaola. Putnam 1998 unp il $16.99; pa $6.99 *

Grades: PreK K 1 2   E

1. Grandmothers—Fiction 2. Death—Fiction

ISBN 0-399-23108-0; 0-698-11836-7 (pa)

LC 96-31908

A newly illustrated edition of the title first published 1973

"Every Sunday four-year-old Tommy's family goes to visit his grandparents. His grandmother is always busy downstairs, but his great-grandmother is always to be found in bed upstairs, because she is 94 years old. . . . [Tommy] is desolate when his upstairs nana dies, but his mother comforts him by explaining that 'she will come back in your memory whenever you think about her.'" Booklist

"The illustrations are vintage dePaola, and the warm palette conveys the boy's love for his elderly relatives." Horn Book Guide

The night of Las Posadas; written and illustrated by Tomie dePaola. Putnam 1999 unp il $15.99; pa $6.99 *

Grades: K 1 2 3   E

1. Mary, Blessed Virgin, Saint—Fiction 2. Joseph, Saint—Fiction 3. Christmas—Fiction 4. Santa Fe (N.M.)—Fiction

ISBN 0-399-23400-4; 0-698-11901-0 (pa)

LC 98-36405

At the annual celebration of Las Posadas in old Santa Fe, the husband and wife slated to play Mary and Joseph are delayed by car trouble, but a mysterious couple appear who seem perfect for the part

"DePaola's talent for crafting folktales is honed to near-perfection, and his pages glow with the soft sun-washed hues of the Southwest." Publ Wkly

Now one foot, now the other. G. P. Putnam's Sons 2005 unp il $14.99; pa $7.99

Grades: PreK K 1 2   E

1. Grandfathers—Fiction 2. Stroke—Fiction

ISBN 0-399-24259-7; 0-14-240104-8 (pa)

A newly illustrated edition of the title first published 1981

When his grandfather suffers a stroke, Bobby teaches him to walk, just as his grandfather had once taught him.

"The illustrations have been digitally colorized in this welcome new edition." Horn Book Guide

Pascual and the kitchen angels; written and illustrated by Tomie dePaola. G.P. Putnam 2004 unp il hardcover o.p. pa $5.99

Grades: PreK K 1 2   E

1. Angels—Fiction 2. Cooking—Fiction 3. Christian life—Fiction

ISBN 0-399-24214-7; 0-14-240536-1 (pa)

LC 2003-8521

Pascual, a boy blessed by angels at his birth, receives divine help when the Franciscan monks make him their cook

"Acrylic illustrations with soft pastel backgrounds show Pascual as a little boy. . . . The winsome paintings capture his serene spirituality as he and the creatures lift their voices toward heaven. Simple, well-chosen words reflect the youngster's sincere love for God and all of His creatures." SLJ

The song of Francis; [by] Tomie dePaola. G.P. Putnam's Sons 2009 unp il $16.99 *

Grades: PreK K 1 2   E

1. Francis, of Assisi, Saint, 1182-1226—Fiction 2. Saints—Fiction 3. Birds—Fiction

ISBN 978-0-399-25210-5; 0-399-25210-X

LC 2008018578

Francis, the Little Poor One, is so filled with the love of God that he bursts into song, and he is joined by birds of every color.

"De Paola's tropical-hued collages convey the magic of this religious interpretation in an appealing way." SLJ

Stagestruck; written and illustrated by Tomie dePaola. G.P. Putnam's Sons 2005 unp il $16.99 *

Grades: PreK K 1 2   E

1. Theater—Fiction 2. School stories

ISBN 0-399-24338-0   LC 2004-9261

Although Tommy fails to get the part of Peter Rabbit in the kindergarten play, he still finds a way to be the center of attention on stage

"The gently delivered lesson at the end does not dampen the fun of watching this aspiring thespian get carried away. . . . With its warm palette, rounded shapes, and clarity of expression, dePaola's signature style makes Tommy's world an inviting place to visit." Booklist

Strega Nona: an old tale. Simon & Schuster 1988 c1975 unp il $18.99; pa $7.99 *

Grades: PreK K 1 2   E

1. Witches—Fiction 2. Italy—Fiction

ISBN 0-671-66283-X; 0-671-66606-1 (pa)

LC 88-11438

A Caldecott Medal honor book, 1976

A reissue of the title first published 1975 by Prentice-Hall

In this Italian folk-tale set in Calabria, "Strega Nona, 'Grandma Witch,' leaves Big Anthony alone with her magic pasta pot. He decides to give the townspeople a treat. . . . Big Anthony doesn't know how to make the pot stop. The town is practically buried in spaghetti before Strega Nona returns to save the day." SLJ

"Tomie de Paola has used simple colors, simple line, and medieval costume and architecture in his spaciously composed humorous pictures." Bull Cent Child Books

Other titles about Strega Nona are:

De Paola, Tomie, 1934-—*Continued*
Big Anthony and the magic ring (1979)
Big Anthony: his story (1998)
Brava, Strega Nona (2008)
Merry Christmas, Strega Nona (1986)
Strega Nona: her story (1996)
Strega Nona meets her match (1993)
Strega Nona takes a vacation (2000)
Strega Nona's harvest (2009)
Strega Nona's magic lessons (1982)

De Regniers, Beatrice Schenk, 1914-2000
May I bring a friend? illustrated by Beni
Montresor. Atheneum Pubs. 1964 unp il hardcover
o.p. pa $7.99 *
Grades: PreK K   E
1. Animals—Fiction
ISBN 0-689-20615-1; 0-689-71353-3 (pa)
Awarded the Caldecott Medal, 1965
"Each time the little boy in this picture book is invited
to take tea or dine with the King and Queen, he brings
along a somewhat difficult animal friend. Their High-
nesses always cope and are wonderfully rewarded in the
end." Publ Wkly
"Rich color and profuse embellishment adorn an opulent setting. Absurdities and contrasts are so imaginatively combined in a hilarious comedy of manners that the
merriment can be enjoyed on several levels." Horn Book

Deacon, Alexis, 1978-
Beegu. Farrar, Straus & Giroux 2003 unp il $16
Grades: PreK K 1 2   E
1. Extraterrestrial beings—Fiction
ISBN 0-374-30667-2   LC 2002-192738
A small creature from space finds no welcome on
Earth, until she meets a group of children on a playground
"Beegu's black outline and solid yellow center evoke
a celestial simplicity. . . . The accomplished artwork underscores the children's easy acceptance of Beegu and
highlights the book's uplifting message that acts of kindness have lasting effects." Publ Wkly

DeFelice, Cynthia C.
Old Granny and the bean thief; pictures by Cat
Bowman Smith. Farrar, Straus and Giroux 2003
unp il $16 *
Grades: K 1 2 3   E
1. Grandmothers—Fiction 2. Thieves—Fiction
ISBN 0-374-35614-9   LC 2002-20770
After a thief steals Old Granny's beans while she is
asleep at night, she gets some surprising help with catching him.
"The down-home narrative is folksy and fun to read
aloud. . . . Smith uses a Southwestern palette in her cartoon-style paintings." SLJ

One potato, two potato; pictures by Andrea
U'Ren. Farrar, Straus and Giroux 2006 unp il $16
*
Grades: K 1 2 3   E
1. Magic—Fiction 2. Potatoes—Fiction
ISBN 978-0-374-35640-8; 0-374-35640-8
                            LC 2004-47217

A very poor, humble couple live so simple a life they
share everything, until the husband discovers a pot with
magical powers buried under the very last potato in the
garden.
"U'Ren's large pen-and-gouache illustrations infuse
the couple's grim situation with humor. . . . An entertaining tale." SLJ

The real, true Dulcie Campbell; [by] Cynthia
DeFelice; pictures by R.W. Alley. Farrar, Straus &
Giroux 2002 unp il $16
Grades: K 1 2 3   E
1. Family life—Fiction 2. Princesses—Fiction
3. Books and reading—Fiction
ISBN 0-374-36220-3   LC 00-58736
Believing that she is a princess, Dulcie Campbell
leaves home to seek her true family, but she finds by
reading a book of fairy tales that being a princess is not
what she thought
"The story radiates good humor as well as sympathy
for the imaginative Dulcie. In Alley's lively, appealing
watercolor paintings, Dulcie's royal fantasies appear in
picture frames alongside homelier scenes of life on the
farm." Booklist

Degen, Bruce, 1945-
Jamberry; story and pictures by Bruce Degen.
Harper & Row 1983 unp il $17.99; pa $7.99; bd
bk $7.99 *
Grades: PreK K 1 2   E
1. Stories in rhyme 2. Berries—Fiction
ISBN   0-06-021416-3;   0-06-443068-5   (pa);
0-694-00651-3 (bd bk)   LC 82-47708
"Boy meets bear, and together they go berry-picking
by canoe, through fields and by pony and 'Boys-in-
Berries' train, all the way to Berryland." Child Book Rev
Serv
"Berries and jam are roundly celebrated in a lilting
rhyme that, coupled with the jaunty colored pictures,
makes it . . . a good pick for sharing one on one, or fun
to read aloud as a poetry introduction." Booklist

Delessert, Étienne, 1941-
Big and Bad; [by] Etienne Delessert. Houghton
Mifflin 2008 32p il $17
Grades: 1 2 3 4   E
1. Pigs—Fiction 2. Cats—Fiction 3. Wolves—Fiction
4. Animals—Fiction
ISBN 978-0-618-88934-1; 0-618-88934-5
                            LC 2007019291
"Walter Lorraine books"
In this variation on the classic tale of the three little
pigs, two clever cats decide to rid their locale of a vicious wolf whose hunger threatens the entire planet, and
enlist the help of assorted animals to build houses for the
bait—three exquisitely pink pigs.
"Surreal watercolor and colored-pencil scenes are rendered in the artist's signature earthy tones against white
backgrounds. . . . Delessert's direct, sophisticated language and unnerving closeups of the 'marauding' felines
and their predator are not for the faint of heart, but the
message—that the powerless can reverse their fortunes if
they unite and use their wits—will resonate with many
readers." SLJ

Delessert, Étienne, 1941-—*Continued*

Moon theater. Creative Editions 2009 unp il $17.95

Grades: K 1 2 3   E
    1. Moon—Fiction 2. Theater—Fiction
ISBN 978-1-56846-208-0; 1-56846-208-5
                  LC 2008-53991

To prepare for the moon's nightly rising, a young stagehand performs such tasks as dressing the birds in long dark coats, training wild dogs to howl, and watering the stars.

"Delessert's distinctive, sophisticated style and a dark palette evoke a nighttime theme that turns the onset of evening into a theatrical production. . . . Inventive and dramatic, this has more child appeal than usual from Delessert; although other man-in-the-moon tales exist, they wane alongside this numinous performance." Booklist

Demarest, Chris L., 1951-

All aboard! a traveling alphabet; concept by Chris L. Demarest; illustrated by Bill Mayer. Simon & Schuster 2008 unp il $17.99

Grades: PreK K 1 2   E
    1. Travel—Fiction 2. Alphabet
ISBN 978-0-689-85249-7; 0-689-85249-5
                  LC 2006103006

An alphabet book provides a presentation of the common structures one sees and uses while getting from place to place, using such images as an 'O' for a looped overpass and a 'B' to denote the arches of a bridge.

"Mayer is a master of airbrush and bold design, using striking perspectives and dynamic angles, often evoking a strong sense of motion in this homage to travel posters of the 1920s." Horn Book Guide

Demas, Corinne, 1947-

Always in trouble; written by Corinne Demas & pictures by Noah Z. Jones. Scholastic Press 2009 unp il $16.99

Grades: K 1 2 3   E
    1. Dogs—Fiction
ISBN 978-0-545-02453-2; 0-545-02453-6
                  LC 2007-36079

Even after attending obedience school, Emma's dog Toby misbehaves until she takes him back to become a "specially trained dog."

"The story is great for reading aloud, but the many humorous details in the cartoon-style illustrations make it fun for individual reading as well. Text, illustration, and design all work together to create a delightful story." SLJ

Saying goodbye to Lulu; illustrated by Ard Hoyt. Little, Brown 2004 unp il hardcover o.p. pa $6.99

Grades: PreK K 1 2   E
    1. Death—Fiction 2. Bereavement—Fiction 3. Dogs—Fiction
ISBN 0-316-70278-1; 0-316-04749-X (pa)
                  LC 2003-44690

When her dog Lulu dies, a girl grieves but then continues with her life

"Hoyt's expressive illustrations, ink-and-colored-pencil drawings washed with watercolors, reflect the tone of the text and show the child's sadness without sentimentality. . . . A sensitive, hopeful portrayal." Booklist

Valentine surprise; [by] Corinne Demas; illustrations by R. W. Alley. Walker & Co. 2008 unp il $12.95

Grades: PreK K 1   E
    1.   Mother-daughter   relationship—Fiction
2. Valentine's Day—Fiction
ISBN 978-0-8027-9664-6; 0-8027-9664-8
                  LC 2007020143

A little girl tries to create the perfect heart-shaped valentine for her mother on Valentine's Day.

"The language is simple enough for beginning readers, and the story will also work well for group sharing. The typeface changes to reflect the adjective relating to each valentine. Cartoon illustrations in pencil, watercolor, and gouache show Lily in a frenzy of activity." SLJ

Demi, 1942-

The boy who painted dragons; [by] Demi. Margaret K. McElderry Books 2007 unp il $21.99 *

Grades: 1 2 3 4   E
    1. Dragons—Fiction 2. Courage—Fiction 3. Artists—Fiction
ISBN 978-1-4169-2469-2; 1-4169-2469-8
                  LC 2005033679

Ping, a painter of dragons—of which he is secretly afraid—is challenged to seek the truth, find the truth, and dare to be true

"Each page contains paintings of gilt-colored creatures and swatches of delicate Chinese silk brocade. The colors range from rich purples and vibrant reds to cool blues and muted beiges. . . . An elegantly told tale, enhanced by exquisite illustrations." SLJ

The emperor's new clothes; a tale set in China. Margaret K. McElderry Bks. 2000 unp il $19.95 *

Grades: K 1 2 3   E
    1. Andersen, Hans Christian, 1805-1875—Adaptations
2. Fairy tales 3. China—Fiction
ISBN 0-689-83068-8   LC 99-24883

In this retelling of Hans Christian Andersen's tale, two rascals sell a vain Chinese emperor an invisible suit of clothes

"Demi's retelling is lucid, graceful, and true to the original. . . . Figures are delicately outlined; they are painted with flat, jewel-like colors and metallic gold and set against subtly patterned grounds that resemble silk damask. . . . A lovely and meticulously wrought rendition." Horn Book Guide

The girl who drew a phoenix; [by] Demi. Margaret K. McElderry Books 2008 unp il $21.99

Grades: 1 2 3   E
    1. Phoenix (Mythical bird)—Fiction 2. Drawing—Fiction 3. China—Fiction
ISBN 978-1-4169-5347-0; 1-4169-5347-7
                  LC 2007015411

Demi, 1942---*Continued*

A young Chinese girl acquires the qualities of the miraculous phoenix—wisdom, clear sight, generosity, and right judgment—by practicing drawing the mythical bird

"Created in paint, ink, and Chinese silk brocade, swirling images of phoenixes with long, feathery tails fill the pages, including elegant horizontal foldouts." Booklist

The greatest power. Margaret K. McElderry Bks. 2004 unp il $19.95
Grades: K 1 2 3   E
1. China—Fiction
ISBN 0-689-84503-0   LC 2002-10869
Companion volume to The empty pot
Long ago, a Chinese emperor challenges the children of his kingdom to show him the greatest power in the world, and all are surprised at what is discovered

"The text and the handsomely designed, richly colored artwork, which is touched with gold leaf, are set within a circular motif that reinforces the idea of eternity. As usual, Demi ably combines striking artwork and a meaningful story, with quiet dignity and wisdom." Booklist

Kites; magic wishes that fly up to the sky. Crown 1999 unp il hardcover o.p. pa $6.99 *
Grades: K 1 2 3   E
1. Kites—Fiction 2. China—Fiction
ISBN 0-517-80050-0; 0-375-81008-0 (pa)
                               LC 98-41372
"In long-ago China, a woman commissioned an artist to paint a special dragon kite for her son. . . . Word of the artist's talent traveled, and he was soon asked to create a wide variety of flyers for other villagers. The small, intricate, colorful kites illustrated in Demi's signature style and set against blues and greens are lovely to look at and will encourage readers to appreciate their beauty. Captions offer brief explanations of the different emblematic figures, creatures, and symbols. . . . There is also mention of a Chinese festival devoted to kites, as well as detailed instructions for making a kite." SLJ

The magic pillow; written and illustrated by Demi. Margaret K. McElderry Books 2008 unp il $19.99
Grades: K 1 2   E
1. Dreams—Fiction 2. Magic—Fiction 3. China—Fiction
ISBN 978-1-4169-2470-8; 1-4169-2470-1
                               LC 2006-029213
A poor young boy in China yearns for wealth and power, until a magician gives him a magic pillow that brings dreams of what would happen if his wishes came true.

"Demi's dainty, jewel-like art is the perfect vehicle for this story, adoped from a Shen Jiji story. Rendered in traditional Chinese paints and inks and framed in her characteristic gold borders." Booklist

Dempsey, Kristy

Me with you; illustrated by Christopher Denise. Philomel Books 2009 unp il $16.99
Grades: PreK K 1   E
1. Bears—Fiction 2. Grandfathers—Fiction 3. Stories in rhyme
ISBN 978-0-399-25017-0; 0-399-25017-4
                               LC 2008-11751
A little girl bear describes her relationship with her beloved grandfather.

"While the rhyming text is delightful, it is the lush, computer-generated illustrations and the two cozy, endearing characters that children will treasure. The enticing, picturesque scenes will make readers want to climb right into the pages to participate in each charming episode." Booklist

Denise, Anika

Pigs love potatoes; illustrated by Christopher Denise. Philomel Books 2007 unp il $15.99
Grades: PreK K   E
1. Cooking—Fiction 2. Pigs—Fiction 3. Counting 4. Stories in rhyme
ISBN 978-0-399-24036-2; 0-399-24036-5
                               LC 2006-20975
A counting book in which increasing numbers of pigs arrive and are recruited to help as Mamma cooks potatoes.

"Charming acrylic and charcoal pictures of a cozy household and a happy family will have wide appeal." SLJ

Denslow, Sharon Phillips, 1947-

In the snow; pictures by Nancy Tafuri. Greenwillow Books 2005 unp il hardcover o.p. lib bdg $16.89
Grades: PreK K 1 2   E
1. Animals—Fiction 2. Snow—Fiction 3. Stories in rhyme
ISBN 0-06-059683-X; 0-06-059684-8 (lib bdg)
                               LC 2003-56861
Forest animals come out after a fresh snow to eat the seeds a thoughtful child has scattered on the ground

"The very short verses of the rhyming text, sometimes limited to one word per page, provide young children with a guide to what is happening in the illustrations. . . . Tafuri works her visual magic, so finely attuned to the sensibilities of young children while challenging them to observe the natural world." Booklist

DePalma, Mary Newell, 1961-

A grand old tree. Arthur A. Levine Books 2005 unp il $16.99
Grades: K 1 2 3   E
1. Trees—Fiction
ISBN 0-439-62334-0
"For many years a tree flourishes. . . . After the old tree dies, it still provides a home to animals and insects as it slowly decomposes. . . . Neither sentimental nor unfeeling, this appealing picture book offers an appreciation of the cycle of life through a story that is accessible to young children." Booklist

DePalma, Mary Newell, 1961-—*Continued*

The Nutcracker doll. Arthur A. Levine Books 2007 unp il $16.99

Grades: K 1 2　　　　　　　　　　　　　　E

1. Ballet—Fiction

ISBN 0-439-80242-0; 978-0-439-80242-0

LC 2006-16466

Kepley, a young ballerina, gets to play a flower doll in a professional production of "The Nutcracker."

"Airy pen-and-wash illustrations convey moments both large and small. The text thoughtfully keeps the spotlight on the young dancer's feelings." Horn Book Guide

The perfect gift. Arthur A. Levine Books 2010 unp il $16.99

Grades: PreK K 1　　　　　　　　　　　　E

1. Parrots—Fiction 2. Animals—Fiction 3. Gifts—Fiction 4. Grandmothers—Fiction 5. Books and reading—Fiction

ISBN 978-0-545-15402-4; 0-545-15402-2

LC 2009006769

Lori the lorikeet wants to give her grandmother a present, but after dropping her beautiful red berry into the river, she and her friends must try to retrieve the berry or find another gift.

"While DePalma uses delightfully expressive, rhythmic language to tell her accessible tale, her acrylic illustrations are the standout." SLJ

Derby, Sally, 1934-

No mush today; by Sally Derby; illustrated by Nicole Tadgell. Lee & Low 2008 unp il $16.95

Grades: PreK　　　　　　　　　　　　　　E

1. African Americans—Fiction 2. Siblings—Fiction 3. Infants—Fiction

ISBN 978-1-60060-238-2; 1-60060-238-X

"Nonie, a young African-American girl, sits at the breakfast table with her parents and a wailing baby, sulking: 'Not gonna eat my mush. Not gonna eat it!' I say. 'Squishy, yucky, yellow stuff-mush is baby food.' She puts on her shiny black shoes, and, with her chin poked out, stomps off to live with Grandma (next door). . . . The spare text deftly conveys Nonie's reactions and emotions, which are clearly reflected in Tadgell's realistic, folksy watercolors sweeping across double pages." SLJ

Whoosh went the wind! written by Sally Derby; illustrated by Vincent Nguyen. Marshall Cavendish Children 2006 unp il $16.99

Grades: PreK K 1 2　　　　　　　　　　　E

1. Teachers—Fiction 2. Winds—Fiction 3. Tall tales

ISBN 978-0-7614-5309-3; 0-7614-5309-1

LC 2005027582

A boy tries to convince his teacher that the reason he is late for school is that, over and over, he had to undo the damage being caused by the wind, from tearing laundry off the line to blowing away street signs

"Derby's dazzling language is accompanied by Nguyen's acrylic and charcoal illustrations that carry the action and add to the story's energy." SLJ

Derom, Dirk, 1980-

Pigeon and Pigeonette; [text by] Dirk Derom; [illustrations by] Sarah Verroken. Enchanted Lion Books 2009 unp il $16.95

Grades: K 1 2　　　　　　　　　　　　　　E

1. Pigeons—Fiction 2. Friendship—Fiction 3. Flight—Fiction 4. Handicapped—Fiction

ISBN 978-1-59270-087-5; 1-59270-087-X

LC 2009-20779

An old, blind pigeon and a young, deformed pigeon become friends as they persevere in their quest to fly.

"The bold woodcuts and limited color palette convey the setting of the woods throughout the seasons. The boot-wearing pigeons are stylized and encourage closer examination. This is a story of overcoming odds and obstacles, and, despite an occasional adult tone, it delivers a positive and important message." SLJ

DeSeve, Randall

The Duchess of Whimsy; an absolutely delicious fairy tale; [by] Randall de Seve; [illustrated by] Peter de Seve. Philomel Books 2009 unp il $17.99

Grades: PreK K 1　　　　　　　　　　　　E

1. Fairy tales

ISBN 978-0-399-25095-8; 0-399-25095-6

LC 2009-2637

The Duchess of Whimsy has absolutely no interest in the Earl of Norm until he makes a sandwich that causes her to look at him in an entirely different way

"Pages burst to life with rich colors whenever the duchess appears and then become comically dull whenever the earl shows up. With a romantic story and smooth art, this charming picture book will appeal to sophisticated young readers who will find the happily-ever-after whimsically ordinary." Booklist

The toy boat; [by] Randall DeSeve; [illustrated by] Loren Long. Philomel Books 2007 unp il $16.99 *

Grades: PreK K　　　　　　　　　　　　　E

1. Toys—Fiction 2. Boats and boating—Fiction

ISBN 978-0-399-24374-5　　　　LC 2006026281

A toy boat gets separated from its owner and has an adventure on the high seas

"The streamlined text is straightforward, letting the amazing art do much of the work. Long's acrylic, hyperrealistic pictures, awash with many shades of blue, are so substantial they seem to be molded from clay." Booklist

Desimini, Lisa, 1965-

My beautiful child; illustrated by Matt Mahurin. Blue Sky Press 2004 unp il $16.95

Grades: PreK K 1 2　　　　　　　　　　　E

1. Parent-child relationship—Fiction

ISBN 0-439-45893-5　　　　　　LC 2003-5566

Parents express their affection and hopes for their beautiful baby.

"Mahurin uses amazing colors in his eye-catching illustrations, the brightest of yellows and the most vivid greens. . . . This volume lends itself to imaginative contemplation in its sense of joy and wonder." SLJ

Dewan, Ted

One true bear. Walker 2009 unp il $14.99

Grades: 1 2 3   E

1. Teddy bears—Fiction

ISBN 978-0-8027-8495-7; 0-8027-8495-X

LC 2009001807

A brave teddy bear puts his fur on the line when he goes to live with a boy who has a long history of destroying his toys.

"Wonderfully rich and detailed illustrations clearly show an active, rambunctious boy who is also capable of some quiet time with his bear. The placement of the text in and around the illustrations reinforces how well they complement one another." SLJ

Dewdney, Anna

Llama, llama red pajama; by Anna Dewdney. Viking 2005 unp il $15.99

Grades: PreK K   E

1. Llamas—Fiction 2. Bedtime—Fiction 3. Mother-child relationship—Fiction 4. Stories in rhyme

ISBN 0-670-05983-8   LC 2004-25149

At bedtime, a little llama worries after his mother puts him to bed and goes downstairs.

"Dewdney gives a wonderfully fresh twist to a familiar nighttime ritual with an adorable bugeyed baby llama, staccato four-line rhymes, and page compositions that play up the drama. The simple rhymes call out for repeating." Booklist

Other titles about Llama are:

Llama Llama mad at Mama (2007)

Llams Llama misses Mama (2009)

Nobunny's perfect; by Anna Dewdney. Viking Childrens Books 2008 32p il $12.99

Grades: PreK K 1   E

1. Etiquette—Fiction 2. Rabbits—Fiction 3. Stories in rhyme

ISBN 978-0-670-06288-1; 0-670-06288-X

LC 2007-24008

Bunnies, who slurp their juice, forget to say "please," and bite their friends, learn about good manners.

"Dewdney's straightforward text, written in short sentences and rhyme, flows well. Full-color artwork effectively captures the facial expressions, conveys the bunnies' changing emotions, and recreates the activity described in the text." SLJ

Roly Poly pangolin. Viking 2010 unp il $16.99

Grades: PreK K   E

1. Pangolins—Fiction 2. Stories in rhyme 3. Shyness—Fiction

ISBN 978-0-670-01160-5; 0-670-01160-6

"In this short rhyming story, a small pangolin is afraid of new experiences, including meeting other animals. When he hears an unexpected sound, he runs off in a panic, trips, and rolls into a tight ball to keep himself safe. . . . Dewdney has created a lovable childlike character with whom most preschoolers can easily identify. Textured full-bleed pages interspersed with some small action drawings on white space convey movement. Expressive closeup illustrations aptly portray Roly Poly's feelings." SLJ

Dewey, Ariane

Splash! [by] Ariane Dewey and Jose Aruego. Harcourt 2001 c2000 unp il $10.95; pa $3.95

Grades: PreK K 1 2   E

1. Bears—Fiction 2. Fishing—Fiction

ISBN 0-15-216256-9; 0-15-216262-3 (pa)

LC 00-9723

"Green Light reader"

Two clumsy bears join in fishing fun at the river

"This combines big, silly ink-and-watercolor pictures with two or three lines of text on each page. New readers will enjoy the slapstick . . . and the sounds of such words as *splash* and *slip* add to the fun of the story." Booklist

Dewey, Jennifer

Once I knew a spider; [by] Jennifer Owens Dewey; illustrated by Jean Cassels. Walker & Co. 2002 unp il $16.95; lib bdg $17.85

Grades: PreK K 1 2   E

1. Spiders—Fiction

ISBN 0-8027-8700-2; 0-8027-8701-0 (lib bdg)

LC 2001-26345

An expectant mother watches as an orb weaver spider spins a web, lays her eggs, and stays with them over the winter

An "eloquent meditation on the cycle of life. The muted tones of Cassels's . . . austere interiors and the detailed paintings of the spider's behavior complement the calm, contemplative tone of the journal-like text." Publ Wkly

Diakité, Penda

I lost my tooth in Africa; by Penda Diakité and Baba Wagué Diakité; illustrated by Baba Wagué Diakité. Scholastic Press 2006 unp il $16.99 *

Grades: PreK K 1 2 3   E

1. Mali—Fiction 2. Teeth—Fiction 3. Chickens—Fiction 4. Family life—Fiction

ISBN 0-439-66226-5   LC 2004-01933

While visiting her father's family in Mali, a young girl loses a tooth, places it under a calabash, and receives a hen and a rooster from the African Tooth Fairy.

"The vivid ceramic-tile illustrations expand the text, revealing a range of animals, houses, and greenery. At the end are the words to Grandma's Good Night Song, the recipe for African Onion Sauce, and a glossary of Bambara words, all of which add to the authentic feel of the story." SLJ

DiCamillo, Kate, 1964-

Great joy; illustrated by Bagram Ibatoulline. Candlewick Press 2007 unp il $16.99 *

Grades: PreK K 1 2   E

1. Christmas—Fiction 2. Homeless persons—Fiction

ISBN 978-0-7636-2920-5; 0-7636-2920-0

LC 2007-29934

Just before Christmas, when Frances sees a sad-eyed organ grinder and his monkey performing near her apartment, she cannot stop thinking about them, wondering where they go at night, and wishing she could do something to help.

DiCamillo, Kate, 1964-—*Continued*

"The plotline is simplicity itself, and the text lacks any sentimentality or fluff, allowing the acrylic paintings . . . to enrich and expand the story." SLJ

Louise; the adventures of a chicken; written by Kate DiCamillo; pictures by Harry Bliss. Joanna Cotler Books 2008 unp il $17.99; lib bdg $18.89 *

Grades: PreK K 1 2   E
1. Chickens—Fiction   2.   Pirates—Fiction
3. Adventure fiction
ISBN   978-0-06-075554-6;   0-06-075554-7;
978-0-06-075555-3 (lib bdg); 0-06-075555-5 (lib bdg)
                                        LC 2008-20091
Longing for adventure, intrepid Louise the chicken leaves her comfortable nest and goes to sea.

"DiCamillo's brisk, comic narrative crackles with read-aloud savoriness, and her respect for Louise makes the book all the funnier. . . . Bliss creates a thrilling sense of place and puts his wide-eyed heroine front and center. An enlarged format does justice to the details in the art—and to the grand sweep of the storytelling." Publ Wkly

Dickinson, Rebecca

Over in the hollow; illustrated by Stephan Britt. Chronicle Books 2009 unp il $15.99

Grades: PreK K 1 2   E
1.   Stories   in   rhyme   2.   Monsters—Fiction
3. Halloween—Fiction 4. Counting
ISBN 978-0-8118-5035-3; 0-8118-5035-8
                                        LC 2009000955
A counting book that features a variety of spooky Halloween creatures, from one spider to thirteen ghosts.

"The rhyme and rhythm flow well, making this a good choice for reading aloud. The mixed-media illustrations have a retro cartoon feel and are spooky, but not scary—just like the text." SLJ

Diesen, Deborah

The pout-pout fish; illustrated by Dan Hanna. Farrar, Straus & Giroux 2008 unp il $16

Grades: PreK K 1   E
1. Fishes—Fiction 2. Marine animals—Fiction
3. Stories in rhyme
ISBN 978-0-374-36096-2; 0-374-36096-0
                                        LC 2007-60730
The pout-pout fish believes he only knows how to frown, even though many of his friends suggest ways to change his expression, until one day a fish comes along that shows him otherwise.

"The bouncy rhythm is appealing [and] . . . the cartoon illustrations of undersea life are bright and clean and the protagonist's exaggerated expressions are entertaining. The layout is attractive, and the three-panel sequences showing the fish moping around during the refrain are especially well done." SLJ

Dillon, Leo, 1933-

Rap a tap tap; here's Bojangles—think of that! [by] Leo & Diane Dillon. Blue Sky Press (NY) 2002 unp il $15.95 *

Grades: PreK K 1 2 3   E
1. Robinson, Bill, 1878-1949 2. Tap dancing
3. African Americans 4. Stories in rhyme
ISBN 0-590-47883-4   LC 2001-43896
In illustrations and rhyme describes the dancing of Bill "Bojangles" Robinson, one of the most famous tap dancers of all time

"The spreads feature a bouncy text and eye-catching art. . . . The paintings have the effect of collage and employ strong city shapes, with bridges, buildings, and park benches pressed against feather-white backgrounds." Booklist

DiPucchio, Kelly S.

Grace for president; written by Kelly DiPucchio; pictures by LeUyen Pham. Hyperion Books for Children 2008 unp il $15.99

Grades: K 1 2 3   E
1. Elections—Fiction
ISBN 978-0-7868-3919-3; 0-7868-3919-8
When Grace discovers that there has never been a female U.S. president, she decides to run for school president.

"The illustrations are colorful, and depict the various aspects of political campaigns. While the readership of this title is elementary students, Social Studies teachers at upper levels might consider this as a good way to introduce a concept that isn't always easily understood. This is a timely title, with a likeable heroine." Libr Media Connect

DiSalvo, DyAnne, 1960-

A castle on Viola Street. HarperCollins Pubs. 2001 unp il $16.95; lib bdg $16.89

Grades: K 1 2 3   E
1. Houses—Fiction
ISBN 0-688-17690-9; 0-688-17691-7 (lib bdg)
                                        LC 00-40889
A hardworking family gets their own house at last by joining a community program that restores old houses

"DiSalvo-Ryan shares an uplifting story of the importance and impact of community pride and support. . . . The colorful gouache, pen, and pencil pictures are folksy and warm." Booklist

A dog like Jack. Holiday House 1999 unp il $17.95 paperback o.p.

Grades: K 1 2 3   E
1. Dogs—Fiction 2. Death—Fiction
ISBN 0-8234-1369-1; 0-8234-1680-1 (pa)
                                        LC 97-41949
After a long life of chasing squirrels, licking ice cream cones, and loving his adoptive family, an old dog comes to the end of his days

"Thoughtful words and tender pictures beautifully convey the special relationship between a young boy and his dog." Booklist

DiSalvo, DyAnne, 1960-—*Continued*

Uncle Willie and the soup kitchen. Morrow Junior Bks. 1991 unp il pa $5.99 hardcover o.p.

Grades: K 1 2 3   E

1. Uncles—Fiction 2. Poverty—Fiction

ISBN 0-688-15285-6 (pa)   LC 90-6375

A boy spends the day with Uncle Willie in the soup kitchen where he works preparing and serving food for the hungry

"The color-pencil and wash illustrations observe . . . [a] balance between attracting the viewer with softly blended colors and avoiding the sentimentality of glamorizing an essentially sad situation. Without sacrifice of story, the total effect leaves young listeners with new considerations of society and social service, a theme too often neglected in picture books." Bull Cent Child Books

Ditchfield, Christin

Cowlick! by Christin Ditchfield; illustrated by Rosalind Beardshaw. Random House 2007 unp il $14.99; lib bdg $17.99

Grades: PreK K 1   E

1. Hair—Fiction 2. Cattle—Fiction

ISBN 0-375-83540-7; 0-375-93540-1 (lib bdg)

"A Golden book"

This "imagines a playful explanation as to how children who go to bed with neat hair wake up with some wild 'dos in the morning. It's all because of a mysterious but kindly bovine nighttime visitor." Publ Wkly

This offers "appealingly rich and textured paintings. . . . The short, lively text makes this fun for sharing aloud." SLJ

Shwatsit! illustrated by Rosalind Beardshaw. Golden Books 2009 unp il $15.99

Grades: PreK K 1   E

1. Toddlers—Fiction 2. Siblings—Fiction

ISBN 978-0-375-84181-1; 0-375-84181-4

As Baby points at everything in sight, she has just one thing to say: "Shwatsit!" But what on earth does it mean? Finally, her older brother solves the mystery.

"The well-designed, expressive illustrations expand on the rhyming text by showing the toddler throughout her day." SLJ

DiTerlizzi, Tony

Jimmy Zangwow's out-of-this-world, moon pie adventure. Simon & Schuster Bks. for Young Readers 2000 unp il $16; pa $4.99

Grades: PreK K 1 2   E

1. Space flight to the moon—Fiction

ISBN 0-689-80076-2; 0-689-87830-3 (pa)

LC 98-16602

When Jimmy's mother won't let him have any moon pies for a snack, he takes a trip to the moon to get some

"The dialogue includes quirky sayings like 'Holy macaroni!' and 'Jumping june bugs!,' which young readers will relish. Large double-page watercolor, gouache, and colored-pencil illustrations enhance the story." SLJ

Dobbins, Jan

Driving my tractor; [text by] Jan Dobbins; [illustrations by] David Sim. Barefoot Books 2009 unp il $16.99

Grades: PreK K   E

1. Stories in rhyme 2. Tractors—Fiction 3. Domestic animals—Fiction 4. Counting 5. Color—Fiction

ISBN 978-1-84686-358-5; 1-84686-358-9

LC 2008051065

The reader is invited to count the animal passengers riding in a tractor traveling on a bumpy road.

"This tale is ideal for storytime with its rhyming text, fun sounds, and refrain, 'Chug, chug, clank, clank, toot! It's a very busy day.' This is a jolly read-aloud, and the accompanying CD with a jazzy version adds to the charm, with both an instrumental track and SteveSongs (of PBS fame) singing the text." SLJ

Docherty, Thomas

Little boat. Templar Books 2009 unp il $15.99

Grades: PreK K   E

1. Boats and boating—Fiction

ISBN 978-0-7636-4428-4; 0-7636-4428-5

Setting off into the big, wide world, Little Boat runs into treacherous waters, turbulent tides, and seafaring friends. After all his nautical adventures, he finds out that he's no longer such a little boat.

"This simple story of friendship and self-esteem is beautifully illustrated in ink-and-watercolor paintings with a wistful, nostalgic flavor." Booklist

To the beach. Templar Books 2009 unp il $15.99

Grades: PreK K 1   E

1. Voyages and travels—Fiction 2. Imagination—Fiction

ISBN 978-0-7636-4429-1; 0-7636-4429-3

"A boy packs up all of the necessary gear for a day at the beach, like goggles, snorkel, flippers, bathing suit, and, of course, a big yellow inner tube. The only problem is: it's raining. His imagination then takes over as he secures an airplane, a sailboat, a truck, a camel, and some sand, and finally arrives at the sea. . . . This clever book is complemented by beautiful ink and watercolor drawings of the landscapes that the boy has created. The simple narrative encourages youngsters to think for themselves and never to limit the places their imaginations will take them." SLJ

Dodd, Emma, 1969-

I don't want a cool cat! Little, Brown 2010 il $15.99 *

Grades: PreK K 1   E

1. Cats—Fiction

ISBN 978-0-316-03674-0; 0-316-03674-9

A little girl "knows what she does not want: 'A stuffy cat. A huffy, over-fluffy cat.' . . . The true-to-life hilarity of the text commands attention, especially when mixed with such smart art. With a combination of paint and collage, the images have a three-dimensional feel as they sit on their smooth, candy-colored backgrounds. . . . Combine the art with the pithy text, and you're got a book that's perfect to read aloud to groups." Booklist

Dodd, Emma, 1969-—*Continued*
I don't want a posh dog! Little, Brown 2009
c2008 unp il $15.99
Grades: PreK K 1   **E**
   1. Stories in rhyme 2. Dogs—Fiction
   ISBN 978-0-316-03390-9; 0-316-03390-1
                                     LC 2008002229
First published 2008 in the United Kingdom
A girl describes in rhyming text the types of dogs she
does not want, and finally arrives at a dog that she can
call her own
   "The rhymes are clever and succinct, and the simple
line art incorporates photo elements . . . that lend the
right touch of surrealism." Booklist

I love bugs. Holiday House 2010 unp il $16.95
Grades: PreK K 1 2   **E**
   1. Insects—Fiction 2. Spiders—Fiction
   ISBN 978-0-8234-2280-7; 0-8234-2280-1
                                     LC 2009-32814
"A small boy with curly hair and a striped T-shirt
sings an extended love song to insects, arachnids, arthro-
pods, and more." Publ Wkly
   "The text juggles sounds and rhymes skillfully. . . .
Varied in composition, palette, and scale, the illustrations
have great vitality. . . . Easy to see from a distance, this
would be an excellent choice for group sharing."
Booklist

Just like you; [by] Emma Dodd. Dutton
Children's Books 2008 unp il $10.99
Grades: PreK   **E**
   1. Father-son relationship—Fiction 2. Bears—Fiction
   3. Stories in rhyme
   ISBN 978-0-525-47933-8; 0-525-47933-3
                                     LC 2007019208
A baby bear describes the ways in which he wants to
be like his father when he grows up.
   "This warm, honest tribute to a child's love for a caring adult is almost flawless in its execution. Dodd's minimalist illustrations feature big, simple shapes with thick
black outlines and blocks of complementary contrasting
colors. . . . The sentiment comes across in just a few
easy words at a time. . . . A sweet, soothing selection
for bedtime sharing." SLJ

No matter what; [by] Emma Dodd. Dutton
Children's Books 2008 unp il $10.99
Grades: PreK   **E**
   1. Elephants—Fiction 2. Parent-child relationship—
   Fiction 3. Stories in rhyme
   ISBN 978-0-525-47932-1; 0-525-47932-5
                                     LC 2007019207
In rhyming text, a baby elephant is assured of being
loved unconditionally.
   "Each phrase is supported by a stylized African landscape in muted colors, but with bright touches. . . . The
young elephant is simply rendered, too, and quite charming. The art, and the padded cover with metallic accents,
is appealing, and the comforting text is perfect for toddlers." SLJ

What pet to get? [by] Emma Dodd. Arthur A.
Levine Books 2008 unp il $16.99
Grades: PreK K 1 2   **E**
   1. Pets—Fiction
   ISBN 0-545-03570-8   LC 2007010106

Jack's mother agrees that he may have a pet, but
when he suggests everything from an elephant to a
tyranosaurus rex, she must explain why each would be
less than ideal
   "Filling in her thick black outlines with a mixture of
digitally manipulated textures and densely saturated colors, Dodd . . . creates a daffy, winning cast of googly-
eyed creatures whose ids run rampant." Publ Wkly

Dodds, Dayle Ann, 1952-
Minnie's Diner; a multiplying menu; illustrated
by John Manders. Candlewick Press 2004 unp il
hardcover o.p. pa $6.99
Grades: K 1 2 3   **E**
   1. Multiplication—Fiction 2. Stories in rhyme
   3. Restaurants—Fiction
   ISBN 0-7636-1736-9; 0-7636-3313-5 (pa)
                                     LC 2002-34756
Rhyming tale of five boys and their father who forget
about their chores on the farm to enjoy Minnie's good
cooking, each requesting double what the previous one
ordered
   "Told in jaunty rhymes with varied type sizes for emphasis, this funny story is illustrated with colorful cartoons done in gouache. Children will appreciate the humor and groan with delight when they recognize the
math pattern." SLJ

The prince won't go to bed; pictures by Kyrsten
Brooker. Farrar, Straus & Giroux 2007 unp il $16
Grades: PreK K 1 2   **E**
   1. Bedtime—Fiction 2. Princes—Fiction 3. Stories in
   rhyme
   ISBN 0-374-36108-8; 978-0-374-36108-2
                                     LC 2005051234
When the young prince refuses to go to bed, assorted
members of the royal household offer their ideas on exactly what he needs, but it is his sister, Princess Kate,
who learns the truth.
   Dodd's "rhymed text abounds with the kind of repetitions in structure and language that make children want
to join in. . . . The fonts grow larger and Brooker's hilarious, cock-eyed collages ever more frantic with each
repetition." Publ Wkly

Teacher's pets; illustrated by Marylin Hafner.
Candlewick Press 2006 unp il $15.99
Grades: PreK K 1 2   **E**
   1. Pets—Fiction 2. School stories
   ISBN 0-7636-2252-4
A teacher invites her students to bring their pets in
each Monday for sharing day, but by the end of the year,
she has a classroom full of "forgotten" animals.
   "This gentle and humorous story has charming watercolor illustrations that reinforce the emotions of the children, the animals, and, of course, the warmhearted teacher." SLJ

Where's Pup? pictures by Pierre Pratt. Dial Bks.
for Young Readers 2003 unp il $12.99
Grades: PreK K 1   **E**
   1. Circus—Fiction 2. Clowns—Fiction 3. Dogs—Fiction 4. Stories in rhyme
   ISBN 0-8037-2744-5   LC 2002-588

Dodds, Dayle Ann, 1952-—*Continued*

A circus clown's search for his partner leads him to the top of an acrobatic pyramid, found by unfolding the book's final page

"Relying on a jeweled palette of acrylic reds and oranges, the images are simple yet arresting and show the action from varying perspectives. A visually exciting charmer." SLJ

Dokas, Dara, 1968-

Muriel's red sweater; illustrations by Bernadette Pons. Dutton Children's Books 2009 unp il $16.99

Grades: PreK K 1   E

1. Birthdays—Fiction 2. Animals—Fiction 3. Gifts—Fiction 4. Clothing and dress—Fiction

ISBN 978-0-525-47962-8; 0-525-47962-7

LC 2008020605

"Unbeknownst to duck Muriel, her sweater is unraveling as she delivers invitations to her birthday party. Luckily, her friends have already been working on the perfect present: a new sweater. The cheery illustrations do a good deal of storytelling; readers can spot hints about the new sweater and chuckle at the uses Muriel's friends find for yarn from the old one." Horn Book Guide

Donaldson, Julia, 1948-

The fish who cried wolf; [by] Julia Donaldson & Axel Scheffler. Arthur A. Levine Books 2008 unp il $15.99

Grades: PreK K 1 2   E

1. Fishes—Fiction 2. Storytelling—Fiction 3. Stories in rhyme

ISBN 978-0-439-92825-0; 0-439-92825-7

LC 2007-12308

Tiddler the fish is always telling tall tales about why he is late for school, but when he is actually caught in a net and taken far from home, it is his stories that help him find his way back.

"Donaldson's rhyming text is crisp and clean, leaving plenty of metaphorical room for Scheffler's expansively imagined art." Publ Wkly

One Ted falls out of bed; illustrated by Anna Currey. Henry Holt 2006 unp il $15.95

Grades: PreK K 1 2   E

1. Teddy bears—Fiction 2. Toys—Fiction 3. Counting 4. Stories in rhyme

ISBN 978-0-8050-7787-2; 0-8050-7787-1

LC 2005-12173

"In this rhythmic counting book, a sleeping child's teddy bear falls out of bed and can't climb back up. Three mice invite him to play, racing four cars, counting five stars, sipping tea with six dolls, and so on. . . . The toys in the airy illustrations that sweep across the pages are packed with personality. Perfect for storytimes or one-on-one lapsits, this book can be counted on for a gentle, cozy read." SLJ

Stick Man; illustrated by Axel Scheffler. Arthur A. Levine Books 2009 c2008 unp il $16.99

Grades: PreK K 1   E

1. Stories in rhyme 2. Santa Claus—Fiction 3. Christmas—Fiction

ISBN 978-0-545-15761-2; 0-545-15761-7

LC 2008-48323

First published 2008 in the United Kingdom

Stick Man ends up far away from his family tree when he is fetched by a dog, thrown by a child, used as a snowman's arm, and even put on a fire, but finally Santa Claus steps in to make sure that Stick Man and his family have a joyous Christmas.

"Scheffler's engaging illustrations, Donaldson's irresistible rhyming text and repeated refrains make this a winning read-aloud that will stick around long after the holiday season." Kirkus

Tyrannosaurus Drip; [by] Julia Donaldson; [illustrations by] David Roberts. Feiwel and Friends 2008 unp il $16.95

Grades: K 1 2   E

1. Dinosaurs—Fiction 2. Stories in rhyme

ISBN 978-0-312-37747-2; 0-312-37747-9

LC 2007-40511

A duckbilled dinosaur, accidentally raised by fierce tyrannosauruses who would eat duckbills if only they could reach them, tries to be like his "family" but finally gives up, runs away, and finds a real home with others of his kind.

"The dinosaurs are rendered in an Art Deco-influenced style, and the lines roll off the tongue like the rhymes of Dr. Seuss. Children will enjoy the repetitive lilt, and adults will appreciate how naturally it reads. Expressive characters enhance the humor, and the limited palette helps emphasize just how different the creatures' worlds are. An enjoyable group read-aloud." SLJ

What the ladybug heard; illustrated by Lydia Monks. Henry Holt and Company 2010 c2009 unp il $16.99

Grades: PreK K 1   E

1. Stories in rhyme 2. Ladybugs—Fiction 3. Domestic animals—Fiction 4. Sounds—Fiction 5. Thieves—Fiction

ISBN 978-0-8050-9028-4; 0-8050-9028-2

LC 2009005266

First published 2009 in the United Kingdom

Although much quieter than the farm animals that moo, cluck, or oink, a gentle ladybug is instrumental in foiling a plan to steal the farm's prize-winning cow.

"Filled with drama, lively action, and a large supporting cast of characters, this is a mini play more than a fully fleshed story. The appealing and brightly colored collage illustrations, rhyming text, and assorted animal sounds make it a natural for individual or group read-alouds." Booklist

Where's my mom? illustrated by Axel Scheffler. Dial Books for Young Readers 2008 unp il $16.99

Grades: PreK K   E

1. Animals—Fiction 2. Butterflies—Fiction 3. Monkeys—Fiction 4. Stories in rhyme

ISBN 978-0-8037-3228-5; 0-8037-3228-7

LC 2007005236

Donaldson, Julia, 1948-—*Continued*

A butterfly tries to help a lost young monkey find its mother in the jungle, meeting many different animals along the way.

"The bouncy rhyming couplets will charm children. . . . Bold cartoon illustrations on full spreads in bright jungle colors feature a host of expressive insects and creatures." SLJ

Donofrio, Beverly

Mary and the mouse, the mouse and Mary; by Beverly Donofrio; illustrated by Barbara McClintock. Schwartz & Wade Books 2007 unp il $16.99

Grades: PreK K 1   E

1. Mice—Fiction 2. Friendship—Fiction

ISBN 978-0-375-83609-1   LC 2006030980

While Mary, a girl whose family lives in a big house, is learning things at school, a young mouse whose family lives in a small house within the big one is learning the same things at her school, and when the two eventually meet they become friends

"The telling is clean, the parallel structure of the tale is pleasing, and McClintock's warm, precisely drawn ink, gouache, and watercolor artwork will fascinate children and adults alike." Booklist

Dorros, Alex

Número uno; by Alex Dorros and Arthur Dorros; illustrated by Susan Guevara. Abrams Books for Young Readers 2007 unp il $16.95

Grades: K 1 2 3   E

1. Mexico—Fiction 2. Spanish language—Vocabulary

ISBN 0-8109-5764-7

Tired of listening to strong Hercules and smart Socrates constantly argue over who is more important to their village, the townspeople devise a test to settle the question once and for all.

"The battle between brains and brawn is entertainingly pitched here. . . . The Spanish dialogue is simple . . . and punctuates the story-hour-ready text with verve. Guevara's tropically accented pastoral oil paintings provide contrast to the often slapstick goings-on but also do their share of storytelling." Horn Book

Dorros, Arthur, 1950-

Abuela; illustrated by Elisa Kleven. Dutton Children's Bks. 1991 unp il $16.99; pa $7.99 *

Grades: PreK K 1 2   E

1. Imagination—Fiction 2. Flight—Fiction 3. Grandmothers—Fiction 4. New York (N.Y.)—Fiction 5. Hispanic Americans—Fiction

ISBN 0-525-44750-4; 0-14-056225-7 (pa)

LC 90-21459

While riding on a bus with her grandmother, a little girl named Rosalba imagines that they are carried up into the sky and fly over the sights of New York City

"Each illustration is a masterpiece of color, line, and form that will mesmerize youngsters. . . . The smooth text, interpesed with Spanish words and phrases, provides ample context clues, so the glossary, while helpful, is not absolutely necessary." Booklist

Another title about Rosalba and her grandmother is:

Isla (1995)

Julio's magic; collages by Ann Grifalconi. HarperCollins 2005 32p il $15.99; lib bdg $16.89

Grades: PreK K 1 2   E

1. Wood carving—Fiction 2. Mexico—Fiction

ISBN 0-06-029004-8; 0-06-029005-6 (lib bdg)

LC 2004-6616

A young artist in a Mexican village discovers the power of friendship when he helps his mentor win a prestigious wood-carving contest

"Grifalconi's photorealistic collages capture the texture, color, and feel of village life. This book will be excellent for art and social studies classrooms. . . . It is also a compassionate intergenerational story." SLJ

Papá and me; by Arthur Dorros; illustrated by Rudy Gutierrez. HarperCollinsPublishers 2008 unp il $16.99; lib bdg $17.89

Grades: PreK K   E

1. Father-son relationship—Fiction 2. Hispanic Americans—Fiction 3. Spanish language—Vocabulary

ISBN 978-0-06-058156-5; 978-0-06-058157-2 (lib bdg)   LC 2007011868

A Pura Belpre Illustrator Award honor book, 2009

"From the time they wake up in the morning, a Latino boy and his father have fun. . . . The simple words, in both Spanish and English, and the bright, exuberant unframed double-page pictures celebrate the loving connection between parent and child. . . . The big, swirling circles in the artwork embrace the characters within the widening arcs of sky and waves." Booklist

Radio Man. Don Radio; a story in English and Spanish; Spanish translation by Sandra Marulanda Dorros. HarperCollins Pubs. 1993 unp il pa $6.99 hardcover o.p. *

Grades: K 1 2 3   E

1. Migrant labor—Fiction 2. Mexican Americans—Fiction 3. Bilingual books—English-Spanish

ISBN 0-06-443482-6 (pa)   LC 92-28369

As he travels with his family of migrant farmworkers, Diego relies on his radio to provide him with companionship and help connect him to all the different places in which he lives

"Spot art separates English and Spanish on text pages that alternate with affecting, primitive-like acrylic paintings." Publ Wkly

Doughty, Rebecca, 1955-

Oh no! Time to go! a book of goodbyes. Schwartz & Wade 2009 unp il $15.99; lib bdg $18.99

Grades: PreK K 1 2   E

1. Stories in rhyme 2. Family life—Fiction

ISBN 978-0-375-84981-7; 0-375-84981-5; 978-0-375-95696-6 (lib bdg); 0-375-95696-4 (lib bdg)   LC 2008022462

A young boy presents the different ways his family members and others say goodbye, then describes the worst goodbye he ever experienced.

"Opaque, brightly colored illustrations outlined in black ink are rendered in a spare, stylized manner. . . . This satisfying tale conveys an important truth about how life's goodbyes often lead to new hellos." SLJ

Downing, Julie, 1956-

No hugs till Saturday; [by] Julie Downing. Clarion Books 2008 31p il lib bdg $16

Grades: PreK K 1   E

1. Hugging—Fiction 2. Mother-son relationship—Fiction 3. Week—Fiction 4. Dragons—Fiction

ISBN 978-0-618-91078-6 (lib bdg); 0-618-91078-6 (lib bdg)   LC 2007010030

When Felix the dragon declares that there will be no hugs, snuggles, or super squeezes for a whole week, both he and his mama have a hard time.

"The soft-edged paintings show a lovable green dragon and humorously depict his antics. . . . Featuring a believably childlike protagonist, a cozy parent-child relationship, and a satisfying resolution, it is a delightfully warmhearted choice for most collections." SLJ

Dowson, Nick

Tigress; illustrated by Jane Chapman. Candlewick Press 2004 27p il $15.99

Grades: PreK K 1   E

1. Tigers—Fiction

ISBN 0-7636-2325-3   LC 2003-55342

A mother tigress raises two cubs and teaches them all they need to know until they are ready to rely on themselves.

"The zoology is as exciting as the story in this action-packed picture book. . . . Chapman's bright, clear, double-page acrylic pictures show the camouflage drama. . . . On each spread, the simple poetic words are in bold type, and small notes in italics add fascinating facts." Booklist

Tracks of a panda; illustrated by Yu Rong. Candlewick Press 2007 unp il $16.99

Grades: PreK K 1 2   E

1. Giant panda—Fiction

ISBN 978-0-7636-3146-8; 0-7636-3146-9   LC 2006051836

A mother panda teaches her cub how to survive in their mountain habitat but as the sound of villagers clearing the forest approaches, she knows they must look for a new home.

"The mother panda's endearing facial features—beautifully rendered in black and white in contrast to the delicate watercolor backgrounds of green, blue, brown, and gray—may well elicit an adoring squeal or two. . . . Dowson leaves the reader with the uncertainty of this pair's future and, on a larger scale, the survival of the species as a whole." Horn Book

Doyen, Denise

Once upon a twice; illustrated by Barry Moser. Random House Children's Books 2009 unp il $16.99; lib bdg $19.99 *

Grades: PreK K 1   E

1. Stories in rhyme 2. Nonsense verses 3. Mice—Fiction 4. Conduct of life—Fiction

ISBN   978-0-375-85612-9;   0-375-85612-9; 978-0-375-95612-6 (lib bdg); 0-375-95612-3 (lib bdg)   LC 2008011125

"A foolish mouse is prone to jamming up the line of fellow night-foragers to smell a rose and wandering off to watch a beetle. After nearly becoming a snake's dinner, 'Jam' lives on to lecture mouslings on the dangers of moonlit meanders." Kirkus

"Doyen's utterly sound and alive story is paired with the perfect illustrator, whose deft touch provides all the eeriness that it begs for. . . . With gloriously nonsensical words and phrases . . . the author manages to get the point across that there is much to fear in the night. . . . This wonderful book is a marvelous read-aloud that children will want to hear again and again." SLJ

Doyle, Malachy, 1954-

Horse; illustrated by Angelo Rinaldi. Margaret K. McElderry Books 2008 unp il $16.99

Grades: K 1 2 3   E

1. Horses—Fiction

ISBN 978-1-4169-2467-8; 1-4169-2467-1   LC 2007-32733

Illustrations and simple text describe the first year of a foal's life, from his birth one warm spring night, through lazy summer days, to the next spring, when he is old enough to be bridled like his mother.

"The photo-realistic oil paintings of the countryside are drenched in sunlight, awash with billowing, John Constable clouds, and startling in their rendering of the sparkling snow. . . . The quiet text, only a sentence or two per page, adds to the book's serene tone, giving readers more time to peruse the elegant paintings." Publ Wkly

Doyle, Roddy, 1958-

Her mother's face; by Roddy Doyle; illustrated by Freya Blackwood. Arthur A. Levine Books 2008 unp il $16.99

Grades: K 1 2 3   E

1. Mothers—Fiction 2. Bereavement—Fiction 3. Ireland—Fiction

ISBN 978-0-439-81501-7; 0-439-81501-0   LC 2007043660

Siobhan and her father continue to feel sad in the years following the death of Siobhan's mother, until Siobhan follows the advice of a mysterious woman

"The storytelling flows gracefully between the naturalistic details . . . and the magical encounter. Blackwood . . . magnifies Doyle's optimism in her limpid watercolor and charcoal art." Publ Wkly

Drescher, Henrik, 1955-

McFig & McFly; a tale of jealousy, revenge, and death (with a happy ending); [by] Henrik Drescher. Candlewick Press 2008 40p il $17.99

Grades: K 1 2 3   E

1. Building—Fiction

ISBN 978-0-7636-3386-8; 0-7636-3386-0   LC 2007-32345

As neighbors McFig and McFly compete to see who can outdo the other in additions to their cottages, they become so involved that they do not realize McFig's daughter and McFly's son have grown up and fallen in love.

"Drescher achieves balance to this outlandish story by swathing his pages in creamy aqua and rosy hues, and using his recognizable rough-line drawings to delineate the characters and buildings. . . . For readers who enjoy the offbeat, this story is sure to generate a laugh." SLJ

Drummond, Allan

Liberty! Farrar, Straus & Giroux 2002 unp il pa $6.95

Grades: K 1 2 3   E

1. Statue of Liberty (New York, N.Y.)—Fiction

ISBN 0-374-34385-3; 0-374-44397-1 (pa)

LC 2001-18777

"Frances Foster books"

"Drummond tells the story of October 28, 1886, the day the Statue of Liberty was first unveiled in New York harbor. A boy, whose name is now lost, is on the ground, ready to signal Bartholdi, the statue's sculptor, to release the tricolor veil that covers the Lady of Liberty's face. . . . This is an unusual offering. Drummond takes a kernel of history . . . and turns it into both a thoughtful lesson and a visual pageant. Scenes of the construction of France's gift to the U.S. are shown in finely wrought, energetic, pen-and-wash images that swirl through the text." Booklist

Tin Lizzie. Farrar, Straus & Giroux 2008 unp il $16.95

Grades: PreK K 1 2   E

1. Automobiles—Fiction 2. Environmental protection—Fiction 3. Grandfathers—Fiction

ISBN 0-374-32000-4; 978-0-374-32000-3

LC 2006-48773

Grandpa loves working on old cars, especially his Model T Ford, and he passes along to his grandchildren not only the history of automobiles and all of their benefits, but also his concerns about traffic, pollution, and the problems of relying on foreign oil.

"The color-washed ink drawings are charming, the book is well-designed, and the text is thought-provoking." Booklist

Dubosarsky, Ursula, 1961-

The terrible plop; pictures by Andrew Joyner. Farrar, Straus and Giroux 2009 unp il $15.95

Grades: PreK K   E

1. Stories in rhyme 2. Rabbits—Fiction 3. Animals—Fiction 4. Fear—Fiction 5. Courage—Fiction

ISBN 978-0-374-37428-0; 0-374-37428-7

LC 2008043323

When a mysterious sound sends the whole forest running away in fear, only the littlest rabbit is courageous enough to discover what really happened.

"Basic, fun rhymes and repetitive, excitable text lend themselves to reading aloud, and the recurring appearance of the word PLOP provides an explosive entree for children to chime in while soaking up Joyner's bouyant mixed-media artwork. In addition, kids will appreciate the easy absurdity of the situation, enjoy the role-reversal in the end, and maybe even come away knowing that most things aren't so scary once you look a little closer." Booklist

Dumbleton, Mike, 1948-

Cat; written by Mike Dumbleton; illustrated by Craig Smith. Kane/Miller 2008 unp il $15.95

Grades: PreK K   E

1. Cats—Fiction

ISBN 978-1-933605-73-9; 1-933605-73-1

First published 2007 in Australia

As a cat navigates the perils of the outside world, it and its prey all find things to be thankful for

"The humor is elucidated in the richly colored green-and brown-tinged gouache and pen-and-ink illustrations that move the action along from one episode to another." Horn Book Guide

Dunbar, Joyce

The monster who ate darkness; illustrated by Jimmy Liao. Candlewick Press 2008 unp il $16.99

Grades: PreK K 1   E

1. Bedtime—Fiction 2. Fear—Fiction 3. Monsters—Fiction 4. Night—Fiction

ISBN 978-0-7636-3859-7; 0-7636-3859-5

LC 2008-928826

"Under Jo-Jo's bed lurks a 'tiny speck of a monster' with a 'big empty feeling.' This endearingly unscary creature discovers a taste for darkness and eats up even the dimmest corners of the room. . . . Jo-Jo, who is normally afraid of the dark, can't fall asleep in the endless daylight. As the compassionate monster cradles the little boy in his arms and soothes him with a lullaby, the evening shades return. Liao's digitally enhanced pen and watercolor illustrations humorously capture the mayhem caused by lack of darkness." SLJ

Oddly. Candlewick Press 2009 unp il $16.99

Grades: K 1 2   E

1. Friendship—Fiction 2. Love—Fiction

ISBN 978-0-7636-4274-7; 0-7636-4274-6

"The Lostlet, the Strangelet and the Oddlet are three furry sui generis critters who wander a desolate beach, pondering the Big Questions: 'What am I?'; 'Where am I?'; 'Who am I?.' [Then] a little boy 'stranger, odder, and more lost than they' stumbles into their melancholy reveries." Publ Wkly

"Patrick Benson's ink-and-watercolor illustrations make this existential questioning pleasant to witness, delivering three appealing imaginary beasts in a quietly bizarre landscape. . . . Dunbar's text is concise and lively, with many memorable touches." Booklist

Dunbar, Polly

Dog Blue. Candlewick Press 2004 unp il hardcover o.p. pa $7.99

Grades: PreK K 1 2   E

1. Dogs—Fiction

ISBN 0-7636-2476-4; 0-7636-3881-1 (pa)

LC 2003-65223

Bertie, who loves the color blue and really wants a dog, finally gets his wish even though the dog he meets is white with black spots

"Dunbar makes clever use of page turns, unfolding the story in pithy, alliterative prose. . . . In the end, the wish fulfillment is gratifying, but it's Bertie's ingenious self-sufficiency that truly resonates." Booklist

Penguin. Candlewick Press 2007 unp il $15.99
*

Grades: PreK K   E

1. Penguins—Fiction 2. Toys—Fiction

ISBN 0-7636-3404-2

"A pajama-clad toddler opens his present to find a toy penguin. Much to Ben's chagrin, the bird doesn't say

Dunbar, Polly—*Continued*

anything, no matter how hard the boy tries to engage it. . . . It isn't until a blue lion chomps on the child that Penguin jumps into action and rescues his new pal. . . . The attractive, spare illustrations in mixed media are focused and centered on a white background." SLJ

Where's Tumpty? Candlewick Press 2009 unp il $12.99

Grades: PreK   E
1. Elephants—Fiction 2. Animals—Fiction 3. Friendship—Fiction
ISBN 978-0-7636-4273-0; 0-7636-4273-8

"After several unsuccessful attempts at hiding, Tumpty the elephant is able to trick his friends into thinking he has disappeared. . . . There are many amusing situations involving Tilly, a little girl, and her animal friends. . . . The background consists of a variety of muted tones, which contrast with the brighter mixed-media drawings. The illustrations are whimsical and detailed. . . . Young children and beginning readers are sure to gravitate to this delightful story that celebrates the joy of friendship." SLJ

Other titles about Tilly and her friends are:
Doodle bites (2009)
Good night, Tiptoe (2009)
Happy Hector (2008)
Hello, Tilly (2008)
Pretty Pru (2009)

Dunn, Todd

We go together! by Todd Dunn; illustrated by Miki Sakamoto. Sterling 2007 unp il $12.95

Grades: PreK K   E
1. Vocabulary—Fiction 2. Stories in rhyme
ISBN 978-1-4027-3260-7; 1-4027-3260-0
                 LC 2006023425

A rhyming picture book with pairs of things that go together exceptionally well, like horse and wagon and fire and dragon.

"Using very readable pictures and predictable scheme, children will easily finish the lines. . . . The colorful illustrations are uncomplicated, yet interesting enough to encourage conversation." SLJ

Dunrea, Olivier, 1953-

Bear Noel. Farrar, Straus & Giroux 2000 unp il hardcover o.p. pa $5.95

Grades: PreK K 1 2   E
1. Bears—Fiction 2. Animals—Fiction 3. Christmas—Fiction
ISBN 0-374-39990-5; 0-374-40001-6 (pa)
                 LC 99-27600

The animals of the North Woods react with excitement as they hear Bear Noel coming to bring them Christmas

"Dunrea beautifully creates the effect of falling snow throughout the pictures and uses a limited palette of browns, grays, and greens with flashes of fox red to lend a celebratory feel." Booklist

Gossie. Houghton Mifflin 2002 unp il $9.95 *

Grades: PreK K 1   E
1. Geese—Fiction
ISBN 0-618-17674-8   LC 2002-214

Gossie is a gosling who likes to wear bright red boots every day, no matter what she is doing, and so she is heartbroken the day the boots are missing and she can't find them anywhere

The succinct text uses "repetition and predictability with great skill and will therefore work equally well with early independent readers and preschoolers. . . . The illustrations, focused against restful white space, are spare and expressive, models of composition and clarity." Horn Book

Other titles about Gossie and her friends are:
BooBoo (2004)
Gossie & Gertie (2002)
Merry Christmas, Ollie (2008)
Ollie (2003)
Ollie the stomper (2003)
Ollie's Easter eggs (2010)
Peedie (2004)

It's snowing! Farrar, Straus & Giroux 2002 unp il hardcover o.p. pa $6.99 *

Grades: PreK K 1   E
1. Snow—Fiction 2. Mothers—Fiction 3. Infants—Fiction
ISBN 0-374-39992-1; 0-312-60216-2 (pa)
                 LC 00-42172

A mother shares the magic of a snowy night with her baby

"The gentle, rhythmical rocking of the text conveys a reassuring message that's beautifully supported by Dunrea's spare, snow-dappled gouache illustrations." Horn Book

Durango, Julia

Angels watching over me; adapted by Julia Durango; illustrated by Elisa Kleven. Simon & Schuster Books for Young Readers 2007 unp il $16.99

Grades: PreK K 1 2   E
1. Angels—Fiction 2. Day—Fiction 3. Stories in rhyme
ISBN 978-0-689-86252-6; 0-689-86252-0

"Rhyming couplets take a child from sunrise to sunset, imagining all the ways . . . that the angels send their vigilant protection. . . . The melody of the language and its reverence for the natural world are sure to spark interest. Kleven's mixed-media compositions—watercolor, ink, collage and colored pencil—convey an appropriately dream-in-flight feeling." Publ Wkly

Cha-cha chimps; illustrated by Eleanor Taylor. Simon & Schuster Books for Young Readers 2006 unp il $15.95

Grades: PreK K 1   E
1. Chimpanzees—Fiction 2. Dance—Fiction 3. Stories in rhyme
ISBN 0-689-86456-6

In this counting book, "10 little chimps sneak out of their tree house to go dancing at Mambo Jambas, where a pig band plays music all night long. . . . The rhymes roll easily off the tongue, making the text fun to read aloud. . . . Done in watercolor and pencil, the illustrations are bright and lively." SLJ

Durango, Julia—*Continued*

Pest fest; by Julia Durango; illustrated by Kurt Cyrus. Simon & Schuster 2007 unp il lib bdg $16.99

Grades: PreK K 1 2   E

1. Insects—Fiction

ISBN 978-0-689-85569-6

In beauty, talent and skills, the housefly can't compete with other bugs. But as a pest he is a winner, Book shows beetle, firefly, cricket, cicada, housefly and spider.

"The rhyming verses capture amusing verbal jousting among the insects. Cyrus's watercolor and colored-pencil illustrations offer stunning closeups of the contestants, showing lush views of the streamside setting from their down-to-earth perspective." SLJ

Durango, Julia, 1967-

Go-go gorillas; illustrated by Eleanor Taylor. Simon & Schuster Books for Young Readers 2010 unp il $15.99

Grades: PreK K 1   E

1. Stories in rhyme 2. Gorillas—Fiction 3. Transportation—Fiction

ISBN 978-1-4169-3779-1; 1-4169-3779-X

LC 2007045160

Summoned to the Great Gorilla Villa by King Big Daddy to meet the newest member of their family, ten gorillas arrive on time using various forms of transportation, including hot-air balloon, taxicab, and pogo stick.

"Durango and Taylor present a bouncy book that will keep little ones counting. . . . The watercolor art, with pictures big enough for groups, has the same sprightly spirit as the text." Booklist

Durant, Alan, 1958-

I love you, Little Monkey; by Alan Durant; illustrated by Katharine McEwen. Simon & Schuster Books for Young Readers 2007 c2006 unp il $15.99

Grades: PreK K   E

1. Monkeys—Fiction 2. Love—Fiction

ISBN 978-1-4169-2481-4; 1-4169-2481-7

First published 2006 in the United Kingdom

"Little Monkey gets into mischief when Big Monkey is too busy to play with him. . . . Little Monkey fears that he is no longer loved when he is sent to bed for punishment, but is reassured that Big Monkey loves him always, even when naughty. . . . The familiar message is always on target for small children. . . . Lively cartoon drawings in watercolor and pencil depict the mischievous animals at play in a colorful jungle setting." SLJ

Duval, Kathy

The Three Bears' Christmas; illustrated by Paul Meisel. Holiday House 2005 unp il $16.95

Grades: PreK K 1   E

1. Bears—Fiction 2. Santa Claus—Fiction 3. Christmas—Fiction

ISBN 0-8234-1871-5   LC 2003-67646

After taking a walk on Christmas Eve while their freshly baked gingerbread cools, Papa, Mama, and Baby Bear arrive home to encounter another "trespasser," who does not have golden hair but wears a red suit and leaves presents

"The old favorite gets wrapped in a Christmas bow, with excellent results. . . . The artwork is utterly childlike." Booklist

Another title about the Three Bears is:
The Three Bears' Halloween (2007)

Duvoisin, Roger, 1904-1980

Petunia. fiftieth anniversary edition. Knopf 2000 c1950 unp il $15.95; pa $6.99 *

Grades: PreK K 1   E

1. Geese—Fiction 2. Books and reading—Fiction

ISBN 0-394-90865-7; 0-394-90865-1 (lib bdg); 0-440-41754-6 (pa)

A reissue of the title first published 1950

Petunia, the goose, learns that possessing knowledge involves more than just carrying a book around under her wing

"Duvoisin's energetic drawings perfectly capture Petunia's growing arrogance." Horn Book Guide

Eastman, P. D. (Philip D.), 1909-1986

Are you my mother? written and illustrated by P. D. Eastman. Beginner Bks. 1960 63p il $8.99; lib bdg $12.99; bd bk $4.99 *

Grades: PreK K 1   E

1. Birds—Fiction 2. Mother-child relationship—Fiction

ISBN 0-394-80018-4; 0-394-90018-9 (lib bdg); 0-679-89047-5 (bd bk)

"A small bird falls from his nest and searches for his mother. He asks a kitten, a hen, a dog, a cow, a boat, [and] a plane . . . 'Are you my mother?' Repetition of words and phrases and funny pictures are just right for beginning readers." Chicago. Public Libr

Eaton, Maxwell, III

Best buds; [by] Maxwell Eaton III. Alfred A. Knopf 2007 unp il (The adventures of Max and Pinky) $12.99; lib bdg $14.99 *

Grades: PreK K 1   E

1. Friendship—Fiction 2. Pigs—Fiction

ISBN 978-0-375-83803-3; 0-375-83803-1; 978-0-375-93803-0 (lib bdg); 0-375-93803-6 (lib bdg)

LC 2006-02037

Best friends Max and Pinky the pig have an adventure together every Saturday, but one week Max looks everywhere and cannot find Pinky.

"The book is offbeat, irreverent, and affectionate, contrasting the pared-down simplicity of the main text with cheerful dialogue in the speech balloons and the sturdy simplicity of of the flat-planed, digitally colored art with the eccentric actions they depict." Horn Book

Other titles about Max and Pinky are:
Superheroes (2007)
The mystery (2008)

Edgemon, Darcie

Seamore, the very forgetful porpoise; by Darcie Edgemon; illustrated by J. Otto Seibold. HarperCollinsPublishers 2008 unp il hardcover o.p. lib bdg $17.89

Grades: K 1 2 3   E
   1. Porpoises—Fiction 2. Memory—Fiction 3. Friendship—Fiction 4. Whales—Fiction
   ISBN   978-0-06-085075-3;   0-06-085075-2; 978-0-06-085076-0 (lib bdg); 0-06-085076-0 (lib bdg)
                           LC 2007010906

Seamore is a very forgetful porpoise and when neither notes to himself nor string around his fins help, he decides to search for his missing memory

This is "effervescent. . . . The straightforward story is buoyed by the polychrome exuberance of Seibold's unmistakable computer-generated illustrations." Booklist

Edwards, David, 1962-

The pen that Pa built; by David Edwards; illustrations by Ashley Wolff. Tricycle Press 2007 unp il $14.95

Grades: PreK K 1 2   E
   1. Sheep—Fiction 2. Weaving—Fiction 3. Wool—Fiction 4. Stories in rhyme
   ISBN 978-1-58246-153-3; 1-58246-153-8
                           LC 2006101994

A cumulative, illustrated tale describing the process of raising sheep and using their wool to make warm woolen blankets.

"The language is pleasant and the rhymes clever. What really works here are Wolff's highly textured gesso-and-gouache illustrations." Booklist

Edwards, Michelle

Papa's latkes; illustrated by Stacey Schuett. Candlewick Press 2004 unp il $15.99 *

Grades: PreK K 1 2   E
   1.   Hanukkah—Fiction   2.   Jews—Fiction 3. Bereavement—Fiction
   ISBN 0-7636-0779-7   LC 00-69801

On the first Hanukkah after Mama died, Papa and his two daughters try to make latkes and celebrate without her.

"The poignant text with touches of humor is nicely matched with warm and richly colored oil paintings. . . . A touching and uplifting story." SLJ

Edwards, Pamela Duncan

Jack and Jill's treehouse; illustrated by Henry Cole. Katherine Tegen Books 2008 unp il $16.99; lib bdg $17.89

Grades: PreK K 1   E
   1. Building—Fiction 2. Tree houses—Fiction 3. Birds—Fiction
   ISBN   978-0-06-009077-7;   0-06-009077-4; 978-0-06-009078-4 (lib bdg); 0-06-009078-2 (lib bdg)

A cumulative tale about Jack and Jill who build a treehouse, as a pair of robins make their own home in the same tree.

"Color, spirit, and a sense of satisfaction fill the soft illustrations, which depict idyllic days spent in outdoor

amusement. . . . The large images lend themselves well to group sharing, and the text includes small rebus pictures of each added item, allowing listeners to chant along." SLJ

The leprechaun's gold; illustrated by Henry Cole. Katherine Tegen Books 2004 unp il $15.99; lib bdg $16.89; pa $6.99

Grades: K 1 2 3   E
   1. Leprechauns—Fiction 2. Musicians—Fiction 3. Ireland—Fiction
   ISBN 0-06-623974-5; 0-06-623975-3 (lib bdg); 0-06-443878-3 (pa)   LC 2002-3150

A leprechaun intervenes with gold and magic when a greedy, boastful young harpist gains an unfair advantage for a royal harping contest

"Cole's imaginative illustrations are a good match for the story, displaying both realism and fantasy. . . . An appealing tale that need not be limited to St. Patrick's Day storytime." Booklist

The mixed-up rooster; written by Pamela Duncan Edwards; illustrated by Megan Lloyd. Katherine Tegen Books 2006 unp il lib bdg $16.89 *

Grades: PreK K 1 2   E
   1. Roosters—Fiction 2. Chickens—Fiction
   ISBN   978-0-06-028999-7;   0-06-028999-6; 978-0-06-029000-9 (lib bdg); 0-06-029000-5 (lib bdg)
                           LC 2005014401

Ned the rooster is fired from his job because he cannot wake up in the morning, but he restores his reputation after discovering his usefulness as a night bird

"This lighthearted story is written in an uncomplicated, comical style and has vibrant illustrations that are full of personality and charm." SLJ

The neat line; scribbling through Mother Goose; illustrated by Diana Cain Bluthenthal. Katherine Tegen Books 2004 unp il hardcover o.p. lib bdg $16.89

Grades: PreK K 1 2   E
   1. Nursery rhymes—Fiction
   ISBN 0-06-623970-2; 0-06-623971-0 (lib bdg)
                           LC 2002-153424

A young scribble matures into a neat line, then wriggles into a book of nursery rhymes where he transforms himself into different objects to assist the characters he meets there

This is a "brilliantly creative romp. . . . The large cartoon paintings . . . are appropriately outlined with thick, bold lines and are framed by book pages on either side." SLJ

The old house; [by] Pamela Duncan Edwards; illustrated by Henry Cole. Dutton Children's Books 2007 unp il $16.99; pa $6.99

Grades: PreK K 1   E
   1. Houses—Fiction
   ISBN 978-0-525-47796-9; 0-14-241480-8 (pa)
                           LC 2006102950

An old empty house feels sorry for itself because it has no family living inside, but with the help of some good friends, its dreams come true

"Edwards colloquial text is accessible for young read-

Edwards, Pamela Duncan—*Continued*

ers to tackle on their own and would make a lively read-aloud. Cole's energetic cartoon-style artwork gives oodles of personality to this house waiting to shine." SLJ

Princess Pigtoria and the pea; illustrated by Henry Cole. Orchard Books 2010 unp il $16.99
Grades: PreK K 1   E
1. Fairy tales 2. Pigs—Fiction 3. Princesses—Fiction
ISBN 978-0-545-15625-7; 0-545-15625-4
LC 2008-52693

To make her pigsty of a palace picturesque again, penniless Princess Pigtoria tries to get the pompous porker Prince Proudfoot to propose marriage.

"Fun for listeners and readers alike. . . The scale of the artwork make this a good choice for storytime." Booklist

Some smug slug; illustrated by Henry Cole. HarperCollins Pubs. 1996 32p il $17.99; pa $6.99
Grades: PreK K 1 2   E
1. Slugs (Mollusks)—Fiction 2. Animals—Fiction
ISBN 0-06-024789-4; 0-06-443502-4 (pa)
LC 94-18682

"A slug senses a slope and saunters on up, against the advice of a sparrow, a spider, and a skink, among others, and meets with a sudden, spontaneous demise. Such is the life of a slug told with a multitude of common and not so common 'S' words. . . . Realistically detailed, earth-toned illustrations focus attention on each scene. . . . This slug is so appealing and full of personality that it will certainly garner sympathy." SLJ

While the world is sleeping; illustrated by Dan Kirk. Orchard Books 2010 unp il lib bdg $16.99
Grades: PreK K 1   E
1. Stories in rhyme 2. Animals—Fiction 3. Night—Fiction 4. Bedtime—Fiction
ISBN 978-0-545-01756-5; 0-545-01756-4
LC 2007040283

A sleepy child is flown through the night sky to see foxes hunting, rabbits playing, raccoons scrounging, and other animals that are active while people sleep.

"Kirk's illustrations are big and bold, featuring the shimmering light of the moon, animals whose every hair seems distinct, and playful faux-Rousseau forests. The book's mix of the realistic and fantastic seems like a perfect prelude to dream time." Booklist

Eeckhout, Emmanuelle, 1976-
There's no such thing as ghosts! Kane/Miller 2008 unp il $13.95
Grades: PreK K 1   E
1. Ghost stories
ISBN 978-1-933605-91-3; 1-933605-91-X

"Eager to explore a neighborhood haunted house, a diminutive boy grabs his butterfly net and sets out to catch a ghost. . . . The joke is that readers see the adorable, playful spirits that cavort, tease, and go about their ghostly business, invisible to the boy. Through a simple palette of black, white, yellow, and pink, Eeckhout uses plenty of white space, full spreads, silhouettes, and small vignettes to great advantage." SLJ

Egan, Tim
Dodsworth in New York; written and illustrated by Tim Egan. Houghton Mifflin 2007 unp il $15 *
Grades: K 1 2   E
1. Voyages and travels—Fiction 2. New York (N.Y.)—Fiction 3. Ducks—Fiction
ISBN 978-0-618-77708-2; 0-618-77708-3
LC 2006-34522

When Dodsworth sets out for adventure, including a stop in New York City before going to Paris, London, and beyond, he does not expect a crazy duck to stow away in his suitcase and lead him on a merry chase.

"Egan favors a palette of golds and clay-browns, and draws pillowy shapes in a gentle, never rigid line. . . . Egan keeps the hijinks low-key, preferring long pauses and slow burns to nutty slapstick." Publ Wkly
Other titles about Dodsworth are:
Dodsworth in Paris (2008)
Dodsworth in London (2009)

The pink refrigerator; [by] Tim Egan. Houghton Mifflin 2007 unp il $16
Grades: K 1 2   E
1. Mice—Fiction
ISBN 978-0-618-63154-4; 0-618-63154-2
LC 2006009816

Dodsworth the mouse does as little work as he can, collecting items from a junkyard and placing them in his thrift store for sale, until he happens upon a pink refrigerator that spurs him to do much more with his life.

"The ink-and-watercolor art mirrors the laid-back tone of the narrative. . . . This offbeat tale is perfect for reading aloud, but will also be appreciated as a read-alone and lap-sit." SLJ

Ehlert, Lois, 1934-
Boo to you! Beach Lane Books 2009 unp il $17.99
Grades: PreK K 1   E
1. Stories in rhyme 2. Mice—Fiction 3. Cats—Fiction 4. Parties—Fiction
ISBN 978-1-4169-8625-6; 1-4169-8625-1
LC 2008-44352

When the neighborhood cat tries to crash the mice's harvest party, the mice have a plan to scare the intruder away

"Ehlert's use of paper, fruit, seeds, and string is labyrinthine enough to have young children tracing their routes, and so vivid they'll want to touch the page to make sure it's not real." Booklist

Circus. HarperCollins Pubs. 1992 unp il $17.99 *
Grades: PreK K 1   E
1. Circus—Fiction 2. Animals—Fiction
ISBN 0-06-020252-1   LC 91-12067

Leaping lizards, marching snakes, a bear on the high wire, and others perform in a somewhat unusual circus

"The book approximates a light show in visual intensity, with neon-bright illustrations set against black or bold backgrounds. . . . The sprightly rhythm of Ms. Ehlert's text complements her Day-Glo palette. Echoing a ringmaster's speech, she's afraid of neither alliteration . . . nor hyperbole." N Y Times Book Rev

Ehlert, Lois, 1934-—*Continued*

Color farm. Lippincott 1990 unp il $17.99; lib bdg $18.89 *

Grades: PreK K 1   E
  1. Color 2. Shape
  ISBN 0-397-32440-5; 0-397-32441-3 (lib bdg)
                          LC 89-13561

"A delightful die-cut exploration of how shapes and colors can be layered and overlapped to create the faces of farm animals. Includes geometric pictures of a rooster, a chicken, a goose, a duck, a cat, a dog, a sheep, a pig, and a cow." Sci Child

Color zoo. Lippincott 1989 unp il $17.99; lib bdg $17.89; bd bk $7.99 *

Grades: PreK K 1   E
  1. Color 2. Shape
  ISBN 0-397-32259-3; 0-397-32260-7 (lib bdg);
  0-694-01067-7 (bd bk)   LC 87-17065

A Caldecott Medal honor book, 1990

This "book features a series of cutouts stacked so that with each page turn, a layer is removed to reveal yet another picture. Each configuration is an animal: a tiger's face (a circle shape) and two ears disappear with a page turn to leave viewers with a square within which is a mouse. . . . There are three such series, and each ends with a small round-up of the shapes used so far. . . . On the reverse of the turned page is the shape cutout previously removed with the shape's printed name." SLJ

"Not only an effective method for teaching basic concepts, the book is also a means for sharpening visual perception, which encourages children to see these shapes in other contexts." Horn Book

Eating the alphabet; fruits and vegetables from A to Z. Harcourt Brace Jovanovich 1989 unp il $17; pa $7; bd bk $6.95 *

Grades: PreK K 1   E
  1. Alphabet 2. Fruit 3. Vegetables
  ISBN 0-15-224435-2; 0-15-224436-0 (pa);
  0-15-201036-X (bd bk)   LC 88-10906

An alphabetical tour of the world of fruits and vegetables, from apricot and artichoke to yam and zucchini

"The objects depicted, shown against a white ground, are easily identifiable for the most part, and represent the more common sounds of the letter shown. . . . Both upper- and lower-case letters are printed in large, black type. A nice added touch is the glossary which includes the pronunciation and interesting facts about the origin of each fruit and vegetable, how it grows, and its uses. An exuberant, eye-catching alphabet book." SLJ

Feathers for lunch. Harcourt Brace Jovanovich 1990 unp il $17; pa $7 *

Grades: PreK K 1 2   E
  1. Cats—Fiction 2. Birds—Fiction 3. Stories in rhyme
  ISBN 0-15-230550-5; 0-15-200986-8 (pa)
                          LC 89-29459

This "book is both a story and a beginning nature guide. A pet cat wants to vary his diet with wild birds, but each attempt gains him only feathers. Twelve different bird species are . . . illustrated. . . . On each page, the bird's typical call is printed and plants pictured are named." SLJ

"Ehlert has attempted many things in these pages—for instance, the birds are all drawn life-size—and has succeeded in all of them; her lavish use of bold color against generous amounts of white space is graphically appealing, and the large type, nearly one-half-inch tall, invites attempts by those just beginning to read. An engaging, entertaining, and recognizably realistic story." Horn Book

Growing vegetable soup; written and illustrated by Lois Ehlert. Harcourt Brace Jovanovich 1987 unp il $17; pa $7; bd bk $6.95 *

Grades: PreK K 1 2   E
  1. Vegetable gardening—Fiction
  ISBN 0-15-232575-1; 0-15-232580-8 (pa);
  0-15-205055-8 (bd bk)   LC 86-22812

"Brightly-colored large illustrations and a boldly-worded text show how to plant and grow vegetables for Dad's soup. Shocking pinks, reds and greens give the illustrations an almost three-dimensional quality and will be good for large audiences of preschoolers." Child Book Rev Serv

Hands; growing up to be an artist. Harcourt 2004 unp il $14.95 *

Grades: PreK K 1 2   E
  ISBN 0-15-205107-4   LC 2004-1237

A reformatted edition of the title first published 1997

When a child works alongside her parents doing carpentry, sewing, and gardening, she thinks of being an artist as well when she grows up

This edition offers "slightly reworked trimmings, but keeps the same die-cut pages—in the shapes of scissors, seed packets and more—as well as a 'paint box' that opens." Publ Wkly

Leaf Man. Harcourt 2005 unp il $16 *

Grades: PreK K 1 2   E
  1. Leaves—Fiction 2. Winds—Fiction
  ISBN 0-15-205304-2   LC 2004-9981

A man made of leaves blows away, traveling wherever the wind may take him.

This is an "eye-popping book. . . . Scalloped edgings on the tops of the pages, cut at varying heights, artfully give the effect of setting the action against a three-dimensional landscape." Booklist

Lots of spots. Beach Lane Books 2010 il $17.99

Grades: PreK K 1   E
  1. Animals
  ISBN 978-1-4424-0289-8; 1-4424-0289-X
                          LC 2009034361

"Each of the 50 featured creatures in Ehlert's . . . offering sports distinctive markings. . . . Each spread freatures a beautiful collage illustration of an animal, accompanied by a poem of four, short, catchy lines. . . . Children will enjoy paging through and identifying the multitude of brilliantly hued animals that make up this visual zoo." Booklist

Ehlert, Lois, 1934——*Continued*

Market day; a story told with folk art; written and designed by Lois Ehlert. Harcourt 2000 unp il $17; pa $7 *
Grades: PreK K 1 2   **E**
  1. Markets—Fiction 2. Farm life—Fiction 3. Stories in rhyme
  ISBN 0-15-202158-2; 0-15-216820-6 (pa)
                  LC 99-6252
On market day, a farm family experiences all the fun and excitement of going to and from the farmers' market
"The very young will enjoy the spare, simple books. . . . All ages will appreciate the illustrations, comprising images of folk art, primitive art, and textiles from around the world. An annotated inventory of the featured items is included." Horn Book Guide

Mole's hill; a woodland tale. Harcourt Brace & Co. 1994 unp il $17; pa $7
Grades: PreK K 1 2   **E**
  1. Moles (Animals)—Fiction
  ISBN 0-15-255116-6; 0-15-201890-5 (pa)
                LC 93-31151
When Fox tells Mole she must move out of her tunnel to make way for a new path, Mole finds an ingenious way to save her home
"Ehlert's language is compact and telling. . . . The art . . . is dark-hued, appropriately nocturnal without losing spirit or contrast, and the beads stippled across the cutout cloth shapes lend interesting texture to the planes of color. . . . The story (which Ehlert says she based on a fragment of a Seneca tale, with source completely cited in the book) has charm and vigor." Bull Cent Child Books

Nuts to you! Harcourt Brace Jovanovich 1993 unp il $17; pa $7 *
Grades: PreK K 1 2   **E**
  1. Squirrels—Fiction 2. Stories in rhyme
  ISBN 0-15-257647-9; 0-15-205064-7 (pa)
                LC 92-19441
"A frisky squirrel digs up bulbs and steals birdseed from a nearby feeder; in his boldest act, he enters the young narrator's apartment through a tear in the window screen. The quick-thinking child entices the mischievous squirrel back outside with some peanuts. . . . The story, told in brisk rhyme, is a fast-paced romp, and the large, dramatically styled collages will dazzle even the largest audiences. . . . The four concluding pages offer basic information about squirrels." Horn Book

Oodles of animals. Harcourt 2008 unp il $17
Grades: PreK K 1 2   **E**
  1. Animals—Fiction 2. Stories in rhyme
  ISBN 978-0-15-206274-3; 0-15-206274-2
                LC 2007-17018
Short, easy to read rhymes reveal what is unique about various animals, from ape to wolf.
"The artist uses scissors, pinking shears, and a hole punch to transform brightly colored papers into squares, rectangles, triangles, circles, diamonds, half circles, ovals, hearts, and teardrops of different sizes, which she then fashions into a menagerie guaranteed to spark readers' imaginations. Each creature is coupled with a short, humorous poem that is sure to delight." SLJ

Pie in the sky. Harcourt 2004 unp il $16 *
Grades: PreK K 1 2   **E**
  1. Cherries—Fiction 2. Pies—Fiction
  ISBN 0-15-216584-3   LC 2003-4986
A father and child watch the cherry tree in their back yard, waiting until there are ripe cherries to bake in a pie. Includes a recipe for cherry pie
"The vibrant collage illustrations, made with an eclectic combination of materials—from paint and handmade papers to sheet metal, wires, and tree branches—celebrate the colors and simplified shapes of birds, insects, the cherry tree, and, yes, kitchen implements." Booklist

Planting a rainbow; written and illustrated by Lois Ehlert. Harcourt Brace Jovanovich 1988 unp il $17; pa $7; bd bk $6.95 *
Grades: PreK K 1   **E**
  1. Gardening—Fiction 2. Flowers—Fiction
  ISBN 0-15-262609-3; 0-15-262610-7 (pa); 0-15-204633-X (bd bk)   LC 87-8528
A mother and daughter plant a rainbow of flowers in the family garden
"The stylized forms of the plants are clearly and beautifully designed, and the primary, blazing colors of the blossoms dazzle in their resplendence. The minimal text, in very large print, is exactly right to set off the glorious illustrations, making a splendid beginning book of colors and flowers cleverly arranged for young readers." Horn Book

Snowballs. Harcourt Brace & Co. 1995 unp il $17; pa $7; bd bk $6.95 *
Grades: PreK K 1   **E**
  1. Snow—Fiction
  ISBN 0-15-200074-7; 0-15-202095-0 (pa); 0-15-216275-5 (bd bk)   LC 94-47183
"Using 'good stuff' like seeds, nuts, corn kernels, and colorful yarn kids create a wonderful snow family. Placed on vertical page spreads, the snow characters extend the full length of the book, a perspective that enhances the drama of their inevitable demise when the sun comes out. Large, well-designed illustrations effectively blend open space, colorful paper cutouts, and real objects." Horn Book Guide

Top cat. Harcourt Brace & Co. 1998 unp il $17; pa $7 *
Grades: PreK K 1 2   **E**
  1. Cats—Fiction 2. Stories in rhyme
  ISBN 0-15-201739-9; 0-15-202425-5 (pa)
                LC 97-8818
The top cat in a household is reluctant to accept the arrival of a new kitten but decides to share various survival secrets with it
"Ehlert creates a memorable cat duo in her trademark cut-paper collage style. . . . Children and other feline fans will quickly warm to this spunky story of rivalry and acceptance." Publ Wkly

Wag a tail; [by] Lois Ehlert. Harcourt, Inc. 2007 unp il $16 *
Grades: PreK K 1 2   **E**
  1. Dogs—Fiction 2. Stories in rhyme
  ISBN 978-0-15-205843-2   LC 2006013318

Ehlert, Lois, 1934-—*Continued*

Assorted graduates of the Bow Wow School meet at a farmers market and a dog park, where most of them remember their obedience training.

"This simple story has a rhythmic, jazzy quality that begs to be read aloud. . . . Collages composed of brightly colored buttons and scraps of paper stand out on vivid green backgrounds." SLJ

Waiting for wings. Harcourt 2001 unp il $17 *
Grades: PreK K 1 2   E
1. Butterflies 2. Stories in rhyme
ISBN 0-15-202608-8   LC 00-9765

Eggs clinging to leaves become caterpillars which become butterflies which lay their eggs

"A brief rhyming text and cheery tone invite readers to explore the full and half pages that form this brilliantly designed book-within-a book." Publ Wkly

Ehrhardt, Karen

This Jazz man; pictures by R. G. Roth. Harcourt 2006 unp il $16 *
Grades: K 1 2 3   E
1. Jazz musicians—Fiction 2. African Americans—Fiction 3. Counting 4. Stories in rhyme
ISBN 0-15-205307-7   LC 2004-21094

Presents an introduction to jazz music and nine well-known jazz musicians, set to the rhythm of the traditional song, "This Old Man." Includes brief facts about each musician.

"The candy-colored collages burst from the pages, making this addition just right as an up-tempo introduction for youngest music lovers." Publ Wkly

Ehrlich, Amy, 1942-

Baby Dragon; [by] Amy Ehrlich; illustrated by Will Hillenbrand. Candlewick Press 2008 unp il $16.99
Grades: PreK K 1 2   E
1. Dragons—Fiction 2. Animals—Fiction 3. Mother-child relationship—Fiction
ISBN 978-0-7636-2840-6; 0-7636-2840-9
                                          LC 2007051883

All day, Baby Dragon turns down other animals' offers to go play or find a snack while he waits for his mother to return for him, but at nightfall, he agrees to go with Crocodile to find her

"Hillenbrand's illustrations, done with ink, colored pencil, finger paint, gouache, and collage, and digitally manipulated, bring to life Baby Dragon's misty tropical forest where water buffaloes wander and storks splash in the river." SLJ

The girl who wanted to dance; by Amy Ehrlich; illustrated by Rebecca Walsh. Candlewick Press 2009 unp il $17.99 *
Grades: 2 3 4   E
1. Dance—Fiction 2. Loss (Psychology)—Fiction 3. Fairy tales
ISBN 978-0-7636-1345-7; 0-7636-1345-2

"Clara lives with her father and grandmother in a little village. More than anything, Clara loves to dance, but her father has had too much sadness in his life to abide dancing. When Clara sees a troupe of dancers performing in the village one June day, she is enchanted enough to follow their wagons deep into the forest—and what she finds there changes her life forever." Publisher's note

"Both a haunting fairy tale and a parable for families separated by divorce or death, this lyrically rendered story also presents art as a vehicle for transcending pain. . . . Working in a representational style, Walsh . . . adds lush paintings of an idealized old world, and her nighttime scenes glow." Publ Wkly

Thumbelina; by Hans Christian Andersen; retold by Amy Ehrlich; [illustrated by Susan Jeffers] Dutton Children's Books 2005 32p il $16.99 *
Grades: K 1 2 3   E
1. Andersen, Hans Christian, 1805-1875—Adaptations 2. Fairy tales
ISBN 0-525-47508-7   LC 2004028979

A reissure of the edition published 1979 by Dial Books for Young Readers

A retelling of Hans Christian Andersen's classic fairy tale about a girl who is only one inch tall.

"This sumptuous picture book version the classic Andersen story has been an adapted text that shows some softening of the tale's harsher edges. . . . [Readers will] be caught up in the action as depicted in Jeffers' striking, pastel-dominated pictures." Booklist

Ehrlich, Fred

Does an elephant take a bath? pictures by Emily Bolan. Blue Apple Books 2005 unp il (Early experiences) lib bdg $13.50; pa $5.95
Grades: PreK K   E
1. Cleanliness 2. Baths 3. Animals
ISBN 1-59354-111-2 (lib bdg); 1-59354-123-5 (pa)

"Does a giraffe take a bath? The question is accompanied by a silly picture showing a giraffe standing in a foaming bathtub. Turn the page and the animal is in its natural habitat, grooming itself with its long tongue. . . . Following similar scenarios for an elephant, a zebra, a black rhino (a mud bath), and more, come several spreads showing how people keep clean and tidy." Booklist

"The humor is just right for the audience . . . and, like the text, the uncluttered illustrations . . . are both informative and amusing." Horn Book Guide

Other titles in the Early experiences series are:
Does a baboon sleep in a bed? (2005)
Does a chimp wear clothes? (2005)
Does a hippo say ahh? (2006)
Does a lion brush? (2005)
Does a panda go to school? (2006)
Does a pig flush? (2005)
Does a seal smile? (2006)
Does a tiger open wide? (2006)
Does a yak get a haircut? (2006)

Ehrlich, H. M.

Louie's goose; illustrated by Emily Bolam. Houghton Mifflin 2000 unp il $15 *
Grades: PreK K 1   E
1. Toys—Fiction 2. Beaches—Fiction
ISBN 0-618-03023-9   LC 99-28566

"Walter Lorraine books"

Ehrlich, H. M.—*Continued*

While spending the summer at the beach with his parents, Louie has a wonderful time playing with his toy goose and even rescues her from a big wave

"This true-to-life look at a preschooler growing more independent is low-key and natural. . . . Bolam's sunny paintings capture the seashore experience of a charming, lovable family." Booklist

Another title about Louie is:

Gotcha, Louie! (2002)

Eichenberg, Fritz, 1901-1990

Ape in a cape; an alphabet of odd animals. Harcourt Brace & Co. 1952 unp il pa $8 hardcover o.p.

Grades: PreK K 1   E

1. Animals 2. Alphabet

ISBN 0-15-607830-9 (pa)

A Caldecott Medal honor book, 1953

"Each letter of the alphabet from A for ape to Z for zoo is represented by a full-page picture of an animal with a brief nonsense rhyme caption explaining it. For example: mouse in a blouse, pig in a wig, toad on the road, whale in a gale." Publ Wkly

"The skill of a craftsman distinguishes this picture book illustrated with bold and lively drawings printed in three colors." N Y Public Libr

Eitzen, Ruth

Tara's flight; [by] Ruth Eitzen; illustrated by Allan Eitzen. Boyds Mills Press 2008 unp il $16.95

Grades: K 1 2 3   E

1. Noah's ark—Fiction 2. Grandfathers—Fiction 3. Birds—Fiction

ISBN 978-1-59078-563-8   LC 2007018815

Aram, a grandson of Noah, is responsible for taking care of the birds on the ark, including his pet dove Tara, who becomes the first creature to leave after the flood

"Decorated with cut-paper pictures of flying white birds, the endpapers celebrate the dove as the elemental peace symbol then and now." Booklist

Elffers, Joost

Do you love me? [by] Joost Elffers + Curious Pictures. Bowen Press 2009 unp il $14.99

Grades: PreK K 1   E

1. Stories in rhyme 2. Love—Fiction

ISBN 978-0-06-166799-2; 0-06-166799-4

LC 2008005939

Playful creatures called Snuzzles explore the idea of unconditional love

"The gentle, rhyming text is the straightforward stuff of bedtime rituals. But while the questions are expected, the answers feel fresh. . . . Set against high-contrast, single-color backgrounds, the action takes place at close range, so that just their heads, or parts of their heads, are visible." Publ Wkly

Ellery, Amanda

If I were a jungle animal; illustrated by Tom Ellery. Simon & Schuster Books for Young Readers 2009 unp il $15.99

Grades: PreK K 1   E

1. Imagination—Fiction 2. Animals—Fiction 3. Baseball—Fiction

ISBN 978-1-4169-3778-4; 1-4169-3778-1

While playing baseball, a boy wonders what it would be like to be different jungle animals.

"Amanda Ellery's tale is simple but delicious, and accessible to very young readers. Husband Tom's expressive, Bill Peet-esque illustrations-in colored pencil, pen and ink-are all they should be: funny, original and so lively they virtually jump off the page." Kirkus

Elliott, David, 1947-

Finn throws a fit; illustrated by Timothy Basil Ering. Candlewick Press 2009 unp il $16.99

Grades: PreK K 1   E

1. Anger—Fiction

ISBN 978-0-7636-2356-2; 0-7636-2356-3

LC 2008-21174

A cranky toddler has an enormous tantrum.

"Elliott . . . and Ering . . . operate like the left and right hands of a single comic mind; each tongue-in-cheek line of text is deftly countered with raw charcoal scrawls, wild strokes of paint and crazed scribbles. Small readers will giggle at the realization of their angry feelings—complete with rippling lengths of toilet paper, floods of tears and flying crockery—while parents will blanch at the brilliant exposition of the power their children hold over them." Publ Wkly

Knitty Kitty; illustrated by Christopher Denise. Candlewick Press 2008 unp il $16.99

Grades: PreK K 1 2   E

1. Cats—Fiction 2. Winter—Fiction

ISBN 978-0-7636-3169-7; 0-7636-3169-8

LC 2007-52160

Knitty Kitty is knitting a scarf, a hat, and some mittens for her kittens, but when night falls and the snow comes down, the kittens request a blanket to keep them warm Knitty Kitty has a better idea.

"The full-bleed illustrations in acrylic and ink portray an idyllic cottage in a snow-covered countryside. Inside the warmth is made evident with soft golds, browns, and touches of soft color here and there." SLJ

On the farm; [by] David Elliott; illustrated by Holly Meade. Candlewick Press 2008 unp il $16.99 *

Grades: PreK K 1 2   E

1. Domestic animals

ISBN 978-0-7636-3322-6; 0-7636-3322-4

LC 2007060857

"Elliott looks at a rooster, a cow, a pony, a dog, sheep, a barn cat, a goat, a pig, a snake, bees, a bull, a turtle, a duck, a hen, and a rabbit in verses that are rich in vocabulary and, for the most part, written in rhyme. Large, black typeface mirrors the black lines in Meade's beautiful, color woodblock prints that superbly reflect the mood and action in the poetry." SLJ

Elliott, David, 1947-—*Continued*

One little chicken; a counting book; by David Elliott; illustrated by Ethan Long. Holiday House 2007 unp il $16.95

Grades: PreK K   E

1. Chickens—Fiction 2. Dance—Fiction 3. Counting

ISBN 978-0-8234-1983-8   LC 2006037046

"For each number up to 10, funny flapping fowls dance up a storm of different steps—from the hula to the cha cha. . . . The computer-generated cartoon art adds shimmy to the text, with egg-eyed pullets wearing silly attire and equally silly expressions." Booklist

What the grizzly knows; [by] David Elliott; illustrated by Max Grafe. Candlewick Press 2008 unp il $16.99

Grades: PreK K   E

1. Stories in rhyme 2. Teddy bears—Fiction 3. Bears—Fiction

ISBN 978-0-7636-2778-2; 0-7636-2778-X
                                   LC 2007052158

When night falls magical things begin to happen to Teddy, taking the reader on an adventure around the countryside and seeing the world through the senses of a bear

"The simple, rhyming text is paired with noteworthy, realistically rendered watercolor art that glows with a dreamlike quality. . . . An engaging fantasy." Booklist

Elliott, Zetta

Bird; illustrated by Shadra Strickland. Lee & Low Books Inc. 2008 unp il $18.95

Grades: 2 3 4 5   E

1. Novels in verse 2. Death—Fiction 3. Drug abuse—Fiction 4. Drawing—Fiction 5. Family life—Fiction 6. African Americans—Fiction

ISBN 978-1-60060-241-2; 1-60060-241-X
                                   LC 2007-49039

Bird, an artistic young African American boy, expresses himself through drawing as he struggles to understand his older brother's drug addiction and death, while a family friend, Uncle Son, provides guidance and understanding

"This picture book tells a poignant story. . . . A complicated weaving of impressive watercolor, gouache, charcoal and ink drawings amplifies the metaphors and action of the poetic text as it combines black-and-white with color." Publ Wkly

Ellis, Sarah, 1952-

Ben over night; illustrated by Kim LaFave. Fitzhenry & Whiteside 2005 unp il $16.95

Grades: PreK K 1   E

1. Fear—Fiction

ISBN 1-55041-807-6

"Little Ben loves to play at his friend Peter's house across the street, but every time he tries to sleep over, he wakens in the night and chickens out. His supportive parents suggest that he take his flashlight and security blanket, but nothing works until his big sister comes up with more imaginative ideas. Ellis tells Ben's story with economy and understanding. . . . With fresh colors and energetic line work, the apparently digital illustrations do a good job of expressing the characters' emotions as well as defining their actions." Booklist

Elvgren, Jennifer Riesmeyer

Josias, hold the book; [by] Jennifer Riesmeyer Elvgren; illustrated by Nicole Tadgell. Boyds Mills Press 2006 unp il $15.95

Grades: PreK K 1 2   E

1.   Haiti—Fiction   2.   Gardening—Fiction 3. Education—Fiction

ISBN 1-59078-318-2   LC 2005024989

Each day Chrislove, who lives in Haiti, asks his friend Josias when he will "hold the book," or join them at school, but Josias can only think of tending the bean garden so that his family will have enough food

"Elvgren has crafted a matter-of-fact snapshot of rural Haitian life. Tadgells muted watercolor spreads set the tone and enhance the text. Emotions are clearly depicted, giving the characters added dimension and believability." SLJ

Elwell, Peter

Adios, Oscar! a butterfly fable. The Blue Sky Press 2009 unp il $16.99

Grades: K 1 2   E

1. Caterpillars—Fiction 2. Books and reading—Fiction 3. Moths—Fiction

ISBN 978-0-545-07159-8; 0-545-07159-3
                                   LC 2007050842

Despite his friends' teasing, Oscar the caterpillar studies to prepare for becoming a butterfly and migrating to Mexico, so when things do not turn out as he expects, he is still able to make his dream come true.

"This charming story about loving oneself and pursuing one's dreams sends an important message to children without being preachy or pedantic. The bright colors and cartoon-style illustrations enhance its ebullient, optimistic tone." SLJ

Elya, Susan Middleton, 1955-

Adios, tricycle; illustrated by Elisabeth Schlossberg. G. P. Putnam's Sons 2009 unp il $16.99

Grades: PreK K   E

1. Stories in rhyme 2. Growth—Fiction 3. Cycling—Fiction 4. Garage sales—Fiction 5. Hispanic Americans—Fiction 6. Spanish language—Vocabulary

ISBN 978-0-399-24522-0; 0-399-24522-7
                                   LC 2008006562

Even though he has outgrown his tricycle, a young pig hides it at his family's yard sale until just the right smaller child comes along.

"Peppy, rhyming text filled with Spanish vocabulary words tells this entertaining, supportive story. . . . Schlossberg's pastel illustrations capture the mixed emotions in scenes of the diverse animal characters." Booklist

Bebé goes shopping; illustrated by Steven Salerno. Harcourt 2006 unp il $16 *

Grades: PreK K 1   E

1. Infants—Fiction 2. Shopping—Fiction 3. Spanish language—Vocabulary 4. Stories in rhyme

ISBN 0-15-205426-X

Rhyming text describes a trip to the grocery store for a mamá and her baby boy. Includes Spanish words.

Elya, Susan Middleton, 1955-—*Continued*

"Almost all the words can be understood from the context or from the pictures. . . . Using gouache, watercolors, colored inks, and pencils, Salerno evokes the hip, retro style of 1950s cartoon-style advertisements. . . . Salerno is also a master at getting motion into his pictures, and his spreads rumble and tumble." Booklist

Another title about Bebé is:

Bebé goes to the beach (2008)

Cowboy José; illustrated by Tim Raglin. Putnam's 2005 unp il $15.99

Grades: PreK K 1 2   E

1. Cowhands—Fiction 2. Mexico—Fiction 3. Stories in rhyme 4. Spanish language—Vocabulary

ISBN 0-399-23570-1   LC 2003-26636

A poor cowboy enters a rodeo to win a date from a pretty señorita, but afterwards wonders if he should spend his winnings on the girl, who is only interested in the money, or on his trusty horse, whose encouragement helped him win.

"Elya's engaging text features snappy rhymes and plenty of contextual clues for the Spanish words that appear in bold type. . . . Raglin's watercolor-and-colored-pencil artwork features bright south-of-the-border colors and characters in traditional dress to accentuate the story's Mexican setting." SLJ

Eight animals on the town; illustrated by Lee Chapman. Putnam 2000 unp il $15.99 *

Grades: PreK K 1 2   E

1. Animals—Fiction 2. Counting 3. Bilingual books—English-Spanish 4. Stories in rhyme

ISBN 0-399-23437-3   LC 99-55269

Eight animals go to market, to supper, and to dance, introducing the numbers from one to eight and vocabulary in English and Spanish

"While the text has wit and whimsy, the illustrations are absolutely delectable. Bright oils on canvas capture qualities of Mexican folk art as tidy borders augment the text." SLJ

Other titles about the Eight animals are:

Eight animals bake a cake (2002)

Eight animals play ball (2003)

F is for fiesta; illustrated by G. Brian Karas. G.P. Putnam's Sons 2006 unp il $11.99 *

Grades: PreK K 1 2   E

1. Spanish language—Vocabulary 2. Alphabet 3. Birthdays 4. Stories in rhyme

ISBN 0-399-24225-2   LC 2004-20478

A rhyming book that outlines the preparations for and celebration of a young boy's birthday, with Spanish words for each letter of the alphabet translated in a glossary.

"At their best, Elya's verses bounce as easily between languages as they did in *Oh, No, Gotta Go!* (2003), which was also buoyantly illustrated by Karas." Booklist

Fairy trails; a story told in English and Spanish; illustrated by Mercedes McDonald. Bloomsbury Children's Books 2005 unp il $17.99

Grades: PreK K 1 2   E

1. Fairy tales 2. Stories in rhyme 3. Spanish language—Vocabulary

ISBN 1-58234-927-4

Miguel and Maria meet various fairy tale characters as they walk to their aunt's house. Includes some Spanish words

"Done in pastels, the warm and colorful illustrations have an appealing folk-art quality. . . . A glossary of the Spanish words is included, but the rhyming text provides ample context clues so that the story is accessible to non-Spanish speakers. Overall, Fairy Trails would be a great storytime choice for both bilingual and English-only audiences." SLJ

N is for Navidad; by Susan Middleton Elya and Merry Banks; illustrated by Joe Cepeda. Chronicle Books 2007 unp il $14.95

Grades: PreK K 1   E

1. Christmas—Fiction 2. Alphabet 3. Stories in rhyme 4. Hispanic Americans—Fiction 5. Spanish language—Vocabulary

ISBN 978-0-8118-5205-0; 0-8118-5205-9

LC 2006008169

A rhyming book that outlines the preparations for and celebration of the Christmas season, with Spanish words for each letter of the alphabet translated in a glossary.

"Cepeda's lively paintings take a colorful, dynamic look at a warm Latino neighborhood celebration of the holiday season. . . . This book has potential to provide a springboard for discussion of holiday traditions while keeping children entertained visually." SLJ

Oh no, gotta go! illustrated by G. Brian Karas. Putnam 2003 unp il $14.99

Grades: PreK K 1 2   E

1. Bathrooms—Fiction 2. Spanish language—Vocabulary 3. Stories in rhyme

ISBN 0-399-23493-4   LC 2002-17703

As soon as she goes out for a drive with her parents, a young girl needs to find a bathroom quickly. Text includes some Spanish words and phrases

"The unexpected rhyming of the English and boldface Spanish words give the rhythmic text an ebullient humor enhanced by Karas' understated gouache, acrylic, pencil, and collage illustrations." Bull Cent Child Books

Another title is:

Oh no, gotta go! #2 (2007)

Tooth on the loose; [by] Susan Middleton Elya; illustrated by Jenny Mattheson. G. P. Putnam's Sons 2008 unp il $16.99

Grades: PreK K 1 2   E

1. Teeth—Fiction 2. Gifts—Fiction 3. Hispanic Americans—Fiction 4. Spanish language—Vocabulary 5. Stories in rhyme

ISBN 978-0-399-24459-9; 0-399-24459-X

LC 2007-7398

A girl hopes her tooth will fall out so that she can have money to buy her father a birthday present. Includes index of Spanish words and phrases used in text.

"Mattheson's illustrations, in oil paint on primed pa-

Elya, Susan Middleton, 1955-—_Continued_
per, are vivd and bright. and they capture a cheerful world." Booklist

Emberley, Barbara, 1932-
Night's nice; [by] Barbara and Ed Emberley. Little, Brown Children 2008 unp il $12.99
Grades: PreK K   E
1. Night—Fiction
ISBN 978-0-316-06623-5; 0-316-06623-0
First published 1962 by Doubleday Books
Moonlit treetops, city lamps aglow, bright fireworks bursting in a dark July sky, and other wondrous illuminated evening sights are captured in a colorful picture book with a die-cut moon and silver foil title type on the cover.
"An inviting exploration of the wonders of nighttime. . . . Thin, sketchlike black line drawings, awash in sumptuous jewel-toned colors, work in tandem with this soothing tale sure to diminish night frights for youngsters concerned about the dark." SLJ

Emberley, Ed
Ed Emberley's bye-bye, big bad bullybug! Little, Brown & Co. 2007 unp il $10.99
Grades: PreK K 1 2   E
1. Monsters—Fiction 2. Insects—Fiction 3. Bullies—Fiction
ISBN 978-0-316-01762-6; 0-316-01762-0
LC 2006-15423
Die-cut pages reveal "a mean and scary 'Big Bad Bullybug' from outer space who threatens to bite, pinch, and tickle itty-bitty baby bugs. Luckily for the small fliers, a human with a huge sneaker is willing to do away with the pink-polka-dotted meanie. The cobolt blue backgrounds create a grand contrast for the electric greens, oranges, and yellows." SLJ

Go away, big green monster! Little, Brown 1992 unp il $10.99 *
Grades: PreK K 1   E
1. Monsters—Fiction 2. Fear—Fiction 3. Bedtime—Fiction
ISBN 0-316-23653-5   LC 92-6231
"In the first half of this fear-dispelling book, graphically distinctive die-cut pages reveal, bit by bit, a monster with 'sharp white teeth' and 'scraggly purple hair.' The process is then reversed as the text commands each scary feature to 'go away,' until there is nothing at all left of the monster but a black page instructing 'Don't Come Back! Until I say so.' Entertaining and empowering for young children." Horn Book Guide

Thanks, Mom! Little, Brown 2003 unp il $11.95
Grades: PreK K 1   E
1. Mice—Fiction 2. Animals—Fiction
ISBN 0-316-24022-2   LC 2001-50715
Kiko the mouse finds some delicious cheese and gets help from his mother when a group of various animals tries to take it
"Using sunny yellow highlights and creatures constructed from bold, geometric shapes, Emberley creates an exciting, chaotic chase with sparse text and an impressive sense of graphic design." SLJ

Where's my sweetie pie? LB Kids 2010 unp il $7.99
Grades: PreK   E
1. Board books for children 2. Stories in rhyme
ISBN 978-0-316-01891-3; 0-316-01891-0
"The book's title becomes a refrain for the short, rhyming text, encouraging kids to lift the flap and discover what's hidden. . . . Bold and colorful, the simple forms that make up the digital illustrations show up clearly against the white backgrounds. . . . As rewarding as a good game of peekaboo." Booklist

Emberley, Rebecca
There was an old monster! [by] Rebecca, Adrian, & Ed Emberley. Orchard Books 2009 unp il lib bdg $16.99 *
Grades: PreK K   E
1. Monsters—Fiction 2. Songs
ISBN 978-0-545-10145-5; 0-545-10145-X
LC 2008007191
In this variation on the traditional cumulative rhyme, a monster swallows ants, a lizard, a bat, and other creatures to try to cure a stomach ache than began when he swallowed a tick.
"Individual readers will pore over the illustrations and enjoy the repetition in the text while the large pictures make this a natural to share with groups. With the song provided as a free download at the publisher's Web site, this jazzy crowd-pleaser will have kids begging for repeat reads." SLJ

Emmett, Jonathan, 1965-
The best gift of all; illustrated by Vanessa Cabban. Candlewick Press 2008 unp il $15.99
Grades: K 1 2   E
1. Moles (Animals)—Fiction 2. Animals—Fiction 3. Gifts—Fiction
ISBN 978-0-7636-3860-3; 0-7636-3860-9
LC 2007-52214
Mole has not seen his friend Rabbit for days because it has been raining, and when he decides to tunnel to her home, he accidentally meets Squirrel and Hedgehog, who would like to visit her, as well
"Children will enjoy this simple tale of friendship. Cabban's cuddly animals drawn in a palette of soft, autumn watercolors reinforce the warm and fuzzy feeling of Emmett's story. A pleasant selection for fall storytimes and a good choice for beginning readers." SLJ

Leaf trouble; illustrated by Caroline Jayne Church. Chicken House 2009 unp il $16.99
Grades: PreK K 1 2   E
1. Autumn—Fiction 2. Leaves—Fiction 3. Squirrels—Fiction
ISBN 978-0-545-16070-4; 0-545-16070-7
LC 2009008268
A young squirrel panics when the leaves on his tree change color and fall, but he feels better when his mother tells him about autumn.
"The colorful and endearing ink illustrations, placed in a layered collage using a variety of textures and perspectives, are a delight." SLJ

Enderle, Judith Ross, 1941-

Smile, Principessa! by Judith Ross Enderle and Stephanie Jacob Gordon; illustrated by Serena Curmi. Margaret K. McElderry Books 2007 unp il $16.99

Grades: PreK K 1   E
    1. Siblings—Fiction   2. Infants—Fiction
    3. Photography—Fiction
    ISBN 978-1-4169-1004-6; 1-4169-1004-2
                            LC 2005012761

A sister is jealous when her baby brother starts getting all the attention in the family photographs

"Featuring characters in snazzy attire, the acrylic and pencil illustrations are delightful. . . . An engaging take on a common family situation." SLJ

English, Karen

The baby on the way; pictures by Sean Qualls. Farrar, Straus and Giroux 2005 unp il $16 *

Grades: PreK K 1 2   E
    1. Grandmothers—Fiction 2. Childbirth—Fiction
    3. Infants—Fiction 4. African Americans—Fiction
    ISBN 0-374-37361-2   LC 2003-49047

Jamal, a young African American boy, asks his grandmother if she was ever a baby, she tells him the story of how she was born.

"The intimate artwork, in earth colors with pencil-thin line details, shows the loving bond between family members stretching back in time and into the future." Booklist

Hot day on Abbott Avenue; illustrated by Javaka Steptoe. Clarion Books 2004 32p il $15 *

Grades: PreK K 1 2   E
    1. Friendship—Fiction   2. Summer—Fiction
    3. African Americans—Fiction 4. Rope skipping—Fiction
    ISBN 0-395-98527-7   LC 2002-09043

After having a fight, two friends spend the day ignoring each other, until the lure of a game of jump rope helps them to forget about being mad.

"Steptoe's found-object and cut-paper collages highlight facial features and depict oppressive summertime weather to perfection. . . . English's simple narrative consists mostly of two to three sentences per page and ends on a gratifying note." SLJ

Speak to me; (and I will listen between the lines); pictures by Amy June Bates. Farrar Straus Giroux 2004 unp il $16 *

Grades: 2 3 4 5   E
    1. School stories 2. San Francisco (Calif.)—Fiction
    3. African Americans—Fiction
    ISBN 0-374-37156-3   LC 2002-192895

Describes events of one day at a San Francisco Bay Area school as perceived by different second-graders, from the observations of first to arrive on the playground to the walk home.

"English's rich descriptions and insights bring readers into the world of six inner-city . . . students. . . . Bates's watercolor-and-ink illustrations capture the characters' expressions and moods vividly." SLJ

Ericsson, Jennifer A.

A piece of chalk; by Jennifer A. Ericsson; illustrated by Michelle Shapiro. Roaring Brook Press 2007 unp il $16.95

Grades: PreK K 1   E
    1. Drawing—Fiction
    ISBN 978-1-59643-057-0; 1-59643-057-5
                            LC 2006032178

"A Neal Porter book"

A little girl creates a colored chalk drawing on her driveway

"This simple, sunny offering captures the delight and escape a child finds in art. . . . The words and rhythms read like poetry, but there are no bouncy rhymes to distract from the story's quiet joy. Shapiro effectively mirrors the girl's art with a childlike style and an appealing palette of bright, opaque colors, muted with chalk white." Booklist

Whoo goes there? illustrated by Bert Kitchen. Roaring Brook Press 2009 unp il $17.99 *

Grades: K 1 2 3   E
    1. Owls—Fiction 2. Animals—Fiction 3. Night—Fiction
    ISBN 978-1-59643-371-7; 1-59643-371-X

"A Neal Porter Book"

"Finding food involves a long night of waiting and listening that's also filled with disappointment for a handsome owl. . . . Ericsson uses a simple repetitive scheme to introduce an array of small animals that travel through the owl's moonlit world. . . . Kitchen's naturalistic paintings are set in attractive alternating sets. . . . The predictive text and handsome pictures are just right for reading with preschoolers." SLJ

Ernst, Lisa Campbell, 1957-

The Gingerbread Girl. Dutton Children's Books 2006 unp il $16.99

Grades: PreK K 1 2   E
    1. Fairy tales
    ISBN 0-525-47667-9; 978-0-525-47667-2
                            LC 2006004193

Like her older brother, the Gingerbread Boy, who was eventually devoured by a fox, the Gingerbread Girl eludes the many people who would like to eat her but also has a plan to escape her sibling's fate.

"Ernst's familiar art . . . utilizes the oversize format to best advantage, with large characters leaping out of their frames." Booklist

Round like a ball! by Lisa Campbell Ernst. Blue Apple Books 2008 unp il $15.95   E
    1. Earth—Fiction
    ISBN 978-1-934706-01-5; 1-934706-01-9

Everyone tries to guess what is round and warm and cold and strong and fragile, until they finally realize it is Earth

"The clues are placed in large letters on the left side of a double-page spread, encircling progressively larger cutout circles. The cutout on each successive page offers a glimpse of the next article guessed. When the pages are flipped, a rainbow of cutout circles, large and small, is created on the previous page. . . . The distinctive illustrations, the guessing element, and the showstopping foldout of the Earth will work well for individual or group viewing." Booklist

Ernst, Lisa Campbell, 1957-—*Continued*

Sam Johnson and the blue ribbon quilt. Lothrop, Lee & Shepard Bks. 1983 32p il lib bdg $17.89; pa $6.99

Grades: K 1 2 3　　　　　　　　　　　　E

　　1. Quilts—Fiction 2. Sex role—Fiction

　　ISBN 0-688-01517-4 (lib bdg); 0-688-11505-5 (pa)

　　　　　　　　　　　　　　　　　LC 82-9980

While mending the awning over the pig pen, Sam discovers that he enjoys sewing the various patches together but meets with scorn and ridicule when he asks his wife if he could join her quilting club

The illustrations "bring an old-timey, bucolic scene to life and show steps in an equal-rights issue." Publ Wkly

Snow surprise. 1st Green Light Readers ed. Harcourt 2008 unp il $12.95; pa $3.95

Grades: 1 2 3　　　　　　　　　　　　E

　　1. Snow—Fiction 2. Siblings—Fiction

　　ISBN 978-0-15-206553-9; 0-15-206553-9; 978-0-15-206559-1 (pa); 0-15-206559-8 (pa)

　　　　　　　　　　　　　　　　LC 2007-42343

Joan makes a surprise for her little brother, Ben, but in the end, she is the one who is surprised.

Sylvia Jean, scout supreme. Dutton Children's Books 2010 unp il $16.99

Grades: PreK K 1 2　　　　　　　　　E

　　1. Costume—Fiction 2. Pigs—Fiction 3. Scouts and scouting—Fiction

　　ISBN 978-0-525-47873-7; 0-525-47873-6

　　　　　　　　　　　　　　　LC 2009017919

Sylvia Jean disguises herself in order to assist a neighbor who does not want her enthusiastic help, but she still might be the only one in her Pig Scout Troop who will not earn a Good Deed Badge.

"Expressive faces enhance the gentle narrative; thin lines indicate a quiet vulnerability. Ernst's scenes feature her signature pastel palette even as humorous details advance the energetic tale." Kirkus

Another title about Sylvia Jean is:

Sylvia Jean, drama queen (2005)

The turn-around upside-down alphabet book. Simon & Schuster Books for Young Readers 2004 unp il $15.95

Grades: PreK K 1 2　　　　　　　　　E

　　1. Alphabet

　　ISBN 0-689-85685-7　　　　　LC 2003-16318

"With touches of humor and a great deal of creativity, Ernst fashioned this book out of cut paper and surrounded each block with a thick black border that sets off white words. Children will enjoy tilting the pages to see the transformations and will be motivated to come up with ideas of their own." SLJ

Zinnia and Dot. Viking 1992 unp il $16.99; pa $5.99

Grades: PreK K 1 2　　　　　　　　　E

　　1. Chickens—Fiction

　　ISBN 0-670-83091-7; 0-14-054199-3 (pa)

　　　　　　　　　　　　　　　　LC 91-36178

Zinnia and Dot, self-satisfied hens who bicker constantly about who lays better eggs, put aside their differ-ences to protect a prime specimen from a marauding weasel.

"Ernst has an easy storytelling style and a flair for grouchy dialogue that clucks to be read aloud, and her line-and-wash paintings, lighted with gentle yellow tones, warm the comedy." Bull Cent Child Books

Esbaum, Jill

Stanza; illustrated by Jack E. Davis. Harcourt Children's Books 2009 unp il $16

Grades: PreK K 1 2　　　　　　　　　E

　　1. Stories in rhyme 2. Poetry—Fiction 3. Contests—Fiction 4. Dogs—Fiction

　　ISBN 978-0-15-205998-9; 0-15-205998-9

　　　　　　　　　　　　　　　LC 2007051078

Stanza the dog and his two rotten brothers terrorize the streets by day, but at night Stanza secretly writes po-etry.

"The message, though well seasoned, is refreshed by lively characterizations of Stanza, his brothers, and the people around them. Children will delight in the details that are often hidden on the page. Rhyming verse makes this an especially fine read-aloud, but the real fun is in upclose scrutiny of the illustrations." SLJ

To the big top; [by] Jill Esbaum; pictures by David Gordon. Farrar Straus Giroux 2008 unp il $16.95

Grades: PreK K 1 2　　　　　　　　　E

　　1. Circus—Fiction 2. Friendship—Fiction

　　ISBN 0-374-39934-4; 978-0-374-39934-4

　　　　　　　　　　　　　　　LC 2006053530

When the circus comes to the small town of Willow Grove in the early 1900s, best friends Benny and Sam enjoy an exciting day helping set up the tent, admiring the various animals, and anticipating the big show.

"Gordon's joyful illustrations capture the appeal traveling entertainers had for small-town residents of the early twentieth century. . . . Esbaum . . . provides a nostalgic trip down memory lane that will give children . . . a good idea of what it was like back then." Booklist

Ets, Marie Hall, 1893-1984

Play with me; story and pictures by Marie Hall Ets. Viking 1955 31p il pa $5.99 hardcover o.p.

Grades: PreK K　　　　　　　　　　E

　　1. Animals—Fiction

　　ISBN 0-14-050178-9 (pa)

A Caldecott Medal honor book, 1956

On a sunny morning in the meadow an excited little girl tries to catch the meadow creatures and play with them. But, one by one, they all run away. Finally, when she learns to sit quietly and wait, there is a happy ending

The "pictures done in muted tones of brown, gray and yellow . . . accurately reflect the little girl's rapidly changing moods of eagerness, bafflement, disappointment and final happiness." N Y Times Book Rev

Evans, Cambria, 1981-

Bone soup. Houghton Miffin 2008 unp il lib
bdg $16

Grades: K 1 2 3   E
  1. Halloween—Fiction 2. Monsters—Fiction
ISBN 978-0-618-80908-0 (lib bdg); 0-618-80908-2 (lib
bdg)   LC 2008001862
The skeletal Finnigin tricks a town's witches, ghouls,
and zombies into helping him make soup
"Even the zombies are lovable in Evans's charming
Halloween-themed rendition of 'Stone Soup.' . . . Seasoned with sprightly, luminescent watercolors and the
perfect dose of gross-out factor, this tale has all the right
ingredients for a hearty storytime." SLJ

Evans, Freddi Williams, 1957-

Hush harbor; praying in secret; illustrated by
Erin Bennett Banks. Carolrhoda Books 2008 c2009
unp il lib bdg $16.95 *

Grades: K 1 2 3   E
  1. Slavery—Fiction 2. African Americans—Fiction
3. Religion—Fiction 4. Christian life—Fiction
ISBN 978-0-8225-7965-6 (lib bdg); 0-8225-7965-0 (lib
bdg)   LC 2007-34777
While Simmy watches for danger from high in a tree,
other slaves gather in a hidden spot in the woods to sing
and pray together in their own way, risking their lives in
pursuit of religious freedom. Includes historical facts
about hush, or brush, arbors and the churches that grew
from them
This is "a moving narrative. . . . Illustrated with extremely stylized pictures that don't prettify their subjects,
this captures some of the fear and horror associated with
slavery." Booklist

Evans, Lezlie

Who loves the little lamb? illustrated by David
McPhail. Disney-Hyperion Books 2010 unp il
$15.99

Grades: PreK   E
  1. Stories in rhyme 2. Mother-child relationship—Fiction 3. Animals—Fiction
ISBN 978-1-4231-1659-2; 1-4231-1659-3
                       LC 2009015896
Rhyming text reveals that, although baby animals are
not always perfect, their mothers love them and help
them through difficult moments.
"This has two things going for it that set it apart: Evans' uncommonly clever text and artwork by McPhail.
. . . What's so terrific about this . . . is the motherly diversity shown in the art." Booklist

Everitt, Betsy

Mean soup. Harcourt Brace Jovanovich 1992
unp il hardcover o.p. pa $8

Grades: PreK K 1 2   E
  1. Anger—Fiction 2. Cooking—Fiction
ISBN 0-15-253146-7; 0-15-200227-8 (pa)
                       LC 91-15244
Horace feels really mean at the end of a bad day, until
he helps his mother make Mean Soup
"The text features short sentences and easy but effec-

tive vocabulary, so the story bubbles with a building excitement. Everitt's . . . stylized paintings and bold palette—hot pinks, purples and black predominate—convey
all of the feisty emotion of a frustrated youngster." Publ
Wkly

Ewart, Claire

Fossil; [by] Claire Ewart. Walker 2004 unp il
$16.89; lib bdg $17.85

Grades: PreK K 1 2   E
  1. Pterosaurs—Fiction 2. Fossils—Fiction 3. Stories in
rhyme
ISBN 0-8027-8890-4; 0-8027-8891-2 (lib bdg)
                       LC 2003-53469
Upon finding a special stone, a child imagines the life
of a pterosaur, the ancient flying reptile that lived, died,
and was fossilized into that stone. Includes facts about
fossils and how they are formed.
"Ewart's inviting text and dramatic artwork work nicely together to describe the fossilization process in an engrossing way." SLJ
Includes bibliographical references

Fackelmayer, Regina

The gifts; illustrated by Christa Unzner.
North-South Books 2009 unp il $16.95

Grades: K 1 2 3   E
  1. Christmas—Fiction 2. Gifts—Fiction
ISBN 978-0-7358-2265-8; 0-7358-2265-4
"Mia buys a turkey for dinner, gifts for her dog and
cat, a hat for herself, and a Christmas tree. Stopping to
help an old man who has slipped on the ice, she leaves
her tree outdoors. . . . The story is written with clarity
and restraint. . . . The sensitive artwork includes a delicately spattered effect that textures all the illustrations
and works particularly well in the snowy outdoor
scenes." Booklist

Falconer, Ian, 1959-

Olivia; written and illustrated by Ian Falconer.
Atheneum Bks. for Young Readers 2000 unp il
$17.99; bd bk $7.99 *

Grades: PreK K 1 2   E
  1. Pigs—Fiction
ISBN 0-689-82953-1; 0-689-87472-3 (bd bk)
                       LC 99-24003
A Caldecott Medal honor book, 2001
"An Anne Schwartz book"
Whether at home getting ready for the day, enjoying
the beach, or at bedtime, Olivia is a feisty pig who has
too much energy for her own good
"The spacious design of the book; the appeal of the
strong, clever art; and the humor that permeates every
page make this a standout. . . . Falconer . . . renders
Olivia's world in charcoal with dollops of red brighten-
ing the pages." Booklist
Other titles about Olivia are:
Olivia . . . and the missing toy (2003)
Olivia forms a band (2006)
Olivia helps with Christmas (2007)
Olivia saves the circus (2001)

Faller, Régis

The adventures of Polo. Roaring Brook Press 2006 75p il $16.95 *

Grades: PreK K 1 2 3   E

1. Dogs—Fiction 2. Stories without words

ISBN 978-1-59643-160-7; 1-59643-160-1

           LC 2005055261

"A Neal Porter book"

Polo the dog sets out from his home and enjoys many adventures, including sailing his boat on top of a whale, roasting hot dogs over a volcano, and taking a ride in a spaceship built from a mushroom.

"Young readers will be charmed by this hound, and be awed by his ingenuity. Somewhat similar to a graphic-novel format, this wordless picture book contains bold, colorful, cartoon panels that are sure to captivate even the most finicky youngster." SLJ

Other titles about Polo are:

Polo: the runaway book (2006)

Polo and the magic flute (2009)

Polo and Lily (2009)

Polo and the dragon (2009)

Polo and the magician (2009)

Falwell, Cathryn

David's drawings; story and pictures by Cathryn Falwell. Lee & Low Bks. 2001 unp il hardcover o.p. pa $8.95

Grades: PreK K 1 2   E

1. School stories 2. Drawing—Fiction 3. Friendship—Fiction 4. African Americans—Fiction

ISBN 1-58430-031-0; 1-58430-261-5 (pa)

           LC 2001-16450

A shy African American boy arriving at a new school makes friends with his classmates by drawing a picture of a tree

"The cut-paper-and-fabric collages are a good choice for the story. . . . Both theme and execution make this a fine choice for classroom read-alouds." Booklist

Scoot! Greenwillow Books 2008 unp il $16.99; lib bdg $17.89 *

Grades: PreK K 1 2   E

1. Turtles—Fiction 2. Ponds—Fiction 3. Stories in rhyme

ISBN 978-0-06-128882-1; 0-06-128882-9; 978-0-06-128883-8 (lib bdg); 0-06-128883-7 (lib bdg)

           LC 2007-18355

Six silent turtles sit still as stones on a log, as energetic movement by the other animals in the pond happens all around them

"Extraordinary paper collages accompany a high-spirited romp. . . . Strong, predictable rhymes bounce across the pages. . . . Unusual, lively words extend vocabulary." SLJ

Shape capers; [by] Cathryn Falwell. Greenwillow Books 2007 unp il $16.99; lib bdg $17.89

Grades: PreK K   E

1. Shape—Fiction 2. Imagination—Fiction 3. Stories in rhyme

ISBN 978-0-06-123699-0; 978-0-06-123700-0 (lib bdg)

           LC 2006043061

A group of children shakes shapes out of a box and discovers the fun of using circles, squares, triangles, semicircles, rectangles, and their imaginations

This is a "bright, playful book, illustrated in whimsical cut-paper collage." Booklist

Turtle splash! countdown at the pond. Greenwillow Bks. 2001 unp il $15.95; lib bdg $15.89 *

Grades: PreK K 1 2   E

1. Turtles—Fiction 2. Counting 3. Stories in rhyme

ISBN 0-06-029462-0; 0-06-029463-9 (lib bdg)

           LC 00-30918

As they are startled by the activities of other nearby creatures, the number of turtles on a log in a pond decreases from ten to one

"The rhyming, alliterative text is energized with a rolling rhythm, suspense, and vivid, descriptive words. . . . Evocative woodland scenes spring to life with well-defined animals that are described in a final appended section." Booklist

Fancher, Lou

Star climbing; by Lou Fancher; paintings by Steve Johnson and Lou Fancher. Laura Geringer Books 2006 unp il hardcover o.p. lib bdg $16.89

Grades: PreK K   E

1. Stars—Fiction 2. Constellations—Fiction 3. Imagination—Fiction 4. Bedtime—Fiction

ISBN 978-0-06-073901-0; 0-06-073901-0; 978-0-06-073902-7 (lib bdg); 0-06-073902-9 (lib bdg)

           LC 2005005048

When he cannot sleep, a little boy imagines himself on a nighttime journey across the sky where he can run and dance with star constellations

"Ethereal, textured paintings accompany Fancher's rhythmic, lyrical poem." Publ Wkly

Farber, Norma

How the hibernators came to Bethlehem; by Norma Farber; illustrated by Barbara Cooney. Walker 2006 c1980 unp il $9.95

Grades: K 1 2 3   E

1. Christmas—Fiction 2. Animals—Fiction 3. Hibernation—Fiction

ISBN 0-8027-9610-9

A reissue of the title first published 1980

The Star of Bethlehem awakens the winter-sleeping creatures, such as Bear, Badger, and Raccoon, to send them to visit a newborn baby.

"The simple, unabashed realism of Cooney's art . . . along with Farber's respectful text, celebrates the hibernators as part of a divine plan." Horn Book Guide

Farooqi, Musharraf, 1968-

The cobbler's holiday, or, why ants don't have shoes; illustrated by Eugene Yelchin. Roaring Brook Press 2008 unp il $16.95

Grades: K 1 2 3   E

1. Shoes—Fiction 2. Ants—Fiction 3. Fashion—Fiction

ISBN 978-1-59643-234-5; 1-59643-234-9

           LC 2007044046

Farooqi, Musharraf, 1968——*Continued*

"A Neal Porter book"

At a time when every ant has at least fifteen pairs of shoes and disputes over footwear are common, the one and only ant cobbler decides to take some time off, which leads to many tears until the Red Ant provides an elegant solution.

This is "a dainty, droll fable. . . . Farooqi builds scenarios ripe with comedy. . . . Yelchin . . . contributes decorative initial caps and a modish Jazz Age aesthetic; his spiky-looking ant flappers and dandies sport ritzy top hats and beaded caps, tailored and fur-collared coats, monocles and, of course, elaborate footwear." Publ Wkly

Farrell, Darren

Doug-Dennis and the flyaway fib; words and pictures by Darren Farrell. Dial Books for Young Readers 2010 unp il $16.95

Grades: K 1 2   E

1. Truthfulness and falsehood—Fiction 2. Honesty—Fiction 3. Friendship—Fiction 4. Circus—Fiction 5. Sheep—Fiction

ISBN 978-0-8037-3437-1; 0-8037-3437-9

LC 2009-12141

Having fibbed about stealing his best friend's popcorn at the circus, Doug-Dennis the sheep finds himself carried far away to a place filled with lies and liars of all sorts and must discover a way to return.

"Sharp-edged irony and wacky cartoon visuals provide newcomer Farrell's moral tale with some serious wattage. . . . Despite the antifib message, the fibs are where all the entertainment is ('I invented the inter-web,' declares a spider), and the ethically unsteady Doug-Dennis has plenty of Homer Simpson–like appeal." Publ Wkly

Faulkner, Matt

A taste of colored water. Simon & Schuster 2008 unp il $16.99

Grades: K 1 2 3   E

1. African Americans—Segregation—Fiction 2. Civil rights demonstrations—Fiction 3. Cousins—Fiction

ISBN 978-1-4169-1629-1; 1-4169-1629-6

In the 1960s two cousins hear of a water fountain labelled "Colored" and imagine a multicolored drink, but they discover the true meaning of the sign when they encounter a Civil Rights demonstration.

"Watercolors decorated with ink crosshatching ably contrast the sweet pastoral fun the children experience with their sudden, terrifying wake up. Faulkner's personal note about his growing up in the north, where segregation was not official but prejudice was always there, will spark discussion." Booklist

Fearnley, Jan

Martha in the middle; [by] Jan Fearnley. Candlewick Press 2008 40p il $16.99

Grades: PreK K 1   E

1. Mice—Fiction 2. Siblings—Fiction 3. Family life—Fiction 4. Frogs—Fiction

ISBN 978-0-7636-3800-9; 0-7636-3800-5

Martha, a young mouse with a sensible big sister and a cute little brother, begins to feel invisible and decides to run away, but at the end of the garden she meets a wise frog who points out just how special the middle can be.

"Fearnley's nimble use of line and uncluttered watercolors focus on character and plenty of action. . . . Witty details . . . ramp up the fun." Publ Wkly

Milo Armadillo. Candlewick Press 2009 unp il $15.99

Grades: PreK K 1 2   E

1. Toys—Fiction 2. Armadillos—Fiction

ISBN 978-0-7636-4575-5; 0-7636-4575-3

LC 2009004231

When no one can find a pink, fluffy rabbit to give to Tallulah for her birthday, her grandmother knits her a pink, fluffy 'thing' that they name Milo Armadillo, which proves to be a great present.

"Mixed-media collages pay homage to all things handmade by incorporating worked yarn and fabric into the illustrations. This candy-colored picture book tells a simple, sweet story about learning to love what you have." SLJ

Mr. Wolf's pancakes; [by] Jan Fearnley. Tiger Tales 2001 c1999 unp il $15.95; pa $6.95

Grades: PreK K 1 2 3   E

1. Wolves—Fiction 2. Fairy tales

ISBN 1-58925-004-4; 1-58925-354-X (pa)

LC 2001-834

First published 1999 in the United Kingdom

"Mr. Wolf seeks assistance from his neighbors, but Chicken Little, Wee Willy Winkle, the Gingerbread Man, Little Red Riding Hood and the Three Little Pigs all nastily refuse. Of course, when Mr. Wolf eventually whips up the pancakes all by himself, they demand a share of his culinary creation. Mr. Wolf . . . lets the marauders into the kitchen-and then gobbles them all up. . . . Chipper watercolors depict a sunny storybook town. . . . A gleeful twist on a nursery staple." Publ Wkly

Another title about Mr. Wolf is:

Mr. Wolf and the three bears (2002)

Feelings, Muriel, 1938-

Jambo means hello; Swahili alphabet book; pictures by Tom Feelings. Dial Bks. for Young Readers 1981 unp il pa $6.99 hardcover o.p. *

Grades: PreK K 1 2   E

1. Alphabet 2. Swahili language 3. East Africa

ISBN 0-14-054652-1 (pa)

A Caldecott Medal honor book, 1975

This book "gives a word for each letter of the alphabet (the Swahili alphabet has 24 letters) save for 'q' and 'x', and a sentence or two provides additional information. A double-page spread of soft black and white drawings illustrates each word." Bull Cent Child Books

"Integrated totally in feeling and mood, the book has been engendered by an intense personal vision of Africa—one that is warm, all-enveloping, quietly strong and filled with love." Horn Book

Feelings, Muriel, 1938-—_Continued_

Moja means one; Swahili counting book; pictures by Tom Feelings. Dial Bks. for Young Readers 1971 unp il pa $6.99 hardcover o.p. *

Grades: PreK K 1 2   E
1. Counting 2. Swahili language 3. East Africa
ISBN 0-14-054662-6 (pa)

A Caldecott Medal honor book, 1972

The book "uses double-page spreads for each number, one to ten, with beautiful illustrations that depict aspects of East African culture as well as numbers of objects in relation to the various numbers." Publ Wkly

"A short introduction explaining the importance of Swahili and providing a map of the areas in which it is spoken expands the book's use beyond the preschool level of the text into the first three school grades." SLJ

Feiffer, Jules

Bark, George. HarperCollins Pubs. 1999 unp il $15.99 *

Grades: PreK K 1 2   E
1. Dogs—Fiction
ISBN 0-06-205185-7

"Michael di Capua books"

"George the puppy has a problem—he just can't bark. He can meow, quack, oink, moo; but not bark." NY Times Book Rev

"Feiffer's characters are unforgettable, the text is brief and easy to follow, and the pictures burst with the sort of broad physical comedy that a lot of children just love." Booklist

Feiffer, Kate

But I wanted a baby brother! illustrated by Diane Goode. Simon & Schuster Books for Young Readers 2010 unp il $16.99

Grades: PreK K 1   E
1. Infants—Fiction 2. Siblings—Fiction 3. Family life—Fiction
ISBN 978-1-4169-3941-2; 1-4169-3941-5

"A Paula Wiseman Book"

Oliver Keaton wants a baby brother more than anything but when he gets a baby sister instead, he sets out with his dog Chaplin to trade his sister for the perfect baby brother.

"Both text and breezy cartoon illustrations are laced with humor, making this an excellent choice for reading aloud. . . . Feiffer's book is a cut above many of its kind." Booklist

Double pink; illustrated by Bruce Ingman. Simon & Schuster Books for Young Readers 2005 unp il $15.95

Grades: PreK K 1   E
1. Color—Fiction
ISBN 0-689-87190-0   LC 2004--06582

"A Paula Wiseman Book"

Madison covers and surrounds herself with her favorite color, pink, until the day her mother has trouble finding her.

"Feiffer's simple text reads easily, and Ingman's playful acrylic-and-ink paintings take a light approach to this look at childhood obsession." SLJ

Henry, the dog with no tail; illustrated by Jules Feiffer. Simon & Schuster Books for Young Readers 2007 unp il $16.99

Grades: PreK K 1 2   E
1. Dogs—Fiction
ISBN 978-1-4169-1614-7; 1-4169-1614-8
     LC 2006-13418

"A Paula Wiseman book."

Envious of the other dogs that have tails, Henry goes in search of a tail of his own, but in the end he decides he is happy the way he is.

"Feiffer's story features droll humor, wonderfully outlandish plot twists, and a satisfying journey of self-discovery. . . . The charcoal and watercolor illustrations use loose lines and color splashes to convey the action and capture the characters' personalities." SLJ

My mom is trying to ruin my life; [by] Kate Feiffer; illustrated by Diane Goode. Simon & Schuster Books for Young Readers 2009 unp il $16.99 *

Grades: PreK K 1 2   E
1. Mother-daughter relationship—Fiction
2. Father-daughter relationship—Fiction
ISBN 978-1-4169-4100-2; 1-4169-4100-2
     LC 2007045351

"A Paula Wiseman book"

A young girl describes all the ways in which her mother and father conspire to ruin her life

"Feiffer and Goode . . . give the old chestnut of a story line an urbane sheen. . . . [Goode's] watercolor vignettes are gems of wry intelligence and comic understatement." Publ Wkly

President Pennybaker; [by] Kate Feiffer; illustrated by Diane Goode. Simon & Schuster Books for Young Readers 2008 unp il $16.99

Grades: PreK K 1 2   E
1. Politics—Fiction
ISBN 978-1-4169-1354-2; 1-4169-1354-8
     LC 2007004815

"A Paula Wiseman book"

Tired of the unfairness of life, young Luke Pennybaker decides to run for president, with his dog Lily as his running mate

"Deadpan narration allows the absurdity of the premise to carry the day, with plenty of help from the illustrations. Goode's breezy watercolors set just the right tone. . . . The humor is deftly understated, both visually and verbally, making this an amusing and appealing send-up of politics and children's chores." SLJ

Feldman, Eve

Billy and Milly, short and silly! written by Eve Feldman; pictures by Tuesday Mourning. G.P. Putnam's Sons 2009 unp il $16.99 *

Grades: PreK K 1 2   E
1. Stories in rhyme
ISBN 978-0-399-24651-7; 0-399-24651-7
     LC 2008-26143

"This picture book presents 13 short rhyming stories about Billy and Milly. Most of them are four words long; some, only three. Every word in each selection

Feldman, Eve—*Continued*

rhymes. . . . The bright cartoon illustrations done in mixed-media collage are the keys to understanding the stories and the humor. . . . Both clever and slapstick, this book can be read for pleasure or used as a jumping-off point for thinking about rhyme, language, and story." SLJ

Fenton, Joe

What's under the bed? written and illustrated by Joe Fenton. Simon & Schuster for Young Readers unp il $15.99

Grades: PreK K 1 2   E

1. Fear—Fiction 2. Bedtime—Fiction 3. Stories in rhyme

ISBN 978-1-4169-4943-5; 1-4169-4943-7

When Fred lays down his head, he imagines there is something monstrous under his bed.

"The narrative is accessible, using uncomplicated rhymes. . . . The brooding illustrations would be more unnerving if Fred, diminutive in outsize glasses, weren't so adorably disarming." Horn Book Guide

Fern, Tracey E.

Buffalo music; illustrated by Lauren Castillo. Clarion Books 2008 31p il $16 *

Grades: 1 2 3 4   E

1. Goodnight, Mollie, 1839-1926—Fiction 2. Texas—Fiction 3. Frontier and pioneer life—Fiction 4. Bison—Fiction

ISBN 978-0-618-72341-6; 0-618-72341-2

LC 2007-18435

After hunters kill off the buffalo around her Texas ranch, a woman begins raising orphan buffalo calves and eventually ships four members of her small herd to Yellowstone National Park, where they form the beginnings of newly thriving buffalo herds. Based on the true story of Mary Ann Goodnight and her husband Charles; includes author's note about her work, with websites and a bibliography.

"Fern's lyrical text and Castillo's folk-style artwork beautifully capture the era and events. Done in warm, earthy hues, the mixed-media illustrations depict a rugged landscape of grays and browns speckled with touches of color-wildflowers or bright blooms on a tree." SLJ

Pippo the Fool; [by] Tracey E. Fern; illustrated by Pau Estrada. Charlesbridge 2009 unp il $15.95 *

Grades: 1 2 3   E

1. Brunelleschi, Filippo, 1377-1446—Fiction 2. Santa Maria del Fiore (Cathedral: Florence, Italy)—Fiction 3. Florence (Italy)—Fiction 4. Italy—History—0-1559—Fiction

ISBN 978-1-57091-655-7; 1-57091-655-1

LC 2007002283

In fifteenth-century Florence, Italy, a contest is held to design a magnificent dome for the town's cathedral, but when Pippo the Fool claims he will win the contest, everyone laughs at him. Based on the true story of Filippo Brunelleschi.

This is "told with a great deal of charm and buttressed by understated humor. . . . Estrada's timeless art highlights Florence's orange-roofed architecture and colorfully attired citizens." Booklist

Finchler, Judy, 1943-

Miss Malarkey leaves no reader behind. Walker & Company 2006 unp il $16.95; lib bdg $17.85 *

Grades: K 1 2 3   E

1. Books and reading—Fiction 2. Teachers—Fiction 3. School stories

ISBN 978-0-8027-8084-3; 0-8027-8084-9; 978-0-8027-8085-0 (lib bdg); 0-8027-8085-7 (lib bdg)

LC 2005037182

Miss Malarkey vows to find each of her students a book to love by the end of the school year, but one video-game loving boy proves to be a challenge.

"O'Malley's illustrations, done in markers and colored pencils, enhance the text with expressive pictures. . . . A must-have for all libraries." SLJ

Other titles about Miss Malarkey are:

Congratulations, Miss Malarkey! (2009)

Miss Malarkey doesn't live in Room 10 (1995)

Miss Malarkey won't be in today (1998)

Miss Malarkey's field trip (2004)

Testing Miss Malarkey (2000)

You're a good sport, Miss Malarkey (2002)

Fine, Edith Hope

Armando and the blue tarp school; [by] Edith Hope Fine & Judith Pinkerton Josephson; illustrated by Hernan Sosa. Lee & Low 2007 unp il lib bdg $16.95

Grades: K 1 2 3   E

1. School stories 2. Mexico—Fiction 3. Poverty—Fiction

ISBN 978-1-58430-278-0

"Armando and his family live in a colonia near the Tiajuana city dump. . . . They eke out a meager living by hunting through the mounds of foul-smelling garbage for anything they can use or sell. Then Señor David arrives, spreads a blue tarp on the ground, and sets up a school." SLJ

"This poignant picture book . . . is based on a true story. . . . [It is illustrated with] clear, unframed, double-page pictures in watercolor and ink with thick white outlines. . . . Without melodrama, Armando's story shows what poverty means and the hope that things can change." Booklist

Fischer, Scott M.

Jump! [by] Scott Fischer. Simon & Schuster Books for Young Readers 2010 unp il $14.99

Grades: PreK K   E

1. Stories in rhyme 2. Animals—Fiction 3. Fear—Fiction

ISBN 978-1-4169-7884-8; 1-4169-7884-4

LC 2008025861

From bugs and frogs to alligators and whales, frightened animals always move out of the way of a larger opponent.

"With simple, rhyming text and action-packed artwork, this picture book will appeal to young preschoolers. . . . Even after kids have figured out what is coming, they will enjoy the animals' shifts in power roles, all depicted in lively drawings, rendered in thick black lines and strong, bright colors against blank white space." Booklist

Fisher, Aileen Lucia, 1906-2002
The story goes on; illustrated by Mique
Moriuchi. Roaring Brook Press 2004 unp il $16.95
Grades: PreK K 1 2   E
1. Food chains (Ecology) 2. Stories in rhyme
ISBN 1-59643-037-0   LC 2003-18143
An illustrated poem about the cycle of life—bug eats
plant, frog eats bug, snake eats frog, hawk eats snake,
and so on
"With bright colors, rhyming text, and collage illustrations, this circular tale points out the interdependence of
life. . . . This offering is a visual treat and an engaging
opportunity to introduce the cycle of life to young readers." SLJ

Fisher, Carolyn, 1968-
The Snow Show; with Chef Kelvin; producer,
Carolyn Fisher. Harcourt 2008 unp il $17
Grades: K 1 2 3   E
1. Snow—Fiction 2. Cooking—Fiction 3. Television
programs—Fiction
ISBN 978-0-15-206019-0; 0-15-206019-7
                               LC 2007031724
A cooking show goes on location to the North Pole to
demonstrate the recipe for making snow.
"The visually dynamic, digitally created art features
lettering that helps tell the story. . . . Fisher includes
collage, dialogue asides, arrows, onomatopoeic descrip-
tors, and fact boxes, yet maintains clarity, cohesion, and
purpose." SLJ

Fisher, Valorie
My big brother. Atheneum Bks. for Young
Readers 2002 unp il $15.95
Grades: PreK K 1   E
1. Brothers—Fiction
ISBN 0-689-84327-5   LC 2001-22947
"An Anne Schwartz book"
Photographs and simple text depict a big brother from
the point of view of his baby sibling
"The design is clean and strong, and the colors, tex-
tures, and lines all lead the eye to the important parts of
the story. Together the text and the pictures tell a funny,
very tender story of sibling relationships." Booklist

Fitzpatrick, Marie-Louise, 1962-
There. Roaring Brook Press 2009 unp il $17.95
Grades: K 1 2   E
1. Growth—Fiction 2. Questions and answers
ISBN 978-1-59643-087-7; 1-59643-087-7
                               LC 2008-54266
"A Neal Porter book"
A young girl asks questions about growing up as she
walks over rolling hills, climbs a ladder up to the stars,
and meets a dragon.
This "is a book for rumination, a rare permission to
ask the unanswerable questions. The thoughts that propel
it and the images that illuminate it make this volume a
small wonder for children." SLJ

Flack, Marjorie, 1897-1958
Ask Mr. Bear. Macmillan 1958 c1932 unp il
$15.95; pa $6.99
Grades: PreK K 1   E
1. Animals—Fiction 2. Birthdays—Fiction
ISBN 0-02-735390-7; 0-02-043090-6 (pa)
First published 1932
Danny did not know what to give his mother for a
birthday present, so he set out to ask various animals—
the hen, the duck, the goose, the lamb, the cow and others, but he met with very little success until he met Mr.
Bear
This "will have a strong appeal to very young children
because of its repetition, its use of the most familiar animals, its gay pictures and the cumulative effect of the
story." N Y Times Book Rev

Flaherty, Alice
The luck of the Loch Ness monster; a tale of
picky eating; [by] A. W. Flaherty; illustrated by
Scott Magoon. Houghton Mifflin 2007 unp il $16
Grades: K 1 2 3   E
1. Ocean travel—Fiction 2. Loch Ness monster—Fiction 3. Scotland—Fiction
ISBN 978-0-618-55644-1; 0-618-55644-3
                               LC 2006026083
"A girl is traveling alone to visit her grandmother in
Scotland. . . . She tosses her dreaded morning oatmeal
overboard, only to attract the attention of a tiny sea
worm that gobbles it up and immediately quadruples in
size. . . . This pourquoi tale about how the Loch Ness
Monster came to be has a lot of imagination and wonderful storytelling techniques. Dark, cartoonlike watercolors exhibit an excellent use of perspective." SLJ

Fleischman, Paul
The animal hedge; illustrated by Bagram
Ibatoulline. Candlewick Press 2003 unp il $16.99
Grades: K 1 2 3   E
1. Animals—Fiction
ISBN 0-7636-1606-0   LC 2002-23751
A newly illustrated edition of the title first published
1983 by Dutton
After being forced to sell the animals he loves, a far-
mer cuts his hedge to look like them and teaches his
sons about following their hearts
"Ibatoulline's watercolor-and-gouache illustrations, in-
spired by 19th-century American folk-art paintings, are
the perfect complement to this simple allegory." SLJ

The birthday tree; illustrated by Barry Root.
Candlewick Press 2008 unp il $16.99
Grades: K 1 2 3   E
1. Trees—Fiction
ISBN 978-0-7636-2604-4   LC 2007-32344
A newly illustrated edition of the title first published
1979 by Harper & Row
When Jack goes to sea, his parents watch as the tree
planted at his birth reflects his fortunes and misfortunes
"Precisely worded and fluid in the telling, the story
has a timeless quality that is echoed in the expressive
watercolor artwork." Booklist

Fleischman, Paul—*Continued*

Sidewalk circus; presented by Paul Fleischman and Kevin Hawkes. Candlewick Press 2004 unp il $15.99

Grades: PreK K 1 2 3   E

1. City and town life—Fiction 2. Circus—Fiction 3. Stories without words

ISBN 0-7636-1107-7   LC 2002-74168

"As posters advertising the world-renowned Garibaldi circus are put up along a busy city block, a girl waiting for a bus watches the circus of everyday life unfold. There is no actual text to the book, just the words of store signs, a scrolling theater marquee, and the show bills. What the girl imagines is revealed through the playful shadows of the people on the street and the corresponding circus flyers. . . . Hawkes's richly colored acrylic paintings sustain interest and pacing throughout the book. . . . This delightful book will fascinate children and help them to see their world with new eyes." SLJ

Weslandia; illustrated by Kevin Hawkes. Candlewick Press 1999 unp il $15.99; pa $5.99 *

Grades: K 1 2 3   E

1. Plants—Fiction 2. Gardening—Fiction

ISBN 0-7636-0006-7; 0-7636-1052-6 (pa)

LC 98-30240

Wesley's garden produces a crop of huge, strange plants which provide him with clothing, shelter, food, and drink, thus helping him create his own civilization and changing his life

"This story about a nonconformist creating his own reality resonates with imagination and humor. . . . His natural creativity is reflected in Hawkes' vivid recreations of Wesley's altered environment, lush illustrations that have a realistic whimsy." Bull Cent Child Books

Fleming, Candace

Boxes for Katje; pictures by Stacey Dressen-McQueen. Farrar, Straus & Giroux 2003 unp il $16 *

Grades: K 1 2 3   E

1. World War, 1939-1945—Fiction 2. Netherlands—Fiction

ISBN 0-374-30922-1   LC 2002-20027

"Melanie Kroupa books"

After a young Dutch girl writes to her new American friend in thanks for the care package sent after World War II, she begins to receive increasingly larger boxes

The story is "moving, and Dressen-McQueen's lively illustrations, in colored pencil, oil pastel, and acrylic, pack lots of color, pattern, and historical details onto every expansive page." Booklist

The hatmaker's sign; a story; by Benjamin Franklin; retold by Candace Fleming; illustrated by Robert Andrew Parker. Orchard Bks. 1998 unp il $16.95; lib bdg $17.99

Grades: K 1 2 3   E

1. Jefferson, Thomas, 1743-1826—Fiction 2. Franklin, Benjamin, 1706-1790—Fiction

ISBN 0-531-30075-7; 0-531-33075-3 (lib bdg)

LC 97-27596

To heal the hurt pride of Thomas Jefferson as Congress makes changes to his Declaration of Independence, Benjamin Franklin tells his friend the story of a hatmaker and his sign

"Based on an anecdote in *The Papers of Thomas Jefferson*, the story has a folktale-like quality that lends itself to being read aloud. The illustrations give dimension to the characters and a sense of times past." Horn Book Guide

Imogene's last stand; written by Candice Fleming; illustrated by Nancy Carpenter. Schwartz & Wade Books 2009 unp il $16.99; lib bdg $19.99 *

Grades: K 1 2   E

1. United States—History—Fiction

ISBN 978-0-375-83607-7; 0-375-83607-1; 978-0-375-93607-4 (lib bdg); 0-375-93607-6 (lib bdg)

LC 2008-22458

Enamored of history, young Imogene Tripp tries to save her town's historical society from being demolished in order to build a shoelace factory.

"Fleming's sense of small-town space is impeccable; Carpenter's pen-and-ink art enjoyably scribbly; and the historical facts and quotes that bookend the story are just the thing to get new Imogenes fired up." Booklist

Muncha! Muncha! Muncha! illustrated by G. Brian Karas. Atheneum Bks. for Young Readers 2002 unp il $16; lib bdg $18.63 *

Grades: PreK K 1 2   E

1. Rabbits—Fiction 2. Gardening—Fiction

ISBN 0-689-83152-8; 0-689-93652-X (lib bdg)

LC 99-24882

"An Anne Schwartz book"

After planting the garden he has dreamed of for years, Mr. McGreely tries to find a way to keep some persistent bunnies from eating all his vegetables

"Fleming's text is lilting and deftly paced, with sound effects . . . strategically and enjoyably employed. . . . Karas' mixed-media (gouache, acrylic, and pencil) illustrations offer a cornucopia of plot-enriching details." Bull Cent Child Books

Another title about Mr. Greely and the bunnies is:

Tippy-tippy-tippy-hide! (2007)

Seven hungry babies; illustrated by Eugene Yelchin. Atheneum Books for Young Readers 2010 unp il $16.99

Grades: PreK K 1   E

1. Stories in rhyme 2. Birds—Fiction

ISBN 978-1-4169-5402-6; 1-4169-5402-3

LC 2008-53481

"Ginee Seo books"

A mother bird frantically tries to keep her seven baby birds fed.

"Fleming's playful text features endearments that will tickle listeners . . . and a rhythm that sweeps the story along. The fresh gouache illustrations are awash in blues and white with fire-bright red and yellow birds and feature expressive faces on the avian stars." SLJ

Fleming, Candace—*Continued*

Sunny Boy! the life and times of a tortoise; pictures by Anne Wilsdorf. Farrar, Straus and Giroux 2005 unp il $16

Grades: PreK K 1 2   E

1. Turtles—Fiction

ISBN 0-374-37297-7   LC 2004-40451

"Melanie Kroupa books"

In this fictionalized account, Sunny Boy, a 100-year-old tortoise, describes various events in his long life including the dangerous barrel ride over Niagara Falls that he takes with his daredevil owner on July 5, 1930

"This saga makes for wildly entertaining reading. . . . The comical cartoon narrative . . . enhances the textual flow of the story. Not to be missed is the author's fascinating historical note." SLJ

This is the baby; pictures by Maggie Smith. Farrar, Straus and Giroux 2004 unp il $16.50 *

Grades: PreK K 1   E

1. Infants—Fiction 2. Clothing and dress—Fiction 3. Stories in rhyme

ISBN 0-374-37486-4   LC 2002-70941

"Melanie Kroupa books"

A cumulative rhyme enumerating all the items of clothing that go on the baby who hates to be dressed, from the diaper often a mess to the jacket woolen and plaid.

"Smith's naive and rosy-cheeked characters, cozy textures, and crayon-box colors are a perfect accompaniment to Fleming's well-constructed, cumulative, 'House That Jack-Built' patterned story that positively insists on reader interaction." SLJ

Fleming, Denise, 1950-

Alphabet under construction. Holt & Co. 2002 unp il $16.95 *

Grades: PreK K 1 2   E

1. Mice—Fiction 2. Alphabet

ISBN 0-8050-6848-1   LC 2001-5210

Companion volume to Lunch

A mouse works his way through the alphabet as he folds the "F," measures the "M," and rolls the "R"

"Fleming has poured colored cotton fiber through hand-cut stencils to make her illustrations, which are thus bold in outline and shape and vivid with an almost incandescent coloring. Although this has the simplicity of many alphabet books, it also has momentum . . . and ingenuity in its execution." Booklist

Barnyard banter. Holt & Co. 1994 unp il $17.95; pa $7.95; bd bk $7.95 *

Grades: PreK K 1 2   E

1. Animals—Fiction 2. Stories in rhyme

ISBN 0-8050-1957-X; 0-8050-5581-9 (pa); 0-8050-6594-6 (bd bk)   LC 93-11032

All the farm animals are where they should be, clucking and mucking, mewing and cooing, except for the missing goose

"Strong rhythm and rhyme, plus fun onomatopoetic animal sounds, demand reading aloud. But even more delightful than the engaging text are Fleming's spectacular illustrations. . . . They create realistically textured, bold, bright settings for the whimsical critters to romp through." SLJ

Beetle bop. Harcourt 2007 unp il $16 *

Grades: PreK K   E

1. Beetles—Fiction 2. Stories in rhyme

ISBN 978-0-15-205936-1   LC 2006-09756

Illustrations and rhyming text reveal the great variety of beetles and their swirling, humming, crashing activities.

"Fleming creates a vibrant exciting portrait of often-overlooked creatures. Here she uses expertly crafted fiber collage to celebrate beetles, and both words and pictures vibrate with the relentless energy of the subject." Booklist

Buster. Holt & Co. 2003 unp il $16.95; pa $6.95

Grades: PreK K 1 2   E

1. Dogs—Fiction 2. Cats—Fiction

ISBN 0-8050-6279-3; 0-8050-8757-5 (pa)

     LC 2002-10857

Buster the dog thinks his perfect life is spoiled when Betty the cat comes to live with him, until he learns not to be afraid of cats

"Fleming's trademark handmade-paper artwork is awash with vibrant colors and dazzling details." SLJ

Another title about Buster is:

Buster goes to Cowboy Camp (2008)

Count! Holt & Co. 1992 unp il $17.95; pa $7.95 *

Grades: PreK K 1 2   E

1. Counting 2. Animals

ISBN 0-8050-1595-7; 0-8050-4252-0 (pa)

     LC 91-25686

The antics of lively and colorful animals present the numbers one to ten, twenty, thirty, forty, and fifty

"A fresh, upbeat concept book. Lizards, giraffes, toucans, butterflies are available for counting—if only they'll hold still long enough! Fuchsias and oranges, teals and purples, roll over the pages blending into each other in Fleming's beautiful couched paper with hand cut-stencil illustrations. Her explosions of color and motion are captivating and energizing." SLJ

The cow who clucked. Henry Holt 2006 unp il $16.95 *

Grades: PreK K 1 2   E

1. Cattle—Fiction 2. Animals—Fiction

ISBN 978-0-8050-7265-5; 0-8050-7265-9

     LC 2005-22676

When a cow loses her moo, she searches to see if another animal in the barn has it

"The gentle inside jokes, the animal sounds, and the repetitive phrase constitute only a fraction of this book's appeal. Fleming is, after all, a thrilling illustrator whose pulp-painting technique brings subtlety and texture to densely colored art. . . . The layers of subtle humor and visual splendor are truly impressive." SLJ

The everything book. Holt & Co. 2000 64p il $18.95 *

Grades: PreK K   E

ISBN 0-8050-6292-0   LC 99-53626

A collection of simple works which introduce colors, shapes, numbers, animals, food, and nursery rhymes

"The book includes everything needed to make it an

Fleming, Denise, 1950-—_Continued_

anthology of preschool interests and concerns. . . . The very attractive illustrations, done in Fleming's characteristic bold and energetic style, were produced by pouring cotton pulp through hand-cut stencils, the result being simple forms that are attractively textured, with edges that are just fuzzy enough to look soft and friendly." SLJ

The first day of winter. Henry Holt and Co. 2005 unp il $16.95 *

Grades: PreK K 1   E
   1. Snow—Fiction 2. Winter—Fiction
   ISBN 0-8050-7384-1   LC 2004-22181

A snowman is built and is given special gifts to put on by his best friend each day for ten days with cumulative items of gifts

"Fleming captures the tranquility and light of snowy days with her unique artistic style. Her paper-pulp and stencil illustrations depict a winter wonderland in which vibrant striped scarves, blue mittens, and red hats provide the color in a white, uncluttered landscape. . . . Quietly told and thoughtfully illustrated." SLJ

In the small, small pond. Holt & Co. 1993 unp il $17.95; pa $7.95 *

Grades: PreK K 1   E
   1. Pond ecology—Fiction 2. Stories in rhyme
   ISBN 0-8050-2264-3; 0-8050-5983-0 (pa)
               LC 92-25770

A Caldecott Medal honor book, 1994

Illustrations and rhyming text describe the activities of animals living in and near a small pond as spring progresses to autumn

"The brilliant, primitive illustrations were made by pouring colored cotton pulp through hand-cut stencils. Against the eye-catching colors, the four-word rhymes in bold black print dance, each double-page spread picturing and describing a different creature. Text, pictures, layout, and design are all beautifully done." SLJ

In the tall, tall grass. Holt & Co. 1991 unp il $17.95; pa $7.99 *

Grades: PreK K 1   E
   1. Animals—Fiction 2. Stories in rhyme
   ISBN 0-8050-1635-X; 0-8050-3941-4 (pa)
               LC 90-26444

Rhymed text (crunch, munch, caterpillars lunch) presents a toddler's view of creatures found in the grass from lunchtime till nightfall, such as bees, ants, and moles

"Boldly colored in grassy greens, sunny yellows, and evening blues, the impressionistic illustrations make this a real treat for eyes as well as ears." Booklist

Lunch. Holt & Co. 1993 unp il $17.99; pa $7.99; bd bk $7.95 *

Grades: PreK K 1   E
   1. Mice—Fiction 2. Color
   ISBN   0-8050-1636-8;   0-8050-4646-1   (pa);
   0-8050-5696-3 (bd bk)   LC 92-178

"A very hungry mouse nibbles and crunches his way through the various components of a vegetarian repast, while the text introduces readers to the individual foods and their respective colors." Publ Wkly

"Fleming continues to work in the medium of handmade paper built from layers of colored pulp that has

been forced through a stencil. A huge typeface and the judicious use of large blocks of bold, solid color give this book a fresh look. Delectable fun, and, with its simple yet engaging plot, sure to be requested over and over by the youngest readers." Horn Book

Mama cat has three kittens. Holt & Co. 1998 unp il $17.95; pa $7.95 *

Grades: PreK K 1   E
   1. Cats—Fiction
   ISBN 0-8050-5745-5; 0-8050-7162-8 (pa)
               LC 98-12249

While two kittens copy everything their mother does, their brother naps

"Fleming's kittens, created by pouring colored cotton pulp through hand-cut stencils, are large and bold and set against colorful backdrops. An excellent choice for reading aloud to groups." SLJ

Pumpkin eye. Holt & Co. 2001 unp il $16.99; pa $7.95 *

Grades: PreK K 1   E
   1. Halloween—Fiction 2. Stories in rhyme
   ISBN 0-8050-6681-0; 0-8050-7635-2 (pa)
               LC 00-44850

Simple rhymes describe the sights, sounds, and smells of Halloween

"Fleming's homemade paper landscapes set off their midnight-blue—well, probably eight-o'clock blue—backdrops with glowing orange and white accents as well as with the rainbow of colors represented in the trick-or-treaters' costumes. . . . This will be just the shivery ticket for kids looking to move from Halloween giggles to genuine spookiness." Bull Cent Child Books

Sleepy, oh so sleepy. Henry Holt 2010 unp il $16.99 *

Grades: PreK   E
   1.   Bedtime—Fiction   2.   Animals—Fiction
   3. Mother-child relationship—Fiction
   ISBN 978-0-8050-8126-8; 0-8050-8126-7
               LC 2009006151

Depicts a number of animal babies sleeping as a mother puts her own baby to bed.

"Formed using Fleming's signature medium of 'pulp painting,' which simultaneously creates the image and the paper that bears it, and accented with pastel pencil, the large-scale illustrations are bold in form and rich in color. With mesmerizing words rolling along, this large-format book does its job so well that it's hard to repress a contented yawn when the story winds down to its quiet ending." Booklist

Time to sleep. Holt & Co. 1997 unp il $17.95; pa $7.95 *

Grades: PreK K 1   E
   1.   Winter—Fiction   2.   Animals—Fiction
   3. Hibernation—Fiction
   ISBN 0-8050-3762-4; 0-8050-6767-1 (pa)
               LC 96-37553

When Bear notices that winter is nearly here he hurries to tell Snail, after which each animal tells another until finally the already sleeping Bear is awakened in his den with the news

"Fleming's simple text is ripe with astute observations

Fleming, Denise, 1950-—*Continued*

of the natural world and animal behavior. . . . Fleming's 'pulp painting' style results in lushly textured handmade paper compositions saturated with earthy browns, reds and golds." Publ Wkly

Fletcher, Ralph, 1953-

The Sandman; [by] Ralph Fletcher; illustrated by Richard Cowdrey. Henry Holt and Company 2008 unp il $16.95

Grades: PreK K 1 2   E

1. Bedtime—Fiction 2. Sleep—Fiction 3. Dragons—Fiction

ISBN 978-0-8050-7726-1; 0-8050-7726-X

LC 2007002831

A tiny little man discovers that sand made from a dragon's scale will send him to dreamland, and begins carrying this magical sand to children each night to give them the gift of sleep

"Fletcher's smoothly written story flows in a thoroughly plausible way and is beautifully served by Cowdrey's vibrant acrylic paintings." SLJ

Fletcher, Susan, 1951-

Dadblamed Union Army cow; [by] Susan Fletcher; illustrated by Kimberly Bulcken Root. Candlewick Press 2007 unp il $16.99

Grades: 2 3 4 5   E

1. United States—History—1861-1865, Civil War—Fiction 2. Cattle—Fiction

ISBN 978-0-7636-2263-3; 0-7636-2263-X

LC 2006051833

During the Civil War, a devoted cow follows her owner when he joins the Union Army and, despite all his efforts to send her home, stays with him and his regiment until the end of the war. Based on a true story

"Root's pencil and watercolor drawings vividly render the Civil War landscape. . . . A terrific read-aloud, and a marvelous approach to history." Publ Wkly

Floca, Brian

The racecar alphabet. Atheneum Bks. for Young Readers 2003 unp il $15.95

Grades: PreK K 1 2   E

1. Automobile racing—Fiction 2. Alphabet

ISBN 0-689-85091-3   LC 2002-2198

"A Richard Jackson book"

Automobile races highlight the letters of the alphabet

"The alphabetical text often uses alliterative phrases. . . . Although a single race appears to proceed throughout the book, the cars, drivers, tracks, and spectators change dramatically from the book's opening in 1901 . . . to the conclusion in 2001. . . . Large in scale, the ink-and-watercolor artwork is bold enough to share with a story hour or classroom group, yet young racing fans will find the details absorbing. Floca's introductory note on the history of racing may interest them as well." Booklist

Flournoy, Valerie, 1952-

The patchwork quilt; pictures by Jerry Pinkney. Dial Bks. for Young Readers 1985 unp il $16.99

Grades: K 1 2 3   E

1. Quilts—Fiction 2. Family life—Fiction 3. African Americans—Fiction

ISBN 0-8037-0097-0   LC 84-1711

Coretta Scott King Award for illustration

Using scraps cut from the family's old clothing, Tanya helps her grandmother and mother make a beautiful quilt that tells the story of her Afro-American family's life

"Plentiful full-page and double-page paintings in pencil, graphite and watercolor are vivid yet delicately detailed. . . . Giving a sense of dramatization to the text, . . . the illustrations provide just the right style and mood for the story." SLJ

Foley, Greg, 1969-

Thank you Bear; by Greg Foley. Viking 2007 unp il $15.99

Grades: PreK K   E

1. Bears—Fiction 2. Mice—Fiction 3. Gifts—Fiction 4. Boxes—Fiction

ISBN 978-0-670-06165-5   LC 2006016881

Despite the criticism of others, a bear finds the perfect gift for his mouse friend

"Bear's journey from euphoria to doubt to euphoria again is gently rendered. . . . Pastels provide the backdrop for the text, while Bear and his detractors stand in contrast on a white page, carrying the story with their expressions and body language." SLJ

Other titles about Bear are:

Don't worry Bear (2008)

Good luck Bear (2009)

Willoughby & the lion. Bowen Press 2009 unp il $17.99; lib bdg $18.89 *

Grades: PreK K 1 2   E

1. Friendship—Fiction 2. Wishes—Fiction 3. Magic—Fiction 4. Lions—Fiction

ISBN   978-0-06-154750-8;   0-06-154750-6; 978-0-06-154751-5 (lib bdg); 0-06-154751-4 (lib bdg)

LC 2008000430

When Willoughby moves to a new house far away from his friends, he meets an enchanted lion who shows him what is truly important in life

Foley "scores points for unique visual presentation in this sumptuously produced, two-color book, instantly distinguished by its heavily embossed jacket. . . . With every wish, the ratio of gold to gray increases and Foley's compositions, mingling line drawings with digitally manipulated b&w photos, become more complex. . . . The elegant combination of the two basic colors boosts the visual impact exponentially." Publ Wkly

Another title about Willoughby is:

Willoughby & the moon (2010)

Ford, Bernette

First snow; illustrated by Sebastien Braun. Holiday House 2005 unp il $16.95 *

Grades: PreK K 1 2   E

1. Rabbits—Fiction 2. Snow—Fiction 3. Night—Fiction

ISBN 0-8234-1937-1   LC 2004-55257

Ford, Bernette—*Continued*

A family of young rabbits goes into a meadow at night to explore and play in winter's first snow.

"Ford's text has a poetic rhythm that emphasizes the senses as the rabbits explore their wintry world. . . . Braun's illustrations . . . are particularly engaging and complement the story wonderfully." SLJ

No more blanket for Lambkin. Boxer Books; distributed by Sterling Pub. 2009 unp il $12.95

Grades: PreK   E

1. Sheep—Fiction 2. Blankets—Fiction 3. Ducks—Fiction 4. Friendship—Fiction

ISBN 978-1-906250-28-7; 1-906250-28-6

"One day Lambkin's friend Ducky comes to visit and decides that they should play laundry day, immediately zeroing in on her friend's much-loved and rather-soiled blanket. Lambkin is none too happy, but she decides it is worth it to play with Ducky. Once the blanket is washed, it's cleaner, but it's also smaller and has some holes. Lambkin is upset, but Ducky surprises her by turning the blanket into a little toy lamb. This is a good story to read to young children when it is nearing the time to give up their blankets. . . . The overall feel is one of gentleness, from the soft style of illustrations to the tone of the dialogue between the two friends." SLJ

No more bottles for Bunny! [by] Bernette Ford and [illustrations by] Sam Williams. Sterling Pub. 2007 unp il $12.95

Grades: PreK   E

1. Rabbits—Fiction 2. Ducks—Fiction 3. Pigs—Fiction 4. Bottle feeding—Fiction 5. Growth—Fiction

ISBN 978-1-905417-34-6; 1-905417-34-9

LC 2007006856

Bunny gives up his bottle so he can have tea and cookies just like the big kids

"This tough topic is handled subtly but the point is made. Complementing this endearing tale are expressive, bright watercolor illustrations with black outlines that make them jump out from the page." SLJ

No more diapers for Ducky! [by] Bernette Ford and [illustrations by] Sam Williams. Sterling Pub. 2006 unp il $12.95

Grades: PreK   E

1. Ducks—Fiction 2. Toilet training—Fiction

ISBN 1-905417-08-X

When Piggy can't come out to play because he is using the potty, Ducky decides it's time for him to learn to use the potty too.

"The interaction between these toddlers and their implicit support of one another is charming. The dynamic characters, done in thick charcoal outlines and watercolor, are set against a white background." SLJ

Ford, Christine, 1953-

Ocean's child; by Chistine Ford and Trish Holland; illustrated by David Diaz. Golden Books 2009 unp il $15.99; lib bdg $18.99

Grades: PreK K 1 2   E

1. Inuit—Fiction 2. Marine animals—Fiction 3. Bedtime—Fiction

ISBN   978-0-375-84752-3;   0-375-84752-9; 978-0-375-95752-9 (lib bdg); 0-375-95752-9 (lib bdg)

"As an Inuit mother paddles her baby home at dusk, she identifies baby ocean animals as they prepare for night. . . . The language is warm and assuring bedtime fare with two free-verse lines introducing each animal, followed by a refrain. . . . Close inspection of mother and child's parkas reveal delicate indigenous designs. . . . The soothing flow of rhythmic language and elegant images creates a serenity just right for bedtimes." Booklist

Foreman, Jack 1986-

Say hello; [by] Jack & Michael Foreman. Candlewick Press 2008 unp il $15.99

Grades: PreK K 1 2   E

1. Stories in rhyme 2. Dogs—Fiction 3. Friendship—Fiction

ISBN 978-0-7636-3657-9; 0-7636-3657-6

"A lone dog comes upon a group of kids playing ball and with leaping ease, joins the game. They're all having so much fun, they don't see a sad little boy standing off by himself." Publisher's note

"A simple story about loneliness and the power of friendliness. Spare charcoal, pastel, and colored pencil drawings illustrate [this book]." SLJ

Foreman, Mark

Grandpa Jack's tattoo tales; [by] Mark Foreman. Farrar, Straus & Giroux 2007 unp il $16

Grades: PreK K 1 2   E

1. Tattooing—Fiction 2. Storytelling—Fiction 3. Grandfathers—Fiction 4. Sea stories

ISBN 978-0-374-32768-2; 0-374-32768-8

LC 2006040853

Chloe loves to spend time at her grandparents' restaurant, where she gets to hear Grandpa Jack's stories about the many tattoos that commemorate events in his life at sea

The illustrations are "done in bright crisp watercolors . . . and the pictures are filled with minute details. . . . Children will relish this amusing tall tale and delight in its visual elements." SLJ

Foreman, Michael, 1938-

The littlest dinosaur's big adventure; written and illustrated by Michael Foreman. Walker & Co. 2009 unp il $16.99

Grades: PreK K 1 2   E

1. Dinosaurs—Fiction 2. Size—Fiction

ISBN 978-0-8027-9545-8; 0-8027-9545-5

LC 2008-40297

The littlest dinosaur discovers the advantages of being small as he frolics among the lily pads with his new frog friends, and then bravely finds his way home after get-

Foreman, Michael, 1938-—*Continued*

ting lost in the woods

"Foreman's soft and gentle cartoon-style illustrations are tailored for young eyes and hearts. Sharing the book aloud will invite discussion as Foreman leaves readers a well-marked trail for inference and reflection, while the twists and turns of the plot will keep even the youngest audiences riveted." SLJ

Another title about the littlest dinosaur is:

The littlest dinosaur (2008)

Mia's story; a sketchbook of hopes and dreams. Candlewick Press 2006 unp il $15.99

Grades: 1 2 3   E

1. Chile—Fiction 2. Flowers—Fiction 3. Dogs—Fiction

ISBN 0-7636-3063-2   LC 2005-53183

"Mia's father harvests scrap metal from the nearby dump and sells it in the city. When Mia's dog Poco disappears one winter day, she rides a horse into the mountains to look for him, gathers some flowering plants she has never seen before, and brings them back to her village, where they change the landscape and her fortunes for the better. . . . This unusual book offers an engaging story, graceful illustrations, and a rare glimpse of a child's life in contemporary Chile." Booklist

Forler, Nan

Bird child. Tundra Books 2009 unp il $19.95

Grades: K 1 2 3   E

1. Bullies—Fiction 2. Friendship—Fiction

ISBN 978-0-88776-894-1; 0-88776-894-6

"Silently, Eliza observes new girl Lainey's ostracism due to her unusual appearance, watching as the bullying increases, refraining from intervention when Lainey is brutally pushed in the snow. The authentic voice portrays bullying's devastating impact. . . . Eliza's mother gently guides her daughter to a moral decision. The symbolism of flight is woven through the narrative. Thisdale's vibrant mixed-media art plays with dominance and size in its compositions; drawings, paintings and digital images add layers of context. . . . This is a sensitive account through an empowered youngster's eyes." Kirkus

Formento, Alison

This tree counts! illustrated by Sarah Snow. Albert Whitman 2010 unp il $16.99

Grades: PreK K 1 2   E

1. Trees—Fiction 2. Counting 3. Ecology—Fiction

ISBN 978-0-8075-7890-2; 0-8075-7890-8

As Mr. Tate's class prepares to plant saplings, they hear the giant oak tree in their schoolyard tell about all the animal life it supports.

"Snow's collage illustrations add texture and natural beauty to the story. . . . The picture of the industrious kids working together in the grassy field under a bright blue sky epitomizes the story's theme of cooperation and friendship." SLJ

Forward, Toby, 1950-

What did you do today? the first day of school; illustrated by Carol Thompson. Clarion Books 2004 29p il $15

Grades: PreK K 1   E

1. School stories 2. Mother-child relationship—Fiction

ISBN 0-618-49586-X   LC 2004-2467

A child describes the events of the first day of school, from making sandwiches for lunch to holding a parent's hand on the walk home

"The parallels between a child's day at school and his mother's day at work are shown with insight and love in this cleverly designed book. . . . Thompson varies her pen-and-watercolor illustrations in surprising and eye-catching ways." Booklist

Fox, F. G. (Frank G.)

Jean Laffite and the big ol' whale; pictures by Scott Cook. Farrar, Straus & Giroux 2003 unp il $16

Grades: K 1 2 3   E

1. Whales—Fiction 2. Mississippi River—Fiction 3. Tall tales

ISBN 0-374-33669-5   LC 99-43733

When a huge white whale gets stuck between the banks of the Mississippi River causing the water to stop flowing, Jean Laffite finds a way to get the river moving again

"This rollicking good yarn is brought to life with Cook's warm, glowing oil paintings full of action and humor." SLJ

Fox, Lee, 1958-

Ella Kazoo will not brush her hair; illustrated by Jennifer Plecas. Walker & Co. 2010 unp il $15.99; lib bdg $16.89

Grades: PreK K 1   E

1. Stories in rhyme 2. Hair—Fiction

ISBN   978-0-8027-8836-8;   0-8027-8836-X; 978-0-8027-8755-2 (lib bdg); 0-8027-8755-X (lib bdg)
                                   LC 2009-13329

First published 2007 in Australia

A little girl refuses to brush her hair until it becomes so unruly that it takes over everything.

"Plecas's creative illustrations bring out quirky Ella and her story of stubbornness. The use of rhyme and its overall energy make this book a terrific read-aloud. . . . This book will definitely find fans in libraries serving the young and the young at heart." Libr Media Connect

Fox, Mem, 1946-

The goblin and the empty chair; [illustrated by] Leo & Diane Dillon. Beach Lane Books 2009 unp il $17.99

Grades: K 1 2 3   E

1. Monsters—Fiction

ISBN 978-1-4169-8585-3; 1-4169-8585-9
                                   LC 2008041862

A goblin who for many years has been hiding himself so that he does not frighten anyone finally finds a family

"The all-star team of Fox and the Dillons brings poise and sensitivity to this folksy tale of the pitfalls of self-

Fox, Mem, 1946-—*Continued*

perception. . . . The ink-and-watercolors are rigidly confined to uniform frames, but even these frames are ornately festooned with not-so-monstrous faces, further developing the story's theme." Booklist

Hattie and the fox; illustrated by Patricia Mullins. Bradbury Press 1987 c1986 unp il $16.95; pa $6.99 *
Grades: PreK K 1 2   E
  1. Chickens—Fiction 2. Foxes—Fiction
  ISBN 0-02-735470-9; 0-689-71611-7 (pa)
                                                  LC 86-18849
First published 1986 in Australia
"Hattie is a fine, portly, and observant hen, and she knows there is something wrong when she spies a sharp foxy nose in the bushes. Her alarmist and ever escalating announcements, however, bring nothing but bored and languid replies." Horn Book
"Bright, whimsical tissue collage and crayon illustrations add zest to this simple cumulative tale, and reveal more action than is expressed by the text alone." SLJ

Hello baby! illustrated by Steve Jenkins. Beach Lane Books 2009 unp il $15.99 *
Grades: PreK K 1   E
  1. Infants—Fiction 2. Animals—Fiction 3. Stories in rhyme
  ISBN 978-1-4169-8513-6; 1-4169-8513-1
                                                  LC 2008-34421
A baby encounters a variety of young animals, including a clever monkey, a hairy warthog, and a dusty lion cub, before discovering the most precious creature of all.
This "has all the marks of a lap-sit classic. . . . While Fox is cooing as only she can, Jenkins . . . works his usual magic with cut paper. In many of his large-scale closeups . . . his subjects' big, expressive eyes seem locked in a gaze with the reader." Publ Wkly

Hunwick's egg; illustrated by Pamela Lofts. Harcourt 2005 unp il $16
Grades: PreK K 1 2   E
  1. Bandicoots—Fiction 2. Australia—Fiction
  ISBN 0-15-216318-2   LC 2003-16385
When a wild storm sends a beautiful egg to Hunwick the bandicoot's burrow, he decides to give it a home and become its friend.
"This slightly offbeat story . . . is accompanied by glowing watercolor pencil illustrations in orange, pink, and violet tones that showcase the flora and fauna of the Australian landscape, adding an interesting element to this charming title." SLJ

Koala Lou; illustrated by Pamela Lofts. Harcourt Brace Jovanovich 1989 c1988 unp il $16.95; pa $6.99 *
Grades: PreK K 1 2   E
  1. Koalas—Fiction
  ISBN 0-15-200502-1; 0-15-200076-3 (pa)
                                                  LC 88-26810
"Gulliver books"
First published 1988 in Australia
This story is "set in the Australian bush. Koala Lou feels bereft when her mother becomes preoccupied with a growing brood of younger koala children. In her desire to recapture her mother's attention and affection, the enterprising Koala Lou decides to become a contestant in the Bush Olympics." Horn Book
"A reassuring story for the child who feels neglected when siblings arrive." Child Book Rev Serv

Night noises; written by Mem Fox; illustrated by Terry Denton. Harcourt Brace Jovanovich 1989 unp il $16; pa $6
Grades: PreK K 1 2   E
  1. Night—Fiction 2. Sleep—Fiction
  ISBN 0-15-200543-9; 0-15-257421-2 (pa)
                                                  LC 89-2162
"Gulliver books"
Old Lily Laceby dozes by the fire with her faithful dog Butch Aggie at her feet as strange night noises herald a surprising awakening
"With an almost joltingly bright palette . . . Denton has divided up many of the double-page spreads into three scenes: the main one depicting Lily Laceby and Butch Aggie in various stages of alertness, another showing the chronology of Lily's life, and the third cleverly revealing clues to the mysterious activity outdoors. The text, in Mem Fox's Houdini-like hands, reads beautifully—the language, pacing, tension, and sparks of excitement absolutely at one with the artwork." Horn Book

A particular cow; [by] Mem Fox; illustrated by Terry Denton. Harcourt 2006 unp il $16
Grades: PreK K 1 2   E
  1. Cattle—Fiction
  ISBN 0-15-200250-2   LC 2004030060
"When a cow decides to take her usual Saturday constitutional, she accidentally steps through a clothesline and ends up with a pair of bloomers covering her head. Unable to see and running off in a panic, the poor bovine wreaks havoc. . . . The story is told with a dry wit and an economy of words, and the illustrations interpret the action with panache." SLJ

Sleepy bears; illustrated by Kerry Argent. Harcourt Brace & Co. 1999 unp il $16; pa $6 *
Grades: PreK K 1 2   E
  1. Bears—Fiction 2. Bedtime—Fiction 3. Stories in rhyme
  ISBN 0-15-202016-0; 0-15-216542-8 (pa)
                                                  LC 98-42640
"Mother Bear tucks in her six cubs, sending them off on dreamy adventures. Baxter dreams of pirates, Bella of the circus, Winifred of the jungle, Tosca of kingdoms, Ali of divine foods, and Baby Bear of moonbeams. . . . The rhymes are well written, and the charming pictures, done in gouache, watercolor, and colored pencil, are full of funny details." SLJ

Sophie; illustrated by Aminah Brenda Lynn Robinson. Harcourt Brace & Co. 1994 c1989 unp il hardcover o.p. pa $7
Grades: PreK K 1 2   E
  1. Grandfathers—Fiction 2. African Americans—Fiction
  ISBN 0-15-277160-3; 0-15-201598-1 (pa)
                                                  LC 94-1976
First published 1989 in Australia

Fox, Mem, 1946——*Continued*

"In this cyclical tale, Grandpa welcomes infant Sophie into the world; much later, Sophie is saddened when 'there was no Grandpa.' The birth of Sophie's own child completes the circle." Publ Wkly

"The artwork is rich, expressionist, heavily lined oil. . . . The oversized hands depicted in many drawings exemplify the handholding theme, and the sunny hues of earth and garden convey with warmth a loving and extended African-American family." Bull Cent Child Books

Ten little fingers and ten little toes; [illustrations by] Helen Oxenbury. Harcourt 2008 unp il $16 *
Grades: PreK K   E
1. Infants—Fiction 2. Stories in rhyme
ISBN 978-0-15-206057-2; 0-15-206057-X
LC 2007-10692

Rhyming text compares babies born in different places and in different circumstances, but they all share the commonality of ten little fingers and ten little toes.

"Given their perfect cadences, the rhymes feel as if they always existed in our collective consciousness and were simply waiting to be written down. . . . Oxenbury . . . once again makes multiculturalism feel utterly natural and chummy. As her global brood of toddlers grows . . . readers can savor each addition both as beguiling individualist and giggly, bouncy co-conspirator." Publ Wkly

Tough Boris; illustrated by Kathryn Brown. Harcourt Brace & Co. 1994 unp il $16; pa $6
Grades: PreK K 1 2   E
1. Pirates—Fiction 2. Parrots—Fiction
ISBN 0-15-289612-0; 0-15-201891-3 (pa)
LC 92-8015

Boris von der Borch is a tough pirate but he weeps when his parrot dies

"The text is deceptively simple, but the observant child will quickly fill in the details, aptly provided in the illustrations. The reassuring message, although understated, is clear and effective." Horn Book Guide

Where is the green sheep? [by] Mem Fox and [illustrated by] Judy Horacek. Harcourt 2004 unp il $15
Grades: PreK K 1 2   E
1. Sheep—Fiction 2. Stories in rhyme
ISBN 0-15-204907-X   LC 2003-4990

A story about many different sheep, and one that seems to be missing.

"Until the lost sheep turns up, children will have fun with the other sheep that make an appearance and perhaps, unbeknownst to them, also get lessons in colors and comparisons. . . . In this neat and satisfying wedding of text and art, the squat, square format uses woolwhite backgrounds to display much of the amusing pen-and-watercolor pictures." Booklist

Where the giant sleeps; [by] Mem Fox; pictures by Vladimir Radunsky. Harcourt 2007 unp il $16
Grades: PreK K 1 2   E
1. Bedtime—Fiction 2. Sleep—Fiction 3. Stories in rhyme
ISBN 978-0-15-205785-5   LC 2006020539

Illustrations and rhyming text portray the different residents of fairyland and where each one goes to sleep.

"The paintings and multifaceted structure of the book inventively translate the puckish text, conjuring misty visions of magical realms." Publ Wkly

Wombat divine; illustrated by Kerry Argent. Harcourt Brace & Co. 1996 unp il $17; pa $7
Grades: PreK K 1 2   E
1. Christmas—Fiction 2. Wombats—Fiction 3. Animals—Fiction
ISBN 0-15-201416-0; 0-15-202096-9 (pa)
LC 96-5480

Wombat auditions for the Nativity play, but has trouble finding the right part

"Fox spiffily combines a witty text with her wonderful art. Here the fun comes with seeing all sorts of Australian animals (emu, bilby, kangaroo) decked out in their Christmas-play garb." Booklist

Fox, Paula

Traces. Front Street 2008 unp il $16.95
Grades: K 1 2 3   E
1. Nature—Fiction
ISBN 978-1-932425-43-7; 1-932425-43-8
LC 2006-11739

Looks at the traces left behind by a turtle on the sand, a jet in the sky, and even a long-gone dinosaur in loose soil.

Fox "gives the book an energetic and distilled poetry. . . . The charming medallion sun, torn-paper clouds and watercolor ribbon of the horizon found on these spreads all feel like the naive and studious work of a dedicated seven-year-old. . . . The pictures are much fun and fit the story perfectly." Publ Wkly

Frame, Jeron Ashford

Yesterday I had the blues; illustrations by R. Gregory Christie. Tricycle Press 2003 unp il $14.95 *
Grades: K 1 2 3   E
1. Emotions—Fiction 2. African Americans—Fiction 3. Family life—Fiction
ISBN 1-58246-084-1   LC 2002-155295

A young African American boy ponders a variety of emotions and how different members of his family experience them, from his own blues to his father's grays and his grandmother's yellows

"Vibrant acrylic-and-gouache spreads give rhythm and meaning to this child's interpretation of everyday life, his neighborhood, and his family. The illustrations effectively express each individual's mood and beautifully capture the cultural and artistic aspects of the family's life, while the expressive text is engaging." SLJ

Franco, Betsy

Bird songs; a backwards counting book; [by] Betsy Franco; [illustrated by] Steve Jenkins. Margaret K. McElderry Books 2006 unp il $16.99
Grades: PreK K 1 2   E
1. Birdsongs—Fiction 2. Birds—Fiction 3. Day—Fiction 4. Counting
ISBN 0-689-87777-3; 978-0-689-87777-3
LC 2004-25056

Franco, Betsy—*Continued*

Throughout the day and into the night various birds sing their songs, beginning with the woodpecker who taps a pole ten times and counting down to the hummingbird who calls once.

"In his vivid, realistic-looking collages, Jenkins uses accurate textures and colors for each species, and creates the appearance of depth, light, and warmth. . . . The writing is lyrical and engaging, and quick 'feathery facts' about the creatures are appended." SLJ

Pond circle; illustrated by Stefano Vitale. Margaret K. McElderry Books 2009 unp il $16.99

Grades: PreK K 1 2 3   E

1. Food chains (Ecology)—Fiction 2. Pond ecology—Fiction 3. Ecology—Fiction 4. Animals—Fiction

ISBN 978-1-4169-4021-0; 1-4169-4021-9

LC 2008016268

In the pond by Anna's house, a food chain begins with algae which is eaten by a mayfly nymph which is eaten by a beetle which is eaten by a bullfrog.

"Vitale's rich, colorful oil-on-wood illustrations are as poetic as the text in their depiction of the natural world. . . . A clear, child-friendly look at ecology." SLJ

Frank, John

How to catch a fish; by John Frank; illustrated by Peter Sylvada. Roaring Brook Press 2007 unp il $17.95

Grades: K 1 2   E

1. Fishing—Fiction 2. Stories in rhyme

ISBN 978-1-59643-163-8; 1-59643-163-6

LC 2006032184

"A Neal Porter book"

Rhyming text and illustrations describe the ways fish are caught in various locations around the world

"The handsome, full-page oil paintings are rendered in an impressionistic style that evokes the atmospheres of watery, misty, aquatic environments. . . . Resonating poetic vignettes spawn a glinting, striking catch." Booklist

Franson, Scott E.

Un-brella. Roaring Brook Press 2007 unp il $15.95

Grades: PreK K   E

1. Weather—Fiction 2. Umbrellas and parasols—Fiction 3. Stories without words 4. Magic—Fiction

ISBN 978-1-59643-179-9; 1-59643-179-2

LC 2006047658

In this wordless book, a little girl uses her magic umbrella to give her the weather she wants, regardless of what the conditions really are outside.

"The crisp, clean pictures have bright colors, exceptional detail, fun patterns, sly repetition, and heaps of whimsy." SLJ

Fraser, Mary Ann

Pet shop lullaby. Boyds Mills Press 2009 unp il $16.95

Grades: PreK K   E

1. Bedtime—Fiction 2. Pets—Fiction 3. Animals—Fiction

ISBN 978-1-59078-618-5; 1-59078-618-1

LC 2009019661

When the pet store closes for the night, a hamster's activities keep the other animals awake as they try to think of some way to put him to sleep.

"Fraser's tale is brief and to the point, and the comical gouache illustrations infuse energy into the telling. Fun touches abound." SLJ

Frasier, Debra, 1953-

A birthday cake is no ordinary cake; written and illustrated by Debra Frasier. Harcourt 2006 unp il $16 *

Grades: PreK K 1 2   E

1. Year—Fiction 2. Birthdays—Fiction 3. Cake—Fiction

ISBN 978-0-15-205742-8; 0-15-205742-0

A lyrical recipe using the changes in the natural world to explain to a child the time that passes between one birthday and the next. Includes recipe for more traditional birthday cake.

"Pop-off-the-page, vibrant-colored cut-paper collage illustrations capture the fanciful and factual concepts." SLJ

On the day you were born. Harcourt Brace Jovanovich 1991 unp il $16 *

Grades: K 1 2 3 4   E

1. Earth 2. Childbirth

ISBN 0-15-302160-8   LC 90-36816

Also available with audio CD $18.95 (ISBN 0-15-205567-3)

This combination of text and paper-collage graphics depicts the earth's preparation for, and celebration of, the birth of a newborn baby

"The text reads like unrhymed poetry, and both parents and educators will find themselves wanting to share this book over and over with individuals and with groups. A three-page appendix that includes miniature versions of each spread elaborates on natural phenomena for older readers—migrating animals, spinning Earth, rising tide, falling rain, growing trees, and more." SLJ

Frazee, Marla, 1958-

A couple of boys have the best week ever; [by] Marla Frazee. Harcourt 2008 32p il $16 *

Grades: K 1 2 3   E

1. Vacations—Fiction 2. Friendship—Fiction 3. Grandparents—Fiction 4. Beaches—Fiction

ISBN 978-0-15-206020-6   LC 2006-25781

A Caldecott Medal honor book, 2009

"After Eamon enrolls in nature camp, he spends nights with his grandparents, Bill and Pam, at their beach cottage. Eamon's friend James joins the sleepover. . . . Humorous contradictions arise between the hand-lettered account . . . and voice-bubble exchanges between the boys. . . . Frazee's narrative resembles a tongue-in-cheek travel journal, with plenty of enticing pencil and gouache illustrations of the characters knocking about the shoreline." Publ Wkly

Roller coaster. Harcourt 2003 unp il lib bdg $16 *

Grades: PreK K 1 2   E

1. Roller coasters

ISBN 0-15-204554-6   LC 2002-7805

Frazee, Marla, 1958-—*Continued*
"Frazee does an extraordinary job of conveying motion by the placement of her images, her use of white space, bright colors, and swooshing speed lines. . . . What will keep children coming back for extra looks, however, is Frazee's clever, dramatic depiction of the 12 riders and their wildly and amusingly different reactions to the stomach-churning experience." Booklist

Santa Claus, the world's number one toy expert. Harcourt 2005 unp il $16 *
Grades: PreK K 1 2   E
1. Santa Claus—Fiction 2. Christmas—Fiction
ISBN 0-15-204970-3   LC 2004-5228
Santa Claus has his own ways of knowing more about children and toys than anyone else in the world.
"Frazee, a master at creating scenes and moods in her energetic drawings and spare text, fills these pages with details and vignettes that readers will want to explore repeatedly." SLJ

Walk on! a guide for babies of all ages. Harcourt, Inc. 2006 unp il $16 *
Grades: PreK K 1 2   E
1. Infants—Fiction 2. Walking—Fiction
ISBN 0-15-205573-8   LC 2004-29895
"In this how-to for little ones, a baby learns to walk for the first time. . . . The pencil-and-gouache art has the delightful feel of self-help pamphlets from an earlier era. . . . This is one of those rare books that speaks to crawling and walking babies who like to look at pictures of creatures like themselves, preschoolers who enjoy stories about what they were like when they were little, and older children and adults who will appreciate the wry humor." SLJ

Frazier, Craig, 1955-
Hank finds inspiration; [by] Craig Frazier. Roaring Brook Press 2008 unp il $16.95 *
Grades: K 1 2   E
1. Snakes—Fiction
ISBN 978-1-59643-358-8; 1-59643-358-2
LC 2007047919
"A Neal Porter book"
Hank the snake and his human friend, Stanley, each go to the city in search of inspiration, but Hank's journey is a failure until he returns home
"Frazier's crisp graphics draw the eye to varied perspectives with bold splashes of color and sharply defined silhouettes and shadings. An 'inspired' addition for all libraries." SLJ

Freedman, Claire
Gooseberry Goose; illustrated by Vanessa Cabban. Tiger Tales 2003 unp il $15.95
Grades: PreK K 1 2   E
1. Geese—Fiction 2. Winter—Fiction 3. Animals—Fiction
ISBN 1-58925-030-3   LC 2003-12960
As Gooseberry Goose practices flying on a beautiful fall morning, his friends are preparing for winter, causing Gooseberry to wonder if there is something else he should be doing

"The text is brought to life through the illustrations, which are loose and lovely. Vibrant red and gold leaves enliven the pages. Gooseberry is a bundle of expression. . . . Readers will be captivated by this irrepressible gosling's infectious charm." SLJ

Freeman, Don, 1908-1978
Corduroy. 40th anniversary edition. Viking Press 2008 c1968 32p il $19.99 *
Grades: PreK K 1   E
1. Teddy bears—Fiction
ISBN 978-0-670-06336-9; 0-670-06336-3
A reissue of the title first published 1968
A toy bear in a department store wants a number of things, but when a little girl finally buys him he finds what he has always wanted most of all. This edition includes copies of letters and the original manuscript.
"The art and story are direct and just right for the very young who like bears and escalators." Book World
Another title about Corduroy is:
A pocket for Corduroy (1978)

Earl the squirrel. Viking 2005 unp il $15.99
Grades: PreK K 1   E
1. Squirrels—Fiction
ISBN 0-670-06019-4   LC 2005-03929
Earl the squirrel learns to gather acorns on his own.
"The pictures are full of energy and detail, and Earl is both cheeky and endearing. . . . The story is gentle, innocent, and funny." SLJ

Quiet! there's a canary in the library; by Don Freeman. Viking Children's Books 2007 unp il $15.99
Grades: PreK K 1   E
1. Libraries—Fiction 2. Animals—Fiction
ISBN 978-0-670-06230-0; 0-670-06230-8
LC 2006-37904
A reissue of the title first published 1969 by Golden Gate
Cary imagines a special day at the library when she invites only animals and birds to browse.
"Freeman contrasts more detailed drawings of the actual library with childlike crayoned depictions of Cary's daydreamed adventures." Horn Book Guide

Freeman, Martha, 1956-
Mrs. Wow never wanted a cow; by Martha Freeman; illustrated by Steven Salerno. Random House 2006 unp il $8.99; lib bdg $11.99
Grades: K 1 2   E
1. Cattle—Fiction 2. Dogs—Fiction 3. Cats—Fiction
ISBN 0-375-83418-4; 0-375-93418-9 (lib bdg)
LC 2005006000
"Beginner books"
When Mrs. Wow takes in a stray cow, her lazy dog and cat hope to train the new household member to catch mice and intimidate the mailman
"The mostly one-syllable words with regular phonetic patterns are spare and natural, and Salerno's brightly colored cartoon illustrations amplify the text's humor." SLJ

French, Jackie, 1950-

Diary of a wombat; illustrated by Bruce Whatley. Clarion Bks. 2003 c2002 unp il $14 *
Grades: PreK K 1 2   E
   1. Wombats—Fiction
   ISBN 0-618-38136-8   LC 2003-829
   First published 2002 in Australia
In his diary, a wombat describes his life of eating, sleeping, and getting to know some new human neighbors
The story is presented in "simple sentences and hilarious yet realistic acrylic illustrations. . . . Whatley gives a sublime balance of the adorable charm of the creature, along with its drawbacks as an acquaintance." SLJ

Pete the sheep-sheep; illustrated by Bruce Whatley. Clarion Books 2005 c2004 32p il $14
Grades: PreK K 1 2   E
   1. Sheep—Fiction 2. Dogs—Fiction
   ISBN 0-618-56862-X   LC 2004-30935
   First published 2004 in Australia with title: Pete the sheep
The sheep-shearers in Shaggy Gully all have a sheep dog, but the new guy Shaun uses an extremely polite sheep named Pete.
"Cleanly designed illustrations work well with French's understated text. Strong lines focus attention on the expressive characters." Horn Book Guide

French, Vivian

The Daddy Goose treasury; as told to Vivian French; illustrated by AnnaLaura Cantone . . . [et al.] Scholastic 2006 93p il $18.99
Grades: K 1 2 3   E
   1. Nursery rhymes—Fiction
   ISBN 0-439-79608-3
   "The Chicken House"
"French includes 12 untold stories that give background and context for such familiar rhymes as Little Miss Muffet, Georgie Porgie, Old King Cole, and Hickory, Dickory, Dock. . . . Four European illustrators contribute lively, colorful, and witty illustrations that adeptly articulate the cozy narratives." SLJ

Yucky worms; illustrated by Jessica Ahlberg. Candlewick Press 2010 28p il $16.99 *
Grades: PreK K 1 2   E
   1. Worms—Fiction 2. Gardening—Fiction 3. Grandmothers—Fiction
   ISBN 978-0-7636-4446-8; 0-7636-4446-3
              LC 2009-17307
While helping Grandma in the garden, a child learns about the important role of the earthworm in helping plants grow.
"The cheerful pencil-and-gouache artwork shows scenes both above and below the ground and weaves facts into each image, as well as humorous cartoon speech bubbles. . . . Friendly and interactive, this is a great choice for sharing at home and in the classroom." Booklist

Freymann, Saxton

Fast food; written and illustrated by Saxton Freymann. Arthur A. Levine Books 2006 32p il $12.99 *
Grades: PreK K 1 2 3   E
   1. Transportation
   ISBN 0-439-11019-X
"This picture book takes a theme (here, transportation) and illustrates it with exceptionally clear color photos of ephemeral, sometimes whimsical sculptures created from fruits and vegetables. As quietly witty as its title, the book is narrated by a little mushroom man who suggests different ways of getting about. . . . The playful text gallops along smoothly in rhymed couplets, while the illustrations work their inimitable charm." Booklist

Food for thought; the complete book of concepts for growing minds; written and illustrated by Saxton Freymann. Arthur A. Levine Books 2005 61p il $14.95 *
Grades: PreK K 1 2 3   E
   1. Concepts 2. Counting 3. Alphabet
   ISBN 0-439-11018-1
This "covers basic shapes, colors, numbers, letters, and opposites—all introduced through images of artfully manipulated fruits and vegetables. . . . The simple, clean design is ideal for demonstrating the concepts. . . . But it's the playful, wonderfully clever transformation of familiar foods that will win an audience." Booklist

How are you peeling? foods with moods; [by] Saxton Freymann and Joost Elffers. Scholastic 1999 unp il $16.95; pa $6.99 *
Grades: PreK K 1 2 3   E
   1. Emotions
   ISBN 0-439-10431-9; 0-439-59841-9 (pa)
              LC 99-18162
"Arthur A. Levine books"
Brief text and photographs of carvings made from vegetables introduce the world of emotions by presenting leading questions such as "Are you feeling angry?"
"Kids will find the inherent silliness irresistible and be drawn in by the book's visual appeal: the colors are strong, the photography is excellent, and the expressions . . . are surprisingly masterful." Booklist

Friedman, Darlene

Star of the Week; a story of love, adoption, and brownies with sprinkles; story by Darlene Friedman; illustrations by Roger Roth. HarperCollins 2009 unp il $17.99; lib bdg $18.89
Grades: PreK K 1 2 3   E
   1. Adoption—Fiction 2. Chinese Americans—Fiction 3. School stories
   ISBN 978-0-06-114136-2; 0-06-114136-4; 978-0-06-114137-9 (lib bdg); 0-06-114137-2 (lib bdg)
              LC 2008-22581
As her turn to be "Star of the Week" in her kindergarten class approaches, Cassidy-Li puts together a poster with pictures of her family, friends, and pets, and wonders about her birthparents in China.
"Roth's vibrant illustrations capture the personality of Cassidy-Li, the six-year-old narrator who tells her story in unaffected language that will appeal to children." SLJ

Friedman, Ina R.
How my parents learned to eat; illustrated by Allen Say. Houghton Mifflin 1984 30p il hardcover o.p. pa $6.99
Grades: K 1 2 3   E
    1. Dining—Fiction 2. Japan—Fiction
    ISBN 0-395-35379-3; 0-395-44235-4 (pa)
                        LC 83-18553
An American sailor courts a Japanese girl and each tries, in secret, to learn the other's way of eating
"The illustrations have precise use of line and soft colors, and the composition is economical. A warm and gentle story of an interracial family." Bull Cent Child Books

Friend, Catherine
Eddie the raccoon; illustrated by Wong Herbert Yee. Candlewick Press 2004 40p il (Brand new readers) hardcover o.p. pa $5.99
Grades: K 1 2   E
    1. Raccoons—Fiction
    ISBN 0-7636-2331-8; 0-7636-2334-2 (pa)
                      LC 2003-69717
Eddie the "raccoon steals Big Chicken's eggs, gets his nose stuck in a jam jar, digs deep holes, and stumbles upon a grumpy bear's cave." SLJ
"Pleasant watercolors . . . provide ample visual clues to the accompanying sentence—usually comprising four or five basic vocabulary words. . . . Each setup packs a gently humorous punch that's easy enough for children to grasp and sweet enough to make their adult helpers chuckle." Booklist

The perfect nest; illustrated by John Manders. Candlewick Press 2007 unp il $16.99
Grades: K 1 2   E
    1. Cats—Fiction 2. Chickens—Fiction
    ISBN 978-0-7636-2430-9; 0-7636-2430-6
                      LC 2006047518
Jack the cat gets much more than he bargained for when he decides to build the perfect nest to attract the perfect chicken
This is "highly comical yet heartwarming tale. . . . Manders's gouache illustrations are a perfect complement to the text." SLJ

Fucile, Tony
Let's do nothing! Candlewick Press 2009 unp il $16.99 *
Grades: PreK K 1 2   E
    1. Imagination—Fiction
    ISBN 978-0-7636-3440-7; 0-7636-3440-9
                      LC 2008-935654
"Frankie and Sal are bored . . . and now there is nothing—which is exactly what they will attempt to do for ten whole seconds. In a series of increasingly hilarious spreads, the two boys . . . are deterred everytime by Frankie's overactive imagination. . . . The imagined scenes employ vibrant color, in effective contrast with the reality sequences. . . . Fucile's figures, ink line with acrylic paints, . . . have a retro touch in their period hues and springy drafting." Bull Cent Child Books

Funke, Cornelia Caroline
The princess knight; by Cornelia Funke; illustrations by Kerstin Meyer; translated by Anthea Bell. Chicken House/Scholastic 2004 unp il $15.95 *
Grades: PreK K 1 2   E
    1. Princesses—Fiction 2. Knights and knighthood—Fiction
    ISBN 0-439-53630-8
    Original German edition 2001
"Raised by a widowed king, Princess Violetta is put through the same paces (swordplay, riding, jousting) as her older, brawnier brothers. Her practice pays off when her father holds a tournament—with Violetta as the grand prize—and she handily scuttles his plans. Bell translates Funke's story from the German with aplomb . . . and Meyer's effervescent line-and-watercolor artwork, as funny as it is lovely, stretches across each spread in horizontal strips." Booklist

Princess Pigsty; by Cornelia Funke; illustrated by Kerstin Meyer; translated by Chantal Wright. Chicken House/Scholastic 2007 unp il $16.99
Grades: K 1 2   E
    1. Princesses—Fiction 2. Fairy tales
    ISBN 0-439-88554-X   LC 2006006294
"Sick of her pampered existence, Princess Isabella tosses aside her tiara, declaring, 'I want to get dirty!' The outraged king prescribes tours of duty in the kitchens and pigsty, but Isabella merely revels in the good, honest work and good, honest mess. . . . Most kids will relate to her spirit of rebellion, especially as embodied in Meyer's ebullient watercolors of the beaming, disheveled girl." Booklist

The wildest brother; [by] Cornelia Funke; illustrated by Kerstin Meyer; translated by Oliver Latsch. The Chicken House/Scholastic 2006 unp il $16.99
Grades: PreK K 1 2   E
    1. Siblings—Fiction
    ISBN 0-439-82862-7
When it comes to protecting his big sister, Anna, young Ben is as brave as a lion. But when the day is over and darkness falls, Ben suddenly doesn't feel quite so brave. Sometimes, he realizes, it's Anna who does the protecting
"Wright's wonderfully expressive acrylic paintings elevate this simple glimpse of sibling play into something special. The animated scenes, filled with Ben's imagined foes, perfectly capture the wild-eyed, physical fun." Booklist

Fusco Castaldo, Nancy, 1962-
Pizza for the queen; by Nancy Castaldo; illustrated by Mélisande Potter. Holiday House 2005 unp il $16.95 *
Grades: PreK K 1 2 3   E
    1. Pizza—Fiction 2. Italy—Fiction 3. Cooking—Fiction
    ISBN 0-8234-1865-0   LC 2004-58134
In 1889 Napoli, Italy, Raffaele Esposito prepares a special pizza for Queen Margherita. Based on a true story. Includes a recipe.

Fusco Castaldo, Nancy, 1962-—*Continued*

"The richly toned, detailed illustrations . . . extend the action and the sense of history in busy scenes in the kitchen and on the picturesque streets." Booklist

Gág, Wanda, 1893-1946

Millions of cats. Putnam 2004 c1928 unp il $13.99 *

Grades: PreK K 1   E
1. Cats—Fiction
ISBN 0-399-23315-6
A Newbery Medal honor book, 1929
A reissue of the title first published 1928 by Coward-McCann

A "story-picture book about a very old man and a very old woman who wanted one little cat and who found themselves with 'millions and billions and trillions of cats.'" St Louis Public Libr

It is "a perennial favorite among children and takes a place of its own, both for the originality and strength of its pictures and the living folktale quality of its text." NY Her Trib Books

Gaiman, Neil, 1960-

Crazy hair; illustrated by Dave McKean. HarperCollins Publishers 2009 unp il $18.99; lib bdg $19.89

Grades: PreK K 1 2 3   E
1. Stories in rhyme 2. Hair—Fiction
ISBN 978-0-06-057908-1;   0-06-057908-0;
978-0-06-057909-8 (lib bdg); 0-06-057909-9 (lib bdg)
LC 2008012791

Bonnie encounters all sorts of exotic animals and marvelous things inside a man's crazy hair.

This is a "chaotic picture book popping with bright collage and multimedia imagery. . . . Each page is a veritable feast for the eyes, with frazzled clumps of hair competing for attention with outlandish elements. . . . There's something a little unsettling and unhinged about the imagery, just on the safe side of nightmarish; but the text, for the most part, is delightful and glib." Booklist

The dangerous alphabet; by Neil Gaiman; illustrated by Gris Grimly. HarperCollinsPublishers 2008 unp il $17.99; lib bdg $18.89

Grades: 2 3 4 5   E
1. Alphabet—Fiction   2.   Monsters—Fiction
3. Pirates—Fiction 4. Stories in rhyme
ISBN 978-0-06-078333-4;   0-06-078333-8;
978-0-06-078334-1 (lib bdg); 0-06-078334-6 (lib bdg)
LC 2007-10893

As two children and their pet gazelle sneak out of the house in search of treasure, they come across a world beneath the city that is inhabited with monsters and pirates.

"A sophisticated, interactive alphabet tale in which even the letters break the expected pattern. . . . Skillful narrative and visual storytelling combine to present a complex adventure that unravels through multilayered text and illustrations, challenging readers to ponder the numerous levels of plot. . . . The gothic illustrations, done in sepia tones and faded color washes, ensure that readers remain riveted throughout the story." SLJ

Instructions; written by Neil Gaiman; illustrated by Charles Vess. Harper 2010 unp il $14.99; lib bdg $15.89

Grades: 1 2 3 4   E
1. Poetry 2. Voyages and travels—Poetry
ISBN 978-0-06-196030-7;   0-06-196030-6;
978-0-06-196031-4 (lib bdg); 0-06-196031-4 (lib bdg)

The poem first published 2000 in *A Wolf at the Door* published by Simon & Schuster

Go on a journey to unknown, but strangely familiar, lands and then travel home again.

"Vess's compositions are distinguished by elegant, winding lines-gnarled vines, plumes of smoke, dragon tails-and intimate frames that evoke moments of gentle wisdom. Young readers should relish the chimerical vision while older Gaiman fans should grasp the underlying suggestion that the compass used to navigate fairy tales can also guide us in the real world." Publ Wkly

The wolves in the walls; written by Neil Gaiman; illustrated by Dave McKean. HarperCollins Pubs. 2003 unp il $16.99

Grades: 2 3 4   E
1. Wolves—Fiction
ISBN 0-380-97827-X   LC 2002-192194

Lucy is sure there are wolves living in the walls of her house, although others in her family disagree, and when the wolves come out, the adventure begins

"Gaiman's text rings with energetic confidence and an inviting tone. . . . McKean . . . expertly matches the tale's funny-scary mood . . . against shadow-filled backdrops that blend paint, digital manipulation and photography, his stylized human figures look right at home. His pen-and-inks of the wolves . . . suggest that they inhabit a world apart—or perhaps unreal?" Publ Wkly

Gal, Susan, 1949-

Night lights. Alfred A. Knopf 2009 unp il $14.99; lib bdg $17.99 *

Grades: PreK K 1   E
1. Night—Fiction 2. Light—Fiction
ISBN 978-0-375-85862-8;   0-375-85862-8;
978-0-375-95862-5 (lib bdg); 0-375-95862-2 (lib bdg)
LC 2008-50909

While preparing for bedtime, a little girl and her dog note all the different kinds of lights that brighten up the night, from headlights to moonlight.

"An appropriately dark palette complements the 15 types of illumination named in this nearly wordless story. Young children will enjoy poring over the rich details in the cozy charcoal and digital collage spreads as they learn to read the simple text." SLJ

Please take me for a walk. Alfred A. Knopf 2010 unp il $15.99; lib bdg $18.99

Grades: PreK K 1   E
1. Dogs—Fiction
ISBN 978-0-375-85863-5;   0-375-85863-6;
978-0-375-95863-2 (lib bdg); 0-375-95863-0 (lib bdg)

A dog gives many good reasons it likes to go for a walk—to chase away the neighbor's cat, to greet people on the street, to watch guys shooting hoops, and to feel the wind lifting its ears.

"Gal celebrates the joys of perambulating the neigh-

Gal, Susan, 1949-—*Continued*

borhood in simple sentences and mixed-media collage illustrations featuring expressive canines and humans, as well as inventive details." Booklist

Galbraith, Kathryn Osebold, 1945-

Arbor Day square; written by Kathryn Galbraith; illustrated by Cyd Moore. Peachtree Publishers 2010 unp $16.95

Grades: K 1 2 3   E

1. Arbor Day—Fiction 2. Trees—Fiction 3. Frontier and pioneer life—Fiction 4. Father-daughter relationship—Fiction

ISBN 978-1-56145-517-1; 1-56145-517-2

LC 2009017017

In the mid-nineteenth century, as young Katie and her father help plant and tend trees in their booming frontier town, she doubts that the spindly saplings will ever grow big. Includes facts about Arbor Day.

"Galbraith's poetic text and Moore's soft watercolor and colored-pencil illustrations recreate those spring days on the prairie when planting trees was cause for celebration." SLJ

Boo, bunny! [by] Kathryn O. Galbraith; illustrated by Jeff Mack. Harcourt 2008 unp il $16

Grades: PreK K   E

1. Fear—Fiction 2. Rabbits—Fiction 3. Halloween—Fiction 4. Stories in rhyme

ISBN 978-0-15-216246-7; 0-15-216246-1

LC 2007021426

Two small bunnies face their fears while trick-or-treating on Halloween night

"With very simple, shivery rhyme and bright shapes on black double-page spreads, this picture book brings toddlers the creepy fun of Halloween." Booklist

Gall, Chris

Dear fish; written and illustrated by Chris Gall. Little, Brown 2006 unp il $16.99

Grades: 1 2 3 4   E

1. Fishes—Fiction 2. Beaches—Fiction

ISBN 0-316-05847-5; 978-0-316-05847-6

LC 2005-03828

One afternoon at the beach, a small boy puts an invitation to the fish to come for a visit in a bottle and throws it into the ocean, and the results are unprecedented.

"The text has a rich vocabulary. . . . Boldly colored illustrations combine clay-engraved art with digital effects to give the pages a three-dimensional look. Readers who enjoy poring over pictures that are layered with meaning on both the literal and figurative levels will find much to explore here." SLJ

Dinotrux. Little, Brown 2009 unp il $16.99 *

Grades: PreK K 1 2   E

1. Trucks—Fiction 2. Dinosaurs—Fiction

ISBN 978-0-316-02777-9; 0-316-02777-4

LC 2008-27531

Millions of years ago, the prehistoric ancestors of today's trucks, such as garbageadon, dozeratops, and craneosaurus, roamed the Earth until they rusted out and

became extinct.

"Blending the endless appeal of dinosaurs and trucks in one hilarious volume, this title will be hard to keep on the shelves." SLJ

There's nothing to do on Mars; written and illustrated by Chris Gall. Little, Brown 2008 unp il $16.99

Grades: PreK K 1 2   E

1. Mars (Planet)—Fiction 2. Science fiction

ISBN 978-0-316-16684-3; 0-316-16684-7

LC 2006025290

After moving to Mars with his family, Davey complains of being bored until he begins exploring the planet with his dog Polaris and uncovers a most unusual "treasure"

"The illustrations, created with an engraving technique, are precisely drawn and appropriately painted in scorching reds and oranges. . . . Amusing details . . . extend the text and play off the deadpan humor." SLJ

Gammell, Stephen, 1943-

Once upon MacDonald's farm. rev format ed. Simon & Schuster Bks. for Young Readers 2000 c1981 unp il $15

Grades: PreK K 1 2   E

1. Farm life—Fiction 2. Animals—Fiction

ISBN 0-689-82885-3   LC 99-30691

First published 1981 by Four Winds Press

MacDonald tries farming with exotic circus animals, but has better luck with his neighbor's cow, horse, and chicken—or does he?

"The accomplished, shaded pencil drawings are well suited to this slyly humorous tale with an unexpected twist." Horn Book Guide

Gannij, Joan

Topsy-turvy bedtime; by Joan Levine; illustrated by Tony Auth. Candlewick 2008 unp il $14.99

Grades: PreK K 1   E

1. Bedtime—Fiction 2. Parent-child relationship—Fiction

ISBN 978-0-7636-3008-9; 0-7636-3008-X

"Arathusela hates going to bed. Her parents are exhausted by day's end, so they reverse roles with her. . . . Kids will appreciate the tables-turned humor ('You forgot to sing us a song') and the reasuring resolution. Auth has a light touch; his watercolors display the particular coziness of domestic life at night." Horn Book Guide

Gantos, Jack

Rotten Ralph; written by Jack B. Gantos; illustrated by Nicole Rubel. Houghton Mifflin 1976 unp il lib bdg $16; pa $7.95 *

Grades: PreK K 1 2   E

1. Cats—Fiction

ISBN 0-395-24276-2 (lib bdg); 0-395-29202-6 (pa)

"The protagonist of this story is a mean and nasty cat, Ralph. As his young owner, Sarah, and her family say, he is very difficult to love. Finally on a trip to the circus his behavior becomes unforgivable and they leave him.

Gantos, Jack—*Continued*

There he is treated as miserably as he has treated everyone else and he comes home a week later a wiser, more benevolent cat—well, almost." Child Book Rev Serv

The "bright watercolor scenes . . . capturing Ralph's demonic meanness and his family's chagrin are a perfect complement to the text." SLJ

Other titles about Rotten Ralph are:
Back to school for Rotten Ralph (1998)
Best in show for Rotten Ralph (2005)
Happy birthday Rotten Ralph (1990)
The nine lives of Rotten Ralph (2009)
Not so Rotten Ralph (1994)
Practice makes perfect for Rotten Ralph (2002)
Rotten Ralph helps out (2001)
Rotten Ralph's rotten Christmas (1984)
Rotten Ralph's rotten romance (1997)
Rotten Ralph's show and tell (1989)
Rotten Ralph's trick or treat! (1986)
Wedding bells for Rotten Ralph (1999)
Worse than rotten, Ralph (1978)

Garcia, Emma, 1969-

Tap tap bang bang. Boxer Books 2010 unp il $16.95

Grades: PreK K   E
1. Building—Fiction 2. Tools—Fiction 3. Sounds—Fiction
ISBN 978-1-907152-00-9; 1-907152-00-8

"A lively introduction to tools and the sounds that they make. . . . They all work together to make a bright, cherry-red go-kart. . . . Garcia's artwork is clear and colorful, and all of the tools stand out against the stark white backgrounds. . . . There are plenty of opportunities to stretch vocabulary with these building-tool words." SLJ

Garden, Nancy, 1938-

Molly's family; pictures by Sharon Wooding. Farrar Straus Giroux 2004 unp il $16

Grades: PreK K 1 2   E
1. Family life—Fiction 2. School stories 3. Lesbians—Fiction
ISBN 0-374-35002-7   LC 2002-29784

When Molly draws a picture of her family for Open School Night, one of her classmates makes her feel bad because he says she cannot have a mommy and a momma

"By tying this specific household to the general diversity within all families, Garden manages to celebrate them all. The soft colored-pencil drawings with their many realistic details depict a room full of active kindergartners." SLJ

Garland, Sherry, 1948-

The buffalo soldier; by Sherry Garland; illustrated by Ronald Himler. Pelican Pub. Co. 2006 unp il $15.95

Grades: 2 3 4   E
1. African American soldiers—Fiction 2. West (U.S.)—Fiction
ISBN 978-1-58980-391-6   LC 2006012484

Realizing that his future lies in owning land, not just being free, a young man raised as a slave becomes a buffalo soldier—a member of an all-black cavalry regiment formed to protect white settlers from Indians, bandits, and outlaws, and that later fought in the Spanish American War. Includes historical note

"Himler's vibrant illustrations capture the broad vistas of western landscape, the excitement of horseback pursuit, and the hardships of the work, at the same time conveying respect for the loyal soldiers who endured it all." Booklist

Includes bibliographical references

Gary, Meredith

Sometimes you get what you want; art by Lisa Brown; words by Meredith Gary. HarperCollinsPublishers 2008 unp il $16.99; lib bdg $17.89

Grades: PreK K   E
1. Conduct of life—Fiction 2. School stories 3. Siblings—Fiction
ISBN 978-0-06-114015-0; 978-0-06-114016-7 (lib bdg)   LC 2007041933

A brother and sister spend a day in preschool learning lessons about boundaries, such as that it is sometimes okay to make a lot of noise, but at other times one must be quiet.

"Gary's concise text conveys an important life lesson about the need to balance fun, responsibility, and respect for others. . . . Appealing illustrations depict each scenario and keep the tone light. Background scenery, props, and adult characters are portrayed in black lines and white and gray shades, while the children are fully fleshed out with a variety of skin tones and bright-hued clothing." SLJ

Garza, Xavier, 1968-

Juan and the Chupacabras; by Xavier Garza; illustrations by April Ward; Spanish translation by Carolina Villarroel. Pinata Books 2006 unp il $15.95

Grades: K 1 2 3   E
1. Monsters—Fiction 2. Grandfathers—Fiction 3. Bilingual books—English-Spanish
ISBN 978-1-55885-454-3; 1-55885-454-1

After hearing about their grandfather's boyhood encounter with the Chupacabras, a green, winged creature with glowing eyes, Juan and his cousin Luz decide to find out if the story could be true.

"The English and Spanish texts appear on the same page, separated by a narrow illustration. The full-page illustration moves the action along nicely. An excellent choice for storytime and classroom sharing." SLJ

Gauch, Patricia Lee

Aaron and the Green Mountain Boys; pictures by Margot Tomes. Boyds Mills Press 2005 c1972 64p il $16.95; pa $9.95

Grades: K 1 2   E
1. United States—History—1775-1783, Revolution—Fiction
ISBN 1-59078-335-2; 1-59078-354-9 (pa)

A reissue of the title first published 1972 by Coward, McCann & Geohegan

Gauch, Patricia Lee—*Continued*

In 1777 nine-year-old Aaron would rather help the Green Mountain Boys fight the British than stay home and bake bread for them.

Tanya and the red shoes; illustrated by Satomi Ichikawa. Philomel Bks. 2002 unp il $16.99 *

Grades: PreK K 1 2   E

1. Ballet—Fiction

ISBN 0-399-23314-8   LC 2001-33916

"Tanya confides her dreams of dancing *en pointe* like the dancer in the movie *The Red Shoes.* She finally gets her wish but discovers that the seemingly effortless beauty of the dance requires much work (and produces many blisters). The use of the present tense underscores the conversational tone, adding verisimilitude matched by Ichikawa's marvelously agile, expressive illustrations." Horn Book

Other titles about Tanya are:

Bravo Tanya (1992)

Dance Tanya (1989)

Presenting Tanya the Ugly Duckling (1999)

Tanya and the magic wardrobe (1997)

Gauch, Sarah

Voyage to the Pharos; illustrated by Roger Roth. Viking 2009 unp il $16.99

Grades: 1 2 3   E

1. Lighthouses—Fiction 2. Egypt—Fiction 3. Sea stories

ISBN 978-0-670-06254-6; 0-670-06254-5

LC 2009012345

A young boy in ancient times embarks on an adventurous sea voyage to Alexandria, Egypt, home of the famous Pharos Lighthouse.

"Large-scale illustrations capture the drama of the events to full effect. . . . Roth varies his palette to increase the intensity of the perilous scenes and to highlight the joy of surviving unharmed." SLJ

Gay, Marie-Louise, 1952-

When Stella was very very small. Groundwood Books 2009 unp il $16.95 *

Grades: PreK K 1 2   E

1. Size—Fiction 2. Growth—Fiction

ISBN 978-0-88899-906-1; 0-88899-906-2

"Stella explores her vantage points from each developmental stage to date. As a crawler, she's eye to eye with a turtle. . . . A goldfish and dog phase follow. Gay's sensitivity to the rich inner life of childhood flows into her art and language. . . . Gay's mixed-media scenes dance with the energy of scribbled butterflies on the walls, teetering objects, and a blanket-turned-turban. . . . Subtle and sweet, yet full of life and humor, the child's world is a place kids will want to visit again and again." SLJ

Other titles about Stella are:

Stella, star of the sea (1999)

Stella, queen of the snow (2000)

Stella, fairy of the forest (2002)

Stella, princess of the sky (2004)

Geeslin, Campbell

Elena's serenade; written by Campbell Geeslin; illustrated by Ana Juan. Atheneum Books for Young Readers 2004 unp il $16.95 *

Grades: K 1 2 3   E

1. Mexico—Fiction 2. Glassblowing—Fiction 3. Sex role—Fiction

ISBN 0-689-84908-7   LC 2002-3233

"An Anne Schwartz book"

In Mexico a little girl disguised as a boy sets out for Monterrey determined to master the art of glassblowing, and in the process, experiences self-discovery along the way

"The story flows well and Spanish words are smoothly incorporated into the text. The alluring acrylic-and-crayon illustrations have a stylized folk-art quality that helps to set the stage for the tale." SLJ

Geisert, Arthur

Country road ABC; an illustrated journey through America's farmland. Houghton Mifflin 2010 unp il $17

Grades: K 1 2 3   E

1. Farm life—Fiction 2. Alphabet

ISBN 978-0-547-19469-1; 0-547-19469-2

Arthur Geisert takes readers on a literal journey following a real road in Iowa through the ins and outs of America's farmland.

"Pastoral charm is not Geisert's aim: . . . he begins with 'A is for ammonia fertilizer.' His finely worked etchings, colored in muted shades, sweep across a sprawl of fields and roads. . . . Much visual information about farming is provided for lovers of tractors and farm animals, but it's more than a simple picture book; it's a deeply personal account." Publ Wkly

Hogwash. Houghton Mifflin 2008 32p il $16

Grades: K 1 2 3   E

1. Pigs—Fiction   2. Cleanliness—Fiction 3. Machinery—Fiction 4. Stories without words

ISBN 978-0-618-77332-9; 0-618-77332-0

LC 2007-21731

"Walter Lorraine books"

Illustrations without words depict the enormous and complicated contraption that Mama Pig uses to get her little piglets clean.

This is illustrated with "intricately detailed colored etchings. . . . A master of the 'page turn,' only Geisert could take a one-word title and create such an engaging scenario." Booklist

Lights out. Houghton Mifflin Co. 2005 32p il $16 *

Grades: 1 2 3 4   E

1. Pigs—Fiction 2. Bedtime—Fiction 3. Inventions—Fiction

ISBN 0-618-47892-2   LC 2005-00555

"Walter Lorraine books"

Told by his parents that his light must be out at eight o'clock, a young piglet who is afraid of the dark devises an ingenious solution to the problem.

"Fans of roller-coaster construction, marble runs, and contraption-like machines will be immediately engaged, and the problem-solving humor is for everyone. The fine

Geisert, Arthur—*Continued*

lines and small scale of Geisert's color art work perfectly to give an effect that is intimate, energetic, and delightful." SLJ

Pigs from 1 to 10. Houghton Mifflin 1992 32p il hardcover o.p. pa $6.95 *

Grades: 1 2 3 4   E

1. Counting 2. Pigs—Fiction

ISBN 0-395-58519-8; 0-618-21611-1 (pa)

LC 92-5097

Ten pigs go on an adventurous quest. The reader is asked to find all ten of them, and the numerals from zero to nine, in each picture

"Geisert's inventiveness knows no bounds, and his illustrations both inspire the imagination and convey a homey charm. The final page, a triumphant aggregation of pigs and numbers, is especially endearing." Publ Wkly

Pigs from A to Z. Houghton Mifflin 1986 unp il $18; pa $8.95 *

Grades: 1 2 3 4   E

1. Alphabet 2. Pigs—Fiction

ISBN 0-395-38509-1; 0-395-77874-3 (pa)

LC 86-18542

Seven piglets cavort through a landscape of hidden letters as they build a tree house

"At the back of the book is a key that shows where the artist has secreted all the letters in each illustration; some are plain, some are subtle and every picture has, in addition to its principal letter, one or two from the alphabetical surroundings. . . . So 'Pigs From A to Z' succeeds as narrative, alphabet book, counting book (are all seven piglets in each etching?), puzzle book and as art." N Y Times Book Rev

George, Jean Craighead, 1919-

Goose and Duck; illustrated by Priscilla Lamont. Laura Geringer Books 2008 48p il (I can read!) $16.99; lib bdg $17.89 *

Grades: PreK K 1 2   E

1. Geese—Fiction 2. Ducks—Fiction

ISBN 978-0-06-117076-8; 0-06-117076-3; 978-0-06-117077-5 (lib bdg); 0-06-117077-1 (lib bdg)

LC 2006-21715

A young boy becomes the "mother" to a goose, who becomes "mother" to a duck, as they learn about the rhythms of nature together.

"Lamont's colorful illustrations combine sensitive line work with appealing color washes. . . . The clearly written story is well suited to beginning readers and, as a read-aloud." Booklist

Luck; the story of a sandhill crane; by Jean Craighead George; paintings by Wendell Minor. Laura Geringer Books 2006 unp il $16.99; lib bdg $17.89

Grades: 1 2 3   E

1. Cranes (Birds)—Fiction

ISBN 0-06-008201-1; 0-06-008202-X (lib bdg)

LC 2004-15628

A young sandhill crane, Luck, finds his place in the ancient crane migration from northern Canada to the Platte River

"Minor's beautifully painted spreads of Luck, including many pictures of the birds in flight, increase the sense of awe that the birds' miraculous journey inspires. A fine title to prompt discussion about local wildlife." Booklist

Morning, noon, and night; paintings by Wendell Minor. HarperCollins Pubs. 1999 unp il $16.99; lib bdg $17.89

Grades: K 1 2 3   E

1. Day—Fiction 2. Animals—Fiction

ISBN 0-06-023628-0; 0-06-023629-9 (lib bdg)

LC 97-28796

Each day as the sun makes its dawn-to-dusk journey from the Eastern seaboard to the Pacific coast, the animals perform their daily activities

This offers "rhythmic, lyrical text. . . . Minor's lushly detailed paintings capture the beauty of both animals and landscape, elucidating the subtle journey the book makes from east coast to west." Horn Book Guide

Nutik, the wolf pup; illustrated by Ted Rand. HarperCollins Pubs. 2001 unp il hardcover o.p. lib bdg $18.89

Grades: K 1 2 3   E

1. Inuit—Fiction 2. Wolves—Fiction 3. Arctic regions—Fiction

ISBN 0-06-028164-2; 0-06-028165-0 (lib bdg)

LC 99-10501

When his older sister Julie brings home two small wolf pups, Amaroq takes care of the one called Nutik and grows to love it, even though Julie tells him it cannot stay

"Rand's realistic paintings establish the Alaska setting and capture the affection between boy and pup. . . . First told in *Julie's Wolf Pack* (1997), the story is skillfully telescoped into a picture book with heart-tugging appeal." Booklist

Another title about Nutik and Amaroq is:

Nutik & Amaroq play ball (2001)

George, Kristine O'Connell

Book! illustrated by Maggie Smith. Clarion Bks. 2001 31p il $9.95; bd bk $5.95

Grades: PreK K   E

1. Books and reading—Fiction 2. Stories in rhyme

ISBN 0-395-98287-1; 0-547-15409-7 (bd bk)

LC 00-65600

"When the toddler narrator opens a present and discovers a volume entitled Bunnies, he and the book immediately become inseparable." Publ Wkly

"Smith's deeply colored, playful acrylics depict the youngster through the day as he puts the book onto the shelf upside down, reads it to his cat, and uses it as a ticket to mom's lap for cozy storytime. Rounded, stiff paper pages ensure that this title will withstand repeated readings." SLJ

Hummingbird nest; a journal of poems; illustrated by Barry Moser. Harcourt 2004 unp il $16

Grades: 2 3 4   E

1. Hummingbirds—Fiction 2. Stories in rhyme

ISBN 0-15-202325-9   LC 99-50909

George, Kristine O'Connell—*Continued*

When a mother hummingbird builds a nest on a family's porch, they watch and record her actions and the birth and development of her fledglings.

"Moser's quiet, exquisitely detailed pictures show the people watching and the small, delicate creatures. . . . The long, beautifully written notes with astonishing facts about hummingbirds make this a fine choice for both language arts and science classes." Booklist

Up! illustrated by Hiroe Nakata. Clarion Books 2005 32p il $15
Grades: PreK K   E
  1. Father-daughter relationship—Fiction 2. Stories in rhyme
  ISBN 0-618-06489-3   LC 2004-10729
Rhyming text and illustrations animate the feeling of "up" as experienced by a little girl with her father.

"Nakata's airy, spirited watercolors beautifully expand on the words' carefree, physical elation with skewed angles, glorious fruit-juice colors, and leaping, tumbling toys and figures." Booklist

George, Lindsay Barrett

In the woods: who's been here? Greenwillow Bks. 1995 unp il hardcover o.p. pa $7.99
Grades: PreK K 1 2   E
  1. Forest animals
  ISBN 0-688-12318-X; 0-688-16163-4 (pa)
                LC 93-16244
A boy and girl in the autumn woods find an empty nest, a cocoon, gnawed bark, and other signs of unseen animals and their activities

"Children will be drawn to George's vivid gouache paintings, especially those depicting the animals in their natural surroundings. . . . For most childen this will be an excellent introduction to classroom nature units and the perfect prelude to a walk in the woods." Booklist
 Other titles in this series are:
Around the pond: who's been here? (1996)
Around the world: who's been here? (1999)
In the garden: who's been here? (2006)
In the snow: who's been here? (1995)

Inside mouse, outside mouse. Greenwillow Books 2004 unp il $15.99; lib bdg $16.89 *
Grades: PreK K 1 2   E
  1. Mice—Fiction
  ISBN 0-06-000466-5; 0-06-000467-3 (lib bdg)
                LC 2003-48497
Two mice, one who sleeps inside the house in a clock and one who sleeps outside the house in a stump, follow complicated but strangely parallel paths and meet each other at a window.

"The pictures are packed with interesting details just waiting to be explored. The simple text . . . compares and contrasts the animals' environments and lifestyles. The overall effect is mesmerizing" SLJ

Maggie's ball. Greenwillow Books 2010 unp il $16.99
Grades: PreK K   E
  1. Dogs—Fiction
  ISBN 978-0-06-172166-3; 0-06-172166-2
                LC 2008052482

When Maggie the dog goes searching for her missing ball, she finds a lot of different things—including a new friend.

"The illustrations are bright and big, as is the minimal text, making the oversize book a winner for preschool storytimes as well as for individual perusings where the ample small details will fascinate children." SLJ

George, William T.

Box Turtle at Long Pond; pictures by Lindsay Barrett George. Greenwillow Bks. 1989 unp il $17.99
Grades: PreK K 1 2   E
  1. Turtles—Fiction
  ISBN 0-688-08184-3   LC 88-18787
On a busy day at Long Pond, Box Turtle searches for food, basks in the sun, and escapes a raccoon

"A beautifully illustrated book that introduces a pond environment. . . . The reader learns of other plants, animals, and insects that inhabit the pond." Sci Child
 Other titles about Long Pond are:
Beaver at Long Pond (1988)
Christmas at Long Pond (1992)
Fishing at Long Pond (1991)

Geras, Adèle

Little ballet star; by Adèle Geras; pictures by Shelagh McNicholas. Dial Books for Young Readers 2008 unp il $16.99 *
Grades: PreK K 1 2   E
  1. Ballet—Fiction 2. Aunts—Fiction
  ISBN 978-0-8037-3237-7; 0-8037-3237-6
Tilly is thrilled when she gets to see her aunt perform in the ballet, "The Sleeping Beauty," especially because she gets to go backstage and even on the stage itself.

"This picture book will charm aspiring young dancers. The large format allows plenty of space for the expressive pencil illustrations, tinted with washes in pastel shades." Booklist
 Another book about about Tilly is:
Time for ballet (2004)

Gerber, Carole

Leaf jumpers; [illustrated by] Leslie Evans. Charlesbridge 2004 32p il $16.95; pa $6.95
Grades: PreK K 1 2   E
  1. Leaves 2. Autumn
  ISBN 1-57091-497-4; 1-57091-498-2 (pa)
                LC 2003-15846
Illustrations and rhyming text describe different leaves and the trees from which they fall

"Gerber's poetic text describes colors, shapes, and characteristics with an abundance of similes and metaphors. . . . Evans' vibrant hand-colored linoleum prints feature scenes of a brother and sister with the family dog enjoying traditional fall activities." Booklist

Gerdner, Linda

Grandfather's story cloth; written by Linda Gerdner and Sarah Langford; illustrated by Stuart Loughridge. Shen's Books 2008 29p il $16.95
Grades: 2 3 4   E
     1. Grandfathers—Fiction 2. Alzheimer's disease—Fiction 3. Quilts—Fiction 4. Laotian Americans—Fiction 5. Hmong (Asian people)—Fiction 6. Bilingual books—English-Hmong
ISBN 978-1-885008-34-3; 1-885008-34-1
Ten-year-old Chersheng helps his beloved grandfather cope with his failing memory, brought on by Alzheimer's disease, by showing him the story quilt Grandfather made after fleeing his homeland, Laos, during wartime.
"The English and Hmong texts face paintings that express the many moods of the characters. Endpapers and the back cover feature numerous geometric patterns that are common in Hmong handicrafts. . . . [The book includes] background information on Alzheimer's disease and the Hmong refugees and their story cloths. . . . A strong family story about difficult social issues relevant to today's society." SLJ

Gerritsen, Paula, 1956-

Nuts; [by] Paula Gerritsen. Front Street 2006 c2005 unp il $15.95
Grades: PreK K 1 2   E
     1. Nuts—Fiction 2. Mice—Fiction 3. Storms—Fiction
ISBN 1-932425-66-7   LC 2005021491
Original Dutch edition 2005
Mouse braves many dangers while trying to collect nuts before winter sets in, including a sudden storm that first brings her disappointment, then a delightful surprise
"The words are well chosen and the repeated refrain will delight readers. The pencil-and-pastel illustrations are charming, displaying the textures and colors of fall and the foreboding energy of the storm." SLJ

Gershator, Phillis, 1942-

Listen, listen; [by] Phillis Gershator; [illustrated by] Alison Jay. Barefoot Books 2007 unp il $16.95 *
Grades: K 1 2 3   E
     1. Sound—Fiction 2. Nature—Fiction 3. Seasons—Fiction 4. Stories in rhyme
ISBN 978-1-84686-084-3   LC 2006100351
Illustrations and rhyming text explore the sights and sounds of nature in each season of the year.
"Jay's magical and occasionally eerie crackle-glaze oil paintings furnish a visual feast. The text is built around a series of rhyming, gentile directives to attune one's ears." Publ Wkly

Sky sweeper; pictures by Holly Meade. Farrar, Straus & Giroux 2007 unp il $16
Grades: 1 2 3 4   E
     1. Gardens—Fiction 2. Work—Fiction 3. Buddhism—Fiction 4. Japan—Fiction
ISBN 978-0-374-37007-7; 0-374-37007-9
     LC 2005-49762
"Melanie Kroupa books"

Despite criticism for his lack of "accomplishments," Takiboki finds contentment sweeping flower blossoms and raking the sand and gravel in the monks' temple garden. Includes a note on the art and beauty of Japanese gardens
"This is a complex, challenging story. . . . But Meade's beautiful collage illustrations of the earthly garden and glorious afterlife greatly enhance the story's accessibility and will help kids get closer to the text's religious and philosophical themes." Booklist

Who's awake in springtime? [by] Phillis Gershator and Mim Green; illustrated by Emilie Chollat. Henry Holt & Co. 2010 unp il $16.99
Grades: PreK K 1 2   E
     1. Stories in rhyme 2. Bedtime—Fiction 3. Animals—Fiction 4. Spring—Fiction
ISBN 978-0-8050-6390-5; 0-8050-6390-0
     LC 2009009224
"Christy Ottaviano books"
Describes, in rhymed cumulative text and illustrations, how various young animals and one small human prepare for sleep at the end of a spring day.
"This cumulative tale is simple and accessible by young readers. . . . Adults who share this book with children can engage the students with the rhythmic text, and repetition throughout the book begs for call-backs and other participation activities. . . . Chollat's illustrations offer bold colors and clear lines and strongly support the story." Libr Media Connect

Zoo day olé! a counting book; illustrated by Santiago Cohen. Marshall Cavendish Children 2009 unp il $17.99
Grades: PreK K 1   E
     1. Animals—Fiction 2. Counting 3. Grandmothers—Fiction 4. Spanish language—Vocabulary 5. Zoos—Fiction
ISBN 978-0-7614-5462-5; 0-7614-5462-4
     LC 2008010783
"Abuelita takes her grandchildren to the zoo, where they count all of the animals in English and in Spanish. The bouncy rhyming text makes for a lively read-aloud, and the method used for introducing Spanish vocabulary adds even more energy to the presentation. . . . The rhyme helps children predict which number comes next, and the page turns add to the excitement. . . . The cartoon illustrations, featuring bright colors outlined in bold black strokes, create a fun-loving atmosphere for the story." SLJ

Gerstein, Mordicai, 1935-

A book. Roaring Brook 2009 unp il $16.95 *
Grades: PreK K 1 2   E
     1. Authorship—Fiction 2. Books and reading—Fiction
ISBN 978-1-59643-251-2; 1-59643-251-9
"This charming story follows a young girl and her family who live in a book, . . . though she doesn't know what kind of story her book is. . . . She dashes though spreads that take her into nursery rhymes, on the trail of a mystery, across pirate waters, and even into outer space before she ultimately decides to write her own story, which is, of course, this story. . . . The concept is executed with . . . cleverness and gentleness." Booklist

Gerstein, Mordicai, 1935-—_Continued_
Carolinda clatter! Roaring Brook Press 2005 unp
il $16.95 *
Grades: PreK K 1 2 3   **E**
  1. Fairy tales 2. Giants—Fiction
  ISBN 1-59643-063-X   LC 2004-24258
The excessively quiet town of Pupickton and the
sleeping lovesick giant upon which it was built, are both
awakened by the joyful noise of a little girl's songs.
  "Gerstein tells his whimsical tale with direct humor,
and his lovely paint-and-ink illustrations extend the comedy." Booklist

Leaving the nest. Farrar, Straus and Giroux
2007 unp il $16
Grades: K 1 2 3   **E**
  1. Cats—Fiction 2. Birds—Fiction 3. Squirrels—Fiction 4. Growth—Fiction
  ISBN 978-0-374-34369-9; 0-374-34369-1
                                   LC 2005-51228
"Frances Foster Books"
The lives of a baby jaybird, a young girl, a kitten, and
a small squirrel intersect as they venture out into the
world.
  "Using dialogue bubbles to reveal conversations and
thoughts, Gerstein's realistic illustrations set the backyard
stage and choreograph the frenzied acts of the drama,
adding touches of humor without diminishing the tension." Booklist

The man who walked between the towers.
Roaring Brook Press 2003 unp il $17.95; lib bdg
$24.90 *
Grades: PreK K 1 2 3   **E**
  1. Petit, Philippe, 1949- 2. Tightrope walking
  ISBN 0-7613-1791-0; 0-7613-2868-8 (lib bdg)
                                   LC 2003-9040
Awarded the Caldecott Medal, 2004
A lyrical evocation of Philippe Petit's 1974 tightrope
walk between the World Trade Center towers
  "The pacing of the narrative is as masterful as the
placement and quality of the oil-and-ink paintings. . . .
Gerstein captures his subject's incredible determination,
profound skill, and sheer joy." SLJ

Minifred goes to school. HarperCollins 2009
unp il $17.99
Grades: PreK K 1 2   **E**
  1. Cats—Fiction 2. Animals—Fiction 3. School stories
  ISBN   978-0-06-075889-9;   0-06-075889-9;
978-0-06-075890-5 (lib bdg); 0-06-075890-2 (lib bdg)
                                   LC 2008-13861
When Mr. Portly finds a kitten, he and his wife raise
her like a child, but unlike a typical child, Minifred the
kitten does not like to follow rules at home or at school.
  "Gerstein matches the story's lighthearted mood with
action-packed scenes, using playful colors, caricatured
figures, and sometimes multiple scenes per page, increasing the sense of action." SLJ

Sparrow Jack. Frances Foster Bks. 2003 unp il
$16
Grades: PreK K 1 2 3   **E**
  1. Bardsley, John, d. 1999—Fiction 2. Sparrows—Fiction 3. Immigrants—Fiction
  ISBN 0-374-37139-3   LC 2001-23829

In 1868, John Bardsley, an immigrant from England,
brought one thousand sparrows from his home country
back to Philadelphia, where he hoped they would help
save the trees from the inch-worms that were destroying
them
  "Though a few imaginative liberties are taken with the
facts, Gerstein's cheerful tale is based on a true story.
The humor of his whimsically witty text is beautifully
captured and expanded by drawings that are filled with
comic action and droll details." Booklist

The white ram; a story of Abraham and Isaac.
Holiday House 2006 unp il $16.95 *
Grades: 1 2 3 4   **E**
  1. Abraham (Biblical figure)—Fiction 2. Sheep—Fiction 3. Rosh ha-Shanah—Fiction
  ISBN 0-8234-1897-9; 978-0-8234-1897-8
                                   LC 2005-46001
A white ram, made on the sixth day of creation, waits
patiently in the garden of Eden until the time is right,
then runs to save a certain child in fulfillment of God's
plan.
  "This stunningly illustrated picture book is based on
a Midrash. . . . The art, done in pen and ink, oils, and
colored pencil, is mesmerizing. [This is told] with a captivating use of language along with true drama." SLJ

Gibbons, Gail
The seasons of Arnold's apple tree. Harcourt
Brace Jovanovich 1984 unp il $17; pa $7
Grades: PreK K 1 2   **E**
  1. Seasons—Fiction 2. Trees—Fiction
  ISBN 0-15-271246-1; 0-15-271245-3 (pa)
                                   LC 84-4484
Arnold enjoys his apple tree through the changing
year: its springtime blossoms, the swing and tree-house
it supports, its summer shade, its autumn harvest; in the
winter, the tree's branches hold strings of popcorn and
berries for the birds
  "Two major concepts emerge here, the first being the
passage of the seasons, the second the valuable resource
Arnold has in his apple tree. . . . Gibbons' crisp pictures
ensure that the multifaceted lesson is explicit, bright and
cheery." Booklist

Gibfried, Diane
Brother Juniper; illustrated by Meilo So. Clarion
Books 2006 unp il $16
Grades: K 1 2 3   **E**
  1. Francis, of Assisi, Saint, 1182-1226—Fiction
  2. Clergy—Fiction
  ISBN 0-618-54361-9; 978-0-618-54361-8
                                   LC 2005-10038
Worried about having left the overly-generous Brother
Juniper in charge of their chapel when they went out to
preach, Father Francis of Assisi and the other friars are
not prepared for what they find upon their return.
  "Filled with delicate details and gentle humor, the accomplished watercolor paintings add greatly to the
book's appeal. . . . This is an excellent choice to open
discussion about generosity." SLJ

Giff, Patricia Reilly

Watch out, Ronald Morgan! illustrated by Susanna Natti. Viking Kestrel 1985 24p il pa $5.99 hardcover o.p.

Grades: PreK K 1 2   E

1. Eyeglasses—Fiction 2. School stories

ISBN 0-14-050638-1 (pa)   LC 84-19623

Ronald has many humorous mishaps until he gets a pair of eyeglasses. Includes a note for adults about children's eye problems

"Told in a forthright manner but with appreciation for children's candor, the book's dialogue rings true with catchy humor. . . . Natti's illustrations show the characters to be bright, colorful informal figures who move with the text." SLJ

Other titles about Ronald Morgan are:
Good luck, Ronald Morgan (1996)
Happy birthday, Ronald Morgan! (1986)
Ronald Morgan goes to bat (1988)
Ronald Morgan goes to camp (1995)
Today was a terrible day (1980)

Giganti, Paul, Jr.

Each orange had 8 slices; a counting book; by Paul Giganti, Jr.; pictures by Donald Crews. Greenwillow Bks. 1992 unp il $16.99; lib bdg $17.89; pa $6.99 *

Grades: PreK K 1 2   E

1. Counting 2. Mathematics

ISBN 0-688-10428-2; 0-688-10429-0 (lib bdg); 0-688-13985-X (pa)   LC 90-24167

This volume presents a series of statements about the illustrations: "'On my way to Grandma's I saw 2 fat cows. Each cow had 2 calves. Each calf had 4 skinny legs,' and the questions follow: 'How many fat cows . . . calves . . . legs were there in all?'" SLJ

"This bright, well-designed book challenges young children to think analytically about what's on its pages. . . . Since the objects are organized into sets and subsets, this could be used to introduce the concept of multiplication as well as counting and addition." Booklist

How many snails? a counting book; by Paul Giganti, Jr.; pictures by Donald Crews. Greenwillow Bks. 1988 unp il $16.99; pa $6.99

Grades: PreK K 1 2   E

1. Counting

ISBN 0-688-06369-1; 0-688-13639-7 (pa)   LC 87-26281

"Instead of inviting children to count static objects, Mr. Giganti poses a series of simple, direct questions designed to encourage youngsters to determine the often subtle differences between those objects. Donald Crews . . . concentrates here on decorating each page with objects that supply the necessary links to the text. Some of the pages—depicting a collection of motley dogs at the park or beautiful toy boats and trucks, cars and airplanes at a toy store—are a joy to look at." N Y Times Book Rev

Gilani-Williams, Fawsia, 1967-

Nabeel's new pants; an Eid tale; retold by Fawzia Gilani-Williams; illustrations by Proiti Roy. Marshall Cavendish Children 2010 c2007 unp il $15.99 *

Grades: K 1 2 3   E

1. Family life—Fiction 2. Id al-Adha—Fiction 3. Muslims—Fiction 4. Turkey—Fiction

ISBN 978-0-7614-5629-2; 0-7614-5629-5

First published 2007 in India

"Turkish shoemaker Nabeel buys Eid gifts for his family. . . . The shopkeeper also persuades Nabeel to buy himself new pants, but the pants are too long. His wife, mother, and daughter are all too busy cooking for Eid to shorten his pants, so he cuts a few inches off himself. Later, the women in the house feel guilty and each secretly trims the pants more. . . . Roy's cheerful gouache, watercolor, and ink illustrations show the bonds among family members as they follow their traditions together. Kids will laugh right along with the loving characters." Booklist

Includes glossary

Gilchrist, Jan Spivey

My America; illustrations by Ashley Bryan and Jan Spivey Gilchrist; poem by Jan Spivey Gilchrist. HarperCollins Pubs. 2007 unp il $16.99; lib bdg $17.89

Grades: PreK K 1 2   E

1. United States—Poetry

ISBN 978-0-06-079104-9; 0-06-079104-7; 978-0-06-079105-6 (lib bdg); 0-06-079105-5 (lib bdg)   LC 2006029867

"This unusual tribute celebrates America's diversity in its landscapes, both urban and rural, its wildlife, but most of all its people. . . . Both Bryan and Gilchrist illustrate the poem in alternating spreads: his signature color swirls work in tandem with her muted, blue-toned tableaux and faces. . . . The words have the potential for choral reading or dramatization." Booklist

Ginsburg, Mirra, 1909-2000

The chick and the duckling; translated [and adapted] from the Russian of V. Suteyev; pictures by Jose & Ariane Aruego. Macmillan 1972 unp il pa $6.99 hardcover o.p. *

Grades: PreK K   E

1. Ducks—Fiction 2. Chickens—Fiction

ISBN 0-689-71226-X (pa)

"The adventures of a duckling who is a leader and a chick who follows suit. When the chick decides that an aquatic life is not for him, this brief selection for reading aloud comes to a humorous conclusion." Wis Libr Bull

"The sunny simplicity of the illustrations is just right for a slight but engaging text, and they add a note of humor that is a nice foil for the bland directness of the story." Bull Cent Child Books

Ginsburg, Mirra, 1909-2000—*Continued*

Good morning, chick; by Mirra Ginsburg, adapted from a story by Korney Chukovsky; pictures by Byron Barton. Greenwillow Bks. 1980 unp il hardcover o.p. pa $6.99
Grades: PreK K   E
1. Chickens—Fiction
ISBN 0-688-84284-4 (lib bdg); 0-688-08741-8 (pa)
LC 80-11352

"In this simple preschool tale . . . a chick hatches out of an egg ('like this'), learns to eat worms ('like this'), is scared by a cat ('like this'), falls in a pond ('like this'), and is coddled back to fluffiness by Mom ('like this')." SLJ

"Based upon a tale by the great Russian poet and storyteller, the totally childlike picture book for the very young employs an engaging device: The text, illustrated with a bright vignette, appears on each of the left-hand pages; then, after pausing briefly and leading the eye to the right, a sentence runs to completion on the opposite page with two words contained in a large storytelling picture done in bold, brilliant color." Horn Book

Giovanni, Nikki
The grasshopper's song; an Aesop's fable revisited; by Nikki Giovanni; illustrated by Chris Raschka. Candlewick Press 2008 44p il $16.99 *
Grades: K 1 2 3   E
1. Grasshoppers—Fiction 2. Ants—Fiction 3. Trials—Fiction
ISBN 978-0-7636-3021-8; 0-7636-3021-7

Every year the Grasshoppers sing and play their instruments and the Ants work in rhythm to the music. But when winter comes, the Ants turn their backs on the Grasshoppers, and Jimmy Grasshopper finds this unfair. He's hired Robin, Robin, Robin, and Wren to sue Abigail and Nestor Ant for what he deserves—R-E-S-P-E-C-T—and a one-half share of the harvest. But will a jury of his peers agree about the worth of art?

"To illustrate Giovanni's detailed and insightful prose, Raschka . . . creates evocative, earth-tone watercolors that suggest camouflage." Publ Wkly

Glaser, Linda
Hoppy Hanukkah! illustrated by Daniel Howarth. Albert Whitman 2009 unp il $15.99
Grades: PreK K   E
1. Hanukkah—Fiction 2. Family life—Fiction 3. Rabbits—Fiction
ISBN 978-0-8075-3378-9; 0-8075-3378-5
LC 2008-55696

Two young bunnies learn about the customs of Hanukkah from their parents and grandparents before they light the menorahs, eat potato latkes, and play dreidel.

"Howarth's soft, bright illustrations of an extended floppy-eared family offer details of a Judaic home in this gentle introduction to the rituals of a traditional celebration that young families can follow as they create a Hanukkah atmosphere in their own homes." Kirkus

Our big home; an Earth poem; illustrated by Elisa Kleven. Millbrook Press 2000 unp il $23.90; pa $7.95
Grades: K 1 2 3   E
1. Nature—Fiction 2. Earth—Fiction
ISBN 0-7613-1650-7; 0-7613-1776-7 (pa)
LC 99-45775

Describes the water, air, soil, sky, sun, and more shared by all living creatures on Earth

"A joyful celebration of the Earth. . . . Kleven's colorful artwork is full of subtle detail. . . . The artist uses an effective mix of media, from collage to chalk, to portray depth of scenes and vibrancy of detail." SLJ

Glass, Eleri, 1969-
The red shoes; by Eleri Glass; illustrated by Ashley Spires. Simply Read 2008 unp il $16.95
Grades: PreK K 1 2   E
1. Shoes—Fiction 2. Shopping—Fiction
ISBN 978-1-894965-78-1; 1-894965-78-7

"Shopping for shoes, a little girl knows that her mother will pick the practical, very dull, lace-ups. Even the palette that Spires uses is dark and drab, and the child's body language screams disappointment. But when she gets to the store, she sees the most wonderful pair of red shoes and wants them more than anything. . . . This sweet story will appeal to little girls who count shoes as something very important indeed." SLJ

Gleeson, Libby, 1950-
Half a world away; by Libby Gleeson; illustrated by Freya Blackwood. Arthur A. Levine Books 2007 unp il $15.99 paperback o.p. *
Grades: PreK K 1 2   E
1. Friendship—Fiction 2. Moving—Fiction
ISBN 0-439-88977-4; 0-439-88978-2 (pa)
LC 2006007712

Previously published under title: Amy and Louis

When Louie's best friend Amy moves to the other side of the world, Louie must find a way to reconnect with her

"Blackwood's tender, realistic watercolors reinforce the friends' sweet closeness and magic. . . . Subtle, direct, and profound." Booklist

Glenn, Sharlee Mullins
Just what Mama needs; [by] Sharlee Glenn; illustrated by Amiko Hirao. Harcourt 2008 unp il lib bdg $16
Grades: PreK K 1 2   E
1. Dogs—Fiction 2. Week—Fiction 3. Imagination—Fiction
ISBN 978-0-15-205759-6; 0-15-205759-5
LC 2005-25440

Abby the dog assumes a different identity for each day of the week until Sunday, when she is just herself.

"Glenn's descriptive text and use of onomatopoeia provide an ideal read-aloud [and] . . . Hirao's collage and colored-pencil art, expressed on a variety of paper surfaces, alternates stark views as Abby introduces a costume, followed by busy scenes of her imagination and the real-life labors. . . . There's something to please nearly everyone in this tale." SLJ

Gliori, Debi

No matter what. Harcourt Brace & Co. 1999 unp il $16; bd bk $6.95

Grades: PreK K 1　　　　　　　　　　　　E

1. Parent-child relationship—Fiction 2. Foxes—Fiction 3. Stories in rhyme

ISBN 0-15-202061-6; 0-15-206343-9 (bd bk)

LC 98-47277

Small, a little fox, seeks reassurance that Large will always provide love, no matter what

"Gliori's whimsical illustrations use warm, inviting color to invoke the same sense of emotional security as the rhyming text." Booklist

Stormy weather; written and illustrated by Debi Gliori. Walker & Co. 2009 unp il $15.99; lib bdg $16.89

Grades: PreK K　　　　　　　　　　　　　E

1. Stories in rhyme 2. Bedtime—Fiction 3. Foxes—Fiction 4. Animals—Fiction 5. Mother-child relationship—Fiction

ISBN　978-0-8027-9419-2;　0-8027-9419-X; 978-0-8027-9422-2 (lib bdg); 0-8027-9422-X (lib bdg)

LC 2008043523

As nighttime approaches, a baby fox and his mother imagine all the different animals around the world preparing for bed and falling asleep.

"The story's lulling pace enhances the quiet bedtime read-aloud. . . . Watercolor-and-ink spreads utilize warm earth tones within the family homes to contrast the sometimes threatening outside elements or cool night backdrops. Nimble lines support the comforting images, and swirling designs and twinkling stars add unique details." SLJ

The trouble with dragons; [by] Debi Gliori. Walker & Co. 2008 unp il $16.99; lib bdg $17.89

Grades: PreK K 1　　　　　　　　　　　　E

1. Stories in rhyme 2. Conservation of natural resources—Fiction 3. Environmental protection—Fiction 4. Dragons—Fiction

ISBN　978-0-8027-9789-6;　0-8027-9789-X; 978-0-8027-9790-2 (lib bdg); 0-8027-9790-3 (lib bdg)

LC 2008005389

When dragons cut down too many trees, blow out too much hot air, and do other environmental damage, the future looks grim, but other animals advise them on how to mend their ways and save the planet

This "is magical, thanks to the playful artwork and bouncy rhymes. Though the text sticks to the basics of taking care of the Earth, the illustrations offer fodder for discussion." SLJ

Global babies; developed by the Global Fund for Children. Charlesbridge 2007 unp il $6.95

Grades: PreK　　　　　　　　　　　　　　E

1. Infants 2. Board books for children

ISBN 978-1-58089-174-5

This board book offers color photographs of babies from 17 cultures around the world.

Goble, Paul

Death of the iron horse; story and illustrations by Paul Goble. Bradbury Press 1987 unp il pa $7.99 hardcover o.p.

Grades: K 1 2 3　　　　　　　　　　　　　E

1. Cheyenne Indians—Fiction 2. Railroads—Fiction

ISBN 0-689-71686-9 (pa)　　　　　　LC 85-28011

The author "has taken several accounts of the 1867 Cheyenne attack of a Union Pacific freight train . . . and combined them into a story from the Indians' viewpoint. As the Cheyenne Prophet Sweet Medicine had foretold, strange hairy people were invading the land, killing women and children and driving off the horses. Descriptions of the iron horse inspired curiosity and fear in the young braves who decided to go out and protect their village from this new menace. Keeping fairly close to actual Indian accounts, Goble presents the braves' bold attack on the train, glossing over the deaths of the train crew." SLJ

Godden, Rumer, 1907-1998

The story of Holly & Ivy; [by] Rumer Godden; [pictures by] Barbara Cooney. Viking 2006 31p il $17.99

Grades: K 1 2 3　　　　　　　　　　　　　E

1. Orphans—Fiction 2. Christmas—Fiction 3. Dolls—Fiction

ISBN 0-670-06219-7; 978-0-670-06219-5

First published 1957; a reissue of the newly illustrated edition published 1985

Orphaned Ivy finds her Christmas wish fulfilled with the help of a lonely couple and a doll named Holly.

"Texturally rich and evocatively wintry, this reissue is timeless." Horn Book Guide

Godwin, Laura

Happy and Honey; written by Laura Godwin; pictures by Jane Chapman. Margaret K. McElderry Bks. 2000 unp il (Happy Honey) $12.95 *

Grades: PreK K 1　　　　　　　　　　　E

1. Dogs—Fiction 2. Cats—Fiction

ISBN 0-689-83406-3　　　　　　　　LC 99-46923

Honey the cat is determined to play with Happy the dog, even though he is trying to sleep

"The text is short and effective, and the delightful acrylic paintings, which are set against an expanse of white space, center on Happy and Honey, keeping children as focused on the goings-on as does the just-right text." Booklist

Other titles about Happy and Honey are:

The best fall of all (2002)

Happy Christmas, Honey (2002)

Honey helps (2000)

Goembel, Ponder

Animal fair; adapted and illustrated by Ponder Goembel. Marshall Cavendish Children 2010 unp il $12.99

Grades: PreK K 1　　　　　　　　　　　E

1. Stories in rhyme 2. Animals—Fiction

ISBN 978-0-7614-5642-1; 0-7614-5642-2

LC 2009005937

Goembel, Ponder—*Continued*

"Based on the children's song Animal Fair, Goembel's adaptation adroitly posits the wild imaginings of a child: what might go on at a fair apparently run by animals? The answer is nonsense, as virtually nothing the animals do makes a whit of sense. That, of course, is what will make young listeners squeal with glee. The text is wonderfully wordy and tied to an irresistible rhythm. . . . Goembel's ink and acrylic-wash artwork has an appealing orderliness to it." Booklist

Gold, August, 1955-

Thank you, God, for everything; by August Gold; illustrated by Wendy Anderson Halperin. G.P. Putnam's Sons 2009 unp il $16.99 *

Grades: PreK K 1 2   E

1. God—Fiction 2. Religious life—Fiction

ISBN 978-0-399-24049-2; 0-399-24049-7

LC 2008016801

As Daisy watches her parents thanking God everyday, she begins to look at everything around her and realizes she is also thankful for many things.

Gold's "goal here is to 'show young readers how to develop their own thankful eyes.' Both she and artist Halperin do that beautifully in this story. . . . In her signature softly colored style . . . Halperin takes everyday doings and elevates them." Booklist

Goldfinger, Jennifer P., 1963-

My dog Lyle. Clarion Books 2007 unp il $16

Grades: PreK K 1 2   E

1. Dogs—Fiction

ISBN 978-0-618-63983-0; 0-618-63983-7

LC 2006-07146

A child provides an ever-increasing list of characteristics that make Lyle a very special dog, despite appearances.

"The lively text matches perfectly with the vibrant, playful illustrations, done in bold, richly hued acrylics and oils." SLJ

Goldman, Judy, 1955-

Uncle monarch and the Day of the Dead; [by] Judy Goldman; illustrated by Rene King Moreno. Boyds Mills Press 2008 unp il $16.95

Grades: K 1 2 3   E

1. Death—Fiction 2. Uncles—Fiction 3. All Souls' Day—Fiction 4. Spanish language—Vocabulary 5. Butterflies—Fiction 6. Mexico—Fiction

ISBN 978-1-59078-425-9; 1-59078-425-1

LC 2007049322

Upon the death of her beloved Tio Urbano, who has taught her that monarch butterflies are the souls of the dead, young Lupita gains a deeper understanding of Dia de los Muertos, the Day of the Dead, as it is observed in rural Mexico. Includes glossary of Spanish terms and facts about the Day of the Dead

"This lovely picture book effectively blends a poignant story about losing a beloved relative with a lucid description of *Día de Muertos*. . . . [This features] lovely, bright-hued colored-pencil illustrations. . . . Spanish words are integrated into the text." SLJ

Golson, Terry

Tillie lays an egg; [by] Terry Golson; with photographs by Ben Fink. Scholastic Press 2009 unp il $16.99

Grades: PreK K 1 2   E

1. Chickens—Fiction

ISBN 978-0-545-00537-1; 0-545-00537-X

LC 2008011737

In search of the perfect place to lay her egg, Tillie the chicken leaves the barnyard and explores the farmhouse

"The photographed scenes are packed with Golson's own chicken-motif treasures—glassware, tins, vintage board games—and invite close exploration. Text and photos appear in bordered boxes; these are set against pastel wallpapers with country patterns—a pleasant contrast to Fink's crisp photography. . . . Full of charm." Publ Wkly

González, Lucía M., 1957-

The storyteller's candle; story by Lucia Gonzalez; illustrations by Lulu Delacre. Children's Book Press 2008 30p il $16.95 *

Grades: K 1 2 3   E

1. Belpré, Pura—Fiction 2. Librarians—Fiction 3. Libraries—Fiction 4. Puerto Ricans—Fiction 5. New York (N.Y.)—Fiction 6. Epiphany—Fiction 7. Bilingual books—English-Spanish

ISBN 978-0-89239-222-3; 0-89239-222-3

A Pura Belpre Author Award honor book, 2009

During the early days of the Great Depression, New York City's first Puerto Rican librarian, Pura Belpré, introduces the public library to immigrants living in El Barrio and hosts the neighborhood's first Three Kings Day fiesta.

"In this large-size, attractive bilingual picture book, Delacre's glowing oil-and-collage artwork depicts early scenes in sepia tones and later ones in a lively color. . . . This is a warm, winning introduction to the work of the first Puerto Rican librarian in New York." Booklist

Gonzalez, Maya Christina, 1964-

I know the river loves me. Children's Book Press 2009 22p il $16.95

Grades: K 1 2   E

1. Rivers—Fiction 2. Bilingual books—English-Spanish

ISBN 978-0-89239-233-9; 0-89239-233-9

LC 2008053194

A girl expresses her love of the river that she visits, plays in, and cares for throughout the year.

This is written "in sweeping lyrical prose—in both English and Spanish. . . . Inspiring and peacefully thought-provoking." Kirkus

My colors, my world = Mis colores, mi mundo. Children's Book Press 2007 23p il $16.95 *

Grades: PreK K 1 2   E

1. Deserts—Fiction 2. Color—Fiction 3. Hispanic Americans—Fiction 4. Bilingual books—English-Spanish

ISBN 978-0-89239-221-6; 0-89239-221-5

LC 2007005297

A Pura Belpré Award honor book, 2008

Gonzalez, Maya Christina, 1964-—*Continued*

Maya, who lives in the dusty desert, opens her eyes wide to find the colors in her world, from Papi's black hair and Mami's orange and purple flowers to Maya's red swing set and the fiery pink sunset

González, Rigoberto, 1970-

Antonio's card; story, Rigoberto González; illustrations, Cecilia Concepción Alvarez. Children's Book Press 2005 30p il $16.95
Grades: 1 2 3   E
   1. Mother-son relationship—Fiction 2. Lesbians—Fiction 3. School stories 4. Bilingual books—English-Spanish
   ISBN 0-89239-204-5   LC 2004-56046
With Mother's Day coming, Antonio finds he has to decide about what is important to him when his classmates make fun of the unusual appearance of his mother's partner, Leslie
"Sensitively written in English, with an excellent translation by Jorge Argueta, the narrative captures the social worries and concerns that children in nontraditional families may experience. The acrylic illustrations are bright and colorful." SLJ

Goode, Diane

The most perfect spot; by Diane Goode. HarperCollins 2006 unp il $16.99; lib bdg $17.89
Grades: PreK K 1 2   E
   1. Mother-son relationship—Fiction 2. Parks—Fiction 3. Brooklyn (New York, N.Y.)—Fiction
   ISBN 0-06-072697-0; 0-06-072698-9 (lib bdg)
                          LC 2004030058
"Young Jack wants to go on a picnic with his mother and thinks that he knows the perfect spot in Prospect Park. Maybe it is, but getting there is fraught with problems. . . . When the rain begins to pour down, Mama and Jack decide there's only one perfect spot for a picnic—back home. . . . Goode's art was inspired by the early years of the last century. . . . Full of amusing details and nice touches . . . this book will sustain more readings than one might expect." Booklist

Thanksgiving is here! HarperCollins Pubs. 2003 unp il $15.99; lib bdg $16.89 *
Grades: PreK K 1 2   E
   1. Thanksgiving Day—Fiction 2. Family life—Fiction
   ISBN 0-06-051588-0; 0-06-051589-9 (lib bdg)
                          LC f002-151781
A family gathers to celebrate Thanksgiving at Grandma's house
"The humorously detailed, pen-and-ink and watercolor, cartoon artwork is exuberant, mischievous, and full of surprises. This Thanksgiving book has something for everyone." SLJ

Goodhart, Pippa

Three little ghosties; illustrated by AnnaLaura Cantone. Bloomsbury Children's Books 2007 unp il $16.95
Grades: PreK K 1 2   E
   1. Ghost stories 2. Stories in rhyme
   ISBN 978-1-58234-711-0; 1-58234-711-5
                          LC 2007-02610

Three mischievous ghosts love scaring little children, until the children decide to take matters into their own hands.
"Goodhart's engagingly silly rhymes are paired with mixed-media illustrations that use dark and spooky colors but feature goofy-looking ghosts." Horn Book

Goodrich, Carter

The hermit crab. Simon & Schuster Books for Young Readers 2009 unp il $16.99
Grades: K 1 2 3   E
   1. Crabs—Fiction 2. Marine animals—Fiction
   ISBN 978-1-4169-3892-7; 1-4169-3892-3
                          LC 2007045240
Absorbed in his search for food, a shy hermit crab, disguised in a fancy new shell, inadvertently rescues a flounder caught beneath a trap and wins the admiration of the other marine animals.
"The personal tone engages the audience, bringing immediacy to the plot, and serves as a warm contrast to the cool illustrations. Goodrich's colored pencil and watercolor spreads predominantly feature greens and blues to convey the watery depth of the sea." SLJ

Gorbachev, Valeri, 1944-

Christopher counting; [by] Valeri Gorbachev. Philomel Books 2008 unp il $15.99 *
Grades: PreK K 1   E
   1. Counting—Fiction 2. Rabbits—Fiction 3. Animals—Fiction
   ISBN 978-0-399-24629-6   LC 2007023642
When Christopher Rabbit learns to count in school, he enjoys it so much that he counts everything in sight, including how many baskets his friends make when they play basketball and how many peas and carrots are on his plate.
"The simplicity of this charming story is what sets it apart from others that aim to introduce this concept. The text's deliberate pace is a perfect match for the pen, ink, and watercolor illustrations." SLJ

Dragon is coming! Harcourt Children's Books 2009 unp il $16
Grades: PreK K 1 2   E
   1. Fear—Fiction 2. Thunderstorms—Fiction 3. Clouds—Fiction 4. Mice—Fiction 5. Animals—Fiction
   ISBN 978-0-15-205196-9; 0-15-205196-1
                          LC 2006101580
Mouse frightens all of the animals she sees by shouting that a dragon is going to eat the sun, and then come after them.
"While the story is familiar, Gorbachev's illustrations revive it with delightful details and humorous poses." SLJ

The missing chick. Candlewick Press 2009 unp il $15.99
Grades: PreK K 1   E
   1. Ducks—Fiction 2. Chickens—Fiction
   ISBN 978-0-7636-3676-0; 0-7636-3676-2
"Mother Hen and her seven chicks are hanging the laundry one sunny morning when neighborly Mrs. Duck

Gorbachev, Valeri, 1944-—*Continued*

observes that one chick is missing. Goat, Sheep, and Dog help to search the premises before being joined by the firefighters and the police on the ground and in helicopters. Amid all this noisy commotion, the missing chick wakes up from its napping spot in the laundry basket. . . . The story's simple premise, just-enough page-turning tension, and comical watercolor and ink illustrations add up to a gentle and satisfying tale that will hold up to repeated readings." SLJ

Molly who flew away. Philomel Books 2009 unp il $16.99

Grades: PreK K 1 2   E

1. Fairs—Fiction 2. Balloons—Fiction 3. Mice—Fiction 4. Animals—Fiction

ISBN 978-0-399-25211-2; 0-399-25211-8

LC 2008-32607

Molly the mouse buys so many balloons for all her animal friends at the fair, she gets carried away into the air.

"Pen-and-ink and watercolor illustrations carry this simple friendship story along to the climactic end. Molly's flight is especially well shown, with a double-page spread with three ascending panels followed by a bird's eye view of the frightened mouse high over the scenery and her friends running to the rescue down below." Booklist

Another title about Molly is:
What's the big idea, Molly? (2010)

Ms. Turtle the babysitter. HarperCollins Pubs. 2005 64p il hardcover o.p. pa $3.99 *

Grades: PreK K 1 2   E

1. Babysitters—Fiction 2. Turtles—Fiction 3. Frogs—Fiction

ISBN 0-06-058073-9; 0-06-058074-7 (lib bdg); 0-06-058075-5 (pa)   LC 2004-6234

"An I can read book"

Ms. Turtle babysits for three little frogs when their parents go out for the evening

"Beginning readers will enjoy this chapter-style book. . . . The pen-and-ink and watercolor cartoons seamlessly complement the text. The expressions on the faces of these endearing frogs are priceless." SLJ

That's what friends are for. Philomel Books 2005 unp il $15.99 *

Grades: PreK K 1 2   E

1. Friendship—Fiction 2. Goats—Fiction 3. Pigs—Fiction

ISBN 0-399-23966-9   LC 2004-18118

When Goat finds his friend Pig crying, he imagines all the terrible things that might have happened to cause his distress

"The book is a warm display of friendship and a caution against unnecessary worry. Soft-colored drawings supply details for the simple text." Horn Book Guide

Turtle's penguin day; [by] Valeri Gorbachev. Alfred A. Knopf 2008 unp il $16.99; lib bdg $19.99 *

Grades: PreK K 1   E

1. Turtles—Fiction 2. Penguins—Fiction 3. Animals—Fiction 4. School stories

ISBN 978-0-375-84374-7; 0-375-84374-4; 978-0-375-94564-9 (lib bdg); 0-375-94564-4 (lib bdg)

LC 2007037078

After hearing a bedtime story about penguins, Turtle dresses as a penguin for school and soon the entire class is having a penguin day.

"Cheerful watercolors and expressive line art imbue the matter-of-fact narrative with personality. . . . This nurturing tale celebrates the inspiration and information found in books, the invention bubbling up from a child who is read to, and the quality of learning that is possible when a teacher seizes the moment." SLJ

Gore, Leonid

Danny's first snow; by Leonid Gore. Atheneum 2007 unp il $16.99

Grades: PreK K   E

1. Snow—Fiction 2. Rabbits—Fiction 3. Imagination—Fiction

ISBN 1-4169-1330-0

When he ventures outside to experience his first snowfall, a young rabbit discovers that his world has greatly changed.

"The exquisite illustrations in this story . . . will delight young readers. . . . Gore achieves remarkable shapes and surfaces, with green pines transformed into bears that gradually melt away as the day advances." Publ Wkly

Mommy, where are you? [by] Leonid Gore. Atheneum Books for Young Readers 2009 unp il $16.99

Grades: PreK K 1   E

1. Mice—Fiction 2. Mother-child relationship—Fiction

ISBN 978-1-4169-5505-4; 1-4169-5505-4

LC 2008-25994

"Ginee Seo Books"

A little mouse wakes up one day and, when he cannot find his mother, goes in search of her.

"Gore skillfully provides both repetition and variety for his audience, so both young listeners and their adults will find the story engaging as well as easy to follow. . . . Acrylic illustrations are simply composed, and the layered colors . . . and textured application of the paint . . . add pleasing depth and sophistication to the images." Bull Cent Child Books

When I grow up. Scholastic Press 2009 unp il $16.99

Grades: PreK   E

1. Growth—Fiction 2. Father-son relationship—Fiction

ISBN 978-0-545-08597-7; 0-545-08597-7

LC 2008014313

At his drawing table on a rainy day, a boy imagines all the ways in which different things might grow up, and comes to the conclusion that he will grow up to be just like his dad.

"The simple and poetic artwork was done in acrylic

Gore, Leonid—*Continued*

and mixed media on die-cut pages. . . . The exploration of his world gives this father-and-son selection a refreshing take on a familiar theme." SLJ

Gourley, Robbin

Bring me some apples and I'll make you a pie; a story about Edna Lewis. Clarion Books 2009 45p il $16 *

Grades: PreK K 1 2   E

1. Lewis, Edna, 1916-2006—Fiction 2. Farm life—Fiction 3. Food—Fiction 4. Family life—Fiction 5. Cooking—Fiction 6. African Americans—Fiction 7. Virginia—Fiction

ISBN 978-0-618-15836-2; 0-618-15836-7

LC 2007-46978

Edna and members of her family gather fruits, berries, and vegetables from the fields, garden, and orchard on their Virginia farm and turn them into wonderful meals. Includes facts about the life of Edna Lewis, a descendant of slaves who grew up to be a famous chef, and five recipes.

"The cheery watercolor spreads follow Edna and various relatives . . . from spring to first snow. . . . Folk sayings or songs accompany mention of each new food. . . . Dynamic paintings, increasingly lush as summer intensifies, add vigor." Publ Wkly

Gower, Catherine

Long-Long's New Year; a story about the Chinese spring festival; illustrated by He Zhihong. Tuttle 2005 unp il $16.95

Grades: K 1 2 3   E

1. Chinese New Year—Fiction 2. China—Fiction 3. Grandfathers—Fiction

ISBN 0-8048-3666-3   LC 2004-111580

"To earn money for the upcoming Spring Festival (also known as Chinese New Year), Long-Long and his grandfather take a bicycle cart loaded with cabbages into town on market day." Booklist

"Gower's simple, appealing story aptly captures the details of the festival as well as specifics of Chinese life. Zhihong's softly colored, detailed drawings on tan rice paper evoke both the bustle of a preholiday marketplace as well as the gentle warmth shared by grandfather and grandchild." SLJ

Graber, Janet, 1942-

Muktar and the camels. Henry Holt and Co. 2009 unp il $16.99

Grades: K 1 2 3   E

1. Orphans—Fiction 2. Refugees—Fiction 3. Camels—Fiction 4. School stories 5. Kenya—Fiction

ISBN 978-0-8050-7834-3; 0-8050-7834-7

LC 2008038217

"Christy Ottaviano books"

Muktar, an eleven-year-old refugee living in a Kenyan orphanage, dreams of tending camels again, as he did with his nomadic family in Somalia, and has a chance to prove himself when a traveling librarian with an injured camel arrives at his school.

"Muktar longs to live the life that is in his blood, and Graber tells his story well. . . . Mack's oil-on-canvas paintings evoke the sun and dust of Kenya, giving readers an impression of the landscape." SLJ

Graham, Bob, 1942-

Dimity Dumpty; the story of Humpty's little sister. Candlewick Press 2006 unp il $15.99

Grades: PreK K 1 2   E

1. Siblings—Fiction 2. Circus—Fiction 3. Eggs—Fiction 4. Nursery rhymes—Fiction

ISBN 0-7636-3078-0   LC 2005-55306

Humpty Dumpty's little sister is too shy to be part of her family's circus act, but she finds courage when her brother needs her help.

"The full-color watercolor illustrations are a delight. . . . The language is lyrical . . . and makes a perfect read-aloud." SLJ

How to heal a broken wing. Candlewick Press 2008 unp il $16.99 *

Grades: PreK K 1 2   E

1. Birds—Fiction 2. Rescue work—Fiction

ISBN 978-0-7636-3903-7; 0-7636-3903-6

LC 2007-40622

When Will finds a bird with a broken wing, he takes it home and cares for it, hoping in time it will be able to return to the sky.

This is a "sparsely worded story. . . . Graham breaks his watercolor-and-ink cartoons into full-bleed spreads and large and small comics-like panels, enabling him to dwell on each moment of tender loving care and to preach patience." Publ Wkly

Let's get a pup, said Kate. Candlewick Press 2001 unp il hardcover o.p. pa $6.99

Grades: PreK K 1 2   E

1. Dogs—Fiction 2. Animal shelters—Fiction

ISBN 0-7636-1452-1; 0-7636-2193-5 (pa)

LC 00-57208

When Kate and her parents visit the animal shelter, an adorable puppy charms them, but it is very hard to leave an older dog behind

"Bob Graham's cozy watercolors, lightly held in place by loose, sketchy outlines, contribute to this story's feelings of warmth, family, and belonging." Horn Book

Another title about Kate and her dog is:

"The trouble with dogs," said Dad (2007)

Oscar's half birthday. Candlewick Press 2005 unp il $16.99 *

Grades: PreK K 1 2   E

1. Racially mixed people—Fiction 2. Birthdays—Fiction 3. Family life—Fiction

ISBN 0-7636-2699-6   LC 2004-57041

"A mixed-race family sets out for a picnic in the park to celebrate baby Oscar's half birthday. . . . The warm, expressive illustrations show a family apartment in which a mop, shoes, and toys all share floor space. . . . This is an effortlessly multicultural story, full of the joy of childhood, family, and community." SLJ

Gralley, Jean

The moon came down on Milk Street; written and illustrated by Jean Gralley. Holt 2004 unp il $16.95

Grades: PreK K 1 2   E

1. Moon—Fiction 2. Rescue work—Fiction 3. Stories in rhyme

ISBN 0-8050-7266-7

When the moon comes down in pieces, different helpers work to set things right again, including the Fire Chief, rescue workers, and helper dogs.

"Gralley presents a perceptive look at how individuals react to an unexpected crisis. . . . Done in gouache and mixed media, the large, uncluttered illustrations on white backgrounds contribute to the gentle nature of the story." SLJ

Gramatky, Hardie, 1907-1979

Little Toot; pictures and story by Hardie Gramatky. G.P. Putnam's Sons 2007 c1939 86p il $17.99

Grades: PreK K   E

1. Tugboats—Fiction

ISBN 978-0-399-24713-2; 0-399-24713-0

First published 1939

"The restored classic" - cover

Little Toot the tugboat conquers his fear of rough seas when he singlehandedly rescues an ocean liner during a storm

"Mr. Gramatky tells his story with humor and enjoyment, giving, too, a genuine sense of the water front in both pictures and story." Horn Book

Grambling, Lois G., 1927-

T. Rex and the Mother's Day hug; by Lois G. Grambling; illustrated by Jack E. Davis. HarperCollins 2008 unp il $16.99; lib bdg $17.89

Grades: K 1 2   E

1. Dinosaurs—Fiction 2. Mother's Day—Fiction

ISBN 978-0-06-053126-3; 0-06-053126-6; 978-0-06-053127-0 (lib bdg); 0-06-053127-4 (lib bdg)

LC 2007-6882

Eager to do something special for Mother's Day, T. Rex decides to surprise his mother by decorating her car.

"Davis's jaunty cartoon illustrations bring these less-than-extinct dinosaurs alive. This fun read-aloud will tickle young children as they prepare for Mother's Day themselves." SLJ

Other titles in this series are:

Here comes T. Rex Cottontail (2007)

T. Rex trick-or-treats (2005)

Grandits, John, 1949-

The travel game; illustrated by R. W. Alley. Clarion Books 2009 32p il $16

Grades: K 1 2 3   E

1. Games—Fiction 2. Imagination—Fiction 3. Hong Kong (China)—Fiction 4. Aunts—Fiction 5. Tailoring—Fiction 6. Buffalo (N.Y.)—Fiction 7. Polish Americans—Fiction

ISBN 978-0-618-56420-0; 0-618-56420-9

LC 2005017646

To avoid a nap, Tad plays his favorite quiet game with his aunt and together their imaginations take them from their home in Buffalo, New York, to Hong Kong.

"Alley's cheery and busy street, home, and shop scenes in ink, watercolor, and acrylic are filled with the sorts of details that are fully appreciated over multiple readings. Children will be charmed by the warmth and humor of Grandits's wonderful tribute to family memories and the power of imagination." SLJ

Grant, Judyann

Chicken said, Cluck! by Judyann Ackerman Grant; pictures by Sue Truesdell. HarperCollins 2008 32p il (My first I can read book) $16.99; lib bdg $17.89 *

Grades: K 1 2   E

1. Chickens—Fiction 2. Gardening—Fiction 3. Grasshoppers—Fiction

ISBN 978-0-06-028723-8; 0-06-028723-3; 978-0-06-028724-5 (lib bdg); 0-06-028724-1 (lib bdg)

LC 2001-24016

A Geisel Award honor book, 2009

"My first shared reading."

Earl and Pearl do not want Chicken's help in the garden, until a swarm of grasshoppers arrives and her true talent shines

"This easy reader has short sentences, a variety of verb tenses, and vowel and consonant blends and digraphs. . . . Emergent readers may chime in with their own 'Shoo, Shoos' and 'Cluck, Cluck.' The funny, expressive pen-and-ink drawings support the reading with simple clarity." SLJ

Grant, Karima, 1972-

Sofie and the city; [by] Karima Grant; illustrated by Janet Montecalvo. Boyds Mills Press 2006 unp il $15.95

Grades: PreK K 1 2   E

1. Immigrants—Fiction 2. African Americans—Fiction 3. City and town life—Fiction 4. Friendship—Fiction

ISBN 1-59078-273-9   LC 2005020116

When Sofie calls her grandmother in Senegal on Sundays, she complains about the ugliness of the city she now lives in, but her life changes when she makes a new friend

"Told in simple language, with dialogue matching that of a child learning English, the text and art show how upsetting any move can be and how it feels to be small in a large and unfamiliar place." SLJ

Gravett, Emily

Dogs. Simon & Schuster 2010 unp il $15.99 *

Grades: PreK K 1   E

1. Dogs—Fiction 2. Opposites 3. Stories in rhyme

ISBN 978-1-4169-8703-1; 1-4169-8703-7

"In minimal, rhyming text, an unidentified narrator describes its favorite kinds of dogs . . . and, along the way, offers a subtle lesson in the meaning of opposites. Expressive pencil drawings, overlaid with soft washes of watercolor on creamy stock, waggishly animate more than a dozen varieties of dogs. . . . The pacing of the simple text and scale of the drawings lend this title equally well to preschool storytimes, lap-sharing, and emergent-reader[s]." SLJ

Gravett, Emily—*Continued*

Little Mouse's big book of fears. Simon & Schuster Books for Young Readers 2008 unp il $17.99 *

Grades: K 1 2 3   E

1. Fear—Fiction 2. Mice—Fiction

ISBN 978-1-4169-5930-4; 1-4169-5930-0

LC 2008-61104

First published 2007 in the United Kingdom with title: Emily Gravett's big book of fears

Little Mouse draws pictures of some of the many things he is afraid of, including creepy crawlies, sharp knives, and having accidents, and provides the correct scientific name for each of his fears

"Spare text and delightful illustrations chronicle this nervous rodent's journey. . . . The striking mixed-media art captures the humorous adventures of the white mouse and his red pencil." SLJ

Meerkat mail. Simon & Schuster Books for Young Readers 2007 unp il $17.99

Grades: PreK K 1   E

1. Meerkats—Fiction 2. Africa—Fiction

ISBN 978-1-4169-3473-8; 1-4169-3473-1

LC 2007001569

Through a series of flip-up postcards addressed to his family, Sunny Meerkat documents his travels as he searches for the perfect place for him to live.

"Gravett neatly incorporates facts about meerkats, mongooses, and their habitats. She employs a spare narrative, allowing Sunny's postcards to tell most of the story through both the character's distinctive voice and each post card's illustrations." Horn Book

Monkey and me. Simon & Schuster 2008 unp il $15.99 *

Grades: PreK K   E

1. Imagination—Fiction 2. Toys—Fiction 3. Animals—Fiction

ISBN 978-1-4169-5457-6; 1-4169-5457-0

"A little girl pretends that she and her adored stuffed monkey fit right in with tribes of penguins, kangaroos, bats, elephants and . . . monkeys. A catchy refrain sets up each scenario. . . . Working in pencil and watercolor, with a palette limited to red, black and brown, Gravett . . . portrays the action in a series of exuberant spot sketches set against a white sweep." Publ Wkly

The odd egg. Simon & Schuster Books for Young Readers 2009 unp il $15.99 *

Grades: PreK K 1   E

1. Eggs—Fiction 2. Ducks—Fiction 3. Birds—Fiction 4. Alligators—Fiction

ISBN 978-1-4169-6872-6; 1-4169-6872-5

LC 2008-61108

Duck is trying to hatch the oddest egg of all.

"Using visual suspense and few words, Gravett depicts an alligator bursting from the shell, snapping its jaws and scattering the naysayers. . . . A witty salute to both nature and nurture." Publ Wkly

Orange pear apple bear. Simon & Schuster Books for Young Readers 2007 unp il $12.99 *

Grades: PreK K   E

1. Bears—Fiction 2. Color—Fiction 3. Shape—Fiction

ISBN 978-1-4169-3999-3; 1-4169-3999-7

LC 2006-17964

A "bear changes color and shape as he balances, juggles, and eventually eats the three pieces of fruit before loping off. The front endpapers show oranges, green pears, and green apples with rosy tinges in a line leading readers into the simple and appealing story. . . . Beautiful, softly hued watercolor illustrations loosely outlined in black pen and ink are delightful." SLJ

Spells. Simon & Schuster Books for Young Readers 2009 unp il $16.99 *

Grades: K 1 2 3 4   E

1. Frogs—Fiction 2. Magic—Fiction

ISBN 978-1-4169-8270-8; 1-4169-8270-1

LC 2008-941243

"A small green frog stumbles on a book of spells, . . . tries to turn himself into a handsome prince, but suffers a series of glitches. Frog transforms himself into a snake, bird, rabbit and other creatures before getting it right. . . . The five pages that show Frog's new forms are cut in half horizontally, and children will delight in turning the half-pages, reading the new spells that appear on the left side of each spread and seeing the combined creatures that emerge (a half-prince, half-newt "prewt," for instance)." Publ Wkly

Wolves; [by] Emily Grrrabbett [i.e. Gravett] Simon & Schuster Books for Young Readers 2006 unp il $15.95

Grades: 1 2 3   E

1. Wolves—Fiction 2. Rabbits—Fiction 3. Books and reading—Fiction

ISBN 978-1-4169-1491-4; 1-4169-1491-9

LC 2005027540

When a young rabbit checks out a library book about wolves, he learns much more about their behavior than he wanted to know

"This imaginative, cleverly designed story unfolds in a delectable blend of spare text and eloquent multimedia illustrations." SLJ

Gray, Libba Moore

My mama had a dancing heart; illustrated by Raúl Colón. Orchard Bks. 1995 unp il hardcover o.p. pa $6.99 *

Grades: K 1 2 3   E

1. Dance—Fiction 2. Mother-daughter relationship—Fiction 3. Seasons—Fiction

ISBN 0-531-09470-7; 0-531-08770-0 (lib bdg); 0-531-07142-1 (pa)   LC 94-48802

"A Melanie Kroupa book"

"In spring, summer, fall and winter, a mother leads her young daughter in dancing a celebratory ballet, a hymn to the season. When the girl is older, she is a ballerina and remembers that her mother gave her a dancing heart. . . . Colón's etched watercolors in earth and muted jewel tones give the book an old-fashioned ambiance. . . . Gray's writing lends itself to reading aloud, but independent readers will also enjoy it." SLJ

Greenberg, David

Crocs! by David T. Greenberg; illustrated by Lynn Munsinger. Little, Brown 2008 unp il $16.99
Grades: K 1 2 3   E
  1. Crocodiles—Fiction 2. Stories in rhyme
  ISBN 978-0-316-07306-6; 0-316-07306-7
                        LC 2006020571
Having moved from the city to a tropical island to escape such horrifying creatures as bugs and cats, a boy encounters a horde of friendly crocodiles, who drink Tabasco sauce, get tangled in dental floss, and turn the house into a swamp
  "The zany illustrations—done in mixed-media, soft-palette watercolors with pen and ink—use plenty of white space and add humor and charm to the perfect-pitch verses." SLJ

Enchanted lions; by David T. Greenberg; illustrated by Kristina Swarner. Dutton Children's Books 2009 unp il $16.99
Grades: PreK K 1 2   E
  1. Stories in rhyme 2. Constellations—Fiction 3. Outer space—Exploration—Fiction
  ISBN 978-0-525-47938-3; 0-525-47938-4
                        LC 2008-34215
One evening, Rose climbs on the back of an enchanted lion who takes her on a tour of outer space, where they race with Monoceros the unicorn, pass by Pegasus and Pisces, and are rescued from a black hole by Cetus the whale.
  "The gentle, rhyming text and the mottled, softly colored scratchboardlike illustrations work together to convey a quiet, calm tone for this heavenly romp." Booklist

Greenfield, Eloise, 1929-

Africa dream; illustrated by Carole Byard. Crowell 1977 unp il hardcover o.p. pa $6.99
Grades: PreK K 1 2   E
  1. Africa—Fiction
  ISBN 0-690-04776-2 (lib bdg); 0-06-443277-7 (pa)
                        LC 77-5080
Coretta Scott King Award for text
  "As ethereal as the title implies, this sparsely worded prose-poem relates the benign dream experience of a young child who transports her mind to 'Long-ago Africa.'" Booklist

Grandpa's face; illustrated by Floyd Cooper. Philomel Bks. 1988 unp il lib bdg $16.99; pa $6.99
Grades: PreK K 1 2   E
  1. Grandfathers—Fiction 2. Actors—Fiction
  ISBN 0-399-21525-5 (lib bdg); 0-399-22106-9 (pa)
                        LC 87-16729
  "Tamika fears that her grandfather, an actor, is incapable of loving her when she sees him practicing a cruel expression. The young girl's turmoil and its resolution are keenly felt through evocative text and striking pictures." SLJ

Gregory, Nan, 1944-

Pink; [illustrated by] Luc Melanson. Groundwood 2007 32p il $17.95
Grades: PreK K 1 2   E
  1. Dolls—Fiction
  ISBN 978-0-88899-781-4
Vivi loves the color pink. She is working and saving her money in order to buy a pink doll from the store. How does she feel when the doll is sold to someone else?
  "Gregory writes with precision and creates apt, sometimes surprising phrases that capture the characters' feelings. Melanson's painterly, digitally assisted pictures create a distinctive look though the elongated forms and faces of the characters." Booklist

Gretz, Susanna

Riley and Rose in the picture. Candlewick Press 2005 unp il $16.99 *
Grades: PreK K 1 2   E
  1. Dogs—Fiction 2. Cats—Fiction 3. Friendship—Fiction
  ISBN 0-7636-2681-3   LC 2004-54569
On a rainy day Reilly the dog and Rosa the cat decide to stay indoors and draw a picture together but have trouble agreeing on how to do it
  "The lively text is read-aloud friendly, incorporating child-familiar dialogue, interactions, and humor. The colorful gouache art is charming, too, filling the pages with expressive characters and distinctive childlike artwork that perfectly matches the story." Booklist

Grey, Mini

The adventures of the dish and the spoon. Knopf 2006 unp il $16.95; lib bdg $18.99 *
Grades: PreK K 1 2   E
  1. Tableware—Fiction 2. Nursery rhymes—Fiction
  ISBN 0-375-83691-8; 0-375-93691-2 (lib bdg)
                        LC 2005017548
Having run away together, the Dish and the Spoon from the nursery rhyme "The Cat and the Fiddle" become vaudeville stars before turning to a life of crime
  "The narrative is packed with tongue-in-cheek humor. The rich art mingles paint with collage, featuring framed scenes and a palette of lush browns dotted with primary reds and blues." Bull Cent Child Books

Egg drop. Alfred A. Knopf 2009 unp il $16.99; lib bdg $19.99
Grades: 1 2 3   E
  1. Eggs—Fiction 2. Flight—Fiction
  ISBN   978-0-375-84260-3;   0-375-84260-8; 978-0-375-94260-0 (lib bdg); 0-375-94260-2 (lib bdg)
                        LC 2008-24534
Tragedy strikes when an egg, eager to fly like birds, airplanes, and insects, steps off of a tall tower.
  "The mixed-media and collage full-color art is quirky and inventive with multiple perspectives, and imbues the Egg with personality." SLJ

Grey, Mini—*Continued*

Traction Man is here! Knopf 2005 unp il $15.95; lib bdg $17.99 *

Grades: PreK K 1 2   E

    1. Toys—Fiction   2. Imagination—Fiction
3. Superheroes—Fiction

    ISBN 0-375-83191-6; 0-375-93191-0 (lib bdg)

                                  LC 2004-4452

Traction Man, a boy's courageous action figure, has a variety of adventures with Scrubbing Brush and other objects in the house

And "imaginative and very funny romp. . . . The angular, full-color art sweeps across the pages and perfectly animates the antics of Traction Man and his enemies." SLJ

Followed by: Traction Man meets Turbodog (2008)

Gribnau, Joe

Kick the cowboy; illustrated by Adrian Tans. Pelican Pub. Co. 2009 unp il $15.95

Grades: PreK K 1 2   E

    1. Cowhands—Fiction 2. Texas—Fiction 3. Tall tales

    ISBN 978-1-58980-605-4; 1-58980-605-0

                                  LC 2009-3950

A cowboy named Kick becomes a mean braggart, driving away all of his friends and terrorizing the people of his Texas town, until a no-nonsense little girl named Belle helps him to mend his ways.

"Gribnau has a real winner here. . . . This above average story will be a real hit with both kids and storytellers. . . . Tans' illustrations are terrific, making the reader really want to see what happens next. This is a fantastic children's story. . . . Highly Recommended." Libr Media Connect

Grifalconi, Ann

Ain't nobody a stranger to me; illustrated by Jerry Pinkney. Hyperion/Jump at the Sun 2007 unp il $16.99 *

Grades: K 1 2 3   E

    1. Grandfathers—Fiction 2. Slavery—Fiction
3. Underground railroad—Fiction 4. African Americans—Fiction

    ISBN 978-0-7868-1857-0

This story spotlights both the loving rapport between a girl and her grandfather, and the story of his family's escape to freedom.

"Pinkney's watercolor double-paged spreads contrast the sepia-toned gloom of slavery and hiding with the abundant light-filled apple orchard today. . . . Caught by the action, children will hear Finger's shining words across time, race, and generations." Booklist

The village that vanished; illustrated by Kadir Nelson. Dial Bks. for Young Readers 2002 unp il $16.99 *

Grades: 1 2 3 4   E

    1. Yao (African people)—Fiction 2. Escapes—Fiction 3. Slave trade—Fiction 4. Southern Africa—Fiction

    ISBN 0-8037-2623-6   LC 00-38416

In southeastern Africa, a young Yao girl and her mother find a way for their fellow villagers to escape approaching slave traders

"This story celebrating resourcefulness, quick thinking, and community solidarity may inspire and empower readers. Nelson's pencil drawings enhanced with oil paints are wonderfully evocative of place, mood, posture, and expression." SLJ

Griffiths, Andy, 1961-

The big fat cow that goes kapow; illustrated by Terry Denton. Feiwel & Friends 2009 123p $14.99 *

Grades: 2 3 4   E

    1. Animals—Fiction

    ISBN 978-0-312-36788-6; 0-312-36788-0

    First published 2008 in Australia

In these ten easy-to-read stories there is a mixed-up cow that says "miaow," a mole called Noel who plays rock 'n' roll in a hole, and a boy named Mike who rides a bike with a very big spike

"Broad slapstick humor and galloping, Seuss-like rhymes are just part of the reason this . . . has strong child appeal. Denton's funny illustrations are full of action, and his use of stick figures and stink lines makes the book look as though it had been illustrated by a cheeky but talented kid." SLJ

The cat on the mat is flat; [by] Andy Griffiths; illustrated by Terry Denton. Feiwel & Friends 2007 166p il pa $9.95

Grades: 2 3 4   E

    1. Animals—Fiction 2. Stories in rhyme

    ISBN 978-0-312-36787-9

This "innovative book for beginning readers collects nine short, intentionally silly snippets propelled by kid-pleasing, tongue-tripping verse. In the title tale, a cat sitting on a mat decides to chase a rat, who grabs a baseball bat. . . . Other protagonists also encounter tongue-in-cheek adversity. . . . Denton's edgy, stick-figure-filled sketches enhance the zaniness factor and the offbeat, ironic humor." Publ Wkly

Grimes, Nikki

Oh, brother! [by] Nikki Grimes; illustrations by Mike Benny. 1st ed. Greenwillow Books 2008 unp il $16.99; lib bdg $17.89

Grades: 2 3 4   E

    1. Stepfamilies—Fiction 2. Brothers—Fiction
3. Remarriage—Fiction 4. Hispanic Americans—Fiction

    ISBN 978-0-688-17294-7;   0-688-17294-6;
978-0-688-17295-4 (lib bdg); 0-688-17295-4 (lib bdg)

                                  LC 2005035645

Xavier is unhappy when his mother suddenly has a new stepbrother, as well as a stepfather, in his home.

"Snappy language and varied rhyme schemes energize Grimes's . . . verses. . . . Benny . . . intersperses surreal illustrations with more realistic scenes. . . . The art and poems capture and memorably convey a range of emotions." Publ Wkly

Grindley, Sally, 1953-

It's my school; [by] Sally Grindley; illustrations by Margaret Chamberlain. Walker & Company 2006 unp il $15.95; lib bdg $16.85

Grades: PreK K 1 2   E

1. School stories 2. Siblings—Fiction

ISBN   978-0-8027-8086-7;   0-8027-8086-5;
978-0-8027-8087-4 (lib bdg); 0-8027-8087-3 (lib bdg)
LC 2005037181

Tom is not happy that his younger sister, Alice, is starting kindergarten at his school

"The large illustrations . . . are depicted in soft pastel hues, capturing the siblings' facial expressions and the varying degress of emotion. . . . This is a new take on first-day-of-school stories, and a realistic choice to help children share their lives with a younger sibling." SLJ

Guarino, Deborah, 1954-

Is your mama a llama? illustrated by Steven Kellogg. Scholastic 1989 unp il hardcover o.p. pa $6.99; bd bk $6.99

Grades: PreK K   E

1. Llamas—Fiction 2. Animals—Fiction 3. Stories in rhyme

ISBN 0-590-41387-2 (lib bdg); 0-439-59842-7 (pa);
0-590-25938-5 (bd bk)   LC 87-32315

A young llama asks his friends if their mamas are llamas and finds out, in rhyme, that their mothers are other types of animals

"The lines are clean as well as exuberant, the colors well-blended as well as bright, and the compositions uncluttered as well as appealing. An ingenious page design invites choral participation, and the ending will encourage a cozy hiatus for bed/nap time." Bull Cent Child Books

Guback, Georgia

Luka's quilt. Greenwillow Bks. 1994 unp il $16.99; lib bdg $13.93

Grades: K 1 2 3   E

1. Quilts—Fiction 2. Grandmothers—Fiction 3. Hawaii—Fiction

ISBN 0-688-12154-3; 0-688-12155-1 (lib bdg)
LC 93-12241

When Luka's grandmother makes a traditional Hawaiian quilt for her, she and Luka disagree over the colors it should include

"Eye-catching collages of brightly painted papers, the illustrations express the characters' emotions and show a delight in the Hawaiian landscape and traditions. . . . An involving story that's all the more satisfying because the ending offers no mere emotional patch up but a real solution." Booklist

Guest, Elissa Haden, 1953-

Harriet's had enough; illustrated by Paul Meisel. Candlewick Press 2009 unp il $15.99

Grades: PreK K 1 2   E

1. Family life—Fiction 2. Raccoons—Fiction

ISBN 978-0-7636-3454-4; 0-7636-3454-9

"Harriet refuses to pick up her toys, and her mother is angry. When she tells her grandmother and father that she will run away because 'Mama's mean', they explain that everyone has chores to complete. Grandma succinctly explains, 'That's life, honey-bun.' . . . Harriet's shifting emotions are conveyed through her varied expressions. Intricate strokes add depth and texture to this raccoon family. Soft watercolor, acrylic, and gouache illustrations suit the subject." SLJ

Iris and Walter; written by Elissa Haden Guest; illustrated by Christine Davenier. Harcourt 2000 43p il $15; pa $5.95 *

Grades: K 1 2   E

1. Country life—Fiction 2. City and town life—Fiction 3. Friendship—Fiction

ISBN 0-15-202122-1; 0-15-216442-1 (pa)
LC 99-6242

"Gulliver books"

When Iris moves to the country, she misses the city where she formerly lived; but with the help of a new friend named Walter, she learns to adjust to her new home

"Christine Davenier's exuberant pen-and-ink drawings reveal all the delightful things Iris discovers with Walter. . . . An easy-to-read chapter book . . . just right for children ready to step up their skills." Booklist

Other titles about Iris and Walter are:

Iris and Walter and Baby Rose (2002)
Iris and Walter and Cousin Howie (2003)
Iris and Walter and the birthday party (2006)
Iris and Walter and the field trip (2005)
Iris and Walter and the substitute teacher (2004)
Iris and Walter, lost and found (2004)
Iris and Walter, the school play (2003)
Iris and Walter, the sleepover (2002)
Iris and Walter, true friends (2001)

Guy, Ginger Foglesong

Fiesta! pictures by Rene King Moreno. Greenwillow Bks. 1996 unp il $15.99 *

Grades: PreK K 1 2   E

1. Parties—Fiction 2. Counting 3. Bilingual books—English-Spanish

ISBN 0-688-14331-8   LC 95-35848

"Three children begin with *una canasta* (one basket) and proceed to fill it with scrumptious candies, trinkets, and toys in preparation for a Mexican fiesta. . . . A simple bilingual text provides numbers in English and Spanish. The soft-edged full-color illustrations done in pencils, pastels, and watercolors have a subtle folkloric quality." SLJ

Perros! Perros! Dogs! Dogs! a story in English and Spanish; by Ginger Foglesong Guy; pictures by Sharon Glick. Greenwillow Books 2006 unp il $15.99; lib bdg $16.89 *

Grades: PreK K 1 2   E

1. Dogs—Fiction 2. Opposites 3. Bilingual books—English-Spanish

ISBN   978-0-06-083574-3;   0-06-083574-5;
978-0-06-083575-0 (lib bdg); 0-06-083575-3 (lib bdg)

This "title makes use of a wide array of breeds to demonstrate the concept of opposites. The story begins with a girl waking up in her bedroom. . . . As she looks out her window, an excited pack of dogs runs by. Big

Guy, Ginger Foglesong—*Continued*

dog. Little dog. . . .Where are they going? . . . What the book lacks in plot development it makes up for in the sheer exuberance of the watercolor cartoons. A must for dog lovers and a good choice for beginning readers in either language." SLJ

Siesta; pictures by René King Moreno. Greenwillow Books 2005 unp il $15.99; lib bdg $16.89; bd bk $7.99 *

Grades: PreK K 1 2   E

1. Color—Fiction 2. Bilingual books—English-Spanish
ISBN 0-06-056061-4; 0-06-056063-0 (lib bdg); 978-0-06-168884-3 (bd bk)   LC 2004-42464

A brother and sister and their teddy bear go through the house gathering items they will need for their siesta in the back yard

This "uses a bilingual approach to reinforce an understanding of colors. . . . Highlighted text in the appropriate hue reinforces the color concept, as do Moreno's soft, appealing illustrations." Booklist

Haas, Jessie

Sugaring; pictures by Jos. A. Smith. Greenwillow Bks. 1996 unp il $17.99

Grades: PreK K 1 2   E

1. Maple sugar—Fiction 2. Grandfathers—Fiction 3. Horses—Fiction
ISBN 0-688-14200-1   LC 95-38139

Nora wants to find a way to give the horses a special treat for helping her grandfather and her gather sap to make maple syrup

"The realistic watercolor illustrations effectively capture the scenes; color and texture are skillfully used to depict the cold, hard job of gathering the sap and the hot steamy atmosphere of the sugar house." SLJ

Haddon, Mark

Footprints on the Moon; illustrated by Christian Birmingham. Candlewick Press 2009 c1996 unp il $16.99 *

Grades: K 1 2 3   E

1. Space flight to the moon—Fiction
ISBN 978-0-7636-4440-6; 0-7636-4440-4

First published 1996 in the United Kingdom with title: The sea of tranquillity

A man remembers his boyhood fascination with the Moon and the night mankind first bounced through the dust in the Sea of Tranquillity.

"Birmingham's nostalgia-tinged illustrations have a dreamlike quality and provide readers a glimpse into both the boy's and astronauts' separate worlds until, in a wonderful spread, both worlds join as a third tiny astronaut is seen bouncing on the Moon with Armstrong and Aldrin. The pairing of text and art creates a wonderful read-aloud." SLJ

Hader, Berta, 1891-1976

The big snow; by Berta and Elmer Hader. Macmillan 1948 unp il $18.99; pa $7.99

Grades: PreK K 1   E

1. Animals—Fiction 2. Winter—Fiction
ISBN 0-02-737910-8; 0-689-71757-1 (pa)
Awarded the Caldecott Medal, 1949

This book shows "the birds and animals which come for the food put out by an old couple after a big snow." Hodges. Books for Elem Sch Libr

Hajdusiewicz, Babs Bell, 1944-

Sputter, sputter, sput! by Babs Bell; illustrated by Bob Staake. HarperCollins 2008 unp il $16.99; lib bdg $17.89

Grades: PreK K   E

1. Automobiles—Fiction 2. Stories in rhyme
ISBN 978-0-06-056222-9; 0-06-056222-6; 978-0-06-056223-6 (lib bdg); 0-06-056223-4 (lib bdg)

A driver happily cruising in his car sputters out of gas, refills his tank, and zooms right out of town.

"Staake's vibrant, computer-generated geometric art perfectly complements the playfulness of the simple, rhyming text. Certain to be a favorite among toddler vehicle enthusiasts." SLJ

Hakala, Marjorie, 1984-

Mermaid dance; by Marjorie Rose Hakala; illustrated by Mark Jones. Blue Apple 2009 unp il $16.99

Grades: PreK K 1 2   E

1. Mermaids and mermen—Fiction 2. Summer solstice—Fiction
ISBN 978-1-934706-47-3; 1-934706-47-7   LC 2008042595

On the first night of summer when high tide brings the ocean to the edge of the forest, woodland animals watch mermaids frolicking under a full moon.

"Jones's pastel illustrations show the dreamlike festivities both above and below water. A magical fantasy to celebrate the summer solstice." SLJ

Hale, Bruce, 1957-

Snoring Beauty; written by Bruce Hale; illustrated by Howard Fine. Harcourt 2008 unp il $16

Grades: PreK K 1 2   E

1. Fairy tales 2. Dragons—Fiction
ISBN 978-0-15-216314-3; 0-15-216314-X   LC 2006022950

"Princess Marge, daughter of King Gluteus and Queen Esophagus, who is nearly doomed by an irate fairy to homicide by a pie wagon, has the harsh sentence modified by another ('half-deaf') fairy, Tintinnitus. The princess will become a sleeping dragon and will 'one day' be awakened by 'a quince.' . . . Enriched by Fine's large, double-page watercolor paintings . . . ; a repetitive refrain ('Yada, yada, hippity-hop'); and those cacophonous snores, this fantastic story is a delightful treat that begs to be read aloud." SLJ

Hall, Bruce Edward

Henry and the kite dragon; illustrated by William Low. Philomel Books 2004 unp il $15.99

Grades: K 1 2 3 4   E

1. Kites—Fiction 2. Chinese Americans—Fiction 3. Italian Americans—Fiction 4. New York (N.Y.)—Fiction
ISBN 0-399-23727-5   LC 2003-16381

Hall, Bruce Edward—*Continued*

In New York City in the 1920s, the children from Chinatown go after the children from Little Italy for throwing rocks at the beautiful kites Grandfather Chin makes, not realizing that they have a reason for doing so.

The author "tells an engaging story about a vibrant community, which is beautifully captured in Low's detailed, dramatic paintings." Booklist

Hall, Donald, 1928-

Ox-cart man; pictures by Barbara Cooney. Viking 1979 unp il $16.99; pa $6.99

Grades: K 1 2 3   E

1. New England—Fiction

ISBN 0-670-53328-9; 0-14-050441-9 (pa)

LC 79-14466

Awarded the Caldecott Medal, 1980

"It is fall and a farmer loads a cart with the year's produce, journeys to market, sells, buys, and returns to his family to begin the year's work anew. The journey, and the ensuing year, unfold at a stately pace against the rich 19th-century New England backdrop alive with the subtly changing colors and activities of the succeeding seasons." SLJ

"The stunning combination of text and illustrations, suggesting early American paintings on wood, depict the countryside through which [the farmer] travels, the jostle of the marketplace, and the homely warmth of family life." Horn Book

Hall, Michael, 1954-

My heart is like a zoo. Greenwillow Books 2010 unp il $16.99; lib bdg $17.89

Grades: PreK K 1   E

1. Stories in rhyme 2. Love—Fiction 3. Animals—Fiction

ISBN 978-0-06-191510-9; 0-06-191510-6; 978-0-06-191511-6 (lib bdg); 0-06-191511-4 (lib bdg)

LC 2009017818

Depicts in rhyming text how love can be many different things, such as eager as a beaver, steady as a yak, or silly as a seal.

"The bold digital collages of zoo animals in this debut picture book are clear and bright, and the simple rhymes about feelings will have preschoolers savoring the words, joining in, and pointing at every playful zoo scene, each featuring one animal per page." Booklist

Hamanaka, Sheila

All the colors of the earth. Morrow Junior Bks. 1994 unp il $17.99; pa $6.99

Grades: 1 2 3 4   E

1. Stories in rhyme

ISBN 0-688-11131-9; 0-688-17062-5 (pa)

LC 93-27118

Reveals in verse that despite outward differences children everywhere are essentially the same and all are lovable

"A poetic picture book and an exemplary work of art. . . . Hamanaka's oil paintings are all double-page spreads filled with the colors of earth, sky, and water, and the texture of the artist's canvas shines through. The text is arranged in undulant waves across each painting." SLJ

Grandparents song. HarperCollins Pubs. 2003 unp il $15.99; lib bdg $16.89

Grades: 1 2 3 4   E

1. Grandparents—Fiction 2. Racially mixed people—Fiction 3. Stories in rhyme

ISBN 0-688-17852-9; 0-688-17853-7 (lib bdg)

LC 00-47952

In verse "a young girl recounts the roots of her family tree. Fondly and respectfully, she describes her grandparents—one American Indian, one Irish, one Mexican, and one a descendent of African slaves. Beautifully rendered in calligraphy, the text is clean, simple, and lilting. . . . Filled with magnificent texture, Hamanaka's oil paintings are substantial and striking." SLJ

Hamilton, K. R., 1958-

Police officers on patrol; by Kersten Hamilton; pictures by R. W. Alley. Viking 2009 unp il $15.99 *

Grades: PreK   E

1. Stories in rhyme 2. Police—Fiction

ISBN 978-0-670-06315-4; 0-670-06315-0

LC 2008023240

"Sergeant Santole dispatches Officers Mike, Jan, and Carl to spots around town that require their expertise. Mike in his police car attends to a broken traffic light, Jan on horseback reconnects a small child with his mom, and Carl runs to a crime scene. . . . The hilarious cartoon illustrations effectively convey excitement and brisk movement. . . . Preschoolers will be reassured that special people are there to assist in a variety of circumstances and see that their jobs require all kinds of cool tools." SLJ

Red Truck; by Kersten Hamilton; illustrated by Valeria Petrone. Viking Childrens Books 2008 unp il $15.99 *

Grades: PreK K   E

1. Trucks—Fiction 2. Buses—Fiction 3. Stories in rhyme

ISBN 978-0-670-06275-1   LC 2007-22902

When a school bus gets stuck in the mud, Red Truck the tow truck saves the day by pulling it out.

"Strong, flowing lines and highly simplified forms create a certain retro look in the digital artwork. . . . With a well-crafted text spiced with sound effects, this appealing picture book is highly recommended for reading aloud to the truck-loving crowd." Booklist

Hamilton, Virginia, 1936-2002

Wee Winnie Witch's Skinny; an original African American scare tale; engravings by Barry Moser. Blue Sky Press 2004 unp il $16.95

Grades: 2 3 4 5   E

1. Witches—Fiction 2. African Americans—Fiction

ISBN 0-590-28880-6   LC 00-67999

James Lee and Uncle Big Anthony become victims of Wee Winnie Witch, who takes them on a ride up into the sky, but Mama Granny saves them.

This "is a wonderful horror story that draws on traditional beliefs about witches. . . . Moser's framed, colored wood engravings do a great job of bringing the wild, shivery adventure close to home, their black backgrounds and strong lines lit with garish Halloween images in green and red." Booklist

Hamm, Mia, 1972-

Winners never quit! illustrated by Carol Thompson. HarperCollins 2004 unp il $15.99; lib bdg $16.89

Grades: PreK K 1 2   E

1. Soccer—Fiction

ISBN 0-06-074050-7; 0-06-074051-5 (lib bdg)

"Mia's favorite sport is soccer but she hates losing. In fact, she dislikes it so much that she quits in the middle of a game. . . . Mia learns quickly that there will be times when she will score a goal and those when she will not, but playing the game is the most fun of all. Bright, energetic cartoons depict the child's ups and downs." SLJ

Hammill, Matt

Sir Reginald's logbook. Kids Can Press 2008 unp il $17.95

Grades: K 1 2 3   E

1. Adventure fiction 2. Imagination—Fiction

ISBN 978-1-55453-202-5; 1-55453-202-7

"Sir Reginald is on a mission to find the Lost Tablet of Illusion. Readers will quickly realize, with the help of Hammill's illustrations, that his dangerous and mysterious quest into the deepest jungle is happening in his imagination. In actuality, he is only searching his home and yard for a missing TV remote control. . . . Hammill's keen sense of humor abounds in both the text and art." SLJ

Hanson, Warren

Bugtown Boogie; illustrated by Steve Johnson and Lou Fancher. Laura Geringer Books 2008 unp il $16.99; lib bdg $17.89

Grades: PreK K 1 2   E

1. Dance—Fiction 2. Insects—Fiction 3. Parties—Fiction 4. Stories in rhyme

ISBN 978-0-06-059937-9; 0-06-059937-5; 978-0-06-059938-6 (lib bdg); 0-06-059938-3 (lib bdg)
LC 2006029207

While strolling home through the woods one evening, a young boy happens upon a rollicking dancing party in Bugtown

This is written "in jazzy rhyming couplets. . . . Vibrant hues and frenetic energy suffuse the artwork." SLJ

Harley, Bill, 1954-

Dirty Joe, the pirate; a true story; words by Bill Harley; pictures by Jack E. Davis. HarperCollinsPublishers 2008 unp il $16.99; lib bdg $17.89

Grades: PreK K 1 2   E

1. Clothing and dress—Fiction 2. Pirates—Fiction 3. Stories in rhyme

ISBN 978-0-06-623780-0; 0-06-623780-7; 978-0-06-623781-7 (lib bdg); 0-06-623781-5 (lib bdg)
LC 2007018377

Dirty Joe and his pirate crew terrorize the seven seas in their quest for dirty socks, but they meet their match in Stinky Annie, whose favorite loot is pilfered underwear

"Davis's balloon-headed, goofy characters are just

right for the tale. The chaotic full-color pictures are jampacked with pirates and dirty laundry. The crews, dressed in a hilarious mishmash of styles, will have readers poring over the pages to spot amusing details." SLJ

Harper, Charise Mericle

Mimi and Lulu; three sweet stories: one forever friendship. Balzer & Bray 2009 unp il $16.99

Grades: PreK K 1   E

1. Friendship—Fiction

ISBN 978-0-06-175583-5; 0-06-175583-4

Mimi and Lulu are best friends despite liking different colors and they love playing together, whether it's pretending to be on a phone or being princesses.

"The dramatic, fuming stand-offs and the fun when things turn around are playfully illustrated in the bright scenes of the cartoonish, animal-like figures, set against spacious white pages. A solid offering to add to the picture-book friendship canon." Booklist

Pink me up. Alfred A. Knopf 2010 unp il $16.99; lib bdg $19.99

Grades: PreK K 1   E

1. Color—Fiction 2. Father-daughter relationship—Fiction

ISBN 978-0-375-85607-5; 0-375-85607-2; 978-0-375-95607-2 (lib bdg); 0-375-95607-7 (lib bdg)
LC 2009-23168

When Mama is too sick to go to the Pink Girls Pinknic with Violet, Daddy offers to take her place but, first, he needs to "pink-up" his clothes.

"Rendered in acrylics, the illustrations are humorous and lively." SLJ

When Randolph turned rotten. Alfred A. Knopf 2007 unp il $16.99; lib bdg $19.99 *

Grades: K 1 2 3   E

1. Friendship—Fiction 2. Beavers—Fiction 3. Geese—Fiction

ISBN 978-0-375-84071-5; 978-0-375-94071-2 (lib bdg)
LC 2006-30572

Best friends Randolph, a beaver, and Ivy, a goose, do everything together until Ivy is invited to a girls-only birthday sleepover party and Randolph, full of bad feelings, tries to spoil her fun

This is "irreverent and fun thanks to Harper's exaggerated situations and signature art, with its brightly colored backgrounds and charmingly simple figures." Booklist

Harper, Dan, 1963-

Sit, Truman! illustrated by Cara Moser & Barry Moser. Harcourt 2001 unp il hardcover o.p. pa $6.99 *

Grades: PreK K 1 2   E

1. Dogs—Fiction

ISBN 0-15-202616-9; 0-15-205068-X (pa)
LC 00-9298

A busy day in the life of Truman the big dog includes walks, play time, and a little dog named Oscar

"Harper's minimal text and the Mosers' watercolor paintings are perfectly paired. Slobbery canine Truman is both exasperating and lovable." SLJ

Harper, Lee, 1960-

Snow! Snow! Snow! Simon & Schuster Books for Young Readers 2009 unp il $14.99
Grades: K 1 2 3 4   E
1. Snow—Fiction 2. Sledding—Fiction 3. Father-son relationship—Fiction 4. Dogs—Fiction
ISBN 978-1-4169-8454-2; 1-4169-8454-2
LC 2008051985
"A Paula Wiseman book"

A dog father and his two sons spend a perfect day sledding together.

"Harper's watercolor illustrations are simple, yet effective. Readers get a good sense of the cold, crisp snow and billowing clouds, and the characters' faces are expressive." SLJ

Harrington, Janice N.

The chicken-chasing queen of Lamar County; pictures by Shelley Jackson. Farrar, Straus and Giroux 2007 unp il $16 *
Grades: K 1 2 3   E
1. Chickens—Fiction 2. Farm life—Fiction 3. African Americans—Fiction
ISBN 0-374-31251-6; 978-0-374-31251-0
LC 2005-52768
"Melanie Kroupa books."

A young farm girl tries to catch her favorite chicken, until she learns something about the hen that makes her change her ways.

"Both words and pictures elevate a simple story about a girl's sly barnyard game into a rollicking, well-told delight." Booklist

Going north; pictures by Jerome Lagarrigue. Farrar, Straus and Giroux 2004 unp il $16
Grades: 2 3 4 5   E
1. African Americans—Fiction 2. Moving—Fiction
ISBN 0-374-32681-9

A young African American girl and her family leave their home in Alabama and head for Lincoln, Nebraska, where they hope to escape segregation and find a better life.

"Lagarrigue's paintings are subdued but powerful and well-suited to Harrington's somber, poetic narrative voice." SLJ

Harris, Joe, 1928-

The belly book; [written and illustrated] by Joe Harris. Random House Children's Books 2008 unp il (Beginner books) $8.99; lib bdg $12.99
Grades: PreK K 1   E
1. Stomach—Fiction 2. Stories in rhyme
ISBN   978-0-375-84340-2;   0-375-84340-X; 978-0-375-94340-9 (lib bdg); 0-375-94340-4 (lib bdg)
LC 2006016630

Bellies can be used for many things, such as dancing the hula and resting your cup, but it is important to feed them healthy foods, too

"This beginning reader has vibrant illustrations, ample white space, and just two to four lines of simple text per page. . . . [This is a] funny, fast-moving, and original romp." SLJ

Harris, Robie H.

The day Leo said I hate you; illustrated by Molly Bang. Little, Brown and Co. 2008 unp il $16.99 *
Grades: PreK K 1 2   E
1. Mother-son relationship—Fiction 2. Anger—Fiction 3. Love—Fiction
ISBN 978-0-316-06580-1; 0-316-06580-3
LC 2007-48371

Leo, upset he has been hearing the word "no" all day, lets three words slip out that he wishes he could take back.

The hero is "evoked via vibrant collages of photos and cut paper." Publ Wkly

Goodbye, Mousie; illustrated by Jan Ormerod. Margaret K. McElderry Bks. 2001 unp il hardcover o.p. pa $6.99 *
Grades: PreK K   E
1. Death—Fiction 2. Mice—Fiction
ISBN 0-689-83217-6; 0-689-87134-1 (pa)
LC 99-89167

A boy grieves for his dead pet Mousie, helps to bury him, and begins to come to terms with his loss

"Ormerod's honest pictures, black-pencil line drawings with watercolor washes on buff-colored paper, capture the emotions of the situation and chronicle the boy's move from disbelief to acceptance. . . . This covers all the bases of a frequently asked-for subject." Booklist

Happy birth day! illustrated by Michael Emberley. Candlewick Press 1996 unp il hardcover o.p. pa $6.99 *
Grades: PreK K   E
1. Childbirth—Fiction 2. Infants—Fiction
ISBN 1-56402-424-5; 0-763609-4-9 (pa)
LC 95-34547

A mother tells her child about its first day of life from the moment of birth through the end of the birth day

"The description of the infant's first sounds and actions is gentle and poetic. Emberley's illustrations in pencil and pastels fill the oversized pages with soft-focused, cozy colors and true-to-life detail." SLJ

I am not going to school today; illustrated by Jan Ormerod. Margaret K. McElderry Bks. 2003 unp il $16.95
Grades: PreK K 1 2   E
1. School stories
ISBN 0-689-83913-8   LC 00-48053

A little boy decides to skip his very first day of school, because on the first day one doesn't know anything, but on the second, one knows everything

"Children with first-day jitters will take comfort in this story. . . . Ormerod's colorful, expressive illustrations capture a child's anxiety and the warmth of family with equal success." Booklist

Mail Harry to the moon! [illustrated by] Michael Emberley. Little, Brown and Co. 2008 unp il $16.99 *
Grades: PreK K 1 2   E
1. Siblings—Fiction 2. Infants—Fiction
ISBN 978-0-316-15376-8; 0-316-15376-1
LC 2007-48369

Harris, Robie H.—*Continued*

Harry's older brother, unhappy that the new baby seems to have taken over, dreams up imaginative ways to get rid of him.

"Harris and Emberley . . . are old hands at striking the right balance between comic Sturm and Drang and genuine poignancy, and their considerable talents make this otherwise familiar tale feel fresh and funny—and psychologically true." Publ Wkly

Maybe a bear ate it! by Robie Harris; illustrated by Michael Emberley. Orchard Books 2007 unp il lib bdg $15.99

Grades: PreK K 1 2   E
  1. Books and reading—Fiction 2. Animals—Fiction 3. Bedtime—Fiction
  ISBN 978-0-439-92961-5   LC 2006102373

At bedtime, a young boy who cannot find his favorite book imagines the various creatures that might have taken it from him

"Plain white backgrounds allow Emberley, who obviously knows how toddlers move and react, to concentrate closely on his character, whose every beautifully calibrated movement and feeling blasts out across the page." Booklist

Harris, Trudy, 1949-

The clock struck one; a time-telling tale; written by Trudy Harris; illustrations by Carrie Hartman. Millbrook Press 2009 31p il (Math is fun) lib bdg $16.95

Grades: K 1 2   E
  1. Stories in rhyme 2. Clocks and watches—Fiction 3. Time—Fiction 4. Animals—Fiction
  ISBN 978-0-8225-9067-5 (lib bdg); 0-8225-9067-0 (lib bdg)   LC 2008041583

Rhyming text expands on the nursery rhyme, "Hickory Dickory Dock," as a cat chases the mouse up the clock, followed by other animals, until midnight arrives and the tired creatures fall asleep. Includes facts about clocks and basic information about telling time

"The animated romp's peppy verse and colorful art capture the comical bedlam with flair. . . . An entertaining addition to beginning time-telling lessons." Booklist

Harrison, Joanna

Grizzly dad. David Fickling Books 2009 unp il $16.99; lib bdg $19.99

Grades: PreK K 1   E
  1. Bears—Fiction 2. Father-son relationship—Fiction
  ISBN 978-0-385-75173-5; 0-385-75173-7; 978-0-385-75174-2 (lib bdg); 0-385-75174-5 (lib bdg)   LC 2007049461

First published 2008 in the United Kingdom

One morning Dad wakes up in such a bad mood that he turns into a bear

This "combines appealing text told from the children's point of view with hilarious illustrations that will ring true to parents and caregivers." Booklist

Harshman, Marc

Only one neighborhood; by Marc Harshman & Barbara Garrison; illustrated by Barbara Garrison. Dutton Children's Books 2007 unp il $15.99

Grades: PreK K 1 2   E
  1. City and town life—Fiction
  ISBN 978-0-525-47468-5   LC 2006035908

Explores a neighborhood that has only one of several kinds of buildings, but within each there are many things, such as different kinds of breads in the bakery, then shows that the neighborhood itself is just one of many in a world united by a single wish

"Like the best celebrations of unity, this picture book is about the exciting diversity that enriches everyone, and the collagraph illustrations, in warm colors, establish the details and the connections." Booklist

Hartfield, Claire, 1957-

Me and Uncle Romie; a story inspired by the life and art of Romare Bearden; paintings by Jerome Lagarrigue. Dial Bks. for Young Readers 2002 unp il $16.99

Grades: 2 3 4   E
  1. Bearden, Romare, 1914-1988—Fiction 2. Artists—Fiction 3. Uncles—Fiction 4. African Americans—Fiction
  ISBN 0-8037-2520-5   LC 99-41390

A boy from North Carolina spends the summer in New York City visiting the neighborhood of Harlem, where his uncle, collage artist Romare Bearden, grew up. Includes a biographical sketch of Bearden and instructions on making a story collage

This is a "vibrant, evocative picture book. . . . Lagarrigue's lush, acrylic illustrations with collage elements recall the tones, brush strokes, and mixture of media that saturate Bearden's groundbreaking work." SLJ

Hartland, Jessie

Night shift. Bloomsbury Children's Books 2007 unp il $16.95; lib bdg $17.85

Grades: PreK K 1 2   E
  1. Occupations—Fiction 2. Night—Fiction
  ISBN 978-1-59990-025-4; 1-59990-025-4; 978-1-59990-138-1 (lib bdg); 1-59990-138-2 (lib bdg)   LC 2006-102092

Late at night after children have gone to bed, people who work the night shift, like street sweepers, window dressers, newspaper printers, road workers, and donut bakers, are doing their jobs.

"Quirky gouache paintings capture the mood of this alternative world with its vibrant life. . . . Text and illustrations are equally unique." SLJ

Harvey, Matt, 1962-

Shopping with Dad; [by] Matt Harvey and [illustrated by] Miriam Latimer. Barefoot Books 2008 unp il $16.99

Grades: PreK K 1 2   E
  1. Stories in rhyme 2. Shopping—Fiction 3. Father-daughter relationship—Fiction
  ISBN 978-1-84686-172-7; 1-84686-172-1
                   LC 2007042763

Harvey, Matt, 1962-—*Continued*

A little girl and her father have a wonderful time in the grocery store until she nearly knocks over a display, then while trying her best to be good she lets out a big sneeze that results in chaos.

"The cartoon mixed-media illustrations depict a lively hubbub amid plenty of color. . . . Funny and warmhearted, this story will be enjoyed one-on-one and handy in classrooms." SLJ

Haseley, Dennis, 1950-

Twenty heartbeats; [illustrated by] Ed Young. Roaring Brook Press 2008 unp il $16.95
Grades: 2 3 4 5   E
1. Artists—Fiction 2. Horses—Fiction
ISBN 978-1-59643-238-3; 1-59643-238-1
LC 2007-13202
"A Neal Porter book"

After waiting for decades for the portrait of his prize horse to be finished, an angry rich man decides to confront the artist.

"Based on a literary anecdote, the story, like its subject, contains only what is essential. Haseley's minimalist text leaves plenty of room for Young's marvelous collages to set the scene and develop the characters." SLJ

Havill, Juanita

Jamaica's find; illustrations by Anne Sibley O'Brien. Houghton Mifflin 1986 32p il $16; pa $6.95 *
Grades: PreK K 1 2   E
1. African Americans—Fiction 2. Toys—Fiction
ISBN 0-395-39376-0; 0-395-45357-7 (pa)
LC 85-14542

"When Jamaica discovers a raggedy stuffed dog at the park, she decides to take it home. Her family's reaction is lukewarm at best . . . and she broods over her mother's suggestion that she return it to the park desk. Reluctantly, she does. Just after that, Jamaica encounters a little girl named Kristin, who has come to search for her missing toy dog." Booklist

"This is a pleasant picture book with warm, expressive pictures and an appealing story line that encourages values clarification." Interracial Books Child Bull
Other titles about Jamaica are:
Brianna, Jamaica, and the Dance of Spring (2002)
Jamaica and Brianna (1993)
Jamaica and the substitute teacher (1999)
Jamaica is thankful (2009)
Jamaica tag-along (1989)
Jamaica's blue marker (1995)

Just like a baby; [by] Juanita Havill; [illustrated by] Christine Davenier. Chronicle Books 2009 unp il $15.99
Grades: PreK K 1   E
1. Infants—Fiction 2. Family life—Fiction
ISBN 978-0-8118-5026-1; 0-8118-5026-9
LC 2008021971

Delighted by the arrival of baby Ellen, extended family members describe their plans for the young one, from becoming a fisherman to playing the saxophone, but baby Ellen prefers other activities.

"Lively dialogue and an upbeat refrain enhance the spare text. Davenier's watercolor-and-ink illustrations seamlessly blend colors; bursts of rosy reds lead to an arresting presentation." Kirkus

Hawkes, Kevin

The wicked big toddlah. Alfred A. Knopf 2007 unp il $16.99; lib bdg $19.99
Grades: PreK K 1 2   E
1. Infants—Fiction 2. Size—Fiction 3. Maine—Fiction
ISBN   978-0-375-82427-2;   0-375-82427-8;
978-0-375-92427-9 (lib bdg); 0-375-92427-2 (lib bdg)
LC 2006-32209

A year in the life of a baby in Maine who is just like any other baby except that he is gigantic.

"Each lush spread . . . uses space and perspective to particular advantage. . . . The many bits of visual humor will keep youngsters poring back and forth over the pages." SLJ

Hayes, Karel, 1949-

The winter visitors; by Karel Hayes. Down East Books 2007 unp il $15.95
Grades: K 1 2 3   E
1. Bears—Fiction 2. Winter—Fiction 3. Houses—Fiction
ISBN 978-0-89272-750-6   LC 2007014051

When the summer visitors leave in the fall, a family of bears moves into the vacation cottage to spend the winter.

"Just five sentences of simple text, spread throughout the book, are a perfect accompaniment to the delightful pen-and-ink and watercolor artwork." SLJ

Hayes, Sarah

Dog day; by Sarah Hayes; illustrated by Hannah Broadway. Farrar Straus and Giroux 2008 unp il $16.95
Grades: PreK K 1 2   E
1. Dogs—Fiction 2. Teachers—Fiction 3. School stories
ISBN 978-0-374-31810-9; 0-374-31810-7

Ben and Ellie's class has a new teacher, and it's a dog named Riff!

"Colorful full-page illustrations add to the doggone good fun. The placement of the illustrations and text lets readers' eyes scamper across the page." SLJ

Hays, Anna Jane

Kindergarten countdown; written by Anna Jane Hays; illustrated by Linda Davick. Alfred A. Knopf 2007 unp il $8.99; lib bdg $11.99
Grades: PreK K   E
1. School stories 2. Stories in rhyme 3. Counting
ISBN 978-0-375-84252-8; 978-0-375-94252-5 (lib bdg)   LC 2006024249

Rhyming text follows an excited little girl as she counts down the days before the start of kindergarten

"Both the rhyming verse and the pictures are filled with humor and energy. . . . The computer-generated illustrations are detailed and vibrant." SLJ

Hays, Anna Jane—*Continued*

Ready, set, preschool! illustrated by True Kelley. Knopf 2005 30p il $16.95; lib bdg $18.99 *

Grades: PreK   E

1. School stories

ISBN 0-375-82519-3; 0-375-92519-8 (lib bdg)

A collection of simple stories, poems, and picture games designed to prepare children for preschool

"With lots of cheerfully illustrated rhymes, stories, and interactive games, this big picture book is an excellent title to prepare kids for preschool." Booklist

Smarty Sara; by Anna Jane Hays; illustrated by Sylvie Wickstrom. Random House 2008 32p il (Step into reading) lib bdg $11.99; pa $3.99

Grades: K 1 2   E

1. Diaries—Fiction 2. Stories in rhyme

ISBN 978-0-375-95054-4 (lib bdg); 0-375-95054-0 (lib bdg); 978-0-375-83512-4 (pa); 0-375-83512-1 (pa)

LC 2007-11068

Everywhere Sara goes she brings along her journal where she jots notes, makes lists, draws pictures and maps, writes poems, and plans a big surprise for her friends.

"The casual, rhyming text has fun with the sound of words as well as their meaning, and the colorful, relaxed pictures, in thick line and watercolor, add to the celebration of reading and writing—not as a duty, but as play." Booklist

Hazen, Barbara Shook, 1930-

Digby; story by Barbara Shook Hazen; pictures by Barbara J. Phillips-Duke. HarperCollins Pubs. 1996 32p il hardcover o.p. lib bdg $15.89; pa $4.99 *

Grades: K 1 2   E

1. Dogs—Fiction 2. Old age—Fiction

ISBN 0-06-026253-2; 0-06-026254-0 (lib bdg); 0-06-444239-X (pa)   LC 95-1689

"An I can read book"

"A boy wants the family dog to play ball, but his big sister explains that Digby is too old now to run and catch. . . . The story of aging and of time passing is told in very simple conversation . . . and the bright contemporary pictures show the bond between the African American brother and sister and their beloved pet." Booklist

Heap, Sue, 1954-

Danny's drawing book; by Sue Heap. Candlewick Press 2008 unp il $9.99

Grades: PreK K 1   E

1. Africa—Fiction 2. Animals—Fiction 3. Zoos—Fiction 4. Drawing—Fiction 5. Imagination—Fiction

ISBN 978-0-7636-3654-8; 0-7636-3654-1

LC 2007040402

On a trip to the zoo with his friend Ettie, Danny draws pictures of some animals, who then lead the two on an imaginary adventure to Africa and back

This is a "charming picture book, illustrated in a childlike style. . . . Heap's colorful acrylic paintings and pencil sketches differentiate between reality and fantasy, but young children will easily recognize that . . . there's plenty of overlap between the worlds." Booklist

Hector, Julian

The Gentleman Bug. Atheneum Books for Young Readers 2010 unp il $16.99

Grades: PreK K 1   E

1. Books and reading—Fiction 2. Insects—Fiction

ISBN 978-1-4169-9467-1; 1-4169-9467-X

LC 2009-13177

Teased because he likes to spend all of his time reading, the Gentleman Bug decides to change in order to catch the eye of the new Lady Bug in the garden, but she is not impressed until he goes back to being himself.

"Hector's crisp, utterly charming watercolor-and-colored pencil illustrations have a classic, timeless feel, and the spectacularly detailed scenes, which demand close-up viewing, do the bulk of the storytelling." Booklist

The Little Matador; words and pictures by Julian Hector. Hyperion Books for Children 2008 unp il $15.99

Grades: PreK K 1 2   E

1. Bullfights—Fiction 2. Artists—Fiction 3. Spain—Fiction

ISBN 978-1-4231-0779-8; 1-4231-0779-9

LC 2007042072

A young matador who would rather draw pictures than fight bulls finds a new way to entertain the townsfolk

"The old-time setting is well conveyed through illustrations using muted colors for the most part, with the hero in a bright red matador's outfit. The succinct text is enriched by numerous visual touches that help tell the story." SLJ

Hegamin, Tonya

Most loved in all the world; illustrated by Cozbi Cabrera. Houghton Mifflin 2009 unp il $17 *

Grades: PreK K 1 2   E

1. Mother-daughter relationship—Fiction 2. Slavery—Fiction 3. African Americans—Fiction

ISBN 0-618-41903-9; 978-0-618-41903-6

LC 2004-13189

Even though Mama is an agent on the Underground Railroad, in order to help others she must remain a slave, but she teaches her daughter the value of freedom through a gift of love and sacrifice.

Cabrera's "broad sweeping paintings—filled with shadowy images, occasionally bordering on the abstract, with some pages merely washes of color—add a deeper note of somberness to the spare text, told in a child's voice." Publ Wkly

Heide, Florence Parry, 1919-

The day of Ahmed's secret; [by] Florence Parry Heide & Judith Heide Gilliland; illustrated by Ted Lewin. Lothrop, Lee & Shepard Bks. 1990 unp il $16; pa $6.99 *

Grades: 1 2 3 4   E

1. Cairo (Egypt)—Fiction

ISBN 0-688-08894-5; 0-688-14023-8 (pa)

LC 90-52694

"Ahmed has monumental news to share with his family, but first he must complete the age-old duties of a butagaz boy, delivering cooking gas to customers all

Heide, Florence Parry, 1919-—*Continued*

over Cairo. . . . Enhanced by Lewin's distinguished photorealistic watercolors, the sights, sounds, and smells of the exotic setting come to life. . . . At home at last, surrounded by his loving family, Ahmed demostrates his newly acquired facility, proudly writing his name in Arabic." SLJ

The one and only Marigold; written by Florence Parry Heide; illustrated by Jill McElmurry. Schwartz & Wade Books 2009 unp il $16.99; lib bdg $19.99

Grades: PreK K 1 2   E

1. Family life—Fiction 2. Friendship—Fiction 3. Monkeys—Fiction 4. Hippopotamus—Fiction

ISBN   978-0-375-84031-9;   0-375-84031-1; 978-0-375-94051-4 (lib bdg); 0-375-94051-0 (lib bdg)
LC 2007-37840

Relates the misadventures of Marigold the monkey, who does not agree with anyone, as she shops with her mother for a coat, becomes interested in a new hobby, finds a way to "bug" her best friend, Maxine (a hippo), and imaginatively copes with finding the right outfit for the first day of school

"As depicted in McElmurry's . . . stylish spreads, a blend of up-to-the-minute humor and nostalgic, folklike patterning, Marigold has a long prehensile tail and spiky rust-colored hair that she sometimes wears in topknots. Heide . . . introduces a stubborn, potentially maddening character, but Marigold's sunny disposition and creativity make up for her mischief." Publ Wkly

Princess Hyacinth; (the surprising tale of a girl who floated); illustrated by Lane Smith. Schwartz & Wade Books 2009 unp il $17.99; lib bdg $20.99
*

Grades: PreK K 1 2   E

1. Princesses—Fiction

ISBN   978-0-375-84501-7;   0-375-84501-1; 978-0-375-93753-8 (lib bdg); 0-375-93753-6 (lib bdg)
LC 2008-39923

Princess Hyacinth is bored and unhappy sitting in her palace every day because, unless she is weighed down by specially-made clothes, she will float away, but her days are made brighter when kite-flying Boy stops to say hello.

"The quirky oil and watercolor illustrations seamlessly match Heide's wry, understated text." Publ Wkly

Sami and the time of the troubles; [by] Florence Parry Heide & Judith Heide Gilliland; illustrated by Ted Lewin. Clarion Bks. 1992 unp il $16; pa $6.95 *

Grades: 1 2 3 4   E

1. Family life—Fiction 2. Lebanon—Fiction

ISBN 0-395-55964-2; 0-395-72085-0 (pa)
LC 91-14343

A ten-year-old Lebanese boy in Beirut goes to school, helps his mother with chores, plays with his friends, and lives with his family in a basement shelter when bombings occur and fighting begins on his street

This is "a powerful, poignant book. Heide and Gilliland's lyrically written, haunting story makes clear that war threatens not only physical existence but affects the human spirit as well. Lewin's watercolor illustrations

capture contemporary Beirut with stunning clarity and drama." SLJ

Heide, Iris van der

A strange day; [by] Iris van der Heide; illustrations by Marijke ten Cate. Lemniscaat 2007 unp il $15.95

Grades: K 1 2   E

1. Letters—Fiction

ISBN 978-1-932425-94-9; 1-932425-94-2
LC 2006029265

Original Dutch edition 2006

Upset when an important letter does not arrive in the mail as expected, Jack wanders through the park not even noticing what he is doing and becomes an unwitting hero

"Dutch artist ten Cate's landscapes may be delicate and winsome, but they also brim with scenes of farce and slapstick. . . . It all adds up to a clever comedy of coincidences and misadventures, with ample rewards for attentive youngsters." Publ Wkly

Heiligman, Deborah

Cool dog, school dog; illustrated by Tim Bowers. Marshall Cavendish Children 2009 unp il $15.99

Grades: PreK K 1   E

1. Stories in rhyme 2. Dogs—Fiction 3. School stories

ISBN 978-0-7614-5561-5; 0-7614-5561-2
LC 2008029398

When Tinka the dog follows her owner to school and creates havoc, the children discover a way to let her stay in the classroom and help.

"Bowers's vivid acrylic illustrations are full of expression. . . . Youngsters will like learning with each turn of the page just what makes this dog so special." SLJ

Helakoski, Leslie Hébert

Big chickens; [by] Leslie Helakoski; illustrated by Henry Cole. Dutton Children's Books 2006 unp il $15.99

Grades: PreK K 1 2   E

1. Chickens—Fiction 2. Fear—Fiction

ISBN 0-525-47575-3   LC 2005003282

While trying to escape from a wolf, four frightened chickens keep getting themselves into the very predicaments they are trying to avoid

"Bright pictures convey the comic events with an exaggerated style just right for the story line. There's a satisfying amount of silliness that will leave children giggling." SLJ

Other titles about the big chickens are:

Big chickens fly the coop (2008)

Big chickens go to town (2009)

Heller, Linda, 1944-

Today is the birthday of the world; by Linda Heller; illustrated by Allison Jay. Dutton Children's Books 2009 unp il $16.99

Grades: PreK K 1   E

1. God—Fiction 2. Animals—Fiction 3. Birthdays—Fiction

ISBN 978-0-525-47905-5; 0-525-47905-8

LC 2008-34216

On the birthday of the world, all of God's creatures pass before Him as He asks whether each has been the best giraffe, or bee, or child they could be, helping to make the world a better place.

Heller's "repeating form lends the soothing tone of a lullaby, well-matched by Jay's . . . bucolic scenes. . . . Readers will be left feeling connected to the larger world, as one of the 'dear little helpers' God praises." Publ Wkly

Hemingway, Edward

Bump in the night; [by] Edward Hemingway. G.P. Putnam's Sons 2008 unp il $15.99

Grades: PreK K 1 2   E

1. Monsters—Fiction 2. Bedtime—Fiction

ISBN 978-0-399-24761-3; 0-399-24761-0

LC 2007013812

After Billy goes to bed one night he hears a scary noise, which, upon investigation turns out to be nothing but a sweet little monster named Bump.

"This lively story meets nighttime fears head-on with the right mix of silliness and reassurance. . . . The acrylic-on-wood illustrations create the perfect mood for this appealing bedtime story." SLJ

Henderson, Kathy

Baby knows best; illustrated by Brita Granström. Little, Brown 2002 c2001 unp il $15.95

Grades: PreK K 1 2   E

1. Infants—Fiction 2. Stories in rhyme

ISBN 0-316-60580-8   LC 00-107325

First published 2001 in the United Kingdom

"For this bubbling baby girl, keys are more fun than toys; newspapers more satisfying than books; a bath plug more engaging than tub toys; a birthday suit more comfortable than any clothes; and cuddles superior to stroller, bouncer, or playpen." SLJ

"The rhyming text is short and fun, and Granström's colorful watercolor illustrations get the point across." Booklist

Look at you! a baby body book; illustrated by Paul Howard. Candlewick Press 2006 unp il $15.99 *

Grades: PreK   E

1. Infants—Fiction 2. Human body—Fiction

ISBN 0-7636-2745-3   LC 2005-50792

This "commemorates a small child's amazing feats, from crawling to clapping to exploring food with their entire bodies. . . . The oversize pencil-and-watercolor illustrations are warm and soft, with perfectly captured body movements and facial expressions." SLJ

Henkes, Kevin, 1960-

Birds; illustrated by Laura Dronzek. Greenwillow Books 2009 unp il $17.99; lib bdg $18.89 *

Grades: PreK K 1 2   E

1. Birds—Fiction

ISBN 978-0-06-136304-7; 0-06-136304-9; 978-0-06-136305-4 (lib bdg); 0-06-136305-7 (lib bdg)

LC 2007-45084

Fascinated by the colors, shapes, sounds, and movements of the many different birds she sees through her window, a little girl is happy to discover that she and they have something in common.

"Henkes' spare, direct words have a lyrical magic, while Dronzek's bright acrylic paintings, in saturated primary color and heavy black outlines, reflect the text's plain elegance while carrying an exuberant energy all their own." Booklist

Chester's way. Greenwillow Bks. 1988 unp il $16.99; lib bdg $17.89; pa $6.99 *

Grades: PreK K 1 2   E

1. Mice—Fiction

ISBN 0-688-07607-6; 0-688-07608-4 (lib bdg); 0-688-15472-7 (pa)   LC 87-14882

The mice Chester and Wilson share the same exact way of doing things, until Lilly moves into the neighborhood and shows them that new ways can be just as good

"Henkes' charming cartoons are drawn with pen-and-ink, washed over with cheerful watercolors. They give witty expressions to his characters." SLJ

Chrysanthemum. Greenwillow Bks. 1991 unp il $16.99; lib bdg $17.89; pa $6.99 *

Grades: PreK K 1 2   E

1. Personal names—Fiction 2. School stories 3. Mice—Fiction

ISBN 0-688-09699-9; 0-688-09700-6 (lib bdg); 0-688-814732-1 (pa)   LC 90-39803

Chrysanthemum, a mouse, loves her name, until she starts going to school and the other children make fun of it

"The text, precise and evocative, uses contrast and repetition to achieve rhythm and balance; the illustrations are forthright yet delicately colored, remarkable for the agility of the fine line which creates setting and characters." Horn Book

Circle dogs; illustrated by Dan Yaccarino. Greenwillow Bks. 1998 unp il $18.99; pa $6.99 *

Grades: PreK K 1 2   E

1. Dogs—Fiction 2. Shape—Fiction

ISBN 0-688-15446-8; 0-06-443757-4 (pa)

LC 97-33037

Circle dogs live in a square house with a square yard and spend a busy day eating circle snacks, digging circle holes, and sleeping

"The text is simple, almost primer-like, with lots of onomatopoetic words. . . . The lively gouache paintings in large flat areas of color have a retro look." SLJ

Henkes, Kevin, 1960-—_Continued_

A good day. Greenwillow Books 2007 unp il $16.99; lib bdg $17.89; bd bk $7.99 *

Grades: PreK K 1   E

1. Animals—Fiction 2. Board books for children

ISBN   978-0-06-114018-1;   0-06-114018-X;
978-0-06-114019-8 (lib bdg); 0-06-114019-8 (lib bdg);
978-0-06-185778-2 (bd bk); 0-06-185778-5 (bd bk)
                                              LC 2005-35923

A bird, a fox, a dog, and a squirrel overcome minor setbacks to have a very good day

"This story works well in every way. As precise, unaffected, and easy for a young child to understand as the text, the illustrations feature forms cleanly defined with thick black lines and brightened with watercolors." Booklist

Jessica. Greenwillow Bks. 1989 unp il $16.99; lib bdg $17.89; pa $6.99 *

Grades: PreK K 1 2   E

1. Imaginary playmates—Fiction

ISBN 0-688-07829-X; 0-688-07830-3 (lib bdg);
0-688-15847-1 (pa)   LC 87-38087

"A shy preschooler insists that her friend Jessica is not imaginary—and, in the end, she's absolutely correct. Henkes' depiction of play-alone and play-together time brims with buoyant camaraderie in this upbeat story of friendship fulfilled." SLJ

Julius, the baby of the world. Greenwillow Bks. 1990 unp il $16.99; lib bdg $16.89; pa $5.99 *

Grades: PreK K 1 2   E

1. Mice—Fiction

ISBN 0-688-08943-7; 0-688-08944-5 (lib bdg);
0-688-14388-1 (pa)   LC 88-34904

Lilly, the girl mouse who debuted in Chester's way "may still be the queen of the world, but her new brother 'Julius is the baby of the world.' Suffering from a severe case of sibling-itis, she warns pregnant strangers: 'You will live to regret that bump under your dress.' While her understanding parents shower her with 'compliments and praise and niceties of all shapes and sizes,' nothing works until snooty Cousin Garland comes for a visit." Booklist

"Magically, Henkes conveys a world of expressions and a wide range of complex emotions with a mere line or two upon the engaging mousey faces of Lilly and her family. A reassuring, funny book for all young children who suffer from new-sibling syndrome." SLJ

Kitten's first full moon. Greenwillow Books 2004 unp il $17.99; lib bdg $16.89 *

Grades: PreK K 1   E

1. Cats—Fiction 2. Moon—Fiction

ISBN 0-06-058828-4; 0-06-058829-2 (lib bdg)
                                              LC 2003-12564

Awarded the Caldecott Medal, 2005

When Kitten mistakes the full moon for a bowl of milk, she ends up tired, wet, and hungry trying to reach it

"Done in a charcoal and cream-colored palette, the understated illustrations feature thick black outlines, pleasing curves, and swiftly changing expressions that are full of nuance. The rhythmic text and delightful artwork ensure storytime success." SLJ

Lilly's purple plastic purse. Greenwillow Bks. 1996 unp il $17.99; lib bdg $18.89 *

Grades: PreK K 1 2   E

1. Mice—Fiction 2. School stories

ISBN 0-688-12897-1; 0-688-12898-X (lib bdg)
                                              LC 95-25085

"Lilly loves everything about school. . . . But most of all, she loves her teacher, Mr. Slinger. . . . The little mouse will do anything for him—until he refuses to allow her to interrupt lessons to show the class her new movie-star sunglasses, three shiny quarters, and purple plastic purse. Seething with anger, she writes a mean story about him and places it in his book bag at the end of the day. . . . Rich vocabulary and just the right amount of repetition fuse perfectly with the watercolor and black-pen illustrations. . . . Clever dialogue and other funny details will keep readers looking and laughing." SLJ

Another title about Lilly is:
Lilly's big day (2006)

My garden. Greenwillow Books 2010 unp il $17.99; lib bdg $18.89 *

Grades: PreK K 1   E

1. Gardens—Fiction 2. Imagination—Fiction

ISBN   978-0-06-171517-4;   0-06-171517-4;
978-0-06-171518-1 (lib bdg); 0-06-171518-2 (lib bdg)
                                              LC 2008-42364

After helping her mother weed, water, and chase the rabbits from their garden, a young girl imagines her dream garden complete with jellybean bushes, chocolate rabbits, and tomatoes the size of beach balls

This is rendered with "thick outlines; boldly applied, ice-cream parlor colors; and simple declarative sentences. . . . [This book is] an enjoyable tour of an imaginary place and will plant creativity in young minds." Booklist

Old Bear. Greenwillow Books 2008 unp il $17.99; lib bdg $18.89 *

Grades: PreK   E

1. Bears—Fiction 2. Dreams—Fiction 3. Seasons—Fiction 4. Hibernation—Fiction

ISBN   978-0-06-155205-2;   0-06-155205-4;
978-0-06-155206-9 (lib bdg); 0-06-155206-2 (lib bdg)
                                              LC 2007-35965

Boston Globe-Horn Book Award honor book: Picture Book (2009)

When Old Bear falls asleep for the winter, he has a dream that he is a cub again, enjoying each of the four seasons.

"Every word, line, color choice, and composition element feels essential and fits beautifully into a common theme. . . . The elemental words and graceful pacing make this a perfect read-aloud. . . . [The illustrations are] rendered in bold outlines and color washes." Booklist

Owen. Greenwillow Bks. 1993 unp il $17.99; lib bdg $16.89 *

Grades: PreK K 1 2   E

1. Blankets—Fiction

ISBN 0-688-11449-0; 0-688-11450-4 (lib bdg)
                                              LC 92-30084

A Caldecott Medal honor book, 1994

Henkes, Kevin, 1960-—*Continued*

Owen's parents try to get him to give up his favorite blanket before he starts school, but when their efforts fail, they come up with a solution that makes everyone happy

This is "imbued with Henkes's characteristically understated humor, spry text and brightly hued watercolor-and-ink pictures." Publ Wkly

Sheila Rae, the brave. Greenwillow Bks. 1987 unp il $16.99; lib bdg $17.89; pa $6.99 *

Grades: PreK K 1 2   E

1. Mice—Fiction

ISBN 0-688-07155-4; 0-688-07156-2 (lib bdg); 0-688-14738-0 (pa)   LC 86-25761

"A mouse both boastful and fearless, Sheila Rae decides to go home from school by taking a new route. She walks backwards with her eyes closed, growls at dogs and cats, climbs trees, turns new corners and crosses different streets—and ends up in the middle of unfamiliar territory." Publ Wkly

"Bouncy watercolors in spring-like colors with some pen-and-ink detailing highlight Sheila Rae's bravado in an engaging and amusing way, and Henkes provides Sheila Rae, Louise, and their school friends with highly expressive faces." SLJ

So happy! pictures by Anita Lobel. Greenwillow Books 2005 unp il $15.99; lib bdg $16.89 *

Grades: PreK K 1 2   E

1. Seeds—Fiction 2. Flowers—Fiction 3. Rabbits—Fiction

ISBN 0-06-056483-0; 0-06-056484-9 (lib bdg)

"A thirsty magic seed, a curious little rabbit, and a bored young boy all experience a great change when rain finally falls." Horn Book

"Lobel's vigorous artwork, a riot of color that pays homage to Van Gogh, locates events in a sun-toasted, south-of-the-border landscape, and captures the rhythm of Henkes' splitting, braided narratives in triptychs alternating with cohesive scenes." Booklist

Wemberly worried. Greenwillow Bks. 2000 unp il lib bdg $16.89 *

Grades: PreK K 1 2   E

1. School stories 2. Mice—Fiction 3. Worry—Fiction

ISBN 0-688-17028-5   LC 99-34341

A mouse named Wemberly, who worries about everything, finds that she has a whole list of things to worry about when she faces the first day of nursery school.

The author combines "good storytelling, careful characterization, and wonderfully expressive artwork to create an entertaining and reassuring picture book that addresses a common concern." SLJ

Hennessy, B. G. (Barbara G.)

Because of you; [by] B.G. Hennessy; illustrated by Hiroe Nakata. Candlewick Press 2005 unp il $15.99 *

Grades: PreK K 1   E

1. Kindness—Fiction 2. Conduct of life—Fiction

ISBN 0-7636-1926-4   LC 2004-45168

"'Because of you,' Hennessy writes, 'there is one more person who will grow and learn,' but also 'one more person who can teach others.' . . . In an empowering conclusion, Hennessy widens the child's sphere of influence, seeing the 'small and precious' acts at home as the first step toward world peace—an ambitious goal made less daunting by Nakata's billowy, cotton candy-hued watercolors of smiling characters exchanging gestures of help and affection." Booklist

Henson, Heather

Grumpy Grandpa; written by Heather Henson; illustrated by Ross MacDonald. Atheneum Books for Young Readers 2009 unp il $16.99

Grades: K 1 2   E

1. Grandfathers—Fiction 2. Old age—Fiction 3. Fishing—Fiction 4. Country life—Fiction

ISBN 978-1-4169-0811-1; 1-4169-0811-0

LC 2008-21543

Jack's grandfather is always grumpy, and a bit scary, too, but during a visit to the country house where "Grumpy Grandpa" lives with the brave Aunt Ellie and Uncle Wilbur, Jack learns that his grandfather was once very different.

"MacDonald's wonderful watercolors have his typical '50s look, and include comic scenes. . . . The pictures are a great match for the text, where the modern elements sit comfortably alongside the old-fashioned ones." SLJ

That Book Woman; pictures by David Small. Atheneum Books for Young Readers 2008 unp il $16.99 *

Grades: K 1 2 3   E

1. Librarians—Fiction 2. Appalachian region—Fiction

ISBN 978-1-4169-0812-8; 1-4169-0812-9

LC 2007-18156

A family living in the Appalachian Mountains in the 1930s gets books to read during the regular visits of the "Book Woman"—a librarian who rides a pack horse through the mountains, lending books to the isolated residents.

"Complementing Cal's authentically childlike thoughts, Small's deft, rough-edged lines and masterful watercolors convey even more than Henson's carefully honed text." Horn Book

Heo, Yumi, 1964-

Ten days and nine nights; an adoption story. Schwartz & Wade Books 2009 unp il $16.99; lib bdg $19.99

Grades: PreK K 1 2   E

1. Adoption—Fiction 2. Sisters—Fiction 3. Family life—Fiction 4. Korean Americans—Fiction

ISBN 978-0-375-84718-9; 0-375-84718-9; 978-0-375-94715-5 (lib bdg); 0-375-94715-9 (lib bdg)

LC 2007044073

A young girl eagerly awaits the arrival of her newly-adopted sister from Korea, while her whole family prepares.

"The exquisite oil, pencil, and collage illustrations dovetail with the quiet, simple tone of the text." SLJ

Herman, Charlotte

First rain; illustrated by Kathryn Mitter. Albert Whitman 2010 unp il $16.99
Grades: 1 2 3   **E**
1. Israel—Fiction 2. Grandmothers—Fiction 3. Rain—Fiction
ISBN 978-0-8075-2453-4; 0-8075-2453-0

When Abby moves with her family to Israel, she misses her grandmother and during the dry Israeli summer, she remembers the fun they used to have splashing in puddles together

"Besides being a realistic look at another culture, this well-written book is heartwarming and reassuring." SLJ

Herold, Maggie Rugg

A very important day; illustrated by Catherine Stock. Morrow Junior Bks. 1995 unp il $17.99 *
Grades: K 1 2 3   **E**
1. Naturalization—Fiction 2. Immigrants—Fiction 3. New York (N.Y.)—Fiction
ISBN 0-688-13065-8   LC 94-16647

Two-hundred nineteen people from thirty-two different countries make their way to downtown New York in a snowstorm to be sworn in as citizens of the United States

"After the first quiet, gray-tone painting . . . this book bursts forth in a riot of color and activity. . . . A glossary supplies guidance for pronouncing names, and a clear, nicely detailed overview of the process of naturalization rounds things out. Pictures and story combine to make the joy of the day contagious." Booklist

Hesse, Karen

The cats in Krasinski Square; illustrated by Wendy Watson. Scholastic Press 2004 unp il $16.95 *
Grades: 2 3 4 5   **E**
1. Poland—Fiction 2. Holocaust, 1933-1945—Fiction 3. Jews—Fiction 4. Cats—Fiction
ISBN 0-439-43540-4   LC 2003-27775

Two Jewish sisters, escapees of the infamous Warsaw ghetto, devise a plan to thwart an attempt by the Gestapo to intercept food bound for starving people behind the dark Wall.

"In luminous free verse [this] book tells a powerful story. . . . In bold black lines and washes of smoky gray and ochre, Watson's arresting images echo the pared-down language as well as the hope that shines like glints of sunlight on Kraskinski Square." Booklist

Come on, rain! pictures by Jon J. Muth. Scholastic Press 1999 unp il $15.95 *
Grades: PreK K 1 2   **E**
1. Rain—Fiction 2. Summer—Fiction
ISBN 0-590-33125-6   LC 98-11575

A young girl eagerly awaits a coming rainstorm to bring relief from the oppressive summer heat

"Beautifully drafted watercolor paintings illustrate the lyrical text, creating a wonderful sense of atmosphere." Horn Book Guide

Spuds; by Karen Hesse; illustrated by Wendy Watson. Scholastic Press 2008 unp il $16.99 *
Grades: PreK K 1 2   **E**
1. Potatoes—Fiction 2. Country life—Fiction 3. Siblings—Fiction 4. Great Depression, 1929-1939—Fiction
ISBN 978-0-439-87993-4; 0-439-87993-0
    LC 2007-24046

Maybelle, Jack, and Eddie want to help Ma by putting something extra on the table, so they set out in the dark to take potatoes from a nearby field, but when they arrive home and empty their potato sacks, they are surprised by what they see.

"This beautifully crafted picture book features panoramic landscapes and intimate pictures. Watson's pencil, ink, watercolor, and gouache illustrations, warmly rendered in earth tones, capture the small figures trudging along under a huge full moon. . . . This sweetly understated affirmation of hard work and honesty, neighborliness and family love, will resonate with a wide audience." SLJ

Hest, Amy

The dog who belonged to no one; by Amy Hest; illustrated by Amy Bates. Abrams Books for Young Readers 2008 unp il $15.95 *
Grades: PreK K 1   **E**
1. Dogs—Fiction
ISBN 978-0-8109-9483-6; 0-8109-9483-6
    LC 2007012763

The hard-working daughter of two bakers and a perfectly nice stray dog live lonely lives in the same town, until they meet one very stormy day.

"The pencil and watercolor illustrations, featuring a palette of golden earth tones, echo the gentle sentiment of the narrative. Lia in her blue dress, pinafore, and jaunty cap and the bright-eyed little dog evoke tender sympathy." SLJ

Guess who, Baby Duck! illustrated by Jill Barton. Candlewick 2004 unp il $15.99 *
Grades: PreK K   **E**
1. Ducks—Fiction 2. Grandfathers—Fiction
ISBN 0-7636-1981-7

"Baby Duck has a cold and Grampa comes to visit, bringing a 'cheering-up present,' an album of her baby photos. Together they look at pictures of her on the day she was born, after her first bath, taking her first steps, and on her first birthday. She feels better and draws a picture of Grampa kissing her cheek, which is just what he does. . . . Barton's watercolor-and-pencil art is as warm and playful as Baby Duck herself." SLJ

Other titles about Baby Duck are:
Baby Duck and the bad eyeglasses (1996)
In the rain with Baby Duck (1995)
Make the team, Baby Duck (2003)
Off to school, Baby Duck (1999)
You're the boss, Baby Duck (1997)

Kiss good night; illustrated by Anita Jeram. Candlewick Press 2001 unp il $15.99
Grades: PreK K   **E**
1. Bears—Fiction 2. Bedtime—Fiction
ISBN 0-7636-0780-0   LC 00-41372

Hest, Amy—*Continued*

Even after a story, being tucked in, and warm milk, Sam the bear is not ready to go to sleep until his mother kisses him good-night

"This is an enchanting little story, with homey illustrations that add to its appeal." SLJ

Other titles about Sam the bear are:

Don't you feel well, Sam? (2002)

You can do it, Sam (2003)

Little Chick; illustrated by Anita Jeram. Candlewick Press 2009 unp il $17.99 *

Grades: PreK K   E

1. Chickens—Fiction 2. Aunts—Fiction

ISBN 978-0-7636-2890-1; 0-7636-2890-5

LC 2008-935296

"Old-Auntie the hen, endlessly patient, marvelously kind, helps Little Chick deal with frustration in three stories. As depicted in Jeram's . . . watercolor washes, Old-Auntie's feathered bulk dwarfs Little Chick, and her gestures . . . are infused with tenderness. Old-Auntie helps Little Chick deal with her eagerness to harvest the carrot she planted; helps Little Chick endure the long wait until her kite finally flies; and assures Little Chick that the star in the night sky that she wants is better off staying just where it is. . . . Hest's . . . light humor and Jeram's visual charm work . . . harmoniously together." Publ Wkly

Mr. George Baker; illustrated by Jon J. Muth. Candlewick Press 2004 unp il hardcover o.p. pa $6.99 *

Grades: K 1 2 3   E

1. Reading—Fiction 2. Old age—Fiction 3. African Americans—Fiction 4. Friendship—Fiction

ISBN 0-7636-1233-2; 0-7636-3308-9 (pa)

Harry sits on the porch with Mr. George Baker, an African American who is one hundred years old but can still dance and play the drums, waiting for the school bus that will take them both to the class where they are learning to read.

This is "beautifully illustrated in subtle watercolors. Hest's understated, unhurried poetry echoes the syncopated rhythms of music. . . . Her book is a simple, sweet, moving portrait of a natural friendship between seniors and children." Booklist

The purple coat; pictures by Amy Schwartz. Four Winds Press 1986 unp il hardcover o.p. pa $6.99

Grades: PreK K 1 2   E

1. Coats—Fiction 2. Grandfathers—Fiction

ISBN 0-02-743640-3; 0-689-71634-6 (pa)

LC 85-29186

"Gabrielle has always gotten a navy coat in the fall, but, this year, to Mama's dismay, she yearns for a purple one. Grandpa, their favorite tailor, discovers a solution to please all." Child Book Rev Serv

"The artwork is full color, and the deep shades and vibrant colors (especially that purple) are arresting. The numerous details and patternings catch the eye and make for pictures that can be looked at over and over; each time the story's satisfying conclusion rings sweetly true." Booklist

When you meet a bear on Broadway; pictures by Elivia Savadier. Farrar, Straus and Giroux 2009 unp il $16.99 *

Grades: PreK K 1   E

1. Bears—Fiction 2. Mother-child relationship—Fiction 3. New York (N.Y.)—Fiction

ISBN 978-0-374-40015-6; 0-374-40015-6

LC 2008026053

"Melanie Kroupa books"

When a little bear becomes separated from its mother in New York, a sympathetic child explains the proper steps that must be taken to reunite them.

"The repetitive beat in the sly, humorous words make this a perfect read-aloud, although the irresistible nuances in Savadier's artwork . . . are best viewed at close range." Booklist

Heyward, DuBose, 1885-1940

The country bunny and the little gold shoes; as told to Jenifer; pictures by Marjorie Flack. Houghton Mifflin 1939 unp il lib bdg $15; pa $5.95

Grades: PreK K   E

1. Rabbits—Fiction 2. Easter—Fiction

ISBN 0-395-15990-3 (lib bdg); 0-395-18557-2 (pa)

This is an Easter story for young readers which grew out of a story the author has told and retold to his young daughter. It is of the little country rabbit who wanted to become one of the five Easter bunnies, and how she managed to realize her ambition

"It is really imaginative and well written. . . . The colored pictures are just right too." New Yorker

Hicks, Barbara Jean

Jitterbug jam; pictures by Alexis Deacon. Farrar, Straus and Giroux 2005 c2004 unp il $16

Grades: K 1 2 3   E

1. Monsters—Fiction

ISBN 0-374-33685-7   LC 2004-46981

First published 2004 in the United Kingdom

Grandpa Boo-Dad not only believes that Bobo has seen a pink-skinned boy with orange fur on his head hiding under the bed, he knows exactly how a little monster can scare off such a horrible creature

"Printed on luxurious, buff-colored paper, Deacon's line-and-watercolor artwork unites cleverly altered Victorian decorative elements . . . with the striking, varied design of contemporary graphic novels. . . . Hicks' folksy, slightly off-kilter language . . . keeps the sense of an exotic, alternate reality watertight." Booklist

Monsters don't eat broccoli; illustrated by Sue Hendra. Alfred A. Knopf 2009 unp il $16.99; lib bdg $19.99

Grades: K 1 2   E

1. Stories in rhyme 2. Food—Fiction 3. Monsters—Fiction

ISBN 978-0-375-85686-0; 0-375-85686-2; 978-0-375-95686-7 (lib bdg); 0-375-95686-7 (lib bdg)

LC 2008-24536

Illustrations and rhyming text reveal how imagination can spice up even the healthiest meal

"With a toe-tapping beat and loud, splashy spreads,

Hicks, Barbara Jean—*Continued*

this paean to mealtime chaos will charm small monsters everywhere. . . . Too much fun to limit to kids who don't like broccoli." Publ Wkly

Hill, Susanna Leonard

Not yet, Rose; written by Susanna Leonard Hill; illustrated by Nicole Rutten. Eerdmans Books for Young Readers 2009 unp il $16.50

Grades: PreK K   E

1.   Infants—Fiction   2.   Siblings—Fiction
3. Imagination—Fiction 4. Hamsters—Fiction
ISBN 978-0-8028-5326-4; 0-8028-5326-9
LC 2008031736

While impatiently waiting for the birth of a new baby brother or sister, Rose the hamster imagines the things they will do together and how her life will change.

"Rutten's cheery watercolor illustrations, depicting the hamsters' life in their cozy country cottage and later in the hospital, are infused with subtle, appropriate humor. With its thoughtful text and playful art, this book gently helps older siblings confidently adjust to their new roles." SLJ

Punxsutawney Phyllis; by Susanna Leonard Hill; illustrated by Jeffrey Ebbeler. Holiday House 2005 unp il $16.95

Grades: K 1 2 3   E

1. Groundhog Day—Fiction 2. Marmots—Fiction
3. Sex role—Fiction
ISBN 0-8234-1872-3   LC 2003-67641

Although she can predict the weather much better than the boys in her family, no one thinks that Phyllis the groundhog has a chance of replacing the aging Punxsutawney Phil when Groundhog Day's official groundhog retires

"Details about the origins of Groundhog Day and Punxsutawney Phil are appended. Ebbeler's full-bleed acrylic illustrations show an exuberant Phyllis skipping through a brook, sunbathing, and munching on berries." SLJ

Hillenbrand, Will, 1960-

Cock-a-doodle Christmas! by Will Hillenbrand. Marshall Cavendish 2007 unp il $16.99

Grades: PreK K 1   E

1. Jesus Christ—Nativity 2. Roosters—Fiction
3. Christmas—Fiction 4. Farm life—Fiction
ISBN 978-0-7614-5354-3   LC 2006030236

Long ago in the town of Bethlehem, young Harold the rooster keeps failing to wake the other farm animals in the morning, but when a young woman gives birth to a very special baby in the stable, Harold is finally able to crow loudly and help spread the good news

"The text, matter-of-fact and unsentimental, reads like a folktale, making this an excellent story to read aloud, and the gouache, ink, and collage illustrations depict a humble but colorful farm." SLJ

Louie! Philomel Books 2009 unp il $16.99 *

Grades: PreK K 1 2   E

1. Pigs—Fiction 2. Artists—Fiction 3. Drawing—Fiction
ISBN 978-0-399-24707-1; 0-399-24707-6
LC 2008-19453

Louie the pig loves to draw but it gets him thrown out of every school he attends, so he goes to live with his aunt and uncle who help him realize he has a wonderful talent.

"Using the bare-bones outline of Ludwig Bemelmans's childhood, Hillenbrand brings to life the experience of countless children whose creativity sets them apart in structured environments, especially school. . . . Hillenbrand's gloriously colored, superbly executed illustrations—collages, fingerpaintings, gouache, inks, pencils—magnetically draw readers from page to page." SLJ

Hills, Tad

Duck & Goose; written and illustrated by Tad Hills. Schwartz & Wade Books 2006 unp il $14.95; lib bdg $17.99 *

Grades: PreK K   E

1. Ducks—Fiction 2. Geese—Fiction
ISBN 0-375-83611-X; 0-375-93611-4 (lib bdg)
LC 2005010849

Duck and Goose learn to work together to take care of a ball, which they think is an egg

"While the narrative is fairly straightforward and has touches of childlike humor throughout, it's the bright and colorful artwork that will attract youngsters' attention. The cartoon-style oil paintings set against soft-focus, almost impressionistic backgrounds keep Duck and Goose center stage, and their expressions are priceless." SLJ

Other titles about Duck and Goose are:

Duck, duck, goose (2007)
Duck & Goose, 1, 2, 3 (2008)
What's up, Duck?: a book of opposites (2008)
Duck & Goose, how are you feeling? (2009)
Duck & Goose find a pumpkin (2009)

How Rocket learned to read. Schwartz & Wade Books 2010 unp il $17.99; lib bdg $20.99

Grades: PreK K 1   E

1. Reading—Fiction 2. Dogs—Fiction 3. Birds—Fiction
ISBN   978-0-375-85899-4;   0-375-85899-7;
978-0-375-95899-1 (lib bdg); 0-375-95899-1 (lib bdg)
LC 2008-51015

A little yellow bird teaches Rocket the dog how to read by first introducing him to the "wondrous, mighty, gorgeous alphabet."

The author "offers up an appealing picture of the learning-to-read process. . . . Hills' oil-paint and colored-pencil illustrations nicely capture both the sweetness of pupil and tutor and the prettiness of the changing seasons." Booklist

Himmelman, John, 1959-

Chickens to the rescue. H. Holt 2006 unp il $16.95 *

Grades: PreK K 1 2   E

1. Chickens—Fiction 2. Farm life—Fiction 3. Days—Fiction
ISBN 978-0-8050-7951-7; 0-8050-7951-3
LC 2005-20044

Six days a week the chickens help the Greenstalk family and their animals recover from mishaps that occur on the farm, but they need one day to rest

Himmelman, John, 1959-—*Continued*

"The simplicity of the text allows the sheer brilliance of the colored-pencil and watercolor illustrations to shine through. The details in each rescue scene will have everyone laughing." SLJ

Another title in this series is:
Pigs to the rescue (2010)

Frog in a bog. Charlesbridge 2004 unp il $15.95; pa $6.95
Grades: K 1 2 3   E
  1. Marshes—Fiction
  ISBN 1-57091-517-2; 1-57091-518-0 (pa)
                     LC 2003-3737

"Himmelman leads children through natural events that occur on a typical day in a bog, beginning with a frog hopping into some moss. . . . Throughout, readers are introduced to plant, insect, and animal names that may not be commonly known and the idea that some events trigger others. Some classification lessons are included at the end of the book. The watercolor illustrations are definitely a draw: the effect is soft and delicate. Detail is beautifully rendered. . . . This book will have broad appeal." SLJ

Includes bibliographical references

Katie loves the kittens. Henry Holt & Co. 2008 unp il $16.95
Grades: PreK K 1 2 3   E
  1. Dogs—Fiction 2. Cats—Fiction 3. Friendship—Fiction
  ISBN 978-0-8050-8682-9; 0-8050-8682-X

When Sara Ann brings home three little kittens, Katie the dog's enthusiasm frightens the kittens away, until she learns that quiet patience is sometimes needed to begin a friendship.

"Himmelman's charming watercolor-and-ink illustrations depict a character sure to earn the affection of young readers. Katie's expressive movements make both her excitement and her dismay palpable and adorable." SLJ

Hindley, Judy

Baby talk; a book of first words and phrases; illustrated by Brita Granström. Candlewick Press 2006 unp il $15.99 *
Grades: PreK   E
  1. Infants—Fiction 2. Stories in rhyme
  ISBN 0-7636-2971-5

Rhyming text describes the the activities in a baby's day and the words he says while going to the playground, eating dinner, and taking a bath.

"Hindley's unfussy rhyme offers on-target opportunities for concept development: low, high, bye, out. Granström's festive gouache-and-pencil cartoons shine." SLJ

Hines, Anna Grossnickle, 1946-

1, 2, buckle my shoe. Harcourt 2008 unp il $16 *
Grades: PreK   E
  1. Nursery rhymes 2. Counting
  ISBN 978-0-15-206305-4; 0-15-206305-6
                     LC 2007007022

A child learns to count with the help of a classic nursery rhyme

"The popular verse, included in numerous collections of nursery rhymes, gets the star treatment in this delightful picture book. Illustrated entirely with quilt patches festooned with buttons, the ditty bounces along in bursts of color." SLJ

Daddy makes the best spaghetti. Clarion Bks. 1986 unp il pa $5.95 hardcover o.p.; bd bk $5.95
Grades: PreK K 1 2   E
  1. Father-son relationship—Fiction
  ISBN 0-89919-794-9 (pa); 0-395-98036-4 (bd bk)
                     LC 85-13993

"Corey and his father enjoy a close relationship that is aptly demonstrated in picture and story. He teases Corey and they spend time together doing things such as shopping for groceries and making a pot of spaghetti or being silly at bath time and getting ready for bed. Hines' simple but warm pencil drawings play out the scenes by capitalizing on the incidents described in the text; the strong sense of family (Mother is here too) is evident." Booklist

Ho, Minfong

Hush! a Thai lullaby; pictures by Holly Meade. Orchard Bks. 1996 unp il pa $6.99 hardcover o.p. *
Grades: PreK K 1 2   E
  1. Thailand—Fiction 2. Lullabies
  ISBN 0-531-07166-9 (pa)   LC 95-23251
  A Caldecott Medal honor book, 1997

"A mother goes to each animal, from lizard to water buffalo to elephant, trying to quiet noises that might wake her child. When the animals are silenced and the mother finally falls asleep, the baby lies awake, with wide eyes and a smile. Ho's rhythmic text is fine for reading aloud. . . . The setting, apparently a remote Thai village, is gently evoked in cut paper and ink pictures that are bold enough to be used with groups. . . . The comforting earth tones suit the quiet nature of the story." Booklist

Hoban, Lillian

Arthur's Christmas cookies; words and pictures by Lillian Hoban. Harper & Row 1972 63p il hardcover o.p. pa $3.99 *
Grades: PreK K 1 2   E
  1. Chimpanzees—Fiction 2. Christmas—Fiction
  ISBN 0-06-022368-5 (lib bdg); 0-06-444055-9 (pa)

"An I can read book"

When Arthur decides to make Christmas cookies for his parents, a "disastrous mistake in the ingredients makes the cookies inedible but the story ends happily when Arthur turns them into holiday decorations." Publ Wkly

The characters are chimpanzees but "are endearingly like human children. . . . The Christmas setting is appealing, the plot has problem, conflict, and solution yet is not too complex for the beginning independent reader, and the simplicity and humor make the book an appropriate one for reading aloud to preschool children also." Bull Cent Child Books

Other titles about Arthur are:

Hoban, Lillian—*Continued*

Arthur's back to school day (1996)
Arthur's birthday party (1999)
Arthur's camp-out (1993)
Arthur's funny money (1981)
Arthur's great big valentine (1989)
Arthur's Halloween costume (1984)
Arthur's Honey Bear (1974)
Arthur's loose tooth (1985)
Arthur's pen pal (1976)
Arthur's prize reader (1978)

Silly Tilly's Thanksgiving dinner; story and pictures by Lillian Hoban. Harper & Row 1990 63p il lib bdg $15.89; pa $3.99 *

Grades: PreK K 1 2   E

1. Thanksgiving Day—Fiction 2. Animals—Fiction

ISBN 0-06-022423-1 (lib bdg); 0-06-444154-7 (pa)
LC 89-29287

"An I can read book"

Forgetful Silly Tilly Mole nearly succeeds in ruining her Thanksgiving dinner, but her animal friends come to the rescue with tasty treats

"Watercolors in vibrant autumn hues accentuate this comedy of errors with quirky characterizations and fine brushwork." Booklist

Other titles about Silly Tilly are:
Silly Tilly and the Easter Bunny (1987)
Silly Tilly's valentine (1998)

Hoban, Russell

Bedtime for Frances; pictures by Garth Williams. HarperCollins Pubs. 1995 c1960 31p il $16.99; lib bdg $17.89; pa $6.99 *

Grades: PreK K 1   E

1. Badgers—Fiction 2. Bedtime—Fiction

ISBN 0-06-027106-X; 0-06-027107-8 (lib bdg); 0-06-443451-6 (pa)   LC 94-43809

A reissue of the title first published 1960

"A little badger with a lively imagination comes up with one scheme after another to put off going to sleep but father badger proves himself as smart as his daughter." Bookmark

"The soft humorous pictures of these lovable animals in human predicaments are delightful." Horn Book

Other titles about Frances are:
A baby sister for Frances (1964)
A bargain for Frances (1970)
Best friends for Frances (1969)
A birthday for Frances (1968)
Bread and jam for Frances (1964)

Hoban, Tana

26 letters and 99 cents. Greenwillow Bks. 1987 unp il $17.99; lib bdg $18.89; pa $6.99 *

Grades: PreK K 1 2   E

1. Alphabet 2. Counting 3. Coins

ISBN 0-688-06361-6; 0-688-06362-4 (lib bdg); 0-688-14389-X (pa)   LC 86-11993

This concept book "is really two books in one. *26 Letters* is a delightful ABC handbook. Each page shows two letters (in both upper- and lowercase) paired with objects from airplane to zipper. Turning the book around reveals

the even more creative *99 Cents*. Here Hoban clearly shows youngsters how to count by pairing photos of numbers with pennies, nickels, dimes and quarters in a variety of combinations. The book counts ones from 1¢ to 30¢, by fives from 30¢ to 50¢, by tens from 50¢ to 90¢, culminating in 99¢. . . . An extremely inventive approach that will be hailed by parents, teachers and librarians." Publ Wkly

Black on white. Greenwillow Bks. 1993 unp il bd bk $5.99 *

Grades: PreK   E

1. Board books for children

ISBN 0-688-11918-2   LC 92-18897

Black illustrations against a white background depict such objects as an elephant, butterfly, and leaf

This board book features "the stunning, sophisticated photography of Tana Hoban. . . . Simply the best for babies." Horn Book Guide

Colors everywhere. Greenwillow Bks. 1995 unp il $18.99; lib bdg $17.89 *

Grades: PreK K   E

1. Color

ISBN 0-688-12762-2; 0-688-12763-0 (lib bdg)
LC 93-24847

"On each page of this wordless picture book is a color photograph accompanied by a bar graph that displays the spectrum of colors found in the photo." Booklist

"Very young children will enjoy naming the pictured objects, while older readers will be drawn into exploring the colors' varying tones. A book children will come back to over and over." Horn Book

Exactly the opposite. Greenwillow Bks. 1990 unp il $17.99; pa $6.99 *

Grades: PreK K   E

1. English language—Synonyms and antonyms

ISBN 0-688-08861-9; 0-688-15473-5 (pa)
LC 89-27227

"Using a variety of people, animals, and objects found in outdoor settings of both the city and the country, [the author] introduces and expands on the concept of opposites in this wordless photographic book. The photographs are clear, bright, and enticing. Pairs of opposites are presented on facing pages." SLJ

Is it larger? Is it smaller? Greenwillow Bks. 1985 unp il pa $6.99 hardcover o.p.

Grades: PreK K   E

1. Size

ISBN 0-688-15287-2 (pa)   LC 84-13719

"In each full-color photograph of the wordless picture book Hoban juxtaposes similar objects of differing size. In the simplest pictures only one kind of object is shown, such as three bright plastic sand cups in graduated sizes or three maple leaves. More complex compositions group several related items: measuring cups, bowls, and utensils; fish, shells, and pebbles in an aquarium. Still others contrast dissimilar objects that have common features. . . . In the photographs, Hoban demonstrates once again her mastery of the elements of composition, such as color, texture, and balance." Horn Book

Hoban, Tana—*Continued*

Is it red? Is it yellow? Is it blue? an adventure in color. Greenwillow Bks. 1978 unp il lib bdg $17.99; pa $6.99 *

Grades: PreK K   E

1. Color 2. Size 3. Shape

ISBN 0-688-84171-6 (lib bdg); 0-688-07034-5 (pa)
LC 78-2549

Illustrations and brief text introduce colors and the concepts of shape and size

"The wordless book is simply designed and opens the eye to the marvelous world of color; each stark-white page contains one photograph which nearly fills it. In the bottom margin the predominant colors in the photograph are indicated by a row of corresponding circles." Horn Book

Is it rough? Is it smooth? Is it shiny? Greenwillow Bks. 1984 unp il $17.99

Grades: PreK K   E

ISBN 0-688-03823-9; 978-0-688-03823-6
LC 83-25460

Color photographs without text introduce objects of many different textures, such as pretzels, foil, hay, mud, kitten, and bubbles

"Extraordinarily crisp, clean color photographs allow Hoban to call attention to textures." Booklist

Let's count. Greenwillow Bks. 1999 unp il $17.99 *

Grades: PreK K   E

1. Counting

ISBN 0-688-16008-5   LC 98-44739

Photographs and dots introduce the numbers one to one hundred

"Hoban brings us another dazzling picture book. . . . Her photos range from the simple—1 hen, 8 Dalmatian puppies—to the more sophisticated—6 twirling rings on the arms of a circus performer; 12 rolls of toilet paper unpacked and stored on a pantry shelf." Booklist

Look book. Greenwillow Bks. 1997 unp il $17.99

Grades: PreK K   E

1. Nature photography

ISBN 0-688-14971-5   LC 96-46268

"Viewers first encounter a piece of an image, viewed through a small, die-cut circle on a black page. The full-color object—be it a flower, a pigeon, or a hot pretzel—is revealed with the turn of a page. Another turn of the page provides a larger view." SLJ

"Hoban presents a dazzling assortment of color photographs that celebrate the rich detail of everyday things." Booklist

Of colors and things. Greenwillow Bks. 1989 unp il pa $7.99 hardcover o.p. *

Grades: PreK K   E

1. Color

ISBN 0-688-04585-5 (pa)   LC 88-11101

Photographs of toys, food, and other common objects are grouped on each page according to color

"Hoban hits on a simple device to heighten a child's awareness, but what lifts this above the average concept book is the quality of its design and illustration." Booklist

Over, under & through, and other spatial concepts. Macmillan 1973 unp il hardcover o.p. pa $8.99

Grades: PreK K   E

1. Vocabulary

ISBN 0-02-744820-7; 1-4169-7541-1 (pa)

In brief text and photographs, the author depicts several spatial concepts—over, under, through, on, in, around, across, between, beside, below, against, and behind

"Children who are confused by these concepts may need help understanding that many of the pictures illustrate more than one concept. However, both the photographs and the format, with the words printed large on broad yellow bands at the beginning of each section, are uncluttered and appealing." Booklist

Shadows and reflections. Greenwillow Bks. 1990 unp il $16.99

Grades: PreK K   E

1. Shades and shadows

ISBN 978-0-688-07089-2; 0-688-07089-2
LC 89-30461

Photographs without text feature shadows and reflections of various objects, animals, and people

"This imaginative, wordless book of color photographs is a visual treat, offering witty and subtle sets of images for enriching the eyes of children and adults." SLJ

Shapes, shapes, shapes. Greenwillow Bks. 1986 unp il $16.99; lib bdg $17.89; pa $6.99

Grades: PreK K   E

1. Shape

ISBN 0-688-05832-9; 0-688-05833-7 (lib bdg); 0-688-14740-2 (pa)   LC 85-17569

Photographs of familiar objects such as chair, barrettes, and manhole cover present a study of rounded and angular shapes

"Tana Hoban has created an excellent concept book that will encourage children to look for specific shapes in everyday urban scenes. . . . The photographs not only serve to teach shapes and colors but are works of art themselves." Appraisal

So many circles, so many squares. Greenwillow Bks. 1998 unp il $16 *

Grades: PreK K   E

1. Shape

ISBN 0-688-15165-5   LC 97-10110

The geometric concepts of circles and squares are shown in photographs of wheels, signs, pots, and other familiar objects

"Teachers and young children will find plenty to talk about as they look at the colorful, well-composed, and clearly defined images." Booklist

White on black. Greenwillow Bks. 1993 unp il bd bk $6.99 *   E

1. Board books for children

ISBN 0-688-11919-0   LC 92-20092

In this board book, white illustrations against a black background depict such objects as a horse, baby bottle, and sailboat

"Hoban's compositions are so supple and her layouts so well balanced that she casts a kind of spell." Publ Wkly

Hobbie, Holly

Toot & Puddle: let it snow. Little, Brown & Co. 2007 unp il $16.99

Grades: PreK K 1 2   E

1. Christmas—Fiction 2. Snow—Fiction 3. Pigs—Fiction 4. Gifts—Fiction 5. Friendship—Fiction

ISBN 978-0-316-16686-7; 0-316-16686-3

Toot and Puddle celebrate Christmas and learn that the best kind of present for the best kind of friend is one that shows just how much you care.

"Hobbie infuses her holiday story of devoted friendship with cozy language . . . all evoked in Hobbie's signature watercolor illustrations." Horn Book

Other titles about Toot & Puddle are:

Toot & Puddle: a present for Toot (1998)

Toot & Puddle: Puddle's ABC (2000)

Toot & Puddle: I'll be home for Christmas (2001)

Toot & Puddle: top of the world (2002)

Toot & Puddle: charming Opal (2003)

Toot & Puddle: one and only (2006)

Hoberman, Mary Ann, 1930-

The two sillies; illustrated by Lynne Cravath. Harcourt 2000 unp il $16

Grades: PreK K 1 2   E

1. Cats—Fiction 2. Mice—Fiction 3. Stories in rhyme

ISBN 0-15-202221-X   LC 98-51844

"Gulliver books"

"When Silly Lilly admires Sammy's cat and asks how to get one, he gives her step-by-step instructions that seem to make no sense at all. . . . Short sentences use mono-syllabic words and rhyme to great effect. The brightly colored cartoon-style art adds just the right touch of exaggerated humor." Horn Book Guide

You read to me, I'll read to you; very short fairy tales to read together (in which wolves are tamed, trolls are transformed, and peas are triumphant); illustrated by Michael Emberley. Little, Brown 2004 32p il $16.95 *

Grades: K 1 2 3   E

1. Fairy tales

ISBN 0-316-14611-0   LC 2003-47445

"Megan Tingley books"

Contents: The three bears; The princess and the pea; Jack and the beanstalk; Little Red Riding Hood; Cinderella; The three little pigs; The little red hen and the grain of wheat; The three billy goats gruff

This is a "picture-book read-aloud with short, rhymed, illustrated scenarios for two voices. . . . The eight stories are . . . fractured fairy tales. . . . Each story ends with former enemies reading together." Booklist

"The two voices join seamlessly together to create a truly delightful reading ensemble. Emberley's humorous illustrations feature expressive characters drawn in pen, watercolor, and pastel." SLJ

Hodges, Margaret

The wee Christmas cabin; retold by Margaret Hodges; illustrated by Kimberly Bulcken Root. Holiday House 2009 unp il $16.95

Grades: K 1 2 3   E

1. Fairies—Fiction 2. Ireland—Fiction 3. Christmas—Fiction

ISBN 978-0-8234-1528-1; 0-8234-1528-7

           LC 00044877

A tinker's child who grows up helping everyone in her Irish village is rewarded in her old age with a cabin built by fairies on Christmas Eve.

"Hodges' elegant prose doesn't spell out exactly what happens to Oona, allowing children's imaginations to fill in the rest, and preserving the wonder of the story. Delicate watercolor paintings emphasize the cool dark blues and greens of wintry Ireland against the warm golds and reds of the cheery cabin's hearth." Booklist

Hodgkins, Fran, 1964-

Who's been here? a tale in tracks; illustrated by Karel Hayes. Down East 2008 unp il $15.95

Grades: PreK K 1 2   E

1. Animal tracks—Fiction 2. Dogs—Fiction

ISBN 978-0-89272-714-8; 0-89272-714-4

           LC 2008015756

"Three children follow golden retriever Willy into the snowy outdoors, seeing not only his paw prints but also those animals he's tracked. Delicate illustrations of snow-covered forest include accurate animal tracks and woodsy borders. The spare text uses repetition effectively in this book for nature lovers." Horn Book Guide

Hodgkinson, Leigh, 1975-

Smile! Balzer & Bray 2010 unp il $16.99

Grades: PreK K 1   E

1. Family life—Fiction

ISBN 978-0-06-185269-5; 0-06-185269-4

           LC 2009-14277

A little girl searches all over the house for the smile that seems to have deserted her.

"The childlike illustrations are done in bright colors with collage elements, occasional labels, and sometimes with sound effects. . . . Sunny's imagination enriches her search." SLJ

Hoff, Syd, 1912-2004

Danny and the dinosaur; story and pictures by Syd Hoff. Harper & Row 1958 64p il (I can read book) $16.99; pa $3.99

Grades: PreK K 1 2   E

1. Dinosaurs—Fiction

ISBN 0-06-022465-7; 0-06-444002-8 (pa)

The story is "about an amiable dinosaur who leaves his home in the museum to stroll about town and play with Danny, a small boy who loves dinosaurs." Bull Cent Child Books

"The bold, humorous, colored pictures convey the imaginative story. . . . Because of the simple vocabulary and sentence structure, first-graders can actually read this story." Libr J

Another title about Danny and the dinosaur is:

Happy birthday, Danny and the dinosaur! (1995)

Hoff, Syd, 1912-2004—*Continued*

The littlest leaguer; story and pictures by Syd Hoff. HarperCollins Childrens Books 2008 48p il (I can read!) $16.99; pa $3.99
Grades: PreK K 1 2   E
   1. Baseball—Fiction
   ISBN 978-0-06-053772-2; 0-06-053772-8; 978-0-06-053774-6 (pa); 0-06-053774-4 (pa)
   A reissue of the title first published 1976
Littlest of all the little leaguers, Harold has a hard time finding some way to really help his team.
"Hoff's ability to tell an interesting story with a minimum of words is unsurpassed." Horn Book Guide

Oliver; story and pictures by Syd Hoff. HarperCollins Pubs. 2000 64p il lib bdg $17.89; pa $3.99
Grades: PreK K 1 2   E
   1. Elephants—Fiction 2. Circus—Fiction
   ISBN 0-06-028709-8 (lib bdg); 0-06-444272-1 (pa)
                            LC 99-25591
"An I can read book"
A newly illustrated edition of the title first published 1960
Oliver the elephant looks elsewhere for employment after learning that the circus already has enough elephants
"One of the most warm-hearted and appealing easy-to-read books available." SLJ

Sammy the seal; story and pictures by Syd Hoff. newly il ed. HarperCollins Pubs. 2000 64p il $16.99; lib bdg $16.89; pa $3.99
Grades: PreK K 1 2   E
   1. Seals (Animals)—Fiction 2. Zoos—Fiction
   ISBN 0-06-028545-1; 0-06-028546-X (lib bdg); 0-06-444270-5 (pa)   LC 99-13805
"An I can read book"
A newly illustrated edition of the title first published 1959
Anxious to see what life is like outside the zoo, Sammy the seal explores the city, goes to school, and plays with the children but decides that there really is no place like home
"Happy adventures told in entertaining colored cartoonlike drawings and in simple vocabulary and short sentences which first graders can read with a minimum of help." Booklist

Hoffman, Mary, 1945-

Amazing Grace; pictures by Caroline Binch. Dial Bks. for Young Readers 1991 unp il $16.99 *
Grades: K 1 2 3   E
   1. African Americans—Fiction 2. Theater—Fiction
   ISBN 0-8037-1040-2   LC 90-25108
Titles about Grace for older readers are also available
Although her classmates say that she cannot play Peter Pan in the school play because she is black and a girl, Grace discovers that she can do anything she sets her mind to do
"Gorgeous watercolor illustrations portraying a deter-mined, talented child and her warm family enhance an excellent text and positive message of self-affirmation. Grace is an amazing girl and this is an amazing book." SLJ
   Other picture book titles about Grace are:
Boundless Grace (1995)
Princess Grace (2008)

The color of home; pictures by Karin Littlewood. Phyllis Fogelman Bks. 2002 unp il $15.99
Grades: K 1 2 3   E
   1. Refugees—Fiction 2. Immigrants—Fiction 3. Somalia—Fiction
   ISBN 0-8037-2841-7   LC 2001-7393
Hassan, newly-arrived in the United States and feeling homesick, paints a picture at school that shows his old home in Somalia as well as the reason his family had to leave
"Readers gain a realistic child's perspective on what it is like to be forced to emigrate from a war-torn country. . . . Littlewood's impressionistic watercolor illustrations . . . beautifully convey Hassan's sadness, fear, and ultimate happiness." SLJ

Hogrogian, Nonny, 1932-
Cool cat. Roaring Brook Press 2009 unp il $17.99
Grades: PreK K 1 2   E
   1. Cats—Fiction 2. Animals—Fiction 3. Painting—Fiction 4. Stories without words
   ISBN 978-1-59643-429-5; 1-59643-429-5
"A Neal Porter Book"
"A vacant lot strewn with garbage is transformed by an artistic and imaginative black cat in this wordless picture book. Using paints and brushes from his wooden art box, the feline covers his drab surroundings with leaves and sky, enlisting the help of some birds and woodland creatures that take up brushes to add flowers, trees, and a pond. . . . Simple, almost childlike art in the lush colors of summer combines with brilliant composition to tell the story. . . . Both visually and conceptually, this is a gem." SLJ

Holabird, Katharine
Angelina Ballerina; story by Katharine Holabird; illustrations by Helen Craig. Viking 2006 c1983 unp il $12.99 *
Grades: PreK K 1 2   E
   1. Mice—Fiction 2. Ballet—Fiction
   ISBN 0-670-06026-7
A reissue of the title first published 1983 by Potter
Angelina the mouse loves to dance and wants to become a ballerina more than anything else in the world.
"Touches of humor, attention to detail, a feel for dance and truly anthropomorphic mice make the illustrations a major part of the book." Child Book Rev Serv
   Other titles about Angelina are:
Angelina and Alice (1987)
Angelina and Henry (2002)
Angelina and the princess (1984)
Angelina and the royal wedding (2010)
Angelina at the fair (1985)

Holabird, Katharine—*Continued*

Angelina on stage (1986)
Angelina, star of the show (2008)
Angelina's baby sister (1991)
Angelina's Christmas (1985)
Angelina's Halloween (2000)

Hole, Stian

Garmann's summer. Eerdmans Books for Young Readers 2008 unp il $17.50 *

Grades: 1 2 3   E

1. Aunts—Fiction 2. Family life—Fiction 3. Fear—Fiction 4. Old age—Fiction 5. Summer—Fiction

ISBN 978-0-8028-5339-4; 0-8028-5339-0

Original Norwegian edition, 2006

Now that summer is nearly over, Garmann is afraid of starting school. He asks his elderly aunts, and his father, and his mother what they are afraid of.

"The illustrations, spacious, quirky mosaic collages comprising photos, old-fashioned etchings, and wallpaper samples are utterly without a trace of sentimentality. In a feat of deceptive simplicity, Hole has crafted an elegant, fanciful, wholly poetic exploration of the nature of fear and the strength and hope required to conquer it." Booklist

Another title about Garmann is:

Garmann's street (2010)

Holmberg, Bo R., 1945-

A day with Dad; illustrations by Eva Eriksson. Candlewick Press 2008 unp il $15.99

Grades: K 1 2 3   E

1. Divorce—Fiction 2. Father-son relationship—Fiction

ISBN 978-0-7636-3221-2; 0-7636-3221-X

LC 2007034228

Tim waits with excitement for a train to bring his father, who lives in another town, then spends an entire day with him, doing all of their favorite things, until it is time for Dad to catch the train home.

"Eriksson's unfussy colored-pencil illustrations are a good match for Holmberg's straightforward text. . . . This gentle, poignant story offers comfort to readers in similar circumstances and leaves them with a hopeful message." Horn Book

Holmes, Mary Tavener

A giraffe goes to Paris; by Mary Tavener Holmes and John Harris; illustrated by Jon Cannell. Marshall Cavendish Children 2010 31p il map $16.95

Grades: K 1 2 3   E

1. Voyages and travels—Fiction 2. Giraffes—Fiction 3. France—Fiction

ISBN 978-0-7614-5595-0; 0-7614-5595-7

LC 2009-19047

Recounts the 1827 journey of a young giraffe named Belle, a gift from the Pasha of Egypt to King Charles X of France, as she makes her way by boat and land to Paris, accompanied by her devoted caretaker, Atir.

"Loopy handwritten script is used for emphasis . . . while old maps, photographs, and potraits supplement Cannell's watercolor-and-ink drawings. . . . This is history for children as it ought to be written." Publ Wkly

Holub, Joan, 1956-

Apple countdown; by Joan Holub; illustrated by Jan Smith. Albert Whitman & Co. 2009 unp il $16.99

Grades: PreK K 1 2   E

1. Stories in rhyme 2. School stories 3. Apples—Fiction 4. Counting

ISBN 978-0-8075-0398-0; 0-8075-0398-3

LC 2008031705

Rhyming text describes a school field trip to an apple orchard, where the students count down all the things they see, from twenty nametags to one apple pie.

"The vibrant watercolor illustrations are dominated by primary colors, and the excitement shows on the smiling faces of the students." SLJ

The garden that we grew; pictures by Hiroe Nakata. Viking 2001 unp il $13.99

Grades: K 1 2   E

1. Pumpkin—Fiction 2. Gardening—Fiction 3. Stories in rhyme

ISBN 0-670-89799-X   LC 00-10966

"A Viking easy-to-read"

Children plant pumpkin seeds, water and weed the garden patch, watch the pumpkins grow, pick them, and enjoy them in various ways

"The text blossoms with the ample warmth, light, and gentle sense of humor in the pictures." Horn Book

Hood, Susan

Pup and Hound hatch an egg; written by Susan Hood; illustrated by Linda Hendry. Kids Can Press 2007 32p il $14.95; pa $3.95

Grades: PreK K 1   E

1. Dogs—Fiction 2. Turtles—Fiction 3. Stories in rhyme

ISBN 978-1-55337-974-4; 1-55337-974-8; 978-1-55337-975-1 (pa); 1-55337-975-6 (pa)

"Kids can read"

"Pup finds an egg in the grass and tries to return it to Duck and then Mother Hen. Both mothers deny ownership, and when the egg eventually hatches, it turns out to be a baby turtle—a new friend for Pup and Hound. [The book has] appealing characters and all of the requisites for a successful beginning reader. . . . Bouncy rhymes add to the fun." SLJ

Other titles about Pup and Hound are:

Pup and Hound (2004)
Pup and Hound at sea (2006)
Pup and Hound catch a thief (2007)
Pup and Hound in trouble (2005)
Pup and Hound lost and found (2006)
Pup and Hound move in (2004)
Pup and Hound play copycats (2007)
Pup and Hound scare a ghost (2007)
Pup and Hound stay up late (2005)

Hooks, Bell

Grump groan growl; illustrated by Chris Raschka. Hyperion Books for Children 2008 unp il $16.99

Grades: PreK K 1   E

1. Emotions—Fiction

ISBN 978-0-7868-0816-8; 0-7868-0816-0

LC 2007022312

Hooks, Bell—*Continued*

Rhythmic text exposes a bad mood on the prowl, and advises the reader not to hide, but to let those feelings be

"Expressionistic art and economical poetry combine smoothly to create an inspiring model of self-control. . . . Thick, almost tactile lines of paint are slathered onto the pages with gusto, capturing a feeling of movement and strong emotion." SLJ

Hopgood, Tim

Wow! said the owl. Farrar, Straus and Giroux 2009 unp il $14.95

Grades: PreK K 1   E

1. Owls—Fiction 2. Day—Fiction 3. Night—Fiction 4. Color—Fiction

ISBN 978-0-374-38518-7; 0-374-38518-1

LC 2008044038

Subtitle on cover: "a book about colors."

A curious little owl decides to stay awake to find out how the things he sees at night look during the daytime.

"Collage-style illustrations done in simple, bright shapes show little owl in her tree while the changing colors and perspectives keep each page turn 'WOW!'-worthy. . . . Straightforward and flowing, this title makes a satisfying introduction to the colors of the day." SLJ

Hopkinson, Deborah

Abe Lincoln crosses a creek; a tall, thin tale (introducing his forgotten frontier friend); pictures by John Hendrix. Schwartz & Wade Books 2008 unp il $16.99; lib bdg $19.99 *

Grades: K 1 2 3   E

1. Lincoln, Abraham, 1809-1865—Fiction 2. Friendship—Fiction

ISBN 978-0-375-83768-5; 0-375-83768-X; 978-0-375-93768-2 (lib bdg); 0-375-93768-4 (lib bdg)

LC 2007-35149

In Knob Creek, Kentucky, in 1816, seven-year-old Abe Lincoln falls into a creek and is rescued by his best friend, Austin Gollaher.

"Hopkinson has created a lively, participatory tale that will surely stand out. . . . Hendrix's illustrations have a naive and rustic flavor that's in perfect harmony with the gravelly, homespun narrator's voice." SLJ

Apples to Oregon; being the (slightly) true narrative of how a brave pioneer father brought apples, peaches, pears, plums, grapes, and cherries (and children) across the plains; illustrated by Nancy Carpenter. Atheneum Books for Young Readers 2004 unp il map $15.95 *

Grades: 1 2 3 4   E

1. Frontier and pioneer life—Fiction 2. Overland journeys to the Pacific—Fiction 3. Fruit culture—Fiction 4. Tall tales

ISBN 0-689-84769-6   LC 2001-22949

"An Anne Schwartz book"

A pioneer father transports his beloved fruit trees and his family to Oregon in the mid-nineteenth century. Based loosely on the life of Henderson Luelling

"Carpenter's oil paintings are filled with vivid shades that reflect the changing scenery. Amusing details abound, and the slightly exaggerated humor of the pictures is in perfect balance with the tone of the text." SLJ

A band of angels; a story inspired by the Jubilee Singers; illustrated by Raúl Colón. Atheneum Bks. for Young Readers 1999 unp il hardcover o.p. pa $7.99 *

Grades: 1 2 3 4   E

1. Moore, Ella Sheppard, 1851-1914—Fiction 2. Jubilee Singers (Musical group)—Fiction 3. African Americans—Fiction 4. Gospel music—Fiction

ISBN 0-689-81062-8; 0-689-84887-0 (pa)

LC 96-20011

"An Anne Schwartz book"

Based on the life of Ella Sheppard Moore. The daughter of a slave forms a gospel singing group and goes on tour to raise money to save Fisk University

"Lilting prose, poignant historical details and arresting portraits of trailblazing singers lost in song contribute to this triumphant tale." Publ Wkly

Billy and the rebel; based on a true Civil War story; illustrated by Brian Floca. Atheneum Books for Young Readers 2002 44p il map $14.95 *

Grades: 1 2 3 4   E

1. Gettysburg (Pa.), Battle of, 1863—Fiction 2. United States—History—1861-1865, Civil War—Fiction

ISBN 0-689-83964-2   LC 2001-22982

"Ready-to-read"

During the Battle of Gettysburg in 1863, a mother and son shelter a young Confederate deserter. Includes a historical note on the incident.

"Based on the real William Bayly and his mother, Harriet Hamilton Bayly, [this book] . . . allows beginning readers and researchers some insight into life during the Civil War. Full-page, full-spread, and spot art, executed mainly in shades of yellow and tan, add detail and expression to this story of courage and an unlikely friendship." SLJ

From slave to soldier; based on a true Civil War story; illustrated by Brian Floca. Atheneum Books for Young Readers 2005 44p il $14.95 *

Grades: 1 2 3   E

1. Slavery—Fiction 2. African American soldiers—Fiction 3. United States—History—1861-1865, Civil War—Fiction

ISBN 0-689-83965-8

A boy who hates being a slave joins the Union Army to fight for freedom, and proves himself brave and capable of handling a mule team when the need arises

This is written "in simple sentences for those who have just begun to read proficiently. . . . Short chapters and detailed watercolors aid the transition to more difficult text, while an exciting plot . . . keeps readers interested." SLJ

Hopkinson, Deborah—*Continued*

Girl wonder; a baseball story in nine innings; with pictures by Terry Widener. Atheneum Bks. for Young Readers 2003 unp il $16.95

Grades: 1 2 3 4   **E**

1. Weiss, Alta, 1890-1964—Fiction 2. Baseball—Fiction

ISBN 0-689-83300-8   LC 99-47052

"An Anne Schwartz book"

In the early 1900s, Alta Weiss, a young woman who knows from an early age that she loves baseball, finds a way to show that she can play, even though she is a girl

"Hopkinson tells her story with practiced skill—vivid details, lively language, varied pacing. . . . The illustrations are . . . broad, somewhat exaggerated, but conveying much emotion and narrative content." Horn Book

The humblebee hunter; pictures by Jen Corace. Disney Hyperion Books 2010 unp il $16.99

Grades: K 1 2   **E**

1. Darwin, Charles, 1809-1882—Fiction 2. Bees—Fiction 3. Great Britain—History—19th century—Fiction

ISBN 978-1-4231-1356-0; 1-4231-1356-X

LC 2009-33987

On a beautiful day, some of Charles Darwin's many children help him study humblebees (bumblebees) in the garden at their home in the English countryside.

"The delicate, stylized illustrations, outlined in black and washed in natural shades of green and brown with spots of color, depict an amiable country Victorian household. . . . [This is an] inspiring read-aloud." SLJ

Sky boys; how they built the Empire State Building; [by] Deborah Hopkinson & James E. Ransome. Schwartz & Wade Books 2006 unp il $16.95 *

Grades: K 1 2 3 4   **E**

1. Empire State Building (New York, N.Y.)—Fiction 2. Building—Fiction 3. New York (N.Y.)—Fiction

ISBN 0-375-83610-1   LC 2005010852

In 1931, a boy and his father watch as the world's tallest building, the Empire State Building, is constructed, step-by-step, near their Manhattan home.

"Crisp, lyrical free verse and bold paintings celebrate the skill and daring of those who constructed the Empire State Building. . . . Ransome's powerful acrylic paintings show the building in all stages of construction, and includes the workers' perilous views. A unique, memorable title." Booklist

Sweet Clara and the freedom quilt; paintings by James Ransome. Knopf 1993 unp il hardcover o.p. pa $6.99 *

Grades: K 1 2 3 4   **E**

1. Slavery—Fiction 2. Quilts—Fiction

ISBN 0-679-82311-5; 0-679-92311-X (lib bdg); 0-679-87472-0 (pa)   LC 91-11601

Clara, a young slave, stitches a quilt with a map pattern which guides her to freedom in the North

"The smooth, optimistic, first-person vernacular of the story is ably accompanied by Ransome's brightly colored, full-page paintings." Horn Book Guide

Another title about Clara is:

Under the quilt of night (2001)

Hoppe, Paul

Hat. Bloomsbury U.S.A Children's Books 2009 unp il $14.99

Grades: PreK K 1   **E**

1. Hats—Fiction 2. Lost and found possessions—Fiction 3. Imagination—Fiction

ISBN 978-1-59990-247-0; 1-59990-247-8; 978-1-59990-248-7 (lib bdg); 1-59990-248-6 (lib bdg)

LC 2008-22357

When Henry finds a hat he is very excited by its possibilities, but becomes worried when he thinks that the hat might belong to someone else

"The text is simple but imaginative. The illustrations bring each imagined scenario to life, and the ink drawings have a slightly retro feel with their subdued colors. The story lends itself to being read aloud, and the red hat pops off the pages." SLJ

Horáček, Petr

Choo choo. Candlewick Press 2008 unp il $5.99 *

Grades: PreK   **E**

1. Railroads—Fiction 2. Board books for children

ISBN 978-0-7636-3477-3; 0-7636-3477-8

"Horáček's cheerful acrylic collage artwork shines in this small, beautifully designed board book about a train that carries cars full of smiling children to the beach. From the sound effects that begin the single line on each spread . . . to the shaped pages that emphasize the curve of mountains or the spikes of treetops, this book begs for interaction." Booklist

Silly Suzy Goose. Candlewick Press 2006 unp il $14.99 *

Grades: PreK K 1 2   **E**

1. Geese—Fiction 2. Lions—Fiction

ISBN 0-7636-3040-3

Suzy longs to be different from all the other geese, but learns that imitating a lion may not be the best way to express her individuality.

"Created in mixed media, the art jumps off the pages, a fitting verb for a clever, clever book, alive in every way." Booklist

Other titles about Suzy Goose are:

Look out, Suzy Goose (2008)

Suzy Goose and the Christmas star (2009)

Horning, Sandra, 1970-

The giant hug; illustrated by Valeri Gorbachev. Knopf 2005 unp il $15.95; lib bdg $17.99

Grades: PreK K 1 2   **E**

1. Grandmothers—Fiction 2. Postal service—Fiction 3. Pigs—Fiction

ISBN 0-375-82477-4; 0-375-92477-9 (lib bdg)

LC 2003-25883

When Owen the pig sends a real hug to his grandmother for her birthday he inadvertently brings cheer to the postal workers as they pass the hug along

"Gorbachev's cast of animal characters, drawn with a . . . sense of whimsy, are well chosen to emphasize the relevant personality traits." Booklist

Horowitz, Dave, 1970-
Twenty-six princesses. Putnam 2008 unp il $15.99
Grades: PreK K 1 2   E
   1. Fairy tales 2. Princesses—Fiction 3. Alphabet
   ISBN 978-0-399-24607-4; 0-399-24607-X
              LC 2007-13233
Twenty-six princesses, one for each letter of the alphabet, go to a party at the prince's castle.
"Horowitz has a light, witty touch, and the text is rich with puns. The words and the pictures play off one another perfectly, encouraging children to pore over each humorously detailed portrait." SLJ
   Includes bibliographical references

Horse, Harry, 1960-2007
Little Rabbit lost. Peachtree Pubs. 2002 unp il $15.95; bd bk $9.95
Grades: PreK K 1   E
   1. Rabbits—Fiction 2. Birthdays—Fiction
   ISBN 1-56145-273-4; 1-56145-345-5 (bd bk)
              LC 2002-2697
On his birthday Little Rabbit thinks that he is now a big rabbit, until he gets lost at the Rabbit World amusement park
"The lovely ink-and-watercolor illustrations are filled with clever details kids will enjoy—carrot-shaped paddleboats and bunny roller-coaster cars. Children will welcome this charming story." Booklist
   Other titles about Little Rabbit are:
Little Rabbit goes to school (2004)
Little Rabbit runaway (2005)
Little Rabbit's Christmas (2007)
Little Rabbit's new baby (2008)

Horstman, Lisa
Squawking Matilda. Marshall Cavendish Children 2009 unp il $17.99
Grades: PreK K 1 2   E
   1. Chickens—Fiction 2. Aunts—Fiction 3. Farm life—Fiction
   ISBN 978-0-7614-5463-2; 0-7614-5463-2
              LC 2008003657
Mae likes starting projects but never seems to finish them, and so when Aunt Susan asks her to take care of a feisty chicken Mae is soon distracted, then must find a way to make up for her neglect before Aunt Susan's visit.
"Handcrafted puppets wearing cheery clothing are posed, photographed, and digitally colored to give this charming selection a down-to-earth quality that matches the story perfectly." SLJ

Houston, Gloria
My great-aunt Arizona; illustrated by Susan Condie Lamb. HarperCollins Pubs. 1992 unp il $15.99; pa $6.99
Grades: K 1 2 3   E
   1. Hughes, Arizona Houston, 1876-1969 2. Teachers 3. Appalachian region
   ISBN 0-06-022606-4; 0-06-022607-2 (lib bdg); 0-06-443374-9 (pa)   LC 90-44112

The author tells the life story of "her great aunt Arizona who never traveled farther than the next town where she trained as a teacher before returning to her small Appalachian community's one-room schoolhouse. Though not well-traveled, Arizona encouraged her students to dream of faraway places and was always there to give them hugs and kisses." Child Book Rev Serv
"The pleasant, conversational rhythm of the prose, the unobtrusive use of repetition, and the ability to sum up the unique quality of a life in a few telling phrases give the writing its substance. . . . Sunny and lively, the watercolor paintings have a naive quality that suits the story well." Booklist

The year of the perfect Christmas tree; an Appalachian story; pictures by Barbara Cooney. Dial Bks. for Young Readers 1988 unp il $15.99; pa $6.99
Grades: K 1 2 3   E
   1. Christmas—Fiction 2. Appalachian region—Fiction
   ISBN 0-8037-0299-X; 0-14-055827-2 (pa)
              LC 87-24551
"It's 1918 in the mountains of North Carolina, and the custom in the village is for one family to select and donate the Christmas tree each year. In the spring Ruthie and her father select a perfect balsam high on a rocky crag. Then Father goes to war. Still, on Christmas Eve the tree is in the church and Ruthie plays the angel. The winning illustrations perfectly match the tone of this affecting story, which comes from the author's family." NY Times Book Rev

Howard, Arthur, 1948-
Hoodwinked. Harcourt 2001 unp il $16
Grades: PreK K 1   E
   1. Pets—Fiction 2. Witches—Fiction
   ISBN 0-15-202656-8   LC 00-8318
Mitzi, a young witch, searches for a creepy pet, but finds that a cute kitten is perfect for her
"The pictures are perfect for this lively story—lots of fangs and slimy, scaly, weird, and wiggly outlines fill the pages." SLJ

Howard, Elizabeth Fitzgerald, 1927-
Aunt Flossie's hats (and crab cakes later); paintings by James Ransome. 10th anniversary ed. Clarion Books 2001 31p il $16; pa $6.95 *
Grades: K 1 2 3   E
   1. Hats—Fiction 2. Aunts—Fiction 3. African Americans—Fiction
   ISBN 0-618-12038-6; 0-395-72077-X (pa)
              LC 00-65757
A reissue of the title first published 1991
   Includes an afterword with biographical information and photographs of the real Aunt Flossie
Sara and Susan share tea, cookies, crab cakes, and stories about hats when they visit their favorite relative, Aunt Flossie.
"This is an affecting portrait of a black American family. . . . Howard's quiet, sure telling is well matched by Ransome's art-elegant, expressive oil paintings that convey warmth, joy, tenderness and love." Publ Wkly

Howard, Elizabeth Fitzgerald, 1927-—*Continued*

Virgie goes to school with us boys; illustrated by E.B. Lewis. Simon & Schuster Bks. for Young Readers 1999 unp il $17.99; pa $7.99 *

Grades: K 1 2 3   E

    1. African Americans—Fiction

    ISBN 0-689-80076-2; 0-689-87793-5 (pa)

                           LC 97-49406

In the post-Civil War South, a young African American girl is determined to prove that she can go to school just like her older brothers

"The story is a superb tribute to the author's great aunt, the inspiration for this book. . . . Lewis's watercolor illustrations capture the characters with warmth and dignity." SLJ

Howard, Reginald

The big, big wall; by Reginald Howard; illustrated by Ariane Dewey and and Jose Aruego; translated by F. Isabel Campoy and Alma Flor Ada. Houghton Mifflin Harcourt 2009 unp il (Green light readers) $12.99; pa $3.99

Grades: K 1 2   E

    1. Stories in rhyme 2. Nursery rhymes—Fiction 3. Eggs—Fiction 4. Friendship—Fiction 5. Animals—Fiction 6. Bilingual books—English-Spanish

    ISBN 978-0-547-25547-7; 0-547-25547-0; 978-0-547-25548-4 (pa); 0-547-25548-9 (pa)

                         LC 2009008751

English language edition first published 2001

Humpty Dumpty's friends help him avoid a big, big fall.

"The text—one or two sentences per page printed in both English and Spanish—is pleasantly rhythmic and repetitive. Smiling animals reassuring a fearful Humpty will entertain your readers." Horn Book Guide

Howe, James, 1946-

Brontorina; illustrated by Randy Cecil. Candlewick Press 2010 il $15.99 *

Grades: PreK K 1 2   E

    1. Dinosaurs—Fiction 2. Ballet—Fiction

    ISBN 978-0-7636-4437-6; 0-7636-4437-4

"Initially turned away from Madame Lucille's Dance Academy for Boys and Girls because she is an enormous dinosaur, Brontorina counters, 'But in my heart I am a ballerina.' . . . Text and illustrations work beautifully together in this witty fantasy. . . . In Cecil's arresting oil paintings, the tawny orange dinosaur stands out boldly against slate blue or white backgrounds, and the unusual texture of the paint creates a distinctive effect." Booklist

Horace and Morris but mostly Dolores; written by James Howe; illustrated by Amy Walrod. Atheneum Bks. for Young Readers 1999 unp il $16; pa $6.99 *

Grades: PreK K 1 2   E

    1. Mice—Fiction 2. Friendship—Fiction 3. Sex role—Fiction

    ISBN 0-689-31874-X; 0-689-85675-X (pa)

                         LC 96-17645

"An Anne Schwartz book"

"Three adventure-loving mice are best friends until gender stereotypes separate them, driving Horace and Morris into a rowdy boys-only clubhouse while Dolores reluctantly goes off to join the ultra-ladylike Cheese Puffs. The bold artwork suits the book's lively protest against conformity." Horn Book Guide

Other titles about Horace, Morris, and Dolores are:

Horace and Morris join the chorus (but what about Dolores?) (2002)

Horace and Morris say cheese (which makes Dolores sneeze!) (2009)

Houndsley and Catina; illustrated by Marie-Louise Gay. Candlewick Press 2006 36p il $14.99 *

Grades: PreK K 1 2   E

    1. Cats—Fiction 2. Dogs—Fiction 3. Friendship—Fiction

    ISBN 0-7636-2404-7   LC 2005-50187

Houndsley, a dog, and Catina, a cat, run into trouble when they decide to prove that they are the best at cooking and writing, respectively.

"The lively, brisk writing is wonderfully extended in Gay's airy watercolor-and-pencil illustrations." Booklist

Other titles about Houndsley and Catina are:

Houndsley and Catina and the birthday surprise (2006)

Houndsley and Catina and the quiet time (2008)

Houndsley and Catina plink and plunk (2009)

Kaddish for Grandpa in Jesus' name, amen; [llustrated by] Catherine Stock. Atheneum Books for Young Readers 2004 unp il $16.95

Grades: K 1 2 3   E

    1. Funeral rites and ceremonies—Fiction 2. Death—Fiction 3. Grandfathers—Fiction 4. Judaism—Fiction 5. Christianity—Fiction

    ISBN 0-689-80185-8   LC 2002-11569

Five-year-old Emily tries to understand her grandfather's death by exploring the Christian and Jewish rituals that her family practices during and after his funeral

"The soft watercolor illustrations, done in pastel colors, are a perfect accompaniment to the story. This book is a good vehicle to explain the rituals of death to children." SLJ

Pinky and Rex; illustrated by Melissa Sweet. Atheneum Pubs. 1990 38p il $15; pa $3.99 *

Grades: K 1 2   E

    1. Museums—Fiction 2. Friendship—Fiction 3. Toys—Fiction

    ISBN 0-689-31454-X; 0-689-82348-7 (pa)

                         LC 89-30786

"Pinky, a boy named for his favorite color, and Rex, a girl whose name reflects her interest in dinosaurs, live next door to each other; they each have twenty-seven stuffed animals and are best friends. . . . They go to the museum and discover that even best friends can vie with each other for the last remaining pink dinosaur in the museum store." Horn Book

"Sweet's gently washed, jovial illustrations reflect the unpretentious sincerity of Rex and Pinky's relationship, while Howe's readable text blending natural dialogue with narrative, is divided into individual chapters." Booklist

Other titles about Pinky and Rex are:

Howe, James, 1946-—*Continued*

Pinky and Rex and the bully (1996)
Pinky and Rex and the double-dad weekend (1995)
Pinky and Rex and the just-right pet (2001)
Pinky and Rex and the mean old witch (1991)
Pinky and Rex and the new baby (1993)
Pinky and Rex and the new neighbors (1997)
Pinky and Rex and the perfect pumpkin (1998)
Pinky and Rex and the school play (1998)
Pinky and Rex and the spelling bee (1991)
Pinky and Rex get married (1990)
Pinky and Rex go to camp (1992)

Howland, Naomi

Latkes, latkes, good to eat; a Chanukah story.
Clarion Bks. 1999 31p il $16; pa $5.95 *
Grades: PreK K 1 2   E
1. Magic—Fiction 2. Hanukkah—Fiction 3. Jews—
Fiction
ISBN 0-395-89903-6; 0-618-49295-X (pa)
LC 97-50616
In an old Russian village, Sadie and her brothers are
poor and hungry until an old woman gives Sadie a frying
pan that will make potato pancakes until it hears the
magic words that make it stop
"Howland effectively sets her story in a Russian
shtetl, using words, intonation, and especially pictures.
Working in gouache and colored pencil, she offers a
snowy landscape peopled with Jewish villagers who
work hard and celebrate harder." Booklist

Princess says goodnight; illustrated by David
Small. HarperCollins 2010 unp il $16.99; lib bdg
$17.89
Grades: PreK K 1 2   E
1. Bedtime—Fiction 2. Princesses—Fiction 3. Stories
in rhyme
ISBN   978-0-06-145525-4;   0-06-145525-3;
978-0-06-145526-1 (lib bdg); 0-06-145526-1 (lib bdg)
Rhyming text presents what a princess might do be-
tween leaving the ball and saying goodnight.
"Sweet and disarmingly infectious without being cloy-
ing, this is a bedtime story full of joy and imagination."
Publ Wkly

Hubbell, Patricia

Airplanes; soaring! diving! turning! by Patricia
Hubbell; illustrated by Megan Halsey and Sean
Addy. Marshall Cavendish Children 2008 unp il
$16.99
Grades: PreK K 1 2   E
1. Airplanes—Fiction 2. Stories in rhyme
ISBN 978-0-7614-5388-8; 0-7614-5388-1
LC 2007011721
Illustrations and rhyming text celebrate different kinds
of airplanes and what they can do
"This picture book features . . . animated, whimsical
art that will delight young would-be jet-setters. . . . The
lively, descriptive prose . . . incorporates peppy sounds
that amp up the energy that's echoed in the vibrant illustrations." Booklist

Boats; speeding! sailing! cruising! illustrated by
Megan Halsey and Sean Addy. Marshall
Cavendish 2009 unp il $17.99 *
Grades: PreK K 1 2   E
1. Boats and boating—Fiction 2. Stories in rhyme
ISBN 978-0-7614-5524-0; 0-7614-5524-8
LC 2007-49522
Illustrations and rhyming text celebrate different kinds
of boats and what they can do.
"The tight, surprisingly informative rhyming text
works so well because it pairs with art that shows off
each of these boats to best advantage. The fun part
comes in the way the design and the mixed-media art
. . . come together." Booklist

Cars; rushing! honking! zooming! illustrated by
Megan Halsey and Sean Addy. Marshall
Cavendish Children 2006 unp il $14.99
Grades: PreK K 1   E
1. Automobiles—Fiction 2. Stories in rhyme
ISBN 978-0-7614-5296-6; 0-7614-5296-6
Illustrations and rhyming text celebrate different kinds
of cars and what they can do
"The rhyming text rolls smoothly along. . . . Color
heightens the appeal of the clip art, stamps, etchings,
maps, and original drawings, which come together in the
paper-collage illustrations." Booklist

Firefighters! speeding! spraying! saving!
illustrated by Viviana Garofoli. Marshall
Cavendish 2007 unp il $14.99; bd bk $7.99
Grades: PreK K 1   E
1. Fire fighters—Fiction 2. Board books for children
3. Stories in rhyme
ISBN   978-0-7614-5337-6;   0-7614-5337-7;
978-0-7614-5615-5 (bd bk); 0-7614-5615-5 (bd bk)
"The tale begins with the 'Clang! Clang! Clang!' of
the alarm. The firefighters rush to get dressed and board
their truck, along with Spot, the firehouse Dalmatian.
Brief, pulsating, rhythmic text follows across the pages.
. . . The digital, cartoon-style artwork is simple. Done in
vibrant hues of predominately primary colors." SLJ

My first airplane ride; by Patricia Hubbell;
illustrated by Nancy Speir. Marshall Cavendish
2008 unp il $16.99
Grades: PreK K 1   E
1. Airplanes—Fiction 2. Stories in rhyme
ISBN 978-0-7614-5436-6; 0-7614-5436-5
"Short, rhyming phrases record the events as a boy
takes his first plane ride. Every incident along the way
is chronicled here: packing, driving to the airport, getting
boarding passes, going through security in stocking feet,
waiting at the gate, etc. . . . The level of detail is well
calibrated to the target audience. . . . Colorful and reassuring." Booklist

Police: hurrying! helping! saving! Marshall
Cavendish Children 2008 unp il $14.99
Grades: PreK K 1   E
1. Police—Fiction 2. Stories in rhyme
ISBN 978-0-7614-5421-2; 0-7614-5421-7
Illustrations and rhyming text celebrate police officers
and what they do.
"A picture book with a rhyming text, bright colors,
and plenty of action." SLJ

Hubbell, Will

Pumpkin Jack; written and illustrated by Will Hubbell. Whitman, A. 2000 unp il $15.95

Grades: PreK K 1 2 3   E

1. Pumpkin—Fiction 2. Halloween—Fiction

ISBN 0-8075-6665-9   LC 00-8282

After Halloween, Tim discards Jack, his jack-o'lantern, in the garden and during the following year it sprouts, blooms, and grows new pumpkins

"Satisfying and surprisingly varied in approach and perspective, Hubbell's colored pencil drawings illustrate the simple story in a series of well-imagined scenes." Booklist

Hucke, Johannes

Pip in the Grand Hotel; illustrated by Daniel Müller. North-South 2009 unp il $16.95

Grades: PreK K 1 2   E

1. Hotels and motels—Fiction 2. Mice—Fiction

ISBN 978-0-7358-2225-2; 0-7358-2225-5

Originally published in Sweden

Mary has a new pet, a mouse named Pip. When she opens the lid to his box, Pip is off straight into the Grand Hotel. The reader can search for Pip in the pictures.

"This lively escapade is heightened by ellipses at the end of each spread, which create dramatic page turns. As the children race through this bustling high-end hotel, Müller's detail-filled watercolor illustrations truly bring the caper to life." SLJ

Huget, Jennifer LaRue

How to clean your room in 10 easy steps; illustrated by Edward Koren. Schwartz & Wade Books 2009 unp il $16.99; lib bdg $19.99

Grades: K 1 2   E

1. Home economics—Fiction

ISBN 978-0-375-84410-2; 0-375-84410-4; 978-0-375-96410-7 (lib bdg); 0-375-96410-X (lib bdg)

LC 2008-48824

A young girl provides unique advice on how to tidy a bedroom.

"Children and their adults are in for a treat with this new showcase for Koren's illustrations. His wry, bushy, squiggly style is well-matched by Huget's puckish and not entirely serious advice. . . . Good for great giggles—and at the end, she promises even more awesome advice on fixing your hair." Kirkus

Thanks a LOT, Emily Post! written by Jennifer LaRue Huget; illustrated by Alexandra Boiger. Schwartz & Wade Books 2009 unp il $16.99; lib bdg $19.99

Grades: K 1 2 3   E

1. Post, Emily, 1873-1960—Fiction 2. Etiquette—Fiction 3. Conduct of life—Fiction 4. Mothers—Fiction

ISBN 978-0-375-83853-8; 0-375-83853-8; 978-0-375-93853-5 (lib bdg); 0-375-93853-2 (lib bdg)

LC 2008004994

When a mother instructs her children to behave according to Emily Post's rules of etiquette, they respond by insisting that Mother follow the rules, as well. Includes information about Post and selected items from her 1922 book.

"Written with clarity and wit. . . . The fresh, expressive watercolors dramatize events through distinctive characters playing out sometimes-chaotic scenes full of energy, elegance, and entertaining details." Booklist

Hughes, Shirley

Alfie and the big boys. Bodley Head 2007 unp il $17.95

Grades: PreK K 1   E

1. School stories 2. Friendship—Fiction

ISBN 978-0-370-32884-3; 0-370-32884-1

Alfie and his friends wish they could play with the bigger boys and one day they get a chance

This "sensitively portrays children's emotional lives through everyday events in familiar settings. Ink drawings, brightened with washes and strokes of color, have the narrative power to tell the basic story on their own. But the book is richer for the inclusion of a straightforward text." Booklist

Annie Rose is my little sister. Candlewick Press 2003 unp il $15.99 *

Grades: PreK K 1 2   E

1. Siblings—Fiction

ISBN 0-7636-1959-0   LC 2002-67695

Alfie describes all the things that he and his younger sister Annie Rose do together

"Few artists have recreated the young child's body language and surroundings as faithfully as Hughes. The gouache-and-oil pastel illustrations teem with well-observed details." Booklist

Ella's big chance; a Jazz-Age Cinderella; [by] Shirley Hughes. Simon & Schuster Books for Young Readers 2004 c2003 unp il $16.95

Grades: K 1 2 3   E

1. Fairy tales

ISBN 0-689-87399-9   LC 2003-27274

In this version of the Cinderella tale set in the 1920s, Ella has two men courting her—the handsome Duke of Arc and Buttons the delivery boy

"Hughes's gouache-and-pen-line illustrations exhibit her usual meticulous attention to detail. . . . This insightful retelling also offers a fascinating visual peek at a glamorous time." SLJ

Hughes, Ted, 1930-1998

My brother Bert; pictures by Tracey Campbell Pearson. Farrar, Straus & Giroux 2009 unp il $16.95

Grades: PreK K 1   E

1. Animals—Fiction 2. Pets—Fiction 3. Siblings—Fiction 4. Stories in rhyme

ISBN 978-0-374-39982-5; 0-374-39982-4

LC 2007034415

Illustrations and rhyming text portray a hobby gone awry, as Bert's collection of exotic pets seems on the verge of breaking into a quarrel, and perhaps a rumpus, as well.

"Full of action, merriment, and wit, the pictures will occupy children with always one more thing to see. . . . Dizzying and delightful." Booklist

Huneck, Stephen

Sally goes to the beach; written and illustrated by Stephen Huneck. Abrams 2000 unp il $17.95 *

Grades: PreK K 1   E

1. Dogs—Fiction 2. Beaches—Fiction

ISBN 0-8109-4186-4   LC 99-28421

Sally, a black Labrador retriever, goes to the beach, where she enjoys various activities with other visiting dogs

"The playful pup's enjoyment is conveyed through a simple but engaging text and beautiful, full-page woodblock prints." SLJ

Other titles about Sally are:

Sally goes to the mountains (2001)

Sally goes to the farm (2002)

Sally goes to the vet (2004)

Sally's snow adventure (2006)

Sally gets a job (2008)

Sally's great balloon adventure (2010)

Hurd, Edith Thacher, 1910-1997

Johnny Lion's book; pictures by Clement Hurd. new ed. HarperCollins Pubs. 2001 63p il (I can read book) hardcover o.p. pa $3.99 *

Grades: PreK K 1   E

1. Lions—Fiction

ISBN 0-06-029334-9 (lib bdg); 0-06-444297-7 (pa)

"An I can read book"

A reissue of the title first published 1965

When his parents go out hunting, Johnny Lion stays home and experiences exciting adventures reading a book about a baby lion who goes out into the world and gets lost

"A subtle boost for the joys of reading in a story with engaging illustrations." Booklist

Other titles about Johnny Lion are:

Johnny Lion's bad day (1970)

Johnny Lion's rubber boots (1972)

Hurd, Thacher, 1949-

Art dog. HarperCollins Pubs. 1996 unp il $15.99; pa $6.99 *

Grades: PreK K 1 2   E

1. Dogs—Fiction 2. Artists—Fiction

ISBN 0-06-024424-0; 0-06-443489-3 (pa)

LC 95-31092

When the Mona Woofa is stolen from the Dogopolis Museum of Art, a mysterious character who calls himself Art Dog tracks down and captures the thieves

"This is exuberantly drawn by Hurd, who has imbued Art Dog with the flash and dash every artist feels at times; but Hurd also captures the shyness that comes with displaying your art. Kids will respond not just to the pictures but also to a story that does as well with characters as with plot." Booklist

Bad frogs. Candlewick Press 2009 unp il $15.99

Grades: PreK K 1 2   E

1. Frogs—Fiction

ISBN 978-0-7636-3253-3; 0-7636-3253-8

"Hurd's bad frogs—170 of them—revel in mischievous conduct and generate chaos wherever they go. Whether jumping in muck, slurping ice cream, burping at the dinner table, fighting with toothbrushes, or skateboarding down stair railings, the delightfully green, yellow-tinged characters prance across the pages in an array of costumes, entertaining viewers with their antics. The artwork gleams with Hurd's shiny bright colors, and his swinging text, presented in bold purple, trumpets the frogs' badness as they romp through the action-packed illustrations." SLJ

Mama don't allow; starring Miles and the Swamp Band. Harper & Row 1984 unp il hardcover o.p. pa $5.99

Grades: PreK K 1 2   E

1. Bands (Music)—Fiction 2. Alligators—Fiction

ISBN 0-06-022690-0 (lib bdg); 0-06-443078-2 (pa)

LC 83-47703

Miles and the Swamp Band have the time of their lives playing at the Alligator Ball, until they discover the menu includes Swamp Band soup

"The multi-colored full-spread watercolor illustrations are stunningly bright and full of movement, far outpacing the story line in energy and imagination." SLJ

The weaver; pictures by Elisa Kleven. Farrar Straus Giroux 2010 unp il $16.99

Grades: PreK K 1 2   E

1. Weaving—Fiction 2. Dreams—Fiction

ISBN 978-0-374-38254-4; 0-374-38254-9

LC 2008028533

High above the world, a weaver spins thread from such things as clouds, dyes it with colors from the sky and grass, and weaves a cloth filled with the emotions she sees throughout the day to make a blanket of dreams.

"The fanciful illustrations reflect the story's sense of celebration, portraying children, their families, and friends sharing small but significant moments in a kaleidoscope of springtime colors. Tiny characters of all nationalities enjoy life in a sun-drenched landscape while the gentle weaver and her adorable gray kitten watch from above. This dreamy story offers a reassuring message of love and security." SLJ

Hurst, Carol Otis

Rocks in his head; pictures by James Stevenson. Greenwillow Bks. 2001 unp il $15.99; lib bdg $15.89

Grades: PreK K 1 2   E

1. Rocks—Collectors and collecting

ISBN 0-06-029403-5; 0-06-029404-3 (lib bdg)

LC 00-56197

Hurst "recounts the story of her father, an avid rock collector from the time he was a boy. . . . Dominated by earth tones, Stevenson's artwork convincingly evokes both the personality of this endearing protagonist and the period in which he lived." Publ Wkly

Terrible storm; [illustrated by] S. D. Schindler. Greenwillow Books 2007 unp il $16.99; lib bdg $17.89 *

Grades: K 1 2 3   E

1. Blizzards—Fiction 2. Grandfathers—Fiction 3. Massachusetts—Fiction

ISBN   978-0-06-009001-2;   0-06-009001-4; 978-0-06-009002-9 (lib bdg); 0-06-009002-2 (lib bdg)

LC 2005-35731

Hurst, Carol Otis—*Continued*

"Walt (a social butterfly) and Fred (his polar opposite) recall New England's Great Blizzard of 1888, when they were young men. . . . Shy Fred found himself stuck in a lively, crowded tavern in town, while Walt was forced to take cover alone in his barn." SLJ

"Humor is everywhere, but the funniest pictures show the men shoveling out of the snow, passing one another through the drifts. This lively, clever story, based on a real storm, neatly captures both the oddities of nature and how differing natures view the same event." Booklist

Hurwitz, Johanna

New shoes for Silvia; illustrated by Jerry Pinkney. Morrow Junior Bks. 1993 unp il $17.99; lib bdg $16.89

Grades: PreK K 1 2   E

1. Shoes—Fiction 2. Latin America—Fiction

ISBN 0-688-05286-X; 0-688-05287-8 (lib bdg)

LC 92-40868

Silvia receives a pair of beautiful red shoes from her Tia Rosita and finds different uses for them until she grows enough for them to fit

"This simple story, told in spare prose, speaks universally to the imagination and emotions. Pinkney's spirited watercolors animate the narrative and are large enough for group sharing." SLJ

Hutchins, H. J. (Hazel J.), 1952-

Mattland; story by Hazel Hutchins and Gail Herbert; art by Dušan Petričic. Annick Press 2008 unp il $19.95; pa $8.95

Grades: K 1 2   E

1. Moving—Fiction 2. Imagination—Fiction 3. Friendship—Fiction

ISBN 978-1-55451-121-1; 1-55451-121-6; 978-1-55451-120-4 (pa); 1-55451-120-8 (pa)

"Matt finds himself in yet another new home. Surrounded by an uninspiring landscape and lacking friends, he begins to poke at the mud outside his house. He quickly notices in his marks the beginning of a landscape. Bit by bit, a miniature world unfolds before Matt. . . . When a rainstorm threatens to flood the newly created 'Mattland,' helping hands appear to route the current safely away. Petričic's understated watercolors are an essential counterpart to Hutchins and Herbert's mature narrative. . . . The illustrator skillfully leads readers from gray, nondescript images to a detailed world brimming with color." SLJ

Hutchins, Pat, 1942-

1 hunter. Greenwillow Bks. 1982 unp il hardcover o.p. pa $6.99

Grades: PreK K 1 2   E

1. Counting 2. Animals—Fiction

ISBN 0-688-00614-0; 0-688-06522-8 (pa)

LC 81-6352

This is "a 1 to 10 and back again counting book. . . . Here, a Mr. Magoo-type hunter blunders through the jungle entirely missing the camouflaged elephants (2), giraffes (3), ostriches (4), etc." SLJ

"Humorous illustrations done in a flat, clear style make an outstanding counting book." Horn Book

The doorbell rang. Greenwillow Bks. 1986 unp il $15.99; lib bdg $16.89; pa $5.99 *

Grades: PreK K 1 2   E

1. Division—Fiction 2. Cookies—Fiction

ISBN 0-688-05251-7; 0-688-05252-5 (lib bdg); 0-688-09234-9 (pa)

LC 85-12615

"Victoria and Sam are delighted when Ma bakes a tray of a dozen cookies, even though Ma insists that her cookies aren't as good as Grandma's. They count them and find that each can have six. But the doorbell rings, friends arrive and the cookies must be re-divided. This happens again and again, and the number of cookies on each plate decreases as the visitors' pile of gear in the corner of the kitchen grows larger." SLJ

"Bright, joyous, dynamic, this wonderfully humorous piece of realism for the young is presented simply but with style and imagination." Horn Book

Rosie's walk. Macmillan 1968 unp il $16.95; pa $6.99 *

Grades: PreK K 1   E

1. Chickens—Fiction 2. Foxes—Fiction

ISBN 0-02-745850-4; 0-02-043750-1 (pa)

"Rosie the hen goes for a walk around the farm and gets home in time for dinner, completely unaware that a fox has been hot on her heels every step of the way. The viewer knows, however, and is not only held in suspense but tickled by the ways in which the fox is foiled at every turn by the unwitting hen. A perfect choice for the youngest." Booklist

Ten red apples. Greenwillow Bks. 2000 unp il $17.99; lib bdg $18.89

Grades: PreK K 1   E

1. Domestic animals—Fiction 2. Apples—Fiction 3. Counting 4. Stories in rhyme

ISBN 0-688-16797-7; 0-688-16798-5 (lib bdg)

LC 99-25065

In rhyming verses, one animal after another neighs, moos, oinks, quacks and makes other appropriate sounds as each eats an apple from the farmer's tree

"A concept book that blends rhyming, counting, repetition, and animal sounds into a charming, folksy story. . . . The gouache paintings are bright and clear." SLJ

We're going on a picnic! Greenwillow Bks. 2002 unp il $15.95; lib bdg $15.89 *

Grades: PreK K 1 2   E

1. Chickens—Fiction 2. Ducks—Fiction

ISBN 0-688-16799-3; 0-688-16800-0 (lib bdg)

LC 00-62225

"Hen, Duck, and Goose intend to enjoy a picnic but are so busy searching for the perfect spot that they don't notice the hungry animals taking up residence in their fruit-filled picnic basket." Horn Book Guide

"With an understated humor infusing both narrative and pictures, Hutchins successfully pulls off the child-pleasing contrivance of letting readers in on the secret." Publ Wkly

Hyde, Heidi Smith

Feivel's flying horses; illustrated by Johanna van der Sterre. Kar-Ben Pub. 2010 unp il lib bdg $17.95; pa $7.95

Grades: PreK K 1 2   E

1. Carousels—Fiction 2. Immigrants—Fiction 3. Wood carving—Fiction 4. Jews—Fiction 5. Coney Island (New York, N.Y.)—Fiction

ISBN   978-0-7613-3957-1;   0-7613-3957-4; 978-0-7613-3959-5 (pa); 0-7613-3959-0 (pa)

LC 2008033480

A Jewish immigrant who is saving money to bring his wife and children to join him in America creates ornate horses for a carousel on Coney Island, one for each member of his family.

"Watercolor illustrations with ink lines illustrate the immigrant experience on New York's Lower East Side in the late 1800s and help bring to life the magic of Coney Island." SLJ

Ichikawa, Satomi, 1949-

Come fly with me; [by] Satomi Ichikawa. Philomel Books 2008 unp il $15.99 *

Grades: PreK K 1   E

1. Airplanes—Fiction 2. Dogs—Fiction 3. Toys—Fiction 4. Paris (France)—Fiction 5. France—Fiction

ISBN 978-0-399-24679-1   LC 2007023643

Woggy and Cosmos, a toy dog and a toy airplane, go on an adventure in Paris.

"The adventure element is perfectly keyed to the age group. . . . The charming watercolors with their everchanging scenes and skies will pull [children] in." Booklist

La La Rose. Philomel Books 2004 unp il $15.99

Grades: PreK K 1 2   E

1. Lost and found possessions—Fiction 2. Paris (France)—Fiction 3. Gardens—Fiction

ISBN 0-399-24029-2   LC 2002-15366

La La Rose, a young girl's stuffed rabbit, gets lost in Luxembourg Gardens in Paris.

"Ichikawa's ink-and-watercolor paintings are a wonderful mix of action and thoughtfulness, sweetness and subtlety that extend the story and give it life past a first reading. . . . A very satisfying story that also captures the magic and excitement of a special place." Booklist

My father's shop. Kane/Miller 2006 unp il $15.95

Grades: K 1 2 3   E

1. Morocco—Fiction 2. Rugs and carpets—Fiction 3. Roosters—Fiction 4. Father-son relationship—Fiction

ISBN 1-929132-99-9

"When given a flawed carpet, Mustafa . . . drums up business for his merchant father by attracting first a similarly colored rooster, then numerous tourists who crow in their own languages: 'Co-co-ri-co!' 'Qui-qui-ri-qui!' and 'Cock-a-doodle-do!' The multicultural message is light and the humor contagious. Bright scenes of the crowded Moroccan marketplace amplify the story." Horn Book Guide

My pig Amarillo. Philomel Bks. 2003 c2002 unp il $15.99

Grades: PreK K 1 2   E

1. Pigs—Fiction 2. Guatemala—Fiction

ISBN 0-399-23768-2   LC 2002-7318

Original French edition, 2002

Pablito, a Guatemalan boy whose pet pig Amarillo has disappeared, uses a kite to send him a message that he still loves him

"Ichikawa uses her Guatemalan setting very effectively, but she also wraps the story in universal emotions: love, longing, grief, hope. The pen-and-watercolor artwork brings children close to all facets of Pablito's story." Booklist

Imai, Ayano, 1980-

Chester. Minedition 2007 unp il $16.99

Grades: PreK K   E

1. Dogs—Fiction

ISBN 978-0-698-40062-7

"Chester, a black-and-white dog with a serious mein, loves his family, but they seem to have forgotten about him. Unhappy, he puts his doghouse on his head and leaves. . . . Imai . . . has produced a small gem. The story . . . is illustrated in delicate watercolors that nonetheless project force both in action and emotion." Booklist

Ingalls, Ann

The little piano girl; by Ann Ingalls & Maryann Macdonald; illustrated by Giselle Potter. Houghton Mifflin Books for Children 2010 unp il $16

Grades: K 1 2 3   E

1. Williams, Mary Lou, 1910-1981—Fiction 2. Pianists—Fiction 3. Jazz musicians—Fiction 4. African American musicians—Fiction

ISBN 978-0-618-95974-7; 0-618-95974-2

LC 2008040457

A child prodigy at the piano sprinkles her music with a little jazz. Based on the life of the twentieth-century jazz musician, Mary Lou Williams.

Potter's "gouache paintings provide a vivid portrait of industrial Pittsburgh at the beginning of the 20th century, yet have an iconic quality too. Ingalls and MacDonald provide a touching memorial to a jazz great who is not a household name—a valuable contribution." Publ Wkly

Innes, Stephanie

A bear in war; [by] Stephanie Innes & Harry Endrulat; illustrated by Brian Deines. Key Porter Books 2009 unp il $19.95

Grades: 1 2 3   E

1. World War, 1914-1918 2. Soldiers—Canada 3. Teddy bears 4. Father-daughter relationship

ISBN 978-1-55470-097-4; 1-55470-097-3

"In Quebec during World War I, Aileen Rogers sent her cherished teddy bear overseas to protect her father, a medic, on the front lines. The bear . . . is the narrator. With sensitivity, he describes his experiences. . . . When Lawrence Browning Rogers is killed at the battle of Passchendaele, his uniform, his medal of bravery, and Teddy are sent to his family. [This is illustrated with]

Innes, Stephanie—*Continued*

Deines's evocative, softly focused pastel illustrations. . . . Inspired by true events, the book includes archival photographs of the Rogers family, a newspaper clipping from 1916, and the Canadian government's report of Lieutenant Rogers's death. A moving remembrance." SLJ

Isaacs, Anne, 1949-

Pancakes for supper! illustrated by Mark Teague. Scholastic Press 2006 unp il $15.99

Grades: PreK K 1   E

1. Animals—Fiction 2. New England—Fiction

ISBN 0-439-64483-6   LC 2005-14532

In the backwoods of New England, a young girl cleverly fends off the threats of wild animals by trading her clothes for her safety.

"Isaacs's clever, respectful take on an iconic tale is testament to its appeal. Teague's pictures are brilliant, cinematic full-bleed oil-paint dramas that capture the essence of a nascent New England spring." SLJ

Swamp Angel; illustrated by Paul O. Zelinsky. Dutton Children's Bks. 1994 unp il $16.99; pa $6.99 *

Grades: K 1 2 3   E

1. Tall tales 2. Frontier and pioneer life—Fiction 3. Tennessee—Fiction

ISBN 0-525-45271-0; 0-14-055908-6 (pa)

         LC 93-43956

A Caldecott Medal honor book, 1995

Along with other amazing feats, Angelica Longrider, also known as Swamp Angel, wrestles a huge bear, known as Thundering Tarnation, to save the winter supplies of the settlers in Tennessee

"Isaacs tells her original story with the glorious exaggeration and uproarious farce of the traditional tall tale and with its typical laconic idiom—you just can't help reading it aloud. . . . Zelinsky's detailed oil paintings in folk-art style are exquisite, framed in cherry, maple, and birch wood grains." Booklist

Isadora, Rachel

Ben's trumpet. Greenwillow Bks. 1979 unp il $17.99; pa $6.99 *

Grades: PreK K 1 2   E

1. Musicians—Fiction 2. African Americans—Fiction

ISBN 0-688-80194-3; 0-688-10988-8 (pa)

         LC 78-12885

A Caldecott Medal honor book, 1980

This is the story of Ben, a boy whose dream is to be a jazz trumpeter but who is too poor to own an instrument until a real musician, remembering his own dreams, puts one into the boy's hands

"The art is astonishingly varied in its brilliant recreation—in the margins, in the urban backgrounds—of the commercial art of the 20's and 30's." N Y Times Book Rev

Happy belly, happy smile. Harcourt Children's Books 2009 unp il $16

Grades: PreK K 1   E

1. Restaurants—Fiction 2. Chinese Americans—Fiction 3. Grandfathers—Fiction

ISBN 978-0-15-206546-1; 0-15-206546-6

         LC 2008046221

Sitting in the kitchen of his grandfather's Chinese restaurant, a young boy enjoys watching the chefs and waiters prepare and serve mouth-watering dishes

"Isadora's characteristic collage-and-oil illustrations [are] attractive as always. . . . This brief bite of Chinese cuisine will add flavor to cuisine-themed story hours." Booklist

Lili at ballet. Putnam 1993 unp il hardcover o.p. pa $6.99 *

Grades: PreK K 1 2   E

1. Ballet—Fiction

ISBN 0-399-22423-8; 0-698-11408-6 (pa)

         LC 92-8429

Lili dreams of becoming a ballerina and goes to her ballet lessons four afternoons a week

"Isadora uses pastel shades of purple, pink, green, and blue with bold splashes of black. This is a prettily illustrated book that captures the magic and hard work involved in ballet." SLJ

Other titles about Lili are:

Lili backstage (1997)

Lili on stage (1995)

Max; story & pictures by Rachel Isadora. Macmillan 1976 unp il pa $5.99 hardcover o.p. *

Grades: PreK K 1 2   E

1. Baseball—Fiction 2. Ballet—Fiction

ISBN 0-02-043800-1 (pa)   LC 76-9088

Max "is the star of his baseball team. On a Saturday morning, he has time to spare before his game and accepts (with some hidden disdain) the invitation of his sister, Lisa, to watch her ballet class in action. Max is surprised to find himself interested and happy to join the students at their teacher's suggestion. . . . The experience pays off at the ball park where Max hits a home run. Now he warms up for the game each week at Lisa's dancing class. The pictures are an ebullient combination of grace and comedy, with the leggy students dipping and soaring, in contrast to Max in his uniform." Publ Wkly

Peekaboo bedtime. G.P. Putnam's Sons 2008 unp il $16.99

Grades: PreK   E

1. Toddlers—Fiction 2. Bedtime—Fiction

ISBN 978-0-399-24384-4; 0-399-24384-4

         LC 2007-34814

Companion volume to: Peekaboo morning (2002)

A toddler plays peekaboo with parents, grandparents, toys, and the moon while getting ready for bed.

"The pastel illustrations are a delight, a visual celebration of family. . . . Perfect for laptime sharing or calm story hours." Kirkus

Say hello! G.P. Putnam's Sons 2010 unp il $16.99

Grades: PreK K 1   E

1. Language and languages—Fiction 2. City and town life—Fiction

ISBN 978-0-399-25230-3; 0-399-25230-4

         LC 2009011318

A little girl greets people in her neighborhood in many different languages.

"The text is paired down to essentials and the striking

Isadora, Rachel—*Continued*

collage-style illustrations are colorful and dynamic. Richly patterned with oil paints as well as printed patterns, the cut-paper shapes show up vividly against the white backgrounds." Booklist

The ugly duckling; written by Hans Christian Andersen; retold and illustrated by Rachel Isadora. G.P. Putnam's Sons 2009 unp il $16.99

Grades: 1 2 3 4   E

1. Andersen, Hans Christian, 1805-1875—Adaptations 2. Fairy tales 3. Ducks—Fiction 4. Swans—Fiction

ISBN 978-0-399-25029-3; 0-399-25029-8

LC 2008036514

In this retelling of the Ugly Duckling, set on the African continent, the duckling spends an unhappy year ostracized by the other animals before he grows into a beautiful swan.

"What shines in this telling are the illustrations, all collage spreads executed in oil on palette paper and printed paper. . . . Isadora's brilliant colors and broad brushstrokes beautifully capture the unnamed African setting." SLJ

Uh-oh! Harcourt 2008 unp il $16

Grades: PreK   E

1. Toddlers—Fiction 2. African Americans—Fiction

ISBN 978-0-15-205765-7; 0-15-205765-X

LC 2006039652

As an African American toddler keeps getting into mischief throughout the day, the reader is invited to discover what the trouble is with each page-turn and to say "uh-oh."

This offers "homey, vibrantly colored pastel illustrations. . . . Young listeners . . . [will] get a charge from each thrilling descent into disarray." Horn Book

Isol, 1972-

It's useful to have a duck; It's useful to have a boy. Groundwood Books 2009 unp il $10

Grades: PreK K 1 2 3   E

1. Ducks—Fiction 2. Board books for children

ISBN 978-0-88899-927-6; 0-88899-927-5

"Why on earth is it useful to have a duck? In a series of accordioned spreads on yellow board, a little boy reveals the answers, accompanied by swift line sketches that illustrate them. . . . The verso, on blue board, . . . is titled *It's Useful to Have a Boy*, [and] the identical images receive a very different gloss in the duck's voice. . . . Do not be deceived by the simple-looking board format: This is not for babies. Rather, it challenges children who have accepted the initial premise with developmentally appropriate narcissism to regard the world from the opposite perspective. Gently mind-bending, this playful Mexican import, packaged in a slipcase, will get readers thinking." Kirkus

Petit, the monster; words and pictures by Isol; translated by Elisa Amado. Groundwood Books 2010 unp il $16.95

Grades: PreK K   E

1. Good and evil—Fiction

ISBN 978-0-88899-947-4; 0-88899-947-X

"Poor Petit is a little confused: sometimes he's a good boy and sometimes he's a bad boy, and that's a hard

contradiction to work out. . . . Argentinian author-illustrator Isol touches imaginatively on the challenging complexities of behavioral morality, and the book gains special traction from going into failed intentions and contrary correlations . . . while keeping the concept easily kid-accessible. Isol's quirky illustrations feature pencil and oil pastels . . . while computer planes of color fill in figures and backgrounds. . . . Kids will appreciate this playful approach to one of their biggest moral conundrums." Bull Cent Child Books

Ives, Penny

Celestine, drama queen. Arthur A. Levine Books 2009 unp il $16.99 *

Grades: PreK K   E

1. Ducks—Fiction 2. Theater—Fiction

ISBN 978-0-545-08149-8; 0-545-08149-1

Celestine the duck is sure that she is destined for stardom, but when her big break comes, she is temporarily stricken with stage fright.

Celestine "captures the essence of children, their emotions, and how they cope. Adorable, annoying, and utterly childlike, Celestine is appealingly portrayed in Ives' funny, sunny watercolors." Booklist

Iwamatsu, Atushi Jun, 1908-1994

Crow Boy; [by] Taro Yashima. Viking 1955 37p il lib bdg $17.99; pa $5.99

Grades: PreK K 1 2   E

1. School stories 2. Japan—Fiction

ISBN 0-670-24931-9 (lib bdg); 0-14-050172-X (pa)

A Caldecott Medal honor book, 1956

"A young boy from the mountain area of Japan goes to school in a nearby village, where he is taunted by his classmates and feels rejected and isolated. Finally an understanding teacher helps the boy gain acceptance. The other students recognize how wrong they have been and nickname him 'Crow Boy' because he can imitate the crow's calls with such perfection." Adventuring with Books. 2d edition

"A moving story interpreted by the author's distinctive illustrations, valuable for human relations and for its picture of Japanese school life." Hodges. Books for Elem Sch Libr

Umbrella; [by] Taro Yashima. Viking 1958 30p il $16.99; pa $6.99

Grades: PreK K 1   E

1. Umbrellas and parasols—Fiction

ISBN 0-670-73858-1; 0-14-050240-8 (pa)

A Caldecott Medal honor book, 1959

"Momo, given an umbrella and a pair of red boots on her third birthday, is overjoyed when at last it rains and she can wear her new rain togs." Hodges. Books for Elem Sch Libr

In this simple tale, young children "will be carried along by their identification with the actions of this very real little girl. . . . The beauty of the book makes this worthwhile." Horn Book

Jackson, Alison, 1953-

The ballad of Valentine; illustrated by Tricia Tusa. Dutton Children's Bks. 2001 unp il $16.99; pa $6.99

Grades: K 1 2 3   E

1. Stories in rhyme

ISBN 0-525-46720-3; 0-14-240400-4 (pa)

LC 2001-42737

An ardent suitor tries various means of communication, from smoke signals to Morse code to skywriting, in order to get his message to his Valentine

"Tusa uses sketchy, wispy lines to create loads of droll details that are both funny and subtle. . . . Jackson and Tusa make perfect harmony here—the cadence and rhythm of text and the watercolor artwork are right on pitch." Booklist

Desert Rose and her highfalutin hog; illustrated by Keith Graves. Walker & Co. 2009 unp il $16.99; lib bdg $17.89

Grades: K 1 2 3   E

1. Tall tales 2. Animals—Fiction 3. Texas—Fiction

ISBN   978-0-8027-9833-6;   0-8027-9833-0; 978-0-8027-9834-3 (lib bdg); 0-8027-9834-9 (lib bdg)

LC 2009000206

Upon finding a large gold nugget on her pig farm, Desert Rose sets out to buy the biggest, fattest hog in Texas to enter in the state fair, but first she must get the hog to Laredo and every animal she asks for help is just as "ornery" as the hog

"The cartoon style of the acrylic illustrations accentuates the alliterative text. Youngsters will laugh out loud." SLJ

Thea's tree; [by] Alison Jackson; illustrated by Janet Pedersen. Dutton Children's Books 2008 unp il $15.99

Grades: K 1 2 3   E

1. Plants—Fiction 2. Science projects—Fiction

ISBN 978-0-525-47443-2; 0-525-47443-9

LC 2007-5220

Thea Teawinkle plants an odd, purple, bean-shaped seed in her backyard for her class science project, with astonishing results that even the experts she writes to—including a botanist, an arborist, a museum curator, and a symphony director—cannot offer any explanations for.

"Pedersen's energetic, full-page watercolor illustrations capture the hilarious consequences of Thea's growing crisis." SLJ

Jackson, Ellen B., 1943-

Cinder Edna; by Ellen Jackson; illustrated by Kevin O'Malley. Lothrop, Lee & Shepard Bks. 1994 unp il $16.99; pa $5.99

Grades: PreK K 1 2   E

1. Fairy tales

ISBN 0-688-12322-8; 0-688-16295-9 (pa)

LC 92-44160

Cinderella and Cinder Edna, who live with cruel stepmothers and stepsisters, have different approaches to life; and, although each ends up with the prince of her dreams, one is a great deal happier than the other

"O'Malley's full-page, full-color illustrations are exuberant and funny. Ella is suitably bubble-headed and self-absorbed while Edna is plain, practical, and bound to enjoy life." SLJ

Jackson, Shelley

Mimi's Dada Catifesto. Clarion Books 2009 41p il $17

Grades: 1 2 3 4   E

1. Dadaism—Fiction 2. Cats—Fiction

ISBN 978-0-547-12681-4; 0-547-12681-6

LC 2008-39486

In Zurich, Switzerland, an artistic cat finds the perfect owner in fellow Dadaist, Mr. Dada. Author's note provides background on the Dadaist art movement.

"Children . . . may not know much about the artistic movement Dada but . . . all (well perhaps not all) becomes clear through Jackson's zingy text and wildly inventive art. . . . With pictures inspired by many artists, including Marcel Duchamp, it's the art that will get kids to sit up and take notice. A mix of collage, fantastical and realistic drawings, and offbeat design work, the illustrations are played against a variety of fonts and typefaces, designed to keep the reader off balance." Booklist

Jacobs, Paul DuBois

Fire drill; [by] Paul DuBois Jacobs and Jennifer Swender; illustrated by Huy Voun Lee. Henry Holt 2010 unp il $15.99

Grades: PreK K 1 2   E

1. Stories in rhyme 2. Fire drills—Fiction 3. Safety education—Fiction 4. School stories

ISBN 978-0-8050-8953-0; 0-8050-8953-5

LC 2009005268

In this story told in brief rhyming text, students in a class follow the proper procedures during a fire drill.

"Simple rhyming text paired with colorful, upbeat art offer children an accessible overview of fire-drill rules. . . . Appealing, cheerful illustrations in elemental shapes and colors and vibrant patterns portray the multicultural group and familiar school settings." Booklist

Jahn-Clough, Lisa, 1967-

Little Dog; by Lisa Jahn-Clough. Houghton Mifflin 2006 unp il $16

Grades: PreK K   E

1. Dogs—Fiction 2. Artists—Fiction

ISBN 978-0-618-57405-6; 0-618-57405-0

LC 2005020455

A lonely stray dog befriends a struggling artist, transforming her art and both their lives.

"The minimal text is accompanied by simple, childlike artwork, framed in and accented by heavy, black brush strokes." SLJ

James, Simon, 1961-

Baby Brains. Candlewick Press 2004 unp il $15.99; pa $6.99 *

Grades: PreK K 1 2   E

1. Infants—Fiction

ISBN 0-7636-2507-8; 0-7636-3682-7 (pa)

LC 2003-65528

Even though the new baby of Mr. and Mrs. Brains is very intelligent, they realize that he is still just a baby

"This tongue-in-cheek tale will tickle the funny bones of young listeners. The loose and playful lines of the watercolor-and-ink illustrations are used judiciously and to great effect." SLJ

James, Simon, 1961-—*Continued*
Other titles about Baby Brains are:
Baby Brains superstar (2005)
Baby Brains and RoboMom (2008)

Little One Step. Candlewick Press 2003 unp il
$15.99; bd bk $6.99
Grades: PreK K 1   E
   1. Ducks—Fiction 2. Brothers—Fiction
   ISBN 0-7636-2070-X; 0-7636-3520-0 (bd bk)
                     LC 2002-71407
As three duckling brothers cross forest and field to return to their mother, the older ones encourage the youngest by teaching him a game that earns him the name of
Little One Step
   "Abundant white space surrounds the line drawings
suffused with buttery yellow and peach watercolor tones.
. . . This satisfying tale about perseverance will find an
eager audience at storytimes, on a parent's lap, and with
independent readers." SLJ

Janni, Rebecca
Every cowgirl needs a horse; illustrations by
Lynne Avril. Dutton Children's Books 2010 unp il
$16.99
Grades: PreK K 1   E
   1. Cowhands—Fiction 2. Imagination—Fiction
   3. Birthdays—Fiction 4. Cycling—Fiction
   ISBN 978-0-525-42164-1; 0-525-42164-5
                     LC 2009-12278
Nellie Sue, who fancies herself a real cowgirl, wants
a horse for her birthday, but she discovers that a brand
new bicycle—her first—takes almost as much taming as
a filly.
   "The bright, sketchy, watercolor and ink illustrations
are suffused with pinks and purples and capture a child
who tries to live up to cowgirl ideals of helping others,
looking on the bright side, and being strong. The lesson
on dealing positively with disappointment is gently delivered." SLJ

Jarka, Jeff
Love that puppy! the story of a boy who wanted
to be a dog. Henry Holt 2009 unp il $12.95
Grades: PreK K 1   E
   1. Dogs—Fiction 2. Imagination—Fiction
   ISBN 978-0-8050-8741-3; 0-8050-8741-9
                     LC 2008018333
When his parents want him to change back into a human boy, Peter the dog comes up with a novel solution.
   "Jarka's colorful comic-strip-style illustrations drive
the humor with one visual joke after another. . . . Children will appreciate both the absurdity of Peter's behavior and Jarka's delivery." SLJ

Jarrett, Clare
Arabella Miller's tiny caterpillar; [by] Clare
Jarrett. Candlewick Press 2008 unp il $16.99 *
Grades: PreK K 1 2   E
   1. Caterpillars—Fiction 2. Butterflies—Fiction
   ISBN 978-0-7636-3660-9; 0-7636-3660-6
Arabella Miller finds a tiny caterpillar and watches
and cares for it until it becomes a butterfly

This is "an engaging, exceptional picture book. . . .
Based on the verse about Little Arabella Miller, the story
arc is simple but the charm lies in the sketchy, pencil-
and-paper collage illustrations." Booklist

Javaherbin, Mina
Goal! illustrated by A.G. Ford. Candlewick
Press 2010 unp il $16.99
Grades: 2 3 4   E
   1. Soccer—Fiction 2. Bullies—Fiction 3. Friendship—
   Fiction 4. South Africa—Fiction
   ISBN 978-0-7636-4571-7; 0-7636-4571-0
                     LC 2008047266
In a dangerous alley in a township in South Africa,
the strength and unity which a group of young friends
feel while playing soccer keep them safe when a gang of
bullies arrives to cause trouble.
   "Illustrations rendered in oil are impressive. Large and
colorful action shots, many full spread, keep the story
moving at a quick pace." SLJ

Javernick, Ellen
The birthday pet; illustrated by Kevin O'Malley.
Marshall Cavendish 2009 unp il $16.99
Grades: PreK K 1 2   E
   1. Stories in rhyme 2. Pets—Fiction 3. Turtles—Fiction 4. Birthdays—Fiction
   ISBN 978-0-7614-5522-6; 0-7614-5522-1
                     LC 2008010740
Danny can have a pet for his birthday and he knows
exactly what he wants, but the other members of his
family think differently.
   "The colorful, animated illustrations incorporate exaggerated close-ups, unusual perspectives, and witty details
that extend the humor in the words. Young readers and
listeners will enjoy the simple, well-paced, rhyming
text." Booklist

Jay, Alison
1 2 3; a child's first counting book. Dutton
Children's Books 2007 unp il $15.99; bd bk $9.99
*
Grades: PreK K 1 2   E
   1. Counting
   ISBN 978-0-525-47836-2; 978-0-525-42165-8 (bd bk)
                     LC 2006035905
   "Jay takes readers on an enchanted journey from 1 to
10 and back again, with help from fairy tale figures. A
quartet of self-satisfied frog princes impressively embody
the number 4, while a plate of gingerbread men . . . represent the number 6. . . . The pictures are a wonder to
behold: Jay's flattened perspectives, gently faded colors,
crackle-glaze finishes and lean, angular characterizations
vaguely evoke the dreamy, ambiguous narrative qualities
of medieval art." Publ Wkly

ABC: a child's first alphabet book. Dutton
Children's Bks. 2003 unp il hardcover o.p. bd bk
$9.99 *
Grades: PreK K 1 2   E
   1. Alphabet
   ISBN 0-525-46951-6; 0-525-47524-9 (bd bk)
                     LC 2003-45218

Jay, Alison—*Continued*

In this alphabet book, a is for apple and z is for zoo

"This imaginative alphabet book offers visual clues to track and a story to tease out in its beautiful paintings. . . . Older children will flip from page to page, finding the simple story, drawing connections, and naming the letter-related objects. Younger ones can simply enjoy the delightful paintings with their crackle-glazed folk art look and touches of humor." Booklist

Red green blue; a first book of colors. Dutton Children's Books 2010 unp il $16.99

Grades: PreK K 1   E

1. Stories in rhyme 2. Color—Fiction 3. Nursery rhymes—Fiction

ISBN 978-0-525-42303-4; 0-525-42303-6

LC 2009-25098

Characters from nursery rhymes populate this tale, which highlights the colorful aspects of the familiar poems. Includes a key to the nursery rhymes referenced in the story.

"There are numerous opportunities for discussing colors, but as ever, it's Jay's luminous images that steal the show." Publ Wkly

Welcome to the zoo. Dial 2008 unp il $16.99

Grades: PreK K 1 2   E

1. Zoos—Fiction 2. Animals—Fiction 3. Stories without words

ISBN 978-0-8037-3177-6; 0-8037-3177-9

"Jay creates a zoo without the usual barriers between the animals and their visitors. . . . The oil paintings reward close attention with amusing visual details and small wordless dramas that carry through from page to page. . . . Polished yet playful, this nearly wordless picture book is a engaging choice." Booklist

Jeffers, Oliver

The great paper caper; [by] Oliver Jeffers. Philomel Books 2009 unp il $17.99

Grades: PreK K   E

1. Trees—Fiction 2. Animals—Fiction

ISBN 978-0-399-25097-2; 0-399-25097-2

LC 2008026192

When tree branches begin disappearing and paper airplanes are left in their place, the forest creatures carry out an investigation to find the culprit who has been stealing their homes.

"Managed forestry is the theme of this book that features folk-art-style animals with funny little stick legs. The mixed-media illustrations nicely complement the spare yet eloquent text." SLJ

The heart and the bottle. Philomel Books 2010 unp il $17.99

Grades: PreK K 1   E

1. Death—Fiction 2. Bereavement—Fiction 3. Emotions—Fiction

ISBN 978-0-399-25452-9; 0-399-25452-8

After safeguarding her heart in a bottle hung around her neck, a girl finds the bottle growing heavier and her interest in things around her becoming smaller.

The "artwork is the sweetness in this bittersweet story. . . . While the subject of loss always has the potential to unsettle young readers, most should find this quietly powerful treatment of grief moving." Publ Wkly

The incredible book eating boy; by Oliver Jeffers. Philomel Books 2007 unp il $16.99

Grades: PreK K 1 2 3   E

1. Books and reading—Fiction 2. Food—Fiction

ISBN 978-0-399-24749-1   LC 2006026279

Henry loves to eat books, until he begins to feel quite ill and decides that maybe he could do something else with the books he has been devouring

"The simple cartoon illustrations twinkle with humor and feeling. Done in paint and pencil on smart backdrops—pages from old books—the pictures set the stage for the quirky story." SLJ

The way back home; [by] Oliver Jeffers. Philomel Books 2008 unp il $16.99

Grades: PreK K 1 2   E

1. Moon—Fiction 2. Space flight—Fiction 3. Extraterrestrial beings—Fiction

ISBN 978-0-399-25074-3; 0-399-25074-3

LC 2007029570

Stranded on the moon after his extraordinary airplane takes him into outer space, a boy meets a marooned young Martian with a broken spacecraft, and the two new friends work together to return to their respective homes

"The charm of this story is how completely it maintains a childlike perspective. . . . This approach continues in the watercolor, graphite, and collage artwork. Figures consist of circle heads, box bodies, and stick legs; the backgrounds are flat colors with a few scribbled-in clouds or puffs of exhaust. Humorous details abound." SLJ

Jeffers, Susan

My Chincoteague pony. Hyperion Books for Children 2008 unp il $16.99

Grades: PreK K 1 2 3   E

1. Horses—Fiction 2. Chincoteague Island (Va.)—Fiction

ISBN 1-4231-0023-9; 978-1-4231-0023-2

Julie's "fondest wish is to have a pony of her own. The child convinces her farm-dwelling parents to take her to Chincoteague Island for Pony Penning Day so that she can bid in the auction. Unfortunately, she is continually outbid and realizes that the money she's earned won't be enough. Then one pony is returned and several people in the crowd pitch in to make her dream come true. . . . The lovely illustrations capture Julie's love of horses, the beauty of the ponies, and the excitement of the roundup." SLJ

The Nutcracker; [retold and illustrated by] Susan Jeffers. HarperCollinsPublishers 2007 unp il $16.99; lib bdg $17.89

Grades: K 1 2   E

1. Fairy tales 2. Toys—Fiction 3. Christmas—Fiction 4. Magic—Fiction

ISBN 978-0-06-074386-4; 0-06-074386-7; 978-0-06-074387-1 (lib bdg); 0-06-074387-5 (lib bdg)

LC 2007012489

An abridged version of the story of Marie Stahlbaum, who helps break the spell on her toy nutcracker and watches him change into a handsome prince

"Children who love the traditional Christmas ballet

Jeffers, Susan—*Continued*

will enjoy this romantic illustrated edition. . . . The illustrations communicate the beauty and the emotional quality of the ballet." SLJ

Jenkins, Emily, 1967-

Daffodil, crocodile; pictures by Tomek Bogacki. Farrar, Straus & Giroux 2007 unp il $16
Grades: PreK K 1 2   E
    1. Sisters—Fiction   2. Imagination—Fiction
3. Triplets—Fiction
    ISBN 978-0-374-39944-3; 0-374-39944-1
                        LC 2005-40163
    "Frances Foster books"
    Tired of being one of three look-alike sisters that no one can tell apart, Daffodil puts on a papier mâché crocodile head and has her own individual adventures
    "Daffodil's words and actions ring kidlike and true. . . . Colorful art, whimsical and expressive, fills the pages with fanciful patterns, perspectives, and details." Booklist

Five creatures; pictures by Tomek Bogacki. Foster Bks. 2001 unp il $16; pa $5.95
Grades: K 1 2 3   E
    1. Family life—Fiction 2. Cats—Fiction
    ISBN 0-374-32341-0; 0-374-42328-8 (pa)
                        LC 00-28771
    In words and pictures, a girl describes the three humans and two cats that live in her house, and details some of the traits that they share
    "This clever, multilayered book is as much for sharing and getting little ones on the path to deductive reasoning as it is for reading. . . . The text encourages readers to be observant. . . . Bogacki's colored chalk art . . . is childlike in the best possible way—immediate, identifiable, and executed with soft colors and simple shapes." Booklist

Skunkdog; pictures by Pierre Pratt. Farrar, Straus and Giroux 2008 unp il $16.95
Grades: K 1 2 3   E
    1. Dogs—Fiction 2. Skunks—Fiction
    ISBN 0-374-37009-5; 978-0-374-37009-1
                        LC 2005-54701
    "Frances Foster books"
    Dumpling, a lonely dog with no sense of smell, moves with his family to the country and makes a new friend who takes some getting used to.
    "Jenkins uses a lot of detail and repetition. Pratt's sunlit illustrations are done in oils and portray a white dog with an elongated nose and a furiously wagging black tail who complements the black-and-white skunk. Children will instantly relate to the pup's skunk encounters. . . . Important themes of loneliness, tolerance, friendship, and family emerge from this funny story." SLJ

That new animal; pictures by Pierre Pratt. Farrar, Straus and Giroux 2005 unp il $16 *
Grades: PreK K 1 2   E
    1. Dogs—Fiction 2. Infants—Fiction
    ISBN 0-374-37443-0   LC 2003-44058
    "Frances Foster Books"

The lives of two dogs change after a new animal, a baby, comes to their house.
    "Both the author and illustrator demonstrate wonderful insight into pet psychology and family dynamics, and the elongated style of the vibrantly colored artwork strikes just the right note of humor and whimsy." SLJ

Jenkins, Steve

Move! [written by Steve Jenkins and Robin Page; illustrated by Steve Jenkins] Houghton Mifflin 2006 unp il $16; bd bk $7.99 *
Grades: PreK K   E
    1. Animal locomotion
    ISBN 0-618-64637-X; 0-547-24000-7 (bd bk)
                        LC 2005-19082
    In this "book illustrated with cut and torn-paper collages, animals leap, swim, slide, swing, and waddle. Each spread contains one action word and two animals for whom that behavior is typical. . . . Jenkins uses brief phrases as captions and provides a well-written, concise appendix. . . . This book is gorgeous and educational." SLJ

Jesset, Aurore

Loopy; by Aurore Jesset; illustrated by Barbara Korthues. North-South 2008 unp il $16.95; pa $7.95
Grades: PreK K 1   E
    1. Toys—Fiction 2. Lost and found possessions—Fiction
    ISBN   978-0-7358-2175-0;   0-7358-2175-5; 978-0-7358-2261-0 (pa); 0-7358-2261-1 (pa)
    "A child leaves her favorite toy at the doctor's office and ponders its fate should they fail to be reunited 'RIGHT NOW!' On each spread, Jesset's speculation about the beloved stuffed animal's current state is matched with Korthues's Tim Burton-esque illustrations rendered in vibrant colors, often muted to depict the nighttime setting. The simple, rhythmic prose recalls a small child's inner dialogue or storytelling voice." SLJ

Ji Zhaohua

No! that's wrong! [by] Zhaohua Ji and Cui Xu. Kane Miller Book Pub. 2008 unp il $15.95
Grades: PreK K 1 2   E
    1. Animals—Fiction 2. Rabbits—Fiction 3. Clothing and dress—Fiction
    ISBN 978-1-933605-66-1; 1-933605-66-9
    "A rabbit has a humorous encounter with a pair of red underpants. Rabbit's not sure how to wear the mysterious garment and tries it on as a hat. He offers the hat in turn to eight different animals until a donkey straightforwardly inquires why the rabbit is wearing underpants on his head. . . . The cartoon-style artwork and the text, consisting primarily of dialogue, work well together. . . . This entertaining picture book stimulates a bit of creative thinking and problem solving." SLJ

Jiménez, Francisco, 1943-

The Christmas gift: El regalo de Navidad; illustrated by Claire B. Cotts. Houghton Mifflin 2000 unp il $15; pa $6.99

Grades: K 1 2 3   E

1. Migrant labor—Fiction 2. Mexican Americans—Fiction 3. Christmas—Fiction 4. Bilingual books—English-Spanish

ISBN 0-395-92869-9; 0-547-13364-2 (pa)

LC 99-26224

When his family has to move again a few days before Christmas in order to find work, Panchito worries that he will not get the ball he has been wanting

"This story, a version of which appeared in Jiménez's . . . *The Circuit,* is presented here in a bilingual picture book format with an excellent Spanish text. . . . Mural-like illustrations soulfully depict the hard life and strong people of the migrant labor camps." Horn Book Guide

Jocelyn, Marthe, 1956-

Eats; [by] Marthe Jocelyn; [illustrations by] Tom Slaughter. Tundra Books 2007 unp il $15.95; bd bk $7.95

Grades: PreK K 1 2   E

1. Animals—Food

ISBN 978-0-88776-820-0; 978-0-88776-988-7 (bd bk)

"Painted paper cuts in jewel colors graphically portray the principal foods eaten by 14 different animals. . . . Using bold, simple, brightly colored shapes . . . [and] placing them on backgrounds of equally bold contrasting colors, the animals and their dinners are easily identified and, thus, will have instant kid appeal." SLJ

Over under; [illustrated by] Tom Slaughter. Tundra Books 2005 unp il $15.95; bd bk $7.95

Grades: PreK   E

1. Opposites

ISBN 0-88776-708-7; 0-88776-790-7 (bd bk)

"Minimal rhyming text and cut-paper illustrations of animals in six basic colors introduce opposites: e.g. 'big' and 'small' are represented by a black elephant and mouse on a vibrant red background." Horn Book Guide

Same same; Tom Slaughter, illustrator. Tundra Books 2009 unp il $15.95; bd bk $7.95 *

Grades: PreK K 1   E

1. Concepts

ISBN   978-0-88776-885-9;   0-88776-885-7; 978-0-88776-987-0 (bd bk); 0-88776-987-X (bd bk)

"Jocelyn and Slaughter . . . strikingly introduce the concept of classification. Slaughter's graphic cut-paper compositions command attention with their paintbox-bright colors. The first spread, for example, shows an apple, a blue-and-green planet Earth and a tambourine. . . 'Round things,' reads the caption. The next pages show the tambourine again, now with a guitar and a bird. This spread is captioned 'things that make music.' Always carrying forward one of the three objects from the previous spread, Jocelyn delivers the vital lesson that everyday objects fall into many categories. The concept is clear and the delivery attractive." Publ Wkly

Johnson, Angela, 1961-

I dream of trains; illustrated by Loren Long. Simon & Schuster Bks. for Young Readers 2003 unp il $16.95 *

Grades: K 1 2 3   E

1. Jones, Casey, 1863-1900—Fiction 2. Railroads—Fiction 3. African Americans—Fiction

ISBN 0-689-82609-5   LC 98-52886

The son of a sharecropper dreams of leaving Mississippi on a train with the legendary engineer Casey Jones

"Long's moody acrylic paintings, mainly in subdued tones, are a sterling accompaniment to the book's provocative prose." SLJ

Just like Josh Gibson; written by Angela Johnson; illustrated by Beth Peck. Simon & Schuster Books for Young Readers 2004 unp il $15.95; pa $6.99

Grades: K 1 2 3   E

1. Baseball—Fiction 2. Grandmothers—Fiction 3. African Americans—Fiction

ISBN 0-689-82628-1; 1-4169-2728-X (pa)

LC 2001-49531

A young girl's grandmother tells her of her love for baseball and the day they let her play in the game even though she was a girl.

"Johnson tempers what could have been a sentimental tale with Grandmama's contagious enthusiasm and sense of empowerment, and her text has a baseball announcer's suspenseful rhythm. . . . Peck's angular pastels . . . skillfully capture the nostalgic sports action and celebration." Booklist

Wind flyers; illustrated by Loren Long. Simon & Schuster 2006 unp il $16.99

Grades: K 1 2 3   E

1. Air pilots—Fiction 2. African Americans—Fiction 3. World War, 1939-1945—Fiction

ISBN 0-689-84879-X

"In spare, poetic lines, a young African American boy introduces his great-great-uncle, who was a Tuskegee airman. . . . Johnson introduces the history in oblique, pared-down words. . . . Long's acrylics beautifully extend the evocative words." Booklist

Johnson, Crockett, 1906-1975

Harold and the purple crayon. Harper & Row 1955 unp il $15.99; lib bdg $15.89; pa $6.99 *

Grades: PreK K   E

1. Drawing—Fiction

ISBN 0-06-022935-7; 0-06-022936-5 (lib bdg); 0-06-443022-7 (pa)

"As Harold goes for a moonlight walk, he uses his purple crayon to draw a path and the things he sees along the way, then draws himself back home." Hodges. Books for Elem Sch Libr

Other titles about Harold are:

Harold's ABC (1963)

Harold's circus (1959)

Harold's fairy tale (1986)

Harold's trip to the sky (1957)

A picture for Harold's room (1960)

Johnson, David, 1951-
Snow sounds; an onomatopoeic story; [by] David A. Johnson. Houghton Mifflin Company 2006 unp il $16
Grades: PreK K 1   E
1. Snow 2. Sound
ISBN 978-0-618-47310-6; 0-618-47310-6
       LC 2006-00333
A nearly-wordless book in which a young boy, eager to reach a much-anticipated holiday party on time, listens to the sounds of the shovels, snow plow, and other equipment used to clear his way.
"Full-bleed watercolor spreads capture the light of a wintry morning perfectly. . . . This accomplished offering has a variety of uses and will appeal to a wide age range." SLJ

Johnson, Dinah
Black magic; illustrated by R. Gregory Christie. Henry Holt and Co. 2010 unp il $15.99 *
Grades: PreK K 1 2   E
1. African Americans—Fiction 2. Black
ISBN 978-0-8050-7833-6; 0-8050-7833-9
       LC 2009-9219
"Christy Ottaviano books"
"This expressive book combines well-matched text and pictures to pay tribute to the myriad qualities of blackness. Buoyant yet reflective, Johnson's . . . free-flowing verse presents an imaginative girl's musings on the essence of black, which she sees as containing multitudinous, even oppositional, dimensions. . . . With vibrant colors offsetting velvety black images, Christie's . . . acrylic gouache illustrations playfully tweak perspective and scale, echoing the verse's energy and fluidity. " Publ Wkly

Johnson, Donald B. (Donald Barton), 1933-
Henry hikes to Fitchburg; [by] D. B. Johnson. Houghton Mifflin 2000 unp il $16; pa $6.95 *
Grades: PreK K 1 2   E
1. Thoreau, Henry David, 1817-1862—Fiction 2. Nature—Fiction 3. Walking—Fiction 4. Bears—Fiction
ISBN 0-395-96867-4; 0-618-73749-9 (pa)
       LC 99-35302
While his friend works hard to earn the train fare to Fitchburg, Henry the bear walks the thirty miles through woods and fields, enjoying nature and the time to think great thoughts. Includes biographical information about Henry David Thoreau
"This splendid book works on several levels. Johnson's adaption of a paragraph taken from Thoreau's *Walden* (set down in an author's note) illuminates the contrast between materialistic and naturalistic views of life without ranting or preaching. His illustrations are breathtakingly rich and filled with lovingly rendered details." Booklist
Other titles about Henry the bear are:
Henry builds a cabin (2002)
Henry climbs a mountain (2003)
Henry works (2004)
Henry's night (2009)

Johnson, Paul Brett
On top of spaghetti; written and illustrated by Paul Brett Johnson; with lyrics by Tom Glazer. Scholastic Press 2006 unp il $15.99 *
Grades: PreK K 1 2   E
1. Dogs—Fiction 2. Animals—Fiction 3. Songs 4. Meatballs—Fiction
ISBN 0-439-74944-1   LC 2005-14311
"Expanding on the popular song, Johnson spins the tale of Yodeler Jones, a hound dog who serves nothing but meatballs and spaghetti at his dining establishment. When business begins to slow, Yodeler concocts a brand-new meatball, but before he can taste it, someone sneezes. . . . With original text printed in black and the lyrics sprinkled throughout in color, this story successfully marries the two. The loony illustrations, full of color and movement, effectively capture the zaniness." SLJ

Johnson, Stephen, 1964-
Alphabet city; [by] Stephen T. Johnson. Viking 1995 unp il $16.99; pa $6.99 *
Grades: PreK K 1   E
1. Alphabet
ISBN 0-670-85631-2; 0-14-055904-3 (pa)
       LC 95-12335
A Caldecott Medal honor book, 1995
"Beginning with the *A* formed by a construction site's sawhorse and ending with the *Z* found in the angle of a fire escape, Johnson draws viewers' eyes to tiny details within everyday objects to find letters." SLJ
"Only after careful scrutiny will viewers realize that these arresting images aren't photographs but compositions of pastels, watercolors, gouache and charcoal. A visual tour de force, Johnson's ingenious alphabet book transcends the genre by demanding close inspection of not just letters, but the world." Publ Wkly

Johnston, Lynn, 1947-
Farley follows his nose; story by Lynn Johnston & Beth Cruikshank; illustrations by Lynn Johnston. Bowen Press 2009 unp il $17.99
Grades: PreK K 1   E
1. Dogs—Fiction 2. Smell—Fiction
ISBN 978-0-06-170234-1; 0-06-170234-X
       LC 2008-24713
Farley the dog follows his nose from one good smell to another all over town.
"Big-eyed, energetic Farley and his 'sniff snorfle SNUFF' nose will be a big hit with storytimers, and it won't matter a bit that they're too young to recognize the characters. A great addition to storytimes on baths, senses and dogs." Kirkus

Johnston, Tony
Day of the Dead; illustrated by Jeanette Winter. Harcourt Brace & Co. 1997 unp il hardcover o.p. pa $6
Grades: PreK K 1 2   E
1. All Souls' Day—Fiction 2. Mexico—Fiction
ISBN 0-15-222863-2; 0-15-202446-8 (pa)
       LC 96-2276

Johnston, Tony—*Continued*

Describes a Mexican family preparing for and celebrating the Day of the Dead

"Spanish phrases are a natural part of the storytelling as the children ask questions about the cooking and preparations. . . . Winter's brilliantly colored, acrylic illustratons in folk-art style express the magic realism that is part of the ceremony under the stars." Booklist

My abuelita; written by Tony Johnston; illustrated by Yuyi Morales; photographed by Tim O'Meara. Harcourt Children's Books 2009 unp il $16 *

Grades: 1 2 3   E

1. Grandmothers—Fiction 2. Storytelling—Fiction 3. Spanish language—Vocabulary

ISBN 978-0-15-216330-3; 0-15-216330-1

ALA ALSC Belpre Illustrator Medal Honor Book (2010)

"A boy describes the morning routine he shares with his grandmother as she prepares for work. Flights of fancy enliven the tasks of bathing, eating breakfast, and dressing. When the pair arrive at her workplace, readers discover that Abuelita is a storyteller—a calling that her grandson shares. Spanish words are sprinkled throughout, often followed by brief definitions. . . . Johnston effectively engages young readers' interest. . . . Morales's bold, innovative illustrations brilliantly reinforce the text. . . . Characters molded from polymer clay are dressed in brightly patterned fabrics and placed among images that evoke Mexican art." SLJ

Uncle Rain Cloud; illustrated by Fabricio Vanden Broeck. Charlesbridge Pub. 2001 unp il $15.95; pa $7.95

Grades: PreK K 1 2   E

1. Uncles—Fiction 2. Mexican Americans—Fiction 3. English language—Fiction

ISBN 0-88106-371-1; 0-88106-372-X (pa)

LC 99-54195

"A Talewinds book"

Carlos tries to help his uncle, who is frustrated and angry at his inability to speak English, adjust to their new home in Los Angeles

"Brisk pacing, sympathetic characters, and clear prose that uses embedded Spanish words effectively make a winner. VandenBroeck's acrylic and colored-pencil illustrations flesh out the narrative in soft, bright colors enhanced by dramatic shading." SLJ

Jonas, Ann

The quilt. Greenwillow Bks. 1984 unp il $16.99

Grades: PreK K 1 2   E

1. Quilts—Fiction

ISBN 0-688-03825-5   LC 83-25385

"A little girl is given a new patchwork quilt, and at bedtime she amuses herself by identifying the materials used in its making. Later, she has a colorful dream in which she almost loses her stuffed dog, Sally (a piece of Sally is in the quilt, too)." Child Book Rev Serv

"The intricate illustrations in Jonas's book can be described only in superlatives. Backed by a length of golden-yellow calico imprinted with small red flowers, a quilt fashioned from squares in a variety of colors is the prize shown to readers by a dear little girl." Publ Wkly

Round trip. Greenwillow Bks. 1983 unp il $15.99; pa $5.99

Grades: PreK K 1 2   E

1. City and town life—Fiction

ISBN 0-688-01772-X; 0-688-09986-6 (pa)

LC 82-12026

Black and white illustrations and text record the sights on a day trip to the city and back home again to the country. The trip to the city is read from front to back and the return trip, from back to front, upside down

"Although one or two pictures too easily suggest their upside-down images and the device is occasionally strained, the author-artist displays a fine sense of graphic design and balance, and pictorial beauty is never sacrificed for mere cleverness." Horn Book

Splash! Greenwillow Bks. 1995 unp il $16.99; pa $6.99 *

Grades: PreK K 1 2   E

1. Counting 2. Animals—Fiction

ISBN 0-688-11051-7; 0-688-15284-8 (pa)

LC 94-4110

A little girl's turtle, fish, frogs, dog, and cat jump in and out of a backyard pond, constantly changing the answer to the question "How many are in my pond?"

"A clever concept book with physical humor and exciting acrylic paintings that capture the heat and drama of a sunny summer day." Booklist

Jones, Sally Lloyd

How to be a baby—by me, the big sister; [by] Sally Lloyd-Jones and [illustrated by] Sue Heap. Schwartz & Wade Books 2007 unp il $15.99; lib bdg $18.99 *

Grades: PreK K 1 2   E

1. Infants—Fiction 2. Siblings—Fiction

ISBN 0-375-83843-0; 978-0-375-83843-9; 0-375-93843-5 (lib bdg); 978-0-375-93843-6 (lib bdg)

LC 2006-02469

"A worldly wise big sister . . . reads from a book she has written for her new sibling. She itemizes a long list of things that babies cannot do. . . . Although she tends to focus on the negatives, in the end the unnamed protagonist admits that babies have some uses. . . . Heap uses acrylic paint, crayon, and felt-tip pen in a pleasing palette of pinks, blues, and yellows to enhance the story with childlike charm." SLJ

Another title about this character is:
How to get married by me, the bride (2009)

The ultimate guide to grandmas and grandpas; by Sally Lloyd-Jones; illustrated by Michael Emberley. HarperCollinsPublishers 2008 unp il $14.99; lib bdg $15.89

Grades: PreK K 1 2 3   E

1. Grandparents—Fiction 2. Family life—Fiction

ISBN 978-0-06-075687-1; 0-06-075687-X; 978-0-06-075688-8 (lib bdg); 0-06-075688-8 (lib bdg)

LC 2007020880

"In this story about how children should treat their elders, grandparents and grandchildren representing all kinds of animal species play together, enjoy snacks, take trips, tell stories, snuggle, and share secrets. Lloyd-Jones's text is both charming and tongue-in-cheek. . . .

Jones, Sally Lloyd—*Continued*
Emberley's enchanting illustrations mirror each character's personality." SLJ

Joosse, Barbara M., 1949-
Higgledy-piggledy chicks; by Barbara Joosse; pictures by Rick Chrustowski. Greenwillow Books 2010 unp il $16.99; lib bdg $17.89
Grades: PreK K 1 2   E
    1. Chickens—Fiction
    ISBN 978-0-06-075042-8; 0-06-075042-1; 978-0-06-075043-5 (lib bdg); 0-06-075043-X (lib bdg)
                               LC 2007047594
Banty Hen keeps her seven new baby chicks safe, even though they like to go exploring.
"Chrustowski's illustrations—done in colorful torn-paper collages—effectively capture the energy of the roaming and curious chicks. Readers will delight in counting the seven chicks on each spread and in predicting what danger might be hiding on the following page." Booklist

Hot city; by Barbara Joosse; illustrated by R. Gregory Christie. Philomel Books 2004 unp il $16.99 *
Grades: PreK K 1 2   E
    1. City and town life—Fiction 2. Summer—Fiction 3. Libraries—Fiction 4. African Americans—Fiction
    ISBN 0-399-23640-6   LC 2002-1254
Mimi and her little brother Joe escape from home and the city's summer heat to read and dream about princesses and dinosaurs in the cool, quiet library.
"This eloquently told story is boldly illustrated with evocative acrylic paintings in shades of orange, red, and yellow." SLJ

Mama, do you love me? illustrated by Barbara Lavallee. Chronicle Bks. 1991 unp il $15.99; bd bk $6.99 *
Grades: PreK K   E
    1. Mother-daughter relationship—Fiction 2. Inuit—Fiction
    ISBN 978-0-87701-759-2; 0-87701-759-X; 978-0-8118-2131-5 (bd bk); 0-8118-2131-5 (bd bk)
                               LC 90-1863
"A young girl asks how much her mother loves her, even when she is naughty, and receives warm, reassuring answers. The twist on this familiar theme is that the two are Inuits, and the text and pictures draw on their unique culture. . . . Two pages of back matter define and explain the functions of various terms in Inuit life past and present. Charming, vibrant watercolor illustrations expand the simple rhythmic text, adding to the characters' personalities and to the cultural information." SLJ

Papa, do you love me? illustrated by Barbara Lavallee. Chronicle Books 2005 unp il $15.95 *
Grades: PreK K   E
    1. Father-son relationship—Fiction 2. Masai (African people)—Fiction 3. Africa—Fiction
    ISBN 0-8118-4265-7   LC 2003-17344
When a Masai father in Africa answers his son's questions, the boy learns that his father's love for him is unconditional.

"Echoing the soothing rhythm of the poetic narrative, Lavallee's graceful watercolors feature a harmoniously balanced palette." Publ Wkly

Please is a good word to say; by Barbara Joosse; pictures by Jennifer Plecas. Philomel Books 2007 unp il $12.99
Grades: PreK K 1 2   E
    1. Etiquette—Fiction
    ISBN 978-0-399-24217-5   LC 2006034508
Harriet gives examples of polite words and expressions to use in various social situations to make them more pleasant.
"Joosse's effective use of speech bubbles in various fonts, in addition to the main text, makes for especially interesting and amusing reading. Plecas's ink-and-watercolor cartoons imbue the already spirited commentary with personality, dimension, and even more energy." SLJ

Roawr! illustrated by Jan Jutte. Philomel Books 2009 unp il $16.99
Grades: PreK K   E
    1. Bears—Fiction
    ISBN 978-0-399-24777-4; 0-399-24777-7
                               LC 2008-16907
When Liam hears a load roar in the middle of the night, he must use all his ingenuity to protect his sleeping mother from a hungry bear.
"This adrenaline-charged romp is, first and foremost, exciting. Jutte's lively cartoon artwork contrasts muted night colors to form powerful images." SLJ

Sleepover at gramma's house; illustrated by Jan Jutte. Philomel Books 2010 unp il $17.99
Grades: PreK K 1   E
    1. Elephants—Fiction 2. Grandmothers—Fiction
    ISBN 978-0-399-25261-7; 0-399-25261-4
                               LC 2009-31549
A little girl and her grandmother have a rollicking good time during a sleepover.
"Jutte's illustrations are jam-packed full of details. Readers get a clear sense of the child's excitement and activity level, but they will never lose sight of the relationship being celebrated. The colors in the ink, watercolor and acrylic illustrations lend the artwork a retro feel, and the elephants may remind many readers of Babar." Kirkus

Wind-wild dog; written by Barbara Joosse; illustrated by Kate Kiesler. Henry Holt and Company 2006 unp il $16.95
Grades: K 1 2 3   E
    1. Dogs—Fiction 2. Alaska—Fiction
    ISBN 978-0-8050-7053-8; 0-8050-7053-2
                               LC 2005020055
Ziva, a "wind-wild" young sled dog, decides whether to stay with the man who has trained her or to run free with the wolves and wind
"In spare, precise prose, Ziva's story drives with understated dramatic tension toward a satisfying conclusion. Kiesler's oil paintings capture the clean beauty of the rural Alaska setting as well as the unique qualities of Ziva and the man." Booklist

Jordan, Deloris

Salt in his shoes; Michael Jordan in pursuit of a dream; by Deloris Jordan with Roslyn M. Jordan; illustrated by Kadir Nelson. Simon & Schuster Bks. for Young Readers 2000 unp il $16.95; pa $7.99 *

Grades: 2 3 4   E

1. Jordan, Michael, 1963- 2. Basketball
ISBN 0-689-83371-7; 0-689-83419-5 (pa)

LC 00-20539

Young Michael Jordan is smaller than the other basketball players, so his mother "recommends salt in his shoes and prayer, and even though the boy can't figure out how the salt's going to help, he takes his mother's advice. Michael doesn't just depend on salt and prayers, though; he constantly practices playing basketball." Bull Cent Child Books

"This readable and entertaining story will delight the superstar's fans. Nelson's illustrations bring the right blend of vivid color, realism, and personality." SLJ

Jordan, Sandra

Mr. and Mrs. Portly and their little dog Snack; pictures by Christine Davenier. Farrar Straus Giroux 2009 unp il $16.99 *

Grades: PreK K 1 2   E

1. Dogs—Fiction 2. Art—Fiction
ISBN 978-0-374-35089-5; 0-374-35089-2

LC 2007046663

Snack is a very happy puppy when Mrs. Portly adopts him but when persnickety Mr. Portly returns from a fishing trip, he banishes Snack to a doghouse until their mutual love of art, and a thief, bring them together.

"Davenport's ink-and-watercolor drawings are a delightful mix of sizes and shapes. . . . Exuding warmth, both narrative and pictures transcend the basic plotline, turning this into an irresistible offering." Booklist

Joyce, William

A day with Wilbur Robinson; by William Joyce. Laura Geringer Books 2006 unp il $16.99

Grades: PreK K 1 2   E

1. Family life—Fiction 2. Eccentrics and eccentricities—Fiction
ISBN 978-0-06-089098-8; 0-06-089098-3

LC 2005037287

An expanded version of the title published 1990

While spending the day in the Robinson household, Wilbur's best friend joins in the search for Grandfather Robinson's missing false teeth and meets one wacky relative after another

"The real fun is in the tension between the deadpan words and the fantastical pictures. . . . Save this for small groups, which will most appreciate the wondrous visual details." Booklist

Dinosaur Bob and his adventures with the family Lazardo. new ed. HarperCollins Pubs. 1995 unp il $16.99 *

Grades: K 1 2 3   E

1. Dinosaurs—Fiction
ISBN 0-06-021074-5   LC 94-19100

"A Laura Geringer book"

A revised and enlarged edition of the title first published 1988

"The Lazardo family goes on safari to Africa where they find a dinosaur. They name him Bob and take him back to Pimlico Hills. . . . Bob soon becomes famous because he can play the trumpet, dance, and most importantly play baseball." Child Book Rev Serv [review of 1988 edition]

George shrinks; story and pictures by William Joyce. Harper & Row 1985 unp il $16.99; pa $6.99 *

Grades: K 1 2 3   E

1. Size—Fiction 2. Fantasy fiction
ISBN 0-06-023070-3; 0-06-443129-0 (pa)

LC 83-47697

"A young boy named George awakes from his nap to discover he has become as small as a mouse. . . . Resting against the alarm clock is a piece of poster-size paper on which parental instructions are written telling George all that he should do after getting up. . . . Most of the book's text consists of this note's contents." N Y Times Book Rev

"The colorful illustrations, executed with painstaking attention to detail, create a surreal landscape from an ordinary breakfast-cereal world, as familiar objects become monumental structures through which the diminutive George moves with panache." Horn Book

Juan, Ana

The Night Eater; by Ana Juan. Arthur A. Levine Books 2004 unp il $16.95

Grades: K 1 2 3   E

1. Night—Fiction
ISBN 0-439-48891-5   LC 2003-20197

The Night Eater, who brings each new day by gobbling up the darkness, decides he is too fat and stops eating, with dire consequences

"The sense of magic realism in this story is matched by in Juan's richly colored acrylic-and-wax paintings. . . . This delightful tale will definitely appeal to children's imaginations." SLJ

Judge, Lita, 1968-

Pennies for elephants. Hyperion Books for Children 2009 unp il $16.99

Grades: PreK K 1 2   E

1. Elephants—Fiction 2. Zoos—Fiction 3. Boston (Mass.)—Fiction
ISBN 978-1-4231-1390-4; 1-4231-1390-X

"In 1914, the children of Boston raised $6,000 to buy three trained elephants for the Franklin Park Zoo. But told through the eyes of siblings (and fund-raisers) Dorothy and Henry, the story expands into an inspired celebration of kid power. . . . Dollops of historical flavor abound, with watercolors of knickers-clad boys and streets bustling with people, horses and horseless carriages. Warm sepia tones lend atmosphere." Publ Wkly

Jules, Jacqueline, 1956-

Duck for Turkey Day; illustrated by Kathyrn Mitter. Albert Whitman 2009 unp il $16.99

Grades: K 1 2 3   E

1. Thanksgiving Day—Fiction 2. Vietnamese Americans—Fiction 3. School stories

ISBN 978-0-8075-1734-5; 0-8075-1734-8

LC 2008055537

When Tuyet finds out that her Vietnamese family is having duck rather than turkey for Thanksgiving dinner, she is upset until she finds out that other children in her class did not eat turkey either.

"Mitter's acrylic illustrations, in clear bright colors and simple shapes, capture the warmth of the holiday bustle and the affection among family members." Booklist

Juster, Norton, 1929-

The hello, goodbye window; story by Norton Juster; pictures by Chris Raschka. Hyperion Books for Children 2005 unp il $15.95 *

Grades: PreK K 1 2   E

1. Grandparents—Fiction

ISBN 0-7868-0914-0

Awarded the Caldecott Medal, 2006

"Michael de Capua Books"

"The window in Nanna and Poppy's kitchen is no ordinary window—it is the place where love and magic happens. . . . The first-person text is both simple and sophisticated, conjuring a perfectly child-centered world. . . . Using a bright rainbow palette of saturated color, Raschka's impressionistic, mixed-media illustrations portray a loving, mixed-race family." SLJ

Another title about Nanna and Poppy and their granddaughter is:

Sourpuss and Sweetie Pie (2008)

Sourpuss and Sweetie Pie; story by Norton Juster; pictures by Chris Raschka. Scholastic 2008 unp il $16.95 *

Grades: PreK K 1 2   E

1. Emotions—Fiction 2. Grandparents—Fiction 3. Racially mixed people—Fiction

ISBN 978-0-439-92943-1; 0-439-92943-1

Companion volume to: The hello, goodbye window (2005)

"Michael di Capua books"

"'Sometimes I'm Sourpuss,' a multiracial girl admits. 'And sometimes I'm Sweetie Pie.' Her grandparents, Poppy and Nanna, accept her dueling dispositions, but when she visits they like to know whom to expect. . . . Both the sunny moments and the tantrums will ring true for readers of any age. Raschka . . . devises competing motifs of light daubs and glowering smears, pairing Sweetie Pie's upbeat sky blue, gold, cantaloupe and pink with Sourpuss's grumpy scarlet, mucky green and purple-blue." Publ Wkly

Kain, Karen

The Nutcracker; paintings by Rajka Kupesic. Tundra Books 2005 unp il $18.95

Grades: K 1 2 3   E

1. Fairy tales 2. Christmas—Fiction

ISBN 0-88776-696-X

Based on The National Ballet of Canada's production

"Misha and Marie are thrilled that Christmas is coming. . . . But there's a disappointment in store. Instead of the beautiful doll she'd hoped for, the only thing strange old Uncle Nikolai has for Marie is a wooden nutcracker. . . . Little does she know that it will lead her and her brother on the adventure of a lifetime." Publisher's note

This is a "striking staging of the classic ballet. . . . The narrative reads smoothly, but it's the art that steals the show. Peopled with doll-like folk-art figures, Kupesic's full-page illustrations . . . are intense with luminous colors." Booklist

Kalan, Robert

Jump, frog, jump! pictures by Byron Baron. Greenwillow Books 1995 c1981 unp il $16.99; pa $6.99 *

Grades: PreK K 1   E

1. Frogs—Fiction 2. Stories in rhyme

ISBN 0-688-13954-X; 0-688-09241-1 (pa)

A reissue of the title first published 1981

"When a frog catches a fly, he sets off a chain of predators. . . . The title answers the repeated refrain 'How did the frog get away?' and children will soon be chanting along with this cumulative tale enhanced by Barton's folk-art-style illustrations." Publ Wkly

Kanevsky, Polly

Sleepy boy; illustrated by Stephanie Anderson. Atheneum Books for Young Readers 2006 unp il $15.95

Grades: PreK K   E

1. Bedtime—Fiction 2. Father-son relationship—Fiction

ISBN 0-689-86735-2

"A Richard Jackson Book"

Unable to fall asleep, a little boy lying next to his father experiences the various sensations of his body and remembers a lion cub he saw that day at the zoo

"Simple, physical words and full-page, unframed, sepia-toned watercolor-and-charcoal images combine to create a portrait of blissful intimacy between a toddler and his father." Booklist

Kanninen, Barbara J.

A story with pictures; story by Barbara Kanninen; pictures by Lynn Rowe Reed. Holiday House 2007 unp il $16.95

Grades: PreK K 1 2   E

1. Authorship—Fiction 2. Illustration of books—Fiction

ISBN 978-0-8234-2049-0; 0-8234-2049-3

LC 2006019535

An author forgets to give her manuscript to an illustrator who begins to paint whatever she herself wants, making the author a character in the book, along with a meddlesome duck and other creatures

Reed's "mixed-media compositions expertly contain the antic action. . . . The artist renders the characters in a childlike style, painting them with skewered proportions and in gumdrop-colored clothes, and enhances her spreads with collage elements. . . . Readers will enjoy the wild ride." Publ Wkly

Karas, G. Brian

The Village Garage. Henry Holt and Company 2010 unp il $16.99

Grades: PreK K 1 2 3   E

1. Garages—Fiction 2. Seasons—Fiction 3. City and town life—Fiction

ISBN 978-0-8050-8716-1; 0-8050-8716-8

LC 2009009223

"Christy Ottaviano books"

Throughout the seasons the workers at the Village Garage are busy taking care of the town and its residents.

"Adding bits of fun along the way, the simple text explains [the workers'] tasks without too much detail. Nicely varied in composition, the appealing pencil, gouache, and acrylic illustrations offer wonderfully child-like depictions of the workers and their machines." Booklist

Kasza, Keiko, 1951-

The dog who cried wolf; [by] Keiko Kasza. G.P. Putnam's Sons 2005 unp il $15.99; pa $6.99 *

Grades: K 1 2 3   E

1. Dogs—Fiction 2. Wolves—Fiction

ISBN 0-399-24247-3; 0-14-241305-4 (pa)

LC 2004-24737

Tired of being a house pet, Moka the dog moves to the mountains to become a wolf but soon misses the comforts of home.

"With an effective variety of page layouts, the expressive pen-and-watercolor pictures show [Moka] dashing off on his adventures. . . . Thanks to excellent pacing, children will get caught up in the childlike Moka's emotions." SLJ

My lucky day. Putnam 2003 unp il $15.99; pa $5.99 *

Grades: PreK K 1 2   E

1. Pigs—Fiction 2. Foxes—Fiction

ISBN 0-399-23874-3; 0-14-240456-X (pa)

LC 2001-57874

When a young pig knocks on a fox's door, the fox thinks dinner has arrived, but the pig has other plans

"Kasza's gouache art is as buoyant and comical as her narrative." Publ Wkly

Ready for anything. G.P. Putnam's Sons 2009 unp il $16.99

Grades: PreK K 1 2   E

1. Worry—Fiction 2. Raccoons—Fiction 3. Ducks—Fiction

ISBN 978-0-399-25235-8; 0-399-25235-5

LC 2008033615

Raccoon is nervous about all of the things that could spoil a picnic, from bees to dragons, until Duck convinces him that surprises can be fun.

"The characters' dialogue is lively and fun to read aloud; Kasza's affable gouache illustrations spotlight action and emotions." Horn Book

The wolf's chicken stew. Putnam 1987 unp il $16.99; pa $6.99 *

Grades: K 1 2 3   E

1. Wolves—Fiction 2. Chickens—Fiction

ISBN 0-399-21400-3; 0-399-22000-9 (pa)

LC 86-12303

"An old plot takes a new turn after the wolf, determined to fatten a chicken for his stew, bakes goodies for her every day only to find them consumed by a horde of baby chicks who shame 'Uncle Wolf' with their adoring gratitude." Bull Cent Child Books

"Kasza combines quivery line and shaded color to turn Wolf and Chicken into scuptural forms. Landscape images are treated similarly. . . . Wolf is comically and suspensefully visualized, making the flimflamming refrains sound just right." Wilson Libr Bull

Katz, Bobbi

Nothing but a dog; illustrated by Jane Manning. Dutton Children's Books 2010 unp il $16.99

Grades: PreK K 1 2   E

1. Dogs—Fiction

ISBN 978-0-525-47858-4; 0-525-47858-2

LC 2009017918

"A young girl wishes for a dog while she engages in everyday activities, exclaiming that once the longing for a pup sets in, nothing stops it. Each page gives examples of other kinds of fun . . . but 'a dog is something else.' Subtle images of canines appear in the delightful watercolor illustrations. . . . This is a sweet addition to the child/pet genre." SLJ

Katz, Karen

My first Chinese New Year; [by] Karen Katz. H. Holt 2004 unp il $14.95

Grades: PreK K   E

1. Chinese New Year—Fiction 2. Chinese Americans—Fiction

ISBN 0-8050-7076-1   LC 2003-23488

In this "picture book, a young girl prepares for and celebrates the Chinese New Year with her extended family. . . . The tale radiates warmth. . . . The collage illustrations, cut from paper with colorful Asian designs, also include paint and other media to capture the joyful celebrants." SLJ

My first Ramadan; [by] Karen Katz. Henry Holt & Co. 2007 unp il $14.95

Grades: PreK K   E

1. Ramadan—Fiction 2. Muslims—Fiction

ISBN 978-0-8050-7894-7; 0-8050-7894-0

LC 2006030768

"A young Muslim boy describes the ways his family celebrates the holy month of Ramadan, explaining some of the rituals and symbols of the holiday. Straightforward, easy-to-read text and bright, friendly collage and mixed-media illustrations make this a solid, approachable resource." Horn Book Guide

Katz, Karen—*Continued*

Princess Baby; [by] Karen Katz. Schwartz & Wade Books 2008 unp il $14.99; lib bdg $17.99
Grades: PreK   E
1. Nicknames—Fiction 2. Princesses—Fiction
ISBN   978-0-375-84119-4;   0-375-84119-9;
978-0-375-94119-1 (lib bdg); 0-375-94119-3 (lib bdg)
LC 2007001913

A little girl does not like any of the nicknames her parents have for her she wants to be called by her "real" name, Princess Baby

"Katz has drawn the human and stuffed-animal characters with perfectly rounded heads, and she uses other softly curving lines in rendering motions. . . . The [predominant] color is fuchsia, while other bright hues complement the rosy tones. . . . Toddlers will ask for repeated readings of this cheerful view of a youngster's world." SLJ

Another title about Princess Baby is:
Princess Baby, night-night (2009)

Ten tiny babies; [by] Karen Katz. Margaret K. McElderry Books 2008 unp il $14.99
Grades: PreK   K   1   E
1. Infants—Fiction 2. Counting 3. Stories in rhyme
ISBN 978-1-4169-3546-9; 1-4169-3546-0
LC 2007-36061

Babies from one to ten enjoy a bouncy, noisy, jiggly day until they are finally fast asleep at night

"The second half of every couplet is split by a page turn, providing a gentle tease that encourages readers to flip the page and complete the rhyme. Ideally suited for read-aloud in both cadence and content." Publ Wkly

Kay, Verla, 1946-

Covered wagons, bumpy trails; illustrated by S.D. Schindler. Putnam 2000 unp il $15.99
Grades: K   1   2   3   E
1. Overland journeys to the Pacific—Fiction 2. Frontier and pioneer life—Fiction 3. Stories in rhyme
ISBN 0-399-22928-0   LC 96-37478

Illustrations and simple rhyming text follow a family as they make the difficult journey by wagon to a new home across the Rocky Mountains

"Schindler handsomely augments the clip-clop rhyme with sweeping vistas and close-up views of the wagons, animals, and people through various stages of the journey." Horn Book Guide

Keane, Dave, 1965-

Sloppy Joe; illustrated by Denise Brunkus. Harper 2009 unp il $16.99; lib bdg $17.89
Grades: PreK   K   1   2   E
1. Cleanliness—Fiction
ISBN   978-0-06-171020-9;   0-06-171020-2;
978-0-06-171021-6 (lib bdg); 0-06-171021-0 (lib bdg)
LC 2008020212

Sloppy Joe determines to do everything he can to surprise his family by becoming Neat Joe.

"The illustrations are hilarious. This charming picture book is a wonderful choice for most libraries." SLJ

Keats, Ezra Jack, 1916-1983

Apt. 3. Viking 1999 unp il hardcover o.p. pa $6.99
Grades: PreK   K   1   2   E
1. City and town life—Fiction 2. Brothers—Fiction 3. Blind—Fiction
ISBN 0-670-88342-5; 0-14-056507-8 (pa)
LC 98-41043

A reissue of the title first published 1971 by Macmillan

On a rainy day two brothers try to discover who is playing the harmonica they hear in their apartment building

"The well-paced text is illustrated with shadowy paintings that capably convey both the dingy surroundings and the brothers' affection." Horn Book Guide

Hi, cat! Viking 1999 unp il $15.99
Grades: PreK   K   1   2   E
1. Cats—Fiction 2. African Americans—Fiction
ISBN 0-670-88546-0   LC 98-37764

A reissue of the title first published 1970 by Macmillan

This book "tells the story of Peter's friend Archie and the inquisitive, nondescript, half-grown alley cat that tags after him and manages to make a shambles out of the boys' street carnival. The text provides an adequate framework for Keats's bold bright paintings of a lively city neighborhood." Horn Book Guide

Another title about Archie is:
Pet show! (1972)

Louie. Viking 2004 unp il pa $6.99
Grades: PreK   K   1   2   E
1. Puppets and puppet plays—Fiction
ISBN 978-0-14-240080-7 (pa); 0-14-240080-7 (pa)
LC 2003-11378

First published 1975 by Greenwillow Books

Susie and Roberto's puppet show is temporarily interrupted when Louis becomes fascinated by one of the puppets

"This story is illustrated with the same glowing colors . . . and with some of the postercollage that is the artist's trademark. The aura is touching without being maudlin, the writing simple and informal." Sutherland. The Best in Child Books

Other titles about Louie are:
Louie's search (1980)
Regards to the man in the moon (1981)
The trip (1978)

Over in the meadow; [written and] illustrated by Ezra Jack Keats. Viking 1999 unp il $16.99; pa $6.99 *
Grades: PreK   K   1   2   E
1. Nursery rhymes 2. Animals—Poetry 3. Counting
ISBN 0-670-88344-1; 0-14-056508-6 (pa)
LC 98-47037

A reissue of the title first published 1971 by Four Winds Press

Based on Southern Appalachian counting rhyme from late 1800's attributed to Olive A. Wadsworth

An old nursery poem introduces animals and their young and the numbers one through ten

"The book features Keats's illustrations that show animals in lively characteristic activity." Horn Book Guide

Keats, Ezra Jack, 1916-1983—*Continued*

The snowy day. Viking 1962 31p il lib bdg $16.99; pa $5.99; bd bk $6.99 *

Grades: PreK K 1 2   E

1. Snow—Fiction

ISBN 0-670-65400-0 (lib bdg); 0-14-050182-7 (pa); 0-670-86733-0 (bd bk)

Awarded the Caldecott Medal, 1963

A small "boy's ecstatic enjoyment of snow in the city is shown in vibrant pictures. Peter listens to the snow crunch under his feet, makes the first tracks in a clean patch of snow, makes angels and a snowman. At night in his warm bed he thinks over his adventures, and in the morning wakens to the promise of another lovely snowy day." Moorachian. What is a City?

Other titles about Peter are:

Goggles (1969)
A letter to Amy (1968)
Peter's chair (1967)
Whistle for Willie (1964)

Keller, Holly

Geraldine's blanket. Greenwillow Bks. 1984 unp il pa $5.99 hardcover o.p. *

Grades: PreK K 1 2   E

1. Blankets—Fiction

ISBN 0-688-07810-9 (pa)   LC 83-14062

"Geraldine's pink blanket was a baby present from Aunt Bessie. It's worn now and patched, and when Aunt Bessie sends her a doll, Geraldine preserves and transfers her affections simultaneously by using the scraps for a doll dress." N Y Times Book Rev

"Simply but wonderfully expressive line drawings washed with pastel colors capture the gentleness and humor of the story." SLJ

Other titles about Geraldine are:

Geraldine and Mrs. Duffy (2000)
Geraldine first (1996)
Geraldine's baby brother (1994)
Geraldine's big snow (1988)
Merry Christmas, Geraldine (1997)

Grandfather's dream. Greenwillow Bks. 1994 unp il $16.99

Grades: PreK K 1 2   E

1. Cranes (Birds)—Fiction 2. Grandfathers—Fiction 3. Vietnam—Fiction

ISBN 0-688-12339-2   LC 93-18186

After the end of the war in Vietnam, a young boy's grandfather dreams of restoring the wetlands of the Mekong delta, hoping that the large cranes that once lived there will return

"Keller uses simple, direct storytelling and vivid watercolor and ink illustrations to present a complex theme in a story of hope and rebirth." Horn Book Guide

Help! a story of friendship. Greenwillow Books 2007 unp il $16.99; lib bdg $17.89 *

Grades: PreK K 1 2   E

1. Fear—Fiction 2. Friendship—Fiction 3. Animals—Fiction

ISBN 978-0-06-123913-7; 0-06-123913-5; 978-0-06-123914-4 (lib bdg); 0-06-123914-3 (lib bdg)
                                       LC 2006-32116

Mouse hears a rumor that snakes do not like mice and while trying to avoid his former friend, Snake, he falls into a hole from which neither Hedgehog, Squirrel, nor Rabbit can help him out

"This story has the simplicity of a fable. The appealing art is done in collographs, which are printed collages, and watercolors." SLJ

Miranda's beach day. Greenwillow Books 2009 unp il $17.99; lib bdg $18.89

Grades: PreK K   E

1. Beaches—Fiction 2. Mother-daughter relationship—Fiction

ISBN 978-0-06-158298-1; 0-06-158298-0; 978-0-06-158300-1 (lib bdg); 0-06-158300-6 (lib bdg)
                                       LC 2008012645

Miranda and Mama spend a fun day at the beach building castles and catching sand crabs, and Miranda learns that just like the sand and the sea, she and her mother will always be together

"Attractive illustrations in watercolors and printed collages on well-designed spreads capture the children's activities and the vastness of the sand and sea. This is a disarmingly simple and reassuring selection." SLJ

Nosy Rosie; [by] Holly Keller. Greenwillow Books 2006 unp il $16.99; lib bdg $17.89

Grades: PreK K 1 2   E

1. Personal names—Fiction 2. Smell—Fiction 3. Foxes—Fiction

ISBN 978-0-06-078758-5; 0-06-078758-9; 978-0-06-078759-2 (lib bdg); 0-06-078759-7 (lib bdg)
                                       LC 2005022183

Rosie the fox's excellent sense of smell is good for finding things, but she stops using it after everyone begins to call her "Nosy Rosie"

"Keller takes on the subject of name calling in a gentle, simple, and compassionate manner. . . . The heartfelt dialogue poignantly conveys the little fox's hurt feelings and reads aloud perfectly. The colorful mixture of robust watercolors and simple black lines touchingly reveals each character's attitude through expressive body movement." SLJ

Pearl's new skates. Greenwillow Books 2005 24p il $15.99

Grades: PreK K 1 2   E

1. Ice skating—Fiction

ISBN 0-06-056280-3   LC 2004-576

Pearl's birthday skates have a single blade and learning to use them is harder than she expects

"With her pitch-perfect text and uncluttered watercolor-and-ink pictures . . . Keller tells a tender story about accepting the failures and frustrations that come with learning something new." Booklist

Keller, Laurie

Do unto otters; (a book about manners); by Laurie Keller. Henry Holt 2007 unp il $16.95 *

Grades: PreK K 1 2   E

1. Etiquette—Fiction 2. Rabbits—Fiction 3. Otters—Fiction

ISBN 978-0-8050-7996-8; 0-8050-7996-3
                                       LC 2006030505

Keller, Laurie—*Continued*

Mr. Rabbit wonders if he will be able to get along with his new neighbors, who are otters, until he is reminded of the golden rule

"From the gleeful title pun to the kenetic illustrations, this clever book . . . introduces the golden rule with irresistible humor." Booklist

Kelley, Ellen A.

My life as a chicken; as told to Ellen A. Kelley; pictures by Michael Slack. Harcourt, Inc. 2007 unp il $16

Grades: PreK K 1 2   E

1. Chickens—Fiction 2. Stories in rhyme

ISBN 0-15-205306-2; 978-0-15-205306-2

LC 2005020051

After escaping the frying pan, Pauline the chicken has an adventure that includes pirates, a typhoon, and a balloon ride before landing happily in a petting zoo.

"Slack's digital mixed-media illustrations are wacky and cartoonish, and the text ripples with big, impressive words befitting the exaggerated nature of Pauline's adventures." SLJ

Kelley, Marty

Twelve terrible things. Tricycle Press 2008 unp il $15.99 *

Grades: 1 2 3 4   E

1. Monsters—Fiction 2. Courage—Fiction

ISBN 978-1-58246-229-5; 1-58246-229-1

LC 2007-46795

Grownups who wax nostalgic about their youth are given a visual tour through twelve terrible experiences of childhood, including bedtime monsters and "atomic wedgies."

"Realistic, double-page watercolor illustrations use a clever first-person perspective to render readers the victims of horrors such as a cheek-pinching lady, an over-the-top birthday clown, and a hairy-moled lunch lady. . . . Minimal text and detailed artwork combine to convey a macabre humor that is bound to ensnare even the most hesitant of readers." SLJ

Kelley, True, 1946-

Dog who saved Santa. Holiday House 2008 unp il $16.95

Grades: PreK K 1 2   E

1. Santa Claus—Fiction 2. Dogs—Fiction 3. Christmas—Fiction

ISBN 978-0-8234-2120-6; 0-8234-2120-1

LC 2007-041180

With the help of his take-charge dog Rodney and a self-help video, young Santa Claus mends his lazy and irresponsible ways.

"The cartoon artwork, done in acrylic, watercolors, and colored pencils, captures the endearing pup's antics and will give readers the giggles." SLJ

Kellogg, Steven, 1941-

Best friends; story and pictures by Steven Kellogg. Dial Bks. for Young Readers 1986 unp il $16.99; pa $6.99 *

Grades: PreK K 1 2   E

1. Friendship—Fiction

ISBN 0-8037-0099-7; 0-14-054607-3 (pa)

LC 85-15971

Kathy feels lonely and betrayed when her best friend Louise goes away for the summer and has a wonderful time

"The watercolor and ink illustrations are appealingly bright and magical. Kathy and Louise's daydreams are vividly and flamboyantly portrayed, with 'reality' just as attractively pictured." SLJ

The missing mitten mystery; story and pictures by Steven Kellogg. Dial Bks. for Young Readers 2000 unp il $15.99; pa $6.99 *

Grades: PreK K 1 2   E

1. Lost and found possessions—Fiction

ISBN 0-8037-2566-3; 0-14-230192-2 (pa)

LC 99-54777

First published 1974 with title: The mystery of the missing red mitten

Annie searches the neighborhood for her red mitten, the fifth she's lost this winter

"Kellogg really outdoes himself with pictures that are filled with good cheer, warm spirits, and happy daydreams. . . . A book that's upbeat and touching by turns." Booklist

The mysterious tadpole; new illustrations and text by Steven Kellogg. 25th anniversary ed. Dial Bks. for Young Readers 2002 unp il $16.99; pa $6.99 *

Grades: PreK K 1 2   E

1. Pets—Fiction

ISBN 0-8037-2788-7; 0-14-240140-4 (pa)

LC 2001-53776

First published 1977

"Louis receives a birthday present from his uncle in Scotland: Alphonse, an amiable tadpole that outgrows his bowl, the bathtub, and even the apartment. . . . The new illustrations are bigger, bolder, brighter, and brimming with lively details." Booklist

The Pied Piper's magic. Dial Books for Young Readers 2009 unp il $16.99

Grades: PreK K 1   E

1. Fairy tales 2. Magic—Fiction 3. Rats—Fiction

ISBN 978-0-8037-2818-9; 0-8037-2818-2

LC 2008-12267

In a story loosely based on The Pied Piper of Hamelin, an elf acquires from a miserable witch a magic pipe that allows him to transform things, including the mean-spirited Grand Duke who rules over a rat-infested town.

"Kellogg depicts the magic-making in bright, buoyant mixed media spreads that show streams of colorful text and corresponding animals pouring from the mouth of the pipe. . . . Far sunnier than the original, this slightly educational adaptation (thanks to the built-in spelling lessons within) should please parents and kids alike." Publ Wkly

Kellogg, Steven, 1941-—*Continued*

Pinkerton, behave! story and pictures by Steven Kellogg. Dial Books for Young Readers 2002 c1979 unp il $17.99; pa $6.99 *

Grades: PreK K 1 2   E

1. Dogs—Fiction

ISBN 0-8037-2722-4; 0-14-230007-1 (pa)

A reissue of the title first published 1979

Pinkerton the Great Dane "doesn't understand his owner's commands. . . . Pinkerton's desperate owner sends him to obedience school, but he flunks out. . . . Then one night a burglar breaks into their house, and Pinkerton is able to put his bad habits to good use." Publisher's note

"Kellogg wittily captures expressions and movements of animal and human, wisely allowing the focal humor to emanate through the faces and action." Booklist

Other titles about Pinkerton are:

A penguin pup for Pinkerton (2001)

Prehistoric Pinkerton (1987)

A Rose for Pinkerton (1981)

Tallyho, Pinkerton (1982)

Kempter, Christa

Wally and Mae; by Christa Kempter; illustrated by Frauke Weldin. North-South 2008 unp il $16.95

Grades: PreK K 1 2   E

1. Bears—Fiction 2. Rabbits—Fiction 3. Friendship—Fiction

ISBN 978-0-7358-2208-5; 0-7358-2208-5

"A capricious bear named Mae befriends a sensible rabbit named Wally, and this unlikely pair shares an idyllic cottage in the woods. . . . Both of the animals are depicted with tenderness. The colors are bright and many of the scenes show one or both of the characters in full action." SLJ

Kenah, Katharine

The best seat in second grade; story by Katharine Kenah; pictures by Abby Carter. HarperCollins Pubs. 2005 48p il $15.99; lib bdg $16.89; pa $3.99

Grades: K 1 2   E

1. Hamsters—Fiction 2. School stories

ISBN 0-06-000734-6; 0-06-000735-4 (lib bdg); 0-06-000736-2 (pa)   LC 2004-178

"An I can read book"

Sam's favorite thing about second grade is the class pet, a hamster named George Washington, so when the class goes on a field trip to a science museum, Sam cannot resist bringing George along

"Kenah has created an appealing cast of characters whose actions ring true. . . . Carter's watercolor illustrations add to the story's appeal." Booklist

Other titles about this second grade are:

The best teacher in second grade (2006)

The best chef in second grade (2007)

Kent, Jack, 1920-1985

There's no such thing as a dragon. Golden Book 2005 c1975 unp il hardcover o.p. pa $6.99

Grades: PreK K 1 2   E

1. Dragons—Fiction

ISBN 0-375-83208-4; 0-375-85137-2 (pa)

          LC 2004-6123

First published 1975 by Western Pub.

"When Billy Bixbee wakes up and finds a dragon in his room, his mother tells him there is no such thing. The neglected dragon grows larger and larger, eventually walking off with the house, and the Bixbee family is forced to admit his existence. Practically a classic. . . for its neat story line and humorous cartoons of expressively surprised characters." Horn Book Guide

Kerby, Mona

Owney, the mail-pouch pooch; pictures by Lynne Barasch. Farrar, Straus and Giroux 2008 unp il $16.95 *

Grades: K 1 2 3   E

1. Dogs—Fiction 2. Postal service—Fiction 3. Voyages and travels—Fiction

ISBN 0-374-35685-8; 978-0-374-35685-9

          LC 2006-47605

"Frances Foster books"

In 1888, Owney, a stray terrier puppy, finds a home in the Albany, New York, post office and becomes its official mascot as he rides the mail train through the Adirondacks and beyond, criss-crossing the United States, into Canada and Mexico, and eventually traveling around the world by mail boat in 132 days.

"The author does an excellent job of introducing readers to the late-19th century and the system used by the postal service to send mail both nationally and internationally via horse-pulled wagons, trains, and steamships. . . . Barasch's ink and watercolor illustrations complement the narrative with period details. A pair of sepia-toned photographs at the end of the book adds to the authenticity of the tale." SLJ

Another title about Owney is:

The further adventures of a lucky dog: Owney, U.S. rail mail mascot (2009)

Kerley, Barbara

You and me together; moms, dads, and kids around the world; with a note by Marian Wright Edelman. National Geographic 2005 32p il $16.95; lib bdg $25.90

Grades: PreK K 1 2   E

1. Parent-child relationship

ISBN 0-7922-8297-3; 0-7922-8298-1 (lib bdg)

"Using a simple rhyming text, Kerley captures the essence of childhood's special moments, accompanied by superb full-color photos. . . . Diverse cultures in various locations around the world are represented. . . . Children and parents engage in activities such as playing an instrument, taking a walk, making a meal, fishing, and dancing. . . . This book is an excellent tool for raising awareness of cultural differences and similarities." SLJ

Kerr, Judith

One night in the zoo. Kane Miller 2010 c2009 unp il $15.99

Grades: PreK K   E

1. Zoos—Fiction 2. Animals—Fiction 3. Magic—Fiction 4. Stories in rhyme

ISBN 978-1-935279-37-2; 1-935279-37-8

One magical night an elephant jumped in the air and flew. Wild antics, high spirits and silly games of the other zoo animals also occur. Will anyone find out?

"Kerr's softly shaded pencil drawings depict the beasts and birds with all the charm of friendly animal characters come to life. Fresh and simple." Booklist

Kessler, Cristina

The best beekeeper of Lalibela; a tale from Africa; by Cristina Kessler; illustrated by Leonard Jenkins. Holiday House 2006 unp il $16.95

Grades: K 1 2 3   E

1. Beekeeping—Fiction 2. Sex role—Fiction 3. Ethiopia—Fiction

ISBN 978-0-8234-1858-9; 0-8234-1858-8

LC 2005046217

In the Ethiopian mountain village of Lalibela a young girl named Almaz determines to find a way to be a beekeeper despite being told that is something only men can do

"Jenkins follows the ups and downs of Almaz's labor in deep-hued, mixed-media scenes spread richly across double pages. . . . Kessler includes well-chosen details about the beekeeping project and a few words from the local Amharic and Tigringna languages." SLJ

Kessler, Leonard P., 1920-

Here comes the strikeout. newly il ed. HarperCollins Pubs. 1992 64p il hardcover o.p. pa $3.99 *

Grades: K 1 2   E

1. Baseball—Fiction

ISBN 0-06-023156-4; 0-06-444011-7 (pa)

LC 91-14717

"An I can read book"

A revised and newly illustrated edition of the title first published 1965

. This "concerns a boy who can't hit a baseball until he follows the advice of a friend. 'Lucky helmets won't do it. Lucky bats won't do it. Only hard work will do it.' . . . A winner." Booklist

Kick, pass, and run; story and pictures by Leonard Kessler. newly il ed. HarperCollins Pubs. 1996 64p il hardcover o.p. pa $3.99 *

Grades: K 1 2   E

1. Football—Fiction

ISBN 0-06-027105-1; 0-06-444210-1 (pa)

LC 95-6185

"An I can read book"

A newly illustrated edition of the title first published 1966

"After a group of animal friends watches a boys' football team play, they are eager to have their own game. An apple serves as a ball until Frog eats it; a paper-bag football works until Duck kicks and pops it. The game

is kept alive when a real football from the boys' game sails into the animals' midst. [A] simply told story with plenty of sports action." Horn Book Guide

Last one in is a rotten egg. newly il ed. HarperCollins Pubs. 1999 64p il hardcover o.p. pa $3.99 *

Grades: K 1 2   E

1. Swimming—Fiction

ISBN 0-06-028485-4; 0-06-444262-4 (pa)

LC 98-50882

"An I can read book"

A newly illustrated edition of the title first published 1969

After Freddy is pushed into deep water by a couple of toughs, he decides to learn to swim

"This lively . . . sports story has been newly illustrated with a multicultural cast in a New York City neighborhood." Booklist

Ketteman, Helen, 1945-

Swamp song; illustrated by Ponder Goembel. Marshall Cavendish Children 2009 unp il $17.99

Grades: PreK K 1 2   E

1. Stories in rhyme 2. Animals—Fiction 3. Marshes—Fiction

ISBN 978-0-7614-5563-9; 0-7614-5563-9

LC 2008013810

Down in the swamp where the cypress grows, the animals all come out to enjoy the day.

"The sunny illustrations are done with colored ink lines and acrylic wash paint against mostly white backgrounds. . . . Children will be tapping their toes with Old Man Gator and creating their own cacophony of swamp sounds as they learn about the inhabitants of this habitat." SLJ

The three little gators; illustrated by Will Terry. Albert Whitman 2009 unp il $16.99

Grades: K 1 2 3   E

1. Folklore 2. Alligators—Folklore

ISBN 978-0-8075-7824-7; 0-8075-7824-X

LC 2008028085

In this adaptation of the traditional folktale, three little gators each build their house in an east Texas swamp, hoping for protection from the Big-bottomed Boar.

"Ketteman's retelling, including a sassy Texas twang, makes the story hilarious and bright. . . . Terry's illustrations work well with the story. The colors are vibrant yet ominous and swampy." SLJ

Khan, Hena

Night of the Moon; a Muslim holiday story; illustrated by Julie Paschkis. Chronicle Books 2008 unp il $16.99 *

Grades: PreK K 1 2   E

1. Ramadan—Fiction 2. Id al-Adha—Fiction 3. Muslims—Fiction 4. Islam—Fiction 5. Pakistani Americans—Fiction

ISBN 978-0-8118-6062-8; 0-8118-6062-0

LC 2007024962

"A new moon is in the sky, and Yasmeen, identified on the jacket as a seven-year-old Pakistani-American,

Khan, Hena—*Continued*

knows that it is time for the holidays of Ramadan and Eid. . . . Paschkis, borrowing from the arabesque motifs and jeweled colors of Islamic art, portrays the Muslim community as warm, welcoming and multiethnic. . . . Sweet and visually striking, this is a good choice both for children who celebrate these holidays and for others seeking a bridge to their culture." Publ Wkly

Khan, Rukhsana, 1962-

Big red lollipop; illustrated by Sophie Blackall. Viking 2010 unp il $16.99 *

Grades: PreK K 1 2   E

1. Sisters—Fiction 2. Parties—Fiction 3. Birthdays—Fiction 4. Pakistani Americans—Fiction

ISBN 978-0-670-06287-4; 0-670-06287-1

"Rubina has been invited to her first birthday party, and her mother, Ami, insists that she bring her little sister along." Publisher's note

"Khan is of Pakistani descent, and this tale of clashing cultural customs is based on an incident from her childhood. The story (and its lesson) comes to like in Blackall's spot-on illustrations. . . . This is an honest, even moving, commentary on sisterly relationships." Booklist

Silly chicken; illustrated by Yunmee Kyong. Viking 2005 unp il $15.99 *

Grades: K 1 2 3   E

1. Chickens—Fiction 2. Pakistan—Fiction

ISBN 0-670-05912-9   LC 2004-15830

In Pakistan, Rani believes that her mother loves their pet chicken Bibi more than she cares for her, until the day that a fluffy chick appears and steals Rani's own affections.

"This picture book clearly depicts a child's jealousy. . . . Kyong . . . paints in a naive style, using fresh, warm colors. A pleasing book with an unusual setting." Booklist

Kimmel, Elizabeth Cody

Glamsters; written by Elizabeth Cody Kimmel; illustrated by Jackie Urbanovic. Hyperion Books for Children 2008 unp il $16.99

Grades: K 1 2   E

1. Hamsters—Fiction

ISBN 978-1-4231-1148-1; 1-4231-1148-6

LC 2008029692

Harriet the hamster is desperate to be adopted, so she gives her sister Patricia and herself glamorous makeovers in hopes they will get more attention when Hamster World has its huge annual sale

"The story is filled with clever details and laugh-out-loud humor, but the underlying message of self-acceptance is an important one for children to hear." SLJ

My penguin Osbert; illustrated by H. B. Lewis. Candlewick Press 2004 unp il $16.99

Grades: PreK K 1 2   E

1. Penguins—Fiction 2. Christmas—Fiction

ISBN 0-7636-1699-0   LC 2003-40981

When a boy finally gets exactly what he wants from Santa, he learns that owning a real penguin may not have

been a good idea after all

"Kimmel sneaks some sly humor into the well-told, nicely paced story, and Lewis' artwork, executed in watercolor and pastels and enhanced with digital renderings, has a soft look, colored in marshmallow tints." Booklist

Another title about Osbert the penguin is:

My penguin Osbert in love (2009)

The top job; by Elizabeth Cody Kimmel; illustrated by Robert Neubecker. Dutton Children's Books 2007 unp il $16.99; pa $6.99

Grades: K 1 2 3   E

1. Empire State Building (New York, N.Y.)—Fiction 2. Occupations—Fiction 3. Father-daughter relationship—Fiction 4. New York (N.Y.)—Fiction

ISBN 978-0-525-47789-1; 0-525-47789-6; 978-0-14-241424-8 (pa); 0-14-241424-7 (pa)

LC 2006039770

On Career Day, a young girl entertains the class with a description of her father's exciting job as light bulb changer at the top of the Empire State Building.

"The pacing and rhythm of the text is impeccable. . . . The stylized, cartoon-style illustrations, rendered in clear colors and bold black outlines, nicely extend the plot." Booklist

Kimmel, Eric A.

The Chanukkah guest; illustrated by Giora Carmi. Holiday House 1990 unp il $15.95; pa $6.95

Grades: K 1 2 3   E

1. Hanukkah—Fiction 2. Bears—Fiction 3. Jews—Fiction

ISBN 0-8234-0788-8; 0-8234-0978-3 (pa)

LC 89-20073

On the first night of Chanukkah, Old Bear wanders into Bubba Brayna's house and receives a delicious helping of potato latkes when she mistakes him for the rabbi

"In this comical story, Kimmel captures the kindness of an old woman and the innocence of a hungry bear in an unusual visit. Carmi's airy pastel illustrations shade the tale with a golden glow appropriate for the Festival of Lights." Publ Wkly

Hershel and the Hanukkah goblins; written by Eric A. Kimmel; illustrated by Trina Schart Hyman. Holiday House 1989 unp il $16.95; pa $6.95 *

Grades: K 1 2 3   E

1. Hanukkah—Fiction 2. Fairies—Fiction 3. Jews—Fiction

ISBN 0-8234-0769-1; 0-8234-1131-1 (pa)

LC 89-1954

A Caldecott Medal honor book, 1990

"The setting is an Eastern European village, and the plot is a little like Halloween Hanukkah—it seems that goblins are occupying the synagogue on the hill. Along comes plucky Hershel of Ostropol, and he cleverly outwits the demons." N Y Times Book Rev

This "will fit companionably with haunted castle variants. Hyman is at her best with windswept landscapes, dark interiors, close portraiture, and imaginatively wicked creatures. Both art and history are charged with energy." Bull Cent Child Books

Kimmel, Eric A.—*Continued*

Joha makes a wish; a Middle Eastern tale; adapted by Eric A. Kimmel; illustrated by Omar Rayyan. Marshall Cavendish Children 2010 unp il $17.99

Grades: 1 2 3 E

 1. Wishes—Fiction 2. Middle East—Fiction
 ISBN 978-0-7614-5599-8; 0-7614-5599-X
          LC 2009006334

An original story, based on the Joha tales of the Arabic-speaking world, in which a hapless man finds a wishing stick that brings him nothing but bad luck. Includes an author's note about the history of Joha tales.

"Kimmel's well-paced text smoothly builds events and dialogue, leaving the character interpretation to the comic portrayals in Rayyan's energetic watercolors." SLJ

Little Britches and the rattlers; by Eric A. Kimmel; illustrated by Vincent Nguyen. Marshall Cavendish Children 2008 unp il $16.99

Grades: PreK K 1 2 E

 1. Cowhands—Fiction 2. Rattlesnakes—Fiction
 3. Texas—Fiction
 ISBN 978-0-7614-5432-8; 0-7614-5432-2
          LC 2007030155

As Little Britches, in her best attire, starts for the rodeo in town, she is waylaid by several rattlesnakes wanting to do her harm, but with some quick thinking she finds a way to outsmart them all

"Kimmel's little yarn makes good use of early counting concepts and introduces some western lingo in a leisurely repetitive structure. . . . Nguyen's artwork complements the glib silliness." Booklist

The mysterious guests; a Sukkot story; by Eric A. Kimmel; illustrated by Katya Krenina. Holiday House 2008 unp il $16.95

Grades: K 1 2 E

 1. Sukkot—Fiction 2. Jews—Fiction 3. Brothers—Fiction
 ISBN 978-0-8234-1893-0; 0-8234-1893-6
          LC 2007-43208

Three mysterious guests appear at generous but impoverished Ezra's table on Sukkot and bless him, while they bring curses upon his rich but selfish brother Eben.

This is "a lyrically rendered tale. . . . Krenina's stylized, harvest-toned acrylics and thoughtful, dark-eyed characters evoke a world where the everyday and mystical are intertwined, and righteousness is clear-cut." Publ Wkly

Rip Van Winkle's return; adapted and retold by Eric A. Kimmel from Rip Van Winkle by Washington Irving; pictures by Leonard Everett Fisher. Farrar, Straus and Giroux 2007 unp il $17

Grades: 1 2 3 4 E

 1. Catskill Mountains (N.Y.)—Fiction 2. New York (State)—Fiction
 ISBN 978-0-374-36308-6; 0-374-36308-0
          LC 2005042922

A man who sleeps for twenty years in the Catskill Mountains wakes to a much-changed world

"Kimmel and Fisher take on an American literary treasure and make it accessible to young children. . . . The drama is nicely played out with Fisher's solid, strategically placed figures." Booklist

Stormy's hat; just right for a railroad man; pictures by Andrea U'Ren. Farrar, Straus and Giroux 2008 unp il $16.95

Grades: PreK K 1 2 E

 1. Hats—Fiction 2. Railroads—Fiction 3. Sewing—Fiction
 ISBN 0-374-37262-4; 978-0-374-37262-0
          LC 2005-51233

As Stormy, a railroad engineer, searches for the perfect hat—one that will not blow off, get too hot, or shade his eyes too much—his wife, Ida, becomes increasingly annoyed that he will not let her help. Includes a historical note about the real Stormy and Ida Kromer.

"U'Ren's vibrant paintings capture the palette and motion of Midwestern landscapes and city scenes. . . . With a snappy, high-interest story and connections to hats, history, trains, gender equality, and industrialism, this book is a gem for libraries and classrooms." SLJ

The three little tamales; by Eric A. Kimmel; illustrated by Valeria Docampo. Marshall Cavendish 2009 unp il $17.99

Grades: K 1 2 3 E

 1. Fairy tales 2. Wolves—Fiction 3. Hispanic Americans—Fiction
 ISBN 978-0-7614-5519-6; 0-7614-5519-1
          LC 2008010738

In this variation of 'The Three Little Pigs' set in the Southwest, three little tamales escape from a restaurant before they can be eaten, and set up homes in the prairie, cornfield, and desert.

"Docampo's oil-on-paper illustrations add dimension to the story and bring the three little tamales to life. An excellent addition to collections of fairy-tale retellings." Booklist

Zigazak! a magical Hanukkah night; illustrated by Jon Goodell. Doubleday Bks. for Young Readers 2001 unp il $15.95; lib bdg $19.99 *

Grades: K 1 2 E

 1. Hanukkah—Fiction 2. Jews—Fiction 3. Magic—Fiction
 ISBN 0-385-32652-1; 0-385-90004-X (lib bdg)
          LC 98-46269

Two evil spirits wreak havoc on the town of Brisk's Hanukkah celebration, until the town's wise rabbi puts a stop to their mischief

"The text is safely boxed away from the devilry in double-page spreads in which intricately detailed art realistically depicts the furnishings, clothing, facial features, and even the townspeople's pets. Storytellers will have fun with the surprise ending." Booklist

Kimmelman, Leslie

Everybody bonjours! by Leslie Kimmelman; illustrated by Sarah McMenemy. Alfred A. Knopf 2008 unp il $16.99; lib bdg $19.99 *

Grades: PreK K E

 1. Paris (France)—Fiction 2. Stories in rhyme
 ISBN 978-0-375-84443-0; 978-0-375-94443-7 (lib bdg)
          LC 2007006899

"On vacation with her parents . . . and little brother, a girl embraces her role as tourist, savoring all the places where one can say 'Bonjour': On a barge trip down the

Kimmelman, Leslie—Continued

Seine, at the top of the Tour Eiffel and Notre Dame, in a chic boutique. . . . McMenemy's . . . mixed-media images, mostly full-page scenes of classic locations, are a stylish yet timeless mélange of fauvist whimsy and affectionate reportage." Publ Wkly

In the doghouse; an Emma and Bo story; by Leslie Kimmelman; illustrated by True Kelley. Holiday House 2006 30p il $14.95

Grades: K 1 2   E

1. Dogs—Fiction 2. Vacations—Fiction

ISBN 0-8234-1882-0   LC 2004047466

"A Holiday House reader"

When the Lewis family goes on vacation to the lake, Emily gets mad at her best friend Bo, the family dog, so he runs away to look for a new best friend

"Kimmelman writes with simplicity and wit, affectionately portraying the main characters' flaws, feelings, and pride. Kelley's cartoonlike ink drawings, brightened with colorful washes, have a carefree air that suits the vacation setting and the tone of the story." Booklist

Mind your manners, Alice Roosevelt! written by Leslie Kimmelman and illustrated by Adam Gustavson. Peachtree Publishers 2009 unp il $16.95

Grades: K 1 2 3   E

1. Longworth, Alice Roosevelt, 1884-1980—Fiction
2. Roosevelt, Theodore, 1858-1919—Fiction
3. Presidents—United States—Fiction

ISBN 978-1-5614-5492-1; 1-5614-5492-3

LC 2008052837

A brief, fictionalized account of what life was like for Theodore Roosevelt during his political career, with his oldest daughter, Alice, a strong-willed and somewhat wild young woman, who loved to do things that shocked the public, even when she lived in the White House

"Gustavson's energetic oil paintings do justice to Alice's shocking escapades, and parts of the text . . . are cleverly incorporated into the art." Booklist

Kinerk, Robert

Clorinda; illustrated by Steven Kellogg. Simon & Schuster Bks. for Young Readers 2003 unp il $15.95; pa $6.99

Grades: PreK K 1 2   E

1. Cattle—Fiction 2. Ballet—Fiction 3. Stories in rhyme

ISBN 0-689-86449-3; 1-4169-3964-4 (pa)

LC 2003-4559

"A Paula Wiseman book"

Defying the odds, Clorinda the cow follows her dream of becoming a ballet dancer

"As fine a mix of story and message as this is, it's the irrepressible art that makes this book shine. Kellogg is at the top of his game, finding the humor in every line." Booklist

Another title about Clorinda is:

Clorinda takes flight (2007)

King, Stephen Michael

Leaf; ideas, sound effects, and pictures. Roaring Brook 2009 unp il $14.95

Grades: K 1 2   E

1. Hair—Fiction 2. Dogs—Fiction 3. Dreams—Fiction

ISBN 978-1-59643-503-2; 1-59643-503-8

"A mopheaded child faces a momlike figure with scissors in her hands—definitely time for a haircut. The child, however, has other ideas and runs out to frolic in the grass. . . . Wonderful squiggly line, patches of green and brown, gold and blue and fabulous use of negative white space make this a joy to reread." Kirkus

Mutt dog! words and pictures by Stephen Michael King. Harcourt 2005 c2004 unp il $16

Grades: PreK K 1 2   E

1. Dogs—Fiction 2. Homeless persons—Fiction

ISBN 0-15-205561-4

First published 2004 in Australia

A lonely dog finally finds a home after he makes friends with a woman who works at a homeless shelter.

"The presentation is well done, and the gentle pen-and-ink and watercolor cartoons tell the story beautifully. . . . The book's oversize format and clear wash illustrations on white backgrounds make this a good choice for storytimes." SLJ

King-Smith, Dick, 1922-

The twin giants; [by] Dick King-Smith; illustrated by Mini Grey. Candlewick Press 2008 67p il $16.99

Grades: K 1 2 3   E

1. Twins—Fiction 2. Giants—Fiction

ISBN 978-0-7636-3529-9; 0-7636-3529-4

Two twin giants do everything together, including looking for the perfect wives.

"This handsomely designed volume offers an original story accompanied by droll illustrations." Booklist

Kinsey-Warnock, Natalie

Nora's ark; illustrated by Emily Arnold McCully. HarperCollins 2005 unp il $15.99; lib bdg $16.89 *

Grades: K 1 2 3   E

1. Floods—Fiction   2. Farm life—Fiction
3. Grandparents—Fiction 4. Vermont—Fiction

ISBN 0-688-17244-X; 0-06-029517-1 (lib bdg)

LC 2004-3444

During the Vermont flood of 1927, a girl and her grandparents share their new hilltop house with neighbors and animals.

This is a "well-told tale, based on an incident from the author's life. . . . [A] stunning picture is the wild, rainy scene showing houses bobbing along as the water pours down." Booklist

Kirk, Connie Ann, 1951-

Sky dancers; illustrations by Christy Hale. Lee & Low Books 2004 unp il $16.95

Grades: 1 2 3 4   E

1. Empire State Building (New York, N.Y.)—Fiction
2. Mohawk Indians—Fiction 3. Steel construction—Fiction 4. Father-son relationship—Fiction

ISBN 1-58430-162-7   LC 2004-1885

Kirk, Connie Ann, 1951-—*Continued*

John Cloud, a Mohawk boy, lives in upstate New York, but he goes to visit his father who is working on the Empire State Building

"Rich, sunlit gouache illustrations establish the 1930s setting for this well-told story." Horn Book Guide

Kirk, Daniel

Keisha Ann can! [by] Daniel Kirk. G.P. Putnam's Sons 2008 unp il $15.99

Grades: PreK K 1 2   E

1. School stories 2. Stories in rhyme
ISBN 978-0-399-24179-6; 0-399-24179-5
                        LC 2007-034815

Keisha Ann is proud of all the things she can do during her day at school.

The "rhyming text . . . is catchy and upbeat. . . . Gouache paintings done in a striking, childlike style are filled with motion and color. . . . The images are clear and crisp, making the book ideal for sharing aloud. The story ends on a positive, all-inclusive note." SLJ

Library mouse. Abrams Books for Young Readers 2007 unp il $15.95 *

Grades: K 1 2 3   E

1. Authorship—Fiction   2.   Mice—Fiction
3. Libraries—Fiction
ISBN 978-0-8109-93464   LC 2006031851

Sam, a shy but creative mouse who lives in a library, decides to write and illustrate his own stories which he places on the shelves with the other library books but when children find the tales, they all want to meet the author.

"In a rainbow of colors, the art, which features a slightly flattened perspective, ranges from small oval pictures of Sam busily sharpening pencils with his teeth to full-page views of the busy library. . . . This is ready-made to introduce a classroom writing activity. . . . This is fun, fun, fun." Booklist

Kirsch, Vincent X.

Natalie & Naughtily. Bloomsbury Children's Books 2008 unp il $16.99; lib bdg $17.89

Grades: K 1 2 3   E

1. Twins—Fiction 2. Sisters—Fiction 3. Department stores—Fiction
ISBN   978-1-59990-269-2;   1-59990-269-9;
978-1-59990-320-0 (lib bdg); 1-59990-320-2 (lib bdg)
                        LC 2007-51098

Natalie and Naughtily Nopps live above their family's department store and love to play there, but one particularly busy day they discover that 'helping' is even better than playing.

"Readers will pore over the intricately detailed watercolor and pencil illustrations of each floor of the department store while chuckling over the girls' ideas of helpfulness." Horn Book Guide

Kirwan, Wednesday

Minerva the monster. Sterling 2008 unp il $14.95

Grades: PreK K 1 2   E

1. Monsters—Fiction 2. Family life—Fiction
ISBN 978-1-4027-5718-1; 1-4027-5718-2
                        LC 2007043376

Feeling out of sorts, Minerva pretends to be a monster, but after realizing that monsters do not eat cookies, read stories, or sleep in nice warm beds, she decides to rejoin her family.

"The gouache and colored-pencil illustrations are crisp, bright, and full of mischief, much like Minerva herself. This book will be a hit with readers." SLJ

Another title about Minerva is:
Nobody notices Minerva (2007)

Kitamura, Satoshi

Stone Age boy. Candlewick Press 2007 32p il $15.99

Grades: K 1 2 3   E

1. Stone Age—Fiction 2. Prehistoric peoples—Fiction
ISBN 978-0-7636-3474-2; 0-7636-3474-3
                        LC 2007025614

"A boy walking in the woods finds himself falling . . . through time and space, landing in the Stone Age. He befriends a girl named Om and learns about prehistoric society by watching her people make fire, prepare food, use tools, and celebrate a successful hunt. . . . Kitmaura makes Om's society come alive. . . . Sentences are concise and easy to read. . . . The well-designed pages make effective use of white space." Horn Book

Kladstrup, Kristin

The gingerbread pirates; illustrated by Matt Tavares. Candlewick Press 2009 unp il $16.99 *

Grades: K 1 2 3   E

1. Cookies—Fiction 2. Pirates—Fiction 3. Christmas—Fiction
ISBN 978-0-7636-3223-6; 0-7636-3223-6
                        LC 2007-23171

When Jim's gingerbread pirate, Captain Cookie, comes alive, the tasty treat prepares to battle Santa Claus, who likes to eat cookies on Christmas Eve.

"An exciting story and full-page, dramatically composed paintings depicting harrowing adventures with a mouse, a cat, and the crew imprisoned in a cookie jar make this a good holiday read-aloud." SLJ

Kleven, Elisa

The apple doll; [by] Elisa Kleven. Farrar, Straus & Giroux 2007 unp il $16 *

Grades: PreK K 1 2   E

1. Dolls—Fiction 2. Apples—Fiction 3. School stories
ISBN 978-0-374-30380-8; 0-374-30380-0
                        LC 2006040981

Lizzy is scared to start school, so she makes a doll out of an apple from her favorite tree to take with her on the first day and keep her company. Includes instructions for making an apple doll

"Kleven's lovely mixed-media collage illustrations

Kleven, Elisa—*Continued*

. . . are filled with eye-catching detail and activity. A sweet story about accepting change, working together, and forming new friendships." SLJ

Klinting, Lars

What do you want? [translated from the Swedish by Maria Lundin] Groundwood Books/House of Anansi Press 2006 unp il $15.95; board book $7.95

Grades: PreK   E

1. Wishes—Fiction 2. Board books for children

ISBN 0-88899-636-5; 978-0-88899-988-7 (board book)

Original Swedish edition 2003

"Each right-hand page of this little picture book begins with a phrase such as, 'The bumblebee wants . . . 'Turn the page, and the rest is revealed: 'its flower.' . . . This simple pattern repeats throughout the book, forming a guessing game." Booklist

"This diminutive book is mesmerizing in its calm simplicity. Cream-colored pages provide the backdrop to clear, precise color illustrations that are executed with artistic aplomb." SLJ

Klise, Kate

Shall I knit you a hat? a Christmas yarn; illustrated by M. Sarah Klise. H. Holt 2004 unp il $16.95; pa $6.99 *

Grades: PreK K 1 2   E

1. Rabbits—Fiction 2. Animals—Fiction 3. Christmas—Fiction 4. Hats—Fiction

ISBN 0-8050-7318-3; 0-312-37139-X (pa)

LC 2003-22497

When Mother Rabbit knits a warm winter hat for Little Rabbit, he likes it so much that he suggests they make hats for all of their friends as Christmas gifts

"The acrylic artwork glows with humor and radiates warmth." Booklist

Other titles about Little Rabbit are:

Why do you cry?: not a sob story (2006)

Imagine Harry (2007)

Little Rabbit and the night mare (2008)

Little Rabbit and the Meanest Mother on Earth (2010)

Stand straight, Ella Kate; the true story of a real giant; pictures by M. Sarah Klise. Dial Books for Young Readers 2010 unp il $16.99 *

Grades: K 1 2 3   E

1. Ewing, Ella Kate, 1872-1913—Fiction 2. Giants—Fiction

ISBN 978-0-8037-3404-3; 0-8037-3404-2

A fictionalized biography of Ella Kate Ewing, born in 1872, who was eight feet tall by the age of seventeen and who became financially independent by traveling the country for nearly twenty years appearing at museums, exhibitions, and in circus shows.

"The story is well told in straightforward prose with lots of dialogue, and Ella's strength of character shines through. The stylized acrylic illustrations add much to the text, using bright colors and emphasizing Ella's height from various perspectives." SLJ

Kloske, Geoffrey

Once upon a time, the end; (asleep in 60 seconds); by Geoffrey Kloske and Barry Blitt. Atheneum Books for Young Readers 2005 25p il $15.95

Grades: PreK K 1 2   E

1. Bedtime—Fiction 2. Fairy tales

ISBN 0-689-86619-4

"An Anne Schwartz Book"

A tired father takes only a few sentences to tell a number of classic tales in order to get the persistent listener to fall asleep.

"Blitt's ink-and-watercolor illustrations are amusing, with fine lines and soothing colors underscoring the comedy in the characters and situations." SLJ

Knapman, Timothy

Guess what I found in Dragon Wood? by Timothy Knapman; illustrated by Gwen Millward. Bloomsbury Children's Books 2008 unp il $16.95

Grades: PreK K 1 2   E

1. Dragons—Fiction

ISBN 978-1-59990-190-9; 1-59990-190-0

LC 2007018847

A young dragon finds a boy and introduces him to his family, friends, and teacher, but it is clear that the boy would like to return to his faraway home

"Executed with humor and cozy, scaly charm. . . . The tidy linework in the line-and-watercolor art adds a certain comic formality to the dragonworld." Bull Cent Child Books

Mungo and the spiders from space; illustrated by Adam Stower. Dial Books for Young Readers 2008 c2007 unp il $16.99

Grades: PreK K 1 2   E

1. Comic books, strips, etc.—Fiction 2. Science fiction

ISBN 978-0-8037-3277-3; 0-8037-3277-5

First published 2007 in the United Kingdom

"Mungo discovers the last page is missing from his secondhand picture book; how will he learn what happens to Captain Galacticus and Gizmo? Mungo himself provides the ending when, suddenly, he is pulled into the book and saves the universe. The brightly colored comic-book format, busy with rocket ships, space creatures, and humorous details, weaves Mungo's story into this metafictional adventure." Horn Book Guide

Knowlton, Laurie Lazzaro

A young man's dance; [by] Laurie Knowlton; paintings by Layne Johnson. Boyds Mills Press 2006 unp il $15.95

Grades: K 1 2 3   E

1. Grandmothers—Fiction 2. Old age—Fiction 3. Alzheimer's disease—Fiction

ISBN 1-59078-259-3   LC 2005021138

Grandma Ronnie's grandson has a hard time adjusting to her needing a wheelchair, living in a nursing home, and not recognizing him when he comes to visit her

"Swirling, dancing colors, both muted and sunny, accompany this lyrical story. . . . Oil paintings reveal clear, expressive faces on soft, fluid backgrounds that breathe action." SLJ

Knudsen, Michelle

Bugged! illustrated by Blanche Sims. Kane Press 2008 32p il (Science solves it!) pa $5.95

Grades: 1 2 3   E

1. Mosquitoes—Fiction

ISBN 978-1-57565-259-7 (pa); 1-57565-259-5 (pa)

LC 2007026567

Tired of being covered in itchy mosquito bites, Riley uses science to investigate why mosquitoes are more attracted to him than to his friends.

"Clear and simple sentences, colorful realistic illustrations, and diverse characters all contribute to this appealing easy reader. . . . Riley's activities serve as a great model of the research process as well as the scientific method." SLJ

Library lion; [by] Michelle Knudsen; illustrated by Kevin Hawkes. Candlewick Press 2006 unp il $15.99; pa $6.99 *

Grades: PreK K 1 2   E

1. Libraries—Fiction 2. Lions—Fiction

ISBN   978-0-7636-2262-6;   0-7636-2262-1; 978-0-7636-3784-2 (pa); 0-7636-3784-X (pa)

LC 2006042578

A lion starts visiting the local library but runs into trouble as he tries to both obey the rules and help his librarian friend

"Hawkes's deft acrylic-and-pencil pictures have appeal for generations of library lovers. They are rich with expression, movement, and detail. . . . This winsome pairing of text and illustration is a natural for storytime and a first purchase for every collection." SLJ

Kohara, Kazuno

Ghosts in the house! [by] Kazuno Kohara. Roaring Brook Press 2008 unp il $12.95 *

Grades: PreK K 1   E

1. Ghost stories 2. Witches—Fiction

ISBN 978-1-59643-427-1; 1-59643-427-9

LC 2008018204

Tired of living in a haunted house, a young witch captures, washes, and turns her pesky ghosts into curtains and a tablecloth

"Kohara's wonderfully distinctive art, all orange and black, has the look of woodcuts. . . . A must-have for Halloween." Booklist

Here comes Jack Frost. Roaring Brook Press 2009 unp il $12.99

Grades: PreK K 1   E

1. Winter—Fiction

ISBN 978-1-59643-442-4; 1-59643-442-2

"A young boy has nobody to play with until a frosty figure named Jack appears. . . . All the boy has to do to ensure more fun is never mention anything warm. . . . The artwork is divine, beginning with the glittered jacket cover. . . . The simple yet creatively rendered shapes are all icy blues and snowy whites. . . . The artful design . . . is what will draw repeat viewers, young and old." Booklist

Kolar, Bob

Big kicks. Candlewick Press 2008 unp il $16.99

Grades: PreK K 1 2   E

1. Bears—Fiction 2. Soccer—Fiction 3. Animals—Fiction

ISBN 978-0-7636-3390-5; 0-7636-3390-9

"Biggie Bear's soccer-playing friends appear at his doorstep . . . begging him to join them. . . . Biggie is a jazz fan who collects stamps. . . . Despite his athletic shortcomings, the score is tied until the bear bends over to grasp a rare stamp on the ground and heads the ball into the net for the winning goal. . . . Kolar's soccer story is just rollicking enough for listeners. . . . Digital cartoons of rounded figures with exaggerated features are brightly hued and presented in detailed scenes that are balanced with less complex spreads." SLJ

Kono, Erin Eitter

Hula lullaby; [by] Erin Eitter Kono. Little, Brown 2005 unp il $15.99

Grades: PreK K 1 2   E

1. Mother-child relationship—Fiction 2. Bedtime—Fiction 3. Hawaii—Fiction

ISBN 0-316-73591-4   LC 2004-10270

Against the backdrop of a beautiful Hawaiian landscape, a young girl cuddles and sleeps in her mother's lap

"The rhyming text becomes almost hypnotic as night deepens around the two and, finally, the girl falls asleep. Glowing with warm colors, which seem all the more brilliant in the night scenes, the gouache-and-pencil illustrations create an idyllic vision of Hawaiian culture." Booklist

Konrad, Marla Stewart

Getting there. Tundra Books 2009 unp il (World vision early readers) $12.95

Grades: PreK K 1 2   E

1. Transportation

ISBN 978-0-88776-867-5; 0-88776-867-9

"This book depicts an ordinary aspect of every child's life—getting from one place to another. . . . What makes it extraordinary are the images that depict the journey: a child in Africa sitting on his mother's shoulders, for example, or a little girl riding a yak for her destination. Each spread includes an easy, large-font sentence or phrase, but it is the stunning color photographs that tell the richer story. Sure to spark questions, observations, and awe." SLJ

Mom and me. Tundra Books 2009 unp il (World vision early readers) $12.95

Grades: PreK K 1 2   E

1. Mother-child relationship

ISBN 978-0-88776-866-8; 0-88776-866-0

"A spare easy-to-read text combined with high-quality, full-color photographs highlights youngsters and mothers throughout the world involved in universal activities such as bathing, feeding, and providing comfort and support. Each spread demonstrates strong emotions and provides evidence of the woman's love and pride in her child. The vivid photos present a variety of settings, including many different cultures, and draw viewers into the pages." SLJ

Kontis, Alethea
Alpha oops! the day Z went first; [by] Alethea Kontis; illustrated by Bob Kolar. Candlewick Press 2006 unp il $15.99
Grades: K 1 2   E
1. Alphabet—Fiction
ISBN 978-0-7636-2728-7; 0-7636-2728-3
                                        LC 2006042310
Chaos ensues when Z thinks that its time for him to go first in the alphabet for a change
"Reflecting the letters' saucy ways, the colorful, stylized artwork dramatizes the action and offers bits of comic byplay for the observant. An alphabet book with attitude." Booklist

Kooser, Ted
Bag in the wind; illustrated by Barry Root. Candlewick 2010 unp il $17.99
Grades: 1 2 3   E
1. Bags—Fiction 2. Recycling—Fiction 3. Landfills—Fiction
ISBN 978-0-7636-3001-0; 0-7636-3001-2
One cold, spring morning, an ordinary grocery bag begins blowing around a landfill, then as it travels down a road, through a stream, and into a town, it is used in various ways by different people, many of whom do not even notice it.
"The muted, dappled colors of Root's gouache and watercolor illustrations are a perfect complement to Kooser's lengthy, meditative passages. . . . An excellent opener for discussions about creative reuse and recycling." Booklist

Kostecki-Shaw, Jenny Sue
My travelin' eye; [by] Jenny Sue Kostecki-Shaw. Henry Holt 2008 unp il $16.95
Grades: K 1 2   E
1. Eye—Fiction 2. Vision—Fiction
ISBN 978-0-8050-8169-5; 0-8050-8169-0
                                        LC 2007007224
Jenny Sue loves that her "travelin' eye" lets her see the world in a special way, and so she is not happy when her teacher suggests that her parents take her to an opthamologist to fix the lazy eye
"Bright colors and patterns warm the realistic story, while graphics-style artwork gives a since of [Jenny] Sue's vision." Booklist

Koster, Gloria
The Peanut-Free Café; illustrated by Maryann Cocca-Leffler. Whitman, A. 2006 unp il $16.95
Grades: K 1 2 3   E
1. Allergy—Fiction 2. Peanuts—Fiction 3. School stories
ISBN 0-8075-6386-2
When a new classmate has a peanut allergy and has to sit in a special area of the lunchroom, Simon reconsiders his love for peanut butter.
"The cartoon-style art is fun, with some moments of exaggerated drama, as when Grant demonstrates what would happen to him if he ate just one peanut." Booklist

Krasnesky, Thad
I always, always get my way; illustrated by David Parkins. Flashlight 2009 unp il $16.95
Grades: PreK K 1 2   E
1. Family life—Fiction
ISBN 978-0-9799746-4-9; 0-9799746-4-X
"Three-year-old Emmy wreaks havoc on her entire household. . . . Krasnesky tells the story with flowing rhyme that accommodates the humor of the plot and heightens Parkins's comical cartoon illustrations." SLJ

Kraus, Robert, 1925-2001
Whose mouse are you? pictures by José Aruego. 30th anniversary ed. Simon & Schuster Books for Young Readers 2000 c1970 unp il $17.95 *
Grades: PreK K   E
1. Mice—Fiction 2. Stories in rhyme
ISBN 0-689-84052-7
A reissue of the title first published 1970 by Macmillan
A lonely little mouse has to be resourceful in order to bring his family back together
"This is an absolute charmer of a picture book, original, tender, and childlike. The rhyming text is so brief, so catchy, and so right that a child will remember the words after one or two readings, and the large, uncluttered illustrations are gay and appealing." Booklist
Other titles about the mouse and his family are:
Come out and play, little mouse (1987)
Mouse in love (2000)
Where are you going, little mouse? (1986)

Krauss, Ruth, 1911-1993
The backward day; story by Ruth Krauss; pictures by Marc Simont. New York Review Children's Collection 2007 unp il (New York Review Children's Collection) $14.95
Grades: PreK K 1   E
1. Morning—Fiction 2. Family—Fiction
ISBN 978-1-59017-237-7; 1-59017-237-X
                                        LC 2007-6747
A reissue of the title first published 1950 by Harper
Having decided that it is backward day, a boy dresses himself first in his coat, last in his socks, and continues in that way with the cooperation of his family.
"The silliness is enhanced by Simont's bold three-color illustrations showing everyone playing along. The universality of Krauss's work assures that a new generation will want to celebrate backward day." Horn Book Guide

Bears; story by Ruth Krauss; pictures by Maurice Sendak. HarperCollins Pubs. 2005 unp il $14.95 *
Grades: PreK   E
1. Bears—Fiction
ISBN 0-06-027994-X
"Michael di Capua Books"
A newly illustrated edition of the title first published 1948
"The 27-word text is full of possibility: 'Bears—Under chairs—Washing hairs—Giving stares—Collecting

Krauss, Ruth, 1911-1993—*Continued*

fares—.' . . . Sendak sets a full-color story in motion on the cover. In a scene both familiar and fresh, a boy in a wolf suit snuggles his stuffed bear in a themed room where the object of his affection is replicated on every conceivable surface. . . . Sure to spark laughter and original wordplay, this is the marriage of two masters." SLJ

The carrot seed; pictures by Crockett Johnson. Harper & Row 1945 unp il $14.99; pa $5.99; bd bk $6.99 *

Grades: PreK K   E

1. Gardening—Fiction

ISBN   0-06-023350-8;   0-06-443210-6   (pa); 0-06-443210-6 (bd bk)

Simple text and picture show how the faith of a small boy, who planted a carrot seed, was rewarded

"Crockett Johnson's pictures are perfect and the brief text is just right." Book Week

The growing story; by Ruth Krauss; illustrated by Helen Oxenbury. HarperCollins 2000 unp il $16.99; lib bdg $17.89 *

Grades: PreK K   E

1. Growth—Fiction

ISBN 0-06-024716-9; 0-06-024717-7 (lib bdg)

LC 97-42822

A newly illustrated edition of the title first published 1947

A little boy worries throughout the summer that he's not getting bigger, but at the end of the season he tries on his winter clothes and realizes that he has grown.

"The story gets right to a child's experiences as it expresses both wondering and wonderment. This comes out beautifully in art that captures the affection between a boy and his hardworking mother who makes a bountiful place of the land they farm." Booklist

A very special house; by Ruth Krauss; pictures by Maurice Sendak. HarperCollins 1981 c1953 unp il $16.95

Grades: PreK K   E

1. Imagination—Fiction

ISBN 0-06-028638-5   LC 2002511422

A Caldecott Medal honor book, 1954

A reissue of the title first published 1953

"The very special house is a house which exists in the imagination of a small boy—a house where the chairs are for climbing, the walls for writing on, and the beds for jumping on; a house where a lion, a giant, or a dead mouse is welcome, and where nobody ever says stop. Told in a chanting rhythm that demands participation by the reader; the imaginary characters, objects, and doings are pictured in line drawings almost as a child would scribble them while the real little boy stands out boldly in bright blue overalls." Booklist

Krebs, Laurie

The Beeman; [text by] Laurie Krebs; [illustrations by] Valeria Cis. Barefoot Books 2008 unp il $16.99

Grades: PreK K 1 2   E

1. Bees—Fiction 2. Grandfathers—Fiction 3. Stories in rhyme

ISBN 978-1-84686-146-8; 1-84686-146-2

A newly illustrated edition of the title first published 2002 by National Geographic

In rhyming text, a child describes the work Grandpa does to take care of honeybees and harvest the honey they make.

"This charming book is visually enticing and just plain fun to read. . . . The acrylic illustrations are done in predominantly muted, pastel shades with occasional touches of bright colors." SLJ

Krensky, Stephen, 1953-

Hanukkah at Valley Forge; illustrated by Greg Harlin. Dutton Children's Books 2006 unp il $17.99

Grades: 1 2 3 4   E

1. Washington, George, 1732-1799—Fiction 2. Hanukkah—Fiction 3. Jews—Fiction 4. United States—History—1775-1783, Revolution—Fiction

ISBN 0-525-47738-1

During the Revolutionary War, a Jewish soldier from Poland lights the menorah on the first night of Hanukkah and tells General George Washington the story of the Maccabees and the miracle that Hanukkah celebrates. Based on factual events.

"Harlin's evocative paintings are rich with period details that successfully bring the settings to life. A well-told story." Booklist

How Santa got his job; illustrated by S.D. Schindler. Simon & Schuster Bks. for Young Readers 1998 unp il hardcover o.p. pa $6.99 *

Grades: PreK K 1 2   E

1. Santa Claus—Fiction

ISBN 0-689-80697-3; 0-689-84668-1 (pa)

LC 97-23474

This "peek at Santa's resume reveals how various odd jobs, like chimney sweep and mail carrier, helped prepare him for his world-famous career. . . . [Schindler's] intricate pen-and-watercolor illustrations make Santa's evolution from boyish redhead to the familiar heavy-set, snowy-bearded character a joy to watch." Publ Wkly

Another title about Santa by this author and illustrator is:

How Santa lost his job (2001)

Noah's bark; illustrated by Roge. Carolrhoda Books 2010 unp il lib bdg $16.95

Grades: K 1 2   E

1. Noah (Biblical figure)—Fiction 2. Noah's ark—Fiction 3. Animals—Fiction 4. Sounds—Fiction

ISBN 978-0-8225-7645-7; 0-8225-7645-7

LC 2007010022

Noah is distracted by animals making whatever sound comes into their heads while he is trying to build, then pilot, the ark, and so he devises a way for each animal to choose only one sound.

Krensky, Stephen, 1953-—*Continued*

"The stylized, brushstroked paintings are embellished with highlighted sound effects and subtle comic expressions. Inventive and sure to elicit a boatload of giggles." Booklist

Sisters of Scituate Light; by Stephen Krensky; illustrated by Stacey Schuett. Dutton Children's Books 2008 unp il $16.99

Grades: 1 2 3   E

1. Massachusetts—Fiction 2. War of 1812—Fiction 3. Lighthouses—Fiction 4. Sisters—Fiction

ISBN 978-0-525-47792-1; 0-525-47792-6

LC 2007028297

In 1814, when their father leaves them in charge of the Scituate lighthouse outside of Boston, two teenaged sisters devise a clever way to avert an attack by a British warship patrolling the Massachusetts coast

"Krensky's fine telling is well matched by Schuett's illustrations, which are especially effective in capturing the colors of the sea and sky." Booklist

Spark the firefighter; by Stephen Krensky; illustrated by Amanda Haley. Dutton Childrens Books 2008 unp il $16.99

Grades: PreK K 1   E

1. Fire fighters—Fiction 2. Dragons—Fiction 3. Fear—Fiction

ISBN 978-0-525-47887-4; 0-525-47887-6

LC 2007050565

Spark's fear of fire has kept him from being a proper dragon, so he takes a job with the Hardscrabble volunteer fire department in hopes of conquering his fear

"Simply told with bright cartoon pictures and a dragon to hold interest, the . . . story teaches fire safety in an appealing way." SLJ

Too many leprechauns; (or how that pot o' gold got to the end of the rainbow); illustrated by Dan Andreasen. Simon & Schuster Books for Young Readers 2007 unp il $12.99 *

Grades: K 1 2 3   E

1. Leprechauns—Fiction 2. Ireland—Fiction

ISBN 0-689-85112-X   LC 2005-20659

Finn O'Finnegan returns home after a year in Dublin and when he finds his village taken over by leprechauns, he must devise a way to get them to leave without making them angry.

"The well-paced story moves along smoothly, enhanced by Andreasen's handsome oil paintings, which picture the setting and characters with equal verve and charm." Booklist

Krishnaswami, Uma, 1956-

Monsoon; pictures by Jamel Akib. Farrar, Straus & Giroux 2003 unp il $16

Grades: K 1 2 3   E

1. Monsoons—Fiction 2. India—Fiction

ISBN 0-374-35015-9   LC 2001-54753

A child in India describes waiting for the monsoon rains to arrive and the worry that they will not come

"Krishnaswami's poetic text rides faithfully on the child's sensibilities. . . . Akib's impressionistic, pastel illustrations make stunning use of extreme perspectives." SLJ

Kroll, Steven

The Hanukkah mice; by Steven Kroll; illustrated by Michelle Shapiro. Marshall Cavendish Children 2008 unp il $14.99

Grades: PreK K 1 2   E

1. Mice—Fiction 2. Hanukkah—Fiction

ISBN 978-0-7614-5428-1; 0-7614-5428-4

LC 2007035003

A family of mice enjoys the doll house and furnishings that Rachel receives as gifts on the eight nights of Hanukkah

"This book would make a wonderful addition to any holiday collection, and will most likely become a new holiday classic that will be cherished by students for years to come." Libr Media Connect

Stuff! reduce, reuse, recycle; illustrated by Steve Cox. Marshall Cavendish 2009 unp il $16.99

Grades: PreK K 1 2   E

1. Rats—Fiction 2. Recycling—Fiction

ISBN 978-0-7614-5570-7; 0-7614-5570-1

LC 2008-12915

Pinch is a pack rat who does not want to give up the possessions that are cluttering his house, but when he finally is persuaded to sell them at a neighborhood tag sale, he discovers the beauty of recycling. Includes tips on "reducing, reusing, and recycling."

"The bright, bold colors convey the friendly tone of the story and ably show the movement from cluttered to clean as Pinch relinquishes his possessions. An admirable introduction to beginning environmentalism for a young audience." Kirkus

Kroll, Virginia L.

Everybody has a teddy; [by] Virginia Kroll; illustrated by Sophie Allsopp. Sterling Pub. 2007 unp il $12.95

Grades: PreK K   E

1. Teddy bears—Fiction 2. Stories in rhyme

ISBN 978-1-4027-3580-6; 1-4027-3580-4

LC 2006005154

A child describes teddy bears owned by other children, from Joshy's giant grizzly to the floppy bear Poppy's grandmother made from socks.

"This light, gentle offering celebrates individuality. . . . The text rolls along with the infectious, easy rhyme and rhythm of a children's song. . . . Cheerful illustrations capture the happy hum of a multicultural classroom filled with kids who paint, play, and look at books." Booklist

Kruusval, Catarina

Franny's friends. R & S Books 2008 unp il $16

Grades: PreK   E

1. Play—Fiction 2. Imagination—Fiction 3. Toys—Fiction

ISBN 978-91-29-66836-0; 91-29-66836-0

"Franny is a sweet little girl who plans a picnic for her seven stuffed animals. The simple outing runs into trouble when the two smallest guests, Itty Bitty Kitty and Little Heddy, fall into a hole and can't get out. . . . Kruusval's pastel-shaded illustrations capture the story's charm. . . . Each animal is drawn with a liveliness that will seem wholly believable to a young child engaged in imaginative play." SLJ

Kulka, Joe, 1965-

Wolf's coming! [by] Joe Kulka. Carolrhoda Books 2007 unp il lib bdg $15.95 *

Grades: PreK K 1   E

1. Animals—Fiction 2. Wolves—Fiction

ISBN 978-1-57505-930-3 (lib. bdg); 1-57505-930-4 (lib bdg)   LC 2006013865

"The simple rhyming text describes the various ways in which the denizens of the forest prepare for Wolf's imminent arrival. . . . Saturated with color, the cartoonlike illustrations depict characters that are more human than animal, but will likely appeal to young children." SLJ

Kurtz, Jane

Faraway home; illustrated by E.B. Lewis. Harcourt Brace & Co. 2000 unp il $16

Grades: PreK K 1 2   E

1. Father-daughter relationship—Fiction 2. African Americans—Fiction 3. Ethiopia—Fiction

ISBN 0-15-200036-4   LC 96-47664

"Gulliver books"

Desta's father, who needs to return briefly to his Ethiopian homeland, describes what it was like for him to grow up there

"Lewis captures the lyricism and rich imagery of the text with his evocative, realistic watercolors." SLJ

Water hole waiting; by Jane and Christopher Kurtz; illustrated by Lee Christiansen. Greenwillow Bks. 2002 unp il $15.95; lib bdg $15.89

Grades: PreK K 1 2   E

1. Monkeys—Fiction 2. Animals—Fiction

ISBN 0-06-029850-2; 0-06-029851-0 (lib bdg)   LC 2001-23040

A thirsty monkey waits as the larger animals drink from the water hole on the African savanna

"Richly colored pastel drawings and precise, surprising word choices make this story a natural for sharing with a group." SLJ

Kushner, Lawrence, 1943-

In God's hands; [by] Lawrence Kushner and Gary Schmidt; illustrated by Matthew J. Baek. Jewish Lights Pub. 2005 unp il $16.99

Grades: K 1 2 3   E

1. Jews—Fiction 2. Miracles—Fiction 3. Prayer—Fiction

ISBN 1-58023-224-8   LC 2005001669

While contemplating their problems in a synagogue, Jacob and David, one man rich, the other poor, come to realize their role in making miracles happen. Inspired by an ancient legend.

"This lovely piece of bookmaking combines a good tale with a strong, easily understood message. Baek's artwork, set against buff-colored pages and highlighted in shades of blue, uses a variety of angles, placements, and design elements to invite interest." Booklist

Kuskin, Karla

A boy had a mother who bought him a hat. Harper 2010 unp il $16.99

Grades: PreK K 1   E

1. Stories in rhyme 2. Mother-son relationship—Fiction

ISBN 978-0-06-075330-6; 0-06-075330-7

A newly illustrated edition of the title first published 1976

After a boy's mother buys him a hat, she buys him a mouse, shoes, boots, skis, mask, cello, and an elephant-none of which he is ever without.

This "showcases the late poet's mastery of verse and her acute awareness of both children's sense of humore and the value they place on special belongings. . . . Hawkes' pictures . . . are skillfully executed and include some hidden surprises." Booklist

Green as a bean. Laura Geringer Books 2007 unp il $16.99; lib bdg $17.89

Grades: PreK K 1 2   E

1. Stories in rhyme

ISBN   978-0-06-075332-0;   0-06-075332-3; 978-0-06-075334-4 (lib bdg); 0-06-075334-X (lib bdg)   LC 2005017881

First published 1960 with title: Square as a house

Questions in verse about the many things you could be if you were square or soft or loud or red or small or fat or fierce or dark

This "is sure to inspire loud crowd participation. . . . Lines in expertly modulated rhyme and meter . . . are nicely extended in Iwai's bright, fanciful acrylic paintings." Booklist

I am me. Simon & Schuster Bks. for Young Readers 2000 unp il $14.95

Grades: PreK K   E

1. Family life—Fiction

ISBN 0-689-81473-9   LC 98-7911

After being told how she resembles other members of her family, a young girl states positively and absolutely that she is "NO ONE ELSE BUT ME"

"The illustrations set the story during a family trip to the beach, and in Wolcott's brightly colored double-page spreads, all the rhythmic curves . . . show the natural connections around us, the loving family embrace across generations, and the child's exuberant energy as her own individual self." Booklist

So what's it like to be a cat? Atheneum Books for Young Readers 2005 unp il $15.95; pa $6.99 *

Grades: PreK K 1 2   E

1. Cats—Fiction

ISBN 0-689-84733-5; 0-689-85930-9 (pa)   LC 2003-27338

A cat answers a young child's questions about such things as how much and where it sleeps, and whether or not it likes living with people.

"Lewin's charming, uncluttered watercolors extend the spare poetry's precise wit with swooping bold lines that beautifully capture both characters' movements and moods." Booklist

Kvasnosky, Laura McGee, 1951-

Really truly Bingo; [by] Laura McGee
Kvasnosky. Candlewick Press 2008 unp il $15.99
Grades: PreK K 1   E
    1. Imaginary playmates—Fiction 2. Dogs—Fiction
    ISBN 978-0-7636-3210-6; 0-7636-3210-4
                             LC 2007-40103
When Bea wants to play, her busy mother tells her to
use her imagination—outside—and soon Bea and a talk-
ing dog, Bingo, are getting into all kinds of mischief.
    "This book, with its child-sized problem and child-
sized solution, is a fresh take on imaginary friends."
Horn Book Guide

Zelda and Ivy, the runaways. Candlewick Press
2006 42p il $14.99; pa $4.99 *
Grades: PreK K 1 2   E
    1. Foxes—Fiction 2. Sisters—Fiction
    ISBN   0-7636-2689-9;   978-0-7636-2689-1;
    0-7636-3061-6 (pa); 978-0-7636-3061-4 (pa)
                             LC 2005-54282
In three short stories, fox sisters Zelda and Ivy run
away from home, bury a time capsule, and take advan-
tage of some creative juice.
    "Bright, expressive cartoon illustrations complement
the fine writing in this beginning reader." SLJ
    Other titles about Zelda and Ivy are:
Zelda and Ivy (1998)
Zelda and Ivy and the boy next door (1999)
Zelda and Ivy one Christmas (2000)
Zelda and Ivy: keeping secrets (2009)

Kwon, Yoon-Duck, 1960-

My cat copies me. Kane/Miller 2007 unp il
$15.95
Grades: PreK K 1 2   E
    1. Cats—Fiction
    ISBN 978-1-933605-26-5
Original Korean edition, 2005
    "Kwon tells the story of a little girl and her cat. The
pet may act coy and shy when the child seeks its affection, but when she turns away, the feline begins to follow her and mimics her actions. . . . The bright, colorful
illustrations feature light gray outlining and accents that
add a luminous quality and increase the imaginative nature of the drawings." SLJ

La Chanze

Little diva; illustrated by Brian Pinkney. Feiwel
and Friends 2010 unp il $16.99
Grades: PreK K   E
    1. Theater—Fiction 2. Mother-daughter relationship—
Fiction
    ISBN 978-0-312-37010-7; 0-312-37010-5
    "LaChanze, a star of stage and screen herself, supplies
a peek at the life of a Broadway performer in this enticing story about a girl's dream of one day conquering the
Great White Way. Nena relates her activities from morning to night as she works as a 'D.I.T.—Diva inTraining.'
After trying on her mother's clothes, dancing and singing
about the house, and watching her mother practice her
yoga, the two spend the afternoon at the theater, where
the woman is the star. . . . Pinkney catches the mood

with sprawling thick black lines and swirling soft hues
of pink, lavender, blue, and tawny, bringing a breezy
lightness that fits this upbeat tale." SLJ

Labatt, Mary, 1944-

Pizza for Sam; written by Mary Labatt;
illustrated by Marisol Sarrazin. Kids Can Press
2003 32p il (Kids can read) $14.95; pa $3.95
Grades: PreK K 1 2   E
    1. Dogs—Fiction
    ISBN 1-55337-329-4; 1-55337-331-6 (pa)
    "Sam the dog watches eagerly as his owners set out
cakes, cookies, and pies for a party. . . . Sam's presented with traditional dog food, but he turns up his
snout, preferring to go hungry . . . until a pizza arrives
and he finds his perfect puppy chow. Winsome pastel illustrations combine with a few large-type sentences per
page in an attractive, uncluttered layout. The basic, repet-
itive text is filled with action, noise, and enough sus-
pense and silliness to engage new readers." Booklist
    Other titles about Sam are:
A friend for Sam (2003)
A parade for Sam (2005)
Sam at the seaside (2006)
Sam finds a monster (2004)
Sam gets lost (2004)
Sam goes next door (2006)
Sam goes to school (2004)
Sam's first Halloween (2003)
Sam's snowy day (2005)

Lacombe, Benjamin, 1982-

Cherry and Olive; [by] Benjamin Lacombe.
Walker & Co. 2007 unp il $16.95
Grades: PreK K 1 2   E
    1. Dogs—Fiction 2. Friendship—Fiction
    ISBN   978-0-8027-9707-0;   0-8027-9707-5;
    978-0-8027-9708-7 (lib bdg); 0-8027-9708-3 (lib bdg)
                             LC 2007006671
Orginial French edition 2006
Cherry, a shy girl who longs for a friend, falls in love
with a lost puppy at the shelter where her father works
and names the dog Olive.
    "The illustrations are somewhat stylized. . . . The art-
ist's palette is dark and rich in the beginning but lightens
as Cherry's world expands. . . . This title will be particularly useful . . . anywhere . . . where lonely children
might need some help fitting in with others." SLJ

LaMarche, Jim

Lost and found. Chronicle Books 2009 unp il
$17.99
Grades: PreK K 1   E
    1. Dogs—Fiction 2. Lost and found possessions—Fic-
tion 3. Short stories
    ISBN 978-0-8118-6401-5; 0-8118-6401-4
                             LC 2008-23009
Contents: Molly; Ginger; Yuki
    "In the first story, Anna's retriever Molly leads the
way home after the girl runs off in anger and gets lost;
in the second, Jules enjoys a happy reunion with his pet
Ginger after the scruffy dog disappears in the woods.
Jack finds a husky named Yuki, whose owner gives

LaMarche, Jim—*Continued*

Jack's single mother a fresh start in the final tale. . . . LaMarche's gentle artwork distinguishes this collection, gracefully rendering the special bond between dogs and children. . . . The soft colors of autumn unite the stories visually, and the pages are full of activity." Publ Wkly

The raft. Lothrop, Lee & Shepard Bks. 2000 unp il $15.99; pa $6.99 *

Grades: 2 3 4 5   E

1. Grandmothers—Fiction 2. Rafting (Sports)—Fiction 3. Animals—Fiction

ISBN 0-688-13977-9; 0-06-443856-2 (pa)

LC 99-35546

Reluctuant Nicky spends a wonderful summer with Grandma who introduces him to the joy of rafting down the river near her home and watching the animals along the banks

"LaMarche introduces young readers to a visually resplendent, magical world. . . . Nicky's descriptive first-person narration supports the radiant, expressive illustrations." SLJ

Up; by Jim LaMarche. Chronicle Books 2006 unp il $16.95

Grades: PreK K 1 2   E

1. Fishing—Fiction 2. Psychokinesis—Fiction 3. Whales—Fiction

ISBN 978-0-8118-4445-1; 0-8118-4445-5

LC 2005029793

Tired of being called Mouse and staying home while his brother helps on their father's fishing boat, Daniel proves himself when a problem arises that he can solve using his newly-developed, extraordinary talent.

"The soft acrylics capture the low light, palpable chill, and blue-gray color scheme of Daniel's fishing village. This is an inspiring and (yes) uplifting title about pursuing one's own talents and possibilities." SLJ

Lamorisse, Albert, 1922-1970

The red balloon. Doubleday 1957 c1956 unp il $16.95; pa $12.95

Grades: PreK K 1 2   E

1. Balloons—Fiction 2. Paris (France)—Fiction

ISBN 0-385-00343-9; 0-385-14297-8 (pa)

Original French edition, 1956

"The chief feature of this book is the stunning photographs, many in color, which were taken during the filming of the French movie of the same name. A little French schoolboy Pascal catches a red balloon which turns out to be magic. The streets of Paris form a backdrop for a charming story and superb photographs." Libr J

Lamstein, Sarah, 1943-

A big night for salamanders; [by] Sarah Marwil Lamstein; art by Carol Benioff. Boyds Mills Press 2010 unp il $17.95

Grades: K 1 2 3   E

1. Salamanders—Fiction

ISBN 978-1-9324-2598-7; 1-9324-2598-5

"One spring evening . . . spotted salamanders emerge from their winter burrows and make their way to a ver-

nal pool. . . . Young Evan and his parents . . . carry salamanders across the road and even stop cars to ask drivers to slow down and watch out for their amphibian neighbors. . . . The dual text offers Evan's story in plain type and information about salamanders in italics. Readers intrigued by salamanders will learn plenty here and more in the back matter. . . . The gouache paintings add color and drama to this informative picture book." Booklist

Includes glossary and bibliographical references

Landolf, Diane Wright

What a good big brother! by Diane Wright Landolf; paintings by Steve Johnson & Lou Fancher. Random House 2009 unp il $16.99; lib bdg $19.99 *

Grades: PreK K 1 2   E

1. Siblings—Fiction 2. Infants—Fiction 3. Family life—Fiction

ISBN 978-0-375-84258-0; 0-375-84258-6; 978-0-375-94258-7 (lib bdg); 0-375-94258-0 (lib bdg)

LC 2006015181

Cameron is always ready to help when his baby sister cries, whether by handing wipes to his father during a diaper change or finding the nursing pillow for his mother, until one day, when no one else can stop Sadie's tears, her big brother succeeds and gets a wonderful reward

Landolf's "simple, descriptive writing should go a long way in alleviating . . . the anxieties of newly minted sibling rivalry. Johnson and Fancher . . . offer a stunning visual counterpoint with their most luxuriant work to date." Publ Wkly

Landry, Leo

Space boy; written and illustrated by Leo Landry. Houghton Mifflin Company 2007 unp il $16

Grades: PreK K 1   E

1. Space flight to the moon—Fiction 2. Family life—Fiction 3. Bedtime—Fiction

ISBN 978-0-618-60568-2; 0-618-60568-1

LC 2006-26081

Having decided not to go to bed because his home is too noisy, Nicholas flies his spaceship to the Moon, where he enjoys a snack, takes a moonwalk, and enjoys the quiet—until he realizes what he is missing at home.

"Simple lines and shapes become much more in the bright watercolor-and-pen paintings. . . . Kids who love outer space and rockets will adore this quiet, imaginative adventure." SLJ

Landström, Lena, 1943-

A hippo's tale; [by] Lena Landström; translated by Joan Sandin. R&S Books 2007 unp il $15

Grades: PreK K 1 2   E

1. Hippopotamus—Fiction 2. Africa—Fiction

ISBN 978-91-29-66603-8; 91-29-66603-1

Original Swedish edition 1993

Deep in the middle of Africa, Mrs. Hippopotamus enjoys having quiet time all to herself, especially when bathing. But then a monkey shows up and disturbs her solitude.

Landström, Lena, 1943-—*Continued*

"This quiet picture book manages to convey a wide range of human emotions through its hippo heroine. . . . The text is simple, and Landstrom's paintings create a pleasing setting and expressive characters with a minimum of fuss." Booklist

Other titles in this series are:
The little hippo's adventure (2002)
The new hippos (2003)

LaReau, Kara

Rabbit & Squirrel; a tale of war & peas; [by] Kara LaReau; Scott Magoon. Harcourt 2008 unp il $16

Grades: K 1 2 3   E
1. Gardening—Fiction   2.   Rabbits—Fiction
3. Squirrels—Fiction
ISBN 978-0-15-206307-8; 0-15-206307-2
LC 2006-101618

Rabbit and Squirrel are neighbors who never even say hello until someone starts damaging their gardens, and then they blame one another and start a fight that continues even after they meet the real culprit.

"The textured, earth-tone illustrations assist in identifying the real garden grabber [and] . . . both text and illustration suggest the bickering may become wearisome and the two may actually become friends." Libr Media Connect

LaRochelle, David, 1960-

The end; story by David LaRochelle; illustrations by Richard Egielski. Arthur A. Levine Books 2007 unp il $16.99 paperback o.p. *

Grades: PreK K 1 2 3   E
1. Fairy tales
ISBN   978-0-439-64011-4;   0-439-64011-3;
978-0-439-64012-1 (pa); 0-439-64012-1 (pa)
LC 2005-24044

When a princess makes some lemonade, she starts a chain of events involving a fire-breathing dragon, one hundred rabbits, a hungry giant, and a handsome knight

"Turning the standard fairy-tale formula on its head, LaRochelle begins his story at the end. . . . The hand-lettered text, enclosed in streaming banners, consists of terse, declarative statements that are lavishly expounded upon by the illustrations." SLJ

Larsen, Andrew

The imaginary garden; [by] Andrew Larsen; [illustrated] by Irene Luxbacher. Kids Can Press 2009 unp il $16.95

Grades: PreK K 1 2   E
1. Gardens—Fiction   2. Grandfathers—Fiction
3. Imagination—Fiction
ISBN 978-1-55453-279-7; 1-55453-279-5

"Theo's Poppa's new apartment has no garden, and the windy balcony does not promise to be a good growing spot. But Theo proposes an imaginary garden, and she and her grandfather begin to fill a large blank canvas with a stone wall for the vines to climb on, early springtime flowers, and a visiting robin. . . . The lively artwork is rendered in pen and ink and multimedia collage. The warmth of the grandparent/grandchild relationship is evident." SLJ

Lasky, Kathryn

Marven of the Great North Woods; written by Kathryn Lasky; illustrated by Kevin Hawkes. Harcourt Brace & Co. 1997 unp il hardcover o.p. pa $7

Grades: K 1 2 3   E
1. Lumber and lumbering—Fiction 2. Minnesota—Fiction 3. Jews—Fiction
ISBN 0-15-200104-2; 0-15-216826-5 (pa)
LC 96-2334

When his Jewish parents send him to a Minnesota logging camp to escape the influenza epidemic of 1918, ten-year-old Marven finds a special friend

"Inspired by her father's childhood, Lasky's handsomely crafted picture book is also a captivating survival story. . . . Contributing to the book's vivid sense of time and place are Hawkes' graphically accomplished paintings." Booklist

Poodle and Hound; illustrated by Mitch Vane. Charlesbridge 2009 48p il $12.95

Grades: 1 2 3 4   E
1. Dogs—Fiction 2. Friendship—Fiction
ISBN 978-1-58089-322-0; 1-58089-322-8
LC 2008025343

In three adventures, Hound and Poodle discover how much they enjoy each other's company, in spite of, or maybe because of, their differences.

"The lively prose, in large, well-spaced print, provides an entertaining, accessible celebration of friendship. . . . The colorful, watercolor-and-ink illustrations incorporate word balloons and amusing, whimsical details." Booklist

Lawrence, John, 1933-

This little chick. Candlewick Press 2002 unp il $15.99; bd bk $6.99 *

Grades: PreK   E
1. Chickens—Fiction 2. Domestic animals—Fiction
3. Stories in rhyme
ISBN 0-7636-1716-4; 0-7636-2882-4 (bd bk)
LC 2001-35633

A little chick shows that he can make the sounds of the animals in his neighborhood

"The silly farce and raucous noises will . . . delight toddlers, and Lawrence coaxes plenty of character from his boisterous, woodcut animal characters." Booklist

Lazo, Caroline Evensen

Someday when my cat can talk; by Caroline Lazo; illustrated by Kyrsten Brooker. Schwartz & Wade Books 2008 unp il $16.99; lib bdg $19.99

Grades: K 1 2   E
1. Cats—Fiction 2. Imagination—Fiction 3. Stories in rhyme 4. Voyages and travels—Fiction 5. Europe—Fiction
ISBN   978-0-375-83754-8;   0-375-83754-X;
978-0-375-93754-5 (lib bdg); 0-375-93754-4 (lib bdg)
LC 2006101809

A girl imagines what her cat would tell her about its exotic travels to such places as the foggy English coast, Spanish bullfights, and an art gallery in Monmartre, France. Includes facts about the places mentioned

"Brooker's illustrations, rendered in collage and oil

Lazo, Caroline Evensen—_Continued_

paint, have the look and feel of a scrapbook. . . . 'The Facts Behind the Story' presents some tidbits about some of the locales, but they seem unnecessary after such a fanciful journey. Rather, the book should be enjoyed as the whimsical daydream that it is." SLJ

Lazo Gilmore, Dorina K.

Cora cooks pancit; written by Dorina Lazo Gilmore; illustrated by Kristi Valiant. Shen's Books 2009 unp il $17.95 *

Grades: PreK K 1 2 3   E

1. Cooking—Fiction 2. Filipino Americans—Fiction

ISBN 978-1-885008-35-0; 1-885008-35-X

LC 2008045836

When all her older siblings are away, Cora's mother finally lets her help make pancit, a Filipino noodle dish. Includes recipe for pancit.

"Clear expository prose explains how to perform kitchen tasks. . . . These scenes effectively model how adults can introduce children to cooking. The simple, direct style also makes the book equally well suited as a read-aloud and for newly independent readers. The artwork nicely complements the text, as Valiant's warm hues of gold, red, and orange highlight the family's loving relationship." SLJ

Le Guin, Ursula K., 1929-

Cat dreams; illustrations by S.D. Schindler. Orchard Books 2009 unp il lib bdg $16.99 *

Grades: PreK K 1   E

1. Stories in rhyme 2. Cats—Fiction 3. Dreams—Fiction

ISBN 978-0-545-04216-1 (lib bdg); 0-545-04216-X (lib bdg)   LC 2008-46299

Presents a feline dreamland where it rains mice, all the dogs have run away, and a big bowl of kibbles and cream is waiting

"Easy rhyming text will be quickly memorized, but the realistic, full-bleed watercolor illustrations will keep youngsters turning the pages. A perfect fit for storytimes on cats, naps and dreams." Kirkus

Leaf, Munro, 1905-1976

The story of Ferdinand; illustrated by Robert Lawson. Viking 1936 unp il $17.99; pa $6.99 *

Grades: PreK K 1 2   E

1. Bulls—Fiction 2. Bullfights—Fiction 3. Spain—Fiction

ISBN 0-670-67424-9; 0-14-050234-3 (pa)

"Ferdinand was a peace-loving little bull who preferred smelling flowers to making a reputation for himself in the bull ring. His story is told irresistibly in pictures and few words." Wis Libr Bull

"The drawings picture not only Ferdinand but Spanish scenes and characters as well." N Y Public Libr

Lechner, John, 1966-

The clever stick. Candlewick Press 2009 unp il $14.99

Grades: K 1 2 3   E

1. Drawing—Fiction 2. Communication—Fiction

ISBN 978-0-7636-3950-1; 0-7636-3950-8

LC 2008024230

"A clever stick longs to express himself but can't find a way to make his thoughts understood. Discouraged, he drags himself home and discovers that the lines he creates in the sand make shapes and even pictures. . . . Lechner's gently funny ink and watercolor pictures convey the story's meaning." Horn Book Guide

Sticky Burr: adventures in Burrwood Forest; [by] John Lechner. Candlewick Press 2007 unp il $15.99; pa $6.99

Grades: K 1 2 3   E

1. Forests and forestry—Fiction 2. Insects—Fiction

ISBN   978-0-7636-3054-6;   0-7636-3054-3; 978-0-7636-3567-1 (pa); 0-7636-3567-7 (pa)

LC 2006049575

Sticky Burr is on the verge of being kicked out of his village in Burrwood Forest because he is not prickly enough to suit some of the other burrs, but when the village is attacked by wild dogs, Sticky Burr and his friends come to the rescue.

"Written in graphic-novel style, the lively and sometimes punny dialogue leads young readers through Sticky's exciting escapades. . . . The illustrations are simple, colorful, and easy to follow." SLJ

Another title about Stick Burr is:

Sticky Burr: the prickly peril

Lee, Ho Baek, 1962-

While we were out. Kane/Miller 2003 unp il $15.95

Grades: PreK K 1 2   E

1. Rabbits—Fiction

ISBN 1-929132-44-1   LC 2002-112325

"A white rabbit who lives on the patio notices that his family has gone to Grandma's, leaving the house empty. Now the house is hers. Simple line-and-wash pictures alternating with radiant full-page paintings follow the rabbit as she indulges in a multitude of obviously long-held wishes. . . . This Korean import is amusing, yes, but there is also a delicacy and intelligence that pervades the tale. A definite cut above." Booklist

Lee, Suzy

Wave. Chronicle Books 2008 unp il $15.99 *

Grades: PreK K   E

1. Beaches—Fiction 2. Ocean—Fiction 3. Stories without words

ISBN 978-0-8118-5924-0; 0-8118-5924-X

LC 2007-62026

A wordless picture book that shows a little girl's first experiences at the beach, as she goes from being afraid of the roaring waves to playing on the shore while gulls soar overhead.

"A panoramic trim size beautifully supports the expansiveness of the beach. . . . Loosely rendered charcoal and acrylic images curl and flow like water and reflect

Lee, Suzy—*Continued*

playfulness, especially in the facial and bodily expressions of the child and seagulls. . . . A simple, well-crafted story." SLJ

Lee, YJ

The little moon princess; written and illustrated by YJ Lee. HarperCollins 2010 unp il $16.99

Grades: K 1 2   E

1. Princesses—Fiction 2. Sparrows—Fiction 3. Stars—Fiction

ISBN 978-0-06-154736-2; 0-06-154736-0

LC 2009-9294

With the help of a friendly sparrow, the Little Moon Princess, who is afraid of the dark, uses the jewels on the surface of her moon to light up the sky.

"Lee's stunning use of watercolor and ink creates the illusion of light, and her art offers readers a breathtaking view of the night sky. A lovely read-aloud." SLJ

Lee-Tai, Amy, 1964-

A place where sunflowers grow; story, Amy Lee-Tai; illustrations by Felicia Hoshino; [Japanese translation, Marc Akio Lee] Children's Book Press 2006 31p il $16.95

Grades: 1 2 3   E

1. Japanese Americans—Evacuation and relocation, 1942-1945—Fiction 2. Bilingual books—English-Japanese

ISBN 978-0-8923-9215-5; 0-8923-9215-0

LC 2005032957

While she and her family are interned at Topaz Relocation Center during World War II, Mari gradually adjusts as she enrolls in an art class, makes a friend, plants sunflowers and waits for them to grow.

"The story is told in both English and Japanese, and the earth-toned illustrations, created using watercolors, ink, tissue paper, and acrylic paint, nicely detail the simple plot." SLJ

Leedy, Loreen, 1959-

Crazy like a fox; a simile story; written and illustrated by Loreen Leedy. Holiday House 2008 unp il lib bdg $16.95; pa $6.95

Grades: K 1 2   E

1. Birthdays—Fiction 2. Parties—Fiction 3. Foxes—Fiction 4. English language—Idioms

ISBN 978-0-8234-1719-3 (lib bdg); 0-8234-1719-0 (lib bdg); 978-0-8234-2248-7 (pa); 0-8234-2248-7 (pa)

LC 2007-051016

"Rufus, a spunky fox in suspenders, rudely startles his friend Babette, a lamb, by roaring 'like...a lion.' She gets 'mad...as a hornet' and chases him, and he eventually leads her to her surprise birthday party. Leedy relates this narrative entirely through similes. Her illustrations emphasize the comparisons as each protagonist is amusingly transformed from one object into another. . . . [Leedy's] vivid illustrations, filled with movement and wide-eyed creatures, will entertain readers." SLJ

The great graph contest; written and illustrated by Loreen Leedy. Holiday House 2005 32p il $16.95; pa $6.95

Grades: 1 2 3   E

1. Graphic methods 2. Frogs—Fiction 3. Lizards—Fiction 4. Snails—Fiction

ISBN 0-8234-1710-7; 0-8234-2029-9 (pa)

LC 2003-62549

Gonk the toad, Chester the snail, and Beezy the lizard hold a contest to see who can make better graphs

"A splashy and colorful offering designed to inform and entertain. . . . The lively text, delivered in large type and contained in dialogue and thought balloons, is engaging and well supported by the vivid, cartoon illustrations." SLJ

Lehman, Barbara, 1963-

Museum trip. Houghton Mifflin 2006 unp il $15

Grades: K 1 2 3   E

1. Art museums—Fiction 2. School stories 3. Stories without words

ISBN 0-618-58125-1   LC 2005052840

In this wordless picture book, a boy imagines himself inside some of the exhibits when he goes on a field trip to an art museum.

"The sturdiness and clarity of the ink-lined, watercolor-and-gouache art juxtaposes wonderfully with the story's airy world of imagination." Booklist

Rainstorm. Houghton Mifflin 2007 unp il $16

Grades: PreK K 1 2   E

1. Play—Fiction 2. Stories without words

ISBN 978-0-618-75639-1; 0-618-75639-6

LC 2006-49318

In this wordless picture book, a boy finds a mysterious key which leads him on an adventure one rainy day.

"Lehman provides purely colored, precisely rendered artwork that capably captures both adventures and emotions." Booklist

The red book. Houghton Mifflin 2004 unp il $12.95 *

Grades: K 1 2 3   E

1. Books and reading—Fiction 2. Stories without words

ISBN 0-618-42858-5

A Caldecott Medal honor book, 2005

This "wordless book tells the complex story of a reader who gets lost, literally, in a little book that has the magic to move her to another place. . . . Done in watercolor, gouache, and ink, the simple, streamlined pictures are rife with invitations to peek inside, to investigate further, and—like a hall of mirrors—reflect, refract, repeat, and reveal. Lehman's story captures the magical possibility that exists every time readers open a book." SLJ

Trainstop. Houghton 2008 unp il $16

Grades: PreK K 1 2   E

1. Railroads—Fiction 2. Imagination—Fiction 3. Stories without words

ISBN 0-618-75640-X

In this wordless picture book, a young girl takes a train and makes a stop at a most unusual place where she has an important task to perform.

Lehman, Barbara, 1963-—*Continued*

Lehman "demonstrates her extraordinary knack for storytelling sans words. . . . Gouache, watercolor, and ink illustrations reveal a bleak cityscape and adults dressed in muted tones—all in pointed contrast to the girl's head-to-toe multicolored outfit. . . . Lehman's true talent is her spot-on depiction of a young child's capacity for criss-crossing the real with the imaginary." Horn Book

Leist, Christina

Jack the bear. Simply Read Books 2009 unp il $16.95

Grades: K 1 2　　　　　　　　　　　　　　E
　　1. Bears—Fiction 2. Friendship—Fiction 3. Kindness—Fiction
　　ISBN 978-1-894965-97-2; 1-894965-97-3

"Nosy Fox wants to know about Jack, the new bear in the area. When Brainy Owl explains that Jack makes the world a better place, Nosy Fox wants to know how Jack can do more than Kings, Queens, philosophers, peace prize winners and scientists to make the world a better place." Libr Media Connect

"It is an earnest message, and Leist spells it out explicitly, but the warmth in the words will hit home with the target audience. The sketchy watercolor-and-crayon illustrations are printed on recycled brown bags, and the visible creases and folded handles add to the book's distinctive look." Booklist

Lendroth, Susan

Ocean wide, ocean deep; illustrated by Raúl Allén. Tricycle Press 2007 unp il $15.99

Grades: K 1 2 3　　　　　　　　　　　　　　E
　　1. Family life—Fiction 2. Sailors—Fiction 3. New England—Fiction 4. Stories in rhyme
　　ISBN 978-1-58246-232-5; 1-58246-232-1
　　　　　　　　　　　　　　　　　LC 2007-18619

In nineteenth-century New England, a young girl watches her baby brother learn to walk and talk while waiting for Papa's return from the sea after he joins the China trade and sails to foreign lands.

"In Allén's American picture book debut, he channels the soft-edged realism and absorption with light shared by 19th-century American painters to create an atmosphere of foreboding. . . . Children in the contemporary equivalent of the narrator's situation—a son or daughter anxious about an absent parent's wellbeing—will appreciate both the distance afforded by the period setting and the comfort of the melodic language and happy ending." Publ Wkly

Lerman, Josh

How to raise Mom and Dad; instructions from someone who figured it out; illustrated by Greg Clarke. Dutton Children's Books 2009 unp il $16.99

Grades: K 1 2　　　　　　　　　　　　　　E
　　1. Parents—Fiction
　　ISBN 978-0-525-47870-6; 0-525-47870-1
　　　　　　　　　　　　　　　　　LC 2008-13886

Advice on how to manipulate your parents in order to avoid eating vegetables, extend your bedtime, or get a puppy.

"The gouache illustrations are as joyful as the text. . . . This is a manual every child will want to read." SLJ

Lester, Helen, 1936-

Hooway for Wodney Wat; illustrated by Lynn Munsinger. Houghton Mifflin 1999 32p il $16; pa $5.95 *

Grades: PreK K 1 2　　　　　　　　　　　　E
　　1. Speech disorders—Fiction 2. School stories
　　ISBN 0-395-92392-1; 0-618-21612-X (pa)
　　　　　　　　　　　　　　　　　LC 98-46149

"Walter Lorraine books"

All his classmates make fun of Rodney because he can't pronounce his name, but it is Rodney's speech impediment that drives away the class bully

"Munsinger's watercolor with pen-and-ink illustrations positively bristle with humor and each rat, mouse, hamster, and capybara is fully realized as both rodent and child." SLJ

The sheep in wolf's clothing; illustrated by Lynn Munsinger. Houghton Mifflin 2007 32p il $16

Grades: PreK K 1 2　　　　　　　　　　　　E
　　1. Sheep—Fiction 2. Wolves—Fiction 3. Clothing and dress—Fiction
　　ISBN 978-0-618-86844-5; 0-618-86844-5
　　　　　　　　　　　　　　　　　LC 2007-00644

"Walter Lorraine books."

Clothing is important to Ewetopia, but her carefully-chosen wolf outfit fails to impress the other sheep at the Woolyones' costume ball until a real wolf appears dressed as a sheep, mistakes her for his mother, and throws a tantrum when she outsmarts him.

"The playful illustrations, suffused with expression and shades of pink, show sheep outfitted in tutus and an Elvis costume, and the wolf having a tantrum. Lester follows a familiar format in this clever tale." SLJ

Three cheers for Tacky; illustrated by Lynn Munsinger. Houghton Mifflin 1994 32p il $16; pa $5.95

Grades: PreK K 1 2　　　　　　　　　　　　E
　　1. Penguins—Fiction 2. Contests—Fiction 3. Cheerleading—Fiction
　　ISBN 0-395-66841-7; 0-395-82-740-X (pa)
　　　　　　　　　　　　　　　　　LC 93-14342

"Practicing with his classmates for a cheerleading contest, Tacky the penguin falls over his own feet, can't remember the right words, and looks simply slovenly. He finally gets it right, but, on the big day, he reverts to his usual form." Horn Book Guide

This "is a smooth, fun read. Munsinger's full-color illustrations are charming and subtle." SLJ

Other titles about Tacky are:

Tacky and the emperor (2000)
Tacky and the winter games (2005)
Tacky goes to camp (2009)
Tacky in trouble (1998)
Tacky the penguin (1988)
Tackylocks and the three bears (2002)

Lester, Julius

Black cowboy, wild horses; a true story; [by] Julius Lester, Jerry Pinkney. Dial Bks. 1998 unp il $18.99 *

Grades: 2 3 4   E

1. Lemmons, Bob—Fiction 2. Horses—Fiction 3. Cowhands—Fiction 4. African Americans—Fiction

ISBN 0-8037-1787-3   LC 97-25210

A black cowboy is so in tune with wild mustangs that they accept him into the herd, thus enabling him singlehandedly to take them to the corral

This story is told in "vivid, poetic prose. . . . Pinkney's magnificent earth-toned paintings bring to life the wild beauty of the horses and the western plains." Horn Book Guide

Sam and the tigers; a new telling of Little Black Sambo; pictures by Jerry Pinkney. Dial Bks. for Young Readers 1996 unp il $16.99; pa $6.99

Grades: K 1 2 3   E

1. Tigers—Fiction

ISBN 0-8037-2028-9; 0-14-056288-5 (pa)

                                   LC 95-43080

A boy named Sam, who lives in the land of Sam-sam-sa-mara, gives his new school clothes to tigers who threaten to eat him, but he re-claims them when the tigers chase one another until they turn into butter

"The rolling, lilting narrative is a model of harmony, clarity, and meticulously chosen detail. . . . Pinkney's lively pencil-and-watercolor illustrations sprawl extravagantly across double spreads and are smoothly integrated with the narrative." SLJ

Leuck, Laura, 1962-

I love my pirate papa; [by] Laura Leuck; illustrated by Kyle M. Stone. Harcourt 2007 unp il $16

Grades: PreK K 1 2   E

1. Pirates—Fiction 2. Father-son relationship—Fiction

ISBN 978-0-15-205664-3   LC 2006009240

A pirate's son shares the things he loves about his father, including climbing the mast together to yell "Land ho" and sharing the booty when they find buried treasure.

This is written "in well cadenced, rhyming verses. . . . The stylized acrylic paintings, using exaggeration and comical details effectively, create one dramatic double-page scene after another." Booklist

One witch; illustrations by S.D. Schindler. Walker & Co. 2003 unp il hardcover o.p. pa $6.95 *

Grades: K 1 2   E

1. Witches—Fiction   2. Halloween—Fiction 3. Counting 4. Stories in rhyme

ISBN 0-8027-8860-2; 0-8027-7729-5 (pa)

                                LC 2002-191049

A witch goes around to her fiendish friends—from two cats to ten werewolves—to gather the ingredients to make gruesome stew for her party

"Eerie yet amusing illustrations and a romping, rhyming text add up to fun in this Halloween counting book. Schindler's ink-and-watercolor artwork is a fine fit for Leuck's action-packed, easy-to-read text." SLJ

Levert, Mireille

The princess who had almost everything; [text by] Mireille Levert; [illustrations by] Josée Masse. Tundra Books 2008 unp il $19.95

Grades: K 1 2 3   E

1. Princesses—Fiction 2. Fairy tales

ISBN 978-0-88776-887-3; 0-88776-887-3

"A princess' parents do everything to make their daughter happy. But Alicia keeps yelling, 'I'M BORED!' . . . When she decides she wants a prince, her parents promise her hand in marriage to anyone who can keep their daughter from tedium. . . . Dramatic angular illustrations in an earth-tone palette let the viewer see the world from contrasting perspectives. . . . The message of the importance of creativity come through loud and clear." Booklist

A wizard in love; [written by] Mireille Levert; [illustrated by] Marie Lafrance. Tundra Books 2009 unp il $17.95

Grades: PreK K 1 2   E

1. Witches—Fiction 2. Noise—Fiction 3. Magic—Fiction

ISBN 978-0-88776-901-6; 0-88776-901-2

Original French edition published 2007 in Canada

Hector, a retired wizard, lives happily and quietly with his cat, Poison, in a dilapidated house at the edge of the forest, until a noisy new neighbor moves into the abandoned house across the road, and things are never the same again.

"Both verbally and visually entirely funny . . . this offbeat import is a sophisticated treat." Kirkus

Levine, Ellen, 1939-

Henry's freedom box; illustrated by Kadir Nelson. Scholastic Press 2007 unp il $16.99 *

Grades: 1 2 3   E

1. Brown, Henry Box, b. 1816—Fiction 2. Slavery—Fiction   3.   African   Americans—Fiction 4. Underground railroad—Fiction

ISBN 0-439-77733-X   LC 2006-09487

A Caldecott Medal honor book, 2008

A fictionalized account of how in 1849 a Virginia slave, Henry "Box" Brown, escapes to freedom by shipping himself in a wooden crate from Richmond to Philadelphia.

"According to the flap copy, an antique lithograph of Brown inspired Nelson's paintings, which use cross-hatched pencil lines layered with watercolors and oil paints. . . . Transcending technique is the humanity Nelson imbues in his characters." Booklist

Levy, Janice

Gonzalo grabs the good life; written by Janice Levy; illustrated by Bill Slavin. Eerdmans Books for Young Readers 2009 unp il $17.50

Grades: K 1 2 3   E

1. Wealth—Fiction 2. Roosters—Fiction

ISBN 978-0-8028-5328-8; 0-8028-5328-5

                                 LC 2008009998

When Gonzalo the rooster wins the lottery, he leaves his job at the farm in search of the good life.

"Acrylic illustrations on gessoed paper animate the hu-

Levy, Janice—*Continued*

mor with fine-feathered cleverness, adding wry details.
. . . A vocabulary list defines the six Spanish words
sprinkled throughout. This is beak-in-cheek fun with an
underlying message." Booklist

Lewis, J. Patrick

Big is big (and little, little); a book of contrasts;
by J. Patrick Lewis; illustrated by Bob Barner.
Holiday House 2007 unp il $16.95

Grades: PreK K 1   E

1. Opposites 2. Animals—Poetry

ISBN 978-0-8234-1909-8; 0-8234-1909-6

LC 2005050341

"Wordplay meets playful art in this clever look at opposites. Lewis's bouncy verse and Barner's rollicking illustrations show the contrasts between various animals.
. . . Done in a combination of cut-paper collage, bright
pastels, and bold black line, Barner's animals cavort
against vivid backgrounds." SLJ

The snowflake sisters; illustrated by Lisa
Desimini. Atheneum Bks. for Young Readers 2003
unp il $16.95

Grades: K 1 2 3   E

1. Snow—Fiction 2. New York (N.Y.)—Fiction

ISBN 0-689-85029-8   LC 2002-6138

"An Anne Schwartz book"

Two snowflakes named Crystal and Ivory travel on
Santa's sleigh and make their way through the wintry
sky until they become part of a snowboy in Central Park

"The setting is New York City, captured through witty
collage illustrations that make use of such materials as
rice paper, maps, newsprint, and Scrabble letters. Lewis's
elegant and fluid rhymed text offers surprises on every
page." SLJ

Lewis, Kim

Good night, Harry. Candlewick Press 2004
c2003 unp il $15.99

Grades: PreK   E

1. Bedtime—Fiction 2. Sleep—Fiction 3. Elephants—
Fiction

ISBN 0-7636-2206-0   LC 2002-41468

First published 2003 in the United Kingdom

When Harry, a toy elephant, has trouble sleeping, his
friends help him.

"Lewis's meticulous illustrations were rendered in colored pencil and pastel, and the vivid, warm textures of
the toys are sure to be appreciated by children. . . . This
is a gentle book with illustrations that hum, and a bedtime story that's as warm as it is irresistible." SLJ

Other titles about Harry are:

Here we go Harry (2005)

Hooray for Harry (2006)

My friend Harry (1997)

Lewis, Rose A.

Every year on your birthday; written by Rose
Lewis; illustrated by Jane Dyer. Little, Brown
2007 unp il $16.99

Grades: PreK K 1 2   E

1. Mother-daughter relationship—Fiction
2. Adoption—Fiction 3. Birthdays—Fiction

ISBN 978-0-316-52552-7; 0-316-52552-9

LC 2006026467

Companion volume to I love you like crazy cakes
(2000)

Each year on the birthday of her adopted Chinese
daughter, a mother recalls the moments they have shared,
from the first toy to the friends left behind in China

"Expressive watercolors evoke vivid memories. . . .
By story's end, readers see a matured parent, secure in
her love for her child." Publ Wkly

I love you like crazy cakes; written by Rose
Lewis; illustrated by Jane Dyer. Little, Brown
2000 unp il $14.95; bd bk $6.99

Grades: PreK K 1 2   E

1. Adoption—Fiction 2. Infants—Fiction

ISBN 0-316-52538-3; 0-316-52576-6 (bd bk)

LC 99-34175

A woman describes how she went to China to adopt
a special baby girl. Based on the author's own experiences

"Dyer's simple watercolor layouts with expressive
characters make this a calming read, befitting the gentle
affection in the text." SLJ

Lexau, Joan M.

Come back, cat; by Joan L. Nodset; pictures by
Steven Kellogg. Harper Collins Childrens Books
2008 unp il $16.99; lib bdg $17.89

Grades: PreK K 1 2   E

1. Cats—Fiction

ISBN 978-0-06-028081-9; 0-06-028081-6;
978-0-06-028082-6 (lib bdg); 0-06-028082-4 (lib bdg)

LC 2007041937

A newly illustrated edition of Come here cat, published 1973

A stray cat and a little girl have their problems getting
acquainted.

"This picture book, originally published in two colors
and out of print for many years, has been reissued with
Kellogg's full-color, mixed-media illustrations. Color is
used quite effectively. . . . The text, which consists exclusively of the child's dialogue, is both fresh and timeless." SLJ

Who took the farmer's [hat]? [by] Joan L.
Nodset; pictures by Fritz Siebel. Harper & Row
1963 unp il lib bdg $17.89; pa $6.99

Grades: PreK K   E

1. Animals—Fiction

ISBN 0-06-024566-2 (lib bdg); 0-06-443174-6 (pa)

"Away flew the farmer's hat. In his search for it he
found that his hat could be many things to many animals
including, most permanently, a bird's nest." Publ Wkly

Lichtenheld, Tom

Bridget's beret. Henry Holt and Company 2010 unp il $16.99 *

Grades: K 1 2   E
1. Drawing—Fiction 2. Artists—Fiction 3. Hats—Fiction
ISBN 978-0-8050-8775-8; 0-8050-8775-3
                                    LC 2009-12220
"Christy Ottaviano books"

When Bridget loses the beret that provides her with artistic inspiration like other great artists, she thinks she will never be able to draw again.

"This smart, saucy book, with its spacious cartoon-style art, is both a spur to artistic endeavor and a message about inspiration and hard work. Yet the motivations are cocooned by a crackin' good tale and tempered by a full-faceted heroine." Booklist

Lies, Brian

Bats at the beach; written and illustrated by Brian Lies. Houghton Mifflin 2006 unp il $16

Grades: PreK K 1 2   E
1. Bats—Fiction 2. Beaches—Fiction
ISBN 978-0-618-55744-8; 0-618-55744-X
                                    LC 2005010757

On a night when the moon can grow no fatter, bats pack their moon-tan lotion and baskets of treats and fly off for some fun on the beach.

"The acrylic paintings capture a moonlit night's deep shadows and reinforce the exuberant rhyming text." Horn Book Guide

Another title about the bats is:
Bats at the library (2008)
Bats at the ballgame (2010)

Lieshout, Maria van

Bloom! a little book about finding love; written and illustrated by Maria van Lieshout. Feiwel and Friends 2008 unp il $12.95

Grades: PreK K 1   E
1. Pigs—Fiction 2. Butterflies—Fiction 3. Love—Fiction 4. Friendship—Fiction
ISBN 978-0-312-36913-2; 0-312-36913-1
                                    LC 2007-33411

Bloom, a pig who prefers flowers to mud puddles, falls in love with a flying flower, but when the butterfly leaves she is brokenhearted until a friend gives her a reason to smile again.

"Van Lieshout's loosely drawn pen and ink illustrations, mostly on stark white pages, wring Oscar-winning expressions from the slenderest curves and squiggles. The minimalist text begins before the title page, when Bloom's faithful friend urges her to join him playing in a puddle. . . . This paper-overboard book's stylish design and small square format designate it as a natural for Valentine's Day." Publ Wkly

Lillegard, Dee

Tiger, tiger; illustrated by Susan Guevara. Putnam 2002 unp il $16.99

Grades: PreK K 1   E
1. Tigers—Fiction 2. Magic—Fiction
ISBN 0-399-22633-8   LC 2002-272

A bored young boy uses a magic feather to form a tiger, and then must use the feather to save his village when the tiger gets hungry

"The suspenseful story reaches a dramatic climax, made all the more vivid by Guevara's highly charged artwork." Booklist

Lin, Grace, 1974-

Bringing in the New Year; [by] Grace Lin. Alfred A. Knopf 2008 unp il $15.99; lib bdg $18.99

Grades: PreK K 1 2   E
1. Chinese New Year—Fiction 2. Chinese Americans—Fiction
ISBN 978-0-375-83745-6; 0-375-83745-0; 978-0-375-93745-3 (lib bdg); 0-375-93745-5
                                    LC 2007011687

A Chinese American family prepares for and celebrates the Lunar New Year. End notes discuss the customs and traditions of Chinese New Year.

"The lustrous gouache illustrations are saturated with bold primary colors and deftly convey the joyousness of the festivities. . . . A wonderful and much-needed addition to Chinese New Year literature." SLJ

Dim sum for everyone! written and illustrated by Grace Lin. Knopf 2001 unp il $14.95; pa $6.99 *

Grades: K 1 2 3   E
1. Chinese Americans—Fiction 2. Restaurants—Fiction
ISBN 0-375-81082-X; 0-440-41770-8 (pa)
                                    LC 00-34813

A child describes the various little dishes of dim sum that she and her family enjoy on a visit to a restaurant in Chinatown

"Lin's paintings are graphically striking. They combine a simplicity of form and design with a delight of patterning that appears in clothing and in backgrounds. . . . Like the pleasures of dim sum, this is a compact treat." Booklist

Kite flying. Knopf 2002 unp il hardcover o.p. pa $6.99

Grades: K 1 2 3   E
1. Kites—Fiction
ISBN 0-375-81520-1; 0-553-11254-6 (pa)
                                    LC 2001-33456

"A Chinese girl describes how the members of her family come together to make and fly a dragon kite. . . . The overall simplicity is effective and appealing, and the spare text is accentuated by bright gouache illustrations, in colorful shapes and painted fabric patterns." Booklist

Ling & Ting: not exactly the same. Little, Brown 2010 43p il $14.99 *

Grades: 1 2   E
1. Twins—Fiction 2. Sisters—Fiction
ISBN 978-0-316-02452-5; 0-316-02452-X

"Sisters Ling and Ting may be twins, but that doesn't mean they're 'exactly the same,' no matter what everyone says upon first meeting them. Children will come to their own conclusions after reading the six short, interconnected stories that make up this pleasing book for be-

Lin, Grace, 1974-—*Continued*

ginning readers. . . . Framed with narrow borders, the paintings illustrate the stories with restrained lines, vivid colors, and clarity." Booklist

Olvina flies; written and illustrated by Grace Lin. Holt & Co. 2003 unp il $15.95
Grades: PreK K 1 2   E
1. Fear—Fiction 2. Voyages and travels—Fiction 3. Pigs—Fiction
ISBN 0-8050-6711-6   LC 2002-8090
When Olvina, a chicken, receives an invitation to the annual Bird Convention in Hawaii, Will the pig and a fellow passenger help her to overcome her fear of flying
"The reassuring story gets a madcap twist from the artwork. Lin's jelly-bean-colored artwork, executed in gouache, finds humor in the small details." Booklist
Another title about Olvina is:
Olvina swims (2007)

Lindbergh, Reeve

My hippie grandmother; illustrated by Abby Carter. Candlewick Press 2003 unp il $15.99
Grades: K 1 2 3   E
1. Grandmothers—Fiction 2. Hippies—Fiction 3. Stories in rhyme
ISBN 0-7636-0671-5   LC 00-37964
A young girl describes all the things she likes about her grandmother, including the purple bus she drives, growing vegetables, picketing City Hall, and playing the banjo
"A wonderful, poetic portrait. . . . Carter's colorful watercolor-and-gouache illustrations capture the happy mood of the verse." SLJ

Lindenbaum, Pija

Mini Mia and her darling uncle; translated by Elizabeth Kallick Dyssegaard. Farrar, Straus & Giroux 2007 unp il $16
Grades: PreK K 1 2   E
1. Uncles—Fiction 2. Homosexuality—Fiction
ISBN 978-91-29-66734-9; 91-29-66734-8
                  LC 2006-93704
"The 'darling uncle' of this . . . title is a gay man, but Lindenbaum . . . focuses not on his identity but on his niece Ella's resentment of his new partner. . . . Lindenbaum paints Uncle Tommy's fabulous shirts and retro furniture with verve, and her pacing is sure. . . . The emotions stay true." Publ Wkly

Lindgren, Barbro, 1937-

Julia wants a pet; [by] Barbro Lindgren & [illustrated by] Eva Eriksson; translated by Elisabeth Kallick Dyssegaard. R & S Books; distributed by Farrar, Straus & Giroux 2003 unp il $15
Grades: K 1 2   E
1. Pets—Fiction
ISBN 91-29-65940-X
Original Swedish edition 2002

"On the lookout for a much-wished-for pet—preferably one that will fit in her baby carriage—Julia darts through town. . . . Lindgren's bracingly straightforward prose makes Julia's yearning and perversity feel immediate and authentic. . . . While Eriksson's brown-and-yellow-toned pictures may seem subdued at first glance, the earthtone colors and subtle pencil textures ground the heroine in the real world, while her yellow tutu and red baby carriage add playful tones." Publ Wkly

Oink, oink Benny; [by] Barbro Lindgren [illustrated by] Olof Lanstrom; translated by Elisabeth Kallick Dyssegaard. R & S Books 2008 unp il $16
Grades: PreK   E
1. Pigs—Fiction 2. Brothers—Fiction
ISBN 978-91-29-66855-1; 91-29-66855-7
"Benny the pig and his toddler brother go outdoors to have some fun. . . . When bullies push Benny's brother in the muck, lovely Klara rescues him and cuddles him close. That makes Benny jealous, so he 'falls' into the mudhole, too. . . . Preschoolers respond to the wry adventure, the envy, and the cozy adventure." Booklist
Other titles about Benny are:
Benny's had enough (2000)
Benny and the binky (2002)

Lindsey, Kat

Sweet potato pie; by Kathleen D. Lindsey; illustrated by Charlotte Riley-Webb. Lee & Low Books 2003 unp il $16.95; pa $7.95
Grades: K 1 2 3   E
1. Farm life—Fiction 2. Family life—Fiction 3. African Americans—Fiction 4. Pies—Fiction
ISBN 1-58430-061-2; 1-60060-277-0 (pa)
                  LC 2002-30164
During a drought in the early 1900s, a large loving African American family finds a delicious way to earn the money they need to save their family farm
"Lindsey's down-home storytelling quality is charming. . . . The artwork's broad, energetic strokes and strong color palette sweep children into this tasty tale, and the included pie recipe makes the experience complete." Booklist

Lionni, Leo, 1910-1999

Alexander and the wind-up mouse; by Leo Lionni. Alfred A. Knopf 2006 c1969 unp il $16.99; lib bdg $18.99; pa $6.99
Grades: PreK K 1 2   E
1. Mice—Fiction
ISBN 0-394-80914-9; 0-394-90914-3 (lib bdg); 0-394-82911-5 (pa)
A Caldecott Medal honor book, 1970
A reissue of the title first published 1969 by Pantheon Books
"Alexander wants to be a wind-up mouse like Willie, who is the little girl's favorite toy. A magic lizard can change him, but then he learns that Willie's key is broken and decides to turn Willie into a real mouse like himself." Adventuring with books, 2nd edition
The author's "collage illustrations are dazzling in their color and bold design and contribute to a beautiful and appealing picture book." Booklist

Lionni, Leo, 1910-1999—*Continued*

Fish is fish. Alfred A. Knopf 2005 c1970 unp il $15.95 *

Grades: PreK K 1 2   E

1. Frogs—Fiction 2. Fishes—Fiction

ISBN 0-394-80440-6

A reissue of the title first published 1970 by Pantheon Bks.

The frog tells the fish all about the world above the sea. The fish, however, can only visualize it in terms of fish-people, fish-birds and fish-cows.

"The story is slight but pleasantly and simply told, the illustrations are page-filling, deft, colorful, and amusing." Bull Cent Child Books

Frederick. Pantheon Bks. 1967 unp il $16.95; lib bdg $18.99; pa $5.99 *

Grades: PreK K 1 2   E

1. Mice—Fiction

ISBN 0-394-81040-6; 0-394-91040-0 (lib bdg); 0-394-82614-0 (pa)

"While other mice are gathering food for the winter, Frederick seems to daydream the summer away. When dreary winter comes, it is Frederick the poet-mouse who warms his friends and cheers them with his words." Wis Libr Bull

"This captivating book . . . sings a hymn of praise to poets in a gentle story that is illustrated with gaiety and charm." Saturday Rev

Inch by inch. Alfred A. Knopf 2010 c1960 unp il $16.99; lib bdg $19.99 *

Grades: PreK K 1 2   E

1. Caterpillars—Fiction 2. Birds—Fiction 3. Measurement—Fiction

ISBN 978-0-375-85764-5; 0-375-85764-8; 978-0-375-95764-2 (lib bdg); 0-375-95764-2 (lib bdg)   LC 2009-1767

A Caldecott Medal honor book, 1961

A reissue of the title first published 1960 by Astor-Honor

To keep from being eaten, an inchworm measures a robin's tail, a flamingo's neck, a toucan's beak, a heron's legs, and a nightingale's song.

"This is a book to look at again and again. The semi-abstract forms are sharply defined, clean and strong, the colors subtle and glowing, and the grassy world of the inchworm is a special place of enchantment." N Y Times Book Rev

Little blue and little yellow; a story for Pippo and Ann and other children. 50th anniversary ed. Alfred A. Knopf 2009 c1959 unp il $15.99; lib bdg $18.99 *

Grades: PreK K 1 2   E

1. Color—Fiction 2. Friendship—Fiction

ISBN 978-0-375-86013-3; 0-375-86013-4; 978-0-375-96013-0 (lib bdg); 0-375-96013-9 (lib bdg)   LC 2008035932

A reissue of the title first published 1959 by Astor-Honor

A little blue spot and a little yellow spot are best friends, and when they hug each other they become green.

"So well are the dots handled on the pages that little blue and little yellow and their parents seem to have real personalities. It should inspire interesting color play and is a very original picture book by an artist." N Y Her Trib Books

Swimmy. Pantheon Bks. 1973 c1963 unp il $16; pa $5.99 *

Grades: PreK K 1 2   E

1. Fishes—Fiction

ISBN 0-394-81713-3; 0-394-82620-5 (pa)

"Swimmy, an insignificant fish, escapes when a whole school of small fish are swallowed by a larger one. As he swims away from danger he meets many wonderful, colorful creatures and later saves another school of fish from the jaws of the enemy." Ont Libr Rev

"To illustrate his clever, but very brief story, Leo Lionni has made a book of astonishingly beautiful pictures, full of undulating, watery nuances of shape, pattern, and color." Horn Book

Lipson, Eden Ross

Applesauce season; illustrated by Mordicai Gerstein. Roaring Brook Press 2009 unp il $17.99

Grades: PreK K 1 2   E

1. Apples—Fiction 2. Family life—Fiction

ISBN 978-1-59643-216-1; 1-59643-216-0

"Flavored with family tradition and spiced with Gerstein's cheerful illustrations, this account of one family's love of applesauce hits the spot. . . . In a crowded orchard of apple books, this one stands out for home or school apple and/or family-tradition projects. Applesauce recipe appended." Kirkus

Lithgow, John, 1945-

Micawber; illustrated by C.F. Payne. Simon & Schuster Bks. for Young Readers 2002 unp il $17.95; pa $6.99 *

Grades: PreK K 1 2   E

1. Artists—Fiction 2. Squirrels—Fiction 3. Stories in rhyme 4. New York (N.Y.)—Fiction

ISBN 0-689-83341-5; 0-689-83542-6 (pa)   LC 2001-20919

Accompanied by CD recording of Lithgow reading his text

Micawber, a squirrel fascinated by art, leaves the Metropolitan Museum of Art with an art student, secretly uses her supplies to make her own paintings, and starts his own art museum atop Central Park's carousel

"The rhymed text sparkles with pleasing sounds. . . . Lithgow's reading on the CD is brimming with texture and playful pomposity. The mixed-media illustrations depict an utterly fetching protagonist displaying a range of moods and poses." SLJ

Little, Jean, 1932-

Emma's yucky brother; story by Jean Little; pictures by Jennifer Plecas. HarperCollins Pubs. 2001 63p il hardcover o.p. pa $3.99 *

Grades: PreK K 1 2   E

1. Siblings—Fiction 2. Adoption—Fiction

ISBN 0-06-028348-3; 0-06-444258-6 (pa)   LC 99-34515

Little, Jean, 1932- —*Continued*

"An I can read book"

Emma finds out how hard it is to be a big sister when her family adopts a four-year-old boy named Max

"Heartfelt and honest. . . . Little's simple words and Plecas' clear, expressive line-and-watercolor illustrations tell an intense story." Booklist

Other titles about Emma are:

Emma's magic winter (1998)

Emma's strange pet (2003)

Liu, Jae Soo

Yellow umbrella; written and illustrated by Jae Soo Liu. Kane/Miller 2002 unp il $19.95

Grades: PreK K 1   E

1. Umbrellas and parasols—Fiction 2. Stories without words

ISBN 1-929132-36-0

Includes audio CD

A story, in pictures and music, of children on their way to school on a rainy day

"Originally published in South Korea, the volume is both delicate and handsome. . . . The joyful hues multiply with each successive spread. Composer Dong II Sheen gracefully glides between rhythms throughout the 15 tracks here [on the CD] . . . maintaining an overall happy tone." Publ Wkly

Livingston, Myra Cohn

Calendar; by Myra Cohn Livingston; illustrated by Will Hillenbrand. Holiday House 2007 unp il $16.95

Grades: PreK K 1 2   E

1. Months—Poetry

ISBN 978-0-8234-1725-4; 0-8234-1725-5

LC 2006012145

"'January shivers / February shines / March blows off the winter ice / April makes / the mornings nice . . .' First published in 1959 in the collection *Wide Awake and Other Poems*, this simple poem by the late Livingston gets its own picture book here with a lively double-page spread for each month of the year. The bright, clear, mixed-media artwork—ink, acrylic, gouache, and collage—extends the words." Booklist

Liwska, Renata

Little panda; written and illustrated by Renata Liwska. Houghton Mifflin Co. 2008 unp il $12.95 *

Grades: PreK K 1 2   E

1. Giant panda—Fiction

ISBN 978-0-618-96627-1; 0-618-96627-7

LC 2007047735

A grandfather tells his grandson an unlikely story about a panda and how it escapes from the tiger that wants to eat it.

"In every word, readers can hear the wise, wry voice of a narrator who knows how to hold a child's attention. The illustrations, a combination of pencil and soft digital color, evoke the simplicity of traditional Chinese art and underscore the intimacy of the book's small format." SLJ

Ljungkvist, Laura

Follow the line; words and art by Laura Ljungkvist. Viking 2006 unp il $16.99 *

Grades: PreK K 1 2   E

1. Counting

ISBN 0-670-06049-6   LC 2005-22701

Invites the reader to visit a wide variety of places and count different objects found in each, from fire hydrants in a big city in the morning, through starfish in the ocean during the day, to babies sleeping in a country village at night.

"An entrancing counting game with a search through detailed art, this title doubles as a vocabulary builder for the youngest readers and includes shapes, colors, and patterns in the search." SLJ

Other titles in this series are:

Follow the line through the house (2007)

Follow the line around the world (2008)

Lloyd, Jennifer

Looking for loons; [by] Jennifer Lloyd; Kirsti Anne Wakelin, illustrator. Simply Read Books 2007 unp il $16.95

Grades: PreK K 1 2 3   E

1. Family life—Fiction 2. Loons—Fiction

ISBN 978-1-894965-54-5

"It's a beautiful September morning, and Patrick awakens when the dim sunlight hits his pillow. He gets out of bed and reaches for his 'cozy housecoat' and binoculars. . . . His patient persistence is rewarded . . . when a group of loons flies into view and lands on the lake. . . . This gentle story is illustrated with warm, muted watercolors that are evocative of unhurried and carefree mornings on a lake in the country." SLJ

Lloyd, Sam, 1971-

Doctor Meow's big emergency. Henry Holt & Co. 2008 unp il (Whoops-a-daisy world) $14.95

Grades: PreK K 1 2   E

1. Physicians—Fiction 2. Cats—Fiction 3. Hospitals—Fiction

ISBN 978-0-8050-8819-9; 0-8050-8819-9

First published 2007 in the United Kingdom

"At Kiss-It-Better Hospital, busy Dr. Meow, a cat wearing a pink coat and stethoscope, receives an emergency call from Tom Cat, who has fallen from a tree after a leap toward Mr. Bird. . . . The cartoon-style animal characters and the spare, animated text, filled with sound effects, make for a light and lively read that doesn't downplay the discomfort of being injured and scared. Vibrant, page-spanning illustrations . . . incorporate playful details." Booklist

Followed by: Chief Rhino to the rescue (2009)

Lobel, Anita, 1934-

Alison's zinnia. Greenwillow Bks. 1990 unp il hardcover o.p. pa $6.99 *

Grades: PreK K 1 2   E

1. Flowers—Fiction 2. Alphabet

ISBN 0-688-08865-1; 0-688-14737-2 (pa)

LC 89-23700

Lobel, Anita, 1934-—*Continued*

"More than two dozen little girls, a full alphabet of them, pick flowers for their friends: 'Alison acquired an Amaryllis for Beryl' and 'Nancy noticed a Narcissus for Olga' and so on till 'Zena zeroed in on a Zinnia for Alison.' Underneath each large handsome floral illustration is a smaller picture of the named child and her flower. Charming." N Y Times Book Rev

Hello, day! Greenwillow Books 2008 unp il $16.99; lib bdg $17.89 *

Grades: PreK   E

1. Sun—Fiction 2. Morning—Fiction 3. Animals—Fiction

ISBN   978-0-06-078765-3;   0-06-078765-1;
978-0-06-078766-0 (lib bdg); 0-06-078766-X (lib bdg)
                                      LC 2007-18361

Various animals greet the sunrise in their own unique voices, except for the owl who welcomes the night.

"The luxuriantly hued, playfully textured portraits will rivet preschoolers and invite them to make animal sounds of their own; the minimal text, set in big, friendly type, may also encourage some simple word recognition." Publ Wkly

Nini here and there. Greenwillow Books 2007 unp il hardcover o.p. lib bdg $17.89

Grades: PreK K 1 2   E

1. Cats—Fiction 2. Moving—Fiction

ISBN 0-06-078767-8; 0-06-078768-6 (lib bdg)
                                      LC 2005-22186

Fearing at first that her family is going on vacation without her, Nini the cat ends up traveling with her owners to their new home.

"The artwork makes this picture book an endearing delight. Irresistible Nini steals the show in full-page portraits painted with Lobel's usual sensitivity in watercolor and gouache." Booklist

One lighthouse, one moon. Greenwillow Bks. 2000 40p il hardcover o.p. pa $6.99 *

Grades: PreK K 1 2   E

1. Days—Fiction 2. Months—Fiction 3. Counting

ISBN 0-688-15539-1; 0-06-000537-8 (pa)
                                      LC 98-50790

This is a "three-part introduction to days, seasons, colors, counting, and other basics. The first section pictures a little girl's feet as they journey through a week, with a different colored shoe marking each day's activity. . . . The second section shows Nini the cat in postcard-size images that reflect those from the 12 months of the year. The title section presents the numbers 1 through 10 in serene images of shoreline activity. . . . The simple phrases are lyrical in places, and Lobel's beautiful paintings, with their rich patterns and textures, luxurious detail, and sophisticated palette, will inspire children to linger over the pages and connect new words with images." Booklist

Lobel, Arnold

Frog and Toad are friends. Harper & Row 1970 64p il $15.99; lib bdg $16.89; pa $3.90 *

Grades: K 1 2   E

1. Frogs—Fiction 2. Toads—Fiction

ISBN 0-06-023957-3; 0-06-023958-1 (lib bdg);
0-06-444020-6 (pa)

A Caldecott Medal honor book, 1971

"An I can read book"

Here are five stories . . . which recount the adventures of two best friends—Toad and Frog. The stories are: Spring; The story; A lost button; A swim; The letter

The stories are told "with humor and perception. Illustrations in soft green and brown enhance the smooth flowing and sensitive story." SLJ

Other titles about Frog and Toad are:
Days with Frog and Toad (1979)
Frog and Toad all year (1976)
Frog and Toad together (1972)

Grasshopper on the road. Harper & Row 1978 62p il lib bdg $17.89; pa $3.99 *

Grades: K 1 2   E

1. Grasshoppers—Fiction 2. Animals—Fiction

ISBN 0-06-023962-X (lib bdg); 0-06-444094-X (pa)
                                      LC 77-25653

"An I can read book"

"Grasshopper's journey is divided into six chapters. In each chapter he meets a different animal or animals attending to a spectrum of tasks. The chapters weave a tale of habit—doing without questioning. Grasshopper gives his need-for-change reaction to each one, but only a worm in his apple home is open to change." Child Book Rev Serv

"The contemporary version of the fable of the ant and the grasshopper is told in a repetitive I-Can-Read text and extended in three-color illustrations which delicately capture the grasshopper's microcosmic world view." Horn Book

Ming Lo moves the mountain; written and illustrated by Arnold Lobel. Greenwillow Bks. 1982 unp il pa $5.99 hardcover o.p.

Grades: K 1 2 3   E

1. Mountains—Fiction 2. Houses—Fiction

ISBN 0-688-10995-0 (pa)   LC 81-13327

"Ming Lo and his wife love their house, but not the mountain that overshadows it. So, at his wife's bidding, Ming Lo undertakes to move the mountain by following the advice of a wise man." Child Book Rev Serv

"An original tale utilizing folkloric motifs, the book is Chinese-like rather than Chinese, for the artist has created an imagined landscape. The setting, shown in flowing lines and tones of delicate watercolors, provides a source of inspiration drawn from an ancient artistic tradition; particularly effective in conveying a sense of distance are the panoramic double-page spreads." Horn Book

Mouse soup. Harper & Row 1977 63p il $15.99; lib bdg $16.89; pa $3.99 *

Grades: K 1 2   E

1. Mice—Fiction

ISBN 0-06-023967-0; 0-06-023968-9 (lib bdg);
0-06-444041-9 (pa)   LC 76-41517

"An I can read book"

Lobel, Arnold—Continued

"In an effort to save himself from a weasel's stew pot, a little mouse tells the weasel four separate stories." West Coast Rev Books

"An artistic triumph with enough suspense, humor and wisdom to hold any reader who has a trace of curiosity and compassion. . . . The little one triumphs over the big one, and every child will rejoice. The exquisite wash drawings in mousey shades of grays, blues, greens and golds, have enough humor and pathos to exact repeated scrutiny. Like the stories, they improve with each reading." N Y Times Book Rev

Mouse tales. Harper & Row 1972 61p il $15.99; lib bdg $16.89; pa $3.99 *
Grades: K 1 2   E
  1. Mice—Fiction
  ISBN 0-06-023941-7; 0-06-023942-5 (lib bdg); 0-06-444013-3 (pa)
  "An I can read book"
Contents: The wishing well; Clouds; Very tall mouse and very short mouse; The mouse and the winds; The journey; The odd mouse; The bath

Papa Mouse tells seven bedtime stories, one for each of his sons

"The illustrations have soft colors and precise, lively little drawings of the imaginative and humorous events in the stories. The themes are familiar to children: cloud shapes, wishing, a tall and a short friend who observe-and greet-natural phenomena on a walk, taking a bath, et cetera." Bull Cent Child Books

On Market Street; pictures by Anita Lobel; words by Arnold Lobel. Greenwillow Bks. 1981 c1980 unp il $16.99; lib bdg $17.89; pa $6.99 *
Grades: K 1 2 3   E
  1. Shopping—Fiction 2. Alphabet 3. Stories in rhyme
  ISBN 0-688-80309-1; 0-688-84309-3 (lib bdg); 0-688-08745-0 (pa)   LC 80-21418
A Caldecott Medal honor book, 1982

In this "alphabet book, a boy trots down Market Street buying presents for a friend, each one starting with a letter of the alphabet. Every letter is illustrated by a figure . . . composed of, for instance, apples or wigs or quilts or Xmas trees." Horn Book

"The artist has adapted the style of old French trade engravings, infusing it with a wonderful sense of color and detail. . . . Arnold Lobel's words ring of old rhymes, but it is these intricate, lovely drawings that take the day, and truly make it brighter." N Y Times Book Rev

Owl at home. Harper & Row 1982 64p il lib bdg $16.89; pa $3.99 *
Grades: K 1 2   E
  1. Owls—Fiction
  ISBN 0-06-023949-2 (lib bdg); 0-06-444034-6 (pa)
  "An I can read book"
Five stories describe the adventures of a lovably foolish owl

"A child reader or listener in a kind of one-upmanship over wide-eyed tufted Owl will bristle with anxiety to have him perceive what causes two bewildering bumps under the blanket at the foot of his bed. The best scope for Lobel's inventiveness in drawing is, however, the

opening episode where 'poor old' Winter makes a pushy entry into Owl's home. Muted browns and greys are countered by an animation that fully reveals Owl's distresses and contentments." Wash Post Child Book World

Small pig; story and pictures by Arnold Lobel. Harper & Row 1969 63p il lib bdg $16.89; pa $3.99 *
Grades: K 1 2   E
  1. Pigs—Fiction
  ISBN 0-06-023932-8 (lib bdg); 0-06-444120-2 (pa)
  "An I can read book"
This "is the story of a pig who, finding the clean farm unbearable, runs away to look for mud—and ends up stuck in cement. His facial expressions alone are worth the price of the book; the illustrations, in blue, green, and gold, are a perfect complement to the story. Humor, adventure, and short, simple sentences provide a real treat for beginning readers." SLJ

A treeful of pigs; pictures by Anita Lobel. Greenwillow Bks. 1979 unp il lib bdg $17.89
Grades: K 1 2 3   E
  1. Pigs—Fiction 2. Farm life—Fiction
  ISBN 0-688-84177-5   LC 78-1810
A "story about a farmer's wife who tries everything to pry her lazy husband out of bed. He says he'll come to help her when the pigs grow on trees, fall from the sky, or 'bloom in the garden like flowers.' His wife knows how to work magic, and she makes each one of them happen with the help of a cooperative brood of piglets." Child Book Rev Serv

"The framed, full-color illustrations, characterized by intricately detailed designs in costumes and setting, are as elaborate as the diction is simple. The total effect, however, is one of unity." Horn Book

Uncle Elephant. Harper & Row 1981 62p il lib bdg $16.89; pa $3.99 *
Grades: K 1 2   E
  1. Elephants—Fiction 2. Uncles—Fiction
  ISBN 0-06-023980-8 (lib bdg); 0-06-444104-0 (pa)
                                                 LC 80-8944
  "An I can read book"
Uncle Elephant takes care of his nephew whose parents are lost at sea. This book describes the way they lived together until the parents are rescued and little elephant rejoins them

"Nine gentle stories for the beginning independent reader; the soft grey, peach, and green tones of the deft pictures are an appropriate echo of the mood." Bull Cent Child Books

Lobel, Gillian

Moonshadow's journey; illustrated by Karin Littlewood. Albert Whitman & Co. 2009 unp il $16.99
Grades: K 1 2 3 4   E
  1. Swans—Fiction 2. Birds—Migration—Fiction 3. Grandfathers—Fiction 4. Death—Fiction
  ISBN 978-0-8075-5273-5; 0-8075-5273-9
                                              LC 2009000004
When his beloved grandfather is killed in a storm while leading the swan flock south for the winter,

Lobel, Gillian—*Continued*

Moonshadow is reassured by his father that the flock will go on with Grandfather always in their hearts

"Lobel skillfully moves the plot forward while creating appropriate character development for Moonshadow. . . . Littlewood's combination of watercolors and gouache on textured paper of light and dark hues adds to the moods and movement of the book. The pictures capture the elements of nature in both harsh and calm circumstances." SLJ

London, Jonathan, 1947-

Baby whale's journey; illustrated by Jon Van Zyle. Chronicle Bks. 1999 unp il $15.95; pa $6.95 *

Grades: K 1 2 3   E
1. Whales—Fiction
ISBN 0-8118-2496-9; 0-8118-5761-1 (pa)
LC 99-13020

Off the Pacific coast of Mexico, a baby sperm whale is born, feeds, speaks to her mother in clicks, and spends her days diving, spy-hopping, lob-tailing, and rolling as she grows and learns the ways of the sea

This book offers "London's lyrical text and Van Zyle's dramatic paintings dominated by blues and purples. . . . An informative afterword supplies additional facts about sperm whales, and a reader's guide offers thoughtful ideas for discussion of both the scientific and poetic aspects of the text." Horn Book Guide

Froggy learns to swim; illustrated by Frank Remkiewicz. Viking 1995 unp il $15.99; pa $5.99 *

Grades: PreK K 1 2   E
1. Swimming—Fiction 2. Frogs—Fiction
ISBN 0-670-85551-0; 0-14-055312-6 (pa)
LC 94-43077

Froggy is afraid of the water until his mother, along with his flippers, snorkel, and mask, help him learn to swim

"Vivid watercolor cartoons add the humor, showing the comical facial expressions and hilarious beachwear. Froggy's childlike dialogue and the sound words—'zook! zik!'; 'flop flop . . . splash!'—make this story a wonderful read-aloud." SLJ

Other titles about Froggy are:
Froggy bakes a cake (2000)
Froggy eats out (2001)
Froggy gets dressed (1992)
Froggy goes to bed (2000)
Froggy goes to camp (2008)
Froggy goes to school (1996)
Froggy goes to the doctor (2002)
Froggy plays in the band (2002)
Froggy plays T-Ball (2007)
Froggy plays soccer (1999)
Froggy's baby sister (2003)
Froggy's best Christmas (2000)
Froggy's day with Dad (2004)
Froggy's first kiss (1998)
Froggy's Halloween (1999)
Froggy's sleepover (2005)
Let's go, Froggy! (1994)

A train goes clickety-clack; by Jonathan London; illustrated by Denis Roche. Henry Holt 2007 unp il $15.95

Grades: PreK K   E
1. Railroads—Fiction 2. Stories in rhyme
ISBN 978-0-8050-7972-2; 0-8050-7972-6
LC 2006030765

Easy-to-read, rhyming text describes the sounds of, and uses for, different kinds of trains

"Brief sentences and bright gouache artwork in primary hues capture the excitement and attraction of trains. The text is filled with appealing rhythms and rhymes." SLJ

A truck goes rattley-bumpa; illustrated by Denis Roche. Henry Holt and Co. 2005 unp il $14.95 *

Grades: PreK K   E
1. Trucks—Fiction 2. Stories in rhyme
ISBN 0-8050-7233-0   LC 2004-22174

"Short, rhyming couplets tell about a variety of trucks: what they look like, what sounds they make, where they go, and what they do. Meanwhile, childlike gouache paintings clearly illustrate the brief sentences or phrases on each page." Booklist

Long, Ethan

Bird & Birdie in a fine day. Ten Speed Press 2010 unp il $14.99

Grades: PreK K 1   E
1. Birds—Fiction 2. Friendship—Fiction
ISBN 978-1-5824-6321-6; 1-5824-6321-2

"Three separate stories introduce two bug-eyed cartoon birds (Bird is blue, while Birdie, who is yellow, sports eyelashes and a pink ribbon) interacting over the course of a day. In 'A Beautiful Morning,' they meet, exchange pleasantries, are briefly separated by a storm, and happily join up again. In 'A Wonderful Afternoon,' Bird tries to concentrate on getting a worm out of the ground but is distracted by Birdie. In 'A Marvelous Night,' Birdie can't get comfortable in her nest until Bird helps out. . . . The fetching Bird and Birdie will hit the right note with many preschoolers and beginning readers." Booklist

Long, Loren

Otis. Philomel Books 2009 unp il $17.99 *
Grades: PreK K 1 2   E
1. Tractors—Fiction 2. Farm life—Fiction
ISBN 978-0-399-25248-8; 0-399-25248-7
LC 2008-50020

When a big new yellow tractor arrives, Otis the friendly little tractor is cast away behind the barn, but when trouble occurs Otis is the only one who can help.

"Long's gouache and pencil artwork is stunning with a red and cream main character against a sepia-toned monochromatic background. The overall effect is nostalgic and comforting." SLJ

Long, Melinda

How I became a pirate; written by Melinda Long; illustrated by David Shannon. Harcourt 2003 unp il $16 *

Grades: K 1 2 3   E

1. Pirates—Fiction

ISBN 0-15-201848-4   LC 2002-6308

"Jeremy spies a pirate ship. When he's asked to join its crew, he can't resist. On board, he does all sorts of fun pirate stuff. . . . But, alas, Jeremy soon discovers, there's no goodnight kiss or bedtime story, so there's something to be said for home. . . . The rollicking tale is a charmer, with a lively, witty, first-person narrative, highly expressive characters, and farcical elements. . . . Shannon's acrylic art is marvelously animated, with bright, bold colors and extraordinary details." Booklist

Another title about Jeremy is:

Pirates don't change diapers (2007)

Look, Lenore

Henry's first-moon birthday; illustrated by Yumi Heo. Atheneum Bks. for Young Readers 2001 unp il $16 *

Grades: PreK K 1 2   E

1. Infants—Fiction 2. Grandmothers—Fiction 3. Chinese Americans—Fiction

ISBN 0-689-82294-4   LC 98-21626

"An Anne Schwartz book"

Jen helps her grandmother with preparations for the traditional Chinese celebration to welcome her new baby brother

"The words are clear and basic as well as creative . . . and Jen's chatty narration infuses the book with the cozy immediacy that's beautifully picked up in Heo's swirling paint-and-paper collages." Booklist

Love as strong as ginger; illustrated by Stephen T. Johnson. Atheneum Pubs. 1999 unp il $15 *

Grades: PreK K 1 2   E

1. Chinese Americans—Fiction 2. Grandmothers—Fiction 3. Work—Fiction

ISBN 0-689-81248-5   LC 96-43459

"An Anne Schwartz book"

A Chinese American girl comes to realize how hard her grandmother works to fulfill her dreams when they spend a day together at the grandmother's job cracking crabs

"Inspired by the author's memories of her grandmother, this gentle story is carefully and precisely told. . . . Johnson's expressive pastel-and-watercolor illustrations are rendered in muted colors and set within wide, softly colored margins." SLJ

Uncle Peter's amazing Chinese wedding; illustrated by Yumi Heo. Atheneum Books for Young Readers 2006 unp il $16.95 *

Grades: PreK K 1 2   E

1. Chinese Americans—Fiction 2. Weddings—Fiction 3. Uncles—Fiction

ISBN 0-689-84458-1   LC 2002-10740

Companion volume to Henry's first-moon birthday

"An Anne Schwartz book"

Jenny, a Chinese American girl, describes the festivities of her uncle's Chinese wedding and the customs behind them.

"Heo's child-inspired illustrations contribute to the story's strong appeal with lively colors, perspectives, and details that accentuate both Jenny's feelings and the wedding traditions. A delightful invitation to learn more about Chinese traditions." SLJ

López, Susana

The best family in the world; [illustrated by] Ulises Wensell. Kane Miller unp il $15.99

Grades: PreK K 1 2   E

1. Adoption—Fiction 2. Family life—Fiction 3. Orphans—Fiction

ISBN 978-1-935279-47-1; 1-935279-47-5

Carlota is anxiously awaiting the arrival of the family who is adopting her. She imagines that they might be astronauts, pastry chiefs or even pirates. And then Carlota finds out that the Lopez family is the best family in the world.

"The telling is clear and lively, while the artwork glows with warmth and light. . . . A lovely, thought-provoking picture book to share and discuss." Booklist

Lorbiecki, Marybeth

Paul Bunyan's sweetheart; written by Marybeth Lorbiecki; illustrated by Renee Graef. Sleeping Bear Press 2007 unp il $16.95

Grades: 1 2 3 4   E

1. Bunyan, Paul (Legendary character) 2. Love—Fiction 3. Nature—Fiction 4. Environmental protection—Fiction 5. Minnesota—Fiction 6. Tall tales

ISBN 1-58536-289-1; 978-1-58536-289-9

LC 2006026583

When legendary logger Paul Bunyan falls in love with Lucette Diana Kensack, he will do whatever it takes to win her heart, including trying to restore the Minnesota environment to its previous condition as part of Lucette's "love test."

"The prose is just right for the genre. . . . The paintings extend the story's humorous images, while firmly placing the action in a mythical time." SLJ

Lord, Cynthia

Hot rod hamster; pictures by Derek Anderson. Scholastic Press 2010 unp il lib bdg $16.99

Grades: PreK K 1   E

1. Automobiles—Fiction 2. Automobile racing—Fiction 3. Hamsters—Fiction 4. Dogs—Fiction 5. Mice—Fiction

ISBN 978-0-545-03530-9 (lib bdg); 0-545-03530-9 (lib bdg)   LC 2009-03930

A hamster, with the help of a canine junkyard dealer and his mouse assistants, builds a hot rod and drives it in a race against some very large dogs.

This "is a rollicking, roaring read. In addition to the rhymed text punctuated by questions, the characters talk in speech balloons that move the story along without breaking the flow. Anderson's fluffy, jaunty illustrations are as full of energy as the rhymes." Kirkus

Lord, Janet

Albert the Fix-it Man; story by Janet Lord; pictures by Julie Paschkis. Peachtree 2008 unp il $15.95 *

Grades: PreK K 1 2   E

1. Repairing—Fiction 2. Community life—Fiction
ISBN 978-1-56145-433-4   LC 2007-29465

A cheerful repairman fixes squeaky doors, leaky roofs, and crumbling fences for his neighbors, who return the kindness when he catches a terrible cold

"Lord's rhythmic, simple text is perfectly cadenced for reading aloud, while Paschkis' cheerful illustrations, filled with scrolling designs and smiling friends, reinforce the sense of the close, busy community working together." Booklist

Here comes Grandma! [by] Janet Lord; illustrated by Julie Paschkis. Henry Holt and Co. 2005 unp il $12.95

Grades: PreK K 1   E

1. Grandmothers—Fiction 2. Transportation—Fiction
ISBN 0-8050-7666-2   LC 2004-22179

Grandma is coming to visit and she will use any possible method of transport, including a horse and a hot air balloon, to get there

"The simple, rhythmic text suits the mood of the story, and the vivid gouache illustrations have a warm, folklike quality." SLJ

Where is Catkin? written by Janet Lord; illustrated by Julie Paschkis. Peachtree Publishers 2010 unp il $16.95

Grades: PreK K 1   E

1. Cats—Fiction 2. Animals—Fiction
ISBN 978-1-56145-523-2; 1-56145-523-7

"In this picture-book hide-and-seek game, feline Catkin jumps off young Amy's lap and goes hunting into the grass, by a pond, through rocks, and up a tree, looking for Cricket, then Frog, Mouse, Snake, and Bird. Where are they? Children will enjoy searching through the busy, bright, stylized pictures in ink and gouache and pointing to the creatures hiding where Catkin doesn't see them." Booklist

Lord, John Vernon, 1939-

The giant jam sandwich; story and pictures by John Vernon Lord, with verses by Janet Burroway. Houghton Mifflin 1973 c1972 32p il lib bdg $17; pa $6.95; bd bk $6.99

Grades: K 1 2 3   E

1. Wasps—Fiction 2. Stories in rhyme
ISBN 0-395-16033-2 (lib bdg); 0-395-44237-0 (pa); 0-547-15077-6 (bd bk)

First published 1972 in the United Kingdom

This is a story in rhymed verse "about the citizens of Itching Down, who, attacked by four million wasps, make a giant jam sandwich to attract and trap the insects. With dump truck, spades, and hoes the people spread butter and strawberry jam across an enormous slice of bread; then, when the wasps settle, they drop the other slice from five helicopters and a flying tractor." Booklist

"Highly amusing in the details of John Vernon Lord's illustrations. . . . The figures are deliciously grotesque, their expressions wickedly accurate and the colours cheerfully vivid." Jr Bookshelf

Lorig, Steffanie

Such a silly baby! by Steffanie and Richard Lorig; illustrated by Amanda Shepherd. Chronicle Books 2008 unp il $15.99

Grades: PreK   E

1. Animals—Fiction 2. Infants—Fiction 3. Stories in rhyme
ISBN 978-0-8118-5134-3; 0-8118-5134-6
         LC 2007-13135

Rhyming text and illustrations follow the adventures of a baby who on excursions to the zoo, the circus, or the farm manages to get switched with an animal.

"Each time [the baby] greets Mom again, he adds a new phrase learned from his animal friends, for a cumulative festival of animal sounds that storytime listeners will love. Shepherd's bright, wildly cartoonlike oil paintings perfectly reflect the wackiness of the text." SLJ

Lottridge, Celia Barker

One watermelon seed. Fitzhenry & Whiteside 2008 unp il $17.95

Grades: PreK K 1 2   E

1. Counting 2. Gardening—Fiction
ISBN 978-1-55455-034-0; 1-55455-034-3

First published 1986 by Oxford University Press

"Numbers, colors, and gardening are combined in this vividly illustrated counting book. The story starts as Max and Josephine plant a garden, first 1 watermelon seed, then 2 pumpkin seeds, and so on all the way to 10. The phrase, 'and they grew' follows mention of each new set of seeds. The graphic-style illustrations depict the seedlings as they grow. . . . The vibrant colors and closeup views of the produce make it look delicious and irresistible." SLJ

Lotu, Denize, 1946-

Running the road to ABC; by Denizé Lauture; illustrated by Reynold Ruffins. Simon & Schuster Bks. for Young Readers 1996 unp il hardcover o.p. pa $6.99 *

Grades: PreK K 1 2   E

1. Haiti—Fiction 2. School stories
ISBN 0-689-80507-1; 0-689-83165-X (pa)
         LC 95-38290

A Coretta Scott King honor book for illustration, 1997

Long before the sun even thinks of rising the Haitian children run to school where they learn the letters, sounds, and words of their beautiful books

"The rich lyrical language used by the author, a Haitian poet, creates a strong sense of place. . . . The lush, green country and sense of hope are reflected and enhanced by stylized, warmly detailed gouache paintings." Horn Book

Loupy, Christophe, 1962-

Hugs and kisses; [by] Christophe Loupy, Eve Tharlet; translated by J. Alison James. North-South Bks. 2001 unp il $15.95; bd bk $6.95

Grades: PreK   E

1. Dogs—Fiction 2. Animals—Fiction
ISBN 0-7358-1484-8; 0-7358-2019-8 (bd bk)
         LC 2001-42595

"A Michael Neugebauer book"

Loupy, Christophe, 1962-—*Continued*

Original German edition published 2001 in Switzerland

Hugs the puppy sets out to collect lots of wonderful kisses from his animal friends, but in the end he discovers that the best kiss of all is the one he gets from his loving mother

"With fur that seems real enough to touch, a sunny disposition, and sweet manners, Hugs is a real charmer." Booklist

Lowell, Susan, 1950-

The elephant quilt; stitch by stitch to California! pictures by Stacey Dressen-McQueen. Farrar, Straus and Giroux 2008 unp il $16.95

Grades: K 1 2 3   E

1. Overland journeys to the Pacific—Fiction
2. Quilts—Fiction

ISBN 0-374-38223-9; 978-0-374-38223-0

LC 2005-51227

Lily Rose and Grandma stitch a quilt that tells the story of their family's journey from Missouri to California by covered wagon in 1859.

"Dramatic, mixed-media paintings portray majestic landscapes and frontier dangers, as well as moments of family merriment. An earthly color palette and brightly patterned quilt pieces add warmth and vibrancy to the 'bodacious' journey." Booklist

Lowry, Lois

Crow call; illustrated by Bagram Ibatoulline. Scholastic Press 2009 unp il $16.99 *

Grades: 1 2 3 4   E

1. Father-daughter relationship—Fiction 2. Hunting—Fiction 3. Crows—Fiction 4. Veterans—Fiction 5. Pennsylvania—Fiction

ISBN 978-0-545-03035-9; 0-545-03035-8

LC 2008-30158

Nine-year-old Liz accompanies the stranger who is her father, just returned from the war, when he goes hunting for crows in Pennsylvania farmland.

"Beautifully written. . . . Lowry's narrative, dense with sensory details, is based on her own life's events. Fittingly, Ibatoulline's muted, earth-toned palette is reminiscent of vintage, faded photographs." Kirkus

Lucas, David, 1966-

The robot and the bluebird. Farrar, Straus and Giroux 2008 unp il $16.95

Grades: PreK K 1 2   E

1. Robots—Fiction 2. Birds—Fiction

ISBN 978-0-374-36330-7; 0-374-36330-7

LC 2007026930

A broken robot makes a home for a cold, tired bluebird trying to fly south for the winter, and eventually he carries the bird to a warmer climate while she rests in the cavity where his heart used to be.

"In characteristically elaborate, warmly lit illustrations, Lucas uses sharp geometrical forms as the basis for his urban scenes; against this backdrop, the bird's more organic form is a welcome contrast. . . . This book's genuine sweetness will easily win over readers." SLJ

Something to do. Philomel Books 2009 unp il $14.99

Grades: PreK K   E

1. Bears—Fiction 2. Parent-child relationship—Fiction 3. Imagination—Fiction

ISBN 978-0-399-25247-1; 0-399-25247-9

LC 2009-1821

A parent and child bear must use their imaginations to find something to do.

"Young readers will instantly relate to the richly textured crayon drawings, which illustrate the expressiveness of the story and complement its softness with their deceptively simple, fuzzy-edged forms. . . . This stands out as a unique work because of its emotionally simple charm." Kirkus

Lucke, Deb

The boy who wouldn't swim. Clarion Books 2008 31p il $16

Grades: K 1 2 3   E

1. Swimming—Fiction 2. Siblings—Fiction 3. Fear—Fiction

ISBN 978-0-618-91484-5; 0-618-91484-6

LC 2007-22120

One very hot summer, Eric Dooley watches his younger sister go from her first swimming lesson all the way to the diving board, while his fear of the water keeps him from joining her and the rest of the people of Clermont County in the pool.

"This fear-of-swimming tale is ideal for kids who are afraid to take that first step. . . . Hot summer yellows and cool watery blues abound in the gouache illustrations, which are filled with action and humor." SLJ

Luebs, Robin

Please pick me up, Mama! Atheneum Books for Young Readers 2009 unp il $15.99

Grades: PreK   E

1. Stories in rhyme 2. Mother-child relationship—Fiction 3. Raccoons—Fiction

ISBN 978-1-4169-7977-7; 1-4169-7977-8

LC 2007052679

A baby raccoon spends the day with its mother enjoying many different experiences, from dressing up the cat to splashing and clapping.

"Warm autumn hues—rich, buttery oranges and crisp, apple greens—permeate the soft acrylic illustrations. Thick brush strokes in blacks, creams and browns naturally blend, adding depth to bushy tails and loving faces. . . . This small selection has both sweetness and spunk." Kirkus

Lum, Kate

What! cried Granny; an almost bedtime story; pictures by Adrian Johnson. Dial Bks. for Young Readers 1999 unp il hardcover o.p. pa $6.99

Grades: K 1 2 3   E

1. Bedtime—Fiction 2. Grandmothers—Fiction

ISBN 0-8037-2382-2; 0-14-230092-6 (pa)

LC 98-19642

First published 1998 in the United Kingdom with title: What!

Lum, Kate—*Continued*

"Sleeping over at Granny's for the first time, Patrick delays the inevitable, saying he can't go to bed because he doesn't even have a bed; or a blanket; or a teddy bear. In response to each legitimate complaint, Granny springs into action, chopping down a tree to build a bed, and so on." Horn Book Guide

This "combines the deadpan and the surreal in wild words and neon-colored acrylic illustrations." Booklist

Lumry, Amanda, 1977-

Safari in South Africa; by Amanda Lumry and Laura Hurwitz; illustrated by Sarah McIntyre. Scholastic 2008 32p il map (Adventures of Riley) $16.99; pa $6.99

Grades: 1 2 3 4   E

1. Wildlife conservation—Fiction 2. Game reserves 3. Animals—Africa 4. South Africa—Fiction

ISBN 978-0-545-06827-7; 0-545-06827-4; 978-0-545-06826-0 (pa); 0-545-06826-6 (pa)

First published 2003 by Eaglemont Press

Riley travels with his Uncle Max to check on the animal population at a South African game reserve.

"Combining whimsical cartoons and striking photographs of animals in the bush, this title is a marvelous intermingling of adventure and science. . . . Boxes presenting significant facts about the animals appear next to their photographs." SLJ

Other titles in this series are:

Amazon River rescue (2004)
Dolphins in danger (2009)
Mission to Madagascar (2005)
Operation Orangutan (2007)
Polar bear puzzle (2008)
Project Panda (2008)
Riddle of the reef (2009)
South Pole penguins (2008)
Tigers in Terai (2009)

Lund, Deb

Monsters on machines; [by] Deb Lund; illustrated by Robert Neubecker. Harcourt 2008 unp il $16

Grades: PreK K 1 2   E

1. Monsters—Fiction 2. Construction workers—Fiction 3. Construction equipment—Fiction 4. Stories in rhyme

ISBN 978-0-15-205365-9; 0-15-205365-4

LC 2006037393

Construction crew monsters arrive on the scene with tractors, cranes, and grader machines, and after a gruesome site is created as their routine, they straighten it up and leave everything clean.

"The India-ink drawings colored digitally in neon-bright hues exude a jazzy, busy look that brings to life the chaos that results when monsters and machines meet." SLJ

Luthardt, Kevin

Peep! Peachtree Pubs. 2003 unp il $15.95

Grades: PreK K   E

1. Ducks—Fiction 2. Pets—Fiction

ISBN 1-56145-046-4   LC 2002-35910

"With just a dozen-plus words, Luthardt tells the story of a young boy's attachment to a duckling ('peep!') who grows up into a duck ('quack!') and grows away from the boy ('it's time'; 'bye bye'). . . . The book's strength is the directness and speed with which art and minimal text tell the story. Pastel and mixed-media illustrations are on colored paper, which imparts warmth and a pleasing texture." Horn Book

Luxbacher, Irene, 1970-

Mattoo, let's play! written and illustrated by Irene Luxbacher. Kids Can Press 2010 unp il $16.95

Grades: PreK K 1   E

1. Cats—Fiction 2. Play—Fiction

ISBN 978-1-55453-424-1; 1-55453-424-0

"Highly imaginative Ruby wants to play with Mattoo, her 'shy' cat, who shuns her attempts at entertainment. As the child crashes and clangs pots and pans, or jumps up and down on her bed . . . readers will understand his 'shyness.' . . . This clever, unique tale illustrates how 'play' can be fun for humans but not so great for pets. Ruby is delightful, full of creativity and imagination. The use of acrylic ink and collage makes for stunning illustrations." SLJ

Lyon, George Ella, 1949-

My friend, the starfinder; by George Ella Lyon; pictures by Stephen Gammell. Atheneum Books for Young Readers 2008 unp il $16.99

Grades: PreK K 1 2   E

1. Storytelling—Fiction

ISBN 978-1-4169-2738-9; 1-4169-2738-7

LC 2006032026

A child relates some of the wondrous tales told by an old man who once found a falling star and stood at the end of a rainbow.

This is a "sumptuously illustrated book. . . . Text and art are sure to evoke wonder in young readers." Publ Wkly

The pirate of kindergarten; illustrated by Lynne Avril. Atheneum Books for Young Readers 2010 il $16.99

Grades: PreK K 1 2   E

1. Vision disorders—Fiction 2. School stories

ISBN 978-1-4169-5024-0; 1-4169-5024-9

Ginny's eyes play tricks on her, making her see everything double, but when she goes to vision screening at school and discovers that not everyone sees this way, she learns that her double vision can be cured.

"Lyon's short, descriptive sentences set up the situation deftly, and Avril's astute chalk, pencil, and acrylic drawings of 'two of everything' provide a vivid window into Ginny's pretreatment world." SLJ

Trucks roll! words by George Ella Lyon; art by Craig Frazier. Atheneum Books for Young Readers 2007 unp il $14.99

Grades: PreK   E

1. Trucks—Fiction 2. Stories in rhyme

ISBN 978-1-4169-2435-7; 1-4169-2435-3

LC 2006-10811

"A Richard Jackson book"

Lyon, George Ella, 1949-—*Continued*

Illustrations and simple, rhyming text reveal many different—and sometimes silly—items that trucks can haul.

"Solid, up-to-date information about a major preschool enthusiasm is leavened with lively verse and touch of whimsy." Horn Book

You and me and home sweet home; illustrated by Stephanie Anderson. Atheneum Books for Young Readers 2009 unp il $17.99
Grades: PreK K 1 2 3   E
  1. Houses—Fiction 2. Building—Fiction 3. Volunteer work—Fiction 4. African Americans—Fiction
  ISBN 978-0-689-87589-2; 0-689-87589-4
                                    LC 2008010414

"A Richard Jackson book"

Third-grader Sharonda and her mother help volunteers from their church to build the house that will be their very own.

"Sharonda narrates in clean, simple prose. . . . Varied in composition and perspective, the watercolor-and-pastel-pencil illustrations center on the nicely individualized characters . . . and readers will share Sharonda's quiet glow of happiness at the end." Booklist

Macaulay, David, 1946-

Black and white. Houghton Mifflin 1990 unp il hardcover o.p. pa $7.99 *
Grades: 1 2 3   E
  1. Railroads—Fiction 2. Cattle—Fiction
  ISBN 0-395-52151-3; 0-618-63687-0 (pa)
                                    LC 89-28888

Awarded the Caldecott Medal, 1990

Four brief "stories" about parents, trains, and cows, or is it really all one story? The author recommends careful inspection of words and pictures to both minimize and enhance confusion

"The magic of *Black and White* comes not from each story, . . . but from the mysterious interactions between them that creates a fifth story. . . . Eventually, the stories begin to merge into a surrealistic tale spanning several levels of reality. . . . *Black and White* challenges the reader to use text and pictures in unexpected ways." Publ Wkly

Shortcut. Houghton Mifflin 1995 unp il $15.95; pa $7.95
Grades: 1 2 3   E
  ISBN 0-395-52436-9; 0-618-00607-9 (pa)
                                    LC 95-2542

"This picture book concerns six humans whose paths cross and recross in the eight chapters of brief text and distinctive artwork. Albert and his horse, June, take their wagon of melons to market, sell them, and go home. . . . Patty's pet pig, Pearl, wanders onto an abandoned railroad line. . . . Professor Tweet is studying birds when suddenly his hot air balloon breaks free and heads toward a nearby cathedral spire. . . . Seemingly inconsequential details in one story become the moving forces in another." Booklist

"Because *Shortcut* is not linear in its progression but rather an exploration of simultaneity and concepts of time and space, it is a picture book for sophisticated readers who enjoy puzzles and unraveling clues. . . .

David Macaulay deserves applause for challenging his readers as well as entertaining them through boldly conceived illustrations with a cast of wonderfully caricatured characters." Horn Book

Why the chicken crossed the road. Houghton Mifflin 1987 31p il lib bdg $16
Grades: 3 4 5   E
  1. Chickens—Fiction
  ISBN 0-395-44241-9 (lib bdg)   LC 87-2908

"A ridiculous chicken sets off a circular story involving a herd of cows, a bridge, a train, a robber, the fire department and some hydrangeas. Chaos. The illustrations are suitably wild—painted with brilliant color and almost palpable energy." N Y Times Book Rev

MacDonald, Ross, 1957-

Another perfect day. Millbrook Press 2002 unp il hardcover o.p. pa $6.95 *
Grades: PreK K 1 2   E
  1. Heroes and heroines—Fiction
  ISBN 0-7613-1595-0; 1-59643-079-6 (pa)
                                    LC 2002-18798

"A Neal Porter book"

What started out as another perfect day for Jack the superhero performing heroic feats suddenly goes awry

"With a beefy hero and graphics inspired by 1930-40s comic books, this impeccably designed volume features a forthright text that comically counterpoints a livelier tale told through the pictures." Publ Wkly

Another title about Jack is:
Bad baby (2005)

Macdonald, Suse, 1940-

Alphabatics. Bradbury Press 1986 unp il $19.95; pa $7.99 *
Grades: PreK K 1 2   E
  1. Alphabet
  ISBN 0-02-761520-0; 0-689-71625-7 (pa)
                                    LC 85-31429

A Caldecott Medal honor book, 1987

MacDonald "maneuvers each letter to create a visual image as well as an object that begins with that letter." Child Book Rev Serv

The "*A* tilts, flops over, and literally becomes an ark as it turns itself around. An *N* turns over, glides up a tree trunk, and becomes a nest for three young birds. Crisp, fresh, and totally effective, it's a unique way of looking at the alphabet. This is a book for creative thinking and sheer enjoyment of MacDonald's precise graphics, rather than for object identification among the very young." SLJ

Alphabet animals; a slide-and-peek adventure. Little Simon 2008 unp il $12.99
Grades: PreK K   E
  1. Alphabet 2. Animals—Fiction 3. Board books for children
  ISBN 978-1-4169-5045-5; 1-4169-5045-1

"A note to parents explains that this book is a guessing game in which animals and birds are drawn in the shapes of letters and children are encouraged to identify them. Each page presents one critter, set against a bright

Macdonald, Suse, 1940-—*Continued*

backdrop, with a pullout panel that reveals the letter represented along with the name of that particular animal. The color combinations are eye-catching and the images are appealing. . . . This is a clever way to help children learn the alphabet and reinforce pre-reading skills." SLJ

Fish, swish! splash, dash! Little Simon 2007 unp il $8.99
Grades: PreK K 1 2   E
1. Fishes—Fiction 2. Counting 3. Stories in rhyme
ISBN 978-1-4169-3605-3; 1-4169-3605-X

Follow the leader and count the fish that live beneath the sea. Turn the book upside-down and count again.
"Vivid hues, clean visual elements, and simple language combine to create a successful and eye-catching concept book." SLJ

Mack, Jeff

Hush little polar bear; [by] Jeff Mack. Roaring Brook Press 2008 unp il $16.95
Grades: PreK K   E
1. Stories in rhyme 2. Bedtime—Fiction 3. Dreams—Fiction 4. Adventure fiction 5. Polar bear—Fiction
ISBN 978-1-59643-368-7; 1-59643-368-X
                                        LC 2007044049

A little girl invites her plush polar bear to dream of all of the places where sleeping bears go, from the high seas to a starry desert and back home
"The richly textured spreads are bright and imaginative, perfectly complementing the simple, lyrical text." SLJ

Mackall, Dandi Daley, 1949-

First day; illustrated by Tiphanie Beeke. Harcourt 2003 unp il $16
Grades: PreK K   E
1. School stories 2. Stories in rhyme
ISBN 0-15-216577-0   LC 2002-933
"Silver Whistle"

The first day of school starts out filled with doubt, but after facing fear of the big kids, reciting the alphabet with ease, and learning about recess, a child can't help but look forward to day two.
"The rhyming text gives the story a sweet, singsong quality. . . . The softly colored, reassuring art works well with the simple text that is set on pastel backgrounds." SLJ

Macken, JoAnn Early, 1953-

Waiting out the storm; illustrated by Susan Gaber. Candlewick Press 2010 unp il $15.99 *
Grades: PreK K 1 2   E
1. Stories in rhyme 2. Storms—Fiction 3. Rain—Fiction 4. Mother-child relationship—Fiction
ISBN 978-0-7636-3378-3; 0-7636-3378-X
                                        LC 2008030746

A mother reassures her child about the wind, lightning, and thunder when a storm passes through.
"The text creates a natural-sounding rhythm and flow of dialogue. . . . Gaber's captivating artwork, combining watercolor, pencil, and charcoal with digital renderings, is simultaneously strong and delicate." Booklist

MacLachlan, Patricia, 1938-

All the places to love; paintings by Mike Wimmer. HarperCollins Pubs. 1994 unp il $16.99; lib bdg $17.89
Grades: K 1 2 3   E
1. Farm life—Fiction 2. Family life—Fiction
ISBN 0-06-021098-2; 0-06-021099-0 (lib bdg)
                                        LC 92-794

A young boy describes the favorite places that he shares with his family on his grandparents' farm and in the nearby countryside
Wimmer's "paintings beautifully convey the splendor of nature, as well as the deep affection binding three generations. This inspired pairing of words and art is a timeless, uplifting portrait of rural family life." Publ Wkly

Bittle; by Patricia MacLachlan & Emily MacLachlan; illustrations by Dan Yaccarino. Joanna Cotler Books 2004 unp il hardcover o.p. lib bdg $16.89 *
Grades: PreK K 1 2   E
1. Infants—Fiction 2. Dogs—Fiction 3. Cats—Fiction
ISBN 0-06-000961-6; 0-06-000962-4 (lib bdg)
                                        LC 2003-2357

Nigel the cat and Julia the dog think they will have no use for the new baby in their house, but after awhile they realize that they have come to love her
"The colors are bright, the lines simple. . . . The authors cleverly highlight the changes a new baby brings to a home, and the animals' growing affection for Bittle is humorous and heartwarming." SLJ

Painting the wind; by Patricia MacLachlan & Emily MacLachlan; illustrated by Katy Schneider. J. Cotler Bks. 2003 unp il $15.99; pa $7.99
Grades: K 1 2 3   E
1. Artists—Fiction 2. Painting—Fiction
ISBN 0-06-029798-0; 0-06-443825-2 (pa)
                                        LC 2001-47549

Several artists who paint different things, with different kinds of paint, and at different times of the day, all paint the same island that they visit each summer
"The gentle prose pairs well with handsome artwork that evokes warm, strong sensory impressions through a combination of thick brushwork, texture, and a vibrant color palette." Booklist

MacLennan, Cathy

Chicky chicky chook chook. Boxer 2007 unp il $12.95; bd bk $7.95 *
Grades: PreK K 1   E
1. Farm life—Fiction 2. Chickens—Fiction 3. Cats—Fiction 4. Bees—Fiction 5. Stories in rhyme
ISBN 978-1-905417-40-3; 1-905417-40-3; 978-1-906250-55-3 (bd bk); 1-906250-55-3 (bd bk)

Chicks, chickens, cats, and bees on a farm enjoy an active, busy day playing, snoozing, and getting drenched in a thunderstorm before finally going to sleep at night
"This rambunctious story has an onomatopoeic rhyming text that children will love to hear again and again. . . . Inspired by the art and culture of her native Zimbabwe, MacLennan dabs, swirls, and sponges bright splashes of paint on brown butcher paper." SLJ

Madison, Alan
Velma Gratch & the way cool butterfly; written by Alan Madison; illustrated by Kevin Hawkes. Schwartz & Wade Books 2007 unp il $16.99; lib bdg $19.99 *
Grades: PreK K 1 2   E
1. Butterflies—Fiction 2. Sisters—Fiction 3. School stories
ISBN 978-0-375-83597-1; 978-0-375-93597-8 (lib bdg)   LC 2006030978
Velma starts first grade in the shadow of her memorable older sisters, and while her newfound interest in butterflies helps her to stand out, it also leads to an interesting complication
"With humorous wordplay and electric cartoon art, this is an uplifting and way-cool look at one child's metamorphosis." SLJ

Madrigal, Antonio Hernandez
Erandi's braids; written by Antonio Hernandez Madrigal; illustrated by Tomie dePaola. Putnam 1999 unp il $15.99; pa $6.99
Grades: K 1 2 3   E
1. Hair—Fiction 2. Mother-daughter relationship—Fiction 3. Mexico—Fiction
ISBN 0-399-23212-5; 0-698-11885-5 (pa)
LC 97-49631
In a poor Mexican village, Erandi surprises her mother by offering to sell her long, beautiful hair in order to raise enough money to buy a new fishing net
"This tale of love and sacrifice is based on an actual Mexican practice in the 1940s and 50s. The facial expressions in dePaola's warm illustrations add to the poignancy of the story." Horn Book Guide

Mahy, Margaret
17 kings and 42 elephants; pictures by Patricia MacCarthy. Dial Bks. for Young Readers 1987 26p il $16.99
Grades: K 1 2 3   E
1. Animals—Fiction 2. Stories in rhyme
ISBN 0-8037-0458-5   LC 87-5311
A newly illustrated edition of the title first published 1972 in the United Kingdom
Seventeen kings and forty-two elephants romp with a variety of jungle animals during their mysterious journey through a wild, wet night
"This book takes you on a jungle journey you will never forget. . . . The text is lyrical, humorous, and full of nonsense and fantasy. Children and adults will be charmed by the melodic use of language and the beautiful batik illustrations." Child Book Rev Serv

Bubble trouble; illustrated by Polly Dunbar. Clarion Books 2009 37p il $16 *
Grades: PreK K 1   E
1. Bubbles—Fiction 2. Stories in rhyme
ISBN 978-0-547-07421-4; 0-547-07421-2
LC 2008-07244
Boston Globe-Horn Book Award: Picture Book (2009)
Mabel blows a bubble that captures Baby and wafts him away, resulting in a wild chase that involves the whole neighborhood.

"Mahy is a master at creating verse that is as light and airy as the baby's bubble. Filled with lovely Briticisms, alliterative nonsense words, double, triple and internal rhymes, it's meant to be read aloud. . . . Dunbar's joyous watercolor-and-cut-paper illustrations are wonderfully expressive, a visual treat moving apace with the text." Kirkus

Mak, Kam
My Chinatown; one year in poems. HarperCollins Pubs. 2002 unp il $16.95 *
Grades: 2 3 4   E
1. Immigrants—Fiction 2. Chinese Americans—Fiction 3. Chinatown (New York, N.Y.)—Fiction
ISBN 0-06-029190-7; 0-06-029191-5 (lib bdg)
LC 2001-16686
A boy adjusts to life away from his home in Hong Kong, in the Chinatown of his new American city
"Extraordinary photo-realistic paintings and spare, free-verse poems bring New York's Chinatown to life in this picture book with appeal to a wide age group." Booklist

Manning, Maurie
Kitchen dance; by Maurie J. Manning. Clarion Books 2008 unp il $16
Grades: PreK K 1   E
1. Bedtime—Fiction 2. Family life—Fiction 3. Dance—Fiction 4. Hispanic Americans—Fiction
ISBN 978-0-618-99110-5; 0-618-99110-7
LC 2007036838
"Drawn from their beds by noises downstairs, the narrator and her little brother, Tito, peer into the kitchen to find that their parents have turned dinner cleanup into a rambunctious, Latin-flavored song and dance number. . . . As the rounded, sculptural bodies of the couple move about the kitchen with humor and grace, the illustrations take on a cinematic sense of motion and space." Publ Wkly

Manning, Mick
Snap! [by] Mick Manning, [illustrated by] Brita Granström. Frances Lincoln 2006 unp il $14.95
Grades: PreK K 1 2   E
1. Food chains (Ecology)—Fiction
ISBN 1-84507-408-4
This "story looks at the food chain, first by introducing a fly who is gobbled up by a frog, who is, in turn, guzzled by a duckling, who is, in turn, eaten by a pike, etc. . . . The comical conclusion is perfect for the younger set, but even the older kids will enjoy the drama in these pages. The bold colorful cartoons are inviting; the text is simple." SLJ

Mannis, Celeste Davidson
One leaf rides the wind; counting in a Japanese garden; by Celeste Davidson Mannis, pictures by Susan Kathleen Hartung. Viking 2002 unp il $15.99; pa $6.99
Grades: PreK K 1 2   E
1. Gardens—Poetry 2. Haiku 3. Counting
ISBN 0-670-03525-4; 0-14-240195-1 (pa)
LC 2002-1024

Mannis, Celeste Davidson—*Continued*

In this collection of haiku poems, a young girl walks through a Japanese garden and discovers many delights, from one leaf to ten stone lanterns. Includes notes about Japanese religion and philosophy

"The book as a whole is elegantly and respectfully presented and the counting aspect is especially well crafted, capturing the meandering focus of a small child. Mannis's simple verses are complemented by Hartung's pleasing and evocative pen-and-ink and watercolor art." SLJ

Manushkin, Fran

How Mama brought the spring; [by] Fran Manushkin; illustrated by Holly Berry. Dutton 2008 unp il $16.99

Grades: K 1 2 3   E

1. Family life—Fiction 2. Cooking—Fiction 3. Russia—Fiction 4. Spring—Fiction

ISBN 978-0-525-42027-9; 0-525-42027-4

LC 2007-05217

A mother in Chicago tells her daughter how Grandma used to make a special surprise on the freezing cold winter mornings in Belarus—so special that it seemed to bring spring with it.

"This tale is filled with rich language and imagery. The illustrations fill the page with great detail and show images of the Russian culture. A recipe for cheese blintzes is included. This book would be a great addition." Libr Media Connect

The Shivers in the fridge; illustrated by Paul O. Zelinsky. Dutton Children's Books 2006 unp il $16.99 *

Grades: PreK K 1 2   E

1. Magnets—Fiction 2. Refrigeration—Fiction

ISBN 0-525-46943-5   LC 2006-03867

One-by-one, the members of the Shivers family disappear from the inside of their chilly refrigerator home

"The story's humor is matched by Zelinsky's inventive artwork, which picks up on the wit and slyness of the text." Booklist

Marceau, Fani

Panorama; a foldout book; [illustrated by] Joëlle Jolivet. Abrams Books for Young Readers 2009 unp il $19.95 *

Grades: 1 2 3   E

1. Travel—Fiction 2. Voyages around the world—Fiction

ISBN 978-0-8109-8332-8; 0-8109-8332-X

LC 2008022166

Original French edition 2007

Illustrations and simple text invite the reader to visit different places around the world, then to view the same scenes at night on the reverse of the fanfolded page.

This is a "stunning travelogue. . . . Each oversize page is grounded by a poetic fragment evoking each locale. . . . A faint ecological bent further enriches the descriptions. But the main event is the alternately dizzying and mysterious black-and-white woodcut illustrations. They can be flipped through like an ordinary book, though the full impact is felt only through unfurling all 15 pages so that they lay flat in a seamless panorama." Booklist

Marcellino, Fred, 1939-2001

I, crocodile. HarperCollins Pubs. 1999 unp il hardcover o.p. pa $6.99

Grades: 1 2 3 4   E

1. Napoleon I, Emperor of the French, 1769-1821—Fiction 2. Crocodiles—Fiction

ISBN 0-06-205168-7; 0-06-008859-1 (pa)

"Michael di Capua books"

"The tale, inspired by a 19th-century French satire by an unknown author, centers on a crocodile captured in Egypt and transported to Paris by Napoleon, who decides to cook and eat the animal. But the crocodile . . . escapes into the sewers and makes his own dinner out of a lady of Napoleon's court." N Y Times Book Rev

"The text is reportorial in tone, a perfect complement to the extravagant, expressive illustrations. . . . A sophisticated picture book, this is one publication with appeal to many different audiences." Horn Book

Mariconda, Barbara

Sort it out! illustrated by Sherry Rogers. Sylvan Dell 2008 unp il $16.95; pa $8.95

Grades: PreK K 1 2   E

1. Rats—Fiction 2. Collectors and collecting—Fiction

ISBN 978-1-934359-11-2; 1-934359-11-4; 978-1-934359-32-7 (pa); 1-934359-32-7 (pa)

"When Pack rat comes home with a cart full of stuff—a locket, a book, an umbrella, a pinecone, and many more random items—his mother admonishes him to sort it all out and put it away. Packy does just that, cleverly sorting things with like characteristics such as where they're found, their color, shape, etc. . . . The illustrations are brightly colored, large, and very clear. Careful readers will notice a subplot in the pictures and find satisfaction in seeing its resolution on the final page. In addition, the rhyming text prompts them to guess the word that defines each collection. Back matter has activities to extend the experience." SLJ

Marino, Gianna

One too many; a seek & find counting book. Chronicle Books 2010 unp il $16.99

Grades: PreK K 1 2   E

1. Animals—Fiction 2. Counting

ISBN 978-0-8118-6908-9; 0-8118-6908-3

Children count from one jumping flea to twelve frisky animals until, at last, they reach one too many.

"Marino's naturalistic illustrations are done in gouache in this remarkable counting book. . . . Young readers will find much to discover as they revisit the book time after time." SLJ

Zoopa; an animal alphabet. Chronicle Books 2005 unp il $14.95

Grades: PreK K 1 2   E

1. Alphabet 2. Animals

ISBN 0-8118-4789-6   LC 2004-63449

"A bowl of tomato soup is the vehicle for introducing the letters of the alphabet and their corresponding animals. Beginning with a playful ant and an orange-and-purple butterfly, two to three animals and their first letters are introduced on each spread. As the menagerie multiplies, the creatures move around the pages, some-

Marino, Gianna—*Continued*

times interacting with humorous results. . . . The playful gouache illustrations depict the colorful crew having as much fun as readers will surely have identifying them." SLJ

Markes, Julie

Good thing you're not an octopus! story by Julie Markes; pictures by Maggie Smith. HarperCollins Pubs. 2001 unp il $14.95; pa $6.99

Grades: PreK K   E

1. Animals—Fiction

ISBN 0-06-028465-X; 0-06-443586-5 (pa)

LC 99-37139

"A boy who complains about getting dressed, riding in his car seat, and more is answered with funny worst-case scenarios: 'You don't like to take a nap? It's a good thing you're not a bear. If you were a bear, you would have to nap all winter long!' The tone is silly, and the cheerful illustrations convey the absurdity in the text." Horn Book Guide

Shhhhh! Everybody's sleeping; illustrated by David Parkins. HarperCollins 2005 unp il $14.99; lib bdg $15.89

Grades: PreK K 1   E

1. Bedtime—Fiction 2. Sleep—Fiction 3. Stories in rhyme

ISBN 0-06-053790-6; 0-06-053791-4 (lib bdg)

LC 2003-27854

A young child is encouraged to go to sleep by the thought of everyone else sleeping, from teacher to baker to postman

"The text satisfyingly moves along while the artwork soars. . . . Glowing with warm colors in subdued hues, the sturdy pictures stretch wide across double-page spreads, offering surprisingly energetic, varied compositions." Booklist

Marlow, Layn

Hurry up and slow down; [by] Layn Marlow. Holiday House 2009 c2008 unp il $16.95 *

Grades: PreK K 1   E

1. Rabbits—Fiction 2. Turtles—Fiction 3. Bedtime—Fiction 4. Books and reading—Fiction

ISBN 978-0-8234-2178-7; 0-8234-2178-3

LC 2008010796

First published 2008 in the United Kingdom

Hare likes to hurry through the day, unlike Tortoise, but manages to slow down for his favorite bedtime story

"This delightful spinoff of 'The Tortoise and the Hare' follows a typical day in the lives of these two friends. . . . The illustrations of Hare, Tortoise, their animal companions, and their environment are rounded and softly colored, creating a comforting world for young children. An endearing story that will no doubt become a bedtime favorite." SLJ

Marshall, Edward, 1942-1992

Fox and his friends; pictures by James Marshall. Dial Bks. for Young Readers 1982 56p il pa $3.99 hardcover o.p. *

Grades: K 1 2   E

1. Foxes—Fiction

ISBN 0-14-037007-2 (pa)   LC 81-68769

"Dial easy-to-read"

"Fox has one objective—having fun with his motley group of friends. Unfortunately, his desires regularly conflict with his mother's insistence that he care for his younger sister Louise or with his responsibilities when assigned to traffic patrol." Horn Book

"The sibling exchanges and situations are comically true to life, as is Fox's duty/pleasure conflict. The red, green and black illustrations, showing a defiant Louise, a beleaguered Fox, a wonderful assortment of creature friends and a hilariously feeble group of old hounds pick the story up and add character embellishment and humor." SLJ

Other titles about Fox are:

Fox all week (1984)

Fox at school (1983)

Fox in love (1982)

Fox on wheels (1983)

Space case; pictures by James Marshall. Dial Bks. for Young Readers 1980 unp il hardcover o.p. pa $6.99 *

Grades: PreK K 1 2   E

1. Science fiction 2. Halloween—Fiction

ISBN 0-8037-8005-2; 0-14-054704-5 (pa)

LC 80-13369

"The 'thing'—a neon yellow robot-like creature from space—arrives on Halloween for a look around and is promptly mistaken for a costumed trick-or-treater. It spends the night with a friendly child . . . visits at school (the teacher takes it for a science project) and leaves promising to return for the next fun holiday, Christmas." SLJ

"The open ending of the brief story is as satisfying as it is original, for the small space traveler is thoroughly childlike in its insouiance, curiosity, and concern for self-gratification. The text is an economical, tongue-in-cheek accompaniment to the various levels of humor depicted in the illustrations." Horn Book

Three by the sea; pictures by James Marshall. Dial Bks. for Young Readers 1981 48p il pa $3.99 hardcover o.p.

Grades: K 1 2   E

1. Storytelling—Fiction

ISBN 0-14-037004-8 (pa)

"Dial easy-to-read"

"When Lolly, on a beach picnic with friends Sam and Spider, reads a story ('The rat saw the cat and the dog.') aloud, it is rated dull. So Sam uses the same rat and cat characters to tell one of his own, and Spider tops Sam's managing to scare the other two with his tale of a monster that passes by the rat and cat to find some tasty kids." SLJ

"The mild lunacy of the illustrations (an almost vertical hill, a neatly striped cat) with their ungainly, comical figures is nicely matched with the bland directness of the writing. This is good-humored and amusing." Bull Cent Child Books

Marshall, Edward, 1942-1992—*Continued*
Other titles about Spider, Sam, and Lolly are:
Four on the shore (1985)
Three up a tree (1986)

Marshall, James, 1942-1992
George and Martha; written and illustrated by
James Marshall. Houghton Mifflin 1972 46p il lib
bdg $16; pa $6.95 *
Grades: PreK K 1 2   E
1. Hippopotamus—Fiction 2. Friendship—Fiction
ISBN 0-395-16619-5 (lib bdg); 0-395-19972-7 (pa)
In these five short episodes which include a misunder-
standing about split pea soup, invasion of privacy and a
crisis over a missing tooth, two not very delicate hippo-
potamuses reveal various aspects of friendship
"The pale pictures of these creatures and their adven-
tures—in yellows, pinks, greens, and grays—capture the
directness and humor of the stories." Horn Book
Other titles about George and Martha are:
George and Martha back in town (1984)
George and Martha encore (1973)
George and Martha, one fine day (1978)
George and Martha rise and shine (1976)
George and Martha round and round (1988)
George and Martha, tons of fun (1980)

Swine Lake; [pictures by] Maurice Sendak.
HarperCollins Pubs. 1999 unp il $16.95 *
Grades: PreK K 1 2   E
1. Ballet—Fiction 2. Wolves—Fiction 3. Pigs—Fiction
ISBN 0-06-205171-7   LC 98-73253
"Michael di Capua books"
A hungry wolf attends a performance of Swine Lake,
performed by the Boarshoi Ballet, intending to eat the
performers, but he is so entranced by the story unfolding
that he forgets about his meal
"Both Marshall and Sendak are cleverly comic here
. . . the text shines. Sendak's art captures the nuance as
well as all the humor of the story." Booklist

Martin, Bill, 1916-2004
Baby Bear, Baby Bear, what do you see? by
Bill Martin, Jr.; pictures by Eric Carle. Henry Holt
2007 unp il $16.95
Grades: PreK K   E
1. Bears—Fiction 2. Animals—Fiction 3. Stories in
rhyme
ISBN 978-0-8050-8336-1; 0-8050-8336-7
LC 2006037769
Illustrations and rhyming text portray a young bear
searching for its mother and meeting many North American animals along the way
"Creative action words and renderings of the various
creatures in motion give the book a pleasing energy,
while Mama Bear's obvious delight at finding her cub
provides an endearing poignancy. [An] elegant balance of
art, text, emotion and exposition." Publ Wkly

Barn dance! by Bill Martin, Jr. and John
Archambault; illustrated by Ted Rand. Holt & Co.
1986 unp il $16.95; pa $6.95
Grades: PreK K 1 2   E
1. Stories in rhyme 2. Dance—Fiction 3. Country
life—Fiction
ISBN 0-8050-0089-5; 0-8050-0799-7 (pa)
LC 86-14225
Unable to sleep on the night of a full moon, a young
boy follows the sound of music across the fields and
finds an unusual barn dance in progress
"The bouncy rhyme will be a pleasure for listeners
and tellers as they pick up the twang and the barn-dance
beat. Rand's raucous two-page watercolor spreads are as
spirited as the story poem." Booklist

A beasty story; [written by] Bill Martin, Jr. &
[illustrated by] Steven Kellogg. Harcourt Brace &
Co. 1999 unp il $16; pa $7 *
Grades: PreK K 1 2   E
1. Mice—Fiction 2. Color—Fiction 3. Stories in
rhyme
ISBN 0-15-201683-X; 0-15-216560-6 (pa)
LC 97-49519
A group of mice venture into a dark, dark woods
where they find a dark brown house with a dark red stair
leading past other dark colors to a spooky surprise
"A rhymed narrative tells the story along the top of
the pages, with the mice commenting in rhymed conversation as they move through the adventure. The silly resolution will appeal to young children. . . . Kellogg's
lively ink-and-watercolor art strikes just the right note for
the gently suspenseful story." Booklist

Brown bear, brown bear what do you see?
pictures by Eric Carle. Holt & Co. 1992 unp il
$16.99; bd bk $7.95 *
Grades: PreK K   E
1. Color—Fiction 2. Animals—Fiction 3. Stories in
rhyme
ISBN 0-8050-1744-5; 0-8050-4790-5 (bd bk)
LC 91-29115
A newly illustrated edition of the title first published
1967 by Holt, Rinehart & Winston
A chant in which a variety of animals, each one a different color, answers the question, "What do you see?"
"Carle's large, brilliantly colored animals set against a
white background make the book perfect for sharing with
a group of preschoolers, while Martin's repetitious text
is eminently chantable—a boon for beginning readers."
Horn Book

Chicka chicka 1, 2, 3; [by] Bill Martin, Jr. &
Michael Sampson; illustrated by Lois Ehlert.
Simon & Schuster Books for Young Readers 2004
unp il $15.95 *
Grades: PreK K 1   E
1. Counting 2. Stories in rhyme
ISBN 0-689-85881-7   LC 2003-19106
Companion volume to Chicka chicka boom boom
Numbers from one to one hundred climb to the top of
an apple tree in this rhyming chant.
"The chanting rhyme and eye-popping images have a
contagious energy youngsters will find irresistible."
Booklist

Martin, Bill, 1916-2004—*Continued*

Chicka chicka boom boom; [by] Bill Martin, Jr. and John Archambault; illustrated by Lois Ehlert. anniversary edition. Beach Lane Books 2009 unp il $17.99 *　　　　　　　　　　　　　　　E
1. Stories in rhyme 2. Alphabet
ISBN 978-1-4169-9091-8; 1-4169-9091-7
LC 2009-626
A reissue of the title first published 1989
An alphabet rhyme/chant that relates what happens when the whole alphabet tries to climb a coconut tree.
"Ehlert's illustrations-bold, colorful shapes-are contained by broad polka-dotted borders, like a proscenium arch through which the action explodes. Tongue-tingling, visually stimulating, with an insistent repetitive chorus of 'chicka chicka boom boom,' the book demands to be read again and again and again." Horn Book

The ghost-eye tree; by Bill Martin, Jr. and John Archambault; illustrated by Ted Rand. Holt & Co. 1985 unp il $16.95; pa $6.95 *
Grades: K 1 2 3　　　　　　　　　　　　　　　E
1. Ghost stories 2. Fear—Fiction
ISBN 0-8050-0208-1; 0-8050-0947-7 (pa)
LC 85-8422
"On a dark and ghostly night a brother and sister are sent to fetch a pail of milk from the other end of town. They must pass the fearful ghost-eye tree, old and horribly twisted, looking like a monster, with a gap in the branches where the moon shines through like an eye. . . . The story is rhythmically told, sometimes rhyming, always moving ahead, sharp with the affectionate teasing of the brother and sister. The realistic watercolor illustrations are superb—strong, striking, very dark, with highlights of moonlight and lantern light that cast a spooky, scary spell. A splendidly theatrical book for storytelling and reading aloud." Horn Book

Knots on a counting rope; by Bill Martin, Jr. and John Archambault; illustrated by Ted Rand. Holt & Co. 1987 unp il $16.95; pa $6.95 *
Grades: K 1 2 3　　　　　　　　　　　　　　　E
1. Native Americans—Fiction 2. Grandfathers—Fiction 3. Blind—Fiction
ISBN 0-8050-0571-4; 0-8050-5479-0 (pa)
LC 87-14858
A different version of the title illustrated by Joe Smith was published in 1966
"Boy-Strength-of-Blue-Horses begs his grandfather to tell him again the story of the night he was born. In a question-and-answer litany, the boy and his grandfather share the telling of the events on that special night." SLJ
"The powerful spare poetic text is done full justice by Rand's fine full-color illustrations, which capture both the drama and brilliance of vast southwestern space and the intimacy of starlit camp-fire scenes." Booklist

The maestro plays; by Bill Martin, Jr.; pictures by Vladimir Radunsky. Holt & Co. 1994 unp il $15.95 *
Grades: K 1 2 3　　　　　　　　　　　　　　　E
1. Musicians—Fiction
ISBN 0-8050-1746-1　　　　　　　　　　　LC 94-1916

"At center stage is a clown-like creature, 'The Maestro,' who plays a progression of instruments. And how does he play? In an intriguing variety of ways, including some that are easy enough to understand ('flowingly, glowingly, knowingly, showingly, goingly') and some that will require youngsters to use their imaginations ('nippingly, drippingly, zippingly, clippingly, pippingly.'" Publ Wkly
"Radunsky's wonderfully bizarre illustrations, created from hand-colored cut paper, are a visual delight. . . . An infectious rhythm builds, at times lapsing into nonsense, but resulting in an almost perfect coupling of text and illustration." SLJ

Panda bear, panda bear, what do you see? by Bill Martin Jr.; pictures by Eric Carle. Holt & Co. 2003 unp il $15.95; bd bk $7.95
Grades: PreK K　　　　　　　　　　　　　　　E
1. Endangered species—Fiction 2. Animals—Fiction 3. Stories in rhyme
ISBN 0-8050-1758-5; 0-8050-8078-3 (bd bk)
LC 2002-10855
Illustrations and rhyming text present ten different endangered animals
"The pictures, featuring animals strolling, splashing, and soaring, are brilliant lessons in the application of color, shape, form, and texture. . . . A fine read-aloud with a subtle, yet clear, message." Booklist

Polar bear, polar bear, what do you hear? by Bill Martin, Jr.; pictures by Eric Carle. Holt & Co. 1991 unp il $16.95; bd bk $7.95
Grades: PreK K　　　　　　　　　　　　　　　E
1. Animals—Fiction 2. Stories in rhyme
ISBN 0-8050-1759-3; 0-8050-5388-3 (bd bk)
LC 91-13322
Zoo animals from polar bear to walrus make their distinctive sounds for each other, while children imitate the sounds for the zookeeper
"Carle's characteristically inventive, jewel-toned artwork forms a seamless succession of images that fairly leap off the pages." Publ Wkly

Trick or treat? [by] Bill Martin, Jr. and Michael Sampson; illustrated by Paul Meisel. Simon & Schuster Bks. for Young Readers 2002 unp il hardcover o.p. pa $6.99 *
Grades: PreK K 1 2　　　　　　　　　　　　　E
1. Halloween—Fiction 2. Magic—Fiction
ISBN 0-689-84968-0; 1-4169-0262-7 (pa)
LC 2002-70646
A child has a wonderful time collecting treats from the wacky neighbors until Magic Merlin decides that a trick would be more fun
"Meisel's cartoon illustrations take full advantage of the topsy-turvy story, adding lots of comic holiday detail to keep little ones alert. The fun is in the pictures, and the challenge is in figuring out the visual joke and the backward names." Booklist

Martin, David, 1944-

Christmas tree; illustrated by Melissa Sweet. Candlewick Press 2009 unp il bd bk $5.99

Grades: PreK   E

1. Christmas—Fiction 2. Trees—Fiction 3. Board books for children

ISBN 978-0-7636-3030-0 (bd bk); 0-7636-3030-6 (bd bk)

At Christmastime, a tree from the outside comes inside, just waiting to be decorated

This "attractive board [book features] simple, [a] clear [concept] and delightful pencil-and-watercolor illustrations enhanced with patterned fabric swatches." SLJ

Hanukkah lights; illustrated by Melissa Sweet. Candlewick Press 2009 unp il bd bk $5.99

Grades: PreK   E

1. Hanukkah—Fiction 2. Board books for children

ISBN 978-0-7636-3029-4 (bd bk); 0-7636-3029-2 (bd bk)

Children celebrate Hanukkah by lighting candles, eating latkes, spinning a dreidel, and giving presents

This "attractive board [book features] simple, clear concepts and delightful pencil-and-watercolor illustrations enhanced with patterned fabric swatches." SLJ

Piggy and Dad go fishing; illustrated by Frank Remkiewicz. Candlewick Press 2005 unp il $14.99

Grades: PreK K 1 2   E

1. Fishing—Fiction 2. Pigs—Fiction 3. Father-son relationship—Fiction

ISBN 0-7636-2506-X   LC 2004-51941

When his dad takes Piggy fishing for the first time and Piggy ends up feeling sorry for the worms and the fish, they decide to make some changes.

"The summery watercolor-and-pencil cartoon illustrations clue listeners into Piggy's emotions and create a bit of tension in the nicely paced story." Horn Book Guide

Other titles about Piggy and Dad are:

Piggy and Dad (2001)

Piggy and Dad play (2002)

Martin, Jacqueline Briggs, 1945-

Grandmother Bryant's pocket; pictures by Petra Mathers. Houghton Mifflin 1996 48p il hardcover o.p. pa $5.95

Grades: K 1 2 3   E

1. Fear—Fiction 2. Grandmothers—Fiction 3. Maine—Fiction

ISBN 0-395-68984-8; 0-618-03309-2 (pa)

LC 94-31309

"In 1787, Sarah Bryant is eight years old and lives on a farm in Maine. She and her spotted dog Patches are inseparable companions until that spring, when the barn burns down and Patches is killed in the fire. Sarah begins to have bad dreams . . . and so she is sent to her grandparents, an herbalist and a woodworker, for solace and healing." Horn Book

"Appealingly structured in one-and two-page chapters, the book is illustrated with watercolor paintings. Executed in naive style, the artwork has an unassuming sweetness." Booklist

On Sand Island; illustrated by David Johnson. Houghton Mifflin 2003 unp il $16

Grades: 1 2 3   E

1. Islands—Fiction

ISBN 0-618-23151-X   LC 2002-5090

In 1916 on an island in Lake Superior, Carl builds himself a boat by bartering with the other islanders for parts and labor

"Martin's simple, poetic text deftly balances small, revealing details about the island's characters and Carl's life with the particulars of boat building. . . . The illustrations . . . capture the lake's translucent light and the story's nostalgic mood in expert, geometric line drawings washed with watery blue-green and sunset-orange colors." Booklist

Martin, Rafe, 1946-

Will's mammoth; illustrated by Stephen Gammell. Putnam 1989 unp il $16.99

Grades: K 1 2 3   E

1. Mammoths—Fiction

ISBN 0-399-21627-8   LC 88-11651

"Will loves mammoths—huge, hairy, woolly mammoths. His parents explain that there are no mammoths left in the world, but Will knows better. Off he goes into an iridescent, snowbound world of his own creation, where he quickly finds all manner of woolly prehistoric beasts." SLJ

"Gammell's depiction of a child's rich imagination is illustrated in vivid colors. The fantasy spreads use winter whites and blues as background for subtly individualized animals who move energetically across the pages." Booklist

Martin, Steve, 1945-

The alphabet from A to Y with bonus letter, Z! by Steve Martin & [illustrated by] Roz Chast. Doubleday/Flying Dolphin Press 2007 unp il $17.95; lib bdg $17.95

Grades: K 1 2 3   E

1. Alphabet 2. Stories in rhyme

ISBN 978-0-385-51662-4; 978-0-385-52377-6 (lib bdg)   LC 2006102543

Presents a rhyming couplet featuring each letter of the alphabet, with such characters as David the dog-faced boy, who dons a derby despite being dirty, and Victor, whose frequent victories have made him vainglorious

"Martin and Chast show their mettle as each other's wacky sidekicks. . . . [A] peculiar and funny book." Publ Wkly

Marzollo, Jean

Ten little Christmas presents. Scholastic 2008 unp il pa $9.99

Grades: PreK K   E

1. Gifts—Fiction 2. Christmas—Fiction 3. Animals—Fiction 4. Santa Claus—Fiction 5. Counting 6. Stories in rhyme

ISBN 978-0-545-02791-5 (pa); 0-545-02791-8 (pa)

LC 2007-21572

"Cartwheel books"

Marzollo, Jean—*Continued*

A counting-down book in which ten forest animals find unexpected Christmas presents, left for them by a Secret Santa

"Toddlers will like the simple, rhyming story and the sketchy, childlike illustrations, and preschoolers will like the reverse counting game. Teachers and librarians will find this a good fit for story hours about counting or Christmas presents." Kirkus

Mathers, Petra

Lottie's new beach towel. Atheneum Bks. for Young Readers 1998 unp il hardcover o.p. pa $6.99 *

Grades: PreK K 1 2   E
    1. Chickens—Fiction 2. Beaches—Fiction
    ISBN 0-689-81606-5; 0-689-84441-7 (pa)
                            LC 97-6689

"An Anne Schwartz book"

Lottie the chicken has a number of adventures at the beach, during which her new towel, a gift from her friend Herbie the duck, comes in handy.

"Pure fun, with a resourceful, big-hearted main character; humor in both text and pictures; and a good story, elegantly shaped." Horn Book

Other titles about Lottie and Herbie are:
A cake for Herbie (2000)
Herbie's secret Santa (2002)
Lottie's new friend (1999)

Matsuoka, Mei

Footprints in the snow. Henry Holt & Co. 2008 unp il $16.95 *

Grades: PreK K 1 2 3   E
    1. Wolves—Fiction 2. Storytelling—Fiction
    ISBN 978-0-8050-8792-5; 0-8050-8792-3

Wolf is feeling offended and indignant: All the wolves he's ever read about are nasty, scary, and greedy! To set the record straight he decides to write a story about a nice wolf. But will his wolfish instincts get the better of him after all?

"Both plot and pictures . . . take a surprising turn, which will delight young readers. Replete with visual allusions to popular wold stories, the folk-art style illustrations set up the scenario for this story-within-stories." Booklist

Matthews, Tina, 1961-

Out of the egg. Houghton Mifflin 2007 unp il $12.95

Grades: K 1 2 3   E
    1. Chickens—Fiction 2. Animals—Fiction
    ISBN 978-0-618-73741-3; 0-618-73741-3
                          LC 2006-09812

When the barnyard animals who refused to help her plant and tend a seed ask to play under the "great green whispery tree" that Little Red Hen grew, she says no, but her chick thinks that answer is mean.

"This gritty, sharply graphic woodcut version of the time-honored tale sets our feathered friend and her slothful sidekicks squarely in the present. . . . Matthews's hand-painted Japanese woodblock illustrations, black and white and red all over—with, of course, an important touch of green—are striking editorial panoramas." SLJ

Mayer, Mercer, 1943-

A boy, a dog, and a frog. Dial Bks. for Young Readers 1967 unp il pa $6.99 hardcover o.p. *

Grades: PreK K 1   E
    1. Frogs—Fiction 2. Stories without words
    ISBN 0-8037-2880-8 (pa)

"Without the need for a single word, humorous, very engaging pictures tell the story of a little boy who sets forth with his dog and a net on a summer day to catch an enterprising and personable frog. Even very young preschoolers will 'read' the tiny book with the greatest satisfaction and pleasure." Horn Book

Other titles in this series are:
A boy, a dog, a frog, and a friend (1971)
Frog goes to dinner (1974)
Frog on his own (1973)
Frog, where are you? (1969)
One frog too many (1975)

The bravest knight; story and pictures by Mercer Mayer. Dial Books for Young Readers 2007 unp il $16.99

Grades: PreK K 1 2   E
    1. Play—Fiction 2. Knights and knighthood—Fiction
    ISBN 978-0-8037-3206-3   LC 2006021321

First published 1968 by Dial Press with title: Terrible Troll

A little boy imagines the adventures he would have if he lived a thousand years ago and was the squire of a bold knight who fought dragons and trolls.

"Funny details abound in every picture. . . . This fresh version of an old favorite should find a place in all picture-book collections." SLJ

There's a nightmare in my closet. Dial Bks. for Young Readers 1968 unp il $16.99; pa $6.99 *

Grades: PreK K 1   E
    1. Fear—Fiction
    ISBN 0-8037-8682-4; 0-14-054712-6 (pa)

"Childhood fear of the dark and the resulting exercise in imaginative exaggeration are given that special Mercer Mayer treatment in this dryly humorous fantasy. Young children will easily empathize with the boy and can be comforted by his experience." SLJ

Another title about this boy is:
There's an alligator under my bed (1987)

Mayo, Margaret, 1935-

Choo choo clickety-clack! written by Margaret Mayo; illustrated by Alex Ayliffe. Carolrhoda Books 2005 unp il lib bdg $14.95

Grades: PreK K   E
    1. Noise—Fiction 2. Transportation—Fiction
    ISBN 1-57505-819-7   LC 2004-11976

First published 2004 in the United Kingdom

Rhythmic sounds imitate trains, planes, and other busy transports that come and go

"Short and snappy, four lines of text encapsulate the excitement that comes with getting in a car, sailing on a lake, or floating in a hot-air balloon. The graphic-style artwork is executed in a melange of pure colors." Booklist

Mayo, Margaret, 1935-—*Continued*

Roar! [by] Margaret Mayo & [illustrated by] Alex Ayliffe. Carolrhoda Books 2007 unp il lib bdg $15.95

Grades: PreK K 1   E

1. Animals—Fiction

ISBN 978-0-7613-9473-0   LC 2006029853

First published 2006 in the United Kingdom

Text and pictures describe the things which different kinds of animals like to do

"The creatures each get a spread with a rhythmic, fun-to-read narrative. . . . The malleable lines of type stretch with the giraffes, wave with the hippos, and jump with the kangaroos. Ayliffe's illustrations have bright, bold colors and simple, but effective depictions of the animals and landscapes that fairly leap off the pages." SLJ

Mayr, Diane, 1949-

Run, Turkey run; [by] Diane Mayr; illustrated by Laura Rader. Walker Pub. Co. 2007 unp il $15.95; lib bdg $16.85

Grades: PreK K 1 2   E

1. Turkeys—Fiction 2. Thanksgiving Day—Fiction

ISBN   978-0-8027-9630-1;   0-8027-9630-3; 978-0-8027-9631-8 (lib bdg); 0-8027-9631-1 (lib bdg)

                         LC 2006036190

The day before Thanksgiving, Turkey tries to disguise himself as other animals in order to avoid being caught by the farmer.

"This fast-paced romp is as much fun to read as it is to listen to. . . . The illustrations are light and humorous." SLJ

Mazer, Norma Fox, 1931-2009

Has anyone seen my Emily Greene? [by] Norma Fox Mazer; illustrated by Christine Davenier. Candlewick Press 2007 unp il $15.99

Grades: PreK K 1 2   E

1. Father-daughter relationship—Fiction 2. Play—Fiction 3. Stories in rhyme

ISBN 978-0-7636-1384-6; 0-7636-1384-3

                         LC 2006051828

Emily decides to play hide and seek when her father calls her for lunch

This is a "picture-book romp that reads with the hand-clapping, foot-stomping rhythm of a rowdy folk song and includes lots of sound effects that kids will want to shout out loud. Davenier's sweeping ink lines, dabbed with watercolors, match the energy in the rhyming words." Booklist

McBratney, Sam

Guess how much I love you; illustrated by Anita Jeram. Candlewick Press 1995 unp il hardcover o.p. bd bk $7.99

Grades: PreK K   E

1. Rabbits—Fiction 2. Father-son relationship—Fiction

ISBN 1-56402-473-3; 0-7636-4264-9 (bd bk)

                         LC 94-1599

During a bedtime game, every time Little Nutbrown Hare demonstrates how much he loves his father, Big Nutbrown Hare gently shows him that the love is re-turned even more

"Neither sugary nor too cartoonlike, the watercolors, in soft shades of brown and greens with delicate ink-line details, warmly capture the loving relationship between parent and child as well as the comedy that stems from little hare's awe of his wonderful dad." Booklist

When I'm big; illustrated by Anita Jeram. Candlewick 2007 unp il bd bk $7.99

Grades: PreK   E

1. Rabbits—Fiction 2. Growth—Fiction 3. Board books for children

ISBN 978-0-7636-3546-6 (bd bk)

Little Nutbrown Hare loves playing in the spring, when everything is growing and changing, but what will a little brown hare grow into?

"Jeram's sunny ink-and-watercolor illustrations—sprightly spot art and spreads—offer subtle yet solid reinforcement of the text." Publ Wkly

McCall, Bruce

Marveltown. Farrar, Straus and Giroux 2008 unp il $16.95

Grades: PreK K 1 2   E

1. Inventions—Fiction 2. Robots—Fiction 3. Science fiction

ISBN 978-0-374-39925-2; 0-374-39925-5

                         LC 2006-38250

Marveltown's adults are outstanding inventors, but when their best engineers create giant but stupid robots that threaten the town, it is the children's outrageous creations that save the day.

"The boldly colored, nostalgic-looking illustrations depict the action with detail, vitality, and humor and will easily grab readers' attention." SLJ

McCarthy, Mary, 1951-

A closer look. Greenwillow Books 2007 unp il $16.99; lib bdg $17.89 *

Grades: PreK K 1 2   E

1. Nature—Fiction

ISBN   978-0-06-124073-7;   0-06-124073-7; 978-0-06-124074-4 (lib bdg); 0-06-124074-5 (lib bdg)

                         LC 2006-29459

Detailed collage illustrations accompanied by simple text present expanding views of familiar objects in nature, such as a bug and a flower.

"Rendered from handmade papers and collage, the bold artwork is elegant and eye-catching. The broad lines, simple graphic images, and textured details suit the magnified perspectives, while the more expansive scenes are beautifully composed." SLJ

McCarty, Peter

Henry in love. Balzer & Bray 2009 unp il $16.99; lib bdg $17.89 *

Grades: PreK K 1   E

1. School stories 2. Love—Fiction 3. Rabbits—Fiction 4. Cats—Fiction

ISBN   978-0-06-114288-8;   0-06-114288-3; 978-0-06-114289-5 (lib bdg); 0-06-114289-1 (lib bdg)

                         LC 2009-14412

McCarty, Peter—*Continued*

On the first day of school, Henry the cat vies for the attention of the most amazing girl in class, Chloe Rabbit.

"This gentle, pitch-perfect romance will have readers' hearts thumping with the thrill of first love." Publ Wkly

Hondo and Fabian. Holt & Co. 2002 unp il $16.95; pa $6.95 *

Grades: PreK K 1 2   E

1. Dogs—Fiction 2. Cats—Fiction

ISBN 0-8050-6352-8; 0-312-36747-3 (pa)

LC 2001-1884

A Caldecott Medal honor book, 2003

Hondo the dog gets to go to the beach and play with his friend Fred, while Fabian the cat spends the day at home

"McCarty's staccato text, one line to a page, captures a lot of action in a few words, but it is the pencil-on-watercolor-paper art that makes this so arresting. Each carefully shaded picture, in muted tones, has a smooth, solid look." Booklist

Another title about Hondo and Fabian is:

Fabian escapes (2007)

Jeremy draws a monster. Henry Holt 2009 unp il $16.99   E

1. Monsters—Fiction 2. Drawing—Fiction

ISBN 978-0-8050-6934-1; 0-8050-6934-8

LC 2008-36813

A young boy who spends most of his time alone in his bedroom makes new friends after the monster in his drawing becomes a monstrous nuisance.

"The finely rendered pen-and-ink and watercolor illustrations skillfully delineate characters and objects. . . . [This is] top-notch." Booklist

Moon plane; written and illustrated by Peter McCarty. Henry Holt 2006 unp il $16.95 *

Grades: PreK K   E

1. Airplanes—Fiction 2. Flight—Fiction 3. Moon—Fiction

ISBN 978-0-8050-7943-2; 0-8050-7943-2

LC 2005016244

A young boy looks at a plane in the sky and imagines flying one all the way to the moon

"Using pencils, McCarty creates soft-edged, silver-tone artwork notable for its elegant simplicity. . . . McCarty catches both the way children's imaginations work and the connections they make." Booklist

T is for terrible; written and illustrated by Peter McCarty. Henry Holt 2004 unp il $15.95; pa $6.99

Grades: PreK K 1   E

1. Dinosaurs—Fiction

ISBN 0-8050-7404-X; 0-312-38423-8 (pa)

LC 2003-18246

A tyrannosaurus rex explains that he cannot help it that he is enormous and hungry and is not a vegetarian.

"Filled with textured lines and soft shading, the artwork glows with warmth and vitality. This beautifully formatted and well-conceived offering has creamy ivory pages that frame the subtle illustrations and spare text." SLJ

McClements, George

Dinosaur Woods; can seven clever critters save their forest home? Beach Lane Books 2009 unp il $16.99 *

Grades: PreK K 1 2   E

1. Endangered species—Fiction 2. Animals—Fiction 3. Dinosaurs—Fiction 4. Environmental protection—Fiction

ISBN 978-1-4169-8626-3; 1-4169-8626-X

LC 2008-33084

"Atheneum Books for Young Readers"

To save their homes from being destroyed by developers, a fanciful group of endangered animals constructs a fearsome dinosaur.

"This title's generous trim size, cleanly rendered illustrations, and fast-paced text are perfect for group read-alouds or one-on-one sharing." SLJ

Night of the Veggie Monster. Bloomsbury Children's Books 2008 unp il $14.95; lib bdg $15.85

Grades: K 1 2 3   E

1. Food—Fiction 2. Family life—Fiction

ISBN 978-1-59990-061-2; 1-59990-061-0; 978-1-59990-234-0 (lib bdg); 1-59990-234-6 (lib bdg)

LC 2007017850

Every Tuesday night, while his parents try to enjoy their dinner, a boy turns into a monster the moment a pea touches his lips

"Illustrations are a creative medley of photographed realia . . . cut-out brown paper . . . and simple pastel lines and textural elements, . . . resulting in a spare vigor that nicely supports the textual humor." Bull Cent Child Books

Ridin' dinos with Buck Bronco; as told to George McClements. Harcourt 2007 unp il $16

Grades: PreK K 1 2   E

1. Dinosaurs—Fiction 2. Cowhands—Fiction

ISBN 978-0-15-205989-7   LC 2006006175

Buck Bronco teaches how to care for and ride a variety of strange dinosaurs.

"Bright, goofy mixed-media collage illustrations demonstrate the cowboy's instructions and will have dinosaur fans chuckling." SLJ

McClintock, Barbara, 1955-

Adèle & Simon. Farrar, Straus & Giroux 2006 unp il $16 *

Grades: PreK K 1 2   E

1. Lost and found possessions—Fiction 2. Siblings—Fiction 3. Paris (France)—Fiction

ISBN 0-374-38044-9   LC 2002-35311

"Frances Foster books"

When Adele walks her little brother Simon home from school he loses one more thing at every stop: his drawing of a cat at the grocer's shop, his books at the park, his crayons at the art museum, and more.

"Set in Paris during the early 20th century, this simple story is the basis for some remarkable illustrations. McClintock's pen-and-ink with watercolor technique has the feel of illustrated children's books from that period. . . . A beautiful example of bookmaking, with plenty to charm children, this is a visual delight." SLJ

Another title about Adele and Simon is:

McClintock, Barbara, 1955-—*Continued*
Adele & Simon in America (2008)

Dahlia. Farrar, Straus & Giroux 2002 unp il $16
*

Grades: PreK K 1   E
 1. Dolls—Fiction
 ISBN 0-374-31678-3   LC 2001-18778
 "Frances Foster books"
 "Charlotte doesn't want a doll for a playmate. . . .
She prefers to climb trees, make mud pies, and dig in the
dirt. When her Aunt Edme sends her a doll that's dressed
in lace, ribbons, and gloves, Charlotte wrinkles her nose
and informs the doll that there will be no tea parties or
riding in 'frilly prams!' . . . McClintock tells an engaging story about an unusual character. . . . In her trademark delicate pen-and-ink outline art—filled with soft
watercolors—McClintock delightfully juxtaposes spirited
Charlotte within the old-fashioned setting." Booklist

McCloskey, Robert, 1914-2003
 Blueberries for Sal. Viking 1948 54p il $16.99;
pa $7.99 *
Grades: PreK K 1 2   E
 1. Bears—Fiction 2. Maine—Fiction
 ISBN 0-670-17591-9; 0-14-050169-X (pa)
 A Caldecott Medal honor book, 1949
 "The author-artist tells what happens on a summer day
in Maine when a little girl and a bear cub, wandering
away from their blueberry-picking mothers, each mistakes the other's mother for its own. The Maine hillside
and meadows are real and lovely, the quiet humor is entirely childlike, and there is just exactly the right amount
of suspense for small children." Wis Libr Bull
 Another title about Sal is:
 One morning in Maine (1952)

Lentil. Viking 1940 unp il $18.99; pa $5.99
Grades: PreK K 1 2   E
 1. Harmonicas—Fiction 2. Ohio—Fiction
 ISBN 0-670-42357-2; 0-14-050287-4 (pa)
 Picture-story book about a small boy who could not
sing, but who could work wonders on a simple harmonica, especially on the day when the great Colonel Carter
returned to his home town
 "Big, vigorous, amusing pictures in black-and-white,
with an Ohio small-town background." New Yorker

Make way for ducklings. Viking 1941 unp il
$17.99; pa $7.99 *
Grades: PreK K 1 2   E
 1. Ducks—Fiction 2. Boston (Mass.)—Fiction
 ISBN 0-670-45149-5; 0-14-056434-9 (pa)
 Awarded the Caldecott Medal, 1942
 "A family of baby ducks was born on the Charles
River near Boston. When they were old enough to follow, Mother Duck, with some help from a friendly policeman, trailed them through Boston traffic to the pond
in the Public Garden." Bookmark
 "There are some very beautiful drawings in this
book." Horn Book

One morning in Maine. Viking 1952 64p il
$17.99; pa $6.99 *
Grades: K 1 2 3   E
 1. Maine—Fiction
 ISBN 0-670-52627-4; 0-14-050174-6 (pa)
 A Caldecott Medal honor book, 1953
 The events of this "story—Sal's discovery of her first
loose tooth, the loss of the tooth while digging clams,
the consequent wish on a gull's feather, and the wish
come true—occur in the course of one morning in
Maine. The lovely Maine seacoast scenes and the doings
of Sal with her family and friends are drawn with enticing detail in beautiful, big double-spread lithographs
printed in dark blue." Booklist

Time of wonder. Viking 1957 63p il $18.99; pa
$6.99 *
Grades: K 1 2 3   E
 1. Maine—Fiction
 ISBN 0-670-71512-3; 0-14-050201-7 (pa)
 Awarded the Caldecott Medal, 1958
 "A summer on an island in Maine is described
through the simple everyday experiences of children, but
also reveals the author's deep awareness of an attachment to all the shifting moods of season and weather,
and the salty, downright character of the New England
people." Top News

McClure, Nikki
 Mama, is it summer yet? Abrams Books for
Young Readers 2010 unp il $17.95
Grades: PreK K 1   E
 1. Summer—Fiction 2. Mother-son relationship—Fiction
 ISBN 978-0-8109-8468-4; 0-8109-8468-7
 "Repetition of this book's title question ties together
responses and scenes of a child and his mother as they
wait for warmer weather. . . . The days pass with a
graceful swirl as the most delicate of paper-cuts detail
budding trees, squirrels nesting, soft earth for seedlings,
young ducklings following their mother, swallows circling overhead, and blossoming trees, culminating in the
anticipated delight of summer berries. . . . Simple black
paper contrasts with a light, neutral background, highlighting spare use of digitally added color accents; solid-
color sheets underscore the repeated text. . . . Children
will appreciate the simple sentences and lyrical verse that
relate the seasonal passing of time." SLJ

McCourt, Frank
 Angela and the baby Jesus; illustrated by Raúl
Colón. Simon & Schuster Books for Young
Readers 2007 unp il $17.99
Grades: K 1 2 3   E
 1. Christmas—Fiction 2. Ireland—Fiction
 ISBN 978-1-4169-3789-0; 1-4169-3789-7
 "The six-year-old heroine is McCourt's mother, Angela, who is disturbed that the Baby Jesus must be cold as
he lies outside in a Nativity scene. . . . Angela steals the
baby so she get him home and warm him in her bed.
. . . McCourt writes with the lilt of the Irish and the
ability to get inside a child's mind. . . . Painted with a
glow that comes from street lamps or candlelight, Colón's artwork showcases the warmth that a caring family
radiates." Booklist

McCully, Emily Arnold

Beautiful warrior; the legend of the nun's kung fu. Levine Bks. 1998 unp il $18.95 *

Grades: 1 2 3 4   E

  1. Martial arts—Fiction 2. China—Fiction

  ISBN 0-590-37487-7   LC 97-3823

"Born near the end of the Ming Dynasty, a girl grows up to become a fighting nun, renowned for her martial arts. Later, when a timid village girl asks for help in deterring her loutish husband-to-be, the nun teaches her kung fu so she can save herself. The story is intriguing, and the watercolors . . . are filled with dramatic motion." Horn Book Guide

First snow. HarperCollins Publishers 2004 unp il $15.99 *

Grades: PreK K   E

  1. Snow—Fiction 2. Sledding—Fiction 3. Mice—Fiction

  ISBN 0-06-623852-8   LC 2003-44971

A timid little mouse discovers the thrill of sledding in the first snow of the winter.

"First published as a wordless picture book in 1985, First Snow is back with a brief text, enhanced illustrations, and a larger trim size. . . . This new edition has brighter, deeper colors. . . . Full of exuberance and excitement." SLJ

Other titles about this young mouse are:

Picnic (2003)

School (2005)

The grandma mix-up; story and pictures by Emily Arnold McCully. Harper & Row 1988 63p il pa $5.99 hardcover o.p. *

Grades: PreK K 1 2   E

  1. Grandmothers—Fiction

  ISBN 0-06-444150-4 (pa)   LC 87-29378

"An I can read book"

Young Pip doesn't know what to do when two very different grandmothers come to baby sit, each with her own way of doing things

"McCully's two-color, line-and-wash drawings emphasize the personality differences by consciously flouting stereotypes: Pip's laid-back Grandma Sal has white hair and glasses, while his strict Grandma Nan dresses like a teenager. Choice of words and sentence length will make the sly humor easy for beginning readers to grasp." Booklist

Other titles about Pip and his grandmothers are:

Grandmas at bat (1993)

Grandmas at the lake (1990)

Mirette on the high wire. Putnam 1992 unp il hardcover o.p. pa $6.99 *

Grades: K 1 2 3   E

  1. Tightrope walking—Fiction 2. Paris (France)—Fiction

  ISBN 0-399-22130-1; 0-698-11443-4 (pa)

                  LC 91-36324

Awarded the Caldecott Medal, 1993

Mirette learns tightrope walking from Monsieur Bellini, a guest in her mother's boarding house, not knowing that he is a celebrated tightrope artist who has withdrawn from performing because of fear

"With a rich palette of deep colors, the artist immerses the reader in 19th-century Paris. Colorful theatrical personalities . . . fill the glowing interiors with robust life. And the exterior scenes . . . are filled with the magic of a Paris night when anything can happen. . . . An exuberant and uplifting picture book." N Y Times Book Rev

Other titles about Mirette and Bellini are:

Mirette & Bellini cross Niagra Falls (2000)

Starring Mirette and Bellini (1997)

Squirrel and John Muir. Farrar Straus Giroux 2004 unp il $16

Grades: K 1 2 3   E

  1. Muir, John, 1838-1914—Fiction 2. California—Fiction

  ISBN 0-374-33697-0   LC 2003-45511

In the early 1900s, a wild little girl nicknamed Squirrel meets John Muir, later to become a famous naturalist, when he arrives at her parents' hotel in Yosemite Valley seeking work and knowledge about the natural world.

"The afterword explains how this fictionalized retelling of an actual relationship reveals much about the compelling founder of the Sierra Club. . . . McCully's sure watercolors capture the stunning natural beauty of the area and provide a majestic backdrop for the small figure of Squirrel." SLJ

Includes bibliographical references

Wonder horse; the true story of the world's smartest horse. Henry Holt 2010 unp il $16.99 *

Grades: PreK K 1 2   E

  1. Key, Bill, 1833-1909—Fiction 2. Horses—Fiction 3. African Americans—Fiction

  ISBN 978-0-8050-8793-2; 0-8050-8793-1

                  LC 2009006208

A fictionalized account of Bill "Doc" Key, a former slave who became a veterinarian, trained his horse, Jim Key, to recognize letters and numbers and to perform in skits around the country, and moved the nation toward a belief in treating animals humanely. Includes an author's note.

"McCully's storytelling is as sensitive, engaging, and well paced as her brightly colored, expressive artwork." Booklist

Includes bibliographical references

McDermott, Gerald

Creation. Dutton Children's Bks. 2003 unp il $16.99

Grades: 2 3 4   E

  1. Creation—Fiction

  ISBN 0-525-46905-2

The author's meditation on the creation story based on Genesis I of Hebrew Bible. In it man and woman are created last to be the keepers of all this beauty

"McDermott casts the story of creation in strong poetic text and sweeping vibrant views. . . . Sumptuous, rhythmic, and mystical, this book is arresting and evocative." SLJ

McDermott, Gerald—*Continued*

Papagayo; the mischief maker; written and illustrated by Gerald McDermott. Harcourt Brace Jovanovich 1992 unp il hardcover o.p. pa $8
Grades: 2 3 4   E
1. Parrots—Fiction
ISBN 0-15-259465-5; 0-15-259464-7 (pa)
       LC 91-40364
A reissue of the title first published 1980 by Windmill Bks.

Papagayo, the noisy parrot, helps the night animals save the moon from being eaten up by the moon dog
"McDermott's original story assumes folktale proportions. . . . Art for the story is striking; deep tropical colors seem intensified by glossy page surfaces, and they nearly vibrate against the intermittent deep-blue backdrop of a night sky." Booklist

McDonald, Megan, 1959-

Hen hears gossip; illustrated by Joung Un Kim. HarperCollins 2008 unp il $17.99; lib bdg $17.89
Grades: PreK K   E
1. Animals—Fiction 2. Gossip—Fiction
ISBN   978-0-06-113876-8;   0-06-113876-2; 978-0-06-113877-5 (lib bdg); 0-06-113877-0 (lib bdg)
       LC 2007027137
When Hen overhears some news on the farm, she runs to tell Duck, who tells another animal, and as the gossip is repeated from one animal to the next, it becomes unrecognizable

"The simple prose incorporates capitals and punctuation that offer guidance for animated read-alouds. The colorful, mixed-media collages . . . blend bold, blocky shapes with vivid, intricate patterns and textures. Children will enjoy the farcical fun." Booklist

It's picture day today! illustrated by Katherine Tillotson. Atheneum Books for Young Readers 2009 unp il $16.99
Grades: PreK K   E
1. Artists' materials—Fiction 2. School stories
ISBN 978-1-4169-2434-0; 1-4169-2434-5
       LC 2007-46435
"A Richard Jackson book"
A classroom of art supplies gathers for their picture day.

"Tillotson's collage work, both creative and endearingly clunky, will awaken the inner cutter-and-paster in almost any young child. An ideal book to pair with a craft session." Booklist

McDonnell, Christine, 1949-

Dog wants to play; illustrated by Jeff Mack. Viking Children's Books 2009 unp il $15.99
Grades: PreK K   E
1. Dogs—Fiction 2. Play—Fiction
ISBN 978-0-670-01126-1; 0-670-01126-6
       LC 2009001955
Dog is eager to have fun, but no one in the barnyard will play with him except one special friend.

"Textured, sun-kissed painted images put bounce into the simple story and capture Dog's realistic body poses." Booklist

McDonnell, Patrick, 1956-

South; [by] Patrick McDonnell. Little, Brown and Co. 2008 unp il $14.99 *
Grades: PreK K 1 2   E
1. Birds—Fiction 2. Cats—Fiction 3. Stories without words
ISBN 978-0-316-00509-8; 0-316-00509-6
       LC 2007048373
Mooch the cat helps a lonely bird find its flock, which has flown south for the winter

"McDonnell's comfort with unfilled expanses, his beautifully balanced compositions, and the nature of his brushwork evoke the feel of traditional Chinese art. Tan recycled paper provides warmth in keeping with this tender, compact story." SLJ

McElligott, Matthew, 1968-

Bean thirteen. G. P. Putnam's Sons 2007 unp il lib bdg $15.99 *
Grades: K 1 2 3   E
1. Division—Fiction 2. Insects—Fiction
ISBN 978-0-399-24535-0 (lib bdg); 0-399-24535-9 (lib bdg)
       LC 2006-26295
Two bugs, Ralph and Flora, try to divide thirteen beans so that the unlucky thirteenth bean disappears, but they soon discover that the math is not so easy.

"Done in pen and ink with digital effects, the cartoon illustrations feature bright hues and slightly off-kilter perspectives that will appeal to children. Youngsters will undoubtedly enjoy this funny tale; teachers will truly appreciate the connections it makes to their curriculum and the use of manipulatives in math." SLJ

The lion's share; [by] Matt McElligott. Walker & Co. 2009 unp il $16.99; lib bdg $17.89 *
Grades: PreK K 1 2   E
1. Etiquette—Fiction 2. Mathematics—Fiction 3. Ants—Fiction 4. Lions—Fiction
ISBN   978-0-8027-9768-1;   0-8027-9768-7; 978-0-8027-9769-8 (lib bdg); 0-8027-9769-5 (lib bdg)
       LC 2008013358
Ant is honored to receive an invitation to lion's annual dinner party, but is shocked when the other guests behave rudely and then accuse her of thinking only of herself.

"McElligott's digitally touched ink-and-watercolor artwork combines expressive animal characters with clear groupings of objects that illustrated the embedded arithmetic exercises. While the story will find an obvious place in early elementary math or character education units, the lively illustrations amplify the story's slapstick humor and will easily entertain story hour crowds." Booklist

McEvoy, Anne

Betsy B. Little; by Anne McEvoy; illustrated by Jacqueline Rogers. HarperCollinsPublishers 2009 unp il $17.99; lib bdg $18.89
Grades: PreK K 1 2   E
1. Stories in rhyme 2. Ballet—Fiction 3. Giraffes—Fiction 4. Size—Fiction
ISBN   978-0-06-059337-7;   0-06-059337-7; 978-0-06-059338-4 (lib bdg); 0-06-059338-5 (lib bdg)
       LC 2008010569

McEvoy, Anne—*Continued*

Betsy the giraffe longs to be a ballerina, so when her dance class does not work out, she discovers another way to make her dreams come true

"The rhyming text is fairly smooth and has a satisfying ending. . . . Watercolor illustrations show Betsy's uniqueness and awkwardness with sympathy and wit." SLJ

McGhee, Alison, 1960-

Always; illustrated by Pascal Lemaitre. Simon & Schuster Books for Young Readers 2009 unp il $15.99

Grades: PreK K 1   E

1. Dogs—Fiction
ISBN 978-1-4169-7481-9; 1-4169-7481-4
LC 2008-42624

"A Paula Wiseman book"

A loyal dog promises to protect his young mistress and her home from any danger.

"Succinct, funny and, in its way, action-packed, this is written in the universal language of affection—only the stonyhearted could withstand its charms." Publ Wkly

Bye-bye, crib; illustrated by Ross MacDonald. Simon & Schuster Books for Young Readers 2008 unp il $16.99 *

Grades: PreK   E

1. Beds—Fiction 2. Growth—Fiction
ISBN 978-1-4169-1621-5; 1-4169-1621-0
LC 2006-10583

"A Paula Wiseman book"

A big boy and his best stuffed friend seek the courage to move to a gigantic new bed.

"MacDonald's evocative art . . . employs the comic-book conventions, visual wit, and pulp-art palette fans know and love, and the animation in both the text and the pictures turns what might have been a ho-hum tale of trepidation into a proactive adventure with a winsome wee hero." SLJ

Mrs. Watson wants your teeth; story by Alison McGhee; pictures by Harry Bliss. Harcourt 2004 unp il $16; pa $6

Grades: K 1 2 3   E

1. School stories 2. Teachers—Fiction 3. Teeth—Fiction
ISBN 0-15-204931-2; 0-15-206348-X (pa)
LC 2003-21267

A first grader is frightened on her first day of school after hearing a rumor that her teacher is a 300-year-old alien with a purple tongue who steals baby teeth from her students.

"McGhee has the pulse of this blue-ribbon worrier. . . . Bliss's watercolor and black-ink illustrations feature distinctive, large-eyed classmates and a number of humorous toothy references on the walls in the hall and in the classroom." SLJ

Only a witch can fly; illustrated by Taeeun Yoo. Feiwel and Friends 2009 unp il $16.99 *

Grades: K 1 2   E

1. Stories in rhyme 2. Witches—Fiction 3. Flight—Fiction
ISBN 978-0-312-37503-4; 0-312-37503-4
LC 2008-28542

A young girl wants to fly like a witch on a broom, and one special night, through enormous effort and with the help of her brother, her black cat, and an owl, she fulfills her dream.

"Yoo's illustrations are linoleum block prints done in shades of green and brown with black and white details, adding a wonderful simplicity to this beautiful story." Libr Media Connect

So many days; with illustrations by Taeeun Yoo. Atheneum Books for Young Readers 2010 unp il $15.99

Grades: PreK K 1   E

1. Parent-child relationship—Fiction 2. Conduct of life—Fiction
ISBN 978-1-4169-5857-4; 1-4169-5857-6
LC 2008038300

Through rhythmic text, a parent reflects on the options and opportunities possible in a beloved child's future.

"This book seamlessly pairs lyrical text and digitally manipulated linocut illustrations in a philosophical offering that encourages youngsters to face life head on." SLJ

Song of middle C; illustrated by Scott Menchin. Candlewick Press 2009 unp il $16.99

Grades: K 1 2 3   E

1. Pianists—Fiction 2. Fear—Fiction
ISBN 978-0-7636-3013-3; 0-7636-3013-6

"One little girl uses imagination, bravado and her lucky underwear to overcome a colossal case of stage fright. She has practiced 'Dance of the Wood Elves' diligently [on the piano]. . . . When she steps confidently onto the stage, however, she totally forgets everything she rehearsed. . . . The only note she can manage is Middle C, so she plays it in several different ways with gusto, verve and true artistry, earning great applause. McGhee . . . employs a first-person narration to tell the story in direct, vivid, fast-paced colloquial language. Menchin's digitally colored pen-and-ink cartoons are remarkably detailed while appearing deceptively simple and childlike." Kirkus

A very brave witch; [by] Alison McGhee; [illustrated by] Harry Bliss. Simon & Schuster Books for Young Readers 2006 unp il lib bdg $12.95

Grades: PreK K 1 2   E

1. Halloween—Fiction 2. Witches—Fiction
ISBN 0-689-86730-1

"A Paula Wiseman book"

"A friendly young witch describes what she likes most about Halloween. . . . After boarding her broom, she zooms in a circle, becomes dizzy, and crashes near some trick-or-treaters. She soon discovers that a brave witch and a brave human girl dressed as a witch are not so very different. . . . The chatty text appears in dialogue balloons. Done in black ink and watercolor, the cartoon artwork captures the holiday's spirit with crisp fall colors and amusing details." SLJ

McGinty, Alice B., 1963-

Eliza's kindergarten surprise; by Alice B. McGinty; illustrated by Nancy Speir. Marshall Cavendish 2007 unp il $14.99

Grades: PreK K   E
1. School stories 2. Mother-daughter relationship—Fiction
ISBN 978-0-7614-5351-2; 0-7614-5351-2
         LC 2006022415

On her first day of school, Eliza fills her pocket with objects—buttons, a pebble, a napkin, and a piece of yarn—that remind her of her mother, whom she misses very much

"McGinty avoids overly sweet clichés with a strong concept and smooth telling, and Speir's cartoonlike illustrations balance scenes showing Eliza's anguish with brightly colored views of a welcoming classroom and pictures of a loving mother and daughter that reinforce the warm, reassuring words." Booklist

McGowan, Michael, 1948-

Sunday is for God; illustrated by Lou Fancher and Steve Johnson. Schwartz & Wade Books 2010 unp il $17.99; lib bdg $20.99

Grades: 1 2 3   E
1. African Americans—Fiction 2. Family life—Fiction 3. Church—Fiction
ISBN 978-0-375-84188-0; 0-375-84188-1; 978-0-375-94591-5 (lib bdg); 0-375-94591-1 (lib bdg)
         LC 2008-48828

"It's Sunday morning and a young African American boy knows what that means: 'Sunday is for God. That's what Momma says.' . . . McGowan unleashes a wealth of sensory details. . . . Johnson and Facher's artwork . . . gets a lift from its textured mix of acrylic and collage. . . . A tender reflection of many children's Sunday experience." Booklist

McGrath, Barbara Barbieri, 1954-

The little red elf; illustrated by Rosalinde Bonnet. Charlesbridge 2009 unp il lib bdg $14.95

Grades: PreK K 1   E
1. Fairies—Fiction 2. North Pole—Fiction 3. Christmas—Fiction
ISBN 978-1-58089-236-0; 1-58089-236-1
         LC 2008-25340

In this version of "The Little Red Hen," set at the North Pole, a penguin and a hare refuse to help an elf plant, grow, and decorate an evergreen tree but nevertheless expect to open the presents found under its branches on Christmas Day.

"The acrylic and ballpoint-pen illustrations are full of childlike humor, depicting cute North Pole characters who look like toys themselves. This is that rare beast— an endearing holiday book without a hint of treacle." SLJ

McGrory, Anik

Kidogo; [by] Anik McGrory. Bloomsbury Children's Books 2005 unp il $15.95

Grades: PreK K 1   E
1. Elephants—Fiction 2. Size—Fiction
ISBN 1-58234-974-6   LC 2004-54729

Sure that he is the smallest creature on earth, a young elephant leaves home and journeys over woodlands, rivers, and plains searching for someone even smaller than he is

"The poetic text is perfectly matched with pencil-and-watercolor illustrations that depict a warm and lovely home." SLJ

McKissack, Patricia C., 1944-

The all-I'll-ever-want Christmas doll; illustrated by Jerry Pinkney. Schwartz & Wade Books 2007 unp il $16.99; lib bdg $19.99 *

Grades: K 1 2 3   E
1. Sisters—Fiction 2. Dolls—Fiction 3. Christmas—Fiction 4. Great Depression, 1929-1939—Fiction 5. African Americans—Fiction
ISBN 978-0-375-83759-3; 0-375-83759-0; 978-0-375-93759-0 (lib bdg); 0-375-93759-5 (lib bdg)
         LC 2006-30981

During the Depression, three young sisters get one baby doll for Christmas and must find a way to share

"McKissack takes a bit of oral history and retells it as a first-person memoir that works well as a picture-book text. Pinkney creates a series of beautiful narrative tableaux, illustrating the characters' feelings as well as their actions with clarity and grace." Booklist

Flossie & the fox; pictures by Rachel Isadora. Dial Bks. for Young Readers 1986 unp il $15.99 *

Grades: K 1 2 3   E
1. Foxes—Fiction 2. African Americans—Fiction
ISBN 0-8037-0250-7   LC 86-2024

A wily fox notorious for stealing eggs meets his match when he encounters a bold little girl in the woods who insists upon proof that he is a fox before she will be frightened

"The watercolor and ink illustrations, with realistic figures set on impressionistic backgrounds, enliven this humorous and well-structured story which is told in the black language of the rural south." SLJ

Goin' someplace special; [illustrated by] Jerry Pinkney. Atheneum Bks. for Young Readers 2001 unp il $16; pa $6.99 *

Grades: K 1 2 3   E
1. Segregation—Fiction 2. African Americans—Fiction 3. Libraries—Fiction 4. Tennessee—Fiction
ISBN 0-689-81885-8; 1-4169-2735-2 (pa)
         LC 99-88258

Coretta Scott King Award for illustration
"An Anne Schwartz book"

In segregated 1950s Nashville, a young African American girl braves a series of indignities and obstacles to get to one of the few integrated places in town: the public library

"Pinkney's watercolor paintings are lush and sprawling as they evoke southern city streets and sidewalks as well as Tricia Ann's inner glow. . . . This book carries a strong message of pride and self-confidence as well as a pointed history lesson." Booklist

McKissack, Patricia C., 1944-—*Continued*

Mirandy and Brother Wind; illustrated by Jerry Pinkney. Knopf 1988 unp il $17; pa $6.99 *
Grades: K 1 2 3   **E**
  1. Dance—Fiction 2. Winds—Fiction 3. African Americans—Fiction
  ISBN 978-0-394-88765-4; 0-394-88765-4; 978-0-679-88333-3 (pa); 0-679-88333-9 (pa)
           LC 87-349

A Caldecott Medal honor book, 1989

"Mirandy is sure that she'll win the cake walk if she can catch Brother Wind for her partner, but he eludes all the tricks her friends advise." Bull Cent Child Books

"Ms. McKissack and Mr. Pinkney's ebullient collaboration captures the texture of rural life and culture 40 years after the end of slavery." N Y Times Book Rev

Precious and the Boo Hag; [by] Patricia C. McKissack and Onawumi Jean Moss; illustrated by Kyrsten Brooker. Atheneum Books for Young Readers 2004 unp il $16.95 *
Grades: K 1 2 3   **E**
  1. Monsters—Fiction 2. African Americans—Fiction
  ISBN 0-689-85194-4   LC 2002-1571

"An Anne Schwartz book"

Home alone with a stomachache while the family works in the fields, a young girl faces up to the horrifying Boo Hag that her brother warned her about.

"With the grand feel of a folktale, this lively story speaks to choosing right in a world full of temptation and peril. . . . Expressive and fluid, Brooker's mixed-media art, comical yet scary, too, pops from the pages." Booklist

McLeod, Bob

SuperHero ABC. HarperCollins Pubs. 2006 40p il $15.99; lib bdg $16.89; pa $7.99 *
Grades: PreK K 1 2   **E**
  1. Superheroes—Fiction 2. Alphabet 3. Graphic novels
  ISBN 0-06-074514-2; 0-06-074515-0 (lib bdg); 0-06-074516-9 (pa)   LC 2004-22180

Humorous SuperHeroes such as Goo Girl and The Volcano represent the letters of the alphabet from A to Z.

"There's strong appeal here for the youngest comic-book fans, with many doses of humor along the way. Each figure has special powers, of course, which readers learn about through alliterative captions and action-packed illustrations." SLJ

McLerran, Alice, 1933-

Roxaboxen; illustrated by Barbara Cooney. Lothrop, Lee & Shepard Bks. 1991 unp il $16.99; pa $6.99
Grades: K 1 2 3   **E**
  1. Imagination—Fiction
  ISBN 0-688-07592-4; 0-06-052633-5 (pa)
           LC 89-8057

A hill covered with rocks and wooden boxes in the desert becomes an imaginary town named Roxaboxen for Marian, her sisters, and their friends

"A celebration of the transforming magic of the imagi-nation, the story was inspired by McLerran's mother's reminiscences of her childhood in Yuma, Arizona. . . . The story, told as though from the memory of a Roxaboxenite, brings their play to life through concrete details and a spare, understated style. Equally vivid, Cooney's full-color artwork evokes the striking variety of colors and moods found in the desert landscape." Booklist

McLimans, David

Gone wild; an endangered animal alphabet. Walker & Company 2006 unp il $16.95; lib bdg $17.85 *
Grades: 1 2 3 4   **E**
  1. Endangered species 2. Alphabet 3. Animals
  ISBN 978-0-8027-9563-2; 978-0-8027-9564-9 (lib bdg); 0-8027-9563-3; 0-8027-9564-1 (lib bdg)
           LC 2006-44702

A Caldecott Medal honor book, 2007

"Although organized as a conventional alphabet book, the letters here are far from ordinary. McLimans has created a black-and-white iconic representation of 26 endangered animals, and his art is striking. . . . The arresting graphics and clean design will hold viewers' attention and create interest in the topic." SLJ

Includes bibliographical references

McMillan, Bruce

Growing colors. Lothrop, Lee & Shepard Bks. 1988 32p il hardcover o.p. pa $5.99 *
Grades: PreK K 1 2   **E**
  1. Color 2. Vegetables 3. Fruit
  ISBN 0-688-07844-3; 0-688-13112-3 (pa)
           LC 88-2767

"A colors book using fruits and vegetables of every hue. Each double-page spread has a small photograph of the whole plant and a large close-up of the fruit or vegetable. The colors are announced in bold type tinted in the appropriate shade. . . . At the end of the book, there is a picture glossary of all the colors and plants used." Publ Wkly

"A luscious-looking book that will help children identify colors. . . . This is notably a treat for kids and an example of photography as an art form in picture books." Bull Cent Child Books

How the ladies stopped the wind; illustrated with paintings by Gunnella. Houghton Mifflin 2007 32p il $16 *
Grades: K 1 2 3   **E**
  1. Trees—Fiction 2. Winds—Fiction 3. Sheep—Fiction 4. Chickens—Fiction 5. Iceland—Fiction
  ISBN 978-0-618-77330-5; 0-618-77330-4
           LC 2007-04207

"Walter Lorraine books."

The women of one village in Iceland decide to plant trees to stop the powerful winds that make it difficult even to go for a walk, but first they must find a ways to prevent sheep from eating all of their saplings, while encouraging chickens to fertilize them.

"The team that made stars of a group of Icelandic ladies in *The Problem with Chickens* returns for another winning round. . . . Gunnella's flat, deadpan oil portraits

McMillan, Bruce—*Continued*

of the ladies, their polka-dot aprons and their hapless chickens are inherently funny, and every page contains another visual poke in the ribs." Publ Wkly

The problem with chickens; illustrated with paintings by Gunnella. Houghton Mifflin 2005 32p il $16 *

Grades: K 1 2 3   E

1. Chickens—Fiction 2. Iceland—Fiction
ISBN 0-618-58581-8   LC 2005-01225
"Walter Lorraine books"

When women in an Icelandic village buy chickens to lay eggs for them to use, the chickens follow them, adopting human ways and forgetting their barnyard roots, until the ladies hatch a clever plan.

"The playful text is both silly and joyous, without a wasted word. Gunnella's enchanting oil paintings are full of childlike humor and saturated with appealing primary colors." SLJ

McMullan, Kate, 1947-

I stink! [by] Kate & Jim McMullan. HarperCollins Pubs. 2002 unp il $15.95; lib bdg $15.89; pa $6.99 *

Grades: PreK K 1 2   E

1. Refuse and refuse disposal—Fiction
ISBN 0-06-029848-0; 0-06-029849-9 (lib bdg);
0-06-443836-8 (pa)   LC 00-54229
"Joanna Cotler books"

A big city garbage truck makes its rounds, consuming everything from apple cores and banana peels to leftover ziti with zucchini

"Kate McMullan creates an automotive beast whose narrative style reeks of personality, and Jim McMullan's renderings are a perfect match, coaxing steely features into flexible, expressive shapes." Bull Cent Child Books

I'm bad; [by] Kate & Jim McMullan. Joanna Cotler Books 2008 unp il $16.99; lib bdg $17.89 *

Grades: PreK K 1   E

1. Dinosaurs—Fiction
ISBN 978-0-06-122971-8; 0-06-122971-7;
978-0-06-122972-5 (lib bdg); 0-06-122972-5 (lib bdg)
     LC 2007032020

A hungry Tyrannosaurus rex searches for food in the prehistoric forest but is thwarted in its attempts to find something to eat

"The high-energy illustrations and macho narrator's words create a rowdy, crowd-pleasing whole. Children will delight in the dinosaur's wild expressions and the dynamic text, filled with comic-book sound effects." Booklist

I'm dirty! [by] Kate & Jim McMullan. Joanna Cotler Books 2006 unp il $16.99; lib bdg $17.89 *

Grades: PreK K 1 2   E

1. Construction equipment—Fiction 2. Cleanliness—Fiction
ISBN 978-0-06-009293-1; 0-06-009293-9;
978-0-06-009294-8 (lib bdg); 0-06-009294-7 (lib bdg)
     LC 2005-17919

A busy backhoe loader describes all the items it hauls off a lot and all the fun it has getting dirty while doing so

"With its saucy tone and dynamic color cartoon illustrations, this picture book exudes energy." SLJ

I'm mighty! [by] Kate & Jim McMullan. Joanna Cotler Bks. 2003 unp il $17.99

Grades: PreK K 1 2   E

1. Tugboats—Fiction
ISBN 0-06-009290-4   LC 2002-7948

A little tugboat shows how he can bring big ships into the harbor even though he is small

"The tugboat that narrates this picture book tells his story with more than a splash of moxie. Strong ink drawings define the harbor setting from a variety of perspectives and show the emotions of the anthropomorphic figures of boats and trucks, while color brightens the scenes and heightens the drama." Booklist

Pearl and Wagner: one funny day; pictures by R. W. Alley. Dial Books for Young Readers 2009 40p il (Dial easy-to-read) $14.99 *

Grades: K 1 2   E

1. April Fools' Day—Fiction 2. School stories 3. Rabbits—Fiction 4. Mice—Fiction 5. Animals—Fiction
ISBN 978-0-8037-3085-4; 0-8037-3085-3
     LC 2008007699
ALA ALSC Geisel Award Honor Book (2010)

April Fools' Day is not a happy one for Wagner the mouse because his best friend, Pearl the rabbit, and other children and adults at school keep tricking him.

"Alley's expressive ink-and-watercolor illustrations portray Wagner's shifting emotions with clarity and finesse." Booklist

Other titles about Pearl and Wagner are:
Pearl and Wagner: two good friends (2003)
Pearl and Wagner: three secrets (2004)

McNamara, Margaret

How many seeds in a pumpkin? illustrated by G. Brian Karas. Schwartz & Wade Books 2007 unp il $14.99

Grades: K 1 2   E

1. Size—Fiction 2. Pumpkin—Fiction 3. Counting—Fiction 4. School stories
ISBN 978-0-375-84014-2; 0-375-84014-1;
978-0-375-94014-9 (lib bdg); 0-375-94014-6 (lib bdg)
     LC 2006-16866

Charlie, the smallest child in his first grade class, is amazed to discover that of the three pumpkins his teacher brings to school, the tiniest one has the most seeds.

"Karas's characteristic watercolor illustrations done in a fall palette depict a diverse, modern classroom full of warm and humorous details. . . . This enjoyable story, sprinkled with math and science lessons, should be a first-purchase consideration." SLJ

McNamara, Margaret—*Continued*

The whistle on the train; [by] Margaret McNamara; illustrated by Richard Egielski; paper engineering by Gene Vosough. Hyperion 2008 unp il $18.99

Grades: PreK   E

1. Pop-up books 2. Railroads—Fiction 3. Songs

ISBN 978-0-7868-4890-4; 0-7868-4890-1

"Here's a great concept, handsomely executed. Take a song known to virtually every preschooler, 'The Wheels on the Bus,' and update it with a vehicle much more widely adored by this group, a train, then soup it up with lavish but resilient paper engineering. Involving plenty of repetition, McNamara's lyrics are easy to learn. . . . The pop-ups, mostly stationary, are multidimensional renderings of Egielski's cheery cartoons." Publ Wkly

McNaughton, Colin, 1951-

Not last night but the night before; illustrated by Emma Chichester Clark. Candlewick Press 2009 unp il $16.99 *

Grades: PreK   K   1   2   E

1. Stories in rhyme 2. Fairy tales 3. Nursery rhymes—Fiction 4. Birthdays—Fiction 5. Parties—Fiction

ISBN 978-0-7636-4420-8; 0-7636-4420-X

"Rhyming, repetitive text tells of a boy who reluctantly welcomes a parade of nursery-rhyme characters into his home. Everyone from the man in the moon to Little Miss Muffet bursts through the entryway wearing party clothes and carrying presents. . . . Colorful pencil and acrylic illustrations alternate between scallop-edged vignettes and full-bleed scenes rife with excitement. Preschoolers will enjoy the predictability of this tale." SLJ

Once upon an ordinary school day; story by Colin McNaughton; pictures by Satoshi Kitamura. Farrar, Straus & Giroux 2005 c2004 unp il $16

Grades: K   1   2   E

1. School stories 2. Teachers—Fiction 3. Imagination—Fiction

ISBN 0-374-35634-3   LC 2004-105656

First published 2004 in the United Kingdom

"An ordinary boy awakens to an ordinary school day. The story opens with drab scenes depicted in shades of gray that turn to Technicolor several pages in, with the arrival of a new teacher in a yellow suit. . . . Deftly rendered cartoon drawings convey the expressive gestures and transformation of the characters and scenes. . . . An excellent selection to start the creative juices flowing or to enliven an ordinary day." SLJ

McNelly McCormack, Caren

The fiesta dress; a quinceañera tale; illustrated by Martha Aviles. Marshall Cavendish 2009 unp il $17.99

Grades: K   1   E

1. Quinceañera (Social custom)—Fiction 2. Sisters—Fiction 3. Family life—Fiction 4. Hispanic Americans—Fiction

ISBN 978-0-7614-5467-0; 0-7614-5467-5

LC 2008-10781

While Eva and her family prepare for her quinceanera, no one is paying attention to her younger sister, but when the dog gets out of the laundry room and steals Eva's sash, her little sister comes to the rescue.

"Aviles incorporates a warm palette of roses, aquas, deep oranges and springy greens to illustrate the story; her acrylic and watercolor compositions have a somewhat old fashioned feel. . . . There is abundant joy in this tale of a big extended family preparing for an exciting event, and audience members will relish being included." Bull Cent Child Books

McPhail, David M.

Big Brown Bear's up and down day; [written and illustrated by] David McPhail. Harcourt 2003 unp il $16; pa $6

Grades: PreK   K   1   2   E

1. Bears—Fiction 2. Rats—Fiction

ISBN 0-15-216407-3; 0-15-205684-X (pa)

LC 2002-15854

Big Brown Bear is visited by a rat who wants to use one of his slippers for a bed

"A warm and gentle story. . . . Beautiful watercolor and pen-and-ink paintings make the most of the size difference between the characters and help to create real personalities by capturing the emotions they experience." SLJ

Other titles about Big Brown Bear are:

Big Brown Bear goes to town (2006)

Big Brown Bear's birthday surprise (2007)

Big Pig and Little Pig; [by] David McPhail. Harcourt 2003 unp il (Green light readers) $11.95; pa $3.95

Grades: PreK   K   1   E

1. Pigs—Fiction

ISBN 978-0-15-204818-1; 0-15-204818-9; 978-0-15-204857-0 (pa); 0-15-204857-X (pa)

A reissue of the title first published 2001

Big Pig and Little Pig enjoy spending time together, though they take different approaches to the same task

"McPhail's signature illustrations fill each page as he once again successfully manages to transfer human emotions to his lovable cartoon pigs. Well-chosen vocabulary and repetition of words make this story a suitable choice for those just learning to read." SLJ

Drawing lessons from a bear; [by] David McPhail. Little, Brown 2000 unp il $14.95 *

Grades: PreK   K   1   E

1. Bears—Fiction 2. Artists—Fiction

ISBN 0-316-56345-5   LC 98-54966

A bear explains how he became an artist, first experimenting with simple drawings, then continuing to draw both things around him and things in his imagination. Includes tips for drawing

"This gentle story combines a humorous tone with warm, cozy watercolors to create inspiration for budding artists." SLJ

Emma in charge; by David McPhail. Dutton Children's Books 2005 unp il $12.99 *

Grades: PreK   K   1   E

1. Bears—Fiction 2. Play—Fiction

ISBN 0-525-47411-0   LC 2004-21580

McPhail, David M.—*Continued*

Emma the bear pretends that she and her dolls spend a day at school.

"McPhail's watercolors are . . . expressive and winsome . . . and the short sentences, printed in bold type, are just right for read-alouds or for emerging readers to follow along." Booklist

Other titles about Emma are:

Emma's pet (1985)

Emma's vacation (1987)

Fix-it (1984)

Mole music; written and illustrated by David McPhail. Holt & Co. 1999 unp il $15.95; pa $7.99

Grades: PreK K 1 2   E

1. Moles (Animals)—Fiction 2. Violins—Fiction 3. Music—Fiction

ISBN 0-8050-2819-6; 0-8050-6766-3 (pa)

LC 98-21318

Feeling that something is missing in his simple life, Mole acquires a violin and learns to make beautiful, joyful music

"McPhail's delicate watercolor-and-ink illustrations work with the simple text to create a lyrical celebration of music and musicians." Booklist

No! Roaring Brook Press 2009 unp il $16.95

Grades: K 1 2 3   E

1. War stories 2. Bullies—Fiction 3. Stories without words

ISBN 978-1-59643-288-8; 1-59643-288-8

LC 2008054607

"In this dark, nearly wordless allegory, the power of a single word ripples outward, stopping a bully, an army, a war. . . . McPhail's . . . delicately tinted crosshatching gives poignancy to the violence the boy witnesses without minimizing it. The idea of taking effective action without fighting is a powerful one, and children and adults alike will find that McPhail's images linger." Publ Wkly

Pigs aplenty, pigs galore! [by] David McPhail. Dutton Children's Bks. 1993 unp il hardcover o.p. pa $6.99 *

Grades: PreK K 1 2   E

1. Pigs—Fiction 2. Stories in rhyme

ISBN 0-525-45079-3; 0-14-055313-4 (pa)

LC 92-27986

"As pigs of every size, shape, and dress (including Elvis) arrive at his house in every possible vehicle, a riotous party begins and lasts through the night as the perplexed narrator looks on." SLJ

"The rhyme is bouncy enough, but it's the pictures that will have parents and kids howling. Using deep watercolors set against a black background, McPhail presents a magnificent group of porkers, whose capacity for costumes and capers is truly wondrous." Booklist

Other titles about the pigs are:

Pigs ahoy! (1995)

Those can-do pigs (1996)

Sylvie & True; [by] David McPhail. Farrar, Straus, & Giroux 2007 31p il lib bdg $15 *

Grades: PreK K 1 2   E

1. Rabbits—Fiction 2. Snakes—Fiction 3. Friendship—Fiction

ISBN 978-0-374-37364-1 (lib bdg); 0-374-37364-7 (lib bdg)

LC 2006048979

In four vignettes, Sylvie the rabbit and her friend True, a giant water snake, share a small apartment in a big city, cook, go bowling, and have a good time together

The scenarios are "simple . . . occasioning affectionate dialogue and terrific sight gags. . . . [This is a] charmer." Publ Wkly

The teddy bear; written and illustrated by David McPhail. Holt & Co. 2002 unp il $15.95; pa $7.99

Grades: PreK K 1 2   E

1. Teddy bears—Fiction 2. Homeless persons—Fiction

ISBN 0-8050-6414-1; 0-8050-7882-7 (pa)

LC 2001-1500

"By accident a boy leaves his beloved bear in a diner. A homeless man finds it in the garbage and loves the bear as much as the boy did. Then one day the boy sees the bear on a park bench and joyfully grabs it. But when he recognizes the lonely man's sorrow at losing his friend, the child returns the toy. . . . It works because McPhail's beautiful soft-toned watercolor pictures with detailed ink cross-hatching tell the elemental story of shelter and love through the child's eyes." Booklist

Water boy; [by] David McPhail. Abrams Books for Young Readers 2007 unp il $15.95

Grades: PreK K 1 2   E

1. Water—Fiction 2. Magic—Fiction

ISBN 978-0-8109-1784-2; 0-8109-1784-X

LC 2006013578

Fascinated by the fact that humans are made mostly of water, a boy develops an unusual relationship with it once he stops being afraid.

"Beautifully written, illustrated, and designed, this small gem of a book calls to be opened, touched, and read from its texturally and visually appealing cover . . . to the rich, color-drenched pictures of the real and the fantastic inside." SLJ

Weezer changes the world; [by] David McPhail. Beach Lane Books 2009 unp il $15.99

Grades: PreK K 1   E

1. Dogs—Fiction

ISBN 978-1-4169-9000-0; 1-4169-9000-3

LC 2009005537

After an ordinary puppyhood, Weezer develops extraordinary skills that make him a major influence in the world.

"McPhail's amusing tale will inspire young children to consider how they can make the world a better place, and his droll ink-and-watercolor illustrations reinforce the book's simple but powerful message." Booklist

McQuinn, Anna

Lola at the library; [by] Anna McQuinn; illustrated by Rosalind Beardshaw. Charlesbridge 2006 unp il lib bdg $15.95; pa $6.95

Grades: PreK K 1 2   E

1. Libraries—Fiction 2. Books and reading—Fiction

ISBN 978-1-58089-113-4 (lib bdg); 1-58089-113-6 (lib bdg); 978-1-58089-142-4 (pa); 1-58089-142-X (pa)

LC 2005019620

Published in the United Kingdom with title: Layla loves the library

Every Tuesday Lola and her mother visit their local library to return and check out books, attend story readings, and share a special treat

"Simple text and large, bright acrylic illustrations of this engaging African-American child make this selection just right for sharing" SLJ

Another title about Lola is:

Lola loves stories (2010)

My friend Jamal; by Anna McQuinn; illustrated by Ben Frey. Annick 2008 unp il (My friend) lib bdg $17.95; pa $8.95

Grades: K 1 2 3   E

1. Friendship—Fiction 2. Immigrants—Fiction 3. Africans—United States—Fiction

ISBN 978-1-55451-123-5 (lib bdg); 1-55451-123-2 (lib bdg); 978-1-55451-122-8 (pa); 1-55451-122-4 (pa)

"Joseph describes his friendship with Jamal, a boy whose family immigrated to the United States from Somalia. . . . He discusses their similarities . . . as well as their differences. . . . The lively, brightly colored collages consist of original photographs of the main characters and stock photos of food or objects with thickly painted outlines and accents added. Both text and pictures project an energetic, friendly tone." SLJ

My friend Mei Jing; text by Anna McQuinn; artwork by Ben Frey; photography by Irvin Cheung. Annick Press 2009 unp il (My friend) $17.95; pa $8.95

Grades: K 1 2 3   E

1. Friendship—Fiction 2. Chinese Americans—Fiction 3. African Americans—Fiction

ISBN   978-1-55451-153-2;   1-55451-153-4; 978-1-55451-152-5 (pa); 1-55451-152-6 (pa)

"In this large, colorful book, a Nigerian-American second-grader tells the story of her best friend from school, who is Chinese-American. The girls share a love of arts and crafts, dressing up, and a desire to become veterinarians. Monifa describes aspects of Mei Jing's culture. . . . The story's authentic voice comes from simple declarative sentences. . . . The brightly colored collages combine photographs of the girls' heads and hands with their cartoon bodies and depict them as they work with clay in arts and crafts at school or walk through an outdoor market with Mei Jing's grandma." SLJ

Meade, Holly

Inside, inside, inside; written and illustrated by Holly Meade. Marshall Cavendish 2005 unp il $16.95

Grades: PreK K 1 2   E

1. Games—Fiction 2. Siblings—Fiction

ISBN 0-7614-5125-0   LC 2004-19321

Noah and Jenny play a game in which they place one item inside another, over and over, until they place it all in the shower, then imagine and draw the shower inside the house, inside the neighborhood, and all the way to the solar system

"Meade cheerfully mixes cut-paper collage and watercolor, and sprinkles many homey details into the large and small scenes. . . . The messy game is fun, and the concept draws a useful lesson from creative play." SLJ

John Willy and Freddy McGee. Marshall Cavendish 1998 unp il hardcover o.p. pa $5.95 *

Grades: PreK K 1 2   E

1. Guinea pigs—Fiction

ISBN 0-7614-5033-5; 0-7614-5143-9 (pa)

LC 97-50362

Two guinea pigs escape from their safe but boring cage and have an adventure in the tunnels of the family's pool table

"Zesty cut-paper collages track all of the details of this funny outing." SLJ

Meddaugh, Susan

The best place. Houghton Mifflin 1999 unp il $15

Grades: PreK K 1 2   E

1. Wolves—Fiction 2. Animals—Fiction

ISBN 0-395-97994-3   LC 98-50184

After traveling around the world to make sure that the view from his screen porch is the best, an old wolf tries drastic measures to get his house back from the rabbit family that had bought it

"Meddaugh combines understated humor with her expressive watercolor illustrations to produce a delightful book." SLJ

Cinderella's rat. Houghton Mifflin 1997 32p il $15; pa $5.95 *

Grades: PreK K 1 2   E

1. Rats—Fiction 2. Fairy tales

ISBN 0-395-86833-5; 0-618-12540-X (pa)

LC 97-2156

One of the rats that was turned into a coachman by Cinderella's fairy godmother saves his rat sister's life, but an inept magician turns her into a girl who says "woof."

"The telling is a perfect example of a successful fractured fairy tale, with switched point of view. . . . The buoyant line drawings capture the whimsy." SLJ

Harry on the rocks. Houghton Mifflin 2003 32p il hardcover o.p. pa $6.95 *

Grades: PreK K 1 2   E

1. Shipwrecks—Fiction

ISBN 0-618-27603-3; 0-618-84068-0 (pa)

LC 2002-9740

"Walter Lorraine books"

Harry and his boat become stranded on an island, where he discovers an egg which hatches into a strange lizard with wings

This is "a well-paced, cleanly wrought piece of storytelling. The cheerful watercolor and colored-pencil art has a sturdy matter-of-factness that makes the fantasy endearingly domestic." Bull Cent Child Books

Meddaugh, Susan—*Continued*

Hog-eye. Houghton Mifflin 1995 32p il hardcover o.p. pa $5.95 *

Grades: PreK K 1 2   E

1. Pigs—Fiction 2. Wolves—Fiction

ISBN 0-395-74276-5; 0-395-93746-9 (pa)

LC 95-3951

Meddaugh presents a "story within a story as a piglet tells her family how she was caught by a wolf and nearly made into soup. Seeing that her captor is illiterate . . . she reads him a recipe that sends him on a wild wolf chase." SLJ

"The little pig's tale is fast-paced, funny, and creatively told. Clear typeface and conversation balloons combine with brightly animated, expressive illustrations that propel readers to the satisfying conclusion of this fresh cautionary tale." Horn Book Guide

Martha speaks. Houghton Mifflin 1992 unp il hardcover o.p. pa $6.99 *

Grades: PreK K 1 2   E

1. Dogs—Fiction

ISBN 0-395-63313-3; 0-395-72952-1 (pa)

LC 91-48455

Problems arise when Martha, the family dog, learns to speak after eating alphabet soup

"Good-natured and amusing, with cheerful illustrations of the delightfully stocky Martha and her amazed family." Horn Book

Other titles about Martha are:

Martha and Skits (2000)

Martha blah blah (1996)

Martha calling (1994)

Martha walks the dog (1998)

Perfectly Martha (2004)

The witch's walking stick. Houghton Mifflin 2005 32p il $16

Grades: K 1 2 3   E

1. Witches—Fiction 2. Magic—Fiction

ISBN 0-618-52948-9   LC 2004-17509

"Walter Lorraine books"

When a witch loses her magic walking stick, which has been used over the years to grant hundreds of miserable wishes, she tricks a young girl into finding and returning it, with unexpected results.

"Illustrated with watercolor and ink in a style that will put readers in mind of William Steig, Meddaugh's dry, quirky tale of the little guy triumphing over adversity will have children smiling and cheering." SLJ

Medearis, Angela Shelf, 1956-

Seven spools of thread; a Kwanzaa story; illustrated by Daniel Minter. Whitman, A. 2001 unp il $15.95; pa $6.95

Grades: K 1 2 3   E

1. Kwanzaa—Fiction 2. Brothers—Fiction 3. Blacks—Fiction 4. Ghana—Fiction

ISBN 0-8075-7315-9; 0-8075-7316-7 (pa)

LC 00-8101

When they are given the seemingly impossible task of turning thread into gold, the seven Ashanti brothers put aside their differences, learn to get along, and embody the principles of Kwanzaa. Includes information on Kwanzaa, West African cloth weaving, and instructions for making a belt

"Well-paced, the story incorporates the Kwanzaa values without spelling them out too much. Minter's attractively composed, dramatic painted linocuts, with strong community images and lively, silhouetted figures, root the story in a sun-drenched, magical landscape." Booklist

Meister, Cari

My pony Jack; illustrated by Amy Young. Viking 2005 32p il $13.99

Grades: PreK K 1 2   E

1. Horses—Fiction 2. Stories in rhyme

ISBN 0-670-05917-X   LC 2004-21417

"Viking easy-to-read"

Easy-to-read, rhyming text follows Lacy as she spends a day with her pony, giving him exercise, grooming him, and feeding him oats and hay.

"The book has an attractive format, with colorful cartoon artwork and a small amount of text on each page. . . . A solid addition to easy-reader collections." SLJ

Other titles about Jack the pony are:

My pony Jack at riding lessons (2005)

My pony Jack at the horse show (2006)

Tiny's bath; illustrated by Rich Davis. Viking 1998 unp il hardcover o.p. pa $3.99 *

Grades: PreK K 1   E

1. Dogs—Fiction 2. Baths—Fiction

ISBN 0-670-87962-2; 0-14-130267-4 (pa)

LC 98-3844

"A Viking easy-to-read"

Tiny is a very big dog who loves to dig, and when it is time for his bath, his owner has trouble finding a place to bathe him

"In this book for the least sophisticated beginning readers, each sentence appears on a single line, and only one sentence appears on a page. Illustrations mirror text, providing clues that support readers as they decipher both words and events. Add Tiny to the roll call of great dogs in children's literature." Horn Book Guide

Other titles about Tiny are:

Tiny goes camping (2006)

Tiny goes to the library (2000)

Tiny on the farm (2008)

Tiny the snow dog (2001)

When Tiny was tiny (1999)

Melanson, Luc

Topsy-Turvy Town. Tundra Books 2010 unp il $17.95

Grades: PreK K   E

1. Imagination—Fiction

ISBN 978-0-88776-920-7; 0-88776-920-9

Original French language edition published 2004 in Canada

A boy lives in a town where it rains broccoli that crunches when it lands on the tops of umbrellas, where police officers march to a very different beat, where you can go fishing in your living room or even juggle a wildcat before bedtime.

"This highly imaginative tale is told in simple text with outstanding illustrations. Round-headed humans and

Melanson, Luc—*Continued*
buildings with harlequin faces abound, as well as a menagerie of animals reminiscent of classic wooden toys." SLJ

Melling, David
The Scallywags. Barron's 2006 unp il $14.99 *
Grades: K 1 2 3   E
1. Wolves—Fiction 2. Animals—Fiction 3. Etiquette—Fiction
ISBN 0-7641-5991-7
"The animals in the neighborhood are disgusted by the Wolf family, known collectively as the Scallywags. . . . After the wolves are sent packing, they finally . . . improve their manners." Booklist
"This hilarious story is accompanied by equally lively and humorous pictures that fill the pages with images worthy of close perusal." SLJ

Melmed, Laura Krauss
Hurry! Hurry! Have you heard? illustrated by Jane Dyer. Chronicle Books 2008 unp il $16.99
Grades: PreK K 1 2   E
1. Jesus Christ—Nativity—Fiction 2. Birds—Fiction 3. Animals—Fiction 4. Stories in rhyme
ISBN 978-0-8118-4225-9   LC 2007021062
A small bird, her heart filled with love, hurries from her perch above the manger to spread the news to creatures of the field and forest that a child, to whom all are precious, has been born.
"This contemporary-set Nativity story, featuring seasonally clad but otherwise realistic-looking animals, has energy and movement." Horn Book Guide

Melvin, Alice, 1982-
Counting birds; written and illustrated by Alice Melvin. Tate 2010 unp il $14.50
Grades: K 1 2   E
1. Counting 2. Birds—Fiction 3. Day—Fiction
ISBN 978-1-85437-855-2; 1-85437-855-4
"This is a charming counting book, replete with lilting text and exquisite illustrations. Beginning at dawn with one cockerel, the narration moves through the day and into the evening, counting birds from 1 to 20. . . . The text, which is composed in couplets, counts birds both inside and outside a stately country house. . . . In her bright and cheerful illustrations, Melvin employs geometric designs and patterns that bring to mind the warmth and comfort of a favorite quilt." SLJ

Merz, Jennifer J.
Playground day! by Jennifer J. Merz. Clarion Books 2007 unp il $16
Grades: PreK K 1   E
1. Play—Fiction 2. Animals—Fiction 3. Stories in rhyme
ISBN 978-0-618-81696-5   LC 2006039215
Children play on the playground, imitating animals from bunnies and squirrels to elephants and penguins.
"The cut- and torn-paper collages are filled with color, depth, and texture, making the pages come alive." SLJ

Meschenmoser, Sebastian
Waiting for winter. Kane Miller 2009 unp il $15.99 *
Grades: PreK K 1 2   E
1. Snow—Fiction 2. Forest animals—Fiction
ISBN 978-1-935279-04-4; 1-935279-04-1
                                    LC 2009-922111
Deer has told Squirrel how wonderful snow is. But Squirrel gets bored with the wait. With his friend Hedgehog they pass the time by singing and waking Bear. Soon things are falling from the sky, but they aren't snow. But eventually they find what snow is.
"The illustrations are deftly drawn in colored pencils, complete with sketching lines that give the renderings depth and maturity. . . . This is a beautiful title to share with children on a lap or with a small group." SLJ

Meyers, Susan
Bear in the air; illustrated by Amy Bates. Abrams Books for Young Readers 2010 il $15.95
Grades: PreK K 1   E
1. Stories in rhyme 2. Teddy bears—Fiction 3. Lost and found possessions—Fiction 4. Adventure fiction
ISBN 978-0-8109-8398-4; 0-8109-8398-2
When a teddy bear is lost by the child who loves him, the bear begins an adventurous journey to get back home again.
"Words are almost unnecessary as the pencil and watercolor illustrations, in appealing beach tones of blue, brown, and tan, tell the story of the lost, bewildered-looking bear and his surprising journey. . . . A sweet story that will capture the imaginations of young children." SLJ

Everywhere babies; illustrated by Marla Frazee. Harcourt 2001 unp il $16; bd bk $6.95 *
Grades: PreK K 1   E
1. Infants 2. Stories in rhyme
ISBN 0-15-202226-0; 0-15-205315-8 (bd bk)
                                    LC 99-6288
Describes babies and the things they do from the time they are born until their first birthday
"The rhythmic rhyming text hums along pleasantly. . . . The many moods, expressions, and body movements of babies are faithfully, gracefully rendered in the pencil drawings, and brightened with watercolors in rather muted hues." Booklist

Kittens! Kittens! Kittens! by Susan Meyers; illustrated by David Walker. Abrams Books for Young Readers 2007 unp il $15.95 *
Grades: PreK K   E
1. Cats—Fiction
ISBN 978-0-8109-1218-2; 0-8109-1218-X
                                    LC 2006013575
Illustrations and rhyming text portray kittens as they go from nestling newborns to proud, independent, and ready to have kittens of their own.
"Cheerful rhymes, with the title used as a satisfying refrain, are expanded on by Walker's acrylic artwork in soft-toned, thickly applied colors that have the look of sunny chalks." Booklist

Michelin, Linda

Zuzu's wishing cake. Houghton Mifflin Company 2006 unp il $16

Grades: PreK K 1   E

1. Friendship—Fiction 2. Gifts—Fiction
ISBN 978-0-618-64640-1; 0-618-64640-X

When Zuzu smiles at the new boy next door and he does not smile back, she makes him a series of gifts that she thinks he needs.

"Zuzu does not understand the language [the new boy's] mother speaks, and the cross-cultural connection is a quiet addition to the warm story. Johnson . . . uses bright, bouncy collage-type pictures to show the fun of making exciting gifts and making a friend." Booklist

Michelson, Richard

Across the alley; [by] Richard Michelson; illustrated by E. B. Lewis. G. P. Putnam's Sons 2006 unp il $16.99

Grades: K 1 2 3   E

1. Friendship—Fiction 2. Jews—Fiction 3. African Americans—Fiction   4.   Baseball—Fiction
5. Violinists—Fiction
ISBN 0-399-23970-7   LC 2005032656

Jewish Abe's grandfather wants him to be a violinist while African-American Wille's father plans for him to be a great baseball pitcher, but it turns out that the two boys are more talented when they switch hobbies.

"The poignancy of two boys who can be friends only at night is revealed brilliantly in both text and rich watercolor art." SLJ

Micklethwait, Lucy

I spy: an alphabet in art; devised & selected by Lucy Micklethwait. Greenwillow Bks. 1992 unp il $19.99; pa $10.99 *

Grades: K 1 2 3   E

1. Art appreciation 2. Alphabet
ISBN 0-688-11679-5; 0-688-14730-5 (pa)
                               LC 91-42212

Presents objects for the letters of the alphabet through paintings by such artists as Magritte, Picasso, Botticelli, and Vermeer

"The author's stated intention of introducing young children to fine art, her choice of paintings, the handsome book design, and the quality of paper and reproduction take this beyond the usual alphabet book." Booklist

Other titles in this series are:

I spy a freight train: transportation in art (1996)
I spy a lion: animals in art (1994)
I spy colors in art (2007)
I spy shapes in art (2004)
I spy two eyes: numbers in art (1993)

Middleton, Charlotte

Nibbles: a green tale. Marshall Cavendish Children 2010 unp il $17.99

Grades: PreK K 1 2   E

1. Guinea pigs—Fiction 2. Dandelions—Fiction
3. Plant conservation—Fiction
ISBN 978-0-7614-5791-6; 0-7614-5791-7

"A guinea pig loves dandelions, just like everyone else in his town. The plants are eaten for breakfast, lunch, dinner, and all snacks in between until they slowly disappear. . . . Luckily Nibbles discovers a lone dandelion survivor growing under his bedroom window. With great patience and the help of a library book, he cares for his secret treasure until it has a full head of billowy white seeds. Then . . . he blows the precious seeds all over Dandeville. . . . Middleton's tale of overconsuming and scarcity is direct but not preachy. . . . The text is simple and age appropriate, but the mixed-media illustrations steal the show." SLJ

Miles, Victoria, 1966-

Old Mother Bear; by Victoria Miles; illustrated by Molly Bang. Chronicle Books 2007 unp il $16.95

Grades: 1 2 3 4   E

1. Bears—Fiction
ISBN 978-0-8118-5033-9; 0-8118-5033-1
                               LC 2006011651

A twenty-four-year-old grizzly bear gives birth to her last litter of cubs, then spends three years teaching them what they need to know to survive in their southern British Columbia home before they go off on their own. Includes facts about grizzlies and the Khutzeymateen Grizzly Bear Sanctuary.

"The detailed zoology facts are the gripping story in this realistic picture book, which is based on true events and illustrated in beautifully textured, closeup, oil-and-chalk artwork by . . . artist Bang." Booklist

Milgrim, David

Amelia makes a movie; by David Milgrim. G.P. Putnam's Sons 2008 unp il $16.99

Grades: K 1 2   E

1. Motion pictures—Production and direction—Fiction
2. Stories in rhyme 3. Siblings—Fiction
ISBN 978-0-399-24670-8   LC 2007018389

Ably assisted by her younger brother Drew, Amelia makes a home video, from writing a script and casting herself as the star to hearing the reviews after their big premiere.

"Each time Amelia calls, 'Action,' Milgrim switches from full-page illustrations to framed comics panels. He works in digital media, yet his draftsmanship suggests traditional pen-and-ink. . . . An entertaining and practical how-to." Publ Wkly

My dog, Buddy. Scholastic 2008 unp il pa $3.99

Grades: K 1 2   E

1. Dogs—Fiction 2. Family life—Fiction
ISBN 978-0-545-03593-4 (pa); 0-545-03593-7 (pa)
                               LC 2007-22795

"Cartwheel Books"

Milgrim, David—*Continued*

Mom, Dad, and brother Pete all try to get Buddy to obey, but only one family member understands how to communicate with the mischievous canine.

"Digitally created art suggests line and watercolor in its smooth planes of color neatly bordered by slightly off-kilter lines. . . . Packed with pithy humor, sly irreverence, and rampant usefulness, this is a beginning reader's best friend." Bull Cent Child Books

Santa Duck. G.P. Putnam's Sons 2008 unp il lib bdg $16.99 *

Grades: PreK K 1 2   E
1. Santa Claus—Fiction 2. Ducks—Fiction 3. Animals—Fiction 4. Christmas—Fiction
ISBN 978-0-399-25018-7 (lib bdg); 0-399-25018-2 (lib bdg)   LC 2007-43162

When Nicholas Duck, wearing a Santa hat and coat he found on his doorstep, goes looking for Santa to tell him what he wants for Christmas, all the other animals mistake him for Mr. Claus.

"Nicholas's silliness and frustration will appeal to youngsters as will the simple message. Milgrim's charming digital ink and oil pastel illustrations use a successful mix of narrative text and cartoon balloons to move the story along at a brisk pace." SLJ

Time to get up, time to go. Clarion Books 2006 32p il $15

Grades: PreK K   E
1. Day—Fiction 2. Dolls—Fiction 3. Stories in rhyme
ISBN 0-618-51998-X; 978-0-618-51998-9
                                    LC 2005011359

"From early morning to bedtime, a boy whirls through his day's activities, taking care of his stuffed blue doll. . . . Milgrim's digital oil-paint illustrations have muted, pleasant shades with the figures crisply outlined in black. They work well with the minimal text, in which not a word is wasted." SLJ

Milich, Zoran

City 1 2 3. Kids Can Press 2005 unp il $15.95; pa $6.95

Grades: PreK K 1 2   E
1. Counting
ISBN 1-55337-540-8; 1-55453-163-2 (pa)

Photographs of objects such as skyscrapers, bags of leaves, fire trucks, and taxis illustrate numbers from 1 to 10

"An excellent, well-constructed concept book. . . . The superb pictures feature not only the required number of items, but the corresponding numeral as well." SLJ

The city ABC book. Kids Can Press 2001 unp il hardcover o.p. pa $5.95

Grades: PreK K 1 2   E
1. Alphabet
ISBN 1-55074-942-0; 1-55074-948-X (pa)

"Milich searched Toronto for hidden geometrics—letters buried in everyday places. From window frames in the shape of As to steel-welded Zs that support a bridge, he finds and documents them—in black and white, highlighting each letter in stop-sign red. . . . Each picture is a wonder and every letter a clear, playful image to consider and behold." Booklist

City colors. Kids Can Press 2004 unp il $14.95; pa $5.95

Grades: PreK K 1 2   E
1. Color
ISBN 1-55337-542-4; 1-55337-981-0 (pa)

This is a collection of color photographs of objects found in cities such as a red bus, a blue warehouse wall, and a yellow highway cone, a green swing, an orange cylindrical curb block, and a purple playground stool.

This is "a dazzling . . . concept book. . . . Precise partial photos inspire speculation on each verso with the recto revealing the complete image." SLJ

City signs. Kids Can Press 2002 unp il $15.95; pa $6.95

Grades: PreK K 1 2   E
1. Signs and signboards
ISBN 1-55337-003-1; 1-55337-748-6 (pa)

"Milich took to the streets with his camera, looking for printed words found in various outdoor environments. The 30 photographs here demonstrate that even children who can't yet read a book understand many of the words they see around them. The quality of the pictures is very good. They are nicely composed, clear, and often colorful." Booklist

Miller, Margaret, 1945-

Big and little. Greenwillow Bks. 1998 unp il $15.99 *

Grades: PreK   E
1. Size
ISBN 0-688-14748-8   LC 97-17242

Photographs and easy text introduce the concepts of size and opposites

"This book uses cheerful, clear color photos of active toddlers to teach basic concepts." Booklist

Guess who? Greenwillow Bks. 1994 unp il $16.99 *

Grades: PreK   E
1. Occupations
ISBN 0-688-12783-5   LC 93-26704

A child is asked who delivers the mail, gives haircuts, flies an airplane, and performs other important tasks. Each question has several different answers from which to choose

"Gender and ethnic representation are deftly handled. The author's sharp, clear full-color photographs are well composed, and her use of cropped photos and white space alternating with bled photos is an effective tool for involving youngsters." SLJ

Miller, Sara Swan

Three more stories you can read to your dog; illustrated by True Kelley. Houghton Mifflin 2000 unp il $14; pa $5.95 *

Grades: PreK K 1 2   E
1. Dogs—Fiction
ISBN 0-395-92293-3; 0-618-15244-X (pa)
                                    LC 99-39880

Stories addressed to dogs and written from a dog's point of view, featuring such topics as going to the vet,

Miller, Sara Swan—*Continued*

making friends with a rocklike creature, and getting a bath

"The witty, believable portrayal of canine thoughts and behavior will amuse readers. . . . True Kelley's lively ink-and-watercolor illustrations brighten every page." Booklist

Other titles in this series are:

Three more stories you can read to your cat (2002)

Three stories you can read to your cat (1997)

Three stories you can read to your dog (1995)

Three stories you can read to your teddy bear (2004)

Miller, William, 1959-

Night golf; illustrated by Cedric Lucas. Lee & Low Bks. 1999 unp il hardcover o.p. pa $8.95 *

Grades: K 1 2 3   E

1. African Americans—Fiction 2. Golf—Fiction 3. Prejudices—Fiction

ISBN 1-880000-79-2; 1-58430-056-6 (pa)

LC 98-47168

Despite being told that only whites can play golf, James becomes a caddy and is befriended by an older African American man who teaches him to play on the course at night

"Gentle paste and pencil illustrations support this quietly powerful story." Horn Book Guide

Rent party jazz; illustrated by Charlotte Riley-Webb. Lee & Low Bks. 2001 unp il $16.95; pa $7.95 *

Grades: K 1 2 3   E

1. Jazz music—Fiction 2. New Orleans (La.)—Fiction

ISBN 1-58430-025-6; 1-60060-344-0 (pa)

LC 2001-16449

When Sonny's mother loses her job in New Orleans during the Depression, Smilin' Jack, a jazz musician, tells him how to organize a rent party to raise the money they need

"Miller uses folksy dialogue to tell the story that celebrates both community and the uplifting power of music. Evocative artwork, done in broad, swirling strokes, fills pages with color and motion." Booklist

Richard Wright and the library card; illustrated by Gregory Christie. Lee & Low Bks. 1997 unp il hardcover o.p. pa $6.95 *

Grades: K 1 2 3   E

1. Wright, Richard, 1908-1960—Fiction 2. African Americans—Fiction 3. Books and reading—Fiction 4. Libraries—Fiction

ISBN 1-880000-57-1; 1-880000-88-1 (pa)

LC 97-6847

Based on a scene from Wright's autobiography, Black boy, in which the seventeen-year-old African-American borrows a white man's library card and devours every book as a ticket to freedom

"Christie's powerful impressionistic paintings in acrylic and colored pencil show the harsh racism in the Jim Crow South. . . . Words and pictures express the young man's loneliness and confinement and, then, the power he found in books." Booklist

Millman, Isaac, 1933-

Moses goes to school. Farrar, Straus & Giroux 2000 unp il $16 *

Grades: PreK K 1 2   E

1. Deaf—Fiction 2. Sign language—Fiction 3. School stories

ISBN 0-374-35069-8   LC 99-40582

"Frances Foster books"

Moses and his friends enjoy the first day of school at their special school for the deaf and hard of hearing, where they use sign language to talk to each other

"Child-friendly cartoon illustrations do a marvelous job of emphasizing the normalcy and charm of these youngsters. . . . The double-page layouts nicely accommodate the primary pictorial action along with written text and ASL inserts. . . . [This is a] great contribution to children's education about disabilities that also succeeds as effective storytelling in its own right." SLJ

Other titles about Moses are:

Moses goes to a concert (1998)

Moses goes to the circus (2003)

Moses sees a play (2004)

Mills, Claudia, 1954-

Gus and Grandpa and the two-wheeled bike; pictures by Catherine Stock. Farrar, Straus & Giroux 1999 47p il hardcover o.p. pa $7.99 *

Grades: K 1 2 3   E

1. Cycling—Fiction 2. Grandfathers—Fiction

ISBN 0-374-32821-8; 0-374-42816-6 (pa)

LC 97-44203

Gus doesn't want to give up the training wheels on his bike, even for a new five-speed bicycle, until Grandpa helps him learn how to get along without them

"Mills conveys strong sentiment without a trace of mawkishness, and Stock's illustrations in loose line and watercolor augment the story of this childhood rite of passage expressively." Horn Book Guide

Other titles about Gus and Grandpa are:

Gus and Grandpa (1997)

Gus and Grandpa and show-and-tell (2000)

Gus and Grandpa and the Christmas cookies (1997)

Gus and Grandpa and the Halloween costume (2002)

Gus and Grandpa and the piano lesson (2004)

Gus and Grandpa at basketball (2001)

Gus and Grandpa at the hospital (1998)

Gus and Grandpa go fishing (2003)

Gus and Grandpa ride the train (1998)

Milord, Susan, 1954-

Love that baby! written and illustrated by Susan Milord. Houghton Mifflin 2005 unp il $7.95

Grades: PreK K 1   E

1. Infants—Fiction

ISBN 0-618-56323-7   LC 2004-25119

"Each folded-over page poses a situation to ponder, while the unfolded spread beneath it suggests what to do next. A drawing of a . . . child . . . is accompanied by the words: 'Baby is hungry,' while the picture of father . . . gives the advice, 'Feed that baby!' Other pages offer suggested actions to take if the baby is napping, hiding, scared, sad, or sleepy. Simple drawings, soft colors in offbeat combinations, and a variety of patterns give

Milord, Susan, 1954-—*Continued*
this simple picture book visual appeal, while the lift-the-flap game will make it enjoyable for toddlers to revisit again and again." Booklist

Milway, Katie Smith

One hen; how one small loan made a big difference; written by Katie Smith Milway; illustrated by Eugenie Fernandes. Kids Can Press 2008 32p il $18.95

Grades: 2 3 4   E
  1. Ghana—Fiction 2. Chickens—Fiction 3. Eggs—Fiction 4. Loans—Fiction
  ISBN 978-1-55453-028-1; 1-55453-028-8
"In Ghana, young Kojo has a business idea, borrowing a small bit of money from his mother to purchase a hen, intending to sell her extra eggs at the market. Slowly his income grows so that he can not only pay his mother back but he can also buy more hens; eventually, he has enough money to go back to school. . . . [This gains] power from its modeling on a real Ghanian entrepeneur, Kwabena Darko. . . . The beneficial effects of small loans and small projects are thoughtfully and carefully explained in the extensive text. . . . Acrylic illustrations, vivid and lively with an emphasis on sunny hues and warm earthtones, balance out the large blocks of text." Bull Cent Child Books
  Includes glossary

Minarik, Else Holmelund

Little Bear; pictures by Maurice Sendak. Harper & Row 1957 63p il $16.95; lib bdg $17.89; pa $3.95 *

Grades: PreK K 1 2   E
  1. Bears—Fiction
  ISBN 0-06-024240-X; 0-06-024241-8 (lib bdg); 0-06-444004-4 (pa)
"An I can read book"
Four episodes "about Little Bear . . . as he persuades his mother to make him a winter outfit—only to discover his fur coat is all he needs; makes himself some birthday soup—and then is surprised with a birthday cake; takes an imaginary trip to the moon, and finally goes happily off to sleep as his mother tells him a story about 'Little Bear.'" Bull Cent Child Books
The pictures "depict all the warmth of feeling and the special companionship that exists between a small child and his mother." Publ Wkly
 Other titles about Little Bear are:
Father Bear comes home (1959)
A kiss for Little Bear (1968)
Little Bear's friend (1960)
Little Bear's visit (1961)

No fighting, no biting! pictures by Maurice Sendak. Harper & Row 1958 62p il lib bdg $17.89; pa $3.95 *

Grades: PreK K 1 2   E
  1. Alligators—Fiction
  ISBN 0-06-024291-4 (lib bdg); 0-06-444015-X (pa)
"An I can read book"
"A young lady who is unable to read in peace because of two children squabbling beside her tells them a story about two little alligators whose fighting and biting almost lead to disastrous consequences with a big hungry alligator. Children are sure to accept and enjoy the lesson in this little adventure tale and be amused by the expressive old-fashioned drawings." Booklist

Miranda, Anne, 1954-

To market, to market; written by Anne Miranda; illustrated by Janet Stevens. Harcourt Brace & Co. 1997 unp il $16; pa $7 *

Grades: PreK K 1 2   E
  1. Stories in rhyme 2. Animals—Fiction
  ISBN 0-15-200035-6; 0-15-216398-0 (pa)
                     LC 95-26326
In this "riff on the old nursery rhyme, 'To market, to market, to buy a fat pig,' a plump matron makes a series of increasingly calamitous purchases of animals at the supermarket. Hungry and cranky after the raucous menagerie turns her house topsy-turvy, the lady . . . wisely decides to make vegetable soup instead." Publ Wkly
"Patterned, staccato verses tell the zany tale, but it is Stevens's wonderfully wild illustrations that bring it to life." SLJ

Mitchell, Margaree King, 1953-

Uncle Jed's barbershop; illustrated by James Ransome. Simon & Schuster Bks. for Young Readers 1993 unp il hardcover o.p. pa $6.99 *

Grades: PreK K 1 2   E
  1. Uncles—Fiction 2. Barbers and barbershops—Fiction 3. African Americans—Fiction
  ISBN 0-671-76969-3; 0-689-81913-7 (pa)
                     LC 91-44148
Despite serious obstacles and setbacks Sarah Jean's Uncle Jed, the only black barber in the county, pursues his dream of saving enough money to open his own barbershop
"The author's convivial depictions of family life are enhanced by Ransome's . . . spirited oil paintings, which set the affectionate intergenerational cast against brightly patterned walls and crisp, leaf-strewn landscapes." Publ Wkly

Mitchell, Stephen, 1943-

The ugly duckling; retold by Stephen Mitchell; illustrated by Steve Johnson and Lou Fancher. Candlewick Press 2008 unp il $16.99

Grades: K 1 2 3   E
  1. Andersen, Hans Christian, 1805-1875—Adaptations 2. Swans—Fiction 3. Fairy tales
  ISBN 978-0-7636-2159-9   LC 2007-34235
An ugly duckling spends an unhappy year ostracized by the other animals before he grows into a beautiful swan.
"Mitchell retells the familiar story, preserving just enough of the character of Andersen's narrative voice to give his adaptation a tart, bracing flavor. . . . Johnson and Fancher's lacy, luminous art, rich with underwaterlike greens, gives [the swan's transformation] all the visual splendor it deserves." Horn Book

Miura, Taro, 1968-

Tools. Chronicle Books 2006 unp il $15.95 *

Grades: PreK K 1   E

1. Tools

ISBN 978-0-8118-5519-8; 0-8118-5519-8

LC 2005-34057

"Miura shows a distinctive set of tools on a double-page spread, identifying items such as a clamp, a saw, and nails. A turn of the page reveals the worker using them. Prereading children will enjoy identifying the tools, but their biggest challenge will be guessing the occupation represented. . . . The guessing-game aspect adds an element of fun to this beautifully designed and distinctively illustrated book." Booklist

Mobin-Uddin, Asma

The best Eid ever; [by] Asma Mobin-Uddin; illustrated by Laura Jacobsen. Boyds Mills Press 2007 unp il $16.95 *

Grades: K 1 2 3   E

1. Id al-Adha—Fiction 2. Muslims—Fiction 3. Pakistani Americans—Fiction 4. Grandmothers—Fiction

ISBN 978-1-59078-431-0; 1-59078-431-6

LC 2006037945

Eid is the Islamic holiday that marks the end of Ramadan. In this story, young Aneesa meets two girls at the prayer hall dressed in ill-fitting clothes and discovers they are refugees. Aneesa comes up with a plan to make this the best Eid ever

"This is a heartwarming tale of a child's generosity, and Jacobsen's illustrations flesh out the warmth and tenderness of the characters' interaction." SLJ

A party in Ramadan; illustrated by Laura Jacobsen. Boyds Mills Press 2009 unp il $16.95

Grades: K 1 2 3   E

1. Ramadan—Fiction 2. Muslims—Fiction 3. Parties—Fiction

ISBN 978-1-59078-604-8; 1-59078-604-1

LC 2008-43890

"With lively pastel-and-pencil artwork, this warm picture book shows and tells the observance and meaning of Ramadan through the viewpoint of a Muslim child. Leena is happy to be invited to her friend's birthday party, although it turns out that the event is on a day during Ramadan when Leena plans to fast with her family. . . . The blend of the upbeat with challenging moments will spark discussion, and a final note fills in more about the holy month." Booklist

Mochizuki, Ken, 1954-

Baseball saved us; written by Ken Mochizuki; illustrated by Dom Lee. Lee & Low Bks. 1993 unp il $16.95; pa $6.95 *

Grades: K 1 2 3   E

1. Japanese Americans—Evacuation and relocation, 1942-1945—Fiction 2. World War, 1939-1945—Fiction 3. Baseball—Fiction 4. Prejudices—Fiction

ISBN 1-880000-01-6; 1-880000-19-9 (pa)

LC 92-73215

A Japanese American boy learns to play baseball when he and his family are forced to live in an internment camp during World War II, and his ability to play helps him after the war is over

"Fences and watchtowers are in the background of many of Lee's moving illustrations, some of which were inspired by Ansel Adams' 1943 photographs of Manzanar. . . . The baseball action will grab kids—and so will the personal experience of bigotry." Booklist

Heroes; written by Ken Mochizuki; illustrated by Dom Lee. Lee & Low Bks. 1995 unp il hardcover o.p. pa $6.95

Grades: K 1 2 3   E

1. Japanese Americans—Fiction 2. Prejudices—Fiction

ISBN 1-880000-16-4; 1-880000-50-4 (pa)

LC 94-26541

"In the 1960's Donnie Okada took a lot of razzing from the other boys in the neighborhood; they insisted that he had to be the enemy in their war games because he looked like the enemy, and they did not believe his father and uncle had served in the American military. Dad and Uncle Yosh give those boys a dignified and effective lesson." N Y Times Book Rev

"The book is a powerful exploration of the cruelty children can inflict upon one another and of the confusion and pain borne by the target of such unthinking racism." Horn Book

Mollel, Tololwa M. (Tololwa Marti)

My rows and piles of coins; illustrated by E. B. Lewis. Clarion Bks. 1999 32p il $15 *

Grades: K 1 2 3   E

1. Money—Fiction 2. Bicycles—Fiction 3. Tanzania—Fiction

ISBN 0-395-75186-1   LC 98-21586

A Coretta Scott King honor book for illustration, 2000

A Tanzanian boy saves his coins to buy a bicycle so that he can help his parents carry goods to market, but then he discovers that in spite of all he has saved, he still does not have enough money

"The story is natural and never excessively moralistic. The fluid, light-splashed watercolor illustrations lend a sense of place and authenticity." SLJ

Monfreid, Dorothée de, 1973-

Dark night. Random House Children's Books 2009 unp il $14.99; lib bdg $17.99

Grades: PreK K 1 2   E

1. Fear—Fiction 2. Night—Fiction 3. Animals—Fiction

ISBN 978-0-375-85687-7; 0-375-85687-0; 978-0-375-95687-4 (lib bdg); 0-375-95687-5 (lib bdg)

LC 2008011257

Original French edition, 2007

When he wanders into the forest at night, Felix, terrified by the ferocious animals he sees, finds refuge in an unusual undergound house.

"De Monfreid's watercolor-and-ink illustrations are simple, charming, and extraordinarily expressive, making this a lovely book to add to any collection." SLJ

Monjo, F. N., 1924-1978

The drinking gourd; a story of the Underground Railroad; pictures by Fred Brenner. newly il ed. HarperCollins Pubs. 1993 62p il pa $3.99 *

Grades: K 1 2 3   E

1. Underground railroad—Fiction
ISBN 0-06-444042-7 (pa)   LC 92-10823
"An I can read book"
First published 1970

Set in New England in the decade before the Civil War. For mischievous behavior in church, Tommy is sent home to his room, but wanders instead into the barn. There he discovers that his father is helping runaway slaves escape to Canada

"The simplicity of dialogue and exposition, the level of concepts, and the length of the story [makes] it most suitable for the primary grades reader. The illustrations are deftly representational, the whole a fine addition to the needed body of historical books for the very young." Bull Cent Child Books

Monroe, Chris

Monkey with a tool belt. Carolrhoda 2008 unp il lib bdg $16.95

Grades: K 1 2 3   E

1. Monkeys—Fiction 2. Tools—Fiction
ISBN 978-0-8225-7631-0; 0-8225-7631-7
LC 2007-10020

Clever monkey Chico Bon Bon builds lots of things with his many tools, and when he is captured by an organ grinder, he uses them to help him escape and get back home.

"Slightly edgy, highly detailed comics-style art will have readers poring over the pages. . . . Not only gadget jockeys will enjoy this visually polished tale." Publ Wkly

Another title about Chico is:
Monkey with a tool belt and the noisy problem (2009)

Montes, Marisa, 1951-

Los gatos black on Halloween; illustrated by Yuyi Morales. Henry Holt and Company 2006 unp il $16.95 *

Grades: PreK K 1 2   E

1. Halloween—Fiction 2. Spanish language—Vocabulary 3. Stories in rhyme
ISBN 978-0-8050-7429-1; 0-8050-7429-5
LC 2005-20049

A Pura Belpré Author Award honor book, 2008

Easy to read, rhyming text about Halloween night incorporates Spanish words, from las brujas riding their broomsticks to los monstruos whose monstrous ball is interrupted by a true horror.

"Montes smoothly incorporates Spanish terms into a rhythmic poem. . . . The full-bleed paintings create a creepy mood with curving lines, fluid textures, and dusky hues. . . . The pictures are eerie enough to tingle spines, but the effect is leavened with bits of humor." SLJ

Moore, Patrick, 1959-

The mighty street sweeper. Holt & Co. 2006 unp il $15.95

Grades: PreK K   E

1. Street cleaning 2. Trucks
ISBN 0-8050-7789-8

"This picture book compares and contrasts the utilitarian street sweeper with a grader, snowplow, bulldozer, and other trucks. While it may not be the largest, most powerful, or fastest machine, it performs an important job. Bright, simple cartoon illustrations of squirrels, cats, dogs, and other animals driving the vehicles are paired with the straightforward text. . . . This offering will delight young truck lovers." SLJ

Mora, Pat

Abuelos; story by Pat Mora; pictures by Amelia Lau Carling. Groundwood Books 2008 unp il $18.95

Grades: PreK K 1 2   E

1. New Mexico—Fiction 2. Winter—Fiction
3. Hispanic Americans—Fiction
ISBN 978-0-88899-716-6; 0-88899-716-7

Mora "introduces the intriguing midwinter New Mexican festival of 'los abuelos' in this playful tale. The narrator, Amelia, is about to experience the spooky-sounding tradition for the first time, and Papá offers reassurances. . . . Played by costumed villagers in scary masks, the abuelos chase the children around bonfires; when one snatches her brother, Amelia grabs the abuelo's mask, only to discover her uncle beneath it. Carling's . . . watercolor and pastel illustrations impart Amelia's apprehension as well as family togetherness." Publ Wkly

Book fiesta! celebrate Children's Day/Book Day; illustrated by Rafael Lopez. HarperCollins 2009 unp il $17.99 *

Grades: PreK K 1 2 3   E

1. Books and reading—Fiction 2. Bilingual books—English-Spanish
ISBN 978-0-06-128877-7; 0-06-128877-2

ALA ALSC Belpre Illustrator Medal (2010)

"Mora encourages teachers, parents, and librarians to celebrate Children's Day/Book Day and includes ideas for observing the festivities. Written in English and Spanish, the text shows children reading in a variety of places, going to the library, listening to stories, and enjoying books. López's acrylic illustrations fill the pages with color. His upbeat iconic style shows how much fun this celebration can be." SLJ

Doña Flor; a tall tale about a giant woman with a great big heart; illustrated by Raul Colón. Knopf 2005 unp il $15.99; lib bdg $17.99 *

Grades: K 1 2 3   E

1. Giants—Fiction 2. Pumas—Fiction 3. Tall tales
ISBN 0-375-82337-9; 0-375-92337-3 (lib bdg)

Doña Flor, a giant woman with a big heart, sets off to protect her neighbors from what they think is a dangerous animal, but soon discovers the tiny secret behind the huge noise.

"A charming tall tale. . . Colón uses his signature mix of watercolor washes, etching, and litho pencils for

Mora, Pat—*Continued*
the art. There is great texture and movement on each
page in the sunbaked tones of the landscape." SLJ

Gracias = Thanks; illustrations by John Parra;
tranlations by Adriana Dominquez. Lee & Low
Books 2009 unp $17.95 *
Grades: PreK K 1 2   E
1. Racially mixed people—Fiction 2. Hispanic Americans—Fiction 3. Bilingual books—English-Spanish
ISBN 978-1-60060-258-0; 1-60060-258-4
LC 2009013060
ALA ALSC Belpre Illustrator Medal Honor Book
(2010)
"From the sun waking him up in the morning to a
cricket chirping him to sleep at night, a young boy gives
thanks for the many things and people who enrich his
life. These blessings are remarkable for their childlike
imagination and fresh imagery. . . . The bilingual format
features Spanish on the left-hand page and English on
the right. . . . Parra's vivid acrylic illustrations have the
feel of folk-art woodcuts and whimsically portray the details of the boy's world." Booklist

Here, kitty, kitty; illustrated by Maribel Suarez.
Rayo 2008 unp il (My family, mi familia) $14.99;
lib bdg $15.89
Grades: PreK K   E
1. Cats—Fiction 2. Bilingual books—English-Spanish
ISBN   978-0-06-085044-9;   0-06-085044-2;
978-0-06-085045-6 (lib bdg); 0-06-085045-0 (lib bdg)
"This joyful picture book tells a lively story of a
young girl who gets a shy new kitten that hides and
makes trouble. With English and Spanish text on each
double-page spread, the line-and-watercolor pictures
show the loving family as the kitten hides under the sofa,
under sister's bed, in a flowerpot, until finally the soft
friend snuggles up on the girl's lap." Booklist

Tomás and the library lady; illustrated by Raúl
Colón. Knopf 1997 unp il $17; pa $6.99
Grades: K 1 2 3   E
1. Rivera, Tomás—Fiction 2. Books and reading—Fiction 3. Libraries—Fiction 4. Migrant labor—Fiction
5. Mexican Americans—Fiction
ISBN 0-679-80401-3; 0-375-80349-1 (pa)
LC 89-37490
While helping his family in their work as migrant laborers far from their home, Tomás finds an entire world
to explore in the books at the local public library
"Mora's story is based on a true incident in the life
of the famous writer Tomás Rivera, the son of migrant
workers who became an education leader and university
president. . . . Colón's beautiful scratchboard illustrations, in his textured, glowingly colored, rhythmic style,
capture the warmth and the dreams that the boy finds in
the world of books." Booklist

Uno, dos, tres: one, two, three; illustrated by
Barbara Lavallee. Clarion Bks. 1996 43p il
hardcover o.p. pa $6.95
Grades: PreK K 1 2   E
1. Mexico—Fiction 2. Counting 3. Stories in rhyme
4. Bilingual books—English-Spanish
ISBN 0-395-67294-5; 0-618-05468-5 (pa)
LC 94-15337

"Two girls search a Mexican market for gifts for their
mother's birthday in this counting book in both English
and Spanish. . . . Cheerful stylized paintings in muted
reds, blues, and yellows depict designs from Mexican art
and use pattern to highlight the number sequence." Horn
Book Guide

Wiggling pockets. Rayo 2009 unp il (My
family, mi familia) $12.99
Grades: PreK K   E
1. Family life—Fiction 2. Frogs—Fiction 3. Bilingual
books—English-Spanish
ISBN 978-0-06-085047-0; 0-06-085047-7
"When Danny comes to the table with wiggling pockets, Mom and Dad ask what he has in them. Four frogs
jump out and cause minor chaos. The simple text in both
English and Spanish and the warm illustrations portray a
loving family." Horn Book Guide

Morales, Yuyi
Just in case; a trickster tale and Spanish
alphabet book. Roaring Brook Press 2008 unp il
$16.95 *
Grades: 1 2 3   E
1. Birthdays—Fiction 2. Gifts—Fiction 3. Ghost stories 4. Alphabet—Fiction
ISBN 978-1-59643-329-8; 1-59643-329-9
LC 2007-44061
A Pura Belpre Author Award honor book, 2009
As Senor Calavera prepares for Grandma Beetle's
birthday he finds an alphabetical assortment of unusual
presents, but with the help of Zelmiro the Ghost, he
finds the best gift of all.
"Luminous, jewel-tone spreads chronicle the collection
of gifts and pay homage to a rich Mexican culture. . . .
Part ghost story and part alphabet book, this trickster
tale transcends both. Librarians will want to share it for the
beautiful language, the spirited artwork, and the rightness
of the ending." SLJ

Little Night. Roaring Brook Press 2006 unp il
$16.95
Grades: PreK K   E
1. Bedtime—Fiction 2. Mother-daughter relationship—
Fiction 3. Night—Fiction 4. Sky—Fiction
ISBN 978-1-59643-088-4; 1-59643-088-5
LC 2006011571
"A Neal Porter book"
At the end of a long day, Mother Sky helps her play-
ful daughter, Little Night, to get ready for bed
"Morales has created a sumptuous feast of metaphors
in her text: a bathtub filled with falling stars, a dress cro-
cheted from clouds. The equally splendid illustrations ef-
fectively convey each of the images and heighten the
comfort and serenity inspired by the text." Booklist

Morris, Richard T., 1969-
Bye-bye, baby! by Richard Morris; illustrated by
Larry Day. Walker & Co. 2009 unp il $16.99; lib
bdg $17.89
Grades: PreK   E
1. Siblings—Fiction 2. Infants—Fiction
ISBN   978-0-8027-9772-8;   0-8027-9772-5;
978-0-8027-9773-5 (lib bdg); 0-8027-9773-3 (lib bdg)
LC 2008044318

Morris, Richard T., 1969-—*Continued*

Felix does not like his new baby sister and thinks his parents should take her back, until a trip to the zoo makes him realize that she might not be as bad as he thought.

"Outstanding illustrations are done in pen, ink, watercolor, and gouache. The characters' expressions and body language could tell this story alone, but wonderfully enhance the strong and simple text." SLJ

Morrow, Barbara Olenyik

A good night for freedom; illustrated by Leonard Jenkins. Holiday House 2004 unp il $16.95

Grades: K 1 2 3   E

1. Coffin, Levi, 1789-1877—Fiction 2. Underground railroad—Fiction 3. Slavery—Fiction

ISBN 0-8234-1709-3   LC 2002-192207

Hallie discovers two runaway slaves hiding in Levi Coffin's home and must decide whether to turn them in or help them escape to freedom. Includes historical notes on the Underground Railroad and abolitionists Levi and Catharine Coffin.

"The well-written text smoothly blends fact and fiction. . . . Jenkins's mixed-media illustrations capture the emotions of the characters as well as the details of pre-Civil War life." SLJ

Includes bibliographical references

Mr. Mosquito put on his tuxedo; illustrated by Ponder Goembel. Holiday House 2009 unp il $16.95

Grades: K 1 2 3   E

1. Mosquitoes—Fiction 2. Insects—Fiction 3. Bears—Fiction 4. Stories in rhyme

ISBN 978-0-8234-2072-8; 0-8234-2072-8

LC 2007025486

Mr. Mosquito saves the insect ball from an intruding bear.

"The abundant and rhyming text is only half of this story; the illustrations tell the rest. Using lush colors befitting a royal ball and excellent attention to detail, Goembel brings this idiosyncratic tale to life." SLJ

Mortensen, Denise Dowling

Good night engines; illustrated by Melissa Iwai. Clarion Bks. 2003 32p il $15

Grades: PreK K   E

1. Vehicles—Fiction 2. Stories in rhyme 3. Bedtime—Fiction

ISBN 0-618-13537-5   LC 2002-155215

Rhyming verses describe how a variety of vehicles, from locomotives to eighteen-wheelers to automobiles, wind down for a night of rest

"The story is as smooth and easy as a familiar lullaby. . . . Iwai's acrylic, full-page spreads match the quiet text." SLJ

A companion to this volume is:

Wake up engines (2007)

Moser, Lisa

Kisses on the wind; illustrated by Kathryn Brown. Candlewick Press 2009 unp il $15.99

Grades: K 1 2 3   E

1. Moving—Fiction 2. Grandmothers—Fiction 3. Frontier and pioneer life—Fiction 4. West (U.S.)—Fiction

ISBN 978-0-7636-3110-9; 0-7636-3110-8

LC 2008-53490

Young Lydia struggles to say goodbye to her grandmother as her parents finish packing their wagon for the long journey to Oregon in the nineteenth century.

"Moser and Brown tell a wise, gentle story about good-byes. . . . The fluid watercolors amplify the story's mood of transition." Booklist

Squirrel's world; illustrated by Valeri Gorbachev. Candlewick Press 2007 44p il $14.99; pa $4.99 *

Grades: 1 2 3   E

1. Squirrels—Fiction 2. Animals—Fiction

ISBN 978-0-7636-2929-8; 0-7636-2929-4; 978-0-7636-4088-0 (pa); 0-7636-4088-3 (pa)

LC 2007-60859

Squirrel's well-meaning attempts to help his forest friends do not always turn out as planned.

"Gorbachev's loosely hatched linework provides appealing informal texture to the forest clan, and his illustrations offer plenty of decoding clues for novices. . . . Early independent readers will revel in the abundant repetition." Bull Cent Child Books

Moss, Lloyd

Zin! zin! zin! a violin; illustrated by Marjorie Priceman. Simon & Schuster Bks. for Young Readers 1995 unp il $17.95; pa $6.99 *

Grades: K 1 2 3   E

1. Musical instruments 2. Counting 3. Stories in rhyme

ISBN 0-671-88239-2; 0-689-83524-8 (pa)

LC 93-37902

A Caldecott Medal honor book, 1996

"Rhyming couplets present 10 instruments and their characteristics. . . . In the process of adding instruments, the book teaches the names of musical groups up to a chamber group of 10 as well as the categories into which the instruments fall: strings, reeds, and brasses. Amazingly, Moss conveys this encyclopedic information while keeping the poem streamlined and peppy. Priceman's sprightly, sunny hued gouache paintings should take a bow, too." Booklist

Moss, Miriam

A babysitter for Billy Bear; [by] Miriam Moss; pictures by Anna Currey. Dial Books for Young Readers 2008 unp il $16.99

Grades: PreK K   E

1. Babysitters—Fiction 2. Worry—Fiction 3. Bears—Fiction

ISBN 978-0-8037-3269-8; 0-8037-3269-4

LC 2007017212

"Billy and his best friend, a small stuffed rabbit, experience their first night with a babysitter while Mama goes

Moss, Miriam—*Continued*

to her pottery class. . . . The gentle watercolor pictures perfectly match the story of the teddy bearish youngster and his Mama-bear-type babysitter." SLJ

Most, Bernard, 1937-

ABC T-Rex. Harcourt Brace & Co. 2000 unp il $14; pa $6

Grades: PreK K 1   E

1. Dinosaurs—Fiction 2. Alphabet
ISBN 0-15-202007-1; 0-15-205028-0 (pa)

LC 98-51128

A young T-Rex loves his ABCs so much that he eats them up, experiencing on each letter a word that begins with that letter

"Heavy black lines define the cartoonlike drawings, brightened with a colorful palette emphasizing shades of green, purple, and orange. Fun for alphabetically inclined preschoolers." Booklist

How big were the dinosaurs. Harcourt Brace & Co. 1994 unp il $16; pa $7

Grades: PreK K 1   E

1. Dinosaurs
ISBN 0-15-236800-0; 0-15-200852-7 (pa)

LC 93-19152

Describes the size of different dinosaurs by comparing them to more familiar objects, such as a school bus, a trombone, or a bowling alley

"The colorful drawings, of children interacting with dinosaurs, will be attractive to children. The text is easy to read. This book will delight young dinosaur lovers." Sci Books Films

Whatever happened to the dinosaurs? written and illustrated by Bernard Most. Harcourt Brace Jovanovich 1984 unp il hardcover o.p. pa $4.95 *

Grades: PreK K 1   E

1. Dinosaurs—Fiction
ISBN 0-15-295295-0; 0-15-295296-9 (pa)

LC 84-3779

The author "offers various fantastic explanations to answer his title question. 'Did the dinosaurs go to another planet? . . . did a magician make them disappear? . . . Are the dinosaurs in the hospital?'" SLJ

"A hilarious book, sure to be popular for individual reading or with groups." Child Book Rev Serv

Munari, Bruno, 1907-1998

Bruno Munari's zoo; [by] Bruno Munari. Chronicle Books 2005 c1963 unp il $17.95

Grades: PreK K   E

1. Zoos 2. Animals
ISBN 0-8118-4830-2   LC 2004-21214

A reissue of the title first published 1963 by World Publishing

Illustrations and brief text introduce more than twenty zoo animals, including a rhinoceros that is always ready to fight and a peacock that struts proudly because he is the peacock.

"A stunning picture book of birds and beasts original in design, brilliant with color, and touched with humor." Booklist

Munro, Roxie, 1945-

Circus. Chronicle Books 2006 unp il $15.95

Grades: PreK K 1 2   E

1. Circus—Fiction 2. Puzzles 3. Stories in rhyme
ISBN 0-8118-5209-1

Flaps open to reveal circus acts, from astounding acrobats to elegant elephants, and rhyming text lists objects hidden within each performance

"The detailed ink and watercolor illustrations are bold and lively." Horn Book Guide

Go! go! go! with more than 70 flaps to uncover & discover. Sterling 2009 unp il $15.95 *

Grades: PreK K 1 2   E

1. Fires—Fiction
ISBN 978-1-4027-3773-2; 1-4027-3773-4

Gatefolds, layers of lift-the-flaps and complex foldouts take the reader on a race of a fire truck to battle a blaze, to gallop to the finish line on the favorite horse and riding the race course in a car.

This is a "fascinating picture book. . . . Text is kept to a minimum while full-spread artwork carries the story. . . . The full-color illustrations are loaded with pertinent details." SLJ

Muntean, Michaela

Do not open this book! illustrated by Pascal LeMaitre. Scholastic Press 2006 unp il $15.99 *

Grades: PreK K 1 2   E

1. Pigs—Fiction 2. Authorship—Fiction 3. Books and reading—Fiction
ISBN 0-439-69839-1

As Pig tries to write a book, he chastises the reader who keeps interrupting him by turning the pages.

"Along with hand lettering Muntean's text, LeMaitre contributes bright, comics-style pictures that clarify the occasionally dizzying concepts. . . . Children will be . . . enraptured by the irreverent, interactive premise and will emerge with a fresh understanding of the powerful qualities of words." Booklist

Murphy, Mary, 1961-

I kissed the baby. Candlewick Press 2003 unp il hardcover o.p. bd bk $6.99 *

Grades: PreK K 1   E

1. Ducks—Fiction 2. Animals—Fiction
ISBN 0-7636-2122-6; 0-7636-2443-8 (bd bk)

LC 2002-31419

Various animals tell how they saw, fed, sang to, tickled, and kissed the new duckling

"Murphy makes creative use of color on the edges of the black-and-white pages, until the duckling appears in a splash of vibrant yellow, and the text changes to hot pink. This is an ideal book for little eyes and ears, for text, illustrations, and design meld perfectly." SLJ

Murphy, Stuart J., 1942-
Leaping lizards; illustrated by JoAnn Adinolfi. HarperCollins Pubs. 2005 33p il (MathStart) hardcover o.p. pa $4.99 *
Grades: 1 2 3   E
1. Counting 2. Addition 3. Lizards—Fiction 4. Stories in rhyme
ISBN 0-06-000130-5; 0-06-000132-1 (pa)
LC 2004-22470
"This book introduces the multiples of five, as lizards of different colors travel through the pages on unicycles, a hot-air balloon, an airplane, and other modes of transport, while a green snake looks on. Finally, the number 50 is reached, and lizards explode in all directions. . . . An intelligent blending of white space and colors make each double-page spread visually stand out. A box on one side of each page helps children keep track of the multiplying lizards, and a closing section offers adults a few more ideas for easy math education." Booklist

Same old horse; illustrated by Steve Björkman. HarperCollins Pubs. 2005 31p il (Mathstart) hardcover o.p. pa $4.99
Grades: K 1 2 3   E
1. Horses—Fiction
ISBN 0-06-055770-2; 0-06-055771-0 (pa)
Hankie wants to be unpredictable, but the other horses are sure he'll always be the same old Hankie. Someone's in for a surprise in this story about making predictions
This "is a lively story that encourages kids to work with numbers to find out what happens next. Bjorkman's clear, funny ink-and-watercolor pictures show horses in a barnyard acting just like children on a school playground." Booklist

Murphy, Yannick
Baby Polar; illustrated by Kristen Balouch. Clarion Books 2009 unp il $16   E
1. Polar bear—Fiction 2. Arctic regions—Fiction 3. Mother-child relationship—Fiction 4. Storms—Fiction
ISBN 978-0-618-99850-0; 0-618-99850-0
LC 2008011619
Even though his mother warns him of a coming storm, Baby Polar goes outside to play, but when he cannot see his own paw he realizes that he now faces danger.
"The illustrations are digitally produced and beautifully designed. Stylized white snowflakes and polar bear figures set against a blue gray background convey well the icy coldness of the storm. . . . The book's reassuring conclusion offers a satisfying story for that audience, as well as an introduction to polar bears and their Arctic world." SLJ

Murray, Marjorie Dennis
Halloween night; by Marjorie Dennis Murray; illustrations by Brandon Dorman. Greenwillow Books 2008 unp il $16.99; lib bdg $17.89
Grades: K 1 2 3   E
1. Halloween—Fiction 2. Monsters—Fiction 3. Parties—Fiction 4. Stories in rhyme
ISBN 978-0-06-135186-0; 0-06-135186-5; 978-0-06-135187-7 (lib bdg); 0-06-135187-3 (lib bdg)
LC 2007027686

Loosely based on "The Night Before Christmas," this rhyming story tells of a group of animals, monsters, and witches who prepare such a frightening Halloween party that their expected trick-or-treaters all run away.
"Murray's smooth rhyming text combines well with Dorman's vibrant and extraordinarily detailed digital art, with surprises on every page. This is an energetic romp with a satisfying conclusion that will be a fun read-aloud." SLJ

Museum shapes. Little, Brown 2005 unp il $16.99 *
Grades: PreK K 1 2   E
1. Shape 2. Art appreciation
ISBN 0-316-05698-7
"Produced by the Department of Special Publications, The Metropolitan Museum of Art"
"An exercise in both art appreciation and recognizing shapes, this book invites children to find one of 10 geometric forms in tiled details taken from several dozen artworks owned by New York's Metropolitan Museum of Art." Booklist
"The concept is simple; what makes this book so wonderful is the art, which is varied in content, style, medium, culture, and period, and is beautifully reproduced." SLJ

Muth, Jon J.
Zen shorts; illustrated by Jon Muth. Scholastic Press 2005 unp il $16.95 *
Grades: K 1 2 3   E
1. Giant panda—Fiction 2. Zen Buddhism—Fiction 3. Storytelling—Fiction
ISBN 0-439-33911-1   LC 2003-20471
A Caldecott Medal honor book, 2006
When Stillwater the panda moves into the neighborhood, the stories he tells to three siblings teach them to look at the world in new ways.
This "is both an accessible, strikingly illustrated story and a thought-provoking mediation." Booklist
Another title about Stillwater the panda is:
Zen ties (2008)

Myers, Christopher
Black cat. Scholastic Press 1999 unp il $16.95 *
Grades: PreK K 1 2   E
1. Cats—Fiction 2. City and town life—Fiction
ISBN 0-590-03375-1   LC 98-28609
A Coretta Scott King honor book for illustration, 2000
A black cat wanders through the streets of a city
"With striking photo-collages enhanced with gouache and ink, this book captures the gritty beauty of the city." Horn Book Guide

Wings. Scholastic Press 2000 unp il $16.95
Grades: K 1 2 3   E
1. Flight—Fiction 2. Classical mythology—Fiction
ISBN 0-590-03377-8   LC 99-87389
"Myers retells the myth of Icarus through the story of Ikarus Jackson, the new boy on the block, who can fly above the rooftops and over the crowd. In this contemporary version, the winged kid nearly falls from the sky

Myers, Christopher—*Continued*

. . . because jeering kids in the schoolyard and repressive adults don't like his being different and try to break his soaring spirit. . . . Myers' beautiful cut-paper collages are eloquent and open." Booklist

Myers, Tim, 1953-

Basho and the river stones; illustrations by Oki S. Han. Marshall Cavendish 2004 unp il $16.95

Grades: K 1 2 3   E

1. Matsuo, Bashō, 1644-1694—Fiction 2. Foxes—Fiction 3. Poetry—Fiction 4. Japan—Fiction

ISBN 0-7614-5165-X   LC 2003-26245

Tricked by a fox into giving up his share of cherries, a famous Japanese poet is inspired to write a haiku and the fox, ashamed of his actions, must devise another trick to set things right

"Han's expressive watercolors, with an unusual variety of perspectives, keep the story lively. A clever original fable." Booklist

Another title about Basho by this author and illustrator is:

Basho and the fox (2000)

Myers, Walter Dean, 1937-

The blues of Flats Brown; illustrated by Nina Laden. Holiday House 2000 unp il $16.95; pa $6.95 *

Grades: 1 2 3 4   E

1. Dogs—Fiction 2. Blues music—Fiction

ISBN 0-8234-1480-9; 0-8234-1679-8 (pa)

                   LC 99-16695

To escape an abusive master, a junkyard dog named Flats runs away and makes a name for himself from Mississippi to New York City playing blues on his guitar

"The narrator's vernacular, rhythmic and easy-rolling, has the feel of a timeless legend, and the vibrant, jewel-toned illustrations, dominated by moody, bittersweet, tonal variations of blue, are filled with rich detail, expressive characters, and fantastic landscapes." Booklist

Looking like me; illustrated by Christopher Myers. Egmont USA 2009 unp il $17.99; lib bdg $21.99 *

Grades: 1 2 3   E

1. Family life—Fiction 2. African Americans—Fiction 3. Harlem (New York, N.Y.)—Fiction

ISBN 978-1-60684-001-6; 1-60684-001-0; 978-1-60684-041-2 (lib bdg); 1-60684-041-X (lib bdg)

                   LC 2009-14640

Jeremy sets out to discover all of the different "people" that make him who he is, including brother, son, writer, and runner

"The innovative art and design represent different identities with colorful silhouettes placed against photos of people, places, and icons. . . . This very contemporary work is encouraging, energetic, and inspired." Booklist

Patrol; an American soldier in Vietnam; collages by Ann Grifalconi. HarperCollins Pubs. 2002 unp il hardcover o.p. lib bdg $16.89; pa $6.99 *

Grades: 3 4 5 6   E

1. Vietnam War, 1961-1975—Fiction 2. African American soldiers—Fiction

ISBN 0-06-028363-7; 0-06-028364-5 (lib bdg); 0-06-073159-1 (pa)   LC 00-35009

A frightened American soldier faces combat in the lush forests of Vietnam and sees a young enemy soldier who is as frightened as he is

The story is told "in free verse that is at once ethereal and white-knuckle tense. . . . Grifalconi's intricate paper and photo collages juxtapose snips of explosion smoke, snapshot images of fleeing villagers, and paper constructions of burning huts against a landscape that approaches fantasy in its lush beauty." Bull Cent Child Books

Na, Il Sung

A book of sleep. Alfred A. Knopf 2009 unp il $15.99; lib bdg $18.99

Grades: PreK K 1   E

1. Sleep—Fiction 2. Owls—Fiction 3. Animals—Fiction

ISBN 978-0-375-86223-6; 0-375-86223-4; 978-0-375-96223-3 (lib bdg); 0-375-96223-9 (lib bdg)

                   LC 2008-47865

First published 2007 in the United Kingdom with title: Zzzz: a book of sleep

While other animals sleep at night, some quietly and others noisily, some alone and others huddled together, a wide-eyed owl watches.

"Na's textural images recall the lightheartedness and limpid charm of Paul Klee. . . . It's the rare picture book that, upon arrival, feels as though it has been around for years already; Na's belongs to this group." Publ Wkly

The thingamabob. Alfred A. Knopf 2010 c2008 unp il $15.99; lib bdg $18.99

Grades: PreK K   E

1. Elephants—Fiction 2. Umbrellas and parasols—Fiction

ISBN 978-0-375-86106-2; 0-375-86106-8; 978-0-375-96106-9 (lib bdg); 0-375-96106-2 (lib bdg)

                   LC 2009003120

First published 2008 in the United Kingdom

An elephant finds a "thingamabob" and experiments until he discovers what to do with it.

"Sumptuous colors and swirling textures turn this slight, silly story into a visual feast, buoyed by a handful of great sight gags and the hands-down adorableness of the animals." Booklist

Nakagawa, Chihiro, 1958-

Who made this cake? text and English translation by Chihiro Nakagawa; illustrations by Junji Koyose. Front Street 2008 unp il $16.95 *

Grades: PreK K 1   E

1. Construction equipment—Fiction 2. Cake—Fiction 3. Baking—Fiction 4. Size—Fiction

ISBN 978-1-59078-595-9; 1-59078-595-9

                   LC 2008003070

Nakagawa, Chihiro, 1958-—*Continued*

While a boy and his parents go for an outing, little people invade the house and use their big construction equipment to bake a cake.

"The understated text is almost unnecessary, as the pictures easily tell the story and then some. . . . Truck fans will naturally pore over every busy, action-filled scene." Horn Book

Namioka, Lensey

The hungriest boy in the world; illustrated by Aki Sogabe. Holiday House 2001 unp il $16.95

Grades: K 1 2 3   E

1. Hunger—Fiction 2. Japan—Fiction

ISBN 0-8234-1542-2   LC 00-25142

After swallowing the Hunger Monster, Jiro begins eating everything in sight, until his family finds a way to lure the monster out of Jiro's stomach

"The story is told economically but with wit and humor. Sogabe's illustrations, created using cut paper over rice paper that has been colored by airbrush or watercolor, complement the text with their elegant simplicity." SLJ

Napoli, Donna Jo, 1948-

Albert; illustrated by Jim LaMarche. Silver Whistle Bks. 2001 unp il $16; pa $7 *

Grades: K 1 2 3   E

1. Birds—Fiction

ISBN 0-15-201572-8; 0-15-205249-6 (pa)

LC 97-7089

One day when Albert is at his window, two cardinals come to build a nest in his hand, an event that changes his life

"Napoli has written a pleasing modern fairy tale, transformed into a picture book by LaMarche's appealing, shaded pencil drawings." Booklist

The Earth shook; a Persian tale; illustrations by Gabi Swiatkowska. Hyperion Books for Children 2009 unp il $15.99

Grades: K 1 2 3   E

1. Iran—Fiction 2. Earthquakes—Fiction 3. Animals—Fiction

ISBN 978-1-4231-0448-3; 1-4231-0448-X

"In this Persian-inspired tale (based on a 2003 earthquake in Bam, Iran), Parisa desperately seeks the company of another human being when her village is destroyed. She knocks on door after door, but hostile animals now occupy any still-standing homes. . . . Swiatkowska's extraordinary artwork—textured oil paintings, decorative designs, splendid palette and artfully spare compositions—adds power and beauty to the poetic text that echoes Rumi. A gorgeous, discussion-provoking read-aloud." Kirkus

The Wishing Club; a story about fractions. Henry Holt 2007 unp il $16.95

Grades: 1 2 3   E

1. Wishes—Fiction 2. Siblings—Fiction 3. Fractions—Fiction

ISBN 978-0-8050-7665-3; 0-8050-7665-4

LC 2006030767

When four siblings wish on a star, each gets only a fraction of what he or she wanted, but when they combine their wishes, they just might get a whole new pet.

"Napoli's story moves smoothly between the magic of wishes granted and the reality of working with fractions. . . . Currey's watercolor-and-ink illustrations evoke summer nights when barefoot youngsters lean on porch railings and look at the stars." SLJ

Nayar, Nandini

What should I make? illustrations by Proiti Roy. Tricycle Press 2009 unp il $12.99

Grades: PreK K 1   E

1. Imagination—Fiction 2. Mother-son relationship—Fiction 3. Cooking—Fiction 4. East Indians—Fiction

ISBN 978-1-58246-294-3; 1-58246-294-1

LC 2008-42803

While his mother makes chapatis (Indian flat bread), Neeraj transforms a piece of dough into different animals.

"Warm-toned illustrations keep attention centered squarely on mother and son. A recipe is included." Horn Book Guide

Nazoa, Aquiles, 1920-1976

A small Nativity; by Aquiles Nazoa; illustrated by Ana Palmero Cáceres; translated by Hugh Hazelton. Groundwood Books 2007 44p il $9.95

Grades: 1 2 3   E

1. Jesus Christ—Nativity

ISBN 0-88899-839-2

"Venezuelan poet Nazoa's unadorned retelling of the Nativity story offers a homely approach to the familiar tale. . . . Palmero Cáceres illustrates this humble text with devotional pictures inspired by medieval illuminated manuscripts. Her richly colored art successfully combines traditional symbols of Christianity with images of Latin American flora and fauna." Horn Book

Nedwidek, John

Ducks don't wear socks; by John Nedwidek; illustrated by Lee White. Viking Childrens Books 2008 unp il $15.99

Grades: PreK K 1 2   E

1. Ducks—Fiction

ISBN 978-0-670-06136-5; 0-670-06136-0

LC 2007023122

Emily, a serious girl, meets a duck who helps her see the more humorous side of life.

"White's colorful illustrations bring the story's humor to life. The cartoon style allows the creature's wackiness to shine while providing visual clues for those just beginning to read independently. A lighthearted lesson on the benefits of laughter, this is just plain fun." SLJ

Neitzel, Shirley

The jacket I wear in the snow; pictures by Nancy Winslow Parker. Greenwillow Bks. 1989 unp il $16.99; pa $6.99

Grades: PreK K 1 2   E

1. Clothing and dress—Fiction 2. Snow—Fiction 3. Stories in rhyme

ISBN 0-688-08028-6; 0-688-04587-1 (pa)

LC 88-18767

A young girl names all the clothes that she must wear to play in the snow

"Written in cheerful, cumulative verse that recalls the well-known favorite nursery rhyme 'The House That Jack Built,' the text, with its easy-going rhythm, will be simple for children to recite from memory. . . . The artist's drawings are executed in . . . watercolor, pencil, and pen; they combine with the large typeface and a generous amount of white space to create a tremendously appealing book." Horn Book

Nelson, Marilyn, 1946-

Snook alone; illustrated by Timothy Basil Ering. Harper 2010 il $16.99

Grades: K 1 2 3   E

1. Dogs—Fiction 2. Monks—Fiction 3. Islands—Fiction

ISBN 978-0-7636-2667-9; 0-7636-2667-8

"Snook is a rat terrier who lives with a monk on an island hermitage. . . . He gleefully munches rats while his companion works and prays. This simple, wonderful life is interrupted when a storm strands Snook on a tiny nearby atoll. Nelson writes in delicate stanzas of effortless poetry. . . . Ering's acrylic-and-ink artwork fades from the bright palette of the monk's abode to a nearly two-tone earthiness and creates a style both realistic and emotional. . . . The final reuniting is sudden yet as genuine as everything else about the book." Booklist

Nelson, Vaunda Micheaux

Who will I be, Lord? illustrated by Sean Qualls. Random House 2009 unp il $16.95; lib bdg $19.99 *

Grades: PreK K 1 2   E

1. African Americans—Fiction 2. Family life—Fiction 3. Occupations—Fiction

ISBN   978-0-375-84342-6;   0-375-84342-6; 978-0-375-94342-3 (lib bdg); 0-375-94342-0 (lib bdg)

LC 2008035186

"An African-American girl looking to the future has a broad range of relatives to emulate—a banjo-playing mailman, a housewife who broke the color barrier, a pool shark, and a burger-flipping aspiring jazzman. Nelson's rhythmic and colloquial first-person narrative introduces the characters not only in terms of the jobs they hold, but also the kind of people they are. . . . Qualls's mixed-media illustrations combine muted and bright elements and feature full-spread renditions of each relative at home or work, followed by a page showing surreal floating heads of the girl and the featured role model as she repeats the title's query. Nelson shows respect for all the ways people live and work." SLJ

Ness, Evaline, 1911-1986

Sam, Bangs & Moonshine; written and illustrated by Evaline Ness. Holt & Co. 1966 unp il $17.95; pa $6.95 *

Grades: PreK K 1 2   E

1. Imagination—Fiction

ISBN 0-8050-0314-2; 0-8050-0315-0 (pa)

Awarded the Caldecott Medal, 1967

Young Samantha, or Sam, "the fisherman's daughter, finally learns to draw the line between reality and the 'moonshine' [her fantasies] in which her mother is a mermaid, she owns a baby kangaroo, and can talk to her cat." Publisher's note

"In this unusually creative story the fantasy in which many, many children indulge is presented in a realistic and sympathetic context. The illustrations in ink and pale color wash (mustard, grayish-aqua) have a touching realism, too. This is an outstanding book." SLJ

Neubecker, Robert

Wow! America! Hyperion Books for Children 2006 unp il $16.99 *

Grades: PreK K 1 2   E

1. United States—Description and travel

ISBN 0-7868-3816-7   LC 2005-44735

"This companion to Wow! City! follows country girl Izzy on another journey, this time with her little sister and dog. Each spread reveals a location in the U.S. . . . Each spread also contains brief informational text. The drawings are as energetic as the exclamation-enhanced text." Horn Book Guide

Wow! city! Hyperion 2004 unp il $16.99 *

Grades: PreK K 1 2   E

1. City and town life—Fiction

ISBN 0-7868-0951-5

Two-year-old toddler Izzy goes on a trip with her father and experiences in what she sees in the hustling-and-bustling, gigantic, crowded, loud, and colorful city.

"Drawn in India ink and vividly colored on a Macintosh computer using Adobe Photoshop, the illustrations are full of life, action, and detail." SLJ

Wow! school! Hyperion Books for Children 2007 unp il $16.99 *

Grades: PreK K 1   E

1. School stories

ISBN 0-7868-3896-5; 978-0-7868-3896-7

LC 2006-49569

Izzy finds many things to be excited about on the first day of school.

"The bold, crayonlike lines of Neubecker's India-ink drawings contrast pleasingly with the computer-generated color. This is a wonderful book for sharing with groups of emergent readers, who will enjoy chiming along, and it is well suited to the attention spans of children just beginning preschool or kindergarten." SLJ

Nevius, Carol, 1955-

Building with Dad; by Carol Nevius; illustrated by Bill Thomson. Marshall Cavendish 2006 unp il $16.99

Grades: PreK K 1 2　　　　　　　　E

1. Building—Fiction 2. Construction equipment—Fiction 3. Father-son relationship—Fiction 4. Stories in rhyme

ISBN 978-0-7614-5312-3; 0-7614-5312-1

LC 2005027311

A father and his young child watch the construction of the new school, from the bulldozing of earth and mixing of the concrete for the foundation to the hanging of the new sign.

This is an "energetic picture book with visual punch. . . . The spreads spill down the page vertically, rather than horizontally, for maximum impact. . . . Thomson uses full color, and his photo-realistic paintings bring viewers close up to, sometimes even under, giant machines." Booklist

Karate hour; illustrated by Bill Thomson. Marshall Cavendish 2004 unp il $14.95 *

Grades: PreK K 1 2　　　　　　　　E

1. Karate—Fiction 2. Stories in rhyme

ISBN 0-7614-5169-2　　　　LC 2003-27122

Rhyming text portrays the exuberance of an hour of karate class. Includes nonfiction information at end

Nevius "deftly captures the excitement and energy of the experience as well as the discipline and commitment required to rise in rank. Thomson's realistic mixed-media artwork is a standout, using light, shadow, and perspective in a variety of interesting ways." SLJ

Newberry, Clare Turlay, 1903-1970

April's kittens. HarperCollins Pubs. 1993 c1940 32p il $16.99

Grades: PreK K 1 2　　　　　　　　E

1. Cats—Fiction

ISBN 0-06-024400-3

A Caldecott Medal honor book, 1941

A reissue of the title first published 1940

"Though old-fashioned, the story of a small girl's yearning to keep both a mother cat and one of her kittens still speaks to pet owners young and old. Newberry's simple, charcoal drawings of the felines are as elegant and endearing as ever." Horn Book

Marshmallow; story and pictures by Clare Turlay Newberry. rev ed. HarperCollinsPublishers 2008 unp il $16.99; lib bdg $17.89; pa $6.99

Grades: K 1 2　　　　　　　　E

1. Rabbits—Fiction 2. Cats—Fiction

ISBN　978-0-06-072486-3;　0-06-072486-2; 978-0-06-072487-0 (lib bdg); 0-06-072487-0 (lib bdg); 978-0-06-072488-7 (pa); 0-06-072488-9 (pa)

LC 2007-30888

A Caldecott Medal honor book, 1943

First published 1942

A cat who is used to being the center of attention learns to share his home with a rabbit

Newbery, Linda, 1952-

Posy! illustrated by Catherine Rayner. Atheneum Books for Young Readers 2009 unp il $16.99 *

Grades: PreK K　　　　　　　　E

1. Stories in rhyme 2. Cats—Fiction

ISBN 978-1-4169-7112-2; 1-4169-7112-2

LC 2008-03807

Posy the kitten has lots of adventures catching spiders, swiping crayons, tangling yarn, and cuddling

"Rendered in watercolor pencil crayons, acrylic, and India inks, [Posy] sometimes dominates the broad cream-colored spreads or divides a page into several vignettes with her actions. . . . While grownups, particularly cat lovers, will be charmed by the stylized art, children will notice in the kitten's daily activities much of what interests them." SLJ

Newcome, Zita, 1959-

Head, shoulders, knees, and toes; and other action counting rhymes. Candlewick Press 2002 60p il $15.99

Grades: PreK K　　　　　　　　E

1. Nursery rhymes 2. Counting 3. Finger play

ISBN 0-7636-1899-3　　　　LC 2002-17508

A collection of approximately fifty nursery and counting rhymes, most accompanied by fingerplays or other activities

"Each page includes the words of one rhyme and energetic watercolor-and-colored pencil illustrations of kids in action. . . . This is exercise and play as well as a lively celebration of the sound and beat of words in the nonsense rhymes that live on." Booklist

Newgarden, Mark

Bow-Wow bugs a bug; [by] Mark Newgarden and Megan Montague Cash. Harcourt 2007 unp il $12.95 *

Grades: K 1 2 3　　　　　　　　E

1. Dogs—Fiction 2. Insects—Fiction 3. Stories without words

ISBN 978-0-15-205813-5　　　　LC 2006-11026

A wordless picture book about a persistent terrier who follows a bug through his neighborhood.

"The clever circular plot is funny, quirky, and even suspenseful. . . . The simple, bold, expressive illustrations, outlined with heavy black line, challenge viewers to follow the visual story line and sequences of events." SLJ

Other titles about Bow-Wow are:

Bow-Wow naps by number (2007)

Bow-Wow orders lunch (2007)

Bow-Wow attracts opposites (2008)

Bow-Wow hears things (2008)

Bow-Wow 12 months running (2009)

Bow-Wow's colorful life (2009)

Newman, Jeff, 1976-

The boys; written by Jeff Newman; illustrated by Jeff Newman. Simon & Schuster Books for Young Readers 2009 unp il $15.99

Grades: 1 2 3   E

1. Shyness—Fiction 2. Baseball—Fiction 3. Old age—Fiction 4. Stories without words

ISBN 978-1-4169-5012-7; 1-4169-5012-5

LC 2007-47985

A shy boy, seeking the courage to play baseball with the other children in a park, is coaxed out of his shell by some "old timers" sitting nearby who, in turn, discover they are still in the game.

"Employing sly visual humor, Newman . . . presents the narrative in sketchy, retro-flavored gouache brushstrokes on a white background. This is a quirky book, but sensitive readers will appreciate the child's shyness and the men's efforts to help him remember what it means to be a kid." Publ Wkly

Newman, Lesléa

The best cat in the world; written by Lesléa Newman; illustrated by Ronald Himler. Eerdmans Books for Young Readers 2004 unp il $16; pa $8

Grades: K 1 2 3   E

1. Cats—Fiction 2. Death—Fiction

ISBN 0-8028-5252-1; 0-8028-5294-7 (pa)

LC 2003-13028

A young boy deals with the loss of his beloved cat Charlie, eventually accepting the arrival of another, very different cat.

"Himler's warm pencil-and-watercolor illustrations generously fill the pages. They portray the casually clad characters with tenderness and contrast the shape of the old and sick animal with that of the young and playful one. . . . For comfort and catharsis, Newman's fine story is the cat's pajamas." SLJ

Daddy, papa, and me; illustrated by Carol Thompson. Tricycle Press 2009 unp il bd bk $7.99

Grades: PreK   E

1. Homosexuality—Fiction 2. Father-child relationship—Fiction 3. Board books for children

ISBN 978-1-58246-262-2 (bd bk); 1-58246-262-3 (bd bk)

ALA GLBTRT Stonewall Book Award Honor Book (2010)

"A smiling tot describes his role within a nurturing two-dad family. . . . Thompson provides warm, mixed-media illustrations of the happy trio against clean white backgrounds as they play and keep house together. . . . It gives children with single-sex parents validation of their family structures in a healthy, positive way." Kirkus

A fire engine for Ruthie; illustrated by Cyd Moore. Clarion Books 2004 32p il $16

Grades: PreK K 1 2   E

1. Play—Fiction 2. Grandmothers—Fiction 3. Sex role—Fiction

ISBN 0-618-15989-4   LC 2003-22791

Ruthie's Nana suggests playing tea party and fashion show during their visit, but Ruthie is much more interested in the vehicles that a neighbor boy is playing with as they pass his house each day.

"This book hits the mark on three solid counts—a real story, good pacing, and deliciously full artwork that has its own momentum." Booklist

Mommy, mama, and me; illustrated by Carol Thompson. Tricycle Press 2009 unp il (My family tree) bd bk $7.99 *

Grades: PreK   E

1. Lesbians—Fiction 2. Mother-child relationship—Fiction 3. Board books for children

ISBN 978-1-58246-263-9 (bd bk); 1-58246-263-1 (bd bk)

ALA GLBTRT Stonewall Book Award Honor Book (2010)

"A curly-haired toddler . . . celebrates 'mommy' and 'mama,' and the activities and tender moments they share. . . . The bright colors . . . and pleasing verse offer a simple lesson about love that same-sex parents should embrace." Publ Wkly

Newman, Patricia, 1958-

Nugget on the flight deck; illustrated by Aaron Zenz. Walker & Co. 2009 unp il $16.99; lib bdg $17.89

Grades: 1 2 3   E

1. Aircraft carriers—Fiction 2. Air pilots—Fiction

ISBN 978-0-8027-9735-3; 0-8027-9735-0; 978-0-8027-9736-0 (lib bdg); 0-8027-9736-9 (lib bdg)

LC 2008044673

Aboard an aircraft carrier, a lieutenant introduces a new aviator to the 'lingo' and layout before taking him on a practice dogfight.

"Military jargon appears in boldface in the text and is defined in a separate pictorial area on each spread. Colored-pencil illustrations show many essential components of the carrier and the planes that take off and land on its deck. . . . Anyone interested in planes will appreciate the high level of information provided in an attractive, accessible format." SLJ

Includes bibliographical references

Nez, John A.

Cromwell Dixon's Sky-Cycle; [by] John Abbott Nez. G.P. Putnam's Sons 2009 unp il $16.99

Grades: 2 3 4 5   E

1. Dixon, Cromwell, 1892-1911—Fiction 2. Air pilots—Fiction 3. Inventors—Fiction 4. Flight—Fiction

ISBN 978-0-399-25041-5; 0-399-25041-7

LC 2008026140

In 1907 Columbus, Ohio, fourteen-year-old Cromwell Dixon, aided by his mother, begins building the flying bicycle he has invented to enter in the St. Louis Air Ship Carnival. Includes facts about Dixon's life as an aviation pioneer.

"Through both text and pictures, Nez conveys a warm mother-son relationship. . . . Detailed watercolor paintings with tremendous kid appeal take readers back in time. . . . [This book tells] a fascinating story." Booklist

Includes bibliographical references

Niemann, Christoph

Pet dragon; a story about adventure, friendship, and Chinese characters; by Christoph Niemann. Greenwillow Books 2008 unp il $16.99; lib bdg $17.89

Grades: K 1 2 3   E
1. Dragons—Fiction 2. Witches—Fiction 3. China—Fiction 4. Chinese language
ISBN   978-0-06-157776-5;   0-06-157776-6;
978-0-06-157777-2 (lib bdg); 0-06-157777-4 (lib bdg)

When Lin's beloved pet dragon disappears, she searches for him far and wide until a witch helps her to reach the dragon's new home. Introduces a different Chinese character on each step of Lin's adventure.

"The book is clever. Its purpose is to introduce the Chinese language, and it succeeds admirably. Each page contains one or more Chinese characters, which appear not only at the bottom with the English translation, but also superimposed on the drawings. . . . The stylized illustrations are jaunty and appealing, and the use of red, a color representing good fortune in China, visually unifies the tale from beginning to end. Playful and humorous." SLJ

The police cloud. Schwartz & Wade Books 2007 unp il $15.99; lib bdg $17.99

Grades: PreK K 1   E
1. Clouds—Fiction 2. Police—Fiction
ISBN   0-375-83963-1;   978-0-375-83963-4;
0-375-93963-6 (lib bdg); 978-0-375-93963-1 (lib bdg)
                                          LC 2006-06415

A small cloud that has always dreamed of becoming a police officer discovers that he might not be suited to the job.

"The computer-enhanced illustrations have a very simple, bold graphic design and feature basic colors. . . . The illustrations do such a good job of telling the story, the concise text is almost unnecessary." Booklist

Subway. Greenwillow Books 2010 unp il $16.99
Grades: PreK K 1 2   E
1. Subways—Fiction 2. New York (N.Y.)—Fiction 3. Stories in rhyme
ISBN 978-0-06-157779-6; 0-06-157779-0

"This colorful, vivacious, child-centered title began with a post on Niemann's blog, Abstract City, in which he describes a day of riding the subway with his two sons just for fun. The artist uses thick gouache paint to render his characters as standard pictograms, akin to those on city signs, with curved edges for hands and feet, and the technique creates a chalky texture that looks like correction fluid. . . . A sure hit with most youngsters, especially those who are transfixed by trains." SLJ

Nikola-Lisa, W.

Magic in the margins; a medieval tale of bookmaking; by W. Nikola-Lisa; illustrated by Bonnie Christensen. Houghton Mifflin 2007 unp il $17

Grades: 1 2 3 4   E
1. Artists—Fiction 2. Illumination of books and manuscripts—Fiction 3. Apprentices—Fiction 4. Orphans—Fiction 5. Middle Ages—Fiction
ISBN 978-0-618-49642-6; 0-618-49642-4
                                          LC 2006017060

At a medieval monastery, orphaned Simon, who is apprenticing in illumination, dreams of the day he can create his own pictures, but finds he must first complete a strange and unusual assignment that Father Anselm has given him.

"Many kids . . . will be drawn in by the appealing story of a child's empowerment and the glimpse of the medieval world. Christensen extends the story with strong, clear scenes, bordered by botanical patterns and executed in ink and egg-tempura pigments." Booklist

Setting the turkeys free; written by W. Nikola-Lisa; illustrated by Ken Wilson-Max. Jump at the Sun/Hyperion Books for Children 2004 unp il $15.99

Grades: PreK K 1   E
1. Turkeys—Fiction 2. Foxes—Fiction 3. Artists—Fiction
ISBN 0-7868-1952-9   LC 2003-50928

When a sly, hungry fox threatens a flock of turkeys, the young artist who drew the birds must find a way to save them.

"Right at a preschooler's level, the artwork . . . has humor as well as momentum. . . . This clever mixing of art and a spot-on text provides a fun story as well as a surefire craft idea that kids will want to try." Booklist

Noble, Trinka Hakes

The day Jimmy's boa ate the wash; pictures by Steven Kellogg. Dial Bks. for Young Readers 1980 unp il $16.99; pa $6.99 *

Grades: PreK K 1 2   E
1. Farm life—Fiction 2. Snakes—Fiction 3. School stories
ISBN 0-8037-1723-7; 0-8037-0094-6 (pa)
                                          LC 80-15098

"One small girl, reporting to her mother after a class visit to a farm . . . describes . . . how Jimmy's boa escaped, set the hens in a flurry, precipitated an egg-throwing match, and so on." Bull Cent Child Books

"The illustrations, which depict disgruntled chickens, expressive pigs, and smiling cats as well as other individualized animal and human characters, show the artist's flair for humorous detail." Horn Book

Other titles about Jimmy's boa are:
Jimmy's boa and the big splash birthday bash (1989)
Jimmy's boa and the bungee jump slam dunk (2003)
Jimmy's boa bounces back (1984)

The last brother; a Civil War tale; illustrated by Robert Papp. Sleeping Bear Press 2006 unp il $17.95

Grades: 2 3 4 5   E
1. Gettysburg (Pa.), Battle of, 1863—Fiction 2. United States—History—1861-1865, Civil War—Fiction 3. Brothers—Fiction
ISBN 1-58536-253-0

Eleven-year-old Gabe enlists in the Union Army in Pennsylvania along with his older brother Davy and, as bugler, does his best to protect Davy during the Battle of Gettysburg.

This "story resonates with courage and fear, love and loyalty. . . . The well-rendered paintings are hauntingly detailed and place readers right in the action." SLJ

Nolen, Jerdine

Big Jabe; illustrations by Kadir Nelson. Lothrop, Lee & Shepard Bks. 2000 unp il hardcover o.p. pa $6.99 *

Grades: K 1 2 3   E
  1. Slavery—Fiction 2. African Americans—Fiction
  ISBN 0-688-13662-1; 0-06-054061-3 (pa)
                           LC 99-38001
Momma Mary tells stories about a special young man who does wondrous things, especially for the slaves on the Plenty Plantation
  "Nolen recounts her original tale with a light touch and lyrical voices that add depth and resonance to its imagery and serious overtones. The gouache and watercolor illustrations convey both the lush summer and the rigorous life of the slaves. This powerful story will be particularly effective shared aloud." Horn Book Guide

Harvey Potter's balloon farm; [illustrated by] Mark Buehner. Lothrop, Lee & Shepard Bks. 1994 unp il $16.99; lib bdg $15.93; pa $5.99

Grades: PreK K 1 2   E
  1. Tall tales 2. Balloons—Fiction 3. Farm life—Fiction
  ISBN 0-688-07887-7; 0-688-07888-5 (lib bdg); 0-688-15845-5 (pa)   LC 91-38129
  "Harvey Potter's unusual crop is balloons—which grow just like corn on long, sturdy stalks. Harvey Potter himself is not at all unusual, and his friend, a young African-American girl, is determined to uncover the secret of his curious harvest. The story is lively, but of even greater attraction are the vivid, air-brushed illustrations of balloons with expressive faces in every size, color, and shape." Horn Book Guide

Hewitt Anderson's great big life; illustrated by Kadir Nelson. Simon & Schuster Books for Young Readers 2005 unp il $16.95 *

Grades: PreK K 1 2   E
  1. Size—Fiction 2. Giants—Fiction
  ISBN 0-689-86866-9   LC 98-14039
  "A Paula Wiseman book"
When tiny Hewitt is born into a family of giants, everyone learns that sometimes small is best of all.
  "Nelson's funny, larger-than-life oil paintings warmly depict this African-American family and give readers a real sense of gigantic proportions. . . . Told in colorful language that begs to be read aloud, this humorous, oversize book offers a gentle look at accepting others as they are." SLJ

Pitching in for Eubie; illustrated by E.B. Lewis. Amistad 2007 unp il $16.99; lib bdg $17.89

Grades: PreK K 1 2   E
  1. Family life—Fiction 2. Money-making projects for children—Fiction 3. Sisters—Fiction 4. African Americans—Fiction
  ISBN 978-0-688-14917-8; 978-0-06-056960-0 (lib bdg)   LC 2007-06995
Lily tries to find a way to pitch in and help her family make enough money to send her older sister, Eubie, to college
  "Imbued with warmth, Nolen's . . . story about a family working together toward a common goal will appeal to many audiences. . . . Each painting helps advance the action and delineate the characters." Publ Wkly

Raising dragons; illustrated by Elise Primavera. Silver Whistle Bks. 1998 unp il $16; pa $7

Grades: PreK K 1 2   E
  1. Dragons—Fiction 2. Farm life—Fiction
  ISBN 0-15-201288-5; 0-15-216536-3 (pa)
                           LC 95-43307
A farmer's young daughter shares numerous adventures with the dragon that she raises from infancy
  "Nolen's chimerical text meets its match in Primavera's imaginative and bold illustrations." Horn Book Guide

Thunder Rose; illustrated by Kadir Nelson. Harcourt 2003 unp il $16; pa $7 *

Grades: K 1 2 3   E
  1. Tall tales 2. African Americans—Fiction 3. West (U.S.)—Fiction
  ISBN 0-15-216472-3; 0-15-206006-5 (pa)
                        LC 2002-12287
Unusual from the day she is born, Thunder Rose performs all sorts of amazing feats, including building fences, taming a stampeding herd of steers, capturing a gang of rustlers, and turning aside a tornado
  "Nolen and Nelson offer up a wonderful tale of joy and love, as robust and vivid as the wide West. The oil, watercolor, and pencil artwork is outstanding." SLJ

Norac, Carl

My daddy is a giant; illustrated by Ingrid Godon. Clarion Books 2005 29p il $16

Grades: PreK K 1 2   E
  1. Father-son relationship—Fiction
  ISBN 0-618-44399-1   LC 2004-12093
A little boy's father seems so large to him that he needs a ladder to cuddle him and birds nest in his father's hair
  "The simple premise captures the little boy's idolization of his dad well. . . . With the man so large that he often has to bend his head or crouch down to fit onto the page, and the full-bleed spreads overflowing the book, these pictures will engage even the children in the last row of storytime." SLJ

My mommy is magic; by Carl Norac; illustrated by Ingrid Godon. Clarion Books 2007 29p il $16

Grades: PreK K   E
  1. Mothers—Fiction
  ISBN 978-0-618-75766-4; 0-618-75766-X
                        LC 2006007149
First published 2006 in the United Kingdom with title: My mummy is magic
A child lists things a mommy does, such as chasing monsters away, that show she is magic, even if she does not have a wand or magic hat
  "Godon's pastel-and-paint, full-bleed spreads in gentle hues exude warmth. They complement the text and the resulting mood is sweet without being cloying." SLJ

Novak, Matt, 1962-
A wish for you. Greenwillow Books 2010 unp il $16.99
Grades: PreK K   E
  1. Stories in rhyme 2. Family life—Fiction 3. Infants—Fiction
  ISBN 978-0-06-155202-1; 0-06-155202-X
                                        LC 2008052485
"In this bouncy story, a man and woman meet, court, marry, and prepare for their new baby. . . . Half-page pictures zip through scenes of preparation for the infant's arrival. Then, when the baby joins them on their vacation adventures. . . . Novak's soft-edged digitally enhanced artwork perfectly portrays the merry mood of his pudgy characters. This is a great choice for cozy sharing with a beloved child." SLJ

Noyes, Deborah, 1965-
Red butterfly; how a princess smuggled the secret of silk out of China; illustrated by Sophie Blackall. Candlewick Press 2007 unp il $16.99 *
Grades: 1 2 3   E
  1. China—Fiction 2. Silkworms—Fiction 3. Princesses—Fiction
  ISBN 978-0-7636-2400-2; 0-7636-2400-4
                                        LC 2006-52931
In long-ago China, as a young princess prepares to leave her parents' kingdom to travel to far-off Khotan where she is to marry the king, she decides to surreptitiously take with her a precious reminder of home.
"Noyes' graceful text includes allusions to nature and the shifting seasons in a style reminiscent of Chinese poetry. . . . [This is illustrated with] beautiful, ink-and-watercolor illustrations in rich, jewel colors." Booklist

Numberman, Neil
Do not build a Frankenstein! Greenwillow Books 2009 unp il $16.99
Grades: K 1   E
  1. Monsters—Fiction 2. Moving—Fiction
  ISBN 978-0-06-156816-9; 0-06-156816-3
                                        LC 2008-20751
A boy warns his new neighbors of the trouble that comes with building a monster, including having to move to a different town in hopes of escaping his creation
"Numberman is a nimble, funny writer, and he opts for showing rather than telling, his naif watercolors scoring a punch line every time." Publ Wkly

Numeroff, Laura Joffe
Beatrice doesn't want to; illustrated by Lynn Munsinger. Candlewick Press 2004 unp il $15.99; pa $6.99
Grades: PreK K 1 2   E
  1. Libraries—Fiction 2. Books and reading—Fiction
  ISBN 0-7636-1160-3; 0-7636-3843-9 (pa)
                                        LC 2002-73908
A newly illustrated edition of the title first published 1981 by Watts
On the third afternoon of going to the library with her brother Henry, Beatrice finally finds something she en-joys doing.
"Done in watercolor, ink, and pencil and featuring floppy-eared canine characters, the expressive illustrations perfectly capture the humor of the text." SLJ

The Chicken sisters; by Laura Numeroff; pictures by Sharleen Collicott. HarperCollins Pubs. 1997 unp il $15.99; pa $6.95
Grades: PreK K 1 2   E
  1. Chickens—Fiction 2. Sisters—Fiction 3. Wolves—Fiction
  ISBN 0-06-026679-1; 0-06-443520-2 (pa)
                                        LC 96-30297
"A Laura Geringer book"
"Violet, Poppy, and Babs, the chicken sisters, possess talents that annoy the neighbors until a threatening wolf moves into the neighborhood. The illustrations achieve a captivating sense of texture that adds immediacy to the humorous story." Horn Book Guide

If you give a mouse a cookie; by Laura Numeroff; illustrated by Felicia Bond. Harper & Row 1985 unp il $15.99; lib bdg $16.89 *
Grades: PreK K 1   E
  1. Mice—Fiction
  ISBN 0-06-024586-7; 0-06-024587-5 (lib bdg)
                                        LC 84-48343
Relating the cycle of requests a mouse is likely to make after you give him a cookie takes the reader through a young child's day
"Children love to indulge in supposition or to ask 'what will happen if . . .?' and here there is a long, satisfying chain of linked and enjoyably nonsensical causes and effects. . . . The illustrations, neatly drawn, spaciously composed, and humorously detailed, extend the story just the way picture book illustrations should." Bull Cent Child Books
Other titles in this series are:
If you give a cat a cupcake (2008)
If you give a moose a muffin (1991)
If you give a pig a pancake (1998)
If you give a pig a party (2005)
If you take a mouse to school (2002)
If you take a mouse to the movies (2000)

When sheep sleep; by Laura Numeroff; illustrated by David McPhail. Abrams Books for Young Readers 2006 unp il $15.95
Grades: PreK K 1 2   E
  1. Animals—Fiction 2. Counting 3. Sleep—Fiction 4. Bedtime—Fiction 5. Stories in rhyme
  ISBN 0-8109-5469-9   LC 2005022544
Rhyming text suggests other options when one tries to count sheep but discovers that they are all asleep.
"McPhail's charming watercolor-and-ink illustrations are infused with warmth and are a lovely complement to the gentle, rhyming lullaby." SLJ

Would I trade my parents? by Laura Numeroff; illustrated by James Bernardin. Abrams Books for Young Readers 2009 unp il $16.95
Grades: PreK K 1 2   E
  1. Parents—Fiction
  ISBN 978-0-8109-0637-2; 0-8109-0637-6
                                        LC 2008030381

Numeroff, Laura Joffe—*Continued*

A young boy considers what is special about all of his friends' parents, and realizes that his own are the most wonderful of all.

"The illustrations are large and clear, made with acrylics and a digital paint program. They simply illustrate the text. . . This is a straightforward retelling of a common childhood exercise in wishful thinking." SLJ

Ó Flatharta, Antoine, 1953-

Hurry and the monarch; illustrated by Meilo So. Knopf 2005 unp il $14.95; pa $7.99 *

Grades: K 1 2   E

1. Butterflies—Fiction 2. Turtles—Fiction

ISBN 0-375-83003-0; 0-385-73719-X (pa)

LC 2004-15984

Hurry the tortoise befriends a monarch butterfly when she stops in his garden in Wichita Falls, Texas, during her migration from Canada to Mexico. Includes facts about monarch butterflies

"Veined with a tracery of inked details, So's subtle watercolors reference both Asian nature-painting traditions and the limited palette of artwork in the early days of color printing. Together with its informative afterword, this is a particularly attractive, affecting introduction to the wonder of species diversity and the elegant continuum of life." Booklist

Obed, Ellen Bryan, 1944-

Who would like a Christmas tree? illustrated by Anne Hunter. Houghton Mifflin Books for Children 2009 unp il $16 *

Grades: 1 2 3   E

1. Christmas—Fiction 2. Trees—Fiction 3. Nature—Fiction 4. Animals—Fiction 5. Months—Fiction

ISBN 978-0-547-04625-9; 0-547-04625-1

LC 2008052302

Describes the flora and fauna that inhabit a Christmas tree farm throughout the year and use the growing trees for a variety of purposes. Includes section on how the farmer takes care of the farm through the year.

"Though presented as a Christmas book, this informative introduction to the different animals inhabiting a Maine tree plantation can be enjoyed year round. . . . The charming watercolor and ink illustrations are rendered in naturalistic fashion using nature's hues and cross-hatching techniques for shading and depth. . . . An excellent resource for getting youngsters enthused about nature." SLJ

Oberman, Sheldon, 1949-2004

The always prayer shawl; illustrated by Ted Lewin. Boyds Mills Press 1994 unp il $15.95; pa $10.95

Grades: 1 2 3 4   E

1. Jews—Fiction 2. Immigrants—Fiction

ISBN 1-878093-22-3; 1-59078-332-8 (pa)

This story "tells of the Jewish boy Adam, growing up in a shtetl, whose life drastically changes when famine and chaos in old Russia force his parents to immigrate to America. At parting, Adam's beloved grandfather gives the boy a gift, a prayer shawl . . . which was pres-

ented to the grandfather by *his* grandfather. . . . The watercolors are abundantly detailed and wonderfully expressive. . . . The pictures enrich the tranquil telling . . . as it movingly depicts how memory and tradition add texture and richness to our lives." Booklist

O'Callahan, Jay, 1938-

Raspberries! [illustrated by] Will Moses. Philomel Books 2009 unp il $17.99 *

Grades: K 1 2 3   E

1. Raspberries—Fiction 2. Baking—Fiction

ISBN 978-0-399-25181-8; 0-399-25181-2

LC 2008048085

Once a famous baker but now down on his luck, Simon makes a living selling eggs until he is given some very special raspberry plants.

"Faithful to narrative details, the energetic folk-art style illustrations capture the personalities, exuberance, and flavor of a story that celebrates a persevering, kindhearted entrepreneur." Booklist

O'Connell, Rebecca, 1968-

Danny is done with diapers; a potty ABC; illustrated by Amanda Gulliver. Albert Whitman & Co. 2010 unp il $16.99

Grades: PreK   E

1. Toilet training—Fiction 2. Alphabet

ISBN 978-0-8075-1466-5; 0-8075-1466-7

"This book gently encourages, commends, and celebrates 26 youngsters who are in the process of being toilet trained. It begins 'A is for Accident, Adam had an accident. It's all right Adam.' Sweet, brightly colored acrylic illustrations discreetly show the kids using a potty chair or a toilet, washing hands, and pulling on clothing, with only a few bare bottoms revealed. . . . Written at a young child's level of understanding, this title will be useful in showing toddlers how others have accomplished this feat." SLJ

O'Connor, Jane, 1947-

Fancy Nancy; by Jane O'Connor; pictures by Robin Preiss Glasser. HarperCollins 2006 unp il $17.99; lib bdg $17.89

Grades: PreK K   E

1. Clothing and dress—Fiction 2. Family life—Fiction

ISBN 0-06-054209-8; 0-06-054210-1 (lib bdg)

LC 2004-28662

"For Nancy, there's no such thing as too, too much; she loves her frilly bedroom, her lace-trimmed socks, and her pen with a plume. Nancy teaches her family how to be fancy, too. . . . Nancy's perky narrative, in short, simple sentences, incorporates some 'fancy' vocabulary for kids to absorb (stupendous, posh), along with a sense of the rewards of a family doing things together. The cheerfully colored art is aptly exuberant, a riotous blending of color and pattern and action." Booklist

Other titles about Fancy Nancy are:

Fancy Nancy and the posh puppy (2007)

Fancy Nancy and the boy from Paris (2008)

Fancy Nancy at the museum (2008)

Fancy Nancy: Bonjour, butterfly (2008)

Fancy Nancy's favorite fancy words (2008)

O'Connor, Jane, 1947-—*Continued*
Fancy Nancy sees stars (2009)
Fancy Nancy: poison ivy expert (2009)
Fancy Nancy: explorer extraordinaire! (2009)
Fancy Nancy tea parties (2009)
Fancy Nancy: the dazzling book report (2009)
Fancy Nancy: splendiferous Christmas (2009)
Fancy Nancy: poet extraordinaire! (2010)
Fancy Nancy: the 100th day of school (2010)
Fancy Nancy: ooh la la! It's beauty day (2010)

The perfect puppy for me; by Jane O'Connor and Jessie Hartland; illustrated by Jessie Hartland. Viking 2003 unp il $15.99
Grades: PreK K 1 2   E
  1. Dogs—Fiction
  ISBN 0-670-03614-5   LC 2002-15568
While waiting to get his very own puppy, a young boy spends time with various dogs and describes what the different breeds are like
"Each page is jam-packed with good advice, useful information, and bright and cleverly detailed paintings that successfully reflect the pertinent traits of the different canines." SLJ

Ready, set, skip! illustrated by Ann James. Viking 2007 unp il $15.99; pa $6.99 *
Grades: PreK K   E
  1. Mother-daughter relationship—Fiction 2. Stories in rhyme
  ISBN 978-0-670-06216-4; 978-0-14-241423-1 (pa)
                                LC 2006-08632
A little girl cannot skip until her mother shows her a special trick.
"Exuberant color and black line illustrations on a white background depict the actions with élan and convey the special camaraderie between girl and dog and mother and daughter." SLJ

Odanaka, Barbara
Crazy day at the Critter Cafe; illustrated by Lee White. Margaret K. McElderry Books 2009 unp il $16.99
Grades: K 1 2   E
  1. Stories in rhyme 2. Animals—Fiction 3. Restaurants—Fiction
  ISBN 978-1-4169-3914-6; 1-4169-3914-8
A quiet morning in a roadside cafe turns to chaos when a bus breaks down and a managerie of noisy, rude animals enters, demanding to be fed.
"The rhymed text emphasizes the zany sound effects as the mixed-media illustrations comically exaggerate the scenes. Kids will giggle over the heightened food mess the animals leave behind." Booklist

Ofanansky, Allison
Harvest of light; by Allison Ofanansky; photos by Eliyahu Alpern. Kar-Ben Pub. 2008 unp il lib bdg $15.95
Grades: 1 2 3   E
  1. Olives—Fiction 2. Hanukkah—Fiction 3. Jews—Fiction 4. Israel—Fiction
  ISBN 978-0-8225-7389-0 (lib bdg); 0-8225-7389-X (lib bdg)   LC 2007-43133

"In this wonderfully different Hanukkah book, an Israeli family harvests olives to be processed into the oil. The daughter provides a simple narrative, which is clearly written and accompanied by full-color photographs depicting each step in the process from gathering and sorting the olives to pressing them and using the oil to light the menorah. Resonating with familial warmth and a shared purpose, this is a fine offering." SLJ

Sukkot treasure hunt; photographs by Eliyahu Alpern. Kar-Ben 2009 unp il $15.95
Grades: PreK K 1 2   E
  1. Sukkot—Fiction 2. Jews—Fiction 3. Israel—Fiction
  ISBN 978-0-8225-8763-7; 0-8225-8763-7
                                LC 2008-31202
In Israel, a young girl and her family go on a scavenger hunt to find the 'four species' they will use in their celebration of the Jewish holiday, Sukkot. Includes facts about plants named in the story.
"Straightforward first-person text and clear photographs encourage readers to join the family on their search for palm, willow, myrtle, and etrog." Horn Book Guide

Offill, Jenny, 1968-
17 things I'm not allowed to do anymore. Schwartz & Wade Books 2006 unp il $15.99 *
Grades: PreK K 1 2   E
  ISBN 0-375-83596-2   LC 2005-16414
A young girl lists the sixteen things she is not allowed to do anymore, including not being able to make ice after freezing a fly in one of the cubes.
"Ingenious artwork—a flawless marriage of digital imagery and pen-and-ink—is indisputably the focus of this winning title." SLJ

Ogburn, Jacqueline K.
The bake shop ghost; illustrated by Marjorie Priceman. Houghton Mifflin 2005 unp il $16; pa $6.99
Grades: K 1 2 3   E
  1. Ghost stories 2. Cake—Fiction 3. Bakers and bakeries—Fiction
  ISBN 0-618-44557-9; 0-547-07677-0 (pa)
Miss Cora Lee Meriweather haunts her bake shop after her death, until Annie Washington, the new shop owner, makes a deal with her.
"Priceman's illustrations are charming, with dashes of color and humor and a sense of action in each one. . . . This is a delightful story with a satisfying conclusion." SLJ

The magic nesting doll; illustrated by Laurel Long. Dial Bks. 2000 unp il $16.99
Grades: K 1 2 3   E
  1. Fairy tales 2. Russia—Fiction
  ISBN 0-8037-2414-4   LC 98-34397
After her grandmother dies, Katya finds herself in a kingdom where the Tsarvitch has been turned into living ice and she uses the magic nesting dolls her babushka had given her to try to break the curse
"The writings is filled with description and poetic images. . . . Created using oil paints on paper primed with

Ogburn, Jacqueline K.—*Continued*

gesso, the illustrations are alive with detail and reminiscent of the miniaturist style used in Russian decorative items." SLJ

O'Hair, Margaret

My pup; by Margaret O'Hair; illustrated by Tammie Lyon. Marshall Cavendish 2008 unp il $14.99; bd bk $7.99

Grades: PreK   E

1. Dogs—Fiction 2. Stories in rhyme
ISBN   978-0-7614-5389-5;   0-7614-5389-X;
978-0-7614-5644-5 (bk bk); 0-7614-5644-9 (bd bk)
LC 2007011719

"Bouncy text and simple rhyming couplets take readers through a day in the life of a little girl and her pet as they play in the mud, enjoy a car ride, get in the way of the cat, go for a walk, and finally cuddle up together in bed. . . . Children will delight in the expressive, brightly colored gouache and pencil spreads of a smiling, round-faced youngster with large, oval animal-print glasses and her pup." SLJ

Oldland, Nicholas

Big bear hug. Kids Can Press 2009 unp il $16.95 *

Grades: PreK K   E

1. Bears—Fiction 2. Trees—Fiction 3. Hugging—Fiction
ISBN 978-1-55453-464-7; 1-55453-464-X

A bear who loves to hug everything meets a human who is about to chop down a tree, and the bear must make a decision on how to save his forest.

"Oldland's rustic-styled digital artwork looks like a hip flannel pajama print . . . and his pictures play sly comic foil to the earnest text." Publ Wkly

O'Malley, Kevin, 1961-

Animal crackers fly the coop. Walker & Co. 2010 unp il $16.99; lib bdg $17.89 *

Grades: 2 3 4   E

1. Animals—Fiction 2. Comedians—Fiction
ISBN   978-0-8027-9837-4;   0-8027-9837-3;
978-0-8027-9838-1 (lib bdg); 0-8027-9838-1 (lib bdg)
LC 2009018188

In this humorous take-off of 'The Bremen Town Musicians,' four animals that aspire to make it big as comedians leave their owners and seek their fortunes.

"Full of puns, this . . . is clever, well executed, and loaded with laughs. O'Malley's expressive black-line illustrations over deep-hued colors bring the large images of the animals and robbers up-front on the page, increasing the interaction with his audience and enhancing the humor." SLJ

Captain Raptor and the moon mystery; illustrations by Patrick O'Brien. Walker & Co. 2005 unp il $16.95; lib bdg $17.85

Grades: PreK K 1 2 3 4   E

1. Graphic novels 2. Science fiction graphic novels
3. Dinosaurs—Graphic novels
ISBN 0-8027-8935-8; 0-8027-8936-6 (lib bdg)
LC 2004-53624

When something lands on one of the moons of the planet Jurassica, Captain Raptor and his spaceship crew go to investigate

"An action-packed science-fiction romp starring a cast of dinosaur characters. . . . Presented in comic-book style, this story blends an eye-catching layout with a quick-moving plot, tongue-in-cheek humor, and an imaginative setting." SLJ

Another title about Captain Raptor is:
Captain Raptor and the space pirates (2007)

Gimme cracked corn and I will share. Walker & Co. 2007 unp il $16.95; lib bdg $17.85 *

Grades: 2 3 4   E

1. Chickens—Fiction
ISBN   978-0-8027-9684-4;   0-8027-9684-2;
978-0-8027-9685-1 (lib bdg); 0-8027-9685-0 (lib bdg)
LC 2007-03706

Chicken dreams about a treasure and sets off on a dangerous journey to find it

"Fans of corny humor and 'punny yolks' will welcome this tale. . . . The unique illustrations are a combination of pen, ink, and Photoshop." SLJ

Lucky leaf. Walker & Co. 2004 unp il hardcover o.p. pa $6.95

Grades: PreK K 1 2   E

1. Leaves—Fiction
ISBN 0-8027-8924-2; 0-8027-8925-0 (lib bdg);
0-8027-9647-8 (pa)   LC 2003-68868

After his mother tells him to stop playing video games and go outside, a young boy tries to catch the last leaf on a tree, thinking it will bring him luck

"Done in pen and ink and colored in PhotoShop, the illustrations feature crisp, vibrant colors that create a vivid setting. . . . The story is told through spare, but effective, dialogue presented in speech bubbles." SLJ

Omololu, Cynthia Jaynes

When it's six o'clock in San Francisco; a trip through time zones; illustrated by Randy DuBurke. Clarion Books 2009 31p il map $16

Grades: K 1 2 3   E

1. Time—Fiction
ISBN 978-0-618-76827-1; 0-618-76827-0
LC 2007012721

When Jared wakes up in San Francisco at six o'clock in the morning, children in other parts of the world are doing other things, like going to school in Buenos Aires, Argentina, playing soccer in London, England, and eating dinner in Lahore, Pakistan, because of the difference in time zones around the globe. Includes factual material about telling time and time zones.

"The diversity and connections across the globe are the story, with warm, colorful, individual portraits that move beyond cultural stereotypes. . . . This is a great choice for science classes and for today's international families." Booklist

O'Neill, Alexis, 1949-

Estela's swap; illustrated by Enrique O. Sanchez. Lee & Low Bks. 2002 unp il hardcover o.p. pa $7.95 *

Grades: K 1 2 3   E

1. Mexican Americans—Fiction

ISBN 1-58430-044-2; 1-60060-253-3 (pa)

LC 2001-38785

A young Mexican American girl accompanies her father to a swap meet, where she hopes to sell her music box for money for dancing lessons

"This is a warm, nicely paced story about sharing and bartering that's filled with sensory descriptions of the vibrant open market. The textured acrylics capture the hum and bustle of the stalls." Booklist

O'Neill, Catharine

Annie and Simon. Candlewick Press 2008 57p il $15.99

Grades: 1 2   E

1. Siblings—Fiction 2. Dogs—Fiction

ISBN 978-0-7636-2688-4; 0-7636-2688-0

LC 2006-47521

Recounts four adventures of Annie, her big brother, Simon, and their dog, Hazel.

"Annie and Simon's four stories collected here will ring true for most newly independent readers. The watercolor illustrations of the two and their bark-full dog Hazel are full of humor and detail. . . . O'Neill's first solo effort in some years is well worth adding to the first-chapter-book collection." Kirkus

Onishi, Satoru

Who's hiding? Kane/Miller 2007 31p il $14.95 *

Grades: PreK K 1 2   E

1. Animals—Fiction 2. Puzzles

ISBN 978-1-933605-24-1

"Eighteen simply drawn, brightly colored animals are laid out in the same order on each spread. . . . The first spread shows the creatures and their names and asks, Who is hiding? The next spread shows all of them except for the reindeer who is invisible except for his antlers. This question alternates with others. . . . This is a clever puzzle book for caregivers and young children to share and to learn animals, colors, concepts." SLJ

Oppel, Kenneth, 1967-

The king's taster; paintings by Steve Johnson & Lou Fancher. HarperCollinsPublishers 2008 unp il $17.99; lib bdg $18.89 *

Grades: K 1 2 3   E

1. Dogs—Fiction 2. Kings and rulers—Fiction 3. Food—Fiction 4. Diet—Fiction

ISBN 978-0-06-075372-6; 0-06-075372-2; 978-0-06-075373-3 (lib bdg); 0-06-075373-0 (lib bdg)

LC 2008000779

The royal chef takes Max the dog, the royal taster, on several international journeys to find a dish for the land's pickiest king.

"The mixed-media illustrations are deliciously capricious with clever collage details. . . . Kids will relish this comic culinary calamity." Booklist

Orloff, Karen Kaufman

I wanna iguana; illustrated by David Catrow. Putnam 2004 unp il $15.99 *

Grades: PreK K 1 2   E

1. Iguanas—Fiction 2. Pets—Fiction

ISBN 0-399-23717-8   LC 2002-10895

Alex and his mother write notes back and forth in which Alex tries to persuade her to let him have a baby iguana for a pet.

"This funny story is told through an amusing exchange of notes. . . . Featuring his signature cartoon characters, Catrow's illustrations provide a hilarious extension of the text." SLJ

Ormerod, Jan

Ballet sisters: the duckling and the swan. Scholastic 2007 32p il $5.99

Grades: PreK K 1 2   E

1. Sisters—Fiction 2. Ballet—Fiction 3. Imagination—Fiction

ISBN 978-0-439-82281-7; 0-439-82281-5

LC 2006-02575

"Cartwheel books"

Sylvie and her older sister dance their way through make-believe adventures that include princesses, fairy queens, swans, and ducklings.

"The language . . . is clear, concise, and descriptive—essential qualities for beginning readers. The watercolor illustrations place the girls and their mother on a clean white background, which effectively highlights the expressive detail in their faces and postures." SLJ

Another title about Sylvie and her sister is:

Ballet sisters: the newest dancer (2008)

If you're happy and you know it! [by] Jan Ormerod, Lindsey Gardiner. Star Bright Books 2003 unp il $15.95; pa $5.95

Grades: PreK   E

1. Animals—Fiction 2. Stories in rhyme

ISBN 1-932065-07-5; 1-932065-10-5 (pa)

LC 2002-13692

A little girl and various animals sing their own versions of this popular rhyme

"Delightful, colorful animal figures cavort through the pages of this book that puts a twist on the familiar song. . . . The action on each spread gives the story a great deal of energy and the backgrounds are washes of color, from dark pink to yellow to blue." SLJ

Lizzie nonsense; a story of pioneer days. Clarion Books 2005 c2004 32p il lib bdg $15 *

Grades: PreK K 1 2   E

1. Imagination—Fiction 2. Family life—Fiction 3. Australia—Fiction

ISBN 0-618-57493-X (lib bdg)   LC 2004-26642

First published 2004 in Australia

"Lizzie lives with her mother, father, and baby brother in a small, isolated house in the Australian bush. Her father has taken his sandalwood into town to sell and will be gone for weeks. Lizzie passes the lonely days by indulging in flights of fancy. . . . The text is simple yet evocative . . . while the skillfully rendered watercolors bring the unique setting to life." SLJ

Ormerod, Jan—*Continued*

Miss Mouse's day. HarperCollins Pubs. 2001 unp il hardcover o.p. lib bdg $14.89

Grades: PreK   E

1. Day—Fiction 2. Mice—Fiction

ISBN 0-688-16333-5; 0-688-16334-3 (lib bdg)

LC 99-27641

"Miss Mouse recounts her day as the stuffed-animal companion of an energetic little girl." Horn Book Guide

"The illustrations, in panels of varying sizes, brim with pattern, detail, and bright splashes of color. . . . Ormerod delightfully and realistically illustrates the challenges of energetic toddlerhood." Booklist

Another title about Miss Mouse is:

Miss Mouse takes off (2001)

Osborne, Mary Pope, 1949-

New York's bravest; paintings by Steve Johnson & Lou Fancher. Knopf 2002 unp il $15.95; pa $6.99 *

Grades: PreK K 1 2   E

1. Fire fighters—Fiction 2. New York (N.Y.)—Fiction

ISBN 0-375-82196-1; 0-375-83841-4 (pa)

LC 2002-455

Tells of the heroic deeds of the legendary New York firefighter, Mose Humphreys

"Boldly executed art supports the tall-tale flavor of a story that is both powerful and humane." Booklist

Otoshi, Kathryn

One. KO Kids Books 2008 unp il $16.95 *

Grades: PreK K 1   E

1. Bullies—Fiction 2. Color—Fiction 3. Counting 4. Courage—Fiction

ISBN 978-0-9723946-4-2; 0-9723946-4-8

Blue is a quiet color. Red's a hothead who likes to pick on Blue. Yellow, Orange, Green, and Purple don't like what they see, but what can they do? When no one speaks up, things get out of hand—until One comes along and shows all the colors how to stand up, stand together, and count.

"The use of colors and numbers gives the story a much-needed universality. . . . Otoshi cleverly offers a way to talk to very young children about the subject of bullying, even as she helps put their imaginations to work on solutions." Booklist

Pak, Soyung

Dear Juno; illustrated by Susan Kathleen Hartung. Viking 1999 unp il hardcover o.p. pa $5.99

Grades: PreK K 1 2   E

1. Grandmothers—Fiction 2. Letters—Fiction 3. Korean Americans—Fiction

ISBN 0-670-88252-6; 0-14-230017-9 (pa)

LC 98-43408

Although Juno, a Korean American boy, cannot read the letter he receives from his grandmother in Seoul, he understands what it means from the photograph and dried flower that are enclosed and decides to send a similar letter back to her

"The handsome layout, featuring ample white space

and illustrations that cover anywhere from one page to an entire spread, perfectly suit the gentle, understated tone of the text." SLJ

Palatini, Margie

Bad boys get henpecked! illustrated by Henry Cole. Katherine Tegen Books 2009 unp il $17.99; lib bdg $18.89

Grades: PreK K 1 2   E

1. Wolves—Fiction 2. Chickens—Fiction

ISBN 978-0-06-074433-5; 0-06-074433-2; 978-0-06-074434-2 (lib bdg); 0-06-074434-0 (lib bdg)

LC 2008-11771

Bad boy wolves Willy and Wally try to get a chicken dinner by disguising themselves as the Handy-Dandy Lupino Brothers and going to work for a hen in need of household help.

"With its fast-paced language and witty narrative paired with lively alliteration and puns, the Bad Boys' latest tale will entertain and capture youngsters' imaginations. Cole deftly expresses humor and the power of understatement in his pencil and watercolor illustrations. Expressive facial expressions and body language tell all." SLJ

Boo-hoo moo; illustrated by Keith Graves. Katherine Tegen Books 2009 unp il $17.99; lib bdg $18.89

Grades: K 1 2   E

1. Cattle—Fiction 2. Farm life—Fiction

ISBN 978-0-06-114375-5; 0-06-114375-8; 978-0-06-114376-2 (lib bdg); 0-06-114376-6 (lib bdg)

LC 2007024417

When Hilda Mae Heifer's trademark 'moo' starts sounding even worse, the other animals decide she is lonely and hold auditions to find her some singing partners.

"Palatini's prose is poetic, quirky, inventive, and just plain fun. . . . Graves escalates the sophisticated silliness with his wacky, superbly crafted, almost 3D illustrations." SLJ

The cheese; paintings by Steve Johnson and Lou Fancher. Katherine Tegan Books 2007 unp il $16.99; lib bdg $17.89 *

Grades: K 1 2 3   E

1. Nursery rhymes—Fiction

ISBN 978-0-06-052630-6; 0-06-052630-0; 978-0-06-052631-3 (lib bdg); 0-06-052631-9 (lib bdg)

LC 2006-18163

After they all agree to ignore the story of "The Farmer in the Dell," the rat, cat, dog, child, farmer, and his wife have a party featuring the tempting hunk of cheese.

"The folk-art quality of the illustrations is rich with country colors—barn reds, field greens, and earthy yellows, and the cartoon animals are funny and expressive. A smattering of words and music from the song is worked in effectively on most pages, and the full lyrics are printed on the last page." SLJ

Palatini, Margie—*Continued*

Earthquack! illustrated by Barry Moser. Simon & Schuster Bks. for Young Readers 2002 unp il $15.95; pa $6.99

Grades: PreK K 1 2   E

1. Domestic animals—Fiction

ISBN 0-689-84280-5; 1-4169-0260-0 (pa)

LC 2001-31302

When Chucky Ducky feels the earth beneath him grumble and rumble, he runs to alert the other barnyard animals to the coming earthquake, but just as a wily weasel is about to take advantage of their fears, the true source of the rumbling is revealed

"Moser captures the essence of Weasel's dark determination as well as the bug-eyed hysteria of the farm animals in his expressive graphite and transparent watercolor illustrations. . . . Palatini's text is funny, with contemporary dialogue, puns, and a fast-paced narrative rich in rhythm and alliteration." SLJ

Gorgonzola; a very stinkysaurus; by Margie Palatini; illustrated by Tim Bowers. Katherine Tegen Books 2008 unp il $16.99; lib bdg $17.89

Grades: PreK K 1 2   E

1. Smell—Fiction 2. Cleanliness—Fiction 3. Dinosaurs—Fiction 4. Birds—Fiction

ISBN 978-0-06-073897-6; 0-06-073897-9; 978-0-06-073898-3 (lib bdg); 0-06-073898-7 (lib bdg)

LC 2006002191

When Gorgonzola the dinosaur learns that everyone runs from him to avoid his smell, rather than out of fear, he is grateful to the little bird who shows him how to brush his teeth and wash

"The over-the-top illustrations of the grossed-out dinosaurs . . . will bring belly laughs to children and inspiration to the grownups who have to wrestle them into the bathtub or dentist's chair. Witty dialogue and an effective layout get the personal hygiene message across without being preachy or didactic." SLJ

Piggie pie! illustrated by Howard Fine. Clarion Bks. 1995 unp il $15; pa $5.95

Grades: PreK K 1 2   E

1. Witches—Fiction 2. Pigs—Fiction 3. Wolves—Fiction

ISBN 0-395-71691-8; 0-395-86618-9 (pa)

LC 94-19726

"Gritch the Witch sets out for Old MacDonald's Farm to get herself a meal of plump piggies. Alerted, however, . . . the swine hastily don sheep, cow, and other barnyard disguises and fool her. . . . The still-hungry Gritch is persuaded to give up by a Big Bad Wolf . . . and the two go off for lunch, each picturing the other made into a sandwich. . . . The exuberant illustrations are colorful and action-filled. Greedy (but not too bright) witch and wolf both get what they deserve in this thoroughly enjoyable romp." SLJ

Three French hens; a holiday tale; illustrations by Richard Egielski. Hyperion Books for Children 2005 unp il $15.99 *

Grades: PreK K 1 2   E

1. Chickens—Fiction 2. Foxes—Fiction 3. Christmas—Fiction 4. New York (N.Y.)—Fiction

ISBN 0-7868-5167-8

"The three French hens from the familiar Christmas song are sent by a Parisian lady to her boyfriend, Philippe Renard, in New York. Alas, the hens wind up in lost mail, and when they can't find Philippe in the phone book, they think perhaps they should translate his name: Phil Fox. They find Phil Fox, but he's a downtrodden fox living in the Bronx. . . . [This] is so much fun, it's hard to imagine an artist milking more laughs from it than Egielski. . . . Something really fresh for the holiday season." Booklist

The three silly billies; illustrated by Barry Moser. Simon & Schuster Books for Young Readers 2005 unp il $15.95

Grades: PreK K 1 2   E

1. Goats—Fiction

ISBN 0-689-85862-0   LC 2002-155835

Three billy goats, unable to cross a bridge because they cannot pay the toll, form a car pool with The Three Bears, Little Red Riding Hood, and Jack of beanstalk fame to get past the rude Troll.

"Painted in cheery watercolors, Moser's figures are in contemporary dress and pop out from the white backgrounds. There is plenty of visual humor. . . . Palatini's hip and punny text is fun to read aloud." SLJ

Pallotta, Jerry

Ocean counting; odd numbers; illustrated by Shennen Bersani. Charlesbridge 2004 unp il $16.95; pa $6.95

Grades: PreK K 1   E

1. Counting 2. Marine animals

ISBN 0-88106-151-4; 0-88106-150-6 (pa)

LC 98-46035

This "offering counts by twos to 50 and includes only odd numbers (except for the deliberate inclusion of 50 and 0). . . . Readers will find creatures from 9 little green crabs to 15 limpets to 33 sand dollars." Booklist

"Bersani's bright, realistic colored-pencil illustrations will lure readers into perusing the factoid-loaded, simple, conversational text. . . . This book offers a colorful, engaging, and intriguing slant on the technique of counting." SLJ

Panahi, H. L.

Bebop Express; illustrated by Steve Johnson and Lou Fancher. Laura Geringer Books 2005 unp il $15.99

Grades: K 1 2 3   E

1. Railroads—Fiction 2. Jazz music—Fiction 3. Stories in rhyme

ISBN 0-06-057190-X   LC 2003-24244

A rollicking rhythmic express train takes passengers on a jazzy journey that celebrates the United States and its unique musical culture.

"The intricate collages use old photographs and vintage fabrics to obtain a unique look. Teeming with life, the art visually complements the noisy text." Booklist

Parenteau, Shirley, 1935-

Bears on chairs; illustrated by David Walker.
Candlewick Press 2009 unp il $15.99

Grades: PreK K   E

1. Bears—Fiction 2. Stories in rhyme
ISBN 978-0-7636-3588-6; 0-7636-3588-X
                 LC 2008-937035

Four bears are happily seated on four chairs until Big
Brown Bear shows up and demands a seat.

"Between the unerringly positive approach to a common early-childhood dilemma and the can't miss rhyme,
this volume will likely find its place on many a daycare
shelf." Kirkus

Parish, Peggy, 1927-1988

Amelia Bedelia; pictures by Fritz Siebel.
HarperFestival 1999 unp il hardcover o.p. pa $6.99
*

Grades: K 1 2   E

1. Household employees—Fiction
ISBN 0-694-01296-3; 0-06-020187-8 (lib bdg);
0-06-444155-5 (pa)   LC 98-31782

"An I can read picture book"

First published 1963; reissued 1992 as an I can read
book

"Amelia Bedelia is a maid whose talent for interpreting instructions literally results in comical situations,
such as dressing the chicken in fine clothes." Hodges.
Books for Elem Sch Libr

Other titles about Amelia Bedelia are:
Amelia Bedelia and the baby (1981)
Amelia Bedelia and the cat (2008)
Amelia Bedelia and the surprise shower (1996)
Amelia Bedelia, bookworm (2003) by Herman Parish
Amelia Bedelia goes camping (1985)
Amelia Bedelia 4 mayor (1999) by Herman Parish
Amelia Bedelia helps out (1979)
Amelia Bedelia, rocket scientist? (2005) by Herman Par-
ish
Amelia Bedelia talks turkey (2008) by Herman Parish
Amelia Bedelia under construction (2006) by Herman
Parish
Amelia Bedelia's family album (1988) by Herman Parish
Amelia Bedelia's first day of school (2009) by Herman
Parish
Amelia Bedelia's masterpiece (2007)
Bravo Amelia Bedelia (1997) by Herman Parish
Calling Doctor Amelia Bedelia (2003) by Herman Parish
Come back, Amelia Bedelia (1971)
Good driving, Amelia Bedelia (1995) by Herman Parish
Good work, Amelia Bedelia (1976)
Happy haunting, Amelia Bedelia (2004) by Herman Par-
ish
Merry Christmas, Amelia Bedelia (1986)
Play ball, Amelia Bedelia (1972)
Teach us, Amelia Bedelia (1977)
Thank you, Amelia Bedelia (1964)

Park, Frances

Good-bye, 382 Shin Dang Dong; [by] Frances
and Ginger Park; illustrated by Yangsook Choi.
National Geographic Soc. 2002 unp il $16.95

Grades: K 1 2 3   E

1. Immigrants—Fiction 2. Korea—Fiction
ISBN 0-7922-7985-9   LC 2001-2976

Jangmi finds it hard to say goodbye to relatives and
friends, plus the food, customs, and beautiful things of
her home in Korea, when her family moves to America

"The oil paintings done in a simple, childlike style are
formally framed with white space. . . . Children will
find the details of cultural differences and the immigrant
experience well evoked." SLJ

Park, Linda Sue, 1960-

Bee-bim bop! illustrated by Ho Baek Lee.
Clarion Books 2005 32p il $15; pa $6.99 *

Grades: PreK K 1 2   E

1. Cooking—Fiction 2. Korean Americans—Fiction
3. Stories in rhyme
ISBN 0-618-26511-2; 0-547-07671-1 (pa)
                 LC 2003027697

"Bee-bim bop . . . is a traditional Korean dish of rice
topped, and then mixed, with meat and vegetables. In
. . . rhyming text, a hungry child tells about helping her
mother make bee-bim bop." Publisher's note

"Playful, cartoonlike drawings portray a round-faced
girl helping her mother. . . . The illustrations . . . are
very appealing. . . . The rhyme works well. A recipe
follows the story." SLJ

The firekeeper's son; illustrated by Julie
Downing. Clarion Books 2004 37p il $16; pa
$6.99 *

Grades: 1 2 3 4   E

1. Korea—Fiction
ISBN 0-618-13337-2; 0-547-23769-3 (pa)
                 LC 2002-13917

In eighteenth-century Korea, after Sang-hee's father
injures his ankle, Sang-hee attempts to take over the task
of lighting the evening fire which signals to the palace
that all is well. Includes historical notes.

"Park's command of place, characterization, and language is as capable and compelling in this picture book
as it is in her novels. . . . [This offers] lyrical prose and
deftly realized watercolors and pastels." SLJ

Parker, Marjorie Blain, 1960-

A paddling of ducks; animals in groups from A
to Z; written by Marjorie Blain Parker; illustrated
by Joseph Kelly. Kids Can Press 2010 il $16.95

Grades: PreK K 1   E

1. Animals 2. Alphabet
ISBN 978-1-55337-682-8; 1-55337-682-X

"This ABC book provides a delightfully offbeat introduction to collective nouns, featuring groups of animals
at a Riviera-like resort locale with palm trees and a seaside Ferris wheel. . . . Even better than learning some of
the unusual ways to refer to multiple animals is the way
Kelly's soft-focus oil and acrylic paintings riff on the
terms themselves. . . . The anthropomorphic animals feel
anatomically authentic, but with exaggerated joie de
vivre to spare." Publ Wkly

Partridge, Elizabeth

Oranges on Golden Mountain; illustrated by Aki Sogabe. Dutton Children's Bks. 2001 unp il hardcover o.p. pa $6.99
Grades: K 1 2 3   E
   1. Immigrants—Fiction 2. Chinese Americans—Fiction 3. San Francisco (Calif.)—Fiction 4. China—Fiction
   ISBN 0-525-46453-0; 0-14-250033-X (pa)
                LC 99-462287
When hard times fall on his family, Jo Lee is sent from China to San Francisco, where he helps his uncle fish and dreams of being reunited with his mother and sister
"The spirited story is beautifully written. . . . The striking, skillful paper-cut illustrations . . . create a vivid sense of place and do much to explain and extend the story's action." Booklist

Patricelli, Leslie

The birthday box. Candlewick Press 2007 unp il $15.99; bd bk $6.99
Grades: PreK   E
   1. Boxes—Fiction 2. Imagination—Fiction 3. Birthdays—Fiction
   ISBN 978-0-7636-2825-3; 0-7636-2825-5; 978-0-7636-4449-9 (bd bk); 0-7636-4449-8 (bd bk)
                LC 2006-49084
"A child wearing only a diaper and a striped party hat gets a present from Grandma. . . . The toddler takes off the wrapping paper . . . and discovers A big brown box! A box is full of possibilities and this child lets imagination reign. . . . Patricelli's simple, first-person narration is refreshing. With bold black outlines, the acrylic paintings are rudimentary but nonetheless expressive and endearing." SLJ

Higher! higher! Candlewick Press 2009 unp il $15.99; bd bk $6.99 *
Grades: PreK K 1   E
   1. Play—Fiction 2. Imagination—Fiction
   ISBN 978-0-7636-3241-0; 0-7636-3241-4; 978-0-7636-4433-8 (bd bk); 0-7636-4433-1 (bd bk)
Boston Globe-Horn Book Award honor book: Picture Book (2009)
"As an adult pushes a pigtailed girl in a striped sweater and socks on a swing, the child calls out: 'Higher! Higher!' The ride gradually takes her from a giraffe's-eye view, to a mountaintop, to an airplane, and finally high enough to trade high fives with a one-eyed, green alien. . . . The repetitive text is ideal for new readers, and the cartoon paintings, though spare, provide plenty of room for imagination." SLJ

Pattison, Darcy S., 1954-

19 girls and me; [by] Darcy Pattison; illustrated by Steven Salerno. Philomel Books 2006 unp il $16.99
Grades: PreK K 1 2   E
   1. Sex role—Fiction 2. School stories
   ISBN 0-399-24336-4   LC 2005020501
John Hercules is worried about being the only boy in his kindergarten class, but after the first week he stops worrying.

"The mixed-media illustrations include wild color combinations and dizzying perspectives that provide the backdrops for the children, drawn in a stylishly simple but endearing cartoon style." SLJ

The journey of Oliver K. Woodman; written by Darcy Pattison; illustrated by Joe Cepeda. Harcourt 2003 unp il $16; pa $6.99
Grades: K 1 2 3   E
   1. Travel—Fiction
   ISBN 0-15-202329-1; 0-15-206118-5 (pa)
                LC 2001-5320
Oliver K. Woodman, a man made of wood, takes a remarkable journey across America, as told through the postcards and letters of those he meets along the way
"The boldly colored, textured illustrations were made with oils over an acrylic under-painting on boards. . . . A fresh, unusual tale." SLJ
Another title about Oliver K. Woodman is:
Searching for Oliver K. Woodman (2005)

Patz, Nancy

Babies can't eat kimchee! by Nancy Patz & [illustrated by] Susan L. Roth. Bloomsbury Children's Books 2007 unp il $16.95
Grades: PreK K 1 2   E
   1. Infants—Fiction 2. Sisters—Fiction 3. Korean Americans—Fiction
   ISBN 1-59990-017-3
A baby sister must wait to grow up before doing big sister things, such as ballet dancing and eating spicy Korean food.
This book's "Korean-American perspective and mixed-media collage illustrations set the title apart. . . . The illustrations use just the right colors and lines to capture the child's changing emotions." SLJ

Paul, Ann Whitford

Count on Culebra; go from 1 to 10 in Spanish. Holiday House 2008 unp il $16.95
Grades: PreK K 1   E
   1. Iguanas—Fiction 2. Rattlesnakes—Fiction 3. Desert animals—Fiction 4. Counting 5. Spanish language—Vocabulary
   ISBN 978-0-8234-2124-4; 0-8234-2124-4
                LC 2007017303
When Iguana stubs her toe and cannot make her popular candies known as cactus butter dulces, Culebra the rattlesnake finds a cure that introduces the Spanish words for the numbers from one to ten.
"The well-paced story exudes a charming silliness and invites participation. Bright cartoon-style illustrations, rendered in gouache and colored pencil, nicely depict the foolishness and are large enough for group sharing. . . . The introduction of Spanish words and counting concepts along with the appealing art and offbeat story make this a treat." Booklist

Fiesta fiasco; illustrated by Ethan Long. Holiday House 2007 unp il $16.95
Grades: PreK K 1 2 3   E
   1. Rabbits—Fiction 2. Desert animals—Fiction 3. Gifts—Fiction 4. Spanish language—Vocabulary
   ISBN 978-0-8234-2037-7; 0-8234-2037-X
                LC 2006-12112

Paul, Ann Whitford—_Continued_

When shopping for Culebra's birthday, Conejo convinces his friends Iguana and Tortuga to buy all the wrong presents. Includes a glossary of Spanish words used.

"A fiery palette enlivens the simple cartoon artwork set in the desert. The scenes are fun to look at." SLJ

Other titles about these characters are:

Mañana Iguana (2004)

Tortuga in trouble (2009)

If animals kissed good night--; [by] Ann Whitford Paul; pictures by David Walker. Farrar, Straus and Giroux 2008 unp il $16.95

Grades: PreK K 1   E
1. Kissing—Fiction 2. Animals—Fiction 3. Parent-child relationship—Fiction 4. Stories in rhyme
ISBN 0-374-38051-1; 978-0-374-38051-9
LC 2006051108

Rhyming text explores what would happen if animals kissed like humans do, from a slow kiss between a sloth and her cub to a mud-happy kiss from a hippo calf to his father

Walker "gets great emotional mileage from his rounded, stuffed toy-like shapes, velvety colors, and tiny dot eyes; the characters radiate unconditional love. There's a lot to go 'Ahhhh' over." Publ Wkly

Snail's good night; by Ann Whitford Paul; illustrated by Rosanne Litzinger. Holiday House 2008 32p il $14.95

Grades: PreK K 1   E
1. Bedtime—Fiction 2. Snails—Fiction
ISBN 978-0-8234-1912-8; 0-8234-1912-6
LC 2007-614

When Snail realizes that his friends are going to bed, he begins a very long, very slow slide to wish them all good night.

"Created using watercolor, gouache, and colored pencil, the fanciful artwork features mild-mannered animal characters and a benevolent moon shining down on the world. . . . The large type and short sentences make this gently amusing story just right for beginning readers." Booklist

Word builder; illustrated by Kurt Cyrus. Simon & Schuster Books for Young Readers 2009 unp il $16.99

Grades: PreK K 1   E
1. Authorship—Fiction
ISBN 978-1-4169-3981-8; 1-4169-3981-4
LC 2007045244

Text explains how putting letters into words, words into sentences, sentences into paragraphs, and paragraphs into chapters ends up creating a book

"This oversize book uses direct language and terrific artwork to show children how literal and figurative construction works. . . . The art, rendered in pencil and digital color, seems almost three-dimensional and will fascinate readers." Booklist

Payne, Emmy, 1919-

Katy No-Pocket; pictures by H. A. Rey. Houghton Mifflin 1944 unp il lib bdg $17; pa $5.95

Grades: PreK K 1 2   E
1. Kangaroos—Fiction 2. Animals—Fiction
ISBN 0-395-17104-0 (lib bdg); 0-395-13717-9 (pa)

Katy Kangaroo was most unfortunately unprovided with a pocket in which to carry her son Freddy. She asked other animals with no pockets how they carried their children but none of their answers seemed satisfactory. Finally a wise old owl advised her to try to find a pocket in the City, and so off she went and in the City she found just what she and Freddy needed

Peacock, Carol Antoinette

Mommy far, Mommy near; an adoption story; written by Carol Antoinette Peacock; illustrated by Shawn Brownell. Whitman, A. 2000 unp il $16.99

Grades: PreK K 1 2   E
1. Adoption—Fiction 2. Mother-child relationship—Fiction 3. Chinese Americans—Fiction
ISBN 0-8075-5234-8   LC 99-36108

Elizabeth, who was born in China, describes the family who has adopted her and tries to sort out her feelings for her mother back in China

"The situation is handled sensitively by the author, who writes from personal experience. . . . The faces deftly show the strong emotional bond between adoptive mother and daughter." Horn Book Guide

Pearce, Philippa, 1920-2006

The squirrel wife; illustrated by Wayne Anderson. Candlewick Press 2007 unp il $16.99

Grades: K 1 2 3   E
1. Fairies—Fiction 2. Squirrels—Fiction 3. Forests and forestry—Fiction 4. Brothers—Fiction 5. Fairy tales
ISBN 978-0-7636-3551-0; 0-7636-3551-0
LC 2006052454

As a reward for saving the life of one of the feared green people, Jack acquires a beautiful and loving squirrel wife, knowledgeable in the secrets of the forest.

"Anderson's mixed-media illustrations strengthen the story's connections while amplifying the sense of enchantment with images of the elfin, lime-colored folk and the forest scenes, rendered in feathery strokes and an earthy green palette of moss and mushrooms. An intriguing, atmospheric offering." Booklist

Pearle, Ida

A child's day; an alphabet of play. Harcourt 2008 unp il $12.95

Grades: PreK K   E
1. Alphabet 2. Play—Fiction
ISBN 978-0-15-206552-2; 0-15-206552-0
LC 2007-33966

"This simple, attractive alphabet of action words and pictures depicts children engaged in play and other activities. . . . The design is particularly effective. Large, colorful cut-paper collages of multiethnic children feature interesting patterns that stand out against solid backgrounds." SLJ

Pearson, Debora

Sophie's wheels; by Debora Pearson; art by Nora Hilb. Annick Press 2006 unp il lib bdg $18.95; pa $6.95

Grades: PreK   E

1. Wheels—Fiction 2. Growth—Fiction
ISBN 978-1-55451-038-2 (lib bdg); 1-55451-038-4 (lib bdg); 978-1-55451-037-5 (pa); 1-55451-037-6 (pa)

This "tale is all about the wheels in Sophie's life, from the 'bouncy baby buggy wheels' of her baby carriage and the wheels of a stroller and shopping cart to the wheels on a tricycle, and, finally, the two big wheels and two small ones on her training bike, which she rides on her own." Booklist

"The language is descriptive. . . . The text is accompanied by simple, soft-washed watercolor illustrations. . . . This [is a] satisfying, peaceful tale." SLJ

Pearson, Tracey Campbell

Bob. Farrar, Straus & Giroux 2002 unp il $16; pa $6.95 *

Grades: PreK K 1 2   E

1. Roosters—Fiction 2. Animals—Fiction
ISBN 0-374-39957-3; 0-374-40871-8 (pa)

LC 2001-40439

While looking for someone to teach him how to crow, a rooster learns to sound like many different animals and finds that his new skills come in handy

"The droll, repetitious text, perfect for reading aloud, is delightfully complemented by bright, lively watercolor illustrations." SLJ

Myrtle. Farrar, Straus and Giroux 2004 unp il $15

Grades: PreK K 1 2   E

1. Mice—Fiction 2. Aunts—Fiction
ISBN 0-374-35157-0   LC 2003-44059

With the help of her favorite Aunt Tizzy, Myrtle learns to overcome her fear of the mean next-door neighbor.

"Pearson uses a fruit-colored palette with lots of design work to showcase her delightful mouse characters, brimming with personality." Booklist

Pedersen, Janet

Houdini the amazing caterpillar; [by] Janet Pedersen. Clarion Books 2008 30p il $16

Grades: PreK K 1 2   E

1. Caterpillars—Fiction 2. Butterflies—Fiction 3. School stories
ISBN 978-0-618-89332-4; 0-618-89332-6

A caterpillar does amazing tricks, like making leaves disappear and shedding its skin, and finally it performs the most amazing trick of all. Includes facts about the life cycle of the monarch butterfly.

"Big, clear artwork in watercolors and liquid inks shows the smiling, hungry little caterpillar basking in the attention from a teacher and pupils. . . . The fantasy and the realism make the nature story fun for home and classroom." Booklist

Peet, Bill

Big bad Bruce. Houghton Mifflin 1977 38p il $17; pa $8.95

Grades: PreK K 1 2   E

1. Bears—Fiction 2. Witches—Fiction
ISBN 0-395-25150-8; 0-395-32922-1 (pa)

LC 76-62502

Bruce, a bear bully, never picks on anyone his own size until he is diminished in more ways than one by a small but very independent witch

"The language of the text is almost musical, with lots of words used for the sheer pleasure or appropriateness of their sounds. The illustrations are colorful and amusing." Child Book Rev Serv

Huge Harold; written and illustrated by Bill Peet. Houghton Mifflin 1961 unp il hardcover o.p. pa $8.95

Grades: PreK K 1 2   E

1. Rabbits—Fiction 2. Stories in rhyme
ISBN 0-395-18449-5; 0-395-32923-X (pa)

"Harold the rabbit grows and grows—to dimensions which deprive him of normal hiding places but help him, after a bizarre chase, to an astonishing and wonderful achievement." Horn Book

This story, "told in rhyming couplets and colored drawings, is action filled and laughable." Booklist

The whingdingdilly; written and illustrated by Bill Peet. Houghton Mifflin 1970 60p il $17; pa $9.95

Grades: PreK K 1 2   E

1. Dogs—Fiction 2. Witches—Fiction
ISBN 0-395-24729-2; 0-395-31381-3 (pa)

"Scamps, the dog, wants to be a horse, but a well-meaning witch turns him into a Whingdingdilly with the hump of a camel, zebra's tail, giraffe's neck, elephant's front legs and ears, rhinoceros' nose, and reindeer's horns." Adventuring With Books. 2d edition

Pelham, David

Trail; paper poetry. Little Simon/Simon & Schuster Books for Young Readers 2007 unp il $26.99 *

Grades: 1 2 3 4   E

1. Pop-up books 2. Snails—Fiction
ISBN 978-1-4169-4894-0

In five pop-up spreads a silver line of poetry on white paper follows a small snail through its day, from roots and leaf on the forest floor to a pond at sunset. Pelham lays the verse out on a paper wheel that must be turned to be read in its entirety.

Pelletier, David

The graphic alphabet. Orchard Bks. 1996 unp il $17.95 *

Grades: PreK K 1 2   E

1. Alphabet
ISBN 0-531-36001-6   LC 96-4001

A Caldecott Medal honor book, 1997

In this alphabet book "a stylized letter Y, pink against a black background, is turned on its side and looks like

Pelletier, David—*Continued*

a mouth open in a yawn. . . . The letter Q is repeated in squares, becoming a handsome quilt, and a three-dimensional golden H hovers over a darkened sky. Even for those who know their letters very well, some of the pictures demand a second look before the artist's view is clear. But that's the point; things can be more than or different from what they seem. An engaging book that will certainly have art-class relevance." Booklist

Pelley, Kathleen T.

Magnus Maximus, a marvelous measurer; [pictures by] S.D. Schindler. Farrar Straus Giroux 2010 unp il $16.99

Grades: K 1 2   E

1. Measurement—Fiction 2. Counting—Fiction

ISBN 978-0-374-34725-3; 0-374-34725-5

                 LC 2006-51714

As the town's official measurer, Magnus Maximus is consumed with measuring and counting everything and everyone, missing out on life's simple pleasures, until one day when he breaks his glasses.

"Children will enjoy the humor in this eccentric's ever-increasing obsession. Fine ink lines and muted watercolors fill the illustrations with small details, add humor, and complete the story. The art firmly places it in the Victorian era, a time of scientific exploration. The style perfectly captures the focus of the marvelous measurer and his scientific obsession." SLJ

Pendziwol, Jean

Marja's skis; [by] Jean E. Pendziwol; pictures by Jirina Marton. Groundwood 2007 unp il $17.95

Grades: 1 2 3   E

1. Skiing—Fiction   2. Immigrants—Fiction
3. Canada—Fiction 4. Lumber and lumbering—Fiction
5. Fathers—Fiction

ISBN 978-0-88899-674-9

"Marja can hardly wait to be big and strong enough to help with Father's horses and attend school. . . . But after her father dies . . . being strong seems too hard. One day . . . Marja sees someone who has fallen through the ice and . . . she finds the courage to help him. . . . Evocative oil-pastels illustrate the text. . . . A simply told, emotionally resonant tale." Booklist

Pennypacker, Sara, 1951-

Pierre in love; pictures by Petra Mathers. Orchard Books 2007 unp il $16.99

Grades: K 1 2   E

1. Love—Fiction 2. Mice—Fiction 3. Rabbits—Fiction

ISBN 0-439-51740-0

Feeling "bloopy and love-swoggled" in the presence of Catherine, the elegant ballet teacher, a humble fisherman tries to muster the courage to reveal his affection for her.

"Subtleties abound, and the emotions may affect adults more than children. But the purity of the love will touch children, too, and both the words and the art are delightful." Booklist

Sparrow girl; illustrated by Yoko Tanaka. Hyperion 2009 unp il $16.99 *

Grades: 1 2 3 4   E

1. Sparrows—Fiction 2. China—History—1949-1976—Fiction 3. Birds—Fiction

ISBN 978-1-4231-1187-0; 1-4231-1187-7

                 LC 2009-6758

When China's leader declares war on sparrows in 1958, everyone makes loud noise in hopes of chasing the hungry birds from their land except for Ming-Li, a young girl whose compassion and foresight prevent a disaster

"Pennypacker strikes a suitably moralistic tone and tells her story with rich, descriptive detail. Tanaka matches the somber elegance of the text with opaque, folk-inspired paintings in a subdued palette. An author's note explains the difficult facts behind the story." Booklist

Pérez, Amada Irma

My very own room; story by Amada Irma Pérez; illustrations by Maya Christina Gonzalez. Children's Bk. Press 2000 30p il $16.95 *

Grades: PreK K 1 2   E

1. Mexican Americans—Fiction 2. Family life—Fiction 3. Bilingual books—English-Spanish

ISBN 0-89239-164-2   LC 00-20769

Title page and text in English and Spanish

With the help of her family, a resourceful Mexican American girl realizes her dream of having a space of her own to read and to think

"Gonzalez' palette is replete with joyfully exuberant colors; rich magentas, purples, and blues contrast with the warm golds of faces and arms, and the dark eyes and hair offer further contrast with the backgrounds and skin colors. Pérez based this story on her own life . . . and the text . . . exudes a comfortably familiar, accessible voice." Bull Cent Child Books

Pérez, L. King

First day in grapes; illustrated by Robert Casilla. Lee & Low Bks. 2002 unp il $16.95

Grades: K 1 2 3   E

1. Migrant labor—Fiction 2. Mexican Americans—Fiction 3. School stories 4. California—Fiction

ISBN 1-58430-045-0   LC 2001-38787

When Chico starts the third grade after his migrant worker family moves to begin harvesting California grapes, he finds that self confidence and math skills help him cope with the first day of school

This story "sheds light on the life of migrant children in a poignant, balanced manner. . . . The watercolor, colored-pencil, and pastel illustrations bring warmth and color to this portrait of life in rural California." SLJ

Pericoli, Matteo

Tommaso and the missing line. Alfred A. Knopf 2008 unp il $15.99; lib bdg $18.99

Grades: K 1 2 3   E

1. Drawing—Fiction 2. Lost and found possessions—Fiction 3. Italy—Fiction

ISBN 978-0-375-84102-6; 0-375-84102-4; 978-0-375-94102-3 (lib bdg); 0-375-94102-9 (lib bdg)

When Tommaso discovers that a line is missing from his favorite drawing, he goes looking for it all around town and notices many lines he never saw before.

Pericoli "demonstrates remarkable draftsmanship and a vivid eye for detail and perspective; the mostly black-and-white pictures combine the elegant extravagance of architectural engravings with the playfulness and spontaneity of a great doodle. The Italian setting adds to the charm. . . . The design is striking. . . . Facing each illustration, the text drops out from solid orange; the effect is eye-popping." Publ Wkly

The true story of Stellina. Knopf 2006 unp il $15.95; lib bdg $17.99

Grades: PreK K 1 2   E

1. Finches 2. New York (N.Y.)

ISBN 0-375-83273-4; 0-375-93273-9 (lib bdg)

The true story of a baby finch rescued and raised by the author and his wife when no zoo would take the abandoned bird fallen from her nest onto a busy street in the middle of New York City.

"A precise linguistic lyricism is at play. . . . The art is sophisticated and spare, but utterly accessible." Booklist

Perkins, Lynne Rae

The cardboard piano. Greenwillow Books 2008 unp il $17.99; lib bdg $18.89 *

Grades: PreK K 1 2   E

1. Friendship—Fiction 2. Pianos—Fiction

ISBN 978-0-06-154265-7; 0-06-154265-2; 978-0-06-154266-4 (lib bdg); 0-06-154266-0 (lib bdg)
LC 2007-39194

When Debbie tries to interest Tina in playing the piano by creating a cardboard keyboard, they find not only does it not have the same appeal but also that they do not need to share everything to be best friends.

"Perkins engages her young audience on three levels: the straightforward yet emotionally complex text; conversational asides in word balloons that develop characterization; and intricate pen-and-ink and watercolor illustrations. . . . Perkins presents the delicate nature of friendship without patronizing." Horn Book

Pictures from our vacation. Greenwillow Books 2007 unp il $16.99; lib bdg $17.89 *

Grades: K 1 2 3   E

1. Vacations—Fiction 2. Family reunions—Fiction 3. Photography—Fiction 4. Canada—Fiction

ISBN 978-0-06-085097-5; 0-06-085097-3; 978-0-06-085098-2 (lib bdg); 0-06-085098-1 (lib bdg)
LC 2006-49256

Given a camera that takes and prints tiny pictures just before leaving for the family farm in Canada, a young girl records a vacation that gets off to a slow start, but winds up being a family reunion filled with good memories.

"Using many overhead perspectives and with an eye for small details, [Perkins] offers watercolors that beautifully capture all that is real about family vacations: boredom, disappointment, fun, and love." Booklist

Snow music. Greenwillow Bks. 2003 unp il $15.99

Grades: PreK K 1   E

1. Snow—Fiction 2. Sound—Fiction

ISBN 0-06-623956-7   LC 2002-192758

When a dog gets loose from the house on a snowy day, his owner searches for him and experiences the sounds of various animals and things in the snow

"With whispery, musical words and detailed, soft-focus images that depict typical winter scenes, this gentle book gives children a sense of what snow is." SLJ

Perlman, Janet, 1954-

The delicious bug. Kids Can Press 2009 unp il $16.95

Grades: PreK K 1 2 3   E

1. Chameleons—Fiction 2. Insects—Fiction

ISBN 978-1-55337-996-6; 1-55337-996-9

"With a flick of the tongue, two hungry chameleons catch the same bumblebug. Neither is willing to let go, and they have a knockdown-dragout fight to claim the snack. Eventually they realize, thanks to some equally hungry crocodiles, how much they need each other. The snappy story . . . is accompanied by cartoony digital illustrations bordered by panel drawings." Horn Book Guide

Perret, Delphine

The Big Bad Wolf and me; [by] Delphine Perret. Sterling Pub. 2006 unp il $9.95

Grades: K 1 2 3   E

1. Wolves—Fiction

ISBN 978-1-4027-3725-1; 1-4027-3725-4
LC 2005031460

Original French edition 2005

When the Big Bad Wolf is mistaken for a dog, he comes to live in a boy's closet and eat chocolate chip cookies.

"Told in witty, thumbnail-size line drawings accompanied by brief text in very small type. . . . The story's humor, absurdity, and heart will please a wide readership." Booklist

Perry, Andrea, 1956-

The Bicklebys' birdbath; illustrated by Roberta Angaramo. Atheneum 2010 unp il $16.99

Grades: PreK K 1 2   E

1. Stories in rhyme

ISBN 978-1-4169-0624-7; 1-4169-0624-X

A cumulative rhyme in the style of "The House That Jack Built," describing the antics that occur when a mailman lands in a birdbath causing it to break.

"This jaunty cumulative tale has a pleasingly playful complexity, both in the wording and in its sense of time. Perry concocts a rhythmic text with unexpected twists and turns, and rather than moving the story forward, it works backward. . . . Sweetly clever." Kirkus

Peters, Lisa Westberg

Cold little duck, duck, duck; pictures by Sam Williams. Greenwillow Bks. 2000 unp il $15.99 *

Grades: PreK K 1   E

1. Ducks—Fiction 2. Spring—Fiction 3. Stories in rhyme

ISBN 0-688-16178-2   LC 99-29880

Early one spring a little duck arrives at her pond and finds it still frozen, but not for long

"The poetic text, well served by expressive watercolors, is set in a large black typeface (inviting letter and word recognition); colorful and playful typefaces are used for the rhythmic three-word refrains." Horn Book Guide

Frankie works the night shift; illustrated by Jennifer Taylor. Greenwillow Books 2010 unp il $16.99

Grades: PreK K   E

1. Cats—Fiction 2. Night—Fiction 3. Counting

ISBN 978-0-06-009095-1; 0-06-009095-2

LC 2008012644

In this counting book, Frankie the cat's night prowling causes a ruckus, waking sleeping neighbors who do not share Frankie's love of the "night shift."

"Peters's spare text, full of exclamatory statements in the second half . . . moves the story forward with energy and speed, but Taylor's artwork is the showstopper, creating a surreal environment for Frankie's nocturnal adventures." Publ Wkly

Phillipps, Julie C.

Wink; the ninja who wanted to be noticed. Viking Children's Books 2009 unp il $15.99 *

Grades: K 1 2 3   E

1. Ninja—Fiction 2. School stories

ISBN 978-0-670-01092-9; 0-670-01092-8

LC 2008-23238

Although ninjas should be silent and use stealth, Wink finds his enthusiasm gets him into trouble with his teacher until he finds the perfect way to express both traits.

"The story's oft-told message of acceptance has been invigorated with originality and humor. The collage-style illustrations often appear to have a three-dimensional effect and Wink practically bounds off the pages with barely contained energy." SLJ

Pichon, Liz

Penguins. Orchard Books 2008 unp il lib bdg $12.99

Grades: PreK K   E

1. Penguins—Fiction 2. Cameras—Fiction 3. Zoos—Fiction

ISBN 978-0-545-02215-6 (lib bdg); 0-545-02215-0 (lib bdg)   LC 2007-40419

Penguins at the zoo have an exciting afternoon when one finds a camera left behind by a visitor.

"The cartoon style of these pastel illustrations is as light and playful as the text. The sweet faces show a lot of expression, while the aqua and purple backgrounds highlight their antics." SLJ

The three horrid little pigs; by Liz Pichon. Tiger Tales 2008 unp il $15.95

Grades: PreK K 1 2   E

1. Pigs—Fiction 2. Wolves—Fiction

ISBN 978-1-58925-077-2; 1-58925-077-X

When their mother sends them packing, three pigs find despicable ways to find new accommodations, but when the big, friendly wolf tries to show them the error of their ways, the pigs respond by huffing and puffing.

"The lively narrative, printed in playfully arranged text of varying size, is well suited for spirited read-alouds, as are the colorful illustrations that add to the hilarity with expressive characters. Children will enjoy the clever twist on a familiar story." Booklist

Pilkey, Dav, 1966-

The Hallo-wiener. Blue Sky Press (NY) 1995 unp il $16.95; pa $5.99

Grades: PreK K 1 2   E

1. Dogs—Fiction 2. Halloween—Fiction

ISBN 0-590-41703-7; 0-439-07946-2 (pa)

LC 94-40949

All the other dogs make fun of Oscar the dachshund until one Halloween when, dressed as a hot dog, Oscar bravely rescues the others

"Pilkey's bold, colorful illustrations add life to his simple tale of courage and friendship." Horn Book Guide

The paperboy; story and paintings by Dav Pilkey. Orchard Bks. 1996 unp il $16.95; pa $6.99 *

Grades: PreK K 1 2   E

1. Newspaper carriers—Fiction

ISBN 0-531-09506-1; 0-531-07139-1 (pa)

LC 95-30641

A Caldecott Medal honor book, 1997

"A Richard Jackson book"

"In the quiet hour before dawn, a boy and his dog get out of their warm bed, eat their breakfasts, and deliver the newspapers. . . . Happy together before the rest of the world awakes, they finish the job and head back home to bed, where they dream of flying across the night sky." Booklist

"The palette of the artwork is rich and inviting, and an emphasis is put on balance and geometric form, giving solidity to this celebration of routine. A meditative evocation of the extraordinary aspects of ordinary living." Horn Book Guide

Pinfold, Levi

The Django. Templar Books 2010 unp il $16.99 *

Grades: K 1 2   E

1. Imaginary playmates—Fiction 2. Banjos—Fiction 3. Gypsies—Fiction 4. Musicians—Fiction

ISBN 978-0-7636-4788-9; 0-7636-4788-8

A young Gypsy boy named Jean has an imaginary friend, Django, who keeps getting him in trouble and eventually is "sent away," but whenever Jean plays the banjo he continues to feel close to Django. Inspired by the life of jazz musician Django Reinhardt; includes facts about his life.

"Fish-eyed perspectives and generous detailing almost

Pinfold, Levi—*Continued*

suck readers' gazes into Pinfold's exotic and pastoral artwork. Once in, children will revel in the bouncy rhythms and nonsense words sprinkled throughout the fun-to-read-and-hear narrative." Booklist

Pinkney, Andrea Davis

Boycott blues; how Rosa Parks inspired a nation; illustrations by Brian Pinkney. Greenwillow Books 2008 unp il $16.99; lib bdg $17.89 *

Grades: 1 2 3 4   E

1. Parks, Rosa, 1913-2005—Fiction 2. African Americans—Fiction 3. Montgomery (Ala.)—Fiction

ISBN 978-0-06-082118-0; 0-06-082118-3; 978-0-06-082119-7 (lib bdg); 0-06-082119-1 (lib bdg)

LC 2006-38273

Illustrations and rhythmic text recall the December, 1955, bus boycott in Montgomery, Alabama.

"Color and movement are vibrant components in this extraordinary book. . . . Text and illustration work in perfect sync. Andrea Pinkney chose the rhythm of the blues as cadence for the guitar-strumming hound-dog narrator. . . . The evocative text is bolstered by Brian Pinkney's perceptive vision. . . . Against electric blues and greens diffused with streaks of black line, Pinkney's artwork rivets the eye." SLJ

Includes bibliographical references

Peggony-Po; a whale of a tale; illustrated by Brian Pinkney. Jump at the Sun/Hyperion Books for Children 2006 unp il $16.99 *

Grades: K 1 2 3   E

1. Whales—Fiction 2. Whaling—Fiction 3. African Americans—Fiction 4. Tall tales

ISBN 0-7868-1958-8   LC 2005047537

Peggony-Po, carved out of wood by his father, a one-legged whaler, determines to catch the huge whale that ate his father's leg.

"Told with humor and verve, this [is a] rollicking tall tale. . . . The illustrations brim with activity and energy." SLJ

Pinkney, Jerry, 1939-

The lion & the mouse. Little, Brown Books for Young Readers 2009 unp il $16.99 *

Grades: PreK K 1 2   E

1. Aesop—Adaptations 2. Fables 3. Folklore 4. Stories without words

ISBN 978-0-316-01356-7; 0-316-01356-0

LC 2008-43852

Awarded the Caldecott Medal (2010)

In this wordless retelling of an Aesop fable, an adventuresome mouse proves that even small creatures are capable of great deeds when he rescues the King of the Jungle.

Young readers will be drawn "into watercolors of . . . detail and splendor. Pinkney's soft, multihued strokes make everything in the jungle seem alive. . . . His luxuriant use of close-ups humanizes his animal characters without idealizing them." Booklist

The little match girl; [by] Hans Christian Andersen; adapted and illustrated by Jerry Pinkney. Phyllis Fogelman Books 1999 unp il hardcover o.p. pa $6.99

Grades: 1 2 3 4   E

1. Andersen, Hans Christian, 1805-1875—Adaptations 2. Fairy tales

ISBN 0-8037-2314-8; 0-14-230188-4 (pa)

LC 99-13814

The wares of the poor little match girl illuminate her cold world, bringing some beauty to her brief, tragic life

"A faithful retelling of a classic tale. . . . The story's haunting death imagery . . . may disturb the very young, but ultimately Pinkney's vision proves as transcendent as Andersen's." Publ Wkly

Rikki-tikki-tavi; by Rudyard Kipling; adapted and illustrated by Jerry Pinkney. Morrow Junior Bks. 1997 unp il $16.99; pa $6.99 *

Grades: 1 2 3 4   E

1. Kipling, Rudyard, 1865-1936—Adaptations 2. Mongooses—Fiction 3. Cobras—Fiction 4. India—Fiction

ISBN 0-688-14320-2; 0-06-058785-7 (pa)

LC 96-51194

This is a retelling of the story from Rudyard Kipling's The jungle book in which a mongoose saves an English boy and his family from cobras in their garden in India

"Dramatic in content, sensitive in line, and rich with color, the illustrations in this picture book make full use of the broad, double-page spreads. Children who are not familiar with the story will be captivated; those who have had the story read to them before will find new things to shiver over." Booklist

The ugly duckling; [by] Hans Christian Andersen; adapted and illustrated by Jerry Pinkney. Morrow Junior Bks. 1999 unp il $16.99; lib bdg $17.89 *

Grades: 1 2 3 4   E

1. Andersen, Hans Christian, 1805-1875—Adaptations 2. Swans—Fiction 3. Fairy tales

ISBN 0-688-15932-X; 0-688-15933-8 (lib bdg)

LC 98-23604

A Caldecott Medal honor book, 2000

An ugly duckling spends an unhappy year ostracized by the other animals before he grows into a beautiful swan

"This is an elegantly accessible retelling, with illustrations full of lively, emotive animals and the kind of vigorous movement that young children are bound to find appealing." Bull Cent Child Books

Pinkney, Sandra L.

Read and rise; photographs by Myles C. Pinkney; foreword by Maya Angelou. Scholastic 2006 unp il $15.99

Grades: PreK K 1   E

1. Reading 2. African American children

ISBN 0-439-30929-8

"Cartwheel books"

Photographs and poetic text celebrate reading as a means of encouraging African American children to pur-

Pinkney, Sandra L.—*Continued*

sue their dreams

"Powerful verbs match the vivid portrayal of children succeeding." SLJ

Shades of black; a celebration of our children; photographs by Myles C. Pinkney. Scholastic 2000 unp il $14.95; bd bk $6.99 *

Grades: PreK K 1   E

1. African Americans

ISBN 0-439-14892-8; 0-439-80251-2 (bd bk)

LC 99-86593

"Cartwheel books"

Photographs and text celebrate the beauty and diversity of African American children

"Wonderful, clear, full-color photographs of youngsters illustrate a poetic, vivid text that describes a range of skin and eye colors and hair textures." SLJ

Pinkwater, Daniel Manus, 1941-

Bear's picture; written by Daniel Pinkwater; illustrated by D. B. Johnson. Houghton Mifflin Company 2008 unp il $16 *

Grades: K 1 2 3   E

1. Bears—Fiction 2. Painting—Fiction

ISBN 978-0-618-75923-1; 0-618-75923-9

LC 2007-15149

A newly illustrated edittion of the title first published 1972 by Holt, Rinehart and Winston

A bear continues to paint what he likes despite criticism from two passing gentlemen.

This is "a quirky, sardonic, and highly entertaining view of what makes art. . . . Johnson . . . provides . . . fabulous mixed-media artwork, including paper sculptures that add both angular dimension and a wry touch to the simple story." Booklist

Piper, Watty

The little engine that could; retold by Watty Piper; illustrated by George & Doris Hauman. Grosset & Dunlap 2009 c1930 unp il $17.99 *

Grades: PreK K 1 2   E

1. Railroads—Fiction 2. Toys—Fiction

ISBN 978-0-448-45257-9; 0-448-45257-X

LC 2009-9031

First published 1930

"When a train carrying good things to children breaks down, the little blue engine proves his courage and determination. The rhythmic, repetitive text encourages children to help tell the story." Hodges. Books for Elem Sch Libr

The little engine that could; illustrated by Loren Long. Philomel 2005 unp il $17.99 *

Grades: PreK K 1 2   E

1. Railroads—Fiction 2. Toys—Fiction

ISBN 0-399-24467-0

A newly illustrated edition of the title first published 1930 by Grosset & Dunlap

Although she is not very big, the Little Blue Engine agrees to try to pull a stranded train full of toys over the mountain.

"Grand in scale but cozy in effect, the impressive acrylic paintings use subtle strokes of rich colors to create a series of narrative scenes large enough to be clearly visible back to the last row of storytime or classroom. . . . This edition provides a brilliant new setting that many readers will prefer to the original picture book." Booklist

Piven, Hanoch, 1963-

My best friend is as sharp as a pencil; and other funny classroom portraits. Schwartz & Wade 2010 unp il $17.99

Grades: K 1 2 3   E

1. Portraits—Fiction

ISBN 978-0-375-85338-8; 0-375-85338-3

"Vibrant portraits in words and realia-collage illustrations, purportedly created by the child narrator in anticipation of her grandmother's inevitable questions about school, will delight readers. One double-page spread gives each new character's traits, expressed in several verbal metaphors . . . and in photos of objects. . . . On the next spread, a painting incorporating those objects forms an eye-catching, idiosyncratic portrait." Booklist

My dog is as smelly as dirty socks; and other funny family portraits. Schwartz & Wade 2007 unp il $16.99; lib bdg $18.99

Grades: PreK K 1 2   E

1. Portraits—Fiction 2. Family life—Fiction

ISBN   978-0-375-84052-4;   0-375-84052-4; 978-0-375-94052-1 (lib bdg); 0-375-94052-9 (lib bdg)

LC 2006-21936

A young girl draws a family portrait, then makes it more accurate by adding common objects to show aspects of each member's personality, such as her father's playfulness, her mother's sweetness, and her brother's strength

"Childlike line drawings are paired with the more creative portraits, in which representational objects are glued on gouache-and-watercolor backgrounds to make the figures. Children will get caught up in this playful, fun, creative, and easy-to-do art concept and will want to follow through with their own creations." Booklist

Plourde, Lynn, 1955-

Field trip day; illustrated by Thor Wickstrom. Dutton Children's Books 2010 unp il $16.99

Grades: PreK K 1 2   E

1. Farm life—Fiction 2. School stories

ISBN 978-0-525-47994-9; 0-525-47994-5

Today is Field Trip Day at school, and everyone in Mrs. Shepherd's class is excited to visit Fandangle's Farm, especially Juan, who loves to explore. But Juan just might be too good at exploring, and Mrs. Shepherd and the chaperones have trouble keeping track of him!

"This good-natured story . . . will appeal to children, especially those who adore farm animals. The watercolor-and-ink cartoons are lively and depict a diverse class that lauds thinking and questioning over strict rule-keeping." SLJ

Plourde, Lynn, 1955-—*Continued*

Grandpappy snippy snappies; illustrated by Christopher Santoro. HarperCollinsPublishers 2009 unp il $17.99

Grades: PreK K 1 2   E
    1. Farmers—Fiction 2. Clothing and dress—Fiction 3. Stories in rhyme
    ISBN 978-0-06-028050-5; 0-06-028050-6
                LC 2001-24328

When things go wrong around his farm Grandpappy sets them right with a snap of his suspenders, but Grandmammy is in trouble and the suspenders are all worn out

"This whimsical tale of an everyday hero has a rhyming text and lively illustrations. . . . Santoro's digital mixed-media illustrations animate the tale in a wonderful way. Together the cartoon and realistic elements add depth, detail, and humor to the tale." SLJ

A mountain of mittens; [by] Lynn Plourde; illustrated by Mitch Vane. Charlesbridge 2007 unp il $15.95; pa $7.95

Grades: PreK K 1   E
    1. Clothing and dress—Fiction 2. Lost and found possessions—Fiction
    ISBN 978-1-57091-585-7; 978-1-57091-466-9 (pa)
                LC 2006021253

Molly's parents try various methods to help her remember her mittens but nothing seems to work.

"Readers will chuckle as they recognize what a problem mateless mittens can become. Vane's watercolor-and-ink drawings have a jaunty air." Booklist

Pochocki, Ethel, 1925-

The blessing of the beasts; by Ethel Pochocki; illustrated by Barry Moser. Paraclete Press 2007 39p il $18.95

Grades: K 1 2 3   E
    1. Cockroaches—Fiction 2. Skunks—Fiction 3. Animals—Fiction 4. Religion—Fiction 5. New York (N.Y.)—Fiction
    ISBN 978-1-55725-502-0; 1-55725-502-4
                LC 2007002231

Martin the skunk and Francesca the cockroach wend their way across the city to attend the blessing of the animals celebration on the Feast of St. Francis at the Cathedral of St. John the Divine.

This is a "a delightful fantasy. . . . Cats and dogs are the usual celebrants at the real service; here they are joined by lions, bears, and falcons. . . . Funny, sly, and noble, the animal pictures range from amusing takeoffs to moving tributes." Booklist

Polacco, Patricia

Babushka's doll. Simon & Schuster Bks. for Young Readers 1990 unp il hardcover o.p. pa $6.95

Grades: K 1 2 3   E
    1. Dolls—Fiction
    ISBN 0-671-68343-8; 0-689-80255-2 (pa)
                LC 89-6122

"When Natasha wants something, she wants it now—not after her grandmother, Babushka, has finished her chores. Babushka gets tired of this attitude, and finally goes off to the market, leaving Natasha to play with a special doll that she keeps on a high shelf. The doll comes to life and subjects Natasha to the same sort of insistent whining that Natasha used on Babushka." SLJ

"Polacco's distinctive artwork interprets the story with style and verve. Using pencil, marker, and paint, she creates a series of varied compositions, highlighting muted shades with an occasional flare of bright colors and strong patterns. . . . A good, original story, illustrated with panache." Booklist

Chicken Sunday. Philomel Bks. 1992 unp il $16.99; pa $6.99 *

Grades: K 1 2 3   E
    1. Easter—Fiction 2. Friendship—Fiction 3. Jews—Fiction 4. African Americans—Fiction
    ISBN 0-399-22133-6; 0-698-11615-1 (pa)
                LC 91-16030

To thank old Eula for her wonderful Sunday chicken dinners, her two grandsons and their friend, a girl who has "adopted" her since her own "babushka" died, sell decorated eggs and buy her a beautiful Easter hat

"Without being heavy-handed, Polacco's text conveys a tremendous pride of heritage as it brims with rich images from her characters' African American and Russian Jewish cultures. Her vibrant pencil-and-wash illustrations glow—actual family photographs have been worked into several spreads." Publ Wkly

G is for goat. Philomel Bks. 2003 unp il $16.99; pa $6.99; bd bk $6.99 *

Grades: PreK K 1 2   E
    1. Goats 2. Alphabet 3. Stories in rhyme
    ISBN   0-399-24018-7;   0-14-240550-7   (pa); 0-399-24530-8 (bd bk)   LC 2002-11551

A rhyming celebration of goats and their antics, from A to Z

"The charming animals will energize any storytime. . . . The pencil-and-watercolor illustrations against white backgrounds steal the spotlight, with charming details." SLJ

Ginger and Petunia; [by] Patricia Polacco. Philomel Books 2007 unp il $16.99 *

Grades: K 1 2 3   E
    1. Pigs—Fiction
    ISBN 978-0-399-24539-8   LC 2006024878

When her beloved Ginger, a piano-playing socialite and very snappy dresser, makes a last-minute trip to London not knowing her housesitter has cancelled, Petunia the pig does more than fend for herself, she becomes Ginger.

"Polacco's comic portrayal of pampered pet and attentive owner is spot-on—and her characteristic watercolor illustrations highlight both characters' sense of fashion and joie de vivre. . . . A delight from start to finish." Booklist

In our mothers' house. Philomel Books 2009 unp il $17.99

Grades: 1 2 3 4   E
    1. Lesbians—Fiction 2. Mothers—Fiction 3. Family life—Fiction 4. Adoption—Fiction
    ISBN 978-0-399-25076-7; 0-399-25076-X
                LC 2008-32615

Polacco, Patricia—*Continued*

"The oldest of three adopted children recalls her childhood with mothers Marmee and Meema, as they raised their African American daughter, Asian American son, and Caucasian daughter in a lively, supportive neighborhood. . . . The energetic illustrations in pencil and marker, . . . teem with family activities and neighborhood festivity." Booklist

John Philip Duck. Philomel Books 2004 unp il $16.99 *
Grades: K 1 2 3   E
1. Ducks—Fiction 2. Hotels and motels—Fiction 3. Memphis (Tenn.)—Fiction
ISBN 0-399-24262-7
During the Depression, a young Memphis boy trains his pet duck to do tricks in the fountain of a grand hotel and ends up becoming the Duck Master of the Peabody Hotel
"This is Polacco at the height of her form in terms of both text and illustration. The story moves smoothly from start to finish and has a refreshing air of innocence. The artwork is simply beautiful as the artist orchestrates a harmonious symphony of color." SLJ

The keeping quilt. rev format ed. Simon & Schuster Bks. for Young Readers 1998 unp il $17.95; pa $6.99 *
Grades: K 1 2 3   E
1. Quilts—Fiction 2. Jews—Fiction
ISBN 0-689-82090-9; 0-689-84447-6 (pa)
LC 97-47690
A reissue of the title first published 1988
A homemade quilt ties together the lives of four generations of an immigrant Jewish family, remaining a symbol of their enduring love and faith
"Jewish customs and the way they've shifted through the years are portrayed unobtrusively in the story, which is illustrated in sepia pencil, except for the quilt, which sparks every page with its strong colors." Booklist

The Lemonade Club; [by] Patricia Polacco. Philomel Books 2007 unp il $16.99 *
Grades: 2 3 4   E
1. Cancer—Fiction 2. Teachers—Fiction 3. School stories 4. Friendship—Fiction
ISBN 978-0-399-24540-4   LC 2007011440
When Marilyn and her teacher, Miss Wichelman, both get cancer, they encourage each other and, aided by medical treatments and support from friends, they get better. Based on a true story.
"Polacco continues to draw from rich family experiences to weave satisfying, inspirations stories. . . . Pencil-and-marker illustrations in Polacco's usual free style gently convey the emotions." Booklist

Mr. Lincoln's way. Philomel Bks. 2001 unp il $16.99 *
Grades: K 1 2 3   E
1. Prejudices—Fiction 2. School stories
ISBN 0-399-23754-2   LC 00-66939
When Mr. Lincoln, "the coolest principal in the whole world," discovers that Eugene, the school bully, knows a lot about birds, he uses this interest to help Eugene overcome his intolerance

"The book may be useful to schools in need of a springboard for discussion of the topic and is graced with impressive watercolors." SLJ

Mrs. Katz and Tush. Doubleday Books for Young Readers 1992 unp il $16.99; lib bdg $19.99; pa $6.99
Grades: K 1 2 3   E
1. Friendship—Fiction 2. Jews—Fiction 3. African Americans—Fiction
ISBN 0-553-08122-5; 0-385-90650-1 (lib bdg); 0-440-40936-5 (pa)   LC 91-18710
A long-lasting friendship develops between Larnel, a young African-American, and Mrs. Katz, a lonely, Jewish widow, when Larnel presents Mrs. Katz with a scrawny kitten without a tail
"Polacco has used loving details in both words and art work to craft a moving and heartfelt story of a friendship that reaches across racial and generational differences." Horn Book

My rotten redheaded older brother. Simon & Schuster Bks. for Young Readers 1994 unp il $17.95; pa $6.99
Grades: PreK K 1 2 3   E
1. Siblings—Fiction
ISBN 0-671-72751-6; 0-689-82036-4 (pa)
LC 93-13980
"Featuring an obnoxious, freckle-faced, bespectacled boy and a comforting, tale-telling grandmother, this autobiographical story is as satisfying as a warm slice of apple pie. Patricia can't quite understand how anyone could possibly like her older brother Richard. Whether picking blackberries or eating raw rhubarb, he always manages to outdo her, rubbing it in with one of his 'extra-rotten, weasel-eyed, greeny-toothed grins.' When their Bubbie teaches Patricia to wish on a falling star, she knows just what to ask for." SLJ

Oh, look! Philomel Books 2004 unp il $16.99 *
Grades: PreK K 1 2   E
1. Goats—Fiction
ISBN 0-399-24223-6
Three goats visit a fair but run home after they seem to encounter a troll.
"In this colorful picture book, the . . . author transfers the rhythms and movement of the traditional bear-hunt chant to safer ground. . . . Polacco's signature pencil-and-watercolor paintings cascade across the pages, creating festive scenes and bright hues." SLJ

Pink and Say. Philomel Bks. 1994 unp il $16.99 *
Grades: 2 3 4   E
1. Friendship—Fiction 2. African American soldiers—Fiction 3. United States—History—1861-1865, Civil War—Fiction
ISBN 0-399-22671-0   LC 93-36340
Say Curtis describes his meeting with Pinkus Aylee, a black soldier, during the Civil War, and their capture by Southern troops
"Polacco pulls out all the stops in this heart-wrenching tale . . . which has been passed through several generations of the author's family. . . . Polacco's signature

Polacco, Patricia—*Continued*
line-and-watercolor paintings epitomize heroism, tenderness, and terror. . . . Unglamorized details of the conventions and atrocities of the Civil War target readers well beyond customary picture book age." Horn Book

Rechenka's eggs; written and illustrated by Patricia Polacco. Philomel Bks. 1988 unp il lib bdg $16.99; pa $6.99 *
Grades: K 1 2 3   E
1. Geese—Fiction 2. Easter—Fiction 3. Eggs—Fiction
ISBN 0-399-21501-8 (lib bdg); 0-698-11385-3 (pa)
LC 87-16588
An injured goose rescued by Babushka, having broken the painted eggs intended for the Easter Festival in Moscva, lays thirteen marvelously colored eggs to replace them, then leaves behind one final miracle in egg form before returning to her own kind
"Polacco achieves optimal dramatic contrast by using bold shapes against uncluttered white space and by contrasting rich colors and design details with faces in black and white." Bull Cent Child Books

Someone for Mr. Sussman; [by] Patricia Polacco. Philomel Books 2008 unp il $16.99
Grades: 2 3 4   E
1. Grandmothers—Fiction 2. Dating (Social customs)—Fiction 3. Jews—United States—Fiction
ISBN 978-0-399-25075-0; 0-399-25075-1
LC 2008000660
Although she is the best matchmaker in the neighborhood, Jerome's Bubbie has a hard time finding a match for the fussy Mr. Sussman
"The author brings in homey, Fiddler on the Roof syntax . . . along with words like 'oy' and 'farklempt,' illustrating the story in her signature style of comfortable caricatures and broad strokes. A good-natured spirit percolates throughout." Publ Wkly

Thank you, Mr. Falker. Philomel Bks. 1998 unp il $16.99 *
Grades: K 1 2 3   E
1. Reading—Fiction 2. Teachers—Fiction 3. Learning disabilities—Fiction
ISBN 0-399-23166-8   LC 97-18685
At first, Trisha loves school, but her difficulty learning to read makes her feel dumb, until, in the fifth grade, a new teacher helps her understand and overcome her problem
"Young readers struggling with learning difficulties will identify with Trisha's situation and find reassurance in her success. Polacco's gouache-and-pencil compositions deftly capture the emotional stages—frustration, pain, elation—of Trisha's journey." Publ Wkly

The trees of the dancing goats. Simon & Schuster Bks. for Young Readers 1996 unp il hardcover o.p. pa $6.99 *
Grades: K 1 2 3   E
1. Hanukkah—Fiction 2. Christmas—Fiction 3. Jews—Fiction
ISBN 0-689-80862-3; 0-689-83857-3 (pa)
LC 95-26670
"On the family farm in Michigan, Trisha and Richard watch as Babushka and Grampa prepare for Hanukkah in

their native Russian way. . . . When scarlet fever debilitates their neighbors, Trisha's whole family pitches in to make and deliver holiday dinners and Christmas trees." Publ Wkly

Polhemus, Coleman
The crocodile blues; [by] Coleman Polhemus. Candlewick Press 2007 unp il $16.99
Grades: PreK K   E
1. Crocodiles—Fiction 2. Eggs—Fiction 3. Stories without words
ISBN 978-0-7636-3543-5; 0-7636-3543-X
LC 2006051848
A wordless tale in which a man and his pet cockatoo discover, much to their dismay, the true nature of the egg they bring home from the store
"Youngsters will laugh at both the story line and the characters depicted in this zany book. The simple royal blue and black silhouettes capture the feeling of the dark night, and the bright yellow of the daylight offers a realistic contrast." SLJ

Politi, Leo, 1908-1996
Emmet. Getty Publications 2009 unp il $16.95
Grades: PreK K 1 2   E
1. Dogs—Fiction
ISBN 978-0-89236-992-8; 0-89236-992-2
A reissue of the title first published 1971 by Scribner
Emmet, one of the many stray dogs taken in by old Mr. Winkel, was always the troublemaker of the lot. Mr. Winkel's neighbors are ready to call the dogcatcher when the rascally dog saves the grocer's shop from a fire set by a prowler.

Juanita. Getty Publications 2009 unp il $16.95
Grades: K 1 2 3   E
1. Mexican Americans—Fiction 2. Los Angeles (Calif.)—Fiction 3. Birthdays—Fiction 4. Easter—Fiction
ISBN 978-0-89236-991-1; 0-89236-991-4
A Caldecott honor book, 1949
A reissue of the title first published 1948 by Scribner
Juanita, a Mexican girl of Olvera Street in Los Angeles, brings the dove she received for her birthday to the Blessing of the Animals on the day before Easter.
"The pictures in soft colors have a warmth and tenderness." Horn Book

Pedro, the angel of Olvera Street. Getty Publications 2009 unp il $14.96
Grades: K 1 2 3   E
1. Mexican Americans—Fiction 2. Los Angeles (Calif.)—Fiction 3. Christmas—Fiction
ISBN 978-0-89236-990-4; 0-89236-990-6
A Caldecott Medal honor book, 1947
A reissue of the title first published 1946 by Scribner
Little Pedro, who sings like an angel, is allowed to lead the Christmas procession, known as La Posada, through the old Mexican section of downtown Los Angeles.
"Beguiling both in text and in the pictures with their soft, rich colors." Bookmark

Politi, Leo, 1908-1996—*Continued*

Song of the swallows. Getty Publications 2009 unp il $16.98

Grades: 2 3 4   E
1. Swallows—Fiction 2. California—Fiction 3. Missions—Fiction
ISBN 978-0-89236-989-8; 0-89236-989-2
Awarded the Caldecott Medal, 1950
A reissue of the title first published 1949 by Scribner

Sad when the swallows leave for the winter, young Juan prepares to welcome them back to the old California Mission at Capistrano on St. Joseph's Day the next spring.

This is a "tender poetic story. . . Lovely pictures in soft colors bring out the charm of the southern California landscape and the melody of the swallow song adds to the feeling of Spring." Horn Book

Pomerantz, Charlotte

The chalk doll; pictures by Frané Lessac. Lippincott 1989 30p il pa $6.99 hardcover o.p.

Grades: K 1 2 3   E
1. Dolls—Fiction 2. Mother-daughter relationship—Fiction 3. Jamaica—Fiction
ISBN 0-06-443333-1 (pa)   LC 88-872

"Rose has a cold and must stay in bed. Before she settles in for a nap, she coaxes her mother to tell stories of her Jamaican childhood. The scene shifts from Rose's colorful room filled with toys to a simple little house in the village where her mother grew up. The stories are touching for the contrast between the poverty and yearning of these childhood memories and the obvious comfort of their present lives." Horn Book

"The stylized illustrations by the West Indian artists Frané Lessac are primitive in bright, oscillating colors, evoking poverty in a tropical paradise as well as mother-daughter affection in a well-appointed home." N Y Times Book Rev

Poole, Amy Lowry

The pea blossom; retold and illustrated by Amy Poole. Holiday House 2005 unp il hardcover o.p. pa $6.95 *

Grades: K 1 2 3   E
1. Andersen, Hans Christian, 1805-1875—Adaptations 2. Fairy tales 3. China—Fiction
ISBN 0-8234-1864-2; 0-8234-2018-3 (pa)
               LC 2003-67544
Based on the Hans Christian Andersen story: Five peas in a pod

In a garden near Beijing, five peas in a shell grow and wait to discover what fate has in store for them.

"Choosing to set her version in Beijing, China, Poole illustrates her simple, elegant prose with watercolors on rice paper that are clearly reminiscent of Chinese paintings." Booklist

Portis, Antoinette

Not a box. HarperCollins 2007 unp il $12.99; lib bdg $14.89 *

Grades: PreK K   E
1. Imagination—Fiction 2. Rabbits—Fiction 3. Boxes—Fiction
ISBN 978-0-06-112322-1; 0-06-112322-6; 978-0-06-112323-8 (lib bdg); 0-06-112323-4 (lib bdg)
               LC 2006002477
To an imaginative bunny, a box is not always just a box.

"The spare, streamlined design and the visual messages about imagination's power will easily draw young children, who will recognize their own flights of fantasy." Booklist

Not a stick. HarperCollinsPublishers 2008 unp il $12.99; lib bdg $14.89 *

Grades: PreK K   E
1. Imagination—Fiction 2. Play—Fiction 3. Pigs—Fiction
ISBN 978-0-06-112325-2; 0-06-112325-0; 978-0-06-112326-9 (lib bdg); 0-06-112326-9 (lib bdg)
               LC 2007-14475
An imaginative young pig shows some of the many things that a stick can be.

"Portis's simple color palette and playful drawings with never a line out of place represent the best in children's illustration." SLJ

A penguin story. HarperCollins 2009 unp il $17.99; lib bdg $18.89 *

Grades: PreK K 1 2   E
1. Penguins—Fiction 2. Color—Fiction
ISBN 978-0-06-145688-6; 0-06-145688-8; 978-0-06-145689-3 (lib bdg); 0-06-145689-6 (lib bdg)
               LC 2008020210
Edna the penguin tries to find something in her surroundings that is not black, white, or blue.

"This gentle tribute to dreamers crackles with quiet humor, and the art's limited palette both parallels the plot and lends the book a classic feel. Portis's ability to convey emotion and character through the slightest change in Edna's beady eyes and flippers is extraordinary, and the interplay of the text and pictures nears perfection. A delightful story, delightfully told." SLJ

Portnoy, Mindy Avra

Tale of two Seders; illustrated by Valeria Cis. Kar-Ben Pub. 2010 32p il lib bdg $17.95; pa $7.95

Grades: PreK K 1 2   E
1. Passover—Fiction 2. Jews—Fiction 3. Divorce—Fiction 4. Family life—Fiction
ISBN 978-0-8225-9907-4; 0-8225-9907-4; 978-0-8225-9931-9 (pa); 0-8225-9931-7 (pa)
               LC 2008033570
After her parents' divorce, a young girl experiences a variety of Passover seders. Includes recipes and facts about Passover.

"Cis's delightful acrylic paintings beautifully complement the text. . . . [This is a] realistic, contemporary story." SLJ

Potter, Beatrix, 1866-1943

The story of Miss Moppet. Warne 2002 32p il $6.99

Grades: PreK K 1 2 3　　　　　　　　E

1. Cats—Fiction 2. Mice—Fiction

ISBN 0-7232-4790-0

First published 1906

Miss Moppet is a kitten who uses her wiles to capture a curious mouse. But her trickery amounts to naught when she herself is outwitted

Other titles about Moppet's brother Tom and sister Mittens are:

The complete adventures of Tom Kitten and his friends (1984)

The roly-poly pudding (1908)

The tale of Tom Kitten (1935)

The tailor of Gloucester. Warne 2002 56p il $6.99 *

Grades: PreK K 1 2 3　　　　　　　　E

1. Tailoring—Fiction 2. Mice—Fiction 3. Christmas—Fiction

ISBN 0-7232-4772-2

First published in 1903

"The cat Simpkin looked after his master when he was ill, but it was the nimble-fingered mice who used snippets of cherry-coloured twist and so finished the embroidered waist coat for the worried tailor. A Christmastime story set in old Gloucester." Four to Fourteen

"A read-aloud classic in polished style, perfectly complemented by the author's exquisite watercolor illustrations." Hodges. Books for Elem Sch Libr

The tale of Jemima Puddle-duck. Warne 2002 56p il $6.99; bd bk $6.99 *

Grades: PreK K 1 2 3　　　　　　　　E

1. Ducks—Fiction

ISBN 0-7232-4778-1; 0-7232-6434-1 (bd bk)

First published 1908

"Jemima Puddle-duck's obstinate determination to hatch her own eggs, makes a story of suspense and sly humor." Toronto Public Libr. Books for Boys & Girls

The tale of Mr. Jeremy Fisher. Warne 2002 56p il $6.99 *

Grades: PreK K 1 2 3　　　　　　　　E

1. Frogs—Fiction

ISBN 0-7232-4776-5

First published 1906

A frog fishing from his lilly pad boat doesn't catch any fish, but one catches him

The tale of Mrs. Tiggy-Winkle. Warne 2002 56p il $6.99 *

Grades: PreK K 1 2 3　　　　　　　　E

1. Hedgehogs—Fiction

ISBN 0-7232-4775-7

First published 1905

Lucie visits the laundry of Mrs. Tiggy-Winkle, a hedgehog, and finds her lost handerchiefs

The tale of Mrs. Tittlemouse. Warne 2002 56p il $6.99

Grades: PreK K 1 2 3　　　　　　　　E

1. Mice—Fiction

ISBN 0-7232-3470-1

First published 1910

The story of a little mouse's funny house, the visitors she has there, and how she finally rids herself of the untidy, messy ones

The tale of Peter Rabbit. Warne 2002 69p il $6.99 *

Grades: PreK K 1 2 3　　　　　　　　E

1. Rabbits—Fiction

ISBN 0-7232-4770-6

First published 1903

All about the famous rabbit family consisting of Flopsy, Mopsy, Cotton-tail and especially Peter Rabbit who disobeys Mother Rabbit's admonishment not to go into Mr. McGregor's garden

"Distinctive writing and a strong appeal to a small child's sense of justice and his sympathies make this an outstanding story. The water color illustrations add charm to the narrative by their simplicity of detail and delicacy of color." Child Books Too Good to Miss

Other titles about Peter Rabbit and his family are:

The tale of Benjamin Bunny (1904)

The tale of Mr. Tod (1912)

The tale of the flopsy bunnies (1909)

The tale of Pigling Bland. Warne 2002 80p il $6.99 *

Grades: PreK K 1 2 3　　　　　　　　E

1. Pigs—Fiction

ISBN 0-7232-4784-6

First published 1913

"Pigling's story ends happily with a perfectly lovely little black Berkshire pig called Pigwig." Toronto Public Libr. Books for Boys & Girls

The tale of Squirrel Nutkin. Warne 2002 56p il $6.99 *

Grades: PreK K 1 2 3　　　　　　　　E

1. Squirrels—Fiction

ISBN 0-7232-4771-4

First published 1903

Each day the squirrels gather nuts, Nutkin propounds a riddle to Mr. Brown, the owl, until impertinent Nutkin, over-estimating Mr. Brown's patience, gets his due

The tale of Timmy Tiptoes. Warne 2002 56p il $6.99 *

Grades: PreK K 1 2 3　　　　　　　　E

1. Squirrels—Fiction

ISBN 0-7232-4781-1

First published 1911

An innocent squirrel accused of stealing nuts is forced down a hole in a tree, where he meets a friendly chipmunk

Potter, Beatrix, 1866-1943—*Continued*
The tale of two bad mice. Warne 2002 56p il
$6.99 *
Grades: PreK K 1 2 3   E
    1. Mice—Fiction
    ISBN 0-7232-4774-9
    First published 1904
    "Two mischievous little mice pilfer a doll's house to
equip their own. They are caught and finally make
amends for what they have done. Perfectly charming illustrations and a most enticing tale." Adventuring With
Books. 2d edition

Pow, Tom, 1950-
Tell me one thing, Dad; illustrated by Ian
Andrew. Candlewick Press 2004 unp il $15.99
Grades: PreK K 1 2 3   E
    1. Father-daughter relationship—Fiction 2. Bedtime—
Fiction
    ISBN 0-7636-2474-8   LC 2003-65272
    Molly and her father play a bedtime game that shows
how much they love each other
    "The sharp yet simple text avoids the obvious, going
for interesting images. . . . The watercolor-and-ink
artwork . . . brims with whimsy in both design and execution." Booklist

Poydar, Nancy
The biggest test in the universe. Holiday House
2005 unp il $16.95 *
Grades: K 1 2 3   E
    1. School stories 2. Examinations—Fiction
    ISBN 0-8234-1944-4
    Sam and his classmates dread Friday, the day they are
to take the infamous Big Test.
    "Enlivened by colorful and humorous illustrations de-
picting the students' worries, this book is fun and cheerful, as well as unique in its subject." SLJ

Fish school. Holiday House 2009 unp il $16.95
Grades: PreK K 1 2   E
    1. Goldfish—Fiction 2. Marine aquariums—Fiction
3. School stories
    ISBN 978-0-8234-2140-4; 0-8234-2140-6
                            LC 2008022576
    Charlie tries to educate his pet goldfish by taking him
to school and to the aquarium on a class trip. Includes
tips on the care and feeding of goldfish.
    "Filled with lively and amusing details, this is a good
choice for one-on-one or independent reading." SLJ

Preller, James, 1961-
Mighty Casey; by James Preller; illustrated by
Matthew Cordell. Feiwel and Friends 2008 unp il
$16.95
Grades: K 1 2 3   E
    1. Stories in rhyme 2. Baseball—Fiction
    ISBN 978-0-312-36764-0; 0-312-36764-3
                            LC 2007-47331
    The Delmar Dogs baseball team is terrible, especially
Casey Jenkins, but with a little bit of faith in themselves,

they finally manage to win a game.
    "Set against ample white space, Cordell's endearingly
geeky kids take center stage. . . . It's hard to envision
a reader who won't take to these underdogs." Publ Wkly

Prelutsky, Jack
The wizard; by Jack Prelutsky; illustrations by
Brandon Dorman. Greenwillow Books 2007 unp il
$16.99; lib bdg $17.89 *
Grades: K 1 2 3   E
    1. Magic—Fiction 2. Stories in rhyme
    ISBN 978-0-06-124076-8; 978-0-06-124077-5 (lib
bdg)
    The verse originally appeared in the 1976 collection
Nightmares: Poems to Trouble Your Sleep
    An illustrated, rhyming tale of a wicked wizard and
his evil deeds, as he uses "elemental sorcery" to change
a bullfrog into a series of objects, from a flea to a flame.
    "The illustrator's digital artwork has all the burnished
lushness and radiance of oil paintings. . . . Dorman
proves his mettle as a marvelous visual storyteller." Publ
Wkly

Preus, Margi
The Peace Bell; illustrated by Hideko
Takahashi. Henry Holt and Co. 2008 unp il $16.95
Grades: K 1 2 3   E
    1. Bells—Fiction 2. Grandmothers—Fiction 3. New
Year—Fiction 4. Friendship—Fiction 5. Japan—Fiction 6. Peace—Fiction
    ISBN 978-0-8050-7800-8; 0-8050-7800-2
                            LC 2007040897
    Yoko's grandmother tells about how the bell in their
town that would ring on New Year's Eve is given up
during the war for scrap metal, finds its way back to
their village, and becomes known as the Peace Bell.
    "The simple plot is clearly developed with descriptive
language, and an author's note provides more historical
details. Done in Japanese acrylic paints, the realistic illustrations accurately portray the setting and capture the
characters' various emotions." SLJ

Prévert, Jacques, 1900-1977
How to paint the portrait of a bird; translated
and illustrated by Mordicai Gerstein. Roaring
Brook 2007 unp il $14.95 *
Grades: K 1 2 3   E
    1. Birds—Fiction
    ISBN 1-59643-215-2; 978-1-59643-215-4
                            LC 2006-32183
    "This petite, elegant picture book . . . delivers a
mind-stretching allegory of artistic creation. First, a
wordless sequence shows a mopheaded boy awakening to
a bluebird's trill. Palette in hand, he follows a peculiar
series of instructions for capturing its likeness: paint a
cage; lure the bird into it; . . . erase the cage, replacing
it with a forest; then see if the bird will sing. It's a delight to see how Gerstein's scribbly lines and loose
washes cohere into playful, accessible images." Booklist

Priceman, Marjorie

Hot air; the (mostly) true story of the first hot-air balloon ride. Atheneum Books for Young Readers 2005 unp il $16.95 *

Grades: K 1 2 3   E

1. Balloons

ISBN 0-689-82642-7   LC 2004-14743

A Caldecott Medal honor book, 2006

"An Anne Schwartz book"

"Combining fact and fancy, Priceman tells the story of the successful 1783 liftoff of a hot-air balloon, invented by the Montgolfier brothers, a flight made even more special because of its passengers: a duck, a sheep, and a rooster." Booklist

"With vibrant colors and varied use of panels, full-page illustrations, and spreads, Priceman paces the tale perfectly." SLJ

How to make a cherry pie and see the U.S.A. Alfred A. Knopf 2008 unp il $16.99; lib bdg $19.99

Grades: PreK K 1 2   E

1. United States—Fiction 2. Voyages and travels—Fiction 3. Baking—Fiction

ISBN 978-0-375-81255-2; 0-375-81255-5; 978-0-375-91255-9 (lib bdg); 0-375-91255-X (lib bdg)

LC 2007-46064

Since the Cook Shop is closed, the reader is led around the United States to gather coal, cotton, granite, and other natural resources needed to make the utensils for preparing a cherry pie

"The trip is a madcap adventure. . . . The art brims with good cheer and excites with detail." Booklist

How to make an apple pie and see the world. Knopf 1994 unp il $16; pa $6.99 *

Grades: PreK K 1 2   E

1. Baking—Fiction 2. Voyages and travels—Fiction

ISBN 0-679-83705-1; 0-679-88083-6 (pa)

LC 93-12341

Since the market is closed, the reader is led around the world to gather the ingredients for making an apple pie

"The perfect blend of whimsical illustrations and tongue-in-cheek humor makes this an irresistible offering. The recipe is included." Child Book Rev Serv

Prigger, Mary Skillings

Aunt Minnie McGranahan; illustrated by Betsy Lewin. Clarion Bks. 1999 31p il $15; pa $5.95

Grades: K 1 2 3   E

1. Aunts—Fiction 2. Orphans—Fiction

ISBN 0-395-82270-X; 0-618-60488-X (pa)

LC 98-33501

The townspeople in St. Clere, Kansas, are sure it will never work out when the neat and orderly spinster, Minnie McGranahan, takes her nine orphaned nieces and nephews into her home in 1920

"In a dexterous style, Prigger employs repetitive elements to establish and maintain a spry tempo in clipped, spruce sentences. . . . The black outlines of Lewin's . . . witty, loose watercolors punctuate the pages in a flurry of scribbles, suggesting the kind of bursting-at-the-seams activity." Publ Wkly

Another title about Aunt Minnie is:

Aunt Minnie and the twister (2002)

Primavera, Elise, 1954-

Louise the big cheese: divine diva; illustrated by Diane Goode. Simon & Schuster Books for Young Readers 2009 unp il $16.99

Grades: PreK K 1 2   E

1. Theater—Fiction 2. Friendship—Fiction

ISBN 978-1-4169-7180-1; 1-4169-7180-7

LC 2008-23608

"A Paula Wiseman book"

When she learns her class will be doing a play, little Louise Cheese has big dreams of being the star, but when her best friend is given the lead she learns that even the small roles count

"Primavera's breezy story . . . and Goode's distinctive artwork intermingle wonderfully. In both story and art, Louise makes a splash. . . . Goode is at her best here." Booklist

Another title about Louise is:

Louise the big cheese and the la-di-da shoes (2009)

Prince, April Jones

Twenty-one elephants and still standing; written by April Jones Prince; illustrated by Francois Roca. Houghton Mifflin 2005 unp il $16 *

Grades: K 1 2 3 4   E

1. Barnum, P. T. (Phineas Taylor), 1810-1891—Fiction 2. Brooklyn Bridge (New York, N.Y.)—Fiction 3. Elephants—Fiction

ISBN 0-618-44887-X   LC 2004-05229

Upon completion of the Brooklyn Bridge, P.T. Barnum and his twenty-one elephants parade across to prove to everyone that the bridge is safe.

A "well-researched, handsomely illustrated picture book. . . . The sparse, yet powerful text contains both alliteration and occasional rhyme, making it a pleasure for readers and listeners alike. Roca's masterful paintings capture both the spirit of the times and of the expansive bridge." SLJ

Pritchett, Dylan, 1959-

The first music; as told by Dylan Pritchett; illustrated by Erin Bennett Banks. August House Little Folk 2006 unp il $16.95 *

Grades: PreK K 1 2   E

1. Music—Fiction 2. Animals—Fiction

ISBN 0-87483-776-6

A series of accidents in the jungle proves that everyone has something special to add when it comes to making music.

"Fresh and intriguing, this African cumulative tale of the origin of music unfolds in a vibrant storyteller's voice. . . . The message (everyone has something to add to the mix) is subtle, but clear enough for children to understand. However, it's the stylized, earth-toned illustrations, resembling carved wooden figures, that really rock and roll, evoking the synergy of the forest animals." Booklist

Proimos, James

Patricia von Pleasantsquirrel. Dial Books for Young Readers 2009 unp il $15.99

Grades: K 1 2   E

1. Princesses—Fiction

ISBN 978-0-8037-3066-3; 0-8037-3066-7

LC 2008015776

After failing to convince her parents that she is a princess, Patricia von Pleasantsquirrel leaves her moatless house in search of a "princessdom."

"Proimos's story plays 'cheeky homage' to Sendak and Max, but the bold-lined, cartoon-style illustrations and Patricia's postmodern sassiness also owe a debt to James Marshall, calling to mind his bossy Goldilocks." SLJ

Paulie Pastrami achieves world peace. Little Brown Books for Young Readers 2009 unp il $15.99

Grades: K 1 2 3   E

1. Conduct of life—Fiction 2. Kindness—Fiction 3. Peace—Fiction

ISBN 978-0-316-03292-6; 0-316-03292-1

LC 2008043800

Seven-year-old Paulie, an ordinary boy, brings peace to his home and school through small acts of kindness, but needs help to achieve his goal of world peace

"The peppy, colorful cartoon art incorporates witty, sometimes hyperbolic details. . . . The positive story conveys how small, individual actions can have a large, ripple effect." Booklist

Todd's TV; words and pictures by James Proimos. Katherine Tegen Books 2010 unp il $15.99

Grades: PreK K 1 2   E

1. Television—Fiction 2. Parents—Fiction

ISBN 978-0-06-170985-2; 0-06-170985-9

LC 2009018507

When Todd's parents are too busy to take care of him, his television steps in to handle the parenting.

"With broad strokes and witty slapdashery, Proimos's light cartoon art and plotline carry some weighty themes. . . . Amusing cartoon drawings in shades of gray, black, and persimmony-red against a white background and a satiric twist at the story's end further enhance this funny-scary cautionary tale." SLJ

Prokofiev, Sergey, 1891-1953

Peter and the wolf; translated by Maria Carlson; illustrated by Charles Mikolaycak. Viking 1982 unp il pa $5.99 hardcover o.p.

Grades: K 1 2 3 4   E

1. Wolves—Fiction 2. Fairy tales

ISBN 0-14-050633-0 (pa)   LC 81-70402

This book retells the orchestral fairy tale of the boy who, ignoring his grandfather's warnings, proceeds to capture a wolf

"Prokofiev's classic, designed to teach children the instruments of an orchestra, has been published in picture book form before, but never better illustrated. The translation is smooth. . . . The paintings are rich in color, dramatic in details of costume or architecture, strong in composition, with distinctive individuality in the faces of people and of the wolf." Bull Cent Child Books

Prosek, James

Bird, butterfly, eel; story and paintings by James Prosek. Simon & Schuster Books for Young Readers 2009 unp il map $16.99 *

Grades: K 1 2 3   E

1. Birds—Fiction 2. Butterflies—Fiction 3. Eels—Fiction

ISBN 978-0-689-86829-0; 0-689-86829-4

LC 2007-15734

Follows a bird, a monarch butterfly, and an eel from summer on a farm until they make their respective fall voyages south, and then later begin to return north again when the weather warms.

"A well-designed and useful resource to pique curiosity about an amazing aspect of the lives of many animals." SLJ

A good day's fishing. Simon & Schuster Bks. for Young Readers 2004 unp il $15.95

Grades: 1 2 3 4   E

1. Fishing—Fiction

ISBN 0-689-85327-0   LC 2003-7383

A child searches through the hooks, lures, bobbers, and other paraphernalia in his tacklebox for the one thing he needs to ensure a good day's fishing. Includes a detailed glossary

"A beautifully illustrated, simple story. . . . Young fishing enthusiasts will certainly learn more about which tackle works best to catch particular kinds of fish, while the wonderfully detailed, gentle watercolor illustrations of fish and gear offer a lovely introduction." Booklist

Provensen, Alice, 1918-

A day in the life of Murphy. Simon & Schuster Bks. for Young Readers 2003 unp il $16.95; pa $6.99 *

Grades: PreK K 1 2 3   E

1. Dogs—Fiction 2. Farm life—Fiction

ISBN 0-689-84884-6; 1-4169-1800-0 (pa)

LC 2002-4309

Murphy, a farm terrier, describes a day in his life as he gets fed in the kitchen, hunts mice, goes to the vet, returns to the house for dinner, investigates a noise outside, and retires to the barn for sleep

"With charming, lively illustrations and peppy, descriptive prose, Provensen portrays the smells, sounds, and activities of a delightful, active pup." Booklist

Pullen, Zachary

Friday my Radio Flyer flew; [by] Zachary Pullen. Simon & Schuster Books for Young Readers 2008 unp il $16.99 *   E

1. Father-son relationship—Fiction 2. Flight—Fiction 3. Imagination—Fiction 4. Days—Fiction

ISBN 978-1-4169-3983-2; 1-4169-3983-0

LC 2007041852

A father and son find an old Radio Flyer wagon when cleaning out the attic and, through the course of a week, turn it back into a wonderful toy

"Subtle alliteration moves the story through the week. . . . Full-color spreads are oversize and beautifully done in oil paints. . . . The final spread . . . is take-your-breath-away wonderful. This is a strong first purchase, affirming the bond between boys and their fathers as well as the power of imagination." SLJ

Pulver, Robin

Never say boo! Holiday House 2009 unp il $16.95

Grades: PreK K 1 2   E

1. Ghost stories 2. School stories

ISBN 978-0-8234-2110-7; 0-8234-2110-4

LC 2008022609

When Gordon, a ghost, moves to a new school, everyone is afraid of him until they learn that he is not as scary as they thought he was.

"In Lucke's creepy and comical gouache illustrations, Gordon's bulging eyes and pasty white skull stand out on the mostly black background and are in contrast to his orange-yellow striped shirt and human classmates. Add in Pulver's straightforward dialogue and you have an amusing read-aloud." SLJ

Nouns and verbs have a field day; illustrated by Lynn Rowe Reed. Holiday House 2006 unp il $16.95; pa $6.95

Grades: 2 3 4   E

1. English language—Fiction 2. School stories

ISBN 978-0-8234-1982-1; 0-8234-1982-7; 978-0-8234-2097-1 (pa); 0-8234-2097-1 (pa)

LC 2005-46207

"In this companion to *Punctuation Takes a Vacation* (2003), the nouns and verbs decide to have some fun of their own while the kids in Mr. Wright's class are away participating in a field day. The nouns pair up with other nouns and the verbs with other verbs, until they realize they must cooperate. . . . Reed's vividly colored cartoons capture the high-energy activity. . . . Although the emphasis is on silliness, Pulver makes her point about the parts of speech; even the youngest listeners will realize that sentences need both nouns and verbs in order to make sense." Booklist

Punctuation takes a vacation; illustrated by Lynn Rowe Reed. Holiday House 2003 unp il $16.95; pa $6.95

Grades: 2 3 4   E

1. Punctuation—Fiction 2. School stories

ISBN 0-8234-1687-9; 0-8234-1820-0 (pa)

LC 2002-68915

When all the punctuation marks in Mr. Wright's class decide to take a vacation, the students discover just how difficult life can be without them

"Pulver's clever story moves along at a nice clip and makes its point without belaboring the matter. Reed's acrylics-on-canvas illustrations are rich in color and texture, and add to the amusement of the story." SLJ

Silent letters loud and clear; written by Robin Pulver; illustrated by Lynn Rowe Reed. Holiday House 2008 unp il $16.95

Grades: 2 3 4   E

1. English language—Fiction 2. School stories

ISBN 978-0-8234-2127-5; 0-8234-2127-9

LC 2007016057

When Mr. Wright's students express a dislike for silent letters, the offended letters decide to teach them a lesson by going on strike.

"Mr Wright's uncertain fate (happily resolved) adds a dose of drama to the absurd situation. The playful design points up the silent letters within the text, and the faux-naive mixed-media illustrations give both human and letter characters lots of personality." Horn Book

Purmell, Ann, 1953-

Apple cider making days; illustrated by Joanne Friar. Millbrook Press 2002 unp il lib bdg $21.90

Grades: K 1 2 3   E

1. Apples—Fiction 2. Farm life—Fiction

ISBN 0-7613-2364-3   LC 2001-44920

Alex and Abigail join the whole family in processing and selling apples and apple cider at their grandfather's farm

"The comfortable, colorful art brings little ones up close to the process and gives them a good look at the conveyor belts and presses and other machinery involved. . . . A double-page spread, 'Cider Lore,' following the story, provides wonderful tidbits about the cider-making process. An excellent resource for autumn units or to use in preparation for a trip to the orchard." Booklist

Christmas tree farm; by Ann Purmell; illustrated by Jill Weber. Holiday House 2006 unp il $16.95

Grades: K 1 2 3   E

1. Christmas tree growing—Fiction 2. Grandfathers—Fiction 3. Farm life—Fiction 4. Family life—Fiction

ISBN 978-0-8234-1886-2; 0-8234-1886-3

LC 2004-47502

A boy describes how he, his grandfather, and the rest of his family work on their tree farm throughout the year to prepare Christmas trees

"Purmell packs the friendly story with plenty of information. . . . The text makes the book interesting; the art gives it charm. The simply drawn, sometimes diminutive characters exude warmth and exemplify the work that goes into any kind of farming." Booklist

Maple syrup season; by Ann Purmell; illustrated by Jill Weber. Holiday House 2008 unp il $16.95

Grades: K 1 2 3   E

1. Grandfathers—Fiction 2. Family life—Fiction 3. Maple sugar—Fiction

ISBN 978-0-8234-1891-6; 0-8234-1891-X

LC 2006-03455

Grandpa leads the way as his family works together to tap maple trees, collect sap, and make syrup.

"This gentle story has a straightforward text and folksy, colorful gouache illustrations. . . . A glossary and two pages of maple syrup lore are appended. This book would be a great addition to units on seasons, farms, or plants and trees." SLJ

Pym, Tasha

Have you ever seen a sneep? pictures by Joel Stewart. Farrar, Straus and Giroux 2009 unp il $16.95 *

Grades: PreK K 1 2   E

1. Stories in rhyme 2. Monsters—Fiction

ISBN 978-0-374-32868-9; 0-374-32868-4

LC 2008042985

"In rhyming text, a boy relates a woeful tale of trying to have fun but being plagued by monsters that ruin his every pleasure. Each encounter begins with the child asking readers if they've experienced a similar situation. . . . The pleasing and unexpected conclusion is sure to be met with a smile. The muted, almost fuzzy-looking illustrations feature the small barefoot and straw-hatted boy. . . . The artwork alternates between full-color

Pym, Tasha—*Continued*

washes that cover the pages completely and spreads that isolate the boy against expanses of white space. Perfectly paced and quietly dramatic." SLJ

Raab, Brigitte

Where does pepper come from? illustrated by Manuela Olten; translated by J. Alison James. North-South 2006 unp il $15.95

Grades: K 1 2 3   E

1. Questions and answers

ISBN 0-7358-2070-8

This is a "humorous cross between a science book and a riddle book. Each of seven questions is first given a funny answer. . . . Readers turn the page to see a child saying, 'No!' followed by a concise, factual answer. Topics range from the color of flamingos to the saltiness of the seas. The pattern works well. . . . The cartoon-style paintings use soft earth tones and subtle humor." SLJ

Raczka, Bob

Snowy, blowy winter; [by] Bob Raczka; illustrated by Judy Stead. Albert Whitman & Co. 2008 unp il $16.99

Grades: PreK K 1 2   E

1. Stories in rhyme 2. Winter—Fiction 3. Snow—Fiction

ISBN 978-0-8075-7526-0; 0-8075-7526-7

LC 2007052608

Illustrations and simple rhyming text portray winter activities, from snowman-building, sledding, and sitting by a fire to feeding birds

"The text is simple and bouncy, and the cartoon illustrations are bright, clear, and inclusive. The book's quick pace and cheerful pictures make it a perfect choice for seasonal storytimes." SLJ

Spring things; by Bob Raczka; illustrated by Judy Stead. Albert Whitman 2007 unp il $16.95

Grades: PreK K 1 2   E

1. Spring—Fiction

ISBN 978-0-8075-7596-3   LC 2006023403

Winter melts into spring with the sights and sounds of hopping and skipping, sowing and mowing, and blading and lemonading

"Stead's paintings add an entertaining element and useful clarification to the active text." SLJ

Summer wonders; illustrated by Judy Stead. Albert Whitman & Co. 2009 unp il $16.99

Grades: PreK K 1 2   E

1. Stories in rhyme 2. Summer—Fiction

ISBN 978-0-8075-7653-3; 0-8075-7653-0

LC 2008031037

Illustrations and rhyming text celebrate the sights and sounds of summer, from days of diving and swimming to nights of stargazing and fireflies.

"Bright-hued acrylic illustrations bring the expressive verbal images to life. The paintings are festive and entertaining." SLJ

Who loves the fall? by Bob Raczka; illustrated by Judy Stead. Albert Whitman 2007 unp il $16.95

Grades: PreK K 1 2   E

1. Autumn—Fiction 2. Stories in rhyme

ISBN 978-0-8075-9037-9; 0-8075-9037-1

LC 2007001506

Rhyming text and illustrations portray the sights and sounds of autumn, from "rakers, leapers, and corn crop reapers" to "trickers, treaters, and turkey eaters"

"The brightly colored, well-designed illustrations pulsate with energy, movement, and charm." SLJ

Radunsky, Vladimir

The mighty asparagus. Silver Whistle/Harcourt 2004 unp il $16

Grades: K 1 2 3   E

1. Asparagus—Fiction 2. Italy—Fiction

ISBN 0-15-216743-9   LC 2003-12241

In Renaissance Italy, a large asparagus appears suddenly in the king's back yard, and he enlists the help of several people and animals, including a songbird, in order to get rid of it

"The lowbrow humor, the blind silliness, and the quirky exaggerations are childishness itself. For older children there is the appeal of random sarcasm and funky, distorted illustrations." SLJ

What does peace feel like? by V. Radunsky and children just like you from around the world. Atheneum Books for Young Readers 2004 unp il $14.95

Grades: K 1 2 3   E

1. Peace

ISBN 0-689-86676-3   LC 2003-11506

"An Anne Schwartz book"

Simple text and illustrations portray what peace looks, sounds, tastes, feels, and smells like to children around the world.

"As much a celebration of the five senses as an antiwar message, this bright picture book combines Radunsky's playful gouache double-page scenarios with quotes from grade-schoolers at an international school in Rome." Booklist

You? translated from Dog-ese to English by my learned dog, Tsetsa. Harcourt, Inc. 2009 unp il $16

Grades: PreK K 1 2   E

1. Dogs—Fiction

ISBN 978-0-15-205177-8; 0-15-205177-5

LC 2008-3281

A lonely girl and a stray dog find one another in a park.

"Radunsky makes the most of his canvas. . . . Thin, energetic lines define the forms minimally on gouache blobs of color, all arrayed on a generous expanse of buff-colored handmade paper. . . . The heartfelt, plaintive dialogue will hold readers' interest, and the wait makes the inevitable discovery—'Woof! YOU!'—all the sweeter." Kirkus

Rahaman, Vashanti, 1953-
Divali rose; [by] Vashanti Rahaman; illustrated by Jamel Akib. Boyds Mills Press 2008 unp il $16.95
Grades: 2 3 4   **E**
    1. Prejudices—Fiction 2. Divali—Fiction 3. Grandparents—Fiction 4. East Indians—Fiction 5. Trinidad—Fiction
ISBN 978-1-59078-524-9; 1-59078-524-X
                          LC 2007049686
As the festival of Divali approaches, Ricki wants to confess that he accidentally broke a rosebud off the bush he and his grandfather planted, but grandfather is busy blaming the neighbors who are newly arrived in Trinidad from India. Includes facts about Divali and the people and language of Trinidad
"This appealing, multilayered story will provoke discussion about resentments between different generations of immigrants. . . . Akib's impressionistic pastel paintings portray the tropical setting and Ricki's feelings of guilt." SLJ

Ramirez, Antonio, 1944-
Napi; story by Antonio Ramirez; pictures by Domi. Groundwood Books 2004 unp il $15.95
Grades: K 1 2 3   **E**
    1. Native Americans—Mexico—Fiction 2. Mazatec Indians—Fiction 3. Mexico—Fiction 4. Herons—Fiction 5. Dreams—Fiction
ISBN 0-88899-610-1
Napi is a Mazatec Indian girl who loves to dream. One day, she dreams of becoming a heron and flying over the river.
"The clear, lyrical prose has a childlike charm that brilliantly recreates the joys of this child's experience. . . . Domi's primitive acrylic artwork enhances the sense of the story." SLJ
Other titles about Napi are:
Napi goes to the mountain (2006)
Napi makes a village (2010)

Ramos, Jorge
I'm just like my mom/I'm just like my dad; illustrated by Akemi Gutierrez. Rayo 2008 unp il $16.99
Grades: PreK K   **E**
    1. Mother-daughter relationship—Fiction 2. Father-son relationship—Fiction 3. Bilingual books—English-Spanish
ISBN 978-0-06-123968-7; 0-06-123968-2
In two stories in English and Spanish, printed back to back, children reflect on how much they resemble their parents.
"This is a comforting celebration of family. . . . Spare illustrations is subtle colors completely fill each double-page spread and feature pleasant figures with enlarged oval heads, giving a happy, open, comfortable feel to the narratives." Booklist

Rand, Ann
I know a lot of things; by Ann & Paul Rand. Chronicle Books 2009 c1956 unp il $16.99
Grades: PreK K 1   **E**
    1. Growth—Fiction
ISBN 978-0-8118-6615-6   LC 2008020680
A reissue of the title first published 1956
Celebrates the many things young children know about their world, while looking forward to a time when they will know more
This is written "in poetic text. . . . Paul Rand's simply composed, ahead-of-their-time illustrations don't look the least bit dated and perfectly reflect the concepts in the text." Horn Book Guide

Sparkle and spin; a book about words; by Ann & Paul Rand. Chronicle Books 2006 c1957 unp il $15.95
Grades: PreK K 1   **E**
    1. English language 2. Communication
ISBN 978-0-8118-5003-2; 0-8118-5003-X
                        LC 2004-23260
A reissue of the title first published 1957 by Harcourt, Brace, and World
Lyrical text explores what words are and how they are used, highlighting such characteristics as that some words are spoken softly, some are shouted, some sound like their meaning, and some evoke certain feelings.
This "is a vibrantly eye-catching collection of visual puns and graphic double-entendres." NY Times Book Rev

Randall, Alison L.
The wheat doll; [by] Alison L. Randall; illustrated by Bill Farnsworth. Peachtree Publishers 2008 30p il $16.95
Grades: K 1 2 3   **E**
    1. Dolls—Fiction 2. Lost and found possessions—Fiction 3. Storms—Fiction 4. Frontier and pioneer life—Fiction
ISBN 978-1-56145-456-3; 1-56145-456-7
                        LC 2008-4562
On the nineteenth-century Utah frontier, Mary Ann is heartbroken when her doll Betty is lost during a fierce storm and her sadness lasts all winter long, until spring brings a wonderful surprise.
"This is a sweet story of loss and renewal told with empathy and feeling that is never heavy-handed. . . . Farnsworth's realistic oil paintings have a warm, soft quality that matches the tone of the text. . . . This picture book is a great addition." SLJ

Rania, Queen, consort of Abdullah, King of Jordan, 1970-
The sandwich swap; by Her Majesty Queen Rania; with Kelly DiPucchio; illustrations by Tricia Tusa. Disney-Hyperion Books 2010 unp il $16.99
Grades: PreK K 1 2   **E**
    1. Food—Fiction 2. Friendship—Fiction 3. Toleration—Fiction 4. School stories
ISBN 978-1-4231-2484-9; 1-4231-2484-7
                        LC 2009018673

Rania, Queen, consort of Abdullah, King of Jordan, 1970-—*Continued*

"The day Lily stops eating her peanut butter and jelly sandwich to tell Salma her hummus and pita sandwich looks yucky—and vice versa—is the day they stop being friends. . . . When the two girls get caught in the middle of a food fight and called to the principal's office, they decide it's time to make some changes. . . . Soft watercolor cartoon illustrations portray a lively student body and a slightly forbidding principal. This engaging title reminds children that having the courage to try new things can result in positive experiences." SLJ

Rankin, Laura

Ruthie and the (not so) teeny tiny lie; [by] Laura Rankin. Bloomsbury Children's Books 2007 unp il $15.95

Grades: PreK K 1 2   E

1. Truthfulness and falsehood—Fiction 2. School stories 3. Foxes—Fiction

ISBN 978-1-59990-010-0; 1-59990-010-6

                  LC 2006013192

Ruthie the fox loves tiny things and when she finds a tiny camera on the playground she is very happy, but after she lies and says the camera belongs to her, nothing seems to go right

"Emotionally authentic in text and art, this story gets its message across without preaching." SLJ

Ransom, Candice F., 1952-

The old blue pickup truck; written by Candice F. Ransom; illustrated by Jenny Mattheson. Walker & Co. 2009 unp il $16.99; lib bdg $17.89

Grades: PreK K 1   E

1. Father-daughter relationship—Fiction 2. Trucks—Fiction

ISBN   978-0-8027-9591-5;   0-8027-9591-9; 978-0-8027-9592-2 (lib bdg); 0-8027-9592-7 (lib bdg)

                  LC 2008-40316

As a girl and her father run errands in their old blue pickup, she discovers how many different ways they can use their truck.

"This enjoyable story is accompanied by oil on primed paper illustrations that have a bright and clean feel." SLJ

Rao, Sandhya

My mother's sari; illustrated by Nina Sabnani. North South Books 2006 unp il $14.95; pa $6.95

Grades: PreK K 1 2   E

1. Clothing and dress—Fiction 2. Mother-daughter relationship—Fiction 3. India—Fiction

ISBN 0-7358-2101-1; 0-7358-2233-6 (pa)

First published in India

A little girl is fascinated by her mother's sari and finds many uses for it.

"Subtle backgrounds, lightly decorated with objects from nature, provide a gentle showcase for the children and the saris. Rao [uses] . . . childlike drawings to represent the kids and photographs of the cloths, bringing the fabric designs, colors, and folds up close. A winsome look at a fresh subject." Booklist

Rappaport, Doreen, 1939-

Dirt on their skirts; the story of the young women who won the world championship; [by] Doreen Rappaport, Lyndall Callan; pictures by E.B. Lewis. Dial Bks. for Young Readers 1999 unp il $16.99

Grades: K 1 2 3   E

1. All-American Girls Professional Baseball League—Fiction 2. Baseball—Fiction

ISBN 0-8037-2042-4   LC 98-47080

Margaret experiences the excitement of watching the 1946 championship game of the All-American Girls Professional Baseball League as it goes into extra innings.

"With its economy of language and telling period details, this book provides an exciting slice of sports history and an appealing bit of Americana. . . . Lewis's finely wrought watercolor paintings deftly capture the crowd and the action on the field." SLJ

The secret seder; illustrated by Emily Arnold McCully. Hyperion Books for Children 2005 unp il $16.99 *

Grades: 2 3 4   E

1. Holocaust, 1933-1945—Fiction 2. Jews—Fiction 3. France—Fiction 4. Passover—Fiction

ISBN 0-7868-0777-6   LC 2003-57115

During the Nazi occupation of France, a boy and his father slip out of their village and into the mountains, where they join a group of fellow Jews at a humble seder table

"Rappaport interweaves themes and descriptive text to create a meaningful story in a distinctive setting. An excellent discussion starter." SLJ

Raschka, Christopher

Five for a little one; [by] Chris Raschka. Atheneum Books for Young Readers 2006 unp il $16.95

Grades: PreK K   E

1. Senses and sensation—Fiction 2. Rabbits—Fiction 3. Counting 4. Stories in rhyme

ISBN 978-0-689-84599-4; 0-689-84599-5

                  LC 2005-08963

"A Richard Jackson book"

"A buoyant bunny, drawn in thick ink outline with a fuzzy body and delightfully mismatched ears (one downy and one plain), introduces readers to the senses, numbering them one through five. The rhyming verses and ebullient artwork convey a child's curiosity and enthusiasm for investigating the world in various ways." SLJ

Hip hop dog; words by Chris Raschka; pictures by Vladimir Radunsky. Harper 2010 unp il $16.99; lib bdg $17.89

Grades: PreK K 1 2   E

1. Stories in rhyme 2. Dogs—Fiction 3. Hip-hop—Fiction 4. Rap music—Fiction

ISBN   978-0-06-123963-2;   0-06-123963-1; 978-0-06-123964-9 (lib bdg); 0-06-123964-X (lib bdg)

                  LC 2008031449

A neglected dog finds his purpose through rapping and rhyming.

"This is great for reading aloud. . . . The well-matched mixed-media illustrations show lively urban

Raschka, Christopher—*Continued*

scenes. . . . Kids will chant along to the text, which slides and whirls across the pages." Booklist

John Coltrane's Giant steps; remixed by Chris Raschka. Atheneum Bks. for Young Readers 2002 33p il $17

Grades: K 1 2 3   E

1. Jazz music

ISBN 0-689-84598-7   LC 2001-33755

"A Richard Jackson book"

John Coltrane's musical composition is performed by a box, a snowflake, some raindrops, and a kitten

"Like Coltrane, Raschka is creating something deeply personal here that we don't need to understand fully to appreciate. Instead, he asks us to trust our own understanding of raindrops, snowflakes, kittens, and music to experience the book. Anyone who's still intimidated by jazz after giving this book a chance is probably just trying too hard." Horn Book

New York is English, Chattanooga is Creek; by Chris Raschka. Atheneum Books for Young Readers 2005 unp il $16.95

Grades: K 1 2 3   E

1. Cities and towns—Fiction 2. Geographic names—Fiction

ISBN 0-689-84600-2   LC 2004-23188

"A Richard Jackson book"

New York City, though a bit boastful, decides to throw a party to make new friends of other unique cities like Chattanooga and Minneapolis

"This is both a fascinating exploration of the etymology and derivation of American city names and a characteristic Raschka farcical flight-of-fancy. . . . Raschka's illustrations rendered in ink and watercolor employ his loose, impressionistic, brushy style to perfect effect, giving the book its humor while artfully delivering his message and entertaining information." SLJ

Peter and the wolf; retold by Chris Raschka. Atheneum Books for Young Readers 2008 unp il $17.99 *

Grades: PreK K 1 2   E

1. Fairy tales 2. Wolves—Fiction

ISBN 978-0-689-85652-5; 0-689-85652-0

LC 2008-04472

"A Richard Jackson book"

Retells the orchestral fairy tale in which a boy ignores his grandfather's warnings and captures a wolf with the help of a bird, a duck, and a cat

"Raschka conveys the mounting suspense in lilting words, swerving zigzags and curves. . . . Raschka's pictures—of characters venturing close to the wolf's beartrap jaws, of the cat's enormous face looming over a tiny Peter—gain extra energy from geometrically shaped color blocks on the same spreads. . . . One reading will not be enough to appreciate the artist's keen attention to detail." Publ Wkly

Yo! Yes? by Chris Raschka. Orchard Bks. 1993 unp il $15.95 *

Grades: PreK K 1 2   E

1. Friendship—Fiction 2. Race relations—Fiction 3. African Americans—Fiction

ISBN 0-531-05469-1   LC 92-25644

A Caldecott Medal honor book, 1994

"A Richard Jackson book"

Two lonely characters, one black and one white, meet on the street and become friends

"The design and drawing are bold, spare and expressive; the language has the strength and rhythm of a playground chant." Bull Cent Child Books

Another title about these characters is:

Ring! Yo? (2000)

Rathmann, Peggy

10 minutes till bedtime. Putnam 1998 unp il $16.99; pa $6.99; bd bk $7.99 *

Grades: PreK K 1 2   E

1. Hamsters—Fiction 2. Bedtime—Fiction

ISBN 0-399-23103-X; 0-14-240024-6 (pa); 0-399-23770-4 (bd bk)   LC 97-51295

A boy's hamster leads an increasingly large group of hamsters on a tour of the boy's house, while his father counts down the minutes to bedtime

"Children will pore over the comical details and follow closely the antics of the numbered hamsters, each one with a personality of its own." SLJ

The day the babies crawled away. Putnam 2003 unp il $16.99 *

Grades: PreK K 1 2   E

1. Infants—Fiction 2. Stories in rhyme

ISBN 0-399-23196-X   LC 2002-152002

A boy follows fives babies who crawl away from a picnic and saves the day by bringing them back

This is a "rollicking rhyming tale, illustrated in needle-sharp, atmospheric silhouettes against twilight skies." Publ Wkly

Good night, Gorilla. Putnam 1994 unp il $14.99; pa $5.99; bd bk $7.99 *

Grades: PreK K 1 2   E

1. Zoos—Fiction 2. Animals—Fiction

ISBN 0-399-22445-9; 0-698-11649-6 (pa); 0-399-23003-3 (bd bk)   LC 92-29020

An unobservant zookeeper is followed home by all the animals he thinks he has left behind in the zoo

"In a book economical in text and simple in illustration, the many amusing, small details, as well as the tranquil tone of the story, make this an outstanding picture book." Horn Book Guide

Officer Buckle and Gloria. Putnam 1995 unp il $16.99 *

Grades: PreK K 1 2   E

1. School stories 2. Dogs—Fiction 3. Safety education—Fiction

ISBN 0-399-22616-8   LC 93-43887

Awarded the Caldecott Medal, 1996

"When rotund, good-natured officer Buckle visits school assemblies to read off his sensible safety tips, the children listen, bored and polite, dozing off one by one. But when the new police dog, Gloria, stands behind him, secretly miming the dire consequences of acting imprudently, the children suddenly become attentive, laughing uproariously and applauding loudly. . . . The deadpan humor of the text and slapstick wit of the illustrations

Rathmann, Peggy—*Continued*

make a terrific combination. Large, expressive line drawings illustrate the characters with finesse, and the Kool-Aid-bright washes add energy and pizzazz." Booklist

Rattigan, Jama Kim

Dumpling soup; illustrated by Lillian Hsu-Flanders. Little, Brown 1993 unp il hardcover o.p. pa $6.99

Grades: K 1 2 3   E

1. Family life—Fiction 2. New Year—Fiction 3. Hawaii—Fiction

ISBN 0-316-73445-4; 0-316-73047-5 (pa)

LC 91-42949

"Marisa, a seven-year-old Asian-American girl who lives in Hawaii, explains the traditions that exist in her family to celebrate the New Year. Her family . . . consists of people who are Japanese, Chinese, Korean, Hawaiian, and *haole* (Hawaiian for white person). . . . A glossary of English, Hawaiian, Japanese, and Korean words provides pronunciations and definitions for many of the possibly unfamiliar terms that weave in and out of the text. A thoroughly enjoyable celebration of family warmth and diverse traditions, illustrated with cheery watercolors." Horn Book

Raven, Margot

Circle unbroken; the story of a basket and its people; [by] Margot Theis Raven; pictures by E. B. Lewis. Farrar, Straus and Giroux 2004 unp il $16; pa $7.99 *

Grades: K 1 2 3   E

1. Baskets—Fiction 2. African Americans—Fiction 3. Gullahs—Fiction

ISBN 0-374-31289-3; 0-312-37603-0 (pa)

LC 2002-24009

"Melanie Kroupa books"

A grandmother tells the tale of Gullahs and their beautiful sweetgrass baskets that keep their African heritage alive

"Raven's text masterfully frames several hundred years of African-American history within the picture-book format. Lewis's double-page, watercolor images are poignant and perfectly matched to the text and mood." SLJ

Night boat to freedom; [by] Margot Theis Raven; pictures by E. B. Lewis. Farrar, Straus and Giroux 2006 unp il $16; pa $6.99 *

Grades: 1 2 3 4   E

1. Slavery—Fiction 2. Underground railroad—Fiction 3. Quilts—Fiction 4. African Americans—Fiction

ISBN 978-0-374-31266-4; 0-374-31266-4; 978-0-312-55018-9 (pa); 0-312-55018-9 (pa)

"Melanie Kroupa Books"

At the request of his fellow slave Granny Judith, Christmas John risks his life to take runaways across a river from Kentucky to Ohio.

"The older mentor is as tough as the young boy, and Lewis' beautiful, unframed double-page spreads depict the bond between them. . . . Words and pictures work perfectly together." Booklist

Ravishankar, Anushka

Elephants never forget; illustrated by Christiane Pieper. Houghton Mifflin Company 2008 unp il $16 *

Grades: PreK K 1 2   E

1. Elephants—Fiction 2. Water buffalo—Fiction 3. Stories in rhyme

ISBN 978-0-618-99784-8; 0-618-99784-9

LC 2007-25745

A lonely elephant meets a herd of buffaloes and decides to stay with them, but when they meet up with some elephants, he must make an important decision

The "story is full of good read-aloud noises. . . . Pieper . . . produces digital woodcuts that . . . [eschew] cuteness in favor of strength and clarity. A two-color scheme—black and periwinkle on cream-colored paper—and bold, simple spreads focus attention on the ponderous forms of the elephant and buffalo. Varied compositions as well as printed letters that grow and shrink and dance across the pages match the dexterity of the text with a visual sprightliness." Publ Wkly

Tiger on a tree; [by] Anushka Ravishankar, Pulak Biswas. Farrar, Straus and Giroux 2004 unp il $15 *

Grades: PreK K 1 2   E

1. Tigers—Fiction 2. Stories in rhyme

ISBN 0-374-37555-0   LC 2003-49050

First published 1997 in India

After trapping a tiger in a tree, a group of men must decide what to do with it

"This very simple chanting story is perfect for reading aloud with young preschoolers. . . . The thickly stroked illustrations, mostly black and white, have occasional splashes of orange." Booklist

Rawlinson, Julia

Fletcher and the falling leaves; by Julia Rawlinson; pictures by Tiphanie Beeke. Greenwillow Books 2006 unp il $16.99; pa $6.99 *

Grades: PreK K 1 2   E

1. Foxes—Fiction 2. Trees—Fiction 3. Leaves—Fiction 4. Autumn—Fiction

ISBN 978-0-06-113401-2; 0-06-113401-5; 978-0-06-157397-2 (pa); 0-06-157397-3 (pa)

LC 2005-34348

When his favorite tree begins to lose its leaves, Fletcher the fox worries that it is sick, but instead a magical sight is in store for him.

"This potent synthesis of art and prose conveys a child's first awareness of the changing seasons with reverence and wonder. . . . Beeke's resplendent watercolors work beautifully with the book's tone, content, layout, and design." SLJ

Another title about Fletcher the fox is:

Fletcher and the springtime blossoms (2009)

Ray, Jane

The apple-pip princess. Candlewick Press 2008 unp il $16.99 *

Grades: PreK K 1 2   E
  1. Fairy tales 2. Princesses—Fiction 3. Seeds—Fiction 4. Apples—Fiction
ISBN 978-0-7636-3747-7; 0-7636-3747-5
LC 2007-34239

In a land that has stood barren, parched by drought and ravaged by frosts since the Queen's death, the King sets his three daughters the task of making the kingdom bloom again, and discovers that sometimes the smallest things can make the biggest difference.

"Ray's rich language and sure pacing create a winning read-aloud, but it's the shining collage artwork that really stands out. Mixing color photos into her typically fine, elaborately decorated illustrations, Ray creates dramatic scenes." Booklist

The dollhouse fairy. Candlewick Press 2009 il $16.99

Grades: PreK K 1 2   E
  1. Dollhouses—Fiction 2. Fairies—Fiction 3. Father-daughter relationship—Fiction 4. Sick—Fiction
ISBN 978-0-7636-4411-6; 0-7636-4411-0
LC 2009-18405

Worried about her father's trip to the hospital, Rosy goes to play with the special dollhouse he built for her and finds Thistle, a very messy and mischievous fairy who needs a place to stay while her injured wing mends.

"The story unfolds with subtlety and sensitivity to the emotional issues at its heart. The book's large format gives plenty of space for the vibrant mixed-media artwork." Booklist

Ray, Mary Lyn

Christmas farm; illustrated by Barry Root. Harcourt 2008 unp il $17 *

Grades: K 1 2   E
  1. Trees—Fiction 2. Gardening—Fiction
ISBN 978-0-15-216290-0; 0-15-216290-9
LC 2007-15216

Wilma decides to plant Christmas trees with the help of her young neighbor, Parker.

"Root's appealing watercolor-and-gouache illustrations invite inspection. . . . [This is] a story that lovingly depicts the hard work, cooperation, and patience necessary to grow crops." Booklist

Recorvits, Helen

My name is Yoon; pictures by Gabi Swiatkowska. Frances Foster Bks. 2002 unp il $16 *

Grades: PreK K 1 2   E
  1. Korean Americans—Fiction 2. Immigrants—Fiction
ISBN 0-374-35114-7   LC 00-51395

Disliking her name as written in English, Korean-born Yoon, or "shining wisdom," refers to herself as "cat," "bird," and "cupcake," as a way to feel more comfortable in her new school and new country

"Swiatkowska's stunningly spare, almost surrealistic paintings enhance the story's message. . . . A powerful and inspiring picture book." SLJ

Other titles about Yoon are:
Yoon and the Christmas mitten (2006)
Yoon and the jade bracelet (2008)

Reed, Lynn Rowe

Basil's birds. Marshall Cavendish Children 2010 unp il $17.99

Grades: K 1 2   E
  1. Birds—Fiction 2. Janitors—Fiction
ISBN 978-0-7614-5627-8; 0-7614-5627-9
LC 2009007071

While Basil the school janitor is napping, birds build a nest atop his head and when the eggs hatch, he becomes a proud 'dad' to the chicks.

"Brightly painted clay birds and photographs of the nest and worms are scanned into Reed's gouache illustrations. Her childlike paintings are done in flat spring colors, often showing faces in profile and bodies so loose jointed that they hardly seem earthbound." SLJ

Reibstein, Mark

Wabi Sabi; art by Ed Young. Little, Brown 2008 unp il $16.99 *

Grades: 2 3 4   E
  1. Cats—Fiction 2. Aesthetics—Fiction 3. Animals—Fiction 4. Japan—Fiction
ISBN 978-0-316-11825-5; 0-316-11825-7
LC 2007-50895

Wabi Sabi, a cat living in the city of Kyoto, learns about the Japanese concept of beauty through simplicity as she asks various animals she meets about the meaning of her name.

"Young's beautiful collages have an almost 3D effect and perfectly complement the spiritual, lyrical text." SLJ

Reid, Barbara

The Subway mouse. Scholastic Press 2005 c2003 unp il $15.95

Grades: PreK K 1 2   E
  1. Mice—Fiction 2. Subways—Fiction
ISBN 0-439-72827-4

First published 2003 in Canada

Remembering childhood stories of a beautiful but dangerous place called Tunnel's End, a mouse named Nib leaves his dirty, crowded home under a busy subway station and sets out on a long journey, joined by Lola, a mouse he meets along the way.

"Reid creates a charming, lively adventure in short, smoothly paced sentences, but it's her marvelous collage illustrations that really bring the characters and richly imagined world to life. Working in found materials and expertly molded, brightly colored plasticine, she sculpts remarkably expressive characters and a vivid, subterranean world." Booklist

Reid, Rob

Comin' down to storytime; pictures by Nadine Bernard Westcott. Upstart Books 2009 32p il $17.95

Grades: PreK K 1   E
    1. Farm life—Fiction 2. Songs 3. Storytelling—Fiction 4. Libraries—Fiction
    ISBN 978-1-60213-039-5; 1-60213-039-6
    "Building on the familiar song 'She'll Be Coming 'Round the Mountain,' Reid's animal version begins, 'We'll be comin' down to storytime when we come. Yee ha!' as all the farm animals run excitedly to the barn. It ends with 'We will check out lots of books when we leave. Bye now!' . . . Illustrations fit the rollicking mood perfectly. Westcott imbues each scene with plenty of color and lively action." SLJ

Reidy, Jean

Too purpley! illustrated by Genevieve Leloup. Bloomsbury Children's Books 2010 unp il $11.99; lib bdg $12.89

Grades: PreK K 1 2   E
    1. Stories in rhyme 2. Clothing and dress—Fiction
    ISBN 978-1-59990-307-1; 1-59990-307-5; 978-1-59990-437-5 (lib bdg); 1-59990-437-3 (lib bdg)
                         LC 2009004741
    A young girl rejects many outfits before finding the perfect clothes to wear
    "This fun book has lots of descriptive words that tickle the ear, great colors and patterns, and a charming protagonist." SLJ

Reiser, Lynn

My baby and me; concept and words by Lynn Reiser; photographs by Penny Gentieu. Alfred A. Knopf 2008 unp il $16.99

Grades: PreK   E
    1. Infants—Fiction 2. Siblings—Fiction 3. Stories in rhyme
    ISBN 978-0-375-85205-3; 0-375-85205-0
                         LC 2007031949
    Photographs and simple text portray interactions between babies and their toddler siblings.
    "The photographs are just right for the very youngest, with each double-page spread foregrounding a pair of siblings and a few baby-friendly objects." Horn Book

My way; a Margaret and Margarita story= A mi manera; un cuento de Margarita y Margaret. Rayo/Greenwillow Books 2007 unp il $15.99

Grades: PreK K 1   E
    1. Friendship—Fiction 2. Bilingual books—English-Spanish
    ISBN 978-0-06-084101-0; 0-06-084101-X
                         LC 2005-35646
    Parallel text in English and Spanish portrays Margaret and Margarita, who mirror one another as they fix their hair, greet their friends, and engage in other routine activities, each in her own special way.
    "The text . . . bears the imprint of childhood in its simple prose. The bright, open watercolor cartoon illustrations are engaging." SLJ

Tortillas and lullabies. Tortillas y cancioncitas; pictures by "Corazones Valientes;" coordinated and translated by Rebecca Hart. Greenwillow Bks. 1998 40p il $16.99; pa $6.99 *

Grades: PreK K 1 2   E
    1.   Mother-daughter   relationship—Fiction 2. Grandmothers—Fiction 3. Bilingual books—English-Spanish
    ISBN 0-688-14628-7; 0-06-089185-8 (pa)
                         LC 97-7096
    Companion volume to Cherry pies and lullabies
    In this "picture book, four everyday activities are depicted—making tortillas, gathering flowers, washing clothes, and singing a lullaby—as they are repeated by the women of a family over the last four generations. . . . Six Costa Rican women worked together to produce the striking acrylic folk-art paintings. With deeply saturated, glowing tones and a decidedly Central American style, the pictures enhance and extend the lyrical narrative, which is printed in English and in Spanish." SLJ

Rennert, Laura Joy

Buying, training & caring for your dinosaur; written by Laura Joy Rennert; pictures by Marc Brown. Alfred A. Knopf 2009 unp il $16.99; lib bdg $19.99

Grades: PreK K 1 2   E
    1. Dinosaurs—Fiction 2. Pets—Fiction
    ISBN 978-0-375-83679-4; 0-375-83679-9; 978-0-375-93679-1 (lib bdg); 0-375-93679-3 (lib bdg)
                         LC 2008-50680
    Includes instructions for choosing and caring for a pet dinosaur
    "This features funny, colorful illustrations. . . . Youngsters will quickly become absorbed in this enjoyable mix of facts, fantasy, and fossils." Booklist

Rex, Adam

Pssst! Harcourt 2007 unp il $16

Grades: PreK K 1 2   E
    1. Zoos—Fiction 2. Animals—Fiction
    ISBN 978-0-15-205817-3; 0-15-205817-6
                         LC 2006-24551
    "A zoo-going girl talks to the animals, but the novelty wears off when the pushy beasts send her on errands. . . . Rex packs increasingly crisp conversations into tight six-panel comics, relaxing into airy spreads as the girl meanders along zoo paths. . . . A very funny excursion." Publ Wkly

Rex, Michael

Goodnight goon; a petrifying parody; [by] Michael Rex. G.P. Putnam's Sons 2008 unp il $14.99

Grades: K 1 2 3   E
    1. Monsters—Fiction 2. Bedtime—Fiction 3. Stories in rhyme
    ISBN 978-0-399-24534-3; 0-399-24534-0
                         LC 2007-16585
    A young monster says goodnight to all of the other monsters in his bedroom.
    "This book is a hilarious adaptation of the classic bed-

Rex, Michael—*Continued*

time story, Goodnight Moon. . . . This is a delightfully funny and witty story containing adorable illustrations with tons of details. . . . Author and illustrator Michael Rex has created a wonderful page-by-page companion to the original." Libr Media Connect

Truck Duck; [by] Michael Rex. G.P. Putnam's Sons 2004 unp il hardcover o.p. bd bk $7.99
Grades: PreK K 1 2   E
  1. Animals—Fiction 2. Vehicles—Fiction 3. Stories in rhyme
ISBN 0-399-24009-8; 0-399-25092-1 (bd bk)
                       LC 2003-707
A variety of animals drive vehicles whose names rhyme with their own
"This is the stuff of toddlers' play, with vrooming action and small characters in charge. The sounds of the words add to the fun, and to little ones' vocabularies. The vehicles are big, bright, and clear." Booklist
 A companion to this title is:
Dunk skunk (2005)

Rey, H. A. (Hans Augusto), 1898-1977

Curious George. Houghton Mifflin 1941 unp il $16; pa $6.95 *
Grades: PreK K 1   E
  1. Monkeys—Fiction
ISBN 0-395-15993-8; 0-395-15023-X (pa)
Curious George goes to the hospital was written by Margret Rey and H. A. Rey in collaboration with the Children's Hospital Medical Center; and Curious George flies a kite was written by Margret Rey with pictures by H. A. Rey
Colored picture book, with simple text, describing the adventures of a curious small monkey, and the difficulties he had in getting used to city life, before he went to live in the zoo
"The bright lithographs in red, yellow, and blue, are gay and lighthearted, following the story closely with the same speed and animated humour." Ont Libr Rev
 Other titles about Curious George are:
Curious George flies a kite (1958)
Curious George gets a medal (1957)
Curious George goes to the hospital (1966)
Curious George learns the alphabet (1963)
Curious George rides a bike (1952)
Curious George takes a job (1947)

Curious George: Cecily G. and the 9 monkeys; written and illustrated by H. A. Rey; afterword by Louise Borden. Houghton Mifflin Company 2007 unp il $16; pa $6.99
Grades: PreK K 1   E
  1. Giraffes—Fiction 2. Monkeys—Fiction
ISBN 978-0-618-80066-7;   0-618-80066-2; 978-0-618-99794-7 (pa); 0-618-99794-6 (pa)
                    LC 2006-38698

First published 1942
A lonely giraffe teams up with the nine playful monkeys.
"This edition of the first story to feature Curious George includes a new afterword." Horn Book Guide

Rey, Margret

Whiteblack the penguin sees the world; [by] Margret & H. A. Rey. Houghton Mifflin 2000 unp il $15; pa $5.95
Grades: PreK K 1   E
  1. Penguins—Fiction
ISBN 0-618-07389-2; 0-618-07390-6 (pa)
                    LC 00-23196
In search of new stories for his radio program, Whiteblack the penguin sets out on a journey and has some interesting adventures
"The plot is very well crafted, and Whiteblack's adventures are appealingly silly, almost slapstick. H. A. Rey's watercolors make great use of the white paper, contrasting it with deep hues of yellow, red, and ultramarine blue and thick black outlines." Booklist

Reynolds, Aaron, 1970-

Back of the bus; illustrated by Floyd Cooper. Philomel Books 2010 unp il $16.99 *
Grades: K 1 2 3   E
  1. Parks, Rosa, 1913-2005—Fiction 2. African Americans—Civil rights—Fiction 3. Race relations—Fiction 4. African Americans—Fiction
ISBN 978-0-399-25091-0; 0-399-25091-3
                  LC 2008018109
From the back of the bus, an African American child watches the arrest of Rosa Parks.
Reynolds's "lyrical yet forceful text conveys the narrator's apprehension and Park's calm resolve. . . . Cooper's . . . filmy oil paintings are characterized by a fine mistlike texture, which results in warm, lifelike portraits that convincingly evoke the era, the intense emotional pitch of this incident, and the everyday heroism it embodied." Publ Wkly

Metal man; illustrated by Paul Hoppe. Charlesbridge 2008 unp il lib bdg $15.95; pa $7.95
Grades: PreK K 1 2   E
  1. African Americans—Fiction 2. Metalwork—Fiction 3. Sculpture—Fiction
ISBN 978-1-58089-150-9 (lib bdg); 1-58089-150-0 (lib bdg); 978-1-58089-151-6 (pa); 1-58089-151-9 (pa)
                  LC 2007-17187
One hot summer day, a man who makes sculpture out of junk helps a boy create what he sees in his mind's eye.
"Beautifully understated, the story is about the capacity of art to empower the artist and to affect how others see the world. The poetic text is visceral. . . . The cartoon illustrations, in rusty browns and shiny blues, depict the metal man as tall, strong, gentle, and wise, a larger-than-life hero. . . . A wonderful example of sensory writing and colloquial storytelling." SLJ

Superhero School; illustrated by Andy Rash. Bloomsbury Children's Books 2009 unp il $16.99; lib bdg $17.89
Grades: K 1 2 3 4   E
  1. Superheroes—Fiction 2. School stories 3. Mathematics—Fiction
ISBN 978-1-59990-166-4;   1-59990-166-8; 978-1-59990-346-0 (lib bdg); 1-59990-346-6 (lib bdg)
                  LC 2008031374

Reynolds, Aaron, 1970-—*Continued*

When Leonard starts attending Superhero School he is disappointed to find that all they learn is math, but when the ice zombies strike, Leonard and his classmates put their newly-acquired knowledge to good use

"Rash's illustrations in digital collage of gouache and Sharpies create his trademark cartoons that pulsate with energy and engage readers. Reynolds creatively blends the use of math skills in word-problem superhero settings that are playful, smart, and positive." SLJ

Reynolds, Peter

The dot; [by] Peter H. Reynolds. Candlewick Press 2003 unp il $14

Grades: PreK K 1 2   E

1. Drawing—Fiction 2. School stories

ISBN 0-7636-1961-2   LC 2002-041113

Vashti believes that she cannot draw, but her art teacher's encouragement leads her to change her mind

"In this engaging, inspiring tale, Reynolds . . . demonstrates the power of a little encouragement. . . . Rendered in watercolor, ink and tea, Reynolds's spare, wispy illustrations exude a fresh, childlike quality pleasingly in sync with his hand-lettered text." Publ Wkly

Ish; [by] Peter H. Reynolds. Candlewick Press 2004 unp il $14

Grades: PreK K 1 2 3   E

1. Drawing—Fiction 2. Siblings—Fiction

ISBN 0-7636-2344-X   LC 2003-66196

Ramon loses confidence in his ability to draw, but his sister gives him a new perspective on things

"The overriding theme about creativity versus exactitude will resonate with many. The line-and-color artwork is simple, but it has great emotion and warmth." Booklist

Rose's garden; [by] Peter H. Reynolds. Candlewick Press 2009 unp il $15.99

Grades: K 1 2 3   E

1. Flowers—Fiction 2. Gardens—Fiction

ISBN 978-0-7636-4641-7; 0-7636-4641-5

LC 2009-24175

Rose finds a neglected patch of earth in the middle of a bustling city where she can plant the flower seeds collected from her travels in her magical teapot

"This inspiring fable will capture the hearts and imaginations of readers and show them that anything is possible. . . . Reynolds's outstanding illustrations done in watercolor and ink begin in shades of gray and then explode with color and joy as the garden evolves and people come to enjoy it." SLJ

Rice, Eve, 1951-

Sam who never forgets. Greenwillow Bks. 1977 unp il pa $5.99 hardcover o.p.

Grades: PreK K   E

1. Zoos—Fiction 2. Animals—Fiction

ISBN 0-688-07335-2 (pa)   LC 76-30370

Sam is "a zoo keeper who 'never, never forgets' to feed the animals promptly at three o'clock. The beasts have their doubts when it looks like Sam has neglected to feed poor Elephant who is both hungry and crestfallen. Happily, Sam returns with a whole wagon of hay."

SLJ

"A simple, unpretentious story with child appeal that lies in the naive, straightforward telling and elemental emotional interactions of the characters. . . . Rice has forsaken her pen drawings for bright, unlined colored shapes. The figures are pleasantly stylized, the scenes evenly composed." Booklist

Richards, Beah, 1926-2000

Keep climbing, girls; by Beah E. Richards; illustrated by R. Gregory Christie; introduction by LisaGay Hamilton. Simon & Schuster Books for Young Readers 2006 unp il $15.95 *

Grades: PreK K 1 2   E

1. Girls—Poetry

ISBN 1-4169-0264-3   LC 2004-29153

"In this picture-book rendition of Richards's 1951 poem of the same name, girls are urged to 'keep climbing' no matter what obstacles get in the way. Bold gouache illustrations create a beguiling green-and-gold landscape with an irresistible tree and a determined little girl who climbs it higher and higher with every page turn." SLJ

Richards, Chuck, 1957-

Critter sitter; [by] Chuck Richards. Walker & Company 2008 unp il $16.99; lib bdg $17.89

Grades: 1 2 3 4   E

1. Pets—Fiction

ISBN   978-0-8027-9595-3;   0-8027-9595-1;
978-0-8027-9596-0 (lib bdg); 0-8027-9596-X (lib bdg)

LC 2008004314

When the Mahoney family hires Henry the Critter Sitter to watch their dog, cat, bird, fish, frog, and snake, he thinks he is up for the challenge since creature control is his game, but the pets have a different idea.

"The storytelling is well paced and amusing, but the artwork is the real grabber here. Created with colored-pencil and watercolor, the illustrations cleverly mix realism with humorous exaggeration." SLJ

Richardson, Justin

And Tango makes three; by Justin Richardson and Peter Parnell; illustrated by Henry Cole. Simon & Schuster Bks. for Young Readers 2005 unp il $14.95 *

Grades: PreK K 1 2   E

1. Penguins—Fiction 2. Homosexuality—Fiction

ISBN 0-689-87845-1

At New York City's Central Park Zoo, two male penguins fall in love and start a family by taking turns sitting on an abandoned egg until it hatches

"Done in soft watercolors, the illustrations set the tone for this uplifting story, and readers will find it hard to resist the penguins' comical expressions. . . . This joyful story about the meaning of family is a must for any library." SLJ

Ries, Lori

Aggie and Ben; three stories; illustrated by Frank W. Dormer. Charlesbridge 2006 48p il lib bdg $12.95; pa $5.95 *

Grades: K 1 2   E

1. Dogs—Fiction

ISBN 978-1-57091-549-9 (lib bdg); 1-57091-594-6 (lib bdg); 978-1-57091-649-6 (pa); 1-57091-649-7 (pa)

LC 2005-28702

After choosing a new dog, Ben describes what the pet Aggie can do and should not do around the house

"Funky but tender, Dormer's pen-and-ink cartoons with watercolor washes add depth to the simple story and provide that perfect illustration-to-text match that one seeks in successful easy readers." SLJ

Other titles about Aggie and Ben are:
Good dog, Aggie (2009)
Aggie the brave (2010)

Punk wig; illustrated by Erin Eitter-Kono. Boyds Mills Press 2008 unp il $16.95

Grades: PreK K 1 2   E

1. Cancer—Fiction 2. Mother-son relationship—Fiction 3. Wigs—Fiction

ISBN 978-1-59078-486-0; 1-59078-486-3

LC 2007-17688

A little boy does helpful things for his mother as she undergoes chemotherapy, and goes with her as she picks out a wig, which together they call her "punk wig."

"The story handles a tough subject with sensitivity, grace, and a sense of fun. It covers some of the issues facing families without giving too much information that might overwhelm a young child, and provides a good introduction to a hard subject. The watercolor pictures fit well with the text, portraying both the mother's treatment and her fun with the family." Libr Media Connect

Riggs, Shannon

Not in Room 204; illustrated by Jaime Zollars. Albert Whitman 2007 unp il $15.95 *

Grades: K 1 2 3   E

1. Child sexual abuse—Fiction 2. School stories

ISBN 978-0-8075-5764-8   LC 2006023402

"Quiet Regina feels comfortable in her classroom, where Mrs. Salvador runs a tight ship and insists on hard work and fair play. When the teacher starts the annual Stranger Danger unit, she departs from the usual script by saying that most often an adult who touches a child inappropriately is not a stranger but someone known to the child. . . . The next morning, Regina arrives early at Room 204 to confide her secret, which involves her father. . . . This picture book's strength is in the forthrightness of its message and the sensitivity of its presentation. . . . The text and digitally enhanced artwork work together well to express the book's message smoothly. . . . This helpful picture book will raise children's awareness of sexual abuse without raising anxiety." Booklist

Riley, Linnea Asplind

Mouse mess; [by] Linnea Riley. Blue Sky Press (NY) 1997 unp il $16.95

Grades: PreK K 1   E

1. Mice—Fiction 2. Food—Fiction 3. Stories in rhyme

ISBN 0-590-10048-3   LC 96-49499

A hungry mouse leaves a huge mess when it goes in search of a snack

"Cut-paper collages, set against black backgrounds, depict a chubby-cheeked mouse spilling, cutting, and eating a variety of colorful foods. . . . The rhyming text, filled with crunching and munching sounds, is rhythmic and fun to read aloud." SLJ

Rim, Sujean

Birdie's big-girl shoes. Little, Brown Books for Young Readers 2009 unp il $15.99

Grades: PreK K   E

1. Shoes—Fiction 2. Play—Fiction 3. Mother-daughter relationship—Fiction

ISBN 978-0-316-04470-7; 0-316-04470-9

LC 2008-43799

Five-year-old Birdie loves her mother's shoes, but when she is finally granted permission to wear some for a little while, she discovers that her 'barefoot shoes' are best of all

"The bold, stylized watercolor and collage illustrations, paired with spare, simple text, are set against ample white space and burst with bright, attractive textile patterns. A light confection for the preschool dress-up set." SLJ

Rinck, Maranke

I feel a foot! [by] Maranke Rinck & Martijn van der Linden. Lemniscaat 2008 unp il $16.95

Grades: PreK K 1   E

1. Animals—Fiction 2. Imagination—Fiction

ISBN 978-1-59078-638-3; 1-59078-638-6

LC 2008000917

Five animal friends, awakened by a strange noise, discover a creature in the dark that seems to be a giant-sized version of each of them.

"With simple wording, Rinck injects personality into each animal and van der Linden's images interact well with the text. His stark black backgrounds spotlight expressively imagined animals that appear in psychedelic colors and patterns reminiscent of a kaleidoscope." SLJ

Ringgold, Faith

Tar Beach. Crown 1991 unp il $18; lib bdg $18.99; pa $6.99 *

Grades: PreK K 1 2   E

1. African Americans—Fiction 2. Dreams—Fiction 3. Harlem (New York, N.Y.)—Fiction

ISBN 0-517-58030-6; 0-517-58031-4 (lib bdg); 0-517-88544-1 (pa)   LC 90-40410

A Caldecott Medal honor book, 1992

Eight-year-old Cassie dreams of flying above her Harlem home, claiming all she sees for herself and her family. Based on the author's quilt painting of the same name

"Part autobiographical, part fictional, this allegorical tale sparkles with symbolic and historical references central to African-American culture. The spectacular artwork, a combination of primitive naive figures in a flattened perspective against a boldly patterned cityscape, resonates with color and texture." Horn Book

Another title about Cassie is:
Cassie's word quilt (2002)

Ritz, Karen
Windows with birds; written and illustrated by
Karen Ritz. Boyds Mills Press 2010 unp il $16.95
Grades: PreK K 1 2   E
  1. Moving—Fiction 2. Cats—Fiction
  ISBN 978-1-59078-656-7; 1-59078-656-4
                                   LC 2009-19504
"This delicate and understated book tells a simple story about a striped cat with green eyes that loves a boy
and a house. All of the feline's comforts are in that
house, but one day the boy takes it to live in an apartment. The cat sulks and hides, while the boy tries to
coax it out. . . . By morning, the cat realizes that the
things it loves best—hiding places, windows with birds,
and the boy—are in the new environment as well. . . .
The realistic, closeup watercolors convey many emotions.
. . . This is a beautiful book for cat lovers and for those
who are uncomfortable with change." SLJ

Robbins, Jacqui
The new girl . . . and me; story by Jacqui
Robbins; with art by Matt Phelan. Atheneum 2006
unp il $16.95
Grades: K 1 2   E
  1. Friendship—Fiction 2. School stories 3. Iguanas—
  Fiction
  ISBN 0-689-86468-X   LC 2004-09931
Two girls named Shakeeta and Mia become friends
when Shakeeta boasts that she has a pet iguana and Mia
learns how to help Shakeeta "feel at home" even when
she is in school.
  "The characters are realistically and sympathetically
portrayed, and the conversations and actions of the children are natural. Phelan's cartoon-style watercolors depict a realistic-looking classroom with a mix of children
from a variety of backgrounds." SLJ

Two of a kind; [by] Jacqui Robbins and Matt
Phelan. Atheneum Books for Young Readers 2008
unp il $16.99
Grades: K 1 2   E
  1. Friendship—Fiction 2. School stories
  ISBN 978-1-4169-2437-1; 1-4169-2437-X
                                   LC 2006033210
When Anna abandons her best friend, Julisa, to spend
time with Kayla and Melanie, whose friendship is considered very special, she soon learns that she has little in
common with her new friends.
  "Phelan's restrained watercolor-and-pencil illustrations
are particularly apt at capturing the emotions at play in
the story, while Kayla and Melanie's devilish expressions
provide a gentle comic lift. A great introduction to early
converations are character, bullying, and peer pressure."
Booklist

Robert, François, 1946-
Find a face; by François and Jean Robert, with
Jane Gittings. Chronicle Books 2004 unp il $15.95
*
Grades: PreK K 1 2   E
  1. Face in art
  ISBN 0-8118-4338-6   LC 2003-17593

Presents, with accompanying rhyming text, photographs of everyday objects depicting faces
  This is "a fun book that demonstrates that faces can
be found anywhere if you look hard enough. . . . The
photographs are clear and bright, and set against boldly
colored backgrounds. Youngsters will never again look at
a light switch in the same way." SLJ

Robert, Na'ima bint
Ramadan moon; by Na'íma B. Robert;
illustrated by Shirin Adl. Frances Lincoln
Children's Books 2009 unp il $17.99
Grades: K 1 2 3   E
  1. Ramadan—Fiction 2. Muslims—Fiction
  ISBN 978-1-84507-922-2; 1-84507-922-1
This "follows a Muslim family through its observance
of the 'Month of Mercy.' . . . This book's poetic words
and playful, patterned collage artwork capture both the
solemnity and joy of religious practice and, in a series of
scenes of worshippers of every type and hue, show the
diversity of the Muslim community around the world."
Booklist

Roberts, Lynn
Little Red; a fizzingly good yarn; retold by
Lynn Roberts; illustrated by David Roberts. Harry
N. Abrams 2005 32p il $16.95
Grades: PreK K 1 2   E
  1. Wolves—Fiction 2. Grandmothers—Fiction
  3. Fairy tales
  ISBN 0-8109-5783-3   LC 2004-29534
In this version of the Grimm fairy tale, Thomas—who
is called Little Red—discovers a wolf in disguise at his
grandmother's house and ingeniously uses ginger ale to
save the day.
  "The real strength of the book is David Roberts' stylish pen-and-ink and watercolor art, which creates a shadowy, detailed work that is deliciously creepy yet packed
with humor." Bull Cent Child Books

Robinson Peete, Holly, 1964-
My brother Charlie; written by Holly Robinson
Peete and Ryan Elizabeth Peete with Denene
Millner; pictures by Shane W. Evans. Scholastic
Press 2010 unp il $16.99
Grades: 1 2 3 4   E
  1. Autism—Fiction 2. Twins—Fiction 3. Siblings—
  Fiction
  ISBN 978-0-545-09466-5; 0-545-09466-6
                                   LC 2009005589
A girl tells what it is like living with her twin brother
who has autism and sometimes finds it hard to communi-
cate with words, but who, in most ways, is just like any
other boy. Includes authors' note about autism
  "The authors, a mother-daughter team, based this story
on personal experience. Evans's bright, mixed-media illustrations skillfully depict the family's warmth and concern." SLJ

Rocco, John

Moonpowder; story and pictures by John Rocco. Hyperion Books for Children 2008 unp il $15.99

Grades: K 1 2　　　　　　　　　　　　E

1. Bedtime—Fiction 2. Dreams—Fiction

ISBN 978-1-4231-0011-9; 1-4231-0011-5

LC 2007-042236

Even though Eli is the "Fixer of all things fixable," one thing he cannot fix is his bad dreams, until one night when Mr. Moon appears and asks him to come fix the Moonpowder factory, where sweet dreams are created.

"Steeped in dreamy sepia tones suffused with golden light and brightened by unexpected patches of electric blue, the illustrations are lush and painterly. Using spreads combined with comic-style panels, Rocco creates a hint of a graphic novel for the youngest readers." SLJ

Wolf! wolf! Hyperion Books for Children 2007 unp il $15.99

Grades: K 1 2 3　　　　　　　　　　　　E

1. Wolves—Fiction 2. Goats—Fiction 3. China—Fiction

ISBN 1-4231-0012-3　　　　　　LC 2007-04636

"This twisted treatment of Aesop's fable flips everything readers know about the boy who cried wolf on its head. . . . Ancient China unfolds as the stage and setting for this story. In this variant, children get a little insight into the wolf's point of view. . . . The purposeful use of frames, unusual setting, and visual humor makes this an excellent addition to any collection." SLJ

Rockwell, Anne F., 1934-

At the supermarket. Henry Holt 2010 unp il $16.99

Grades: PreK　　　　　　　　　　　　E

1. Supermarkets—Fiction 2. Shopping—Fiction 3. Birthdays—Fiction

ISBN 978-0-8050-7662-2; 0-8050-7662-X

LC 2009009221

"Christy Ottaviano books"

A revised and newly illustrated edition of *The Supermarket*, published 1979 by MacMillan

A boy and his mother fill a cart at the supermarket with everything from grapes to paper towels, finishing off with ingredients for a birthday cake.

"The well-written narration explains their trip from start to finish, including how the checkout line works. The brightly colored gouache illustrations on white backgrounds show the child helping to fill the cart and feature such items as produce and a container of ice cream alone on the page, making identification easy. This is a fun, educational read-aloud." SLJ

Big wheels; by Anne Rockwell. Walker & Co. 2003 c1986 unp il $14.95; bd bk $6.95

Grades: PreK K 1　　　　　　　　　　　　E

1. Vehicles 2. Machinery

ISBN 0-8027-8882-3; 0-8027-8903-X (bd bk)

LC 2002-34348

A reissue of the title first published 1986 by Dutton Children's Bks.

Introduces a number of big-wheeled trucks, such as bulldozers, power shovels, and dump trucks, and explains what they do

"Although the author-artist has supplied a very brief text, she uses active, vivid verbs, such as *dig, dump*, and *chop up*, effectively conveying a sense of the machinery in the fewest words necessary. Likewise, her illustrations contain exactly the right amount of detail to satisfy but not confuse." Horn Book

Father's Day; by Anne Rockwell; pictures by Lizzy Rockwell. HarperCollins 2005 unp il $14.99 *

Grades: PreK K 1　　　　　　　　　　　　E

1. Father's Day—Fiction 2. Fathers—Fiction

ISBN 0-06-051377-2　　　　　　LC 2004-6243

For Fathers' Day, the students in Mrs. Madoff's class write and illustrate books about their dads.

"The best part of the book is the way it reflects the differences in dads. . . . The artwork, with rounded shapes and smooth colors, has a simple, friendly look that puts the focus on the characters." Booklist

Other titles about Mrs. Madoff's class are:

100 school days (2002)

Career day (2000)

Halloween day (1997)

Mother's Day (2004)

Presidents' Day (2007)

St. Patrick's Day (2010)

Thanksgiving Day (1999)

Valentine's Day (2001)

Four seasons make a year; pictures by Megan Halsey. Walker & Co. 2004 unp il $15.95; lib bdg $16.85 *

Grades: PreK K 1　　　　　　　　　　　　E

1. Seasons

ISBN 0-8027-8883-1; 0-8027-8885-8 (lib bdg)

LC 2003-57171

Describes the passing of the seasons through the changes in plants and animals that occur on a farm

"The first-person text is simple and childlike, a tone reflected in the clearly delineated collages. Combining ink drawings with acrylic paintings on torn paper, these illustrations create eye-catching compositions." Booklist

My preschool; [by] Anne Rockwell. Holt 2008 unp il $16.95

Grades: PreK　　　　　　　　　　　　E

1. School stories

ISBN 978-0-8050-7955-5; 0-8050-7955-6

LC 2007002834

Follows a little boy during his day at preschool, from cheerful hellos in circle time, to painting colorful pictures and playing at the water table, to passing out paper cups for snack

In the illustrations Rockwell uses "colorful inks and traditional Japanese woodblock printing. . . . The detail and realistic depiction of the preschool experience will help to calm some newcomers' trepidations about attending school for the first time." SLJ

The toolbox; by Anne & Harlow Rockwell. Walker & Company 2004 unp il hardcover o.p. bd bk $6.95 *

Grades: PreK K 1　　　　　　　　　　　　E

1. Tools

ISBN 0-8027-8930-7; 0-8027-9609-5 (bd bk)

LC 2003-66562

Rockwell, Anne F., 1934-—*Continued*

A reissue of the title first published 1971 by Macmillan

An easy-to-read description of the basic tools found in a toolbox

"The brief text is printed in clear, handsome type. . . . [The illustrations] make ingenious use of watercolor to show textures and surfaces of wood and metal." Horn Book

Rodman, Mary Ann

First grade stinks; written by Mary Ann Rodman; illustrated by Beth Spiegel. Peachtree 2006 unp il $15.95; pa $8.95

Grades: K 1 2   E

1. School stories

ISBN 1-56145-377-3; 1-56145-462-1 (pa)

LC 2006-02711

First-grader Haley wishes she were back having fun in kindergarten with her old teacher, until she finds out that first-grade is special, too

"The scratchy, fluid, full-color watercolor-and-ink illustrations feature plenty of white space. Perfect as a read-aloud." SLJ

My best friend; illustrated by E.B. Lewis. Viking 2005 unp il $14.99; pa $5.99 *

Grades: PreK K 1   E

1. Friendship—Fiction

ISBN 0-670-05989-7; 0-14-240806-9 (pa)

LC 2004-22778

Six-year-old Lily has a best friend all picked out for play group day, but unfortunately the differences between first-graders and second-graders are sometimes very large

"Rodman's honest text captures the girl's heartbroken disappointment and makes it real for young readers, and Lewis's shining, sun-drenched illustrations convey both the harshness and warmth of the bright days at the pool." SLJ

Surprise soup; illustrated by G. Brian Karas. Viking 2009 unp il $15.99 *

Grades: PreK K 1   E

1. Brothers—Fiction 2. Family life—Fiction 3. Soups—Fiction 4. Cooking—Fiction 5. Bears—Fiction

ISBN 978-0-670-06274-4; 0-670-06274-X

LC 2008-22548

"Mama Bear's on the way home with a new baby, and middle brother Kevie does his best to help big Josh and Daddy make homecoming Saturday Soup." SLJ

"Frequent, playful sound effects . . . will make read-alouds fun, and Rodman perfectly captures the rhythm and words of family dialogue. . . . Kara's collage artwork combines thickly lined, expressive figures with patterned details." Booklist

A tree for Emmy; written by Mary Ann Rodman; illustrated by Tatjana Mai-Wyss. Peachtree 2009 unp il $15.95

Grades: K 1 2   E

1. Trees—Fiction 2. Birthdays—Fiction

ISBN 978-1-56145-475-4; 1-56145-475-3

LC 2008036745

Emmy loves the mimosa tree in her grandmother's yard and asks for one for her birthday, only to find that stores do not sell wild trees.

"The repetition of phrases, the cadence of the text, and the understanding of a child's emotions make this picture book a fine choice for reading aloud." Booklist

Rodriguez, Beatrice, 1969-

The chicken thief. Enchanted Lion Books 2010 unp il $14.95

Grades: PreK K 1   E

1. Stories without words 2. Chickens—Fiction 3. Foxes—Fiction

ISBN 978-1-59270-092-9; 1-59270-092-6

"In Rodriguez's wordless debut, a bear and rabbit are enjoying a peaceful lunch in the garden outside their cottage when a fox makes off with one of their hens. The rooster wrings his wings melodramatically, and all three give chase. . . . Rodriguez succeeds in creating a distinctive personality for each of the characters, and her ability to capture the players' emotions via body language is masterful. . . . For readers who love a good chase—and who doesn't?—this one is a delight from beginning to end." Publ Wkly

Rodriguez, Edel

Sergio makes a splash. Little, Brown 2008 unp il $15.99 *

Grades: PreK K 1 2   E

1. Penguins—Fiction 2. Swimming—Fiction

ISBN 978-0-316-06616-7

Even though he loves water, Sergio the penguin is afraid to swim in the deep water until he learns how.

"The simple woodblock and digital art is stunningly rendered in bright orange, stark white, and cool aquamarine. Rodriquez uses bold graphics, lines, and angles to create a sense of play and space that draws in readers. The text is great fun for storytimes or for reading alone." SLJ

Another title about Sergio is:

Sergio saves the game! (2009)

Rogers, Gregory

Midsummer knight. Roaring Brook Press 2007 unp il $16.95 *

Grades: K 1 2 3 4 5   E

1. Fairies—Fiction 2. Bears—Fiction 3. Heroes and heroines—Fiction 4. Stories without words

ISBN 978-1-59643-183-6; 1-59643-183-0

LC 2006-51013

Companion volume to: The boy, the bear, the baron, the bard (2004)

First published in Australia 2006

A bear is rescued by a fairy in an enchanted wood and agrees to return the favor by leading the battle against a usurper who has imprisoned the king and queen, along with their loyal subjects, in the dungeon of their castle

"This is another wordless adventure, depicted in colorful, comics-style panels that will delight young readers." Booklist

Rohmann, Eric, 1957-

Clara and Asha. Roaring Brook 2005 unp il $16.95 *

Grades: PreK K 1 2   E

1. Imaginary playmates—Fiction 2. Fishes—Fiction 3. Bedtime—Fiction

ISBN 1-59643-031-1   LC 2005-04677

Young Clara would rather play with her imaginary giant fish, Asha, than settle down to sleep.

"The oil paintings portray a natural world in all its glorious seasons, brimming with mystery and delight. . . . Children will revel in the opportunity to see their dreams and longings realized so enchantingly." SLJ

A kitten tale. Alfred A. Knopf 2008 unp il $15.99; lib bdg $18.99 *

Grades: PreK   E

1. Cats—Fiction 2. Seasons—Fiction 3. Snow—Fiction

ISBN 978-0-517-70915-3; 978-0-517-70916-0 (lib bdg)   LC 2007-11093

As four kittens who have never seen winter watch the seasons pass, three of them declare the reasons they will dislike snow when it arrives, while the fourth cannot wait to experience it for himself

This is a "marvel of sly simplicity for the very young. . . . [Rohmann's] uncluttered, inventive scenes masterfully echo the repetitive rhythm in the words." Booklist

My friend Rabbit. Roaring Brook Press 2002 unp il $15; pa $6.99 *

Grades: PreK K 1 2   E

1. Friendship—Fiction 2. Rabbits—Fiction 3. Mice—Fiction

ISBN 0-7613-1535-7; 0-312-36752-X (pa)   LC 2002-17764

Awarded the Caldecott Medal, 2003

Something always seems to go wrong when Rabbit is around, but Mouse lets him play with his toy plane anyway because he is his good friend

"The double-page, hand-colored relief prints with heavy black outlines are magnificent, and children will enjoy the comically expressive pictures of the animals." SLJ

Time flies. Crown 1994 unp il $17; lib bdg $17.99; pa $6.99

Grades: PreK K 1 2   E

1. Stories without words 2. Birds—Fiction 3. Dinosaurs—Fiction

ISBN 0-517-59598-2; 0-517-59599-0 (lib bdg); 0-517-88555-7 (pa)   LC 93-28200

A Caldecott Medal honor book, 1995

A wordless tale in which a bird flying around the dinosaur exhibit in a natural history museum has an unsettling experience when the dinosaur seems to come alive and view the bird as a potential meal

"The handsome, atmospheric paintings heighten the drama as they tell their simple, somewhat mysterious, and quite short story." Booklist

Roosa, Karen

Pippa at the parade; illustrated by Julie Fortenberry. Boyds Mills Press 2009 unp il $16.95

Grades: PreK K   E

1. Stories in rhyme 2. Parades—Fiction

ISBN 978-1-59078-567-6; 1-59078-567-3   LC 2008028127

A young child has a fun-filled day with her parents at the big parade

"Bursting with movement, the spirited and freeflowing watercolors capture cartwheeling gymnasts and marching scout troops. . . . The brief rhyming verses . . . include a few onomatopoeic phrases that invite young listeners to join in." Booklist

Root, Phyllis, 1949-

Big Momma makes the world; written by Phyllis Root; illustrated by Helen Oxenbury. Candlewick Press 2003 unp il $16.99; pa $6.99

Grades: PreK K 1 2   E

1. Creation—Fiction

ISBN 0-7636-1132-8; 0-7636-2600-7 (pa)   LC 2002-17498

Big Momma, with a baby on her hip and laundry piling up, makes the world and everything in it and, at the end of the sixth day, tells the people she has made that they must take care of her creation

"Root's text is strong and sassy, with a down-home cadence that has immediate appeal, and Oxenbury's Big Momma is the perfect embodiment of the story's earth mother." Booklist

Creak! said the bed; illustrated by Regan Dunnick. Candlewick Press 2010 unp il $15.99

Grades: PreK K   E

1. Beds—Fiction 2. Noise—Fiction

ISBN 978-0-7636-2004-2; 0-7636-2004-1

"The increasingly crowded bed . . . is by now a standard picture-book plotline. Fresh takes on the subject are hard to come by, but Root manages to make it feel new by punctuating the story with the sounds of impending disaster. . . . The economy of the story line is paralleled by gouache illustrations . . . that reinforce the bed-centered tale but also pull in and zoom out on its inhabitants for different perspectives. The lantern-jawed, snub-nosed family is cartoon cute, making for a perfect storytime read." Booklist

Flip, flap, fly! illustrated by David Walker. Candlewick 2009 unp il $14.99

Grades: PreK   E

1. Animals—Fiction 2. Stories in rhyme

ISBN 978-0-7636-3109-3; 0-7636-3109-4

An "assortment of baby animals flap, wiggle and splash their way through the forest, spotting each other in turn as they play with their mamas. Human babies and toddlers will love guessing which animal comes next as they follow clues from Root's contagious, rhyming text and Walker's bright and warm acrylic illustrations." Kirkus

Root, Phyllis, 1949—*Continued*

Kiss the cow; illustrated by Will Hillenbrand. Candlewick Press 2000 unp il hardcover o.p. pa $6.99

Grades: K 1 2 3   E
  1. Cattle—Fiction
  ISBN 0-7636-0298-1; 0-7636-2003-3 (pa)
                                    LC 00-20926

Annalisa, the most curious and stubborn of Mama May's children, disobeys her mother and upsets the family's magic cow by refusing to kiss her in return for the milk she gives

"Elements of folklore echo through the story that reads aloud rhythmically with a satisfying, folksy sound. . . . The well-conceived illustrations, warm in color and graceful in line, depict a variety of scenes with style and panache." Booklist

Lucia and the light; illustrated by Mary Grandpré. Candlewick Press 2006 unp il $16.99 *

Grades: PreK K 1 2   E
  1. Sun—Fiction 2. Winter—Fiction 3. Trolls—Fiction
  4. Cats—Fiction
  ISBN 978-0-7636-2296-1; 0-7636-2296-6

One winter in the Far North the sun disappears and Lucia, accompanied by her milk-white cat, braves the freezing cold and trolls who want to eat her, trying to find the sun and bring it back.

"Grandpré's evocative, dimly lit acrylics capture the eerie mystery and shivery suspense of the adventure. . . . Root's rich language and well-paced story are sure to capture a young crowd of eager listeners." Booklist

The name quilt; pictures by Margot Apple. Farrar, Straus & Giroux 2003 unp il $16

Grades: K 1 2 3   E
  1. Quilts—Fiction 2. Grandmothers—Fiction
  ISBN 0-374-35484-7   LC 2002-69328

One of Sadie's favorite things to do when she visits her grandmother is to hear stories about the family members whose names are on a special quilt that Grandma had made, so Sadie is very sad when the quilt is blown away in a storm

"Root makes the most of the simple, intimate anecdotes that flow between generations, and the crayon-looking drawings bespeak a rustic informality." Publ Wkly

Paula Bunyan; illustrated by Kevin O'Malley. Farrar, Straus and Giroux 2009 unp il $16.95

Grades: K 1 2 3   E
  1. Tall tales 2. Size—Fiction
  ISBN 978-0-374-35759-7; 0-374-35759-5
                                    LC 2007-43728

Recounts the exploits of Paul Bunyan's "little" sister, Paula, who lived in the North Woods, sang three-part harmony with the wolves, and used an angry bear for a foot warmer.

"O'Malley's white-framed, woodcutlike pictures, heavily outlined with intricate line shading, appear throughout this appropriately tall book. Sweeping panoramic views, Paula's thunderous voice depicted in large speech bubbles, bear-carrying mosquitoes, comical animal expressions, and energetic black-and-white drawings add to the fun. The timely environmental message is an added plus." SLJ

Thirsty Thursday; illustrated by Helen Craig. Candlewick Press 2009 unp il $9.99

Grades: PreK K   E
  1. Flowers—Fiction 2. Rain—Fiction 3. Farm life—Fiction
  ISBN 978-0-7636-3628-9; 0-7636-3628-2

"It's Thursday on Bonnie Bumble's farm, and everyone is thirsty—especially the flowers. . . . Not a drop of rain is in sight, but luckily Bonnie has an idea. She puts the sheep on top of the cow and the pig on top of the sheep, and she climbs on top of the pig . . . and tickles the cloud with a feather. . . . Short, sweet and unabashedly darling, Root's text employs just the right amount of repetition to get toddlers chiming in by the second reading. Craig's ink, watercolor and pencil illustrations lend Bonnie, animals and flowers expressive personalities." Kirkus

Toot toot zoom! illustrated by Matthew Cordell. Candlewick Press 2009 unp il $15.99

Grades: PreK K   E
  1. Animals—Fiction 2. Automobiles—Fiction
  3. Friendship—Fiction
  ISBN 978-0-7636-3452-0; 0-7636-3452-2
                                    LC 2008-934781

"Pierre, a red fox, lives alone at the foot of a mountain. One day he drives off in his little red sports convertible, hoping to make a friend on the other side." SLJ

"A simple storyline, great sound effects, a touch of humor, and big, bold illustrations make this a lively choice for storytime." Bull Cent Child Books

Rose, Deborah Lee, 1955-

Birthday zoo; written by Lee Rose; illustrated by Lynn Munsinger. Whitman, A. 2002 unp il $15.95; pa $6.95

Grades: PreK K 1 2   E
  1. Zoos—Fiction 2. Birthdays—Fiction 3. Animals—Fiction 4. Stories in rhyme
  ISBN 0-8075-0776-8; 0-8075-0777-6 (pa)
                                    LC 2002-1726

Rhyming text describes the preparations made for a boy's birthday party by his hosts, the animals at the zoo

"While Rose's strong rhythm and rhymes will charm youngsters in a storytime, Munsinger's lively pen-and-ink and watercolor illustrations beg for closer inspection." SLJ

One nighttime sea; an ocean counting rhyme; pictures by Steve Jenkins. Scholastic 2003 unp il $16.95 *

Grades: PreK K 1 2   E
  1. Counting 2. Marine animals 3. Night
  ISBN 0-439-33906-5   LC 2002-8127

A counting book featuring nocturnal sea creatures, from one blue whale calf to ten turtle hatchlings, and back down to one seal pup. Includes facts about each of the twenty featured animals

"In a lapping, sealike rhythm, this enchanting counting book lulls its audience into the world beneath the waves. . . . Vivid cut-paper collages beautifully interplay with the rhymes." SLJ

Rose, Deborah Lee, 1955-—*Continued*

The twelve days of winter; a school counting book; illustrated by Carey Armstrong-Ellis. Abrams 2006 unp il lib bdg $14.95

Grades: PreK K 1 2   E

1. Winter—Fiction 2. Counting

ISBN 0-8109-5472-9

A cumulative counting verse in which a child lists items pertaining to winter given to him by his teacher, from twelve treats for tasting to one bird feeder in a snowy tree.

"While the book would work well as a read or sing-aloud, with so much to pore over and absorb in the art, it is best used for one-on-one sharing. A surefire choice to spice up the dreariest winter day." SLJ

Rosen, Michael, 1946-

I'm number one; illustrated by Bob Graham. Candlewick Press 2009 unp il $16.99

Grades: PreK K 1 2   E

1. Toys—Fiction

ISBN 978-0-7636-4535-9; 0-7636-4535-4

LC 2009004246

A wind-up soldier bosses and berates the other toys, making them feel terrible, until they suddenly start to rebel.

"The pen-and-watercolor illustrations are filled with expressive characters and Graham's signature, whimsical details, such as the stuffed pig's snout ring. This simple, affecting story will be welcome anywhere that more than two young kids are gathered together and where laughter, not mean words, is the lingua franca." Booklist

Michael Rosen's sad book; words by Michael Rosen; pictures by Quentin Blake. Candlewick Press 2005 unp il $16.99; pa $6.99 *

Grades: K 1 2 3   E

1. Bereavement—Fiction

ISBN 0-7636-2597-3; 0-7636-4104-9 (pa)

LC 2004-45787

A man tells about all the emotions that accompany his sadness over the death of his son, and how he tries to cope

"Blake's evocative watercolor-and-ink illustrations use shades of gray for the pictures where sadness has taken hold but brighten with color at the memory of happy times. This story is practical and universal and will be of comfort to those who are working through their bereavement. A brilliant and distinguished collaboration." SLJ

Red Ted and the lost things; illustrated by Joel Stewart. Candlewick Press 2009 40p il $16.99; pa $8.99

Grades: PreK K 1 2   E

1. Teddy bears—Fiction 2. Toys—Fiction 3. Lost and found possessions—Fiction

ISBN 978-0-7636-4537-3; 0-7636-4537-0; 978-0-7636-4624-0 (pa); 0-7636-4624-5 (pa)

LC 2009-02992

When a teddy bear is accidentally left on the seat of a train, he uses his ingenuity—and some new friends—to search for the little girl who lost him.

"Rosen's quirky combination of characters is matched by Stewart's muted colors and deliberately hazy back-grounds, which nicely spotlight the stuffed animals. . . . The plucky and determined Red Ted deserves a place among the many lost-toys books on library shelves." SLJ

Totally wonderful Miss Plumberry; [by] Michael Rosen; illustrated by Chinlun Lee. Candlewick Press 2006 unp il $15.99 *

Grades: PreK K 1 2   E

1. Teachers—Fiction 2. School stories

ISBN 0-7636-2744-5   LC 2005045392

Molly's day turns from totally wonderful to totally horrible when her classmates are not interested in the special crystal she has brought to school, until Miss Plumberry steps in to help

"This gentle picture book captures the impact a sensitive teacher has on the lives of her students. . . . The soft watercolor-and-pencil illustrations reveal [Molly's] emotions and expose the fickle attention of children in engaging . . . spreads." SLJ

We're going on a bear hunt; anniversary edition of a modern classic; retold by Michael Rosen; illustrated by Helen Oxenbury. Margaret K. McElderry Books 2009 unp il $18.99 *

Grades: PreK K 1 2   E

1. Bears—Fiction 2. Hunting—Fiction

ISBN 978-1-4169-8711-6; 1-4169-8711-8

LC 2008-53214

First published 1989

Brave bear hunters go through grass, a river, mud, and other obstacles before the inevitable encounter with the bear forces a headlong retreat

"Glorious puddles of watercolor alternate with impish charcoal sketches in this refreshing interpretation of an old hand rhyme in which a man, four children, and a dog stalk the furry beast through mud and muck, high and low. A book with a genuine atmosphere of togetherness and boundless enthusiasm for the hunt." SLJ

Rosenberg, Liz

Nobody; illustrated by Julie Downing. Roaring Brook Press 2010 unp il $16.99

Grades: PreK K   E

1. Imaginary playmates—Fiction 2. Morning—Fiction 3. Parent-child relationship—Fiction

ISBN 978-1-59643-120-1; 1-59643-120-2

"A Neal Porter book"

"Young George wakes up early one morning while his parents are asleep. His imaginary companion, Nobody, is there to keep him company and inspires plenty of mischief. . . . Color pops off the page with playful illustrations done in watercolor, colored pencil, pastels, and china marker. Downing cleverly contrasts Nobody in black and white. The visual impact is strong but simple and underscores the tightly written text, and the facial expressions are priceless. Perspective is creatively used, particularly in a spread where George and Nobody are exploring the contents of the refrigerator. Kids and their parents will love this one." SLJ

Rosenberry, Vera, 1948-

Vera's first day of school. Holt & Co. 1999 unp il hardcover o.p. pa $6.95 *

Grades: PreK K 1 2   E

1. School stories

ISBN 0-8050-5936-9; 0-8050-7269-1 (pa)

LC 98-43347

Vera cannot wait for the day when she starts school, but the first day does not go exactly as she has anticipated

"Rosenberry's playful, brightly colored gouache illustrations capture Vera's jubilation-turned-dismay." Horn Book Guide

Other titles about Vera are:

Vera goes to the dentist (2002)

Vera rides a bike (2004)

Vera runs away (2000)

Vera's baby sister (2005)

Vera's Halloween (2008)

Vera's new school (2006)

When Vera was sick (1998)

Rosenthal, Amy Krouse

Bedtime for Mommy; illustrated by LeUyen Pham. Bloomsbury 2010 unp il $16.99; lib bdg $17.89

Grades: PreK K 1 2   E

1. Bedtime—Fiction 2. Mother-daughter relationship—Fiction

ISBN   978-1-59990-341-5;   1-59990-341-5; 978-1-59990-465-8 (lib bdg); 1-59990-465-9 (lib bdg)

LC 2009-18205

In a reversal of the classic bedtime story, a child helps her mommy get ready for bed, enduring pleas for one more book, five more minutes of play time, and a glass of water before the lights go out.

"The facial expressions throughout are priceless, and the final illustration showing the parents peeking in at a sleeping daughter round out this tale. This very visual story will appeal to beginning readers as well as parents and librarians looking for a fun bedtime read-aloud." Libr Media Connect

Cookies; bite-size life lessons; written by Amy Krouse Rosenthal; illustrated by Jane Dyer. HarperCollins Publishers 2006 unp il $12.99; lib bdg $13.89 *

Grades: PreK K 1 2   E

1. Conduct of life 2. Cookies

ISBN   978-0-06-058081-0;   0-06-058081-X; 978-0-06-058082-7 (lib bdg); 0-06-058082-8 (lib bdg)

LC 2005-15134

"Using the activity of making and eating cookies, the author defines some important concepts for young children, such as respect, trustworthiness, patience, politeness, loyalty, etc. . . . Lovely pastel watercolor illustrations show appealing children and anthropomorphic animals interacting with one another and the treats. . . . The utilization of the cookies to explain the concepts is a brilliant idea and works well on a child's level. The text is short and clear, and the book is delightful to look at and browse through." SLJ

Other titles in this series are:

Christmas cookies (2008)

Sugar cookies (2009)

One smart cookie (2010)

Duck! Rabbit! [illustrated by] Tom Lichtenheld. Chronicle Books 2009 unp il $16.99 *

Grades: PreK K 1 2   E

1. Ducks—Fiction 2. Rabbits—Fiction

ISBN 978-0-8118-6865-5; 0-8118-6865-6

LC 2008-28102

Rosenthal and Lichtenheld play "with perspective and visual trickery, . . . using a classic image that looks like either a rabbit (with long ears) or a duck (with a long bill). . . . Two off-stage speakers, their words appearing on either side of the animal's head, argue their points of view. The snappy dialogue makes for [a] fine read-aloud." Publ Wkly

Little Hoot; illustrated by Jen Corace. Chronicle Books 2008 unp il $12.99 *

Grades: PreK K   E

1. Bedtime—Fiction 2. Owls—Fiction

ISBN 978-0-8118-6023-9; 0-8118-6023-X

LC 2007-24960

Little Hoot wants to go to bed early, like all of his friends do, and he is hopping mad when Mama and Papa Owl insist that he stay up late and play.

The "owl family . . . feels recognizable. . . . This outing is not to be missed." Publ Wkly

Other titles in the series are:

Little oink (2009)

Little pea (2005)

The OK book; [by] Amy Krouse Rosenthal & Tom Lichtenheld. HarperCollins 2007 unp il $12.99

Grades: PreK K 1 2   E

1. Ability—Fiction 2. Self-acceptance—Fiction

ISBN 978-0-06-115255-9; 0-06-115255-2

LC 2006030432

"The book's hero is a little stick figure whose head is the O of OK, and whose arms and legs are the K. . . . I like to try a lot of different things, the OK figure says. I'm not great at all of them, but I enjoy them all the same. . . . One day, I'll grow up to be really excellent at something, OK says, while lying in bed. . . . It can't hurt to remind kids that the pleasure we take in simple activities is what makes life worthwhile." Publ Wkly

Yes Day! [by] Amy Krouse Rosenthal & [illustrated by] Tom Lichtenheld. HarperCollins 2009 unp il $14.99; lib bdg $15.89

Grades: PreK K 1   E

1. Wishes—Fiction 2. Day—Fiction

ISBN   978-0-06-115259-7;   0-06-115259-5; 978-0-06-115260-3 (lib bdg); 0-06-115260-9 (lib bdg)

LC 2008-20219

A little boy gets everything he asks for on Yes Day, a special day that only comes once a year.

"Lichtenheld's bright and funny cartoons bring the story to life, with character expressions that are right on the mark." SLJ

Rosenthal, Betsy R.

Which shoes would you choose? illustrated by Nancy Cote. G. P. Putnam's Sons 2010 unp il $15.99

Grades: PreK   E

1. Shoes—Fiction

ISBN 978-0-399-25013-2; 0-399-25013-1

"This picture book invites children to enjoy a shoe-themed guessing game as they follow a boy named Sherman through his day. The question-and-answer text alternates between two types of queries. The first asks Which shoes does he choose? A situation is described, followed by an answer and a reason for the choice. The second sort of question begins with the last shoes chosen and asks if they are worn in an amusingly inappropriate situation. . . . The questions are sure to garner responses from individual children or story hour crowds. . . . Almost cartoonlike in their simplicity, the pleasant gouache and watercolor-pencil drawings feature tousle-haired Sherman sporting an extraordinarily large wardrobe of footwear." Booklist

Rosenthal, Marc, 1949-

Archie and the pirates. Joanna Cotler Books 2009 unp il $16.99

Grades: K 1 2 3   E

1. Monkeys—Fiction   2. Islands—Fiction 3. Friendship—Fiction 4. Pirates—Fiction

ISBN 978-0-06-144164-6; 0-06-144164-3

LC 2008-35251

When Archie the monkey finds himself on a strange island, he makes a multitude of new friends who help him defend their home from intruding pirates.

"Rosenthal relates the adventure in a simple, matter-of-fact way and pairs the narrative to neatly drawn . . . cartoons. . . . Loaded with child appeal." Booklist

Rosoff, Meg

Jumpy Jack and Googily; [by] Meg Rosoff; illustrated by Sophie Blackall. Henry Holt 2008 unp il $16.95 *

Grades: PreK K 1   E

1. Fear—Fiction 2. Monsters—Fiction 3. Snails—Fiction 4. Friendship—Fiction

ISBN 978-0-8050-8066-7; 0-8050-8066-X

LC 2007-07227

Jumpy Jack the snail is terrified that there are monsters around every corner despite the reassurances of his best friend, Googily.

"The interplay between the two creates a wonderfully safe space for children to explore their fears. . . . The text . . . employs a formal elevated tone that gently chides Jumpy Jack's childish fears, adding an element of dry humor. The illustrations are filled with whimsical details." SLJ

Meet wild boars; [written by] Meg Rosoff and [illustrated by] Sophie Blackall. Henry Holt & Co. 2005 unp il $15.95; pa $6.99 *

Grades: PreK K 1 2   E

1. Boars—Fiction

ISBN 0-8050-7488-0; 0-312-37963-3 (pa)

LC 2004-8985

It is very hard to be friends with wild boars because they are dirty and smelly, bad-tempered, and rude

This is "bitingly funny and deeply satisfying. . . . Blackall's roll-on-the-ground-in-laughter illustrations are incisively rendered in ink and gouache." Booklist

Another title about the wild boars is:

Wild boars cook (2008)

Ross, Michael Elsohn, 1952-

Mama's milk; by Michael Elsohn Ross; illustrated by Ashley Wolff. Tricycle Press 2007 unp il $12.95

Grades: PreK K   E

1. Breast feeding—Fiction 2. Mammals—Fiction 3. Animals—Fiction 4. Stories in rhyme

ISBN 978-1-58246-181-6; 1-58246-181-3

LC 2006020873

"From humans to a variety of aquatic and land animals, Ross's rhyming text describes the different ways that mothers nurse their babies. . . . The pastel-infused watercolor illustrations tastefully depict the nursing pairs." SLJ

Ross, Pat

Meet M and M; pictures by Marylin Hafner. Pantheon Bks. 1980 41p il pa $4.99 hardcover o.p.

Grades: K 1 2   E

1. Friendship—Fiction

ISBN 0-14-038731-5 (pa)

LC 79-190

"An I am reading book"

"Because they look so much alike, Mandy and Mimi like to pretend they're twins. . . . Then, 'one crabby day,' they have a squabble, it takes several miserable days more before they make up." Bull Cent Child Books

"Beginning readers will have no difficulty with the humorously told, very real incidents. . . . The many black-and-white pencil drawings capture the girls' facial expressions especially well." Horn Book

Other titles about M and M (Mandy and Mimi) are:

M and M and the bad news babies (1983)

M and M and the Halloween monster (1991)

M and M and the haunted house game (1980)

M and M and the mummy mess (1986)

Ross, Tony, 1938-

I want two birthdays! Andersen Press 2010 unp il $16.95

Grades: PreK K 1 2   E

1. Birthdays—Fiction 2. Princesses—Fiction

ISBN 978-0-76135-495-6; 0-76135-495-6

First published 2008 in the United Kingdom

A little princess decides that two birthdays would be better than one, and three better than two, until every day becomes her birthday, but she soon realizes that the more birthdays she has, the less special they are.

"Ross's bright, cheerful trademark watercolor illustrations add much humor to this already funny tale about having too much of a good thing." SLJ

Rostoker-Gruber, Karen

Bandit; illustrated by Vincent Nguyen. Marshall Cavendish Children's Books 2008 unp il $15.99 *
Grades: PreK K 1 2   E
1. Cats—Fiction 2. Moving—Fiction
ISBN 978-0-7614-5382-6; 0-7614-5382-2
                                      LC 2007011720
When Bandit's family moves to a new house, the cat runs away and returns to the only home he knows, but after he is brought back, he understands that the new house is now home

"By telling the story from the point of view of an extremely territorial pet, Rostoker-Gruber approaches the issue of moving in a fresh way. . . . Nguyen's mixed-media illustrations have an attractive Pop Art style. . . . A funny, stylish book." SLJ

Another title about Bandit is:
Bandit's surprise (2010)

Roth, Carol

The little school bus; illustrated by Pamela Paparone. North-South Bks. 2002 unp il hardcover o.p. pa $6.95
Grades: PreK K   E
1. Animals—Fiction 2. Buses—Fiction 3. Stories in rhyme
ISBN 0-7358-1646-8; 0-7358-1905-X (pa)
                                      LC 2002-71417
An assortment of animals, including a goat in a coat, a quick chick, and a hairy bear, ride the bus to and from school

"Paparone's bright, sprightly illustrations feature plenty of cheery mugging out the windows and other amusing side business. . . . This will take children on a verbal and visual ride that they'll want to repeat as often as possible." Booklist

Will you still love me? illustrated by Daniel Howarth. Albert Whitman 2010 unp il $15.99
Grades: PreK K   E
1. Animals—Fiction 2. Siblings—Fiction 3. Love—Fiction 4. Parent-child relationship—Fiction
ISBN 978-0-8075-9114-7; 0-8075-9114-9
Young animals and a little boy are reassured that their mothers will still love them after a new baby arrives.

"Howarth's sunny watercolor and ink illustrations match the upbeat tone of the bouncy, rhyming text." SLJ

Roth, Susan L.

Hard hat area; [by] Susan Roth. Bloomsbury Children's Books 2004 unp il $17.95
Grades: PreK K 1 2   E
1. Construction workers—Fiction 2. Building—Fiction
ISBN 1-58234-946-0   LC 2003-65343
Construction workers ask Kristen, a young apprentice, to bring them snacks and supplies

"Stunning collages showcase the workers, their jobs, and their equipment *in situ*; clear explanatory notes describe the work and responsibilities for each person involved in the construction." Horn Book Guide

Rotner, Shelley

Senses at the seashore. Millbrook Press 2006 unp il lib bdg $22.60
Grades: PreK K 1 2   E
1. Senses and sensation 2. Seashore
ISBN 978-0-7613-2897-1 (lib bdg); 0-7613-2897-1 (lib bdg)
                                      LC 2005-06151
"This picture book tells what children see, hear, smell, touch, and taste at the beach. . . . A few of the clear, colorful photos show adults (fishermen, a lifeguard) at work, but most of the illustrations are closeups of children at play. An inviting, kid-friendly introduction to the senses and the seashore." Booklist

Senses in the city; by Shelley Rotner. Millbrook Press 2008 unp il (Shelley Rotner's early childhood library) lib bdg $23.93
Grades: PreK K 1   E
1. City and town life 2. Senses and sensation
ISBN 978-0-8225-7502-3 (lib bdg); 0-8225-7502-7 (lib bdg)
"Both an exciting celebration of city life and a show-and-tell about the five senses, this photo-essay will draw even very young children. Clear, direct words and unframed pictures show children in the packed streets of an unnamed city, where they see the skyline and hear trains passing by, go inside tall buildings, and travel in a subway car." Booklist

Shades of people; by Shelley Rotner and Sheila M. Kelly; photographs by Shelley Rotner. Holiday House 2009 unp il $16.95
Grades: PreK K 1   E
1. Color 2. Skin 3. Race
ISBN 978-0-8234-2191-6; 0-8234-2191-0
                                      LC 2008022574
Explores the many different shades of human skin, and points out that skin is just a covering that does not reveal what someone is like inside.

"Filled with smiles and hugs, the pictures prove an upbeat confirmation of the book's central idea. . . . This will enrich and spark discussions of diversity." Booklist

Rubin, Alan

How many fish? Yellow Umbrella Bks. 2003 17p il $14.60
Grades: PreK K 1 2   E
1. Counting 2. Fishes
ISBN 0-7368-2013-2   LC 2003-924
"Yellow umbrella books for early readers"
Introduces counting by showing different numbers of fish and other creatures swimming in the sea

"Not only can beginning readers feel successful at mastering the short, repetitive sentences, but they can also excel at counting the human feet and fish under the water. Colorful illustrations enhance the text." SLJ

Rueda, Claudia

My little polar bear. Scholastic Press 2009 unp il $16.99
Grades: PreK K 1 2   E
1. Polar bear—Fiction 2. Mother-child relationship—Fiction
ISBN 978-0-545-14600-5; 0-545-14600-3
                                      LC 2008043079

Rueda, Claudia—*Continued*

When a cub asks if he is a polar bear, his mother describes what a polar bear is and does, reassuring him that she will teach him to hunt, walk securely on ice, and otherwise be true to his breed, and that she will always love him.

"The striking, minimalist style of illustration seem well suited to the Arctic scenes. Despite the cold setting, the story generates its own warmth." Booklist

Ruelle, Karen Gray, 1957-

The Thanksgiving beast feast. Holiday House 1999 32p il $15.95 *

Grades: PreK K 1 2   E

1. Thanksgiving Day—Fiction 2. Cats—Fiction 3. Animals—Fiction

ISBN 0-8234-1511-2   LC 98-51339

"A Holiday House reader"

Harry the cat and his sister Emily celebrate Thanksgiving by making a holiday feast for the animals in their yard

"Simple and child-centered, the story reads well and uses repetition in ways that sound natural, while reinforcing word recognition. Pleasantly childlike, the naive ink drawings are tinted with gentle washes." Booklist

Other titles about Harry and Emily are:

April fool (2002)

The crunchy, munchy Christmas tree (2003)

Dear Tooth Fairy (2006)

Easter egg disaster (2004)

Easy as apple pie (2002)

Great groundhogs! (2005)

Just in time for New Year's (2004)

The monster in Harry's backyard (1999)

Mother's Day mess (2003)

Snow valentines (2000)

Spookier than a ghost (2001)

Rumford, James, 1948-

Silent music; a story of Baghdad. Roaring Brook Press 2008 unp il $17.95 *

Grades: K 1 2 3   E

1. Calligraphy—Fiction 2. Iraq War, 2003—Fiction 3. Baghdad (Iraq)—Fiction 4. Iraq—Fiction

ISBN 978-1-59643-276-5; 1-59643-276-4

LC 2007-23600

"A Neal Porter book"

As bombs and missiles fall on Baghdad in 2003, a young boy named Ali uses the art of calligraphy to distance himself from the horror of war.

"Art sings on the pages of this visual celebration of Arabic calligraphy as Rumford's . . . collages of floral and geometric designs and flowing lines deftly echo Arabic language and patterns. . . . Spreads incorporating stamps, money and postcards reinforce the Baghdad setting and complement representational scenes." Publ Wkly

Tiger and turtle. Roaring Brook 2010 unp il $17.99

Grades: 1 2 3   E

1. Tigers—Fiction 2. Turtles—Fiction 3. Friendship—Fiction

ISBN 978-1-59643-416-5; 1-59643-416-3

"A Neal Porter book"

When a tiger and a turtle both want a flower that has fallen to the ground, they argue over it until a fight breaks out between them.

"The brief text is well paced, with repeated rising and falling action, and the resolution of the most suspenseful moments requires a page turn. Read this tale aloud . . . for a lively storyhour." SLJ

Russell, Natalie, 1972-

Moon rabbit. Viking Children's Books 2009 unp il $16.99

Grades: PreK K 1   E

1. Rabbits—Fiction 2. Friendship—Fiction 3. City and town life—Fiction

ISBN 978-0-670-01170-4; 0-670-01170-3

LC 2008022799

A city rabbit befriends a country rabbit, but soon she misses her home with its cafes and bright lights

"The story's considerable appeal is amplified by Russell's exceptional artwork. Using her skills as a printmaker, she places her endearing characters on beautifully colored backgrounds so smooth they resemble suede." Booklist

Another title about these rabbits is:

Brown Rabbit in the city (2010)

Russo, Marisabina, 1950-

The big brown box. Greenwillow Bks. 2000 unp il $16.99 *

Grades: PreK K 1 2   E

1. Boxes—Fiction 2. Brothers—Fiction

ISBN 0-688-17096-X   LC 99-14871

As he plays in a very large box in his room and turns it into a house, then a cave, then a boat, Sam is reluctant to let his little brother Ben join him, but then he finds the perfect way for them to share.

"The well-paced, child-centered text is complemented by Russo's trademark two-dimensional gouache illustrations that realistically capture the creative play of children." SLJ

A very big bunny. Schwartz & Wade Books 2010 unp il $17.99; lib bdg $20.99

Grades: PreK K 1 2   E

1. Size—Fiction 2. School stories 3. Friendship—Fiction 4. Rabbits—Fiction

ISBN 978-0-375-84463-8; 0-375-84463-5; 978-0-375-94463-5 (lib bdg); 0-375-94463-X (lib bdg)

LC 2008-39924

Amelia is so big that she is always last in line at school and none of the other students will play with her, but a special new classmate teaches her that size is not always the most important thing.

"Russo's tale about unlikely friends executes a familiar theme with abundant charm and humor. . . . Featuring a saturated palate, Russo's matte gouache illustrations amplify the snappy storytelling." Publ Wkly

Ruzzier, Sergio

Amandina. Roaring Brook Press 2008 unp il
$16.95

Grades: K 1 2 3   E
1. Dogs—Fiction 2. Theater—Fiction
ISBN 978-1-59643-236-9; 1-59643-236-5
LC 2007047914

"A Neal Porter Book"

Amandina decides to overcome her shyness and show
the town what a talented little dog she is, but when no
one shows up for her performance, she finds that she
also has a lot of perseverance.

"The artwork combines delicate lines and faded colors
to create a fanciful stage for this likable character." SLJ

Hey rabbit! Roaring Brook Press 2010 unp il
$16.99

Grades: K 1 2   E
1. Magic—Fiction 2. Rabbits—Fiction 3. Animals—
Fiction 4. Gifts—Fiction
ISBN 978-1-59643-502-5; 1-59643-502-X

"Instead of a magician pulling a rabbit out of a hat,
here we have a rabbit magically producing all sorts of
things from a suitcase. An ode to gift giving, Ruzzier's
latest picture book showcases his charming illustrations
without letting a complicated plot get in the way. . . .
Ruzzier's animals are a very appealing group . . . and
each wish leads to a colorful and lively scene." Booklist

Ryder, Joanne, 1946-

Dance by the light of the moon; written by
Joanne Ryder; illustrated by Guy Francis.
Hyperion Books for Children 2007 unp il $15.99

Grades: PreK K 1 2   E
1. Animals—Fiction 2. Dance—Fiction
ISBN 0-7868-1820-4

"Buffalo Flo gets an invitation to 'come out tonight
and dance by the light of the moon' and proceeds to collect her friends Goose, Cat, and Pig for the occasion.
. . . The rhymes dance, and so do Francis's paintings.
Detailed moonlit landscapes are filled with animal characters that seem to leap from the pages." SLJ

Each living thing; illustrations by Ashley Wolff.
Harcourt 2000 unp il $16

Grades: K 1 2 3   E
1. Animals—Fiction 2. Stories in rhyme
ISBN 0-15-201898-0   LC 98-51832

"Gulliver Books"

Celebrates the creatures of the earth, from spiders dan-
gling in their webs to owls hooting and hunting out of
sight, and asks that we respect and care for them

"Wolff's intense gouache paintings, outlined in black,
are as lyrical as the text, with just the right balance of
simplicity and subtle detail." Booklist

My father's hands; illustrated by Mark Graham.
Morrow Junior Bks. 1994 unp il $16.99

Grades: PreK K 1 2   E
1. Father-daughter relationship—Fiction
2. Gardening—Fiction
ISBN 0-688-09189-X   LC 93-27116

"A little girl and her father share the wonders of nature as they examine several small creatures in the gar-

den—a pink worm, a golden beetle, a sliding snail, and
a praying mantis. Graham's lovely double-page, impressionistic oil paintings clearly focus on the man and his
daughter, with closeups of faces and hands in nearly every illustration. The garden in the background, lush with
flowers and vegetable plants, provides a picturesque setting for this simple, straightforward description of a special parent/child outing." SLJ

Rylant, Cynthia

All in a day; illustrated by Nikki McClure.
Abrams Books for Young Readers 2009 unp il
$17.95 *

Grades: PreK K 1 2   E
1. Stories in rhyme 2. Day—Fiction
ISBN 978-0-8109-8321-2; 0-8109-8321-4
LC 2008030527

Illustrations and rhyming text pay homage to a new
day, with promises for the future in its "perfect piece of
time."

"Alternating backdrops of color, finch-yellow and a
soft, muted blue, allow for a whole new outlook with every page turn. This uplifting picture book succeeds in introducing children to the perennial promise of tomorrow
through lithe language and honed imagery." Kirkus

Alligator boy; [by] Cynthia Rylant & [illustrated
by] Diane Goode. Harcourt 2007 unp il $16

Grades: PreK K   E
1. Alligators—Fiction 2. Stories in rhyme
ISBN 978-0-15-206092-3   LC 2006006049

A boy puts on an alligator head and tail and is transformed into an alligator boy.

"Goode's watercolor and gouache cartoon vignettes on
white ground are reminiscent of the artist's other work
in which she evokes a former time. . . . [A] charming
story." SLJ

Annie and Snowball and the dress-up birthday;
the first book of their adventures; [by] Cynthia
Rylant; illustrated by Suçie Stevenson. Simon &
Schuster Books for Young Readers 2007 40p il
(Ready-to-read) $15.95; pa $3.99 *

Grades: K 1 2   E
1. Birthdays—Fiction 2. Parties—Fiction 3. Rabbits—
Fiction
ISBN   978-1-4169-0938-5;   1-4169-0938-9;
978-1-4169-1459-4 (pa); 1-4169-1459-5 (pa)
LC 2006-02516

Annie and her pet bunny, Snowball, love living next
door to Annie's favorite cousin, Henry and his dog,
Mudge. Whether it's playing Frisbee or watching old
movies, there's no shortage of fun to be had when these
four are together.

"Stevenson's lively pen-and-ink and watercolor illustrations depict lots of action in the story's four short
chapters, and amplify the characters' warmth, affection,
and laughter." SLJ

Other titles about Annie and Snowball are:

Annie and Snowball and the prettiest house (2007)
Annie and Snowball and the dress-up birthday (2007)
Annie and Snowball and the pink surprise (2008)
Annie and Snowball and the teacup club (2008)
Annie and Snowball and the cozy nest (2009)
Annie and Snowball and the shining star (2009)
Annie and Snowball and the magical house (2010)

Rylant, Cynthia—*Continued*

Brownie & Pearl step out; pictures by Brian Biggs. Beach Lane Books 2010 unp il $12.99
Grades: PreK K   **E**
1. Parties—Fiction 2. Birthdays—Fiction 3. Cats—Fiction
ISBN 978-1-4169-8632-4; 1-4169-8632-4
LC 2008032804
A little girl named Brownie arrives at a birthday party feeling shy while her cat Pearl confidently enters through the "kitty door."
"Rylant addresses the challenges and rewards of facing new social situations in short, conversational text perfectly suited to its young audience. Biggs' digitally rendered, cartoonlike illustrations . . . make this first title in the Brownie and Pearl series as delicious and appealing as a triple-layered birthday cake." Booklist
Another title about Brownie & Pearl is:
Brownie & Pearl get dolled up (2010)

The case of the missing monkey; story by Cynthia Rylant; pictures by G. Brian Karas. Greenwillow Bks. 2000 48p il (High-rise private eyes) pa $3.99 *
Grades: K 1 2   **E**
1. Mystery fiction
ISBN 0-06-444306-X   LC 99-16878
While having breakfast at their favorite diner, two detectives, Bunny and Jack, find a missing glass monkey
"The full-color illustrations, rendered in acrylic gouache, and pencil, capture the cartoonlike animals' animated expressions and poses. . . . Children will enjoy searching the pages for the reported clues." SLJ
Other titles in the High-rise private eyes series are:
The case of the baffled bear (2004)
The case of the climbing cate (2000)
The case of the desperate duck (2005)
The case of the fidgety fox (2003)
The case of the puzzling possum (2001)
The case of the sleepy sloth (2002)
The case of the troublesome turtle (2001)

Henry and Mudge; the first book of their adventures; story by Cynthia Rylant; pictures by Suçie Stevenson. Bradbury Press 1987 39p il $15 paperback o.p. *
Grades: K 1 2   **E**
1. Dogs—Fiction
ISBN 0-689-81004-0; 0-689-71399-1 (pa)
LC 86-13615
This book tells "about a boy named Henry and his dog, Mudge. . . . Henry yearns for a dog and convinces his parents to get one. Mudge is small at first, but soon grows 'out of seven collars in a row' to become enormous, and Henry's best friend. Then comes a day when Mudge is lost, and boy and dog realize what they mean to each other." N Y Times Book Rev
"The stories are lighthearted and affectionate. Backed by line-and-wash cartoon drawings, they celebrate the familiar in a down-to-earth way that will please young readers." Booklist
Other titles about Henry and Mudge are:
Henry and Mudge and a very Merry Christmas (2004)
Henry and Mudge and Annie's good move (1998)

Henry and Mudge and Annie's perfect pet (2000)
Henry and Mudge and Mrs. Hopper's house (2003)
Henry and Mudge and the bedtime thumps (1991)
Henry and Mudge and the best day of all (1995)
Henry and Mudge and the big sleepover (2006)
Henry and Mudge and the careful cousin (1994)
Henry and Mudge and the forever sea (1989)
Henry and Mudge and the funny lunch (2004)
Henry and Mudge and the great grandpas (2005)
Henry and Mudge and the happy cat (1990)
Henry and Mudge and the long weekend (1992)
Henry and Mudge and the sneaky crackers (1998)
Henry and Mudge and the Snowman plan (1999)
Henry and Mudge and the starry night (1998)
Henry and Mudge and the tall tree house (1999)
Henry and Mudge and the tumbling trip (2005)
Henry and Mudge and the wild goose chase (2003)
Henry and Mudge and the wild wind (1993)
Henry and Mudge get the cold shivers (1989)
Henry and Mudge in puddle trouble (1987)
Henry and Mudge in the family trees (1997)
Henry and Mudge in the green time (1987)
Henry and Mudge in the sparkle days (1988)
Henry and Mudge take the big test (1991)
Henry and Mudge under the yellow moon (1987)

Moonlight: the Halloween cat; illustrated by Melissa Sweet. HarperCollins Pubs. 2003 unp il $14.99; lib bdg $15.89; pa $6.99
Grades: PreK K 1 2   **E**
1. Halloween—Fiction 2. Cats—Fiction
ISBN 0-06-029711-5; 0-06-029712-3 (lib bdg); 0-06-443814-7 (pa)   LC 2001-39511
Moonlight the cat loves everything about Halloween, from pumpkins to children to candy
"In simple, poetic prose, Rylant tracks the meandering cat's night journey. . . . Sweet's endearingly childlike, color-rich paintings convey an appreciation for the ever-deepening night. . . . A soothing, ghoul-free, utterly noncreepy Halloween picture book for the preschool set." Booklist

Mr. Putter & Tabby pour the tea; illustrated by Arthur Howard. Harcourt Brace & Co. 1994 unp il $14; pa $5.95 *
Grades: K 1 2   **E**
1. Cats—Fiction 2. Old age—Fiction
ISBN 0-15-256255-9; 0-15-200901-9 (pa)
LC 93-21470
"Mr. Putter, a lonely old man, finds a friend in Tabby, an elderly cat he gets from the pound." Booklist
"Rylant's charming story of two elderly characters is complemented and enhanced by Howard's delightful illustrations, done in pencil, watercolor, and gouache." SLJ
Other titles about Mr. Putter and Tabby are:
Mr. Putter & Tabby bake the cake (1994)
Mr. Putter & Tabby catch the cold (2002)
Mr. Putter & Tabby feed the fish (2001)
Mr. Putter & Tabby fly the plane (1997)
Mr. Putter & Tabby make a wish (2005)
Mr. Putter & Tabby paint the porch (2000)
Mr. Putter & Tabby pick the pears (1995)
Mr. Putter & Tabby row the boat (1997)
Mr. Putter & Tabby run the race (2008)
Mr. Putter & Tabby see the stars (2007)
Mr. Putter & Tabby spill the beans (2009)

Rylant, Cynthia—*Continued*

Mr. Putter & Tabby spin the yarn (2006)
Mr. Putter & Tabby stir the soup (2003)
Mr. Putter & Tabby take the train (1998)
Mr. Putter & Tabby toot the horn (1998)
Mr. Putter & Tabby walk the dog (1994)
Mr. Putter & Tabby write the book (2004)

Poppleton; book one; illustrated by Mark Teague. Blue Sky Press (NY) 1997 48p il hardcover o.p. pa $3.99 *

Grades: K 1 2   E
   1. Pigs—Fiction 2. Friendship—Fiction
   ISBN 0-590-84783-X; 0-590-84782-1 (pa)
                                        LC 96-3365

"City pig Poppleton adjusts to small-town life in this . . . chapter book. In 'Neighbors,' the polite Poppleton tries to think up a polite way to say 'no thanks' to Cherry Sue, a friendly llama who invites him to breakfast, lunch and dinner every single day. . . . The second vignette, 'The Library,' details Poppleton's reading ritual, which demands solitude. Finally, 'The Pill' introduces Fillmore, a sick goat who refuses to take his pill unless Poppleton hides it in a cake. . . . [Rylant's] concise sentences mimic the characters' good manners and wryly point up the failures of etiquette. Teague contributes fetching watercolor-and-pencil images of the pudgy pig, slender llama and dignified goat." Publ Wkly

   Other titles about Poppleton are:
Poppleton and friends (1997)
Poppleton everyday (1998)
Poppleton forever (1998)
Poppleton has fun (2000)
Poppleton in Fall (1999)
Poppleton in Spring (1999)
Poppleton in Winter (2001)
Poppleton through and through (2000)

Puppies and piggies; illustrated by Ivan Bates. Harcourt 2008 32p il $16

Grades: PreK   E
   1. Animals—Fiction 2. Stories in rhyme
   ISBN 978-0-15-202321-8; 0-15-202321-6
                                        LC 2004-3136

Rhyming text describes what various animals do and what they love, as well as a baby who loves his bed and his mother.

"Told in reassuring rhyme, the simple upbeat text showcases happy animals doing what comes naturally while Bates's idyllic watercolor and crayon illustrations present a bucolic barnyard teeming with contented critters. . . . Comforting and carefree fare for tiny tots." Kirkus

The relatives came; story by Cynthia Rylant; illustrated by Stephen Gammell. rev format ed. Atheneum Books for Young Readers 2001 c1985 unp il $16.95; pa $6.99 *

Grades: PreK K 1 2   E
   1. Family life—Fiction
   ISBN 0-689-84508-1; 0-689-71738-5 (pa)
   A Caldecott Medal honor book, 1986
   A reformatted edition of the title first published 1985 by Bradbury Press

"The relatives have come . . . bringing with them hugs and laughs, quiet talk, and, at night when all are asleep hither and yon." Booklist

"If there's anything more charming than the tone of voice in this story, it's the drawings that go with it. Stephen Gammell . . . fills the pages with bright, crayony pictures teeming with details that children should enjoy poring over for hours." NY Times Book Rev

Snow; illustrated by Lauren Stringer. Harcourt 2008 unp il $17 *

Grades: PreK K 1 2   E
   1. Snow—Fiction
   ISBN 978-0-15-205303-1; 0-15-205303-4
                                        LC 2006-06171

Celebrates the beauty of a snowfall and its happy effects on children.

"Snow is not an uncommon subject in picture books, but few have both the grace and exuberance of this lovely collaboration featuring Rylant's evocative words and Stringer's entrancing paintings." Booklist

When I was young in the mountains; illustrated by Diane Goode. Dutton 1982 unp il $15.99; pa $6.99

Grades: K 1 2 3   E
   1. Appalachian region—Fiction
   ISBN 0-525-42525-X; 0-525-44198-0 (pa)
                                        LC 81-5359

   A Caldecott Medal honor book, 1983

"Based on the author's memories of an Appalachian childhood. . . . The author reminisces about the busy, peaceful life of an extended family and their community." Bull Cent Child Books

"The people in the story are poor in material things, but rich in family pleasures. The title becomes a pleasing refrain. . . . Illustrations and text are placed on a bed of white space, without borders, which makes them look uncrowded and imparts a great feeling of freedom." SLJ

Rymond, Lynda Gene

Oscar and the mooncats; by Lynda Gene Rymond; illustrated by Nicoletta Ceccoli. Houghton Mifflin Company 2007 unp il $16

Grades: PreK K 1 2   E
   1. Cats—Fiction 2. Moon—Fiction
   ISBN 978-0-618-56316-6; 0-618-56316-4
                                        LC 2006026079

Feeling more than a little wild, Oscar the cat leaps from one high spot to another until he lands on the Moon, where he plays with the mooncats until his boy begins to call and he must find a way back home or risk becoming a mooncat, himself.

"Mixed-media illustrations created with plasticine, acrylics, and computer graphics beautifully depict scenes. . . . The 3-D effect of the pictures and the unusual perspectives . . . are in perfect keeping with the surreal nature of the story." Booklist

Sabuda, Robert

Alice's adventures in Wonderland; a pop-up adaptation of Lewis Carroll's original tale; illustrated by Robert Sabuda. Little Simon 2003 unp il $25.95

Grades: 1 2 3 4   E

    1. Fantasy fiction 2. Pop-up books

    ISBN 0-689-84743-2

A pop-up version of Lewis Carroll's classic tale of Alice who falls down the rabbit hole to find a new world.

"Sabuda brings Alice's world to life with breathtaking, three-dimensional images that are incredibly imaginative, intricately detailed, and perfectly executed. Carroll's text has been significantly abridged, and . . . the quickly paced narrative retains the flavor of the original." SLJ

The Christmas alphabet. deluxe anniversary edition. Orchard Books 2004 unp il $22.95

Grades: K 1 2 3 4   E

    1. Alphabet 2. Christmas 3. Pop-up books

    ISBN 0-439-67256-2

    First published 1994

"Four large flaps per spread—each representing a letter of the alphabet—open to reveal sophisticated 3D images, some with parts that move in uncommonly inventive ways. Many of the pop-ups are obvious Christmas symbols. . . . Others have ambiguous—but resourceful—ties to the holiday. . . . A yuletide gem." Publ Wkly

The Chronicles of Narnia pop-up; based on the books by C. S. Lewis; pop-ups by Robert Sabuda. HarperCollinsPublishers 2007 unp il $29.99

Grades: 3 4 5   E

    1. Pop-up books 2. Fantasy fiction

    ISBN 978-0-06-117612-8

"Sabuda works his pop-up magic once again, designing for each of the seven Narnia books a multilayered scene that unfolds and rears up dramatically as the spread is opened. Four spreads also contain a smaller pop-up behind a corner flap. The painted art is equal to the complex articulations, depicting Aslan and the rest of the cast as colorful, boldly drawn figures." SLJ

Peter Pan: a classic collectible pop-up. Simon & Schuster Children's Pub. 2008 unp il $29.99 *

Grades: 2 3 4 5 6   E

    1. Fairy tales 2. Pop-up books

    ISBN 978-0-689-85364-7; 0-689-85364-5

"Sabuda enhances the already powerful enchantments of J. M. Barrie's classic 1902 tale with astonishing paper engineering. Illustrations suggest a hybrid of period styles, somewhere between arts and crafts, with their rich patterning, and art nouveau, with their Tiffany glass-like outlines and colorations. . . . Not to be missed." Publ Wkly

Saenz, Benjamin Alire

The dog who loved tortillas; La perrita que le encantaban las tortillas; illustrations by Geronimo Garcia. Cinco Puntos Press 2009 36p il $17.95

Grades: K 1 2   E

    1. Dogs—Fiction 2. Family life—Fiction 3. Mexican Americans—Fiction 4. Bilingual books—English-Spanish

    ISBN 978-1-933693-54-5; 1-933693-54-1

                    LC 2008-56036

When Gabriela and her brother Little Diego get a puppy named Sofie, they fight over who she belongs to, but when Sofie gets very sick they find the answer

"A captivating bilingual book with close family relationships and unconditional love at its core. . . . Full-page innovative and colorful clay illustrations will hold the attention of young readers." SLJ

A perfect season for dreaming; Un tiempo perfecto para soñar; written by Benjamin Alire Saenz; illustrated by Esau Andrade Valencia [translation by Luis Humberto Crosthwaite] Cinco Puntos Press 2008 unp il $17.95

Grades: 2 3 4   E

    1. Dreams—Fiction 2. Animals—Fiction 3. Bilingual books—English-Spanish

    ISBN 978-1-933693-01-9; 1-933693-01-0

                    LC 2007019442

Ninety-two-year-old Octavio Rivera has been visited by some very interesting dreams—dreams about pinatas that spill their treasures before him revealing kissing turtles, winged pigs, hitchhiking armadillos and many more fantastic things

This "haunting work, presented in English and Spanish, is part short story, part fable. . . . Children . . . will respond to Sáenz's elemental warmth and rhythmic storytelling." Publ Wkly

Saint-Lot, Katia Novet, 1963-

Amadi's snowman; illustrated by Dimitrea Tokunbo. Tilbury House 2008 unp il $16.95

Grades: PreK K 1 2   E

    1. Books and reading—Fiction 2. Igbo (African people)—Fiction 3. Nigeria—Fiction

    ISBN 978-0-88448-298-7; 0-88448-298-7

                    LC 2007043343

As a young Igbo man, Amadi does not understand why his mother insists he learn to read, since he already knows his numbers and will be a businessman one day, but an older boy teaches him the value of learning about the world through books

"Children will enjoy reading about Amadi's life in the village, depicted in the earth-toned, intimate scenes." Booklist

Sakai, Komako, 1966-

Emily's balloon. Chronicle Books 2006 unp il $14.95

Grades: PreK K 1   E

    1. Balloons—Fiction

    ISBN 0-8118-5219-9   LC 2005-11283

A little girl's new friend is round, lighter than air, and looks like the moon at night.

Sakai, Komako, 1966-—*Continued*

"The yellow balloon and its blue string stand out in a simple color palette of white, gray, and tan with a few accents of red. The illustrations, rendered in watercolor and charcoal, are placed on tan pages and surrounded by unadorned thin, round-edged black frames. A tale of a common childhood experience, tenderly and sweetly told." SLJ

The snow day. Arthur A. Levine Books 2009 unp il $16.99 *

Grades: PreK K   E

1. Snow—Fiction 2. Rabbits—Fiction
ISBN 978-0-545-01321-5; 0-545-01321-6
                                       LC 2007-49949

Original Japanese edition 2005

A little rabbit enjoys having a day off from kindergarten and spending time with his mother during a snowstorm, but his father's flight home is cancelled until the snow stops falling.

Sakai's "subdued palette and minimalist text suggest the blanketed sound produced by a heavy snowfall. . . . The layers of paint are applied to a black ground with a combination of wet and dry brushes, producing a convincing depth and texture. . . . The sentences are appropriately concise, yet with lovely rhythms and interesting details." SLJ

Salerno, Steven, 1958-

Harry hungry! written and illustrated by Steven Salerno. Harcourt 2009 unp il $16

Grades: PreK K   E

1. Hunger—Fiction 2. Infants—Fiction
ISBN 978-0-15-206257-6; 0-15-206257-2
                                       LC 2007-04375

Harry is a baby so hungry that he eats all the food in his house, then goes outside to find more.

"Done in his trademark retro style, Salerno's bright, sweeping illustrations and offbeat perspectives instantly capture this tiny tot's insatiable energy. . . . Children will delight in growling loudly along with Harry's tummy." Kirkus

Salley, Coleen

Epossumondas saves the day; written by Coleen Salley; illustrated by Janet Stevens. Harcourt 2006 unp il $16

Grades: K 1 2 3   E

1. Opossums—Fiction 2. Turtles—Fiction
3. Birthdays—Fiction
ISBN 0-15-205701-3   LC 2005-27538

In this variation on the folktale, Sody Salyraytus, each of Epossumondas's birthday guests disappears until it is finally up to him to rescue them all and bring home the "sody" for his birthday biscuits.

"Salley's text is alive with the colorful expressions of the South . . . which make the story a delight to read aloud. Stevens's hilarious mixed-media illustrations are a perfect match for the narrative." SLJ

Saltzberg, Barney

I want a dog! Random House Children's Books 2009 unp il $11.99

Grades: PreK K   E

1. Dogs—Fiction 2. Pop-up books
ISBN 978-0-375-85783-6; 0-375-85783-4

"The earnest speaker in this fun story, based on the author's song of the same title, pleads for a dog, promising that it 'will never, ever make a mess' (via a pull tab, she sweeps his 'mess' into a dustpan as she holds her nose). Other animals—a hippo, a pig—won't do (turning a wheel helps the girl feed an endless bucket of slop to a tubby swine). On a final pop-up spread, she embraces a dog, surrounded by blooming, red hearts. Effective interactive elements and simple humor will charm." Publ Wkly

Stanley and the class pet; [by] Barney Saltzberg. Candlewick Press 2008 unp il $16.99

Grades: PreK K 1 2   E

1. Birds—Fiction 2. School stories 3. Hamsters—Fiction
ISBN 978-0-7636-3595-4; 0-7636-3595-2
                                       LC 2007-40541

Stanley is excited about bringing the class pet, a bird, home for the weekend, but when his friend Larry urges him to open the cage and let Figgy out to fly, it is hard to know who is to blame for the ensuing disaster.

"With clearly lined acrylic paintings and a smoothly paced text that avoids a too-heavy message, Saltzberg deftly turns a common classroom scenario into a gentle story about peer pressure and responsibility." Booklist

Other titles about Stanley are:
Crazy hair day (2003)
Star of the week (2006)

Samuels, Barbara

The trucker. Farrar, Straus and Giroux 2010 unp il $16.99

Grades: PreK K 1   E

1. Trucks—Fiction 2. Toys—Fiction 3. Cats—Fiction
ISBN 978-0-374-37804-2; 0-374-37804-5
                                       LC 2007029266

"Melanie Kroupa books"

A boy who loves trucks is disappointed when he receives a cat named Lola instead of a toy fire truck, but Lola proves to be a "trucker" after all.

"A winner for young children, this offers a real story along with all of the vehicle action. Kids will enjoy the combination of active play and cozy snuggling." Booklist

Sandburg, Carl, 1878-1967

The Huckabuck family and how they raised popcorn in Nebraska and quit and came back; pictures by David Small. Farrar, Straus & Giroux 1999 unp il $16; pa $6.95

Grades: 1 2 3 4   E

1. Farm life—Fiction
ISBN 0-374-33511-7; 0-374-43449-2 (pa)
                                       LC 98-6676

The text was originally published in 1923 by Harcourt, Brace & Company in the book Rootabaga stories

Sandburg, Carl, 1878-1967—*Continued*

After the popcorn the Huckabucks had raised explodes in a fire and Pony Pony Huckabuck finds a silver buckle inside a squash, the family decides it is time for a change

"Small's watercolors have a translucent, airy quality that suits the fantastical elements of Sandburg's story. . . . Sandburg's language is as bracing as a tonic, and the inherent humor and rhythms of his tale are as invigorating today as when it was first written." Bull Cent Child Books

Sandemose, Iben

Gracie & Grandma & the itsy, bitsy seed; translated from Norwegian by Tonje Vetleseter. MacKenzie Smiles 2009 unp il $14.95
Grades: PreK K 1 2   E
1. Grandmothers—Fiction 2. Plants—Fiction 3. Growth—Fiction
ISBN 978-0-9790347-5-6; 0-9790347-5-2

"Spunky and imaginative Gracie presents her equally exuberant grandmother with a surprise–an itsy, bitsy seed. But what will it grow into? As the plant gets larger and larger, Grandma incorrectly guesses that it is a banana, lemon, fried mackerel, balloon, jungle, cow, or ghost tree until she spots a large red dot growing at the top and shouts: 'A big tomato!' . . . The simple yet expressive text, in a large, bold typeface, perfectly complements the wacky, exaggerated, dazzlingly bright colored ink and marker cartoon illustrations." SLJ

Other titles in this series are:
Gracie & Grandma (2008)
Gracie & Grandma under water (2008)

Sanders-Wells, Linda

Maggie's monkeys; illustrated by Abby Carter. Candlewick Press 2009 unp il $16.99
Grades: K 1 2   E
1. Imagination—Fiction 2. Siblings—Fiction 3. Family life—Fiction
ISBN 978-0-7636-3326-4; 0-7636-3326-7
LC 2008-28711

When Maggie reports that pink monkeys have moved into the refrigerator, her mother and father play along and accomodate the invisible visitors, much to the frustration of Maggie's older, reality-obsessed brother.

"Sanders-Wells wonderfully encapsulates the difficulties of being a middle child—simultaneously too old and too young. Carter's masterful facial expressions reflects this inner battle. Her gouache artwork is done in a bright, tropical palette that emphasizes the imaginative theme. . . . A humorous tale sure to make siblings smile, even as they inwardly groan." Kirkus

Sandin, Joan, 1942-

At home in a new land. HarperCollinsPublishers 2007 64p il (I can read!) $15.99; lib bdg $16.89
Grades: 1 2 3   E
1. Immigrants—Fiction 2. Frontier and pioneer life—Fiction 3. Swedish Americans—Fiction 4. Minnesota—Fiction
ISBN 978-0-06-058077-3; 0-06-058077-1; 978-0-06-058078-0 (lib bdg); 0-06-058078-X (lib bdg)
LC 2006-36251

Carl Erik, a recent immigrant from Sweden, becomes the man of the house when his father and uncle go to work in a logging camp, and he learns many things about life in Minnesota while attending school, doing his chores, and trying to put meat on the table

"Watercolor and ink illustrations add realistic detail to a story that reveals Carl's lifestyle and warm bonds with his family and friends. . . . This book provides a solid introduction to historical fiction for early readers." SLJ

Santiago, Esmeralda

A doll for Navidades; illustrated by Enrique O. Sánchez. Scholastic Press 2005 unp il $16.99
Grades: PreK K 1 2   E
1. Christmas—Fiction 2. Puerto Rico—Fiction 3. Gifts—Fiction
ISBN 0-439-55398-9

While preparing for Christmas in Puerto Rico, seven-year-old Esmeralda asks the Three Magi for a baby doll like her cousin's, but when they bring something else instead she gains a deeper understanding of the meaning of the holiday

"Santiago's autobiographical tale is both a universal story of holiday disappointment and a rich sensory portrait. . . . Sánchez's acrylic-on-canvas paintings add to the exotic flavor and the familiarity of the large family." SLJ

Santore, Charles

The Silk Princess. Random House Children's Books 2007 unp il $17.99; lib bdg $20.99
Grades: 1 2 3   E
1. China—Fiction 2. Silk—Fiction 3. Princesses—Fiction
ISBN 978-0-375-83664-0; 978-0-375-93664-7 (lib bdg)
LC 2007-04764

After a cocoon falls into her tea cup and unravels to form a long, delicate thread, Hsi-Ling Chi, a princess in ancient China, meets a mysterious man who reveals how to transform the cocoons into silk.

The text "tells an exciting, vivid tale, but it's Santore's exquisitely detailed artwork, combining beautiful character close-ups with scenes resembling traditional Chinese landscapes, that is so extraordinary." Booklist

Sarcone-Roach, Julia

The secret plan. Alfred A. Knopf 2009 unp il $16.99; lib bdg $19.99
Grades: PreK K 1 2   E
1. Play—Fiction 2. Bedtime—Fiction 3. Elephants—Fiction 4. Cats—Fiction
ISBN 978-0-375-85858-1; 0-375-85858-X; 978-0-375-95858-8 (lib bdg); 0-375-95858-4 (lib bdg)
LC 2008-39291

Continually thwarted in their efforts to escape bedtime and continue playing, Milo the elephant and three kittens named Henry, Hildy, and Harriet finally find a "perfect late night bedtime-free hideout."

"The age-old dilemma of wanting to stay up and play just a bit longer finds a gently humorous treatment in this tale, accompanied by swirly acrylic paintings that evoke dreamy nighttime fantasy." SLJ

Sartell, Debra

Time for bed, baby Ted; illustrations by Kay Chorao. Holiday House 2010 unp il $16.95

Grades: PreK   E

1. Stories in rhyme 2. Bedtime—Fiction

ISBN 978-0-8234-1968-5; 0-8234-1968-1

LC 2008-48652

At bedtime, Baby Ted finds many ways to avoid going to bed.

"The various animal sounds and action words in the short text, coupled with Chorao's pleasing illustrations, featuring a mop-topped Ted and his pretend menagerie, make this a fun read-aloud for parent and child and a natural for sharing with a young group of children." Booklist

Sattler, Jennifer

Sylvie. Random House 2009 unp il $15.99; lib bdg $18.99

Grades: PreK K 1   E

1. Flamingos—Fiction 2. Color—Fiction 3. Food—Fiction

ISBN 978-0-375-85708-9; 0-375-85708-7; 978-0-375-95708-6 (lib bdg); 0-375-95708-1 (lib bdg)

LC 2008-11259

When Sylvie the pink flamingo learns her color comes from the little pink shrimp she eats, she decides to expand her choices, trying everything under the sun and, unfortunately, overdoing it.

"Sattler's art steals the show; the colors are eye-popping and vibrant, right to the swirling bright endpapers. . . . This title is sure to create storytime magic." SLJ

Sauer, Tammi

Chicken dance; illustrated by Dan Santat. Sterling 2009 unp il $14.95

Grades: PreK K 1   E

1. Contests—Fiction 2. Chickens—Fiction 3. Domestic animals—Fiction

ISBN 978-1-4027-5366-4; 1-4027-5366-7

LC 2008-50578

Determined to win tickets to an Elvis Poultry concert, hens Marge and Lola enter the Barnyard Talent Show, then, while the ducks who usually win the contest jeer, they test out their abilities.

"The zippy narrative features punchy dialogue and witty interactions. . . . Santat's rich ink-and-acrylic designs provide a humorous context through animated expressions. . . . Fly the coop to enjoy this hilarious adventure." Kirkus

Savadier, Elivia

Time to get dressed! Roaring Brook Press 2006 unp il $14.95

Grades: PreK K   E

1. Clothing and dress—Fiction 2. Father-son relationship—Fiction

ISBN 978-1-59643-161-4; 1-59643-161-X

LC 2005-19923

"Solomon likes to dress himself ('ME!'), but thirty minutes later—pants on his head, sock on his hand, and shoe tied around his ankle—it's his weary-looking dad's turn to say 'ME!'" Horn Book Guide

"Savadier's skillfully rendered watercolors use thick, supple lines and soft colors set against lots of white space. With a rhythmic, lean text and charming pictures, this will be great for sharing, either in groups or one-on-one." SLJ

Will Sheila share? Roaring Brook Press 2008 unp il $12.95

Grades: PreK   E

1. Grandmothers—Fiction

ISBN 978-1-59643-289-5; 1-59643-289-6

LC 2007-10039

"A Neal Porter Book"

Nana helps teach her toddler granddaughter to share.

"Savadier's watercolor and ink pictures are particularly energetic. . . . The author shows a shrewd understanding of how an uncooperative child can unnerve everyone—including the kid in question. Her pithy text and expressive, economical pictures deliver a reassuring response along with solid comedy." Publ Wkly

Say, Allen, 1937-

Allison. Houghton Mifflin 1997 32p il $17; pa $6.95 *

Grades: PreK K 1 2   E

1. Adoption—Fiction 2. Japanese Americans—Fiction

ISBN 0-395-85895-X; 0-618-49537-1 (pa)

LC 97-7528

When Allison realizes that she looks more like her Japanese doll than like her parents, she comes to terms with this unwelcomed discovery through the help of a stray cat

"A subtle, sensitive probing of interracial adoption, this exquisitely illustrated story will encourage thoughtful adult-child dialogue on a potentially difficult issue." Publ Wkly

The bicycle man. Parnassus Press 1982 unp il lib bdg $16; pa $5.95

Grades: K 1 2 3   E

1. Cycling—Fiction 2. Japan—Fiction

ISBN 0-395-32254-5 (lib bdg); 0-395-50652-2 (pa)

LC 82-2980

The amazing tricks two American soldiers do on a borrowed bicycle are a fitting finale for the school sports day festivities in a small village in occupied Japan

"The kindly, openhearted story is beautifully pictured in a profusion of delicate pen-and-ink drawings washed in gentle colors." Horn Book

Erika-san. Houghton Mifflin Books for Children 2009 unp il $17 *

Grades: 2 3 4   E

1. Japan—Fiction 2. Teachers—Fiction

ISBN 978-0-618-88933-4; 0-618-88933-7

LC 2008-00601

After falling in love with Japan as a little girl, Erika becomes a teacher and fulfills her childhood dream by moving to a remote Japanese island.

"With luminous watercolors and economical text . . . Say . . . tells of an American girl whose ingenuous hopes of reaching 'old Japan' are finally realized." Publ Wkly

Say, Allen, 1937-—*Continued*

Grandfather's journey; written and illustrated by Allen Say. Houghton Mifflin 1993 32p il $16.95; pa $7.99 *
Grades: 1 2 3 4   E
1. Japanese Americans—Fiction 2. Grandfathers—Fiction 3. Voyages and travels—Fiction 4. Japan—Fiction
ISBN 0-395-57035-2; 0-547-07680-0 (pa)
LC 93-18836
Awarded the Caldecott Medal, 1994
A Japanese American man recounts his grandfather's journey to America which he later also undertakes, and the feelings of being torn by a love for two different countries
"The brief text is simple and unaffected, but the emotions expressed are deeply complex. The paintings are astonishingly still, like the captured moments found in a family photo album. Each translucent watercolor is suffused with light." SLJ

Kamishibai man; written and illustrated by Allen Say. Houghton Mifflin Co. 2005 32p il $17 *
Grades: PreK K 1 2 3   E
1. Entertainers—Fiction 2. Japan—Fiction
ISBN 0-618-47954-6
"Walter Lorraine books."
After many years of retirement, an old Kamishibai man—a Japanese street performer who tells stories and sells candies—decides to make his rounds once more even though such entertainment declined after the advent of television.
"The quietly dramatic, beautifully evocative tale contains a cliffhanger of its own, and its exquisite art, in the style of Kamishibai picture cards, will attract even the most jaded kid away from the TV to enjoy a good, good book." Booklist

The lost lake. Houghton Mifflin 1989 32p il $16; pa $6.95
Grades: K 1 2 3   E
1. Father-son relationship—Fiction 2. Camping—Fiction
ISBN 0-395-50933-5; 0-395-63036-3 (pa)
LC 89-11026
"Luke is disappointed in his relationship with his taciturn, work-absorbed father, with whom he is spending the summer. Early one morning his father awakens him with exciting news of a camping trip: they are going to find the Lost Lake, a very special and secret place Luke's father used to visit with his own father." Horn Book
"Using colors as crisp and clean as the outdoors, Say effectively alternates between scenes where father and son are the focus and those where the landscape predominates. Both in story and art, a substantial piece." Booklist

Tea with milk. Houghton Mifflin 1999 32p il $17; pa $6.99 *
Grades: K 1 2 3 4   E
1. Japanese Americans—Fiction 2. Japan—Fiction
ISBN 0-395-90495-1; 0-547-23747-2 (pa)
LC 98-11667
"Walter Lorraine books"

After growing up near San Francisco, Masako (or May) returns with her parents to their native Japan, but she feels foreign and out of place until she finds a job in Osaka and marries a man with a similarly mixed background
"Say's masterfully executed watercolors tell as much of this story . . . as his eloquent prose." Publ Wkly

Tree of cranes; written and illustrated by Allen Say. Houghton Mifflin 1991 32p il $17.95; pa $7.99
Grades: K 1 2 3   E
1. Christmas—Fiction 2. Mother-son relationship—Fiction 3. Japan—Fiction
ISBN 0-395-52024-X; 0-547-24830-X (pa)
LC 91-14107
A Japanese boy learns of Christmas when his mother decorates a pine tree with paper cranes
"The quiet, graciously told picture book is a perfect blend of text and art. Fine-lined and handsome, Say's watercolors not only capture fascinating details of the boy's far away home . . . but also depict, with simple grace, the rich and complex bond between mother and child that underlies the story." Booklist

Sayre, April Pulley
Dig, wait, listen; a desert toad's tale; pictures by Barbara Bash. Greenwillow Bks. 2001 unp il $15.95
Grades: PreK K 1 2   E
1. Toads—Fiction 2. Desert animals—Fiction
ISBN 0-688-16614-8   LC 00-32111
A spadefoot toad waits under the sand for the rain, hears the sounds of other desert animals, and eventually mates and spawns other toads
"Created with pencil, pen and ink, and watercolor, Bash's pictures illustrate the desert scenes with pleasingly varied colors, perspectives, and layouts. Preschool and primary-grade children will find this well-crafted book a wholly satisfying introduction to the spadefoot toad in particular and desert animals and the idea of life cycles in general." Booklist

One is a snail, ten is a crab; a counting by feet book; [by] April Pulley Sayre and Jeff Sayre; illustrated by Randy Cecil. Candlewick Press 2003 unp il hardcover o.p. pa $6.99
Grades: PreK K 1 2   E
1. Counting 2. Animals 3. Foot
ISBN 0-7636-1406-8; 0-7636-2631-7 (pa)
LC 2001-52494
A counting book featuring animals with different numbers of feet
"Very simple text in large type is appropriate for group use as well as beginning readers. Uncluttered, black-outlined, oil-on-paper pictures clearly illustrate the concepts, and Cecil's googly-eyed snails, sports-minded crabs, and other animals add a touch of humor." SLJ

Turtle, turtle, watch out! illustrated by Annie Patterson. Charlesbridge 2010 unp il lib bdg $17.95
Grades: K 1 2   E
1. Sea turtles—Fiction
ISBN 978-1-580-89148-6; 1-580-89148-9
LC 2008025338

Sayre, April Pulley—*Continued*

A newly illustrated edition of the title first published 2000 by Orchard Books

From before the time she hatches until she returns to the same beach to lay eggs of her own, a sea turtle is helped to escape from danger many times by different human hands.

"The simple, direct text reads aloud well, drawing readers into the turtles' story without anthropomorphism. Impressive pastel illustrations, including many dramatic double-page spreads, depict with power and beauty the turtles' world of sand and shore." Booklist

Schachner, Judith Byron

The Grannyman. Dutton Children's Bks. 1999 unp il $15.99; pa $6.99

Grades: PreK K 1 2   E

1. Cats—Fiction 2. Old age—Fiction

ISBN 0-525-46122-1; 0-14-250062-3 (pa)

LC 98-52964

Simon the cat is so old that most of his parts have stopped working, but just when he is ready to breathe his last breath, his family brings home a new kitten for him to raise

"Schachner's expressive watercolor-and-mixed-media artwork mirrors the affection, humor, and warmth of her finely crafted text." Booklist

Schaefer, Carole Lexa

Big Little Monkey; illustrated by Pierre Pratt. Candlewick Press 2008 unp il $16.99

Grades: PreK K 1 2   E

1. Monkeys—Fiction

ISBN 978-0-7636-2006-6; 0-7636-2006-8

LC 2007052024

When Little Monkey decides to venture out into the jungle alone, beyond the gaze of his watchful Mama, he discovers that other animals are not as friendly and warm as his own family and that independence is not altogether a good thing

"Schaefer's text has the style and cadences of a folktale with the effective refrain 'bim-ba-lah, bim-ba-lah' appearing as the protagonist swings through the trees. . . . Pratt's stylized animals, done in sweeping, brightly colored acrylics . . . and the mostly full-bleed illustrations with their color-saturated backgrounds are eye-catching and will carry well in storytimes." SLJ

The biggest soap; pictures by Stacey Dressen-McQueen. Farrar, Straus and Giroux 2004 unp il $16

Grades: K 1 2 3   E

1. Oceania—Fiction 2. Storytelling—Fiction 3. Soap—Fiction

ISBN 0-374-30690-7   LC 2003-48512

When Kessy, who lives in the Truk Islands, is sent by his mother to buy laundry soap, he hurries back to listen to her storytelling, discovering that his own experience is a good story too

"Both the text and the pencil, oil pastel, and acrylic artwork, alive with the sun-drenched colors and patterns of the South Pacific, bubble with happiness. Refreshing, engaging, and thoroughly delightful." Booklist

Dragon dancing; illustrated by Pierr Morgan. Viking 2007 unp il $16.99

Grades: PreK K 1   E

1. Dragons—Fiction 2. Imagination—Fiction 3. Birthdays—Fiction 4. School stories

ISBN 0-670-06084-9

A group of children pretend that they are a dragon to celebrate their classmate's birthday.

"An excellent choice for storytime, the text features . . . many fun sounds. . . . The color of the gouache-and-marker illustrations increases in brightness as the students transition gradually from the classroom into their imaginative fantasy. . . . Pleasing to the eye and the ear." SLJ

Schaefer, Lola M., 1950-

Loose tooth; story by Lola M. Schaefer; pictures by Sylvie Wickstrom. HarperCollinsPublishers 2004 31p il (My first I can read book) hardcover o.p. pa $3.99 *

Grades: PreK K 1 2   E

1. Teeth—Fiction 2. Stories in rhyme

ISBN 0-06-052776-5; 0-06-052778-1 (pa)

LC 2003-6322

A young child experiences a loose tooth for the first time and eagerly waits for it to come out

"With a few words, lots of repetition, some rhyme, and good rhythm, this story is perfect for beginning readers. The cartoon illustrations add details to the plot and create interest." SLJ

Mittens; story by Lola M. Schaefer; pictures by Susan Kathleen Hartung. HarperCollinsPublishers 2006 25p il (I can read!) $16.99; lib bdg $15.89; pa $3.99

Grades: PreK K 1 2   E

1. Cats—Fiction

ISBN 0-06-054659-X; 0-06-054660-3 (lib bdg); 0-06-054661-1 (pa)

Nick helps Mittens the kitten adjust to life in a new home

"The controlled vocabulary in this gentle, unassuming story is made up primarily of one-syllable words, and the sentence structure is very basic. The soft pastel illustrations are simple and uncluttered and enhance the quiet tone of the text." SLJ

Other titles about Mittens are:

Follow me, Mittens (2007)

What's that, Mittens (2008)

This is the sunflower; pictures by Donald Crews. Greenwillow Bks. 2000 unp il $15.99

Grades: PreK K 1 2   E

1. Sunflowers—Fiction 2. Stories in rhyme

ISBN 0-688-16413-7   LC 98-46682

A cumulative verse describing how a sunflower in a garden blossoms and, with the help of the birds, spreads its seeds to create an entire patch of sunflowers

"A beautiful, noteworthy title. The velvety watercolors are clearly defined and saturated with color. . . . This is perfect for story hours; also recommend it to budding ornithologists, who will appreciate the illustrated key identifying the birds pictured in the text." Booklist

Schaefer, Lola M., 1950-—*Continued*

What's up, what's down? pictures by Barbara Bash. Greenwillow Bks. 2002 unp il $15.99; lib bdg $17.89

Grades: PreK K 1 2   E

1. Nature

ISBN 0-06-029757-3; 0-06-029758-1 (lib bdg)

"On each page is the question 'What's up if you're ...?' from the viewpoint of various flora and fauna: a mole, a root, grass, a toad. . . . The highest thing 'up' is the moon, and then it's time to turn the book upside down and move down through sky and water to see 'what's down.' Children will have a chance to stretch their imaginations as they get a rudimentary idea of how the natural world works. The artwork, executed in chalks, has a muscular look that brings nature home." Booklist

Scheer, Julian, 1926-2001

Rain makes applesauce; by Julian Scheer & Marvin Bileck. Holiday House 1964 unp il $16.95

Grades: PreK K 1 2   E

ISBN 0-8234-0091-3

A Caldecott Medal honor book, 1965

"A book of original nonsense, illustrated with intricate drawings. Small children live the refrains, 'Rain makes applesauce' and 'You're just talking silly talk,' and enjoy the fantastic details in the pictures." Hodges. Books for Elem Sch Libr

Schertle, Alice, 1941-

1, 2, I love you; illustrated by Emily Arnold McCully. Chronicle Books 2004 unp il $16.95

Grades: PreK K   E

1. Counting 2. Stories in rhyme 3. Elephants—Fiction

ISBN 0-8118-3518-9   LC 2003-21245

"A mother elephant addresses her little one as they engage in a variety of child-centered activities. . . . The numbers climb from 1 to 10 in the first half of the book, then descend until the end, when the little elephant goes to bed and to sleep. The rhythmic, rhyming verses are . . . engaging. . . . The colorful artwork features playful, large-scale paintings." Booklist

Down the road; illustrated by E. B. Lewis. Browndeer Press 1995 unp il $16; pa $6

Grades: PreK K 1 2   E

1. Eggs—Fiction 2. Country life—Fiction

ISBN 0-15-276622-7; 0-15-202471-9 (pa)

     LC 94-9901

Hetty "makes her first solo jaunt to Mr. Birdie's store for fresh eggs, determined to prove how responsible she is. On the way home, temptation beckons in the guise of an apple tree; Hetty breaks the eggs while picking fruit, then hides among the branches in shame. Papa and Mama take her failure better than she expects and, instead of scolding, join her in the tree and share apple pie for breakfast." Bull Cent Child Books

"The story is remarkable for its evocative imagery, and the loving interchange between the characters set a charming tone. The words are perfectly complemented by Lewis' dazzling, impressionistic watercolors." Booklist

Little Blue Truck; illustrated by Jill McElmurry. Harcourt Children's Books 2008 unp il $16 *

Grades: PreK K 1 2   E

1. Trucks—Fiction 2. Friendship—Fiction 3. Animals—Fiction

ISBN 978-0-15-205661-2; 0-15-205661-0

     LC 2006-29445

"Schertle contrasts a huge dump truck, hurtling self-importantly down a country road, with a small pickup that greets each farm animal. . . . When the dump truck bogs down in a deep slough, its cries of distress go unanswered. When the pickup gets stuck while trying to help, the animals rush in to lend a hearty push. . . . McElmurry creates crisply drawn rural scenes. . . . Along with being a natural for storytime, this upbeat tale may spark a discussion about friendships and helping one another." Booklist

Another title about Little Blue Truck is:

Little Blue Truck leads the way (2009)

Schmitz, Tamara

Standing on my own two feet; a child's affirmation of love in the midst of divorce. Price Stern Sloan 2008 unp il $9.99

Grades: PreK K 1   E

1. Divorce—Fiction

ISBN 978-0-8431-3221-2; 0-8431-3221-3

"When Addison's parents get divorced, he ends up with two homes, and he feels safe in both of them. He knows that his mom and dad will always love him. The text uses simple straightforward statements. . . . The brightly colored illustrations have exactly the right images to support the story. Due to its positive feel, easy-to-understand message, and topical nature, this book is an excellent choice for most libraries." SLJ

Schnur, Steven, 1952-

Autumn; an alphabet acrostic; illustrated by Leslie Evans. Clarion Bks. 1997 unp il $16

Grades: K 1 2 3   E

1. Autumn 2. Acrostics 3. Alphabet

ISBN 0-395-77043-2   LC 96-50219

"A fall riddle is presented for each letter of the alphabet. The answer is spelled out in the first letter of each line. The riddles are spare with striking images. . . . Evans's stunning hand-colored linoleum block prints are clear, bright, and provide sharp clues for the riddles. . . . This delightful alphabet book with a new twist will provide inspiration and challenges for a wide audience." SLJ

Spring; an alphabet acrostic; illustrated by Leslie Evans. Clarion Bks. 1999 unp il $15

Grades: K 1 2 3   E

1. Spring 2. Acrostics 3. Alphabet

ISBN 0-395-82269-6   LC 98-22704

Describes spring, with its animals, green smells, and renewed outside activities. When read vertically, the first letters of the lines of text spell related words arranged alphabetically, from "April" to "zenith"

"The evocative free verse captures the season's promise, as do the colorful block-print illustrations." Horn Book Guide

Schnur, Steven, 1952-—*Continued*

Summer; an alphabet acrostic; illustrated by Leslie Evans. Clarion Books 2001 unp il $16

Grades: K 1 2 3   E

1. Summer 2. Acrostics 3. Alphabet

ISBN 0-618-02372-0   LC 00-31674

"This concept book features a short poem in which the first letter of each line spells out the word it represents. 'Daisy' becomes 'Dragonflies dart/And hover,/Inspecting white flowers with/Sunlike/Yellow centers.' The sheer inventiveness of each poem is impressive. . . . Neatly framed linoleum-block illustrations feature rich colors and bold lines that capture the brightness of the days." SLJ

Winter; an alphabet acrostic; illustrated by Leslie Evans. Clarion Bks. 2002 unp il $15

Grades: K 1 2 3   E

1. Winter 2. Acrostics 3. Alphabet

ISBN 0-618-02374-7   LC 2001-17358

"On each page, a winter-related word provides the basis for an acrostic that reads like a short poem. . . . A striking, hand-colored linoleum print illustrates each small, boxed acrostic." Booklist

Schoenherr, Ian

Cat & mouse; [by] Ian Schoenherr. Greenwillow Books 2008 unp il $16.95; lib bdg $17.89

Grades: PreK K 1 2   E

1. Mice—Fiction 2. Cats—Fiction 3. Play—Fiction 4. Nursery rhymes—Fiction 5. Stories in rhyme

ISBN 978-0-06-136313-9; 0-06-136313-8; 978-0-06-136314-6 (lib bdg); 0-06-136314-6 (lib bdg)

LC 2007036145

"Adapting and combining 'Hickory, Dickory, Dock,' 'Eeny Meeny Miney Mo,' and 'I Love Little Pussy,' Schoenherr crafts a wild romp featuring a paper-parasol-equipped mouse leading a cat on a merry chase. . . . The dynamic and realistic ink and acrylic illustrations feature a stop-action energy and changing perspectives that make the characters appear to actually move across the pages. This [is a] bright, funny book." SLJ

Don't spill the beans! Greenwillow Books 2010 unp il $16.99; lib bdg $17.89 *

Grades: PreK   E

1. Stories in rhyme 2. Birthdays—Fiction 3. Bears—Fiction 4. Animals—Fiction

ISBN 978-0-06-172457-2; 0-06-172457-2; 978-0-06-172458-9 (lib bdg); 0-06-172458-0 (lib bdg)

LC 2008042363

A bear tries hard to keep a birthday surprise a secret.

"The story is told in short rhyming sentences of large, colorful, hand-lettered text. The ink and acrylic paint illustrations depict cheerfully clothed animals with expressive faces." SLJ

Read it, don't eat it! Greenwillow Books 2009 unp il $17.99; lib bdg $18.89 *

Grades: PreK K   E

1. Stories in rhyme 2. Books and reading—Fiction

ISBN 978-0-06-172455-8; 0-06-172455-6; 978-0-06-178034-9 (lib bdg); 0-06-178034-0 (lib bdg)

LC 2008027716

Rhyming advice on how to take care of a library book

"One white, hand-lettered sentence per page is set against a bold color, and the ink and acrylic art features endearing animal library users on an expansive white space. The book is simple enough to use with preschool children and funny enough to be appreciated by early readers." SLJ

Schotter, Roni

The boy who loved words; pictures by Giselle Potter. Schwartz & Wade Books 2006 unp il $16.95; lib bdg $18.99 *

Grades: K 1 2 3   E

1. English language—Fiction

ISBN 0-375-83601-2; 0-375-93601-7 (lib bdg)

LC 2005-10850

Selig, who loves words and copies them on pieces of paper that he carries with him, goes on a trip to discover his purpose.

"Potter's signature naive-style art is light and comical, while Schotter's words are a lovely celebration of the power and the music of language." Booklist

Doo-Wop Pop; by Roni Schotter; illustrated by Bryan Collier. Amistad/HarperCollins 2008 unp il $16.99; lib bdg $17.89 *

Grades: K 1 2 3   E

1. Stories in rhyme 2. Singing—Fiction 3. Janitors—Fiction 4. School stories

ISBN 978-0-06-057968-5; 0-06-057968-4; 978-0-06-057974-6 (lib bdg); 0-06-057974-9 (lib bdg)

LC 2008015212

A school janitor teaches children to sing and have confidence in themselves

"Schotter stacks the prose with rhymes, giving the first-person narrative an authentic, contemporary freestyle flow that begs to be read aloud. Collier's trademark collage paintings, shaded with bursts of yellow and green, hum with the students' energy and pride." Booklist

Mama, I'll give you the world; by Roni Schotter; illustrated by S. Saelig Gallagher. Schwartz & Wade Books 2006 unp il $16.95 *

Grades: K 1 2 3   E

1. Birthdays—Fiction 2. Mother-daughter relationship—Fiction 3. Beauty shops—Fiction

ISBN 978-0-375-83612-1; 0-375-83612-8

At Walter's World of Beauty, Luisa's secret plans are underway to create a very special birthday celebration for her hardworking, single mother who is employed there as a stylist.

"Gallagher's bright-eyed, smiling, subtly modeled faces light up this loving mother-daughter tale." Booklist

Schroeder, Alan, 1961-

Minty: a story of young Harriet Tubman; pictures by Jerry Pinkney. Dial Bks. for Young Readers 1996 unp il hardcover o.p. pa $6.99

Grades: 1 2 3 4   E

1. Tubman, Harriet, 1820?-1913—Fiction 2. Slavery—Fiction

ISBN 0-8037-1888-8; 0-14-056196-X (pa)

LC 95-23499

Coretta Scott King Award for illustration

Schroeder, Alan, 1961-—*Continued*

"Young Araminta, or 'Minty,' who will later in life be known as Harriet Tubman, proves too clumsy and defiant to be a house slave and is sent by Mistress Brodas to work in the fields. . . . The child purposely frees the muskrats from the traps she has been ordered to empty and is cruelly whipped and threatened to be sold 'downriver.' Certain that his headstrong daughter will one day attempt to run away, Minty's father begins to instruct her in outdoor survival and navigation." Bull Cent Child Books

Pinkney's "paintings, done in pencil, colored-pencils, and watercolor, use light and shadow to great effect. . . . This is a dramatic story that will hold listeners' interest and may lead them to biographical material." SLJ

Satchmo's blues; illustrated by Floyd Cooper. Doubleday Bks. for Young Readers 1996 unp il hardcover o.p. pa $6.99 *

Grades: 1 2 3 4   E
1. Armstrong, Louis, 1900-1971—Fiction 2. African American musicians—Fiction 3. New Orleans (La.)—Fiction
ISBN 0-385-32046-9; 0-440-41472-5 (pa)
LC 93-41082

A fictional recreation of the youth of trumpeter Louis Armstrong in New Orleans

"This book is full of gorgeous writing, accompanied by Cooper's atmospheric paintings." SLJ

Schubert, Leda

Feeding the sheep; pictures by Andrea U'Ren. Farrar Straus Giroux 2010 unp il $16.99

Grades: PreK K 1 2   E
1. Stories in rhyme 2. Sheep—Fiction 3. Weaving—Fiction 4. Wool—Fiction 5. Mother-daughter relationship—Fiction
ISBN 978-0-374-32296-0; 0-374-32296-1
LC 2007048843

In pictures and rhythmic text, a mother relates to her daughter all the steps involved in making her a snug, wooly sweater, starting at the very beginning with feeding the sheep

"The physicality of the words, . . . the fascinating facts, and the action-filled, brightly colored illustrations will capture kids' attention, as will the cozy family bond between parent and child." Booklist

Schuch, Steve

A symphony of whales; illustrated by Peter Sylvada. Harcourt Brace & Co. 1999 unp il hardcover o.p. pa $7 *

Grades: 1 2 3 4   E
1. Whales—Fiction 2. Music—Fiction
ISBN 0-15-201670-8; 0-15-216548-7 (pa)
LC 98-17248

Young Glashka's dream of the singing of whales, accompanied by a special kind of music, leads to the rescue of thousands of whales stranded in a freezing Siberian bay

"This is a quiet, powerful story, beautifully extended by Sylvada's paintings of ghostly whale shapes and glowing, fin-shaped skies." Booklist

Schwartz, Amy, 1954-

A beautiful girl. Roaring Brook Press 2006 unp il $16.95

Grades: PreK K   E
1. Animals—Fiction 2. Human body—Fiction
ISBN 978-1-59643-165-2; 1-59643-165-2
LC 2005-33022

"A Neal Porter book"

On her way to the market, Jenna encounters an elephant, a robin, a fly, and a goldfish who discover some of the things that make little girls different from each of them.

"The short and snappy story line and dialogue will hold the attention of young audiences, as will the naive cartoon illustrations in bright, candy-colored watercolors on white backgrounds." SLJ

Things I learned in second grade. Katherine Tegen Books 2004 unp il $15.99; lib bdg $16.89 *

Grades: K 1 2 3   E
1. School stories
ISBN 0-06-050936-8; 0-06-050937-6 (lib bdg)
LC 2002-155507

A young boy shares all of the things he learned and how he changed in second grade, what he still wonders about, and what he hopes to accomplish when he is in third grade.

"This sweet story is accompanied by precisely drawn, softly colored illustrations of the boy engaged in a variety of activities at home and in the classroom, and the optimistic and cheerful ending pulls it together to a satisfactory conclusion." SLJ

Tiny and Hercules. Roaring Brook Press 2009 unp il $16.95

Grades: K 1 2 3   E
1. Friendship—Fiction 2. Elephants—Fiction 3. Mice—Fiction
ISBN 978-1-59643-253-6; 1-59643-253-5
LC 2008-54268

"A Neal Porter book"

Five short stories about the lives of two unusual friends: Tiny, an elephant with a fear of ice skating and a newfound love of knitting, and Hercules, a mouse with a heart of gold and a desire to learn to paint.

"Even the most sidesplitting moments in these stories . . . are secondary to the touching portrait of a devoted friendship." SLJ

What James likes best. Atheneum Bks. for Young Readers 2003 unp il $16.95 *

Grades: PreK K 1 2   E
1. Transportation—Fiction
ISBN 0-689-84059-4   LC 2001-22988
"A Richard Jackson book"

James goes with his parents on an express bus to visit twins, in a taxi to visit Grandma, and in a car to see the county fair, then walks next door with his mother for a play date

"Schwartz's pristine illustrations are streamlined and clean; the lucid, transparent colors make her gouache and pen-and-ink illustrations . . . seem almost weightless. This is a terrifically simple, successful way to get readers and listeners to interact with printed text." Bull Cent Child Books

Schwartz, David M., 1951-

How much is a million? pictures by Steven Kellogg. Lothrop, Lee & Shepard Bks. 1985 unp il $16.99; lib bdg $17.89; pa $6.99 *

Grades: PreK K 1 2 3   E

1. Million (The number) 2. Billion (The number) 3. Trillion (The number)

ISBN 0-688-04049-7; 0-688-04050-0 (lib bdg); 0-688-09933-5 (pa)   LC 84-5736

"Marvelosissimo the Mathematical Magician leads the reader through Steven Kellogg's scenes of fantasy to express the concepts of a million, a billion and a trillion. The text is all printed in capital letters to point out the expanding scenes portrayed in the fabulous illustrations. The idea is to make possible to children the awesome concept of large numbers. It is a delightful fantasy as a picture book, but it is even more compelling as a first reader." Okla State Dept of Educ

If you made a million; pictures by Steven Kellogg. Lothrop, Lee & Shepard Bks. 1989 unp il hardcover o.p. pa $6.99

Grades: PreK K 1 2 3   E

1. Personal finance

ISBN 0-688-07017-5; 0-688-13634-6 (pa)

       LC 88-12819

The author examines "how one earns money, how checks are used instead of cash, why banks pay interest on money deposited, [and] why interest is charged on loans." Booklist

"The concepts of banks and banking . . . are all explained with absurd and humorous examples involving Ferris wheels, ogres, and rhinoceroses. . . . The best advice of all is 'Enjoying your work is more important than money.' Steven Kellogg's splendidly funny illustrations contain a troupe of two cats, one dog, numerous kids, a unicorn, and the wonderful magician Marvelosissimo." Horn Book

Schwartz, Joanne, 1960-

City alphabet; words by Joanne Schwartz; photos by Matt Beam. Groundwood Books 2009 unp il $18.95; pa $12.95 *

Grades: K 1 2 3 4   E

1. Alphabet 2. City and town life

ISBN   978-0-88899-928-3;   0-88899-928-3; 978-0-88899-962-7 (pa); 0-88899-962-3 (pa)

"This art book follows the letters of the alphabet found in words printed on signs, etched in concrete, and painted on various surfaces in downtown Toronto. Each photograph is paired with a clean white page containing the particular letter (in both upper and lowercase) and the featured word (printed in a clean bold font)." SLJ

"Stark, metallic and urban, these images may encourage children to think about alternate ways of seeing their surroundings." Publ Wkly

Our corner grocery store; illustrated by Laura Beingessner. Tundra Books 2009 unp il $19.95 *

Grades: K 1 2 3   E

1. Family life—Fiction 2. Grandparents—Fiction 3. Italian Americans—Fiction 4. Retail trade—Fiction

ISBN 978-0-88776-868-2; 0-88776-868-7

"This sweet story takes readers through young Anna Maria's Saturday as she helps her grandparents in their neighborhood store. The day is special for its simplicity; the book is special for its rich evocation of the delights of a little Italian market and the loving relationships between a girl and her grandparents. Beingessner's folksy illustrations and Schwartz's easy text fit well together and are filled with details." SLJ

Schwarz, Viviane, 1977-

There are cats in this book. Candlewick Press 2008 unp il $16.99 *

Grades: PreK   E

1. Cats—Fiction 2. Play—Fiction

ISBN 978-0-7636-3923-5; 0-7636-3923-0

       LC 2007-52165

The reader is invited to lift the flaps and follow the cats as they play with yarn, boxes, pillows, and fish.

"Interactive pages colored with ink, paint and photo collage invite readers to revel in what felines already know: that the mere existence of cats is cause for festivity. . . . The whirlwind of pure kinetic energy ensures that readers are wholly part of the impenitent kitty world and will be reluctant to say goodbye." Publ Wkly

Timothy and the strong pajamas; a superhero adventure. Arthur A. Levine Books 2008 unp il $16.99

Grades: PreK K 1 2   E

1. Superheroes—Fiction

ISBN 978-0-545-03329-9; 0-545-03329-2

       LC 2007-06812

After his mother mends his favorite pajamas, Timothy finds that he has super strength and decides to use it to help others, but when the pajamas rip again, he loses his strength just when he needs it most.

"The watercolor illustrations vary from small vignettes, to vertical and horizontal paneled scenes, to full pages and spreads. . . . Youngsters who long to be strong and powerful will enter into this fantasy with gusto." SLJ

Scieszka, Jon, 1954-

Baloney (Henry P.); received and decoded by Jon Scieszka; visual recreation by Lane Smith. Viking 2001 unp il $15.99 *

Grades: K 1 2 3   E

1. Life on other planets—Fiction

ISBN 0-670-89248-3   LC 00-12041

A transmission received from outer space in a combination of different Earth languages tells of an alien schoolboy's fantastic excuse for being late to school again

"Every Earth kid will immediately recognize a soul mate in this extraterrestrial truth-stretcher and tall-tale teller. . . . Illustrator Smith has been having equal fun stretching the visual truth to create a vision of space that is not only artfully outer but also utterly outre. The result is wacky fun for everyone." Booklist

The Frog Prince continued; story by Jon Scieszka; paintings by Steve Johnson. Viking 1991 unp il $15.99; pa $6.99 *

Grades: 2 3 4 5   E

1. Fairy tales 2. Frogs—Fiction

ISBN 0-670-83421-1; 0-14-054285-X (pa)

       LC 90-26537

Scieszka, Jon, 1954-—*Continued*

After the frog turns into a prince, he and the Princess do not live happily ever after and the Prince decides to look for a witch to help him turn back into a frog

"The dialogue is witty; the plot, as logical as it is offbeat. Steve Johnson's paintings, executed in a rich and somber palette, are like stage settings; his depiction of the various characters is inspired." Horn Book

Math curse; illustrated by Lane Smith. Viking 1995 unp il $16.99 *

Grades: 2 3 4 5   E

1. Mathematics—Fiction

ISBN 0-670-86194-4   LC 95-12341

When the teacher tells her class that they can think of almost everything as a math problem, one student acquires a math anxiety which becomes a real curse

"Bold in design and often bizarre in expression, Smith's paintings clearly express the child's feelings of bemusement, frustration, and panic as well as her eventual joy when she overcomes the math curse. . . . A child-centered, witty picture book." Booklist

Pete's party; written by Jon Scieszka; characters and environments developed by the Design Garage: David Gordon, Loren Long, David Shannon. Aladdin 2008 unp il (John Scieszka's Trucktown: Ready-to-roll) lib bdg $13.89; pa $3.99

Grades: PreK K 1   E

1. Signs and signboards—Fiction 2. Trucks—Fiction

ISBN 978-1-4169-4149-1 (lib bdg); 1-4169-4149-5 (lib bdg); 978-1-4169-4138-5 (pa); 1-4169-4138-X (pa)

LC 2007027154

The Trucktown trucks follow the road signs directing them to Pete's party

This title "will draw beginning readers into the zany world of anthropomorphic trucks, whose distinct personalities and endearing facial expressions roll across the colorful pages." SLJ

Other titles in this series are:

Dizzy Izzy (2010)
Kat's mystery (2009)
Melvin's valentine (2009)
Snow trucking! (2008)
Zoom! boom? bully (2008)
The spooky tire (2009)
Uh-oh Max (2009)

Robot Zot! illustrated by David Shannon. Simon & Schuster Books for Young Readers 2009 unp il $17.99 *

Grades: K 1 2   E

1. Robots—Fiction

ISBN 978-1-4169-6394-3; 1-4169-6394-4

LC 2008-20031

On a mission to conquer planet Earth, tiny but fearless Robot Zot and his mechanical sidekick leave a path of destruction as they battle kitchen appliances.

"Scieszka laces his action-filled narrative with rhymes and repetitive robot phrases. . . . Shannon's acrylic artwork offers bright colors and plenty of humor." Publ Wkly

Science verse; illustrated by Lane Smith. Viking 2004 unp il $16.99 *

Grades: 2 3 4 5   E

1. Poetry—Fiction 2. Science—Fiction

ISBN 0-670-91057-0   LC 2004-1641

Companion volume to Math curse

When the teacher tells his class that they can hear the poetry of science in everything, a student is struck with a curse and begins hearing nothing but science verses that sound very much like some well known poems.

"Children need not be familiar with the works upon which the spoofs are based to enjoy the humor, but this is a perfect opportunity to introduce the originals and to discuss parody as a poetic form. The dynamic cartoons are an absolute delight." SLJ

Smash! crash! illustrated by David Shannon, Loren Long, and David Gordon. Simon & Schuster 2008 unp il (Jon Scieszka's Trucktown) $16.99

Grades: PreK K   E

1. Trucks—Fiction

ISBN 1-4169-4133-9

"Jack Truck, a red flatbed with chrome exhaust stacks, and best friend Dump Truck Dan, a blue guy with a yellow cab and mud flaps, adore the smash and crash of work in progress. . . . Scieszka . . . revs readers up with gear-grinding noise and rowdy antics. . . . Illustrators Shannon, Long and Gordon embed mechanical shapes in their punchy display type, and they contribute panoramic vistas." Publ Wkly

Other titles in this series are:

Melvin might? (2008)
Truckery rhymes (2009)

The Stinky Cheese Man and other fairly stupid tales; [by Jon Scieszka & Lane Smith] Viking 1992 unp il $17.99 *

Grades: 2 3 4 5   E

1. Fairy tales 2. Short stories

ISBN 0-670-84487-X   LC 91-48194

A Caldecott Medal honor book, 1993

"Cinderumpelstiltskin and The Really Ugly Duckling are among the tales that Jack the narrator tries to present. But the Dedication is upside down; the Table of Contents is late; and Little Red Running Shorts and the wolf quit." Publisher's note

"The picture-book set will probably recognize the stories enough to know that what's going on isn't what's 'supposed' to happen. But *The Stinky Cheese Man* isn't a book for little ones. It will take older children (that's teens along with 10s) to follow the disordered story lines and appreciate the narrative's dry wit, wordplay, and wacky, sophomoric jokes. . . . Smith's New Wave art is an intricate part of the whole, extending as well as reinforcing the narrative; the pictures are every bit as comically insolent and deliberately clever as the words." Booklist

The true story of the 3 little pigs; pictures by Lane Smith. Viking Kestrel 1989 unp il $16.99; pa $7.99 *

Grades: K 1 2 3 4   E

1. Wolves—Fiction 2. Pigs—Fiction

ISBN 0-670-82759-2; 0-14-054451-8 (pa)

LC 89-8953

Scieszka, Jon, 1954-—*Continued*

The wolf gives his own outlandish version of what really happened when he tangled with the three little pigs

"The 'excited and funky' illustrations match the hilarious revisionist text to a standard story." N Y Times Book Rev

Scillian, Devin

Pappy's handkerchief; by Devin Scillian; illustrated by Chris Ellison. Sleeping Bear Press 2007 unp il (Tales of young Americans) $17.95

Grades: 2 3 4   E

1. Oklahoma—Fiction 2. African Americans—Fiction 3. Frontier and pioneer life—Fiction 4. Family life—Fiction

ISBN 978-1-58536-316-2   LC 2007006394

In 1889, young Moses and his family sell everything they own and leave their Baltimore, Maryland, home to join many other settlers—black and white—in a race to claim land in the newly-opened territory of Oklahoma.

"This history of a unique and interesting part of the settling of the West is illustrated in beautiful paintings of warm, soft browns, yellows, and blues that complement the narrative, together creating a fascinating look at the past." SLJ

Scott, Ann Herbert, 1926-

Brave as a mountain lion; illustrated by Glo Coalson. Clarion Bks. 1996 31p il $16

Grades: K 1 2 3   E

1. School stories 2. Shoshoni Indians—Fiction

ISBN 0-395-66760-7   LC 94-42906

Spider is afraid to get up on stage in front of everybody in the school spelling bee, but after listening to his father's advice, decides that he too will try to be as brave as his Shoshoni ancestors

"This story is well shaped and rhythmically told. Coalson's subdued watercolor and pastel illustrations depict the wintry landscapes and interiors with sensitivity and detail." SLJ

On Mother's lap; illustrated by Glo Coalson. Clarion Bks. 1992 32p il $16; pa $6.95; bd bk $5.95

Grades: PreK K   E

1. Inuit—Fiction 2. Mother-child relationship—Fiction

ISBN 0-395-58920-7; 0-395-62976-4 (pa); 0-618-05159-7 (bd bk)   LC 91-17765

A newly illustrated edition of the title first published 1972 by McGraw-Hill

"Sitting on his mother's lap, a young Eskimo boy gathers his belongings until he, some toys, his puppy, and a blanket are all crowded together in the rocking chair. When his baby sister cries, the boy claims there is no room for her, but Mother proves him wrong, and the threesome settle comfortably in the chair. Soft illustrations depict a cozy scene and a loving family." Horn Book

Scotton, Rob

Russell the sheep; by Rob Scotton. HarperCollins 2005 unp il $17.99; lib bdg $18.89

Grades: PreK K 1 2   E

1. Sheep—Fiction 2. Bedtime—Fiction

ISBN 0-06-059848-4; 0-06-059849-2 (lib bdg)
                                LC 2003-24274

Russell the sheep tries all different ways to get to sleep

"Scotton makes a captivating debut with this comical tale. He illustrates it with a witty, engaging, and fluffy character bathed in calming blue hues." SLJ

Other titles about Russell are:
Russell and the lost treasure (2006)
Russell's Christmas magic (2007)

Splat the cat. HarperCollins 2008 unp il $16.99; lib bdg $17.89

Grades: K 1 2   E

1. Cats—Fiction 2. School stories 3. Friendship—Fiction

ISBN 978-0-06-083154-7; 0-06-083154-5; 978-0-06-083155-4 (lib bdg); 0-06-083155-3 (lib bdg)
                                LC 2008-20218

"The fuzzy black feline is worried about his first day of school, and despite determined attempts to avoid the inevitable, he ends up there. . . . This lighthearted story, told with a generous helping of humor and goofy characterizations, will have broad appeal." SLJ

Other titles about Splat are:
Love, Splat (2008)
Merry Christmas, Splat (2009)

Seder, Rufus Butler

Gallop! [by] Rufus Butler Seder. Workman Pub. 2007 unp il $12.95

Grades: PreK K 1 2   E

1. Animal locomotion—Fiction 2. Animals—Fiction 3. Stories in rhyme

ISBN 978-0-7611-4763-3   LC 2007024247

"A Scanimation picture book"

"A first book of motion for kids, [this book] shows a horse in full gallop and a turtle swimming up the page. A dog runs, a cat springs, an eagle soars, and a butterfly flutters. Created by Rufus Butler Seder . . . Scanimation is a state-of-the-art six-phase animation process that combines the 'persistence of vision' principle with a striped acetate overlay to give the illusion of movement." Publisher's note

"Readers will gasp with delight when they open this book." Publ Wkly

Swing! Workman Pub. 2008 unp il $12.95

Grades: PreK K 1 2   E

1. Sports—Fiction

ISBN 978-0-7611-5127-2; 0-7611-5127-3

"A Scanimation picture book"

"Open the die-cut cover and see a baseball player swing his bat at a ball, then watch as the ball zooms ever-larger to fit the acetate window showcasing all this action. . . . Colored fonts and multicolored borders offset the severity of the b&w pictures and generate reader participation. . . . On other spreads, child athletes perform soccer drills, run, cartwheel, twirl on ice skates,

Seder, Rufus Butler—*Continued*

shoot hoops, swim and lead cheers—it's all jaw-dropping, even if the novelty technology has yet to find its most imaginative application." Publ Wkly

Waddle! Workman Pub. 2009 unp il $12.95
Grades: PreK K 1 2   E
    1. Animal locomotion—Fiction 2. Animals—Fiction
    ISBN 978-0-7611-5112-8; 0-7611-5112-5
    "A Scanimation picture book"
    Text asks if the reader can move like a variety of animals. Striped acetate overlays on board pages give illustrations the illusion of movement.
    "The level of detail . . . is striking . . . [and the] readers should find the animations mesmerizing." Publ Wkly

Sederman, Marty

    Casey and Derek on the ice; illustrated by Zachary Pullen. Chronicle Books 2008 unp il $15.99
Grades: PreK K 1 2   E
    1. Hockey—Fiction 2. Stories in rhyme
    ISBN 978-0-8118-5132-9; 0-8118-5132-X
                       LC 2007021063
    A rhyming tale of an underdog hockey team's last minute attempt to win a big game.
    "Hockey jargon abounds, but any sports enthusiast can enjoy this simple tale with basic brotherly concern. The oil-on-canvas illustrations show how the action intensifies as the illustrator uses varying angles and perspectives." SLJ

Sedgwick, Marcus

    The emperor's new clothes; retold by Marcus Sedgwick; illustrated by Alison Jay. Chronicle Books 2004 unp il $16.95
Grades: K 1 2 3 4   E
    1. Andersen, Hans Christian, 1805-1875—Adaptations 2. Animals—Fiction 3. Fairy tales 4. Stories in rhyme
    ISBN 0-8118-4569-9   LC 2004-2855
    In this retelling of the Hans Christian Andersen story in which two rascals sell a vain emperor an invisible suit of clothes, all the characters are animals
    "Sedgwick's . . . jaunty rhymed couplets and Jay's . . . signature stylized artwork ably accentuate the wry humor of this . . . tale." Publ Wkly
    Includes bibliographical references

Seeger, Laura Vaccaro

    Black? white! day? night! a book of opposites. Roaring Brook Press 2006 20p il $16.95 *
Grades: PreK K 1 2   E
    1. Opposites
    ISBN 978-1-59643-185-0; 1-59643-185-7
                       LC 2005-32378
    On the first page of this picture book "a large black flap with a cutout [reveals] a black bat set against a pure white background. The single word *black?* printed in white, stands out clearly on the page. When kids lift the flap, they'll see the word *white!* (in white type) and discover that what appeared to be a bat is really the mouth

of a ghost. Each of 18 opposites is similarly conveyed using only one word and the lift of a flap. . . . Each flap is a different bold color . . . and the scenes under the flaps are in keeping with the simple yet sophisticated graphic design of the book. Thick, shiny pages add to the sense of richness." Booklist

    Dog and Bear: two friends, three stories. Roaring Brook Press 2007 unp il $12.95 *
Grades: PreK K   E
    1. Friendship—Fiction 2. Dogs—Fiction 3. Bears—Fiction
    ISBN 978-1-59643-053-2; 1-59643-053-2
                       LC 2006-11687
    "Bear is a multicolored stuffed toy; Dog is a playful, rowdy dachshund. . . . In the first episode, Dog helps timid Bear down from a high stool. In the second, Dog wants to play, but Bear needs some quiet time alone. And in the final story, Dog suffers a small identity crisis, but Bear helps him recognize that he is just fine as he is. . . . Seeger's minimal text is perfectly paced for new readers, who will love the dose of humor at each story's close. In pictures as spare and charming as the text, Seeger captures preschoolers' expressions and body language." Booklist
    Other titles about Dog and Bear are:
    Dog and Bear: two's company (2008)
    Dog and Bear: three to get ready (2009)

    First the egg. Roaring Brook Press 2007 unp il $14.95 *
Grades: PreK K   E
    1. Growth
    ISBN 978-1-59643-272-7; 1-59643-272-1
                       LC 2006-32924
    A Caldecott Medal honor book, 2008
    "A Neal Porter book"
    Seeger "introduces a chicken-or-egg dilemma on her book's cover, picturing a plump white egg in a golden-brown nest. Remove the die-cut dust jacket, and a hen appears on the glossy inner cover. The eggshell, thickly brushed in bluish-white and cream, also serves as the chicken's feathers. This 'first/then' pattern is repeated . . . with a die-cut on every other page." Publ Wkly
    "Pages are color-saturated and as minimalist as the text. . . . Cleverly conceived and executed cutouts reinforce the book's tactile appeal. . . . The best picture books creat a world in themselves, and this tour de force is one of them." Horn Book

    The hidden alphabet. Roaring Brook Press 2003 unp il $17.95
Grades: PreK K 1 2   E
    1. Alphabet
    ISBN 0-7613-1941-7   LC 2002-152838
    "A Neal Porter book"
    An alphabet book in which windows open to reveal the letters hidden within each picture
    "From the black book jacket with cutout openings for each letter of the title to the vibrant, painterly strokes of yellow on the endpapers, Hidden Alphabet is a visual delight." SLJ

Seeger, Laura Vaccaro—*Continued*

Lemons are not red. Roaring Brook Press 2004 unp il $14.95 *

Grades: PreK K 1 2   E

1. Color

ISBN 1-59643-008-7

"A Neal Porter book"

"The first spread reads, 'Lemons are not/ RED.' The word 'RED' appears on a bright yellow page beneath the die-cut shape of a lemon with a red background showing through. When the page is turned, the die-cut shape falls on the correct yellow background, with the words 'Lemons are YELLOW' underneath. . . . This framework continues throughout the book. . . . Illustrated with richly colored yet simple oil paintings, this offering will delight preschoolers." SLJ

One boy. Roaring Brook Press 2008 unp il $14.95 *

Grades: PreK K 1 2   E

1. Vocabulary—Fiction   2. Painting—Fiction   3. Counting

ISBN 978-1-59643-274-1; 1-59643-274-8

LC 2007-45941

A Geisel Award honor book, 2009

A boy creates ten paintings in this counting book that also explores the relationship of words within words.

Seeger "crafts another nifty peek-a-boo book, counting to 10 and identifying new words by exposing or covering letters with die-cuts. . . . Seeger uses pared-down digital art and flat saturated colors." Publ Wkly

Walter was worried. Roaring Book Press 2005 unp il $15.95 *

Grades: PreK K 1 2   E

1. Storms—Fiction   2. Emotions—Fiction

ISBN 1-59643-066-8   LC 2004-024558

"A Neal Porter book."

Children's faces, depicted with letters of the alphabet, react to the onset of a storm and its aftermath in this picture book, accompanied by simple alliterative text.

"The artwork uses bold colors with wide brush marks as backdrops and primary colors with almost graphic shapes to represent rain, snow flakes, leaves, and branches. With only one sentence per page, there is surprising depth in this wonderful collaboration of art and story." SLJ

What if? Roaring Brook Press 2010 unp il $15.99 *

Grades: PreK K   E

1. Seals (Animals)—Fiction   2. Beaches—Fiction

ISBN 978-1-59643-398-4; 1-59643-398-1

"A Neal Porter book"

"What if a boy found a beach ball and kicked it into the ocean? What if two seals found it and began to play? What if a third seal appeared on the beach looking for a friend? In this . . . book, Laura Vaccaro Seeger shows us the same story with three different outcomes, each highlighting the possibility in possibilities." Publisher's note

"It's simplicity itself, but the emotions are exactixely executed by careful placement of characters upon the page and the slightest hints of emotions. . . . The brushstrokes and possibly even finger strokes evident in the colorful paint give it an ever deeper sense of intimacy." Booklist

Seeger, Pete

The deaf musicians; by Pete Seeger and Paul DuBois Jacobs; illustrations by R. Gregory Christie. Putnam 2006 unp il $16.99

Grades: K 1 2 3   E

1. Deaf—Fiction   2. Musicians—Fiction   3. Jazz music—Fiction

ISBN 0-399-24316-X   LC 2005026901

Lee, a jazz pianist, has to leave his band when he begins losing his hearing, but he meets a deaf saxophone player in a sign language class and together they form a snazzy new band.

"Christie's snazzy style matches perfectly with the book's vivacity. The expressive faces and bold use of color make the story sing. . . . Both uplifting and inclusive, it is a celebration of music and resilience." SLJ

Segal, John

Alistair and Kip's great adventure; written and illustrated by John Segal. Margaret K. McElderry Books 2008 unp il $15.99

Grades: PreK K 1 2   E

1. Boats and boating—Fiction   2. Cats—Fiction   3. Dogs—Fiction   4. Whales—Fiction

ISBN 978-1-4169-0280-5; 1-4169-0280-5

LC 2006019870

Alistair the cat and Kip the dog build a boat and soon find themselves sailing down the creek to the river to the bay and out to sea where a violent storm threatens to capsize them

"The quick-paced story is told through both dialogue and simple narrative. Beautifully rendered watercolors in bright hues comically depict the self-confident cat and his smaller canine pal." SLJ

Carrot soup; written and illustrated by John Segal. Margaret K. McElderry Books 2006 unp il $12.95

Grades: PreK K 1 2   E

1. Carrots—Fiction   2. Rabbits—Fiction   3. Gardening—Fiction

ISBN 0-689-87702-1   LC 2004-16963

After working hard on his garden all spring and summer, Rabbit looks forward to harvest time when he can make soup, but every carrot disappears and Rabbit must find out who has taken them. Includes a recipe for carrot soup

"The clues are in Segal's stylized pencil and watercolor pictures, and observant children won't have any trouble determining where the carrots went. The delicate springtime greens and browns used in the background contrast nicely with Rabbit's comically expressive face." Booklist

Far far away. Philomel Books 2009 unp il $16.99

Grades: PreK K 1   E

1. Mother-child relationship—Fiction   2. Runaway children—Fiction   3. Pigs—Fiction

ISBN 978-0-399-25007-1; 0-399-25007-7

LC 2008035855

Segal, John—*Continued*

When an unhappy young pig decides to run away, his mother helps him to see that everything he needs and wants is right there at home.

"Segal's art, executed in pencil and watercolors, features stylized pigs set against backgrounds that alternate between mottled colors and pure white. The pictures make good use of space and squeeze every bit of humor out of a familiar situation." Booklist

Segal, Lore Groszmann

Morris the artist; [by] Lore Segal; pictures by Boris Kulikov. Farrar, Straus & Giroux 2003 unp il $16

Grades: PreK K 1 2   E

1. Birthdays—Fiction

ISBN 0-374-35063-9   LC 2002-66295

"Frances Foster books"

Morris buys a set of paints as a birthday present for Benjamin, but he wants to keep them for himself

"This simple and realistic tale is made fantastical by Kulikov's bizarrely sophisticated paintings. . . . Youngsters will enjoy the story, take the odd perspectives in stride, and maybe even learn a thing or two about friendship and generosity." SLJ

Seibold, J. Otto, 1960-

Olive the other reindeer; by J. Otto Seibold and Vivian Walsh. Chronicle Bks. 1997 unp il $15.99 *

Grades: PreK K 1 2   E

1. Reindeer—Fiction 2. Dogs—Fiction 3. Christmas—Fiction 4. Santa Claus—Fiction

ISBN 0-8118-1807-1   LC 97-9876

Thinking that "all of the other reindeer" she hears people singing about include her, Olive the dog reports to the North Pole to help Santa Claus on Christmas Eve

"Seibold has developed a signature style with computer digitized art, and his playful skewed lines and warm shades of ochre, pimento and olive green are user-friendly." Publ Wkly

Sendak, Maurice

Alligators all around; an alphabet. Harper & Row 1962 unp il lib bdg $16.89; pa $5.95 *

Grades: PreK K 1 2   E

1. Alphabet

ISBN 0-06-025530-7 (lib bdg); 0-06-443254-8 (pa)

Originally published in smaller format as volume one of the "Nutshell library"

An alphabet book of alligators doing dishes, juggling jelly beans, throwing tantrums and wearing wigs, all from A to Z

Chicken soup with rice; a book of months. Harper & Row 1962 30p il lib bdg $16.89; pa $5.95 *

Grades: PreK K 1 2   E

1. Seasons—Fiction 2. Stories in rhyme

ISBN 0-06-025535-8 (lib bdg); 0-06-443253-X (pa)

Originally published in smaller format as volume two of the "Nutshell library"

Pictures and verse illustrate the delight of eating chicken soup with rice in every season of the year

In the night kitchen. 25th anniversary ed. HarperCollins Pubs. 1996 c1970 unp il $17.95; lib bdg $18.89; pa $6.95 *

Grades: PreK K 1 2 3   E

1. Fantasy fiction

ISBN 0-06-026668-6; 0-06-026669-4 (lib bdg); 0-06-443436-2 (pa)

A Caldecott Medal honor book, 1971

First published 1970

"A small boy falls through the dark, out of his clothes, and into the bright, night kitchen where he is stirred into the cake batter and almost baked, jumps into the bread dough, kneads and shapes it into an airplane, and flies up over the top of the Milky Way to get milk for the bakers." Booklist

"A perfect midnight fantasy. The feelings, smells, sights, and comforting emotions which young children experience are here in lovely dream colors." Brooklyn. Art Books for Child

Mommy? [art by Maurice Sendak; scenario by Arthur Yorinks; paper engineering by Matthew Reinhart] Scholastic 2006 unp il $24.95 *

Grades: PreK K 1 2   E

1. Monsters—Fiction 2. Pop-up books

ISBN 0-439-88050-5

A boy "wanders into a haunted house and naively calls, 'Mommy?' . . . Characters . . . unfold in 3D to menace the child, but . . . he pulls pranks on everyone." Publ Wkly

"This pop-up tour de force abounds with humor, vibrant artwork, and visual fireworks." SLJ

One was Johnny; a counting book. Harper & Row 1962 unp il lib bdg $16.89; pa $5.95 *

Grades: PreK K 1 2   E

1. Counting

ISBN 0-06-025540-4 (lib bdg); 0-06-443251-3 (pa)

Originally published in smaller format as volume three of the "Nutshell library"

Counting from one to ten and back again to one, Johnny, who starts off alone, acquires too many numbered visitors for his own comfort, until they disappear one by one

Outside over there. Harper & Row 1981 unp il $22.95; pa $9.95 *

Grades: K 1 2 3   E

1. Fairy tales 2. Sisters—Fiction

ISBN 0-06-025523-4; 0-06-443185-1 (pa)

LC 79-2682

A Caldecott Medal honor book, 1982

"An Ursula Nordstrom book"

With Papa off to sea and Mama despondent, Ida must go outside over there to rescue her baby sister from goblins who steal her to be a goblin's bride

"A gentle yet powerful story in the romantic tradition. . . . Soft in tones, rich in the use of light and color . . . the pictures are particularly distinctive for the tenderness with which the children's faces are drawn, the classic handling of texture, the imaginative juxtaposition of in-

Sendak, Maurice—*Continued*

fant faces and the baroque landscape details that might have come from Renaissance paintings." Bull Cent Child Books

Pierre; a cautionary tale in five chapters and a prologue. Harper & Row 1962 48p il lib bdg $16.89; pa $5.95 *

Grades: PreK K 1 2   E

1. Stories in rhyme

ISBN 0-06-025965-5 (lib bdg); 0-06-443252-1 (pa)

Originally published in smaller format as volume four of the "Nutshell library"

A story in verse about a little boy called Pierre who insisted upon saying 'I don't care' until he said it once too often and learned a well needed lesson

Where the wild things are; story and pictures by Maurice Sendak. Harper & Row 1963 unp il $17.95; lib bdg $18.89; pa $8.95 *

Grades: PreK K 1 2   E

1. Fantasy fiction

ISBN 0-06-025492-0; 0-06-025493-9 (lib bdg); 0-06-443178-9 (pa)

Awarded the Caldecott Medal, 1964

"A tale of very few words about Max, sent to his room for cavorting around in his wolf suit, who dreamed of going where the wild things are, to rule them and share their rumpus. Then a longing to be 'where someone loved him best of all' swept over him." Book Week

"This vibrant picture book in luminous, understated full color has proved utterly engrossing to children with whom it has been shared. . . . A sincere, preceptive contribution which bears repeated examination." Horn Book

Senir, Mirik, 1948-

When I first held you; a lullaby from Israel; [by] Mirik Snir; [illustrated by] Eleyor Snir; translated from the Hebrew by Mary Jane Shubow. Kar-Ben 2009 unp il $9.95

Grades: PreK K 1   E

1. Stories in rhyme 2. Parent-child relationship—Fiction 3. Nature—Fiction 4. Lullabies

ISBN 978-0-7613-5098-9; 0-7613-5098-5

LC 2008-53741

A parent describes, in rhyming text, the beauty of the world on the day a young child is born

"The unassuming and calming melodious text, fluidly translated by Shubow, will certainly encourage serenity and comfort at the end of each day." Kirkus

Serfozo, Mary

Plumply, dumply pumpkin; written by Mary Serfozo; illustrated by Valeria Petrone. Margaret K. McElderry Bks. 2001 unp il hardcover o.p. pa $6.99; bd bk $6.99

Grades: PreK K 1 2   E

1. Pumpkin—Fiction 2. Halloween—Fiction 3. Stories in rhyme

ISBN 0-689-83834-4; 0-689-87135-X (pa); 0-689-86277-6 (bd bk)   LC 00-32421

Peter finds the perfect pumpkin so that he and his Dad can make a jack-o-lantern

"Toddlers will relish the bouncy, rhyming stanzas and silly wordplay, which help make this a great, nonspooky Halloween storytime choice. The subtly textured computer-generated art has solid child appeal." Booklist

Whooo's there? by Mary Serfozo; illustrated by Jeffrey Scherer. Random House 2007 unp il $9.99; lib bdg $12.99

Grades: PreK K 1   E

1. Owls—Fiction 2. Animals—Fiction 3. Stories in rhyme

ISBN 978-0-375-84050-0; 978-0-375-94050-7 (lib bdg)   LC 2006014438

An inquisitive owl keeps track of the comings and goings of woodland creatures all night long

"The story is told in pleasing verse made up of quatrains. . . . Illustrations have thick lines of color that accentuate outlines, and the animals feature mostly friendly cartoonlike visages that are quite appealing." SLJ

Seuss, Dr.

The 500 hats of Bartholomew Cubbins. Random House 1990 c1938 unp il $14.95

Grades: PreK K 1 2 3   E

1. Hats—Fiction

ISBN 0-394-84484-X   LC 88-38412

"A Vanguard Press book"

A reissue of the title first published 1938 by Vanguard Press

"A read-aloud story telling what happened to Bartholomew Cubbins when he couldn't take his hat off before the King." Hodges. Books for Elem Sch Libr

"It is a lovely bit of tomfoolery which keeps up the suspense and surprise until the last page, and of the same ingenious and humorous imagination are the author's black and white illustrations in which a red cap and then an infinite number of red caps titillate the eye." N Y Times Book Rev

And to think that I saw it on Mulberry Street. Random House 1989 c1937 unp il $14.95; lib bdg $15.99 *

Grades: PreK K 1 2   E

1. Stories in rhyme

ISBN 0-394-84494-7; 0-394-94494-1 (lib bdg)

LC 88-38411

"A Vanguard Press book"

A reissue of the title first published 1937 by Vanguard Press

This book tells in rhyme accompanied by pictures how little Marco saw a horse and wagon on Mulberry Street. Then "how that horse became a zebra, then a reindeer, then an elephant, and how the cart turned into a band wagon with a retinue of police to guide it through the traffic on Mulberry Street, only the book can properly explain." Christ Sci Monit

"A fresh, inspiring picture-story book in bright colors. . . . As convincing to a child as to the psychologist in quest of a book with an appeal to the child's imaginations." Horn Book

Seuss, Dr.—*Continued*

Bartholomew and the oobleck; written and illustrated by Dr. Seuss. Random House 1949 unp il $14.95; lib bdg $15.99
Grades: PreK K 1 2   E
  ISBN 0-394-80075-3; 0-394-90075-8 (lib bdg)
  A Caldecott Medal honor book, 1950
  "Bored with the same old kinds of weather, the King of Didd commanded his magicians to stir up something new and different. What they produced was a gooey, gummy green stuff which might have wrecked the kingdom had it not been for Bartholomew Cubbins, the page boy." Booklist

The cat in the hat; by Dr. Seuss. 50th anniversary ed. Random House 2007 c1957 61p il $8.99 *   E
  1. Cats—Fiction 2. Stories in rhyme
  ISBN 978-0-394-80001-1
  "Beginner books"
  A reissue of the title first published 1957
  A nonsense story in verse illustrated by the author about an unusual cat and his tricks which he displayed for the children one rainy day
  Another title about The cat in the hat is:
  The cat in the hat returns! (1958)

Green eggs and ham. Beginner Bks. 1960 62p il $8.99; lib bdg $11.99; pa $9.95 *   E
  1. Food—Fiction 2. Stories in rhyme
  ISBN 0-394-80016-8; 0-394-90016-2 (lib bdg); 0-394-89220-8 (pa)
  This book is about "Sam-I-Am who wins a determined campaign to make another Seuss character eat a plate of green eggs and ham." Libr J
  "The happy theme of refusal-to-eat changing to relish will be doubly enjoyable to the child who finds many common edibles as nauseating as the title repast. The pacing throughout is magnificent, and the opening five pages, on which the focal character introduces himself with a placard: 'I am Sam,' are unsurpassed in the controlled-vocabulary literature." Saturday Rev

Hooray for Diffendoofer Day! [by] Dr. Seuss with some help from Jack Prelutsky & Lane Smith. Knopf 1998 unp il $17; lib bdg $18.99
Grades: PreK K 1 2   E
  1. School stories 2. Stories in rhyme
  ISBN 0-679-89008-4; 0-679-99008-9 (lib bdg)
                  LC 97-39725
  The students of Diffendoofer School celebrate their unusual teachers and curriculum, including Miss Fribble who teaches laughing, Miss Bonkers who teaches frogs to dance, and Mr. Katz who builds robotic rats
  "Given an unfinished manuscript (some sketches, snippets of verse, and jottings of names—but no plot) retrieved after Seuss's death, Prelutsky and Smith have brought this fragment to fruition in a style that does credit to all three artists." Horn Book Guide

Horton hatches the egg. Random House 1940 unp il $14.95; lib bdg $15.99 *
Grades: PreK K 1 2   E
  1. Elephants—Fiction 2. Stories in rhyme
  ISBN 0-394-80077-X; 0-394-90077-4 (lib bdg)
  "Horton, the elephant, is faithful one hundred percent as he carries out his promise to watch a bird's egg while she takes a rest. Hilarious illustrations and a surprise ending." Adventuring with Books. 2d edition

Horton hears a Who! Random House 1954 unp il $14.95; lib bdg $16.99 *
Grades: PreK K 1 2   E
  1. Elephants—Fiction 2. Stories in rhyme
  ISBN 0-394-80078-8; 0-394-90078-2 (lib bdg)
  "Although considered the biggest blame fool in the Jungle of Nool, the faithful and kindhearted elephant of 'Horton hatches the egg' believing that a person's a person no matter how small, stanchly defends the Whos, too-small-to-be-seen inhabitants of Whoville, a town which exists on a dust speck." Booklist
  "The verses are full of the usual lively, informal language and amazing rhymes that have delighted such a world-wide audience in the good 'doctor's' other books." N Y Her Trib Books

How the Grinch stole Christmas. Random House 1957 unp il $15; lib bdg $18 *
Grades: PreK K 1 2   E
  1. Christmas—Fiction 2. Stories in rhyme
  ISBN 0-394-80079-6; 0-394-90079-0 (lib bdg)
  "The Grinch lived on a mountain where it was able to ignore the people of the valley except at Christmas time when it had to endure the sound of their singing. One year it decided to steal all the presents so there would be no Christmas, but much to its amazement discovered that people did not need presents to enjoy Christmas. It thereupon reformed, returned the presents and joined in the festivities." Bull Cent Child Books
  "The verse is as lively and the pages are as bright and colorful as anyone could wish." Saturday Rev

If I ran the circus. Random House 1956 unp il $14.95; lib bdg $15.99 *
Grades: PreK K 1 2   E
  1. Circus—Fiction 2. Stories in rhyme
  ISBN 0-394-80080-X; 0-394-90080-4 (lib bdg)
  The author-illustrator "presents the fabulous Circus McGurkus with its highly imaginative young owner, Morris McGurk and its intrepid performer, Sneelock, behind whose store the circus is to be housed. There are the expected number of strange creatures with nonsensical names, but the real humor lies in the situations, and especially those involving Mr. Sneelock. There is fun for the entire family here." Bull Cent Child Books

If I ran the zoo. Random House 1950 unp il $14.95; lib bdg $16.99 *
Grades: PreK K 1 2   E
  1. Zoos—Fiction 2. Stories in rhyme
  ISBN 0-394-80081-8; 0-394-90081-2 (lib bdg)
  A Caldecott Medal honor book, 1951
  "Assembled here are the rare and wonderful creatures which young Gerald McGrew collects from far and un-

Seuss, Dr.—*Continued*

usual places for the 'gol-darndest zoo on the face of the earth.'" Booklist

"As you turn the pages, the imaginings get wilder and funnier, the rhymes more hilarious. There will be no age limits for this book, because families will be forced to share rereading and quotation, for a long long time." NY Her Trib Books

McElligot's pool; written and illustrated by Dr. Seuss. Random House 1947 unp il $14.95; lib bdg $16.99

Grades: PreK K 1 2   E

1. Fishing—Fiction 2. Stories in rhyme

ISBN 0-394-80083-4; 0-394-90083-9 (lib bdg)

A Caldecott Medal honor book, 1948

"In spite of warnings that there are no fish in McElligot's Pool, a boy continues to fish and to imagine the rare and wonderful denizens of the deep which he just 'might' catch." Hodges. Books for Elem Sch Libr

"Fine color surrounding a host of strange creatures enlivens this amazing fish story for all ages." Horn Book

Oh, the places you'll go! Random House 1990 unp il $17; lib bdg $20.99

Grades: PreK K 1 2   E

1. Stories in rhyme

ISBN 0-679-80527-3; 0-679-90527-8 (lib bdg)

LC 89-36892

Advice in rhyme for proceeding in life; weathering fear, loneliness, and confusion; and being in charge of your actions

"The combination of the lively text and wacky, off-beat pictures will delight both children and their parents." Child Book Rev Serv

Yertle the turtle and other stories; A 50th anniversary retrospective; with 32 pages of rarely seen Seuss images and commentary by Charles D. Cohen. 50th anniversary ed. Random House 2008 114p il $24.99; lib bdg $27.99

Grades: PreK K 1 2   E

1. Stories in rhyme 2. Turtles—Fiction

ISBN 978-0-375-83850-7; 0-375-83850-3; 978-0-375-93850-4 (lib bdg); 0-375-93850-8 (lib bdg)

LC 2007033486

A reissue of the title first published 1958

Includes three humorous stories in verse, Yertle the Turtle, Gertrude McFuzz, and The Big Brag, followed by commentary and end notes, reproductions of illustrations from other Dr. Seuss books, and two poems, 'The Ruckus' and 'The Kindly Snather'

Includes bibliographical references

Seymour, Tres

Hunting the white cow; story by Tres Seymour; pictures by Wendy Anderson Halperin. Orchard Bks. 1993 unp il $16.95

Grades: K 1 2 3   E

1. Cattle—Fiction 2. Farm life—Fiction

ISBN 0-531-05496-9   LC 92-43757

"A Richard Jackson book"

A child watches as more and more people join in the attempts to catch the family cow that has gotten loose, each remarking on how special the cow is

"Wendy Halperin's soft colored-pencil drawings of fields and woods that drift far back into the distant hills add to the mythic aura. A unique and imaginative book." Horn Book

Shahan, Sherry, 1949-

Spicy hot colors: colores picantes; illustrated by Paula Barragan. August House 2004 unp il $16.95

Grades: PreK K 1 2   E

1. Color 2. Bilingual books—English-Spanish

ISBN 0-87483-741-3

This is an "introduction to the names of nine colors in Spanish. Snappy, image-filled verses bring to life some of the hues and traditions of Latino culture. . . . Vibrant paintings that have both ethnic and fine-art references are appealing and attention grabbing." SLJ

Shange, Ntozake

Ellington was not a street; written by Ntozake Shange; illustrations by Kadir Nelson. Simon & Schuster Bks. for Young Readers 2004 unp il $15.95 *

Grades: K 1 2 3 4   E

1. African Americans—Poetry

ISBN 0-689-82884-5   LC 00-45060

"Nelson illustrates the noted poet's 'Mood Indigo,' from her collection entitled *A Daughter's Geography*. . . . In the poem, Shange recalls her childhood when her family entertained many of the . . . 'men/who changed the world,' including Paul Robeson, W.E.B. DuBois, Ray Barretto, Dizzy Gillespie, 'Sonny Til' Tilghman, Kwame Nkrumah, and Duke Ellington. Both the words and the rich, nostalgic illustrations are a tribute to these visionaries. . . . A biographical sketch of each man appears at the end, along with the poem reprinted on a single page." SLJ

Shannon, David, 1959-

Alice the fairy. Blue Sky Press 2004 unp il $15.95 *

Grades: PreK K 1 2   E

1. Imagination—Fiction 2. Fairies—Fiction

ISBN 0-439-49025-1   LC 2003-23478

Alice, who claims to be a Temporary Fairy, still has a lot to learn, such as how to make her clothes put themselves away in the closet.

"Kids will find most of the humor right at their level, in terms of both wit and imagination. The pictures are richly colored, some almost effervescent in their playfulness." Booklist

Duck on a bike. Blue Sky Press (NY) 2002 unp il $15.95 *

Grades: PreK K 1 2   E

1. Ducks—Fiction 2. Domestic animals—Fiction 3. Cycling—Fiction

ISBN 0-439-05023-5   LC 2001-35992

A duck decides to ride a bike and soon influences all the other animals on the farm to ride bikes too

Shannon, David, 1959-—*Continued*

"This delightful story will have youngsters chiming in on the repeated phrases and predicting, in no time, what will happen next, and the many animal sounds provide ample opportunities for role-playing. Shannon's brightly colored spreads are filled with humor." SLJ

Good boy, Fergus! Blue Sky Press 2006 unp il $15.99 *

Grades: PreK K 1 2   E

  1. Dogs—Fiction

    ISBN 0-439-49027-8   LC 2005-08541

Except for his bath, Fergus experiences the perfect doggy day, from chasing cats and motorcycles to being scratched on his favorite tickle spot.

"This book is all about the impressive, oversize visuals—pictures that show the adorable doggie in full canine-caper mode." Booklist

No, David! Blue Sky Press (NY) 1998 unp il $16.99 *

Grades: PreK K 1 2   E

  1. Mother-son relationship—Fiction

    ISBN 0-590-93002-8   LC 97-35125

  A Caldecott Medal honor book, 1999

"All little David hears from his mother as he writes on the wall, runs naked down the road, lets water pour over the side of the tub, sticks his finger far, far up his nose, and the like is 'No, David!.'" Booklist

"The vigorous and wacky full-color acrylic paintings portray a lively and imaginative boy whose stick-figure body conveys every nuance of anger, exuberance, defiance, and best of all, the reassurance of his mother's love." SLJ

  Other titles about David are:

David gets in trouble (2002))

David goes to school (1999)

The rain came down. Blue Sky Press (NY) 2000 unp il lib bdg $15.95 *

Grades: PreK K 1 2   E

  1. Rain—Fiction

    ISBN 0-439-05021-9   LC 99-86363

"When the rain starts falling, a whole neighborhood is soon honking, bickering, and snapping at one another. . . . Calm and goodwill are finally restored when the rain stops and the sun comes out." Horn Book Guide

"This deceptively simple story showcases Shannon's quirky humor and offbeat illustrations." SLJ

Too many toys. Blue Sky Press 2008 unp il $16.99 *

Grades: PreK K 1 2   E

  1. Toys—Fiction

    ISBN 978-0-439-49029-0; 0-439-49029-4

                 LC 2007-44753

Although he finally agrees that he has too many toys and needs to give them away, there is one toy that Spencer absolutely cannot part with.

"A master at capturing the workings of a young mind, Shannon combines realistic dialogue with his boisterous illustrations to create another surefire hit." SLJ

Shannon, George, 1952-

Tippy-toe chick, go! pictures by Laura Dronzek. Greenwillow Bks. 2003 unp il $15.99; lib bdg $16.89

Grades: PreK K 1 2   E

  1. Chickens—Fiction 2. Dogs—Fiction

    ISBN 0-06-029823-5; 0-06-029824-3 (lib bdg)

                 LC 2002-17509

When a mean dog blocks the path to the garden where a delicious breakfast awaits, Little Chick shows her family how brave and clever she is

"The narrative has a fresh, buoyant vitality that begs to be read aloud. . . . The bright, uncluttered acrylic illustrations neatly match the spare text." Booklist

Tomorrow's alphabet; pictures by Donald Crews. Greenwillow Bks. 1996 unp il $17; pa $6.99 *

Grades: PreK K 1 2 3   E

  1. Alphabet

    ISBN 0-688-13504-8; 0-688-16424-2 (pa)

                 LC 94-19484

"In 26 double-page spreads, the letters of the alphabet are used to demonstrate where things come from. 'A is for seed' is followed on the next page with 'tomorrow's APPLE.' 'D is for puppy—tomorrow's DOG.'. . . All of the combinations are clever, well chosen, and well within youngsters' experience. . . . Each two-page spread offers brightly colored, large and realistic depictions of the objects named." SLJ

White is for blueberry; pictures by Laura Dronzek. Greenwillow Books 2005 unp il $17.99; lib bdg $17.89 *

Grades: PreK K 1 2 3   E

  1. Color

    ISBN 0-06-029275-X; 0-06-029276-8 (lib bdg)

                 LC 2004-10147

"Shannon challenges color associations that become ingrained in early life by using unusual combinations of words and images. . . . Red poppies, for example, are black 'when we take the time to look inside.'" Booklist

"The bold, uncluttered scenes, rendered in acrylics, have a sweetness and strength that is quite pleasing to the eye. Easy to read and fun to share, this paean to the wonder of cycles and the rewards of close observation is the perfect prelude to a thoughtful excursion." SLJ

Shannon, Margaret, 1966-

The red wolf; written and illustrated by Margaret Shannon. Houghton Mifflin 2002 unp il $15

Grades: K 1 2 3   E

  1. Fairy tales 2. Princesses—Fiction

    ISBN 0-618-05544-4   LC 00-56742

Roselupin, a princess locked in a tower by her overprotective father, uses yarn to knit a red wolf suit to free herself

"Shannon's brightly colored illustrations and the creative design and layout enrich this original, delightful tale. A thoroughly enjoyable story of empowerment." SLJ

Shapiro, Zachary

We're all in the same boat; [by] Zachary Shapiro; illustrated by Jack E. Davis. G.P. Putnam's Sons 2008 unp il $16.99 *

Grades: PreK K 1 2   E

1. Noah's ark—Fiction 2. Animals—Fiction 3. Alphabet

ISBN 978-0-399-24393-6; 0-399-24393-3

                         LC 2007041316

After being on the ark for months and months, the ants get antsy, the bees bored, and the llamas livid, and Noah must find a way to make everyone get along.

"Davis's hilarious illustrations of the facial expressions and actions of the various animals add to the liveliness and humor. Lots of interactions occur simultaneously, giving readers much to explore visually. . . . Shapiro has crafted a humorous alphabet story with an underlying message of cooperation—a winning combination." SLJ

Sharmat, Marjorie Weinman, 1928-

Gila monsters meet you at the airport; pictures by Byron Barton. Macmillan 1980 unp il hardcover o.p. pa $5.99

Grades: PreK K 1 2   E

1. Moving—Fiction 2. West (U.S.)—Fiction

ISBN 0-02-782450-0; 0-689-71383-5 (pa)

                         LC 80-12264

A New York City boy's preconceived ideas of life in the West make him very apprehensive about the family's move there

"The exaggeration is amusing, the style yeasty, with a nice final touch; the illustrations are comic and awkward, but add little that's not inherent in the story." Bull Cent Child Books

Nate the Great; illustrated by Marc Simont. Delacorte Press 2002 c1972 60p il $13.95; pa $4.50 *

Grades: K 1 2   E

1. Mystery fiction

ISBN 978-0-385-73017-4;   0-385-73017-9; 978-0-440-46126-5 (pa); 0-440-46126-X (pa)

A reissue of the title first published 1972 by McCann & Geoghegan

Nate the Great, a junior detective who has found missing balloons, books, slippers, chickens and even a goldfish, is now in search of a painting of a dog by Annie, the girl down the street.

"The illustrations capture the exaggerated, tongue-in-cheek humor of the story." Booklist

Other titles about Nate the Great are:

Nate the Great and me: the case of the fleeing fang (1998)

Nate the Great and the big sniff (2001)

Nate the Great and the boring beach bag (1987)

Nate the Great and the crunchy Christmas (1996)

Nate the Great and the fishy prize (1985)

Nate the Great and the Halloween hunt (1989)

Nate the Great and the hungry book club (2009)

Nate the Great and the lost list (1975)

Nate the Great and the missing key (1981)

Nate the Great and the monster mess (1999)

Nate the Great and the mushy valentine (1994)

Nate the Great and the musical note (1990)

Nate the Great and the phony clue (1977)

Nate the Great and the pillowcase (1993)

Nate the Great and the snowy trail (1982)

Nate the Great and the sticky case (1978)

Nate the Great and the stolen base (1992)

Nate the Great and the tardy tortoise (1995)

Nate the Great goes down in the dumps (1989)

Nate the Great goes undercover (1974)

Nate the Great on the Owl Express (2003)

Nate the Great, San Francisco detective (2000)

Nate the Great saves the King of Sweden (1997)

Nate the Great stalks stupidweed (1986)

Nate the Great talks turkey (2006)

Sharmat, Mitchell, 1927-

Gregory, the terrible eater; illustrated by Jose Aruego and Ariane Dewey. Four Winds Press 1985 c1980 unp il $16.95

Grades: PreK K 1 2   E

1. Goats—Fiction 2. Diet—Fiction

ISBN 0-02-782250-8   LC 85-29290

Also available in paperback from Scholastic

A reissue of the title first published 1980

"Gregory is not your average goat. In fact, he's the original goat gourmet, abandoning bottle caps in favor of bananas and trading last year's boots for bread and butter." SLJ

"Aruego and Dewey's illustrations are highly amusing, thanks to their goats' dot-eyed facial expressions. . . . There is energy in the pictures; they are beguiling and help to carry the humor." Booklist

Shaw, Charles, 1892-1974

It looked like spilt milk. Harper & Row 1947 unp il $16.99; lib bdg $18.89; pa $6.99; bd bk $6.99 *

Grades: PreK K 1   E

ISBN 0-06-025566-8; 0-06-025565-X (lib bdg); 0-06-443159-2 (pa); 0-694-00491-X (bd bk)

White silhouettes on a blue background with simple captions: "sometimes it looked like a tree," "Sometimes it looked like a bird," etc. lead to a surprise ending "sometimes it looked like split milk, but what it was was—"

"What one thing could look like all of these? On the last page you are told, and I could no more tell you now than I could spoil an adult mystery by a review that gives away its solution." N Y Her Trib Books

Shaw, Hannah

Sneaky weasel. Alfred A. Knopf 2009 unp il $15.99; lib bdg $18.99 *

Grades: K 1 2 3   E

1. Weasels—Fiction 2. Bullies—Fiction 3. Parties—Fiction 4. Friendship—Fiction

ISBN 978-0-375-85625-9;   0-375-85625-0; 978-0-375-95625-6 (lib bdg); 0-375-95625-5 (lib bdg)

"Sneaky Weasel's schemes and scams have made him rich, but when nobody comes to his big party, Weasel determines to discover why. . . . The descriptive, lively narrative offers an entertaining exploration of bullying. . . . The animated, colorful illustrations feature Weasel in intricately rendered scenes that are filled with clever details." Booklist

Shaw, Nancy

Raccoon tune; illustrated by Howard Fine. Holt & Co. 2003 unp il $15.95

Grades: PreK K 1 2   E

1. Raccoons—Fiction 2. Stories in rhyme
ISBN 0-8050-6544-X   LC 2002-5945

A family of raccoons prowls around a neighborhood making a ruckus until they find supper

"Playful illustrations expand the lighthearted mood of the story. Fine's use of blues, greens, and light makes nighttime scenes almost as bright as the white of the raccoons' markings, and such objects as the metal trash cans shine with reflected moonlight." SLJ

Sheep in a jeep; illustrated by Margot Apple. Houghton Mifflin 1986 32p il lib bdg $15; pa $5.95; bd bk $5.95 *

Grades: PreK K 1 2   E

1. Sheep—Fiction 2. Stories in rhyme
ISBN 0-395-41105-X (lib bdg); 0-395-47030-7 (pa); 0-395-86786-X (bd bk)   LC 86-3101

"When five sheep pile into one little jeep, there is trouble . . . [as] the poor woolly travelers push, shove, and attempt to drive their way from one calamity to another." Horn Book

"Shaw demonstrates a promising capacity for creating nonsense rhymes. . . . Veteran illustrator Apple's whimsical portraits of the sheep bring the story to life. Pleasing and lighthearted, this has much appeal for young readers." Publ Wkly

Other titles about the sheep are:

Sheep blast off! (2008)
Sheep in a shop (1991)
Sheep on a ship (1989)
Sheep out to eat (1992)
Sheep take a hike (1994)
Sheep trick or treat (1997)

Shea, Bob

Big plans; [illustrated by] Lane Smith. Hyperion 2008 42p il $17.99 *

Grades: 1 2 3 4   E

1. Imagination—Fiction 2. School stories
ISBN 1-4231-1100-1; 978-1-4231-1100-9
     LC 2008-00707

A little boy sits in the corner of his classroom dreaming about his big plans for his future.

"Smith is the perfect artist for this illogically logical scenario, with retro tones of gold and avocado predominating in his carefully disorganized oversized compositions. . . . An escapist adventure, a victory over important adults, and a new catch-phrase to triumphantly wield." Bull Cent Child Books

Dinosaur vs. bedtime. Hyperion Books for Children 2008 unp il $15.99 *

Grades: PreK   E

1. Dinosaurs—Fiction 2. Bedtime—Fiction
ISBN 978-1-4231-1335-5; 1-4231-1335-7

"Nothing can stop little dinosaur—not talking grownups, spaghetti, or even bath time. But what happens when he faces the biggest challenge of all . . . bedtime?" Publisher's note

"Incorporating paper, paint, photo collage and quick strokes of crayon, Shea's freewheeling compositions convey both a beguiling spontaneity and a preschooler's sense of invincibility." Publ Wkly

New socks; by Bob Shea. Little, Brown 2007 unp il $12.99

Grades: PreK K 1 2   E

1. Clothing and dress—Fiction 2. Chickens—Fiction
ISBN 978-0-316-01357-4; 0-316-01357-9
     LC 2006013741

A chicken is filled with excitement and self-confidence when he dons a new pair of orange socks

"The text, which presents a childlike blend of fervor and silliness, is wonderfully extended through the artwork. . . . The chick's body is a yellow lima-bean-shaped blob; black-dot eyes, a beak fashioned from two half-moons, and thick-rimmed glasses define his face and add expression." SLJ

Oh, Daddy! Balzer + Bray 2010 unp il $16.99 *

Grades: PreK K   E

1. Father-child relationship—Fiction
2. Hippopotamus—Fiction
ISBN 978-0-06-173080-1; 0-06-173080-7

A young hippopotamus shows his father the right way to do things, such as getting dressed, watering the flowers, and especially giving big hugs.

"The concise text captures the child's voice perfectly. . . . The mixed-media illustrations incorporate collage elements into a spare, cartoonlike world. . . . The gentle humor . . . will keep kids entertained." SLJ

Race you to bed. Katherine Tegen Books 2010 unp il $16.99

Grades: PreK K 1   E

1. Stories in rhyme 2. Rabbits—Fiction 3. Bedtime—Fiction
ISBN 978-0-06-170417-8; 0-06-170417-2
     LC 2008044525

"A fuzzy white rabbit with an oversize head races readers to bed, but he finds many reasons to delay bedtime. Animals, toys, and other objects divert his attention. . . . The singsong rhyme flows as the rabbit cavorts through the flat colored pages. The backgrounds are all done in soothing pastel colors, with the exuberant youngster cavorting across the pages. Clever details in the art enhance the telling." SLJ

Shelby, Anne

The man who lived in a hollow tree; by Anne Shelby and Cor Hazelaar. Atheneum Books for Young Readers 2009 unp il $17.99 *

Grades: K 1 2 3   E

1. Carpentry—Fiction 2. Trees—Fiction 3. Ecology—Fiction 4. Tall tales
ISBN 978-0-689-86169-7; 0-689-86169-9
     LC 2008-10369

"A Richard Jackson Book"

Carpenter Harlan Burch, who builds everything from cradle to casket, plants two trees for every one he cuts down, and when he is very old his sap begins to rise, he grows young again, and starts a family that still lives all over the mountains.

Shelby, Anne—*Continued*
"The storyteller's voice is vibrant, and the earth-toned acrylics on textured backgrounds of cardboard and linen have a quaint, collage-like feel." Booklist

Sherman, Pat
Ben and the Emancipation Proclamation; written by Pat Sherman; illustrated by Floyd Cooper. Eerdmans Books for Young Readers 2010 unp il $16.99
Grades: 3 4 5   E
  1. Holmes, Benjamin C., fl. 1846-1870—Fiction
2. Emancipation Proclamation (1863)—Fiction
3. Slavery—Fiction 4. African Americans—Fiction
5. Books and reading—Fiction
ISBN 978-0-8028-5319-6; 0-8028-5319-6
"Based on the life of Benjamin Holmes, a slave who taught himself to read at a young age, this picture book is an inspiring account of overcoming oppression. Sherman's fictionalized telling is stirring, especially when Holmes revels in the discovery of new words. . . . Sherman's text has a stately simplicity. Cooper's paintings glow with a hopeful, golden warmth. . . . This is a powerful tale of a bright ray of light in a very dark period in America." SLJ
Includes bibliographical references

Sherry, Kevin
I'm the biggest thing in the ocean. Dial Books for Young Readers 2007 unp il $16.99
Grades: PreK   E
  1. Squids—Fiction 2. Marine animals—Fiction
3. Size—Fiction
ISBN 978-0-8037-3192-9; 0-8037-3192-2
                           LC 2006-27815
A giant squid brags about being bigger than everything else in the ocean—almost.
"A lighthearted, clever story presented in an oversize, colorful package." SLJ
Another title about the giant squid is:
I'm the best artist in the ocean (2008)

Sheth, Kashmira
Monsoon afternoon; written by Kashmira Sheth; illustrated by Yoshiko Jaeggi. Peachtree 2008 unp il $16.95
Grades: PreK K 1 2   E
  1. Rain—Fiction 2. Monsoons—Fiction
3. Grandfathers—Fiction 4. India—Fiction
ISBN 978-1-56145-455-6; 1-56145-455-9
                           LC 2008004565
A young boy and his grandfather find much they can do together on a rainy day during monsoon season in India
"Jaeggi's atmospheric watercolors nicely translate the sensory details in the words. . . . The scenes give a strong sense of everyday life in the boy's Indian community, as well as the sweet bond between grandfather and grandson." Booklist

My Dadima wears a sari; written by Kashmira Sheth; illustrated by Yoshiko Jaeggi. Peachtree 2007 unp il $16.95
Grades: K 1 2 3   E
  1. Clothing and dress—Fiction 2. Grandmothers—Fiction 3. East Indians—United States—Fiction
ISBN 1-56145-392-7   LC 2006024334
Two young sisters raised in America learn about the beauty and art of wearing a sari from their wise Indian grandmother.
"Soft watercolor paintings capture the magnificent fabrics of Dadima's saris and accentuate the loving story." SLJ

Shields, Carol Diggory
Lucky pennies and hot chocolate; illustrated by Hiroe Nakata. Dutton Children's Bks. 2000 unp il $13.99
Grades: PreK K 1 2   E
  1. Grandfathers—Fiction
ISBN 0-525-46450-6   LC 00-20967
A grandfather and his grandson enjoy sharing knock-knock jokes, playing games, hot chocolate, watching movies, reading books, playing baseball and just spending time together
"The illustrations are as warm, colorful, and winning as the story." Booklist

Wombat walkabout; illustrated by Sophie Blackall. Dutton Children's Books 2009 unp il $16.99
Grades: PreK K   E
  1. Stories in rhyme 2. Wombats—Fiction
3. Animals—Fiction 4. Australia—Fiction
5. Counting
ISBN 978-0-525-47865-2; 0-525-47865-5
                         LC 2008013885
Rhyming text follows six little wombats on walkabout and a hungry dingo following, envisioning them as his lunch until the wombats turn the tables on him.
"This picture book offers a nicely cadenced, rhyming story with a solid base in folklore and a distinctive locale. . . . The pleasing double-page paintings . . . use color sparingly but well." Booklist

Shields, Gillian
When the world is ready for bed. Bloomsbury 2009 unp il $14.99; lib bdg $15.89
Grades: PreK K   E
  1. Stories in rhyme 2. Bedtime—Fiction 3. Rabbits—Fiction
ISBN   978-1-59990-339-2;   1-59990-339-3;
978-1-59990-385-9 (lib bdg); 1-59990-385-7 (lib bdg)
                         LC 2009002858
"This calming tale follows three brown bunnies as their day draws to a close. They have dinner, tidy up, tell dad about the fun they've had, brush their teeth, and listen to one last story. . . . The gentle singsong text makes for excellent bedtime reading, and the homey watercolors are equally pleasant. The bunnies wear distinctive outfits and have a variety of expressions." SLJ

Shipton, Jonathan

Baby baby blah blah blah! illustrated by Francesca Chessa. Holiday House 2009 unp il $16.95 *

Grades: PreK K 1 2   E

1. Infants—Fiction 2. Family life—Fiction 3. Siblings—Fiction 4. Twins—Fiction

ISBN 978-0-8234-2213-5; 0-8234-2213-5

LC 2008-34895

When her parents tell her that they are expecting a baby, Emily sets to work on a list of pros and cons.

"No matter how many new baby books you have on your shelves, you'll want to make room for this bright and bubbling treasure. . . . Chessa's colorfully messy, childlike illustrations perfectly match the breezy tone of the story." SLJ

Shirley, Debra

Best friend on wheels; by Debra Shirley; illustrated by Judy Stead. Albert Whitman & Co. 2008 unp il $15.95

Grades: K 1 2 3   E

1. Friendship—Fiction 2. Physically handicapped children—Fiction 3. Stories in rhyme

ISBN 978-0-8075-8868-0; 0-8075-8868-7

LC 2007024252

A young girl relates all the ways she and her best friend, Sarah, are alike, in spite of the fact that Sarah uses a wheelchair.

"The colorful cartoon illustrations delightfully capture [the friends] in their favorite activities. . . . The rhyme moves quickly yet touches on many aspects of life for people in wheelchairs. . . . The artwork conveys the same positive fun as the text. The book's lesson is evident without being didactic." SLJ

Shulevitz, Uri, 1935-

How I learned geography. Farrar, Straus & Giroux 2008 unp il $16.95 *

Grades: PreK K 1 2   E

1. Refugees—Fiction 2. Maps—Fiction 3. Geography—Fiction 4. Kazakhstan—Fiction 5. Imagination—Fiction

ISBN 978-0-374-33499-4; 0-374-33499-4

LC 2007-11889

A Caldecott Medal honor book, 2009

As he spends hours studying his father's world map, a young boy escapes the hunger and misery of refugee life. Based on the author's childhood in Kazakhstan, where he lived as a Polish refugee during World War II.

The "text is clear and straightforward but vivid, and small memorable touches . . . add dimensionality. Watercolor illustrations avoid demonizing the boy's real-life: the town (Turkestan, according to Shulevitz' note) looks like an interesting place. . . . Chunky lines and sweeps of washy watercolor gain additional textures in the map worlds." Bull Cent Child Books

Snow. Farrar, Straus & Giroux 1998 unp il $16; pa $6.99 *

Grades: PreK K 1 2   E

1. Snow—Fiction

ISBN 0-374-37092-3; 0-374-46862-1 (pa)

LC 97-37257

A Caldecott Medal honor book, 1999

As snowflakes slowly come down, one by one, people in the city ignore them, and only a boy and his dog think that the snowfall will amount to anything

"Passersby are caricatured into humorous figures bent into impossible postures, their tall hats, parasols, and funny shoes giving them an almost circus-clown appearance. . . . The elegantly stark text suits the elegant architectural lines of the cityscape." Bull Cent Child Books

So sleepy story. Farrar Straus Giroux 2006 unp il $16 *

Grades: PreK K 1 2   E

1. Night—Fiction 2. Sleep—Fiction

ISBN 0-374-37031-1   LC 2005-51146

"A sleepy sleepy boy is fast asleep in his sleepy sleepy bed along with everything else in his sleepy sleepy house until music comes drifting in, in ever louder tones. Then the child and his surroundings gradually come alive, dance, and shake to the beat, and drift back to sleep as the notes and instruments depart. The brief repetitive text takes a backseat to the whimsical watercolor-and-ink cartoon illustrations." SLJ

When I wore my sailor suit. Farrar, Straus & Giroux 2009 unp il $16.95

Grades: K 1 2 3   E

1. Adventure fiction 2. Sailors—Fiction 3. Imagination—Fiction

ISBN 978-0-374-34749-9; 0-374-34749-2

LC 2008016187

A young child spends the day imagining himself to be a sailor on a grand adventure.

"Shulevitz combines child-size sentences with words that stretch and please. . . . The artist's mastery of the medium produces both warm, dappled interiors and Old Master severity, with convincing fades into the fantastic. . . . This is the work of a wise and wonderful storyteller." SLJ

Shulman, Lisa

The moon might be milk; [by] Lisa Shulman; illustrated by Will Hillenbrand. Dutton Children's Books 2007 unp il $16.99 *

Grades: PreK K   E

1. Moon—Fiction 2. Cookies—Fiction 3. Grandmothers—Fiction 4. Animals—Fiction

ISBN 978-0-525-47647-4; 0-525-47647-4

LC 2005032750

A young girl asks her animal friends what they think the moon is made of, and her grandmother proves that each theory is partly correct. Includes recipe

"The mixed-media artwork features Hillenbrand's strong, distinctive lines that define the characters, colors that range in intensity from brilliant to muted, and a rich array of patterned surfaces that make the settings varied and vivid. . . . The story reads aloud well." Booklist

Shulman, Mark, 1962-

Mom and Dad are palindromes; a dilemma for words . . . and backwards; by Mark Shulman; illustrated by Adam McCauley. Chronicle Books 2006 unp il $15.95 *

Grades: 1 2 3 4   E

  1. Palindromes—Fiction

ISBN 978-0-8118-4328-7; 0-8118-4328-9

                        LC 2005023614

When Bob realizes that he is surrounded by palindromes, from his mom, dad, and sis Anna to his dog Otto, he discovers a way to deal with the palindrome puzzle

"In all, Shulman cleverly weaves over 101 palindromes into the text. . . . The mixed-media cartoon art amplifies the zany situation." SLJ

Siddals, Mary McKenna

Compost stew; an A to Z recipe for the earth; illustrated by Ashley Wolff. Tricycle Press 2010 unp il $15.99; lib bdg $18.99

Grades: PreK K 1 2   E

  1. Stories in rhyme 2. Compost—Fiction 3. Alphabet

ISBN   978-1-58246-316-2;   1-58246-316-6;
978-1-58246-341-4 (lib bdg); 1-58246-341-7 (lib bdg)

                        LC 2009016300

"With bouncing, rhyming lines, this cheerful title uses the alphabet to introduce children to ingredients that make great compost, from apple cores to zinnias. . . . A short supplementary note about what compost is and why it is beneficial is included. . . . This title . . . provides a lighthearted introduction to an earth- and kid-friendly activity. The brightly patterned collage artwork featuring a cast of multicultural kids working together will easily draw a young audience." Booklist

I'll play with you; illustrated by David Wisniewski. Clarion Bks. 2000 28p il $14

Grades: PreK K 1 2   E

  1. Play—Fiction

ISBN 0-395-90373-4   LC 99-57849

Children speak to the sun, wind, clouds, rain, stars, and moon, asking to play with them

"Despite the simplicity of the text, which is well suited for beginning readers, the words are poetic, mixing humor and glee into the reverence for nature. In his familiar cut-paper artwork, Wisniewski shows the children's profound satisfaction at play." Booklist

Sidman, Joyce, 1956-

Red sings from treetops; a year in colors; illustrated by Pamela Zagarenski. Houghton Mifflin Harcourt 2009 unp il $16 *

Grades: PreK K 1   E

  1. Color—Fiction 2. Nature—Fiction 3. Seasons—Fiction

ISBN 978-0-547-01494-4; 0-547-01494-5

                        LC 2008-35947

ALA ALSC Caldecott Medal Honor Book (2010)

Nature displays different colors to announce the seasons of the year.

"Fresh descriptions and inventive artistry are a charming inspiration to notice colors and correlate emotions. Details in the artwork will invite repeated readings and challenge kids to muse about other color icons." Kirkus

Sierra, Judy

Ballyhoo Bay; illustrated by Derek Anderson. Simon & Schuster Books for Young Readers 2009 unp il $16.99

Grades: K 1 2   E

  1. Stories in rhyme 2. Social action—Fiction 3. Beaches—Fiction 4. Environmental protection—Fiction 5. Artists—Fiction

ISBN 978-1-4169-5888-8; 1-4169-5888-6

                        LC 2007-49720

"A Paula Wiseman Book"

Mira Bella mobilizes her art students, from grandmothers to children, crabs to seagulls, to stop a dastardly plan for turning the beach at Ballyhoo Bay into an exclusive resort, and offers an alternative—leave the beach as it is

"Lively, humorous acrylic cartoons have a buoyancy that captures the sparkle of the seaside setting and the exaggerated antics of the characters. This upbeat ecological message is delivered with plenty of panache. Told in rhyming couplets, the story reads aloud well." SLJ

Born to read; story by Judy Sierra; pictures by Marc Brown. Alfred A. Knopf 2008 unp il $16.99; lib bdg $19.99

Grades: PreK K 1 2   E

  1. Reading—Fiction 2. Stories in rhyme

ISBN   978-0-375-84687-8;   0-375-84687-5;
978-0-375-94687-5 (lib bdg); 0-375-94687-X (lib bdg)

                        LC 2007-2306

A little boy named Sam discovers the many unexpected ways in which a love of reading can come in handy, and sometimes even save the day

This is written "in quick, quirky rhymed couplets. . . . Brown's gouache illustrations are cheery, and each page pours into the next through the use of subtly repeated background motifs. . . . This is an easy, obvious choice for events with literacy and early learning as their themes." SLJ

Preschool to the rescue; illustrated by Will Hillenbrand. Harcourt 2001 unp il $15

Grades: PreK   E

  1. Vehicles—Fiction 2. Stories in rhyme

ISBN 0-15-202035-7   LC 99-6475

"Gulliver books"

When a mud puddle traps a pizza van, police car, tow truck, and other vehicles, a group of preschoolers comes along and saves the day

"The repetition and rhyme carry the story along and the fun doesn't stop until the book is closed. The artwork is perfect." SLJ

Sleepy little alphabet; a bedtime story from Alphabet Town; written by Judy Sierra; illustrated by Melissa Sweet. Alfred A. Knopf 2009 unp il $16.99; lib bdg $19.99

Grades: PreK K 1   E

  1. Stories in rhyme 2. Alphabet 3. Bedtime—Fiction

ISBN   978-0-375-84002-9;   0-375-84002-8;
978-0-375-94002-6 (lib bdg); 0-375-94002-2 (lib bdg)

                        LC 2008-24526

Sleepy letters of the alphabet get ready for bed

"The bounce of Sierra's meter, the time-for-bed theme and Sweet's offhand pencil and watercolor drawings

Sierra, Judy—*Continued*

make the story feel fresh. Throughout, Sierra inserts vocabulary items that incorporate the letters . . . while Sweet provides the laughs." Pub Wkly

Thelonius Monster's sky-high fly pie; illustrations by Edward Koren. Knopf 2006 unp il $16.95; lib bdg $18.99 *

Grades: K 1 2 3   E

1. Monsters—Fiction 2. Pies—Fiction 3. Flies—Fiction 4. Stories in rhyme

ISBN 0-375-83218-1; 0-375-93218-6 (lib bdg)

LC 2005-16773

A good-natured monster thinks a pie made out of flies would be a good dessert, and invites all his friends and relatives over to try it.

"An incomparable rhymester has teamed up with a master cartoonist to conjure up some haute cuisine on the fly. . . . The words are carefully chosen. . . . A lovable and entertaining work of art." SLJ

Wild about books; by Judy Sierra; pictures by Marc Brown. Knopf 2004 unp il $16.95 *

Grades: PreK K 1 2   E

1. Animals—Fiction 2. Books and reading—Fiction 3. Libraries—Fiction 4. Stories in rhyme

ISBN 0-375-82538-X

A librarian named Mavis McGrew introduces the animals in the zoo to the joy of reading when she drives her bookmobile to the zoo by mistake.

"Sierra's text has a wacky verve and enough clever asides and allusions to familiar characters to satisfy bibliophiles of all ages. . . . Brown's cheerful, full-color illustrations stretch his trademark art with ever-so-slightly stylized spreads that are rich in pattern, texture, and nuance." SLJ

Silsbe, Brenda, 1953-

The bears we know; [text by] Brenda Silsbe; [art by] Vlasta van Kampen. Annick Press 2009 unp il $19.95; pa $7.95

Grades: PreK K 1 2   E

1. Bears—Fiction

ISBN   978-1-55451-167-9;   1-55451-167-4; 978-1-55451-166-2 (pa); 1-55451-166-6 (pa)

Nobody has seen the bears, but everybody knows where they live that their house is a mess, they eat bagfuls of chips, jump on the furniture, decorate with sawdust, and sing songs that make them cry.

"The warm, funny watercolors are a great match for the goofy creatures and their various antics. Their great brown bodies sprawl across the page (and the couches), and the simple text is clearly printed on a field of white." SLJ

Silverman, Erica

Cowgirl Kate and Cocoa; written by Erica Silverman; painted by Betsy Lewin. Harcourt 2005 unp il $15 *

Grades: K 1 2   E

1. Horses—Fiction 2. Cowhands—Fiction

ISBN 0-15-202124-8   LC 2004-5739

Cowgirl Kate and her cowhorse Cocoa, who is always hungry, count cows, share a story, and help each other fall asleep.

"Children will . . . recognize the friends' good-natured banter and lively dialogue. . . . Lewin's bold-lined illustrations extend the comedy and the affectionate friendship." Booklist

Other titles about Kate and Cocoa are:

Cowgirl Kate and Cocoa: partners (2006)

Cowgirl Kate and Cocoa: school days (2007)

Cowgirl Kate and Cocoa: rain or shine (2008)

Cowgirl Kate and Cocoa: horse in the house (2009)

Cowgirl Kate and Cocoa: spring babies (2010)

Silverstein, Shel

Who wants a cheap rhinoceros? Simon & Schuster 2009 unp il $9.99

Grades: K 1 2 3   E

1. Rhinoceros—Fiction

ISBN 978-1-4169-9613-2; 1-4169-9613-3

A revised and expanded edition of the title first published 1964

"Silverstein's economical black-line drawings illustrate the joys of owning a rhinoceros. . . . The deadpan text belies the goofiness of the pictures, with the rhinoceros jumping rope, playing pirates, and opening a soda can with his horn." Horn Book Guide

Siminovich, Lorena

Alex and Lulu: two of a kind. Templar Books 2009 unp il $14.99 *

Grades: PreK K 1   E

1. Friendship—Fiction 2. Dogs—Fiction 3. Cats—Fiction

ISBN 978-0-7636-4423-9; 0-7636-4423-4

"Alex, a white dog with a large black spot over one eye, is best friends with a white cat with black markings. One day, Lulu gets her pal thinking about the ways in which they are different. . . . He worries that their relationship is in jeopardy. To reassure him, Lulu offers several examples of true opposites . . . and reminds Alex that they share many interests in common. . . . Siminovich's spare scenes offer patterned backgrounds and an occasional charming detail. . . . With their retro feel and lack of fuss, the artwork is delectable." SLJ

Simmons, Jane

Together; [by] Jane Simmons. Alfred A. Knopf 2007 unp il $15.95; lib bdg $18.99

Grades: PreK K 1   E

1. Dogs—Fiction 2. Friendship—Fiction

ISBN 978-0-375-84339-6; 978-0-375-94339-3 (lib bdg)   LC 2006022734

Two dogs, Mousse and Nut, learn that even though they may like different things, they can still be best friends

"Fat, rusty-colored Mousse and tiny Nut are utterly charming as they frolic across the well-designed pages. This is a book that is not only artistically pleasing but also offers something to talk about." Booklist

Simms, Laura, 1947-
Rotten teeth; illustrated by David Catrow. Houghton Mifflin 1998 unp il $16
Grades: K 1 2 3   E
  1. School stories 2. Teeth—Fiction
  ISBN 0-395-82850-3   LC 97-2528
When Melissa takes a big glass bottle of authentic pulled teeth from her father's dental office for a show-and-tell presentation, she becomes a first-grade celebrity
"Catrow's watercolors are a suitably twisted complement to Simms' somewhat warped sense of humor (actually, it's perfect for this audience)." Bull Cent Child Books

Simont, Marc, 1915-
The stray dog; retold and illustrated by Marc Simont from a true story by Reiko Sassa. HarperCollins Pubs. 2001 unp il $16.99; lib bdg $18.89 *
Grades: PreK K 1 2   E
  1. Dogs—Fiction
  ISBN 0-06-028933-3; 0-06-028934-1 (lib bdg)
A Caldecott Medal honor book, 2002
"Two children play with a stray dog in the country one Saturday. The whole family thinks about him all week, and the next Saturday they return to the same picnic spot, where the children save the dog from the dogcatcher and adopt him." Horn Book Guide
"Simont's art and narrative play off each other strategically, together imparting the tale's humor and tenderness." Publ Wkly

Singer, Marilyn, 1948-
I'm your bus; pictures by Evan Polenghi. Scholastic Press 2009 unp il $16.99
Grades: PreK   E
  1. Buses—Fiction
  ISBN 978-0-545-08918-0; 0-545-08918-2
               LC 2008017870
In rhyming text, a school bus describes its busy day transporting children to and from school.
"The digitally rendered pictures, composed of bold black outlines and bright colors, create a wholly endearing character. . . . Both energetic and reassuring." Booklist

Shoe bop! by Marilyn Singer; illustrated by Hiroe Nakata. Dutton Children's Books 2008 32p il $15.99
Grades: PreK K 1 2   E
  1. Shoes—Fiction 2. Shopping—Fiction 3. Stories in rhyme
  ISBN 978-0-525-47939-0; 0-525-47939-2
               LC 2007028296
When her favorite purple tennis shoes fall apart, an almost-second-grader visits a shoe store, where she tries on footwear of all colors and styles before finding the pair that is right for her
Singer and Nakata "extol the joys of shoe shopping in a compendium of rhymed verses accompanied by a dizzying display of possibilities . . . in the watercolor spot illustrations. . . . The busy pages have the breathless feel of a shopping spree." Publ Wkly

Siomades, Lorianne
Katy did it! Boyds Mills Press 2009 unp il $16.95
Grades: PreK K 1   E
  1. Katydids—Fiction
  ISBN 978-1-59078-602-4; 1-59078-602-5
               LC 2008028133
A katydid named Katy, who upsets other insects as she bounces through the garden, saves the day for a colony of ants
"Digitally created jewel-tone illustrations are airy and uncluttered against a pure white background. . . . Sound effects . . . mimic Katy's hops, ever advancing the story, and the insect's simplified face with round, googly eyes is especially expressive. This bright, bouncy story will be a favorite with youngsters." SLJ

Sís, Peter, 1949-
Ballerina! Greenwillow Bks. 2001 unp il $14.95; bd bk $7.99 *
Grades: PreK K 1   E
  1. Ballet—Fiction 2. Color
  ISBN 0-688-17944-4; 0-06-075966-6 (bd bk)
               LC 00-35401
A little girl puts on costumes of different colors and imagines herself dancing on stage
Sis "creates a beautifully realized spot-on view of creative kids at play." Booklist

Dinosaur! Greenwillow Bks. 2000 unp il $15.99; bd bk $7.99 *
Grades: PreK K 1   E
  1. Dinosaurs 2. Stories without words
  ISBN 0-688-17049-8; 0-06-075967-4 (bd bk)
               LC 99-32923
While taking a bath, a young boy is joined by all sorts of dinosaurs
"A wordless picture book that takes readers on a wild adventure of the imagination. . . . This imaginative story with wonderful end-papers naming the creatures should appeal to all young dinosaur lovers. Sis's barely fleshed-out, cookie-cutter cartoons tell the story." SLJ

Fire truck. Greenwillow Bks. 1998 unp il $15.99; bd bk $6.99 *
Grades: PreK K 1   E
  1. Fire engines—Fiction
  ISBN 0-688-15878-1; 0-06-056259-5 (bd bk)
               LC 97-29320
Matt, who loves fire trucks, wakes up one morning to find that he has become a fire truck, with one driver, two ladders, three hoses, and ten boots. Features a gate-fold illustration that opens into a three-page spread
"Sis blends simple text with bold pictures to give insight into one boy's vivid imagination." SLJ

Madlenka. Farrar, Straus & Giroux 2000 unp il $17
Grades: PreK K 1 2 3   E
  1. New York (N.Y.)—Fiction 2. Teeth—Fiction
  ISBN 0-374-39969-7   LC 99-57730
"Frances Foster books"
Madlenka, whose New York City neighbors include the French baker, the Indian news vendor, the Italian ice-

Sís, Peter, 1949—*Continued*

cream man, the South American grocer, and the Chinese shopkeeper, goes around the block to show her friends her loose tooth and finds that it is like taking a trip around the world

"The real magic comes in the cleverly cut-away windows in each storefront through which children glimpse complex, global dreamscapes. Madlenka journeys through these mystical places, too, and it is these surreal, wordless stories-within-the-story that will excite a wide range of children, launching them in their own imagined departures." Booklist

Another title about Madlenka is:

Madlenka's dog (2002)

Trucks, trucks, trucks. Greenwillow Bks. 1999 unp il $16.99; bd bk $7.99 *

Grades: PreK K   E

1. Trucks—Fiction

ISBN 0-688-16276-2; 0-06-056258-7 (bd bk)

LC 98-4482

A little boy cleans up his room using a variety of trucks and gives a one word description of their work such as hauling, plowing, and loading. Features a gatefold illustration that opens into a three-page spread

"Sís creates a simple, bold look. . . . Gouache paints in yellow, black, and gray are set off by plenty of white space. The single verbs on each page are rendered in shades of blue, purple, green, and orange. This cheery romp is perfect for toddlers." SLJ

Skeers, Linda, 1958-

Tutus aren't my style; pictures by Anne Wilsdorf. Dial Books for Young Readers 2010 unp il $16.99

Grades: K 1 2   E

1. Ballet—Fiction

ISBN 978-0-8037-3212-4; 0-8037-3212-0

LC 2009009284

When she receives a ballerina costume from her uncle, Emma, who does not know how to be a ballerina, gets a lot of advice from friends and family.

"The simple but expressive illustrations are perfect for the story. The artwork, done in watercolor with images outlined in black ink, is very funny." SLJ

Sklansky, Amy E., 1971-

The duck who played the kazoo; illustrated by Tiphanie Beeke. Clarion Books 2008 unp il $16.99

Grades: PreK K 1   E

1. Ducks—Fiction 2. Musicians—Fiction 3. Friendship—Fiction 4. Stories in rhyme

ISBN 978-0-618-42854-0; 0-618-42854-2

LC 2006-29204

After a hurricane blows through and with only his kazoo for company, a lonely duck searches for friends but soon realizes there is no place like home.

"Told in rhyming couplets, the simple story is graced with sweet watercolor and mixed-media art. . . . The illustrations add a humorous touch. . . . This is a tender and charming tale of looking for and finding friendship." SLJ

Slate, Joseph, 1928-

I want to be free; illustrated by E. B. Lewis. G.P. Putnam's Sons 2009 unp il $16.99 *

Grades: 2 3 4   E

1. Slavery—Fiction 2. African Americans—Fiction 3. Stories in rhyme

ISBN 978-0-399-24342-4; 0-399-24342-9

LC 2007-38356

Based on a sacred Buddhist tale as related in Rudyard Kipling's novel "Kim," tells of an escaped slave who rescues an abandoned baby from slave hunters

"The spare words and pictures never sensationalize the drama or the universal themes of cruelty, courage, and kindness." Booklist

Miss Bindergarten celebrates the 100th day of kindergarten; illustrated by Ashley Wolff. Dutton Children's Bks. 1998 unp il $16.99; pa $6.99

Grades: PreK K 1   E

1. Kindergarten—Fiction 2. Animals—Fiction 3. Stories in rhyme

ISBN 0-525-46000-4; 0-14-250005-4 (pa)

LC 98-10486

To celebrate one hundred days in Miss Bindergarten's kindergarten class, all her students bring one hundred of something to school, including a one-hundred-year-old relative, one hundred candy hearts, and one hundred polka dots

"Wolff's sturdy, genially observed illustrations prove a perfect match for Slate's rhyming text." Publ Wkly

Other titles about Miss Bindergarten are:

Miss Bindergarten celebrates the last day of kindergarten (2006)

Miss Bindergarten gets ready for kindergarten (1996)

Miss Bindergarten has a wild day in kindergarten (2005)

Miss Bindergarten stays home from kindergarten (2000)

Miss Bindergarten takes a field trip with kindergarten (2001)

Miss Bindergarten's craft center (1999)

Slater, Dashka

Baby shoes; by Dashka Slater; pictures by Hiroe Nakata. Bloomsbury Children's Books 2006 unp il $15.95

Grades: PreK   E

1. Shoes—Fiction 2. Color—Fiction 3. Stories in rhyme

ISBN 978-1-58234-684-7; 1-58234-684-4

LC 2005053581

After taking a walk with his mother, Baby's new white shoes with the blue stripe are covered with a variety of colors

"In the text, loping lines of rhymed couplets are interspersed with staccato sections, followed by a refrain that reins in the pace. . . . The changing rhythm creates a pleasing pattern and gives listeners places to chime in. Setting a sunny tone for the excursion, Nakata's airy watercolor artwork sympathetically depicts an increasingly scruffy toddler and his tired but resilient mother." Booklist

Slater, Dashka—*Continued*

The sea serpent and me; by Dashka Slater; illustrated by Catia Chien. Houghton Mifflin Company 2008 unp il $17

Grades: PreK K 1 2   E

1. Sea monsters—Fiction 2. Growth—Fiction

ISBN 978-0-618-72394-2; 0-618-72394-3

LC 2007015577

One day a small sea serpent falls from the faucet into the tub as a child is about to take a bath, and as the days go by and the serpent grows, they both realize that he needs to go back to the sea where he belongs.

"The lovely watercolor illustrations are lush with vivid blues and greens, and the bathtub and underwater scenes are full of movement and life. . . . The text flows well and highlights the strong bond between the child and the serpent." SLJ

Sloat, Teri

Berry magic; written by Teri Sloat and Betty Huffmon; illustrated by Teri Sloat. Alaska Northwest Books 2004 unp il $15.95 paperback o.p.

Grades: K 1 2 3   E

1. Berries—Fiction 2. Alaska—Fiction 3. Inuit—Fiction

ISBN 0-88240-575-6; 0-88240-576-4 (pa)

LC 2003-70851

Long ago, the only berries on the tundra were hard, tasteless, little crowberries. When Anana sings, she turns four dolls into little girls who run and tumble over the tundra creating patches of fat, juicy berries: blueberries, cranberries, salmonberries, and raspberries

"Done in a palette of deep, earthy hues, ethereal blues, and bright highlights, Sloat's pictures are vibrant and engaging. . . . The rich language enlightens readers to different elements of the Eskimo culture." SLJ

I'm a duck! story and pictures by Teri Sloat. G.P. Putnam's Sons 2006 unp il hardcover o.p. pa $6.99

Grades: PreK K 1 2   E

1. Ducks—Fiction 2. Stories in rhyme

ISBN 0-399-24274-0; 0-14-241062-4 (pa)

LC 2004-20479

"From the moment he hatches, a duckling celebrates his duck-ness–his webbed feet, his perfect waddle, his strong quack, and his flapping wings. As he grows, he meets a mate, becomes a father, and continues his zestful take on life. Sloat's rhymed text captures the exuberance of this eternal optimist and gives a glimpse into the life cycle of a mallard. The full-color art is rendered in pastels and has bold lines and a variety of perspectives and page layouts." SLJ

There was an old man who painted the sky; illustrated by Stefano Vitale. Henry Holt 2009 32p il $16.95

Grades: PreK K 1 2   E

1. Cave drawings and paintings—Fiction 2. Prehistoric art—Fiction 3. Songs

ISBN 978-0-8050-6751-4; 0-8050-6751-5

LC 2008-18340

In this song based on 'The Old Woman Who Swallowed a Fly,' a prehistoric man, contemplating the creation of the world, paints images on the ceiling of a cave, that are later discovered by a young Spanish girl in 1879

"Vitale's vibrant illustrations, in mixed media on board, reference both cave drawings and folk art. Appropriate for a wide audience, this will find its ideal fit with families wishing to impart diverse beliefs about the Earth's beginnings to their children." Booklist

Slobodkina, Esphyr, 1908-2002

Caps for sale; a tale of a peddler, some monkeys & their monkey business; told and illustrated by Esphyr Slobodkina. Addison Wesley Longman 1947 unp il $17.99; pa $6.99 *

Grades: PreK K   E

1. Monkeys—Fiction 2. Peddlers and peddling—Fiction

ISBN 0-201-09147-X; 0-06-443143-6 (pa)

A picture book story which "provides hilarious confusion. A cap peddler takes a nap under a tree. When he wakes up, his caps have disappeared. He looks up in the tree and sees countless monkeys, each wearing a cap and grinning." Parent's Guide To Child Read

Small, David, 1945-

George Washington's cows. Farrar, Straus and Giroux 1994 unp il hardcover o.p. pa $6.95

Grades: PreK K 1 2   E

1. Washington, George, 1732-1799—Fiction 2. Animals—Fiction 3. Stories in rhyme

ISBN 0-374-32535-9; 0-374-42534-5 (pa)

LC 93-39989

Humorous rhymes about George Washington's farm where the cows wear dresses, the pigs wear wigs, and the sheep are scholars

"Small's watercolors immeasurably extend his zany poem and make maximum use of the double-page spreads. Cleverly designed and well-executed scenes are filled with silly details that children will love." Booklist

Imogene's antlers; written and illustrated by David Small. Crown 2000 c1985 unp il $16.99; pa $6.99

Grades: PreK K 1 2   E

ISBN 0-375-81048-X; 0-517-56242-1 (pa)

First published 1985

One Thursday Imogene wakes up with a pair of antlers growing out of her head and causes a sensation wherever she goes

The author "maximizes the inherent humor of the absurd situation by allowing the imaginative possibilities of Imogene's predicament to run rampant. The brief text is supported by Small's expansive watercolors. They brim with humorous details." SLJ

Smee, Nicola

Clip-clop. Boxer Books 2006 unp il $12.95; bd bk $6.95

Grades: PreK K   E

1. Animals—Fiction

ISBN   978-1-905417-09-4;   1-905417-09-8; 978-1-905417-60-5 (bd bk); 1-905417-60-8 (bd bk)

When Mr. Horse gives a ride to his friends, Cat, Dog, Pig, and Duck, they urge him to go faster and faster

"With its simplicity of plot and design, lovable characters, repetitive sound effects, and captivating color illustrations, this laugh-out-loud picture book is first-rate." SLJ

Another title about Mr. Horse and his friends is; Jingle-jingle (2008)

What's the matter, Bunny Blue? Boxer Books 2010 unp il $14.95

Grades: PreK   E

1.   Animals—Fiction   2.   Rabbits—Fiction 3. Grandmothers—Fiction

ISBN 978-1-906250-91-1; 1-906250-91-X

"A wide-eyed little blue bunny . . . calls, 'Granny! Granny! Where are you?' No sooner does he explain his dilemma to Duck and Bee than the tears begin. A series of animals—a tiger, alligator, bear, and fox—ask the despondent bunny what Granny looks like. . . . All the animals join the ultimately successful search for Granny. The very real, small details of twinkly eyes, a big smile, and soft furry arms are just what matter to children when they experience separation anxiety. The uncluttered pages with lots of white space and sympathetic, childlike animals are perfect for the toddler set." Booklist

Smith, Charles R., 1969-

Dance with me; [by] Charles R. Smith Jr.; illustrated by Noah Z. Jones. Candlewick Press 2008 unp il (Super sturdy picture book) $8.99

Grades: PreK K 1 2   E

1. Stories in rhyme 2. Dance—Fiction 3. Board books for children

ISBN 978-0-7636-2246-6; 0-7636-2246-X

LC 2007-51886

Illustrations and simple, rhyming text encourage the reader to wiggle, shake, and twirl to the beat.

"This features thick pages and large type aimed at emerging readers. The book's small trim size and abundant visual details make it best suited for small groups of preschoolers, who will find it hard to resist the story's encouragement to move and groove." Booklist

Smith, Cynthia Leitich

Jingle dancer; illustrated by Cornelius Van Wright and Ying-Hwa Hu. Morrow Junior Bks. 2000 unp il $17.99; lib bdg $18.89

Grades: K 1 2 3   E

1. Creek Indians—Fiction 2. Native American dance—Fiction

ISBN 0-688-16241-X; 0-688-16242-8 (lib bdg)

LC 99-15503

Jenna, a member of the Muscogee, or Creek, Nation, borrows jingles from the dresses of several friends and relatives so that she can perform the jingle dance at the powwow. Includes a note about the jingle dance tradition and its regalia

"The colorful, well-executed watercolor illustrations lend warmth to the story." Booklist

Smith, Danna

Two at the zoo; illustrated by Valeria Petrone. Clarion 2009 32p il $16

Grades: PreK K   E

1.   Animals—Fiction 2.   Grandfathers—Fiction 3. Stories in rhyme 4. Zoos—Fiction

ISBN 978-0-547-04982-3; 0-547-04982-X

A grandfather and grandchild go to the zoo, where they count animals from one to ten.

"The digital gouache illustrations have vibrant colors, clean lines, and palpable texture. . . . An engaging read-aloud for storytime and one-on-one sharing." SLJ

Smith, Lane

The big elephant in the room. Hyperion Books for Children 2009 unp il $16.99

Grades: K 1 2 3 4   E

1. Donkeys—Fiction 2. Communication—Fiction

ISBN 978-1-4231-1667-7; 1-4231-1667-4

When one donkey tells his friend that they need to talk about 'the big elephant in the room,' his friend wonders what this embarrassing issue could possibly be.

"Done in muted tones, the droll artwork tells much of the story through lively layouts and funny details. With the roll of an eye or the flick of an ear, the animals convey a range of emotions. . . . Kids will get a kick out of this book (while also learning about idioms)." SLJ

John, Paul, George & Ben. Hyperion Books for Children 2006 unp il $16.99 *

Grades: 2 3 4   E

1. United States—History—1775-1783, Revolution—Fiction

ISBN 0-7868-4893-6   LC 2005-52735

"Describing each man in turn as either bold, noisy, honest, clever, or independent, and taking many liberties with the truth, Smith relates how the Founding Fathers of the title [John Hancock, Paul Revere, George Washington, Benjamin Franklin]—and [Thomas] Jefferson, too—played a part in securing America's freedom. . . . The pen-and-ink cartoon illustrations, richly textured with various techniques, add to the fun. . . . A true-and-false section in the back separates fact from fiction." SLJ

Madam President. Hyperion Books for Children 2008 unp il lib bdg $16.99 *

Grades: K 1 2   E

1. Presidents—Fiction 2. Sex role—Fiction

ISBN 978-1-4231-0846-7 (lib bdg); 1-4231-0846-9 (lib bdg)   LC 2008-04509

A little girl imagines what her day would be like if she were President of the United States.

This is a "sly, witty recitation of a president's responsibilities. . . . The list . . . does grow rather long. But the stretch can be forgiven because it provides more opportunity to enjoy Smith's amazing artwork. Madam President, with her boxy head and triangular body appears against a variety of backgrounds . . . with disparate uses of materials and images that often give the look of collage." Booklist

Smith, Linda, 1949-2007

The inside tree; illustrated by David Parkins. HarperCollins 2010 unp il $16.99; lib bdg $17.89

Grades: K 1 2   E

1. Trees—Fiction 2. Dogs—Fiction

ISBN   978-0-06-028241-7;   0-06-028241-X; 978-0-06-029818-0 (lib bdg); 0-06-029818-9 (lib bdg)

          LC 2005019699

When Mr. Potter decides to bring both his dog and a tree inside to share his cozy house, there are unexpected repercussions.

"Smith's text is perfectly complemented by the illustrations. . . . Parkins uses a mix of realistic details, excellent facial expressions, and varying perspectives to bring the story to life. This kindhearted tale is best read aloud with plenty of extra time for laughter and bemusement." SLJ

Snell, Gordon

The King of Quizzical Island; illustrated by David McKee. Candlewick Press 2009 unp il $16

Grades: K 1 2 3   E

1. Explorers—Fiction 2. Voyages and travels—Fiction 3. Kings and rulers—Fiction 4. Earth—Fiction 5. Stories in rhyme

ISBN 978-0-7636-3857-3; 0-7636-3857-9

          LC 2008-26510

When no one can answer his question about what is at the edge of the world, the King of Quizzical Island builds a boat and sets sail to find out for himself, despite the objections of his fearful people.

"The text is a case study in clever rhyme, and the pen-and-ink and watercolor illustrations—in black-and-white except for the king—show readers that curiosity is like a light in the darkness." Horn Book Guide

Snicket, Lemony, 1970-

The composer is dead; written by Lemony Snicket; with music composed by Nathaniel Stookey and illustrations by Carson Ellis. HarperCollinsPublishers 2008 unp il $17.99; lib bdg $18.89 *

Grades: K 1 2 3   E

1. Musical instruments—Fiction 2. Orchestra—Fiction 3. Mystery fiction

ISBN   978-0-06-123627-3;   0-06-123627-6; 978-0-06-123628-0 (lib bdg); 0-06-123628-4 (lib bdg)

          LC 2007-20834

An inspector seeks to solve a murder mystery at the symphony by questioning each of the musical instruments.

This offers "witty wordplay. . . . Ellis . . . brightens the heavily black stage scenes with coral, gold and sepia accents against expansive white backgrounds. . . . The accompanying CD features Snicket narrating and the San Francisco Symphony Orchestra performing Stookey's original score." Publ Wkly

The latke who couldn't stop screaming; a Christmas story; by Lemony Snicket; illustrations by Lisa Brown. McSweeney's Books 2007 43p il $9.95 *

Grades: K 1 2 3 4   E

1. Hanukkah—Fiction 2. Christmas—Fiction

ISBN 978-1-932416-87-9

"The miraculous birth here is of a potato pancake, which . . . begins screaming the moment it gets cooked. Leaping out of the frying pan and into the great white spaces of Brown's retro-cool graphics, the latke screams even louder as it tries in vain to explain itself and its role at Hanukkah to flashing colored lights . . . and an equally Christmas-centric candy cane and tree. Embedding the satirical sting in his elegantly cadenced prose, the author . . . up-ends any number of conventions in what may be his funniest book yet." Publ Wkly

Solheim, James

Born yesterday; the diary of a young journalist; illustrated by Simon James. Philomel Books 2010 unp il lib bdg $15.99

Grades: PreK K   E

1. Infants—Fiction 2. Siblings—Fiction 3. Diaries—Fiction

ISBN 978-0-399-25155-9 (lib bdg); 0-399-25155-3 (lib bdg)   LC 2009006251

A baby who plans to grow up to be a writer records thoughts and events in a private journal.

"The watercolor and ink illustrations . . . faithfully follow the humorous text. . . . The book is a fresh and amusing slant on sibling adjustment." SLJ

Soman, David

Ladybug Girl; [by] David Soman and Jacky Davis. Dial Books for Young Readers 2008 unp il $16.99

Grades: PreK K   E

1. Imagination—Fiction 2. Play—Fiction 3. Siblings—Fiction 4. Superheroes—Fiction

ISBN 978-0-8037-3195-0   LC 2007008619

After her brother tells her she is too little to play with him, Lulu, dressed as Ladybug Girl, makes her own fun.

"Readers' eyes are inexorably drawn to Lulu's red ladybug costume, which sets off the subdues earth tones. . . . Simple sentences throughout the story usually express just one thought or directive at a time, usually in just one sentence per page. A super book for lapsits and storyhours." SLJ

Other titles about Ladybug Girl are:
Ladybug Girl and Bumblebee Boy (2009)
Ladybug Girl at the beach (2010)

Soto, Gary

Chato's kitchen; illustrated by Susan Guevara. Putnam 1995 unp il $16.99; pa $6.99

Grades: PreK K 1 2   E

1. Cats—Fiction 2. Mice—Fiction

ISBN 0-399-22658-3; 0-698-11600-3 (pa)

          LC 93-43503

To get the "ratoncitos," little mice, who have moved into the barrio to come to his house, Chato the cat pre-

Soto, Gary—*Continued*

pares all kinds of good food: fajitas, frijoles, salsa, enchiladas, and more

"Soto adeptly captures the flavor of life in *el barrio* in this amusing tale. The animal characters have distinct personalities, and their language, sprinkled with Spanish phrases and expressions, credibly brings them to life. Best of all, though, are Guevara's striking illustrations that enrich the text with delightful, witty details." SLJ

Other titles about Chato are:

Chato and the party animals (2000)

Chato goes cruisin' (2005)

Too many tamales; illustrated by Ed Martinez. Putnam 1992 unp il $16.99; pa $7.99

Grades: PreK K 1 2   E

1. Christmas—Fiction 2. Mexican Americans—Fiction

ISBN 0-399-22146-8; 0-698-11412-4 (pa)

LC 91-19229

Maria tries on her mother's wedding ring while helping make tamales for a Christmas family get together, but panic ensues when hours later, she realizes the ring is missing

This is "a very funny story, full of delicious surprise. The handsome, realistic oil paintings, in rich shades of brown, red, and purple, are filled with light, evoking the togetherness of an extended family." Booklist

Spangler, Brie

Peg Leg Peke; [by] Brie Spangler. Alfred A. Knopf 2008 unp il $15.99; lib bdg $18.99

Grades: PreK K 1   E

1. Dogs—Fiction 2. Imagination—Fiction 3. Pirates—Fiction

ISBN 978-0-375-84888-9; 0-375-84888-6; 978-0-375-94888-6 (lib bdg); 0-375-94888-0 (lib bdg)

LC 2007033241

When Peke, a pekingese puppy breaks his leg, he fantasizes that he is a pirate in search of buried treasure.

"Spangler keeps her pictures simple, with just enough details and splashes of colors to set a scene. Kids, empowered by their role as speaker, should find the drawings sweet and chummy." Publ Wkly

Spanyol, Jessica, 1965-

Little neighbors on Sunnyside Street; [by] Jessica Spanyol. Candlewick Press 2007 unp il $16.99 *

Grades: PreK K   E

1. Animals—Fiction 2. Day—Fiction

ISBN 978-0-7636-2986-1; 0-7636-2986-3

LC 2005053641

On Sunnyside Street "the animal and insect residents enjoy doing their own things. . . . [The] peek into their everyday activities is accompanied with boisterous word sounds [and] playful typefaces. . . . Pen-and-gouache illustrations are a melding of . . . simple shapes, flat dimension, and busy pages with plenty of preschool child appeal." SLJ

Spiegelman, Art

Jack and the box; a toon book. Raw Junior 2008 32p il (Toon books) $12.95

Grades: K 1   E

1. Rabbits—Fiction 2. Toys—Fiction

ISBN 978-0-9799238-3-8; 0-9799238-3-2

"Spiegelman has produced a polished and fun story following a young bunny's struggle with his new jack-in-the-box, which proves to be hyperactive and rather argumentative. [This is filled] with plenty of word repetition and age-appropriate humor to keep pre- and early readers engaged and curious." Booklist

Spinelli, Eileen, 1942-

The best story; [by] Eileen Spinelli; illustrations by Anne Wilsdorf. Dial Books for Young Readers 2008 unp il $16.99

Grades: 1 2 3   E

1. Authorship—Fiction

ISBN 978-0-8037-3055-7; 0-8037-3055-1

LC 2007028478

When a contest at the local library offers a prize for the best story, a girl tries to write one using her family's suggestions, but her story does not seem right until she listens to her heart.

"Lively energy and imagination permeate both the watercolor and ink illustrations and the warm text." Horn Book Guide

Heat wave; written by Eileen Spinelli; illustrated by Betsy Lewin. Harcourt 2007 unp il $16 *

Grades: K 1 2 3   E

1. Heat—Fiction 2. City and town life—Fiction

ISBN 0-15-216779-X; 978-0-15-216779-0

LC 2005-18946

Abigail, Ralphie, and the other citizens of Lumberville struggle to endure a week-long heat wave in the days before air conditioning.

"While the story is simple and straightforward, the sun-drenched illustrations provide a spirited and evocative look back in time." SLJ

I know it's autumn; illustrated by Nancy Hayashi. HarperCollinsPublishers 2004 unp il $15.99; lib bdg $16.89

Grades: PreK K 1 2   E

1. Autumn—Fiction 2. Stories in rhyme

ISBN 0-06-029422-1; 0-06-029423-X (lib bdg)

LC 2003-4099

A rhyming celebration of the sights, smells, and sounds of autumn, such as pumpkin muffins, turkey stickers on spelling papers, and piles of raked leaves

"Large enough for group sharing and as quiet and comfortable as the text, Hayashi's illustrations feature rounded lines, soft shading, and gentle colors." Booklist

Miss Fox's class goes green; illustrated by Anne Kennedy. Albert Whitman 2009 unp il $16.99

Grades: K 1 2   E

1. Environmental protection—Fiction 2. School stories 3. Animals—Fiction

ISBN 978-0-8075-5166-0; 0-8075-5166-X

LC 2008055693

Spinelli, Eileen, 1942-—*Continued*

The students in Miss Fox's class lead their school in making choices to help keep the planet healthy, such as turning off lights when leaving a room, taking shorter showers, and using cloth bags instead of plastic ones

"The best part of this, besides Kennedy's exuberant watercolor pictures, is the way the kids consider their actions." Booklist

Other titles about Miss Fox's class are:
Peace Week in Miss Fox's class (2009)
Miss Fox's class earns a field trip (2010)

Night shift daddy; illustrated by Melissa Iwai. Hyperion Bks. for Children 2000 unp il $14.99
Grades: PreK K 1 2   E
    1. Father-daughter relationship—Fiction 2. Bedtime—Fiction 3. Stories in rhyme
    ISBN 0-7868-0495-5   LC 98-52499
A father shares dinner and bedtime rituals with his daughter before going out to work the night shift

"The rhyming text manages to convey many feelings—love, loneliness, anticipation—in few words; the mood is reinforced beautifully by the rich, detailed illustrations, especially those depicting a child's room at night." Horn Book Guide

Silly Tilly; by Eileen Spinelli; illustrated by David Slonim. Marshall Cavendish Children 2009 unp il $16.99
Grades: PreK K 1 2   E
    1. Stories in rhyme 2. Geese—Fiction 3. Animals—Fiction
    ISBN 978-0-7614-5525-7; 0-7614-5525-6
                  LC 2008022880

"Tilly, a goose, bathes in apple juice, wears a pancake as a hat, and likes to tickle frogs. But her ways raise the ire of the other farm animals, who demand that she cease all silliness. . . . The acrylic, pencil, and ballpoint pen illustrations complement the rhyming text and do a nice job of conveying the animals' varying levels of frustration. Some pictures are laugh-out-loud funny." SLJ

Sophie's masterpiece; a spider's tale; illustrations by Jane Dyer. Simon & Schuster Bks. for Young Readers 2001 unp il $16 *
Grades: PreK K 1 2   E
    1. Spiders—Fiction
    ISBN 0-689-80112-2   LC 95-44063
Sophie the spider makes wondrous webs, but the residents of Beekman's Boarding House do not appreciate her until at last, old and tired, she weaves her final masterpiece

"The graceful telling glimmers with feeling and occasional humor, while the full-page watercolors and lacy spot art capture the delicate magic of Sophie's webs and enhance the tale's quiet mood." Horn Book Guide

Three pebbles and a song; pictures by S.D. Schindler. Dial Bks. for Young Readers 2003 unp il $16.99 *
Grades: PreK K 1 2   E
    1. Mice—Fiction 2. Winter—Fiction
    ISBN 0-8037-2528-0   LC 2002-6822
As his mouse family endures a long, cold winter, Moses's contributions of a dance, a juggling act, and a little

song prove more useful than he had supposed

"The plot is well developed, the text contains many descriptive words, and emergent readers will appreciate the repetitive and predictable language. Done in gouache, watercolors, inks, pastels, and chalk, Schindler's painterly artwork captures perfectly the chill of the coming winter and the warmth of a happy home." SLJ

Wanda's monster; written by Eileen Spinelli; illustrated by Nancy Hayashi. Whitman, A. 2002 unp il $15.95; pa $6.95
Grades: PreK K 1 2   E
    1. Monsters—Fiction 2. Grandmothers—Fiction
    ISBN 0-8075-8656-0; 0-8075-8657-9 (pa)
                  LC 2002-1955
When Wanda fears that she has a monster in her closet, she takes her grandmother's advice and begins to look at things from the monster's point of view

"Hayashi's watercolor and colored-pencil illustrations do a great job of melding the real and the imaginary in Spinelli's story, staying true to the child's fearful fantasies and transforming them with warmth and affection." Booklist

When Papa comes home tonight; illustrated by David McPhail. Simon & Schuster Books for Young Readers 2009 unp il $16.99
Grades: PreK   E
    1. Stories in rhyme 2. Father-child relationship—Fiction 3. Bedtime—Fiction
    ISBN 978-1-4169-1028-2; 1-4169-1028-X
                  LC 2008008860
A father and child enjoy a range of activities together before bedtime.

"A sweet ode to family life, beautifully illustrated in pencil, pen-and-ink, and watercolor. . . . The rhyming phrases are gentle but not cloying." SLJ

When you are happy; illustrated by Geraldo Valério. Simon & Schuster Books for Young Readers 2006 unp il $16.95
Grades: PreK K 1   E
    1. Emotions—Fiction 2. Family life—Fiction
    ISBN 0-689-86251-2
"Using a comforting refrain (When you are . . .), each member of the young girl's family reassures her when she is cold, sick, lonely, tired, grumpy, lost, and happy. . . . Appealingly offbeat, whimsical illustrations characterize the girl's emotions." Booklist

Spinelli, Jerry, 1941-

I can be anything; illustrated by Jimmy Liao. Little, Brown 2010 unp il $16.99
Grades: PreK K   E
    1. Stories in rhyme 2. Occupations—Fiction
    ISBN 978-0-316-16226-5; 0-316-16226-4
A little boy ponders the many possible jobs in his future, from paper-plane folder and puppy-dog holder to mixing-bowl licker and tin-can kicker.

"Aided by Liao's cleverly integrated full-bleed mixed-media illustrations, which radiate every hue of the rainbow, and dynamic typesetting with words that swoop and dive, the author's perspective on this adult-inspired question yields some refreshingly child-oriented answers. . . . An inspired take on a timeless question." Kirkus

Spinner, Stephanie, 1943-

It's a miracle! a Hanukkah storybook; written by Stephanie Spinner; illustrated by Jill McElmurry. Atheneum Bks. for Young Readers 2003 unp il $16.95

Grades: K 1 2 3　　　　　　　　　　E

1. Hanukkah—Fiction 2. Grandmothers—Fiction
ISBN 0-689-84493-X　　　　LC 2002-6137

"An Anne Schwartz book"

"Owen Block, aged six and a half, has just been named O.C.L.-Official Candle Lighter. Each night, as he performs his duty, he listens to Grandma Karen's cozy stories of family life. . . . A brief retelling of the Hanukkah legend and blessings in Hebrew, English, and transliteration appear at the end of the book. McElmurry's gouache illustrations add a light, humorous touch. Adults will appreciate the lessons gracefully imparted, and children will enjoy the silliness of Grandma's fanciful, zany family stories." SLJ

The Nutcracker; retold by Stephanie Spinner; illustrated by Peter Malone; with a fully orchestrated CD of Peter Ilyich Tchaikovsky music. Alfred A. Knopf 2008 unp il $16.99; lib bdg $19.99

Grades: K 1 2 3 4　　　　　　　　E

1. Fairy tales 2. Christmas—Fiction
ISBN 978-0-375-84464-5; 0-375-84464-3; 978-0-375-94464-2 (lib bdg); 0-375-94464-8 (lib bdg)
　　　　　　　　　　LC 2007041524

In this retelling of the original 1816 German story, Godfather Drosselmeier gives young Marie a nutcracker for Christmas, and she finds herself in a magical realm where she saves the nutcracker and sees him change into a handsome prince

"Malone's richly colored, opaque watercolors embellish the dancers' magic. . . . This book, which comes with a CD, provides a good entry-point before attending a performance as well as a chance to relive the experience afterward." Horn Book

Spirin, Gennadiĭ

A apple pie; art by Gennady Spirin. Philomel Books 2005 unp il $16.99

Grades: PreK K 1 2　　　　　　　E

1. Alphabet 2. Nursery rhymes
ISBN 0-399-23981-2　　　　LC 2004030497

Introduces the letters A to Z while following the fortunes of an apple pie.

"Whimsically detailed watercolors revitalize an alphabet verse dating from the 1600s. . . . Delicately rendered vines and flowers are reminiscent of Victorian botanical prints. Busy details offer new discoveries with each reading. The letters, text, and paintings are unified in style and become a single work of art." SLJ

Martha. Philomel Books 2005 unp il $14.99

Grades: K 1 2 3　　　　　　　　　E

1. Crows 2. Russia
ISBN 0-399-23980-4　　　　LC 2004-6735

The author relates how he and his Moscow family rescued Martha, a crow with a broken wing, and how she joined their household.

"The story will appeal to the picture book audience.

. . . The lush art set in plentiful white space beautifully portrays a Moscow of a few decades ago." Horn Book Guide

Spiro, Ruth

Lester Fizz, bubble-gum artist; illustrated by Thor Wickstrom. Dutton 2008 unp il $16.99

Grades: 1 2 3　　　　　　　　　　E

1. Artists—Fiction 2. Chewing gum—Fiction 3. Art—Fiction
ISBN 978-0-525-47861-4; 0-525-47861-2

Everyone in the Fizz family is an artist. Everyone, that is, except Lester, whose paintings are pitiful and doodles are drab. He can't seem to find a way to fit in with the illustrious Fizzes, until one day a mouthful of gum becomes a work of art in Lester's talented lips.

"Spiro's droll text is infused with alliteration and punning that adds to the sense of fun, which is extended in colorful, whimsical illustrations. Wickstrom's playful images portray scenarios both realistic and fantastical and incorporate classic works by famous artists, including Joseph Cornell and Dorothea Lange." Booklist

Spohn, Kate

Turtle and Snake's day at the beach. Viking 2003 32p il hardcover o.p. pa $3.99 *

Grades: K 1 2　　　　　　　　　　E

1. Beaches—Fiction 2. Turtles—Fiction 3. Snakes—Fiction
ISBN 0-670-03628-5; 0-14-240157-9 (pa)
　　　　　　　　　　LC 2002-153376

"A Viking easy-to-read"

Turtle and Snake go to the beach, where they and some other animals participate in a sandcastle-making contest

"Brightly colored, simple drawings capture the pleasure of this fun-in-the-sun day at the beach. . . . It's difficult to find easy-to-read books that have charm and a real story, and this one does." SLJ

Other titles about Turtle and Snake are:
Turtle and Snake and the Christmas tree (2000)
Turtle and Snake at work (1999)
Turtle and Snake fix it (2002)
Turtle and Snake go camping (2000)
Turtle and Snake's spooky Halloween (2002)
Turtle and Snake's Valentine's Day (2003)

Staake, Bob

The donut chef. Random House 2008 unp il $14.99; lib bdg $17.99

Grades: PreK K 1 2　　　　　　　E

1. Baking—Fiction 2. Stories in rhyme
ISBN 978-0-375-84403-4; 0-375-84403-1; 978-0-375-94716-2 (lib bdg); 0-375-94716-7 (lib bdg)

"A Golden book"

A baker hangs out his shingle on a small street and soon the line for his donuts stretches down the block. But it's not long before the competition arrives and a battle of the bakers ensues.

"The entire book has a retro tone, from its lengthy rhyming text to its Art Deco-style illustrations, which are updated with more modern-looking graphic shapes and a multicolored palette. . . . The story's lively rhythmic text and colorful artwork should make it a good pick for storytime." SLJ

Staake, Bob—*Continued*

The red lemon. Golden Books 2006 unp il $14.95; lib bdg $16.99

Grades: PreK K 1   **E**

1. Lemons—Fiction 2. Stories in rhyme

ISBN 0-375-83593-8; 0-375-93593-2 (lib bdg)

LC 2005-09854

Farmer McPhee's yellow lemons are ready to be picked and made into lemonade, pies, and muffins, but when a red lemon is found in the crop and discarded, it eventually yields some surprises.

"Bold, enticing illustrations dominate the pages. Staake creates a fun, dynamic world . . . in its sweeping arcs, bright colors, multicolored cartoon people, and effortlessly rhyming text." SLJ

Stainton, Sue

I love cats; [written by] Sue Stainton; [illustrated by] Anne Mortimer. Katherine Tegen Books 2007 unp il $15.99

Grades: PreK K   **E**

1. Cats—Fiction

ISBN 978-0-06-085154-5; 0-06-085154-6; 978-0-06-085156-9 (lib bdg); 0-06-085156-2 (lib bdg)

LC 2005018100

"The unseen narrator likes all kinds of cats, and there are plenty of cats to be seen: big cats, little cats, hairy cats, scaredy-cats. Using an almost photo-realistic technique, Mortimer offers more than two dozen cats to 'ooh' and 'ahh' over." Booklist

Stamp, Jørgen, 1969-

Flying high. Enchanted Lion 2009 unp il $16.95

Grades: K 1 2   **E**

1. Giraffes—Fiction 2. Turtles—Fiction 3. Air pilots—Fiction

ISBN 978-1-59270-089-9; 1-59270-089-6

"Walter is a giraffe who wishes he could fly. He finds himself a book, and begins to build an airplane for himself. When Sonny the turtle meanders over and asks if he, too, can go flying, Walter tells his friend he's too slow and cowardly and hurts his feelings. . . . When his plane is hit by lightning and crashes into the lake, it is Sonny who swims out and saves him. . . . The colorful cartoon illustrations convey the fast pace of the tale and do a suitable job of moving things along to a satisfying conclusion." SLJ

Stanley, Diane, 1943-

The Giant and the beanstalk; written and illustrated by Diane Stanley. HarperCollinsPublishers 2004 unp il $17.99; lib bdg $17.89

Grades: K 1 2 3   **E**

1. Fairy tales

ISBN 0-06-000010-4; 0-06-000011-2 (lib bdg)

LC 2003-1818

In this version of the traditional tale, a young giant chases Jack down the beanstalk to rescue his beloved hen and meets other Jacks from various nursery rhymes along the way

"Stanley injects her characteristic, understated humor into both text and art, and young ones will take pleasure in identifying the individual elements of the thoroughly mixed-up story." Booklist

Goldie and the three bears. HarperCollins Pubs. 2003 unp il $15.99; lib bdg $17.89; pa $6.99

Grades: K 1 2 3   **E**

1. Friendship—Fiction 2. Bears—Fiction

ISBN 0-06-000008-2; 0-06-000009-0 (lib bdg); 0-06-113611-5 (pa)   LC 2002-23843

In this story, loosely based on that of Goldilocks, Goldie, who has yet to find a friend to "love with all her heart," makes an unplanned visit to the house of some bears

"The writing is smooth, concise, and rhythmic. . . . The pictures are marvelous, with fine lines; soft, glowing colors; and winsome, telling details." SLJ

Rumpelstiltskin's daughter. Morrow Junior Bks. 1997 unp il $17.99; lib bdg $16.89; pa $7.99 *

Grades: K 1 2 3   **E**

1. Fairy tales

ISBN 0-688-14327-X; 0-688-14328-8 (lib bdg); 0-06-441095-1 (pa)   LC 96-14834

"Rumpelstiltskin's daughter relies on her cleverness instead of magic. When the king orders her to spin straw into gold, she tricks him out of his greedy ways and becomes prime minister of his kingdom. The illustrations provide splendid, detailed palace interiors and endow the characters, especially the king and his minions, with comically exaggerated features." Horn Book Guide

Saving Sweetness; illustrated by G. Brian Karas. Putnam 1996 unp il $16.99; pa $5.99

Grades: K 1 2 3   **E**

1. Orphans—Fiction 2. West (U.S.)—Fiction

ISBN 0-399-22645-1; 0-698-11767-0 (pa)

LC 95-10621

The sheriff of a dusty western town rescues Sweetness, an unusually resourceful orphan, from nasty old Mrs. Sump and her terrible orphanage

"Telling the tale from the sheriff's point of view, Stanley packs this fast-paced adventure full of language that begs to be read aloud. . . . Combining gouache, acrylic, and pencil drawings with cyanotype photographs, Karas's illustrations evoke the arid landscape of the West yet remain wonderfully original." SLJ

Another title about Sweetness is:

Raising Sweetness (1999)

The trouble with wishes. HarperCollins Pubs. 2007 unp il $16.99; lib bdg $17.89 *

Grades: 1 2 3 4   **E**

1. Sculpture—Fiction 2. Wishes—Fiction 3. Classical mythology—Fiction

ISBN 0-06-055451-7; 0-06-055452-5 (lib bdg)

Jane wishes she were more like her friend Pyg the sculptor until Pyg's statue of a beautiful goddess comes to life and teaches them both to be careful what they wish for. Based on the Greek myth of Pygmalion

"Stanley's fresh artwork, which mixes the grandeur of old classical forms and the absurdity of the new, is in perfect balance with the parody." Booklist

Stanton, Karen, 1960-

Papi's gift; by Karen Stanton; illustrated by Rene King Moreno. Boyds Mills Press 2007 unp il $16.95

Grades: K 1 2 3   E

1. Father-daughter relationship—Fiction 2. Birthdays—Fiction 3. Droughts—Fiction 4. Latin America—Fiction

ISBN 978-1-59078-422-8; 1-59078-422-7

LC 2006011569

Graciela's Papi has been working in the United States for so long that she has almost forgotten his face, so when the box he promised for her seventh birthday does not arrive, she is very upset and nearly loses hope that he— and the rain—will someday return

"A few Spanish words and phrases add authenticity to the engaging text. Moreno uses pastels to render soothing, warm illustrations that have a Latin American flavor and elements of folk art." SLJ

Stauffacher, Sue, 1961-

Bessie Smith and the night riders; illustrated by John Holyfield. G. P. Putnam's Sons 2006 unp il $16.99 *

Grades: K 1 2 3 4   E

1. Smith, Bessie, 1894-1937—Fiction 2. Ku Klux Klan—Fiction 3. Blues music—Fiction 4. African Americans—Fiction 5. North Carolina—Fiction

ISBN 0-399-24237-6   LC 2005010399

Black blues singer Bessie Smith singlehandedly scares off Ku Klux Klan members who are trying to disrupt her show one hot July night in Concord, North Carolina. Includes historical note

"Holyfield's brilliantly colored acrylic spreads aptly depict a larger-than-life individual. . . . The book is based on a true event. . . . This tale of courage would make a fine addition to units on the Civil Rights movement." SLJ

Includes bibliographical references

Stead, Philip C.

A sick day for Amos McGee; written by Philip C. Stead; illustrated by Erin E. Stead. Roaring Brook Press 2010 unp il $16.99

Grades: PreK K 1 2   E

1. Zoos—Fiction 2. Animals—Fiction 3. Sick—Fiction

ISBN 978-1-59643-402-8; 1-59643-402-3

Amos McGee he spends a little bit of time each day with each of his friends at the zoo, running races with the tortoise, keeping the shy penguin company, and even reading bedtime stories to the owl. But when Amos is too sick to make it to the zoo, his animal friends decide it's time they returned the favor.

"The artwork in this quiet tale of good deeds rewarded uses woodblock-printing techniques, soft flat colors, and occasional bits of red. Illustrations are positioned on the white space to move the tale along and underscore the bonds of friendship and loyalty. Whether read individually or shared, this gentle story will resonate with youngsters." SLJ

Steffensmeier, Alexander

Millie waits for the mail; [by] Alexander Steffensmeier. Walker & Co. 2007 unp il $16.95; lib bdg $17.85 *

Grades: PreK K 1 2   E

1. Cattle—Fiction 2. Letter carriers—Fiction

ISBN 978-0-8027-9662-2; 0-8027-9662-1; 978-0-8027-9663-9 (lib bdg); 0-8027-9663-X (lib bdg)

LC 2006035326

Millie the cow loves to scare the mailman and chase him off the farm, until the mailman comes up with a plan that ends up pleasing everyone.

"While the text is both lively and concise, most of the book's considerable charm emanates from the droll visual humor." Publ Wkly

Another title about Millie is:
Millie in the snow (2008)

Steggall, Susan

Rattle and rap; [illustrated by Susan Steggall] Frances Lincoln 2009 unp il $15.95 *

Grades: PreK K 1   E

1. Railroads—Fiction

ISBN 978-1-84507-703-7; 1-84507-703-2

Steggall's "virtuoso torn-paper collages follow a boy and his family on a train trip through the British countryside to the coast, where an unnamed (but grandmotherly) relative greets them with open arms. . . . The detail-rich, full-spread pictures . . . are stunning in their evocation of the real world." Publ Wkly

Steig, Jeanne

Fleas; illustrated by Britt Spencer. Philomel 2008 unp il $16.99

Grades: PreK K 1 2   E

1. Barter—Fiction 2. Circus—Fiction

ISBN 978-0-399-24756-9; 0-399-24756-4

A cumulative tale in which Quantz, who is repaid in fleas for scratching a stray dog, makes a series of trades that turn one person's burden into the next one's joy and ultimately brings them all together for a circus performance.

Steig's "shaggy dog story, like the swapping stories found in folk or fairy tales, takes readers on a hilarious journey. . . . In Spencer's . . . capable hands, the intrepid hero looks like Ichabod Crane, and part of the joy is in seeing each new outlandish personage." Publ Wkly

Steig, William, 1907-2003

The amazing bone. Farrar, Straus & Giroux 1976 unp il $17.99; pa $7.99 *

Grades: PreK K 1 2 3   E

1. Pigs—Fiction 2. Bones—Fiction

ISBN 0-374-30248-0; 0-374-40358-9 (pa)

A Caldecott Medal honor book, 1977

On her way home from school, Pearl finds an unusual bone that has unexpected powers

"Steig's marvelously straightfaced telling comes with a panoply of ultra-spring landscapes for pink-dressed Pearl to tiptoe through. And there's no holding back the chortles at the wonderfully expressive faces the artist delights in. This is a tight mesh of witty storytelling and art bound to please any audience." Booklist

Steig, William, 1907-2003—*Continued*

Brave Irene. Farrar, Straus & Giroux 1986 unp
il $17; pa $7.95 *

Grades: PreK K 1 2 3   E

1. Blizzards—Fiction 2. Courage—Fiction

ISBN 0-374-30947-7; 0-374-40927-7 (pa)

LC 86-80957

"Mrs. Bobbin has just finished a beautiful ballgown
for the duchess, but she has a headache and can't deliver
it. Brave and devoted daughter Irene takes charge . . .
determinedly marching out into a raging snowstorm with
the dress." Publ Wkly

"With sure writing and well-composed, riveting art,
Steig keeps readers with Irene every step of the long
way. The pictures . . . are done in winter blues, purples,
and grays that gradually get darker as Irene trudges on."
Booklist

Caleb & Kate. Farrar, Straus & Giroux 1977
unp il pa $6.95 hardcover o.p.

Grades: PreK K 1 2 3   E

1. Dogs—Fiction 2. Witches—Fiction

ISBN 0-374-41038-0 (pa)   LC 77-4947

"Though Caleb the carpenter loves Kate the weaver
very much, he leaves her one day because of a quarrel.
In the deep woods where he is resting Yedida the witch
turns him into a dog. The tale of his faithfulness and
love for his wife, even though he is a dog, is . . . told.
Their love is shared to the end, when a remarkable turn
of events enables him to return to his former self." Child
Book Rev Serv

"The well-cadenced storytelling has a certain old-
fashioned elegance of language, and the humor is emphasized by an atmosphere of mock-pathos." Horn Book

Doctor De Soto. Farrar, Straus & Giroux 1982
unp il $17; pa $7.99 *

Grades: PreK K 1 2   E

1. Dentists—Fiction 2. Mice—Fiction 3. Animals—
Fiction

ISBN 0-374-31803-4; 0-374-41810-1 (pa)

LC 82-15701

A Newbery Medal honor book, 1983

"Dr. De Soto is a mouse dentist who . . . treats all
creatures large and small but none that are injurious to
mice. When Fox begs for help, the couple face a dilemma. He is in pain and professional ethics demand that
they pull his aching tooth and replace it with a sound
one." Publ Wkly

"The story achieves comic heights partly through the
delightful irony of the situation. . . . Watercolor paintings, with the artist's firm line and luscious color, depict
with aplomb the eminently dentistlike mouse as he goes
about his business." Horn Book

Another title about Doctor De Soto is:

Doctor De Soto goes to Africa (1992)

Pete's a pizza. HarperCollins Pubs. 1998 unp il
$16.99; lib bdg $17.89 *

Grades: PreK K 1 2   E

1. Father-son relationship—Fiction

ISBN 0-06-205157-1; 0-06-205158-X (lib bdg)

LC 97-78384

"Michael di Capua books"

Pete "moodily contemplates a rain-drenched landscape
when his understanding father decides to cheer him up
by transforming him into a pizza. The recipe: plenty of
kneading, stretching, twirling, and decorating with delicacies such as cheese (in reality pieces of paper) and tomatoes (checkers), plus tickling and obviously lots of love."
Horn Book

"The watercolor illustrations are executed in a clean
palette with precise lines in tightly controlled compositions, the semi-formality of which only add to the hilarity. . . . This is a jolly, affectionate story." Bull Cent
Child Books

Potch & Polly; with pictures by Jon Agee.
Farrar, Straus & Giroux 2002 unp il $16

Grades: K 1 2 3   E

1. Love—Fiction

ISBN 0-374-36090-1   LC 00-29544

Lively Potch pursues the girl of his dreams, the darling Polly Pumpernickel

"This irresistible picture book has it all: a tongue-in-
cheek text brimming with deliciously alliterative phrases,
wry cartoons that mix visual gags with a comic-book
punch, and a plot featuring two lovers who are taunted
by twists of fate and turns of slapstick humor." SLJ

Shrek! twentieth anniversary edition. Farrar
Straus Giroux 2010 c1990 unp il $16.99

Grades: K 1 2 3 4   E

1. Monsters—Fiction

ISBN 978-0-374-36879-1; 0-374-36879-1

A reissue of the title first published 1990

"Shrek is the ugliest monster around and this is the
tale of his encounters with a witch, dragon, knight, lightening and thunder on his quest to find the ugly princess."
Child Book Rev Serv

"The pictures are just as nutty as the story, blending
with the text so thoroughly, sometimes echoing, sometimes expanding it, that it's hard to imagine one without
the other. . . . The fast-forward movement of the story
and the inventive challenging language, full of surprises,
make this especially fun to read aloud." SLJ

Sylvester and the magic pebble. Simon &
Schuster Books for Young Readers 2005 c1969
unp il $16.95 *

Grades: PreK K 1 2 3   E

1. Donkeys—Fiction

ISBN 1-4169-0206-6   LC 2004-15445

Awarded the Caldecott Medal, 1970

A reissue of the title first published 1969

This edition includes William Steig's Caldecott Award
acceptance speech

In a moment of fright, Sylvester the donkey asks his
magic pebble to turn him into a rock but then can not
hold the pebble to wish himself back to normal again

"A remarkable atmosphere of childlike innocence pervades the book; beautiful pictures in full, natural color
show daily and seasonal changes in the lush countryside
and greatly extend the kindly humor and the warm, unselfconscious tenderness." Horn Book

When everybody wore a hat. Joanna Cotler Bks.
2003 unp il $17.99; pa $8.99

Grades: PreK K 1 2 3   E

ISBN 0-06-009700-0; 0-06-009702-7 (pa)

LC 2002-6512

Steig, William, 1907-2003—*Continued*

"In 1916, Steig was eight years old. This autobiography describes that year of his life. . . . The childlike, watercolor artwork that accompanies the memories features flattened tables, nostrils on the sides of noses, and a sidewalk extending up into the air. Yet the illustrations' naiveté belies their underlying sophistication. With a few spare lines, the artist manages to convey body language, facial expression, and gesture." SLJ

Stein, David Ezra

Cowboy Ned and Andy; [by] David Ezra Stein. Simon & Schuster Books for Young Readers 2006 unp il $14.95

Grades: PreK K 1 2   E

1. Cowhands—Fiction 2. Horses—Fiction 3. West (U.S.)—Fiction 4. Birthdays—Fiction

ISBN 978-1-4169-0041-2; 1-4169-0041-1

LC 2005006969

"A Paula Wiseman book"

On a cattle drive in the desert on the night before Cowboy Ned's birthday, his horse Andy goes in search of a birthday cake, which he thinks will make Ned's birthday complete

"Stein's language is simple yet expressive. . . . Done in ink and watercolor, the cartoon illustrations make the most of the Western landscape." SLJ

Another title about Cowboy Ned and Andy is:
Ned's new friend (2007)

Leaves. Putnam 2007 unp il $15.99 *

Grades: PreK K 1 2   E

1. Bears—Fiction 2. Leaves—Fiction 3. Seasons—Fiction

ISBN 978-0-399-24636-4; 0-399-24636-3

LC 2006-24753

A curious bear observes how leaves change throughout the seasons.

"Bamboo pen and earth-toned watercolors are used to great effect. . . . The serene scenes and streamlined story line reflect perfectly the gentle passage of time." SLJ

Monster hug! [by] David Ezra Stein. G.P. Putnam's Sons 2007 unp il $15.99

Grades: PreK K 1 2   E

1. Monsters—Fiction 2. Play—Fiction

ISBN 978-0-399-24637-1   LC 2007008196

Two rambunctious young monsters have an action-packed day together

"Stein's rambunctious watercolors are as joyously messy as the characters they bring to life. His primary-color palette stands out boldly against the white backgrounds." SLJ

Pouch! G.P. Putnam's Sons 2009 unp il $15.99 *

Grades: PreK K 1   E

1. Growth—Fiction 2. Kangaroos—Fiction 3. Mother-child relationship—Fiction

ISBN 978-0-399-25051-4; 0-399-25051-4

LC 2008-53558

A baby kangaroo takes his first tentative hops outside of his mama's pouch, meeting other creatures and growing bolder each time.

"The short, pithy text tells a story young listeners will immediately understand. . . . Done in marker, watercolor, and crayon, the artwork has a fresh energetic quality that suits the story well." Booklist

Stevens, April, 1963-

Waking up Wendell; written by April Stevens; illustrated by Tad Hills. Schwartz & Wade Books 2007 unp il $15.99; lib bdg $18.99 *

Grades: PreK K 1 2   E

1. Sounds—Fiction 2. Counting

ISBN 978-0-375-83621-3;   0-375-83621-7; 978-0-375-83893-1 (lib bdg); 0-375-93893-1 (lib bdg)

LC 2006030979

Early in the morning, a bird begins to sing at number One Fish Street, waking the man next door and his dog, and before long, as one noise leads to another, everyone on the street is awake.

"Hills's bright oil paint and colored pencil illustrations, done with simple lines and contrasting colors, enliven the text and add extra humor. This picture book is both a clever and original counting book and a great read-aloud." SLJ

Stevens, Janet, 1953-

Cook-a-doodle-doo! [by] Janet Stevens and Susan Stevens Crummel; illustrated by Janet Stevens. Harcourt Brace & Co. 1999 unp il $17; pa $7 *

Grades: PreK K 1 2   E

1. Cooking—Fiction 2. Animals—Fiction

ISBN 0-15-201924-3; 0-15-205658-0 (pa)

LC 98-8853

With the questionable help of his friends, Big Brown Rooster manages to bake a strawberry shortcake which would have pleased his great-grandmother, Little Red Hen

"With the main story and each hilarious, mouthwatering double-page picture of pandemonium, there is a quiet sidebar in small type that explains what recipes are, what ingredients are, what measuring and baking means, and how to make a strawberry shortcake, step by step. The luscious illustrations on hand-made paper are beautifully drawn and deliciously textured. . . . The full recipe is printed on the last page." Booklist

The great fuzz frenzy; written by Janet Stevens and Susan Stevens Crummel; illustrated by Janet Stevens. Harcourt 2005 unp il $17 *

Grades: PreK K 1 2 3   E

1. Prairie dogs—Fiction

ISBN 0-15-204626-7

When a fuzzy tennis ball lands in a prairie-dog town, the prairie dogs discover that their newfound frenzy for fuzz creates no end of trouble.

"The marvelously rendered mixed-media illustrations, with vivid blues, earthy browns, and that luminescent green, capture the true fuzzy nature and greenish glow of the ball." SLJ

Stevens, Janet, 1953-—*Continued*

Help me, Mr. Mutt! expert answers for dogs with people problems; written by Janet Stevens and Susan Stevens Crummel; illustrated by Janet Stevens. Harcourt 2008 unp il $17

Grades: 1 2 3   E
1. Dogs—Fiction
ISBN 978-0-15-204628-6; 0-15-204628-3
LC 2007020549

Dogs across the United States write to Mr. Mutt, a people expert, for help with their humans.

"Art and text work seemlessly, with plenty of visual and verbal jokes . . . to entice repeated readings." Booklist

Stevenson, James, 1929-

Flying feet; a Mud Flat story. Greenwillow Books 2004 47p il $15.99; lib bdg $16.89 *

Grades: K 1 2   E
1. Tap dancing—Fiction 2. Animals—Fiction
ISBN 0-06-051975-4; 0-06-051976-2 (lib bdg)
LC 2002-29785

Stanley and the the other animals of Mud Flat take dance lessons from some touring tap dancers and prepare for a big show

"Stevenson's trademark pen-and-watercolor illustrations lovingly depict exuberant characters and provide lots of special details. . . . Children will enjoy this zany story." SLJ

Other titles about Mud Flat are:
Christmas at Mud Flat (2000)
Heat wave at Mud Flat (1997)
Mud Flat April Fool (1998)
The Mud Flat mystery (1997)
Mud Flat Olympics (1994)
Mud Flat spring (1999)
Yard sale (1996)

No laughing, no smiling, no giggling. Farrar, Straus and Giroux 2004 unp il $16

Grades: PreK K 1 2   E
1. Animals—Fiction
ISBN 0-374-31829-8   LC 2003-45508

Companion volume to Don't make me laugh (1999)

"Frances Foster books"

The reader joins Freddy Fafnaffer the pig as he deals with Mr. Frimdimpny, a crocodile who never laughs and who decides on the rules for reading this book.

"Children will enjoy the humorous cartoons and delight in helping Freddy out of his predicament. The act of inviting readers to actively participate in the plot has great appeal." SLJ

Stevenson, Robert Louis, 1850-1894

Block city; illustrated by Daniel Kirk. Simon & Schuster Books for Young Readers 2005 unp il $14.95

Grades: PreK K 1   E
1. Play—Fiction
ISBN 0-689-86964-9

A child creates a world of his own which has mountains and sea, a city and ships, all from toy blocks.

"This colorfully illustrated version of Stevenson's poem is as relevant today as when it was written for *A Child's Garden of Verses* in 1883. . . . Done in colored pencils and gouache in rich, deep colors, the large, clear pictures have a retro feel." SLJ

The moon; [by] Robert Louis Stevenson; pictures by Tracey Campbell Pearson. Farrar, Straus and Giroux 2006 unp il $16 *

Grades: PreK K 1 2   E
1. Moon—Poetry
ISBN 0-374-35046-9   LC 2005040067

"Stevenson's famous 12-line poem, which begins 'The moon has a face / like the clock in the hall,' becomes the text of a picture-book depiction of the nighttime outing of a contemporary father and his child. Leaving Mother and Baby behind, they climb into a truck with the dog, the cat, and some provisions; travel to the dock; and take their boat across a cove and back again while they watch the places and creatures illuminated by the moon. The pictured journey creates a vivid, visual counterpoint to the poetry, which flows as magically as an incantation. . . . The luminous ink-and-watercolor illustrations reflect Pearson's creative imagination and her sure sense of what is visually interesting to young children." Booklist

Stewart, Amber

Bedtime for Button; [by] Amber Stewart & [illustrated by] Layn Marlow. Orchard Books 2009 c2008 unp il lib bdg $12.99

Grades: PreK K   E
1. Bedtime—Fiction 2. Bears—Fiction 3. Father-son relationship—Fiction
ISBN 978-0-545-12991-6 (lib bdg); 0-545-12991-5 (lib bdg)   LC 2008-29859

First published 2008 in the United Kingdom with title: Just like tonight

When Button the bear remembers something frightening that happened during the day, he worries that he will have bad dreams until his father gives him something nice to think about—the day he was born.

"The soft colors and brushstrokes of Marlow's illustrations underscore the sweet, gentle nature of the tale." SLJ

Little by little; [by] Amber Stewart; [illustrated by] Layn Marlow. Orchard Books 2008 unp il $12.99

Grades: PreK K 1   E
1. Otters—Fiction 2. Siblings—Fiction 3. Swimming—Fiction
ISBN 978-0-545-06163-6; 0-545-06163-6
LC 2007033288

Otto is a young otter who can do many things well, but swimming is not one of them until his older sister tells him to start small and, little by little, he is able to reach his goal, adding swimming to his 'I can do' list

"The message will resonate with children learning this skill and others 'little by little,' and Marlow's expressive watercolor and ink illustrations will capture their interest. The real star here, however, is the peppy text, which bounces along with all the energy of Otto rolling through the water." SLJ

Stewart, Joel

Addis Berner Bear forgets; [by] Joel Stewart. Farrar, Straus and Giroux 2008 unp il $16.95

Grades: K 1 2 3   E

1. City and town life—Fiction 2. Memory—Fiction 3. Musicians—Fiction 4. Bears—Fiction

ISBN 978-0-374-30036-4; 0-374-30036-4

LC 2007044778

A musical bear visits the city and finds the experience a bit overwhelming until he remembers the reason for his trip

"The delicate artwork fascinates, sometimes exacerbating, sometimes ameliorating the bleakest parts of the story. But there's happiness here as well in the vignettes and full-page art." Booklist

Stewart, Sarah

The friend; pictures by David Small. Farrar, Straus and Giroux 2004 unp il $16 *

Grades: K 1 2 3   E

1. Household employees—Fiction

ISBN 0-374-32463-8   LC 2003-64352

With Mom too busy and Dad away much of the time, Belle finds companionship with a household employee who after each day's work takes Belle "hand in hand" to the beach

"David Small's elegant, moving illustrations . . . show the twosome touchingly small on the vast beach. . . . In both illustrations and text, Bea is not merely a playmate but her own person." NY Times Book Rev

The gardener; pictures by David Small. Farrar, Straus & Giroux 1997 unp il $16; pa $6.95 *

Grades: K 1 2 3   E

1. Gardening—Fiction 2. Letters—Fiction 3. Great Depression, 1929-1939—Fiction

ISBN 0-374-32517-0; 0-374-42518-3 (pa)

LC 96-30894

A Caldecott Medal honor book, 1998

"In the depth of the Depression, Lydia Grace Finch is sent to the big city to live with her dour Uncle Jim and cultivates an urban garden." N Y Times Book Rev

"Stewart's quiet story, relayed in the form of letters written by a little girl, focuses on a child who literally makes joy blossom. Small's illustrations . . . [offer] wonderfully expressive characters, ink-line details, and patches of pastel." Booklist

The journey; pictures by David Small. Farrar, Straus & Giroux 2001 unp il $16; pa $6.95 *

Grades: K 1 2 3   E

1. Amish—Fiction 2. City and town life—Fiction

ISBN 0-374-33905-8; 0-374-40010-5 (pa)

LC 99-31001

A young Amish girl tells her "silent friend," her diary, about all the wonderous experiences she has on her first trip to the city

"This title offers so much: a glimpse into Amish culture and Chicago treasures; a winsome main character and many sensitively depicted supporting personalities; a fresh, authentic voice; and a design perfectly melded to its subtle message." SLJ

The library; pictures by David Small. Farrar, Straus & Giroux 1995 unp il $16.50; pa $6.95

Grades: K 1 2 3   E

1. Books and reading—Fiction 2. Stories in rhyme

ISBN 0-374-34388-8; 0-374-44394-7 (pa)

LC 94-30320

Elizabeth Brown loves to read more than anything else, but when her collection of books grows and grows, she must make a change in her life

"Framed watercolors give the book an old-fashioned, scrapbooklike appearance. . . . Small black-ink line drawings decorate the verses below and often add an additional touch of humor. This is a funny, heartwarming story about a quirky woman with a not-so-peculiar obsession." SLJ

Stiegemeyer, Julie

Gobble-gobble crash! by Julie Stiegemeyer; illustrated by Valeri Gorbachev. Dutton Childrens Books 2008 unp il $16.99

Grades: PreK K 1   E

1. Stories in rhyme 2. Turkeys—Fiction 3. Domestic animals—Fiction 4. Counting

ISBN 978-0-525-47959-8; 0-525-47959-7

LC 2008003012

A flock of clumsy turkeys disrupts a quiet night on the farm, but when the farmer threatens them, all the barnyard animals help the noisy birds hide

"In rhythmic couplets, a numbers game unfolds. . . . Gorbachev's action-filled illustrations add to the fun. His animals cavort against moonlit teal backgrounds, with the text printed in white." SLJ

Stier, Catherine

Bugs in my hair?! written by Catherine Stier; illustrated by Tammie Lyon. Albert Whitman & Co. 2008 unp il $15.95

Grades: K 1 2 3   E

1. Lice—Fiction 2. School stories

ISBN 978-0-8075-0908-1; 0-8075-0908-6

LC 2007024250

When immaculately groomed Ellie gets head lice she is terribly upset, but once she learns some facts about the creatures, she calms down and figures out a way to help her classmates.

"Stier has taken a difficult topic and turned it into a charming story that demystifies the fears and false information surrounding lice infestation. The writing . . . comes across simply without sounding didactic. Cartoon illustrations capture Ellie's emotions." SLJ

Stinson, Kathy, 1952-

Big or little? Kathy Stinson [text]; Toni Goffe [illustrations] Annick Press 2009 unp il $19.95; pa $6.95

Grades: PreK   E

1. Size—Fiction 2. Growth—Fiction

ISBN   978-1-55451-169-3;   1-55451-169-0; 978-1-55451-168-6 (pa); 1-55451-168-2 (pa)

"Toby, a preschooler with flyaway hair, considers the benefits and responsibilities of being big, as well as the frustrations of being small. The mishaps of spilled milk

Stinson, Kathy, 1952-—*Continued*
or a wet bed, for instance, are balanced by the joys of helping to wash the car and remembering to return library books. Goffe's line drawings in a pastel palette depict a traditional family of five in a messy home. . . . Plenty of children will relate to [Toby]." SLJ

Stock, Catherine
Gugu's house. Clarion Bks. 2001 31p il $14 *
Grades: PreK K 1 2   E
1. Grandmothers—Fiction 2. Zimbabwe—Fiction
ISBN 0-618-00389-4   LC 00-43009
Kukamba loves helping her grandmother decorate her mud home in a dusty Zimbabwe village, but when the annual rains partially destroy all her art work, Kukamba learns to see the goodness of the rains
"Stock's watercolors capture not only the bright hues of landscape and traditional dress but also a clear sense of Gugu's deep serenity and the shared purpose that sends her and Kukamba striding back from their walk to restore the house to its former glory." Booklist

A porc in New York; [by] Catherine Stock. Holiday House 2007 unp il $16.95
Grades: PreK K 1 2   E
1. Animals—Fiction 2. Vacations—Fiction 3. New York (N.Y.)—Fiction
ISBN 978-0-8234-1994-4; 0-8234-1994-0
                                      LC 2006002015
Monsieur Monmouton and his dog Cabot fly from France to New York City in pursuit of his farm animals, who are taking a vacation to see such sights as Blooming Dells and MOOMA
"The story is fun, and the expansive, exuberant artwork shows Stock at the top of her game." Booklist

Stoeke, Janet Morgan
The bus stop; [by] Janet Morgan Stoeke. Dutton Children's Books 2007 unp il $12.99
Grades: PreK K   E
1. Buses—Fiction 2. School stories 3. Stories in rhyme
ISBN 978-0-525-47805-8   LC 2006024469
Kindergartners gather for their exciting first ride on the school bus.
"The cartoon artwork is colorful and inviting, showing characters with sweetly delineated features. The repetitive text invites participation while portraying this rite of passage in an upbeat manner." SLJ

A hat for Minerva Louise. Dutton Children's Bks. 1994 unp il hardcover o.p. pa $5.99 *
Grades: PreK K 1 2   E
1. Chickens—Fiction 2. Hats—Fiction
ISBN 0-525-45328-8; 0-14-055666-4 (pa)
                                      LC 94-2139
Minerva Louise, a snow-loving chicken, mistakes a pair of mittens for two hats to keep both ends warm
This "is a rare find: a picture book exactly on target for preschoolers that sacrifices none of the essential elements of plot, character, and humor. . . . The pictures, in large rectangles of bright primary colors, are easy for preschoolers to 'read' and contain most of the book's considerable humor." Horn Book

Other titles about Minerva Louise are:
A friend for Minerva Louise (1997)
Minerva Louise (1988)
Minerva Louise and the colorful eggs (2006)
Minerva Louise at school (1996)
Minerva Louise at the fair (2000)
Minerva Louise on Christmas Eve (2007)
Minerva Louise on Halloween (2009)

It's library day; [by] Janet Morgan Stoeke. Dutton Children's Books 2008 unp il $12.99
Grades: K 1 2   E
1. Stories in rhyme 2. Books and reading—Fiction 3. Libraries—Fiction 4. School stories
ISBN 978-0-525-47944-4; 0-525-47944-9
                                      LC 2007040589
"In short bursts of rhyme, this introduces kids who read . . . and captures the excitement they feel when it's library day at school. . . . The pure-colored illustrations, with an almost graphic edge, have tons of appeal." Booklist

Waiting for May. Dutton Children's Bks. 2005 unp il $16.99
Grades: PreK K 1 2   E
1. Adoption—Fiction 2. Siblings—Fiction
ISBN 0-525-47098-0
A young boy looks forward to the day when a new sister, who will be adopted from China, joins his family.
"The smoothly flowing text . . . imparts a surprising amount of information about requirements unique to international adoptions. . . . The colorful paintings enhance the narrative and capture the various emotions of the characters. . . . An excellent addition to all collections." SLJ

Stohner, Anu
Brave Charlotte; [illustrated by Henrike Wilson; translated from the German by Alyson Cole] Bloomsbury Children's Bks. 2005 unp il $16.95
Grades: PreK K 1 2   E
1. Sheep—Fiction
ISBN 1-58234-690-9
Charlotte, a headstrong sheep, rescues the flock when their shepherd is injured.
"There is a lot to like in 'Brave Charlotte': the gentle way the story unfolds, and the lovely way the illustrator . . . expresses an inviting, dingy fluffiness. . . . Each dreamlike image is suffused with colors that are rich yet subdued." NY Times Book Rev
Another title about Charlotte is:
Brave Charlotte and the wolves (2009)

Stojic, Manya
Rain; written and illustrated by Manya Stojic. Crown 2000 unp il $15.95 *
Grades: PreK K 1 2   E
1. Rain—Fiction 2. Animals—Fiction 3. Africa—Fiction
ISBN 0-517-80085-3; 0-517-80086-1 (lib bdg)
                                      LC 99-35298
The animals of the African savanna use their senses to predict and then enjoy the rain

Stojic, Manya—*Continued*

"The brilliant double-page spreads, the play on the five senses, and a text that invites participation make this one trip to Africa you can't afford to miss!" SLJ

Storad, Conrad J.

Rattlesnake rules; illustrated by Nathaniel P. Jensen. Five Star Publications 2009 40p il $16.95
Grades: PreK K 1   E
1. Stories in rhyme 2. Rattlesnakes—Fiction
3. Snakes—Fiction
ISBN 978-1-58985-161-0; 1-58985-161-7
LC 2009-27518

A mother rattlesnake who can locate food with her tongue and swallow prey in one gulp shares survival tips with her babies—and with humans.

"Nathaniel Jensen's illustrations are playfully rendered showcasing the love a mother rattlesnake has for her babies. The skillful combination of fiction and fact in this cleverly conceived story is sure to engage children and teachers alike." Libr Media Connect

Stott, Ann, 1964-

Always; illustrated by Matt Phelan. Candlewick Press 2008 unp il $15.99
Grades: PreK   E
1. Love—Fiction 2. Mother-son relationship—Fiction
ISBN 978-0-7636-3232-8; 0-7636-3232-5
LC 2007052020

A child is reassured by his mother that she will love him even when he misbehaves.

"A sweet, understated story. . . . Phelan's illustrations bring this quiet text to exuberant life with pastel watercolors." SLJ

Straaten, Harmen van, 1961-

Duck's tale; by Harmen van Straaten; translated by Marianne Martens. North-South Books 2007 unp il $16.95
Grades: K 1 2   E
1. Ducks—Fiction 2. Toads—Fiction 3. Reading—Fiction 4. Authorship—Fiction
ISBN 978-0-7358-2133-0; 0-7358-2133-X
LC 2006100310

When Toad finds some reading glasses and Duck finds a pen, they also acquire some skills they never knew they had

"The warm, softly colored illustrations suit the calm atmosphere of the story. Children will be drawn to these appealing creatures." SLJ

Another title about Duck and his friends is:
For me? (2008)

Strauss, Linda L., 1942-

The princess gown; by Linda Leopold Strauss; illustrated by Malene Reynolds Laugesen. Houghton Mifflin Company 2008 unp il $16
Grades: K 1 2 3   E
1. Dressmaking—Fiction 2. Princesses—Fiction
3. Clothing and dress—Fiction 4. Embroidery—Fiction
5. Fairy tales
ISBN 978-0-618-86259-7; 0-618-86259-5
LC 2007012923

If the wedding dress young Hanna's family is making is not chosen for the princess, they will go to the poor house but thanks to Hanna's sharp eyes and artistic ability, her father stands a very good chance of becoming Embroiderer to the Princess.

Laugesen's "animation-style illustrations . . . are rendered in oil crayon and linseed oil on colored paper, creating a nearly tangible, saturated texture. . . . The pictures keep step with the well-paced tale." Publ Wkly

Stringer, Lauren, 1957-

Winter is the warmest season; by Lauren Stringer. Harcourt 2006 unp il $16 *
Grades: PreK K 1 2   E
1. Winter—Fiction
ISBN 0-15-204967-3   LC 2005005723

A child describes pleasant ways to stay warm during the winter, from sipping hot chocolate and eating grilled cheese sandwiches to wearing wooly sweaters and sitting near a glowing fireplace.

"It takes special art to accentuate the evocative words, and Stringer . . . provides distinctive pictures for herself. . . . The deeply hued acrylic artwork ranges from friendly to joyous. . . . A special book worthy of many readings, this radiates warmth." Booklist

Strøm, Kellie, 1967-

Sadie the air mail pilot. David Fickling Books 2007 unp il $17.78
Grades: K 1 2 3   E
1. Air pilots—Fiction 2. Cats—Fiction
ISBN 978-0-385-60506-9; 0-385-60506-4

Although her day got off to a bad start, Sadie, a highflying cat, is confident that she can make the air mail run to Knuckle Peak Weather Station, even after the station reports that a storm is headed their way.

"Strom peppers the narrative with memorable rhymes. . . . Children will be fascinated by the courage of this determined pilot. They will pore over the antique-appearing illustrations that glow in an orangish-red palette with rusty browns and golden yellows." SLJ

Stroud, Bettye, 1939-

The patchwork path; a quilt map to freedom; illustrated by Erin Susanne Bennett. Candlewick Press 2005 32p il $15.99
Grades: K 1 2 3   E
1. Slavery—Fiction 2. Underground railroad—Fiction
3. Quilts—Fiction 4. African Americans—Fiction
ISBN 0-7636-2423-3   LC 2004-45786

While her father leads her toward Canada and away from the plantation where they have been slaves, a young girl thinks of the quilt her mother used to teach her a code that will help guide them to freedom.

"The exciting escape story makes the history immediate, and the fascinating quilt-code messages will have children revisiting the page that shows each symbol and its secret directions. Bennett's bright oil paintings make dramatic use of collage." Booklist

Stryer, Andrea Stenn, 1938-
Kami and the yaks; [by] Andrea Stenn Stryer; illustrated by Bert Dodson. Bay Otter Press 2007 unp il $15.95 paperback o.p.
Grades: K 1 2 3   E
1. Deaf—Fiction 2. Himalaya Mountains—Fiction 3. Nepal—Fiction 4. Yaks—Fiction
ISBN 978-0-977896-10-3; 978-0-977896-11-0 (pa)
"Readers will be transported to the rugged Himalayas with this story of a deaf Sherpa boy in Nepal, who braves a storm in search of his family's yaks. . . . Although Kami's disability plays an important role in the story, the author focuses on his strength. . . . Dark, yet vivid watercolors extend the text." SLJ

Sturges, Philemon
How do you make a baby smile? by Philemon Sturges; illustrated by Bridget Strevens-Marzo. HarperCollinsPublishers 2007 unp il $16.99 *
Grades: PreK   E
1. Animals—Fiction 2. Infants—Fiction 3. Stories in rhyme
ISBN 978-0-06-076072-4; 0-06-076072-9; 978-0-06-076073-1 (lib bdg); 0-06-076073-7 (lib bdg)
LC 2007012488
Animal parents use their best tricks to make their babies smile, laugh, coo, and grin.
This is written "in catchy verse with large-scale, eye-catching artwork. . . . Broad black outlines and flat areas of bold colors clearly define the characters and settings with wit and style." Booklist

I love planes! illustrated by Shari Halpern. HarperCollins Pubs. 2003 unp il $12.99; lib bdg $14.89
Grades: PreK K   E
1. Airplanes—Fiction
ISBN 0-06-028898-1; 0-06-028899-X (lib bdg)
LC 2001-26483
A child celebrates his love of planes by naming his favorite kinds and their notable characteristics
"The simplicity of the child's words is well matched by the colorful, uncluttered images, outlined in black." Booklist

I love school! illustrated by Shari Halpern. HarperCollins Pubs. 2004 unp il $12.99; lib bdg $14.89
Grades: PreK K   E
1. School stories 2. Stories in rhyme
ISBN 0-06-009284-X; 0-06-009285-8 (lib bdg)
LC 2002-68554
A brother and sister describe the things they love to do during their day at kindergarten
This book "is a good way to prepare nervous new preschoolers and kindergartners. . . . [It features] simple, rhymed text and big, clear color pictures outlined in thick black line." Booklist

I love trains! illustrated by Shari Halpern. HarperCollins Pubs. 2001 unp il $12.95; lib bdg $13.89
Grades: PreK K   E
1. Railroads—Fiction 2. Stories in rhyme
ISBN 0-06-028900-7; 0-06-028901-5 (lib bdg)
LC 99-86367
A boy expresses his love of trains, describing many kinds of train cars and their special jobs
This offers "clear, bright, double-page pictures with thick black lines and neon colors. . . . Toddlers will enjoy making the hoot, roar, and rumble sounds and identifying the various cars." Booklist

Stutson, Caroline
By the light of the Halloween moon; illustrated by Kevin Hawkes. Marshall Cavendish 2009 c1993 unp il $16.99 *
Grades: PreK K 1 2   E
1. Halloween—Fiction 2. Stories in rhyme
ISBN 978-0-7614-5553-0; 0-7614-5553-1
LC 2008022965
A reissue of the title first published 1993 by Lothrop, Lee, & Shepherd Books
In this cumulative tale, a host of Halloween spooks, including a cat, a witch, and a ghoul, are drawn to the tapping of a little girl's toe.
"Not only is the text rhythmically bouncy and appealing, but the illustrations are of the least fearful and most amusing of ghastly creatures, very effectively set against a black and gloomy background. A sure Halloween hit." Horn Book

Cats' night out; illustrated by J. Klassen. Simon & Schuster Books for Young Readers 2010 unp il $15.99
Grades: K 1 2 3   E
1. Stories in rhyme 2. Cats—Fiction 3. Dance—Fiction 4. City and town life—Fiction
ISBN 978-1-4169-4005-0; 1-4169-4005-7
LC 2008-52268
"A Paula Wiseman book"
Cats dance the night away out on the town, doing the tango, rumba, twist, fox trot, and more
"Klassen's eye-catching digitally rendered urban streetscapes resemble the sets of classic musical theater. . . . The finely detailed illustrations feature a subdued palette of brown, gray, and charcoal enlivened by splashes of color. The subtle charms of this lighter-than-air confection should delight young connoisseurs of dance and style." SLJ

Suen, Anastasia
Red light, green light; written by Anastasia Suen; illustrated by Ken Wilson-Max. Harcourt 2005 unp il $16 *
Grades: PreK K 1   E
1. Transportation—Fiction 2. Stories in rhyme
ISBN 0-15-202582-0
"Gulliver Books"
A young boy creates an imaginary world filled with zooming cars, flashing traffic lights, and racing fire engines.

Suen, Anastasia—*Continued*

"The flowing text rhymes and has a good pace and rhythm, which makes it an ideal read-aloud for transportation fans. The illustrations are bright and full of detail." SLJ

Subway; written by Anastasia Suen; illustrated by Karen Katz. Viking 2004 unp il $15.99 *

Grades: PreK K 1 2   E

   1. Subways—Fiction 2. Stories in rhyme

   ISBN 0-670-03622-6   LC 2003-14020

"In brief, rhyming verses, an African-American child describes her ride on the subway. . . . The rhythmic language captures the feel of her journey and a repeated refrain invites readers to participate in the telling of the story. The bright, bold artwork depicts each scene in a realistic manner from the child's point of view." SLJ

Sullivan, Sarah, 1953-

Once upon a baby brother; pictures by Tricia Tusa. Farrar Straus Giroux 2010 unp il $16.99

Grades: PreK K 1 2   E

   1. Storytelling—Fiction 2. Authorship—Fiction 3. Siblings—Fiction 4. Infants—Fiction

   ISBN 978-0-374-34635-5; 0-374-34635-6

                   LC 2008016791

"Melanie Kroupa books"

Lizzie, who loves to tell and write stories, is surprised to discover that much of her storytelling inspiration comes from her messy baby brother.

"Sullivan has found an oblique way to write about the ups and downs of a school-age child adjusting to a much younger sibling, and she carries it out with skill. Bringing the story to life, Tusa's strong, quirky line-and-wash drawings define characters and settings, add bits of visual humor, amplify the book's emotional content, and give the jacket its winsome appeal." Booklist

Sussman, Michael B.

Otto grows down; illustrated by Scott Magoon. Sterling Pub. Co. 2009 unp il $14.95

Grades: PreK K 1   E

   1. Wishes—Fiction 2. Growth—Fiction 3. Infants—Fiction 4. Siblings—Fiction

   ISBN 978-1-4027-4703-8; 1-4027-4703-9

                   LC 2008028229

When time goes backwards, granting six-year-old Otto his wish that his attention-stealing baby sister was never born, it keeps going backwards, and Otto finds himself getting younger and younger.

"A refreshing take on the arrival of a new sibling and the rivalry that frequently follows. . . . Exaggerated cartoon art captures his predicament. With humor and poignancy, author and illustrator portray an age-old rite of passage." SLJ

Sutton, Jane, 1950-

Don't call me Sidney; illustrated by Renata Gallio. Dial Books for Young Readers 2010 unp il $16.99

Grades: K 1 2 3   E

   1. Personal names—Fiction 2. Friendship—Fiction 3. Pigs—Fiction 4. Animals—Fiction

   ISBN 978-0-8037-2753-3; 0-8037-2753-4

                   LC 2008054962

Unable to find a rhyme for his name, Sidney the pig decides to become Joe, much to the dismay of his mother and friends.

"This amusing story about a poetic pig's search for his true identity is accompanied by humorous acrylic and pencil collage illustrations in which large figures of the characters dominate the subtly detailed scenes." SLJ

Sutton, Sally

Roadwork! [by] Sally Sutton; illustrated by Brian Lovelock. Candlewick Press 2008 32p il $15.99

Grades: PreK   E

   1. Construction equipment—Fiction 2. Trucks—Fiction 3. Stories in rhyme

   ISBN 978-0-7636-3912-9; 0-7636-3912-5

"Kids who love trucks and construction will find an ideal vehicle for their passions in this exuberant book from New Zealand, which uses full-bleed art and rhyming text to show how each of seven machines functions in the building of a road. Sutton's rhythms invite audience participation, as do the sound effects that end each verse . . . Using ink, acrylics and colored pencils, Lovelock conjures artful landscapes with visible brushwork, reserving a speckling effect not unlike concrete for the road." Publ Wkly

Swaim, Jessica

The hound from the pound; illustrated by Jill McElmurry. Candlewick Press 2007 unp il $15.99

Grades: K 1 2   E

   1. Dogs—Fiction

   ISBN 978-0-7636-2330-2; 0-7636-2330-X

                   LC 2006051851

When lonely Miss Mary Lynn MacIntosh decides to adopt Blue, a basset hound from the pound, she gets far more companionship than she ever expected.

"Swaim's playful poetry, dog puns, and refreshingly sophisticated vocabulary . . . make for a lively and substantial read-aloud. McElmurry's gouache paintings project a retro sensibility yet feel modern and fresh. Her warm, color-washed scenes extend the humor." Booklist

Swain, Gwenyth, 1961-

Riding to Washington; written by Gwenyth Swain; illustrated by David Geister. Sleeping Bear Press 2008 unp il (Tales of young Americans) $17.95

Grades: 1 2 3 4   E
1. King, Martin Luther, Jr., 1929-1968—Fiction 2. African Americans—Fiction 3. Race relations—Fiction
ISBN 978-1-58536-324-7; 1-58536-324-3
"A young white girl rides the bus with her father to the March on Washington in 1963—at which Dr. Martin Luther King, Jr., would give his 'I Have a Dream' speech. She comes to see that Dr. King's dream belongs not just to Blacks but to all Americans." Publisher's note
"The illustrations provide a strong sense of the period. The soft earth tones and rounded forms create a mood of safety and stability. This heartfelt tale provides an unusual and compelling perspective on a historical event." SLJ

Swallow, Pamela Curtis

Groundhog gets a say; as told to Pamela Curtis Swallow; illustrated by Denise Brunkus. G.P. Putnam's Sons 2005 unp il $15.99

Grades: PreK K 1 2   E
1. Marmots—Fiction 2. Squirrels—Fiction 3. Crows—Fiction
ISBN 0-399-23876-X
A groundhog describes his various characteristics to a skeptical squirrel and crow. Text includes various facts about groundhogs
"The humorous text is completed by Brunkus's finely executed, animated, watercolor-and-colored-pencil drawings." SLJ

Swanson, Susan Marie

The first thing my mama told me; illustrated by Christine Davenier. Harcourt 2002 unp il $16

Grades: PreK K 1 2   E
1. Personal names—Fiction 2. Growth—Fiction
ISBN 0-15-201075-0   LC 2001-986
"Seven-year-old Lucy recounts childhood memories that all center on the importance of her name: her uncle building her a stool and painting her name on it, eating alphabet pancakes that spell her name, stomping her name in the snow." Horn Book Guide
"Davenier's delightful pictures are a great match for the text. Using a combination of pencil, ink, and pastel, she achieves a spunky, free-spirited look." Booklist

The house in the night; written by Susan Marie Swanson and illustrated by Beth Krommes. Houghton Mifflin Company 2008 unp il $16 *

Grades: PreK K 1   E
1. Houses—Fiction 2. Light—Fiction 3. Night—Fiction
ISBN 978-0-618-86244-3; 0-618-86244-7
     LC 2007012921
Awarded the Caldecott Medal, 2009
Illustrations and easy-to-read text explore the light that makes a house in the night a home filled with light.
"Inspired by traditional cumulative poetry, Swanson weaves a soothing song that is as luminescent and soulful as the gorgeous illustrations that accompany her words. . . . Krommes's folk-style black-and-white etchings with touches of yellow-orange make the world of the poem an enchanted place." SLJ

To be like the sun; [by] Susan Marie Swanson; [illustrated by] Margaret Chodos-Irvine. Harcourt 2008 unp il $16

Grades: K 1 2 3   E
1. Seeds—Fiction 2. Sunflowers—Fiction
ISBN 978-0-15-205796-1; 0-15-205796-X
     LC 2006103262
A child reflects on how a small, striped gray seed eventually becomes a strong, beautiful sunflower
"The lyrical free verse is enhanced by Chodos-Irvine's colorful linocuts. The blocky yet realistic prints fit the mood perfectly and bring subtle layers of interpretation to the words." SLJ

Sweet, Melissa

Carmine; a little more red; by Melissa Sweet. Houghton Mifflin 2005 unp il $16

Grades: PreK K 1 2   E
1. Wolves—Fiction 2. Dogs—Fiction 3. Fairy tales 4. Alphabet
ISBN 0-618-38794-3   LC 2004-9212
While a little girl who loves red—and loves to dilly-dally—stops to paint a picture on the way to visit her grandmother, her dog Rufus meets a wolf and leads him directly to Granny's house.
"A fetching retelling of 'Little Red Riding Hood' that also works as an effective alphabet book. . . . The fresh and imaginative mixed-media art imitates the sketchbook of a child artist." SLJ

Tupelo rides the rails; written and illustrated by Melissa Sweet. Houghton Mifflin Company 2008 unp il $17 *

Grades: K 1 2 3   E
1. Dogs—Fiction 2. Stars—Fiction 3. Wishes—Fiction 4. Tramps—Fiction 5. Railroads—Fiction
ISBN 978-0-618-71714-9; 0-618-71714-5
     LC 2007012924
After being left by the side of a road with nothing but her favorite sock toy, Tupelo meets a pack of dogs named the BONEHEADS (The Benevolent Order of Nature's Exalted Hounds Earnest And Doggedly Sublime), led by a hobo named Garbage Pail Tex. Tupelo joins them as they are wishing on Sirius, the Dog Star, for new homes, and as they catch a passing train.
"Sweet's beautifully detailed artwork, in watercolor and mixed-media, is packed with feeling and story." Booklist

Swift, Hildegarde Hoyt, d. 1977

The little red lighthouse and the great gray bridge; by Hildegarde H. Swift and [illustrated by] Lynd Ward. Harcourt 2002 c1942 unp il $16 *

Grades: PreK K 1 2   E
1. George Washington Bridge (N.Y. and N.J.)—Fiction 2. Lighthouses—Fiction
ISBN 0-15-204571-6   LC 2001-7106
A reissue of the title first published 1942

Swift, Hildegarde Hoyt, d. 1977—*Continued*

"After the great beacon atop the . . . George Washington Bridge was installed, the little red lighthouse feared he would no longer be useful, but when an emergency arose, the little lighthouse proved that he was still important." Hodges. Books for Elem Sch Libr

"The story is written with imagination and a gift for bringing alive this little lighthouse and its troubles. . . . [Lynd Ward's] illustrations have some distinction and one in particular, the fog creeping over the river clutching at the river boats, has atmosphere, rhythm and good colour." Ont Libr Rev

Swinburne, Stephen R.

Whose shoes? a shoe for every job. Boyds Mills Press 2010 unp il $16.95
Grades: PreK   E
1. Shoes
ISBN 978-1-59078-569-0; 1-59078-569-X
Swinburne "offers a guessing game in which a photo on the right-hand page shows a person below the knees and asks, Whose shoes? A turn of the page gives the answer and a full-length photo of a ballerina (or farmer, Army National Guard soldier, post office worker, clown . . .) on the left. The facing page repeats the question Whose Shoes? with a new photo. . . . The clear, colorful photos provide plenty of talking points, while the short text flows in a conversational way." Booklist

Swope, Sam

Gotta go! Gotta go! pictures by Sue Riddle. Farrar, Straus & Giroux 2000 unp il hardcover o.p. pa $5.95
Grades: PreK K 1 2   E
1. Butterflies—Fiction 2. Caterpillars—Fiction
ISBN 0-374-32757-2; 0-374-427867-0 (pa)
LC 99-28503
Although she does not know why or how, a caterpillar who becomes a monarch butterfly is certain that she must make her way to Mexico

"The rhythm and repetition are infectious; and the pen-and-ink and watercolor illustrations, set against expanses of white space, enlarge the book remarkably." Horn Book Guide

Sydor, Colleen

Timmerman was here; illustrated by Nicolas Debon. Tundra Books 2009 unp il $19.95
Grades: K 1 2 3   E
1. Friendship—Fiction
ISBN 978-0-88776-890-3; 0-88776-890-3
"A little girl is forced to contend with a boarder, Timmerman, when he temporarily occupies the bedroom of her Granddad, who has moved to a senior citizens' home. Despite her resentment, the little girl begins to appreciate the boarder's kindness, diligence, helpfulness and soft-spoken demeanor. But Timmerman's mysterious late-night walks, carrying a spade and burlap sack, raise everyone's suspicions. . . . Debon's deep, dark, Depression-era-style paintings rendered in gouache and colored and wax pencils show one man's work ethic opposite a child's intuitive yet waning confidence in a story filled with mystery, misperceptions, doubt and friendship. . . . Readers' and listeners' predictions will abound as will discussion of how one's actions should be interpreted and noted. Provocative." Kirkus

Symes, Ruth, 1962-

Harriet dancing; by Ruth Symes; illustrated by Caroline Jayne Church. Chicken House 2008 unp il $16.99
Grades: PreK K 1   E
1. Dance—Fiction 2. Hedgehogs—Fiction
3. Butterflies—Fiction
ISBN 978-0-545-03204-9; 0-545-03204-0
LC 2007015258
Harriet the hedgehog learns that dancing is for everyone, big and small

"Church's collage illustrations are charming and vibrant, and children will love the depictions of the protagonist as she progresses through the story." SLJ

Taback, Simms, 1932-

I miss you every day; by Simms Taback. Viking Children's Books 2007 unp il $16.99 *
Grades: PreK K 1 2   E
1. Stories in rhyme 2. Postal service—Fiction
ISBN 978-0-670-06192-1   LC 2007008046
A little girl misses someone so much that she wraps herself up like a package and sends herself through the mail.

"Anyone who has ever yearned for an absent loved one will treasure this beautifully simple picture book. . . . Taback's trademark wavy outlines and simple shapes . . . add both whimsy and wide appeal." SLJ

Joseph had a little overcoat. Viking 1999 unp il music $15.99 *
Grades: K 1 2 3   E
1. Clothing and dress—Fiction 2. Jews—Fiction
ISBN 0-670-87855-3   LC 98-47721
Awarded the Caldecott Medal, 2000
A newly illustrated edition of the title first published 1977 by Random House
A very old overcoat is recycled numerous times into a variety of garments. Based on a Yiddish folk song, which is included

"Taback's inventive use of die-cut pages shows off his signature artwork. . . . This diverting, sequential story unravels as swiftly as the threads of Joseph's well-loved, patch-covered plaid coat." Publ Wkly

Simms Taback's big book of words. Blue Apple Books 2004 unp il $12.95
Grades: PreK K   E
1. Reference books 2. Vocabulary 3. Picture dictionaries
ISBN 1-59354-035-3
Illustrations and text present common toys, articles of clothing, foods and animals.

"A superb choice for emergent readers. The book's simple elegance is eye-catching. . . . The vibrant colors . . . draw children's attention to each picture." SLJ

Taback, Simms, 1932-—*Continued*

Simms Taback's city animals. Blue Apple Books 2009 unp il $12.99

Grades: PreK K 1   E

1. Animals—Fiction 2. City and town life—Fiction
ISBN 978-1-934706-52-7; 1-934706-52-3
                                    LC 2008044713

The reader is invited to guess which animal is hiding beneath fold-outs that reveal a succession of clues

"Children will love this bright, bold foldout book. . . . The text is simple and direct, with a typeface that is easy to read." SLJ

Simms Taback's Safari animals. Blue Apple Books 2008 unp il $12.95 *

Grades: PreK K   E

1. Animals—Fiction
ISBN 978-1-934706-19-0; 1-934706-19-1

"This book is boldly illustrated and cheerful, with fold-out pages that contain guessing games. On the first verso, 'Who am I?' is written in a childlike, chunky font next to a pair of huge gray legs with pink-toed feet. The facing page is black, with the words 'I have big feet' in white letters. Open it upward and a larger view of the animal is unveiled. . . . The newly opened flap is a vivid blue and contains the words, 'I have a long nose.' The page folds out once again to reveal the whole animal: . . . 'I'm an ELEPHANT!' That's the formula for six creatures—but the formula doesn't begin to describe the wonder of opening up each page into a satisfyingly enormous illustration in the master designer/illustrator's typically pleasing shapes with thick, black outlines and wildly contrasting colors." SLJ

Tafolla, Carmen, 1951-

Fiesta babies; illustrated by Amy Cordova. Tricycle Press 2010 unp il $12.99

Grades: PreK K   E

1. Stories in rhyme 2. Infants—Fiction 3. Mexican Americans—Fiction
ISBN 978-1-5824-6319-3; 1-5824-6319-0
                                    LC 2009016301

"Short lines of bouncy, rhyming text describe how several adorable, chubby babies and toddlers participate in their local Hispanic celebration. . . . The length and rhythm of the text make this book an excellent choice for toddler and preschool storytimes. Córdova once again demonstrates how her award-winning style brilliantly brings an author's words to life. Her bold acrylic colors and brisk brushstrokes capture the fiesta's energy and good cheer." SLJ

What can you do with a rebozo? by Carmen Tafolla; illustrations by Amy Cordova. Tricycle Press 2007 unp il $14.95

Grades: PreK K 1   E

1. Clothing and dress—Fiction 2. Mexican Americans—Fiction 3. Stories in rhyme
ISBN 978-1-58246-220-2; 1-58246-220-8
                                    LC 2006-39624

A Pura Belpre Illustrator Award honor book, 2009

A spunky, young Mexican American girl explains the many uses of her mother's red rebozo, or long scarf.

"Bright, textured acrylic illustrations with a strong sense of line decorate this celebration of cultural heritage. An author's note gives more information about the rebozo as well as asking readers what they might do with one." Horn Book Guide

Tafuri, Nancy

The big storm; a very soggy counting book. Simon & Schuster Books for Young Readers 2009 unp il $15.99

Grades: PreK K   E

1. Animals—Fiction 2. Storms—Fiction 3. Counting
ISBN 978-1-4169-6795-8; 1-4169-6795-8
                                    LC 2007047989

Ten animals find shelter in a hill hollow one by one, but when the storm is over, a rumbling tells them there is still danger afoot.

"This title accomplishes much with simplicity. Repetitive words . . . add tension to the plot. Dramatic poses picture the animals' wariness of the storm ahead. . . . An autumn-colored palette with orange-and-yellow leaves swirling across a spread is rendered in watercolor and watercolor pencils." SLJ

Blue Goose. Simon & Schuster Books for Young Readers 2008 unp il $15.99 *

Grades: PreK K   E

1. Animals—Fiction 2. Farm life—Fiction 3. Color—Fiction
ISBN 978-1-4169-2834-8; 1-4169-2834-0
                                    LC 2006-38368

When Farmer Gray goes away for the day, Blue Goose, Red Hen, Yellow Chick, and White Duck get together and paint their black and white farm.

"The scenes have the bold, graphic punch of murals. . . . [The] generously sized animals and pithy text extend a warm welcome to readers." Publ Wkly

The busy little squirrel; [by] Nancy Tafuri. Simon & Schuster Books for Young Readers 2007 unp il $15.99

Grades: PreK K   E

1. Squirrels—Fiction 2. Animals—Fiction 3. Autumn—Fiction
ISBN 978-0-689-87341-6; 0-689-87341-7
                                    LC 2005015520

Squirrel is too busy getting ready for winter to nibble a pumpkin with Mouse, run in the field with Dog, or otherwise play with any of the other animals

"The ink-and-watercolor pictures show squirrel's flurry of activity. . . . The basic words and large, clearly defined pictures of familiar animals are perfectly suited for preschool read-alouds." Booklist

Five little chicks. Simon & Schuster Books for Young Readers 2006 unp il $14.95 *

Grades: PreK K   E

1. Chickens—Fiction
ISBN 0-689-87342-5

Five chicks and their mother peck in the corn patch in search of breakfast.

"Created with brush pen, watercolor pencils, and ink, the gorgeous double-page spreads, in warm shades of red, yellow, and brown, manage to be both clear and fuzzy, simple and rich." Booklist

Tafuri, Nancy—*Continued*

Have you seen my duckling? Greenwillow Bks. 1984 unp il $16.99; lib bdg $17.89; pa $6.99; bd bk $6.99 *

Grades: PreK K   E

1. Ducks—Fiction
ISBN 0-688-02797-0; 0-688-02798-9 (lib bdg); 0-688-10994-2 (pa); 0-688-14899-9 (bd bk)

LC 83-17196

A Caldecott Medal honor book, 1985

"In a picture book virtually wordless except for the repeated question of the title, seven ducklings obediently cluster in their nest, while the eighth—more daring and more curious—scrambles after an errant butterfly." Horn Book

"Tafuri's artwork . . . features clean lines, generous figures, and clear, cool colors. She also adds nice detail—feathers, for instance, that you can almost feel under your hands." Booklist

Spots, feathers, and curly tails. Greenwillow Bks. 1988 unp il $16.95 *

Grades: PreK K 1 2   E

1. Domestic animals
ISBN 0-688-07536-3; 0-688-07537-1 (lib bdg)

LC 87-15638

Questions and answers highlight some outstanding characteristics of farm animals, such as a chicken's feathers and a horse's mane

"In the watercolor illustrations with black pen outline, Nancy Tafuri manages in the simplest style to give energy and personality to the animals through the angle of a head or the set of a snout. The story will provide a successful experience for both child and adult reader and is an ideal book for the beginning reader to entertain a younger sibling in a game they'll both enjoy." Horn Book

This is the farmer. Greenwillow Bks. 1994 unp il $16.99 *

Grades: PreK K 1 2   E

1. Farm life—Fiction
ISBN 0-688-09468-6

LC 92-30082

A farmer's kiss causes an amusing chain of events on the farm

"The well-defined, watercolor-and-ink double-spread illustrations are . . . of the highest quality. The brief story is rhythmic, predictable, and printed in extra-large type." SLJ

Whose chick are you? Greenwillow Books 2007 unp il $16.99; lib bdg $17.89

Grades: PreK K   E

1. Birds—Fiction 2. Swans—Fiction
ISBN 0-06-082514-6; 0-06-082515-4 (lib bdg)

Goose, Duck, Hen, Bird and the little chick, itself, cannot tell to whom a new hatchling belongs, but its mother knows.

"The artwork's close-up perspective and the combination of large type, onomatopoeia, and the clues to Little Chick's parents scattered through the pictures will draw children into the scenes." Booklist

You are special, little one. Scholastic Press 2003 unp il $16.95; bd bk $7.99 *

Grades: PreK K   E

1. Animals—Fiction
ISBN 0-439-39879-7; 0-439-68613-X (bd bk)

LC 2002-151459

A variety of baby animals ask the question, "How am I special?" and receive loving answers from their mothers and fathers

"Tafuri's colored-pencil-and-watercolor art fills the oversize pages, depicting tranquil panoramas of various animal habitats as well as plenty of cozy close-ups of parents and children snuggling. Young children will be comforted by the text's rhythmic reassurances." Booklist

Tankard, Jeremy

Grumpy Bird. Scholastic Press 2007 unp il $12.99

Grades: K 1 2 3   E

1. Birds—Fiction 2. Emotions—Fiction
ISBN 0-439-85147-5; 978-0-439-85147-3

LC 2006-03770

Feeling too grumpy to fly, Bird begins to walk and finds that his mood changes as other animals join him.

"This straightforward story is enlivened by unusual mixed-media illustrations. Each scene consists of sketches of farmland or trees, layered over photographs of real farms and trees. Cheerful flowers and stars are scribbled throughout. The animal characters are simplistic cartoons with thick black outlines and comical facial expressions." SLJ

Another title about Bird is:
Boo hoo Bird (2009)

Me hungry! Candlewick Press 2008 unp il $15.99

Grades: PreK K   E

1. Prehistoric peoples—Fiction 2. Animals—Fiction
ISBN 978-0-7636-3360-8; 0-7636-3360-7

LC 2007-35735

A little prehistoric boy decides to hunt for his own food, and makes a new friend in the process.

"Tankard's bold, thick black lines, done in ink and digital media, outline the youngster and his many choices for a snack, allowing the characters to jump off the monochromatic pages. Minimal but effective text perfectly complements the expressive prehistoric family. This energetic story comes full circle with a humorous punch line that will make all children with busy parents laugh out loud." SLJ

Tarlow, Ellen

Pinwheel days; by Ellen Tarlow; art by Gretel Parker. Star Bright Books 2007 56p il pa $6.95

Grades: K 1 2   E

1. Donkeys—Fiction 2. Squirrels—Fiction 3. Animals—Fiction 4. Friendship—Fiction
ISBN 978-1-59572-059-7 (pa); 1-59572-059-6 (pa)

In four separate stories, Pinwheel the donkey learns about friendship when his loneliness ends after meeting his "echo," a lovely picnic stems from a mistake, his rubbing on a tree seems to break it, and his best dream ever comes true

Tarlow, Ellen—*Continued*

"The four easy-to-read chapters feature abundant dialogue and humorous plots. Complementing the text, the watercolor illustrations are characterized by round figures, warm earth tones, and decorative elements such as multiple patterns." SLJ

Tarpley, Natasha, 1971-

Bippity Bop barbershop; by Natasha Anastasia Tarpley; illustrated by E.B. Lewis. Little, Brown 2002 unp il $15.95

Grades: PreK K 1 2   E

1. Barbers and barbershops—Fiction 2. African Americans—Fiction

ISBN 0-316-52284-8   LC 00-30188

"Megan Tingley books"

A story celebrating a young African-American boy's first trip to the barbershop

"Expressive watercolors showcase [the child's] curiosity, fear, and satisfaction, as well as a close father-son relationship." Horn Book Guide

Tashiro, Chisato

Five nice mice; [by] Chisato Tashiro; translated from the Japanese by Sayako Uchida; adapted by Kate Westerlund. Penguin/Minedition 2007 unp il $16.99

Grades: PreK K 1 2   E

1. Mice—Fiction 2. Frogs—Fiction 3. Music—Fiction

ISBN 978-0-698-40058-0

"After five little mice sneak into the park to hear the frog chorus, they are enthralled; then they are thrown out of the frogs-only concert. Haunted by what they have heard, the mice decide to form their own orchestra. . . . When the mice perform to wild applause, frogs in the audience join in, and then they play music together. Filled with light and color, the double-page spreads, executed in watercolor and pastels, are crowded yet clear, and they extend the story of each individual. " Booklist

Taulbert, Clifton L.

Little Cliff and the porch people; paintings by E.B. Lewis. Dial Bks. for Young Readers 1999 unp il $16.99 *

Grades: K 1 2 3   E

1. African Americans—Fiction 2. Mississippi—Fiction

ISBN 0-8037-2174-9; 0-8037-2175-7 (lib bdg)

LC 98-5503

Sent to buy special butter for Mama Pearl's candied sweet potatoes and told to get back lickety-split, Little Cliff is delayed by all his neighbors when they want to contribute their own ingredients

"The old Mississippi setting is authentic, the intergenerational relationships are realistic, and Lewis's illustrations add warmth to the simply told story." Horn Book Guide

Other titles about Little Cliff are:

Little Cliff and the cold place (2002)

Little Cliff's first day of school (2001)

Tavares, Matt

Mudball; [by] Matt Tavares. Candlewick Press 2005 unp il $15.99

Grades: K 1 2 3   E

1. Baseball—Fiction

ISBN 0-7636-2387-3   LC 2004-40671

During a rainy Minneapolis Millers baseball game in 1903, Little Andy Oyler has the chance to become a hero by hitting the shortest and muddiest home run in history

"The large-scale, softly shaded pencil drawings have plenty of motion, just right for a sports story. . . . An attractive book for baseball fans who enjoy watching small heroes triumph and don't mind a bit of nostalgia." Booklist

Taylor, Debbie A., 1955-

Sweet music in Harlem; illustrated by Frank Morrison. Lee & Low Books 2004 unp il $16.95

Grades: K 1 2 3   E

1. Jazz musicians—Fiction 2. Harlem (New York, N.Y.)—Fiction 3. African Americans—Fiction

ISBN 1-58430-165-1   LC 2003-8994

C.J., who aspires to be as great a jazz musician as his uncle, searches for Uncle Click's hat in preparation for an important photograph and inadvertently gathers some of the greatest musicians of 1950s Harlem to join in on the picture

"This dazzling tale is filled with energy, rhythm, and style from its attention-grabbing cover to its satisfying ending. . . . The acrylic illustrations make the text come alive." SLJ

Taylor, Sean

When a monster is born; [illustrated by] Nick Sharratt. Roaring Brook Press 2007 unp il $16.95

Grades: PreK K 1   E

1. Monsters—Fiction

ISBN 978-1-59643-254-3; 1-59643-254-3

LC 2006-20890

Explores the options available to a monster from the time it is born, such as becoming the scary monster under someone's bed or playing on the school basketball team.

"The words have the rhythm of a chant. . . . Sharratt's neon-toned artwork, which has the look of computer-generated collage, features a furry, round, lime-green monster, whose pink horns and buck teeth make an endearingly goofy star. Bright, funny, and interactive." Booklist

Teague, David

Franklin's big dreams; pictures by Boris Kulikov. Disney/Hyperion Books 2010 il $16.99 *

Grades: PreK K 1   E

1. Dreams—Fiction 2. Night—Fiction 3. Building—Fiction

ISBN 978-1-4231-1919-7; 1-4231-1919-3

LC 2010004520

"Teague imagines how dreams are made from the point of view of a young boy and his dog. Night after night, construction crews break into Franklin's bedroom to build train tracks, a runway, a canal; they're all

Teague, David—*Continued*

deconstructed before the break of day. . . . It's the mystery that makes this so imaginative and fresh. Kulikov's dramatic paintings freature a chiaroscruo effect; Franklin's nighttime room is portrayed in navy blues and subdued colors, while warm yellow light pours from the towering forms of the train, jet, and boat." Booklist

Teague, Mark, 1963-

Dear Mrs. LaRue; letters from obedience school; written and illustrated by Mark Teague. Scholastic Press 2002 unp il $15.95
Grades: PreK K 1 2 3   E
  1. Dogs—Fiction
  ISBN 0-439-20663-4   LC 2001-43479
Gertrude LaRue receives typewritten and paw-written letters from her dog Ike, entreating her to let him leave the Igor Brotweiler Canine Academy and come back home
"The humorous acrylic illustrations are, at times, a howl and the over-sized format is well-suited to storytelling." SLJ
Other titles about Mrs. LaRue and her dog Ike are:
Detective LaRue (2004)
LaRue for mayor (2008)

Funny Farm. Orchard Books 2009 unp il $16.99
Grades: PreK K   E
  1. Farm life—Fiction 2. Dogs—Fiction 3. Animals—Fiction
  ISBN 978-0-439-91499-4; 0-439-91499-X
                                LC 2008-02477
"When Edward, a city-slicker dog, arrives at his canine relatives' farm for a visit, Teague provides the perfect setup for this goofily sweet fish-out-of-water tale. . . . The narrative nature of the crisp oil illustrations reveals a much more entertaining version of the story than does the straightforward text. . . . Young readers will find plenty to revisit in the humorous bucolic scenes of barnyard creatures at work and play." Publ Wkly
Another title about Edward is:
Firehouse! (2010)

Pigsty. Scholastic 1994 unp il hardcover o.p. pa $6.99
Grades: PreK K 1 2 3   E
  1. Pigs—Fiction 2. Cleanliness—Fiction
  ISBN 0-590-45915-5; 0-439-59843-5 (pa)
                                LC 93-21179
When Wendell doesn't clean up his room, a whole herd of pigs comes to live with him
"Much of the tale's fun resides in Teague's quirky acrylic art. . . . Whether Wendell and his friends are jumping on the bed or playing Monopoly on the rug, their antics are rendered in the bold palette of a gleefully inventive imagination. Highly recommended for neat-freaks and mess-makers alike." Publ Wkly

Teckentrup, Britta

Big Smelly Bear; [by] Britta Teckentrup. Sterling Pub. 2007 unp il $12.95
Grades: PreK K   E
  1. Bears—Fiction 2. Cleanliness—Fiction
  ISBN 978-1-905417-37-7   LC 2006101350

Big Fluffy Bear insists that Big Smelly Bear visit the pond for a bath before she will scratch the itch he cannot reach
"This charming oversize book is accompanied by watercolor illustrations." SLJ

Grumpy cat; by Britta Teckentrup. Boxer 2008 unp il $14.95 *
Grades: PreK K   E
  1. Cats—Fiction
  ISBN 978-1-905417-69-8; 1-905417-69-1
"The frowning, brown cat with black stripes sits alone, eats alone, and is considered grumpy by other cats. . . . One stormy night a tiny, orange kitten shows up, wet and soggy. . . . The characters are appealing, the story is short and linear, and the ending is warm and satisfactory. But the highpoint is the art: graphically inspired, textured, and large in scale." Booklist

Tekavec, Heather, 1969-

Storm is coming! pictures by Margaret Spengler. Dial Bks. for Young Readers 2002 unp il $14.99
Grades: PreK K 1 2   E
  1. Storms—Fiction 2. Domestic animals—Fiction
  ISBN 0-8037-2626-0   LC 00-34622
The animals misunderstand the farmer's "Storm" warning and expect someone scary and mean
"Children will giggle over the animals' confusion and enjoy the well-paced buildup of suspense. Inviting pastel illustrations feature round, cartoonlike animals and dramatic use of perspective." Horn Book Guide

Tenzing Norbu, 1971-

Secret of the snow leopard; [by] Tenzing Norbu, Lama with Stéphane Frattini. Douglas & McIntyre 2004 unp il $16.95
Grades: 1 2 3 4   E
  1. Nepal—Fiction 2. Himalaya Mountains—Fiction
  ISBN 0-88899-544-X
Tsering, a boy from a small Nepali village, and "his stepfather accompany the village healer, who is gravely ill, on a journey to the monastery where he will seek a cure. . . . On the way home, Tsering . . . asserts his independence by climbing the dangerous pass where his father . . . lost his life. . . . Handsome earth-tone paintings, stylized and carefully composed, portray the people and animals that belong to this stark landscape. . . . The quiet authority of the artwork and the drama of the story will engage children emotionally." SLJ
Another title about Tsering is:
Himalaya (2002)

Thayer, Jane, 1904-

The popcorn dragon; written by Jane Thayer; illustrated by Lisa McCue. Morrow Junior Bks. 1989 unp il $17.99
Grades: PreK K 1 2   E
  1. Dragons—Fiction
  ISBN 0-688-08340-4   LC 88-39855
A newly illustrated edition of the title first published 1953

Thayer, Jane, 1904—*Continued*

Though his hot breath is the envy of all the other animals, a young dragon learns that showing off does not make friends

"McCue's new full-color illustrations capture the whimsical mood of the fable. The animals, although too coy, have appealing humanlike expressions which convey their envy and contempt." SLJ

The puppy who wanted a boy; illustrated by Lisa McCue. HarperCollins Pubs. 2003 unp il $14.99; lib bdg $15.89

Grades: PreK K 1 2   E

1. Dogs—Fiction 2. Christmas—Fiction

ISBN 0-06-052696-3; 0-06-052697-1 (lib bdg)

A reissue of the edition published 1986 by Morrow; story first published 1958 with different illustrations

When Petey the puppy decides that he wants a boy for Christmas, he discovers that he must go out and find one on his own

"It is the same, somewhat sentimental but certainly appealing tale that Thayer fashioned in 1958, when this was originally published; however, McCue's affectionately drawn, warmly colored illustrations go a long way toward perking up the story." Booklist

Thierry, Raphaël, 1972-

Green butterfly; a Superdog adventure; [by] Raphael Thierry. Handprint Books 2007 unp il $7.95

Grades: 2 3 4   E

1. Butterflies—Fiction 2. Dogs—Fiction

ISBN 978-1-59354-198-9; 1-59354-198-8

Original French edition, 2000; first English language edition published 2005 in the United Kingdom

"Green Butterfly alights on Superdog's nose, notices that the white pup is tied to a post, and proceeds to flutter about, flaunting his own freedom. But wise Superdog is not to be bothered; he uses his imagination and a little optimism to find flexibility in his fetters. . . . Minimal text and a subdued, mostly mauve palette draw attention to Superdog's red choker and the white butterfly's wings in spring green. . . . Children . . . will innately understand that there is more to Superdog than meets the eye and delight in uncovering the meaning in this small gem." SLJ

Thiesing, Lisa

The Aliens are coming! Dutton Children's Books 2004 32p il $13.99 *

Grades: K 1 2   E

1. Pigs—Fiction 2. Rock musicians—Fiction

ISBN 0-525-47277-0   LC 2003-19303

Peggy the pig becomes very worried when she hears that the Aliens are coming, but then she learns that they are a rock band.

"This clever tale will appeal to newly independent readers." SLJ

Other titles about Peggy are:

A dark and noisy night (2005)

The scarecrow's new clothes (2006)

The Viper (2002)

Thomas, Jan, 1958-

Can you make a scary face? Beach Lane Books 2009 unp il $12.99

Grades: PreK K 1   E

1. Imagination—Fiction 2. Ladybugs—Fiction 3. Frogs—Fiction

ISBN 978-1-4169-8581-5; 1-4169-8581-6

         LC 2008-38288

A ladybug invites the reader to play a game of "let's pretend."

"This book will have youngsters jumping, wiggling, dancing, pretending, and laughing. . . . The expressive ladybug is outlined in broad black lines and seems only inches away from readers. Adults will enjoy using this title to encourage lively activity and imaginative games. Children will love everything about it—especially the surprise ending." SLJ

The doghouse. Harcourt 2008 unp il $12.95

Grades: PreK K   E

1. Animals—Fiction 2. Fear—Fiction 3. Dogs—Fiction

ISBN 978-0-15-206533-1; 0-15-206533-4

         LC 2007038355

Cow, Pig, Duck, and Mouse are afraid to retrieve their ball when it goes into the dog's house, but when they do go in they are pleasantly surprised.

"The simple cartoon characters, scenery, and dialogue balloons are outlined in thick, bold lines. Colors are smooth and flat, with backgrounds done in bright blues, purple, and lime green. The pictures are large and distinct, and will work well with a group." SLJ

Another title about Cow, Pig, Duck, and Mouse is:

A birthday for Cow! (2008)

Rhyming dust bunnies. Atheneum Books for Young Readers 2009 unp il $12.99 *

Grades: K 1 2   E

1. Rhyme—Fiction 2. Dust—Fiction

ISBN 978-1-4169-7976-0; 1-4169-7976-X

         LC 2008-28779

As three dust bunnies, Ed, Ned, and Ted, are demonstrating how much they love to rhyme, a fourth, Bob, is trying to warn them of approaching danger.

"The simple text and rhyming game-playing make this a natural as an early reader while also offering entertaining opportunities for readers-aloud. Digitally rendered art offers coloring-book strength and simplicity." Bull Cent Child Books

Another title about the dust bunnies is:

Here comes the big, mean dust bunny! (2009)

What will Fat Cat sit on? Harcourt 2007 unp il $12.95

Grades: PreK K   E

1. Cats—Fiction 2. Animals—Fiction

ISBN 978-0-15-206051-0; 0-15-206051-0

         LC 2006-24558

A group of animals is terrified at the prospect of being sat upon by the imposing Fat Cat, until the mouse comes up with a solution that satisfies everyone.

"Thomas . . . makes this book a laugh-out-loud pas de deux between Dick-and-Jane-get-stylish typography . . . and the supremely silly visual evocation of high anxiety. . . . She renders her barnyard characters in super-saturated colors and thick, bold outlines." Publ Wkly

Thomas, Joyce Carol

I have heard of a land; illustrated by Floyd Cooper. HarperCollins Pubs. 1998 unp il hardcover o.p. pa $6.99

Grades: K 1 2 3   E
1. Oklahoma—Fiction 2. Frontier and pioneer life—Fiction 3. African Americans—Fiction
ISBN 0-06-023477-6; 0-06-023478-4 (lib bdg); 0-06-443617-9 (pa)   LC 95-48791
A Coretta Scott King honor book for illustration, 1999
"Joanna Cotler books"

Describes the joys and hardships experienced by an African-American pioneer woman who staked a claim for free land in the Oklahoma territory

"The strength and tenderness of Thomas' text are matched by Cooper's always evocative artwork." Booklist

Thomas, Patricia J., 1934-

Red sled; [by] Patricia Thomas; illustrated by Chris L. Demarest. Boyds Mills Press 2008 unp il $16.95

Grades: PreK K 1   E
1. Stories in rhyme 2. Sledding—Fiction 3. Father-son relationship—Fiction
ISBN 978-1-59078-559-1; 1-59078-559-2
LC 2007-50838

A boy and his father lift one another's spirits by going sledding on a winter's night.

"The brief text consists of easy-to-read words in rhyming pairs. . . . Bright watercolor pictures capture perfectly the downcast faces of the characters when they are stuck inside during a snowstorm, . . . their expressions of happiness and excitement during their nocturnal adventure on the red sled." SLJ

Thomas, Shelley Moore

Good night, Good Knight; pictures by Jennifer Plecas. Dutton Children's Bks. 2000 47p il (Dutton easy reader) $13.99 *

Grades: PreK K 1 2   E
1. Knights and knighthood—Fiction 2. Dragons—Fiction 3. Bedtime—Fiction
ISBN 0-525-46326-7   LC 99-28415
A Good Knight helps three little dragons who are having trouble getting to sleep.

"The short, simple, repetitive phrases are sure to capture the imaginations of young children. . . . With a palette dominated by the blues, grays, and purples of the nighttime setting, Plecas's illustrations are a wonderful complement to this endearing tale." SLJ

Other titles about the Good Knight are:
A cold winter's Good Knight (2008)
Get well, Good Knight (2002)
Happy birthday, Good Knight (2006)
Take care Good Knight (2006)

Thomassie, Tynia

Feliciana Feyra LeRoux; a Cajun tall tale; illustrated by Cat Bowman Smith. Pelican 2005 c1995 unp il $15.95

Grades: K 1 2 3   E
1. Alligators—Fiction 2. Cajuns—Fiction 3. Louisiana—Fiction
ISBN 1-58980-286-1
A reissue of the title first published 1995 by Little, Brown

"Feliciana's grandpa won't let her go alligator hunting in the Louisiana Cajun bajou. When she sneaks out, Feliciana causes fun and excitement, and even becomes a heroine." Soc Educ

This "combines breezy watercolors and a swinging text that's perfect for reading aloud. A note on Cajun culture, a glossary, and a pronunciation guide are included." Booklist

Another title about Feliciana is:
Feliciana meets d'Loup Garou (1998)

Thompson, Lauren, 1962-

The apple pie that Papa baked; illustrated by Jonathan Bean. Simon & Schuster Books for Young Readers 2007 unp il $15.99 *

Grades: PreK K 1   E
1. Apples—Fiction 2. Pies—Fiction 3. Trees—Fiction
ISBN 1-4169-1240-1; 978-1-4169-1240-8

"A pigtailed girl introduces the apple pie 'warm and sweet that Papa baked.' Then moving backward, the girl runs . . . out to the tree 'crooked and strong,' where shiny red apples are waiting to be picked. The roots 'deep and fine,' feed the tree. . . . Rain waters the roots, clouds drop the rain, the sky carries the clouds, the sun lights the sky. . . . The text is clear, and it's well matched by delightful illustrations . . . The intricately detailed art is reminiscent of the time when picture books were rarely full color." Booklist

The Christmas magic; illustrated by Jon J. Muth. Scholastic Press 2009 unp il $16.99

Grades: K 1 2 3   E
1. Magic—Fiction 2. Santa Claus—Fiction 3. Christmas—Fiction
ISBN 978-0-439-77497-0; 0-439-77497-7
LC 2008-43308

As Santa prepares for the upcoming holiday season, it is the Christmas magic that truly makes everything happen.

"Muth's haunting watercolor and pastel illustrations bring the simple story to magical life. . . . This gentle and lovely book is sheer enchantment." SLJ

How many cats? pictures by Robin Eley. Disney Hyperion Books 2009 unp il $15.99

Grades: K 1 2   E
1. Stories in rhyme 2. Cats—Fiction 3. Counting
ISBN 978-1-4231-0801-6; 1-4231-0801-9
LC 2008-46540

From zero to twenty, a house becomes filled with frolicking cats, who then leave alone or in groups

"Eley paints exuberant bundles of fun that dance and leap across the pages of Thompson's joyous and slyly math-infused counting tale. . . . Sure to be a call-and-response crowd-pleaser at any kitty-cat storytime." Kirkus

Thompson, Lauren, 1962- — *Continued*

Little Quack; pictures by Derek Anderson. Simon & Schuster Bks. for Young Readers 2003 unp il $14.95

Grades: PreK K   E
  1. Ducks—Fiction 2. Counting
  ISBN 0-689-84723-8   LC 2002-5567
One by one, four ducklings find the courage to jump into the pond and paddle with Mama Duck, until only Little Quack is left in the nest, trying to be brave

"Here's a familiar story kicked up a notch by a counting element and irresistible art. The story is reassuring and utterly straightforward. . . . The charm is in Anderson's comical, eye-commanding acrylics." Booklist

Other titles about Little Quack are:
Little Quack's bedtime (2005)
Little Quack's hide and seek (2004)
Little Quack's new friend (2006)

Polar bear night; illustrated by Stephen Savage. Scholastic Press 2004 unp il $15.95

Grades: PreK K 1 2   E
  1. Polar bear—Fiction 2. Night—Fiction
  ISBN 0-439-49524-5   LC 2003-27538
After wandering out at night to watch a magical star shower, a polar bear cub returns home to snuggle with her mother in their warm den.

"With comforting, carefully chosen words and soft pastels shading linocut prints, this book has all the elements to make it a bedtime favorite." SLJ

Wee little bunny; illustrated by John Butler. Simon & Schuster Books for Young Readers 2010 unp il $14.99

Grades: PreK   E
  1. Rabbits—Fiction 2. Animals—Fiction
  ISBN 978-1-4169-7937-1; 1-4169-7937-9
                                       LC 2008044911
A young rabbit enjoys a 'busy, dizzy' day of playing in the meadow near his home

"This sweet follow-up to *Little Chick* and *Little Lamb* is ideal for kids who like adventures, but like coming home even more." Publ Wkly

Wee little chick; by Lauren Thompson; illustrated by John Butler. Simon & Schuster Books for Young Readers 2008 unp il $14.99

Grades: PreK   E
  1. Chickens—Fiction 2. Size—Fiction 3. Animals—Fiction
  ISBN 978-1-4169-3468-4; 1-4169-3468-5
                                       LC 2007016411
When the other barnyard animals comment on how tiny the littlest chick is, the proud little one peeps louder, stands taller, and runs faster than any of them

"Thompson's simple, rhythmic text moves the action along at a brisk, even pace. Butler's bright acrylic and pencil illustrations artistically portray the story's springtime mood and warmhearted tone." SLJ

Wee little lamb; by Lauren Thompson; illustrated by John Butler. Simon & Schuster Books for Young Readers 2009 unp il $14.99

Grades: PreK   E
  1. Sheep—Fiction 2. Animals—Fiction
  ISBN 978-1-4169-3469-1; 1-4169-3469-3
                                       LC 2008004428
A little, newborn lamb, too shy to say hello to the rabbit or sing with the robin, is finally drawn out by a tiny fieldmouse

"This gentle, reassuring tale tells youngsters that they can explore their world at their own speed. The eye-catching spreads and simple language make this book a natural for toddler storytime." SLJ

Thomson, Bill, 1963-
  Chalk. Marshall Cavendish Children 2010 unp il $15.99 *

Grades: PreK K 1 2   E
  1. Drawing—Fiction 2. Stories without words
  ISBN 978-0-7614-5526-4; 0-7614-5526-4
                                       LC 2009014141
A wordless picture book about three children who go to a park on a rainy day, find some chalk, and draw pictures that come to life.

"With eye-catching, realistic illustrations, clever details, and some dramatic suspense, this wordless picture book offers a fresh take on the drawings-come-to-life theme. . . . Vibrant acrylic and colored-pencil illustrations, rendered with intricate precision, nearly leap off the page." Booklist

Thomson, Sarah L.
  Imagine a night; paintings by Rob Gonsalves; text by Sarah L. Thomson. Atheneum Books for Young Readers 2003 unp il $16.95

Grades: 2 3 4 5 6   E
  1. Night—Fiction 2. Imagination—Fiction
  ISBN 0-689-85218-5   LC 2002-10718
Presents a night when imagination takes over and gravity does not work quite as expected.

"Magical realism permeates Gonsalves's large acrylic paintings, and they are essential to the lyrical text. . . . This is a fascinating foray into the imagination and a fine discussion starter for older children." SLJ

Other titles in this series are:
Imagine a day (2005)
Imagine a place (2008)

Pirates, ho! by Sarah L. Thomson; illustrated by Stephen Gilpin. Marshall Cavendish 2008 unp il $14.99

Grades: K 1 2   E
  1. Pirates—Fiction 2. Stories in rhyme
  ISBN 978-0-7614-5435-9; 0-7614-5435-7
                                       LC 2007-29792
Pirates Peg-Leg Tom, Angus Black, Dreadful Nell, and One-Eyed Jack chase ships on the high seas, tell ghost stories, and fall asleep counting gold instead of sheep.

"Gilpin's wacky cartoons have a retro, take-no-prisoners abandon. . . . This funny, fabulously illustrated rhyme is certainly worth adding." SLJ

Thomson, Sarah L.—*Continued*

The sound of colors; a journey of imagination; [by] Jimmy Liao; English text adapted by Sarah L. Thomson. Little, Brown 2006 unp il $16.99

Grades: K 1 2 3 4   E
    1. Blind—Fiction
    ISBN 0-316-93992-7   LC 2004-025100

"A young girl's eyesight began slipping away a year ago. With her white cane in hand, she ventures on a subway trip using her imagination to take herself and readers on a journey. . . . Poetic, lyrical language is used in this translation from Chinese. The girl is strong and admirable. . . . Liao's watercolor illustrations invite readers to take time, slow down, and pore over the details." SLJ

Thong, Roseanne

Fly free! illustrated by Eujin Kim Neilan. Boyds Mills Press 2010 unp il $17.95

Grades: 3 4 5   E
    1. Kindness—Fiction 2. Conduct of life—Fiction 3. Buddhism—Fiction 4. Vietnam—Fiction
    ISBN 978-1-59078-550-8; 1-59078-550-9
                            LC 2009020248

When Mai feeds the caged birds at a Buddhist temple in Vietnam, her simple act of kindness starts a chain of thoughtful acts that ultimately comes back to her. Includes author's note explaining the Buddhist concepts of karma and samsara, or the wheel of life.

"The lesson of this simple story, that helping others is helpful to you, is universal. The muted and warm watercolor-on-board illustrations glow with gold, orange, red, and brown tones." SLJ

One is a drummer; written by Roseanne Thong; illustrated by Grace Lin. Chronicle Books 2004 unp il $14.95; pa $6.99

Grades: PreK K 1 2   E
    1. Counting 2. Chinese Americans—Fiction 3. Stories in rhyme
    ISBN 0-8118-3772-6; 0-8118-6482-4 (pa)
                            LC 2003-10810

A young girl numbers her discoveries in the world around her, from one dragon boat to four mahjong players to ten bamboo stalks

"The rhymes provide a pleasing framework for the book, and Lin's striking artwork gives it great visual appeal. . . . An appealing counting book, particularly for Chinese American children who want to learn a little about their heritage." Booklist

Red is a dragon; a book of colors; written by Roseanne Thong; illustrated by Grace Lin. Chronicle Bks. 2001 unp il hardcover o.p. pa $6.99

Grades: PreK K 1 2   E
    1. Color 2. Chinese Americans—Fiction 3. Stories in rhyme
    ISBN 0-8118-3177-9; 0-8118-6481-2 (pa)
                            LC 2001-93

A Chinese American girl provides rhyming descriptions of the great variety of colors she sees around her, from the red of a dragon, firecrackers, and lychees to the brown of her teddy bear

"Lin's simply drawn gouache illustrations, outlined in black, fairly explode with color. . . . This is a must-have for libraries serving Chinese American populations, and it will be a welcome addition to preschool story hours for children of all backgrounds." Booklist

Round is a mooncake; a book of shapes; written by Roseanne Thong; illustrated by Grace Lin. Chronicle Books 2000 unp il $15.99

Grades: PreK K 1 2   E
    1. Shape 2. Chinese Americans—Fiction 3. Stories in rhyme
    ISBN 0-8118-2676-7   LC 99-50852

As a little girl discovers things round, square, and rectangular in her urban neighborhood, she is reminded of her Chinese American culture

"Lin's gouache paintings are bright and arresting, presenting scenes that have an interest beyond shape identification." Booklist

Thurber, James, 1894-1961

Many moons; illustrated by Louis Slobodkin. Harcourt Brace Jovanovich 1943 unp il $17; pa $7 *

Grades: 1 2 3 4   E
    1. Fairy tales 2. Princesses—Fiction 3. Moon—Fiction
    ISBN 0-15-251873-8; 0-15-656980-9 (pa)
    Awarded the Caldecott Medal, 1944

This is "the story of a little princess who fell ill of a surfeit of raspberry tarts and would get well only if she could have the moon." Booklist

"Louis Slobodkin's pictures float on the pages in four colors: black and white cannot represent them. They are the substance of dreams . . . the long thoughts little children, and some adults wise as they, have about life." N Y Her Trib Books

Many moons; illustrated by Marc Simont. Harcourt Brace Jovanovich 1990 unp il $17 *

Grades: 1 2 3 4   E
    1. Fairy tales 2. Princesses—Fiction 3. Moon—Fiction
    ISBN 0-15-251872-X   LC 89-36465

A newly illustrated edition of the title first published 1943

Though many try, only the court jester is able to fulfill Princess Lenore's wish for the moon.

"Simont proves a noble successor to Louis Slobodkin, and his buoyant watercolors, full of poignancy and subtle merriment, more than do justice to Thurber's beloved tale. . . . Even staunch traditionalists will find it hard to resist this new version." Publ Wkly

Tidholm, Anna-Clara, 1946-

Knock! knock! adaptation by MaryChris Bradley. MacKenzie Smiles 2009 unp il $9.95

Grades: PreK   E
    1. Doors—Fiction 2. Animals—Fiction 3. Color—Fiction 4. Stories in rhyme
    ISBN 978-0-9815761-6-9; 0-9815761-6-8

"Young children are invited to knock on and then enter a succession of different colored doors. Behind the full-page panels are rooms filled with people or animals performing such simple daily actions as playing, eating, and, in the end, snoring. . . . Each color is introduced

Tidholm, Anna-Clara, 1946-—*Continued*
with a rhyming couplet. . . . Little hands will love turning the pages to see a cozy family of rabbits around a kitchen table, silly monkeys engaged in a pillow fight, and bears brushing their teeth. . . . The charming story offers an excellent rhythm and rhyme scheme, a review of colors, bright and playful cartoon illustrations, and an opportunity for listener participation." SLJ

Tierney, Fiona
Lion's lunch? illustrated by Margaret Chamberlain. Chicken House 2010 unp il $17.99
Grades: K 1 2 3   E
   1. Lions—Fiction 2. Animals—Fiction 3. Drawing—Fiction
ISBN 978-0-545-17691-0; 0-545-17691-3
                            LC 2009-08267
When Lion comes upon Sarah walking in the jungle, he threatens to eat her unless she shows that she can do something none of the other animals can do.
   "Vibrant, brightly colored illustrations of the lively animals and cheerful child fill every bit of space on the spreads and are sure to engage readers. This clever tale of courage and confidence teaches an important life lesson in a fun way." SLJ

Tillman, Nancy
On the night you were born. Feiwel & Friends 2006 unp il $16.95
Grades: K 1 2   E
   1. Childbirth—Fiction 2. Nature—Fiction 3. Stories in rhyme
ISBN 0-312-34606-9
First published 2005 by Darling Press
The moon, wind, rain, and a variety of animals celebrate the special occasion that is the birth of a child.
   Tillman's "writing has the authenticity of whispered conversation. . . . The pictures subtly radiate golden glints of moonlight, and her almost sculptural rendering style gives her characters a hefty physicality that counterbalances the ethereal sentiments being expressed." Publ Wkly

The spirit of Christmas. Feiwel and Friends 2009 unp il $16.99
Grades: PreK K 1 2   E
   1. Stories in rhyme 2. Christmas—Fiction
ISBN 978-0-312-54965-7; 0-312-54965-2
                            LC 2008-48139
Despite the arrival of the Spirit of Christmas, who brings all sorts of trimmings and reminders of seasonal joys, something is still lacking.
   "Realism and fantasy are satisfyingly paired to bring the mixed-media illustrations of treasured holiday scenes to life. . . . A beautiful and timeless book." SLJ

Timberlake, Amy
The dirty cowboy; pictures by Adam Rex. Farrar, Straus & Giroux 2003 unp il $16
Grades: K 1 2 3   E
   1. Cowhands—Fiction 2. Dogs—Fiction
ISBN 0-374-31791-7   LC 2001-53224

Telling his faithful dog to make sure nobody touches his clothes but him, a cowboy jumps into a New Mexico river for a bath, not realizing just how much the scrubbing will change his scent
   "Told in descriptive language that rolls off the tongue, this story makes the most of a humorous situation. . . . The paintings have a gritty, sinewy look that matches the earthy tone of the tale." SLJ

Timmers, Leo, 1970-
Who is driving? [by] Leo Timmers. Bloomsbury Children's Books 2007 unp il $12.95
Grades: PreK K   E
   1. Vehicles—Fiction 2. Animals—Fiction
ISBN 978-1-59990-021-6; 1-59990-021-1
                            LC 2006009541
Easy-to-read text invites the reader to guess which animal is driving each of seven vehicles based on how they are dressed, then reveals their destinations and the vehicles' sounds
   "The vivid acrylic illustrations in primary colors have a three-dimensional look and will delight toddlers." SLJ

Tinkham, Kelly
Hair for Mama; [by] Kelly A. Tinkham; illustrated by Amy June Bates. Dial Books for Young Readers 2007 unp il $16.99
Grades: K 1 2 3   E
   1. Cancer—Fiction 2. Hair—Fiction 3. Mother-son relationship—Fiction 4. African Americans—Fiction
ISBN 0-8037-2955-3; 978-0-8037-2955-1
                            LC 2005-10621
When Marcus's mother has chemotherapy for her cancer and loses her hair, he tries to find new hair for her to make her well again.
   "This is a beautifully written story about an African-American family dealing with cancer. . . . The lovely watercolor illustrations fit the text well, using gold, brown, orange, and green tones to show a family going through tough times together." SLJ

Titherington, Jeanne, 1951-
Pumpkin, pumpkin. Greenwillow Bks. 1986 23p il $16.99; pa $6.99
Grades: PreK K 1 2   E
   1. Gardening—Fiction 2. Pumpkin—Fiction
ISBN 0-688-05695-4; 0-688-09930-0 (pa)
                            LC 84-25334
Jamie "plants a seed, then grows and harvests a pumpkin from which he saves seeds for next year. The large, detailed drawings capture Jamie's anticipation and pleasure just right. . . . Nonreaders can easily follow the story in pictures alone. Very large, clear print on facing pages makes the simple narrative inviting for beginning readers, too." SLJ

Tobin, Jim, 1956-
Sue MacDonald had a book; illustrated by Dave Coverly. Holt & Co. 2009 unp il $16.95
Grades: K 1 2   E
   1. Books and reading—Fiction 2. Alphabet—Fiction
ISBN 978-0-8050-8766-6; 0-8050-8766-4
   "Christy Ottaviano books"

Tobin, Jim, 1956-—*Continued*

"This lively grammar-related adventure is a sing-along to the tune of 'Old MacDonald Had a Farm' with the repeated refrain, 'AEIOU.' Sue MacDonald has a book called My Farm by O. MacDonald but can no longer read it after the vowels escape. . . . Done in vivid colors, the ink-and-watercolor illustrations feature high-energy cartoon figures. . . . This educational romp . . . is a strong choice for classroom and library collections." SLJ

Tolman, Marije, 1976-

The tree house; [by] Marije Tolman & Ronald Tolman. Lemniscaat unp il $17.95

Grades: PreK K 1   E

1. Animals—Fiction 2. Stories without words

ISBN 978-1-59078-806-6; 1-59078-806-0

Original Dutch edition 2009

"A wordless picture book about an elaborate wooden structure in the tree. Three stories tall, it soaks up the water surrounding its base as animals inhabit its various nooks and crannies. Bears, peacocks, and owls, and a hippo all find different ways to amuse themselves while up so high. . . . Soft pastel spreads allow readers to see all the activity in and around the tree. . . . Children will gaze in wonder at this tree house. . . . This oversize picture book celebrates acceptance of others and the splendor of nature." SLJ

Tonatiuh, Duncan

Dear Primo; a letter to my cousin. Abrams 2010 unp il $15.95

Grades: 1 2 3   E

1. Cousins—Fiction 2. Mexican Americans—Fiction 3. Mexico—Fiction 4. Country life—Fiction 5. City and town life—Fiction

ISBN 978-0-81093-872-4; 0-81093-872-3

Two cousins, one in Mexico and one in New York City, write to each other and learn that even though their daily lives differ, at heart the boys are very similar.

"The digitally enhanced collage illustrations are based on traditional Mixtec art, and show the characters posed in profile in simply composed scenes. This useful method of comparing and contrasting can serve as a fine general introduction to contemporary rural life in Mexico, while it also demonstrates the fun of having a pen pal and reinforces the sense that kids around the world are more alike than different." Booklist

Torrey, Rich

Almost. HarperCollinsPublishers 2009 unp il $17.99; lib bdg $18.89

Grades: PreK K   E

1. Growth—Fiction

ISBN 978-0-06-156166-5; 0-06-156166-5; 978-0-06-156167-2 (lib bdg); 0-06-156167-3 (lib bdg)

LC 2008011724

Companion to: Why? (2010)

Almost six-year-old Jack lists all the ways in which he is almost a grown-up.

"The large, cartoonlike spreads have plenty of pleasing color and detail, and expand on the simple text. . . . This simple story addresses both the desire of children to be older and sibling rivalry. It's sure to be a hit at storytime." SLJ

Tougas, Chris

Art's supplies; by Chris Tougas. Orca Book Publishers 2008 unp il $19.95

Grades: 1 2 3   E

1. Art—Fiction

ISBN 978-1-55143-920-4; 1-55143-920-4

"Bright colors, heavy doses of humor, and puns to make readers groan fill the pages as a boy's art supplies prepare for a personality-plus party. . . . Art's endearing, off-centered features combine with google-eyed markers, crayons, boxes, brushes, tapes, scissors, and glue. . . . This lively title is sure to be a favorite of youngsters learning to appreciate both subtle humor and engaging cartoon art." SLJ

Townsend, Michael, 1981-

Billy Tartle in Say Cheese! Alfred A. Knopf 2007 unp il $15.99; lib bdg $18.99

Grades: K 1 2 3   E

1. Photography—Fiction 2. School stories

ISBN 978-0-375-83932-0; 0-375-83932-1; 978-0-375-93932-7 (lib bdg); 0-375-93932-6 (lib bdg)

LC 2006-24354

Billy is determined to find a way to make his school picture day less boring than usual.

The story "unfolds in comic-strip panels that effectively juggle their multitude of elements and palette of high-voltage colors with strategic design. Billy's . . . adventurous take on reality fits the comic-strip medium perfectly." Bull Cent Child Books

Trachtenberg, Stanley

The Elevator Man; illustrated by Paul Cox. Eerdmans Books for Young Readers 2009 unp il $18

Grades: PreK K 1   E

1. Elevators—Fiction 2. Apartment houses—Fiction

ISBN 978-0-8028-5315-8; 0-8028-5315-3

LC 2008-31737

When the elevator in a building in the 1950s is modernized, a young resident misses the operator

"Rich, appealing illustrations sketch the characters in broad, quick strokes of black filled in with warm golds, blues, greens, and maroons, against the backdrop of the building's ongoing activities." SLJ

Trapani, Iza

Haunted party. Charlesbridge 2009 unp il lib bdg $15.95; pa $7.95

Grades: PreK K 1 2   E

1. Stories in rhyme 2. Halloween—Fiction 3. Parties—Fiction 4. Supernatural—Fiction 5. Ghost stories 6. Counting

ISBN 978-1-58089-246-9 (lib bdg); 1-58089-246-9 (lib bdg); 978-1-58089-247-6 (pa); 1-58089-247-7 (pa)

LC 2008025330

In this counting book that introduces the numbers from one to ten, a ghost and his supernatural friends have a party on Halloween night.

This is a "rollicking Halloween tale. . . . Rhyming stanzas build steadily then shrink to single lines, adding to the guests' speedy departure. Humor abounds . . . in the watercolor, colored-pencil, and ink illustrations." Horn Book Guide

Tresselt, Alvin R., 1916-2000

Hide and seek fog; by Alvin Tresselt; illustrated by Roger Duvoisin. Lothrop, Lee & Shepard Bks. 1965 unp il lib bdg $18.89; pa $6.99

Grades: PreK K 1   E

1. Fog

ISBN 0-688-51169-4 (lib bdg); 0-688-07813-3 (pa)

A Caldecott Medal honor book, 1966

"This is . . . a mood picture book . . . describing a fog which rolls in from the sea to veil an Atlantic seacoast village for three days. The beautiful paintings . . . and the brief, poetic text sensitively and effectively evoke the atmosphere of the 'worst fog in twenty years' and depict the reactions of children and grown-ups to it." Booklist

White snow, bright snow; by Alvin Tresselt; illustrated by Roger Duvoisin. Lothrop, Lee & Shepard Bks. 1988 c1947 unp il $17.99; lib bdg $18.89; pa $6.99 *

Grades: PreK K 1   E

1. Snow—Fiction

ISBN 0-688-41161-4; 0-688-51161-9 (lib bdg); 0-688-08294-7 (pa)   LC 88-10018

Awarded the Caldecott Medal, 1948

A reissue of the title first published 1947

When it begins to look, feel, and smell like snow, everyone prepares for a winter blizzard

Trewin, Trudie

I lost my kisses; [by] Trudie Trewin; illustrations by Nick Bland. Scholastic 2008 32p il $14.99

Grades: PreK K   E

1. Kissing—Fiction 2. Lost and found possessions—Fiction

ISBN 0-545-05557-1; 978-0-545-05557-4

Matilda Rose loves to kiss hello, goodbye, good morning, and goodnight, but on the day her father is to return from a trip, she cannot find her kisses anywhere, despite knowing how they feel, taste, and sound.

"Bland's striking black-and-white pencil illustrations have splashes of watercolor highlighting the wide-eyed cow's polka-dotted tights as she searches high and low. . . . Matilda Rose has a whimsical charm." SLJ

Trivizas, Eugene, 1946-

The three little wolves and the big bad pig; illustrated by Helen Oxenbury. Margaret K. McElderry Bks. 1993 unp il $18.99; pa $7.99

Grades: PreK K 1 2   E

1. Pigs—Fiction 2. Wolves—Fiction

ISBN 0-689-50569-8; 0-689-81528-X (pa)

LC 92-24829

"In this reverse of 'The Three Little Pigs' the wolves build with cement, barbed wire and reinforced chains. In response, the 'big bad pig' uses a sledgehammer, pneumatic drill and dynamite." Child Book Rev Serv

"Trivizas laces the text with funny, clever touches. . . . Oxenbury's watercolors capture the story's broad humor and add a wealth of supplementary details, with exquisite renderings of the wolves' comic temerity and the pig's bellicose stances." Publ Wkly

Trottier, Maxine

The paint box; [illustrations by] Stella East. Fitzhenry & Whiteside 2003 32p il $16.95; pa $8.95

Grades: 2 3 4   E

1. Tintoretto, Marietta, d. 1590—Fiction 2. Artists—Fiction 3. Venice (Italy)—Fiction

ISBN 1-55041-801-7; 1-55041-808-4 (pa)

LC 2003-464840

"'Long ago in Venice there was a girl named Marietta who loved to paint. She was the daughter of the great artist Tintoretto.' With her father's help, she disguises herself as a boy in order to explore the art world of Venice. . . . Marietta befriends an enslaved cabin boy and they spend their days sketching and exploring the city, and telling one another about their lives. When it is time for Piero's owner to leave the city, Marietta helps him escape and return to his family. This poignant tale has its roots in historical fact. . . . Trottier's fictional story about Marietta and her friend seems plausible, due in part to her descriptive and expressive writing style. East's painterly illustrations are magnificent. Each spread captures the feeling of Renaissance Venice and supports the accompanying text." SLJ

Tryon, Leslie

Albert's birthday; written and illustrated by Leslie Tryon. Atheneum Bks. for Young Readers 1999 unp il $16; pa $6.99

Grades: PreK K 1 2   E

1. Birthdays—Fiction 2. Animals—Fiction

ISBN 0-689-82296-0; 0-689-85251-7 (pa)

LC 98-36621

Patsy Pig plans a surprise birthday party for her friend Albert, giving careful instructions to all their friends, but she forgets to invite the guest of honor

"The prose is personable and engaging, and colorful, exquisitely detailed illustrations portray the animal cast in such familiar human settings as a classroom and a town." Booklist

Other titles about Albert are:

Albert's alphabet (1991)

Albert's ballgame (1996)

Albert's Christmas (1997)

Albert's field trip (1993)

Albert's Halloween (1998)

Albert's play (1992)

Albert's Thanksgiving (1994)

Tseng, Kevin, 1973-

Ned's new home. Tricycle Press 2009 unp il $14.99

Grades: PreK K 1   E

1. Worms—Fiction 2. Fruit—Fiction 3. Home—Fiction

ISBN 978-1-58246-297-4; 1-58246-297-6

LC 2008-42385

A worm tries out a variety of new homes when the apple he has been living in starts to rot, but none—from a lemon to a watermelon—is satisfactory.

"The cartoon illustrations are filled with warm colors and comic touches. Endpapers depict the life cycle of the apple from seed to fruit and back to seed. This reassuring tale will be appreciated by the read-aloud crowd while also supplying a subtle lesson in ecology." SLJ

Tucker, Kathy

The seven Chinese sisters; written by Kathy Tucker; illustrated by Grace Lin. Whitman, A. 2003 unp il $15.95; pa $6.99

Grades: K 1 2 3   E

1. Sisters—Fiction 2. Dragons—Fiction 3. China—Fiction

ISBN 0-8075-7309-4; 0-8075-7310-5 (pa)

LC 2002-11330

When a dragon snatches the youngest of seven talented Chinese sisters, the other six come to her rescue

Lin "expertly captures the drama and humor of the story with delightful paintings that reveal lovely Chinese landscapes and a quirky, not-too-scary dragon. A wonderful read-aloud." Booklist

Tudor, Tasha, 1915-2008

1 is one. Simon & Schuster Bks. for Young Readers 2000 unp il $16

Grades: PreK K 1 2   E

1. Counting

ISBN 0-689-82843-8   LC 99-31290

A Caldecott Medal honor book, 1957

A reissue of the title first published 1956 by Oxford University Press

"The author-artist has with characteristic charming quaintness written and illustrated a counting book. Delicately tinted, decoratively bordered pictures and rhyming lines of text count from one to twenty." Booklist

Turner, Ann Warren, 1945-

Dust for dinner; story by Ann Turner; pictures by Robert Barrett. HarperCollins Pubs. 1995 64p il (I can read book) hardcover o.p. pa $3.99 *

Grades: K 1 2 3   E

1. Great Depression, 1929-1939—Fiction 2. Family life—Fiction 3. Farm life—Fiction

ISBN 0-06-023377-X (lib bdg); 0-06-444225-X (pa)

LC 93-34634

Jake narrates the story of his family's life in the Oklahoma dust bowl and the journey from their ravaged farm to California during the Great Depression

"Turner takes a sad episode in history and fashions it into a story that has some depth as well as some drama. . . . Realistic, nicely executed illustrations decorate every page." Booklist

Turner, Pamela S.

Hachiko; written by Pamela S. Turner; illustrated by Yan Nascimbene. Houghton Mifflin 2004 unp il $15 *

Grades: K 1 2 3   E

1. Dogs—Fiction 2. Japan—Fiction

ISBN 0-618-14094-8   LC 2002-155546

This "picture book pays tribute to one of the world's lesser-known animal heroes: Hachiko, a dog who kept vigil for nearly 10 years at a Tokyo train station, waiting for his deceased master to return from work. Turner unfolds this poignant true story in the natural, unaffected voice of Kentaro, a fictional little boy, who wonders at the dog's unswerving devotion. Unobtrusive details evoke a sense of place . . . as does Nascimbene's spare line-and-watercolor artwork, reminiscent of Japanese woodblock prints. . . . This will resonate with any child who has loved a dog and been loved in return." Booklist

Turner-Denstaedt, Melanie, 1963-2007

The hat that wore Clara B.; pictures by Frank Morrison. Farrar, Straus & Giroux 2009 unp il $16.95

Grades: K 1 2   E

1. Hats—Fiction 2. Grandmothers—Fiction 3. African Americans—Fiction

ISBN 978-0-374-32794-1; 0-374-32794-7

LC 2006-47606

In church on Mothers' Sunday when all the older ladies dress in white and wear their most beautiful hats, Clara B., sitting in the pew behind her grandmother and admiring her every move, determines to find a way to wear her grandmother's hat.

"Morrison's large and expressive paintings are suffused with warmth and reflect the text beautifully. This is a wonderful family story that celebrates the bond between generations." SLJ

Uchida, Yoshiko, 1921-1992

The bracelet; story by Yoshiko Uchida; illustrated by Joanna Yardley. Philomel Bks. 1993 unp il $17.99; pa $6.99

Grades: K 1 2 3   E

1. Japanese Americans—Evacuation and relocation, 1942-1945—Fiction 2. World War, 1939-1945—Fiction 3. Friendship—Fiction

ISBN 0-399-22503-X; 0-698-11390-X (pa)

LC 92-26196

Emi, a Japanese American in the second grade, is sent with her family to an internment camp during World War II, but the loss of the bracelet her best friend has given her proves that she does not need a physical reminder of that friendship

This "is a gentle, honest introduction to the treatment of the Japanese-Americans during the war, and Yardley's delicate pencil-and-watercolor paintings are cleanly drawn and richly colored." Bull Cent Child Books

Udry, Janice May

A tree is nice; pictures by Marc Simont. Harper & Row 1956 unp il $17.99; lib bdg $18.89; pa $6.99 *

Grades: PreK K 1 2   E

1. Trees—Fiction

ISBN 0-06-026155-2; 0-06-026156-0 (lib bdg); 0-06-443147-9 (pa)

Awarded the Caldecott Medal, 1957

"In childlike terms and in enticing pictures, colored and black and white, author and artist set forth reasons why trees are nice to have around—trees fill up the sky, they make everything beautiful, cats get away from dogs in them, leaves come down and can be played in, and trees are nice to climb in, to hang a swing in, or to plant. A picture book sure to please young children." Booklist

Uegaki, Chieri

Rosie and Buttercup; written by Chieri Uegaki; illustrated by Stéphane Jorisch. Kids Can Press 2008 unp il $17.95

Grades: PreK K 1 2   E

1. Sisters—Fiction

ISBN 978-1-55337-997-3

"At first Rosie's perfect life seems even more perfect when little sister Buttercup arrives. . . . In time, Rosie becomes disenchanted and gives Buttercup away—to her sitter, Oxford. . . . Predictably, she is soon sorry. . . . Uegaki's assured text assumes an intelligent reader. . . . Jorisch's watercolor illustrations, uncluttered but dense with patterns, are crisp against generous fields of white space." Publ Wkly

Suki's kimono; written by Chieri Uegaki; illustrated by Stephane Jorisch. Kids Can Press 2003 unp il hardcover o.p. pa $7.95

Grades: PreK K 1 2   E

ISBN 1-55337-084-8; 1-55337-752-4 (pa)

LC 2003-495264

"On her first day of first grade [Suki] chooses to wear her beloved Japanese kimono to school, despite the objections of her older sisters and the initial laughter of other children on the playground. . . . Her day ends in triumph, with her teacher and classmates won over by her impromptu dance performance. . . . This is an appealing story of courage and independence. Delicate, playful watercolor-and-ink illustrations perfectly capture the child's neighborhood and the characters' facial expressions." SLJ

Uhlberg, Myron

Dad, Jackie, and me; illustrated by Colin Bootman. Peachtree Publishers 2005 unp il $16.95

Grades: K 1 2 3   E

1. Robinson, Jackie, 1919-1972—Fiction 2. Deaf—Fiction 3. Father-son relationship—Fiction 4. Baseball—Fiction 5. Brooklyn (New York, N.Y.)—Fiction

ISBN 1-56145-329-3   LC 2004-16711

In Brooklyn, New York, in 1947, a boy learns about discrimination and tolerance as he and his deaf father share their enthusiasm over baseball and the Dodgers' first baseman, Jackie Robinson.

"Bootman's lovely watercolor paintings add detail and wistful nostalgia. . . . [Readers] will appreciate the story's insightful treatment of deafness as viewed through the eyes of a child." SLJ

Ulmer, Wendy K., 1950-

A isn't for fox; an isn't alphabet; written by Wendy K. Ulmer; illustrated by Laura Knorr. Sleeping Bear Press 2008 unp il $16.95

Grades: PreK K   E

1. Alphabet

ISBN 978-1-58536-319-3; 1-58536-319-7

LC 2007006436

"This book points out first what each letter of the alphabet is not for and then gives an example of a word that does begin with the letter." Publisher's note

"Though the entertaining non-examples show an ap-

preciation for the audience's sense of the silly, Knorr's charming paintings of winking cats, smiling jellyfish, trumpeting lions, and pillow-fighting llamas are worth the purchase price alone." SLJ

Underwood, Deborah, 1962-

A balloon for Isabel; illustrations by Laura Rankin. Greenwillow Books 2010 unp il $16.99

Grades: K 1 2   E

1. Porcupines—Fiction 2. Balloons—Fiction 3. School stories 4. Candy—Fiction

ISBN 978-0-06-177987-9; 0-06-177987-3

LC 2009018759

As graduation day approaches, Isabel tries to convince her teacher that she and Walter, both porcupines, should receive balloons on the big day just like the other children.

"Illustrations full of color and personality add to the story's depth and appeal. Authentic dialogue, a touch of humor, and Isabel's ingenious invention make this title of desire and determination a keeper." SLJ

Granny Gomez & Jigsaw; illustrated by Scott Magoon. Disney Hyperion Books 2009 unp il $16.99

Grades: PreK K 1 2   E

1. Pigs—Fiction 2. Pets—Fiction

ISBN 978-0-7868-5216-1; 0-7868-5216-X

LC 2008-46225

Granny Gomez's pet pig grows too big to live in the house, so she builds him his own barn but discovers that she is lonely without him.

"Colorful, cartoon-style illustrations ratchet up the laughs with comic details . . . but are equally endearing at other times. Jigsaw's floppy ears and lopsided grin are irresistible, as is Granny's spunk, in humorous contrast with her conventional, demure appearance (including a tidy gray bun)—further proof that friends can come in all kinds of packages." Publ Wkly

The quiet book; illustrated by Renata Liwska. Houghton Mifflin Books for Children 2010 unp il $12.95 *

Grades: PreK K   E

1. Noise—Fiction 2. Animals—Fiction

ISBN 978-0-547-21567-9; 0-547-21567-3

From the quiet of being the first one awake in the morning to "sweet dreams quiet" when the last light is turned off, simple text explores the many kinds of quiet that can exist during the day.

"The soft, matte feel of the illustrations, created with pencil, are digitally enhanced, and are priceless. The animals' facial expressions and body language are endearing. . . . All of the scenarios are child-centric and realistic." SLJ

Ungerer, Tomi, 1931-

Crictor. Harper & Row 1958 32p il $17.99; pa $6.99 *

Grades: PreK K 1 2   E

1. Snakes—Fiction

ISBN 0-06-026180-3; 0-06-443044-8 (pa)

A story "about the boa constrictor that was sent to Madame Bodot, who lived and taught school in a little

Ungerer, Tomi, 1931-—*Continued*

French town. . . . The boys used him for a slide and the girls for a jump-rope. When Crictor captured a burglar by coiling around him until the police came, he was awarded impressive tokens of esteem and affection of the townspeople. Engaging line drawings echo the restrained and elegant absurdities of the text." Bull Cent Child Books

Urban, Linda

Mouse was mad; illustrated by Henry Cole. Harcourt Children's Books 2009 unp il $16
Grades: PreK K 1 2   E
  1. Anger—Fiction 2. Mice—Fiction 3. Animals—Fiction
  ISBN 978-0-15-205337-6; 0-15-205337-9
                      LC 2007045081
Mouse struggles to find the right way to express his anger, modeling the behavior of Hare, Bear, Hedgehog, and Bobcat, only to discover that his own way may be the best way of all.
"Through playful language and expressive watercolors with colored pencil and ink, this story about anger management proves to be both entertaining and therapeutic." SLJ

Urbanovic, Jackie

Duck at the door. HarperCollins 2007 unp il $16.99; lib bdg $17.89
Grades: PreK K 1 2   E
  1. Ducks—Fiction 2. Winter—Fiction 3. Animals—Fiction
  ISBN 0-06-121438-8; 0-06-121439-6 (lib bdg)
When Max the duck decides to stay behind when his flock flies south, Irene invites him to stay with her for the winter.
"Urbanovic's animals, with their expressive, engaging facial features, take center stage in the open, cheery illustrations. . . . Great fun for storyhours." SLJ
 Other titles about Max the duck are:
Duck soup (2008)
Duck and cover (2009)

U'Ren, Andrea, 1968-

Mary Smith. Farrar, Straus & Giroux 2003 unp il $16
Grades: K 1 2 3   E
  1. City and town life—Fiction
  ISBN 0-374-34842-1   LC 2002-69775
Early in the morning Mary Smith walks through the town, waking people up by shooting at their windows with her peashooter
"Outlined in black, U'Ren's art has a clean, graphic appearance that perfectly complements the simplicity of the story. . . . A historical note gives supplemental information about the real Mrs. Mary Smith and the role of the knocker-ups. A rollicking read." SLJ

Vail, Rachel

Jibberwillies at night; illustrated by Yumi Heo. Scholastic Press 2008 unp il $16.99
Grades: PreK K 1 2   E
  1. Fear—Fiction 2. Bedtime—Fiction
  ISBN 978-0-439-42070-9; 0-439-42070-9
                      LC 2007-34087
Katie is almost always happy, but sometimes at night, when the Jibberwillies come and scare her, her mother must catch them in a bucket and throw them out the window before Katie can fall asleep
"Katie's personality leaps off the page via Vail's evocative language . . . and Heo's bright and kicky mixed-media compositions." Publ Wkly

Righty & Lefty; a tale of two feet; by Rachel Vail; illustrations by Matthew Cordell. Scholastic Press 2007 unp il $16.99
Grades: PreK K   E
  1. Foot—Fiction
  ISBN 978-0-439-63629-2; 0-439-63629-9
                      LC 2006-28840
Even though Lefty and Righty like different things, they find they must learn to get along together without tripping over each other.
"It's a wonderfully weird story, filled with hilarious detail and deadpan humor. . . . Cordell's easygoing line-and-watercolor illustrations . . . [keep] the feet so sustainedly in focus that they gain character through sheer persistance." Bull Cent Child Books

Sometimes I'm Bombaloo; illustrated by Yumi Heo. Scholastic Press 2001 unp il $15.95
Grades: PreK K 1 2   E
  1. Anger—Fiction
  ISBN 0-439-08755-4   LC 99-58709
 When Katie Honors feels angry and out of control, her mother helps her to be herself again
"Vail captures the intensity of emotion that children (and many adults) feel when they are angry, and then distills it with laughter. Heo uses lots of stripes and splotches of color to match Katie's emotions. . . . Kudos to Vail and Heo for making a scary subject manageable." Booklist

Valckx, Catharina

Lizette's green sock. Clarion Books 2005 unp il $15
Grades: PreK K 1 2   E
  1. Clothing and dress—Fiction 2. Birds—Fiction
  ISBN 0-618-45298-2   LC 2004-12042
  Original French edition, 2002
Lizette, a young bird, tries to figure out what to do with the one green sock that she finds while out walking one day
"Utterly simple and springtime fresh. . . . Valckx conveys an impressive range of mood and action through spare, swooping brushstrokes, and pale tones of lemon, mint, and sky blue allow the kelly green of the sock to draw the eye instantly." Booklist

Vamos, Samantha R.

Before you were here, mi amor; illustrated by Santiago Cohen. Viking 2009 unp il $15.99

Grades: PreK K 1 E

1. Family life—Fiction 2. Infants—Fiction 3. Spanish language—Vocabulary

ISBN 978-0-670-06301-7; 0-670-06301-0

LC 2008-21548

Family members lovingly prepare for arrival of a new baby. Spanish words are woven throughout the text.

"Cohen uses the texture of the paper and his watercolor paints to create depth and movement in the vividly colored illustrations. This lovely story may encourage discussions of individual birth preparations in readers' own families." SLJ

Van Allsburg, Chris

Ben's dream; story and pictures by Chris Van Allsburg. Houghton Mifflin 1982 31p il lib bdg $16.95 *

Grades: K 1 2 3 4 E

1. Dreams—Fiction

ISBN 0-395-32084-4 LC 81-20029

"When rain spoils Ben's ball game with Margaret, he returns to an empty house, falls asleep in his father's chair, and embarks on a dream. In a marvelous series of double-page black-and-white pictures meticulously textured with hatching, one shares Ben's voyage past such sights as the Statue of Liberty, the Sphinx, and the Mount Rushmore presidents, all with flood waters lapping about their respective chins and waists. . . . A visual tour de force." Horn Book

The garden of Abdul Gasazi; written and illustrated by Chris Van Allsburg. Houghton Mifflin 1979 unp il lib bdg $18.95

Grades: 1 2 3 4 E

1. Magic—Fiction 2. Dogs—Fiction

ISBN 0-395-27804-X

A Caldecott Medal honor book, 1980

When the dog he is caring for runs away from Alan into the forbidden garden of a retired dog-hating magician, a spell seems to be cast over the contrary dog

The full page "lithographlike drawings are astonishing—eerie, monumental, surreal and witty all at once—and the effect of the whole is original and unforgettable." Books of the Times

Jumanji; written and illustrated by Chris Van Allsburg. Houghton Mifflin 1981 unp il $18.95 *

Grades: K 1 2 3 4 E

1. Games—Fiction

ISBN 0-395-30448-2 LC 80-29632

Awarded the Caldecott Medal, 1982

Left on their own for an afternoon, two bored and restless children find more excitement than they bargained for in a mysterious and mystical jungle adventure board game.

"Through the masterly use of light and shadow, the interplay of design elements, and audacious changes in perspective and composition, the artist conveys an impression of color without losing the dramatic contrast of black and white." Horn Book

Just a dream. Houghton Mifflin 1990 unp il $18.95

Grades: K 1 2 3 4 E

1. Environmental protection—Fiction 2. Pollution—Fiction 3. Dreams—Fiction

ISBN 0-395-53308-2 LC 90-41343

When he has a dream about a future Earth devastated by pollution, Walter begins to understand the importance of taking care of the environment.

"Van Allsburg demonstrates his unique artistic magic in combining foresight, wisdom and striking artwork to deliver an ecological message concerning conservation and renewal." Child Book Rev Serv

The mysteries of Harris Burdick. Houghton Mifflin 1984 unp il lib bdg $18.95

Grades: 1 2 3 4 E

1. Storytelling—Fiction 2. Imagination—Fiction

ISBN 0-395-35393-9 LC 84-9006

Presents a series of loosely related drawings each accompanied by a title and a caption which the reader may use to make up his or her own story

Rendered in the author's "signature velvet black and white . . . the pictures are nothing short of spectacular. . . . While some may find this just an excuse for handsome artwork, others will see its great potential for stretching a child's imagination. Although the book could be used in countless ways, primarily it will make storytellers of children." Booklist

The Polar Express; written and illustrated by Chris Van Allsburg. Twentieth anniversary ed. Houghton Mifflin 2005 unp il $35 *

Grades: PreK K 1 2 3 E

1. North Pole—Fiction 2. Santa Claus—Fiction 3. Christmas—Fiction

ISBN 978-0-618-61169-0; 0-618-61169-X

LC 2005281613

Awarded the Caldecott Medal, 1986

A reissue of the title first published 1985

A magical train ride on Christmas Eve takes a boy to the North Pole to receive a special gift from Santa Claus.

This offers "stunning paintings in which Van Allsburg uses dark, rich colors and misty shapes in contrast with touches of bright white-gold light to create scenes, interior and exterior, that have a quality of mystery that imbues the strong composition to achieve a soft, evocative mood." Bull Cent Child Books

The stranger. Houghton Mifflin 1986 unp il lib bdg $18.95

Grades: 1 2 3 4 E

1. Seasons—Fiction

ISBN 0-395-42331-7 LC 86-15235

The enigmatic origins of the stranger Farmer Bailey hits with his truck and brings home to recuperate seem to have a mysterious relation to the weather.

"The full-color illustrations, framed in white, evoke an old-fashioned New England landscape at the end of summer; some are remarkably peaceful in tone, others slightly spooky by virtue of brooding colors, unexpected perspectives, or the stranger's peculiar expressions." Bull Cent Child Books

Van Allsburg, Chris—*Continued*

The sweetest fig. Houghton Mifflin 1993 unp il $18.95

Grades: 1 2 3 4   E
1. Dreams—Fiction 2. Magic—Fiction 3. Dogs—Fiction
ISBN 0-395-67346-1   LC 93-12692

After being given two magical figs that make his dreams come true, Monsieur Bibot sees his plans for future wealth upset by his long-suffering dog

"The full-color, expressive illustrations are filled with nuance, detail and mystery. Once again, Van Allsburg weaves a spell with ultimate skill and creativity." Child Book Rev Serv

The widow's broom. Houghton Mifflin 1992 unp il $18.95

Grades: 1 2 3 4   E
1. Magic—Fiction 2. Witchcraft—Fiction
ISBN 0-395-64051-2   LC 92-7110

A witch's worn-out broom serves a widow well, until her neighbors decide the thing is wicked and dangerous

"In addition to being a neatly understated piece of storytelling, this fuels Van Allsburg's best kind of illustration—darkly rounded, speckle-textured art with eerie effects." Bull Cent Child Books

The wreck of the Zephyr; written and illustrated by Chris Van Allsburg. Houghton Mifflin 1983 unp il lib bdg $18.95

Grades: 1 2 3 4   E
1. Imagination—Fiction 2. Boats and boating—Fiction
ISBN 0-395-33075-0   LC 82-23371

A boy's ambition to be the greatest sailor in the world brings him to ruin when he misuses his new ability to sail his boat in the air.

This "displays recognizable hallmarks of the artist's work: beauty of composition, striking contrasts of light and shadow, and especially the fascinating ambiguity of illusion and reality." Horn Book

The wretched stone. Houghton Mifflin 1991 unp il $18.95

Grades: 1 2 3 4   E
1. Sea stories
ISBN 0-395-53307-4   LC 91-11525

A strange glowing stone picked up on a sea voyage captivates a ship's crew and has a terrible transforming effect on them

"Although Van Allsburg clearly has a message to convey, he has added to the book an enjoyable and necessary dollop of humor. The story has a quiet, understated, yet suspenseful tone; most of the plot's considerable drama is conveyed in the impressive illustrations." Horn Book

The Z was zapped; a play in twenty-six acts; performed by the Caslon Players; written and directed by Chris Van Allsburg. Houghton Mifflin 1987 unp il $18.95 *

Grades: K 1 2 3   E
1. Alphabet
ISBN 0-395-44612-0   LC 87-14988

At head of title: The Alphabet Theatre proudly presents

Depicts how A was in an avalanche, B was badly bitten, C was cut to ribbons, and the other letters of the alphabet suffered similar mishaps.

"Children can try to guess what action has occured, thereby increasing their vocabulary and the fun, or they can turn the page and read the text, or better yet—do both. This clever romp resembles old vaudeville theater, with one curious act following the next." SLJ

Zathura; a space adventure; written and illustrated by Chris Van Allsburg. Houghton Mifflin 2002 unp il $18

Grades: 1 2 3 4   E
1. Games—Fiction
ISBN 0-618-25396-3   LC 2002-1751

"Danny and Walter Budwing, last seen on the final page of *Jumanji*, find the magical game box in the park. They discover a second game board inside, decorated with space images. Once home, they begin to play, and . . . they are instantly catapulted into the game's parallel universe, which . . . involves meteor showers, pirate aliens, violent robots, wild shifts in gravity, and a black hole." Booklist

"Van Allsburg illustrates the surreal events in a grainy charcoal-black that seems to shimmer on a rough, cream-colored ground. His deathly quiet images . . . have a frozen stillness that leaves all color and activity to the imagination; with each new threat, the book seems to hold its breath. . . . Zathura, like Jumanji, is a satisfying enigma." Publ Wkly

Van Camp, Katie

Harry and Horsie; illustrated by Lincoln Agnew. Balzer & Bray 2009 unp il $16.99

Grades: PreK K 1 2   E
1. Imagination—Fiction
ISBN 978-0-06-175598-9; 0-06-175598-2

When a boy named Harry sneaks out of bed one night with his best friend, Horsie, to play with his Super Duper Bubble Blooper—an out-of-this-world adventure begins!

"Agnew's art uses an effectively limited color palette, faded dot patterns, and crisp lines to create a retro-cartoon feel. . . . With dashing visuals that capture Harry's deep-space adventure with verve to spare, and a comforting resolution, this has potential to be a bedtime favorite." Booklist

Van Dusen, Chris

The circus ship. Candlewick Press 2009 unp il $16.99

Grades: PreK K 1 2 3   E
1. Animals—Fiction 2. Shipwrecks—Fiction 3. Circus—Fiction 4. Stories in rhyme
ISBN 978-0-7636-3090-4; 0-7636-3090-X
                                        LC 2008938402

"When a circus ship runs aground off the coast of Maine, the poor animals are left on their own to swim the chilly waters. Staggering onto a nearby island, they soon win over the wary townspeople with their kind, courageous ways. So well do the critters blend in that when the greedy circus owner returns to claim them, villagers of all species conspire to outsmart the bloated blowhard." Publisher's note

Van Dusen, Chris—*Continued*

Van Dusen "uses an actual 1836 shipwreck as the seed for this charming and humorous picture book. . . . The rhyming text provides the structure for the story; however, the vividly colored, meticulously drawn illustrations articulate the story so well that they could practically stand on their own." Booklist

Van Laan, Nancy

Nit-pickin'; [by] Nancy Van Laan and [illustrated by] George Booth. Atheneum Books for Young Readers 2008 unp il $15.99
Grades: PreK K 1   E
1. Lice—Fiction 2. Stories in rhyme
ISBN 0-689-83898-0; 978-0-689-83898-9
LC 00-062077
Family members go to great lengths to rid their child of head lice.
"The lively text is complemented by the over-the-top antics observed in Booth's cartoon illustrations." SLJ

Teeny tiny tingly tales; illustrated by Victoria Chess. Atheneum Bks. for Young Readers 2001 unp il $16
Grades: PreK K 1 2   E
1. Horror fiction 2. Short stories 3. Stories in rhyme
ISBN 0-689-81875-0   LC 97-37452
"An Anne Schwartz book"
Three rhyming scary stories, including 'Old Doctor Wango Tango,' 'It,' and 'The Hairy Toe'
"Victoria Chess's squat figures, all teeth and beady eyes and unkempt hair, complement the zany, but a teeny-tiny bit scary, nature of these tales." Horn Book

When winter comes; illustrated by Susan Gaber. Atheneum Bks. for Young Readers 2000 unp il $16
Grades: PreK K 1 2   E
1. Winter—Fiction 2. Animals—Fiction 3. Stories in rhyme
ISBN 0-689-81778-9   LC 97-32914
"An Anne Schwartz book"
Rhyming text asks what happens to different animals and plants "when winter comes and the cold wind blows"
"The rhyming answers use simple and accessible language. Gaber's exuberant acrylic paintings show a child, mother, father, and dog taking a walk through the woods during a snowfall." SLJ

Van Leeuwen, Jean

Amanda Pig and the awful, scary monster; pictures by Ann Schweninger. Phyllis Fogelman Bks. 2003 48p il (PJF easy-to-read) hardcover o.p. pa $3.99 *
Grades: K 1 2   E
1. Monsters—Fiction 2. Bedtime—Fiction 3. Pigs—Fiction
ISBN 0-8037-2766-6; 0-14-240203-6 (pa)
LC 2001-33519
Amanda pig sees monsters at night, but her parents and her brother find different ways to convince her that

there are no monsters
"Van Leeuwen captures childhood emotions perfectly and includes just the right amount of humor. With bright illustrations done in carbon pencil, colored pencils, and watercolor washes on every page, this book will delight the piglet's many fans." SLJ
Other titles about Amanda Pig are:
Amanda Pig and her big brother Oliver (1982)
Tales of Amanda Pig (1983)
More tales of Amanda Pig (1985)
Oliver, Amanda, and Grandmother Pig (1987)
Oliver and Amanda's Christmas (1989)
Amanda Pig on her own (1991)
Oliver and Amanda's Halloween (1992)
Oliver and Amanda and the big snow (1995)
Amanda Pig, school girl (1997)
Amanda Pig and her best friend Lollipop (1998)
Amanda Pig and the really hot day (2005)
Amanda Pig, first grader (2007)
Amanda Pig and the wiggly tooth (2008)

Benny & beautiful baby Delilah; pictures by LeUyen Pham. Dial Books for Young Readers 2006 32p il $16.99
Grades: PreK K 1 2   E
1. Infants—Fiction 2. Siblings—Fiction
ISBN 0-8037-2891-3   LC 2004-19412
"Benny gets his very own little sister, but realizes pretty quickly that shes not much fun. . . . In the end, after a long session of crying, Benny takes charge and is able to get Delilah to smile. . . . While this well-paced story doesn't break any new ground thematically, it is realistic and heartwarming. What makes it truly shine is the art. . . . The characterizations, created with a heavy ink line, are expressive, jaunty, and lively." SLJ

Chicken soup; by Jean Van Leeuwen; illustrated by David Gavril. Abrams Books for Young Readers 2009 unp il $16.95
Grades: PreK K 1   E
1. Chickens—Fiction 2. Farm life—Fiction
ISBN 978-0-8109-8326-7; 0-8109-8326-5
LC 2008030824
When they hear that Mrs. Farmer is making soup, all the frightened chickens run for their lives, but Mr. Farmer finds Little Chickie, who has a bad cold, and he takes her to the kitchen for some nice hot vegetable soup.
"This simple, just-scary-enough story will appeal to preschoolers with its repetition and bright, childlike pen and watercolor illustrations." SLJ

Oliver the Mighty Pig; pictures by Ann Schweninger. Dial Bks. for Young Readers 2004 48p il lib bdg $14.99 *
Grades: K 1 2   E
1. Pigs—Fiction 2. Superheroes—Fiction
ISBN 0-8037-2886-7   LC 2002-7310
"Dial easy-to-read"
Oliver feels like the superhero Mighty Pig when he wears his Mighty Pig cape, but he finds that being a superhero in the real world has some complications.
"Van Leeuwen's text is filled with lively dialogue and simple sentences that are just right for beginning readers. . . . The bright, uncluttered pictures on each page reinforce the meaning in the words and add layers of humor." Booklist

Van Leeuwen, Jean—*Continued*
Other titles about Oliver Pig are:
Tales of Oliver Pig (1979)
More tales of Oliver Pig (1981)
Amanda Pig and her big brother Oliver (1982)
Oliver, Amanda, and Grandmother Pig (1987)
Oliver and Amanda's Christmas (1989)
Oliver Pig at school (1990)
Oliver and Amanda's Halloween (1992)
Oliver and Amanda and the big snow (1995)
Oliver and Albert, friends forever (2000)
Oliver Pig and the best fort ever (2006)

Papa and the pioneer quilt; [by] Jean Van
Leeuwen; pictures by Rebecca Bond. Dial Books
for Young Readers 2007 unp il $16.99
Grades: K 1 2 3   E
1. Quilts—Fiction 2. Overland journeys to the Pacific—Fiction 3. Frontier and pioneer life—Fiction
4. West (U.S.)—Fiction
ISBN 0-8037-3028-4   LC 2005022983
As her family travels by wagon train to Oregon, a
young girl gathers scraps of cloth so that she can make
a quilt. Includes historical note.
"Bond's excellent illustrations, done in acrylics on watercolor paper, provide an ideal dreamy background for
the story. The smooth first-person narrative, appealing dialogue, and sunny artwork vividly capture a child's experience in the early days of the United States." SLJ

Van Steenwyk, Elizabeth, 1928-
Prairie Christmas; written by Elizabeth Van
Steenwyk; illustrated by Ronald Himler. Eerdmans
2006 unp il $17
Grades: 1 2 3 4   E
1. Christmas—Fiction   2. Midwives—Fiction
3. Mother-daughter   relationship—Fiction
4. Nebraska—Fiction
ISBN 0-8028-5280-7
On the Nebraska prairie in 1880, eleven-year-old
Emma finds a way to celebrate the spirit of Christmas
while her mother, a midwife, delivers a baby on Christmas Eve.
"This memorable tale is beautifully told in clear and
simple prose, which is complemented perfectly by the
uncluttered, colored-pencil and watercolor drawings."
SLJ

Vander Zee, Ruth
Always with you; written by Ruth Vander Zee;
illustrated by Ronald Himler. Eerdmans Books for
Young Readers 2008 unp il $17
Grades: 2 3 4   E
1. Mother-daughter relationship—Fiction 2. Orphans—
Fiction 3. Vietnam—Fiction
ISBN 978-0-8028-5295-3   LC 2007009354
Orphaned at the age of four when her village in Viet-
nam is bombed, Kim is rescued by soldiers and raised in
an orphanage, always finding comfort in her mother's
last words "Don't be afraid. I will always be with you."

Mississippi morning; written by Ruth Vander
Zee; illustrated by Floyd Cooper. Eerdmans Books
for Young Readers 2004 unp il $16
Grades: 1 2 3 4   E
1. Ku Klux Klan—Fiction 2. Race relations—Fiction
3. Father-son relationship—Fiction 4. Mississippi—
Fiction
ISBN 0-8028-5211-4   LC 2002-151212
Amidst the economic depression and the racial tension
of the 1930s, a boy discovers a horrible secret of his father's involvement in the Ku Klux Klan
"Cooper's large, warm oil paintings create the perfect
sense of time, place, and atmosphere. . . . A sad and
poignant story." SLJ

VanHecke, Susan
An apple pie for dinner; retold by Susan
VanHecke; illustrated by Carol Baicker-McKee.
Marshall Cavendish Children 2009 unp il $17.99
Grades: K 1 2 3   E
1. Apples—Fiction 2. Barter—Fiction 3. Baking—Fic-
tion
ISBN 978-0-7614-5452-6; 0-7614-5452-7
                               LC 2008003664
Wishing to bake an apple pie, Old Granny Smith sets
out with a full basket, trading its contents for a series of
objects until she gets the apples she needs.
"The bas-relief illustrations, made from baked clay
and mixed-media of found objects, create a 3-D,
Claymation effect. . . . The fascinating tactile details
will have young and old poring over the pages. . . .
Complete with a pie recipe and notes from both the author and illustrator that cite the origin of the tale (the English folktale 'An Apple Dumpling') and directions on
how to make bas-reliefs, the book is a delicious treat to
be shared anytime. " Booklist

Varela, Barry
Gizmo; [by] Barry Varela; illustrations by Ed
Briant. Roaring Brook Press 2007 unp il $16.95
Grades: K 1 2 3   E
1. Machinery—Fiction 2. Stories in rhyme
ISBN 978-1-59643-115-7; 1-59643-115-6
                               LC 2006012007
"A Neal Porter book"
When Professor Ludwig von Glink's contraption gets
so out of hand that the City Buildings and Permits In-
spector condemns his home, the City Contemporary Art
Museum comes to the rescue
"The animation inherent in Briant's colorful line-and-
wash artwork bolsters the humor, while Varela's playful
sense of language leads to some inspired wordplay."
Booklist

Varennes, Monique de, 1947-
The jewel box ballerinas; [by] Monique de
Varennes; pictures by Ana Juan. Schwartz &
Wade Books 2007 unp il $16.99; lib bdg $19.99
Grades: K 1 2 3   E
1. Magic—Fiction 2. Wealth—Fiction 3. Friendship—
Fiction
ISBN   978-0-375-83605-3;   0-375-83605-5;
978-0-375-93605-0 (lib bdg); 0-375-93605-X (lib bdg)
                               LC 2004-19622

Varennes, Monique de, 1947-—*Continued*

Wealthy Bibi purchases a magic jewel box and sets out to make the two tiny ballerinas within it smile again

"The richly colored, jewel-toned art suits the surreal tale, gently spoofing Bibi and her possessions. . . . This story of transformation is made twice as nice by the pairing of equally witty text and illustrations." Horn Book

Varon, Sara, 1971-

Chicken and Cat; by Sara Varon. Scholastic Press 2006 unp il $16.99

Grades: PreK K 1 2   **E**

1. Cats—Fiction 2. Chickens—Fiction 3. City and town life—Fiction 4. Stories without words

ISBN 0-439-63406-7   LC 2003025297

When Cat feels sad about living in the hustle and bustle of the city, Chicken finds colorful ways to make Cat feel better

"In this wordless story, bold, full-bleed cartoon illustrations are amiably cluttered. . . . This book has a funny, big-eyed sweetness, and is packed with details that kids will relish discovering in successive readings." SLJ

Another title about Chicken and Cat is:

Chicken and Cat clean up (2009)

Vere, Ed

Chick. Holt & Co. 2010 c2009 unp il $9.99

Grades: PreK   **E**

1. Chickens—Fiction 2. Pop-up books

ISBN 978-0-8050-9168-7; 0-8050-9168-8

First published 2009 in the United Kingdom

"A beak cracks through an orange pop-up egg—'crick crack crickety crack'—and out pops a yellow chick whose loud 'cheep!' brings its mother rushing to its side. She's a red chicken with a three-fingered crest, and together they eat and rest. . . . Humor, bold colors, and clever engineering make for a simple, memorable package." Publ Wkly

Vestergaard, Hope

Potty animals; what to know when you've gotta go! illustrated by Valeria Petrone. Sterling Pub. 2010 unp il $14.95

Grades: PreK   **E**

1. Toilet training—Fiction 2. Animals—Fiction 3. Stories in rhyme

ISBN 978-1-4027-5996-3; 1-4027-5996-7

"Petrone's cheery digital characters and Vestergaard's decorous yet humorous rhymes invite readers to help civilize the bathroom habits of some uncouth preschool-age animals. . . . Petrone's wide-eyed cartoon animals capture a broad spectrum of toddler emotions." Publ Wkly

Vidal, Beatriz

Federico and the Magi's gift; a Latin American Christmas story; by Beatriz Vidal. Knopf 2004 unp il $15.95; lib bdg $17.99

Grades: PreK K 1 2   **E**

1. Epiphany—Fiction 2. Magi—Fiction 3. Latin America—Fiction

ISBN 0-375-82518-5; 0-375-92518-X (lib bdg)

LC 2003-25880

Because he has misbehaved, four-year-old Federico is afraid the three kings will not bring him the toy horse he asked them for and, unable to sleep, he goes outside to await their arrival

"Decoratively patterned, the gouache-and-watercolor paintings employ naive forms and glowing colors. . . . With its quiet narrative and beautiful illustrations, this celebrates the end of the Christmas season in a distinctly Latin American way." Booklist

Vigil-Piñón, Evangelina, 1949-

Marina's muumuu; illustrations by Pablo Torrecilla. Arte Público Press 2001 unp il $14.95

Grades: PreK K 1 2   **E**

1. Clothing and dress—Fiction 2. Bilingual books—English-Spanish

ISBN 1-55885-350-2   LC 2001-21487

Title page and text in English and Spanish

Marina has always dreamed of having a colorful muumuu, the traditional dress of the Hawaiian people, and finally goes to the bustling downtown with her grandmother to buy the fabric

"Gloriously bright tropical colors and patterns fill these gaily decorated pages." Booklist

Villeneuve, Anne

The red scarf. Tundra Books 2010 unp il $17.95

Grades: PreK K 1   **E**

1. Moles (Animals)—Fiction 2. Taxicabs—Fiction 3. Circus—Fiction 4. Animals—Fiction 5. Lost and found possessions—Fiction

ISBN 978-0-88776-989-4; 0-88776-989-6

"In this nearly wordless book, Turpin, a white mole, serves as taxi driver to a mysterious caped man who leaves behind a scarlet, fringed scarf. Determined to return the property, kind Turpin follows a trail leading to a circus. . . . Villeneuve's muted crayon palette gracefully swirls and smears scenes from city to center ring. The cartoons keep the action at forefront, with minimal backgrounds and energetic compositions. This gentle comedy with familiar adventures at the big top will please young audiences." SLJ

Viorst, Judith

Alexander and the terrible, horrible, no good, very bad day; illustrated by Ray Cruz; with a new preface by Judith Viorst and Ray Cruz. Special limited ed. Atheneum Books for Young Readers 2009 unp il $17.99 *

Grades: PreK K 1 2   **E**

1. Day—Fiction

ISBN 978-1-4169-8595-2; 1-4169-8595-6

LC 2008049478

A reissue of the title first published 1972

On a day when everything goes wrong for him, Alexander is consoled by the thought that other people have bad days too.

"Small listeners can enjoy the litany of disaster, and perhaps be stimulated to discuss the possibility that one contributes by expectation. The illustrations capture the grumpy dolor of the story, ruefully funny." Sutherland. The Best In Child Books

Other titles about Alexander are:

Viorst, Judith—*Continued*

Alexander, who is not (do you hear me?) going (I mean it) to move (1995)

Alexander, who used to be rich last Sunday (1978)

Just in case; written by Judith Viorst; illustrated by Diana Cain Bluthenthal. Atheneum Books for Young Readers 2006 unp il $15.95

Grades: PreK K 1 2   E

1. Worry—Fiction

ISBN 0-689-87164-3   LC 2003-26068

"Ginee Seo books"

Charlie likes to be ready for anything, imagining that his house could be flooded or a mermaid might kidnap him, but he learns that it is sometimes good to be unprepared

"Blumenthal's colorful, mixed-media illustrations add some good cheer, sly wit, . . . and a companionable canine to the catalog of Charlie's hypothetical 'just in case' concerns." Booklist

Nobody here but me; [by] Judith Viorst; pictures by Christine Davenier. Farrar, Straus and Giroux 2008 unp il $16.95

Grades: PreK K 1   E

1. Family life—Fiction

ISBN 978-0-374-35540-1; 0-374-35540-1

LC 2006-101606

With his mother on the phone, his father checking e-mail, and his sister playing with her friends, a little boy feels as if he is all alone in the house, and no matter how badly he behaves, no one comes to stop him

"Davenier's watercolor-and-ink illustrations place the boy in his pleasant house with his busy family. The muted colors reflect his mood. . . . This book addresses a universal childhood experience." SLJ

The tenth good thing about Barney; illustrated by Erik Blegvad. Atheneum Pubs. 1971 25p il $15.95; pa $5.99

Grades: PreK K 1 2   E

1. Death—Fiction 2. Cats—Fiction

ISBN 0-689-20688-7; 0-689-71203-0 (pa)

"A little boy saddened by the death of his cat thinks of nine good things about Barney to say at his funeral. Later his father helps him discover a tenth good thing: Barney is in the ground helping grow flowers and trees and grass." Booklist

"The author succinctly and honestly handles both the emotions stemming from the loss of a beloved pet and the questions about the finality of death . . . An unusually good book that handles a difficult subject straightforwardly." Horn Book

Voake, Charlotte

Hello, twins. Candlewick Press 2006 unp il $15.99

Grades: PreK K   E

1. Twins—Fiction 2. Siblings—Fiction

ISBN 0-7636-3003-9   LC 2005-50185

Although twins Charlotte and Simon do everything differently and do not look alike, they still share a special bond.

"The lithesome watercolor-and-ink illustrations are amusing and consistently expand the simple text." SLJ

Vogel, Amos

How little Lori visited Times Square; pictures by Maurice Sendak. HarperCollins Pubs. 2001 unp il $14.95 *

Grades: PreK K 1 2   E

1. New York (N.Y.)—Fiction

ISBN 0-06-028462-5

A reissue of the title first published 1963

This "tells the story of Lori's many misadventures trying to get to Times Square on various modes of transportation, with a slow-moving turtle finally bearing him off." Horn Book Guide

Vries, Anke de, 1936-

Raf; [illustrated by] Charlotte Dematons. Lemniscaat 2009 unp il $16.95

Grades: PreK K   E

1. Toys—Fiction 2. Voyages and travels—Fiction 3. Africa—Fiction

ISBN 978-1-59078-749-6

Original Dutch edition, 2008

This "follows a toy giraffe that spontaneously disappears from his child's room to travel through Africa. . . . In postcards sent to his owner/pal, Ben . . . Raf tells of encounters with camels, flamingos, elephants, monkeys, and giraffes. . . . Just in time for Ben's birthday, the toy arrives in the mail, dressed in kente cloth and colored beads. . . . In addition to being a great success with preschool fans of toy tales, this story could also be shared with primary-grade children in conjunction with units on biome study or continents." SLJ

Waber, Bernard

Evie & Margie. Houghton Mifflin 2003 32p il $15

Grades: PreK K 1 2   E

1. Friendship—Fiction 2. Theater—Fiction 3. Hippopotamus—Fiction

ISBN 0-618-34124-2   LC 2003-533

"Walter Lorraine books"

Best friends hippopotamuses, Evie and Margie, are surprised to experience jealousy when they try out for the same part in the school play

"The book gets to the heart of what is important to children, and the color illustrations are vintage Waber with great facial expressions and humorous, child-friendly images." SLJ

Ira sleeps over. Houghton Mifflin 1972 48p il lib bdg $16; pa $6.95 *

Grades: PreK K 1 2   E

1. Teddy bears—Fiction 2. Friendship—Fiction

ISBN 0-395-13893-0 (lib bdg); 0-395-20503-4 (pa)

Ira is excited at the prospect of spending the night at his friend's house but worries how he'll get along without his teddy bear

"An appealing picture book which depicts common childhood qualms with empathy and humor in brief text and colorful illustrations." Booklist

Another title about Ira is:

Ira says goodbye (1988)

Waber, Bernard—*Continued*

Lyle, Lyle, crocodile. Houghton Mifflin 1965
48p il $16; pa $6.95 *

Grades: PreK K 1 2   E

1. Crocodiles—Fiction 2. New York (N.Y.)—Fiction

ISBN 0-395-16995-X; 0-395-13720-9 (pa)

Lyle the crocodile who lives in New York City
"wants desperately to win the friendship of the cat Loretta two doors away but every time Loretta catches a
glimpse of him she flings herself into a nervous fit."
Booklist

"The illustrations are cartoon-like, lively, and colorful.
. . . The situation is nicely exploited with a bland
daffiness." Bull Cent Child Books

Other titles about Lyle are:

Funny, funny Lyle (1987)

The house on East 88th Street (1962)

Lovable Lyle (1969)

Lyle and the birthday party (1966)

Lyle at Christmas (1998)

Lyle at the office (1994)

Lyle finds his mother (1974)

Lyle walks the dogs (2010)

The mouse that snored. Houghton Mifflin 2000
unp il $15; pa $5.95

Grades: PreK K 1 2   E

1. Noise—Fiction 2. Mice—Fiction 3. Stories in
rhyme

ISBN 0-395-97518-2; 0-618-43954-4 (pa)

LC 98-47276

"Walter Lorraine books"

A loudly snoring mouse disturbs the residents of a
quiet country house

"Using characteristically humorous pictures and a delightful, rhyming text, Waber creates a world-weary
mouse with a snore that moves furniture." Booklist

Waddell, Martin

Can't you sleep, Little Bear? illustrated by
Barbara Firth. special anniversary edition.
Candlewick Press 2002 unp il $15.99

Grades: PreK   E

1. Bears—Fiction 2. Bedtime—Fiction

ISBN 978-0-76361-929-9; 0-76361-929-9

First published 1988 in the United Kingdom

When bedtime comes Little Bear is afraid of the dark,
until Big Bear brings him lights and love.

"Firth's brightly lit watercolor and soft pencil illustrations, framed in the dark blue of the night, capture the
cozy, physical affection of the story, the playfulness of
Little Bear, . . . the shadowy mystery of the moonlit
landscape, and the huge comforting presence of a parent
who is always there when you call." Booklist

Other titles about Little Bear are:

Good job, Little Bear! (1999)

Let's go home, Little Bear (1993)

Little Bear's baby book (2000)

Sleep tight Little Bear (2005)

Well done, Little Bear (1999)

You and me, Little Bear (1996)

Captain Small Pig; illustrated by Susan Varley.
Peachtree Pubs. 2009 unp il $15.95 *

Grades: PreK K   E

1. Pigs—Fiction 2. Goats—Fiction 3. Turkeys—Fiction 4. Boats and boating—Fiction

ISBN 978-1-56145-519-5; 1-56145-519-9

Small Pig persuades Old Goat and Turkey to go out
on Blue Lake in a row boat with him and fish for whales

"This book pleases at every level. The simplicity of its
concept, the ease of its words, and the ink-and-
watercolor art's subtle mix of wit and whimsy combine
in a comfortable way." Booklist

Farmer duck; illustrated by Helen Oxenbury.
Candlewick Press 1992 c1991 unp il hardcover
o.p. pa $5.99; bd bk $6.99 *

Grades: PreK K 1 2   E

1. Ducks—Fiction 2. Farm life—Fiction

ISBN 1-56402-009-6; 1-56402-596-9 (pa);
0-7636-2167-6 (bd bk)   LC 91-71855

First published 1991 in the United Kingdom

When a kind and hardworking duck nearly collapses
from overwork, while taking care of a farm because the
owner is too lazy to do so, the rest of the animals get
together and chase the farmer out of town

"Hilarious art masterfully captures the expressions of
the put-upon duck, the supportive cast, and the slovenly
ergophobic who reads the newspaper and chomps on
bonbons in bed. . . . With its lilting, large-print text and
satisfying resolution, it's as perfect for beginning readers
as it is for story hours." SLJ

It's quacking time! illustrated by Jill Barton.
Candlewick Press 2005 unp il $15.99

Grades: PreK K 1   E

1. Ducks—Fiction 2. Eggs—Fiction

ISBN 0-7636-2738-0   LC 2004-57039

A duckling and all his family happily await the hatching of his parents' new egg

"A warm tale. . . . Barton's expressive watercolor and
pencil illustrations are appropriately full of life." Horn
Book Guide

Owl babies; illustrated by Patrick Benson.
Candlewick Press 1992 unp il hardcover o.p. pa
$6.99; bd bk $6.99 *

Grades: PreK K 1 2   E

1. Owls—Fiction

ISBN 1-56402-101-7; 0-7636-1710-5 (pa);
1-56402-965-4 (bd bk)   LC 91-58750

Three owl babies whose mother has gone out in the
night try to stay calm while she is gone

"The illustrations, executed in black ink and watercol-
or, capture in every feather and expression the little
owls' worry and watchfulness as well as their complete
joy when Owl Mother returns." Horn Book

Snow bears; illustrated by Sarah Fox-Davies.
Candlewick Press 2002 unp il hardcover o.p. bd
bk $6.99

Grades: PreK K 1 2   E

1. Bears—Fiction 2. Snow—Fiction

ISBN 0-7636-1906-X; 0-7636-2441-1 (bd bk)

LC 2001-58258

Waddell, Martin—*Continued*

When three little bears play in the snow, they pretend to be "snow bears" and their mother goes along with the game

"Waddell's affectionate text offers an idyllic frosty gambol, and youngsters will appreciate the lulling repetition, the gentle trickery, and the smallest baby bear's struggles to keep up with her elder siblings." Bull Cent Child Books

The super hungry dinosaur; pictures by Leonie Lord. Dial Books for Young Readers 2009 unp il $16.99

Grades: PreK K 1   E

1. Dinosaurs—Fiction

ISBN 978-0-8037-3446-3; 0-8037-3446-8

LC 2008-51099

"When a Super Hungry Dinosaur charges into Hal's backyard, it's up to Hal to teach it some manners and keep himself, his parents, and even his dog from becoming lunch. The charming, naive illustrations look as though they are done in pencil and crayon. . . . Great fun." Booklist

Tiny's big adventure; illustrated by John Lawrence. Candlewick Press 2004 unp il $15.99; pa $6.99 *

Grades: PreK K   E

1. Mice—Fiction 2. Country life—Fiction 3. Siblings—Fiction

ISBN 0-7636-2170-6; 0-7636-3819-6 (pa)

LC 2002-35004

Katy Mouse teaches her younger brother, Tiny, the names of some of the things they see, including a boot, a snail, and a pheasant, when they go to the cornfield to play games

"The rich mixture of vinyl engravings, watercolor washes, and printed wood textures gives a timeless flavor to the adventure, as do Waddell's sweet story line and clear sentences." Booklist

Wadsworth, Olive A.

Over in the meadow; a counting rhyme; illustrated by Anna Vojtech. North-South Bks. 2002 unp il $15.95 *

Grades: PreK K 1 2   E

1. Counting 2. Nursery rhymes

ISBN 0-7358-1596-8; 0-7358-1597-6 (lib bdg)

LC 2001-51434

"A Cheshire Studio book"

An old nursery poem introduces animals and their young and the number one through ten

"Although many versions of the verse, both traditional and nontraditional, are available, this is an accessible rendition that children will enjoy in storytime and on their own." SLJ

Wahl, Jan, 1933-

Candy shop; illustrated by Nicole Wong. Charlesbridge 2004 unp il lib bdg $15.95 *

Grades: K 1 2 3   E

1. Toleration—Fiction 2. Taiwanese Americans—Fiction 3. African Americans—Fiction

ISBN 1-57091-508-3   LC 2003-3695

When a boy and his aunt find that a bigot has written hurtful words on the sidewalk just outside the candy shop owned by "Miz Chu," a new immigrant from Taiwan, they set out to comfort her

"The clean hues and supple lines of the pictures support Wahl's gentle message of comfort and tolerance." Booklist

Waldron, Kevin, 1979-

Mr. Peek and the misunderstanding at the zoo. Candlewick Press 2010 il $15.99

Grades: PreK K 1 2   E

1. Animals—Fiction 2. Zoos—Fiction 3. Worry—Fiction

ISBN 978-0-7636-4549-6; 0-7636-4549-4

LC 2009015137

"A Templar book"

First published 2008 in the United Kingdom

"Poor Mr. Peek thinks he has suddenly gained a tremendous amount of weight when he puts on his zookeeper jacket and a button pops off. As he makes his morning rounds, he complains to himself about how fat and wrinkled he is. . . . He does not notice that the zoo animals are worried because they think he is talking to them. Luckily, he returns home to discover that he had inadvertently switched jackets with his son. . . . Waldron's digital-media illustrations humorously convey the alarmed expressions of the animals while the quirky font and creative text placement reinforce Mr. Peek's stream-of-consciousness muttering." SLJ

Walker, Anna

I love Christmas. Simon & Schuster Books for Young Readers 2009 unp il $9.99

Grades: PreK K 1   E

1. Christmas—Fiction 2. Dogs—Fiction 3. Zebras—Fiction 4. Stories in rhyme

ISBN 978-1-4169-8317-0; 1-4169-8317-1

"A zebra named Ollie runs down some of his favorite holiday activities. Sweet, soft watercolors show Ollie and his dog decorating the Christmas tree, baking holiday treats with Nanna, and waiting for Santa, creating a cozy, merry accompaniment to the simple rhyming text. This is a great choice for a lap-sit and also as a read-alone for beginning readers." SLJ

Other titles about Ollie are:

I love my dad (2010)

I love my mom (2010)

Walker, Rob D.

Mama says; a book of love for mothers and sons; by Rob D. Walker; illustrations by Leo & Diane Dillon. The Blue Sky Press 2008 unp il $16.99 *

Grades: K 1 2 3   E

1. Conduct of life—Fiction 2. Faith 3. Mother-son relationship—Fiction 4. Stories in rhyme

ISBN 978-0-439-93208-0; 0-439-93208-4

LC 2007029827

"This elegantly designed book pairs a series of poems with stunning illustrations to celebrate the bond between mothers and sons. . . . The poems appear in English as

Walker, Rob D.—*Continued*

well as another language (among them Cherokee, Danish, Hebrew, and Inuktitut). . . . The illustrations . . . are well-researched and lavish, showing mothers in traditional dress lovingly engaged with their sons. . . . The Dillons' breathtaking paintings and the quiet dignity of the poems merit a wide audience." Publ Wkly

Walker, Sally M.

Druscilla's Halloween; illustrations by Lee White. Carolrhoda Books 2009 unp il lib bdg $16.95

Grades: PreK K   E
  1. Witches—Fiction   2. Old age—Fiction
3. Halloween—Fiction
  ISBN 978-0-8225-8941-9 (lib bdg); 0-8225-8941-9 (lib bdg)   LC 2008-41163

In the time when witches tiptoe about to have their Halloween fun, ancient Druscilla knows her creaking knees will prevent her from being sneaky and sets out to find a silent conveyance for herself, her cat, and her jack-o-lantern

"Walker shows her lighter side in this witty picture book. White's expressive paintings, wonderfully varied in size and approach but unified by style, capture both the comedy and the pathos of Druscillas's predicament." Booklist

The Vowel family; a tale of lost letters; by Sally M. Walker; illustrated by Kevin Luthardt. Carolrhoda Books 2008 unp il lib bdg $16.95

Grades: 1 2 3   E
  1. English language—Fiction
  ISBN 978-0-8225-7982-3 (lib bdg); 0-8225-7982-0 (lib bdg)   LC 2007-9952

The members of the Vowel family have a hard time talking until their children, Alan, Ellen, Iris, Otto, and Ursula, are born, and when one of them gets lost one day, it takes their Aunt Cyndy to fix the problem

"Luthardt's bright illustrations, featuring people with cartoonish balloon heads, ably echo the story's silliness. This clever approach to learning vowels will prove far more fun than just the basic recitation that's commonly taught." Booklist

Wallace, Carol

One nosy pup; illustrated by Steve Björkman. Holiday House 2005 40p il $15.95 *

Grades: K 1 2   E
  1. Dogs—Fiction 2. Hamsters—Fiction
  ISBN 0-8234-1917-7

"A Holiday House reader"

After moving to a new house, Poky the beagle befriends Charlie the hamster, who was accidentally left behind by the previous owners

"Wallace writes in short, simply constructed sentences and uses a brisk, basic vocabulary just right for new readers, and the expressive, color-washed art hums with activity and emotion." Booklist

The Santa secret; by Carol Wallace; illustrated by Steve Björkman. Holiday House 2007 40p il (Holiday House reader) $15.95

Grades: K 1 2   E
  1. Christmas—Fiction 2. Santa Claus—Fiction
3. Family life—Fiction 4. Dogs—Fiction
  ISBN 978-0-8234-2022-3; 0-8234-2022-1

With the help of the family bloodhound, a little girl's secret Christmas wish, known only to Santa, finally comes true

This is a "well-paced story. . . . The full-color, expressive cartoon drawings . . . play an integral part in helping youngsters decode and understand the text. This should be a popular choice for newly independent readers." SLJ

Turkeys together; illustrated by Jacqueline Rogers. Holiday House 2005 38p il $15.95 *

Grades: K 1 2   E
  1. Dogs—Fiction 2. Turkeys—Fiction 3. Eggs—Fiction
  ISBN 0-8234-1895-2   LC 2004-52392

"A Holiday House reader"

A pointer dog puppy helps a mother turkey figure out how to protect her eggs from being stolen.

"A sweet tale about cooperation and friendship, with a satisfying conclusion. . . . Soft watercolor illustrations add meaning to the text and provide clues for some of the more difficult words. . . . The expressive animal faces are charming and realistic." SLJ

Wallace, Nancy Elizabeth

Look! look! look! by Nancy Elizabeth Wallace with Linda K. Friedlaender; illustrated by Nancy Elizabeth Wallace. Marshall Cavendish 2006 unp il $16.95

Grades: K 1 2 3   E
  1. Art—Fiction 2. Mice—Fiction
  ISBN 978-0-7614-5282-9; 0-7614-5282-6
                        LC 2005-16934

Three mice "borrow" a postcard which is a reproduction of a painting, and from it they learn about color, pattern, line, and shape. Includes instructions for making and sending a postcard.

"This is not only an amusing, creative story, but also an adventure into art that encourages originality while inspiring creativity." SLJ

Pumpkin day! written and illustrated by Nancy Elizabeth Wallace. Marshall Cavendish 2002 unp il $16.95

Grades: PreK K 1 2   E
  1. Pumpkin—Fiction 2. Rabbits—Fiction
  ISBN 0-7614-5128-5   LC 2002-834

Companion volume to Apples, apples, apples (2000)

A bunny family picks pumpkins at a local farm and learns pumpkin facts in the process

"Although there are many other books on the topic, this one stands apart because of its simple, yet dynamic collage artwork and the quality and quantity of information that is tucked into the text in all sorts of interesting ways." Booklist

Wallace, Nancy Elizabeth—*Continued*

Recycle every day! written and illustrated by Nancy Elizabeth Wallace. Marshall Cavendish 2003 unp il $16.95

Grades: PreK K 1 2   E
    1. Recycling—Fiction 2. Rabbits—Fiction
    ISBN 0-7614-5149-8   LC 2001-26050

When Minna has a school assignment to make a poster about recycling, her entire rabbit family spends the week practicing various kinds of recycling and suggesting ideas for her poster

"Using found materials to create the lovely art, the author/illustrator practices what she preaches and invites readers to search for the recycled materials. An activity and a game are appended. While the book's message is obvious, there is enough of a story to keep youngsters interested." SLJ

Other titles about Minna are:
The kindness quilt (2006)
Stars! Stars! Stars! (2009)

Seeds! Seeds! Seeds! written and illustrated by Nancy Elizabeth Wallace. Marshall Cavendish 2004 unp il hardcover o.p. pa $5.99

Grades: PreK K 1 2   E
    1. Seeds—Fiction 2. Bears—Fiction
    ISBN 0-7614-5159-5; 0-7614-5366-0 (pa)
                         LC 2003-9318

Buddy Bear learns about different kinds of seeds and their uses when he opens a package sent by his grandfather

"The artwork consists of cut-paper collages with shadowing and life-sized photos of real seeds that look as though they can be picked right off the pages. The story is entertaining and educational." SLJ

Walsh, Ellen Stoll, 1942-

Dot & Jabber and the big bug mystery. Harcourt 2003 unp il $15

Grades: PreK K 1 2   E
    1. Mice—Fiction 2. Insects—Fiction 3. Mystery fiction
    ISBN 0-15-216518-5   LC 2002-11386

Dot and Jabber, mouse detectives, try to solve the mystery of the disappearing insects

"The distinctive cut-paper collages step nicely off the page for a 3-D look, and the earthy greens and browns are gentle and calming. A note on insects and camouflage is included." SLJ

Other titles about Dot & Jabber are:
Dot & Jabber and the great acorn mystery (2001)
Dot & Jabber and the mystery of the missing stream (2002)

For Pete's sake. Harcourt Brace & Co. 1998 unp il $16

Grades: PreK K 1 2   E
    1. Alligators—Fiction 2. Flamingos—Fiction
    ISBN 0-15-200324-X   LC 97-25677

Pete, an alligator who thinks that he is a flamingo, worries when he begins to notice the differences between him and his flamingo friends

"Walsh's precise paper-cut collages are just right. Subtly textured and with spacious, stark white backgrounds,

they are pleasingly simple, giving the comedy and the message plenty of unencumbered opportunity to sink in." Booklist

Mouse shapes. Harcourt 2007 unp il $16 *

Grades: PreK K   E
    1. Shape—Fiction 2. Mice—Fiction
    ISBN 978-0-15-206091-6   LC 2006-13695

Three mice make a variety of things out of different shapes as they hide from a scary cat

"The collage technique works well for distinguishing the brightly colored shapes, and the simple story is pitched perfectly for sharing with the youngest of listeners." SLJ

Other titles about the mice are:
Mouse paint (1989)
Mouse count (1991)

Walter, Mildred Pitts, 1922-

Alec's primer; illustrated by Larry Johnson. Vermont Folklife Center 2004 unp il (Vermont Folklife Center children's book series) $15.95

Grades: K 1 2 3   E
    1. Slavery—Fiction 2. African Americans—Fiction
    3. Reading—Fiction
    ISBN 0-916718-20-4   LC 2003-27716

A young slave's journey to freedom begins when a plantation owner's granddaughter teaches him how to read. Based on the childhood of Alec Turner (1845-1923) who escaped from slavery by joining the Union Army during the Civil War and later became a landowner in Vermont

"Walter's spare, dramatic words and Johnson's stirring double-page paintings present a glimpse of the history in a brutal world." Booklist

Walters, Catherine, 1965-

Time to sleep, Alfie Bear. Dutton Children's Bks. 2003 unp il $15.99

Grades: PreK K   E
    1. Bedtime—Fiction 2. Bears—Fiction
    ISBN 0-525-47204-5   LC 2003-40962

On a night when Alfie Bear is not sleepy, he tries to join various nocturnal animals so that he can stay up later

"The sweet story is set off nicely by the lush, realistic single and double-page artwork. Young observers will appreciate the detailed illustrations." SLJ

Other titles about Alfie Bear are:
Are you there, Baby Bear? (1999)
Play gently, Alfie Bear (2002)
When will it be spring? (1998)
Where are you, Alfie Bear? (2002)

Walters, Virginia

Are we there yet, Daddy? illustrated by S.D. Schindler. Viking 1999 unp il hardcover o.p. pa $6.99

Grades: PreK K 1 2   E
    1. Automobile travel—Fiction 2. Maps—Fiction
    3. Stories in rhyme
    ISBN 0-670-87402-7; 0-14-230013-6 (pa)
                         LC 97-18220

Walters, Virginia—*Continued*
Colored map on folded page preceding t.p
A young boy describes the trip he and his father make to Grandma's house, measuring how many miles are left at various points on the trip
"This unique picture book combines maps and counting skills with a bouncy refrain that invites kids to join in. . . . The flat, pastel pictures add enlivening details to the repetitive text." SLJ

Wang Xiaohong, 1966-
One year in Beijing; written by Xiaohong Wang; illustrated by Grace Lin. ChinaSprout 2006 unp il map $16.95
Grades: PreK K 1 2   E
1. China—Fiction
ISBN 0-97473-025-4; 978-0-97473-025-7
In this introduction to China and Chinese culture, an eight-year-old girl named "Ling Ling points out famous places as well as some of her favorite spots, describes foods eaten during special occasions, and explains traditions associated with particular celebrations throughout the year. . . . Grace Lin's bright, colorful illustrations and accompanying cartoonlike ink sketches accentuate the narrative's informality and make this engaging personal tour an excellent supplement to classroom textbooks." Booklist

Warburton, Tom
1000 times no; as told by Mr. Warburton. Laura Geringer Books 2009 unp il $17.99
Grades: PreK K 1   E
1. Polyglot materials
ISBN 978-0-06-154263-3; 0-06-154263-6
                                    LC 2007044270
When Noah's mother tells him that it is time to go, he finds more than a few ways to refuse.
"Gouache cartoon scenes visually reinforce Noah's multilingual vetoes, from a full-page sphinx and hieroglyphics to a small square panel with a text message. Endpapers provide identification of the languages, pronunciations, and cultures that the precocious youngster employs. Delightful fun in its theme and delivery, this story will be asked for again and again." SLJ

Ward, Helen, 1962-
The rooster and the fox; retold & illustrated by Helen Ward. Millbrook Press 2003 unp il $16.95; lib bdg $24.90
Grades: K 1 2 3   E
1. Chaucer, Geoffrey, d. 1400—Adaptations 2. Roosters—Fiction 3. Fables
ISBN 0-7613-1846-1; 0-7613-2920-X (lib bdg)
"A Templar book"
First published 2002 in the United Kingdom
An adaptation of the "Nun's priest's tale" from Geoffrey Chaucer's Canterbury tales
"After being outsmarted by a cunning fox, a cocky rooster gathers his wits and turns the tables on his captor. Chaucer's Chanticleer is brought to life through a riveting retelling and magnificent, edge-of-your-seat artwork." SLJ

Ward, Jennifer, 1963-
The busy tree; illustrated by Lisa Falkenstern. Marshall Cavendish Children 2009 unp il $17.99
Grades: PreK K 1 2   E
1. Stories in rhyme 2. Trees—Fiction 3. Forest animals—Fiction
ISBN 978-0-7614-5550-9; 0-7614-5550-7
                                    LC 2008006005
"In rhyming couplets, an old oak introduces children to the wildlife that lives and feeds in and around it. . . . Handsome realistic oil paintings set on white pages show details of the tree and its denizens in daytime, at sunset, and at night, in fall and in summer. . . . Children will enjoy this brief glimpse at a familiar species that reinforces much that they have already observed." SLJ

Ward, Lynd Kendall, 1905-1985
The biggest bear; by Lynd Ward. Houghton Mifflin 1988 84p il lib bdg $16; pa $6.95
Grades: PreK K 1 2   E
1. Bears—Fiction
ISBN 0-395-14806-5 (lib bdg); 0-395-15024-8 (pa)
                                    LC 88-176366
Awarded the Caldecott Medal, 1953
A reissue of the title first published 1952
"Johnny Orchard never did acquire the bearskin for which he boldly went hunting. Instead, he brought home a cuddly bear cub, which grew in size and appetite to mammoth proportions and worried his family and neighbors half to death." Child Books Too Good to Miss

Wargin, Kathy-Jo, 1965-
Moose on the loose; written by Kathy-jo Wargin; illustrated by John Bendall-Brunello. Sleeping Bear Press 2009 unp il $15.95
Grades: PreK K 1   E
1. Stories in rhyme 2. Moose—Fiction
ISBN 978-1-58536-427-5; 1-58536-427-4
                                    LC 2009004803
Rhyming text poses a series of questions about how the reader would deal with a moose that is on the loose, in the yard, in the house, or taking a bath
"Children will delight in the antics of both the moose and its young human companion. Bold, bright, cartoonlike illustrations capture the action in a humorous style." SLJ

Warhola, James
Uncle Andy's. Putnam 2003 unp il $16.99
Grades: K 1 2 3   E
1. Warhol, Andy, 1928?-1987 2. Artists—United States
ISBN 0-399-23869-7   LC 2002-7766
The author describes a trip to see his uncle, the soon-to-be-famous artist Andy Warhol, and the fun that he and his family had on the visit
"This catches the excitement that the creative process can engender, both for the established artist and for the dreamer." Booklist
Another title about Uncle Andy is:
Uncle Andy's cats (2009)

Waring, Geoffrey

Oscar and the bat; a book about sound; [by] Geoff Waring. Candlewick Press 2008 27p il (Start with science) $14.99

Grades: PreK K 1 2   E

1. Cats—Fiction 2. Bats—Fiction 3. Sound—Fiction

ISBN 978-0-7636-4025-5; 0-7636-4025-5

LC 2007052195

First published 2006 in the United Kingdom

Bat teaches Oscar the kitten to hear and identify the sounds around him, whether they are made by animals and birds or by a passing thunderstorm

This is "clear and immediate. . . . Spacious digital color illustrations show Oscar the Cat in a meadow with his friend, Bat, who answers Oscar's questions with fascinating scientific detail." Booklist

Other titles about Oscar are:

Oscar and the bird (2009)

Oscar and the cricket (2008)

Oscar and the frog (2007)

Oscar and the moth (2007)

Oscar and the snail (2009)

Waring, Richard

Hungry hen; illustrated by Caroline Jayne Church. HarperCollins Pubs. 2001 unp il $14.95 *

Grades: PreK K 1 2   E

1. Chickens—Fiction 2. Foxes—Fiction

ISBN 0-06-623880-3   LC 2001-24044

A greedy fox watches a hungry hen growing bigger every day, knowing that the longer he waits to eat her, the bigger she will be

"The story is simple and dramatic, with a perfect blend of words and pictures. . . . This is elemental storytelling, with tension rising until it's almost unbearable, and then the great surprise. The art is beautiful, with big, bright, clear shapes of the rosy hen and the sneaky fox on backgrounds of handmade paper." Booklist

Warnes, Tim

Chalk and Cheese. Simon & Schuster Books for Young Readers 2008 unp il $16.99

Grades: K 1 2   E

1. Mice—Fiction 2. Dogs—Fiction 3. Friendship—Fiction 4. New York (N.Y.)—Fiction

ISBN 978-1-4169-1378-8; 1-4169-1378-5

LC 2007-18332

Cheese, an English country mouse, goes to visit his best friend, Chalk, a dog who lives in New York City, and even though the two of them are very different, they have a great time.

This is illustrated with "expansive, humor-laden art, some drawn in cartoon-strip style. . . . What's best is the sheer exuberance both feel about New York. . . . Kids . . . will enjoy both the travelogue and the unlikely friendship." Booklist

Daddy hug; by Tim Warnes; illustrated by Jane Chapman. HarperCollins 2008 unp il $16.99; lib bdg $17.89

Grades: PreK K   E

1. Fathers—Fiction 2. Animals—Fiction 3. Stories in rhyme

ISBN 978-0-06-058950-9; 0-06-058950-7; 978-0-06-058951-6 (lib bdg); 0-06-058951-5 (lib bdg)

LC 2005017867

"In a jolly, rhyming text, this book describes various animal fathers. . . . The vibrant, painterly illustrations, featuring fathers interacting with their offspring, are filled with action and color. . . . The simple text and warm-hued artwork create a feeling of security that will appeal to children." SLJ

Watson, Renée

A place where hurricanes happen; illustrated by Shadra Strickland. Random House 2010 unp il $17.99; lib bdg $20.99

Grades: 1 2 3 4   E

1. Hurricane Katrina, 2005—Fiction 2. New Orleans (La.)—Fiction

ISBN 978-0-375-85609-9; 0-375-85609-9; 978-0-375-95609-6 (lib bdg); 0-375-95609-3 (lib bdg)

LC 2009017826

Told in alternating voices, four friends from the same New Orleans neighborhood describe what happens to them and their community when they are separated, then reunited, as a result of Hurricane Katrina.

"The text is lyrical and realistically portrays a child's point of view, deftly describing in a few words how the children are affected. . . . The evocative watercolor-and-ink illustrations in soft pastels and grays limn the devastation but also the good times of the neighborhood to great effect." SLJ

Watt, Melanie, 1975-

Chester; written and illustrated by Melanie Watt. Kids Can Press 2007 unp il $16.95

Grades: PreK K 1 2   E

1. Cats—Fiction 2. Authorship—Fiction

ISBN 978-1-55453-140-0; 1-55453-140-3

"Watt presents audiences with the story of a mouse—or she tries to, but her cat Chester has a red marker and his own idea about the subject of the story: himself. . . . The notion is entertaining and its execution . . . is frequently hilarious. . . . This entertains both as a cat story and as an entry-level metatextual narrative." Bull Cent Child Books

Other titles about Chester are:

Chester's back! (2008)

Chester's masterpiece (2010)

Have I got a book for you! Kids Can Press 2009 unp il $16.95

Grades: PreK K 1 2   E

1. Selling—Fiction 2. Books and reading—Fiction

ISBN 978-1-55453-289-6; 1-55453-289-2

Mr. Al Foxword is one persistent salesman! He will do just about anything to sell you this book. Al tries every trick of the trade. But just when you're ready to close the book on him, he comes up with a clever tactic

Watt, Melanie, 1975-—_Continued_
you simply can't refuse!

"Charcoal pencil illustrations are digitally assembled and feature bright orange, yellow, and green. Foxword's clever sales techniques make this book funny to the hilt." SLJ

Scaredy Squirrel. Kids Can Press 2006 unp il $14.95

Grades: PreK K 1 2   E
   1. Squirrels—Fiction 2. Fear—Fiction
   ISBN 1-55337-959-4

Scaredy Squirrel never leaves his nut tree because he's afraid of the unknown "out there." But then, something unexpected happens that may just change his outlook.

"With his iconic nervous grin and over-the-top punctiliousness, Scaredy Squirrel is an endearing character. Thick-lined cartoons with bold patches of color, quirky charts and graphs, and clever asides provide humor that will appeal to children." SLJ

Other titles about Scaredy Squirrel are:
Scaredy Squirrel makes a friend (2007)
Scaredy Squirrel at the beach (2008)
Scaredy Squirrel at night (2009)

Watts, Bernadette, 1942-
The Smallest Snowflake. North-South 2009 unp il $16.95

Grades: PreK K 1 2   E
   1. Snow—Fiction 2. Winter—Fiction 3. Spring—Fiction
   ISBN 978-0-7358-2258-0; 0-7358-2258-1

"Smallest Snowflake, longing for 'someplace special,' drifts along through the air until she lands in the window box of a little cottage. . . . Finally, green shoots push up through the dirt and snowdrop flowers open on the stalks. . . . Watts writes a tale as sturdy yet delicate as her artwork. . . . This quiet yet involving picture book is highly recommended for reading aloud as winter turns to spring." Booklist

The ugly duckling; by Hans Christian Andersen; adapted and illustrated by Bernadette Watts. North-South Bks. 2000 unp il $15.95; lib bdg $16.95

Grades: K 1 2 3 4   E
   1. Andersen, Hans Christian, 1805-1875—Adaptations 2. Swans—Fiction 3. Fairy tales
   ISBN 0-7358-1388-4; 0-7358-1389-2 (lib bdg)
                                          LC 00-35125

An ugly duckling spends an unhappy year ostracized by the other animals before he grows into a beautiful swan

The "detailed double-paged spreads are beautiful. . . . Watts' active pastoral landscapes, filled with light and movement, capture the changing seasons and the sturdy, unwanted outsider's search for home." Booklist

Wax, Wendy, 1963-
City witch, country switch; illustrated by Scott Gibala-Broxholm. Marshall Cavendish 2008 unp il $16.99

Grades: K 1 2 3   E
   1. Witches—Fiction 2. Cousins—Fiction 3. City and town life—Fiction 4. Country life—Fiction 5. Stories in rhyme
   ISBN 978-0-7614-5429-8; 0-7614-5429-2
                                       LC 2007-28355

While paying a surprise visit to her city-dwelling cousin, Muffletump misses her home in the country but when Mitzi leaves the city to see where Muffletump lives, she is just as uncomfortable until the two, together, conjure a solution.

"Told in rollicking, lyrical text accompanied by bright, colorful illustrations. . . . Children will want to check this book out again and again." Libr Media Connect

Wayland, April Halprin, 1954-
New Year at the pier; a Rosh Hashanah story; illustrated by Stephane Jorisch. Dial Books for Young Readers 2009 unp il $16.99

Grades: K 1 2 3   E
   1. Jews—Fiction 2. Rosh ha-Shanah—Fiction
   ISBN 978-0-8037-3279-7; 0-8037-3279-1
                                       LC 2007039812

On Rosh Hashanah, Izzy and his family make lists of the wrongs they have committed over the past year, and after they have apologized, they throw pieces of bread into the water to 'clean their hearts' in a ceremony called tashlich.

"The empathetic, low-key prose makes important points about personal responsibility without pummeling readers, while the stylish, keenly observed watercolors convey both Izzy's sheepish chagrin and the joys of communal tradition." Publ Wkly

Weatherby, Brenda
The trucker; written by Brenda Weatherby; illustrated by Mark Weatherby. Scholastic 2004 unp il $15.95

Grades: PreK K 1 2   E
   1. Trucks—Fiction
   ISBN 0-439-39877-0   LC 2002-70787

Wesley dreams his toy semi-flatbed rig grows big enough for him to have a trucking adventure but wakes to find he is in the back of his father's truck.

"The brief, simple text is filled with the lively sounds of the big machine on the road. . . . Using acrylic, sand, and, appropriately, road dirt, the pictures convey something of the story's blurry, dreamlike quality, while supplying plenty of realistic details of the trucker's life." Booklist

Weatherford, Carole Boston, 1956-

Champions on the bench; the Cannon Street YMCA all-stars; by Carole Boston Weatherford; illustrations by Leonard Jenkins. Dial Books for Young Readers 2007 unp il $16.99

Grades: 1 2 3 4   E

1. Baseball—Fiction 2. African Americans—Fiction 3. Race relations—Fiction 4. South Carolina—Fiction

ISBN 0-8037-2987-1; 978-0-8037-2987-2

LC 2003-19385

Story based on the discrimination faced by the 1955 Cannon Street YMCA Little League All-Stars when the white teams refused to play them in the series tournament.

"Done in pencil, acrylic, and spray paint, Jenkins's color-saturated illustrations imbue the text with warmth, passion, and nostalgia. This is a powerful story, well told." SLJ

Freedom on the menu; the Greensboro sit-ins; paintings by Jerome Lagarrigue. Dial Books for Young Readers 2005 unp il $16.99 *

Grades: K 1 2 3   E

1. African Americans—Fiction 2. Civil rights demonstrations—Fiction 3. Race relations—Fiction 4. North Carolina—Fiction

ISBN 0-8037-2860-3   LC 2002-13226

The 1960 civil rights sit-ins at the Woolworth's lunch counter in Greensboro, North Carolina, are seen through the eyes of a young Southern black girl.

"Simple and straightforward, the first-person narrative relates events within the context of one close-knit family. . . . The well-composed, painterly illustrations show up well from a distance. A handsome book." Booklist

Weatherly, Lee

The scariest monster in the world; [by] Lee Weatherly & [illustrated by] Algy Craig Hall. Boxer Books 2009 unp il $14.95

Grades: K 1 2   E

1. Monsters—Fiction

ISBN 978-1-906250-40-9; 1-906250-40-5

"A scary, hairy monster with green teeth chases and frightens all of the woodland creatures. One day, he comes down with the hiccups. . . . When the other animals see him sitting on a rock and crying, they develop a novel idea for curing the problem. . . . The large illustrations, done in graphite stick and watercolor paints, are lively, fresh, and expressive, giving personality to the story." SLJ

Weaver, Tess

Cat jumped in! by Tess Weaver; illustrated by Emily Arnold McCully. Clarion Books 2007 32p il $16

Grades: PreK K 1 2   E

1. Cats—Fiction

ISBN 978-0-618-61488-2   LC 2006039217

An inquisitive feline walks through the rooms of a house, jumping into one mess after another, before landing in the loving arms of its owner.

"Some 26 different verbs describe the cat's movements, infusing the story with plenty of action, and the bright watercolors seem quickly carefully rendered." Booklist

Frederick Finch, loudmouth; by Tess Weaver; illustrated by Debbie Tilley. Clarion Books 2008 unp il $16

Grades: K 1 2   E

1. Contests—Fiction 2. Fairs—Fiction

ISBN 0-618-45239-7; 978-0-618-45239-2

LC 2007019114

After trying and trying to win a ribbon at the state fair, Frederick finally is rewarded for his true talent.

"This title uses humor to illustrate how even an unusual and often-considered-negative talent can be useful. . . . The watercolor-and-ink illustrations humorously depict the boy's trials without giving away the surprise ending." SLJ

Weeks, Sarah

Drip, drop; story by Sarah Weeks; pictures by Jane Manning. HarperCollins Pubs. 2000 32p il (I can read book) hardcover o.p. pa $3.99

Grades: PreK K 1 2   E

1. Mice—Fiction 2. Rain—Fiction 3. Stories in rhyme

ISBN 0-06-028523-0; 0-06-028524-9 (lib bdg); 0-06-443597-0 (pa)   LC 00-21652

Pip Squeak the mouse is kept awake all night by the drips from his leaky roof

"Short, simple sentences keep the action moving along while a single problem focuses readers' attention. The snappy narrative is coupled with expressive, silly illustrations." SLJ

Another title about Pip Squeak is:

Pip Squeak (2007)

Ella, of course! written by Sarah Weeks; illustrated by Doug Cushman. Harcourt 2007 unp il $16

Grades: PreK K   E

1. Pigs—Fiction 2. Dance—Fiction

ISBN 978-0-15-204943-0; 0-15-204943-6

LC 2005-25910

When Ella the pig is banned from bringing her umbrella to the dance recital, she comes up with an ingenious solution to the problem

"Weeks' short text includes lots of repetitive phrases and sound effects that will easily encourage participation. Cushman adds slapstick humor with double-page scenes." Booklist

Overboard! by Sarah Weeks; illustrated by Sam Williams. Harcourt, Inc. 2006 unp il $14

Grades: PreK   E

1. Play—Fiction 2. Rabbits—Fiction 3. Stories in rhyme

ISBN 0-15-205046-9

From morning to night, a little bunny playfully grabs and throws items, including a bathtime rubber ducky and snacktime raisins.

"Bright and sunny as only a toddler's book on the subject could be, the rhyming, rhythmic text bounces merrily along, while the broad lines and bold colors of the artwork express the same carefree sense of exuberance." Booklist

Another title about this bunny is:

Bunny fun (2007)

Weeks, Sarah—*Continued*

Sophie Peterman tells the truth! illustrated by Robert Neubecker. Beach Lane Books 2009 unp il $16.99 *

Grades: PreK K 1 2   **E**
    1. Infants—Fiction 2. Siblings—Fiction
    ISBN 978-1-4169-8686-7; 1-4169-8686-3
                      LC 2008-51058

A disgruntled big sister reveals unpleasant facts about babies.

This offers "thick-lined cartoon illustrations in bright colors and clear bold type that gets bigger and bigger. . . . The details of messy daily life and the honest, un-sentimental expressions of rage and bonding are just right for young children to recognize and laugh about to-gether." Booklist

Two eggs, please; written by Sarah Weeks; illustrated by Betsy Lewin. Atheneum Bks. for Young Readers 2003 unp il $15.95

Grades: PreK K 1 2   **E**
    1. Eggs—Fiction 2. Restaurants—Fiction 3. Animals—Fiction
    ISBN 0-689-83196-X   LC 2002-5291

"An all-night diner attracts a wide variety of custom-ers in the middle of the night, including a rhino cab driv-er, two wolf police officers, and a crocodile street per-former and his snake. One by one, they take stools at the counter and order the same thing, 'Two eggs, please,' but each order is different: soft-boiled, hard-boiled, poached, raw (for the snake). The premise is as basic as fried eggs, and handled with a light touch, but Lewin's inviting watercolor and ink illustrations add flavor and expand the story to involve young listeners and readers." Horn Book

Woof; a love story; illustrated by Holly Berry. Laura Geringer Books 2009 unp il $16.99 *

Grades: PreK K 1 2   **E**
    1.   Dogs—Fiction   2.   Cats—Fiction
    3. Communication—Fiction 4. Love—Fiction
    5. Stories in rhyme
    ISBN 978-0-06-025007-2; 0-06-025007-0
                      LC 2006022295

Despite a language barrier, a dog and cat fall in love with the help of a buried trombone.

"This affectionate and funny story is told almost musi-cally, in rhythmic . . . verse by expert storyteller Weeks. Berry's exuberant collage illustrations spill over the pages, gorgeously chaotic and filled with heart." SLJ

Weigel, Jeff, 1958-

Atomic Ace; (he's just my dad); written and illustrated by Jeff Weigel. Albert Whitman & Co. 2004 unp il $15.95

Grades: PreK K 1 2   **E**
    1. Fathers—Fiction 2. Superheroes—Fiction
    3. Stories in rhyme 4. Science fiction
    ISBN 0-8075-3216-9   LC 2003-17523

In this rhyming story told in comic book format, a boy considers his family normal, though his superhero dad, Atomic Ace, does amazing feats, even battling the evil Insect King

"The juxtapositions between superheroics and regular-guy domesticity are clever, and Weigl's confident artwork . . . is guaranteed to satisfy children obsessed with caped crusaders." Booklist

    Another title about Atomic Ace is:

Atomic Ace and the robot rampage (2006)

Weigelt, Udo

Super Guinea Pig to the rescue; [by] Udo Weigelt; illustrations by Nina Spranger. Walker & Co. 2007 unp il $16.95

Grades: K 1 2 3   **E**
    1. Guinea pigs—Fiction 2. Pets—Fiction
    3. Superheroes—Fiction
    ISBN 0-8027-9705-9; 978-0-8027-9705-6
                      LC 2007-06668

A guinea pig gets upset when his fellow pets make fun of his favorite television superhero, and so he makes a costume and pretends to be Super Guinea Pig himself.

"Using lively language, Weigelt compassionately and humorously relates the guinea pig's earnest efforts, as expressive watercolor-and-acrylic illustrations show char-acters and events from a variety of perspectives." Booklist

Weill, Cynthia, 1959-

ABeCedarios; Mexican folk art ABCs in English and Spanish; [by] Cynthia Weill and K.B. Basseches; wood sculptures from Oaxaca by Moises and Armando Jimenez. Cinco Puntos Press 2008 unp il $14.95

Grades: PreK K 1 2 3 4   **E**
    1. Folk art 2. Alphabet 3. Mexican art 4. Animals in art 5. Bilingual books—English-Spanish
    ISBN 1-933693-13-4; 978-1-933693-13-2
                      LC 2007019441

"Mexican folk-art figures are the focus of this colorful alphabet book. Each page presents a small Oaxacan woodcarving of an animal done in a rainbow of colors. The only text is the animals' names in Spanish and in English. . . . The sculpted figures display personality and enough vibrant energy to leap off the pages." SLJ

Opuestos; Mexican folk art opposites in English and Spanish; wood sculptures from Oaxaca by Quirino and Martin Santiago. Cinco Puntos Press 2009 unp il $14.95

Grades: PreK K 1 2 3 4   **E**
    1. Folk art 2. Opposites 3. Mexican art 4. Animals in art 5. Bilingual books—English-Spanish
    ISBN 978-1-933693-56-9; 1-933693-56-8
                      LC 2008-56039

"Oaxacan folk art in the form of hand-carved wood sculptures abounds in this bilingual concept book about opposites. Contrasting concepts include inside and out-side, high and low, and left and right, to name a few. At the turn of each page, readers see brightly painted wood characters set against equally vibrantly colored back-ground pages that effortlessly convey the concept the au-thor sets out to teach." SLJ

Weinstein, Muriel Harris

When Louis Armstrong taught me scat; by Muriel Harris Weinstein; illustrated by R. Gregory Christie. Chronicle Books 2008 unp il $16.99
Grades: PreK K 1 2   E
    1. Armstrong, Louis, 1900-1971—Fiction 2. Jazz music—Fiction 3. Singing—Fiction 4. African Americans—Fiction
    ISBN 978-0-8118-5131-2; 0-8118-5131-1
                        LC 2007044305

After dancing to music on the radio before she goes to bed, a young girl learns how to sing scat when Louis Armstrong comes to her in a dream. Includes facts about Louis Armstrong and scat singing.

"Decked out in bubble-gum pinks and soulful blues, scenes of the little girl and Satchmo cool-catting it across the pages will [get] kids moving, but it's the bop-happy nonsense words themselves that highlight the art." Booklist

Weis, Carol

When the cows got loose; [by] Carol Weis; [illustrated by] Ard Hoyt. Simon & Schuster Books for Young Readers 2006 unp il $16.95
Grades: K 1 2 3   E
    1. Cattle—Fiction 2. Circus—Fiction
    ISBN 0-689-85166-9

"When a family of big-top performers' eccentric cow herd is on the loose, it's young Ida Mae's job to perform the roundup. . . . Ida Mae narrates in a droll, colloquial voice . . . and the tension between what her words leave out and what the pictures show makes most of the fun. . . . The expressive mixed-media images . . . will easily draw interest, giggles, and requests for repeated viewings." Booklist

Weiss, Ellen, 1953-

The taming of Lola; a shrew story; a picture book in five acts; illustrated by Jerry Smath. Abrams Books for Young Readers 2010 unp il $15.95
Grades: PreK K 1 2   E
    1. Cousins—Fiction   2. Shrews—Fiction 3. Grandmothers—Fiction
    ISBN 978-0-8109-4066-6; 0-8109-4066-3
                        LC 2009-00617

Lola, a shrew, is famous all over West Meadow for her temper tantrums, but when her cousin Lester comes for a visit and gets special treatment just because he demands it, Lola begins to rethink her behavior.

"Screwball dialogue and banter, . . . asides from the narrator, and details about the shrew diet . . . combine to keep action and laughs coming. The pacing is even, the goody-goody peacemaking is leavened by the wisecracks, and there's even a surprise ending." Publ Wkly

Weitzman, Jacqueline Preiss

You can't take a balloon into the Metropolitan Museum; story by Jacqueline Preiss Weitzman; pictures by Robin Preiss Glasser. Dial Bks. for Young Readers 1998 37p il hardcover o.p. pa $7.99 *
Grades: K 1 2 3   E
    1. Metropolitan Museum of Art (New York, N.Y.)—Fiction 2. New York (N.Y.)—Fiction 3. Stories without words
    ISBN 0-8037-2301-6; 0-14-056816-6 (pa)
                        LC 97-31629

In this wordless story, a young girl and her grandmother view works inside the Metropolitan Museum of Art, while the balloon she has been forced to leave outside floats around New York City causing a series of mishaps that mirror scenes in the museum's artworks

"Lively, squiggly ink sketches with characters picked out in watercolor and gouache for accent, along with reproductions of art from the Met . . . tell a vivid, happy tale." Booklist
Other titles in this series are:
You can't take a balloon into the Museum of Fine Arts (2002)
You can't take a balloon into the National Gallery (2000)

Weller, Frances Ward

The day the animals came; a story of Saint Francis Day; illustrated by Loren Long. Philomel Bks. 2003 unp il $16.99
Grades: K 1 2 3   E
    1. Animals—Fiction 2. Hispanic Americans—Fiction 3. New York (N.Y.)—Fiction
    ISBN 0-399-23630-9   LC 2002-6297

A young girl who misses her former home and her animal friends left behind in the West Indies makes new friends at the blessing of the animals at a cathedral in New York City on the Feast of St. Francis

"The acrylic paintings soar as Long looks at goings-on from many different perspectives. . . . Children will like seeing so many animals in such an unexpected place, and Ria's feeling of acceptance makes for a satisfying conclusion." Booklist

Wellington, Monica

Apple farmer Annie. Dutton Children's Bks. 2001 unp il $14.99
Grades: PreK K 1 2   E
    1. Apples—Fiction
    ISBN 0-525-46727-0   LC 00-46203

Annie the apple farmer saves her most beautiful apples to sell fresh at the farmers' market

"Charming and cheery, [this] story makes a great read-aloud. The illustrations seem to step right out of a coloring book with simple shapes, objects, and bright, crayon-box colors." SLJ

Mr. Cookie Baker; [by] Monica Wellington. rev ed. Dutton Children's Books 2006 unp il $15.99 *
Grades: PreK   E
    1. Baking—Fiction 2. Cookies—Fiction
    ISBN 0-525-47763-2
    First published 1992

Wellington, Monica—*Continued*

After a day of making and selling cookies, Mr. Baker gets to enjoy one himself. Includes cookie recipes.

"Done in gouache and colored pencil, the artwork features clean lines and flat colors that are as cheery as the cookies' sugar sprinkles." Booklist

Pizza at Sally's; [by] Monica Wellington. Dutton Children's Books 2006 unp il $14.99

Grades: PreK K 1 2   E
  1. Cooking—Fiction   2. Pizza—Fiction
3. Restaurants—Fiction
  ISBN 978-0-525-47715-0; 0-525-47715-2
                               LC 2005026498

With vegetables from her own garden and other fresh ingredients, Sally mixes and bakes hot and bubbly pizzas for her customers to take home or eat in her pizzeria

"Cheerful, precisely composed gouache paintings accented with photo collages of fresh ingredients add warmth and humor to the story." SLJ

Riki's birdhouse. Dutton Children's Books 2009 unp il $15.99

Grades: PreK K 1 2   E
  1. Birdhouses—Fiction 2. Birds—Fiction
  ISBN 978-0-525-42079-8; 0-525-42079-7
                               LC 2008013890

Riki, who loves to watch, feed, and listen to the birds that come to his garden, decides to build a birdhouse

"Riki's passion for birds is evident, and likely to be contagious. . . . The bold colors, simple shapes and clean lines of the gouache illustrations are in sharp contrast to the details found in the photographic elements cut out and glued onto the artwork. . . . Backmatter includes instructions for building and installing a birdhouse, a recipe for bird-food cupcakes and information about birdbaths, feeders and bluebirds." Kirkus

Truck driver Tom; [by] Monica Wellington. Dutton Children's Books 2007 unp il $15.99

Grades: PreK K   E
  1. Trucks—Fiction
  ISBN 978-0-525-47831-7   LC 2006035911

The driver of a tractor-trailer picks up a load of fresh fruits and vegetables, then drives through the countryside, past small towns, and into the big city, passing farms, construction sites, and many other vehicles, then delivers the produce and relaxes with other drivers

"The simple text is printed in a large block font that is just right for beginning readers. . . . Clearly drawn gouache paintings are enhanced with meticulously cut photos to add texture and character to the scene." SLJ

Wells, Rosemary, 1943-

Emily's first 100 days of school. Hyperion Bks. for Children 2000 unp il hardcover o.p. pa $7.99 *

Grades: PreK K   E
  1. School stories 2. Rabbits—Fiction 3. Counting
  ISBN 0-7868-0507-2; 0-7868-1354-7 (pa)
                               LC 99-27021

Starting with number one for the first day of school, Emily the rabbit learns the numbers to one hundred in many different ways

"Wells manages to find fresh, engaging presentations for that many numbers. Alive with color and thematically relevant decoration, the oversized pages are sometimes divided into several panels, but never feel too busy." Horn Book Guide

Another title about Emily and her school is:
My kindergarten (2004)

McDuff moves in; pictures by Susan Jeffers. Hyperion Books for Children 2005 c1997 unp il $9.99 *

Grades: PreK K 1 2   E
  1. Dogs—Fiction
  ISBN 0-7868-5677-7

A reissue of the title first published 1997

A white terrier "is rejected at several doors before finding a loving home, complete with an herbal bath and vanilla rice pudding." SLJ

"This collaboration by Wells and Jeffers is as sweet, substantial, and comforting as that bowl of rice pudding and will suit the many children who like stories with simple words, clear story lines, and happily-ever-after endings." Booklist

Other titles about McDuff are:
McDuff and the baby (1997)
McDuff comes home (1997)
McDuff goes to school (2001)
McDuff saves the day (2001)
McDuff's Christmas (2005)
McDuff's favorite things (2004)
McDuff's new friend (1998)
McDuff's wild romp (2005)

The miraculous tale of the two Maries; illustrated by Petra Mathers. Viking 2006 unp il $16.99

Grades: 1 2 3 4   E
  1. Miracles—Fiction 2. France—Fiction
  ISBN 0-670-05960-9   LC 2005017743

After perishing in a boating accident, two sixteen-year-old girls, both named Marie, ask God to allow them to return to the earth and intervene in the lives of villagers.

"Anchoring the story's ethereal themes are palpable south-of-France details, from the narrative's occasional French phrases to Mathers' alluring artwork, which captures the region's azure skies and sunbaked, salt-cured colors." Booklist

Morris's disappearing bag. Viking 1999 unp il hardcover o.p. pa $6.99 *

Grades: PreK K 1 2   E
  1. Christmas—Fiction 2. Rabbits—Fiction
  ISBN 0-670-88721-8; 0-14-230004-7 (pa)
                               LC 00-267633

First published 1975 by Dial Bks. for Young Readers
New illustrations by the author

Morris is so disappointed with his Christmas present that he invents a disappearing bag, which gives him a chance to share his brother's and sister's gifts

In this version "Morris re-appears in a full-color, full-size edition of the Christmas day story." Horn Book Guide

Wells, Rosemary, 1943-—*Continued*

My shining star; raising a child who is ready to learn; [by] Rosemary Wells. Scholastic Press 2006 unp il $8.99

Grades: PreK K   E

1. Parenting

ISBN 0-439-84701-X   LC 2005010481

"Young children will enjoy the adorable bunny characters and the small size that is just right for their little hands. But this gem of a picture book is directed to adults—and it belongs in the big hands of every teacher and parent. On each colorful spread, Wells expands on 10 principles to help any child succeed. The direct, simple advice is illustrated with Wells' favorite rabbits demonstrating the recommendations." Booklist

Noisy Nora; with all new illustrations [by] Rosemary Wells. Dial Bks. for Young Readers 1997 unp il $15.99; pa $6.99 *

Grades: PreK K 1 2   E

1. Mice—Fiction 2. Stories in rhyme

ISBN 0-670-88722-6; 0-14-056728-3 (pa)

A newly illustrated edition of the title first published 1973

Little Nora, tired of being ignored, tries to gain her family's attention by being noisy. When this doesn't work Nora disappears but returns when she is sure she has been missed

"All new illustrations infuse this much-loved picture book . . . with energy. Vibrant colors and a larger format make the characters seem to jump out at readers." SLJ

Only you. Viking 2003 unp il $14.99

Grades: PreK K   E

1. Mother-child relationship—Fiction 2. Bears—Fiction

ISBN 0-670-03634-X   LC 2002-15570

A little bear describes how much his mother means to him

"Wells's illustrations are right on target. Most of them feature parent and child as the central characters, cozily enclosed in a square and surrounded by a soft, pastel border. . . . Perfect for one-on-one sharing." SLJ

Otto runs for President. Scholastic Press 2008 unp il $15.99

Grades: K 1 2   E

1. Dogs—Fiction 2. Politics—Fiction 3. School stories

ISBN 978-0-545-03722-8; 0-545-03722-0

LC 2007024816

While the popular Tiffany and athletic Charles make increasingly outrageous promises in their campaigns for President of Canine Country Day School, Otto quietly enters the race, vowing only to try to do what students really want.

"Wells' canine coterie . . . is satisfyingly personable and appealing, and kids will find the knowledge they accrue from the book very useful." Booklist

Read to your bunny. Scholastic 1998 c1997 unp il $7.95; pa $3.99

Grades: PreK K   E

1. Rabbits—Fiction 2. Books and reading—Fiction 3. Stories in rhyme

ISBN 0-590-30284-1; 0-439-08717-1 (pa)

LC 97-17704

Brief rhyming text and colorful illustrations tell what happens when parents and children share twenty minutes a day reading

"Each line of text gets one of Wells' delightful bordered pictures of parents and children at all sorts of activities, from bathing to skating, but always with a book in hand." Booklist

Ruby's beauty shop. Viking 2002 unp il $16.99; pa $6.99 *

Grades: PreK K 1 2   E

1. Beauty shops—Fiction 2. Siblings—Fiction 3. Rabbits—Fiction

ISBN 0-670-03553-X; 0-14-240194-3 (pa)

LC 2001-7730

Board books about Max and Ruby are also available

Louise and Ruby use Louise's "Deluxe Beauty Kit" to give Max a make-over, but when Grandma calls to schedule her own make-over, she makes an appointment with Max

"Wells is in top form. . . . The author's affinity for kid-based glee is playfully evident." Bull Cent Child Books

Other titles about Max and Ruby are:

Bunny cakes (1997)
Bunny mail (2004)
Bunny money (1997)
Bunny party (2001)
Max and Ruby's first Greek myth: Pandora's box (1993)
Max and Ruby's Midas: another Greek myth (1995)
Max cleans up (2000)
Max counts his chickens (2007)
Max's ABC (2006)
Max's bath (1985)
Max's bedtime (1985)
Max's birthday (1985)
Max's breakfast (1985)
Max's bunny business (2008)
Max's chocolate chicken (1989)
Max's Christmas (1986)
Max's dragon shirt (1991)
Max's first word (1979)
Max's new suit (1979)
Max's ride (1979)
Max's toys (1979)

Shy Charles; [by] Rosemary Wells. Viking 2001 c1988 unp il hardcover o.p. pa $5.99

Grades: PreK K 1 2   E

1. Mice—Fiction 2. Stories in rhyme

ISBN 0-670-88729-3; 0-14-056843-3 (pa)

LC 2001-271649

A reissue of the title first published 1988 by Dial Books for Young Readers

"Charles, a young mouse, is perfectly happy playing by himself, and social contacts are an endless ordeal. . . . But when the baby sitter falls down the stairs, Charles is able to comfort her and call for help, before resuming his shy silence." NY Times Book Rev

"Wells' illustrations . . . show the plump, large-eared cast to be full of charm and cleverness. Facial expressions, posture, and background details substantially extend the humor of the story. The simple rhythm of the rhyming text is subtle and playful." SLJ

Wells, Rosemary, 1943-—*Continued*
Timothy's tales from Hilltop School. Viking 2002 64p il hardcover o.p. pa $7.99
Grades: K 1 2   **E**
1. School stories 2. Animals—Fiction
ISBN 0-670-03554-8; 0-14-240156-0 (pa)
LC 2001-7360
Companion volume to Timothy goes to school (1992)
A collection of six stories featuring the teachers and students of Hilltop School as they learn about taking turns, working together, and never giving up
"The language is evocative, the dilemmas are real, and the solutions are satisfying. Watercolor personality portraits and spot art throughout feature Wells' familiar and beloved animal characters." Bull Cent Child Books

Yoko. Hyperion Bks. for Children 1998 unp il $14.95; pa $6.99 *
Grades: PreK K 1 2   **E**
1. Food—Fiction 2. Japanese Americans—Fiction 3. Cats—Fiction 4. School stories
ISBN 0-7868-0395-9; 1-4231-1983-5 (pa)
LC 98-12342
When Yoko the cat brings sushi to school for lunch, her classmates make fun of what she eats—until one of them tries it for himself
"Wells sets the story in an active preschool classroom, and her clear ink-and-watercolor pictures have never been more expressive and tender, with a range of animal characters that are endearingly human in body language and expression." Booklist
Other titles about Yoko are:
Yoko writes her name (2008)
Yoko's paper cranes (2001)
Yoko's world of kindness (2005)

Wentworth, Marjory, 1958-
Shackles; by Marjory Heath Wentworth; illustration by Leslie Darwin Pratt-Thomas. Legacy 2009 unp il $16.99
Grades: 2 3 4 5   **E**
1. African Americans—Fiction 2. Slavery—Fiction 3. South Carolina—Fiction
ISBN 978-0-93310-106-7; 0-93310-106-6
"Hunter, 11, watches his pesky little brothers dig for buried treasure in their backyard on Sullivan's Island, South Carolina. When they dig up 'an armful of mud and metal,' their neighbor . . . explains to them that what they have found are shackles used on slaves to prevent their escape. . . . Based on a true story, this compelling picture book speaks in clear, lyrical prose, true to Hunter's perspective, with beautiful oil paintings." Booklist

We're going on a lion hunt; [illustrated by] David Axtell. Holt & Co. 2000 c1999 unp il $15.95
Grades: PreK K 1 2   **E**
1. Lions—Fiction 2. Africa—Fiction
ISBN 0-8050-6159-2   LC 98-47507
First published 1999 in the United Kingdom
Two girls set out bravely in search of a lion, going through long grass, a swamp, and a cave before they find what they're looking for
"Axtell takes a storytime classic to the African savan-

na. . . . [His] sun-soaked, impressionistic oil paintings offer beautiful landscapes and engaging details. . . . Large figures on the page make this a good choice for storytimes as well as lap times." SLJ

Weston, Carrie
If a chicken stayed for supper; by Carrie Weston; illustrated by Sophie Fatus. Holiday House 2007 unp il $16.95
Grades: PreK K 1 2   **E**
1. Foxes—Fiction 2. Chickens—Fiction 3. Night—Fiction
ISBN 978-0-8234-2067-4   LC 2006049511
First published 2006 in the United Kingdom
Even though they promise not to leave the den when their mother goes out hunting for a chicken for supper, five little foxes are unable to resist going outside to play in the dark.
"The language is engaging and precise, complemented by the vibrant and cheerful illustrations, rich with folk-art inspiration and a pleasing page layout." SLJ

Weston, Tamson
Hey, pancakes! words by Tamson Weston; pictures by Stephen Gammell. Harcourt 2003 unp il $16
Grades: PreK K 1 2   **E**
1. Family life—Fiction 2. Stories in rhyme
ISBN 0-15-216502-9   LC 2001-6867
The day gets off to a rough start, but soon the smell of pancakes fills the air and a family gathers for a breakfast feast
"Weston's paean to pancakes has a bouncy breakfast beat that lends itself to reading aloud. . . . Gammell's pastel, pencil, and watercolor illustrations swirl around like food coloring in an enthusiastic blend." Bull Cent Child Books

Whatley, Bruce
Clinton Gregory's secret; [by] Bruce Whatley. Abrams Books for Young Readers 2008 unp il $15.95
Grades: K 1 2   **E**
1. Dreams—Fiction
ISBN 978-0-8109-9364-8; 0-8109-9364-3
LC 2007012760
Clinton Gregory has fantastic adventures every night, from fighting dragons to flying around the world with his friends, and he keeps each one a secret.
"Everything is big in Whatley's colorful and fantastical spreads, which include details sure to appeal to children. . . . An entertaining addition to help wind down the day." SLJ

Wait! No paint! written and illustrated by Bruce Whatley. HarperCollins Pubs. 2001 31p il hardcover o.p. pa $6.99
Grades: PreK K 1 2   **E**
1. Pigs—Fiction 2. Wolves—Fiction 3. Illustrators—Fiction
ISBN 0-06-028270-3; 0-06-028271-1 (lib bdg); 0-06-443546-6 (pa)   LC 00-61351

Whatley, Bruce—_Continued_

The three little pigs are in their usual trouble with the big bad wolf, until a mysterious Voice gets involved and mixes things up

"The 'Voice' is the careless illustrator of the story, and . . . he's run out of red paint! . . . A quirky retelling of a perennial favorite, this may appeal most to early-elementary-age children, who will delight in the picture's conceptual surprises." Booklist

Wheeler, Lisa, 1963-

Boogie knights; words by Lisa Wheeler; pictures by Mark Siegel. Atheneum Books for Young Readers 2008 unp il $16.99 *

Grades: PreK K 1   E

1. Monsters—Fiction 2. Knights and knighthood—Fiction 3. Parties—Fiction 4. Stories in rhyme

ISBN 978-0-689-87639-4; 0-689-87639-4

                LC 2007-24158

"A Richard Jackson book"

When the knights of the castle are awakened by the noise from the Madcap Monster Ball, they decide to join the party.

"Wheeler's rhythmic text is filled with taut rhymes, alliteration, and vivid images. . . . Done in charcoal, pencil, and Photoshop, Siegel's sophisticated, graphic-novel-style artwork . . . demands a second look. . . . Sepia tones, splashes of color, silhouettes, and outline sketches cleverly underscore the plot elements and keep the pages interesting." SLJ

Bubble gum, bubble gum; illustrated by Laura Huliska-Beith. Little, Brown and Co. 2004 unp il $15.99

Grades: PreK K 1 2   E

1. Animals—Fiction 2. Stories in rhyme

ISBN 0-316-98894-4   LC 2002-16268

After a variety of animals get stuck one by one in bubble gum melting in the road, they must survive encounters with a big blue truck and a burly black bear.

"A fast-paced, rhyming story with vibrant, bouncing illustrations." SLJ

Castaway cats; story by Lisa Wheeler; art by Ponder Goembel. Atheneum Books for Young Readers 2006 unp il $16.95

Grades: PreK K 1 2   E

1. Cats—Fiction 2. Survival after airplane accidents, shipwrecks, etc.—Fiction 3. Stories in rhyme

ISBN 0-689-86232-6   LC 2004-541

"A Richard Jackson book."

Fifteen felines find themselves marooned on an island and are not sure what to do.

"This delightful book is told in verses that become smoother as the cats cooperate and find their groove. . . . Goembel's illustrations, done in acrylic and ink, are fantastic and provide wonderful insight into the side stories developing as the book progresses." SLJ

Jazz baby; illustrations by R. Gregory Christie. Harcourt 2007 unp il $16 *

Grades: PreK K 1   E

1. Jazz music—Fiction 2. Infants—Fiction 3. Family life—Fiction 4. Stories in rhyme

ISBN 978-0-15-202522-9; 0-15-202522-7

                LC 2006-09236

Baby and his family make some jazzy music.

"The percussive text scans like a musical dream, a nearly flawless scat on music, dance, and the contagious joy of jazz. Christie's gouache illustrations—in a sixties palette of olive, gold, and brick—feature characters with fluid bodies and mobile faces that fill the images with movement and energy." Booklist

Old Cricket; illustrations by Ponder Goembel. Atheneum Bks. for Young Readers 2003 unp il $16.95 *

Grades: PreK K 1 2   E

1. Crickets—Fiction

ISBN 0-689-84510-3   LC 2002-2199

"A Richard Jackson book"

Old Cricket doesn't feel like helping his wife and neighbors to prepare for winter and so he pretends to have all sorts of ailments that require the doctor's care, but hungry Old Crow has other ideas

"Wheeler invests her delightful tale with all the characteristics of a good fable, and Goembel's sharp, highly detailed acrylic artwork gives a clever, humorous bug's-eye view of the world." Booklist

Te amo, Bebé, little one; illustrated by Maribel Suárez. Little, Brown 2004 unp il $15.95

Grades: PreK K 1   E

1. Mother-child relationship—Fiction 2. Infants—Fiction 3. Stories in rhyme

ISBN 0-316-61410-6

In this picture book "verses describe a baby's first year of life. As the seasons change, the infant and mother are shown engaging in a variety of activities including a trip to the beach, dancing to fiesta music at the country fair, and enjoying a winter's night. . . . Spanish words are smoothly incorporated into the text. The illustrations are done in bright, bold colors. . . . This is a good choice for intimate sharing with little ones." SLJ

Whelan, Gloria

The listeners; written by Gloria Whelan; illustrated by Mike Benny. Sleeping Bear Press 2009 unp il $17.95

Grades: 1 2 3   E

1. Slavery—Fiction 2. African Americans—Fiction

ISBN 978-1-58536-419-0; 1-58536-419-3

                LC 2009005436

After a day of picking cotton in late 1860, Ella May, a young slave, joins her friends Bobby and Sue at their second job of listening outside the windows of their master's house for useful information

This is "a spare, lyrical narrative. . . . Benny's unframed, dusk-toned, double-page paintings emphasize the stark contrast between slave shacks and plantation mansion." Booklist

Waiting for the owl's call; [illustrated by] Pascal Milelli. Sleeping Bear Press 2009 unp il (Tales of the world) $17.95

Grades: 2 3 4 5   E

1. Weaving—Fiction 2. Afghanistan—Fiction 3. Rugs and carpets—Fiction 4. Child labor—Fiction

ISBN 978-1-58536-418-3; 1-58536-418-5

                LC 2009005437

Whelan, Gloria—*Continued*

For generations the women of Zulviya's family have earned their living by weaving rugs by hand. During one work day, Zulviya will tie thousands of knots. As she sits at her work, Zulviya weaves not one but two patterns. The pattern on the loom will become a fine rug. She weaves a second pattern in her mind.

"Impressionistic paintings in muted colors accompany Zulviya's lyrical description of her Afghan homeland and her yearning to escape 'the shadow of the loom.' An author's note provides details about illiegal child labor in the Afghani rug-making industry." Horn Book Guide

Yuki and the one thousand carriers; written by Gloria Whelan; illustrated by Yan Nascimbene. Sleeping Bear Press 2008 unp il (Tales of the world) $17.95

Grades: 1 2 3   **E**

1. Voyages and travels—Fiction 2. Haiku—Fiction 3. Japan—Fiction

ISBN 978-1-58536-352-0; 1-58536-352-9

LC 2007046318

In Japan, as a provincial governor, his wife, and daughter Yuki, followed by 1,000 attendants, travel the historic Tokaido Road to the Shogun's palace in Edo, Yuki keeps up with her lessons by writing poems describing the journey

"Nascimbene stays true to Yuki's childish perspective. . . . Accompanying the simple prose narrative, are haiku . . . that express intense feelings in clear, casual words." Booklist

Whitaker, Zai, 1954-

Kali and the rat snake; story by Zai Whitaker; illustrations by Srividya Natarajan. Kane/Miller 2006 c2000 unp il $15.95

Grades: 1 2 3   **E**

1. Snakes—Fiction 2. India—Fiction 3. Prejudices—Fiction 4. School stories

ISBN 1-933605-10-3

First published 2000 in India

"Kali has always been proud of his father, who is the best snake catcher in their Indian village. But when he attends school, the children make fun of his Irula ways. . . . But one day the classroom is visited by a six-foot-long rat snake. . . . Kali grabs it and becomes the class hero. The text is smoothly written, with lots of cultural details. . . . Natarajan's stylized illustrations are a mixture of smaller pencil drawings and luscious larger paintings that seem to be done on silk." SLJ

Whiting, Sue

The firefighters; [by] Sue Whiting; illustrated by Donna Rawlins. Candlewick Press 2008 unp il $15.99

Grades: PreK K 1 2   **E**

1. Fire fighters—Fiction 2. Imagination—Fiction 3. School stories

ISBN 978-0-7636-4019-4; 0-7636-4019-0

LC 2007051895

After dressing up as fire fighters, building a fire truck out of a cardboard box, and extinguishing imaginary fires on the playground, Mrs. Iverson's students are surprised

by the arrival of a real fire engine with real fire fighters on board

"Rawlins's acrylic illustrations feature bright, primary colors that stand out against the clean, white backgrounds. . . . A great choice for introducing not only fire safety, but also creative play." SLJ

Whitman, Candace, 1958-

Lines that wiggle; illustrations by Steve Wilson. Blue Apple Books 2009 unp il $14.99

Grades: K 1 2 3   **E**

1. Stories in rhyme 2. Monsters—Fiction

ISBN 978-1-934706-54-1; 1-934706-54-X

LC 2008042383

A variety of monsters and other creatures demonstrate some of the different things that lines can do, from curve and curl to zig-zag

"Through bouncy verse and lively artwork, this creative collaboration explores the many different ways that lines are used. . . . Children will enjoy this book on many levels." SLJ

Whitman, Walt, 1819-1892

When I heard the learn'd astronomer; words by Walt Whitman; pictures by Loren Long. Simon & Schuster Books for Young Readers 2004 unp il $16.95

Grades: 1 2 3 4   **E**

1. Astronomy—Poetry

ISBN 0-689-86397-7   LC 2004-7538

"A little boy obsessed with outer space has been dragged to an astronomy lecture. . . . The fidgety youngster takes his toy rocket ship outside, where he marvels at the 'perfect silence of the stars, casting a decisive vote for creative speculation over chilly analysis.' The painterly artwork . . . gets its own injection of childlike wonder through playful doodles contributed by Long's two children." Booklist

Why did the chicken cross the road? [by] Jon Agee . . . [et al.] Dial Books for Young Readers 2006 unp il $16.99 *

Grades: 1 2 3 4   **E**

1. Chickens—Fiction

ISBN 0-8037-3094-2   LC 2005-16196

"What is perhaps the world's most tired joke becomes fresh and inspired in this lively collection of work by well-known contemporary children's book artists. On each double-page spread, a different contributor offers a new, illustrated punch line to the title question. . . . Lots of fun for young children, this collection, which demonstrates the impressive artistic range and talent featured in today's picture books, will also attract older art students and children's book enthusiasts." Booklist

Whybrow, Ian

The noisy way to bed; illustrated by Tiphanie Beeke. Arthur A. Levine Books 2004 unp il $15.95

Grades: PreK K 1 2   **E**

1. Bedtime—Fiction 2. Animals—Fiction 3. Stories in rhyme

ISBN 0-439-55689-9   LC 2003-2785

Whybrow, Ian—*Continued*

As a sleepy boy decides it is bedtime and sets out across the farm toward home, he meets several animals who, in their noisy way, express the same idea

"This engaging bedtime story begs for participation from children. . . . [Beeke's] full-page, mixed-media pictures are captivating, providing an eye-pleasing blend of colors, textures, and facial expressions." SLJ

Wickberg, Susan

Hey Mr. Choo-Choo, where are you going? [by] Susan Wickberg; illustrated by Yumi Heo. G.P. Putnam's Sons 2008 unp il $16.99 *

Grades: PreK K   E

1. Railroads—Fiction 2. Stories in rhyme

ISBN 978-0-399-23993-9; 0-399-23993-6

LC 2006034459

A train engine hauls his cars from the city to the sea, answering questions about what he is pulling, seeing, and hearing along the way.

"Heo's collages and oil paintings are chock-full of friendly facets that will keep children coming back. Done in a primitive style, the artwork sports a striped coal car, a robot toy, a billboard of a fish, and a lamb rolling in the meadow. . . . Readers will be anxious to climb back on Mr. Choo-Choo for another energetic ride." SLJ

Wiesner, David

Flotsam. Clarion Books 2006 unp il $17 *

Grades: K 1 2 3 4   E

1. Cameras—Fiction 2. Beaches—Fiction 3. Stories without words

ISBN 0-618-19457-6

Awarded the Caldecott Medal, 2007

"A wave deposits an old-fashioned contraption at the feet of an inquisitive young beachcomber. It's a Melville underwater camera, and the excited boy quickly develops the film he finds inside. The photos are amazing. . . . This wordless books vivid watercolor paintings have a crisp realism that anchors the elements of fantasy. . . . Filled with inventive details and delightful twists, each snapshot is a tale waiting to be told." SLJ

Free fall. Lothrop, Lee & Shepard Bks. 1988 unp il lib bdg $18.89; pa $6.99

Grades: K 1 2 3 4   E

1. Dreams—Fiction 2. Stories without words

ISBN 0-688-05584-2 (lib bdg); 0-688-10990-X (pa)

LC 87-22834

A Caldecott Medal honor book, 1989

A young boy dreams of daring adventures in the company of imaginary creatures inspired by the things surrounding his bed

"Technical virtuosity is the trademark of the double-page watercolor spreads. Especially notable is the solidity of forms and architectural details." SLJ

Hurricane. Clarion Bks. 1990 unp il $16; pa $6.95

Grades: K 1 2 3   E

1. Hurricanes—Fiction 2. Brothers—Fiction

ISBN 0-395-54382-7; 0-395-62974-8 (pa)

LC 90-30070

"A family weathers a hurricane; the next day, in the post-hurricane yard, the two boys in the family play on a great fallen elm, imagining it to be a jungle, a pirate ship, and a space ship. A handsome book, affording opportunities for sharing fears and dreams of adventure." Horn Book Guide

June 29, 1999. Clarion Bks. 1992 unp il $16; pa $5.95

Grades: K 1 2 3 4   E

1. Vegetables—Fiction

ISBN 0-395-59762-5; 0-395-72767-7 (pa)

LC 91-34854

"Either Holly Evans's science project that sent vegetable seedlings into the ionosphere is enormously successful—or else something unearthly is going on." SLJ

"Here an understated, fairly straightforward text is a perfect foil for the outrageous scenes of vegetables run amok. Realistic watercolors reveal red peppers that need to be roped down, beans with bemused Arizona sheep clambering over them, and gargantuan peas floating down the Mississippi like logs to the sawmill. Fans of Wiesner's offbeat sense of humor will be delighted." Horn Book

Sector 7. Clarion Bks. 1999 unp il $16 *

Grades: K 1 2 3 4   E

1. Empire State Building (New York, N.Y.)—Fiction 2. Clouds—Fiction 3. Stories without words

ISBN 0-395-74656-6   LC 96-40343

A Caldecott Medal honor book, 2000

While on a school trip to the Empire State Building, a boy is taken by a friendly cloud to visit Sector 7, where he discovers how clouds are shaped and channeled throughout the country

"Wiesner's lofty watercolors render words superfluous as he transforms the sky into magical scenes of marine life, reminding children of the innate power of their own imagination." Publ Wkly

The three pigs. Clarion Bks. 2001 unp il $16 *

Grades: K 1 2 3 4   E

1. Pigs—Fiction

ISBN 0-618-00701-6   LC 00-57016

Awarded the Caldecott Medal, 2002

The three pigs escape the wolf by going into another world where they meet the cat and the fiddle, the cow that jumped over the moon, and a dragon

"Wiesner's brilliant use of white space and perspective evokes a feeling that the characters can navigate endless possibilities—and that the range of story itself is limitless." Publ Wkly

Tuesday. Clarion Bks. 1991 unp il $17; pa $6.95 *

Grades: K 1 2 3 4   E

1. Frogs—Fiction

ISBN 0-395-55113-7; 0-395-87082-8 (pa)

LC 90-39358

Awarded the Caldecott Medal, 1992

Frogs rise on their lily pads, float through the air, and explore the nearby houses while their inhabitants sleep

"Wiesner offers a fantasy watercolor journey accomplished with soft-edged realism. Studded with bits of humor, the narrative artwork tells a simple, pleasant story with a consistency and authenticity that makes the fantasy convincing." Booklist

Wilcoxen, Chuck

Niccolini's song; illustrated by Mark Buehner. Dutton Children's Books 2004 unp il $16.99

Grades: PreK K 1 2   **E**
1. Railroads—Fiction 2. Lullabies—Fiction 3. Bedtime—Fiction
ISBN 0-525-46805-6

A gentle night watchman at the railroad yard lulls anxious train engines to sleep by singing just the right song.

"The rhythmic pace of the text, short sentences, and alliterative phrases make this creative bedtime story ideal for reading aloud. Buehner's soft paintings are imbued with dusky, nighttime hues." SLJ

Wild, Margaret, 1948-

Kiss kiss! [by] Margaret Wild & Bridget Strevens-Marzo. Simon & Schuster Books for Young Readers 2004 c2003 unp il $12.95

Grades: PreK K   **E**
1. Hippopotamus—Fiction 2. Mother-child relationship—Fiction
ISBN 0-689-86279-2   LC 2002-154516

First published 2003 in Australia

Baby Hippo is in such a rush to play one morning he forgets to kiss his mama, but strangely all the jungle noises seem to remind him

"This is a story filled with movement and physical affection. The lap-sit audience will love the squishy, lumpy sounds and the repetition of the text as they point to the animals in the clear, bright pictures." Booklist

The little crooked house; illustrated by Jonathan Bentley. Simply Read Books 2006 unp il $16.95

Grades: PreK K 1 2 3   **E**
1. Houses—Fiction 2. Moving—Fiction
ISBN 1-894965-59-0

"Wild adds her own inimitable touch to this offering about a crooked man, his crooked cat, and their crooked mouse, all living in their crooked little house. The residents cannot remain in their home because of its unfortunate location at the side of the railroad tracks. Thus, one move leads to another, from a desert vicinity to riverside property. . . . Bentley's rollicking, rowdy watercolor illustrations beckon readers to come along on this topsy-turvy trip." SLJ

Midnight babies; illustrated by Ann James. Clarion Bks. 2001 c1999 unp il $15

Grades: PreK K   **E**
1. Infants—Fiction
ISBN 0-618-10412-7   LC 00-58978

First published 1999 in Australia

Baby Brenda and her friends have fun at the Midnight Cafe, enjoying a "wibble wobble" dance, a "jiggly-joggly" treat, and a dip in the sprinklers before going home to bed

"The art is bold and delicious; the text captures the pure exuberance of the sweet, silly action." Booklist

Our granny; story by Margaret Wild; pictures by Julie Vivas. Ticknor & Fields 1994 c1993 unp il $17; pa $6.95 *

Grades: PreK K 1 2   **E**
1. Grandmothers—Fiction
ISBN 0-395-67023-3; 0-395-88395-4 (pa)
      LC 93-11950

First published 1993 in Australia

"Two young children present a catalog of all the varying sizes, shapes, and types of grandmothers, interspersed with loving comments about their own granny, who has 'a wobbly bottom' and wears a funny bathing suit. . . . Vivas's lively illustrations capture the grandmothers in their most comic moments." Horn Book Guide

Piglet and Mama; illustrated by Stephen Michael King. Harry N. Abrams 2005 unp il $14.95 *

Grades: PreK K   **E**
1. Mothers—Fiction 2. Pigs—Fiction 3. Farm life—Fiction
ISBN 0-8109-5869-4   LC 2004-19497

When Piglet cannot find her mother, all of the barnyard animals try to make her feel better, but Piglet wants nothing but Mama.

"The text is reassuring and rhythmic. . . . The cheery watercolor cartoons depict farm life on a bright, sunny day, and the gentle pastel color scheme matches the tender tone of the text." SLJ

Other titles about Piglet are:
Piglet and Papa (2007)
Piglet and Granny (2009)

Puffling; illustrated by Julie Vivas. Feiwel and Friends 2009 unp il $16.99 *

Grades: PreK K 1 2   **E**
1. Puffins—Fiction 2. Growth—Fiction 3. Parent-child relationship—Fiction
ISBN 978-0-312-56570-1; 0-312-56570-4
      LC 2008048137

As his affectionate parents nourish and protect him, a plucky young puffin impatiently waits—but not without some reservations—for the day when he is "strong enough and tall enough and brave enough" to leave his nest on the rocky cliff-face and waddle off to the sea

"The beautiful, spare illustrations, rendered in pastel and watercolor pencil on textured paper, show the tender bonds between family members while showcasing actual facts about puffin life." Booklist

Tom goes to kindergarten; [illustrated by] David Legge. Whitman, A. 2000 unp il $15.95

Grades: PreK K   **E**
1. Giant panda—Fiction 2. School stories
ISBN 0-8075-8012-0   LC 99-50420

When Tom, a young panda, goes to his very first day of kindergarten, his whole family stays and plays and wishes they could be in kindergarten too

"Large, bright, whimsical watercolors make this a perfect book both for group storytelling and for one-on-one sharing." SLJ

Wildsmith, Brian, 1930-

Brian Wildsmith's ABC. Star Bright Bks. 1995 unp bd bk $6.95

Grades: PreK K   E

1. Alphabet 2. Board books for children

ISBN 978-1-88773-402-8 (bd bk); 1-88773-402-3 (bd bk)   LC 95-31730

First published 1962 in the United Kingdom; first U.S. edition 1963 by Watts

"From A/apple to Z/zebra, Wildsmith's 26 playful renderings of objects and animals are highlighted with an eye-catching, colorful design; kaleidoscopic animals constructed from bold circles, triangles and squares add an unexpected geometric element to the counting book." Publ Wkly

Brian Wildsmith's Amazing animal alphabet. Star Bright Books 2009 unp $17.95; pa $7.95

Grades: PreK K   E

1. Alphabet 2. Animals

ISBN 978-1-59572-104-4; 1-59572-104-5; 978-1-59572-185-3 (pa); 1-59572-185-1 (pa)   LC 2007033811

"Wildsmith's distinctive, detailed animals pop against brightly colored backgrounds as they illustrate each letter of the alphabet. Preschoolers will easily recognize most of the creatures, with a few refreshingly unusual exceptions (*quetzel* for *Q*, *vole* for *V*, *xenops* for *X*). Four pages of 'Amazing Animal Facts' conclude the animal parade." Horn Book Guide

Jungle party. Star Bright Books 2006 unp il $16.95; pa $6.95

Grades: PreK K 1 2   E

1. Pythons—Fiction 2. Animals—Fiction 3. Parties—Fiction

ISBN 978-1-59572-052-8; 1-59572-052-9; 978-1-59572-053-5 (pa); 1-59572-053-7 (pa)

First published 1974 by Oxford University Press with title: Python's party

Although he is hungry, Python tries to prove his goodwill by throwing a party for all the jungle animals

"Wildsmith excels at bold, brightly colored illustrations of animals, and this cautionary tale is a visual delight." Horn Book Guide

Wiles, Deborah

Freedom Summer; illustrated by Jerome Lagarrigue. Atheneum Bks. for Young Readers 2001 unp il $16

Grades: K 1 2 3   E

1. African Americans—Fiction 2. Race relations—Fiction 3. Friendship—Fiction

ISBN 0-689-87829-X   LC 98-52805

"An Anne Schwartz book"

In 1964, Joe is pleased that a new law will allow his best friend John Henry, who is colored, to share the town pool and other public places with him, but he is dismayed to find that prejudice still exists

"The text, though concise, is full of nuance, and the oil paintings shimmer with the heat of the South in summer." Horn Book Guide

Wilkes, Angela

My first word book. DK Pub. 1999 64p il hardcover o.p. bd bk $5.99 *

Grades: PreK   E

1. Vocabulary

ISBN 0-7894-3977-8; 0-7894-9905-3 (bd bk)   LC 99-206690

A slightly revised edition of the title first published 1991

"Common, familiar objects, animals, and activities—featured in clear, bright photos set against a white background or in small drawings—are grouped together on double-page spreads with such headings as 'On the farm' and 'Colors, shapes, and numbers.' Children will be drawn to the bright, cheerful pages of this first vocabulary lesson." Horn Book Guide

Willans, Tom

Wait! I want to tell you a story; written and illustrated by Tom Willans. Simon & Schuster Books for Young Readers 2005 c2004 unp il $15.95

Grades: PreK K 1 2   E

1. Storytelling—Fiction 2. Animals—Fiction

ISBN 0-689-87166-X

First published 2004 in the United Kingdom

"To avoid being eaten by a tiger, a fast-talking muskrat spins a tale about a frog who's about to be eaten by a shark who tells a story about a lizard who's about to be eaten by a snake, and so on. This bouncy repetitive tale with a twist is made all the funnier by the zany ink and watercolor illustrations." Horn Book Guide

Willems, Mo

Big Frog can't fit in; a pop out book; paper engineering by Bruce Foster. Hyperion 2009 unp il $19.99

Grades: PreK K 1   E

1. Pop-up books 2. Frogs—Fiction

ISBN 978-1-4231-1436-9; 1-4231-1436-1

Big Frog really wants to fit in, but even this pop-up book can't hold her, so it takes a lot of work from some good friends to help her.

"A sunny tribute to the power of friendship to provide ingenuity, help and cheer." Publishers Weekly

Cat the Cat, who is that? Balzer & Bray 2010 unp il $12.99; lib bdg $14.89 *

Grades: PreK K 1   E

1. Cats—Fiction 2. Animals—Fiction 3. Friendship—Fiction

ISBN 978-0-06-172840-2; 0-06-172840-3; 978-0-06-172841-9 (lib bdg); 0-06-172841-1 (lib bdg)   LC 2008-46187

An exuberant cat introduces readers to her friends.

"Willems provides just enough humor and surprise to entertain youngest audiences and . . . Cat could become another favorite; her personality sparkles in expansive gestures and gleeful interactions." Publ Wkly

Other titles about Cat the Cat and her friends are:

Let's say hi to friends who fly! (2010)

What's your sound, Hound the Hound ?(2010)

Time to sleep, Sheep the Sheep! (2010)

Willems, Mo—*Continued*

City Dog, Country Frog; illustrated by Jon J. Muth. Hyperion 2010 unp il $17.99 *

Grades: PreK K 1 2   E

1. Seasons—Fiction 2. Friendship—Fiction 3. Dogs—Fiction 4. Frogs—Fiction

ISBN 978-1-4231-0300-4; 1-4231-0300-9

City Dog and Country Frog play together in the spring and summer and fall, but in winter Country Frog is gone. Then when spring comes again City Dog makes a new friend.

Willems "is gracefully spare here, making every word count. That leaves room for Muth's watercolors, richly seasonal, which fill every page. The pictures are imbued with hope and happiness, leaving and longing. This wonderful collaboration makes a significant impact with subtlety and wit." Booklist

Don't let the pigeon drive the bus! words and pictures by Mo Willems. Hyperion Bks. for Children 2003 unp il $12.99 *

Grades: PreK K 1 2   E

1. Pigeons—Fiction 2. Buses—Fiction

ISBN 0-7868-1988-X

A Caldecott Medal honor book, 2004

"When a bus driver goes on break, he asks the audience to keep an eye on his vehicle and the daft, bug-eyed pigeon who desperately wants to drive it. The pigeon then relentlessly begs readers for some time behind the wheel." Publ Wkly

"An unflinching and hilarious look at a child's potential for mischief. In a plain palette, with childishly elemental line drawings, Willems has captured the essence of unreasonableness in the very young." SLJ

Other titles about the pigeon are:

The pigeon finds a hot dog! (2004)

Don't let the pigeon stay up late (2006)

The pigeon wants a puppy (2008)

Edwina, the dinosaur who didn't know she was extinct; words and pictures by Mo Willems. Hyperion 2006 unp il $16.99

Grades: PreK K 1   E

1. Dinosaurs—Fiction

ISBN 0-7868-3748-9

Everyone in town loves Edwina the dinosaur except Reginald, who is determined to prove to everyone, including Edwina, that dinosaurs are extinct.

"Set against plain, light-blue backdrops, the pictures, in Willem's familiar cartoon style, show Reginald up to his dastardly deeds. . . . Consider this an enjoyable visit to a happy community that has no room for curmudgeons." Booklist

Knuffle Bunny; a cautionary tale. Hyperion Books for Children 2004 unp il $15.99 *

Grades: PreK K 1 2   E

1. Lost and found possessions—Fiction

ISBN 0-7868-1870-0

A Caldecott Medal honor book, 2005

After Trixie and daddy leave the laundromat, something very important turns up missing.

A "concise, deftly told narrative. . . . Printed on olive-green backdrops, the illustrations are a combination of muted, sepia-toned photographs upon which bright cartoon drawings of people have been superimposed. . . . A seamless and supremely satisfying presentation of art and text." SLJ

Another title about Knuffle Bunny is:

Knuffle Bunny too (2007)

Leonardo, the terrible monster. Hyperion 2005 unp il $16.99 *

Grades: PreK K 1 2   E

1. Monsters—Fiction

ISBN 0-7868-5294-1

Leonardo is a terrible monster he can't seem to frighten anyone. When he discovers the perfect nervous little boy, will he scare the lunch out of him? Or will he think of something better?

"Willems's familiar cartoon drawings work hand in glove with the brief text to tell this perfectly paced story." SLJ

Naked Mole Rat gets dressed; words and pictures by Mo Willems. Hyperion Books for Children 2009 unp il $16.99 *

Grades: PreK K 1 2   E

1. Naked mole rat—Fiction

ISBN 978-1-4231-1437-6; 1-4231-1437-X

LC 2008-48251

Willems "informs readers that 'for this story' they need only know three things about naked mole rats: '1. They are a little bit rat. 2. They are a little bit mole. 3. They are all naked.' The exception to point number three, however, is Wilbur, who revels in a wardrobe that ranges from a turtleneck and beret to an astronaut suit—infuriating his brethren. . . . [Willems'] legion of emotive, square-headed rodents . . . are paired successfully with droll prose." Publ Wkly

Today I will fly! Hyperion Books for Children 2007 57p il $8.99 *

Grades: PreK K 1 2   E

1. Friendship—Fiction 2. Pigs—Fiction 3. Elephants—Fiction

ISBN 978-14231-0295-3; 1-4231-0295-9

LC 2006-49621

While Piggie is determined to fly, Elephant is skeptical, but when Piggie gets a little help from others, amazing things happen.

"Characters zip in and out of white space, proffer speech-bubble remarks, and express emotion through spot-on body language. . . . Accessible, appealing, and full of authentic emotions." Booklist

Other titles in this series are:

My friend is sad (2007)

I am invited to a party! (2007)

There is a bird on your head (2007)

I love my new toy! (2008)

I will surprise my friend! (2008)

Are you ready to play outside? (2008)

Elephants cannot dance! (2009)

Pigs make me sneeze! (2009)

Watch me throw the ball! (2009)

I am going! (2010)

Williams, Barbara

Albert's impossible toothache; illustrated by Doug Cushman. Candlewick Press 2003 unp il $15.99

Grades: PreK K 1 2   E

1. Turtles—Fiction

ISBN 0-7636-1723-7   LC 2002-67059

A newly illustrated edition of Albert's toothache, published 1974 by Dutton

When Albert the turtle complains of a toothache, no one in his family believes him, until his grandmother takes the time to really listen to him

"This title is a worthwhile addition to any picture-book collection." SLJ

Another title about Albert is:

Albert's gift for grandmother (2006)

Williams, Brenda, 1946-

Lin Yi's lantern; a Moon Festival tale; [text by] Brenda Williams; [illustrations by] Benjamin Lacombe. Barefoot Books 2009 unp il $16.99

Grades: K 1 2 3   E

1. Shopping—Fiction 2. Festivals—Fiction 3. China—Fiction

ISBN 978-1-84686-147-5; 1-84686-147-0   LC 2008043900

When his mother sends him to the market to buy necessities for the upcoming festival, Lin Yi is certain his bargaining skills will get him the best prices and he will have money left over for his coveted red rabbit lantern

"Handsome, stylized gouache illustrations portray the Chinese characters and scenes from a variety of perspectives. . . . The length of the narrative and accompanying cultural information make this an excellent supplement for primary multicultural units." Booklist

Williams, Karen Lynn

A beach tail; illustrated by Floyd Cooper. Boyds Mills Press 2010 unp il $17.95 *

Grades: PreK K 1 2   E

1. Beaches—Fiction 2. Father-son relationship—Fiction 3. African Americans—Fiction

ISBN 978-1-59078-712-0; 1-59078-712-9

"At the beach with his father, Greg strays from his beach umbrella, but stays calm and remembers the two things Dad told him: 'Don't go in the water, and don't leave Sandy.' Sandy is a lion Greg has drawn in the sand, and because Greg hasn't lifted the stick with which he has drawn Sandy's long, long tail . . . he's able to retrace his steps to find his father. . . . Cooper . . . draws a startlingly real Greg in a series of tight closeups. . . . Grainy pastel and washed-out color evoke the seashore's bleached palette. . . . Williams's . . . even pacing and soothing text reassure children without losing momentum." Publ Wkly

Four feet, two sandals; written by Karen Lynn Williams and Khadra Mohammed; illustrated by Doug Chayka. Eerdmans Books for Young Readers 2007 unp il $17

Grades: 2 3 4   E

1. Refugees—Fiction 2. Afghanistan—Fiction 3. Pakistan—Fiction 4. Friendship—Fiction 5. Shoes—Fiction

ISBN 978-0-8028-5296-0   LC 2006002635

Two young Afghani girls living in a refugee camp in Pakistan share a precious pair of sandals brought by relief workers

"The thickly brushed, double-page paintings show the long lines of desperate refugees and then close-ups of the two Muslim girls. . . . This is a personal drama behind the daily news." Booklist

Galimoto; illustrated by Catherine Stock. Lothrop, Lee & Shepard Bks. 1990 unp il $16.95; pa $6.99

Grades: PreK K 1 2   E

1. Toys—Fiction 2. Malawi—Fiction

ISBN 0-688-08789-2; 0-688-10991-8 (pa)   LC 89-2258

"In Malawi, Africa, according to the author's note, galimoto are intricate and popular push toys crafted by children. Williams tells the story of seven-year-old Kondi's quest to find ample scrap material to fashion his own toy pickup truck. . . . Kondi's perseverance and the pleasure he takes in his accomplishment are just two of the delights of this appealing story. Stock's graceful watercolors portray life in a bustling village and include enough detail . . . to give readers the flavor of a day in this southern African nation." Horn Book

My name is Sangoel; written by Karen Lynn Williams and Khadra Mohammed; illustrated by Catherine Stock. Eerdmans Books for Young Readers 2009 unp il $17

Grades: 1 2 3   E

1. Immigrants—Fiction 2. Refugees—Fiction 3. Sudanese Americans—Fiction 4. Personal names—Fiction

ISBN 978-0-8028-5307-3; 0-8028-5307-2   LC 2008-31735

As a refugee from Sudan to the United States, Sangoel is frustrated that no one can pronounce his name correctly until he finds a clever way to solve the problem.

"Stock's bright watercolor scenarios, accentuated with thick black lines, express the wrenching leave-taking and then the combination of exciting new things, . . . as well as disorienting ones. . . . [This is a] moving story." Booklist

Painted dreams; pictures by Catherine Stock. Lothrop, Lee & Shepard Bks. 1998 unp il hardcover o.p. lib bdg $15.93

Grades: PreK K 1 2   E

1. Haiti—Fiction 2. Artists—Fiction

ISBN 0-688-13901-9; 0-688-13902-7 (lib bdg)   LC 97-32920

Because her Haitian family is too poor to be able to buy paints for her, eight-year-old Ti Marie finds her own way to create pictures that make the heart sing

"Beautifully composed and full of life, Stock's watercolors suggest the personalities of the characters through their expressions and gestures." Booklist

Williams, Laura E.

The Can Man; illustrated by Craig Orback. Lee & Low 2010 unp il $18.95

Grades: K 1 2 3   E

1. Homeless persons—Fiction

ISBN 978-1-60060-266-5; 1-60060-266-5

"Tim wants a skateboard badly, but money is tight. Watching a homeless man every calls the Can Man . . . collect cans to redeem for cash, Tim decides to do the same to bankroll his skateboard. . . . Orback's . . . realistic oil paintings on canvas bring the tale's urban setting into clear focus in warmly lit scenes that illuminate the characters' feelings." Publ Wkly

Williams, Linda

The little old lady who was not afraid of anything; illustrated by Megan Lloyd. Crowell 1986 unp il $16.99; lib bdg $18.89; pa $6.99 *

Grades: PreK K 1 2   E

1. Fear—Fiction

ISBN 0-690-04584-0; 0-690-04586-7 (lib bdg); 0-06-443183-5 (pa)   LC 85-48250

A little old lady who is not afraid of anything must deal with a pumpkin head, a tall black hat, and other spooky objects that follow her through the dark woods trying to scare her

"A delightful picture book, perfect for both independent reading pleasure and for telling aloud." SLJ

Williams, Sherley Anne, 1944-1999

Working cotton; written by Sherley Anne Williams; illustrated by Carole Byard. Harcourt Brace Jovanovich 1992 unp il hardcover o.p. pa $7

Grades: PreK K 1 2   E

1. Migrant labor—Fiction 2. Cotton—Fiction 3. African Americans—Fiction

ISBN 0-15-299624-9; 0-15-201482-9 (pa)

LC 91-21586

A Caldecott Medal honor book, 1993

A young black girl relates the daily events of her family's migrant life in the cotton fields of central California

"Byard's acrylic paintings contribute weight and emotion to Williams's spare text. The fields and family members fill each full-page spread, drawing the reader very close to the action of the story. The mural-like paintings glow with blue and brown tones, recreating the textures and hues of the cotton fields. Williams's text, based on her poems, has a lyrical, rhythmic quality." Horn Book

Williams, Sue, 1948-

Let's go visiting; written by Sue Williams; illustrated by Julie Vivas. Harcourt Brace & Co. 1998 unp il hardcover o.p. pa $7; bd bk $6.95

Grades: PreK K   E

1. Domestic animals—Fiction 2. Counting 3. Stories in rhyme

ISBN 0-15-201823-9; 0-15-202410-7 (pa); 0-15-204638-0 (bd bk)   LC 97-34398

"Gulliver books"

A counting story in which a boy visits his farmyard friends, from one brown foal to six yellow puppies

"The bold illustrations, simple yet full of motion, combine with a lively text to make this perfect for toddler story hours." Booklist

Williams, Suzanne

Library Lil; illustrated by Steven Kellogg. Dial Bks. for Young Readers 1997 unp il $16.99; pa $6.99

Grades: PreK K 1 2 3   E

1. Librarians—Fiction 2. Books and reading—Fiction 3. Tall tales

ISBN 0-8037-1698-2; 0-14-056837-9 (pa)

LC 95-23490

A formidable librarian makes readers not only out of the once resistant residents of her small town, but out of a tough-talking, television-watching motorcycle gang as well

"The silliness of both story and pictures are perfectly matched. Kellogg's distinctive toothy kids and laughing cats crowd the pages, fitting right in with the baby-faced biker banditos." SLJ

Williams, Treat, 1951-

Air show! pictures by Robert Neubecker. Disney Hyperion 2010 unp il $16.99

Grades: PreK K   E

1. Airplanes—Fiction 2. Siblings—Fiction

ISBN 978-1-4231-1185-6; 1-4231-1185-0

"Williams' story follows a sister and brother, Ellie and Gill, as their father flies them to the show, gives them a grand tour, and surprises Ellie with a trip in a stunt plane. . . . It's Neubecker's artwork that really shines here. . . . The large-scale, double page spreads pack in interest, and the foldout, which features almost two dozen aircraft, from a 1916 Spad to a 2009 Boeing 787, provides enough detail for aviation buffs to pore over for hours." Booklist

Williams, Vera B.

A chair for my mother. Greenwillow Bks. 1982 unp il $15.99; lib bdg $16.89; pa $6.99 *

Grades: PreK K 1 2 3   E

1. Family life—Fiction 2. Saving and investment—Fiction 3. Chairs—Fiction

ISBN 0-688-00914-X; 0-688-00915-8 (lib bdg); 0-688-04074-8 (pa)   LC 81-7010

A Caldecott Medal honor book, 1983

Rosa, her waitress mother, and her grandmother save dimes to buy a comfortable armchair after all their furniture is lost in a fire

"The cheerful paintings take up the full left-hand page and face, in most cases, a small chunk of the text set against a modulated wash of a complementing color; a border containing a pertinent motif surrounds the two pages, further unifying the design. The result is a superbly conceived picture book expressing the joyful spirit of a loving family." Horn Book

Other titles about Rosa and her family are:

Music, music for everyone (1984)

Something special for me (1983)

A chair for always (2009)

Williams, Vera B.—*Continued*

Cherries and cherry pits. Greenwillow Bks. 1986 unp il $17.99 hardcover o.p.; pa $6.99 *

Grades: PreK K 1 2 3   E

1. African Americans—Fiction 2. Drawing—Fiction
ISBN 0-688-05145-6; 0-688-05146-4 (lib bdg); 0-688-10478-9 (pa)   LC 85-17156

"Bidemmi, a young black child, draws splendid pictures. 'As she draws, she tells the story of what she is drawing,' always starting with the word 'this.' . . . Finally, Bidemmi tells her story, revealing her wish for her neighborhood and her world. Each story involves cherries—buying, sharing, and enjoying them." SLJ

"Williams' portraits of Bidemmi drawing are done in watercolor; the drawings Bidemmi makes are done with bright markers, some being simple sketches, others filling the page with color, looking like naive, but glorious icons. The interior stories are well integrated with each other, and the whole adds up to a study of child as artist that is fresh, vibrant, and exciting." Bull Cent Child Books

Lucky song. Greenwillow Bks. 1997 unp il $16.99

Grades: PreK K 1   E

1. Day—Fiction 2. Kites—Fiction 3. Songs—Fiction
ISBN 0-688-14459-4   LC 96-7151

"Evie flies the kite made by her grandfather until it's time to go home for supper all tired and ready for bed. This patterned story, showing a little girl surrounded by a loving family, ends by circling back to the beginning. It is illustrated using brilliantly colored watercolors." Child Book Rev Serv

"More more more" said the baby; 3 love stories. Greenwillow Bks. 1990 unp il $17.99; lib bdg $18.89; pa $6.99; bd bk $7.99 *

Grades: PreK K 1   E

1. Infants—Fiction 2. Family life—Fiction
ISBN 0-688-09173-3; 0-688-09174-1 (lib bdg); 0-688-814736-4 (pa); 0-688-15634-7 (bd bk)
                                             LC 89-2023

A Caldecott Medal honor book, 1991

Three babies are caught up in the air and given loving attention by a father, grandmother, and mother

"The pages reverberate with bright colors and vigorous forms, and the rhythmic language begs to be read aloud." Horn Book Guide

Music, music for everyone. Greenwillow Bks. 1984 unp il $17.99; pa $6.99 *

Grades: PreK K 1 2   E

1. Family life—Fiction 2. Bands (Music)—Fiction 3. Grandmothers—Fiction
ISBN 0-688-02603-6; 0-688-07811-7 (pa)
                                            LC 83-14196

Rosa plays her accordion with her friends in the Oak Street Band and earns money to help her mother with expenses while her grandmother is sick

"In Miss Williams's lovely watercolor illustrations, everyday things look special. . . . [This] is a gently exuberant book." NY Times Book Rev

Stringbean's trip to the shining sea; greetings from Vera B. Williams, story and pictures; and Jennifer Williams, more pictures. Greenwillow Bks. 1987 unp il $18.99 hardcover o.p.; pa $7.99 *

Grades: K 1 2 3   E

1. West (U.S.)—Fiction 2. Automobile travel—Fiction
ISBN 0-688-07161-9; 0-688-07162-7 (lib bdg); 0-688-16701-2 (pa)   LC 86-29502

"Stringbean and big brother Fred (joined en route by Potato, Stringbean's dog) take a car trip from their home in Kansas to the Pacific Ocean, and their pilgrimage is recorded herein in the form of a mock photo and postcard album." Bull Cent Child Books

"The use of mixed media—watercolors, Magic Markers, and colored pencils—is as aesthetically pleasing as it is skillful. Nothing has been forgotten; nothing more needs to be added. Not for the usual picture-book set, this travelogue storybook will appeal to slightly older audiences." Horn Book

Three days on a river in a red canoe. Greenwillow Bks. 1984 unp il hardcover o.p. pa $6.99

Grades: K 1 2 3   E

1. Canoes and canoeing—Fiction 2. Camping—Fiction
ISBN 0-688-84307-7 (lib bdg); 0-688-04072-1 (pa)
                                             LC 80-23893

In this book, a "canoe trip for two children and two adults is recorded with all its interesting detail in a spontaneous first-person account and engaging full-color drawings on carefully designed pages. Driving to a river site, making camp, paddling the craft, negotiating a waterfall, swimming, fishing, dealing with a sudden storm, and even rescuing one overboard child are all described as important incidents in a summertime adventure." Horn Book

Willis, Jeanne, 1959-

The bog baby; written by Jeanne Willis; illustrated by Gwen Millward. Schwartz & Wade Books 2009 c2008 unp il $16.99; lib bdg $19.99 *

Grades: K 1 2 3   E

1. Magic—Fiction 2. Sisters—Fiction
ISBN 978-0-375-86176-5; 0-375-86176-9; 978-0-375-96176-2 (lib bdg); 0-375-96176-3 (lib bdg)
                                            LC 2008-47635

First published 2008 in the United Kingdom

When two sisters go fishing in a magic pond, they find a winged blue bog baby and take it home with them.

"The glorious illustrations reveal a lush dreamscape of a backyard flush with tendrils, bluebells, Queen Anne's lace, birch trees, cherry trees, dragonflies, ladybugs, and more, all delicately and minutely drawn, and painted in watercolors. The child-voiced, economical narrative transports readers into the squelches and squeaks of tromping through the mud and spring plants." SLJ

Willis, Jeanne, 1959-—*Continued*

Cottonball Colin; illustrated by Tony Ross. Eerdmans Books for Young Readers 2008 unp il $16 *

Grades: PreK K 1 2   **E**

  1. Mother-son relationship—Fiction 2. Mice—Fiction 3. Size—Fiction

  ISBN 978-0-8028-5331-8; 0-8028-5331-5

                 LC 2007009356

Afraid that her smallest child, Colin, will be hurt if he goes outside or plays, a mother mouse insists that he sit quietly indoors until his grandmother suggests wrapping him in cotton wool, which proves to be effective, but in a most unexpected way.

"Ross's elegant watercolor and ink drawings take Colin from domestic comedy to thrilling action-adventure without a hitch, and make his transformation from nebbish to cool dude totally believable." Publ Wkly

Gorilla! Gorilla! [by] Jeanne Willis and [illustrated by] Tony Ross. Simon & Schuster 2006 unp il $15.95

Grades: PreK K 1 2   **E**

  1. Mice—Fiction 2. Gorillas—Fiction

  ISBN 978-1-4169-1490-7; 1-4169-1490-0

"While searching for her lost baby, a mouse is chased by a great, big, hairy, scary ape! . . . Young readers will guess what the mother mouse, in her terror, can't see—that the seemingly fierce gorilla is simply trying to return her baby to her. The brief, lively text and the melodramatic refrain make for a humorous and boisterous readaloud. Ross's bright pastel illustrations capture the mouse's fear and the gorilla's determination with verve." SLJ

Mommy, do you love me? [by] Jeanne Willis; illustrated by Jan Fearnley. Candlewick Press 2008 unp il $15.99

Grades: PreK   **E**

  1. Chickens—Fiction 2. Mother-child relationship—Fiction 3. Love—Fiction

  ISBN 978-0-7636-3470-4; 0-7636-3470-0

"Through a series of tests—deliberate and not—a chick becomes almost totally convinced that his mother's affections are unshakable. Then, provoked by her son's almost manic cheeping, his mother momentarily loses it, and Little Chick is himself shaken. The mother hen repairs the breach with some unconditional reassurance. . . . Working in warm, translucent watercolors and velvety black outlines, Fearnley . . . gives her characters an endearing depth of expression and personality." Publ Wkly

Susan laughs; illustrated by Tony Ross. Holt & Co. 2000 unp il $15 *

Grades: PreK K 1   **E**

  1. Play—Fiction 2. Physically handicapped—Fiction 3. Stories in rhyme

  ISBN 0-8050-6501-6   LC 99-59560

Rhyming couplets describe a wide range of common emotions and activities experienced by a little girl who uses a wheelchair

"Without being condescending or preachy, the words, pictures, and design of this very simple picture book show that a physically disabled child is 'just like me, just like you.' Only on the very last page do we discover that Susan uses a wheelchair." Booklist

Wilson, Karma

Bear snores on; illustrations by Jane Chapman. Margaret K. McElderry Bks. 2002 unp il $16; bd bk $7.99 *

Grades: PreK K 1   **E**

  1. Bears—Fiction 2. Animals—Fiction 3. Parties—Fiction 4. Stories in rhyme

  ISBN 0-689-83187-0; 1-4169-0272-4 (bd bk)

                 LC 00-28371

On a cold winter night many animals gather to party in the cave of a sleeping bear, who then awakes and protests that he has missed the food and the fun

"The characters are infused with warmth and humor. . . . The warm, soft tones of these acrylic illustrations perfectly capture the coziness of Bear's lair and capture the action." SLJ

Other titles in this series are:

Bear feels scared (2008)

Bear feels sick (2007)

Bear stays up for Christmas (2004)

Bear wants more (2003)

Bear's new friend (2006)

The cow loves cookies; illustrated by Marcellus Hall. Margaret K. McElderry Books 2010 il $16.99

Grades: PreK K 1 2   **E**

  1. Stories in rhyme 2. Cattle—Fiction 3. Domestic animals—Fiction 4. Farmers—Fiction 5. Cookies—Fiction

  ISBN 978-1-4169-4206-1; 1-4169-4206-8

                 LC 2009000742

While all the other animals on the farm enjoy eating their regular food, the cow chooses to eat the one thing that she loves best.

"The big, clear watercolor pictures with thick ink lines leave lots of white space, and the simple rhyming lines, with descriptive words and messy action, will encourage preschoolers to join in." Booklist

A frog in the bog; [illustrated by] Joan Rankin. Margaret K. McElderry Bks. 2003 unp il $16.95

Grades: PreK K 1   **E**

  1. Frogs—Fiction 2. Insects—Fiction 3. Stories in rhyme 4. Counting

  ISBN 0-689-84081-0   LC 2002-5903

A frog in the bog grows larger and larger as he eats more and more bugs, until he attracts the attention of an alligator who puts an end to his eating

"This gastronomic adventure is told in catchy rhyming verse, complemented by soft, dreamy watercolors that perfectly recreate the bog. The illustrations are enhanced by humorous details." SLJ

How to bake an American pie; illustrated by Raul Colón. Simon & Schuster 2007 unp il $16.99

Grades: K 1 2 3   **E**

  1. Patriotism—Fiction 2. Stories in rhyme

  ISBN 0-689-86506-6; 978-0-689-86506-0

Rhyming text and illustrations present a recipe for how to bake a pie from all the things that make America

Wilson, Karma—*Continued*

great.

"In these watercolor-and-ink paintings, the action rolls across the spreads in all sorts of fantastical ways. Purple mountain majesties grow out of teacups, and the cooks pull rainbows out of a sky studded with stars and stripes. . . . [This is a] wild, wonderful celebration." Booklist

Mama always comes home; illustrated by Brooke Dyer. HarperCollins 2005 unp il $15.99; lib bdg $16.89

Grades: PreK K 1   E

1. Mother-child relationship—Fiction 2. Animals—Fiction 3. Stories in rhyme

ISBN 0-06-057505-0; 0-06-057506-9 (lib bdg)
                                   LC 2003-26979

From Mama Bird to Mama Cat, mothers of all kinds come home to their children

"The consistently tender illustrations follow the text's well-crafted rhymes. . . . Presented with a delicate and loving touch, this book embodies the power of thoughtful text supported by insightful pictures." SLJ

Where is home, Little Pip? [by] Karma Wilson; illustrated by Jane Chapman. Margaret K. McElderry Books 2008 unp il $16.99

Grades: PreK K 1   E

1. Penguins—Fiction 2. Animals—Fiction 3. Antarctica—Fiction

ISBN 978-0-689-85983-0; 0-689-85983-X
                                   LC 2006019094

After Little Pip the penguin gets lost she meets a whale, a kelp gull, and sled dogs who cannot help her, but with the aid of her family's song, home finds her

"Well-structured text, genuine emotions, and beautiful full-bleed illustrations in a palette that ranges from cool whites and blues to warm pinks, corals, and tans combine to produce a wonderful story of a loving family separated and then reunited." SLJ

Other titles about Little Pip are:
Don't be afraid, Little Pip (2009)
What's in the egg, Little Pip? (2010)

Whopper cake; [by] Karma Wilson; [illustrated by] Will Hillenbrand. Margaret K. McElderry Books 2007 unp il $16.99

Grades: PreK K 1 2   E

1. Birthdays—Fiction 2. Cake—Fiction 3. Tall tales 4. Stories in rhyme

ISBN 0-689-83844-1   LC 00058742

Grandad bakes Grandma a whopper of a birthday cake. Includes recipe and directions for chocolate cake

"Rendered in ink and egg tempera, Hillenbrand's illustrations spill off the spreads." SLJ

Wilson, Sarah, 1934-

The day we danced in underpants; by Sarah Wilson; illustrations by Catherine Stock. Tricycle Press 2008 unp il $14.95

Grades: PreK K 1   E

1. Dance—Fiction 2. Kings and rulers—Fiction 3. France—Fiction 4. Stories in rhyme

ISBN 978-1-58246-205-9; 1-58246-205-4
                                   LC 2007018172

When Papa's pants—worn thin from dancing on his visit to France—split as he sits down to picnic with the king, the embarrassing moment provides both cooling and comic relief for the guests, prompting them to take off their hot clothes and dance.

"Jaunty rhymed text and colorful pen-and-ink, watercolor, and collage illustrations evoke the joyous movement of dance." Horn Book Guide

Friends and pals and brothers, too; illustrated by Leo Landry. Holt 2008 unp il $16.95

Grades: PreK K 1 2   E

1. Brothers—Fiction 2. Friendship—Fiction 3. Seasons—Fiction 4. Stories in rhyme

ISBN 978-0-8050-7643-1; 0-8050-7643-3
                                   LC 2007002829

Two brothers who are best friends have fun together throughout the year

"Told in uncomplicated verse, one short line per page, this unassuming book captures the warmth and delight of being best friends. The rhyming is easy and predictable. . . . The childlike, unembellished watercolor and pencil illustrations fit the text perfectly, and the muted colors underscore the simplicity and joyful intimacy of the boys' relationship." SLJ

Wing, Natasha, 1960-

Go to bed, monster! written by Natasha Wing; illustrated by Sylvie Kantorovitz. Harcourt 2007 unp il $16

Grades: PreK K 1   E

1. Monsters—Fiction 2. Bedtime—Fiction

ISBN 978-0-15-205775-6   LC 2006010849

Trying to avoid bedtime, Lucy uses her imagination and some crayons to draw a monster to play with.

"Kantorovitz's whimsical ink-and-watercolor pictures on open white backgrounds . . . are perfectly paired to Wing's engaging and breezy text and characters." SLJ

Winter, Jeanette, 1939-

Angelina's island. Farrar, Straus & Giroux 2007 unp il $16

Grades: K 1 2 3   E

1. Jamaica—Fiction 2. New York (N.Y.)—Fiction 3. Immigrants—Fiction

ISBN 978-0-374-30349-5; 0-374-30349-5
                                   LC 2005052752

"Frances Foster books"

Every day, Angelina dreams of her home in Jamaica and imagines she is there, until her mother finds a wonderful way to convince her that New York is now their home

"Using simple, poetic text and small, framed, brilliantly colored pictures, Winter sets the child's two worlds on opposite sides of each double-page spread." Booklist

Biblioburro; a true story from Colombia. Beach Lane Books 2010 il $16.99 *

Grades: PreK K 1 2   E

1. Soriano, Luis 2. Colombia 3. Books and reading 4. Libraries

ISBN 978-1-416-99778-8; 1-416-99778-4

"After amassing piles of books, Luis, a voracious reader, dreams up a way to share his collection with 'far-

Winter, Jeanette, 1939-—*Continued*

away villages.' He starts with two burros—one for himself, one for books—and heads off. Tough terrain and menacing bandits challenge him along the way, but at last he reaches a remote town, where he holds a story hour and loans titles to eager kids before returning home to his wife and reading late into the night. Winter's captivating paintings evoke a South American feel in their brilliant palette and dense, green tropical scenes teeming with creatures, including large, orange-winged butterflies on every page. . . . Winter's text is spare and streamlined, as usual, and here it has a particularly engaging, repetitive rhythm that builds into a lulling bedtime beat." Booklist

Calavera abecedario; a Day of the Dead alphabet. Harcourt 2004 unp il $16 *

Grades: PreK K 1 2   E

1. All Souls' Day—Fiction 2. Alphabet 3. Spanish language—Vocabulary 4. Mexico—Social life and customs

ISBN 0-15-205110-4   LC 2004-1554

Every year Don Pedro makes papier-mache skeletons, or calaveras, for Mexico's Day of the Dead fiesta. From Angel to Unicornio, each letter of the alphabet has its own special calavera. Spanish words illustrate each letter of the alphabet.

This "features jaunty illustrations inspired by Mexican folk art. . . . This is a lovely book that approaches the Day of the Dead from an unusual angle." SLJ

Follow the drinking gourd; story and pictures by Jeanette Winter. Alfred A. Knopf 2008 c1988 unp il hardcover o.p. pa $7.99 *

Grades: K 1 2 3   E

1. Slavery—Fiction 2. Underground railroad—Fiction 3. African Americans—Fiction

ISBN 978-0-394-89694-6; 978-0-679-81997-4 (pa)

A reissue of the title first published 1988

By following directions in a song, taught them by an old sailor, runaway slaves journey north along the Underground Railroad to freedom in Canada.

"Complementing the few lines of text per page are dark-hued illustrations horizontally framed with a fine black line and plenty of white space. . . . The art carries the weight of introducing children to a riveting piece of U.S. history, and the music included at the end of the book will fix it in their minds." Bull Cent Child Books

Josefina. Harcourt Brace & Co. 1996 unp il $16

Grades: PreK K 1 2   E

1. Women artists—Fiction 2. Mexico—Fiction 3. Counting

ISBN 0-15-201091-2   LC 95-34110

"In a sunny patio in Mexico, there is one rising sun in a sky where two angels keep watch over three houses. . . . Throughout her life—from her childhood through the deaths of her parents, her marriage to José, and the birth of their nine children, Josefina works the soft clay into figures to create this world. . . . Inspired by the painted clay figures decorating Josefina Aguilar's patio in Ocotlán, Mexico, Winter has crafted a picture-book vision of the folk artist's life that cleverly turns into a bilingual counting story. . . . Paired with a simple prose narrative, the artwork creates an effect that is both elegant and soothing." Booklist

The librarian of Basra; a true story from Iraq. Harcourt, Inc. 2004 c2005 32p il $16 *

Grades: PreK K 1 2 3   E

1. Baker, Alia Muhammad 2. Librarians 3. Books 4. Libraries

ISBN 0-15-205445-6   LC 2004-12969

The story of Alia Muhammad Baker, a librarian in Basra, Iraq, who managed to rescue seventy percent of the library's collection before the library burned in the Iraq War in 2003

"Winter's bright, folk-art style does much to mute the horrific realties of war. . . . The librarian's quiet bravery serves as a point of entry into a freighted topic." Booklist

Mama; a true story in which a baby hippo loses his mama during a tsunami, but finds a new home, and a new mama. Harcourt 2006 unp il $16 *

Grades: PreK K 1 2   E

1. Hippopotamus 2. Turtles 3. Indian Ocean earthquake and tsunami, 2004

ISBN 978-0-15-205495-3; 0-15-205495-2

                    LC 2005-20905

Set against the backdrop of the devastating 2004 tsunami, this book reveals the true story of a rescued baby hippo who adopts a new "mother" —a 130-year-old male tortoise

"This visually poetic book's subtitle is longer than its entire text. . . . Winter reassuringly portrays how friendship can ease a devastating loss." Publ Wkly

September roses. Farrar, Straus & Giroux 2004 unp il $14 *

Grades: PreK K 1 2 3   E

1. September 11 terrorist attacks, 2001 2. Roses 3. New York (N.Y.)

ISBN 0-374-36736-1   LC 2003-54877

"Frances Foster books"

"Two sisters fly to New York from South Africa with thousands of roses meant for a flower show. The day they fly is September 11, 2001, and after the attack they are stranded at the airport with their flowers. They are offered shelter and offer their roses in return: at Union Square, they design two fallen towers made of roses. Winter . . . makes beautiful patterns with her figures and her roses using her signature thick black outlines. . . . This is understated and full of tenderness." Booklist

Winter, Jonah

The fabulous feud of Gilbert & Sullivan; illustrated by Richard Egielski. Arthur A. Levine Books 2009 unp il $16.99 paperback o.p. *

Grades: K 1 2 3   E

1. Gilbert, W. S. (William Schwenck), 1836-1911—Fiction 2. Sullivan, Sir Arthur, 1842-1900—Fiction 3. Composers—Fiction 4. Authors—Fiction 5. Operetta—Fiction 6. Great Britain—History—19th century—Fiction

ISBN 978-0-439-93050-5; 0-439-93050-2; 978-0-439-93051-2 (pa); 0-439-93051-0 (pa)

                    LC 2008-27027

In the late nineteenth century, Mr. Gilbert and Mr. Sullivan, who write operas together for a theater called Topsy-Turvydom, have a falling-out when Mr. Sullivan

Winter, Jonah—*Continued*

refuses to write music for another ridiculous story that is like all the others.

"The clearly written story comes alive in a series of distinctive ink-and-watercolor illustrations that are full of intriguing details and show great skill in the use of color, shading, and composition." Booklist

Here comes the garbage barge! written by Jonah Winter; illustrated by Red Nose Studio. Schwartz & Wade Books 2010 unp il $17.99; lib bdg $20.99 *

Grades: K 1 2   E
  1. Refuse and refuse disposal—Fiction 2. Voyages and travels—Fiction 3. Long Island (N.Y.)—Fiction
  ISBN   978-0-375-85218-3;   0-375-85218-2;
  978-0-375-95218-0 (lib bdg); 0-375-95218-7 (lib bdg)
                                        LC 2008-40709
In the spring of 1987, the town of Islip, New York, with no place for its 3,168 tons of garbage, loads it on a barge that sets out on a 162-day journey along the east coast, around the Gulf of Mexico, down to Belize, and back again, in search of a place willing to accept and dispose of its very smelly cargo

"A fictionalized account of real events. . . . The illustrations are photographs of objects made from garbage. The people, full of personality and expression, were made from polymer clay, and wire, wood scraps, and leftover materials of all kinds were used for the tugboat and barge. The inside of the paper jacket explains how the art was done. This title should be a part of every elementary school ecology unit." SLJ

Steel Town; illustrated by Terry Widener. Atheneum Books for Young Readers 2008 unp il $16.99 *

Grades: 2 3 4   E
  1. Cities and towns—Fiction 2. Factories—Fiction 3. Steel industry—Fiction
  ISBN 978-1-4169-4081-4; 1-4169-4081-2
                                        LC 2006-29284
In Steel Town, it's always raining, freight trains come and go, the big furnace roars, and the steel mill never sleeps.

"The acrylic artwork creates an atmosphere of gloom with fiery furnaces and gray skies. Against this backdrop is the rhythmic, repetitive language detailing a day in the life of Steel Town. . . . Both informative and visually stunning, . . . beautifully written and powerfully illustrated." SLJ

Winters, Kay

My teacher for President; illustrated by Denise Brunkus. Dutton Children's Books 2004 unp il $14.99

Grades: PreK K 1 2   E
  1. Teachers—Fiction 2. Presidents—Fiction
  ISBN 0-525-47186-3   LC 2003-19222
A second-grader writes a television station with reasons why his teacher would make a good president, but only if she can continue teaching till the end of the year

"Brunkus' cheerful illustrations show a gray-haired woman in large, round glasses. . . . The humorous tone brings lofty ideals about desirable presidential qualities down to an everyday, accessible level." Booklist

Whooo's that? Harcourt Children's Book 2009 unp il $9.99

Grades: PreK   E
  1. Halloween—Fiction
  ISBN 978-0-15-206480-8; 0-15-206480-X
                                        LC 2007039823
"A lift-the-flap pumpkin fun book."—Cover

"'Whooo's that prancing . . . in the park?/Whooo's that . . . prowling in the dark?' Why, it's trick-or-treaters, of course, as revealed on the book's final page. The volume is enhanced by its appealing trim size, the many engaging lift-the-flaps, and the softly spooky and expressive characters waiting to be uncovered from behind toothy jack-o-lanterns." Horn Book Guide

Winthrop, Elizabeth

The biggest parade; [by] Elizabeth Winthrop; illustrated by Mark Ulriksen. Henry Holt 2006 unp il $16.95

Grades: K 1 2 3   E
  1. Parades—Fiction 2. Dogs—Fiction
  ISBN 978-0-8050-7685-1; 0-8050-7685-9
                                        LC 2005019753
Harvey is so excited when the mayor appoints him Parade Chairman for a big celebration that he forgets something very important but, fortunately, his dog, Fred, remembers

"Winthrop's tale . . . is fun and quirky, with lots of humor. . . . The acrylic paintings almost resemble photographs in their detail, and Fred's expressions are priceless." SLJ

Shoes; illustrated by William Joyce. Harper & Row 1986 19p il lib bdg $16.89; pa $6.99

Grades: PreK K   E
  1. Shoes—Fiction 2. Stories in rhyme
  ISBN 0-06-026592-2 (lib bdg); 0-06-443171-1 (pa)
                                        LC 85-45841
"A jaunty rhyme about shoes of all kinds—'shoes for fishing, shoes for wishing, shoes for muddy squishing.' The roly-poly figures are drawn from a child's perspective." N Y Times Book Rev

"This lilting rhyme about shoes and feet easily pleases. . . . Backing the verses are full-color drawings of children busily involved with one kind of shoe or another. Joyce's pictures are animated, energetic, and warmly colored." Booklist

Squashed in the middle; illustrated by Pat Cummings. Holt 2005 unp il $16.95

Grades: PreK K 1 2   E
  1. Family life—Fiction 2. African Americans—Fiction
  ISBN 0-8050-6497-4
When Daisy, a middle child, is invited to spend the night at her friend's house, her family finally pays attention to her.

"Cummings' recognizable robust style and intense palette are evident in the engaging design here, a bright amalgamation of bold full-page closeups that clearly reflect Daisy's feelings. . . . Homey and whimsical details . . . give Daisy and her African American family a thoroughly modern, familiar look." Booklist

Wise, William, 1923-

Ten sly piranhas; a counting story in reverse (a tale of wickedness—and worse!); pictures by Victoria Chess. Dial Bks. for Young Readers 1993 unp il hardcover o.p. pa $5.99

Grades: PreK K 1 2   E

1. Fishes—Fiction 2. Counting 3. Stories in rhyme

ISBN 0-8037-1200-6; 0-14-240074-2 (pa)

LC 91-33704

A school of ten sly piranhas gradually dwindles as they waylay and eat each other, and the last is eaten by a crocodile

"The combination of a jaunty, rhymed text and gleefully fiendish illustrations demonstrates with delicious derring-do that the wicked frequently receive their just deserts." Horn Book

Wiseman, Bernard

Morris and Boris at the circus; by B. Wiseman. Harper & Row 1988 64p il (I can read book) hardcover o.p. pa $3.99

Grades: PreK K 1 2   E

1. Moose—Fiction 2. Bears—Fiction 3. Circus—Fiction

ISBN 0-06-026478-0 (lib bdg); 0-06-444143-1 (pa)

LC 87-45682

"Morris the Moose and his friend Boris the Bear . . . take a trip to the circus. Morris has never gone before, so he doesn't quite have the big picture. He thinks the clown's nose is red because he has a cold, and when they join the performers in the ring, Morris rides 'bearback' on Boris, instead of on a horse." Booklist

"The cartoon illustrations with bold colors provide ample context clues for beginning readers. This delightful combination of text and illustrations will entice children to read and re-read this book." SLJ

Wishinsky, Frieda

Maggie can't wait; illustrated by Dean Griffiths. Fitzhenry & Whiteside 2009 unp il $17.95

Grades: PreK K 1   E

1. Cats—Fiction 2. Adoption—Fiction 3. Infants—Fiction 4. Sisters—Fiction

ISBN 978-1-55455-103-3; 1-55455-103-X

Maggie the cat "is excited about the arrival of her newly adopted baby sister. But when she takes a picture of Rose to school, a mean-spirited nemesis dubs the baby ugly. . . . The drama of a cruel comment is fully realized in a manner and tone that children will identify with; Maggie's mortification is as believable as her triumph." SLJ

Another title about Maggie is:

Give Maggie a chance (2002)

Please, Louise! [by] Frieda Wishinsky; illustrated by Marie-Louise Gay. Groundwood Books 2007 unp il $17.95

Grades: PreK K 1 2   E

1. Siblings—Fiction 2. Dogs—Fiction

ISBN 0-88899-796-5; 978-0-88899-796-8

Jake is annoyed that his little sister Louise won't leave him alone. He wishes Louise were a dog. Suddenly Louise is gone and a little dog appears to be in her

place. Jake is worried that his wish may have come true.

"Deft pencil drawings, brightened with watercolor washes and collage elements, capture every nuance of the characters' emotions. . . . [The] story . . . unfolds with surprise and wit." Booklist

Wisniewski, David

Rain player; story and pictures by David Wisniewski. Clarion Bks. 1991 unp il $17; pa $7.95

Grades: 1 2 3 4   E

1. Mayas—Fiction 2. Games—Fiction

ISBN 0-395-55112-9; 0-395-72083-4 (pa)

LC 90-44101

To bring rain to his thirsty village, Pik challenges the rain god to a game of pok-a-tok

"This original tale combines research on Mayan history and legend with a suspenseful sports story. . . . Intricate and dramatic cut-paper illustrations powerfully recreate the foliage, landscape, architecture, and clothing of the Mayan classical period. . . . An author's note provides fascinating background information on Mayan civilization and gives in-depth explanations of some of the words and phrases used in the text." Horn Book

Witte, Anna

The parrot Tico Tango; written and illustrated by Anna Witte. Barefoot Books 2004 unp il $15.99; pa $6.99

Grades: PreK K 1 2   E

1. Parrots—Fiction 2. Rain forest animals—Fiction 3. Stories in rhyme

ISBN 1-84148-243-9; 1-84148-890-9 (pa)

LC 2004-17922

A cumulative rhyme in which a greedy parrot keeps taking fruit from the other creatures of the rainforest until he can hold no more.

"The rhymes are unusually taut and rhythmic, and the mixed-media art, which features fabric swatches, amounts to a feast of tropical colors." Horn Book Guide

Wiviott, Meg

Benno and the Night of Broken Glass; illustrated by Josee Bisaillon. Kar-Ben Pub. 2010 unp il lib bdg $17.95; pa $7.95 *

Grades: 2 3 4 5   E

1. Germany—History—1933-1945—Fiction 2. Kristallnacht, 1938—Fiction 3. Holocaust, 1933-1945—Fiction 4. Jews—Germany—Fiction 5. Cats—Fiction

ISBN 978-0-8225-9929-6; 0-8225-9929-5; 978-0-8225-9975-3 (pa); 0-8225-9975-9 (pa)

LC 2008033482

In 1938 Berlin, Germany, a cat sees Rosenstrasse change from a peaceful neighborhood of Jews and Gentiles to an unfriendly place where, one November night, men in brown shirts destroy Jewish-owned businesses and arrest or kill Jewish people. Includes facts about Kristallnacht and a list of related books and web resources.

"The straightforward text describes events without sentimentality. . . . But what truly distinguishes this

Wiviott, Meg—*Continued*

book is the striking multimedia artwork composed of paper, fabric, and drawn images in hues of olive, brown, and red. Interesting angles, textures, and patterns add to the visual effect throughout. . . . The message of terror and sadness that marks the beginning of the Holocaust is transmitted in a way that is both meaningful and comprehensible." SLJ

Includes bibliographical references

Wojciechowski, Susan

The Christmas miracle of Jonathan Toomey; illustrated by P. J. Lynch. Candlewick Press 2004 c1995 unp il $12.99

Grades: 1 2 3 4   E

1. Wood carving—Fiction 2. Christmas—Fiction 3. Friendship—Fiction

ISBN 0-7636-2621-X

A reissue of the title first published 1995

Includes audio CD, with story read aloud by James Earl Jones

The widow McDowell and her seven-year-old son Thomas ask the gruff Jonathan Toomey, the best woodcarver in the valley, to carve the figures for a Christmas creche

"The story verges on the sentimental, but it's told with feeling and lyricism. . . . Lynch's sweeping illustrations, in shades of wood grain, are both realistic and gloriously romantic, focusing on faces and hands at work before the fire and in the lamplight." Booklist

A fine St. Patrick's day; illustrated by Tom Curry. Random House 2004 unp il hardcover o.p. pa $6.99

Grades: K 1 2 3   E

1. Saint Patrick's Day—Fiction 2. Ireland—Fiction

ISBN 0-375-82386-7; 978-0-385-73640-4 (pa); 0-385-73640-1 (pa)   LC 2002-11684

Two towns, Tralee and Tralah, compete in an annual St. Patrick's Day decorating contest which Tralah boastfully always wins, but when their hearts are put to the test by a little man with pointed ears, Tralee wins with no effort at all

"Wojciechowski's charming tale is beautifully complemented by Curry's stylized depictions of green rolling hills and thatched-roof houses. Both text and art convey a sturdy feeling about community and charity, brushed with touch of whimsy." Booklist

Wolf, Sallie, 1950-

Truck stuck; illustrated by Andy Robert Davies. Charlesbridge 2008 unp il $14.95

Grades: PreK K 1   E

1. Trucks—Fiction 2. Vehicles—Fiction 3. Stories in rhyme

ISBN 978-1-58089-119-6; 1-58089-119-5

"A red 18-wheeler gets stuck under a viaduct and causes a huge traffic jam. Nearby, two children who have a lemonade stand observe the incident and try to keep everyone cool by selling their wares. . . . Eventually, a huge tow truck arrives and, after the air has been let out of the semi's tires, the road is cleared for traffic to resume just in time, because the children are out of lemonade. The bright, flat, cartoon art brings the minimal rhyming text to life and really tells the story." SLJ

Wolff, Ashley, 1956-

Me baby, you baby. Dutton Children's Books 2004 unp il $14.99

Grades: PreK   E

1. Infants—Fiction 2. Zoos—Fiction 3. Stories in rhyme

ISBN 0-525-46952-4   LC 2003-45219

Simple rhyming text describes a day in the life of two babies as they greet the day, go to the zoo with their mothers, and return home at night.

"With its rhythmic text and delicate gouache artwork, this is a delightful book to share with two and three-year-olds." SLJ

Wolff, Ferida, 1946-

It is the wind; illustrated by James Ransome. HarperCollins 2005 unp il $14.99; lib bdg $15.89

Grades: PreK K 1 2   E

1. Bedtime—Fiction 2. Sound—Fiction

ISBN 0-06-028191-X; 0-06-028192-8 (lib bdg)   LC 00-63197

"In his room at night, a boy looks outside and tries to imagine what is making the noise he hears. . . . The mesmerizing effect of the verse makes this a good bedtime story. . . . Ransome makes the most of the simple story with graceful scenes of the African American boy and the rural night scenes he sees and imagines." Booklist

The story blanket; [written by Ferida Wolff and Harriet May Savitz; illustrated by Elena Odriozola] Peachtree 2008 unp il $16.95

Grades: K 1 2 3   E

1. Blankets—Fiction 2. Storytelling—Fiction 3. Gifts—Fiction

ISBN 978-1-56145-466-2; 1-56145-466-4   LC 2008-08627

With no wool to be found in the village, Babba Zarrah, the storyteller, starts unraveling her story blanket bit by bit, to secretly supply the needs of the community, and when the villagers realize what is happening they return the favor.

"Colorful illustrations accompany this story of generosity and ingenuity. Rosy-cheeked children and the bright folk art quilt suggest a timelessness to the story as well as the underlying message." Libr Media Connect

Wong, Janet S., 1962-

Apple pie 4th of July; pictures by Margaret Chodos-Irvine. Harcourt 2002 unp il $16

Grades: PreK K 1 2   E

1. Fourth of July—Fiction 2. Chinese Americans—Fiction

ISBN 0-15-202543-X   LC 2001-1313

A Chinese American girl fears that the food her parents are preparing to sell on the Fourth of July will not be eaten

"An appealing story with believable characters and emotions, written in the girl's spare, lyrical voice. Chodos-Irvine . . . captures the story's uncluttered, elemental qualities in opaque prints that resemble paper cutouts." Booklist

Wong, Janet S., 1962-—*Continued*

Buzz; illustrated by Margaret Chodos-Irvine. Harcourt 2000 unp il $15

Grades: PreK K 1 2   E
   1. Morning—Fiction 2. Bees—Fiction
   ISBN 0-15-201923-5   LC 99-6148
   "A young child relates the simple morning events that happen in his house, all of which seem to make a buzz." Booklist
   "Chodos-Irvine's use of various print-making techniques results in illustrations that are strongly geometric and graphically clean, in springtime colors that suit the cheerful tone of the text. The humor in both text and pictures contributes to the light-hearted atmosphere." Bull Cent Child Books

Hide & seek; pictures by Margaret Chodos-Irvine. Harcourt 2005 unp il $16

Grades: PreK K   E
   1. Counting
   ISBN 0-15-204934-7   LC 2003-27737
   In this counting book, a child and parent play hide-and-seek while they bake cookies
   "The rhythmic words capture the breathless excitement of searching and hiding, and Chodos-Irvine's prints, in her signature style of simple, dynamic shapes and bright, saturated hues, match the vibrant energy and elemental sounds in the simple words." Booklist

Homegrown house; illustrated by E.B. Lewis. Margaret K. McElderry Books 2009 unp il $16.99

Grades: K 1 2 3   E
   1.   Home—Fiction   2.   Moving—Fiction
   3. Grandmothers—Fiction
   ISBN 978-0-689-84718-9; 0-689-84718-1
                                          LC 2006038599
   A young girl describes her grandmother's comfortable, long-time home, and wishes that she and her parents could stay in the same house instead of moving so often.
   "Wong's poignant poem nicely captures a child's sense of powerlessness and disorientation. With his usual mastery and sensitivity, Lewis creates a true story from the words in sensitive scenes." Booklist

This next New Year; pictures by Yangsook Choi. Foster Bks. 2000 unp il $16

Grades: PreK K 1 2   E
   1. Chinese New Year—Fiction
   ISBN 0-374-35503-7   LC 99-22377
   "A Chinese-Korean boy reflects on what Chinese New Year means to him. By sweeping last year's mistakes and bad luck out of the house, he hopes to make room for 'a fresh start, my second chance.'" Horn Book Guide
   "Choi's smooth, brightly colored paintings . . . ably illustrate the optimistic activity and the yearning in the accessible, rhythmic text." Booklist

Wood, Audrey

The Bunyans; illustrated by David Shannon. Blue Sky Press (NY) 1996 unp il $16.95

Grades: K 1 2 3 4   E
   1. Bunyan, Paul (Legendary character) 2. Tall tales
   ISBN 0-590-48089-8   LC 95-26170

Paul Bunyan "meets a gigantic woman, and he and Carrie are soon married. Two oversize children arrive and play a important role in the formation of many of America's natural wonders: Niagara Falls, Bryce Canyon, and Big Sur, among others. . . . Wood captures the tongue-in-cheek tone and the exaggeration bordering on the ridiculous that characterize American tall tales. . . . Shannon's realistic, full-color paintings provide a counterpoint to the text, serving to make it seem almost believable. The artist's figures are large and solid." SLJ

The deep blue sea; a book of colors; story by Audrey Wood; pictures of Bruce Wood. Blue Sky Press 2005 unp il $15.99

Grades: PreK K   E
   1. Color
   ISBN 0-439-75382-1
   Introduces various colors by presenting a colorful scene on a rock in the deep blue sea.
   "Sharply focused, vividly hued artwork makes this concept book a standout. . . . The rhythmic text is enticing and reads aloud smoothly." SLJ

A dog needs a bone; story and pictures by Audrey Wood. Blue Sky Press 2007 unp il $16.99

Grades: PreK K 1   E
   1. Dogs—Fiction 2. Stories in rhyme
   ISBN   978-0-545-00005-5;   0-545-00005-X;
   978-0-545-00006-2 (pa); 0-545-00006-8 (pa)
                                          LC 2006035625
   In this rhyming tale, a dog makes extravagant promises to its mistress if only she will give it a bone.
   "Jovial, cartoonlike illustrations, drawn using crayons on brown paper bags, create a comfortable, homelike atmosphere and perfectly capture the animal's antics and expressions. . . . Filled with child appeal, it's sure to be a winner." SLJ

Elbert's bad word; illustrated by Audrey and Don Wood. Harcourt Brace Jovanovich 1988 unp il hardcover o.p. pa $7

Grades: K 1 2 3 4   E
   1. Parties—Fiction
   ISBN 0-15-225320-3; 0-15-201367-9 (pa)
                                          LC 86-7557
   "A bad word, spoken by a small boy at a fashionable garden party, creates havoc, and the child, Elbert, gets his mouth scrubbed out with soap. The bad word, in the shape of a long-tailed furry monster, will not go away until a wizard-gardener cooks up some really delicious, super-long words that everyone at the party applauds. This single-idea cautionary tale has lively, absurdist pictures of tiara-crowned, formally dressed adults recoiling in horror or cavorting with glee when Elbert, the only child at the party, speaks a word." SLJ

Heckedy Peg; illustrated by Don Wood. Harcourt Brace Jovanovich 1987 unp il lib bdg $17; pa $7 *

Grades: K 1 2 3 4   E
   1. Fairy tales 2. Witches—Fiction
   ISBN 0-15-233678-8 (lib bdg); 0-15-233679-6 (pa)
                                          LC 86-33639
   "The poor mother of seven children, each named for a day of the week, goes off to market promising to re-

Wood, Audrey—*Continued*

turn with individual gifts that each child has requested and admonishing them to lock the door to strangers and not to touch the fire. The gullible children are tricked into disobeying their mother by the witch, Heckedy Peg, who turns them all into various kinds of food. The mother can rescue her children only by guessing which child is the fish, the roast rib, the bread. . . . This story, deep and rich with folk wisdom, is stunningly illustrated with Don Wood's luminous paintings. . . . With variety of color and line he enhances every nuance of the text." SLJ

King Bidgood's in the bathtub; written by Audrey Wood; illustrated by Don Wood. Harcourt Brace Jovanovich 1985 unp il lib bdg $17 *

Grades: K 1 2 3 4   E

1. Kings and rulers—Fiction 2. Baths—Fiction
ISBN 0-15-242730-9   LC 85-5472

A Caldecott Medal honor book, 1986

Despite pleas from his court, a fun-loving king refuses to get out of his bathtub to rule his kingdom

"The few simple words of text per large, well-designed page invite story-telling—but keep the group very small, so the children can be close enough to pore over the brilliant, robust illustrations." SLJ

Wood, Don, 1945-

The napping house. Harcourt Children's Books 2009 unp il $17.99 *

Grades: K 1 2 3   E

1. Sleep—Fiction
ISBN 978-0-15-256708-8; 0-15-256708-9

A reissue, with new audio CD, of the title first published 1984

"In this sleepytime cumulative tale, all are pleasantly napping until a pesky flea starts the clamor that wakes up the whole family-mouse, cat, dog, child, and granny." Child Book Rev Serv

"The cool blues and greens are superseded by warm colors and bursts of action as each sleeper wakes, ending in an eruption of color and energy as naptime ends. A deft matching of text and pictures adds to the appeal of cumulation, and to the silliness of the mound of sleepers—just the right kind of humor for the lap audience." Bull Cent Child Books

Piggies; written by Don and Audrey Wood; illustrated by Don Wood. Harcourt Brace Jovanovich 1991 unp il $17; pa $8; bd bk $5.95 *

Grades: PreK K 1 2   E

1. Bedtime—Fiction 2. Pigs—Fiction
ISBN 0-15-256341-5; 0-15-200217-0 (pa); 0-15-202638-X (bd bk)   LC 89-24598

Ten little piggies dance on a young child's fingers and toes before finally going to sleep

"A happy text and luxuriant, witty pictures make this a book to pore over again and again." Booklist

Wood, Douglas, 1951-

Miss Little's gift; illustrated by Jim Burke. Candlewick Press 2009 unp il $16.99

Grades: 1 2 3   E

1. Teachers 2. Hyperactive children 3. Reading 4. Attention deficit disorder
ISBN 978-0-7636-1686-1; 0-7636-1686-9
                                       LC 2008-17915

"This autobiographical picture book chronicles the author's struggles in second grade. Smaller than everyone else, new in town, and speaking with an unfamiliar Southern accent, Wood also found reading to be a chore. . . . . The story works as a tribute to those unsung teacher heroes whose dedication to their craft and native intuition about children have changed lives. . . . Burke's large, realistic oils, with their rich greens and blues, complement the story nicely." SLJ

What dads can't do; pictures by Doug Cushman. Simon & Schuster Bks. for Young Readers 2000 unp il $14

Grades: PreK K   E

1. Fathers—Fiction
ISBN 0-689-82620-6   LC 98-41773

"The young, green, reptilian narrator enumerates all the things dads—and especially the green reptilian one pictured—can never do. Dads 'can't cross the street without holding hands,' they 'lose at checkers and cards,' and 'Dads can push, but they can't swing.'" Horn Book Guide

"This amusing picture book will tickle youngsters' funny bones and make every parent and child smile with recognition. . . . Cushman's large, delightful, pen-and-ink and watercolor cartoons . . . capture perfectly the father-and-son interactions." SLJ

Other titles in this series are:
What grandmas can't do (2005)
What moms can't do (2000)
What Santa can't do (2003)
What teachers can't do (2000)

Where the sunrise begins; words by Douglas Wood; art by Wendy Popp. Simon & Schuster Books for Young Readers 2010 unp il $16.99

Grades: PreK K 1   E

1. Sun—Fiction 2. Nature—Fiction
ISBN 978-0-689-86172-7; 0-689-86172-9

Reveals the part that each of us plays in the beginning of every day.

"Science is in full view as the author searches for the place where the sunrise begins. The beautiful watercolor drawings complement the simple but rich text. Not only are different cultures revealed, but geography is also put on display as the author, a naturalist, explores the world trying to find exactly where the sunrise begins. What the book unveils will amaze and delight the reader." Libr Media Connect

Wood, Nancy C.

Mr. and Mrs. God in the Creation Kitchen; illustrated by Timothy Basil Ering. Candlewick Press 2006 unp il $16.99

Grades: K 1 2   E

1. Creation—Fiction
ISBN 0-7636-1258-8   LC 2005-53187

Wood, Nancy C.—*Continued*

"Mr. and Mrs. God putter in the Creation Kitchen, first roasting Sun and Earth in their enormous oven, then whipping up Earth's creatures in between marital tiffs, finishing off with two jut-jawed humans and speculations about 'how they'll turn out.' . . . Ering's artwork captures the puckish spirit of Wood's telling. Spattered with dribbles and cluttered with gadgets, this chaotic kitchen reinforces the creators' portrayal as anything but perfect." Booklist

Woodruff, Elvira

The memory coat; story by Elvira Woodruff; illustrations by Michael Dooling. Scholastic Press 1999 unp il $17.99

Grades: K 1 2 3   E

1. Ellis Island Immigration Station—Fiction 2. Immigrants—Fiction 3. Jews—Fiction

ISBN 0-590-67717-9   LC 95-30048

In the early 1900s, cousins Rachel and Grisha leave their Russian shtetl with the rest of their family to come to America, hopeful that they will all pass the dreaded inspection at Ellis Island

This offers "warm, realistic period paintings, some in color, some in sepia shades. . . . In a long, interesting author's note, Woodruff discusses the shtetl and immigrant history." Booklist

Small beauties; the journey of Darcy Heart O'Hara; by Elvira Woodruff; pictures by Adam Rex. Alfred A. Knopf 2006 unp il $15.95

Grades: 1 2 3 4   E

1. Ireland—Fiction 2. Immigrants—Fiction 3. Family life—Fiction

ISBN 0-375-82686-6   LC 2005016038

Darcy Heart O'Hara, a young Irish girl who neglects her chores to observe the beauties of nature and everyday life, shares "family memories" with her homesick parents and siblings after the O'Haras are forced to emigrate to America in the 1840s

"Woodruff's simple, poetic storytelling combines with Rex's illustrations in charcoal, graphite pencils, and oil to present the drama through Darcy's eyes." Booklist

Woodson, Jacqueline

Coming on home soon; illustrated by E.B. Lewis. Putnam's 2004 unp il $16.99 *

Grades: K 1 2 3   E

1. Mother-child relationship—Fiction 2. Grandmothers—Fiction 3. World War, 1939-1945—Fiction 4. African Americans—Fiction

ISBN 0-399-23748-8   LC 2003-21949

A Caldecott Medal honor book, 2005

After Mama takes a job in Chicago during World War II, Ada Ruth stays with Grandma but misses her mother who loves her more than rain and snow.

"Woodson and Lewis tell a moving historical story of longing and separation. . . . Lewis' beautiful watercolors establish the setting. . . . Period and place are wonderfully specific." Booklist

The other side; illustrations by E. B. Lewis. Putnam 2001 unp il $16.99 *

Grades: K 1 2 3   E

1. Race relations—Fiction 2. Friendship—Fiction 3. African Americans—Fiction

ISBN 0-399-23116-1   LC 99-42055

Two girls, one white and one black, gradually get to know each other as they sit on the fence that divides their town

"Lewis' watercolors provide a telling backdrop to the action. . . . This is an emotionally intricate tale presented simply and intimately." Bull Cent Child Books

Show way; illustrated by Hudson Talbott. G. P. Putnam's Sons 2005 unp il $16.99 *

Grades: K 1 2 3   E

1. Quilts—Fiction 2. Slavery—Fiction 3. African Americans—Fiction

ISBN 0-399-23749-6   LC 2004-28093

A Newbery Medal honor book, 2006

The making of "Show ways," or quilts which once served as secret maps for freedom-seeking slaves, is a tradition passed from mother to daughter in the author's family.

"The gorgeous, multimedia art includes chalk, watercolors, and muslin. An outstanding tribute, perfectly executed in terms of text, design, and illustration." SLJ

Visiting day; illustrated by James E. Ransome. Scholastic Press 2002 unp il $15.95

Grades: K 1 2 3   E

1. Prisoners—Fiction 2. Fathers—Fiction 3. African Americans—Fiction

ISBN 0-590-40005-3   LC 00-35772

A young girl and her grandmother visit the girl's father in prison

"The text is spare, gentle, and reassuring. . . . Ransome's vibrant acrylic paintings fill each page at home with intense pinks, yellows, greens, and blues in contrast to the monotone hue of the prison walls. Both author and illustrator provide notes that relate this story to their own personal experiences." SLJ

We had a picnic this Sunday past; illustrated by Diane Greenseid. Hyperion Bks. for Children 1998 c1997 unp il pa $5.99

Grades: K 1 2 3   E

1. Family life—Fiction 2. African Americans—Fiction

ISBN 0-7868-0242-1; 1-4231-0681-4 (pa)

LC 96-16312

Teeka describes her various relatives and the foods they bring to the annual family picnic

"If this is more character sketch than actual story, the solid acrylic paintings help bring all the people in this African American family to life." Booklist

Wormell, Christopher

George and the dragon; [by] Chris Wormell. Knopf 2006 c2002 unp il $16.95

Grades: PreK K 1 2   E

1. Dragons—Fiction 2. Mice—Fiction

ISBN 0-375-83315-3

First published in 2002 in the United Kingdom

A dragon terrorizes the kingdom until he is frightened by George the mouse.

Wormell, Christopher—*Continued*

Henry and the fox; [by] Chris Wormell. Random House 2008 unp il hardcover o.p. pa $9.95

Grades: K 1 2   **E**
1. Roosters—Fiction 2. Foxes—Fiction 3. Courage—Fiction
ISBN   978-0-224-07044-7;   0-224-07044-4; 978-0-09-948383-0 (pa); 0-09-948383-1 (pa)
First published 2006 in the United Kingdom

"Henry is a cowardly cockerel who won't even say 'poo!' to a piglet, and his crowing is awful. Luckily for Henry, little Buffy Bantam . . . has come up with a brilliant plan and with just a red sock and a red woolly jumper." Publisher's note

This "is gorgeously illustrated and delightfully written. . . . Wormell's lovely watercolors are reminiscent of the radiant work of Jerry Pinkney." SLJ

Teeth, tails, & tentacles; an animal counting book. Running Press 2004 64p il $18.95
Grades: PreK K 1 2   **E**
1. Animals 2. Counting
ISBN 0-7624-2100-2

The first portion of the work is a counting book covering the numbers one to twenty with block prints of animals. The second portion of the work has factual information concerning the animals.

"Within the art, limpid colors melt into single-hue light-to-dark continuums or flash in arresting contrast, while surprising shifts in perspective and shadow create an almost tangible visual texture and depth which invite repeated viewing." Bull Cent Child Books

Wright, Betty Ren

The blizzard; illustrated by Ronald Himler. Holiday House 2003 unp il $16.95
Grades: PreK K 1 2 3   **E**
1. Birthdays—Fiction
ISBN 0-8234-1656-9   LC 2002-190764

Although a blizzard prevents his cousins from visiting for his birthday, a disappointed Billy ends up having a very special day when his teacher and classmates must stay overnight at his family's house to wait out the snowstorm

"This evocative story harkens back to an earlier, simpler time. . . . The feelings the events engender are tender and strong. Himler's artwork alternates between the white-gray of the blowing snow and the golden glow that comes from both inside the house and the hearts of those who live there." Booklist

Wright, Johanna

The secret circus. Roaring Brook Press 2009 unp il $16.95
Grades: PreK K 1   **E**
1. Circus—Fiction 2. Mice—Fiction 3. Paris (France)—Fiction 4. France—Fiction
ISBN 978-1-59643-403-5; 1-59643-403-1
      LC 2008-54261
"A Neal Porter Book"

Mice carefully dress for an evening out, journey across Paris in a hot air balloon, and finally arrive at a secret place to see the circus.

This is written in "simple, rhythmic prose. . . . Rustic canvas paintings done in a subdued palette cast a mood of quiet mystery over the nocturnal activities of the mice. The artwork provides the clever details that the text never reveals." SLJ

Wright, Maureen, 1961-

Sleep, Big Bear, sleep! illustrated by Will Hillenbrand. Marshall Cavendish Children 2009 unp il $16.99 *
Grades: PreK K 1   **E**
1. Stories in rhyme 2. Bears—Fiction 3. Winter—Fiction 4. Hibernation—Fiction
ISBN 978-0-7614-5560-8; 0-7614-5560-4
      LC 2008029402

As winter comes and Big Bear prepares to hibernate, he keeps thinking he hears Old Man Winter giving him exhausting orders that prevent him from sleeping.

"The text moves at a steady clip, and the refrain will encourage child participation. . . . The story reads aloud well, and the limited text and oversize illustrations will be effective in storytime. The artwork is the real star here, though. Hillenbrand imbues his characters with motion and personality." SLJ

Wright, Randall

The geezer in the freezer; illustrated by Thor Wickstrom. Bloomsbury USA Children's Books 2009 unp il $16.99; lib bdg $17.89
Grades: PreK K 1 2   **E**
1. Stories in rhyme
ISBN   978-1-59990-135-0;   1-59990-135-8; 978-1-59990-390-3 (lib bdg); 1-59990-390-3 (lib bdg)
      LC 2009004631

Stuck between a rump roast and a pie, the old man living in the freezer finally gets to tell his tale of woe.

"The horror-story premise is played beautifully for laughs, thanks to the expertly sustained country-flavored rhymes. Wickstrom's slathered-on oils capture the situation's absurdity—and tenderness, when the geezer is telling his tale of star-crossed love." Horn Book Guide

Xinran, 1958-

Motherbridge of love; text provided by Mother Bridge of Love; illustrated by Josee Masse. Barefoot 2007 unp il $16.99 *
Grades: PreK K 1 2   **E**
1. Adoption—Fiction 2. Mothers—Fiction
ISBN 978-1-84686-047-8

Celebrates the bond between parent and child as the adoptive parent of a little Chinese girl speaks about her love for her adopted daughter.

"Simple, lyrical language and gorgeous art make this more than just another adoption story. . . . The sentiment is exactly right—loving, caring, and thoughtful—and the stylized acrylic illustrations, in thick brush strokes and swirling shapes, evoke the lyrical tone with grace and elegance." Booklist

Yaccarino, Dan

Every Friday. Henry Holt and Company 2007 32p il $16.95

Grades: PreK K 1 2   E

1. Father-son relationship—Fiction

ISBN 978-0-8050-7724-7; 0-8050-7724-3

LC 2005020253

A "boy describes the route that he and his dad walk on their way to their weekly Friday breakfast at the corner diner. . . . Yaccarino's clean lines, saturated colors, and very simple words distill the story's emotions into clear, understated sweetness that's not too sugary." Booklist

Lawn to lawn. Alfred A. Knopf 2010 unp il $17.99; lib bdg $20.99

Grades: K 1 2 3   E

1. Gardens—Fiction 2. Adventure fiction 3. Voyages and travels—Fiction

ISBN 978-0-375-85574-0; 0-375-85574-2; 978-0-375-95574-7 (lib bdg); 0-375-95574-7 (lib bdg)

LC 2009002303

When their family moves away and leaves them behind, a group of lawn ornaments sets out on a dangerous trek across the country to try to find them.

"Yaccarino's clean, bright illustrations have an appealing retro look, and the trek through suburbs, swamps, fields, and city is a visual treat." Booklist

Yang, Belle

Foo, the flying frog of Washtub Pond. Candlewick 2009 unp il $16.99

Grades: PreK K 1 2   E

1. Animals—Fiction 2. Friendship—Fiction 3. Frogs—Fiction 4. Ponds—Fiction 5. Size—Fiction

ISBN 978-0-7636-3615-9; 0-7636-3615-0

"On the banks of Washtub Pond, Foo Frog, Sue-Lin Salamander, and MaoMao Mudpuppy live as friends the same size until Foo starts growing. Unfortunately, his ego grows as well, and soon he is convinced that he is the biggest animal in the world." SLJ

"Gouache illustrations made up of buoyant, spontaneous, and comedic strokes match the exaggeration of this foolish frog." Booklist

Hannah is my name. Candlewick Press 2004 unp il $16.99

Grades: K 1 2 3   E

1. Chinese Americans—Fiction 2. Immigrants—Fiction 3. San Francisco (Calif.)—Fiction

ISBN 0-7636-2223-0   LC 2003-69675

A young Chinese girl and her parents emigrate to the United States and try their best to assimilate into their San Francisco neighborhood while anxiously awaiting the arrival of their green cards.

"The bright gouache pictures of San Francisco draw strongly on Chinese and American traditions. . . . The struggle with documentation and the celebration when the green cards finally arrive in the mail is a drama many immigrant families will recognize." Booklist

Yates, Louise

A small surprise. Alfred A. Knopf 2009 unp il $16.99; lib bdg $19.99

Grades: PreK K 1   E

1. Size—Fiction 2. Rabbits—Fiction 3. Circus—Fiction

ISBN 978-0-375-85698-3; 0-375-85698-6; 978-0-375-95698-0 (lib bdg); 0-375-95698-0 (lib bdg)

LC 2008024535

A little rabbit, too small even to wipe his own nose, is just the right size to do one very special thing

"The illustrations are rendered in soft hues that are soothing yet colorful. The animals . . . have wonderfully expressive eyes and gestures. There are a few words in a large font on each page, making it easy for young children to follow along." SLJ

Yee, Wong Herbert, 1953-

Detective Small in the amazing banana caper; written and illustrated by Wong Herbert Yee. Houghton Mifflin 2007 unp il $15

Grades: PreK K 1 2   E

1. Mystery fiction 2. Animals—Fiction 3. Stories in rhyme

ISBN 978-0-618-47285-7; 0-618-47285-1

LC 2006009821

When shop owners call on Detective Small to track down a banana thief, he follows the clues to a likely suspect, then learns that the real culprit is still on the loose

"The rhyming text creates an infectious, bouncing rhythm that will appeal to many young listeners. It's Yee's pencil-and-watercolor illustrations, though, that really extend the action and humor." Booklist

Mouse and Mole, fine feathered friends. Houghton Mifflin Books for Children 2009 unp il $15 *

Grades: K 1 2 3   E

1. Bird watching—Fiction 2. Birds—Fiction 3. Mice—Fiction 4. Moles (Animals)—Fiction 5. Spring—Fiction

ISBN 978-0-5471-5222-6; 0-5471-5222-1

LC 2008040465

When spring arrives, Mole and Mouse find a unique way to bird watch.

"Transitional readers will enjoy the well-paced text's wordplay (including lots of puns); the gentle, realistic friendship conflicts; and the ink-and-watercolor artwork that captures the story's humor, action, and feeling." Booklist

Tracks in the snow. H. Holt 2003 unp il $15.95

Grades: PreK K 1 2   E

1. Animal tracks—Fiction 2. Snow—Fiction 3. Stories in rhyme

ISBN 0-8050-6771-X   LC 2002-10854

A little girl investigates tracks in the snow, trying to determine what could have made them.

"The gentle, rhyming text makes an ideal read-aloud, and young listeners will chime in on the repeated phrases. The soft-focus, colored-pencil illustrations portray a small Asian girl exploring her safe world, but a world transformed by the fresh snowfall." SLJ

Yee, Wong Herbert, 1953-—*Continued*
Upstairs Mouse, downstairs Mole. Houghton Mifflin Co. 2005 unp il $15
Grades: K 1 2 3   E
1. Mice—Fiction 2. Moles (Animals)—Fiction 3. Friendship—Fiction
ISBN 0-618-47313-0   LC 2004-5238
Mouse and her downstairs neighbor, Mole, discover that when they help each other, housecleaning and other daily tasks are much easier
"The expressive bamboo-pen and watercolor with colored-pencil illustrations capture the humor of the situations as well as the emotions of the characters. . . . A real winner." SLJ
Other titles about Mouse and Mole are:
Abracadabra! Magic with Mouse and Mole (2007)
A brand-new day with Mouse and Mole (2008)
Mouse and Mole: fine feathered friends (2009)

Who likes rain? Holt & Co. 2007 unp il $14.95
Grades: PreK K 1   E
1. Rain—Fiction
ISBN 978-0-8050-7734-6; 0-8050-7734-0
    LC 2006-03429
As a young girl splashes in the rain, she plays a guessing game with the reader about other living things that enjoy a cloudburst.
"The rhyming text tells the story as naturally as if the rhythm and rhyme just fell into place. . . . Fine strokes of color softly define the shapes of characters and settings." Booklist

Yeoman, John
The wild washerwomen; illustrated by Quentin Blake. Andersen; distributed by Lerner 2009 unp il lib bdg $16.95
Grades: K 1 2 3   E
1. Laundresses—Fiction
ISBN 978-0-7613-5152-8; 0-7613-5152-3
    LC 2008055432
A reissue of the title first published 1979 by Greenwillow Books
Seven washerwomen, sick of their work, go on an uncontrollable rampage, only to meet their match in seven very dirty woodcutters.
"The expressive illustrations—caricature line drawings washed with color—continuously echo and expand the preposterous, joyful text's often understated humor." Horn Book Guide

Yep, Laurence
Auntie Tiger; pictures by Insu Lee. HarperCollinsPublishers 2009 unp il $17.99; lib bdg $18.89
Grades: K 1 2 3   E
1. Fairy tales 2. China—Fiction 3. Tigers—Fiction 4. Sisters—Fiction
ISBN 978-0-06-029551-6; 0-06-029551-1; 978-0-06-029552-3 (lib bdg); 0-06-029552-X (lib bdg)
    LC 2006-28649
In this version of Red Riding Hood set in China, Big Sister sets aside her differences with Little Sister to rescue her from a tiger in disguise.

"Bright, energetic illustrations done in jewel tones bring this story to life. The cunning tiger with his large head, bulging eyes, and small pointy teeth is scarcely contained in three of the spreads." SLJ

Yin
Brothers; by Yin; paintings by Chris Soentpiet. Philomel Books 2006 unp il $16.99
Grades: 2 3 4   E
1. Chinese Americans—Fiction 2. Irish Americans—Fiction 3. Friendship—Fiction 4. San Francisco (Calif.)—Fiction
ISBN 0-399-23406-3
Companion volume to Coolies (2000)
Having arrived in San Francisco from China to work in his brother's store, Ming is lonely until an Irish boy befriends him.
"Soentpiet's luminescent, photo-realistic paintings, which provide many vivid setting details, perfectly complement Yin's thoughtful text." Booklist
Includes bibliographical references

Coolies; illustrated by Chris K. Soentpiet. Philomel Bks. 2001 unp il $16.99
Grades: 2 3 4   E
1. Central Pacific Railroad—Fiction 2. Chinese Americans—Fiction 3. Brothers—Fiction
ISBN 0-399-23227-3   LC 98-40403
A young boy hears the story of his great-great-great-grandfather and his brother who came to the United States to make a better life for themselves helping to build the transcontinental railroad
"Soentpiet's strong, realistic watercolor paintings, in shades of blue and gold, show the bond between the brothers. . . . The American history is powerful. Yin provides notes and a bibliography for readers who want to know more." Booklist

Yolen, Jane
Baby Bear's books; written by Jane Yolen; illustrated by Melissa Sweet. Harcourt 2006 unp il $16 *
Grades: PreK K   E
1. Bears—Fiction 2. Books and reading—Fiction 3. Stories in rhyme
ISBN 0-15-205290-9   LC 2005019203
Throughout the day, Baby Bear finds a book to fit every special moment.
"Mixed-media and collage illustrations create a warm and comfortable world. . . . The charming double-page pictures are large enough to share with groups, and the rhymes will engage listeners." SLJ
Other titles about Baby Bear are:
Baby Bear's chairs (2005)
Baby Bear's big dreams (2007)

Come to the fairies' ball; illustrated by Gary Lippincott. Wordsong 2009 unp il $17.95
Grades: 1 2 3 4   E
1. Stories in rhyme 2. Fairies—Fiction
ISBN 978-1-59078-464-8; 1-59078-464-2
    LC 2009018247

Yolen, Jane—*Continued*

All the fairies are excited to be invited to the King's ball, except for one young fairy whose only party dress is in tatters.

"An enchanting picture book full of whimsy and magic. . . . Lippincott's paintings take the forefront in this book, while Yolen's clever verse adds to the unfolding pictorial drama." SLJ

Commander Toad and the voyage home; pictures by Bruce Degen. Putnam 1998 64p il hardcover o.p. pa $5.99

Grades: 1 2 3 4   E

1. Toads—Fiction 2. Science fiction
ISBN 0-399-23122-6; 0-698-11602-X (pa)
                                         LC 96-21739

Commander Toad leads the lean green space machine "Star Warts" to find new worlds but runs into trouble when he sets course for home

"Yolen captures the high drama of space fiction in a delightful story that never loses sight of developing readers, who will be old enough to get the jokes but still young enough to relish the goofiness." Booklist

Other titles about Commander Toad are:
Commander Toad and the big black hole (1996)
Commander Toad and the dis-asteroid (1996)
Commander Toad and the intergalactic spy (1997)
Commander Toad and the Planet of the Grapes (1996)
Commander Toad and the space pirates (1997)
Commander Toad in space (1996)

Dimity Duck; illustrated by Sebastien Braun. Philomel Books 2006 unp il $15.99

Grades: PreK K   E

1. Ducks—Fiction 2. Frogs—Fiction 3. Friendship—Fiction 4. Stories in rhyme
ISBN 0-399-24532-0

Dimity Duck and Frumity Frog have a fun day together in the pond, then go home when it gets dark outside.

"There's an appealing, old-fashioned sound to the verses that is reminiscent of nursery rhymes. . . . The pleasing artwork focuses on Dimity and Frumity as the main inhabitants of the simplified, sunlit world of the pond." Booklist

How do dinosaurs say goodnight? illustrated by Mark Teague. Blue Sky Press (NY) 2000 unp il $15.95 *

Grades: PreK K 1 2 3   E

1. Bedtime—Fiction 2. Dinosaurs—Fiction 3. Stories in rhyme
ISBN 0-590-31681-8   LC 98-56134

Mother and child ponder the different ways a dinosaur can say goodnight, from slamming his tail and pouting to giving a big hug and kiss

"The text is sweet and simple—just right for the wonderful pictures that really make this picture book special. . . . Endpapers introduce the critter cast in all their gorgeous glory: tyrannosaurus rex, dimetrodon, and more, in vivid, yet still earthbound colors." Booklist

Other titles in this series are:
How do dinosaurs eat their food? (2005)
How do dinosaurs get well soon? (2003)
How do dinosaurs go to school? (2007)
How do dinosaurs say I love you? (2009)

Mama's kiss; by Jane Yolen; illustrations by Daniel Baxter. Handprint Books 2008 unp il $14.99

Grades: PreK K 1   E

1. Stories in rhyme 2. Kissing—Fiction
ISBN 978-0-8118-6683-5; 0-8118-6683-1
                                        LC 2008021177

A kiss from Mama misses its intended target and instead embarks on a merry adventure as it slips, slides, and twists its way around the world.

"Yolen's jaunty rhymes are short and sweet; debut illustrator Baxter's droll, cartoonlike pictures practically jump from page to page." Publ Wkly

My father knows the names of things; illustrated by Stephane Jorisch. Simon & Schuster Books for Young Readers 2010 unp il $15.99

Grades: PreK K 1   E

1. Stories in rhyme 2. Father-child relationship—Fiction
ISBN 978-1-4169-4895-7; 1-4169-4895-3
                                        LC 2007-41840

Rhyming text depicts a father sharing with his child such things as seven words that all mean blue and the name of every kind of cloud.

"Yolen's easeful rhymes and Jorisch's warm illustrations craft a bighearted tribute to fathers' seemingly infinite capacities for information—and their willingness to share it." Publ Wkly

My Uncle Emily; illustrated by Nancy Carpenter. Philomel Books 2009 unp il $17.99 *

Grades: K 1 2   E

1. Dickinson, Emily, 1830-1886—Fiction 2. Poets—Fiction 3. Massachusetts—Fiction
ISBN 978-0-399-24005-8; 0-399-24005-5
                                         LC 2008-32614

In 1881 Amherst, Massachusetts, six-year-old Gilbert finds it both challenging and wonderful to spend time with his aunt, the reclusive poet Emily Dickinson, who lives next door.

"Yolen artfully incorporates elements from Dickinson's poetry and life to give readers an inside look at the enigmatic poet from her nephew's fresh and loving perspective. Carpenter's nostalgic, pastel-hued pen, ink and digital-media illustrations capture the atmosphere of late-19th-century Amherst as well as Gil's special relationship with his famous aunt in this poetic vignette." Kirkus

Naming Liberty; by Jane Yolen; illustrated by Jim Burke. Philomel Books 2008 unp il $16.99

Grades: 1 2 3   E

1. Bartholdi, Frédéric Auguste, 1834-1904—Fiction 2. Statue of Liberty (New York, N.Y.)—Fiction 3. Immigrants—Fiction 4. Jews—Fiction 5. United States—History—1865-1898—Fiction
ISBN 978-0-399-24250-2; 0-399-24250-3

In parallel stories, a Ukrainian Jewish family prepares to emigrate to the United States in the late 1800s, and Frederic Auguste Bartholdi designs, raises funds for, and builds the Statue of Liberty in honor of the United States' centennial.

"Burke's luminous paintings, designed on burnt sienna oil-washed boards, convey the landscapes and details of nineteenth-century Europe and New York. . . . An ideal choice for introducing the concepts of immigration and liberty to young listeners." Booklist

Yolen, Jane—*Continued*

Off we go! illustrated by Laurel Molk. Little, Brown 2000 unp il lib bdg $12.95

Grades: PreK K   E

1. Animals—Fiction 2. Grandmothers—Fiction 3. Stories in rhyme

ISBN 0-316-90228-4   LC 98-6893

One by one, baby woodland creatures leave home and sing their way to visit grandma

"Rhyme, repetition, and the playful, onomatopoeic language make this especially appealing for read-alouds. Large watercolors in earthy tones of gray, green, and brown are soft and fluid." Horn Book Guide

Owl moon; illustrated by John Schoenherr. 20th anniversary edition. Philomel 2007 c1987 unp il $16.99 *

Grades: PreK K 1 2   E

1. Owls—Fiction 2. Father-daughter relationship—Fiction

ISBN 978-0-399-24799-6; 0-399-24799-8

Awarded the Caldecott Medal, 1988

A reissue of the title first published 1987

On a winter's night under a full moon, a father and daughter trek into the woods to see the great horned owl

This book "conveys the scary majesty of winter woods at night in language that seldom overreaches either character or subject. . . . This book has a magic that is extremely rare in books for any age." NY Times Book Rev

Sleep, black bear, sleep; by Jane Yolen and Heidi E. Y. Stemple; illustrated by Brooke Dyer. HarperCollins 2007 unp il $15.99; lib bdg $16.89

Grades: PreK K 1   E

1. Hibernation—Fiction 2. Animals—Fiction 3. Winter—Fiction 4. Bedtime—Fiction 5. Stories in rhyme

ISBN 978-0-06-081560-8; 0-06-081560-4; 978-0-06-081561-5 (lib bdg); 0-06-081561-2 (lib bdg)   LC 2006000344

As winter's chill spreads, different animals settle into their cozy homes for a long sleep

"The rhyme scheme is as lilting as a lullaby, and Dyer's ineffably sweet watercolor illustrations enrich this bedtime story." Booklist

Yolleck, Joan

Paris in the spring with Picasso; illustrated by Marjorie Priceman. Schwartz & Wade Books 2010 unp il $17.99; lib bdg $20.99 *

Grades: K 1 2 3   E

1. Picasso, Pablo, 1881-1973—Fiction 2. Stein, Gertrude, 1874-1946—Fiction 3. Toklas, Alice B.—Fiction 4. Apollinaire, Guillaume, 1880-1918—Fiction 5. Jacob, Max, 1876-1944—Fiction 6. Paris (France)—Fiction

ISBN 978-0-375-83756-2; 0-375-83756-6; 978-0-375-93756-9 (lib bdg); 0-375-93756-0 (lib bdg)   LC 2008-05867

Describes how some of Paris's famous artists and writers, such as Pablo Picasso, Max Jacob, and Guillaume Apollinaire, spend their day before preparing to attend a party at Gertrude Stein's apartment.

"Priceman's brightly colored illustrations exhibit energy, creativity, and general joie de vivre. . . . This whirlwind tour flows easily thanks to clear writing and carefully chosen details." SLJ

Yoo, Tae-Eun, 1977-

The little red fish. Dial Books for Young Readers 2007 unp il $15.99 *

Grades: PreK K 1 2   E

1. Libraries—Fiction 2. Fishes—Fiction 3. Magic—Fiction

ISBN 978-0-8037-3145-5   LC 2006018427

A little boy named JeJe explores a magical library with his friend, a little red fish.

"Detailed hand-colored etchings match well with the quiet, mysterious story that unfolds. . . . The boy's fantastical experiences will resonate with readers." SLJ

Yoon, Salina, 1972-

Opposnakes; a lift-the-flap book about opposites. Little Simon 2009 unp il $9.99

Grades: PreK K   E

1. Snakes—Fiction 2. Opposites

ISBN 978-1-4169-7875-6; 1-4169-7875-5

"Yoon introduces opposites via friendly snakes. The spare text focuses on simple concepts: 'Cold snake/Hot snake,' 'Skinny snake/Plump snake,' 'One snake/Many snakes!' Brightly colored, cartoonlike reptiles stretch across the double-foldout spreads and are set against a white background. They are full of amusing details. . . . A book that entertains as it informs." SLJ

Super babies on the move; Mia on the move. G.P. Putnam's Sons 2009 unp il $14.99

Grades: PreK   E

1. Infants—Fiction

ISBN 978-0-399-24755-2; 0-399-24755-6   LC 2008000706

Two stories bound back to back and inverted.

Mia on the move; Max on the move

After following Baby Mia as she sneaks out during naptime to go to the playground, the reader may turn the book upside down to watch Baby Max skip bathtime to join in a backyard animal chase.

"Toddlers will like these stories, both for the bright but simply styled visuals and the text." SLJ

Yorinks, Arthur, 1953-

Happy bees; by Arthur Yorinks; illustrated by Carey Armstrong-Ellis. Harry N. Abrams 2005 unp il $15.95 *

Grades: PreK K 1 2   E

1. Bees—Fiction

ISBN 0-8109-5866-X   LC 2004-15454

Rhythmic text describes the carefree life of bees as they sting knees, munch on Swiss cheese, and laugh in the breeze.

"The nonsensical text doubles as the lyrics of the first tune on the accompanying CD. . . . The happy-go-lucky insects have loads of personality. . . . Listeners will enjoy the romp, whether spoken or sung, and can discover more bee-guiling silliness in the other selections on the CD." SLJ

Yorinks, Arthur, 1953-—*Continued*

Hey, Al; story by Arthur Yorinks; pictures by Richard Egielski. Farrar, Straus & Giroux 1986 unp il $17; pa $7.99 *
Grades: PreK K 1 2 3   E
  1. Fantasy fiction 2. Birds—Fiction
  ISBN 0-374-33060-3; 0-374-42985-5 (pa)
                       LC 86-80955
Awarded the Caldecott Medal, 1987
"Al, a janitor, and his faithful dog, Eddie, live in a single room on the West Side. . . . Their tiny home is crowded and cramped; their life is an endless struggle. Al and Eddie are totally miserable until a large and mysterious bird offers them a change of fortune." Publisher's note
"Egielski's solid naturalism provides just the visual foil needed to establish the surreal character of this fantasy. . . . Text and pictures work together to challenge readers' concept of reality." SLJ

Homework; illustrations by Richard Egielski. Walker & Co. 2009 unp il $16.99; lib bdg $17.89
Grades: K 1 2   E
  1. Homework—Fiction 2. Writing—Materials and instruments—Fiction
  ISBN 978-0-8027-9585-4; 0-8027-9585-4; 978-0-8027-9586-1 (lib bdg); 0-8027-9586-2 (lib bdg)
                      LC 2008-28011
When Tony's pens, along with his pencil and eraser, come to life, the squabbling set of writing tools tries to complete Tony's neglected homework
"Yorinks has devised a pleasing homage to the creative process and uses a light touch to show how inspiration can derive from the unlikeliest of places. . . . A simple but amusing winner." Booklist

The witch's child; by Arthur Yorinks; illustrated by Jos. A. Smith. Abrams Books for Young Readers 2007 unp il $16.95
Grades: K 1 2 3   E
  1. Witches—Fiction 2. Fairy tales
  ISBN 978-0-8109-9349-5   LC 2006031980
Desiring a child of her own, Rosina the witch fashions one out of straw and scraps, but when she cannot bring the rag child to life she becomes enraged and turns the village children into shrubs, where they stay until a kind girl discovers the discarded doll and saves her.
"Yorinks's flowing language is evocative, and the plot builds steadily to an exciting climax. Smith's detailed paintings depict Rosina with jet-black standing-on-end hair and exaggerated facial features that vividly—and frighteningly—express her emotions." SLJ

You read to me & I'll read to you; 20th-century stories to share; selected by Janet Schulman. Knopf 2001 250p il $34.95 *
Grades: PreK K 1 2   E
  1. Short stories
  ISBN 0-375-81083-8   LC 2001-29211
Companion volume to The 20th century children's book treasury (1998)
This is a collection of 26 picture books and selections from early chapter books by such authors as Maurice Sendak, William Steig, Dr. Seuss, and Florence Parry

Heide
"A great choice for family or classroom sharing." SLJ

Young, Amy
Belinda, the ballerina. Viking 2002 unp il $15.99
Grades: PreK K 1 2   E
  1. Ballet—Fiction
  ISBN 0-670-03549-1   LC 2001-8395
When Belinda auditions for the Spring Ballet Recital and the judges tell her she can not be a ballerina because her feet are too big, she tries to forget about dancing
This offers "spirited gouache paintings that capture the sadness, the humor and the triumph of Belinda's story. . . . The story puts physical defects into perspective and offers something to laugh about at the same time." Booklist
  Other titles about Belinda are:
Belinda and the glass slipper (2006)
Belinda begins ballet (2008)
Belinda in Paris (2005)

Young, Ed
Hook. Roaring Brook Press 2009 unp il $17.95 *
Grades: PreK K 1   E
  1. Birds—Fiction 2. Flight—Fiction
  ISBN 978-1-59643-363-2; 1-59643-363-9
                      LC 2008-49331
"A Neal Porter book"
A chick hatched by hens turns out to be an eagle who must get help from a boy in learning how to fly.
"Vibrant, minimal chalk drawings—hardly more than sketches, but glorious ones—utilize shifting perspectives to enhance the sky's imposing vastness. . . . Arresting and absorbing, this tale soars." Kirkus

My Mei Mei. Philomel Books 2006 unp il $16.99 *
Grades: PreK K 1 2   E
  1. Adoption—Fiction 2. Sisters—Fiction 3. Chinese Americans—Fiction 4. China—Fiction
  ISBN 0-399-24339-9
Antonia gets her wish when her parents return to China to bring home a Mei Mei, or younger sister, for her.
"Young's vibrant collage illustrations joyously extend the spare, direct words." Booklist

Yum, Hyewon
Last night. Farrar, Straus & Giroux 2008 unp il $15.95 *
Grades: K 1 2 3   E
  1. Stories without words 2. Dreams—Fiction 3. Toys—Fiction
  ISBN 978-0-374-34358-3; 0-374-34358-6
                      LC 2007030386
"Frances Foster books"
Sent to her room for refusing to eat her dinner, a little girl soon falls asleep and together with her bear friend begins a fantastic voyage deep into the forest where they dance and play all night
"Yum's evocative linocut illustrations offer ample

Yum, Hyewon—*Continued*

context for a child to imagine what the little girl is feeling, and how her mood changes over the course of the night. White, pink, and yellow tones blend and contrast in her face to sometimes resemble a mask." SLJ

Zalben, Jane Breskin

Baby shower. Roaring Brook Press 2010 unp il $16.99 *

Grades: PreK K 1 2   **E**

1. Animals—Fiction 2. Pets—Fiction 3. Dogs—Fiction 4. Aunts—Fiction

ISBN 978-1-5964-3465-3; 1-5964-3465-1

"A Neal Porter book"

"Zoe wants a pet. . . . To get her mind off dogs . . . and cats . . . Mama suggests that Zoe help with her aunt's baby shower. That night in bed Zoe . . . [dreams] about a baby shower—of puppies, kittens, and even piglets and ducklings. . . . Much of the charm comes from Zalben's sweet and funny ink-and-watercolor pictures, filled with delicious detail in both the homey scenes and windswept expanses of tumbling babies." Booklist

Zemach, Kaethe, 1958-

Just enough and not too much. Levine Bks. 2003 unp il $16.95 *

Grades: K 1 2 3   **E**

1. Musicians—Fiction

ISBN 0-439-37724-2   LC 2003-399

Simon the fiddler decides he needs more—more chairs, more hats, more stuffed animals—until he discovers that his house is too full and must think of a way to get back to having just enough

"The rich watercolor-and-gouache illustrations, many emphasizing rounded forms, are full of movement and joy. . . . Perfect for storyhours or individual readings." SLJ

Ms. McCaw learns to draw; by Kaethe Zemach. Arthur A. Levine Books 2008 unp il $16.99

Grades: 1 2 3   **E**

1. Teachers—Fiction 2. Learning disabilities—Fiction 3. School stories 4. Drawing—Fiction

ISBN 978-0-439-82914-4; 0-439-82914-3

LC 2006016465

Dudley Ellington struggles to learn anything at school, but when his very patient teacher, Mrs. McGraw, is unable to draw a face on the board, he helps her figure out how to do it

"Because the text is simple and straightforward, the book is a good choice to read aloud. . . . The pen and watercolor illustrations are expressive and full of energy." SLJ

Zemach, Margot

Eating up Gladys; illustrated by Kaethe Zemach. Arthur A. Levine Books 2005 unp il $16.99

Grades: PreK K 1 2   **E**

1. Sisters—Fiction

ISBN 0-439-66490-X

When Hilda and Rose get fed up with their older sister's bossiness, they get revenge by threatening to have her for dinner

"The dialogue captures the essence of sibling interaction, and children will easily recognize themselves in these characters. The charming watercolor illustrations ensure the story remains lighthearted while clearly depicting the characters' many emotions." SLJ

Another title about Hilda and her sisters is:
To Hilda for helping (1977)

Zepeda, Gwendolyn, 1971-

Growing up with tamales = Los Tamales de Ana; [by] Gwendolyn Zepeda; with illustrations by April Ward; Spanish translation by Gabriela Baeza Ventura. Piñata Books 2008 unp il $15.95

Grades: PreK K 1 2   **E**

1. Growth—Fiction 2. Cooking—Fiction 3. Hispanic Americans—Fiction   4.   Christmas—Fiction 5. Bilingual books—English-Spanish

ISBN 978-1-55885-493-2; 1-55885-493-2

LC 2007061477

Six-year-old Ana looks forward to growing older and being allowed more responsibility in making the tamales for the family's Christmas celebrations

"This is an upbeat multicultural family story with brilliantly colored artwork." SLJ

Ziefert, Harriet

The big, bigger, biggest book; illustrated by SAMi. Chronicle Books 2008 unp il $14.95

Grades: PreK K   **E**

1. English language—Grammar

ISBN 978-1-934706-39-8; 1-934706-39-6

"Using the most minimal text, this novelty book engagingly explores adjectives and adverbs in their absolute, comparative and superlative forms. Each spread incorporates a gatefold flap: at first, readers see only a single word, e.g., 'deep,' which accompanies a scuba diver in an underwater setting. This particular flap unfolds from the bottom of the page, once to show the diver swimming 'deeper' and again to show him 'deepest.'" Publ Wkly

A bunny is funny; and so is this book! [by] Harriet Ziefert and Fred Ehrlich; paintings by Todd McKie. Blue Apple Books 2008 unp il $16.95

Grades: PreK K 1 2 3   **E**

1. Animals—Fiction 2. Stories in rhyme

ISBN 978-1-934706-03-9; 1-934706-03-5

LC 2007031196

Short rhymes point out traits that characterize different animals, such as an owl's keen eyesight or the beauty of a butterfly's wings

"Each witty rhyme is accompanied by a highly stylized and vibrantly colored illustration of the animal set against a solid-colored background. The charm of each poem is perfectly matched with the boldness of the art. The two pages that feature large flaps with die cuts increase the level of humor and appeal. This book is an excellent choice to share with a group of young children, as well as with an elementary class embarking on a creative-writing unit." SLJ

Ziefert, Harriet—*Continued*

By the light of the harvest moon; illustrations by Mark Jones. Blue Apple Books 2009 unp il $16.99

Grades: K 1 2   E

1. Leaves—Fiction 2. Autumn—Fiction

ISBN 978-1-934706-69-5; 1-934706-69-8

LC 2009-12658

As the fall harvest moon shines on the farm, leaf families gather to celebrate the autumnal equinox.

"This warm picture-book fantasy celebrates fall, especially the amazing movement, light, color, and sounds of autumn leaves. . . . The combination of fantasy and realism in the crisp autumn night will spark children's imagination about the leaf piles they find in their city, suburb, or country roads." Booklist

A dozen ducklings lost and found; illustrated by Donald Dreifuss. Houghton Mifflin 2003 unp il $15

Grades: PreK K   E

1. Ducks—Fiction 2. Counting

ISBN 0-618-14175-8   LC 2002-9403

Between the pond and the farm house some of Mother Duck's new babies get lost

"Dreifuss' naive, impressionistic paintings have a simplicity of composition that makes them easy to for group viewing, with the fluffy yellow ducklings standing out against the verdant background." Bull Cent Child Books

Home for Navidad; paintings by Santiago Cohen. Houghton Mifflin 2003 unp il $15

Grades: K 1 2 3   E

1. Mothers—Fiction 2. Christmas—Fiction 3. Mexico—Fiction

ISBN 0-618-34976-6   LC 2002-156430

Ten-year-old Rosa hopes that her mother, whom she has not seen for three years, will leave her job in New York and come home to Santa Catarina, Mexico, for Christmas and maybe even longer. Includes a glossary of Spanish words used

"The combination of simple words and bold, vibrant art relays the wrenching family separation from the child's viewpoint." Booklist

Mighty Max; by Harriet Ziefert; illustrated by Elliot Kreloff. Blue Apple Books 2008 unp il $15.95

Grades: PreK K 1 2   E

1. Imagination—Fiction 2. Play—Fiction 3. Beaches—Fiction 4. Superheroes—Fiction

ISBN 978-1-934706-36-7; 1-934706-36-1

LC 2008009662

As Max imagines himself as the super hero—Mighty Max—while at the beach, he saves a game, a castle, and his lunch from some hungry gulls

"Maxwell is a lively little boy with an active imagination. . . . The collage and crayon illustrations are colorful and exuberant." SLJ

One smart skunk; [by] Harriet Ziefert; illustrated by Santiago Cohen. Blue Apple Books 2004 unp il $15.95

Grades: PreK K 1 2   E

1. Skunks—Fiction

ISBN 1-59354-064-7   LC 2004-10533

Rebecca the skunk lives under a suburban family's deck, eluding the traps set to ensnare her, but the smell of moth balls and the noise of rap music finally convince her that the suburbs are no place to raise her family

"Cohen's illustrations are luminous, and the layout effectively varies text location and illustration size to create an appealing and modern background for this charming, informative text." SLJ

Snow party; illustrated by Mark Jones. Blue Apple Books 2008 unp il $16.95

Grades: PreK K 1 2   E

1. Snow—Fiction 2. Winter—Fiction

ISBN 978-1-934706-28-2; 1-934706-28-0

LC 2008005874

A newly illustrated edition of Snow magic, first published 1988 by Viking Kestrel

When the first snow of the year falls on the first day of winter, all the snow people have a snow party.

"Jones provides an emotional and fantasy counterpoint to the quiet intensity of Ziefert's . . . reportorial text. Jones takes full advantage of the book's horizontal format, varying his perspectives and infusing his pictures with a sense of bustle and plenty of detail. . . . He confers individuality upon the members of the snow people community—quite an accomplishment." Publ Wkly

Zimmerman, Andrea Griffing, 1950-

Dig! [by] Andrea Zimmerman and David Clemesha; illustrated by Marc Rosenthal. Harcourt 2004 unp il $16 *

Grades: PreK K   E

1. Excavating machinery—Fiction 2. Construction workers—Fiction 3. Dogs—Fiction

ISBN 0-15-216785-4   LC 2003-4373

"Silver Whistle"

Follows Mr. Rally and his dog, Lightning, as they travel the town on a big yellow digging machine, taking care of five important jobs

"Earth-tone illustrations are created with watercolor and Prismacolor pencil. . . . The pace, repetition, and word choices make the book appropriate for beginning readers. The uncluttered art, catchy refrain, and focus on heavy machinery make it a natural for storytimes." SLJ

Digger man; [by] Andrea Zimmerman & David Clemesha. Holt & Co. 2003 unp il $15.95 *

Grades: PreK K   E

1. Steam-shovels—Fiction 2. Brothers—Fiction

ISBN 0-8050-6628-4   LC 2002-10856

"Silver Whistle"

A young boy imagines how he will use his digger to make a park where he and his little brother can play

"The joyful acrylic illustrations and the sparse, confident text will delight other digger-wannabes." Booklist

Fire engine man; [by] Andrea Zimmerman & [illustrated by] David Clemesha. Henry Holt 2007 unp il $15.95

Grades: PreK K   E

1. Fire fighters—Fiction 2. Brothers—Fiction 3. Imagination—Fiction

ISBN 978-0-8050-7905-0   LC 2006007909

Zimmerman, Andrea Griffing, 1950-—*Continued*

A young boy imagines the work he will do and the safety gear he will wear when he becomes a fireman some day, as his younger brother first watches then joins him on the job

"The brothers from *Digger Man* (Holt, 2003) are back. . . . The same colorful acrylic illustrations greet readers, and have enough detail to interest yet not overwhelm them. The text moves at a brisk pace." SLJ

Trashy town; [by] Andrea Zimmerman and David Clemesha; illustrated by Dan Yaccarino. HarperCollins Pubs. 1999 unp il $17.99 *

Grades: PreK K   E

1. Refuse and refuse disposal—Fiction

ISBN 0-06-027139-6   LC 98-27495

Little by little, can by can, Mr. Gillie, the trash man, cleans up his town

"Short energetic sentences propel the tale. . . . Employing primary colors dominated by bold blues, Yaccarino's vibrant art has a retro look." Booklist

Zion, Gene

Harry the dirty dog; pictures by Margaret Bloy Graham. Harper & Row 1956 unp il $17.99; lib bdg $17.89; pa $6.99; bd bk $7.99 *

Grades: PreK K   E

1. Dogs—Fiction

ISBN 0-06-026865-4; 0-06-026866-2 (lib bdg); 0-06-443009-X (pa); 0-06-084244-X (bd bk)

"A runaway dog becomes so dirty his family almost doesn't recognize him. Harry's flight from scrubbing brush and bath water takes him on a tour of the city." Moorachian. What is a City?

"Harry's fun and troubles are told simply, and the drawings are full of action and humor. The combination will have great appeal for the very young." Horn Book

Other titles about Harry are:

Harry and the lady next door (1960)

Harry by the sea (1965)

No roses for Harry! (1958)

Zolotow, Charlotte, 1915-

The beautiful Christmas tree; illustrated by Yan Nacimbene. Houghton Mifflin 1999 32p il $15

Grades: K 1 2 3   E

1. City and town life—Fiction 2. Trees—Fiction 3. Christmas—Fiction

ISBN 0-395-91365-9   LC 98-50006

A newly illustrated edition of the title first published 1972 by Parnassus Press

Although his elegant neighbors do not appreciate his efforts, a kind old man transforms his rundown house and a small neglected pine tree into the best on the street

"In handsome depictions of the urban setting, Nascimbene's delicate watercolors convey the emotional warmth of Zolotow's testament to a simple man's faith and love." Horn Book Guide

A father like that; by Charlotte Zolotow; illustrated by LeUyen Pham. HarperCollinsPublishers 2007 unp il $16.99; lib bdg $17.89

Grades: PreK K 1 2   E

1. Father-son relationship—Fiction 2. Single parent family—Fiction

ISBN 978-0-06-027864-9; 0-06-027864-1; 978-0-06-027865-6 (lib bdg); 0-06-027865-X (lib bdg)

LC 2006000353

A newly illustrated edition of the title first published 1971

A young boy shares with his mother his daydreams about the father who left before he was born

"Zolotow's powerful story . . . has been updated with Pham's realistic, mixed-media illustrations featuring African-American characters. . . . The expressive artwork depicts the characters' emotions and the love they share." SLJ

If it weren't for you; by Charlotte Zolotow; pictures by G. Brian Karas. HarperCollins Pubs. 2006 unp il $15.99; lib bdg $16.89

Grades: PreK K 1 2   E

1. Sisters—Fiction

ISBN 0-06-027875-7; 0-06-027876-5 (lib bdg)

A newly illustrated edition of the title first published 1966

"Big sister is feeling sorry for herself as she imagines how good life would be without her younger sibling. . . . As she sulks, little sister gradually works her way into her sibling's heart with small acts of kindness. Finally big sister concedes that having a younger sister is not all bad. . . . The new illustrations not only change the gender of the main characters, but also give the story a fresh, contemporary look." SLJ

Mr. Rabbit and the lovely present; pictures by Maurice Sendak. Harper & Row 1962 unp il $16.99; pa $5.99

Grades: PreK K 1 2   E

1. Birthdays—Fiction 2. Color—Fiction 3. Rabbits—Fiction

ISBN 0-06-026945-6; 0-06-443020-0 (pa)

A Caldecott Medal honor book, 1963

"A serious little girl and a tall, other-worldly white rabbit converse about a present for her mother. 'But what?' said the little girl. 'Yes, what?' said Mr. Rabbit. It requires a day of searching—for red, yellow, green, and blue, all things the mother likes, to make a basket of fruit for the present." Horn Book

"The quiet story, told in dialogue, is illustrated in richly colored pictures which exactly fit the fanciful mood." Hodges. Books for Elem Sch Libr

The old dog; paintings by James Ransome. rev and newly illustrated ed. HarperCollins Pubs. 1995 unp il $16.99

Grades: K 1 2   E

1. Dogs—Fiction 2. Death—Fiction

ISBN 0-06-024409-7   LC 93-41081

A revised and newly illustrated edition of the title first published 1972 by Coward, McCann & Geoghegan under the author's pseudonym Sarah Abbott

Zolotow, Charlotte, 1915-—*Continued*

When Ben finds his old dog dead one morning, he spends the rest of the day thinking about all the good times they had together

"Zolotow's elemental story . . . is newly illustrated here with rich oil paintings. . . . An unsentimental story about connection and loss and renewal." Booklist

The seashore book; paintings by Wendell Minor. HarperCollins Pubs. 1992 unp il $16.99; pa $6.99
Grades: K 1 2   E
  1. Seashore—Fiction 2. Mother-son relationship—Fiction
  ISBN 0-06-020213-0; 0-06-443364-1 (pa)
                                              LC 91-22783
A mother's words help a little boy imagine the sights and sounds of the seashore, even though he's never seen the ocean

"Minor's crisply detailed watercolors evoke place with imaginative accuracy and visual grace, and Zolotow's . . . spare, poetic text provides a lyrical and nostalgic paean to the wonders of seaside life." Publ Wkly

When the wind stops; illustrated by Stefano Vitale. rev and newly illustrated ed. HarperCollins Pubs. 1995 unp il hardcover o.p. pa $6.99
Grades: PreK K   E
  1. Nature—Fiction
  ISBN 0-06-025425-4; 0-06-443472-9 (pa)
                                              LC 94-14477
A revised and newly illustrated edition of the title first published 1962 by Abelard-Schuman

A mother explains to her son that in nature an end is also a beginning as day gives way to night, winter ends and spring begins, and, after it stops falling, rain makes clouds for other storms

"The full-color scenes, painted on wood, gloriously depict heaven and earth and give concrete meaning to abstract concepts. Not only wonderful for lap sharing,

this beautiful book will also be a rich supplement for a science unit on the elements or the seasons." Booklist

William's doll; pictures by William Pène Du Bois. Harper & Row 1972 30p il $16.99; pa $6.99
*
Grades: PreK K 1 2   E
  1. Dolls—Fiction 2. Sex role—Fiction
  ISBN 0-06-027047-0; 0-06-027048-9 (lib bdg); 0-06-443067-7 (pa)
When little William asks for a doll, the other boys scorn him and his father tries to interest him in conventional boys' playthings such as a basketball and a train. His sympathetic grandmother buys him the doll, explaining his need to have it to love and care for so that he can practice being a father

"Very, very special. The strong, yet delicate pictures . . . convey a gentleness of spirit and longing most effectively, as William pantomimes his craving." N Y Times Book Rev

Zuckerman, Andrew

Creature ABC. Chronicle Books 2009 unp il $19.99 *
Grades: PreK K 1 2   E
  1. Animals 2. Alphabet
  ISBN 978-0-8118-6978-2; 0-8118-6978-4
                                              LC 2009-04365
"This adaption of Zuckerman's adult pictorial *Creature* (2007) uses white backdrops in striking juxtaposition with brilliantly detailed photographs to introduce animals and the ABCs." Kirkus

"This is a first choice for libraries." Bull Cent Child Books

Includes glossary

AUTHOR, TITLE, AND SUBJECT INDEX

This index to the books in the Classified Collection includes author, title, and subject entries; added entries for publishers' series, illustrators, joint authors, and editors of works entered under title; and name and subject cross-references; all arranged in one alphabet.

The number or symbol in bold face type at the end of each entry refers to the Dewey Decimal Classification or to the Fiction (Fic) or Story Collection (S C), or Easy Books (E) section where the main entry for the book will be found. Works classed in 92 are entered under the name of the person written about.

For further directions for the use of this index and for examples of entries, see How to Use Children's Core Collection.

Abigail Iris: the one and only. Glatt, L. **Fic**

Abigail spells. Alter, A. **E**

Ability
Fiction
Rosenthal, A. K. The OK book **E**

Abiyoyo. Seeger, P. **398.2**

Ablow, Gail, 1962-
A horse in the house, and other strange but true animal stories **590**

Abnaki Indians
Fiction
Bruchac, J. Night wings **Fic**
Bruchac, J. The winter people **Fic**
Folklore
Bruchac, J. Raccoon's last race **398.2**

Abolafia, Yossi, 1944-
(il) Prelutsky, J. It's snowing! it's snowing! **811**
(il) Prelutsky, J. It's Valentine's Day **811**

Abolitionists
Adler, D. A. A picture book of Harriet Beecher Stowe **92**
Adler, D. A. A picture book of Sojourner Truth **92**
Clinton, C. When Harriet met Sojourner [biography of Harriet Tubman and Sojourner Truth] **92**
Ford, C. T. Slavery and the underground railroad **326**
Fritz, J. Harriet Beecher Stowe and the Beecher preachers **92**
Hendrix, J. John Brown **92**
Horn, G. Sojourner Truth **92**
Huey, L. M. American archaeology uncovers the Underground Railroad **973.7**
Jurmain, S. The forbidden schoolhouse [biography of Prudence Crandall] **92**
Landau, E. Fleeing to freedom on the Underground Railroad **973.7**
McKissack, P. C. Frederick Douglass **92**
McKissack, P. C. Sojourner Truth **92**
Pinkney, A. D. Sojourner Truth's step-stomp stride **92**
Rockwell, A. F. Only passing through: the story of Sojourner Truth **92**
Roop, P. Sojourner Truth **92**
Rossi, A. Freedom struggle **973.7**
See/See also pages in the following book(s):
McKissack, P. C. Black hands, white sails **639.2**

Aboriginal Australians
Arnold, C. Uluru, Australia's Aboriginal heart **994**
Connolly, S. The Americas and the Pacific **970.004**
Folklore
Marshall, J. V. Stories from the Billabong **398.2**

Aborigines, Australian *See* Aboriginal Australians

About crustaceans. Sill, C. P. **595.3**

About habitats [series]
Sill, C. P. Wetlands **577.6**

About marsupials. Sill, C. P. **599.2**

About rodents. Sill, C. P. **599.35**

About the author [series]
McGinty, A. B. Meet Daniel Pinkwater **92**
McGinty, A. B. Meet Jane Yolen **92**

About time. Koscielniak, B. **529**

The **abracadabra** kid. Fleischman, S. **92**

Abraham (Biblical figure)
About
Jules, J. Abraham's search for God **222**
Jules, J. Sarah laughs **222**
Fiction
Gerstein, M. The white ram **E**

Abraham, Denise Gonzales, 1949-
(jt. auth) Abraham, S. G. Cecilia's year **Fic**

Abraham, Susan Gonzales, 1951-
Cecilia's year **Fic**

Abraham Lincoln comes home. Burleigh, R. **92**

Abraham Lincoln for kids. Herbert, J. **92**

Abraham's search for God. Jules, J. **222**

Abrams, Dennis, 1960-
Gary Soto **92**

Abrams, Douglas Carlton
(jt. auth) Tutu, D. God's dream **231.7**

Abramson, Andra Serlin
Fighter planes up close **623.74**
Fire engines up close **628.9**
Heavy equipment up close **629.225**
Submarines up close **623.82**

Abramson, Jill, 1954-
Obama **92**

Absolutely normal chaos. Creech, S. **Fic**

Abstract art
Johnson, S. A is for art **709**
Raimondo, J. What's the big idea? **709.04**

Abuela. Dorros, A. **E**

Abuela's weave. Castañeda, O. S. **E**

Abuelos. Mora, P. **E**

Abuse of children *See* Child abuse

Abuse of wives *See* Wife abuse

Abused women
Fiction
Cassidy, C. Indigo Blue **Fic**
Galante, C. Hershey herself **Fic**

Academic achievement
Farmer, L. S. J. Student success and library media programs **027.8**

Academic freedom
Pipkin, G. At the schoolhouse gate **373.1**

Accadians (Sumerians) *See* Sumerians

Accidents
See also types of accidents and subjects with the subdivision *Accidents*
Fiction
Bauer, M. D. On my honor **Fic**
Prevention
See also Safety education

Acclimatization *See* Adaptation (Biology)

Ace it! information literacy [series]
Bullard, L. Ace your oral or multimedia presentation **808.5**
Gaines, A. Ace your Internet research **001.4**

Adventure graphic novels—*Continued*

Hergé. The adventures of Tintin, vol. 1
741.5

Kibuishi, K. Amulet, book one: The Stonekeeper **741.5**

Kibuishi, K. Copper **741.5**

Kim, S. City of spies **741.5**

Macdonald, F. Journey to the Center of the Earth **741.5**

Macdonald, F. Kidnapped **741.5**

O'Donnell, L. Wild ride: a graphic guide adventure **741.5**

Parker, J. Missile Mouse: the star crusher **741.5**

Phelan, M. The storm in the barn **741.5**

Renier, A. The Unsinkable Walker Bean **741.5**

Sava, S. C. Hyperactive **741.5**

Weigel, J. Thunder from the sea **741.5**

Adventure sports [series]

Wurdinger, S. D. Kayaking **797.1**

Adventures in cartooning. Sturm, J. **741.5**

Adventures in memory [series]

Cleary, B. P. "Mrs. Riley Bought Five Itchy Aardvarks" and other painless tricks for memorizing science facts **507**

The **adventures** of Ali Baba Bernstein. Hurwitz, J. **Fic**

The **adventures** of Brer Rabbit. See Lester, J. The tales of Uncle Remus **398.2**

The adventures of Chance Fortune [series]

Berryhill, S. Chance Fortune and the Outlaws **Fic**

Adventures of Daniel Boom AKA Loud Boy [series]

Steinberg, D. Sound off! **741.5**

The **adventures** of Hershel of Ostropol. Kimmel, E. A. **398.2**

The **adventures** of High John the Conqueror. Sanfield, S. **398.2**

The **adventures** of Jack Lime. Leck, J. **Fic**

The **adventures** of Marco Polo. Freedman, R. **92**

The adventures of Max and Pinky [series]

Eaton, M., III. Best buds **E**

The **adventures** of Molly Whuppie and other Appalachian folktales. Shelby, A. **398.2**

The **adventures** of Odysseus. Lupton, H. **292**

The **adventures** of Pinocchio [illustrated by Roberto Innocenti] Collodi, C. **Fic**

The **adventures** of Polo. Faller, R. **E**

Adventures of Riley [series]

Lumry, A. Safari in South Africa **E**

The **adventures** of Sir Lancelot the Great. Morris, G. **Fic**

The **adventures** of Taxi Dog. Barracca, D. **E**

The **adventures** of the dish and the spoon. Grey, M. **E**

The **adventures** of Thor the Thunder God. Lunge-Larsen, L. **293**

The **adventures** of Tintin, vol. 1. Hergé **741.5**

The **adventures** of Tom Sawyer. Twain, M. **Fic**

Adventuring with books **011.6**

The **adventurous** book of outdoor games. Strother, S. **796**

The **adventurous** deeds of Deadwood Jones. Hemphill, H. **Fic**

The **adventurous** life of Myles Standish. Harness, C. **92**

Adventurous women. Colman, P. **920**

Advertising

Fiction

Williams, M. The Fizzy Whiz kid **Fic**

Libraries

Imhoff, K. R. Library contests **021.7**

Aerial photography

Delannoy, I. Our living Earth **779**

Aeronautics

See also Airplanes; Flight; Rocketry

Bailey, G. Flight **629.13**

Clark, W. Planes on the move **629.133**

Crowther, R. Flight: a pop-up book of aircraft **629.13**

Hense, M. How fighter pilots use math **629.13**

Hodgkins, F. How people learned to fly **629.13**

Skurzynski, G. This is rocket science **629.4**

Accidents

See Aircraft accidents

Flights

Burleigh, R. Flight: the journey of Charles Lindbergh **92**

History

Borden, L. Touching the sky **629.13**

Carson, M. K. The Wright Brothers for kids **629.13**

Collins, M. Airborne: a photobiography of Wilbur and Orville Wright **92**

Dixon-Engel, T. The Wright brothers **92**

Freedman, R. The Wright brothers: how they invented the airplane **92**

Nahum, A. Flying machine **629.133**

Old, W. To fly: the story of the Wright brothers **92**

O'Sullivan, R. The Wright brothers fly **92**

Aerospace engineers

Skurzynski, G. This is rocket science **629.4**

Aesop

Adaptations

Brett, J. Town mouse, country mouse **398.2**

Forest, H. The contest between the Sun and the Wind **398.2**

Morpurgo, M. The McElderry book of Aesop's fables **398.2**

Palatini, M. Lousy rotten stinkin' grapes **398.2**

Pinkney, J. The lion & the mouse **E**

Ward, H. The hare and the tortoise **398.2**

Ward, H. Unwitting wisdom **398.2**

Wormell, C. Mice, morals, & monkey business **398.2**

African American athletes—*Continued*

Stauffacher, S. Nothing but trouble [biography of Althea Gibson] **92**

Tavares, M. Henry Aaron's dream **92**

Trollinger, P. B. Perfect timing [biography of Isaac Murphy] **92**

Wade, M. D. Amazing Olympic athlete Wilma Rudolph **92**

Weatherford, C. B. Jesse Owens **92**

Weatherford, C. B. A Negro league scrapbook **796.357**

Weatherford, C. B. Racing against the odds [biography of Wendell Scott] **92**

Winter, J. Muhammad Ali **92**

African American authors

Bryan, A. Ashley Bryan **92**

Burleigh, R. Langston's train ride **92**

Clinton, C. Phillis's big test [biography of Phillis Wheatley] **92**

Cooper, F. Coming home [biography of Langston Hughes] **92**

Haskins, J. Toni Morrison **92**

Houghton, G. Mildred Taylor **92**

Lasky, K. A voice of her own: the story of Phillis Wheatley, slave poet **92**

Miller, W. Zora Hurston and the chinaberry tree **92**

Parker-Rock, M. Christopher Paul Curtis **92**

Parker-Rock, M. Patricia and Fredrick McKissack **92**

Porter, A. P. Jump at de sun: the story of Zora Neale Hurston **92**

Walker, A. Langston Hughes, American poet **92**

Bio-bibliography

Wilkinson, B. S. African American women writers **810.9**

African-American biography library [series]

Schuman, M. Barack Obama **92**

Shichtman, S. H. Colin Powell **92**

Westen, R. Oprah Winfrey **92**

African American businesspeople

Lasky, K. Vision of beauty: the story of Sarah Breedlove Walker **92**

McKissack, P. C. Madam C.J. Walker **92**

African American children

Bolden, T. Tell all the children our story **305.8**

Pinkney, S. L. Read and rise **E**

African American dancers

Barasch, L. Knockin' on wood [biography of Peg Leg Bates] **92**

Gladstone, V. A young dancer **792.8**

Miller, N. Stompin' at the Savoy [biography of Norma Miller] **92**

Nelson, M. Beautiful ballerina **792.8**

African American educators

McKissack, P. C. Booker T. Washington **92**

The **African** American family album. Hoobler, D. **305.8**

African American folklore *See* African Americans—Folklore

African-American heroes [series]

Feinstein, S. Barack Obama **92**

African American inventors

Mitchell, B. Shoes for everyone: a story about Jan Matzeliger **92**

African American literature *See* American literature—African American authors

African American music

> *See also* Gospel music; Rap music; Soul music

Igus, T. I see the rhythm **780.89**

Johnson, J. W. Lift every voice and sing **782.42**

African American musicians

Harris, A. R. Tupac Shakur **92**

Kimmel, E. A. A horn for Louis [biography of Louis Armstrong] **92**

Parker, R. A. Piano starts here: the young Art Tatum **92**

Stein, S. Duke Ellington **92**

Troupe, Q. Little Stevie Wonder **92**

Weatherford, C. B. Before John was a jazz giant: a song of John Coltrane **92**

Winter, J. Dizzy [biography of Dizzy Gillespie] **92**

Fiction

Ingalls, A. The little piano girl **E**

Schroeder, A. Satchmo's blues **E**

African American pilots

De Capua, S. The Tuskegee airmen **940.54**

Grimes, N. Talkin' about Bessie: the story of aviator Elizabeth Coleman **92**

African American poetry *See* American poetry—African American authors

African American singers

Freedman, R. The voice that challenged a nation [biography of Marian Anderson] **92**

Orgill, R. Skit-scat raggedy cat: Ella Fitzgerald **92**

Pinkney, A. D. Ella Fitzgerald **92**

Ryan, P. M. When Marian sang: the true recital of Marian Anderson, the voice of a century **92**

African American soldiers

Clinton, C. The Black soldier **355**

Clinton, C. Hold the flag high **973.7**

Myers, W. D. The Harlem Hellfighters **940.4**

Fiction

Garland, S. The buffalo soldier **E**

Hopkinson, D. From slave to soldier **E**

Myers, W. D. Patrol **E**

Polacco, P. Pink and Say **E**

The **African** American story. Masoff, J. **305.8**

African American women

Angelou, M. Maya Angelou **811**

Katz, W. L. Black women of the Old West **978**

Biography

Adler, D. A. A picture book of Harriet Tubman **92**

Adler, D. A. A picture book of Sojourner Truth **92**

Bolden, T. Maritcha [biography of Maritcha Rémond Lyons] **92**

Brophy, D. Michelle Obama **92**

African American women—Biography—*Continued*

Clinton, C. When Harriet met Sojourner [biography of Harriet Tubman and Sojourner Truth] **92**

Colbert, D. Michelle Obama **92**

Dray, P. Yours for justice, Ida B. Wells **92**

Fradin, D. B. Ida B. Wells **92**

Freedman, R. The voice that challenged a nation [biography of Marian Anderson] **92**

Giovanni, N. Rosa [biography of Rosa Parks] **92**

Hopkinson, D. Michelle [Obama] **92**

Horn, G. Sojourner Truth **92**

Jemison, M. C. Find where the wind goes **92**

Jones, L. Mrs. Lincoln's dressmaker: the unlikely friendship of Elizabeth Keckley and Mary Todd Lincoln **92**

Lasky, K. Vision of beauty: the story of Sarah Breedlove Walker **92**

Lowery, L. Aunt Clara Brown **92**

McKissack, P. C. Madam C.J. Walker **92**

McKissack, P. C. Sojourner Truth **92**

Miller, N. Stompin' at the Savoy [biography of Norma Miller] **92**

Myers, W. D. Ida B. Wells **92**

Orgill, R. Skit-scat raggedy cat: Ella Fitzgerald **92**

Parks, R. Rosa Parks: my story **92**

Pinkney, A. D. Ella Fitzgerald **92**

Pinkney, A. D. Let it shine **920**

Pinkney, A. D. Sojourner Truth's step-stomp stride **92**

Rockwell, A. F. Only passing through: the story of Sojourner Truth **92**

Roop, P. Sojourner Truth **92**

Ryan, P. M. When Marian sang: the true recital of Marian Anderson, the voice of a century **92**

Shange, N. Coretta Scott [King] **92**

Turner, G. T. An apple for Harriet Tubman **92**

Weatherford, C. B. Moses [biography of Harriet Tubman] **92**

Weatherford, C. B. Oprah [biography of Oprah Winfrey] **92**

Westen, R. Oprah Winfrey **92**

African American women writers. Wilkinson, B. S. **810.9**

African Americans

See also Gullahs

Barbour, K. Mr. Williams **92**

Dillon, L. Rap a tap tap **E**

Hoobler, D. The African American family album **305.8**

Keedle, J. West African Americans **305.8**

Kuklin, S. How my family lives in America **305.8**

McKissack, P. C. Black hands, white sails **639.2**

Pinkney, S. L. Shades of black **E**

Bibliography

The Black experience in children's books **016.3058**

Biography

Abramson, J. Obama **92**

Adler, D. A. Heroes for civil rights **920**

Adler, D. A. A picture book of Thurgood Marshall **92**

Altman, S. Extraordinary African-Americans **920**

Blumberg, R. York's adventures with Lewis and Clark **978**

Bolden, T. George Washington Carver **92**

Bolden, T. Portraits of African-American heroes **920**

Brimner, L. D. Booker T. Washington **92**

Brimner, L. D. We are one: the story of Bayard Rustin **92**

Cook, M. Our children can soar **920**

Crews, D. Bigmama's **92**

Farris, C. My brother Martin [biography of Martin Luther King] **92**

Feinstein, S. Barack Obama **92**

Figley, M. R. Prisoner for liberty [biography of James Forten] **92**

Greenfield, E. Paul Robeson **92**

Grimes, N. Barack Obama **92**

Halfmann, J. Seven miles to freedom **92**

Harness, C. The groundbreaking, chance-taking life of George Washington Carver and science & invention in America **92**

Hopkinson, D. Keep on! **92**

Hopkinson, D. Sweet land of liberty [biography of Oscar L. Chapman] **92**

Hudson, W. Powerful words **808.8**

Johnson, D. Onward [biography of Matthew Henson] **92**

Kennedy, R. F. Robert Smalls **92**

Marzollo, J. Happy birthday, Martin Luther King **92**

Maupin, M. Benjamin Banneker **92**

McKissack, P. C. Frederick Douglass **92**

Michelson, R. As good as anybody: Martin Luther King Jr. and Abraham Joshua Heschel's amazing march toward freedom **92**

Myers, W. D. I've seen the promised land [biography of Martin Luther King] **92**

Myers, W. D. Malcolm X **92**

Nelson, S. R. Ain't nothing but a man [biography of John William Henry] **92**

Nelson, V. M. Bad news for outlaws **92**

Pinkney, A. D. Bill Pickett, rodeo-ridin' cowboy **92**

Pinkney, A. D. Dear Benjamin Banneker **92**

Pinkney, A. D. Duke Ellington **92**

Rappaport, D. Freedom river [biography of John P. Parker] **92**

Rappaport, D. Martin's big words: the life of Dr. Martin Luther King, Jr. **92**

Rembert, W. Don't hold me back **92**

Schuman, M. Barack Obama **92**

Shichtman, S. H. Colin Powell **92**

Tillage, L. Leon's story **92**

Waxman, L. H. Colin Powell **92**

Whiting, J. W.E.B. Du Bois **92**

Yates, E. Amos Fortune, free man **92**

Civil rights

Adler, D. A. Heroes for civil rights **920**

Aretha, D. Sit-ins and freedom rides **323.1**

Bausum, A. Freedom Riders **323.1**

African Americans—Civil rights—*Continued*

Bridges, R. Through my eyes: the autobiography of Ruby Bridges **92**
Brimner, L. D. Birmingham Sunday **323.1**
Brimner, L. D. We are one: the story of Bayard Rustin **92**
Crewe, S. The Scottsboro case **345**
Donaldson, M. Ruby Bridges **92**
Dray, P. Yours for justice, Ida B. Wells **92**
Farris, C. March on! [biography of Martin Luther King] **92**
Farris, C. My brother Martin [biography of Martin Luther King] **92**
Fradin, D. B. Ida B. Wells **92**
Freedman, R. Freedom walkers **323.1**
Freedman, R. The voice that challenged a nation [biography of Marian Anderson] **92**
Giovanni, N. Rosa [biography of Rosa Parks] **92**
Halfmann, J. Seven miles to freedom **92**
Haskins, J. Delivering justice [biography of Westley Wallace Law] **92**
Haskins, J. John Lewis in the lead **92**
Holland, L. J. Dr. Martin Luther King Jr.'s I have a dream speech in translation **323.1**
Hopkinson, D. Sweet land of liberty [biography of Oscar L. Chapman] **92**
Jeffrey, L. S. Celebrate Martin Luther King, Jr., Day **394.26**
Kennedy, R. F. Robert Smalls **92**
King, C. Oh, freedom! **323.1**
King, M. L., Jr. I have a dream **323.1**
Marzollo, J. Happy birthday, Martin Luther King **92**
McClaurin, I. The civil rights movement **323.1**
McWhorter, D. A dream of freedom **323.1**
Michelson, R. As good as anybody: Martin Luther King Jr. and Abraham Joshua Heschel's amazing march toward freedom **92**
Myers, W. D. Ida B. Wells **92**
Myers, W. D. I've seen the promised land [biography of Martin Luther King] **92**
Parks, R. Rosa Parks: my story **92**
Pinkney, A. D. Let it shine **920**
Pinkney, A. D. Sit-in **323.1**
Rappaport, D. Free at last! **305.8**
Rappaport, D. Martin's big words: the life of Dr. Martin Luther King, Jr. **92**
Rappaport, D. Nobody gonna turn me 'round **323.1**
Shange, N. Coretta Scott [King] **92**
Shelton, P. Y. Child of the civil rights movement **323.1**
Weatherford, C. B. The beatitudes **323.1**
Whiting, J. W.E.B. Du Bois **92**

Civil rights—Fiction
Reynolds, A. Back of the bus **E**
Williams-Garcia, R. One crazy summer **Fic**

Civil rights—Poetry
Shange, N. We troubled the waters **811**
Shore, D. Z. This is the dream **811**
Weatherford, C. B. Birmingham, 1963 **811**

Civil rights—Songs
Stotts, S. We shall overcome **782.42**

Education
Haskins, J. Separate, but not equal **379**

Jurmain, S. The forbidden schoolhouse [biography of Prudence Crandall] **92**
Morrison, T. Remember **379**
Walker, P. R. Remember Little Rock **379**

Employment
See also African American businesspeople
Fiction
Allen, D. Dancing in the wings **E**
Anderson, L. H. Chains **Fic**
Armstrong, W. H. Sounder **Fic**
Aston, D. H. Moon over Star **E**
Belton, S. Beauty, her basket **E**
Belton, S. The tallest tree **Fic**
Bildner, P. The Hallelujah Flight **E**
Birtha, B. Grandmama's pride **E**
Birtha, B. Lucky beans **E**
Blue, R. Ron's big mission **E**
Boles, P. M. Little divas **Fic**
Bradby, M. Momma, where are you from? **E**
Bradby, M. More than anything else **E**
Brandeis, G. My life with the Lincolns **Fic**
Brenner, B. Wagon wheels **E**
Broyles, A. Priscilla and the hollyhocks **E**
Bunting, E. Smoky night **E**
Cameron, A. Gloria's way **Fic**
Cameron, A. The stories Julian tells **Fic**
Campbell, B. M. Sometimes my mommy gets angry **E**
Campbell, B. M. Stompin' at the Savoy **E**
Carbone, E. L. Night running **E**
Carbone, E. L. Storm warriors **Fic**
Cohen, B. Thank you, Jackie Robinson **Fic**
Collier, B. Uptown **E**
Collier, J. L. Jump ship to freedom **Fic**
Collier, J. L. War comes to Willy Freeman **Fic**
Cooke, T. Full, full, full of love **E**
Cooper, F. Willie and the All-Stars **E**
Cotten, C. Rain play **E**
Crews, D. Shortcut **E**
Cummings, P. Harvey Moon, museum boy **E**
Curtis, C. P. Bucking the Sarge **Fic**
Curtis, C. P. Bud, not Buddy **Fic**
Curtis, C. P. Mr. Chickee's funny money **Fic**
Curtis, C. P. The Watsons go to Birmingham—1963 **Fic**
Curtis, G. The bat boy & his violin **E**
Dahlberg, M. F. The story of Jonas **Fic**
DeGross, M. Donavan's double trouble **Fic**
Derby, S. No mush today **E**
Draper, S. M. Little Sister is not my name **Fic**
Dudley, D. L. The bicycle man **Fic**
Ehrhardt, K. This Jazz man **E**
Elliott, Z. Bird **E**
Emerson, K. Carlos is gonna get it **Fic**
English, K. The baby on the way **E**
English, K. Francie **Fic**
English, K. Hot day on Abbott Avenue **E**
English, K. Nikki & Deja **Fic**
English, K. Speak to me **E**
Evans, F. W. Hush harbor **E**
Falwell, C. David's drawings **E**

African Americans—Fiction—*Continued*

Fenner, C. Yolonda's genius   **Fic**
Flake, S. G. The broken bike boy and the Queen of 33rd Street   **Fic**
Flournoy, V. The patchwork quilt   **E**
Fox, M. Sophie   **E**
Frame, J. A. Yesterday I had the blues   **E**
Fuqua, J. S. Darby   **Fic**
Gourley, R. Bring me some apples and I'll make you a pie   **E**
Grant, K. Sofie and the city   **E**
Greene, B. Philip Hall likes me, I reckon maybe   **Fic**
Greenfield, E. The friendly four   **Fic**
Greenfield, E. Sister   **Fic**
Grifalconi, A. Ain't nobody a stranger to me   **E**
Grimes, N. Make way for Dyamonde Daniel   **Fic**
Hamilton, V. The bells of Christmas   **Fic**
Hamilton, V. Drylongso   **Fic**
Hamilton, V. The house of Dies Drear   **Fic**
Hamilton, V. M.C. Higgins, the great   **Fic**
Hamilton, V. The planet of Junior Brown   **Fic**
Hamilton, V. Wee Winnie Witch's Skinny   **E**
Hamilton, V. Zeely   **Fic**
Harrington, J. N. The chicken-chasing queen of Lamar County   **E**
Harrington, J. N. Going north   **E**
Hartfield, C. Me and Uncle Romie   **E**
Havill, J. Jamaica's find   **E**
Hegamin, T. Most loved in all the world   **E**
Hemphill, H. The adventurous deeds of Deadwood Jones   **Fic**
Hest, A. Mr. George Baker   **E**
Hoffman, M. Amazing Grace   **E**
Hoffman, M. Starring Grace   **Fic**
Hopkinson, D. A band of angels   **E**
Howard, E. F. Aunt Flossie's hats (and crab cakes later)   **E**
Howard, E. F. Virgie goes to school with us boys   **E**
Isadora, R. Ben's trumpet   **E**
Isadora, R. Uh-oh!   **E**
Johnson, A. Bird   **Fic**
Johnson, A. I dream of trains   **E**
Johnson, A. Just like Josh Gibson   **E**
Johnson, A. Wind flyers   **E**
Johnson, D. Black magic   **E**
Joosse, B. M. Hot city   **E**
Jordan, R. Lost Goat Lane   **Fic**
Keats, E. J. Hi, cat!   **E**
Konigsburg, E. L. Jennifer, Hecate, Macbeth, William McKinley, and me, Elizabeth   **Fic**
Kurtz, J. Faraway home   **E**
Latham, I. Leaving Gee's Bend   **Fic**
Lester, J. Black cowboy, wild horses   **E**
Lester, J. The old African   **Fic**
Levine, E. Henry's freedom box   **E**
Levine, G. C. Dave at night   **Fic**
Lindsey, K. Sweet potato pie   **E**
Lombard, J. Drita, my homegirl   **Fic**
Lyon, G. E. You and me and home sweet home   **E**
Lyons, M. E. Letters from a slave girl   **Fic**
McCully, E. A. Wonder horse   **E**

McGowan, M. Sunday is for God   **E**
McKissack, P. C. Abby takes a stand   **Fic**
McKissack, P. C. The all-I'll-ever-want Christmas doll   **E**
McKissack, P. C. The dark-thirty   **S C**
McKissack, P. C. Flossie & the fox   **E**
McKissack, P. C. Goin' someplace special   **E**
McKissack, P. C. Let my people go   **Fic**
McKissack, P. C. Mirandy and Brother Wind   **E**
McKissack, P. C. Porch lies   **S C**
McKissack, P. C. Precious and the Boo Hag   **E**
McKissack, P. C. Stitchin' and pullin'   **Fic**
McKissack, P. C. Tippy Lemmey   **Fic**
McQuinn, A. My friend Mei Jing   **E**
Mead, A. Junebug   **Fic**
Michelson, R. Across the alley   **E**
Miller, W. Night golf   **E**
Miller, W. Richard Wright and the library card   **E**
Mitchell, M. K. Uncle Jed's barbershop   **E**
Moses, S. P. Sallie Gal and the Wall-a-kee man   **Fic**
Myers, W. D. Looking like me   **E**
Nelson, V. M. Who will I be, Lord?   **E**
Neri, G. Chess rumble   **Fic**
Nolen, J. Big Jabe   **E**
Nolen, J. Pitching in for Eubie   **E**
Nolen, J. Thunder Rose   **E**
Paratore, C. Sunny Holiday   **Fic**
Paterson, K. Jip   **Fic**
Paulsen, G. The legend of Bass Reeves   **Fic**
Pinkney, A. D. Boycott blues   **E**
Pinkney, A. D. Peggony-Po   **E**
Polacco, P. Chicken Sunday   **E**
Polacco, P. January's sparrow   **Fic**
Polacco, P. Mrs. Katz and Tush   **E**
Quattlebaum, M. Jackson Jones and Mission Greentop   **Fic**
Rappaport, D. Freedom ship   **Fic**
Raschka, C. Yo! Yes?   **E**
Raven, M. Circle unbroken   **E**
Raven, M. Night boat to freedom   **E**
Reeder, C. Across the lines   **Fic**
Reynolds, A. Back of the bus   **E**
Reynolds, A. Metal man   **E**
Ringgold, F. Tar Beach   **E**
Robinet, H. G. Forty acres and maybe a mule   **Fic**
Robinet, H. G. Walking to the bus-rider blues   **Fic**
Robinson, S. Safe at home   **Fic**
Scillian, D. Pappy's handkerchief   **E**
Sebestyen, O. Words by heart   **Fic**
Sherman, P. Ben and the Emancipation Proclamation   **E**
Slate, J. I want to be free   **E**
Slote, A. Finding Buck McHenry   **Fic**
Smith, H. A. Keeping the night watch   **Fic**
Smith, H. A. The way a door closes   **Fic**
Stauffacher, S. Bessie Smith and the night riders   **E**
Stroud, B. The patchwork path   **E**
Swain, G. Riding to Washington   **E**
Tarpley, N. Bippity Bop barbershop   **E**

African Americans—Fiction—*Continued*

Tate, E. E. Celeste's Harlem Renaissance **Fic**

Taulbert, C. L. Little Cliff and the porch people **E**

Taylor, D. A. Sweet music in Harlem **E**

Taylor, M. D. The friendship **Fic**

Taylor, M. D. The gold Cadillac **Fic**

Taylor, M. D. Let the circle be unbroken **Fic**

Taylor, M. D. Mississippi bridge **Fic**

Taylor, M. D. The road to Memphis **Fic**

Taylor, M. D. Roll of thunder, hear my cry **Fic**

Taylor, M. D. Song of the trees **Fic**

Taylor, M. D. The well **Fic**

Thomas, J. C. I have heard of a land **E**

Thomson, M. Keena Ford and the second-grade mixup **Fic**

Tingle, T. Crossing Bok Chitto **Fic**

Tinkham, K. Hair for Mama **E**

Turner-Denstaedt, M. The hat that wore Clara B. **E**

Wahl, J. Candy shop **E**

Walter, M. P. Alec's primer **E**

Walter, M. P. Justin and the best biscuits in the world **Fic**

Weatherford, C. B. Champions on the bench **E**

Weatherford, C. B. Dear Mr. Rosenwald **Fic**

Weatherford, C. B. Freedom on the menu **E**

Weinstein, M. H. When Louis Armstrong taught me scat **E**

Wentworth, M. Shackles **E**

Whelan, G. The listeners **E**

Whittenberg, A. Sweet Thang **Fic**

Wiles, D. Freedom Summer **E**

Williams, K. L. A beach tail **E**

Williams, S. A. Working cotton **E**

Williams, V. B. Cherries and cherry pits **E**

Winter, J. Follow the drinking gourd **E**

Winthrop, E. Squashed in the middle **E**

Woods, B. My name is Sally Little Song **Fic**

Woods, B. The red rose box **Fic**

Woodson, J. Coming on home soon **E**

Woodson, J. Feathers **Fic**

Woodson, J. Locomotion **Fic**

Woodson, J. The other side **E**

Woodson, J. Peace, Locomotion **Fic**

Woodson, J. Show way **E**

Woodson, J. Visiting day **E**

Woodson, J. We had a picnic this Sunday past **E**

Folklore

Hamilton, V. Bruh Rabbit and the tar baby girl **398.2**

Hamilton, V. The people could fly: American Black folktales **398.2**

Hamilton, V. The people could fly: the picture book **398.2**

Keats, E. J. John Henry **398.2**

Krensky, S. John Henry **398.2**

Lester, J. John Henry **398.2**

Lester, J. The tales of Uncle Remus **398.2**

Lester, J. Uncle Remus, the complete tales **398.2**

Lyons, M. E. Roy makes a car **398.2**

McGill, A. Sure as sunrise **398.2**

McGill, A. Way up and over everything **398.2**

Myers, C. Lies and other tall tales **398.2**

San Souci, R. The secret of the stones **398.2**

San Souci, R. Sukey and the mermaid **398.2**

Sanfield, S. The adventures of High John the Conqueror **398.2**

Stevens, J. Tops and bottoms **398.2**

Thomas, J. C. The six fools **398.2**

Thomas, J. C. The skull talks back and other haunting tales **398.2**

Thomas, J. C. The three witches **398.2**

History

Cook, M. Our children can soar **920**

Haskins, J. Africa **967**

Haskins, J. The rise of Jim Crow **305.8**

Hudson, W. Powerful words **808.8**

Jordan, A. D. The Civil War **973.7**

Masoff, J. The African American story **305.8**

McClaurin, I. Facing the future **305.8**

McKissack, P. C. Days of Jubilee **973.7**

Myers, W. D. Now is your time! **305.8**

Rappaport, D. Free at last! **305.8**

Sanders, N. I. America's black founders **973.3**

Schomp, V. Marching toward freedom **305.8**

Stroud, B. The Reconstruction era **973.8**

Weatherford, C. B. The beatitudes **323.1**

See/See also pages in the following book(s):

Clinton, C. The Black soldier **355**

History—Sources

The Black Americans **305.8**

Music

See African American music

Poetry

Angelou, M. Maya Angelou **811**

Ashley Bryan's ABC of African-American poetry **811.008**

Brooks, G. Bronzeville boys and girls **811**

Dant, T. Some kind of love **811**

Giovanni, N. Spin a soft black song: poems for children **811**

Grant, S. Up home **811**

Greenfield, E. Brothers & sisters **811**

Greenfield, E. Honey, I love, and other love poems **811**

Grimes, N. Meet Danitra Brown **811**

Grimes, N. When Gorilla goes walking **811**

Hughes, L. The dream keeper and other poems **811**

Hughes, L. Langston Hughes **811**

Hughes, L. My people **811**

Hughes, L. The Negro speaks of rivers **811**

I, too, sing America **811.008**

In daddy's arms I am tall **811.008**

In the hollow of your hand **782.42**

Johnson, D. Hair dance! **811**

Myers, W. D. Blues journey **811**

Myers, W. D. Harlem **811**

Shange, N. Ellington was not a street **E**

Smith, H. A. Mother poems **811**

Soul looks back in wonder **811.008**

Ahlberg, Jessica—*Continued*
(il) Tellegen, T. Letters to anyone and everyone
Fic

Ahmed, Hany El Saed
(jt. auth) Johnson-Davies, D. Goha the wise fool
398.2

AIDS (Disease)
Ballard, C. AIDS and other epidemics **614.5**
Silverstein, A. The AIDS update **616.97**

AIDS and other epidemics. Ballard, C. **614.5**

The **AIDS** update. Silverstein, A. **616.97**

Aiello, Laurel
(il) Sabbeth, A. Rubber-band banjos and a java
jive bass **781**

Aiken, Joan, 1924-2004
Shadows and moonshine **S C**
The wolves of Willoughby Chase **Fic**

Aillaud, Cindy Lou, 1955-
Recess at 20 below **370.9**

Ain't nobody a stranger to me. Grifalconi, A.
E

Ain't nothing but a man [biography of John William Henry] Nelson, S. R. **92**

Air
Branley, F. M. Air is all around you **551.5**
Meiani, A. Air **533**
Parker, S. The science of air **533**

Air, Moisture of *See* Humidity

Air is all around you. Branley, F. M. **551.5**

Air pilots

See also African American pilots; Women
air pilots

Burleigh, R. Flight: the journey of Charles Lindbergh **92**
Hense, M. How fighter pilots use math
629.13
Maurer, R. The Wright sister [biography of
Katharine Wright Haskell] **92**
Provensen, A. The glorious flight: across the
Channel with Louis Blériot, July 25, 1909
92
Tunnell, M. O. Candy bomber [biography of
Gail Halvorsen] **92**
Fiction
Bildner, P. The Hallelujah Flight **E**
Breen, S. Violet the pilot **E**
Ferrari, M. Born to fly **Fic**
Johnson, A. Wind flyers **E**
Newman, P. Nugget on the flight deck **E**
Nez, J. A. Cromwell Dixon's Sky-Cycle **E**
Saint-Exupéry, A. d. The little prince **Fic**
Saint-Exupéry, A. d. The little prince: deluxe
pop-up book **Fic**
Stamp, J. Flying high **E**
Strøm, K. Sadie the air mail pilot **E**

Air pollution
Bridges, A. Clean air **363.7**
Rapp, V. Protecting Earth's air quality **363.7**
Rockwell, A. F. What's so bad about gasoline?
665.5

Air show!. Williams, T. **E**

Airborne: a photobiography of Wilbur and Orville
Wright. Collins, M. **92**

Aircraft. Graham, I. **629.133**
Aircraft accidents
Vogel, C. G. The man who flies with birds
598
Aircraft carriers
Sutherland, J. Aircraft carriers **623.82**
Fiction
Newman, P. Nugget on the flight deck **E**
Airman. Colfer, E. **Fic**
Airplanes
Barton, B. Airplanes **387.7**
Barton, B. Airport **387.7**
Clark, W. Planes on the move **629.133**
Goldish, M. Freaky-big airplanes **629.13**
Graham, I. Aircraft **629.133**
Oxlade, C. Airplanes **629.133**
Accidents
See Aircraft accidents
Design and construction
Provensen, A. The glorious flight: across the
Channel with Louis Blériot, July 25, 1909
92
Fiction
Colfer, E. Airman **Fic**
Hubbell, P. Airplanes **E**
Hubbell, P. My first airplane ride **E**
Ichikawa, S. Come fly with me **E**
McCarty, P. Moon plane **E**
Sturges, P. I love planes! **E**
Williams, T. Air show! **E**
Models
Harbo, C. L. The kids' guide to paper airplanes
745.592
Simon, S. The paper airplane book **745.592**
Models—**Fiction**
Polacco, P. The junkyard wonders **Fic**
Airports
Barton, B. Airport **387.7**
Fiction
Bunting, E. Fly away home **E**
Ajmera, Maya
Be my neighbor **307**
Faith **200**
To be an artist **700**
Akaba, Suekichi, 1910-
(il) Ōtsuka, Y. Suho's white horse **398.2**
Akib, Jamel
(il) Iyengar, M. M. Tan to tamarind **811**
(il) Krishnaswami, U. Monsoon **E**
(il) Markle, S. Animals Christopher Columbus
saw **970.01**
(il) Rahaman, V. Divali rose **E**
Akkadians (Sumerians) *See* Sumerians
Al Adely, Laith Muhmood
(jt. auth) Hassig, S. M. Iraq **956.7**
Al Capone does my shirts. Choldenko, G. **Fic**
Al-Hazza, Tami Craft
Books about the Middle East **016.3058**
ALA fundamentals series
Sullivan, M. Fundamentals of children's services
027.62
ALA readers' advisory series
Goldsmith, F. The readers' advisory guide to
graphic novels **025.2**

Alabama

Fiction

Collard, S. B., III. Double eagle	**Fic**
English, K. Francie	**Fic**
Johnson, A. Bird	**Fic**
Key, W. Alabama moon	**Fic**
Latham, I. Leaving Gee's Bend	**Fic**
Levine, K. The best bad luck I ever had	**Fic**
McKissack, P. C. Stitchin' and pullin'	**Fic**
Ray, D. Singing hands	**Fic**

Alabama moon. Key, W.   **Fic**

Aladdin and the enchanted lamp. Pullman, P.   **398.2**

Aladdin and the magic lamp = Aladino y la lámpara marvillosa. Vallverdú, J.   **398.2**

Alalou, Ali
(jt. auth) Alalou, E. The butter man   **E**

Alalou, Elizabeth
The butter man   **E**

Alamo (San Antonio, Tex.)
Fradin, D. B. The Alamo	**976.4**
Walker, P. R. Remember the Alamo	**976.4**

Alaniz, Adam
(il) Kornberg, A. Germ stories   **616.9**

Alarcón, Francisco X., 1954-
Animal poems of the Iguazu	**811**
From the bellybutton of the moon and other summer poems	**811**
Iguanas in the snow and other winter poems	**811**
Poems to dream together	**811**
(jt. auth) Garza, C. L. In my family	**306.8**

Alaska
Aillaud, C. L. Recess at 20 below	**370.9**
Lourie, P. Arctic thaw	**998**
Lourie, P. Whaling season	**599.5**
McMillan, B. Salmon summer	**639.2**
Miller, D. S. Big Alaska	**979.8**
Miller, D. S. The great serum race	**798.8**
Webb, S. Looking for seabirds	**598**

Fiction

Bauer, M. D. A bear named Trouble	**Fic**
Blake, R. J. Togo	**E**
Hill, K. The year of Miss Agnes	**Fic**
Joosse, B. M. Wind-wild dog	**E**
Morey, W. Gentle Ben	**Fic**
Sloat, T. Berry magic	**E**

Natural history
See Natural history—Alaska

Nome
See Nome (Alaska)

Albania
Knowlton, M. Albania   **949.65**

Albanians

Fiction
Lombard, J. Drita, my homegirl   **Fic**

Albee, Sarah
Poop happened!   **363.7**

Albers, Josef, 1888-1976

About
Wing, N. An eye for color: the story of Josef Albers   **92**

Albert. Napoli, D. J.   **E**

Albert Einstein. Venezia, M.   **92**

Albert Einstein and his theory of relativity. Herweck, D.   **92**

Albert the Fix-it Man. Lord, J.   **E**

Albert's birthday. Tryon, L.   **E**

Albert's impossible toothache. Williams, B.   **E**

Albert's toothache. See Williams, B. Albert's impossible toothache   **E**

Albino animals. Racanelli, M.   **591.6**

Albinos and albinism
Racanelli, M. Albino animals   **591.6**

Alborough, Jez, 1959-
Duck in the truck	**E**
Some dogs do	**E**
Tall	**E**
Where's my teddy?	**E**

Alcatraz Island (Calif.)
Murphy, C. R. Children of Alcatraz   **979.4**

Fiction
Choldenko, G. Al Capone does my shirts   **Fic**

Alcatraz versus the evil Librarians. Sanderson, B.   **Fic**

The **alchemist's** cat. Jarvis, R.   **Fic**

Alchemy

Fiction
Cushman, K. Alchemy and Meggy Swann   **Fic**

Alchemy and Meggy Swann. Cushman, K.   **Fic**

Alcohol

Physiological effect
Gottfried, T. Alcohol   **362.292**

Alcohol as fuel
Benduhn, T. Ethanol and other new fuels   **662**

Alcoholic beverages
See also Drinking of alcoholic beverages

Alcoholism
See also Drinking of alcoholic beverages
Gottfried, T. Alcohol   **362.292**

Fiction
Conly, J. L. Crazy lady!	**Fic**
Day, K. Tall tales	**Fic**
Fogelin, A. The sorta sisters	**Fic**

Alcorn, Stephen, 1958-
A gift of days	**808.88**
(il) America at war. See America at war	**811.008**
(il) Dray, P. Yours for justice, Ida B. Wells	**92**
(jt. auth) Hopkins, L. B. Days to celebrate	**051**
(il) Hopkinson, D. Keep on!	**92**
(il) I, too, sing America. See I, too, sing America	**811.008**
(il) My America. See My America	**811.008**
(il) Pinkney, A. D. Let it shine	**920**

Alcott, Louisa May, 1832-1888
Little women   **Fic**

About
McDonough, Y. Z. Louisa   **92**

Alice's adventures in Wonderland. See Carroll, L. Lewis Carroll's Alice in Wonderland **Fic**

Alice's birthday pig. Kennemore, T. **Fic**

Alien Eraser to the rescue. Moss, M. **Fic**

Alien invaders. Drake, J. **578.6**

Alien invasion. Jackson, C. **578.6**

Aliens

  See also Illegal aliens; Immigrants

United States

  See also United States—Immigration and emigration

Aliens are coming!. McCarthy, M. **791.44**

The Aliens are coming!. Thiesing, L. **E**

Aliens ate my homework. Coville, B. **Fic**

Aliens from Earth. Batten, M. **578.6**

Aliens from outer space *See* Extraterrestrial beings

Aliki

  Ah, music! **780**
  All by myself! **E**
  Corn is maize **633.1**
  Feelings **152.4**
  Fossils tell of long ago **560**
  The gods and goddesses of Olympus **292**
  Manners **395**
  A medieval feast **940.1**
  Milk from cow to carton **637**
  My feet **612**
  My five senses **612.8**
  My hands **612**
  My visit to the aquarium **639.34**
  My visit to the zoo **590.73**
  Painted words: Marianthe's story one **E**
  A play's the thing **E**
  Push button **E**
  Quiet in the garden **E**
  The two of them **E**
  We are best friends **E**
  Wild and woolly mammoths **569**
  William Shakespeare & the Globe **822.3**

Alire, Camila

  Serving Latino communities **027.6**

Alison's zinnia. Lobel, A. **E**

Alistair and Kip's great adventure. Segal, J. **E**

Alive. Ganeri, A. **612**

All aboard!. Demarest, C. L. **E**

All aboard!. Zimmermann, K. R. **385**

All about Braille. Jeffrey, L. S. **411**

All about electric and hybrid cars. Bearce, S. **629.222**

All about frogs. Arnosky, J. **597.8**

All about sharks. Arnosky, J. **597**

All about sign language. Lowenstein, F. **419**

All about sleep from A to ZZZZ. Scott, E. **612.8**

All about teeth. Schuh, M. C. **617.6**

All about tide pools. Halpern, M. **577.6**

All-action classics [series]

  Mucci, T. The odyssey **741.5**

All alone in the universe. Perkins, L. R. **Fic**

All-American Girls Professional Baseball League

Fiction

  Corey, S. Players in pigtails **E**
  Rappaport, D. Dirt on their skirts **E**

All by myself!. Aliki **E**

All God's critters. Staines, B. **782.42**

All Hallows' Eve *See* Halloween

The all-I'll-ever-want Christmas doll. McKissack, P. C. **E**

All in a day. Rylant, C. **E**

All in just one cookie. Goodman, S. **641.8**

All in the family. Otfinoski, S. **292**

All kinds of . . . [series]

  Miller, S. S. All kinds of ears **591.4**
  Miller, S. S. All kinds of eyes **591.4**
  Miller, S. S. All kinds of feet **591.4**
  Miller, S. S. All kinds of mouths **591.4**
  Miller, S. S. All kinds of noses **591.4**
  Miller, S. S. All kinds of skin **591.4**

All kinds of ears. Miller, S. S. **591.4**

All kinds of eyes. Miller, S. S. **591.4**

All kinds of feet. Miller, S. S. **591.4**

All kinds of mouths. Miller, S. S. **591.4**

All kinds of noses. Miller, S. S. **591.4**

All kinds of skin. Miller, S. S. **591.4**

All night, all day **782.25**

All-of-a-kind family. Taylor, S. **Fic**

All of baby, nose to toes. Adler, V. **E**

All of me!. Bang, M. **E**

All of our noses are here, and other noodle tales. Schwartz, A. **398.2**

All of the above. Pearsall, S. **Fic**

All our relatives. Goble, P. **970.004**

All pigs are beautiful. King-Smith, D. **636.4**

All Souls' Day

  Ancona, G. Pablo remembers **394.26**
  McGee, R. Paper crafts for Day of the Dead **745.594**

Fiction

  Goldman, J. Uncle monarch and the Day of the Dead **E**
  Johnston, T. Day of the Dead **E**
  Winter, J. Calavera abecedario **E**

All-star! [biography of Honus Wagner] Yolen, J. **92**

All stations! distress!. Brown, D. **910.4**

All terrain cycling *See* Mountain biking

All the colors of the earth. Hamanaka, S. **E**

All the lovely bad ones. Hahn, M. D. **Fic**

All the places to love. MacLachlan, P. **E**

All the small poems and fourteen more. Worth, V. **811**

All the way home. Giff, P. R. **Fic**

All the way to Lhasa. Berger, B. **398.2**

All the world. Scanlon, L. G. **811**

All things bright and beautiful. Alexander, C. F. **264**

Allard, Harry, 1928-

  Miss Nelson is missing! **E**

Amazing magic tricks: expert level. Barnhart, N. **793.8**

Amazing magic tricks: master level. Barnhart, N. **793.8**

Amazing Olympic athlete Wilma Rudolph. Wade, M. D. **92**

Amazing peace. Angelou, M. **811**

Amazing planet earth [series]
Green, J. Mighty rivers **551.48**
Green, J. The world's oceans **551.46**
Jennings, T. Earthquakes and tsunamis **551.2**
Jennings, T. Extreme weather **551.55**
Jennings, T. Massive mountains **551.4**
Jennings, T. Violent volcanoes **551.2**

Amazing president Theodore Roosevelt. Wade, M. D. **92**

Amazing rubber band cars. Rigsby, M. **745.592**

Amazing science. Animal classification [series]
Salas, L. P. Amphibians **597.8**

Amazing ships [series]
Sutherland, J. Aircraft carriers **623.82**
Sutherland, J. Container ships and oil tankers **623.82**
Sutherland, J. Cruise ships **623.82**
Sutherland, J. Submarines **623.82**

The **amazing** trail of Seymour Snail. Hazen, L. E. **Fic**

Amazing water frogs. Goldish, M. **597.8**

Amazing whales!. Thomson, S. L. **599.5**

Amazing you. Saltz, G. **612.6**

Amazon River
Fitzpatrick, A. Amazon River **981**

Amazon River valley
Berkenkamp, L. Discover the Amazon **981**
Fitzpatrick, A. Amazon River **981**
Fiction
Nelson, N. Bringing the boy home **Fic**
Folklore
McDermott, G. Jabuti the tortoise **398.2**
Taylor, S. The great snake **398.2**

Amazons!. Clayton, S. P. **398.2**

Amber Brown is not a crayon. Danziger, P. **Fic**

Amber was brave, Essie was smart. Williams, V. B. **811**

Ambrose, Stephen E.
The good fight **940.53**

Amelia Bedelia. Parish, P. **E**

Amelia makes a movie. Milgrim, D. **E**

Amelia rules!: the whole world's crazy!. Gownley, J. **741.5**

Amelia's 6th-grade notebook. Moss, M. **Fic**

Amendola, Dana
A day at the New Amsterdam Theatre **792.6**

America
See also Latin America; North America; South America
Antiquities
Huey, L. M. American archaeology uncovers the Dutch colonies **974.7**

Huey, L. M. American archaeology uncovers the earliest English colonies **973.2**
Huey, L. M. American archaeology uncovers the Vikings **970.01**
Mann, C. C. Before Columbus **970.01**
Wyatt, V. Who discovered America? **970.01**
Exploration
Bodden, V. Columbus reaches the New World **970.01**
Collier, J. L. Christopher Columbus **92**
Englar, M. French colonies in America **970.01**
Faber, H. Samuel de Champlain **92**
Fritz, J. Brendan the Navigator **398.2**
Fritz, J. Where do you think you're going, Christopher Columbus? **92**
Hernández, R. E. Early explorations: the 1500s **970.01**
Huey, L. M. American archaeology uncovers the earliest English colonies **973.2**
Huey, L. M. American archaeology uncovers the Vikings **970.01**
Lilly, A. Spanish colonies in America **970.01**
Lourie, P. On the Texas trail of Cabeza de Vaca **92**
MacLeod, E. Samuel de Champlain **92**
Maestro, B. The discovery of the Americas **970.01**
Maestro, B. Exploration and conquest **970.01**
Markle, S. Animals Christopher Columbus saw **970.01**
Meltzer, M. Francisco Pizarro **92**
Otfinoski, S. Juan Ponce de Leon **92**
Weaver, J. Hudson **92**
Wyatt, V. Who discovered America? **970.01**
Exploration—Fiction
Dorris, M. Morning Girl **Fic**
Howard, E. The crimson cap **Fic**

America at war **811.008**

America in today's world (1969-2004). Stanley, G. E. **973.92**

America the beautiful. Bates, K. L. **E**

America the Beautiful, third series **973**

American alligators. Feigenbaum, A. **597.98**

American archaeology [series]
Huey, L. M. American archaeology uncovers the Dutch colonies **974.7**
Huey, L. M. American archaeology uncovers the earliest English colonies **973.2**
Huey, L. M. American archaeology uncovers the Underground Railroad **973.7**
Huey, L. M. American archaeology uncovers the Vikings **970.01**
Huey, L. M. American archaeology uncovers the westward movement **978**

American archaeology uncovers the Dutch colonies. Huey, L. M. **974.7**

American archaeology uncovers the earliest English colonies. Huey, L. M. **973.2**

American archaeology uncovers the Underground Railroad. Huey, L. M. **973.7**

American archaeology uncovers the Vikings. Huey, L. M. **970.01**

American poetry

African American authors—Collections

Ashley Bryan's ABC of African-American poetry **811.008**

The entrance place of wonders **811.008**

Hip hop speaks to children **811.008**

I am the darker brother **811.008**

I, too, sing America **811.008**

Soul looks back in wonder **811.008**

Words with wings **811.008**

Collections

The 20th century children's poetry treasury **811.008**

Amazing faces **811.008**

America at war **811.008**

Behind the museum door **811.008**

The Bill Martin Jr. Big book of poetry **811.008**

Carnival of the animals **811.008**

Every second something happens **811.008**

Falling down the page **811.008**

For laughing out loud **811.008**

Got geography! **811.008**

Hamsters, shells, and spelling bees **811.008**

Hanukkah lights **811.008**

Heart to heart **811.008**

Here's a little poem **811.008**

Hip hop speaks to children **811.008**

In daddy's arms I am tall **811.008**

Incredible inventions **811.008**

It rained all day that night **811.008**

A kick in the head **811.008**

Knock at a star **811.008**

Lives: poems about famous Americans **811.008**

Marvelous math **811.008**

More pocket poems **811.008**

My America **811.008**

The Oxford book of children's verse in America **811.008**

The Place my words are looking for **811.008**

Poetry from A to Z **808.1**

Poetry speaks to children **811.008**

A Poke in the I **811.008**

The Random House book of poetry for children **811.008**

Read a rhyme, write a rhyme **811.008**

Read-aloud rhymes for the very young **821.008**

Salting the ocean **811.008**

Sharing the seasons **811.008**

She's all that! **811.008**

Sky magic **811.008**

Hispanic American authors—Collections

Cool salsa **811.008**

American Red Cross

Somervill, B. A. Clara Barton **92**

Wade, M. D. Amazing civil war nurse Clara Barton **92**

The **American** Revolution for kids. Herbert, J. **973.3**

American science See Science—United States

American songs

See also Folk songs—United States; Spirituals (Songs)

American speeches

Holland, L. J. Dr. Martin Luther King Jr.'s I have a dream speech in translation **323.1**

American story series

Maestro, B. Liberty or death **973.3**

Maestro, B. A new nation **973.3**

Maestro, B. Struggle for a continent **973.2**

American tall tales. Osborne, M. P. **398.2**

Americanization

See also Naturalization

Americans from India and other South Asian countries. Park, K. **305.8**

Americans from Russia and Eastern Europe. Weiss, G. G. **305.8**

Americans from the Caribbean and Central America. Keedle, J. **305.8**

Americans: the spirit of a nation [series]

Worth, R. Johnny Appleseed **92**

The **Americas** and the Pacific. Connolly, S. **970.004**

America's animal comebacks [series]

Caper, W. American bison **599.64**

Feigenbaum, A. American alligators **597.98**

Goldish, M. California condors **598**

Goldish, M. Florida manatees **599.5**

Goldish, M. Red wolves **599.77**

Greene, J. D. Grizzly bears **599.78**

Leardi, J. Southern sea otters **599.7**

America's black founders. Sanders, N. I. **973.3**

America's champion swimmer: Gertrude Ederle. Adler, D. A. **92**

America's ecosystems [series]

Wallace, M. D. America's forests **578.7**

America's forests. Wallace, M. D. **578.7**

America's living history [series]

Kent, D. Witchcraft trials **133.4**

McNeese, T. The fascinating history of American Indians **970.004**

Stein, R. C. Cuban Missile Crisis **972.91**

Worth, R. The Harlem Renaissance **700**

America's national parks [series]

Graham, A. Great Smoky Mountains National Park **976.8**

Jankowski, S. Everglades National Park **975.9**

Jankowski, S. Olympic National Park **979.7**

Reed, J. Cape Hatteras National Seashore **975.6**

America's westward expansion [series]

Steele, C. Cattle ranching in the American West **978**

Steele, C. Famous wagon trails **978**

Steele, C. Pioneer life in the American West **978**

Ames, Gerald, 1906-1993

(jt. auth) Wyler, R. Magic secrets **793.8**

Ames, Lee J., 1921-

[Draw 50 series] **743**

Amish

Bial, R. Amish home **289.7**

Fiction

Stewart, S. The journey **E**

Ancient Egypt. Rubalcaba, J. 932

The **ancient** Egyptians. Perl, L. 932

Ancient Greece!. Hart, A. 938

Ancient Greece. Langley, A. 709.38

Ancient Greece. McGee, M. 938

Ancient Greece. Pearson, A. 938

The **ancient** Greeks. Lassieur, A. 938

The **ancient** Inca. Calvert, P. 985

Ancient Inca. Gruber, B. 985

Ancient India. Schomp, V. 934

Ancient Iraq. Gruber, B. 935

The **ancient** Kushites. Sonneborn, L. 939

Ancient Maya. Harris, N. 972

The **ancient** Maya. Perl, L. 972

The **ancient** Mediterranean. Stefoff, R. 938

Ancient Mesopotamia. Schomp, V. 935

Ancient Mexico. Campbell-Hinshaw, K. 709.39

The **ancient** Near East. Stefoff, R. 939

Ancient Pueblo. Croy, A. 978

The **ancient** Romans. Lassieur, A. 937

Ancient Rome. James, S. 937

Ancona, George, 1929-
Capoeira 793.3
The fiestas 394.26
Pablo remembers 394.26
The piñata maker: El piñatero 745.594
Powwow 970.004

And if the moon could talk. Banks, K. E

And Tango makes three. Richardson, J. E

And the train goes. . . Bee, W. E

And then comes Halloween. Brenner, T. E

And then what happened, Paul Revere? Fritz, J. 92

And to think that I saw it on Mulberry Street. Seuss, Dr. E

And what comes after a thousand? Bley, A. E

Ander, 1967-
Me and my bike E

Andersen, Bethanne
(il) McDonough, Y. Z. Louisa 92
(il) Meltzer, M. Ten kings 920
(il) Meltzer, M. Ten queens 920
(il) Sasso, S. E. But God remembered 221.9
(il) Shea, P. D. Patience Wright 92

Andersen, Hans Christian, 1805-1875
The emperor's new clothes [illustrated by Virginia Lee Burton] E
Hans Christian Andersen's Fairy Tales [illustrated by Lisbeth Zwerger] S C
The little match girl [illustrated by Rachel Isadora] Fic
The princess and the pea [illustrated by Dorothee Duntze] Fic
Thumbeline [illustrated by Lisbeth Zwerger] E
The ugly duckling [illustrated by Pirkko Vainio] E

Andersen, Hans Christian, 1805-1875
About
Varmer, H. Hans Christian Andersen 92
Yolen, J. The perfect wizard [biography of Hans Christian Andersen] 92
See/See also pages in the following book(s):
Krull, K. Lives of the writers 920
Adaptations
Alderson, B. Thumbelina E
Braun, S. The ugly duckling E
Cech, J. The princess and the pea E
Demi. The emperor's new clothes E
Ehrlich, A. The Snow Queen Fic
Ehrlich, A. Thumbelina E
Ensor, B. Thumbelina Fic
Isadora, R. The ugly duckling E
Mitchell, S. The nightingale Fic
Mitchell, S. The tinderbox Fic
Mitchell, S. The ugly duckling E
Pinkney, J. The little match girl E
Pinkney, J. The nightingale Fic
Pinkney, J. The ugly duckling E
Poole, A. L. The pea blossom E
Reichenstetter, F. Andersen's fairy tales S C
Sedgwick, M. The emperor's new clothes E
Watts, B. The ugly duckling E

Andersen's fairy tales. Reichenstetter, F. S C

Anderson, Bethanne
(il) Bryant, J. Georgia's bones [biography of Georgia O'Keefe] 92

Anderson, Cynthia, 1945-
Write grants, get money 025.1

Anderson, Dale, 1953-
Ancient China 709.51
The Cold War years 973.92
World Almanac library of the Civil War [series] 973.7

Anderson, Derek
(il) Sierra, J. Ballyhoo Bay E
(il) Thompson, L. Little Quack E

Anderson, Derek, 1969-
(il) Lord, C. Hot rod hamster E

Anderson, Janet, 1946-
The last treasure Fic

Anderson, Jennifer Joline
John Lennon 92

Anderson, Jill, 1968-
Giraffes 599.63

Anderson, Jodi Lynn
May Bird and The Ever After Fic

Anderson, Judith *See* Heneghan, Judith, 1965-

Anderson, Laurie Halse, 1961-
Chains Fic
Fever, 1793 Fic
The hair of Zoe Fleefenbacher goes to school E
Independent dames 973.3

Anderson, M. T., 1968-
The Game of Sunken Places Fic
Handel, who knew what he liked 92
Strange Mr. Satie 92
Whales on stilts Fic

Anderson, Margaret Jean, 1931-
Carl Linnaeus 92

Angels

Fiction

Arrigan, M. Mario's Angels   **E**

Chaikin, M. Angels sweep the desert floor

    296.1

Creech, S. The unfinished angel   **Fic**

De Paola, T. Pascual and the kitchen angels

    E

Durango, J. Angels watching over me   **E**

Morpurgo, M. On angel wings   **Fic**

Richter, J. Beyond the station lies the sea

    Fic

Angel's mother's wedding. Delton, J.   **Fic**

Angels sweep the desert floor. Chaikin, M.

    296.1

Angels watching over me. Durango, J.   **E**

Anger

Fiction

Bang, M. When Sophie gets angry—really, really angry   **E**

Elliott, D. Finn throws a fit   **E**

Everitt, B. Mean soup   **E**

Harris, R. H. The day Leo said I hate you

    E

Urban, L. Mouse was mad   **E**

Vail, R. Sometimes I'm Bombaloo   **E**

Angle, Kimberly Greene

Hummingbird   **Fic**

Angles

Murphy, S. J. Hamster champs   **516**

Anglo-American cataloguing rules

Gorman, M. The concise AACR2   **025.3**

Anglo-American invasion of Iraq, 2003 *See* Iraq War, 2003-

Angola

Sheehan, S. Angola   **967.3**

Angulo, Teresa Cárdenas *See* Cárdenas, Teresa, 1970-

Anholt, Laurence

Cézanne and the apple boy   **E**

Matisse   **92**

Animal abuse *See* Animal welfare

Animal aha!. Swanson, D.   **590**

Animal attack and defense [series]

Pryor, K. J. Amazing armor   **591.47**

Pryor, K. J. Clever camouflage   **591.47**

Pryor, K. J. Mimicry and relationships

    591.47

Pryor, K. J. Tricky behavior   **591.47**

Pryor, K. J. Venom, poison, and electricity

    591.6

Pryor, K. J. Warning colors   **591.47**

Animal babies

Arnosky, J. Babies in the bayou   **E**

Ashman, L. Babies on the go   **E**

Baillie, M. Small wonders   **591.3**

Bredeson, C. Baby animals of the desert

    591.7

Bredeson, C. Baby animals of the frozen tundra

    591.7

Bredeson, C. Baby animals of the grasslands

    591.7

Bredeson, C. Baby animals of the ocean

    591.7

Bredeson, C. Baby animals of the tropical rain forest   **591.7**

Bredeson, C. Baby animals of the woodland forest   **591.7**

Fraser, M. A. How animal babies stay safe

    591.56

Hengel, K. It's a baby Australian fur seal!

    599.79

Hickman, P. M. Animals and their young

    591.56

Kajikawa, K. Close to you   **591.3**

Markle, S. How many baby pandas?   **599.78**

Markle, S. Sneaky, spinning, baby spiders

    595.4

Rose, D. L. Ocean babies   **591.3**

Swinburne, S. R. Safe, warm, and snug

    591.56

Animal baths. Fielding, B.   **591.5**

Animal behavior

See also Animal defenses; Animals—Food

Bancroft, H. Animals in winter   **591.56**

Batten, M. Please don't wake the animals

    591.5

Benbow, A. Awesome animal science projects

    590.7

Bishop, N. The secrets of animal flight

    591.47

Buckley, C. Tarra & Bella   **599.67**

Burnie, D. How animals work   **591.4**

Collard, S. B., III. Animal dads   **591.56**

Collard, S. B., III. Animals asleep   **591.56**

Fielding, B. Animal baths   **591.5**

Fraser, M. A. Where are the night animals?

    591.5

Gardner, R. Ace your animal science project

    590.7

Goodman, S. The truth about poop   **573.4**

Hickman, P. M. Animals and their mates

    591.56

Himmelman, J. Who's at the seashore?

    591.7

Jenkins, S. How many ways can you catch a fly?   **591.5**

Jenkins, S. Sisters & brothers   **591.56**

Pipe, J. Swarms   **591.5**

Racanelli, M. Animal mimics   **591.5**

Schubert, I. Like people   **591.56**

Schuette, S. L. Let's look at fall   **508.2**

Schuette, S. L. Let's look at spring   **508.2**

Schuette, S. L. Let's look at summer   **508.2**

Schuette, S. L. Let's look at winter   **508.2**

Settel, J. Exploding ants   **591.5**

Stewart, M. Under the snow   **591.7**

Stewart, M. When rain falls   **591.7**

Stockdale, S. Carry me!   **591.56**

Swinburne, S. R. Safe, warm, and snug

    591.56

Animal body-part regenerators. Mitchell, S. K.

    571.8

Animal chemical combat. Mitchell, S. K.

    591.47

Animal colors. Fielding, B.   **591.47**

Animal communication

Baines, R. What did one elephant say to the other   **591.59**

Animal tracks—*Continued*
Fiction
Hodgkins, F. Who's been here?   E
Yee, W. H. Tracks in the snow   E
Animal tracks & signs. Johnson, J.   590
Animal welfare
    See also Animal shelters
Laidlaw, R. Wild animals in captivity
       636.088
Fiction
Correa, S. Gaff   Fic
Animals
    See also Dangerous animals; Exotic animals; Pets; Poisonous animals; Predatory animals; Prehistoric animals; Rare animals; Wildlife and names of orders and classes of the animal kingdom; kinds of animals characterized by their environments; and names of individual species. Animals of the Bible
       220.8
Ablow, G. A horse in the house, and other strange but true animal stories   590
Aliki. My visit to the zoo   590.73
Aston, D. H. An egg is quiet   591.4
Baines, R. What's in that egg?   591.4
Bayrock, F. Bubble homes and fish farts
       590
Boutignon, B. Not all animals are blue   E
Burnie, D. How animals work   591.4
Carle, E. Does a kangaroo have a mother, too?
       E
Collard, S. B., III. Teeth   591.47
Collard, S. B., III. Wings   591.47
Cusick, D. Animal tongues   591.4
Davies, N. Extreme animals   590
Davies, N. Just the right size   591.4
Eamer, C. Super crocs & monster wings
       591.3
Ehlert, L. Lots of spots   E
Ehrlich, F. Does an elephant take a bath?   E
Eichenberg, F. Ape in a cape   E
Fielding, B. Animal colors   591.47
Fleming, D. Count!   E
Gannij, J. Hidden hippo   590
Goodman, S. Claws, coats, and camouflage
       591.4
Guiberson, B. Z. Earth feeling the heat
       363.7
Higginson, M. Feathers and fur   591.47
James, R. H. Teeth and fangs   591.47
Jenkins, S. Actual size   591.4
Jenkins, S. Big & little   591.4
Jenkins, S. Biggest, strongest, fastest   590
Jenkins, S. I see a kookaburra!   591.7
Johnson, J. Animal tracks & signs   590
Jones, C. F. The king who barked   636
Komiya, T. Life-size zoo   590
Krautwurst, T. Night science for kids   591.5
Marino, G. Zoopa   E
Markle, S. Animal heroes   636.088
Markle, S. Animals Charles Darwin saw   92
McLimans, D. Gone wild   E
Miller, S. S. All kinds of ears   591.4
Miller, S. S. All kinds of eyes   591.4
Miller, S. S. All kinds of feet   591.4
Miller, S. S. All kinds of mouths   591.4

Miller, S. S. All kinds of noses   591.4
Miller, S. S. All kinds of skin   591.4
Munari, B. Bruno Munari's zoo   E
Myers, J. The puzzle of the platypus   590
Parker, M. B. A paddling of ducks   E
Patkau, K. Creatures great and small   591.4
Patkau, K. Creatures yesterday and today
       591.3
Posada, M. Guess what is growing inside this egg   591.4
Post, H. Creepy crawlies   590
Racanelli, M. Camouflaged creatures   591.47
Racanelli, M. Underground animals   591.5
Rau, D. M. Animals   590
Sayre, A. P. One is a snail, ten is a crab   E
Schwartz, D. M. Where else in the wild?
       591.4
Schwartz, D. M. Where in the wild?   591.4
Seuling, B. Cows sweat through their noses
       590
Singer, M. Eggs   591.4
Siwanowicz, I. Animals up close   590
Slade, S. What's new at the zoo?   513
Souza, D. M. Look what feet can do   573.9
Souza, D. M. Look what mouths can do
       573.9
Souza, D. M. Look what tails can do   573.9
Swanson, D. Animal aha!   590
Walker, R. Animal life   590
Werner, S. Alphabeasties and other amazing types   411
Wildsmith, B. Brian Wildsmith's Amazing animal alphabet   E
Wormell, C. Teeth, tails, & tentacles   E
Zuckerman, A. Creature ABC   E
Camouflage
    See Camouflage (Biology)
Classification
BishopRoby, J. Animal kingdom   590
Levine, S. Animals   590
Color
Jenkins, S. Living color   591.47
Racanelli, M. Albino animals   591.6
Encyclopedias
Animals   590.3
Animals: a visual encyclopedia   590.3
McGhee, K. Encyclopedia of animals   590.3
Wildlife and plants   578
Fiction
Alborough, J. Duck in the truck   E
Alexander, C. Lucy and the bully   E
Aliki. Quiet in the garden   E
Allen, J. The little rabbit who liked to say moo
       E
Arnosky, J. Gobble it up!   E
Asher, S. Here comes Gosling!   E
Avi. Poppy   Fic
Baddiel, I. Cock-a-doodle quack! quack!   E
Baker, K. Hickory dickory dock   E
Barrett, J. Never take a shark to the dentist and other things not to do   E
Bartlett, T. C. Tuba lessons   E
Bauer, M. D. The longest night   E
Bauer, M. D. One brown bunny   E
Beaumont, K. Duck, duck, goose!   E
Beaumont, K. Move over, Rover   E

Animals—Fiction—*Continued*

Beaumont, K. Who ate all the cookie dough? **E**

Benedictus, D. Return to the Hundred Acre Wood **Fic**

Bergman, M. Yum yum! What fun! **E**

Black, M. I. Chicken cheeks **E**

Blackstone, S. Octopus opposites **E**

Blomgren, J. Where do I sleep? **E**

Bloom, S. A mighty fine time machine **E**

Boyle, B. Hugo and the really, really, really long string **E**

Brett, J. The hat **E**

Briant, E. If you lived here you'd be home by now **E**

Broach, E. Gumption! **E**

Brown, L. How to be **E**

Brown, M. W. Big red barn **E**

Brown, M. W. A child's good morning book **E**

Brown, M. W. Where have you been? **E**

Brown, R. The old tree **E**

Buehner, C. I did it, I'm sorry **E**

Bunting, E. Our library **E**

Burningham, J. Mr. Gumpy's outing **E**

Butler, J. Bedtime in the jungle **E**

Cabral, O. The seven sneezes **E**

Cabrera, J. If you're happy and you know it **E**

Cabrera, J. Kitty's cuddles **E**

Cabrera, J. Mommy, carry me please! **E**

Cabrera, J. One, two, buckle my shoe **E**

Calmenson, S. Jazzmatazz! **E**

Campbell, R. Dear zoo **E**

Carle, E. "Slowly, slowly, slowly," said the sloth **E**

Carle, E. The very clumsy click beetle **E**

Carle, E. Where are you going? To see my friend! **E**

Carlson, N. L. Henry and the Valentine surprise **E**

Carrick, C. Mothers are like that **E**

Carris, J. D. Welcome to the Bed & Biscuit **Fic**

Cauley, L. B. Clap your hands **E**

Chatterton, M. The Brain finds a leg **Fic**

Chichester-Clark, E. Little Miss Muffet counts to ten **E**

Chick, B. The secret zoo **Fic**

Church, C. Digby takes charge **E**

Cole, H. I took a walk **E**

Conover, C. Over the hills & far away **E**

Costello, D. I can help **E**

Cousins, L. I'm the best **E**

Craig, L. Dancing feet! **E**

Cushman, D. Mystery at the Club Sandwich **E**

Dahl, R. The enormous crocodile **Fic**

De Paola, T. Four friends at Christmas **E**

De Regniers, B. S. May I bring a friend? **E**

Delessert, É. Big and Bad **E**

Denslow, S. P. In the snow **E**

DePalma, M. N. The perfect gift **E**

Dokas, D. Muriel's red sweater **E**

Donaldson, J. Where's my mom? **E**

Dubosarsky, U. The terrible plop **E**

Dunbar, P. Where's Tumpty? **E**

Dunrea, O. Bear Noel **E**

Edwards, P. D. Some smug slug **E**

Edwards, P. D. While the world is sleeping **E**

Ehlert, L. Circus **E**

Ehlert, L. Oodles of animals **E**

Ehrlich, A. Baby Dragon **E**

Ellery, A. If I were a jungle animal **E**

Elya, S. M. Eight animals on the town **E**

Emberley, E. Thanks, Mom! **E**

Emmett, J. The best gift of all **E**

Ericsson, J. A. Whoo goes there? **E**

Ets, M. H. Play with me **E**

Evans, L. Who loves the little lamb? **E**

Farber, N. How the hibernators came to Bethlehem **E**

Fischer, S. M. Jump! **E**

Flack, M. Ask Mr. Bear **E**

Fleischman, P. The animal hedge **E**

Fleming, D. Barnyard banter **E**

Fleming, D. The cow who clucked **E**

Fleming, D. In the tall, tall grass **E**

Fleming, D. Sleepy, oh so sleepy **E**

Fleming, D. Time to sleep **E**

Fox, M. Hello baby! **E**

Fox, M. Wombat divine **E**

Franco, B. Pond circle **E**

Fraser, M. A. Pet shop lullaby **E**

Freedman, C. Gooseberry Goose **E**

Freeman, D. Quiet! there's a canary in the library **E**

Gammell, S. Once upon MacDonald's farm **E**

Gannett, R. S. My father's dragon **Fic**

George, J. C. Morning, noon, and night **E**

Gershator, P. Who's awake in springtime? **E**

Gershator, P. Zoo day olé! **E**

Gerstein, M. Minifred goes to school **E**

Gliori, D. Stormy weather **E**

Goembel, P. Animal fair **E**

Gorbachev, V. Christopher counting **E**

Gorbachev, V. Dragon is coming! **E**

Gorbachev, V. Molly who flew away **E**

Gorbachev, V. Turtle's penguin day **E**

Grabien, D. Dark's tale **Fic**

Grahame, K. The wind in the willows **Fic**

Grahame, K. The wind in the willows [illustrated by Robert R. Ingpen] **Fic**

Grahame, K. The wind in the willows [abridged and illustrated by Inga Moore] **Fic**

Gravett, E. Monkey and me **E**

Griffiths, A. The big fat cow that goes kapow **E**

Griffiths, A. The cat on the mat is flat **E**

Guarino, D. Is your mama a llama? **E**

Hader, B. The big snow **E**

Hale, B. From Russia with lunch **Fic**

Hall, M. My heart is like a zoo **E**

Harris, R. H. Maybe a bear ate it! **E**

Harris, T. The clock struck one **E**

Heap, S. Danny's drawing book **E**

Heller, L. Today is the birthday of the world **E**

Henkes, K. A good day **E**

Hoban, L. Silly Tilly's Thanksgiving dinner **E**

Hoeye, M. Time stops for no mouse **Fic**

Animals—Fiction—*Continued*

Smee, N. Clip-clop   E
Smee, N. What's the matter, Bunny Blue?   E
Smith, D. Two at the zoo   E
Spanyol, J. Little neighbors on Sunnyside Street   E
Spinelli, E. Miss Fox's class goes green   E
Spinelli, E. Silly Tilly   E
Stead, P. C. A sick day for Amos McGee   E
Steig, W. Doctor De Soto   E
Steig, W. The real thief   **Fic**
Stevens, J. Cook-a-doodle-doo!   E
Stevenson, J. Flying feet   E
Stevenson, J. No laughing, no smiling, no giggling   E
Stock, C. A porc in New York   E
Stojic, M. Rain   E
Sturges, P. How do you make a baby smile?   E
Sutton, J. Don't call me Sidney   E
Taback, S. Simms Taback's city animals   E
Taback, S. Simms Taback's Safari animals   E
Tafuri, N. The big storm   E
Tafuri, N. Blue Goose   E
Tafuri, N. The busy little squirrel   E
Tafuri, N. You are special, little one   E
Tankard, J. Me hungry!   E
Tarlow, E. Pinwheel days   E
Teague, M. Funny Farm   E
Tellegen, T. Letters to anyone and everyone   **Fic**
Thomas, J. The doghouse   E
Thomas, J. What will Fat Cat sit on?   E
Thompson, L. Wee little bunny   E
Thompson, L. Wee little chick   E
Thompson, L. Wee little lamb   E
Tidholm, A.-C. Knock! knock!   E
Tierney, F. Lion's lunch?   E
Timmers, L. Who is driving?   E
Tolman, M. The tree house   E
Tryon, L. Albert's birthday   E
Underwood, D. The quiet book   E
Urban, L. Mouse was mad   E
Urbanovic, J. Duck at the door   E
Van Dusen, C. The circus ship   E
Van Laan, N. When winter comes   E
Vestergaard, H. Potty animals   E
Villeneuve, A. The red scarf   E
Voake, S. Daisy Dawson is on her way!   **Fic**
Waldron, K. Mr. Peek and the misunderstanding at the zoo   E
Warnes, T. Daddy hug   E
Weeks, S. Two eggs, please   E
Weller, F. W. The day the animals came   E
Wells, R. Timothy's tales from Hilltop School   E
Wheeler, L. Bubble gum, bubble gum   E
Whybrow, I. The noisy way to bed   E
Wildsmith, B. Jungle party   E
Willans, T. Wait! I want to tell you a story   E
Willems, M. Cat the Cat, who is that?   E
Wilson, K. Bear snores on   E
Wilson, K. Mama always comes home   E
Wilson, K. Where is home, Little Pip?   E

Yang, B. Foo, the flying frog of Washtub Pond   E
Yee, W. H. Detective Small in the amazing banana caper   E
Yolen, J. Off we go!   E
Yolen, J. Sleep, black bear, sleep   E
Zalben, J. B. Baby shower   E
Ziefert, H. A bunny is funny   E

Folklore

See also Dragons; Monsters; Mythical animals

Aardema, V. Rabbit makes a monkey of lion   **398.2**
Aardema, V. Who's in Rabbit's house?   **398.2**
Aardema, V. Why mosquitoes buzz in people's ears   **398.2**
Aylesworth, J. The mitten   **398.2**
Blackstone, S. Storytime   **398.2**
Brett, J. The mitten   **398.2**
Bruchac, J. The great ball game   **398.2**
Casey, D. The great race   **398.2**
Emberley, E. Chicken Little   **398.2**
Forest, H. The little red hen   **398.2**
French, V. Henny Penny   **398.2**
Galdone, P. Henny Penny   **398.2**
Hamilton, V. A ring of tricksters   **398.2**
Kellogg, S. Chicken Little   **398.2**
Kimmel, E. A. Anansi and the moss-covered rock   **398.2**
Leedy, L. There's a frog in my throat   **428**
Lester, J. The tales of Uncle Remus   **398.2**
Lester, J. Uncle Remus, the complete tales   **398.2**
MacDonald, M. R. Bat's big game   **398.2**
Puttapipat, N. The musicians of Bremen   **398.2**
San Souci, R. Sister tricksters   **398.2**
Scott, N. K. The sacred banana leaf   **398.2**
Shannon, G. Rabbit's gift   **398.2**
Thomas, J. C. What's the hurry, Fox?   **398.2**

Food

Jocelyn, M. Eats   E

Graphic novels

Venable, C. A. Hamster and cheese   **741.5**

Habitations

Ashman, L. Castles, caves, and honeycombs   E
Halpern, M. Underground towns, treetops, and other animal hiding places   **591.47**
Hickman, P. M. It's moving day!   **591.56**
Roemer, H. B. Whose nest is this?   **591.56**

Hibernation

See Hibernation

Infancy

See Animal babies

Migration

Kaner, E. Animals migrating   **591.5**
Kant, T. The migration of a whale   **599.5**
Rylant, C. The journey   **591.56**

Pictorial works

See also Animals in art

Poetry

Alarcón, F. X. Animal poems of the Iguazu   **811**

Appalachian Mountains

Folklore

See Folklore—Appalachian Mountains

Appalachian region

Houston, G. My great-aunt Arizona — E
Rylant, C. Appalachia — 974

Fiction

Cleaver, V. Where the lillies bloom — Fic
Hamilton, V. M.C. Higgins, the great — Fic
Henson, H. That Book Woman — E
Houston, G. The year of the perfect Christmas tree — E
Naylor, P. R. Faith, hope, and Ivy June — Fic
Rylant, C. When I was young in the mountains — E
White, R. Belle Prater's boy — Fic

Appelbaum, Susannah

The Hollow Bettle — Fic

Appelt, Kathi, 1954-

Bats around the clock — E
Brand-new baby blues — E
Bubba and Beau, best friends — E
Keeper — Fic
Oh my baby, little one — E
The underneath — Fic

Appetite disorders *See* Eating disorders

Apple, Margot, 1946-

(il) Baehr, P. G. Boo Cow — E
(il) Delton, J. Angel's mother's wedding — Fic
(il) Haas, J. Birthday pony — Fic
(il) Root, P. The name quilt — E
(il) Shaw, N. Sheep in a jeep — E

Apple cider making days. Purmell, A. — E

Apple countdown. Holub, J. — E

The **apple** doll. Kleven, E. — E

Apple farmer Annie. Wellington, M. — E

An **apple** for Harriet Tubman. Turner, G. T. — 92

Apple for the teacher. Yolen, J. — 782.42

Apple is my sign. Riskind, M. — Fic

Apple pie 4th of July. Wong, J. S. — E

An **apple** pie for dinner. VanHecke, S. — E

The **apple** pie that Papa baked. Thompson, L. — E

The **apple** pie tree. Hall, Z. — 634

The **apple-pip** princess. Ray, J. — E

Applegate, K. A. *See* Applegate, Katherine

Applegate, Katherine

The buffalo storm — E
Home of the brave — Fic

Apples

Bulla, C. R. A tree is a plant — 582.16
Esbaum, J. Apples for everyone — 634
Farmer, J. Apples — 634
Ganeri, A. From seed to apple — 583
Gibbons, G. Apples — 634
Hall, Z. The apple pie tree — 634
Landau, E. Apples — 634
Maestro, B. How do apples grow? — 634
Smucker, A. E. Golden delicious — 634
Turner, G. T. An apple for Harriet Tubman — 92

Worth, R. Johnny Appleseed — 92
Yolen, J. Johnny Appleseed — 92
Ziefert, H. One red apple — 634

Fiction

Bunting, E. One green apple — E
Giff, P. R. All the way home — Fic
Holub, J. Apple countdown — E
Hutchins, P. Ten red apples — E
Kleven, E. The apple doll — E
Lipson, E. R. Applesauce season — E
Purmell, A. Apple cider making days — E
Ray, J. The apple-pip princess — E
Thompson, L. The apple pie that Papa baked — E
VanHecke, S. An apple pie for dinner — E
Wellington, M. Apple farmer Annie — E

Apples for everyone. Esbaum, J. — 634

Apples to Oregon. Hopkinson, D. — E

Applesauce season. Lipson, E. R. — E

Appleseed, Johnny, 1774-1845

About

Kellogg, S. Johnny Appleseed — 92
Moses, W. Johnny Appleseed — 92
Worth, R. Johnny Appleseed — 92
Yolen, J. Johnny Appleseed — 92

Appliances, Electric *See* Electric apparatus and appliances

Applied arts *See* Decorative arts

Appomattox Campaign, 1865

Stark, K. Marching to Appomattox — 973.7

Apprentices

Fiction

Cowley, M. The golden bull — Fic
Helgerson, J. Crows & cards — Fic
Higgins, F. E. The Black Book of Secrets — Fic
Nikola-Lisa, W. Magic in the margins — E
Prineas, S. The magic thief — Fic

Approximate computation

Goldstone, B. Great estimations — 519.5
Goldstone, B. Greater estimations — 519.5
Murphy, S. J. Betcha! — 519.5
Murphy, S. J. Coyotes all around — 519.5

April foolishness. Bateman, T. — E

April Fools' Day

Fiction

Bateman, T. April foolishness — E
McMullan, K. Pearl and Wagner: one funny day — E

April's kittens. Newberry, C. T. — E

Apt. 3. Keats, E. J. — E

Apte, Sunita

The Aztec empire — 972
Eating green — 630
India — 954

Aquanauts *See* Underwater exploration

Aquariums

See also Marine aquariums

Bozzo, L. My first fish — 639.34
Buckmaster, M. L. Freshwater fishes — 639.34
Jeffrey, L. S. Fish — 639.34
Murphy, S. J. Room for Ripley — 530.8
Rau, D. M. Top 10 fish for kids — 639.34

Aquariums—*Continued*

Richardson, A. Caring for your fish   **639.34**

Aquatic animals *See* Marine animals

Aquatic birds *See* Water birds

Aquatic plants *See* Marine plants

Arab Americans

Wolf, B. Coming to America   **305.8**

The **Arab-Israeli** conflict. Senker, C.   **956.04**

Arab-Israeli conflicts *See* Israel-Arab conflicts

Arab-Jewish relations *See* Jewish-Arab relations

Arabella Miller's tiny caterpillar. Jarrett, C.   **E**

The **Arabian** nights entertainments   **398.2**

Arabian Peninsula

See also Oman

Arabs

See also Bedouins; Palestinian Arabs

Folklore

The Arabian nights entertainments   **398.2**

MacDonald, M. R. How many donkeys?   **398.2**

Mitchell, S. Genies, meanies, and magic rings   **398.2**

Pullman, P. Aladdin and the enchanted lamp   **398.2**

Vallverdú, J. Aladdin and the magic lamp = Aladino y la lámpara marvillosa   **398.2**

Arachnida *See* Mites; Spiders

Araminta Spookie [series]

Sage, A. My haunted house   **Fic**

The **Arapaho**. Burgan, M.   **978**

Arapaho Indians

Burgan, M. The Arapaho   **978**

See/See also pages in the following book(s):

Ehrlich, A. Wounded Knee: an Indian history of the American West   **970.004**

Arato, Rona

Protists   **579**

Arawak Indians *See* Taino Indians

Arbo, Cris, 1950-

(il) Mortensen, L. In the trees, honeybees!   **595.7**

Arbor Day

Fiction

Galbraith, K. O. Arbor Day square   **E**

Arbor Day square. Galbraith, K. O.   **E**

Arcella, Steve

(il) Sandburg, C. Carl Sandburg   **811**

Archaea. Barker, D. M.   **579.3**

Archaeology *See* Archeology

Archaeology for kids. Panchyk, R.   **930.1**

Archaeopteryx

Zoehfeld, K. W. Did dinosaurs have feathers?   **568**

Archambault, Ariane

(jt. auth) Corbeil, J.-C. My first French English visual dictionary   **443**

(jt. auth) Corbeil, J.-C. My first Spanish English visual dictionary   **463**

Archambault, John

(jt. auth) Martin, B. Barn dance!   **E**

(jt. auth) Martin, B. Chicka chicka boom boom   **E**

(jt. auth) Martin, B. The ghost-eye tree   **E**

(jt. auth) Martin, B. Knots on a counting rope   **E**

Archeological specimens *See* Antiquities

Archeologists

Schlitz, L. A. The hero Schliemann   **92**

Archeology

See also Antiquities; Excavations (Archeology); Prehistoric peoples names of extinct cities; and names of groups of people and of cities (except extinct cities), countries, regions, etc., with the subdivision Antiquities

Aronson, M. If stones could speak   **936**

Clifford, B. Real pirates   **910.4**

Croy, A. Ancient Pueblo   **978**

Deckker, Z. Ancient Rome   **937**

Deem, J. M. Bodies from the bog   **930.1**

Getz, D. Frozen man   **930.1**

Hawass, Z. A. Curse of the pharaohs   **932**

McIntosh, J. Archeology   **930.1**

Panchyk, R. Archaeology for kids   **930.1**

Peterson, J. M. Digging up history   **930.1**

See/See also pages in the following book(s):

Arnold, C. Stone Age farmers beside the sea   **936.1**

Fiction

Barrett, T. On Etruscan time   **Fic**

Rollins, J. Jake Ransom and the Skull King's shadow   **Fic**

Archer, Peggy

From dawn to dreams   **811**

Name that dog!   **811**

Archers, alchemists, and 98 other medieval jobs you might have loved or loathed. Galloway, P.   **940.1**

Archery

Fiction

Lloyd, A. Year of the tiger   **Fic**

Archie and the pirates. Rosenthal, M.   **E**

Archie's war. Williams, M.   **Fic**

Archimedes, ca. 287-212 B.C.

About

Hightower, P. The greatest mathematician [biography of Archimedes]   **92**

Architects

Bodden, V. Frank Gehry   **92**

Rodriguez, R. Building on nature   **92**

Zaunders, B. Gargoyles, girders, & glass houses   **720.9**

Architectural decoration and ornament

Hill, I. Urban animals   **729**

Architectural engineering *See* Building

Architecture

See also Sustainable architecture

Hosack, K. Buildings   **720**

Laroche, G. What's inside   **720**

Macaulay, D. Building big   **720**

Roeder, A. 13 buildings children should know   **720**

Spilsbury, L. Can buildings speak?   **720**

Architecture—*Continued*

Thorne-Thomsen, K. Greene & Greene for kids [biography of Charlie & Henry Greene]
92

Details

See also Woodwork

History

Zaunders, B. Gargoyles, girders, & glass houses
720.9

Architecture, Gothic *See* Gothic architecture

Architecture, Roman *See* Roman architecture

Arctic. Lynch, W. 998

Arctic adventures. Rivera, R. 920

Arctic appetizers. Hooks, G. 577.5

Arctic fox. Person, S. 599.77

Arctic lights, arctic nights. Miller, D. S. 591.4

Arctic regions

Poetry

Spinelli, E. Polar bear, arctic hare 811

Arctic regions

See also North Pole

Arnold, C. Global warming and the dinosaurs
567.9

Baker, S. In the Arctic 971.9

Beattie, O. Buried in ice 998

Foster, K. Atlas of the Poles and Oceans
998

Guiberson, B. Z. Ice bears 599.78

Heuer, K. Being caribou 599.65

Hooks, G. Arctic appetizers 577.5

Kirkpatrick, K. A. Snow baby [biography of Marie Ahnighito Peary] 92

Levy, J. Discovering the Arctic tundra 577.5

Love, A. The kids book of the Far North
998

Lynch, W. Arctic 998

Martin, J. B. The lamp, the ice, and the boat called Fish 998

Scott, E. Poles apart 998

Thomson, S. L. Where do polar bears live?
599.78

Wallace, M. Inuksuk journey 971.9

Wells, R. E. Polar bear, why is your world melting? 363.7

Fiction

Fardell, J. The 7 professors of the Far North
Fic

George, J. C. Julie Fic

George, J. C. Julie of the wolves Fic

George, J. C. Nutik, the wolf pup E

Murphy, Y. Baby Polar E

Taylor, T. Ice drift Fic

Arctic thaw. Lourie, P. 998

Arctic tundra. Tocci, S. 577.5

Ardizzone, Edward, 1900-1979

(il) Estes, E. The Alley Fic

(il) Estes, E. The witch family Fic

Ardley, Neil, 1937-

(jt. auth) Macaulay, D. The new way things work 600

Are we alone? Skurzynski, G. 576.8

Are we there yet, Daddy? Walters, V. E

Are you afraid yet? the science behind scary stuff. O'Meara, S. J. 500

Are you going to be good? Best, C. E

Are you my mother? Eastman, P. D. E

Are you ready for fall? Anderson, S. 508.2

Are you ready for spring? Anderson, S. 508.2

Are you there God?, it's me, Margaret. Blume, J.
Fic

Area, distance, and volume. Sullivan, N. 516

Arellano, Juan Estevan, 1947-

(jt. auth) Lamadrid, E. R. Juan the bear and the water of life 398.2

Arena, Jill

(il) Colato Laínez, R. Playing loteria E

Aretha, David

Sit-ins and freedom rides 323.1

Argent, Kerry, 1960-

(il) Fox, M. Sleepy bears E

(y) Fox, M. Wombat divine E

Argentina

Gofen, E. Argentina 982

Folklore

See Folklore—Argentina

Argueta, Jorge

Moony Luna E

A movie in my pillow 861

Sopa de frijoles = Bean soup 811

Talking with Mother Earth 811

Arid regions

See also Deserts

Arihara, Shino, 1973-

(il) Franco, B. Zero is the leaves on the tree
513

(il) Lord, M. A song for Cambodia [biography of Arn Chorn-Pond] 92

Arithme-tickle. Lewis, J. P. 513

Arithmetic

See also Addition; Fractions; Multiplication; Percentage; Subtraction

Fisher, V. How high can a dinosaur count?
513

Lewis, J. P. Arithme-tickle 513

Markel, M. Tyrannosaurus math 513

Marsico, K. Football 796.332

Marsico, K. Running 796.42

Marsico, K. Speed skating 796.91

Marsico, K. Tennis 796.342

Minden, C. Swimming 797.2

Murphy, S. J. Betcha! 519.5

Murphy, S. J. Less than zero 513

Murphy, S. J. More or less 513

Robinson, E. K. Making cents 332.4

Estimation

See Approximate computation

Arizona

Fiction

Kadohata, C. Weedflower Fic

Arkansas

Fiction

Greene, B. Philip Hall likes me, I reckon maybe
Fic

The **Arnold** Lobel book of Mother Goose
398.8

Arnosky, Jim
All about frogs 597.8
All about sharks 597
Babies in the bayou E
Beachcombing 578.7
The brook book 577.6
Dolphins on the sand E
Gobble it up! E
Grandfather Buffalo E
I'm a turkey! E
Jim Arnosky's All about manatees 599.5
Parrotfish and sunken ships 578.7
The pirates of Crocodile Swamp Fic
Slither and crawl 597.9
Slow down for manatees E
Turtle in the sea E
Watching desert wildlife 591.7
Watching water birds 598
Wild tracks! 590

Aron, Bill
(il) Hoffman, L. A. What you will see inside a
synagogue 296.4

Aronin, Miriam
The ant's nest 595.7
Aye-aye 599.8
The prairie dog's town 599.3

Aronson, Billy
Richard M. Nixon 92
Ulysses S. Grant 92

Aronson, Marc
For boys only 031.02
If stones could speak 936
The world made new 910.4
(jt. auth) Nelson, S. R. Ain't nothing but a man
[biography of John William Henry] 92

Arora Lal, Sunandini
(jt. auth) Seward, P. Netherlands 949.2

Around-the-house history [series]
Lauber, P. What you never knew about beds,
bedrooms, and pajamas 392
Lauber, P. What you never knew about fingers,
forks, & chopsticks 394.1

Around-the-world art & activities. Press, J.
745.5

Around the world cookbook. Dodge, A. J.
641.5

Around the world in a hundred years. Fritz, J.
910.4

Arrasmith, Patrick
(il) Delaney, J. Revenge of the witch Fic
(il) Delaney, J. The Spook's tale and other horrors S C

Arrigan, Mary, 1943-
Mario's Angels E

Arrorró mi niño 398.8

The **arrow** over the door. Bruchac, J. Fic

Arrow to the sun. McDermott, G. 398.2

Arroyo, Sheri L.
How chefs use math 641.5
How crime fighters use math 363.2
How deep sea divers use math 797.2
How race car drivers use math 796.72

Arroz con leche 782.42

Art
See also Children's art; Composition (Art);
Folk art
Henry, S. Making amazing art 745.5
Luxbacher, I. The jumbo book of outdoor art
704.9
Rissman, R. Shapes in art 516
See/See also pages in the following book(s):
Bauer, C. F. Celebrations 808.8

19th century
See also Impressionism (Art)

20th century
Heart to heart 811.008

Encyclopedias
One million things 031

Fiction
Balliett, B. Chasing Vermeer Fic
Brennan-Nelson, D. Willow E
Cottrell Boyce, F. Framed Fic
Daly, N. Bettina Valentino and the Picasso Club
Fic
De Paola, T. The art lesson E
Jordan, S. Mr. and Mrs. Portly and their little
dog Snack E
Runholt, S. The mystery of the third Lucretia
Fic
Spiro, R. Lester Fizz, bubble-gum artist E
Tougas, C. Art's supplies E
Wallace, N. E. Look! look! look! E

History
Ayres, C. Lives of the great artists 709
Children's book of art 709
Raczka, B. Name that style 709
Wenzel, A. 13 artists children should know
709

Museums
See Art museums

Poetry
Behind the museum door 811.008

Study and teaching
Luxbacher, I. The jumbo book of art 702.8

Technique
Fitzgerald, S. What is texture? 701

Art, Abstract *See* Abstract art
Art, African *See* African art
Art, African American *See* African American art
Art, American *See* American art
Art, Asian *See* Asian art
Art, Chinese *See* Chinese art
Art, Egyptian *See* Egyptian art
Art, Greek *See* Greek art
Art, Indian *See* Native American art
Art, Islamic *See* Islamic art
Art, Jewish *See* Jewish art and symbolism
Art, Latin American *See* Latin American art
Art, Mexican *See* Mexican art
Art, Prehistoric *See* Prehistoric art

Art across the ages [series]
Campbell-Hinshaw, K. Ancient Mexico
709.39

Art adventures [series]
Raczka, B. Name that style 709

Art adventures—*Continued*
Raczka, B. The Vermeer interviews
759.9492

Art and music
Lach, W. Can you hear it? **780**

Art appreciation
Bingham, J. Emotion & relationships **704.9**
Bingham, J. Landscape & the environment
704.9
Bingham, J. Science & technology **704.9**
Bingham, J. Society & class **704.9**
Children's book of art **709**
Coyne, J. T. Come look with me: discovering
women artists for children **704**
Cressy, J. Can you find it? **750**
D'Harcourt, C. Masterpieces up close **750**
Guéry, A. Alphab'art **709**
Lane, K. Come look with me: Asian art
709.5
Lane, K. Come look with me: Latin American
art **709.8**
Micklethwait, L. Children **750**
Micklethwait, L. I spy: an alphabet in art **E**
Monet, C. Monet's impressions **759.4**
Museum shapes **E**
Niepold, M. Oooh! Picasso **730.9**
Raczka, B. Action figures **704.9**
Raczka, B. The art of freedom **704.9**
Raczka, B. Artful reading **750**
Raczka, B. More than meets the eye **750**
Raczka, B. No one saw **759.06**
Raczka, B. Unlikely pairs **750**
Raczka, B. The Vermeer interviews
759.9492
Raczka, B. Where in the world? **709**
Raimondo, J. Express yourself! **709.04**
Raimondo, J. Imagine that! **709.04**
Raimondo, J. Make it pop! **709.04**
Raimondo, J. Picture this! **759.05**
Raimondo, J. What's the big idea? **709.04**
Renshaw, A. The art book for children **701**
Renshaw, A. The art book for children: book
two **701**
Richardson, J. Looking at pictures **750.1**
Rolling, J. H., Jr. Come look with me: discover-
ing African American art for children **704**
Sabbeth, C. Monet and the impressionists for
kids **759.05**
Schümann, B. 13 women artists children should
know **709**
Tang, G. Math-terpieces **510**
Thomson, R. Portraits **757**
Wenzel, A. 13 artists children should know
709
Wenzel, A. 13 paintings children should know
750
Wolfe, G. Look! Drawing the line in art
750.1
Wolfe, G. Look! Seeing the light in art
750.1
Fiction
Scieszka, J. Seen Art? **Fic**

Art around the world [series]
Finley, C. The art of African masks **391**
The **art** book for children. Renshaw, A. **701**

The **art** book for children: book two. Renshaw, A.
701
Art dog. Hurd, T. **E**
Art explorers [series]
Raimondo, J. Express yourself! **709.04**
Raimondo, J. Imagine that! **709.04**
Raimondo, J. Make it pop! **709.04**
Raimondo, J. Picture this! **759.05**
Raimondo, J. What's the big idea? **709.04**
Art for kids [series]
Roche, A. Cartooning **741.5**
Temple, K. Drawing **741.2**
Art from her heart: folk artist Clementine Hunter.
Whitehead, K. **92**
Art industries and trade *See* Decorative arts
The **art** lesson. De Paola, T. **E**
Art museums
See also names of individual art museums
Fiction
Bragg, G. Matisse on the loose **Fic**
Konigsburg, E. L. The mysterious edge of the
heroic world **Fic**
Lehman, B. Museum trip **E**
The **art** of African masks. Finley, C. **391**
The **art** of Eric Carle. Carle, E. **741.6**
The **art** of freedom. Raczka, B. **704.9**
The **art** of keeping cool. Lisle, J. T. **Fic**
The **art** of Maurice Sendak. Kushner, T. **741.6**
The **art** of reading **741.6**
The **art** of the catapult. Gurstelle, W. **623.4**
Art on the wall [series]
Spilsbury, R. Pop art **709.04**
Art profiles for kids [series]
Somervill, B. A. Pierre-Auguste Renoir **92**
Art revelations [series]
Ward, E. M. Old Testament women **221.9**
Artell, Mike, 1948-
Funny cartooning for kids **741.5**
Artemis Fowl. Colfer, E. **Fic**
Artemis Fowl: the graphic novel. Colfer, E.
741.5
Artful reading. Raczka, B. **750**
Arthritis
Gray, S. H. Living with juvenile rheumatoid ar-
thritis **616.7**
Arthropoda
Bonotaux, G. Dirty rotten bugs? **595**
Arthur, King
Fiction
Gilman, L. A. Grail quest: the Camelot spell
Fic
Llewellyn, S. The well between the worlds
Fic
Morris, G. The adventures of Sir Lancelot the
Great **Fic**
White, T. H. The sword in the stone **Fic**
Legends
Green, R. L. King Arthur and his Knights of the
Round Table **398.2**
Hodges, M. Merlin and the making of the king
398.2

Ashevak, Kenojuak *See* Kenojuak, 1927-
Ashley Bryan. Bryan, A.   **92**
Ashley Bryan's ABC of African-American poetry
   811.008
Ashley Bryan's African tales, uh-huh. Bryan, A.
   398.2

Ashman, Linda, 1960-
  Babies on the go   **E**
  Castles, caves, and honeycombs   **E**
  Come to the castle!   **940.1**
  Creaky old house   **E**
  M is for mischief   **E**
  Mama's day   **E**
  Stella, unleashed   **E**
  To the beach!   **E**
  When I was king   **E**

Asia
   See also names of individual countries, e.g.
   China
  Law, F. Atlas of Southwest and Central Asia
   950
  Law, F. Atlas of the Far East and Southeast
  Asia   **950**
  Peoples of Western Asia   **950**
    Description and travel
  Markle, S. Animals Marco Polo saw   **92**
    Folklore
   See Folklore—Asia

Asian Americans
  Park, K. Americans from India and other South
  Asian countries   **305.8**
  Wachtel, A. Southeast Asian Americans
   305.8
    Biography
  Sinnott, S. Extraordinary Asian Americans and
  Pacific Islanders   **920**
    Fiction
  Sonnenblick, J. Zen and the art of faking it
   Fic

Asian art
  Lane, K. Come look with me: Asian art
   709.5

Asian arts & crafts for creative kids [series]
  Hosking, W. Asian kites   **629.133**
Asian kites. Hosking, W.   **629.133**
Asia's most amazing animals. Ganeri, A.
   591.9

Asimov, Isaac, 1920-1992
  The life and death of stars   **523.8**
  The Milky Way and other galaxies   **523.1**
Ask Mr. Bear. Flack, M.   **E**
Ask the bones: scary stories from around the
  world. Olson, A. N.   **398.2**
Asking about sex & growing up. Cole, J.
   613.9

Asparagus
    Fiction
  Radunsky, V. The mighty asparagus   **E**

Asperger's syndrome
  Snedden, R. Explaining autism   **616.85**
  Van Niekerk, C. Understanding Sam and
  Asperger Syndrome   **616.85**

    Fiction
  Crowley, S. The very ordered existence of
  Merilee Marvelous   **Fic**
  Dowd, S. The London Eye mystery   **Fic**
  Erskine, K. Mockingbird   **Fic**
  Henson, H. Here's how I see it, here's how it
  is   **Fic**
Assessing learning. Harada, V. H.   **027.8**
**Association for Educational Communications
and Technology**
  American Association of School Librarians. In-
  formation power   **027.8**
**Association for Library Collections and Techni-
cal Services**
  Cataloging correctly for kids. See Cataloging
  correctly for kids   **025.3**
Association for Library Service to Children
  The Newbery and Caldecott awards. See The
  Newbery and Caldecott awards   **028.5**
Associations
   See also Clubs
Astaire, Adele, 1896-1981
    About
  Orgill, R. Footwork [biography of Fred & Adele
  Astaire]   **92**
Astaire, Fred
    About
  Orgill, R. Footwork [biography of Fred & Adele
  Astaire]   **92**
Asterix the Gaul. Goscinny   **741.5**
Asteroids
  Sherman, J. Asteroids, meteors, and comets
   523.4
  Simon, S. Comets, meteors, and asteroids
   523.6
Asteroids, meteors, and comets. Sherman, J.
   523.4
Asthma
  Landau, E. Asthma   **616.2**
  Moore-Mallinos, J. I have asthma   **616.2**
  Robbins, L. How to deal with asthma   **616.2**
  Royston, A. Asthma   **616.2**
  Royston, A. Explaining asthma   **616.2**
  Silverstein, A. The asthma update   **616.2**
    Fiction
  Hurwitz, J. Mostly Monty   **Fic**
The **asthma** update. Silverstein, A.   **616.2**
Aston, Dianna Hutts, 1964-
  An egg is quiet   **591.4**
  Moon over Star   **E**
  Not so tall for six   **E**
  An orange in January   **E**
  A seed is sleepy   **581.4**
Astrobiology. Bortz, A. B.   **576.8**
Astronaut handbook. McCarthy, M.   **629.45**
Astronautics
   See also Space flight
  Aldrin, B. Look to the stars   **629.4**
  Barchers, S. I. Revolution in space   **629.4**
  Bredeson, C. What do astronauts do   **629.45**
  Burleigh, R. One giant leap   **629.45**
  Chaikin, A. Mission control, this is Apollo
   629.45

Atlas of Australia. Foster, K. **994**

Atlas of Europe. Foster, K. **940**

Atlas of North America. Foster, K. **970**

Atlas of South America. Foster, K. **980**

Atlas of Southwest and Central Asia. Law, F. **950**

Atlas of the Poles and Oceans. Foster, K. **998**

Atlas of the universe. Garlick, M. A. **520**

Atlas of the world **912**

Atlases

Adams, S. The most fantastic atlas of the whole wide world by the Brainwaves **912**

Atlas of the world **912**

Beginner's United States atlas **912**

Britannica's student atlas **912**

Goode, J. P. Goode's world atlas **912**

National Geographic beginner's world atlas **912**

National Geographic United States atlas for young explorers **912**

National Geographic world atlas for young explorers **912**

Rubel, D. Scholastic atlas of the United States **912**

Steele, P. Scholastic atlas of the world **912**

Student Atlas **912**

Wilkinson, P. The Kingfisher student atlas **912**

Atlases, Historical *See* Historical atlases

Atmosphere

See also Air; Sky

Cosgrove, B. Weather **551.5**

Gallant, R. A. Atmosphere **551.51**

Atmospheric humidity *See* Humidity

Atocha (Ship) *See* Nuestra Señora de Atocha (Ship)

Atomic Ace. Weigel, J. **E**

Atomic bomb

Allman, T. J. Robert Oppenheimer **92**

Lawton, C. Hiroshima **940.54**

Fiction

Klages, E. The green glass sea **Fic**

Physiological effect

Coerr, E. Sadako [biography of Sadako Sasaki] **92**

Coerr, E. Sadako and the thousand paper cranes [biography of Sadako Sasaki] **92**

Atomic energy *See* Nuclear energy

Atomic power plants *See* Nuclear power plants

Atomic theory

Cregan, E. R. The atom **539.7**

Atomic universe. Jerome, K. B. **539.7**

Atoms

Baxter, R. The particle model of matter **530**

Cregan, E. R. The atom **539.7**

Fox, K. Older than the stars **523.1**

Woodford, C. Atoms and molecules **540**

Atoms and molecules. Woodford, C. **540**

Atonement, Day of *See* Yom Kippur

The **attack** of the frozen woodchucks. Elish, D. **Fic**

Attack of the killer video book. Shulman, M. **778.59**

Attack of the Turtle. Carlson, D. **Fic**

Atteberry, Kevan

(il) Fields, B. W. Lunchbox and the aliens **Fic**

Attention deficit disorder

Capaccio, G. ADD and ADHD **616.85**

Kraus, J. Annie's plan **371.3**

Quinn, P. O. Attention, girls! **616.85**

Robbins, L. How to deal with ADHD **616.85**

Silverstein, A. The ADHD update **616.85**

Taylor, J. F. The survival guide for kids with ADD or ADHD **616.85**

Wood, D. Miss Little's gift **E**

Fiction

Cheaney, J. B. The middle of somewhere **Fic**

Gantos, J. Joey Pigza swallowed the key **Fic**

Attention, girls!. Quinn, P. O. **616.85**

Attica. Kilworth, G. **Fic**

Attila, King of the Huns, d. 453

See/See also pages in the following book(s):

Meltzer, M. Ten kings **920**

Attoe, Steve

(il) Becker, H. What's the big idea? **609**

Atwater, Florence Carroll, 1896-1979

(jt. auth) Atwater, R. T. Mr. Popper's penguins **Fic**

Atwater, Richard Tupper, 1892-1948

Mr. Popper's penguins **Fic**

Auch, Herm

(jt. auth) Auch, M. J. Beauty and the beaks **E**

(il) Auch, M. J. I was a third grade science project **Fic**

(jt. auth) Auch, M. J. The plot chickens **E**

Auch, Mary Jane

Beauty and the beaks **E**

A dog on his own **Fic**

I was a third grade science project **Fic**

Journey to nowhere **Fic**

One-handed catch **Fic**

Peeping Beauty **E**

The plot chickens **E**

Wing nut **Fic**

Auden, Scott

Medical mysteries **610**

Audio cassettes *See* Sound recordings

Audiobooks

Coville, B. William Shakespeare's A midsummer night's dream **822.3**

Audubon, John James, 1785-1851

About

Davies, J. The boy who drew birds: a story of John James Audubon **92**

Fiction

Cole, H. A nest for Celeste **Fic**

August, Louise

(il) Jaffe, N. The way meat loves salt **398.2**

The **August** House book of scary stories
398.2

Augustin, Byron
Andorra 946

Augustyn, Frank
Footnotes 792.8

Ault, Kelly
Let's sign! 419

Aung San Suu Kyi
See/See also pages in the following book(s):
Krull, K. Lives of extraordinary women 920

Aunt Clara Brown. Lowery, L. 92

Aunt Flossie's hats (and crab cakes later). Howard, E. F. E

Aunt Minnie McGranahan. Prigger, M. S. E

Aunt Nancy and the bothersome visitors. Root, P.
S C

Auntie Tiger. Yep, L. E

Aunts
Fiction
Alvarez, J. How Tía Lola came to visit/stay
Fic
Avi. Prairie school Fic
Cates, K. The Secret Remedy Book E
Chen, Y. A gift E
Couloumbis, A. Getting near to baby Fic
Da Costa, D. Hanukkah moon E
Geras, A. Little ballet star E
Grandits, J. The travel game E
Hest, A. Little Chick E
Hole, S. Garmann's summer E
Horstman, L. Squawking Matilda E
House, S. Eli the Good Fic
Howard, E. F. Aunt Flossie's hats (and crab cakes later) E
Kennedy, M. Me and the pumpkin queen
Fic
MacDonald, A. Too much flapdoodle! Fic
MacLachlan, P. Seven kisses in a row Fic
Marsden, C. When heaven fell Fic
Mathews, E. The linden tree Fic
Paros, J. Violet Bing and the Grand House
Fic
Pearson, T. C. Myrtle E
Prigger, M. S. Aunt Minnie McGranahan E
Root, P. Aunt Nancy and the bothersome visitors S C
Tate, E. E. Celeste's Harlem Renaissance
Fic
Waite, M. P. The witches of Dredmoore Hollow
Fic
Weeks, S. Jumping the scratch Fic
Zalben, J. B. Baby shower E

The **Aurora** County All-Stars. Wiles, D. Fic

Austen, Jane, 1775-1817
See/See also pages in the following book(s):
Krull, K. Lives of the writers 920

Austin, Michael
(il) Cummins, J. Sam Patch 92

Austin, Michael, 1965-
(il) Deedy, C. A. Martina the beautiful cockroach 398.2

Australia
Arnold, C. Uluru, Australia's Aboriginal heart
994
Foster, K. Atlas of Australia 994
Gordon, S. Australia 994
Lewin, T. Top to bottom down under 994
Rajendra, V. Australia 994
Rau, D. M. Australia 994
Turner, K. Australia 994
Fiction
Baker, J. Where the forest meets the sea E
Baker, J. Window E
Bateson, C. Being Bee Fic
Bateson, C. Magenta McPhee Fic
Bateson, C. Stranded in Boringsville Fic
Blake, R. J. Little devils E
Chatterton, M. The Brain finds a leg Fic
Cohn, R. The Steps Fic
Fox, M. Hunwick's egg E
Godwin, J. Falling from Grace Fic
Herrick, S. Naked bunyip dancing Fic
Millard, G. The naming of Tishkin Silk Fic
Ormerod, J. Lizzie nonsense E
Roberts, M. Sunny side up Fic
Shields, C. D. Wombat walkabout E
Thomason, M. Moonrunner Fic

Natural history
See Natural history—Australia
Australia, Hawaii, and the Pacific. Underwood, D.
780.9

Australian Aborigines
Folklore
See Aboriginal Australians—Folklore
An **Australian** outback food chain. Wojahn, R. H.
577.5

Austria
Grahame, D. A. Austria 943.6
Sheehan, S. Austria 943.6

Auth, Tony, 1942-
(il) Gannij, J. Topsy-turvy bedtime E
(il) Pinkwater, D. M. The Hoboken chicken emergency Fic

Auth, William Anthony *See* Auth, Tony, 1942-
Author. Lester, H. 92
The **author** event primer. Langemack, C.
021.2

Authors
See also Women authors
Christelow, E. What do authors do? 808
Cotter, C. Born to write 920
Funny business 920
Gillespie, J. T. The Newbery/Printz companion
028.5
Hey! listen to this 028.5
Krull, K. Lives of the writers 920
Langemack, C. The author event primer
021.2
Recycle this book 333.72
Dictionaries
Eighth book of junior authors and illustrators
920.003
Favorite children's authors and illustrators
920.003

Authors—Dictionaries—*Continued*
Ninth book of junior authors and illustrators
920.003
Something about the author **920.003**
Something about the author: autobiography series **920.003**
Tenth book of junior authors and illustrators
920.003

Fiction
Bunting, E. My special day at Third Street School **E**
Howe, J. Bunnicula meets Edgar Allan Crow **Fic**
Klise, K. Dying to meet you **Fic**
Poblocki, D. The stone child **Fic**
Winter, J. The fabulous feud of Gilbert & Sullivan **E**

Authors, African American *See* African American authors

Authors, American
Abrams, D. Gary Soto **92**
Ada, A. F. Under the royal palms **92**
Adler, D. A. A picture book of Harriet Beecher Stowe **92**
Anderson, W. T. Pioneer girl: the story of Laura Ingalls Wilder **92**
Berne, E. C. Laura Ingalls Wilder **92**
Borden, L. The journey that saved Curious George [biography of Margret Rey and H. A. Rey] **92**
Brown, D. American boy: the adventures of Mark Twain **92**
Bryan, A. Ashley Bryan **92**
Cohen, C. D. The Seuss, the whole Seuss, and nothing but the Seuss **92**
Collier, J. L. The Mark Twain you never knew **92**
Crews, D. Bigmama's **92**
De Paola, T. 26 Fairmount Avenue **92**
De Paola, T. Christmas remembered **92**
De Paola, T. For the duration **92**
De Paola, T. Here we all are **92**
De Paola, T. I'm still scared **92**
De Paola, T. On my way **92**
De Paola, T. Things will never be the same **92**
De Paola, T. What a year! **92**
De Paola, T. Why? **92**
Engel, D. Ezra Jack Keats **92**
Fleischman, S. The abracadabra kid **92**
Fleischman, S. The trouble begins at 8 **92**
Fletcher, R. Marshfield dreams **92**
Fritz, J. Harriet Beecher Stowe and the Beecher preachers **92**
George, J. C. A tarantula in my purse **92**
Giff, P. R. Don't tell the girls **92**
Greene, M. Louis Sachar **92**
Harness, C. The literary adventures of Washington Irving **92**
Haskins, J. Toni Morrison **92**
Haugen, H. M. Daniel Handler [biography of Lemony Snicket] **92**
Kehret, P. Five pages a day **92**
Kehret, P. Small steps **92**
Kerley, B. The extraordinary Mark Twain (according to Susy) **92**

Krull, K. The boy on Fairfield Street: how Ted Geisel grew up to become Dr. Seuss **92**
Krull, K. The road to Oz [biography of L. Frank Baum] **92**
Lasky, K. A brilliant streak: the making of Mark Twain **92**
Lowry, L. Looking back **92**
MacLeod, E. Mark Twain **92**
Marcus, L. S. Pass it down **920**
Marcus, L. S. Side by side **070.5**
McDonough, Y. Z. Louisa **92**
McGinty, A. B. Meet Daniel Pinkwater **92**
McGinty, A. B. Meet Jane Yolen **92**
Medina, J. Tomás Rivera **92**
Parker-Rock, M. Alma Flor Ada **92**
Parker-Rock, M. Bruce Coville **92**
Parker-Rock, M. Bruce Hale **92**
Parker-Rock, M. Christopher Paul Curtis **92**
Parker-Rock, M. Jack Gantos **92**
Parker-Rock, M. Joseph Bruchac **92**
Parker-Rock, M. Linda Sue Park **92**
Parker-Rock, M. Patricia and Fredrick McKissack **92**
Parker-Rock, M. Sid Fleischman **92**
Paulsen, G. Caught by the sea **92**
Paulsen, G. How Angel Peterson got his name **92**
Paulsen, G. My life in dog years **92**
Peet, B. Bill Peet: an autobiography **92**
Ray, D. K. Wanda Gag **92**
Reed, J. Paula Danziger **92**
Scieszka, J. Knucklehead [biography of Jon Scieszka] **92**
Seidman, D. Jerry Spinelli **92**
Spinelli, J. Knots in my yo-yo string **92**
Wilder, L. I. A Little House traveler **92**
Wilder, L. I. West from home **92**
Winter, J. Gertrude is Gertrude is Gertrude is Gertrude [biography of Gertude Stein] **92**
Yep, L. The lost garden **92**

Authors, Canadian
Wallner, A. Lucy Maud Montgomery **92**

Authors, Chinese
Demi. Su Dongpo **92**

Authors, Colombian
Brown, M. My name is Gabito: the life of Gabriel Garcia Márquez **92**

Authors, Danish
Varmer, H. Hans Christian Andersen **92**
Yolen, J. The perfect wizard [biography of Hans Christian Andersen] **92**

Authors, English
Burningham, J. John Burningham **92**
Chippendale, L. A. Triumph of the imagination: the story of writer J.K. Rowling **92**
Dahl, R. More about Boy **92**
Harmin, K. L. J. K. Rowling **92**
Rosen, M. Dickens **92**
Winter, J. Beatrix: various episodes from the life of Beatrix Potter **92**

Authors, Mexican
Mora, P. A library for Juana: the world of Sor Juana Inés **92**

Authors, Scottish

Murphy, J. Across America on an emigrant train [biography of Robert Louis Stevenson]   **92**

Yolen, J. Lost boy [biography of J. M. Barrie]
92

Authors, Yiddish

Silverman, E. Sholom's treasure [biography of Sholem Aleichem]   **92**

Authors kids love [series]

Parker-Rock, M. Alma Flor Ada   **92**
Parker-Rock, M. Bruce Coville   **92**
Parker-Rock, M. Bruce Hale   **92**
Parker-Rock, M. Christopher Paul Curtis   **92**
Parker-Rock, M. Jack Gantos   **92**
Parker-Rock, M. Joseph Bruchac   **92**
Parker-Rock, M. Linda Sue Park   **92**
Parker-Rock, M. Patricia and Fredrick McKissack   **92**
Parker-Rock, M. Sid Fleischman   **92**

Authors teens love [series]

Reed, J. Paula Danziger   **92**

Authorship

See also Creative writing; Journalism
Bullard, L. You can write a story!   **808.3**
Christelow, E. What do authors do?   **808**
Fletcher, R. How to write your life story
808
Funny business   **920**
Hamilton, V. Virginia Hamilton: speeches, essays, and conversations   **813.009**
Hershenhorn, E. S is for story   **808.3**
Kerley, B. The extraordinary Mark Twain (according to Susy)   **92**
Leedy, L. Look at my book   **808**
Levine, G. C. Writing magic   **808.3**
Mazer, A. Spilling ink   **808.3**
Otfinoski, S. Extraordinary short story writing
808.3
Stevens, J. From pictures to words   **741.6**
Trueit, T. S. Keeping a journal   **808**
See/See also pages in the following book(s):
Lester, H. Author   **92**
Fiction
Auch, M. J. The plot chickens   **E**
Baskin, N. R. Anything but typical   **Fic**
Bateson, C. Magenta McPhee   **Fic**
Child, L. Clarice Bean spells trouble   **Fic**
Clements, A. The school story   **Fic**
Davis, K. The curse of Addy McMahon   **Fic**
DiSalvo, D. The sloppy copy slipup   **Fic**
Gerstein, M. A book   **E**
Grindley, S. Dear Max   **Fic**
Haddix, M. P. Dexter the tough   **Fic**
Kanninen, B. J. A story with pictures   **E**
Kirk, D. Library mouse   **E**
Kladstrup, K. The book of story beginnings
Fic
MacLachlan, P. Word after word after word
Fic
Muntean, M. Do not open this book!   **E**
Murphy, P. The wild girls   **Fic**
Nicholls, S. Ways to live forever   **Fic**
Paul, A. W. Word builder   **E**
Russell, C. Y. Tofu quilt   **Fic**
Snyder, Z. K. The bronze pen   **Fic**
Spinelli, E. The best story   **E**

Straaten, H. v. Duck's tale   **E**
Sullivan, S. Once upon a baby brother   **E**
Venuti, K. C. Leaving the Bellweathers   **Fic**
Watt, M. Chester   **E**
Handbooks, manuals, etc.
Children's writer's & illustrator's market
808

Autism

Brill, M. T. Autism   **616.85**
Robbins, L. How to deal with autism
616.85
Shapiro, O. Autism and me   **616.85**
Snedden, R. Explaining autism   **616.85**
Fiction
Altman, A. Waiting for Benjamin   **E**
Baskin, N. R. Anything but typical   **Fic**
Choldenko, G. Al Capone does my shirts
Fic
Lord, C. Rules   **Fic**
Robinson Peete, H. My brother Charlie   **E**

Autism and me. Shapiro, O.   **616.85**

Autobiographical graphic novels

Siegel, S. C. To dance   **92**
Telgemeier, R. Smile   **741.5**

Autobiography

Authorship
Fletcher, R. How to write your life story
808

Automania! [series]

Eagen, R. NASCAR   **796.72**

Automata *See* Robots

An **automation** primer for school library media centers and small libraries. Schultz-Jones, B.
027.8

Automobile accidents *See* Traffic accidents

Automobile industry

Mitchell, D. Driven   **92**
Weston, M. Honda [biography of Soichiro Honda]   **92**

Automobile racing

Arroyo, S. L. How race car drivers use math
796.72
Caldwell, D. Speed show   **796.72**
Eagen, R. NASCAR   **796.72**
Egan, E. Hottest race cars   **796.72**
Gigliotti, J. Hottest dragsters and funny cars
796.72
Kelley, K. C. Hottest NASCAR machines
796.72
Rex, M. My race car   **629.228**
Weatherford, C. B. Racing against the odds [biography of Wendell Scott]   **92**
Fiction
Floca, B. The racecar alphabet   **E**
Lord, C. Hot rod hamster   **E**

Automobile travel

Koehler-Pentacoff, E. Jackson and Bud's bumpy ride   **917.3**
Fiction
Cheaney, J. B. The middle of somewhere
Fic
Soup, C. A whole nother story   **Fic**
Walters, V. Are we there yet, Daddy?   **E**
Williams, V. B. Stringbean's trip to the shining sea   **E**

Automobiles

See also Electric automobiles

Clark, W. Cars on the move	629.222
Court, R. How to draw cars and trucks	743
Crowther, R. Cars	629.222
Mitchell, J. S. Crashed, smashed, and mashed	629.222
Rex, M. My race car	629.228
Steggall, S. The life of a car	629.222
Woods, B. Hottest muscle cars	629.222
Woods, B. Hottest sports cars	629.222

Fiction

Barton, B. My car	E
Berger, C. OK go	E
Cottrell Boyce, F. Framed	Fic
D'Aulaire, I. The two cars	E
Drummond, A. Tin Lizzie	E
Hajdusiewicz, B. B. Sputter, sputter, sput!	E
Hubbell, P. Cars	E
Lord, C. Hot rod hamster	E
Peck, R. Here lies the librarian	Fic
Root, P. Toot toot zoom!	E

Folklore

Lyons, M. E. Roy makes a car	398.2

Models

Rigsby, M. Amazing rubber band cars	745.592

Touring

See Automobile travel

Autumn

Anderson, S. Are you ready for fall?	508.2
Gerber, C. Leaf jumpers	E
Hawk, F. Count down to Fall	508.2
Maestro, B. Why do leaves change color?	582.16
Pfeffer, W. We gather together	394.26
Schnur, S. Autumn	E
Schuette, S. L. Let's look at fall	508.2
Smith, S. Fall	508.2

Fiction

Berger, C. The little yellow leaf	E
Brenner, T. And then comes Halloween	E
Emmett, J. Leaf trouble	E
Raczka, B. Who loves the fall?	E
Rawlinson, J. Fletcher and the falling leaves	E
Spinelli, E. I know it's autumn	E
Tafuri, N. The busy little squirrel	E
Ziefert, H. By the light of the harvest moon	E

Poetry

Florian, D. Autumnblings	811

Autumn Street. Lowry, L. — Fic

Autumnblings. Florian, D. — 811

Ava Tree and the wishes three. Betancourt, J. — Fic

Avalanches

Schuh, M. C. Avalanches	551.57

Aver, Kate *See* Avraham, Kate Aver

Averbeck, Jim

In a blue room	E

Avi, 1937-

The barn	Fic
Blue heron	Fic
The Book Without Words	Fic
Crispin: the cross of lead	Fic
Don't you know there's a war on?	Fic
The end of the beginning	Fic
The fighting ground	Fic
Finding Providence: the story of Roger Williams	92
The good dog	Fic
Hard gold	Fic
Iron thunder	Fic
Midnight magic	Fic
Never mind!	Fic
Poppy	Fic
Prairie school	Fic
S.O.R. losers	Fic
The secret school	Fic
The seer of shadows	Fic
Silent movie	E
Strange happenings	S C
Traitor's gate	Fic
The true confessions of Charlotte Doyle	Fic
What do fish have to do with anything? and other stories	S C
(ed) Best shorts. See Best shorts	S C

Aviation *See* Aeronautics

Aviators *See* Air pilots

Avilés Junco, Martha

(il) Kimmel, E. A. The fisherman and the turtle	398.2
(il) McNelly McCormack, C. The fiesta dress	E

Avraham, Kate Aver

What will you be, Sara Mee?	E

Avril, Lynne, 1951-

(il) Giff, P. R. Kidnap at the Catfish Cafe	Fic
(il) Hoberman, M. A. The two sillies	E
(il) Janni, R. Every cowgirl needs a horse	E
(il) Lyon, G. E. The pirate of kindergarten	E
(il) Saltz, G. Amazing you	612.6
(il) Saltz, G. Changing you!	612.6
(il) Stier, C. If I ran for president	324

Awesome animal science projects. Benbow, A. — 590.7

Awful Ogre running wild. Prelutsky, J. — 811

Awful Ogre's awful day. Prelutsky, J. — 811

Axles

De Medeiros, M. Wheels and axles	621.8
Thales, S. Wheels and axles to the rescue	621.8

Axtell, David

(il) We're going on a lion hunt. See We're going on a lion hunt	E

Ayala, Jacqueline

(jt. auth) Alire, C. Serving Latino communities	027.6

Aye-aye (Animal)

Aronin, M. Aye-aye	599.8

Aye-aye. Aronin, M. — 599.8

Aylesworth, Jim, 1943-

The full belly bowl	E
The Gingerbread man	398.2
Goldilocks and the three bears	398.2
Little Bitty Mousie	E

Aylesworth, Jim, 1943-—*Continued*
The mitten | 398.2
Old black fly | E
Our Abe Lincoln | 92
The tale of Tricky Fox | 398.2
Ayliffe, Alex
(il) Mayo, M. Choo choo clickety-clack! | E
(il) Mayo, M. Roar! | E
Ayres, Charlie
Lives of the great artists | 709
Ayres, Katherine
Macaroni boy | Fic
Up, down, and around | E
Ayto, Russell, 1960-
(il) Burgess, M. Where teddy bears come from | E
(il) Cutbill, A. The cow that laid an egg | E
(il) McBratney, S. One voice, please | 398.2
Azarian, Mary
(il) Connor, L. Miss Bridie chose a shovel | E
(il) Martin, J. B. Snowflake Bentley [biography of Wilson Alwyn Bentley] | 92
(il) McGinty, A. B. Darwin | 92
(il) Michelson, R. Tuttle's Red Barn | 630.9
Azerbaijan
King, D. C. Azerbaijan | 947.5
The **Aztec** empire. Apte, S. | 972
The **Aztec** empire. Stein, R. C. | 972
Aztecs
Apte, S. The Aztec empire | 972
Cooke, T. Ancient Aztec | 972
Coulter, L. Ballplayers and bonesetters | 972
Lourie, P. Hidden world of the Aztec | 972
Serrano, F. The poet king of Tezcoco [biography of Nezahualcóyotl] | 92
Sonneborn, L. The ancient Aztecs | 972
Stein, R. C. The Aztec empire | 972
Folklore
Kimmel, E. A. The fisherman and the turtle | 398.2

B

Baasansuren, Bolormaa
My little round house | E
Baba Yaga and Vasilisa the brave. Mayer, M. | 398.2
Babbitt, Natalie
The Devil's storybook | S C
The eyes of the Amaryllis | Fic
Kneeknock Rise | Fic
The search for delicious | Fic
Tuck everlasting | Fic
(il) Worth, V. All the small poems and fourteen more | 811
(il) Worth, V. Peacock and other poems | 811
Babe. King-Smith, D. | Fic
The **Babe** & I. Adler, D. A. | E
Baber, Maxwell
Map basics | 912
Babies *See* Infants
Babies can't eat kimchee!. Patz, N. | E

Babies don't eat pizza. Danzig, D. | 649
Babies in the bayou. Arnosky, J. | E
Babies in the library!. Marino, J. | 027.62
Babies on the go. Ashman, L. | E
Babin, Claire
Gus is a fish | E
Baboons
Fiction
Banks, K. Baboon | E
Baboushka and the three kings. Robbins, R. | 398.2
Babushka's doll. Polacco, P. | E
Babushka's Mother Goose. Polacco, P. | 398.8
Baby animals of the desert. Bredeson, C. | 591.7
Baby animals of the frozen tundra. Bredeson, C. | 591.7
Baby animals of the grasslands. Bredeson, C. | 591.7
Baby animals of the ocean. Bredeson, C. | 591.7
Baby animals of the tropical rain forest. Bredeson, C. | 591.7
Baby animals of the woodland forest. Bredeson, C. | 591.7
Baby Australian animals [series]
Doudna, K. It's a baby kangaroo! | 599.2
Hengel, K. It's a baby Australian fur seal! | 599.79
Baby baby blah blah blah!. Shipton, J. | E
Baby Bear, Baby Bear, what do you see? Martin, B. | E
Baby Bear's books. Yolen, J. | E
Baby Beluga. Raffi | 782.42
Baby Bird's first nest. Asch, F. | E
Baby blessings. Jordan, D. | 242
Baby Brains. James, S. | E
Baby can. Bunting, E. | E
Baby danced the polka. Beaumont, K. | E
Baby Dragon. Ehrlich, A. | E
Baby face. Rylant, C. | 811
The **baby** in the hat. Ahlberg, A. | E
Baby knows best. Henderson, K. | E
The **baby** on the way. English, K. | E
Baby on the way. Sears, W. | 612.6
Baby Polar. Murphy, Y. | E
Baby rhyming time. Ernst, L. L. | 027.62
Baby sea otter. Tatham, B. | 599.7
Baby shoes. Slater, D. | E
Baby shower. Zalben, J. B. | E
The **baby** sister. De Paola, T. | E
The **Baby-sitter's** Club: Kristy's great idea. Martin, A. M. | 741.5
Baby talk. Hindley, J. | E
Baby whales drink milk. Esbensen, B. J. | 599.5
Baby whale's journey. London, J. | E

Bardhan-Quallen, Sudipta—*Continued*
The hog prince | E
Last-minute science fair projects | 507.8
The real monsters | 001.9

Bardoe, Cheryl
Gregor Mendel | 92
Mammoths and mastodons | 569

Bardsley, John, d. 1999
Fiction
Gerstein, M. Sparrow Jack | E

Barefoot. Weisburd, S. | 811
The **Barefoot** book of Buddhist tales. See Chödzin, S. The wisdom of the crows and other Buddhist tales | 294.3
The **Barefoot** book of classic poems | 821.008
The **Barefoot** book of Earth tales. Casey, D. | 398.2

Barger, Jan, 1948-
(il) Ross, K. Crafts for kids who are learning about dinosaurs | 745.5

Bark, George. Feiffer, J. | E

Barker, Dan
Maybe right, maybe wrong | 370.1

Barker, David, 1959-
Compost it | 631.8
Top 50 reasons to care about great apes | 599.8

Barker, David M.
Archaea | 579.3

Barker, M. P., 1960-
A difficult boy | Fic

Barkley, James
(il) Armstrong, W. H. Sounder | Fic

Barlas, Robert
Bahamas | 972.96
Latvia | 947.96
Uganda | 967.61

The **barn**. Avi | Fic

Barn dance!. Martin, B. | E

Barnaby Grimes [series]
Stewart, P. The curse of the night wolf | Fic

Barnard, Alan
(il) Brewster, H. Dinosaurs in your backyard | 567.9
(il) Tanaka, S. New dinos | 567.9

Barnard, Bryn
Outbreak | 614.4
(il) Redmond, S.-R. Tentacles! | 594

Barner, Bob
Bears! bears! bears! | E
Bug safari | E
Dem bones | 612.7
Dinosaurs roar, butterflies soar! | 560
Fish wish | E
Penguins, penguins, everywhere! | 598
(il) Lewis, J. P. Big is big (and little, little) | E

Barnes, Julia, 1955-
Camels and llamas at work | 636.2
Elephants at work | 636.9
Horses at work | 636.1
Pet cats | 636.8
Pet dogs | 636.7
Pet guinea pigs | 636.9
Pet rabbits | 636.9

Barnes, Karen
(il) Berger, M. Why don't haircuts hurt? | 612

Barnett, Ida B. Wells- *See* Wells-Barnett, Ida B., 1862-1931

Barnett, Mac
The case of the case of mistaken identity | Fic
Guess again! | E
Oh no!, or, How my science project destroyed the world | E
(jt. auth) Teplin, S. The clock without a face | Fic

Barnett, Moneta, 1922-1976
(il) Greenfield, E. Sister | Fic

Barnett, Paul, 1949-
See also Grant, John, 1949-

Barnham, Kay
Protect nature | 333.95
Recycle | 363.7
Save energy | 333.79
Save water | 333.91

Barnhart, Norm
Amazing magic tricks: a beginner level | 793.8
Amazing magic tricks: apprentice level | 793.8
Amazing magic tricks: expert level | 793.8
Amazing magic tricks: master level | 793.8

Barnhill, Kelly Regan
Monsters of the deep | 591.7

Barnum, Jay Hyde, d. 1962
(il) Tunis, J. R. The Kid from Tomkinsville | Fic

Barnum, P. T. (Phineas Taylor), 1810-1891
About
Fleming, C. The great and only Barnum | 92
Fiction
Prince, A. J. Twenty-one elephants and still standing | E

Barnum, Phineas Taylor *See* Barnum, P. T. (Phineas Taylor), 1810-1891

Barnyard banter. Fleming, D. | E

Barr, Catherine
Best books for children: preschool through grade 6 | 011.6
Best new media, K-12 | 011.6
(jt. auth) Thomas, R. L. Popular series fiction for K-6 readers | 016.8

Barracca, Debra
The adventures of Taxi Dog | E

Barracca, Sal
(jt. auth) Barracca, D. The adventures of Taxi Dog | E

Barraclough, Sue
Fair play | 175
Honesty | 179
Leadership | 303.3
Reusing things | 363.7
Sharing | 177

Barton, Jill, 1940-—*Continued*
(il) Waddell, M. It's quacking time! E
Barton, Otis
About
Matsen, B. The incredible record-setting deep-sea dive of the bathysphere **551.46**
Barton, Patrice, 1955-
(il) Millard, G. The naming of Tishkin Silk **Fic**
Bartone, Elisa
Peppe the lamplighter E
Bartram, Simon
Bob's best ever friend E
(il) Lewis, J. P. Once upon a tomb **811**
Baruzzi, Agnese
The true story of Little Red Riding Hood E
Bas mitzvah *See* Bat mitzvah
Base, Graeme, 1958-
Enigma **Fic**
Uno's garden E
Baseball
See also Negro leagues; Softball
Bertoletti, J. C. How baseball managers use math **796.357**
Bonnet, R. L. Home run! **530**
Bow, J. Baseball science **796.357**
Buckley, J., Jr. Ultimate guide to baseball **796.357**
Coleman, J. W. Baseball for everyone **796.357**
Cook, S. Hey batta batta swing! **796.357**
Curlee, L. Ballpark **796.357**
Doeden, M. The greatest baseball records **796.357**
Kisseloff, J. Who is baseball's greatest pitcher? **796.357**
Krasner, S. Play ball like the hall of famers **796.357**
Krasner, S. Play ball like the pros **796.357**
McKissack, P. C. Black diamond **796.357**
Nelson, K. We are the ship **796.357**
Smith, C. R. Diamond life **796.357**
Stewart, M. Long ball **796.357**
Teitelbaum, M. Baseball **796.357**
Weatherford, C. B. A Negro league scrapbook **796.357**
See/See also pages in the following book(s):
Bauer, C. F. Celebrations **808.8**
Biography
Adler, D. A. Campy [biography of Roy Campanella] **92**
Adler, D. A. Lou Gehrig **92**
Adler, D. A. A picture book of Jackie Robinson **92**
Adler, D. A. Satchel Paige **92**
Bowen, F. No easy way **92**
Burleigh, R. Stealing home [biography of Jackie Robinson] **92**
Cline-Ransome, L. Satchel Paige **92**
Golenbock, P. Hank Aaron **92**
Golenbock, P. Teammates [biography of Jackie Robinson] **92**
Green, M. Y. A strong right arm: the story of Mamie "Peanut" Johnson **92**
Lipsyte, R. Heroes of baseball **796.357**

Marlin, J. Mickey Mantle **92**
McDonough, Y. Z. Hammerin' Hank [biography of Hank Greenberg] **92**
Needham, T. Albert Pujols **92**
O'Sullivan, R. Jackie Robinson plays ball **92**
Perdomo, W. Clemente! **92**
Robinson, S. Promises to keep: how Jackie Robinson changed America **92**
Robinson, S. Testing the ice: a true story about Jackie Robinson **92**
Tavares, M. Henry Aaron's dream **92**
Viola, K. Lou Gehrig **92**
Winter, J. Roberto Clemente **92**
Winter, J. You never heard of Sandy Koufax!? **92**
Wise, B. Louis Sockalexis **92**
Yolen, J. All-star! [biography of Honus Wagner] **92**
Collectibles
Wong, S. Baseball treasures **796.357**
Fiction
Baggott, J. The Prince of Fenway Park **Fic**
Baseball crazy: ten short stories that cover all the bases **S C**
Bildner, P. Shoeless Joe & Black Betsy E
Burleigh, R. Home run E
Chabon, M. Summerland **Fic**
Cohen, B. Thank you, Jackie Robinson **Fic**
Cooper, F. Willie and the All-Stars E
Corbett, S. Free baseball **Fic**
Corey, S. Players in pigtails E
Coy, J. Top of the order **Fic**
Curtis, G. The bat boy & his violin E
Ellery, A. If I were a jungle animal E
Gratz, A. The Brooklyn nine **Fic**
Green, T. Baseball great **Fic**
Gutman, D. Shoeless Joe & me **Fic**
Haven, P. Two hot dogs with everything **Fic**
Heldring, T. Roy Morelli steps up to the plate **Fic**
Hoff, S. The littlest leaguer E
Hopkinson, D. Girl wonder E
Hurwitz, J. Baseball fever **Fic**
Isadora, R. Max E
Jennings, P. Out standing in my field **Fic**
Johnson, A. Just like Josh Gibson E
Kessler, L. P. Here comes the strikeout E
Lupica, M. The batboy **Fic**
Lupica, M. Heat **Fic**
Michelson, R. Across the alley E
Mochizuki, K. Baseball saved us E
Newman, J. The boys E
Preller, J. Mighty Casey E
Preller, J. Six innings **Fic**
Rappaport, D. Dirt on their skirts E
Roberts, K. Thumb on a diamond **Fic**
Robinson, S. Safe at home **Fic**
Rockliff, M. The case of the stinky socks **Fic**
Slote, A. Finding Buck McHenry **Fic**
Tavares, M. Mudball E
Tocher, T. Bill Pennant, Babe Ruth, and me **Fic**
Tunis, J. R. The Kid from Tomkinsville **Fic**
Uhlberg, M. Dad, Jackie, and me E

Bateman, Teresa—*Continued*

Red, white, blue, and Uncle who? **929.9**

Bates, Amy June

(il) Bryant, J. Abe's fish **E**

(il) DeGross, M. Donavan's double trouble **Fic**

(il) English, K. Speak to me **E**

(il) Hest, A. The dog who belonged to no one **E**

(il) Krull, K. The brothers Kennedy **920**

(il) Meyers, S. Bear in the air **E**

(il) Rodowsky, C. F. The next-door dogs **Fic**

(il) Tinkham, K. Hair for Mama **E**

(il) Tolan, S. S. Wishworks, Inc. **Fic**

(il) Weatherford, C. B. First pooch **973.932**

Bates, Ivan

Five little ducks **782.42**

(il) Bauer, M. D. One brown bunny **E**

(il) Rylant, C. Puppies and piggies **E**

Bates, Katharine Lee, 1859-1929

America the beautiful **E**

Bates, Martin Van Buren, 1837-1919

About

Andreasen, D. The giant of Seville **E**

Bates, Peg Leg, 1907-1998

About

Barasch, L. Knockin' on wood [biography of Peg Leg Bates] **92**

Bateson, Catherine, 1960-

Being Bee **Fic**

Magenta McPhee **Fic**

Stranded in Boringsville **Fic**

Bathrooms

Fiction

Elya, S. M. Oh no, gotta go! **E**

Poetry

Shields, C. D. Someone used my toothbrush! **811**

Baths

Ehrlich, F. Does an elephant take a bath? **E**

Fielding, B. Animal baths **591.5**

Fiction

Andreasen, D. The treasure bath **E**

Babin, C. Gus is a fish **E**

Meister, C. Tiny's bath **E**

Wood, A. King Bidgood's in the bathtub **E**

Bathtub science. Levine, S. **507.8**

Batman (Fictional character)

Cosentino, R. Batman: the story of the Dark Knight **E**

Dahl, M. The man behind the mask **Fic**

Fein, E. My frozen valentine **Fic**

Batman: the story of the Dark Knight. Cosentino, R. **E**

Batmanglij, Najmieh

See/See also pages in the following book(s):

Major, J. S. Caravan to America **920**

Batmanglij, Najmieh, 1947-

Happy Nowruz **641.5**

Bats

Berman, R. Let's look at bats **599.4**

Dornfeld, M. Bats **599.4**

Earle, A. Zipping, zapping, zooming bats **599.4**

Gibbons, G. Bats **599.4**

Gonzales, D. Bats in the dark **599.4**

Lockwood, S. Bats **599.4**

Lunde, D. P. Hello, bumblebee bat **599.4**

Markovics, J. L. The bat's cave **599.4**

Rodriguez, C. Bats **599.4**

Stewart, M. How do bats fly in the dark? **599.4**

Vogel, J. Bats **599.4**

Fiction

Appelt, K. Bats around the clock **E**

Buhler, C. v. But who will bell the cats? **E**

Cannon, J. Stellaluna **E**

Davies, N. Bat loves the night **E**

Holub, J. Bed, bats, and beyond **Fic**

Jarrell, R. The bat-poet **Fic**

Lies, B. Bats at the beach **E**

Oppel, K. Silverwing **Fic**

Waring, G. Oscar and the bat **E**

Folklore

MacDonald, M. R. Bat's big game **398.2**

Bats around the clock. Appelt, K. **E**

Bats at the beach. Lies, B. **E**

Bat's big game. MacDonald, M. R. **398.2**

The **bat's** cave. Markovics, J. L. **599.4**

Bats in the dark. Gonzales, D. **599.4**

Batten, John D. (John Dickson), 1860-1932

(il) Jacobs, J. English fairy tales **398.2**

Batten, Mary

Aliens from Earth **578.6**

Please don't wake the animals **591.5**

Battered children *See* Child abuse

Battered women *See* Abused women

Battering of wives *See* Wife abuse

The **battle** of Iwo Jima. Hama, L. **940.54**

The **Battle** of the Little Bighorn. Uschan, M. V. **973.8**

Battles & weapons: exploring history through art. Chapman, C. **355**

Battling in the Pacific. Beller, S. P. **940.54**

Battut, Eric

The fox and the hen **E**

Bauer, A. C. E.

No castles here **Fic**

Bauer, Caroline Feller, 1935-

Caroline Feller Bauer's new handbook for storytellers **372.6**

Celebrations **808.8**

Leading kids to books through crafts **027.62**

Leading kids to books through magic **027.62**

Leading kids to books through puppets **027.62**

This way to books **028.5**

Bauer, Marion Dane, 1938-

A bear named Trouble **Fic**

The blue ghost **Fic**

The double-digit club **Fic**

The longest night **E**

On my honor **Fic**

One brown bunny **E**

Runt **Fic**

Beaks!. Collard, S. B., III   **598**

Beaks and bills. Higginson, M.   **598**

Beale, Deborah, 1958-
(jt. auth) Williams, T. The dragons of Ordinary Farm   **Fic**

Bealer, Alex W.
Only the names remain   **970.004**

Beam, Matt, 1970-
(il) Schwartz, J. City alphabet   **E**

Bean, Alan
(il) Chaikin, A. Mission control, this is Apollo   **629.45**

Bean, Jonathan, 1979-
At night   **E**
(il) Jonell, L. Emmy and the incredible shrinking rat   **Fic**
(il) Orr, W. Mokie & Bik   **Fic**
(il) Thompson, L. The apple pie that Papa baked   **E**

Bean, Rachel
United Kingdom   **941**

Bean thirteen. McElligott, M.   **E**

Beane, Allan L., 1950-
(jt. auth) Fox, D. Good-bye bully machine   **302.3**

Beans
Ganeri, A. From bean to bean plant   **583**
Rockwell, A. F. One bean   **635**
Fiction
Birtha, B. Lucky beans   **E**

A **bear** called Paddington. Bond, M.   **Fic**

Bear dancer. Wyss, T. H.   **Fic**

Bear dreams. Cooper, E.   **E**

Bear in the air. Meyers, S.   **E**

A **bear** in war. Innes, S.   **E**

The **bear** makers. Cheng, A.   **Fic**

A **bear** named Trouble. Bauer, M. D.   **Fic**

Bear Noel. Dunrea, O.   **E**

Bear rescue. Thomas, K.   **599.78**

Bear snores on. Wilson, K.   **E**

Bearce, Stephanie
All about electric and hybrid cars   **629.222**
How to harness solar power for your home   **621.47**
A kid's guide to container gardening   **635.9**
A kid's guide to making a terrarium   **635.9**

Beard, Darleen Bailey, 1961-
Annie Glover is not a tree lover   **Fic**
Operation Clean Sweep   **Fic**
Twister   **E**

Bearden, Romare, 1914-1988
Fiction
Hartfield, C. Me and Uncle Romie   **E**

Beardshaw, Rosalind
(il) Ditchfield, C. Cowlick!   **E**
(il) Ditchfield, C. Shwatsit!   **E**
(il) McQuinn, A. Lola at the library   **E**

Beardsley, Aubrey, 1872-1898
(il) Green, R. L. King Arthur and his Knights of the Round Table   **398.2**

Bearn, Emily
Tumtum & Nutmeg   **Fic**

Bears
See also Grizzly bear; Polar bear
Baines, R. A den is a bed for a bear   **599.78**
Berman, R. Let's look at brown bears   **599.78**
Guiberson, B. Z. Moon bear   **599.78**
Hirschi, R. Our three bears   **599.78**
Hirschi, R. Searching for grizzlies   **599.78**
Montgomery, S. Search for the golden moon bear   **599.78**
Schwabacher, M. Bears   **599.78**
Swinburne, S. R. Black bear   **599.78**
Thomas, K. Bear rescue   **599.78**
Fiction
Agee, J. Milo's hat trick   **E**
Alborough, J. Where's my teddy?   **E**
Asch, F. Happy birthday, Moon   **E**
Baek, M. J. Panda and polar bear   **E**
Baker, B. One Saturday evening   **E**
Barner, B. Bears! bears! bears!   **E**
Bauer, M. D. A bear named Trouble   **Fic**
Beaty, A. Doctor Ted   **E**
Becker, B. A visitor for Bear   **E**
Bond, M. A bear called Paddington   **Fic**
Braun, S. On our way home   **E**
Bruchac, J. Bearwalker   **Fic**
Bruins, D. The legend of Ninja Cowboy Bear   **E**
Bunting, E. Little Bear's little boat   **E**
Carlstrom, N. W. Jesse Bear, what will you wear?   **E**
Cooper, E. Bear dreams   **E**
Dalgliesh, A. The bears on Hemlock Mountain   **Fic**
Dempsey, K. Me with you   **E**
Dewey, A. Splash!   **E**
Dodd, E. Just like you   **E**
Dunrea, O. Bear Noel   **E**
Duval, K. The Three Bears' Christmas   **E**
Elliott, D. What the grizzly knows   **E**
Foley, G. Thank you Bear   **E**
Fox, M. Sleepy bears   **E**
Gravett, E. Orange pear apple bear   **E**
Harrison, J. Grizzly dad   **E**
Hayes, K. The winter visitors   **E**
Henkes, K. Old Bear   **E**
Hest, A. Kiss good night   **E**
Hest, A. When you meet a bear on Broadway   **E**
Johnson, D. B. Henry hikes to Fitchburg   **E**
Joosse, B. M. Roawr!   **E**
Kempter, C. Wally and Mae   **E**
Kimmel, E. A. The Chanukkah guest   **E**
Kolar, B. Big kicks   **E**
Krauss, R. Bears   **E**
Leist, C. Jack the bear   **E**
Lucas, D. Something to do   **E**
Martin, B. Baby Bear, Baby Bear, what do you see?   **E**
McCloskey, R. Blueberries for Sal   **E**
McPhail, D. M. Big Brown Bear's up and down day   **E**
McPhail, D. M. Drawing lessons from a bear   **E**
McPhail, D. M. Emma in charge   **E**

Bears—Fiction—*Continued*

Miles, V. Old Mother Bear   E
Milne, A. A. The House at Pooh Corner   **Fic**
Milne, A. A. Winnie-the-Pooh   **Fic**
Minarik, E. H. Little Bear   E
Morey, W. Gentle Ben   **Fic**
Morrow, B. O. Mr. Mosquito put on his tuxedo   E
Moss, M. A babysitter for Billy Bear   E
Oldland, N. Big bear hug   E
Parenteau, S. Bears on chairs   E
Paver, M. Wolf brother   **Fic**
Peet, B. Big bad Bruce   E
Pinkwater, D. M. Bear's picture   E
Rodman, M. A. Surprise soup   E
Rogers, G. Midsummer knight   E
Rosen, M. We're going on a bear hunt   E
Schoenherr, I. Don't spill the beans!   E
Seeger, L. V. Dog and Bear: two friends, three stories   E
Silsbe, B. The bears we know   E
Stanley, D. Goldie and the three bears   E
Stein, D. E. Leaves   E
Stewart, A. Bedtime for Button   E
Stewart, J. Addis Berner Bear forgets   E
Teckentrup, B. Big Smelly Bear   E
Tripp, J. Pete & Fremont   **Fic**
Waddell, M. Can't you sleep, Little Bear?   E
Waddell, M. Snow bears   E
Wallace, N. E. Seeds! Seeds! Seeds!   E
Walters, C. Time to sleep, Alfie Bear   E
Ward, L. K. The biggest bear   E
Wells, R. Only you   E
Wilson, K. Bear snores on   E
Wiseman, B. Morris and Boris at the circus   E
Wright, M. Sleep, Big Bear, sleep!   E
Yolen, J. Baby Bear's books   E

Folklore

Aylesworth, J. Goldilocks and the three bears   **398.2**
Barton, B. The three bears   **398.2**
Bruchac, J. How Chipmunk got his stripes   **398.2**
Buehner, C. Goldilocks and the three bears   **398.2**
Chichester-Clark, E. Goldilocks and the three bears   **398.2**
Galdone, P. The three bears   **398.2**
James, E. The woman who married a bear   **398.2**
Lamadrid, E. R. Juan the bear and the water of life   **398.2**
Marshall, J. Goldilocks and the three bears   **398.2**
Sanderson, R. Goldilocks   **398.2**
Spirin, G. Goldilocks and the three bears   **398.2**
Stevens, J. Tops and bottoms   **398.2**
Willey, M. The 3 bears and Goldilocks   **398.2**

Bears (Football team) *See* Chicago Bears (Football team)

Bears! bears! bears!. Barner, B.   E
Bears on chairs. Parenteau, S.   E

The **bears** on Hemlock Mountain. Dalgliesh, A.   **Fic**
Bear's picture. Pinkwater, D. M.   E
The **bears** we know. Silsbe, B.   E
The **Bearskinner**. Schlitz, L. A.   398.2
The **beasts** of Clawstone Castle. Ibbotson, E.   **Fic**
A **beasty** story. Martin, B.   E
The **beatitudes**. Weatherford, C. B.   323.1

Beatles
    Rappaport, D. John's secret dreams [biography of John Lennon]   92

Beaton, Clare, 1947-
    (il) Blackstone, S. Secret seahorse   E
    (il) Gannij, J. Hidden hippo   590

Beatrice doesn't want to. Numeroff, L. J.   E
Beatrix: various episodes from the life of Beatrix Potter. Winter, J.   92

Beattie, Owen
    Buried in ice   998

Beatty, Richard
    (ed) Exploring the world of mammals. See Exploring the world of mammals   599

Beaty, Andrea
    Cicada summer   **Fic**
    Doctor Ted   E
    When giants come to play   E

Beaudoin, Marie-Nathalie
    Responding to the culture of bullying and disrespect   371.5

Beaufort, Sir Francis, 1774-1857
About
    Malone, P. Close to the wind   551.51

Beaumont, Karen
    Baby danced the polka   E
    Doggone dogs!   E
    Duck, duck, goose!   E
    I ain't gonna paint no more!   E
    Move over, Rover   E
    Who ate all the cookie dough?   E

Beautiful ballerina. Nelson, M.   792.8
Beautiful beads. Ross, K.   745.58
Beautiful blackbird. Bryan, A.   398.2
The **beautiful** Christmas tree. Zolotow, C.   E
A **beautiful** girl. Schwartz, A.   E
The **beautiful** stories of life. Rylant, C.   292
Beautiful warrior. McCully, E. A.   E
Beauty and the beaks. Auch, M. J.   E
Beauty and the beast. Brett, J.   398.2
Beauty and the beast. Eilenberg, M.   398.2
Beauty and the beast = La bella y la bestia. Ros, R.   398.2
Beauty, her basket. Belton, S.   E
The **Beauty** of the beast   811.008
Beauty shops
Fiction
    Choung, E.-H. Minji's salon   E
    Schotter, R. Mama, I'll give you the world   E
    Wells, R. Ruby's beauty shop   E

Beaver is lost. Cooper, E.   **E**

Beavers
Kalman, B. The life cycle of a beaver
    599.3
Mara, W. Beavers   **599.3**
Reingold, A. The beaver's lodge   **599.3**
Fiction
Cooper, E. Beaver is lost   **E**
Harper, C. M. When Randolph turned rotten
    E
Folklore
Bruchac, J. Turtle's race with Beaver   **398.2**

The **beaver's** lodge. Reingold, A.   **599.3**

Bebé goes shopping. Elya, S. M.   **E**

Bebop Express. Panahi, H. L.   **E**

Because of Winn-Dixie. DiCamillo, K.   **Fic**

Because of you. Hennessy, B. G.   **E**

Becca at sea. Baker, D. F.   **Fic**

Beccia, Carlyn
The raucous royals   **920**

Bechtold, Lisze
Sally and the purple socks   **E**

Beck, Andrea, 1956-
Pierre Le Poof!   **E**
(il) Beck, C. Buttercup's lovely day   **811**

Beck, Carolyn
Buttercup's lovely day   **811**

Beck, Ian
The secret history of Tom Trueheart   **Fic**

Beck, Scott
Monster sleepover!   **E**

Becker, Bonny
Holbrook   **Fic**
The magical Ms. Plum   **Fic**
A visitor for Bear   **E**

Becker, Helaine
Magic up your sleeve   **793.8**
Science on the loose   **507.8**
What's the big idea?   **609**

Becker, John E., 1942-
Wild cats: past & present   **599.75**

Becker, Paula, 1958-
(il) MacGregor, C. Think for yourself   **170**

Becker, Suzy
Manny's cows   **E**

The **beckoning** cat. Nishizuka, K.   **398.2**

Becoming a citizen. Hamilton, J.   **323.6**

Becoming butterflies. Rockwell, A. F.   **595.7**

Becoming Naomi León. Ryan, P. M.   **Fic**

Bed, bats, and beyond. Holub, J.   **Fic**

Bed-knob and broomstick. Norton, M.   **Fic**

Beddows, Eric, 1951-
(il) Fleischman, P. I am phoenix: poems for two
voices   **811**
(il) Fleischman, P. Joyful noise: poems for two
voices   **811**

Bedford, David, 1969-
The way I love you   **E**

Bednar, Sylvie
Flags of the world   **929.9**

Bedouins
Fiction
La Fevers, R. L. Flight of the phoenix   **Fic**

Beds
Fiction
Bergstein, R. M. Your own big bed   **E**
McGhee, A. Bye-bye, crib   **E**
Root, P. Creak! said the bed   **E**

Bedtime
Fiction
Adams, D. I can do it myself!   **E**
Adler, D. A. It's time to sleep, it's time to
dream   **E**
Averbeck, J. In a blue room   **E**
Bang, M. Ten, nine, eight   **E**
Banks, K. And if the moon could talk   **E**
Bass, L. G. Boom boom go away!   **E**
Bluemle, E. Dogs on the bed   **E**
Bogan, P. Goodnight Lulu   **E**
Braun, S. Back to bed, Ed!   **E**
Brown, M. W. Goodnight moon   **E**
Butler, J. Bedtime in the jungle   **E**
Cooper, E. A good night walk   **E**
Crow, K. Bedtime at the swamp   **E**
Daddo, A. Goodnight, me   **E**
Dewdney, A. Llama, llama red pajama   **E**
Dodds, D. A. The prince won't go to bed   **E**
Dunbar, J. The monster who ate darkness   **E**
Edwards, P. D. While the world is sleeping
    E
Emberley, E. Go away, big green monster!
    E
Fancher, L. Star climbing   **E**
Fenton, J. What's under the bed?   **E**
Fleming, D. Sleepy, oh so sleepy   **E**
Fletcher, R. The Sandman   **E**
Ford, C. Ocean's child   **E**
Fox, M. Sleepy bears   **E**
Fox, M. Where the giant sleeps   **E**
Fraser, M. A. Pet shop lullaby   **E**
Gannij, J. Topsy-turvy bedtime   **E**
Geisert, A. Lights out   **E**
Gershator, P. Who's awake in springtime?   **E**
Gliori, D. Stormy weather   **E**
Harris, R. H. Maybe a bear ate it!   **E**
Hemingway, E. Bump in the night   **E**
Hest, A. Kiss good night   **E**
Hoban, R. Bedtime for Frances   **E**
Holub, J. Bed, bats, and beyond   **Fic**
Howland, N. Princess says goodnight   **E**
Isadora, R. Peekaboo bedtime   **E**
Kanevsky, P. Sleepy boy   **E**
Kloske, G. Once upon a time, the end   **E**
Kono, E. E. Hula lullaby   **E**
Landry, L. Space boy   **E**
Lewis, K. Good night, Harry   **E**
Lum, K. What! cried Granny   **E**
Mack, J. Hush little polar bear   **E**
Manning, M. Kitchen dance   **E**
Markes, J. Shhhhh! Everybody's sleeping   **E**
Marlow, L. Hurry up and slow down   **E**
Morales, Y. Little Night   **E**
Mortensen, D. D. Good night engines   **E**
Numeroff, L. J. When sheep sleep   **E**
Paul, A. W. Snail's good night   **E**
Pow, T. Tell me one thing, Dad   **E**

Belpré, Pura
Fiction
González, L. M. The storyteller's candle   E

Belton, Sandra, 1939-
Beauty, her basket   E
The tallest tree   Fic

Bemelmans, Ludwig, 1898-1962
Madeline   E

Ben-Ami, Doron
(il) Byars, B. C. Tornado   Fic

Ben and me. Lawson, R.   Fic

Ben and the Emancipation Proclamation. Sherman, P.   E

Ben Franklin's almanac. Fleming, C.   92

Ben over night. Ellis, S.   E

Ben-Zvi, Rebecca Tova *See* O'Connell, Rebecca, 1968-

Benbow, Ann
Awesome animal science projects   590.7
Lively plant science projects   580.7
Sprouting seed science projects   580.7

Benchley, Nathaniel, 1915-1981
A ghost named Fred   E

Benchmark all stars [series]
Bradley, M. Lance Armstrong   92

Benchmark rebus. Creepy critters [series]
Trueit, T. S. Ants   595.7
Trueit, T. S. Beetles   595.7
Trueit, T. S. Caterpillars   595.7
Trueit, T. S. Grasshoppers   595.7
Trueit, T. S. Spiders   595.4
Trueit, T. S. Worms   592

Benchmark rockets. Animals [series]
Greenberg, D. A. Chimpanzees   599.8
Greenberg, D. A. Whales   599.5

Bendall-Brunello, John
(il) Braun, T. My goose Betsy   E
(il) Wargin, K.-J. Moose on the loose   E

Bender, Lionel
Explaining blindness   617.7
Explaining epilepsy   616.8
Invention   609

Bender, Robert
(il) Hall, K. Ribbit riddles   793.73

Benduhn, Tea
Ethanol and other new fuels   662
Nuclear power   621.48
Oil, gas, and coal   665.5
Solar power   621.47
Water power   621.31
What is color?   701
What is shape?   701
Wind power   621.31

Beneath the streets of Boston. McKendry, J.   625.4

Benedict, of Nursia, Saint *See* Benedict, Saint, Abbot of Monte Cassino

Benedict, Saint, Abbot of Monte Cassino
About
Norris, K. The holy twins: Benedict and Scholastica   92

Benedictus, David, 1938-
Return to the Hundred Acre Wood   Fic

Beneduce, Ann
Jack and the beanstalk   398.2

Benin
Kneib, M. Benin   966.83

Benioff, Carol
(il) Lamstein, S. A big night for salamanders   E

Benjamin (Biblical figure)
About
Jules, J. Benjamin and the silver goblet   222

Benjamin and the silver goblet. Jules, J.   222

Benjamin Franklin, American genius. Miller, B. M.   92

Benjamin Pratt and the Keepers of the School [series]
Clements, A. We the children   Fic

Bennett, Belva Ann *See* Lockwood, Belva Ann, 1830-1917

Bennett, Erin Susanne
(il) Stroud, B. The patchwork path   E

Bennett, Kelly
Dad and Pop   E
Your daddy was just like you   E

Bennett, Nneka
(il) Lasky, K. Vision of beauty: the story of Sarah Breedlove Walker   92

Bennett, Richard, 1899-
(il) Farshtey, G. Bionicle #1: rise of the Toa Nuva   741.5

Benno and the Night of Broken Glass. Wiviott, M.   E

Benny, Mike, 1964-
(il) Grimes, N. Oh, brother!   E
(il) Whelan, G. The listeners   E

Benny and Omar. Colfer, E.   Fic

Benny and Penny in just pretend. Hayes, G.   741.5

Benoit, Renné, 1977-
(il) Barclay, J. Proud as a peacock, brave as a lion   E

Ben's dream. Van Allsburg, C.   E

Ben's trumpet. Isadora, R.   E

Benson, Kathleen, 1947-
(jt. auth) Haskins, J. Africa   967
(jt. auth) Haskins, J. John Lewis in the lead   92
(jt. auth) Haskins, J. The rise of Jim Crow   305.8

Benson, Patrick, 1956-
(il) Waddell, M. Owl babies   E
(il) Wise, W. Christopher Mouse   Fic

Bentley, Jonathan
(il) Wild, M. The little crooked house   E

Bentley, Wilson Alwyn, 1865-1931
About
Martin, J. B. Snowflake Bentley [biography of Wilson Alwyn Bentley]   92

Benton, Gail, 1950-
Ready-to-go storytimes   027.62

Benton, Mike
The Kingfisher dinosaur encyclopedia   567.9

Beowulf
　Morpurgo, M. Beowulf　　　　　398.2
　Rumford, J. Beowulf　　　　　　398.2
　　　　　　Graphic novels
　Storrie, P. D. Beowulf　　　　　741.5
Beowulf. Storrie, P. D.　　　　741.5
Bereal, JaeMe
　(il) Schroeder, A. In her hands　　92
Bereavement
　Brown, L. K. When dinosaurs die　155.9
　Krementz, J. How it feels when a parent dies
　　　　　　　　　　　　　　　155.9
　Murphy, P. J. Death　　　　　　155.9
　　　　　　　Fiction
　Angle, K. G. Hummingbird　　　　Fic
　Banerjee, A. Looking for Bapu　　Fic
　Beaty, A. Cicada summer　　　　　Fic
　Bley, A. And what comes after a thousand?
　　　　　　　　　　　　　　　　E
　Brallier, J. M. Tess's tree　　　　E
　Brisson, P. I remember Miss Perry　E
　Charles, V. M. The birdman　　　E
　Cochran, B. The forever dog　　　E
　Cohen, M. Jim's dog Muffins　　　E
　Cotten, C. Fair has nothing to do with it
　　　　　　　　　　　　　　　　Fic
　Crowe, C. Turtle girl　　　　　　E
　Davis, K. The curse of Addy McMahon　Fic
　De Guzman, M. Henrietta Hornbuckle's circus
　　of life　　　　　　　　　　　Fic
　Demas, C. Saying goodbye to Lulu　E
　Doyle, R. Her mother's face　　　E
　Edwards, M. Papa's latkes　　　　E
　Erskine, K. Mockingbird　　　　　Fic
　Going, K. L. The garden of Eve　　Fic
　Graff, L. Umbrella summer　　　　Fic
　Hemingway, E. M. Road to Tater Hill　Fic
　Henkes, K. Bird Lake moon　　　　Fic
　Jeffers, O. The heart and the bottle　E
　Kennedy, M. Me and the pumpkin queen
　　　　　　　　　　　　　　　　Fic
　Kuhlman, E. The last invisible boy　Fic
　LaFleur, S. M. Love, Aubrey　　　Fic
　Lopez, D. Confetti girl　　　　　Fic
　Mathews, E. The linden tree　　　Fic
　Nuzum, K. A. The leanin' dog　　　Fic
　Potter, E. Slob　　　　　　　　　Fic
　Ransom, C. F. Finding Day's Bottom　Fic
　Roberts, W. D. The one left behind　Fic
　Rosen, M. Michael Rosen's sad book　E
　Tilly, M. Porcupine　　　　　　　Fic
　Tolan, S. S. Listen!　　　　　　　Fic
　　　　　　　Poetry
　Smith, H. A. Mother poems　　　　811
Berenzy, Alix, 1957-
　Sammy the classroom guinea pig　　E
　(il) Guiberson, B. Z. Into the sea　597.92
Berg, Elizabeth, 1953-
　Senegal　　　　　　　　　　　966.3
Berg, Michelle
　(il) Sidman, J. Meow ruff　　　　811
Bergen, David
　Life-size dinosaurs　　　　　　　567.9
Berger, Barbara, 1945-
　All the way to Lhasa　　　　　　398.2

Berger, Carin
　Forever friends　　　　　　　　　E
　The little yellow leaf　　　　　　E
　OK go　　　　　　　　　　　　E
　(il) Prelutsky, J. Behold the bold umbrellaphant
　　　　　　　　　　　　　　　811
Berger, Gilda
　(jt. auth) Berger, M. How do flies walk upside
　　down?　　　　　　　　　　　595.7
　(jt. auth) Berger, M. Penguins swim but don't
　　get wet　　　　　　　　　　591.7
　(jt. auth) Berger, M. The real Vikings　948
　(jt. auth) Berger, M. Why don't haircuts hurt?
　　　　　　　　　　　　　　　612
Berger, Joe, 1970-
　Bridget Fidget and the most perfect pet!　E
Berger, Lou
　The elephant wish　　　　　　　E
Berger, Melvin, 1927-
　Chirping crickets　　　　　　　595.7
　Germs make me sick!　　　　　　616.9
　How do flies walk upside down?　595.7
　Look out for turtles!　　　　　　597.92
　Penguins swim but don't get wet　591.7
　The real Vikings　　　　　　　　948
　Spinning spiders　　　　　　　　595.4
　Switch on, switch off　　　　　　537
　Why don't haircuts hurt?　　　　612
　Why I sneeze, shiver, hiccup, and yawn
　　　　　　　　　　　　　　　612.7
Berger, Samantha, 1969-
　Martha doesn't say sorry!　　　　E
Bergin, Joseph III
　(il) Sava, S. C. Hyperactive　　　741.5
Bergin, Mark
　(il) Adams, S. The Kingfisher atlas of explora-
　　tion & empires　　　　　　　911
　(il) Kant, T. The migration of a whale
　　　　　　　　　　　　　　　599.5
Bergman, Mara
　Snip snap!　　　　　　　　　　E
　Yum yum! What fun!　　　　　　E
Bergren, Lisa Tawn
　God found us you　　　　　　　E
Bergstein, Rita M.
　Your own big bed　　　　　　　E
Bergum, Constance Rummel, 1952-
　(il) Stewart, M. Under the snow　591.7
　(il) Stewart, M. When rain falls　591.7
Berk, Ariel
　Secret history of mermaids and creatures of the
　　deep　　　　　　　　　　　398
Berkeley, Jon
　The hidden boy　　　　　　　　Fic
　The Palace of Laughter　　　　　Fic
　(il) Harper, J. Uh-oh, Cleo　　　Fic
Berkenkamp, Lauri
　See also Anderson, Maxine
　Discover the Amazon　　　　　　981
Berkes, Marianne Collins, 1939-
　Over in the jungle　　　　　　　E
Berkowitz, Jacob
　Jurassic poop　　　　　　　　　567.9
　Out of this world　　　　　　　576.8

Berlin, Eric
The puzzling world of Winston Breen   **Fic**

Berlin (Germany)
  History—Blockade, 1948-1949
  Tunnell, M. O. Candy bomber [biography of Gail Halvorsen]   **92**

Berman, Len
The greatest moments in sports   **796**

Berman, Rachel
(il) Beiser, T. Bradley McGogg, the very fine frog   **E**

Berman, Ruth, 1958-
Let's look at bats   **599.4**
Let's look at brown bears   **599.78**

Bermuda
Karwoski, G. Miracle   **972.9**

Bernadette and the lunch bunch. Glickman, S.   **Fic**

Bernadorne, Francis *See* Francis, of Assisi, Saint, 1182-1226

Bernardin, James, 1966-
(il) Kimmel, E. A. A horn for Louis [biography of Louis Armstrong]   **92**
(il) Kinsey-Warnock, N. Lumber camp library   **Fic**
(il) Numeroff, L. J. Would I trade my parents?   **E**

Bernay, Emma *See* Berne, Emma Carlson

Berne, Emma Carlson
Laura Ingalls Wilder   **92**

Berne, Jennifer
Manfish: a story of Jacques Cousteau   **92**

Berner, Rotraut Susanne, 1948-
Definitely not for little ones   **398.2**
In the town all year 'round   **E**

Berner, Susanne *See* Berner, Rotraut Susanne, 1948-

Bernheimer, Kate
The girl in the castle inside the museum   **E**

Bernier-Grand, Carmen T.
César   **811**

Bernstein, Zena
(il) O'Brien, R. C. Mrs. Frisby and the rats of NIMH   **Fic**

Berries
  See also Strawberries
Gibbons, G. The berry book   **634**
  Fiction
Degen, B. Jamberry   **E**
Sloat, T. Berry magic   **E**

Berry, Holly, 1952-
(il) Manushkin, F. How Mama brought the spring   **E**
(il) Rascol, S. I. The impudent rooster   **398.2**
(il) Stanley, D. Roughing it on the Oregon Trail   **Fic**
(il) Weeks, S. Woof   **E**

Berry, Lynne
Duck skates   **E**

Berry, Matt
Up on Daddy's shoulders   **E**

The **berry** book. Gibbons, G.   **634**

Berry magic. Sloat, T.   **E**

Berryhill, Shane
Chance Fortune and the Outlaws   **Fic**

Bersani, Shennen
(jt. auth) Pallotta, J. Ocean counting   **E**

Berthod, Anne
(jt. auth) Ali, R. Slumgirl dreaming [biography of Rubina Ali]   **92**

Bertholf, Bret
Long gone lonesome history of country music   **781.642**

Bertoletti, John C.
How baseball managers use math   **796.357**
How fashion designers use math   **746.9**

Bertrand, Lynne
Granite baby   **E**

Beryl. Simmons, J.   **Fic**

Beshore, George W.
Science in ancient China   **509**

Bessie Smith and the night riders. Stauffacher, S.   **E**

Best, Cari, 1951-
Are you going to be good?   **E**
Easy as pie   **E**
Goose's story   **E**
Sally Jean, the Bicycle Queen   **E**
Shrinking Violet   **E**
Three cheers for Catherine the Great!   **E**
What's so bad about being an only child?   **E**

The **best** bad luck I ever had. Levine, K.   **Fic**

The **best** beekeeper of Lalibela. Kessler, C.   **E**

Best best friends. Chodos-Irvine, M.   **E**

The **best** birthday parties ever!. Ross, K.   **793.2**

Best books
Adventuring with books   **011.6**
Barr, C. Best books for children: preschool through grade 6   **011.6**
Barstow, B. Beyond picture books   **011.6**
Freeman, J. Books kids will sit still for 3   **011.6**
Helbig, A. Dictionary of American children's fiction, 1995-1999   **028.5**
Notable social studies trade books for young people   **016.3**
Outstanding science trade books for students K-12   **016.5**
Pearl, N. Book crush   **028.5**
Silvey, A. 100 best books for children   **011.6**
What do children and young adults read next?   **016.8**
Zbaracki, M. D. Best books for boys   **028.5**

Best books for boys. Zbaracki, M. D.   **028.5**

Best books for children: preschool through grade 6. Barr, C.   **011.6**

Best buds. Eaton, M., III   **E**

The **best** cat in the world. Newman, L.   **E**

The **best** children's books of the year   **016.3**

The **best** Christmas pageant ever. Robinson, B.   **Fic**

The **best** Eid ever. Mobin-Uddin, A.   **E**

The **best** family in the world. López, S.   E

Best friend on wheels. Shirley, D.   E

Best friends. Kellogg, S.   E

Best friends. Wilson, J.   Fic

Best friends forever. Patt, B.   Fic

The **best** gift of all. Emmett, J.   E

Best holiday books [series]
MacMillan, D. M. Diwali—Hindu festival of lights   394.26
MacMillan, D. M. Ramadan and Id al-Fitr   297.3

The **best** horse ever. DeLaCroix, A.   Fic

The **best** nest. Mueller, D. L.   398.2

Best new media, K-12. Barr, C.   011.6

The **best** of times. Tang, G.   513

The **best** place. Meddaugh, S.   E

Best practices for school library media professionals [series]
Farmer, L. S. J. Collaborating with administrators and educational support staff   027.8
Hart, T. L. The school library media facilities planner   027.8

The **best** seat in second grade. Kenah, K.   E

Best shorts   S C

The **best** story. Spinelli, E.   E

Bestiaries
Baynes, P. Questionable creatures   398.2

Betancourt, Jeanne, 1941-
Ava Tree and the wishes three   Fic
My name is brain Brian   Fic

Betcha!. Murphy, S. J.   519.5

Bethune, Mary Jane McLeod, 1875-1955
See/See also pages in the following book(s):
Colman, P. Adventurous women   920
Pinkney, A. D. Let it shine   920

Betsy B. Little. McEvoy, A.   E

Betsy-Tacy. Lovelace, M. H.   Fic

Bettina Valentino and the Picasso Club. Daly, N.   Fic

Betting *See* Gambling

Bettoli, Delana
(il) Cotten, C. This is the stable   E

Between earth & sky. Bruchac, J.   398.2

Between heaven and earth. Norman, H.   398.2

Beverages
See also Tea

Bevis, Mary Elizabeth, 1939-
Wolf song   E

Beware, take care. Moore, L.   811

Beyl, Charles
(il) Kraus, J. Annie's plan   371.3

Beyond Old MacDonald. Hoce, C.   811

Beyond picture books. Barstow, B.   011.6

Beyond Pluto. Landau, E.   523.4

Beyond the Deepwoods. Stewart, P.   Fic

Beyond the dinosaurs. Brown, C. L.   560

Beyond the great mountains. Young, E.   811

Beyond the ridge. Goble, P.   Fic

Beyond The Spiderwick Chronicles [series]
DiTerlizzi, T. The Nixie's song   Fic

Beyond the station lies the sea. Richter, J.   Fic

The **BFG**. Dahl, R.   Fic

Bhargava, Neirah
(il) Jani, M. What you will see inside a Hindu temple   294.5

Bhatia, Mohini Kaur
(jt. auth) Hawker, F. Sikhism in India   294.6

Bhushan, Rahul
(il) Arnold, C. Taj Mahal   954

Bi-racial people *See* Racially mixed people

Bial, Raymond
Amish home   289.7
Ellis Island   325.73
Ghost towns of the American West   978
A handful of dirt   577.5
Nauvoo   289.3
The strength of these arms   326
The super soybean   633.3
Tenement   974.7
The Underground Railroad   326
Where Washington walked   92

Biamonte, Edward
(il) Harrison, D. L. Cave detectives   560

Bianco, Margery Williams, 1881-1944
The velveteen rabbit   Fic

Bias crimes *See* Hate crimes

Bible

Natural history
. Animals of the Bible   220.8

Bible. O.T. Genesis
Fischer, C. In the beginning: the art of Genesis   222

Bible. O.T. Psalms
Delval, M.-H. Psalms for young children   223
Lindbergh, R. On morning wings   223
Moser, B. Psalm 23   223

Bible. N.T.
Jesus   232.9

Bible. O.T. Ecclesiastes
To every thing there is a season   223

Bible
The Bible: Authorized King James Version   220.5
The Holy Bible [New Revised Standard Version]   220.5

Bible (as subject)
Brown, A. The Bible and Christianity   220
Feiler, B. S. Walking the Bible   222

The **Bible** and Christianity. Brown, A.   220

The **Bible** for children from Good Books. Watts, M.   220.9

Bible stories. Tomie dePaola's book of Bible stories   220.9
Brown, L. The Children's illustrated Jewish Bible   220.9
Chaikin, M. Angels sweep the desert floor   296.1
Fischer, C. In the beginning: the art of Genesis   222
Graham, L. B. How God fix Jonah   398.2

Big Jabe. Nolen, J. — E
Big kicks. Kolar, B. — E
Big Little Monkey. Schaefer, C. L. — E
Big Momma makes the world. Root, P. — E
Big Nate. Peirce, L. — Fic
A **big** night for salamanders. Lamstein, S. — E
Big or little? Stinson, K. — E
Big Pig and Little Pig. McPhail, D. M. — E
Big plans. Shea, B. — E
Big red barn. Brown, M. W. — E
Big red drawing book, Ed Emberley's. Emberley, E. — 741.2
Big red lollipop. Khan, R. — E
Big rig bugs. Cyrus, K. — E
Big sister now. Sheldon, A. — 306.8
Big Smelly Bear. Teckentrup, B. — E
The **big** snow. Hader, B. — E
The **big** splash. Ferraiolo, J. D. — Fic
The **big** storm. Tafuri, N. — E
Big talk. Fleischman, P. — 811
Big tracks, little tracks. Selsam, M. E. — 590
Big wheels. Rockwell, A. F. — E
Big Wolf & Little Wolf. Brun-Cosme, N. — E
Big words for little people. Curtis, J. L. — E
Bigda, Diane
  (il) Park, L. S. Mung-mung! — 413
Bigger, Better, BEST!. Murphy, S. J. — 516
The **biggest** bear. Ward, L. K. — E
The **biggest** parade. Winthrop, E. — E
The **biggest** soap. Schaefer, C. L. — E
Biggest, strongest, fastest. Jenkins, S. — 590
The **biggest** test in the universe. Poydar, N. — E
Biggs, Brian
  (il) Brunelle, L. Camp out! — 796.54
  (il) Draanen, W. v. Shredderman: Secret identity — Fic
  (il) Nix, G. One beastly beast — S C
  (il) Rylant, C. Brownie & Pearl step out — E
Bigmama's. Crews, D. — 92
Bigotry *See* Toleration
Bikes on the move. Clark, W. — 629.227
Bildner, Phil
  The greatest game ever played — E
  The Hallelujah Flight — E
  Shoeless Joe & Black Betsy — E
  Turkey Bowl — E
Bileck, Marvin, 1920-
  (jt. auth) Scheer, J. Rain makes applesauce — E
Bilingual books
English-Chinese
Keister, D. To grandmother's house — 951
English-Hmong
Gerdner, L. Grandfather's story cloth — E
English-Japanese
Carle, E. Where are you going? To see my friend! — E
Lee-Tai, A. A place where sunflowers grow — E

English-Spanish
Acosta Gonzalez, A. Mayte and the Bogeyman — E
Ada, A. F. Gathering the sun — 811
Ada, A. F. Merry Navidad! — 394.26
Alarcón, F. X. Animal poems of the Iguazu — 811
Alarcón, F. X. From the bellybutton of the moon and other summer poems — 811
Alarcón, F. X. Iguanas in the snow and other winter poems — 811
Alarcón, F. X. Poems to dream together — 811
Anaya, R. A. The first tortilla — Fic
Ancona, G. The piñata maker: El piñatero — 745.594
Argueta, J. Moony Luna — E
Argueta, J. A movie in my pillow — 861
Argueta, J. Sopa de frijoles = Bean soup — 811
Argueta, J. Talking with Mother Earth — 811
Arrorró mi niño — 398.8
Arroz con leche — 782.42
Brown, M. My name is Gabito: the life of Gabriel Garcia Márquez — 92
Brown, M. Pele, king of soccer — 92
Cárdenas, T. Oloyou — 398.2
Carrasco, X. Rumpelstiltskin — 398.2
Chapra, M. Sparky's bark — E
Colato Laínez, R. Playing loteria — E
Cool salsa — 811.008
Cruz, A. The woman who outshone the sun — 398.2
Cumpiano, I. Quinito's neighborhood — E
De colores = Bright with colors — 782.42
De colores and other Latin-American folk songs for children — 782.42
Diez deditos. Ten little fingers & other play rhymes and action songs from Latin America — 782.42
Dorros, A. Radio Man. Don Radio — E
Ehlert, L. Cuckoo. Cucú — 398.2
Ehlert, L. Moon rope. Un lazo a la luna — 398.2
Elya, S. M. Eight animals on the town — E
Fiestas: a year of Latin American songs of celebration — 782.42
Garza, C. L. Family pictures — 306.8
Garza, C. L. In my family — 306.8
Garza, X. Juan and the Chupacabras — E
Garza, X. Lucha libre: the Man in the Silver Mask — Fic
González, L. M. The storyteller's candle — E
Gonzalez, M. C. I know the river loves me — E
Gonzalez, M. C. My colors, my world = Mis colores, mi mundo — E
González, R. Antonio's card — E
Guy, G. F. Fiesta! — E
Guy, G. F. Perros! Perros! Dogs! Dogs! — E
Guy, G. F. Siesta — E
Hayes, J. Dance, Nana, dance — 398.2
Hayes, J. Little Gold Star — 398.2
Herrera, J. F. Laughing out loud, I fly — 811
Herrera, J. F. The upside down boy — 92
Hinojosa, T. Cada niño/Every child — 782.42
Howard, R. The big, big wall — E

Bird houses *See* Birdhouses

Bird Lake moon. Henkes, K.   **Fic**

Bird song *See* Birdsongs

Bird songs. Franco, B.   **E**

Bird watching
    Thompson, B., III. The young birder's guide to birds of eastern North America   **598**
        Fiction
    Yee, W. H. Mouse and Mole, fine feathered friends   **E**

Bird Woman *See* Sacagawea, b. 1786

Birdhouses
    Schwarz, R. Birdhouses   **690**
        Fiction
    Wellington, M. Riki's birdhouse   **E**

Birdie's big-girl shoes. Rim, S.   **E**

Birdie's lighthouse. Hopkinson, D.   **Fic**

The **birdman**. Charles, V. M.   **E**

Birds
    See also Cage birds; Finches; State birds; Woodpeckers
    Bishop, N. Digging for bird-dinosaurs   **567.9**
    Burnie, D. Bird   **598**
    Collard, S. B., III. Beaks!   **598**
    Davies, J. The boy who drew birds: a story of John James Audubon   **92**
    Holub, J. Why do birds sing?   **598**
    Jeffrey, L. S. Birds   **636.6**
    Kenyon, L. Rainforest bird rescue   **598**
    Lessem, D. Feathered dinosaurs   **567.9**
    MacLeod, E. Monster fliers   **567.9**
    Prap, L. Dinosaurs?!   **567.9**
    Rodriguez, A. M. Secret of the puking penguins . . . and more!   **591.4**
    Sloan, C. How dinosaurs took flight   **567.9**
    Solway, A. Eagles and other birds   **598**
    Stewart, M. A place for birds   **598**
    Thompson, B., III. The young birder's guide to birds of eastern North America   **598**
    Webb, S. Looking for seabirds   **598**
    Zoehfeld, K. W. Did dinosaurs have feathers?   **568**

        Eggs and nests
    See Birds—Nests
        Encyclopedias
    Birds of the world   **598**
        Fiction
    Asch, F. Baby Bird's first nest   **E**
    Auch, M. J. Wing nut   **Fic**
    Baker, K. Just how long can a long string be!?   **E**
    Berger, C. Forever friends   **E**
    Bruel, N. Little red bird   **E**
    Charles, V. M. The birdman   **E**
    De Paola, T. The song of Francis   **E**
    Eastman, P. D. Are you my mother?   **E**
    Edwards, P. D. Jack and Jill's treehouse   **E**
    Ehlert, L. Feathers for lunch   **E**
    Eitzen, R. Tara's flight   **E**
    Fleming, C. Seven hungry babies   **E**
    Franco, B. Bird songs   **E**
    Gerstein, M. Leaving the nest   **E**
    Graham, B. How to heal a broken wing   **E**
    Gravett, E. The odd egg   **E**

Henkes, K. Birds   **E**
Hills, T. How Rocket learned to read   **E**
Lionni, L. Inch by inch   **E**
Loizeaux, W. Wings   **Fic**
Long, E. Bird & Birdie in a fine day   **E**
Lucas, D. The robot and the bluebird   **E**
McDonnell, P. South   **E**
Melmed, L. K. Hurry! Hurry! Have you heard?   **E**
Melvin, A. Counting birds   **E**
Napoli, D. J. Albert   **E**
Palatini, M. Gorgonzola   **E**
Paulsen, G. The amazing life of birds   **Fic**
Pennypacker, S. Sparrow girl   **E**
Prévert, J. How to paint the portrait of a bird   **E**
Prosek, J. Bird, butterfly, eel   **E**
Reed, L. R. Basil's birds   **E**
Rohmann, E. Time flies   **E**
Saltzberg, B. Stanley and the class pet   **E**
Tafuri, N. Whose chick are you?   **E**
Tankard, J. Grumpy Bird   **E**
Valckx, C. Lizette's green sock   **E**
Wellington, M. Riki's birdhouse   **E**
Wolf-Morgenlander, K. Ragtag   **Fic**
Yee, W. H. Mouse and Mole, fine feathered friends   **E**
Yorinks, A. Hey, Al   **E**
Young, E. Hook   **E**

        Flight
Arnold, C. Birds   **598**
See/See also pages in the following book(s):
Bishop, N. The secrets of animal flight   **591.47**

        Folklore
Bryan, A. Beautiful blackbird   **398.2**
Climo, S. Tuko and the birds   **398.2**
Mueller, D. L. The best nest   **398.2**
Norman, H. Between heaven and earth   **398.2**
Polacco, P. Luba and the wren   **398.2**
Spirin, G. The tale of the Firebird   **398.2**
        Migration
Hiscock, B. Ookpik   **598**
Vogel, C. G. The man who flies with birds   **598**
Willis, N. C. Red knot   **598**
        Migration—Fiction
Cuffe-Perez, M. Skylar   **Fic**
Lobel, G. Moonshadow's journey   **E**
        Nests
Bash, B. Urban roosts: where birds nest in the city   **598**
Bond, R. In the belly of an ox: the unexpected photographic adventures of Richard and Cherry Kearton   **92**
Kelly, I. Even an ostrich needs a nest   **598**
Mueller, D. L. The best nest   **398.2**
Roemer, H. B. Whose nest is this?   **591.56**
        Photography
See Photography of birds
        Poetry
Fleischman, P. I am phoenix: poems for two voices   **811**
Rosen, M. J. The cuckoo's haiku   **811**

Bisallion, Josée
(il) Wiviott, M. Benno and the Night of Broken Glass   **E**

Biscuit's new trick. Capucilli, A.   **E**

Bishop, Gavin, 1946-
(il) Cowley, J. Snake and Lizard   **Fic**

Bishop, Kay, 1942-
The collection program in schools   **027.8**

Bishop, Nic, 1955-
Digging for bird-dinosaurs   **567.9**
Nic Bishop butterflies and moths   **595.7**
Nic Bishop frogs   **597.8**
Nic Bishop marsupials   **599.2**
The secrets of animal flight   **591.47**
Spiders   **595.4**
(il) Cowley, J. Chameleon chameleon   **597.95**
(il) Cowley, J. Red-eyed tree frog   **E**
(il) Jackson, E. B. Looking for life in the universe   **576.8**
(il) Jackson, E. B. The mysterious universe   **523.8**
(il) Montgomery, S. Kakapo rescue   **639.9**
(il) Montgomery, S. Quest for the tree kangaroo   **599.2**
(il) Montgomery, S. Saving the ghost of the mountain   **599.75**
(il) Montgomery, S. The snake scientist   **597.96**
(il) Montgomery, S. The tarantula scientist   **595.4**

Bishop, Rudine Sims, 1937-
Free within ourselves   **028.5**

BishopRoby, Joshua
Animal kingdom   **590**

Bison
Bruchac, J. Buffalo song [biography of Walking Coyote]   **92**
Caper, W. American bison   **599.64**
Freedman, R. Buffalo hunt   **970.004**
George, J. C. The buffalo are back   **599.64**
Marrin, A. Saving the buffalo   **599.64**
Patent, D. H. The buffalo and the Indians   **978**
Perry, P. J. Buffalo   **599.64**
    Fiction
Arnosky, J. Grandfather Buffalo   **E**
Baker, O. Where the buffaloes begin   **Fic**
Fern, T. E. Buffalo music   **E**
    Folklore
Goble, P. Buffalo woman   **398.2**

Biswas, Pulak, 1941-
(jt. auth) Ravishankar, A. Tiger on a tree   **E**

Bites and stings
Landau, E. Bites and stings   **617.1**

Bittle. MacLachlan, P.   **E**

Bix, Cynthia Overbeck
(jt. auth) Rauzon, M. J. Water, water everywhere   **551.48**

Bizarre dinosaurs. Sloan, C.   **567.9**

Bjorklund, Ruth
Cerebral palsy   **616.8**
Cystic fibrosis   **616.3**
Eating disorders   **616.85**
Epilepsy   **616.8**

Food-borne illnesses   **615.9**
The Hopi   **970.004**
Lizards   **639.3**
Rabbits   **636.9**
Venus   **523.4**

Björkman, Steve
(il) Cochran, B. My parents are divorced, my elbows have nicknames, and other facts about me   **E**
(il) Cox, J. Puppy power   **Fic**
(il) Murphy, S. J. Coyotes all around   **519.5**
(il) Murphy, S. J. The Grizzly Gazette   **513**
(il) Murphy, S. J. Safari Park   **512**
(il) Murphy, S. J. Same old horse   **E**
(il) Post, P. Emily Post's table manners for kids   **395**
(jt. auth) Post, P. Emily's everyday manners   **395**
(il) Wallace, C. One nosy pup   **E**
(il) Wallace, C. The Santa secret   **E**

Black, Angela
(jt. auth) Sheehan, S. Jamaica   **972.92**

Black, Ann N.
Readers theatre for middle school boys   **812**

Black, Holly, 1971-
(jt. auth) DiTerlizzi, T. The Nixie's song   **Fic**

Black, Michael Ian
Chicken cheeks   **E**
The purple kangaroo   **E**

Black
Johnson, D. Black magic   **E**

Black Americans *See* African Americans

The **Black** Americans   **305.8**

Black and white. Macaulay, D.   **E**

Black art (Magic) *See* Witchcraft

Black authors
    See also African American authors

Black authors and illustrators of books for children and young adults. Murphy, B. T.   **920.003**

Black authors and illustrators of children's books. See Murphy, B. T. Black authors and illustrators of books for children and young adults   **920.003**

Black bear. Swinburne, S. R.   **599.78**

Black Beauty. Sewell, A.   **Fic**

The **black** book of colors. Cottin, M.   **E**

The **Black** Book of Secrets. Higgins, F. E.   **Fic**

The **Black** Canary. Curry, J. L.   **Fic**

Black cat. Myers, C.   **E**

Black cowboy, wild horses. Lester, J.   **E**

Black death *See* Plague

The **Black** Death. Ollhoff, J.   **616.9**

Black diamond. McKissack, P. C.   **796.357**

Black Elk, 1863-1950
    About
Nelson, S. D. Black Elk's vision   **92**

Black Elk's vision. Nelson, S. D.   **92**

The **Black** experience in children's books
016.3058

Black hands, white sails. McKissack, P. C.
639.2

Black history in the pages of children's literature. Casement, R. **028.5**

Black holes (Astronomy)
Jackson, E. B. The mysterious universe
523.8
Rau, D. M. Black holes **523.8**
Solway, A. What's inside a black hole?
523.1

Black is brown is tan. Adoff, A. **E**

Black Jack. Smith, C. R. **92**

Black literature (American) See American literature—African American authors

Black magic (Witchcraft) See Magic

Black magic. Johnson, D. **E**

Black music
See also African American music

Black musicians
See also African American musicians

Black on white. Hoban, T. **E**

Black Panther Party
Fiction.
Williams-Garcia, R. One crazy summer **Fic**

The **black** pearl. O'Dell, S. **Fic**

Black pearls. Hawes, L. **S C**

Black poetry (American) See American poetry—African American authors

The **Black** soldier. Clinton, C. **355**

The **Black** Stallion. Farley, W. **Fic**

Black stars [series]
Wilkinson, B. S. African American women writers **810.9**

Black stars in a white night sky. Lawson, J.
811

Black? white! day? night!. Seeger, L. V. **E**

Black women of the Old West. Katz, W. L.
978

Blackaby, Susan
Cleopatra **92**
Nest, nook & cranny **811**

Blackall, Sophie
(il) Barrows, A. Ivy + Bean **Fic**
(jt. auth) Best, C. What's so bad about being an only child? **E**
(il) Bridges, S. Y. Ruby's wish **E**
(il) Khan, R. Big red lollipop **E**
(il) Noyes, D. Red butterfly **E**
(il) Rosoff, M. Jumpy Jack and Googily **E**
(il) Rosoff, M. Meet wild boars **E**
(il) Shields, C. D. Wombat walkabout **E**

Blackbeard, 1680?-1718
Poetry
Lewis, J. P. Blackbeard, the pirate king **811**

Blackbeard, the pirate king. Lewis, J. P. **811**

Blackburn, G. Meredith
(comp) Index to poetry for children and young people. See Index to poetry for children and young people **808.81**

Blackburn, Lorraine A.
(comp) Index to poetry for children and young people. See Index to poetry for children and young people **808.81**

The **blacker** the berry. Thomas, J. C. **811**

Blackford, Harriet
Elephant's story **E**
Tiger's story **E**

Blacklock, Dyan, 1951-
The Roman Army **937**

Blacks
Bibliography
The Black experience in children's books
016.3058
Biography
See also African Americans—Biography
Rockwell, A. F. Open the door to liberty!: a biography of Toussaint L'Ouverture **92**
Fiction
Medearis, A. S. Seven spools of thread **E**
Poetry
Dawes, K. S. N. I saw your face **811**
United States
See African Americans

Blacks in art
See also African Americans in art

Blacks in literature
See also African Americans in literature

Blackstone, Stella
My granny went to market **E**
Octopus opposites **E**
Secret seahorse **E**
Storytime **398.2**

Blackwater. Bunting, E. **Fic**

Blackwater Ben. Durbin, W. **Fic**

Blackwood, Freya
(il) Doyle, R. Her mother's face **E**
(il) Gleeson, L. Half a world away **E**

Blackwood, Gary L.
Debatable deaths **920**
Enigmatic events **904**
The just-so woman **E**
Legends or lies? **398.2**
Mysterious messages **652**
Second sight **Fic**
The Shakespeare stealer **Fic**

Blair, Chris, 1968-
(il) Clements, A. Room one **Fic**

Blake, Francis
(il) Andrews, J. Stories at the door **398.2**

Blake, Quentin, 1932-
(il) Dahl, R. The BFG **Fic**
(il) Dahl, R. Charlie and the chocolate factory
Fic
(il) Dahl, R. The enormous crocodile **Fic**
(il) Dahl, R. The magic finger **Fic**
(il) Dahl, R. Matilda **Fic**
(il) Fleischman, S. Here comes McBroom!
Fic
(il) Morpurgo, M. On angel wings **Fic**
(il) Rosen, M. Michael Rosen's sad book **E**
(il) Walliams, D. The boy in the dress **Fic**
(il) Yeoman, J. The wild washerwomen **E**

Blake, Robert J.
Little devils — E
Togo — E

Blake, Stephanie
I don't want to go to school! — E

Blakemore, Catherine
Faraway places — 011.6

Blakley Kinsler, Gwen, 1947-
Crocheting — 746.43

Blanchette, Peg, 1949-
12 easy knitting projects — 746.43

Bland, Nick
(il) Trewin, T. I lost my kisses — E

Blankets
Fiction
Bynum, J. Kiki's blankie — E
Cote, N. Jackson's blanket — E
Ford, B. No more blanket for Lambkin — E
Henkes, K. Owen — E
Keller, H. Geraldine's blanket — E
Wolff, F. The story blanket — E

Blashfield, Jean F.
England — 942

Blass, Rosanne J., 1937-
Celebrate with books — 028.1

Blauer, Ettagale
Mali — 966.2
Mauritania — 966.1

Blauweiss, Stephen
(jt. auth) Steiner, J. Look-alikes around the world — 793.73

Blaxland, Beth
Centipedes, millipedes, and their relatives — 595.6
Crabs, crayfishes, and their relatives — 595.3
Octopuses, squids, and their relatives — 594
Sea stars, sea urchins, and their relatives — 593.9
Snails, clams, and their relatives — 594

Blaxland, Wendy
Basketballs — 688.7
Guitars — 787.87
Helmets — 621.9
Sneakers — 685
Sweaters — 746.9

Blecha, Aaron
(il) Bolger, K. Zombiekins — Fic

Bleck, Linda
(il) A children's treasury of poems. See A children's treasury of poems — 808.81
(il) Pfeffer, W. The longest day — 394.26
(il) Pfeffer, W. A new beginning — 394.26
(il) Pfeffer, W. We gather together — 394.26

Bledsoe, Karen E., 1962-
Chinese New Year crafts — 745.594
Genetically engineered foods — 664

Bledsoe, Lucy Jane
Cougar canyon — Fic
How to survive in Antarctica — 998

Blegvad, Erik
(il) Borden, L. Sea clocks — 526
(il) Kendall, C. The Gammage Cup — Fic
(il) Norton, M. Bed-knob and broomstick — Fic

(il) Viorst, J. The tenth good thing about Barney — E

Blériot, Louis, 1872-1936
About
Provensen, A. The glorious flight: across the Channel with Louis Blériot, July 25, 1909 — 92

Blessed Virgin Mary, Saint See Mary, Blessed Virgin, Saint

Blessen, Karen
(il) Gilley, J. Peace one day — 303.6

Blessing, Charlotte
New old shoes — E

The **blessing** of the beasts. Pochocki, E. — E

Bley, Anette
And what comes after a thousand? — E

Blia Xiong
Nine-in-one, Grr! Grr! — 398.2

Bligh, William, 1754-1817
About
O'Brien, P. The mutiny on the Bounty — 910.4

Blind
Alexander, S. H. She touched the world: Laura Bridgman, deaf-blind pioneer — 92
Bender, L. Explaining blindness — 617.7
Cline-Ransome, L. Helen Keller — 92
Delano, M. F. Helen's eyes — 92
Garrett, L. Helen Keller — 92
Lawlor, L. Helen Keller: rebellious spirit — 92
Sullivan, G. Helen Keller — 92
Tingle, T. Saltypie — 92
Troupe, Q. Little Stevie Wonder — 92
Books and reading
Adler, D. A. A picture book of Louis Braille — 92
Freedman, R. Out of darkness: the story of Louis Braille — 92
Jeffrey, L. S. All about Braille — 411
Fiction
Cole, B. H. Anna & Natalie — E
Cottin, M. The black book of colors — E
Keats, E. J. Apt. 3 — E
Kinsey-Warnock, N. Lumber camp library — Fic
Kurtz, J. The storyteller's beads — Fic
Martin, B. Knots on a counting rope — E
Taylor, T. The cay — Fic
Taylor, T. Timothy of the cay — Fic
Taylor, T. The trouble with Tuck — Fic
Thomson, S. L. The sound of colors — E

Blind, Dogs for the See Guide dogs

Blind mountain. Thomas, J. R. — Fic

Bliss, Corinne Demas See Demas, Corinne, 1947-

Bliss, Harry
Luke on the loose — 741.5
(jt. auth) Cronin, D. Diary of a spider — E
(il) Cronin, D. Diary of a worm — E
(il) McGhee, A. Mrs. Watson wants your teeth — E
(il) McGhee, A. A very brave witch — E

Bliss, Harry, 1964-
(il) Cronin, D. Diary of a fly — E
(il) DiCamillo, K. Louise — E

Blitt, Barry
(jt. auth) Kloske, G. Once upon a time, the end
                                              E
(il) Wilson, K. What's the weather inside?
                                            811
The **blizzard**. Wright, B. R.   E
Blizzards
Stewart, M. Blizzards and winter storms
                                      551.55
Fiction
Clifford, E. Help! I'm a prisoner in the library
                                      Fic
Hurst, C. O. Terrible storm   E
Steig, W. Brave Irene   E
Blizzards and winter storms. Stewart, M.
                                      551.55
Blobaum, Cindy, 1966-
Geology rocks!   **551**
Insectigation!   **595.7**
Bloch, Serge
Butterflies in my stomach and other school hazards   E
(il) Cali, D. The enemy   E
(il) Lewis, J. P. The underwear salesman
                                      811
(il) Morgenstern, S. H. A book of coupons
                                      Fic
Block, Francesca Lia
House of dolls   Fic
Block, Ira
(il) Lange, K. E. 1607   975.5
Block city. Stevenson, R. L.   E
Blockhead. D'Agnese, J.   92
Blogs See Weblogs
Blomgren, Jennifer, 1954-
Where do I sleep?   E
Blood
Showers, P. A drop of blood   612.1
Circulation
See also Cardiovascular system
Corcoran, M. K. The circulatory story   612.1
Yount, L. William Harvey   92
Diseases
See also Leukemia
Blood moon rider. Waters, Z. C.   Fic
Blood on the river. Carbone, E. L.   Fic
Bloom, Suzanne, 1950-
A mighty fine time machine   E
A splendid friend, indeed   E
(il) Bunting, E. Girls A to Z   E
(il) Bunting, E. My special day at Third Street School   E
Bloom!. Lieshout, M. v.   E
Bloomability. Creech, S.   Fic
Bloomfield, Jill
Jewish holidays cookbook   641.5
Blos, Joan W., 1928-
A gathering of days: a New England girl's journal, 1830-32   Fic
Letters from the corrugated castle   Fic

Blough, Paula
(jt. auth) Dixon, T. The sound of storytime
                                      027.62
Blowers, Helene
Weaving a library Web   025.04
Blue, Rose
Ron's big mission   E
(jt. auth) Naden, C. J. James Monroe   92
Blue. Hostetter, J.   Fic
Blue 2. Carter, D. A.   E
The **blue** book on information age inquiry, instruction and literacy. Callison, D.   028.7
Blue collar workers *See* Working class
A **blue-eyed** daisy. Rylant, C.   Fic
The **Blue** fairy book   398.2
The **blue** ghost. Bauer, M. D.   Fic
Blue Goose. Tafuri, N.   E
Blue heron. Avi   Fic
Blue jasmine. Sheth, K.   Fic
Blue like Friday. Parkinson, S.   Fic
Blue lipstick. Grandits, J.   811
Blue Moo. Boynton, S.   782.42
Blue potatoes, orange tomatoes. Creasy, R.
                                      635
Blue Ridge Mountains region
Fiction
McDowell, M. T. Carolina Harmony   Fic
The **blue** shoe. Townley, R.   Fic
Blue whales up close. Rake, J. S.   599.5
Blue willow. Gates, D.   Fic
Blue zoo guides [series]
Phillips, D. Mammals   599
Blueberries for Sal. McCloskey, R.   E
Bluemel Oldfield, Dawn
Leaping ground frogs   597.8
Bluemle, Elizabeth
Dogs on the bed   E
How do you wokka-wokka?   E
Blues. Handyside, C.   781.643
Blues journey. Myers, W. D.   811
Blues music
See also Jazz music; Soul music
Handyside, C. Blues   781.643
Fiction
Crow, K. The middle-child blues   E
Myers, W. D. The blues of Flats Brown   E
Stauffacher, S. Bessie Smith and the night riders
                                      E
Poetry
Myers, W. D. Blues journey   811
The **blues** of Flats Brown. Myers, W. D.   E
Blumberg, Rhoda, 1917-
Commodore Perry in the land of the Shogun
                                      952
Shipwrecked!: the true adventures of a Japanese boy [biography of Manjiro Nakahama]   92
York's adventures with Lewis and Clark
                                      978
Blume, Judy
Are you there God?, it's me, Margaret   Fic
Freckle juice   Fic

Blume, Judy—*Continued*

Otherwise known as Sheila the Great   **Fic**

The Pain and the Great One   **E**

Soupy Saturdays with The Pain and The Great One   **Fic**

Tales of a fourth grade nothing   **Fic**

Blume, Lesley M. M.

Cornelia and the audacious escapades of the Somerset sisters   **Fic**

The rising star of Rusty Nail   **Fic**

Tennyson   **Fic**

Blumenthal, Karen

Let me play   **796**

Bluthenthal, Diana Cain

(il) Edwards, P. D. The neat line   **E**

(il) Viorst, J. Just in case   **E**

Bly, Nellie, 1864-1922
About
Macy, S. Bylines: a photobiography of Nellie Bly   **92**

Blythe, Gary, 1959-

(il) Davies, N. Ice bear   **599.78**

(il) Ehrlich, A. A treasury of princess stories   **398.2**

Bo & Mzzz Mad. Fleischman, S.   **Fic**

Boadicea, Queen, d. 62

See/See also pages in the following book(s):

Meltzer, M. Ten queens   **920**

Boake, Kathy

(il) Swanson, D. You are weird   **612**

Board books for children

American babies   **E**

Anderson, S. A day at the market   **E**

Emberley, E. Where's my sweetie pie?   **E**

Emberley, R. My big book of Spanish words   **468**

Global babies   **E**

Henkes, K. A good day   **E**

Hoban, T. Black on white   **E**

Hoban, T. White on black   **E**

Horáček, P. Choo choo   **E**

Hubbell, P. Firefighters! speeding! spraying! saving!   **E**

Isol. It's useful to have a duck   **E**

Klinting, L. What do you want?   **E**

Macdonald, S. Alphabet animals   **E**

Martin, D. Christmas tree   **E**

Martin, D. Hanukkah lights   **E**

McBratney, S. When I'm big   **E**

Newman, L. Daddy, papa, and me   **E**

Newman, L. Mommy, mama, and me   **E**

Sellier, M. Renoir's colors   **759.05**

Smith, C. R. Dance with me   **E**

Wildsmith, B. Brian Wildsmith's ABC   **E**

Boars
Fiction
Rosoff, M. Meet wild boars   **E**

Boat book. Gibbons, G.   **387.2**

Boats, Submarine *See* Submarines

Boats. Barton, B.   **387.2**

Boats and boating

See also Rafting (Sports); Sailing; Ships

Barton, B. Boats   **387.2**

Gibbons, G. Boat book   **387.2**

Paulsen, G. Caught by the sea   **92**

Sandler, M. W. On the waters of the USA   **387.2**
Fiction
Buell, J. Sail away, Little Boat   **E**

DeSeve, R. The toy boat   **E**

Docherty, T. Little boat   **E**

Hiaasen, C. Flush   **Fic**

Hubbell, P. Boats   **E**

Orr, W. Mokie & Bik   **Fic**

Segal, J. Alistair and Kip's great adventure   **E**

Van Allsburg, C. The wreck of the Zephyr   **E**

Waddell, M. Captain Small Pig   **E**

Zimmer, T. V. The floating circus   **Fic**
Poetry
Sturges, P. Down to the sea in ships   **811**

Boats on the move. Clark, W.   **623.82**

Bob. Pearson, T. C.   **E**

Bob and Otto. Bruel, R. O.   **E**

Bobak, Cathy

(il) Poetry from A to Z. See Poetry from A to Z   **808.1**

The **bobbin** girl. McCully, E. A.   **Fic**

Bobby vs. girls (accidentally). Yee, L.   **Fic**

Bobrick, Benson, 1947-

Fight for freedom   **973.3**

Bob's best ever friend. Bartram, S.   **E**

Bochner, Arthur Berg

The new totally awesome business book for kids (and their parents)   **658**

The new totally awesome money book for kids (and their parents)   **332.024**

Bochner, Rose

(jt. auth) Bochner, A. B. The new totally awesome business book for kids (and their parents)   **658**

(jt. auth) Bochner, A. B. The new totally awesome money book for kids (and their parents)   **332.024**

Bockenhauer, Mark H.

Our fifty states   **973**

Bodach, Vijaya

Bar graphs   **510**

Pictographs   **510**

Pie graphs   **510**

Tally charts   **510**

Bodden, Valerie

Columbus reaches the New World   **970.01**

Concrete poetry   **809.1**

Frank Gehry   **92**

Haiku   **809.1**

Limericks   **809.1**

Man walks on the Moon   **629.45**

Nursery rhymes   **398.8**

Vincent van Gogh   **92**

Bode, N. E.

The Anybodies   **Fic**

The slippery map   **Fic**

Bodecker, N. M., 1922-1988

(il) Eager, E. Half magic   **Fic**

(il) Eager, E. Magic or not?   **Fic**

(il) Eager, E. Seven-day magic   **Fic**

Books and reading—Fiction—*Continued*
Kinsey-Warnock, N. Lumber camp library
             Fic
Lehman, B. The red book   **E**
MacLachlan, P. The true gift   **Fic**
Marlow, L. Hurry up and slow down   **E**
McQuinn, A. Lola at the library   **E**
Miller, W. Richard Wright and the library card
             E
Mora, P. Book fiesta!   **E**
Mora, P. Tomás and the library lady   **E**
Muntean, M. Do not open this book!   **E**
Numeroff, L. J. Beatrice doesn't want to   **E**
Poblocki, D. The stone child   **Fic**
Saint-Lot, K. N. Amadi's snowman   **E**
Schoenherr, I. Read it, don't eat it!   **E**
Shelf life: stories by the book   **S C**
Sherman, P. Ben and the Emancipation Proclamation   **E**
Sierra, J. Wild about books   **E**
Skelton, M. Endymion Spring   **Fic**
Spinelli, J. The library card   **S C**
Stanley, D. The mysterious matter of I.M. Fine
             Fic
Stellings, C. The contest   **Fic**
Stewart, S. The library   **E**
Stoeke, J. M. It's library day   **E**
Tobin, J. Sue MacDonald had a book   **E**
Walker, K. I hate books!   **Fic**
Watt, M. Have I got a book for you!   **E**
Wells, R. Read to your bunny   **E**
Williams, S. Library Lil   **E**
Yolen, J. Baby Bear's books   **E**
         Poetry
Lewis, J. P. Please bury me in the library
             811
Lewis, J. P. Spot the plot   **811**
Books and reading for children *See* Children—
  Books and reading
Books for children *See* Children's literature
Books kids will sit still for 3. Freeman, J.
             011.6
Books of Ember [series]
DuPrau, J. The city of Ember   **Fic**
The books of Umber [series]
Catanese, P. W. Happenstance found   **Fic**
Books on cassette *See* Audiobooks
Books on tape *See* Audiobooks
Booksellers and bookselling
         Fiction
Caple, K. Duck & company   **E**
Booktalking *See* Book talks
Booktalking authentic multicultural literature.
  York, S.   **021**
Booktalking bonanza. Diamant-Cohen, B.
             028.5
Bookworms. Nature's cycles [series]
Rau, D. M. Animals   **590**
Rau, D. M. Day and night   **508**
Rau, D. M. Food chains   **577**
Rau, D. M. Plants   **580**
Rau, D. M. Seasons   **508.2**
Boom!. Haddon, M.   **Fic**
Boom bah!. Cummings, P.   **E**

Boom boom go away!. Bass, L. G.   **E**
Boomhower, Ray E., 1959-
Fighting for equality   **92**
Boone, Daniel, 1734-1820
         About
Calvert, P. Daniel Boone   **92**
Spradlin, M. P. Daniel Boone's great escape
             92
Boonyadhistarn, Thiranut
Beading   **745.58**
Fingernail art   **646.7**
Stamping art   **761**
Boo's dinosaur. Byars, B. C.   **Fic**
Booth, Edwin, 1833-1893
         About
Giblin, J. Good brother, bad brother [biography
  of John Wilkes Booth and Edwin Booth]
             92
Booth, George, 1926-
(il) Van Laan, N. Nit-pickin'   **E**
Booth, John Wilkes, 1838-1865
         About
Giblin, J. Good brother, bad brother [biography
  of John Wilkes Booth and Edwin Booth]
             92
Boothroyd, Jennifer, 1972-
What is a gas?   **530.4**
What is a liquid?   **530.4**
What is a solid?   **530.4**
What is hearing?   **612.8**
What is sight?   **612.8**
What is smell?   **612.8**
What is taste?   **612.8**
What is touch?   **612.8**
Bootman, Colin
Steel pan man of Harlem   **E**
(il) Adler, D. A. A picture book of Harriet Bee-
  cher Stowe   **92**
(il) Birtha, B. Grandmama's pride   **E**
(il) Flake, S. G. The broken bike boy and the
  Queen of 33rd Street   **Fic**
(il) Uhlberg, M. Dad, Jackie, and me   **E**
Boots *See* Shoes
Bootsie Barker bites. Bottner, B.   **E**
Borden, Louise, 1949-
The A+ custodian   **E**
A. Lincoln and me   **E**
Across the blue Pacific   **Fic**
Good luck, Mrs. K!   **E**
The greatest skating race   **Fic**
The John Hancock Club   **E**
The journey that saved Curious George [biogra-
  phy of Margret Rey and H. A. Rey]   **92**
The last day of school   **Fic**
The little ships   **E**
The lost-and-found tooth   **Fic**
Off to first grade   **E**
Sea clocks   **526**
Touching the sky   **629.13**
Boring, Mel, 1939-
(jt. auth) Dendy, L. A. Guinea pig scientists
             616
Born to be giants. Judge, L.   **567.9**

Born to be wild [series]
Costa-Prades, B. Little gorillas — 599.8

Born to fly. Ferrari, M. — Fic

Born to read. Sierra, J. — E

Born to write. Cotter, C. — 920

Born yesterday. Solheim, J. — E

Borns, Steven
(il) Mitchell, J. S. Crashed, smashed, and mashed — 629.222

Borrego, Diana
(jt. auth) Pavon, A.-E. 25 Latino craft projects — 027.62

Borreguita and the coyote. Aardema, V. — 398.2

Borrowing. Tomljanovic, T. — 332.7

Borrowing money See Loans

Bortolotti, Dan
Exploring Saturn — 523.4
Panda rescue — 599.78
Tiger rescue — 333.95

Borton, Elizabeth See Treviño, Elizabeth Borton de, 1904-

Bortz, Alfred B., 1944-
Astrobiology — 576.8

Bortz, Fred See Bortz, Alfred B., 1944-

Bosch, Nicole in den
(il) Ross, K. Beautiful beads — 745.58
(il) Ross, K. Bedroom makeover crafts — 745.5
(il) Ross, K. One-of-a-kind stamps and crafts — 761

Bosch, Pseudonymous
The name of this book is secret — Fic

Bosco, Don
(jt. auth) Levy, P. Tibet — 951

Bosnia and Hercegovina
See also Sarajevo (Bosnia and Hercegovina)

Bostock, Mike
(il) Wallace, K. Think of an eel — 597

Boston, L. M. (Lucy Maria), 1892-1990
The children of Green Knowe — Fic

Boston, Lucy Maria See Boston, L. M. (Lucy Maria), 1892-1990

Boston, Peter, 1918-
(il) Boston, L. M. The children of Green Knowe — Fic

Boston (Mass.)
Fiction
Corriveau, A. How I, Nicky Flynn, finally get a life (and a dog) — Fic
Emerson, K. Carlos is gonna get it — Fic
Judge, L. Pennies for elephants — E
McCloskey, R. Make way for ducklings — E
Wolf-Morgenlander, K. Ragtag — Fic
History
Krensky, S. What's the big idea? — 974.4
McKendry, J. Beneath the streets of Boston — 625.4
Winters, K. Colonial voices — 973.3

Boston Massacre, 1770
Decker, T. For liberty — 973.3

Boston Red Sox (Baseball team)
Fiction
Baggott, J. The Prince of Fenway Park — Fic

Boston Tea Party, 1773
Fradin, D. B. The Boston Tea Party — 973.3
Winters, K. Colonial voices — 973.3

Boswell, Addie K.
The rain stomper — E

Botany
See also Plants
Benbow, A. Lively plant science projects — 580.7
VanCleave, J. P. Janice VanCleave's plants — 580.7
United States
See Plants—United States

Botswana
LeVert, S. Botswana — 968.83

Bott, C. J., 1947-
The bully in the book and in the classroom — 371.5
More bullies in more books — 371.5

Bottle feeding
Fiction
Ford, B. No more bottles for Bunny! — E

Bottner, Barbara, 1943-
Bootsie Barker bites — E
Miss Brooks loves books (and I don't) — E
Raymond and Nelda — E

Botzakis, Stergios
Pretty in print — 050

Bouchard, Dave
The gift of reading — 372.4

Bouchard, Jocelyne
(il) Love, A. The kids book of the Far North — 998

Boucher, Jerry, 1941-
(il) Wilcox, C. Bald eagles — 598

Boudicca See Boadicea, Queen, d. 62

Boudreau, Helene
Swimming science — 797.2

Boueri, Marijean
Lebanon A to Z — 956.92

Boughn, Michael
Into the world of the dead — 398.2

Boulanger, Nadia, 1887-1979
See/See also pages in the following book(s):
Krull, K. Lives of the musicians — 920

Boulogne, Joseph See Saint-Georges, Joseph Boulogne, chevalier de, 1745-1799

Bouma, Paddy, 1947-
(il) Mandela, N. Nelson Mandela: long walk to freedom — 92

Bound for Oregon. Van Leeuwen, J. — Fic

Bounty (Ship)
O'Brien, P. The mutiny on the Bounty — 910.4

Bourgeois, Paulette
The dirt on dirt — 631.4

Bourguignon, Laurence
Heart in the pocket — E

Bourseiller, Philippe
(il) Burleigh, R. Volcanoes 551.2

Boursin, Didier
Folding for fun 736

Boutignon, Beatrice
Not all animals are blue E

Boutros, Jill
(jt. auth) Boueri, M. Lebanon A to Z
956.92

Bouwman, H. M.
The remarkable and very true story of Lucy and Snowcap Fic

Bow, James
Baseball science 796.357
Cycling science 796.6

Bow, Patricia
Chimpanzee rescue 599.8

Bow, Patricia, 1946-
Tennis science 796.342

Bow and arrow
See also Archery

Bow-Wow bugs a bug. Newgarden, M. E

Bowden, Rob
African culture 960
Ancient Africa 960
Changing Africa 960
Energy 333.79
Food and farming 363.8
Jerusalem 956.94
Modern Africa 960
The Nile 962
Waste 363.7

Bowe, Julie, 1962-
My last best friend Fic

Bowen, Anne, 1952-
The great math tattle battle E
I know an old teacher E

Bowen, Betsy
(il) Lunge-Larsen, L. The troll with no heart in his body and other tales of trolls from Norway 398.2
(il) Van Laan, N. Shingebiss 398.2

Bowen, Fred, 1953-
No easy way 92
Touchdown trouble Fic

Bowers, Nathan, 1988-
4-H guide to training horses 636.1

Bowers, Sharon
Ghoulish goodies 641.5

Bowers, Tim
(il) Clements, A. Dogku 811
(il) Heiligman, D. Cool dog, school dog E
(il) Palatini, M. Gorgonzola E

Bowers, Vivien, 1951-
Crazy about Canada! 971

Bowman, Leslie W.
(il) Loizeaux, W. Wings Fic

A **box** full of tales. MacMillan, K. 027.6

Box Turtle at Long Pond. George, W. T. E

Box turtles. Stone, L. M. 597.92

Boxes
Walsh, D. The cardboard box book 745.54

Fiction
Bloom, S. A mighty fine time machine E
Foley, G. Thank you Bear E
Patricelli, L. The birthday box E
Portis, A. Not a box E
Russo, M. The big brown box E
The **boxes**. Sleator, W. Fic
Boxes for Katje. Fleming, C. E

Boxing
Lewin, T. At Gleason's gym 796.8
Smith, C. R. Black Jack 92
Biography
Adler, D. A. Joe Louis 92
Bolden, T. The champ! [biography of Muhammad Ali] 92
Myers, W. D. Muhammad Ali 92
Smith, C. R. Twelve rounds to glory: the story of Muhammad Ali 92
Winter, J. Muhammad Ali 92
Fiction
Morris, T. Total knockout Fic

A **boy**, a dog, and a frog. Mayer, M. E

A **boy** called Slow: the true story of Sitting Bull. Bruchac, J. 92

Boy dumplings. Compestine, Y. C. E

A **boy** had a mother who bought him a hat. Kuskin, K. E

The **boy** in the dress. Walliams, D. Fic

A **boy** named Beckoning: the true story of Dr. Carlos Montezuma, Native American hero. Capaldi, G. 92

The **boy** of the three-year nap. Snyder, D. 398.2

The **boy** on Fairfield Street: how Ted Geisel grew up to become Dr. Seuss. Krull, K. 92

Boy on the lion throne [biography of the Dalai Lama] Kimmel, E. C. 92

Boy Scouts of America
Fiction
Salisbury, G. Night of the howling dogs Fic

Boy, were we wrong about dinosaurs!. Kudlinski, K. V. 567.9

Boy were we wrong about the solar system!. Kudlinski, K. V. 523.2

The **boy** who climbed into the moon. Almond, D. Fic

The **boy** who cried wolf. Hennessy, B. G. 398.2

The **boy** who dared. Bartoletti, S. C. Fic

The **boy** who drew birds: a story of John James Audubon. Davies, J. 92

The **boy** who invented TV: the story of Philo Farnsworth. Krull, K. 92

The **boy** who loved to draw: Benjamin West. Brenner, B. 92

The **boy** who loved words. Schotter, R. E

The **boy** who painted dragons. Demi E

The **boy** who saved Cleveland. Giblin, J. Fic

The **boy** who wouldn't swim. Lucke, D. E

Bradman, Tony
Daddy's lullaby   E
(ed) Give me shelter. See Give me shelter
    S C

Brady, Hana
About
Levine, K. Hana's suitcase   940.53
Levine, K. Hana's suitcase on stage   812

Braeuner, Shellie
The great dog wash   E

Bragg, Georgia
Matisse on the loose   Fic

Brahms, Johannes, 1833-1897
See/See also pages in the following book(s):
Krull, K. Lives of the musicians   920

A **Braid** of lives   970.004

Braille, Louis, 1809-1852
About
Adler, D. A. A picture book of Louis Braille
    92
Freedman, R. Out of darkness: the story of Louis Braille   92

Braille books See Blind—Books and reading

Brain
Fleischman, J. Phineas Gage: a gruesome but true story about brain science   362.1
Funston, S. It's all in your head   612.8
Simon, S. The brain   612.8
Simpson, K. The human brain   612.8
Woodward, J. How to be a genius   152
Diseases
See also Stroke
Wounds and injuries—Fiction
Hartry, N. Watching Jimmy   Fic
Warner, S. It's only temporary   Fic

The **brain**. Simon, S.   612.8

The **Brain** finds a leg. Chatterton, M.   Fic

Brainboy and the Deathmaster. Seidler, T.   Fic

Brainwaves [series]
Adams, S. The most fantastic atlas of the whole wide world by the Brainwaves   912

Braley, Shawn
(il) Reilly, K. M. The human body   612

Brallier, Jess M.
Tess's tree   E

Braman, Arlette N., 1952-
Kids around the world cook!   641.5

Brand-new baby blues. Appelt, K.   E

Brand new readers [series]
Friend, C. Eddie the raccoon   E

Brandeis, Gayle, 1968-
My life with the Lincolns   Fic

Brandenberg, Aliki See Aliki

Brandenburg, Jim
Face to face with wolves   599.77
(il) Swinburne, S. R. Once a wolf   333.95

Brandenburg, Judith Berman
(jt. auth) Brandenburg, J. Face to face with wolves   599.77

Brandon See Brendan, Saint, the Voyager, ca. 483-577

Branford, Henrietta, 1946-
Fire, bed, & bone   Fic

Branley, Franklyn Mansfield, 1915-2002
Air is all around you   551.5
The Big Dipper   523.8
Day light, night light   535
Down comes the rain   551.57
Earthquakes   551.2
Flash, crash, rumble, and roll   551.55
Floating in space   629.45
The International Space Station   629.44
Is there life in outer space?   576.8
Mission to Mars   629.45
The moon seems to change   523.3
Snow is falling   551.57
The sun, our nearest star   523.7
Sunshine makes the seasons   508.2
Volcanoes   551.2
What makes a magnet?   538
What the moon is like   523.3

Brannen, Sarah S.
Uncle Bobby's wedding   E

Braren, Loretta Trezzo
(il) Press, J. The little hands big fun craft book
    745.5

Braun, Sebastien
Back to bed, Ed!   E
Meeow and the big box   E
On our way home   E
The ugly duckling   E
(jt. auth) Ford, B. First snow   E
(il) Yolen, J. Dimity Duck   E

Braun, Trudi
My goose Betsy   E

Brave as a mountain lion. Scott, A. H.   E

Brave Charlotte. Stohner, A.   E

Brave dogs, gentle dogs. Urbigkit, C.   636.7

Brave Harriet [biography of Harriet Quimby]
Moss, M.   92

Brave Irene. Steig, W.   E

The **brave** little seamstress. Osborne, M. P.
    398.2

The **brave** women and children of the American Revolution. Micklos, J.   973.3

The **bravest** knight. Mayer, M.   E

Bravo! brava! a night at the opera. Siberell, A.
    792.5

Brazil
Deckker, Z. Brazil   981
Reiser, R. Brazil   981
Richard, C. Brazil   981
Walters, T. Brazil   981
Folklore
See Folklore—Brazil

Brazilian Americans
Fiction
Giff, P. R. Wild girl   Fic

Bread
Morris, A. Bread, bread, bread   641.8
Raum, E. The story behind bread   641.8

Bread and roses, too. Paterson, K.   Fic

Bread, bread, bread. Morris, A.   641.8

Brisson, Pat
I remember Miss Perry   E
Tap-dance fever   E
Bristow, M. J.
(ed) National anthems of the world. See National anthems of the world   782.42
Britannica illustrated science library   503
Britannica student encyclopedia   031
Britannica's student atlas   912
British Cameroons See Cameroon
British Columbia
Harvey, S. N. The West is calling   811
Fiction
Baker, D. F. Becca at sea   Fic
Horvath, P. Everything on a waffle   Fic
Roberts, K. Thumb on a diamond   Fic
British Empire See Great Britain—Colonies
Britt, Stephan
(il) Dickinson, R. Over in the hollow   E
Brittain, Bill
The wish giver   Fic
Brittney, L.
Dangerous times   Fic
Brittney, Lynn See Brittney, L.
The Brixton Brothers [series]
Barnett, M. The case of the case of mistaken identity   Fic
Broach, Elise, 1963-
Gumption!   E
Masterpiece   Fic
Shakespeare's secret   Fic
When dinosaurs came with everything   E
Broadcasting
See also Television broadcasting
Broadway, Hannah
(il) Hayes, S. Dog day   E
Brockmeier, Kevin
Grooves   Fic
Brodie, Carolyn S., 1958-
(jt. auth) Latrobe, K. H. The children's literature dictionary   028.5
Brøgger, Lilian, 1950-
(il) Varmer, H. Hans Christian Andersen   92
The broken bike boy and the Queen of 33rd Street. Flake, S. G.   Fic
Broken bones. Landau, E.   617.1
Broken song. Lasky, K.   Fic
Bromann, Jennifer
More storytime action!   027.62
Storytime action!   027.62
Bronchial asthma See Asthma
Brontë, Charlotte, 1816-1855
See/See also pages in the following book(s):
Krull, K. Lives of the writers   920
Brontë, Emily, 1818-1848
See/See also pages in the following book(s):
Krull, K. Lives of the writers   920
Bronte's book club. Gregory, K.   Fic
Brontorina. Howe, J.   E

Bronx (New York, N.Y.)
Fiction
Adler, D. A. Don't talk to me about the war   Fic
Bronx Zoo
Caper, W. American bison   599.64
The **bronze** bow. Speare, E. G.   Fic
The **bronze** pen. Snyder, Z. K.   Fic
Bronzes
Fritz, J. Leonardo's horse   730.9
Bronzeville boys and girls. Brooks, G.   811
Brook, Larry
Daily life in ancient and modern Timbuktu   966.23
The **brook** book. Arnosky, J.   577.6
Brooker, Kyrsten
(il) Davies, J. The night is singing   E
(il) Dodds, D. A. The prince won't go to bed   E
(il) Lazo, C. E. Someday when my cat can talk   E
(il) McKissack, P. C. Precious and the Boo Hag   E
Brooklyn (New York, N.Y.)
Fiction
Avi. Don't you know there's a war on?   Fic
Avi. Iron thunder   Fic
Dee, B. Solving Zoe   Fic
Estes, E. The Alley   Fic
Giff, P. R. All the way home   Fic
Giff, P. R. A house of tailors   Fic
Giff, P. R. Water Street   Fic
Goode, D. The most perfect spot   E
Gratz, A. The Brooklyn nine   Fic
Hesse, K. Brooklyn Bridge   Fic
Schirripa, S. R. Nicky Deuce   Fic
Scieszka, J. Spaceheadz   Fic
Uhlberg, M. Dad, Jackie, and me   E
Poetry
Frampton, D. Mr. Ferlinghetti's poem   811
Brooklyn Bridge (New York, N.Y.)
Curlee, L. Brooklyn Bridge   624.2
Fiction
Prince, A. J. Twenty-one elephants and still standing   E
Brooklyn Bridge. Hesse, K.   Fic
Brooklyn Dodgers (Baseball team)
Golenbock, P. Teammates [biography of Jackie Robinson]   92
The **Brooklyn** nine. Gratz, A.   Fic
Brooks, Bruce, 1950-
Everywhere   Fic
Brooks, Erik, 1972-
(il) Byars, B. C. Boo's dinosaur   Fic
(il) Byars, B. C. Cat diaries   S C
(il) Byars, B. C. Dog diaries   S C
(il) Climo, S. Monkey business   398.2
(il) Giblin, J. Did Fleming rescue Churchill?   Fic
Brooks, Gwendolyn
Bronzeville boys and girls   811
See/See also pages in the following book(s):
Wilkinson, B. S. African American women writers   810.9

Brown, Tricia
Salaam   297.3

Brown, William Wells, 1815-1884
See/See also pages in the following book(s):
Currie, S. Escapes from slavery   326

Brown bear, brown bear what do you see? Martin, B.   E

Brown honey in broomwheat tea. Thomas, J. C.   811

Brown v. Board of Education. Good, D. L.   344

Browne, Anthony
Little Beauty   E
My brother   E
My dad   E
My mom   E
Piggybook   E
Silly Billy   E
Voices in the park   E

Brownell, Shawn
(il) Peacock, C. A. Mommy far, Mommy near   E

Brownie & Pearl step out. Rylant, C.   E

Browning, Diane
Signed, Abiah Rose   E

Brownstone, David M.
Frontier America   973.03

Broxholm, Scott Gibala- *See* Gibala-Broxholm, Scott

Broyles, Anne, 1953-
Priscilla and the hollyhocks   E

Bruchac, James
The girl who helped thunder and other Native American folktales   398.2
(jt. auth) Bruchac, J. How Chipmunk got his stripes   398.2
(jt. auth) Bruchac, J. Raccoon's last race   398.2
(jt. auth) Bruchac, J. Turtle's race with Beaver   398.2

Bruchac, Joseph, 1942-
The arrow over the door   Fic
Bearwalker   Fic
Between earth & sky   398.2
A boy called Slow: the true story of Sitting Bull   92
Buffalo song [biography of Walking Coyote]   92
Children of the longhouse   Fic
Crazy Horse's vision   E
The dark pond   Fic
The first strawberries   398.2
The great ball game   398.2
How Chipmunk got his stripes   398.2
My father is taller than a tree   E
Night wings   Fic
Pushing up the sky: seven Native American plays for children   812
Raccoon's last race   398.2
Skeleton man   Fic
Thirteen moons on a turtle's back   811
The Trail of Tears   970.004
Turtle's race with Beaver   398.2
Whisper in the dark   Fic

The winter people   Fic
About
Parker-Rock, M. Joseph Bruchac   92
(jt. auth) Bruchac, J. The girl who helped thunder and other Native American folktales   398.2
(jt. auth) Caduto, M. J. Keepers of the night   398.2

Bruchac, Margaret M.
(jt. auth) Grace, C. O. 1621   394.26

Bruel, Nick
Bad Kitty   E
Boing!   E
Little red bird   E
(il) Bruel, R. O. Bob and Otto   E
(il) King-Smith, D. Clever duck   Fic
(il) King-Smith, D. Dinosaur trouble   Fic
(il) King-Smith, D. The mouse family Robinson   Fic

Bruel, Robert O.
Bob and Otto   E

Bruh Rabbit and the tar baby girl. Hamilton, V.   398.2

Bruins, David
The legend of Ninja Cowboy Bear   E

Brun-Cosme, Nadine
Big Wolf & Little Wolf   E
No, I want daddy!   E

Brunelle, Lynn
Camp out!   796.54
(jt. auth) Shannon, G. Chicken scratches   811

Brunelleschi, Filippo, 1377-1446
Fiction
Fern, T. E. Pippo the Fool   E

Brunello, John Bendall- *See* Bendall-Brunello, John

Brunhoff, Jean de, 1899-1937
The story of Babar, the little elephant   E

Brunkus, Denise
(il) Keane, D. Sloppy Joe   E
(il) Park, B. Junie B. Jones and her big fat mouth   Fic
(il) Swallow, P. C. Groundhog gets a say   E
(il) Winters, K. My teacher for President   E

Bruno, Elsa Knight
A punctuation celebration!   428

Bruno, Iacopo
(il) Baccalario, P. The door to time   Fic
(il) Baccalario, P. Ring of fire   Fic

Bruno Munari's zoo. Munari, B.   E

Brushing Mom's hair. Cheng, A.   Fic

Bruss, Deborah
Book! book! book!   E

Bryan, Ashley, 1923-
Ashley Bryan   92
Ashley Bryan's African tales, uh-huh   398.2
Beautiful blackbird   398.2
Sing to the sun   811
(il) Alexander, C. F. All things bright and beautiful   264
(comp) All night, all day. See All night, all day   782.25

Bryan, Ashley, 1923-—*Continued*
(il) Ashley Bryan's ABC of African-American poetry. See Ashley Bryan's ABC of African-American poetry **811.008**
(il) Gilchrist, J. S. My America **E**
(il) Giovanni, N. The sun is so quiet **811**
(il) Graham, L. B. How God fix Jonah **398.2**
(il) Let it shine. See Let it shine **782.25**
(comp) The Night has ears. See The Night has ears **398.9**
(il) Salting the ocean. See Salting the ocean **811.008**

Bryan, Kim
One million things. See One million things **031**

Bryan, Nichol, 1958-
Exxon Valdez oil spill **363.7**

Bryan, Robin
(jt. auth) Blowers, H. Weaving a library Web **025.04**

Bryant, Jennifer
Abe's fish **E**
Georgia's bones [biography of Georgia O'Keefe] **92**
A river of words: the story of William Carlos Williams **92**

Bryant, Laura J.
(il) Bergren, L. T. God found us you **E**

Bryant, Megan E.
Oh my gods! **292**
She's all that! **292**

Bryson, Bill
A really short history of nearly everything **500**

Bstan-'dzin-rgya-mtsho *See* Dalai Lama XIV, 1935-

Bubba and Beau, best friends. Appelt, K. **E**

Bubble gum
McCarthy, M. Pop! **664**

Bubble gum, bubble gum. Wheeler, L. **E**

Bubble homes and fish farts. Bayrock, F. **590**

Bubble trouble. Mahy, M. **E**

Bubbles
Bayrock, F. Bubble homes and fish farts **590**
Bradley, K. B. Pop! **530.4**
Fiction
Mahy, M. Bubble trouble **E**

Bubonic plague *See* Plague

Buchanan, Andrea J.
The daring book for girls **031.02**

Bucher, Katherine Toth, 1947-
(jt. auth) Al-Hazza, T. C. Books about the Middle East **016.3058**

Bucking the Sarge. Curtis, C. P. **Fic**

Buckingham, Royce
Demonkeeper **Fic**

Buckley, Annie, 1968-
Be a better babysitter **649**
Be a better biker **796.6**

Buckley, Carol
Just for elephants **639.9**

Tarra & Bella **599.67**

Buckley, Helen E. (Helen Elizabeth), 1918-
Grandfather and I **E**
Grandmother and I **E**

Buckley, James, Jr.
Ultimate guide to baseball **796.357**
Ultimate guide to football **796.332**
The Child's World encyclopedia of the NFL. See The Child's World encyclopedia of the NFL **796.332**

Buckley, Michael
The fairy-tale detectives **Fic**
NERDS **Fic**

Buckley, Susan
Journeys for freedom **973**
Kids make history **973**
(jt. auth) Leacock, E. Journeys in time **973**
(jt. auth) Leacock, E. Places in time **911**

Buckley-Archer, Linda
Gideon the cutpurse **Fic**

Buckmaster, Marjorie L.
Freshwater fishes **639.34**
Skin cancer **616.99**

Bud, not Buddy. Curtis, C. P. **Fic**

Buddha, Gautama *See* Gautama Buddha

Buddha. Demi **294.3**

Buddha stories. Demi **294.3**

The **Buddha's** diamonds. Marsden, C. **Fic**

Buddhism

See also Zen Buddhism
Brown, D. Far beyond the garden gate: Alexandra David-Neel's journey to Lhasa **92**
Chödzin, S. The wisdom of the crows and other Buddhist tales **294.3**
Demi. The Dalai Lama **92**
Ganeri, A. Buddhism **294.3**
George, C. What makes me a Buddhist? **294.3**
Hawker, F. Buddhism in Thailand **294.3**
Kimmel, E. C. Boy on the lion throne [biography of the Dalai Lama] **92**
Levin, J. Japanese mythology **299.5**
Nardo, D. Buddhism **294.3**
See/See also pages in the following book(s):
Osborne, M. P. One world, many religions **200**

Fiction
Gershator, P. Sky sweeper **E**
Marsden, C. The Buddha's diamonds **Fic**
Thong, R. Fly free! **E**

Buddhism in Thailand. Hawker, F. **294.3**

The Buddy files [series]
Butler, D. H. The case of the lost boy **Fic**

Budget
Wiseman, B. Budgeting **332.024**

Budgeting. Wiseman, B. **332.024**

Budgets, Personal *See* Personal finance

Buehner, Caralyn
Fanny's dream **E**
Goldilocks and the three bears **398.2**
I did it, I'm sorry **E**
Snowmen at night **E**
Superdog **E**

Buehner, Mark
  (il) Barracca, D. The adventures of Taxi Dog
                                     E
  (il) Buehner, C. Fanny's dream   E
  (il) Buehner, C. Goldilocks and the three bears
                                 398.2
  (il) Buehner, C. I did it, I'm sorry   E
  (jt. auth) Buehner, C. Snowmen at night E
  (il) Buehner, C. Superdog   E
  (il) Nolen, J. Harvey Potter's balloon farm
                                     E
  (il) Wilcoxen, C. Niccolini's song   E
Buell, Janet, 1945-
  Sail away, Little Boat   E
Buening, Alice P. *See* Pope, Alice
Buffalo, American *See* Bison
Buffalo (N.Y.)
               Fiction
  Grandits, J. The travel game   E
Buffalo. Perry, P. J.   599.64
The **buffalo** and the Indians. Patent, D. H.
                                   978
The **buffalo** are back. George, J. C.   599.64
Buffalo Bill, 1846-1917
               Fiction
  Peck, R. Fair weather   Fic
Buffalo hunt. Freedman, R.   970.004
Buffalo music. Fern, T. E.   E
The **buffalo** soldier. Garland, S.   E
Buffalo song [biography of Walking Coyote]
  Bruchac, J.   92
The **buffalo** storm. Applegate, K.   E
Buffalo woman. Goble, P.   398.2
Buffam, Leslie
  (jt. auth) Harvey, S. N. The West is calling
                                   811
Bug butts. Cusick, D.   595.7
Bug in a rug. Gilson, J.   Fic
Bug safari. Barner, B.   E
The **bug** scientists. Jackson, D. M.   595.7
Bug zoo. Baker, N.   595.7
Bugged!. Knudsen, M.   E
Bugs. Harrison, D. L.   811
Bugs. Martin, R.   595.7
Bugs [series]
  Povey, K. D. Centipede   595.6
Bugs and bugsicles. Hansen, A.   595.7
Bugs and spiders. Stradling, J.   595.7
Bugs are insects. Rockwell, A. F.   595.7
Bugs before time. Camper, C.   560
Bugs in my hair?!. Stier, C.   E
Bugs on your body. Perritano, J.   595.7
Bugs up close. Swanson, D.   595.7
Bugtown Boogie. Hanson, W.   E
Buhler, Cynthia von
  But who will bell the cats?   E
  (il) Fradin, D. B. Nicolaus Copernicus   92
  (il) Rockwell, A. F. They called her Molly
  Pitcher   92
Build it!. Mason, A.   624.1

Build it yourself [series]
  Mooney, C. Amazing Africa   960
Build it yourself series
  Van Vleet, C. Great Ancient Egypt projects you
  can build yourself   932
Building
     See also Carpentry; House construction;
  Steel construction
  Barton, B. Machines at work   690
  Caney, S. Steven Caney's ultimate building
  book   624
  Gibbons, G. How a house is built   690
  Hudson, C. W. Construction zone   690
  Macaulay, D. Unbuilding   690
  Mason, A. Build it!   624.1
  Sandvold, L. B. Revolution in construction
                                   624
  See/See also pages in the following book(s):
  Macaulay, D. Underground   624
              Fiction
  Banks, K. The night worker   E
  Drescher, H. McFig & McFly   E
  Edwards, P. D. Jack and Jill's treehouse E
  Garcia, E. Tap tap bang bang   E
  Hopkinson, D. Sky boys   E
  Lyon, G. E. You and me and home sweet home
                                       E
  Nevius, C. Building with Dad   E
  Roth, S. L. Hard hat area   E
  Teague, D. Franklin's big dreams   E
Building a house. Barton, B.   690
Building big. Macaulay, D.   720
Building greenscrapers. Stern, S. L.   720
Building machinery *See* Construction equipment
Building Manhattan. Vila, L.   974.7
Building on nature. Rodriguez, R.   92
Building the book Cathedral. Macaulay, D.
                                   726
Building with Dad. Nevius, C.   E
Buildings
     See also Apartment houses; Garages; His-
  toric buildings; Houses; Skyscrapers
  Hosack, K. Buildings   720
  Rissman, R. Shapes in buildings   516
  Spilsbury, L. Can buildings speak?   720
Built by angels. Podwal, M. H.   296.4
Built to last. Sullivan, G.   624
Bulimia
  Silverstein, A. The eating disorders update
                               616.85
Bulion, Leslie, 1958-
  Hey there, stink bug!   811
  The trouble with rules   Fic
Bull, Jane, 1957-
  Make it!   745.5
Bull Run, 1st Battle of, 1861
               Fiction
  Fleischman, P. Bull Run   Fic
  Hemphill, M. Stonewall Hinkleman and the Bat-
  tle of Bull Run   Fic
Bulla, Clyde Robert, 1914-2007
  The chalk box kid   E
  Daniel's duck   E

California condors *See* Condors

California condors. Goldish, M.   598

Calisthenics *See* Gymnastics

Call, Greg
  (jt. auth) Abbott, T. Kringle   Fic
  (il) Barry, D. Peter and the starcatchers   Fic
  (il) Elish, D. The attack of the frozen wood-chucks   Fic
  (il) Rappaport, D. Victory or death!   973.3

Call it courage. Sperry, A.   Fic

Callan, Lyndall
  (jt. auth) Rappaport, D. Dirt on their skirts
    E

Callen, Liz
  (il) Seabrooke, B. Wolf pie   Fic

Callie's rules. Zucker, N. F.   Fic

Calligraphy
  Hanson, A. Cool calligraphy   745.6
  Winters, E. 1 2 3 calligraphy!   745.6
     Fiction
  Rumford, J. Silent music   E

Callison, Daniel, 1948-
  The blue book on information age inquiry, instruction and literacy   028.7

Calmenson, Stephanie
  Good for you!   811
  Jazzmatazz!   E
  Late for school!   E
  May I pet your dog?   636.7
  Rosie   636.7
  Welcome, baby!   811
  (jt. auth) Cole, J. Why did the chicken cross the road? and other riddles, old and new
    793.73
  (comp) The Eentsy, weentsy spider: fingerplays and action rhymes. See The Eentsy, weentsy spider: fingerplays and action rhymes
    796.1
  (comp) Miss Mary Mack and other children's street rhymes. See Miss Mary Mack and other children's street rhymes   796.1

Calvert, Pam, 1966-
  Multiplying menace   E
  Princess Peepers   E

Calvert, Patricia, 1931-
  The ancient Celts   936
  The ancient Inca   985
  Daniel Boone   92
  Kit Carson   92
  Robert E. Peary   92
  Sir Ernest Shackleton   92
  Vasco da Gama   92
  Zebulon Pike   92

Calvin Coconut: trouble magnet. Salisbury, G.
    Fic

Cam Jansen and the mystery of the stolen diamonds. Adler, D. A.   Fic

Cambodia
  Lord, M. A song for Cambodia [biography of Arn Chorn-Pond]   92
  Sheehan, S. Cambodia   959.6
     Fiction
  Smith, I. Half spoon of rice   Fic

Cambodian Americans
     Fiction
  Ly, M. Home is east   Fic

Camels
  Barnes, J. Camels and llamas at work   636.2
  Jango-Cohen, J. Camels   599.63
     Fiction
  Graber, J. Muktar and the camels   E
     Poetry
  Carryl, C. E. The camel's lament   E

Camels and llamas at work. Barnes, J.   636.2

The **camel's** lament. Carryl, C. E.   E

Cameras
     Fiction
  Pichon, L. Penguins   E
  Wiesner, D. Flotsam   E

Cameron, Ann, 1943-
  Colibri   Fic
  Gloria's way   Fic
  The stories Julian tells   Fic

Cameron, Eleanor, 1912-1996
  The wonderful flight to the Mushroom Planet
    Fic

Cameron, Marie
  (il) Chödzin, S. The wisdom of the crows and other Buddhist tales   294.3

Cameroon
     Fiction
  Alexander, L. The fortune-tellers   E
     Folklore
   See Folklore—Cameroon

Camille McPhee fell under the bus. Tracy, K.
    Fic

Camisa, Kathryn
  Hairy tarantulas   595.4

Cammuso, Frank
  Knights of the lunch table: the dodgeball chronicles   741.5
  Otto's orange day   741.5

Camouflage (Biology)
  Cooper, J. Camouflage and disguise   591.47
  Helman, A. Hide and seek   591.47
  Mitchell, S. K. Animals with crafty camouflage
    591.47
  Pryor, K. J. Clever camouflage   591.47
  Racanelli, M. Camouflaged creatures   591.47
  Schwartz, D. M. Where else in the wild?
    591.4
  Schwartz, D. M. Where in the wild?   591.4

Camouflage and disguise. Cooper, J.   591.47

Camouflaged creatures. Racanelli, M.   591.47

Camp Harmony Assembly Center (Puyallup, Wash.) *See* Puyallup Assembly Center (Wash.)

Camp out!. Brunelle, L.   796.54

Campanella, Roy, 1921-1993
     About
  Adler, D. A. Campy [biography of Roy Campanella]   92

Campbell, Andrew C. (Andrew Campbell)
  (jt. auth) Dawes, J. Exploring the world of aquatic life   591.7

Campbell, Bebe Moore
Sometimes my mommy gets angry   E
Stompin' at the Savoy   E

Campbell, Bruce, 1950-
(il) Hawker, F. Buddhism in Thailand   **294.3**
(il) Hawker, F. Christianity in Mexico   **282**
(il) Hawker, F. Hinduism in Bali   **294.5**
(il) Hawker, F. Islam in Turkey   **297**
(il) Hawker, F. Judaism in Israel   **296**
(il) Hawker, F. Sikhism in India   **294.6**

Campbell, Nicola I.
Shi-shi-etko   E

Campbell, Richard P.
(il) Campbell, S. C. Growing patterns   **513**
(il) Campbell, S. C. Wolfsnail   **594**

Campbell, Rod, 1945-
Dear zoo   E

Campbell, Sarah C.
Growing patterns   **513**
Wolfsnail   **594**

Campbell-Hinshaw, Kelly
Ancient Mexico   **709.39**

Camper, Cathy
Bugs before time   **560**

Campfire Mallory. Friedman, L. B.   **Fic**

Camping
Brunelle, L. Camp out!   **796.54**
George, J. C. Pocket guide to the outdoors   **796.5**

Fiction
Barshaw, R. M. Ellie McDoodle: have pen, will travel   **Fic**
Bruchac, J. Bearwalker   **Fic**
Gilson, J. 4B goes wild   **Fic**
Salisbury, G. Night of the howling dogs   **Fic**
Say, A. The lost lake   E
Williams, V. B. Three days on a river in a red canoe   E

Poetry
George, K. O. Toasting marshmallows   **811**

Camping with the president [biography of Theodore Roosevelt] Wadsworth, G.   **92**

Campion, Pascal
(il) They Might Be Giants (Musical group). Kids go!   **782.42**

Campoy, F. Isabel, 1946-
Tales our abuelitas told   **398.2**
Muu, moo! See Muu, moo!   **398.8**
(jt. auth) Ada, A. F. Merry Navidad!   **394.26**
(comp) ¡Pio peep! See ¡Pio peep!   **398.8**

Camps

Fiction
Danziger, P. There's a bat in bunk five   **Fic**
Ferber, B. A. Jemma Hartman, camper extraordinaire   **Fic**
Friedman, L. B. Campfire Mallory   **Fic**
Larson, H. Chiggers   **741.5**
Pogue, D. Abby Carnelia's one and only magical power   **Fic**
Wedekind, A. A horse of her own   **Fic**

Campy [biography of Roy Campanella] Adler, D. A.   **92**

Can buildings speak? Spilsbury, L.   **720**
The **Can** Man. Williams, L. E.   E

Can we get along? Burstein, J.   **179**
Can you find it? Cressy, J.   **750**
Can you greet the whole wide world? Evans, L.   **413**
Can you guess my name? Sierra, J.   **398.2**
Can you hear it? Lach, W.   **780**
Can you make a scary face? Thomas, J.   E
Can you see the chalkboard? Silverstein, A.   **617.7**
Can you see what I see? Wick, W.   **793.73**

Canada
Bowers, V. Crazy about Canada!   **971**
Junior Worldmark encyclopedia of the Canadian provinces   **971**
Murphy, P. J. Canada   **971**
Pang, G.-C. Canada   **971**
Penn, B. The kids book of Canadian geography   **971**
Wallace, M. Inuksuk journey   **971.9**
Williams, B. Canada   **971**

Children
See Children—Canada
Fiction
Beha, E. Tango   **Fic**
Campbell, N. I. Shi-shi-etko   E
Cooper, S. The Boggart   **Fic**
Curtis, C. P. Elijah of Buxton   **Fic**
Cutler, J. Guttersnipe   E
Jocelyn, M. Mable Riley   **Fic**
Johnston, J. A very fine line   **Fic**
Pendziwol, J. Marja's skis   E
Perkins, L. R. Pictures from our vacation   E
Stellings, C. The contest   **Fic**
Wynne-Jones, T. Rex Zero and the end of the world   **Fic**
History—0-1763 (New France)
Maestro, B. The new Americans   **973.2**

Canada goose *See* Geese

Canadian Arctic Expedition (1913-1918)
Martin, J. B. The lamp, the ice, and the boat called Fish   **998**

Canadian authors *See* Authors, Canadian

Canadian geographic kids [series]
Baillie, M. Small wonders   **591.3**
Bowers, V. Crazy about Canada!   **971**

Canadian Indians *See* Native Americans—Canada

Canadians
See also French Canadians

Canals
Fiction
Howard, E. The gate in the wall   **Fic**

Cancer
See also Breast cancer; Leukemia
Buckmaster, M. L. Skin cancer   **616.99**
Watters, D. Where's Mom's hair?   **616.99**
Fiction
Borden, L. Good luck, Mrs. K!   E
Cheng, A. Brushing Mom's hair   **Fic**
Hannigan, K. Ida B   **Fic**
Hobbs, V. Defiance   **Fic**
MacLachlan, P. Word after word after word   **Fic**
Paulsen, G. Notes from the dog   **Fic**

Cancer—Fiction—*Continued*

Pearce, E. S. Isabel and the miracle baby
Fic

Polacco, P. The Lemonade Club   **E**

Preller, J. Six innings   **Fic**

Ries, L. Punk wig   **E**

Sneve, V. D. H. Lana's Lakota moons   **Fic**

Sonnenblick, J. After ever after   **Fic**

Tinkham, K. Hair for Mama   **E**

Candle Man [series]

Dakin, G. The Society of Unrelenting Vigilance
Fic

Candles

Check, L. Create your own candles   **745.5**

Candlewick illustrated classics [series]

Grahame, K. The wind in the willows   **Fic**

Candy

Love, A. Sweet!   **641.8**

Fiction

Lane, K. Nana cracks the case!   **Fic**

Underwood, D. A balloon for Isabel   **E**

Candy bomber [biography of Gail Halvorsen]
Tunnell, M. O.   **92**

Candy shop. Wahl, J.   **E**

Candyfloss. Wilson, J.   **Fic**

Cane toad. Somervill, B. A.   **597.8**

Caney, Steven

Steven Caney's ultimate building book   **624**

Canfield, Dorothy *See* Fisher, Dorothy Canfield, 1879-1958

Canfield, Jack, 1944-

Chicken soup for the soul: kids in the kitchen
641.5

Canga, Chris

(il) Santopolo, J. The Niña, the Pinta, and the vanishing treasure   **Fic**

The **canine** connection: stories about dogs and people. Hearne, B. G.   **S C**

Cann, Helen, 1969-

(il) Guo Yue. Little Leap Forward   **Fic**

(il) Matthews, C. Fireside stories   **398.2**

(il) Milligan, B. Brigid's cloak   **398.2**

(il) Watts, M. The Bible for children from Good Books   **220.9**

Canned. Shearer, A.   **Fic**

Cannell, Jon

(il) Holmes, M. T. A giraffe goes to Paris
E

(il) Holmes, M. T. My travels with Clara
599.66

(il) McCutcheon, M. The kid who named Pluto
509

Cannon, Annie

(il) Crenson, V. Horseshoe crabs and shorebirds
577.7

Cannon, Janell, 1957-

Crickwing   **E**

Stellaluna   **E**

Cannon, Kevin

(il) Ottaviani, J. T-Minus: the race to the moon
741.5

Cannon, Zander, 1972-

(il) Ottaviani, J. T-Minus: the race to the moon
741.5

Canoes and canoeing

Fiction

Williams, V. B. Three days on a river in a red canoe   **E**

Can't you make them behave, King George? [biography of George III, King of Great Britain]
Fritz, J.   **92**

Can't you sleep, Little Bear? Waddell, M.   **E**

Canterbury tales. Cohen, B.   **821**

Canto familiar. Soto, G.   **811**

Cantone, Anna-Laura

(il) French, V. The Daddy Goose treasury   **E**

(il) Goodhart, P. Three little ghosties   **E**

Canwell, Diane

(jt. auth) Sutherland, J. Aircraft carriers
623.82

(jt. auth) Sutherland, J. Container ships and oil tankers   **623.82**

(jt. auth) Sutherland, J. Cruise ships   **623.82**

(jt. auth) Sutherland, J. Submarines   **623.82**

Canyon, Jeanette, 1965-

(il) Berkes, M. C. Over in the jungle   **E**

(il) Rammell, S. K. City beats   **811**

Capaccio, George

ADD and ADHD   **616.85**

Jupiter   **523.4**

Mars   **523.4**

The sun   **523.7**

Capaldi, Gina

A boy named Beckoning: the true story of Dr. Carlos Montezuma, Native American hero
92

Caparo, Antonio Javier

(il) Prineas, S. The magic thief   **Fic**

Cape Cod (Mass.)

Clifford, B. Real pirates   **910.4**

Cape Hatteras National Seashore (N.C.)

Reed, J. Cape Hatteras National Seashore
975.6

Caper, William

American bison   **599.64**

Capital. Curlee, L.   **975.3**

Caple, Kathy

Duck & company   **E**

The friendship tree   **E**

Caple, Laurie A.

(il) Arnold, C. Giant sea reptiles of the dinosaur age   **567.9**

(il) Arnold, C. Giant shark: megalodon, prehistoric super predator   **567**

(il) Arnold, C. Global warming and the dinosaurs   **567.9**

(il) Arnold, C. Pterosaurs   **567.9**

(il) Arnold, C. When mammoths walked the earth   **569**

Capoeira (Dance)

Ancona, G. Capoeira   **793.3**

Cappon, Manuela

(il) Platt, R. London   **942.1**

Caps for sale. Slobodkina, E.   **E**

Captain Invincible and the space shapes. Murphy, S. J. **516**

Captain Nobody. Pitchford, D. **Fic**

Captain Raptor and the moon mystery. O'Malley, K. **E**

Captain Small Pig. Waddell, M. **E**

Capucilli, Alyssa, 1957-
Biscuit's new trick **E**
Katy duck is a caterpillar **E**
Pedro's burro **E**

Caravan to America. Major, J. S. **920**

Carbohydrates
King, H. Carbohydrates for a healthy body **613.2**

Carbohydrates for a healthy body. King, H. **613.2**

Carbon dioxide greenhouse effect See Greenhouse effect

Carbone, Elisa Lynn, 1954-
Blood on the river **Fic**
Night running **E**
Storm warriors **Fic**

The **cardboard** box book. Walsh, D. **745.54**

The **cardboard** piano. Perkins, L. R. **E**

Cárdenas, Teresa, 1970-
Oloyou **398.2**

Cardiovascular system
See also Blood—Circulation; Heart
Corcoran, M. K. The circulatory story **612.1**
Jakab, C. The circulatory system
Simon, S. The heart **612.1**

Cards, Debit See Debit cards

Cardwell, Ken
(jt. auth) Brown, T. Salaam **297.3**

Care, Medical See Medical care

Career guidance See Vocational guidance

Careers See Occupations

Carey, Bob, 1961-
(il) Jackson, E. A home for Dixie **636.7**

Caribbean Americans
Keedle, J. Americans from the Caribbean and Central America **305.8**

Caribbean region
Fiction
Cherry, L. The sea, the storm, and the mangrove tangle **E**
Taylor, T. The cay **Fic**
Taylor, T. Timothy of the cay **Fic**
Folklore
See Folklore—Caribbean region

Caribou
Heuer, K. Being caribou **599.65**

Caricatures See Cartoons and caricatures

Caricaturists See Cartoonists

Caring for nature. Guillain, C. **333.95**

Caring for your fish. Richardson, A. **639.34**

Caring for your hamster. Richardson, A. **636.9**

Caring for your hermit crab. Richardson, A. **639**

Carle, Eric
10 little rubber ducks **E**
The art of Eric Carle **741.6**
Do you want to be my friend? **E**
Does a kangaroo have a mother, too? **E**
The grouchy ladybug **E**
A house for Hermit Crab **E**
Mister Seahorse **E**
The mixed-up chameleon **E**
Papa, please get the moon for me **E**
"Slowly, slowly, slowly," said the sloth **E**
Today is Monday **782.42**
The very busy spider **E**
The very clumsy click beetle **E**
The very hungry caterpillar **E**
The very lonely firefly **E**
The very quiet cricket **E**
Where are you going? To see my friend! **E**
(il) Eric Carle's animals, animals. See Eric Carle's animals, animals **808.81**
(il) Eric Carle's dragons dragons and other creatures that never were. See Eric Carle's dragons dragons and other creatures that never were **808.81**
(il) Martin, B. Baby Bear, Baby Bear, what do you see? **E**
(il) Martin, B. Brown bear, brown bear what do you see? **E**
(il) Martin, B. Panda bear, panda bear, what do you see? **E**
(il) Martin, B. Polar bear, polar bear, what do you hear? **E**

Carling, Amelia Lau, 1949-
Mama & Papa have a store **E**
(il) Mora, P. Abuelos **E**

Carlos is gonna get it. Emerson, K. **Fic**

Carlow, Regina
Exploring the connection between children's literature and music **372**

Carls, Claudia
(il) Bell, A. The porridge pot **398.2**

Carl's sleepy afternoon. Day, A. **E**

Carlson, Drew
Attack of the Turtle **Fic**

Carlson, Laurie M., 1952-
Harry Houdini for kids **92**
Thomas Edison for kids **92**

Carlson, Lori M.
(ed) Cool salsa. See Cool salsa **811.008**

Carlson, Maria
(jt. auth) Prokofiev, S. Peter and the wolf **E**

Carlson, Nancy L., 1953-
Get up and go! **E**
Harriet and the roller coaster **E**
Henry and the Valentine surprise **E**
Hooray for Grandparent's Day **E**
I like me! **E**

Carlson, Natalie Savage, 1906-
The family under the bridge **Fic**

Carlson-Voiles, Polly, 1943-
Someone walks by **591.7**

Carlstrom, Nancy White, 1948-
It's your first day of school, Annie Claire **E**
Jesse Bear, what will you wear? **E**

Carluccio, Maria
The sounds around town   E

Carman, Patrick
The Dark Hills divide   Fic
The house of power   Fic

Carmi, Giora, 1944-
(il) Kimmel, E. A. The Chanukkah guest   E
(il) Schwartz, H. A journey to paradise and other Jewish tales   398.2

Carmichael, Clay
Wild things   Fic

Carmine. Sweet, M.   E

Carnation, Lily, Lily, Rose. Brewster, H.   Fic

Carney, Elizabeth, 1981-
Frogs!   597.8
(jt. auth) Johns, C. Face to face with cheetahs   599.75
(jt. auth) Nichols, M. Face to face with gorillas   599.8
(jt. auth) Rosing, N. Face to face with polar bears   599.78

Carney, William, 1840-1908
About
Clinton, C. Hold the flag high   973.7

Carnival
Hoyt-Goldsmith, D. Mardi Gras: a Cajun country celebration   394.25

Carnival of the animals   811.008

Carolina Harmony. McDowell, M. T.   Fic

Carolinda clatter!. Gerstein, M.   E

Caroline Arnold's animals [series]
Arnold, C. A platypus' world   599.2
Arnold, C. A wombat's world   599.2

Caroline Feller Bauer's new handbook for storytellers. Bauer, C. F.   372.6

Carolrhoda creative minds book [series]
Mitchell, B. Shoes for everyone: a story about Jan Matzeliger   92

Carolrhoda nature watch book [series]
Johnson, S. A. Crows   598
Stewart, M. Sloths   599.3
Stone, L. M. Tigers   599.75
Walker, S. M. Rays   597
Wilcox, C. Bald eagles   598

Carols
Ada, A. F. Merry Navidad!   394.26
Spirin, G. We three kings   782.28

Caron, Romi, 1967-
(il) Baillie, M. Small wonders   591.3

Carousels
Fiction
Hyde, H. S. Feivel's flying horses   E

Carpenter, Humphrey
The Oxford companion to children's literature   809

Carpenter, Nancy
(il) Ashman, L. M is for mischief   E
(il) Beard, D. B. Twister   E
(il) Bunting, E. Little Bear's little boat   E
(il) Bunting, E. A picnic in October   E
(il) Fleming, C. Imogene's last stand   E
(il) Hopkinson, D. Apples to Oregon   E

(il) Hopkinson, D. Fannie in the kitchen   641.5
(il) Offill, J. 17 things I'm not allowed to do anymore   E
(il) Yolen, J. My Uncle Emily   E

Carpentry
Walker, L. Carpentry for children   694
Fiction
Shelby, A. The man who lived in a hollow tree   E

Carpentry for children. Walker, L.   694

Carpetbag rule See Reconstruction (1865-1876)

Carpets See Rugs and carpets; Weaving

Carr, Jan, 1953-
Greedy Apostrophe   E

Carrasco, Xavier
Rumpelstiltskin   398.2

Carrel, Douglas
(il) Steer, D. The dragon diary   Fic

Carriages and carts
Ammon, R. Conestoga wagons   388.3

Carrick, Carol
Mothers are like that   E
Patrick's dinosaurs   E

Carrick, Donald
(il) Bunting, E. The Wednesday surprise   E
(il) Hooks, W. H. Moss gown   398.2
(il) Uchida, Y. Journey to Topaz   Fic

Carrick, Paul, 1946-
(il) Carrick, C. Mothers are like that   E
(il) Carrick, C. Patrick's dinosaurs   E
(il) Suen, A. Wired   621.319
(il) Zoehfeld, K. W. Dinosaur parents, dinosaur young   567.9

Carriers, Aircraft See Aircraft carriers

Carrilho, André
(il) McKissack, P. C. Porch lies   S C
(il) Winter, J. You never heard of Sandy Koufax!?   92

Carris, Joan Davenport, 1938-
Welcome to the Bed & Biscuit   Fic

Carroll, Lewis, 1832-1898
Alice through the looking glass   Fic
Alice's adventures in Wonderland [illustrated by Alison Jay]   Fic

[illustrated by Helen Oxenbury]   Fic

[illustrated by John Tenniel]   Fic

[illustrated by Robert Ingpen]   Fic
Alice's adventures in Wonderland; adaptation. See Sabuda, R. Alice's adventures in Wonderland   E
Jabberwocky   821
Lewis Carroll's Alice in Wonderland   Fic

Carroll, Lewis, 1832-1898
See/See also pages in the following book(s):
Ellis, S. From reader to writer   372.6

The **carrot** seed. Krauss, R.   E

Carrot soup. Segal, J.   E

Carrots

Fiction

Segal, J. Carrot soup   E

Carry me!. Stockdale, S.   **591.56**

Carryl, Charles E., 1841-1920
The camel's lament   E

Cars (Automobiles) *See* Automobiles

Cars. Crowther, R.   **629.222**

Cars. Hubbell, P.   E

Cars on Mars. Siy, A.   **629.43**

Cars on the move. Clark, W.   **629.222**

Carson, Kit, 1809-1868

About

Calvert, P. Kit Carson   **92**

Carson, Mary Kay, 1964-
Alexander Graham Bell   **92**
Emi and the rhino scientist   **599.66**
Exploring the solar system   **523.2**
Weather projects for young scientists   **551.5**
The Wright Brothers for kids   **629.13**

Carson, Rachel, 1907-1964

About

Ehrlich, A. Rachel   **92**
Gow, M. Rachel Carson   **92**
Scherer, G. Who on earth is Rachel Carson?   **92**

Carter, Abby
(il) Becker, B. Holbrook   **Fic**
(il) Dodds, D. A. Full house   **513**
(il) Jacobson, J. Andy Shane and the very bossy Dolores Starbuckle   **Fic**
(il) Kenah, K. The best seat in second grade   E
(il) Lindbergh, R. My hippie grandmother   E
(il) Sanders-Wells, L. Maggie's monkeys   E

Carter, David A.
600 black spots   E
Blue 2   E
One red dot   E
White noise   E
Yellow square   E

Cartlidge, Cherese
Home windmills   **621.4**
Water from air   **628.1**

Cartography *See* Maps

Cartooning

Technique

Artell, M. Funny cartooning for kids   **741.5**
Caldwell, B. Fantasy! cartooning   **741.5**
Roche, A. Cartooning   **741.5**

Cartooning. Roche, A.   **741.5**

Cartoonists
Gherman, B. Sparky: the life and art of Charles Schulz   **92**
Nobleman, M. T. Boys of steel [biography of Jerry Siegel and Joe Shuster]   **92**

The **cartoonist's** big book of drawing animals. Hart, C.   **741.5**

Cartoons and caricatures

See also Cartooning; Comic books, strips, etc.

Hart, C. The cartoonist's big book of drawing animals   **741.5**

Hart, C. Drawing the new adventure cartoons   **741.5**
Hart, C. Kids draw Manga Shoujo   **741.5**
Hart, C. You can draw cartoon animals   **741.5**
Stephens, J. Heroes!   **741.5**
Stephens, J. Monsters!   **741.5**
Stephens, J. Robots!   **741.5**

Fiction

Davis, K. The curse of Addy McMahon   **Fic**

Cartoons and comics *See* Cartoons and caricatures

Carts *See* Carriages and carts

Carus, Marianne
(ed) Celebrate Cricket. See Celebrate Cricket   **808.8**

Carver, George Washington, 1864?-1943

About

Bolden, T. George Washington Carver   **92**
Harness, C. The groundbreaking, chance-taking life of George Washington Carver and science & invention in America   **92**

Carville, James
Lu and the swamp ghost   E

Carving, Wood *See* Wood carving

Casanova, Mary
The hunter   **398.2**
The klipfish code   **Fic**
Some dog!   E
Utterly otterly day   E

Case, Chris, 1976-
Sophie and the next-door monsters   E

A **case** for Jenny Archer. Conford, E.   **Fic**

The **case** of the case of mistaken identity. Barnett, M.   **Fic**

The **case** of the hungry stranger. Bonsall, C. N.   E

The **case** of the lost boy. Butler, D. H.   **Fic**

The **case** of the missing marquess. Springer, N.   **Fic**

The **case** of the missing monkey. Rylant, C.   E

The **case** of the purloined professor. Cox, J.   **Fic**

The **case** of the stinky socks. Rockliff, M.   **Fic**

Caseley, Judith, 1951-
On the town   E

Casement, Rose
Black history in the pages of children's literature   **028.5**

Casey, Carolyn
Mary Cassatt   **92**

Casey, Dawn
The great race   **398.2**

Casey, Dawn, 1975-
The Barefoot book of Earth tales   **398.2**

Casey and Derek on the ice. Sederman, M.   E

Casey at the bat. Thayer, E. L.   **811**

Casey back at bat. Gutman, D.   **811**

Cash, Megan Montague
(jt. auth) Newgarden, M. Bow-Wow bugs a bug   E

Celebrate! It's cinco de mayo!. Levy, J.
394.26

Celebrate Kwanzaa. Altman, L. J. **394.26**

Celebrate Kwanzaa. Otto, C. **394.26**

Celebrate Martin Luther King, Jr., Day. Jeffrey,
L. S. **394.26**

Celebrate Passover. Heiligman, D. **296.4**

Celebrate Ramadan. Jeffrey, L. S. **297.3**

Celebrate Ramadan & Eid al-Fitr. Heiligman, D.
297.3

Celebrate Rosh Hashanah and Yom Kippur.
Heiligman, D. **296.4**

Celebrate Tet. Jeffrey, L. S. **394.26**

Celebrate Thanksgiving. Heiligman, D. **394.26**

Celebrate the 50 states. Leedy, L. **973**

Celebrate the states **973**

Celebrate the USA. Kuntz, L. **973**

Celebrate Valentine's Day. Otto, C. **394.26**

Celebrate with books. Blass, R. J. **028.1**

Celebrating a Quinceañera. Hoyt-Goldsmith, D.
392

Celebrating Chinese New Year. Hoyt-Goldsmith,
D. **394.26**

Celebrating culture in your library [series]
Pavon, A.-E. 25 Latino craft projects **027.62**

Celebrating Hanukkah. Hoyt-Goldsmith, D.
296.4

Celebrating Passover. Hoyt-Goldsmith, D.
296.4

Celebrating Ramadan. Hoyt-Goldsmith, D.
297.3

Celebrations. Bauer, C. F. **808.8**

Celebrations. Kindersley, A. **394.26**

Celebrities
Alcorn, S. A gift of days **808.88**
Fiction
Palmer, R. Yours truly, Lucy B. Parker: girl vs.
superstar **Fic**

Celenza, Anna Harwell
Gershwin's Rhapsody in Blue **E**

Celeste's Harlem Renaissance. Tate, E. E. **Fic**

Celestine, drama queen. Ives, P. **E**

Celia Cruz, Queen of salsa. Chambers, V. **92**

Celia's robot. Chang, M. S. **Fic**

Cells
Johnson, R. L. Mighty animal cells **571.6**
Lee, K. F. Cells **571.6**

Celtic civilization
Green, J. Ancient Celts **936**

Celts
Calvert, P. The ancient Celts **936**
Green, J. Ancient Celts **936**

Cemeteries
Fiction
Gaiman, N. The graveyard book **Fic**

Cendrars, Blaise, 1887-1961
Shadow **841**

Cendrillon. San Souci, R. **398.2**

Censorship
Adams, H. R. Ensuring intellectual freedom and
access to information in the school library
media program **027.8**
Pipkin, G. At the schoolhouse gate **373.1**

Census
Fiction
Davies, J. Tricking the Tallyman **E**

Centipedes
Blaxland, B. Centipedes, millipedes, and their
relatives **595.6**
Povey, K. D. Centipede **595.6**

Centipedes, millipedes, and their relatives.
Blaxland, B. **595.6**

Central America
Shields, C. J. Central America: facts and figures
972.8
Fiction
Colato Laínez, R. My shoes and I **E**

Central American Americans
Keedle, J. Americans from the Caribbean and
Central America **305.8**

Central heating. Singer, M. **811**

Central High School (Little Rock, Ark.)
Walker, P. R. Remember Little Rock **379**

Central Pacific Railroad
Halpern, M. Railroad fever **385.09**
Perritano, J. The transcontinental railroad
385.09
Fiction
Yin. Coolies **E**

Central Utah Relocation Center
Tunnell, M. O. The children of Topaz
940.53

Centsibility. Roderick, S. **332.024**

Cepeda, Joe
(il) Elya, S. M. N is for Navidad **E**
(il) Gauthier, G. A girl, a boy, and three robbers
Fic
(il) Montes, M. Juan Bobo goes to work
398.2
(il) Pattison, D. S. The journey of Oliver K.
Woodman **E**
(il) Reiche, D. I, Freddy **Fic**

Cephalopods
Blaxland, B. Octopuses, squids, and their relatives **594**

Cephalopods: octopuses, squids, and their relatives. See Blaxland, B. Octopuses, squids, and
their relatives **594**

Ceramics
Llimós, A. Easy clay crafts in 5 steps **738.1**

Cerebral palsy
Bjorklund, R. Cerebral palsy **616.8**
Levete, S. Explaining cerebral palsy **616.8**
Thompson, L. Ballerina dreams **792.8**
Fiction
Draper, S. M. Out of my mind **Fic**
Wait, L. Finest kind **Fic**

Cerebrovascular disease *See* Stroke

Cerniglia, Carlyn
(il) Matthews, T. L. Danger in the dark **Fic**

Cheaney, J. B.
The middle of somewhere   **Fic**
My friend, the enemy   **Fic**

Cheating in sports See Sports—Corrupt practices

Check, Laura, 1958-
Create your own candles   **745.5**

Checkerboard science library [series]
Wheeler, J. C. Alternative cars   **629.222**

Chedru, Delphine
Spot it!   **793.73**

Chee, Cheng-khee, 1934-
(il) Esbensen, B. J. Swing around the sun
    811

Chee-lin. Rumford, J.   **599.63**

Cheerleading
Fiction
Lester, H. Three cheers for Tacky   **E**

Cheese
Peterson, C. Extra cheese, please!   **637**

The **cheese.** Palatini, M.   **E**

Cheetah math. Nagda, A. W.   **513**

Cheetahs
Estigarribia, D. Cheetahs   **599.75**
Johns, C. Face to face with cheetahs   **599.75**
Nagda, A. W. Cheetah math   **513**
Nuzzolo, D. Cheetahs   **599.75**
Squire, A. Cheetahs   **599.75**

Chefs See Cooks

Chemical elements
Dingle, A. The periodic table   **546**
The Elements [Benchmark Bks. series]   **546**
Van Gorp, L. Elements   **540**

Chemical pollution See Pollution

Chemical reaction. Baxter, R.   **540**

Chemical reactions
Oxlade, C. Changing materials   **530.4**

Chemistry
Ballard, C. Mixtures and solutions   **541**
Baxter, R. Chemical reaction   **540**
Gardner, R. Ace your chemistry science project
    540.7
Gardner, R. Ace your science project using
chemistry magic and toys   **540.7**
Gardner, R. Easy genius science projects with
chemistry   **540.7**
Juettner, B. Molecules   **540**
Meiani, A. Chemistry   **540.7**
Newmark, A. Chemistry   **540**
Rhatigan, J. Cool chemistry concoctions
    540.7
Townsend, J. Crazy chemistry   **540**

Chemists
Cregan, E. R. Marie Curie   **92**
Krull, K. Marie Curie   **92**
McClafferty, C. K. Something out of nothing
[biography of Marie Curie]   **92**
Steele, P. Marie Curie   **92**

Chen, Chih-Yuan
Guji Guji   **E**
On my way to buy eggs   **E**

Chen, Jiang Hong, 1963-
The magic horse of Han Gan   **398.2**
Mao and me   **951.05**

Chen, Pauline, 1966-
Peiling and the chicken-fried Christmas   **Fic**

Chen, Yong, 1963-
A gift   **E**

Cheng, Andrea, 1957-
The bear makers   **Fic**
Brushing Mom's hair   **Fic**
Eclipse   **Fic**
Honeysuckle house   **Fic**
The lace dowry   **Fic**
Only one year   **Fic**
Shanghai messenger   **Fic**
Where the steps were   **Fic**

Cheong-Lum, Roseline Ng, 1962-
Haiti   **972.94**

Cheops, King of Egypt, fl. 2900-2877 B.C.
About
Weitzman, D. L. Pharaoh's boat   **932**

Chernaik, Judith
(ed) Carnival of the animals. See Carnival of the
animals   **811.008**

Chernick, Miriam
(jt. auth) Clark, D. C. A kid's guide to Washington, D.C.   **917.53**

Cherokee Indians
Bealer, A. W. Only the names remain
    970.004
Bruchac, J. The Trail of Tears   **970.004**
Dennis, Y. W. Sequoyah, 1770?-1843   **92**
Rumford, J. Sequoyah   **92**
Wade, M. D. Amazing Cherokee writer
Sequoyah   **92**
Folklore
Bruchac, J. The first strawberries   **398.2**
Bushyhead, R. H. Yonder mountain   **398.2**

Cherries
Fiction
Ehlert, L. Pie in the sky   **E**
Farmer, N. Clever Ali   **Fic**

Cherries and cherry pits. Williams, V. B.   **E**

Cherry, Lynne, 1952-
Flute's journey   **598**
The great kapok tree   **E**
How Groundhog's garden grew   **E**
How we know what we know about our chang-
ing climate   **363.7**
The sea, the storm, and the mangrove tangle
    E
(il) Viorst, J. If I were in charge of the world
and other worries   **811**

Cherry and Olive. Lacombe, B.   **E**

Cheryl Harness history [series]
Harness, C. The adventurous life of Myles Standish   **92**
Harness, C. The tragic tale of Narcissa Whitman
and a faithful history of the Oregon Trail
    92

Cheshire, Simon
The curse of the ancient mask and other case
files   **Fic**

Chess, Victoria, 1939-
(il) Schwartz, A. Ghosts!   **398.2**
(il) Van Laan, N. Teeny tiny tingly tales   **E**
(il) Wise, W. Ten sly piranhas   **E**

Children's literature—Bibliography—*Continued*
Zbaracki, M. D. Best books for boys   **028.5**
Bio-bibliography
Eighth book of junior authors and illustrators
  920.003
The Essential guide to children's books and their creators   **028.5**
McElmeel, S. L. 100 most popular picture book authors and illustrators   **810.3**
Murphy, B. T. Black authors and illustrators of books for children and young adults
  920.003
Ninth book of junior authors and illustrators
  920.003
Something about the author   **920.003**
Something about the author: autobiography series   **920.003**
Tenth book of junior authors and illustrators
  920.003
Vardell, S. M. Poetry people   **811**
Dictionaries
Carpenter, H. The Oxford companion to children's literature   **809**
Helbig, A. Dictionary of American children's fiction, 1995-1999   **028.5**
Latrobe, K. H. The children's literature dictionary   **028.5**
Encyclopedias
The Oxford encyclopedia of children's literature
  809

History and criticism
Baxter, K. A. From cover to cover   **028.1**
Bishop, R. S. Free within ourselves   **028.5**
Casement, R. Black history in the pages of children's literature   **028.5**
Children's books in children's hands   **028.5**
The Coretta Scott King awards, 1970-2009
  028.5
Embracing, evaluating, and examining African American children's and young adult literature   **028.5**
The Essential guide to children's books and their creators   **028.5**
Everything I need to know I learned from a children's book   **808.8**
Gillespie, J. T. The children's and young adult literature handbook   **011.6**
Gillespie, J. T. The Newbery/Printz companion
  028.5
Gilton, D. L. Multicultural and ethnic children's literature in the United States   **028.5**
Hamilton, V. Virginia Hamilton: speeches, essays, and conversations   **813.009**
Lerer, S. Children's literature   **028.5**
Marcus, L. S. Golden legacy   **070.5**
Marcus, L. S. Minders of make-believe
  070.5
The Norton anthology of children's literature
  808.8
Stephens, C. G. Coretta Scott King Award books   **028.5**
Sutherland, Z. Children & books   **028.5**
Vardell, S. M. Children's literature in action
  028.5
Wilkin, B. T. African and African American images in Newbery Award winning titles
  810.9

Yolen, J. Touch magic   **028.5**
Study and teaching
Ellis, S. From reader to writer   **372.6**
Scales, P. R. Teaching banned books   **323.44**
Children's literature. Lerer, S.   **028.5**
The **children's** literature dictionary. Latrobe, K. H.
  028.5
Children's literature gems. Bird, E.   **027.62**
Children's literature in action. Vardell, S. M.
  028.5
Children's moneymaking projects *See* Moneymaking projects for children
Children's Museum (Boston, Mass.)
Simonds, N. Moonbeams, dumplings & dragon boats   **394.26**
Children's poetry
  See also Lullabies; Nonsense verses; Nursery rhymes; Tongue twisters
Vardell, S. M. Poetry people   **811**
Children's stories from the Bible. Pirotta, S.
  220.9
Children's traditional games. Sierra, J.   **796**
A **children's** treasury of poems   **808.81**
Children's writer's & illustrator's market   **808**
Children's writer's & illustrator's market. See Children's writer's & illustrator's market
  808
Children's writings
Falvey, D. Letters to a soldier   **956.7**
—I never saw another butterfly—   **741.9**
River of words   **808.81**
Salting the ocean   **811.008**
Childress, Diana
The War of 1812   **973.5**
A **child's** book of prayers   **242**
A **child's** calendar. Updike, J.   **811**
A **child's** Christmas in Wales. Thomas, D.
  828
A **child's** Christmas in Wales [illustrated by Trina Schart Hyman] Thomas, D.   **828**
A **child's** day. Pearle, I.   **E**
A **child's** garden of verses. Stevenson, R. L.
  821
A **child's** good morning book. Brown, M. W.
  E
A **child's** introduction to poetry. Driscoll, M.
  808.81
The **Child's** World encyclopedia of the NFL
  796.332
Chile
Rau, D. M. Chile   **983**
Ray, D. K. To go singing through the world [biography of Pablo Neruda]   **92**
Winter, J. K. Chile   **983**
Fiction
Foreman, M. Mia's story   **E**
Chilean poets *See* Poets, Chilean
Chimp math. Nagda, A. W.   **529**
Chimpanzee rescue. Bow, P.   **599.8**
Chimpanzees
Bow, P. Chimpanzee rescue   **599.8**

Chimpanzees—*Continued*
Coxon, M. Termites on a stick	**599.8**
Goodall, J. The chimpanzees I love	**599.8**
Greenberg, D. A. Chimpanzees	**599.8**
Jankowski, C. Jane Goodall	**92**
Lockwood, S. Chimpanzees	**599.8**
Nagda, A. W. Chimp math	**529**

Fiction
Alborough, J. Tall	**E**
Durango, J. Cha-cha chimps	**E**
Hoban, L. Arthur's Christmas cookies	**E**

The **chimpanzees** I love. Goodall, J.	**599.8**

Chin, Jason, 1978-
Redwoods	**585**
(il) Jango-Cohen, J. Chinese New Year	**394.26**
(il) Thomson, S. L. Where do polar bears live?	**599.78**

Ch'in Shih-huang, Emperor of China, 259-210 B.C.
Tomb
Dean, A. Terra-cotta soldiers	**931**
O'Connor, J. The emperor's silent army	**931**

China
Asher, S. China	**951**
Ferroa, P. G. China	**951**
Fritz, J. Homesick: my own story	**92**
Keister, D. To grandmother's house	**951**
Li Cunxin. Dancing to freedom [biography of Li Cunxin]	**92**
Marx, T. Elephants and golden thrones	**951**
Quan, E. Once upon a full moon	**92**
Riehecky, J. China	**951**
Rumford, J. Chee-lin	**599.63**

Antiquities
Ball, J. A. Ancient China	**931**
Dean, A. Terra-cotta soldiers	**931**
O'Connor, J. The emperor's silent army	**931**
Shuter, J. Ancient China	**931**

Children
See Children—China
Civilization
Anderson, D. Ancient China	**709.51**
Ball, J. A. Ancient China	**931**
Cole, J. Ms. Frizzle's adventures: Imperial China	**931**
Schomp, V. The ancient Chinese	**931**
Shuter, J. Ancient China	**931**

Communism
See Communism—China
Fiction
Alexander, L. The remarkable journey of Prince Jen	**Fic**
Bridges, S. Y. Ruby's wish	**E**
Chen, Y. A gift	**E**
Cheng, A. Shanghai messenger	**Fic**
Compestine, Y. C. Boy dumplings	**E**
Compestine, Y. C. The runaway rice cake	**E**
DeJong, M. The house of sixty fathers	**Fic**
Demi. The emperor's new clothes	**E**
Demi. The girl who drew a phoenix	**E**
Demi. The greatest power	**E**
Demi. Kites	**E**
Demi. The magic pillow	**E**
Gower, C. Long-Long's New Year	**E**

Gunderson, J. The emperor's painting	**Fic**
Gunderson, J. The jade dragon	**Fic**
Gunderson, J. Stranger on the silk road	**Fic**
Gunderson, J. The terracotta girl	**Fic**
Lewis, E. F. Young Fu of the upper Yangtze	**Fic**
Lloyd, A. Year of the tiger	**Fic**
McCaughrean, G. The kite rider	**Fic**
McCully, E. A. Beautiful warrior	**E**
Muth, J. J. Stone soup	**398.2**
Niemann, C. Pet dragon	**E**
Noyes, D. Red butterfly	**E**
Partridge, E. Oranges on Golden Mountain	**E**
Poole, A. L. The pea blossom	**E**
Rocco, J. Wolf! wolf!	**E**
Santore, C. The Silk Princess	**E**
Tucker, K. The seven Chinese sisters	**E**
Wang Xiaohong. One year in Beijing	**E**
Williams, B. Lin Yi's lantern	**E**
Yep, L. Auntie Tiger	**E**
Yep, L. The dragon's child	**Fic**
Young, E. My Mei Mei	**E**

Folklore
See Folklore—China
Graphic novels
Jolley, D. Guan Yu	**741.5**

History
Cole, J. Ms. Frizzle's adventures: Imperial China	**931**

History—1949-1976—**Fiction**
Compestine, Y. C. Revolution is not a dinner party	**Fic**
Guo Yue. Little Leap Forward	**Fic**
Pennypacker, S. Sparrow girl	**E**

History—1949-1976—**Personal narratives**
Chen, J. H. Mao and me	**951.05**
Jiang, J.-l. Red scarf girl	**951.05**
Zhang, A. Red land, yellow river	**951.05**

Poetry
Young, E. Beyond the great mountains	**811**

Religion
Fisher, L. E. The gods and goddesses of ancient China	**299**

Science
See Science—China
Social life and customs
Demi. Happy, happy Chinese New Year!	**394.26**
Otto, C. Celebrate Chinese New Year	**394.26**

China (Republic of China, 1949-) *See* Taiwan

Chinatown (New York, N.Y.)
Fiction
Mak, K. My Chinatown	**E**

Chincoteague Island (Va.)
Fiction
Henry, M. Misty of Chincoteague	**Fic**
Jeffers, S. My Chincoteague pony	**E**

Chinese
Quan, E. Once upon a full moon	**92**

Fiction
Carling, A. L. Mama & Papa have a store	**E**

Chinese—*Continued*
United States—Fiction
Namioka, L. Yang the youngest and his terrible ear **Fic**

The **Chinese** American family album. Hoobler, D. **305.8**

Chinese Americans
See also Chinese—United States

Hoobler, D. The Chinese American family album **305.8**

Kuklin, S. How my family lives in America **305.8**

Biography
Yep, L. The lost garden **92**

Yoo, P. Shining star: the Anna May Wong story **92**

Fiction
Chang, M. S. Celia's robot **Fic**
Chen, Y. A gift **E**
Cheng, A. Honeysuckle house **Fic**
Cheng, A. Only one year **Fic**
Cheng, A. Shanghai messenger **Fic**
Chinn, K. Sam and the lucky money **E**
Coerr, E. Chang's paper pony **E**
Cummings, M. Three names of me **Fic**
Friedman, D. Star of the Week **E**
Hall, B. E. Henry and the kite dragon **E**
Isadora, R. Happy belly, happy smile **E**
Katz, K. My first Chinese New Year **E**
Lee, M. Landed **Fic**
Lin, G. Bringing in the New Year **E**
Lin, G. Dim sum for everyone! **E**
Look, L. Alvin Ho: allergic to girls, school, and other scary things **Fic**
Look, L. Henry's first-moon birthday **E**
Look, L. Love as strong as ginger **E**
Look, L. Ruby Lu, brave and true **Fic**
Look, L. Uncle Peter's amazing Chinese wedding **E**
Lord, B. B. In the Year of the Boar and Jackie Robinson **Fic**
Mak, K. My Chinatown **E**
McQuinn, A. My friend Mei Jing **E**
Partridge, E. Oranges on Golden Mountain **E**
Peacock, C. A. Mommy far, Mommy near **E**
Thong, R. One is a drummer **E**
Thong, R. Red is a dragon **E**
Thong, R. Round is a mooncake **E**
Wong, J. S. Apple pie 4th of July **E**
Yang, B. Hannah is my name **E**
Yee, L. Millicent Min, girl genius **Fic**
Yep, L. The dragon's child **Fic**
Yep, L. The magic paintbrush **Fic**
Yep, L. The traitor **Fic**
Yep, L. When the circus came to town **Fic**
Yin. Brothers **E**
Yin. Coolies **E**
Young, E. My Mei Mei **E**
Social life and customs
Hoyt-Goldsmith, D. Celebrating Chinese New Year **394.26**
Waters, K. Lion dancer: Ernie Wan's Chinese New Year **394.26**

Chinese art
Anderson, D. Ancient China **709.51**

Chinese authors *See* Authors, Chinese

Chinese civilization *See* China—Civilization

Chinese cooking
Lee, F. Fun with Chinese cooking **641.5**
See/See also pages in the following book(s):
Simonds, N. Moonbeams, dumplings & dragon boats **394.26**

Chinese language
Lee, H. V. 1, 2, 3 go! **495.1**
Lee, H. V. At the beach **495.1**
Niemann, C. Pet dragon **E**

The **Chinese** mirror. Ginsburg, M. **398.2**

Chinese New Year
Bledsoe, K. E. Chinese New Year crafts **745.594**
Demi. Happy, happy Chinese New Year! **394.26**
Hoyt-Goldsmith, D. Celebrating Chinese New Year **394.26**
Jango-Cohen, J. Chinese New Year **394.26**
Kule, E. A. Celebrate Chinese New Year **394.26**
McGee, R. Paper crafts for Chinese New Year **745.594**
Otto, C. Celebrate Chinese New Year **394.26**
Waters, K. Lion dancer: Ernie Wan's Chinese New Year **394.26**
See/See also pages in the following book(s):
Simonds, N. Moonbeams, dumplings & dragon boats **394.26**
Fiction
Chen, Y. A gift **E**
Chinn, K. Sam and the lucky money **E**
Compestine, Y. C. The runaway rice cake **E**
Gower, C. Long-Long's New Year **E**
Katz, K. My first Chinese New Year **E**
Lin, G. Bringing in the New Year **E**
Lin, G. The Year of the Dog **Fic**
Wong, J. S. This next New Year **E**
Yep, L. When the circus came to town **Fic**

Chinese New Year crafts. Bledsoe, K. E. **745.594**

Chinese science *See* Science—China

Chinn, Karen, 1959-
Sam and the lucky money **E**

Chinook Indians
Folklore
Taylor, H. P. Coyote places the stars **398.2**

Chipmunks
Folklore
Bruchac, J. How Chipmunk got his stripes **398.2**

Chippendale, Lisa A.
Triumph of the imagination: the story of writer J.K. Rowling **92**

Chippewa Indians *See* Ojibwa Indians

Chirping crickets. Berger, M. **595.7**

Chisholm, Penny *See* Chisholm, Sallie

Chisholm, Sallie
(jt. auth) Bang, M. Living sunlight **572**

Chisholm, Shirley, 1924-2005
See/See also pages in the following book(s):
Pinkney, A. D. Let it shine **920**

Chivalry
See also Medieval civilization

Chmara, Theresa
Privacy and confidentiality issues　344

Cho, Michael
(il) Ali, D. Media madness　302.23

Chock full of chocolate. MacLeod, E.　641.6

Chocolate, Debbi, 1954-
El barrio　E
My first Kwanzaa book　394.26

Chocolate
Burleigh, R. Chocolate　641.3
MacLeod, E. Chock full of chocolate　641.6
Price, S. The story behind chocolate　641.3
Ridley, S. A chocolate bar　664
Fiction
Cali, D. I love chocolate　E
Smith, R. K. Chocolate fever　Fic

A **chocolate** bar. Ridley, S.　664

Chocolate fever. Smith, R. K.　Fic

The **Choctaw**. De Capua, S.　970.004

Choctaw Indians
De Capua, S. The Choctaw　970.004
Tingle, T. Saltypie　92
Fiction
Tingle, T. Crossing Bok Chitto　Fic

Chodos-Irvine, Margaret
Best best friends　E
Ella Sarah gets dressed　E
(il) Cruise, R. Only you　E
(il) Swanson, S. M. To be like the sun　E
(il) Wong, J. S. Apple pie 4th of July　E
(il) Wong, J. S. Buzz　E
(il) Wong, J. S. Hide & seek　E

Chödzin, Sherab
The wisdom of the crows and other Buddhist tales　294.3

Choi, Sook Nyul
Halmoni and the picnic　E

Choi, Yangsook
Behind the mask　E
(il) Park, F. Good-bye, 382 Shin Dang Dong　E
(il) Wong, J. S. This next New Year　E

Choice (Psychology)
See also Decision making
Parker, V. Making choices　170

Choirs (Music)
Fiction
Bauer, A. C. E. No castles here　Fic
Payne, C. C. Something to sing about　Fic

Choksi, Nishant
(il) Law, S. Really, really big questions　100

Choldenko, Gennifer, 1957-
Al Capone does my shirts　Fic
If a tree falls at lunch period　Fic
Louder, Lili　E
Notes from a liar and her dog　Fic

Chollat, Emilie
(il) Gershator, P. Who's awake in springtime?　E

Choo choo. Horáček, P.　E

Choo choo clickety-clack!. Mayo, M.　E

Choosing books for children. Hearne, B. G.　028.5

Chopin, Frédéric, 1810-1849
See/See also pages in the following book(s):
Krull, K. Lives of the musicians　920

Choral societies
See also Choirs (Music)

Chorao, Kay, 1936-
D is for drums　975.5
(il) Adler, D. A. It's time to sleep, it's time to dream　E
(comp) Rhymes round the world. See Rhymes round the world　808.81
(il) Sartell, D. Time for bed, baby Ted　E

Choreographers
Reich, S. José! [biography of José Limón]　92

Chorn-Pond, Arn *See* Arn Chorn-Pond

Choung, Euh-Hee
Minji's salon　E

Chowder. Brown, P.　E

Chrisp, Peter
Atlas of ancient worlds　911
Welcome to the Globe　822.3

Christ *See* Jesus Christ

Christelow, Eileen, 1943-
Five little monkeys jumping on the bed　E
Letters from a desperate dog　E
Vote!　324
What do authors do?　808

Christensen, Bonnie, 1951-
Django [Reinhardt]　92
Woody Guthrie, poet of the people　92
(il) Myers, W. D. Ida B. Wells　92
(il) Nikola-Lisa, W. Magic in the margins　E
(il) Osborne, M. P. Pompeii　937

Christian X, King of Denmark, 1870-1947
Fiction
Deedy, C. A. The yellow star　Fic

Christian, Fletcher, 1764-1793
About
O'Brien, P. The mutiny on the Bounty　910.4

Christian life
Fiction
Bergren, L. T. God found us you　E
De Paola, T. Pascual and the kitchen angels　E
Dutton, S. Mary Mae and the gospel truth　Fic
Evans, F. W. Hush harbor　E
Kuijer, G. The book of everything　Fic
Parry, R. Heart of a shepherd　Fic
Payne, C. C. Something to sing about　Fic
Smiley, J. The Georges and the Jewels　Fic

Christian saints
De Paola, T. Patrick: patron saint of Ireland　92
Demi. The legend of Saint Nicholas　92
Hodges, M. Joan of Arc　92
Kennedy, R. F. Saint Francis of Assisi　271
Norris, K. The holy twins: Benedict and Scholastica　92
Sabuda, R. Saint Valentine　92

Clarabelle. Peterson, C.   **636.2**

Clare, of Assisi, Saint, 1194-1253
About
Visconti, G. Clare and Francis   **271**

Clare and Francis. Visconti, G.   **271**

Clarence Cochran, a human boy. Loizeaux, W.   **Fic**

Clarice Bean spells trouble. Child, L.   **Fic**

Clark, Christopher Stuart- *See* Stuart-Clark, Christopher

Clark, Clara Gillow, 1951-
Hill Hawk Hattie   **Fic**

Clark, Diane C.
A kid's guide to Washington, D.C.   **917.53**

Clark, Emma Chichester- *See* Chichester-Clark, Emma, 1955-

Clark, Warren
(il) Swanson, D. Nibbling on Einstein's brain   **500**

Clark, William, 1770-1838
About
Faber, H. Lewis and Clark   **978**
Perritano, J. The Lewis and Clark Expedition   **978**
Schanzer, R. How we crossed the West   **978**
Fiction
Myers, L. Lewis and Clark and me   **Fic**

Clark, Willow
Bikes on the move   **629.227**
Boats on the move   **623.82**
Cars on the move   **629.222**
Motorcycles on the move   **629.227**
Planes on the move   **629.133**
Trains on the move   **625.1**

Clark R. Bavin National Fish and Wildlife Forensics Laboratory *See* U.S. Fish and Wildlife Service. Forensics Laboratory

Clarke, Gregory, 1959-
(il) Lerman, J. How to raise Mom and Dad   **E**

Clarke, J. (Jane), 1954-
Stuck in the mud   **E**

Clarke, Jane *See* Clarke, J. (Jane)

Clarke, Penny
Hippos   **599.63**

Clarkson, Karen
(il) Tingle, T. Saltypie   **92**

Class clown. Hurwitz, J.   **Fic**

A class of their own [series]
Arato, R. Protists   **579**
Barker, D. M. Archaea   **579.3**
Levine, S. Animals   **590**
Levine, S. Plants   **580**
Wearing, J. Bacteria   **579.3**
Wearing, J. Fungi   **579**

Classic collectible pop-up [series]
Reinhart, M. A pop-up book of nursery rhymes   **398.8**

Classic fairy tale collection [series]
Cech, J. Puss in boots   **398.2**

Classical antiquities
See also Greece—Antiquities; Rome—Antiquities; Rome (Italy)—Antiquities

Classical civilization
See also Rome—Civilization

Classical music *See* Music

Classical mythology
See also Eros (Greek deity); Greek mythology; Persephone (Greek deity); Psyche (Greek deity); Zeus (Greek deity)
Aliki. The gods and goddesses of Olympus   **292**
Bryant, M. E. Oh my gods!   **292**
Bryant, M. E. She's all that!   **292**
Burleigh, R. Pandora   **398.2**
Byrd, R. The hero and the minotaur   **398.2**
Craft, M. Cupid and Psyche   **292**
Curlee, L. Mythological creatures   **292**
Harris, J. Strong stuff   **398.2**
Karas, G. B. Young Zeus   **292**
Kelly, S. What a beast!   **398**
Kimmel, E. A. The McElderry book of Greek myths   **292**
Lupton, H. The adventures of Odysseus   **292**
Mayer, M. Pegasus   **292**
McCaughrean, G. Hercules   **292**
McCaughrean, G. Odysseus   **292**
McCaughrean, G. Perseus   **292**
Mitton, J. Once upon a starry night   **523.8**
O'Connor, G. Zeus   **741.5**
Osborne, M. P. Favorite Greek myths   **292**
Otfinoski, S. All in the family   **292**
Rylant, C. The beautiful stories of life   **292**
Steer, D. The mythology handbook   **292**
Fiction
Collins, R. Medusa Jones   **Fic**
Coville, B. Juliet Dove, Queen of Love   **Fic**
Hennesy, C. Pandora gets jealous   **Fic**
Myers, C. Wings   **E**
Springer, N. Dusssie   **Fic**
Stanley, D. The trouble with wishes   **E**

Claws
Cooper, J. Hooves and claws   **591.47**

Claws, coats, and camouflage. Goodman, S.   **591.4**

Clay, Cassius *See* Ali, Muhammad, 1942-

Clay
Kenney, K. L. Super simple clay projects   **738.1**
Llimós, A. Easy clay crafts in 5 steps   **738.1**

Clay boy. Ginsburg, M.   **398.2**

Claybourne, Anna
Forms of energy   **531**
The nature of matter   **530.4**

Clayman, Deborah Paula *See* Da Costa, Deborah

Clayton, Elaine, 1961-
(jt. auth) Smiley, J. The Georges and the Jewels   **Fic**
(il) Zimmer, T. V. 42 miles   **Fic**

Clayton, Sally Pomme
Amazons!   **398.2**
Persephone   **292**
Tales told in tents   **398.2**

Clean air. Bridges, A.   **363.7**

Clean water. Geiger, B.   363.7

Cleanliness

See also Hygiene; Sanitation

Ehrlich, F. Does an elephant take a bath?   E

Fielding, B. Animal baths   591.5

Murphy, S. J. Mighty Maddie   389

Fiction

Cuyler, M. Monster mess!   E

Geisert, A. Hogwash   E

Hannigan, K. Emmaline and the bunny   Fic

Keane, D. Sloppy Joe   E

McMullan, K. I'm dirty!   E

Palatini, M. Gorgonzola   E

Teague, M. Pigsty   E

Teckentrup, B. Big Smelly Bear   E

Wight, E. Frankie Pickle and the closet of doom
    741.5

Cleary, Beverly

Dear Mr. Henshaw   Fic

Ellen Tebbits   Fic

Henry Huggins   Fic

The hullabaloo ABC   E

Mitch and Amy   Fic

The mouse and the motorcycle   Fic

Muggie Maggie   Fic

Otis Spofford   Fic

Ramona the pest   Fic

Socks   Fic

Strider   Fic

Cleary, Brian P., 1959-

The action of subtraction   513

But and for, yet and nor   425

Hairy, scary, ordinary   428

How long or how wide?   530.8

How much can a bare bear bear?   428

I and you and don't forget who   428

The laugh stand   817

Lazily, crazily, just a bit nasally   428

"Mrs. Riley Bought Five Itchy Aardvarks" and
other painless tricks for memorizing science
facts   507

On the scale   530.8

The punctuation station   428

Quirky, jerky, extra-perky   428

Stop and go, yes and no   428

Stroll and walk, babble and talk   428

Cleaver, Bill

(jt. auth) Cleaver, V. Where the lillies bloom
    Fic

Cleaver, Vera

Where the lillies bloom   Fic

Clemens, Samuel Langhorne *See* Twain, Mark,
1835-1910

Clemens, Susy, 1872-1894

About

Kerley, B. The extraordinary Mark Twain (according to Susy)   92

Clément, Frédéric

(il) Freedman, R. Confucius   92

Clement, Gary

(il) Funston, S. It's all in your head   612.8

(il) King, T. A Coyote solstice tale   Fic

(il) Lottridge, C. B. Stories from Adam and Eve
to Ezekiel   220.9

(il) Shepard, A. One-Eye! Two-Eyes! Three-
Eyes!   398.2

Clement, Nathan, 1966-

Drive   E

Clemente, Roberto, 1934-1972

About

Perdomo, W. Clemente!   92

Winter, J. Roberto Clemente   92

See/See also pages in the following book(s):

Krull, K. Lives of the athletes   920

Clemente!. Perdomo, W.   92

Clementine. Pennypacker, S.   Fic

Clements, Andrew, 1949-

Circus family dog   E

Dogku   811

Extra credit   Fic

Frindle   Fic

The handiest things in the world   E

The janitor's boy   Fic

The Landry News   Fic

Lost and found   Fic

Lunch money   Fic

A million dots   513

No talking   Fic

The report card   Fic

Room one   Fic

The school story   Fic

We the children   Fic

Workshop   621.9

Clemesha, David

(jt. auth) Zimmerman, A. G. Dig!   E

(jt. auth) Zimmerman, A. G. Digger man   E

(il) Zimmerman, A. G. Fire engine man   E

(jt. auth) Zimmerman, A. G. Trashy town   E

Clemmons, Brad

(jt. auth) Harris, P. K. Welcome to Switzerland
    949.4

Cleopatra, Queen of Egypt, d. 30 B.C.

About

Blackaby, S. Cleopatra   92

Stanley, D. Cleopatra   92

See/See also pages in the following book(s):

Krull, K. Lives of extraordinary women   920

Meltzer, M. Ten queens   920

Clergy

See also Priests

Granfield, L. Out of slavery   264

Jackson Issa, K. Howard Thurman's great hope
    92

Fiction

Gibfried, D. Brother Juniper   E

Ray, D. Singing hands   Fic

Cleveland (Ohio)

Fiction

Merrill, J. The toothpaste millionaire   Fic

Clever Ali. Farmer, N.   Fic

Clever Beatrice. Willey, M.   398.2

Clever camouflage. Pryor, K. J.   591.47

Clever duck. King-Smith, D.   Fic

Clever Rachel. Waldman, D.   398.2

The **clever** stick. Lechner, J.   E

Click, clack, moo. Cronin, D.   E

Cochran, Bill, 1966-
The forever dog   E
My parents are divorced, my elbows have nicknames, and other facts about me   E

Cochran, Josh
(il) Bardhan-Quallen, S. The real monsters   **001.9**
(il) Wetzel, C. Haunted U.S.A.   **133.1**

Cochran, Thomas, 1955-
Running the dogs   Fic

Cochrane, Elizabeth See Bly, Nellie, 1864-1922

Cock-a-doodle Christmas!. Hillenbrand, W.   E

Cock-a-doodle quack! quack!. Baddiel, I.   E

Cockcroft, Jason
Counter clockwise   Fic
(il) Bradman, T. Daddy's lullaby   E

Cockroaches
Merrick, P. Cockroaches   **595.7**
    Fiction
Cannon, J. Crickwing   E
Loizeaux, W. Clarence Cochran, a human boy   Fic
Pochocki, E. The blessing of the beasts   E
    Folklore
Deedy, C. A. Martina the beautiful cockroach   **398.2**

CoConis, Constantinos See CoConis, Ted

CoConis, Ted
(il) Byars, B. C. The summer of the swans   Fic

Cocovini, Abby
What's inside your tummy, Mommy?   **612.6**

Code deciphering See Cryptography

Code red [series]
Feigenbaum, A. Emergency at Three Mile Island   **621.48**

Codell, Esmé Raji, 1968-
How to get your child to love reading   **028.5**

Codes See Ciphers

Codes and ciphers. Gilbert, A.   **652**

Codfish
Kurlansky, M. The cod's tale   **639.2**

The **cod's** tale. Kurlansky, M.   **639.2**

Cody, Matthew
Powerless   Fic

Cody, William Frederick See Buffalo Bill, 1846-1917

Coelacanth
Walker, S. M. Fossil fish found alive   **597**

Coerr, Eleanor, 1922-
The big balloon race   E
Chang's paper pony   E
The Josefina story quilt   E
Sadako [biography of Sadako Sasaki]   **92**
Sadako and the thousand paper cranes [biography of Sadako Sasaki]   **92**

Coffelt, Nancy
Dogs in space   E
Fred stays with me   E

Coffey, Tim
(il) MacDonald, M. R. Mabela the clever   **398.2**

Coffin, Levi, 1789-1877
    Fiction
Morrow, B. O. A good night for freedom   E

Cogswell, Matthew
(il) Coville, B. Thor's wedding day   Fic

Cogswell, Alice
    About
McCully, E. A. My heart glow: Alice Cogswell, Thomas Gallaudet and the birth of American sign language   **92**

Cohagan, Carolyn
The lost children   Fic

Cohen, Barbara, 1932-1992
Canterbury tales   **821**
Molly's pilgrim   E
Thank you, Jackie Robinson   Fic

Cohen, Betsy Diamant- See Diamant-Cohen, Betsy

Cohen, Caron Lee
The mud pony   **398.2**

Cohen, Charles D.
The Seuss, the whole Seuss, and nothing but the Seuss   **92**
(jt. auth) Seuss, Dr. Yertle the turtle and other stories   E

Cohen, Deborah Bodin, 1968-
Nachshon, who was afraid to swim   E

Cohen, Jacqueline M.
(il) Stampler, A. R. Shlemazel and the remarkable spoon of Pohost   **398.2**

Cohen, Judith Jango- See Jango-Cohen, Judith

Cohen, Lisa
(il) Troupe, Q. Little Stevie Wonder   **92**

Cohen, Lisa, 1963-
(il) Tokunbo, D. The sound of Kwanzaa   **394.26**

Cohen, Miriam, 1926-
First grade takes a test   E
Jim's dog Muffins   E
Mimmy and Sophie all around the town   Fic
My big brother   E
Will I have a friend?   E

Cohen, Santiago
(il) Gershator, P. Zoo day olé!   E
(il) Vamos, S. R. Before you were here, mi amor   E
(il) Ziefert, H. Home for Navidad   E
(il) Ziefert, H. One smart skunk   E

Cohen, Tish, 1963-
The invisible rules of the Zoë Lama   Fic

Cohn, Diana
Namaste!   E

Cohn, Rachel
The Steps   Fic

Cohn, Scotti
One wolf howls   **599.77**

Coins
Hoban, T. 26 letters and 99 cents   E
Leedy, L. Follow the money!   **332.4**
Orr, T. Coins and other currency   **332.4**

Collins-Philippe, Jane
  (ed) Sail away with me. *See* Sail away with me
      808.81

Collodi, Carlo, 1826-1890
  The adventures of Pinocchio [illustrated by Roberto Innocenti]   **Fic**

Colman, Penny
  Adventurous women   **920**
  Rosie the riveter   **331.4**

Colombia
  Croy, A. Colombia   **986.1**
  De Capua, S. Colombia   **986.1**
  DuBois, J. Colombia   **986.1**
  Winter, J. Biblioburro   **E**
          Fiction
  Durango, J. The walls of Cartagena   **Fic**

Colombian authors *See* Authors, Colombian

Colombo, Cristoforo *See* Columbus, Christopher

Colón, Raúl
  (il) Burleigh, R. Pandora   **398.2**
  (il) Gray, L. M. My mama had a dancing heart   **E**
  (il) Grimes, N. What is goodbye?   **811**
  (il) Hopkinson, D. A band of angels   **E**
  (il) Johnston, T. Any small goodness   **Fic**
  (il) Martinez, R. Once upon a time   **398.2**
  (il) McCourt, F. Angela and the baby Jesus   **E**
  (il) Michelson, R. As good as anybody: Martin Luther King Jr. and Abraham Joshua Heschel's amazing march toward freedom   **92**
  (il) Mora, P. Doña Flor   **E**
  (il) Mora, P. Tomás and the library lady   **E**
  (il) Reich, S. José! [biography of José Limón]   **92**
  (il) Shelton, P. Y. Child of the civil rights movement   **323.1**
  (il) Storace, P. Sugar Cane   **398.2**
  (il) Wilson, K. How to bake an American pie   **E**
  (il) Winter, J. Roberto Clemente   **92**
  (il) Yolen, J. Mightier than the sword   **398.2**

Colonial America and the Revolutionary War   **973.2**

Colonial craftsmen and the beginnings of American industry. Tunis, E.   **680**

Colonial days. King, D. C.   **973.2**

Colonial living. Tunis, E.   **973.2**

Colonial voices. Winters, K.   **973.3**

Colonial Williamsburg (Williamsburg, Va.)
  Chorao, K. D is for drums   **975.5**
  Kostyal, K. M. 1776   **973.3**

Colonial Williamsburg Foundation
  Kostyal, K. M. 1776   **973.3**

Color
  Barton, C. The Day-Glo brothers   **535.6**
  Color   **535.6**
  Ehlert, L. Color farm   **E**
  Ehlert, L. Color zoo   **E**
  Farndon, J. Color   **535.6**
  Fielding, B. Animal colors   **591.47**
  Fleming, D. Lunch   **E**

  Gardner, R. Dazzling science projects with light and color   **535**
  Hoban, T. Colors everywhere   **E**
  Hoban, T. Is it red? Is it yellow? Is it blue?   **E**
  Hoban, T. Of colors and things   **E**
  Houblon, M. A world of colors   **535.6**
  McMillan, B. Growing colors   **E**
  Milich, Z. City colors   **E**
  Rotner, S. Shades of people   **E**
  Seeger, L. V. Lemons are not red   **E**
  Shahan, S. Spicy hot colors: colores picantes   **E**
  Shannon, G. White is for blueberry   **E**
  Sís, P. Ballerina!   **E**
  Stewart, M. Why do we see rainbows?   **612.8**
  Thong, R. Red is a dragon   **E**
  Wood, A. The deep blue sea   **E**
  See/See also pages in the following book(s):
  Luxbacher, I. The jumbo book of art   **702.8**
          Fiction
  Averbeck, J. In a blue room   **E**
  Chessa, F. Holly's red boots   **E**
  Cottin, M. The black book of colors   **E**
  Dobbins, J. Driving my tractor   **E**
  Feiffer, K. Double pink   **E**
  Gonzalez, M. C. My colors, my world = Mis colores, mi mundo   **E**
  Gravett, E. Orange pear apple bear   **E**
  Guy, G. F. Siesta   **E**
  Harper, C. M. Pink me up   **E**
  Hopgood, T. Wow! said the owl   **E**
  Jay, A. Red green blue   **E**
  Lionni, L. Little blue and little yellow   **E**
  Martin, B. A beasty story   **E**
  Martin, B. Brown bear, brown bear what do you see?   **E**
  Otoshi, K. One   **E**
  Portis, A. A penguin story   **E**
  Sattler, J. Sylvie   **E**
  Sidman, J. Red sings from treetops   **E**
  Slater, D. Baby shoes   **E**
  Tafuri, N. Blue Goose   **E**
  Tidholm, A.-C. Knock! knock!   **E**
  Zolotow, C. Mr. Rabbit and the lovely present   **E**

          Graphic novels
  Cammuso, F. Otto's orange day   **741.5**
          Poetry
  Iyengar, M. M. Tan to tamarind   **811**
  Larios, J. H. Yellow elephant   **811**
  Luján, J. Colors! Colores!   **861**
  O'Neill, M. L. D. Hailstones and halibut bones   **811**

Color   **535.6**

Color farm. Ehlert, L.   **E**

Color in art
  Benduhn, T. What is color?   **701**
  Gogh, V. v. Vincent's colors   **759.9492**
  Gonyea, M. A book about color   **701**
  Sellier, M. Renoir's colors   **759.05**
  Wing, N. An eye for color: the story of Josef Albers   **92**

The **color** of home. Hoffman, M.   **E**

The **color** of my words. Joseph, L.   **Fic**

Color zoo. Ehlert, L.   E

Colorado

Fiction

Avi. The secret school   Fic
Danneberg, J. Family reminders   Fic
Eboch, C. The ghost on the stairs   Fic
Ferris, J. Much ado about Grubstake   Fic
Mason, T. The last synapsid   Fic
Mills, C. How Oliver Olson changed the world   Fic
Nuzum, K. A. The leanin' dog   Fic
Oswald, N. Nothing here but stones   Fic
Ramthun, B. The White Gates   Fic

Gold discoveries—Fiction

Avi. Hard gold   Fic

Colorado River (Colo.-Mexico)

Ray, D. K. Down the Colorado [biography of John Wesley Powell]   92
Waldman, S. The last river   978

Colorful peacocks. Underwood, D.   598

Colors! Colores!. Luján, J.   861

Colors everywhere. Hoban, T.   E

Colosseum (Rome, Italy)

Mann, E. The Roman Colosseum   937
Nardo, D. Roman amphitheaters   725

Coltrane, John, 1926-1967

About

Weatherford, C. B. Before John was a jazz giant: a song of John Coltrane   92
(jt. auth) Raschka, C. John Coltrane's Giant steps   E

Columbia (Space shuttle)

Cole, M. D. The Columbia space shuttle disaster   629.44

Columbia. See Cole, M. D. The Columbia space shuttle disaster   629.44

The Columbia space shuttle disaster. Cole, M. D.   629.44

Columbus, Christopher

About

Bodden, V. Columbus reaches the New World   970.01
Collier, J. L. Christopher Columbus   92
Fritz, J. Where do you think you're going, Christopher Columbus?   92
Markle, S. Animals Christopher Columbus saw   970.01
See/See also pages in the following book(s):
Fritz, J. Around the world in a hundred years   910.4

Columbus reaches the New World. Bodden, V.   970.01

Colvin, Claudette
See/See also pages in the following book(s):
Freedman, R. Freedom walkers   323.1

Coman, Carolyn
What Jamie saw   Fic

The Comanche. De Capua, S.   970.004

Comanche Indians
De Capua, S. The Comanche   970.004
See/See also pages in the following book(s):
Freedman, R. Indian chiefs   920

Come and play   305.23

Come back, cat. Lexau, J. M.   E

Come back, salmon. Cone, M.   639.3

Come fly with me. Ichikawa, S.   E

Come here cat. See Lexau, J. M. Come back, cat   E

Come look with me: Asian art. Lane, K.   709.5

Come look with me: discovering African American art for children. Rolling, J. H., Jr.   704

Come look with me: discovering women artists for children. Coyne, J. T.   704

Come look with me: Latin American art. Lane, K.   709.8

Come on, rain!. Hesse, K.   E

Come sing, Jimmy Jo. Paterson, K.   Fic

Come to the castle!. Ashman, L.   940.1

Come to the fairies' ball. Yolen, J.   E

Come to the ocean's edge. Pringle, L. P.   577.7

Come with me. Nye, N. S.   811

Comeback kids [series]
Lupica, M. Hot hand   Fic

Comedians
Fleischman, S. Sir Charlie [biography of Charlie Chaplin]   92

Fiction

O'Malley, K. Animal crackers fly the coop   E

Comerford, Lynda B.
Rissa Bartholomew's declaration of independence   Fic

Comets
Cole, M. D. Comets and asteroids   523.6
Sherman, J. Asteroids, meteors, and comets   523.4
Simon, S. Comets, meteors, and asteroids   523.6

Comets and asteroids. Cole, M. D.   523.6

Comets, meteors, and asteroids. Simon, S.   523.6

Comets, stars, the Moon, and Mars. Florian, D.   811

Comic books, strips, etc.
See also Cartoons and caricatures; Graphic novels
Davis, J. Garfield: 30 years of laughs & lasagna   741.5
Miller, R. H. Stan Lee   92
The TOON treasury of classic children's comics   741.5

Authorship

Sturm, J. Adventures in cartooning   741.5

Fiction

David, P. Mascot to the rescue!   Fic
Knapman, T. Mungo and the spiders from space   E

History and criticism

Graphic novels beyond the basics   025.2
Rosinsky, N. M. Graphic content!   741.5

Comics crash course. Giarrano, V.   741.5

Comin' down to storytime. Reid, R.   E

Coming home [biography of Langston Hughes] Cooper, F.   **92**

The **coming** of dragons. Lake, A. J.   **Fic**

Coming on home soon. Woodson, J.   **E**

Coming to America. Wolf, B.   **305.8**

The **coming** to America cookbook. D'Amico, J.   **641.5**

Coming to America: the story of immigration. Maestro, B.   **325.73**

Comins, Andy
   (il) Turner, P. S. The frog scientist   **597.8**

Commander Toad and the voyage home. Yolen, J.   **E**

Commercial fishing
   Kurlansky, M. The cod's tale   **639.2**

Commodore Perry in the land of the Shogun. Blumberg, R.   **952**

The **common** cold. Landau, E.   **616.2**

Commonwealth countries
   See also Great Britain—Colonies

Communicable diseases
   See also Smallpox
   Ballard, C. AIDS and other epidemics   **614.5**

Communication
   See also Telecommunication
   Rand, A. Sparkle and spin   **E**
   Solway, A. Communication   **303.4**
       Fiction
   Lechner, J. The clever stick   **E**
   Smith, L. The big elephant in the room   **E**
   Weeks, S. Woof   **E**

Communication among animals *See* Animal communication

Communication arts *See* Language arts

Communication systems, Computer *See* Computer networks

Communism
       Fiction
   Compestine, Y. C. Revolution is not a dinner party   **Fic**
   Guo Yue. Little Leap Forward   **Fic**
       China
   See/See also pages in the following book(s):
   Jiang, J.-l. Red scarf girl   **951.05**

Community and libraries *See* Libraries and community

Community development
   See also City planning

Community life
   Ajmera, M. Be my neighbor   **307**
       Fiction
   Caseley, J. On the town   **E**
   Chocolate, D. El barrio   **E**
   Lord, J. Albert the Fix-it Man   **E**

Comora, Madeleine
   (jt. auth) Arnold, C. Taj Mahal   **954**
   (jt. auth) Chandra, D. George Washington's teeth   **E**

Compact discs
   Sirrine, C. Cool crafts with old CDs   **745.58**

Companies *See* Business enterprises

Comparative government
   Giesecke, E. Governments around the world   **320.3**

Comparative religion *See* Religions

Compestine, Ying Chang
   Boy dumplings   **E**
   Revolution is not a dinner party   **Fic**
   The runaway rice cake   **E**

Competitions *See* Contests

The **Complete** dog book for kids   **636.7**

The **complete** verse and other nonsense. Lear, E.   **821**

Comport, Sally Wern
   (il) Bruchac, J. Bearwalker   **Fic**
   (il) Bruchac, J. The dark pond   **Fic**
   (il) Bruchac, J. Night wings   **Fic**
   (il) Bruchac, J. Whisper in the dark   **Fic**

The **composer** is dead. Snicket, L.   **E**

Composers
   See also Women composers
   Anderson, M. T. Handel, who knew what he liked   **92**
   Anderson, M. T. Strange Mr. Satie   **92**
   Brewster, H. The other Mozart [biography of Joseph Bologne Saint-Georges]   **92**
   Frisch, A. Dark fiddler: the life and legend of Nicolo Paganini   **92**
   Gerstein, M. What Charlie heard [biography of Charles Edward Ives]   **92**
   Krull, K. Lives of the musicians   **920**
   Martin, R. The mysteries of Beethoven's hair   **92**
   Norton, J. R. Haydn's world   **92**
   Riggs, K. Wolfgang Amadeus Mozart   **92**
   Shefelman, J. J. I, Vivaldi   **92**
   Sís, P. Play, Mozart, play!   **92**
   Stanley, D. Mozart, the wonder child   **92**
   Viegas, J. Beethoven's world   **92**
   Weeks, M. Mozart   **92**
       Fiction
   Celenza, A. H. Gershwin's Rhapsody in Blue   **E**
   Winter, J. The fabulous feud of Gilbert & Sullivan   **E**

Composition (Art)
   Meredith, S. What is form?   **701**

Composition (Rhetoric) *See* Rhetoric

Compost
   Barker, D. Compost it   **631.8**
   Glaser, L. Garbage helps our garden grow   **631.8**
       Fiction
   Siddals, M. M. Compost stew   **E**

Compost it. Barker, D.   **631.8**

Compost stew. Siddals, M. M.   **E**

Compulsory labor *See* Slavery

Computation, Approximate *See* Approximate computation

Computer animation
   Egan, J. How video game designers use math   **794.8**

Computer-assisted instruction
Bell, A. Handheld computers in schools and media centers **371.3**

Computer-based information systems *See* Information systems

Computer crimes
Jakubiak, D. J. A smart kid's guide to Internet privacy **005.8**

Computer games
Egan, J. How video game designers use math **794.8**
Jakubiak, D. J. A smart kid's guide to playing online games **794.8**
Fiction
Pratchett, T. Only you can save mankind **Fic**

Computer network resources *See* Internet resources

Computer networks
See also Internet
Gordon, R. S. Teaching the Internet in libraries **025.04**

Computer software
See also Presentation software

Computers
Oxlade, C. My first computer guide **004**
Rooney, A. Computers **004**
History
Jackson, C. Revolution in computers **004**
Sherman, J. The history of the personal computer **004**

Computers and children
Jakubiak, D. J. A smart kid's guide to playing online games **794.8**

Con artists *See* Swindlers and swindling

Conahan, Carolyn, 1961-
(il) Bayrock, F. Bubble homes and fish farts **590**

Concentration camps
See also Holocaust, 1933-1945; Japanese Americans—Evacuation and relocation, 1942-1945

Concepts
See also Shape
Freymann, S. Food for thought **E**
Jocelyn, M. Same same **E**

The **conch** bearer. Divakaruni, C. B. **Fic**

The **concise** AACR2. Gorman, M. **025.3**

Concord (Mass.), Battle of, 1775
Brown, D. Let it begin here! **973.3**
Fradin, D. B. Let it begin here! **973.3**

Concrete poetry. Bodden, V. **809.1**

Condors
Goldish, M. California condors **598**

Conduct of life
Barker, D. Maybe right, maybe wrong **370.1**
MacGregor, C. Think for yourself **170**
McIntyre, T. The behavior survival guide for kids **158**
Pryor, K. J. Cooperation **177**
Pryor, K. J. Courage **179**
Pryor, K. J. Honesty **177**
Pryor, K. J. Kindness **177**
Pryor, K. J. Respect **177**
Pryor, K. J. Tolerance **177**
Rimm, S. B. See Jane win for girls **305.23**
Rosenthal, A. K. Cookies **E**
Spinelli, E. Today I will **808.8**
Fiction
Brown, L. How to be **E**
Cooper, I. The golden rule **E**
Curtis, J. L. Big words for little people **E**
Curtis, J. L. Is there really a human race? **E**
Dahl, R. Charlie and the chocolate factory **Fic**
Doyen, D. Once upon a twice **E**
Gary, M. Sometimes you get what you want **E**
Hennessy, B. G. Because of you **E**
Huget, J. L. Thanks a LOT, Emily Post! **E**
Mass, W. Jeremy Fink and the meaning of life **Fic**
McGhee, A. So many days **E**
Proimos, J. Paulie Pastrami achieves world peace **E**
Thong, R. Fly free! **E**
Walker, R. D. Mama says **E**

Conducting basic and advanced searches. Porterfield, J. **025.04**

Cone, Molly, 1918-
Come back, salmon **639.3**

Conejito. MacDonald, M. R. **398.2**

Cones
Olson, N. Cones **516**

Conestoga wagons. Ammon, R. **388.3**

Coney Island (New York, N.Y.)
Fiction
Hyde, H. S. Feivel's flying horses **E**

Confectionery
See also Candy

Confessions of a closet Catholic. Littman, S. **Fic**

Confetti girl. Lopez, D. **Fic**

Conflict, Ethnic *See* Ethnic relations

Conflict management
Polland, B. K. We can work it out **303.6**

Conflict resolution *See* Conflict management

Conford, Ellen
Annabel the actress starring in "Gorilla my dreams" **Fic**
A case for Jenny Archer **Fic**

Confucianism
See/See also pages in the following book(s):
Osborne, M. P. One world, many religions **200**

Confucius
About
Freedman, R. Confucius **92**

Congo (Brazzaville) *See* Congo (Republic)
Congo (Republic)
Heale, J. Democratic Republic of the Congo **967.51**
Willis, T. Democratic Republic of the Congo **967.51**
Fiction
Smith, R. Cryptid hunters **Fic**

Cooking—*Continued*
Taylor, G. George Crum and the Saratoga chip **92**
Walker, B. M. The Little House cookbook **641.5**
Webb, L. S. Holidays of the world cookbook for students **641.5**
Yolen, J. Fairy tale feasts **641.5**
See/See also pages in the following book(s):
Erlbach, A. Merry Christmas, everywhere! **394.26**
Gibbons, G. The berry book **634**
King, D. C. Colonial days **973.2**
King, D. C. Pioneer days **978**

Fiction
Compestine, Y. C. Boy dumplings **E**
Cooper, H. Pumpkin soup **E**
De Paola, T. Pascual and the kitchen angels **E**
Denise, A. Pigs love potatoes **E**
Everitt, B. Mean soup **E**
Fisher, C. The Snow Show **E**
Fusco Castaldo, N. Pizza for the queen **E**
Gourley, R. Bring me some apples and I'll make you a pie **E**
Lazo Gilmore, D. K. Cora cooks pancit **E**
Manushkin, F. How Mama brought the spring **E**
Nayar, N. What should I make? **E**
Park, L. S. Bee-bim bop! **E**
Rodman, M. A. Surprise soup **E**
Stevens, J. Cook-a-doodle-doo! **E**
Wellington, M. Pizza at Sally's **E**
Zepeda, G. Growing up with tamales = Los Tamales de Ana **E**

Natural foods
See also Natural foods
Poetry
Argueta, J. Sopa de frijoles = Bean soup **811**

Cooking through time [series]
Ichord, L. F. Double cheeseburgers, quiche, and vegetarian burritos **394.1**

Cooks
Arroyo, S. L. How chefs use math **641.5**

Cool art [series]
Hanson, A. Cool calligraphy **745.6**
Hanson, A. Cool collage **702.8**
Hanson, A. Cool drawing **741.2**
Hanson, A. Cool painting **751.4**
Hanson, A. Cool printmaking **760.2**
Hanson, A. Cool sculpture **731.4**
Cool beaded jewelry. Scheunemann, P. **745.58**
Cool calligraphy. Hanson, A. **745.6**
Cool cat. Hogrogian, N. **E**
Cool chemistry concoctions. Rhatigan, J. **540.7**
Cool collage. Hanson, A. **702.8**
Cool costumes. Kenney, K. L. **792**
Cool crafts [series]
Price, P. S. Cool rubber stamp art **761**
Price, P. S. Cool scrapbooks **745.593**
Scheunemann, P. Cool beaded jewelry **745.58**
Wagner, L. Cool melt & pour soap **668**

Wagner, L. Cool painted stuff **745.7**
Cool crafts with old CDs. Sirrine, C. **745.58**
Cool crafts with old jeans. Sirrine, C. **745.5**
Cool crafts with old t-shirts. Sirrine, C. **745.5**
Cool crafts with old wrappers, cans and bottles. Sirrine, C. **745.5**
Cool Daddy Rat. Crow, K. **E**
Cool distance assistants. Hopwood, J. **507.8**
Cool dog, school dog. Heiligman, D. **E**
Cool drawing. Hanson, A. **741.2**
A **cool** drink of water. Kerley, B. **363.6**
Cool dry ice devices. Hopwood, J. **507.8**
Cool gravity activities. Hopwood, J. **531**
Cool makeup. Kenney, K. L. **792**
Cool melons—turn to frogs!: the life and poems of Issa [Kobayashi] Gollub, M. **92**
Cool melt & pour soap. Wagner, L. **668**
A **cool** moonlight. Johnson, A. **Fic**
Cool painted stuff. Wagner, L. **745.7**
Cool painting. Hanson, A. **751.4**
Cool performances [series]
Kenney, K. L. Cool costumes **792**
Kenney, K. L. Cool makeup **792**
Kenney, K. L. Cool productions **792**
Kenney, K. L. Cool scripts & acting **792**
Kenney, K. L. Cool sets & props **792**
Kenney, K. L. Cool special effects **792**
Cool printmaking. Hanson, A. **760.2**
Cool productions. Kenney, K. L. **792**
Cool rubber stamp art. Price, P. S. **761**
Cool salsa **811.008**
Cool science [series]
Bortz, A. B. Astrobiology **576.8**
Firestone, M. Wireless technology **621.384**
Fridell, R. Forensic science **363.2**
Fridell, R. Genetic engineering **660.6**
Fridell, R. Military technology **623.4**
Fridell, R. Sports technology **688.7**
Fridell, R. Spy technology **327.12**
Goldsmith, C. Cutting-edge medicine **610**
Hopwood, J. Cool distance assistants **507.8**
Hopwood, J. Cool dry ice devices **507.8**
Hopwood, J. Cool gravity activities **531**
Jango-Cohen, J. Bionics **617.9**
Johnson, R. L. Satellites **629.46**
Miller, J. Food science **641.3**
Ward, D. J. Exploring Mars **523.4**
Ward, D. J. Materials science **620.1**
Winner, C. Cryobiology **571.4**
Winner, C. Life on the edge **578.7**
Cool science careers [series]
Somervill, B. A. Marine biologist **578.7**
Cool scrapbooks. Price, P. S. **745.593**
Cool scripts & acting. Kenney, K. L. **792**
Cool sculpture. Hanson, A. **731.4**
Cool sets & props. Kenney, K. L. **792**
Cool special effects. Kenney, K. L. **792**
Cool story programs for the school-age crowd. Reid, R. **028.5**

Cool Stuff 2.0 and how it works. Woodford, C. **600**

Coolies. Yin **E**

Cooling. Oxlade, C. **530.4**

Coombs, Kate
The runaway princess **Fic**
The secret-keeper **E**

Cooney, Barbara, 1917-2000
Chanticleer and the fox **E**
Eleanor [biography of Eleanor Roosevelt] **92**
(il) Farber, N. How the hibernators came to Bethlehem **E**
(il) Godden, R. The story of Holly & Ivy **E**
(il) Hall, D. Ox-cart man **E**
(il) Houston, G. The year of the perfect Christmas tree **E**
(il) McLerran, A. Roxaboxen **E**
(il) Salten, F. Bambi **Fic**
(il) Seeger, R. C. American folk songs for children in home, school, and nursery school **782.42**
(il) Tortillitas para mamá and other nursery rhymes. See Tortillitas para mamá and other nursery rhymes **398.8**

Cooper, Bob, 1963-
(jt. auth) Greiner, T. Analyzing library collection use with Excel **025.2**

Cooper, Deborah, 1951-
(jt. auth) Hirschi, R. Searching for grizzlies **599.78**

Cooper, Elisha
Beach **E**
Bear dreams **E**
Beaver is lost **E**
Farm **E**
A good night walk **E**
Magic thinks big **E**

Cooper, Floyd
Coming home [biography of Langston Hughes] **92**
Jump! [biography of Michael Jordan] **92**
Mandela **92**
Willie and the All-Stars **E**
(il) Greenfield, E. Grandpa's face **E**
(il) Grimes, N. Meet Danitra Brown **811**
(il) Reynolds, A. Back of the bus **E**
(il) Schroeder, A. Satchmo's blues **E**
(il) Sherman, P. Ben and the Emancipation Proclamation **E**
(il) Thomas, J. C. The blacker the berry **811**
(il) Thomas, J. C. Brown honey in broomwheat tea **811**
(il) Thomas, J. C. I have heard of a land **E**
(il) Vander Zee, R. Mississippi morning **E**
(il) Williams, K. L. A beach tail **E**

Cooper, Helen, 1963-
Dog biscuit **E**
Pumpkin soup **E**

Cooper, Ilene, 1948-
The golden rule **E**
Jewish holidays all year round **296.4**
Look at Lucy! **Fic**

Cooper, Jason, 1942-
Camouflage and disguise **591.47**

Hooves and claws **591.47**

Cooper, Jenny, 1961-
(il) Buxton, J. The littlest llama **E**

Cooper, Martha
(il) Waters, K. Lion dancer: Ernie Wan's Chinese New Year **394.26**

Cooper, Michael L., 1950-
Dust to eat **973.917**
Hero of the high seas [biography of John Paul Jones] **92**

Cooper, Robert, 1945-
Croatia **949.7**

Cooper, Susan, 1935-
The Boggart **Fic**
The grey king **Fic**
King of shadows **Fic**
The magician's boy **Fic**
Over sea, under stone **Fic**
Victory **Fic**

Cooper, Susan, 1935-
See/See also pages in the following book(s):
Ellis, S. From reader to writer **372.6**

Cooper, Wade
On the road **629.2**

Cooperation
Pryor, K. J. Cooperation **177**

Coots, John Frederick, 1897-1985
Santa Claus is comin' to town **782.42**

Coovert, J. P.
(il) Kuhlman, E. The last invisible boy **Fic**

Cope, E. D. (Edward Drinker), 1840-1897
About
Goldish, M. The fossil feud **560**

Cope, Edward Drinker See Cope, E. D. (Edward Drinker), 1840-1897

Copeland, Gregory
(il) Collier, J. L. The Tecumseh you never knew **92**

Copernicus, Nicolaus, 1473-1543
About
Andronik, C. M. Copernicus **92**
Fradin, D. B. Nicolaus Copernicus **92**

Copp, Jim, 1913-1999
Jim Copp, will you tell me a story? **E**

Coppendale, Jean
The great big book of mighty machines **621.8**

Copper. Kibuishi, K. **741.5**

Coppola, Angela
(il) Bloomfield, J. Jewish holidays cookbook **641.5**
(il) Chryssicas, M. K. I love yoga **613.7**

Copsey, Sue, 1960-
(jt. auth) Kindersley, B. Children just like me **305.23**

Copyright
See also Fair use (Copyright)
Butler, R. P. Copyright for teachers and librarians **346.04**
Butler, R. P. Smart copyright compliance for schools **346.04**
Crews, K. D. Copyright law for librarians and educators **346.04**

Copyright essentials for librarians and educators. See Crews, K. D. Copyright law for librarians and educators **346.04**

Copyright for teachers and librarians. Butler, R. P. **346.04**

Copyright law for librarians and educators. Crews, K. D. **346.04**

Cora cooks pancit. Lazo Gilmore, D. K. **E**

Corace, Jen
(il) Hopkinson, D. The humblebee hunter **E**
(il) Rosenthal, A. K. Little Hoot **E**
(il) Rylant, C. Hansel and Gretel **398.2**

The **coral** reef. Johansson, P. **577.7**

The **coral** reef. Person, S. **578.7**

Coral reefs. Gibbons, G. **577.7**

Coral reefs and islands
Arnosky, J. Parrotfish and sunken ships **578.7**
Collard, S. B., III. On the coral reefs **577.7**
Collard, S. B., III. One night in the Coral Sea **593.6**
Gibbons, G. Coral reefs **577.7**
Johansson, P. The coral reef **577.7**
Kummer, P. K. The Great Barrier Reef **578.7**
Person, S. The coral reef **578.7**
Pfeffer, W. Life in a coral reef **577.7**
Taylor-Butler, C. A home in the coral reef **577.7**
Tocci, S. Coral reefs **577.7**
Fiction
Barner, B. Fish wish **E**
Blackstone, S. Secret seahorse **E**

Coraline. Gaiman, N. **Fic**

Coraline [graphic novel] Russell, P. C. **741.5**

Corals
Collard, S. B., III. One night in the Coral Sea **593.6**

Corazones Valientes (Organization)
Reiser, L. Tortillas and lullabies. Tortillas y cancioncitas **E**

Corbeil, Jean-Claude
My first French English visual dictionary **443**
My first Spanish English visual dictionary **463**

Corbett, Sue
Free baseball **Fic**
The last newspaper boy in America **Fic**

Corbishley, Mike
The Middle Ages **940.1**

Corcoran, Mary K.
The circulatory story **612.1**
The quest to digest **612.3**

Cordell, Matthew, 1975-
Trouble gum **E**
(il) Preller, J. Mighty Casey **E**
(il) Root, P. Toot toot zoom! **E**
(il) Vail, R. Justin Case **Fic**
(il) Vail, R. Righty & Lefty **E**

Corder, Zizou
Lionboy **Fic**

Cordi, Kevin
(jt. auth) Sima, J. Raising voices **027.62**

Córdova, Amy, 1953-
(il) Anaya, R. A. The first tortilla **Fic**
(il) Cohn, D. Namaste! **E**
(il) Lamadrid, E. R. Juan the bear and the water of life **398.2**
(il) Tafolla, C. Fiesta babies **E**
(il) Tafolla, C. What can you do with a rebozo? **E**

Cordsen, Carol Foskett
Market day **E**
The milkman **E**

Corduroy. Freeman, D. **E**

Coren, Stanley
Why do dogs have wet noses? **636.7**

Coretta Scott [King] Shange, N. **92**

Coretta Scott King Award
The Coretta Scott King awards, 1970-2009 **028.5**
Stephens, C. G. Coretta Scott King Award books **028.5**

Coretta Scott King Award books. Stephens, C. G. **028.5**

The **Coretta** Scott King awards, 1970-2009 **028.5**

Corey, Shana, 1974-
Mermaid Queen [biography of Annette Kellerman] **92**
Monster parade **E**
Players in pigtails **E**

Corio, Paul
(il) Matsen, B. Go wild in New York City **974.7**

Cork & Fuzz. Chaconas, D. **E**

Corn
Aliki. Corn is maize **633.1**
Gibbons, G. Corn **633.1**
Landau, E. Corn **633.1**
Micucci, C. The life and times of corn **633.1**

Corn-fed. Stevenson, J. **811**

Corn is maize. Aliki **633.1**

Cornelia and the audacious escapades of the Somerset sisters. Blume, L. M. M. **Fic**

Cornell, Laura
(il) Curtis, J. L. Big words for little people **E**
(il) Curtis, J. L. I'm gonna like me **E**
(il) Curtis, J. L. Is there really a human race? **E**
(il) Curtis, J. L. Tell me again about the night I was born **E**
(il) Fleischman, S. The ghost on Saturday night **Fic**

A **corner** of the universe. Martin, A. M. **Fic**

Cornerstones of freedom [series]
Davis, L. Medicine in the American West **610.9**
Richards, N. Monticello **975.5**

Cornerstones of freedom, Second series
Good, D. L. Brown v. Board of Education **344**

Creatures yesterday and today. Patkau, K.   **591.3**

Crebbin, June, 1938-
(comp) Horse tales. See Horse tales   **S C**

Credit
> *See also* Consumer credit

Tomljanovic, T. Borrowing   **332.7**

Credit cards
Hall, M. Credit cards and checks   **332.7**

Credit cards and checks. Hall, M.   **332.7**

Creech, Sharon
Absolutely normal chaos   **Fic**
Bloomability   **Fic**
Chasing Redbird   **Fic**
Granny Torrelli makes soup   **Fic**
Heartbeat   **Fic**
Love that dog   **Fic**
Ruby Holler   **Fic**
The unfinished angel   **Fic**
Walk two moons   **Fic**
The Wanderer   **Fic**

Creek Indians
Fiction
Smith, C. L. Jingle dancer   **E**
Folklore
Bruchac, J. The great ball game   **398.2**

Creepy crawlies. Post, H.   **590**

Creepy crawly animal origami. Nguyen, D.   **736**

Creepy riddles. Hall, K.   **793.73**

Cregan, Elizabeth R.
The atom   **539.7**
Marie Curie   **92**

The **cremation** of Sam McGee. Service, R. W.   **811**

Crenson, Victoria
Horseshoe crabs and shorebirds   **577.7**

Cressy, Judith
Can you find it?   **750**

Crete (Greece)
Scarre, C. The Palace of Minos at Knossos   **728.8**

Crew, Hilary S., 1942-
Women engaged in war in literature for youth   **016.3**

Crewe, Sabrina
The Scottsboro case   **345**

Crews, Donald
Bigmama's   **92**
Harbor   **E**
Night at the fair   **E**
Parade   **E**
Sail away   **E**
School bus   **E**
Shortcut   **E**
Ten black dots   **E**
Truck   **E**
(il) Giganti, P., Jr. Each orange had 8 slices   **E**
(il) Giganti, P., Jr. How many snails?   **E**
(il) Schaefer, L. M. This is the sunflower   **E**
(il) Shannon, G. Tomorrow's alphabet   **E**

Crews, Jeanne Lee
See/See also pages in the following book(s):
Thimmesh, C. Girls think of everything   **920**

Crews, Kenneth D.
Copyright law for librarians and educators   **346.04**

Crews, Nina
Below   **E**

Cribb, Joe
Money   **332.4**

Crick, Francis, 1916-2004
See/See also pages in the following book(s):
Phelan, G. Double helix   **572.8**

Cricket (Periodical)
Celebrate Cricket   **808.8**

The **cricket** in Times Square. Selden, G.   **Fic**

Crickets
Berger, M. Chirping crickets   **595.7**
Gonzales, D. Crickets in the dark   **595.7**
Fiction
Bunting, E. Christmas cricket   **E**
Carle, E. The very quiet cricket   **E**
Selden, G. The cricket in Times Square   **Fic**
Wheeler, L. Old Cricket   **E**

Crickets in the dark. Gonzales, D.   **595.7**

Crickwing. Cannon, J.   **E**

Crictor. Ungerer, T.   **E**

Crime
> *See also* Computer crimes; Hate crimes; Homicide; Trials

Somervill, B. A. Graphing crime   **364**

Crime prevention
Raatma, L. Safety in your neighborhood   **613.6**

Criminal investigation
> *See also* Forensic anthropology; Forensic sciences

Arroyo, S. L. How crime fighters use math   **363.2**
Denega, D. Gut-eating bugs   **363.2**
Denega, D. Have you seen this face?   **363.2**
Fridell, R. Forensic science   **363.2**
Platt, R. Forensics   **363.2**

Criminalistics *See* Forensic sciences

Criminals
> *See also* Thieves
Fiction
Horowitz, A. The switch   **Fic**
Kehret, P. Don't tell anyone   **Fic**
Walden, M. H.I.V.E   **Fic**

The **crimson** cap. Howard, E.   **Fic**

Crisis management
> *See also* Conflict management

Crispin: the cross of lead. Avi   **Fic**

Criss cross. Perkins, L. R.   **Fic**

Crist, James J.
Siblings   **306.8**
What to do when you're sad & lonely   **158**
What to do when you're scared & worried   **158**

Critter sitter. Richards, C.   **E**

Cultures of the world—*Continued*

Spilling, M. Georgia	**947.5**
Srinivasan, R. India	**954**
Tan, C. L. Finland	**948.97**
Tope, L. R. R. Philippines	**959.9**
Wanasundera, N. P. Sri Lanka	**954.93**
Wilcox, J. Iceland	**949.12**
Winter, J. K. Chile	**983**
Winter, J. K. Italy	**945**
Winter, J. K. Venezuela	**987**

Cummings, Mary, 1951-
Three names of me **Fic**

Cummings, Michael, 1945-
(il) In the hollow of your hand. See In the hollow of your hand **782.42**

Cummings, Pat, 1950-
Ananse and the lizard **398.2**
Harvey Moon, museum boy **E**
(jt. auth) Winthrop, E. Squashed in the middle **E**

Cummings, Phil, 1957-
Boom bah! **E**

Cummings, Terrance
(il) Stotts, S. We shall overcome **782.42**

Cummings, Troy
The eensy weensy spider freaks out (big time!) **E**

Cummins, Julie
Sam Patch **92**
Women daredevils **920**
(jt. auth) Munro, R. The inside-outside book of libraries **027**

Cumpiano, Ina
Quinito's neighborhood **E**

Cunha, Stephen F.
National Geographic Bee **910**
(jt. auth) Bockenhauer, M. H. Our fifty states **973**

Cunnane, Kelly
For you are a Kenyan child **E**

Cupcakes of doom!. Friesen, R. **741.5**

Cupid (Roman deity) *See* Eros (Greek deity)

Cupid and Psyche. Craft, M. **292**

Cupples, Pat
(il) Wyatt, V. The math book for girls and other beings who count **510**

Cure quest. Nardo, D. **616**

Curie, Maria Sklodowska *See* Curie, Marie, 1867-1934

Curie, Marie, 1867-1934
About
Cregan, E. R. Marie Curie **92**
Krull, K. Marie Curie **92**
McClafferty, C. K. Something out of nothing [biography of Marie Curie] **92**
Steele, P. Marie Curie **92**

Curiosities and wonders
See also Eccentrics and eccentricities; Monsters; World records
Allen, J. Unexplained **001.9**
Aronson, M. For boys only **031.02**
Blackwood, G. L. Enigmatic events **904**

Buchanan, A. J. The daring book for girls **031.02**
Farndon, J. Do not open **031.02**
Guinness world records **032.02**
Iggulden, C. The dangerous book for boys **031.02**
Masoff, J. Oh, yuck! **031.02**
One million things **031**
Thomas, K. Planet Earth News presents: super humans **031.02**
Turner, T. World of the weird **031**

The **curious** adventures of the abandoned toys. Fellowes, J. **Fic**

A **curious** collection of cats. Franco, B. **811**

The **curious** garden. Brown, P. **E**

Curious George. Rey, H. A. **E**

Curious George: Cecily G. and the 9 monkeys. Rey, H. A. **E**

Curious Pictures (Firm)
Elffers, J. Do you love me? **E**

Curlee, Lynn, 1947-

Ballpark	**796.357**
Brooklyn Bridge	**624.2**
Capital	**975.3**
Liberty	**974.7**
Mythological creatures	**292**
Parthenon	**726**
Skyscraper	**720**
Trains	**385.09**

Curmi, Serena
(il) Enderle, J. R. Smile, Principessa! **E**

Currency. Kummer, P. K. **332.4**

Current science [series]
Jackson, C. Alien invasion **578.6**
Perritano, J. Bugs on your body **595.7**

Currents, Ocean *See* Ocean currents

Currey, Anna
(il) Donaldson, J. One Ted falls out of bed **E**
(il) Moss, M. A babysitter for Billy Bear **E**
(il) Napoli, D. J. The Wishing Club **E**

Curricula (Courses of study) *See* Education—Curricula

Curriculum materials centers *See* Instructional materials centers

Currie, Stephen, 1960-
Escapes from slavery **326**

Curry, Jane Louise, 1932-
The Black Canary **Fic**
Hold up the sky: and other Native American tales from Texas and the Southern Plains **398.2**

Curry, Tom
(il) Wojciechowski, S. A fine St. Patrick's day **E**

Curry-Rood, Leah
(jt. auth) Raines, S. C. Story stretchers for infants, toddlers, and twos **372.4**

The **curse** of Addy McMahon. Davis, K. **Fic**

The **curse** of the ancient mask and other case files. Cheshire, S. **Fic**

The **curse** of the blue figurine. Bellairs, J. **Fic**

Dalal, A. Kamala
India   **954**
Laos   **959.4**

Dale, Doris Cruger
Bilingual children's books in English and Spanish   **011.6**

Dale, Penny, 1954-
(il) Fine, A. Jamie and Angus together   **Fic**

Daley, Michael J.
Space station rat   **Fic**

Dalgleish, Sharon
Exercise and rest   **613.7**

Dalgliesh, Alice, 1893-1979
The bears on Hemlock Mountain   **Fic**

Dall, Mary Doerfler, 1949-
Little Hands create!   **745.5**

Dalston, Teresa R., 1965-
(jt. auth) Hallam, A. Managing budgets and finances   **025.1**

D'Aluisio, Faith, 1957-
(jt. auth) Menzel, P. What the world eats   **641.3**

Daly, James
(jt. auth) Zuckerman, A. 2030   **600**

Daly, Jude
(il) Brooks, J. Let there be peace   **242**
(il) Conway, D. Lila and the secret of rain   **E**
(il) McGill, A. Way up and over everything   **398.2**

Daly, Niki, 1946-
Bettina Valentino and the Picasso Club   **Fic**
Pretty Salma   **E**
Ruby sings the blues   **E**
Welcome to Zanzibar Road   **E**
(il) Borden, L. The greatest skating race   **Fic**
(il) Gregorowski, C. Fly, eagle, fly!   **398.2**
(il) Moses, S. P. Sallie Gal and the Wall-a-kee man   **Fic**

Damerum, Kanako
(il) Horowitz, A. Stormbreaker: the graphic novel   **741.5**

D'Amico, Carmela
Ella the Elegant Elephant   **E**

D'Amico, Joan, 1957-
The coming to America cookbook   **641.5**
The healthy body cookbook   **641.5**
The math chef   **641.5**
The science chef   **641.3**

D'Amico, Steven
(jt. auth) D'Amico, C. Ella the Elegant Elephant   **E**

Dams
See/See also pages in the following book(s):
Macaulay, D. Building big   **720**

Dance
See also Ballet; Modern dance; Tap dancing
Collins, P. L. I am a dancer   **792.8**
Nathan, A. Meet the dancers   **920**
Reid, R. Shake & shout   **027.62**
Veitch, C. Dancing   **792.8**
Fiction
Arnold, M. D. Prancing, dancing Lily   **E**

Bell, K. If the shoe fits   **Fic**
Bluemle, E. How do you wokka-wokka?   **E**
Campbell, B. M. Stompin' at the Savoy   **E**
Capucilli, A. Katy duck is a caterpillar   **E**
Craig, L. Dancing feet!   **E**
Durango, J. Cha-cha chimps   **E**
Ehrlich, A. The girl who wanted to dance   **E**
Elliott, D. One little chicken   **E**
Gray, L. M. My mama had a dancing heart   **E**
Hanson, W. Bugtown Boogie   **E**
Manning, M. Kitchen dance   **E**
Martin, B. Barn dance!   **E**
McKissack, P. C. Mirandy and Brother Wind   **E**
Ryder, J. Dance by the light of the moon   **E**
Smith, C. R. Dance with me   **E**
Stutson, C. Cats' night out   **E**
Symes, R. Harriet dancing   **E**
Weeks, S. Ella, of course!   **E**
Wilson, S. The day we danced in underpants   **E**
Folklore
Quattlebaum, M. Sparks fly high   **398.2**
Africa
Keeler, P. A. Drumbeat in our feet   **793.3**

Dance [series]
Solway, A. Modern dance   **792.8**
Dance by the light of the moon. Ryder, J.   **E**
Dance, Nana, dance. Hayes, J.   **398.2**
Dance with me. Smith, C. R.   **E**

Dancers
See also African American dancers
Nathan, A. Meet the dancers   **920**
Orgill, R. Footwork [biography of Fred & Adele Astaire]   **92**
Reich, S. José! [biography of José Limón]   **92**

Dancing *See* Dance
Dancing. Veitch, C.   **792.8**
Dancing feet!. Craig, L.   **E**
Dancing in Cadillac light. Holt, K. W.   **Fic**
Dancing in the wings. Allen, D.   **E**
The **Dancing** Pancake. Spinelli, E.   **Fic**
Dancing teepees: poems of American Indian youth   **897**
Dancing through fire. Lasky, K.   **Fic**
Dancing to freedom [biography of Li Cunxin] Li Cunxin   **92**

D'Anda, Carlos
(il) Farshtey, G. Bionicle #1: rise of the Toa Nuva   **741.5**

Dandelions
Johnson, J. Dandelion   **583**
Posada, M. Dandelions   **583**
Fiction
Middleton, C. Nibbles: a green tale   **E**
Dandelions. Bunting, E.   **E**

Daneshvari, Gitty
School of Fear   **Fic**
Danger in the dark. Matthews, T. L.   **Fic**

Danger zone: dieting and eating disorders [series]

    Zahensky, B. A. Diet fads   **613.2**

The **dangerous** alphabet. Gaiman, N.   **E**

Dangerous animals

    See also Poisonous animals

    Gilpin, D. Life-size killer creatures   **591.6**

    Jenkins, S. Never smile at a monkey   **591.6**

    Lewin, T. Tooth and claw   **590**

    Wilkes, A. Dangerous creatures   **591.6**

The **dangerous** book for boys. Iggulden, C.   **031.02**

Dangerous creatures. Wilkes, A.   **591.6**

Dangerous crossing. Krensky, S.   **Fic**

Dangerous times. Brittney, L.   **Fic**

Dangles and bangles. Haab, S.   **745.5**

Daniel, Alan, 1939-

    (il) Howe, D. Bunnicula   **Fic**

    (il) Naylor, P. R. The grand escape   **Fic**

Daniel Boone's great escape. Spradlin, M. P.   **92**

Daniel Handler [biography of Lemony Snicket] Haugen, H. M.   **92**

Daniel's duck. Bulla, C. R.   **E**

Danish authors *See* Authors, Danish

Danks, Fiona

    (jt. auth) Schofield, J. Make it wild   **796.5**

Dann, Geoff

    (il) Gravett, C. Knight   **940.1**

    (il) Greenaway, T. Jungle   **577.3**

Danneberg, Julie, 1958-

    Family reminders   **Fic**

Danny and the dinosaur. Hoff, S.   **E**

Danny is done with diapers. O'Connell, R.   **E**

Danny's drawing book. Heap, S.   **E**

Danny's first snow. Gore, L.   **E**

Dant, Traci

    Some kind of love   **811**

D'Antona, Robin, 1946-

    (jt. auth) Kevorkian, M. 101 facts about bullying   **302.3**

Danzig, Dianne

    Babies don't eat pizza   **649**

Danziger, Paula, 1944-2004

    Amber Brown is not a crayon   **Fic**

    The cat ate my gymsuit   **Fic**

    It's Justin Time, Amber Brown   **E**

    P.S. Longer letter later   **Fic**

    Snail mail no more   **Fic**

    There's a bat in bunk five   **Fic**

    About

    Reed, J. Paula Danziger   **92**

Darby. Fuqua, J. S.   **Fic**

Darbyshire, Kristen

    Put it on the list   **E**

Dare to be scared. San Souci, R.   **S C**

Dare to be scared 4. San Souci, R.   **S C**

D'Argo, Laura

    (il) Carson, M. K. The Wright Brothers for kids   **629.13**

The **daring** adventures of Penhaligon Brush. Rogan, S. J.   **Fic**

The **daring** book for girls. Buchanan, A. J.   **031.02**

The **daring** Miss Quimby [biography of Harriet Quimby] Whitaker, S.   **92**

Dark Ages *See* Middle Ages

A **dark,** dark tale. Brown, R.   **E**

Dark Emperor and other poems of the night. Sidman, J.   **811**

Dark fiddler: the life and legend of Nicolo Paganini. Frisch, A.   **92**

The **Dark** Hills divide. Carman, P.   **Fic**

Dark life. Falls, K.   **Fic**

Dark night. Monfried, D. d.   **E**

The **dark** pond. Bruchac, J.   **Fic**

The **dark** stairs. Byars, B. C.   **Fic**

The **dark-thirty.** McKissack, P. C.   **S C**

Darkest age [series]

    Lake, A. J. The coming of dragons   **Fic**

Darkness creeping. Shusterman, N.   **S C**

Dark's tale. Grabien, D.   **Fic**

Darkwood. Breen, M. E.   **Fic**

Darling, Kathy, 1943-

    (jt. auth) Cobb, V. We dare you!   **507.8**

Darling, Louis, 1916-1970

    (il) Butterworth, O. The enormous egg   **Fic**

    (il) Cleary, B. Ellen Tebbits   **Fic**

    (il) Cleary, B. Henry Huggins   **Fic**

    (il) Cleary, B. The mouse and the motorcycle   **Fic**

    (il) Cleary, B. Otis Spofford   **Fic**

    (il) Cleary, B. Ramona the pest   **Fic**

Darwin, Beatrice

    (il) Cleary, B. Socks   **Fic**

Darwin, Charles, 1809-1882

    About

    Ashby, R. Young Charles Darwin and the voyage of the Beagle   **92**

    Lasky, K. One beetle too many: the extraordinary adventures of Charles Darwin   **92**

    Markle, S. Animals Charles Darwin saw   **92**

    McGinty, A. B. Darwin   **92**

    Schanzer, R. What Darwin saw   **92**

    Sís, P. The tree of life: a book depicting the life of Charles Darwin, naturalist, geologist & thinker   **92**

    Weaver, A. H. The voyage of the beetle   **576.8**

    Wood, A. J. Charles Darwin and the Beagle adventure   **508**

    Fiction

    Hopkinson, D. The humblebee hunter   **E**

Darwinism *See* Evolution

Das, Prodeepta

    (jt. auth) Cheung, H. K is for Korea   **951.9**

Dash, Joan

    The longitude prize [biography of John Harrison]   **92**

Data storage and retrieval systems *See* Information systems

Davis, Eleanor
The secret science alliance and the copycat crook **741.5**
Stinky **741.5**

Davis, Jack E.
(il) Esbaum, J. Stanza **E**
(il) Grambling, L. G. T. Rex and the Mother's Day hug **E**
(il) Harley, B. Dirty Joe, the pirate **E**
(il) Shapiro, Z. We're all in the same boat **E**
(il) Sierra, J. Monster Goose **811**

Davis, Jacky, 1966-
(jt. auth) Soman, D. Ladybug Girl **E**

Davis, Jane
Crochet **746.43**

Davis, Jill
The first rule of little brothers **E**

Davis, Jim, 1945-
Garfield: 30 years of laughs & lasagna **741.5**

Davis, Katie
The curse of Addy McMahon **Fic**

Davis, Lambert
(il) Esbensen, B. J. Baby whales drink milk **599.5**
(il) Hamilton, V. The bells of Christmas **Fic**
(il) Rylant, C. The journey **591.56**

Davis, Lucile
Medicine in the American West **610.9**

Davis, Nancy, 1949-
A garden of opposites **E**
(il) Fox, K. Older than the stars **523.1**
(il) Graham, J. B. Flicker flash **811**

Davis, Rich, 1958-
(il) Meister, C. Tiny's bath **E**

Davis, Tony, 1961-
Roland Wright: future knight **Fic**

Davy Crockett gets hitched. Miller, B. **398.2**

Dawdle Duckling. Buzzeo, T. **E**

Dawes, John
Exploring the world of aquatic life **591.7**

Dawes, Kwame Senu Neville, 1962-
I saw your face **811**

Dawson, Arthur L.
(il) Jackson Issa, K. Howard Thurman's great hope **92**

Day, Alexandra
Carl's sleepy afternoon **E**

Day, Betsy
(il) Press, J. Around-the-world art & activities **745.5**

Day, Jeff, 1980-
Don't touch that! **615.9**

Day, Karen
Tall tales **Fic**

Day, Larry, 1921-
(jt. auth) Jurmain, S. George did it [biography of George Washington] **92**

Day, Larry, 1956-
(il) Crowley, N. Nanook & Pryce **E**
(il) Fradin, D. B. Duel! **973.4**
(il) Fradin, D. B. Let it begin here! **973.3**

(il) Morris, R. T. Bye-bye, baby! **E**
(jt. auth) Winters, K. Colonial voices **973.3**

Day
See also Night
Bailey, J. Sun up, sun down **525**
Murphy, S. J. It's about time! **529**
Rau, D. M. Day and night **508**
Fiction
Carluccio, M. The sounds around town **E**
Durango, J. Angels watching over me **E**
Franco, B. Bird songs **E**
George, J. C. Morning, noon, and night **E**
Hopgood, T. Wow! said the owl **E**
Melvin, A. Counting birds **E**
Milgrim, D. Time to get up, time to go **E**
Ormerod, J. Miss Mouse's day **E**
Rosenthal, A. K. Yes Day! **E**
Rylant, C. All in a day **E**
Spanyol, J. Little neighbors on Sunnyside Street **E**
Viorst, J. Alexander and the terrible, horrible, no good, very bad day **E**
Williams, V. B. Lucky song **E**

Day and night. Rau, D. M. **508**

A **day** at the market. Anderson, S. **E**

A **day** at the New Amsterdam Theatre. Amendola, D. **792.6**

The **Day-Glo** brothers. Barton, C. **535.6**

The **day** I had to play with my sister. Bonsall, C. N. **E**

A **day** in the life of Murphy. Provensen, A. **E**

The **day** Jimmy's boa ate the wash. Noble, T. H. **E**

The **day** Leo said I hate you. Harris, R. H. **E**

Day light, night light. Branley, F. M. **535**

The **day** of Ahmed's secret. Heide, F. P. **E**

Day of Atonement *See* Yom Kippur

Day of the Dead *See* All Souls' Day

Day of the Dead. Johnston, T. **E**

The **day** the animals came. Weller, F. W. **E**

The **day** the babies crawled away. Rathmann, P. **E**

The **day** the dinosaurs died. Brown, C. L. **567.9**

The **day** we danced in underpants. Wilson, S. **E**

A **day** with Dad. Holmberg, B. R. **E**

A **day** with Wilbur Robinson. Joyce, W. **E**

Dayenu!. Leon, C. B. **296.4**

Dayrell, Elphinstone, 1869-1917
Why the Sun and the Moon live in the sky **398.2**

Days
Fiction
Himmelman, J. Chickens to the rescue **E**
Lobel, A. One lighthouse, one moon **E**
Pullen, Z. Friday my Radio Flyer flew **E**

Days of change [series]
Bodden, V. Columbus reaches the New World **970.01**
Bodden, V. Man walks on the Moon **629.45**
Riggs, K. The French Revolution **944.04**

Defensive backs. Gigliotti, J.   **796.332**

Defiance. Hobbs, V.   **Fic**

Definitely not for little ones. Berner, R. S.   **398.2**

Degas, Edgar, 1834-1917
About
Cocca-Leffler, M. Edgar Degas: paintings that dance   **92**
Rubin, S. G. Degas and the dance   **92**

Degas, Hilaire Germain Edgar See Degas, Edgar, 1834-1917

Degas and the dance. Rubin, S. G.   **92**

Degen, Bruce, 1945-
Jamberry   **E**
(il) Calmenson, S. Jazzmatazz!   **E**
(il) Carlstrom, N. W. Jesse Bear, what will you wear?   **E**
(il) Coerr, E. The Josefina story quilt   **E**
(il) Cole, J. The magic school bus and the climate challenge   **363.7**
(il) Cole, J. The magic school bus and the electric field trip   **621.319**
(il) Cole, J. The magic school bus and the science fair expedition   **509**
(il) Cole, J. The magic school bus at the waterworks   **551.48**
(il) Cole, J. The magic school bus explores the senses   **612.8**
(il) Cole, J. The magic school bus: in the time of the dinosaurs   **567.9**
(il) Cole, J. The magic school bus inside a beehive   **595.7**
(il) Cole, J. The magic school bus inside a hurricane   **551.55**
(il) Cole, J. The magic school bus inside the Earth   **551.1**
(il) Cole, J. The magic school bus inside the human body   **612**
(il) Cole, J. The magic school bus, lost in the solar system   **523**
(il) Cole, J. The magic school bus on the ocean floor   **591.7**
(il) Cole, J. Ms. Frizzle's adventures: Imperial China   **931**
(il) Yolen, J. Commander Toad and the voyage home   **E**

DeGroat, Diane, 1947-
(il) Gilson, J. Bug in a rug   **Fic**

DeGross, Monalisa
Donavan's double trouble   **Fic**

Deines, Brian
(il) Innes, S. A bear in war   **E**

Deities See Gods and goddesses

DeJong, Meindert, 1906-1991
The house of sixty fathers   **Fic**
The wheel on the school   **Fic**

Del Negro, Janice
Passion and poison   **S C**
(jt. auth) Greene, E. Storytelling: art & technique   **372.6**

Delacre, Lulu, 1957-
Golden tales   **398.2**
Salsa stories   **S C**

(comp) Arrorró mi niño. See Arrorró mi niño   **398.8**
(il) Arroz con leche. See Arroz con leche   **782.42**
(il) González, L. M. Señor Cat's romance and other favorite stories from Latin America   **398.2**
(il) González, L. M. The storyteller's candle   **E**

DeLaCroix, Alice, 1940-
The best horse ever   **Fic**

Delahunty, Andrew
Barron's first thesaurus   **423**

Delaney, Joseph, 1904-1991
Revenge of the witch   **Fic**

Delaney, Joseph, 1945-
The Spook's tale and other horrors   **S C**

Delannoy, Isabelle
Our living Earth   **779**

Delano, Marfe Ferguson
Earth in the hot seat   **363.7**
Genius [biography of Albert Einstein]   **92**
Helen's eyes   **92**
Inventing the future: a photobiography of Thomas Alva Edison   **92**

Délano, Poli, 1936-
When I was a boy Neruda called me Policarpo   **92**

Delaware Bay (Del. and N.J.)
Crenson, V. Horseshoe crabs and shorebirds   **577.7**

Delessert, Étienne, 1941-
Big and Bad   **E**
Moon theater   **E**

The **delicious** bug. Perlman, J.   **E**

Delinois, Alix
(il) Myers, W. D. Muhammad Ali   **92**

Delinquency, Juvenile See Juvenile delinquency

Dell, Pamela
Protecting the planet   **333.72**

The **Delta** is my home. McLeod, T.   **970.004**

Delton, Judy, 1932-2001
Angel's mother's wedding   **Fic**

Delval, Marie-Hélène
Psalms for young children   **223**

Dem bones. Barner, B.   **612.7**

Demarest, Chris L., 1951-
All aboard!   **E**
Firefighters A to Z   **628.9**
Hurricane hunters!   **551.55**
(il) Murphy, S. J. Beep beep, vroom vroom!   **515**
(il) Thomas, P. J. Red sled   **E**

Demas, Corinne, 1947-
Always in trouble   **E**
Saying goodbye to Lulu   **E**
Valentine surprise   **E**

Dematons, Charlotte, 1957-
(il) Vries, A. d. Raf   **E**

DeMauro, Lisa
Thomas Edison. See Thomas Edison   **92**

Dembicki, Matt
  (ed) Trickster: Native American tales. See
    Trickster: Native American tales   **398.2**

Demi, 1942-
  The boy who painted dragons   **E**
  Buddha   **294.3**
  Buddha stories   **294.3**
  The Dalai Lama   **92**
  The emperor's new clothes   **E**
  The empty pot   **398.2**
  Gandhi   **92**
  Genghis Khan   **92**
  The girl who drew a phoenix   **E**
  The greatest power   **E**
  Happy, happy Chinese New Year!   **394.26**
  The hungry coat   **398.2**
  Jesus   **232.9**
  King Midas   **398.2**
  Kites   **E**
  The legend of Lao Tzu and the Tao te ching
    299.5
  The legend of Saint Nicholas   **92**
  The magic pillow   **E**
  Marco Polo   **92**
  Mary   **232.91**
  Mother Teresa   **92**
  Muhammad   **297**
  Rumi [biography if Jalāl al-Dîn Rūmî]   **92**
  Su Dongpo   **92**
  Tutankhamun   **92**

Democracy
  Thomas, W. D. What is a constitution?   **342**

Democratic Republic of the Congo. Heale, J.
    967.51

Democratic Republic of the Congo. Willis, T.
    967.51

Demoniac possession
        Fiction
  Paver, M. Wolf brother   **Fic**

Demonkeeper. Buckingham, R.   **Fic**

Demonology
        Fiction
  Milford, K. The Boneshaker   **Fic**

Demonstrations
    See also Civil rights demonstrations; Riots

Dempsey, Kristy
  Me with you   **E**

A **den** is a bed for a bear. Baines, R.   **599.78**

Dendy, Leslie A., 1946-
  Guinea pig scientists   **616**

Denega, Danielle, 1978-
  Gut-eating bugs   **363.2**
  Have you seen this face?   **363.2**

Denenberg, Barry
  Lincoln shot!   **92**

Denise, Anika
  Pigs love potatoes   **E**

Denise, Christopher, 1968-
  (il) Dempsey, K. Me with you   **E**
  (il) Denise, A. Pigs love potatoes   **E**
  (il) Elliott, D. Knitty Kitty   **E**

Denman, Michael L.
  (il) Tourville, A. D. A giraffe grows up
    599.63
  (il) Tourville, A. D. A jaguar grows up
    599.75

Denmark
  Pateman, R. Denmark   **948.9**
        Fiction
  Bredsdorff, B. The Crow-girl   **Fic**
  Bredsdorff, B. Eidi   **Fic**
  Deedy, C. A. The yellow star   **Fic**
  Lowry, L. Number the stars   **Fic**
  Stuchner, J. B. Honey cake   **Fic**
  Toksvig, S. Hitler's canary   **Fic**
        Folklore
    See Folklore—Denmark

Dennis, Brian, 1971-
  Nubs   **636.7**

Dennis, Wesley, 1903-1966
  (il) Henry, M. Brighty of the Grand Canyon
    Fic
  (il) Henry, M. Justin Morgan had a horse
    Fic
  (il) Henry, M. King of the wind   **Fic**
  (il) Henry, M. Misty of Chincoteague   **Fic**

Dennis, Yvonne Wakim
  Children of native America today   **970.004**
  A kid's guide to native American history
    970.004
  Sequoyah, 1770?-1843   **92**
  (jt. auth) Molin, P. F. American Indian stereo-
    types in the world of children   **970.004**

Denos, Julia
  (il) Madison, A. 100 days and 99 nights   **Fic**

Denslow, Sharon Phillips, 1947-
  In the snow   **E**

Denslow, William Wallace, 1856-1915
  (il) Baum, L. F. The wonderful Wizard of Oz
    Fic

Denstaedt, Melanie Turner- *See* Turner-
  Denstaedt, Melanie, 1963-2007

Dent, Charlie, 1919-1994
        About
  Fritz, J. Leonardo's horse   **730.9**

Dentistry
  Landau, E. Cavities and toothaches   **617.6**
  Miller, E. The tooth book   **617.6**
  Royston, A. Why do I brush my teeth?
    617.6
  Thomas, P. Do I have to go to the dentist?
    617.6
  Ziefert, H. ABC dentist   **617.6**
        Graphic novels
  Telgemeier, R. Smile   **741.5**

Dentists
        Fiction
  Steig, W. Doctor De Soto   **E**

Denton, Kady MacDonald
  (il) Becker, B. A visitor for Bear   **E**
  (il) Hutchins, H. J. A second is a hiccup
    529

Denton, Terry
  (il) Fox, M. Night noises   **E**
  (il) Fox, M. A particular cow   **E**

Denton, Terry—*Continued*
(il) Griffiths, A. The big fat cow that goes kapow   **E**
(il) Griffiths, A. The cat on the mat is flat   **E**

DePalma, Mary Newell, 1961-
A grand old tree   **E**
The Nutcracker doll   **E**
The perfect gift   **E**

DePaola, Tomie *See* De Paola, Tomie, 1934-

Department stores
     Fiction
Kirsch, V. X. Natalie & Naughtily   **E**

Depression (Psychology)
     See also Manic-depressive illness
Crist, J. J. What to do when you're sad & lonely   **158**
Roy, J. R. Depression   **616.85**
     Fiction
Bell, J. Breaking trail   **Fic**
Hemingway, E. M. Road to Tater Hill   **Fic**
LaFleur, S. M. Love, Aubrey   **Fic**

Depressions
     1929
     See Great Depression, 1929-1939

Derby, Ethel Roosevelt, 1891-1977
     Fiction
Bradley, K. B. The President's daughter   **Fic**

Derby, Sally, 1934-
Kyle's island   **Fic**
No mush today   **E**
Whoosh went the wind!   **E**

Deriso, Christine Hurley, 1961-
The Right-Under Club   **Fic**
Talia Talk   **Fic**

DerKazarian, Susan, 1969-
You have head lice!   **616.5**

Derom, Dirk, 1980-
Pigeon and Pigeonette   **E**

DeRoy, Craig
(il) Polland, B. K. We can work it out   **303.6**

Derzipilski, Kathleen
Beetles   **595.7**

DeSaix, Debbi Durland
(jt. auth) Ruelle, K. G. The grand mosque of Paris   **940.53**

DeSalle, Rob
(jt. auth) Tattersall, I. Bones, brains and DNA   **599.93**

Desegregation *See* Segregation

Desegregation in education *See* School integration

Desert animals
     See also Camels
Arnosky, J. Watching desert wildlife   **591.7**
Bredeson, C. Baby animals of the desert   **591.7**
Hodge, D. Desert animals   **591.7**
Landstrom, L. A. Nature's yucky! 2: the desert southwest   **591.7**
     Fiction
Paul, A. W. Count on Culebra   **E**

Paul, A. W. Fiesta fiasco   **E**
Sayre, A. P. Dig, wait, listen   **E**

Desert dinners. Lundgren, J. K.   **577.5**

Desert ecology
Bash, B. Desert giant   **583**
Fridell, R. Life in the desert   **577.5**
Guiberson, B. Z. Cactus hotel   **583**
Jackson, K. Explore the desert   **577.5**
Johansson, P. The dry desert   **577.5**
Johnson, R. L. A walk in the desert   **577.5**
Levinson, N. S. Death Valley   **577.5**
Lundgren, J. K. Desert dinners   **577.5**
Lynch, W. Sonoran Desert   **577.5**
Stille, D. R. Deserts   **577.5**

Desert giant. Bash, B.   **583**

Desert plants
     See also Cactus

Desert Rose and her highfalutin hog. Jackson, A.   **E**

Deserts
Fridell, R. Life in the desert   **577.5**
Serafini, F. Looking closely across the desert   **578.7**
     Fiction
Gonzalez, M. C. My colors, my world = Mis colores, mi mundo   **E**

Deserts. Stille, D. R.   **577.5**

DeSeve, Randall
The Duchess of Whimsy   **E**
The toy boat   **E**

Design
Gonyea, M. Another book about design   **745.4**
Gonyea, M. A book about design   **745.4**
Henry, S. Making amazing art   **745.5**
Oldham, T. Kid made modern   **745.5**

Design, Industrial *See* Industrial design

Design your own butterfly garden. Harkins, S. S.   **638**

Designer drugs
LeVert, S. Ecstasy   **362.29**

Designing a school library media center for the future. Erikson, R.   **027.8**

Desimini, Lisa, 1965-
My beautiful child   **E**
(il) Aardema, V. Anansi does the impossible!   **398.2**
(il) Adoff, A. Touch the poem   **811**
(il) Alda, A. Iris has a virus   **E**
(il) Annino, J. G. She sang promise: the story of Betty Mae Jumper, Seminole tribal leader   **92**
(il) Lewis, J. P. Doodle dandies   **811**
(il) Lewis, J. P. The snowflake sisters   **E**

Desperate journey. Murphy, J.   **Fic**

Despite all obstacles: La Salle and the conquest of the Mississippi. Goodman, J. E.   **92**

Desrocher, Jack
(il) Doeden, M. Eat right!   **613.2**
(il) Johnson, R. L. Amazing DNA   **572.8**
(il) Johnson, R. L. Mighty animal cells   **571.6**

A **difficult** boy. Barker, M. P.   Fic
Difficult origami. Alexander, C.   **736**
Dig!. Zimmerman, A. G.   E
Dig, wait, listen. Sayre, A. P.   E
Digby. Hazen, B. S.   E
Digby and Kate and the beautiful day. Baker, B.   E
Digby takes charge. Church, C.   E
Digestion
   Corcoran, M. K. The quest to digest   **612.3**
   Jakab, C. The digestive system   **612.3**
   Simon, S. Guts   **612.3**
The **digestive** system. Jakab, C.   **612.3**
Digger man. Zimmerman, A. G.   E
Digging for bird-dinosaurs. Bishop, N.   **567.9**
Digging for the past [series]
   Scarre, C. The Palace of Minos at Knossos   **728.8**
Digging up history. Peterson, J. M.   **930.1**
Digging up the past [series]
   Dean, A. Terra-cotta soldiers   **931**
Digital and information literacy [series]
   Cefrey, H. Researching people, places, and events   **001.4**
   Furgang, A. Searching online for image, audio, and video files   **025.04**
   Orr, T. Creating multimedia presentations   **005**
   Porterfield, J. Conducting basic and advanced searches   **025.04**
Digital libraries
   The whole digital library handbook   **025.1**
Digital photography
   Bidner, J. The kids' guide to digital photography   **775**
   Johnson, D. 4-H guide to digital photography   **775**
A **dignity** of dragons. Ogburn, J. K.   **398**
Dillon, Diane
   (il) Aardema, V. Who's in Rabbit's house?   **398.2**
   (il) Aardema, V. Why mosquitoes buzz in people's ears   **398.2**
   (il) Bible. O.T. Ecclesiastes. To every thing there is a season   **223**
   (il) Brown, M. W. Two little trains   E
   (il) Brown, M. W. Where have you been?   E
   (jt. auth) Dillon, L. Jazz on a Saturday night   **781.65**
   (jt. auth) Dillon, L. Mother Goose numbers on the loose   **398.8**
   (jt. auth) Dillon, L. Rap a tap tap   E
   (il) Fox, M. The goblin and the empty chair   E
   (il) Greenfield, E. Honey, I love, and other love poems   **811**
   (il) Hamilton, V. The girl who spun gold   **398.2**
   (il) Hamilton, V. Many thousand gone   **326**
   (il) Hamilton, V. The people could fly: American Black folktales   **398.2**
   (il) Hamilton, V. The people could fly: the picture book   **398.2**

   (il) Musgrove, M. Ashanti to Zulu: African traditions   **960**
   (il) Norman, H. Between heaven and earth   **398.2**
   (il) Paterson, K. The tale of the mandarin ducks   **398.2**
   (il) Verne, J. 20,000 leagues under the sea   Fic
   (il) Walker, R. D. Mama says   E
Dillon, Leo, 1933-
   Jazz on a Saturday night   **781.65**
   Mother Goose numbers on the loose   **398.8**
   Rap a tap tap   E
   (il) Aardema, V. Who's in Rabbit's house?   **398.2**
   (il) Aardema, V. Why mosquitoes buzz in people's ears   **398.2**
   (il) Bible. O.T. Ecclesiastes. To every thing there is a season   **223**
   (il) Brown, M. W. Two little trains   E
   (il) Brown, M. W. Where have you been?   E
   (jt. auth) Burns, K. Mansa Musa   Fic
   (il) Fox, M. The goblin and the empty chair   E
   (il) Greenfield, E. Honey, I love, and other love poems   **811**
   (il) Hamilton, V. The girl who spun gold   **398.2**
   (il) Hamilton, V. Many thousand gone   **326**
   (il) Hamilton, V. The people could fly: American Black folktales   **398.2**
   (il) Hamilton, V. The people could fly: the picture book   **398.2**
   (il) Musgrove, M. Ashanti to Zulu: African traditions   **960**
   (il) Norman, H. Between heaven and earth   **398.2**
   (il) Paterson, K. The tale of the mandarin ducks   **398.2**
   (il) Verne, J. 20,000 leagues under the sea   Fic
   (il) Walker, R. D. Mama says   E
Dillon Dillon. Banks, K.   Fic
Dim sum for everyone!. Lin, G.   E
Dimity Duck. Yolen, J.   E
Dimity Dumpty. Graham, B.   E
Dingle, Adrian
   The periodic table   **546**
Dining
            Fiction
   Ahlberg, A. The runaway dinner   E
   Friedman, I. R. How my parents learned to eat   E
            History
   Aliki. A medieval feast   **940.1**
Dino riddles. Hall, K.   **793.73**
Dino–why?. Funston, S.   **567.9**
Dinomummy. Manning, P. L.   **567.9**
Dinosaur!. Sís, P.   E
Dinosaur Bob and his adventures with the family Lazardo. Joyce, W.   E
Dinosaur hour!, vol. 1. Shioya, H.   **741.5**
Dinosaur hunt. Catrow, D.   E
Dinosaur mountain. Ray, D. K.   **567.9**

Discovering women artists for children. See Coyne, J. T. Come look with me: discovering women artists for children **704**

Discoverology [series]
Woodward, J. Creatures of the deep **591.7**

Discovery! [series]
Goldenberg, L. Little people and a lost world **599.93**

The **discovery** and mystery of a dinosaur named Jane. Williams, J. **567.9**

The **discovery** of the Americas. Maestro, B. **970.01**

Discrimination
See also Hate crimes; Sex discrimination

Discrimination in education
See also Segregation in education
Morrison, T. Remember **379**

Discs, Compact See Compact discs

Disease germs See Bacteria; Germ theory of disease

Disease update [series]
Silverstein, A. The ADHD update **616.85**
Silverstein, A. The AIDS update **616.97**
Silverstein, A. The asthma update **616.2**
Silverstein, A. The breast cancer update **616.99**
Silverstein, A. The diabetes update **616.4**
Silverstein, A. The eating disorders update **616.85**
Silverstein, A. The flu and pneumonia update **616.2**
Silverstein, A. The food poisoning update **615.9**
Silverstein, A. The sickle cell anemia update **616.1**
Silverstein, A. The tuberculosis update **616.2**

Diseases
See also Chickenpox; Mouth—Diseases; Sick names of specific diseases and groups of diseases; and subjects with the subdivision Diseases
Auden, S. Medical mysteries **610**
Barnard, B. Outbreak **614.4**
Bjorklund, R. Food-borne illnesses **615.9**
Murphy, P. J. Illness **616**
Piddock, C. Outbreak **614.4**
Walker, R. Epidemics & plagues **614.4**

Dishonesty See Honesty

Disney (Walt) Productions See Walt Disney Productions

Dispezio, Michael A.
Eye-popping optical illusions **152.14**

Displaced persons See Refugees

Dispute settlement See Conflict management

Ditchfield, Christin
Cowlick! **E**
Golf **796.352**
Memorial Day **394.26**
Shwatsit! **E**
Tennis **796.342**
Wrestling **796.8**

DiTerlizzi, Tony
Jimmy Zangwow's out-of-this-world, moon pie adventure **E**
Kenny & the dragon **Fic**
The Nixie's song **Fic**
(il) Howitt, M. B. The spider and the fly **821**

Divakaruni, Chitra Banerjee, 1956-
The conch bearer **Fic**

Divali
Heiligman, D. Celebrate Diwali **294.5**
MacMillan, D. M. Diwali—Hindu festival of lights **394.26**
Plum-Ucci, C. Celebrate Diwali **294.5**
Fiction
Rahaman, V. Divali rose **E**

Divali rose. Rahaman, V. **E**

Dive!. Earle, S. A. **551.46**

Divers, Sonia Hernandez- See Hernandez-Divers, Sonia, 1969-

Diversity, Biological See Biological diversity

Divide and ride. Murphy, S. J. **513**

Diving
Yoo, P. Sixteen years in sixteen seconds [biography of Sammy Lee] **92**

Diving, Scuba See Scuba diving

Diving, Submarine See Submarine diving

Diving to a deep-sea volcano. Mallory, K. **551.46**

Division
Murphy, S. J. Divide and ride **513**
Murphy, S. J. Jump, kangaroo, jump! **513**
Nagda, A. W. Cheetah math **513**
Fiction
Hutchins, P. The doorbell rang **E**
McElligott, M. Bean thirteen **E**

DiVito, Anna
(il) Holub, J. Why do birds sing? **598**
(il) Holub, J. Why do cats meow? **636.8**
(il) Holub, J. Why do horses neigh? **636.1**
(il) Holub, J. Why do rabbits hop? **636.9**
(il) Holub, J. Why do snakes hiss? **597.96**
(il) Krull, K. A kid's guide to America's Bill of Rights **342**

Divorce
See also Children of divorced parents; Remarriage
Brown, L. K. Dinosaurs divorce **306.89**
Holyoke, N. A smart girl's guide to her parents' divorce **306.89**
Krementz, J. How it feels when parents divorce **306.89**
Murphy, P. J. Divorce and separation **306.89**
Rogers, F. Divorce **306.89**
Fiction
Alvarez, J. How Tía Lola came to visit/stay **Fic**
Bateman, C. Running with the Reservoir Pups **Fic**
Bateson, C. Stranded in Boringsville **Fic**
Boles, P. M. Little divas **Fic**
Brown, J. R. 13 **Fic**
Brown, S. T. Hugging the rock **Fic**

Divorce—Fiction—*Continued*

Bunting, E. Some frog! **Fic**
Cleary, B. Dear Mr. Henshaw **Fic**
Cleary, B. Strider **Fic**
Cochran, B. My parents are divorced, my elbows have nicknames, and other facts about me **E**
Coffelt, N. Fred stays with me **E**
Corriveau, A. How I, Nicky Flynn, finally get a life (and a dog) **Fic**
Coy, J. Top of the order **Fic**
Heldring, T. Roy Morelli steps up to the plate **Fic**
Henkes, K. Bird Lake moon **Fic**
Holmberg, B. R. A day with Dad **E**
Ly, M. Home is east **Fic**
Portnoy, M. A. Tale of two Seders **E**
Schmitz, T. Standing on my own two feet **E**
Smith, Y. I, Lorelei **Fic**
Spinelli, E. The Dancing Pancake **Fic**
Tolan, S. S. Wishworks, Inc. **Fic**
Wilson, J. Candyfloss **Fic**
Zimmer, T. V. 42 miles **Fic**
Zimmer, T. V. Sketches from a spy tree **Fic**

Divorce and separation. Murphy, P. J. **306.89**

Diwali—Hindu festival of lights. MacMillan, D. M. **394.26**

Dixon, Cromwell, 1892-1911
Fiction
Nez, J. A. Cromwell Dixon's Sky-Cycle **E**

Dixon, Debra Spina
(il) Jacobs, P. D. Putting on a play **792**

Dixon, Dougal, 1947-
Amazing dinosaurs **567.9**
Dougal Dixon's dinosaurs **567.9**
World of dinosaurs and other prehistoric life **567.9**

Dixon, Norma
Focus on flies **595.7**
Lowdown on earthworms **592**

Dixon, Tiara
The sound of storytime **027.62**

Dixon-Engel, Tara
The Wright brothers **92**

Dizin, Pascal
(il) Kim, S. City of spies **741.5**

Dizzy. Cassidy, C. **Fic**

Dizzy [biography of Dizzy Gillespie] Winter, J. **92**

The **Django**. Pinfold, L. **E**

Django [Reinhardt] Christensen, B. **92**

DK biography [series]
Garrett, L. Helen Keller **92**
Wills, C. A. Annie Oakley: a photographic story of a life **92**

DK Children's illustrated dictionary. McIllwain, J. **423**

DK eyewitness books [series]
Adams, S. World War I **940.3**
Adams, S. World War II **940.53**
Bender, L. Invention **609**
Burnie, D. Bird **598**
Burnie, D. Light **535**

Byam, M. Arms & armor **355.8**
Challoner, J. Hurricane & tornado **551.55**
Clutton-Brock, J. Cat **599.75**
Cosgrove, B. Weather **551.5**
Cribb, J. Money **332.4**
Fortey, J. Great scientists **920**
Gamlin, L. Evolution **576.8**
Gravett, C. Knight **940.1**
Greenaway, T. Jungle **577.3**
Hill, D. Witches & magic-makers **133.4**
Hornby, H. Soccer **796.334**
James, S. Ancient Rome **937**
Langley, A. Medieval life **940.1**
Macquitty, M. Shark **597**
McCarthy, C. Reptile **597.9**
McIntosh, J. Archeology **930.1**
Murdoch, D. H. North American Indian **970.004**
Nahum, A. Flying machine **629.133**
Newmark, A. Chemistry **540**
Parker, S. Electricity **537**
Parker, S. Seashore **577.7**
Pearson, A. Ancient Greece **938**
Platt, R. Shipwreck **910.4**
Redmond, I. Gorilla, monkey & ape **599.8**
Rowland-Warne, L. Costume **391**
Stanchak, J. E. Civil War **973.7**
Stott, C. Space exploration **629.4**
Symes, R. F. Crystal & gem **548**
Taylor, P. D. Fossil **560**
Walker, R. Human body **612**
Whalley, P. E. S. Butterfly & moth **595.7**

DK first dinosaur encyclopedia **567.9**

DK first science encyclopedia **503**

DK Merriam-Webster children's dictionary **423**

DNA
Johnson, R. L. Amazing DNA **572.8**
Phelan, G. Double helix **572.8**

Do I have to go to the dentist? Thomas, P. **617.6**

Do it yourself [series]
Hurd, W. Changing states **530.4**
Oxlade, C. Experiments with sound **534**

Do it yourself projects! [series]
D'Cruz, A.-M. Make your own books **686**
D'Cruz, A.-M. Make your own masks **646.4**
D'Cruz, A.-M. Make your own musical instruments **784.19**
D'Cruz, A.-M. Make your own puppets **791.5**
D'Cruz, A.-M. Make your own purses and bags **646.4**
D'Cruz, A.-M. Make your own slippers and shoes **685**

Do not build a Frankenstein!. Numberman, N. **E**

Do not open. Farndon, J. **031.02**

Do not open this book!. Muntean, M. **E**

Do rabbits have Christmas? Fisher, A. L. **811**

Do tell!. Weissman, A. **027.62**

Do unto otters. Keller, L. **E**

Do you love me? Elffers, J. **E**

Do you want to be my friend? Carle, E. **E**

Dobbins, Jan
Driving my tractor   E
Dobbs, Kathy
(il) Raines, S. C. Story stretchers for infants, toddlers, and twos   **372.4**
Doc Wilde and the frogs of doom. Byrd, T.   Fic
Docampo, Valeria, 1976-
(il) Kimmel, E. A. The three little tamales   E
Docherty, Thomas
Little boat   E
To the beach   E
Doctor All-Knowing. Orgel, D.   **398.2**
Doctor De Soto. Steig, W.   E
Doctor Meow's big emergency. Lloyd, S.   E
Doctor Proctor's fart powder. Nesbø, J.   Fic
Doctor Ted. Beaty, A.   E
Doctors See Physicians
Documentary photography
Sandler, M. W. The Dust Bowl through the lens   **973.9**
Documents that shaped the nation [series]
Armentrout, D. The Mayflower Compact   **974.4**
Dodd, Emma, 1969-
I don't want a cool cat!   E
I don't want a posh dog!   E
I love bugs   E
Just like you   E
No matter what   E
What pet to get?   E
Dodds, Dayle Ann, 1952-
Full house   **513**
Minnie's Diner   E
The prince won't go to bed   E
Teacher's pets   E
Where's Pup?   E
Doder, Joshua, 1968-
A dog called Grk   Fic
Dodge, Abigail Johnson
Around the world cookbook   **641.5**
Dodge, Mary Mapes, 1830-1905
Hans Brinker; adaptation. See Coville, B. Hans Brinker   E
Hans Brinker, or, The silver skates   Fic
Dodgers (Baseball team) See Brooklyn Dodgers (Baseball team); Los Angeles Dodgers (Baseball team)
Dodgson, Charles Lutwidge See Carroll, Lewis, 1832-1898
Dodson, Bert
(il) Stryer, A. S. Kami and the yaks   E
Dodsworth in New York. Egan, T.   E
Doeden, Matt, 1974-
Eat right!   **613.2**
The greatest baseball records   **796.357**
The greatest basketball records   **796.323**
Does a kangaroo have a mother, too? Carle, E.   E
Does an elephant take a bath? Ehrlich, F.   E

Dog and Bear: two friends, three stories. Seeger, L. V.   E
Dog biscuit. Cooper, H.   E
Dog Blue. Dunbar, P.   E
A **dog** called Grk. Doder, J.   Fic
Dog crafts. Hendry, L.   **745.5**
Dog day. Hayes, S.   E
The **dog** days of Charlotte Hayes. Kennedy, M.   Fic
Dog diaries. Byars, B. C.   S C
A **dog** for life. Matthews, L. S.   Fic
Dog Friday. McKay, H.   Fic
A **dog** like Jack. DiSalvo, D.   E
A **dog** needs a bone. Wood, A.   E
A **dog** on his own. Auch, M. J.   Fic
Dog racing
    See also Iditarod Trail Sled Dog Race, Alaska; Sled dog racing
Dog train. Boynton, S.   **782.42**
Dog wants to play. McDonnell, C.   E
The **dog** who belonged to no one. Hest, A.   E
The **dog** who cried wolf. Kasza, K.   E
The **dog** who loved tortillas. Saenz, B. A.   E
Dog who saved Santa. Kelley, T.   E
Dogboy. Russell, C.   Fic
Dogerella. Boelts, M.   E
Doggone dogs!. Beaumont, K.   E
The **doghouse**. Thomas, J.   E
Dogku. Clements, A.   **811**
Dogs
    See also Sheep dogs; Working dogs
Altman, L. J. Big dogs   **636.7**
Barnes, J. Pet dogs   **636.7**
Bidner, J. Is my dog a wolf?   **636.7**
Bozzo, L. My first dog   **636.7**
Buckley, C. Tarra & Bella   **599.67**
Calmenson, S. May I pet your dog?   **636.7**
Calmenson, S. Rosie   **636.7**
The Complete dog book for kids   **636.7**
Coren, S. Why do dogs have wet noses?   **636.7**
Crosby, J. Little lions, bull baiters & hunting hounds   **636.7**
Dennis, B. Nubs   **636.7**
Gaines, A. Top 10 dogs for kids   **636.7**
George, J. C. How to talk to your dog   **636.7**
Gibbons, G. Dogs   **636.7**
Grogan, J. Marley   **636.7**
Hart, J. Big dogs   **636.7**
Hart, J. Small dogs   **636.7**
Hendry, L. Dog crafts   **745.5**
Holub, J. Why do dogs bark?   **636.7**
Houston, D. Bulu, African wonder dog   **636.7**
Jackson, E. A home for Dixie   **636.7**
Jeffrey, L. S. Dogs   **636.7**
Jenkins, S. Dogs and cats   **636.7**
Johnson, J. Dogs and puppies   **636.7**
Kehret, P. Shelter dogs   **636.7**
Larson, K. Two Bobbies   **636.08**

Dogs—*Continued*

Leedy, L. Measuring Penny	**530.8**
Mehus-Roe, K. Dogs for kids!	**636.7**
Miller, D. S. The great serum race	**798.8**
Paulsen, G. My life in dog years	**92**
Simon, S. Dogs	**636.7**
Weatherford, C. B. First pooch	**973.932**
Whitehead, S. How to speak dog	**636.7**

Fiction

Alborough, J. Some dogs do	**E**
Appelt, K. Bubba and Beau, best friends	**E**
Appelt, K. The underneath	**Fic**
Armstrong, W. H. Sounder	**Fic**
Ashman, L. Stella, unleashed	**E**
Auch, M. J. A dog on his own	**Fic**
Avi. The good dog	**Fic**
Baker, B. Digby and Kate and the beautiful day	**E**
Bansch, H. I want a dog!	**E**
Barracca, D. The adventures of Taxi Dog	**E**
Bartram, S. Bob's best ever friend	**E**
Beaumont, K. Doggone dogs!	**E**
Beaumont, K. Move over, Rover	**E**
Beck, A. Pierre Le Poof!	**E**
Bedford, D. The way I love you	**E**
Beha, E. Tango	**Fic**
Behrens, A. The fast and the furriest	**Fic**
Beil, K. M. Jack's house	**E**
Bell, C. Itty bitty	**E**
Blake, R. J. Togo	**E**
Bluemle, E. Dogs on the bed	**E**
Bodeen, S. A. A small, brown dog with a wet, pink nose	**E**
Boelts, M. Before you were mine	**E**
Boelts, M. Dogerella	**E**
Braeuner, S. The great dog wash	**E**
Branford, H. Fire, bed, & bone	**Fic**
Breathed, B. Flawed dogs	**Fic**
Breen, S. Violet the pilot	**E**
Brown, P. Chowder	**E**
Buehner, C. Superdog	**E**
Burleigh, R. Good-bye, Sheepie	**E**
Butler, D. H. The case of the lost boy	**Fic**
Byars, B. C. Dog diaries	**S C**
Byars, B. C. Tornado	**Fic**
Capucilli, A. Biscuit's new trick	**E**
Carbone, E. L. Night running	**E**
Carlson, N. L. Harriet and the roller coaster	**E**
Carlstrom, N. W. It's your first day of school, Annie Claire	**E**
Casanova, M. Some dog!	**E**
Catrow, D. Dinosaur hunt	**E**
Catusanu, M. The strange case of the missing sheep	**E**
Cazet, D. The octopus	**E**
Chall, M. W. One pup's up	**E**
Chapra, M. Sparky's bark	**E**
Chichester-Clark, E. Melrose and Croc: an adventure to remember	**E**
Chichester-Clark, E. Piper	**E**
Child, L. Who wants to be a poodle I don't	**E**
Choung, E.-H. Minji's salon	**E**
Christelow, E. Letters from a desperate dog	**E**
Church, C. Digby takes charge	**E**

Cleary, B. Strider	**Fic**
Clements, A. Circus family dog	**E**
Cochran, B. The forever dog	**E**
Cochran, T. Running the dogs	**Fic**
Coffelt, N. Dogs in space	**E**
Coffelt, N. Fred stays with me	**E**
Cooper, H. Dog biscuit	**E**
Cooper, I. Look at Lucy!	**Fic**
Corriveau, A. How I, Nicky Flynn, finally get a life (and a dog)	**Fic**
Cousins, L. I'm the best	**E**
Cox, J. Puppy power	**Fic**
Cronin, D. Wiggle	**E**
D'Aulaire, I. Foxie	**E**
Day, A. Carl's sleepy afternoon	**E**
De Paola, T. Meet the Barkers	**E**
Demas, C. Always in trouble	**E**
Demas, C. Saying goodbye to Lulu	**E**
DiCamillo, K. Because of Winn-Dixie	**Fic**
DiSalvo, D. A dog like Jack	**E**
Dodd, E. I don't want a posh dog!	**E**
Dodds, D. A. Where's Pup?	**E**
Doder, J. A dog called Grk	**Fic**
Dunbar, P. Dog Blue	**E**
Ehlert, L. Wag a tail	**E**
Esbaum, J. Stanza	**E**
Estes, E. Ginger Pye	**Fic**
Faller, R. The adventures of Polo	**E**
Feiffer, J. Bark, George	**E**
Feiffer, K. Henry, the dog with no tail	**E**
Feiffer, K. The problem with the Puddles	**Fic**
Fields, B. W. Lunchbox and the aliens	**Fic**
Fine, A. Notso hotso	**Fic**
Fleming, D. Buster	**E**
Foreman, J. Say hello	**E**
Foreman, M. Mia's story	**E**
Fox, P. The stone-faced boy	**Fic**
Freeman, M. Mrs. Wow never wanted a cow	**E**
French, J. Pete the sheep-sheep	**E**
French, J. Rover	**Fic**
Gal, S. Please take me for a walk	**E**
Gardiner, J. R. Stone Fox	**Fic**
George, L. B. Maggie's ball	**E**
Gipson, F. B. Old Yeller	**Fic**
Glenn, S. M. Just what Mama needs	**E**
Godwin, L. Happy and Honey	**E**
Goldfinger, J. P. My dog Lyle	**E**
Graham, B. Let's get a pup, said Kate	**E**
Gravett, E. Dogs	**E**
Gretz, S. Riley and Rose in the picture	**E**
Guy, G. F. Perros! Perros! Dogs! Dogs!	**E**
Haig, M. Samuel Blink and the forbidden forest	**Fic**
Harlow, J. H. Secret of the night ponies	**Fic**
Harlow, J. H. Star in the storm	**Fic**
Harper, D. Sit, Truman!	**E**
Harper, L. Snow! Snow! Snow!	**E**
Hayes, S. Dog day	**E**
Hazen, B. S. Digby	**E**
Hearne, B. G. The canine connection: stories about dogs and people	**S C**
Heiligman, D. Cool dog, school dog	**E**
Henkes, K. Circle dogs	**E**
Henkes, K. Protecting Marie	**Fic**

Dogs—Fiction—*Continued*

Hest, A. The dog who belonged to no one   E

Hills, T. How Rocket learned to read   E

Himmelman, J. Katie loves the kittens   E

Hobbs, V. Sheep   Fic

Hodgkins, F. Who's been here?   E

Hood, S. Pup and Hound hatch an egg   E

Howe, J. Houndsley and Catina   E

Howe, P. Waggit's tale   Fic

Huneck, S. Sally goes to the beach   E

Hurd, T. Art dog   E

Ichikawa, S. Come fly with me   E

Imai, A. Chester   E

Jahn-Clough, L. Little Dog   E

Jarka, J. Love that puppy!   E

Jenkins, E. Skunkdog   E

Jenkins, E. That new animal   E

Johnson, P. B. On top of spaghetti   E

Johnston, L. Farley follows his nose   E

Joosse, B. M. Wind-wild dog   E

Jordan, S. Mr. and Mrs. Portly and their little dog Snack   E

Kadohata, C. Cracker!   Fic

Kasza, K. The dog who cried wolf   E

Katz, B. Nothing but a dog   E

Kelley, T. Dog who saved Santa   E

Kellogg, S. Pinkerton, behave!   E

Kennedy, M. The dog days of Charlotte Hayes   Fic

Kerby, M. Owney, the mail-pouch pooch   E

Kimmelman, L. In the doghouse   E

King, S. M. Leaf   E

King, S. M. Mutt dog!   E

Kvasnosky, L. M. Really truly Bingo   E

Labatt, M. Pizza for Sam   E

Lacombe, B. Cherry and Olive   E

LaMarche, J. Lost and found   E

Langston, L. The trouble with Cupid   Fic

Lasky, K. Poodle and Hound   E

Leonard, E. A coyote's in the house   Fic

Lord, C. Hot rod hamster   E

Loupy, C. Hugs and kisses   E

Lowry, L. Stay!   Fic

MacLachlan, P. Bittle   E

Matthews, L. S. A dog for life   Fic

McCarty, P. Hondo and Fabian   E

McDonnell, C. Dog wants to play   E

McGhee, A. Always   E

McGhee, A. Julia Gillian (and the art of knowing)   Fic

McKay, H. Dog Friday   Fic

McKissack, P. C. Tippy Lemmey   Fic

McPhail, D. M. Weezer changes the world   E

Meddaugh, S. Martha speaks   E

Meister, C. Tiny's bath   E

Milgrim, D. My dog, Buddy   E

Miller, S. S. Three more stories you can read to your dog   E

Myers, L. Lewis and Clark and me   Fic

Myers, W. D. The blues of Flats Brown   E

Myers, W. D. Three swords for Granada   Fic

Naylor, P. R. Shiloh   Fic

Nelson, M. Snook alone   E

Newgarden, M. Bow-Wow bugs a bug   E

Newman, L. Hachiko waits   Fic

Nolan, L. A. On the road   Fic

Nuzum, K. A. The leanin' dog   Fic

O'Connor, B. How to steal a dog   Fic

O'Connor, B. The small adventure of Popeye and Elvis   Fic

O'Connor, J. The perfect puppy for me   E

O'Hair, M. My pup   E

O'Neill, C. Annie and Simon   E

Oppel, K. The king's taster   E

Patterson, N. R. The winner's walk   Fic

Peet, B. The whingdingdilly   E

Pilkey, D. The Hallo-wiener   E

Politi, L. Emmet   E

Provensen, A. A day in the life of Murphy   E

Radunsky, V. You?   E

Raschka, C. Hip hop dog   E

Rathmann, P. Officer Buckle and Gloria   E

Rawls, W. Where the red fern grows   Fic

Resau, L. Star in the forest   Fic

Riddell, C. Ottoline and the yellow cat   Fic

Ries, L. Aggie and Ben   E

Rodowsky, C. F. The next-door dogs   Fic

Russell, C. Dogboy   Fic

Russell, C. Hunted   Fic

Ruzzier, S. Amandina   E

Rylant, C. Henry and Mudge   E

Saenz, B. A. The dog who loved tortillas   E

Saltzberg, B. I want a dog!   E

Seeger, L. V. Dog and Bear: two friends, three stories   E

Segal, J. Alistair and Kip's great adventure   E

Seibold, J. O. Olive the other reindeer   E

Seidler, T. Gully's travels   Fic

Sendak, M. Higglety pigglety pop!   Fic

Shannon, D. Good boy, Fergus!   E

Shannon, G. Tippy-toe chick, go!   E

Sherlock, P. Letters from Wolfie   Fic

Siminovich, L. Alex and Lulu: two of a kind   E

Simmons, J. Together   E

Simont, M. The stray dog   E

Smith, L. The inside tree   E

Spangler, B. Peg Leg Peke   E

Staples, S. F. The green dog   Fic

Steig, W. Caleb & Kate   E

Steig, W. Dominic   Fic

Stevens, J. Help me, Mr. Mutt!   E

Swaim, J. The hound from the pound   E

Sweet, M. Carmine   E

Sweet, M. Tupelo rides the rails   E

Taylor, T. The trouble with Tuck   Fic

Teague, M. Dear Mrs. LaRue   E

Teague, M. Funny Farm   E

Thayer, J. The puppy who wanted a boy   E

Thierry, R. Green butterfly   E

Thomas, J. The doghouse   E

Timberlake, A. The dirty cowboy   E

Tolan, S. S. Listen!   Fic

Tolan, S. S. Wishworks, Inc.   Fic

Tripp, J. Pete & Fremont   Fic

Turner, P. S. Hachiko   E

Van Allsburg, C. The garden of Abdul Gasazi   E

Van Allsburg, C. The sweetest fig   E

Dogs—Fiction—*Continued*

Vande Velde, V. Smart dog	Fic
Voake, S. Daisy Dawson is on her way!	Fic
Walker, A. I love Christmas	E
Wallace, C. One nosy pup	E
Wallace, C. The Santa secret	E
Wallace, C. Turkeys together	E
Warnes, T. Chalk and Cheese	E
Weeks, S. Woof	E
Wells, R. McDuff moves in	E
Wells, R. Otto runs for President	E
Willems, M. City Dog, Country Frog	E
Winthrop, E. The biggest parade	E
Wishinsky, F. Please, Louise!	E
Wood, A. A dog needs a bone	E
Ylvisaker, A. Little Klein	Fic
Zalben, J. B. Baby shower	E
Zimmerman, A. G. Dig!	E
Zion, G. Harry the dirty dog	E
Zolotow, C. The old dog	E

Folklore

MacDonald, M. R. The great smelly, slobbery, small-tooth dog **398.2**

Graphic novels

Kibuishi, K. Copper	741.5
Varon, S. Robot dreams	741.5

Poetry

Archer, P. Name that dog!	811
Clements, A. Dogku	811
George, K. O. Little Dog and Duncan	811
George, K. O. Little dog poems	811
Gottfried, M. Good dog	811
MacLachlan, P. Once I ate a pie	811
Sidman, J. Meow ruff	811

Training

Rogers, T. 4-H guide to dog training and dog tricks **636.7**

Dogs. Gravett, E.	E
Dogs and cats. Jenkins, S.	636.7
Dogs and puppies. Johnson, J.	636.7
Dogs for kids!. Mehus-Roe, K.	636.7

Dogs for the blind *See* Guide dogs

A **dog's** gotta do what a dog's gotta do. Singer, M. **636.7**

Dogs in space. Coffelt, N.	E
Dogs on the bed. Bluemle, E.	E

Doherty, Berlie

Fairy tales	398.2
The goblin baby	Fic

Dokas, Dara, 1968-

Muriel's red sweater	E

Dolan, Edward F., 1924-

George Washington	92

Doll, Carol Ann

Managing and analyzing your collection **025.2**

A **doll** for Navidades. Santiago, E.	E
The **doll** in the garden. Hahn, M. D.	Fic
The **doll** people. Martin, A. M.	Fic
The **doll** shop downstairs. McDonough, Y. Z.	Fic

The **doll** with the yellow star. McDonough, Y. Z. **Fic**

Dollar

Forest, C. The dollar bill in translation	332.4

The **dollar** bill in translation. Forest, C. **332.4**

Dolley Madison saves George Washington. Brown, D. **92**

The **dollhouse** fairy. Ray, J.	E
The **dollhouse** murders. Wright, B. R.	Fic

Dollhouses

Fiction

Godden, R. The doll's house	Fic
Ray, J. The dollhouse fairy	E

Dolls

Fiction

Block, F. L. House of dolls	Fic
Browne, A. Silly Billy	E
De Guzman, M. Finding Stinko	Fic
Field, R. Hitty: her first hundred years	Fic
Godden, R. The doll's house	Fic
Godden, R. The story of Holly & Ivy	E
Gregory, N. Pink	E
Kleven, E. The apple doll	E
Martin, A. M. The doll people	Fic
McClintock, B. Dahlia	E
McDonough, Y. Z. The doll shop downstairs	Fic
McDonough, Y. Z. The doll with the yellow star	Fic
McKissack, P. C. The all-I'll-ever-want Christmas doll	E
Milgrim, D. Time to get up, time to go	E
Polacco, P. Babushka's doll	E
Pomerantz, C. The chalk doll	E
Randall, A. L. The wheat doll	E
Zolotow, C. William's doll	E

The **doll's** house. Godden, R. **Fic**

Dolphin talk. Pfeffer, W. **599.5**

Dolphins

Christopherson, S. C. Top 50 reasons to care about whales and dolphins	599.5
Dudzinski, K. Meeting dolphins	599.5
Hatkoff, J. Winter's tail	639.9
Nicklin, F. Face to face with dolphins	599.5
Pfeffer, W. Dolphin talk	599.5
Simon, S. Dolphins	599.5

Fiction

Arnosky, J. Dolphins on the sand	E

Dolphins on the sand. Arnosky, J. **E**

Domenico, Gino

(il) Amendola, D. A day at the New Amsterdam Theatre **792.6**

Domestic animals

See also Pets; Working animals

Elliott, D. On the farm	E
Tafuri, N. Spots, feathers, and curly tails	E

Fiction

Anderson, P. P. Chuck's truck	E
Armstrong, A. Whittington	Fic
Banks, K. What's coming for Christmas?	E
Battut, E. The fox and the hen	E
Bruss, D. Book! book! book!	E
Bunting, E. Hurry! hurry!	E

Doolittle, Michael J.
  (il) Goodman, S. Claws, coats, and camouflage
                        591.4
  (il) Goodman, S. Life on the ice   **998**
  (il) Goodman, S. Seeds, stems, and stamens
                        581.4
The **doom** machine. Teague, M.   **Fic**
The **door** in the wall. De Angeli, M. L.   **Fic**
The **door** to time. Baccalario, P.   **Fic**
The **doorbell** rang. Hutchins, P.   **E**
Doors
              Fiction
  Tidholm, A.-C. Knock! knock!   **E**
Doran, Colleen, 1963-
  (il) David, P. Mascot to the rescue!   **Fic**
Doran, Ella
  (il) Color. See Color   **535.6**
Dorjee, Yeshi *See* Yeshi Dorjee
The **Dorling** Kindersley children's illustrated dictionary. See McIllwain, J. DK Children's illustrated dictionary   **423**
Dorling Kindersley readers [series]
  Chrisp, P. Welcome to the Globe   **822.3**
  Hayden, K. Horse show   **798.2**
Dorman, Brandon
  (il) Berkeley, J. The Palace of Laughter   **Fic**
  (il) Bode, N. E. The slippery map   **Fic**
  (il) Murray, M. D. Halloween night   **E**
  (il) Prelutsky, J. Be glad your nose is on your face and other poems   **811**
  (il) Prelutsky, J. The wizard   **E**
Dormer, Frank W.
  (il) Aston, D. H. Not so tall for six   **E**
  (il) Cadena, B. Supersister   **E**
  (il) Ries, L. Aggie and Ben   **E**
Dormia. Halpern, J.   **Fic**
Dornfeld, Margaret
  Bats   **599.4**
Dorris, Michael
  Morning Girl   **Fic**
  Sees Behind Trees   **Fic**
Dorros, Alex
  Número uno   **E**
Dorros, Arthur, 1950-
  Abuela   **E**
  Ant cities   **595.7**
  Follow the water from brook to ocean
                    551.48
  Julio's magic   **E**
  Papá and me   **E**
  Radio Man. Don Radio   **E**
  (jt. auth) Dorros, A. Número uno   **E**
  (il) Wyler, R. Magic secrets   **793.8**
The **dot**. Reynolds, P.   **E**
Dot & Jabber and the big bug mystery. Walsh, E. S.   **E**
Dotlich, Rebecca Kai
  Over in the pink house   **811**
  What is science?   **500**
Doubilet, David
  Face to face with sharks   **597**
Double cheeseburgers, quiche, and vegetarian burritos. Ichord, L. F.   **394.1**

Double-dare to be scared: another thirteen chilling tales. San Souci, R.   **S C**
The **double-digit** club. Bauer, M. D.   **Fic**
Double eagle. Collard, S. B., III   **Fic**
Double helix. Phelan, G.   **572.8**
Double pink. Feiffer, K.   **E**
Double the ducks. Murphy, S. J.   **513**
Doudna, Kelly, 1963-
  It's a baby kangaroo!   **599.2**
Doug-Dennis and the flyaway fib. Farrell, D.
                    E
Dougal Dixon's amazing dinosaurs. See Dixon, D. Amazing dinosaurs   **567.9**
Dougal Dixon's dinosaurs. Dixon, D.   **567.9**
The **doughboys** over there. Beller, S. P.   **940.4**
Dougherty, Terri, 1964-
  The greatest football records   **796.332**
Doughty, Rebecca, 1955-
  Oh no! Time to go!   **E**
Douglas, Amy
  (ed) English folktales. See English folktales
                    398.2
Douglass, Ali
  (il) Holyoke, N. A smart girl's guide to money
                332.024
Douglass, Earl, 1862-1931
            About
  Ray, D. K. Dinosaur mountain   **567.9**
Douglass, Frederick, 1817?-1895
            About
  McKissack, P. C. Frederick Douglass   **92**
Douglass, Susan L., 1950-
  Ramadan   **297.3**
Doves *See* Pigeons
Dovey Coe. Dowell, F. O.   **Fic**
Dowd, Siobhan
  The London Eye mystery   **Fic**
Dowdle, Mary
  (il) Friedman, L. Break a leg!   **792**
Dowell, Frances O'Roark
  Chicken boy   **Fic**
  Dovey Coe   **Fic**
  Falling in   **Fic**
  The kind of friends we used to be   **Fic**
  Phineas L. Macguire erupts!   **Fic**
  The secret language of girls   **Fic**
  Shooting the moon   **Fic**
  Where I'd like to be   **Fic**
Down by the bay. Raffi   **782.42**
Down by the station. Hillenbrand, W.   **782.42**
Down by the station. Vetter, J. R.   **782.42**
Down comes the rain. Branley, F. M.   **551.57**
Down, down, down. Jenkins, S.   **591.7**
Down Girl and Sit [series]
  Nolan, L. A. On the road   **Fic**
Down syndrome
  Brill, M. T. Down syndrome   **616.85**
  Routh, K. Down syndrome   **616.85**
  Royston, A. Explaining down syndrome
                616.85
  Skotko, B. Fasten your seatbelt   **616.85**

Down syndrome—*Continued*
Fiction
Hobbs, V. The last best days of summer
    Fic

Down the Colorado [biography of John Wesley Powell] Ray, D. K.   **92**

Down the road. Schertle, A.   **E**

The **down-to-earth** guide to global warming. David, L.   **363.7**

Down to the sea in ships. Sturges, P.   **811**

Downard, Barry
The race of the century   **398.2**

Downer, Ann, 1960-
Hatching magic   **Fic**

Downing, Julie, 1956-
No hugs till Saturday   **E**
(il) Park, L. S. The firekeeper's son   **E**
(il) Rosenberg, L. Nobody   **E**

Downs, Elizabeth, 1953-
The school library media specialist's policy & procedure writer   **027.8**

Dowson, Nick
Tigress   **E**
Tracks of a panda   **E**

Doyen, Denise
Once upon a twice   **E**

Doyle, Beverly, 1963-
(il) Batten, M. Aliens from Earth   **578.6**

Doyle, Malachy, 1954-
Horse   **E**
Tales from old Ireland   **398.2**

Doyle, Roddy, 1958-
Her mother's face   **E**

A **dozen** ducklings lost and found. Ziefert, H.
    E

Dr. Frankenstein's human body book. Walker, R.
    612

Dr. Jenner and the speckled monster. Marrin, A.
    614.5

Dr. Martin Luther King Jr.'s I have a dream speech in translation. Holland, L. J.   **323.1**

Dr. Seuss *See* Seuss, Dr.

Draanen, Wendelin van
Flipped   **Fic**
Sammy Keyes and the hotel thief   **Fic**
Shredderman: Secret identity   **Fic**

Dragon bones and dinosaur eggs: a photobiography of Roy Chapman Andrews. Bausum, A.   **92**

Dragon condices [series]
Henham, R. D. The red dragon codex   **Fic**

Dragon dancing. Schaefer, C. L.   **E**

The **dragon** diary. Steer, D.   **Fic**

The **dragon** emperor. Wang Ping   **398.2**

The **dragon** in the sock drawer. Klimo, K.
    Fic

Dragon is coming!. Gorbachev, V.   **E**

Dragon keepers [series]
Klimo, K. The dragon in the sock drawer
    Fic

The **dragon** of Krakow and other Polish stories. Monte, R.   **398.2**

The **dragon** of Trelian. Knudsen, M.   **Fic**

Dragon Puncher. Kochalka, J.   **741.5**

Dragon rider. Funke, C. C.   **Fic**

DragonArt. Peffer, J.   **743**

Dragonflies
Glaser, L. Dazzling dragonflies   **595.7**
Lockwood, S. Dragonflies   **595.7**
Miller, H. This is your life cycle   **595.7**
Fiction
Breen, S. Stick   **E**

The **dragonfly** pool. Ibbotson, E.   **Fic**

Dragons
Gibbons, G. Behold . . . the dragons!   **398**
Grant, J. Life-size dragons   **398**
Malam, J. Dragons   **398.2**
Peffer, J. DragonArt   **743**
Penner, L. R. Dragons   **398.2**
Pringle, L. P. Imagine a dragon   **398.2**
Fiction
Ashburn, B. Over at the castle   **E**
The Book of dragons   **S C**
Coombs, K. The runaway princess   **Fic**
Coville, B. Jeremy Thatcher, dragon hatcher
    Fic
De Mari, S. The last dragon   **Fic**
Demi. The boy who painted dragons   **E**
DiTerlizzi, T. Kenny & the dragon   **Fic**
Downer, A. Hatching magic   **Fic**
Downing, J. No hugs till Saturday   **E**
Drake, S. Dragonsdale   **Fic**
Ehrlich, A. Baby Dragon   **E**
Fletcher, R. The Sandman   **E**
Funke, C. C. Dragon rider   **Fic**
Gannett, R. S. My father's dragon   **Fic**
Gliori, D. The trouble with dragons   **E**
Grahame, K. The reluctant dragon   **Fic**
Hale, B. Snoring Beauty   **E**
Henham, R. D. The red dragon codex   **Fic**
Kent, J. There's no such thing as a dragon
    E
Klimo, K. The dragon in the sock drawer
    Fic
Knapman, T. Guess what I found in Dragon Wood?   **E**
Knudsen, M. The dragon of Trelian   **Fic**
Krensky, S. Spark the firefighter   **E**
Lairamore, D. Ivy's ever after   **Fic**
Lake, A. J. The coming of dragons   **Fic**
Lin, G. Where the mountain meets the moon
    Fic
Niemann, C. Pet dragon   **E**
Nigg, J. How to raise and keep a dragon
    Fic
Nolen, J. Raising dragons   **E**
Schaefer, C. L. Dragon dancing   **E**
Steer, D. The dragon diary   **Fic**
Thayer, J. The popcorn dragon   **E**
Thomas, S. M. Good night, Good Knight   **E**
Thomson, S. L. Dragon's egg   **Fic**
Tucker, K. The seven Chinese sisters   **E**
Wormell, C. George and the dragon   **E**
Wrede, P. C. Dealing with dragons   **Fic**
Yep, L. City of fire   **Fic**

Drawing lessons from a bear. McPhail, D. M.
E

Drawing the new adventure cartoons. Hart, C.
741.5

Dray, Philip
Yours for justice, Ida B. Wells **92**

The **dreadful** revenge of Ernest Gallen. Collier, J.
L. **Fic**

Dream big [series]
Troupe, T. K. If I were a ballerina **792.8**

The **dream** keeper and other poems. Hughes, L.
811

A **dream** of freedom. McWhorter, D. **323.1**

The **dream** stealer. Fleischman, S. **Fic**

The **dreamer**. Ryan, P. M. **Fic**

Dreamer from the village [biography of Marc
Chagall] Markel, M. **92**

Dreams

See also Sleep
Fiction
Banks, K. Close your eyes **E**
Briggs, R. The snowman **E**
Demi. The magic pillow **E**
Fleischman, S. The dream stealer **Fic**
Henkes, K. Old Bear **E**
Hurd, T. The weaver **E**
King, S. M. Leaf **E**
Le Guin, U. K. Cat dreams **E**
Mack, J. Hush little polar bear **E**
Orlev, U. The song of the whales **Fic**
Ramirez, A. Napi **E**
Ringgold, F. Tar Beach **E**
Rocco, J. Moonpowder **E**
Saenz, B. A. A perfect season for dreaming
E
Teague, D. Franklin's big dreams **E**
Van Allsburg, C. Ben's dream **E**
Van Allsburg, C. Just a dream **E**
Van Allsburg, C. The sweetest fig **E**
Whatley, B. Clinton Gregory's secret **E**
Wiesner, D. Free fall **E**
Yum, H. Last night **E**

Dreifuss, Donald
(il) Ziefert, H. A dozen ducklings lost and found
E

Drescher, Henrik, 1955-
McFig & McFly **E**
(il) Sierra, J. The gruesome guide to world monsters **398**

Dress, Robert
(il) Thompson, K. Highway robbery **Fic**

Dress *See* Clothing and dress

Dress accessories
Warwick, E. Everywear **745.5**

Dressen-McQueen, Stacey
(il) Behind the museum door. See Behind the
museum door **811.008**
(il) Cruise, R. Little Mama forgets **E**
(il) Fleming, C. Boxes for Katje **E**
(il) Lowell, S. The elephant quilt **E**
(il) Schaefer, C. L. The biggest soap **E**

Dressmaking

See also Needlework
Fiction
Strauss, L. L. The princess gown **E**

Dreyer, Francis
(jt. auth) Plisson, P. Lighthouses **387.1**

Drez, Ronald J.
Remember D-day **940.54**

Drinker, Susan G.
(il) Marino, J. Mother Goose time **027.62**

The **drinking** gourd. Monjo, F. N. **E**

Drinking of alcoholic beverages
Gottfried, T. Alcohol **362.292**

Drinking problem *See* Alcoholism; Drinking of
alcoholic beverages

Drip, drop. Weeks, S. **E**

Driscoll, Michael, 1973-
A child's introduction to poetry **808.81**

Drita, my homegirl. Lombard, J. **Fic**

Drive. Clement, N. **E**

Driven. Mitchell, D. **92**

Driving my tractor. Dobbins, J. **E**

Drizzle. Van Cleve, K. **Fic**

Dronzek, Laura
(il) Henkes, K. Birds **E**
(il) Shannon, G. Rabbit's gift **398.2**
(il) Shannon, G. Tippy-toe chick, go! **E**
(il) Shannon, G. White is for blueberry **E**

A **drop** of blood. Showers, P. **612.1**

A **drop** of water. Wick, W. **553.7**

Droughts
Cooper, M. L. Dust to eat **973.917**
Fradin, J. B. Droughts **363.34**
Fiction
Conway, D. Lila and the secret of rain **E**
Hamilton, V. Drylongso **Fic**
Jackson, A. Rainmaker **Fic**
McKinnon, H. R. Franny Parker **Fic**
Stanton, K. Papi's gift **E**
Van Cleve, K. Drizzle **Fic**
Folklore
Aardema, V. Bringing the rain to Kapiti Plain
398.2

A **drowned** maiden's hair. Schlitz, L. A. **Fic**

Drucker, Malka, 1945-
Portraits of Jewish American heroes **920**

Drug abuse
LeVert, S. Ecstasy **362.29**
Fiction
Elliott, Z. Bird **E**

Drug facts [series]
Gottfried, T. Alcohol **362.292**
Gottfried, T. Marijuana **362.29**
LeVert, S. Ecstasy **362.29**
LeVert, S. Steroids **362.29**
Menhard, F. R. The facts about inhalants
362.29

Drugs

See also Designer drugs; Steroids

Drugs, Designer *See* Designer drugs

Druids and Druidism
Fiction
Farmer, N. The Sea of Trolls   Fic

Drumbeat in our feet. Keeler, P. A.   793.3

Drummer Hoff. Emberley, B.   398.8

Drummond, Allan
Liberty!   E
Tin Lizzie   E
(il) Borden, L. The journey that saved Curious George [biography of Margret Rey and H. A. Rey]   92

Drummond, Karen Eich
(jt. auth) D'Amico, J. The coming to America cookbook   641.5
(jt. auth) D'Amico, J. The healthy body cookbook   641.5
(jt. auth) D'Amico, J. The math chef   641.5
(jt. auth) D'Amico, J. The science chef   641.3

Drums
Fiction
Bynum, E. Jamari's drum   E

Druscilla's Halloween. Walker, S. M.   E

The **dry** desert. Johansson, P.   577.5

Drylongso. Hamilton, V.   Fic

Du Bois, W. E. B. (William Edward Burghardt), 1868-1963
About
Whiting, J. W.E.B. Du Bois   92

Du Bois, William Edward Burghardt *See* Du Bois, W. E. B. (William Edward Burghardt), 1868-1963

Du Bois, William Pène, 1916-1993
The twenty-one balloons   Fic
(il) Zolotow, C. William's doll   E

DuBois, Jill, 1952-
Colombia   986.1
Greece   949.5
Israel   956.94
Korea   951.9

Dubosarsky, Ursula, 1961-
The terrible plop   E
The word snoop   420

DuBurke, Randy
(il) Omololu, C. J. When it's six o'clock in San Francisco   E

The **Duchess** of Whimsy. DeSeve, R.   E

Duck. Cecil, R.   E

Duck & company. Caple, K.   E

Duck & Goose. Hills, T.   E

Duck at the door. Urbanovic, J.   E

Duck-billed platypus *See* Platypus

Duck, duck, goose!. Beaumont, K.   E

Duck for President. Cronin, D.   E

Duck for Turkey Day. Jules, J.   E

Duck in the truck. Alborough, J.   E

Duck on a bike. Shannon, D.   E

Duck! Rabbit!. Rosenthal, A. K.   E

Duck skates. Berry, L.   E

The **duck** who played the kazoo. Sklansky, A. E.   E

Duckie's ducklings. Barry, F.   E

Ducks
Baker, K. Quack and count   E
Goldin, A. R. Ducks don't get wet   598
Johnson, J. Duck   598
Mara, W. Ducks   598
McMillan, B. Days of the ducklings   598
Minden, C. Ducks   636.5
Savage, S. Duck   598
Fiction
Alborough, J. Duck in the truck   E
Andersen, H. C. The ugly duckling [illustrated by Pirkko Vainio]   E
Aruego, J. The last laugh   E
Barry, F. Duckie's ducklings   E
Berry, L. Duck skates   E
Braun, S. The ugly duckling   E
Buzzeo, T. Dawdle Duckling   E
Caple, K. Duck & company   E
Capucilli, A. Katy duck is a caterpillar   E
Cecil, R. Duck   E
Chen, C.-Y. Guji Guji   E
Cooper, H. Pumpkin soup   E
Cronin, D. Duck for President   E
Egan, T. Dodsworth in New York   E
Ford, B. No more blanket for Lambkin   E
Ford, B. No more bottles for Bunny!   E
Ford, B. No more diapers for Ducky!   E
George, J. C. Goose and Duck   E
Ginsburg, M. The chick and the duckling   E
Gorbachev, V. The missing chick   E
Gravett, E. The odd egg   E
Hest, A. Guess who, Baby Duck!   E
Hills, T. Duck & Goose   E
Hutchins, P. We're going on a picnic!   E
Isadora, R. The ugly duckling   E
Isol. It's useful to have a duck   E
Ives, P. Celestine, drama queen   E
James, S. Little One Step   E
Kasza, K. Ready for anything   E
King-Smith, D. Clever duck   Fic
King-Smith, D. Funny Frank   Fic
Luthardt, K. Peep!   E
McCloskey, R. Make way for ducklings   E
Milgrim, D. Santa Duck   E
Murphy, M. I kissed the baby   E
Nedwidek, J. Ducks don't wear socks   E
Peters, L. W. Cold little duck, duck, duck   E
Polacco, P. John Philip Duck   E
Potter, B. The tale of Jemima Puddle-duck   E
Rosenthal, A. K. Duck! Rabbit!   E
Shannon, D. Duck on a bike   E
Sklansky, A. E. The duck who played the kazoo   E
Sloat, T. I'm a duck!   E
Straaten, H. v. Duck's tale   E
Tafuri, N. Have you seen my duckling?   E
Thompson, L. Little Quack   E
Urbanovic, J. Duck at the door   E
Waddell, M. Farmer duck   E
Waddell, M. It's quacking time!   E
Yolen, J. Dimity Duck   E

Durango, Julia
Angels watching over me — E
Cha-cha chimps — E
Pest fest — E
(jt. auth) Park, L. S. Yum! Yuck! — 413

Durango, Julia, 1967-
Go-go gorillas — E
The walls of Cartagena — Fic

Durant, Alan, 1958-
I love you, Little Monkey — E

Durbin, William, 1951-
Blackwater Ben — Fic

Dusssie. Springer, N. — Fic

Dussutour, Olivier
(jt. auth) Guéry, A. Alphab'art — 709

Dust
Sayre, A. P. Stars beneath your bed — 551.51
Fiction
Thomas, J. Rhyming dust bunnies — E
The **Dust** Bowl through the lens. Sandler, M. W. — 973.9

Dust for dinner. Turner, A. W. — E

Dust storms
Sandler, M. W. The Dust Bowl through the lens — 973.9
Fiction
Hesse, K. Out of the dust — Fic
Graphic novels
Phelan, M. The storm in the barn — 741.5

Dust to eat. Cooper, M. L. — 973.917

Dutch Americans
Englar, M. Dutch colonies in America — 974.7
Huey, L. M. American archaeology uncovers the Dutch colonies — 974.7

Dutch artists *See* Artists, Dutch

Dutch colonies in America. Englar, M. — 974.7

DuTemple, Lesley A., 1952-
The New York subways — 388.4

Dutton, Sandra
Mary Mae and the gospel truth — Fic

Dutton easy reader [series]
Thomas, S. M. Good night, Good Knight — E

Duval, Kathy
The Three Bears' Christmas — E

Duvoisin, Roger, 1904-1980
Petunia — E
(il) Tresselt, A. R. Hide and seek fog — E
(il) Tresselt, A. R. White snow, bright snow — E

Duwel, Lucretia I., 1948-
(jt. auth) Simpson, M. S. Bringing classes into the public library — 027.62

The **dwarf** planet Pluto. Lew, K. — 523.4

Dwarfism
Fiction
Graff, L. The thing about Georgie — Fic

Dyer, Alan, 1953-
Mission to the moon — 629.45

Dyer, Brooke
(il) Wilson, K. Mama always comes home — E
(il) Yolen, J. Sleep, black bear, sleep — E

Dyer, Heather, 1970-
Ibby's magic weekend — Fic

Dyer, Jane
(il) Appelt, K. Oh my baby, little one — E
(il) Ashman, L. Babies on the go — E
(il) Beaumont, K. Move over, Rover — E
(il) Krull, K. A woman for president [biography of Victoria C. Woodhull] — 92
(il) Lewis, R. A. Every year on your birthday — E
(il) Lewis, R. A. I love you like crazy cakes — E
(il) Melmed, L. K. Hurry! Hurry! Have you heard? — E
(il) The Random House book of bedtime stories. See The Random House book of bedtime stories — S C
(il) Rosenthal, A. K. Cookies — E
(il) Spinelli, E. Sophie's masterpiece — E

Dying patients *See* Terminally ill

Dying to meet you. Klise, K. — Fic

Dyslexia
Landau, E. Dyslexia — 616.85
Fiction
Betancourt, J. My name is brain Brian — Fic

Dyson, Marianne J.
Home on the moon — 629.45

E

E-mail systems *See* Electronic mail systems

E.S.P. *See* Extrasensory perception

Each living thing. Ryder, J. — E

Each orange had 8 slices. Giganti, P., Jr. — E

Eagen, Rachel, 1979-
NASCAR — 796.72

Eager, Edward, 1911-1964
Half magic — Fic
Magic or not? — Fic
Seven-day magic — Fic

Eager. Fox, H. — Fic

Eagles
See also Bald eagle
Bardhan-Quallen, S. Flying eagle — 598
Markle, S. Eagles — 598
Nobleman, M. T. Eagles — 598
Folklore
Gregorowski, C. Fly, eagle, fly! — 398.2

Eagles and other birds. Solway, A. — 598

Eamer, Claire
Super crocs & monster wings — 591.3

Ear
Larsen, C. S. Crust and spray — 612.8
Miller, S. S. All kinds of ears — 591.4
Simon, S. Eyes and ears — 612.8

Ear infections
Cobb, V. Your body battles an earache — 617.8

The **Ear,** the Eye, and the Arm. Farmer, N. — Fic

Earhart, Amelia, 1898-1937
About
Adler, D. A. A picture book of Amelia Earhart
92

Lauber, P. Lost star: the story of Amelia Earhart
92

Tanaka, S. Amelia Earhart **92**
Graphic novels
Taylor, S. S. Amelia Earhart **741.5**

Earle, Ann
Zipping, zapping, zooming bats **599.4**

Earle, Sylvia A., 1935-
Dive! **551.46**
About
Reichard, S. E. Who on earth is Sylvia Earle?
92

Early bird Earth science [series]
Storad, C. J. Earth's crust **551.1**

Early bird food webs [series]
Fleisher, P. Forest food webs **577.3**

Early bird nature books [series]
Patent, D. H. White-tailed deer **599.65**
Walker, S. M. Fireflies **595.7**

Early experiences [series]
Ehrlich, F. Does an elephant take a bath? **E**

Early explorations: the 1500s. Hernández, R. E.
970.01

Early I can read book [series]
Bonsall, C. N. Who's afraid of the dark? **E**

Early literacy programming en Español. Diamant-Cohen, B. **027.6**

Earnest, Peter
The real spy's guide to becoming a spy
327.12

Earning, saving, spending [series]
Hall, M. Banks **332.1**
Hall, M. Credit cards and checks **332.7**
Hall, M. Your allowance **332.024**

Earth
Gravity
See Gravity

Earth
Bailey, J. Sun up, sun down **525**
Frasier, D. On the day you were born **E**
Fuoco, G. D. Earth **333.72**
Gaff, J. Looking at earth **550**
Gardner, R. Earth-shaking science projects about planet Earth **550**
Gibbons, G. Planet earth/inside out **550**
Gibbons, G. The reasons for seasons **525**
Hicks, T. A. Earth and the moon **525**
Karas, G. B. On Earth **525**
Kelly, E. Evolving planet **551**
Landau, E. Earth **525**
Martin, B. I love our Earth **525**
Miller, R. Earth and the moon **525**
Ride, S. K. Mission: planet Earth **525**
Ross, M. E. Earth cycles **525**
Simon, S. Earth: our planet in space **525**
Solway, A. Understanding cycles and systems
550
Wells, R. E. What's so special about planet Earth? **525**
Woodward, J. Planet Earth **550**

Crust
Storad, C. J. Earth's crust **551.1**
Fiction
Ernst, L. C. Round like a ball! **E**
Glaser, L. Our big home **E**
Snell, G. The King of Quizzical Island **E**
Internal structure
Cole, J. The magic school bus inside the Earth
551.1
Surface
Snedden, R. Earth's shifting surface **551.1**
Earth and the moon. Hicks, T. A. **525**
Earth and the moon. Miller, R. **525**
The **Earth** book. Parr, T. **333.72**
Earth cycles. Ross, M. E. **525**
Earth Day-hooray!. Murphy, S. J. **513**
Earth feeling the heat. Guiberson, B. Z. **363.7**
Earth fills *See* Landfills
Earth-friendly crafts. Ross, K. **745.5**
Earth-friendly design. Welsbacher, A. **745.2**
Earth in action [series]
Schuh, M. C. Avalanches **551.57**
Schuh, M. C. Tornadoes **551.55**
Schuh, M. C. Tsunamis **551.46**
Earth in the hot seat. Delano, M. F. **363.7**
Earth science for every kid, Janice VanCleave's. VanCleave, J. P. **550**
Earth sciences
See also Geology
Lauber, P. You're aboard Spaceship Earth
550
Solway, A. Understanding cycles and systems
550
VanCleave, J. P. Janice VanCleave's earth science for every kid **550**
Earth-shaking science projects about planet Earth. Gardner, R. **550**
The **Earth** shook. Napoli, D. J. **E**
Earthenware *See* Pottery
Earthquack!. Palatini, M. **E**
Earthquake sea waves *See* Tsunamis
Earthquakes
Branley, F. M. Earthquakes **551.2**
Fradin, J. B. Earthquakes **551.2**
Grace, C. O. Forces of nature **551.2**
Jennings, T. Earthquakes and tsunamis **551.2**
Levy, M. Earthquakes, volcanoes, and tsunamis
551.2
Silverstein, A. Earthquakes **551.2**
Simon, S. Earthquakes **551.2**
Stille, D. R. Great shakes **551.2**
Tagliaferro, L. How does an earthquake become a tsunami? **551.46**
Fiction
Carman, P. The house of power **Fic**
Hopkinson, D. Into the firestorm **Fic**
Napoli, D. J. The Earth shook **E**
Salisbury, G. Night of the howling dogs **Fic**
Earthquakes and tsunamis. Jennings, T. **551.2**
Earthquakes, volcanoes, and tsunamis. Levy, M.
551.2
Earth's crust. Storad, C. J. **551.1**

Easy paper crafts in 5 steps. Llimós, A.
    745.54

Eat right!. Doeden, M.   **613.2**

Eating *See* Dining

Eating customs

 See also Table etiquette
Batmanglij, N. Happy Nowruz **641.5**
Ichord, L. F. Double cheeseburgers, quiche, and
 vegetarian burritos   **394.1**
Lauber, P. What you never knew about fingers,
 forks, & chopsticks   **394.1**
Menzel, P. What the world eats **641.3**
Solheim, J. It's disgusting—and we ate it!
    641.3

Eating disorders

 See also Anorexia nervosa; Bulimia
Bjorklund, R. Eating disorders **616.85**
Silverstein, A. The eating disorders update
    616.85

The **eating** disorders update. Silverstein, A.
    616.85

Eating green. Apte, S.   **630**

Eating the alphabet. Ehlert, L.   **E**

Eating up Gladys. Zemach, M.   **E**

Eaton, Maxwell, III
Best buds   **E**

Eats. Jocelyn, M.   **E**

Eats, shoots & leaves. Truss, L.   **428**

Ebbeler, Jeffrey
(il) Cox, J. One is a feast for Mouse **E**
(il) Hill, S. L. Punxsutawney Phyllis **E**

Ebert, Len
(il) Allen, K. President George Washington
    92

Ebner, Aviva
(ed) Science activities for all students. See Science activities for all students **507.8**

Eboch, Chris
The ghost on the stairs   **Fic**

Eccentrics and eccentricities
Fiction
Atkinson, E. From Alice to Zen and everyone in
 between   **Fic**
Joyce, W. A day with Wilbur Robinson **E**
Nesbø, J. Doctor Proctor's fart powder **Fic**
Railsback, L. Noonie's masterpiece **Fic**
Riddleburger, S. The strange case of Origami
 Yoda   **Fic**
Tolan, S. S. Surviving the Applewhites **Fic**
Venuti, K. C. Leaving the Bellweathers **Fic**
Weeks, S. Oggie Cooder   **Fic**

Echinoderms
Blaxland, B. Sea stars, sea urchins, and their
 relatives   **593.9**

Echinoderms: sea stars, sea urchins, and their relatives. See Blaxland, B. Sea stars, sea urchins, and their relatives **593.9**

Eckert, Allan W., 1931-
Incident at Hawk's Hill   **Fic**

Eclipse. Cheng, A.   **Fic**

Eclipses, Solar *See* Solar eclipses

Ecocrafts [series]
Jazzy jewelry   **745.594**

Ecological movement *See* Environmental movement

Ecologists. Housel, D. J.   **920**

Ecology

 See also Biological diversity; Environmen-
tal protection; Food chains (Ecology); Habitat
(Ecology) types of ecology
Gardner, R. Ace your ecology and environmen-
 tal science project   **577**
Gibbons, G. Marshes & swamps **577.6**
Godkin, C. Wolf island   **577**
Goodman, S. Seeds, stems, and stamens
    581.4
Housel, D. J. Ecologists   **920**
Housel, D. J. Ecosystems   **577**
Latham, D. Ecology   **577**
Munro, R. Ecomazes   **577**
Pollock, S. Ecology   **577**
Rockwell, A. F. Who lives in an alligator hole?
    597.98
Rompella, N. Ecosystems   **577**
Somervill, B. A. Our living world **577**
Stille, D. R. Nature interrupted **577**
Tocci, S. Coral reefs   **577.7**
VanCleave, J. P. Janice Vancleave's ecology for
 every kid   **577**
See/See also pages in the following book(s):
Patent, D. H. Biodiversity **333.95**
Fiction
Cherry, L. The sea, the storm, and the mangrove
 tangle   **E**
Cole, H. On the way to the beach **E**
Formento, A. This tree counts! **E**
Franco, B. Pond circle   **E**
Shelby, A. The man who lived in a hollow tree
    E
Folklore
Casey, D. The Barefoot book of Earth tales
    398.2
MacDonald, M. R. Surf war! **398.2**

Ecology, Human *See* Human ecology

Ecomazes. Munro, R.   **577**

Economic botany
 See also Plant conservation

Economic recessions *See* Recessions

Economic zoology
 See also Working animals

Ecosystems. Housel, D. J.   **577**

Ecosystems. Rompella, N.   **577**

Ecstasy (Drug)
LeVert, S. Ecstasy   **362.29**

Ecuador
Foley, E. Ecuador   **986.6**

Ed Emberley's big green drawing book. Emberley,
 E.   **741.2**

Ed Emberley's big red drawing book. Emberley,
 E.   **741.2**

Ed Emberley's bye-bye, big bad bullybug!.
 Emberley, E.   **E**

The **Eentsy,** weentsy spider: fingerplays and action rhymes **796.1**

Effler, James M., 1956-
(il) Berger, M. How do flies walk upside down? **595.7**

Egan, Erin
Hottest race cars **796.72**

Egan, Jill
How video game designers use math **794.8**

Egan, Tim
Dodsworth in New York **E**
The pink refrigerator **E**

Egg drop. Grey, M. **E**

An **egg** is quiet. Aston, D. H. **591.4**

Eggs
Aston, D. H. An egg is quiet **591.4**
Baines, R. What's in that egg? **591.4**
Posada, M. Guess what is growing inside this egg **591.4**
Singer, M. Eggs **591.4**
Sklansky, A. E. Where do chicks come from? **636.5**

Fiction
Battut, E. The fox and the hen **E**
Brett, J. The Easter egg **E**
Bunting, E. Hurry! hurry! **E**
Cutbill, A. The cow that laid an egg **E**
Graham, B. Dimity Dumpty **E**
Gravett, E. The odd egg **E**
Grey, M. Egg drop **E**
Howard, R. The big, big wall **E**
Klimo, K. The dragon in the sock drawer **Fic**
Milway, K. S. One hen **E**
Polacco, P. Rechenka's eggs **E**
Polhemus, C. The crocodile blues **E**
Schertle, A. Down the road **E**
Waddell, M. It's quacking time! **E**
Wallace, C. Turkeys together **E**
Weeks, S. Two eggs, please **E**

Egielski, Richard
The gingerbread boy **398.2**
Saint Francis and the wolf **398.2**
(il) Broach, E. Gumption! **E**
(il) Brown, M. W. The fierce yellow pumpkin **E**
(il) LaRochelle, D. The end **E**
(il) McNamara, M. The whistle on the train **E**
(il) Palatini, M. Three French hens **E**
(il) Winter, J. The fabulous feud of Gilbert & Sullivan **E**
(il) Yorinks, A. Hey, Al **E**
(il) Yorinks, A. Homework **E**

Egoff, Sheila A.
Once upon a time **92**

An **egret's** day. Yolen, J. **811**

Egypt
Bolton, A. Pyramids and mummies **932**
Parker, L. K. Egypt **962**
Pateman, R. Egypt **962**

Antiquities
Biesty, S. Egypt in spectacular cross-section **932**
Giblin, J. Secrets of the Sphinx **932**

Harris, G. Ancient Egypt **932**
Hawass, Z. A. Curse of the pharaohs **932**
Rubalcaba, J. Ancient Egypt **932**
Sabuda, R. Tutankhamen's gift **92**
Taylor, J. H. Mummy **932**
Whiting, J. Threat to ancient Egyptian treasures **932**

Civilization
Adams, S. Ancient Egypt **932**
Biesty, S. Egypt in spectacular cross-section **932**
Galford, E. Hatshepsut **92**
Giblin, J. Secrets of the Sphinx **932**
Harris, G. Ancient Egypt **932**
Hawass, Z. A. Tutankhamun **932**
Kennett, D. Pharaoh **932**
Langley, A. Ancient Egypt **932**
Logan, C. The 5,000-year-old puzzle **932**
Macaulay, D. Pyramid **726**
Park, L. The Pharaohs' armies **355**
Perl, L. The ancient Egyptians **932**
Rubalcaba, J. Ancient Egypt **932**
Trumble, K. The Library of Alexandria **027**
Van Vleet, C. Great Ancient Egypt projects you can build yourself **932**
Weitzman, D. L. Pharaoh's boat **932**

Fiction
Farmer, N. Clever Ali **Fic**
Gauch, S. Voyage to the Pharos **E**
La Fevers, R. L. Theodosia and the Serpents of Chaos **Fic**
Riordan, R. The red pyramid **Fic**
Snyder, Z. K. The Egypt game **Fic**

Folklore
See Folklore—Egypt

History
Blackaby, S. Cleopatra **92**
Demi. Tutankhamun **92**
Galford, E. Hatshepsut **92**
Hawass, Z. A. Tutankhamun **932**
Kramer, A. Egyptian myth **299**
Stanley, D. Cleopatra **92**

Religion
Kennett, D. Pharaoh **932**

Science
See Science—Egypt

The **Egypt** game. Snyder, Z. K. **Fic**

Egypt in spectacular cross-section. Biesty, S. **932**

Egyptian art
Kramer, A. Egyptian myth **299**
Langley, A. Ancient Egypt **932**

The **Egyptian** Cinderella. Climo, S. **398.2**

Egyptian language
Giblin, J. The riddle of the Rosetta Stone **493**

Egyptian myth. Kramer, A. **299**

Egyptian mythology
Kramer, A. Egyptian myth **299**

Egyptian science *See* Science—Egypt

Ehlert, Lois, 1934-
Boo to you! **E**
Circus **E**
Color farm **E**

Elections—Fiction—*Continued*

Cronin, D. Duck for President   E

DiPucchio, K. S. Grace for president   E

United States

Thomas, W. D. How do we elect our leaders?   **324**

Electric apparatus and appliances

Bartholomew, A. Electric mischief   **621.31**

Electric automobiles

Bearce, S. All about electric and hybrid cars   **629.222**

Juettner, B. Hybrid cars   **629.222**

Electric guitar man: the genius of Les Paul. Wyckoff, E. B.   **92**

Electric lamps

Nolan, J. The firehouse light   **363.3**

Electric lines

See/See also pages in the following book(s):

Macaulay, D. Underground   **624**

Electric mischief. Bartholomew, A.   **621.31**

Electric power

Cole, J. The magic school bus and the electric field trip   **621.319**

Suen, A. Wired   **621.319**

Electric power plants

See also Nuclear power plants

Electrical engineering

Price, S. The story behind electricity   **621.3**

Electricity

Bang, M. My light   **621.47**

Bartholomew, A. Electric mischief   **621.31**

Berger, M. Switch on, switch off   **537**

Cole, J. The magic school bus and the electric field trip   **621.319**

Farndon, J. Electricity   **537**

Gardner, R. Easy genius science projects with electricity and magnetism   **537**

Gardner, R. Energizing science projects with electricity and magnetism   **537**

Graf, M. How does a waterfall become electricity?   **621.31**

Meiani, A. Electricity   **537**

Parker, S. Electricity   **537**

Price, S. The story behind electricity   **621.3**

Spilsbury, R. What is electricity and magnetism?   **537**

Suen, A. Wired   **621.319**

VanCleave, J. P. Janice VanCleave's electricity   **537**

Woodford, C. Electricity   **537**

Electronic journals *See* Weblogs

Electronic libraries *See* Digital libraries

Electronic mail systems

Oxlade, C. My first E-Mail guide   **004.6**

Electronic surveillance

Gilbert, A. Top technology   **621.389**

Electronic toys

See also Computer games

Elementary school libraries

See also Children's libraries

The **Elements** [Benchmark Bks. series]   **546**

Elena's serenade. Geeslin, C.   E

An **elephant** in the backyard. Sobol, R.   **636.9**

Elephant quest. Lewin, T.   **591.9**

The **elephant** quilt. Lowell, S.   E

Elephant rescue. Morgan, J.   **599.67**

The **elephant** wish. Berger, L.   E

Elephants

Arnold, K. Elephants can paint, too!   **599.67**

Barnes, J. Elephants at work   **636.9**

Buckley, C. Just for elephants   **639.9**

Buckley, C. Tarra & Bella   **599.67**

Firestone, M. Top 50 reasons to care about elephants   **599.67**

Gibbons, G. Elephants of Africa   **599.67**

Helfer, R. The world's greatest elephant   **791.3**

Joubert, B. Face to face with elephants   **599.67**

Lewin, T. Balarama   **636.9**

Morgan, J. Elephant rescue   **599.67**

Schubert, L. Ballet of the elephants   **791.8**

Schwabacher, M. Elephants   **599.67**

Sobol, R. An elephant in the backyard   **636.9**

See/See also pages in the following book(s):

Sayre, A. P. Secrets of sound   **591.59**

Fiction

Bachelet, G. My cat, the silliest cat in the world   E

Berger, L. The elephant wish   E

Blackford, H. Elephant's story   E

Breathed, B. Pete & Pickles   E

Brunhoff, J. d. The story of Babar, the little elephant   E

Cushman, D. Mystery at the Club Sandwich   E

Daly, N. Welcome to Zanzibar Road   E

D'Amico, C. Ella the Elegant Elephant   E

DiCamillo, K. The magician's elephant   Fic

Dodd, E. No matter what   E

Dunbar, P. Where's Tumpty?   E

Fleischman, S. The white elephant   Fic

Hoff, S. Oliver   E

Joosse, B. M. Sleepover at gramma's house   E

Judge, L. Pennies for elephants   E

Kadohata, C. A million shades of gray   Fic

Kipling, R. The elephant's child   Fic

Lewis, K. Good night, Harry   E

Lobel, A. Uncle Elephant   E

McGrory, A. Kidogo   E

Na, I. S. The thingamabob   E

Prince, A. J. Twenty-one elephants and still standing   E

Ravishankar, A. Elephants never forget   E

Sarcone-Roach, J. The secret plan   E

Schertle, A. 1, 2, I love you   E

Schwartz, A. Tiny and Hercules   E

Seuss, Dr. Horton hatches the egg   E

Seuss, Dr. Horton hears a Who!   E

Willems, M. Today I will fly!   E

Folklore

Young, E. Seven blind mice   **398.2**

Elephants and golden thrones. Marx, T.   **951**

Elephants at work. Barnes, J.   **636.9**

Elephants can paint, too!. Arnold, K.   **599.67**

The **elephant's** child. Kipling, R.   Fic

Elephants never forget. Ravishankar, A.   **E**
Elephants of Africa. Gibbons, G.   **599.67**
Elephant's story. Blackford, H.   **E**
Elevator magic. Murphy, S. J.   **513**
The **Elevator** Man. Trachtenberg, S.   **E**
Elevators
       Fiction
  Trachtenberg, S. The Elevator Man   **E**
Eleven. Giff, P. R.   **Fic**
Eleven. Myracle, L.   **Fic**
Eleven planets. See Aguilar, D. A. 11 planets
       523.4
Eley, Robin
  (il) Thompson, L. How many cats?   **E**
Elf Realm [series]
  Kirk, D. The low road   **Fic**
Elffers, Joost
  Do you love me?   **E**
  (jt. auth) Freymann, S. How are you peeling?
       E
Eli the Good. House, S.   **Fic**
Elias, Marie Louise
  (jt. auth) Kohen, E. Spain   **946**
Elijah of Buxton. Curtis, C. P.   **Fic**
Elijah's angel. Rosen, M. J.   **Fic**
Eliot, T. S. (Thomas Stearns), 1888-1965
  Old Possum's book of practical cats   **811**
Eliot, Thomas Stearns *See* Eliot, T. S. (Thomas
  Stearns), 1888-1965
Eliot Jones, midnight superhero. Cottringer, A.
       E
Elish, Dan, 1960-
  The attack of the frozen woodchucks   **Fic**
  Franklin Delano Roosevelt   **92**
  James Madison   **92**
  Theodore Roosevelt   **92**
  (jt. auth) Brown, J. R. 13   **Fic**
Elissa's quest. Verrillo, E. F.   **Fic**
Elizabeth I, Queen of England, 1533-1603
       About
  Adams, S. Elizabeth I   **92**
  Stanley, D. Good Queen Bess: the story of Eliz-
    abeth I of England   **92**
  See/See also pages in the following book(s):
  Krull, K. Lives of extraordinary women   **920**
  Meltzer, M. Ten queens   **920**
       Fiction
  Lasky, K. Elizabeth I   **Fic**
Elizabeth leads the way. Stone, T. L.   **92**
Elizabeti's doll. Bodeen, S. A.   **E**
Eliza's kindergarten surprise. McGinty, A. B.
       E
Elk
       Fiction
  Steinhöfel, A. An elk dropped in   **Fic**
An **elk** dropped in. Steinhöfel, A.   **Fic**
Ella enchanted. Levine, G. C.   **Fic**
Ella Kazoo will not brush her hair. Fox, L.   **E**
Ella, of course!. Weeks, S.   **E**
Ella Sarah gets dressed. Chodos-Irvine, M.   **E**
Ella the Elegant Elephant. D'Amico, C.   **E**

Ellabbad, Mohieddine, 1940-
  The illustrator's notebook   **741.6**
Ella's big chance. Hughes, S.   **E**
Ellen Tebbits. Cleary, B.   **Fic**
Ellery, Amanda
  If I were a jungle animal   **E**
Ellery, Tom
  (il) Ellery, A. If I were a jungle animal   **E**
Ellie McDoodle: have pen, will travel. Barshaw,
  R. M.   **Fic**
Ellington, Duke, 1899-1974
       About
  Pinkney, A. D. Duke Ellington   **92**
  Stein, S. Duke Ellington   **92**
Ellington was not a street. Shange, N.   **E**
Elliot, David, 1952-
  (il) Cowley, J. Chicken feathers   **Fic**
Elliott, David, 1947-
  Finn throws a fit   **E**
  Knitty Kitty   **E**
  On the farm   **E**
  One little chicken   **E**
  What the grizzly knows   **E**
Elliott, Laura
  Give me liberty   **Fic**
Elliott, Mark
  (il) Clements, A. Extra credit   **Fic**
  (il) Clements, A. Lost and found   **Fic**
  (il) Clements, A. No talking   **Fic**
  (jt. auth) Pateman, R. Belgium   **949.3**
Elliott, Randy
  (il) Farshtey, G. Bionicle #1: rise of the Toa
  Nuva   **741.5**
Elliott, Zetta
  Bird   **E**
Ellis, Carol, 1945-
  Hamsters and gerbils   **636.9**
Ellis, Carson, 1975-
  (il) Rylant, C. The beautiful stories of life
       292
  (il) Snicket, L. The composer is dead   **E**
  (il) Stewart, T. L. The mysterious Benedict So-
    ciety   **Fic**
Ellis, Deborah, 1960-
  I am a taxi   **Fic**
  Off to war   **303.6**
  Three wishes   **956.94**
Ellis, Jan Davey
  (il) Ichord, L. F. Double cheeseburgers, quiche,
    and vegetarian burritos   **394.1**
  (il) Ichord, L. F. Skillet bread, sourdough, and
    vinegar pie   **641.5**
Ellis, Sarah, 1952-
  Ben over night   **E**
  From reader to writer   **372.6**
  The several lives of Orphan Jack   **Fic**
Ellis Island Immigration Station
  Bial, R. Ellis Island   **325.73**
  I was dreaming to come to America   **325.73**
  Kroll, S. Ellis Island   **325.73**
  Levine, E. . . . if your name was changed at
    Ellis Island   **325.73**
  Sandler, M. W. Island of hope   **325.73**

Ellis Island Immigration Station—*Continued*
Staton, H. Ellis Island   **325.73**
See/See also pages in the following book(s):
Maestro, B. Coming to America: the story of immigration   **325.73**
Fiction
Woodruff, E. The memory coat   **E**

Ellison, Chris
(il) Scillian, D. Pappy's handkerchief   **E**

Ellison, Elizabeth Stow, 1970-
Flight   **Fic**

Elly. Gross, E. B.   **92**

Elocution *See* Public speaking

The Elsewhere chronicles [series]
Bannister (Person). The shadow door   **741.5**

The elves and the shoemaker. Galdone, P.
      398.2

Elvgren, Jennifer Riesmeyer
Josias, hold the book   **E**

Elvis & Olive. Watson, S. E.   **Fic**

Elvis the rooster almost goes to heaven. Cazet, D.
      E

Elwell, Peter
Adios, Oscar!   **E**

Elya, Susan Middleton, 1955-
Adios, tricycle   **E**
Bebé goes shopping   **E**
Cowboy José   **E**
Eight animals on the town   **E**
F is for fiesta   **E**
Fairy trails   **E**
N is for Navidad   **E**
Oh no, gotta go!   **E**
Say hola to Spanish, otra vez   **468**
Tooth on the loose   **E**

Emancipation Proclamation (1863)
Fiction
Sherman, P. Ben and the Emancipation Proclamation   **E**

Emberley, Adrian, 1985-
(jt. auth) Emberley, R. There was an old monster!   **E**

Emberley, Barbara, 1932-
Drummer Hoff   **398.8**
Night's nice   **E**
(il) Branley, F. M. The moon seems to change   **523.3**

Emberley, Ed
Chicken Little   **398.2**
Ed Emberley's big green drawing book   **741.2**
Ed Emberley's big red drawing book   **741.2**
Ed Emberley's bye-bye, big bad bullybug!   **E**
Ed Emberley's drawing book: make a world   **741.2**
Ed Emberley's drawing book of faces   **743**
Ed Emberley's fingerprint drawing book   **741.2**
Ed Emberley's great thumbprint drawing book   **741.2**
Go away, big green monster!   **E**
Thanks, Mom!   **E**
Where's my sweetie pie?   **E**

(il) Branley, F. M. The moon seems to change   **523.3**
(il) Emberley, B. Drummer Hoff   **398.8**
(jt. auth) Emberley, B. Night's nice   **E**
(jt. auth) Emberley, R. There was an old monster!   **E**

Emberley, Michael, 1960-
(il) Bottner, B. Miss Brooks loves books (and I don't)   **E**
(il) Harris, R. H. Happy birth day!   **E**
(il) Harris, R. H. It's not the stork!   **612.6**
(il) Harris, R. H. It's perfectly normal   **613.9**
(il) Harris, R. H. It's so amazing!   **612.6**
(il) Harris, R. H. Mail Harry to the moon!   **E**
(il) Harris, R. H. Maybe a bear ate it!   **E**
(il) Hoberman, M. A. You read to me, I'll read to you [very short fairy tales to read together]   **E**
(il) Hoberman, M. A. You read to me, I'll read to you [very short Mother Goose tales to read together]   **811**
(il) Hoberman, M. A. You read to me, I'll read to you [very short stories to read together]   **811**
(il) Hoberman, M. A. You read to me, I'll read to you: very short scary tales to read together   **811**
(il) Jones, S. L. The ultimate guide to grandmas and grandpas   **E**

Emberley, Rebecca
My big book of Spanish words   **468**
There was an old monster!   **E**
(jt. auth) Emberley, E. Chicken Little   **398.2**

Emblems *See* Signs and symbols

Emblems, National *See* National emblems

Embracing *See* Hugging

Embracing, evaluating, and examining African American children's and young adult literature   **028.5**

Embroidery
Sadler, J. A. Embroidery   **746.44**
Fiction
Strauss, L. L. The princess gown   **E**

Embryology
    See also Fetus; Reproduction

Emerald ash borer
Gray, S. H. Emerald ash borer   **595.7**

Emergency at Three Mile Island. Feigenbaum, A.
      621.48

Emergency survival *See* Survival skills

An **emerging** world power (1900-1929). Stanley, G. E.   **973.91**

Emeril's there's a chef in my family!. Lagasse, E.
      641.5

Emeril's there's a chef in my world!. Lagasse, E.
      641.5

Emerson, Kevin
Carlos is gonna get it   **Fic**

Emi and the rhino scientist. Carson, M. K.
      599.66

Emigrants *See* Immigrants

Emigration *See* Immigration and emigration

Emil and Karl. Glatstein, J.   Fic

Emily Gravett's big book of fears. See Gravett, E.
Little Mouse's big book of fears   E

Emily Post's table manners for kids. Post, P.
395

Emily Post's The guide to good manners for kids.
Post, P.   395

Emily Stew. Rockwell, T.   811

Emily's art. Catalanotto, P.   E

Emily's balloon. Sakai, K.   E

Emily's everyday manners. Post, P.   395

Emily's first 100 days of school. Wells, R.   E

Emily's fortune. Naylor, P. R.   Fic

Emma Dilemma and the new nanny. Hermes, P.
Fic

Emma in charge. McPhail, D. M.   E

Emma-Jean Lazarus fell out of a tree. Tarshis, L.
Fic

Emmaline and the bunny. Hannigan, K.   Fic

Emma's poem. Glaser, L.   974.7

Emma's yucky brother. Little, J.   E

Emmet. Politi, L.   E

Emmett, Jonathan, 1965-
The best gift of all   E
Leaf trouble   E

Emmy and the incredible shrinking rat. Jonell, L.
Fic

Emotion & relationships. Bingham, J.   704.9

Emotions

> *See also* Anxiety

Aliki. Feelings   152.4
Freymann, S. How are you peeling?   E
> **Fiction**

Frame, J. A. Yesterday I had the blues   E
Hooks, B. Grump groan growl   E
Jeffers, O. The heart and the bottle   E
Juster, N. Sourpuss and Sweetie Pie   E
Seeger, L. V. Walter was worried   E
Spinelli, E. When you are happy   E
Tankard, J. Grumpy Bird   E

Emotions in art
Bingham, J. Emotion & relationships   704.9

The emperor lays an egg. Guiberson, B. Z.
598

Emperors
> **Rome**

Galford, E. Julius Caesar   92

The emperor's new clothes. Demi   E

The emperor's new clothes. Sedgwick, M.   E

The emperor's new clothes [illustrated by Virginia
Lee Burton] Andersen, H. C.   E

The emperor's painting. Gunderson, J.   Fic

The emperor's silent army. O'Connor, J.   931

Empire State Building (New York, N.Y.)
Macaulay, D. Unbuilding   690
> **Fiction**

Hopkinson, D. Sky boys   E
Kimmel, E. C. The top job   E

Kirk, C. A. Sky dancers   E
Wiesner, D. Sector 7   E

Employees
> **Training**
> *See also* Apprentices

Employment
> *See also* Summer employment

Employment guidance *See* Vocational guidance

Employment of children *See* Child labor

Employment of women *See* Women—Employment

The empty mirror. Collier, J. L.   Fic

The empty pot. Demi   398.2

The enchanted castle. Nesbit, E.   Fic

Enchanted lions. Greenberg, D.   E

Enchantment of the world, second series
Blashfield, J. F. England   942
Foster, L. M. Oman   953
Orr, T. Bangladesh   954.92
Willis, T. Democratic Republic of the Congo
967.51

Encyclopedia Brown, boy detective. Sobol, D. J.
Fic

Encyclopedia horrifica. Gee, J.   001.9

Encyclopedia mythologica [series]
Reinhart, M. Fairies and magical creatures
398
Reinhart, M. Gods & heroes   201

Encyclopedia of animals. McGhee, K.   590.3

Encyclopedia of health   610.3

The encyclopedia of junior science. Jakab, C.
503

Encyclopedia of people and places. See The
World Book encyclopedia of people and
places   910.3

The encyclopedia of U.S. presidential elections
324

Encyclopedia prehistorica [series]
Sabuda, R. Dinosaurs   567.9
Sabuda, R. Mega beasts   569
Sabuda, R. Sharks and other sea monsters
560

Encyclopedias and dictionaries
> *See also* Picture dictionaries names of languages with the subdivision *Dictionaries* and subjects with the subdivision *Dictionaries* or *Encyclopedias*

Britannica student encyclopedia   031
Grolier student encyclopedia   031
Heinemann first encyclopedia   031
Kane, J. N. Famous first facts   031.02
The New book of knowledge   031
One million things   031
Scholastic children's encyclopedia   031
Wilkes, A. My world of discovery   031
The World Book encyclopedia   031

The end. LaRochelle, D.   E

The end of the beginning. Avi   Fic

End of the world
> **Fiction**
Rex, A. The true meaning of Smekday   Fic

Endangered species

See also Rare animals; Wildlife conservation

Barker, D. Top 50 reasons to care about great apes **599.8**

Barry, F. Let's save the animals **591.68**

Christopherson, S. C. Top 50 reasons to care about marine turtles **597.92**

Christopherson, S. C. Top 50 reasons to care about whales and dolphins **599.5**

Collard, S. B., III. In the wild **591.68**

Firestone, M. Top 50 reasons to care about elephants **599.67**

Firestone, M. Top 50 reasons to care about giant pandas **599.78**

Firestone, M. Top 50 reasons to care about rhinos **599.66**

Firestone, M. Top 50 reasons to care about tigers **599.75**

Hamilton, G. Frog rescue **597.8**

Harkins, S. S. Threat to the whooping crane **598**

Hickman, P. M. Turtle rescue **597.92**

Hirsch, R. E. Helping endangered animals **591.68**

Hirsch, R. E. Top 50 reasons to care about polar bears **599.78**

Jenkins, S. Almost gone **591.68**

Juettner, B. The seed vault **631.5**

McLimans, D. Gone fishing **591.7**

McLimans, D. Gone wild **E**

Montgomery, S. Kakapo rescue **639.9**

O'Neal, C. Threat to the Bengal tiger **599.75**

Pobst, S. Animals on the edge **578.68**

Salmansohn, P. Saving birds **333.95**

Sheehan, S. Endangered species **333.95**

Taylor, B. Planet animal **591.68**

Thomas, K. Bear rescue **599.78**

Fiction

Bracegirdle, P. J. Fiendish deeds **Fic**

George, J. C. There's an owl in the shower **Fic**

Martin, B. Panda bear, panda bear, what do you see? **E**

McClements, G. Dinosaur Woods **E**

Enderle, Judith Ross, 1941-

Smile, Principessa! **E**

Endle, Kate

(il) Sayre, A. P. Trout are made of trees **577**

Endredy, James

The journey of Tunuri and the Blue Deer **398.2**

Endrulat, Harry

(jt. auth) Innes, S. A bear in war **E**

Endurance, Physical *See* Physical fitness

Endurance (Ship)

Calvert, P. Sir Ernest Shackleton **92**

Kimmel, E. C. Ice story **998**

Endymion Spring. Skelton, M. **Fic**

The **enemy**. Cali, D. **E**

Energizing science projects with electricity and magnetism. Gardner, R. **537**

Energy *See* Force and energy

Energy. Bowden, R. **333.79**

Energy. Herweck, D. **621**

Energy. Juettner, B. **333.79**

Energy conservation

Barnham, K. Save energy **333.79**

Guillain, C. Saving energy **333.79**

Hewitt, S. Using energy **333.79**

Rockwell, A. F. What's so bad about gasoline? **665.5**

Fiction

Connor, L. Crunch **Fic**

Energy conversion from waste *See* Waste products as fuel

Energy development

Bowden, R. Energy **333.79**

Slade, S. What can we do about the energy crisis? **333.79**

Energy for today [series]

Benduhn, T. Ethanol and other new fuels **662**

Benduhn, T. Nuclear power **621.48**

Benduhn, T. Oil, gas, and coal **665.5**

Benduhn, T. Solar power **621.47**

Benduhn, T. Water power **621.31**

Benduhn, T. Wind power **621.31**

Energy makes things happen. Bradley, K. B. **531**

Energy resources

See also Hydrogen as fuel

Barnham, K. Save energy **333.79**

Benduhn, T. Ethanol and other new fuels **662**

Benduhn, T. Oil, gas, and coal **665.5**

Benduhn, T. Water power **621.31**

Benduhn, T. Wind power **621.31**

Herweck, D. Energy **621**

Hewitt, S. Using energy **333.79**

Juettner, B. Energy **333.79**

Leedy, L. The shocking truth about energy **333.79**

Rau, D. M. Alternative energy beyond fossil fuels **333.79**

Rockwell, A. F. What's so bad about gasoline? **665.5**

Slade, S. What can we do about the energy crisis? **333.79**

Spilsbury, R. What is energy? **621**

VanCleave, J. P. Janice VanCleave's energy for every kid **531**

Woodford, C. Energy **333.79**

Fiction

Jonell, L. The secret of zoom **Fic**

Energy revolution [series]

Walker, N. Generating wind power **621.4**

Walker, N. Hydrogen **665**

Engel, Dean, 1943-

Ezra Jack Keats **92**

Engels, Christiane

(il) Knick knack paddy whack. See Knick knack paddy whack **782.42**

Engineering

See also Electrical engineering; Steel construction

English language—*Continued*
Slang
O'Reilly, G. Slangalicious   427
Spelling
See also Spellers
Study and teaching
Roth, R. The story road to literacy   372.6
Synonyms and antonyms
Bollard, J. K. Scholastic children's thesaurus
    423
Cleary, B. P. Stop and go, yes and no   428
Cleary, B. P. Stroll and walk, babble and talk
    428
Delahunty, A. Barron's first thesaurus   423
Hellweg, P. The American Heritage children's
thesaurus   423
Hellweg, P. The American Heritage student the-
saurus   423
Hoban, T. Exactly the opposite   E
The McGraw-Hill children's thesaurus   423
Simon & Schuster thesaurus for children
    423
Terms and phrases
Leedy, L. There's a frog in my throat   428
Terban, M. Mad as a wet hen! and other funny
idioms   423
Usage
O'Conner, P. T. Woe is I Jr   428
Vocabulary
See Vocabulary

English poetry
Collections
I saw Esau   398.8
Knock at a star   811.008
The Random House book of poetry for children
    811.008
Read-aloud rhymes for the very young
    821.008

Enigma. Base, G.   Fic

Enigmas *See* Curiosities and wonders

Enigmatic events. Blackwood, G. L.   904

The **enormous** crocodile. Dahl, R.   Fic

The **enormous** egg. Butterworth, O.   Fic

Enright, Elizabeth, 1909-1968
Gone-Away Lake   Fic

Ensor, Barbara
Thumbelina   Fic

Ensuring intellectual freedom and access to information in the school library media program.
Adams, H. R.   027.8

Entertainers
See also Comedians
Keating, F. Will Rogers: an American legend
    92
Macy, S. Bulls-eye: a photobiography of Annie
Oakley   92
Weatherford, C. B. Oprah [biography of Oprah
Winfrey]   92
Wills, C. A. Annie Oakley: a photographic story
of a life   92
Fiction
Ackerman, K. Song and dance man   E
Byars, B. C. The Golly sisters go West   E
Krull, K. Fartiste   Fic

Say, A. Kamishibai man   E

The **entrance** place of wonders   811.008

Environment
See also Environmental degradation
The **environment**. Sohn, E.   363.7

Environment action! [series]
Barnham, K. Protect nature   333.95
Barnham, K. Recycle   363.7
Barnham, K. Save energy   333.79
Barnham, K. Save water   333.91

Environmental degradation
Stille, D. R. Nature interrupted   577
Fiction
Diamand, E. Raiders' ransom   Fic

Environmental disasters [series]
Bryan, N. Exxon Valdez oil spill   363.7

Environmental movement
Dell, P. Protecting the planet   333.72
Raatma, L. Green living   333.72
Smalley, C. P. Green changes you can make
around your home   333.72
Wadsworth, G. Camping with the president [bi-
ography of Theodore Roosevelt]   92

Environmental pollution *See* Pollution

Environmental protection
See also Conservation of natural resources
Bang, M. Nobody particular   363.7
Barnham, K. Protect nature   333.95
Barraclough, S. Reusing things   363.7
Cole, J. The magic school bus and the climate
challenge   363.7
Dell, P. Protecting the planet   333.72
Harris, E. S. Save the Earth science experiments
    507.8
Hewitt, S. Your local environment   333.72
Kelsey, E. Not your typical book about the en-
vironment   333.72
Lorbiecki, M. Planet patrol   363.7
McKay, K. True green kids   333.72
Metz, L. What can we do about global warm-
ing?   363.7
Parr, T. The Earth book   333.72
Raatma, L. Green living   333.72
Recycle this book   333.72
Ride, S. K. Mission: save the planet   333.72
Sirett, D. Love your world   333.72
Smalley, C. P. Green changes you can make
around your home   333.72
Try this at home   333.72
Welsbacher, A. Earth-friendly design   745.2
Welsbacher, A. Protecting Earth's rain forests
    577.3
Bibliography
Wesson, L. P. Green reads   016.3
Fiction
Beard, D. B. Annie Glover is not a tree lover
    Fic
Berger, C. OK go   E
Drummond, A. Tin Lizzie   E
Gliori, D. The trouble with dragons   E
Greenwald, L. My life in pink and green
    Fic
Hiaasen, C. Flush   Fic
Hiaasen, C. Hoot   Fic

Everett, Ron *See* Karenga, Maulana, 1941-

Everglades (Fla.)
George, J. C. Everglades   975.9
Lynch, W. The Everglades   508
Marx, T. Everglades forever   577.6
         Poetry
Van Wassenhove, S. The seldom-ever-shady
glades   811

Everglades forever. Marx, T.   577.6

Everglades National Park (Fla.)
Jankowski, S. Everglades National Park
    975.9

Everitt, Betsy
Mean soup   E

Evert, Laura, 1967-
Birds of prey   598

Every child. *See* Hinojosa, T. Cada niño/Every
child   782.42

Every cowgirl needs a horse. Janni, R.   E

Every Friday. Yaccarino, D.   E

Every human has rights   323

Every planet has a place. Baines, R.   523.2

Every season. Rotner, S.   508.2

Every second something happens   811.008

Every soul a star. Mass, W.   Fic

Every year on your birthday. Lewis, R. A.   E

Everybody bonjours!. Kimmelman, L.   E

Everybody has a bellybutton. Pringle, L. P.
    612.6

Everybody has a teddy. Kroll, V. L.   E

Everybody was a baby once, and other poems.
Ahlberg, A.   811

Everybody's revolution. Fleming, T. J.   973.3

Everyday economics [series]
Morrison, J. Investing   332.6
Morrison, J. Saving   332.024
Tomljanovic, T. Borrowing   332.7
Wiseman, B. Budgeting   332.024

Everyday living skills *See* Life skills

Everyday materials [series]
Langley, A. Glass   620.1
Langley, A. Metal   620.1
Langley, A. Paper products   676
Langley, A. Plastic   668.4
Langley, A. Wood   620.1
Langley, A. Wool   677

The **everything** book. Fleming, D.   E

Everything I need to know I learned from a children's book   808.8

Everything on a waffle. Horvath, P.   Fic

Everything spring. Esbaum, J.   508.2

Everything you need to know   503

Everything you need to know about science.
Goldsmith, M.   500

Everywear. Warwick, E.   745.5

Everywhere. Brooks, B.   Fic

Everywhere babies. Meyers, S.   E

Everywhere the cow says "Moo!". Weinstein, E.
    413

Evie & Margie. Waber, B.   E

Evil *See* Good and evil

Evil spirits *See* Demonology

Evolution
Ashby, R. Young Charles Darwin and the voy-
age of the Beagle   92
Burton, V. L. Life story   560
Eamer, C. Super crocs & monster wings
    591.3
Gamlin, L. Evolution   576.8
Hartman, E. Changing life on Earth   576.8
Jenkins, S. Life on earth: the story of evolution
    576.8
Kelly, E. Evolving planet   551
Lasky, K. One beetle too many: the extraordi-
nary adventures of Charles Darwin   92
Markle, S. Animals Charles Darwin saw   92
McGinty, A. B. Darwin   92
Patkau, K. Creatures yesterday and today
    591.3
Prap, L. Dinosaurs?!   567.9
Schanzer, R. What Darwin saw   92
Tattersall, I. Bones, brains and DNA   599.93
Weaver, A. H. The voyage of the beetle
    576.8
Winston, R. M. L. Evolution revolution
    576.8
Wood, A. J. Charles Darwin and the Beagle ad-
venture   508
See/See also pages in the following book(s):
Patent, D. H. Biodiversity   333.95
         Study and teaching
Olson, S. P. The trial of John T. Scopes
    345

The **evolution** of Calpurnia Tate. Kelly, J.   Fic

Evolution revolution. Winston, R. M. L.   576.8

Evolving planet. Kelly, E.   551

Ewart, Claire
Fossil   E

Ewing, Ella Kate, 1872-1913
         Fiction
Klise, K. Stand straight, Ella Kate   E

Ex-service men *See* Veterans

Exactly the opposite. Hoban, T.   E

Examinations
         Fiction
Cohen, M. First grade takes a test   E
Poydar, N. The biggest test in the universe
    E

Excavating machinery
         Fiction
Zimmerman, A. G. Dig!   E

Excavating the past [series]
Quigley, M. Mesa Verde   978.8
Shuter, J. Ancient China   931
Shuter, J. Mesopotamia   935

Excavations (Archeology)
Peterson, J. M. Digging up history   930.1
Schlitz, L. A. The hero Schliemann   92
         Canada
Huey, L. M. American archaeology uncovers the
Vikings   970.01
         China
Shuter, J. Ancient China   931

Explore winter!. Anderson, M. 508.2

Explorers

Aronson, M. The world made new 910.4
Calvert, P. Robert E. Peary 92
Calvert, P. Sir Ernest Shackleton 92
Calvert, P. Vasco da Gama 92
Calvert, P. Zebulon Pike 92
Collier, J. L. Christopher Columbus 92
Demi. Marco Polo 92
Faber, H. Samuel de Champlain 92
Freedman, R. The adventures of Marco Polo
92
Fritz, J. Around the world in a hundred years
910.4
Fritz, J. Where do you think you're going,
Christopher Columbus? 92
Goodman, J. E. Despite all obstacles: La Salle
and the conquest of the Mississippi 92
Goodman, J. E. A long and uncertain journey:
the 27,000 mile voyage of Vasco da Gama
92
Hernández, R. E. Early explorations: the 1500s
970.01
Hopkinson, D. Keep on! 92
Jackson, D. M. Extreme scientists 509
Johnson, D. Onward [biography of Matthew
Henson] 92
Jones, C. F. Westward ho! 920
Kirkpatrick, K. A. Snow baby [biography of
Marie Ahnighito Peary] 92
Kostyal, K. M. Trial by ice: a photobiography
of Sir Ernest Shackleton 92
Levinson, N. S. Magellan and the first voyage
around the world 92
Lilly, A. Spanish colonies in America
970.01
Lourie, P. On the Texas trail of Cabeza de Vaca
92
MacLeod, E. Samuel de Champlain 92
Markle, S. Animals Marco Polo saw 92
Markle, S. Animals Robert Scott saw 998
McCarty, N. Marco Polo 92
Meltzer, M. Francisco Pizarro 92
Nelson, S. P. Jedediah Smith 92
Otfinoski, S. David Livingstone 92
Otfinoski, S. Juan Ponce de Leon 92
Otfinoski, S. Marco Polo 92
Perritano, J. The Lewis and Clark Expedition
978
Ray, D. K. Down the Colorado [biography of
John Wesley Powell] 92
Schanzer, R. John Smith escapes again! 92
Sheldon, D. Into the deep [biography of William
Beebe] 92
Spradlin, M. P. Daniel Boone's great escape
92
Weaver, J. Hudson 92

Dictionaries

Biography for beginners: world explorers
920.003

Fiction

Howard, E. The crimson cap Fic
Snell, G. The King of Quizzical Island E

Explorers [series]

Markle, S. Animals Robert Scott saw 998

Exploring citizenship [series]

Barraclough, S. Fair play 175
Barraclough, S. Honesty 179
Barraclough, S. Leadership 303.3
Barraclough, S. Sharing 177
Parker, V. Acting responsibly 179
Parker, V. Good relationships 177
Parker, V. Making choices 170

Exploring life science 570

Exploring mammals 599

Exploring Mars. Ward, D. J. 523.4

Exploring our solar system [series]

Jefferis, D. Galaxies 523.1
Jefferis, D. Space probes 629.43
Jefferis, D. Star spotters 522
Jefferis, D. The stars 523.8

Exploring planet earth [series]

Friend, S. Earth's wild winds 551.51

Exploring Saturn. Bortolotti, D. 523.4

Exploring the connection between children's literature and music. Carlow, R. 372

Exploring the deep, dark sea. Gibbons, G.
551.46

Exploring the elements [series]

Kaner, E. Who likes the rain? 551.57
Kaner, E. Who likes the snow? 551.57
Kaner, E. Who likes the wind? 551.51

Exploring the solar system. Carson, M. K.
523.2

Exploring the world of mammals 599

Exploring tough issues [series]

Woolf, A. Why are people terrorists? 303.6

Explosions

Richardson, G. Kaboom! 500

Express yourself!. Raimondo, J. 709.04

Expressionism (Art)

Raimondo, J. Express yourself! 709.04

Extinct animals

See also Mass extinction of species; Prehistoric animals; Rare animals

Extinct cities

See also Ghost towns

Extinction of species, Mass *See* Mass extinction
of species

Extra cheese, please!. Peterson, C. 637

Extra credit. Clements, A. Fic

The extraordinary adventures of Ordinary Boy
[series]

Boniface, W. The hero revealed Fic

Extraordinary African-Americans. Altman, S.
920

Extraordinary Asian Americans and Pacific Islanders. Sinnott, S. 920

Extraordinary Asian-Pacific Americans. See
Sinnott, S. Extraordinary Asian Americans
and Pacific Islanders 920

Extraordinary Black Americans. See Altman, S.
Extraordinary African-Americans 920

Extraordinary Ernie and Marvelous Maud. Watts,
F. Fic

Extraordinary Hispanic Americans. Alegre, C.
920

The **extraordinary** Mark Twain (according to Susy). Kerley, B. 92

Extraordinary people [series]
Alegre, C. Extraordinary Hispanic Americans
920
Altman, S. Extraordinary African-Americans
920
Sinnott, S. Extraordinary Asian Americans and Pacific Islanders 920

Extraordinary short story writing. Otfinoski, S.
808.3

Extrasensory perception
See also Clairvoyance; Telepathy
Fiction
Lester, J. The old African Fic
Nelson, N. Bringing the boy home Fic

Extrasolar planetary systems *See* Extrasolar planets

Extrasolar planets
Wittenstein, V. O. Planet hunter 523.2
Poetry
Prelutsky, J. The swamps of Sleethe 811

Extraterrestrial bases
See also Space colonies

Extraterrestrial beings
Nardo, D. Martians 001.9
Fiction
Arnold, T. Green Wilma, frog in space E
Byrd, T. Doc Wilde and the frogs of doom
Fic
Coville, B. Aliens ate my homework Fic
Deacon, A. Beegu E
Elish, D. The attack of the frozen woodchucks
Fic
Fields, B. W. Lunchbox and the aliens Fic
Haddon, M. Boom! Fic
Jeffers, O. The way back home E
Klass, D. Stuck on Earth Fic
Moss, M. Alien Eraser to the rescue Fic
Rex, A. The true meaning of Smekday Fic
Saint-Exupéry, A. d. The little prince Fic
Saint-Exupéry, A. d. The little prince: deluxe pop-up book Fic
Scieszka, J. Spaceheadz Fic
Stadler, A. Julian Rodriguez: episode one, Trash crisis on earth Fic
Teague, M. The doom machine Fic
Poetry
Prelutsky, J. The swamps of Sleethe 811

Extravehicular activity (Space flight)
Vogt, G. Spacewalks 629.45

Extreme animals. Davies, N. 590

Extreme balloon tying. Levine, S. 745.594

Extreme dinosaurs! Q & A. Thomson, S. L.
567.9

Extreme rocks & minerals! 552

Extreme scientists. Jackson, D. M. 509

Extreme scientists [series]
Peterson, J. M. Digging up history 930.1

Extreme weather. Jennings, T. 551.55

Extreme weather. Simpson, K. 551.6

Exxon Valdez (Ship)
Bryan, N. Exxon Valdez oil spill 363.7

Exxon Valdez oil spill. Bryan, N. 363.7

Eye
Cobb, V. Open your eyes 612.8
Larsen, C. S. Crust and spray 612.8
Miller, S. S. All kinds of eyes 591.4
Silverstein, A. Can you see the chalkboard?
617.7
Simon, S. Eyes and ears 612.8
Stewart, M. Why do we see rainbows?
612.8
Fiction
Kostecki-Shaw, J. S. My travelin' eye E

An **eye** for color: the story of Josef Albers. Wing, N. 92

Eye on energy [series]
Wheeler, J. C. Alternative cars 629.222

Eye-popping optical illusions. Dispezio, M. A.
152.14

Eye to eye with endangered species [series]
Rodriguez, C. Bats 599.4
Rodriguez, C. Cougars 599.75
Rodriguez, C. Sea turtles 597.92
Stearns, P. M. Manatees 599.5
Stearns, P. M. Steller sea lions 599.79
Stearns, P. M. Whooping cranes 598

Eyeglasses
Fiction
Calvert, P. Princess Peepers E
Giff, P. R. Watch out, Ronald Morgan! E

Eyes and ears. Simon, S. 612.8

The **eyes** of the Amaryllis. Babbitt, N. Fic

Eyewitness books [series]
Mound, L. A. Insect 595.7
Steele, P. Vote 324

F

F is for fiesta. Elya, S. M. E

F is for firefighting. Butler, D. H. 628.9

F.W. prep [series]
Otfinoski, S. Extraordinary short story writing
808.3

Faber, Harold
Lewis and Clark 978
Samuel de Champlain 92

Fables
Bolt, R. The hare and the tortoise and other fables of La Fontaine 398.2
Brett, J. Town mouse, country mouse 398.2
Brown, M. Once a mouse 398.2
Cooney, B. Chanticleer and the fox E
D'Aulaire, I. The two cars E
Downard, B. The race of the century 398.2
Forest, H. The contest between the Sun and the Wind 398.2
Galdone, P. The monkey and the crocodile
398.2
MacDonald, M. R. Bat's big game 398.2
Morpurgo, M. The McElderry book of Aesop's fables 398.2

The **facts** about inhalants. Menhard, F. R.
362.29

The **facts** and fictions of Minna Pratt. MacLachlan, P. **Fic**

Facts of life. Soto, G. **S C**

Fagan, Deva
Fortune's folly **Fic**
The magical misadventures of Prunella Bogthistle **Fic**

Faidley, Warren
(il) Kramer, S. Lightning **551.56**

Fair has nothing to do with it. Cotten, C. **Fic**

Fair play. Barraclough, S. **175**

Fair use (Copyright)
Butler, R. P. Copyright for teachers and librarians **346.04**
Butler, R. P. Smart copyright compliance for schools **346.04**

Fair weather. Peck, R. **Fic**

Fairies
Knudsen, S. Fairies and elves **398**
Malam, J. Fairies **398.2**
Reinhart, M. Fairies and magical creatures **398**

Fiction
Colato Laínez, R. The Tooth Fairy meets El Ratón Pérez **E**
Colfer, E. Artemis Fowl **Fic**
Doherty, B. The goblin baby **Fic**
Hahn, M. D. Witch catcher **Fic**
Harrison, M. 13 treasures **Fic**
Hodges, M. The wee Christmas cabin **E**
Kessler, L. Philippa Fisher's fairy godsister **Fic**
Kimmel, E. A. Hershel and the Hanukkah goblins **E**
Kirk, D. The low road **Fic**
McGrath, B. B. The little red elf **E**
McGraw, E. J. The moorchild **Fic**
Nesbit, E. Five children and it **Fic**
Pearce, P. The squirrel wife **E**
Ray, J. The dollhouse fairy **E**
Rogers, G. Midsummer knight **E**
Schlitz, L. A. The night fairy **Fic**
Shannon, D. Alice the fairy **E**
Yolen, J. Come to the fairies' ball **E**
Folklore
MacDonald, M. R. Too many fairies **398.2**

Fairies and elves. Knudsen, S. **398**

Fairies and magical creatures. Reinhart, M.
398

Fairman, Jennifer E.
(il) Johnson, R. L. Mighty animal cells
571.6

Fairs
Fiction
Crews, D. Night at the fair **E**
Gorbachev, V. Molly who flew away **E**
Weaver, T. Frederick Finch, loudmouth **E**

The **fairy-tale** detectives. Buckley, M. **Fic**

Fairy tale feasts. Yolen, J. **641.5**

Fairy tales
See also Fantasy fiction
Ahlberg, A. Previously **E**
Ahlberg, J. The jolly postman **E**
Alderson, B. Thumbelina **E**
Andersen, H. C. The emperor's new clothes [illustrated by Virginia Lee Burton] **E**
Andersen, H. C. Hans Christian Andersen's Fairy Tales [illustrated by Lisbeth Zwerger] **S C**
Andersen, H. C. The princess and the pea [illustrated by Dorothee Duntze] **Fic**
Andersen, H. C. Thumbeline [illustrated by Lisbeth Zwerger] **E**
Andersen, H. C. The ugly duckling [illustrated by Pirkko Vainio] **E**
The Arabian nights entertainments **398.2**
Aylesworth, J. The full belly bowl **E**
Bardhan-Quallen, S. The hog prince **E**
Barrie, J. M. Peter Pan **Fic**
Barry, D. Peter and the starcatchers **Fic**
Baruzzi, A. The true story of Little Red Riding Hood **E**
Bateman, T. Harp o' gold **E**
Beck, I. The secret history of Tom Trueheart **Fic**
Bell, A. The porridge pot **398.2**
Beneduce, A. Jack and the beanstalk **398.2**
Berner, R. S. Definitely not for little ones **398.2**
Bianco, M. W. The velveteen rabbit **Fic**
The big book for toddlers **808.8**
The Blue fairy book **398.2**
Boelts, M. Dogerella **E**
Braun, S. The ugly duckling **E**
Brett, J. Beauty and the beast **398.2**
Buckley, M. The fairy-tale detectives **Fic**
Burns, B. The king with horse's ears and other Irish folktales **398.2**
Calvert, P. Multiplying menace **E**
Carrasco, X. Rumpelstiltskin **398.2**
Cech, J. Jack and the beanstalk **398.2**
Cech, J. The nutcracker **E**
Cech, J. The princess and the pea **E**
Cech, J. Puss in boots **398.2**
Cech, J. The twelve dancing princesses **398.2**
Claflin, W. The uglified ducky **E**
Climo, S. The Egyptian Cinderella **398.2**
Climo, S. The Korean Cinderella **398.2**
Cole, B. Good enough to eat **E**
Collodi, C. The adventures of Pinocchio [illustrated by Roberto Innocenti] **Fic**
Coombs, K. The runaway princess **Fic**
Coombs, K. The secret-keeper **E**
Cooper, S. The magician's boy **Fic**
Cousins, L. Yummy **398.2**
Daly, N. Pretty Salma **E**
D'Aulaire, I. The terrible troll-bird **398.2**
De Paola, T. Adelita **398.2**
De Regniers, B. S. Little sister and the month brothers **398.2**
Demi. The emperor's new clothes **E**
DeSeve, R. The Duchess of Whimsy **E**
DiCamillo, K. The tale of Despereaux **Fic**
Doherty, B. Fairy tales **398.2**

Fairy tales—*Continued*

Sabuda, R. Peter Pan: a classic collectible pop-up   **E**
San Souci, R. Cendrillon   **398.2**
San Souci, R. Little Gold Star   **398.2**
Sandburg, C. Rootabaga stories   **S C**
Schlitz, L. A. The Bearskinner   **398.2**
Schram, P. The magic pomegranate   **398.2**
Schulman, J. The nutcracker   **Fic**
Scieszka, J. The Frog Prince continued   **E**
Scieszka, J. The Stinky Cheese Man and other fairly stupid tales   **E**
Sedgwick, M. The emperor's new clothes   **E**
Sendak, M. Outside over there   **E**
Shannon, M. The red wolf   **E**
Sharpe, L. M. The goat-faced girl   **398.2**
Shepard, A. One-Eye! Two-Eyes! Three-Eyes!   **398.2**
Shepard, A. The princess mouse   **398.2**
Sierra, J. The gift of the Crocodile   **398.2**
Silverman, E. Raisel's riddle   **398.2**
Spinner, S. The Nutcracker   **E**
Spirin, G. The tale of the Firebird   **398.2**
Stanley, D. Bella at midnight   **Fic**
Stanley, D. The Giant and the beanstalk   **E**
Stanley, D. Rumpelstiltskin's daughter   **E**
Stockton, F. The bee-man of Orn   **Fic**
Strauss, L. L. The princess gown   **E**
Sweet, M. Carmine   **E**
Thurber, J. Many moons [illustrated by Louis Slobodkin]   **E**
Thurber, J. Many moons [illustrated by Marc Simont]   **E**
Townley, R. The blue shoe   **Fic**
Troll's eye view   **S C**
Tseng, G. White tiger, blue serpent   **398.2**
Vallverdú, J. Aladdin and the magic lamp = Aladino y la lámpara marvillosa   **398.2**
Wargin, K.-J. The frog prince   **398.2**
Watts, B. The ugly duckling   **E**
Wisnewski, A. Little Red Riding Hood   **398.2**
Wood, A. Heckedy Peg   **E**
Wrede, P. C. Dealing with dragons   **Fic**
Yep, L. Auntie Tiger   **E**
Yolen, J. Not one damsel in distress   **398.2**
Yorinks, A. The witch's child   **E**
Zahler, D. The thirteenth princess   **Fic**
Zelinsky, P. O. Rapunzel   **398.2**
Zelinsky, P. O. Rumpelstiltskin   **398.2**
Ziefert, H. Little Red Riding Hood   **398.2**

Bibliography

Lynn, R. N. Fantasy literature for children and young adults   **016.8**

Graphic novels

Hale, S. Rapunzel's revenge   **741.5**
Hoena, B. A. Jack and the beanstalk: the graphic novel   **741.5**
Medley, L. Castle waiting   **741.5**

Poetry

Singer, M. Mirror mirror   **811**
Whipple, L. If the shoe fits   **811**

Fairy trails. Elya, S. M.   **E**

Faith

Walker, R. D. Mama says   **E**

Faith. Ajmera, M.   **200**

Faith, hope, and Ivy June. Naylor, P. R.   **Fic**
A **faith** like mine. Buller, L.   **200**
The **faithful** friend. San Souci, R.   **398.2**

Falconer, Ian, 1959-

Olivia   **E**

Falconer, Kieran, 1970-

Peru   **985**

Falcons

Fiction

George, J. C. My side of the mountain trilogy   **Fic**

Falkenstern, Lisa

(il) Ward, J. The busy tree   **E**

Fall *See* Autumn

Fall. Smith, S.   **508.2**

The **fall** of the Amazing Zalindas. Mack, T.   **Fic**

Faller, Régis

The adventures of Polo   **E**

Falling down the page   **811.008**
Falling from Grace. Godwin, J.   **Fic**
Falling in. Dowell, F. O.   **Fic**
Falling stars *See* Meteors
Falling up. Silverstein, S.   **811**

Falls, Kat

Dark life   **Fic**

Falsehood *See* Truthfulness and falsehood

Falvey, David

Letters to a soldier   **956.7**

Correspondence.

Falvey, D. Letters to a soldier   **956.7**

Falwell, Cathryn

David's drawings   **E**
Scoot!   **E**
Shape capers   **E**
Turtle splash!   **E**

Fame and glory in Freedom, Georgia. O'Connor, B.   **Fic**

Families. Kuklin, S.   **306.8**

Families and their faiths [series]

Hawker, F. Buddhism in Thailand   **294.3**
Hawker, F. Christianity in Mexico   **282**
Hawker, F. Hinduism in Bali   **294.5**
Hawker, F. Islam in Turkey   **297**
Hawker, F. Judaism in Israel   **296**
Hawker, F. Sikhism in India   **294.6**

Family

See also types of family members
Charlip, R. Hooray for me!   **306.8**
Garza, C. L. Family pictures   **306.8**
Garza, C. L. In my family   **306.8**
Kuklin, S. Families   **306.8**
Kuklin, S. How my family lives in America   **305.8**
Parr, T. We belong together   **362.7**

Fiction

Dutton, S. Mary Mae and the gospel truth   **Fic**
Krauss, R. The backward day   **E**
Riordan, R. The maze of bones   **Fic**
Simmons, J. Beryl   **Fic**

A **family** apart. Nixon, J. L.   **Fic**

Family life—Fiction—*Continued*

Gantos, J. Heads or tails — **Fic**

García, C. I wanna be your shoebox — **Fic**

Garden, N. Molly's family — **E**

Geisert, B. Prairie summer — **Fic**

Gephart, D. How to survive middle school — **Fic**

Gifaldi, D. Listening for crickets — **Fic**

Giff, P. R. Water Street — **Fic**

Giff, P. R. Wild girl — **Fic**

Gifford, P. E. Moxy Maxwell does not love Stuart Little — **Fic**

Gilani-Williams, F. Nabeel's new pants — **E**

Glaser, L. Hoppy Hanukkah! — **E**

Glatt, L. Abigail Iris: the one and only — **Fic**

Goode, D. Thanksgiving is here! — **E**

Gourley, R. Bring me some apples and I'll make you a pie — **E**

Graff, L. The thing about Georgie — **Fic**

Graham, B. Oscar's half birthday — **E**

Gratz, A. The Brooklyn nine — **Fic**

Greenwald, S. Rosy Cole's worst ever, best yet tour of New York City — **Fic**

Gregory, K. My darlin' Clementine — **Fic**

Gregory, N. I'll sing you one-o — **Fic**

Guest, E. H. Harriet's had enough — **E**

Guo Yue. Little Leap Forward — **Fic**

Gwaltney, D. Homefront — **Fic**

Hahn, M. D. Anna all year round — **Fic**

Hamilton, V. The bells of Christmas — **Fic**

Hamilton, V. M.C. Higgins, the great — **Fic**

Hannigan, K. Ida B — **Fic**

Harper, J. Uh-oh, Cleo — **Fic**

Havill, J. Just like a baby — **E**

Hayter, R. The witchy worries of Abbie Adams — **Fic**

Heide, F. P. The one and only Marigold — **E**

Heide, F. P. Sami and the time of the troubles — **E**

Henkes, K. Bird Lake moon — **Fic**

Henkes, K. The birthday room — **Fic**

Henkes, K. Olive's ocean — **Fic**

Heo, Y. Ten days and nine nights — **E**

Hermes, P. Emma Dilemma and the new nanny — **Fic**

Hesse, K. Brooklyn Bridge — **Fic**

Hesse, K. Just Juice — **Fic**

Hirahara, N. 1001 cranes — **Fic**

Hodgkinson, L. Smile! — **E**

Hole, S. Garmann's summer — **E**

Holm, J. L. Middle school is worse than meatloaf — **Fic**

Holm, J. L. Our only May Amelia — **Fic**

Holm, J. L. Penny from heaven — **Fic**

Holm, J. L. Turtle in paradise — **Fic**

Holt, K. A. Mike Stellar: nerves of steel — **Fic**

Holt, K. W. Piper Reed, Navy brat — **Fic**

Horvath, P. The Pepins and their problems — **Fic**

House, S. Eli the Good — **Fic**

Hurst, C. O. You come to Yokum — **Fic**

Hurwitz, J. Rip-roaring Russell — **Fic**

Jenkins, E. Five creatures — **E**

Jones, K. K. Sand dollar summer — **Fic**

Jones, S. L. The ultimate guide to grandmas and grandpas — **E**

Joseph, L. The color of my words — **Fic**

Joyce, W. A day with Wilbur Robinson — **E**

Kelly, J. The evolution of Calpurnia Tate — **Fic**

Kelly, K. Lucy Rose, here's the thing about me — **Fic**

Kelsey, M. Tracking Daddy down — **Fic**

Kennedy, M. The dog days of Charlotte Hayes — **Fic**

Kennemore, T. Alice's birthday pig — **Fic**

Kerley, B. Greetings from planet Earth — **Fic**

King-Smith, D. The mouse family Robinson — **Fic**

Kirwan, W. Minerva the monster — **E**

Krasnesky, T. I always, always get my way — **E**

Kuhlman, E. The last invisible boy — **Fic**

Kuijer, G. The book of everything — **Fic**

Kuskin, K. I am me — **E**

Landolf, D. W. What a good big brother! — **E**

Landry, L. Space boy — **E**

Law, I. Savvy — **Fic**

Lendroth, S. Ocean wide, ocean deep — **E**

L'Engle, M. Meet the Austins — **Fic**

Levine, K. The best bad luck I ever had — **Fic**

Levitin, S. Journey to America — **Fic**

Lindo, E. Manolito Four-Eyes — **Fic**

Lindsey, K. Sweet potato pie — **E**

Lipson, E. R. Applesauce season — **E**

Lloyd, J. Looking for loons — **E**

López, S. The best family in the world — **E**

Love, D. A. Semiprecious — **Fic**

Lowry, L. Anastasia Krupnik — **Fic**

Lowry, L. The Willoughbys — **Fic**

MacLachlan, P. All the places to love — **E**

MacLachlan, P. Seven kisses in a row — **Fic**

Madden, K. Gentle's Holler — **Fic**

Manning, M. Kitchen dance — **E**

Manushkin, F. How Mama brought the spring — **E**

Marsden, C. Silk umbrellas — **Fic**

Marsden, C. When heaven fell — **Fic**

Mason, S. The Quigleys — **Fic**

Mathews, E. The linden tree — **Fic**

Mazer, N. F. Ten ways to make my sister disappear — **Fic**

McClements, G. Night of the Veggie Monster — **E**

McDonough, Y. Z. The doll shop downstairs — **Fic**

McGhee, A. Julia Gillian (and the art of knowing) — **Fic**

McGowan, M. Sunday is for God — **E**

McKay, H. Saffy's angel — **Fic**

McKinnon, H. R. Franny Parker — **Fic**

McKissack, P. C. Stitchin' and pullin' — **Fic**

McNelly McCormack, C. The fiesta dress — **E**

Meehl, B. Out of Patience — **Fic**

Milgrim, D. My dog, Buddy — **E**

Millard, G. The naming of Tishkin Silk — **Fic**

Mills, C. The totally made-up Civil War diary of Amanda MacLeish — **Fic**

Mora, P. Wiggling pockets — **E**

Morris, T. Total knockout — **Fic**

Moses, S. P. Sallie Gal and the Wall-a-kee man — **Fic**

Fantasy fiction—*Continued*

Coville, B. The skull of truth	**Fic**
Dahl, R. James and the giant peach	**Fic**
De Mari, S. The last dragon	**Fic**
DiTerlizzi, T. The Nixie's song	**Fic**
Doherty, B. The goblin baby	**Fic**
Dowell, F. O. Falling in	**Fic**
Drake, S. Dragonsdale	**Fic**
Eager, E. Half magic	**Fic**
Eager, E. Magic or not?	**Fic**
Eager, E. Seven-day magic	**Fic**
Etchemendy, N. The power of Un	**Fic**
Farmer, N. The Sea of Trolls	**Fic**
Flanagan, J. The ruins of Gorlan	**Fic**
Fleischman, S. The 13th floor	**Fic**
Fletcher, C. Stoneheart	**Fic**
Fombelle, T. d. Toby alone	**Fic**
Funke, C. C. Dragon rider	**Fic**
Funke, C. C. Igraine the brave	**Fic**
Funke, C. C. Inkheart	**Fic**
Gannett, R. S. My father's dragon	**Fic**
Gardner, L. Into the woods	**Fic**
Halpern, J. Dormia	**Fic**
Haptie, C. Otto and the flying twins	**Fic**
Hardinge, F. Fly by night	**Fic**
Hardy, J. The shifter	**Fic**
Haydon, E. The Floating Island	**Fic**
Henham, R. D. The red dragon codex	**Fic**
Ibbotson, E. The secret of platform 13	**Fic**
Iggulden, C. Tollins	**Fic**
Jacques, B. Redwall	**Fic**
Jansson, T. Moominsummer madness	**Fic**
Jarrell, R. The animal family	**Fic**
Johnston, T. The spoon in the bathroom wall	**Fic**
Jones, D. W. Castle in the air	**Fic**
Jones, D. W. House of many ways	**Fic**
Jones, D. W. Howl's moving castle	**Fic**
Joyce, W. George shrinks	**E**
Juster, N. The phantom tollbooth	**Fic**
Kendall, C. The Gammage Cup	**Fic**
Kessler, L. Philippa Fisher's fairy godsister	**Fic**
Kilworth, G. Attica	**Fic**
Kirk, D. The low road	**Fic**
Knudsen, M. The dragon of Trelian	**Fic**
Lake, A. J. The coming of dragons	**Fic**
Landy, D. Skulduggery Pleasant	**Fic**
Langton, J. The fledgling	**Fic**
Lasky, K. Lone wolf	**Fic**
Le Guin, U. K. Catwings	**Fic**
L'Engle, M. A wrinkle in time	**Fic**
Lennon, J. Questors	**Fic**
Levine, G. C. Ella enchanted	**Fic**
Levine, G. C. The two princesses of Bamarre	**Fic**
Lewis, C. S. The lion, the witch, and the wardrobe	**Fic**
Lisle, H. The Ruby Key	**Fic**
Llewellyn, S. The well between the worlds	**Fic**
Lofting, H. The voyages of Doctor Dolittle	**Fic**
Mahy, M. Maddigan's Fantasia	**Fic**
McGraw, E. J. The moorchild	**Fic**
Moloney, J. The Book of Lies	**Fic**

Myers, W. D. Three swords for Granada	**Fic**
Nesbit, E. The enchanted castle	**Fic**
Nix, G. One beastly beast	**S C**
Norton, M. Bed-knob and broomstick	**Fic**
Pearce, P. Tom's midnight garden	**Fic**
Pierce, T. Magic steps	**Fic**
Prineas, S. The magic thief	**Fic**
Pullman, P. I was a rat!	**Fic**
Rodda, E. The key to Rondo	**Fic**
Rodda, E. Rowan of Rin	**Fic**
Ruby, L. The chaos king	**Fic**
Ruby, L. The Wall and the Wing	**Fic**
Rutkoski, M. The Cabinet of Wonders	**Fic**
Sabuda, R. Alice's adventures in Wonderland	**E**
Sabuda, R. The Chronicles of Narnia pop-up	**E**
Sage, A. Magyk	**Fic**
Saint-Exupéry, A. d. The little prince	**Fic**
Saint-Exupéry, A. d. The little prince: deluxe pop-up book	**Fic**
Sanderson, B. Alcatraz versus the evil Librarians	**Fic**
Scieszka, J. Knights of the kitchen table	**Fic**
Sendak, M. In the night kitchen	**E**
Sendak, M. Where the wild things are	**E**
Sensel, J. The Farwalker's quest	**Fic**
Sensel, J. The timekeeper's moon	**Fic**
Sherman, D. Changeling	**Fic**
Snow, A. Here be monsters!	**Fic**
Steer, D. The dragon diary	**Fic**
Stewart, P. Beyond the Deepwoods	**Fic**
Thomson, S. L. Dragon's egg	**Fic**
Tolkien, J. R. R. The hobbit, or, There and back again	**Fic**
Travers, P. L. Mary Poppins	**Fic**
Verrillo, E. F. Elissa's quest	**Fic**
Wharton, T. The shadow of Malabron	**Fic**
Wolf-Morgenlander, K. Ragtag	**Fic**
Yep, L. City of fire	**Fic**
Yorinks, A. Hey, Al	**E**

Bibliography

Lynn, R. N. Fantasy literature for children and young adults	**016.8**

History and criticism

Colbert, D. The magical worlds of Harry Potter	**823.009**

Fantasy for children. *See* Lynn, R. N. Fantasy literature for children and young adults
016.8

Fantasy graphic novels

Cavallaro, M. L. Frank Baum's The Wizard of Oz	**741.5**
Colfer, E. Artemis Fowl: the graphic novel	**741.5**
Crane, J. The clouds above	**741.5**
Espinosa, R. The courageous princess	**741.5**
Flight explorer	**741.5**
Frampton, O. Oddly Normal	**741.5**
Fuji, M. The big adventures of Majoko, volume 1	**741.5**
Hale, S. Rapunzel's revenge	**741.5**
Hastings, J. Terrabella Smoot and the unsung monsters	**741.5**

Fantasy graphic novels—*Continued*

Kibuishi, K. Amulet, book one: The Stonekeeper **741.5**

Kovac, T. Wonderland **741.5**

Medley, L. Castle waiting **741.5**

Petersen, D. Mouse Guard: Fall 1152 **741.5**

Thompson, J. Magic Trixie **741.5**

Fantasy in art

Caldwell, B. Fantasy! cartooning **741.5**

Fantasy literature for children and young adults. Lynn, R. N. **016.8**

Far beyond the garden gate: Alexandra David-Neel's journey to Lhasa. Brown, D. **92**

Far far away. Segal, J. **E**

Far-flung adventures [series]

Stewart, P. Fergus Crane **Fic**

Far-out science projects about Earth's sun and moon. Gardner, R. **523**

Far-out science projects with height and depth. Gardner, R. **530.8**

Faraway home. Kurtz, J. **E**

A **faraway** island. Thor, A. **Fic**

Faraway places. Blakemore, C. **011.6**

Farber, Norma

How the hibernators came to Bethlehem **E**

Fardell, John, 1967-

The 7 professors of the Far North **Fic**

Faria, Rosana

(il) Cottin, M. The black book of colors **E**

Faricy, Patrick

(il) Kennedy, R. F. Robert Smalls **92**

Farley, Walter, 1915-1989

The Black Stallion **Fic**

Farley follows his nose. Johnston, L. **E**

Farlow, James Orville, 1951-

Bringing dinosaur bones to life **567.9**

Farm. Cooper, E. **E**

Farm animals *See* Domestic animals

Farm engines *See* Agricultural machinery

Farm laborers *See* Agricultural laborers

Farm life

See also Family farms

Siegal, A. Memories of Babi **92**

Fiction

Alvarez, J. Return to sender **Fic**

Angle, K. G. Hummingbird **Fic**

Aston, D. H. Moon over Star **E**

Avi. The barn **Fic**

Baddiel, I. Cock-a-doodle quack! quack! **E**

Baehr, P. G. Boo Cow **E**

Bateman, T. April foolishness **E**

Birdseye, T. A tough nut to crack **Fic**

Blackwood, G. L. The just-so woman **E**

Brown, M. W. Big red barn **E**

Buehner, C. Fanny's dream **E**

Cleary, B. The hullabaloo ABC **E**

Cooper, E. Farm **E**

Cordsen, C. F. Market day **E**

Cowley, J. Chicken feathers **Fic**

Cronin, D. Click, clack, moo **E**

Crum, S. Thunder-Boomer! **E**

Ehlert, L. Market day **E**

Fisher, D. C. Understood Betsy **Fic**

Fleischman, S. Here comes McBroom! **Fic**

Gammell, S. Once upon MacDonald's farm **E**

Geisert, A. Country road ABC **E**

Geisert, B. Prairie summer **Fic**

Gourley, R. Bring me some apples and I'll make you a pie **E**

Hamilton, V. Drylongso **Fic**

Harrington, J. N. The chicken-chasing queen of Lamar County **E**

Hesse, K. Out of the dust **Fic**

Hillenbrand, W. Cock-a-doodle Christmas! **E**

Himmelman, J. Chickens to the rescue **E**

Horstman, L. Squawking Matilda **E**

Hunt, I. Across five Aprils **Fic**

King-Smith, D. Clever duck **Fic**

King-Smith, D. The golden goose **Fic**

Kinsey-Warnock, N. Nora's ark **E**

Lindsey, K. Sweet potato pie **E**

Lobel, A. A treeful of pigs **E**

Long, L. Otis **E**

MacDonald, A. Too much flapdoodle! **Fic**

MacLachlan, P. All the places to love **E**

MacLachlan, P. The true gift **Fic**

MacLennan, C. Chicky chicky chook chook **E**

Martínez, A. O. Pedrito's world **Fic**

Mathews, E. The linden tree **Fic**

McDowell, M. T. Carolina Harmony **Fic**

McMullan, M. When I crossed No-Bob **Fic**

Noble, T. H. The day Jimmy's boa ate the wash **E**

Nolen, J. Harvey Potter's balloon farm **E**

Nolen, J. Raising dragons **E**

Palatini, M. Boo-hoo moo **E**

Paterson, K. Park's quest **Fic**

Paulsen, G. The winter room **Fic**

Plourde, L. Field trip day **E**

Provensen, A. A day in the life of Murphy **E**

Purmell, A. Apple cider making days **E**

Purmell, A. Christmas tree farm **E**

Reid, R. Comin' down to storytime **E**

Root, P. Thirsty Thursday **E**

Sandburg, C. The Huckabuck family and how they raised popcorn in Nebraska and quit and came back **E**

Seredy, K. The Good Master **Fic**

Seymour, T. Hunting the white cow **E**

Tafuri, N. Blue Goose **E**

Tafuri, N. This is the farmer **E**

Teague, M. Funny Farm **E**

Turner, A. W. Dust for dinner **E**

Van Leeuwen, J. Chicken soup **E**

Waddell, M. Farmer duck **E**

Wild, M. Piglet and Mama **E**

Zimmer, T. V. 42 miles **Fic**

Poetry

Beck, C. Buttercup's lovely day **811**

Gottfried, M. Our farm **811**

Hoce, C. Beyond Old MacDonald **811**

Songs

Cabrera, J. Old MacDonald had a farm **782.42**

Canada

Kurelek, W. A prairie boy's winter **971.27**

Fast food. Freymann, S.   **E**

Fasten your seatbelt. Skotko, B.   **616.85**

The **fastest** dinosaurs. Lessem, D.   **567.9**

The **fastest** game on two feet and other poems about how sports began. Low, A.   **811**

Fasts and feasts

Hinduism

See Hindu holidays

Judaism

See Jewish holidays

Fat cat. MacDonald, M. R.   **398.2**

Fatally ill patients *See* Terminally ill

Fate and fatalism

Fiction

Levine, G. C. Ever   **Fic**

McCaughrean, G. The death-defying Pepper Roux   **Fic**

Father and child *See* Father-child relationship

Father-child relationship

Fiction

Braun, S. On our way home   **E**

Newman, L. Daddy, papa, and me   **E**

Shea, B. Oh, Daddy!   **E**

Spinelli, E. When Papa comes home tonight   **E**

Yolen, J. My father knows the names of things   **E**

Father-daughter relationship

Innes, S. A bear in war   **E**

Fiction

Banks, K. That's Papa's way   **E**

Bateson, C. Being Bee   **Fic**

Bateson, C. Magenta McPhee   **Fic**

Bennett, K. Dad and Pop   **E**

Boles, P. M. Little divas   **Fic**

Brown, S. T. Hugging the rock   **Fic**

Clark, C. G. Hill Hawk Hattie   **Fic**

Cole, B. Buttons   **E**

Cushman, K. Alchemy and Meggy Swann   **Fic**

Erskine, K. Mockingbird   **Fic**

Feiffer, K. My mom is trying to ruin my life   **E**

Fitzmaurice, K. The year the swallows came early   **Fic**

Galbraith, K. O. Arbor Day square   **E**

George, K. O. Up!   **E**

Hahn, M. D. Witch catcher   **Fic**

Harper, C. M. Pink me up   **E**

Harvey, M. Shopping with Dad   **E**

Henkes, K. Protecting Marie   **Fic**

Hest, A. Remembering Mrs. Rossi   **Fic**

Kadohata, C. Outside beauty   **Fic**

Kelsey, M. Tracking Daddy down   **Fic**

Kimmel, E. C. The top job   **E**

Kurtz, J. Faraway home   **E**

Lawrence, I. The giant-slayer   **Fic**

Lopez, D. Confetti girl   **Fic**

Lowry, L. Crow call   **E**

Madison, A. 100 days and 99 nights   **Fic**

Mazer, N. F. Has anyone seen my Emily Greene?   **E**

Ormerod, J. Molly and her dad

Pow, T. Tell me one thing, Dad   **E**

Railsback, L. Noonie's masterpiece   **Fic**

Ransom, C. F. The old blue pickup truck   **E**

Ray, J. The dollhouse fairy   **E**

Ryder, J. My father's hands   **E**

Spinelli, E. Night shift daddy   **E**

Stanton, K. Papi's gift   **E**

Verrillo, E. F. Elissa's quest   **Fic**

Wilson, J. Candyfloss   **Fic**

Wilson, J. Cookie   **Fic**

Yolen, J. Owl moon   **E**

Zahler, D. The thirteenth princess   **Fic**

A **father** like that. Zolotow, C.   **E**

Father-son relationship

Fiction

Anholt, L. Cézanne and the apple boy   **E**

Avi. The barn   **Fic**

Baggott, J. The Prince of Fenway Park   **Fic**

Berry, M. Up on Daddy's shoulders   **E**

Bildner, P. The greatest game ever played   **E**

Bruchac, J. My father is taller than a tree   **E**

Bunting, E. Some frog!   **Fic**

Burleigh, R. Good-bye, Sheepie   **E**

Charlip, R. A perfect day   **E**

Clements, A. The janitor's boy   **Fic**

Cockcroft, J. Counter clockwise   **Fic**

Colato Laínez, R. My shoes and I   **E**

Cole, S. Z. Rex   **Fic**

Corriveau, A. How I, Nicky Flynn, finally get a life (and a dog)   **Fic**

Curtis, G. The bat boy & his violin   **E**

Dodd, E. Just like you   **E**

Dorros, A. Papá and me   **E**

Durbin, W. Blackwater Ben   **Fic**

Gore, L. When I grow up   **E**

Green, T. Baseball great   **Fic**

Harper, L. Snow! Snow! Snow!   **E**

Harrison, J. Grizzly dad   **E**

Hines, A. G. Daddy makes the best spaghetti   **E**

Holmberg, B. R. A day with Dad   **E**

Holmes, E. A. Tracktown summer   **Fic**

Hurwitz, J. Baseball fever   **Fic**

Ichikawa, S. My father's shop   **E**

Jennings, P. Out standing in my field   **Fic**

Joosse, B. M. Papa, do you love me?   **E**

Kanevsky, P. Sleepy boy   **E**

Kerley, B. Greetings from planet Earth   **Fic**

Kirk, C. A. Sky dancers   **E**

Kuhlman, E. The last invisible boy   **Fic**

Lawlor, L. He will go fearless   **Fic**

Leuck, L. I love my pirate papa   **E**

Lupica, M. Hot hand   **Fic**

Martin, D. Piggy and Dad go fishing   **E**

Mass, W. Jeremy Fink and the meaning of life   **Fic**

McBratney, S. Guess how much I love you   **E**

Nevius, C. Building with Dad   **E**

Nimmo, J. The snow spider   **Fic**

Norac, C. My daddy is a giant   **E**

Pullen, Z. Friday my Radio Flyer flew   **E**

Ramos, J. I'm just like my mom/I'm just like my dad   **E**

Ryan, P. M. The dreamer   **Fic**

Savadier, E. Time to get dressed!   **E**

Say, A. The lost lake   **E**

Father-son relationship—Fiction—*Continued*

Steig, W. Pete's a pizza	E
Stewart, A. Bedtime for Button	E
Thomas, J. R. Blind mountain	Fic
Thomas, P. J. Red sled	E
Uhlberg, M. Dad, Jackie, and me	E
Vander Zee, R. Mississippi morning	E
Wells, R. Lincoln and his boys	Fic
Williams, K. L. A beach tail	E
Yaccarino, D. Every Friday	E
Zolotow, C. A father like that	E

Fathers

See also Stepfathers

Herb, S. Connecting fathers, children, and reading **028.5**

Fiction

Almond, D. My dad's a birdman	Fic
Bennett, K. Dad and Pop	E
Bennett, K. Your daddy was just like you	E
Bradman, T. Daddy's lullaby	E
Browne, A. My dad	E
Bunting, E. Pop's bridge	E
Carle, E. Mister Seahorse	E
Clement, N. Drive	E
Hof, M. Against the odds	Fic
Pendziwol, J. Marja's skis	E
Resau, L. Star in the forest	Fic
Rockwell, A. F. Father's Day	E
Smith, H. A. Keeping the night watch	Fic
Smith, H. A. The way a door closes	Fic
Warnes, T. Daddy hug	E
Weigel, J. Atomic Ace	E
Wood, D. What dads can't do	E
Woodson, J. Visiting day	E

Poetry

In daddy's arms I am tall **811.008**

Fathers, Single parent *See* Single parent family

Fathers and sons *See* Father-son relationship

Father's Day

Fiction

Rockwell, A. F. Father's Day	E

Fats for a healthy body. Powell, J. **613.2**

Fattouh, Hamdy Mohamed

(jt. auth) Johnson-Davies, D. Goha the wise fool
398.2

Fatus, Sophie

Here we go round the mulberry bush
782.42

(il) Weston, C. If a chicken stayed for supper
E

Faulkner, Matt

A taste of colored water	E

(il) Anderson, L. H. Independent dames
973.3

(il) St. George, J. Stand tall, Abe Lincoln
92

(il) St. George, J. You're on your way, Teddy
Roosevelt! **92**

Faulkner, Rebecca

Fossils	560
Igneous rock	552
Metamorphic rock	552
Sedimentary rock	552

Fauteux, Nicole

(jt. auth) Simon, S. Let's try it out in the water
532

Favorite children's authors and illustrators	**920.003**
Favorite folk songs	**782.42**
Favorite Greek myths. Osborne, M. P.	**292**
Favorite nursery rhymes from Mother Goose	**398.8**
Favorite nursery tales, Tomie dePaola's	**398.2**

Fawcett, Katie Pickard

To come and go like magic	Fic

Fazio, Wende

Saudi Arabia	953.8

Fear

See also Anxiety; Phobias

Crist, J. J. What to do when you're scared &
worried **158**

Fiction

Acosta Gonzalez, A. Mayte and the Bogeyman	E
Applegate, K. The buffalo storm	E
Blume, J. Otherwise known as Sheila the Great	Fic
Bonsall, C. N. Who's afraid of the dark?	E
Bunting, E. The Banshee	E
Cohen, D. B. Nachshon, who was afraid to swim	E
Cummings, T. The eensy weensy spider freaks out (big time!)	E
Dubosarsky, U. The terrible plop	E
Dunbar, J. The monster who ate darkness	E
Ellis, S. Ben over night	E
Emberley, E. Go away, big green monster!	E
Fenton, J. What's under the bed?	E
Fischer, S. M. Jump!	E
Galbraith, K. O. Boo, bunny!	E
Gorbachev, V. Dragon is coming!	E
Gravett, E. Little Mouse's big book of fears	E
Greene, S. Princess Posey and the first grade parade	Fic
Helakoski, L. H. Big chickens	E
Hole, S. Garmann's summer	E
Keller, H. Help!	E
Krensky, S. Spark the firefighter	E
Leach, S. Jake Reynolds: chicken or eagle?	Fic
Lin, G. Olvina flies	E
Look, L. Alvin Ho: allergic to girls, school, and other scary things	Fic
Lucke, D. The boy who wouldn't swim	E
Martin, B. The ghost-eye tree	E
Martin, J. B. Grandmother Bryant's pocket	E
Mayer, M. There's a nightmare in my closet	E
McGhee, A. Julia Gillian (and the art of know-ing)	Fic
McGhee, A. Song of middle C	E
Monfried, D. d. Dark night	E
Payne, C. C. Something to sing about	Fic
Rodowsky, C. F. The next-door dogs	Fic
Rosoff, M. Jumpy Jack and Googily	E

Fishes

See also Aquariums; Codfish; Coelacanth; Eels; Goldfish; Rays (Fishes); Salmon

Bozzo, L. My first fish   **639.34**
Buckmaster, M. L. Freshwater fishes   **639.34**
Jeffrey, L. S. Fish   **639.34**
Pfeffer, W. What's it like to be a fish?   **597**
Rau, D. M. Top 10 fish for kids   **639.34**
Richardson, A. Caring for your fish   **639.34**
Rodriguez, A. M. Secret of the suffocating slime trap . . . and more!   **597**
Rubin, A. How many fish?   **E**
Stockdale, S. Fabulous fishes   **597**
Wilkes, S. Fish   **597**

Fiction

Babin, C. Gus is a fish   **E**
Carle, E. Mister Seahorse   **E**
Cousins, L. Hooray for fish!   **E**
Diesen, D. The pout-pout fish   **E**
Donaldson, J. The fish who cried wolf   **E**
Gall, C. Dear fish   **E**
Lionni, L. Fish is fish   **E**
Lionni, L. Swimmy   **E**
Macdonald, S. Fish, swish! splash, dash!   **E**
Rohmann, E. Clara and Asha   **E**
Wise, W. Ten sly piranhas   **E**
Yoo, T.-E. The little red fish   **E**

Folklore

Bunting, E. Finn McCool and the great fish   **398.2**
Partridge, E. Kogi's mysterious journey   **398.2**

Fishing

McMillan, B. Going fishing   **949.12**
McMillan, B. Salmon summer   **639.2**
See/See also pages in the following book(s):
Bauer, C. F. Celebrations   **808.8**

Fiction

Banks, K. That's Papa's way   **E**
Butler, D. H. My grandpa had a stroke   **E**
DeFelice, C. C. The missing manatee   **Fic**
Dewey, A. Splash!   **E**
Frank, J. How to catch a fish   **E**
Henson, H. Grumpy Grandpa   **E**
LaMarche, J. Up   **E**
Marsden, C. The Buddha's diamonds   **Fic**
Martin, D. Piggy and Dad go fishing   **E**
Philbrick, W. R. The young man and the sea   **Fic**
Prosek, J. A good day's fishing   **E**
Salisbury, G. Lord of the deep   **Fic**
Seuss, Dr. McElligot's pool   **E**

Fishkin, Rebecca Love, 1972-
English colonies in America   **973.2**

Fishman, Cathy, 1951-
On Hanukkah   **296.4**
On Rosh Hashanah and Yom Kippur   **296.4**
On Sukkot and Simchat Torah   **296.4**

Fisk Jubilee Singers (Musical group) *See* Jubilee Singers (Musical group)

A **fistful** of pearls. Laird, E.   **398.2**

Fitch, Florence Mary, 1875-1959
A book about God   **231**

Fitzgerald, Dawn
Soccer chick rules   **Fic**

Vinnie and Abraham [biography of Vinnie Ream]   **92**

Fitzgerald, Ella
About
Orgill, R. Skit-scat raggedy cat: Ella Fitzgerald   **92**
Pinkney, A. D. Ella Fitzgerald   **92**

Fitzgerald, Joanne, 1956-
Yum! yum!!   **398.8**

Fitzgerald, John D., 1907-1988
The Great Brain   **Fic**

Fitzgerald, Stephanie
What is texture?   **701**

Fitzhugh, Louise, 1928-1974
Harriet, the spy   **Fic**

Fitzmaurice, Kathryn
The year the swallows came early   **Fic**

Fitzpatrick, Anne, 1978-
Amazon River   **981**

Fitzpatrick, Jim, 1948-
Skateboarding   **796.22**

Fitzpatrick, Marie-Louise, 1962-
There   **E**

Five children and it. Nesbit, E.   **Fic**
Five creatures. Jenkins, E.   **E**
Five for a little one. Raschka, C.   **E**
The **five** hundred hats of Batholomew Cubbins. See Seuss, Dr. The 500 hats of Bartholomew Cubbins   **E**
Five little chicks. Tafuri, N.   **E**
Five little ducks. Bates, I.   **782.42**
Five little ducks. Raffi   **782.42**
Five little monkeys jumping on the bed. Christelow, E.   **E**
Five-minute tales. MacDonald, M. R.   **398.2**
Five nice mice. Tashiro, C.   **E**
Five pages a day. Kehret, P.   **92**

Five senses [series]
Cobb, V. Feeling your way   **612.8**
Cobb, V. Follow your nose   **612.8**
Cobb, V. Open your eyes   **612.8**
Cobb, V. Perk up your ears   **612.8**

The **five-thousand-year-old** puzzle. See Logan, C. The 5,000-year-old puzzle   **932**

Fivr senses [series]
Cobb, V. Your tongue can tell   **612.8**

Fixing *See* Repairing

The **Fizzy** Whiz kid. Williams, M.   **Fic**

Flack, Marjorie, 1897-1958
Ask Mr. Bear   **E**
(il) Heyward, D. The country bunny and the little gold shoes   **E**

The **flag** with fifty-six stars. Rubin, S. G.   **940.53**

Flags
Bednar, S. Flags of the world   **929.9**
World Book's encyclopedia of flags   **929.9**
United States
Allen, K. The first American flag   **929.9**
Rubin, S. G. The flag with fifty-six stars   **940.53**

Flowers

See also Roses; Sunflowers

Pascoe, E. Flowers	582.13
Schaefer, L. M. Pick, pull, snap!	582
Souza, D. M. Freaky flowers	582.13
Wade, M. D. Flowers bloom!	582.13

Fiction

Bunting, E. Flower garden	E
Ehlert, L. Planting a rainbow	E
Foreman, M. Mia's story	E
Henkes, K. So happy!	E
Lobel, A. Alison's zinnia	E
Reynolds, P. Rose's garden	E
Root, P. Thirsty Thursday	E

Folklore

De Paola, T. The legend of the poinsettia	398.2

Flowers bloom!. Wade, M. D.   582.13

Flu *See* Influenza

The **flu**. Hoffmann, G.	616.2
The **flu**. Ollhoff, J.	616.2
The **flu** and pneumonia update. Silverstein, A.	616.2

Fluid mechanics

See also Hydrodynamics

The **flunking** of Joshua T. Bates. Shreve, S. R.   Fic

Fluorescence

Barton, C. The Day-Glo brothers	535.6

Flush. Hiaasen, C.   Fic

Flute's journey. Cherry, L.   598

Fly away home. Bunting, E.	E
Fly by night. Hardinge, F.	Fic
Fly, Cher Ami, fly!. Burleigh, R.	940.4
Fly, eagle, fly!. Gregorowski, C.	398.2
Fly free!. Thong, R.	E

Flying *See* Flight

Flying eagle. Bardhan-Quallen, S.	598
Flying feet. Stevenson, J.	E
Flying giants of dinosaur time. Lessem, D.	567.9
Flying high. Stamp, J.	E
Flying machine. Nahum, A.	629.133
Flying solo. Fletcher, R.	Fic

Focus on flies. Dixon, N.   595.7

Fog

Tresselt, A. R. Hide and seek fog	E

Fogelin, Adrian, 1951-

The sorta sisters	Fic

Fold me a poem. George, K. O.   811

Folding for fun. Boursin, D.   736

Foley, Erin, 1967-

Costa Rica	972.86
Dominican Republic	972.93
Ecuador	986.6
El Salvador	972.84

Foley, Greg, 1969-

Thank you Bear	E
Willoughby & the lion	E

Foliage *See* Leaves

Folk. Handyside, C.   781.62

Folk art

See also Decorative arts

Weill, C. ABeCedarios	E
Weill, C. Opuestos	E
Whitehead, K. Art from her heart: folk artist Clementine Hunter	92

Folk dancing

See also Native American dance

The **Folk** Keeper. Billingsley, F.   Fic

Folk lore *See* Folklore

Folk music

Handyside, C. Folk	781.62

United States

See also Country music

Seeger, R. C. American folk songs for children in home, school, and nursery school   782.42

Folk songs

The 12 days of Christmas	782.42
Arroz con leche	782.42
De colores and other Latin-American folk songs for children	782.42
Favorite folk songs	782.42
Knick knack paddy whack	782.42
Langstaff, J. M. Frog went a-courtin'	782.42
Langstaff, J. M. Oh, a-hunting we will go	782.42
Langstaff, J. M. Over in the meadow	782.42
Leodhas, S. N. Always room for one more	782.42
Let's sing together	782.42
Rueda, C. Let's play in the forest while the wolf is not around	782.42
Taback, S. There was an old lady who swallowed a fly	782.42
The twelve days of Christmas [illustrated by Ilse Plume]	782.42

United States

See also Spirituals (Songs)

Cabrera, J. Old MacDonald had a farm	782.42
The Farmer in the dell	782.42
The Fox went out on a chilly night	782.42
Hopkinson, D. Home on the range	92
Hush, little baby	782.42
I hear America singing!	782.42
Pinkney, B. Hush, little baby	782.42
Sleepytime songs	782.42
Voake, C. Tweedle dee dee	782.42

Folk songs, English *See* English folk songs

Folklore

See also Animals—Folklore; Dragons; Legends; Tongue twisters topics as themes in folklore and names of ethnic or national groups with the subdivision *Folklore*

Andrews, J. Stories at the door	398.2
The August House book of scary stories	398.2
Aylesworth, J. The Gingerbread man	398.2
Aylesworth, J. Goldilocks and the three bears	398.2

Folklore—*Continued*

Barton, B. The little red hen	398.2
Barton, B. The three bears	398.2
Berner, R. S. Definitely not for little ones	
	398.2
Blackstone, S. Storytime	398.2
The Blue fairy book	398.2
Brett, J. Gingerbread baby	398.2
Buehner, C. Goldilocks and the three bears	
	398.2
Casey, D. The Barefoot book of Earth tales	
	398.2
Cech, J. The twelve dancing princesses	
	398.2
Chichester-Clark, E. Goldilocks and the three bears	398.2
Clayton, S. P. Amazons!	398.2
Climo, S. Monkey business	398.2
Cousins, L. Yummy	398.2
Doherty, B. Fairy tales	398.2
Egielski, R. The gingerbread boy	398.2
Ehrlich, A. A treasury of princess stories	
	398.2
Emberley, E. Chicken Little	398.2
Ernst, L. C. Little Red Riding Hood: a newfangled prairie tale	398.2
Fleischman, P. Glass slipper, gold sandal	
	398.2
Forest, H. The contest between the Sun and the Wind	398.2
Forest, H. The little red hen	398.2
French, V. Henny Penny	398.2
Galdone, P. The gingerbread boy	398.2
Galdone, P. Henny Penny	398.2
Galdone, P. The little red hen	398.2
Galdone, P. The three bears	398.2
Gibbons, G. Behold . . . the dragons!	398
Greene, E. The little golden lamb	398.2
Hamilton, V. A ring of tricksters	398.2
Hausman, G. Horses of myth	398.2
Hennessy, B. G. The boy who cried wolf	
	398.2
Isadora, R. The fisherman and his wife	
	398.2
Isadora, R. Hansel and Gretel	398.2
Isadora, R. The twelve dancing princesses	
	398.2
Jaffe, N. The cow of no color: riddle stories and justice tales from around the world	398.2
Karlin, B. James Marshall's Cinderella	398.2
Kellogg, S. Chicken Little	398.2
Kellogg, S. The three little pigs	398.2
Ketteman, H. The three little gators	E
Kimmel, E. A. The fisherman and the turtle	
	398.2
Kimmel, E. A. The gingerbread man	398.2
Kimmel, E. A. The runaway tortilla	398.2
Kimmelman, L. The Little Red Hen and the Passover matzah	398.2
Livo, N. J. Tales to tickle your funny bone	
	398.2
Lunge-Larsen, L. The hidden folk	398.2
MacDonald, M. R. Five-minute tales	398.2
MacDonald, M. R. Look back and see	
	372.6
MacDonald, M. R. Shake-it-up tales!	372.6

MacDonald, M. R. The storyteller's start-up book	372.6
MacDonald, M. R. Three-minute tales	398.2
MacDonald, M. R. When the lights go out	
	372.6
Maddern, E. The cow on the roof	398.2
Maddern, E. Nail soup	398.2
Marshall, J. Goldilocks and the three bears	
	398.2
Matthews, C. Fireside stories	398.2
Matthews, J. Trick of the tale	398.2
McBratney, S. One voice, please	398.2
McGovern, A. Too much noise	398.2
Mitton, T. The storyteller's secrets	398.2
Muth, J. J. Stone soup	398.2
Norman, H. Between heaven and earth	
	398.2
Olson, A. N. Ask the bones: scary stories from around the world	398.2
Olson, A. N. More bones	398.2
Osborne, M. P. The brave little seamstress	
	398.2
Palatini, M. Lousy rotten stinkin' grapes	
	398.2
Penner, L. R. Dragons	398.2
Pinkney, J. The lion & the mouse	E
Pinkney, J. The little red hen	398.2
Princess stories	398.2
The Random House book of bedtime stories	
	S C
Rapunzel and other magic fairy tales	398.2
Rylant, C. Hansel and Gretel	398.2
San Souci, R. Short & shivery	398.2
Sanderson, R. Goldilocks	398.2
Schwartz, A. All of our noses are here, and other noodle tales	398.2
Schwartz, A. Ghosts!	398.2
Schwartz, A. I saw you in the bathtub, and other folk rhymes	398.2
Schwartz, A. In a dark, dark room, and other scary stories	398.2
Schwartz, A. There is a carrot in my ear, and other noodle tales	398.2
Shannon, G. More stories to solve	398.2
Shannon, G. Stories to solve	398.2
Shepard, A. One-Eye! Two-Eyes! Three-Eyes!	
	398.2
Shulevitz, U. The treasure	398.2
Sierra, J. Can you guess my name?	398.2
Sierra, J. The gruesome guide to world monsters	398
Sierra, J. Nursery tales around the world	
	398.2
Souhami, J. King Pom and the fox	398.2
Souhami, J. Sausages	398.2
Spirin, G. Goldilocks and the three bears	
	398.2
Sturges, P. The Little Red Hen (makes a pizza)	
	398.2
Tchana, K. H. Changing Woman and her sisters	
	398.2
Tomie dePaola's Favorite nursery tales	
	398.2
Valeri, M. E. The hare and the tortoise = La liebre y la tortuga	398.2
Van Kampen, V. It couldn't be worse!	
	398.2

Folklore—Germany—*Continued*

Grimm, J. Hansel and Gretel	398.2
Grimm, J. Little Red Cap	398.2
Grimm, J. Little Red Riding Hood	398.2
Grimm, J. Snow White	398.2
Hettinga, D. R. The Brothers Grimm	92
Hyman, T. S. Little Red Riding Hood	398.2
Isadora, R. Rapunzel	398.2
Kimmel, E. A. Iron John	398.2
Lesser, R. Hansel and Gretel	398.2
Long, L. The lady & the lion	398.2
Marshall, J. Hansel and Gretel	398.2
Marshall, J. Red Riding Hood	398.2
Mitchell, S. Iron Hans	398.2
Morpurgo, M. Hansel and Gretel	398.2
Orgel, D. Doctor All-Knowing	398.2
Osborne, W. Sleeping Bobby	398.2
Pinkney, J. Little Red Riding Hood	398.2
Pirotta, S. The McElderry book of Grimms' fairy tales	398.2
Puttapipat, N. The musicians of Bremen	398.2
Ray, J. Snow White	398.2
San Souci, R. As luck would have it	398.2
Schlitz, L. A. The Bearskinner	398.2
Wargin, K.-J. The frog prince	398.2
Wisnewski, A. Little Red Riding Hood	398.2
Zelinsky, P. O. Rumpelstiltskin	398.2
Ziefert, H. Little Red Riding Hood	398.2

Ghana

Cummings, P. Ananse and the lizard	398.2
McDermott, G. Anansi the spider	398.2
Mollel, T. M. Ananse's feast	398.2

Great Britain

Beneduce, A. Jack and the beanstalk	398.2
Cech, J. Jack and the beanstalk	398.2
English folktales	398.2
Galdone, P. The teeny-tiny woman	398.2
Hodges, M. Dick Whittington and his cat	398.2
I saw Esau	398.8
Jacobs, J. English fairy tales	398.2
Kellogg, S. Jack and the beanstalk	398.2
MacDonald, M. R. The great smelly, slobbery, small-tooth dog	398.2
Marshall, J. The three little pigs	398.2
Mueller, D. L. The best nest	398.2
Nesbit, E. Jack and the beanstalk	398.2
Osborne, M. P. Kate and the beanstalk	398.2
Zemach, M. The three little pigs	398.2

Guatemala

Menchú, R. The secret legacy	398.2

Haiti

Wolkstein, D. The magic orange tree, and other Haitian folktales	398.2

Hawaii

Martin, R. The Shark God	398.2
McDermott, G. Pig-Boy	398.2

Hungary

MacDonald, M. R. Little Rooster's diamond button	398.2

India

Brown, M. Once a mouse	398.2
Galdone, P. The monkey and the crocodile	398.2

Hamilton, M. The ghost catcher	398.2
Nanji, S. Indian tales	398.2
Young, E. Seven blind mice	398.2

Indonesia

MacDonald, M. R. Go to sleep, Gecko!	398.2
Scott, N. K. The sacred banana leaf	398.2
Sierra, J. The gift of the Crocodile	398.2

Iraq

Henderson, K. Lugalbanda	398.2
Hickox, R. The golden sandal	398.2
Laird, E. A fistful of pearls	398.2
McCaughrean, G. The epic of Gilgamesh	398.2

Ireland

Bunting, E. Finn McCool and the great fish	398.2
Burns, B. The king with horse's ears and other Irish folktales	398.2
De Paola, T. Jamie O'Rourke and the big potato	398.2
Doyle, M. Tales from old Ireland	398.2
Krull, K. A pot o' gold	820.8
Milligan, B. Brigid's cloak	398.2
Souhami, J. Mrs. McCool and the giant Cuhullin	398.2

Italy

Langton, J. Saint Francis and the wolf	398.2
Sharpe, L. M. The goat-faced girl	398.2

Japan

Bodkin, O. The crane wife	398.2
Kajikawa, K. Tsunami!	398.2
Mosel, A. The funny little woman	398.2
Myers, T. The furry-legged teapot	398.2
Nishizuka, K. The beckoning cat	398.2
Partridge, E. Kogi's mysterious journey	398.2
Paterson, K. The tale of the mandarin ducks	398.2
Sakade, F. Japanese children's favorite stories	398.2
Sierra, J. Tasty baby belly buttons	398.2
Snyder, D. The boy of the three-year nap	398.2
Wada, S. Momotaro and the island of ogres	398.2

Korea

Climo, S. The Korean Cinderella	398.2
Ginsburg, M. The Chinese mirror	398.2
Han, S. C. The rabbit's tail	398.2
Heo, Y. The green frogs	398.2
Kim, S.-U. Korean children's favorite stories	398.2
McClure, G. The land of the dragon king and other Korean stories	398.2
Park, J. J. The love of two stars	398.2

Laos

Blia Xiong. Nine-in-one, Grr! Grr!	398.2

Latin America

Arroz con leche	782.42
Campoy, F. I. Tales our abuelitas told	398.2
De colores and other Latin-American folk songs for children	782.42
Delacre, L. Golden tales	398.2

Folklore—Latin America—*Continued*

Diez deditos. Ten little fingers & other play rhymes and action songs from Latin America **782.42**

González, L. M. Señor Cat's romance and other favorite stories from Latin America **398.2**

Martinez, R. Once upon a time **398.2**

Perl, L. Piñatas and paper flowers **394.26**

Tortillitas para mamá and other nursery rhymes **398.8**

Liberia

Paye, W.-L. Head, body, legs **398.2**

Paye, W.-L. Mrs. Chicken and the hungry crocodile **398.2**

Mali

Wagué Diakité, B. The magic gourd **398.2**

Wagué Diakité, B. Mee-An and the magic serpent **398.2**

Marshall Islands

MacDonald, M. R. Surf war! **398.2**

Martinique

San Souci, R. Cendrillon **398.2**

San Souci, R. The faithful friend **398.2**

Mexico

Aardema, V. Borreguita and the coyote **398.2**

Coburn, J. R. Domitila **398.2**

De Paola, T. Adelita **398.2**

De Paola, T. The legend of the poinsettia **398.2**

Ehlert, L. Cuckoo. Cucú **398.2**

Lowery, L. The tale of La Llorona **398.2**

McDermott, G. Musicians of the sun **398.2**

Morales, Y. Just a minute **398.2**

Philip, N. Horse hooves and chicken feet: Mexican folktales **398.2**

Ryan, P. M. Nacho and Lolita **398.2**

Middle East

Smith, C. One city, two brothers **398.2**

Young, E. What about me? **398.2**

Mongolia

Ōtsuka, Y. Suho's white horse **398.2**

Morocco

Fowles, S. The bachelor and the bean **398.2**

New England

Aylesworth, J. The tale of Tricky Fox **398.2**

De Paola, T. Tomie dePaola's front porch tales and North Country whoppers **398.2**

New Mexico

Lamadrid, E. R. Juan the bear and the water of life **398.2**

Nicaragua

Rohmer, H. Uncle Nacho's hat **398.2**

Nigeria

Dayrell, E. Why the Sun and the Moon live in the sky **398.2**

Gerson, M.-J. Why the sky is far away **398.2**

Norway

Brett, J. Who's that knocking on Christmas Eve **398.2**

D'Aulaire, I. The terrible troll-bird **398.2**

Galdone, P. The three Billy Goats Gruff **398.2**

Lunge-Larsen, L. The troll with no heart in his body and other tales of trolls from Norway **398.2**

Pakistan

L'Homme, E. Tales of a lost kingdom **398.2**

Panama

MacDonald, M. R. Conejito **398.2**

Peru

Ehlert, L. Moon rope. Un lazo a la luna **398.2**

Knutson, B. Love and roast chicken **398.2**

Philippines

Climo, S. Tuko and the birds **398.2**

Poland

Monte, R. The dragon of Krakow and other Polish stories **398.2**

Puerto Rico

Montes, M. Juan Bobo goes to work **398.2**

Romania

Rascol, S. I. The impudent rooster **398.2**

Russia

See also Folklore—Ukraine

Ginsburg, M. Clay boy **398.2**

Mayer, M. Baba Yaga and Vasilisa the brave **398.2**

McCaughrean, G. Grandma Chickenlegs **398.2**

Polacco, P. Luba and the wren **398.2**

Robbins, R. Baboushka and the three kings **398.2**

Shepard, A. The sea king's daughter **398.2**

Spirin, G. The tale of the Firebird **398.2**

Scotland

Lupton, H. Pirican Pic and Pirican Mor **398.2**

MacDonald, M. R. Too many fairies **398.2**

South Africa

Seeger, P. Abiyoyo **398.2**

South America

Bateman, T. The Frog with the Big Mouth **398.2**

Southern States

Bushyhead, R. H. Yonder mountain **398.2**

Chase, R. The Jack tales **398.2**

Curry, J. L. Hold up the sky: and other Native American tales from Texas and the Southern Plains **398.2**

Grandfather tales **398.2**

Salley, C. Epossumondas **398.2**

San Souci, R. Little Gold Star **398.2**

San Souci, R. Sister tricksters **398.2**

San Souci, R. The talking eggs **398.2**

Thomas, J. C. The three witches **398.2**

Thomas, J. C. What's the hurry, Fox? **398.2**

Wooldridge, C. N. Wicked Jack **398.2**

Spain

Martinez, R. Once upon a time **398.2**

Tibet (China)

Berger, B. All the way to Lhasa **398.2**

Rose, N. C. Tibetan tales from the top of the world **398.2**

Turkey

Demi. The hungry coat **398.2**

Johnson-Davies, D. Goha the wise fool **398.2**

Ukraine

Aylesworth, J. The mitten **398.2**

Brett, J. The mitten **398.2**

Foster home care—Fiction—*Continued*
  Shafer, A. The mailbox **Fic**
  Wolfson, J. Home, and other big, fat lies
    Fic
  Wolfson, J. What I call life **Fic**
  Woodson, J. Locomotion **Fic**
  Woodson, J. Peace, Locomotion **Fic**
Fotheringham, Edwin, 1965-
  (il) Corey, S. Mermaid Queen [biography of Annette Kellerman] **92**
  (il) Kerley, B. The extraordinary Mark Twain (according to Susy) **92**
  (il) Kerley, B. What to do about Alice? [biography of Alice Roosevelt Longworth] **92**
Found. Haddix, M. P. **Fic**
The **founders**. Fradin, D. B. **920**
The **foundling** and other tales of Prydain. Alexander, L. **S C**
Fountain, Joanna F.
  (ed) Cataloging correctly for kids. See Cataloging correctly for kids **025.3**
Four feet, two sandals. Williams, K. L. **E**
Four friends at Christmas. De Paola, T. **E**
Four-H guide to digital photography. See Johnson, D. 4-H guide to digital photography **775**
Four-H guide to raising chickens. See Kindschi, T. 4-H guide to raising chickens **636.5**
Four-H guide to training horses. See Bowers, N. 4-H guide to training horses **636.1**
Four perfect pebbles. Perl, L. **940.53**
Four seasons make a year. Rockwell, A. F. **E**
Fourth dimension
  See also Time travel
Fourth of July
  Heiligman, D. Celebrate Independence Day **394.26**
  Hess, D. The Fourth of July **394.26**
Fiction
  Wong, J. S. Apple pie 4th of July **E**
Fowles, Shelley
  The bachelor and the bean **398.2**
  (il) Laird, E. A fistful of pearls **398.2**
Fox, Annie, 1950-
  Real friends vs. the other kind **158**
Fox, Debbie, 1958-
  Good-bye bully machine **302.3**
Fox, F. G. (Frank G.)
  Jean Laffite and the big ol' whale **E**
Fox, Frank G. See Fox, F. G. (Frank G.)
Fox, Helen
  Eager **Fic**
Fox, Janet S.
  Get organized without losing it **371.3**
Fox, Karen
  Older than the stars **523.1**
Fox, Lee, 1958-
  Ella Kazoo will not brush her hair **E**
Fox, Mem, 1946-
  The goblin and the empty chair **E**
  Hattie and the fox **E**
  Hello baby! **E**
  Hunwick's egg **E**

  Koala Lou **E**
  Night noises **E**
  A particular cow **E**
  Reading magic **028.5**
  Sleepy bears **E**
  Sophie **E**
  Ten little fingers and ten little toes **E**
  Tough Boris **E**
  Where is the green sheep? **E**
  Where the giant sleeps **E**
  Wombat divine **E**
Fox, Merrion Frances See Fox, Mem, 1946-
Fox, Paula
  The slave dancer **Fic**
  The stone-faced boy **Fic**
  Traces **E**
Fox, Tom
  Snowball launchers, giant-pumpkin growers, and other cool contraptions **745.5**
Fox. Banks, K. **E**
Fox. Johnson, J. **599.77**
Fox and his friends. Marshall, E. **E**
The **fox** and the hen. Battut, E. **E**
Fox-Davies, Sarah
  (il) Davies, N. Bat loves the night **E**
  (il) Fisher, A. L. Do rabbits have Christmas? **811**
  (il) Waddell, M. Snow bears **E**
The **Fox** went out on a chilly night **782.42**
Foxes
  Johnson, J. Fox **599.77**
  Nobleman, M. T. Foxes **599.77**
  Person, S. Arctic fox **599.77**
Fiction
  Banks, K. Fox **E**
  Battut, E. The fox and the hen **E**
  Beha, E. Tango **Fic**
  Bergren, L. T. God found us you **E**
  Brun-Cosme, N. No, I want daddy! **E**
  Church, C. One smart goose **E**
  Cooney, B. Chanticleer and the fox **E**
  Fox, M. Hattie and the fox **E**
  Gliori, D. No matter what **E**
  Gliori, D. Stormy weather **E**
  Hutchins, P. Rosie's walk **E**
  Kasza, K. My lucky day **E**
  Keller, H. Nosy Rosie **E**
  Kvasnosky, L. M. Zelda and Ivy, the runaways **E**
  Leedy, L. Crazy like a fox **E**
  Marshall, E. Fox and his friends **E**
  McKissack, P. C. Flossie & the fox **E**
  Myers, T. Basho and the river stones **E**
  Nikola-Lisa, W. Setting the turkeys free **E**
  Palatini, M. Three French hens **E**
  Rankin, L. Ruthie and the (not so) teeny tiny lie **E**
  Rawlinson, J. Fletcher and the falling leaves **E**
  Rodriguez, B. The chicken thief **E**
  Rogan, S. J. The daring adventures of Penhaligon Brush **Fic**
  Waring, R. Hungry hen **E**
  Weston, C. If a chicken stayed for supper **E**
  Wormell, C. Henry and the fox **E**

Foxes—*Continued*
Folklore
Aylesworth, J. The tale of Tricky Fox   398.2
Hogrogian, N. One fine day   398.2
Knutson, B. Love and roast chicken   398.2
Palatini, M. Lousy rotten stinkin' grapes
   398.2
Graphic novels
Luciani, B. The meeting   741.5
Songs
The Fox went out on a chilly night   782.42
Foxie. D'Aulaire, I.   E
Fraction action. Leedy, L.   513
Fraction fun. Adler, D. A.   513
Fractions
Adler, D. A. Fraction fun   513
Adler, D. A. Fractions, decimals, and percents
   513
Dodds, D. A. Full house   513
Leedy, L. Fraction action   513
Long, L. Fabulous fractions   513
Murphy, S. J. Jump, kangaroo, jump!   513
Nagda, A. W. Polar bear math   513
Fiction
Napoli, D. J. The Wishing Club   E
Fractions, decimals, and percents. Adler, D. A.
   513
Fractures
Cobb, V. Your body battles a broken bone
   617.1
Landau, E. Broken bones   617.1
Fradin, Dennis B.
The Alamo   976.4
The Boston Tea Party   973.3
The Declaration of Independence   973.3
Duel!   973.4
The founders   920
Ida B. Wells   92
Let it begin here!   973.3
Nicolaus Copernicus   92
Samuel Adams   92
September 11, 2001   973.931
The signers   920
With a little luck   509
(jt. auth) Fradin, J. B. Droughts   363.34
(jt. auth) Fradin, J. B. Earthquakes   551.2
(jt. auth) Fradin, J. B. Hurricane Katrina
   363.34
(jt. auth) Fradin, J. B. Hurricanes   551.55
(jt. auth) Fradin, J. B. Tsunamis   551.46
(jt. auth) Fradin, J. B. Volcanoes   551.2
Fradin, Judith Bloom
Droughts   363.34
Earthquakes   551.2
Hurricane Katrina   363.34
Hurricanes   551.55
Tsunamis   551.46
Volcanoes   551.2
(jt. auth) Fradin, D. B. Ida B. Wells   92
Frame, Jeron Ashford
Yesterday I had the blues   E
Framed. Cottrell Boyce, F.   Fic
Frampton, David
Mr. Ferlinghetti's poem   811

(il) Fleischman, P. Bull Run   Fic
(il) Grimes, N. At Jerusalem's gate   811
Frampton, Otis
Oddly Normal   741.5
France
NgCheong-Lum, R. France   944
Tidmarsh, C. France   944
Colonies
Englar, M. French colonies in America
   970.01
Fiction
Banks, K. The cat who walked across France
   E
Hartnett, S. The silver donkey   Fic
Holmes, M. T. A giraffe goes to Paris   E
Ichikawa, S. Come fly with me   E
Knight, J. Charlotte in Giverny   Fic
McCaughrean, G. The death-defying Pepper
Roux   Fic
Morpurgo, M. Waiting for Anya   Fic
Mourlevat, J.-C. The pull of the ocean   Fic
Polacco, P. The butterfly   Fic
Rappaport, D. The secret seder   E
Wells, R. The miraculous tale of the two Maries
   E
Wilson, S. The day we danced in underpants
   E
Wright, J. The secret circus   E
Folklore
See Folklore—France
History—0-1328
Kramer, A. Eleanor of Aquitaine   92
History—1328-1589, House of Valois
Hodges, M. Joan of Arc   92
Stanley, D. Joan of Arc   92
Wilkinson, P. Joan of Arc   92
History—1789-1799, Revolution
Riggs, K. The French Revolution   944.04
History—1789-1799, Revolution—Fiction
Bradley, K. B. The lacemaker and the princess
   Fic
History—1799-1815
Burleigh, R. Napoleon   92
History—1940-1945, German occupation
Ruelle, K. G. The grand mosque of Paris
   940.53
History—Graphic novels
Goscinny. Asterix the Gaul   741.5
Kings and rulers
Burleigh, R. Napoleon   92
St. George, J. Zarafa   599.63
Francie. English, K.   Fic
Francis, of Assisi, Saint, 1182-1226
About
Kennedy, R. F. Saint Francis of Assisi   271
Visconti, G. Clare and Francis   271
Fiction
De Paola, T. The song of Francis   E
Gibfried, D. Brother Juniper   E
Legends
Egielski, R. Saint Francis and the wolf
   398.2
Langton, J. Saint Francis and the wolf
   398.2

Francis, Guy
(il) Ryder, J. Dance by the light of the moon
    E
Franck, Irene M.
(jt. auth) Brownstone, D. M. Frontier America
    973.03
Franco
(jt. auth) Baltazar, A. Tiny Titans: welcome to
    the treehouse   **741.5**
Franco, Betsy
Bees, snails, and peacock tails shapes—naturally
    811
Bird songs   E
A curious collection of cats   **811**
Messing around on the monkey bars   **811**
Pond circle   E
Zero is the leaves on the tree   **513**
Frank, Anne, 1929-1945
The diary of a young girl: the definitive edition
    92
About
Hurwitz, J. Anne Frank: life in hiding   **92**
Metselaar, M. Anne Frank: her life in words and
    pictures   **92**
Poole, J. Anne Frank   **92**
Rol, R. v. d. Anne Frank, beyond the diary
    92
Frank, John
How to catch a fish   E
Keepers   **811**
Frank, Otto, 1889-1980
(ed) Frank, A. The diary of a young girl: the de-
    finitive edition   **92**
Frankenstein makes a sandwich. Rex, A.   **811**
Frankenstein takes the cake. Rex, A.   **811**
Frankfurters
Sylver, A. Hot diggity dog   **641.3**
Frankie Pickle and the closet of doom. Wight, E.
    741.5
Frankie works the night shift. Peters, L. W.   E
Frankland, David
(il) Lisle, J. T. Highway cats   Fic
Franklin, Benjamin, 1706-1790
About
Adler, D. A. B. Franklin, printer   **92**
Barretta, G. Now & Ben   **609**
Fleming, C. Ben Franklin's almanac   **92**
Fritz, J. What's the big idea, Ben Franklin?
    92
Harness, C. The remarkable Benjamin Franklin
    92
McCurdy, M. So said Ben [biography of Benja-
    min Franklin]   **92**
Miller, B. M. Benjamin Franklin, American ge-
    nius   **92**
Rushby, P. Ben Franklin   **92**
Fiction
Fleming, C. The hatmaker's sign   E
Lawson, R. Ben and me   Fic
See/See also pages in the following book(s):
Smith, L. John, Paul, George & Ben   E
Franklin, Sir John, 1786-1847
About
Beattie, O. Buried in ice   **998**

Franklin, Patricia, 1951-
(jt. auth) Stephens, C. G. Library 101   **027.8**
Franklin Delano Roosevelt for kids. Panchyk, R.
    92
Franklin's big dreams. Teague, D.   E
Franny Parker. McKinnon, H. R.   Fic
Franny's friends. Kruusval, C.   E
Franson, Leanne, 1963-
(il) Roberts, K. Thumb on a diamond   Fic
Franson, Scott E.
Un-brella   E
Fraser, Mary Ann
How animal babies stay safe   **591.56**
Pet shop lullaby   E
Where are the night animals?   **591.5**
Frasier, Debra, 1953-
A birthday cake is no ordinary cake   E
On the day you were born   E
Frattini, Stéphane
(jt. auth) Tenzing Norbu. Secret of the snow
    leopard   E
Fraud
Hoaxed!   **500**
Spilsbury, R. Counterfeit!   **363.2**
Fiction
Curtis, C. P. Bucking the Sarge   Fic
Fraud, Computer *See* Computer crimes
Frazee, Marla, 1958-
A couple of boys have the best week ever
    E
Roller coaster   E
Santa Claus, the world's number one toy expert
    E
Walk on!   E
(il) Hush, little baby. See Hush, little baby
    782.42
(il) Meyers, S. Everywhere babies   E
(il) Pennypacker, S. Clementine   Fic
(il) Scanlon, L. G. All the world   **811**
Frazier, Craig, 1955-
Hank finds inspiration   E
(il) Lyon, G. E. Trucks roll!   E
Frazier, Sundee Tucker, 1968-
Brendan Buckley's universe and everything in it
    Fic
Freaky-big airplanes. Goldish, M.   **629.13**
Freaky facts [series]
Morley, C. Freaky facts about spiders   **595.4**
Seuling, B. Cows sweat through their noses
    590
Seuling, B. Your skin weighs more than your
    brain   **612**
Freaky facts about spiders. Morley, C.   **595.4**
Freaky flowers. Souza, D. M.   **582.13**
Freaky Friday. Rodgers, M.   Fic
Freckle juice. Blume, J.   Fic
Fred stays with me. Coffelt, N.   E
Frederick, Heather Vogel
The voyage of Patience Goodspeed   Fic
Frederick. Lionni, L.   E
Frederick Finch, loudmouth. Weaver, T.   E

Frederick-Frost, Alexis
   (il) Anderson, M. Explore spring! 508.2
   (il) Anderson, M. Explore winter! 508.2
   (jt. auth) Sturm, J. Adventures in cartooning
   741.5
Fredericks, Anthony D.
   African legends, myths, and folktales for readers
   theatre 812
Fredericks, Karen
   (il) Wyatt, V. How to build your own country
   320.4
Free at last!. Rappaport, D. 305.8
Free baseball. Corbett, S. Fic
Free fall. Wiesner, D. E
Free within ourselves. Bishop, R. S. 028.5
Freedman, Claire
   Gooseberry Goose E
Freedman, Florence B. (Florence Bernstein)
   (jt. auth) Engel, D. Ezra Jack Keats 92
Freedman, Russell
   The adventures of Marco Polo 92
   Babe Didrikson Zaharias 92
   Buffalo hunt 970.004
   Children of the Great Depression 305.23
   Children of the wild West 978
   Confucius 92
   Eleanor Roosevelt 92
   Franklin Delano Roosevelt 92
   Freedom walkers 323.1
   Give me liberty! 973.3
   Immigrant kids 325.73
   In the days of the vaqueros 636.2
   Indian chiefs 920
   An Indian winter 978
   Kids at work 331.3
   Lincoln: a photobiography 92
   Out of darkness: the story of Louis Braille
   92
   The voice that challenged a nation [biography of
   Marian Anderson] 92
   Washington at Valley Forge 973.3
   The Wright brothers: how they invented the air-
   plane 92
   (jt. auth) Bad Heart Buffalo, A. The life and
   death of Crazy Horse 92
Freedom, Academic See Academic freedom
Freedom marches for civil rights See Civil rights
   demonstrations
Freedom of information
      See also Censorship
   Adams, H. R. Ensuring intellectual freedom and
   access to information in the school library
   media program 027.8
Freedom on the menu. Weatherford, C. B. E
Freedom Riders. Bausum, A. 323.1
Freedom river [biography of John P. Parker]
   Rappaport, D. 92
Freedom ship. Rappaport, D. Fic
Freedom struggle. Rossi, A. 973.7
Freedom Summer. Wiles, D. E
Freedom walkers. Freedman, R. 323.1
Freeman, Don, 1908-1978
   Corduroy E

Earl the squirrel E
Quiet! there's a canary in the library E
Freeman, Evelyn B.
   Children's books in children's hands. See Chil-
   dren's books in children's hands 028.5
Freeman, Judy
   Books kids will sit still for 3 011.6
Freeman, Laura
   (il) English, K. Nikki & Deja Fic
Freeman, Martha, 1956-
   Mrs. Wow never wanted a cow E
   The trouble with cats Fic
   Who stole Halloween? Fic
Freeze frame. Macy, S. 796.98
French, Jackie, 1950-
   Diary of a wombat E
   How to scratch a wombat 599.2
   Pete the sheep-sheep E
   Rover Fic
French, Martin
   (il) Miller, N. Stompin' at the Savoy [biography
   of Norma Miller] 92
French, Paul See Asimov, Isaac, 1920-1992
French, Vivian
   The Daddy Goose treasury E
   Henny Penny 398.2
   T. Rex 567.9
   Yucky worms E
French Americans
   Englar, M. French colonies in America
   970.01
French and Indian War See United States—His-
   tory—1755-1763, French and Indian War
French artists See Artists, French
French Cameroons See Cameroon
French Canadians
   Englar, M. French colonies in America
   970.01
French colonies in America. Englar, M.
   970.01
French language
      Dictionaries
   Corbeil, J.-C. My first French English visual
   dictionary 443
   Kudela, K. R. My first book of French words
   443
French painting
   Sellier, M. Renoir's colors 759.05
French poetry
   Cendrars, B. Shadow 841
The **French** Revolution. Riggs, K. 944.04
Fresco painting See Mural painting and decora-
   tion
Freshwater animals
   Aliki. My visit to the aquarium 639.34
   Hodge, D. Wetland animals 591.7
Freshwater ecology
   Arnosky, J. The brook book 577.6
   Hooks, G. Freshwater feeders 577.6
   Johansson, P. Lakes and rivers 577.6
   Toupin, L. Freshwater habitats 577.6
Freshwater feeders. Hooks, G. 577.6

Friendship—Fiction—*Continued*

Konigsburg, E. L. The view from Saturday	
	Fic
Koss, A. G. The girls	**Fic**
Krumgold, J. Onion John	**Fic**
Kurtz, J. The storyteller's beads	**Fic**
Lacombe, B. Cherry and Olive	**E**
LaFleur, S. M. Love, Aubrey	**Fic**
Lasky, K. Poodle and Hound	**E**
Leist, C. Jack the bear	**E**
Levine, K. The best bad luck I ever had	
	Fic
Lieshout, M. v. Bloom!	**E**
Lionni, L. Little blue and little yellow	**E**
Lisle, J. T. Afternoon of the elves	**Fic**
Lombard, J. Drita, my homegirl	**Fic**
Long, E. Bird & Birdie in a fine day	**E**
Lopez, D. Confetti girl	**Fic**
Lovelace, M. H. Betsy-Tacy	**Fic**
Lowry, L. Autumn Street	**Fic**
Lowry, L. Number the stars	**Fic**
Mackel, K. MadCat	**Fic**
Marino, N. Neil Armstrong is my uncle	**Fic**
Marsden, C. Moon runner	**Fic**
Marsden, C. Take me with you	**Fic**
Marshall, J. George and Martha	**E**
Martin, A. M. A corner of the universe	**Fic**
Mass, W. 11 birthdays	**Fic**
Mass, W. Every soul a star	**Fic**
Mazer, N. F. Ten ways to make my sister disappear	**Fic**
McGhee, A. Snap	**Fic**
McPhail, D. M. Sylvie & True	**E**
McQuinn, A. My friend Jamal	**E**
McQuinn, A. My friend Mei Jing	**E**
Michelin, L. Zuzu's wishing cake	**E**
Michelson, R. Across the alley	**E**
Millard, G. The naming of Tishkin Silk	**Fic**
Morgan, N. Chicken friend	**Fic**
Murphy, P. The wild girls	**Fic**
Myracle, L. Eleven	**Fic**
Myracle, L. Luv ya bunches	**Fic**
Naylor, P. R. Patches and scratches	**Fic**
Naylor, P. R. Starting with Alice	**Fic**
Nesbø, J. Doctor Proctor's fart powder	**Fic**
Nielsen, S. Word nerd	**Fic**
O'Connor, B. The small adventure of Popeye and Elvis	**Fic**
O'Dell, K. Agnes Parker . . . girl in progress	**Fic**
Paros, J. Violet Bing and the Grand House	**Fic**
Paterson, K. Bridge to Terabithia	**Fic**
Patt, B. Best friends forever	**Fic**
Pennypacker, S. Clementine	**Fic**
Perkins, L. R. All alone in the universe	**Fic**
Perkins, L. R. The cardboard piano	**E**
Polacco, P. Chicken Sunday	**E**
Polacco, P. The Lemonade Club	**E**
Polacco, P. Mrs. Katz and Tush	**E**
Polacco, P. Pink and Say	**E**
Preus, M. The Peace Bell	**E**
Primavera, E. Louise the big cheese: divine diva	**E**
Rania, Queen, consort of Abdullah, King of Jordan. The sandwich swap	**E**
Raschka, C. Yo! Yes?	**E**

Reiser, L. My way	**E**
Resau, L. Star in the forest	**Fic**
Robbins, J. The new girl . . . and me	**E**
Robbins, J. Two of a kind	**E**
Roberts, M. Sunny side up	**Fic**
Rodman, M. A. My best friend	**E**
Rohmann, E. My friend Rabbit	**E**
Root, P. Toot toot zoom!	**E**
Rosenthal, M. Archie and the pirates	**E**
Rosoff, M. Jumpy Jack and Googily	**E**
Ross, P. Meet M and M	**E**
Roy, J. Max Quigley	**Fic**
Rumford, J. Tiger and turtle	**E**
Runholt, S. The mystery of the third Lucretia	**Fic**
Russell, N. Moon rabbit	**E**
Russo, M. A very big bunny	**E**
Rylant, C. A fine white dust	**Fic**
Rylant, C. Poppleton	**E**
Sachar, L. Holes	**Fic**
Schertle, A. Little Blue Truck	**E**
Schlitz, L. A. The night fairy	**Fic**
Schwartz, A. Tiny and Hercules	**E**
Scotton, R. Splat the cat	**E**
Seabrooke, B. Wolf pie	**Fic**
Seeger, L. V. Dog and Bear: two friends, three stories	**E**
Shaw, H. Sneaky weasel	**E**
Shimko, B. The private thoughts of Amelia E. Rye	**Fic**
Shirley, D. Best friend on wheels	**E**
Shreve, S. R. Under the Watsons' porch	**Fic**
Siminovich, L. Alex and Lulu: two of a kind	**E**
Simmons, J. Together	**E**
Sklansky, A. E. The duck who played the kazoo	**E**
Smith, D. B. A taste of blackberries	**Fic**
Sonnenblick, J. After ever after	**Fic**
Speare, E. G. The sign of the beaver	**Fic**
Spinelli, J. Crash	**Fic**
St. Anthony, J. The summer Sherman loved me	**Fic**
Stanley, D. Goldie and the three bears	**E**
Stauffacher, S. Donuthead	**Fic**
Stellings, C. The contest	**Fic**
Stier, C. The terrible secrets of the Tell-All Club	**Fic**
Stone, P. Deep down popular	**Fic**
Sutton, J. Don't call me Sidney	**E**
Sydor, C. Timmerman was here	**E**
Tacang, B. Bully-be-gone	**Fic**
Tarlow, E. Pinwheel days	**E**
Tarshis, L. Emma-Jean Lazarus fell out of a tree	**Fic**
Tingle, T. Crossing Bok Chitto	**Fic**
Tolan, S. S. Wishworks, Inc.	**Fic**
Townsend, M. Kit Feeny: on the move	
	741.5
Tracy, K. Camille McPhee fell under the bus	**Fic**
Uchida, Y. The bracelet	**E**
Varennes, M. d. The jewel box ballerinas	**E**
Waber, B. Evie & Margie	**E**
Waber, B. Ira sleeps over	**E**
Warnes, T. Chalk and Cheese	**E**
Watson, S. E. Elvis & Olive	**Fic**

Frogs—*Continued*

Firestone, M. What's the difference between a frog and a toad? **597.8**
Gibbons, G. Frogs **597.8**
Goldish, M. Amazing water frogs **597.8**
Hamilton, G. Frog rescue **597.8**
Haney, J. Frogs **639.3**
Johnson, J. Frog **597.8**
Lunis, N. Tricky tree frogs **597.8**
Magloff, L. Frog **597.8**
Markle, S. Hip-pocket papa **597.8**
Markle, S. Slippery, slimy baby frogs **597.8**
Moffett, M. W. Face to face with frogs **597.8**
Pfeffer, W. From tadpole to frog **597.8**
Schwabacher, M. Frogs **597.8**
Stewart, M. A place for frogs **597.8**
Turner, P. S. The frog scientist **597.8**
Wechsler, D. Frog heaven **577.6**
Whiting, J. Frogs in danger **597.8**
Winer, Y. Frogs sing songs **597.8**

Fiction

Anderson, P. P. Joe on the go **E**
Arnold, T. Green Wilma, frog in space **E**
Asch, F. Baby Bird's first nest **E**
Beiser, T. Bradley McGogg, the very fine frog **E**
Billout, G. The frog who wanted to see the sea **E**
Breen, S. Stick **E**
Byrd, T. Doc Wilde and the frogs of doom **Fic**
Cowley, J. Red-eyed tree frog **E**
Cyrus, K. Tadpole Rex **E**
De Paola, T. Four friends at Christmas **E**
Donovan, G. In loving memory of Gorfman T. Frog **Fic**
Fearnley, J. Martha in the middle **E**
Gorbachev, V. Ms. Turtle the babysitter **E**
Gravett, E. Spells **E**
Hurd, T. Bad frogs **E**
Kalan, R. Jump, frog, jump! **E**
Leedy, L. The great graph contest **E**
Lionni, L. Fish is fish **E**
Lobel, A. Frog and Toad are friends **E**
London, J. Froggy learns to swim **E**
Mayer, M. A boy, a dog, and a frog **E**
Mora, P. Wiggling pockets **E**
Napoli, D. J. The prince of the pond **Fic**
Potter, B. The tale of Mr. Jeremy Fisher **E**
Scieszka, J. The Frog Prince continued **E**
Tashiro, C. Five nice mice **E**
Thomas, J. Can you make a scary face? **E**
Wiesner, D. Tuesday **E**
Willems, M. Big Frog can't fit in **E**
Willems, M. City Dog, Country Frog **E**
Wilson, K. A frog in the bog **E**
Yang, B. Foo, the flying frog of Washtub Pond **E**
Yolen, J. Dimity Duck **E**

Folklore

Bateman, T. The Frog with the Big Mouth **398.2**
Heo, Y. The green frogs **398.2**
Kimmel, E. A. The frog princess **398.2**

Poetry

Lobel, A. The frogs and toads all sang **811**

Songs

Langstaff, J. M. Frog went a-courtin' **782.42**
The **frogs** and toads all sang. Lobel, A. **811**
Frogs in danger. Whiting, J. **597.8**
Frogs sing songs. Winer, Y. **597.8**
The **frogs** wore red suspenders. Prelutsky, J. **811**

From Alice to Zen and everyone in between. Atkinson, E. **Fic**
From bean to bean plant. Ganeri, A. **583**
From boneshakers to choppers. Smedman, L. **629.227**
From caterpillar to butterfly. Heiligman, D. **595.7**
From cover to cover. Baxter, K. A. **028.1**
From dawn to dreams. Archer, P. **811**
From egg to butterfly. Knudsen, S. **595.7**
From pictures to words. Stevens, J. **741.6**
From rags to riches. Sills, L. **391**
From reader to writer. Ellis, S. **372.6**
From Russia with lunch. Hale, B. **Fic**
From seed to apple. Ganeri, A. **583**
From seed to pumpkin. Pfeffer, W. **583**
From seed to sunflower. Ganeri, A. **583**
From slave ship to freedom road. Lester, J. **326**
From slave to soldier. Hopkinson, D. **E**
From tadpole to frog. Pfeffer, W. **597.8**
From the bellybutton of the moon and other summer poems. Alarcón, F. X. **811**

From the highly scientific notebooks of Phineas L. MacGuire [series]
Dowell, F. O. Phineas L. Macguire erupts! **Fic**

From the mixed-up files of Mrs. Basil E. Frankweiler. Konigsburg, E. L. **Fic**

Frontera, Antonio
(jt. auth) Canfield, J. Chicken soup for the soul: kids in the kitchen **641.5**

Frontier America. Brownstone, D. M. **973.03**

Frontier and pioneer life
Anderson, W. T. Pioneer girl: the story of Laura Ingalls Wilder **92**
Berne, E. C. Laura Ingalls Wilder **92**
Friedman, M. The Oregon Trail **978**
Greenwood, B. A pioneer sampler **971.3**
Hailstone, R. The white ox **92**
Halpern, M. Railroad fever **385.09**
Harness, C. The tragic tale of Narcissa Whitman and a faithful history of the Oregon Trail **92**
Kellogg, S. Johnny Appleseed **92**
Lowery, L. Aunt Clara Brown **92**
Moses, W. Johnny Appleseed **92**
Nelson, V. M. Bad news for outlaws **92**
Olson, T. How to get rich on the Oregon Trail **978**
Spradlin, M. P. Daniel Boone's great escape **92**
Spradlin, M. P. Texas Rangers **976.4**
Steele, C. Famous wagon trails **978**

Fuji, Machiko
The big adventures of Majoko, volume 1
741.5

Fujiwara, Murasaki *See* Murasaki Shikibu, b. 978?

Fujiwara, Yumiko
Honey **638**

Fukuda, Toyofumi
(il) Komiya, T. Life-size zoo **590**

The **full** belly bowl. Aylesworth, J. **E**

Full, full, full of love. Cooke, T. **E**

Full house. Dodds, D. A. **513**

Fuller, Barbara, 1961-
Germany **943**

Fulton, Robert, 1765-1815
About
Herweck, D. Robert Fulton **92**

Fun holiday crafts kids can do [series]
Bledsoe, K. E. Chinese New Year crafts
745.594
Gnojewski, C. Cinco de Mayo crafts
745.594

Fun with Chinese cooking. Lee, F. **641.5**

Fun with Roman numerals. Adler, D. A. **513**

Fundamental life skills *See* Life skills

Fundamentalism and evolution *See* Creationism

Fundamentals of children's services. Sullivan, M.
027.62

Funeral directors *See* Undertakers and undertaking

Funeral rites and ceremonies
Sloan, C. Bury the dead **393**
Fiction
Bartek, M. Funerals & fly fishing **Fic**
Howe, J. Kaddish for Grandpa in Jesus' name, amen **E**

Funerals & fly fishing. Bartek, M. **Fic**

Fungi
See also Mushrooms
Wearing, J. Fungi **579**

Funke, Cornelia Caroline
Dragon rider **Fic**
Igraine the brave **Fic**
Inkheart **Fic**
The princess knight **E**
Princess Pigsty **E**
The wildest brother **E**

Funky junk. Schwarz, R. **745.5**

Funnies *See* Comic books, strips, etc.

Funny business **920**

Funny cartooning for kids. Artell, M. **741.5**

Funny Farm. Teague, M. **E**

Funny Frank. King-Smith, D. **Fic**

The **funny** little woman. Mosel, A. **398.2**

Funston, Sylvia
Dino–why? **567.9**
It's all in your head **612.8**

Fuoco, Gina Dal
Earth **333.72**

Fuqua, Jonathon Scott
Darby **Fic**

Fur
Higginson, M. Feathers and fur **591.47**

Furgang, Adam
Searching online for image, audio, and video files **025.04**

Furrow, Robert, 1985-
(jt. auth) Napoli, D. J. Sly the Sleuth and the pet mysteries **Fic**

Furry ferrets. Lunis, N. **636.97**

The **furry-legged** teapot. Myers, T. **398.2**

Fusco Castaldo, Nancy, 1962-
Pizza for the queen **E**
Rainforests **577.3**
River wild **577.6**

Future life
Folklore
Boughn, M. Into the world of the dead
398.2

Future tech. Piddock, C. **600**

Futurology *See* Forecasting

G

G.I.'s *See* Soldiers—United States

G is for goat. Polacco, P. **E**

G is for googol. Schwartz, D. M. **510**

Gaber, Susan
(il) Forest, H. The contest between the Sun and the Wind **398.2**
(il) Forest, H. The little red hen **398.2**
(il) Macken, J. E. Waiting out the storm **E**
(il) Silverman, E. Raisel's riddle **398.2**
(il) Van Laan, N. When winter comes **E**

Gable, Brian, 1949-
(il) Cleary, B. P. The action of subtraction
513
(il) Cleary, B. P. But and for, yet and nor
425
(il) Cleary, B. P. How long or how wide?
530.8
(il) Cleary, B. P. How much can a bare bear bear? **428**
(il) Cleary, B. P. I and you and don't forget who **428**
(il) Cleary, B. P. Lazily, crazily, just a bit nasally **428**
(il) Cleary, B. P. On the scale **530.8**
(il) Cleary, B. P. Quirky, jerky, extra-perky
428
(il) Cleary, B. P. Stop and go, yes and no
428
(il) Cleary, B. P. Stroll and walk, babble and talk **428**

Gabriel, Andrea
(il) Blomgren, J. Where do I sleep? **E**

Gabrielson, Curt
Stomp rockets, catapults, and kaleidoscopes
507.8

Gaff, Jackie
Looking at earth **550**
Looking at growing up **612.6**
Looking at solids, liquids, and gases **530**

Gaff. Correa, S. **Fic**

Gardening for kids—*Continued*

Bearce, S. A kid's guide to making a terrarium
635.9

Harkins, S. S. Design your own butterfly garden
638

Gardens

See also Butterfly gardens

Rissman, R. Shapes in the garden   **516**

Serafini, F. Looking closely inside the garden
578.7

Fiction

Aliki. Quiet in the garden   **E**

Arnold, C. Wiggle and Waggle   **E**

Brenner, B. Good morning, garden   **E**

Brown, P. The curious garden   **E**

Burnett, F. H. The secret garden   **Fic**

Davis, N. A garden of opposites   **E**

Fleischman, P. Seedfolks   **Fic**

Gershator, P. Sky sweeper   **E**

Henkes, K. My garden   **E**

Ichikawa, S. La La Rose   **E**

Larsen, A. The imaginary garden   **E**

Quattlebaum, M. Jackson Jones and Mission
Greentop   **Fic**

Reynolds, P. Rose's garden   **E**

Yaccarino, D. Lawn to lawn   **E**

Poetry

Havill, J. I heard it from Alice Zucchini
811

Mannis, C. D. One leaf rides the wind   **E**

Songs

Mallett, D. Inch by inch   **782.42**

Gardiner, John Reynolds, 1944-2006

Stone Fox   **Fic**

Gardiner, Lindsey, 1971-

(il) Ormerod, J. If you're happy and you know
it!   **E**

Gardiner, Lynton

(il) Murdoch, D. H. North American Indian
970.004

Gardner, Lyn

Into the woods   **Fic**

Gardner, Robert, 1929-

Ace your animal science project   **590.7**

Ace your chemistry science project   **540.7**

Ace your ecology and environmental science
project   **577**

Ace your exercise and nutrition science project:
great science fair ideas   **613**

Ace your food science project   **664**

Ace your forces and motion science project
531

Ace your human biology science project
612

Ace your math and measuring science project
530.8

Ace your physical science project   **530**

Ace your plant science project   **580.7**

Ace your science project about the senses
612.8

Ace your science project using chemistry magic
and toys   **540.7**

Ace your space science project   **520**

Ace your weather science project   **551.5**

Dazzling science projects with light and color
535

Earth-shaking science projects about planet
Earth   **550**

Easy genius science projects with chemistry
540.7

Easy genius science projects with electricity and
magnetism   **537**

Easy genius science projects with temperature
and heat   **536**

Easy genius science projects with weather
551.5

Energizing science projects with electricity and
magnetism   **537**

Far-out science projects about Earth's sun and
moon   **523**

Far-out science projects with height and depth
530.8

Heavy-duty science projects with weight
530.8

It's about time! Science projects   **529**

Jazzy science projects with sound and music
534

Melting, freezing, and boiling science projects
with matter   **530.4**

Really hot science projects with temperature
536

Science project ideas about trees   **582.16**

Science projects about physics in the home
530

Sensational science projects with simple machines   **621.8**

Sizzling science projects with heat and energy
536

Slam dunk! science projects with basketball
530

Smashing science projects about Earth's rocks
and minerals   **552**

Split-second science projects with speed   **531**

Stellar science projects about Earth's sky
551.5

Super science projects about Earth's soil and
water   **631.4**

Super-sized science projects with volume
530.8

Wild science projects about Earth's weather
551.5

(jt. auth) Goodstein, M. Ace your sports science
project   **507.8**

Gareth (Legendary character)

Hodges, M. The kitchen knight   **398.2**

Gareth Stevens vital science: life science [series]

Somervill, B. A. The human body   **612**

Gareth Stevens vital science: physical science
[series]

Claybourne, A. The nature of matter   **530.4**

Garfield, James A., 1831-1881

See/See also pages in the following book(s):

St. George, J. In the line of fire   **364.1**

Garfield: 30 years of laughs & lasagna. Davis, J.
741.5

Gargoyles, girders, & glass houses. Zaunders, B.
720.9

Garland, Sherry, 1948-

The buffalo soldier   **E**

Gentieu, Penny
(il) Reiser, L. My baby and me   **E**

Gentle Ben. Morey, W.   **Fic**

Gentle reads. McDaniel, D.   **028.5**

The **Gentleman** Bug. Hector, J.   **E**

Gentle's Holler. Madden, K.   **Fic**

Geographic names
Fiction
Raschka, C. New York is English, Chattanooga is Creek   **E**

Geographical distribution of people See Human geography

Geography
    See also Maps; Voyages and travels
Bednar, S. Flags of the world   **929.9**
Cunha, S. F. National Geographic Bee   **910**
Jenkins, S. Hottest, coldest, highest, deepest   **910**
Rockwell, A. F. Our earth   **910**
Dictionaries
The World Book encyclopedia of people and places   **910.3**
Encyclopedias
Gifford, C. The Kingfisher geography encyclopedia   **910.3**
Junior Worldmark encyclopedia of the nations   **910.3**
Fiction
Shulevitz, U. How I learned geography   **E**
Poetry
Got geography!   **811.008**

Geography, Historical See Historical geography

Geology
Blobaum, C. Geology rocks!   **551**
Cole, J. The magic school bus inside the Earth   **551.1**
Gibbons, G. Planet earth/inside out   **550**
Zoehfeld, K. W. How mountains are made   **551.4**

Geology rocks!. Blobaum, C.   **551**

Geology rocks! [series]
Faulkner, R. Fossils   **560**
Faulkner, R. Igneous rock   **552**
Faulkner, R. Metamorphic rock   **552**
Faulkner, R. Sedimentary rock   **552**

Geometric patterns See Patterns (Mathematics)

Geometry
    See also Shape; Volume (Cubic content)
Adler, D. A. Shape up!   **516**
Murphy, S. J. Captain Invincible and the space shapes   **516**
Olson, N. Cones   **516**
Olson, N. Cubes   **516**
Olson, N. Cylinders   **516**
Olson, N. Pyramids   **516**
Olson, N. Spheres   **516**
Sullivan, N. Area, distance, and volume   **516**
VanCleave, J. P. Janice VanCleave's geometry for every kid   **516**

Geophysics
Gardner, R. Earth-shaking science projects about planet Earth   **550**

George III, King of Great Britain, 1738-1820
About
Fritz, J. Can't you make them behave, King George? [biography of George III, King of Great Britain]   **92**
Schanzer, R. George vs. George   **973.3**

George, Saint, d. 303
About
Hodges, M. Saint George and the dragon   **398.2**

George, Charles, 1949-
What makes me a Buddhist?   **294.3**
What makes me a Hindu?   **294.5**
What makes me a Mormon?   **289.3**

George, Craig See George, John Craighead

George, Jean Craighead, 1919-
The buffalo are back   **599.64**
The cats of Roxville Station   **Fic**
Charlie's raven   **Fic**
Everglades   **975.9**
Goose and Duck   **E**
How to talk to your cat   **636.8**
How to talk to your dog   **636.7**
Julie   **Fic**
Julie of the wolves   **Fic**
Luck   **E**
Morning, noon, and night   **E**
My side of the mountain trilogy   **Fic**
Nutik, the wolf pup   **E**
Pocket guide to the outdoors   **796.5**
A tarantula in my purse   **92**
There's an owl in the shower   **Fic**
The wolves are back   **599.77**

George, John Craighead
About
Lourie, P. Whaling season   **599.5**

George, Kristine O'Connell
Book!   **E**
Fold me a poem   **811**
The great frog race and other poems   **811**
Hummingbird nest   **E**
Little Dog and Duncan   **811**
Little dog poems   **811**
Old Elm speaks   **811**
Toasting marshmallows   **811**
Up!   **E**

George, Lindsay Barrett
In the woods: who's been here?   **E**
Inside mouse, outside mouse   **E**
Maggie's ball   **E**
(il) George, W. T. Box Turtle at Long Pond   **E**
(il) Schaefer, L. M. Pick, pull, snap!   **582**

George, Twig C., 1950-
Seahorses   **597**

George, William T.
Box Turtle at Long Pond   **E**

George and Martha. Marshall, J.   **E**

George and the dragon. Wormell, C.   **E**

George Crum and the Saratoga chip. Taylor, G.   **92**

George did it [biography of George Washington] Jurmain, S.   **92**

George shrinks. Joyce, W.   **E**

Ghost stories—*Continued*

Hearne, B. G. Hauntings, and other tales of danger, love, and sometimes loss **S C**

Ibbotson, E. The beasts of Clawstone Castle **Fic**

Ibbotson, E. Dial-a-ghost **Fic**

Irving, W. The Legend of Sleepy Hollow **Fic**

Kehret, P. The ghost's grave **Fic**

Kimmel, E. C. School spirit **Fic**

Klise, K. Dying to meet you **Fic**

Kohara, K. Ghosts in the house! **E**

Lowery, L. The tale of La Llorona **398.2**

Martin, B. The ghost-eye tree **E**

McKissack, P. C. The dark-thirty **S C**

Morales, Y. Just in case **E**

Newbery, L. Lost boy **Fic**

Ogburn, J. K. The bake shop ghost **E**

Pinkwater, D. M. The Yggyssey **Fic**

Pulver, R. Never say boo! **E**

Ruby, L. Lily's ghosts **Fic**

Sage, A. My haunted house **Fic**

San Souci, R. Short & shivery **398.2**

Schwartz, A. Ghosts! **398.2**

Schwartz, A. In a dark, dark room, and other scary stories **398.2**

Schwartz, A. More scary stories to tell in the dark **398.2**

Schwartz, A. Scary stories 3 **398.2**

Schwartz, A. Scary stories to tell in the dark **398.2**

Stringer, H. Spellbinder **Fic**

Trapani, I. Haunted party **E**

Vande Velde, V. There's a dead person following my sister around **Fic**

Wright, B. R. Princess for a week **Fic**

Ghost towns

Bial, R. Ghost towns of the American West **978**

Ghost towns of the American West. Bial, R. **978**

Ghosts

Bardhan-Quallen, S. The real monsters **001.9**

Gee, J. Encyclopedia horrifica **001.9**

Stefoff, R. Ghosts and spirits **133.1**

Wetzel, C. Haunted U.S.A. **133.1**

Folklore

Hamilton, M. The ghost catcher **398.2**

Graphic novels

Kochalka, J. Johnny Boo: the best little ghost in the world! **741.5**

Watson, A. Glister and the haunted teapot **741.5**

Ghosts!. Schwartz, A. **398.2**

Ghosts and spirits. Stefoff, R. **133.1**

The **ghost's** grave. Kehret, P. **Fic**

Ghosts in the house!. Kohara, K. **E**

Ghoulish goodies. Bowers, S. **641.5**

Giacobbe, Beppe

(il) Burleigh, R. Clang-clang! Beep-beep! **E**

(il) Fleischman, P. Big talk **811**

Giant African snail. Gray, S. H. **594**

The **Giant** and the beanstalk. Stanley, D. **E**

The **giant** hug. Horning, S. **E**

The **giant** jam sandwich. Lord, J. V. **E**

The **giant** of Seville. Andreasen, D. **E**

Giant panda

Bortolotti, D. Panda rescue **599.78**

Firestone, M. Top 50 reasons to care about giant pandas **599.78**

Gibbons, G. Giant pandas **599.78**

Markle, S. How many baby pandas? **599.78**

Nagda, A. W. Panda math **513**

Ryder, J. Little panda **599.78**

Fiction

Baek, M. J. Panda and polar bear **E**

Dowson, N. Tracks of a panda **E**

Liwska, R. Little panda **E**

Muth, J. J. Zen shorts **E**

Wild, M. Tom goes to kindergarten **E**

The **Giant** Rat of Sumatra. Fleischman, S. **Fic**

Giant sea reptiles of the dinosaur age. Arnold, C. **567.9**

Giant shark: megalodon, prehistoric super predator. Arnold, C. **567**

The **giant-slayer**. Lawrence, I. **Fic**

Giant snakes. Simon, S. **597.96**

Giants

Andreasen, D. The giant of Seville **E**

Fiction

Aguiar, N. The lost island of Tamarind **Fic**

Beaty, A. When giants come to play **E**

Coville, B. Thor's wedding day **Fic**

Dahl, R. The BFG **Fic**

Gerstein, M. Carolinda clatter! **E**

King-Smith, D. The twin giants **E**

Klise, K. Stand straight, Ella Kate **E**

Mora, P. Doña Flor **E**

Nolen, J. Hewitt Anderson's great big life **E**

Folklore

Bunting, E. Finn McCool and the great fish **398.2**

Cech, J. Jack and the beanstalk **398.2**

Johnson, P. B. Jack outwits the giants **398.2**

Kellogg, S. Jack and the beanstalk **398.2**

Malam, J. Giants **398.2**

Nesbit, E. Jack and the beanstalk **398.2**

Osborne, M. P. Kate and the beanstalk **398.2**

Seeger, P. Abiyoyo **398.2**

Souhami, J. Mrs. McCool and the giant Cuhullin **398.2**

Willey, M. Clever Beatrice **398.2**

Giants (Baseball team) *See* New York Giants (Baseball team)

Giants of science [series]

Allman, T. J. Robert Oppenheimer **92**

Krull, K. Albert Einstein **92**

Krull, K. Isaac Newton **92**

Krull, K. Leonardo da Vinci **92**

Krull, K. Marie Curie **92**

Krull, K. Sigmund Freud **92**

Giarrano, Vince, 1960-

Comics crash course **741.5**

Gibala-Broxholm, Scott

(il) Wax, W. City witch, country switch **E**

Gibbon, Rebecca

(il) Corey, S. Players in pigtails **E**

Gilton, Donna L.
Multicultural and ethnic children's literature in the United States **028.5**

Gimme cracked corn and I will share. O'Malley, K. **E**

Ginger and Petunia. Polacco, P. **E**

Ginger Pye. Estes, E. **Fic**

Gingerbread baby. Brett, J. **398.2**

The **gingerbread** boy. Egielski, R. **398.2**

The **gingerbread** boy. Galdone, P. **398.2**

Gingerbread friends. Brett, J. **E**

The **Gingerbread** Girl. Ernst, L. C. **E**

The **Gingerbread** man. Aylesworth, J. **398.2**

The **gingerbread** man. Kimmel, E. A. **398.2**

The **gingerbread** pirates. Kladstrup, K. **E**

Ginsburg, David W., 1971-
(il) Heller, E. S. Menorah under the sea **296.4**

Ginsburg, Max
(il) Taylor, M. D. The friendship **Fic**
(il) Taylor, M. D. Mississippi bridge **Fic**

Ginsburg, Mirra, 1909-2000
The chick and the duckling **E**
The Chinese mirror **398.2**
Clay boy **398.2**
Good morning, chick **E**

Giotto, di Bondone, 1266?-1337
Fiction
Arrigan, M. Mario's Angels **E**

Giovanni, Nikki
The grasshopper's song **E**
Rosa [biography of Rosa Parks] **92**
Spin a soft black song: poems for children **811**
The sun is so quiet **811**
See/See also pages in the following book(s):
Wilkinson, B. S. African American women writers **810.9**
(ed) Hip hop speaks to children. See Hip hop speaks to children **811.008**

Gipsies See Gypsies

Gipson, Frederick Benjamin, 1903-1973
Old Yeller **Fic**

A **giraffe** goes to Paris. Holmes, M. T. **E**

A **giraffe** grows up. Tourville, A. D. **599.63**

Giraffes
Anderson, J. Giraffes **599.63**
Bredeson, C. Giraffes up close **599.63**
Rumford, J. Chee-lin **599.63**
St. George, J. Zarafa **599.63**
Tourville, A. D. A giraffe grows up **599.63**
Fiction
Holmes, M. T. A giraffe goes to Paris **E**
McEvoy, A. Betsy B. Little **E**
Rey, H. A. Curious George: Cecily G. and the 9 monkeys **E**
St. John, L. The white giraffe **Fic**
Stamp, J. Flying high **E**

Giraffes up close. Bredeson, C. **599.63**

Girard, Rogé See Rogé, 1972-

Giraudon, David
(il) Burleigh, R. Volcanoes **551.2**

A **girl,** a boy, and three robbers. Gauthier, G. **Fic**

Girl crafts [series]
Ross, K. Bedroom makeover crafts **745.5**
Ross, K. One-of-a-kind stamps and crafts **761**

The **girl** from Chimel. Menchú, R. **92**

The **girl** in the castle inside the museum. Bernheimer, K. **E**

Girl in the know. Katz, A. **612.6**

A **girl** named Disaster. Farmer, N. **Fic**

The **girl** who could fly. Forester, V. **Fic**

The **girl** who drew a phoenix. Demi **E**

The **girl** who helped thunder and other Native American folktales. Bruchac, J. **398.2**

The **girl** who loved wild horses. Goble, P. **398.2**

The **girl** who spun gold. Hamilton, V. **398.2**

The **girl** who wanted to dance. Ehrlich, A. **E**

Girl wonder. Hopkinson, D. **E**

Girls
Buchanan, A. J. The daring book for girls **031.02**
Jukes, M. Growing up: it's a girl thing **612.6**
Movsessian, S. Puberty girl **612.6**
Rimm, S. B. See Jane win for girls **305.23**
Sills, L. From rags to riches **391**
Education
Winter, J. Nasreen's secret school **371.82**
Employment
See Child labor
Health and hygiene
American Medical Association girl's guide to becoming a teen **613**
Birkemoe, K. Strike a pose **613.7**
Cheung, L. W. Y. Be healthy! it's a girl thing **613**
Katz, A. Girl in the know **612.6**
Madaras, L. Ready, set, grow! **612.6**
Madaras, L. The "what's happening to my body?" book for girls **612.6**
Poetry
Johnson, D. Hair dance! **811**
Richards, B. Keep climbing, girls **E**
She's all that! **811.008**

Girls, Teenage See Teenagers

The **girls.** Koss, A. G. **Fic**

Girls A to Z. Bunting, E. **E**

The **girl's** like spaghetti. Truss, L. **428**

Girls rock! [series]
Buckley, A. Be a better babysitter **649**
Buckley, A. Be a better biker **796.6**

Girls think of everything. Thimmesh, C. **920**

Girouard, Patrick
(il) Caffey, D. Yikes-lice! **616.5**

GIs See Soldiers—United States

Gish, Steven, 1963-
Ethiopia **963**

Gist, E. M.
(il) Olson, A. N. More bones **398.2**

The **glorious** flight: across the Channel with Louis Blériot, July 25, 1909. Provensen, A.　**92**

Glossaries *See* Encyclopedias and dictionaries

Glossop, Jennifer
(jt. auth) Gillies, J. The jumbo vegetarian cookbook　**641.5**
(jt. auth) Gillies, J. The Kids Can Press jumbo cookbook　**641.5**

Gnash, gnaw, dinosaur!. Mitton, T.　**811**

Gnat Stokes and the Foggy Bottom Swamp Queen. Keehn, S. M.　**Fic**

Gnojewski, Carol
Cinco de Mayo crafts　**745.594**

Gnus
Walden, K. Wildebeests　**599.64**

Go away, big green monster!. Emberley, E.　**E**

Go figure!. Ball, J.　**793.74**

Go fly a bike!. Haduch, B.　**629.227**

Go, go America. Yaccarino, D.　**973**

Go! go! go!. Munro, R.　**E**

Go-go gorillas. Durango, J.　**E**

Go long!. Barber, T.　**Fic**

Go to bed, monster!. Wing, N.　**E**

Go to sleep, Gecko!. MacDonald, M. R.　**398.2**

Go to sleep, Groundhog!. Cox, J.　**E**

Go wild in New York City. Matsen, B.　**974.7**

Goal!. Javaherbin, M.　**E**

Goal! science projects with soccer. Goodstein, M.　**507.8**

Goal!: the fire and fury of soccer's greatest moment. Stewart, M.　**796.334**

The **goat-faced** girl. Sharpe, L. M.　**398.2**

Goats
Polacco, P. G is for goat　**E**
Fiction
Cole, H. Trudy　**E**
Gorbachev, V. That's what friends are for　**E**
Jordan, R. Lost Goat Lane　**Fic**
Palatini, M. The three silly billies　**E**
Polacco, P. Oh, look!　**E**
Rocco, J. Wolf! wolf!　**E**
Sharmat, M. Gregory, the terrible eater　**E**
Waddell, M. Captain Small Pig　**E**
Westera, M. Sheep and Goat　**Fic**
Folklore
Galdone, P. The three Billy Goats Gruff　**398.2**

Gobble-gobble crash!. Stiegemeyer, J.　**E**

Gobble it up!. Arnosky, J.　**E**

Goble, Paul
All our relatives　**970.004**
Beyond the ridge　**Fic**
Buffalo woman　**398.2**
Death of the iron horse　**E**
The girl who loved wild horses　**398.2**
The legend of the White Buffalo Woman　**398.2**
Song of creation　**242**

The **goblin** and the empty chair. Fox, M.　**E**

The **goblin** baby. Doherty, B.　**Fic**

God
Fitch, F. M. A book about God　**231**
Jules, J. Abraham's search for God　**222**
Lindbergh, R. On morning wings　**223**
Tutu, D. God's dream　**231.7**
Fiction
Gold, A. Thank you, God, for everything　**E**
Heller, L. Today is the birthday of the world　**E**

God found us you. Bergren, L. T.　**E**

Godden, Rumer, 1907-1998
The doll's house　**Fic**
The story of Holly & Ivy　**E**

Goddesses *See* Gods and goddesses

Godkin, Celia, 1948-
Fire!　**577.2**
Hurricane!　**551.55**
Wolf island　**577**

Godon, Ingrid
(il) Norac, C. My daddy is a giant　**E**
(il) Norac, C. My mommy is magic　**E**

Gods & heroes. Reinhart, M.　**201**

Gods and goddesses
See also Religions names of individual gods and goddesses
Bryant, M. E. Oh my gods!　**292**
Bryant, M. E. She's all that!　**292**
Fisher, L. E. The gods and goddesses of ancient China　**299**
Reinhart, M. Gods & heroes　**201**
Tchana, K. H. Changing Woman and her sisters　**398.2**
Fiction
Levine, G. C. Ever　**Fic**
Riordan, R. The red pyramid　**Fic**

The **gods** and goddesses of ancient China. Fisher, L. E.　**299**

The **gods** and goddesses of Olympus. Aliki　**292**

Gods and goddesses of the ancient Norse. Fisher, L. E.　**293**

God's dream. Tutu, D.　**231.7**

Godwin, Jane, 1964-
Falling from Grace　**Fic**

Godwin, Laura
Happy and Honey　**E**
(jt. auth) Martin, A. M. The doll people　**Fic**

Goebel, Nancy Andrews- *See* Andrews-Goebel, Nancy

Goede, Irene
(il) Post, H. Creepy crawlies　**590**
(il) Post, H. Sparrows　**598**

Goembel, Ponder
Animal fair　**E**
(il) Ketteman, H. Swamp song　**E**
(il) Morrow, B. O. Mr. Mosquito put on his tuxedo　**E**
(il) Wheeler, L. Castaway cats　**E**
(il) Wheeler, L. Old Cricket　**E**

Gofen, Ethel, 1937-
Argentina　**982**

Goffe, Toni
(il) Stinson, K. Big or little?　**E**

Goldszmit, Henryk *See* Korczak, Janusz, 1878-1942

Goldwork
Fiction
Cowley, M. The golden bull   **Fic**
The **golem**. Rogasky, B.   **398.2**
Golem. Wisniewski, D.   **398.2**
Golembe, Carla
  (il) Gerson, M.-J. Why the sky is far away   **398.2**
Golenbock, Peter, 1946-
  Hank Aaron   **92**
  Teammates [biography of Jackie Robinson]   **92**
Golf
  Ditchfield, C. Golf   **796.352**
  Kelley, K. C. Golf   **796.352**
Fiction
Miller, W. Night golf   **E**
Gollub, Matthew, 1960-
  Cool melons—turn to frogs!: the life and poems of Issa [Kobayashi]   **92**
The **Golly** sisters go West. Byars, B. C.   **E**
Golson, Terry
  Tillie lays an egg   **E**
Gombe Stream National Park (Tanzania)
  Jankowski, C. Jane Goodall   **92**
Gomez, Elena, 1971-
  (il) Brooks, J. A world of prayers   **242**
Gómez, Elizabeth
  (il) Argueta, J. Moony Luna   **E**
  (il) Argueta, J. A movie in my pillow   **861**
  (il) Herrera, J. F. The upside down boy   **92**
Gone-Away Lake. Enright, E.   **Fic**
Gone fishing. McLimans, D.   **591.7**
Gone wild. McLimans, D.   **E**
Gonna sing my head off! See I hear America singing!   **782.42**
Gonsalves, Rob
  (il) Thomson, S. L. Imagine a night   **E**
Gonyea, Mark
  Another book about design   **745.4**
  A book about color   **701**
  A book about design   **745.4**
Gonzales, Doreen
  Bats in the dark   **599.4**
  Crickets in the dark   **595.7**
  Owls in the dark   **598**
  Raccoons in the dark   **599.7**
  Scorpions in the dark   **595.4**
  Skunks in the dark   **599.7**
Gonzalez, Emiliano Thomas, 1959- *See* Gonzalez, Thomas, 1959-
González, Lucía M., 1957-
  Señor Cat's romance and other favorite stories from Latin America   **398.2**
  The storyteller's candle   **E**
Gonzalez, Maya Christina, 1964-
  I know the river loves me   **E**
  My colors, my world = Mis colores, mi mundo   **E**
  (il) Alarcón, F. X. Animal poems of the Iguazu   **811**

  (il) Alarcón, F. X. From the bellybutton of the moon and other summer poems   **811**
  (il) Alarcón, F. X. Iguanas in the snow and other winter poems   **811**
  (il) Pérez, A. I. My diary from here to there   **Fic**
  (il) Pérez, A. I. My very own room   **E**
González, Rigoberto, 1970-
  Antonio's card   **E**
Gonzalez, Thomas, 1959-
  (il) Deedy, C. A. 14 cows for America   **327**
Gonzalez, Ada Acosta *See* Acosta Gonzalez, Ada
Gonzalo grabs the good life. Levy, J.   **E**
Good, Diane L.
  Brown v. Board of Education   **344**
Good and evil
Fiction
Baccalario, P. Ring of fire   **Fic**
Cooper, S. The grey king   **Fic**
Cooper, S. Over sea, under stone   **Fic**
Isol. Petit, the monster   **E**
Kirov, E. Magickeepers: the eternal hourglass   **Fic**
Good boy, Fergus!. Shannon, D.   **E**
Good brother, bad brother [biography of John Wilkes Booth and Edwin Booth] Giblin, J.   **92**
Good-bye, 382 Shin Dang Dong. Park, F.   **E**
Good-bye bully machine. Fox, D.   **302.3**
Good-bye, Sheepie. Burleigh, R.   **E**
A **good** day. Henkes, K.   **E**
A **good** day's fishing. Prosek, J.   **E**
The **good** dog. Avi   **Fic**
Good dog. Gottfried, M.   **811**
Good enough to eat. Cole, B.   **E**
The **good** fight. Ambrose, S. E.   **940.53**
Good for you!. Calmenson, S.   **811**
The **Good** Master. Seredy, K.   **Fic**
Good masters! Sweet ladies!. Schlitz, L. A.   **940.1**
Good morning, chick. Ginsburg, M.   **E**
Good morning, garden. Brenner, B.   **E**
Good neighbors. Thompson, C.   **Fic**
Good night engines. Mortensen, D. D.   **E**
A **good** night for freedom. Morrow, B. O.   **E**
Good night, Good Knight. Thomas, S. M.   **E**
Good night, Gorilla. Rathmann, P.   **E**
Good night, Harry. Lewis, K.   **E**
A **good** night walk. Cooper, E.   **E**
Good Queen Bess: the story of Elizabeth I of England. Stanley, D.   **92**
Good relationships. Parker, V.   **177**
Good sports. Prelutsky, J.   **811**
The **good,** the bad, the slimy. Latta, S. L.   **579**
Good thing you're not an octopus!. Markes, J.   **E**
Goodall, Jane, 1934-
  The chimpanzees I love   **599.8**

Goodall, Jane, 1934-
About
Jankowski, C. Jane Goodall   92

Goodbody, Slim *See* Burstein, John, 1949-

Goodbye, gasoline. Lew, K.   621.31

Goodbye, Mousie. Harris, R. H.   E

The **goodbye** time. Conway, C.   Fic

Goode, Diane
The most perfect spot   E
Thanksgiving is here!   E
(il) Feiffer, K. But I wanted a baby brother!   E
(il) Feiffer, K. My mom is trying to ruin my life   E
(il) Feiffer, K. President Pennybaker   E
(il) Primavera, E. Louise the big cheese: divine diva   E
(il) Rylant, C. Alligator boy   E
(il) Rylant, C. Baby face   811
(il) Rylant, C. When I was young in the mountains   E

Goode, J. Paul, 1862-1932
Goode's world atlas   912

Goodell, Jon
(il) Kimmel, E. A. Zigazak!   E

Goode's school atlas. See Goode, J. P. Goode's world atlas   912

Goode's world atlas. Goode, J. P.   912

Goodhart, Pippa
Three little ghosties   E

Gooding, La Chanze *See* La Chanze

Goodman, David
(il) Color. See Color   535.6

Goodman, Emily
Plant secrets   580

Goodman, Jim, 1947-
Thailand   959.3

Goodman, Joan E., 1950-
Ballet bunnies   792.8
Despite all obstacles: La Salle and the conquest of the Mississippi   92
A long and uncertain journey: the 27,000 mile voyage of Vasco da Gama   92

Goodman, Susan, 1952-
All in just one cookie   641.8
Claws, coats, and camouflage   591.4
Gee whiz! it's all about pee!   612.4
Life on the ice   998
See how they run   324
Seeds, stems, and stamens   581.4
The truth about poop   573.4

Goodman, Katherine Noble- *See* Noble-Goodman, Katherine

Goodnight, Mollie, 1839-1926
Fiction
Fern, T. E. Buffalo music   E

Goodnight goon. Rex, M.   E

Goodnight Lulu. Bogan, P.   E

Goodnight, me. Daddo, A.   E

Goodnight moon. Brown, M. W.   E

Goodrich, Carter
The hermit crab   E

Goodstein, Madeline
Ace your sports science project   507.8
Goal! science projects with soccer   507.8
Wheels!   530
(jt. auth) Gardner, R. Ace your forces and motion science project   531
(jt. auth) Gardner, R. Ace your physical science project   530
(jt. auth) Gardner, R. Ace your space science project   520

GoodWeather, Hartley *See* King, Thomas, 1943-

Goodyear, Charles, 1800-1860
See/See also pages in the following book(s):
Fradin, D. B. With a little luck   509

Gooney Bird Greene. Lowry, L.   Fic

Goose and Duck. George, J. C.   E

The **goose** man. Greenstein, E.   92

Gooseberry Goose. Freedman, C.   E

Goose's story. Best, C.   E

Gorbachev, Valeri, 1944-
Christopher counting   E
Dragon is coming!   E
The missing chick   E
Molly who flew away   E
Ms. Turtle the babysitter   E
That's what friends are for   E
Turtle's penguin day   E
(il) Horning, S. The giant hug   E
(il) Moser, L. Squirrel's world   E
(il) Stiegemeyer, J. Gobble-gobble crash!   E

Gordon, Cambria
(jt. auth) David, L. The down-to-earth guide to global warming   363.7

Gordon, David
(il) Esbaum, J. To the big top   E
(jt. auth) Scieszka, J. Pete's party   E
(il) Scieszka, J. Smash! crash!   E
(jt. auth) Scieszka, J. Truckery rhymes   811

Gordon, Rachel Singer
Teaching the Internet in libraries   025.04

Gordon, Sharon
Argentina   982
Australia   994
Cuba   972.91
Germany   943
Great Britain   941
Greece   949.5
Philippines   959.9
Poland   943.8

Gordon, Stephanie Jacob, 1940-
(jt. auth) Enderle, J. R. Smile, Principessa!   E

Gore, Al, Jr., 1948-
An inconvenient truth   363.7

Gore, Leonid
Danny's first snow   E
Mommy, where are you?   E
When I grow up   E
(jt. auth) Anderson, J. L. May Bird and The Ever After   Fic
(il) Bauer, M. D. The secret of the painted house   Fic
(il) Pullman, P. Clockwork   Fic
(il) Quattlebaum, M. Sparks fly high   398.2

Gore, Leonid—*Continued*
(il) Shepard, A. The princess mouse   **398.2**

Gorey, Edward, 1925-2000
(il) Bellairs, J. The house with a clock in its
walls   **Fic**
(il) Ciardi, J. You read to me, I'll read to you
811
(jt. auth) Heide, F. P. The shrinking of Treehorn
Fic

Gorge-purge syndrome *See* Bulimia

Gorgonzola. Palatini, M.   **E**

Gorilla doctors. Turner, P. S.   **333.95**

Gorilla! Gorilla!. Willis, J.   **E**

Gorilla, monkey & ape. Redmond, I.   **599.8**

Gorillas
Costa-Prades, B. Little gorillas   **599.8**
Kushner, J. M. Who on earth is Dian Fossey?
92
Looking for Miza   **599.8**
Nichols, M. Face to face with gorillas   **599.8**
Simon, S. Gorillas   **599.8**
Turner, P. S. Gorilla doctors   **333.95**
Fiction
Browne, A. Little Beauty   **E**
Browne, A. Voices in the park   **E**
Durango, J. Go-go gorillas   **E**
Willis, J. Gorilla! Gorilla!   **E**

Gorman, Michael, 1941-
The concise AACR2   **025.3**

Gorrell, Gena K. (Gena Kinton), 1946-
Heart and soul: the story of Florence Nightin-
gale   **92**
In the land of the jaguar   **980**
Working like a dog   **636.7**

Gorski, Jason
(il) Murphy, P. Exploratopia   **507.8**

Gorton, Julia
(il) Cobb, V. I face the wind   **551.51**
(il) Cobb, V. I fall down   **531**
(il) Cobb, V. I get wet   **532**
(il) Cobb, V. I see myself   **535**

Gorton, Steve
(il) Stott, C. Space exploration   **629.4**

Goscinny, 1926-1977
Asterix the Gaul   **741.5**
Nicholas   **Fic**

Gospel music
See also Spirituals (Songs)
Fiction
Hopkinson, D. A band of angels   **E**

Goss, Gary, 1947-
(jt. auth) Rotner, S. Where does food come
from?   **664**

Gossie. Dunrea, O.   **E**

Gossip
Fiction
McDonald, M. Hen hears gossip   **E**
Folklore
Waldman, D. A sack full of feathers   **398.2**

Got geography!   **811.008**

Gotama Siddhatta *See* Gautama Buddha

Gotcha covered!. Baxter, K. A.   **028.5**

Gotcha for guys!. Baxter, K. A.   **028.5**

Gotcha good!. Baxter, K. A.   **028.5**

Gothic architecture
Macaulay, D. Building the book Cathedral
726
Macaulay, D. Cathedral: the story of its construction   **726**

Goths
Kroll, S. Barbarians!   **940.1**

Goto, Scott
The perfect sword   **Fic**

Gotta go! Gotta go!. Swope, S.   **E**

Gottfried, Maya
Good dog   **811**
Our farm   **811**

Gottfried, Ted, 1928-
Alcohol   **362.292**
Marijuana   **362.29**
Millard Fillmore   **92**

Gourley, Robbin
Bring me some apples and I'll make you a pie
E

Gouveia, Pedro Alvares de *See* Cabral, Pedro
Alvares, 1460?-1526?

Govenar, Alan B., 1952-
(jt. auth) Miller, N. Stompin' at the Savoy [bi-
ography of Norma Miller]   **92**

Government *See* Political science

Government, Local *See* Local government

Government in action! [series]
Hamilton, J. Becoming a citizen   **323.6**
Hamilton, J. How a bill becomes a law
328.73
Hamilton, J. Running for office   **324**

Governments around the world. Giesecke, E.
320.3

Gow, Mary
Rachel Carson   **92**

Gower, Catherine
Long-Long's New Year   **E**

Gownley, Jimmy
Amelia rules!: the whole world's crazy!
741.5

Grabenstein, Chris
The crossroads   **Fic**

Graber, Janet, 1942-
Muktar and the camels   **E**

Grabien, Deborah
Dark's tale   **Fic**

Grace, Catherine O'Neill, 1950-
1621   **394.26**
Forces of nature   **551.2**
The White House   **975.3**

Grace for president. DiPucchio, K. S.   **E**

Gracias = Thanks. Mora, P.   **E**

Gracie & Grandma & the itsy, bitsy seed.
Sandemose, I.   **E**

Graef, Renée
(il) Lorbiecki, M. Paul Bunyan's sweetheart
E
(il) Schulman, J. The nutcracker   **Fic**

Graf, Mike
How does a waterfall become electricity?
621.31

Grafe, Max
(il) Elliott, D. What the grizzly knows   **E**
(il) Schlitz, L. A. The Bearskinner   **398.2**

Graff, Lisa, 1981-
The life and crimes of Bernetta Wallflower
Fic
The thing about Georgie   **Fic**
Umbrella summer   **Fic**

Graffiti
Bingham, J. Graffiti   **751.7**

Graham, Amy
Great Smoky Mountains National Park   **976.8**

Graham, Bette Nesmith, 1924-1980
See/See also pages in the following book(s):
Thimmesh, C. Girls think of everything   **920**

Graham, Bob, 1942-
Dimity Dumpty   **E**
How to heal a broken wing   **E**
Let's get a pup, said Kate   **E**
Oscar's half birthday   **E**
(il) King-Smith, D. The nine lives of Aristotle
Fic
(il) Rosen, M. I'm number one   **E**

Graham, Elspeth, 1953-
(jt. auth) Peet, M. Cloud Tea monkeys   **Fic**

Graham, Ian, 1953-
Aircraft   **629.133**
Microscopic scary creatures   **591.6**
(jt. auth) Coppendale, J. The great big book of
mighty machines   **621.8**

Graham, Joan Bransfield
Flicker flash   **811**

Graham, Kennon *See* Harrison, David Lee, 1937-

Graham, Lorenz B., 1902-1989
How God fix Jonah   **398.2**

Graham, Margaret Bloy, 1920-
(il) Zion, G. Harry the dirty dog   **E**

Graham, Mark, 1952-
(il) Collins, P. L. I am a dancer   **792.8**
(il) Ryder, J. My father's hands   **E**

Grahame, Deborah A.
Austria   **943.6**
Sweden   **948.5**

Grahame, Kenneth, 1859-1932
The reluctant dragon   **Fic**
The wind in the willows
Fic
[abridged and illustrated by Inga Moore]
Fic
[illustrated by Robert R. Ingpen]   **Fic**

Grail quest: the Camelot spell. Gilman, L. A.
Fic

Grajnert, Paul
(jt. auth) Heale, J. Poland   **943.8**

Gralley, Jean
The moon came down on Milk Street   **E**

Gramatky, Hardie, 1907-1979
Little Toot   **E**

Grambling, Lois G., 1927-
T. Rex and the Mother's Day hug   **E**

Grammar
    See also English language—Grammar

Grand, Carmen T. Bernier- *See* Bernier-Grand,
Carmen T.

Grand Canyon (Ariz.)
Brown, C. M. Mule train mail   **383**
Fiction
Henry, M. Brighty of the Grand Canyon   **Fic**

The **grand** escape. Naylor, P. R.   **Fic**

The **grand** mosque of Paris. Ruelle, K. G.
940.53

A **grand** old tree. DePalma, M. N.   **E**

Grandfather and I. Buckley, H. E.   **E**

Grandfather Buffalo. Arnosky, J.   **E**

Grandfather tales   **398.2**

Grandfathers
Fiction
Ackerman, K. Song and dance man   **E**
Aliki. The two of them   **E**
Banerjee, A. Looking for Bapu   **Fic**
Barclay, J. Proud as a peacock, brave as a lion
E
Bartek, M. Funerals & fly fishing   **Fic**
Base, G. Enigma   **Fic**
Brooks, B. Everywhere   **Fic**
Buckley, H. E. Grandfather and I   **E**
Bunting, E. Butterfly house   **E**
Butler, D. H. My grandpa had a stroke   **E**
Cheaney, J. B. The middle of somewhere
Fic
Choi, Y. Behind the mask   **E**
Cotten, C. Fair has nothing to do with it
Fic
Creech, S. Heartbeat   **Fic**
Cruise, R. Bartleby speaks!   **E**
De Paola, T. Now one foot, now the other
E
Dempsey, K. Me with you   **E**
Drummond, A. Tin Lizzie   **E**
Eitzen, R. Tara's flight   **E**
Foreman, M. Grandpa Jack's tattoo tales   **E**
Fox, M. Sophie   **E**
Frazier, S. T. Brendan Buckley's universe and
everything in it   **Fic**
García, C. I wanna be your shoebox   **Fic**
Garza, X. Juan and the Chupacabras   **E**
George, J. C. Charlie's raven   **Fic**
Gerdner, L. Grandfather's story cloth   **E**
Gower, C. Long-Long's New Year   **E**
Greenfield, E. Grandpa's face   **E**
Grifalconi, A. Ain't nobody a stranger to me
E
Haas, J. Sugaring   **E**
Henson, H. Grumpy Grandpa   **E**
Hest, A. Guess who, Baby Duck!   **E**
Hest, A. The purple coat   **E**
Holt, K. W. Dancing in Cadillac light   **Fic**
Howe, J. Kaddish for Grandpa in Jesus' name,
amen   **E**
Hurst, C. O. Terrible storm   **E**
Isadora, R. Happy belly, happy smile   **E**
Jones, M. T. Ratfink   **Fic**
Keller, H. Grandfather's dream   **E**
Kelly, J. The evolution of Calpurnia Tate
Fic

Graphic myths and legends [series]

Jolley, D. Guan Yu	**741.5**
Storrie, P. D. Beowulf	**741.5**

Graphic novels

See also Adventure graphic novels; Autobiographical graphic novels; Biographical graphic novels; Fantasy graphic novels; Horror graphic novels; Humorous graphic novels; Manga; Mystery graphic novels; Science fiction graphic novels; Superhero graphic novels

Abadzis, N. Laika	**741.5**
Alley, Z. B. There's a wolf at the door	**398.2**
Baltazar, A. Tiny Titans: welcome to the treehouse	**741.5**
Bannister (Person). The shadow door	**741.5**
Barba, C. Yam: bite-size chunks	**741.5**
Big fat Little Lit	**741.5**
Bliss, H. Luke on the loose	**741.5**
Bullock, M. Lions, tigers, and bears, vol. 1: Fear and pride	**741.5**
Cammuso, F. Knights of the lunch table: the dodgeball chronicles	**741.5**
Cammuso, F. Otto's orange day	**741.5**
Cavallaro, M. L. Frank Baum's The Wizard of Oz	**741.5**
Colfer, E. Artemis Fowl: the graphic novel	**741.5**
Collicutt, P. City in peril!	**741.5**
Craddock, E. Stone rabbit: Pirate Palooza	**741.5**
Crane, J. The clouds above	**741.5**
Davis, E. The secret science alliance and the copycat crook	**741.5**
Davis, E. Stinky	**741.5**
De Campi, A. Kat & Mouse: Teacher torture	**741.5**
Espinosa, R. The courageous princess	**741.5**
Farshtey, G. Bionicle #1: rise of the Toa Nuva	**741.5**
Flight explorer	**741.5**
Frampton, O. Oddly Normal	**741.5**
Friesen, R. Cupcakes of doom!	**741.5**
Fuji, M. The big adventures of Majoko, volume 1	**741.5**
Goscinny. Asterix the Gaul	**741.5**
Gownley, J. Amelia rules!: the whole world's crazy!	**741.5**
Grant, A. Robert Louis Stevenson's Strange case of Dr. Jekyll and Mr. Hyde	**741.5**
Guibert, E. Sardine in outer space	**741.5**
Hale, S. Rapunzel's revenge	**741.5**
Hama, L. The battle of Iwo Jima	**940.54**
Hastings, J. Terrabella Smoot and the unsung monsters	**741.5**
Hayes, G. Benny and Penny in just pretend	**741.5**
Hergé. The adventures of Tintin, vol. 1	**741.5**
Hoena, B. A. Jack and the beanstalk: the graphic novel	**741.5**
Holm, J. L. Babymouse: queen of the world	**741.5**
Horowitz, A. Stormbreaker: the graphic novel	**741.5**
Jolley, D. Guan Yu	**741.5**

Kibuishi, K. Amulet, book one: The Stonekeeper	**741.5**
Kibuishi, K. Copper	**741.5**
Kim, S. City of spies	**741.5**
Kochalka, J. Dragon Puncher	**741.5**
Kochalka, J. Johnny Boo: the best little ghost in the world!	**741.5**
Kovac, T. Wonderland	**741.5**
Krosoczka, J. J. Lunch Lady and the League of Librarians	**741.5**
Larson, H. Chiggers	**741.5**
Lemke, D. Zinc Alloy: Super Zero	**741.5**
Lepp, R. David: Shepard's song, vol. 1	**741.5**
Luciani, B. The meeting	**741.5**
Lynch, J. Mo and Jo: fighting together forever	**741.5**
Macdonald, F. Journey to the Center of the Earth	**741.5**
Macdonald, F. Kidnapped	**741.5**
Martin, A. M. The Baby-sitter's Club: Kristy's great idea	**741.5**
McLeod, B. SuperHero ABC	**E**
Medley, L. Castle waiting	**741.5**
Meister, C. Clues in the attic	**741.5**
Morse, S. Magic Pickle	**741.5**
Mortensen, L. The missing monster card	**741.5**
Mucci, T. The odyssey	**741.5**
O'Brien, A. S. The legend of Hong Kil Dong, the Robin Hood of Korea	**741.5**
O'Connor, G. Zeus	**741.5**
O'Donnell, L. Wild ride: a graphic guide adventure	**741.5**
O'Malley, K. Captain Raptor and the moon mystery	**E**
Ottaviani, J. T-Minus: the race to the moon	**741.5**
Parker, J. Missile Mouse: the star crusher	**741.5**
Petersen, D. Mouse Guard: Fall 1152	**741.5**
Phelan, M. The storm in the barn	**741.5**
Pien, L. Long Tail Kitty	**741.5**
Renier, A. Spiral-bound	**741.5**
Renier, A. The Unsinkable Walker Bean	**741.5**
Reynolds, A. Joey Fly, private eye in Creepy crawly crime	**741.5**
Roberts, S. Patty-cake and friends: color collection	**741.5**
Rosenstiehl, A. Silly Lilly and the four seasons	**741.5**
Runton, A. Owly: The way home and The bittersweet summer	**741.5**
Russell, P. C. Coraline [graphic novel]	**741.5**
Sava, S. C. Hyperactive	**741.5**
Serchay, D. S. The librarian's guide to graphic novels for children and tweens	**025.2**
Sfar, J. Little Vampire	**741.5**
Shiga, J. Meanwhile	**741.5**
Shioya, H. Dinosaur hour!, vol. 1	**741.5**
Siegel, S. C. To dance	**92**
Smith, J. Little Mouse gets ready	**741.5**
Sonishi, K. Leave it to PET!: the misadventures of a recycled super robot, vol. 1	**741.5**
Spires, A. Binky the space cat	**741.5**

Graphic novels—*Continued*

Stanley, J. Little Lulu, vol. 1: My dinner with Lulu **741.5**

Steinberg, D. Sound off! **741.5**

Storrie, P. D. Beowulf **741.5**

Sturm, J. Adventures in cartooning **741.5**

Telgemeier, R. Smile **741.5**

Thompson, J. Magic Trixie **741.5**

Townsend, M. Kit Feeny: on the move **741.5**

Trickster: Native American tales **398.2**

Trondheim, L. Tiny Tyrant **741.5**

Varon, S. Robot dreams **741.5**

Watson, A. Glister and the haunted teapot **741.5**

Weigel, J. Thunder from the sea **741.5**

Wight, E. Frankie Pickle and the closet of doom **741.5**

Administration
Lyga, A. A. W. Graphic novels in your media center **025.2**

Miller, S. Developing and promoting graphic novel collections **025.2**

Authorship
Rosinsky, N. M. Write your own graphic novel **741.5**

Sturm, J. Adventures in cartooning **741.5**

Bibliography
Goldsmith, F. The readers' advisory guide to graphic novels **025.2**

Pawuk, M. G. Graphic novels **016.7**

History and criticism
Graphic novels beyond the basics **025.2**

Graphic novels. Pawuk, M. G. **016.7**

Graphic novels beyond the basics **025.2**

Graphic novels in your media center. Lyga, A. A. W. **025.2**

Graphing crime. Somervill, B. A. **364**

Graphing immigration. Solway, A. **325.73**

Graphing war and conflict. Solway, A. **355**

Grasses

See also Grasslands

Grasshopper on the road. Lobel, A. **E**

Grasshopper summer. Turner, A. W. **Fic**

Grasshoppers

Trueit, T. S. Grasshoppers **595.7**

Fiction
Giovanni, N. The grasshopper's song **E**

Grant, J. Chicken said, Cluck! **E**

Lobel, A. Grasshopper on the road **E**

The **grasshopper's** song. Giovanni, N. **E**

Grassian, Esther Stampfer

Information literacy instruction **025.5**

Grassland buffet. Lundgren, J. K. **577.4**

Grassland ecology

Dunphy, M. Here is the African savanna **577.4**

Hoare, B. Temperate grasslands **577.4**

Hodge, D. Savanna animals **591.7**

Jackson, K. Explore the grasslands **577.4**

Levy, J. Discovering the tropical savanna **577.4**

Lundgren, J. K. Grassland buffet **577.4**

Stille, D. R. Grasslands **577.4**

Toupin, L. Life in the temperate grasslands **577.4**

Toupin, L. Savannas **577.4**

Grasslands

See also Prairies

Bredeson, C. Baby animals of the grasslands **591.7**

Grasslands. Stille, D. R. **577.4**

Gratsaniti, Olga

(jt. auth) DuBois, J. Greece **949.5**

Gratz, Alan, 1972-

The Brooklyn nine **Fic**

Gravelle, Jennifer

(jt. auth) Gravelle, K. The period book **612.6**

Gravelle, Karen

The period book **612.6**

Graven images. Fleischman, P. **S C**

Graves, Keith

(il) Asher, S. Here comes Gosling! **E**

(il) Jackson, A. Desert Rose and her highfalutin hog **E**

(il) Lewis, J. P. The World's Greatest **811**

(il) Palatini, M. Boo-hoo moo **E**

Gravett, Christopher, 1951-

Knight **940.1**

Gravett, Emily

Dogs **E**

Little Mouse's big book of fears **E**

Meerkat mail **E**

Monkey and me **E**

The odd egg **E**

Orange pear apple bear **E**

Spells **E**

Wolves **E**

The **graveyard** book. Gaiman, N. **Fic**

Graveyards *See* Cemeteries

Gravitation

Gardner, R. Heavy-duty science projects with weight **530.8**

Parker, B. R. The mystery of gravity **531**

Gravity

Bradley, K. B. Forces make things move **531**

Cobb, V. I fall down **531**

Hopwood, J. Cool gravity activities **531**

Macdonald, W. Galileo's leaning tower experiment **531**

Phelan, G. Invisible force **531**

Sullivan, N. Weight **531**

Gray, Leon, 1974-

Iran **955**

Gray, Libba Moore

My mama had a dancing heart **E**

Gray, Paula

(il) Warner, P. Signing fun **419**

Gray, Susan Heinrichs

Emerald ash borer **595.7**

Giant African snail **594**

The human body [series] **612**

Living with juvenile rheumatoid arthritis **616.7**

Walking catfish **597**

Great Britain—History—1485-1603, Tudors—
History—19th century—Fiction—*Continued*

Winter, J. The fabulous feud of Gilbert & Sullivan **E**

Kings and rulers

Adams, S. Elizabeth I **92**

Fritz, J. Can't you make them behave, King
George? [biography of George III, King of
Great Britain] **92**

Stanley, D. Good Queen Bess: the story of Elizabeth I of England **92**

Great Britain. Navy *See* Great Britain. Royal
Navy

Great Britain. Royal Navy

Graphic novels

Weigel, J. Thunder from the sea **741.5**

Great building feats [series]

DuTemple, L. A. The New York subways
388.4

Great cities of the world [series]

Barber, N. Istanbul **949.6**

Bowden, R. Jerusalem **956.94**

Rowe, P. Toronto **971**

Stacey, G. London **942.1**

Great Depression, 1929-1939

Cooper, M. L. Dust to eat **973.917**

Freedman, R. Children of the Great Depression
305.23

Stanley, J. Children of the Dust Bowl **371.9**

Fiction

Adler, D. A. The Babe & I **E**

Ayres, K. Macaroni boy **Fic**

Birtha, B. Lucky beans **E**

Blume, L. M. M. Tennyson **Fic**

Burch, R. Ida Early comes over the mountain
Fic

Carville, J. Lu and the swamp ghost **E**

Collier, J. L. The dreadful revenge of Ernest
Gallen **Fic**

Curtis, C. P. Bud, not Buddy **Fic**

Hale, M. The truth about sparrows **Fic**

Hesse, K. Out of the dust **Fic**

Hesse, K. Spuds **E**

Hoberman, M. A. Strawberry Hill **Fic**

Holm, J. L. Turtle in paradise **Fic**

Jackson, A. Rainmaker **Fic**

McKissack, P. C. The all-I'll-ever-want Christmas doll **E**

Peck, R. A long way from Chicago **Fic**

Peck, R. A year down yonder **Fic**

Stewart, S. The gardener **E**

Taylor, M. D. Let the circle be unbroken
Fic

Taylor, M. D. Song of the trees **Fic**

Turner, A. W. Dust for dinner **E**

Wyatt, L. J. Poor is just a starting place
Fic

Great displays for your library step by step. Phillips, S. P. **021.7**

The **great** dog wash. Braeuner, S. **E**

The **great** doughnut parade. Bond, R. **E**

Great escapes [series]

Currie, S. Escapes from slavery **326**

Great estimations. Goldstone, B. **519.5**

Great explorations [series]

Calvert, P. Daniel Boone **92**

Calvert, P. Kit Carson **92**

Calvert, P. Robert E. Peary **92**

Calvert, P. Sir Ernest Shackleton **92**

Calvert, P. Vasco da Gama **92**

Calvert, P. Zebulon Pike **92**

Collier, J. L. Christopher Columbus **92**

Faber, H. Lewis and Clark **978**

Faber, H. Samuel de Champlain **92**

Meltzer, M. Francisco Pizarro **92**

Otfinoski, S. David Livingstone **92**

Otfinoski, S. Juan Ponce de Leon **92**

Otfinoski, S. Marco Polo **92**

Great explorers book [series]

Goodman, J. E. Despite all obstacles: La Salle
and the conquest of the Mississippi **92**

Goodman, J. E. A long and uncertain journey:
the 27,000 mile voyage of Vasco da Gama
92

Great extinctions of the past. Mehling, R.
576.8

The **great** fire. Murphy, J. **977.3**

The **great** frog race and other poems. George, K.
O. **811**

The **great** fuzz frenzy. Stevens, J. **E**

The **great** Gilly Hopkins. Paterson, K. **Fic**

The **great** graph contest. Leedy, L. **E**

Great horned owl *See* Owls

A great idea [series]

Allman, T. The Jaws of Life **628.9**

Allman, T. The Nexi robot **629.8**

Allman, T. Recycled tires **678**

Cartlidge, C. Home windmills **621.4**

Cartlidge, C. Water from air **628.1**

Hirschmann, K. LEGO toys **688.7**

Juettner, B. Hybrid cars **629.222**

Juettner, B. The seed vault **631.5**

Mooney, C. Sunscreen for plants **632**

Woog, A. The bionic hand **617**

Woog, A. YouTube **006.7**

Great idea series

Kulling, M. It's a snap! **92**

Great inventions of the 20th century. Jedicke, P.
609

Great joy. DiCamillo, K. **E**

The **great** kapok tree. Cherry, L. **E**

Great Lakes

Kummer, P. K. The Great Lakes **977**

Great Lakes region

Fiction

Holling, H. C. Paddle-to-the-sea **Fic**

The **great** little Madison. Fritz, J. **92**

The **great** math tattle battle. Bowen, A. **E**

The **great** migration. Lawrence, J. **759.13**

Great minds of ancient science and math [se-
ries]

Hightower, P. The greatest mathematician
92

Great minds of science [series]

Anderson, M. J. Carl Linnaeus **92**

Anderson, M. J. Isaac Newton **92**

Andronik, C. M. Copernicus **92**

Green, Robert, 1969-
Coal   553.2

Green, Roger Lancelyn, 1918-1987
King Arthur and his Knights of the Round Table   398.2

Green, Sheila Ellen *See* Greenwald, Sheila, 1934-

Green, Tim
Baseball great   **Fic**
Football genius   **Fic**
Football hero   **Fic**

Green architecture *See* Sustainable architecture

Green as a bean. Kuskin, K.   **E**

Green Belt Movement (Kenya)
Johnson, J. C. Seeds of change [biography of Wangari Maathai]   92
Napoli, D. J. Mama Miti: Wangari Maathai and the trees of Kenya   92
Nivola, C. A. Planting the trees of Kenya   92
Winter, J. Wangari's trees of peace [biography of Wangari Maathai]   92

Green butterfly. Thierry, R.   **E**

Green changes you can make around your home. Smalley, C. P.   333.72

Green-collar careers [series]
Gazlay, S. Managing green spaces   333.7

The **green** dog. Staples, S. F.   **Fic**

Green eggs and ham. Seuss, Dr.   **E**

The **green** frogs. Heo, Y.   398.2

Green generation [series]
Dell, P. Protecting the planet   333.72
Hanel, R. Climate fever   363.7
Raatma, L. Green living   333.72
Rau, D. M. Alternative energy beyond fossil fuels   333.79

The **green** glass sea. Klages, E.   **Fic**

Green grass and white milk. See Aliki. Milk from cow to carton   637

Green iguanas. Lunis, N.   639.3

Green Light readers [series]
Bunting, E. My robot   **E**
Dewey, A. Splash!   **E**
Howard, R. The big, big wall   **E**
McPhail, D. M. Big Pig and Little Pig   **E**
Medina, J. Tomás Rivera   92

Green living. Raatma, L.   333.72

Green reads. Wesson, L. P.   016.3

Green team [series]
Hewitt, S. Using energy   333.79
Hewitt, S. Your food   641.3
Hewitt, S. Your local environment   333.72

Green Wilma, frog in space. Arnold, T.   **E**

Greenaway, Theresa, 1947-
Crabs   595.3
Jungle   577.3
Whales   599.5

Greenberg, Daniel A.
Chimpanzees   599.8
Whales   599.5

Greenberg, David
Crocs!   **E**
Enchanted lions   **E**

Greenberg, Hank, 1911-1986
About
McDonough, Y. Z. Hammerin' Hank [biography of Hank Greenberg]   92

Greenberg, Jan, 1942-
Action Jackson [biography of Jackson Pollock]   92
(ed) Heart to heart. See Heart to heart   811.008

Greenberg, Melanie Hope
(il) Krull, K. Supermarket   381

Greenberg, Suzanne
(jt. auth) Glatt, L. Abigail Iris: the one and only   **Fic**

Greene, Bette, 1934-
Philip Hall likes me, I reckon maybe   **Fic**
Summer of my German soldier   **Fic**

Greene, Charles Sumner, 1868-1957
About
Thorne-Thomsen, K. Greene & Greene for kids [biography of Charlie & Henry Greene]   92

Greene, Ellin, 1927-
The little golden lamb   398.2
Storytelling: art & technique   372.6

Greene, Henry Mather, 1870-1954
About
Thorne-Thomsen, K. Greene & Greene for kids [biography of Charlie & Henry Greene]   92

Greene, Jacqueline Dembar
Grizzly bears   599.78
The secret shofar of Barcelona   **Fic**

Greene, Meg
Louis Sachar   92

Greene, Nathanael, 1742-1786
About
Mierka, G. A. Nathanael Greene   92

Greene, Stephanie
Moose's big idea   **Fic**
Owen Foote, frontiersman   **Fic**
Princess Posey and the first grade parade   **Fic**

Greene & Greene for kids [biography of Charlie & Henry Greene] Thorne-Thomsen, K.   92

Greenelsh, Susan
(il) Fielding, B. Animal baths   591.5

Greenfeld, Howard
The hidden children   940.53

Greenfeld, Marsha D.
(jt. auth) Hutchins, D. J. Family reading night   372.4

Greenfield, Eloise, 1929-
Africa dream   **E**
Brothers & sisters   811
The friendly four   **Fic**
Grandpa's face   **E**
Honey, I love, and other love poems   811
Paul Robeson   92
Sister   **Fic**
When the horses ride by   811

Greenhouse effect
Baker, S. Climate change in the Antarctic   508

Greenhouse effect—*Continued*
Baker, S. In temperate zones   **551.6**
Baker, S. In the Antarctic   **508**
Baker, S. In the Arctic   **971.9**
Baker, S. In the tropics   **508**
Bridges, A. Clean air   **363.7**
Cherry, L. How we know what we know about our changing climate   **363.7**
Cole, J. The magic school bus and the climate challenge   **363.7**
David, L. The down-to-earth guide to global warming   **363.7**
Delano, M. F. Earth in the hot seat   **363.7**
Gore, A., Jr. An inconvenient truth   **363.7**
Guiberson, B. Z. Earth feeling the heat   **363.7**
Hanel, R. Climate fever   **363.7**
Hartman, E. Climate change   **551.6**
Lourie, P. Arctic thaw   **998**
Metz, L. What can we do about global warming?   **363.7**
Morris, N. Global warming   **363.7**
Nardo, D. Climate crisis   **363.7**
Parks, P. J. Global warming   **363.7**
Pringle, L. P. Global warming   **363.7**
Rockwell, A. F. What's so bad about gasoline?   **665.5**
Rockwell, A. F. Why are the ice caps melting?   **363.7**
Royston, A. Global warming   **363.7**
Simon, S. Global warming   **363.7**
Simpson, K. Extreme weather   **551.6**
Thornhill, J. This is my planet   **363.7**
Wells, R. E. Polar bear, why is your world melting?   **363.7**
Fiction
Stead, R. First light   **Fic**

Greenland
Fiction
Stead, R. First light   **Fic**

Greenseid, Diane
(il) Woodson, J. We had a picnic this Sunday past   **E**

Greenstein, Elaine, 1959-
The goose man   **92**

Greenwald, Lisa
My life in pink and green   **Fic**

Greenwald, Sheila, 1934-
Rosy Cole's worst ever, best yet tour of New York City   **Fic**

Greenwillow read-alone books [series]
Prelutsky, J. It's Valentine's Day   **811**

Greenwood, Barbara
A pioneer sampler   **971.3**

Greenwood, Mark, 1958-
The donkey of Gallipoli   **940.4**

Greeting card making. Hufford, D.   **745.59**

Greeting cards
Hufford, D. Greeting card making   **745.59**

Greetings from planet Earth. Kerley, B.   **Fic**

Gregor the Overlander. Collins, S.   **Fic**

Gregorowski, Christopher, 1940-
Fly, eagle, fly!   **398.2**

Gregory, Adair
(jt. auth) Peacock, C. A. Sugar was my best food   **362.1**

Gregory, Kristiana
Bronte's book club   **Fic**
My darlin' Clementine   **Fic**

Gregory, Kyle Carney
(jt. auth) Peacock, C. A. Sugar was my best food   **362.1**

Gregory, Nan, 1944-
I'll sing you one-o   **Fic**
Pink   **E**

Gregory, the terrible eater. Sharmat, M.   **E**

Greiner, Tony
Analyzing library collection use with Excel   **025.2**

Grenier, Daniel
(il) Daigle, E. The world of penguins   **598**

Greste, Peter
(il) Hatkoff, I. Owen & Mzee   **599.63**
(il) Hatkoff, I. Owen & Mzee: the language of friendship   **599.63**
(il) Looking for Miza. See Looking for Miza   **599.8**

Gretz, Susanna
Riley and Rose in the picture   **E**

Grey, Mini
The adventures of the dish and the spoon   **E**
Egg drop   **E**
Traction Man is here!   **E**
(il) Gardner, L. Into the woods   **Fic**
(il) King-Smith, D. The twin giants   **E**

The grey king. Cooper, S.   **Fic**

Gribnau, Joe
Kick the cowboy   **E**

Gridzbi spudvetch. See Haddon, M. Boom!   **Fic**

Griego, Margot C.
(comp) Tortillitas para mamá and other nursery rhymes. See Tortillitas para mamá and other nursery rhymes   **398.8**

Grifalconi, Ann
Ain't nobody a stranger to me   **E**
The village of round and square houses   **398.2**
The village that vanished   **E**
(il) Dorros, A. Julio's magic   **E**
(il) Myers, W. D. Patrol   **E**

Griff Carver, hallway patrol. Krieg, J.   **Fic**

Griffin, Peni R.
The ghost sitter   **Fic**

Griffin, Rachel, 1962-
(il) Mhlophe, G. African tales   **398.2**

Griffin, Robert, 1951-
(ed) Junior Worldmark encyclopedia of world holidays. See Junior Worldmark encyclopedia of world holidays   **394.26**

Griffith, Gershom, 1960-
(il) Adler, D. A. A picture book of Sojourner Truth   **92**

Griffiths, Andy, 1961-
The big fat cow that goes kapow   **E**
The cat on the mat is flat   **E**

Groundhog Day
Gibbons, G. Groundhog day!   **394.26**
Fiction
Cox, J. Go to sleep, Groundhog!   E
Hill, S. L. Punxsutawney Phyllis   E
Groundhog gets a say. Swallow, P. C.   E
Grow it, cook it   **635**
Growing colors. McMillan, B.   E
Growing patterns. Campbell, S. C.   **513**
The **growing** story. Krauss, R.   E
Growing up in coal country. Bartoletti, S. C.
    331.3
Growing up in pioneer America, 1800 to 1890.
Josephson, J. P.   **978**
Growing up in revolution and the new nation,
1775 to 1800. Miller, B. M.   **973.3**
Growing up: it's a girl thing. Jukes, M.   **612.6**
Growing up with tamales = Los Tamales de Ana.
Zepeda, G.   E
Growing vegetable soup. Ehlert, L.   E
Growing your own garden. Hirsch, R. E.   **635**
Growth
Gaff, J. Looking at growing up   **612.6**
Parker, S. Reproduction   **612.6**
Saltz, G. Amazing you   **612.6**
Schwartz, J. Short   **612.6**
Seeger, L. V. First the egg   E
Silverstein, A. Growth and development
    571.8
Wade, M. D. Plants grow!   **571.8**
Fiction
Bergstein, R. M. Your own big bed   E
Brown, M. W. Another important book   E
Bunting, E. Baby can   E
Bunting, E. Little Bear's little boat   E
Cruise, R. Bartleby speaks!   E
Cyrus, K. Tadpole Rex   E
Elya, S. M. Adios, tricycle   E
Fitzpatrick, M.-L. There   E
Ford, B. No more bottles for Bunny!   E
Gay, M.-L. When Stella was very very small
    E
Gerstein, M. Leaving the nest   E
Gore, L. When I grow up   E
Krauss, R. The growing story   E
McBratney, S. When I'm big   E
McGhee, A. Bye-bye, crib   E
Pearson, D. Sophie's wheels   E
Rand, A. I know a lot of things   E
Sandemose, I. Gracie & Grandma & the itsy,
bitsy seed   E
Slater, D. The sea serpent and me   E
Stein, D. E. Pouch!   E
Stinson, K. Big or little?   E
Sussman, M. B. Otto grows down   E
Swanson, S. M. The first thing my mama told
me   E
Torrey, R. Almost   E
Wild, M. Puffling   E
Zepeda, G. Growing up with tamales = Los Ta-
males de Ana   E
Growth and development. Silverstein, A.
    571.8

Growth disorders
See also Dwarfism
Growth retardation *See* Dwarfism
Gruber, Beth
Ancient Inca   **985**
Ancient Iraq   **935**
Mexico   **972**
Gruen, John
(il) Ronci, K. Kids crochet   **746.43**
The **gruesome** guide to world monsters. Sierra, J.
    398
Grump groan growl. Hooks, B.   E
Grumpy Bird. Tankard, J.   E
Grumpy cat. Teckentrup, B.   E
Grumpy Grandpa. Henson, H.   E
Grupper, Jonathan
Destination: deep sea   **591.7**
Destination: Rocky Mountains   **978**
Grutter, Alexandra
About
Collard, S. B., III. On the coral reefs   **577.7**
Guan Yu *See* Kuan, Yu, 160-220
Guan Yu. Jolley, D.   **741.5**
Guarino, Deborah, 1954-
Is your mama a llama?   E
Guatemala
Croy, A. Guatemala   **972.81**
Menchú, R. The girl from Chimel   **92**
Fiction
Carling, A. L. Mama & Papa have a store
    E
Castañeda, O. S. Abuela's weave   E
Ichikawa, S. My pig Amarillo   E
Guay, Rebecca
(il) Hawes, L. Black pearls   S C
Guback, Georgia
Luka's quilt   E
Gudeon, Karla
(il) Ziefert, H. Hanukkah haiku   **296.4**
(il) Ziefert, H. One red apple   **634**
(il) Ziefert, H. Passover   **296.4**
Guéry, Anne
Alphab'art   **709**
Guess, George *See* Sequoyah, 1770?-1843
Guess again!. Barnett, M.   E
Guess how much I love you. McBratney, S.   E
Guess what I found in Dragon Wood? Knapman,
T.   E
Guess what is growing inside this egg. Posada, M.
    591.4
Guess who? Miller, M.   E
Guess who, Baby Duck!. Hest, A.   E
Guess who's coming to Santa's for dinner? De
Paola, T.   E
Guest, Elissa Haden, 1953-
Harriet's had enough   E
Iris and Walter   E
Guevara, Susan
(il) Dorros, A. Número uno   E
(il) Johnston, T. Voice from afar   **811**
(il) Lillegard, D. Tiger, tiger   E

Guevara, Susan—*Continued*
  (il) Soto, G. Chato's kitchen   **E**
  (il) Yolen, J. Not one damsel in distress
        398.2

Gugu's house. Stock, C.   **E**

Guiberson, Brenda Z., 1946-
  Cactus hotel   **583**
  Disasters   **904**
  Earth feeling the heat   **363.7**
  The emperor lays an egg   **598**
  Ice bears   **599.78**
  Into the sea   **597.92**
  Life in the boreal forest   **578.7**
  Moon bear   **599.78**
  Mud city   **598**
  Rain, rain, rain forest   **577.3**

Guibert, Emmanuel, 1964-
  Sardine in outer space   **741.5**

Guida, Liisa Chauncy
  (jt. auth) Tomecek, S. Moon   **523.3**

Guidance, Vocational *See* Vocational guidance

Guide dogs
  Kent, D. Animal helpers for the disabled
        636.088
  Patent, D. H. The right dog for the job
        362.4

Fiction
  Cole, B. H. Anna & Natalie   **E**

Guide to collective biographies for children and
  young adults. Barancik, S.   **016.9**

Guile, Melanie, 1949-
  Culture in India   **954**
  Culture in Malaysia   **959.5**
  Culture in Vietnam   **959.7**

Guillain, Charlotte
  Caring for nature   **333.95**
  Cycling   **796.6**
  Different sounds   **534**
  How do we hear?   **612.8**
  Making sounds   **534**
  Saving energy   **333.79**
  Saving water   **333.91**
  Soccer   **796.334**
  Swimming   **797.2**
  What is sound?   **534**

Guilt

Fiction
  Bunting, E. Blackwater   **Fic**

Guinea PIG, Pet shop private eye [series]
  Venable, C. A. Hamster and cheese   **741.5**

Guinea pig scientists. Dendy, L. A.   **616**

Guinea pigs
  Barnes, J. Pet guinea pigs   **636.9**
  Foran, J. Guinea pig   **636.9**
  Holub, J. Why do rabbits hop?   **636.9**
  Jeffrey, L. S. Hamsters, gerbils, guinea pigs,
    rabbits, ferrets, mice, and rats   **636.9**
  Johnson, J. Guinea pigs   **636.9**
  Newcomb, R. Is my hamster wild?   **636.9**
  Petrylak, A. Guinea pigs   **636.9**
  See/See also pages in the following book(s):
  Bozzo, L. My first guinea pig and other small
    pets   **636.9**

Fiction
  Bateson, C. Being Bee   **Fic**
  Berenzy, A. Sammy the classroom guinea pig
        E
  Brannen, S. S. Uncle Bobby's wedding   **E**
  Meade, H. John Willy and Freddy McGee   **E**
  Middleton, C. Nibbles: a green tale   **E**
  Weigelt, U. Super Guinea Pig to the rescue
        E

Folklore
  Knutson, B. Love and roast chicken   **398.2**
Graphic novels
  Venable, C. A. Hamster and cheese   **741.5**
Poetry
  Katz, S. Oh, Theodore!   **811**

Guinea pigs. Petrylak, A.   **636.9**
Guinness book of records. See Guinness world re-
  cords   **032.02**
Guinness book of world records. See Guinness
  world records   **032.02**
Guinness world records   **032.02**

Guitarists
  Christensen, B. Django [Reinhardt]   **92**
  Wyckoff, E. B. Electric guitar man: the genius
    of Les Paul   **92**

Guitars
  Blaxland, W. Guitars   **787.87**

Guji Guji. Chen, C.-Y.   **E**
Gullahs

Fiction
  Belton, S. Beauty, her basket   **E**
  Raven, M. Circle unbroken   **E**

Gullible Gus. Schur, M.   **Fic**

Gulliver, Amanda
  (il) O'Connell, R. Danny is done with diapers
        E

Gulls
  Gibbons, G. Gulls—gulls—gulls   **598**
Gulls—gulls—gulls. Gibbons, G.   **598**
Gully's travels. Seidler, T.   **Fic**
Gumption!. Broach, E.   **E**

Gunderson, Jessica, 1976-
  The emperor's painting   **Fic**
  The jade dragon   **Fic**
  Stranger on the silk road   **Fic**
  The terracotta girl   **Fic**

Gunnella, 1956-
  (il) McMillan, B. How the ladies stopped the
    wind   **E**
  (il) McMillan, B. The problem with chickens
        E

Gunter, Veronika Alice
  Pet science   **636**
  The ultimate indoor games book   **793**
  (jt. auth) Rhatigan, J. Cool chemistry concoc-
    tions   **540.7**

Gunzi, Christiane
  (jt. auth) Murrell, D. J. Mega trucks
        629.224

Guo Yue, 1958-
  Little Leap Forward   **Fic**
Gurstelle, William
  The art of the catapult   **623.4**

Gus and Grandpa and the two-wheeled bike. Mills, C. **E**

Gus is a fish. Babin, C. **E**

Gustafson, Scott, 1956-
(il) Barrie, J. M. Peter Pan **Fic**
(il) Favorite nursery rhymes from Mother Goose. See Favorite nursery rhymes from Mother Goose **398.8**

Gustavson, Adam
(il) Borden, L. The A+ custodian **E**
(il) Borden, L. Good luck, Mrs. K! **E**
(il) Borden, L. The John Hancock Club **E**
(il) Borden, L. The last day of school **Fic**
(il) Borden, L. The lost-and-found tooth **Fic**
(il) Kay, V. Rough, tough Charley [biography of Charley Parkhurst] **92**
(il) Kimmelman, L. Mind your manners, Alice Roosevelt! **E**
(il) Weber, E. The Yankee at the seder **Fic**

Gut-eating bugs. Denega, D. **363.2**

Gutenberg, Johann, 1397?-1468
About
Koscielniak, B. Johann Gutenberg and the amazing printing press **686.2**
Fiction
Skelton, M. Endymion Spring **Fic**

Guthrie, Woody, 1912-1967
About
Christensen, B. Woody Guthrie, poet of the people **92**
See/See also pages in the following book(s):
Krull, K. Lives of the musicians **920**

Gutierrez, Akemi
(il) Ramos, J. I'm just like my mom/I'm just like my dad **E**

Gutierrez, Rudy
(il) Brown, M. Pele, king of soccer **92**
(il) Dorros, A. Papá and me **E**

Gutman, Dan
Casey back at bat **811**
The Christmas genie **Fic**
Coach Hyatt is a riot! **Fic**
The homework machine **Fic**
Shoeless Joe & me **Fic**
(ed) Recycle this book. See Recycle this book **333.72**

Guts. Simon, S. **612.3**

Guttersnipe. Cutler, J. **E**

Guy, Ginger Foglesong
Fiesta! **E**
Perros! Perros! Dogs! Dogs! **E**
Siesta **E**

Guy, Lucinda
Kids learn to crochet **746.43**
Kids learn to knit **746.43**

Guyana
Jermyn, L. Guyana **988.1**

Gwaltney, Doris
Homefront **Fic**

Gym shorts [series]
Hicks, B. Basketball Bats **Fic**

Gymnastics
Veitch, C. Gymnastics **796.44**

Gypsies
Fiction
Pinfold, L. The Django **E**
Rutkoski, M. The Cabinet of Wonders **Fic**

H

H.I.V.E. Walden, M. **Fic**

Haab, Michelle
(jt. auth) Haab, S. Dangles and bangles **745.5**

Haab, Sherri, 1964-
Dangles and bangles **745.5**

Haake, Martin
(il) Donovan, S. Pingpong Perry experiences how a book is made **070.5**

Haas, Jessie
Birthday pony **Fic**
Chase **Fic**
Jigsaw pony **Fic**
Sugaring **E**

Haas, Robert B.
African critters **591.9**

Habitat (Ecology)
See also types of ecology, e.g. Desert ecology; Marine ecology
Blackaby, S. Nest, nook & cranny **811**
Fleming, D. Where once there was a wood **639.9**
Habitats of the world **577**
Jenkins, S. I see a kookaburra! **591.7**
Parker, S. Animal habitats **591.7**
Stetson, E. Kids' easy-to-create wildlife habitats **639.9**
Toft, K. M. The world that we want **577**
VanCleave, J. P. Janice Vancleave's ecology for every kid **577**

Habitats of the world **577**

Hachiko. Turner, P. S. **E**

Hachiko waits. Newman, L. **Fic**

Had gadya **296.4**

Haddix, Margaret Peterson, 1964-
Dexter the tough **Fic**
Found **Fic**

Haddon, Mark
Boom! **Fic**
Footprints on the Moon **E**

Hader, Berta, 1891-1976
The big snow **E**

Hader, Elmer Stanley, 1889-1973
(jt. auth) Hader, B. The big snow **E**

Haduch, Bill
Go fly a bike! **629.227**
Science fair success secrets **507.8**

Haefele, Steve
(il) Cobb, V. Squirts and spurts **507.8**

Hafner, Marylin, 1925-
(il) Berger, M. Germs make me sick! **616.9**
(il) Dodds, D. A. Teacher's pets **E**
(il) Horvath, P. The Pepins and their problems **Fic**
(il) Prelutsky, J. It's Christmas! **811**

Halkin, Hillel, 1939-
(jt. auth) Orlev, U. The man from the other side **Fic**

Hall, Algy Craig
(il) Weatherly, L. The scariest monster in the world **E**

Hall, Alvin
Show me the money **332.024**

Hall, August
(il) Appelt, K. Keeper **Fic**

Hall, Bruce Edward
Henry and the kite dragon **E**

Hall, Donald, 1928-
Ox-cart man **E**
(ed) The Oxford book of children's verse in America. See The Oxford book of children's verse in America **811.008**

Hall, Eleanor J.
Recycling **363.7**

Hall, François
(jt. auth) Guy, L. Kids learn to crochet **746.43**
(jt. auth) Guy, L. Kids learn to knit **746.43**

Hall, Greg, 1963-
(il) Thomas, K. Planet Earth News presents: super humans **031.02**

Hall, Katy, 1947-
See also McMullan, Kate, 1947-
Creepy riddles **793.73**
Dino riddles **793.73**
Ribbit riddles **793.73**
Simms Taback's great big book of spacey, snakey, buggy riddles **793.73**
Snakey riddles **793.73**
Turkey riddles **793.73**

Hall, Kirsten, 1974-
Leatherback turtle **597.92**

Hall, Marcellus
(il) Hopkins, L. B. City I love **811**
(il) Wilson, K. The cow loves cookies **E**

Hall, Margaret, 1947-
Banks **332.1**
Credit cards and checks **332.7**
Your allowance **332.024**

Hall, Melanie W.
(il) Every second something happens. See Every second something happens **811.008**
(il) Fishman, C. On Hanukkah **296.4**
(il) Fishman, C. On Rosh Hashanah and Yom Kippur **296.4**
(il) Fishman, C. On Sukkot and Simchat Torah **296.4**
(il) Hanukkah lights. See Hanukkah lights **811.008**
(il) Schram, P. The magic pomegranate **398.2**

Hall, Michael, 1954-
My heart is like a zoo **E**

Hall, Ruby Bridges *See* Bridges, Ruby

Hall, Susan, 1940-
Using picture storybooks to teach literary devices **016.8**

Hall, Teri
The Line **Fic**

Hall, Zoe, 1957-
The apple pie tree **634**

Hall-Ellis, Sylvia Dunn, 1949-
Grants for school libraries **025.1**

Hallam, Arlita
Managing budgets and finances **025.1**

The **Hallelujah** Flight. Bildner, P. **E**

Hallensleben, Georg
(il) Banks, K. And if the moon could talk **E**
(il) Banks, K. Baboon **E**
(il) Banks, K. The cat who walked across France **E**
(il) Banks, K. Close your eyes **E**
(il) Banks, K. Fox **E**
(il) Banks, K. A gift from the sea **E**
(il) Banks, K. The night worker **E**
(il) Banks, K. What's coming for Christmas? **E**

Hallett, Mark, 1947-
(il) Becker, J. E. Wild cats: past & present **599.75**

The **Hallo-wiener**. Pilkey, D. **E**

Halloran, Josh
(il) Walsh, D. The cardboard box book **745.54**

Halloween
Barth, E. Witches, pumpkins, and grinning ghosts **394.26**
Bowers, S. Ghoulish goodies **641.5**
Gibbons, G. Halloween is— **394.26**
Heiligman, D. Celebrate Halloween **394.26**
McGee, R. Paper crafts for Halloween **745.594**
Old, W. The Halloween book of facts and fun **394.26**
See/See also pages in the following book(s):
Bauer, C. F. Celebrations **808.8**

Fiction
Brenner, T. And then comes Halloween **E**
Bunting, E. The bones of Fred McFee **E**
Choi, Y. Behind the mask **E**
Corey, S. Monster parade **E**
De Groat, D. Trick or treat, smell my feet **E**
Dickinson, R. Over in the hollow **E**
Evans, C. Bone soup **E**
Fleming, D. Pumpkin eye **E**
Freeman, M. Who stole Halloween? **Fic**
Galbraith, K. O. Boo, bunny! **E**
Hubbell, W. Pumpkin Jack **E**
Leuck, L. One witch **E**
Marshall, E. Space case **E**
Martin, B. Trick or treat? **E**
McGhee, A. A very brave witch **E**
Montes, M. Los gatos black on Halloween **E**
Murray, M. D. Halloween night **E**
Pilkey, D. The Hallo-wiener **E**
Pitchford, D. Captain Nobody **Fic**
Rylant, C. Moonlight: the Halloween cat **E**
Serfozo, M. Plumply, dumply pumpkin **E**
Stutson, C. By the light of the Halloween moon **E**

Handwriting

See also Calligraphy

Fiction

Borden, L. The John Hancock Club	E
Cleary, B. Muggie Maggie	Fic

Handyside, Chris, 1972-

Blues	781.643
Country	781.642
Folk	781.62
Jazz	781.65
Rock	781.66
Soul and R&B	781.644

Hanel, Rachael

Climate fever	363.7
Gladiators	937
Knights	940.1
Penguins	598
Samurai	952
Tigers	599.75

Haney, Johannah

Ferrets	636.97
Frogs	639.3
Parrots	636.6
Small birds	636.6
Turtles	639.3

Hanft, Joshua E., 1956-

The miracles of Passover	296.4
Miracles of the Bible	221.9

Hank finds inspiration. Frazier, C.   E

Hankin, Rosie

Crafty kids	745.5

Hanna, Dan

(il) Diesen, D. The pout-pout fish	E

Hannah, Julie

The man who named the clouds [biography of Luke Howard]   92

Hannah is my name. Yang, B.   E

Hanne's quest. Dunrea, O.   Fic

Hannigan, Katherine

Emmaline and the bunny	Fic
Ida B	Fic

Hans Brinker. Coville, B.   E

Hans Brinker, or, The silver skates. Dodge, M. M.   Fic

Hans Christian Andersen's Fairy Tales [illustrated by Lisbeth Zwerger] Andersen, H. C.   S C

Hansel and Gretel. Grimm, J.	398.2
Hansel and Gretel. Isadora, R.	398.2
Hansel and Gretel. Lesser, R.	398.2
Hansel and Gretel. Marshall, J.	398.2
Hansel and Gretel. Morpurgo, M.	398.2
Hansel and Gretel. Rylant, C.	398.2

Hansen, Amy

Bugs and bugsicles	595.7

Hansen, Mark Victor

(jt. auth) Canfield, J. Chicken soup for the soul: kids in the kitchen   641.5

Hanson, Anders, 1980-

Cool calligraphy	745.6
Cool collage	702.8
Cool drawing	741.2
Cool painting	751.4
Cool printmaking	760.2
Cool sculpture	731.4

Hanson, Mary Elizabeth

How to save your tail	Fic

Hanson, Warren

Bugtown Boogie	E

Hantula, Richard

(jt. auth) Asimov, I. The life and death of stars   523.8

(jt. auth) Asimov, I. The Milky Way and other galaxies   523.1

Hanukkah

Fishman, C. On Hanukkah	296.4
Heiligman, D. Celebrate Hanukkah	296.4
Heller, E. S. Menorah under the sea	296.4
Hoyt-Goldsmith, D. Celebrating Hanukkah	296.4
Lehman-Wilzig, T. Hanukkah around the world	296.4
Ziefert, H. Hanukkah haiku	296.4

Fiction

Bunting, E. One candle	E
Da Costa, D. Hanukkah moon	E
Edwards, M. Papa's latkes	E
Glaser, L. Hoppy Hanukkah!	E
Howland, N. Latkes, latkes, good to eat	E
Kimmel, E. A. The Chanukkah guest	E
Kimmel, E. A. Hershel and the Hanukkah goblins	E
Kimmel, E. A. The jar of fools: eight Hanukkah stories from Chelm	S C
Kimmel, E. A. Zigazak!	E
Krensky, S. Hanukkah at Valley Forge	E
Kroll, S. The Hanukkah mice	E
Kushner, E. The golden dreydl	Fic
Martin, D. Hanukkah lights	E
Ofanansky, A. Harvest of light	E
Polacco, P. The trees of the dancing goats	E
Rosen, M. J. Elijah's angel	Fic
Snicket, L. The latke who couldn't stop screaming	E
Spinner, S. It's a miracle!	E

Poetry

Hanukkah lights	811.008

Songs

Baum, M. I have a little dreidel	782.42
Roth, S. L. Hanukkah, oh Hanukkah	782.42

Hanukkah around the world. Lehman-Wilzig, T.   296.4

Hanukkah at Valley Forge. Krensky, S.   E

Hanukkah haiku. Ziefert, H.   296.4

Hanukkah lights   811.008

Hanukkah lights. Martin, D.   E

The **Hanukkah** mice. Kroll, S.   E

Hanukkah moon. Da Costa, D.   E

Hanukkah, oh Hanukkah. Roth, S. L.   782.42

Hapipi, Rafiz

(jt. auth) Foley, E. El Salvador   972.84

Happenstance found. Catanese, P. W.   Fic

Happy and Honey. Godwin, L.   E

Happy bees. Yorinks, A.   E

Happy belly, happy smile. Isadora, R.   E

Happy birth day!. Harris, R. H.   E

Happy birthday, Martin Luther King. Marzollo, J.
92

Happy birthday, Moon. Asch, F.   E

Happy birthday to you!. Raven, M.   782.42

Happy, happy Chinese New Year!. Demi
394.26

Happy Honey [series]
Godwin, L. Happy and Honey   E

Happy New Year! Kung-Hsi Fa-ts'ai! See Demi.
Happy, happy Chinese New Year!   394.26

Happy Nowruz. Batmanglij, N.   641.5

Haptie, Charlotte
Otto and the flying twins   Fic

Harada, Violet H.
Assessing learning   027.8
Inquiry learning through librarian-teacher partnerships   371.1
(jt. auth) Hughes-Hassell, S. School reform and the school library media specialist   027.8

Harbo, Christopher L.
The kids' guide to paper airplanes   745.592

Harbors
Crews, D. Harbor   E

Harburg, E. Y. (Edgar Yipsel), 1896-1981
Over the rainbow   782.42

Harburg, Edgar Yipsel *See* Harburg, E. Y. (Edgar Yipsel), 1896-1981

Harburg, Yip *See* Harburg, E. Y. (Edgar Yipsel), 1896-1981

Hard gold. Avi   Fic

Hard hat area. Roth, S. L.   E

Harding, R. R., 1938-
(jt. auth) Symes, R. F. Crystal & gem   548

Hardinge, Frances
Fly by night   Fic
Well witched   Fic

Hardy, Janice
The shifter   Fic

The **hare** and the lion. See Aardema, V. Rabbit makes a monkey of lion   398.2

The **hare** and the tortoise. Ward, H.   398.2

The **hare** and the tortoise and other fables of La Fontaine. Bolt, R.   398.2

The **hare** and the tortoise = La liebre y la tortuga. Valeri, M. E.   398.2

Hargis, Wes
(il) Koehler-Pentacoff, E. Jackson and Bud's bumpy ride   917.3

Hargraves, Orin
(jt. auth) Seward, P. Morocco   964

Hariton, Anca, 1955-
(il) Richards, J. A fruit is a suitcase for seeds
581.4

Harker, Christa
Library research with emergent readers
027.62

Harker, Lesley
(il) Doherty, B. The goblin baby   Fic
(il) Thomas, P. Do I have to go to the dentist?
617.6
(il) Thomas, P. I think I am going to sneeze
616.97

Harkins, Susan Sales
Design your own butterfly garden   638
Threat to the whooping crane   598

Harkins, William H.
(jt. auth) Harkins, S. S. Design your own butterfly garden   638
(jt. auth) Harkins, S. S. Threat to the whooping crane   598

Harkrader, L. D. *See* Harkrader, Lisa

Harkrader, Lisa
(jt. auth) Gottfried, T. Marijuana   362.29

Harlan, Mary Ann
Personal learning networks   027.8

Harlem (New York, N.Y.)
     Fiction
Bootman, C. Steel pan man of Harlem   E
Campbell, B. M. Stompin' at the Savoy   E
Collier, B. Uptown   E
Myers, W. D. Looking like me   E
Ringgold, F. Tar Beach   E
Tate, E. E. Celeste's Harlem Renaissance
Fic
Taylor, D. A. Sweet music in Harlem   E
     Poetry
Myers, W. D. Harlem   811

The **Harlem** Hellfighters. Myers, W. D.   940.4

Harlem Renaissance
The entrance place of wonders   811.008
Johnson, D. The Harlem Renaissance   700
Schroeder, A. In her hands   92
Worth, R. The Harlem Renaissance   700
     Fiction
Tate, E. E. Celeste's Harlem Renaissance
Fic

Harley, Avis
African acrostics   811
The monarch's progress   811
Sea stars   811

Harley, Bill, 1954-
Dirty Joe, the pirate   E

Harlin, Greg
(il) Krensky, S. Hanukkah at Valley Forge
E

Harlin, Gregory
(il) Krensky, S. Dangerous crossing   Fic

Harlow, Joan Hiatt
Secret of the night ponies   Fic
Star in the storm   Fic

Harmin, Karen Leigh
J. K. Rowling   92

Harmon, Charles T., 1960-
(jt. auth) Symons, A. K. Protecting the right to read   025.2

Harmonicas
     Fiction
McCloskey, R. Lentil   E

Harms, Jeanne McLain
Picture books to enhance the curriculum
011.6

Harness, Cheryl
Abe Lincoln goes to Washington, 1837-1865
92
The adventurous life of Myles Standish   92
The amazing impossible Erie Canal   386

Hassell, Sandra Hughes- *See* Hughes-Hassell, Sandra

Hassig, Susan M., 1969-
Iraq   **956.7**
Panama   **972.87**
Somalia   **967.73**

Hastings, Jon
Terrabella Smoot and the unsung monsters
    741.5

The **hat**. Brett, J.   **E**

Hat. Hoppe, P.   **E**

A **hat** for Minerva Louise. Stoeke, J. M.   **E**

The **hat** that wore Clara B. Turner-Denstaedt, M.
    E

Hatasu *See* Hatshepsut, Queen of Egypt

Hatchepset *See* Hatshepsut, Queen of Egypt

Hatching magic. Downer, A.   **Fic**

Hate crimes
Brimner, L. D. Birmingham Sunday   **323.1**

Hatha yoga *See* Yoga

Hatkoff, Craig
Looking for Miza. See Looking for Miza
    599.8
(jt. auth) Hatkoff, I. Owen & Mzee   **599.63**
(jt. auth) Hatkoff, I. Owen & Mzee: the language of friendship   **599.63**
(jt. auth) Hatkoff, J. Knut   **599.78**
(jt. auth) Hatkoff, J. Winter's tail   **639.9**

Hatkoff, Isabella
Owen & Mzee   **599.63**
Owen & Mzee: the language of friendship
    599.63
Looking for Miza. See Looking for Miza
    599.8
(jt. auth) Hatkoff, J. Knut   **599.78**
(jt. auth) Hatkoff, J. Winter's tail   **639.9**

Hatkoff, Juliana
Knut   **599.78**
Winter's tail   **639.9**
Looking for Miza. See Looking for Miza
    599.8

The **hatmaker's** sign. Fleming, C.   **E**

Hats
Morris, A. Hats, hats, hats   **391**
    Fiction
D'Amico, C. Ella the Elegant Elephant   **E**
Hoppe, P. Hat   **E**
Howard, E. F. Aunt Flossie's hats (and crab cakes later)   **E**
Kimmel, E. A. Stormy's hat   **E**
Klise, K. Shall I knit you a hat?   **E**
Lichtenheld, T. Bridget's beret   **E**
Seuss, Dr. The 500 hats of Bartholomew Cubbins   **E**
Stoeke, J. M. A hat for Minerva Louise   **E**
Turner-Denstaedt, M. The hat that wore Clara B.   **E**

Hats, hats, hats. Morris, A.   **391**

The **hatseller** and the monkeys. Wagué Diakité, B.
    398.2

Hatshepsut, Queen of Egypt
    About
Galford, E. Hatshepsut   **92**

Hattie and the fox. Fox, M.   **E**

Haugen, Hayley Mitchell, 1968-
Daniel Handler [biography of Lemony Snicket]
    92

Hauman, Doris, 1898-
(il) Piper, W. The little engine that could [illustrated by George & Doris Hauman]   **E**

Hauman, George, 1890-1961
(il) Piper, W. The little engine that could [illustrated by George & Doris Hauman]   **E**

Haunted [series]
Eboch, C. The ghost on the stairs   **Fic**

Haunted party. Trapani, I.   **E**

Haunted U.S.A. Wetzel, C.   **133.1**

The **haunting** hour. Stine, R. L.   **S C**

Hauntings, and other tales of danger, love, and sometimes loss. Hearne, B. G.   **S C**

Hauser, Jill Frankel
Super science concoctions   **507.8**

Hausman, Gerald
Horses of myth   **398.2**

Hausman, Loretta
(jt. auth) Hausman, G. Horses of myth
    398.2

Have I got a book for you!. Watt, M.   **E**

Have you ever seen a sneep? Pym, T.   **E**

Have you seen my duckling? Tafuri, N.   **E**

Have you seen this face? Denega, D.   **363.2**

Haven, Kendall F.
Reluctant heroes   **920**

Haven, Paul
Two hot dogs with everything   **Fic**

Havill, Juanita
I heard it from Alice Zucchini   **811**
Jamaica's find   **E**
Just like a baby   **E**

Hawaii
Feeney, S. Sun and rain   **996.9**
Karwoski, G. Tsunami   **363.34**
    Fiction
Correa, S. Gaff   **Fic**
Guback, G. Luka's quilt   **E**
Kono, E. E. Hula lullaby   **E**
Rattigan, J. K. Dumpling soup   **E**
Salisbury, G. Calvin Coconut: trouble magnet
    Fic
Salisbury, G. Lord of the deep   **Fic**
Salisbury, G. Night of the howling dogs   **Fic**
Yep, L. City of fire   **Fic**
    Folklore
See Folklore—Hawaii
    History
Stanley, F. The last princess: the story of Princess Ka'iulani of Hawai'i   **92**
    Poetry
Peters, L. W. Volcano wakes up!   **811**

Hawass, Zahi A.
Curse of the pharaohs   **932**
Tutankhamun   **932**

Hawcock, David
(il) Platt, R. Moon landing   **629.45**

Headline science—*Continued*

Nardo, D. Climate crisis 363.7
Nardo, D. Cure quest 616
Stille, D. R. Great shakes 551.2
Stille, D. R. Nature interrupted 577
VanVoorst, J. Rise of the thinking machines 629.8

Heads of state

See also Kings and rulers; Presidents

Heads or tails. Gantos, J. Fic

Heale, Jay

Democratic Republic of the Congo 967.51
Madagascar 969.1
Poland 943.8
Portugal 946.9
Tanzania 967.8

Healing stories. Golding, J. M. 028.5

The Healing Wars [series]

Hardy, J. The shifter Fic

Health

See also Hygiene; Physical fitness

Miller, E. The monster health book 613
Read, L. Keeping well 613
Rooney, A. Health and medicine 610
Schaefer, A. Staying healthy 613

Health alert [series]

Bjorklund, R. Cerebral palsy 616.8
Bjorklund, R. Cystic fibrosis 616.3
Bjorklund, R. Eating disorders 616.85
Bjorklund, R. Epilepsy 616.8
Bjorklund, R. Food-borne illnesses 615.9
Brill, M. T. Autism 616.85
Brill, M. T. Down syndrome 616.85
Brill, M. T. Multiple sclerosis 616.8
Buckmaster, M. L. Skin cancer 616.99
Calamandrei, C. Fever 616
Capaccio, G. ADD and ADHD 616.85
Colligan, L. H. Sleep disorders 616.8
Colligan, L. H. Tick-borne illnesses 616.9
Hicks, T. A. Allergies 616.97
Hicks, T. A. Obesity 616.3
Hoffmann, G. Chicken pox 616.9
Hoffmann, G. The flu 616.2
Hoffmann, G. Mononucleosis 616.9
Hoffmann, G. Osteoporosis 616.7
Klosterman, L. Meningitis 616.8
Klosterman, L. Rabies 616.9
Petreycik, R. Headaches 616.8
Roy, J. R. Depression 616.85

Health and fitness [series]

Schaefer, A. Exercise 613.7
Schaefer, A. Healthy food 613.2
Schaefer, A. Staying healthy 613
Schaefer, A. Staying safe 613.6

Health and medicine. Rooney, A. 610

Health care *See* Medical care

Health foods *See* Natural foods

Health insurance

Lynette, R. What to do when your family can't afford healthcare 368.3

Health zone [series]

Doeden, M. Eat right! 613.2

The **healthy** body cookbook. D'Amico, J. 641.5

Healthy choices [series]

Dalgleish, S. Exercise and rest 613.7

Healthy food. Schaefer, A. 613.2

Heap, Sue, 1954-

Danny's drawing book E
(il) Jones, S. L. How to be a baby—by me, the big sister E

Hear the wind blow. Hahn, M. D. Fic

Hear this!. Hewitt, S. 612.8

Hear your heart. Showers, P. 612.1

Heard, Georgia

(comp) Falling down the page. See Falling down the page 811.008

Hearing

Boothroyd, J. What is hearing? 612.8
Cobb, V. Perk up your ears 612.8
Farndon, J. Sound and hearing 534
Guillain, C. How do we hear? 612.8
Hewitt, S. Hear this! 612.8
Simon, S. Eyes and ears 612.8
Veitch, C. Sound and hearing 612.8

Hearing impaired

See also Deaf

Hearn, Diane Dawson

(il) Levinson, N. S. Death Valley 577.5
(il) Levinson, N. S. North Pole, South Pole 998
(il) Levinson, N. S. Rain forests 577.3

Hearn, Lafcadio, 1850-1904

The old woman and her dumpling; adaptation. See Mosel, A. The funny little woman 398.2

Hearne, Betsy Gould, 1942-

The canine connection: stories about dogs and people S C
Choosing books for children 028.5
Hauntings, and other tales of danger, love, and sometimes loss S C

Hearne, Elizabeth G. *See* Hearne, Betsy Gould, 1942-

Hen hears gossip. McDonald, M. E

Heart

See also Blood—Circulation

Showers, P. Hear your heart 612.1
Simon, S. The heart 612.1

The **heart**. Simon, S. 612.1

Heart and soul: the story of Florence Nightingale. Gorrell, G. K. 92

The **heart** and the bottle. Jeffers, O. E

Heart in the pocket. Bourguignon, L. E

Heart of a shepherd. Parry, R. Fic

Heart of a tiger. Arnold, M. D. E

Heart to heart 811.008

Heartbeat. Creech, S. Fic

Hearts, cupids, and red roses. Barth, E. 394.26

Heat

Gardner, R. Easy genius science projects with temperature and heat 536
Gardner, R. Really hot science projects with temperature 536

Hello, day!. Lobel, A. **E**

Hello, good-bye. Alda, A. **E**

The **hello,** goodbye window. Juster, N. **E**

Hello, squirrels!. Glaser, L. **599.3**

Hello, twins. Voake, C. **E**

Hello world!. Stojic, M. **413**

Hellweg, Paul
The American Heritage children's thesaurus **423**

The American Heritage student thesaurus **423**

Helman, Andrea, 1946-
Hide and seek **591.47**

Helmets
Blaxland, W. Helmets **621.9**

Help!. Keller, H. **E**

Help! I'm a prisoner in the library. Clifford, E. **Fic**

Help me, Mr. Mutt!. Stevens, J. **E**

Help the environment [series]
Guillain, C. Caring for nature **333.95**
Guillain, C. Saving energy **333.79**
Guillain, C. Saving water **333.91**

Helping behavior
   Fiction
Costello, D. I can help **E**

Helping endangered animals. Hirsch, R. E. **591.68**

Helquist, Brett
(il) Balliett, B. Chasing Vermeer **Fic**
(il) Dickens, C. A Christmas carol **Fic**
(il) Gaiman, N. Odd and the Frost Giants **Fic**
(il) Haydon, E. The Floating Island **Fic**
(il) Snicket, L. The bad beginning **Fic**

Helsby, Genevieve
Those amazing musical instruments **784.19**

Hemingway, Edith Morris, 1950-
Road to Tater Hill **Fic**

Hemingway, Edward
Bump in the night **E**

Hemp jewelry. Sadler, J. A. **746.42**

Hemphill, Helen, 1955-
The adventurous deeds of Deadwood Jones **Fic**

Hemphill, Michael
Stonewall Hinkleman and the Battle of Bull Run **Fic**

Henderson, Kathy
Baby knows best **E**
Look at you! **E**
Lugalbanda **398.2**

Henderson, Meryl
(il) Pringle, L. P. Alligators and crocodiles! **597.98**
(il) Pringle, L. P. Penguins! strange and wonderful **598**
(il) Pringle, L. P. Sharks!: strange and wonderful **597**
(il) Pringle, L. P. Snakes! **597.96**

Hendra, Sue
(il) Hicks, B. J. Monsters don't eat broccoli **E**

Hendricks, Jeff
(jt. auth) LeVert, S. Ecstasy **362.29**

Hendrix, John
John Brown **92**
(il) Fleischman, S. The Giant Rat of Sumatra **Fic**
(il) Hanson, M. E. How to save your tail **Fic**
(il) Hopkinson, D. Abe Lincoln crosses a creek **E**

Hendry, Linda
Cat crafts **745.5**
Dog crafts **745.5**
Horse crafts **745.5**
(il) Hood, S. Pup and Hound hatch an egg **E**

Heneghan, Judith, 1965-
The magician's apprentice **Fic**

Hengel, Katherine, 1982-
It's a baby Australian fur seal! **599.79**

Henham, R. D.
The red dragon codex **Fic**

Henie, Sonja, 1912-1969
See/See also pages in the following book(s):
Krull, K. Lives of the athletes **920**

Henkes, Kevin, 1960-
Bird Lake moon **Fic**
Birds **E**
The birthday room **Fic**
Chester's way **E**
Chrysanthemum **E**
Circle dogs **E**
A good day **E**
Jessica **E**
Julius, the baby of the world **E**
Kitten's first full moon **E**
Lilly's purple plastic purse **E**
My garden **E**
Old Bear **E**
Olive's ocean **Fic**
Owen **E**
Protecting Marie **Fic**
Sheila Rae, the brave **E**
So happy! **E**
Sun & Spoon **Fic**
Wemberly worried **E**
Words of stone **Fic**

Henneberger, Robert, 1921-
(il) Cameron, E. The wonderful flight to the Mushroom Planet **Fic**

Hennessy, B. G. (Barbara G.)
Because of you **E**
The boy who cried wolf **398.2**

Hennessy, Barbara G. *See* Hennessy, B. G. (Barbara G.)

Hennesy, Carolyn, 1962-
Pandora gets jealous **Fic**

Henny Penny. French, V. **398.2**

Henny Penny. Galdone, P. **398.2**

Henrietta Hornbuckle's circus of life. De Guzman, M. **Fic**

Hereditary succession *See* Inheritance and succession

Heredity
Gallant, R. A. The treasure of inheritance   **576.5**

Here's a little poem   **811.008**

Here's how I see it, here's how it is. Henson, H.   **Fic**

Here's looking at me. Raczka, B.   **757**

Hergé, 1907-1983
The adventures of Tintin, vol. 1   **741.5**

Herman, Charlotte
First rain   **E**

Hermes, Patricia, 1936-
Emma Dilemma and the new nanny   **Fic**

Hermetic art and philosophy *See* Alchemy

The **hermit** crab. Goodrich, C.   **E**

Hermit crabs *See* Crabs

Hernández, Roger E.
1898 to World War II   **305.8**
The Civil War, 1840s-1890s   **973.7**
Early explorations: the 1500s   **970.01**
New Spain: 1600-1760s   **973.1**

Hernandez, Romel
Trinidad & Tobago   **972.983**

Hernández de la Cruz, Maria
(il) Endredy, J. The journey of Tunuri and the Blue Deer   **398.2**

Hernandez-Divers, Sonia, 1969-
Geckos   **639.3**

The **hero** and the minotaur. Byrd, R.   **398.2**

Hero of the high seas [biography of John Paul Jones] Cooper, M. L.   **92**

The **hero** revealed. Boniface, W.   **Fic**

The **hero** Schliemann. Schlitz, L. A.   **92**

Heroes. Mochizuki, K.   **E**

Heroes!. Stephens, J.   **741.5**

Heroes [series]
McCaughrean, G. Hercules   **292**
McCaughrean, G. Odysseus   **292**
McCaughrean, G. Perseus   **292**

Heroes and heroines
Haven, K. F. Reluctant heroes   **920**
Winter, J. Peaceful heroes   **920**
Fiction
MacDonald, R. Another perfect day   **E**
Rogers, G. Midsummer knight   **E**

Heroes for civil rights. Adler, D. A.   **920**

Heroes of baseball. Lipsyte, R.   **796.357**

Heroes of the environment. Rohmer, H.   **333.72**

Heroines *See* Heroes and heroines

Heroism *See* Courage

Herold, Maggie Rugg
A very important day   **E**

Herons
Fiction
Avi. Blue heron   **Fic**
Ramirez, A. Napi   **E**
Poetry
Yolen, J. An egret's day   **811**

Herrera, Diego *See* Yayo

Herrera, Juan Felipe, 1948-
Laughing out loud, I fly   **811**
The upside down boy   **92**
About
Herrera, J. F. The upside down boy   **92**

Herrick, Steven, 1958-
Naked bunyip dancing   **Fic**

Herschel, Frederick William *See* Herschel, Sir William, 1738-1822

Herschel, Sir William, 1738-1822
About
Sherman, J. Uranus   **523.4**

Hershel and the Hanukkah goblins. Kimmel, E. A.   **E**

Hershenhorn, Esther, 1945-
S is for story   **808.3**

Hershey, Mary
10 lucky things that have happened to me since I nearly got hit by lightning   **Fic**

Hershey herself. Galante, C.   **Fic**

Herweck, Don
Albert Einstein and his theory of relativity   **92**
Energy   **621**
Robert Fulton   **92**

Herxheimer, Sophie
(il) Clayton, S. P. Amazons!   **398.2**
(il) Clayton, S. P. Tales told in tents   **398.2**

He's got the whole world in his hands. Nelson, K.   **782.25**

Heschel, Abraham Joshua, 1907-1972
About
Michelson, R. As good as anybody: Martin Luther King Jr. and Abraham Joshua Heschel's amazing march toward freedom   **92**

Heslop, Michael
(il) Cooper, S. The grey king   **Fic**

Hess, Debra
The Fourth of July   **394.26**

Hess, Nina
(jt. auth) Greenberg, D. A. Whales   **599.5**

Hess, Paul, 1961-
(il) Maddern, E. The cow on the roof   **398.2**
(il) Maddern, E. Nail soup   **398.2**
(il) Monte, R. The dragon of Krakow and other Polish stories   **398.2**

Hesse, Karen
Brooklyn Bridge   **Fic**
The cats in Krasinski Square   **E**
Come on, rain!   **E**
Just Juice   **Fic**
Letters from Rifka   **Fic**
Out of the dust   **Fic**
Spuds   **E**
Stowaway   **Fic**
Witness   **Fic**

Hest, Amy
The dog who belonged to no one   **E**
Guess who, Baby Duck!   **E**
Kiss good night   **E**
Little Chick   **E**
Mr. George Baker   **E**

Hest, Amy—*Continued*

The purple coat	E
Remembering Mrs. Rossi	Fic
When you meet a bear on Broadway	E

Hestler, Anna

Yemen	953.3

Hettinga, Donald R.

The Brothers Grimm	92

Heuer, Karsten

Being caribou	599.65

Heur, Valerie d'

(il) Bourguignon, L. Heart in the pocket	E

Hewett, Richard

(il) Arnold, C. The ancient cliff dwellers of Mesa Verde	970.004

Hewitt, Kathryn

(il) Bunting, E. Flower garden	E
(il) Krull, K. Lives of extraordinary women	920
(il) Krull, K. Lives of the artists	920
(il) Krull, K. Lives of the athletes	920
(il) Krull, K. Lives of the musicians	920
(il) Krull, K. Lives of the presidents	920
(il) Krull, K. Lives of the writers	920

Hewitt, Sally

Hear this!	612.8
Look here!	612.8
Smell it!	612.8
Tastes good!	612.8
Touch that!	612.8
Using energy	333.79
Your food	641.3
Your local environment	333.72

Hewitt Anderson's great big life. Nolen, J.   E

Hey, Al. Yorinks, A.   E

Hey batta batta swing!. Cook, S.   796.357

Hey! listen to this   028.5

Hey Mr. Choo-Choo, where are you going? Wickberg, S.   E

Hey, pancakes!. Weston, T.   E

Hey rabbit!. Ruzzier, S.   E

Hey there, stink bug!. Bulion, L.   811

Heyman, Alissa

The big book of horror	S C

Heyman, Ken, 1930-

(il) Morris, A. Bread, bread, bread	641.8
(il) Morris, A. Hats, hats, hats	391

Heyward, DuBose, 1885-1940

The country bunny and the little gold shoes	E

Heyworth, Heather

(il) Troupe, T. K. If I were a ballerina	792.8

Hi, cat!. Keats, E. J.   E

Hi, Fly Guy!. Arnold, T.   E

Hiaasen, Carl, 1953-

Flush	Fic
Hoot	Fic
Scat	Fic

Hiawatha. Longfellow, H. W.   811

Hibernation

Baines, R. A den is a bed for a bear	599.78

Fiction

Farber, N. How the hibernators came to Bethlehem	E
Fleming, D. Time to sleep	E
Henkes, K. Old Bear	E
Wright, M. Sleep, Big Bear, sleep!	E
Yolen, J. Sleep, black bear, sleep	E

Hiccups

Fiction

Cuyler, M. Skeleton hiccups	E

Hickman, Pamela M., 1958-

Animals and their mates	591.56
Animals and their young	591.56
Animals in motion	591.47
It's moving day!	591.56
Turtle rescue	597.92

Hickory dickory dock. Baker, K.   E

Hickox, Rebecca

The golden sandal	398.2

Hicks, Barbara Jean

Jitterbug jam	E
Monsters don't eat broccoli	E

Hicks, Betty

Basketball Bats	Fic
Out of order	Fic

Hicks, Kelli L.

(ed) Rourke's complete history of our presidents encyclopedia. See Rourke's complete history of our presidents encyclopedia   920.003

Hicks, Mark A.

(il) Kuntz, L. Celebrate the USA	973

Hicks, Terry Allan

Allergies	616.97
The Chumash	970.004
Earth and the moon	525
Obesity	616.3
Saturn	523.4

The **hidden** alphabet. Seeger, L. V.   E

The **hidden** boy. Berkeley, J.   Fic

Hidden child. Millman, I.   940.53

The **hidden** children. Greenfeld, H.   940.53

The **hidden** folk. Lunge-Larsen, L.   398.2

Hidden hippo. Gannij, J.   590

Hidden world of the Aztec. Lourie, P.   972

Hidden worlds: looking through a scientist's microscope. Kramer, S.   502.8

Hide & seek. Wong, J. S.   E

Hide and seek. Helman, A.   591.47

Hide and seek fog. Tresselt, A. R.   E

Hiding Edith. Kacer, K.   940.53

Hiding from the Nazis. Adler, D. A.   940.53

Hiding to survive. Rosenberg, M. B.   940.53

Hieroglyphics

Giblin, J. The riddle of the Rosetta Stone	493
Rumford, J. Seeker of knowledge [biography of Jean François Champollion]	92

Higgins, F. E.

The Black Book of Secrets	Fic

Hinduism—*Continued*
George, C. What makes me a Hindu?   294.5
Hawker, F. Hinduism in Bali   294.5
Jani, M. What you will see inside a Hindu temple   294.5
Rasamandala Das. Hinduism   294.5
See/See also pages in the following book(s):
Osborne, M. P. One world, many religions
   200

Hinduism in Bali. Hawker, F.   294.5

Hindus
Festivals
See Hindu holidays
Fiction
Banerjee, A. Looking for Bapu   Fic

Hine, Lewis Wickes, 1874-1940
About
Freedman, R. Kids at work   331.3
Fiction
Winthrop, E. Counting on Grace   Fic

Hines, Anna Grossnickle, 1946-
1, 2, buckle my shoe   E
Daddy makes the best spaghetti   E
Pieces   811
Winter lights   811

Hines, Gary, 1944-
Midnight forests [biography of Gifford Pinchot]
   92

Hines-Stephens, Sarah
Show off   790.1

Hinojosa, Tish
Cada niño/Every child   782.42

Hinshaw, Kelly Campbell- *See* Campbell-Hinshaw, Kelly

Hip & Hop, don't stop. Czekaj, J.   E

Hip-hop
Fiction
Raschka, C. Hip hop dog   E

Hip hop dog. Raschka, C.   E

Hip hop speaks to children   811.008

Hip-pocket papa. Markle, S.   597.8

Hippies
Fiction
Lindbergh, R. My hippie grandmother   E

Hippopotamus
Clarke, P. Hippos   599.63
Gannij, J. Hidden hippo   590
Hatkoff, I. Owen & Mzee   599.63
Hatkoff, I. Owen & Mzee: the language of friendship   599.63
Jango-Cohen, J. Hippopotamuses   599.63
Winter, J. Mama   E
Fiction
Heide, F. P. The one and only Marigold   E
Landström, L. A hippo's tale   E
Marshall, J. George and Martha   E
Shea, B. Oh, Daddy!   E
Waber, B. Evie & Margie   E
Wild, M. Kiss kiss!   E

Hippopotamuses. Jango-Cohen, J.   599.63

Hippos. Clarke, P.   599.63

A **hippo's** tale. Landström, L.   E

Hirahara, Naomi, 1962-
1001 cranes   Fic

Hirao, Amiko
(il) Glenn, S. M. Just what Mama needs   E

Hiromi's hands [biography of Hiromi Suzuki]
Barasch, L.   92

Hiroshima (Japan)
Bombardment, 1945
Coerr, E. Sadako [biography of Sadako Sasaki]
   92
Coerr, E. Sadako and the thousand paper cranes [biography of Sadako Sasaki]   92
Lawton, C. Hiroshima   940.54

Hirsch, Rebecca E., 1969-
Growing your own garden   635
Helping endangered animals   591.68
Protecting our natural resources   333.72
Top 50 reasons to care about polar bears
   599.78

Hirschfelder, Arlene B.
(jt. auth) Dennis, Y. W. Children of native America today   970.004
(jt. auth) Dennis, Y. W. A kid's guide to native American history   970.004
(jt. auth) Molin, P. F. American Indian stereotypes in the world of children   970.004

Hirschi, Ron
Lions, tigers, and bears   591.5
Our three bears   599.78
Searching for grizzlies   599.78

Hirschmann, Kris, 1967-
LEGO toys   688.7
Lice   616.5
Solar energy   333.79

Hirsh, Marilyn, 1944-1988
The rabbi and the twenty-nine witches   398.2

Hiscock, Bruce, 1940-
Ookpik   598
(il) Swinburne, S. R. Armadillo trail   599.3
(il) Swinburne, S. R. Turtle tide   597.92

Hispanic America [series]
Hernández, R. E. 1898 to World War II
   305.8
Hernández, R. E. The Civil War, 1840s-1890s
   973.7
Hernández, R. E. Early explorations: the 1500s
   970.01
Hernández, R. E. New Spain: 1600-1760s
   973.1
Otfinoski, S. The new republic: 1760-1840s
   973.3

Hispanic-American crafts kids can do!. Robinson, F.   745.5

Hispanic American poetry *See* American poetry—Hispanic American authors

Hispanic Americans
Hernández, R. E. The Civil War, 1840s-1890s
   973.7
Otfinoski, S. The new republic: 1760-1840s
   973.3
Wáchale! poetry and prose on growing up Latino in America   810.8

Hoffmann, Ernst Theodor Amadeus *See* Hoffmann, E. T. A. (Ernst Theodor Amadeus), 1776-1822

Hoffmann, Gretchen
Chicken pox   **616.9**
The flu   **616.2**
Mononucleosis   **616.9**
Osteoporosis   **616.7**

Hog-eye. Meddaugh, S.   **E**

The **hog** prince. Bardhan-Quallen, S.   **E**

Hogan, Jamie
(il) Blackaby, S. Nest, nook & cranny   **811**
(il) Perkins, M. Rickshaw girl   **Fic**

Hogan, Sophie
(il) Watters, D. Where's Mom's hair?   **616.99**

Hogrogian, Nonny, 1932-
The contest   **398.2**
Cool cat   **E**
One fine day   **398.2**
(il) Leodhas, S. N. Always room for one more   **782.42**

Hogwash. Geisert, A.   **E**

Hokanson, Lars
(il) Finkelstein, N. H. Remember not to forget   **940.53**

Hokanson, Lois
(il) Finkelstein, N. H. Remember not to forget   **940.53**

Hokusai (Katsushika Hokusai), 1760-1849
About
Ray, D. K. Hokusai   **92**
Fiction
Place, F. The old man mad about drawing   **Fic**

Holabird, Katharine
Angelina Ballerina   **E**

Holbrook. Becker, B.   **Fic**

Hold the flag high. Clinton, C.   **973.7**

Hold up the sky: and other Native American tales from Texas and the Southern Plains. Curry, J. L.   **398.2**

Holderness, Grizelda, 1953-
(il) Koralek, J. The story of Queen Esther   **222**

Hole, Stian
Garmann's summer   **E**

Holes. Sachar, L.   **Fic**

Holgate, Douglas
(il) Lemke, D. Zinc Alloy: Super Zero   **741.5**

Holiday cooking
Bowers, S. Ghoulish goodies   **641.5**

Holiday House reader [series]
Caple, K. The friendship tree   **E**
Kimmelman, L. In the doghouse   **E**
Levinson, N. S. Death Valley   **577.5**
Levinson, N. S. Rain forests   **577.3**
Ruelle, K. G. The Thanksgiving beast feast   **E**
Wallace, C. One nosy pup   **E**
Wallace, C. The Santa secret   **E**
Wallace, C. Turkeys together   **E**

Holiday stew. Whitehead, J.   **811**

Holidays
See also Christmas; Father's Day; Fourth of July; Kwanzaa; Martin Luther King Day; Memorial Day; Mother's Day; New Year; Saint Patrick's Day; Thanksgiving Day; Valentine's Day
Bauer, C. F. Celebrations   **808.8**
Chase's calendar of events   **394.26**
Hopkins, L. B. Days to celebrate   **051**
Jones, L. Kids around the world celebrate!   **394.26**
Junior Worldmark encyclopedia of world holidays   **394.26**
Kindersley, A. Celebrations   **394.26**
Perl, L. Piñatas and paper flowers   **394.26**
Webb, L. S. Holidays of the world cookbook for students   **641.5**
Bibliography
Blass, R. J. Celebrate with books   **028.1**
Matthew, K. I. Neal-Schuman guide to celebrations & holidays around the world   **394.26**
Poetry
Hines, A. G. Winter lights   **811**
Whitehead, J. Holiday stew   **811**

Holidays, Hindu *See* Hindu holidays

Holidays, Jewish *See* Jewish holidays

Holidays around the world [series]
Heiligman, D. Celebrate Christmas   **394.26**
Heiligman, D. Celebrate Diwali   **294.5**
Heiligman, D. Celebrate Halloween   **394.26**
Heiligman, D. Celebrate Hanukkah   **296.4**
Heiligman, D. Celebrate Independence Day   **394.26**
Heiligman, D. Celebrate Passover   **296.4**
Heiligman, D. Celebrate Ramadan & Eid al-Fitr   **297.3**
Heiligman, D. Celebrate Rosh Hashanah and Yom Kippur   **296.4**
Heiligman, D. Celebrate Thanksgiving   **394.26**
Otto, C. Celebrate Chinese New Year   **394.26**
Otto, C. Celebrate Cinco de Mayo   **394.26**
Otto, C. Celebrate Kwanzaa   **394.26**
Otto, C. Celebrate Valentine's Day   **394.26**

Holidays of the world cookbook for students. Webb, L. S.   **641.5**

Holland, Gay W., 1941-
(il) Glaser, L. Brilliant bees   **595.7**
(il) Glaser, L. Hello, squirrels!   **599.3**

Holland, Kevin Crossley- *See* Crossley-Holland, Kevin

Holland, Leslie J.
Dr. Martin Luther King Jr.'s I have a dream speech in translation   **323.1**

Holland, Richard
(il) Jenkins, M. The time book   **529**
(il) Mark, J. The museum book   **069**

Holland, Trish
(jt. auth) Ford, C. Ocean's child   **E**

Holland *See* Netherlands

Hollihan, Kerrie Logan
Isaac Newton and physics for kids   **92**

Holling, Holling C., 1900-1973
Paddle-to-the-sea — Fic

The **Hollow** Bettle. Appelbaum, S. — Fic

Holly, reindeer, and colored lights. Barth, E. — 394.26

Hollyer, Beatrice
Our world of water — 363.6

Hollyer, Belinda
River song — Fic
(comp) She's all that! See She's all that! — 811.008

Holly's red boots. Chessa, F. — E

Hollywood (Calif.)
Fiction
Leonard, E. A coyote's in the house — Fic
Pinkwater, D. M. The Yggyssey — Fic
Williams, M. The Fizzy Whiz kid — Fic

Holm, Jennifer L.
Babymouse: queen of the world — 741.5
Middle school is worse than meatloaf — Fic
Our only May Amelia — Fic
Penny from heaven — Fic
Turtle in paradise — Fic

Holm, Matthew, 1974-
(jt. auth) Holm, J. L. Babymouse: queen of the world — 741.5

Holm, Sharon Lane, 1955-
(il) Erlbach, A. Merry Christmas, everywhere! — 394.26
(il) Ross, K. The best birthday parties ever! — 793.2

Holmberg, Bo R., 1945-
A day with Dad — E

Holmes, Benjamin C., fl. 1846-1870
Fiction
Sherman, P. Ben and the Emancipation Proclamation — E

Holmes, Elizabeth Ann, 1957-
Tracktown summer — Fic

Holmes, Mary Tavener
A giraffe goes to Paris — E
My travels with Clara — 599.66

Holmes, Sara Lewis
Operation Yes — Fic

Holmes, Thom
Dinosaur scientist — 560

Holmes, Timothy
Zambia — 968.94

Holocaust, 1933-1945
See also Holocaust survivors; World War, 1939-1945—Jews
Adler, D. A. Hiding from the Nazis — 940.53
Bachrach, S. D. Tell them we remember — 940.53
Bogacki, T. The champion of children — 92
Finkelstein, N. H. Remember not to forget — 940.53
Frank, A. The diary of a young girl: the definitive edition — 92
Hurwitz, J. Anne Frank: life in hiding — 92
—I never saw another butterfly— — 741.9
Kacer, K. Hiding Edith — 940.53
Levine, K. Hana's suitcase — 940.53

Meltzer, M. Never to forget: the Jews of the Holocaust — 940.53
Meltzer, M. Rescue: the story of how Gentiles saved Jews in the Holocaust — 940.53
Metselaar, M. Anne Frank: her life in words and pictures — 92
Mochizuki, K. Passage to freedom — 940.53
Poole, J. Anne Frank — 92
Rol, R. v. d. Anne Frank, beyond the diary — 92
Rubin, S. G. The Anne Frank Case: Simon Wiesenthal's search for the truth — 92
Rubin, S. G. The cat with the yellow star — 940.53
Rubin, S. G. The flag with fifty-six stars — 940.53
Ruelle, K. G. The grand mosque of Paris — 940.53
Russo, M. Always remember me — 940.53
Talbott, H. Forging freedom — 940.53
Taylor, P. L. The secret of Priest's Grotto — 940.53
Warren, A. Surviving Hitler — 940.53
Whiteman, D. B. Lonek's journey — 940.53
Drama
Levine, K. Hana's suitcase on stage — 812
Fiction
Ackerman, K. The night crossing — Fic
Bunting, E. One candle — E
Deedy, C. A. The yellow star — Fic
Glatstein, J. Emil and Karl — Fic
Hesse, K. The cats in Krasinski Square — E
McDonough, Y. Z. The doll with the yellow star — Fic
Orlev, U. The man from the other side — Fic
Rappaport, D. The secret seder — E
Roy, J. R. Yellow star — Fic
Stuchner, J. B. Honey cake — Fic
Wiviott, M. Benno and the Night of Broken Glass — E
Personal narratives
Greenfeld, H. The hidden children — 940.53
Gross, E. B. Elly — 92
Krinitz, E. N. Memories of survival — 940.53
Millman, I. Hidden child — 940.53
Perl, L. Four perfect pebbles — 940.53
Reiss, J. The upstairs room — 92
Rosenberg, M. B. Hiding to survive — 940.53
Poetry
Levy, D. The year of goodbyes — 811

Holocaust Museum (U.S.) *See* United States Holocaust Memorial Museum

Holocaust remembrance book for young readers [series]
Kacer, K. Hiding Edith — 940.53
Levine, K. Hana's suitcase on stage — 812

Holocaust survivors
Gross, E. B. Elly — 92
Rubin, S. G. The Anne Frank Case: Simon Wiesenthal's search for the truth — 92

Holt, K. A.
Mike Stellar: nerves of steel — Fic

Holt, Kimberly Willis
Dancing in Cadillac light — Fic
Piper Reed, Navy brat — Fic
When Zachary Beaver came to town — Fic

Holt, Leslie Edmonds
  (jt. auth) Fasick, A. M. Managing children's services in the public library   **027.62**

Holub, Joan, 1956-
  Apple countdown   **E**
  Bed, bats, and beyond   **Fic**
  The garden that we grew   **E**
  Why do birds sing?   **598**
  Why do cats meow?   **636.8**
  Why do dogs bark?   **636.7**
  Why do horses neigh?   **636.1**
  Why do rabbits hop?   **636.9**
  Why do snakes hiss?   **597.96**
  (jt. auth) Hannah, J. The man who named the clouds [biography of Luke Howard]   **92**

The **Holy** Bible [New Revised Standard Version] Bible   **220.5**

The **holy** twins: Benedict and Scholastica. Norris, K.   **92**

Holyfield, John
  (il) Bildner, P. The Hallelujah Flight   **E**
  (il) Stauffacher, S. Bessie Smith and the night riders   **E**

Holyoke, Nancy
  A smart girl's guide to her parents' divorce   **306.89**
  A smart girl's guide to money   **332.024**

Holzer, Harold
  The president is shot!   **973.7**

Hom, Nancy
  (il) Blia Xiong. Nine-in-one, Grr! Grr!   **398.2**

Home
  Ashman, L. Castles, caves, and honeycombs   **E**
Fiction
  Cole, H. A nest for Celeste   **Fic**
  Tseng, K. Ned's new home   **E**
  Wong, J. S. Homegrown house   **E**

Home. Baker, J.   **E**

Home, and other big, fat lies. Wolfson, J.   **Fic**

Home decoration See Interior design

Home economics
Fiction
  Huget, J. L. How to clean your room in 10 easy steps   **E**

A **home** for Dixie. Jackson, E.   **636.7**

Home for Navidad. Ziefert, H.   **E**

A **home** in the coral reef. Taylor-Butler, C.   **577.7**

Home is east. Ly, M.   **Fic**

Home life See Family life

Home of the brave. Applegate, K.   **Fic**

Home on the moon. Dyson, M. J.   **629.45**

A **home** on the prairie. Lion, D. C.   **577.4**

Home on the range. Hopkinson, D.   **92**

A **home** on the tundra. Marsico, K.   **577.5**

Home run!. Bonnet, R. L.   **530**

Home run. Burleigh, R.   **E**

Home video systems
  See also Video recording

Home windmills. Cartlidge, C.   **621.4**

Homefront. Gwaltney, D.   **Fic**

Homegrown house. Wong, J. S.   **E**

Homeless bird. Whelan, G.   **Fic**

Homeless persons
  See also Refugees; Runaway children; Runaway teenagers; Tramps
  Lynette, R. What to do when your family loses its home   **362.5**
Fiction
  Bunting, E. Fly away home   **E**
  Clements, A. Room one   **Fic**
  Cole, B. Good enough to eat   **E**
  DiCamillo, K. Great joy   **E**
  Hesse, K. Brooklyn Bridge   **Fic**
  Howe, J. Dew drop dead   **Fic**
  King, S. M. Mutt dog!   **E**
  McPhail, D. M. The teddy bear   **E**
  O'Connor, B. How to steal a dog   **Fic**
  Richter, J. Beyond the station lies the sea   **Fic**
  Sachar, L. Holes   **Fic**
  Spinelli, J. Maniac Magee   **Fic**
  Williams, L. E. The Can Man   **E**

Homer
Adaptations
  Landmann, B. The incredible voyage of Ulysses   **883**
  Mucci, T. The odyssey   **741.5**

Homer Price. McCloskey, R.   **Fic**

Homesick: my own story. Fritz, J.   **92**

Homework
  Kraus, J. Annie's plan   **371.3**
Fiction
  Yorinks, A. Homework   **E**

Homework. Yorinks, A.   **E**

The **homework** machine. Gutman, D.   **Fic**

Homicide
Fiction
  Hahn, M. D. Closed for the season   **Fic**

Homosexual parents See Gay parents

Homosexuality
Fiction
  Brannen, S. S. Uncle Bobby's wedding   **E**
  Lindenbaum, P. Mini Mia and her darling uncle   **E**
  Newman, L. Daddy, papa, and me   **E**
  Richardson, J. And Tango makes three   **E**

Homosexuals, Female See Lesbians

Honda, Sōichirō, 1906-1991
About
  Weston, M. Honda [biography of Soichiro Honda]   **92**

Hondo and Fabian. McCarty, P.   **E**

Honduras
  McGaffey, L. Honduras   **972.83**
  Shields, C. J. Honduras   **972.83**
Fiction
  Trueman, T. Hurricane   **Fic**

Honest pretzels. Katzen, M.   **641.5**

Honesty
  See also Truthfulness and falsehood
  Barraclough, S. Honesty   **179**
  Pryor, K. J. Honesty   **177**

Horror fiction—*Continued*

Shusterman, N. Darkness creeping   **S C**
Stine, R. L. The haunting hour   **S C**
Thomas, J. C. The skull talks back and other haunting tales   **398.2**
Van Laan, N. Teeny tiny tingly tales   **E**

Horror graphic novels

Bannister (Person). The shadow door   **741.5**
Grant, A. Robert Louis Stevenson's Strange case of Dr. Jekyll and Mr. Hyde   **741.5**
Russell, P. C. Coraline [graphic novel]   **741.5**

Horse, Harry, 1960-2007

Little Rabbit lost   **E**

Horse & pony breeds. Ransford, S.   **636.1**

Horse & pony care. Ransford, S.   **636.1**

Horse crafts. Hendry, L.   **745.5**

Horse hooves and chicken feet: Mexican folktales. Philip, N.   **398.2**

A **horse** in the house, and other strange but true animal stories. Ablow, G.   **590**

A **horse** of her own. Wedekind, A.   **Fic**

Horse racing

Hubbard, C. The last Black king of the Kentucky Derby   **92**
Lewin, T. Horse song   **951.7**
McCarthy, M. Seabiscuit   **798.4**
Tate, N. Behind the scenes: the racehorse   **798.4**
Trollinger, P. B. Perfect timing [biography of Isaac Murphy]   **92**

Horse show. Hayden, K.   **798.2**

Horse show handbook for kids. Kimball, C.   **798.2**

Horse showing for kids. See Kimball, C. Horse show handbook for kids   **798.2**

Horse song. Lewin, T.   **951.7**

Horse tales   **S C**

Horse: the essential guide for young equestrians. Hamilton, L.   **636.1**

Horseback riding *See* Horsemanship

Horsemanship

See also Rodeos

Draper, J. My first horse and pony book   **636.1**
Draper, J. My first horse and pony care book   **636.1**
Gibbons, G. Horses!   **636.1**
Hayden, K. Horse show   **798.2**
Kimball, C. Horse show handbook for kids   **798.2**
Ransford, S. The Kingfisher illustrated horse & pony encyclopedia   **636.1**

Fiction

Haas, J. Birthday pony   **Fic**
Wedekind, A. A horse of her own   **Fic**

Horsepower. Peterson, C.   **636.1**

Horses

Barnes, J. Horses at work   **636.1**
Bozzo, L. My first horse   **636.1**
Draper, J. My first horse and pony book   **636.1**

Draper, J. My first horse and pony care book   **636.1**
Gibbons, G. Horses!   **636.1**
Hamilton, L. Horse: the essential guide for young equestrians   **636.1**
Hendry, L. Horse crafts   **745.5**
Holub, J. Why do horses neigh?   **636.1**
Jeffrey, L. S. Horses   **636.1**
Lomberg, M. Horse   **636.1**
Lunis, N. Miniature horses   **636.1**
Mack, G. Horses   **636.1**
MacLeod, E. Why do horses have manes?   **636.1**
Momatiuk, Y. Face to face with wild horses   **599.66**
Peterson, C. Horsepower   **636.1**
Ransford, S. Horse & pony breeds   **636.1**
Ransford, S. Horse & pony care   **636.1**
Ransford, S. The Kingfisher illustrated horse & pony encyclopedia   **636.1**
Simon, S. Horses   **636.1**

Fiction

Adler, C. S. One unhappy horse   **Fic**
Armstrong, J. Magnus at the fire   **E**
Bradley, K. B. The perfect pony   **E**
Byars, B. C. Little Horse   **Fic**
Coerr, E. Chang's paper pony   **E**
Cowley, J. Where horses run free   **E**
DeLaCroix, A. The best horse ever   **Fic**
Doyle, M. Horse   **E**
Duey, K. Lara and the gray mare   **Fic**
Farley, W. The Black Stallion   **Fic**
Giff, P. R. Wild girl   **Fic**
Haas, J. Birthday pony   **Fic**
Haas, J. Jigsaw pony   **Fic**
Haas, J. Sugaring   **E**
Harlow, J. H. Secret of the night ponies   **Fic**
Haseley, D. Twenty heartbeats   **E**
Henry, M. Justin Morgan had a horse   **Fic**
Henry, M. King of the wind   **Fic**
Henry, M. Misty of Chincoteague   **Fic**
Horse tales   **S C**
Jeffers, S. My Chincoteague pony   **E**
Lawson, R. Mr. Revere and I   **Fic**
Lester, J. Black cowboy, wild horses   **E**
McCully, E. A. Wonder horse   **E**
Meister, C. My pony Jack   **E**
Morpurgo, M. War horse   **Fic**
Murphy, S. J. Same old horse   **E**
Sewell, A. Black Beauty   **Fic**
Silverman, E. Cowgirl Kate and Cocoa   **E**
Smiley, J. The Georges and the Jewels   **Fic**
Stein, D. E. Cowboy Ned and Andy   **E**
Thomason, M. Moonrunner   **Fic**
Thompson, K. Highway robbery   **Fic**
Wedekind, A. A horse of her own   **Fic**
Wedekind, A. Wild Blue   **Fic**

Folklore

Chen, J. H. The magic horse of Han Gan   **398.2**
Cohen, C. L. The mud pony   **398.2**
Goble, P. The girl who loved wild horses   **398.2**
Hausman, G. Horses of myth   **398.2**
Ōtsuka, Y. Suho's white horse   **398.2**

Household moving *See* Moving

Household pests

    See also Cockroaches

Housel, Debra J., 1961-

    Ecologists   920

    Ecosystems   577

Houses

    Gibbons, G. How a house is built   690

        Fiction

    Ashman, L. Creaky old house   E

    Burton, V. L. The little house   E

    DiSalvo, D. A castle on Viola Street   E

    Edwards, P. D. The old house   E

    Hayes, K. The winter visitors   E

    Jones, D. W. House of many ways   Fic

    Lobel, A. Ming Lo moves the mountain   E

    Lyon, G. E. You and me and home sweet home   E

    Murphy, R. Bird   Fic

    Paros, J. Violet Bing and the Grand House   Fic

    Swanson, S. M. The house in the night   E

    Wild, M. The little crooked house   E

        Poetry

    Lewis, J. P. The house   811

Houses, Historic *See* Historic buildings

Houston, Dick

    Bulu, African wonder dog   636.7

Houston, Gloria

    My great-aunt Arizona   E

    The year of the perfect Christmas tree   E

Houston, James A., 1921-2005

    James Houston's Treasury of Inuit legends   398.2

Houston, Samuel, 1793-1863

        About

    Fritz, J. Make way for Sam Houston   92

Houston (Tex.)

        Fiction

    Papademetriou, L. Chasing normal   Fic

Hovemann, Anisa Claire

    (il) Myers, T. If you give a T-rex a bone   567.9

How a bill becomes a law. Hamilton, J.   328.73

How a house is built. Gibbons, G.   690

How Angel Peterson got his name. Paulsen, G.   92

How animal babies stay safe. Fraser, M. A.   591.56

How animals work. Burnie, D.   591.4

How are they made? [series]

    Blaxland, W. Basketballs   688.7

    Blaxland, W. Guitars   787.87

    Blaxland, W. Helmets   621.9

    Blaxland, W. Sneakers   685

    Blaxland, W. Sweaters   746.9

How are you peeling? Freymann, S.   E

How astronauts use math. Hense, M.   629.45

How baseball managers use math. Bertoletti, J. C.   796.357

How basketball works. Thomas, K.   796.323

How big is it? Hillman, B.   153.7

How big were the dinosaurs. Most, B.   E

How chefs use math. Arroyo, S. L.   641.5

How Chipmunk got his stripes. Bruchac, J.   398.2

How crime fighters use math. Arroyo, S. L.   363.2

How deep sea divers use math. Arroyo, S. L.   797.2

How dinosaurs took flight. Sloan, C.   567.9

How do apples grow? Maestro, B.   634

How do bats fly in the dark? Stewart, M.   599.4

How do bees make honey? Stewart, M.   595.7

How do caterpillars become butterflies? Bailer, D.   595.7

How do chameleons change color? Stewart, M.   597.95

How do dinosaurs say goodnight? Yolen, J.   E

How do flies walk upside down? Berger, M.   595.7

How do spiders make webs? Stewart, M.   595.4

How do we elect our leaders? Thomas, W. D.   324

How do we hear? Guillain, C.   612.8

How do you make a baby smile? Sturges, P.   E

How do you wokka-wokka? Bluemle, E.   E

How does a bone become a fossil? Stewart, M.   560

How does a plant become oil? Tagliaferro, L.   553.2

How does a volcano become an island? Tagliaferro, L.   551.2

How does a waterfall become electricity? Graf, M.   621.31

How does an earthquake become a tsunami? Tagliaferro, L.   551.46

How does it grow? [series]

    Johnson, J. Butterfly   595.7

    Johnson, J. Dandelion   583

    Johnson, J. Duck   598

    Johnson, J. Frog   597.8

    Johnson, J. Oak tree   583

How does it happen? [series]

    Graf, M. How does a waterfall become electricity?   621.31

    Stewart, M. How does a bone become a fossil?   560

    Stewart, M. How does sand become glass?   666

    Tagliaferro, L. How does a plant become oil?   553.2

    Tagliaferro, L. How does a volcano become an island?   551.2

    Tagliaferro, L. How does an earthquake become a tsunami?   551.46

How does it work? [series]

    Johnson, J. Fox   599.77

How-to-do-it manuals for librarians [series]
Alire, C. Serving Latino communities   **027.6**
Curzon, S. C. Managing change   **025.1**
Duncan, D. I-search for success   **025.5**
Hallam, A. Managing budgets and finances
   025.1
Herb, S. Connecting fathers, children, and reading   **028.5**
Imhoff, K. R. Library contests   **021.7**
Symons, A. K. Protecting the right to read
   025.2

How-to-do it manuals for libraries [series]
Butler, R. P. Smart copyright compliance for schools   **346.04**
Martin, B. S. Fundamentals of school library media management   **025.1**

How to do "The three bears" with two hands. Minkel, W.   **791.5**

How to draw cars and trucks. Court, R.   **743**

How to eat fried worms. Rockwell, T.   **Fic**

How to get rich [series]
Olson, T. How to get rich in the California Gold Rush   **979.4**
Olson, T. How to get rich on the Oregon Trail
   978

How to get rich in the California Gold Rush. Olson, T.   **979.4**

How to get rich on a Texas cattle drive. Olson, T.   **978**

How to get rich on the Oregon Trail. Olson, T.   **978**

How to get your child to love reading. Codell, E. R.   **028.5**

How to harness solar power for your home. Bearce, S.   **621.47**

How to heal a broken wing. Graham, B.   **E**

How to make a cherry pie and see the U.S.A. Priceman, M.   **E**

How to make an apple pie and see the world. Priceman, M.   **E**

How to paint the portrait of a bird. Prévert, J.
   E

How to raise and keep a dragon. Nigg, J.   **Fic**

How to raise Mom and Dad. Lerman, J.   **E**

How to really fool yourself. Cobb, V.   **152.1**

How to save your tail. Hanson, M. E.   **Fic**

How to scratch a wombat. French, J.   **599.2**

How to speak cat. Whitehead, S.   **636.8**

How to speak dog. Whitehead, S.   **636.7**

How to steal a dog. O'Connor, B.   **Fic**

How to survive in Antarctica. Bledsoe, L. J.
   998

How to survive middle school. Gephart, D.
   Fic

How to talk to your cat. George, J. C.   **636.8**

How to talk to your dog. George, J. C.   **636.7**

How to think like a scientist. Kramer, S.   **507**

How to use waste energy to heat and light your home. O'Neal, C.   **621.1**

How to use wind power to light and heat your home. O'Neal, C.   **621.31**

How to write your life story. Fletcher, R.   **808**

How underwear got under there. Shaskan, K.
   391

How video game designers use math. Egan, J.
   794.8

How we crossed the West. Schanzer, R.   **978**

How we know what we know about our changing climate. Cherry, L.   **363.7**

How weird is it. Hillman, B.   **500**

How you were born. Cole, J.   **612.6**

How your body works. Stewart, D. E.   **612**

Howard, Arthur, 1948-
Hoodwinked   **E**
(il) Appelt, K. Bubba and Beau, best friends
   E
(il) Byars, B. C. The SOS file   **Fic**
(il) Cuyler, M. 100th day worries   **E**
(il) Rylant, C. Mr. Putter & Tabby pour the tea
   E

Howard, Elizabeth Fitzgerald, 1927-
Aunt Flossie's hats (and crab cakes later)   **E**
Virgie goes to school with us boys   **E**

Howard, Ellen
The crimson cap   **Fic**
The gate in the wall   **Fic**

Howard, Luke, 1772-1864
About
Hannah, J. The man who named the clouds [biography of Luke Howard]   **92**

Howard, Paul, 1967-
(il) Cooke, T. Full, full, full of love   **E**
(il) Henderson, K. Look at you!   **E**

Howard, Reginald
The big, big wall   **E**

Howard Thurman's great hope. Jackson Issa, K.
   92

Howarth, Daniel
(il) Glaser, L. Hoppy Hanukkah!   **E**
(il) Roth, C. Will you still love me?   **E**

Howe, Deborah, 1946-1978
Bunnicula   **Fic**

Howe, James, 1946-
Brontorina   **E**
Bunnicula meets Edgar Allan Crow   **Fic**
Dew drop dead   **Fic**
Horace and Morris but mostly Dolores   **E**
Houndsley and Catina   **E**
Kaddish for Grandpa in Jesus' name, amen
   E
Pinky and Rex   **E**
When you go to kindergarten   **372.2**
(jt. auth) Howe, D. Bunnicula   **Fic**

Howe, Peter, 1942-
Waggit's tale   **Fic**

Howe, Samuel Gridley, 1801-1876
About
Alexander, S. H. She touched the world: Laura Bridgman, deaf-blind pioneer   **92**

Howell, Troy
(il) Osborne, M. P. Favorite Greek myths
   292

Howitt, Mary Botham, 1799-1888
The spider and the fly   **821**

Howland, Naomi
Latkes, latkes, good to eat   E
Princess says goodnight   E
Howl's moving castle. Jones, D. W.   Fic
How's your health? [series]
Royston, A. Allergies   **616.97**
Royston, A. Asthma   **616.2**
Royston, A. Colds, the flu, and other infections   **616.2**
Royston, A. Cuts, bruises, and breaks   **617.1**
Royston, A. Head lice   **616.5**
Royston, A. Tooth decay   **617.6**
Howse, Jennifer
Inclined planes   **621.8**
Levers   **621.8**
Hoxie, Vinnie Ream *See* Ream, Vinnie, 1847-1914
Hoyt, Ard
(il) Anderson, L. H. The hair of Zoe Fleefenbacher goes to school   E
(il) Brendler, C. Winnie Finn, worm farmer   E
(il) Casanova, M. Some dog!   E
(il) Casanova, M. Utterly otterly day   E
(il) Demas, C. Saying goodbye to Lulu   E
(il) Spradlin, M. P. Daniel Boone's great escape   **92**
(il) Weis, C. When the cows got loose   E
Hoyt, Erich, 1950-
Whale rescue   **599.5**
Hoyt-Goldsmith, Diane
Celebrating a Quinceañera   **392**
Celebrating Chinese New Year   **394.26**
Celebrating Hanukkah   **296.4**
Celebrating Passover   **296.4**
Celebrating Ramadan   **297.3**
Cinco de Mayo   **394.26**
Mardi Gras: a Cajun country celebration   **394.25**
Las Posadas   **394.26**
Pueblo storyteller   **970.004**
Three Kings Day   **394.26**
Hreljac, Ryan
About
Shoveller, H. Ryan and Jimmy   **361.7**
Hsu-Flanders, Lillian
(il) Rattigan, J. K. Dumpling soup   E
Hu, Caroline
(il) Gunderson, J. The emperor's painting   Fic
(il) Gunderson, J. The jade dragon   Fic
(il) Gunderson, J. Stranger on the silk road   Fic
(il) Gunderson, J. The terracotta girl   Fic
Hu, Ying-hwa
(il) Chinn, K. Sam and the lucky money   E
(il) Haas, J. Jigsaw pony   Fic
(il) Miller, W. Zora Hurston and the chinaberry tree   **92**
(il) Pringle, L. P. American slave, American hero [biography of York]   **92**
(il) Rappaport, D. We are the many   **920**
(il) Smith, C. L. Jingle dancer   E

Hubbard, Crystal
The last Black king of the Kentucky Derby   **92**
Hubbell, Patricia
Airplanes   E
Boats   E
Cars   E
Firefighters! speeding! spraying! saving!   E
My first airplane ride   E
Police: hurrying! helping! saving!   E
Hubbell, Will
Pumpkin Jack   E
Hubble Space Telescope
Cole, M. D. Hubble Space Telescope   **522**
Hübener, Helmuth, 1925-1942
Fiction
Bartoletti, S. C. The boy who dared   Fic
Huck, Charlotte S., 1922-2005
Princess Furball   **398.2**
The **Huckabuck** family and how they raised popcorn in Nebraska and quit and came back. Sandburg, C.   E
Hucke, Johannes
Pip in the Grand Hotel   E
Hudson, Cheryl Willis
Construction zone   **690**
Hudson, Henry, d. 1611
About
Weaver, J. Hudson   **92**
Hudson, Wade
Powerful words   **808.8**
Hudson. Weaver, J.   **92**
Hudson River (N.Y. and N.J.)
Talbott, H. River of dreams   **974.7**
Huey, Lois Miner
American archaeology uncovers the Dutch colonies   **974.7**
American archaeology uncovers the earliest English colonies   **973.2**
American archaeology uncovers the Underground Railroad   **973.7**
American archaeology uncovers the Vikings   **970.01**
American archaeology uncovers the westward movement   **978**
Huffmon, Betty
(jt. auth) Sloat, T. Berry magic   E
Hufford, Deborah
Greeting card making   **745.59**
Huge Harold. Peet, B.   E
Huget, Jennifer LaRue
How to clean your room in 10 easy steps   E
Thanks a LOT, Emily Post!   E
Hugging
Fiction
Downing, J. No hugs till Saturday   E
Oldland, N. Big bear hug   E
Hugging the rock. Brown, S. T.   Fic
Hughes, Arizona Houston, 1876-1969
About
Houston, G. My great-aunt Arizona   E
Hughes, Edward James *See* Hughes, Ted, 1930-1998

Hughes, George
  (il) Clifford, E. Help! I'm a prisoner in the library   **Fic**

Hughes, Langston, 1902-1967
  The dream keeper and other poems   **811**
  Langston Hughes   **811**
  My people   **811**
  The Negro speaks of rivers   **811**
      About
  Burleigh, R. Langston's train ride   **92**
  Cooper, F. Coming home [biography of Langston Hughes]   **92**
  Walker, A. Langston Hughes, American poet   **92**
  See/See also pages in the following book(s):
  Krull, K. Lives of the writers   **920**

Hughes, Monica
  See/See also pages in the following book(s):
  Ellis, S. From reader to writer   **372.6**

Hughes, Neal
  (il) Sachar, L. Marvin Redpost, kidnapped at birth?   **Fic**

Hughes, Pat
  Seeing the elephant   **Fic**

Hughes, Patrice Raccio *See* Hughes, Pat

Hughes, Shirley
  Alfie and the big boys   **E**
  Annie Rose is my little sister   **E**
  Ella's big chance   **E**

Hughes, Ted, 1930-1998
  Collected poems for children   **821**
  The iron giant   **Fic**
  My brother Bert   **E**

Hughes-Hassell, Sandra
  Collection management for youth   **025.2**
  School reform and the school library media specialist   **027.8**
  (ed) The Information-powered school. See The Information-powered school   **027.8**

Hugo and the really, really, really long string. Boyle, B.   **E**

Hugs and kisses. Loupy, C.   **E**

Huiett, William J., 1943-
  (il) Tourville, A. D. A giraffe grows up   **599.63**
  (il) Tourville, A. D. A jaguar grows up   **599.75**

Hula lullaby. Kono, E. E.   **E**

Huliska-Beith, Laura
  (il) Lear, E. Edward Lear   **821**
  (il) Wheeler, L. Bubble gum, bubble gum   **E**

Hull, Henrietta Goodnough, 1889-1967
  See/See also pages in the following book(s):
  Colman, P. Adventurous women   **920**

Hull, Peggy *See* Hull, Henrietta Goodnough, 1889-1967

The **hullabaloo** ABC. Cleary, B.   **E**

Hulme, John, 1970-
  The glitch in sleep   **Fic**

Human anatomy
  See also Human body
  Walker, R. Body   **611**

Human behavior
  See also Behaviorism; Risk-taking (Psychology); Sportsmanship

Human body
  See also Body image
  Bailey, G. Body and health   **612**
  Berger, M. Why don't haircuts hurt?   **612**
  Calabresi, L. Human body   **612**
  Cole, J. The magic school bus inside the human body   **612**
  Ganeri, A. Alive   **612**
  Gray, S. H. The human body [series]   **612**
  Johnson, R. L. Ultra-organized cell systems   **612**
  Lew, K. Human organs   **611**
  Manning, M. Under your skin   **612**
  Parker, N. W. Organs!   **612**
  Podesto, M. The body   **612**
  Rau, D. M. What's inside me? [series]   **612**
  Reilly, K. M. The human body   **612**
  Seuling, B. Your skin weighs more than your brain   **612**
  Simon, S. The human body   **612**
  Somervill, B. A. The human body   **612**
  Stewart, D. E. How your body works   **612**
  Stradling, J. The human body   **612**
  Swanson, D. You are weird   **612**
  VanCleave, J. P. Janice VanCleave's the human body for every kid   **612**
  Walker, R. Dr. Frankenstein's human body book   **612**
  Walker, R. How the incredible human body works—by the Brainwaves   **612**
  Walker, R. Human body   **612**
  Walker, R. Ouch!   **612**
      Fiction
  Bang, M. All of me!   **E**
  Bauer, M. D. Thank you for me!   **E**
  Henderson, K. Look at you!   **E**
  Schwartz, A. A beautiful girl   **E**

Human body [series]
  Ballard, C. The skeleton and muscular system   **612.7**

The **human** brain. Simpson, K.   **612.8**

Human ecology
  Lourie, P. Arctic thaw   **998**
  Mason, P. Population   **363.9**
  Parker, S. Population   **363.7**
  See/See also pages in the following book(s):
  Swamp, J. Giving thanks   **299.7**
      Fiction
  Baker, J. Window   **E**

Human geography
  Delannoy, I. Our living Earth   **779**
  Smith, D. J. If the world were a village   **304.6**

The **human** head. Allen, K.   **611**

Human impact. Vogel, C. G.   **333.91**

Human influence on nature
  Parker, S. Population   **363.7**
  Vogel, C. G. Human impact   **333.91**
  See/See also pages in the following book(s):
  Patent, D. H. Biodiversity   **333.95**

Human muscles. Wheeler-Toppen, J.   **611**

Human organs. Lew, K.   **611**

Human origins

     See also Evolution; Fossil hominids; Prehistoric peoples

     Poynter, M. The Leakeys   **92**

     Tattersall, I. Bones, brains and DNA   **599.93**

     Thimmesh, C. Lucy long ago   **599.93**

Human relations *See* Interpersonal relations

Human reproduction. Rand, C.   **612.6**

Human rights

     Barker, D. Maybe right, maybe wrong   **370.1**

     Every human has rights   **323**

     We are all born free   **323**

The **human** skeleton. Rake, J. S.   **611**

Humanitarian intervention

     Mortenson, G. Listen to the wind   **371.82**

     Mortenson, G. Three cups of tea   **371.82**

The **humblebee** hunter. Hopkinson, D.   **E**

Humbug witch. Balian, L.   **E**

Humidity

     Cartlidge, C. Water from air   **628.1**

Hummingbird. Angle, K. G.   **Fic**

Hummingbird nest. George, K. O.   **E**

Hummingbirds

     Kelly, I. It's a hummingbird's life   **598**

     Otfinoski, S. Hummingbirds   **598**

         Fiction

     George, K. O. Hummingbird nest   **E**

Humor *See* Wit and humor

Humorists

     Keating, F. Will Rogers: an American legend   **92**

Humorous graphic novels

     Alley, Z. B. There's a wolf at the door   **398.2**

     Baltazar, A. Tiny Titans: welcome to the treehouse   **741.5**

     Barba, C. Yam: bite-size chunks   **741.5**

     Bliss, H. Luke on the loose   **741.5**

     Cammuso, F. Knights of the lunch table: the dodgeball chronicles   **741.5**

     Craddock, E. Stone rabbit: Pirate Palooza   **741.5**

     Davis, E. The secret science alliance and the copycat crook   **741.5**

     Davis, E. Stinky   **741.5**

     Flight explorer   **741.5**

     Frampton, O. Oddly Normal   **741.5**

     Friesen, R. Cupcakes of doom!   **741.5**

     Goscinny. Asterix the Gaul   **741.5**

     Gownley, J. Amelia rules!: the whole world's crazy!   **741.5**

     Guibert, E. Sardine in outer space   **741.5**

     Hale, S. Rapunzel's revenge   **741.5**

     Holm, J. L. Babymouse: queen of the world   **741.5**

     Kochalka, J. Johnny Boo: the best little ghost in the world!   **741.5**

     Krosoczka, J. J. Lunch Lady and the League of Librarians   **741.5**

     Lemke, D. Zinc Alloy: Super Zero   **741.5**

     Lynch, J. Mo and Jo: fighting together forever   **741.5**

     Morse, S. Magic Pickle   **741.5**

     Pien, L. Long Tail Kitty   **741.5**

     Roberts, S. Patty-cake and friends: color collection   **741.5**

     Rosenstiehl, A. Silly Lilly and the four seasons   **741.5**

     Sava, S. C. Hyperactive   **741.5**

     Shioya, H. Dinosaur hour!, vol. 1   **741.5**

     Smith, J. Little Mouse gets ready   **741.5**

     Sonishi, K. Leave it to PET!: the misadventures of a recycled super robot, vol. 1   **741.5**

     Spires, A. Binky the space cat   **741.5**

     Stanley, J. Little Lulu, vol. 1: My dinner with Lulu   **741.5**

     Thompson, J. Magic Trixie   **741.5**

     Trondheim, L. Tiny Tyrant   **741.5**

     Wight, E. Frankie Pickle and the closet of doom   **741.5**

Humorous poetry

     Agee, J. Orangutan tongs   **811**

     Brown, C. Flamingoes on the roof   **811**

     Brown, C. Soup for breakfast   **811**

     Ciardi, J. You read to me, I'll read to you   **811**

     Dahl, R. Vile verses   **821**

     Florian, D. Laugh-eteria   **811**

     For laughing out loud   **811.008**

     Katz, A. Oops!   **811**

     Lawson, J. Black stars in a white night sky   **811**

     Levy, D. Maybe I'll sleep in the bathtub tonight   **811**

     Lobel, A. Odd owls & stout pigs   **811**

     Prelutsky, J. Behold the bold umbrellaphant   **811**

     Prelutsky, J. The new kid on the block: poems   **811**

     Prelutsky, J. A pizza the size of the sun   **811**

     Prelutsky, J. Something big has been here   **811**

     Shapiro, K. J. I must go down to the beach again   **811**

     Shields, C. D. Almost late to school and more school poems   **811**

     Silverstein, S. Don't bump the glump and other fantasies   **811**

     Silverstein, S. Falling up   **811**

     Silverstein, S. A light in the attic   **811**

     Silverstein, S. Runny Babbit   **811**

     Silverstein, S. Where the sidewalk ends   **811**

     Viorst, J. If I were in charge of the world and other worries   **811**

     Wilson, K. What's the weather inside?   **811**

     Zobel, A. Smelly feet sandwich   **811**

Humpback whales up close. Rake, J. S.   **599.5**

The **hundred** dresses. Estes, E.   **Fic**

The **hundred-year-old** secret. See Barrett, T. The 100-year-old secret   **Fic**

Hundred Years' War, 1339-1453

         Fiction

     Russell, C. Dogboy   **Fic**

Hundreth day worries. See Cuyler, M. 100th day worries   **E**

Huneck, Stephen

     Sally goes to the beach   **E**

Hungarian Americans
    Fiction
Cheng, A. Eclipse   Fic
Hungary
Esbenshade, R. S. Hungary   943.9
    Fiction
Cheng, A. The bear makers   Fic
Cheng, A. The lace dowry   Fic
Seredy, K. The Good Master   Fic
Seredy, K. The white stag   Fic
    Folklore
    See Folklore—Hungary
Hunger
    Fiction
Namioka, L. The hungriest boy in the world
    E
Salerno, S. Harry hungry!   E
The **hungriest** boy in the world. Namioka, L.
    E
The **hungry** coat. Demi   398.2
Hungry hen. Waring, R.   E
Huns
Kroll, S. Barbarians!   940.1
Hunt, Charlotte Dumaresq *See* Demi, 1942-
Hunt, Irene, 1907-2001
Across five Aprils   Fic
Hunt, Judith A.
(il) McKay, S. Animals under our feet   590
Hunt, Robert
(il) Ashby, R. Rocket man [biography of John
Glenn]   92
Hunted. Russell, C.   Fic
Hunter, Anne
(il) Obed, E. B. Who would like a Christmas
tree?   E
Hunter, Clementine, 1886?-1988
    About
Whitehead, K. Art from her heart: folk artist
Clementine Hunter   92
Hunter, Linzie
(il) Bodeen, S. A. A small, brown dog with a
wet, pink nose   E
The **hunter.** Casanova, M.   398.2
The **hunterman** and the crocodile. Wagué Diakité,
B.   398.2
Hunting
    See also Tracking and trailing
    Fiction
Dahl, R. The magic finger   Fic
Lowry, L. Crow call   E
Rosen, M. We're going on a bear hunt   E
The **hunting** [series]
Cole, S. Z. Rex   Fic
Hunting the white cow. Seymour, T.   E
Hunwick's egg. Fox, M.   E
Hurd, Clement, 1908-1988
(il) Brown, M. W. Goodnight moon   E
(il) Brown, M. W. The runaway bunny   E
(il) Hurd, E. T. Johnny Lion's book   E
Hurd, Edith Thacher, 1910-1997
Johnny Lion's book   E

Hurd, Owen
Chicago history for kids   977.3
Hurd, Thacher, 1949-
Art dog   E
Bad frogs   E
Mama don't allow   E
The weaver   E
Hurd, Will
Changing states   530.4
Hurling (Game)
    Fiction
Colfer, E. Benny and Omar   Fic
Huron Indians
King, D. C. The Huron   970.004
Hurricane. Trueman, T.   Fic
Hurricane. Wiesner, D.   E
Hurricane & tornado. Challoner, J.   551.55
Hurricane force. Treaster, J. B.   551.55
Hurricane hunters!. Demarest, C. L.   551.55
Hurricane Katrina, 2005
Fradin, J. B. Hurricane Katrina   363.34
Larson, K. Two Bobbies   636.08
Miller, M. Hurricane Katrina strikes the Gulf
Coast   363.34
    Fiction
Watson, R. A place where hurricanes happen
    E
Hurricane Katrina strikes the Gulf Coast. Miller,
M.   363.34
Hurricanes
    See also Typhoons
Ceban, B. J. Hurricanes, typhoons, and cyclones
    551.55
Cole, J. The magic school bus inside a hurricane
    551.55
Demarest, C. L. Hurricane hunters!   551.55
Fradin, J. B. Hurricanes   551.55
Gibbons, G. Hurricanes!   551.55
Godkin, C. Hurricane!   551.55
Miller, M. Hurricane Katrina strikes the Gulf
Coast   363.34
Silverstein, A. Hurricanes   551.55
Simon, S. Hurricanes   551.55
Treaster, J. B. Hurricane force   551.55
    Fiction
Collard, S. B., III. Double eagle   Fic
Morrison, P. R. Wind tamer   Fic
Trueman, T. Hurricane   Fic
Wiesner, D. Hurricane   E
Hurricanes, tsunamis, and other natural disasters.
Langley, A.   363.34
Hurricanes, typhoons, and cyclones. Ceban, B. J.
    551.55
Hurry and the monarch. Ó Flatharta, A.   E
Hurry! hurry!. Bunting, E.   E
Hurry! Hurry! Have you heard? Melmed, L. K.
    E
Hurry up and slow down. Marlow, L.   E
Hurst, Carol Otis
Rocks in his head   E
Terrible storm   E
You come to Yokum   Fic

Hypnotism

Fiction

Auch, M. J. I was a third grade science project
Fic

I

I ain't gonna paint no more!. Beaumont, K.   **E**

I always, always get my way. Krasnesky, T.   **E**

I am a dancer. Collins, P. L.   **792.8**

I am a taxi. Ellis, D.   **Fic**

I am Jack. Gervay, S.   **Fic**

I am me. Kuskin, K.   **E**

I am not going to school today. Harris, R. H.
E

I am phoenix: poems for two voices. Fleischman, P.   **811**

I am the darker brother   **811.008**

I am too absolutely small for school. Child, L.
E

I and I [biography of Bob Marley] Medina, T.
92

I and you and don't forget who. Cleary, B. P.
428

I can be anything. Spinelli, J.   **E**

I can do it myself!. Adams, D.   **E**

I can help. Costello, D.   **E**

I can read! [series]
  Brown, C. L. After the dinosaurs   **569**
  Brown, C. L. Beyond the dinosaurs   **560**
  Capucilli, A. Pedro's burro   **E**
  Cazet, D. The octopus   **E**
  George, J. C. Goose and Duck   **E**
  Hamsters, shells, and spelling bees   **811.008**
  Hoff, S. The littlest leaguer   **E**
  Prelutsky, J. It's Christmas!   **811**
  Prelutsky, J. It's Thanksgiving!   **811**
  Sandin, J. At home in a new land   **E**
  Schaefer, L. M. Mittens   **E**

I can read book [series]
  Blackwood, G. L. The just-so woman   **E**
  Bonsall, C. N. The case of the hungry stranger
E
  Brenner, B. Wagon wheels   **E**
  Brown, C. L. The day the dinosaurs died
567.9
  Bulla, C. R. Daniel's duck   **E**
  Byars, B. C. The Golly sisters go West   **E**
  Cazet, D. Elvis the rooster almost goes to heaven   **E**
  Cazet, D. Minnie and Moo, wanted dead or alive   **E**
  Coerr, E. The big balloon race   **E**
  Coerr, E. Chang's paper pony   **E**
  Coerr, E. The Josefina story quilt   **E**
  Cushman, D. Dirk Bones and the mystery of the haunted house   **E**
  Cushman, D. Inspector Hopper   **E**
  Gorbachev, V. Ms. Turtle the babysitter   **E**
  Hanukkah lights   **811.008**
  Hazen, B. S. Digby   **E**
  Hoban, L. Arthur's Christmas cookies   **E**

Hoban, L. Silly Tilly's Thanksgiving dinner
E
Hoff, S. Danny and the dinosaur   **E**
Hoff, S. Oliver   **E**
Hoff, S. Sammy the seal   **E**
Hurd, E. T. Johnny Lion's book   **E**
Kenah, K. The best seat in second grade   **E**
Kessler, L. P. Here comes the strikeout   **E**
Kessler, L. P. Kick, pass, and run   **E**
Kessler, L. P. Last one in is a rotten egg   **E**
Little, J. Emma's yucky brother   **E**
Lobel, A. Frog and Toad are friends   **E**
Lobel, A. Grasshopper on the road   **E**
Lobel, A. Mouse soup   **E**
Lobel, A. Mouse tales   **E**
Lobel, A. Owl at home   **E**
Lobel, A. Small pig   **E**
Lobel, A. Uncle Elephant   **E**
Maestro, M. What do you hear when cows sing?
793.73
McCully, E. A. The grandma mix-up   **E**
Minarik, E. H. Little Bear   **E**
Minarik, E. H. No fighting, no biting!   **E**
Monjo, F. N. The drinking gourd   **E**
Prelutsky, J. It's snowing! it's snowing!   **811**
Schwartz, A. All of our noses are here, and other noodle tales   **398.2**
Schwartz, A. Ghosts!   **398.2**
Schwartz, A. I saw you in the bathtub, and other folk rhymes   **398.2**
Schwartz, A. In a dark, dark room, and other scary stories   **398.2**
Schwartz, A. There is a carrot in my ear, and other noodle tales   **398.2**
Thomson, S. L. Amazing whales!   **599.5**
Turner, A. W. Dust for dinner   **E**
Weeks, S. Drip, drop   **E**
Wiseman, B. Morris and Boris at the circus
E
Wyler, R. Magic secrets   **793.8**

I can read chapter book [series]
  Avi. Finding Providence: the story of Roger Williams   **92**
  Avi. Prairie school   **Fic**

I can read mystery book [series]
  Benchley, N. A ghost named Fred   **E**

I can read picture book [series]
  Parish, P. Amelia Bedelia   **E**

I, crocodile. Marcellino, F.   **E**

I did it, I'm sorry. Buehner, C.   **E**

I don't want a cool cat!. Dodd, E.   **E**

I don't want a posh dog!. Dodd, E.   **E**

I don't want to go to school!. Blake, S.   **E**

I dream of trains. Johnson, A.   **E**

I face the wind. Cobb, V.   **551.51**

I fall down. Cobb, V.   **531**

I feel a foot!. Rinck, M.   **E**

I fooled you   **S C**

I, Freddy. Reiche, D.   **Fic**

I get wet. Cobb, V.   **532**

I hate books!. Walker, K.   **Fic**

I have a dream. King, M. L., Jr.   **323.1**

I have a little dreidel. Baum, M.   **782.42**

I have asthma. Moore-Mallinos, J.   **616.2**

I have heard of a land. Thomas, J. C.   **E**

I hear America singing!   **782.42**

I heard it from Alice Zucchini. Havill, J.   **811**

I, Juan de Pareja. Treviño, E. B. d.   **Fic**

I kissed the baby. Murphy, M.   **E**

I know a lot of things. Rand, A.   **E**

I know an old lady who swallowed a fly. See Taback, S. There was an old lady who swallowed a fly   **782.42**

I know an old teacher. Bowen, A.   **E**

I know here. Croza, L.   **E**

I know it's autumn. Spinelli, E.   **E**

I know the river loves me. Gonzalez, M. C.   **E**

I like me!. Carlson, N. L.   **E**

I like plants! [series]
Wade, M. D. Flowers bloom!   **582.13**
Wade, M. D. People need plants!   **581.6**
Wade, M. D. Plants grow!   **571.8**
Wade, M. D. Plants live everywhere!   **581**
Wade, M. D. Seeds sprout!   **581.4**
Wade, M. D. Trees, weeds, and vegetables—so many kinds of plants!   **580**

I like space! [series]
Bredeson, C. What do astronauts do   **629.45**
Bredeson, C. What is the solar system?   **523.2**

I live in Tokyo. Takabayashi, M.   **952**

I, Lorelei. Smith, Y.   **Fic**

I lost my kisses. Trewin, T.   **E**

I lost my tooth in Africa. Diakité, P.   **E**

I love. See Bedford, D. The way I love you   **E**

I love bugs. Dodd, E.   **E**

I love cats. Stainton, S.   **E**

I love chocolate. Cali, D.   **E**

I love Christmas. Walker, A.   **E**

I love my pirate papa. Leuck, L.   **E**

I love our Earth. Martin, B.   **525**

I love planes!. Sturges, P.   **E**

I love school!. Sturges, P.   **E**

I love to draw horses!. Lipsey, J.   **743**

I love to finger paint!. Lipsey, J.   **751.4**

I love to paint!. Lipsey, J.   **751.4**

I love trains!. Sturges, P.   **E**

I love yoga. Chryssicas, M. K.   **613.7**

I love you like crazy cakes. Lewis, R. A.   **E**

I love you, Little Monkey. Durant, A.   **E**

I miss you every day. Taback, S.   **E**

I must go down to the beach again. Shapiro, K. J.   **811**

—I never saw another butterfly—   **741.9**

I put a spell on you. Selzer, A.   **Fic**

I, Q.: book one, Indepedence Hall. Smith, R.   **Fic**

I read signs. Hoban, T.   **659.1**

I remember Miss Perry. Brisson, P.   **E**

I said no!. Burstein, J.   **158**

I saw Esau   **398.8**

I saw you in the bathtub, and other folk rhymes. Schwartz, A.   **398.2**

I saw your face. Dawes, K. S. N.   **811**

I-search for success. Duncan, D.   **025.5**

I see a kookaburra!. Jenkins, S.   **591.7**

I see myself. Cobb, V.   **535**

I see the rhythm. Igus, T.   **780.89**

I spy. Wick, W.   **793.73**

I spy: an alphabet in art. Micklethwait, L.   **E**

I stink!. McMullan, K.   **E**

I think I am going to sneeze. Thomas, P.   **616.97**

I, too, sing America   **811.008**

I took a walk. Cole, H.   **E**

I took the moon for a walk. Curtis, C.   **E**

I, Vivaldi. Shefelman, J. J.   **92**

I wanna be your shoebox. García, C.   **Fic**

I wanna iguana. Orloff, K. K.   **E**

I want a dog!. Bansch, H.   **E**

I want a dog!. Saltzberg, B.   **E**

I want to be free. Slate, J.   **E**

I want two birthdays!. Ross, T.   **E**

I was a rat!. Pullman, P.   **Fic**

I was a third grade science project. Auch, M. J.   **Fic**

I was dreaming to come to America   **325.73**

I witness [series]
Avi. Hard gold   **Fic**

Ibatoulline, Bagram
(il) Alderson, B. Thumbelina   **E**
(il) Bass, L. G. Boom boom go away!   **E**
(il) DiCamillo, K. Great joy   **E**
(jt. auth) DiCamillo, K. The miraculous journey of Edward Tulane   **Fic**
(il) Fleischman, P. The animal hedge   **E**
(il) Fleischman, P. Graven images   **S C**
(il) Freedman, R. The adventures of Marco Polo   **92**
(il) Giblin, J. Secrets of the Sphinx   **932**
(il) Lowry, L. Crow call   **E**
(il) Mitchell, S. The nightingale   **Fic**
(il) Mitchell, S. The tinderbox   **Fic**
(il) Rabin, S. Mr. Lincoln's boys   **92**
(il) Stanley, D. Bella at midnight   **Fic**

Ibbotson, Eva
The beasts of Clawstone Castle   **Fic**
Dial-a-ghost   **Fic**
The dragonfly pool   **Fic**
The secret of platform 13   **Fic**
The star of Kazan   **Fic**

Ibby's magic weekend. Dyer, H.   **Fic**

Ibn Battuta, 1304-1377
About
Rumford, J. Traveling man: the journey of Ibn Battuta, 1325-1354   **92**

Ibo (African people) See Igbo (African people)

Ice
Wells, R. E. Polar bear, why is your world melting?   **363.7**

Ice Age
   Harrison, D. L. Cave detectives   **560**
Ice bear. Davies, N.   **599.78**
Ice bears. Guiberson, B. Z.   **599.78**
Ice cream, ices, etc.
   Fleisher, P. Ice cream treats   **641.8**
   Gibbons, G. Ice cream   **641.8**
Ice cream treats. Fleisher, P.   **641.8**
Ice drift. Taylor, T.   **Fic**
Ice hockey *See* Hockey
Ice skating
   Marsico, K. Speed skating   **796.91**
   Thomas, K. How figure skating works
      796.91
         Fiction
   Borden, L. The greatest skating race   **Fic**
   Coville, B. Hans Brinker   **E**
   Dodge, M. M. Hans Brinker, or, The silver
      skates   **Fic**
   Keller, H. Pearl's new skates   **E**
   Yep, L. Mia   **Fic**
Ice story. Kimmel, E. C.   **998**
Ice time. McKinley, M.   **796.962**
Icebergs
   Simon, S. Icebergs and glaciers   **551.3**
Icebergs and glaciers. Simon, S.   **551.3**
Iceland
   McMillan, B. Going fishing   **949.12**
   Wilcox, J. Iceland   **949.12**
         Fiction
   McMillan, B. How the ladies stopped the wind
      E
   McMillan, B. The problem with chickens   **E**
Ichikawa, Satomi, 1949-
   Come fly with me   **E**
   La La Rose   **E**
   My father's shop   **E**
   My pig Amarillo   **E**
   (il) Gauch, P. L. Tanya and the red shoes   **E**
Ichord, Loretta Frances
   Double cheeseburgers, quiche, and vegetarian
      burritos   **394.1**
   Skillet bread, sourdough, and vinegar pie
      641.5
Iconography *See* Religious art
Id al-Adha
   Douglass, S. L. Ramadan   **297.3**
   Heiligman, D. Celebrate Ramadan & Eid al-Fitr
      297.3
   Jeffrey, L. S. Celebrate Ramadan   **297.3**
   MacMillan, D. M. Ramadan and Id al-Fitr
      297.3
   Marchant, K. Id-ul-Fitr   **297.3**
         Fiction
   Gilani-Williams, F. Nabeel's new pants   **E**
   Khan, H. Night of the Moon   **E**
   Mobin-Uddin, A. The best Eid ever   **E**
Id-ul-Fitr. Marchant, K.   **297.3**
Ida B. Hannigan, K.   **Fic**
Ida Early comes over the mountain. Burch, R.
      Fic

Idaho
         Fiction
   Gregory, K. My darlin' Clementine   **Fic**
   Tracy, K. Camille McPhee fell under the bus
      Fic
Identification
      See also Forensic anthropology
Idioms *See* English language—Idioms
Iditarod dream. Wood, T.   **798.8**
Iditarod Trail Sled Dog Race, Alaska
   Miller, D. S. The great serum race   **798.8**
If. Kipling, R.   **821**
If a chicken stayed for supper. Weston, C.   **E**
If a tree falls at lunch period. Choldenko, G.
      Fic
If America were a village. Smith, D. J.   **973**
If animals kissed good night--. Paul, A. W.   **E**
If I ran for president. Stier, C.   **324**
If I ran the circus. Seuss, Dr.   **E**
If I ran the zoo. Seuss, Dr.   **E**
If I were a ballerina. Troupe, T. K.   **792.8**
If I were a jungle animal. Ellery, A.   **E**
If I were in charge of the world and other worries.
   Viorst, J.   **811**
If it weren't for you. Zolotow, C.   **E**
If not for the cat. Prelutsky, J.   **811**
If stones could speak. Aronson, M.   **936**
If the shoe fits. Bell, K.   **Fic**
If the shoe fits. Whipple, L.   **811**
If the world were a village. Smith, D. J.
      304.6
If you decide to go to the moon. McNulty, F.
      629.45
If you give a mouse a cookie. Numeroff, L. J.
      E
If you give a T-rex a bone. Myers, T.   **567.9**
If you lived here you'd be home by now. Briant,
   E.   **E**
If you love a nursery rhyme   **398.8**
If you made a million. Schwartz, D. M.   **E**
If you were there in 1776. Brenner, B.   **973.3**
. . . if your name was changed at Ellis Island.
   Levine, E.   **325.73**
If you're happy and you know it. Cabrera, J.
      E
If you're happy and you know it!. Ormerod, J.
      E
Igbo (African people)
         Fiction
   Saint-Lot, K. N. Amadi's snowman   **E**
Iggulden, Conn, 1971-
   The dangerous book for boys   **031.02**
   Tollins   **Fic**
Iggulden, Hal, 1972-
   (jt. auth) Iggulden, C. The dangerous book for
      boys   **031.02**
Ignatow, Amy
   The popularity papers   **Fic**
Igneous rock. Faulkner, R.   **552**

I'm mighty!. McMullan, K.   E
I'm number one. Rosen, M.   E
I'm still scared. De Paola, T.   92
I'm the best. Cousins, L.   E
I'm the biggest thing in the ocean. Sherry, K.   E
I'm your bus. Singer, M.   E
The **imaginary** garden. Larsen, A.   E
Imaginary menagerie. Larios, J. H.   811

Imaginary playmates
Fiction
Henkes, K. Jessica   E
Kvasnosky, L. M. Really truly Bingo   E
Martin, P. Lulu Atlantis and the quest for true blue love   Fic
Pinfold, L. The Django   E
Rohmann, E. Clara and Asha   E
Rosenberg, L. Nobody   E

Imagination
Feinberg, B. Welcome to Lizard Motel   028.5
Fiction
Ahlberg, A. The shopping expedition   E
Andreasen, D. The treasure bath   E
Babin, C. Gus is a fish   E
Beaty, A. Doctor Ted   E
Black, M. I. The purple kangaroo   E
Bloom, S. A mighty fine time machine   E
Bode, N. E. The slippery map   Fic
Braun, S. Meeow and the big box   E
Brennan-Nelson, D. Willow   E
Cooper, H. Dog biscuit   E
Crews, N. Below   E
Crumpacker, B. Alexander's pretending day   E
David, P. Mascot to the rescue!   Fic
Docherty, T. To the beach   E
Dorros, A. Abuela   E
Ellery, A. If I were a jungle animal   E
Falwell, C. Shape capers   E
Fancher, L. Star climbing   E
Fucile, T. Let's do nothing!   E
Gauthier, G. A girl, a boy, and three robbers   Fic
Glenn, S. M. Just what Mama needs   E
Gore, L. Danny's first snow   E
Grandits, J. The travel game   E
Gravett, E. Monkey and me   E
Grey, M. Traction Man is here!   E
Hammill, M. Sir Reginald's logbook   E
Heap, S. Danny's drawing book   E
Henkes, K. My garden   E
Hill, S. L. Not yet, Rose   E
Hoppe, P. Hat   E
Hutchins, H. J. Mattland   E
Janni, R. Every cowgirl needs a horse   E
Jarka, J. Love that puppy!   E
Jenkins, E. Daffodil, crocodile   E
Krauss, R. A very special house   E
Kruusval, C. Franny's friends   E
Larsen, A. The imaginary garden   E
Lawrence, I. The giant-slayer   Fic
Lazo, C. E. Someday when my cat can talk   E
Lehman, B. Trainstop   E

Lucas, D. Something to do   E
Madison, A. 100 days and 99 nights   Fic
McLerran, A. Roxaboxen   E
McNaughton, C. Once upon an ordinary school day   E
Melanson, L. Topsy-Turvy Town   E
Nayar, N. What should I make?   E
Ness, E. Sam, Bangs & Moonshine   E
Ormerod, J. Ballet sisters: the duckling and the swan   E
Ormerod, J. Lizzie nonsense   E
Patricelli, L. The birthday box   E
Patricelli, L. Higher! higher!   E
Portis, A. Not a box   E
Portis, A. Not a stick   E
Pullen, Z. Friday my Radio Flyer flew   E
Rinck, M. I feel a foot!   E
Sanders-Wells, L. Maggie's monkeys   E
Schaefer, C. L. Dragon dancing   E
Shannon, D. Alice the fairy   E
Shea, B. Big plans   E
Shulevitz, U. How I learned geography   E
Shulevitz, U. When I wore my sailor suit   E
Snyder, Z. K. The Egypt game   Fic
Soman, D. Ladybug Girl   E
Spangler, B. Peg Leg Peke   E
Thomas, J. Can you make a scary face?   E
Thomson, S. L. Imagine a night   E
Tolan, S. S. Wishworks, Inc.   Fic
Van Allsburg, C. The mysteries of Harris Burdick   E
Van Allsburg, C. The wreck of the Zephyr   E
Van Camp, K. Harry and Horsie   E
Weston, R. P. Zorgamazoo   Fic
Whiting, S. The firefighters   E
Wight, E. Frankie Pickle and the closet of doom   741.5
Ziefert, H. Mighty Max   E
Zimmerman, A. G. Fire engine man   E

Imaginative inventions. Harper, C. M.   609
Imagine a dragon. Pringle, L. P.   398.2
Imagine a night. Thomson, S. L.   E
Imagine that!. Raimondo, J.   709.04

Imai, Ayano, 1980-
Chester   E

Imershein, Betsy, 1953-
(il) Howe, J. When you go to kindergarten   372.2

Imhoff, Kathleen R.
Library contests   021.7

Immersed in verse. Wolf, A.   808.1

Immigrant kids. Freedman, R.   325.73

Immigrants
Hailstone, R. The white ox   92
Fiction
Aliki. Painted words: Marianthe's story one   E
Applegate, K. Home of the brave   Fic
Avi. Silent movie   E
Brown, J. Little Cricket   Fic
Bunting, E. One green apple   E
Bunting, E. A picnic in October   E
Cheng, A. Eclipse   Fic
Cheng, A. Honeysuckle house   Fic

Immigrants—Fiction—*Continued*

Cohen, B. Molly's pilgrim	E
Colato Laínez, R. My shoes and I	E
Connor, L. Miss Bridie chose a shovel	E
Cornwell, N. Christophe's story	Fic
Cutler, J. Guttersnipe	E
Fleming, C. Lowji discovers America	Fic
Gerstein, M. Sparrow Jack	E
Giff, P. R. A house of tailors	Fic
Giff, P. R. Wild girl	Fic
Glaser, L. Bridge to America	Fic
Grant, K. Sofie and the city	E
Herold, M. R. A very important day	E
Hesse, K. Brooklyn Bridge	Fic
Hesse, K. Letters from Rifka	Fic
Hoffman, M. The color of home	E
Hyde, H. S. Feivel's flying horses	E
Jaramillo, A. La linea	Fic
Lee, M. Landed	Fic
Mak, K. My Chinatown	E
McDonough, Y. Z. The doll shop downstairs	Fic
McQuinn, A. My friend Jamal	E
Napoli, D. J. The king of Mulberry Street	Fic
Oberman, S. The always prayer shawl	E
Oswald, N. Nothing here but stones	Fic
Park, F. Good-bye, 382 Shin Dang Dong	E
Partridge, E. Oranges on Golden Mountain	E
Paterson, K. Bread and roses, too	Fic
Pendziwol, J. Marja's skis	E
Pérez, A. I. My diary from here to there	Fic
Recorvits, H. My name is Yoon	E
Sandin, J. At home in a new land	E
Sheth, K. Blue jasmine	Fic
Stanley, D. Saving Sky	Fic
Williams, K. L. My name is Sangoel	E
Winter, J. Angelina's island	E
Woodruff, E. The memory coat	E
Woodruff, E. Small beauties	E
Yang, B. Hannah is my name	E
Yep, L. The dragon's child	Fic
Yolen, J. Naming Liberty	E

Poetry

Argueta, J. A movie in my pillow	861

United States

Bial, R. Tenement	974.7
Glaser, L. Emma's poem	974.7
Hopkinson, D. Shutting out the sky	974.7
Keedle, J. Americans from the Caribbean and Central America	305.8
Keedle, J. Mexican Americans	305.8
Keedle, J. West African Americans	305.8
Park, K. Americans from India and other South Asian countries	305.8
Thomas, W. D. Korean Americans	305.8
Wachtel, A. Southeast Asian Americans	305.8
Weiss, G. G. Americans from Russia and Eastern Europe	305.8

Immigration and emigration

See also Children of immigrants; Immigrants; Refugees names of countries with the subdivision *Immigration and emigration*; and names of nationality groups

Andryszewski, T. Walking the earth	304.8

See/See also pages in the following book(s):

Bauer, C. F. Celebrations	808.8

Immortality

See also Future life

Fiction

Bosch, P. The name of this book is secret	Fic
Levine, G. C. Ever	Fic

Immune system

Cobb, V. Your body battles a cavity	617.6
Cobb, V. Your body battles a cold	616.2
Cobb, V. Your body battles a skinned knee	617.1
Cobb, V. Your body battles a stomachache	616.3
Cobb, V. Your body battles an earache	617.8

Immunization *See* Vaccination

Immunological system *See* Immune system

Imogene's antlers. Small, D.	E
Imogene's last stand. Fleming, C.	E

Imperial Palace (Beijing, China) *See* Forbidden City (Beijing, China)

Imperial Trans-Antarctic Expedition (1914-1917)

Calvert, P. Sir Ernest Shackleton	92
Kimmel, E. C. Ice story	998

Impressionism (Art)

Monet, C. Monet's impressions	759.4
Raimondo, J. Picture this!	759.05
Sabbeth, C. Monet and the impressionists for kids	759.05

The **impudent** rooster. Rascol, S. I.	398.2
In a blue room. Averbeck, J.	E
In a dark, dark room, and other scary stories. Schwartz, A.	398.2
In a word. Baker, R. F.	422
In Aunt Giraffe's green garden. Prelutsky, J.	811
In daddy's arms I am tall	811.008
In den Bosch, Nicole *See* Bosch, Nicole in den
In God's hands. Kushner, L.	E
In her hands. Schroeder, A.	92
In loving memory of Gorfman T. Frog. Donovan, G.	Fic
In my family. Garza, C. L.	306.8
In my own words [series]	
Custer, E. B. The diary of Elizabeth Bacon Custer	973.8
Leeper, D. R. The diary of David R. Leeper	92
In our mothers' house. Polacco, P.	E
In temperate zones. Baker, S.	551.6
In the Antarctic. Baker, S.	508
In the Arctic. Baker, S.	971.9

Infants—Fiction—*Continued*

Pearce, E. S. Isabel and the miracle baby **Fic**

Rathmann, P. The day the babies crawled away **E**

Reiser, L. My baby and me **E**

Salerno, S. Harry hungry! **E**

Shipton, J. Baby baby blah blah blah! **E**

Solheim, J. Born yesterday **E**

Sturges, P. How do you make a baby smile? **E**

Sullivan, S. Once upon a baby brother **E**

Sussman, M. B. Otto grows down **E**

Tafolla, C. Fiesta babies **E**

Vamos, S. R. Before you were here, mi amor **E**

Van Leeuwen, J. Benny & beautiful baby Delilah **E**

Weeks, S. Sophie Peterman tells the truth! **E**

Wheeler, L. Jazz baby **E**

Wheeler, L. Te amo, Bebé, little one **E**

Wild, M. Midnight babies **E**

Williams, V. B. "More more more" said the baby **E**

Wishinsky, F. Maggie can't wait **E**

Wolff, A. Me baby, you baby **E**

Yoon, S. Super babies on the move **E**

Poetry

Ahlberg, A. Everybody was a baby once, and other poems **811**

Archer, P. From dawn to dreams **811**

Calmenson, S. Welcome, baby! **811**

Rylant, C. Baby face **811**

Infection and infectious diseases *See* Communicable diseases

Influenza

Hoffmann, G. The flu **616.2**

Ollhoff, J. The flu **616.2**

Royston, A. Colds, the flu, and other infections **616.2**

Silverstein, A. The flu and pneumonia update **616.2**

Fiction

Collier, J. L. The empty mirror **Fic**

Moss, J. Winnie's war **Fic**

Information literacy

Callison, D. The blue book on information age inquiry, instruction and literacy **028.7**

Gaines, A. Master the library and media center **020**

Grassian, E. S. Information literacy instruction **025.5**

Harker, C. Library research with emergent readers **027.62**

Standards for the 21st-century learner in action **025.5**

Taylor, J. Information literacy and the school library media center **028.7**

Wan Guofang. Virtually true **025.04**

Study and teaching

Eisenberg, M. The Super3 **025.04**

Information literacy and the school library media center. Taylor, J. **028.7**

Information literacy instruction. Grassian, E. S. **025.5**

Information networks

See also Computer networks; Internet

Information power. American Association of School Librarians **027.8**

The **Information-powered** school **027.8**

Information resources

See also Internet resources

Gaines, A. Master the library and media center **020**

Information society

See also Information technology

Information storage and retrieval systems *See* Information systems

Information systems

See also Digital libraries; Multimedia

Wolinsky, A. Internet power research using the Big6 approach **025.04**

Information technology

Keane, N. J. The tech-savvy booktalker **021.7**

Solway, A. Communication **303.4**

Ingalls, Ann

The little piano girl **E**

Ingman, Bruce, 1963-

(il) Ahlberg, A. Everybody was a baby once, and other poems **811**

(il) Ahlberg, A. The pencil **E**

(il) Ahlberg, A. Previously **E**

(il) Ahlberg, A. The runaway dinner **E**

(il) Cabral, O. The seven sneezes **E**

(il) Feiffer, K. Double pink **E**

Ingpen, Robert R.

(il) Carroll, L. Alice's adventures in Wonderland [illustrated by Robert Ingpen] **Fic**

(il) Grahame, K. The wind in the willows [illustrated by Robert R. Ingpen] **Fic**

(il) Rosen, M. Dickens **92**

Ingraham, Erick, 1950-

(il) Calhoun, M. Cross-country cat **E**

Ingram, Jay

(jt. auth) Funston, S. It's all in your head **612.8**

Ingram, Scott, 1948-

A basketball all-star **796.323**

A football all-pro **796.332**

Inhalant abuse

Menhard, F. R. The facts about inhalants **362.29**

Inheritance and succession

Fiction

Naylor, P. R. Emily's fortune **Fic**

Injeanuity. Warwick, E. **746**

Injuries *See* Accidents; Wounds and injuries

Inkheart. Funke, C. C. **Fic**

Innerst, Stacy

(il) Krull, K. Lincoln tells a joke **92**

Innes, Stephanie

A bear in war **E**

Innocenti, Roberto

(il) Collodi, C. The adventures of Pinocchio [illustrated by Roberto Innocenti] **Fic**

(il) Lewis, J. P. The house **811**

Innovation in sports [series]
Fitzpatrick, J. Skateboarding   **796.22**
Gigliotti, J. Football   **796.332**
Kelley, K. C. Golf   **796.352**
Kelley, K. C. Soccer   **796.334**
Labrecque, E. Basketball   **796.323**
Teitelbaum, M. Baseball   **796.357**
Timblin, S. Swimming   **797.2**

Innovators [series]
Woog, A. Mark Zuckerberg, Facebook creator   **92**

Inns *See* Hotels and motels

Innuit *See* Inuit

Inoculation *See* Vaccination

Inquiry learning through librarian-teacher partnerships. Harada, V. H.   **371.1**

Insane *See* Mentally ill

Hospitals
See Psychiatric hospitals

Inscriptions
See also Graffiti

Insect detective. Voake, S.   **595.7**

Insect world [series]
Markle, S. Hornets   **595.7**
Markle, S. Luna moths   **595.7**
Markle, S. Praying mantises   **595.7**
Markle, S. Termites   **595.7**

Insectigation!. Blobaum, C.   **595.7**

Insects
See also Ants; Butterflies; Dragonflies; Grasshoppers; Moths; Wasps
Baker, N. Bug zoo   **595.7**
Berger, M. How do flies walk upside down?   **595.7**
Blobaum, C. Insectigation!   **595.7**
Bradley, T. J. Paleo bugs   **560**
Camper, C. Bugs before time   **560**
Cusick, D. Bug butts   **595.7**
Davies, A. Super-size bugs   **595.7**
Denega, D. Gut-eating bugs   **363.2**
Hansen, A. Bugs and bugsicles   **595.7**
Jackson, D. M. The bug scientists   **595.7**
Johnson, J. Simon & Schuster children's guide to insects and spiders   **595.7**
Markle, S. Insects   **595.7**
Martin, R. Bugs   **595.7**
Mound, L. A. Insect   **595.7**
Perritano, J. Bugs on your body   **595.7**
Rockwell, A. F. Bugs are insects   **595.7**
Rodriguez, A. M. Secret of the plant-killing ants . . . and more!   **595.7**
Rompella, N. Don't squash that bug!   **595.7**
Stradling, J. Bugs and spiders   **595.7**
Swanson, D. Bugs up close   **595.7**
Tait, N. Insects & spiders   **595.7**
VanCleave, J. P. Janice VanCleave's insects and spiders   **595.7**
Voake, S. Insect detective   **595.7**
Wilkes, S. Insects   **595.7**
See/See also pages in the following book(s):
Bishop, N. The secrets of animal flight   **591.47**

Fiction
Barner, B. Bug safari   **E**

Cushman, D. Inspector Hopper   **E**
Cyrus, K. Big rig bugs   **E**
Dodd, E. I love bugs   **E**
Durango, J. Pest fest   **E**
Emberley, E. Ed Emberley's bye-bye, big bad bullybug!   **E**
Hanson, W. Bugtown Boogie   **E**
Hector, J. The Gentleman Bug   **E**
Lechner, J. Sticky Burr: adventures in Burrwood Forest   **E**
McElligott, M. Bean thirteen   **E**
Morrow, B. O. Mr. Mosquito put on his tuxedo   **E**
Newgarden, M. Bow-Wow bugs a bug   **E**
Perlman, J. The delicious bug   **E**
Walsh, E. S. Dot & Jabber and the big bug mystery   **E**
Wilson, K. A frog in the bog   **E**

Poetry
Bulion, L. Hey there, stink bug!   **811**
Fleischman, P. Joyful noise: poems for two voices   **811**
Harrison, D. L. Bugs   **811**

Insects & spiders. Tait, N.   **595.7**

Inservice training *See* Librarians—In-service training

Inside, inside, inside. Meade, H.   **E**

Inside mouse, outside mouse. George, L. B.   **E**

The **inside-outside** book of libraries. Munro, R.   **027**

Inside-outside dinosaurs. Munro, R.   **567.9**

Inside the Titanic. Marschall, K.   **910.4**

The **inside** tree. Smith, L.   **E**

Insiders [series]
Calabresi, L. Human body   **612**
Garlick, M. A. Atlas of the universe   **520**
Long, J. A. Dinosaurs   **567.9**
Tait, N. Insects & spiders   **595.7**
Vogt, R. C. Rain forests   **577.3**

Insignia
See also National emblems

Inspector Hopper. Cushman, D.   **E**

Instruction *See* Teaching

Instructional materials *See* Teaching—Aids and devices

Instructional materials centers
See also School libraries
American Association of School Librarians. Information power   **027.8**
Bell, A. Handheld computers in schools and media centers   **371.3**
Farmer, L. S. J. Collaborating with administrators and educational support staff   **027.8**
Gaines, A. Master the library and media center   **020**
Harada, V. H. Assessing learning   **027.8**
Hughes-Hassell, S. Collection management for youth   **025.2**
The Information-powered school   **027.8**
Kaplan, A. G. Catalog it!   **025.3**
Martin, A. M. 7 steps to an award-winning school library program   **027.8**
Martin, B. S. Fundamentals of school library media management   **025.1**

Islands—Fiction—*Continued*

Buzzeo, T. The sea chest	E
Derby, S. Kyle's island	Fic
Jones, K. K. Sand dollar summer	Fic
Leach, S. Jake Reynolds: chicken or eagle?	Fic
Martin, J. B. On Sand Island	E
Nelson, M. Snook alone	E
Rosenthal, M. Archie and the pirates	E
Thor, A. A faraway island	Fic

Isol, 1972-

It's useful to have a duck	E
Petit, the monster	E

Israel

See also Jerusalem

DuBois, J. Israel	956.94
Hawker, F. Judaism in Israel	296
Marx, T. Sharing our homeland	956.04
Roy, J. R. Israel	956.94
Young, E. Israel	956.94

Fiction

Herman, C. First rain	E
Ofanansky, A. Harvest of light	E
Ofanansky, A. Sukkot treasure hunt	E
Orlev, U. The song of the whales	Fic

Israel-Arab conflicts

Ellis, D. Three wishes	956.94
Senker, C. The Arab-Israeli conflict	956.04

Israeli-Arab relations *See* Jewish-Arab relations

Issues in focus today [series]

Winkler, K. Bullying	371.5

Istanbul (Turkey)

Barber, N. Istanbul	949.6
It couldn't be worse!. Van Kampen, V.	398.2
It is the wind. Wolff, F.	E
It looked like spilt milk. Shaw, C.	E
It rained all day that night	811.008

It works! [series]

Barchers, S. I. Revolution in space	629.4
Jackson, C. Revolution in computers	004
Perritano, J. Revolution in communications	621.382
Perritano, J. Revolution in transportation	629.04
Sandvold, L. B. Revolution in construction	624
Sandvold, L. B. Revolution in medicine	610.9

The **Italian** American family album. Hoobler, D.	305.8

Italian Americans

Hoobler, D. The Italian American family album	305.8

Fiction

Bartone, E. Peppe the lamplighter	E
Bunting, E. A picnic in October	E
Hall, B. E. Henry and the kite dragon	E
Holm, J. L. Penny from heaven	Fic
Kent, R. Kimchi & calamari	Fic
Napoli, D. J. The king of Mulberry Street	Fic
Schirripa, S. R. Nicky Deuce	Fic
Schwartz, J. Our corner grocery store	E

Italian artists *See* Artists, Italian

Italy

Malone, M. G. Italy	945
Winter, J. K. Italy	945

Fiction

Alexander, L. The rope trick	Fic
Arrigan, M. Mario's Angels	E
Avi. Midnight magic	Fic
Baccalario, P. Ring of fire	Fic
Barrett, T. On Etruscan time	Fic
De Paola, T. Strega Nona: an old tale	E
Egielski, R. Saint Francis and the wolf	398.2
Fusco Castaldo, N. Pizza for the queen	E
Marsden, C. Take me with you	Fic
Pericoli, M. Tommaso and the missing line	E
Radunsky, V. The mighty asparagus	E
Shefelman, J. J. Anna Maria's gift	Fic
Weston, C. The diary of Melanie Martin; or, How I survived Matt the Brat, Michelangelo, and the Leaning Tower of Pizza	Fic

Folklore

See Folklore—Italy

History—0-1559—Fiction

Fern, T. E. Pippo the Fool	E
Itch & ooze. Lew, K.	616.5
It's a baby Australian fur seal!. Hengel, K.	599.79
It's a baby kangaroo!. Doudna, K.	599.2
It's a hummingbird's life. Kelly, I.	598
It's a miracle!. Spinner, S.	E
It's a secret. Burningham, J.	E
It's a snap! [biography of George Eastman] Kulling, M.	92
It's about time!. Murphy, S. J.	529
It's about time! Science projects. Gardner, R.	529
It's all in your head. Funston, S.	612.8
It's Christmas!. Prelutsky, J.	811
It's disgusting—and we ate it!. Solheim, J.	641.3
It's Justin Time, Amber Brown. Danziger, P.	E
It's library day. Stoeke, J. M.	E
It's like this, Cat. Neville, E. C.	Fic
It's moving day!. Hickman, P. M.	591.56
It's my school. Grindley, S.	E
It's my state! [series]	973
It's not the stork!. Harris, R. H.	612.6
It's only temporary. Warner, S.	Fic
It's perfectly normal. Harris, R. H.	613.9
It's picture day today!. McDonald, M.	E
It's probably Penny. Leedy, L.	519.2
It's quacking time!. Waddell, M.	E
It's snowing!. Dunrea, O.	E
It's snowing! it's snowing!. Prelutsky, J.	811
It's so amazing!. Harris, R. H.	612.6
It's Thanksgiving!. Prelutsky, J.	811

James, Gordon C.
(il) Adler, D. A. Campy [biography of Roy Campanella] **92**
(jt. auth) McKissack, P. C. Abby takes a stand **Fic**

James, Matt, 1973-
(il) Croza, L. I know here **E**

James, Raymond H., 1917-2001
Teeth and fangs **591.47**

James, Simon, 1957-
Ancient Rome **937**

James, Simon, 1961-
Baby Brains **E**
Little One Step **E**
(il) Solheim, J. Born yesterday **E**

James and the giant peach. Dahl, R. **Fic**

James Houston's Treasury of Inuit legends. Houston, J. A. **398.2**

James Marshall's Cinderella. Karlin, B. **398.2**

James Towne: struggle for survival. Sewall, M. **975.5**

Jamestown (Va.)
History
Karwoski, G. Miracle **972.9**
Lange, K. E. 1607 **975.5**
Rosen, D. New beginnings **975.5**
Sewall, M. James Towne: struggle for survival **975.5**

See/See also pages in the following book(s):
Huey, L. M. American archaeology uncovers the earliest English colonies **973.2**
History—Fiction
Carbone, E. L. Blood on the river **Fic**
Jamestown and the Virginia Colony. See Rosen, D. New beginnings **975.5**

Jamie and Angus together. Fine, A. **Fic**

Jamie O'Rourke and the big potato. De Paola, T. **398.2**

Jamie O'Rourke and the pooka. De Paola, T. **E**

Janeczko, Paul B., 1945-
Top secret **652**
Wing nuts **811**
(ed) A foot in the mouth. See A foot in the mouth **808.81**
(comp) A kick in the head. See A kick in the head **811.008**
(jt. auth) Lewis, J. P. Birds on a wire **811**
(comp) The Place my words are looking for. See The Place my words are looking for **811.008**
(comp) Poetry from A to Z. See Poetry from A to Z **808.1**
(comp) A Poke in the I. See A Poke in the I **811.008**

Jango-Cohen, Judith
Armadillos **599.3**
Bees **595.7**
Bionics **617.9**
Camels **599.63**
Chinese New Year **394.26**
Hippopotamuses **599.63**
The history of food **641.3**
Kangaroos **599.2**

Let's look at iguanas **597.95**
Octopuses **594**
Porcupines **599.35**
Rhinoceroses **599.66**

Jani, Mahendra
What you will see inside a Hindu temple **294.5**

Jani, Vandana
(jt. auth) Jani, M. What you will see inside a Hindu temple **294.5**

Janice VanCleave's 201 awesome, magical, bizarre & incredible experiments. VanCleave, J. P. **507.8**

Janice VanCleave's 202 oozing, bubbling, dripping & bouncing experiments. VanCleave, J. P. **507.8**

Janice VanCleave's 203 icy, freezing, frosty, cool & wild experiments. VanCleave, J. P. **507.8**

Janice VanCleave's big book of play and find out science projects. VanCleave, J. P. **507.8**

Janice VanCleave's earth science for every kid. VanCleave, J. P. **550**

Janice Vancleave's ecology for every kid. VanCleave, J. P. **577**

Janice VanCleave's electricity. VanCleave, J. P. **537**

Janice VanCleave's energy for every kid. VanCleave, J. P. **531**

Janice VanCleave's engineering for every kid. VanCleave, J. P. **507.8**

Janice VanCleave's geometry for every kid. VanCleave, J. P. **516**

Janice VanCleave's guide to more of the best science fair projects. VanCleave, J. P. **507.8**

Janice VanCleave's guide to the best science fair projects. VanCleave, J. P. **507.8**

Janice VanCleave's insects and spiders. VanCleave, J. P. **595.7**

Janice VanCleave's oceans for every kid. VanCleave, J. P. **551.46**

Janice VanCleave's plants. VanCleave, J. P. **580.7**

Janice VanCleave's play and find out about math. VanCleave, J. P. **513**

Janice VanCleave's play and find out about nature. VanCleave, J. P. **570**

Janice VanCleave's rocks and minerals. VanCleave, J. P. **552**

Janice VanCleave's science around the year. VanCleave, J. P. **507.8**

Janice VanCleave's solar system. VanCleave, J. P. **523.2**

Janice VanCleave's the human body for every kid. VanCleave, J. P. **612**

Janice VanCleave's weather. VanCleave, J. P. **551.5**

Janitors
Fiction
Borden, L. The A+ custodian **E**
Reed, L. R. Basil's birds **E**
Schotter, R. Doo-Wop Pop **E**

Jewish New Year *See* Rosh ha-Shanah

Jewish refugees

Borden, L. The journey that saved Curious George [biography of Margret Rey and H. A. Rey] **92**

Whiteman, D. B. Lonek's journey **940.53**

Fiction

Levitin, S. Journey to America **Fic**

Jewish wit and humor

See/See also pages in the following book(s):

Bauer, C. F. Celebrations **808.8**

Jews

Biography

Markel, M. Dreamer from the village [biography of Marc Chagall] **92**

McDonough, Y. Z. Hammerin' Hank [biography of Hank Greenberg] **92**

Michelson, R. As good as anybody: Martin Luther King Jr. and Abraham Joshua Heschel's amazing march toward freedom **92**

Rubin, S. G. The Anne Frank Case: Simon Wiesenthal's search for the truth **92**

Siegal, A. Memories of Babi **92**

Silverman, E. Sholom's treasure [biography of Sholem Aleichem] **92**

Waldman, N. Out of the shadows **92**

Winter, J. You never heard of Sandy Koufax!? **92**

Festivals

See Jewish holidays

Fiction

Ackerman, K. The night crossing **Fic**

Baskin, N. R. The truth about my Bat Mitzvah **Fic**

Brown, J. R. 13 **Fic**

Bunting, E. One candle **E**

Cohen, B. Molly's pilgrim **E**

Cohen, D. B. Nachshon, who was afraid to swim **E**

Cutler, J. Guttersnipe **E**

Da Costa, D. Hanukkah moon **E**

Edwards, M. Papa's latkes **E**

García, C. I wanna be your shoebox **Fic**

Glaser, L. Bridge to America **Fic**

Glatstein, J. Emil and Karl **Fic**

Hesse, K. The cats in Krasinski Square **E**

Hesse, K. Letters from Rifka **Fic**

Howland, N. Latkes, latkes, good to eat **E**

Hyde, H. S. Feivel's flying horses **E**

Kimmel, E. A. The Chanukkah guest **E**

Kimmel, E. A. Hershel and the Hanukkah goblins **E**

Kimmel, E. A. The jar of fools: eight Hanukkah stories from Chelm **S C**

Kimmel, E. A. The mysterious guests **E**

Kimmel, E. A. Zigazak! **E**

Krensky, S. Hanukkah at Valley Forge **E**

Kushner, E. The golden dreydl **Fic**

Kushner, L. In God's hands **E**

Lasky, K. Broken song **Fic**

Lasky, K. Marven of the Great North Woods **E**

Lasky, K. The night journey **Fic**

Levine, G. C. Dave at night **Fic**

Littman, S. Confessions of a closet Catholic **Fic**

Lowry, L. Number the stars **Fic**

McDonough, Y. Z. The doll with the yellow star **Fic**

Michelson, R. Across the alley **E**

Morpurgo, M. Waiting for Anya **Fic**

Napoli, D. J. The king of Mulberry Street **Fic**

Oberman, S. The always prayer shawl **E**

O'Connell, R. Penina Levine is a hard-boiled egg **Fic**

Ofanansky, A. Harvest of light **E**

Ofanansky, A. Sukkot treasure hunt **E**

Orlev, U. The song of the whales **Fic**

Oswald, N. Nothing here but stones **Fic**

Polacco, P. The butterfly **Fic**

Polacco, P. Chicken Sunday **E**

Polacco, P. The keeping quilt **E**

Polacco, P. Mrs. Katz and Tush **E**

Polacco, P. The trees of the dancing goats **E**

Portnoy, M. A. Tale of two Seders **E**

Rappaport, D. The secret seder **E**

Rosen, M. J. Elijah's angel **Fic**

Roy, J. R. Yellow star **Fic**

Schwabach, K. A pickpocket's tale **Fic**

Schwartz, E. Stealing home **Fic**

Singer, I. B. Stories for children **S C**

Stuchner, J. B. Honey cake **Fic**

Taback, S. Joseph had a little overcoat **E**

Taylor, S. All-of-a-kind family **Fic**

Thor, A. A faraway island **Fic**

Toksvig, S. Hitler's canary **Fic**

Wayland, A. H. New Year at the pier **E**

Weber, E. The Yankee at the seder **Fic**

Woodruff, E. The memory coat **E**

Yolen, J. Naming Liberty **E**

Folklore

Fowles, S. The bachelor and the bean **398.2**

Hirsh, M. The rabbi and the twenty-nine witches **398.2**

Jaffe, N. The way meat loves salt **398.2**

Kimmel, E. A. Even higher! **398.2**

Kimmel, E. A. Gershon's monster **398.2**

Kimmelman, L. The Little Red Hen and the Passover matzah **398.2**

Oberman, S. Solomon and the ant **398.2**

Rogasky, B. The golem **398.2**

Schram, P. The magic pomegranate **398.2**

Schwartz, H. Before you were born **398.2**

Schwartz, H. A coat for the moon and other Jewish tales **398.2**

Schwartz, H. A journey to paradise and other Jewish tales **398.2**

Silverman, E. Raisel's riddle **398.2**

Singer, I. B. Zlateh the goat, and other stories **398.2**

Souhami, J. The little, little house **398.2**

Stampler, A. R. Shlemazel and the remarkable spoon of Pohost **398.2**

Taback, S. Kibitzers and fools **398.2**

Waldman, D. Clever Rachel **398.2**

Waldman, D. A sack full of feathers **398.2**

Wisniewski, D. Golem **398.2**

History

Finkelstein, N. H. Remember not to forget **940.53**

Jules, Jacqueline, 1956-
  Abraham's search for God   222
  Benjamin and the silver goblet   222
  Duck for Turkey Day   E
  Sarah laughs   222
  Unite or die   973.3

Julia Gillian (and the art of knowing). McGhee, A.   **Fic**

Julia Morgan built a castle. Mannis, C. D.   92

Julia wants a pet. Lindgren, B.   E

Julian Rodriguez: episode one, Trash crisis on earth. Stadler, A.   **Fic**

Julie. George, J. C.   **Fic**

Julie Andrews' collection of poems, songs, and lullabies   808.8

Julie of the wolves. George, J. C.   **Fic**

Juliet Dove, Queen of Love. Coville, B.   **Fic**

Julio's magic. Dorros, A.   E

Julius, the baby of the world. Henkes, K.   E

Jumanji. Van Allsburg, C.   E

The **jumbo** book of art. Luxbacher, I.   702.8

The **jumbo** book of needlecrafts   746.4

The **jumbo** book of outdoor art. Luxbacher, I.   704.9

The **jumbo** vegetarian cookbook. Gillies, J.   641.5

Jump!. Fischer, S. M.   E

Jump! [biography of Michael Jordan] Cooper, F.   92

Jump at de sun: the story of Zora Neale Hurston. Porter, A. P.   92

Jump, frog, jump!. Kalan, R.   E

Jump into science [series]
  Tomecek, S. Moon   523.3

Jump, kangaroo, jump!. Murphy, S. J.   513

Jump rope See Rope skipping

Jump rope rhymes
  Anna Banana: 101 jump-rope rhymes   398.8
  Dotlich, R. K. Over in the pink house   811
  Sierra, J. Schoolyard rhymes   398.8

Jump ship to freedom. Collier, J. L.   **Fic**

Jumper, Betty Mae, 1923-
        About
  Annino, J. G. She sang promise: the story of Betty Mae Jumper, Seminole tribal leader   92

Jumping the scratch. Weeks, S.   **Fic**

Jumpy Jack and Googily. Rosoff, M.   E

Junco, Martha Avilés See Avilés Junco, Martha

June 29, 1999. Wiesner, D.   E

Junebug. Mead, A.   **Fic**

Juneteenth
  Nelson, V. M. Juneteenth   394.26

Jungle. Greenaway, T.   577.3

The **jungle** book: Mowgli's story. Kipling, R.   **S C**

The **jungle** book: the Mowgli stories. Kipling, R.   **S C**

Jungle party. Wildsmith, B.   E

Jungles
        Fiction
  Broach, E. Gumption!   E

Junie B. Jones and her big fat mouth. Park, B.   **Fic**

Junior authors & illustrators series
  Eighth book of junior authors and illustrators   920.003
  Ninth book of junior authors and illustrators   920.003
  Tenth book of junior authors and illustrators   920.003

Junior high schools
    See also Middle schools

Junior state maps on file   973

Junior Worldmark encyclopedia of the Canadian provinces   971

Junior Worldmark encyclopedia of the Mexican states   972

Junior Worldmark encyclopedia of the nations   910.3

Junior Worldmark encyclopedia of the states   973.03

Junior Worldmark encyclopedia of world holidays   394.26

Junk drawer jewelry. Di Salle, R.   745.594

Junk food. Cobb, V.   664

The **junkyard** wonders. Polacco, P.   **Fic**

Jupiter (Planet)
  Capaccio, G. Jupiter   523.4
  Landau, E. Jupiter   523.4

Jupiter (Roman deity) *See* Zeus (Greek deity)

Jurassic poop. Berkowitz, J.   567.9

Jurmain, Suzanne
  The forbidden schoolhouse [biography of Prudence Crandall]   92
  George did it [biography of George Washington]   92

Just a dream. Van Allsburg, C.   E

Just a minute. Morales, Y.   398.2

Just add water   546

Just enough and not too much. Zemach, K.   E

Just enough carrots. Murphy, S. J.   513

Just for elephants. Buckley, C.   639.9

Just for kids! [series]
  Hart, C. You can draw cartoon animals   741.5

Just Grace. Harper, C. M.   **Fic**

Just how long can a long string be!? Baker, K.   E

Just in case. Morales, Y.   E

Just in case. Viorst, J.   E

Just Juice. Hesse, K.   **Fic**

Just like a baby. Havill, J.   E

Just like Josh Gibson. Johnson, A.   E

Just like tonight. See Stewart, A. Bedtime for Button   E

Just like you. Dodd, E.   E

Just so stories. Kipling, R.   **S C**

The **just-so** woman. Blackwood, G. L.   E

Kidhaven science library [series]
Baxter, R. Chemical reaction   540
Juettner, B. Molecules   540
Nardo, D. Telescopes   522
Kidnap at the Catfish Cafe. Giff, P. R.   Fic
Kidnapped. Macdonald, F.   741.5
The **kidnappers**. Roberts, W. D.   Fic
Kidnapping
Fiction
Bruchac, J. Skeleton man   Fic
Cameron, A. Colibri   Fic
Corder, Z. Lionboy   Fic
Cox, J. The case of the purloined professor   Fic
Diamand, E. Raiders' ransom   Fic
Fleischman, P. The Half-a-Moon Inn   Fic
Giff, P. R. Eleven   Fic
Kehret, P. Abduction!   Fic
Malaghan, M. Greek ransom   Fic
Roberts, W. D. The kidnappers   Fic
Roberts, W. D. The one left behind   Fic
Yohalem, E. Escape under the forever sky   Fic
Kidogo. McGrory, A.   E
Kids around the world celebrate!. Jones, L.   394.26
Kids around the world cook!. Braman, A. N.   641.5
Kids at work. Freedman, R.   331.3
The **kids'** book club book. Gelman, J.   028.5
The **kids** book of Canadian geography. Penn, B.   971
The **kids** book of the Far North. Love, A.   998
The **kids'** book of weather forecasting. Breen, M.   551.63
The **kids'** building workshop. Robertson, J. C.   694
Kids can [series]
Henry, S. Making amazing art   745.5
Kids can do it [series]
Bartholomew, A. Electric mischief   621.31
Blakley Kinsler, G. Crocheting   746.43
Di Salle, R. Junk drawer jewelry   745.594
Friedman, D. Picture this   770
Hendry, L. Cat crafts   745.5
Hendry, L. Dog crafts   745.5
Hendry, L. Horse crafts   745.5
MacLeod, E. Bake and make amazing cakes   641.8
MacLeod, E. Bake and make amazing cookies   641.8
Sadler, J. A. Christmas crafts from around the world   745.594
Sadler, J. A. Embroidery   746.44
Sadler, J. A. Hemp jewelry   746.42
Sadler, J. A. Knitting   746.43
Sadler, J. A. Knotting   746.42
Sadler, J. A. Quick knits   746.43
Sadler, J. A. Simply sewing   646.2
Schwarz, R. Birdfeeders   690
Schwarz, R. Birdhouses   690
Schwarz, R. Funky junk   745.5
Schwarz, R. Making masks   646.4

Schwarz, R. Wind chimes and whirligigs   745.592
Silver, P. Face painting   745.5
Storms, B. Quilting   746.46
The **Kids** Can Press jumbo book of easy crafts. See Sadler, J. A. The new jumbo book of easy crafts   745.5
The **Kids** Can Press jumbo book of gardening. Morris, K.   635
The **Kids** Can Press jumbo cookbook. Gillies, J.   641.5
Kids Can Press wildlife series
Mason, A. Skunks   599.7
Kids can read [series]
Hood, S. Pup and Hound hatch an egg   E
Labatt, M. Pizza for Sam   E
MacLeod, E. Samuel de Champlain   92
Kids care!. Olien, R.   361.2
Kids cook 1-2-3. Gold, R.   641.5
Kids' crafts [series]
Davis, J. Crochet   746.43
Rhatigan, J. Soapmaking   668
Kids crochet. Ronci, K.   746.43
Kids draw [series]
Hart, C. Kids draw Manga Shoujo   741.5
Kids draw Manga Shoujo. Hart, C.   741.5
Kids' easy-to-create wildlife habitats. Stetson, E.   639.9
Kids' first cookbook   641.5
Kids go!. They Might Be Giants (Musical group)   782.42
A **kid's** guide to America's Bill of Rights. Krull, K.   342
The **kids'** guide to building cool stuff. Bell-Rehwoldt, S.   745.5
The **kids'** guide to classic games. Bell-Rehwoldt, S.   790.1
A **kid's** guide to container gardening. Bearce, S.   635.9
Kid's guide to creating Web pages for home and school. See Selfridge, B. A teen's guide to creating Web pages and blogs   006.7
The **kids'** guide to digital photography. Bidner, J.   775
A **kid's** guide to earning money. Orr, T.   650.1
Kids' guide to government [series]
Giesecke, E. Governments around the world   320.3
Giesecke, E. Local government   320.8
Giesecke, E. National government   320
Giesecke, E. State government   352.13
A **kid's** guide to Latino history. Petrillo, V.   305.8
A **kid's** guide to making a terrarium. Bearce, S.   635.9
The **kids** guide to money cent$. Thomas, K.   332.024
A **kid's** guide to native American history. Dennis, Y. W.   970.004
The **kids'** guide to paper airplanes. Harbo, C. L.   745.592

The **kid's** guide to social action. Lewis, B. A.
361.2

A **kid's** guide to the brain. See Funston, S. It's all in your head **612.8**

Kid's guide to the classification of living things [series]
Pascoe, E. Plants without seeds **586**

A **kid's** guide to Washington, D.C. Clark, D. C.
917.53

Kids' guides [series]
Bass, S. Kayaking **797.1**
Bell-Rehwoldt, S. The kids' guide to building cool stuff **745.5**
Bell-Rehwoldt, S. The kids' guide to classic games **790.1**
Harbo, C. L. The kids' guide to paper airplanes **745.592**
Schoenherr, A. Mountain biking **796.6**
Spencer, R. Skateboarding **796.22**
Woods, B. Snowboarding **796.9**

Kids' health [series]
Robbins, L. How to deal with ADHD
616.85
Robbins, L. How to deal with allergies
616.97
Robbins, L. How to deal with asthma **616.2**
Robbins, L. How to deal with autism
616.85
Robbins, L. How to deal with diabetes
616.4
Robbins, L. How to deal with obesity **616.3**

Kids knit!. Bradberry, S. **746.43**

Kids learn to crochet. Guy, L. **746.43**

Kids learn to knit. Guy, L. **746.43**

Kids make history. Buckley, S. **973**

Kids on strike!. Bartoletti, S. C. **331.8**

Kids online [series]
Jakubiak, D. J. A smart kid's guide to avoiding online predators **004.6**
Jakubiak, D. J. A smart kid's guide to doing Internet research **001.4**
Jakubiak, D. J. A smart kid's guide to Internet privacy **005.8**
Jakubiak, D. J. A smart kid's guide to online bullying **302.3**
Jakubiak, D. J. A smart kid's guide to playing online games **794.8**
Jakubiak, D. J. A smart kid's guide to social networking online **006.7**

Kids weaving. Swett, S. **746.41**

Kids who rule. Cotter, C. **920**

The **kids** winter handbook. Drake, J. **790.1**

Kidslabel (Firm)
Spot 7 School. See Spot 7 School **793.73**

Kiefte, Kees de
(il) Namioka, L. Yang the youngest and his terrible ear **Fic**

Kiernan, Denise
Signing our lives away **920**

Kiesler, Kate, 1971-
(il) Freedman, R. Out of darkness: the story of Louis Braille **92**

(il) George, K. O. The great frog race and other poems **811**
(il) George, K. O. Old Elm speaks **811**
(il) George, K. O. Toasting marshmallows
811
(il) Joosse, B. M. Wind-wild dog **E**

Kiki Strike: inside the shadow city. Miller, K.
Fic

Kiki's blankie. Bynum, J. **E**

Kikuyu (African people)
Fiction
Barasch, L. First come the zebra **E**

Killer ants. Nirgiotis, N. **595.7**

Killer whales. Markle, S. **599.5**

Killing germs, saving lives. Phelan, G. **615**

Kilworth, Garry
Attica **Fic**

Kim, Doug
See/See also pages in the following book(s):
Major, J. S. Caravan to America **920**

Kim, F. S.
Constellations **523.8**

Kim, Joung Un
(il) McDonald, M. Hen hears gossip **E**

Kim, So-Un
Korean children's favorite stories **398.2**

Kim, Susan
City of spies **741.5**

Kimball, Cheryl
Horse show handbook for kids **798.2**

Kimchi & calamari. Kent, R. **Fic**

Kimmel, Elizabeth Cody
Balto and the great race **636.7**
Boy on the lion throne [biography of the Dalai Lama] **92**
Glamsters **E**
Ice story **998**
Ladies first **920**
My penguin Osbert **E**
The reinvention of Moxie Roosevelt **Fic**
School spirit **Fic**
The top job **E**

Kimmel, Eric A.
The adventures of Hershel of Ostropol **398.2**
Anansi and the magic stick **398.2**
Anansi and the moss-covered rock **398.2**
Anansi and the talking melon **398.2**
Anansi goes fishing **398.2**
Anansi's party time **398.2**
The Chanukkah guest **E**
Even higher! **398.2**
The fisherman and the turtle **398.2**
The frog princess **398.2**
Gershon's monster **398.2**
The gingerbread man **398.2**
Hershel and the Hanukkah goblins **E**
A horn for Louis [biography of Louis Armstrong] **92**
Iron John **398.2**
The jar of fools: eight Hanukkah stories from Chelm **S C**
Joha makes a wish **E**
Little Britches and the rattlers **E**
The McElderry book of Greek myths **292**

Kimmel, Eric A.—*Continued*

The mysterious guests — E
A picture for Marc — **Fic**
Rip Van Winkle's return — E
The runaway tortilla — 398.2
Stormy's hat — E
The three little tamales — E
Three sacks of truth — 398.2
Wonders and miracles — 296.4
Zigazak! — E

Kimmelman, Leslie

Everybody bonjours! — E
In the doghouse — E
The Little Red Hen and the Passover matzah — 398.2
Mind your manners, Alice Roosevelt! — E

The **kind** of friends we used to be. Dowell, F. O. — **Fic**

Kindergarten

Howe, J. When you go to kindergarten — 372.2

Fiction

Cleary, B. Ramona the pest — **Fic**
Slate, J. Miss Bindergarten celebrates the 100th day of kindergarten — E

Kindergarten countdown. Hays, A. J. — E

Kindersley, Anabel

Celebrations — 394.26
(jt. auth) Kindersley, B. Children just like me — 305.23

Kindersley, Barnabas

Children just like me — 305.23
(il) Kindersley, A. Celebrations — 394.26

Kindness

Barraclough, S. Sharing — 177
Pryor, K. J. Kindness — 177

Fiction

Hennessy, B. G. Because of you — E
Leist, C. Jack the bear — E
Proimos, J. Paulie Pastrami achieves world peace — E
Thong, R. Fly free! — E

Kindschi, Tara, 1970-

4-H guide to raising chickens — 636.5

Kinerk, Robert

Clorinda — E

King, B. B.

Fiction

Boynton, S. Sandra Boynton's One shoe blues — 782.42

King, Casey

Oh, freedom! — 323.1

King, Coretta Scott, 1927-2006

About

Shange, N. Coretta Scott [King] — 92

King, Daniel, 1963-

Chess — 794.1

King, Dave

(il) Whalley, P. E. S. Butterfly & moth — 595.7

King, David C., 1933-

Azerbaijan — 947.5
Children's encyclopedia of American history — 973.03

Colonial days — 973.2
First people — 970.004
The Haida — 970.004
The Huron — 970.004
The Inuit — 970.004
Jellyfish — 593.5
Kyrgyzstan — 958.4
The Mohawk — 970.004
Monaco — 944
Mozambique — 967.9
The Nez Perce — 970.004
The Ojibwe — 970.004
Pioneer days — 978
The Powhatan — 970.004
Rwanda — 967.571
The Seminole — 970.004
Serbia and Montenegro — 949.7
The United Arab Emirates — 953

King, Hazel, 1962-

Carbohydrates for a healthy body — 613.2

King, Martin Luther, Jr., 1929-1968

I have a dream — 323.1

About

Farris, C. March on! [biography of Martin Luther King] — 92
Farris, C. My brother Martin [biography of Martin Luther King] — 92
Holland, L. J. Dr. Martin Luther King Jr.'s I have a dream speech in translation — 323.1
Jeffrey, L. S. Celebrate Martin Luther King, Jr., Day — 394.26
Marzollo, J. Happy birthday, Martin Luther King — 92
Michelson, R. As good as anybody: Martin Luther King Jr. and Abraham Joshua Heschel's amazing march toward freedom — 92
Myers, W. D. I've seen the promised land [biography of Martin Luther King] — 92
Rappaport, D. Martin's big words: the life of Dr. Martin Luther King, Jr. — 92
Shange, N. Coretta Scott [King] — 92

See/See also pages in the following book(s):
Freedman, R. Freedom walkers — 323.1

Fiction

Swain, G. Riding to Washington — E

King, Riley B. *See* King, B. B.

King, Sandra

Shannon: an Ojibway dancer — 970.004

King, Stephen Michael

Leaf — E
Mutt dog! — E
(il) Wild, M. Piglet and Mama — E

King, Thomas, 1943-

A Coyote solstice tale — **Fic**

King, Martin Luther, holiday *See* Martin Luther King Day

King Arthur and his Knights of the Round Table. Green, R. L. — 398.2

King Arthur and the Round Table. Talbott, H. — 398.2

King Bidgood's in the bathtub. Wood, A. — E

King George: what was his problem? Sheinkin, S. — 973.3

King Midas. Demi — 398.2

King Midas. Stewig, J. W.   398.2
King Midas and the golden touch. Craft, C.
     398.2
The king of Mulberry Street. Napoli, D. J.
     Fic
The King of Quizzical Island. Snell, G.   E
King of shadows. Cooper, S.   Fic
The king of the Golden River. Ruskin, J.   Fic
King of the wind. Henry, M.   Fic
King Pom and the fox. Souhami, J.   398.2

King-Smith, Dick, 1922-
  All pigs are beautiful   636.4
  Babe   Fic
  The Catlady   Fic
  Clever duck   Fic
  Dinosaur trouble   Fic
  Funny Frank   Fic
  The golden goose   Fic
  Lady Lollipop   Fic
  The mouse family Robinson   Fic
  The nine lives of Aristotle   Fic
  The twin giants   E

The king who barked. Jones, C. F.   636
The king with horse's ears and other Irish folk-tales. Burns, B.   398.2

Kingfisher, Rupert
  Madame Pamplemousse and her incredible edibles   Fic

The **Kingfisher** atlas of exploration & empires. Adams, S.   911
The **Kingfisher** atlas of the medieval world. Adams, S.   909.07
The **Kingfisher** atlas of the modern world. Adams, S.   909.8
The **Kingfisher** dinosaur encyclopedia. Benton, M.   567.9
The **Kingfisher** geography encyclopedia. Gifford, C.   910.3
The **Kingfisher** history encyclopedia   909
The **Kingfisher** illustrated horse & pony encyclopedia. Ransford, S.   636.1

Kingfisher knowledge [series]
  Adams, S. Castles & forts   355.7
  Butterfield, M. Pirates & smugglers   910.4
  Hynes, M. Rocks & fossils   552
  Langley, A. Hurricanes, tsunamis, and other natural disasters   363.34
  Platt, R. Forensics   363.2
  Robinson, J. Inventions   609
  Smith, M. Speed machines   629.2
  Steele, P. Middle East   956
  Walker, R. Epidemics & plagues   614.4
  Walker, R. Genes & DNA   576.5
  Walker, R. Microscopic life   579
  Wilkes, A. Dangerous creatures   591.6

Kingfisher riding club [series]
  Ransford, S. Horse & pony breeds   636.1
  Ransford, S. Horse & pony care   636.1

The **Kingfisher** science encyclopedia   503
The **Kingfisher** soccer encyclopedia. Gifford, C.   796.334

The **Kingfisher** student atlas. Wilkinson, P.   912

Kingfisher voyages [series]
  Adams, S. Ancient Egypt   932
  Harris, C. Wild weather   551.55

Kings and rulers
    See also Emperors; Queens
  Beccia, C. The raucous royals   920
  Cotter, C. Kids who rule   920
  Demi. Genghis Khan   92
  Demi. Tutankhamun   92
  Galford, E. Hatshepsut   92
  Geyer, F. Saladin   92
  Gifford, C. 10 kings & queens who changed the world   920
  Meltzer, M. Ten kings   920
  Ross, S. Monarchs   940.1
  Stanley, D. Saladin: noble prince of Islam   92

          Fiction
  Farmer, N. Clever Ali   Fic
  Oppel, K. The king's taster   E
  Snell, G. The King of Quizzical Island   E
  Wilson, S. The day we danced in underpants   E
  Wood, A. King Bidgood's in the bathtub   E

The **King's** fifth. O'Dell, S.   Fic
The **king's** taster. Oppel, K.   E

Kingsley, Ben
  (jt. auth) Ganeri, A. The young person's guide to the orchestra   784.2

Kinkor, Kenneth J.
  (jt. auth) Clifford, B. Real pirates   910.4

Kinney, Jeff
  Diary of a wimpy kid: Greg Heffley's journal   Fic

Kinsey-Warnock, Natalie
  Lumber camp library   Fic
  Nora's ark   E

Kiowa Indians
  See/See also pages in the following book(s):
  Freedman, R. Indian chiefs   920

Kipling, Rudyard, 1865-1936
  A collection of Rudyard Kipling's Just so stories   S C
  The elephant's child   Fic
  If   821
  The jungle book: Mowgli's story   S C
  The jungle book: the Mowgli stories   S C
  Just so stories   S C
          Adaptations
  Pinkney, J. Rikki-tikki-tavi   E

Kira-Kira. Kadohata, C.   Fic

Kirk, Connie Ann, 1951-
  Sky dancers   E

Kirk, Daniel
  Keisha Ann can!   E
  Library mouse   E
  The low road   Fic
  (il) Edwards, P. D. While the world is sleeping   E
  (il) Stevenson, R. L. Block city   E

Kirk, Shoshanna
  T is for tugboat   623.82

Kirk, Steve
  (il) Camper, C. Bugs before time   **560**
Kirker, Christine
  (jt. auth) MacMillan, K. Storytime magic   **027.62**
Kirkpatrick, John Simpson, 1892-1915
  About
  Greenwood, M. The donkey of Gallipoli   **940.4**
Kirkpatrick, Katherine A., 1964-
  Snow baby [biography of Marie Ahnighito Peary]   **92**
Kirov, Erica
  Magickeepers: the eternal hourglass   **Fic**
Kirsch, Vincent X.
  Natalie & Naughtily   **E**
Kirwan, Wednesday
  Minerva the monster   **E**
Kiss good night. Hest, A.   **E**
Kiss kiss!. Wild, M.   **E**
Kiss the cow. Root, P.   **E**
Kissel, Richard
  (jt. auth) Kelly, E. Evolving planet   **551**
Kisseloff, Jeff
  Who is baseball's greatest pitcher?   **796.357**
Kisses on the wind. Moser, L.   **E**
Kissing
  Fiction
  Paul, A. W. If animals kissed good night--   **E**
  Trewin, T. I lost my kisses   **E**
  Yolen, J. Mama's kiss   **E**
Kit Feeny: on the move. Townsend, M.   **741.5**
Kitain, Sandra
  Shelf-esteem   **028.5**
Kitamura, Satoshi
  Stone Age boy   **E**
  (il) Carnival of the animals. See Carnival of the animals   **811.008**
  (il) McNaughton, C. Once upon an ordinary school day   **E**
Kitchel, JoAnn E.
  (il) Celenza, A. H. Gershwin's Rhapsody in Blue   **E**
Kitchen, Bert
  (il) Ericsson, J. A. Whoo goes there?   **E**
  (il) Tagholm, S. The rabbit   **599.3**
Kitchen dance. Manning, M.   **E**
The kitchen knight. Hodges, M.   **398.2**
Kite flying. Lin, G.   **E**
The kite rider. McCaughrean, G.   **Fic**
Kites
  Hosking, W. Asian kites   **629.133**
  Murphy, S. J. Let's fly a kite   **516**
  Fiction
  Demi. Kites   **E**
  Hall, B. E. Henry and the kite dragon   **E**
  Lin, G. Kite flying   **E**
  McCaughrean, G. The kite rider   **Fic**
  Murphy, R. Bird   **Fic**
  Williams, V. B. Lucky song   **E**

Kites sail high: a book about verbs. Heller, R.   **428**
A kitten tale. Rohmann, E.   **E**
Kitten's first full moon. Henkes, K.   **E**
Kittens! Kittens! Kittens!. Meyers, S.   **E**
Kitty's cuddles. Cabrera, J.   **E**
KKK See Ku Klux Klan
Kladstrup, Kristin
  The book of story beginnings   **Fic**
  The gingerbread pirates   **E**
Klaffke, Ben
  (il) Landau, E. Smokejumpers   **628.9**
Klages, Ellen, 1954-
  The green glass sea   **Fic**
Klare, Roger
  Gregor Mendel   **92**
Klass, David, 1960-
  Stuck on Earth   **Fic**
Klassen, J.
  (il) Stutson, C. Cats' night out   **E**
  (il) Wood, M. The mysterious howling   **Fic**
Klassen, Jon See Klassen, J.
Klavan, Laurence
  (jt. auth) Kim, S. City of spies   **741.5**
Kleven, Elisa
  The apple doll   **E**
  (il) De colores and other Latin-American folk songs for children. See De colores and other Latin-American folk songs for children   **782.42**
  (il) Diez deditos. Ten little fingers & other play rhymes and action songs from Latin America. See Diez deditos. Ten little fingers & other play rhymes and action songs from Latin America   **782.42**
  (il) Dorros, A. Abuela   **E**
  (il) Durango, J. Angels watching over me   **E**
  (il) Fiestas: a year of Latin American songs of celebration. See Fiestas: a year of Latin American songs of celebration   **782.42**
  (il) Glaser, L. Our big home   **E**
  (il) Hurd, T. The weaver   **E**
  (il) Jaskol, J. City of angels   **979.4**
  (il) Thong, R. Wish   **398**
Klimley, A. Peter
  About
  Mallory, K. Swimming with hammerhead sharks   **597**
Klimo, Kate
  The dragon in the sock drawer   **Fic**
Kline, Michael P.
  (il) Blobaum, C. Geology rocks!   **551**
  (il) Breen, M. The kids' book of weather forecasting   **551.63**
  (il) Hart, A. Ancient Greece!   **938**
  (il) Hauser, J. F. Super science concoctions   **507.8**
  (il) Johmann, C. Bridges!   **624.2**
  (il) Milord, S. Mexico!   **972**
  (il) Olien, R. Kids care!   **361.2**
Kline, Suzy, 1943-
  Herbie Jones   **Fic**
  Horrible Harry in room 2B   **Fic**

Kratter, Paul, 1956-
The living rain forest   **591.7**
(il) Collard, S. B., III. Butterfly count   **E**

Kraus, Jeanne, 1950-
Annie's plan   **371.3**

Kraus, Robert, 1925-2001
Whose mouse are you?   **E**

Krauss, Ruth, 1911-1993
The backward day   **E**
Bears   **E**
The carrot seed   **E**
The growing story   **E**
A very special house   **E**

Krautwurst, Terry, 1946-
Night science for kids   **591.5**

Kray, Robert Clement, 1930-
(il) Hansen, A. Bugs and bugsicles   **595.7**

Krebs, Laurie
The Beeman   **E**
Up and down the Andes   **985**

Kreiter, Eshel
John Singer Sargent   **92**

Kreloff, Elliot
(il) Ziefert, H. Mighty Max   **E**

Krementz, Jill
How it feels to be adopted   **362.7**
How it feels when a parent dies   **155.9**
How it feels when parents divorce   **306.89**

Krenina, Katya, 1968-
(il) Kimmel, E. A. The mysterious guests   **E**

Krensky, Stephen, 1953-
Anansi and the box of stories   **398.2**
Dangerous crossing   **Fic**
Hanukkah at Valley Forge   **E**
How Santa got his job   **E**
John Henry   **398.2**
Noah's bark   **E**
Paul Bunyan   **398.2**
Pecos Bill   **398.2**
Sisters of Scituate Light   **E**
Spark the firefighter   **E**
Too many leprechauns   **E**
What's the big idea?   **974.4**

Kresh, Diane
(ed) The whole digital library handbook. See
The whole digital library handbook   **025.1**

Kress, Adrienne
Alex and the Ironic Gentleman   **Fic**

Kress, Stephen W.
(jt. auth) Salmansohn, P. Saving birds
  333.95

Krieg, Jim
Griff Carver, hallway patrol   **Fic**

Krier, Ann Kristen, 1962-
Totally cool origami animals   **736**

Kringle. Abbott, T.   **Fic**

Krinitz, Esther Nisenthal
Memories of survival   **940.53**

Krishnaswami, Uma, 1956-
Monsoon   **E**

Kristallnacht, 1938
Fiction
Wiviott, M. Benno and the Night of Broken
Glass   **E**

Kristina, Queen of Sweden, 1626-1689 *See*
Christina, Queen of Sweden, 1626-1689

Kristo, Janice V.
(ed) Adventuring with books. See Adventuring
with books   **011.6**

Krog, Hazlitt
(jt. auth) Shulman, M. Attack of the killer video
book   **778.59**

Kroll, Steven
Barbarians!   **940.1**
Ellis Island   **325.73**
The Hanukkah mice   **E**
Stuff!   **E**
William Penn   **92**

Kroll, Virginia L.
Everybody has a teddy   **E**

Krommes, Beth, 1956-
(il) Lunge-Larsen, L. The hidden folk   **398.2**
(il) Martin, J. B. The lamp, the ice, and the boat
called Fish   **998**
(il) Sidman, J. Butterfly eyes and other secrets
of the meadow   **811**
(il) Swanson, S. M. The house in the night
  E

Kronheimer, Ann
(il) King-Smith, D. The golden goose   **Fic**

The Kronos Chronicles [series]
Rutkoski, M. The Cabinet of Wonders   **Fic**

Kronquist, Burleigh *See* Burleigh, Robert, 1936-

Krosoczka, Jarrett J.
Lunch Lady and the League of Librarians
  741.5

Krull, Kathleen, 1952-
Albert Einstein   **92**
The boy on Fairfield Street: how Ted Geisel
grew up to become Dr. Seuss   **92**
The boy who invented TV: the story of Philo
Farnsworth   **92**
The brothers Kennedy   **920**
Fartiste   **Fic**
Harvesting hope   **92**
Houdini   **92**
Isaac Newton   **92**
A kid's guide to America's Bill of Rights
  342
Leonardo da Vinci   **92**
Lincoln tells a joke   **92**
Lives of extraordinary women   **920**
Lives of the artists   **920**
Lives of the athletes   **920**
Lives of the musicians   **920**
Lives of the presidents   **920**
Lives of the writers   **920**
Marie Curie   **92**
Pocahontas   **92**
A pot o' gold   **820.8**
The road to Oz [biography of L. Frank Baum]
  92
Sigmund Freud   **92**
Supermarket   **381**

Kurisu, Jane—*Continued*
  (il) Morris, K. The Kids Can Press jumbo book
    of gardening   **635**
  (il) Sadler, J. A. Simply sewing   **646.2**
Kurlansky, Mark
  The cod's tale   **639.2**
  The story of salt   **553.6**
Kurosaki, Yoshisuke
  (il) Sakade, F. Japanese children's favorite sto-
    ries   **398.2**
Kurtti, Jeff
  (jt. auth) Schumacher, T. L. How does the show
    go on?   **792**
Kurtz, Christopher
  (jt. auth) Kurtz, J. Water hole waiting   **E**
Kurtz, Jane
  Faraway home   **E**
  Fire on the mountain   **398.2**
  The storyteller's beads   **Fic**
  Water hole waiting   **E**
Kushites *See* Cushites
Kushner, Ellen, 1955-
  The golden dreydl   **Fic**
Kushner, Jill Menkes, 1951-
  Who on earth is Dian Fossey?   **92**
Kushner, Lawrence, 1943-
  In God's hands   **E**
Kushner, Tony
  The art of Maurice Sendak   **741.6**
Kuskin, Karla
  A boy had a mother who bought him a hat
        E
  Green as a bean   **E**
  I am me   **E**
  So what's it like to be a cat?   **E**
  (il) Fox, P. Traces   **E**
Kusugak, Michael
  See/See also pages in the following book(s):
  Ellis, S. From reader to writer   **372.6**
Kuwait
  O'Shea, M. Kuwait   **953.67**
    Fiction
  Addasi, M. The white nights of Ramadan   **E**
Kvasnosky, Laura McGee, 1951-
  Really truly Bingo   **E**
  Zelda and Ivy, the runaways   **E**
Kwanzaa
  Altman, L. J. Celebrate Kwanzaa   **394.26**
  Chocolate, D. My first Kwanzaa book
        394.26
  McGee, R. Paper crafts for Kwanzaa
        745.594
  Otto, C. Celebrate Kwanzaa   **394.26**
  Tokunbo, D. The sound of Kwanzaa   **394.26**
    Fiction
  Medearis, A. S. Seven spools of thread   **E**
Kwolek, Stephanie L., 1923-
  See/See also pages in the following book(s):
  Thimmesh, C. Girls think of everything   **920**
Kwon, Yoon-Duck, 1960-
  My cat copies me   **E**
Kyle's island. Derby, S.   **Fic**

Kyong, Yunmee
  (il) Khan, R. Silly chicken   **E**
Kyrgyzstan
  King, D. C. Kyrgyzstan   **958.4**
Kyvelos, Peter
  See/See also pages in the following book(s):
  Major, J. S. Caravan to America   **920**

L

L. Frank Baum's The Wizard of Oz. Cavallaro, M.
      741.5
L is for lollygag   **428**
La Chanze
  Little diva   **E**
La Fevers, R. L.
  Flight of the phoenix   **Fic**
  Theodosia and the Serpents of Chaos   **Fic**
La Fontaine, Jean de, 1621-1695
    Adaptations
  Bolt, R. The hare and the tortoise and other fa-
    bles of La Fontaine   **398.2**
La La Rose. Ichikawa, S.   **E**
La Salle, René Robert Cavelier *See* La Salle,
  Robert Cavelier, sieur de, 1643-1687
La Salle, Robert Cavelier, sieur de, 1643-1687
    About
  Goodman, J. E. Despite all obstacles: La Salle
    and the conquest of the Mississippi   **92**
    Fiction
  Howard, E. The crimson cap   **Fic**
LaBaff, Tom
  (il) Benbow, A. Awesome animal science proj-
    ects   **590.7**
  (il) Benbow, A. Lively plant science projects
        580.7
  (il) Benbow, A. Sprouting seed science projects
        580.7
  (il) Gardner, R. Earth-shaking science projects
    about planet Earth   **550**
  (il) Gardner, R. Far-out science projects about
    Earth's sun and moon   **523**
  (il) Gardner, R. Smashing science projects about
    Earth's rocks and minerals   **552**
  (il) Gardner, R. Stellar science projects about
    Earth's sky   **551.5**
  (il) Gardner, R. Super science projects about
    Earth's soil and water   **631.4**
  (il) Gardner, R. Wild science projects about
    Earth's weather   **551.5**
  (il) Gunter, V. A. Pet science   **636**
  (il) Rhatigan, J. Cool chemistry concoctions
        540.7
Labatt, Mary, 1944-
  Pizza for Sam   **E**
Labor
  See also Agricultural laborers; Migrant la-
    bor; Work; Working class

Labor and laboring classes *See* Working class

Labor disputes

 See also Strikes

Labor movement
     History
 Tafolla, C. That's not fair! [biography of Emma Tenayuca] **92**

Labrecque, Ellen
 Basketball **796.323**

Lace and lace making
     Fiction
 Bradley, K. B. The lacemaker and the princess **Fic**

The **lace** dowry. Cheng, A. **Fic**

The **lacemaker** and the princess. Bradley, K. B. **Fic**

Lacey, Josh *See* Doder, Joshua, 1968-

Lach, William, 1968-
 Can you hear it? **780**

Lacombe, Benjamin, 1982-
 Cherry and Olive **E**
 (il) Williams, B. Lin Yi's lantern **E**

Ladd, London
 (il) Farris, C. March on! [biography of Martin Luther King] **92**
 (il) Weatherford, C. B. Oprah [biography of Oprah Winfrey] **92**

Laden, Nina, 1962-
 (il) Myers, W. D. The blues of Flats Brown **E**

Ladies first. Kimmel, E. C. **920**

Ladwig, Tim
 (il) Weatherford, C. B. The beatitudes **323.1**

The **lady** & the lion. Long, L. **398.2**

Lady Liberty. Rappaport, D. **974.7**

Lady Lollipop. King-Smith, D. **Fic**

Ladybirds *See* Ladybugs

Ladybug Girl. Soman, D. **E**

Ladybugs
 Posada, M. Ladybugs **595.7**
 Thomson, R. The life cycle of a ladybug **595.7**

     Fiction
 Berger, J. Bridget Fidget and the most perfect pet! **E**
 Carle, E. The grouchy ladybug **E**
 Cummings, T. The eensy weensy spider freaks out (big time!) **E**
 Donaldson, J. What the ladybug heard **E**
 Thomas, J. Can you make a scary face? **E**

LaFave, Kim, 1955-
 (il) Campbell, N. I. Shi-shi-etko **E**
 (il) Ellis, S. Ben over night **E**

LaFaye, A., 1970-
 Water steps **Fic**
 Worth **Fic**

Lafayette, Marie Joseph Paul Yves Roch Gilbert du Motier, marquis de, 1757-1834
     About
 Fritz, J. Why not, Lafayette? **92**

LaFleur, Suzanne M., 1983-
 Love, Aubrey **Fic**

Lafrance, Marie
 (il) Kaner, E. Who likes the rain? **551.57**
 (il) Kaner, E. Who likes the snow? **551.57**
 (il) Kaner, E. Who likes the wind? **551.51**
 (il) Levert, M. A wizard in love **E**
 (il) Nolan, J. The firehouse light **363.3**

Lagarrigue, Jerome
 (il) Angelou, M. Maya Angelou **811**
 (il) Harrington, J. N. Going north **E**
 (il) Hartfield, C. Me and Uncle Romie **E**
 (il) Trollinger, P. B. Perfect timing [biography of Isaac Murphy] **92**
 (il) Weatherford, C. B. Freedom on the menu **E**
 (il) Wiles, D. Freedom Summer **E**

Lagasse, Emeril
 Emeril's there's a chef in my family! **641.5**
 Emeril's there's a chef in my world! **641.5**

Laidlaw, Rob
 Wild animals in captivity **636.088**

Laika. Abadzis, N. **741.5**

Lairamore, Dawn
 Ivy's ever after **Fic**

Laird, Elizabeth
 A fistful of pearls **398.2**

Lake, A. J.
 The coming of dragons **Fic**

Lake, Kate
 (il) Matsen, B. Go wild in New York City **974.7**

Lakes
 Johansson, P. Lakes and rivers **577.6**
     Fiction
 Derby, S. Kyle's island **Fic**
 Henkes, K. Bird Lake moon **Fic**
 Holmes, E. A. Tracktown summer **Fic**

Lakes and rivers. Johansson, P. **577.6**

Lakota Indians *See* Teton Indians

Lal, Sunandini Arora *See* Arora Lal, Sunandini

Lalicki, Tom *See* Matthews, Tom L., 1949-

Lamadrid, Enrique R., 1948-
 Juan the bear and the water of life **398.2**

Laman, Tim
 Face to face with orangutans **599.8**

Lamanna, Paolo, 1973-
 (il) Colfer, E. Artemis Fowl: the graphic novel **741.5**

LaMarche, Jim
 Lost and found **E**
 The raft **E**
 Up **E**
 (il) Napoli, D. J. Albert **E**

Lamb, Susan Condie
 (il) Houston, G. My great-aunt Arizona **E**

Lamont, Priscilla
 (il) George, J. C. Goose and Duck **E**
 (il) Stauffacher, S. Gator on the loose! **Fic**

Lamorisse, Albert, 1922-1970
 The red balloon **E**

The **lamp**, the ice, and the boat called Fish. Martin, J. B. **998**

Lamps

See also Electric lamps

Lamstein, Sarah, 1943-
A big night for salamanders ... E

Lana's Lakota moons. Sneve, V. D. H. ... Fic

Lancelot (Legendary character)
Fiction
Morris, G. The adventures of Sir Lancelot the Great ... Fic

The **land** I lost: adventures of a boy in Vietnam. Huynh, Q. N. ... 92

The land is our storybook [series]
Andre, J.-A. We feel good out here ... 970.004
McLeod, T. The Delta is my home ... 970.004
Zoe, T. Living stories ... 970.004

The land of Elyon [series]
Carman, P. The Dark Hills divide ... Fic

The **land** of the dragon king and other Korean stories. McClure, G. ... 398.2

Land surveying *See* Surveying

Landau, Elaine
Apples ... 634
Asthma ... 616.2
Bananas ... 634
Beyond Pluto ... 523.4
Big cats ... 599.75
Bites and stings ... 617.1
Broken bones ... 617.1
Bumps, bruises, and scrapes ... 617.1
Cavities and toothaches ... 617.6
Chickenpox ... 616.9
The common cold ... 616.2
Corn ... 633.1
Dyslexia ... 616.85
Earth ... 525
Easter ... 394.26
Fleeing to freedom on the Underground Railroad ... 973.7
Food allergies ... 616.97
The history of everyday life ... 609
Jupiter ... 523.4
Mars ... 523.4
Mercury ... 523.4
The moon ... 523.3
Neptune ... 523.4
Pluto ... 523.4
Popcorn ... 641.3
Saturn ... 523.4
Smokejumpers ... 628.9
St. Patrick's Day ... 394.26
The sun ... 523.7
Uranus ... 523.4
Valentine's day ... 394.26
Venus ... 523.4
Wheat ... 633.1

Landfills
Fiction
Kooser, T. Bag in the wind ... E

Landforms [series]
Sepehri, S. Continents ... 910
Sepehri, S. Glaciers ... 551.3
Sepehri, S. Rivers ... 551.48
Sheehan, T. F. Islands ... 551.4
Sheehan, T. F. Mountains ... 551.4

Landmann, Bimba
The incredible voyage of Ulysses ... 883

Landmark events in American history [series]
Uschan, M. V. The Battle of the Little Bighorn ... 973.8

Landolf, Diane Wright
What a good big brother! ... E

Landry, Leo
Space boy ... E
(il) Ault, K. Let's sign! ... 419
(il) Wilson, S. Friends and pals and brothers, too ... E

The **Landry** News. Clements, A. ... Fic

Landscape & the environment. Bingham, J. ... 704.9

Landscape in art
Bingham, J. Landscape & the environment ... 704.9

Landstrom, Lee Ann, 1954-
Nature's yucky! 2: the desert southwest ... 591.7

Landström, Lena, 1943-
A hippo's tale ... E

Landström, Olof, 1943-
(il) Lindgren, B. Oink, oink Benny ... E

Landy, Derek
Skulduggery Pleasant ... Fic

Lane, Kathleen, 1967-
Nana cracks the case! ... Fic

Lane, Kimberly
Come look with me: Asian art ... 709.5
Come look with me: Latin American art ... 709.8

Lang, Andrew, 1844-1912
(ed) The Arabian nights entertainments. See The Arabian nights entertainments ... 398.2
(ed) The Blue fairy book. See The Blue fairy book ... 398.2

Lang, Aubrey
(jt. auth) Lynch, W. Sonoran Desert ... 577.5

Langdo, Bryan, 1973-
(jt. auth) Burell, S. Diamond Jim Dandy and the sheriff ... E

Lange, Dorothea, 1895-1965
About
Partridge, E. Restless spirit: the life and work of Dorothea Lange ... 92

Lange, Karen E.
1607 ... 975.5

Langemack, Chapple
The author event primer ... 021.2

Langford, Sarah
(jt. auth) Gerdner, L. Grandfather's story cloth ... E

Langley, Andrew
Ancient Egypt ... 932
Ancient Greece ... 709.38
Glass ... 620.1
Hurricanes, tsunamis, and other natural disasters ... 363.34
Medieval life ... 940.1
Metal ... 620.1
Paper products ... 676

Lassieur, Allison—*Continued*
The ancient Romans   **937**

The last apprentice [series]
Delaney, J. Revenge of the witch   **Fic**
Delaney, J. The Spook's tale and other horrors   **S C**

The **last** best days of summer. Hobbs, V.   **Fic**

The **last** Black king of the Kentucky Derby. Hubbard, C.   **92**

The **last** brother. Noble, T. H.   **E**

The **last** day of school. Borden, L.   **Fic**

The **last** dragon. De Mari, S.   **Fic**

The **last** invisible boy. Kuhlman, E.   **Fic**

The **last** laugh. Aruego, J.   **E**

Last-minute science fair projects. Bardhan-Quallen, S.   **507.8**

The **last** newspaper boy in America. Corbett, S.   **Fic**

Last night. Yum, H.   **E**

Last one in is a rotten egg. Kessler, L. P.   **E**

The **last** princess: the story of Princess Ka'iulani of Hawai'i. Stanley, F.   **92**

The **last** river. Waldman, S.   **978**

The **last** synapsid. Mason, T.   **Fic**

The **last** treasure. Anderson, J.   **Fic**

Late for school!. Calmenson, S.   **E**

Latham, Donna
Ecology   **577**

Latham, Irene
Leaving Gee's Bend   **Fic**

Lathrop, Dorothy P., 1891-1980
(il). Animals of the Bible   **220.8**
(il) Field, R. Hitty: her first hundred years   **Fic**

Latif, Zawiah Abdul
(jt. auth) Gish, S. Ethiopia   **963**
(jt. auth) Hassig, S. M. Somalia   **967.73**
(jt. auth) Heale, J. Madagascar   **969.1**
(jt. auth) Kagda, F. Algeria   **965**
(jt. auth) Kagda, S. Lithuania   **947.93**
(jt. auth) Levy, P. Sudan   **962.4**
(jt. auth) Sheehan, S. Lebanon   **956.92**
(jt. auth) Wilcox, J. Iceland   **949.12**

Latimer, Jonathan P.
Butterflies   **595.7**
Caterpillars   **595.7**
(ed) Simon & Schuster thesaurus for children. See Simon & Schuster thesaurus for children   **423**

Latimer, Miriam
(il) Harvey, M. Shopping with Dad   **E**

Latin America

See also South America
Fiction
Delacre, L. Salsa stories   **S C**
Hurwitz, J. New shoes for Silvia   **E**
Stanton, K. Papi's gift   **E**
Vidal, B. Federico and the Magi's gift   **E**

Folklore
See Folklore—Latin America
Social life and customs
Ada, A. F. Merry Navidad!   **394.26**
Fiestas: a year of Latin American songs of celebration   **782.42**
Robinson, F. Hispanic-American crafts kids can do!   **745.5**

Latin America and the Caribbean. Solway, A.   **780.9**

Latin American art
Lane, K. Come look with me: Latin American art   **709.8**

Latin American literature
Bibliography
Schon, I. Recommended books in Spanish for children and young adults, 2004-2008   **011.6**
Treviño, R. Z. Read me a rhyme in Spanish and English = Léame una rima en español e inglés   **027.62**

Latin American music *See* Music—Latin America

Latin American poetry
Collections
Muu, moo!   **398.8**

Latin Americans
Fiction
Chapra, M. Sparky's bark   **E**
Songs
Mora, P. A pinata in a pine tree   **782.42**

Latinos (U.S.) *See* Hispanic Americans

The **latke** who couldn't stop screaming. Snicket, L.   **E**

Latkes, latkes, good to eat. Howland, N.   **E**

Latrobe, Kathy Howard
The children's literature dictionary   **028.5**

Latta, Sara L.
The good, the bad, the slimy   **579**

Latter-day Saints *See* Church of Jesus Christ of Latter-day Saints

Latvia
Barlas, R. Latvia   **947.96**

Lau, Ruth
(jt. auth) Berg, E. Senegal   **966.3**

Lauber, Patricia, 1924-
Be a friend to trees   **582.16**
Lost star: the story of Amelia Earhart   **92**
What you never knew about beds, bedrooms, and pajamas   **392**
What you never knew about fingers, forks, & chopsticks   **394.1**
Who eats what?   **577**
You're aboard Spaceship Earth   **550**

Laugesen, Malene
(il) Strauss, L. L. The princess gown   **E**

Laugh & learn [series]
Crist, J. J. Siblings   **306.8**
Fox, J. S. Get organized without losing it   **371.3**

Laugh-eteria. Florian, D.   **811**

The **laugh** stand. Cleary, B. P.   **817**

Laugh till you cry. Nixon, J. L.   **Fic**

Laughing out loud, I fly. Herrera, J. F.   **811**

Laundresses
Fiction
Yeoman, J. The wild washerwomen   **E**

Laura Secord: a story of courage. Lunn, J. L. S.   **Fic**

Lauré, Jason, 1940-
(jt. auth) Blauer, E. Mali   **966.2**
(jt. auth) Blauer, E. Mauritania   **966.1**

Lauren, Jill, 1961-
That's like me!   **371.9**

Laurent, Richard
(il) Bauer, C. F. Leading kids to books through magic   **027.62**
(il) Bauer, C. F. Leading kids to books through puppets   **027.62**

Lautrec, Henri de Toulouse- *See* Toulouse-Lautrec, Henri de, 1864-1901

Lauture, Denize *See* Lotu, Denize, 1946-

Lauw, Darlene
Light   **535**
Water   **553.7**
Weather   **551.5**

Lavallee, Barbara
(il) Joosse, B. M. Mama, do you love me?   **E**
(jt. auth) Joosse, B. M. Papa, do you love me?   **E**
(il) Mora, P. Uno, dos, tres: one, two, three   **E**

Law, Felicia
Atlas of Southwest and Central Asia   **950**
Atlas of the Far East and Southeast Asia   **950**

Law, Ingrid, 1970-
Savvy   **Fic**

Law, Ruth, b. 1887
About
Brown, D. Ruth Law thrills a nation   **629.13**

Law, Stephen
Really, really big questions   **100**

Law, Westley Wallace, 1923-2002
About
Haskins, J. Delivering justice [biography of Westley Wallace Law]   **92**

Law
Hamilton, J. How a bill becomes a law   **328.73**

Law enforcement
Nelson, V. M. Bad news for outlaws   **92**

Lawlor, Laurie
He will go fearless   **Fic**
Helen Keller: rebellious spirit   **92**
Muddy as a duck puddle and other American similes   **425**
The school at Crooked Creek   **Fic**

Lawlor, Veronica
(il) I was dreaming to come to America. See I was dreaming to come to America   **325.73**

Lawn Boy. Paulsen, G.   **Fic**
Lawn to lawn. Yaccarino, D.   **E**

Lawrence, George, 1953-
(il) Weaver, A. H. The voyage of the beetle   **576.8**

Lawrence, Iain, 1955-
The convicts   **Fic**
The giant-slayer   **Fic**
Lord of the nutcracker men   **Fic**
The wreckers   **Fic**

Lawrence, Jack
(jt. auth) Bullock, M. Lions, tigers, and bears, vol. 1: Fear and pride   **741.5**

Lawrence, Jacob, 1917-2000
The great migration   **759.13**
Harriet and the Promised Land   **811**
About
Collard, S. B., III. Jacob Lawrence   **92**
Duggleby, J. Story painter: the life of Jacob Lawrence   **92**

Lawrence, John, 1933-
This little chick   **E**
(il) Butterworth, C. Sea horse   **597**
(il) Stevenson, R. L. Treasure Island   **Fic**
(il) Waddell, M. Tiny's big adventure   **E**

Lawrence (Mass.)
Fiction
Paterson, K. Bread and roses, too   **Fic**

Lawson, JonArno, 1968-
Black stars in a white night sky   **811**

Lawson, Robert, 1892-1957
Ben and me   **Fic**
Mr. Revere and I   **Fic**
Rabbit Hill   **Fic**
(il) Atwater, R. T. Mr. Popper's penguins   **Fic**
(il) Leaf, M. The story of Ferdinand   **E**
(il) Vining, E. G. Adam of the road   **Fic**

Lawton, Clive, 1951-
Hiroshima   **940.54**

Lawyers
See also Judges; Women lawyers

Lay-ups and long shots   **S C**
Layla loves the library. See McQuinn, A. Lola at the library   **E**

Layton, Lesley, 1954-
Singapore   **959.57**

Layton, Neal
(il) Cowell, C. That rabbit belongs to Emily Brown   **E**
(il) Davies, N. Extreme animals   **590**
(il) Davies, N. Just the right size   **591.4**
(il) Davies, N. What's eating you?   **591.6**

Lazan, Marion Blumenthal
(jt. auth) Perl, L. Four perfect pebbles   **940.53**

Lazar, Ralph
(il) Adams, S. The most fantastic atlas of the whole wide world by the Brainwaves   **912**
(il) Walker, R. How the incredible human body works—by the Brainwaves   **612**
(il) Watts, C. The most explosive science book in the universe   **500**

Lazare, Jerry, 1927-
(il) Burch, R. Queenie Peavy   **Fic**

Leprosy
Lynette, R. Leprosy   616.9
Fiction
Durango, J. The walls of Cartagena   Fic

Lerer, Seth, 1955-
Children's literature   028.5

Lerman, Josh
How to raise Mom and Dad   E

Lerner, Carol, 1927-
Butterflies in the garden   595.7

Lesbians
See also Gay parents
Fiction
Garden, N. Molly's family   E
González, R. Antonio's card   E
Newman, L. Mommy, mama, and me   E
Polacco, P. In our mothers' house   E

Leshem, Yossi
(jt. auth) Vogel, C. G. The man who flies with
birds   598

Less is more. Baumbach, D.   025.2

Less than zero. Murphy, S. J.   513

Lessac, Frané, 1954-
(il) Greenwood, M. The donkey of Gallipoli
    940.4
(il) Melmed, L. K. Heart of Texas   976.4
(il) Melmed, L. K. New York, New York
    974.7
(il) Pomerantz, C. The chalk doll   E
(il) Rockwell, A. F. Clouds   551.57

Lessem, Don
The fastest dinosaurs   567.9
Feathered dinosaurs   567.9
Flying giants of dinosaur time   567.9
Sea giants of dinosaur time   567.9
The smartest dinosaurs   567.9

Lesser, Rika
Hansel and Gretel   398.2

Lester, Helen, 1936-
Author   92
Hooway for Wodney Wat   E
The sheep in wolf's clothing   E
Three cheers for Tacky   E

Lester, Julius
Black cowboy, wild horses   E
From slave ship to freedom road   326
John Henry   398.2
Let's talk about race   305.8
The old African   Fic
Sam and the tigers   E
The tales of Uncle Remus   398.2
To be a slave   326
Uncle Remus, the complete tales   398.2

Lester, Mike, 1955-
(il) Crow, K. Cool Daddy Rat   E

Lester Fizz, bubble-gum artist. Spiro, R.   E

Let it begin here!. Brown, D.   973.3

Let it begin here!. Fradin, D. B.   973.3

Let it shine   782.25

Let it shine. Pinkney, A. D.   920

Let me play. Blumenthal, K.   796

Let my people go. McKissack, P. C.   Fic

Let the circle be unbroken. Taylor, M. D.   Fic

Let there be peace. Brooks, J.   242

Let there be peace on earth. Jackson, J.
    782.42

Let's count. Hoban, T.   E

Let's do nothing!. Fucile, T.   E

Let's fly a kite. Murphy, S. J.   516

Let's get a pup, said Kate. Graham, B.   E

Let's get cooking! [series]
Lee, F. Fun with Chinese cooking   641.5

Let's go!. Flatt, L.   388

Let's go rock collecting. Gans, R.   552

Let's go visiting. Williams, S.   E

Let's look at animals [series]
Cooper, J. Camouflage and disguise   591.47
Cooper, J. Hooves and claws   591.47
Higginson, M. Beaks and bills   598
Higginson, M. Feathers and fur   591.47
James, R. H. Teeth and fangs   591.47

Let's look at bats. Berman, R.   599.4

Let's look at brown bears. Berman, R.   599.78

Let's look at fall. Schuette, S. L.   508.2

Let's look at iguanas. Jango-Cohen, J.   597.95

Let's look at pigeons. Piehl, J.   598

Let's look at prairie dogs. Zuchora-Walske, C.
    599.3

Let's look at snails. Waxman, L. H.   594

Let's look at spring. Schuette, S. L.   508.2

Let's look at summer. Schuette, S. L.   508.2

Let's look at winter. Schuette, S. L.   508.2

Let's play in the forest while the wolf is not
around. Rueda, C.   782.42

Let's-read-and-find-out science [series]
Bancroft, H. Animals in winter   591.56
Berger, M. Chirping crickets   595.7
Berger, M. Germs make me sick!   616.9
Berger, M. Spinning spiders   595.4
Berger, M. Why I sneeze, shiver, hiccup, and
yawn   612.7
Bradley, K. B. Energy makes things happen
    531
Bradley, K. B. Forces make things move
    531
Bradley, K. B. Pop!   530.4
Branley, F. M. Air is all around you   551.5
Branley, F. M. Day light, night light   535
Branley, F. M. Down comes the rain   551.57
Branley, F. M. Earthquakes   551.2
Branley, F. M. Flash, crash, rumble, and roll
    551.55
Branley, F. M. Floating in space   629.45
Branley, F. M. The International Space Station
    629.44
Branley, F. M. Is there life in outer space?
    576.8
Branley, F. M. Mission to Mars   629.45
Branley, F. M. Snow is falling   551.57
Branley, F. M. The sun, our nearest star
    523.7
Branley, F. M. Volcanoes   551.2
Branley, F. M. What makes a magnet?   538
Branley, F. M. What the moon is like   523.3

Lew, Kristi, 1968-—*Continued*
Human organs   611
Itch & ooze   **616.5**

Lew-Vriethoff, Joanne
(il) Cleary, B. P. The punctuation station
    428
(il) Spinelli, E. The Dancing Pancake   **Fic**

Lewandowski, Christine Laura *See* Lew, Kristi, 1968-

Lewin, Betsy, 1937-
Animal snackers   **811**
(il) Cronin, D. Click, clack, moo   **E**
(il) Cronin, D. Duck for President   **E**
(il) Kuskin, K. So what's it like to be a cat?
    E
(jt. auth) Lewin, T. Balarama   **636.9**
(jt. auth) Lewin, T. Elephant quest   **591.9**
(jt. auth) Lewin, T. Horse song   **951.7**
(jt. auth) Lewin, T. Top to bottom down under
    994
(il) Prigger, M. S. Aunt Minnie McGranahan
    E
(il) Silverman, E. Cowgirl Kate and Cocoa
    E
(il) Spinelli, E. Heat wave   **E**
(il) Weeks, S. Two eggs, please   **E**

Lewin, Ted, 1935-
At Gleason's gym   **796.8**
Balarama   **636.9**
Elephant quest   **591.9**
Horse song   **951.7**
How much?   **381**
Lost city   **985**
Market!   **381**
Tooth and claw   **590**
Top to bottom down under   **994**
(il) Bartone, E. Peppe the lamplighter   **E**
(il) Bauer, M. D. The longest night   **E**
(il) Borden, L. A. Lincoln and me   **E**
(il) Bunting, E. One green apple   **E**
(il) Heide, F. P. The day of Ahmed's secret
    E
(il) Heide, F. P. Sami and the time of the troubles
    E
(il) Oberman, S. The always prayer shawl   **E**
(il) O'Dell, S. Island of the Blue Dolphins
    Fic
(il) Scott, A. H. Cowboy country   **978**

Lewis, Barbara A., 1943-
The kid's guide to social action   **361.2**

Lewis, Bobby *See* Moore, Bobbie, 1944-

Lewis, Brian, 1963-
(jt. auth) Jaskol, J. City of angels   **979.4**

Lewis, C. S. (Clive Staples), 1898-1963
The Chronicles of Narnia; adaptation. See Sabuda, R. The Chronicles of Narnia pop-up
    E
The lion, the witch, and the wardrobe   **Fic**
See/See also pages in the following book(s):
Ellis, S. From reader to writer   **372.6**

Lewis, Clive Staples *See* Lewis, C. S. (Clive Staples), 1898-1963

Lewis, Cynthia Copeland, 1960-
(il) Cobb, V. Feeling your way   **612.8**
(il) Cobb, V. Follow your nose   **612.8**

(jt. auth) Cobb, V. Open your eyes   **612.8**
(il) Cobb, V. Your tongue can tell   **612.8**

Lewis, E. B. (Earl B.), 1956-
(il) Bass, H. The secret world of Walter Anderson   **92**
(il) Campbell, B. M. Sometimes my mommy gets angry   **E**
(il) Carbone, E. L. Night running   **E**
(il) Curtis, G. The bat boy & his violin   **E**
(il) Grimes, N. Talkin' about Bessie: the story of aviator Elizabeth Coleman   **92**
(il) Howard, E. F. Virgie goes to school with us boys   **E**
(il) Hughes, L. The Negro speaks of rivers
    811
(il) Kurtz, J. Faraway home   **E**
(il) Kurtz, J. Fire on the mountain   **398.2**
(il) Michelson, R. Across the alley   **E**
(il) Mollel, T. M. My rows and piles of coins
    E
(il) Nolen, J. Pitching in for Eubie   **E**
(il) Rappaport, D. Dirt on their skirts   **E**
(il) Raven, M. Circle unbroken   **E**
(il) Raven, M. Night boat to freedom   **E**
(il) Rodman, M. A. My best friend   **E**
(il) Schertle, A. Down the road   **E**
(il) Slate, J. I want to be free   **E**
(il) Smith, H. A. Keeping the night watch
    Fic
(il) Tarpley, N. Bippity Bop barbershop   **E**
(il) Taulbert, C. L. Little Cliff and the porch people   **E**
(il) This little light of mine. See This little light of mine   **782.25**
(il) Wong, J. S. Homegrown house   **E**
(il) Woodson, J. Coming on home soon   **E**
(il) Woodson, J. The other side   **E**

Lewis, Earl B. *See* Lewis, E. B. (Earl B.), 1956-

Lewis, Edna, 1916-2006
Fiction
Gourley, R. Bring me some apples and I'll make you a pie   **E**

Lewis, Elizabeth Foreman, 1892-1958
Young Fu of the upper Yangtze   **Fic**

Lewis, H. B.
(il) Kimmel, E. C. My penguin Osbert   **E**

Lewis, J. Patrick
Arithme-tickle   **513**
Big is big (and little, little)   **E**
Birds on a wire   **811**
Blackbeard, the pirate king   **811**
The brothers' war   **811**
Countdown to summer   **811**
Doodle dandies   **811**
The house   **811**
Monumental verses   **811**
Once upon a tomb   **811**
Please bury me in the library   **811**
The snowflake sisters   **E**
Spot the plot   **811**
Under the kissletoe   **811**
The underwear salesman   **811**
The World's Greatest   **811**
(jt. auth) Janeczko, P. B. Wing nuts   **811**

Lewis, John, 1940-
About
Bausum, A. Freedom Riders   323.1
Haskins, J. John Lewis in the lead   92
Lewis, Kim
Good night, Harry   E
Lewis, Maggie
Morgy makes his move   Fic
Lewis, Meriwether, 1774-1809
About
Faber, H. Lewis and Clark   978
Perritano, J. The Lewis and Clark Expedition
    978
Schanzer, R. How we crossed the West   978
Fiction
Myers, L. Lewis and Clark and me   Fic
Lewis, Rose A.
Every year on your birthday   E
I love you like crazy cakes   E
Lewis and Clark. Faber, H.   978
Lewis and Clark and me. Myers, L.   Fic
Lewis and Clark Expedition (1804-1806)
Adler, D. A. A picture book of Sacagawea
    92
Blumberg, R. York's adventures with Lewis and
Clark   978
Faber, H. Lewis and Clark   978
Patent, D. H. Animals on the trail with Lewis
and Clark   978
Patent, D. H. Plants on the trail with Lewis and
Clark   978
Perritano, J. The Lewis and Clark Expedition
    978
Pringle, L. P. American slave, American hero
[biography of York]   92
Schanzer, R. How we crossed the West   978
St. George, J. Sacagawea   92
Fiction
Myers, L. Lewis and Clark and me   Fic
O'Dell, S. Streams to the river, river to the sea
    Fic
Lewis Carroll's Alice in Wonderland. Carroll, L.
    Fic
Lexau, Joan M.
Come back, cat   E
Who took the farmer's [hat]?   E
Lexington (Mass.), Battle of, 1775
Brown, D. Let it begin here!   973.3
Fradin, D. B. Let it begin here!   973.3
L'Homme, Erik
Tales of a lost kingdom   398.2
Li Cunxin, 1961-
Dancing to freedom [biography of Li Cunxin]
    92
Liano, Dante, 1948-
(jt. auth) Menchú, R. The girl from Chimel
    92
(jt. auth) Menchú, R. The honey jar   398.2
(jt. auth) Menchú, R. The secret legacy
    398.2
Liao, Jimmy, 1958-
(jt. auth) Dunbar, J. The monster who ate dark-
ness   E
(il) Spinelli, J. I can be anything   E

(jt. auth) Thomson, S. L. The sound of colors
    E
Libbrecht, Kenneth G., 1958-
The secret life of a snowflake   551.57
Libel and slander
See also Gossip
Liberia
Folklore
See Folklore—Liberia
Liberty. Curlee, L.   974.7
Liberty!. Drummond, A.   E
Liberty Bell
Magaziner, H. J. Our Liberty Bell   974.8
Liberty or death. Maestro, B.   973.3
Liberty rising. Shea, P. D.   974.7
The **librarian** of Basra. Winter, J.   E
The **librarian** who measured the earth [biography
of Eratosthenes] Lasky, K.   92
Librarians
Egoff, S. A. Once upon a time   92
Kenney, K. L. Librarians at work   020
Walter, V. A. Twenty-first-century kids, twenty-
first-century librarians   027.62
Winter, J. The librarian of Basra   E
Fiction
Barnett, M. The case of the case of mistaken
identity   Fic
Bottner, B. Miss Brooks loves books (and I
don't)   E
González, L. M. The storyteller's candle   E
Henson, H. That Book Woman   E
Peck, R. Here lies the librarian   Fic
Sanderson, B. Alcatraz versus the evil Librarians
    Fic
Williams, S. Library Lil   E
Graphic novels
Krosoczka, J. J. Lunch Lady and the League of
Librarians   741.5
In-service training
Harlan, M. A. Personal learning networks
    027.8
Librarians at work. Kenney, K. L.   020
A **librarian's** guide to cultivating an elementary
school garden. Mackey, B.   372
The **librarian's** guide to graphic novels for chil-
dren and tweens. Serchay, D. S.   025.2
Librarian's guide to online searching. Bell, S. S.
    025.5
Libraries
See also Digital libraries; Instructional ma-
terials centers; Public libraries
Duncan, D. I-search for success   025.5
Gaines, A. Master the library and media center
    020
Munro, R. The inside-outside book of libraries
    027
Myron, V. Dewey the library cat   636.8
Sawa, M. The library book   027
Winter, J. Biblioburro   E
Winter, J. The librarian of Basra   E
Administration
Curzon, S. C. Managing change   025.1

Lisker, Sonia O., 1933-
(il) Blume, J. Freckle juice   **Fic**
Lisle, Holly, 1960-
The Ruby Key   **Fic**
Lisle, Janet Taylor, 1947-
Afternoon of the elves   **Fic**
The art of keeping cool   **Fic**
Highway cats   **Fic**
Listen!. Tolan, S. S.   **Fic**
Listen, listen. Gershator, P.   **E**
Listen to the wind. Mortenson, G.   **371.82**
The **listeners**. Whelan, G.   **E**
Listening for crickets. Gifaldi, D.   **Fic**
Listening for lions. Whelan, G.   **Fic**
Lister, Joseph, Baron, 1827-1912
About
Ollhoff, J. The germ detectives   **616.9**
Literacy
Fiction
Ellison, E. S. Flight   **Fic**
Hesse, K. Just Juice   **Fic**
Literacy, Information *See* Information literacy
The **literary** adventures of Washington Irving.
Harness, C.   **92**
Literary prizes
See also Caldecott Medal; Coretta Scott
King Award; Newbery Medal
Literary recreations
See also Word games
Literature
See also African Americans in literature;
Children's literature; Native American litera-
ture; Teenagers' writings; Young adult litera-
ture names of national literatures, e.g. *English
literature*
Collections
Bauer, C. F. Celebrations   **808.8**
Celebrate Cricket   **808.8**
Hey! listen to this   **028.5**
The Norton anthology of children's literature
    808.8
Sawyer, R. The way of the storyteller   **372.6**
History and criticism
See also Authors
Study and teaching
Hall, S. Using picture storybooks to teach liter-
ary devices   **016.8**
Literature for youth [series]
Crew, H. S. Women engaged in war in literature
for youth   **016.3**
Garcha, R. The world of Islam in literature for
youth   **016.3058**
Leeper, A. Poetry in literature for youth
    016.8
Lithgow, John, 1945-
Micawber   **E**
Lithuania
Kagda, S. Lithuania   **947.93**
Little, Jean, 1932-
Emma's yucky brother   **E**
See/See also pages in the following book(s):
Ellis, S. From reader to writer   **372.6**

Little, Malcolm *See* Malcolm X, 1925-1965
Little Audrey. White, R.   **Fic**
Little ballet star. Geras, A.   **E**
Little Bear. Minarik, E. H.   **E**
Little Bear's little boat. Bunting, E.   **E**
Little Beauty. Browne, A.   **E**
Little Bighorn, Battle of the, 1876
Anderson, P. C. George Armstrong Custer
    92
January, B. Little Bighorn, June 25, 1876
    973.8
Turner, A. W. Sitting Bull remembers   **92**
Uschan, M. V. The Battle of the Little Bighorn
    973.8
Walker, P. R. Remember Little Bighorn
    973.8
Little Bighorn, June 25, 1876. January, B.
    973.8
Little Bitty Mousie. Aylesworth, J.   **E**
Little Black Sambo, The story of. See Bannerman,
H. The story of Little Babaji   **E**
Little blue and little yellow. Lionni, L.   **E**
Little Blue Truck. Schertle, A.   **E**
Little boat. Docherty, T.   **E**
Little Britches and the rattlers. Kimmel, E. A.
    E
Little by little. Stewart, A.   **E**
Little Chick. Hest, A.   **E**
Little Cliff and the porch people. Taulbert, C. L.
    E
Little Cricket. Brown, J.   **Fic**
The **little** crooked house. Wild, M.   **E**
Little devils. Blake, R. J.   **E**
Little diva. La Chanze   **E**
Little divas. Boles, P. M.   **Fic**
Little Dog. Jahn-Clough, L.   **E**
Little Dog and Duncan. George, K. O.   **811**
Little dog poems. George, K. O.   **811**
The **little** dump truck. Cuyler, M.   **E**
The **little** engine that could [illustrated by George
& Doris Hauman] Piper, W.   **E**
The **little** engine that could [illustrated by Loren
Long] Piper, W.   **E**
Little Gold Star. Hayes, J.   **398.2**
Little Gold Star. San Souci, R.   **398.2**
The **little** golden lamb. Greene, E.   **398.2**
Little gorillas. Costa-Prades, B.   **599.8**
The **little** hands big fun craft book. Press, J.
    745.5
Little Hands create!. Dall, M. D.   **745.5**
Little Hoot. Rosenthal, A. K.   **E**
Little Horse. Byars, B. C.   **Fic**
The **little** house. Burton, V. L.   **E**
The **Little** House cookbook. Walker, B. M.
    641.5
Little house in the big woods. Wilder, L. I.
    Fic
A **Little** House traveler. Wilder, L. I.   **92**
The **little** island. Brown, M. W.   **E**

Lobel, Gillian
Moonshadow's journey — E
Lobster learners [series]
Rompella, N. Don't squash that bug! — 595.7
Local farms and sustainable foods. Vogel, J. — 630
Local government
Giesecke, E. Local government — 320.8
Local news. Soto, G. — S C
Loch Ness monster
Fiction
Flaherty, A. The luck of the Loch Ness monster — E
The **locked** garden. Whelan, G. — Fic
Locker, Thomas, 1937-
(il) Bruchac, J. Between earth & sky — 398.2
(il) Bruchac, J. Thirteen moons on a turtle's back — 811
Lockhart, Laura
(jt. auth) Duncan, D. I-search for success — 025.5
Lockheart, Susanna
(il) If you love a nursery rhyme. See If you love a nursery rhyme — 398.8
Lockouts See Strikes
Lockwood, Belva Ann, 1830-1917
About
Bardhan-Quallen, S. Ballots for Belva [biography of Belva Ann Lockwood] — 92
Lockwood, Sophie
Ants — 595.7
Bats — 599.4
Chimpanzees — 599.8
Dragonflies — 595.7
Flies — 595.7
Polar Bears — 599.78
Sea turtles — 597.92
Whales — 599.5
Zebras — 599.66
Locomotion. Woodson, J. — Fic
Locomotives
Zimmermann, K. R. Steam locomotives — 385.09
Locricchio, Matthew
The international cookbook for kids — 641.5
The 2nd international cookbook for kids — 641.5
Loertscher, David V., 1940-
(ed) The Whole school library handbook. See The Whole school library handbook — 027.8
Lofting, Hugh, 1886-1947
The voyages of Doctor Dolittle — Fic
Lofts, Pamela
(il) Fox, M. Hunwick's egg — E
(il) Fox, M. Koala Lou — E
Logan, Claudia
The 5,000-year-old puzzle — 932
Logging See Lumber and lumbering
A **log's** life. Pfeffer, W. — 577.3
Loizeaux, William
Clarence Cochran, a human boy — Fic
Wings — Fic

Lola at the library. McQuinn, A. — E
Lomas Garza, Carmen See Garza, Carmen Lomas, 1948-
Lomax, John Avery, 1867-1948
About
Hopkinson, D. Home on the range — 92
Lombard, Jenny
Drita, my homegirl — Fic
Lomberg, Michelle
Horse — 636.1
Spider — 639
Lon Po Po. Young, E. — 398.2
London, Jack, 1876-1916
See/See also pages in the following book(s):
Krull, K. Lives of the writers — 920
London, Jonathan, 1947-
Baby whale's journey — E
Froggy learns to swim — E
A train goes clickety-clack — E
A truck goes rattley-bumpa — E
(jt. auth) Bruchac, J. Thirteen moons on a turtle's back — 811
London (England)
Stacey, G. London — 942.1
Fiction
Avi. Traitor's gate — Fic
Cockcroft, J. Counter clockwise — Fic
Curry, J. L. The Black Canary — Fic
Cushman, K. Alchemy and Meggy Swann — Fic
Dowd, S. The London Eye mystery — Fic
Jarvis, R. The alchemist's cat — Fic
La Fevers, R. L. Theodosia and the Serpents of Chaos — Fic
Skelton, M. The story of Cirrus Flux — Fic
Springer, N. The case of the missing marquess — Fic
Stewart, P. The curse of the night wolf — Fic
Woodruff, E. The Ravenmaster's secret — Fic
History
Platt, R. London — 942.1
London (England). Tower See Tower of London (England)
The **London** Eye mystery. Dowd, S. — Fic
Lone wolf. Lasky, K. — Fic
Lonek's journey. Whiteman, D. B. — 940.53
Loneliness
Fiction
Brun-Cosme, N. Big Wolf & Little Wolf — E
DeFelice, C. C. Signal — Fic
Hannigan, K. Emmaline and the bunny — Fic
Long, Ethan
Bird & Birdie in a fine day — E
(il) Amato, M. Stinky and successful — Fic
(il) Carr, J. Greedy Apostrophe — E
(il) Elliott, D. One little chicken — E
(il) Lawlor, L. Muddy as a duck puddle and other American similes — 425
(il) Lewis, J. P. Countdown to summer — 811
(il) Nesbitt, K. My hippo has the hiccups — 811
(il) Paul, A. W. Count on Culebra — E
(il) Paul, A. W. Fiesta fiasco — E

Luján, Jorge
  Colors! Colores!   861
Luka's quilt. Guback, G.   E
Luke on the loose. Bliss, H.   741.5
Lukenbill, W. Bernard
  Biography in the lives of youth   028.5
Lullabies
  Arrorró mi niño   398.8
  Ho, M. Hush!   E
  Hush, little baby   782.42
  In the hollow of your hand   782.42
  Julie Andrews' collection of poems, songs, and
    lullabies   808.8
  Pinkney, B. Hush, little baby   782.42
  Senir, M. When I first held you   E
  Sleepytime songs   782.42
  Starry night, sleep tight   808.81
  Weave little stars into my sleep   782.42
      Fiction
  Wilcoxen, C. Niccolini's song   E
Lulu Atlantis and the quest for true blue love.
  Martin, P.   Fic
Lulu's hat. Meddaugh, S.   Fic
Lum, Bernice
  (il) Murphy, S. J. Mighty Maddie   389
  (il) Warwick, E. Everywear   745.5
  (il) Warwick, E. Injeanuity   746
Lum, Kate
  What! cried Granny   E
Lum, Roseline NgCheong- *See* NgCheong-Lum,
  Roseline, 1962-
Lumber and lumbering
      Fiction
  Durbin, W. Blackwater Ben   Fic
  Kinsey-Warnock, N. Lumber camp library
     Fic
  Lasky, K. Marven of the Great North Woods
     E
  Pendziwol, J. Marja's skis   E
Lumber camp library. Kinsey-Warnock, N.
     Fic
Lumry, Amanda, 1977-
  Safari in South Africa   E
Luna moths. Markle, S.   595.7
Lunar expeditions *See* Space flight to the moon
Lunch. Fleming, D.   E
Lunch Lady and the League of Librarians.
  Krosoczka, J. J.   741.5
Lunch money. Clements, A.   Fic
Lunchbox and the aliens. Fields, B. W.   Fic
Lund, Deb
  Monsters on machines   E
Lunde, Darrin P.
  Hello, bumblebee bat   599.4
Lundgren, Julie K.
  Desert dinners   577.5
  Forest fare   577.3
  Grassland buffet   577.4
Lundgren, Orrin
  (il) Harris, E. S. Save the Earth science experi-
    ments   507.8

Lundquist, David R., 1950-
  (il) Peterson, C. Clarabelle   636.2
  (jt. auth) Peterson, C. Fantastic farm machines
     631.3
Lunge-Larsen, Lise
  The adventures of Thor the Thunder God
     293
  The hidden folk   398.2
  The troll with no heart in his body and other
    tales of trolls from Norway   398.2
Lungs
      Diseases
    See also Asthma
Lungs. Simon, S.   612.2
Lunis, Natalie
  Deadly black widows   595.4
  Furry ferrets   636.97
  Green iguanas   639.3
  Miniature horses   636.1
  Prickly sea stars   593.9
  Tricky tree frogs   597.8
Lunn, Janet Louise Swoboda, 1928-
  Laura Secord: a story of courage   Fic
Lupica, Mike
  The batboy   Fic
  Heat   Fic
  Hot hand   Fic
Lupton, Hugh
  The adventures of Odysseus   292
  Pirican Pic and Pirican Mor   398.2
Lushington, Nolan, 1929-
  Libraries designed for kids   025.1
Luthardt, Kevin
  Peep!   E
  (il) Walker, S. M. The Vowel family   E
Lutz, Richard A.
      About
  Mallory, K. Diving to a deep-sea volcano
     551.46
Luv ya bunches. Myracle, L.   Fic
Luxbacher, Irene, 1970-
  1 2 3 I can build!   731.4
  1 2 3 I can collage!   702.8
  1 2 3 I can draw!   741.2
  1 2 3 I can make prints!   760.2
  1 2 3 I can paint!   751.4
  1 2 3 I can sculpt!   731.4
  The jumbo book of art   702.8
  The jumbo book of outdoor art   704.9
  Mattoo, let's play!   E
  (il) Larsen, A. The imaginary garden   E
Luxembourg
  Sheehan, P. Luxembourg   949.35
Ly, Many
  Home is east   Fic
Lyddie. Paterson, K.   Fic
Lyga, Allyson A. W.
  Graphic novels in your media center   025.2
Lyga, Barry
  (jt. auth) Lyga, A. A. W. Graphic novels in
    your media center   025.2
Lying *See* Truthfulness and falsehood
Lyle, Lyle, crocodile. Waber, B.   E

Lynch, Chris
Cyberia   Fic

Lynch, Jay
Mo and Jo: fighting together forever   **741.5**
(jt. auth) Cammuso, F. Otto's orange day   **741.5**

Lynch, P. J., 1962-
(il) Stockton, F. The bee-man of Orn   Fic
(il) Wells, R. Lincoln and his boys   Fic
(il) Wojciechowski, S. The Christmas miracle of Jonathan Toomey   E

Lynch, Wayne
Arctic   **998**
The Everglades   **508**
Penguins!   **598**
Sonoran Desert   **577.5**
(jt. auth) Evert, L. Birds of prey   **598**

Lynette, Rachel
Anorexia   **616.85**
Leprosy   **616.9**
What to do when your family can't afford healthcare   **368.3**
What to do when your family has to cut costs   **332.024**
What to do when your family is in debt   **332.024**
What to do when your family is on welfare   **362.7**
What to do when your family loses its home   **362.5**
What to do when your parent is out of work   **331.1**

Lynn, Ruth Nadelman, 1948-
Fantasy literature for children and young adults   **016.8**

Lyon, George Ella, 1949-
Mother to tigers [biography of Helen Martini]   **92**
My friend, the starfinder   E
The pirate of kindergarten   E
Trucks roll!   E
You and me and home sweet home   E

Lyon, Tammie, 1965-
(il) O'Hair, M. My pup   E
(il) Stier, C. Bugs in my hair?!   E

Lyonesse [series]
Llewellyn, S. The well between the worlds   Fic

Lyons, Maritcha Rémond, 1848-1929
About
Bolden, T. Maritcha [biography of Maritcha Rémond Lyons]   **92**

Lyons, Mary E.
Letters from a slave girl   Fic
Roy makes a car   **398.2**

M

M.C. Higgins, the great. Hamilton, V.   Fic
M is for mischief. Ashman, L.   E
Maass, Robert
Little trucks with big jobs   **629.224**

Maathai, Wangari, 1940-
About
Johnson, J. C. Seeds of change [biography of Wangari Maathai]   **92**
Napoli, D. J. Mama Miti: Wangari Maathai and the trees of Kenya   **92**
Nivola, C. A. Planting the trees of Kenya   **92**
Winter, J. Wangari's trees of peace [biography of Wangari Maathai]   **92**

Mabela the clever. MacDonald, M. R.   **398.2**

Mable Riley. Jocelyn, M.   Fic

Mably, Colin, 1942-
(jt. auth) Benbow, A. Awesome animal science projects   **590.7**
(jt. auth) Benbow, A. Lively plant science projects   **580.7**
(jt. auth) Benbow, A. Sprouting seed science projects   **580.7**

Macaroni boy. Ayres, K.   Fic

Macaulay, David, 1946-
Black and white   E
Building big   **720**
Building the book Cathedral   **726**
Castle   **728.8**
Cathedral: the story of its construction   **726**
City: a story of Roman planning and construction   **711**
Mill   **690**
Mosque   **726**
The new way things work   **600**
Pyramid   **726**
Rome antics   **945**
Shortcut   E
Unbuilding   **690**
Underground   **624**
Why the chicken crossed the road   E

Macaulay, Ellen
(jt. auth) Murphy, P. Exploratopia   **507.8**

Maccabbees, Feast of the See Hanukkah

MacCarthy, Patricia
(il) Mahy, M. 17 kings and 42 elephants   E

MacDonald, Alan, 1958-
Trolls go home!   Fic

MacDonald, Amy
Too much flapdoodle!   Fic

MacDonald, Bailey
Wicked Will   Fic

Macdonald, Fiona
Journey to the Center of the Earth   **741.5**
Kidnapped   **741.5**

MacDonald, George, 1824-1905
The light princess   Fic

Macdonald, John
(il) Karwoski, G. Tsunami   **363.34**

MacDonald, Margaret Read
Bat's big game   **398.2**
Conejito   **398.2**
Fat cat   **398.2**
Five-minute tales   **398.2**
Go to sleep, Gecko!   **398.2**
The great smelly, slobbery, small-tooth dog   **398.2**
How many donkeys?   **398.2**

Maestro, Marco
What do you hear when cows sing? **793.73**
The **maestro** plays. Martin, B. **E**

Mafia
Fiction
Green, T. Football hero **Fic**

Magarian, La Verne J.
See/See also pages in the following book(s):
Major, J. S. Caravan to America **920**

Magaziner, Henry J.
Our Liberty Bell **974.8**

Magazines *See* Periodicals

Magellan, Ferdinand, 1480?-1521
About
Levinson, N. S. Magellan and the first voyage
around the world **92**
See/See also pages in the following book(s):
Fritz, J. Around the world in a hundred years
910.4

Magellan and the first voyage around the world.
Levinson, N. S. **92**

Magenta McPhee. Bateson, C. **Fic**

Maggie can't wait. Wishinsky, F. **E**

Maggie's ball. George, L. B. **E**

Maggie's monkeys. Sanders-Wells, L. **E**

Magi
Fiction
Menotti, G. C. Amahl and the night visitors
Fic
Vidal, B. Federico and the Magi's gift **E**

Magic
Hill, D. Witches & magic-makers **133.4**
Stefoff, R. Magic **133.4**
Fiction
Aguiar, N. The lost island of Tamarind **Fic**
Avi. The Book Without Words **Fic**
Bauer, A. C. E. No castles here **Fic**
Becker, B. The magical Ms. Plum **Fic**
Billingsley, F. Well wished **Fic**
Bode, N. E. The Anybodies **Fic**
Bouwman, H. M. The remarkable and very true
story of Lucy and Snowcap **Fic**
Brittain, B. The wish giver **Fic**
Brown, M. Chavela and the Magic Bubble
E
Catanese, P. W. Happenstance found **Fic**
Chabon, M. Summerland **Fic**
Coville, B. Juliet Dove, Queen of Love **Fic**
Crabtree, J. Discovering pig magic **Fic**
Dahl, R. The magic finger **Fic**
DeFelice, C. C. One potato, two potato **E**
Demi. The magic pillow **E**
Divakaruni, C. B. The conch bearer **Fic**
Downer, A. Hatching magic **Fic**
Dyer, H. Ibby's magic weekend **Fic**
Fagan, D. The magical misadventures of Prunel-
la Bogthistle **Fic**
Foley, G. Willoughby & the lion **E**
Franson, S. E. Un-brella **E**
Funke, C. C. Igraine the brave **Fic**
Gilman, L. A. Grail quest: the Camelot spell
Fic
Gliori, D. Pure dead frozen **Fic**
Going, K. L. The garden of Eve **Fic**

Gravett, E. Spells **E**
Haig, M. Samuel Blink and the forbidden forest
Fic
Haptie, C. Otto and the flying twins **Fic**
Hardinge, F. Well witched **Fic**
Hayter, R. The witchy worries of Abbie Adams
Fic
Helgerson, J. Horns & wrinkles **Fic**
Howland, N. Latkes, latkes, good to eat **E**
Jeffers, S. The Nutcracker **E**
Jennings, R. W. Orwell's luck **Fic**
Johnson, G. Thora **Fic**
Johnston, T. The spoon in the bathroom wall
Fic
Jones, D. W. House of many ways **Fic**
Keehn, S. M. Gnat Stokes and the Foggy Bot-
tom Swamp Queen **Fic**
Kellogg, S. The Pied Piper's magic **E**
Kerr, J. One night in the zoo **E**
Kessler, L. Philippa Fisher's fairy godsister
Fic
Kimmel, E. A. Zigazak! **E**
Kirk, D. The low road **Fic**
Kirov, E. Magickeepers: the eternal hourglass
Fic
Kladstrup, K. The book of story beginnings
Fic
Knudsen, M. The dragon of Trelian **Fic**
Kushner, E. The golden dreydl **Fic**
La Fevers, R. L. Theodosia and the Serpents of
Chaos **Fic**
Lake, A. J. The coming of dragons **Fic**
Landy, D. Skulduggery Pleasant **Fic**
Law, I. Savvy **Fic**
Levert, M. A wizard in love **E**
Lillegard, D. Tiger, tiger **E**
Mahy, M. Maddigan's Fantasia **Fic**
Martin, B. Trick or treat? **E**
McPhail, D. M. Water boy **E**
Meddaugh, S. The witch's walking stick **E**
Moloney, J. The Book of Lies **Fic**
Nimmo, J. Midnight for Charlie Bone **Fic**
Nimmo, J. The snow spider **Fic**
Pearce, P. A finder's magic **Fic**
Pogue, D. Abby Carnelia's one and only magi-
cal power **Fic**
Prelutsky, J. The wizard **E**
Prineas, S. The magic thief **Fic**
Rodda, E. The key to Rondo **Fic**
Rowling, J. K. The tales of Beedle the Bard
S C
Rutkoski, M. The Cabinet of Wonders **Fic**
Ruzzier, S. Hey rabbit! **E**
Sage, A. Magyk **Fic**
Schlitz, L. A. The night fairy **Fic**
Selfors, S. Fortune's magic farm **Fic**
Skelton, M. Endymion Spring **Fic**
Snyder, L. Any which wall **Fic**
Snyder, Z. K. The bronze pen **Fic**
Stanley, D. The mysterious matter of I.M. Fine
Fic
Strickland, B. The sign of the sinister sorcerer
Fic
Thompson, C. Good neighbors **Fic**
Thompson, L. The Christmas magic **E**
Umansky, K. Clover Twig and the magical cot-
tage **Fic**

Magic—Fiction—*Continued*

Van Allsburg, C. The garden of Abdul Gasazi   **E**

Van Allsburg, C. The sweetest fig   **E**

Van Allsburg, C. The widow's broom   **E**

Van Cleve, K. Drizzle   **Fic**

Vande Velde, V. Wizard at work   **Fic**

Varennes, M. d. The jewel box ballerinas   **E**

Verrillo, E. F. Elissa's quest   **Fic**

Willis, J. The bog baby   **E**

Wilson, N. D. 100 cupboards   **Fic**

Yep, L. City of fire   **Fic**

Yep, L. The magic paintbrush   **Fic**

Yoo, T.-E. The little red fish   **E**

Zahler, D. The thirteenth princess   **Fic**

Graphic novels

Cammuso, F. Otto's orange day   **741.5**

Thompson, J. Magic Trixie   **741.5**

The **magic** bean tree. Van Laan, N.   **398.2**

The **magic** finger. Dahl, R.   **Fic**

The **magic** gourd. Wagué Diakité, B.   **398.2**

The **magic** half. Barrows, A.   **Fic**

The **magic** horse of Han Gan. Chen, J. H.   **398.2**

Magic in the margins. Nikola-Lisa, W.   **E**

The **magic** nesting doll. Ogburn, J. K.   **E**

Magic or not? Eager, E.   **Fic**

The **magic** orange tree, and other Haitian folktales. Wolkstein, D.   **398.2**

The **magic** paintbrush. Yep, L.   **Fic**

Magic Pickle. Morse, S.   **741.5**

The **magic** pillow. Demi   **E**

The **magic** pomegranate. Schram, P.   **398.2**

The **magic** rabbit. Cate, A. L.   **E**

The **magic** school bus and the climate challenge. Cole, J.   **363.7**

The **magic** school bus and the electric field trip. Cole, J.   **621.319**

The **magic** school bus and the science fair expedition. Cole, J.   **509**

The **magic** school bus at the waterworks. Cole, J.   **551.48**

The **magic** school bus explores the senses. Cole, J.   **612.8**

The **magic** school bus: in the time of the dinosaurs. Cole, J.   **567.9**

The **magic** school bus inside a beehive. Cole, J.   **595.7**

The **magic** school bus inside a hurricane. Cole, J.   **551.55**

The **magic** school bus inside the Earth. Cole, J.   **551.1**

The **magic** school bus inside the human body. Cole, J.   **612**

The **magic** school bus, lost in the solar system. Cole, J.   **523**

The **magic** school bus on the ocean floor. Cole, J.   **591.7**

Magic secrets. Wyler, R.   **793.8**

Magic steps. Pierce, T.   **Fic**

The **magic** thief. Prineas, S.   **Fic**

Magic thinks big. Cooper, E.   **E**

Magic tricks

Barnhart, N. Amazing magic tricks: a beginner level   **793.8**

Barnhart, N. Amazing magic tricks: apprentice level   **793.8**

Barnhart, N. Amazing magic tricks: expert level   **793.8**

Barnhart, N. Amazing magic tricks: master level   **793.8**

Bauer, C. F. Leading kids to books through magic   **027.62**

Becker, H. Magic up your sleeve   **793.8**

Carlson, L. M. Harry Houdini for kids   **92**

Wyler, R. Magic secrets   **793.8**

Fiction

Graff, L. The life and crimes of Bernetta Wallflower   **Fic**

Magic Tricks [series]

Barnhart, N. Amazing magic tricks: a beginner level   **793.8**

Barnhart, N. Amazing magic tricks: apprentice level   **793.8**

Barnhart, N. Amazing magic tricks: expert level   **793.8**

Barnhart, N. Amazing magic tricks: master level   **793.8**

Magic Trixie. Thompson, J.   **741.5**

Magic up your sleeve. Becker, H.   **793.8**

Magical library lessons. Stover, L. F.   **027.62**

Magical math [series]

Long, L. Fabulous fractions   **513**

Long, L. Marvelous multiplication   **513**

Long, L. Measurement mania   **530.8**

The **magical** misadventures of Prunella Bogthistle. Fagan, D.   **Fic**

The **magical** Monkey King. Jiang, J.-l.   **398.2**

The **magical** Ms. Plum. Becker, B.   **Fic**

The **magical** worlds of Harry Potter. Colbert, D.   **823.009**

Magician trilogy [series]

Nimmo, J. The snow spider   **Fic**

Magicians

Carlson, L. M. Harry Houdini for kids   **92**

Fleischman, S. Escape! [biography of Harry Houdini]   **92**

Krull, K. Houdini   **92**

MacLeod, E. Harry Houdini   **92**

Fiction

Agee, J. Milo's hat trick   **E**

Alexander, L. The rope trick   **Fic**

Avi. Midnight magic   **Fic**

Base, G. Enigma   **Fic**

Cate, A. L. The magic rabbit   **E**

Cooper, S. The magician's boy   **Fic**

Dyer, H. Ibby's magic weekend   **Fic**

Fleischman, S. The midnight horse   **Fic**

Heneghan, J. The magician's apprentice   **Fic**

Higgins, F. E. The bone magician   **Fic**

Kirov, E. Magickeepers: the eternal hourglass   **Fic**

Matthews, T. L. Danger in the dark   **Fic**

Meddaugh, S. Lulu's hat   **Fic**

March of the penguins. Jacquet, L.   598

Marchant, Kerena
Id-ul-Fitr   297.3

Marching to Appomattox. Stark, K.   973.7

Marching toward freedom. Schomp, V.   305.8

Marco Polo. Demi   92

Marcus, Leonard S., 1950-
A Caldecott celebration   741.6
Golden legacy   070.5
Minders of make-believe   070.5
Pass it down   920
Side by side   070.5
(comp) Funny business. See Funny business   920

Marcy, Geoffrey W.
About
Wittenstein, V. O. Planet hunter   523.2

Mardi Gras *See* Carnival

Mardi Gras: a Cajun country celebration. Hoyt-Goldsmith, D.   394.25

Maren, Julie, 1970-
(il) Aston, D. H. An orange in January   E
(il) Chambers, V. Celia Cruz, Queen of salsa   92

Margeson, John
(il) Rosen, M. J. Balls!: round 2   796.3

Maria Theresa, Empress of Austria, 1717-1780
See/See also pages in the following book(s):
Meltzer, M. Ten queens   920

Marianthe's story. See Aliki. Painted words: Marianthe's story one   E

Mariconda, Barbara
Sort it out!   E

Marie Antoinette, Queen, consort of Louis XVI, King of France, 1755-1793
See/See also pages in the following book(s):
Krull, K. Lives of extraordinary women   920
Fiction
Bradley, K. B. The lacemaker and the princess   Fic

Marijuana
Gottfried, T. Marijuana   362.29

Marín, Guadalupe Rivera *See* Rivera Marín, Guadalupe, 1924-

Marina's muumuu. Vigil-Piñón, E.   E

Marine animals
   See also Corals; Freshwater animals; Marine mammals
Aliki. My visit to the aquarium   639.34
Arnold, C. Giant sea reptiles of the dinosaur age   567.9
Barnhill, K. R. Monsters of the deep   591.7
Bredeson, C. Baby animals of the ocean   591.7
Cerullo, M. M. Life under ice   578.7
Cerullo, M. M. The truth about dangerous sea creatures   591.7
Cole, J. The magic school bus on the ocean floor   591.7
Collard, S. B., III. Reign of the sea dragons   567.9
Ganeri, A. The oceans' most amazing animals   591.7

Grupper, J. Destination: deep sea   591.7
Jenkins, S. Down, down, down   591.7
Johnson, J. Simon & Schuster children's guide to sea creatures   591.7
Mannis, C. D. Snapshots   591.7
McLimans, D. Gone fishing   591.7
O'Neill, M. P. Ocean magic   578.7
Pallotta, J. Ocean counting   E
Parker, S. Seashore   577.7
Rose, D. L. Into the A, B, sea   591.7
Rose, D. L. Ocean babies   591.3
Rose, D. L. One nighttime sea   E
Swinburne, S. R. Ocean soup   591.7
Turner, P. S. Prowling the seas   591.7
Woodward, J. Creatures of the deep   591.7
Young, K. R. Across the wide ocean   623.89
Encyclopedias
Dawes, J. Exploring the world of aquatic life   591.7
Fiction
Cherry, L. The sea, the storm, and the mangrove tangle   E
Crowley, N. Nanook & Pryce   E
Diesen, D. The pout-pout fish   E
Ford, C. Ocean's child   E
Goodrich, C. The hermit crab   E
Sherry, K. I'm the biggest thing in the ocean   E
Poetry
Harley, A. Sea stars   811

Marine animals in art
Nguyen, D. Under the sea origami   736

Marine aquariums
Aliki. My visit to the aquarium   639.34
Fiction
Poydar, N. Fish school   E

Marine biologist. Somervill, B. A.   578.7

Marine biology
Conlan, K. Under the ice   578.7
Gibbons, G. Exploring the deep, dark sea   551.46
Heller, E. S. Menorah under the sea   296.4
Kudlinski, K. V. The seaside switch   577.6
Mallory, K. Diving to a deep-sea volcano   551.46
Reichard, S. E. Who on earth is Sylvia Earle?   92
Somervill, B. A. Marine biologist   578.7

Marine ecology
Collard, S. B., III. On the coral reefs   577.7
Hooks, G. Makers and takers   577.7
Jackson, K. Explore the ocean   577.7

Marine mammals
   See also Dolphins; Porpoises; Seals (Animals); Whales
Arnold, C. Super swimmers   599.5
Malam, J. Pinnipeds   599.79

Marine plants
Cerullo, M. M. Life under ice   578.7
Parker, S. Seashore   577.7

Marine pollution
   See also Oil spills
Conlan, K. Under the ice   578.7
Vogel, C. G. Human impact   333.91

Marino, Gianna
  One too many   E
  Zoopa   E

Marino, Jane
  Babies in the library!   027.62
  Mother Goose time   027.62

Marino, Nan
  Neil Armstrong is my uncle   Fic

Marinsky, Jane
  (il) Sharpe, L. M. The goat-faced girl   398.2

Mario's Angels. Arrigan, M.   E

Maritcha [biography of Maritcha Rémond Lyons]
  Bolden, T.   92

Marja's skis. Pendziwol, J.   E

Mark, Jan, 1943-2006
  The museum book   069

Mark, Steve
  (il) Crist, J. J. Siblings   306.8

The **Mark** Twain you never knew. Collier, J. L.
      92

Mark Zuckerberg, Facebook creator. Woog, A.
      92

Markel, Michelle
  Dreamer from the village [biography of Marc
    Chagall]   92
  Tyrannosaurus math   513

Markes, Julie
  Good thing you're not an octopus!   E
  Shhhhh! Everybody's sleeping   E

Market day. Cordsen, C. F.   E

Market day. Ehlert, L.   E

Markets
  Lewin, T. How much?   381
  Lewin, T. Market!   381
        Fiction
  Anderson, S. A day at the market   E
  Cordsen, C. F. Market day   E
  Ehlert, L. Market day   E

Markey, Penny S.
  (jt. auth) Cerny, R. Outstanding library service
    to children   027.62

Markle, Sandra, 1946-
  Animal heroes   636.088
  Animals Charles Darwin saw   92
  Animals Christopher Columbus saw   970.01
  Animals Marco Polo saw   92
  Animals Robert Scott saw   998
  Crocodiles   597.98
  Eagles   598
  Finding home   599.2
  Great white sharks   597
  Grizzly bears   599.78
  Hip-pocket papa   597.8
  Hornets   595.7
  How many baby pandas?   599.78
  Insects   595.7
  Killer whales   599.5
  Lions   599.75
  Luna moths   595.7
  A mother's journey   598
  Octopuses   594
  Outside and inside big cats   599.75
  Outside and inside dinosaurs   567.9
  Outside and inside giant squid   594
  Outside and inside killer bees   595.7
  Outside and inside mummies   393
  Outside and inside rats and mice   599.35
  Outside and inside woolly mammoths   569
  Polar bears   599.78
  Porcupines   599.35
  Prairie dogs   599.3
  Praying mantises   595.7
  Rattlesnakes   597.96
  Rescues!   363.34
  Sharks   597
  Slippery, slimy baby frogs   597.8
  Sneaky, spinning, baby spiders   595.4
  Spiders   595.4
  Termites   595.7
  Wolves   599.77

Marklew, Gilly
  (il) Drake, S. Dragonsdale   Fic

Markovics, Joyce L.
  The bat's cave   599.4
  The honey bee's hive   595.7
  Tasmanian devil   599.2
  Weddell seal   599.79

Marks, Alan, 1957-
  (il) Markle, S. Finding home   599.2
  (il) Markle, S. Hip-pocket papa   597.8
  (il) Markle, S. A mother's journey   598

Marks, Diana F.
  Children's book award handbook   028.5

Markuson, Carolyn A.
  (jt. auth) Erikson, R. Designing a school library
    media center for the future   027.8

Marley, Bob
        About
  Medina, T. I and I [biography of Bob Marley]
      92

Marley. Grogan, J.   636.7

Marlin, John, 1977-
  Mickey Mantle   92

Marlow, Layn
  Hurry up and slow down   E
  (il) Stewart, A. Bedtime for Button   E
  (il) Stewart, A. Little by little   E

Marmots
  Gibbons, G. Groundhog day!   394.26
        Fiction
  Cherry, L. How Groundhog's garden grew   E
  Cox, J. Go to sleep, Groundhog!   E
  Elish, D. The attack of the frozen woodchucks
      Fic
  Hill, S. L. Punxsutawney Phyllis   E
  Swallow, P. C. Groundhog gets a say   E

Marooned [biography of Alexander Selkirk]
  Kraske, R.   92

Márquez, Gabriel García *See* García Márquez,
  Gabriel, 1928-

Marrella, Maria Pia
  (il) MacLachlan, P. Seven kisses in a row
      Fic

Marriage
    See also Divorce; Family; Remarriage;
  Weddings

Martin, Barbara Stein, 1947-
Fundamentals of school library media management **025.1**

Martin, Bill, 1916-2004
Baby Bear, Baby Bear, what do you see? **E**
Barn dance! **E**
A beasty story **E**
Brown bear, brown bear what do you see? **E**
Chicka chicka 1, 2, 3 **E**
Chicka chicka boom boom **E**
The ghost-eye tree **E**
I love our Earth **525**
Knots on a counting rope **E**
The maestro plays **E**
Panda bear, panda bear, what do you see? **E**
Polar bear, polar bear, what do you hear? **E**
Trick or treat? **E**
(ed) The Bill Martin Jr. Big book of poetry. See The Bill Martin Jr. Big book of poetry **811.008**

Martin, Courtney A.
(il) Bardhan-Quallen, S. Ballots for Belva [biography of Belva Ann Lockwood] **92**

Martin, David, 1944-
Christmas tree **E**
Hanukkah lights **E**
Piggy and Dad go fishing **E**

Martin, Jacqueline Briggs, 1945-
Grandmother Bryant's pocket **E**
The lamp, the ice, and the boat called Fish **998**
On Sand Island **E**
Snowflake Bentley [biography of Wilson Alwyn Bentley] **92**

Martin, Joseph Plumb, 1760-1850
About
Murphy, J. A young patriot **973.3**

Martin, Laura C.
Recycled crafts box **363.7**

Martin, Patricia
Lulu Atlantis and the quest for true blue love **Fic**

Martin, Pedro, 1967-
(il) Murphy, S. J. Hamster champs **516**

Martin, Rafe, 1946-
The Shark God **398.2**
Will's mammoth **E**
The world before this one **398.2**

Martin, Russell, 1952-
The mysteries of Beethoven's hair **92**

Martin, Ruth
Bugs **595.7**

Martin, Sarah Catherine, 1768-1826
Old Mother Hubbard. See Cabrera, J. Old Mother Hubbard **398.8**

Martin, Steve, 1945-
The alphabet from A to Y with bonus letter, Z! **E**

Martin, Stuart
(il) Harpur, J. Mythical creatures **398**

Martin, William Ivan *See* Martin, Bill, 1916-2004

Martin Bridge: ready for takeoff!. Kerrin, J. S. **Fic**

Martin-Jourdenais, Norma Jean
(il) Blanchette, P. 12 easy knitting projects **746.43**
(il) Check, L. Create your own candles **745.5**

Martin Luther King Day
Jeffrey, L. S. Celebrate Martin Luther King, Jr., Day **394.26**

Martina the beautiful cockroach. Deedy, C. A. **398.2**

Martínez, Arturo O., 1933-
Pedrito's world **Fic**

Martinez, Ed, 1954-
(il) Medina, J. Tomás Rivera **92**
(il) Soto, G. Too many tamales **E**

Martinez, Miriam G., 1948-
Children's books in children's hands. See Children's books in children's hands **028.5**

Martinez, Rueben, 1940-
Once upon a time **398.2**

Martinez, Sergio, 1937-
(il) San Souci, R. Little Gold Star **398.2**

Martini, Angela
(il) Stout, S. K. Fiona Finkelstein, big-time ballerina! **Fic**

Martini, Helen, 1912-
About
Lyon, G. E. Mother to tigers [biography of Helen Martini] **92**

Martinique
Folklore
See Folklore—Martinique

Martins, George
(il) Giovanni, N. Spin a soft black song: poems for children **811**

Martin's big words: the life of Dr. Martin Luther King, Jr. Rappaport, D. **92**

Marton, Jirina, 1946-
(il) Pendziwol, J. Marja's skis **E**
(il) Rivera, R. Arctic adventures **920**

Marvelous math **811.008**

Marvelous Mattie [biography of Margaret Knight]. McCully, E. A. **92**

Marvelous multiplication. Long, L. **513**

The **marvelous** toy. Paxton, T. **782.42**

Marvels in the muck. Wechsler, D. **578.7**

Marveltown. McCall, B. **E**

Marven of the Great North Woods. Lasky, K. **E**

Marvin Redpost, kidnapped at birth? Sachar, L. **Fic**

Marx, Trish, 1948-
Elephants and golden thrones **951**
Everglades forever **577.6**
Sharing our homeland **956.04**
(jt. auth) Borden, L. Touching the sky **629.13**

Marxism

See also Communism

Mary, Blessed Virgin, Saint
About
Demi. Mary   232.91
Fiction
De Paola, T. The night of Las Posadas   E

Mary, Queen of Scots, 1542-1587
See/See also pages in the following book(s):
Cotter, C. Kids who rule   920

Mary and the mouse, the mouse and Mary. Donofrio, B.   E

Mary had a little lamb. Hoberman, M. A.
782.42

Mary Mae and the gospel truth. Dutton, S.
Fic

Mary on horseback [biography of Mary Breckinridge] Wells, R.   92

Mary Poppins. Travers, P. L.   Fic

Mary Smith. U'Ren, A.   E

Maryland
Fiction
Mills, C. The totally made-up Civil War diary of Amanda MacLeish   Fic
Stout, S. K. Fiona Finkelstein, big-time ballerina!   Fic

Marzel, Pepi, 1957-
(il) Groner, J. S. My first Hebrew word book
492.4
(il) Sussman, J. K. My first Yiddish word book
439

Marzollo, Jean
Happy birthday, Martin Luther King   92
Ten little Christmas presents   E
(jt. auth) Wick, W. I spy   793.73

Masai (African people)
Deedy, C. A. 14 cows for America   327
Fiction
Barasch, L. First come the zebra   E
Joosse, B. M. Papa, do you love me?   E
Folklore
Aardema, V. Who's in Rabbit's house?
398.2
Mollel, T. M. The orphan boy   398.2

Mascot to the rescue!. David, P.   Fic

Masih, Iqbal, d. 1995
Fiction
D'Adamo, F. Iqbal   Fic

Masks (Facial)
D'Cruz, A.-M. Make your own masks   646.4
Finley, C. The art of African masks   391
Schwarz, R. Making masks   646.4
Fiction
Choi, Y. Behind the mask   E

Masks (Sculpture)
Kenney, K. L. Super simple masks   731

Maslin, Ruthie, 1966-
(jt. auth) Imhoff, K. R. Library contests
021.7

Masoff, Joy, 1951-
The African American story   305.8
Oh, yuck!   031.02
We are all Americans   325.73

Mason, Adrienne
Build it!   624.1
Change it!   530
Move it!   531
Skunks   599.7
Touch it!   530.4
(ed) Robots: from everyday to out of this world. See Robots: from everyday to out of this world   629.8

Mason, Biddy, 1818-1891
See/See also pages in the following book(s):
Colman, P. Adventurous women   920
Pinkney, A. D. Let it shine   920

Mason, Bob
About
Montgomery, S. The snake scientist   597.96

Mason, Joseph, 1807-1883
Fiction
Cole, H. A nest for Celeste   Fic

Mason, Paul, 1967-
Judo   796.8
Population   363.9
Poverty   362.5

Mason, Simon, 1962-
The Quigleys   Fic

Mason, Timothy
The last synapsid   Fic

Mass, Wendy, 1967-
11 birthdays   Fic
Every soul a star   Fic
Jeremy Fink and the meaning of life   Fic

Mass communication See Communication; Telecommunication

Mass extinction of species
Mehling, R. Great extinctions of the past
576.8

Mass media
Ali, D. Media madness   302.23

Massachusetts
Fiction
Atkinson, E. From Alice to Zen and everyone in between   Fic
Barker, M. P. A difficult boy   Fic
Clements, A. We the children   Fic
Hurst, C. O. Terrible storm   E
Hurst, C. O. You come to Yokum   Fic
Krensky, S. Sisters of Scituate Light   E
Lewis, M. Morgy makes his move   Fic
Look, L. Alvin Ho: allergic to girls, school, and other scary things   Fic
McCully, E. A. The bobbin girl   Fic
Paterson, K. Lyddie   Fic
Sanchez, A. The invasion of Sandy Bay   Fic
Yolen, J. My Uncle Emily   E

History—1600-1775, Colonial period
See also Plymouth Rock
Armentrout, D. The Mayflower Compact
974.4
Atkins, J. Anne Hutchinson's way   92
Harness, C. The adventurous life of Myles Standish   92
Kent, D. Witchcraft trials   133.4
Sewall, M. The pilgrims of Plimoth   974.4
Waters, K. Sarah Morton's day   974.4

Massachusetts—History—1600-1775, Colonial period—*Continued*

Yero, J. L. The Mayflower Compact   **974.4**

Masse, Josée

(il) Chaconas, D. Mousie love   **E**

(il) Levert, M. The princess who had almost everything   **E**

(il) Singer, M. Mirror mirror   **811**

(il) Xinran. Motherbridge of love   **E**

Massey, Cal

(il) Chocolate, D. My first Kwanzaa book   **394.26**

Massive mountains. Jennings, T.   **551.4**

Master the library and media center. Gaines, A.   **020**

Masterpiece. Broach, E.   **Fic**

Masterpieces up close. D'Harcourt, C.   **750**

Mastodons

Bardoe, C. Mammoths and mastodons   **569**

Materials

See also Strength of materials

Mason, A. Touch it!   **530.4**

Oxlade, C. Changing shape   **620.1**

Oxlade, C. Joining materials   **620.1**

Oxlade, C. Mixing and separating   **546**

Oxlade, C. Mixing and separating   **541**

Oxlade, C. Shaping materials   **620.1**

Ward, D. J. Materials science   **620.1**

Materials science. Ward, D. J.   **620.1**

Math appeal. Tang, G.   **793.74**

The **math** book for girls and other beings who count. Wyatt, V.   **510**

The **math** chef. D'Amico, J.   **641.5**

Math curse. Scieszka, J.   **E**

Math doesn't suck. McKellar, D.   **510**

Math fables. Tang, G.   **513**

Math fables too. Tang, G.   **513**

Math for the very young   **793.74**

Math in the real world [series]

Arroyo, S. L. How chefs use math   **641.5**

Arroyo, S. L. How crime fighters use math   **363.2**

Arroyo, S. L. How deep sea divers use math   **797.2**

Arroyo, S. L. How race car drivers use math   **796.72**

Bertoletti, J. C. How baseball managers use math   **796.357**

Bertoletti, J. C. How fashion designers use math   **746.9**

Egan, J. How video game designers use math   **794.8**

Glasscock, S. How nurses use math   **610.73**

Hense, M. How astronauts use math   **629.45**

Hense, M. How fighter pilots use math   **629.13**

Math is categorical [series]

Cleary, B. P. How long or how wide?   **530.8**

Cleary, B. P. On the scale   **530.8**

Math is fun [series]

Harris, T. The clock struck one   **E**

Math potatoes. Tang, G.   **793.74**

Math-terpieces. Tang, G.   **510**

Mathematical recreations

Ball, J. Go figure!   **793.74**

Lewis, J. P. Arithme-tickle   **513**

Math for the very young   **793.74**

Tang, G. The grapes of math   **793.74**

Tang, G. Math appeal   **793.74**

Tang, G. Math potatoes   **793.74**

Mathematicians

See also Women mathematicians

D'Agnese, J. Blockhead   **92**

Hightower, P. The greatest mathematician [biography of Archimedes]   **92**

Mathematics

See also Arithmetic; Fractions; Patterns (Mathematics); Pi

Anno, M. Anno's mysterious multiplying jar   **512**

Anno, M. Anno's magic seeds   **513**

Arroyo, S. L. How chefs use math   **641.5**

Arroyo, S. L. How crime fighters use math   **363.2**

Arroyo, S. L. How deep sea divers use math   **797.2**

Arroyo, S. L. How race car drivers use math   **796.72**

Ball, J. Go figure!   **793.74**

Ball, J. Why pi   **530.8**

Bertoletti, J. C. How baseball managers use math   **796.357**

Bertoletti, J. C. How fashion designers use math   **746.9**

D'Amico, J. The math chef   **641.5**

Egan, J. How video game designers use math   **794.8**

Giganti, P., Jr. Each orange had 8 slices   **E**

Glasscock, S. How nurses use math   **610.73**

Hense, M. How astronauts use math   **629.45**

Hense, M. How fighter pilots use math   **629.13**

Lee, C. The great number rumble   **510**

Markel, M. Tyrannosaurus math   **513**

McKellar, D. Math doesn't suck   **510**

Merriam, E. 12 ways to get to 11   **510**

Murphy, S. J. The sundae scoop   **511**

Schmandt-Besserat, D. The history of counting   **513**

Schwartz, D. M. G is for googol   **510**

VanCleave, J. P. Janice VanCleave's play and find out about math   **513**

Wyatt, V. The math book for girls and other beings who count   **510**

Fiction

Birtha, B. Lucky beans   **E**

Bowen, A. The great math tattle battle   **E**

McElligott, M. The lion's share   **E**

Merrill, J. The toothpaste millionaire   **Fic**

Mills, C. 7 x 9 = trouble!   **Fic**

Reynolds, A. Superhero School   **E**

Scieszka, J. Math curse   **E**

Poetry

Marvelous math   **811.008**

Mathers, Petra

Lottie's new beach towel   **E**

Mattoo, let's play!. Luxbacher, I.　　　　**E**

Matzeliger, Jan, 1852-1889
About
　Mitchell, B. Shoes for everyone: a story about Jan Matzeliger　　**92**

Maupin, Melissa, 1958-
　Benjamin Banneker　　**92**

Maurer, Richard, 1950-
　The Wright sister [biography of Katharine Wright Haskell]　　**92**

Maurer, Tracy, 1965-
　Scrapbook starters　　**745.593**

Mauritania
　Blauer, E. Mauritania　　**966.1**

Max, Ken Wilson- *See* Wilson-Max, Ken, 1965-

Max. Isadora, R.　　**E**

Max and the dumb flower picture. Alexander, M. G.　　**E**

Max Disaster [series]
　Moss, M. Alien Eraser to the rescue　　**Fic**

Max Quigley. Roy, J.　　**Fic**

Max Spaniel [series]
　Catrow, D. Dinosaur hunt　　**E**

Maximilian, Prince of Wied-Neuwied *See* Wied, Maximilian, Prinz von, 1782-1867

Maxims *See* Proverbs

Max's words. Banks, K.　　**E**

May, Katie
　(il) Kessler, L. Philippa Fisher's fairy godsister　　**Fic**

May Bird and The Ever After. Anderson, J. L.　　**Fic**

May I bring a friend? De Regniers, B. S.　　**E**

May I pet your dog? Calmenson, S.　　**636.7**

Mayall, Beth
　(jt. auth) Farrell, J. Middle school, the real deal　　**373.1**

Mayas
　Coulter, L. Ballplayers and bonesetters　　**972**
　Harris, N. Ancient Maya　　**972**
　Kops, D. Palenque　　**972**
　Menchú, R. The girl from Chimel　　**92**
　Orr, T. The Maya　　**972**
　Perl, L. The ancient Maya　　**972**
Antiquities
　Mann, E. Tikal　　**972.81**
Fiction
　Cameron, A. Colibri　　**Fic**
　Rollins, J. Jake Ransom and the Skull King's shadow　　**Fic**
　Wisniewski, D. Rain player　　**E**
Folklore
　Ehlert, L. Cuckoo. Cucú　　**398.2**
　Menchú, R. The honey jar　　**398.2**
　Menchú, R. The secret legacy　　**398.2**

Maybe a bear ate it!. Harris, R. H.　　**E**

Maybe I'll sleep in the bathtub tonight. Levy, D.　　**811**

Maybe right, maybe wrong. Barker, D.　　**370.1**

Maybe yes, maybe no, maybe maybe. Patron, S.　　**Fic**

Mayer, Bill
　(il) Demarest, C. L. All aboard!　　**E**

Mayer, Marianna, 1945-
　Baba Yaga and Vasilisa the brave　　**398.2**
　Pegasus　　**292**

Mayer, Mercer, 1943-
　A boy, a dog, and a frog　　**E**
　The bravest knight　　**E**
　There's a nightmare in my closet　　**E**
　(il) Fitzgerald, J. D. The Great Brain　　**Fic**

Mayflower (Ship)
　Armentrout, D. The Mayflower Compact　　**974.4**

Mayflower Compact (1620)
　Yero, J. L. The Mayflower Compact　　**974.4**
The **Mayflower** Compact. Armentrout, D.　　**974.4**

Mayo, Margaret, 1935-
　Choo choo clickety-clack!　　**E**
　Roar!　　**E**

Mayr, Diane, 1949-
　Run, Turkey run　　**E**

Mayte and the Bogeyman. Acosta Gonzalez, A.　　**E**

Mazatec Indians
Fiction
　Ramirez, A. Napi　　**E**
The **maze** of bones. Riordan, R.　　**Fic**

Maze puzzles
　Lankford, M. D. Mazes around the world　　**793.73**
　Munro, R. Amazement park　　**793.73**
　Munro, R. Ecomazes　　**577**
　Munro, R. Mazeways: A to Z　　**793.73**

Mazer, Anne, 1953-
　Spilling ink　　**808.3**

Mazer, Norma Fox, 1931-2009
　Has anyone seen my Emily Greene?　　**E**
　Ten ways to make my sister disappear　　**Fic**

Mazes *See* Maze puzzles

Mazes around the world. Lankford, M. D.　　**793.73**

Mazeways: A to Z. Munro, R.　　**793.73**

McArdle, Paula, 1971-
　(il) Shelby, A. The adventures of Molly Whuppie and other Appalachian folktales　　**398.2**

McBratney, Sam
　Guess how much I love you　　**E**
　One voice, please　　**398.2**
　When I'm big　　**E**

McCain, John S., 1936-
About
　Wells, C. John McCain　　**92**

McCall, Bruce
　Marveltown　　**E**

McCarthy, Colin, 1951-
　Reptile　　**597.9**

McCarthy, Mary, 1951-
　A closer look　　**E**

McCarthy, Meghan
　Aliens are coming!　　**791.44**

McCully, Emily Arnold—*Continued*
(il) Weaver, T. Cat jumped in!   E

McCurdy, Michael, 1942-
So said Ben [biography of Benjamin Franklin]   92
(il) Fradin, D. B. The founders   920
(il) Fradin, D. B. The signers   920
(il) Osborne, M. P. American tall tales   398.2
(il) War and the pity of war. See War and the pity of war   808.81

McCutcheon, Marc
The kid who named Pluto   509

McDaniel, Deanna
Gentle reads   028.5

McDaniel, Melissa
Monkeys   599.8

McDermott, Gerald
Anansi the spider   398.2
Arrow to the sun   398.2
Coyote: a trickster tale from the American Southwest   398.2
Creation   E
Jabuti the tortoise   398.2
Musicians of the sun   398.2
Papagayo   E
Pig-Boy   398.2
Raven   398.2
Zomo the Rabbit   398.2

McDonald, Megan, 1959-
Hen hears gossip   E
It's picture day today!   E
Judy Moody   Fic
Stink: the incredible shrinking kid   Fic

McDonald, Mercedes
(il) Elya, S. M. Fairy trails   E

McDonnell, Christine, 1949-
Dog wants to play   E

McDonnell, Patrick, 1956-
South   E

McDonough, Yona Zeldis
The doll shop downstairs   Fic
The doll with the yellow star   Fic
Hammerin' Hank [biography of Hank Greenberg]   92
Louisa   92
Peaceful protest: the life of Nelson Mandela   92

McDowell, Marilyn Taylor
Carolina Harmony   Fic

McDuff moves in. Wells, R.   E

The **McElderry** book of Aesop's fables. Morpurgo, M.   398.2

The **McElderry** book of Greek myths. Kimmel, E. A.   292

The **McElderry** book of Grimms' fairy tales. Pirotta, S.   398.2

McElligot's pool. Seuss, Dr.   E

McElligott, Matthew, 1968-
Bean thirteen   E
The lion's share   E

McElmeel, Sharron L.
100 most popular picture book authors and illustrators   810.3

McElmurry, Jill
(il) Heide, F. P. The one and only Marigold   E
(il) Schertle, A. Little Blue Truck   E
(il) Spinner, S. It's a miracle!   E
(il) Swaim, J. The hound from the pound   E

McElrath-Eslick, Lori
(il) Weisburd, S. Barefoot   811

McElroy, Lisa Tucker
Sonia Sotomayor   92

McEvoy, Anne
Betsy B. Little   E

McEwen, Katharine
(il) Durant, A. I love you, Little Monkey   E

McFig & McFly. Drescher, H.   E

McGaffey, Leta
Honduras   972.83

McGee, John F.
(il) Evert, L. Birds of prey   598

McGee, Marni
Ancient Greece   938

McGee, Randel
Paper crafts for Chinese New Year   745.594
Paper crafts for Christmas   745.594
Paper crafts for Day of the Dead   745.594
Paper crafts for Halloween   745.594
Paper crafts for Kwanzaa   745.594
Paper crafts for Valentine's Day   745.594

McGhee, Alison, 1960-
Always   E
Bye-bye, crib   E
Julia Gillian (and the art of knowing)   Fic
Mrs. Watson wants your teeth   E
Only a witch can fly   E
Snap   Fic
So many days   E
Song of middle C   E
A very brave witch   E

McGhee, Karen
Encyclopedia of animals   590.3

McGill, Alice
Sure as sunrise   398.2
Way up and over everything   398.2
(comp) In the hollow of your hand. See In the hollow of your hand   782.42

McGillian, Jamie Kyle
Sleepover party!   793.2

McGinty, Alice B., 1963-
Darwin   92
Eliza's kindergarten surprise   E
Meet Daniel Pinkwater   92
Meet Jane Yolen   92

McGovern, Ann
Too much noise   398.2

McGowan, Michael, 1948-
Sunday is for God   E

McGrath, Barbara Barbieri, 1954-
The little red elf   E

McGraw, Eloise Jarvis, 1915-2000
The moorchild   Fic

McLaren, Chesley—*Continued*
(il) McLaren, C. When royals wore ruffles
391

McLarney, Rose, 1982-
(jt. auth) Newcomb, R. Is my hamster wild?
636.9

McLaughlin, Julie
(il) Rohmer, H. Heroes of the environment
333.72

McLean family
About
Friedman, R. The silent witness **973.7**

McLennan, Connie
(il) Coburn, J. R. Domitila **398.2**
(il) Roemer, H. B. Whose nest is this?
591.56

McLeod, Bob
SuperHero ABC **E**

McLeod, Tom
The Delta is my home **970.004**

McLerran, Alice, 1933-
Roxaboxen **E**

McLimans, David
Gone fishing **591.7**
Gone wild **E**

McMahon, Bob, 1956-
(il) Robinson, E. K. Making cents **332.4**

McMenemy, Sarah, 1965-
(il) Davis, J. The first rule of little brothers
E
(il) Kimmelman, L. Everybody bonjours! **E**

McMillan, Bruce
Days of the ducklings **598**
Going fishing **949.12**
Growing colors **E**
How the ladies stopped the wind **E**
Nights of the pufflings **598**
Penguins at home **598**
The problem with chickens **E**
Salmon summer **639.2**
Summer ice **508**
Wild flamingos **598**

McMillan, Naomi *See* Grimes, Nikki

McMillan, Terry, 1951-
See/See also pages in the following book(s):
Wilkinson, B. S. African American women writers **810.9**

McMullan, James, 1934-
(il) Julie Andrews' collection of poems, songs, and lullabies. See Julie Andrews' collection of poems, songs, and lullabies **808.8**

McMullan, Jim, 1934-
(jt. auth) McMullan, K. I stink! **E**
(jt. auth) McMullan, K. I'm bad **E**
(jt. auth) McMullan, K. I'm dirty! **E**
(il) McMullan, K. I'm mighty! **E**

McMullan, Kate, 1947-
See also Hall, Katy, 1947-
I stink! **E**
I'm bad **E**
I'm dirty! **E**
I'm mighty! **E**
Pearl and Wagner: one funny day **E**

McMullan, Margaret
How I found the Strong **Fic**
When I crossed No-Bob **Fic**

McNair, Jonda C., 1970-
(ed) Embracing, evaluating, and examining African American children's and young adult literature. See Embracing, evaluating, and examining African American children's and young adult literature **028.5**

McNair, Ronald E.
Fiction
Blue, R. Ron's big mission **E**

McNall, Belva Ann *See* Lockwood, Belva Ann, 1830-1917

McNamara, Margaret
How many seeds in a pumpkin? **E**
The whistle on the train **E**

McNaughton, Colin, 1951-
Not last night but the night before **E**
Once upon an ordinary school day **E**

McNeely, Tom
(il) Goodman, J. E. Despite all obstacles: La Salle and the conquest of the Mississippi
92
(il) Goodman, J. E. A long and uncertain journey: the 27,000 mile voyage of Vasco da Gama **92**
(il) Mann, E. Tikal **972.81**

McNeese, Tim
The fascinating history of American Indians
970.004

McNelly McCormack, Caren
The fiesta dress **E**

McNicholas, June, 1956-
Rats **636.9**

McNicholas, Shelagh
(il) Bradley, K. B. The perfect pony **E**
(il) Geras, A. Little ballet star **E**

McNulty, Faith
If you decide to go to the moon **629.45**

McPhail, David M.
Big Brown Bear's up and down day **E**
Big Pig and Little Pig **E**
Drawing lessons from a bear **E**
Emma in charge **E**
Mole music **E**
No! **E**
Pigs aplenty, pigs galore! **E**
Sylvie & True **E**
The teddy bear **E**
Water boy **E**
Weezer changes the world **E**
(il) Ashman, L. When I was king **E**
(il) Byars, B. C. Little Horse **Fic**
(il) Evans, L. Who loves the little lamb? **E**
(il) Krull, K. A pot o' gold **820.8**
(il) Numeroff, L. J. When sheep sleep **E**
(il) Plourde, L. Margaret Chase Smith **92**
(jt. auth) Rockwell, T. Emily Stew **811**
(il) Spinelli, E. When Papa comes home tonight
E

McPherson, James M.
Fields of fury **973.7**

McQueen, Stacey Dressen- *See* Dressen-
McQueen, Stacey

McQuinn, Anna
Lola at the library   E
My friend Jamal   E
My friend Mei Jing   E
(jt. auth) McQuinn, C. Ireland   941.5

McQuinn, Colm
Ireland   941.5

McSwigan, Marie, 1907-1962
Snow treasure   Fic

McWhorter, Diane
A dream of freedom   323.1

McWhorter, Heather
(il) Willey, M. Clever Beatrice   398.2

MDMA (Drug)
    See also Ecstasy (Drug)

Me and Billy. Collier, J. L.   Fic
Me and my bike. Ander   E
Me and the pumpkin queen. Kennedy, M.   Fic
Me and Uncle Romie. Hartfield, C.   E
Me and you. Côté, G.   E
Me baby, you baby. Wolff, A.   E
Me hungry!. Tankard, J.   E
Me with you. Dempsey, K.   E

Mead, Alice, 1952-
Junebug   Fic

Mead, Wendy
Top 10 birds for kids   636.6

Meade, Holly
Inside, inside, inside   E
John Willy and Freddy McGee   E
(il) Best, C. Goose's story   E
(il) Brenner, T. And then comes Halloween   E
(il) Elliott, D. On the farm   E
(il) Gershator, P. Sky sweeper   E
(il) Ho, M. Hush!   E
(il) Lindbergh, R. On morning wings   223

Meadows
    Fiction
Cole, H. On Meadowview Street   E
    Poetry
Sidman, J. Butterfly eyes and other secrets of
the meadow   811

Meal planning *See* Nutrition

Meals for school children *See* School children—
Food

Mean soup. Everitt, B.   E
Meanwhile. Shiga, J.   741.5

Measure up! [series]
Sullivan, N. Area, distance, and volume   516
Sullivan, N. Speed   531
Sullivan, N. Temperature   536
Sullivan, N. Weight   531

Measurement
    See also Volume (Cubic content)
Adler, D. A. How tall, how short, how faraway   530.8
Ball, J. Why pi   530.8
Cleary, B. P. How long or how wide?   530.8

Gardner, R. Ace your math and measuring sci-
ence project   530.8
Gardner, R. Far-out science projects with height
and depth   530.8
Gardner, R. Heavy-duty science projects with
weight   530.8
Gardner, R. Super-sized science projects with
volume   530.8
Glass, S. Watch out!   502.8
Leedy, L. Measuring Penny   530.8
Long, L. Measurement mania   530.8
Murphy, S. J. Bigger, Better, BEST!   516
Murphy, S. J. Polly's pen pal   516
Murphy, S. J. Room for Ripley   530.8
Robbins, K. For good measure   530.8
Schwartz, D. M. Millions to measure   530.8
Sullivan, N. Area, distance, and volume   516
Sullivan, N. Speed   531
    Fiction
Lionni, L. Inch by inch   E
Pelley, K. T. Magnus Maximus, a marvelous
measurer   E

Measurement mania. Long, L.   530.8
Measures *See* Weights and measures
Measuring Penny. Leedy, L.   530.8
Meatballs
    Fiction
Johnson, P. B. On top of spaghetti   E

Meddaugh, Susan
The best place   E
Cinderella's rat   E
Harry on the rocks   E
Hog-eye   E
Lulu's hat   Fic
Martha speaks   E
The witch's walking stick   E

Medearis, Angela Shelf, 1956-
Seven spools of thread   E

Media *See* Mass media

Media literacy [series]
Botzakis, S. Pretty in print   050
Wan Guofang. TV takeover   384.55

Media madness. Ali, D.   302.23

Medicaid
Lynette, R. What to do when your family can't
afford healthcare   368.3

Medical care
Barber, N. Going to the hospital   362.1
Murphy, L. ABC doctor   610
Rogers, F. Going to the hospital   362.1
Singer, M. I'm getting a checkup   610
    Fiction
Harper, J. Uh-oh, Cleo   Fic
Lawrence, I. The giant-slayer   Fic

Medical insurance *See* Health insurance
Medical mysteries. Auden, S.   610
Medical technology
Rooney, A. Health and medicine   610
Sandvold, L. B. Revolution in medicine   610.9

Medicine
    See also and names of diseases and groups
of diseases
Goldsmith, C. Cutting-edge medicine   610

Medicine—*Continued*
  Murphy, L. ABC doctor 610
  Rooney, A. Health and medicine 610
  Singer, M. I'm getting a checkup 610
    Encyclopedias
  Encyclopedia of health 610.3
    History
  Davis, L. Medicine in the American West
    610.9
  Sandvold, L. B. Revolution in medicine
    610.9
  Woolf, A. Death and disease 610.9
    Research
  Auden, S. Medical mysteries 610
  Dendy, L. A. Guinea pig scientists 616
  Piddock, C. Outbreak 614.4

Medicine, Veterinary *See* Veterinary medicine

Medicine in the American West. Davis, L.
    610.9

Medieval civilization
  Adams, S. The Kingfisher atlas of the medieval
    world 909.07
  Adkins, J. What if you met a knight? 940.1
  Aliki. A medieval feast 940.1
  Ashman, L. Come to the castle! 940.1
  Corbishley, M. The Middle Ages 940.1
  Galloway, P. Archers, alchemists, and 98 other
    medieval jobs you might have loved or
    loathed 940.1
  Gibbons, G. Knights in shining armor 940.1
  Gravett, C. Knight 940.1
  Hanel, R. Knights 940.1
  Hart, A. Knights & castles 940.1
  Langley, A. Medieval life 940.1
  Park, L. The medieval knights 940.1
  Ross, S. Monarchs 940.1
  Woolf, A. Death and disease 610.9

A **medieval** feast. Aliki 940.1

The **medieval** knights. Park, L. 940.1

Medieval life. Langley, A. 940.1

Medieval realms [series]
  Ross, S. Monarchs 940.1
  Woolf, A. Death and disease 610.9

Medina, Jane, 1953-
  Tomás Rivera 92

Medina, Tony
  I and I [biography of Bob Marley] 92
  (ed) Hip hop speaks to children. See Hip hop
    speaks to children 811.008

Meditation
  Andrews, L. W. Meditation 158

Mediterranean region
    History
  Stefoff, R. The ancient Mediterranean 938

Medley, Linda
  Castle waiting 741.5

Medlock, Scott
  (il) Bunting, E. Some frog! Fic

Medusa (Greek mythology)
    Fiction
  Collins, R. Medusa Jones Fic

Medusa Jones. Collins, R. Fic

Mee-An and the magic serpent. Wagué Diakité, B.
    398.2

Meehl, Brian
  Out of Patience Fic

Meeow and the big box. Braun, S. E

Meerkat mail. Gravett, E. E

Meerkats
  Walden, K. Meerkats 599.74
    Fiction
  Gravett, E. Meerkat mail E

Meet Daniel Pinkwater. McGinty, A. B. 92

Meet Danitra Brown. Grimes, N. 811

Meet Jane Yolen. McGinty, A. B. 92

Meet M and M. Ross, P. E

Meet Mr. and Mrs. Green. Baker, K. E

Meet the Austins. L'Engle, M. Fic

Meet the Barkers. De Paola, T. E

Meet the dancers. Nathan, A. 920

Meet the dinosaurs [series]
  Lessem, D. The fastest dinosaurs 567.9
  Lessem, D. Feathered dinosaurs 567.9
  Lessem, D. Flying giants of dinosaur time
    567.9
  Lessem, D. Sea giants of dinosaur time
    567.9
  Lessem, D. The smartest dinosaurs 567.9

Meet the howlers. Sayre, A. P. 599.8

Meet the musicians. Nathan, A. 780

Meet wild boars. Rosoff, M. E

Meet your community! [series]
  Kenney, K. L. Mail carriers at work 383

Meet your community workers! [series]
  Kenney, K. L. Firefighters at work 628.9
  Kenney, K. L. Librarians at work 020
  Kenney, K. L. Nurses at work 610.73
  Kenney, K. L. Police officers at work 363.2
  Kenney, K. L. Teachers at work 371.1

The **meeting**. Luciani, B. 741.5

Meeting dolphins. Dudzinski, K. 599.5

Mega beasts. Sabuda, R. 569

Mega trucks. Murrell, D. J. 629.224

Megatooth!. O'Brien, P. 567

Mehling, Randi
  Great extinctions of the past 576.8

Mehus-Roe, Kristin
  Dogs for kids! 636.7

Meiani, Antonella
  Air 533
  Chemistry 540.7
  Electricity 537
  Light 535
  Magnetism 538
  Water 532

Meinking, Mary
  Easy origami 736
  Not-quite-so-easy origami 736

Meir, Golda, 1898-1978
  See/See also pages in the following book(s):
  Krull, K. Lives of extraordinary women 920

Meisel, Paul
  (il) Ashman, L. Stella, unleashed E
  (il) Bennett, K. Dad and Pop E

Meshbesher, Wendy—*Continued*
    (jt. auth) Hartman, E. Climate change   **551.6**
    (jt. auth) Hartman, E. Fossil fuels   **333.8**
    (jt. auth) Hartman, E. Light and sound   **530**
    (jt. auth) Hartman, E. Science ethics and controversies   **174**

Mesmerism *See* Hypnotism

Mesopotamia *See* Iraq

Mesopotamia. Shuter, J.   **935**

Messages from Mars. Leedy, L.   **523.4**

Messengers of rain and other poems from Latin America   **861.008**

Messiness *See* Cleanliness

Messing around on the monkey bars. Franco, B.   **811**

Metal man. Reynolds, A.   **E**

Metals
    Langley, A. Metal   **620.1**

Metals, Transmutation of *See* Alchemy

Metalwork
    See also Metals
        Fiction
    Reynolds, A. Metal man   **E**

Metamorphic rock. Faulkner, R.   **552**

Meteorites
        Fiction
    Gutman, D. The Christmas genie   **Fic**
    Patneaude, D. A piece of the sky   **Fic**

Meteorological instruments
    See also Thermometers

Meteorology
    See also Climate; Droughts; Weather; Weather forecasting
    Cole, J. The magic school bus inside a hurricane   **551.55**
    Gallant, R. A. Atmosphere   **551.51**

Meteors
    Sherman, J. Asteroids, meteors, and comets   **523.4**
    Simon, S. Comets, meteors, and asteroids   **523.6**

Metric system
    Murphy, S. J. Polly's pen pal   **516**
    See/See also pages in the following book(s):
    Schwartz, D. M. Millions to measure   **530.8**

Metropolitan Museum of Art (New York, N.Y.)
    Cressy, J. Can you find it?   **750**
    Gogh, V. v. Vincent's colors   **759.9492**
    Monet, C. Monet's impressions   **759.4**
    Museum shapes. See Museum shapes   **E**
        Fiction
    Konigsburg, E. L. From the mixed-up files of Mrs. Basil E. Frankweiler   **Fic**
    Weitzman, J. P. You can't take a balloon into the Metropolitan Museum   **E**

Metselaar, Menno
    Anne Frank: her life in words and pictures   **92**

Metter, Bert
    Bar mitzvah, bat mitzvah   **296.4**

Metz, Lorijo
    What can we do about global warming?   **363.7**
    What can we do about invasive species?   **578.6**
    What can we do about trash and recycling?   **363.7**

Mexican American authors
    Abrams, D. Gary Soto   **92**
    Medina, J. Tomás Rivera   **92**

The **Mexican** American family album. Hoobler, D.   **305.8**

The **Mexican-American** War. Feldman, R. T.   **973.6**

Mexican Americans
    Freedman, R. In the days of the vaqueros   **636.2**
    Garza, C. L. Family pictures   **306.8**
    Hoobler, D. The Mexican American family album   **305.8**
    Keedle, J. Mexican Americans   **305.8**
        Biography
    Abrams, D. Gary Soto   **92**
    Herrera, J. F. The upside down boy   **92**
    Krull, K. Harvesting hope   **92**
    Medina, J. Tomás Rivera   **92**
    Reich, S. José! [biography of José Limón]   **92**
    Tafolla, C. That's not fair! [biography of Emma Tenayuca]   **92**
    Wadsworth, G. Cesar Chavez   **92**
        Fiction
    Bledsoe, L. J. Cougar canyon   **Fic**
    Blos, J. W. Letters from the corrugated castle   **Fic**
    Brown, M. Chavela and the Magic Bubble   **E**
    Bulla, C. R. The Paint Brush Kid   **Fic**
    Colato Laínez, R. Playing loteria   **E**
    Colato Laínez, R. The Tooth Fairy meets El Ratón Pérez   **E**
    Cruise, R. Little Mama forgets   **E**
    Da Costa, D. Hanukkah moon   **E**
    Dorros, A. Radio Man. Don Radio   **E**
    Estevis, A. Chicken Foot Farm   **Fic**
    Jiménez, F. The Christmas gift: El regalo de Navidad   **E**
    Johnston, T. Any small goodness   **Fic**
    Johnston, T. Uncle Rain Cloud   **E**
    Lopez, D. Confetti girl   **Fic**
    Martínez, A. O. Pedrito's world   **Fic**
    Mora, P. Tomás and the library lady   **E**
    O'Neill, A. Estela's swap   **E**
    Pérez, A. I. My diary from here to there   **Fic**
    Pérez, A. I. My very own room   **E**
    Pérez, L. K. First day in grapes   **E**
    Politi, L. Juanita   **E**
    Politi, L. Pedro, the angel of Olvera Street   **E**
    Resau, L. Star in the forest   **Fic**
    Ryan, P. M. Becoming Naomi León   **Fic**
    Ryan, P. M. Esperanza rising   **Fic**
    Saenz, B. A. The dog who loved tortillas   **E**
    Soto, G. Baseball in April, and other stories   **S C**

Mice—*Continued*

Fiction

Asch, F. Mrs. Marlowe's mice	E
Avi. Poppy	Fic
Aylesworth, J. Little Bitty Mousie	E
Bearn, E. Tumtum & Nutmeg	Fic
Becker, B. A visitor for Bear	E
Billingsley, F. Big Bad Bunny	E
Braun, S. Back to bed, Ed!	E
Buhler, C. v. But who will bell the cats?	E
Bunting, E. Mouse island	E
Calmenson, S. Jazzmatazz!	E
Carle, E. Do you want to be my friend?	E
Carlson, N. L. Henry and the Valentine surprise	E
Chaconas, D. Mousie love	E
Cleary, B. The mouse and the motorcycle	Fic
Colato Laínez, R. The Tooth Fairy meets El Ratón Pérez	E
Cole, H. A nest for Celeste	Fic
Cousins, L. Maisy goes to preschool	E
Cox, J. One is a feast for Mouse	E
DiCamillo, K. The tale of Despereaux	Fic
Donofrio, B. Mary and the mouse, the mouse and Mary	E
Doyen, D. Once upon a twice	E
Egan, T. The pink refrigerator	E
Ehlert, L. Boo to you!	E
Emberley, E. Thanks, Mom!	E
Fearnley, J. Martha in the middle	E
Fleming, D. Alphabet under construction	E
Fleming, D. Lunch	E
Foley, G. Thank you Bear	E
George, L. B. Inside mouse, outside mouse	E
Gerritsen, P. Nuts	E
Gorbachev, V. Dragon is coming!	E
Gorbachev, V. Molly who flew away	E
Gore, L. Mommy, where are you?	E
Gravett, E. Little Mouse's big book of fears	E
Harris, R. H. Goodbye, Mousie	E
Henkes, K. Chester's way	E
Henkes, K. Chrysanthemum	E
Henkes, K. Julius, the baby of the world	E
Henkes, K. Lilly's purple plastic purse	E
Henkes, K. Sheila Rae, the brave	E
Henkes, K. Wemberly worried	E
Hoberman, M. A. The two sillies	E
Hoeye, M. Time stops for no mouse	Fic
Holabird, K. Angelina Ballerina	E
Howe, J. Horace and Morris but mostly Dolores	E
Hucke, J. Pip in the Grand Hotel	E
Jacques, B. Redwall	Fic
King-Smith, D. The mouse family Robinson	Fic
Kirk, D. Library mouse	E
Kraus, R. Whose mouse are you?	E
Kroll, S. The Hanukkah mice	E
Lawson, R. Ben and me	Fic
Lionni, L. Alexander and the wind-up mouse	E
Lionni, L. Frederick	E
Lobel, A. Mouse soup	E
Lobel, A. Mouse tales	E

Lord, C. Hot rod hamster	E
Martin, B. A beasty story	E
McCully, E. A. First snow	E
McMullan, K. Pearl and Wagner: one funny day	E
Numeroff, L. J. If you give a mouse a cookie	E
O'Brien, R. C. Mrs. Frisby and the rats of NIMH	Fic
Ormerod, J. Miss Mouse's day	E
Pearson, T. C. Myrtle	E
Pennypacker, S. Pierre in love	E
Potter, B. The story of Miss Moppet	E
Potter, B. The tailor of Gloucester	E
Potter, B. The tale of Mrs. Tittlemouse	E
Potter, B. The tale of two bad mice	E
Reid, B. The Subway mouse	E
Riley, L. A. Mouse mess	E
Rohmann, E. My friend Rabbit	E
Schoenherr, I. Cat & mouse	E
Schwartz, A. Tiny and Hercules	E
Selden, G. The cricket in Times Square	Fic
Shea, P. D. Ten mice for Tet!	394.26
Soto, G. Chato's kitchen	E
Spinelli, E. Three pebbles and a song	E
Steig, W. Abel's island	Fic
Steig, W. Doctor De Soto	E
Tashiro, C. Five nice mice	E
Urban, L. Mouse was mad	E
Waber, B. The mouse that snored	E
Waddell, M. Tiny's big adventure	E
Wallace, N. E. Look! look! look!	E
Walsh, E. S. Dot & Jabber and the big bug mystery	E
Walsh, E. S. Mouse shapes	E
Warnes, T. Chalk and Cheese	E
Weeks, S. Drip, drop	E
Wells, R. Noisy Nora	E
Wells, R. Shy Charles	E
White, E. B. Stuart Little	Fic
Willis, J. Cottonball Colin	E
Willis, J. Gorilla! Gorilla!	E
Wise, W. Christopher Mouse	Fic
Wormell, C. George and the dragon	E
Wright, J. The secret circus	E
Yee, W. H. Mouse and Mole, fine feathered friends	E
Yee, W. H. Upstairs Mouse, downstairs Mole	E

Folklore

Brett, J. Town mouse, country mouse	398.2
MacDonald, M. R. Fat cat	398.2
MacDonald, M. R. Mabela the clever	398.2
Shepard, A. The princess mouse	398.2
Steptoe, J. The story of Jumping Mouse	398.2
Young, E. Seven blind mice	398.2

Graphic novels

Hayes, G. Benny and Penny in just pretend	741.5
Holm, J. L. Babymouse: queen of the world	741.5
Parker, J. Missile Mouse: the star crusher	741.5
Petersen, D. Mouse Guard: Fall 1152	741.5
Smith, J. Little Mouse gets ready	741.5

Mice—*Continued*
Songs
Langstaff, J. M. Frog went a-courtin' **782.42**

Mice, morals, & monkey business. Wormell, C. **398.2**

Michael, Pamela
(ed) River of words. See River of words **808.81**

Michael L. Printz award
Gillespie, J. T. The Newbery/Printz companion **028.5**

Michael Rosen's sad book. Rosen, M. **E**

Michael Townsend's amazing Greek myths of wonder and blunders. Townsend, M. **292**

Michelangelo Buonarroti, 1475-1564
About
Stanley, D. Michelangelo **92**
Wilkinson, P. Michelangelo **92**

Michelin, Linda
Zuzu's wishing cake **E**

Michelle [Obama] Hopkinson, D. **92**

Michelson, Richard
Across the alley **E**
As good as anybody: Martin Luther King Jr. and Abraham Joshua Heschel's amazing march toward freedom **92**
Tuttle's Red Barn **630.9**

Michigan
Fiction
Derby, S. Kyle's island **Fic**
Strickland, B. The sign of the sinister sorcerer **Fic**
Whelan, G. The locked garden **Fic**

Mick Harte was here. Park, B. **Fic**

Micklethwait, Lucy
Children **750**
I spy: an alphabet in art **E**

Micklos, John, 1956-
The brave women and children of the American Revolution **973.3**

Micro mania. Brown, J. **579**

Microbes See Bacteria

Microbiology
Kornberg, A. Germ stories **616.9**
Ollhoff, J. The germ detectives **616.9**

Microorganisms
See also Bacteria
Brown, J. Micro mania **579**
Graham, I. Microscopic scary creatures **591.6**
Latta, S. L. The good, the bad, the slimy **579**
Walker, R. Microscopic life **579**
Zamosky, L. Simple organisms **579**

Microquests [series]
Johnson, R. L. Amazing DNA **572.8**
Johnson, R. L. Mighty animal cells **571.6**
Johnson, R. L. Ultra-organized cell systems **612**

Microscopes
Kramer, S. Hidden worlds: looking through a scientist's microscope **502.8**

Levine, S. The ultimate guide to your microscope **502.8**

Microscopic life. Walker, R. **579**

Microscopic scary creatures. Graham, I. **591.6**

Microsoft Excel (Computer program) *See* Excel (Computer program)

Micucci, Charles, 1959-
The life and times of corn **633.1**
The life and times of the ant **595.7**
The life and times of the honeybee **595.7**
The life and times of the peanut **641.3**

Midas (Legendary character)
Craft, C. King Midas and the golden touch **398.2**
Demi. King Midas **398.2**
Stewig, J. W. King Midas **398.2**

Middle Ages
See also Medieval civilization
Cohen, B. Canterbury tales **821**
Corbishley, M. The Middle Ages **940.1**
Hart, A. Knights & castles **940.1**
Kroll, S. Barbarians! **940.1**
Williams, M. Chaucer's Canterbury Tales **821**
Drama
Schlitz, L. A. Good masters! Sweet ladies! **940.1**
Fiction
Ashburn, B. Over at the castle **E**
Avi. The Book Without Words **Fic**
Avi. Crispin: the cross of lead **Fic**
Branford, H. Fire, bed, & bone **Fic**
Cushman, K. Catherine, called Birdy **Fic**
Cushman, K. Matilda Bone **Fic**
Cushman, K. The midwife's apprentice **Fic**
Davis, T. Roland Wright: future knight **Fic**
De Angeli, M. L. The door in the wall **Fic**
Gilman, L. A. Grail quest: the Camelot spell **Fic**
Karr, K. Fortune's fool **Fic**
Lindgren, A. Ronia, the robber's daughter **Fic**
Nikola-Lisa, W. Magic in the margins **E**
Russell, C. Dogboy **Fic**
Russell, C. Hunted **Fic**
Springer, N. Rowan Hood, outlaw girl of Sherwood Forest **Fic**
Vining, E. G. Adam of the road **Fic**

The **middle-child** blues. Crow, K. **E**

Middle East
Feiler, B. S. Walking the Bible **222**
Law, F. Atlas of Southwest and Central Asia **950**
Steele, P. Middle East **956**
Bibliography
Al-Hazza, T. C. Books about the Middle East **016.3058**
Civilization
Stefoff, R. The ancient Near East **939**
Fiction
Alexander, L. The golden dream of Carlo Chuchio **Fic**
Kimmel, E. A. Joha makes a wish **E**
La Fevers, R. L. Flight of the phoenix **Fic**

Milich, Zoran
City 1 2 3   E
The city ABC book   E
City colors   E
City signs   E
Military aeronautics
   See also World War, 1939-1945—Aerial operations
Military airplanes
   See also Fighter planes
Military art and science
   See also Naval art and science
Chapman, C. Battles & weapons: exploring history through art   355
Fridell, R. Military technology   623.4
History
Murrell, D. J. Greek warrior   355
Park, L. The Japanese samurai   355
Park, L. The Pharaohs' armies   355
Military bases
Fiction
Holmes, S. L. Operation Yes   Fic
Military history
Chapman, C. Battles & weapons: exploring history through art   355
Solway, A. Graphing war and conflict   355
Military personnel
   See also Admirals; Soldiers
Military technology. Fridell, R.   623.4
Milk
Aliki. Milk from cow to carton   637
Gibbons, G. The milk makers   637
Milk from cow to carton. Aliki   637
The **milk** makers. Gibbons, G.   637
The **milkman**. Cordsen, C. F.   E
Milky Way
Asimov, I. The Milky Way and other galaxies   523.1
Jefferis, D. Galaxies   523.1
Rau, D. M. The Milky Way and other galaxies   523.1
The **Milky** Way and other galaxies. Asimov, I.   523.1
The **Milky** Way and other galaxies. Rau, D. M.   523.1
Mill. Macaulay, D.   690
Millar, H. R., 1869-ca. 1940
(il) Nesbit, E. Five children and it   Fic
Millard, Glenda
The naming of Tishkin Silk   Fic
Miller, Bobbi
Davy Crockett gets hitched   398.2
One fine trade   398.2
Miller, Brandon Marie
Benjamin Franklin, American genius   92
Declaring independence   973.3
George Washington for kids   92
Growing up in revolution and the new nation, 1775 to 1800   973.3
Miller, Debbie S.
Arctic lights, arctic nights   591.4
Big Alaska   979.8

The great serum race   798.8
Survival at 40 below   591.7
Miller, Donalyn, 1967-
The book whisperer   372.6
Miller, Edward, 1964-
Fireboy to the rescue!   613.6
The monster health book   613
The tooth book   617.6
(il) Adler, D. A. Fractions, decimals, and percents   513
(il) Adler, D. A. Fun with Roman numerals   513
(il) Adler, D. A. Money madness   332.4
(il) Branley, F. M. Is there life in outer space?   576.8
(il) Branley, F. M. The sun, our nearest star   523.7
(il) Showers, P. A drop of blood   612.1
(il) Showers, P. What happens to a hamburger?   612.3
Miller, Heather, 1971-
Subway ride   388.4
This is your life cycle   595.7
Miller, Jeanne
Food science   641.3
Miller, Joseph, 1946-
(ed) Sears list of subject headings. See Sears list of subject headings   025.4
Miller, Karen, 1942-
(jt. auth) Raines, S. C. Story stretchers for infants, toddlers, and twos   372.4
Miller, Kirsten, 1963-
Kiki Strike: inside the shadow city   Fic
Miller, Lee
Roanoke   975.6
Miller, Linda L., 1943-
(jt. auth) Baumbach, D. Less is more   025.2
Miller, Mara, 1968-
Hurricane Katrina strikes the Gulf Coast   363.34
Miller, Marcia
(il) Math for the very young. See Math for the very young   793.74
Miller, Margaret, 1945-
Big and little   E
Guess who?   E
(il) Bradley, K. B. Pop!   530.4
(il) Cole, J. How you were born   612.6
(il) Cole, J. The new baby at your house   306.8
Miller, Norma, 1919-
Stompin' at the Savoy [biography of Norma Miller]   92
Miller, Pat
Library skills   025.5
Reading activities   025.5
Research skills   025.5
Miller, Raymond H., 1967-
Stan Lee   92
Miller, Ron, 1947-
Earth and the moon   525
Robot explorers   629.43
Saturn   523.4

Minerals—*Continued*

Green, D. Rocks and minerals 552
Pellant, C. Minerals 549
Royston, A. Vitamins and minerals for a healthy body 613.2
Trueit, T. S. Rocks, gems, and minerals 552
VanCleave, J. P. Janice VanCleave's rocks and minerals 552

Minerals, rocks, and soil. Davis, B. J. 552

Miners

See also Coal miners

Fiction

Gregory, K. My darlin' Clementine Fic
Wiseman, D. Jeremy Visick Fic

Minerva the monster. Kirwan, W. E

Mines and mineral resources

See also Coal mines and mining

Mine's the best. Bonsall, C. N. E

Ming Lo moves the mountain. Lobel, A. E

Mini Mia and her darling uncle. Lindenbaum, P. E

Miniature horses. Lunis, N. 636.1

Minifred goes to school. Gerstein, M. E

Minister, Peter

(il) Woodward, J. Dinosaurs eye to eye 567.9

Minji's salon. Choung, E.-H. E

Minkel, Walter

How to do "The three bears" with two hands 791.5

Minn and Jake. Wong, J. S. Fic

Minnesota

Fiction

Applegate, K. Home of the brave Fic
Blume, L. M. M. The rising star of Rusty Nail Fic
Brown, J. Little Cricket Fic
Durbin, W. Blackwater Ben Fic
Lasky, K. Marven of the Great North Woods E
Lorbiecki, M. Paul Bunyan's sweetheart E
Lovelace, M. H. Betsy-Tacy Fic
McGhee, A. Julia Gillian (and the art of knowing) Fic
Paulsen, G. The winter room Fic
Sandin, J. At home in a new land E

Minnie and Moo, wanted dead or alive. Cazet, D. E

Minnie's Diner. Dodds, D. A. E

Minnow and Rose. Young, J. Fic

Minor, Wendell

Yankee Doodle America 973.3
(il) Aldrin, B. Look to the stars 629.4
(il) Aldrin, B. Reaching for the moon 92
(il) Brown, M. W. Nibble nibble 811
(il) Burleigh, R. Abraham Lincoln comes home 92
(jt. auth) Ehrlich, A. Rachel 92
(il) George, J. C. The buffalo are back 599.64
(il) George, J. C. Everglades 975.9
(il) George, J. C. Julie Fic
(il) George, J. C. Luck E

(il) George, J. C. Morning, noon, and night E
(il) George, J. C. The wolves are back 599.77
(il) Turner, A. W. Abe Lincoln remembers 92
(il) Turner, A. W. Sitting Bull remembers 92
(il) Zolotow, C. The seashore book E

Minorities

See also Ethnic relations

Minorities in literature

Gilton, D. L. Multicultural and ethnic children's literature in the United States 028.5

Minotaur (Greek mythology)

Byrd, R. The hero and the minotaur 398.2

Minstrels

Fiction

Vining, E. G. Adam of the road Fic

Minter, Daniel

(il) Medearis, A. S. Seven spools of thread E
(il) Reynolds, S. The first marathon: the legend of Pheidippides 938

Minty: a story of young Harriet Tubman. Schroeder, A. E

Miracle. Karwoski, G. 972.9

Miracles

Hanft, J. E. Miracles of the Bible 221.9

Fiction

Kushner, L. In God's hands E
Wells, R. The miraculous tale of the two Maries E

Folklore

De Paola, T. The clown of God 398.2

The **miracles** of Passover. Hanft, J. E. 296.4

Miracles of the Bible. Hanft, J. E. 221.9

The **miraculous** journey of Edward Tulane. DiCamillo, K. Fic

The **miraculous** tale of the two Maries. Wells, R. E

Miranda, Anne, 1954-

To market, to market E

Miranda's beach day. Keller, H. E

Mirandy and Brother Wind. McKissack, P. C. E

Mirette on the high wire. McCully, E. A. E

Miriam (Biblical figure)

About

Manushkin, F. Miriam's cup 222

Miriam's cup. Manushkin, F. 222

Mirror mirror. Singer, M. 811

A **mirror** to nature. Yolen, J. 811

The **misadventures** of Maude March. Couloumbis, A. Fic

Misadventures of Millicent Madding [series]

Tacang, B. Bully-be-gone Fic

Misakian, Jo Ellen Priest

The essential school library glossary 020

Miscellaneous facts *See* Curiosities and wonders

Misenta, Marisol *See* Isol, 1972-

Miss Bindergarten celebrates the 100th day of kindergarten. Slate, J. **E**

Miss Bridie chose a shovel. Connor, L. **E**

Miss Brooks loves books (and I don't). Bottner, B. **E**

Miss Fox's class goes green. Spinelli, E. **E**

Miss Little's gift. Wood, D. **E**

Miss Malarkey leaves no reader behind. Finchler, J. **E**

Miss Mary Mack. Hoberman, M. A. **398.8**

Miss Mary Mack and other children's street rhymes **796.1**

Miss Mouse's day. Ormerod, J. **E**

Miss Nelson is missing!. Allard, H. **E**

Missile Mouse [series]
  Parker, J. Missile Mouse: the star crusher **741.5**

Missile Mouse: the star crusher. Parker, J. **741.5**

The missing [series]
  Haddix, M. P. Found **Fic**

The missing chick. Gorbachev, V. **E**

Missing children
  See also Runaway children
    Fiction
  Berkeley, J. The hidden boy **Fic**
  Butler, D. H. The case of the lost boy **Fic**
  DiCamillo, K. The magician's elephant **Fic**
  Dowd, S. The London Eye mystery **Fic**
  Godwin, J. Falling from Grace **Fic**
  Harris, L. A taste for red **Fic**

The missing manatee. DeFelice, C. C. **Fic**

Missing May. Rylant, C. **Fic**

The missing mitten mystery. Kellogg, S. **E**

The missing monster card. Mortensen, L. **741.5**

Missing persons
  See also Runaway teenagers
    Fiction
  Armstrong, A. Looking for Marco Polo **Fic**
  Byrd, T. Doc Wilde and the frogs of doom **Fic**
  Hiaasen, C. Scat **Fic**
  Parkinson, S. Blue like Friday **Fic**
  Prévost, G. The book of time **Fic**
  Santopolo, J. The Niña, the Pinta, and the vanishing treasure **Fic**
  Sheth, K. Boys without names **Fic**
  Springer, N. The case of the missing marquess **Fic**
  Wilson, N. D. Leepike Ridge **Fic**

Mission: addition. Leedy, L. **513**

Mission control, this is Apollo. Chaikin, A. **629.45**

Mission: planet Earth. Ride, S. K. **525**

Mission: save the planet. Ride, S. K. **333.72**

Mission: science [series]
  BishopRoby, J. Animal kingdom **590**
  Cregan, E. R. The atom **539.7**
  Cregan, E. R. Marie Curie **92**
  Fuoco, G. D. Earth **333.72**
  Greathouse, L. E. Solar system **523.2**
  Herweck, D. Albert Einstein and his theory of relativity **92**
  Herweck, D. Energy **621**
  Herweck, D. Robert Fulton **92**
  Housel, D. J. Ecologists **920**
  Housel, D. J. Ecosystems **577**
  Jankowski, C. Astronomers **920**
  Jankowski, C. Jane Goodall **92**
  Jankowski, C. Space exploration **520**
  Lee, K. F. Cells **571.6**
  Van Gorp, L. Elements **540**
  Van Gorp, L. Gregor Mendel **92**
  Weir, J. Matter **530**
  Weir, J. Max Planck **92**
  Zamosky, L. Louis Pasteur **92**
  Zamosky, L. Simple organisms **579**

Mission to Mars. Branley, F. M. **629.45**

Mission to the moon. Dyer, A. **629.45**

Missions
    Fiction
  Politi, L. Song of the swallows **E**

Mississippi
    Fiction
  McMullan, M. How I found the Strong **Fic**
  McMullan, M. When I crossed No-Bob **Fic**
  Rodman, M. A. Yankee girl **Fic**
  Taulbert, C. L. Little Cliff and the porch people **E**
  Taylor, M. D. The friendship **Fic**
  Taylor, M. D. Let the circle be unbroken **Fic**
  Taylor, M. D. Mississippi bridge **Fic**
  Taylor, M. D. The road to Memphis **Fic**
  Taylor, M. D. Roll of thunder, hear my cry **Fic**
  Taylor, M. D. Song of the trees **Fic**
  Taylor, M. D. The well **Fic**
  Tingle, T. Crossing Bok Chitto **Fic**
  Vander Zee, R. Mississippi morning **E**
  Wiles, D. The Aurora County All-Stars **Fic**
  Wiles, D. Love, Ruby Lavender **Fic**

Mississippi bridge. Taylor, M. D. **Fic**

Mississippi morning. Vander Zee, R. **E**

Mississippi River
    Fiction
  Fox, F. G. Jean Laffite and the big ol' whale **E**
  Helgerson, J. Horns & wrinkles **Fic**
  Twain, M. The adventures of Tom Sawyer **Fic**

Mississippi River valley
  Goodman, J. E. Despite all obstacles: La Salle and the conquest of the Mississippi **92**

Mississippi valley *See* Mississippi River valley

Missouri
    Fiction
  Milford, K. The Boneshaker **Fic**
  Twain, M. The adventures of Tom Sawyer **Fic**

Missouri River valley
  Freedman, R. An Indian winter **978**

Mister Seahorse. Carle, E.   **E**

Misty of Chincoteague. Henry, M.   **Fic**

Mitch and Amy. Cleary, B.   **Fic**

Mitchell, Barbara, 1941-
Shoes for everyone: a story about Jan Matzeliger   **92**

Mitchell, Don, 1957-
Driven   **92**
Liftoff [biography of John Glenn]   **92**

Mitchell, Hetty
(il) Mitchell, B. Shoes for everyone: a story about Jan Matzeliger   **92**

Mitchell, Joyce Slayton, 1933-
Crashed, smashed, and mashed   **629.222**

Mitchell, Margaree King, 1953-
Uncle Jed's barbershop   **E**

Mitchell, Stephen, 1943-
Genies, meanies, and magic rings   **398.2**
Iron Hans   **398.2**
The nightingale   **Fic**
The tinderbox   **Fic**
The ugly duckling   **E**

Mitchell, Susan, 1962-
(il) Deen, P. H. Paula Deen's my first cookbook   **641.5**
(il) MacDonald, M. R. Too many fairies   **398.2**

Mitchell, Susan K., 1972-
Animal body-part regenerators   **571.8**
Animal chemical combat   **591.47**
Animal mimics   **591.47**
Animals with awesome armor   **591.47**
Animals with crafty camouflage   **591.47**
Animals with wicked weapons   **591.47**

Mitchell, Tracy
(il) Avi. What do fish have to do with anything? and other stories   **S C**

Mites
Jarrow, G. Chiggers   **616.9**

The **mitten**. Aylesworth, J.   **398.2**

The **mitten**. Brett, J.   **398.2**

Mittens. Schaefer, L. M.   **E**

Mitter, Kathryn
(il) Herman, C. First rain   **E**

Mitter, Kathy
(il) Jules, J. Duck for Turkey Day   **E**

Mitton, Jacqueline
Once upon a starry night   **523.8**
Zodiac   **398**

Mitton, Tony, 1951-
Gnash, gnaw, dinosaur!   **811**
Rainforest romp   **591.7**
Rumble, roar, dinosaur!   **811**
The storyteller's secrets   **398.2**

Miura, Taro, 1968-
Tools   **E**

Mixed beasts. Cox, K.   **811**

Mixed race people See Racially mixed people

The **mixed-up** chameleon. Carle, E.   **E**

The **mixed-up** rooster. Edwards, P. D.   **E**

Mixing and separating. Oxlade, C.   **541**

Mixing and separating. Oxlade, C.   **546**

Mixter, Helen
(jt. auth) Baasansuren, B. My little round house   **E**

Mixtures and solutions. Ballard, C.   **541**

Mizuna, Tomomi
(il) Fuji, M. The big adventures of Majoko, volume 1   **741.5**

Mobin-Uddin, Asma
The best Eid ever   **E**
A party in Ramadan   **E**

Mobs See Riots

Mochizuki, Ken, 1954-
Baseball saved us   **E**
Be water, my friend [biography of Bruce Lee]   **92**
Heroes   **E**
Passage to freedom   **940.53**

Mockingbird. Erskine, K.   **Fic**

Model airplanes See Airplanes—Models

Model cars See Automobiles—Models

Models and modelmaking
See also Airplanes—Models

Modern Africa. Bowden, R.   **960**

Modern art
1900-1999 (20th century)
See Art—20th century

Modern dance
Solway, A. Modern dance   **792.8**

Modern painting
Raczka, B. No one saw   **759.06**

The **Moffats**. Estes, E.   **Fic**

Moffett, Mark W.
Face to face with frogs   **597.8**

Mogul Empire
Arnold, C. Taj Mahal   **954**
Mann, E. Taj Mahal   **954**

Mohammed See Muḥammad, d. 632

Mohammed, Khadra
(jt. auth) Williams, K. L. Four feet, two sandals   **E**
(jt. auth) Williams, K. L. My name is Sangoel   **E**

Mohammedanism See Islam

Mohammedans See Muslims

Mohapatra, Jyotirmayee, 1978-
About
Woog, A. Jyotirmayee Mohapatra   **92**

The **Mohawk**. King, D. C.   **970.004**

Mohawk Indians
King, D. C. The Mohawk   **970.004**
Swamp, J. Giving thanks   **299.7**
Fiction
Bruchac, J. Bearwalker   **Fic**
Bruchac, J. Children of the longhouse   **Fic**
Bruchac, J. Skeleton man   **Fic**
Kirk, C. A. Sky dancers   **E**

Mohr, Nicholasa, 1935-
Going home   **Fic**

Moiz, Azra, 1963-
Taiwan   **951.2**

Moja means one. Feelings, M.   **E**

Mojave Desert (Calif.)
Fiction
Fleischman, S. Bo & Mzzz Mad **Fic**
Mokie & Bik. Orr, W. **Fic**
Moldova
Sheehan, P. Moldova **947.6**
Mole music. McPhail, D. M. **E**
Molecules
Ballard, C. Mixtures and solutions **541**
Juettner, B. Molecules **540**
Woodford, C. Atoms and molecules **540**
Moles (Animals)
Fiction
Ehlert, L. Mole's hill **E**
Emmett, J. The best gift of all **E**
McPhail, D. M. Mole music **E**
Villeneuve, A. The red scarf **E**
Yee, W. H. Mouse and Mole, fine feathered friends **E**
Yee, W. H. Upstairs Mouse, downstairs Mole **E**
Mole's hill. Ehlert, L. **E**
Molin, Paulette Fairbanks
American Indian stereotypes in the world of children **970.004**
Molk, Laurel
(il) Yolen, J. Off we go! **E**
Mollel, Tololwa M. (Tololwa Marti)
Ananse's feast **398.2**
My rows and piles of coins **E**
The orphan boy **398.2**
Mollusks
See also Cephalopods; Slugs (Mollusks); Snails; Squids
Blaxland, B. Snails, clams, and their relatives **594**
Mollusks: snails, clams, and their relatives. See Blaxland, B. Snails, clams, and their relatives **594**
Molly and her dad. Ormerod, J.
Molly who flew away. Gorbachev, V. **E**
Molly's family. Garden, N. **E**
Molly's pilgrim. Cohen, B. **E**
Molnar, Leslie, 1955-
(jt. auth) Barstow, B. Beyond picture books **011.6**
Moloney, James, 1954-
The Book of Lies **Fic**
Mom and Dad are palindromes. Shulman, M. **E**
Mom and me. Konrad, M. S. **E**
MoMA *See* Museum of Modern Art (New York, N.Y.)
Momatiuk, Yva, 1940-
Face to face with penguins **598**
Face to face with wild horses **599.66**
Momma, where are you from? Bradby, M. **E**
Mommy?. Sendak, M. **E**
Mommy, carry me please!. Cabrera, J. **E**
Mommy, do you love me? Willis, J. **E**
Mommy far, Mommy near. Peacock, C. A. **E**

Mommy, mama, and me. Newman, L. **E**
Mommy, where are you? Gore, L. **E**
Momotaro and the island of ogres. Wada, S. **398.2**
Monaco
King, D. C. Monaco **944**
Monaghan, Kimberly
Organic crafts **745.5**
Monarch butterflies up close. Bredeson, C. **595.7**
Monarch butterfly. Gibbons, G. **595.7**
Monarchs *See* Kings and rulers
Monarchs. Ross, S. **940.1**
The **monarch's** progress. Harley, A. **811**
Monarchy
See also Queens
Monasticism and religious orders for women
See also Nuns
Monday's troll. Prelutsky, J. **811**
Monet, Claude, 1840-1926
Monet's impressions **759.4**
About
Kelley, T. Claude Monet: sunshine and waterlilies **92**
Monet and the impressionists for kids. Sabbeth, C. **759.05**
Monet's impressions. Monet, C. **759.4**
Money
See also Dollar; Paper money
Adler, D. A. Money madness **332.4**
Cribb, J. Money **332.4**
Forest, C. The dollar bill in translation **332.4**
Hall, A. Show me the money **332.024**
Kummer, P. K. Currency **332.4**
Leedy, L. Follow the money! **332.4**
Maestro, B. The story of money **332.4**
Orr, T. Coins and other currency **332.4**
Robinson, E. K. Making cents **332.4**
Fiction
Cottrell Boyce, F. Millions **Fic**
Mollel, T. M. My rows and piles of coins **E**
Money madness. Adler, D. A. **332.4**
Money-making projects for children
Bochner, A. B. The new totally awesome business book for kids (and their parents) **658**
Orr, T. A kid's guide to earning money **650.1**
Fiction
Clements, A. Lunch money **Fic**
Davies, J. The lemonade war **Fic**
Graff, L. The life and crimes of Bernetta Wallflower **Fic**
Nolen, J. Pitching in for Eubie **E**
Money matters: a kid's guide to money [series]
Orr, T. Coins and other currency **332.4**
Orr, T. A kid's guide to earning money **650.1**
Monfreid, Dorothée de, 1973-
Dark night **E**
Mongolia
Lewin, T. Horse song **951.7**

Monsters—Fiction—*Continued*

Hicks, B. J. Monsters don't eat broccoli   E
Kelley, M. Twelve terrible things   E
Kirwan, W. Minerva the monster   E
Lund, D. Monsters on machines   E
McCarty, P. Jeremy draws a monster   E
McKissack, P. C. Precious and the Boo Hag
   E
Murray, M. D. Halloween night   E
Numberman, N. Do not build a Frankenstein!
   E
Poblocki, D. The stone child   Fic
Pym, T. Have you ever seen a sneep?   E
Rex, M. Goodnight goon   E
Rosoff, M. Jumpy Jack and Googily   E
Sendak, M. Mommy?   E
Sierra, J. Thelonius Monster's sky-high fly pie
   E
Snow, A. Here be monsters!   Fic
Spinelli, E. Wanda's monster   E
Steig, W. Shrek!   E
Stein, D. E. Monster hug!   E
Taylor, S. When a monster is born   E
Van Leeuwen, J. Amanda Pig and the awful,
   scary monster   E
Weatherly, L. The scariest monster in the world
   E
Wheeler, L. Boogie knights   E
Whitman, C. Lines that wiggle   E
Willems, M. Leonardo, the terrible monster
   E
Wing, N. Go to bed, monster!   E

Folklore
Morpurgo, M. Beowulf   398.2
Rogasky, B. The golem   398.2
Rumford, J. Beowulf   398.2
Wisniewski, D. Golem   398.2

Graphic novels
Davis, E. Stinky   741.5
Hastings, J. Terrabella Smoot and the unsung
   monsters   741.5
Phelan, M. The storm in the barn   741.5
Storrie, P. D. Beowulf   741.5

Poetry
Hoberman, M. A. You read to me, I'll read to
   you: very short scary tales to read together
   811
Moore, L. Beware, take care   811
Prelutsky, J. Awful Ogre running wild   811
Prelutsky, J. Awful Ogre's awful day   811
Prelutsky, J. The Headless Horseman rides to-
   night   811
Prelutsky, J. Nightmares: poems to trouble your
   sleep   811
Rex, A. Frankenstein makes a sandwich   811
Rex, A. Frankenstein takes the cake   811
Sierra, J. Monster Goose   811

Monsters!. Stephens, J.   741.5

Monsters [series]
Nardo, D. Martians   001.9

Monsters don't eat broccoli. Hicks, B. J.   E

Monsters in art
Stephens, J. Monsters!   741.5

Monsters of the deep. Barnhill, K. R.   591.7

Monsters on machines. Lund, D.   E

Montana
Fiction
Thomas, J. R. Blind mountain   Fic

Montardre, Hélène
(jt. auth) Burleigh, R. Volcanoes   551.2

Monte, Richard
The dragon of Krakow and other Polish stories
   398.2

Montecalvo, Janet
(il) Grant, K. Sofie and the city   E

Montenegro
King, D. C. Serbia and Montenegro   949.7

Monterey (Calif.)
Mannis, C. D. Snapshots   591.7

Montes, Marisa, 1951-
Los gatos black on Halloween   E
Juan Bobo goes to work   398.2

Montezuma, Carlos, 1866?-1923
About
Capaldi, G. A boy named Beckoning: the true
   story of Dr. Carlos Montezuma, Native American hero   92

Montgomery, L. M. (Lucy Maud), 1874-1942
About
Wallner, A. Lucy Maud Montgomery   92
See/See also pages in the following book(s):
Ellis, S. From reader to writer   372.6

Montgomery, Lucy Maud *See* Montgomery, L.
M. (Lucy Maud), 1874-1942

Montgomery, Sy
Kakapo rescue   639.9
The man-eating tigers of Sundarbans   599.75
Quest for the tree kangaroo   599.2
Saving the ghost of the mountain   599.75
Search for the golden moon bear   599.78
The snake scientist   597.96
The tarantula scientist   595.4

Montgomery (Ala.)
Fiction
Pinkney, A. D. Boycott blues   E
Race relations
Freedman, R. Freedom walkers   323.1
Parks, R. Rosa Parks: my story   92

Months
Cohn, S. One wolf howls   599.77
Fiction
Lobel, A. One lighthouse, one moon   E
Obed, E. B. Who would like a Christmas tree?
   E
Poetry
Bunting, E. Sing a song of piglets   811
Livingston, M. C. Calendar   E
Updike, J. A child's calendar   811

Monticello. Richards, N.   975.5

Montileaux, Don
(il) Tatanka and the Lakota people. See Tatanka
   and the Lakota people   398.2

Montresor, Beni, 1926-2001
(il) De Regniers, B. S. May I bring a friend?
   E

Montserrat, Pep, 1966-
(il) Kimmel, E. A. The McElderry book of
   Greek myths   292

Montserrat, Pep, 1966-—*Continued*
(il) Vallverdú, J. Aladdin and the magic lamp = Aladino y la lámpara marvillosa **398.2**

Monumental verses. Lewis, J. P. **811**

Monuments
Bullard, L. The Gateway Arch **977.8**
Poetry
Lewis, J. P. Monumental verses **811**

Monuments, National *See* National monuments

Moominsummer madness. Jansson, T. **Fic**

Moon
Bailey, J. Sun up, sun down **525**
Branley, F. M. The moon seems to change **523.3**
Branley, F. M. What the moon is like **523.3**
Dyson, M. J. Home on the moon **629.45**
Gardner, R. Far-out science projects about Earth's sun and moon **523**
Gibbons, G. The moon book **523.3**
Hicks, T. A. Earth and the moon **525**
Landau, E. The moon **523.3**
McNulty, F. If you decide to go to the moon **629.45**
Miller, R. Earth and the moon **525**
Simon, S. The moon **523.3**
Stewart, M. Why does the moon change shape? **523.3**
Tomecek, S. Moon **523.3**
Whitman, S. Under the Ramadan moon **297.3**
Exploration
Dyer, A. Mission to the moon **629.45**
Ross, S. Moon: science, history, and mystery **629.45**
Vogt, G. Apollo moonwalks **629.45**
Fiction
Almond, D. The boy who climbed into the moon **Fic**
Asch, F. Happy birthday, Moon **E**
Banks, K. And if the moon could talk **E**
Bartram, S. Bob's best ever friend **E**
Carle, E. Papa, please get the moon for me **E**
Curtis, C. I took the moon for a walk **E**
Da Costa, D. Hanukkah moon **E**
Delessert, É. Moon theater **E**
Gralley, J. The moon came down on Milk Street **E**
Henkes, K. Kitten's first full moon **E**
Jeffers, O. The way back home **E**
Lin, G. Where the mountain meets the moon **Fic**
McCarty, P. Moon plane **E**
Rymond, L. G. Oscar and the mooncats **E**
Shulman, L. The moon might be milk **E**
Thurber, J. Many moons [illustrated by Louis Slobodkin] **E**
Thurber, J. Many moons [illustrated by Marc Simont] **E**
Folklore
Dayrell, E. Why the Sun and the Moon live in the sky **398.2**
Ehlert, L. Moon rope. Un lazo a la luna **398.2**
Hirsh, M. The rabbi and the twenty-nine witches **398.2**

Poetry
Sky magic **811.008**
Stevenson, R. L. The moon **E**

Moon, Voyages to *See* Space flight to the moon

The **moon**. Stevenson, R. L. **E**

Moon & sun [series]
Lisle, H. The Ruby Key **Fic**

Moon bear. Guiberson, B. Z. **599.78**

The **moon** book. Gibbons, G. **523.3**

The **moon** came down on Milk Street. Gralley, J. **E**

Moon Indigo. See Shange, N. Ellington was not a street **E**

Moon landing. Platt, R. **629.45**

The **moon** might be milk. Shulman, L. **E**

Moon over Star. Aston, D. H. **E**

Moon plane. McCarty, P. **E**

Moon rabbit. Russell, N. **E**

Moon rope. Un lazo a la luna. Ehlert, L. **398.2**

Moon runner. Marsden, C. **Fic**

Moon: science, history, and mystery. Ross, S. **629.45**

The **moon** seems to change. Branley, F. M. **523.3**

Moon theater. Delessert, É. **E**

Moonbeams, dumplings & dragon boats. Simonds, N. **394.26**

Mooney, Carla, 1970-
Amazing Africa **960**
Sunscreen for plants **632**

Moonlight: the Halloween cat. Rylant, C. **E**

Moonpowder. Rocco, J. **E**

Moonrunner. Thomason, M. **Fic**

Moonshadow's journey. Lobel, G. **E**

Moonshot. Floca, B. **629.45**

Moony Luna. Argueta, J. **E**

The **moorchild.** McGraw, E. J. **Fic**

Moore, Ann
See/See also pages in the following book(s):
Thimmesh, C. Girls think of everything **920**

Moore, Bobbie, 1944-
(il) King, D. C. Colonial days **973.2**

Moore, Clement Clarke, 1779-1863
The night before Christmas [illustrated by Rachel Isadora] **811**
[illustrated by Richard Jesse Watson] **811**

Moore, Cyd
(il) Brennan-Nelson, D. Willow **E**
(il) Galbraith, K. O. Arbor Day square **E**
(il) Newman, L. A fire engine for Ruthie **E**

Moore, Ella Sheppard, 1851-1914
Fiction
Hopkinson, D. A band of angels **E**

Moore, Gustav
(il) Ross, M. E. Earth cycles **525**

Moore, Heidi, 1976-
The story behind cotton **633.5**
The story behind diamonds **553.8**

Moore, Heidi, 1976-—*Continued*
The story behind salt   **553.6**
Moore, Inga
(il) Burnett, F. H. The secret garden   **Fic**
(il) Grahame, K. The wind in the willows
  [abridged and illustrated by Inga Moore]
                                                        Fic
(il) Horse tales. See Horse tales   **S C**
Moore, Lilian, 1909-2004
Beware, take care   **811**
Mural on Second Avenue, and other city poems
                                                        811
(jt. auth) Charlip, R. Hooray for me!   **306.8**
Moore, Margie
(il) Carlstrom, N. W. It's your first day of
  school, Annie Claire   **E**
Moore, Patrick, 1959-
The mighty street sweeper   **E**
Moore-Mallinos, Jennifer
I have asthma   **616.2**
Moose
Estigarribia, D. Moose   **599.65**
Fiction
Greene, S. Moose's big idea   **Fic**
Wargin, K.-J. Moose on the loose   **E**
Wiseman, B. Morris and Boris at the circus
                                                          E

Moose and Hildy [series]
Greene, S. Moose's big idea   **Fic**
Moose on the loose. Wargin, K.-J.   **E**
Moose's big idea. Greene, S.   **Fic**
Mora, Francisco X.
(il) Climo, S. Tuko and the birds   **398.2**
Mora, Pat
Abuelos   **E**
Book fiesta!   **E**
Doña Flor   **E**
Gracias = Thanks   **E**
Here, kitty, kitty   **E**
A library for Juana: the world of Sor Juana Inés
                                                          92
A pinata in a pine tree   **782.42**
Tomás and the library lady   **E**
Uno, dos, tres: one, two, three   **E**
Wiggling pockets   **E**
Yum! mmmm! que rico!   **811**
Moral and philosophic stories *See* Fables
Moral education
Barker, D. Maybe right, maybe wrong   **370.1**
Moral philosophy *See* Ethics
Morales, Magaly
(il) Brown, M. Chavela and the Magic Bubble
                                                          E
(il) Mora, P. A pinata in a pine tree   **782.42**
Morales, Yuyi
Just a minute   **398.2**
Just in case   **E**
Little Night   **E**
(il) Johnston, T. My abuelita   **E**
(il) Krull, K. Harvesting hope   **92**
(il) Montes, M. Los gatos black on Halloween
                                                          E

Moran, Barbara B.
(jt. auth) Stueart, R. D. Library and information
  center management   **025.1**
Moran, Thomas, 1837-1926
About
Judge, L. Yellowstone Moran   **92**
Mordan, C. B.
(il) Avi. Silent movie   **E**
(il) Dendy, L. A. Guinea pig scientists   **616**
(il) Marrin, A. Oh, rats!   **599.35**
Morden, Daniel
(jt. auth) Lupton, H. The adventures of Odys-
  seus   **292**
Mordhorst, Heidi
Pumpkin butterfly   **811**
More about Boy. Dahl, R.   **92**
More bones. Olson, A. N.   **398.2**
More bullies in more books. Bott, C. J.   **371.5**
More family storytimes. Reid, R.   **027.62**
"**More** more more" said the baby. Williams, V. B.
                                                          E
More or less. Murphy, S. J.   **513**
A **more** perfect union. Maestro, B.   **342**
More pocket poems   **811.008**
More reading connections. Knowles, E.   **028.5**
More scary stories to tell in the dark. Schwartz,
  A.   **398.2**
More simple science fair projects, grades 3-5.
  Tocci, S.   **507.8**
More stories to solve. Shannon, G.   **398.2**
More storytime action!. Bromann, J.   **027.62**
More than anything else. Bradby, M.   **E**
More than meets the eye. Raczka, B.   **750**
Moreillon, Judi
Collaborative strategies for teaching reading
  comprehension   **372.4**
Moreno, Rene King
(il) Goldman, J. Uncle monarch and the Day of
  the Dead   **E**
(il) Guy, G. F. Fiesta!   **E**
(il) Guy, G. F. Siesta   **E**
(il) Stanton, K. Papi's gift   **E**
Morey, Walt, 1907-1992
Gentle Ben   **Fic**
Morgan, Jody
Elephant rescue   **599.67**
Morgan, Julia
About
Mannis, C. D. Julia Morgan built a castle
                                                          92
Morgan, Nicola, 1961-
Chicken friend   **Fic**
Morgan, Pierr, 1952-
(jt. auth) Schaefer, C. L. Dragon dancing   **E**
Morgenstern, Susie Hoch
A book of coupons   **Fic**
Morgy makes his move. Lewis, M.   **Fic**
Morin, Paul, 1959-
(il) Mollel, T. M. The orphan boy   **398.2**
Moriuchi, Mique
(il) Fisher, A. L. The story goes on   **E**

Morley, Christine
Freaky facts about spiders   **595.4**

Morley, Taia
(il) Tang, G. Math fables too   **513**

Mormon Church *See* Church of Jesus Christ of Latter-day Saints

The **Mormon** Trail. Sonneborn, L.   **978**

Mormons
Bial, R. Nauvoo   **289.3**
George, C. What makes me a Mormon?   **289.3**
Hailstone, R. The white ox   **92**
Sonneborn, L. The Mormon Trail   **978**

Morning
Fiction
Brown, M. W. A child's good morning book   **E**
Krauss, R. The backward day   **E**
Lobel, A. Hello, day!   **E**
Rosenberg, L. Nobody   **E**
Wong, J. S. Buzz   **E**

Morning Girl. Dorris, M.   **Fic**

Morning, noon, and night. George, J. C.   **E**

Morocco
Seward, P. Morocco   **964**
Fiction
Alalou, E. The butter man   **E**
Ichikawa, S. My father's shop   **E**
Folklore
See Folklore—Morocco

Morpurgo, Michael
Beowulf   **398.2**
Hansel and Gretel   **398.2**
Kensuke's kingdom   **Fic**
The McElderry book of Aesop's fables   **398.2**
On angel wings   **Fic**
Sir Gawain and the Green Knight   **398.2**
Waiting for Anya   **Fic**
War horse   **Fic**

Morris, Ann
Bread, bread, bread   **641.8**
Hats, hats, hats   **391**
Shoes, shoes, shoes   **391**
Tsunami   **959.3**

Morris, Christopher G.
(ed) Macmillan dictionary for children. *See* Macmillan dictionary for children   **423**
(ed) Macmillan first dictionary. *See* Macmillan first dictionary   **423**

Morris, Gerald, 1963-
The adventures of Sir Lancelot the Great   **Fic**

Morris, Jackie
(comp) The Barefoot book of classic poems. *See* The Barefoot book of classic poems   **821.008**
(il) Jones, S. L. Little one, we knew you'd come   **232.9**

Morris, Karyn
The Kids Can Press jumbo book of gardening   **635**

Morris, Neil, 1946-
Global warming   **363.7**

Morris, Richard T., 1969-
Bye-bye, baby!   **E**

Morris, Steveland *See* Wonder, Stevie

Morris, Taylor
Total knockout   **Fic**

Morris and Boris at the circus. Wiseman, B.   **E**

Morris the artist. Segal, L. G.   **E**

Morrison, Frank
(il) Taylor, D. A. Sweet music in Harlem   **E**
(il) Thomson, M. Keena Ford and the second-grade mixup   **Fic**
(il) Turner-Denstaedt, M. The hat that wore Clara B.   **E**

Morrison, Frank, 1971-
(il) Taylor, G. George Crum and the Saratoga chip   **92**

Morrison, Gordon
Nature in the neighborhood   **508**
Pond   **577.6**

Morrison, Jessica
Investing   **332.6**
Saving   **332.024**

Morrison, Lillian, 1917-
(comp) It rained all day that night. *See* It rained all day that night   **811.008**

Morrison, P. R.
Wind tamer   **Fic**

Morrison, Phillip
(il) Morley, C. Freaky facts about spiders   **595.4**

Morrison, Taylor, 1971-
The coast mappers   **623.89**
Wildfire   **634.9**

Morrison, Toni, 1931-
Remember   **379**
About
Haskins, J. Toni Morrison   **92**

Morris's disappearing bag. Wells, R.   **E**

Morrow, Barbara Olenyik
A good night for freedom   **E**
Mr. Mosquito put on his tuxedo   **E**

Morse, Scott
Magic Pickle   **741.5**

Morse, Susan
(jt. auth) Swinburne, S. R. The woods scientist   **591.7**

Mortensen, Denise Dowling
Good night engines   **E**

Mortensen, Lori, 1955-
In the trees, honeybees!   **595.7**
The missing monster card   **741.5**
Paul Revere's ride   **92**
Writing the U.S. Constitution   **342**
(jt. auth) Schwabacher, M. Elephants   **599.67**

Mortenson, Greg, 1957-
Listen to the wind   **371.82**
Three cups of tea   **371.82**

Morticians *See* Undertakers and undertaking

Mortimer, Anne, 1958-
(il) Lear, E. The owl and the pussycat [illustrated by Anne Mortimer]   **821**
(il) Stainton, S. I love cats   **E**

Mosaics
Harris, N. Mosaics   **738.5**

Mosel, Arlene
The funny little woman   **398.2**
Tikki Tikki Tembo   **398.2**

Moser, Barry
Psalm 23   **223**
(il) Doyen, D. Once upon a twice   **E**
(il) George, K. O. Hummingbird nest   **E**
(il) Hamilton, V. In the beginning; creation stories from around the world   **201**
(il) Hamilton, V. A ring of tricksters   **398.2**
(il) Hamilton, V. Wee Winnie Witch's Skinny   **E**
(il) Harper, D. Sit, Truman!   **E**
(il) Hodges, M. Moses   **222**
(il) Kipling, R. Just so stories   **S C**
(il) Lasky, K. A brilliant streak: the making of Mark Twain   **92**
(il) Palatini, M. Earthquack!   **E**
(il) Palatini, M. Lousy rotten stinkin' grapes   **398.2**
(jt. auth) Palatini, M. The three silly billies   **E**
(il) Pochocki, E. The blessing of the beasts   **E**
(il) Rylant, C. Appalachia   **974**
(il) Twain, M. The adventures of Tom Sawyer   **Fic**

Moser, Cara
(il) Harper, D. Sit, Truman!   **E**

Moser, Lisa
Kisses on the wind   **E**
Squirrel's world   **E**

Moses (Biblical figure)
About
Chaikin, M. Angels sweep the desert floor   **296.1**
Hodges, M. Moses   **222**

Moses, Shelia P.
Sallie Gal and the Wall-a-kee man   **Fic**

Moses, Will, 1956-
Johnny Appleseed   **92**
Raining cats and dogs   **428**
(il) O'Callahan, J. Raspberries!   **E**
(il) Will Moses Mother Goose. See Will Moses Mother Goose   **398.8**

Moses [biography of Harriet Tubman] Weatherford, C. B.   **92**

Moses goes to school. Millman, I.   **E**

Moslemism *See* Islam

Moslems *See* Muslims

Mosque. Macaulay, D.   **726**

Mosques
Khan, A. K. What you will see inside a mosque   **297.3**
Design and construction
Macaulay, D. Mosque   **726**

Mosquito bite. Siy, A.   **595.7**

Mosquitoes
Siy, A. Mosquito bite   **595.7**
Fiction
Knudsen, M. Bugged!   **E**

Morrow, B. O. Mr. Mosquito put on his tuxedo   **E**
Folklore
Aardema, V. Why mosquitoes buzz in people's ears   **398.2**

Moss, Jenny, 1958-
Winnie's war   **Fic**

Moss, Lloyd
Zin! zin! zin! a violin   **E**

Moss, Marissa
Alien Eraser to the rescue   **Fic**
Amelia's 6th-grade notebook   **Fic**
Brave Harriet [biography of Harriet Quimby]   **92**
Sky high: the true story of Maggie Gee   **92**
(il) Schwartz, D. M. G is for googol   **510**

Moss, Miriam
A babysitter for Billy Bear   **E**

Moss, Onawumi Jean
(jt. auth) McKissack, P. C. Precious and the Boo Hag   **E**

Moss gown. Hooks, W. H.   **398.2**

Mosses
Pascoe, E. Plants without seeds   **586**

Most, Bernard, 1937-
ABC T-Rex   **E**
How big were the dinosaurs   **E**
Whatever happened to the dinosaurs?   **E**

The **most** beautiful roof in the world. Lasky, K.   **577.3**

The **most** explosive science book in the universe. Watts, C.   **500**

The **most** fantastic atlas of the whole wide world by the Brainwaves. Adams, S.   **912**

The **most** important gift of all. Conway, D.   **E**

Most loved in all the world. Hegamin, T.   **E**

The **most** perfect spot. Goode, D.   **E**

Mostly Monty. Hurwitz, J.   **Fic**

The **mostly** true adventures of Homer P. Figg. Philbrick, W. R.   **Fic**

Mosz, Gosia
(il) Da Costa, D. Hanukkah moon   **E**

Motels *See* Hotels and motels

Mother and child *See* Mother-child relationship

Mother-child relationship
Konrad, M. S. Mom and me   **E**
Fiction
Appelt, K. Oh my baby, little one   **E**
Ashman, L. Mama's day   **E**
Billingsley, F. Big Bad Bunny   **E**
Bourguignon, L. Heart in the pocket   **E**
Cabrera, J. Mommy, carry me please!   **E**
Campbell, B. M. Sometimes my mommy gets angry   **E**
Carrick, C. Mothers are like that   **E**
Crumpacker, B. Alexander's pretending day   **E**
Dewdney, A. Llama, llama red pajama   **E**
Eastman, P. D. Are you my mother?   **E**
Ehrlich, A. Baby Dragon   **E**
Evans, L. Who loves the little lamb?   **E**
Fleming, D. Sleepy, oh so sleepy   **E**
Forward, T. What did you do today?   **E**

Mother-child relationship—Fiction—*Continued*

Gliori, D. Stormy weather   E
Gore, L. Mommy, where are you?   E
Hest, A. When you meet a bear on Broadway   E
Kono, E. E. Hula lullaby   E
Luebs, R. Please pick me up, Mama!   E
Macken, J. E. Waiting out the storm   E
Murphy, Y. Baby Polar   E
Newman, L. Mommy, mama, and me   E
Peacock, C. A. Mommy far, Mommy near   E
Rueda, C. My little polar bear   E
Scott, A. H. On Mother's lap   E
Segal, J. Far far away   E
Stein, D. E. Pouch!   E
Wells, R. Only you   E
Wheeler, L. Te amo, Bebé, little one   E
Wild, M. Kiss kiss!   E
Willis, J. Mommy, do you love me?   E
Wilson, K. Mama always comes home   E
Woodson, J. Coming on home soon   E

Mother-daughter relationship
Fiction

Appelt, K. Keeper   Fic
Averbeck, J. In a blue room   E
Blos, J. W. Letters from the corrugated castle   Fic
Bradby, M. Momma, where are you from?   E
Brown, S. T. Hugging the rock   Fic
Brun-Cosme, N. No, I want daddy!   E
Cadena, B. Supersister   E
Carlstrom, N. W. It's your first day of school, Annie Claire   E
Cassidy, C. Dizzy   Fic
Cheng, A. Brushing Mom's hair   Fic
Cohen, T. The invisible rules of the Zoë Lama   Fic
Demas, C. Valentine surprise   E
Deriso, C. H. Talia Talk   Fic
Dutton, S. Mary Mae and the gospel truth   Fic
Feiffer, K. My mom is trying to ruin my life   E
Gephart, D. As if being 12 3/4 isn't bad enough, my mother is running for president!   Fic
Gray, L. M. My mama had a dancing heart   E
Greenwald, L. My life in pink and green   Fic
Hahn, M. D. Deep and dark and dangerous   Fic
Hegamin, T. Most loved in all the world   E
Hollyer, B. River song   Fic
Joosse, B. M. Mama, do you love me?   E
Kadohata, C. Outside beauty   Fic
Keller, H. Miranda's beach day   E
Kimmel, E. C. School spirit   Fic
Koss, A. G. The not-so-great depression   Fic
La Chanze. Little diva   E
Lewis, R. A. Every year on your birthday   E
MacLachlan, P. Word after word after word   Fic
Madrigal, A. H. Erandi's braids   E

McGinty, A. B. Eliza's kindergarten surprise   E
Morales, Y. Little Night   E
O'Connor, J. Ready, set, skip!   E
Paratore, C. Sunny Holiday   Fic
Pearce, E. S. Isabel and the miracle baby   Fic
Peet, M. Cloud Tea monkeys   Fic
Pomerantz, C. The chalk doll   E
Ramos, J. I'm just like my mom/I'm just like my dad   E
Rao, S. My mother's sari   E
Reiser, L. Tortillas and lullabies. Tortillas y cancioncitas   E
Rim, S. Birdie's big-girl shoes   E
Rodgers, M. Freaky Friday   Fic
Rosenthal, A. K. Bedtime for Mommy   E
Schotter, R. Mama, I'll give you the world   E
Schubert, L. Feeding the sheep   E
Shimko, B. The private thoughts of Amelia E. Rye   Fic
Springer, N. Dusssie   Fic
St. Anthony, J. The summer Sherman loved me   Fic
Stauffacher, S. Harry Sue   Fic
Van Steenwyk, E. Prairie Christmas   E
Vander Zee, R. Always with you   E
Wilson, J. The illustrated Mum   Fic
Yohalem, E. Escape under the forever sky   Fic

Mother Goose

The Arnold Lobel book of Mother Goose   398.8
Favorite nursery rhymes from Mother Goose   398.8
Fitzgerald, J. Yum! yum!!   398.8
Here comes Mother Goose   398.8
Knick knack paddy whack   782.42
My very first Mother Goose   398.8
The neighborhood Mother Goose   398.8
Opie, I. A. Mother Goose's little treasures   398.8
Polacco, P. Babushka's Mother Goose   398.8
The real Mother Goose   398.8
Reinhart, M. A pop-up book of nursery rhymes   398.8
Rufus and friends: rhyme time   398.8
Sylvia Long's Mother Goose   398.8
Tomie dePaola's Mother Goose   398.8
Will Moses Mother Goose   398.8

Mother Goose numbers on the loose. Dillon, L.   398.8
Mother Goose time. Marino, J.   027.62
Mother Goose's little treasures. Opie, I. A.   398.8
Mother Jones *See* Jones, Mother, 1830-1930
Mother nature, designer. Spilsbury, L.   738
Mother poems. Smith, H. A.   811

Mother-son relationship
Fiction

Broach, E. When dinosaurs came with everything   E
Cadow, K. M. Alfie runs away   E
Downing, J. No hugs till Saturday   E

Mount Everest (China and Nepal)—*Continued*
Jenkins, S. The top of the world **796.52**
Kalz, J. Mount Everest **954.96**
Skreslet, L. To the top of Everest **796.52**
Taylor-Butler, C. Sacred mountain **954.96**

Mount Rushmore National Memorial (S.D.)
Thomas, W. Mount Rushmore **978.3**

Mountain biking
Schoenherr, A. Mountain biking **796.6**

Mountain ecology
Levy, J. Discovering mountains **577.5**

Mountain life
Fiction
Dowell, F. O. Dovey Coe **Fic**
Hemingway, E. M. Road to Tater Hill **Fic**

Mountain lions *See* Pumas

A **mountain** of mittens. Plourde, L. **E**

Mountain pose. Wilson, N. H. **Fic**

Mountaineering
Burleigh, R. Tiger of the snows [biography of Tenzing Norgay] **92**
Coburn, B. Triumph on Everest: a photobiography of Sir Edmund Hillary **92**
Jenkins, S. The top of the world **796.52**
Skreslet, L. To the top of Everest **796.52**
Fiction
Patneaude, D. A piece of the sky **Fic**
Thomas, J. R. Blind mountain **Fic**

Mountains

See also Adirondack Mountains (N.Y.); Andes; Catskill Mountains (N.Y.); Himalaya Mountains; Ozark Mountains; Rocky Mountains

Jennings, T. Massive mountains **551.4**
Levy, J. Discovering mountains **577.5**
Sheehan, T. F. Mountains **551.4**
Simon, S. Mountains **551.4**
Zoehfeld, K. W. How mountains are made **551.4**
Fiction
Lobel, A. Ming Lo moves the mountain **E**

Mourlevat, Jean-Claude
The pull of the ocean **Fic**

Mourning, Tuesday
(il) Calvert, P. Princess Peepers **E**
(il) Feldman, E. Billy and Milly, short and silly! **E**
(il) Wolf, A. Immersed in verse **808.1**

Mouse *See* Mice

Mouse. Savage, S. **599.35**

Mouse and Mole, fine feathered friends. Yee, W. H. **E**

The **mouse** and the motorcycle. Cleary, B. **Fic**

The **mouse** family Robinson. King-Smith, D. **Fic**

Mouse Guard: Fall 1152. Petersen, D. **741.5**

Mouse island. Bunting, E. **E**

Mouse mess. Riley, L. A. **E**

Mouse shapes. Walsh, E. S. **E**

Mouse soup. Lobel, A. **E**

Mouse tales. Lobel, A. **E**

The **mouse** that snored. Waber, B. **E**

Mouse was mad. Urban, L. **E**

Mousie love. Chaconas, D. **E**

Mouth
Miller, S. S. All kinds of mouths **591.4**
Souza, D. M. Look what mouths can do **573.9**
Diseases
Donovan, S. Hawk & Drool **612.3**

Mouth organs *See* Harmonicas

Move it!. Mason, A. **531**

Move over, Rover. Beaumont, K. **E**

A **movie** in my pillow. Argueta, J. **861**

Moving
Barber, N. Moving to a new house **648**
Fiction
Atkinson, E. From Alice to Zen and everyone in between **Fic**
Auch, M. J. Wing nut **Fic**
Bateson, C. Stranded in Boringsville **Fic**
Bauer, M. D. The secret of the painted house **Fic**
Cabot, M. Moving day **Fic**
Cassidy, C. Indigo Blue **Fic**
Clements, A. Lost and found **Fic**
Cody, M. Powerless **Fic**
Corriveau, A. How I, Nicky Flynn, finally get a life (and a dog) **Fic**
Croza, L. I know here **E**
Danziger, P. Amber Brown is not a crayon **Fic**
DeFelice, C. C. Signal **Fic**
Fleming, C. Lowji discovers America **Fic**
Galante, C. Willowood **Fic**
Gleeson, L. Half a world away **E**
Grimes, N. Make way for Dyamonde Daniel **Fic**
Hale, M. The truth about sparrows **Fic**
Harrington, J. N. Going north **E**
Hoberman, M. A. Strawberry Hill **Fic**
Holt, K. W. Piper Reed, Navy brat **Fic**
Hutchins, H. J. Mattland **E**
Kelly, K. Lucy Rose, here's the thing about me **Fic**
Lasky, K. Felix takes the stage **Fic**
Lewis, M. Morgy makes his move **Fic**
Lobel, A. Nini here and there **E**
Ly, M. Home is east **Fic**
Moser, L. Kisses on the wind **E**
Nixon, J. L. Laugh till you cry **Fic**
Numberman, N. Do not build a Frankenstein! **E**
Patron, S. Maybe yes, maybe no, maybe maybe **Fic**
Peck, R. A season of gifts **Fic**
Polikoff, B. G. Why does the coqui sing? **Fic**
Ritz, K. Windows with birds **E**
Rostoker-Gruber, K. Bandit **E**
Scieszka, J. Spaceheadz **Fic**
Sharmat, M. W. Gila monsters meet you at the airport **E**
Siebold, J. My nights at the Improv **Fic**
Soup, C. A whole nother story **Fic**
Spinelli, E. Where I live **Fic**
Tolan, S. S. Wishworks, Inc. **Fic**

Moving—Fiction—*Continued*
Townsend, M. Kit Feeny: on the move
    741.5
Wild, M. The little crooked house   **E**
Williams, M. The Fizzy Whiz kid   **Fic**
Wong, J. S. Homegrown house   **E**
Wynne-Jones, T. Rex Zero and the end of the world   **Fic**
Moving day. Cabot, M.   **Fic**
Moving pictures *See* Motion pictures
Moving to a new house. Barber, N.   **648**
Movsessian, Shushann
  Puberty girl   **612.6**
Moxy Maxwell does not love Stuart Little. Gifford, P. E.   **Fic**
Mozambique
  King, D. C. Mozambique   **967.9**
        Fiction
  Farmer, N. A girl named Disaster   **Fic**
Mozart, Johann Chrysostom Wolfgang Amadeus *See* Mozart, Wolfgang Amadeus, 1756-1791
Mozart, Wolfgang Amadeus, 1756-1791
        About
  Riggs, K. Wolfgang Amadeus Mozart   **92**
  Sís, P. Play, Mozart, play!   **92**
  Stanley, D. Mozart, the wonder child   **92**
  Weeks, M. Mozart   **92**
  See/See also pages in the following book(s):
  Krull, K. Lives of the musicians   **920**
Mozart, the wonder child. Stanley, D.   **92**
Mr. and Mrs. God in the Creation Kitchen. Wood, N. C.   **E**
Mr. and Mrs. Portly and their little dog Snack. Jordan, S.   **E**
Mr. Badger and Mrs. Fox [series]
  Luciani, B. The meeting   **741.5**
Mr. Chickee's funny money. Curtis, C. P.   **Fic**
Mr. Cookie Baker. Wellington, M.   **E**
Mr. Ferlinghetti's poem. Frampton, D.   **811**
Mr. George Baker. Hest, A.   **E**
Mr. Gumpy's outing. Burningham, J.   **E**
Mr. Lincoln's boys. Rabin, S.   **92**
Mr. Lincoln's way. Polacco, P.   **E**
Mr. Mosquito put on his tuxedo. Morrow, B. O.   **E**
Mr. Peek and the misunderstanding at the zoo. Waldron, K.   **E**
Mr. Popper's penguins. Atwater, R. T.   **Fic**
Mr. Putter & Tabby pour the tea. Rylant, C.   **E**
Mr. Rabbit and the lovely present. Zolotow, C.   **E**
Mr. Revere and I. Lawson, R.   **Fic**
Mr. Tucket. Paulsen, G.   **Fic**
Mr. Williams. Barbour, K.   **92**
Mr. Wolf's pancakes. Fearnley, J.   **E**
Mrs. Chicken and the hungry crocodile. Paye, W.-L.   **398.2**
Mrs. Frisby and the rats of NIMH. O'Brien, R. C.   **Fic**

Mrs. Katz and Tush. Polacco, P.   **E**
Mrs. Lincoln's dressmaker: the unlikely friendship of Elizabeth Keckley and Mary Todd Lincoln. Jones, L.   **92**
Mrs. Marlowe's mice. Asch, F.   **E**
Mrs. McCool and the giant Cuhullin. Souhami, J.   **398.2**
"**Mrs.** Riley Bought Five Itchy Aardvarks" and other painless tricks for memorizing science facts. Cleary, B. P.   **507**
Mrs. Watson wants your teeth. McGhee, A.   **E**
Mrs. Wow never wanted a cow. Freeman, M.   **E**
Ms. Frizzle's adventures: Imperial China. Cole, J.   **931**
Ms. McCaw learns to draw. Zemach, K.   **E**
Ms. Turtle the babysitter. Gorbachev, V.   **E**
Mucci, Tim
  The odyssey   **741.5**
Much ado about Grubstake. Ferris, J.   **Fic**
Mud city. Guiberson, B. Z.   **598**
The **mud** pony. Cohen, C. L.   **398.2**
Mudball. Tavares, M.   **E**
Mudd-Ruth, Maria
  Owls   **598**
Muddy as a duck puddle and other American similes. Lawlor, L.   **425**
Mudshark. Paulsen, G.   **Fic**
Mueller, Doris L.
  The best nest   **398.2**
Mufaro's beautiful daughters. Steptoe, J.   **398.2**
Muggie Maggie. Cleary, B.   **Fic**
Muḥammad, d. 632
        About
  Demi. Muhammad   **297**
Muhammad Ali. Winter, J.   **92**
Muhammad ibn 'Abd Allāh ibn Baṭūṭah *See* Ibn Battuta, 1304-1377
Muhammedanism *See* Islam
Muhammedans *See* Muslims
Muir, John, 1838-1914
        About
  Lasky, K. John Muir   **92**
  Wadsworth, G. Camping with the president [biography of Theodore Roosevelt]   **92**
        Fiction
  McCully, E. A. Squirrel and John Muir   **E**
Muktar and the camels. Graber, J.   **E**
Mule train mail. Brown, C. M.   **383**
Müller, Daniel
  (il) Hucke, J. Pip in the Grand Hotel   **E**
Mullins, Patricia
  (il) Fox, M. Hattie and the fox   **E**
Multicultural and ethnic children's literature in the United States. Gilton, D. L.   **028.5**
Multicultural crafts kids can do! [series]
  Robinson, F. Hispanic-American crafts kids can do!   **745.5**

Musgrove, Margaret, 1943-
Ashanti to Zulu: African traditions 960
Mushrooms
See also Fungi
Royston, A. Life cycle of a mushroom
579.6
Music
Aliki. Ah, music! 780
Nathan, A. Meet the musicians 780
Parker, S. The science of sound 534
Sabbeth, A. Rubber-band banjos and a java jive bass 781
Analysis, appreciation
See Music appreciation
Fiction
Bass, L. G. Boom boom go away! E
Celenza, A. H. Gershwin's Rhapsody in Blue
E
Cummings, P. Boom bah! E
Galante, C. Hershey herself Fic
McPhail, D. M. Mole music E
Pritchett, D. The first music E
Schuch, S. A symphony of whales E
Tashiro, C. Five nice mice E
Poetry
Carnival of the animals 811.008
Study and teaching
Carlow, R. Exploring the connection between children's literature and music 372
Australia
Underwood, D. Australia, Hawaii, and the Pacific 780.9
Caribbean region
Solway, A. Latin America and the Caribbean
780.9
Europe
Allen, P. Europe 780.94
Hawaii
Underwood, D. Australia, Hawaii, and the Pacific 780.9
Latin America
Solway, A. Latin America and the Caribbean
780.9
Oceania
Underwood, D. Australia, Hawaii, and the Pacific 780.9
Music, African *See* African music
Music, African American *See* African American music
Music, Gospel *See* Gospel music
Music and art *See* Art and music
Music appreciation
Ganeri, A. The young person's guide to the orchestra 784.2
Music education *See* Music—Study and teaching
Music industry
Vocational guidance
Miles, L. Making a recording 781.49
Music, music for everyone. Williams, V. B. E
Music throughout history [series]
Norton, J. R. Haydn's world 92
Viegas, J. Beethoven's world 92

Musical instruments
D'Cruz, A.-M. Make your own musical instruments 784.19
Ganeri, A. The young person's guide to the orchestra 784.2
Helsby, G. Those amazing musical instruments
784.19
Koscielniak, B. The story of the incredible orchestra 784.2
Moss, L. Zin! zin! zin! a violin E
Rissman, R. Shapes in music 516
Sabbeth, A. Rubber-band banjos and a java jive bass 781
Wiseman, A. S. Making music 784.19
Fiction
Bartlett, T. C. Tuba lessons E
Cox, J. My family plays music E
Snicket, L. The composer is dead E
Folkore
Ōtsuka, Y. Suho's white horse 398.2
Musicals
See also Operetta
Boynton, S. Philadelphia chickens 782.42
Musicians
See also Composers; Women musicians
George-Warren, H. Honky-tonk heroes & hillbilly angels 920
George-Warren, H. Shake, rattle, & roll 920
Lord, M. A song for Cambodia [biography of Arn Chorn-Pond] 92
Nathan, A. Meet the musicians 780
Fiction
Bateman, T. Harp o' gold E
Blume, L. M. M. The rising star of Rusty Nail
Fic
Calmenson, S. Jazzmatazz! E
Conover, C. Over the hills & far away E
Cox, J. My family plays music E
Crow, K. Cool Daddy Rat E
Edwards, P. D. The leprechaun's gold E
Fenner, C. Yolonda's genius Fic
Greene, J. D. The secret shofar of Barcelona
Fic
Isadora, R. Ben's trumpet E
MacLachlan, P. The facts and fictions of Minna Pratt Fic
Martin, B. The maestro plays E
Pinfold, L. The Django E
Seeger, P. The deaf musicians E
Sklansky, A. E. The duck who played the kazoo
E
Stewart, J. Addis Berner Bear forgets E
Urban, L. A crooked kind of perfect Fic
Zemach, K. Just enough and not too much
E
Folklore
Shepard, A. The sea king's daughter 398.2
Musicians, African American *See* African American musicians
The **musicians** of Bremen. Puttapipat, N.
398.2
Musicians of the sun. McDermott, G. 398.2
Muskrats
Fiction
Chaconas, D. Cork & Fuzz E

My first Hebrew word book. Groner, J. S.
492.4

My first horse. Bozzo, L.   636.1

My first horse and pony book. Draper, J.
636.1

My first horse and pony care book. Draper, J.
636.1

My first I can read book [series]
  Bonsall, C. N. The day I had to play with my
  sister   E
  Bonsall, C. N. Mine's the best   E
  Capucilli, A. Biscuit's new trick   E
  Grant, J. Chicken said, Cluck!   E
  Schaefer, L. M. Loose tooth   E

My first Internet guide. Oxlade, C.   004.6

My first Kwanzaa book. Chocolate, D.   394.26

My first monologue book. Dabrowski, K.   812

My first pet library from the American Humane Association [series]
  Bozzo, L. My first bird   636.6
  Bozzo, L. My first cat   636.8
  Bozzo, L. My first dog   636.7
  Bozzo, L. My first fish   639.34
  Bozzo, L. My first guinea pig and other small
  pets   636.9
  Bozzo, L. My first horse   636.1

My first prayers. Brooks, J.   242

My first Ramadan. Katz, K.   E

My first Spanish English visual dictionary. Corbeil, J.-C.   463

My first word book. Wilkes, A.   E

My five senses. Aliki   612.8

My football book. Gibbons, G.   796.332

My friend [series]
  McQuinn, A. My friend Jamal   E
  McQuinn, A. My friend Mei Jing   E

My friend Jamal. McQuinn, A.   E

My friend Mei Jing. McQuinn, A.   E

My friend Rabbit. Rohmann, E.   E

My friend, the enemy. Cheaney, J. B.   Fic

My friend, the starfinder. Lyon, G. E.   E

My frozen valentine. Fein, E.   Fic

My garden. Henkes, K.   E

My goose Betsy. Braun, T.   E

My grandpa had a stroke. Butler, D. H.   E

My granny went to market. Blackstone, S.   E

My great-aunt Arizona. Houston, G.   E

My hands. Aliki   612

My haunted house. Sage, A.   Fic

My health [series]
  Silverstein, A. Can you see the chalkboard?
     617.7
  Silverstein, A. Sleep   612.8

My heart glow: Alice Cogswell, Thomas Gallaudet and the birth of American sign language. McCully, E. A.   92

My heart is like a zoo. Hall, M.   E

My hippie grandmother. Lindbergh, R.   E

My hippo has the hiccups. Nesbitt, K.   811

My last best friend. Bowe, J.   Fic

My life as a chicken. Kelley, E. A.   E

My life as a fifth-grade comedian. Levy, E.
Fic

My life in dog years. Paulsen, G.   92

My life in pink and green. Greenwald, L.   Fic

My life with the Lincolns. Brandeis, G.   Fic

My light. Bang, M.   621.47

My little polar bear. Rueda, C.   E

My little round house. Baasansuren, B.   E

My lucky day. Kasza, K.   E

My mama had a dancing heart. Gray, L. M.   E

My Mei Mei. Young, E.   E

My mom. Browne, A.   E

My mom is trying to ruin my life. Feiffer, K.
E

My mommy is magic. Norac, C.   E

My mom's having a baby!. Butler, D. H.
612.6

My mother's sari. Rao, S.   E

My mummy is magic. See Norac, C. My mommy is magic   E

My name is brain Brian. Betancourt, J.   Fic

My name is Gabito: the life of Gabriel Garcia Márquez. Brown, M.   92

My name is Georgia [biography of Georgia O'Keeffe] Winter, J.   92

My name is Sally Little Song. Woods, B.   Fic

My name is Sangoel. Williams, K. L.   E

My name is Yoon. Recorvits, H.   E

My nights at the Improv. Siebold, J.   Fic

My one hundred adventures. Horvath, P.   Fic

My papa Diego and me [biography of Diego Rivera] Rivera Marín, G.   92

My parents are divorced, my elbows have nicknames, and other facts about me. Cochran, B.
E

My penguin Osbert. Kimmel, E. C.   E

My people. Hughes, L.   811

My pet [series]
  Craats, R. Gecko   639.3
  Foran, J. Guinea pig   636.9
  Hamilton, L. Ferret   636.97
  Hamilton, L. Turtle   639.3
  Lomberg, M. Horse   636.1

My pets [series]
  Lomberg, M. Spider   639

My pig Amarillo. Ichikawa, S.   E

My pony Jack. Meister, C.   E

My preschool. Rockwell, A. F.   E

My pup. O'Hair, M.   E

My race car. Rex, M.   629.228

My robot. Bunting, E.   E

My rotten life. Lubar, D.   Fic

My rotten redheaded older brother. Polacco, P.
E

My rows and piles of coins. Mollel, T. M.   E

My school in the rain forest. Ruurs, M.   370.9

Native Americans

See also Taino Indians; Zapotec Indians names of Native American peoples and linguistic families

A Braid of lives · **970.004**

Dennis, Y. W. Children of native America today · **970.004**

Goble, P. All our relatives · **970.004**

January, B. Native American art & culture · **709.7**

January, B. Native Americans · **709.7**

King, D. C. First people · **970.004**

McNeese, T. The fascinating history of American Indians · **970.004**

Molin, P. F. American Indian stereotypes in the world of children · **970.004**

Murdoch, D. H. North American Indian · **970.004**

Swamp, J. Giving thanks · **299.7**

See/See also pages in the following book(s):

Freedman, R. Children of the wild West · **978**

Antiquities

Quigley, M. Mesa Verde · **978.8**

Biography

Brimner, L. D. Chief Crazy Horse · **92**

Brown, D. Bright path [biography of Jim Thorpe] · **92**

Bruchac, J. Buffalo song [biography of Walking Coyote] · **92**

Capaldi, G. A boy named Beckoning: the true story of Dr. Carlos Montezuma, Native American hero · **92**

Freedman, R. Indian chiefs · **920**

Rappaport, D. We are the many · **920**

Weber, E. N. R. Rattlesnake Mesa · **92**

Wise, B. Louis Sockalexis · **92**

Fiction

Armstrong, A. Raleigh's page · **Fic**

Baker, O. Where the buffaloes begin · **Fic**

Broyles, A. Priscilla and the hollyhocks · **E**

Bruchac, J. The arrow over the door · **Fic**

Campbell, N. I. Shi-shi-etko · **E**

Dorris, M. Sees Behind Trees · **Fic**

Goble, P. Beyond the ridge · **Fic**

Helgerson, J. Crows & cards · **Fic**

Howard, E. The crimson cap · **Fic**

Martin, B. Knots on a counting rope · **E**

O'Dell, S. Island of the Blue Dolphins · **Fic**

O'Dell, S. Streams to the river, river to the sea · **Fic**

Smith, C. L. Indian shoes · **Fic**

Speare, E. G. The sign of the beaver · **Fic**

Young, J. Minnow and Rose · **Fic**

Folklore

Bruchac, J. The girl who helped thunder and other Native American folktales · **398.2**

Bruchac, J. Between earth & sky · **398.2**

Bruchac, J. How Chipmunk got his stripes · **398.2**

Bruchac, J. Thirteen moons on a turtle's back · **811**

Caduto, M. J. Keepers of the night · **398.2**

Curry, J. L. Hold up the sky: and other Native American tales from Texas and the Southern Plains · **398.2**

De Paola, T. The legend of the Indian paintbrush · **398.2**

Delacre, L. Golden tales · **398.2**

Goble, P. Buffalo woman · **398.2**

Goble, P. The girl who loved wild horses · **398.2**

Goble, P. The legend of the White Buffalo Woman · **398.2**

James, E. The woman who married a bear · **398.2**

Longfellow, H. W. Hiawatha · **811**

McDermott, G. Coyote: a trickster tale from the American Southwest · **398.2**

McDermott, G. Jabuti the tortoise · **398.2**

McDermott, G. Raven · **398.2**

Steptoe, J. The story of Jumping Mouse · **398.2**

Taylor, C. J. Spirits, fairies, and merpeople · **398.2**

Trickster: Native American tales · **398.2**

Van Laan, N. The magic bean tree · **398.2**

Zoe, T. Living stories · **970.004**

Folklore—Mexico

Endredy, J. The journey of Tunuri and the Blue Deer · **398.2**

History

Connolly, S. The Americas and the Pacific · **970.004**

Dennis, Y. W. A kid's guide to native American history · **970.004**

Mann, C. C. Before Columbus · **970.01**

Origin

Mann, C. C. Before Columbus · **970.01**

Poetry

Bruchac, J. Thirteen moons on a turtle's back · **811**

Dancing teepees: poems of American Indian youth · **897**

Longfellow, H. W. Hiawatha · **811**

Rites and ceremonies

Ancona, G. Powwow · **970.004**

Wars

See also United States—History—1755-1763, French and Indian War

Anderson, P. C. George Armstrong Custer · **92**

Custer, E. B. The diary of Elizabeth Bacon Custer · **973.8**

Ehrlich, A. Wounded Knee: an Indian history of the American West · **970.004**

Canada

Andre, J.-A. We feel good out here · **970.004**

McLeod, T. The Delta is my home · **970.004**

Zoe, T. Living stories · **970.004**

Central America

See also Mayas

Great Plains

Freedman, R. Buffalo hunt · **970.004**

January, B. Little Bighorn, June 25, 1876 · **973.8**

Patent, D. H. The buffalo and the Indians · **978**

Terry, M. B. H. Daily life in a Plains Indian village, 1868 · **970.004**

Naval history

    See also Military history

Navigation

  Borden, L. Sea clocks   **526**

  Kirk, S. T is for tugboat   **623.82**

  Lasky, K. The man who made time travel
    526

  Young, K. R. Across the wide ocean   **623.89**

        Fiction

  Frederick, H. V. The voyage of Patience

  Goodspeed   **Fic**

Nayar, Nandini

  What should I make?   **E**

Naylor, Phyllis Reynolds, 1933-

  Emily's fortune   **Fic**

  Faith, hope, and Ivy June   **Fic**

  The grand escape   **Fic**

  Patches and scratches   **Fic**

  Roxie and the Hooligans   **Fic**

  Shiloh   **Fic**

  Starting with Alice   **Fic**

Nazism *See* National socialism

Nazoa, Aquiles, 1920-1976

  A small Nativity   **E**

NBA *See* National Basketball Association

Neal-Schuman guide to celebrations & holidays

  around the world. Matthew, K. I.   **394.26**

Near East *See* Middle East

The **neat** line. Edwards, P. D.   **E**

Neatness *See* Cleanliness

Nebraska

        Fiction

  Bunting, E. Dandelions   **E**

  Clements, A. Room one   **Fic**

  Conrad, P. My Daniel   **Fic**

  LaFaye, A. Worth   **Fic**

  Van Steenwyk, E. Prairie Christmas   **E**

Nebulae, Extragalactic *See* Galaxies

The **Neddiad**. Pinkwater, D. M.   **Fic**

Ned's new home. Tseng, K.   **E**

Nedwidek, John

  Ducks don't wear socks   **E**

Needham, Tom

  Albert Pujols   **92**

Needlework

  The jumbo book of needlecrafts   **746.4**

Neel, Alexandra David- *See* David-Neel, Alexandra, 1868-1969

Neely, Keith, 1943-

  (il) Krasner, S. Play ball like the hall of famers
    796.357

Negotiation

    See also Conflict management

A **Negro** league scrapbook. Weatherford, C. B.
    796.357

Negro leagues

  Nelson, K. We are the ship   **796.357**

  Weatherford, C. B. A Negro league scrapbook
    796.357

The **Negro** speaks of rivers. Hughes, L.   **811**

Neidigh, Sherry

  (il) Evert, L. Birds of prey   **598**

  (il) Hawk, F. Count down to Fall   **508.2**

  (il) Mueller, D. L. The best nest   **398.2**

Neighborhood *See* Community life

The **neighborhood** Mother Goose   **398.8**

Neighborhood odes. Soto, G.   **811**

Neil Armstrong is my uncle. Marino, N.   **Fic**

Neilan, Eujin Kim

  (il) Pringle, L. P. Imagine a dragon   **398.2**

  (il) Thong, R. Fly free!   **E**

Neitzel, Shirley

  The jacket I wear in the snow   **E**

Nelson, Annika

  (il) Soto, G. Canto familiar   **811**

Nelson, Drew, 1952-

  (jt. auth) Nelson, V. M. Juneteenth   **394.26**

Nelson, Horatio Nelson, Viscount, 1758-1805

        Fiction

  Cooper, S. Victory   **Fic**

Nelson, Jon, Ph.D.

  (jt. auth) Cassino, M. The story of snow
    551.57

Nelson, Kadir

  He's got the whole world in his hands
    782.25

  We are the ship   **796.357**

  (il) Allen, D. Dancing in the wings   **E**

  (il) Grifalconi, A. The village that vanished
    E

  (il) Jordan, D. Salt in his shoes   **E**

  (il) Levine, E. Henry's freedom box   **E**

  (il) Napoli, D. J. Mama Miti: Wangari Maathai
    and the trees of Kenya   **92**

  (il) Nolen, J. Big Jabe   **E**

  (il) Nolen, J. Hewitt Anderson's great big life
    E

  (il) Nolen, J. Thunder Rose   **E**

  (il) Obama, B. Change has come   **328.73**

  (jt. auth) Rappaport, D. Abe's honest words
    92

  (il) Robinson, S. Testing the ice: a true story
    about Jackie Robinson   **92**

  (il) Shange, N. Coretta Scott [King]   **92**

  (il) Shange, N. Ellington was not a street   **E**

  (il) Staines, B. All God's critters   **782.42**

  (il) Weatherford, C. B. Moses [biography of
    Harriet Tubman]   **92**

Nelson, Marilyn, 1946-

  Beautiful ballerina   **792.8**

  Snook alone   **E**

  Sweethearts of rhythm   **811**

Nelson, Nina

  Bringing the boy home   **Fic**

Nelson, S. D.

  Black Elk's vision   **92**

  (il) Bruchac, J. Crazy Horse's vision   **E**

Nelson, Scott Reynolds

  Ain't nothing but a man [biography of John
    William Henry]   **92**

Nelson, Sharlene P.

  Jedediah Smith   **92**

Nelson, Ted W.

  (jt. auth) Nelson, S. P. Jedediah Smith   **92**

Newberry, Clare Turlay, 1903-1970—*Continued*
Marshmallow   E
Newbery, Linda, 1952-
At the firefly gate   Fic
Lost boy   Fic
Posy!   E
The **Newbery/Printz** companion. Gillespie, J. T.
    028.5
The **Newbery** and Caldecott awards   028.5
Newbery Medal
Gillespie, J. T. The Newbery/Printz companion
    028.5
The Newbery and Caldecott awards   028.5
Wilkin, B. T. African and African American images in Newbery Award winning titles
    810.9

Newbery Medal titles
Armstrong, W. H. Sounder   Fic
Avi. Crispin: the cross of lead   Fic
Blos, J. W. A gathering of days: a New England girl's journal, 1830-32   Fic
Brink, C. R. Caddie Woodlawn   Fic
Byars, B. C. The summer of the swans   Fic
Cleary, B. Dear Mr. Henshaw   Fic
Coatsworth, E. J. The cat who went to heaven
    Fic
Cooper, S. The grey king   Fic
Creech, S. Walk two moons   Fic
Curtis, C. P. Bud, not Buddy   Fic
Cushman, K. The midwife's apprentice   Fic
De Angeli, M. L. The door in the wall   Fic
DeJong, M. The wheel on the school   Fic
DiCamillo, K. The tale of Despereaux   Fic
Du Bois, W. P. The twenty-one balloons
    Fic
Estes, E. Ginger Pye   Fic
Field, R. Hitty: her first hundred years   Fic
Fleischman, P. Joyful noise: poems for two voices   811
Fleischman, S. The whipping boy   Fic
Freedman, R. Lincoln: a photobiography   92
George, J. C. Julie of the wolves   Fic
Hamilton, V. M.C. Higgins, the great   Fic
Henry, M. King of the wind   Fic
Hesse, K. Out of the dust   Fic
Kadohata, C. Kira-Kira   Fic
Keith, H. Rifles for Watie   Fic
Konigsburg, E. L. From the mixed-up files of Mrs. Basil E. Frankweiler   Fic
Konigsburg, E. L. The view from Saturday
    Fic
Krumgold, J. Onion John   Fic
Lawson, R. Rabbit Hill   Fic
L'Engle, M. A wrinkle in time   Fic
Lowry, L. The giver   Fic
Lowry, L. Number the stars   Fic
MacLachlan, P. Sarah, plain and tall   Fic
Naylor, P. R. Shiloh   Fic
Neville, E. C. It's like this, Cat   Fic
O'Brien, R. C. Mrs. Frisby and the rats of NIMH   Fic
O'Dell, S. Island of the Blue Dolphins   Fic
Park, L. S. A single shard   Fic
Paterson, K. Bridge to Terabithia   Fic
Patron, S. The higher power of Lucky   Fic
Peck, R. A year down yonder   Fic

Perkins, L. R. Criss cross   Fic
Raskin, E. The Westing game   Fic
Rylant, C. Missing May   Fic
Sachar, L. Holes   Fic
Sawyer, R. Roller skates   Fic
Schlitz, L. A. Good masters! Sweet ladies!
    940.1
Seredy, K. The white stag   Fic
Speare, E. G. The bronze bow   Fic
Speare, E. G. The witch of Blackbird Pond
    Fic
Sperry, A. Call it courage   Fic
Spinelli, J. Maniac Magee   Fic
Taylor, M. D. Roll of thunder, hear my cry
    Fic
Treviño, E. B. d. I, Juan de Pareja   Fic
Vining, E. G. Adam of the road   Fic
Voigt, C. Dicey's song   Fic
Willard, N. A visit to William Blake's inn
    811
Wojciechowska, M. Shadow of a bull   Fic
Yates, E. Amos Fortune, free man   92
Newbigging, Martha
(il) Bourgeois, P. The dirt on dirt   631.4
(il) Coulter, L. Ballplayers and bonesetters
    972
(il) Coulter, L. Cowboys and coffin makers
    331.7
(il) Galloway, P. Archers, alchemists, and 98 other medieval jobs you might have loved or loathed   940.1
(il) Shulman, M. Attack of the killer video book
    778.59
Newcomb, Rain
Is my hamster wild?   636.9
Smash it! crash it! launch it!   507.8
(jt. auth) Gunter, V. A. Pet science   636
(jt. auth) Rhatigan, J. Out-of-this-world astronomy   520
(jt. auth) Rhatigan, J. Prize-winning science fair projects for curious kids   507.8
Newcome, Zita, 1959-
Head, shoulders, knees, and toes   E
Newfoundland
    Fiction
Harlow, J. H. Secret of the night ponies   Fic
Harlow, J. H. Star in the storm   Fic
Tilly, M. Porcupine   Fic
Newgarden, Mark
Bow-Wow bugs a bug   E
Newhouse, Maxwell, 1947-
The house that Max built   690
(il) Lunn, J. L. S. Laura Secord: a story of courage   Fic
Newland, Gillian
(il) Bogart, J. E. Big and small, room for all
    E
Newman, Colin
(il) Greenaway, T. Crabs   595.3
(il) Greenaway, T. Whales   599.5
Newman, Jeff, 1976-
The boys   E
Newman, Lesléa
The best cat in the world   E
Daddy, papa, and me   E

Newman, Lesléa—*Continued*
A fire engine for Ruthie   E
Hachiko waits   Fic
Mommy, mama, and me   E
Newman, Patricia, 1958-
Nugget on the flight deck   E
Newman, Sandra, 1965-
The Inca empire   985
Newman, Shirlee Petkin, 1924-
Child slavery in modern times   326
Newmark, Ann
Chemistry   540
Newquist, H. P. (Harvey P.)
(jt. auth) Aronson, M. For boys only   031.02
Newquist, Harvey P. *See* Newquist, H. P. (Harvey P.)
Newsboys *See* Newspaper carriers
Newsgirl. Ketchum, L.   Fic
Newspaper carriers
Brown, D. Kid Blink beats the world   331.3
Fiction
Corbett, S. The last newspaper boy in America   Fic
Pilkey, D. The paperboy   E
Newspapers
See also Journalism; Periodicals
Fiction
Butler, D. H. The truth about Truman School   Fic
Clements, A. The Landry News   Fic
Newton, Sir Isaac, 1642-1727
About
Anderson, M. J. Isaac Newton   92
Hollihan, K. L. Isaac Newton and physics for kids   92
Krull, K. Isaac Newton   92
Steele, P. Isaac Newton   92
See/See also pages in the following book(s):
Fradin, D. B. With a little luck   509
Newton, John, 1725-1807
About
Granfield, L. Out of slavery   264
Newts
Goldish, M. Little newts   597.8
The **Nexi** robot. Allman, T.   629.8
The **next-door** dogs. Rodowsky, C. F.   Fic
Nez, John A.
Cromwell Dixon's Sky-Cycle   E
The **Nez** Perce. King, D. C.   970.004
Nez Percé Indians
Englar, M. Chief Joseph, 1840-1904   92
King, D. C. The Nez Perce   970.004
See/See also pages in the following book(s):
Freedman, R. Indian chiefs   920
Nezahualcóyotl, King of Texcoco, 1402-1472
About
Serrano, F. The poet king of Tezcoco [biography of Nezahualcóyotl]   92
NFL *See* National Football League
NFL today [series]
LeBoutillier, N. The story of the Chicago Bears   796.332

Ngawang Lobsang Yishey Tenzing Gyatso *See* Dalai Lama XIV, 1935-
NgCheong-Lum, Roseline, 1962-
France   944
Tahiti   996
Nguyen, Duy
Creepy crawly animal origami   736
Monster origami   736
Origami birds   736
Under the sea origami   736
Nguyen, Vincent
(il) Derby, S. Whoosh went the wind!   E
(il) Kimmel, E. A. Little Britches and the rattlers   E
(il) Rostoker-Gruber, K. Bandit   E
Nhem, Sopaul, 1987-
(il) Smith, I. Half spoon of rice   Fic
Niagara Falls (N.Y. and Ont.)
Fiction
Becker, S. Manny's cows   E
Nibble nibble. Brown, M. W.   811
Nibbles: a green tale. Middleton, C.   E
Nibbling on Einstein's brain. Swanson, D.   500
Nibley, Lydia
(jt. auth) Martin, R. The mysteries of Beethoven's hair   92
Nic Bishop butterflies and moths. Bishop, N.   595.7
Nic Bishop frogs. Bishop, N.   597.8
Nic Bishop marsupials. Bishop, N.   599.2
Nicaragua
Kott, J. Nicaragua   972.85
Folklore
See Folklore—Nicaragua
Niccolini's song. Wilcoxen, C.   E
Nicholas, Saint, Bishop of Myra
About
Demi. The legend of Saint Nicholas   92
Nicholas. Goscinny   Fic
Nicholls, Calvin
(il) Martin, R. The world before this one   398.2
Nicholls, Sally, 1983-
Ways to live forever   Fic
Nichols, Judy, 1947-
Storytimes for two-year-olds   027.62
Nichols, Michael, 1952-
Face to face with gorillas   599.8
Nicholson, Dorinda Makanaōnalani
Remember World War II   940.53
Nicholson, Sir William, 1872-1949
(il) Bianco, M. W. The velveteen rabbit   Fic
Nickle, John
Alphabet explosion!   793.73
(il) Barrett, J. Never take a shark to the dentist and other things not to do   E
Nicklin, Flip
Face to face with dolphins   599.5
Face to face with whales   599.5
Nicklin, Linda
(jt. auth) Nicklin, F. Face to face with dolphins   599.5

Nicklin, Linda—*Continued*
  (jt. auth) Nicklin, F. Face to face with whales
                        599.5

Nicknames
              Fiction
  Katz, K. Princess Baby   E
  Korman, G. The sixth grade nickname game
                        Fic
Nicky Deuce. Schirripa, S. R.   **Fic**
Nicola, Christos
  (jt. auth) Taylor, P. L. The secret of Priest's
    Grotto   **940.53**
Nielsen, Susin
  Word nerd   **Fic**
Niem, Thay Phap
  (jt. auth) Marsden, C. The Buddha's diamonds
                        Fic
Niemann, Christoph
  Pet dragon   E
  The police cloud   E
  Subway   E
Niepold, Mil
  Oooh! Matisse   **759.4**
  Oooh! Picasso   **730.9**
Niger
  Seffal, R. Niger   **966.26**
Nigeria
  Giles, B. Nigeria   **966.9**
  Levy, P. Nigeria   **966.9**
  Murphy, P. J. Nigeria   **966.9**
  Oluonye, M. N. Nigeria   **966.9**
  Onyefulu, I. Ikenna goes to Nigeria **966.9**
              Fiction
  Saint-Lot, K. N. Amadi's snowman E
             Folklore
    See Folklore—Nigeria
Nigg, Joe
  How to raise and keep a dragon **Fic**
Night
    See also Bedtime; Day
  Bailey, J. Sun up, sun down   **525**
  Fraser, M. A. Where are the night animals?
                     591.5
  Krautwurst, T. Night science for kids **591.5**
  Murphy, S. J. It's about time!   **529**
  Rau, D. M. Day and night   **508**
  Rose, D. L. One nighttime sea E
             Fiction
  Banks, K. And if the moon could talk E
  Banks, K. The night worker   E
  Bauer, M. D. The longest night   E
  Bean, J. At night   E
  Bonsall, C. N. Who's afraid of the dark? E
  Burningham, J. It's a secret   E
  Davies, J. The night is singing   E
  Dunbar, J. The monster who ate darkness E
  Edwards, P. D. While the world is sleeping
                    E
  Emberley, B. Night's nice   E
  Ericsson, J. A. Whoo goes there? E
  Ford, B. First snow   E
  Fox, M. Night noises   E
  Gal, S. Night lights   E
  Hartland, J. Night shift   E

Hopgood, T. Wow! said the owl   E
Juan, A. The Night Eater   E
Monfreid, D. d. Dark night   E
Morales, Y. Little Night   E
Peters, L. W. Frankie works the night shift
                     E
Shulevitz, U. So sleepy story   E
Swanson, S. M. The house in the night E
Teague, D. Franklin's big dreams   E
Thompson, L. Polar bear night   E
Thomson, S. L. Imagine a night   E
Weston, C. If a chicken stayed for supper E
              Folklore
Caduto, M. J. Keepers of the night   **398.2**
              Poetry
Sidman, J. Dark Emperor and other poems of
  the night   **811**
Night at the fair. Crews, D.   E
The **night** before Christmas [illustrated by Rachel
  Isadora] Moore, C. C.   **811**
The **night** before Christmas [illustrated by Richard
  Jesse Watson] Moore, C. C.   **811**
Night boat to freedom. Raven, M.   E
The **night** crossing. Ackerman, K.   **Fic**
The **Night** Eater. Juan, A.   E
The **night** fairy. Schlitz, L. A.   **Fic**
Night golf. Miller, W.   E
The **Night** has ears   **398.9**
The **night** is singing. Davies, J.   E
The **night** journey. Lasky, K.   **Fic**
Night lights. Gal, S.   E
Night noises. Fox, M.   E
The **night** of Las Posadas. De Paola, T. E
Night of the howling dogs. Salisbury, G. **Fic**
Night of the Moon. Khan, H.   E
Night of the Veggie Monster. McClements, G.
                     E
Night running. Carbone, E. L.   E
Night science for kids. Krautwurst, T. **591.5**
Night shift. Hartland, J.   E
Night shift daddy. Spinelli, E.   E
Night wings. Bruchac, J.   **Fic**
The **night** worker. Banks, K.   E
Nightingale, Florence, 1820-1910
              About
  Gorrell, G. K. Heart and soul: the story of Flor-
    ence Nightingale   **92**
The **nightingale**. Mitchell, S.   **Fic**
The **nightingale**. Pinkney, J.   **Fic**
Nightingales
              Fiction
  Mitchell, S. The nightingale   **Fic**
  Pinkney, J. The nightingale   **Fic**
Nightmares: poems to trouble your sleep.
  Prelutsky, J.   **811**
Night's nice. Emberley, B.   E
Nights of the pufflings. McMillan, B. **598**
Nikki & Deja. English, K.   **Fic**
Nikola-Lisa, W.
  Magic in the margins   E

Nikola-Lisa, W.—*Continued*
Setting the turkeys free — E
The **Nile**. Bowden, R. — 962
The **Nile**. Heinrichs, A. — 962

Nile River
Bowden, R. The Nile — 962
Heinrichs, A. The Nile — 962

Nile River valley
Bowden, R. The Nile — 962
Heinrichs, A. The Nile — 962

Nimmo, Jenny, 1944-
Midnight for Charlie Bone — Fic
The snow spider — Fic

The **Niña**, the Pinta, and the vanishing treasure. Santopolo, J. — Fic

Nine-in-one, Grr! Grr!. Blia Xiong — 398.2

The **nine** lives of Aristotle. King-Smith, D. — Fic

Nineteen girls and me. See Pattison, D. S. 19 girls and me — E

Ninety miles to Havana. See Flores-Galbis, E. 90 miles to Havana — Fic

Nini here and there. Lobel, A. — E

Ninja
Fiction
Bruins, D. The legend of Ninja Cowboy Bear — E
Phillipps, J. C. Wink — E

Ninth book of junior authors and illustrators — 920.003

Nirgiotis, Nicholas
Killer ants — 595.7

Nishizuka, Koko
The beckoning cat — 398.2

Nit-pickin'. Van Laan, N. — E

Niven, Penelope
Carl Sandburg: adventures of a poet — 92

Nivola, Claire A., 1947-
Planting the trees of Kenya — 92
(il) Friedman, R. The silent witness — 973.7
(il) Glaser, L. Emma's poem — 974.7

Nix, Garth, 1963-
One beastly beast — S C
The **Nixie's** song. DiTerlizzi, T. — Fic

Nixon, Joan Lowery, 1927-2003
A family apart — Fic
Laugh till you cry — Fic

Nixon, Richard M. (Richard Milhous), 1913-1994
About
Aronson, B. Richard M. Nixon — 92

Njinga *See* Nzinga, Queen of Matamba, 1582-1663

No!. McPhail, D. M. — E

No backbone!: The world of invertebrates [series]
Camisa, K. Hairy tarantulas — 595.4
Goldish, M. Deadly praying mantises — 595.7
Goldish, M. Smelly stink bugs — 595.7
Lunis, N. Deadly black widows — 595.4

No backbones! the world of invertebrates [series]
Lunis, N. Prickly sea stars — 593.9

No better hope. Ashabranner, B. K. — 975.3

No castles here. Bauer, A. C. E. — Fic

No, David!. Shannon, D. — E

No easy way. Bowen, F. — 92

No fighting, no biting!. Minarik, E. H. — E

No girls allowed (dogs okay). Trueit, T. S. — Fic

No hugs till Saturday. Downing, J. — E

No, I want daddy!. Brun-Cosme, N. — E

No laughing, no smiling, no giggling. Stevenson, J. — E

No matter what. Dodd, E. — E

No matter what. Gliori, D. — E

No more!. Rappaport, D. — 326

No more blanket for Lambkin. Ford, B. — E

No more bottles for Bunny!. Ford, B. — E

No more diapers for Ducky!. Ford, B. — E

No more pumpkins. Catalanotto, P. — Fic

No mush today. Derby, S. — E

No one saw. Raczka, B. — 759.06

No talking. Clements, A. — Fic

No! that's wrong!. Ji Zhaohua — E

Noah (Biblical figure)
See/See also pages in the following book(s):
Brett, J. On Noah's ark — E
Fiction
Krensky, S. Noah's bark — E

Noah's ark
Spier, P. Noah's ark — 222
Stewig, J. W. The animals watched — 222
Fiction
Brett, J. On Noah's ark — E
Eitzen, R. Tara's flight — E
Krensky, S. Noah's bark — E
Shapiro, Z. We're all in the same boat — E

Noah's bark. Krensky, S. — E

Noakes, Vivien, 1937-
(ed) Lear, E. The complete verse and other nonsense — 821

Nobati, Eugenia
(il) MacDonald, M. R. Bat's big game — 398.2

Nobility
Beccia, C. The raucous royals — 920
Brewster, H. The other Mozart [biography of Joseph Bologne Saint-Georges] — 92

Noble, Trinka Hakes
The day Jimmy's boa ate the wash — E
The last brother — E

Noble-Goodman, Katherine
Zebras — 599.66

Nobleman, Marc Tyler
Boys of steel [biography of Jerry Siegel and Joe Shuster] — 92
Eagles — 598
Foxes — 599.77

Nobody. Rosenberg, L. — E

Nubs. Dennis, B.   636.7

Nuclear energy
  Benduhn, T. Nuclear power   621.48
  Cregan, E. R. The atom   539.7

Nuclear physics
  Jerome, K. B. Atomic universe   539.7

Nuclear power. Benduhn, T.   621.48

Nuclear power plants
      See also Nuclear energy
  Feigenbaum, A. Emergency at Three Mile Island
                                                             621.48

Nuclear weapons
      See also Atomic bomb

Nuestra Señora de Atocha (Ship)
  Gibbons, G. Sunken treasure   910.4

Nugent, Cynthia
  (il) Stuchner, J. B. Honey cake   Fic

Nugget on the flight deck. Newman, P.   E

Number patterns *See* Patterns (Mathematics)

Number systems *See* Numbers

Number the stars. Lowry, L.   Fic

Number theory
      See also Factorials

Numberman, Neil
  Do not build a Frankenstein!   E
  (il) Reynolds, A. Joey Fly, private eye in
      Creepy crawly crime   741.5

Numbers
      See also Counting; Pi
  Campbell, S. C. Growing patterns   513
  D'Agnese, J. Blockhead   92
  Murphy, S. J. Henry the fourth   513

Numerals
      See also Numbers; Roman numerals

Numeration *See* Numbers

Numerical analysis
      See also Approximate computation

Número uno. Dorros, A.   E

Numeroff, Laura Joffe
  Beatrice doesn't want to   E
  The Chicken sisters   E
  If you give a mouse a cookie   E
  When sheep sleep   E
  Would I trade my parents?   E

Numismatics
      See also Coins

Nuñez Cabeza de Vaca, Alvar, 16th cent.
                          About
  Lourie, P. On the Texas trail of Cabeza de Vaca
                                                                92

Nunn, Laura Silverstein, 1968-
  (jt. auth) Silverstein, A. Adaptation   578.4
  (jt. auth) Silverstein, A. The ADHD update
                                                             616.85
  (jt. auth) Silverstein, A. The AIDS update
                                                             616.97
  (jt. auth) Silverstein, A. The asthma update
                                                              616.2
  (jt. auth) Silverstein, A. The breast cancer up-
      date   616.99

  (jt. auth) Silverstein, A. Can you see the
      chalkboard?   617.7
  (jt. auth) Silverstein, A. The diabetes update
                                                              616.4
  (jt. auth) Silverstein, A. Earthquakes   551.2
  (jt. auth) Silverstein, A. The eating disorders up-
      date   616.85
  (jt. auth) Silverstein, A. The flu and pneumonia
      update   616.2
  (jt. auth) Silverstein, A. The food poisoning up-
      date   615.9
  (jt. auth) Silverstein, A. Forces and motion
                                                                531
  (jt. auth) Silverstein, A. Growth and develop-
      ment   571.8
  (jt. auth) Silverstein, A. Hurricanes   551.55
  (jt. auth) Silverstein, A. Matter   530
  (jt. auth) Silverstein, A. The sickle cell anemia
      update   616.1
  (jt. auth) Silverstein, A. Sleep   612.8
  (jt. auth) Silverstein, A. Tornadoes   551.55
  (jt. auth) Silverstein, A. The tuberculosis update
                                                              616.2
  (jt. auth) Silverstein, A. Volcanoes   551.2
  (jt. auth) Silverstein, A. Wildfires   634.9

Nuns
  Demi. Mother Teresa   92
  Mora, P. A library for Juana: the world of Sor
      Juana Inés   92

Nursery rhymes
      See also Jump rope rhymes
  The Arnold Lobel book of Mother Goose
                                                              398.8
  Arrorró mi niño   398.8
  Baker, K. Big fat hen   398.8
  Baker, K. Potato Joe   E
  The big book for toddlers   808.8
  Bodden, V. Nursery rhymes   398.8
  Cabrera, J. Old Mother Hubbard   398.8
  Chapman, J. Sing a song of sixpence   398.8
  Collins, H. Out came the sun   398.8
  Diamant-Cohen, B. Early literacy programming
      en Español   027.6
  Dillon, L. Mother Goose numbers on the loose
                                                              398.8
  Emberley, B. Drummer Hoff   398.8
  Favorite nursery rhymes from Mother Goose
                                                              398.8
  Fitzgerald, J. Yum! yum!!   398.8
  Galdone, P. The cat goes fiddle-i-fee   398.8
  Galdone, P. Three little kittens   398.8
  The Helen Oxenbury nursery collection
                                                              398.8
  Here comes Mother Goose   398.8
  Hines, A. G. 1, 2, buckle my shoe   E
  Hoberman, M. A. Miss Mary Mack   398.8
  If you love a nursery rhyme   398.8
  Keats, E. J. Over in the meadow   E
  Marino, J. Mother Goose time   027.62
  Miss Mary Mack and other children's street
      rhymes   796.1
  Muu, moo!   398.8
  My very first Mother Goose   398.8
  The neighborhood Mother Goose   398.8
  Newcome, Z. Head, shoulders, knees, and toes
                                                                E

Nursery rhymes—*Continued*

Opie, I. A. Mother Goose's little treasures
398.8

¡Pio peep! **398.8**

Polacco, P. Babushka's Mother Goose **398.8**

Prelutsky, J. The frogs wore red suspenders
811

Prelutsky, J. Ride a purple pelican **811**

Read-aloud rhymes for the very young
821.008

The real Mother Goose **398.8**

Reinhart, M. A pop-up book of nursery rhymes
398.8

Ross, T. Three little kittens and other favorite
nursery rhymes **398.8**

Rufus and friends: rhyme time **398.8**

Scieszka, J. Truckery rhymes **811**

Spirin, G. A apple pie **E**

Sylvia Long's Mother Goose **398.8**

Taback, S. This is the house that Jack built
398.8

This little piggy **398.8**

Tomie dePaola's Mother Goose **398.8**

Tortillitas para mamá and other nursery rhymes
398.8

Wadsworth, O. A. Over in the meadow **E**

Will Moses Mother Goose **398.8**

Winter, J. The house that Jack built **398.8**

Dictionaries

The Oxford dictionary of nursery rhymes
398.8

Fiction

Chichester-Clark, E. Little Miss Muffet counts
to ten **E**

Conway, D. The great nursery rhyme disaster
E

Edwards, P. D. The neat line **E**

French, V. The Daddy Goose treasury **E**

Graham, B. Dimity Dumpty **E**

Grey, M. The adventures of the dish and the
spoon **E**

Hoberman, M. A. You read to me, I'll read to
you [very short Mother Goose tales to read
together] **811**

Howard, R. The big, big wall **E**

Jay, A. Red green blue **E**

McNaughton, C. Not last night but the night before **E**

Palatini, M. The cheese **E**

Schoenherr, I. Cat & mouse **E**

Nursery schools

See also Preschool education

Nursery tales around the world. Sierra, J.
398.2

Nurses

Glasscock, S. How nurses use math **610.73**

Gorrell, G. K. Heart and soul: the story of Florence Nightingale **92**

Kenney, K. L. Nurses at work **610.73**

Somervill, B. A. Clara Barton **92**

Wade, M. D. Amazing civil war nurse Clara
Barton **92**

Wells, R. Mary on horseback [biography of
Mary Breckinridge] **92**

Nurses at work. Kenney, K. L. **610.73**

Nursing (Infant feeding) *See* Breast feeding

The **nutcracker**. Cech, J. **E**

Nutcracker. Hoffmann, E. T. A. **Fic**

The **Nutcracker**. Jeffers, S. **E**

The **Nutcracker**. Kain, K. **E**

The **Nutcracker**. Koppe, S. **Fic**

The **nutcracker**. Schulman, J. **Fic**

The **Nutcracker**. Spinner, S. **E**

The **Nutcracker** doll. DePalma, M. N. **E**

Nutik, the wolf pup. George, J. C. **E**

Nutrition

See also Diet; Eating customs

Cheung, L. W. Y. Be healthy! it's a girl thing
613

D'Amico, J. The healthy body cookbook
641.5

Doeden, M. Eat right! **613.2**

Gardner, R. Ace your exercise and nutrition science project: great science fair ideas **613**

King, H. Carbohydrates for a healthy body
613.2

Leedy, L. The edible pyramid **613.2**

Miller, E. The monster health book **613**

Powell, J. Fats for a healthy body **613.2**

Royston, A. Proteins for a healthy body
613.2

Royston, A. Vitamins and minerals for a healthy
body **613.2**

Royston, A. Water and fiber for a healthy body
613.2

Schaefer, A. Healthy food **613.2**

Nuts

Fiction

Gerritsen, P. Nuts **E**

Nuts. Cook, K. **Fic**

Nuts. Gerritsen, P. **E**

Nuts to you!. Ehlert, L. **E**

Nutt, Ken *See* Beddows, Eric, 1951-

Nutzhorn, Dorothea *See* Lange, Dorothea, 1895-
1965

Nuzum, K. A.

The leanin' dog **Fic**

Nuzzolo, Deborah

Cheetahs **599.75**

Nye, Naomi Shihab, 1952-

Come with me **811**

(comp) Salting the ocean. See Salting the ocean
811.008

Nykko

(jt. auth) Bannister (Person). The shadow door
741.5

Nyquist, Kate *See* Jerome, Kate Boehm

Nzinga, Queen of Matamba, 1582-1663
See/See also pages in the following book(s):
Krull, K. Lives of extraordinary women **920**

O

Ó Flatharta, Antoine, 1953-
Hurry and the monarch **E**

Ocean—Fiction—*Continued*

Falls, K. Dark life — **Fic**

Lee, S. Wave — **E**

Poetry

Harrison, D. L. Vacation — **811**

Ocean babies. Rose, D. L. — **591.3**

Ocean bottom

Barnhill, K. R. Monsters of the deep — **591.7**

Collard, S. B., III. In the deep sea — **572**

Gibbons, G. Exploring the deep, dark sea — **551.46**

Jenkins, S. Down, down, down — **591.7**

Lindop, L. Venturing the deep sea — **551.46**

Mallory, K. Diving to a deep-sea volcano — **551.46**

Matsen, B. The incredible record-setting deep-sea dive of the bathysphere — **551.46**

Ocean counting. Pallotta, J. — **E**

Ocean currents

See also El Niño Current

Burns, L. G. Tracking trash — **551.46**

Ocean liners

Sutherland, J. Cruise ships — **623.82**

Zimmermann, K. R. Ocean liners — **387.2**

Ocean magic. O'Neill, M. P. — **578.7**

Ocean soup. Swinburne, S. R. — **591.7**

Ocean travel

O'Brien, P. The mutiny on the Bounty — **910.4**

Paulsen, G. Caught by the sea — **92**

Zimmermann, K. R. Ocean liners — **387.2**

Fiction

Flaherty, A. The luck of the Loch Ness monster — **E**

Ocean waves

See also Tsunamis

Ocean wide, ocean deep. Lendroth, S. — **E**

Oceania

Fiction

Schaefer, C. L. The biggest soap — **E**

Oceanography

VanCleave, J. P. Janice VanCleave's oceans for every kid — **551.46**

Ocean's child. Ford, C. — **E**

The **oceans'** most amazing animals. Ganeri, A. — **591.7**

O'Connell, Rebecca, 1968-

Danny is done with diapers — **E**

Penina Levine is a hard-boiled egg — **Fic**

O'Conner, Patricia T.

Woe is I Jr — **428**

O'Connor, Barbara

Fame and glory in Freedom, Georgia — **Fic**

How to steal a dog — **Fic**

Leonardo da Vinci — **92**

The small adventure of Popeye and Elvis — **Fic**

O'Connor, George

Zeus — **741.5**

O'Connor, Jane, 1947-

The emperor's silent army — **931**

Fancy Nancy — **E**

The perfect puppy for me — **E**

Ready, set, skip! — **E**

(jt. auth) Gore, A., Jr. An inconvenient truth — **363.7**

The **octopus**. Cazet, D. — **E**

Octopus opposites. Blackstone, S. — **E**

Octopuses

Coldiron, D. Octopuses — **594**

Jango-Cohen, J. Octopuses — **594**

Markle, S. Octopuses — **594**

Fiction

Cazet, D. The octopus — **E**

Octopuses, squids, and their relatives. Blaxland, B. — **594**

Odanaka, Barbara

Crazy day at the Critter Cafe — **E**

Odd and the Frost Giants. Gaiman, N. — **Fic**

Odd boy out: young Albert Einstein. Brown, D. — **92**

The **odd** egg. Gravett, E. — **E**

Odd owls & stout pigs. Lobel, A. — **811**

Oddities *See* Curiosities and wonders

Oddly. Dunbar, J. — **E**

Oddly Normal. Frampton, O. — **741.5**

O'Dell, Kathleen

Agnes Parker . . . girl in progress — **Fic**

O'Dell, Scott, 1898-1989

The black pearl — **Fic**

Island of the Blue Dolphins — **Fic**

The King's fifth — **Fic**

Sing down the moon — **Fic**

Streams to the river, river to the sea — **Fic**

O'Donnell, Kerri, 1972-

The gold rush — **979.4**

O'Donnell, Liam, 1970-

Wild ride: a graphic guide adventure — **741.5**

Odriozola, Elena

(il) Wolff, F. The story blanket — **E**

Odysseus (Greek mythology)

Lupton, H. The adventures of Odysseus — **292**

McCaughrean, G. Odysseus — **292**

The **odyssey**. Mucci, T. — **741.5**

Of colors and things. Hoban, T. — **E**

Of numbers and stars [biography of Hypatia] Love, D. A. — **92**

Ofanansky, Allison

Harvest of light — **E**

Sukkot treasure hunt — **E**

Off like the wind!. Spradlin, M. P. — **383**

Off to first grade. Borden, L. — **E**

Off to war. Ellis, D. — **303.6**

Off we go!. Yolen, J. — **E**

Offenses against public safety

See also Bombings

Offenses against the person

See also Homicide; Kidnapping

Offermann, Andrea

(il) Milford, K. The Boneshaker — **Fic**

Officer Buckle and Gloria. Rathmann, P. — **E**

Offill, Jenny, 1968-

17 things I'm not allowed to do anymore — **E**

Ogburn, Jacqueline K.
The bake shop ghost   E
A dignity of dragons   398
The magic nesting doll   E
(jt. auth) Long, L. The lady & the lion
  398.2

Oggie Cooder. Weeks, S.   Fic

Ogilvy, Stephen
(il) Levine, S. Sports science   507.8

Oglala Indians
Freedman, R. The life and death of Crazy Horse
  92
Nelson, S. D. Black Elk's vision   92
See/See also pages in the following book(s):
Freedman, R. Indian chiefs   920
Fiction
Bruchac, J. Crazy Horse's vision   E

Ogle, Nancy Gray
(il) Mason, A. Skunks   599.7

Oh, a-hunting we will go. Langstaff, J. M.
  782.42

Oh, brother!. Grimes, N.   E

Oh, Daddy!. Shea, B.   E

Oh, freedom!. King, C.   323.1

Oh, look!. Polacco, P.   E

Oh my baby, little one. Appelt, K.   E

Oh my gods!. Bryant, M. E.   292

Oh no, gotta go!. Elya, S. M.   E

Oh no!, or, How my science project destroyed the
world. Barnett, M.   E

Oh no! Time to go!. Doughty, R.   E

Oh, rats!. Marrin, A.   599.35

Oh, the places you'll go!. Seuss, Dr.   E

Oh, Theodore!. Katz, S.   811

Oh, yuck!. Masoff, J.   031.02

O'Hair, Margaret
My pup   E

Ohio
Rosen, M. J. Our farm   630.9
Fiction
Cheng, A. Eclipse   Fic
Clements, A. Lost and found   Fic
Cook, K. Nuts   Fic
DeFelice, C. C. Weasel   Fic
Dutton, S. Mary Mae and the gospel truth
  Fic
Giblin, J. The boy who saved Cleveland   Fic
Hamilton, V. The bells of Christmas   Fic
Hamilton, V. The house of Dies Drear   Fic
Kuhlman, E. The last invisible boy   Fic
McCloskey, R. Lentil   E
Pearsall, S. Crooked river   Fic
Van Leeuwen, J. Cabin on Trouble Creek
  Fic

Oil *See* Petroleum

Oil, gas, and coal. Benduhn, T.   665.5

Oil painting *See* Painting

Oil spills
Bryan, N. Exxon Valdez oil spill   363.7

Oils and fats
Hartman, E. Fossil fuels   333.8
Powell, J. Fats for a healthy body   613.2

Oink, oink Benny. Lindgren, B.   E

Ojibwa Indians
King, D. C. The Ojibwe   970.004
King, S. Shannon: an Ojibway dancer
  970.004
Fiction
Erdrich, L. The birchbark house   Fic
Erdrich, L. The game of silence   Fic
Erdrich, L. The porcupine year   Fic
Pearsall, S. Crooked river   Fic
Folklore
San Souci, R. Sootface   398.2
Van Laan, N. Shingebiss   398.2

The Ojibwe. King, D. C.   970.004

The OK book. Rosenthal, A. K.   E

OK go. Berger, C.   E

O'Keeffe, Georgia, 1887-1986
About
Bryant, J. Georgia's bones [biography of Georgia O'Keefe]   92
Rodriguez, R. Through Georgia's eyes [biography of Georgia O'Keeffe]   92
Winter, J. My name is Georgia [biography of Georgia O'Keeffe]   92

Oklahoma
Nelson, V. M. Bad news for outlaws   92
Fiction
Hesse, K. Out of the dust   Fic
Love, D. A. Semiprecious   Fic
McKinnon, H. R. Franny Parker   Fic
Scillian, D. Pappy's handkerchief   E
Thomas, J. C. I have heard of a land   E

Ol' Paul, the mighty logger. Rounds, G.   398.2

Old, Wendie
The Halloween book of facts and fun
  394.26
To fly: the story of the Wright brothers   92

The old African. Lester, J.   Fic

Old age
Fiction
Agee, J. The retired kid   E
Arnosky, J. Grandfather Buffalo   E
Auch, M. J. Wing nut   Fic
Best, C. Are you going to be good?   E
Giff, P. R. Pictures of Hollis Woods   Fic
Hazen, B. S. Digby   E
Henson, H. Grumpy Grandpa   E
Hest, A. Mr. George Baker   E
Hobbs, V. The last best days of summer
  Fic
Hole, S. Garmann's summer   E
Holt, K. W. Dancing in Cadillac light   Fic
Kennedy, M. The dog days of Charlotte Hayes
  Fic
Knowlton, L. L. A young man's dance   E
Newman, J. The boys   E
Orlev, U. The song of the whales   Fic
Rylant, C. Mr. Putter & Tabby pour the tea
  E
Schachner, J. B. The Grannyman   E
Walker, S. M. Druscilla's Halloween   E

Old bag of bones. Stevens, J.   398.2

Old Bear. Henkes, K.   E

Old black fly. Aylesworth, J.   E

The **old** blue pickup truck. Ransom, C. F. — E

Old Cricket. Wheeler, L. — E

The **old** dog. Zolotow, C. — E

Old Elm speaks. George, K. O. — 811

Old Granny and the bean thief. DeFelice, C. C. — E

The **old** house. Edwards, P. D. — E

Old MacDonald had a farm. Cabrera, J. — 782.42

The **old** man mad about drawing. Place, F. — Fic

Old Mother Bear. Miles, V. — E

Old Mother Hubbard. Cabrera, J. — 398.8

Old Penn Station. Low, W. — 725

Old Possum's book of practical cats. Eliot, T. S. — 811

Old Testament women. Ward, E. M. — 221.9

The **old** tree. Brown, R. — E

The **old** Willis place. Hahn, M. D. — Fic

Old Yeller. Gipson, F. B. — Fic

Older, Jules, 1940-
Telling time — 529

Older than the stars. Fox, K. — 523.1

Oldfield, Dawn Bluemel *See* Bluemel Oldfield, Dawn

Oldham, Todd
Kid made modern — 745.5

Oldland, Nicholas
Big bear hug — E

Oldroyd, Mark
(il) Krensky, S. John Henry — 398.2

Oleynikov, Igor, 1953-
(il) Burns, B. The king with horse's ears and other Irish folktales — 398.2

Olien, Rebecca
Kids care! — 361.2

Olive the other reindeer. Seibold, J. O. — E

Oliver, Jenni
(il) Lowry, L. A summer to die — Fic

Oliver, Tony
(il) Winer, Y. Frogs sing songs — 597.8

Oliver. Hoff, S. — E

Oliver the Mighty Pig. Van Leeuwen, J. — E

Olivera, Francisco E.
(il) Cruz, A. The woman who outshone the sun — 398.2

Olives
Fiction
Ofanansky, A. Harvest of light — E

Olive's ocean. Henkes, K. — Fic

Olivia. Falconer, I. — E

Olivia Kidney. Potter, E. — Fic

Ollhoff, Jim, 1959-
The Black Death — 616.9
The flu — 616.2
The germ detectives — 616.9
Malaria — 616.9
Smallpox — 616.9
What are germs? — 616

Oloyou. Cárdenas, T. — 398.2

Olson, Arielle North, 1932-
Ask the bones: scary stories from around the world — 398.2
More bones — 398.2

Olson, Nathan
Cones — 516
Cubes — 516
Cylinders — 516
Pyramids — 516
Spheres — 516

Olson, Steven P.
The trial of John T. Scopes — 345

Olson, Tod, 1962-
How to get rich in the California Gold Rush — 979.4
How to get rich on a Texas cattle drive — 978
How to get rich on the Oregon Trail — 978

Olten, Manuela
(il) Raab, B. Where does pepper come from? — E

Oluonye, Mary N., 1955-
Nigeria — 966.9

Olvina flies. Lin, G. — E

Olympians [series]
O'Connor, G. Zeus — 741.5

Olympic games
Macy, S. Freeze frame — 796.98
Macy, S. Swifter, higher, stronger — 796.48

Olympic National Park (Wash.)
Jankowski, S. Olympic National Park — 979.7

O'Malley, Kevin, 1961-
Animal crackers fly the coop — E
Captain Raptor and the moon mystery — E
Gimme cracked corn and I will share — E
Lucky leaf — E
(jt. auth) Finchler, J. Miss Malarkey leaves no reader behind — E
(il) Jackson, E. B. Cinder Edna — E
(il) Javernick, E. The birthday pet — E
(il) Murphy, S. J. Jump, kangaroo, jump! — 513
(il) Root, P. Paula Bunyan — E

Oman
Foster, L. M. Oman — 953

O'Meara, Stephen James, 1956-
Are you afraid yet? the science behind scary stuff — 500

O'Meara, Tim, 1966-
(il) Johnston, T. My abuelita — E

Ommen, Sylvia van
(il) Westera, M. Sheep and Goat — Fic

Omnibeasts. Florian, D. — 811

Omololu, Cynthia Jaynes
When it's six o'clock in San Francisco — E

On a road in Africa. Doner, K. — 636.08

On angel wings. Morpurgo, M. — Fic

On beyond a million. Schwartz, D. M. — 513

On Earth. Karas, G. B. — 525

On Etruscan time. Barrett, T. — Fic

On Hanukkah. Fishman, C. — 296.4

On Market Street. Lobel, A. — E

On Meadowview Street. Cole, H. — E

On morning wings. Lindbergh, R. — 223

On Mother's lap. Scott, A. H. — E

On my honor. Bauer, M. D. — Fic

On my own biography [series]
  Lowery, L. Aunt Clara Brown — 92
  Wadsworth, G. Cesar Chavez — 92

On my own folklore [series]
  Krensky, S. Anansi and the box of stories — 398.2
  Krensky, S. John Henry — 398.2
  Krensky, S. Paul Bunyan — 398.2
  Krensky, S. Pecos Bill — 398.2
  Lowery, L. The tale of La Llorona — 398.2
  Schram, P. The magic pomegranate — 398.2
  Wang Ping. The dragon emperor — 398.2

On my own history [series]
  Figley, M. R. Prisoner for liberty — 92

On my own holidays [series]
  Douglass, S. L. Ramadan — 297.3
  Jango-Cohen, J. Chinese New Year — 394.26
  Nelson, V. M. Juneteenth — 394.26

On my way. De Paola, T. — 92

On my way to buy eggs. Chen, C.-Y. — E

On Noah's ark. Brett, J. — E

On our way home. Braun, S. — E

On Rosh Hashanah and Yom Kippur. Fishman, C. — 296.4

On Sand Island. Martin, J. B. — E

On Sukkot and Simchat Torah. Fishman, C. — 296.4

On the coral reefs. Collard, S. B., III — 577.7

On the day you were born. Frasier, D. — E

On the farm. Elliott, D. — E

On the night you were born. Tillman, N. — E

On the road. Cooper, W. — 629.2

On the road. Nolan, L. A. — Fic

On the scale. Cleary, B. P. — 530.8

On the Texas trail of Cabeza de Vaca. Lourie, P. — 92

On the town. Caseley, J. — E

On the verge of extinction: crisis in the environment [series]
  Harkins, S. S. Threat to the whooping crane — 598
  Leathers, D. Polar bears on the Hudson Bay — 599.78
  O'Neal, C. Threat to the Bengal tiger — 599.75
  Whiting, J. Frogs in danger — 597.8
  Whiting, J. Threat to ancient Egyptian treasures — 932

On the waters of the USA. Sandler, M. W. — 387.2

On the way to the beach. Cole, H. — E

On the wings of heroes. Peck, R. — Fic

On time. Skurzynski, G. — 529

On top of spaghetti. Johnson, P. B. — E

On top of the potty and other get-up-and-go songs. Katz, A. — 782.42

On your mark, get set, grow!. Madaras, L. — 612.6

Once a mouse. Brown, M. — 398.2

Once a wolf. Swinburne, S. R. — 333.95

Once I ate a pie. MacLachlan, P. — 811

Once I knew a spider. Dewey, J. — E

Once upon a baby brother. Sullivan, S. — E

Once upon a banana. Armstrong, J. — E

Once upon a full moon. Quan, E. — 92

Once upon a starry night. Mitton, J. — 523.8

Once upon a time. Egoff, S. A. — 92

Once upon a time. Heitman, J. — 372.6

Once upon a time. Martinez, R. — 398.2

Once upon a time, the end. Kloske, G. — E

Once upon a tomb. Lewis, J. P. — 811

Once upon a twice. Doyen, D. — E

Once upon an ordinary school day. McNaughton, C. — E

Once upon MacDonald's farm. Gammell, S. — E

One. Otoshi, K. — E

The **one** and only Marigold. Heide, F. P. — E

One bean. Rockwell, A. F. — 635

One beastly beast. Nix, G. — S C

One beetle too many: the extraordinary adventures of Charles Darwin. Lasky, K. — 92

One boy. Seeger, L. V. — E

One brown bunny. Bauer, M. D. — E

One candle. Bunting, E. — E

One child, one seed. Cave, K. — E

One city, two brothers. Smith, C. — 398.2

One crazy summer. Williams-Garcia, R. — Fic

One-Eye! Two-Eyes! Three-Eyes!. Shepard, A. — 398.2

One fine day. Hogrogian, N. — 398.2

One fine trade. Miller, B. — 398.2

One giant leap. Burleigh, R. — 629.45

One giant leap: the story of Neil Armstrong. Brown, D. — 92

One green apple. Bunting, E. — E

One-handed catch. Auch, M. J. — Fic

One hen. Milway, K. S. — E

One hundred and one facts about bullying. See Kevorkian, M. 101 facts about bullying — 302.3

One hundred cupboards. See Wilson, N. D. 100 cupboards — Fic

One hundred days and ninety-nine nights. See Madison, A. 100 days and 99 nights — Fic

One hundred most popular picture book authors and illustrators. See McElmeel, S. L. 100 most popular picture book authors and illustrators — 810.3

One hundreth day worries. See Cuyler, M. 100th day worries — E

One hunter. See Hutchins, P. 1 hunter — E

One is a drummer. Thong, R. — E

One is a feast for Mouse. Cox, J. — E

One is a snail, ten is a crab. Sayre, A. P. — E

One leaf rides the wind. Mannis, C. D. — E

The **one** left behind. Roberts, W. D. — Fic

One lighthouse, one moon. Lobel, A.   E

One little chicken. Elliott, D.   E

One million things   031

One million things [series]
   Walker, R. Animal life   590
   Woodward, J. Planet Earth   550

One morning in Maine. McCloskey, R.   E

One night in the Coral Sea. Collard, S. B., III   **593.6**

One night in the zoo. Kerr, J.   E

One nighttime sea. Rose, D. L.   E

One nosy pup. Wallace, C.   E

One-of-a-kind stamps and crafts. Ross, K.   **761**

One parent family *See* Single parent family

One peace. Wilson, J.   **305.23**

One potato, two potato. DeFelice, C. C.   E

One pup's up. Chall, M. W.   E

One red apple. Ziefert, H.   **634**

One red dot. Carter, D. A.   E

One Saturday evening. Baker, B.   E

One small place by the sea. Brenner, B.   **577.6**

One small place in a tree. Brenner, B.   **577.3**

One smart goose. Church, C.   E

One smart skunk. Ziefert, H.   E

One Ted falls out of bed. Donaldson, J.   E

One thousand times no. See Warburton, T. 1000 times no   E

One thousand tracings. Judge, L.   **940.53**

One tiny turtle. Davies, N.   **597.92**

One too many. Marino, G.   E

One true bear. Dewan, T.   E

One, two, buckle my shoe. Cabrera, J.   E

One, two, buckle my shoe. See Hines, A. G. 1, 2, buckle my shoe   E

One, two, I love you. See Schertle, A. 1, 2, I love you   E

One, two, three. See Mora, P. Uno, dos, tres: one, two, three   E

One two three calligraphy. See Winters, E. 1 2 3 calligraphy!   **745.6**

One, two, three go! See Lee, H. V. 1, 2, 3 go!   **495.1**

One, two, three I can build! See Luxbacher, I. 1 2 3 I can build!   **731.4**

One two three I can collage! See Luxbacher, I. 1 2 3 I can collage!   **702.8**

One, two, three I can draw! See Luxbacher, I. 1 2 3 I can draw!   **741.2**

One two three I can make prints! See Luxbacher, I. 1 2 3 I can make prints!   **760.2**

One two three I can paint! See Luxbacher, I. 1 2 3 I can paint!   **751.4**

One two three I can sculpt! See Luxbacher, I. 1 2 3 I can sculpt!   **731.4**

One unhappy horse. Adler, C. S.   Fic

One voice, please. McBratney, S.   **398.2**

One was Johnny. Sendak, M.   E

One watermelon seed. Lottridge, C. B.   E

One well. Strauss, R.   **553.7**

One witch. Leuck, L.   E

One wolf howls. Cohn, S.   **599.77**

One world, many religions. Osborne, M. P.   **200**

One world, one day. Kerley, B.   **305.23**

One year in Beijing. Wang Xiaohong   E

O'Neal, Claire
   How to use waste energy to heat and light your home   **621.1**
   How to use wind power to light and heat your home   **621.31**
   Threat to the Bengal tiger   **599.75**

O'Neill, Alexis, 1949-
   Estela's swap   E

O'Neill, Catharine
   Annie and Simon   E

O'Neill, Mary Le Duc, 1908-1990
   Hailstones and halibut bones   **811**

O'Neill, Michael Patrick
   Ocean magic   **578.7**

Onion John. Krumgold, J.   Fic

Onishi, Satoru
   Who's hiding?   E

Online catalogs
   See also Libraries—Automation

Only a witch can fly. McGhee, A.   E

Only child
Fiction
   Best, C. What's so bad about being an only child?   E

Only Emma. Warner, S.   Fic

Only one neighborhood. Harshman, M.   E

Only one year. Cheng, A.   Fic

Only passing through: the story of Sojourner Truth. Rockwell, A. F.   **92**

Only the names remain. Bealer, A. W.   **970.004**

Only you. Cruise, R.   E

Only you. Wells, R.   E

Only you can save mankind. Pratchett, T.   Fic

Ontario
   Greenwood, B. A pioneer sampler   **971.3**

Onward [biography of Matthew Henson] Johnson, D.   **92**

Onyefulu, Ifeoma, 1959-
   Ikenna goes to Nigeria   **966.9**
   Welcome Dede!   **392**

Oobleck, slime, & dancing spaghetti. Williams, J.   **507.8**

Oodles of animals. Ehlert, L.   E

Ookpik. Hiscock, B.   **598**

Oonark, Jessie, 1906-1985
See/See also pages in the following book(s):
   Rivera, R. Arctic adventures   **920**

The Oooh! artist [series]
   Niepold, M. Oooh! Picasso   **730.9**

Oooh! Matisse. Niepold, M.   **759.4**

Oooh! Picasso. Niepold, M.   **730.9**

Oops!. Katz, A.   **811**

Out of bounds: seven stories of conflict and hope. Naidoo, B. **S C**

Out of darkness: the story of Louis Braille. Freedman, R. **92**

Out of my mind. Draper, S. M. **Fic**

Out of order. Hicks, B. **Fic**

Out of Patience. Meehl, B. **Fic**

Out of slavery. Granfield, L. **264**

Out of the dust. Hesse, K. **Fic**

Out of the egg. Matthews, T. **E**

Out of the shadows. Waldman, N. **92**

Out of this world. Berkowitz, J. **576.8**

Out-of-this-world astronomy. Rhatigan, J. **520**

Out-of-work people See Unemployed

Out standing in my field. Jennings, P. **Fic**

Outbreak. Piddock, C. **614.4**

Outdoor life

See also Camping

George, J. C. Pocket guide to the outdoors **796.5**

Schofield, J. Make it wild **796.5**

Fiction

Greene, S. Owen Foote, frontiersman **Fic**

Outdoor photography

See also Nature photography

Outdoor survival See Wilderness survival

Outer space

Exploration—Fiction

Cottrell Boyce, F. Cosmic **Fic**

Greenberg, D. Enchanted lions **E**

Outer space

Aldrin, B. Look to the stars **629.4**

Rockwell, A. F. Our stars **523.8**

Colonies

See Space colonies

Exploration

See also Space probes

Barchers, S. I. Revolution in space **629.4**

Berkowitz, J. Out of this world **576.8**

Branley, F. M. Is there life in outer space? **576.8**

Carson, M. K. Exploring the solar system **523.2**

Cole, J. The magic school bus, lost in the solar system **523**

Cole, M. D. NASA space vehicles **629.44**

Harris, J. Space exploration **629.4**

Jankowski, C. Space exploration **520**

Jedicke, P. Great moments in space exploration **629.4**

Jefferis, D. Star spotters **522**

Sparrow, G. Cosmic! **520**

Stott, C. Space exploration **629.4**

Outer space travel See Interplanetary voyages

The **outlandish** adventures of Liberty Aimes. Easton, K. **Fic**

Outside and inside big cats. Markle, S. **599.75**

Outside and inside dinosaurs. Markle, S. **567.9**

Outside and inside giant squid. Markle, S. **594**

Outside and inside killer bees. Markle, S. **595.7**

Outside and inside mummies. Markle, S. **393**

Outside and inside rats and mice. Markle, S. **599.35**

Outside and inside woolly mammoths. Markle, S. **569**

Outside beauty. Kadohata, C. **Fic**

Outside over there. Sendak, M. **E**

Outstanding library service to children. Cerny, R. **027.62**

Outstanding science trade books for students K-12 **016.5**

Over at the castle. Ashburn, B. **E**

Over in the hollow. Dickinson, R. **E**

Over in the jungle. Berkes, M. C. **E**

Over in the meadow. Keats, E. J. **E**

Over in the meadow. Langstaff, J. M. **782.42**

Over in the meadow. Wadsworth, O. A. **E**

Over in the pink house. Dotlich, R. K. **811**

Over sea, under stone. Cooper, S. **Fic**

Over the hills & far away. Conover, C. **E**

Over the rainbow. Harburg, E. Y. **782.42**

Over under. Jocelyn, M. **E**

Over, under & through, and other spatial concepts. Hoban, T. **E**

Overboard!. Weeks, S. **E**

Overcoming adversity [series]

Chippendale, L. A. Triumph of the imagination: the story of writer J.K. Rowling **92**

Overland journeys to the Pacific

See also West (U.S.)—Exploration

Calabro, M. The perilous journey of the Donner Party **978**

Friedman, M. The Oregon Trail **978**

Harness, C. The tragic tale of Narcissa Whitman and a faithful history of the Oregon Trail **92**

Leeper, D. R. The diary of David R. Leeper **92**

Olson, T. How to get rich on the Oregon Trail **978**

Steele, C. Famous wagon trails **978**

See/See also pages in the following book(s):

Freedman, R. Children of the wild West **978**

Fiction

Applegate, K. The buffalo storm **E**

Coerr, E. The Josefina story quilt **E**

Hopkinson, D. Apples to Oregon **E**

Kay, V. Covered wagons, bumpy trails **E**

Lawlor, L. He will go fearless **Fic**

Lowell, S. The elephant quilt **E**

Stanley, D. Roughing it on the Oregon Trail **Fic**

Van Leeuwen, J. Bound for Oregon **Fic**

Van Leeuwen, J. Papa and the pioneer quilt **E**

Owen, Cheryl

Gifts for kids to make **745.5**

Owen. Henkes, K. **E**

Parmenter, Wayne
(il) Levine, E. . . . if your name was changed at Ellis Island **325.73**

Parnall, Peter
(il) Miles, M. Annie and the Old One **Fic**

Parnell, Peter
(jt. auth) Richardson, J. And Tango makes three **E**

Parodies
Shapiro, K. J. I must go down to the beach again **811**

Paros, Jennifer
Violet Bing and the Grand House **Fic**

Parr, Todd
The Earth book **333.72**
We belong together **362.7**

Parra, John, 1972-
(il) Mora, P. Gracias = Thanks **E**
The **parrot** Tico Tango. Witte, A. **E**

Parrotfish and sunken ships. Arnosky, J.
578.7

Parrots
Altman, L. J. Parrots **636.6**
Haney, J. Parrots **636.6**
Montgomery, S. Kakapo rescue **639.9**
Fiction
Agee, J. Terrific **E**
Bee, W. And the train goes. . . **E**
DePalma, M. N. The perfect gift **E**
Fox, M. Tough Boris **E**
McDermott, G. Papagayo **E**
Witte, A. The parrot Tico Tango **E**

Parry, Rosanne
Heart of a shepherd **Fic**

Parsons, Garry
(il) Clarke, J. Stuck in the mud **E**

Parthenon (Athens, Greece)
Curlee, L. Parthenon **726**
Mann, E. The Parthenon **726**

Participatory web *See* Web 2.0

The **particle** model of matter. Baxter, R. **530**

A **particular** cow. Fox, M. **E**

Parties
McGillian, J. K. Sleepover party! **793.2**
Ross, K. The best birthday parties ever!
793.2
Fiction
Avraham, K. A. What will you be, Sara Mee?
E
Beck, S. Monster sleepover! **E**
Best, C. Are you going to be good? **E**
Best, C. Three cheers for Catherine the Great!
E
Betancourt, J. Ava Tree and the wishes three
Fic
Cabrera, J. One, two, buckle my shoe **E**
Conford, E. Annabel the actress starring in "Gorilla my dreams" **Fic**
Ehlert, L. Boo to you! **E**
Guy, G. F. Fiesta! **E**
Hanson, W. Bugtown Boogie **E**
Khan, R. Big red lollipop **E**
Leedy, L. Crazy like a fox **E**

McNaughton, C. Not last night but the night before **E**
Mobin-Uddin, A. A party in Ramadan **E**
Murray, M. D. Halloween night **E**
Rylant, C. Annie and Snowball and the dress-up birthday **E**
Rylant, C. Brownie & Pearl step out **E**
Shaw, H. Sneaky weasel **E**
Trapani, I. Haunted party **E**
Wheeler, L. Boogie knights **E**
Wildsmith, B. Jungle party **E**
Wilson, K. Bear snores on **E**
Wood, A. Elbert's bad word **E**

Partridge, Elizabeth
Kogi's mysterious journey **398.2**
Oranges on Golden Mountain **E**
Restless spirit: the life and work of Dorothea Lange **92**

A **party** in Ramadan. Mobin-Uddin, A. **E**

Parzival. Paterson, K. **398.2**

Pasachoff, Naomi E., 1947-
Barbara McClintock **92**
Niels Bohr **92**

Paschen, Elise
(ed) Poetry speaks to children. See Poetry speaks to children **811.008**
(ed) Poetry speaks: who I am. See Poetry speaks: who I am **808.81**

Paschkis, Julie
(il) Baum, M. I have a little dreidel **782.42**
(il) Engle, M. Summer birds: the butterflies of Maria Merian **92**
(il) Fleischman, P. Glass slipper, gold sandal
398.2
(il) Khan, H. Night of the Moon **E**
(il) Larios, J. H. Imaginary menagerie **811**
(jt. auth) Larios, J. H. Yellow elephant **811**
(il) Lord, J. Albert the Fix-it Man **E**
(il) Lord, J. Here comes Grandma! **E**
(il) Lord, J. Where is Catkin? **E**
(il) MacDonald, M. R. Fat cat **398.2**
(il) MacDonald, M. R. The great smelly, slobbery, small-tooth dog **398.2**
(il) Paye, W.-L. Head, body, legs **398.2**
(il) Paye, W.-L. Mrs. Chicken and the hungry crocodile **398.2**
(il) Paye, W.-L. The talking vegetables
398.2
(il) Rodriguez, R. Building on nature **92**
(il) Rodriguez, R. Through Georgia's eyes [biography of Georgia O'Keeffe] **92**
(il) Wong, J. S. Knock on wood **811**
(il) Wong, J. S. Twist **811**

Pascoe, Elaine
Flowers **582.13**
Mice **599.35**
Plants without seeds **586**
Soil **577.5**

Pascual and the kitchen angels. De Paola, T.
E

Pass it down. Marcus, L. S. **920**

Passage to freedom. Mochizuki, K. **940.53**

Passion and poison. Del Negro, J. **S C**

Pearl fisheries
Fiction
O'Dell, S. The black pearl — Fic

Pearl Harbor (Oahu, Hawaii), Attack on, 1941
Allen, T. B. Remember Pearl Harbor — 940.54

Pearle, Ida
A child's day — E

Pearl's new skates. Keller, H. — E

Pearsall, Shelley
All of the above — Fic
Crooked river — Fic

Pearson, Anne
Ancient Greece — 938

Pearson, Debora
Sophie's wheels — E

Pearson, Kit
See/See also pages in the following book(s):
Ellis, S. From reader to writer — 372.6

Pearson, Mike Parker
About
Aronson, M. If stones could speak — 936

Pearson, Ridley
(jt. auth) Barry, D. Peter and the starcatchers
— Fic

Pearson, Tracey Campbell
Bob — E
Myrtle — E
(il) Cutler, J. Rats! — Fic
(il) Hughes, T. My brother Bert — E
(il) Stevenson, R. L. The moon — E

Peary, Marie Ahnighito, 1893-1978
About
Kirkpatrick, K. A. Snow baby [biography of
Marie Ahnighito Peary] — 92

Peary, Robert Edwin, 1856-1920
About
Calvert, P. Robert E. Peary — 92
Kirkpatrick, K. A. Snow baby [biography of
Marie Ahnighito Peary] — 92

Pebble plus. Healthy teeth [series]
Schuh, M. C. All about teeth — 617.6
Schuh, M. C. Loose tooth — 617.6

Peck, Beth
(il) Bunting, E. How many days to America?
— E
(il) Johnson, A. Just like Josh Gibson — E

Peck, Penny
Crash course in storytime fundamentals
— 027.62

Peck, Richard, 1934-
Fair weather — Fic
Here lies the librarian — Fic
A long way from Chicago — Fic
On the wings of heroes — Fic
A season of gifts — Fic
The teacher's funeral — Fic
A year down yonder — Fic

Pecos Bill (Legendary character)
Kellogg, S. Pecos Bill — 398.2
Krensky, S. Pecos Bill — 398.2

Peculiar pets [series]
Lunis, N. Furry ferrets — 636.97
Lunis, N. Green iguanas — 639.3

Lunis, N. Miniature horses — 636.1

Pedagogy *See* Teaching

Peddlers and peddling
Fiction
Slobodkina, E. Caps for sale — E
Folklore
Miller, B. One fine trade — 398.2

Pedersen, Janet
Houdini the amazing caterpillar — E
(il) Breznak, I. Sneezy Louise — E
(il) Donovan, G. In loving memory of Gorfman
T. Frog — Fic
(il) Jackson, A. Thea's tree — E

Pedersen, Judy
(il) Fleischman, P. Seedfolks — Fic

Pedrito's world. Martínez, A. O. — Fic

Pedro, the angel of Olvera Street. Politi, L. — E

Pedro's burro. Capucilli, A. — E

Peekaboo bedtime. Isadora, R. — E

Peep!. Luthardt, K. — E

Peeping Beauty. Auch, M. J. — E

Peer group influence *See* Peer pressure

Peer pressure
Burstein, J. I said no! — 158

Peet, Bill
Big bad Bruce — E
Bill Peet: an autobiography — 92
Huge Harold — E
The whingdingdilly — E

Peet, Mal
Cloud Tea monkeys — Fic

Peete, Holly Robinson *See* Robinson Peete, Holly

Peete, Ryan Elizabeth, 1997-
(jt. auth) Robinson Peete, H. My brother Charlie
— E

Peffer, Jessica, 1983-
DragonArt — 743

Peg Leg Peke. Spangler, B. — E

Pegasus (Greek mythology)
Mayer, M. Pegasus — 292

Peggony-Po. Pinkney, A. D. — E

Peiling and the chicken-fried Christmas. Chen, P.
— Fic

Peirce, Lincoln
Big Nate — Fic

Pelé, 1940-
About
Brown, M. Pele, king of soccer — 92
Cline-Ransome, L. Young Pelé — 92
See/See also pages in the following book(s):
Krull, K. Lives of the athletes — 920

Pele, king of soccer. Brown, M. — 92

Pelham, David
Trail — E

Pellant, Chris
Fossils — 560
Minerals — 549

Pellant, Helen
(jt. auth) Pellant, C. Fossils — 560
(jt. auth) Pellant, C. Minerals — 549

Pets—*Continued*

Fiction

Arnold, T. Hi, Fly Guy!　E

Baicker-McKee, C. Mimi　E

Berger, J. Bridget Fidget and the most perfect pet!　E

Best, C. What's so bad about being an only child?　E

Bowen, A. I know an old teacher　E

Chamberlain, M. Please don't tease Tootsie　E

Cook, K. Nuts　Fic

Dodd, E. What pet to get?　E

Dodds, D. A. Teacher's pets　E

Feiffer, J. A room with a zoo　Fic

Fraser, M. A. Pet shop lullaby　E

Howard, A. Hoodwinked　E

Howe, J. Bunnicula meets Edgar Allan Crow　Fic

Hughes, T. My brother Bert　E

Javernick, E. The birthday pet　E

Jennings, P. We can't all be rattlesnakes　Fic

Kellogg, S. The mysterious tadpole　E

Lindgren, B. Julia wants a pet　E

Luthardt, K. Peep!　E

Napoli, D. J. Sly the Sleuth and the pet mysteries　Fic

Naylor, P. R. Patches and scratches　Fic

Orloff, K. K. I wanna iguana　E

Rennert, L. J. Buying, training & caring for your dinosaur　E

Richards, C. Critter sitter　E

Underwood, D. Granny Gomez & Jigsaw　E

Weigelt, U. Super Guinea Pig to the rescue　E

Zalben, J. B. Baby shower　E

Pets and the handicapped *See* Animals and the handicapped

A pet's life [series]

Ganeri, A. Rabbits　636.9

Petty crimes. Soto, G.　S C

Petunia. Duvoisin, R.　E

Pfeffer, Wendy, 1929-

Dolphin talk　599.5

From seed to pumpkin　583

From tadpole to frog　597.8

Life in a coral reef　577.7

A log's life　577.3

The longest day　394.26

A new beginning　394.26

The shortest day　394.26

We gather together　394.26

What's it like to be a fish?　597

Wiggling worms at work　592

Pfeifer, Kate Gruenwald

American Medical Assocation boy's guide to becoming a teen. See American Medical Assocation boy's guide to becoming a teen　613

Pham, LeUyen

(il) DiPucchio, K. S. Grace for president　E

(il) Look, L. Alvin Ho: allergic to girls, school, and other scary things　Fic

(il) Rosenthal, A. K. Bedtime for Mommy　E

(il) Snyder, L. Any which wall　Fic

(il) Tutu, D. God's dream　231.7

(il) Van Leeuwen, J. Benny & beautiful baby Delilah　E

(il) Zolotow, C. A father like that　E

Pham, Viet Dinh

(il) Shea, P. D. Ten mice for Tet!　394.26

The **phantom** tollbooth. Juster, N.　Fic

Pharaoh. Kennett, D.　932

The **Pharaohs'** armies. Park, L.　355

Pharaoh's boat. Weitzman, D. L.　932

Pheidippides, fl. 490 B.C.

About

Reynolds, S. The first marathon: the legend of Pheidippides　938

Phelan, Glen

Double helix　572.8

Invisible force　531

Killing germs, saving lives　615

Phelan, Matt

The storm in the barn　741.5

(il) Birney, B. G. The seven wonders of Sassafras Springs　Fic

(il) Mazer, A. Spilling ink　808.3

(il) Patron, S. The higher power of Lucky　Fic

(il) Robbins, J. The new girl . . . and me　E

(il) Robbins, J. Two of a kind　E

(il) Rockwell, A. F. Big George: how a shy boy became President Washington　92

(il) Spinelli, E. Where I live　Fic

(il) Stott, A. Always　E

Phelps, Michael, 1985-

About

Torsiello, D. P. Michael Phelps　92

Philadelphia (Pa.)

Staton, H. Independence Hall　974.8

Fiction

Anderson, L. H. Fever, 1793　Fic

De Angeli, M. L. Thee, Hannah!　Fic

Philadelphia chickens. Boynton, S.　782.42

Philbrick, Rodman *See* Philbrick, W. R. (W. Rodman)

Philbrick, W. R. (W. Rodman)

The mostly true adventures of Homer P. Figg　Fic

The young man and the sea　Fic

Philip, Neil

Horse hooves and chicken feet: Mexican folktales　398.2

The pirate princess and other fairy tales　398.2

(ed) A Braid of lives. See A Braid of lives　970.004

(ed) Stockings of buttermilk: American folktales. See Stockings of buttermilk: American folktales　398.2

(ed) War and the pity of war. See War and the pity of war　808.81

(ed) Weave little stars into my sleep. See Weave little stars into my sleep　782.42

Philip Hall likes me, I reckon maybe. Greene, B.　Fic

Philippa Fisher's fairy godsister. Kessler, L.　Fic

Philippides *See* Pheidippides, fl. 490 B.C.

Philippines

Gordon, S. Philippines **959.9**

Tope, L. R. R. Philippines **959.9**

Folklore

See Folklore—Philippines

Phillipps, Julie C.

Wink **E**

Phillips, Charles

Japan **952**

Sweden **948.5**

Phillips, Dee, 1967-

Mammals **599**

Phillips, Gary R.

(il) Blessing, C. New old shoes **E**

Phillips, John

Leonardo da Vinci **92**

Phillips, Louise

(il) Gillies, J. The jumbo vegetarian cookbook **641.5**

(il) Gillies, J. The Kids Can Press jumbo cookbook **641.5**

(il) Silver, P. Face painting **745.5**

Phillips, Susan P., 1945-

Great displays for your library step by step **021.7**

Phillips-Duke, Barbara J.

(il) Hazen, B. S. Digby **E**

Phillis's big test [biography of Phillis Wheatley] Clinton, C. **92**

Philology *See* Language and languages

Philosophers

Freedman, R. Confucius **92**

Love, D. A. Of numbers and stars [biography of Hypatia] **92**

Philosophers' stone *See* Alchemy

Philosophy

Law, S. Really, really big questions **100**

Philosophy, Moral *See* Ethics

Philosophy of nature

Goble, P. All our relatives **970.004**

Phineas Gage: a gruesome but true story about brain science. Fleischman, J. **362.1**

Phineas L. Macguire erupts!. Dowell, F. O. **Fic**

Phobias

Fiction

Daneshvari, G. School of Fear **Fic**

LaFaye, A. Water steps **Fic**

Phoenix (Mythical bird)

Fiction

Demi. The girl who drew a phoenix **E**

La Fevers, R. L. Flight of the phoenix **Fic**

Phoenix rising [series]

Verrillo, E. F. Elissa's quest **Fic**

Phonograph records *See* Sound recordings

Photographers

See also Women photographers

Bond, R. In the belly of an ox: the unexpected photographic adventures of Richard and Cherry Kearton **92**

Fiction

Winthrop, E. Counting on Grace **Fic**

Photography

See also Aerial photography; Digital photography; Nature photography

Friedman, D. Picture this **770**

Digital techniques

See Digital photography

Equipment and supplies

See also Cameras

Fiction

Avi. The seer of shadows **Fic**

Enderle, J. R. Smile, Principessa! **E**

Perkins, L. R. Pictures from our vacation **E**

Townsend, M. Billy Tartle in Say Cheese! **E**

History

Kulling, M. It's a snap! [biography of George Eastman] **92**

Photography, Aerial *See* Aerial photography

Photography, Documentary *See* Documentary photography

Photography of birds

Bond, R. In the belly of an ox: the unexpected photographic adventures of Richard and Cherry Kearton **92**

Photosynthesis

Bang, M. Living sunlight **572**

Phusomsai, Sunantha *See* Sunantha Phusomsai

Physical anthropology

See also Human origins

Physical appearance *See* Personal appearance

Physical fitness

Cheung, L. W. Y. Be healthy! it's a girl thing **613**

Royston, A. Why do I run? **613.7**

Physically handicapped

See also Blind; Deaf

Fiction

Avi. Prairie school **Fic**

Fletcher, S. Shadow spinner **Fic**

Konigsburg, E. L. The view from Saturday **Fic**

Willis, J. Susan laughs **E**

Physically handicapped children

Fiction

De Angeli, M. L. The door in the wall **Fic**

Fleischman, P. The Half-a-Moon Inn **Fic**

Shirley, D. Best friend on wheels **E**

Physicians

Bryant, J. A river of words: the story of William Carlos Williams **92**

Capaldi, G. A boy named Beckoning: the true story of Dr. Carlos Montezuma, Native American hero **92**

Yount, L. William Harvey **92**

Fiction

Beaty, A. Doctor Ted **E**

Cushman, K. Matilda Bone **Fic**

Hof, M. Against the odds **Fic**

Lloyd, S. Doctor Meow's big emergency **E**

Ramthun, B. The White Gates **Fic**

Stewart, P. The curse of the night wolf **Fic**

Whelan, G. Listening for lions **Fic**

Pigs—Fiction—*Continued*

Denise, A. Pigs love potatoes	E
DiCamillo, K. Mercy Watson to the rescue	Fic
Eaton, M., III. Best buds	E
Edwards, P. D. Princess Pigtoria and the pea	E
Ernst, L. C. Sylvia Jean, scout supreme	E
Falconer, I. Olivia	E
Ford, B. No more bottles for Bunny!	E
Geisert, A. Hogwash	E
Geisert, A. Lights out	E
Geisert, A. Pigs from 1 to 10	E
Geisert, A. Pigs from A to Z	E
Gorbachev, V. That's what friends are for	E
Greene, S. Moose's big idea	Fic
Hillenbrand, W. Louie!	E
Hobbie, H. Toot & Puddle: let it snow	E
Horning, S. The giant hug	E
Ichikawa, S. My pig Amarillo	E
Kasza, K. My lucky day	E
Kennemore, T. Alice's birthday pig	Fic
King-Smith, D. Babe	Fic
King-Smith, D. Clever duck	Fic
King-Smith, D. Lady Lollipop	Fic
Lieshout, M. v. Bloom!	E
Lin, G. Olvina flies	E
Lindgren, B. Oink, oink Benny	E
Lobel, A. Small pig	E
Lobel, A. A treeful of pigs	E
Marshall, J. Swine Lake	E
Martin, D. Piggy and Dad go fishing	E
McPhail, D. M. Big Pig and Little Pig	E
McPhail, D. M. Pigs aplenty, pigs galore!	E
Meddaugh, S. Hog-eye	E
Muntean, M. Do not open this book!	E
Palatini, M. Piggie pie!	E
Pichon, L. The three horrid little pigs	E
Polacco, P. Ginger and Petunia	E
Portis, A. Not a stick	E
Potter, B. The tale of Pigling Bland	E
Rylant, C. Poppleton	E
Scieszka, J. The true story of the 3 little pigs	E
Seabrooke, B. Wolf pie	Fic
Segal, J. Far far away	E
Simmons, J. Beryl	Fic
Steig, W. The amazing bone	E
Sutton, J. Don't call me Sidney	E
Teague, M. Pigsty	E
Thiesing, L. The Aliens are coming!	E
Trivizas, E. The three little wolves and the big bad pig	E
Underwood, D. Granny Gomez & Jigsaw	E
Van Leeuwen, J. Amanda Pig and the awful, scary monster	E
Van Leeuwen, J. Oliver the Mighty Pig	E
Waddell, M. Captain Small Pig	E
Weeks, S. Ella, of course!	E
Whatley, B. Wait! No paint!	E
White, E. B. Charlotte's web	Fic
Wiesner, D. The three pigs	E
Wild, M. Piglet and Mama	E
Willems, M. Today I will fly!	E
Wood, D. Piggies	E

Folklore

Kellogg, S. The three little pigs	398.2
Marshall, J. The three little pigs	398.2
McDermott, G. Pig-Boy	398.2
Zemach, M. The three little pigs	398.2

Poetry

Bunting, E. Sing a song of piglets	811
Lobel, A. Odd owls & stout pigs	811

Pigs aplenty, pigs galore!. McPhail, D. M.	E
Pigs from 1 to 10. Geisert, A.	E
Pigs from A to Z. Geisert, A.	E
Pigs love potatoes. Denise, A.	E
Pigsty. Teague, M.	E

Pikas

Bill, T. Pika	599.35

Pike, Zebulon Montgomery, 1779-1813
About

Calvert, P. Zebulon Pike	92

Pike Place Market (Seattle, Wash.)
Fiction

Anderson, S. A day at the market	E

Pilger, Mary Anne

Science experiments index for young people	507.8

Pilgrims (New England colonists)

Armentrout, D. The Mayflower Compact	974.4
Barth, E. Turkeys, Pilgrims, and Indian corn	394.26
Grace, C. O. 1621	394.26
Harness, C. The adventurous life of Myles Standish	92
Sewall, M. The pilgrims of Plimoth	974.4
Waters, K. Sarah Morton's day	974.4
Yero, J. L. The Mayflower Compact	974.4

Fiction

Lasky, K. Two bad pilgrims	Fic
The **pilgrims** of Plimoth. Sewall, M.	974.4

Pilkey, Dav, 1966-

The Hallo-wiener	E
The paperboy	E

Pilots, Airplane *See* Air pilots

Pilots and pilotage *See* Navigation

A **pinata** in a pine tree. Mora, P.	782.42
The **piñata** maker: El piñatero. Ancona, G.	745.594
Piñatas and paper flowers. Perl, L.	394.26
Piñatero. See Ancona, G. The piñata maker: El piñatero	745.594
The **pinballs**. Byars, B. C.	Fic

Pinchot, Gifford, 1865-1946
About

Hines, G. Midnight forests [biography of Gifford Pinchot]	92

Pinfold, Levi

The Django	E

Pingpong Perry experiences how a book is made. Donovan, S.	070.5
Pink. Gregory, N.	E
Pink and Say. Polacco, P.	E
Pink me up. Harper, C. M.	E
The **pink** refrigerator. Egan, T.	E
Pinkerton, behave!. Kellogg, S.	E

Poisons and poisoning

See also Food poisoning

Day, J. Don't touch that! **615.9**

Fiction

Appelbaum, S. The Hollow Bettle **Fic**

The Poisons of Caux [series]

Appelbaum, S. The Hollow Bettle **Fic**

A **Poke** in the I **811.008**

Polacco, Patricia

Babushka's doll **E**

Babushka's Mother Goose **398.8**

The butterfly **Fic**

Chicken Sunday **E**

G is for goat **E**

Ginger and Petunia **E**

In our mothers' house **E**

January's sparrow **Fic**

John Philip Duck **E**

The junkyard wonders **Fic**

The keeping quilt **E**

The Lemonade Club **E**

Luba and the wren **398.2**

Mr. Lincoln's way **E**

Mrs. Katz and Tush **E**

My rotten redheaded older brother **E**

Oh, look! **E**

Pink and Say **E**

Rechenka's eggs **E**

Someone for Mr. Sussman **E**

Thank you, Mr. Falker **E**

The trees of the dancing goats **E**

When lightning comes in a jar **Fic**

Poland

Deckker, Z. Poland **943.8**

Gordon, S. Poland **943.8**

Heale, J. Poland **943.8**

Fiction

Hesse, K. The cats in Krasinski Square **E**

Roy, J. R. Yellow star **Fic**

Folklore

See Folklore—Poland

Polar animals. Hodge, D. **591.7**

Polar bear

Davies, N. Ice bear **599.78**

Gibbons, G. Polar bears **599.78**

Guiberson, B. Z. Ice bears **599.78**

Hatkoff, J. Knut **599.78**

Hirsch, R. E. Top 50 reasons to care about polar bears **599.78**

Leathers, D. Polar bears on the Hudson Bay **599.78**

Lockwood, S. Polar Bears **599.78**

Markle, S. Polar bears **599.78**

Nagda, A. W. Polar bear math **513**

Rosing, N. Face to face with polar bears **599.78**

Ryder, J. A pair of polar bears **599.78**

Thomson, S. L. Where do polar bears live? **599.78**

Fiction

Baek, M. J. Panda and polar bear **E**

Bloom, S. A splendid friend, indeed **E**

Mack, J. Hush little polar bear **E**

Murphy, Y. Baby Polar **E**

Rueda, C. My little polar bear **E**

Thompson, L. Polar bear night **E**

Folklore

Brett, J. The three snow bears **398.2**

Dabcovich, L. The polar bear son **398.2**

Polar bear, arctic hare. Spinelli, E. **811**

Polar bear math. Nagda, A. W. **513**

Polar bear night. Thompson, L. **E**

Polar bear, polar bear, what do you hear? Martin, B. **E**

The **polar** bear son. Dabcovich, L. **398.2**

Polar bear, why is your world melting? Wells, R. E. **363.7**

Polar bears on the Hudson Bay. Leathers, D. **599.78**

Polar expeditions *See* Antarctica—Exploration

The **Polar** Express. Van Allsburg, C. **E**

Polar regions

See also Antarctica; Arctic regions; North Pole; South Pole

Conlan, K. Under the ice **578.7**

Goodman, S. Life on the ice **998**

Polenghi, Evan

(jt. auth) Singer, M. I'm your bus **E**

Poles apart. Scott, E. **998**

Polette, Nancy, 1930-

Find someone who **011.6**

Polhemus, Coleman

The crocodile blues **E**

Police

Kenney, K. L. Police officers at work **363.2**

Fiction

Barnett, M. The case of the case of mistaken identity **Fic**

Hamilton, K. R. Police officers on patrol **E**

Hubbell, P. Police: hurrying! helping! saving! **E**

Niemann, C. The police cloud **E**

The **police** cloud. Niemann, C. **E**

Police: hurrying! helping! saving!. Hubbell, P. **E**

Police officers at work. Kenney, K. L. **363.2**

Police officers on patrol. Hamilton, K. R. **E**

Polikoff, Barbara Garland

Why does the coqui sing? **Fic**

Poliomyelitis

Kehret, P. Small steps **92**

Fiction

Giff, P. R. All the way home **Fic**

Hostetter, J. Blue **Fic**

Lawrence, I. The giant-slayer **Fic**

Poliomyelitis vaccine

Tocci, S. Jonas Salk **92**

Polish Americans

Fiction

Cushman, K. Rodzina **Fic**

Grandits, J. The travel game **E**

Politi, Leo, 1908-1996

Emmet **E**

Juanita **E**

Pedro, the angel of Olvera Street **E**

Song of the swallows **E**

Porch lies. McKissack, P. C. **S C**
Porcupine. Tilly, M. **Fic**
The **porcupine** year. Erdrich, L. **Fic**
Porcupines
Jango-Cohen, J. Porcupines **599.35**
Markle, S. Porcupines **599.35**
Fiction
Underwood, D. A balloon for Isabel **E**
Porpoises
Fiction
Edgemon, D. Seamore, the very forgetful porpoise **E**
The **porridge** pot. Bell, A. **398.2**
Porter, A. P., 1945-
Jump at de sun: the story of Zora Neale Hurston **92**
Porter, Janice Lee
(il) Lowery, L. Aunt Clara Brown **92**
(il) Lowery, L. The tale of La Llorona **398.2**
Porter, Sue
(il) Ibbotson, E. The secret of platform 13 **Fic**
Porter, Tracey
Billy Creekmore **Fic**
Porterfield, Jason
Conducting basic and advanced searches **025.04**
Portis, Antoinette
Not a box **E**
Not a stick **E**
A penguin story **E**
Portland (Steamer)
Cerullo, M. M. Shipwrecks **910.4**
Portnoy, Amy
(il) Becker, B. The magical Ms. Plum **Fic**
Portnoy, Mindy Avra
Tale of two Seders **E**
Portraits
Thomson, R. Portraits **757**
Fiction
Piven, H. My best friend is as sharp as a pencil **E**
Piven, H. My dog is as smelly as dirty socks **E**
Portraits [series]
Lasky, K. Dancing through fire **Fic**
Portraits of African-American heroes. Bolden, T. **920**
Portraits of Jewish American heroes. Drucker, M. **920**
Ports *See* Harbors
Portugal
Deckker, Z. Portugal **946.9**
Heale, J. Portugal **946.9**
Posada, Mia
Dandelions **583**
Guess what is growing inside this egg **591.4**
Ladybugs **595.7**
(il) Glaser, L. Dazzling dragonflies **595.7**
Las Posadas. Hoyt-Goldsmith, D. **394.26**

Positively pets [series]
Richardson, A. Caring for your fish **639.34**
Richardson, A. Caring for your hamster **636.9**
Richardson, A. Caring for your hermit crab **639**
Possessions, Lost and found *See* Lost and found possessions
Post, Emily, 1873-1960
Fiction
Huget, J. L. Thanks a LOT, Emily Post! **E**
Post, Hans, 1959-
Creepy crawlies **590**
Sparrows **598**
Post, Peggy, 1945-
Emily Post's table manners for kids **395**
Emily Post's The guide to good manners for kids **395**
Emily's everyday manners **395**
Post-traumatic stress disorder
Fiction
House, S. Eli the Good **Fic**
Postal service
Kay, V. Whatever happened to the Pony Express? **383**
Spradlin, M. P. Off like the wind! **383**
Fiction
Ahlberg, J. The jolly postman **E**
Horning, S. The giant hug **E**
Kerby, M. Owney, the mail-pouch pooch **E**
Taback, S. I miss you every day **E**
West (U.S.)
Brown, C. M. Mule train mail **383**
The **postcard**. Abbott, T. **Fic**
Postier, Jim
(il) Crowe, C. Turtle girl **E**
Postlethwaite, Mark, 1964-
(il) Parker, M. H. David and the Mighty Eighth **Fic**
Posy!. Newbery, L. **E**
A **pot** o' gold. Krull, K. **820.8**
The **pot** of wisdom: Ananse stories. Badoe, A. **398.2**
The **pot** that Juan built [biography of Juan Quezada] Andrews-Goebel, N. **92**
Potato Joe. Baker, K. **E**
Potatoes
Fiction
DeFelice, C. C. One potato, two potato **E**
Hesse, K. Spuds **E**
Potch & Polly. Steig, W. **E**
Potter, Beatrix, 1866-1943
The story of Miss Moppet **E**
The tailor of Gloucester **E**
The tale of Jemima Puddle-duck **E**
The tale of Mr. Jeremy Fisher **E**
The tale of Mrs. Tiggy-Winkle **E**
The tale of Mrs. Tittlemouse **E**
The tale of Peter Rabbit **E**
The tale of Pigling Bland **E**
The tale of Squirrel Nutkin **E**
The tale of Timmy Tiptoes **E**
The tale of two bad mice **E**

Prehistoric man *See* Fossil hominids
Prehistoric peoples
  Andryszewski, T. Walking the earth   **304.8**
  Arnold, C. Stone Age farmers beside the sea
                              936.1
  Deem, J. M. Bodies from the bog   **930.1**
  Getz, D. Frozen man   **930.1**
             Fiction
  Kitamura, S. Stone Age boy   **E**
  Paver, M. Wolf brother   **Fic**
  Tankard, J. Me hungry!   **E**
Preiss-Glasser, Robin *See* Glasser, Robin Preiss
Prejudices
  Lester, J. Let's talk about race   **305.8**
  Schwartz, J. Short   **612.6**
             Fiction
  Bunting, E. Walking to school   **E**
  Conly, J. L. Crazy lady!   **Fic**
  Curtis, C. P. The Watsons go to Birmingham—
    1963   **Fic**
  Hesse, K. Witness   **Fic**
  Ketchum, L. Where the great hawk flies   **Fic**
  Kurtz, J. The storyteller's beads   **Fic**
  Levine, K. The best bad luck I ever had
                      Fic
  Marsden, C. The gold-threaded dress   **Fic**
  Miller, W. Night golf   **E**
  Mochizuki, K. Baseball saved us   **E**
  Mochizuki, K. Heroes   **E**
  Polacco, P. Mr. Lincoln's way   **E**
  Rahaman, V. Divali rose   **E**
  Stanley, D. Saving Sky   **Fic**
  Taylor, M. D. The gold Cadillac   **Fic**
  Taylor, M. D. Mississippi bridge   **Fic**
  Uchida, Y. A jar of dreams   **Fic**
  Whitaker, Z. Kali and the rat snake   **E**
  Williams, L. E. Slant   **Fic**
  Yep, L. The traitor   **Fic**
Preller, James, 1961-
  Mighty Casey   **E**
  Six innings   **Fic**
Prelutsky, Jack
  Awful Ogre running wild   **811**
  Awful Ogre's awful day   **811**
  Be glad your nose is on your face and other po-
    ems   **811**
  Behold the bold umbrellaphant   **811**
  The dragons are singing tonight   **811**
  The frogs wore red suspenders   **811**
  Good sports   **811**
  The Headless Horseman rides tonight   **811**
  If not for the cat   **811**
  In Aunt Giraffe's green garden   **811**
  It's Christmas!   **811**
  It's snowing! it's snowing!   **811**
  It's Thanksgiving!   **811**
  It's Valentine's Day   **811**
  Monday's troll   **811**
  My dog may be a genius   **811**
  The new kid on the block: poems   **811**
  Nightmares: poems to trouble your sleep
                      811
  Pizza, pigs, and poetry   **808.1**
  A pizza the size of the sun   **811**
  Ride a purple pelican   **811**
  Scranimals   **811**

  Something big has been here   **811**
  The swamps of Sleethe   **811**
  Tyrannosaurus was a beast   **811**
  What a day it was at school!   **811**
  The wizard   **E**
  (comp) The 20th century children's poetry trea-
    sury. See The 20th century children's poetry
    treasury   **811.008**
  (comp) The Beauty of the beast. See The Beau-
    ty of the beast   **811.008**
  (comp) For laughing out loud. See For laughing
    out loud   **811.008**
  (ed) The Random House book of poetry for
    children. See The Random House book of po-
    etry for children   **811.008**
  (comp) Read a rhyme, write a rhyme. See Read
    a rhyme, write a rhyme   **811.008**
  (comp) Read-aloud rhymes for the very young.
    See Read-aloud rhymes for the very young
                      821.008
  (jt. auth) Seuss, Dr. Hooray for Diffendoofer
    Day!   **E**
Preschool education
    See also Kindergarten
  Raines, S. C. Story stretchers for infants, tod-
    dlers, and twos   **372.4**
Preschool favorites. Briggs, D.   **372.6**
Preschool to the rescue. Sierra, J.   **E**
Presentation software
  Orr, T. Creating multimedia presentations
                      005
Preservation of wildlife *See* Wildlife conservation
Preserve our planet [series]
  Delano, M. F. Earth in the hot seat   **363.7**
The **presidency**. Horn, G.   **352.23**
President George Washington. Allen, K.   **92**
The **president** is shot!. Holzer, H.   **973.7**
President Pennybaker. Feiffer, K.   **E**
Presidents
             Fiction
  Bradley, K. B. The President's daughter   **Fic**
  Smith, L. Madam President   **E**
  Wells, R. Lincoln and his boys   **Fic**
  Winters, K. My teacher for President   **E**
          United States
  Abramson, J. Obama   **92**
  Adler, D. A. George Washington   **92**
  Adler, D. A. A picture book of Dolley and
    James Madison   **92**
  Adler, D. A. A picture book of John and Abi-
    gail Adams   **92**
  Adler, D. A. A picture book of John F. Kenne-
    dy   **92**
  Adler, D. A. A picture book of Thomas Jeffer-
    son   **92**
  Allen, K. President George Washington   **92**
  Aronson, B. Richard M. Nixon   **92**
  Aronson, B. Ulysses S. Grant   **92**
  Aylesworth, J. Our Abe Lincoln   **92**
  Bausum, A. Our country's presidents   **920**
  Bial, R. Where Washington walked   **92**
  Brown, D. Teedie   **92**
  Burleigh, R. Abraham Lincoln comes home
                      92

Presley, Elvis, 1935-1977
About
Stamaty, M. A. Shake, rattle & turn that noise
down! **781.66**
Press, Judy, 1944-
Around-the-world art & activities **745.5**
ArtStarts for little hands! **745.5**
The little hands big fun craft book **745.5**
Press
See also Newspapers
Pressler, Mirjam
(ed) Frank, A. The diary of a young girl: the de-
finitive edition **92**
Pressure groups *See* Lobbying
Pretty in print. Botzakis, S. **050**
Pretty Salma. Daly, N. **E**
Preus, Margi
The Peace Bell **E**
Prévert, Jacques, 1900-1977
How to paint the portrait of a bird **E**
Previously. Ahlberg, A. **E**
Prévost, Guillaume, 1964-
The book of time **Fic**
Price, Caroline
(il) Sadler, J. A. The new jumbo book of easy
crafts **745.5**
Price, Geoff
Puberty boy **612.6**
Price, Nick
(il) Bearn, E. Tumtum & Nutmeg **Fic**
Price, Pamela S.
Cool rubber stamp art **761**
Cool scrapbooks **745.593**
Price, Sean, 1963-
The story behind chocolate **641.3**
The story behind electricity **621.3**
The story behind skyscrapers **720**
Priceman, Marjorie
Hot air **E**
How to make a cherry pie and see the U.S.A.
E
How to make an apple pie and see the world
E
(il) For laughing out loud. See For laughing out
loud **811.008**
(il) Moss, L. Zin! zin! zin! a violin **E**
(il) Ogburn, J. K. The bake shop ghost **E**
(il) Yolleck, J. Paris in the spring with Picasso
E
Prichard, Mari
(jt. auth) Carpenter, H. The Oxford companion
to children's literature **809**
Prickly sea stars. Lunis, N. **593.9**
A **pride** of African tales. Washington, D. L.
398.2
Priestley, Chris, 1958-
Tales of terror from the Black Ship **Fic**
Uncle Montague's tales of terror **S C**
Priests
Fiction
Hershey, M. 10 lucky things that have happened
to me since I nearly got hit by lightning
Fic

Prigger, Mary Skillings
Aunt Minnie McGranahan **E**
Prigmore, Shane
(il) Scieszka, J. Spaceheadz **Fic**
Primary physical science [series]
Mason, A. Build it! **624.1**
Mason, A. Change it! **530**
Mason, A. Move it! **531**
Mason, A. Touch it! **530.4**
Primary source history of the United States [se-
ries]
Stanley, G. E. America in today's world (1969-
2004) **973.92**
Stanley, G. E. An emerging world power (1900-
1929) **973.91**
Primary sources in American history [series]
O'Donnell, K. The gold rush **979.4**
Primary sources in the library. Johnson, M.
027.8
Primates
Collard, S. B., III. In the wild **591.68**
Redmond, I. Gorilla, monkey & ape **599.8**
Primavera, Elise, 1954-
Louise the big cheese: divine diva **E**
(il) Fritz, J. Make way for Sam Houston **92**
(il) Nolen, J. Raising dragons **E**
Primitive societies
See also Nomads
Primm, E. Russell, 1958-
(ed) Favorite children's authors and illustrators.
See Favorite children's authors and illustrators
920.003
Prince, April Jones
Twenty-one elephants and still standing **E**
Prince Edward Island
Fiction
Beha, E. Tango **Fic**
The **Prince** of Fenway Park. Baggott, J. **Fic**
The **prince** of the pond. Napoli, D. J. **Fic**
The **prince** won't go to bed. Dodds, D. A. **E**
Princes
Fiction
Arnold, T. The twin princes **E**
Dodds, D. A. The prince won't go to bed **E**
Rutkoski, M. The Cabinet of Wonders **Fic**
Saint-Exupéry, A. d. The little prince **Fic**
Saint-Exupéry, A. d. The little prince: deluxe
pop-up book **Fic**
Princes and princesses *See* Princesses
The **princess** and the pea. Cech, J. **E**
The **princess** and the pea [illustrated by Dorothee
Duntze] Andersen, H. C. **Fic**
The **princess** and the Peabodys. Birney, B. G.
Fic
Princess Baby. Katz, K. **E**
Princess Bess gets dressed. Cuyler, M. **E**
Princess for a week. Wright, B. R. **Fic**
Princess Furball. Huck, C. S. **398.2**
The **princess** gown. Strauss, L. L. **E**
Princess Hyacinth. Heide, F. P. **E**

Princess K.I.M. and the lie that grew. Cocca-Leffler, M.   **E**

The **princess** knight. Funke, C. C.   **E**

The **princess** mouse. Shepard, A.   **398.2**

Princess Peepers. Calvert, P.   **E**

Princess Pigsty. Funke, C. C.   **E**

Princess Pigtoria and the pea. Edwards, P. D.   **E**

The **princess** plot. Boie, K.   **Fic**

Princess Posey and the first grade parade. Greene, S.   **Fic**

Princess says goodnight. Howland, N.   **E**

Princess stories   **398.2**

The **princess** who had almost everything. Levert, M.   **E**

Princesses

  Stanley, F. The last princess: the story of Princess Ka'iulani of Hawai'i   **92**

Fiction

  Andrews, J. The very fairy princess   **E**

  Birney, B. G. The princess and the Peabodys   **Fic**

  Boie, K. The princess plot   **Fic**

  Buhler, C. v. But who will bell the cats?   **E**

  Calvert, P. Princess Peepers   **E**

  Coombs, K. The runaway princess   **Fic**

  Cuyler, M. Princess Bess gets dressed   **E**

  DeFelice, C. C. The real, true Dulcie Campbell   **E**

  Edwards, P. D. Princess Pigtoria and the pea   **E**

  Ehrlich, A. A treasury of princess stories   **398.2**

  Funke, C. C. The princess knight   **E**

  Funke, C. C. Princess Pigsty   **E**

  Heide, F. P. Princess Hyacinth   **E**

  Horowitz, D. Twenty-six princesses   **E**

  Howland, N. Princess says goodnight   **E**

  Katz, K. Princess Baby   **E**

  King-Smith, D. Lady Lollipop   **Fic**

  Knudsen, M. The dragon of Trelian   **Fic**

  Lairamore, D. Ivy's ever after   **Fic**

  Lee, Y. The little moon princess   **E**

  Levert, M. The princess who had almost everything   **E**

  Levine, G. C. The two princesses of Bamarre   **Fic**

  Lowry, L. Birthday ball   **Fic**

  Noyes, D. Red butterfly   **E**

  Proimos, J. Patricia von Pleasantsquirrel   **E**

  Ray, J. The apple-pip princess   **E**

  Ross, T. I want two birthdays!   **E**

  Santore, C. The Silk Princess   **E**

  Shannon, M. The red wolf   **E**

  Strauss, L. L. The princess gown   **E**

  Thurber, J. Many moons [illustrated by Louis Slobodkin]   **E**

  Thurber, J. Many moons [illustrated by Marc Simont]   **E**

  Vande Velde, V. Wizard at work   **Fic**

  Zahler, D. The thirteenth princess   **Fic**

Graphic novels

  Espinosa, R. The courageous princess   **741.5**

Principles and practice series

  Hughes-Hassell, S. School reform and the school library media specialist   **027.8**

Prineas, Sarah

  The magic thief   **Fic**

Pringle, Laurence P.

  Alligators and crocodiles!   **597.98**

  American slave, American hero [biography of York]   **92**

  Come to the ocean's edge   **577.7**

  Everybody has a bellybutton   **612.6**

  Global warming   **363.7**

  Imagine a dragon   **398.2**

  Penguins! strange and wonderful   **598**

  Sharks!: strange and wonderful   **597**

  Snakes!   **597.96**

Printing

  Hanson, A. Cool printmaking   **760.2**

  Luxbacher, I. 1 2 3 I can make prints!   **760.2**

History

  Koscielniak, B. Johann Gutenberg and the amazing printing press   **686.2**

Prints

  Hanson, A. Cool printmaking   **760.2**

  Luxbacher, I. 1 2 3 I can make prints!   **760.2**

Printup, Erwin, 1956-

  (il) Swamp, J. Giving thanks   **299.7**

Prischmann, Deirdre A.

  Poop-eaters   **595.7**

Priscilla and the hollyhocks. Broyles, A.   **E**

Prisoner for liberty [biography of James Forten] Figley, M. R.   **92**

Prisoners

Fiction

  Colfer, E. Airman   **Fic**

  Fitzmaurice, K. The year the swallows came early   **Fic**

  Lawrence, I. The convicts   **Fic**

  Stauffacher, S. Harry Sue   **Fic**

  Woodson, J. Visiting day   **E**

Prisoners of war, German *See* German prisoners of war

Pritchett, Dylan, 1959-

  The first music   **E**

Privacy, Right of *See* Right of privacy

Privacy and confidentiality issues. Chmara, T.   **344**

Private Joel and the Sewell Mountain seder. Fireside, B. J.   **Fic**

The **private** thoughts of Amelia E. Rye. Shimko, B.   **Fic**

Prize-winning science fair projects for curious kids. Rhatigan, J.   **507.8**

Probabilities

  Leedy, L. It's probably Penny   **519.2**

  Murphy, S. J. Probably pistachio   **519.2**

Probably pistachio. Murphy, S. J.   **519.2**

Problem drinking *See* Alcoholism

Problem solving

  See also Conflict management; Decision making

The **problem** with chickens. McMillan, B.   **E**

The **problem** with the Puddles. Feiffer, K.   **Fic**

Proch, Gregory
   (il) Olson, T. How to get rich on a Texas cattle drive   **978**
   (il) Olson, T. How to get rich on the Oregon Trail   **978**

Professions
   See also Occupations

Programmed instruction
   See also Computer-assisted instruction

Programs, Television *See* Television programs

Proimos, James
   Patricia von Pleasantsquirrel   **E**
   Paulie Pastrami achieves world peace   **E**
   Todd's TV   **E**

Project Apollo
   Bodden, V. Man walks on the Moon   **629.45**
   Chaikin, A. Mission control, this is Apollo   **629.45**
   Dyer, A. Mission to the moon   **629.45**
   Ross, S. Moon: science, history, and mystery   **629.45**
   Vogt, G. Apollo moonwalks   **629.45**

Project Apollo *See* Apollo project

Project Apollo (U.S.)
   History
   Burleigh, R. One giant leap   **629.45**

Project Gemini *See* Gemini project

Project Mercury
   Ashby, R. Rocket man [biography of John Glenn]   **92**

Project Mulberry. Park, L. S.   **Fic**

Project UltraSwan. Osborn, E.   **598**

Projects you can build yourself [series]
   Reilly, K. M. Planet Earth   **333.72**

Prokofiev, Sergey, 1891-1953
   Peter and the wolf   **E**
   See/See also pages in the following book(s):
   Krull, K. Lives of the musicians   **920**
   (jt. auth) Raschka, C. Peter and the wolf   **E**

Promises to keep: how Jackie Robinson changed America. Robinson, S.   **92**

Prophecies
   Stefoff, R. Prophets and prophecy   **133.3**
   Fiction
   Fagan, D. Fortune's folly   **Fic**

Prophets
   Stefoff, R. Prophets and prophecy   **133.3**

Prophets and prophecy. Stefoff, R.   **133.3**

Pros and cons [series]
   Harris, J. Space exploration   **629.4**
   Rooney, A. Health and medicine   **610**
   Solway, A. Communication   **303.4**

Prosek, James
   Bird, butterfly, eel   **E**
   A good day's fishing   **E**

Proserpina (Roman deity) *See* Persephone (Greek deity)

Prosmitsky, Jenya, 1974-
   (il) Cleary, B. P. Hairy, scary, ordinary   **428**

Prosthesis *See* Artificial organs

Protect nature. Barnham, K.   **333.95**

Protect our planet [series]
   Royston, A. Global warming   **363.7**

Protecting Earth's air quality. Rapp, V.   **363.7**

Protecting Earth's rain forests. Welsbacher, A.   **577.3**

Protecting intellectual freedom in your school library. Scales, P. R.   **025.2**

Protecting Marie. Henkes, K.   **Fic**

Protecting our natural resources. Hirsch, R. E.   **333.72**

Protecting our planet [series]
   Metz, L. What can we do about global warming?   **363.7**
   Metz, L. What can we do about invasive species?   **578.6**
   Metz, L. What can we do about trash and recycling?   **363.7**
   Slade, S. What can we do about the energy crisis?   **333.79**

Protecting the planet. Dell, P.   **333.72**

Protecting the right to read. Symons, A. K.   **025.2**

Protection of birds *See* Birds—Protection

Protection of environment *See* Environmental protection

Protection of game *See* Game protection

Protection of wildlife *See* Wildlife conservation

Proteins
   Royston, A. Proteins for a healthy body   **613.2**

Proteins for a healthy body. Royston, A.   **613.2**

Protists
   Arato, R. Protists   **579**

Protoctista
   Zabludoff, M. The protoctist kingdom   **579**

Protozoa
   Arato, R. Protists   **579**
   Graham, I. Microscopic scary creatures   **591.6**

Proud as a peacock, brave as a lion. Barclay, J.   **E**

A **proud** taste for scarlet and miniver. Konigsburg, E. L.   **Fic**

Prove it!. Glass, S.   **507**

Provensen, Alice, 1918-
   A day in the life of Murphy   **E**
   The glorious flight: across the Channel with Louis Blériot, July 25, 1909   **92**
   (il) Willard, N. A visit to William Blake's inn   **811**

Provensen, Martin, 1916-1987
   (jt. auth) Provensen, A. The glorious flight: across the Channel with Louis Blériot, July 25, 1909   **92**
   (il) Willard, N. A visit to William Blake's inn   **811**

Proverbs
   McCurdy, M. So said Ben [biography of Benjamin Franklin]   **92**

Punishment in schools *See* School discipline

Punk wig. Ries, L.   **E**

Punxsutawney Phyllis. Hill, S. L.   **E**

Pup and Hound hatch an egg. Hood, S.   **E**

Puppet magic. Lowe, J. L.   **027.62**

Puppet mania. Kennedy, J. E.   **791.5**

Puppet planet. Kennedy, J. E.   **791.5**

Puppets and puppet plays

Bauer, C. F. Leading kids to books through puppets   **027.62**

Champlin, C. Storytelling with puppets   **372.6**

D'Cruz, A.-M. Make your own puppets   **791.5**

Exner, C. R. Practical puppetry A-Z   **791.5**

Kennedy, J. E. Puppet mania   **791.5**

Kennedy, J. E. Puppet planet   **791.5**

Lowe, J. L. Puppet magic   **027.62**

Minkel, W. How to do "The three bears" with two hands   **791.5**

Stanley, D. Mozart, the wonder child   **92**

Fiction

Boynton, S. Sandra Boynton's One shoe blues   **782.42**

Collodi, C. The adventures of Pinocchio [illustrated by Roberto Innocenti]   **Fic**

Keats, E. J. Louie   **E**

Riddleburger, S. The strange case of Origami Yoda   **Fic**

Puppies and piggies. Rylant, C.   **E**

Puppy power. Cox, J.   **Fic**

The **puppy** who wanted a boy. Thayer, J.   **E**

Pura Belpré award

The Pura Belpré Awards   **028.5**

The **Pura** Belpré Awards   **028.5**

Pure dead frozen. Gliori, D.   **Fic**

Puritans

Fiction

Speare, E. G. The witch of Blackbird Pond   **Fic**

Purmell, Ann, 1953-

Apple cider making days   **E**

Christmas tree farm   **E**

Maple syrup season   **E**

The **purple** balloon. Raschka, C.   **155.9**

The **purple** coat. Hest, A.   **E**

The **purple** kangaroo. Black, M. I.   **E**

Push button. Aliki   **E**

The **pushcart** war. Merrill, J.   **Fic**

Pushing up the sky: seven Native American plays for children. Bruchac, J.   **812**

Puss in boots. Cech, J.   **398.2**

Puss in boots. Galdone, P.   **398.2**

Puss in boots. Light, S.   **398.2**

Puss in boots. Perrault, C.   **398.2**

Put it on the list. Darbyshire, K.   **E**

Putonti, Dorette

(jt. auth) Harker, C. Library research with emergent readers   **027.62**

Puttapipat, Niroot

The musicians of Bremen   **398.2**

Putting on a play. Jacobs, P. D.   **792**

Puyallup Assembly Center (Wash.)

Fiction

Patt, B. Best friends forever   **Fic**

Puybaret, Eric

(il) Berne, J. Manfish: a story of Jacques Cousteau   **92**

(il) Cech, J. The nutcracker   **E**

(il) Harburg, E. Y. Over the rainbow   **782.42**

(il) Yarrow, P. Puff, the magic dragon   **782.42**

The **puzzle** of the platypus. Myers, J.   **590**

Puzzles

See also Maze puzzles; Picture puzzles; Riddles

Carter, D. A. 600 black spots   **E**

Carter, D. A. Blue 2   **E**

Carter, D. A. One red dot   **E**

Clark, D. C. A kid's guide to Washington, D.C.   **917.53**

Munro, R. Circus   **E**

Nickle, J. Alphabet explosion!   **793.73**

Onishi, S. Who's hiding?   **E**

Spot 7 School   **793.73**

Steiner, J. Look-alikes around the world   **793.73**

Wick, W. Can you see what I see?   **793.73**

Wick, W. I spy   **793.73**

Fiction

Beil, M. D. The Red Blazer Girls: the ring of Rocamadour   **Fic**

Berlin, E. The puzzling world of Winston Breen   **Fic**

The **puzzling** world of Winston Breen. Berlin, E.   **Fic**

Pygmies

Goldenberg, L. Little people and a lost world   **599.93**

Pyle, Chuck, 1954-

(il) Bowen, F. No easy way   **92**

Pym, Tasha

Have you ever seen a sneep?   **E**

Pyramids

Bolton, A. Pyramids and mummies   **932**

Hyman, T. L. Pyramids   **726**

Macaulay, D. Pyramid   **726**

Olson, N. Pyramids   **516**

Pyramids. Olson, N.   **516**

Pyramids and mummies. Bolton, A.   **932**

Pythons

Fiction

Wildsmith, B. Jungle party   **E**

Python's party. See Wildsmith, B. Jungle party   **E**

Q

Q is for quark. Schwartz, D. M.   **500**

Qatar

Orr, T. Qatar   **953.6**

QEB changes in . . . [series]

Parker, S. Animal habitats   **591.7**

Parker, S. Climate   **551.6**

Quimby, Harriet, 1875-1912—About—*Continued*
Whitaker, S. The daring Miss Quimby [biography of Harriet Quimby]   **92**
Quinceañera (Social custom)
Hoyt-Goldsmith, D. Celebrating a Quinceañera   **392**

Fiction
McNelly McCormack, C. The fiesta dress   E
Quinito's neighborhood. Cumpiano, I.   E
Quinn, Patricia O.
Attention, girls!   **616.85**
Quirky, jerky, extra-perky. Cleary, B. P.   **428**
Quotations
See also Proverbs
Alcorn, S. A gift of days   **808.88**
Spinelli, E. Today I will   **808.8**

R

Raab, Brigitte
Where does pepper come from?   E
Raatma, Lucia
Green living   **333.72**
Islam   **297**
Safety for babysitters   **649**
Safety in your neighborhood   **613.6**
The **rabbi** and the twenty-nine witches. Hirsh, M.   **398.2**
Rabbit (Legendary character)
Johnston, T. The tale of Rabbit and Coyote   **398.2**
Rabbit & Squirrel. LaReau, K.   E
Rabbit Hill. Lawson, R.   Fic
Rabbit makes a monkey of lion. Aardema, V.   **398.2**
Rabbits
Barnes, J. Pet rabbits   **636.9**
Bjorklund, R. Rabbits   **636.9**
Ganeri, A. Rabbits   **636.9**
Gibbons, G. Rabbits, rabbits, & more rabbits!   **599.3**
Holub, J. Why do rabbits hop?   **636.9**
Jeffrey, L. S. Hamsters, gerbils, guinea pigs, rabbits, ferrets, mice, and rats   **636.9**
Johnson, J. Rabbits   **636.9**
Stewart, M. Rabbits   **599.3**
Tagholm, S. The rabbit   **599.3**
See/See also pages in the following book(s):
Bozzo, L. My first guinea pig and other small pets   **636.9**

Fiction
Adams, R. Watership Down   Fic
Allen, J. The little rabbit who liked to say moo   E
Base, G. Enigma   Fic
Bauer, M. D. One brown bunny   E
Berger, C. Forever friends   E
Bianco, M. W. The velveteen rabbit   Fic
Blake, S. I don't want to go to school!   E
Brett, J. The Easter egg   E
Brown, M. W. Goodnight moon   E
Brown, M. W. The runaway bunny   E
Carlson, N. L. Get up and go!   E

Carlson, N. L. Harriet and the roller coaster   E
Cate, A. L. The magic rabbit   E
Côté, G. Me and you   E
Cowell, C. That rabbit belongs to Emily Brown   E
Czekaj, J. Hip & Hop, don't stop   E
Dewdney, A. Nobunny's perfect   E
DiCamillo, K. The miraculous journey of Edward Tulane   Fic
DiTerlizzi, T. Kenny & the dragon   Fic
Dubosarsky, U. The terrible plop   E
Fleming, C. Muncha! Muncha! Muncha!   E
Ford, B. First snow   E
Ford, B. No more bottles for Bunny!   E
Galbraith, K. O. Boo, bunny!   E
Glaser, L. Hoppy Hanukkah!   E
Gorbachev, V. Christopher counting   E
Gore, L. Danny's first snow   E
Gravett, E. Wolves   E
Hannigan, K. Emmaline and the bunny   Fic
Hazen, L. E. Cinder Rabbit   Fic
Henkes, K. So happy!   E
Heyward, D. The country bunny and the little gold shoes   E
Horse, H. Little Rabbit lost   E
Jennings, R. W. Orwell's luck   Fic
Ji Zhaohua. No! that's wrong!   E
Keller, L. Do unto otters   E
Kempter, C. Wally and Mae   E
Klise, K. Shall I knit you a hat?   E
LaReau, K. Rabbit & Squirrel   E
Lawson, R. Rabbit Hill   Fic
Lee, H. B. While we were out   E
Marlow, L. Hurry up and slow down   E
McBratney, S. Guess how much I love you   E
McBratney, S. When I'm big   E
McCarty, P. Henry in love   E
McMullan, K. Pearl and Wagner: one funny day   E
McPhail, D. M. Sylvie & True   E
Newberry, C. T. Marshmallow   E
Paul, A. W. Fiesta fiasco   E
Peet, B. Huge Harold   E
Pennypacker, S. Pierre in love   E
Portis, A. Not a box   E
Potter, B. The tale of Peter Rabbit   E
Raschka, C. Five for a little one   E
Rohmann, E. My friend Rabbit   E
Rosenthal, A. K. Duck! Rabbit!   E
Russell, N. Moon rabbit   E
Russo, M. A very big bunny   E
Ruzzier, S. Hey rabbit!   E
Rylant, C. Annie and Snowball and the dress-up birthday   E
Sakai, K. The snow day   E
Segal, J. Carrot soup   E
Shea, B. Race you to bed   E
Shields, G. When the world is ready for bed   E
Smee, N. What's the matter, Bunny Blue?   E
Spiegelman, A. Jack and the box   E
Thompson, L. Wee little bunny   E
Wallace, N. E. Pumpkin day!   E
Wallace, N. E. Recycle every day!   E
Weeks, S. Overboard!   E

Rabbits—Fiction—*Continued*
Wells, R. Emily's first 100 days of school
        E
Wells, R. Morris's disappearing bag   E
Wells, R. Read to your bunny   E
Wells, R. Ruby's beauty shop   E
Yates, L. A small surprise   E
Zolotow, C. Mr. Rabbit and the lovely present
        E
Folklore
Downard, B. The race of the century   **398.2**
Hamilton, V. Bruh Rabbit and the tar baby girl
        398.2
Han, S. C. The rabbit's tail   **398.2**
MacDonald, M. R. Conejito   **398.2**
McDermott, G. Zomo the Rabbit   **398.2**
Shannon, G. Rabbit's gift   **398.2**
Stevens, J. Tops and bottoms   **398.2**
Valeri, M. E. The hare and the tortoise = La
    liebre y la tortuga   **398.2**
Wagué Diakité, B. The magic gourd   **398.2**
Ward, H. The hare and the tortoise   **398.2**
Poetry
Brown, M. W. Nibble nibble   **811**

Rabbit's gift. Shannon, G.   **398.2**

Rabbits, rabbits, & more rabbits!. Gibbons, G.
        599.3

The **rabbit's** tail. Han, S. C.   **398.2**

Rabies
Klosterman, L. Rabies   **616.9**

Rabin, Staton, 1958-
Mr. Lincoln's boys   **92**

Rabinovitch, Sholem *See* Sholem Aleichem,
    1859-1916

Rabinowitz, Sholem Yakov *See* Sholem
    Aleichem, 1859-1916

Rabinowitz, Solomon *See* Sholem Aleichem,
    1859-1916

Racanelli, Marie
Albino animals   **591.6**
Animal mimics   **591.5**
Animals with armor   **591.47**
Animals with pockets   **599.2**
Camouflaged creatures   **591.47**
Underground animals   **591.5**

Raccoon tune. Shaw, N.   E

Raccoons
Gonzales, D. Raccoons in the dark   **599.7**
Fiction
Bunting, E. Our library   E
Friend, C. Eddie the raccoon   E
Guest, E. H. Harriet's had enough   E
Kasza, K. Ready for anything   E
Luebs, R. Please pick me up, Mama!   E
Shaw, N. Raccoon tune   E
Folklore
Bruchac, J. Raccoon's last race   **398.2**

Raccoons in the dark. Gonzales, D.   **599.7**

Raccoon's last race. Bruchac, J.   **398.2**

Race, Pat
(il) Symons, A. K. Protecting the right to read
        025.2

Race
Rotner, S. Shades of people   E

Race awareness
Molin, P. F. American Indian stereotypes in the
    world of children   **970.004**
The **race** of the century. Downard, B.   **398.2**
Race relations
    See also Ethnic relations; Multiculturalism
    names of countries, cities, etc., with the sub-
    division *Race relations*
Fiction
Brandeis, G. My life with the Lincolns   **Fic**
Choldenko, G. If a tree falls at lunch period
        Fic
Cooper, F. Willie and the All-Stars   E
English, K. Francie   **Fic**
Fuqua, J. S. Darby   **Fic**
Hemphill, H. The adventurous deeds of Dead-
    wood Jones   **Fic**
Jordan, R. Lost Goat Lane   **Fic**
Levine, K. The best bad luck I ever had
        Fic
Martin, A. M. Belle Teal   **Fic**
McMullan, M. When I crossed No-Bob   **Fic**
Raschka, C. Yo! Yes?   E
Reeder, C. Across the lines   **Fic**
Reynolds, A. Back of the bus   E
Robinet, H. G. Walking to the bus-rider blues
        Fic
Rodman, M. A. Yankee girl   **Fic**
Sebestyen, O. Words by heart   **Fic**
Spinelli, J. Maniac Magee   **Fic**
Swain, G. Riding to Washington   E
Taylor, M. D. The friendship   **Fic**
Taylor, M. D. The gold Cadillac   **Fic**
Taylor, M. D. Mississippi bridge   **Fic**
Taylor, M. D. The road to Memphis   **Fic**
Taylor, M. D. The well   **Fic**
Taylor, T. The cay   **Fic**
Taylor, T. Timothy of the cay   **Fic**
Vander Zee, R. Mississippi morning   E
Weatherford, C. B. Champions on the bench
        E
Weatherford, C. B. Freedom on the menu   E
Wiles, D. The Aurora County All-Stars   **Fic**
Wiles, D. Freedom Summer   E
Woodson, J. Feathers   **Fic**
Woodson, J. The other side   E

Race you to bed. Shea, B.   E

The **racecar** alphabet. Floca, B.   E

Races of people *See* Ethnology

Rachel. Ehrlich, A.   **92**

Racial balance in schools *See* School integration

Racially mixed people
Abramson, J. Obama   **92**
Brewster, H. The other Mozart [biography of
    Joseph Bologne Saint-Georges]   **92**
Feinstein, S. Barack Obama   **92**
Grimes, N. Barack Obama   **92**
Schuman, M. Barack Obama   **92**
Taylor, G. George Crum and the Saratoga chip
        92
Fiction
Adoff, A. Black is brown is tan   E
Chang, M. S. Celia's robot   **Fic**
Curry, J. L. The Black Canary   **Fic**

Racially mixed people—Fiction—*Continued*

Frazier, S. T. Brendan Buckley's universe and everything in it — **Fic**
García, C. I wanna be your shoebox — **Fic**
Graham, B. Oscar's half birthday — **E**
Grimes, N. The road to Paris — **Fic**
Hamanaka, S. Grandparents song — **E**
Juster, N. Sourpuss and Sweetie Pie — **E**
Marsden, C. Take me with you — **Fic**
Mora, P. Gracias = Thanks — **E**
Paterson, K. Jip — **Fic**
Schwartz, E. Stealing home — **Fic**
Stauffacher, S. Gator on the loose! — **Fic**
Stellings, C. The contest — **Fic**

Racing against the odds [biography of Wendell Scott] Weatherford, C. B. — **92**

Racism
Lester, J. Let's talk about race — **305.8**
Poetry
Argueta, J. Talking with Mother Earth — **811**

Rackham, Arthur, 1867-1939
(il) Grimm, J. Grimm's fairy tales — **398.2**
(il) Irving, W. Washington Irving's Rip van Winkle — **Fic**

Racz, Michael
(il) Mann, E. The Roman Colosseum — **937**

Raczka, Bob
3-D ABC — **730**
Action figures — **704.9**
The art of freedom — **704.9**
Artful reading — **750**
Here's looking at me — **757**
More than meets the eye — **750**
Name that style — **709**
No one saw — **759.06**
Snowy, blowy winter — **E**
Spring things — **E**
Summer wonders — **E**
Unlikely pairs — **750**
The Vermeer interviews — **759.9492**
Where in the world? — **709**
Who loves the fall? — **E**

Rader, Laura
(il) Mayr, D. Run, Turkey run — **E**

Radio Man. Don Radio. Dorros, A. — **E**

Radioactivity
Jerome, K. B. Atomic universe — **539.7**

Radunsky, Vladimir
The mighty asparagus — **E**
What does peace feel like? — **E**
You? — **E**
(il) Fox, M. Where the giant sleeps — **E**
(il) Martin, B. The maestro plays — **E**
(il) Raschka, C. Hip hop dog — **E**

Raf. Vries, A. d. — **E**

Raffi, 1948-
Baby Beluga — **782.42**
Down by the bay — **782.42**
Five little ducks — **782.42**

Raffi songs to read [series]
Raffi. Baby Beluga — **782.42**
Raffi. Down by the bay — **782.42**
Raffi. Five little ducks — **782.42**

The **raft**. LaMarche, J. — **E**

Rafting (Sports)
Fiction
LaMarche, J. The raft — **E**
Rage *See* Anger
Raglin, Tim
(il) Coville, B. William Shakespeare's Twelfth night — **822.3**
(il) Elya, S. M. Cowboy José — **E**
Ragtag. Wolf-Morgenlander, K. — **Fic**
Rahaman, Vashanti, 1953-
Divali rose — **E**
Raible, Alton, 1918-
(il) Snyder, Z. K. The Egypt game — **Fic**
(il) Snyder, Z. K. The headless cupid — **Fic**
(il) Snyder, Z. K. The witches of Worm — **Fic**
Raiders' ransom. Diamand, E. — **Fic**
Railroad fever. Halpern, M. — **385.09**
Railroad stations
Low, W. Old Penn Station — **725**
Railroads
Barton, B. Trains — **625.1**
Big book of trains — **625.1**
Clark, W. Trains on the move — **625.1**
Crowther, R. Trains: a pop-up railroad book — **625.1**
Simon, S. Seymour Simon's book of trains — **625.1**
Zimmermann, K. R. All aboard! — **385**
Fiction
Barton, C. Shark vs. train — **E**
Bee, W. And the train goes. . . — **E**
Brown, M. W. Two little trains — **E**
Crews, D. Shortcut — **E**
Goble, P. Death of the iron horse — **E**
Horáček, P. Choo choo — **E**
Johnson, A. I dream of trains — **E**
Kimmel, E. A. Stormy's hat — **E**
Lehman, B. Trainstop — **E**
London, J. A train goes clickety-clack — **E**
Macaulay, D. Black and white — **E**
McNamara, M. The whistle on the train — **E**
Panahi, H. L. Bebop Express — **E**
Piper, W. The little engine that could [illustrated by Loren Long] — **E**
Piper, W. The little engine that could [illustrated by George & Doris Hauman] — **E**
Steggall, S. Rattle and rap — **E**
Sturges, P. I love trains! — **E**
Sweet, M. Tupelo rides the rails — **E**
Wickberg, S. Hey Mr. Choo-Choo, where are you going? — **E**
Wilcoxen, C. Niccolini's song — **E**
History
Curlee, L. Trains — **385.09**
Halpern, M. Railroad fever — **385.09**
Murphy, J. Across America on an emigrant train [biography of Robert Louis Stevenson] — **92**
Nelson, S. R. Ain't nothing but a man [biography of John William Henry] — **92**
Perritano, J. The transcontinental railroad — **385.09**
Songs
Hillenbrand, W. Down by the station — **782.42**
Railsback, Lisa
Noonie's masterpiece — **Fic**

Raimondo, Joyce
Express yourself!   **709.04**
Imagine that!   **709.04**
Make it pop!   **709.04**
Picture this!   **759.05**
What's the big idea?   **709.04**

Rain
    See also Droughts
Branley, F. M. Down comes the rain   **551.57**
Feeney, S. Sun and rain   **996.9**
Kaner, E. Who likes the rain?   **551.57**
Stewart, M. When rain falls   **591.7**
       Fiction
Beaumont, K. Move over, Rover   E
Boswell, A. K. The rain stomper   E
Conway, D. Lila and the secret of rain   E
Cotten, C. Rain play   E
Herman, C. First rain   E
Hesse, K. Come on, rain!   E
Hirsh, M. The rabbi and the twenty-nine witches   **398.2**
Macken, J. E. Waiting out the storm   E
Root, P. Thirsty Thursday   E
Shannon, D. The rain came down   E
Sheth, K. Monsoon afternoon   E
Stojic, M. Rain   E
Van Cleve, K. Drizzle   Fic
Weeks, S. Drip, drop   E
Yee, W. H. Who likes rain?   E
       Poetry
Sidman, J. Meow ruff   **811**
Rain. Stojic, M.   E
Rain & hail. See Branley, F. M. Down comes the rain   **551.57**
The **rain** came down. Shannon, D.   E

Rain forest animals
Berkes, M. C. Over in the jungle   E
Bredeson, C. Baby animals of the tropical rain forest   **591.7**
Hodge, D. Rain forest animals   **591.7**
Kenyon, L. Rainforest bird rescue   **598**
Kratter, P. The living rain forest   **591.7**
Mitton, T. Rainforest romp   **591.7**
       Fiction
Witte, A. The parrot Tico Tango   E
       Folklore
Bateman, T. The Frog with the Big Mouth   **398.2**

Rain forest ecology
Fusco Castaldo, N. Rainforests   **577.3**
Gibbons, G. Nature's green umbrella   **577.3**
Greenaway, T. Jungle   **577.3**
Guiberson, B. Z. Rain, rain, rain forest   **577.3**
Jackson, K. Rain forests   **577.3**
Jackson, T. Tropical forests   **577.3**
Johansson, P. The tropical rain forest   **577.3**
Lasky, K. The most beautiful roof in the world   **577.3**
Levinson, N. S. Rain forests   **577.3**
Levy, J. Discovering rain forests   **577.3**
Stille, D. R. Tropical rain forest   **577.3**
Tagliaferro, L. Explore the tropical rain forest   **577.3**
Tocci, S. Life in the tropical forests   **577.3**

Rain forests
    See also Jungles
Collard, S. B., III. In the rain forest canopy   **578**
Jackson, K. Rain forests   **577.3**
Levy, J. Discovering rain forests   **577.3**
Vogt, R. C. Rain forests   **577.3**
Welsbacher, A. Protecting Earth's rain forests   **577.3**
       Fiction
Baker, J. Where the forest meets the sea   E
Byrd, T. Doc Wilde and the frogs of doom   Fic
Cherry, L. The great kapok tree   E
Cowley, J. Red-eyed tree frog   E
Nelson, N. Bringing the boy home   Fic
       Poetry
Alarcón, F. X. Animal poems of the Iguazu   **811**
Rain makes applesauce. Scheer, J.   E
Rain play. Cotten, C.   E
Rain player. Wisniewski, D.   E
Rain, rain, rain forest. Guiberson, B. Z.   **577.3**
The **rain** stomper. Boswell, A. K.   E

Rainbow
Stewart, M. Why do we see rainbows?   **612.8**
Rainbows are made: poems. Sandburg, C.   **811**

Raines, Shirley C., 1945-
Story stretchers for infants, toddlers, and twos   **372.4**

Rainfall *See* Rain

Rainforest bird rescue. Kenyon, L.   **598**

Rainforest romp. Mitton, T.   **591.7**

Rainforests. Fusco Castaldo, N.   **577.3**

Raining cats and dogs. Moses, W.   **428**

Rainis, Kenneth G.
(jt. auth) Gardner, R. Ace your animal science project   **590.7**
(jt. auth) Gardner, R. Ace your chemistry science project   **540.7**

Rainmaker. Jackson, A.   Fic

Rainstorm. Lehman, B.   E

Raisel's riddle. Silverman, E.   **398.2**

Raising dragons. Nolen, J.   E

Raising voices. Sima, J.   **027.62**

Rajendra, Rudi
(jt. auth) Rajendra, V. Iran   **955**

Rajendra, Sundran, 1967-
(jt. auth) Rajendra, V. Australia   **994**

Rajendra, Vijeya, 1936-
Australia   **994**
Iran   **955**

Rake, Jody Sullivan, 1961-
Blue whales up close   **599.5**
The human skeleton   **611**
Humpback whales up close   **599.5**

Rakitin, Sarah *See* Cole, Sarah Rakitin

Ralegh, Walter *See* Raleigh, Sir Walter, 1552?-1618

Raleigh, Sir Walter, 1552?-1618
Fiction
Armstrong, A. Raleigh's page   **Fic**
Raleigh's page. Armstrong, A.   **Fic**
Ramá, Sue
  (il) Miller, H. Subway ride   **388.4**
  (il) Park, L. S. Yum! Yuck!   **413**
Ramadan
  Douglass, S. L. Ramadan   **297.3**
  Heiligman, D. Celebrate Ramadan & Eid al-Fitr
             297.3
  Hoyt-Goldsmith, D. Celebrating Ramadan
             297.3
  Jeffrey, L. S. Celebrate Ramadan   **297.3**
  MacMillan, D. M. Ramadan and Id al-Fitr
             297.3
  Whitman, S. Under the Ramadan moon
             297.3
Fiction
  Addasi, M. The white nights of Ramadan   **E**
  Katz, K. My first Ramadan   **E**
  Khan, H. Night of the Moon   **E**
  Mobin-Uddin, A. A party in Ramadan   **E**
  Robert, N. b. Ramadan moon   **E**
Ramadan and Id al-Fitr. MacMillan, D. M.
             297.3
Ramadan moon. Robert, N. b.   **E**
The **Ramayana** and Hinduism. Ganeri, A.
             294.5
Ramirez, Antonio, 1944-
  Napi   **E**
Ramirez, José
  (il) Cumpiano, I. Quinito's neighborhood   **E**
Rammell, S. Kelly
  City beats   **811**
Ramon, Ilan, 1954-2003
About
  Stone, T. L. Ilan Ramon, Israel's first astronaut
             92
Ramona the pest. Cleary, B.   **Fic**
Ramos, Jorge
  I'm just like my mom/I'm just like my dad
             E
Rampersad, Arnold
  (ed) Hughes, L. Langston Hughes   **811**
Ramsey, Marcy Dunn
  (il) Naylor, P. R. Patches and scratches   **Fic**
Ramthun, Bonnie
  The White Gates   **Fic**
Ranch life
  Freedman, R. In the days of the vaqueros
             636.2
  Steele, C. Cattle ranching in the American West
             978
Fiction
  Estevis, A. Chicken Foot Farm   **Fic**
  Parry, R. Heart of a shepherd   **Fic**
  Smiley, J. The Georges and the Jewels   **Fic**
  Stanley, D. Saving Sky   **Fic**
  Waters, Z. C. Blood moon rider   **Fic**
Rand, Ann
  I know a lot of things   **E**
  Sparkle and spin   **E**

Rand, Casey
  Human reproduction   **612.6**
Rand, Paul, 1914-1996
  (jt. auth) Rand, A. I know a lot of things   **E**
  (jt. auth) Rand, A. Sparkle and spin   **E**
Rand, Ted, 1915-2005
  (il) Bunting, E. The memory string   **E**
  (il) Bunting, E. Secret place   **E**
  (il) Cleary, B. The hullabaloo ABC   **E**
  (il) George, J. C. Nutik, the wolf pup   **E**
  (il) Martin, B. Barn dance!   **E**
  (il) Martin, B. The ghost-eye tree   **E**
  (il) Martin, B. Knots on a counting rope   **E**
  (il) Prelutsky, J. If not for the cat   **811**
Rand McNally Goode's world atlas. See Goode, J.
  P. Goode's world atlas   **912**
Randall, Alison L.
  The wheat doll   **E**
Randall, Ron
  (il) Jolley, D. Guan Yu   **741.5**
  (il) Storrie, P. D. Beowulf   **741.5**
The **Random** House book of bedtime stories
             S C
The **Random** House book of Bible stories. Os-
  borne, M. P.   **220.9**
The **Random** House book of Mother Goose. See
  The Arnold Lobel book of Mother Goose
             398.8
The **Random** House book of poetry for children
             811.008
Ranger's apprentice [series]
  Flanagan, J. The ruins of Gorlan   **Fic**
**Rania, Queen, consort of Abdullah, King of
  Jordan, 1970-**
  The sandwich swap   **E**
Rankin, Jeannette, 1880-1973
  See/See also pages in the following book(s):
  Krull, K. Lives of extraordinary women   **920**
Rankin, Joan, 1940-
  (il) Borden, L. Off to first grade   **E**
  (il) Ruddell, D. A whiff of pine, a hint of skunk
             811
  (il) Wilson, K. A frog in the bog   **E**
Rankin, Laura
  The handmade alphabet   **419**
  Ruthie and the (not so) teeny tiny lie   **E**
  (il) Underwood, D. A balloon for Isabel   **E**
Ransford, Sandy
  Horse & pony breeds   **636.1**
  Horse & pony care   **636.1**
  The Kingfisher illustrated horse & pony ency-
  clopedia   **636.1**
Ransom, Candice F., 1952-
  Finding Day's Bottom   **Fic**
  The old blue pickup truck   **E**
Ransome, Arthur, 1884-1967
  See/See also pages in the following book(s):
  Ellis, S. From reader to writer   **372.6**
Ransome, James
  (il) Cline-Ransome, L. Helen Keller   **92**
  (il) Cline-Ransome, L. Satchel Paige   **92**
  (il) Cline-Ransome, L. Young Pelé   **92**
  (il) Hamilton, V. Bruh Rabbit and the tar baby
  girl   **398.2**

Ransome, James—_Continued_
- (jt. auth) Hopkinson, D. Sky boys   **E**
- (il) Hopkinson, D. Sweet Clara and the freedom quilt   **E**
- (il) Howard, E. F. Aunt Flossie's hats (and crab cakes later)   **E**
- (il) Jordan, D. Baby blessings   **242**
- (il) McKissack, P. C. Let my people go   **Fic**
- (il) Mitchell, M. K. Uncle Jed's barbershop   **E**
- (il) San Souci, R. The secret of the stones   **398.2**
- (il) Shore, D. Z. This is the dream   **811**
- (il) Thomson, S. L. What Lincoln said   **92**
- (il) Washington, D. L. A pride of African tales   **398.2**
- (il) Wolff, F. It is the wind   **E**
- (il) Woodson, J. Visiting day   **E**
- (il) Zolotow, C. The old dog   **E**

Ransome, Lesa Cline- _See_ Cline-Ransome, Lesa

Rao, Sandhya
- My mother's sari   **E**

Rap a tap tap. Dillon, L.   **E**

Rap music
- Harris, A. R. Tupac Shakur   **92**
  ### Fiction
- Czekaj, J. Hip & Hop, don't stop   **E**
- Raschka, C. Hip hop dog   **E**

Rapp, Valerie
- Protecting Earth's air quality   **363.7**

Rappaport, Doreen, 1939-
- Abe's honest words   **92**
- Dirt on their skirts   **E**
- Eleanor, quiet no more [biography of Eleanor Roosevelt]   **92**
- Free at last!   **305.8**
- Freedom river [biography of John P. Parker]   **92**
- Freedom ship   **Fic**
- John's secret dreams [biography of John Lennon]   **92**
- Lady Liberty   **974.7**
- Martin's big words: the life of Dr. Martin Luther King, Jr.   **92**
- No more!   **326**
- Nobody gonna turn me 'round   **323.1**
- The secret seder   **E**
- United no more!   **973.7**
- Victory or death!   **973.3**
- We are the many   **920**

Rapparlie, Leslie
- (jt. auth) Wurdinger, S. D. Kayaking   **797.1**

Raptor. Henry, M.   **567.9**

Rapunzel. Isadora, R.   **398.2**

Rapunzel. Zelinsky, P. O.   **398.2**

Rapunzel and other magic fairy tales   **398.2**

Rapunzel's revenge. Hale, S.   **741.5**

Rare animals
- _See also_ Endangered species
- Jenkins, S. Almost gone   **591.68**
- Lasky, K. Interrupted journey   **639.9**
- Taylor, B. Planet animal   **591.68**

Rare plants
- _See also_ Endangered species

Rare treasure: Mary Anning and her remarkable discoveries. Brown, D.   **92**

Rasamandala Das
- Hinduism   **294.5**

Raschka, Christopher
- Five for a little one   **E**
- Hip hop dog   **E**
- John Coltrane's Giant steps   **E**
- New York is English, Chattanooga is Creek   **E**
- Peter and the wolf   **E**
- The purple balloon   **155.9**
- Yo! Yes?   **E**
- (il) Best shorts. See Best shorts   **S C**
- (il) Brown, M. W. Another important book   **E**
- (il) Creech, S. Granny Torrelli makes soup   **Fic**
- (il) A foot in the mouth. See A foot in the mouth   **808.81**
- (il) Giovanni, N. The grasshopper's song   **E**
- (il) Hooks, B. Grump groan growl   **E**
- (il) Juster, N. The hello, goodbye window   **E**
- (il) Juster, N. Sourpuss and Sweetie Pie   **E**
- (il) A kick in the head. See A kick in the head   **811.008**
- (il) A Poke in the I. See A Poke in the I   **811.008**
- (il) Prelutsky, J. Good sports   **811**
- (il) Thomas, D. A child's Christmas in Wales   **828**

Rascol, Sabina I.
- The impudent rooster   **398.2**

Rash, Andy
- (il) Reynolds, A. Superhero School   **E**

Rashkin, Rachel
- Feeling better   **616.89**

Raskin, Ellen, 1928-1984
- The mysterious disappearance of Leon (I mean Noel)   **Fic**
- The Westing game   **Fic**

Rasmussen, Wendy
- (il) Poetry speaks to children. See Poetry speaks to children   **811.008**

Raspberries
  ### Fiction
- O'Callahan, J. Raspberries!   **E**

Raspberries!. O'Callahan, J.   **E**

The Ratbridge chronicles [series]
- Snow, A. Here be monsters!   **Fic**

Ratfink. Jones, M. T.   **Fic**

Rathmann, Peggy
- 10 minutes till bedtime   **E**
- The day the babies crawled away   **E**
- Good night, Gorilla   **E**
- Officer Buckle and Gloria   **E**
- (il) Bottner, B. Bootsie Barker bites   **E**

Rats
- Jeffrey, L. S. Hamsters, gerbils, guinea pigs, rabbits, ferrets, mice, and rats   **636.9**
- Johnson, J. Rats and mice   **636.9**

Rats—*Continued*

Markle, S. Outside and inside rats and mice
599.35

Marrin, A. Oh, rats! **599.35**

McNicholas, J. Rats **636.9**

Savage, S. Rat **599.35**

See/See also pages in the following book(s):

Bozzo, L. My first guinea pig and other small pets **636.9**

Fiction

Bondoux, A.-L. Vasco leader of the tribe
Fic

Bootman, C. Steel pan man of Harlem **E**

Caple, K. Duck & company **E**

Cox, J. The case of the purloined professor
Fic

Crow, K. Cool Daddy Rat **E**

Daley, M. J. Space station rat **Fic**

Hanson, M. E. How to save your tail **Fic**

Jonell, L. Emmy and the incredible shrinking rat
Fic

Kellogg, S. The Pied Piper's magic **E**

Kroll, S. Stuff! **E**

Mariconda, B. Sort it out! **E**

McPhail, D. M. Big Brown Bear's up and down day **E**

Meddaugh, S. Cinderella's rat **E**

O'Brien, R. C. Mrs. Frisby and the rats of NIMH **Fic**

Folklore

Young, E. Cat and Rat **398.2**

Rats!. Cutler, J. **Fic**

Rats and mice. Johnson, J. **636.9**

Rats on the roof, and other stories. Marshall, J.
S C

Rattigan, Jama Kim

Dumpling soup **E**

Rattle and rap. Steggall, S. **E**

Rattlesnake Mesa. Weber, E. N. R. **92**

Rattlesnake rules. Storad, C. J. **E**

Rattlesnakes

Markle, S. Rattlesnakes **597.96**

Fiction

Burell, S. Diamond Jim Dandy and the sheriff
E

Kimmel, E. A. Little Britches and the rattlers
E

Paul, A. W. Count on Culebra **E**

Storad, C. J. Rattlesnake rules **E**

Rau, Dana Meachen, 1971-

Ace your creative writing project **808**

Ace your writing assignment **808**

Alternative energy beyond fossil fuels
333.79

Animals **590**

Australia **994**

Black holes **523.8**

Chile **983**

Day and night **508**

Food chains **577**

The Milky Way and other galaxies **523.1**

Plants **580**

Quilting for fun! **746.46**

Seasons **508.2**

Singapore **959.57**

Thailand **959.3**

Top 10 cats for kids **636.8**

Top 10 fish for kids **639.34**

What's inside me? [series] **612**

The **raucous** royals. Beccia, C. **920**

Raum, Elizabeth

The Pledge of Allegiance in translation
323.6

The story behind bread **641.8**

The story behind gold **553.4**

The story behind time **529**

The story behind toilets **696**

Raut, Radhashyam

(il) Scott, N. K. The sacred banana leaf
398.2

Rauzon, Mark J.

Water, water everywhere **551.48**

Raven, Margot

Circle unbroken **E**

Happy birthday to you! **782.42**

Night boat to freedom **E**

Raven. McDermott, G. **398.2**

The **Ravenmaster's** secret. Woodruff, E. **Fic**

Ravens

Fiction

George, J. C. Charlie's raven **Fic**

Woodruff, E. The Ravenmaster's secret **Fic**

Ravishankar, Anushka

Elephants never forget **E**

Tiger on a tree **E**

Rawlings, Marjorie Kinnan, 1896-1953

The yearling **Fic**

Rawlins, Donna

(il) Whiting, S. The firefighters **E**

Rawlinson, Julia

Fletcher and the falling leaves **E**

Rawls, Wilson, 1913-1984

Where the red fern grows **Fic**

Rawls, Woodrow Wilson *See* Rawls, Wilson, 1913-1984

Ray, Deborah Kogan, 1940-

Dinosaur mountain **567.9**

Down the Colorado [biography of John Wesley Powell] **92**

Hokusai **92**

To go singing through the world [biography of Pablo Neruda] **92**

Wanda Gag **92**

(il) Bardhan-Quallen, S. Flying eagle **598**

(il) Coerr, E. Chang's paper pony **E**

Ray, Delia

Ghost girl **Fic**

Singing hands **Fic**

Ray, Jane

Adam and Eve and the Garden of Eden **222**

The apple-pip princess **E**

The dollhouse fairy **E**

Snow White **398.2**

(il) Doherty, B. Fairy tales **398.2**

(il) Henderson, K. Lugalbanda **398.2**

Ray, Mary Lyn

Christmas farm **E**

Ray, Virginia Lawrence
  School wide book events   **027.8**

Rayevsky, Robert
  (il) Hodges, M. Joan of Arc   **92**
  (il) Kimmel, E. A. Three sacks of truth
    398.2

Raymond and Graham rule the school. Knudson,
  M.   **Fic**

Raymond and Nelda. Bottner, B.   **E**

Rayner, Catherine
  (il) Newbery, L. Posy!   **E**

Rays (Fishes)
  Coldiron, D. Stingrays   **597**
  Walker, S. M. Rays   **597**
  Wearing, J. Manta rays   **597**

Rayyan, Omar
  (il) Cox, J. The case of the purloined professor
    Fic
  (il) Howe, P. Waggit's tale   **Fic**
  (il) Kimmel, E. A. Joha makes a wish   **E**
  (il) Stewig, J. W. King Midas   **398.2**

Reaching for the moon. Aldrin, B.   **92**

Read, Leon
  Keeping well   **613**
  My senses   **612.8**

Read a rhyme, write a rhyme   **811.008**

The **read-aloud** handbook. Trelease, J.   **028.5**

Read-aloud rhymes for the very young
    821.008

Read and rise. Pinkney, S. L.   **E**

Read and wonder [series]
  King-Smith, D. All pigs are beautiful   **636.4**

Read-it! chapter books: historical tales [series]
  Gunderson, J. The emperor's painting   **Fic**
  Gunderson, J. The jade dragon   **Fic**
  Gunderson, J. Stranger on the silk road   **Fic**
  Gunderson, J. The terracotta girl   **Fic**

Read it, don't eat it!. Schoenherr, I.   **E**

Read me a rhyme in Spanish and English =
  Léame una rima en español e inglés. Treviño,
  R. Z.   **027.62**

Read to your bunny. Wells, R.   **E**

The **readers'** advisory guide to graphic novels.
  Goldsmith, F.   **025.2**

Readers' theater
  Black, A. N. Readers theatre for middle school
  boys   **812**
  Fredericks, A. D. African legends, myths, and
  folktales for readers theatre   **812**
  Shepard, A. Stories on stage   **812**

Readers theatre [series]
  Black, A. N. Readers theatre for middle school
  boys   **812**
  Fredericks, A. D. African legends, myths, and
  folktales for readers theatre   **812**

Reading
  Bacon, P. S. 100+ literacy lifesavers   **428**
  Bouchard, D. The gift of reading   **372.4**
  Bradbury, J. Children's book corner: a read-
  aloud resource with tips, techniques, and
  plans for teachers, librarians and parents:
  grades 5 and 6   **372.4**

Bradbury, J. Children's book corner: a read-
  aloud resource with tips, techniques, and
  plans for teachers, librarians, and parents:
  level grades 1 and 2   **372.4**
Bradbury, J. Children's book corner: a read-
  aloud resource with tips, techniques, and
  plans for teachers, librarians, and parents:
  level grades 3 and 4   **372.4**
Bradbury, J. Children's book corner: a read-
  aloud resource with tips, techniques, and
  plans for teachers, librarians, and parents:
  level pre-K–K   **372.4**
Buzzeo, T. Collaborating to meet literacy stan-
  dards   **372.4**
Heitman, J. Once upon a time   **372.6**
Hutchins, D. J. Family reading night   **372.4**
Pinkney, S. L. Read and rise   **E**
Wood, D. Miss Little's gift   **E**
      Fiction
Bunting, E. The Wednesday surprise   **E**
Hest, A. Mr. George Baker   **E**
Hills, T. How Rocket learned to read   **E**
Polacco, P. Thank you, Mr. Falker   **E**
Sierra, J. Born to read   **E**
Straaten, H. v. Duck's tale   **E**
Walter, M. P. Alec's primer   **E**

Reading activities. Miller, P.   **025.5**

Reading comprehension
  Grimes, S. Reading is our business   **027.8**
  Moreillon, J. Collaborative strategies for teach-
  ing reading comprehension   **372.4**

Reading in art
  Raczka, B. Artful reading   **750**

Reading interests of children *See* Children—
  Books and reading

Reading Is Fundamental, Inc.
  The art of reading. See The art of reading
    741.6

Reading is our business. Grimes, S.   **027.8**

Reading magic. Fox, M.   **028.5**

Reading raps. Soltan, R.   **027.62**

Ready for anything. Kasza, K.   **E**

Ready-for-chapters [series]
  McKissack, P. C. Tippy Lemmey   **Fic**

Ready set grow!   **635**

Ready, set, grow!. Madaras, L.   **612.6**

Ready, set, preschool!. Hays, A. J.   **E**

Ready, set, skip!. O'Connor, J.   **E**

Ready-to-go storytimes. Benton, G.   **027.62**

Ready-to-read [series]
  Hopkinson, D. Billy and the rebel   **E**
  Rylant, C. Annie and Snowball and the dress-up
  birthday   **E**

Ready-to-read: Wonders of America [series]
  Bauer, M. D. The Statue of Liberty   **974.7**

Real friends vs. the other kind. Fox, A.   **158**

Real life science experiments [series]
  Benbow, A. Awesome animal science projects
    590.7
  Benbow, A. Lively plant science projects
    580.7
  Benbow, A. Sprouting seed science projects
    580.7

The **real** monsters. Bardhan-Quallen, S.   **001.9**

The **real** Mother Goose   **398.8**

Real pirates. Clifford, B.   **910.4**

The **real** spy's guide to becoming a spy. Earnest, P.   **327.12**

The **real** thief. Steig, W.   **Fic**

The **real,** true Dulcie Campbell. DeFelice, C. C.   **E**

The **real** Vikings. Berger, M.   **948**

Real world data [series]
Solway, A. Graphing immigration   **325.73**
Solway, A. Graphing war and conflict   **355**
Somervill, B. A. Graphing crime   **364**

Real world math: personal finance [series]
Minden, C. Investing   **332.6**

Real world math: Sports [series]
Marsico, K. Football   **796.332**
Marsico, K. Running   **796.42**
Marsico, K. Speed skating   **796.91**
Marsico, K. Tennis   **796.342**
Minden, C. Swimming   **797.2**

Really hot science projects with temperature. Gardner, R.   **536**

Really, really big questions. Law, S.   **100**

A **really** short history of nearly everything. Bryson, B.   **500**

Really truly Bingo. Kvasnosky, L. M.   **E**

Ream, Vinnie, 1847-1914
About
Fitzgerald, D. Vinnie and Abraham [biography of Vinnie Ream]   **92**

Reardon, Mary
(il) McSwigan, M. Snow treasure   **Fic**

The **reasons** for seasons. Gibbons, G.   **525**

Rebels against slavery. McKissack, P. C.   **326**

Rebman, Renee C., 1961-
Anteaters   **599.3**
Cats   **636.8**
Turtles and tortoises   **597.92**

RebuildingBooks, relationships, divorce and beyond [series]
MacGregor, C. Jigsaw puzzle family   **306.8**

Receivers. Gigliotti, J.   **796.332**

Recess at 20 below. Aillaud, C. L.   **370.9**

Recessions
See also names of countries, states, cities, etc., with the subdivision Economic conditions, to be added as needed
Fiction
Koss, A. G. The not-so-great depression   **Fic**

Rechenka's eggs. Polacco, P.   **E**

Recher, Andrew
(il) Vogel, J. Bats   **599.4**

A **recipe** 4 robbery. Kelsey, M.   **Fic**

Recipes *See* Cooking

Recitations *See* Monologues

Recommended books in Spanish for children and young adults, 2004-2008. Schon, I.   **011.6**

Reconstruction (1865-1876)
Stroud, B. The Reconstruction era   **973.8**

Fiction
McMullan, M. When I crossed No-Bob   **Fic**
Robinet, H. G. Forty acres and maybe a mule   **Fic**

The **Reconstruction** era. Stroud, B.   **973.8**

Recorded books *See* Audiobooks

Recordings, Sound *See* Sound recordings

Records, World *See* World records

Recorvits, Helen
My name is Yoon   **E**

Recreation
See also Amusements
Buchanan, A. J. The daring book for girls   **031.02**
Drake, J. The kids winter handbook   **790.1**
Hines-Stephens, S. Show off   **790.1**
Iggulden, C. The dangerous book for boys   **031.02**

Recycle. Barnham, K.   **363.7**

Recycle every day!. Wallace, N. E.   **E**

Recycle this book   **333.72**

Recycled crafts box. Martin, L. C.   **363.7**

Recycled tires. Allman, T.   **678**

Recycling
Allman, T. Recycled tires   **678**
Alter, A. What can you do with an old red shoe?   **745.5**
Barnham, K. Recycle   **363.7**
Barraclough, S. Reusing things   **363.7**
Bull, J. Make it!   **745.5**
Hall, E. J. Recycling   **363.7**
Jazzy jewelry   **745.594**
Llimós, A. Easy earth-friendly crafts in 5 steps   **745.5**
Martin, L. C. Recycled crafts box   **363.7**
Metz, L. What can we do about trash and recycling?   **363.7**
Minden, C. Reduce, reuse, and recycle   **363.7**
Murphy, S. J. Earth Day-hooray!   **513**
O'Neal, C. How to use waste energy to heat and light your home   **621.1**
Recycle this book   **333.72**
Ross, K. Earth-friendly crafts   **745.5**
Sirrine, C. Cool crafts with old jeans   **745.5**
Fiction
Kooser, T. Bag in the wind   **E**
Kroll, S. Stuff!   **E**
Wallace, N. E. Recycle every day!   **E**
Graphic novels
Sonishi, K. Leave it to PET!: the misadventures of a recycled super robot, vol. 1   **741.5**

The **red** balloon. Lamorisse, A.   **E**

The **Red** Blazer Girls: the ring of Rocamadour. Beil, M. D.   **Fic**

The **red** book. Lehman, B.   **E**

Red butterfly. Noyes, D.   **E**

Red Cloud, Sioux Chief, 1822-1909
See/See also pages in the following book(s):
Ehrlich, A. Wounded Knee: an Indian history of the American West   **970.004**
Freedman, R. Indian chiefs   **920**

Red Cross of the United States *See* American
   Red Cross

The **red** dragon codex. Henham, R. D.   Fic

Red-eyed tree frog. Cowley, J.   E

Red green blue. Jay, A.   E

Red is a dragon. Thong, R.   E

Red knot. Willis, N. C.   598

Red land, yellow river. Zhang, A.   951.05

Red leaf, yellow leaf. Ehlert, L.   582.16

The **red** lemon. Staake, B.   E

The **red** pyramid. Riordan, R.   Fic

Red Riding Hood. Marshall, J.   398.2

The **red** rose box. Woods, B.   Fic

The **red** scarf. Villeneuve, A.   E

Red scarf girl. Jiang, J.-l.   951.05

The **red** shoes. Glass, E.   E

Red sings from treetops. Sidman, J.   E

Red Sox (Baseball team) *See* Boston Red Sox
   (Baseball team)

Red Ted and the lost things. Rosen, M.   E

Red Truck. Hamilton, K. R.   E

Red, white, blue, and Uncle who? Bateman, T.
   929.9

The **red** wolf. Shannon, M.   E

Red wolves. Goldish, M.   599.77

Redmond, Ian
   Gorilla, monkey & ape   599.8

Redmond, Shirley-Raye
   Tentacles!   594

Reduce, reuse, and recycle. Minden, C.   363.7

Reducing *See* Weight loss

Redwall. Jacques, B.   Fic

Redwood
   Chin, J. Redwoods   585

Redwoods. Chin, J.   585

Reed, Jennifer
   Cape Hatteras National Seashore   975.6
   Paula Danziger   92

Reed, Lynn Rowe
   Basil's birds   E
   (il) Kanninen, B. J. A story with pictures   E
   (il) Pulver, R. Nouns and verbs have a field day
      E
   (il) Pulver, R. Punctuation takes a vacation
      E
   (il) Pulver, R. Silent letters loud and clear   E

Reed, Mike, 1951-
   (il) Bollard, J. K. Scholastic children's thesaurus
      423
   (il) Clements, A. A million dots   513
   (il) Nolan, L. A. On the road   Fic

Reeder, Carolyn, 1937-
   Across the lines   Fic

Reese, Harold *See* Reese, Pee Wee, 1919-1999

Reese, Pee Wee, 1919-1999
      About
   Golenbock, P. Teammates [biography of Jackie
      Robinson]   92

Reeve, Joan B.
   (jt. auth) Nespeca, S. M. Picture books plus
      028.5

Reeve, Philip, 1966-
   Larklight   Fic

Reeves, Bass, 1838-1910
      About
   Nelson, V. M. Bad news for outlaws   92
      Fiction
   Paulsen, G. The legend of Bass Reeves   Fic

Reeves, Jeni, 1947-
   (il) Douglass, S. L. Ramadan   297.3
   (il) Krensky, S. Anansi and the box of stories
      398.2

Reeves, Rick, 1959-
   (il) Rappaport, D. United no more!   973.7

Reference books
   Adams, S. The Kingfisher atlas of exploration &
      empires   911
   Adams, S. The Kingfisher atlas of the ancient
      world   930
   Adams, S. The Kingfisher atlas of the medieval
      world   909.07
   Adams, S. The Kingfisher atlas of the modern
      world   909.8
   Adams, S. The most fantastic atlas of the whole
      wide world by the Brainwaves   912
   Adventuring with books   011.6
   Al-Hazza, T. C. Books about the Middle East
      016.3058
   The American Heritage children's dictionary
      423
   The American Heritage first dictionary   423
   The American Heritage picture dictionary
      423
   Animals   590.3
   Animals: a visual encyclopedia   590.3
   Atlas of the world   912
   Barancik, S. Guide to collective biographies for
      children and young adults   016.9
   Barr, C. Best books for children: preschool
      through grade 6   011.6
   Barr, C. Best new media, K-12   011.6
   Barstow, B. Beyond picture books   011.6
   Bauer, C. F. Leading kids to books through
      crafts   027.62
   Bauer, C. F. Leading kids to books through
      magic   027.62
   Bauer, C. F. Leading kids to books through pup-
      pets   027.62
   Beginner's United States atlas   912
   The best children's books of the year   016.3
   Biology matters!   570
   Birds of the world   598
   The Black experience in children's books
      016.3058
   Blakemore, C. Faraway places   011.6
   Blass, R. J. Celebrate with books   028.1
   Bockenhauer, M. H. Our fifty states   973
   Bollard, J. K. Scholastic children's thesaurus
      423
   Bott, C. J. The bully in the book and in the
      classroom   371.5
   Bott, C. J. More bullies in more books
      371.5
   Britannica illustrated science library   503

Reference books—*Continued*

Rourke's complete history of our presidents encyclopedia **920.003**

Rubel, D. Scholastic atlas of the United States **912**

Scholastic children's dictionary **423**

Scholastic children's encyclopedia **031**

Scholastic first dictionary **423**

Scholastic first picture dictionary **423**

Schon, I. Recommended books in Spanish for children and young adults, 2004-2008 **011.6**

Serving young teens and 'tweens **027.62**

Silvey, A. 100 best books for children **011.6**

Simon & Schuster thesaurus for children **423**

Somervill, B. A. Our living world **577**

Something about the author **920.003**

Something about the author: autobiography series **920.003**

Space science **500.5**

Steele, P. Scholastic atlas of the world **912**

Student Atlas **912**

Sussman, J. K. My first Yiddish word book **439**

Tenth book of junior authors and illustrators **920.003**

Terban, M. Scholastic dictionary of idioms **423**

Terban, M. Scholastic dictionary of spelling **428**

Thomas, R. L. Popular series fiction for K-6 readers **016.8**

Timelines of history **902**

Van Orden, P. J. Library service to children **027.62**

Walter, V. A. War & peace **016.3**

Webster's New World children's dictionary **423**

Wesson, L. P. Green reads **016.3**

What do children and young adults read next? **016.8**

Wildlife and plants **578**

Wilkes, A. My world of discovery **031**

The world almanac and book of facts, 2010 **031.02**

The World Book encyclopedia **031**

The World Book encyclopedia of people and places **910.3**

World Book's encyclopedia of flags **929.9**

York, S. Ethnic book awards **011.6**

Reflexes

Berger, M. Why I sneeze, shiver, hiccup, and yawn **612.7**

Reformers

Boomhower, R. E. Fighting for equality **92**

Refrigeration

Fiction

Manushkin, F. The Shivers in the fridge **E**

Refugees

Making it home **305.23**

Fiction

Applegate, K. Home of the brave **Fic**

Bunting, E. How many days to America? **E**

Cornwell, N. Christophe's story **Fic**

Give me shelter **S C**

Graber, J. Muktar and the camels **E**

Hoffman, M. The color of home **E**

Lombard, J. Drita, my homegirl **Fic**

Shulevitz, U. How I learned geography **E**

Thor, A. A faraway island **Fic**

Williams, K. L. Four feet, two sandals **E**

Williams, K. L. My name is Sangoel **E**

Williams, M. Brothers in hope **Fic**

Refugees, Cuban *See* Cuban refugees

Refugees, Jewish *See* Jewish refugees

Refuse and refuse disposal

See also Recycling

Albee, S. Poop happened! **363.7**

Bowden, R. Waste **363.7**

Fiction

McMullan, K. I stink! **E**

Winter, J. Here comes the garbage barge! **E**

Zimmerman, A. G. Trashy town **E**

Regan, Sally

The vampire book **398**

Regarding the sink. Klise, K. **Fic**

Regeneration (Biology)

Mitchell, S. K. Animal body-part regenerators **571.8**

Regular Guy. Weeks, S. **Fic**

Rehwoldt, Sheri Bell- *See* Bell-Rehwoldt, Sheri, 1962-

Reibstein, Mark

Wabi Sabi **E**

Reich, Susanna, 1954-

Clara Schumann **92**

José! [biography of José Limón] **92**

Reichard, Susan E.

Who on earth is Sylvia Earle? **92**

Reiche, Dietlof, 1941-

I, Freddy **Fic**

Reichenstetter, Friederun, 1940-

Andersen's fairy tales **S C**

Reid, Alastair, 1926-

Ounce, dice, trice **428**

Reid, Barbara

The Subway mouse **E**

Reid, Rob

Children's jukebox **782.42**

Comin' down to storytime **E**

Cool story programs for the school-age crowd **028.5**

More family storytimes **027.62**

Reid's read-alouds **011.6**

Shake & shout **027.62**

Something funny happened at the library **027.62**

Reid Banks, Lynne *See* Banks, Lynne Reid, 1929-

Reid's read-alouds. Reid, R. **011.6**

Reidy, Jean

Too purpley! **E**

Reiff, Katie Bowers, 1984-

(jt. auth) Bowers, N. 4-H guide to training horses **636.1**

Reign of the sea dragons. Collard, S. B., III **567.9**

Rey, H. A. (Hans Augusto), 1898-1977—*Continued*

About

Borden, L. The journey that saved Curious George [biography of Margret Rey and H. A. Rey]   **92**

(il) Payne, E. Katy No-Pocket   **E**

(jt. auth) Rey, M. Whiteblack the penguin sees the world   **E**

Rey, Hans Augusto *See* Rey, H. A. (Hans Augusto), 1898-1977

Rey, Margret

Whiteblack the penguin sees the world   **E**

About

Borden, L. The journey that saved Curious George [biography of Margret Rey and H. A. Rey]   **92**

Reynish, Jenny

(il) Mordhorst, H. Pumpkin butterfly   **811**

Reynolds, Aaron, 1970-

Back of the bus   **E**

Joey Fly, private eye in Creepy crawly crime   **741.5**

Metal man   **E**

Superhero School   **E**

Reynolds, David West

Star wars: incredible cross sections   **791.43**

Reynolds, Jan, 1956-

Cycle of rice, cycle of life   **633.1**

Reynolds, Peter

The dot   **E**

Ish   **E**

Rose's garden   **E**

(il) McDonald, M. Judy Moody   **Fic**

(il) McDonald, M. Stink: the incredible shrinking kid   **Fic**

(il) Potter, E. Olivia Kidney   **Fic**

Reynolds, Peter, 1961-

(il) Brallier, J. M. Tess's tree   **E**

Reynolds, Susan

The first marathon: the legend of Pheidippides   **938**

Rhatigan, Joe

Cool chemistry concoctions   **540.7**

Out-of-this-world astronomy   **520**

Prize-winning science fair projects for curious kids   **507.8**

Soapmaking   **668**

Rhetoric

Study and teaching

Ellis, S. From reader to writer   **372.6**

Rhinoceros

Carson, M. K. Emi and the rhino scientist   **599.66**

Firestone, M. Top 50 reasons to care about rhinos   **599.66**

Holmes, M. T. My travels with Clara   **599.66**

Jango-Cohen, J. Rhinoceroses   **599.66**

Walden, K. Rhinoceroses   **599.66**

Fiction

Silverstein, S. Who wants a cheap rhinoceros?   **E**

Rhode Island

Fiction

Bruchac, J. Whisper in the dark   **Fic**

Ferrari, M. Born to fly   **Fic**

Lisle, J. T. The art of keeping cool   **Fic**

History

Avi. Finding Providence: the story of Roger Williams   **92**

Rhodesia, Northern *See* Zambia

Rhodesia, Southern *See* Zimbabwe

Rhyme

See also English language—Rhyme; Stories in rhyme

Fiction

Thomas, J. Rhyming dust bunnies   **E**

Rhymes round the world   **808.81**

Rhyming dust bunnies. Thomas, J.   **E**

Rhythm and blues music

Handyside, C. Soul and R&B   **781.644**

Ribbit riddles. Hall, K.   **793.73**

Rice, Eve, 1951-

Sam who never forgets   **E**

Rice, John, 1958-

(il) Myers, J. The puzzle of the platypus   **590**

Rice

Reynolds, J. Cycle of rice, cycle of life   **633.1**

Rich, Susan, 1969-

(ed) Half-minute horrors. See Half-minute horrors   **S C**

Richard, Christopher, 1959-

Brazil   **981**

Richard, Maurice, 1921-2000

See/See also pages in the following book(s):

Krull, K. Lives of the athletes   **920**

Richard Wright and the library card. Miller, W.   **E**

Richards, Beah, 1926-2000

Keep climbing, girls   **E**

Richards, Chuck, 1957-

Critter sitter   **E**

Richards, Jean, 1940-

A fruit is a suitcase for seeds   **581.4**

Richards, Norman, 1932-

Monticello   **975.5**

Richardson, Adele, 1966-

Caring for your fish   **639.34**

Caring for your hamster   **636.9**

Caring for your hermit crab   **639**

Richardson, Gillian

Kaboom!   **500**

Richardson, Joy

Looking at pictures   **750.1**

Richardson, Justin

And Tango makes three   **E**

Richter, Jutta, 1955-

Beyond the station lies the sea   **Fic**

Rickshaw girl. Perkins, M.   **Fic**

Riddell, Chris, 1962-

Ottoline and the yellow cat   **Fic**

(il) Jenkins, M. Don Quixote   **Fic**

Riddell, Chris, 1962-—*Continued*
(jt. auth) Stewart, P. Beyond the Deepwoods
Fic
(jt. auth) Stewart, P. The curse of the night wolf
Fic
(jt. auth) Stewart, P. Fergus Crane **Fic**
Riddle, Sue, 1966-
(il) Swope, S. Gotta go! Gotta go! **E**
Riddle, Tohby, 1965-
(il) Dubosarsky, U. The word snoop **420**
Riddle, Bonnie *See* Ceban, Bonnie J.
The **riddle** of the Rosetta Stone. Giblin, J.
493
Riddle roundup. Maestro, G. **793.73**
Riddleburger, Sam
The strange case of Origami Yoda **Fic**
(jt. auth) Hemphill, M. Stonewall Hinkleman
and the Battle of Bull Run **Fic**
Riddles
Brewer, P. You must be joking! **817**
Brewer, P. You must be joking, two! **817**
Cole, J. Why did the chicken cross the road?
and other riddles, old and new **793.73**
Hall, K. Creepy riddles **793.73**
Hall, K. Dino riddles **793.73**
Hall, K. Ribbit riddles **793.73**
Hall, K. Simms Taback's great big book of
spacey, snakey, buggy riddles **793.73**
Hall, K. Snakey riddles **793.73**
Hall, K. Turkey riddles **793.73**
Lewis, J. P. Spot the plot **811**
Maestro, G. Riddle roundup **793.73**
Maestro, M. What do you hear when cows sing?
793.73
Shannon, G. More stories to solve **398.2**
Shannon, G. Stories to solve **398.2**
Fiction
Waldman, D. Clever Rachel **398.2**
Ride, Sally K.
Mission: planet Earth **525**
Mission: save the planet **333.72**
Ride a purple pelican. Prelutsky, J. **811**
Ridin' dinos with Buck Bronco. McClements, G.
E
Riding *See* Horsemanship
Riding to Washington. Swain, G. **E**
Riding with the mail. Thompson, G. **383**
Ridley, Sarah, 1963-
A chocolate bar **664**
Riedling, Ann Marlow, 1952-
(jt. auth) Kaplan, A. G. Catalog it! **025.3**
Riehecky, Janet, 1953-
China **951**
Rielly, Robin L.
Karate for kids **796.8**
Ries, Lori
Aggie and Ben **E**
Punk wig **E**
Rieth, Elizabeth, 1957-
(jt. auth) Johmann, C. Bridges! **624.2**
Rifles for Watie. Keith, H. **Fic**

Rigano, Giovanni
(il) Colfer, E. Artemis Fowl: the graphic novel
741.5
Rigg, Sharon *See* Creech, Sharon
Riggle, Judith
(jt. auth) Barstow, B. Beyond picture books
011.6
Riggs, Kate
The French Revolution **944.04**
Wolfgang Amadeus Mozart **92**
Riggs, Shannon
Not in Room 204 **E**
The **right** dog for the job. Patent, D. H. **362.4**
Right of privacy
Chmara, T. Privacy and confidentiality issues
344
Jakubiak, D. J. A smart kid's guide to Internet
privacy **005.8**
Right to know *See* Freedom of information
The **Right-Under** Club. Deriso, C. H. **Fic**
Rights, Civil *See* Civil rights
Rights, Human *See* Human rights
Righty & Lefty. Vail, R. **E**
Riglietti, Serena
(il) Cooper, S. The magician's boy **Fic**
Rigsby, Mike
Amazing rubber band cars **745.592**
Riki's birdhouse. Wellington, M. **E**
Rikki-tikki-tavi. Pinkney, J. **E**
Riley, Linnea Asplind
Mouse mess **E**
Riley and Rose in the picture. Gretz, S. **E**
Riley-Webb, Charlotte
(il) The entrance place of wonders. See The entrance place of wonders **811.008**
(il) Lindsey, K. Sweet potato pie **E**
(il) Miller, W. Rent party jazz **E**
Rim, Sujean
Birdie's big-girl shoes **E**
Rimm, Sylvia B., 1935-
See Jane win for girls **305.23**
Rinaldi, Angelo
(il) Doyle, M. Horse **E**
Rinaldo, Denise
White House Q & A **975.3**
Rinck, Maranke
I feel a foot! **E**
Ring of fire. Baccalario, P. **Fic**
A **ring** of tricksters. Hamilton, V. **398.2**
Ringgold, Faith
Tar Beach **E**
About
Venezia, M. Faith Ringgold **92**
(il) Brooks, G. Bronzeville boys and girls
811
(il) Thomas, J. C. The three witches **398.2**
Rio Grande valley
Lourie, P. Rio Grande **976.4**
Riordan, Rick
The maze of bones **Fic**
The red pyramid **Fic**

The Riot Brothers [series]
Amato, M. Stinky and successful   Fic
Riots
Fiction
Bunting, E. Smoky night   E
Rip-roaring Russell. Hurwitz, J.   Fic
Rip Van Winkle's return. Kimmel, E. A.   E
The **rise** of Jim Crow. Haskins, J.   305.8
Rise of the thinking machines. VanVoorst, J.   629.8
The **rising** star of Rusty Nail. Blume, L. M. M.   Fic
Risk-taking (Psychology)
Burstein, J. I said no!   158
Riskind, Mary, 1944-
Apple is my sign   Fic
Rissa Bartholomew's declaration of independence. Comerford, L. B.   Fic
Rissik, Dee
(jt. auth) Rosmarin, I. South Africa   968
Rissman, Rebecca
Shapes in art   516
Shapes in buildings   516
Shapes in music   516
Shapes in sports   516
Shapes in the garden   516
Ritchie, Scot
(il) Flatt, L. Let's go!   388
Ritz, Karen
Windows with birds   E
(il) Adler, D. A. Hiding from the Nazis   940.53
(il) Kroll, S. Ellis Island   325.73
River animals See Stream animals
River ecology
Fusco Castaldo, N. River wild   577.6
River journey [series]
Bowden, R. The Nile   962
River of dreams. Talbott, H.   974.7
River of words   808.81
A **river** of words: the story of William Carlos Williams. Bryant, J.   92
River plants See Stream plants
River song. Hollyer, B.   Fic
River wild. Fusco Castaldo, N.   577.6
Rivera, Diego, 1886-1957
About
Rivera Marín, G. My papa Diego and me [biography of Diego Rivera]   92
Sabbeth, C. Frida Kahlo and Diego Rivera: their lives and ideas   92
Winter, J. Diego [biography of Diego Rivera]   92
(il) Rivera Marín, G. My papa Diego and me [biography of Diego Rivera]   92
Rivera, Frida Kahlo See Kahlo, Frida, 1907-1954
Rivera, Raquel, 1966-
Arctic adventures   920
Rivera, Tomás
About
Medina, J. Tomás Rivera   92

Fiction
Mora, P. Tomás and the library lady   E
Rivera Marín, Guadalupe, 1924-
My papa Diego and me [biography of Diego Rivera]   92
About
Rivera Marín, G. My papa Diego and me [biography of Diego Rivera]   92
Rivers
See also Amazon River; Colorado River (Colo.-Mexico); Hudson River (N.Y. and N.J.); Mississippi River; Nile River
Chambers, C. Rivers   551.48
Fusco Castaldo, N. River wild   577.6
Green, J. Mighty rivers   551.48
Johansson, P. Lakes and rivers   577.6
Sepehri, S. Rivers   551.48
Fiction
Gonzalez, M. C. I know the river loves me   E
Poetry
Hughes, L. The Negro speaks of rivers   811
Rivers of North America [series]
Harris, T. The Mackenzie River   971
Roach, Marilynne K.
In the days of the Salem witchcraft trials   133.4
Roach (Insect) See Cockroaches
Road runner See Roadrunners
The **road** to Memphis. Taylor, M. D.   Fic
The **road** to Oz [biography of L. Frank Baum] Krull, K.   92
The **road** to Paris. Grimes, N.   Fic
Road to Tater Hill. Hemingway, E. M.   Fic
Roadrunners
Murphy, S. J. Coyotes all around   519.5
Fiction
Wallace, B. The legend of thunderfoot   Fic
Roadwork!. Sutton, S.   E
Roald Amundsen and Robert Scott race to the South Pole. Thompson, G.   998
Roanoke. Miller, L.   975.6
Roanoke Island (N.C.)
History
Fritz, J. The Lost Colony of Roanoke   975.6
Miller, L. Roanoke   975.6
See/See also pages in the following book(s):
Huey, L. M. American archaeology uncovers the earliest English colonies   973.2
Roar!. Mayo, M.   E
Roawr!. Joosse, B. M.   E
Robb, Don
Ox, house, stick   411
Robbers and outlaws See Thieves
Robbins, Jacqui
The new girl . . . and me   E
Two of a kind   E
Robbins, Ken, 1945-
For good measure   530.8
Pumpkins   635
Seeds   581.4
(il) Frank, J. Keepers   811

Robot City [series]
Collicutt, P. City in peril!   741.5
Robot dreams. Varon, S.   741.5
Robot explorers. Miller, R.   629.43
Robot Zot!. Scieszka, J.   E
Robotics *See* Robots
Robots
Allman, T. The Nexi robot   629.8
Miller, R. Robot explorers   629.43
Robots: from everyday to out of this world
    629.8
VanVoorst, J. Rise of the thinking machines
    629.8
Fiction
Barnett, M. Oh no!, or, How my science project
destroyed the world   E
Bunting, E. My robot   E
Chang, M. S. Celia's robot   Fic
Fox, H. Eager   Fic
Lucas, D. The robot and the bluebird   E
McCall, B. Marveltown   E
Scieszka, J. Robot Zot!   E
Selznick, B. The invention of Hugo Cabret
    Fic
Graphic novels
Collicutt, P. City in peril!   741.5
Lemke, D. Zinc Alloy: Super Zero   741.5
Varon, S. Robot dreams   741.5
Robots!. Stephens, J.   741.5
Robots: from everyday to out of this world
    629.8
Robots in art
Stephens, J. Robots!   741.5
Robusti, Marietta *See* Tintoretto, Marietta, d.
1590
Roca, François
(il) Paterson, K. The light of the world
    232.9
(jt. auth) Prince, A. J. Twenty-one elephants and
still standing   E
(il) Winter, J. Muhammad Ali   92
Rocco, John
Moonpowder   E
Wolf! wolf!   E
(il) Kudlinski, K. V. Boy were we wrong about
the solar system!   523.2
Roche, Art
Cartooning   741.5
Roche, Denis
(il) Evans, L. Can you greet the whole wide
world?   413
(il) London, J. A train goes clickety-clack   E
(il) London, J. A truck goes rattley-bumpa   E
Rochelle, Belinda
(ed) Words with wings. See Words with wings
    811.008
Rock. Handyside, C.   781.66
Rock and roll music *See* Rock music
Rock collecting. See Gans, R. Let's go rock collecting   552

Rock drawings, paintings, and engravings
See also Cave drawings and paintings
Rock, Michelle Parker- *See* Parker-Rock, Mi-
chelle
Rock music
Boynton, S. Dog train   782.42
George-Warren, H. Shake, rattle, & roll   920
Handyside, C. Rock   781.66
Stamaty, M. A. Shake, rattle & turn that noise
down!   781.66
Fiction
Appelt, K. Bats around the clock   E
Rock musicians
Anderson, J. J. John Lennon   92
Rappaport, D. John's secret dreams [biography
of John Lennon]   92
Fiction
Thiesing, L. The Aliens are coming!   E
Rock stars [series]
Pellant, C. Fossils   560
Pellant, C. Minerals   549
Rocketry
Skurzynski, G. This is rocket science   629.4
Rockin' earth science experiments [series]
Gardner, R. Earth-shaking science projects about
planet Earth   550
Gardner, R. Far-out science projects about
Earth's sun and moon   523
Gardner, R. Smashing science projects about
Earth's rocks and minerals   552
Gardner, R. Stellar science projects about
Earth's sky   551.5
Gardner, R. Super science projects about Earth's
soil and water   631.4
Gardner, R. Wild science projects about Earth's
weather   551.5
Rockliff, Mara
The case of the stinky socks   Fic
Rockman, Connie C.
(ed) Eighth book of junior authors and illustra-
tors. See Eighth book of junior authors and il-
lustrators   920.003
(ed) Ninth book of junior authors and illustra-
tors. See Ninth book of junior authors and il-
lustrators   920.003
(ed) Tenth book of junior authors and illustra-
tors. See Tenth book of junior authors and il-
lustrators   920.003
Rocks
Davis, B. J. Minerals, rocks, and soil   552
Extreme rocks & minerals!   552
Farndon, J. Rocks and minerals   549
Faulkner, R. Igneous rock   552
Faulkner, R. Metamorphic rock   552
Faulkner, R. Sedimentary rock   552
Gardner, R. Smashing science projects about
Earth's rocks and minerals   552
Green, D. Rocks and minerals   552
Hynes, M. Rocks & fossils   552
Trueit, T. S. Rocks, gems, and minerals   552
VanCleave, J. P. Janice VanCleave's rocks and
minerals   552
Collectors and collecting
Gans, R. Let's go rock collecting   552
Hurst, C. O. Rocks in his head   E

Root, Barry
  (il) Fleischman, P. The birthday tree   E
  (il) Kay, V. Whatever happened to the Pony Express?   383
  (il) Kooser, T. Bag in the wind   E
  (il) Ray, M. L. Christmas farm   E
Root, Kimberly Bulcken
  (il) Fisher, D. C. Understood Betsy   Fic
  (il) Fletcher, S. Dadblamed Union Army cow   E
  (il) Hodges, M. The wee Christmas cabin   E
  (il) Hopkinson, D. Birdie's lighthouse   Fic
  (il) Kay, V. Whatever happened to the Pony Express?   383
  (il) McDonough, Y. Z. The doll with the yellow star   Fic
Root, Phyllis, 1949-
  Aunt Nancy and the bothersome visitors   S C
  Big Momma makes the world   E
  Creak! said the bed   E
  Flip, flap, fly!   E
  Kiss the cow   E
  Lucia and the light   E
  The name quilt   E
  Paula Bunyan   E
  Thirsty Thursday   E
  Toot toot zoom!   E
Rootabaga stories. Sandburg, C.   S C
Roots (Botany)
  Farndon, J. Roots   581.4
Rope skipping
           Fiction
  English, K. Hot day on Abbott Avenue   E
Rope skipping rhymes *See* Jump rope rhymes
The **rope** trick. Alexander, L.   Fic
Roraff, Susan
  (jt. auth) Winter, J. K. Chile   983
Ros, Roser
  Beauty and the beast = La bella y la bestia   398.2
Rosa [biography of Rosa Parks] Giovanni, N.   92
Rose, Deborah Lee, 1955-
  Birthday zoo   E
  Into the A, B, sea   591.7
  Ocean babies   591.3
  One nighttime sea   E
  The twelve days of winter   E
Rose, Naomi C.
  Tibetan tales from the top of the world   398.2
Rose and Riley. Cutler, J.   E
Rosen, Daniel
  New beginnings   975.5
Rosen, Elizabeth, 1961-
  (il) Drucker, M. Portraits of Jewish American heroes   920
Rosen, Michael, 1946-
  Dickens   92
  I'm number one   E
  Michael Rosen's sad book   E
  Red Ted and the lost things   E
  Totally wonderful Miss Plumberry   E

  We're going on a bear hunt   E
Rosen, Michael J., 1954-
  Balls!: round 2   796.3
  The cuckoo's haiku   811
  Elijah's angel   Fic
  Our farm   630.9
Rosenberg, Liz
  Nobody   E
Rosenberg, Maxine B., 1939-
  Hiding to survive   940.53
Rosenberry, Vera, 1948-
  Vera's first day of school   E
  (il) Hurwitz, J. Anne Frank: life in hiding   92
Rosenstiehl, Agnès
  Silly Lilly and the four seasons   741.5
Rosenthal, Amy Krouse
  Bedtime for Mommy   E
  Cookies   E
  Duck! Rabbit!   E
  Little Hoot   E
  The OK book   E
  The wonder book   817
  Yes Day!   E
Rosenthal, Betsy R.
  Which shoes would you choose?   E
Rosenthal, Marc
  (il) Zimmerman, A. G. Dig!   E
Rosenthal, Marc, 1949-
  Archie and the pirates   E
Rosenwald, Julius, 1862-1932
           Fiction
  Weatherford, C. B. Dear Mr. Rosenwald   Fic
Roses
  Winter, J. September roses   E
Rose's garden. Reynolds, P.   E
Rosetta stone
  Giblin, J. The riddle of the Rosetta Stone   493
Rosewarne, Graham
  (il) Johnson, J. Dandelion   583
  (il) Johnson, J. Fox   599.77
  (il) Johnson, J. Frog   597.8
  (il) Johnson, J. Oak tree   583
Rosh, Mair
  (jt. auth) DuBois, J. Israel   956.94
Rosh ha-Shanah
  Fishman, C. On Rosh Hashanah and Yom Kippur   296.4
  Heiligman, D. Celebrate Rosh Hashanah and Yom Kippur   296.4
           Fiction
  Gerstein, M. The white ram   E
  Greene, J. D. The secret shofar of Barcelona   Fic
  Kimmel, E. A. Even higher!   398.2
  Kimmel, E. A. Gershon's monster   398.2
  Wayland, A. H. New Year at the pier   E
Rosh Hodesh
           Fiction
  Da Costa, D. Hanukkah moon   E
Rosie. Calmenson, S.   636.7
Rosie and Buttercup. Uegaki, C.   E

Rueda, Claudia
Let's play in the forest while the wolf is not
around **782.42**
My little polar bear **E**
(il) Ryan, P. M. Nacho and Lolita **398.2**
Ruelle, Karen Gray, 1957-
The grand mosque of Paris **940.53**
The Thanksgiving beast feast **E**
Ruffins, Reynold, 1930-
(il) Lotu, D. Running the road to ABC **E**
(il) Sierra, J. The gift of the Crocodile
398.2
Rufus and friends: rhyme time **398.8**
Ruggi, Gilda Williams See Williams Ruggi, Gilda
Rugs and carpets
Fiction
Ichikawa, S. My father's shop **E**
Whelan, G. Waiting for the owl's call **E**
Rui, Paolo
(il) Macdonald, W. Galileo's leaning tower ex-
periment **531**
Ruins See Excavations (Archeology)
The **ruins** of Gorlan. Flanagan, J. **Fic**
Rulers See Emperors; Kings and rulers; Queens
Rules. Lord, C. **Fic**
Rules of the game. Maddox, M. **811**
The **rules** of the universe by Austin W. Hale.
Vaupel, R. **Fic**
Rumble & spew. Donovan, S. **612.3**
Rumble, roar, dinosaur!. Mitton, T. **811**
Rumford, James, 1948-
Beowulf **398.2**
Chee-lin **599.63**
Seeker of knowledge [biography of Jean Fran-
çois Champollion] **92**
Sequoyah **92**
Silent music **E**
Tiger and turtle **E**
Traveling man: the journey of Ibn Battuta,
1325-1354 **92**
(jt. auth) Alexander, M. G. Max and the dumb
flower picture **E**
Rumi See Jalāl al-Dīn Rūmī, Maulana, 1207-1273
Rūmī, Jalāl al-Dīn See Jalā̄l al-Dīn Rūmī,
Maulana, 1207-1273
Rumi [biography if Jalāl al-Dīn Rumî] Demi
92
Rumpelstiltskin. Carrasco, X. **398.2**
Rumpelstiltskin. Zelinsky, P. O. **398.2**
Rumpelstiltskin's daughter. Stanley, D. **E**
Run, Turkey run. Mayr, D. **E**
The **runaway** bunny. Brown, M. W. **E**
Runaway children
Fiction
Arnosky, J. The pirates of Crocodile Swamp
Fic
Cadow, K. M. Alfie runs away **E**
Corriveau, A. How I, Nicky Flynn, finally get a
life (and a dog) **Fic**
De Guzman, M. Finding Stinko **Fic**
Easton, K. The outlandish adventures of Liberty
Aimes **Fic**

Matthews, L. S. A dog for life **Fic**
Patron, S. The higher power of Lucky **Fic**
Segal, J. Far far away **E**
The **runaway** dinner. Ahlberg, A. **E**
The **runaway** princess. Coombs, K. **Fic**
The **runaway** rice cake. Compestine, Y. C. **E**
Runaway teenagers
Fiction
Johnson, A. Bird **Fic**
The **runaway** tortilla. Kimmel, E. A. **398.2**
Runholt, Susan, 1948-
The mystery of the third Lucretia **Fic**
Running
See also Marathon running
Marsico, K. Running **796.42**
Royston, A. Why do I run? **613.7**
Fiction
Creech, S. Heartbeat **Fic**
Marsden, C. Moon runner **Fic**
Running backs. Kelley, K. C. **796.332**
Running for office. Hamilton, J. **324**
Running the dogs. Cochran, T. **Fic**
Running the road to ABC. Lotu, D. **E**
Running with the Reservoir Pups. Bateman, C.
Fic
Runny Babbit. Silverstein, S. **811**
Runt. Bauer, M. D. **Fic**
Runton, Andy
Owly: The way home and The bittersweet sum-
mer **741.5**
Rupp, Rebecca
Sarah Simpson's Rules for Living **Fic**
Weather **551.6**
Rural life See Country life; Farm life
Rush, Barbara
(jt. auth) Schwartz, H. A coat for the moon and
other Jewish tales **398.2**
Rushby, Pamela
Ben Franklin **92**
Discovering Supercroc **567.9**
Ruskin, John, 1819-1900
The king of the Golden River **Fic**
Russell, Ching Yeung, 1945-
Tofu quilt **Fic**
Russell, Christopher, 1947-
Dogboy **Fic**
Hunted **Fic**
Russell, Henry, 1954-
Germany **943**
Russia **947**
Russell, Lillian, 1861-1922
Fiction
Peck, R. Fair weather **Fic**
Russell, Natalie, 1972-
Moon rabbit **E**
Russell, P. Craig, 1951-
Coraline [graphic novel] **741.5**
Russell, Patricia Yates, 1937-
(jt. auth) Garcha, R. The world of Islam in liter-
ature for youth **016.3058**
Russell the sheep. Scotton, R. **E**

Sail away with me   808.81

Sailing

Fiction

Appelt, K. Keeper   **Fic**

Creech, S. The Wanderer   **Fic**

Crews, D. Sail away   **E**

Ferber, B. A. Jemma Hartman, camper extraordinaire   **Fic**

Mead, A. Junebug   **Fic**

Sailors

Fiction

Lendroth, S. Ocean wide, ocean deep   **E**

Shulevitz, U. When I wore my sailor suit   **E**

Sailors' life *See* Seafaring life

Saint-Exupéry, Antoine de, 1900-1944

The little prince   **Fic**

The little prince: deluxe pop-up book   **Fic**

Saint Francis and the wolf. Egielski, R.   398.2

Saint Francis and the wolf. Langton, J.   398.2

Saint Francis of Assisi. Kennedy, R. F.   271

Saint George and the dragon. Hodges, M.   398.2

Saint-Georges, Joseph Boulogne, chevalier de, 1745-1799

About

Brewster, H. The other Mozart [biography of Joseph Bologne Saint-Georges]   92

Saint-Lot, Katia Novet, 1963-

Amadi's snowman   **E**

Saint Louis (Mo.)

Fiction

Helgerson, J. Crows & cards   **Fic**

Saint Lucia

Orr, T. Saint Lucia   972.98

Saint Patrick's Day

Barth, E. Shamrocks, harps, and shillelaghs   394.26

Gibbons, G. St. Patrick's Day   394.26

Landau, E. St. Patrick's Day   394.26

See/See also pages in the following book(s):

Bauer, C. F. Celebrations   808.8

Fiction

Wojciechowski, S. A fine St. Patrick's day   **E**

Saint Valentine. Sabuda, R.   92

Saint Valentine's Day *See* Valentine's Day

Saints

See also Christian saints

Fiction

Alvarez, J. A gift of gracias   **E**

De Paola, T. The song of Francis   **E**

Sakade, Florence

Japanese children's favorite stories   398.2

Sakai, Komako, 1966-

Emily's balloon   **E**

The snow day   **E**

Sakamoto, Miki

(il) Dunn, T. We go together!   **E**

Sakyamuni *See* Gautama Buddha

Salaam. Brown, T.   297.3

Salad people and more real recipes. Katzen, M.   641.5

Saladin, Sultan of Egypt and Syria, 1137-1193

About

Geyer, F. Saladin   92

Stanley, D. Saladin: noble prince of Islam   92

Saladin: noble prince of Islam. Stanley, D.   92

Salamanders

Goldish, M. Slimy salamanders   597.8

Fiction

Lamstein, S. A big night for salamanders   **E**

Salariya, David

(il) Graham, I. Microscopic scary creatures   591.6

(jt. auth) Malam, J. Pinnipeds   599.79

(jt. auth) Pipe, J. Swarms   591.5

Salas, Laura Purdie, 1966-

Amphibians   597.8

(jt. auth) Menhard, F. R. The facts about inhalants   362.29

Salem (Mass.)

History

Jackson, S. The witchcraft of Salem Village   133.4

Kent, D. Witchcraft trials   133.4

Roach, M. K. In the days of the Salem witchcraft trials   133.4

Salerno, Steven, 1958-

Harry hungry!   **E**

(jt. auth) Elya, S. M. Bebé goes shopping   **E**

(il) Freeman, M. Mrs. Wow never wanted a cow   **E**

(il) Pattison, D. S. 19 girls and me   **E**

Salesmanship *See* Selling

Salisbury, Graham, 1944-

Calvin Coconut: trouble magnet   **Fic**

Lord of the deep   **Fic**

Night of the howling dogs   **Fic**

Saliva

Donovan, S. Hawk & Drool   612.3

Salk, Jonas, 1914-1995

About

Tocci, S. Jonas Salk   92

Salk vaccine *See* Poliomyelitis vaccine

Salley, Coleen

Epossumondas   398.2

Epossumondas saves the day   **E**

Sallie Gal and the Wall-a-kee man. Moses, S. P.   **Fic**

Sally and the purple socks. Bechtold, L.   **E**

Sally Ann Thunder Ann Whirlwind Crockett. Kellogg, S.   398.2

Sally goes to the beach. Huneck, S.   **E**

Sally Jean, the Bicycle Queen. Best, C.   **E**

Sally Ride science [series]

Bridges, A. Clean air   363.7

Geiger, B. Clean water   363.7

Ride, S. K. Mission: planet Earth   525

Ride, S. K. Mission: save the planet   333.72

Salmansohn, Pete, 1947-

Saving birds   333.95

Salmon

Cone, M. Come back, salmon   639.3

McMillan, B. Salmon summer   639.2

Salmon summer. McMillan, B.   **639.2**

Salsa stories. Delacre, L.   **S C**

Salt
  Kurlansky, M. The story of salt   **553.6**
  Moore, H. The story behind salt   **553.6**

Salt in his shoes. Jordan, D.   **E**

Salt marshes
  Wechsler, D. Marvels in the muck   **578.7**

Salten, Felix, 1869-1945
  Bambi   **Fic**

Salting the ocean   **811.008**

Saltypie. Tingle, T.   **92**

Saltz, Gail
  Amazing you   **612.6**
  Changing you!   **612.6**

Saltzberg, Barney
  I want a dog!   **E**
  Stanley and the class pet   **E**
  (il) Murphy, S. J. Sluggers' car wash   **513**

Salvadori, Mario George, 1907-1997
  (jt. auth) Levy, M. Earthquakes, volcanoes, and tsunamis   **551.2**

Salvage
  Alter, A. What can you do with an old red shoe?   **745.5**
  Mitchell, J. S. Crashed, smashed, and mashed   **629.222**
  Sirrine, C. Cool crafts with old CDs   **745.58**
  Sirrine, C. Cool crafts with old t-shirts   **745.5**
  Sirrine, C. Cool crafts with old wrappers, cans and bottles   **745.5**

Salzmann, Siegmund *See* Salten, Felix, 1869-1945

Sam and the lucky money. Chinn, K.   **E**

Sam and the tigers. Lester, J.   **E**

Sam, Bangs & Moonshine. Ness, E.   **E**

Sam Johnson and the blue ribbon quilt. Ernst, L. C.   **E**

Sam who never forgets. Rice, E.   **E**

Same old horse. Murphy, S. J.   **E**

Same same. Jocelyn, M.   **E**

The **same** stuff as stars. Paterson, K.   **Fic**

SAMi, 1950-
  (il) Ziefert, H. The big, bigger, biggest book   **E**

Sami and the time of the troubles. Heide, F. P.   **E**

Samiuddin, Shahrezad
  (jt. auth) Sheehan, S. Pakistan   **954.91**

Samms, Tara *See* Cole, Stephen, 1971-

Sammy Keyes and the hotel thief. Draanen, W. v.   **Fic**

Sammy the classroom guinea pig. Berenzy, A.   **E**

Sammy the seal. Hoff, S.   **E**

Sampson, Michael, 1952-
  (ed) The Bill Martin Jr. Big book of poetry. See The Bill Martin Jr. Big book of poetry   **811.008**

Sampson, Michael R.
  (jt. auth) Martin, B. Chicka chicka 1, 2, 3   **E**
  (jt. auth) Martin, B. I love our Earth   **525**
  (jt. auth) Martin, B. Trick or treat?   **E**

Samuel (Biblical figure)
Graphic novels
  Lepp, R. David: Shepard's song, vol. 1   **741.5**

Samuel Blink and the forbidden forest. Haig, M.   **Fic**

Samuels, Barbara
  The trucker   **E**

Samuels, Charlie, 1961-
  Iraq   **956.7**

Samurai
  Hanel, R. Samurai   **952**
  Park, L. The Japanese samurai   **355**
  Turnbull, S. R. Real samurai   **952**
Fiction
  Bradford, C. Young samurai: the way of the warrior   **Fic**
  Goto, S. The perfect sword   **Fic**
  Snow, M. Sisters of the sword   **Fic**

San Francisco (Calif.)
Fiction
  Bunting, E. Pop's bridge   **E**
  English, K. Speak to me   **E**
  Freeman, M. The trouble with cats   **Fic**
  Grabien, D. Dark's tale   **Fic**
  Hopkinson, D. Into the firestorm   **Fic**
  Ketchum, L. Newsgirl   **Fic**
  Lee, M. Landed   **Fic**
  Partridge, E. Oranges on Golden Mountain   **E**
  Yang, B. Hannah is my name   **E**
  Yin. Brothers   **E**

San José, Christine
  (ed) Every second something happens. See Every second something happens   **811.008**

San Nicolas Island (Calif.)
Fiction
  O'Dell, S. Island of the Blue Dolphins   **Fic**

San Souci, Daniel
  (il) San Souci, R. As luck would have it   **398.2**
  (il) San Souci, R. Sister tricksters   **398.2**
  (il) San Souci, R. Sootface   **398.2**

San Souci, Robert, 1946-
  As luck would have it   **398.2**
  Cendrillon   **398.2**
  Cut from the same cloth   **398.2**
  Dare to be scared 4   **S C**
  Double-dare to be scared: another thirteen chilling tales   **S C**
  The faithful friend   **398.2**
  Little Gold Star   **398.2**
  The secret of the stones   **398.2**
  Short & shivery   **398.2**
  Sister tricksters   **398.2**
  Sootface   **398.2**
  Sukey and the mermaid   **398.2**
  The talking eggs   **398.2**
  Triple-dare to be scared   **S C**
  (jt. auth) Ouimet, D. Dare to be scared   **S C**

Sanchez, Anita, 1956-
The invasion of Sandy Bay   Fic

Sanchez, Enrique O., 1942-
(il) Castañeda, O. S. Abuela's weave   E
(il) O'Neill, A. Estela's swap   E
(il) Santiago, E. A doll for Navidades   E

Sanctuary movement
    See also Refugees

Sand
Stewart, M. How does sand become glass?
        666

Sand Creek, Battle of, 1864
    See/See also pages in the following book(s):
Ehrlich, A. Wounded Knee: an Indian history of
    the American West   970.004

Sand dollar summer. Jones, K. K.   Fic

Sandburg, Carl, 1878-1967
Carl Sandburg   811
The Huckabuck family and how they raised
    popcorn in Nebraska and quit and came back
        E
Rainbows are made: poems   811
Rootabaga stories   S C
The Sandburg treasury   818
      About
Niven, P. Carl Sandburg: adventures of a poet
        92
    See/See also pages in the following book(s):
Krull, K. Lives of the writers   920
(jt. auth) Niven, P. Carl Sandburg: adventures of
    a poet   92

The **Sandburg** treasury. Sandburg, C.   818

Sandemose, Iben
Gracie & Grandma & the itsy, bitsy seed   E

Sanders, Brian
(il) Jenkins, M. Titanic   910.4

Sanders, Nancy I., 1960-
America's black founders   973.3

Sanders-Wells, Linda
Maggie's monkeys   E

Sanderson, Brandon, 1975-
Alcatraz versus the evil Librarians   Fic

Sanderson, Ruth, 1951-
Goldilocks   398.2

Sandford, John, 1953-
(il) Maddox, M. Rules of the game   811

Sandin, Joan, 1942-
At home in a new land   E
(il) Bulla, C. R. Daniel's duck   E

Sandler, Martin W.
The Dust Bowl through the lens   973.9
Island of hope   325.73
On the waters of the USA   387.2
Trapped in ice!   639.2

The **Sandman**. Fletcher, R.   E

Sandpipers
Willis, N. C. Red knot   598

Sandra Boynton's One shoe blues. Boynton, S.
        782.42

Sandvold, Lynnette Brent
Revolution in construction   624
Revolution in medicine   610.9

The **sandwich** swap. Rania, Queen, consort of
    Abdullah, King of Jordan   E

Sandy, J. P.
(il) Cleary, B. P. The laugh stand   817
(il) Cleary, B. P. "Mrs. Riley Bought Five Itchy
    Aardvarks" and other painless tricks for mem-
    orizing science facts   507

Sandy's circus. Stone, T. L.   92

Sanfield, Steve
The adventures of High John the Conqueror
        398.2

Sanitary landfills See Landfills

Sanitation
Albee, S. Poop happened!   363.7

Sanna, Ellyn, 1957-
    See also Simons, Rae, 1957-

Santa Claus
Demi. The legend of Saint Nicholas   92
      Fiction
Abbott, T. Kringle   Fic
De Paola, T. Guess who's coming to Santa's for
    dinner?   E
Donaldson, J. Stick Man   E
Duval, K. The Three Bears' Christmas   E
Frazee, M. Santa Claus, the world's number one
    toy expert   E
Kelley, T. Dog who saved Santa   E
Krensky, S. How Santa got his job   E
Marzollo, J. Ten little Christmas presents   E
Milgrim, D. Santa Duck   E
Seibold, J. O. Olive the other reindeer   E
Steinhöfel, A. An elk dropped in   Fic
Thompson, L. The Christmas magic   E
Van Allsburg, C. The Polar Express   E
Wallace, C. The Santa secret   E
      Poetry
Moore, C. C. The night before Christmas [illus-
    trated by Richard Jesse Watson]   811
Moore, C. C. The night before Christmas [illus-
    trated by Rachel Isadora]   811
      Songs
Coots, J. F. Santa Claus is comin' to town
        782.42

Santa Claus is comin' to town. Coots, J. F.
        782.42

Santa Claus, the world's number one toy expert.
    Frazee, M.   E

Santa Duck. Milgrim, D.   E

Santa Fe (N.M.)
      Fiction
De Paola, T. The night of Las Posadas   E

**Santa Maria del Fiore (Cathedral: Florence, It-
aly)**
      Fiction
Fern, T. E. Pippo the Fool   E

The **Santa** secret. Wallace, C.   E

Santat, Dan
(il) Barnett, M. Oh no!, or, How my science
    project destroyed the world   E
(il) Gutman, D. The Christmas genie   Fic
(il) Sauer, T. Chicken dance   E
(il) Yee, L. Bobby vs. girls (accidentally)
        Fic

Savadier, Elivia—*Continued*
(il) Hest, A. When you meet a bear on Broadway   **E**

Savage, Augusta Christine, 1892-1962
About
Schroeder, A. In her hands   **92**

Savage, Stephen, 1965-
Duck   **598**
Mouse   **599.35**
Rat   **599.35**
(il) Thompson, L. Polar bear night   **E**

Savage, Steve, 1965- *See* Savage, Stephen, 1965-

Savage safari   **591.7**

Savanna animals. Hodge, D.   **591.7**

Savannas. Toupin, L.   **577.4**

Save energy. Barnham, K.   **333.79**

Save the Earth science experiments. Harris, E. S.   **507.8**

Save the planet [series]
Barker, D. Compost it   **631.8**
Farrell, C. Keeping water clean   **363.7**
Farrell, C. Using alternative energies   **333.79**
Hirsch, R. E. Growing your own garden   **635**
Hirsch, R. E. Helping endangered animals   **591.68**
Hirsch, R. E. Protecting our natural resources   **333.72**
Minden, C. Reduce, reuse, and recycle   **363.7**
Vogel, J. Local farms and sustainable foods   **630**

Save water. Barnham, K.   **333.91**

Saving. Morrison, J.   **332.024**

Saving and investment
Morrison, J. Saving   **332.024**
Fiction
Williams, V. B. A chair for my mother   **E**

Saving birds. Salmansohn, P.   **333.95**

Saving energy. Guillain, C.   **333.79**

Saving our living Earth [series]
Rapp, V. Protecting Earth's air quality   **363.7**
Welsbacher, A. Earth-friendly design   **745.2**
Welsbacher, A. Protecting Earth's rain forests   **577.3**

Saving Sky. Stanley, D.   **Fic**

Saving Sweetness. Stanley, D.   **E**

Saving the Baghdad Zoo. Halls, K. M.   **636.088**

Saving the buffalo. Marrin, A.   **599.64**

Saving the ghost of the mountain. Montgomery, S.   **599.75**

Saving water. Guillain, C.   **333.91**

Savitz, Harriet May, 1933-2008
(jt. auth) Wolff, F. The story blanket   **E**

Savvy. Law, I.   **Fic**

Sawa, Maureen
The library book   **027**

Sawdust and spangles: the amazing life of W.C. Coup. Covert, R.   **92**

Sawyer, Ruth, 1880-1970
Long Christmas. See Hodges, M. The wee Christmas cabin   **E**
Roller skates   **Fic**
The way of the storyteller   **372.6**

Saxby Smart, private detective [series]
Cheshire, S. The curse of the ancient mask and other case files   **Fic**

Say, Allen, 1937-
Allison   **E**
The bicycle man   **E**
Erika-san   **E**
Grandfather's journey   **E**
Kamishibai man   **E**
The lost lake   **E**
Tea with milk   **E**
Tree of cranes   **E**
(il) Friedman, I. R. How my parents learned to eat   **E**
(il) Snyder, D. The boy of the three-year nap   **398.2**

Say hello. Foreman, J.   **E**

Say hello!. Isadora, R.   **E**

Say hola to Spanish, otra vez. Elya, S. M.   **468**

Sayad, Joanne Keratsos
(jt. auth) Boueri, M. Lebanon A to Z   **956.92**

Sayago, Mauricio Trenard, 1963-
(il) Hayes, J. Dance, Nana, dance   **398.2**

Saying goodbye to Lulu. Demas, C.   **E**

Sayles, Elizabeth
(il) Ackerman, K. The night crossing   **Fic**

Sayre, April Pulley
Dig, wait, listen   **E**
Honk, honk, goose!   **598**
Meet the howlers   **599.8**
One is a snail, ten is a crab   **E**
Secrets of sound   **591.59**
Stars beneath your bed   **551.51**
Trout are made of trees   **577**
Turtle, turtle, watch out!   **E**
Vulture view   **598**

Sayre, Jeff, 1963-
(jt. auth) Sayre, A. P. One is a snail, ten is a crab   **E**

Scales, Pat R.
Protecting intellectual freedom in your school library   **025.2**
Teaching banned books   **323.44**

The **Scallywags**. Melling, D.   **E**

Scandinavia
Civilization
Park, L. The Scandinavian Vikings   **948**

The **Scandinavian** American family album. Hoobler, D.   **305.8**

Scandinavian Americans
Hoobler, D. The Scandinavian American family album   **305.8**

Scandinavian civilization *See* Scandinavia—Civilization

The **Scandinavian** Vikings. Park, L.   **948**

School stories—*Continued*

Birney, B. G. The princess and the Peabodys **Fic**

Birney, B. G. The world according to Humphrey **Fic**

Blake, S. I don't want to go to school! **E**

Bloch, S. Butterflies in my stomach and other school hazards **E**

Bolger, K. Zombiekins **Fic**

Borden, L. The A+ custodian **E**

Borden, L. Good luck, Mrs. K! **E**

Borden, L. The John Hancock Club **E**

Borden, L. The last day of school **Fic**

Borden, L. The lost-and-found tooth **Fic**

Borden, L. Off to first grade **E**

Bottner, B. Miss Brooks loves books (and I don't) **E**

Bowe, J. My last best friend **Fic**

Bowen, A. The great math tattle battle **E**

Bowen, A. I know an old teacher **E**

Brisson, P. I remember Miss Perry **E**

Brown, J. R. 13 **Fic**

Buckley, M. NERDS **Fic**

Bulion, L. The trouble with rules **Fic**

Bunting, E. Cheyenne again **E**

Bunting, E. My special day at Third Street School **E**

Bunting, E. One green apple **E**

Bunting, E. Spying on Miss Müller **Fic**

Burnett, F. H. A little princess **Fic**

Burningham, J. John Patrick Norman McHennessy **E**

Butler, D. H. The truth about Truman School **Fic**

Byars, B. C. The burning questions of Bingo Brown **Fic**

Byars, B. C. The SOS file **Fic**

Cabot, M. Moving day **Fic**

Calmenson, S. Late for school! **E**

Carlson, N. L. Henry and the Valentine surprise **E**

Carlson, N. L. Hooray for Grandparent's Day **E**

Carlstrom, N. W. It's your first day of school, Annie Claire **E**

Catalanotto, P. No more pumpkins **Fic**

Chatterton, M. The Brain finds a leg **Fic**

Cheng, A. Where the steps were **Fic**

Child, L. I am too absolutely small for school **E**

Chodos-Irvine, M. Best best friends **E**

Choldenko, G. If a tree falls at lunch period **Fic**

Choldenko, G. Louder, Lili **E**

Cleary, B. Dear Mr. Henshaw **Fic**

Cleary, B. Ellen Tebbits **Fic**

Cleary, B. Henry Huggins **Fic**

Cleary, B. Mitch and Amy **Fic**

Cleary, B. Muggie Maggie **Fic**

Cleary, B. Otis Spofford **Fic**

Cleary, B. Ramona the pest **Fic**

Clements, A. Frindle **Fic**

Clements, A. The janitor's boy **Fic**

Clements, A. The Landry News **Fic**

Clements, A. Lost and found **Fic**

Clements, A. Lunch money **Fic**

Clements, A. No talking **Fic**

Clements, A. The report card **Fic**

Clements, A. Room one **Fic**

Clements, A. We the children **Fic**

Cocca-Leffler, M. Jack's talent **E**

Cody, M. Powerless **Fic**

Cohen, B. Molly's pilgrim **E**

Cohen, M. First grade takes a test **E**

Cohen, M. Jim's dog Muffins **E**

Cohen, M. Will I have a friend? **E**

Cohen, T. The invisible rules of the Zoë Lama **Fic**

Cole, B. H. Anna & Natalie **E**

Comerford, L. B. Rissa Bartholomew's declaration of independence **Fic**

Cooper, I. Look at Lucy! **Fic**

Cornwell, N. Christophe's story **Fic**

Cousins, L. Maisy goes to preschool **E**

Cox, J. Butterfly buddies **Fic**

Cox, J. Puppy power **Fic**

Coy, J. Top of the order **Fic**

Crabtree, J. Discovering pig magic **Fic**

Creech, S. Bloomability **Fic**

Creech, S. Love that dog **Fic**

Crews, D. School bus **E**

Cuyler, M. 100th day worries **E**

Dahl, R. Matilda **Fic**

Daly, N. Bettina Valentino and the Picasso Club **Fic**

D'Amico, C. Ella the Elegant Elephant **E**

Daneshvari, G. School of Fear **Fic**

Danziger, P. Amber Brown is not a crayon **Fic**

Danziger, P. The cat ate my gymsuit **Fic**

Davis, E. The secret science alliance and the copycat crook **741.5**

De Paola, T. Meet the Barkers **E**

De Paola, T. Stagestruck **E**

Dee, B. Solving Zoe **Fic**

DeGross, M. Donavan's double trouble **Fic**

DeJong, M. The wheel on the school **Fic**

Deriso, C. H. Talia Talk **Fic**

DiSalvo, D. The sloppy copy slipup **Fic**

Dodds, D. A. Teacher's pets **E**

Donofrio, B. Thank you, Lucky Stars **Fic**

Donovan, G. In loving memory of Gorfman T. Frog **Fic**

Dowell, F. O. The kind of friends we used to be **Fic**

Dowell, F. O. Phineas L. Macguire erupts! **Fic**

Dowell, F. O. The secret language of girls **Fic**

Draanen, W. v. Shredderman: Secret identity **Fic**

Durand, H. Dessert first **Fic**

Dutton, S. Mary Mae and the gospel truth **Fic**

Edwards, M. The talent show **Fic**

Emerson, K. Carlos is gonna get it **Fic**

English, K. Nikki & Deja **Fic**

English, K. Speak to me **E**

Erskine, K. Mockingbird **Fic**

Falwell, C. David's drawings **E**

Ferraiolo, J. D. The big splash **Fic**

Finchler, J. Miss Malarkey leaves no reader behind **E**

School stories—*Continued*

McDonald, M. Stink: the incredible shrinking kid **Fic**

McGhee, A. Mrs. Watson wants your teeth **E**

McGinty, A. B. Eliza's kindergarten surprise **E**

McMullan, K. Pearl and Wagner: one funny day **E**

McNamara, M. How many seeds in a pumpkin? **E**

McNaughton, C. Once upon an ordinary school day **E**

Millman, I. Moses goes to school **E**

Mills, C. 7 x 9 = trouble! **Fic**

Mills, C. Being Teddy Roosevelt **Fic**

Mills, C. How Oliver Olson changed the world **Fic**

Mills, C. The totally made-up Civil War diary of Amanda MacLeish **Fic**

Morgenstern, S. H. A book of coupons **Fic**

Morris, T. Total knockout **Fic**

Moss, M. Amelia's 6th-grade notebook **Fic**

Murphy, P. The wild girls **Fic**

Myracle, L. Luv ya bunches **Fic**

Nagda, A. W. The perfect cat-sitter **Fic**

Nagda, A. W. Tarantula power! **Fic**

Naylor, P. R. Faith, hope, and Ivy June **Fic**

Naylor, P. R. Starting with Alice **Fic**

Neubecker, R. Wow! school! **E**

Nimmo, J. Midnight for Charlie Bone **Fic**

Nixon, J. L. Laugh till you cry **Fic**

Noble, T. H. The day Jimmy's boa ate the wash **E**

O'Connell, R. Penina Levine is a hard-boiled egg **Fic**

O'Connor, B. Fame and glory in Freedom, Georgia **Fic**

O'Dell, K. Agnes Parker . . . girl in progress **Fic**

Ormerod, J. Molly and her dad

Palatini, M. Geek Chic **Fic**

Park, B. Junie B. Jones and her big fat mouth **Fic**

Pattison, D. S. 19 girls and me **E**

Paulsen, G. Mudshark **Fic**

Pearsall, S. All of the above **Fic**

Pedersen, J. Houdini the amazing caterpillar **E**

Peirce, L. Big Nate **Fic**

Pennypacker, S. Clementine **Fic**

Pérez, L. K. First day in grapes **E**

Phillipps, J. C. Wink **E**

Plourde, L. Field trip day **E**

Polacco, P. The junkyard wonders **Fic**

Polacco, P. The Lemonade Club **E**

Polacco, P. Mr. Lincoln's way **E**

Poydar, N. The biggest test in the universe **E**

Poydar, N. Fish school **E**

Pulver, R. Never say boo! **E**

Pulver, R. Nouns and verbs have a field day **E**

Pulver, R. Punctuation takes a vacation **E**

Pulver, R. Silent letters loud and clear **E**

Railsback, L. Noonie's masterpiece **Fic**

Rania, Queen, consort of Abdullah, King of Jordan. The sandwich swap **E**

Rankin, L. Ruthie and the (not so) teeny tiny lie **E**

Rathmann, P. Officer Buckle and Gloria **E**

Ray, D. Ghost girl **Fic**

Reynolds, A. Superhero School **E**

Reynolds, P. The dot **E**

Riddleburger, S. The strange case of Origami Yoda **Fic**

Riggs, S. Not in Room 204 **E**

Robbins, J. The new girl . . . and me **E**

Robbins, J. Two of a kind **E**

Rockwell, A. F. My preschool **E**

Rodman, M. A. First grade stinks **E**

Rodman, M. A. Yankee girl **Fic**

Rosen, M. Totally wonderful Miss Plumberry **E**

Rosenberry, V. Vera's first day of school **E**

Rupp, R. Sarah Simpson's Rules for Living **Fic**

Russo, M. A very big bunny **E**

Sachar, L. Wayside School gets a little stranger **Fic**

Salisbury, G. Calvin Coconut: trouble magnet **Fic**

Saltzberg, B. Stanley and the class pet **E**

Schaefer, C. L. Dragon dancing **E**

Schmidt, G. D. The Wednesday wars **Fic**

Schneider, R. Knightley Academy **Fic**

Schotter, R. Doo-Wop Pop **E**

Schwartz, A. Things I learned in second grade **E**

Scieszka, J. Spaceheadz **Fic**

Scott, A. H. Brave as a mountain lion **E**

Scotton, R. Splat the cat **E**

Selzer, A. I put a spell on you **Fic**

Seuss, Dr. Hooray for Diffendoofer Day! **E**

Shea, B. Big plans **E**

Shefelman, J. J. Anna Maria's gift **Fic**

Shreve, S. R. The flunking of Joshua T. Bates **Fic**

Siebold, J. My nights at the Improv **Fic**

Simms, L. Rotten teeth **E**

Slade, A. G. Jolted **Fic**

Sonnenblick, J. After ever after **Fic**

Sonnenblick, J. Zen and the art of faking it **Fic**

Spinelli, E. Miss Fox's class goes green **E**

Spinelli, J. Loser **Fic**

Spinelli, J. There's a girl in my hammerlock **Fic**

Stier, C. Bugs in my hair?! **E**

Stier, C. The terrible secrets of the Tell-All Club **Fic**

Stoeke, J. M. The bus stop **E**

Stoeke, J. M. It's library day **E**

Stone, P. Deep down popular **Fic**

Sturges, P. I love school! **E**

Tarshis, L. Emma-Jean Lazarus fell out of a tree **Fic**

Thomson, M. Keena Ford and the second-grade mixup **Fic**

Timberlake, A. That girl Lucy Moon **Fic**

Townsend, M. Billy Tartle in Say Cheese! **E**

Tracy, K. Camille McPhee fell under the bus **Fic**

School stories—*Continued*

Trueit, T. S. No girls allowed (dogs okay) **Fic**

Underwood, D. A balloon for Isabel **E**
Urban, L. A crooked kind of perfect **Fic**
Vail, R. Justin Case **Fic**
Walker, K. I hate books! **Fic**
Walliams, D. The boy in the dress **Fic**
Weatherford, C. B. Dear Mr. Rosenwald **Fic**
Weeks, S. Oggie Cooder **Fic**
Wells, R. Emily's first 100 days of school **E**
Wells, R. Otto runs for President **E**
Wells, R. Timothy's tales from Hilltop School **E**
Wells, R. Yoko **E**
Whitaker, Z. Kali and the rat snake **E**
Whiting, S. The firefighters **E**
Whittenberg, A. Sweet Thang **Fic**
Wild, M. Tom goes to kindergarten **E**
Wilson, J. Best friends **Fic**
Winerip, M. Adam Canfield of the Slash **Fic**
Wolf, J. M. Someone named Eva **Fic**
Wong, J. S. Minn and Jake **Fic**
Yee, L. Bobby vs. girls (accidentally) **Fic**
Yee, L. Millicent Min, girl genius **Fic**
Zemach, K. Ms. McCaw learns to draw **E**
Zucker, N. F. Callie's rules **Fic**

Graphic novels

Cammuso, F. Knights of the lunch table: the dodgeball chronicles **741.5**
Krosoczka, J. J. Lunch Lady and the League of Librarians **741.5**
Sfar, J. Little Vampire **741.5**

The **school** story. Clements, A. **Fic**

School wide book events. Ray, V. L. **027.8**

Schools

See also Education; Public schools

Barber, N. First day of school **372**
Ruurs, M. My school in the rain forest **370.9**
A school like mine **371.82**

Administration

Farmer, L. S. J. Collaborating with administrators and educational support staff **027.8**

Fiction

See School stories

Poetry

Bagert, B. School fever **811**
Franco, B. Messing around on the monkey bars **811**
Hamsters, shells, and spelling bees **811.008**
Lewis, J. P. Countdown to summer **811**
Prelutsky, J. What a day it was at school! **811**
Shields, C. D. Almost late to school and more school poems **811**
Singer, M. First food fight this fall and other school poems **811**

Songs

Katz, A. Smelly locker **782.42**

Afghanistan

Mortenson, G. Three cups of tea **371.82**
Winter, J. Nasreen's secret school **371.82**

Alaska

Aillaud, C. L. Recess at 20 below **370.9**

Pakistan

Mortenson, G. Listen to the wind **371.82**
Mortenson, G. Three cups of tea **371.82**

Schools and libraries *See* Libraries and schools

Schoolyard rhymes. Sierra, J. **398.8**

Schoonmaker, Frances

(ed) Sandburg, C. Carl Sandburg **811**

Schories, Pat

(il) Capucilli, A. Biscuit's new trick **E**

Schotter, Roni

The boy who loved words **E**
Doo-Wop Pop **E**
Mama, I'll give you the world **E**

Schram, Peninnah, 1934-

The magic pomegranate **398.2**
(ed) Oberman, S. Solomon and the ant **398.2**

Schroades, John

(il) Klimo, K. The dragon in the sock drawer **Fic**

Schroder, Mark

(il) Nelson, V. M. Juneteenth **394.26**
(il) Wadsworth, G. Cesar Chavez **92**

Schroeder, Alan, 1961-

In her hands **92**
Minty: a story of young Harriet Tubman **E**
Satchmo's blues **E**

Schroeder, Becky

See/See also pages in the following book(s):
Thimmesh, C. Girls think of everything **920**

Schubert, Dieter, 1947-

(jt. auth) Schubert, I. Like people **591.56**

Schubert, Ingrid, 1953-

Like people **591.56**

Schubert, Leda

Ballet of the elephants **791.8**
Feeding the sheep **E**

Schuch, Steve

A symphony of whales **E**

Schuckett, Sandy

Political advocacy for school librarians **027.8**

Schuerger, Andrew

(jt. auth) Leedy, L. Messages from Mars **523.4**

Schuett, Stacey

(il) Branley, F. M. Day light, night light **535**
(il) Bulla, C. R. A tree is a plant **582.16**
(il) Edwards, M. Papa's latkes **E**
(il) Katz, S. Oh, Theodore! **811**
(il) Krensky, S. Sisters of Scituate Light **E**

Schuette, Sarah L., 1976-

Let's look at fall **508.2**
Let's look at spring **508.2**
Let's look at summer **508.2**
Let's look at winter **508.2**

Schuh, Mari C., 1975-

All about teeth **617.6**
Avalanches **551.57**
Loose tooth **617.6**

Science—*Continued*

Experiments—Indexes

Pilger, M. A. Science experiments index for young people **507.8**

Fiction

Scieszka, J. Science verse **E**

History

Cole, J. The magic school bus and the science fair expedition **509**

Fradin, D. B. With a little luck **509**

Methodology

Challen, P. C. What just happened? **507.8**

Challen, P. C. What's going to happen? **507.8**

Glass, S. Analyze this! **507**

Glass, S. Prove it! **507**

Hyde, N. What's the plan? **507.8**

Kramer, S. How to think like a scientist **507**

Science detectives **507**

Swanson, D. Nibbling on Einstein's brain **500**

Moral and religious aspects

See Science—Ethical aspects

Poetry

The tree that time built **808.81**

China—History

Beshore, G. W. Science in ancient China **509**

Egypt—History

Woods, G. Science in ancient Egypt **509**

Rome—History

Harris, J. L. Science in ancient Rome **509**

United States—History

January, B. Science in colonial America **509**

Science & technology. Bingham, J. **704.9**

Science activities for all students **507.8**

Science adventures [series]

Collard, S. B., III. In the deep sea **572**

Collard, S. B., III. In the rain forest canopy **578**

Collard, S. B., III. In the wild **591.68**

Collard, S. B., III. On the coral reefs **577.7**

Science alive! [series]

Lauw, D. Light **535**

Lauw, D. Water **553.7**

Lauw, D. Weather **551.5**

Science and civilization

Beshore, G. W. Science in ancient China **509**

Harris, J. L. Science in ancient Rome **509**

January, B. Science in colonial America **509**

Woods, G. Science in ancient Egypt **509**

The science behind natural disasters [series]

Silverstein, A. Earthquakes **551.2**

Silverstein, A. Hurricanes **551.55**

Silverstein, A. Tornadoes **551.55**

Silverstein, A. Volcanoes **551.2**

Silverstein, A. Wildfires **634.9**

The **science** chef. D'Amico, J. **641.3**

Science concepts [series]

Silverstein, A. Adaptation **578.4**

Silverstein, A. Forces and motion **531**

Silverstein, A. Growth and development **571.8**

Silverstein, A. Matter **530**

Science detectives **507**

Science detectives [series]

Rene, E. Investigating why leaves change their color **582.16**

Science ethics and controversies. Hartman, E. **174**

Science experiments [series]

Farndon, J. Color **535.6**

Farndon, J. Electricity **537**

Farndon, J. Light and optics **535**

Farndon, J. Magnetism **538**

Farndon, J. Rocks and minerals **549**

Farndon, J. Sound and hearing **534**

Farndon, J. Water **532**

Science experiments index for young people. Pilger, M. A. **507.8**

Science experiments on file. Walker, P. **507.8**

Science experiments you can eat. Cobb, V. **507.8**

Science fair projects *See* Science projects

Science fair projects [series]

Rompella, N. Ecosystems **577**

Whitehouse, P. Plants **580.7**

Science fair success secrets. Haduch, B. **507.8**

Science fiction

See also Fantasy fiction

Anderson, M. T. Whales on stilts **Fic**

Berryhill, S. Chance Fortune and the Outlaws **Fic**

Buckley-Archer, L. Gideon the cutpurse **Fic**

Cameron, E. The wonderful flight to the Mushroom Planet **Fic**

Carman, P. The house of power **Fic**

Christopher, J. The White Mountains **Fic**

Cole, S. Z. Rex **Fic**

Coville, B. Aliens ate my homework **Fic**

Daley, M. J. Space station rat **Fic**

Diamand, E. Raiders' ransom **Fic**

DuPrau, J. The city of Ember **Fic**

Elish, D. The attack of the frozen woodchucks **Fic**

Falls, K. Dark life **Fic**

Fardell, J. The 7 professors of the Far North **Fic**

Farmer, N. The Ear, the Eye, and the Arm **Fic**

Fields, B. W. Lunchbox and the aliens **Fic**

Forester, V. The girl who could fly **Fic**

Fox, H. Eager **Fic**

Gall, C. There's nothing to do on Mars **E**

Haddix, M. P. Found **Fic**

Haddon, M. Boom! **Fic**

Hall, T. The Line **Fic**

Holt, K. A. Mike Stellar: nerves of steel **Fic**

Hughes, T. The iron giant **Fic**

Hulme, J. The glitch in sleep **Fic**

Klass, D. Stuck on Earth **Fic**

Knapman, T. Mungo and the spiders from space **E**

Lowry, L. The giver **Fic**

Lynch, C. Cyberia **Fic**

Marshall, E. Space case **E**

Science projects—*Continued*

Gardner, R. Easy genius science projects with weather **551.5**

Gardner, R. Far-out science projects about Earth's sun and moon **523**

Gardner, R. Far-out science projects with height and depth **530.8**

Gardner, R. Heavy-duty science projects with weight **530.8**

Gardner, R. It's about time! Science projects **529**

Gardner, R. Really hot science projects with temperature **536**

Gardner, R. Science project ideas about trees **582.16**

Gardner, R. Science projects about physics in the home **530**

Gardner, R. Slam dunk! science projects with basketball **530**

Gardner, R. Smashing science projects about Earth's rocks and minerals **552**

Gardner, R. Split-second science projects with speed **531**

Gardner, R. Stellar science projects about Earth's sky **551.5**

Gardner, R. Super science projects about Earth's soil and water **631.4**

Gardner, R. Super-sized science projects with volume **530.8**

Gardner, R. Wild science projects about Earth's weather **551.5**

Goodstein, M. Ace your sports science project **507.8**

Goodstein, M. Goal! science projects with soccer **507.8**

Goodstein, M. Wheels! **530**

Haduch, B. Science fair success secrets **507.8**

Harris, E. S. Save the Earth science experiments **507.8**

Harris, E. S. Yikes! wow! yuck! **507.8**

Hopwood, J. Cool distance assistants **507.8**

Hopwood, J. Cool dry ice devices **507.8**

Hopwood, J. Cool gravity activities **531**

Reilly, K. M. Planet Earth **333.72**

Rhatigan, J. Prize-winning science fair projects for curious kids **507.8**

Rompella, N. Ecosystems **577**

Science activities for all students **507.8**

Tocci, S. More simple science fair projects, grades 3-5 **507.8**

VanCleave, J. P. Janice VanCleave's big book of play and find out science projects **507.8**

VanCleave, J. P. Janice VanCleave's electricity **537**

VanCleave, J. P. Janice VanCleave's energy for every kid **531**

VanCleave, J. P. Janice VanCleave's engineering for every kid **507.8**

VanCleave, J. P. Janice VanCleave's guide to more of the best science fair projects **507.8**

VanCleave, J. P. Janice VanCleave's guide to the best science fair projects **507.8**

VanCleave, J. P. Janice VanCleave's insects and spiders **595.7**

VanCleave, J. P. Janice VanCleave's plants **580.7**

VanCleave, J. P. Janice VanCleave's rocks and minerals **552**

VanCleave, J. P. Janice VanCleave's solar system **523.2**

VanCleave, J. P. Janice VanCleave's weather **551.5**

Whitehouse, P. Plants **580.7**

Fiction

Barnett, M. Oh no!, or, How my science project destroyed the world **E**

Jackson, A. Thea's tree **E**

Mills, C. How Oliver Olson changed the world **Fic**

Science projects [Enslow series]

Gardner, R. Science projects about physics in the home **530**

Science projects about physics in the home. Gardner, R. **530**

Science quest [series]

Jerome, K. B. Atomic universe **539.7**

Phelan, G. Double helix **572.8**

Phelan, G. Invisible force **531**

Phelan, G. Killing germs, saving lives **615**

Science solves it! [series]

Knudsen, M. Bugged! **E**

Science verse. Scieszka, J. **E**

Science warriors. Collard, S. B., III **578.6**

Science wizardry for kids. Kenda, M. **507.8**

Science works [series]

Bailey, J. Monster bones **567.9**

Bailey, J. Sun up, sun down **525**

Scientific American [series]

Jedicke, P. Great inventions of the 20th century **609**

Jedicke, P. Great moments in space exploration **629.4**

Mehling, R. Great extinctions of the past **576.8**

Scientific American winning science fair projects [series]

Tocci, S. More simple science fair projects, grades 3-5 **507.8**

Scientific apparatus and instruments

Glass, S. Watch out! **502.8**

Scientific expeditions

See also Exploration

Scientific experiments *See* Science—Experiments

Scientific recreations

Cleary, B. P. "Mrs. Riley Bought Five Itchy Aardvarks" and other painless tricks for memorizing science facts **507**

Hauser, J. F. Super science concoctions **507.8**

Kenda, M. Science wizardry for kids **507.8**

Scientists

See also Environmentalists; Women scientists

Anderson, M. J. Isaac Newton **92**

Anderson, M. Amazing Leonardo da Vinci inventions you can build yourself **92**

Bardoe, C. Gregor Mendel **92**

Sea stories

Avi. The true confessions of Charlotte Doyle **Fic**

Babbitt, N. The eyes of the Amaryllis **Fic**
Cooper, S. Victory **Fic**
Creech, S. The Wanderer **Fic**
Foreman, M. Grandpa Jack's tattoo tales **E**
Fox, P. The slave dancer **Fic**
Gauch, S. Voyage to the Pharos **E**
Hesse, K. Stowaway **Fic**
Priestley, C. Tales of terror from the Black Ship **Fic**
Van Allsburg, C. The wretched stone **E**
The **sea,** the storm, and the mangrove tangle. Cherry, L. **E**

Sea turtles

Christopherson, S. C. Top 50 reasons to care about marine turtles **597.92**
Gibbons, G. Sea turtles **597.92**
Guiberson, B. Z. Into the sea **597.92**
Hall, K. Leatherback turtle **597.92**
Lasky, K. Interrupted journey **639.9**
Lockwood, S. Sea turtles **597.92**
Rodriguez, C. Sea turtles **597.92**
Swinburne, S. R. Turtle tide **597.92**
Wearing, J. Sea turtle **597.92**
Fiction
Arnosky, J. Turtle in the sea **E**
Crowe, C. Turtle girl **E**
Sayre, A. P. Turtle, turtle, watch out! **E**

Sea Venture (Ship)
Karwoski, G. Miracle **972.9**

Seabiscuit (Race horse)
McCarthy, M. Seabiscuit **798.4**

Seabrook, Alexis
(il) Buchanan, A. J. The daring book for girls **031.02**

Seabrooke, Brenda, 1941-
Wolf pie **Fic**

Seafaring life
Fiction
Ahlberg, A. The baby in the hat **E**
Frederick, H. V. The voyage of Patience Goodspeed **Fic**

Seaglass summer. Banerjee, A. **Fic**

Seah, Audrey, 1958-
Vietnam **959.704**

Seals (Animals)
Hengel, K. It's a baby Australian fur seal! **599.79**
Malam, J. Pinnipeds **599.79**
Markovics, J. L. Weddell seal **599.79**
Stearns, P. M. Steller sea lions **599.79**
Fiction
Hoff, S. Sammy the seal **E**
Seeger, L. V. What if? **E**
The **seals** on the bus. Hort, L. **782.42**

Seamen See Sailors

Seamore, the very forgetful porpoise. Edgemon, D. **E**

Search and rescue operations See Rescue work

The **search** for delicious. Babbitt, N. **Fic**

Search for the golden moon bear. Montgomery, S. **599.78**

Searching for grizzlies. Hirschi, R. **599.78**

Searching online for image, audio, and video files. Furgang, A. **025.04**

Searching the internet See Internet searching

Sears, Martha
(jt. auth) Sears, W. Baby on the way **612.6**
(jt. auth) Sears, W. What baby needs **649**

Sears, William
Baby on the way **612.6**
What baby needs **649**

Sears children's library [series]
Sears, W. Baby on the way **612.6**
Sears, W. What baby needs **649**

Sears list of subject headings **025.4**

Seashore
Arnosky, J. Beachcombing **578.7**
Parker, S. Seashore **577.7**
Rotner, S. Senses at the seashore **E**
Serafini, F. Looking closely along the shore **578.7**
Fiction
Cooper, E. Beach **E**
Zolotow, C. The seashore book **E**
The **seashore** book. Zolotow, C. **E**

Seashore ecology
Himmelman, J. Who's at the seashore? **591.7**
Johansson, P. The seashore **577.6**
The **seaside** switch. Kudlinski, K. V. **577.6**

A **season** of gifts. Peck, R. **Fic**

Seasons
See also Autumn; Spring; Summer; Winter
Branley, F. M. Sunshine makes the seasons **508.2**
Feeney, S. Sun and rain **996.9**
Gibbons, G. The reasons for seasons **525**
Lin, G. Our seasons **508.2**
Morrison, G. Nature in the neighborhood **508**
Rau, D. M. Seasons **508.2**
Rockwell, A. F. Four seasons make a year **E**
Rotner, S. Every season **508.2**
Royston, A. Looking at weather and seasons **551.6**
Fiction
Adler, D. A. It's time to sleep, it's time to dream **E**
Anno, M. Anno's counting book **E**
Berger, C. Forever friends **E**
Berner, R. S. In the town all year 'round **E**
Gershator, P. Listen, listen **E**
Gibbons, G. The seasons of Arnold's apple tree **E**
Gray, L. M. My mama had a dancing heart **E**
Henkes, K. Old Bear **E**
Karas, G. B. The Village Garage **E**
Rohmann, E. A kitten tale **E**
Sendak, M. Chicken soup with rice **E**
Sidman, J. Red sings from treetops **E**
Stein, D. E. Leaves **E**
Van Allsburg, C. The stranger **E**
Willems, M. City Dog, Country Frog **E**

Señor Cat's romance and other favorite stories from Latin America. González, L. M.
398.2

Sensational science experiments [series]
Gardner, R. Far-out science projects with height and depth **530.8**
Gardner, R. Heavy-duty science projects with weight **530.8**
Gardner, R. It's about time! Science projects **529**
Gardner, R. Really hot science projects with temperature **536**
Gardner, R. Split-second science projects with speed **531**
Gardner, R. Super-sized science projects with volume **530.8**

Sensational science projects with simple machines. Gardner, R. **621.8**

Sense Pass King. Tchana, K. H. **398.2**

Sensel, Joni, 1962-
The Farwalker's quest **Fic**
The timekeeper's moon **Fic**

Senses and sensation
Aliki. My five senses **612.8**
Cobb, V. How to really fool yourself **152.1**
Cole, J. The magic school bus explores the senses **612.8**
Gardner, R. Ace your science project about the senses **612.8**
Jenkins, S. What do you do with a tail like this? **573.8**
Read, L. My senses **612.8**
Rotner, S. Senses at the seashore **E**
Rotner, S. Senses in the city **E**
Fiction
Cole, H. On the way to the beach **E**
Nelson, N. Bringing the boy home **Fic**
Raschka, C. Five for a little one **E**
Poetry
Walker, A. There is a flower at the tip of my nose smelling me **811**

Senses at the seashore. Rotner, S. **E**

Senses in the city. Rotner, S. **E**

Separate, but not equal. Haskins, J. **379**

Sepehri, Sandy
Continents **910**
Glaciers **551.3**
Rivers **551.48**

September 11, 2001. Fradin, D. B. **973.931**

September 11 terrorist attacks, 2001
Deedy, C. A. 14 cows for America **327**
Fradin, D. B. September 11, 2001 **973.931**
Kalman, M. Fireboat **974.7**
Winter, J. September roses **E**
See/See also pages in the following book(s):
Ganci, C. Chief **92**

September roses. Winter, J. **E**

Sequoia *See* Redwood

Sequoyah, 1770?-1843
About
Dennis, Y. W. Sequoyah, 1770?-1843 **92**
Rumford, J. Sequoyah **92**
Wade, M. D. Amazing Cherokee writer Sequoyah **92**

Serafini, Frank
Looking closely across the desert **578.7**
Looking closely along the shore **578.7**
Looking closely inside the garden **578.7**
Looking closely through the forest **578.7**

Serbia
King, D. C. Serbia and Montenegro **949.7**

Serbia and Montenegro. King, D. C. **949.7**

Serchay, David S., 1971-
The librarian's guide to graphic novels for children and tweens **025.2**

Seredy, Kate, 1899-1975
The Good Master **Fic**
The white stag **Fic**

Serfozo, Mary
Plumply, dumply pumpkin **E**
Whooo's there? **E**

Sergio makes a splash. Rodriguez, E. **E**

Serial publications
See also Newspapers

A series of unfortunate events [series]
Snicket, L. The bad beginning **Fic**

The serpent slayer: and other stories of strong women. Tchana, K. H. **398.2**

Serrano, Francisco, 1949-
The poet king of Tezcoco [biography of Nezahualcóyotl] **92**

Serrano, Pablo, 1910-1985
(il) Serrano, F. The poet king of Tezcoco [biography of Nezahualcóyotl] **92**

Servants *See* Household employees

Service, Robert W., 1874-1958
The cremation of Sam McGee **811**

Serving Latino communities. Alire, C. **027.6**

Serving young teens and 'tweens **027.62**

Servitude *See* Slavery

Seskin, Steve
Sing my song **782.42**

Set theory
Murphy, S. J. Dave's down-to-earth rock shop **511.3**
Murphy, S. J. Seaweed soup **511.3**
Tang, G. Math-terpieces **510**

Settel, Joanne
Exploding ants **591.5**

Setting the turkeys free. Nikola-Lisa, W. **E**

Seuling, Barbara
Cows sweat through their noses **590**
Your skin weighs more than your brain **612**

Seuss, Dr.
The 500 hats of Bartholomew Cubbins **E**
And to think that I saw it on Mulberry Street **E**
Bartholomew and the oobleck **E**
The cat in the hat **E**
Green eggs and ham **E**
Hooray for Diffendoofer Day! **E**
Horton hatches the egg **E**
Horton hears a Who! **E**
How the Grinch stole Christmas **E**
If I ran the circus **E**
If I ran the zoo **E**

Shape—*Continued*

Murphy, S. J. Captain Invincible and the space shapes   **516**

Museum shapes   **E**

Olson, N. Cones   **516**

Olson, N. Cubes   **516**

Olson, N. Cylinders   **516**

Olson, N. Pyramids   **516**

Olson, N. Spheres   **516**

Rissman, R. Shapes in art   **516**

Rissman, R. Shapes in buildings   **516**

Rissman, R. Shapes in music   **516**

Rissman, R. Shapes in sports   **516**

Rissman, R. Shapes in the garden   **516**

Thong, R. Round is a mooncake   **E**

Fiction

Falwell, C. Shape capers   **E**

Gravett, E. Orange pear apple bear   **E**

Henkes, K. Circle dogs   **E**

Walsh, E. S. Mouse shapes   **E**

Poetry

Franco, B. Bees, snails, and peacock tails shapes—naturally   **811**

Shape capers. Falwell, C.   **E**

Shape up!. Adler, D. A.   **516**

Shapes in art. Rissman, R.   **516**

Shapes in buildings. Rissman, R.   **516**

Shapes in music. Rissman, R.   **516**

Shapes in sports. Rissman, R.   **516**

Shapes in the garden. Rissman, R.   **516**

Shapes, shapes, shapes. Hoban, T.   **E**

Shaping materials. Oxlade, C.   **620.1**

Shapiro, Karen Jo, 1964-

I must go down to the beach again   **811**

Shapiro, Michelle, 1961-

(il) Ericsson, J. A. A piece of chalk   **E**

(il) Kroll, S. The Hanukkah mice   **E**

Shapiro, Ouisie

Autism and me   **616.85**

Shapiro, Zachary

We're all in the same boat   **E**

Sharing. Barraclough, S.   **177**

A sharing nature with children book [series]

Myers, T. If you give a T-rex a bone   **567.9**

Sharing our homeland. Marx, T.   **956.04**

Sharing the seasons   **811.008**

The **Shark** God. Martin, R.   **398.2**

Shark vs. train. Barton, C.   **E**

Sharkey, Niamh

(il) Doyle, M. Tales from old Ireland   **398.2**

Sharks

Arnold, C. Giant shark: megalodon, prehistoric super predator   **567**

Arnosky, J. All about sharks   **597**

Bradley, T. J. Paleo sharks   **567**

Cerullo, M. M. The truth about great white sharks   **597**

De la Bédoyère, C. Sharks   **597**

Doubilet, D. Face to face with sharks   **597**

Gibbons, G. Sharks   **597**

Macquitty, M. Shark   **597**

Mallory, K. Swimming with hammerhead sharks   **597**

Markle, S. Great white sharks   **597**

Markle, S. Sharks   **597**

O'Brien, P. Megatooth!   **567**

Pringle, L. P. Sharks!: strange and wonderful   **597**

Rockwell, A. F. Little shark   **597**

Simon, S. Sharks   **597**

Fiction

Barton, C. Shark vs. train   **E**

Folklore

Martin, R. The Shark God   **398.2**

Sharks and other sea monsters. Sabuda, R.   **560**

Sharks!: strange and wonderful. Pringle, L. P.   **597**

Sharmat, Marjorie Weinman, 1928-

Gila monsters meet you at the airport   **E**

Nate the Great   **E**

Sharmat, Mitchell, 1927-

Gregory, the terrible eater   **E**

Sharp, S. Pearl

The slave trade and the middle passage   **326**

Sharp, Saundra *See* Sharp, S. Pearl

Sharpe, Leah Marinsky

The goat-faced girl   **398.2**

Sharratt, Nick

(il) Taylor, S. When a monster is born   **E**

(il) Wilson, J. Candyfloss   **Fic**

(il) Wilson, J. Cookie   **Fic**

Shaskan, Kathy

How underwear got under there   **391**

Shattil, Wendy

(il) Jackson, D. M. The wildlife detectives   **363.2**

Shaw, Charles, 1892-1974

It looked like spilt milk   **E**

Shaw, Hannah

Sneaky weasel   **E**

Shaw, Nancy

Raccoon tune   **E**

Sheep in a jeep   **E**

Shaw, Jenny Sue Kostecki- *See* Kostecki-Shaw, Jenny Sue

The **Shawnee.** De Capua, S.   **970.004**

Shawnee Indians

Collier, J. L. The Tecumseh you never knew   **92**

De Capua, S. The Shawnee   **970.004**

Spradlin, M. P. Daniel Boone's great escape   **92**

Fiction

Bruchac, J. The dark pond   **Fic**

She sang promise: the story of Betty Mae Jumper, Seminole tribal leader. Annino, J. G.   **92**

She sells sea shells. Chwast, S.   **398.8**

She touched the world: Laura Bridgman, deaf-blind pioneer. Alexander, S. H.   **92**

Shea, Bob

Big plans   **E**

Dinosaur vs. bedtime   **E**

New socks   **E**

Shea, Bob—*Continued*

Oh, Daddy!	E
Race you to bed	E

Shea, Pegi Deitz, 1960-

Liberty rising	974.7
Patience Wright	92
Ten mice for Tet!	394.26

Shearer, Alex

Canned	Fic

Shecter, Ben

(il) Benchley, N. A ghost named Fred	E

Shed, Greg

(il) Bunting, E. Butterfly house	E

Shed, Greg, 1928-

(il) Bunting, E. Dandelions	E

Shedd, Blair

(il) Berkenkamp, L. Discover the Amazon	981
(il) Brown, C. L. Discover National Monuments, National Parks	363.6

Sheehan, Patricia, 1954-

Luxembourg	949.35
Moldova	947.6

Sheehan, Sean, 1951-

Angola	967.3
Austria	943.6
Cambodia	959.6
Cuba	972.91
Endangered species	333.95
Jamaica	972.92
Lebanon	956.92
Malta	945
Pakistan	954.91
Zimbabwe	968.91

Sheehan, Thomas F., 1928-

Islands	551.4
Mountains	551.4

Sheep

Minden, C. Sheep	636.3
Urbigkit, C. The shepherd's trail	636.3
Urbigkit, C. A young shepherd	636.3

Fiction

Caple, K. The friendship tree	E
Catusanu, M. The strange case of the missing sheep	E
Church, C. Digby takes charge	E
Edwards, D. The pen that Pa built	E
Farrell, D. Doug-Dennis and the flyaway fib	E
Ford, B. No more blanket for Lambkin	E
Fox, M. Where is the green sheep?	E
French, J. Pete the sheep-sheep	E
Gerstein, M. The white ram	E
Hobbs, V. Sheep	Fic
Lester, H. The sheep in wolf's clothing	E
McMillan, B. How the ladies stopped the wind	E
Schubert, L. Feeding the sheep	E
Scotton, R. Russell the sheep	E
Shaw, N. Sheep in a jeep	E
Stohner, A. Brave Charlotte	E
Thompson, L. Wee little lamb	E
Watts, F. Extraordinary Ernie and Marvelous Maud	Fic
Westera, M. Sheep and Goat	Fic

Folklore

Aardema, V. Borreguita and the coyote	398.2
Greene, E. The little golden lamb	398.2
Hennessy, B. G. The boy who cried wolf	398.2

Songs

Hoberman, M. A. Mary had a little lamb	782.42

Sheep and Goat. Westera, M.	Fic

Sheep dogs

Urbigkit, C. Brave dogs, gentle dogs	636.7

Sheep herders *See* Shepherds

Sheep in a jeep. Shaw, N.	E
The **sheep** in wolf's clothing. Lester, H.	E
The **sheep-pig**. See King-Smith, D. Babe	Fic

Shefelman, Janice Jordan, 1930-

Anna Maria's gift	Fic
I, Vivaldi	92

Shefelman, Tom, 1927-

(il) Shefelman, J. J. I, Vivaldi	92

Sheila Rae, the brave. Henkes, K.	E

Sheinkin, Steve, 1968-

King George: what was his problem?	973.3
Two miserable presidents	973.7
Which way to the wild West?	978

Shelby, Anne

The adventures of Molly Whuppie and other Appalachian folktales	398.2
The man who lived in a hollow tree	E

Shelby, Uncle *See* Silverstein, Shel

Sheldon, Annette

Big sister now	306.8

Sheldon, David

Into the deep [biography of William Beebe]	92

Shelf-esteem. Kitain, S.	028.5
Shelf life: stories by the book	S C

Shelley, John

(il) Danneberg, J. Family reminders	Fic

Shelley, Rebecca *See* Henham, R. D.

Shelley Rotner's early childhood library [series]

Rotner, S. Senses in the city	E

Shellfish

See also Crabs; Mollusks

Shells

Zoehfeld, K. W. What lives in a shell?	591.4

Shelter dogs. Kehret, P.	636.7

Shelters, Animal *See* Animal shelters

Shelton, Paula Young

Child of the civil rights movement	323.1

Shepard, Aaron

One-Eye! Two-Eyes! Three-Eyes!	398.2
The princess mouse	398.2
The sea king's daughter	398.2
Stories on stage	812

Shepard, Alan B., Jr.

About

Orr, T. Alan Shepard	92

Shepard, Ernest H. (Ernest Howard), 1879-1976

(il) Grahame, K. The reluctant dragon	Fic

Shepard, Ernest H. (Ernest Howard), 1879-1976—*Continued*
(il) Grahame, K. The wind in the willows
Fic
(il) Milne, A. A. The House at Pooh Corner
Fic
(il) Milne, A. A. Now we are six **821**
(il) Milne, A. A. When we were very young
821
(il) Milne, A. A. Winnie-the-Pooh **Fic**
Shepard, Mary Eleanor, 1909-2000
(il) Travers, P. L. Mary Poppins **Fic**
Shepherd, Amanda
(il) Lorig, S. Such a silly baby! **E**
Shepherds
Urbigkit, C. The shepherd's trail **636.3**
Urbigkit, C. A young shepherd **636.3**
Fiction
Morpurgo, M. On angel wings **Fic**
The **shepherd's** trail. Urbigkit, C. **636.3**
Sheppard, Ella *See* Moore, Ella Sheppard, 1851-1914
Shepperson, Rob
(il) Harrison, D. L. Bugs **811**
(il) Harrison, D. L. Vacation **811**
(il) Lewis, J. P. Under the kissletoe **811**
Sher, Emil, 1959-
(jt. auth) Levine, K. Hana's suitcase on stage
812
Sherlock, Patti
Letters from Wolfie **Fic**
The **Sherlock files** [series]
Barrett, T. The 100-year-old secret **Fic**
Sherlock Holmes and the Baker Street irregulars [series]
Mack, T. The fall of the Amazing Zalindas
Fic
Sherman, Delia
Changeling **Fic**
Sherman, Josepha
Asteroids, meteors, and comets **523.4**
The history of the personal computer **004**
Neptune **523.4**
Uranus **523.4**
Sherman, Pat
Ben and the Emancipation Proclamation **E**
The sun's daughter **398.2**
Sherman, Patsy O., 1930-
See/See also pages in the following book(s):
Thimmesh, C. Girls think of everything **920**
Sherman, Whitney
(il) Jaffe, N. The cow of no color: riddle stories and justice tales from around the world
398.2
Sherrard, Valerie, 1957-
Tumbleweed skies **Fic**
Sherrow, Victoria
Ancient Africa **939**
Sherry, Kevin
I'm the biggest thing in the ocean **E**
She's all that! **811.008**
She's all that!. Bryant, M. E. **292**

Sheth, Kashmira
Blue jasmine **Fic**
Boys without names **Fic**
Monsoon afternoon **E**
My Dadima wears a sari **E**
Shhh! we're writing the Constitution. Fritz, J.
342
Shhhhh! Everybody's sleeping. Markes, J. **E**
Shi-shi-etko. Campbell, N. I. **E**
Shichtman, Sandra H.
Colin Powell **92**
Shields, Carol Diggory
Almost late to school and more school poems
811
English, fresh squeezed! **811**
Lucky pennies and hot chocolate **E**
Someone used my toothbrush! **811**
Wombat walkabout **E**
Shields, Charles J., 1951-
Belize **972.82**
Central America: facts and figures **972.8**
Honduras **972.83**
Shields, Gillian
When the world is ready for bed **E**
Shields, Sarah D., 1955-
Turkey **956.1**
The **shifter.** Hardy, J. **Fic**
Shiga, Jason
Meanwhile **741.5**
Shih Huang-ti, Emperor of China *See* Ch'in Shih-huang, Emperor of China, 259-210 B.C.
Shikibu, Murasaki *See* Murasaki Shikibu, b. 978?
Shillinglaw, Bruce
(il) Zoehfeld, K. W. Dinosaur parents, dinosaur young **567.9**
Shiloh. Naylor, P. R. **Fic**
Shimin, Symeon, 1902-
(il) Hamilton, V. Zeely **Fic**
(il) Krumgold, J. Onion John **Fic**
Shimko, Bonnie
The private thoughts of Amelia E. Rye **Fic**
Shingebiss. Van Laan, N. **398.2**
Shining star: the Anna May Wong story. Yoo, P.
92
Shinto
Levin, J. Japanese mythology **299.5**
Shioya, Hitoshi, 1969-
Dinosaur hour!, vol. 1 **741.5**
Shipping
United States
Sandler, M. W. On the waters of the USA
387.2
Ships
See also Steamboats
Barton, B. Boats **387.2**
Crews, D. Harbor **E**
Gibbons, G. Boat book **387.2**
Kirk, S. T is for tugboat **623.82**
Lindeen, M. Ships **623.82**
O'Brien, P. The great ships **387.2**
Sandler, M. W. On the waters of the USA
387.2

Shurgin, Ann H., 1952-
(ed) Junior Worldmark encyclopedia of world holidays. See Junior Worldmark encyclopedia of world holidays **394.26**

Shuster, Joe, 1914-1992
About
Nobleman, M. T. Boys of steel [biography of Jerry Siegel and Joe Shuster] **92**

Shusterman, Neal
Darkness creeping **S C**

Shute, Carolyn
(ed) Best shorts. See Best shorts **S C**

Shuter, Jane, 1955-
Ancient China **931**
Mesopotamia **935**

Shutting out the sky. Hopkinson, D. **974.7**

Shuttles, Space *See* Space shuttles

Shy Charles. Wells, R. **E**

Shyness
Fiction
Alexander, C. Small Florence, piggy pop star **E**
Dewdney, A. Roly Poly pangolin **E**
Newman, J. The boys **E**

Siberell, Anne
Bravo! brava! a night at the opera **792.5**

Sibling sequence *See* Birth order

Siblings
See also Twins
Cole, J. The new baby at your house **306.8**
Crist, J. J. Siblings **306.8**
Danzig, D. Babies don't eat pizza **649**
Jenkins, S. Sisters & brothers **591.56**
Sears, W. What baby needs **649**
Shapiro, O. Autism and me **616.85**
Sheldon, A. Big sister now **306.8**
Skotko, B. Fasten your seatbelt **616.85**
Fiction
Aguiar, N. The lost island of Tamarind **Fic**
Appelt, K. Brand-new baby blues **E**
Avraham, K. A. What will you be, Sara Mee? **E**
Barrett, T. The 100-year-old secret **Fic**
Beard, D. B. Twister **E**
Bearn, E. Tumtum & Nutmeg **Fic**
Beaty, A. Cicada summer **Fic**
Berkeley, J. The hidden boy **Fic**
Berlin, E. The puzzling world of Winston Breen **Fic**
Betancourt, J. Ava Tree and the wishes three **Fic**
Blume, J. The Pain and the Great One **E**
Blume, J. Soupy Saturdays with The Pain and The Great One **Fic**
Bodeen, S. A. Elizabeti's doll **E**
Bonsall, C. N. The day I had to play with my sister **E**
Bracegirdle, P. J. Fiendish deeds **Fic**
Brown, M. T. D.W. all wet **E**
Bruchac, J. Children of the longhouse **Fic**
Byars, B. C. The not-just-anybody family **Fic**
Byars, B. C. The summer of the swans **Fic**

Cheaney, J. B. The middle of somewhere **Fic**
Cheng, A. Only one year **Fic**
Chick, B. The secret zoo **Fic**
Child, L. I am too absolutely small for school **E**
Choldenko, G. Al Capone does my shirts **Fic**
Cleaver, V. Where the lillies bloom **Fic**
Connor, L. Crunch **Fic**
Conway, D. The most important gift of all **E**
Coville, B. Hans Brinker **E**
Cowley, M. The golden bull **Fic**
Crow, K. The middle-child blues **E**
Davies, J. The lemonade war **Fic**
De Groat, D. Trick or treat, smell my feet **E**
De Paola, T. The baby sister **E**
Derby, S. Kyle's island **Fic**
Derby, S. No mush today **E**
DiCamillo, K. The magician's elephant **Fic**
Ditchfield, C. Shwatsit! **E**
Dowd, S. The London Eye mystery **Fic**
Eboch, C. The ghost on the stairs **Fic**
Ellison, E. S. Flight **Fic**
Enderle, J. R. Smile, Principessa! **E**
Ernst, L. C. Snow surprise **E**
Erskine, K. Mockingbird **Fic**
Fearnley, J. Martha in the middle **E**
Feiffer, K. But I wanted a baby brother! **E**
Fenner, C. Yolonda's genius **Fic**
Fox, P. The stone-faced boy **Fic**
Funke, C. C. The wildest brother **E**
Gary, M. Sometimes you get what you want **E**
Gifaldi, D. Listening for crickets **Fic**
Glatt, L. Abigail Iris: the one and only **Fic**
Graham, B. Dimity Dumpty **E**
Gregory, N. I'll sing you one-o **Fic**
Grimes, N. The road to Paris **Fic**
Grindley, S. It's my school **E**
Hahn, M. D. All the lovely bad ones **Fic**
Hahn, M. D. Hear the wind blow **Fic**
Haig, M. Samuel Blink and the forbidden forest **Fic**
Harper, J. Uh-oh, Cleo **Fic**
Harris, R. H. Mail Harry to the moon! **E**
Hesse, K. Spuds **E**
Hill, S. L. Not yet, Rose **E**
Horvath, P. My one hundred adventures **Fic**
Hughes, S. Annie Rose is my little sister **E**
Hughes, T. My brother Bert **E**
Jaramillo, A. La linea **Fic**
Jennings, P. The weeping willow **Fic**
Jones, S. L. How to be a baby—by me, the big sister **E**
Joseph, L. The color of my words **Fic**
Kennemore, T. Alice's birthday pig **Fic**
Landolf, D. W. What a good big brother! **E**
Lisle, H. The Ruby Key **Fic**
Little, J. Emma's yucky brother **E**
Lord, C. Rules **Fic**
Lowry, L. The Willoughbys **Fic**
Lucke, D. The boy who wouldn't swim **E**
MacLachlan, P. The true gift **Fic**
Malaghan, M. Greek ransom **Fic**

Silverstein, Alvin—*Continued*

Earthquakes	**551.2**
The eating disorders update	**616.85**
The flu and pneumonia update	**616.2**
The food poisoning update	**615.9**
Forces and motion	**531**
Growth and development	**571.8**
Hurricanes	**551.55**
Matter	**530**
The sickle cell anemia update	**616.1**
Sleep	**612.8**
Tornadoes	**551.55**
The tuberculosis update	**616.2**
Volcanoes	**551.2**
Wildfires	**634.9**

Silverstein, Shel

Don't bump the glump and other fantasies	**811**
Falling up	**811**
A light in the attic	**811**
Runny Babbit	**811**
Where the sidewalk ends	**811**
Who wants a cheap rhinoceros?	**E**

Silverstein, Virginia B.

(jt. auth) Silverstein, A. Adaptation	**578.4**
(jt. auth) Silverstein, A. The ADHD update	**616.85**
(jt. auth) Silverstein, A. The AIDS update	**616.97**
(jt. auth) Silverstein, A. The asthma update	**616.2**
(jt. auth) Silverstein, A. The breast cancer update	**616.99**
(jt. auth) Silverstein, A. Can you see the chalkboard?	**617.7**
(jt. auth) Silverstein, A. The diabetes update	**616.4**
(jt. auth) Silverstein, A. Earthquakes	**551.2**
(jt. auth) Silverstein, A. The eating disorders update	**616.85**
(jt. auth) Silverstein, A. The flu and pneumonia update	**616.2**
(jt. auth) Silverstein, A. The food poisoning update	**615.9**
(jt. auth) Silverstein, A. Forces and motion	**531**
(jt. auth) Silverstein, A. Growth and development	**571.8**
(jt. auth) Silverstein, A. Hurricanes	**551.55**
(jt. auth) Silverstein, A. Matter	**530**
(jt. auth) Silverstein, A. The sickle cell anemia update	**616.1**
(jt. auth) Silverstein, A. Sleep	**612.8**
(jt. auth) Silverstein, A. Tornadoes	**551.55**
(jt. auth) Silverstein, A. The tuberculosis update	**616.2**
(jt. auth) Silverstein, A. Volcanoes	**551.2**
(jt. auth) Silverstein, A. Wildfires	**634.9**

Silverwing. Oppel, K. **Fic**

Silvey, Anita

100 best books for children	**011.6**
(ed) The Essential guide to children's books and their creators. See The Essential guide to children's books and their creators	**028.5**

(ed) Everything I need to know I learned from a children's book. See Everything I need to know I learned from a children's book **808.8**

Sim, David, 1953-
(jt. auth) Dobbins, J. Driving my tractor **E**

Sima, Judy
Raising voices **027.62**

Simard, Rémy

(il) Meister, C. Clues in the attic	**741.5**
(il) Mortensen, L. The missing monster card	**741.5**
(il) Murphy, S. J. Captain Invincible and the space shapes	**516**
(il) Murphy, S. J. Polly's pen pal	**516**

Simchath Torah
Fishman, C. On Sukkot and Simchat Torah **296.4**

Simile
Lawlor, L. Muddy as a duck puddle and other American similes **425**

Siminovich, Lorena
Alex and Lulu: two of a kind **E**

Simmons, Jane

Beryl	**Fic**
Together	**E**

Simmons, Nancy B.
(ed) Exploring the world of mammals. See Exploring the world of mammals **599**

Simms, Laura, 1947-
Rotten teeth **E**

Simms Taback's big book of words. Taback, S. **E**

Simms Taback's city animals. Taback, S. **E**

Simms Taback's great big book of spacey, snakey, buggy riddles. Hall, K. **793.73**

Simms Taback's Safari animals. Taback, S. **E**

Simon, Francesca
Horrid Henry **Fic**

Simon, Seymour, 1931-

Big cats	**599.75**
Bones	**612.7**
The brain	**612.8**
Cats	**636.8**
Comets, meteors, and asteroids	**523.6**
Crocodiles & alligators	**597.98**
Dogs	**636.7**
Dolphins	**599.5**
Earth: our planet in space	**525**
Earthquakes	**551.2**
Eyes and ears	**612.8**
Galaxies	**523.1**
Giant snakes	**597.96**
Global warming	**363.7**
Gorillas	**599.8**
Guts	**612.3**
The heart	**612.1**
Horses	**636.1**
The human body	**612**
Hurricanes	**551.55**
Icebergs and glaciers	**551.3**
Let's try it out in the water	**532**
Lightning	**551.56**
Lungs	**612.2**

Simon, Seymour, 1931-—*Continued*

The moon	523.3
Mountains	551.4
Muscles	612.7
Now you see it, now you don't	152.14
Oceans	551.46
Our solar system	523.2
The paper airplane book	745.592
Penguins	598
Seymour Simon's book of trains	625.1
Seymour Simon's book of trucks	629.224
Sharks	597
Spiders	595.4
Storms	551.55
Tornadoes	551.55
The universe	523.1
Wildfires	577.2

Simon & Schuster children's guide to insects and spiders. Johnson, J. **595.7**

Simon & Schuster children's guide to sea creatures. Johnson, J. **591.7**

Simon & Schuster thesaurus for children **423**

Simon says gold: Simon Whitfield's pursuit of athletic excellence. Whitfield, S. **92**

Simonds, Nina
Moonbeams, dumplings & dragon boats **394.26**

Simons, Rae, 1957-
Survival skills **155.9**

Simont, Marc, 1915-
The stray dog **E**
(il) Krauss, R. The backward day **E**
(il) Lord, B. B. In the Year of the Boar and Jackie Robinson **Fic**
(il) Sharmat, M. W. Nate the Great **E**
(il) Thurber, J. Many moons [illustrated by Marc Simont] **E**
(il) Udry, J. M. A tree is nice **E**

Simple machines
Gardner, R. Sensational science projects with simple machines **621.8**
Solway, A. Castle under siege! **621.8**
Thales, S. Inclined planes to the rescue **621.8**
Thales, S. Levers to the rescue **621.8**
Thales, S. Pulleys to the rescue **621.8**
Thales, S. Screws to the rescue **621.8**
Thales, S. Wedges to the rescue **621.8**
Thales, S. Wheels and axles to the rescue **621.8**

Simple machines to the rescue [series]
Thales, S. Inclined planes to the rescue **621.8**
Thales, S. Levers to the rescue **621.8**
Thales, S. Pulleys to the rescue **621.8**
Thales, S. Screws to the rescue **621.8**
Thales, S. Wedges to the rescue **621.8**
Thales, S. Wheels and axles to the rescue **621.8**

Simple organisms. Zamosky, L. **579**

Simply Sarah [series]
Naylor, P. R. Patches and scratches **Fic**

Simply science [series]
Bailey, G. Body and health **612**

Bailey, G. Flight **629.13**
Simply sewing. Sadler, J. A. **646.2**
Simpson, Kathleen
Extreme weather **551.6**
Genetics **576.5**
The human brain **612.8**
Simpson, Martha Seif, 1954-
Bringing classes into the public library **027.62**
Simpson, Sharon
(jt. auth) Clifford, B. Real pirates **910.4**
Sims, Blanche
(il) Cox, J. Butterfly buddies **Fic**
(il) Knudsen, M. Bugged! **E**
Sing a song of piglets. Bunting, E. **811**
Sing a song of sixpence. Chapman, J. **398.8**
Sing-along stories [series]
Hoberman, M. A. Mary had a little lamb **782.42**
Sing down the moon. O'Dell, S. **Fic**
Sing my song. Seskin, S. **782.42**
Sing to the sun. Bryan, A. **811**
Singapore
Layton, L. Singapore **959.57**
Rau, D. M. Singapore **959.57**
Singer, Isaac Bashevis, 1904-1991
Stories for children **S C**
Zlateh the goat, and other stories **398.2**
See/See also pages in the following book(s):
Krull, K. Lives of the writers **920**
Singer, Marilyn, 1948-
Central heating **811**
A dog's gotta do what a dog's gotta do **636.7**
Eggs **591.4**
First food fight this fall and other school poems **811**
I'm getting a checkup **610**
I'm your bus **E**
Mirror mirror **811**
Shoe bop! **E**
Venom **591.6**
Singers
See also African American singers
Chambers, V. Celia Cruz, Queen of salsa **92**
Christensen, B. Woody Guthrie, poet of the people **92**
Greenfield, E. Paul Robeson **92**
Medina, T. I and I [biography of Bob Marley] **92**
Fiction
Alexander, C. Small Florence, piggy pop star **E**
Curry, J. L. The Black Canary **Fic**
Daly, N. Ruby sings the blues **E**
Singh, Vandana
Younguncle comes to town **Fic**
Singing
Fiction
Payne, C. C. Something to sing about **Fic**
Schotter, R. Doo-Wop Pop **E**

Sisters—Fiction—*Continued*

Patron, S. Maybe yes, maybe no, maybe maybe   **Fic**

Patz, N. Babies can't eat kimchee!   **E**

Roberts, W. D. The one left behind   **Fic**

Schwabach, K. The Hope Chest   **Fic**

Sendak, M. Outside over there   **E**

Snow, M. Sisters of the sword   **Fic**

Thor, A. A faraway island   **Fic**

Tucker, K. The seven Chinese sisters   **E**

Uegaki, C. Rosie and Buttercup   **E**

Williams-Garcia, R. One crazy summer   **Fic**

Willis, J. The bog baby   **E**

Wilson, J. The illustrated Mum   **Fic**

Wishinsky, F. Maggie can't wait   **E**

Yep, L. Auntie Tiger   **E**

Young, E. My Mei Mei   **E**

Zahler, D. The thirteenth princess   **Fic**

Zemach, M. Eating up Gladys   **E**

Zimmer, T. V. Sketches from a spy tree   **Fic**

Zolotow, C. If it weren't for you   **E**

Poetry

Williams, V. B. Amber was brave, Essie was smart   **811**

Sisters (in religious orders, congregations, etc.)
See Nuns

Sisters & brothers. Jenkins, S.   **591.56**

Sisters and brothers *See* Siblings

The sisters Grimm [series]

Buckley, M. The fairy-tale detectives   **Fic**

Sisters of Scituate Light. Krensky, S.   **E**

Sisters of the sword. Snow, M.   **Fic**

Sisters of the sword [series]

Snow, M. Sisters of the sword   **Fic**

Sit-in. Pinkney, A. D.   **323.1**

Sit-ins and freedom rides. Aretha, D.   **323.1**

Sit, Truman!. Harper, D.   **E**

Sitarski, Anita

Cold light   **572**

Sitting Bull, Dakota Chief, 1831-1890

About

Bruchac, J. A boy called Slow: the true story of Sitting Bull   **92**

Turner, A. W. Sitting Bull remembers   **92**

See/See also pages in the following book(s):

Ehrlich, A. Wounded Knee: an Indian history of the American West   **970.004**

Freedman, R. Indian chiefs   **920**

Sitting Bull remembers. Turner, A. W.   **92**

Siwanowicz, Igor

Animals up close   **590**

The six fools. Thomas, J. C.   **398.2**

Six innings. Preller, J.   **Fic**

Sixteen twenty one. See Grace, C. O. 1621   **394.26**

Sixteen years in sixteen seconds [biography of Sammy Lee] Yoo, P.   **92**

Sixteenth Street Baptist Church (Birmingham, Ala.)

Brimner, L. D. Birmingham Sunday   **323.1**

The sixth grade nickname game. Korman, G.   **Fic**

Siy, Alexandra

Cars on Mars   **629.43**

Mosquito bite   **595.7**

Sneeze!   **612.2**

Size

Davies, N. Just the right size   **591.4**

Hillman, B. How big is it?   **153.7**

Hoban, T. Is it larger? Is it smaller?   **E**

Hoban, T. Is it red? Is it yellow? Is it blue?   **E**

Jenkins, S. Actual size   **591.4**

Jenkins, S. Big & little   **591.4**

Komiya, T. Life-size zoo   **590**

Markle, S. Insects   **595.7**

Markle, S. Sharks   **597**

Markle, S. Spiders   **595.4**

Miller, M. Big and little   **E**

Murphy, S. J. Bigger, Better, BEST!   **516**

Patkau, K. Creatures great and small   **591.4**

Schwartz, J. Short   **612.6**

Fiction

Alborough, J. Tall   **E**

Aston, D. H. Not so tall for six   **E**

Bechtold, L. Sally and the purple socks   **E**

Bell, C. Itty bitty   **E**

Berry, M. Up on Daddy's shoulders   **E**

Bogart, J. E. Big and small, room for all   **E**

Cottrell Boyce, F. Cosmic   **Fic**

Draper, S. M. Little Sister is not my name   **Fic**

Foreman, M. The littlest dinosaur's big adventure   **E**

Gay, M.-L. When Stella was very very small   **E**

Hawkes, K. The wicked big toddlah   **E**

Joyce, W. George shrinks   **E**

McEvoy, A. Betsy B. Little   **E**

McGrory, A. Kidogo   **E**

McNamara, M. How many seeds in a pumpkin?   **E**

Mourlevat, J.-C. The pull of the ocean   **Fic**

Nakagawa, C. Who made this cake?   **E**

Nolen, J. Hewitt Anderson's great big life   **E**

Root, P. Paula Bunyan   **E**

Russo, M. A very big bunny   **E**

Sherry, K. I'm the biggest thing in the ocean   **E**

Stinson, K. Big or little?   **E**

Thompson, L. Wee little chick   **E**

Willis, J. Cottonball Colin   **E**

Yang, B. Foo, the flying frog of Washtub Pond   **E**

Yates, L. A small surprise   **E**

Ylvisaker, A. Little Klein   **Fic**

Size and shape *See* Shape; Size

Sizzling science projects with heat and energy. Gardner, R.   **536**

Skaggs, Gayle, 1952-

Look, it's books!   **021.7**

Skateboarding

Fitzpatrick, J. Skateboarding   **796.22**

Spencer, R. Skateboarding   **796.22**

Skating *See* Ice skating

Skeens, Matthew
  (il) Seuling, B. Cows sweat through their noses **590**
  (il) Seuling, B. Your skin weighs more than your brain **612**

Skeers, Linda, 1958-
  Tutus aren't my style **E**

Skeletal system. Jakab, C. **612.7**

Skeleton
  Baines, R. The bones you own **612.7**
  Ballard, C. The skeleton and muscular system **612.7**
  Barner, B. Dem bones **612.7**
  Jakab, C. Skeletal system **612.7**
  Rake, J. S. The human skeleton **611**
  Simon, S. Bones **612.7**
             Fiction
  Cuyler, M. Skeleton hiccups **E**

The skeleton and muscles. Parker, S. **612.7**

The skeleton and muscular system. Ballard, C. **612.7**

Skeleton hiccups. Cuyler, M. **E**

Skeleton man. Bruchac, J. **Fic**

Skellig. Almond, D. **Fic**

Skelton, Matthew
  Endymion Spring **Fic**
  The story of Cirrus Flux **Fic**

Sketches from a spy tree. Zimmer, T. V. **Fic**

Skevington, Andrea
  The story of Jesus **232.9**

Skiing
             Fiction
  Pendziwol, J. Marja's skis **E**

Skillet bread, sourdough, and vinegar pie. Ichord, L. F. **641.5**

Skills, Life *See* Life skills

Skin
  Baines, R. Your skin holds you in **612.7**
  Cobb, V. Your body battles a skinned knee **617.1**
  Lew, K. Itch & ooze **616.5**
  Miller, S. S. All kinds of skin **591.4**
  Rotner, S. Shades of people **E**
             Diseases
  Buckmaster, M. L. Skin cancer **616.99**
  Lew, K. Itch & ooze **616.5**
       Diseases—Fiction
  Johnson, A. A cool moonlight **Fic**

Skin cancer. Buckmaster, M. L. **616.99**

Skin diving
      See also Scuba diving
  Berne, J. Manfish: a story of Jacques Cousteau **92**
  Yaccarino, D. The fantastic undersea life of Jacques Cousteau **92**

Skinny-dipping at Monster Lake. Wallace, B. **Fic**

The skirt. Soto, G. **Fic**

Skis and skiing *See* Skiing

Skit-scat raggedy cat: Ella Fitzgerald. Orgill, R. **92**

Skittagetan Indians *See* Haida Indians

Sklansky, Amy E., 1971-
  The duck who played the kazoo **E**
  Where do chicks come from? **636.5**

Skotko, Brian
  Fasten your seatbelt **616.85**

Skoura, Xenia
  (jt. auth) DuBois, J. Greece **949.5**

Skreslet, Laurie
  To the top of Everest **796.52**

Skulduggery Pleasant. Landy, D. **Fic**

The skull of truth. Coville, B. **Fic**

The skull talks back and other haunting tales. Thomas, J. C. **398.2**

Skunkdog. Jenkins, E. **E**

Skunks
  Gonzales, D. Skunks in the dark **599.7**
  Mason, A. Skunks **599.7**
  Otfinoski, S. Skunks **599.7**
             Fiction
  Jenkins, E. Skunkdog **E**
  Pochocki, E. The blessing of the beasts **E**
  Ziefert, H. One smart skunk **E**

Skunks in the dark. Gonzales, D. **599.7**

Skurzynski, Gloria, 1930-
  Are we alone? **576.8**
  On time **529**
  This is rocket science **629.4**

Sky
  Gardner, R. Stellar science projects about Earth's sky **551.5**
             Fiction
  Morales, Y. Little Night **E**

Sky boys. Hopkinson, D. **E**

Sky dancers. Kirk, C. A. **E**

Sky high: the true story of Maggie Gee. Moss, M. **92**

Sky magic **811.008**

Sky sweeper. Gershator, P. **E**

Skylar. Cuffe-Perez, M. **Fic**

The sky's the limit. Thimmesh, C. **500**

Skyscrapers
  Curlee, L. Skyscraper **720**
  Macaulay, D. Unbuilding **690**
  Oxlade, C. Skyscrapers **720**
  Price, S. The story behind skyscrapers **720**
  Stern, S. L. Building greenscrapers **720**
  See/See also pages in the following book(s):
  Macaulay, D. Building big **720**

Slack, Michael H., 1969-
  (il) Donovan, S. Hawk & Drool **612.3**
  (il) Donovan, S. Rumble & spew **612.3**
  (il) Kelley, E. A. My life as a chicken **E**
  (il) Larsen, C. S. Crust and spray **612.8**
  (il) Lew, K. Clot & scab **617.1**
  (il) Lew, K. Itch & ooze **616.5**

Slade, Arthur G., 1967-
  Jolted **Fic**

Slade, Christian, 1974-
  (il) Rogan, S. J. The daring adventures of Penhaligon Brush **Fic**

Slade, Suzanne, 1964-
What can we do about the energy crisis?
333.79
What's new at the zoo? **513**

Slam dunk! science projects with basketball. Gardner, R. **530**

Slangalicious. O'Reilly, G. **427**

Slant. Williams, L. E. **Fic**

Slate, Joseph, 1928-
I want to be free **E**
Miss Bindergarten celebrates the 100th day of kindergarten **E**

Slater, Dashka
Baby shoes **E**
The sea serpent and me **E**

Slaughter, Tom
(il) Jocelyn, M. Eats **E**
(il) Jocelyn, M. Over under **E**
(il) Jocelyn, M. Same same **E**

The **slave** dancer. Fox, P. **Fic**

Slave trade
Clifford, B. Real pirates **910.4**
Granfield, L. Out of slavery **264**
Sharp, S. P. The slave trade and the middle passage **326**

Fiction
Fox, P. The slave dancer **Fic**
Grifalconi, A. The village that vanished **E**

The **slave** trade and the middle passage. Sharp, S. P. **326**

Slavery
Haskins, J. Africa **967**
Newman, S. P. Child slavery in modern times **326**
Rappaport, D. No more! **326**
Sharp, S. P. The slave trade and the middle passage **326**

Fiction
Anderson, L. H. Chains **Fic**
Broyles, A. Priscilla and the hollyhocks **E**
Carbone, E. L. Night running **E**
Cohen, D. B. Nachshon, who was afraid to swim **E**
Collier, J. L. Jump ship to freedom **Fic**
Collier, J. L. War comes to Willy Freeman **Fic**
Cowley, M. The golden bull **Fic**
Curtis, C. P. Elijah of Buxton **Fic**
Dahlberg, M. F. The story of Jonas **Fic**
Durango, J. The walls of Cartagena **Fic**
Evans, F. W. Hush harbor **E**
French, J. Rover **Fic**
Grifalconi, A. Ain't nobody a stranger to me **E**
Hegamin, T. Most loved in all the world **E**
Helgerson, J. Crows & cards **Fic**
Hopkinson, D. From slave to soldier **E**
Hopkinson, D. Sweet Clara and the freedom quilt **E**
Lester, J. The old African **Fic**
Levine, E. Henry's freedom box **E**
Lyons, M. E. Letters from a slave girl **Fic**
McKissack, P. C. Let my people go **Fic**
McMullan, M. How I found the Strong **Fic**
Morrow, B. O. A good night for freedom **E**

Nolen, J. Big Jabe **E**
Paterson, K. Jip **Fic**
Paulsen, G. The legend of Bass Reeves **Fic**
Polacco, P. January's sparrow **Fic**
Rappaport, D. Freedom ship **Fic**
Raven, M. Night boat to freedom **E**
Schroeder, A. Minty: a story of young Harriet Tubman **E**
Sherman, P. Ben and the Emancipation Proclamation **E**
Sheth, K. Boys without names **Fic**
Slate, J. I want to be free **E**
Stroud, B. The patchwork path **E**
Tingle, T. Crossing Bok Chitto **Fic**
Treviño, E. B. d. I, Juan de Pareja **Fic**
Vande Velde, V. There's a dead person following my sister around **Fic**
Walter, M. P. Alec's primer **E**
Wentworth, M. Shackles **E**
Whelan, G. The listeners **E**
Winter, J. Follow the drinking gourd **E**
Woods, B. My name is Sally Little Song **Fic**
Woodson, J. Show way **E**

Folklore
Hamilton, V. The people could fly: the picture book **398.2**
McGill, A. Way up and over everything **398.2**

Poetry
In the hollow of your hand **782.42**

United States
See also Abolitionists
Bial, R. The strength of these arms **326**
Bial, R. The Underground Railroad **326**
Clinton, C. Phillis's big test [biography of Phillis Wheatley] **92**
Clinton, C. When Harriet met Sojourner [biography of Harriet Tubman and Sojourner Truth] **92**
Currie, S. Escapes from slavery **326**
Ford, C. T. Slavery and the underground railroad **326**
Halfmann, J. Seven miles to freedom **92**
Hamilton, V. Many thousand gone **326**
Haskins, J. Get on board: the story of the Underground Railroad **326**
Heinrichs, A. The Underground Railroad **326**
Hendrix, J. John Brown **92**
Huey, L. M. American archaeology uncovers the Underground Railroad **973.7**
Jones, L. Mrs. Lincoln's dressmaker: the unlikely friendship of Elizabeth Keckley and Mary Todd Lincoln **92**
Jordan, A. D. Slavery and resistance **326**
Kennedy, R. F. Robert Smalls **92**
Landau, E. Fleeing to freedom on the Underground Railroad **973.7**
Lasky, K. A voice of her own: the story of Phillis Wheatley, slave poet **92**
Lester, J. From slave ship to freedom road **326**
Lester, J. To be a slave **326**
McKissack, P. C. Days of Jubilee **973.7**

Slobodkin, Louis, 1903-1975
  (il) Estes, E. The hundred dresses   **Fic**
  (il) Estes, E. The Moffats   **Fic**
  (il) Thurber, J. Many moons [illustrated by Louis Slobodkin]   **E**
Slobodkina, Esphyr, 1908-2002
  Caps for sale   **E**
Slonim, David
  (il) Spinelli, E. Silly Tilly   **E**
The **sloppy** copy slipup. DiSalvo, D.   **Fic**
Sloppy Joe. Keane, D.   **E**
Slote, Alfred
  Finding Buck McHenry   **Fic**
Sloths
  Stewart, M. Sloths   **599.3**
        Fiction
  Carle, E. "Slowly, slowly, slowly," said the sloth   **E**
Slovenz-Low, Madeline
  (jt. auth) Waters, K. Lion dancer: Ernie Wan's Chinese New Year   **394.26**
Slow down for manatees. Arnosky, J.   **E**
Slow learning children
  See also Mentally handicapped children
"**Slowly,** slowly, slowly," said the sloth. Carle, E.   **E**
Sluggers' car wash. Murphy, S. J.   **513**
Slugs (Mollusks)
        Fiction
  Edwards, P. D. Some smug slug   **E**
Slumdog millionaire (Motion picture)
  Ali, R. Slumgirl dreaming [biography of Rubina Ali]   **92**
Slumgirl dreaming [biography of Rubina Ali] Ali, R.   **92**
Sly the Sleuth and the pet mysteries. Napoli, D. J.   **Fic**
Small, David, 1945-
  George Washington's cows   **E**
  Imogene's antlers   **E**
  (il) Appelt, K. The underneath   **Fic**
  (jt. auth) Armstrong, J. Once upon a banana   **E**
  (il) Broach, E. When dinosaurs came with everything   **E**
  (il) Henson, H. That Book Woman   **E**
  (il) Howland, N. Princess says goodnight   **E**
  (il) Sandburg, C. The Huckabuck family and how they raised popcorn in Nebraska and quit and came back   **E**
  (il) St. George, J. So you want to be an inventor?   **609**
  (il) St. George, J. So you want to be president?   **973**
  (il) Stewart, S. The friend   **E**
  (il) Stewart, S. The gardener   **E**
  (il) Stewart, S. The journey   **E**
  (il) Stewart, S. The library   **E**
Small, Ernest *See* Lent, Blair, 1930-2009
The **small** adventure of Popeye and Elvis. O'Connor, B.   **Fic**
Small beauties. Woodruff, E.   **E**
Small birds. Haney, J.   **636.6**

A **small,** brown dog with a wet, pink nose. Bodeen, S. A.   **E**
Small business
  Bochner, A. B. The new totally awesome business book for kids (and their parents)   **658**
Small dogs. Hart, J.   **636.7**
Small Florence, piggy pop star. Alexander, C.   **E**
A **small** Nativity. Nazoa, A.   **E**
Small pig. Lobel, A.   **E**
Small steps. Kehret, P.   **92**
A **small** surprise. Yates, L.   **E**
Small wonders. Baillie, M.   **591.3**
The **Smallest** Snowflake. Watts, B.   **E**
Smalley, Carol Parenzan, 1960-
  Green changes you can make around your home   **333.72**
Smallpox
  Marrin, A. Dr. Jenner and the speckled monster   **614.5**
  Ollhoff, J. Smallpox   **616.9**
Smalls, Robert, 1839-1915
        About
  Halfmann, J. Seven miles to freedom   **92**
  Kennedy, R. F. Robert Smalls   **92**
        Fiction
  Rappaport, D. Freedom ship   **Fic**
Smart, Denise
  The children's baking book   **641.8**
Smart about art [series]
  Cocca-Leffler, M. Edgar Degas: paintings that dance   **92**
  Frith, M. Frida Kahlo   **92**
  Kelley, T. Claude Monet: sunshine and waterlilies   **92**
Smart copyright compliance for schools. Butler, R. P.   **346.04**
Smart dog. Vande Velde, V.   **Fic**
Smart feller fart smeller & other Spoonerisms. Agee, J.   **793.73**
A **smart** girl's guide to her parents' divorce. Holyoke, N.   **306.89**
A **smart** girl's guide to money. Holyoke, N.   **332.024**
A **smart** kid's guide to avoiding online predators. Jakubiak, D. J.   **004.6**
A **smart** kid's guide to doing Internet research. Jakubiak, D. J.   **001.4**
A **smart** kid's guide to Internet privacy. Jakubiak, D. J.   **005.8**
A **smart** kid's guide to online bullying. Jakubiak, D. J.   **302.3**
A **smart** kid's guide to playing online games. Jakubiak, D. J.   **794.8**
A **smart** kid's guide to social networking online. Jakubiak, D. J.   **006.7**
The **smartest** dinosaurs. Lessem, D.   **567.9**
Smarty Sara. Hays, A. J.   **E**
Smash! crash!. Scieszka, J.   **E**
Smash it! crash it! launch it!. Newcomb, R.   **507.8**

Smashing science projects about Earth's rocks and minerals. Gardner, R.   **552**

Smath, Jerry
(il) Weiss, E. The taming of Lola   **E**

Smedman, Lisa
From boneshakers to choppers   **629.227**

Smee, Nicola
Clip-clop   **E**
What's the matter, Bunny Blue?   **E**

Smell
Boothroyd, J. What is smell?   **612.8**
Cobb, V. Follow your nose   **612.8**
Hewitt, S. Smell it!   **612.8**
Fiction
Johnston, L. Farley follows his nose   **E**
Keller, H. Nosy Rosie   **E**
Palatini, M. Gorgonzola   **E**

Smell it!. Hewitt, S.   **612.8**
Smelly feet sandwich. Zobel, A.   **811**
Smelly locker. Katz, A.   **782.42**
Smelly stink bugs. Goldish, M.   **595.7**

Smelt, Roselynn
New Zealand   **993**

Smile!. Hodgkinson, L.   **E**
Smile. Telgemeier, R.   **741.5**
Smile, Principessa!. Enderle, J. R.   **E**

Smiles, Eileen Michaelis
(jt. auth) Yolen, J. Apple for the teacher   **782.42**

Smiley, Jane, 1949-
The Georges and the Jewels   **Fic**

Smith, Alex T.
(il) Cottringer, A. Eliot Jones, midnight superhero   **E**

Smith, Alvin
(il) Wojciechowska, M. Shadow of a bull   **Fic**

Smith, Andy
(il) Woodward, J. How to be a genius   **152**

Smith, Anne, 1958-
(il) Robb, D. Ox, house, stick   **411**

Smith, Bessie, 1894-1937
Fiction
Stauffacher, S. Bessie Smith and the night riders   **E**

Smith, Brian, 1975-
(il) Steinberg, D. Sound off!   **741.5**

Smith, Cat Bowman
(il) DeFelice, C. C. Old Granny and the bean thief   **E**
(il) Freeman, M. The trouble with cats   **Fic**
(il) MacDonald, A. Too much flapdoodle!   **Fic**
(il) Murphy, S. J. Dave's down-to-earth rock shop   **511.3**
(il) Swain, R. F. Hairdo!   **391**
(il) Thomassie, T. Feliciana Feyra LeRoux   **E**

Smith, Charles R.
Black Jack   **92**
Diamond life   **796.357**
Hoop kings   **811**
Hoop queens   **811**
Winning words   **S C**

(il) Kipling, R. If   **821**

Smith, Charles R., 1969-
Dance with me   **E**
Twelve rounds to glory: the story of Muhammad Ali   **92**
(il) Hughes, L. My people   **811**

Smith, Chris, 1947-
One city, two brothers   **398.2**

Smith, Craig, 1955-
(il) Bell, K. If the shoe fits   **Fic**
(il) Dumbleton, M. Cat   **E**

Smith, Cynthia Leitich
Indian shoes   **Fic**
Jingle dancer   **E**

Smith, Danna
Two at the zoo   **E**

Smith, David J.
If America were a village   **973**
If the world were a village   **304.6**

Smith, Dick King- *See* King-Smith, Dick, 1922-

Smith, Doris Buchanan
A taste of blackberries   **Fic**

Smith, Duane, 1974-
(il) Halfmann, J. Seven miles to freedom   **92**

Smith, Elwood H., 1941-
(il) Goodman, S. Gee whiz! it's all about pee!   **612.4**
(il) Goodman, S. See how they run   **324**
(il) Goodman, S. The truth about poop   **573.4**
(il) Sylver, A. Hot diggity dog   **641.3**

Smith, Henrietta M.
(ed) The Coretta Scott King awards, 1970-2009. *See* The Coretta Scott King awards, 1970-2009   **028.5**

Smith, Hope Anita
Keeping the night watch   **Fic**
Mother poems   **811**
The way a door closes   **Fic**

Smith, Icy, 1966-
Half spoon of rice   **Fic**

Smith, Jan
(il) Holub, J. Apple countdown   **E**

Smith, Jedediah Strong, 1799-1831
About
Nelson, S. P. Jedediah Smith   **92**

Smith, Jeff, 1960 Feb. 27-
Little Mouse gets ready   **741.5**

Smith, Jessie Willcox, 1863-1935
(il) Spyri, J. Heidi   **Fic**

Smith, John, 1580-1631
About
Schanzer, R. John Smith escapes again!   **92**

Smith, Jos. A. *See* Smith, Joseph A., 1936-

Smith, Joseph A., 1936-
(jt. auth) Bardoe, C. Gregor Mendel   **92**
(il) Fleischman, S. Bandit's moon   **Fic**
(il) Ginsburg, M. Clay boy   **398.2**
(il) Haas, J. Sugaring   **E**
(jt. auth) Yorinks, A. The witch's child   **E**

Smith, Lane
The big elephant in the room   **E**
John, Paul, George & Ben   **E**

Snow music. Perkins, L. R.   **E**

Snow party. Ziefert, H.   **E**

The **Snow** Queen. Ehrlich, A.   **Fic**

The **Snow** Show. Fisher, C.   **E**

Snow! Snow! Snow!. Harper, L.   **E**

Snow sounds. Johnson, D.   **E**

The **snow** spider. Nimmo, J.   **Fic**

Snow surprise. Ernst, L. C.   **E**

Snow treasure. McSwigan, M.   **Fic**

Snow White. Grimm, J.   **398.2**

Snow White. Ray, J.   **398.2**

Snowball launchers, giant-pumpkin growers, and other cool contraptions. Fox, T.   **745.5**

Snowballs. Ehlert, L.   **E**

Snowboarding
    Woods, B. Snowboarding   **796.9**
Fiction
    Ramthun, B. The White Gates   **Fic**

Snowed in with Grandmother Silk. Fenner, C.   **Fic**

The **snowflake**. Waldman, N.   **551.48**

Snowflake Bentley [biography of Wilson Alwyn Bentley] Martin, J. B.   **92**

The **snowflake** sisters. Lewis, J. P.   **E**

The **snowman**. Briggs, R.   **E**

Snowmen at night. Buehner, C.   **E**

Snowy, blowy winter. Raczka, B.   **E**

The **snowy** day. Keats, E. J.   **E**

Snowy weather days. Marsico, K.   **551.57**

Snyder, Dianne
    The boy of the three-year nap   **398.2**

Snyder, Grace, 1882-1982
About
    Warren, A. Pioneer girl [biography of Grace McCance Snyder]   **92**

Snyder, Laurel
    Any which wall   **Fic**

Snyder, Trish
    Alligator & crocodile rescue   **597.98**

Snyder, Zilpha Keatley
    The bronze pen   **Fic**
    The Egypt game   **Fic**
    The headless cupid   **Fic**
    William S. and the great escape   **Fic**
    The witches of Worm   **Fic**

So, Meilo
    (il) The 20th century children's poetry treasury. See The 20th century children's poetry treasury   **811.008**
    (il) The Beauty of the beast. See The Beauty of the beast   **811.008**
    (il) Gibfried, D. Brother Juniper   **E**
    (il) Ó Flatharta, A. Hurry and the monarch   **E**
    (il) Read a rhyme, write a rhyme. See Read a rhyme, write a rhyme   **811.008**
    (il) Schulman, J. Pale Male   **598**
    (il) Sierra, J. Tasty baby belly buttons   **398.2**
    (il) Simonds, N. Moonbeams, dumplings & dragon boats   **394.26**
    (il) Singer, M. Central heating   **811**

So B. it. Weeks, S.   **Fic**

So far from the bamboo grove. Watkins, Y. K.   **Fic**

So far from the sea. Bunting, E.   **E**

So happy!. Henkes, K.   **E**

So many circles, so many squares. Hoban, T.   **E**

So many days. McGhee, A.   **E**

So said Ben [biography of Benjamin Franklin] McCurdy, M.   **92**

So sleepy story. Shulevitz, U.   **E**

So what's it like to be a cat? Kuskin, K.   **E**

So you want to be an inventor? St. George, J.   **609**

So you want to be president? St. George, J.   **973**

Soap
    Rhatigan, J. Soapmaking   **668**
    Wagner, L. Cool melt & pour soap   **668**
Fiction
    Schaefer, C. L. The biggest soap   **E**

Soapmaking. Rhatigan, J.   **668**

Soaring with the wind. Gibbons, G.   **598**

Sobol, Donald J., 1924-
    Encyclopedia Brown, boy detective   **Fic**

Sobol, Richard
    An elephant in the backyard   **636.9**
    (il) Hudson, C. W. Construction zone   **690**

Soccer
    Gifford, C. Soccer [Personal best series]   **796.334**
    Gifford, C. Soccer [Know your sport series]   **796.334**
    Goodstein, M. Goal! science projects with soccer   **507.8**
    Guillain, C. Soccer   **796.334**
    Hornby, H. Soccer   **796.334**
    Hyde, N. Soccer science   **796.334**
    Kelley, K. C. Soccer   **796.334**
    Stewart, M. Goal!: the fire and fury of soccer's greatest moment   **796.334**
Biography
    Brown, M. Pele, king of soccer   **92**
    Cline-Ransome, L. Young Pelé   **92**
Encyclopedias
    Gifford, C. The Kingfisher soccer encyclopedia   **796.334**
Fiction
    Avi. S.O.R. losers   **Fic**
    Fitzgerald, D. Soccer chick rules   **Fic**
    Hamm, M. Winners never quit!   **E**
    Javaherbin, M. Goal!   **E**
    Kolar, B. Big kicks   **E**
    Walliams, D. The boy in the dress   **Fic**
Folkore
    MacDonald, M. R. Bat's big game   **398.2**

Soccer chick rules. Fitzgerald, D.   **Fic**

Soccer science. Hyde, N.   **796.334**

Social action
    Houle, M. E. Lindsey Williams   **92**
    Lewis, B. A. The kid's guide to social action   **361.2**
    Olien, R. Kids care!   **361.2**

Social action—*Continued*

Schwartz, H. E. Political activism 322.4
Shoveller, H. Ryan and Jimmy 361.7
Woog, A. Jyotirmayee Mohapatra 92

Fiction

Sierra, J. Ballyhoo Bay E
Timberlake, A. That girl Lucy Moon Fic

Social anthropology *See* Ethnology

Social classes

See also Nobility; Working class

Fiction

Amado, E. Tricycle E
Carman, P. The house of power Fic
Hesse, K. Brooklyn Bridge Fic
Lloyd, A. Year of the tiger Fic

Social classes in art

Bingham, J. Society & class 704.9

Social conflict

See also Conflict management

Social drinking *See* Drinking of alcoholic beverages

Social problems

Lewis, B. A. The kid's guide to social action 361.2

Social sciences

Bibliography

Notable social studies trade books for young people 016.3

Societies

See also Clubs; Secret societies

Society & class. Bingham, J. 704.9

Society in art

Bingham, J. Society & class 704.9

Society of Friends

Kroll, S. William Penn 92
Mierka, G. A. Nathanael Greene 92
Woog, A. What makes me a Quaker? 289.6

Fiction

Bruchac, J. The arrow over the door Fic
De Angeli, M. L. Thee, Hannah! Fic

The **Society** of Unrelenting Vigilance. Dakin, G. Fic

Sockalexis, Chief *See* Sockalexis, Louis, 1871-1913

Sockalexis, Louis, 1871-1913

About

Wise, B. Louis Sockalexis 92

Socks. Cleary, B. Fic

Sodium chloride *See* Salt

Soentpiet, Chris K.

(il) Amazing faces. See Amazing faces 811.008
(il) Bradby, M. Momma, where are you from? E
(il) Bradby, M. More than anything else E
(il) Bunting, E. Jin Woo E
(il) Bunting, E. So far from the sea E
(il) Farris, C. My brother Martin [biography of Martin Luther King] 92
(il) Raven, M. Happy birthday to you! 782.42
(il) Yin. Brothers E
(il) Yin. Coolies E

Soesbee, Ree *See* Henham, R. D.

Sofie and the city. Grant, K. E

Softball

Fiction

Mackel, K. MadCat Fic

Sogabe, Aki

(il) Namioka, L. The hungriest boy in the world E
(il) Partridge, E. Kogi's mysterious journey 398.2
(il) Partridge, E. Oranges on Golden Mountain E

Sohn, Emily

The environment 363.7

Soil. Pascoe, E. 577.5

Soil ecology

Bial, R. A handful of dirt 577.5
Bourgeois, P. The dirt on dirt 631.4
Pascoe, E. Soil 577.5

Soils

Bial, R. A handful of dirt 577.5
Bourgeois, P. The dirt on dirt 631.4
Gardner, R. Super science projects about Earth's soil and water 631.4

Sojourner Truth *See* Truth, Sojourner, d. 1883

Sojourner Truth's step-stomp stride. Pinkney, A. D. 92

Solar eclipses

Fiction

Mass, W. Every soul a star Fic

Solar energy

Bang, M. My light 621.47
Bearce, S. How to harness solar power for your home 621.47
Benduhn, T. Solar power 621.47
Hirschmann, K. Solar energy 333.79

Solar power. Benduhn, T. 621.47

Solar radiation

See also Greenhouse effect

Solar system

Fiction

Coffelt, N. Dogs in space E
Mills, C. How Oliver Olson changed the world Fic

Solar system

Aguilar, D. A. 11 planets 523.4
Aguilar, D. A. Planets, stars, and galaxies 520
Baines, R. Every planet has a place 523.2
Bredeson, C. What is the solar system? 523.2
Carson, M. K. Exploring the solar system 523.2
Croswell, K. Ten worlds 523.4
Greathouse, L. E. Solar system 523.2
Kudlinski, K. V. Boy were we wrong about the solar system! 523.2
Simon, S. Our solar system 523.2
Trammel, H. K. The solar system 523.2
VanCleave, J. P. Janice VanCleave's solar system 523.2

Solbert, Ronni

(il) Merrill, J. The pushcart war Fic

Soldiers
Falvey, D. Letters to a soldier   956.7
Greenwood, M. The donkey of Gallipoli
    940.4
Park, L. The Spartan hoplites   938
Fiction
Cali, D. The enemy   E
Cohen, M. My big brother   E
Dowell, F. O. Shooting the moon   Fic
Hartnett, S. The silver donkey   Fic
Hughes, P. Seeing the elephant   Fic
Madison, A. 100 days and 99 nights   Fic
Rodman, M. A. Jimmy's stars   Fic
Weber, E. The Yankee at the seder   Fic
Canada
Innes, S. A bear in war   E
Rome
Beller, S. P. Roman legions on the march
    937
United States
Beller, S. P. Battling in the Pacific   940.54
Beller, S. P. Billy Yank and Johnny Reb
    973.7
Beller, S. P. The doughboys over there
    940.4

Soldiers on the battlefront [series]
Beller, S. P. Battling in the Pacific   940.54
Beller, S. P. Billy Yank and Johnny Reb
    973.7
Beller, S. P. The doughboys over there
    940.4
Beller, S. P. Roman legions on the march
    937

Solheim, James
Born yesterday   E
It's disgusting—and we ate it!   641.3
Solids
Boothroyd, J. What is a solid?   530.4
Hurd, W. Changing states   530.4
Solitude
Crist, J. J. What to do when you're sad & lonely   158
Solomon, Heather
(il) Coombs, K. The secret-keeper   E
(il) Willey, M. The 3 bears and Goldilocks
    398.2
Solomon and the ant. Oberman, S.   398.2
Soltan, Rita
Reading raps   027.62
Summer reading renaissance   027.62
Solve that crime! [series]
Spilsbury, R. Bones speak!   614
Spilsbury, R. Counterfeit!   363.2
Solving Zoe. Dee, B.   Fic
Solway, Andrew
Africa   780.9
Castle under siege!   621.8
Communication   303.4
Eagles and other birds   598
Graphing immigration   325.73
Graphing war and conflict   355
Inventions and investigations   600
Latin America and the Caribbean   780.9
Modern dance   792.8
Renewable energy sources   333.79

Understanding cycles and systems   550
What's inside a black hole?   523.1
(jt. auth) Biesty, S. Rome: in spectacular cross section   937
Somalia
Hassig, S. M. Somalia   967.73
Fiction
Hoffman, M. The color of home   E
Soman, David
Ladybug Girl   E
Some dog!. Casanova, M.   E
Some dogs do. Alborough, J.   E
Some frog!. Bunting, E.   Fic
Some kind of love. Dant, T.   811
Some smug slug. Edwards, P. D.   E
Someday a tree. Bunting, E.   E
Someday when my cat can talk. Lazo, C. E.
    E
Someone for Mr. Sussman. Polacco, P.   E
Someone named Eva. Wolf, J. M.   Fic
Someone used my toothbrush!. Shields, C. D.
    811
Someone walks by. Carlson-Voiles, P.   591.7
Somervill, Barbara A., 1948-
Cane toad   597.8
Clara Barton   92
Graphing crime   364
The human body   612
Marine biologist   578.7
Our living world   577
Pierre-Auguste Renoir   92
Something about the author   920.003
Something about the author: autobiography series
    920.003
Something big has been here. Prelutsky, J.
    811
Something funny happened at the library. Reid, R.
    027.62
Something out of nothing [biography of Marie Curie] McClafferty, C. K.   92
Something to do. Lucas, D.   E
Something to sing about. Payne, C. C.   Fic
Something wickedly weird [series]
Mould, C. The wooden mile   Fic
Sometimes I'm Bombaloo. Vail, R.   E
Sometimes my mommy gets angry. Campbell, B. M.   E
Sometimes you get what you want. Gary, M.
    E
Sommer, Shelley
John F. Kennedy   92
Song and dance man. Ackerman, K.   E
A **song** for Cambodia [biography of Arn Chorn-Pond] Lord, M.   92
Song of creation. Goble, P.   242
The **song** of Francis. De Paola, T.   E
Song of middle C. McGhee, A.   E
Song of the swallows. Politi, L.   E
Song of the trees. Taylor, M. D.   Fic
Song of the water boatman. Sidman, J.   811

The **song** of the whales. Orlev, U.   **Fic**

Songhai Empire
  McKissack, P. C. The royal kingdoms of Ghana, Mali, and Songhay   **966.2**

Songs
    See also Carols; National songs; Spirituals (Songs)
  Aylesworth, J. Our Abe Lincoln   **92**
  Bates, I. Five little ducks   **782.42**
  Baum, M. I have a little dreidel   **782.42**
  Boynton, S. Blue Moo   **782.42**
  Boynton, S. Dog train   **782.42**
  Boynton, S. Philadelphia chickens   **782.42**
  Boynton, S. Sandra Boynton's One shoe blues   **782.42**
  Cabrera, J. If you're happy and you know it   **E**
  Carle, E. Today is Monday   **782.42**
  Coots, J. F. Santa Claus is comin' to town   **782.42**
  De colores = Bright with colors   **782.42**
  Deck the halls   **782.42**
  Diez deditos. Ten little fingers & other play rhymes and action songs from Latin America   **782.42**
  DiPucchio, K. S. Sipping spiders through a straw   **782.42**
  The Eentsy, weentsy spider: fingerplays and action rhymes   **796.1**
  Emberley, R. There was an old monster!   **E**
  Fatus, S. Here we go round the mulberry bush   **782.42**
  Fiestas: a year of Latin American songs of celebration   **782.42**
  Had gadya   **296.4**
  Harburg, E. Y. Over the rainbow   **782.42**
  Hillenbrand, W. Down by the station   **782.42**
  Hinojosa, T. Cada niño/Every child   **782.42**
  Hoberman, M. A. The eensy-weensy spider   **782.42**
  Hoberman, M. A. Mary had a little lamb   **782.42**
  Hort, L. The seals on the bus   **782.42**
  Jackson, J. Let there be peace on earth   **782.42**
  Johnson, J. W. Lift every voice and sing   **782.42**
  Johnson, P. B. On top of spaghetti   **E**
  Julie Andrews' collection of poems, songs, and lullabies   **808.8**
  Katz, A. On top of the potty and other get-up-and-go songs   **782.42**
  Katz, A. Smelly locker   **782.42**
  Katz, A. Take me out of the bathtub and other silly dilly songs   **782.42**
  Mallett, D. Inch by inch   **782.42**
  McNamara, M. The whistle on the train   **E**
  Mora, P. A pinata in a pine tree   **782.42**
  Paxton, T. The marvelous toy   **782.42**
  Raffi. Baby Beluga   **782.42**
  Raffi. Down by the bay   **782.42**
  Raffi. Five little ducks   **782.42**
  Raven, M. Happy birthday to you!   **782.42**
  Reid, R. Comin' down to storytime   **E**
  Reid, R. Shake & shout   **027.62**
  Roth, S. L. Hanukkah, oh Hanukkah   **782.42**

  Seeger, R. C. American folk songs for children in home, school, and nursery school   **782.42**
  Sloat, T. There was an old man who painted the sky   **E**
  Staines, B. All God's critters   **782.42**
  They Might Be Giants (Musical group). Kids go!   **782.42**
  This little piggy   **398.8**
  Vetter, J. R. Down by the station   **782.42**
  Yarrow, P. Puff, the magic dragon   **782.42**
  Yolen, J. Apple for the teacher   **782.42**
  Zelinsky, P. O. Knick-knack paddywhack!   **782.42**
    Fiction
  Williams, V. B. Lucky song   **E**
    Indexes
  Reid, R. Children's jukebox   **782.42**
    United States
  Bates, K. L. America the beautiful   **E**

Songs from the loom. Roessel, M.   **970.004**

Songwriters *See* Composers

Songwriters and songwriting
  Seskin, S. Sing my song   **782.42**

Sonishi, Kenji, 1969-
  Leave it to PET!: the misadventures of a recycled super robot, vol. 1   **741.5**

Sonneborn, Liz
  The ancient Aztecs   **972**
  The ancient Kushites   **939**
  The Mormon Trail   **978**
  Pompeii   **937**

Sonnenblick, Jordan
  After ever after   **Fic**
  Zen and the art of faking it   **Fic**

Sonoran Desert
  Lynch, W. Sonoran Desert   **577.5**
    Natural history
    See Natural history—Sonoran Desert

Sonoran Desert. Lynch, W.   **577.5**

Sons and fathers *See* Father-son relationship

Sons and mothers *See* Mother-son relationship

The **sons** of the Dragon King. Young, E.   **398.2**

Sootface. San Souci, R.   **398.2**

Sopa de frijoles = Bean soup. Argueta, J.   **811**

Sophie. Fox, M.   **E**

Sophie and the next-door monsters. Case, C.   **E**

Sophie Peterman tells the truth!. Weeks, S.   **E**

Sophie's masterpiece. Spinelli, E.   **E**

Sophie's wheels. Pearson, D.   **E**

Sorcery *See* Magic

Sorensen, Henri, 1950-
  (il) Deedy, C. A. The yellow star   **Fic**
  (il) Fitch, F. M. A book about God   **231**
  (il) Frost, R. Robert Frost   **811**

Soriano, Luis
    About
  Winter, J. Biblioburro   **E**

Sorra, Kristin
  (il) Hall, K. Turkey riddles   **793.73**

Sort it out!. Mariconda, B.   **E**

South Africa—Race relations—*Continued*
Mandela, N. Nelson Mandela: long walk to freedom **92**
McDonough, Y. Z. Peaceful protest: the life of Nelson Mandela **92**
    Race relations—Fiction
Naidoo, B. Journey to Jo'burg **Fic**
Naidoo, B. Out of bounds: seven stories of conflict and hope **S C**
    Social life and customs
Cave, K. One child, one seed **E**
South America
Foster, K. Atlas of South America **980**
Gorrell, G. K. In the land of the jaguar **980**
    Fiction
Byrd, T. Doc Wilde and the frogs of doom **Fic**

    Folklore
    See Folklore—South America
South American Indians *See* Native Americans—South America
South America's most amazing animals. Ganeri, A. **591.9**
South Carolina
    Fiction
Blue, R. Ron's big mission **E**
Fuqua, J. S. Darby **Fic**
O'Connor, B. The small adventure of Popeye and Elvis **Fic**
Weatherford, C. B. Champions on the bench **E**
Wentworth, M. Shackles **E**
South Dakota
    Fiction
Geisert, B. Prairie summer **Fic**
Turner, A. W. Grasshopper summer **Fic**
South Korea *See* Korea (South)
South Pacific Region *See* Oceania
South Pole
    See also Antarctica
Levinson, N. S. North Pole, South Pole **998**
Thompson, G. Roald Amundsen and Robert Scott race to the South Pole **998**
South Sea Islands *See* Oceania
South Seas *See* Oceania
Southeast Asian Americans. Wachtel, A. **305.8**

Southern Africa
    Fiction
Grifalconi, A. The village that vanished **E**
Southern Rhodesia *See* Zimbabwe
Southern sea otters. Leardi, J. **599.7**
Southern States
    Folklore
    See Folklore—Southern States
    History
Hernández, R. E. Early explorations: the 1500s **970.01**
Hernández, R. E. New Spain: 1600-1760s **973.1**
    Race relations
Aretha, D. Sit-ins and freedom rides **323.1**
Bausum, A. Freedom Riders **323.1**

Pinkney, A. D. Sit-in **323.1**
Rappaport, D. Free at last! **305.8**
Southwest, New *See* Southwestern States
Southwest Pacific Region *See* Oceania
Southwestern States
    Antiquities
Croy, A. Ancient Pueblo **978**
    History
Hernández, R. E. Early explorations: the 1500s **970.01**
Hernández, R. E. New Spain: 1600-1760s **973.1**
Southwestern States
Freedman, R. In the days of the vaqueros **636.2**

    Natural history
    See Natural history—Southwestern States
Souza, D. M. (Dorothy M.)
Freaky flowers **582.13**
Look what feet can do **573.9**
Look what mouths can do **573.9**
Look what tails can do **573.9**
Plant invaders **581.6**
Souza, Dorothy M. *See* Souza, D. M. (Dorothy M.)
Sovereigns *See* Emperors; Kings and rulers; Queens
Soviet Union
    See also Russia
Soybean
Bial, R. The super soybean **633.3**
Space, Outer *See* Outer space
Space! [series]
Bjorklund, R. Venus **523.4**
Capaccio, G. Jupiter **523.4**
Capaccio, G. Mars **523.4**
Capaccio, G. The sun **523.7**
Colligan, L. H. Mercury **523.4**
Hicks, T. A. Earth and the moon **525**
Hicks, T. A. Saturn **523.4**
Lew, K. The dwarf planet Pluto **523.4**
Mack, G. The stars **523.8**
Sherman, J. Asteroids, meteors, and comets **523.4**
Sherman, J. Neptune **523.4**
Sherman, J. Uranus **523.4**
Space and time
    See also Time travel
    Fiction
Hahn, M. D. The doll in the garden **Fic**
Hahn, M. D. Time for Andrew **Fic**
Kladstrup, K. The book of story beginnings **Fic**
Mason, T. The last synapsid **Fic**
Pearce, P. Tom's midnight garden **Fic**
Snyder, L. Any which wall **Fic**
Stead, R. When you reach me **Fic**
Teague, M. The doom machine **Fic**
Winterson, J. Tanglewreck **Fic**
Wiseman, D. Jeremy Visick **Fic**
Space and time in art
Meredith, S. What is space? **701**

Spanfeller, Jim (James J.), 1930--—*Continued*
Folklore
See Folklore—Spain
History—1898, War of 1898
See Spanish-American War, 1898
Spanfeller, Jim (James J.), 1930-
(jt. auth) Cleaver, V. Where the lillies bloom **Fic**

Spangler, Brie
Peg Leg Peke   **E**
Spaniards
United States
Hernández, R. E. New Spain: 1600-1760s
    973.1
Lilly, A. Spanish colonies in America
    970.01
Otfinoski, S. The new republic: 1760-1840s
    973.3

Spanish America *See* Latin America
Spanish-American War, 1898
Kupferberg, A. E. The Spanish-American War
    973.8

Spanish artists *See* Artists, Spanish
Spanish colonies in America. Lilly, A.   **970.01**
Spanish-English bilingual books *See* Bilingual books—English-Spanish

Spanish language
Dictionaries
Corbeil, J.-C. My first Spanish English visual dictionary   **463**
Kudela, K. R. My first book of Spanish words
    463
Vocabulary
Dorros, A. Número uno   **E**
Dorros, A. Papá and me   **E**
Elya, S. M. Adios, tricycle   **E**
Elya, S. M. Bebé goes shopping   **E**
Elya, S. M. Cowboy José   **E**
Elya, S. M. F is for fiesta   **E**
Elya, S. M. Fairy trails   **E**
Elya, S. M. N is for Navidad   **E**
Elya, S. M. Oh no, gotta go!   **E**
Elya, S. M. Say hola to Spanish, otra vez
    468
Elya, S. M. Tooth on the loose   **E**
Emberley, R. My big book of Spanish words
    468
Gershator, P. Zoo day olé!   **E**
Goldman, J. Uncle monarch and the Day of the Dead   **E**
Johnston, T. My abuelita   **E**
Montes, M. Los gatos black on Halloween
    E
Mora, P. A pinata in a pine tree   **782.42**
Paul, A. W. Count on Culebra   **E**
Paul, A. W. Fiesta fiasco   **E**
Vamos, S. R. Before you were here, mi amor
    E
Winter, J. Calavera abecedario   **E**
Spanish literature
Bibliography
Schon, I. Recommended books in Spanish for children and young adults, 2004-2008
    011.6

Spanish poetry
Collections
Messengers of rain and other poems from Latin America   **861.008**
Spanyol, Jessica, 1965-
Little neighbors on Sunnyside Street   **E**
Spark the firefighter. Krensky, S.   **E**
Sparkle and spin. Rand, A.   **E**
Sparks, Timothy *See* Dickens, Charles, 1812-1870
Sparks fly high. Quattlebaum, M.   **398.2**
Sparky: the life and art of Charles Schulz. Gherman, B.   **92**
Sparky's bark. Chapra, M.   **E**
Sparrow, Giles
Cosmic!   **520**
Sparrow girl. Pennypacker, S.   **E**
Sparrow Jack. Gerstein, M.   **E**
Sparrows
Post, H. Sparrows   **598**
Fiction
Gerstein, M. Sparrow Jack   **E**
Lee, Y. The little moon princess   **E**
Pennypacker, S. Sparrow girl   **E**
Sparta (Extinct city)
Park, L. The Spartan hoplites   **938**
The **Spartan** hoplites. Park, L.   **938**
Spastic paralysis *See* Cerebral palsy
The **Spatulatta** cookbook. Gerasole, I.   **641.5**
Speak to me. English, K.   **E**
Speaking *See* Public speaking
Speaking volumes. Gilmore, B.   **028.5**
Speare, Elizabeth George, 1908-1994
The bronze bow   **Fic**
The sign of the beaver   **Fic**
The witch of Blackbird Pond   **Fic**
Spears, Rick
(jt. auth) Halls, K. M. Tales of the cryptids
    001.9

Special collections in libraries *See* Libraries—Special collections
Special education
Fiction
Polacco, P. The junkyard wonders   **Fic**
Spectacular animal towns [series]
Aronin, M. The ant's nest   **595.7**
Aronin, M. The prairie dog's town   **599.3**
Markovics, J. L. The bat's cave   **599.4**
Markovics, J. L. The honey bee's hive
    595.7
Person, S. The coral reef   **578.7**
Reingold, A. The beaver's lodge   **599.3**
Spectacular science projects series
VanCleave, J. P. Janice VanCleave's insects and spiders   **595.7**
VanCleave, J. P. Janice VanCleave's plants
    580.7
VanCleave, J. P. Janice VanCleave's rocks and minerals   **552**
VanCleave, J. P. Janice VanCleave's weather
    551.5

Stoberock, Martha
(il) Pellowski, A. The storytelling handbook
372.6

Stock, Catherine
Gugu's house   E
A porc in New York   E
(il) Fitzgerald, D. Vinnie and Abraham [biography of Vinnie Ream]   **92**
(il) Herold, M. R. A very important day   E
(il) Howe, J. Kaddish for Grandpa in Jesus' name, amen   E
(il) Mills, C. Gus and Grandpa and the two-wheeled bike   E
(il) Walter, M. P. Justin and the best biscuits in the world   Fic
(il) Whitaker, S. The daring Miss Quimby [biography of Harriet Quimby]   **92**
(il) Williams, K. L. Galimoto   E
(jt. auth) Williams, K. L. My name is Sangoel   E
(il) Williams, K. L. Painted dreams   E
(il) Wilson, S. The day we danced in underpants   E

Stockdale, Susan, 1954-
Carry me!   **591.56**
Fabulous fishes   **597**

Stockings of buttermilk: American folktales   **398.2**

Stockton, Frank, 1834-1902
The bee-man of Orn   Fic

Stoeke, Janet Morgan
The bus stop   E
A hat for Minerva Louise   E
It's library day   E
Waiting for May   E

Stohner, Anu
Brave Charlotte   E

Stojic, Manya
Hello world!   **413**
Rain   E
(il) Blackford, H. Elephant's story   E
(il) Blackford, H. Tiger's story   E

Stomach
Cobb, V. Your body battles a stomachache   **616.3**

Fiction
Harris, J. The belly book   E

Stomp rockets, catapults, and kaleidoscopes. Gabrielson, C.   **507.8**

Stompin' at the Savoy. Campbell, B. M.   E

Stompin' at the Savoy [biography of Norma Miller] Miller, N.   **92**

Stone, Kazuko G.
(il) Gollub, M. Cool melons—turn to frogs!: the life and poems of Issa [Kobayashi]   **92**

Stone, Kyle M.
(il) Leuck, L. I love my pirate papa   E

Stone, Lynn M.
Box turtles   **597.92**
Tigers   **599.75**

Stone, Phoebe, 1947-
Deep down popular   Fic

Stone, Tanya Lee
Elizabeth leads the way   **92**

Ilan Ramon, Israel's first astronaut   **92**
Sandy's circus   **92**

Stone Age
Fiction
Kitamura, S. Stone Age boy   E
Stone Age boy. Kitamura, S.   E
Stone Age farmers beside the sea. Arnold, C.   **936.1**

The **stone** child. Poblocki, D.   Fic
The **stone-faced** boy. Fox, P.   Fic
Stone Fox. Gardiner, J. R.   Fic
Stone soup. Brown, M.   **398.2**
Stone soup. Muth, J. J.   **398.2**
Stonecipher. See Heneghan, J. The magician's apprentice   Fic
Stoneheart. Fletcher, C.   Fic
Stoneheart trilogy [series]
Fletcher, C. Stoneheart   Fic
Stonehenge (England)
Aronson, M. If stones could speak   **936**
Stones in water. Napoli, D. J.   Fic
Stonewall [biography of Stonewall Jackson] Fritz, J.   **92**
Stonewall Hinkleman and the Battle of Bull Run. Hemphill, M.   Fic
Stoneware See Pottery
Stop and go, yes and no. Cleary, B. P.   **428**
Storace, Patricia
Sugar Cane   **398.2**
Storad, Conrad J.
Earth's crust   **551.1**
Rattlesnake rules   E
Stores See Retail trade; Supermarkets
Stories at the door. Andrews, J.   **398.2**
Stories for children. Singer, I. B.   S C
Stories from Adam and Eve to Ezekiel. Lottridge, C. B.   **220.9**
Stories from the Billabong. Marshall, J. V.   **398.2**
Stories from the life of Jesus. Lottridge, C. B.   **232.9**
Stories in art [series]
Harris, N. Mosaics   **738.5**
Harris, N. Wall paintings   **751.7**
Stories in rhyme
Aardema, V. Bringing the rain to Kapiti Plain   **398.2**
Adams, D. I can do it myself!   E
Adler, V. All of baby, nose to toes   E
Ahlberg, J. The jolly postman   E
Alborough, J. Duck in the truck   E
Alborough, J. Some dogs do   E
Alborough, J. Where's my teddy?   E
Alda, A. Here a face, there a face   E
Aliki. Push button   E
Anderson, P. P. Chuck's truck   E
Anderson, P. P. Joe on the go   E
Anderson, S. A day at the market   E
Andreasen, D. The baker's dozen   E
Appelt, K. Bats around the clock   E
Appelt, K. Brand-new baby blues   E
Appelt, K. Oh my baby, little one   E

Stories in rhyme—*Continued*

Arnold, T. Green Wilma, frog in space   E
Arnosky, J. Gobble it up!   E
Arnosky, J. I'm a turkey!   E
Ashburn, B. Over at the castle   E
Ashman, L. Castles, caves, and honeycombs   E
Ashman, L. Come to the castle!   **940.1**
Ashman, L. Creaky old house   E
Ashman, L. M is for mischief   E
Ashman, L. Mama's day   E
Ashman, L. Stella, unleashed   E
Ashman, L. When I was king   E
Aylesworth, J. Little Bitty Mousie   E
Aylesworth, J. Old black fly   E
Ayres, K. Up, down, and around   E
Baker, K. Hickory dickory dock   E
Baker, K. Just how long can a long string be!?   E
Baker, K. LMNO peas   E
Barnett, M. Guess again!   E
Barracca, D. The adventures of Taxi Dog   E
Base, G. Enigma   **Fic**
Bateman, T. April foolishness   E
Bauer, M. D. One brown bunny   E
Bayer, J. A my name is Alice   E
Beaumont, K. Doggone dogs!   E
Beaumont, K. Duck, duck, goose!   E
Beaumont, K. I ain't gonna paint no more!   E
Beaumont, K. Move over, Rover   E
Beaumont, K. Who ate all the cookie dough?   E
Beiser, T. Bradley McGogg, the very fine frog   E
Bemelmans, L. Madeline   E
Bergman, M. Yum yum! What fun!   E
Berry, L. Duck skates   E
Black, M. I. Chicken cheeks   E
Blackstone, S. My granny went to market   E
Blackstone, S. Octopus opposites   E
Blackstone, S. Secret seahorse   E
Blomgren, J. Where do I sleep?   E
Bluemle, E. How do you wokka-wokka?   E
Bond, R. The great doughnut parade   E
Bowen, A. I know an old teacher   E
Boyle, B. Hugo and the really, really, really long string   E
Braeuner, S. The great dog wash   E
Brenner, B. Good morning, garden   E
Brown, M. W. Another important book   E
Brown, M. W. Big red barn   E
Brown, M. W. Goodnight moon   E
Brown, M. W. Where have you been?   E
Bruchac, J. My father is taller than a tree   E
Bruel, N. Little red bird   E
Buehner, C. Snowmen at night   E
Buell, J. Sail away, Little Boat   E
Bunting, E. The bones of Fred McFee   E
Bunting, E. Butterfly house   E
Bunting, E. Flower garden   E
Burleigh, R. Clang-clang! Beep-beep!   E
Butler, J. Bedtime in the jungle   E
Buxton, J. The littlest llama   E
Cabrera, J. One, two, buckle my shoe   E
Calmenson, S. Jazzmatazz!   E
Calmenson, S. Late for school!   E

Carlstrom, N. W. It's your first day of school, Annie Claire   E
Carlstrom, N. W. Jesse Bear, what will you wear?   E
Carluccio, M. The sounds around town   E
Casanova, M. Utterly otterly day   E
Cauley, L. B. Clap your hands   E
Chall, M. W. One pup's up   E
Chamberlain, M. Please don't tease Tootsie   E
Charlip, R. A perfect day   E
Chichester-Clark, E. Little Miss Muffet counts to ten   E
Clarke, J. Stuck in the mud   E
Cleary, B. The hullabaloo ABC   E
Clements, A. The handiest things in the world   E
Cohn, S. One wolf howls   **599.77**
Conover, C. Over the hills & far away   E
Copp, J. Jim Copp, will you tell me a story?   E
Cordsen, C. F. Market day   E
Cordsen, C. F. The milkman   E
Corey, S. Monster parade   E
Cote, N. Jackson's blanket   E
Cotten, C. Rain play   E
Cotten, C. This is the stable   E
Craig, L. Dancing feet!   E
Crews, D. Ten black dots   E
Cronin, D. Wiggle   E
Crow, K. Cool Daddy Rat   E
Crow, K. The middle-child blues   E
Crowley, N. Nanook & Pryce   E
Cummings, P. Harvey Moon, museum boy   E
Curtis, C. I took the moon for a walk   E
Curtis, J. L. Big words for little people   E
Curtis, J. L. I'm gonna like me   E
Curtis, J. L. Is there really a human race?   E
Cuyler, M. The little dump truck   E
Cuyler, M. Monster mess!   E
Cuyler, M. Princess Bess gets dressed   E
Cyrus, K. Big rig bugs   E
Cyrus, K. Tadpole Rex   E
Davies, J. The night is singing   E
Degen, B. Jamberry   E
Dempsey, K. Me with you   E
Denise, A. Pigs love potatoes   E
Denslow, S. P. In the snow   E
Dewdney, A. Llama, llama red pajama   E
Dewdney, A. Nobunny's perfect   E
Dewdney, A. Roly Poly pangolin   E
Dickinson, R. Over in the hollow   E
Diesen, D. The pout-pout fish   E
Dillon, L. Rap a tap tap   E
Dobbins, J. Driving my tractor   E
Dodd, E. I don't want a posh dog!   E
Dodd, E. Just like you   E
Dodd, E. No matter what   E
Dodds, D. A. Full house   **513**
Dodds, D. A. Minnie's Diner   E
Dodds, D. A. The prince won't go to bed   E
Dodds, D. A. Where's Pup?   E
Donaldson, J. The fish who cried wolf   E
Donaldson, J. One Ted falls out of bed   E
Donaldson, J. Stick Man   E
Donaldson, J. Tyrannosaurus Drip   E

Storytelling: art & technique. Greene, E.
372.6

The **storytelling** handbook. Pellowski, A.
372.6

Storytelling with puppets. Champlin, C.   372.6
Storytime. Blackstone, S.   398.2
Storytime action!. Bromann, J.   027.62
Storytime magic. MacMillan, K.   027.62
The **storytime** sourcebook II. Cullum, C. N.
027.62

Storytimes for two-year-olds. Nichols, J.
027.62

Stott, Ann, 1964-
　Always   E

Stott, Carole
　Space exploration   629.4

Stotts, Stuart, 1957-
　We shall overcome   782.42

Stout, Shawn K.
　Fiona Finkelstein, big-time ballerina!   Fic

Stover, Lynne Farrell
　Magical library lessons   027.62
Stowaway. Hesse, K.   Fic

Stowe, Harriet Beecher, 1811-1896
About
　Adler, D. A. A picture book of Harriet Beecher
　Stowe   92
　Fritz, J. Harriet Beecher Stowe and the Beecher
　preachers   92

Stowe, Harriet Elizabeth *See* Stowe, Harriet Beecher, 1811-1896

Stower, Adam
　(il) Clements, A. We the children   Fic
　(il) Knapman, T. Mungo and the spiders from
　space   E

Straaten, Harmen van, 1961-
　Duck's tale   E

Stradling, Jan
　Bugs and spiders   595.7
　The human body   612
Stranded in Boringsville. Bateson, C.   Fic
The **strange** case of Origami Yoda. Riddleburger,
　S.   Fic
The **strange** case of the missing sheep. Catusanu,
　M.   E
A **strange** day. Heide, I. v. d.   E
Strange happenings. Avi   S C
Strange Mr. Satie. Anderson, M. T.   92
The **stranger.** Van Allsburg, C.   E
Stranger on the silk road. Gunderson, J.   Fic

Strassburg, Brian
　(il) Barker, D. Maybe right, maybe wrong
370.1

Strauss, Linda L., 1942-
　The princess gown   E

Strauss, Lindy *See* Edwards, Linda
Strauss, Rochelle, 1967-
　One well   553.7
　Tree of life   578

Stravinsky, Igor, 1882-1971
　See/See also pages in the following book(s):
　Krull, K. Lives of the musicians   920
　Schubert, L. Ballet of the elephants   791.8
Strawberries
Folklore
　Bruchac, J. The first strawberries   398.2
Strawberry Hill. Hoberman, M. A.   Fic
The **stray** dog. Simont, M.   E
Stream animals
　Arnosky, J. The brook book   577.6
Stream plants
　Arnosky, J. The brook book   577.6
Streams to the river, river to the sea. O'Dell, S.
Fic

Street, Pat
　(jt. auth) Leedy, L. There's a frog in my throat
428

Street cleaning
　Moore, P. The mighty street sweeper   E
Street gangs *See* Gangs
Street people *See* Homeless persons
Strega Nona: an old tale. De Paola, T.   E

Streiffert, Kristi
　(jt. auth) Kott, J. Nicaragua   972.85

Streissguth, Thomas, 1958-
　Mexico   972

Strength of materials
　Oxlade, C. Changing materials   530.4
The **strength** of these arms. Bial, R.   326

Stress (Psychology)
　See also Anxiety; Post-traumatic stress dis-
　order

Stretchy library lessons [series]
　Miller, P. Library skills   025.5
　Miller, P. Reading activities   025.5
　Miller, P. Research skills   025.5

Strevens-Marzo, Bridget
　(il) Sturges, P. How do you make a baby smile?
E
　(il) Wild, M. Kiss kiss!   E

Strickland, Brad
　The sign of the sinister sorcerer   Fic

Strickland, Shadra
　(il) Elliott, Z. Bird   E
　(il) Watson, R. A place where hurricanes happen
E

Strider. Cleary, B.   Fic
Strike a pose. Birkemoe, K.   613.7
Strikes
　Bartoletti, S. C. Kids on strike!   331.8
　Brown, D. Kid Blink beats the world   331.3
Fiction
　McCully, E. A. The bobbin girl   Fic
　Paterson, K. Bread and roses, too   Fic
A **string** in the harp. Bond, N.   Fic
Stringbean's trip to the shining sea. Williams, V.
　B.   E
Stringer, Helen
　Spellbinder   Fic

Stringer, Lauren, 1957-
Winter is the warmest season   E
(il) Ashman, L. Castles, caves, and honeycombs
    E
(il) George, K. O. Fold me a poem   **811**
(il) Rylant, C. Snow   E

Stroke

Fiction
Butler, D. H. My grandpa had a stroke   E
De Paola, T. Now one foot, now the other
    E

Stroll and walk, babble and talk. Cleary, B. P.
    428

Strøm, Kellie, 1967-
Sadie the air mail pilot   E

Strong man: the story of Charles Atlas. McCarthy,
M.   **92**

A **strong** right arm: the story of Mamie "Peanut"
Johnson. Green, M. Y.   **92**

Strong stuff. Harris, J.   **398.2**

Strong to the hoop. Coy, J.   E

Strother, Scott
The adventurous book of outdoor games
    796

Stroud, Bettye, 1939-
The patchwork path   E
The Reconstruction era   **973.8**

Structural engineering
Mason, A. Build it!   **624.1**

Struggle for a continent. Maestro, B.   **973.2**

Strugnell, Ann
(il) Cameron, A. The stories Julian tells   Fic

Stryer, Andrea Stenn, 1938-
Kami and the yaks   E

Stuart-Clark, Christopher
(ed) The Oxford book of story poems. See The
Oxford book of story poems   **808.81**

Stuart Little. White, E. B.   Fic

Stuchner, Joan Betty
Honey cake   Fic

Stuck in the mud. Clarke, J.   E

Stuck on Earth. Klass, D.   Fic

Stuckenschneider, Dan
(il) Tomecek, S. What a great idea!   **609**

Student Atlas   **912**

The **student** encyclopedia of the United States
    973.03

Student success and library media programs. Farmer, L. S. J.   **027.8**

Students
See also School children
Ruurs, M. My school in the rain forest
    370.9

Students and libraries *See* Libraries and students

Study, Method of *See* Study skills

Study skills
Fox, J. S. Get organized without losing it
    371.3
Kraus, J. Annie's plan   **371.3**

Studying food webs [series]
Hooks, G. Arctic appetizers   **577.5**

Hooks, G. Freshwater feeders   **577.6**
Hooks, G. Makers and takers   **577.7**
Lundgren, J. K. Desert dinners   **577.5**
Lundgren, J. K. Forest fare   **577.3**
Lundgren, J. K. Grassland buffet   **577.4**

Stueart, Robert D.
Library and information center management
    025.1

Stuff!. Kroll, S.   E

Stunt men and women *See* Stunt performers

Stunt performers
Cummins, J. Sam Patch   **92**
Cummins, J. Women daredevils   **920**

Sturges, Philemon
Down to the sea in ships   **811**
How do you make a baby smile?   E
I love planes!   E
I love school!   E
I love trains!   E
The Little Red Hen (makes a pizza)   **398.2**

Sturm, Brian W.
(jt. auth) MacDonald, M. R. The storyteller's
sourcebook   **398**

Sturm, James, 1965-
Adventures in cartooning   **741.5**

Stutson, Caroline
By the light of the Halloween moon   E
Cats' night out   E

Stuve-Bodeen, Stephanie *See* Bodeen, S. A.,
1965-

Su, Shih, 1036 or 7-1101

About
Demi. Su Dongpo   **92**

Su, Tung-p'o *See* Su, Shih, 1036 or 7-1101

Su Dongpo *See* Su, Shih, 1036 or 7-1101

Su Dongpo. Demi   **92**

Su-Kennedy, Hui Hui
(il) Jiang, J.-l. The magical Monkey King
    398.2

Suárez, Maribel, 1952-
(il) Mora, P. Here, kitty, kitty   E
(il) Mora, P. Wiggling pockets   E
(il) Wheeler, L. Te amo, Bebé, little one   E

Subject headings
Sears list of subject headings   **025.4**

Submarine diving
Earle, S. A. Dive!   **551.46**

Submarine exploration *See* Underwater exploration

Submarines
Abramson, A. S. Submarines up close
    623.82
Sutherland, J. Submarines   **623.82**

Fiction
Carlson, D. Attack of the Turtle   Fic
Verne, J. 20,000 leagues under the sea   Fic

Submarines up close. Abramson, A. S.   **623.82**

Substance abuse *See* Drug abuse

Subtraction
Cleary, B. P. The action of subtraction   **513**
Leedy, L. Subtraction action   **513**
Murphy, S. J. Elevator magic   **513**
Nagda, A. W. Panda math   **513**

Subtraction action. Leedy, L. 513
Suburban life
    Fiction
    Cole, H. On Meadowview Street E
Subway. Niemann, C. E
Subway. Suen, A. E
A **subway** for New York. Weitzman, D. L. 625.4
The **Subway** mouse. Reid, B. E
Subway ride. Miller, H. 388.4
Subways
    DuTemple, L. A. The New York subways 388.4
    McKendry, J. Beneath the streets of Boston 625.4
    Miller, H. Subway ride 388.4
    Weitzman, D. L. A subway for New York 625.4
    See/See also pages in the following book(s):
    Macaulay, D. Underground 624
    Fiction
    Niemann, C. Subway E
    Reid, B. The Subway mouse E
    Suen, A. Subway E
Success
    See also Academic achievement
    Rimm, S. B. See Jane win for girls 305.23
Such a silly baby!. Lorig, S. E
Sudan
    Levy, P. Sudan 962.4
    Fiction
    Williams, M. Brothers in hope Fic
Sudanese Americans
    Fiction
    Williams, K. L. My name is Sangoel E
Suddenly supernatural [series]
    Kimmel, E. C. School spirit Fic
Sue MacDonald had a book. Tobin, J. E
Suen, Anastasia
    Red light, green light E
    Subway E
    Wired 621.319
Suffrage
    See also Women—Suffrage
Suffragists
    Stone, T. L. Elizabeth leads the way 92
Sugar
    See also Maple sugar
Sugar Cane. Storace, P. 398.2
Sugar was my best food. Peacock, C. A. 362.1
Sugaring. Haas, J. E
Sugihara, Chiune *See* Sugihara, Sempo, 1900-1986
Sugihara, Sempo, 1900-1986
    About
    Mochizuki, K. Passage to freedom 940.53
Suho's white horse. Ōtsuka, Y. 398.2
Sukey and the mermaid. San Souci, R. 398.2
Suki's kimono. Uegaki, C. E

Sukkot
    Fishman, C. On Sukkot and Simchat Torah 296.4
    Fiction
    Kimmel, E. A. The mysterious guests E
    Ofanansky, A. Sukkot treasure hunt E
Sukkot treasure hunt. Ofanansky, A. E
Sullivan, Anne, 1866-1936
    About
    Cline-Ransome, L. Helen Keller 92
    Delano, M. F. Helen's eyes 92
Sullivan, Sir Arthur, 1842-1900
    See/See also pages in the following book(s):
    Krull, K. Lives of the musicians 920
    Fiction
    Winter, J. The fabulous feud of Gilbert & Sullivan E
Sullivan, George
    Built to last 624
    Helen Keller 92
    Journalists at risk 070.4
    Abraham Lincoln 92
Sullivan, Jody *See* Rake, Jody Sullivan, 1961-
Sullivan, Michael
    Fundamentals of children's services 027.62
    Connecting boys with books 2 028.5
Sullivan, Mike
    (jt. auth) O'Brien, T. Afghan dreams 958.1
Sullivan, Navin
    Area, distance, and volume 516
    Speed 531
    Temperature 536
    Weight 531
Sullivan, Sarah, 1953-
    Once upon a baby brother E
Sullivan, Simon
    (il) Madaras, L. The "what's happening to my body?" book for boys 612.6
    (il) Madaras, L. The "what's happening to my body?" book for girls 612.6
Sultanate of Oman *See* Oman
Sumerians
    Shuter, J. Mesopotamia 935
Summer
    Pfeffer, W. The longest day 394.26
    Schnur, S. Summer E
    Schuette, S. L. Let's look at summer 508.2
    Smith, S. Summer 508.2
    Fiction
    English, K. Hot day on Abbott Avenue E
    Gifford, P. E. Moxy Maxwell does not love Stuart Little Fic
    Greenfield, E. The friendly four Fic
    Hesse, K. Come on, rain! E
    Hole, S. Garmann's summer E
    Horvath, P. My one hundred adventures Fic
    Joosse, B. M. Hot city E
    McClure, N. Mama, is it summer yet? E
    Raczka, B. Summer wonders E
    Staples, S. F. The green dog Fic

Supercroc and the origin of crocodiles. Sloan, C.
    567.9

Superdog. Buehner, C.   **E**

SuperHero ABC. McLeod, B.   **E**

Superhero graphic novels
  Baltazar, A. Tiny Titans: welcome to the
    treehouse   **741.5**
  Lemke, D. Zinc Alloy: Super Zero   **741.5**
  Lynch, J. Mo and Jo: fighting together forever
    741.5
  Morse, S. Magic Pickle   **741.5**
  Sava, S. C. Hyperactive   **741.5**
  Steinberg, D. Sound off!   **741.5**

Superhero School. Reynolds, A.   **E**

Superheroes
  Stephens, J. Heroes!   **741.5**
        Fiction
  Boniface, W. The hero revealed   **Fic**
  Buzzeo, T. Adventure Annie goes to work   **E**
  Catusanu, M. The strange case of the missing
    sheep   **E**
  Cody, M. Powerless   **Fic**
  Cosentino, R. Batman: the story of the Dark
    Knight   **E**
  Cosentino, R. Superman: the story of the man of
    steel   **E**
  Cottringer, A. Eliot Jones, midnight superhero
    E
  Dahl, M. The man behind the mask   **Fic**
  Dakin, G. The Society of Unrelenting Vigilance
    Fic
  David, P. Mascot to the rescue!   **Fic**
  Draanen, W. v. Shredderman: Secret identity
    Fic
  Fein, E. My frozen valentine   **Fic**
  Grey, M. Traction Man is here!   **E**
  McLeod, B. SuperHero ABC   **E**
  Reynolds, A. Superhero School   **E**
  Schwarz, V. Timothy and the strong pajamas
    E
  Sniegoski, T. Billy Hooten, Owlboy   **Fic**
  Soman, D. Ladybug Girl   **E**
  Van Leeuwen, J. Oliver the Mighty Pig   **E**
  Watts, F. Extraordinary Ernie and Marvelous
    Maud   **Fic**
  Weigel, J. Atomic Ace   **E**
  Weigelt, U. Super Guinea Pig to the rescue
    E
  Ziefert, H. Mighty Max   **E**
Superhumans. See Thomas, K. Planet Earth News
  presents: super humans   **031.02**

Superman (Fictional character)
  Cosentino, R. Superman: the story of the man of
    steel   **E**
  Nobleman, M. T. Boys of steel [biography of
    Jerry Siegel and Joe Shuster]   **92**

Superman: the story of the man of steel.
  Cosentino, R.   **E**

The **supermarket.** See Rockwell, A. F. At the supermarket   **E**

Supermarkets
  Krull, K. Supermarket   **381**
        Fiction
  Rockwell, A. F. At the supermarket   **E**

Supernatural
  See also Spiritualism
  O'Meara, S. J. Are you afraid yet? the science
    behind scary stuff   **500**
        Fiction
  Avi. The Book Without Words   **Fic**
  Avi. Strange happenings   **S C**
  Baggott, J. The Prince of Fenway Park   **Fic**
  Buckingham, R. Demonkeeper   **Fic**
  Cody, M. Powerless   **Fic**
  Collier, J. L. The dreadful revenge of Ernest
    Gallen   **Fic**
  Cooper, S. The Boggart   **Fic**
  Del Negro, J. Passion and poison   **S C**
  Delaney, J. Revenge of the witch   **Fic**
  Delaney, J. The Spook's tale and other horrors
    S C
  Farmer, N. A girl named Disaster   **Fic**
  Fleischman, P. Graven images   **S C**
  Gaiman, N. Coraline   **Fic**
  Gaiman, N. The graveyard book   **Fic**
  Hearne, B. G. Hauntings, and other tales of dan-
    ger, love, and sometimes loss   **S C**
  Horowitz, A. The switch   **Fic**
  Jarvis, R. The Whitby witches   **Fic**
  Milford, K. The Boneshaker   **Fic**
  Mould, C. The wooden mile   **Fic**
  Murphy, R. Bird   **Fic**
  Newbery, L. At the firefly gate   **Fic**
  Poblocki, D. The stone child   **Fic**
  Pullman, P. Clockwork   **Fic**
  Skelton, M. The story of Cirrus Flux   **Fic**
  Stead, R. First light   **Fic**
  Strickland, B. The sign of the sinister sorcerer
    Fic
  Trapani, I. Haunted party   **E**
  Williams, T. The dragons of Ordinary Farm
    Fic
  Wiseman, D. Jeremy Visick   **Fic**
        Poetry
  Moore, L. Beware, take care   **811**
  Prelutsky, J. Monday's troll   **811**

Supernovas
  Jackson, E. B. The mysterious universe
    523.8

Supersister. Cadena, B.   **E**

Superstition
        Fiction
  Babbitt, N. Kneeknock Rise   **Fic**
  Bunting, E. The Banshee   **E**
  Haven, P. Two hot dogs with everything
    Fic
        Poetry
  Wong, J. S. Knock on wood   **811**

Supreme Court (U.S.) *See* United States. Supreme Court

The **Supreme** Court. Horn, G.   **347**

Sure as sunrise. McGill, A.   **398.2**

Surf war!. MacDonald, M. R.   **398.2**

Surface of the earth *See* Earth—Surface

Surfer of the century. Crowe, E.   **92**

Surfing
  Crowe, E. Surfer of the century   **92**

Surgery, Plastic *See* Plastic surgery

Surprise soup. Rodman, M. A.   **E**

Surrealism
     Raimondo, J. Imagine that!   **709.04**

Surveillance, Electronic *See* Electronic surveillance

Surveying
     Morrison, T. The coast mappers   **623.89**

Survival after airplane accidents, shipwrecks, etc.
     Blumberg, R. Shipwrecked!: the true adventures of a Japanese boy [biography of Manjiro Nakahama]   **92**
     Kraske, R. Marooned [biography of Alexander Selkirk]   **92**
     Markle, S. Rescues!   **363.34**
     McCully, E. A. Manjiro [biography of Manjiro Nakahama]   **92**
Fiction
     Morpurgo, M. Kensuke's kingdom   **Fic**
     Salisbury, G. Night of the howling dogs   **Fic**
     Steig, W. Abel's island   **Fic**
     Taylor, T. The cay   **Fic**
     Taylor, T. Timothy of the cay   **Fic**
     Trueman, T. Hurricane   **Fic**
     Wheeler, L. Castaway cats   **E**
     Wyss, J. D. The Swiss family Robinson   **Fic**

Survival at 40 below. Miller, D. S.   **591.7**

The **survival** guide for kids with ADD or ADHD. Taylor, J. F.   **616.85**

Survival skills
     Simons, R. Survival skills   **155.9**

Surviving Hitler. Warren, A.   **940.53**

Surviving the Applewhites. Tolan, S. S.   **Fic**

Survivors: ordinary people, extraordinary circumstances [series]
     Simons, R. Survival skills   **155.9**

Susan laughs. Willis, J.   **E**

Sussman, Joni Kibort
     My first Yiddish word book   **439**

Sussman, Michael B.
     Otto grows down   **E**

Sustainable agriculture
     Apte, S. Eating green   **630**
     Reynolds, J. Cycle of rice, cycle of life   **633.1**
     Vogel, J. Local farms and sustainable foods   **630**

Sustainable architecture
     Stern, S. L. Building greenscrapers   **720**

Sustainable buildings *See* Sustainable architecture

Sustainable world [series]
     Bowden, R. Energy   **333.79**
     Bowden, R. Food and farming   **363.8**
     Bowden, R. Waste   **363.7**

Sutcliffe, Justin
     (il) Calmenson, S. Rosie   **636.7**

Sutherland, Jonathan, 1958-
     Aircraft carriers   **623.82**
     Container ships and oil tankers   **623.82**
     Cruise ships   **623.82**
     Submarines   **623.82**

Sutherland, Zena, 1915-2002
     Children & books   **028.5**

Sutton, Jane, 1950-
     Don't call me Sidney   **E**

Sutton, Sally
     Roadwork!   **E**

Sutton, Wendy K.
     (jt. auth) Bouchard, D. The gift of reading   **372.4**
     (jt. auth) Egoff, S. A. Once upon a time   **92**

Suu Kyi *See* Aung San Suu Kyi

Suvanjieff, Ivan
     (jt. auth) Engle, D. PeaceJam   **303.6**

Suzuki, Hiromi
About
     Barasch, L. Hiromi's hands [biography of Hiromi Suzuki]   **92**

Swahili language
     Feelings, M. Jambo means hello   **E**
     Feelings, M. Moja means one   **E**

Swaim, Jessica
     The hound from the pound   **E**

Swain, Gwenyth, 1961-
     Riding to Washington   **E**

Swain, Ruth Freeman
     Hairdo!   **391**
     Underwear   **391**

Swallow, Pamela Curtis
     Groundhog gets a say   **E**

Swallowing the sun. See Trueman, T. Hurricane   **Fic**

Swallows
Fiction
     Politi, L. Song of the swallows   **E**
Folklore
     Ryan, P. M. Nacho and Lolita   **398.2**

Swamp, Jake, 1941-
     Giving thanks   **299.7**

Swamp Angel. Isaacs, A.   **E**

Swamp animals
     Bateman, D. M. Deep in the swamp   **591.7**

Swamp song. Ketteman, H.   **E**

Swamps *See* Marshes; Wetlands

The **swamps** of Sleethe. Prelutsky, J.   **811**

Swans
     Helget, N. L. Swans   **598**
     Osborn, E. Project UltraSwan   **598**
     Stewart, M. Swans   **598**
Fiction
     Andersen, H. C. The ugly duckling [illustrated by Pirkko Vainio]   **E**
     Braun, S. The ugly duckling   **E**
     Isadora, R. The ugly duckling   **E**
     Lobel, G. Moonshadow's journey   **E**
     Mitchell, S. The ugly duckling   **E**
     Pinkney, J. The ugly duckling   **E**
     Tafuri, N. Whose chick are you?   **E**
     Watts, B. The ugly duckling   **E**
     White, E. B. The trumpet of the swan   **Fic**

Swanson, Diane, 1944-
     Animal aha!   **590**
     Bugs up close   **595.7**
     Nibbling on Einstein's brain   **500**

Swanson, Diane, 1944-—*Continued*
You are weird **612**

Swanson, Maggie
(il) The American Heritage picture dictionary.
See The American Heritage picture dictionary
423

Swanson, Susan Marie
The first thing my mama told me **E**
The house in the night **E**
To be like the sun **E**

Swarms. Pipe, J. **591.5**

Swarner, Kristina
(jt. auth) Greenberg, D. Enchanted lions **E**
(il) Schwartz, H. Before you were born
398.2

Swartz, Leslie
(jt. auth) Simonds, N. Moonbeams, dumplings &
dragon boats **394.26**

Swearingen, Greg, 1976-
(il) Dakin, G. The Society of Unrelenting Vigilance **Fic**
(jt. auth) Easton, K. The outlandish adventures
of Liberty Aimes **Fic**
(il) Williams, T. The dragons of Ordinary Farm
Fic

Sweaters
Blaxland, W. Sweaters **746.9**

Sweden
Gan, D. Sweden **948.5**
Grahame, D. A. Sweden **948.5**
Phillips, C. Sweden **948.5**
Fiction
Lindgren, A. Pippi Longstocking **Fic**
Thor, A. A faraway island **Fic**

Swedish Americans
Fiction
Sandin, J. At home in a new land **E**

Sweet, Melissa
Carmine **E**
Tupelo rides the rails **E**
(il) Appelt, K. Bats around the clock **E**
(il) Calmenson, S. Good for you! **811**
(il) Calmenson, S. Welcome, baby! **811**
(il) Davies, J. The boy who drew birds: a story
of John James Audubon **92**
(il) Howe, J. Pinky and Rex **E**
(il) Knight, J. Charlotte in Giverny **Fic**
(il) Logan, C. The 5,000-year-old puzzle
932
(il) Martin, D. Christmas tree **E**
(il) Martin, D. Hanukkah lights **E**
(il) Rupp, R. Weather **551.6**
(il) Rylant, C. Moonlight: the Halloween cat
E
(il) Sierra, J. Schoolyard rhymes **398.8**
(il) Thimmesh, C. Girls think of everything
920
(il) Thimmesh, C. The sky's the limit **500**
(il) Yolen, J. Baby Bear's books **E**

(il) Best, C. Easy as pie **E**
(il) Bryant, J. A river of words: the story of
William Carlos Williams **92**
(il) Sierra, J. Sleepy little alphabet **E**

Sweet!. Love, A. **641.8**
Sweet Clara and the freedom quilt. Hopkinson, D.
E
Sweet eats. Dunnington, R. **641.8**
Sweet land of liberty [biography of Oscar L.
Chapman] Hopkinson, D. **92**
Sweet music in Harlem. Taylor, D. A. **E**
Sweet potato pie. Lindsey, K. **E**
Sweet Thang. Whittenberg, A. **Fic**
A **sweet** year. Podwal, M. H. **296.4**
The **sweetest** fig. Van Allsburg, C. **E**
Sweethearts of rhythm. Nelson, M. **811**

Swender, Jennifer
(jt. auth) Jacobs, P. D. Fire drill **E**
(jt. auth) Jacobs, P. D. Putting on a play
792

Swerling, Lisa
(il) Adams, S. The most fantastic atlas of the
whole wide world by the Brainwaves **912**
(il) Walker, R. How the incredible human body
works—by the Brainwaves **612**
(il) Watts, C. The most explosive science book
in the universe **500**

Swett, Sarah
Kids weaving **746.41**

Swiatkowska, Gabriela
(il) Cooper, I. The golden rule **E**
(il) Napoli, D. J. The Earth shook **E**
(il) Recorvits, H. My name is Yoon **E**

Swift, Hildegarde Hoyt, d. 1977
The little red lighthouse and the great gray
bridge **E**
Swifter, higher, stronger. Macy, S. **796.48**

Swimming
Adler, D. A. America's champion swimmer:
Gertrude Ederle **92**
Boudreau, H. Swimming science **797.2**
Corey, S. Mermaid Queen [biography of An-
nette Kellerman] **92**
Crowe, E. Surfer of the century **92**
Gifford, C. Swimming **797.2**
Guillain, C. Swimming **797.2**
Minden, C. Swimming **797.2**
Timblin, S. Swimming **797.2**
Torsiello, D. P. Michael Phelps **92**
Fiction
Kessler, L. P. Last one in is a rotten egg **E**
London, J. Froggy learns to swim **E**
Lucke, D. The boy who wouldn't swim **E**
Rodriguez, E. Sergio makes a splash **E**
Stewart, A. Little by little **E**
Swimming science. Boudreau, H. **797.2**
Swimming with hammerhead sharks. Mallory, K.
597

Swimmy. Lionni, L. **E**

Swinburne, Stephen R.
Armadillo trail **599.3**
Black bear **599.78**
Coyote **599.77**
Ocean soup **591.7**
Once a wolf **333.95**
Safe, warm, and snug **591.56**
Turtle tide **597.92**

Tabori, Lena
(ed) The big book for toddlers. See The big book for toddlers **808.8**

Tacang, Brian
Bully-be-gone **Fic**

Tadgell, Nicole, 1969-
(il) Birtha, B. Lucky beans **E**
(il) Derby, S. No mush today **E**
(il) Elvgren, J. R. Josias, hold the book **E**

Tadjo, Véronique, 1955-
(ed) Talking drums. See Talking drums **896**

Tadpole Rex. Cyrus, K. **E**

Tadpoles *See* Frogs

Tafolla, Carmen, 1951-
Fiesta babies **E**
That's not fair! [biography of Emma Tenayuca] **92**
What can you do with a rebozo? **E**

Tafuri, Nancy
The big storm **E**
Blue Goose **E**
The busy little squirrel **E**
Five little chicks **E**
Have you seen my duckling? **E**
Spots, feathers, and curly tails **E**
This is the farmer **E**
Whose chick are you? **E**
You are special, little one **E**
(il) Denslow, S. P. In the snow **E**

Tagholm, Sally
The rabbit **599.3**

Tagliaferro, Linda
Explore the tropical rain forest **577.3**
Explore the tundra **577.5**
How does a plant become oil? **553.2**
How does a volcano become an island? **551.2**
How does an earthquake become a tsunami? **551.46**

Tahiti (French Polynesia)
NgCheong-Lum, R. Tahiti **996**

Tai, Amy Lee-, 1964- *See* Lee-Tai, Amy, 1964-

Taibah, Nadia Jameel
(jt. auth) MacDonald, M. R. How many donkeys? **398.2**

Tail-end Charlie. Manning, M. **940.54**

The **tailor** of Gloucester. Potter, B. **E**

Tailoring
Fiction
Grandits, J. The travel game **E**
Potter, B. The tailor of Gloucester **E**

Tails
Souza, D. M. Look what tails can do **573.9**

The **tailypo**. Galdone, J. **398.2**

Taino Indians
Fiction
Dorris, M. Morning Girl **Fic**

Tait, Noel
Insects & spiders **595.7**

Taiwan
Moiz, A. Taiwan **951.2**

Taiwanese Americans
Fiction
Chen, P. Peiling and the chicken-fried Christmas **Fic**
Lin, G. The Year of the Dog **Fic**
Wahl, J. Candy shop **E**

Taj Mahal (Agra, India)
Arnold, C. Taj Mahal **954**
Mann, E. Taj Mahal **954**

Tajikistan
Abazov, R. Tajikistan **958.6**

Takabayashi, Mari, 1960-
I live in Tokyo **952**

Takahashi, Hideko
(il) Preus, M. The Peace Bell **E**

Takahashi, Kiyoshi, 1940-
(il) Tokuda, Y. I'm a pill bug **595.3**

Takasaki, Yuzuru
(il) Horowitz, A. Stormbreaker: the graphic novel **741.5**

Take action [series]
Schwartz, H. E. Political activism **322.4**

Take me out of the bathtub and other silly dilly songs. Katz, A. **782.42**

Take me with you. Marsden, C. **Fic**

Taking risks *See* Risk-taking (Psychology)

Taking sides. Soto, G. **Fic**

Talbott, Hudson
Forging freedom **940.53**
King Arthur and the Round Table **398.2**
River of dreams **974.7**
United tweets of America **973**
(il) Fritz, J. Leonardo's horse **730.9**
(il) Fritz, J. The Lost Colony of Roanoke **975.6**
(il) Woodson, J. Show way **E**

The **tale** of Despereaux. DiCamillo, K. **Fic**

A **tale** of gold. Wyss, T. H. **Fic**

The **tale** of Jemima Puddle-duck. Potter, B. **E**

The **tale** of La Llorona. Lowery, L. **398.2**

The **tale** of Mr. Jeremy Fisher. Potter, B. **E**

The **tale** of Mrs. Tiggy-Winkle. Potter, B. **E**

The **tale** of Mrs. Tittlemouse. Potter, B. **E**

The **tale** of Pale Male. Winter, J. **598**

The **tale** of Peter Rabbit. Potter, B. **E**

The **tale** of Pigling Bland. Potter, B. **E**

The **tale** of Rabbit and Coyote. Johnston, T. **398.2**

The **tale** of Squirrel Nutkin. Potter, B. **E**

The **tale** of the Firebird. Spirin, G. **398.2**

The **tale** of the mandarin ducks. Paterson, K. **398.2**

The **tale** of Timmy Tiptoes. Potter, B. **E**

The **tale** of Tricky Fox. Aylesworth, J. **398.2**

The **tale** of two bad mice. Potter, B. **E**

Tale of two Seders. Portnoy, M. A. **E**

The **talent** show. Edwards, M. **Fic**

Tales from old Ireland. Doyle, M. **398.2**

Tales from Shakespeare. Packer, T. **822.3**

Tales of a fourth grade nothing. Blume, J. **Fic**

Tales of a lost kingdom. L'Homme, E.   **398.2**
The **tales** of Beedle the Bard. Rowling, J. K.
S C
Tales of famous Americans. Roop, C.   **920**
Tales of terror from the Black Ship. Priestley, C.
Fic
Tales of the cryptids. Halls, K. M.   **001.9**
Tales of the world [series]
Whelan, G. Waiting for the owl's call   **E**
Whelan, G. Yuki and the one thousand carriers
E
The **tales** of Uncle Remus. Lester, J.   **398.2**
Tales of young Americans [series]
Scillian, D. Pappy's handkerchief   **E**
Swain, G. Riding to Washington   **E**
Young, J. Minnow and Rose   **Fic**
Tales our abuelitas told. Campoy, F. I.   **398.2**
Tales to tickle your funny bone. Livo, N. J.
398.2
Tales told in tents. Clayton, S. P.   **398.2**
Talia Talk. Deriso, C. H.   **Fic**
Taliesin
Fiction
Bond, N. A string in the harp   **Fic**
Talk about books!. Knowles, E.   **372.4**
Talkin' about Bessie: the story of aviator Elizabeth Coleman. Grimes, N.   **92**
Talking books *See* Audiobooks
Talking drums   **896**
The **talking** eggs. San Souci, R.   **398.2**
Talking tails. Love, A.   **636**
The **talking** vegetables. Paye, W.-L.   **398.2**
Talking walls. Knight, M. B.   **909**
Talking with Mother Earth. Argueta, J.   **811**
Tall. Alborough, J.   **E**
Tall tales
Bertrand, L. Granite baby   **E**
Derby, S. Whoosh went the wind!   **E**
Fleischman, S. Here comes McBroom!   **Fic**
Fox, F. G. Jean Laffite and the big ol' whale
E
Gribnau, J. Kick the cowboy   **E**
Hopkinson, D. Apples to Oregon   **E**
Isaacs, A. Swamp Angel   **E**
Jackson, A. Desert Rose and her highfalutin hog
E
Kellogg, S. Mike Fink   **398.2**
Kellogg, S. Paul Bunyan   **398.2**
Kellogg, S. Pecos Bill   **398.2**
Kellogg, S. Sally Ann Thunder Ann Whirlwind
Crockett   **398.2**
Krensky, S. Paul Bunyan   **398.2**
Krensky, S. Pecos Bill   **398.2**
Lamadrid, E. R. Juan the bear and the water of
life   **398.2**
Lorbiecki, M. Paul Bunyan's sweetheart   **E**
Lyons, M. E. Roy makes a car   **398.2**
Miller, B. Davy Crockett gets hitched   **398.2**
Mora, P. Doña Flor   **E**
Myers, C. Lies and other tall tales   **398.2**
Nolen, J. Harvey Potter's balloon farm   **E**
Nolen, J. Thunder Rose   **E**

Osborne, M. P. American tall tales   **398.2**
Pinkney, A. D. Peggony-Po   **E**
Root, P. Paula Bunyan   **E**
San Souci, R. Cut from the same cloth
398.2
Schur, M. Gullible Gus   **Fic**
Shelby, A. The man who lived in a hollow tree
E
Williams, S. Library Lil   **E**
Wilson, K. Whopper cake   **E**
Wood, A. The Bunyans   **E**
Tall tales. Day, K.   **Fic**
Tallchief, Maria
Tallchief   **92**
About
Tallchief, M. Tallchief   **92**
Tallec, Olivier, 1970-
(il) Babin, C. Gus is a fish   **E**
(il) Brun-Cosme, N. Big Wolf & Little Wolf
E
The **tallest** tree. Belton, S.   **Fic**
Tally charts. Bodach, V.   **510**
The **taming** of Lola. Weiss, E.   **E**
Tan, Chung Lee, 1949-
Finland   **948.97**
Tan to tamarind. Iyengar, M. M.   **811**
Tanaka, Shelley
Amelia Earhart   **92**
Mummies   **393**
New dinos   **567.9**
(jt. auth) Augustyn, F. Footnotes   **792.8**
(jt. auth) Beattie, O. Buried in ice   **998**
Tanaka, Yoko
(il) DiCamillo, K. The magician's elephant
Fic
(il) La Fevers, R. L. Theodosia and the Serpents
of Chaos   **Fic**
(il) Pennypacker, S. Sparrow girl   **E**
Tang, Greg
The best of times   **513**
The grapes of math   **793.74**
Math appeal   **793.74**
Math fables   **513**
Math fables too   **513**
Math potatoes   **793.74**
Math-terpieces   **510**
Tang Ge
(il) Wang Ping. The dragon emperor   **398.2**
Tanglewreck. Winterson, J.   **Fic**
Tango. Beha, E.   **Fic**
Tanguy, Elara
(il) Brunelle, L. Camp out!   **796.54**
Tankard, Jeremy
Grumpy Bird   **E**
Me hungry!   **E**
Tankers
Sutherland, J. Container ships and oil tankers
623.82
Tanksley, Ann
(il) Thomas, J. C. The six fools   **398.2**
Tans, Adrian
(jt. auth) Gribnau, J. Kick the cowboy   **E**

Tantalizing tidbits for middle schoolers. Cox
Clark, R. E. **028.5**

Tanya and the red shoes. Gauch, P. L. **E**

Tanzania
Heale, J. Tanzania **967.8**
Fiction
Bodeen, S. A. Elizabeti's doll **E**
Mollel, T. M. My rows and piles of coins **E**

Taoism
Demi. The legend of Lao Tzu and the Tao te
ching **299.5**
See/See also pages in the following book(s):
Osborne, M. P. One world, many religions
  200

Tap-dance fever. Brisson, P. **E**

Tap dancing
Barasch, L. Knockin' on wood [biography of
Peg Leg Bates] **92**
Dillon, L. Rap a tap tap **E**
Fiction
Brisson, P. Tap-dance fever **E**
Stevenson, J. Flying feet **E**

Tap dancing on the roof. Park, L. S. **811**

Tap tap bang bang. Garcia, E. **E**

Tape recordings, Audio *See* Sound recordings

Tar Beach. Ringgold, F. **E**

A **tarantula** in my purse. George, J. C. **92**

Tarantula power!. Nagda, A. W. **Fic**

The **tarantula** scientist. Montgomery, S. **595.4**

Tarantulas
Bredeson, C. Tarantulas up close **595.4**
Camisa, K. Hairy tarantulas **595.4**
Montgomery, S. The tarantula scientist **595.4**
Fiction
Nagda, A. W. Tarantula power! **Fic**

Tarantulas up close. Bredeson, C. **595.4**

Tara's flight. Eitzen, R. **E**

Tarlow, Ellen
Pinwheel days **E**

Tarpley, Natasha, 1971-
Bippity Bop barbershop **E**

Tarra & Bella. Buckley, C. **599.67**

Tarshis, Lauren
Emma-Jean Lazarus fell out of a tree **Fic**

Tarter, Jill Cornell, 1944-
About
Jackson, E. B. Looking for life in the universe
  576.8

Tashiro, Chisato
Five nice mice **E**

Tasmanian devils
Markovics, J. L. Tasmanian devil **599.2**
Fiction
Blake, R. J. Little devils **E**

Taste
Boothroyd, J. What is taste? **612.8**
Cobb, V. Your tongue can tell **612.8**
Hewitt, S. Tastes good! **612.8**

A **taste** for red. Harris, L. **Fic**

A **taste** of blackberries. Smith, D. B. **Fic**

A **taste** of colored water. Faulkner, M. **E**

A **taste** of culture [series] **641.5**

Tastes good!. Hewitt, S. **612.8**

Tasty baby belly buttons. Sierra, J. **398.2**

Tatanka and the Lakota people **398.2**

Tatanka Iyotake *See* Sitting Bull, Dakota Chief,
1831-1890

Tate, Don
(il) Blue, R. Ron's big mission **E**
(il) McGill, A. Sure as sunrise **398.2**

Tate, Eleanora E., 1948-
Celeste's Harlem Renaissance **Fic**

Tate, Lindsey
Kate Larkin, bone expert **Fic**

Tate, Nikki, 1962-
Behind the scenes: the racehorse **798.4**

Tatham, Betty
Baby sea otter **599.7**
Penguin chick **598**

Tattersall, Ian
Bones, brains and DNA **599.93**

Tattooing
Fiction
Foreman, M. Grandpa Jack's tattoo tales **E**
Wilson, J. The illustrated Mum **Fic**

Tatum, Art, 1910-1956
About
Parker, R. A. Piano starts here: the young Art
Tatum **92**

Taub, Daniel, 1962-
(jt. auth) Hawker, F. Judaism in Israel **296**

Taulbert, Clifton L.
Little Cliff and the porch people **E**

Tavares, Matt
Henry Aaron's dream **92**
Mudball **E**
(il) Kladstrup, K. The gingerbread pirates **E**
(il) Mitchell, S. Iron Hans **398.2**
(il) Nesbit, E. Jack and the beanstalk **398.2**
(il) Rappaport, D. Lady Liberty **974.7**

Taxicabs
Fiction
Barracca, D. The adventures of Taxi Dog **E**
Villeneuve, A. The red scarf **E**

Taylor, Barbara, 1954-
Planet animal **591.68**

Taylor, C. J. (Carrie J.), 1952-
Spirits, fairies, and merpeople **398.2**

Taylor, Debbie A., 1955-
Sweet music in Harlem **E**

Taylor, Eleanor, 1969-
(jt. auth) Durango, J. Cha-cha chimps **E**
(il) Durango, J. Go-go gorillas **E**

Taylor, Gaylia
George Crum and the Saratoga chip **92**

Taylor, Harriet Peck
Coyote places the stars **398.2**

Taylor, Jennifer, 1979-
(il) Peters, L. W. Frankie works the night shift
  E

Taylor, John F., 1944-
The survival guide for kids with ADD or
ADHD **616.85**

Teaching the Internet in libraries. Gordon, R. S.
025.04

Teague, David
  Franklin's big dreams   E
Teague, Mark, 1963-
  Dear Mrs. LaRue   E
  The doom machine   Fic
  Funny Farm   E
  Pigsty   E
  (il) Isaacs, A. Pancakes for supper!   E
  (il) Rylant, C. Poppleton   E
  (il) Yolen, J. How do dinosaurs say goodnight?
                                                 E
Team moon. Thimmesh, C.   629.45
Team teaching See Teaching teams
Teammates [biography of Jackie Robinson]
  Golenbock, P.   92
The **tech-savvy** booktalker. Keane, N. J.   021.7
Technically, it's not my fault. Grandits, J.   811
Technologies for education   371.3
Technology
    See also Engineering
  Fridell, R. Sports technology   688.7
  Macaulay, D. The new way things work
                                                 600
  Murphy, G. Why is snot green   500
  Piddock, C. Future tech   600
  Woodford, C. Cool Stuff 2.0 and how it works
                                                 600
  Zuckerman, A. 2030   600
                  Encyclopedias
  Everything you need to know   503
  One million things   031
                  History
  Jedicke, P. Great inventions of the 20th century
                                                 609
  Robinson, J. Inventions   609
Technology, Information See Information tech-
  nology
Technology and civilization
                  Fiction
  Lynch, C. Cyberia   Fic
Technology in art
  Bingham, J. Science & technology   704.9
Teckentrup, Britta
  Big Smelly Bear   E
  Grumpy cat   E
Tecumseh, Shawnee Chief, 1768-1813
                  About
  Collier, J. L. The Tecumseh you never knew
                                                 92
The **Tecumseh** you never knew. Collier, J. L.
                                                 92
Teddy bears
  Innes, S. A bear in war   E
                  Fiction
  Alborough, J. Where's my teddy?   E
  Burgess, M. Where teddy bears come from
                                                 E
  Dewan, T. One true bear   E
  Donaldson, J. One Ted falls out of bed   E
  Elliott, D. What the grizzly knows   E

  Fellowes, J. The curious adventures of the aban-
    doned toys   Fic
  Freeman, D. Corduroy   E
  Kroll, V. L. Everybody has a teddy   E
  McPhail, D. M. The teddy bear   E
  Meyers, S. Bear in the air   E
  Rosen, M. Red Ted and the lost things   E
  Waber, B. Ira sleeps over   E
Teedie. Brown, D.   92
Teen age See Adolescence
Teenage gangs See Gangs
Teenagers
    See also Internet and teenagers; Runaway
    teenagers
              Books and reading
  Gelman, J. The kids' book club book   028.5
  Larson, J. C. Bringing mysteries alive for chil-
    dren and young adults   028.5
  Lukenbill, W. B. Biography in the lives of
    youth   028.5
  Serving young teens and 'tweens   027.62
  York, S. Booktalking authentic multicultural lit-
    erature   021
                  Employment
    See also Summer employment
                  Afghanistan
  O'Brien, T. Afghan dreams   958.1
Teenagers and the Internet See Internet and
  teenagers
Teenagers' library services See Young adults' li-
  braries
Teenagers' writings
  River of words   808.81
A **teen's** guide to creating Web pages and blogs.
  Selfridge, B.   006.7
Teens @ the library series
  Miller, S. Developing and promoting graphic
    novel collections   025.2
Teeny tiny tingly tales. Van Laan, N.   E
The **teeny-tiny** woman. Galdone, P.   398.2
Teeth
  Chandra, D. George Washington's teeth   E
  Cobb, V. Your body battles a cavity   617.6
  Collard, S. B., III. Teeth   591.47
  James, R. H. Teeth and fangs   591.47
  Landau, E. Cavities and toothaches   617.6
  Miller, E. The tooth book   617.6
  Royston, A. Tooth decay   617.6
  Royston, A. Why do I brush my teeth?
                                                 617.6
  Schuh, M. C. All about teeth   617.6
  Schuh, M. C. Loose tooth   617.6
  Thomas, P. Do I have to go to the dentist?
                                                 617.6
                  Fiction
  Borden, L. The lost-and-found tooth   Fic
  Colato Laínez, R. The Tooth Fairy meets El Ra-
    tón Pérez   E
  Diakité, P. I lost my tooth in Africa   E
  Elya, S. M. Tooth on the loose   E
  McGhee, A. Mrs. Watson wants your teeth
                                                 E
  Schaefer, L. M. Loose tooth   E
  Simms, L. Rotten teeth   E

Teeth—Fiction—*Continued*
Sís, P. Madlenka   E
Folklore
Beeler, S. B. Throw your tooth on the roof   398

Teeth and fangs. James, R. H.   591.47

Teeth, tails, & tentacles. Wormell, C.   E

Teetoncey. Taylor, T.   Fic

Teitelbaum, Michael, 1953-
Baseball   796.357

Tekavec, Heather, 1969-
Storm is coming!   E

Telecommunication
    See also Computer networks; Electronic mail systems
Perritano, J. Revolution in communications   621.382
Solway, A. Communication   303.4

Telekinesis *See* Psychokinesis

Telemarking *See* Skiing

Telepathy
Fiction
Black, M. I. The purple kangaroo   E

Teleprocessing networks *See* Computer networks

Telescopes
    See also Hubble Space Telescope
Jefferis, D. Star spotters   522
Nardo, D. Telescopes   522

Television
Krull, K. The boy who invented TV: the story of Philo Farnsworth   92
See/See also pages in the following book(s):
Bauer, C. F. Celebrations   808.8
Equipment and supplies
    See also Video recording
Fiction
Proimos, J. Todd's TV   E

Television actors *See* Actors

Television broadcasting
Wan Guofang. TV takeover   384.55

Television industry *See* Television broadcasting

Television programs
Fiction
Deriso, C. H. Talia Talk   Fic
Eboch, C. The ghost on the stairs   Fic
Fisher, C. The Snow Show   E

Telgemeier, Raina
Smile   741.5
(il) Martin, A. M. The Baby-sitter's Club: Kristy's great idea   741.5

Tell all the children our story. Bolden, T.   305.8

Tell me about sports [series]
Gifford, C. Basketball   796.323
Gifford, C. Football   796.332
Gifford, C. Martial arts   796.8

Tell me again about the night I was born. Curtis, J. L.   E

Tell me one thing, Dad. Pow, T.   E

Tell me, tree. Gibbons, G.   582.16

Tell me why, tell me how [series]
Bailer, D. How do caterpillars become butterflies?   595.7
Stewart, M. How do bats fly in the dark?   599.4
Stewart, M. How do bees make honey?   595.7
Stewart, M. How do chameleons change color?   597.95
Stewart, M. How do spiders make webs?   595.4
Stewart, M. Why do we see rainbows?   612.8
Stewart, M. Why does the moon change shape?   523.3

Tell them we remember. Bachrach, S. D.   940.53

Tell your parents [series]
Bearce, S. All about electric and hybrid cars   629.222
Bearce, S. How to harness solar power for your home   621.47
O'Neal, C. How to use waste energy to heat and light your home   621.1
O'Neal, C. How to use wind power to light and heat your home   621.31
Smalley, C. P. Green changes you can make around your home   333.72

Tellegen, Toon, 1941-
Letters to anyone and everyone   Fic

Telling time. Older, J.   529

Temperance
    See also Drinking of alcoholic beverages

The **temperate** forest. Johansson, P.   577.3

Temperate grasslands. Hoare, B.   577.4

Temperature
Gardner, R. Easy genius science projects with temperature and heat   536
Gardner, R. Melting, freezing, and boiling science projects with matter   530.4
Gardner, R. Really hot science projects with temperature   536
Sullivan, N. Temperature   536

Temple, Charles A., 1947-
Children's books in children's hands. See Children's books in children's hands   028.5

Temple, Kathryn
Drawing   741.2

Ten black dots. Crews, D.   E

Ten days and nine nights. Heo, Y.   E

Ten inventors who changed the world. See Gifford, C. 10 inventors who changed the world   920

Ten kings. Meltzer, M.   920

Ten kings & queens who changed the world. See Gifford, C. 10 kings & queens who changed the world   920

Ten little Christmas presents. Marzollo, J.   E

Ten little fingers. See Diez deditos. Ten little fingers & other play rhymes and action songs from Latin America   782.42

Ten little fingers and ten little toes. Fox, M.   E

Thay, Winnie
(jt. auth) Gish, S. Ethiopia   **963**
Thayer, Ernest Lawrence, 1863-1940
Casey at the bat   **811**
Casey at the bat. See Gutman, D. Casey back at bat   **811**
Ernest L. Thayer's Casey at the bat   **811**
Thayer, Jane, 1904-
The popcorn dragon   **E**
The puppy who wanted a boy   **E**
The 2nd international cookbook for kids. Locricchio, M.   **641.5**
The 3 bears and Goldilocks. Willey, M.   **398.2**
The second international cookbook for kids. See Locricchio, M. The 2nd international cookbook for kids   **641.5**
Thea's tree. Jackson, A.   **E**
Theater
See also Acting; Musicals; Readers' theater
Amendola, D. A day at the New Amsterdam Theatre   **792.6**
Friedman, L. Break a leg!   **792**
Kenney, K. L. Cool costumes   **792**
Schumacher, T. L. How does the show go on?   **792**

Fiction
Aliki. A play's the thing   **E**
Best, C. Shrinking Violet   **E**
Blackwood, G. L. The Shakespeare stealer   **Fic**
De Paola, T. Stagestruck   **E**
Delessert, É. Moon theater   **E**
Hazen, L. E. Cinder Rabbit   **Fic**
Henson, H. Here's how I see it, here's how it is   **Fic**
Hoffman, M. Amazing Grace   **E**
Ives, P. Celestine, drama queen   **E**
Knudson, M. Raymond and Graham rule the school   **Fic**
La Chanze. Little diva   **E**
MacDonald, B. Wicked Will   **Fic**
Primavera, E. Louise the big cheese: divine diva   **E**
Ruzzier, S. Amandina   **E**
Tolan, S. S. Surviving the Applewhites   **Fic**
Waber, B. Evie & Margie   **E**

Production and direction
See also Motion pictures—Production and direction
Jacobs, P. D. Putting on a play   **792**
Kenney, K. L. Cool productions   **792**
Kenney, K. L. Cool scripts & acting   **792**
Underwood, D. Staging a play   **792**
Theaters
Stage setting and scenery
Kenney, K. L. Cool sets & props   **792**
Kenney, K. L. Cool special effects   **792**
Theatrical costume See Costume
Theatrical makeup
Kenney, K. L. Cool makeup   **792**
Thee, Hannah!. De Angeli, M. L.   **Fic**
Theft
Fiction
Amado, E. Tricycle   **E**

MacDonald, M. R. Tunjur! Tunjur! Tunjur!   **398.2**
Santopolo, J. The Niña, the Pinta, and the vanishing treasure   **Fic**
Teplin, S. The clock without a face   **Fic**
Thelen, Laurie Noble
Essentials of elementary library management   **025.1**
Thelonius Monster's sky-high fly pie. Sierra, J.   **E**
Thematic inquiry through fiction and nonfiction, PreK to grade 6. MacDonell, C.   **372**
Theodore [biography of Theodore Roosevelt] Keating, F.   **92**
Theodosia and the Serpents of Chaos. La Fevers, R. L.   **Fic**
Theology
See also Faith
Therapy, Psychological *See* Psychotherapy
There. Fitzpatrick, M.-L.   **E**
There are cats in this book. Schwarz, V.   **E**
There is a carrot in my ear, and other noodle tales. Schwartz, A.   **398.2**
There is a flower at the tip of my nose smelling me. Walker, A.   **811**
There was an old lady who swallowed a fly. Taback, S.   **782.42**
There was an old man who painted the sky. Sloat, T.   **E**
There was an old monster!. Emberley, R.   **E**
There's a bat in bunk five. Danziger, P.   **Fic**
There's a dead person following my sister around. Vande Velde, V.   **Fic**
There's a frog in my throat. Leedy, L.   **428**
There's a girl in my hammerlock. Spinelli, J.   **Fic**
There's a nightmare in my closet. Mayer, M.   **E**
There's a wolf at the door. Alley, Z. B.   **398.2**
There's an owl in the shower. George, J. C.   **Fic**
There's no such thing as a dragon. Kent, J.   **E**
There's no such thing as ghosts!. Eeckhout, E.   **E**
There's nothing to do on Mars. Gall, C.   **E**
Thermal waters *See* Geothermal resources
Thermometers
Sullivan, N. Temperature   **536**
Thermometry *See* Thermometers
Theseus (Greek mythology)
Byrd, R. The hero and the minotaur   **398.2**
They called her Molly Pitcher. Rockwell, A. F.   **92**
They Might Be Giants (Musical group)
Kids go!   **782.42**
They wore what?!. Platt, R.   **391**
Thibault, Terri, 1954-
(jt. auth) Blanchette, P. 12 easy knitting projects   **746.43**

Threatened species *See* Endangered species

The **three** bears. Barton, B.   **398.2**

The **three** bears. Galdone, P.   **398.2**

The **Three** Bears' Christmas. Duval, K.   **E**

The **three** Billy Goats Gruff. Galdone, P.   **398.2**

Three by the sea. Marshall, E.   **E**

Three cheers for Catherine the Great!. Best, C.   **E**

Three cheers for Tacky. Lester, H.   **E**

Three cups of tea. Mortenson, G.   **371.82**

Three-D ABC. *See* Raczka, B. 3-D ABC   **730**

Three days on a river in a red canoe. Williams, V. B.   **E**

Three French hens. Palatini, M.   **E**

Three good deeds. Vande Velde, V.   **Fic**

The **three** horrid little pigs. Pichon, L.   **E**

Three Kings Day. Hoyt-Goldsmith, D.   **394.26**

The **three** little gators. Ketteman, H.   **E**

Three little ghosties. Goodhart, P.   **E**

Three little kittens. Galdone, P.   **398.8**

The **three** little pigs. Kellogg, S.   **398.2**

The **three** little pigs. Marshall, J.   **398.2**

The **three** little pigs. Zemach, M.   **398.2**

The **three** little tamales. Kimmel, E. A.   **E**

The **three** little wolves and the big bad pig. Trivizas, E.   **E**

Three Mile Island Nuclear Power Plant (Pa.)
Feigenbaum, A. Emergency at Three Mile Island   **621.48**

Three-minute tales. MacDonald, M. R.   **398.2**

Three more stories you can read to your dog. Miller, S. S.   **E**

Three names of me. Cummings, M.   **Fic**

Three pebbles and a song. Spinelli, E.   **E**

The **three** pigs. Wiesner, D.   **E**

Three sacks of truth. Kimmel, E. A.   **398.2**

The **three** silly billies. Palatini, M.   **E**

The **three** snow bears. Brett, J.   **398.2**

Three swords for Granada. Myers, W. D.   **Fic**

Three wise men (Magi) *See* Magi

Three wishes. Ellis, D.   **956.94**

The **three** witches. Thomas, J. C.   **398.2**

Thrift *See* Saving and investment

Throat
Larsen, C. S. Crust and spray   **612.8**

Through artists' eyes [series]
Bingham, J. Emotion & relationships   **704.9**
Bingham, J. Landscape & the environment   **704.9**
Bingham, J. Science & technology   **704.9**
Bingham, J. Society & class   **704.9**

Through Georgia's eyes [biography of Georgia O'Keeffe] Rodriguez, R.   **92**

Through my eyes: the autobiography of Ruby Bridges. Bridges, R.   **92**

Through the eyes of your ancestors. Taylor, M.   **929**

Through the looking-glass and what Alice found there. See Carroll, L. Alice through the looking glass   **Fic**

Through time [series]
Platt, R. London   **942.1**
Platt, R. Pompeii   **937**

Throw your tooth on the roof. Beeler, S. B.   **398**

Thumb on a diamond. Roberts, K.   **Fic**

Thumbelina. Alderson, B.   **E**

Thumbelina. Ehrlich, A.   **E**

Thumbelina. Ensor, B.   **Fic**

Thumbeline [illustrated by Lisbeth Zwerger] Andersen, H. C.   **E**

Thunder at Gettysburg. Gauch, P. L.   **Fic**

Thunder-Boomer!. Crum, S.   **E**

Thunder from the sea. Weigel, J.   **741.5**

Thunder Rose. Nolen, J.   **E**

Thunderstorms
Branley, F. M. Flash, crash, rumble, and roll   **551.55**

Fiction
Crum, S. Thunder-Boomer!   **E**
Gorbachev, V. Dragon is coming!   **E**

Thurber, James, 1894-1961
Many moons [illustrated by Louis Slobodkin]   **E**
[illustrated by Marc Simont]   **E**

Thurian, Max
(il) Valeri, M. E. The hare and the tortoise = La liebre y la tortuga   **398.2**

Thurman, Howard, 1900-1981
About
Jackson Issa, K. Howard Thurman's great hope   **92**

Thurman, Mark, 1948-
(il) Drake, J. Alien invaders   **578.6**

Tibet (China)
Brown, D. Far beyond the garden gate: Alexandra David-Neel's journey to Lhasa   **92**
Demi. The Dalai Lama   **92**
Kimmel, E. C. Boy on the lion throne [biography of the Dalai Lama]   **92**
Levy, P. Tibet   **951**
Sís, P. Tibet   **951**

Folklore
See Folklore—Tibet (China)

Tibetan tales from the top of the world. Rose, N. C.   **398.2**

Tick-borne diseases
Colligan, L. H. Tick-borne illnesses   **616.9**

Tick-borne illnesses. Colligan, L. H.   **616.9**

Tidal waves, Seismic *See* Tsunamis

Tide pool ecology
Brenner, B. One small place by the sea   **577.6**
Halpern, M. All about tide pools   **577.6**
Kudlinski, K. V. The seaside switch   **577.6**
Swinburne, S. R. Ocean soup   **591.7**

Tidholm, Anna-Clara, 1946-
Knock! knock!   **E**

The **trouble** with wishes. Stanley, D.   E

Troupe, Quincy
   Little Stevie Wonder   92

Troupe, Thomas Kingsley
   If I were a ballerina   792.8

Trout are made of trees. Sayre, A. P.   577

Troy (Extinct city)
   Schlitz, L. A. The hero Schliemann   92

Truce. Murphy, J.   940.4

Truck. Crews, D.   E

Truck driver Tom. Wellington, M.   E

Truck Duck. Rex, M.   E

A **truck** goes rattley-bumpa. London, J.   E

Truck stuck. Wolf, S.   E

The **trucker**. Samuels, B.   E

The **trucker**. Weatherby, B.   E

Truckery rhymes. Scieszka, J.   811

Trucks
   Barton, B. Trucks   629.224
   Court, R. How to draw cars and trucks   743
   Lindeen, M. Trucks   629.224
   Maass, R. Little trucks with big jobs
          629.224
   Moore, P. The mighty street sweeper   E
   Murrell, D. J. Mega trucks   629.224
   Simon, S. Seymour Simon's book of trucks
          629.224
   Stille, D. R. Trucks   629.224

Fiction
   Anderson, P. P. Chuck's truck   E
   Clement, N. Drive   E
   Crews, D. Truck   E
   Cuyler, M. The little dump truck   E
   Gall, C. Dinotrux   E
   Hamilton, K. R. Red Truck   E
   London, J. A truck goes rattley-bumpa   E
   Lyon, G. E. Trucks roll!   E
   Merrill, J. The pushcart war   Fic
   Ransom, C. F. The old blue pickup truck   E
   Samuels, B. The trucker   E
   Schertle, A. Little Blue Truck   E
   Scieszka, J. Pete's party   E
   Scieszka, J. Smash! crash!   E
   Sís, P. Trucks, trucks, trucks   E
   Sutton, S. Roadwork!   E
   Weatherby, B. The trucker   E
   Wellington, M. Truck driver Tom   E
   Wolf, S. Truck stuck   E

Poetry
   Scieszka, J. Truckery rhymes   811

Trucks. Stille, D. R.   629.224

Trucks roll!. Lyon, G. E.   E

Trucks, trucks, trucks. Sís, P.   E

Trudy. Cole, H.   E

True book [series]
   Apte, S. The Aztec empire   972
   Apte, S. India   954
   Brimner, L. D. Caves   551.4
   Ditchfield, C. Golf   796.352
   Ditchfield, C. Memorial Day   394.26
   Ditchfield, C. Tennis   796.342
   Ditchfield, C. Wrestling   796.8
   Fazio, W. Saudi Arabia   953.8

Flanagan, A. K. The Pueblos   970.004
Flanagan, A. K. The Zunis   970.004
Friedman, M. The Oregon Trail   978
Kim, F. S. Constellations   523.8
Knotts, B. Track and field   796.42
Knotts, B. Weightlifting   796.41
Landau, E. Apples   634
Landau, E. Bananas   634
Landau, E. Beyond Pluto   523.4
Landau, E. Corn   633.1
Landau, E. Earth   525
Landau, E. Jupiter   523.4
Landau, E. Mars   523.4
Landau, E. Mercury   523.4
Landau, E. The moon   523.3
Landau, E. Neptune   523.4
Landau, E. Pluto   523.4
Landau, E. Saturn   523.4
Landau, E. The sun   523.7
Landau, E. Uranus   523.4
Landau, E. Venus   523.4
Landau, E. Wheat   633.1
Newman, S. The Inca empire   985
Perritano, J. The Lewis and Clark Expedition
          978
Perritano, J. The transcontinental railroad
          385.09
Squire, A. Cheetahs   599.75
Stille, D. R. Deserts   577.5
Stille, D. R. Grasslands   577.4
Stille, D. R. Oceans   551.46
Stille, D. R. Tropical rain forest   577.3
Stille, D. R. Trucks   629.224
Taylor-Butler, C. Food allergies   616.97
Than, K. Stars   523.8
Trammel, H. K. The solar system   523.2
Walters, T. Brazil   981

The **true** confessions of Charlotte Doyle. Avi
          Fic

The **true** gift. MacLachlan, P.   Fic

True green kids. McKay, K.   333.72

The **true** meaning of Smekday. Rex, A.   Fic

True stories [series]
   Moore, H. The story behind cotton   633.5
   Moore, H. The story behind diamonds   553.8
   Moore, H. The story behind salt   553.6
   Price, S. The story behind electricity   621.3
   Price, S. The story behind skyscrapers   720
   Raum, E. The story behind bread   641.8
   Raum, E. The story behind gold   553.4
   Raum, E. The story behind time   529
   Raum, E. The story behind toilets   696

The **true** story of Little Red Riding Hood.
   Baruzzi, A.   E

The **true** story of Stellina. Pericoli, M.   E

The **true** story of the 3 little pigs. Scieszka, J.
          E

Trueit, Trudi Strain
   Ants   595.7
   Beetles   595.7
   Caterpillars   595.7
   Grasshoppers   595.7
   Keeping a journal   808
   No girls allowed (dogs okay)   Fic
   Rocks, gems, and minerals   552

Trueit, Trudi Strain—*Continued*
Spiders **595.4**
Worms **592**

Trueman, Matthew
(il) Kimmel, E. A. A picture for Marc **Fic**
(il) Lasky, K. One beetle too many: the extraordinary adventures of Charles Darwin **92**

Trueman, Terry
Hurricane **Fic**

Truesdell, Sue
(il) Byars, B. C. The Golly sisters go West **E**
(il) Clements, A. Circus family dog **E**
(il) George, J. C. How to talk to your dog **636.7**
(il) Grant, J. Chicken said, Cluck! **E**

Trumble, Kelly
(jt. auth) Marshall, R. M. The Library of Alexandria **027**

The **trumpet** of the swan. White, E. B. **Fic**

Truss, Lynne
Eats, shoots & leaves **428**
The girl's like spaghetti **428**
Twenty-odd ducks **428**

Truth, Sojourner, d. 1883
About
Adler, D. A. A picture book of Sojourner Truth **92**
Clinton, C. When Harriet met Sojourner [biography of Harriet Tubman and Sojourner Truth] **92**
Horn, G. Sojourner Truth **92**
McKissack, P. C. Sojourner Truth **92**
Pinkney, A. D. Sojourner Truth's step-stomp stride **92**
Rockwell, A. F. Only passing through: the story of Sojourner Truth **92**
Roop, P. Sojourner Truth **92**
See/See also pages in the following book(s):
Pinkney, A. D. Let it shine **920**

The **truth** about dangerous sea creatures. Cerullo, M. M. **591.7**

The **truth** about great white sharks. Cerullo, M. M. **597**

The **truth** about my Bat Mitzvah. Baskin, N. R. **Fic**

The **truth** about poop. Goodman, S. **573.4**

The **truth** about sparrows. Hale, M. **Fic**

The **truth** about Truman School. Butler, D. H. **Fic**

Truthfulness and falsehood
See also Honesty
Fiction
Amado, E. Tricycle **E**
Burningham, J. John Patrick Norman McHennessy **E**
Choldenko, G. Notes from a liar and her dog **Fic**
Cocca-Leffler, M. Princess K.I.M. and the lie that grew **E**
Coville, B. The skull of truth **Fic**
Farrell, D. Doug-Dennis and the flyaway fib **E**

Rankin, L. Ruthie and the (not so) teeny tiny lie **E**

Try this at home **333.72**

Tryon, Leslie
Albert's birthday **E**

Tseng, Grace
White tiger, blue serpent **398.2**

Tseng, Jean
(il) Huynh, Q. N. Water buffalo days **92**
(il) Mahy, M. The seven Chinese brothers **398.2**
(il) Tseng, G. White tiger, blue serpent **398.2**

Tseng, Kevin, 1973-
Ned's new home **E**

Tseng, Mou-sien
(il) Huynh, Q. N. Water buffalo days **92**
(il) Mahy, M. The seven Chinese brothers **398.2**
(il) Tseng, G. White tiger, blue serpent **398.2**

Tsunami!. Kajikawa, K. **398.2**

Tsunamis
Adamson, T. K. Tsunamis **551.46**
Fradin, J. B. Tsunamis **551.46**
Hamilton, J. Tsunamis **551.46**
Jennings, T. Earthquakes and tsunamis **551.2**
Karwoski, G. Tsunami **363.34**
Levy, M. Earthquakes, volcanoes, and tsunamis **551.2**
Morris, A. Tsunami **959.3**
Schuh, M. C. Tsunamis **551.46**
Silverstein, A. Earthquakes **551.2**
Tagliaferro, L. How does an earthquake become a tsunami? **551.46**
Fiction
Salisbury, G. Night of the howling dogs **Fic**
Folklore
Kajikawa, K. Tsunami! **398.2**

Tuba lessons. Bartlett, T. C. **E**

Tuberculosis
Silverstein, A. The tuberculosis update **616.2**

The **tuberculosis** update. Silverstein, A. **616.2**

Tubman, Harriet, 1820?-1913
About
Adler, D. A. A picture book of Harriet Tubman **92**
Clinton, C. When Harriet met Sojourner [biography of Harriet Tubman and Sojourner Truth] **92**
Haskins, J. Get on board: the story of the Underground Railroad **326**
Turner, G. T. An apple for Harriet Tubman **92**
Weatherford, C. B. Moses [biography of Harriet Tubman] **92**
See/See also pages in the following book(s):
Currie, S. Escapes from slavery **326**
Krull, K. Lives of extraordinary women **920**
Pinkney, A. D. Let it shine **920**
Fiction
Schroeder, A. Minty: a story of young Harriet Tubman **E**

Tubman, Harriet, 1820?-1913—About—*Continued*

Poetry
Lawrence, J. Harriet and the Promised Land
811

Tuck everlasting. Babbitt, N.   Fic

Tucker, Kathy
The seven Chinese sisters   E

Tudor, Tasha, 1915-2008
1 is one   E
(il) Burnett, F. H. A little princess   Fic
(il) Godden, R. The doll's house   Fic
(il) Stevenson, R. L. A child's garden of verses
821

Tuesday. Wiesner, D.   E

Tugboats
Fiction
Gramatky, H. Little Toot   E
McMullan, K. I'm mighty!   E

Tugeau, Jeremy
(il) Butler, D. H. The case of the lost boy
Fic

Tuko and the birds. Climo, S.   398.2

Tumbleweed skies. Sherrard, V.   Fic

Tumtum & Nutmeg. Bearn, E.   Fic

Tundra ecology
Johansson, P. The frozen tundra   577.5
Johnson, R. L. A walk in the tundra   577.5
Levy, J. Discovering the Arctic tundra   577.5
Marsico, K. A home on the tundra   577.5
Tagliaferro, L. Explore the tundra   577.5
Tocci, S. Alpine tundra   577.5
Tocci, S. Arctic tundra   577.5
Wojahn, R. H. A tundra food chain   577.5

A **tundra** food chain. Wojahn, R. H.   577.5

Tunis, Edwin, 1897-1973
Colonial craftsmen and the beginnings of American industry   680
Colonial living   973.2

Tunis, John R., 1889-1975
The Kid from Tomkinsville   Fic

Tunisia
Brown, R. V. Tunisia   961.1
Fiction
Colfer, E. Benny and Omar   Fic

Tunjur! Tunjur! Tunjur!. MacDonald, M. R.
398.2

Tunnell, Michael O.
Candy bomber [biography of Gail Halvorsen]
92
The children of Topaz   940.53

Tunnels
See/See also pages in the following book(s):
Macaulay, D. Building big   720

Tupac Shakur *See* Shakur, Tupac

Tupelo rides the rails. Sweet, M.   E

Turkey
Hawker, F. Islam in Turkey   297
Shields, S. D. Turkey   956.1
Fiction
Gilani-Williams, F. Nabeel's new pants   E

Folklore
See Folklore—Turkey

Turkey Bowl. Bildner, P.   E
Turkey riddles. Hall, K.   793.73
Turkey vultures *See* Vultures

Turkeys
Fiction
Arnosky, J. I'm a turkey!   E
Auch, M. J. Beauty and the beaks   E
Mayr, D. Run, Turkey run   E
Nikola-Lisa, W. Setting the turkeys free   E
Stiegemeyer, J. Gobble-gobble crash!   E
Waddell, M. Captain Small Pig   E
Wallace, C. Turkeys together   E

Turkeys, Pilgrims, and Indian corn. Barth, E.
394.26

Turkeys together. Wallace, C.   E

Turkmenistan
Knowlton, M. Turkmenistan   958.5

The **turn-around** upside-down alphabet book.
Ernst, L. C.   E

Turnbull, Stephen R.
Real samurai   952

Turner, Alan, 1947-
National Geographic prehistoric mammals
569

Turner, Ann Warren, 1945-
Abe Lincoln remembers   92
Dust for dinner   E
Grasshopper summer   Fic
Sitting Bull remembers   92

Turner, Glennette Tilley
An apple for Harriet Tubman   92

Turner, Kate
Australia   994

Turner, Pamela S.
The frog scientist   597.8
Gorilla doctors   333.95
Hachiko   E
A life in the wild [biography of George Schaller]   92
Life on earth—and beyond   576.8
Prowling the seas   591.7

Turner, Tracey
World of the weird   031

Turner-Denstaedt, Melanie, 1963-2007
The hat that wore Clara B.   E

Turning points in U.S. history [series]
Fradin, D. B. The Alamo   976.4
Fradin, D. B. The Boston Tea Party   973.3
Fradin, D. B. The Declaration of Independence
973.3
Fradin, D. B. September 11, 2001   973.931
Fradin, J. B. Hurricane Katrina   363.34

Turpin, Dick *See* Turpin, Richard, 1706-1739

Turpin, Richard, 1706-1739
Fiction
Thompson, K. Highway robbery   Fic

Turtle and Snake's day at the beach. Spohn, K.
E

Turtle girl. Crowe, C.   E

Turtle in paradise. Holm, J. L.   Fic

Vainio, Pirkko, 1957-
(il) Andersen, H. C. The ugly duckling [illustrated by Pirkko Vainio]   E

Valckx, Catharina
Lizette's green sock   E

Valdez (Ship) *See* Exxon Valdez (Ship)

Valencia, Esau Andrade *See* Andrade Valencia, Esau

Valentine, Saint
About
Sabuda, R. Saint Valentine   92

Valentine surprise. Demas, C.   E

Valentine's Day
Barth, E. Hearts, cupids, and red roses   394.26
Landau, E. Valentine's day   394.26
McGee, R. Paper crafts for Valentine's Day   745.594
Otto, C. Celebrate Valentine's Day   394.26
See/See also pages in the following book(s):
Bauer, C. F. Celebrations   808.8
Fiction
Carlson, N. L. Henry and the Valentine surprise   E
Demas, C. Valentine surprise   E
Fein, E. My frozen valentine   Fic

Valeri, M. Eulalia
The hare and the tortoise = La liebre y la tortuga   398.2

Valério, Geraldo, 1970-
(il) Hickman, P. M. It's moving day!   591.56
(il) MacDonald, M. R. Conejito   398.2
(il) MacDonald, M. R. Go to sleep, Gecko!   398.2
(il) MacDonald, M. R. Surf war!   398.2
(il) Spinelli, E. When you are happy   E

Valiant, Kristi
(il) Lazo Gilmore, D. K. Cora cooks pancit   E

Valley Forge (Pa.)
History
Allen, T. B. Remember Valley Forge   973.3
Freedman, R. Washington at Valley Forge   973.3

Vallverdú, Josep, 1923-
Aladdin and the magic lamp = Aladino y la lámpara marvillosa   398.2

Values [series]
Pryor, K. J. Cooperation   177
Pryor, K. J. Courage   179
Pryor, K. J. Honesty   177
Pryor, K. J. Kindness   177
Pryor, K. J. Respect   177
Pryor, K. J. Tolerance   177

Vamos, Samantha R.
Before you were here, mi amor   E

The **vampire** book. Regan, S.   398

Vampires
Gee, J. Encyclopedia horrifica   001.9
Regan, S. The vampire book   398
Fiction
Collins, R. Dear Vampa   E
Harris, L. A taste for red   Fic

Graphic novels
Sfar, J. Little Vampire   741.5

Van Allsburg, Chris
Ben's dream   E
The garden of Abdul Gasazi   E
Jumanji   E
Just a dream   E
The mysteries of Harris Burdick   E
The Polar Express   E
The stranger   E
The sweetest fig   E
The widow's broom   E
The wreck of the Zephyr   E
The wretched stone   E
The Z was zapped   E
Zathura   E

Van Beethoven, Ludwig *See* Beethoven, Ludwig van, 1770-1827

Van Camp, Katie
Harry and Horsie   E

Van Cleve, Kathleen
Drizzle   Fic

Van der Linden, Martijn *See* Linden, Martijn van der

Van der Meer, Jan *See* Vermeer, Johannes, 1632-1675

Van der Sterre, Johanna
(il) Hyde, H. S. Feivel's flying horses   E

Van Draanen, Wendelin *See* Draanen, Wendelin van

Van Dusen, Chris
The circus ship   E
(il) DiCamillo, K. Mercy Watson to the rescue   Fic

Van Gelder, Richard George, 1928-1994
(jt. auth) Bancroft, H. Animals in winter   591.56

Van Gogh, Vincent *See* Gogh, Vincent van, 1853-1890

Van Gorp, Lynn
Elements   540
Gregor Mendel   92

Van Kampen, Vlasta, 1943-
It couldn't be worse!   398.2
(il) Silsbe, B. The bears we know   E

Van Laan, Nancy
The magic bean tree   398.2
Nit-pickin'   E
Shingebiss   398.2
Teeny tiny tingly tales   E
When winter comes   E

Van Leeuwen, Jean
Amanda Pig and the awful, scary monster   E
Benny & beautiful baby Delilah   E
Bound for Oregon   Fic
Cabin on Trouble Creek   Fic
Chicken soup   E
Oliver the Mighty Pig   E
Papa and the pioneer quilt   E

Van Lieshout, Maria *See* Lieshout, Maria van

Van Niekerk, Clarabelle, 1952-
Understanding Sam and Asperger Syndrome   616.85

Van Orden, Phyllis J.
Library service to children   **027.62**

Van Steenwyk, Elizabeth, 1928-
Prairie Christmas   **E**

Van Straaten, Harmen *See* Straaten, Harmen van, 1961-

Van Vleet, Carmella
Great Ancient Egypt projects you can build yourself   **932**

Van Wassenhove, Sue, 1951-
The seldom-ever-shady glades   **811**

Van Wright, Cornelius
(il) Chinn, K. Sam and the lucky money   **E**
(il) Miller, W. Zora Hurston and the chinaberry tree   **92**
(il) Pringle, L. P. American slave, American hero [biography of York]   **92**
(il) Rappaport, D. We are the many   **920**
(il) Smith, C. L. Jingle dancer   **E**

Van Wyk, Christopher, 1957-
(jt. auth) Mandela, N. Nelson Mandela: long walk to freedom   **92**

Van Wyk, Rupert, 1971-
(il) Foster, J. Barron's junior rhyming Dictionary   **423**

Van Zyle, Jon, 1942-
(il) London, J. Baby whale's journey   **E**
(il) Miller, D. S. Arctic lights, arctic nights   **591.4**
(il) Miller, D. S. Big Alaska   **979.8**
(il) Miller, D. S. The great serum race   **798.8**
(il) Miller, D. S. Survival at 40 below   **591.7**

VanCleave, Janice Pratt
Janice VanCleave's 201 awesome, magical, bizarre & incredible experiments   **507.8**
Janice VanCleave's 202 oozing, bubbling, dripping & bouncing experiments   **507.8**
Janice VanCleave's 203 icy, freezing, frosty, cool & wild experiments   **507.8**
Janice VanCleave's big book of play and find out science projects   **507.8**
Janice VanCleave's earth science for every kid   **550**
Janice Vancleave's ecology for every kid   **577**
Janice VanCleave's electricity   **537**
Janice VanCleave's energy for every kid   **531**
Janice VanCleave's engineering for every kid   **507.8**
Janice VanCleave's geometry for every kid   **516**
Janice VanCleave's guide to more of the best science fair projects   **507.8**
Janice VanCleave's guide to the best science fair projects   **507.8**
Janice VanCleave's insects and spiders   **595.7**
Janice VanCleave's oceans for every kid   **551.46**
Janice VanCleave's plants   **580.7**
Janice VanCleave's play and find out about math   **513**

Janice VanCleave's play and find out about nature   **570**
Janice VanCleave's rocks and minerals   **552**
Janice VanCleave's science around the year   **507.8**
Janice VanCleave's solar system   **523.2**
Janice VanCleave's the human body for every kid   **612**
Janice VanCleave's weather   **551.5**

Vande Velde, Vivian, 1951-
Smart dog   **Fic**
There's a dead person following my sister around   **Fic**
Three good deeds   **Fic**
Wizard at work   **Fic**

Vanden Broeck, Fabricio *See* Vandenbroeck, Fabricio, 1954-

Vandenbroeck, Fabricio, 1954-
(il) Colato Laínez, R. My shoes and I   **E**
(il) Johnston, T. Uncle Rain Cloud   **E**

Vander Zee, Ruth
Always with you   **E**
Mississippi morning   **E**

Vanderlinden, Kathy
(jt. auth) Bourgeois, P. The dirt on dirt   **631.4**

Vane, Mitch
(il) Lasky, K. Poodle and Hound   **E**
(il) Plourde, L. A mountain of mittens   **E**

VanHecke, Susan
An apple pie for dinner   **E**

Vanishing species *See* Endangered species

VanVoorst, Jennifer, 1972-
Rise of the thinking machines   **629.8**

Vardell, Sylvia M.
Children's literature in action   **028.5**
Poetry people   **811**

Varela, Barry
Gizmo   **E**

Varennes, Monique de, 1947-
The jewel box ballerinas   **E**

Varley, Susan
(il) Waddell, M. Captain Small Pig   **E**

Varmer, Hjørdis, 1936-
Hans Christian Andersen   **92**

Varon, Sara, 1971-
Chicken and Cat   **E**
Robot dreams   **741.5**

Vasco leader of the tribe. Bondoux, A.-L.   **Fic**

Vaupel, Robin
The rules of the universe by Austin W. Hale   **Fic**

VCRs *See* Video recording

Vegetable gardening
Creasy, R. Blue potatoes, orange tomatoes   **635**
Grow it, cook it   **635**
Hirsch, R. E. Growing your own garden   **635**

Fiction
Ehlert, L. Growing vegetable soup   **E**

Vegetables

See also names of vegetables

Creasy, R. Blue potatoes, orange tomatoes
635

Ehlert, L. Eating the alphabet — E
Gibbons, G. The vegetables we eat — 635
McMillan, B. Growing colors — E
Mora, P. Yum! mmmm! que rico! — 811

Fiction

Wiesner, D. June 29, 1999 — E

Folklore

Paye, W.-L. The talking vegetables — 398.2

The **vegetables** we eat. Gibbons, G. — 635

Vegetarian cooking

Gillies, J. The jumbo vegetarian cookbook
641.5

Katzen, M. Honest pretzels — 641.5

Vehicles

Cooper, W. On the road — 629.2
Coppendale, J. The great big book of mighty machines — 621.8
Rockwell, A. F. Big wheels — E
Smith, M. Speed machines — 629.2
Vetter, J. R. Down by the station — 782.42

Fiction

Mortensen, D. D. Good night engines — E
Rex, M. Truck Duck — E
Sierra, J. Preschool to the rescue — E
Timmers, L. Who is driving? — E
Wolf, S. Truck stuck — E

Veitch, Catherine

Dancing — 792.8
Gymnastics — 796.44
Sound and hearing — 612.8

Velasquez, Eric

(il) Boswell, A. K. The rain stomper — E
(il) Brewster, H. The other Mozart [biography of Joseph Bologne Saint-Georges] — 92
(il) Dant, T. Some kind of love — 811
(il) Krull, K. Houdini — 92
(il) Naidoo, B. Journey to Jo'burg — Fic
(il) Soto, G. The skirt — Fic
(il) Weatherford, C. B. Jesse Owens — 92
(il) Weatherford, C. B. Racing against the odds [biography of Wendell Scott] — 92

Velázquez, Diego, 1599-1660

About

Venezia, M. Diego Velázquez — 92

Fiction

Treviño, E. B. d. I, Juan de Pareja — Fic

Velma Gratch & the way cool butterfly. Madison, A. — E

Velocity *See* Speed

The **velveteen** rabbit. Bianco, M. W. — Fic

Venable, Colleen AF

Hamster and cheese — 741.5

Venezia, Mike, 1945-

Albert Einstein — 92
Diego Velázquez — 92
Faith Ringgold — 92
Horace Pippin — 92
Luis Alvarez — 92
Thomas Edison — 92

Venezuela

Winter, J. K. Venezuela — 987

Venice (Italy)

Fiction

Armstrong, A. Looking for Marco Polo — Fic
Shefelman, J. J. Anna Maria's gift — Fic
Trottier, M. The paint box — E

Vennema, Peter

(jt. auth) Stanley, D. Bard of Avon: the story of William Shakespeare — 822.3
(jt. auth) Stanley, D. Cleopatra — 92
(jt. auth) Stanley, D. Good Queen Bess: the story of Elizabeth I of England — 92

Venom. Singer, M. — 591.6

Venom, poison, and electricity. Pryor, K. J.
591.6

Venter, Liezl

(jt. auth) Van Niekerk, C. Understanding Sam and Asperger Syndrome — 616.85

Venti, Anthony Bacon

(il) Fritz, J. Around the world in a hundred years — 910.4

Ventriloquism

Fiction

De Guzman, M. Finding Stinko — Fic

Venturing the deep sea. Lindop, L. — 551.46

Venus (Planet)

Bjorklund, R. Venus — 523.4
Landau, E. Venus — 523.4

Venuti, Kristin Clark

Leaving the Bellweathers — Fic

Vera's first day of school. Rosenberry, V. — E

Verbal learning

See also Reading comprehension

Verdi, Giuseppe, 1813-1901

See/See also pages in the following book(s):
Krull, K. Lives of the musicians — 920

Verdick, Elizabeth

Words are not for hurting — 177
(jt. auth) Crist, J. J. Siblings — 306.8

Verdu, Jean-Yves

(jt. auth) Niepold, M. Oooh! Matisse — 759.4
(jt. auth) Niepold, M. Oooh! Picasso — 730.9

Vere, Ed

Chick — E

Veregin, Howard

(ed) Goode, J. P. Goode's world atlas — 912

Verhoeven, Rian

(jt. auth) Rol, R. v. d. Anne Frank, beyond the diary — 92

Vermeer, Johannes, 1632-1675

About

Raczka, B. The Vermeer interviews
759.9492

Fiction

Balliett, B. Chasing Vermeer — Fic

The **Vermeer** interviews. Raczka, B. — 759.9492

Vermeer van Delft, Jan *See* Vermeer, Johannes, 1632-1675

Vocational guidance—*Continued*

Arroyo, S. L. How race car drivers use math
796.72

Bertoletti, J. C. How baseball managers use math **796.357**

Bertoletti, J. C. How fashion designers use math **746.9**

Egan, J. How video game designers use math **794.8**

Gazlay, S. Managing green spaces **333.7**

Glasscock, S. How nurses use math **610.73**

Harlan, M. A. Personal learning networks **027.8**

Hense, M. How astronauts use math **629.45**

Hense, M. How fighter pilots use math **629.13**

Holmes, T. Dinosaur scientist **560**

Kenney, K. L. Firefighters at work **628.9**

Kenney, K. L. Librarians at work **020**

Kenney, K. L. Mail carriers at work **383**

Kenney, K. L. Nurses at work **610.73**

Kenney, K. L. Police officers at work **363.2**

Kenney, K. L. Teachers at work **371.1**

Somervill, B. A. Marine biologist **578.7**

Vocations *See* Occupations

Vogel, Amos

How little Lori visited Times Square **E**

Vogel, Carole Garbuny

Human impact **333.91**

The man who flies with birds **598**

Vogel, Jennifer

A library story **727**

Vogel, Julia, 1958-

Bats **599.4**

Local farms and sustainable foods **630**

Vogt, Gregory

Apollo moonwalks **629.45**

Spacewalks **629.45**

Vogt, Richard Carl

Rain forests **577.3**

Voice from afar. Johnston, T. **811**

A **voice** of her own: the story of Phillis Wheatley, slave poet. Lasky, K. **92**

The **voice** that challenged a nation [biography of Marian Anderson] Freedman, R. **92**

Voices for freedom: abolitionist heroes [series]

Horn, G. Sojourner Truth **92**

Voices from colonial America [series] **973.2**

Voices in the park. Browne, A. **E**

Voigt, Cynthia

Dicey's song **Fic**

Vojtech, Anna, 1946-

(il) Bruchac, J. The first strawberries **398.2**

(il) Wadsworth, O. A. Over in the meadow **E**

Volavková, Hana

(ed) —I never saw another butterfly—. See —I never saw another butterfly— **741.9**

Volcano wakes up!. Peters, L. W. **811**

Volcanoes

Branley, F. M. Volcanoes **551.2**

Burleigh, R. Volcanoes **551.2**

Fradin, J. B. Volcanoes **551.2**

Grace, C. O. Forces of nature **551.2**

Harrison, D. L. Volcanoes: nature's incredible fireworks **551.2**

Jennings, T. Violent volcanoes **551.2**

Levy, M. Earthquakes, volcanoes, and tsunamis **551.2**

Silverstein, A. Volcanoes **551.2**

Tagliaferro, L. How does a volcano become an island? **551.2**

Waldron, M. Volcanoes **551.2**

Woods, M. Volcanoes **551.2**

Fiction

Bynum, E. Jamari's drum **E**

Poetry

Peters, L. W. Volcano wakes up! **811**

Volcanoes. Woods, M. **551.2**

Volleyball

Crossingham, J. Spike it volleyball **796.325**

Volume (Cubic content)

Gardner, R. Super-sized science projects with volume **530.8**

Volunteer work

Fiction

Lyon, G. E. You and me and home sweet home **E**

Von Buhler, Cynthia *See* Buhler, Cynthia von

Von Linné, Carl *See* Linné, Carl von, 1707-1778

Von Schmidt, Eric, 1931-2007

(il) Fleischman, S. By the Great Horn Spoon! **Fic**

Voodooism

See also Zombies

Vossmeyer, Gabriele

(jt. auth) Fuller, B. Germany **943**

Vote!. Christelow, E. **324**

Vote. Steele, P. **324**

Voting *See* Elections

The **Vowel** family. Walker, S. M. **E**

Voyage: Ocean: a full-speed-ahead tour of the oceans. Woodward, J. **551.46**

The **voyage** of Patience Goodspeed. Frederick, H. V. **Fic**

The **voyage** of the beetle. Weaver, A. H. **576.8**

Voyage to the Pharos. Gauch, S. **E**

Voyages and travels

See also Travel

Demi. Marco Polo **92**

Freedman, R. The adventures of Marco Polo **92**

Markle, S. Animals Marco Polo saw **92**

McCarty, N. Marco Polo **92**

Otfinoski, S. Marco Polo **92**

Quan, E. Once upon a full moon **92**

Rumford, J. Traveling man: the journey of Ibn Battuta, 1325-1354 **92**

Fiction

Alexander, L. The golden dream of Carlo Chuchio **Fic**

Blackstone, S. My granny went to market **E**

Bondoux, A.-L. Vasco leader of the tribe **Fic**

Cohagan, C. The lost children **Fic**

Voyages and travels—Fiction—*Continued*

Corder, Z. Lionboy	Fic
Crowley, N. Nanook & Pryce	E
DeFelice, C. C. Bringing Ezra back	Fic
Docherty, T. To the beach	E
Egan, T. Dodsworth in New York	E
Erdrich, L. The porcupine year	Fic
Hobbs, W. Jason's gold	Fic
Holmes, M. T. A giraffe goes to Paris	E
Kerby, M. Owney, the mail-pouch pooch	E
Krensky, S. Dangerous crossing	Fic
Law, I. Savvy	Fic
Lazo, C. E. Someday when my cat can talk	E
Lin, G. Olvina flies	E
Naylor, P. R. Emily's fortune	Fic
Priceman, M. How to make a cherry pie and see the U.S.A.	E
Priceman, M. How to make an apple pie and see the world	E
Riordan, R. The red pyramid	Fic
Say, A. Grandfather's journey	E
Seidler, T. Gully's travels	Fic
Snell, G. The King of Quizzical Island	E
Vries, A. d. Raf	E
Weston, C. The diary of Melanie Martin; or, How I survived Matt the Brat, Michelangelo, and the Leaning Tower of Pizza	Fic
Whelan, G. Yuki and the one thousand carriers	E
Winter, J. Here comes the garbage barge!	E
Yaccarino, D. Lawn to lawn	E

Poetry

Gaiman, N. Instructions	E

Voyages around the world

Levinson, N. S. Magellan and the first voyage around the world	92

Fiction

Hesse, K. Stowaway	Fic
Marceau, F. Panorama	E

The **voyages** of Doctor Dolittle. Lofting, H.

	Fic

Vries, Anke de, 1936-

Raf	E

Vriethoff, Joanne Lew- *See* Lew-Vriethoff, Joanne

Vulture view. Sayre, A. P.   598

Vultures

Sayre, A. P. Vulture view	598

W

Waber, Bernard

Evie & Margie	E
Ira sleeps over	E
Lyle, Lyle, crocodile	E
The mouse that snored	E

Wabi Sabi. Reibstein, M.   E

Wáchale! poetry and prose on growing up Latino in America   810.8

Wachtel, Alan

Southeast Asian Americans	305.8

Wada, Stephanie

Momotaro and the island of ogres	398.2

Waddell, Martin

Can't you sleep, Little Bear?	E
Captain Small Pig	E
Farmer duck	E
It's quacking time!	E
Owl babies	E
Snow bears	E
The super hungry dinosaur	E
Tiny's big adventure	E

Waddle!. Seder, R. B.   E

Wade, Mary Dodson, 1930-

Amazing Cherokee writer Sequoyah	92
Amazing civil war nurse Clara Barton	92
Amazing Olympic athlete Wilma Rudolph	92
Amazing president Theodore Roosevelt	92
Flowers bloom!	582.13
People need plants!	581.6
Plants grow!	571.8
Plants live everywhere!	581
Seeds sprout!	581.4
Trees, weeds, and vegetables—so many kinds of plants!	580

Wadsworth, Ginger

Camping with the president [biography of Theodore Roosevelt]	92
Cesar Chavez	92
Up, up, and away	595.4

Wadsworth, Olive A.

Over in the meadow	E

Wag a tail. Ehlert, L.   E

Waggit's tale. Howe, P.   Fic

Wagner, Heather Lehr

How the president is elected	324

Wagner, Honus, 1874-1955

About

Yolen, J. All-star! [biography of Honus Wagner]	92

Wagner, Lisa, 1961-

Cool melt & pour soap	668
Cool painted stuff	745.7

Wagon wheels. Brenner, B.   E

Wagons *See* Carriages and carts

Wagué Diakité, Baba

The hatseller and the monkeys	398.2
The hunterman and the crocodile	398.2
The magic gourd	398.2
Mee-An and the magic serpent	398.2
(il) Badoe, A. The pot of wisdom: Ananse stories	398.2
(il) Bynum, E. Jamari's drum	E
(jt. auth) Diakité, P. I lost my tooth in Africa	E

Wahl, Jan, 1933-

Candy shop	E

Waichulaitis, Trisha, 1954-

(jt. auth) Benton, G. Ready-to-go storytimes	027.62

The **Wainscott** weasel. Seidler, T.   Fic

Wait, Lea, 1946-

Finest kind	Fic

Wait! I want to tell you a story. Willans, T.   E

Wait! No paint!. Whatley, B.   E

Wait till Helen comes. Hahn, M. D.   Fic

Waite, Michael P., 1960-
The witches of Dredmoore Hollow   Fic

Waites, Joan C.
(il) Butler, D. H. F is for firefighting   628.9
(il) Slade, S. What's new at the zoo?   513

Waiting for Anya. Morpurgo, M.   Fic

Waiting for Benjamin. Altman, A.   E

Waiting for May. Stoeke, J. M.   E

Waiting for normal. Connor, L.   Fic

Waiting for the owl's call. Whelan, G.   E

Waiting for wings. Ehlert, L.   E

Waiting for winter. Meschenmoser, S.   E

Waiting out the storm. Macken, J. E.   E

Wakefield, Ruth
See/See also pages in the following book(s):
Thimmesh, C. Girls think of everything   920

Wakelin, Kirsti Anne
(il) Lloyd, J. Looking for loons   E

Waking up Wendell. Stevens, A.   E

Wakiyama, Hanako
(il) Archer, P. From dawn to dreams   811

Walden, Katherine
Meerkats   599.74
Rhinoceroses   599.66
Warthogs   599.63
Wildebeests   599.64

Walden, Mark
H.I.V.E   Fic

Waldman, Debby
Clever Rachel   398.2
A sack full of feathers   398.2

Waldman, Neil, 1947-
Out of the shadows   92
The snowflake   551.48
(il) Schecter, E. The family Haggadah   296.4

Waldman, Stuart, 1941-
The last river   978

Waldrep, Richard
(il) Crowe, E. Surfer of the century   92

Waldron, Kevin, 1979-
Mr. Peek and the misunderstanding at the zoo   E

Waldron, Melanie, 1972-
Volcanoes   551.2

Wales
Fiction
Bond, N. A string in the harp   Fic
Cooper, S. The grey king   Fic
Cottrell Boyce, F. Framed   Fic
Newbery, L. Lost boy   Fic
Nimmo, J. The snow spider   Fic

A walk in New York. Rubbino, S.   917.47

A walk in the boreal forest. Johnson, R. L.   577.3

A walk in the deciduous forest. Johnson, R. L.   577.3

A walk in the desert. Johnson, R. L.   577.5

A walk in the prairie. Johnson, R. L.   577.4

A walk in the tundra. Johnson, R. L.   577.5

Walk on!. Frazee, M.   E

Walk two moons. Creech, S.   Fic

Walker, Alice, 1944-
Langston Hughes, American poet   92
There is a flower at the tip of my nose smelling me   811
Why war is never a good idea   811

Walker, Anna
I love Christmas   E

Walker, Barbara Muhs, 1928-
The Little House cookbook   641.5

Walker, C. J., Madame, 1867-1919
About
Lasky, K. Vision of beauty: the story of Sarah Breedlove Walker   92
McKissack, P. C. Madam C.J. Walker   92

Walker, David, 1965-
(il) Bennett, K. Your daddy was just like you   E
(il) Boelts, M. Before you were mine   E
(il) Meyers, S. Kittens! Kittens! Kittens!   E
(il) Parenteau, S. Bears on chairs   E
(il) Paul, A. W. If animals kissed good night--   E
(il) Root, P. Flip, flap, fly!   E

Walker, Jane, 1956-
(jt. auth) Steele, P. Scholastic atlas of the world   912

Walker, Kate, 1950-
I hate books!   Fic

Walker, Lester
Carpentry for children   694

Walker, Madame C. J. *See* Walker, C. J., Madame, 1867-1919

Walker, Niki, 1972-
Generating wind power   621.4
Hydrogen   665

Walker, Pamela, 1958-
Science experiments on file   507.8

Walker, Paul Robert
Remember Little Bighorn   973.8
Remember Little Rock   379
Remember the Alamo   976.4

Walker, Richard, 1951-
Body   611
Dr. Frankenstein's human body book   612
Epidemics & plagues   614.4
Genes & DNA   576.5
How the incredible human body works—by the Brainwaves   612
Human body   612
Microscopic life   579
Ouch!   612
Animal life   590

Walker, Rob D.
Mama says   E

Walker, Sally M.
Druscilla's Halloween   E
Fireflies   595.7
Fossil fish found alive   597
Rays   597
The Vowel family   E

Walker, Sarah Breedlove See Walker, C. J., Madame, 1867-1919

Walking

Fiction
Cooper, E. A good night walk   **E**
Frazee, M. Walk on!   **E**
Johnson, D. B. Henry hikes to Fitchburg   **E**

Walking catfish. Gray, S. H.   **597**

Walking Coyote

About
Bruchac, J. Buffalo song [biography of Walking Coyote]   **92**

Walking the Bible. Feiler, B. S.   **222**

Walking the earth. Andryszewski, T.   **304.8**

Walking to school. Bunting, E.   **E**

Walking to the bus-rider blues. Robinet, H. G.   **Fic**

The **Wall**. Bunting, E.   **E**

The **wall**. Sís, P.   **92**

The **Wall** and the Wing. Ruby, L.   **Fic**

Wall painting See Mural painting and decoration

Wall paintings. Harris, N.   **751.7**

Wallace, Bill, 1947-
The legend of thunderfoot   **Fic**
Skinny-dipping at Monster Lake   **Fic**

Wallace, Carol
One nosy pup   **E**
The Santa secret   **E**
Turkeys together   **E**

Wallace, Chad
(il) Guiberson, B. Z. Earth feeling the heat   **363.7**

Wallace, Daisy See Cuyler, Margery

Wallace, John, 1966-
(il) Bauer, M. D. The Statue of Liberty   **974.7**
(il) Bauer, M. D. Wind   **551.51**

Wallace, Karen
Think of an eel   **597**

Wallace, Marianne D.
America's forests   **578.7**

Wallace, Mary, 1950-
Inuksuk journey   **971.9**

Wallace, Nancy Elizabeth
Look! look! look!   **E**
Pumpkin day!   **E**
Recycle every day!   **E**
Seeds! Seeds! Seeds!   **E**

Walliams, David, 1971-
The boy in the dress   **Fic**

Wallner, Alexandra, 1946-
Abigail Adams   **92**
Grandma Moses   **92**
Lucy Maud Montgomery   **92**
(il) Adler, D. A. A picture book of Louis Braille   **92**
(il) Adler, D. A. A picture book of Thomas Jefferson   **92**
(il) The Farmer in the dell. See The Farmer in the dell   **782.42**

Wallner, John C.
(il) Adler, D. A. A picture book of Louis Braille   **92**
(il) Adler, D. A. A picture book of Thomas Jefferson   **92**
(il) O'Neill, M. L. D. Hailstones and halibut bones   **811**

Walls
Knight, M. B. Talking walls   **909**

The **walls** of Cartagena. Durango, J.   **Fic**

Wally and Mae. Kempter, C.   **E**

Walrod, Amy
(il) Howe, J. Horace and Morris but mostly Dolores   **E**
(il) Sturges, P. The Little Red Hen (makes a pizza)   **398.2**

Walruses
Malam, J. Pinnipeds   **599.79**

Walsh, Danny
The cardboard box book   **745.54**

Walsh, Ellen Stoll, 1942-
Dot & Jabber and the big bug mystery   **E**
For Pete's sake   **E**
Mouse shapes   **E**

Walsh, Jake
(jt. auth) Walsh, D. The cardboard box book   **745.54**

Walsh, Melanie
10 things I can do to help my world   **333.72**

Walsh, Niall
(jt. auth) Walsh, D. The cardboard box book   **745.54**

Walsh, Patricia, 1951-
(jt. auth) Fridell, R. Life cycle of a pumpkin   **635**

Walsh, Rebecca
(il) Ehrlich, A. The girl who wanted to dance   **E**

Walsh, Tina Cash- See Cash-Walsh, Tina, 1960-

Walsh, Vivian
(il) Seibold, J. O. Olive the other reindeer   **E**

Walsingham, Sir Francis, 1530?-1590
Fiction
Brittney, L. Dangerous times   **Fic**

Walske, Christine Zuchora- See Zuchora-Walske, Christine

Walt Disney Productions
Peet, B. Bill Peet: an autobiography   **92**

Walter, Mildred Pitts, 1922-
Alec's primer   **E**
Justin and the best biscuits in the world   **Fic**

Walter, Virginia A.
Children and libraries   **027.62**
Twenty-first-century kids, twenty-first-century librarians   **027.62**
War & peace   **016.3**

Walter was worried. Seeger, L. V.   **E**

Walter Wick's optical tricks. Wick, W.   **152.14**

Walters, Catherine, 1965-
Time to sleep, Alfie Bear   **E**

Walters, Tara, 1973-
Brazil   981

Walters, Virginia
Are we there yet, Daddy?   E

Wampanoag Indians
Grace, C. O. 1621   394.26
Peters, R. M. Clambake   970.004

Wan Guofang
TV takeover   384.55
Virtually true   025.04

Wanasundera, Nanda P., 1932-
Sri Lanka   954.93

Wanda's monster. Spinelli, E.   E

The **Wanderer**. Creech, S.   Fic

Wang, Lin, 1973-
(il) Cummings, M. Three names of me   Fic
(il) Yoo, P. Shining star: the Anna May Wong story   92

Wang, Su-ling See Wang Suling

Wang Ping, 1957-
The dragon emperor   398.2

Wang Suling
(jt. auth) Bauer, M. D. The blue ghost   Fic
(il) Yep, L. The magic paintbrush   Fic
(il) Yep, L. When the circus came to town   Fic

Wang Xiaohong, 1966-
One year in Beijing   E

Wangari's trees of peace [biography of Wangari Maathai] Winter, J.   92

Waniek, Marilyn Nelson See Nelson, Marilyn, 1946-

War
Sullivan, G. Journalists at risk   070.4
Bibliography
Crew, H. S. Women engaged in war in literature for youth   016.3
Walter, V. A. War & peace   016.3
Fiction
See War stories

War & peace. Walter, V. A.   016.3

War and children See Children and war

War and the pity of war   808.81

War comes to Willy Freeman. Collier, J. L.   Fic

War games. Couloumbis, A.   Fic

War horse. Morpurgo, M.   Fic

War in art
Chapman, C. Battles & weapons: exploring history through art   355

War of 1812
Brown, D. Dolley Madison saves George Washington   92
Childress, D. The War of 1812   973.5
Edelman, R. The War of 1812   973.5
Fiction
Krensky, S. Sisters of Scituate Light   E
Lunn, J. L. S. Laura Secord: a story of courage   Fic
Sanchez, A. The invasion of Sandy Bay   Fic

War of the worlds (Radio program)
McCarthy, M. Aliens are coming!   791.44

War on terrorism
Fradin, D. B. September 11, 2001   973.931

War poetry
America at war   811.008
Greenfield, E. When the horses ride by   811
Johnston, T. Voice from afar   811
Walker, A. Why war is never a good idea   811
War and the pity of war   808.81

War stories
Aguiar, N. The lost island of Tamarind   Fic
Cali, D. The enemy   E
Hardy, J. The shifter   Fic
Hof, M. Against the odds   Fic
McPhail, D. M. No!   E
Pratchett, T. Only you can save mankind   Fic
Williams, M. Brothers in hope   Fic
Wolf-Morgenlander, K. Ragtag   Fic

Warburton, Tom
1000 times no   E

Ward, April
(il) Fletcher, R. A writing kind of day   811
(il) Garza, X. Juan and the Chupacabras   E
(il) Zepeda, G. Growing up with tamales = Los Tamales de Ana   E

Ward, David J. (David John)
Exploring Mars   523.4
Materials science   620.1

Ward, Elaine M.
Old Testament women   221.9

Ward, Helen, 1962-
The hare and the tortoise   398.2
The rooster and the fox   E
Unwitting wisdom   398.2

Ward, Jennifer, 1963-
The busy tree   E

Ward, John
(il) Sanfield, S. The adventures of High John the Conqueror   398.2

Ward, Keith
(il) Farley, W. The Black Stallion   Fic

Ward, Lynd Kendall, 1905-1985
The biggest bear   E
(il) Coatsworth, E. J. The cat who went to heaven   Fic
(il) Swift, H. H. The little red lighthouse and the great gray bridge   E
(il) Wyss, J. D. The Swiss family Robinson   Fic

Ward, Patricia Layzell
(jt. auth) Evans, G. E. Leadership basics for librarians and information professionals   303.3

Wargin, Kathy-Jo, 1965-
The frog prince   398.2
Moose on the loose   E

Warhol, Andy, 1928?-1987
About
Rubin, S. G. Andy Warhol   92
Warhola, J. Uncle Andy's   E

Warhola, James
Uncle Andy's   E

Watson, Wendy
(il) Hesse, K. The cats in Krasinski Square
E
(il) Hesse, K. Spuds **E**
(il) Showers, P. Sleep is for everyone **612.8**
The **Watsons** go to Birmingham—1963. Curtis, C.
P. **Fic**
Watt, Melanie, 1975-
Chester **E**
Have I got a book for you! **E**
Scaredy Squirrel **E**
Wattenberg, Jane
(il) Lear, E. Edward Lear's The duck & the
kangaroo **821**
Watters, Debbie, 1961-
Where's Mom's hair? **616.99**
Watters, Emmett
(jt. auth) Watters, D. Where's Mom's hair?
616.99
Watters, Haydn
(jt. auth) Watters, D. Where's Mom's hair?
616.99
Watts, Bernadette, 1942-
The Smallest Snowflake **E**
The ugly duckling **E**
(il) Grimm, J. Little Red Riding Hood
398.2
Watts, Claire
The most explosive science book in the universe
500
Watts, Frances
Extraordinary Ernie and Marvelous Maud
Fic
Watts, James, 1955-
(il) Curry, J. L. Hold up the sky: and other Na-
tive American tales from Texas and the
Southern Plains **398.2**
Watts, Murray
The Bible for children from Good Books
220.9
Watts library [series]
Kent, D. Animal helpers for the disabled
636.088
Nardo, D. Roman amphitheaters **725**
Nelson, S. P. Jedediah Smith **92**
Newman, S. P. Child slavery in modern times
326
Orr, T. The Maya **972**
Schlaepfer, G. G. The Louisiana Purchase
973.4
Sherman, J. The history of the personal comput-
er **004**
Sonneborn, L. The Mormon Trail **978**
Souza, D. M. Freaky flowers **582.13**
Souza, D. M. Plant invaders **581.6**
Trueit, T. S. Rocks, gems, and minerals **552**
Watts reference [series]
The encyclopedia of U.S. presidential elections
324
Wave. Lee, S. **E**
Waves
Tagliaferro, L. How does an earthquake become
a tsunami? **551.46**

Wax, Wendy, 1963-
City witch, country switch **E**
Waxman, Laura Hamilton
Colin Powell **92**
Let's look at snails **594**
Way, Steve
(jt. auth) Bailey, G. Body and health **612**
The **way** a door closes. Smith, H. A. **Fic**
The **way** back home. Jeffers, O. **E**
Way Down Deep. White, R. **Fic**
The **way** I love you. Bedford, D. **E**
The **way** meat loves salt. Jaffe, N. **398.2**
The **way** of the storyteller. Sawyer, R. **372.6**
The **way** things work. See Macaulay, D. The new
way things work **600**
Way up and over everything. McGill, A.
398.2
Wayland, April Halprin, 1954-
New Year at the pier **E**
Ways to live forever. Nicholls, S. **Fic**
Wayside School gets a little stranger. Sachar, L.
Fic
We are all Americans. Masoff, J. **325.73**
We are all born free **323**
We are best friends. Aliki **E**
We are one: the story of Bayard Rustin. Brimner,
L. D. **92**
We are still here [series]
King, S. Shannon: an Ojibway dancer
970.004
Peters, R. M. Clambake **970.004**
Roessel, M. Songs from the loom **970.004**
We are the many. Rappaport, D. **920**
We are the ship. Nelson, K. **796.357**
We belong together. Parr, T. **362.7**
We both read [series]
McKay, S. Animals under our feet **590**
We can work it out. Polland, B. K. **303.6**
We can't all be rattlesnakes. Jennings, P. **Fic**
We dare you!. Cobb, V. **507.8**
We feel good out here. Andre, J.-A. **970.004**
We gather together. Pfeffer, W. **394.26**
We go together!. Dunn, T. **E**
We had a picnic this Sunday past. Woodson, J.
E
We rode the orphan trains. Warren, A. **362.7**
We shall overcome. Stotts, S. **782.42**
We the children. Clements, A. **Fic**
We the people [series]
Englar, M. Dutch colonies in America **974.7**
Englar, M. French colonies in America
970.01
Fishkin, R. L. English colonies in America
973.2
Heinrichs, A. The Underground Railroad
326
Lilly, A. Spanish colonies in America
970.01
Santella, A. The Korean War **951.9**
We three kings. Spirin, G. **782.28**

Whales—*Continued*
Fiction
Edgemon, D. Seamore, the very forgetful porpoise **E**
Fox, F. G. Jean Laffite and the big ol' whale **E**
LaMarche, J. Up **E**
London, J. Baby whale's journey **E**
Pinkney, A. D. Peggony-Po **E**
Schuch, S. A symphony of whales **E**
Segal, J. Alistair and Kip's great adventure **E**

Songs
Raffi. Baby Beluga **782.42**

Whales on stilts. Anderson, M. T. **Fic**

Whaling
Foster, M. Whale port **639.2**
Lourie, P. Arctic thaw **998**
McKissack, P. C. Black hands, white sails **639.2**
Sandler, M. W. Trapped in ice! **639.2**
Fiction
Frederick, H. V. The voyage of Patience Goodspeed **Fic**
Pinkney, A. D. Peggony-Po **E**

Whaling season. Lourie, P. **599.5**

Whalley, Paul Ernest Sutton
Butterfly & moth **595.7**

Wharton, Thomas, 1963-
The shadow of Malabron **Fic**
What!. See Lum, K. What! cried Granny **E**
What a beast!. Kelly, S. **398**
What a day it was at school!. Prelutsky, J. **811**
What a good big brother!. Landolf, D. W. **E**
What a great idea!. Tomecek, S. **609**
What a year!. De Paola, T. **92**
What about me? Young, E. **398.2**
What are citizens' basic rights? Thomas, W. D. **323**
What are forces and motion? Spilsbury, R. **531**
What are germs? Ollhoff, J. **616**
What are solids, liquids, and gases? Spilsbury, R. **530.4**
What baby needs. Sears, W. **649**
What can we do about global warming? Metz, L. **363.7**
What can we do about invasive species? Metz, L. **578.6**
What can we do about the energy crisis? Slade, S. **333.79**
What can we do about trash and recycling? Metz, L. **363.7**
What can you do with a rebozo? Tafolla, C. **E**
What can you do with an old red shoe? Alter, A. **745.5**
What Charlie heard [biography of Charles Edward Ives] Gerstein, M. **92**
What! cried Granny. Lum, K. **E**

What dads can't do. Wood, D. **E**
What Darwin saw. Schanzer, R. **92**
What did one elephant say to the other. Baines, R. **591.59**
What did you do today? Forward, T. **E**
What do astronauts do. Bredeson, C. **629.45**
What do authors do? Christelow, E. **808**
What do children and young adults read next? **016.8**
What do children read next? See What do children and young adults read next? **016.8**
What do fish have to do with anything? and other stories. Avi **S C**
What do I know about? [series]
Moore-Mallinos, J. I have asthma **616.2**
What do you do, dear? Joslin, S. **395**
What do you do when something wants to eat you? Jenkins, S. **591.47**
What do you do with a tail like this? Jenkins, S. **573.8**
What do you hear when cows sing? Maestro, M. **793.73**
What do you say, dear? Joslin, S. **395**
What do you want? Klinting, L. **E**
What do young adults read next? See What do children and young adults read next? **016.8**
What does peace feel like? Radunsky, V. **E**
What every girl (except me) knows. Baskin, N. R. **Fic**
What happens to a hamburger? Showers, P. **612.3**
What I call life. Wolfson, J. **Fic**
What if? Seeger, L. V. **E**
What if we do nothing? [series]
Ballard, C. AIDS and other epidemics **614.5**
Morris, N. Global warming **363.7**
Sheehan, S. Endangered species **333.95**
What if you met a knight? Adkins, J. **940.1**
What is a constitution? Thomas, W. D. **342**
What is a gas? Boothroyd, J. **530.4**
What is a liquid? Boothroyd, J. **530.4**
What is a solid? Boothroyd, J. **530.4**
What is art? [series]
Hosack, K. Buildings **720**
What is color? Benduhn, T. **701**
What is electricity and magnetism? Spilsbury, R. **537**
What is energy? Spilsbury, R. **621**
What is form? Meredith, S. **701**
What is goodbye? Grimes, N. **811**
What is hearing? Boothroyd, J. **612.8**
What is light? Spilsbury, R. **535**
What is line? Meredith, S. **701**
What is science? Dotlich, R. K. **500**
What is sculpture? Spilsbury, L. **731.4**
What is shape? Benduhn, T. **701**
What is sight? Boothroyd, J. **612.8**
What is smell? Boothroyd, J. **612.8**

When the horses ride by. Greenfield, E.　　811
When the lights go out. MacDonald, M. R.
　　372.6
When the wind stops. Zolotow, C.　　E
When the wolves returned. Patent, D. H.
　　599.77
When the world is ready for bed. Shields, G.
　　E
When we were very young. Milne, A. A.　　821
When winter comes. Van Laan, N.　　E
When you are happy. Spinelli, E.　　E
When you go to kindergarten. Howe, J.　　372.2
When you meet a bear on Broadway. Hest, A.
　　E
When you reach me. Stead, R.　　Fic
When you were inside Mommy. Cole, J.
　　612.6
When Zachary Beaver came to town. Holt, K. W.
　　Fic
Where are the night animals? Fraser, M. A.
　　591.5
Where are you going? To see my friend!. Carle,
　　E.　　E
Where did you fall from? See Weave little stars
　　into my sleep　　782.42
Where do chicks come from? Sklansky, A. E.
　　636.5
Where do I sleep? Blomgren, J.　　E
Where do polar bears live? Thomson, S. L.
　　599.78
Where do you think you're going, Christopher
　　Columbus? Fritz, J.　　92
Where does food come from? Rotner, S.　　664
Where does pepper come from? Raab, B.　　E
Where else in the wild? Schwartz, D. M.
　　591.4
Where have you been? Brown, M. W.　　E
Where horses run free. Cowley, J.　　E
Where I live. Spinelli, E.　　Fic
Where I'd like to be. Dowell, F. O.　　Fic
Where in the wild? Schwartz, D. M.　　591.4
Where in the world? Raczka, B.　　709
Where is Catkin? Lord, J.　　E
Where is home, Little Pip? Wilson, K.　　E
Where is the green sheep? Fox, M.　　E
Where once there was a wood. Fleming, D.
　　639.9
Where teddy bears come from. Burgess, M.　　E
Where the bald eagles gather. See Patent, D. H.
　　The bald eagle returns　　598
Where the buffaloes begin. Baker, O.　　Fic
Where the forest meets the sea. Baker, J.　　E
Where the giant sleeps. Fox, M.　　E
Where the great hawk flies. Ketchum, L.　　Fic
Where the lillies bloom. Cleaver, V.　　Fic
Where the mountain meets the moon. Lin, G.
　　Fic
Where the red fern grows. Rawls, W.　　Fic

Where the sidewalk ends. Silverstein, S.　　811
Where the steps were. Cheng, A.　　Fic
Where the sunrise begins. Wood, D.　　E
Where the wild things are. Sendak, M.　　E
Where was Patrick Henry on the 29th of May?
　　Fritz, J.　　92
Where Washington walked. Bial, R.　　92
Where's Mom's hair? Watters, D.　　616.99
Where's my mom? Donaldson, J.　　E
Where's my sweetie pie? Emberley, E.　　E
Where's my teddy? Alborough, J.　　E
Where's Pup? Dodds, D. A.　　E
Where's the science here? [series]
　　Cobb, V. Fireworks　　662
　　Cobb, V. Junk food　　664
　　Cobb, V. Sneakers　　685
Where's Tumpty? Dunbar, P.　　E
Which shoes would you choose? Rosenthal, B. R.
　　E
Which way to the wild West? Sheinkin, S.
　　978

Whidah (Ship)
　　Clifford, B. Real pirates　　910.4
A whiff of pine, a hint of skunk. Ruddell, D.
　　811
While the world is sleeping. Edwards, P. D.　　E
While we were out. Lee, H. B.　　E
The whingdingdilly. Peet, B.　　E
The whipping boy. Fleischman, S.　　Fic
Whipple, Catherine
　　(il) King, S. Shannon: an Ojibway dancer
　　970.004
Whipple, Laura
　　If the shoe fits　　811
　　(comp) Eric Carle's animals, animals. See Eric
　　Carle's animals, animals　　808.81
　　(comp) Eric Carle's dragons dragons and other
　　creatures that never were. See Eric Carle's
　　dragons dragons and other creatures that nev-
　　er were　　808.81
Whirligigs
　　Schwarz, R. Wind chimes and whirligigs
　　745.592
Whisper in the dark. Bruchac, J.　　Fic
The whistle on the train. McNamara, M.　　E
Whitaker, Suzanne
　　The daring Miss Quimby [biography of Harriet
　　Quimby]　　92
Whitaker, Zai, 1954-
　　Kali and the rat snake　　E
The Whitby witches. Jarvis, R.　　Fic
Whitcraft, James E.
　　(il) Farlow, J. O. Bringing dinosaur bones to life
　　567.9
White, E. B. (Elwyn Brooks), 1899-1985
　　Charlotte's web　　Fic
　　Stuart Little　　Fic
　　The trumpet of the swan　　Fic
　　See/See also pages in the following book(s):
　　Krull, K. Lives of the writers　　920

White, Elwyn Brooks *See* White, E. B. (Elwyn Brooks), 1899-1985

White, Lee, 1970-
  (il) Nedwidek, J. Ducks don't wear socks   E
  (il) Odanaka, B. Crazy day at the Critter Cafe   E
  (il) Walker, S. M. Druscilla's Halloween   E

White, Linda
  I could do that! [biography of Esther Hobart Morris]   92

White, Maureen
  (jt. auth) Latrobe, K. H. The children's literature dictionary   028.5

White, Nancy, 1942-
  Using Earth's underground heat   333.8

White, Ruth
  Belle Prater's boy   Fic
  Little Audrey   Fic
  Way Down Deep   Fic

White, T. H. (Terence Hanbury), 1906-1964
  The sword in the stone   Fic

White, Terence Hanbury *See* White, T. H. (Terence Hanbury), 1906-1964

White, Vicky
  (il) Jenkins, M. Ape   599.8

The **white** elephant. Fleischman, S.   Fic

The **White** Gates. Ramthun, B.   Fic

The **white** giraffe. St. John, L.   Fic

White House (Washington, D.C.)
  Grace, C. O. The White House   975.3
  Our White House   975.3
  Rinaldo, D. White House Q & A   975.3

White House Q & A. Rinaldo, D.   975.3

White is for blueberry. Shannon, G.   E

The **White** Mountains. Christopher, J.   Fic

The **white** nights of Ramadan. Addasi, M.   E

White noise. Carter, D. A.   E

White on black. Hoban, T.   E

White owl, barn owl. Davies, N.   E

The **white** ox. Hailstone, R.   92

The **white** ram. Gerstein, M.   E

White snow, bright snow. Tresselt, A. R.   E

The **white** stag. Seredy, K.   Fic

White-tailed deer. Patent, D. H.   599.65

White tiger, blue serpent. Tseng, G.   398.2

Whiteblack the penguin sees the world. Rey, M.   E

Whitehead, Jenny
  Holiday stew   811
  (il) Bruno, E. K. A punctuation celebration!   428

Whitehead, Kathy, 1957-
  Art from her heart: folk artist Clementine Hunter   92

Whitehead, Sarah
  How to speak cat   636.8
  How to speak dog   636.7

Whitehouse, Patricia, 1958-
  Plants   580.7

Whiteman, Dorit Bader
  Lonek's journey   940.53

Whitfield, Simon, 1975-
  Simon says gold: Simon Whitfield's pursuit of athletic excellence   92

Whitfield, Susan
  Afghanistan   958.1

Whitford, Rebecca
  Little yoga   613.7

Whiting, Jim
  W.E.B. Du Bois   92

  Frogs in danger   597.8
  Threat to ancient Egyptian treasures   932
  (jt. auth) LeVert, S. Steroids   362.29

Whiting, Sue
  The firefighters   E

Whitman, Candace, 1958-
  Lines that wiggle   E

Whitman, Narcissa Prentiss, 1808-1847
About
  Harness, C. The tragic tale of Narcissa Whitman and a faithful history of the Oregon Trail   92

Whitman, Sylvia, 1961-
  Under the Ramadan moon   297.3

Whitman, Walt, 1819-1892
  When I heard the learn'd astronomer   E
About
  Kerley, B. Walt Whitman   92

Whittenberg, Allison
  Sweet Thang   Fic

Whittington, Richard, d. 1423
Legends
  Hodges, M. Dick Whittington and his cat   398.2

Whittington. Armstrong, A.   Fic

Whittling *See* Wood carving

Who ate all the cookie dough? Beaumont, K.   E

Who discovered America? Wyatt, V.   970.01

Who eats what? Lauber, P.   577

Who is baseball's greatest pitcher? Kisseloff, J.   796.357

Who is driving? Timmers, L.   E

Who likes rain? Yee, W. H.   E

Who likes the rain? Kaner, E.   551.57

Who likes the snow? Kaner, E.   551.57

Who likes the wind? Kaner, E.   551.51

Who lives here? [series]
  Hodge, D. Desert animals   591.7
  Hodge, D. Forest animals   591.7
  Hodge, D. Polar animals   591.7
  Hodge, D. Rain forest animals   591.7
  Hodge, D. Savanna animals   591.7
  Hodge, D. Wetland animals   591.7

Who lives in an alligator hole? Rockwell, A. F.   597.98

Who loves the fall? Raczka, B.   E

Who loves the little lamb? Evans, L.   E

Who made this cake? Nakagawa, C.   E

Who on earth is Dian Fossey? Kushner, J. M.   92

Who on earth is Rachel Carson? Scherer, G. **92**

Who on earth is Sylvia Earle? Reichard, S. E. **92**

Who stole Halloween? Freeman, M. **Fic**

Who took the farmer's [hat]? Lexau, J. M. **E**

Who wants a cheap rhinoceros? Silverstein, S. **E**

Who wants to be a poodle I don't. Child, L. **E**

Who was the woman who wore the hat? Patz, N. **811**

Who will I be, Lord? Nelson, V. M. **E**

Who will plant a tree? Pallotta, J. **582.16**

Who would like a Christmas tree? Obed, E. B. **E**

Who wrote that? [series]
  Abrams, D. Gary Soto **92**

The **whole** digital library handbook **025.1**

A **whole** nother story. Soup, C. **Fic**

The **Whole** school library handbook **027.8**

Whoo goes there? Ericsson, J. A. **E**

Whooo's that? Winters, K. **E**

Whooo's there? Serfozo, M. **E**

Whooping cranes *See* Cranes (Birds)

Whooping cranes. Stearns, P. M. **598**

Whoops-a-daisy world [series]
  Lloyd, S. Doctor Meow's big emergency **E**

Whoosh went the wind!. Derby, S. **E**

Whopper cake. Wilson, K. **E**

Who's afraid of the dark? Bonsall, C. N. **E**

Who's at the seashore? Himmelman, J. **591.7**

Who's awake in springtime? Gershator, P. **E**

Who's been here? Hodgkins, F. **E**

Who's hiding? Onishi, S. **E**

Who's in Rabbit's house? Aardema, V. **398.2**

Who's that knocking on Christmas Eve. Brett, J. **398.2**

Who's that stepping on Plymouth Rock? Fritz, J. **974.4**

Whose chick are you? Tafuri, N. **E**

Whose mouse are you? Kraus, R. **E**

Whose nest is this? Roemer, H. B. **591.56**

Whose shoes? Swinburne, S. R. **E**

Why are people terrorists? Woolf, A. **303.6**

Why are the ice caps melting? Rockwell, A. F. **363.7**

Why are you picking on me? Burstein, J. **302.3**

Why did the chicken cross the road? **E**

Why did the chicken cross the road? and other riddles, old and new. Cole, J. **793.73**

Why do birds sing? Holub, J. **598**

Why do cats have whiskers? MacLeod, E. **636.8**

Why do cats meow? Holub, J. **636.8**

Why do dogs bark? Holub, J. **636.7**

Why do dogs have wet noses? Coren, S. **636.7**

Why do horses have manes? MacLeod, E. **636.1**

Why do horses neigh? Holub, J. **636.1**

Why do I brush my teeth? Royston, A. **617.6**

Why do I run? Royston, A. **613.7**

Why do I sleep? Royston, A. **612.8**

Why do I wash my hands? Royston, A. **613**

Why do leaves change color? Maestro, B. **582.16**

Why do rabbits hop? Holub, J. **636.9**

Why do snakes hiss? Holub, J. **597.96**

Why do we see rainbows? Stewart, M. **612.8**

Why does the coqui sing? Polikoff, B. G. **Fic**

Why does the moon change shape? Stewart, M. **523.3**

Why don't haircuts hurt? Berger, M. **612**

Why don't you get a horse, Sam Adams? Fritz, J. **92**

Why I cough, sneeze, shiver, hiccup & yawn. See Berger, M. Why I sneeze, shiver, hiccup, and yawn **612.7**

Why I sneeze, shiver, hiccup, and yawn. Berger, M. **612.7**

Why is snot green. Murphy, G. **500**

Why mosquitoes buzz in people's ears. Aardema, V. **398.2**

Why not, Lafayette? Fritz, J. **92**

Why pi. Ball, J. **530.8**

Why the chicken crossed the road. Macaulay, D. **E**

Why the sky is far away. Gerson, M.-J. **398.2**

Why the Sun and the Moon live in the sky. Dayrell, E. **398.2**

Why war is never a good idea. Walker, A. **811**

Whybrow, Ian
  The noisy way to bed **E**

Whydah (Ship) *See* Whidah (Ship)

Wiacek, Bob
  (il) Tocci, S. More simple science fair projects, grades 3-5 **507.8**

Wick, Walter, 1953-
  Can you see what I see? **793.73**
  A drop of water **553.7**
  I spy **793.73**
  Walter Wick's optical tricks **152.14**

Wickberg, Susan
  Hey Mr. Choo-Choo, where are you going? **E**

The **wicked** big toddlah. Hawkes, K. **E**

Wicked Jack. Wooldridge, C. N. **398.2**

Wicked Will. MacDonald, B. **Fic**

Wickenheiser, Hayley, 1978-
  About
  Etue, E. Hayley Wickenheiser **92**

Wickstrom, Sylvie *See* Kantorovitz, Sylvie

Wickstrom, Thor
  (il) Plourde, L. Field trip day **E**

Wilkin, Binnie Tate, 1933-
African and African American images in Newbery Award winning titles **810.9**

Wilkins, Mary Huiskamp Calhoun *See* Calhoun, Mary, 1926-

Wilkinson, Brenda Scott, 1946-
African American women writers **810.9**

Wilkinson, Philip, 1955-
Gandhi **92**
Joan of Arc **92**
The Kingfisher student atlas **912**
Michelangelo **92**

Wilkinson, Steve
(jt. auth) Knudson, M. Raymond and Graham rule the school **Fic**

Will I have a friend? Cohen, M. **E**

Will Moses Mother Goose **398.8**

Will Rogers: an American legend. Keating, F. **92**

Will Sheila share? Savadier, E. **E**

Will you read to me? Cazet, D. **E**

Will you sign here, John Hancock? Fritz, J. **92**

Will you still love me? Roth, C. **E**

Willans, Tom
Wait! I want to tell you a story **E**

Willard, Nancy, 1936-
A visit to William Blake's inn **811**

Willems, Mo
Big Frog can't fit in **E**
Cat the Cat, who is that? **E**
City Dog, Country Frog **E**
Don't let the pigeon drive the bus! **E**
Edwina, the dinosaur who didn't know she was extinct **E**
Knuffle Bunny **E**
Leonardo, the terrible monster **E**
Naked Mole Rat gets dressed **E**
Today I will fly! **E**

Willett, Mindy, 1968-
(jt. auth) Andre, J.-A. We feel good out here **970.004**
(jt. auth) McLeod, T. The Delta is my home **970.004**
(jt. auth) Zoe, T. Living stories **970.004**

Willey, Margaret
Clever Beatrice **398.2**
The 3 bears and Goldilocks **398.2**

William, Kate *See* Armstrong, Jennifer, 1961-

William S. and the great escape. Snyder, Z. K. **Fic**

William Shakespeare & the Globe. Aliki **822.3**

William Shakespeare's A midsummer night's dream. Coville, B. **822.3**

William Shakespeare's Macbeth. Coville, B. **822.3**

William Shakespeare's Romeo and Juliet. Coville, B. **822.3**

William Shakespeare's Twelfth night. Coville, B. **822.3**

Williams, Amanda, 1953-
(jt. auth) Cerny, R. Outstanding library service to children **027.62**

Williams, Anthony, 1964-
(il) Hama, L. The battle of Iwo Jima **940.54**

Williams, Barbara
Albert's impossible toothache **E**
World War II, Pacific **940.54**

Williams, Berkeley
(il) Grandfather tales. See Grandfather tales **398.2**
(il) Chase, R. The Jack tales **398.2**

Williams, Brenda, 1946-
Lin Yi's lantern **E**

Williams, Brian, 1943-
Canada **971**

Williams, Carla, 1965-
The Underground Railroad **973.7**

Williams, Dar
Amalee **Fic**

Williams, David *See* Walliams, David, 1971-

Williams, Garth, 1912-1996
(il) Carlson, N. S. The family under the bridge **Fic**
(il) Hoban, R. Bedtime for Frances **E**
(il) Prelutsky, J. Ride a purple pelican **811**
(il) Selden, G. The cricket in Times Square **Fic**
(il) Walker, B. M. The Little House cookbook **641.5**
(il) White, E. B. Charlotte's web **Fic**
(il) White, E. B. Stuart Little **Fic**
(il) Wilder, L. I. Little house in the big woods **Fic**

Williams, J. W., 1929-
About
Barbour, K. Mr. Williams **92**

Williams, Jennifer
(il) Williams, V. B. Stringbean's trip to the shining sea **E**

Williams, Jennifer, 1971-
Oobleck, slime, & dancing spaghetti **507.8**

Williams, Judith
The discovery and mystery of a dinosaur named Jane **567.9**

Williams, Karen Lynn
A beach tail **E**
Four feet, two sandals **E**
Galimoto **E**
My name is Sangoel **E**
Painted dreams **E**

Williams, Laura E.
The Can Man **E**
Slant **Fic**

Williams, Linda
The little old lady who was not afraid of anything **E**

Williams, Lindsey, 1987-
About
Houle, M. E. Lindsey Williams **92**

Wilsdorf, Anne
  (il) Bluemle, E. Dogs on the bed   **E**
  (il) Fleming, C. Sunny Boy!   **E**
  (il) Loizeaux, W. Clarence Cochran, a human
    boy   **Fic**
  (il) Look, L. Ruby Lu, brave and true   **Fic**
  (jt. auth) Skeers, L. Tutus aren't my style   **E**
  (il) Spinelli, E. The best story   **E**

Wilson, Alex
  (il) Hill, D. Witches & magic-makers   **133.4**
  (il) Platt, R. Shipwreck   **910.4**

Wilson, Anne, 1974-
  (il) Blackstone, S. Storytime   **398.2**
  (il) Casey, D. The great race   **398.2**
  (il) Casey, D. The Barefoot book of Earth tales
    398.2

Wilson, Diane
        About
  Bang, M. Nobody particular   **363.7**

Wilson, Edwin Graves
  (ed) Angelou, M. Maya Angelou   **811**

Wilson, Hannah
  Life-size reptiles   **597.9**

Wilson, Henrike
  (jt. auth) Stohner, A. Brave Charlotte   **E**

Wilson, Jacqueline
  Best friends   **Fic**
  Candyfloss   **Fic**
  Cookie   **Fic**
  The illustrated Mum   **Fic**

Wilson, Janet, 1962-
  One peace   **305.23**
  (il) Granfield, L. Out of slavery   **264**

Wilson, Karma
  Bear snores on   **E**
  The cow loves cookies   **E**
  A frog in the bog   **E**
  How to bake an American pie   **E**
  Mama always comes home   **E**
  What's the weather inside?   **811**
  Where is home, Little Pip?   **E**
  Whopper cake   **E**

Wilson, Nancy Hope, 1947-
  Mountain pose   **Fic**

Wilson, Nathan D.
  100 cupboards   **Fic**
  Leepike Ridge   **Fic**

Wilson, Phil
  (il) Ashby, R. Pteranodon   **567.9**
  (il) Brown, C. L. After the dinosaurs   **569**
  (il) Brown, C. L. Beyond the dinosaurs   **560**
  (il) Brown, C. L. The day the dinosaurs died
    567.9

Wilson, Rosie
  (jt. auth) Bowden, R. African culture   **960**
  (jt. auth) Bowden, R. Ancient Africa   **960**
  (jt. auth) Bowden, R. Changing Africa   **960**
  (jt. auth) Bowden, R. Modern Africa   **960**

Wilson, Sarah, 1934-
  The day we danced in underpants   **E**
  Friends and pals and brothers, too   **E**

Wilson, Steve, 1972-
  (il) Whitman, C. Lines that wiggle   **E**

Wilson-Max, Ken, 1965-
  (il) Nikola-Lisa, W. Setting the turkeys free
    E
  (il) Suen, A. Red light, green light   **E**

Wimmer, Mike
  (il) Burleigh, R. Flight: the journey of Charles
    Lindbergh   **92**
  (il) Burleigh, R. Home run   **E**
  (il) Burleigh, R. One giant leap   **629.45**
  (il) Burleigh, R. Stealing home [biography of
    Jackie Robinson]   **92**
  (il) Fritz, J. Bully for you, Teddy Roosevelt!
    92
  (il) Keating, F. Theodore [biography of Theo-
    dore Roosevelt]   **92**
  (il) Keating, F. Will Rogers: an American leg-
    end   **92**
  (il) MacLachlan, P. All the places to love   **E**

Winborn, Marsha
  (il) Baker, B. Digby and Kate and the beautiful
    day   **E**
  (il) Murphy, S. J. Bigger, Better, BEST!
    516
  (il) Murphy, S. J. Probably pistachio   **519.2**

Wind chimes
  Schwarz, R. Wind chimes and whirligigs
    745.592

Wind chimes and whirligigs. Schwarz, R.
    745.592

Wind flyers. Johnson, A.   **E**

The **wind** in the willows. Grahame, K.   **Fic**

The **wind** in the willows [abridged and illustrated
  by Inga Moore] Grahame, K.   **Fic**

The **wind** in the willows [illustrated by Robert R.
  Ingpen] Grahame, K.   **Fic**

Wind power
  Benduhn, T. Wind power   **621.31**
  O'Neal, C. How to use wind power to light and
    heat your home   **621.31**
  Walker, N. Generating wind power   **621.4**

Wind tamer. Morrison, P. R.   **Fic**

Wind-wild dog. Joosse, B. M.   **E**

Windham, Sophie
  (il) French, V. Henny Penny   **398.2**

Windling, Terri, 1958-
  (ed) Troll's eye view. See Troll's eye view
    S C

Windmills
  Cartlidge, C. Home windmills   **621.4**

Window. Baker, J.   **E**

Window gardening
    See also Container gardening

Windows with birds. Ritz, K.   **E**

Winds
  Bauer, M. D. Wind   **551.51**
  Cobb, V. I face the wind   **551.51**
  Friend, S. Earth's wild winds   **551.51**
  Kaner, E. Who likes the wind?   **551.51**
  Malone, P. Close to the wind   **551.51**
        Fiction
  Asch, F. Like a windy day   **E**
  Derby, S. Whoosh went the wind!   **E**
  Ehlert, L. Leaf Man   **E**

A **wizard** from the start: the incredible boyhood & amazing inventions of Thomas Edison. Brown, D. **92**

A **wizard** in love. Levert, M. **E**

The **Wizard** of Oz. Baum, L. F. **Fic**

Wizards and witches. Kerns, A. **133.4**

Woe is I Jr. O'Conner, P. T. **428**

Wohnoutka, Mike
(il) Beil, K. M. Jack's house **E**

Wojahn, Donald
(jt. auth) Wojahn, R. H. An Australian outback food chain **577.5**
(jt. auth) Wojahn, R. H. A tundra food chain **577.5**

Wojahn, Rebecca Hogue
An Australian outback food chain **577.5**
A tundra food chain **577.5**

Wojciechowska, Maia, 1927-2002
Shadow of a bull **Fic**

Wojciechowski, Susan
The Christmas miracle of Jonathan Toomey **E**
A fine St. Patrick's day **E**

Wolcott, Dyanna
(il) Kuskin, K. I am me **E**

Wolf, Allan
Immersed in verse **808.1**

Wolf, Bernard, 1930-
Coming to America **305.8**

Wolf, Joan M., 1966-
Someone named Eva **Fic**

Wolf, Sallie, 1950-
Truck stuck **E**

Wolf brother. Paver, M. **Fic**

Wolf children *See* Wild children

Wolf island. Godkin, C. **577**

Wolf-Morgenlander, Karl
Ragtag **Fic**

Wolf pie. Seabrooke, B. **Fic**

Wolf song. Bevis, M. E. **E**

Wolf! wolf!. Rocco, J. **E**

Wolfe, Gillian
Look! Drawing the line in art **750.1**
Look! Seeing the light in art **750.1**

Wolff, Ashley, 1956-
Me baby, you baby **E**
(il) Edwards, D. The pen that Pa built **E**
(il) Raffi. Baby Beluga **782.42**
(il) Ross, M. E. Mama's milk **E**
(il) Ryder, J. Each living thing **E**
(il) Siddals, M. M. Compost stew **E**
(il) Slate, J. Miss Bindergarten celebrates the 100th day of kindergarten **E**

Wolff, Ferida, 1946-
It is the wind **E**
The story blanket **E**

Wolff, Jason, 1972-
(il) Bardhan-Quallen, S. The hog prince **E**

Wolfram, von Eschenbach, 12th cent.
Parzival; adaptation. See Paterson, K. Parzival **398.2**

The **wolf's** chicken stew. Kasza, K. **E**

Wolf's coming!. Kulka, J. **E**

Wolfsgruber, Linda, 1961-
(il) Lottridge, C. B. Stories from the life of Jesus **232.9**

Wolfsnail. Campbell, S. C. **594**

Wolfson, Jill
Home, and other big, fat lies **Fic**
What I call life **Fic**

Wolfson, Ron
(jt. auth) Hoffman, L. A. What you will see inside a synagogue **296.4**

Wolinsky, Art
Internet power research using the Big6 approach **025.04**

Wolk-Stanley, Jessica
(il) Cobb, V. How to really fool yourself **152.1**

Wolkstein, Diane
The magic orange tree, and other Haitian folktales **398.2**

Wolves
Bidner, J. Is my dog a wolf? **636.7**
Brandenburg, J. Face to face with wolves **599.77**
Cohn, S. One wolf howls **599.77**
George, J. C. The wolves are back **599.77**
Gibbons, G. Wolves **599.77**
Goldish, M. Red wolves **599.77**
Markle, S. Wolves **599.77**
Patent, D. H. When the wolves returned **599.77**
Swinburne, S. R. Once a wolf **333.95**

Fiction
Avi. The good dog **Fic**
Bauer, M. D. Runt **Fic**
Bevis, M. E. Wolf song **E**
Breen, M. E. Darkwood **Fic**
Brun-Cosme, N. Big Wolf & Little Wolf **E**
Burgess, M. Where teddy bears come from **E**
Catusanu, M. The strange case of the missing sheep **E**
Delessert, É. Big and Bad **E**
Fearnley, J. Mr. Wolf's pancakes **E**
Gaiman, N. The wolves in the walls **E**
George, J. C. Julie **Fic**
George, J. C. Julie of the wolves **Fic**
George, J. C. Nutik, the wolf pup **E**
Gravett, E. Wolves **E**
Kasza, K. The dog who cried wolf **E**
Kasza, K. The wolf's chicken stew **E**
Kimmel, E. A. The three little tamales **E**
Knight, R. J. Winter Shadow **Fic**
Kulka, J. Wolf's coming! **E**
Lasky, K. Lone wolf **Fic**
Leach, S. Jake Reynolds: chicken or eagle? **Fic**
Lester, H. The sheep in wolf's clothing **E**
Marshall, J. Swine Lake **E**
Matsuoka, M. Footprints in the snow **E**
Meddaugh, S. The best place **E**
Meddaugh, S. Hog-eye **E**
Melling, D. The Scallywags **E**
Numeroff, L. J. The Chicken sisters **E**
Palatini, M. Bad boys get henpecked! **E**

Wood, Douglas, 1951-
Miss Little's gift   E
What dads can't do   E
Where the sunrise begins   E
Wood, Elaine, 1950-
(jt. auth) Walker, P. Science experiments on file
    507.8
Wood, Maryrose
The mysterious howling   **Fic**
Wood, Michele
(il) Igus, T. I see the rhythm   **780.89**
Wood, Nancy C.
Mr. and Mrs. God in the Creation Kitchen
    E
Wood, Ted, 1965-
Iditarod dream   **798.8**
Wood
Langley, A. Wood   **620.1**
Wood carving
Fiction
Bulla, C. R. Daniel's duck   E
Dorros, A. Julio's magic   E
Hyde, H. S. Feivel's flying horses   E
Wojciechowski, S. The Christmas miracle of
    Jonathan Toomey   E
Wood lice See Woodlice
Wood thrush
Cherry, L. Flute's journey   **598**
Woodchucks See Marmots
Woodcock, Jon
(jt. auth) Woodford, C. Cool Stuff 2.0 and how
    it works   **600**
The **wooden** mile. Mould, C.   **Fic**
Woodford, Chris, 1943-
Atoms and molecules   **540**
Cool Stuff 2.0 and how it works   **600**
Electricity   **537**
Energy   **333.79**
Woodhull, Anne
(jt. auth) Rotner, S. Every season   **508.2**
Woodhull, Anne Love
(jt. auth) Rotner, S. The buzz on bees   **595.7**
Wooding, Sharon, 1943-
(il) Garden, N. Molly's family   E
Woodlice
Tokuda, Y. I'm a pill bug   **595.3**
Woodpeckers
Miller, S. S. Woodpeckers, toucans, and their
    kin   **598**
Woodpeckers, toucans, and their kin. Miller, S. S.
    598
Woodruff, Elvira
Fearless   **Fic**
The memory coat   E
The Ravenmaster's secret   **Fic**
Small beauties   E
Woods, Bob
Hottest motorcycles   **629.227**
Hottest muscle cars   **629.222**
Hottest sports cars   **629.222**
Snowboarding   **796.9**
Woods, Brenda
My name is Sally Little Song   **Fic**

The red rose box   **Fic**
Woods, Geraldine, 1948-
Science in ancient Egypt   **509**
Woods, Mary B., 1946-
(jt. auth) Woods, M. Volcanoes   **551.2**
Woods, Michael, 1943-
(il) Johnson, J. Butterfly   **595.7**
(il) Johnson, J. Duck   **598**
Woods, Michael, 1946-
Volcanoes   **551.2**
Woods, Rosemary
(il) Strauss, R. One well   **553.7**
Woods See Forests and forestry
The **woods** scientist. Swinburne, S. R.   **591.7**
Woodson, Jacqueline
Coming on home soon   E
Feathers   **Fic**
Locomotion   **Fic**
The other side   E
Peace, Locomotion   **Fic**
Show way   E
Visiting day   E
We had a picnic this Sunday past   E
Woodward, John, 1954-
Creatures of the deep   **591.7**
Dinosaurs eye to eye   **567.9**
How to be a genius   **152**
Planet Earth   **550**
Voyage: Ocean: a full-speed-ahead tour of the
    oceans   **551.46**
Woodwork
    See also Carpentry
Robertson, J. C. The kids' building workshop
    694
Schwarz, R. Birdhouses   **690**
Fiction
Giff, P. R. Eleven   **Fic**
Woody Guthrie, poet of the people. Christensen,
    B.   **92**
Woof. Weeks, S.   E
Woog, Adam, 1953-
The bionic hand   **617**
Jyotirmayee Mohapatra   **92**
Mark Zuckerberg, Facebook creator   **92**
What makes me a Jew?   **296.4**
What makes me a Quaker?   **289.6**
YouTube   **006.7**
Wool
Blaxland, W. Sweaters   **746.9**
Langley, A. Wool   **677**
Fiction
Edwards, D. The pen that Pa built   E
Schubert, L. Feeding the sheep   E
Wooldridge, Connie Nordhielm, 1950-
Wicked Jack   **398.2**
Woolf, Alex
Death and disease   **610.9**
Why are people terrorists?   **303.6**
Woolley, Catherine
    See also Thayer, Jane, 1904-
Woolls, E. Blanche
(ed) The Whole school library handbook. See
    The Whole school library handbook   **027.8**

Worms—Fiction—*Continued*
Brendler, C. Winnie Finn, worm farmer   **E**
Bruel, R. O. Bob and Otto   **E**
Cronin, D. Diary of a worm   **E**
French, V. Yucky worms   **E**
Rockwell, T. How to eat fried worms   **Fic**
Tseng, K. Ned's new home   **E**

Worry
    See also Anxiety
Crist, J. J. What to do when you're scared & worried   **158**
       Fiction
Browne, A. Silly Billy   **E**
Cuyler, M. 100th day worries   **E**
Graff, L. Umbrella summer   **Fic**
Henkes, K. Wemberly worried   **E**
Hof, M. Against the odds   **Fic**
Kasza, K. Ready for anything   **E**
Moss, M. A babysitter for Billy Bear   **E**
Stout, S. K. Fiona Finkelstein, big-time ballerina!   **Fic**
Viorst, J. Just in case   **E**
Waldron, K. Mr. Peek and the misunderstanding at the zoo   **E**

Worth, Richard, 1945-
The Harlem Renaissance   **700**
Johnny Appleseed   **92**

Worth, Valerie
All the small poems and fourteen more   **811**
Animal poems   **811**
Peacock and other poems   **811**

Worth. LaFaye, A.   **Fic**

Wortis, Avi *See* Avi, 1937-

Would I trade my parents? Numeroff, L. J.   **E**
Would you believe in 1500, platform shoes were outlawed? See Platt, R. They wore what?!   **391**

Wounded Knee: an Indian history of the American West. Ehrlich, A.   **970.004**

Wounds and injuries
    See also Brain—Wounds and injuries; Burns and scalds; Fractures; Wounds and injuries
Cobb, V. Your body battles a skinned knee   **617.1**
Landau, E. Bumps, bruises, and scrapes   **617.1**
Lew, K. Clot & scab   **617.1**
Royston, A. Cuts, bruises, and breaks   **617.1**
       Fiction
Harper, J. Uh-oh, Cleo   **Fic**
Tolan, S. S. Listen!   **Fic**

Wow! America!. Neubecker, R.   **E**
Wow! city!. Neubecker, R.   **E**
Wow! said the owl. Hopgood, T.   **E**
Wow! school!. Neubecker, R.   **E**

Wrath *See* Anger

The **wreck** of the Zephyr. Van Allsburg, C.   **E**

The **wreckers**. Lawrence, I.   **Fic**

Wrede, Patricia C., 1953-
Dealing with dragons   **Fic**

Wrestling
Ditchfield, C. Wrestling   **796.8**

       Fiction
Garza, X. Lucha libre: the Man in the Silver Mask   **Fic**
Spinelli, J. There's a girl in my hammerlock   **Fic**

The **wretched** stone. Van Allsburg, C.   **E**

Wright, Amy Bartlett
(il) Latimer, J. P. Butterflies   **595.7**
(il) Latimer, J. P. Caterpillars   **595.7**

Wright, Betty Ren
The blizzard   **E**
The dollhouse murders   **Fic**
Princess for a week   **Fic**

Wright, Blanche Fisher
(il) The real Mother Goose. See The real Mother Goose   **398.8**

Wright, Johanna
The secret circus   **E**
(il) Umansky, K. Clover Twig and the magical cottage   **Fic**

Wright, Katharine *See* Haskell, Katharine Wright, 1874-1929

Wright, Maureen, 1961-
Sleep, Big Bear, sleep!   **E**

Wright, Orville, 1871-1948
       About
Borden, L. Touching the sky   **629.13**
Carson, M. K. The Wright Brothers for kids   **629.13**
Collins, M. Airborne: a photobiography of Wilbur and Orville Wright   **92**
Dixon-Engel, T. The Wright brothers   **92**
Freedman, R. The Wright brothers: how they invented the airplane   **92**
Maurer, R. The Wright sister [biography of Katharine Wright Haskell]   **92**
Old, W. To fly: the story of the Wright brothers   **92**
O'Sullivan, R. The Wright brothers fly   **92**

Wright, Patience Lovell, 1725-1786
       About
Shea, P. D. Patience Wright   **92**

Wright, Randall
The geezer in the freezer   **E**

Wright, Richard, 1908-1960
       Fiction
Miller, W. Richard Wright and the library card   **E**

Wright, Wilbur, 1867-1912
       About
Borden, L. Touching the sky   **629.13**
Carson, M. K. The Wright Brothers for kids   **629.13**
Collins, M. Airborne: a photobiography of Wilbur and Orville Wright   **92**
Dixon-Engel, T. The Wright brothers   **92**
Freedman, R. The Wright brothers: how they invented the airplane   **92**
Maurer, R. The Wright sister [biography of Katharine Wright Haskell]   **92**
Old, W. To fly: the story of the Wright brothers   **92**
O'Sullivan, R. The Wright brothers fly   **92**
The **Wright** brothers. Dixon-Engel, T.   **92**

Yachts and yachting
See also Sailing

Yaks
Fiction
Stryer, A. S. Kami and the yaks   E

Yam: bite-size chunks. Barba, C.   741.5

Yamasaki, James
(il) Compestine, Y. C. Boy dumplings   E

Yamasaki, Katie
(il) Weston, M. Honda [biography of Soichiro Honda]   92

Yang, Belle
Foo, the flying frog of Washtub Pond   E
Hannah is my name   E

Yang the youngest and his terrible ear. Namioka, L.   Fic

The Yankee at the seder. Weber, E.   Fic

Yankee Doodle America. Minor, W.   973.3

Yankee girl. Rodman, M. A.   Fic

Yankees (Baseball team) *See* New York Yankees (Baseball team)

Yao (African people)
Fiction
Grifalconi, A. The village that vanished   E

Yard sales *See* Garage sales

Yarde, Richard, 1939-
(il) Campbell, B. M. Stompin' at the Savoy   E

Yardley, Joanna
(il) Uchida, Y. The bracelet   E

Yarrow, Peter, 1938-
Puff, the magic dragon   782.42
(comp) Favorite folk songs. See Favorite folk songs   782.42
(comp) Let's sing together. See Let's sing together   782.42
(comp) Sleepytime songs. See Sleepytime songs   782.42

Yashima, Taro *See* Iwamatsu, Atushi Jun, 1908-1994

Yassin, Rania *See* Rania, Queen, consort of Abdullah, King of Jordan, 1970-

Yates, Elizabeth, 1905-2001
Amos Fortune, free man   92

Yates, Louise
A small surprise   E

Yayo
(il) Bateman, T. Keeper of soles   E
(il) Jones, C. F. The king who barked   636

Ybáñez, Terry
(il) Tafolla, C. That's not fair! [biography of Emma Tenayuca]   92

Year
Fiction
Berner, R. S. In the town all year 'round   E
Frasier, D. A birthday cake is no ordinary cake   E

A **year** down yonder. Peck, R.   Fic
The **year** of goodbyes. Levy, D.   811
The **year** of Miss Agnes. Hill, K.   Fic
The **Year** of the Dog. Lin, G.   Fic

The **year** of the perfect Christmas tree. Houston, G.   E
Year of the tiger. Lloyd, A.   Fic
The **year** the swallows came early. Fitzmaurice, K.   Fic
The **yearling**. Rawlings, M. K.   Fic

Yee, Lisa
Bobby vs. girls (accidentally)   Fic
Millicent Min, girl genius   Fic

Yee, Paul
See/See also pages in the following book(s):
Ellis, S. From reader to writer   372.6

Yee, Wong Herbert, 1953-
Detective Small in the amazing banana caper   E
Mouse and Mole, fine feathered friends   E
Tracks in the snow   E
Upstairs Mouse, downstairs Mole   E
Who likes rain?   E
(il) Friend, C. Eddie the raccoon   E

Yeh-Shen. Louie, A.-L.   398.2

Yelchin, Eugene, 1956-
(il) Beaumont, K. Who ate all the cookie dough?   E
(il) Farooqi, M. The cobbler's holiday, or, why ants don't have shoes   E
(il) Fleming, C. Seven hungry babies   E
(il) Hodgman, A. The house of a million pets   92

Yellow fever
Murphy, J. An American plague   614.5
Fiction
Anderson, L. H. Fever, 1793   Fic

Yellow square. Carter, D. A.   E
The **yellow star. Deedy, C. A.**   Fic
Yellow star. Roy, J. R.   Fic
Yellow umbrella. Liu, J. S.   E

Yellow umbrella books for early readers [series]
Rubin, A. How many fish?   E

Yellowstone Moran. Judge, L.   92

Yellowstone National Park
George, J. C. The wolves are back   599.77
Judge, L. Yellowstone Moran   92
Patent, D. H. When the wolves returned   599.77

Yemen
Hestler, A. Yemen   953.3

Yeoman, John
The wild washerwomen   E

Yep, Kathleen S.
(jt. auth) Yep, L. The dragon's child   Fic

Yep, Laurence
Auntie Tiger   E
City of fire   Fic
The dragon's child   Fic
The lost garden   92
The magic paintbrush   Fic
Mia   Fic
The traitor   Fic
When the circus came to town   Fic

Yero, Judith Lloyd
The Mayflower Compact   974.4

Yerrill, Gail
  (il) Starry night, sleep tight. See Starry night, sleep tight   **808.81**

Yertle the turtle and other stories. Seuss, Dr.   **E**

Yes Day!. Rosenthal, A. K.   **E**

YES mag (Periodical)
  Hoaxed!   **500**

Yeshi Dorjee
  See/See also pages in the following book(s):
  Major, J. S. Caravan to America   **920**

Yesterday I had the blues. Frame, J. A.   **E**

Yezerski, Thomas
  (il) Cohen, M. Mimmy and Sophie all around the town   **Fic**
  (il) Cutler, J. Rose and Riley   **E**
  (il) Patterson, N. R. The winner's walk   **Fic**

The Yggyssey. Pinkwater, D. M.   **Fic**

Yiddish language
  Sussman, J. K. My first Yiddish word book   **439**

Yikes-lice!. Caffey, D.   **616.5**

Yikes! wow! yuck!. Harris, E. S.   **507.8**

Yin
  Brothers   **E**
  Coolies   **E**

Ylvisaker, Anne
  Little Klein   **Fic**

Yo! Yes? Raschka, C.   **E**

Yockteng, Rafael
  (il) Argueta, J. Sopa de frijoles = Bean soup   **811**
  (il) Messengers of rain and other poems from Latin America. See Messengers of rain and other poems from Latin America   **861.008**

Yoga
  Birkemoe, K. Strike a pose   **613.7**
  Chryssicas, M. K. I love yoga   **613.7**
  Whitford, R. Little yoga   **613.7**
      Poetry
  Wong, J. S. Twist   **811**

Yohalem, Eve
  Escape under the forever sky   **Fic**

Yoko. Wells, R.   **E**

Yokota, Junko
  Children's books in children's hands. See Children's books in children's hands   **028.5**

Yolen, Jane
  All-star! [biography of Honus Wagner]   **92**
  Apple for the teacher   **782.42**
  Baby Bear's books   **E**
  Come to the fairies' ball   **E**
  Commander Toad and the voyage home   **E**
  Dimity Duck   **E**
  An egret's day   **811**
  Fairy tale feasts   **641.5**
  Here there be dragons   **810.8**
  How do dinosaurs say goodnight?   **E**
  Johnny Appleseed   **92**
  Lost boy [biography of J. M. Barrie]   **92**
  Mama's kiss   **E**
  Meow   **398.2**
  Mightier than the sword   **398.2**

  A mirror to nature   **811**
  My father knows the names of things   **E**
  My Uncle Emily   **E**
  Naming Liberty   **E**
  Not one damsel in distress   **398.2**
  Off we go!   **E**
  Owl moon   **E**
  The perfect wizard [biography of Hans Christian Andersen]   **92**
  Sea queens   **920**
  Sleep, black bear, sleep   **E**
  Touch magic   **028.5**
      About
  McGinty, A. B. Meet Jane Yolen   **92**
  (ed) Here's a little poem. See Here's a little poem   **811.008**
  (ed) This little piggy. See This little piggy   **398.8**

Yolleck, Joan
  Paris in the spring with Picasso   **E**

Yolonda's genius. Fenner, C.   **Fic**

Yom Kippur
  Fishman, C. On Rosh Hashanah and Yom Kippur   **296.4**
  Heiligman, D. Celebrate Rosh Hashanah and Yom Kippur   **296.4**

Yonder mountain. Bushyhead, R. H.   **398.2**

Yong, Jui Lin
  (jt. auth) Barlas, R. Uganda   **967.61**
  (jt. auth) Heale, J. Democratic Republic of the Congo   **967.51**
  (jt. auth) Jermyn, L. Paraguay   **989.2**
  (jt. auth) Sheehan, S. Angola   **967.3**

Yoo, Paula
  Shining star: the Anna May Wong story   **92**
  Sixteen years in sixteen seconds [biography of Sammy Lee]   **92**

Yoo, Tae-Eun, 1977-
  The little red fish   **E**
  (il) Bridges, S. Y. The Umbrella Queen   **E**
  (il) McGhee, A. Only a witch can fly   **E**
  (il) McGhee, A. So many days   **E**

Yoon, Salina, 1972-
  Opposnakes   **E**
  Super babies on the move   **E**

Yorinks, Adrienne
  Quilt of states   **973**

Yorinks, Arthur, 1953-
  Happy bees   **E**
  Hey, Al   **E**
  Homework   **E**
  The witch's child   **E**
  (jt. auth) Sendak, M. Mommy?   **E**

York, ca. 1775-ca. 1815
      About
  Blumberg, R. York's adventures with Lewis and Clark   **978**
  Pringle, L. P. American slave, American hero [biography of York]   **92**

York, Sherry, 1947-
  Booktalking authentic multicultural literature   **021**
  Children's and young adult literature by Latino writers   **028.5**

YouTube, Inc.—*Continued*
Employment
See also Summer employment

YouTube, Inc.
Woog, A. YouTube   **006.7**
Yucky worms. French, V.   **E**
Yue, Stephanie
(il) Venable, C. A. Hamster and cheese   **741.5**
Yuen, Charles
(il) Lagasse, E. Emeril's there's a chef in my family!   **641.5**
(il) Lagasse, E. Emeril's there's a chef in my world!   **641.5**
Yugoslav War, 1991-1995
Halilbegovich, N. My childhood under fire   **949.7**

Yugoslavia
> *See also* Croatia; Serbia
> ### History—Civil War, 1991-1995
> *See* Yugoslav War, 1991-1995

Yuki and the one thousand carriers. Whelan, G.   **E**
Yukon River valley (Yukon and Alaska)
Fiction
Bell, J. Breaking trail   **Fic**
Yukon Territory
History
> *See also* Klondike River valley (Yukon)—Gold discoveries
Poetry
Service, R. W. The cremation of Sam McGee   **811**

Yum, Hyewon
Last night   **E**
Yum! mmmm! que rico!. Mora, P.   **811**
Yum! Yuck!. Park, L. S.   **413**
Yum! yum!!. Fitzgerald, J.   **398.8**
Yum yum! What fun!. Bergman, M.   **E**
Yummy. Cousins, L.   **398.2**

Z

Z goes home. Agee, J.   **E**
Z. Rex. Cole, S.   **Fic**
The **Z** was zapped. Van Allsburg, C.   **E**
Zabludoff, Marc
The protoctist kingdom   **579**
The reptile class   **597.9**
(jt. auth) Kreiter, E. John Singer Sargent   **92**
Zagarenski, Pamela
(il) Sidman, J. Red sings from treetops   **E**
(il) Sidman, J. This is just to say   **811**
Zahares, Wade
(il) Addy, S. Lucky Jake   **E**
(il) Shea, P. D. Liberty rising   **974.7**
Zaharias, Babe Didrikson, 1911-1956
About
Freedman, R. Babe Didrikson Zaharias   **92**

See/See also pages in the following book(s):
Krull, K. Lives of the athletes   **920**
Zahensky, Barbara A.
Diet fads   **613.2**
Zahler, Diane
The thirteenth princess   **Fic**
Zakanitch, Robert Rahway, 1935-
(il) Gottfried, M. Good dog   **811**
(il) Gottfried, M. Our farm   **811**
Zalben, Jane Breskin
Baby shower   **E**
Brenda Berman, wedding expert   **Fic**
Zallinger, Jean
(il) Sattler, H. R. The book of North American owls   **598**
Zambia
Holmes, T. Zambia   **968.94**
Houston, D. Bulu, African wonder dog   **636.7**
Folklore
> *See* Folklore—Zambia
Zamosky, Lisa
Louis Pasteur   **92**
Simple organisms   **579**
Zannier, Marco, 1972-
(jt. auth) Martin, B. S. Fundamentals of school library media management   **025.1**
Zanzibar
Folklore
> *See* Folklore—Zanzibar
Zapotec Indians
Folklore
Cruz, A. The woman who outshone the sun   **398.2**
Johnston, T. The tale of Rabbit and Coyote   **398.2**
Zarafa. St. George, J.   **599.63**
Zathura. Van Allsburg, C.   **E**
Zaunders, Bo
Gargoyles, girders, & glass houses   **720.9**
Zbaracki, Matthew D.
Best books for boys   **028.5**
Zebras
Lockwood, S. Zebras   **599.66**
Noble-Goodman, K. Zebras   **599.66**
Fiction
Walker, A. I love Christmas   **E**
Zeely. Hamilton, V.   **Fic**
Zeitlin, Steven J.
(jt. auth) Jaffe, N. The cow of no color: riddle stories and justice tales from around the world   **398.2**
Zelda and Ivy, the runaways. Kvasnosky, L. M.   **E**
Zeldis, Malcah, 1931-
(il) McDonough, Y. Z. Hammerin' Hank [biography of Hank Greenberg]   **92**
(il) McDonough, Y. Z. Peaceful protest: the life of Nelson Mandela   **92**
Zelinsky, Paul O.
Knick-knack paddywhack!   **782.42**
Rapunzel   **398.2**

Zelinsky, Paul O.—*Continued*
Rumpelstiltskin   **398.2**
(il) Cleary, B. Dear Mr. Henshaw   **Fic**
(il) Cleary, B. Strider   **Fic**
(il) Isaacs, A. Swamp Angel   **E**
(il) Jenkins, E. Toys go out   **Fic**
(il) Lesser, R. Hansel and Gretel   **398.2**
(il) Manushkin, F. The Shivers in the fridge
   E
(il) Nesbit, E. The enchanted castle   **Fic**
(il) Prelutsky, J. Awful Ogre running wild
   811
(il) Prelutsky, J. Awful Ogre's awful day
   811
Zemach, Kaethe, 1958-
Just enough and not too much   **E**
Ms. McCaw learns to draw   **E**
(il) Zemach, M. Eating up Gladys   **E**
Zemach, Margot
Eating up Gladys   **E**
The little red hen   **398.2**
The three little pigs   **398.2**
(il) Ginsburg, M. The Chinese mirror   **398.2**
Zemke, Deborah
(il) More pocket poems. See More pocket poems   **811.008**
Zemlicka, Shannon *See* Knudsen, Shannon, 1971-
Zen and the art of faking it. Sonnenblick, J.
   Fic
Zen Buddhism
Fiction
Muth, J. J. Zen shorts   **E**
Sonnenblick, J. Zen and the art of faking it
   Fic
Zen shorts. Muth, J. J.   **E**
Zenobia, Queen of Palmyra
See/See also pages in the following book(s):
Meltzer, M. Ten queens   **920**
Zenz, Aaron
(il) Newman, P. Nugget on the flight deck
   E
Zepeda, Gwendolyn, 1971-
Growing up with tamales = Los Tamales de
Ana   **E**
Zero (The number)
Franco, B. Zero is the leaves on the tree
   513
Murphy, S. J. Less than zero   **513**
Zero is the leaves on the tree. Franco, B.   **513**
Zeus (Greek deity)
Karas, G. B. Young Zeus   **292**
O'Connor, G. Zeus   **741.5**
Zeus. O'Connor, G.   **741.5**
Zhang, Ange
Red land, yellow river   **951.05**
Zich, John
(il) Gerasole, I. The Spatulatta cookbook
   641.5
Zickefoose, Julie
(il) Thompson, B., III. The young birder's guide
to birds of eastern North America   **598**
Ziefert, Harriet
ABC dentist   **617.6**

The big, bigger, biggest book   **E**
A bunny is funny   **E**
By the light of the harvest moon   **E**
A dozen ducklings lost and found   **E**
Hanukkah haiku   **296.4**
Home for Navidad   **E**
Little Red Riding Hood   **398.2**
Mighty Max   **E**
One red apple   **634**
One smart skunk   **E**
Passover   **296.4**
Snow party   **E**
Ziegler, Mark *See* Dahl, Michael, 1954-
Zig zag [series]
Baines, R. A den is a bed for a bear
   599.78
Baines, R. Every planet has a place   **523.2**
Baines, R. What did one elephant say to the
other   **591.59**
Zigazak!. Kimmel, E. A.   **E**
Zigzag [series]
Baines, R. The bones you own   **612.7**
Baines, R. Your skin holds you in   **612.7**
Zimbabwe
Sheehan, S. Zimbabwe   **968.91**
Fiction
Farmer, N. The Ear, the Eye, and the Arm
   Fic
Farmer, N. A girl named Disaster   **Fic**
Stock, C. Gugu's house   **E**
Zimmer, Dirk, 1943-
(il) Maguire, G. Seven spiders spinning   **Fic**
(il) Schwartz, A. In a dark, dark room, and other scary stories   **398.2**
Zimmer, Tracie Vaughn
42 miles   **Fic**
The floating circus   **Fic**
Sketches from a spy tree   **Fic**
Steady hands   **811**
Zimmerman, Andrea Griffing, 1950-
Dig!   **E**
Digger man   **E**
Fire engine man   **E**
Trashy town   **E**
Zimmermann, Karl R.
All aboard!   **385**
Ocean liners   **387.2**
Steam locomotives   **385.09**
Zin! zin! zin! a violin. Moss, L.   **E**
Zinnia and Dot. Ernst, L. C.   **E**
Zion, Gene
Harry the dirty dog   **E**
Zipes, Jack David
(ed) The Norton anthology of children's literature. See The Norton anthology of children's
literature   **808.8**
(ed) The Oxford encyclopedia of children's literature. See The Oxford encyclopedia of children's literature   **809**
Zipping, zapping, zooming bats. Earle, A.
   599.4
Zlateh the goat, and other stories. Singer, I. B.
   398.2

Zwerg, Jim, 1939-
About
Bausum, A. Freedom Riders   **323.1**
Zwerger, Lisbeth
(ed) Andersen, H. C. Hans Christian Andersen's
Fairy Tales [illustrated by Lisbeth Zwerger]
S C

(il) Andersen, H. C. Thumbeline [illustrated by
Lisbeth Zwerger]   **E**
(il) Baum, L. F. The Wizard of Oz   **Fic**
(il) Grimm, J. Little Red Cap   **398.2**
(il) Koppe, S. The Nutcracker   **Fic**
Zzzz: a book of sleep. See Na, I. S. A book of
sleep   **E**